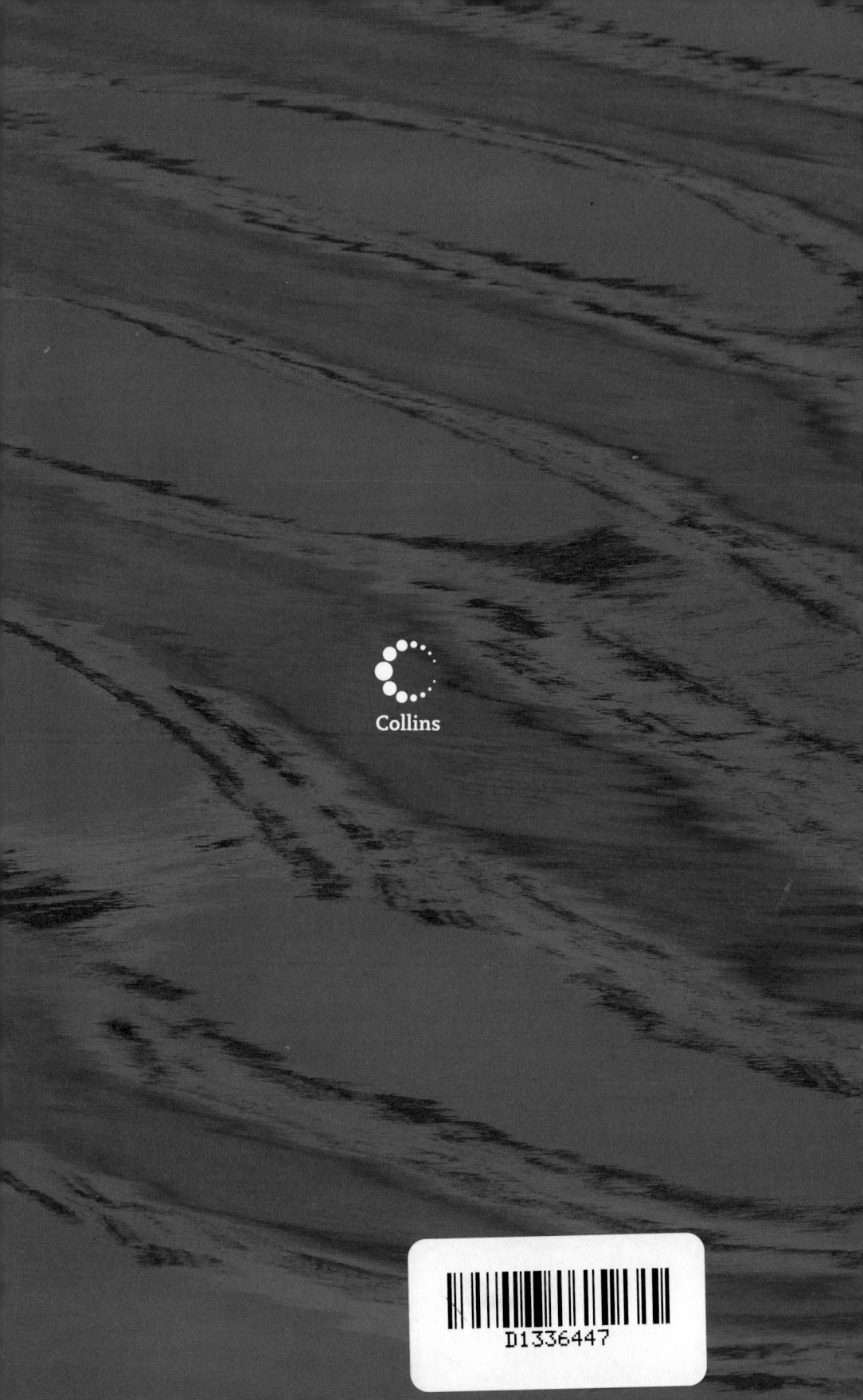

Collins

175 YEARS OF DICTIONARY PUBLISHING

Collins

Collins

175 YEARS OF DICTIONARY PUBLISHING

Dictionary

Collins

HarperCollins Publishers
Westerhill Road
Bishopbriggs
Glasgow
G64 2QT

Seventh Edition 2008

Reprint 10 9 8 7 6 5 4 3 2 1 0

UK EDITION
ISBN 978-0-00-726112-3

NEW ZEALAND EDITION
ISBN 978-0-00-782467-0

AUSTRALIAN EDITION
ISBN 978-0-7322-8806-8

www.collinslanguage.com

A catalogue record for this book is available
from the British Library.

Designed by Mark Thomson

This edition typeset by
Interactive Sciences Ltd,
Gloucester, England

Printed and bound in Italy by
Rotolito Lombarda S.p.A.

Acknowledgements
We would like to thank those authors and
publishers who kindly gave permission
for copyright material to be used in the
Collins Word Web. We would also like to
thank Times Newspapers Ltd for providing
valuable data.

When you buy this Collins title and
register with your unique serial
number (see inside front cover) on
www.collinslanguage.com for the
online services, you will not be charged
by HarperCollins for access to this title
on that website. However, your operator's
charges for using the internet on your
computer will apply. Costs vary from
operator to operator. HarperCollins is
not responsible for any charges levied by
online service providers for accessing this
Collins title on **www.collinslanguage.com**
using these services.

HarperCollins does not warrant that
the functions contained in
www.collinslanguage.com content will
be uninterrupted or error free, that
defects will be corrected, or that
www.collinslanguage.com or the server
that makes it available are free of viruses
or bugs. HarperCollins is not responsible
for any access difficulties that may
be experienced due to problems with
network, web, online or mobile phone
connections. This offer runs for the
lifetime of this edition.

About the type

This dictionary is typeset in CollinsFedra, a special version of the Fedra family of types designed by Peter Bil'ak. CollinsFedra has been customized especially for Collins dictionaries; it includes both sans serif (for headwords) and serif (entries) versions, in several different weights. Its large x-height, its open 'eye', and its basis in the tradition of humanist letterforms make CollinsFedra both familiar and easy to read at small sizes. It has been designed to use the minimum space without sacrificing legibility, as well as including a number of characters and signs that are specific to dictionary typography. Its companion phonetic type is the first of its kind to be drawn according to the same principles as the regular typeface, rather than assembled from rotated and reflected characters from other types.

Peter Bil'ak (born 1973, Slovakia) is a graphic and type designer living in the Netherlands. He is the author of two books, *Illegibility* and *Transparency*. As well as the Fedra family, he has designed several other typefaces including Eureka. His typotheque.com website has become a focal point for research and debate around contemporary type design.

Contents

Foreword

The best dictionaries are snapshots of the language they define at the moment they go to press. At Collins our priority is simple: to make those pictures the sharpest and most true to life available. To achieve this goal consistently, we have had to position ourselves at the very forefront of language monitoring. Collins editors have initiated an extensive reading, listening, and viewing programme, taking in all kinds of broadcasts and publications – from the *British Medical Journal* to *Viz*, from the *Sopranos* to the *Six O'clock News*.

But what keeps users of our dictionaries firmly up to speed with the latest developments in English is our close analysis of **Collins Word Web**, an unparalleled 2.5-billion-word "corpus" of lexical data. A constant flow of text is fed into it from sources around the globe – newspapers, books, websites, and even transcripts of radio and tv shows. Every month, Collins Word Web grows by 35 million words, making it the largest resource of its kind in the world. When we suggest an expression is growing in popularity, we can back it up with hard figures. If it appears to be shifting in meaning we can call up reams of usage examples from the real world.

It's in the discovery of new words and phrases, however, that this way of working really comes into its own. Rather than relying solely on contributors noticing the emergence of a new coinage, Collins editors are automatically alerted to it at the moment of its acceptance, however fleetingly, into the language.

While this Collins dictionary draws on the latest available technology, it also relies on the experience of editors who are able to interpret the data they receive and who follow the established values which have underpinned Collins dictionaries for the best part of two centuries.

The dictionary offers some features that are not found in other concise dictionaries: most notably, it includes a host of biographical and geographical entries which offer reliable information on people and places in the news. In addition to the main dictionary text, a special section called *Defining the Moment* offers a glimpse of the very latest words and meanings being captured by our language monitoring system. Furthermore, a supplement on writing reports and giving presentations offers advice on using language in a professional context.

Moreover, the information in the dictionary is now available in a range of formats to suit your needs. We understand that the requirements of dictionary users are constantly changing, and so now, when you buy a Collins dictionary, you can access the full dictionary online, browse the WAP site, or download it to your desktop. To find out more, visit **www.collinslanguage.com**. However you choose to use your Collins dictionary, we are confident that it offers an ideal resource for anyone seeking information about current English.

Guide to the Use of the Dictionary

This dictionary is designed to be easy to use so that you can go straight to the word you want. The Guide that follows sets out the main principles on which the dictionary is arranged and enables you to make full use of the dictionary by showing the range of information that it contains.

HEADWORD

All main entries, including place names, biographies, abbreviations, prefixes, and suffixes, are printed in large bold type and are listed in strict alphabetical order. This applies even if the headword consists of more than one word.

Order of entries

Words that have the same spelling but are derived from different sources (homographs) are entered separately with superscript numbers after the headwords.

> **saw**[1] (sɔː) *n* **1** any of various hand tools ...
> **saw**[2] (sɔː) *vb* the past tense of **see**[1]
> **saw**[3] (sɔː) *n* a wise saying, maxim, or proverb ...

A word with a capital initial letter, if entered separately, follows the lowercase form. For example, **Arras** follows **arras**.

Place names

If a place has more than one name, its main entry is given at the name most often used in modern English, with a cross-reference at other names. Thus, the main entry for the capital of Bavaria is at **Munich**, with a cross-reference at **München**. If a place name has no current anglicized form, its main entry is at the form of the name used in the official language of the area. Thus, the main entry is at **Brno**, with a cross-reference at **Brünn**. Historical names of importance are also given, with dates where these can be ascertained.

> **Paris**[1] ('pærɪs; *French* pari) *n* ... Ancient name:
> Lutetia
> **Volgograd** (*Russian* vəlga'grat; English 'vɒlgəg,ræd) *n*
> ... Former names: Tsaritsyn (until 1925), Stalingrad
> (1925–61)

Statistical information about places has been obtained from the most up-to-date and reliable sources available. Population figures are derived from the most recent census available, the date of which is always given.

Biographical entries

Biographical entries are entered separately from and immediately following place names of the same spelling. They are entered at the surname of the subject or at his or her title if that is the name by which he or she is better known and are grouped under one headword when the spelling of the surname (or title) is identical.

Abbreviations, acronyms, and symbols

Abbreviations, acronyms, and symbols are entered as headwords in the main alphabetical list. In line with modern practice, full stops are generally not used but it can be assumed that nearly all abbreviations are equally acceptable with or without stops.

Prefixes, suffixes, and combining forms

Prefixes (eg **in-**, **pre-**, **sub-**), suffixes (eg **-able**, **-ation**, **-ity**), and combining forms (eg **psycho-**, **-iatry**) have been entered as headwords if they are still used freely to produce new words in English.

Plural headwords

Words that have a standard use or uses in the plural may be entered as separate headwords at both singular and plural forms, with a cross-reference to the plural form at the singular entry if other headwords intervene.

> **air** (ɛə) *n* **1** the mixture of gases ...
> ▷ See also **airs**
> **airs** (ɛəz) *pl n* affected manners ...

Variant spellings

Common acceptable variant spellings of English words are given as alternative forms of the headword.

> **capitalize** *or* **capitalise** ('kæpɪtəˌlaiz) *vb* ...

US spellings

Where different, US spellings are also recorded in the headword.

> **centre** *or US* **center** ('sɛntə) *n* ...

PRONUNCIATIONS

Pronunciations of words in this dictionary represent those that are common in educated British English speech. They are transcribed in the International Phonetic Alphabet (IPA). A *Pronunciation Key* is printed at the end of this Guide. The pronunciation is normally given in brackets immediately after the headword.

> **abase** (ə'beis) *vb* (*tr*) **1** to humble ...

The stress pattern is marked by the symbols ' for primary stress and , for secondary stress. The stress mark precedes the syllable to which it applies.

Variant pronunciations

When a headword has an acceptable variant pronunciation or stress pattern, the variant is given by repeating only the syllable or syllables that change.

> **economic** (ˌiːkə'nɒmik, ˌɛkə-) *adj* **1** of or relating
> to ...

Pronunciations with different parts of speech

When two or more parts of speech of a word have different pronunciations, the pronunciations are shown in brackets before the relevant group of senses.

> **record** *n* ('rɛkɔːd) **1** an account in permanent
> form...
> ▷ *vb* (rɪ'kɔːd) (*mainly tr*) **18** to set down in some
> permanent form ...

Pronunciation of individual senses

If one sense of a headword is pronounced differently from the other senses, the pronunciation is given in brackets after the sense number.

> **conjure** ('kʌndʒə) *vb* **1** (*intr*) to practise conjuring
> or be a conjuror **2** (*intr*) to call upon supposed
> supernatural forces by spells and incantations
> **3** (kən'dʒʊə) (*tr*) to appeal earnestly or strongly to:
> *I conjure you to help me*

Foreign words and phrases

Foreign words or phrases are printed in bold italic type and are given foreign-language pronunciations only, unless they are regarded as having become accepted into English.

> ***Zeitgeist*** *German* ('tsaitgaist) *n* ...

INFLECTED FORMS

Where inflections are not shown, it may be assumed that they are formed as follows:

nouns regular plurals are formed by the addition of -s (eg pencils, monkeys) or, in the case of nouns ending in -s, -x, -z, -ch, or -sh, by the addition of -es (eg losses).

verbs in regular inflected verbs: the third person singular of the present tense is formed by the addition of -s to the infinitve (eg plays) or, for verbs ending in -s, -x, -z, -ch, or -sh, by the addition of -es (eg passes, reaches); the past tense and past participle are formed by the addition of -ed to the infinitive (eg played); the present participle is formed by the addition of -ing to the infinitive (eg playing). Verbs that end in a consonant plus -e (eg locate, snare) regularly lose the final -e before the addition of -ed and -ing.

adjectives regular comparatives and superlatives of adjectives are formed by adding -er and -est to the base (eg short, shorter, shortest). Adjectives that end in a consonant plus -e regularly lose the -e before -er and -est (eg fine, finer, finest).

PARTS OF SPEECH

A part-of-speech label in italics precedes the sense or senses relating to that part of speech.

Standard parts of speech

The standard parts of speech, with the abbreviations used, are as follows: adjective (*adj*), adverb (*adv*), conjunction (*conj*), interjection (*interj*), noun (*n*), preposition (*prep*), pronoun (*pron*), verb (*vb*).

Less traditional parts of speech

Some less traditional parts of speech have been used in this dictionary:
determiner this denotes such words as *the, a, some, any, that, this*, as well as the numerals, and possessives such as *my* and *your*. Many determiners can have a pronoun function without a change of meaning:

> **some** (sʌm; *unstressed* səm) *determiner* ... **2 a** an unknown or
> unspecified quantity or amount of: *there's some rice on*
> *the table; he owns some horses* **b** (*as pronoun; functioning as*
> *sing or plural*): *we'll buy some* ...

sentence connector this description replaces the traditional classification of certain words, such as therefore and however, as adverbs or conjunctions. These words link sentences together rather in the manner of conjunctions; however, they are not confined to the first position in a clause as conjunctions are.

sentence substitute these are words such as yes, no, perhaps, definitely, and maybe. They can stand alone as meaningful utterances.

Words used as more than one part of speech

If a word can be used as more than one part of speech, the senses of one part of speech are separated from the others by an empty arrow (▷):

> **lure** (lʊə) *vb* (*tr*) ... **2** *falconry* to entice (a hawk
> or falcon) from the air to the falconer by a lure
> ▷ *n* **3** a person or thing that lures ...

GRAMMATICAL INFORMATION

Grammatical information is provided in brackets and typically in italics to distinguish it from other types of information.

Adjectives and determiners

Some adjectives and determiners are restricted by usage to a particular position relative to the nouns they qualify. This is indicated by the following labels:

postpositive (used predicatively or after the noun, but not before it):

> **ablaze** (ə'bleiz) *adj, adv* (*postpositive*) **1** on fire;
> burning ...

immediately postpositive (always used immediately following the noun qualified and never used predicatively):

> **galore** (gə'lɔː) *determiner* (*immediately postpositive*) in
> great numbers or quantity: *there were daffodils galore*
> *in the park* ...

prenominal (used before the noun, and never used predicatively):

> **chief** (tʃiːf) ... *adj* **4** (*prenominal*) **a** most important;
> principal ...

Intensifiers

Adjectives and adverbs that perform an exclusively intensifying function, with no addition of meaning, are described as (intensifier) without further explanation:

> **blooming** ('bluːmɪŋ) *adv, adj* *Brit informal*
> (*intensifier*): *a blooming genius; blooming painful*

Conjunctions

Conjunctions are divided into two classes, marked by the following labels:

coordinating coordinating conjunctions connect words, phrases, or clauses that perform an identical function and are not dependent on each other. They include *and*, *but*, and *or*.

subordinating subordinating conjunctions introduce clauses that are dependent on a main clause in a complex sentence. They include *where*, *until*, and *if*.

Some conjunctions, such as *while* and *whereas*, can function as either coordinating or subordinating conjunctions.

Singular and plural labelling of nouns

Headwords and senses that are apparently plural in form but that take a singular verb, etc, are marked (*functioning as sing*):

> **physics** ('fiziks) *n* (*functioning as singular*) **1** the branch
> of science ...

Headwords and senses that appear to be singular, such as collective nouns, but that take a plural verb, etc, are marked (*functioning as plural*):

> **cattle** ('kæt³l) *n (functioning as plural)* **1** bovid
> mammals of the tribe *Bovini* ...

Headwords and senses that may take either a singular or a plural verb, etc, are marked (*functioning as sing or plural*):

> **bellows** ('bɛləʊz) *n (functioning as sing or plural)* **1** Also
> called: pair of bellows an instrument consisting of
> an air chamber ...

Modifiers

A noun that is commonly used as if it were an adjective is labelled modifier. If the sense of the modifier can be understood from the sense of the noun, the modifier is shown without further explanation, with an example to illustrate its use. Otherwise its meaning and/or usage is explained separately.

> **key**¹ (ki:) *n* ... **18** (*modifier*) of great importance: *a key*
> *issue*

Verbs

The principal parts given are: 3rd person singular of the present tense; present participle; past tense; past participle (if different from the past tense).

Intransitive and transitive verbs

When a sense of a verb (*vb*) is restricted to transitive use, it is labelled (*tr*); if it is intransitive only, it is labelled (*intr*). If all the senses of a verb are transitive or all are intransitive, the appropriate label appears before the first numbered sense and is not repeated.
Absence of a label is significant: it indicates that the sense may be used both transitively and intransitively.

If nearly all the senses of a verb are transitive, the label (*mainly tr*) appears immediately before the first numbered sense. This indicates that, unless otherwise labelled, any given sense of the verb is transitive. Similarly, all the senses of a verb may be labelled (*mainly intr*).

Copulas

A verb that takes a complement is labelled (*copula*).

> **seem** (si:m) *vb* (may take an infinitive) **1** (*copula*) to
> appear to the mind or eye; look: *this seems nice; the car*
> *seems to be running well* ...

Phrasal verbs

Verbal constructions consisting of a verb and a prepositional or an adverbial particle are given headword status if the meaning of the phrasal verb cannot be deduced from the separate meanings of the verb and the particle.

Phrasal verbs are labelled to show four possible distinctions:
a transitive verb with an adverbial particle (*tr, adverb*); a transitive verb with a prepositional particle (*tr, preposition*); an intransitive verb with an adverbial particle (*intr, adverb*); an intransitive verb with a prepositional particle (*intr, preposition*):

> **turn on** ... **4** (*tr, adverb*) *informal* to produce (charm,
> tears, etc) suddenly or automatically
> **take for** *vb* (*tr, preposition*) *informal* to consider or suppose
> to be, esp mistakenly: *the fake coins were taken for*
> *genuine; who do you take me for?*

break off ... **3** *(intr, adverb)* to stop abruptly; halt: *he broke off in the middle of his speech*

turn on ... **2** *(intr, preposition)* to depend or hinge on: *the success of the party turns on you*

The absence of a label is significant. If there is no label *(tr)* or *(intr)*, the verb may be used either transitively or intransitively. If there is no label *(adverb)* or *(preposition)*, the particle may be either adverbial or prepositional.

Any noun, adjective, or modifier formed from a phrasal verb is entered under the phrasal-verb headword. In some cases, where the noun or adjective is more common than the verb, the phrasal verb is entered after the noun or adjective form:

breakaway ('breɪkə,weɪ) *n* **1 a** loss or withdrawal of a group of members from an association, club, etc **b** *(as modifier)*: *a breakaway faction* ... *vb* **break away** *(intr, adverb)* **3** (often foll by *from*) to leave hastily or escape

RESTRICTIVE LABELS

If a particular sense is restricted as to appropriateness, connotation, subject field, etc, an italic label is placed immediately before the relevant definition:

hang on *vb (intr)* ... **5** *(adverb) informal* to wait or remain: *hang on for a few minutes*

If a label applies to all senses of one part of speech, it is placed immediately after the part-of-speech label.

assured (ə'ʃʊəd) *adj* ... ▷ *n* **4** *chiefly Brit* **a** the beneficiary under a life assurance policy **b** the person whose life is insured ...

If a label applies to all senses of a headword, it is placed immediately after the pronunciation (or inflections).

con[1] (kɒn) *informal* ▷ *n* **1 a** short for **confidence trick b** *(as modifier)*: *con man* ▷ *vb* **cons, conning, conned 2** *(tr)* to swindle or defraud

Usage labels

slang refers to words or senses that are informal and restricted in context, for example, to members of a particular social or cultural group. Slang words are inappropriate in formal speech or writing.

informal applies to words or senses that may be widely used, especially in conversation, letter-writing, etc, but that are not common in formal writing. Such words are subject to fewer contextual restrictions than slang words.

taboo indicates words that are not acceptable in polite use.

offensive indicates that a word might be regarded as offensive by the person described or referred to, even if the speaker uses the word without any malicious intention.

derogatory implies that the connotations of a word are unpleasant with intent on the part of the speaker or writer.

not standard indicates words or senses that are frequently encountered but widely regarded as incorrect.

archaic denotes a word or sense that is no longer in common use but that may be found in literary works or used to impart a historical colour to contemporary writing.

obsolete denotes a word or sense that is no longer in use. In specialist or technical fields the label often implies that the term has been superseded.

The word 'formerly' is placed in brackets before a sense when the practice, concept, etc, being described, rather than the word itself, is obsolete or out of date.
A number of other usage labels, such as *ironic, facetious,* and *euphemistic,* are used where appropriate.
Further help on usage is provided in usage notes after certain entries.

Subject-field labels
A number of italic labels are used to indicate that a word or sense is used in a particular specialist or technical field.

National and regional labels
Words or senses restricted to or associated with a particular country or region are labelled accordingly. The following labels are the ones most frequently used: *Austral* (Australian), *Brit* (British), *Canadian, Caribbean, Irish,* NZ (New Zealand), *Scot* (Scottish), *South African,* US (United States).

The label *Brit* is used mainly to distinguish a particular word or sense from its North American equivalent or to identify a term or concept that does not exist in North American English. The North American equivalent may be given in bold type after the appropriate numbered sense.

Regional dialects (*Scot and Northern English dialect, Midland dialect,* etc) have been specified as precisely as possible, even at the risk of overrestriction, in order to give the reader an indication of the appropriate regional flavour.

MEANING

The meaning of each headword in this dictionary is explained in one or more definitions, together with information about context and typical use.

Order of senses
As a general rule, where a headword has more than one sense, the first sense given is the one most common in current usage.

> **complexion** (kəmˈplɛkʃən) *n* **1** the colour
> and general appearance of a person's skin, esp
> of the face **2** aspect, character, or nature: *the*
> *general complexion of a nation's finances* **3** *obsolete* **a** the
> temperament of a person ...

Where the lexicographers consider that a current sense is the 'core meaning', in that it illuminates the meaning of other senses, the core meaning may be placed first.

> **competition** (ˌkɒmpɪˈtɪʃən) *n* **1** the act of competing;
> rivalry **2** a contest in which a winner is selected
> from among two or more entrants **3** a series of
> games, sports events, etc **4** the opposition offered
> by a competitor or competitors

Subsequent senses are arranged so as to give a coherent account of the meaning of a headword. If a word is used as more than one part of speech, all the senses of each part of speech are grouped together in a single block. Within a part-of-speech block, closely related senses are grouped together; technical senses usually follow general senses; archaic and obsolete senses follow technical senses; idioms and fixed phrases are generally placed last.

Scientific and technical definitions

Units, physical quantities, formulas, etc In accordance with the recommendations of the International Standards Organization, all scientific measurements are expressed in si units (Système International d'Unités). Measurements and quantities in more traditional units are often given as well as si units. The entries for chemical compounds give the systematic names as well as the more familiar popular names.

Plants and animals When the scientific (Latin) names of phyla, divisions, classes, orders, families, genera, and species are used in defintions, they are printed in italic type and all except the specific name have an initial capital letter. Taxonomic information is always given.

> **moss** (mɒs) *n* **1** any bryophyte of the phylum
> *Bryophyta*, typically growing in dense mats
> on trees …

CROSS-REFERENCES

The main entry is always given at the most common spelling or form of the word. Cross-reference entries refer to this main entry. Thus the entry for **deoxyribonucleic acid** cross-refers to **DNA**, where the full explanantion is given.

Comparisons

Cross-references introduced by the words 'See also' or 'Compare' refer the reader to additional information elsewhere in the Dictionary. If the crossreference is preceded by an empty arrow ▷, it applies to all senses of the headword that have gone before it, unless otherwise stated. If there is no empty arrow, the cross-reference applies only to the sense immediately preceding it.

Variant spellings

Variant spellings (eg **foetus** … a variant spelling of **fetus**) are generally entered as cross-references if their place in the alphabetical lists is more than ten entries distant from the main entry.

Alternative names

Alternative names or terms are printed in bold type and introduced by the words 'Also' or 'Also called'. If the alternative name or term is preceded by an empty arrow, it applies to the entire entry.

RELATED ADJECTIVES

Certain nouns, especially of Germanic origin, have related adjectives that are derived from Latin or French. For example, **mural** (from Latin) is an adjective related in meaning to **wall**. Such adjectives are shown in a number of cases after the sense (or part-of-speech block) to which they are related.

> **wall** (wɔːl) *n* **1 a** a vertical construction made of
> stone, brick,wood, etc … Related adj: **mural** …

IDIOMS

Fixed noun phrases, such as **dark horse**, and certain other idioms are given full headword status. Other idioms are placed under the key word of the idiom, as a separate sense, generally at the end of the appropriate part-ofspeech block.

> **ground¹** (graʊnd) *n* … **17** break new ground to do
> something that has not been done before …

ETYMOLOGIES

Etymologies are within square brackets and appear after the definition. They are given for most headwords except those that are derivative forms (consisting of a base word and a suffix or prefix), compound words, inflected forms, and proper names.

Many headwords, such as **enlighten** and **prepossess**, consist of a prefix and a base word and are not accompanied by etymologies since the essential etymological information is shown for the component parts, all of which are entered in the dictionary as headwords in their own right.

The purpose of the etymologies is to trace briefly the history of the word back from the present day, through its first recorded appearance in English, to its origin, often in some source language other than English. The etymologies show the history of the word both in English (wherever there has been significant change in form or sense) and in its pre-English source languages. Words printed in SMALL CAPITALS refer to other headwords where relevant or additional information, either in the definition or in the etymology, may be found.

Dating

The etymology records the first known occurrence (a written citation) of a word in English. Words first appearing in the language during the Middle English period or later are dated by century, abbreviated c.

> **mantis** ... [c17 New Latin, from Greek: prophet, alluding to its praying posture]

This indicates that there is a written citation for mantis in the seventeenth century. The absence of a New Latin or Greek form in the etymology means that the form of the word was the same in those languages as in English.

Old English

Native words from Old English are not dated, written records of Old English being scarce, but are simply identified as being of Old English origin.

DERIVED WORDS

Words derived from a base word by the addition of suffixes such as *-ly*, *-ness*, etc, are entered in bold type immediately after the etymology or after the last definition if there is no etymology.

They are preceded by the icon >. The meanings of such words may be deduced from the meanings of the suffix and the headword.

USAGE NOTES

A brief note introduced by the label usage has been added after some entries in order to comment on matters of usage.

Abbreviations

adj	adjective	N	north(ern)
adv	adverb(ial)	NE	northeast(ern)
anthropol	anthropology	*no*	number
archaeol	archaeology	NW	northwest(ern)
architect	architecture	NZ	New Zealand
Austral	Australian	*ornithol*	ornithology
biochem	biochemistry	*pathol*	pathology
Brit	Britain; British	*pharmacol*	pharmacology
c	century (e.g. c14 = 14th century)	*photog*	photography
°C	degrees Celsius	*physiol*	physiology
conj	conjunction	*Pop*	population
crystallog	crystallography	*prep*	preposition(al)
E	east(ern)	*pron*	pronoun
embryol	embryology	*psychol*	psychology
e.g.	for example	*pt*	point
entomol	entomology	RC	Roman Catholic
esp	especially	S	south(ern)
est	estimate	*Scot*	Scottish; Scots
foll	followed	SE	southeast(ern)
ft	foot or feet	*sing*	singular
i.e.	that is	*sq*	square
in	inch(es)	SW	southwest(ern)
interj	interjection	*telecom*	telecommunications
intr	intransitive	*theol*	theology
km	kilometre(s)	*tr*	transitive
m	metre(s)	US	United States
maths	mathematics	*vb*	verb
myth	mythology	W	west(ern)
n	noun	*wt*	weight

Pronunciation Key

The symbols used in the pronunciation transcriptions are those of the International Phonetic Alphabet.The following consonant symbols have their usual English values: b, d, f, h, k, l, m, n, p, r, s, t, v, w, z.
The remaining symbols and their interpretations are listed below.

English Sounds

ɑː   as in *father* ('fɑːðə), *alms* (ɑːmz), *clerk* (klɑːk), *heart* (hɑːt), *sergeant* ('sɑːdʒənt)

æ   as in *act* (ækt), *Caedmon* ('kædmən), *plait* (plæt)

aɪ   as in *dive* (daɪv), *aisle* (aɪl), *guy* (gaɪ), *might* (maɪt), *rye* (raɪ)

aɪə   as in *fire* ('faɪə), *buyer* ('baɪə), *liar* ('laɪə), *tyre* ('taɪə)

aʊ   as in *out* (aʊt), *bough* (baʊ), *crowd* (kraʊd), *slouch* (slaʊtʃ)

aʊə   as in *flour* ('flaʊə), *cower* ('kaʊə), *flower* ('flaʊə), *sour* ('saʊə)

ɛ   as in *bet* (bɛt), *bury* ('bɛrɪ), *heifer* ('hɛfə), *said* (sɛd), *says* (sɛz)

eɪ   as in *paid* (peɪd), *day* (deɪ), *deign* (deɪn), *gauge* (geɪdʒ), *grey* (greɪ), *neigh* (neɪ)

ɛə   as in *bear* (bɛə), *dare* (dɛə), *prayer* (prɛə), *stairs* (stɛəz), *where* (wɛə)

g   as in *get* (gɛt), *give* (gɪv), *ghoul* (guːl), *guard* (gɑːd), *examine* (ɪg'zæmɪn)

ɪ   as in *pretty* ('prɪtɪ), *build* (bɪld), *busy* ('bɪzɪ), *nymph* (nɪmf), *pocket* ('pɒkɪt), *sieve* (sɪv), *women* ('wɪmɪn)

iː   as in *see* (siː), *aesthete* ('iːsθiːt), *evil* ('iːvᵊl), *magazine* (ˌmægə'ziːn), *receive* (rɪ'siːv), *siege* (siːdʒ)

ɪə   as in *fear* (fɪə), *beer* (bɪə), *mere* (mɪə), *tier* (tɪə)

j   as in *yes* (jɛs), *onion* ('ʌnjən), *vignette* (vɪ'njɛt)

ɒ   as in *pot* (pɒt), *botch* (bɒtʃ), *sorry* ('sɒrɪ)

əʊ   as in *note* (nəʊt), *beau* (bəʊ), *dough* (dəʊ), *hoe* (həʊ), *slow* (sləʊ), *yeoman* ('jəʊmən)

ɔː   as in *thaw* (θɔː), *broad* (brɔːd), *drawer* ('drɔːə), *fault* (fɔːlt), *halt* (hɔːlt), *organ* ('ɔːgən)

ɔɪ   as in *void* (vɔɪd), *boy* (bɔɪ), *destroy* (dɪ'strɔɪ)

ʊ   as in *pull* (pʊl), *good* (gʊd), *should* (ʃʊd), *woman* ('wʊmən)

uː   as in *zoo* (zuː), *do* (duː), *queue* (kjuː), *shoe* (ʃuː), *spew* (spjuː), *true* (truː), *you* (juː)

ʊə   as in *poor* (pʊə), *skewer* ('skjʊə), *sure* (ʃʊə)

ə   as in *potter* ('pɒtə), *alone* (ə'ləʊn), *furious* ('fjʊərɪəs), *nation* ('neɪʃən), *the* (ðə)

ɜː   as in *fern* (fɜːn), *burn* (bɜːn), *fir* (fɜː), *learn* (lɜːn), *term* (tɜːm), *worm* (wɜːm)

ʌ   as in *cut* (kʌt), *flood* (flʌd), *rough* (rʌf), *son* (sʌn)

ʃ   as in *ship* (ʃɪp), *election* (ɪ'lɛkʃən), *machine* (mə'ʃiːn), *mission* ('mɪʃən), *pressure* ('prɛʃə), *schedule* ('ʃɛdjuːl), *sugar* ('ʃʊgə)

ʒ   as in *treasure* ('trɛʒə), *azure* ('æʒə), *closure* ('kləʊʒə), *evasion* (ɪ'veɪʒən)

tʃ   as in *chew* (tʃuː), *nature* ('neɪtʃə)

dʒ   as in *jaw* (dʒɔː), *adjective* ('ædʒɪktɪv), *lodge* (lɒdʒ), *soldier* ('səʊldʒə), *usage* ('juːsɪdʒ)

θ   as in *thin* (θɪn), *strength* (strɛŋθ), *three* (θriː)

ð   as in *these* (ðiːz), *bathe* (beɪð), *lather* ('lɑːðə)

ŋ   as in *sing* (sɪŋ), *finger* ('fɪŋgə), *sling* (slɪŋ)

ᵊ   indicates that the following consonant (l or n) is syllabic, as in *bundle* ('bʌndᵊl), *button* ('bʌtᵊn)

Foreign Sounds

The symbols above are also used to represent foreign sounds where these are similar to English sounds. However, certain common foreign sounds require symbols with markedly different values, as follows:

a   *a* in French *ami*, German *Mann*, Italian *pasta*: a sound between English (æ) and (ɑː), similar to the vowel in Northern English *cat* or London *cut*

ɑ   *a* in French *bas*: a sound made with the tongue position similar to that of English

	(ɑː), but shorter
e	*é* in French *été*, *eh* in German *sehr*, *e* in Italian *che*: a sound similar to the first part of the English diphthong (eɪ) in *day* or to the Scottish vowel in *day*
i	*i* in French *il*, German *Idee*, Spanish *filo*, Italian *signore*: a sound made with a tongue position similar to that of English (iː), but shorter
ɔ	*o* in Italian *no*, French *bonne*, German *Sonne*: a vowel resembling English (ɒ), but with a higher tongue position and more rounding of the lips
o	*o* in French *rose*, German *so*, Italian *voce*: a sound between English (ɔː) and (uː) with closely rounded lips, similar to the Scottish vowel in *so*
u	*ou* in French *genou*, *u* in German *kulant*, Spanish *puna*: a sound made with a tongue position similar to that of English (uː), but shorter
y	*u* in French *tu*, *ü* in German *über* or *fünf*: a sound made with a tongue position similar to that of English (iː), but with closely rounded lips
ø	*eu* in French *deux*, *ö* in German *schön*: a sound made with the tongue position of (e), but with closely rounded lips
œ	*oeu* in French *oeuf*, *ö* in German *zwölf*: a sound made with a tongue position similar to that of English (ɛ), but with open rounded lips
˜	above a vowel indicates nasalization, as in French *un* (œ̃), *bon* (bɔ̃), *vin* (vɛ̃), *blanc* (blɑ̃)
x	*ch* in Scottish *loch*, German *Buch*, *j* in Spanish *Juan*
ç	*ch* in German *ich*: a (j) sound as in *yes*, said without voice; similar to the first sound in *huge*
β	*b* in Spanish *Habana*: a voiced fricative sound similar to (v), but made by the two lips
ʎ	*ll* in Spanish *llamar*, *gl* in Italian *consiglio*: similar to the (lj) sequence in *million*, but with the tongue tip lowered and the sounds said simultaneously
ɥ	*u* in French *lui*: a short (y)
ɲ	*gn* in French *vigne*, Italian *gnocchi*, *ñ* in Spanish *España*: similar to the (nj) sequence in *onion*, but with the tongue tip lowered and the two sounds said simultaneously
ɣ	*g* in Spanish *luego*: a weak (g) made with voiced friction

Length
The symbol : denotes length and is shown together with certain vowel symbols when the vowels are typically long.

Stress
Three grades of stress are shown in the transcriptions by the presence or absence of marks placed immediately *before* the affected syllable. Primary or strong stress is shown by ', while secondary or weak stress is shown by ˌ. Unstressed syllables are not marked. In *photographic* (ˌfəʊtəˈgræfɪk), for example, the first syllable carries secondary stress and the third primary stress, while the second and fourth are unstressed.

Notes
(i) Though words like *castle*, *path*, and *fast* are shown as pronounced with an /ɑː/ sound, many speakers use an /æ/. Such variations are acceptable and are to be assumed by the reader.

(ii) The letter 'r' in some positions is not sounded in the speech of Southern England and elsewhere. However, many speakers in other areas do sound the 'r' in such positions with varying degrees of distinctness. Again such variations are to be assumed, and in such words as *fern*, *fear*, and *arm* the reader will sound or not sound the 'r' according to his or her speech habits.

(iii) Though the widely received pronunciation of words like which and why is with a simple /w/ sound and is so shown in the dictionary, many speakers in Scotland and elsewhere preserve an aspirated sound: /hw/. Once again this variation is to be assumed.

Aa

a¹ or **A** (eɪ) *n*, *pl* **a's**, **A's** or **As** **1** the first letter and first vowel of the modern English alphabet **2** any of several speech sounds represented by this letter, in English as in *take, bag, calm, shortage,* or *cobra* **3** Also called: **alpha** the first in a series, esp the highest grade or mark, as in an examination **4** **from A to Z** from start to finish, thoroughly and in detail

a² (ə; *stressed or emphatic* eɪ) *determiner* (*indefinite article*; used before an initial consonant) See **an¹** **1** used preceding a singular countable noun, if the noun is not previously specified or known: *a dog; a terrible disappointment* **2** used preceding a noun or determiner of quantity: *a cupful; a dozen eggs; a great many; to read a lot* **3** (preceded by *once, twice, several times,* etc) each or every; per: *once a day; fifty pence a pound* **4** a certain; one: *to change policy at a stroke; a Mr Jones called* **5** (preceded by *not*) any at all: *not a hope* ▷ See **the¹**

A *symbol for* **1** *music* **a** a note having a frequency of 440 hertz (**A above middle C**) or this value multiplied or divided by any power of 2; the sixth note of the scale of C major **b** the major or minor key having this note as its tonic **2** a human blood type of the ABO group, containing the A antigen **3** (in Britain) a major arterial road **4** ampere(s) **5** absolute (temperature) **7** (*in combination*) atomic: *an A-bomb; an A-plant* **8 a** a person whose job is in top management, or who holds a senior administrative or professional position **b** (*as modifier*): *an A worker.* See also **occupation groupings**

Å *symbol for* angstrom unit

A. *abbreviation* **1** acre(s) or acreage **2** America(n) **3** answer

a-¹ or before a vowel **an-** *prefix* not; without; opposite to: *atonal; asocial* [from Greek *a-, an-* not, without]

a-² *prefix* **1** on; in; towards: *afoot; abed; aground; aback* **2** in the condition or state of: *afloat; alive; asleep*

A1, A-1 or **A-one** ('eɪ'wan) *adj* **1** in good health; physically fit **2** *informal* first class; excellent **3** (of a vessel) with hull and equipment in first-class condition

A2 *n Brit* an advanced level of a subject taken for the General Certificate of Education, forming the second part of an A level course, after the AS level

A4 *n* a standard paper size, 210 × 297 mm

AA *abbreviation* **1** Alcoholics Anonymous **2** anti-aircraft **3** (in Britain) Automobile Association **4** (in Britain) Advertising Association

AAA *abbreviation* **1** *Brit* Amateur Athletic Association **2** *US* Automobile Association of America **3** Automobile Association of Australia

Aachen ('ɑːkən; *German* 'aːxən) *n* a city and spa in W Germany, in North Rhine-Westphalia: the northern capital of Charlemagne's empire. Pop: 256 605 (2003 est). French name: **Aix-la-Chapelle**

Aalborg or **Ålborg** (*Danish* 'ɔlbɔr) *n* a city and port in Denmark, in N Jutland. Pop: 121 549 (2004 est)

Aalesund (*Norwegian* 'oːləsun) *n* a variant spelling of **Ålesund**

Aalto (*Finnish* 'ɑːltɔ) *n* **Alvar** ('alvar). 1898–1976, Finnish architect and furniture designer, noted particularly for his public and industrial buildings, in which wood is much used. He invented bent plywood furniture (1932)

A & E *abbreviation* Accident and Emergency (department in hospitals)

A & R *abbreviation* artists and repertoire

AAP *abbreviation* **1** Australian Associated Press **2** (in the US) affirmative action program

Aarau (*German* 'aːrau) *n* a town in N Switzerland, capital of Aargau canton: capital of the Helvetic Republic from 1798 to 1803. Pop: 15 470 (2000)

aardvark ('ɑːd,vɑːk) *n* a nocturnal mammal, *Orycteropus afer,* the sole member of its family (*Orycteropodidae*) and order (*Tubulidentata*). It inhabits the grasslands of Africa, has long ears and snout, and feeds on termites. Also called: **ant bear** [C19: from obsolete Afrikaans, from *aarde* earth + *varken* pig]

aardwolf ('ɑːd,wʊlf) *n*, *pl* **-wolves** a nocturnal mammal, *Proteles cristatus,* that inhabits the plains of southern Africa and feeds on termites and insect larvae: family *Hyaenidae* (hyenas), order *Carnivora* (carnivores) [C19: from Afrikaans, from *aarde* earth + *wolf* wolf]

Aargau (*German* 'aːrgau) *n* a canton in N Switzerland. Capital: Aarau. Pop: 556 200 (2002 est). Area: 1404 sq km (542 sq miles). French name: **Argovie**

Aarhus (*Danish* 'ɔhuːs) *n* a variant spelling of **Århus**

Aaron ('ɛərən) *n* *Old Testament* the first high priest of the Israelites, brother of Moses (Exodus 4:14)

Aaron's beard *n* another name for **rose of Sharon** (sense 1)

Aaron's rod *n* a widespread Eurasian scrophulariaceous plant, *Verbascum thapsus*, having woolly leaves and tall erect spikes of yellow flowers

aarti ('ɑːtɪ) *n* a Hindu ceremony in which lights with wicks soaked in ghee are lit and offered up to one or more deities [c21: Hindi]

A'asia *abbreviation* Australasia

AB *abbreviation* **1** Also called: a.b. able-bodied seaman **2** (in the US) Bachelor of Arts **3** (esp in postal addresses) Alberta (Canada) ▷ *symbol for* **4** a human blood type of the ABO group, containing both the A antigen and the B antigen

ab-¹ *prefix* away from; off; outside of; opposite to: *abnormal; abaxial; aboral* [from Latin *ab* away from]

ab-² *prefix* denoting a cgs unit of measurement in the electromagnetic system: *abvolt* [abstracted from ABSOLUTE]

aba ('æbə) *n* **1** a type of cloth from Syria, made of goat hair or camel hair **2** a sleeveless outer garment of such cloth [from Arabic]

abaca ('æbəkə) *n* **1** a Philippine plant, *Musa textilis*, related to the banana: family *Musaceae*. Its leafstalks are the source of Manila hemp **2** another name for **Manila hemp** [via Spanish from Tagalog *abaká*]

aback (ə'bæk) *adv* taken aback **a** startled or disconcerted **b** *nautical* (of a vessel or sail) having the wind against the forward side so as to prevent forward motion [Old English *on bæc* to the back]

abacus ('æbəkəs) *n*, *pl* -ci (-ˌsaɪ) or -cuses a counting device that consists of a frame holding rods on which a specific number of beads are free to move. Each rod designates a given denomination, such as units, tens, hundreds, etc, in the decimal system, and each bead represents a digit or a specific number of digits [c16: from Latin, from Greek *abax* board covered with sand for tracing calculations, from Hebrew *ābhāq* dust]

Abaddon (ə'bædˀn) *n* **1** the Devil (Revelation 9:11) **2** (in rabbinical literature) a part of Gehenna; Hell [Hebrew: literally, destruction]

abaft (ə'bɑːft) *nautical* ▷ *adv*, *adj* (*postpositive*) **1** closer to the stern than to another place on a vessel ▷ *prep* **2** behind; aft of [c13: *on baft; baft* from Old English *beæftan*, from *be* by + *æftan* behind]

Abakan (*Russian* aba'kan) *n* a city in S central Russia, capital of the Khakass Republic, at the confluence of the Yenisei and Abakan Rivers. Pop: 167 000 (2005 est)

abalone (ˌæbə'ləʊnɪ) *n* any of various edible marine gastropod molluscs of the genus *Haliotis*, having an ear-shaped shell that is perforated with a row of respiratory holes. The shells are used for ornament or decoration. Also called: **ear shell** [c19: from American Spanish *abulón*; origin unknown]

abandon (ə'bændən) *vb* (*tr*) **1** to forsake completely; desert; leave behind **2** to give up completely: *to abandon a habit; to abandon hope* **3** to give up (something begun) before completion: *to abandon a job; the game was abandoned* **4** to surrender (oneself) to emotion without restraint **5** to give (insured property that has suffered partial loss or damage) to the insurers in order that a claim for a total loss may be made ▷ *n* **6** freedom from inhibitions, restraint, concern, or worry: *she danced with abandon* [c14: *abandounen* (vb), from Old French, from *a bandon* under one's control, in one's power, from *a* at, to + *bandon* control, power] > a'bandonment *n*

abandoned (ə'bændənd) *adj* **1** deserted: *an abandoned windmill* **2** forsaken: *an abandoned child* **3** unrestrained; uninhibited

abase (ə'beɪs) *vb* (*tr*) **1** to humble or belittle (oneself, etc) **2** to lower or reduce, as in rank or estimation [c15: *abessen*, from Old French *abaissier* to make low. See BASE²] > a'basement *n*

abash (ə'bæʃ) *vb* (*tr; usually passive*) to cause to feel ill at ease, embarrassed, or confused; make ashamed [c14: via Norman French from Old French *esbair* to be astonished, from *es-* out + *bair* to gape, yawn]

abashed (ə'bæʃt) *adj* ill at ease, embarrassed, or confused; ashamed > a'bashedly *adv*

abate (ə'beɪt) *vb* **1** to make or become less in amount, intensity, degree, etc **2** (*tr*) *law* **a** to remove, suppress, or terminate (a nuisance) **b** to suspend or extinguish (a claim or action) **c** to annul (a writ) **3** (*intr*) *law* (of a writ, legal action, etc) to become null and void [c14: from Old French *abatre* to beat down, fell] > a'batement *n*

abatis *or* **abattis** ('æbətɪs, æbə'tiː) *n* *fortifications* **1** a rampart of felled trees bound together placed with their branches outwards **2** a barbed-wire entanglement before a position [c18: from French, from *abattre* to fell]

abattoir (ˈæbəˌtwɑː) *n* another name for **slaughterhouse** [c19: French, from *abattre* to fell]

abaya (ə'baɪə) *n* a long black long-sleeved robe worn by Muslim women in Arabic-speaking countries, often with a headscarf or veil [Arabic]

Abba¹ ('æbə) *n* Swedish pop group (1972–82): comprised Benny Andersson (born 1946), Agnetha Faltskog (born 1950), Anni-Frid Lyngstad (born 1945), and Bjorn Ulvaeus (born 1945); numerous hit singles included "Waterloo" (1974), "Dancing Queen" (1977), and "The Winner Takes It All" (1980)

Abba² ('æbə) *n* **1** *New Testament* father (used of God) **2** a title given to bishops and patriarchs in the Syrian, Coptic, and Ethiopian Churches [from Aramaic]

abbacy ('æbəsɪ) *n*, *pl* -cies the office, term of office, or jurisdiction of an abbot or abbess [c15: from Church Latin *abbātia*, from *abbāt-* ABBOT]

Abbado (ə'bɑːdəʊ) *n* **Claudio**. born 1933, Italian conductor; principal conductor of the London Symphony Orchestra (1979–88); director of the Vienna State Opera (1986–91), and the Berlin Philharmonic (1989–2001)

Abbas ('æbəs) *n* **Ferhat**. 1899–1985, Algerian nationalist leader: joined the National Liberation Front (1956); president of the provisional government of the Algerian republic (1958–61)

Abbas I called *the Great*. 1557–1628, shah of Persia. He greatly extended Persian territory by defeating the Uzbeks and the Ottomans

Abbasid ('æbəˌsɪd, ə'bæsɪd) *n* **a** any caliph of the dynasty that ruled the Muslim empire from Baghdad (750–1258) and claimed descent from Abbas, uncle of Mohammed **b** (*as modifier*): *the Abbasid dynasty*

abbatial (ə'beɪʃəl) *adj* of or relating to an abbot, abbess, or abbey [c17: from Church Latin *abbātiālis*, from *abbāt-* ABBOT; see -AL¹]

abbé ('æbeɪ; *French* abe) *n* **1** a French abbot **2** a title used in addressing any other French cleric, such as a priest

Abbe ('æbɪ; *German* 'aːbə) *n* **Ernst**. 1840–1905, German physicist, noted for his work in optics and the microscope condenser known as the **Abbe condenser**

abbed (æbd) *adj informal* displaying well-developed abdominal muscles

abbess ('æbɪs) *n* the female superior of a convent [c13: from Old French, from Church Latin *abbātissa*]

Abbeville (*French* abəvil) *n* a town in N France: brewing, sugar-refining, and carpet industries. Pop: 24 567 (1999)

Abbevillian (æb'vɪlɪən, -jən) *archaeol* ▷ *n* **1** the period represented by Lower Palaeolithic European sites containing the earliest hand axes, dating from the Mindel glaciation ▷ *adj* **2** of or relating to this period [c20: after ABBEVILLE, where the stone tools were discovered]

abbey ('æbɪ) *n* **1** a building inhabited by a community of monks or nuns governed by an abbot or abbess **2** a church built in conjunction with such a building **3** such a community of monks or nuns [c13: via Old French *abeie* from Church Latin *abbātia* ABBACY]

abbot ('æbət) *n* the superior of an abbey of monks [Old English *abbod*, from Church Latin *abbāt-* (stem of *abbas*), ultimately from Aramaic *abbā* ABBA] > 'abbot,ship *or* 'abbotcy *n*

abbreviate (ə'briːvɪˌeɪt) *vb* (*tr*) **1** to shorten (a word or phrase) by contraction or omission of some letters or words **2** to cut short [c15: from the past participle of Late Latin *abbreviāre*, from Latin *brevis* brief]

abbreviation (əˌbriːvɪ'eɪʃən) *n* **1** a shortened or contracted form of a word or phrase used in place of the whole **2** the process or result of abbreviating

ABC[1] *n* **1** (*plural in US*) the rudiments of a subject **2** an alphabetical guide to a subject **3** (*often plural in US*) the alphabet

ABC[2] *abbreviation* **1** Australian Broadcasting Corporation **2** American Broadcasting Company

Abd Allah (æbd ˈælə) *n* 1846–99, Sudanese leader; he led the uprising against the Egyptian government of the Sudan; defeated by Kitchener in 1898

Abd al-Malik ibn Marwan (æbd ʊlˈmælɪk ɪbᵊn mærˈwɑːn) *n* ?646–705 AD, fifth caliph (685–705) of the Omayyad Arab dynasty. He pacified the Muslim empire and extended its territory in North Africa

Abdelkader (ˌæbdʊlˈkɑːdə) *n* ?1807–83, Algerian nationalist, who resisted the French invasion of Algeria and established (1837) an independent state. He surrendered to the French in 1847

Abd-el-Krim (ˌæbdʊlˈkrɪm) *n* 1882–1963, Moroccan chief who led revolts against Spain and France, surrendered before their combined forces in 1926, but later formed the North African independence movement

Abdias (æbˈdaɪəs) *n Bible* the Douay form of **Obadiah**

abdicate (ˈæbdɪˌkeɪt) *vb* to renounce (a throne, power, responsibility, rights, etc), esp formally [c16: from the past participle of Latin *abdicāre* to proclaim away, disclaim] > ˌabdiˈcation *n* > ˈabdiˌcator *n*

abdomen (ˈæbdəmən, æbˈdəʊ-) *n* **1** the region of the body of a vertebrate that contains the viscera other than the heart and lungs. In mammals it is separated from the thorax by the diaphragm **2** the front or surface of this region; belly **3** (in arthropods) the posterior part of the body behind the thorax, consisting of up to ten similar segments [c16: from Latin; origin obscure] > abdominal (æbˈdɒmɪnᵊl) *adj*

abdominoplasty (æbˈdɒmɪnəʊˌplæstɪ) *n, pl* -ies the surgical removal of excess skin and fat from the abdomen

abduct (æbˈdʌkt) *vb* (*tr*) **1** to remove (a person) by force or cunning; kidnap **2** (of certain muscles) to pull (a leg, arm, etc) away from the median axis of the body [c19: from the past participle of Latin *abdūcere* to lead away] > abˈductor *n* > abˈduction *n*

Abdul-Hamid II (ˌæbdʊlhæˈmiːd) *n* 1842–1918, sultan of Turkey (1876–1909), deposed by the Young Turks, noted for his brutal suppression of the Armenian revolt (1894–96)

Abdullah (æbˈdʌlə) *n* 1882–1951, emir of Transjordan (1921–46) and first king of Jordan (1946–51). He joined the Arab revolt against Turkish rule in World War I; assassinated 1951

Abdullah II *n* born 1962, King of Jordan from 1999, son of King **Hussein**. See **Hussein** (sense 1)

Abdul Rahman (ˈæbdʊl ˈrɑːmən) *n* **Tunku.** 1903–90, Malaysian statesman; prime minister of Malaya (1957–63) and of Malaysia (1963–70)

abeam (əˈbiːm) *adv, adj* (*postpositive*) at right angles to the length and directly opposite the centre of a vessel or aircraft [c19: A-² + BEAM]

abed (əˈbɛd) *adv archaic* in bed

Abednego (əˈbɛdnɪˌgəʊ) *n Old Testament* one of Daniel's three companions who, together with Shadrach and Meshach, was miraculously saved from destruction in Nebuchadnezzar's fiery furnace (Daniel 3:12–30)

Abel (ˈeɪbᵊl) *n Old Testament* the second son of Adam and Eve, a shepherd, murdered by his brother Cain (Genesis 4:1–8)

Abelard (ˈæbəˌlɑːd) *n* **Peter.** French name *Pierre Abélard*. 1079–1142, French scholastic philosopher and theologian whose works include *Historia Calamitatum* and *Sic et Non* (1121). His love for Héloïse is recorded in their correspondence

Abelson (ˈeɪbᵊlsən) *n* **Philip.** 1913–2004, US physical chemist. He created (with Edwin McMillan) the first transuranic element, neptunium (1940)

Abeokuta (ˌæbɪəʊˈkuːtə) *n* a town in W Nigeria, capital of Ogun state. Pop: 487 000 (2005 est)

Abercrombie (ˈæbəˌkrɒmbɪ) *n* Sir (**Leslie**) **Patrick.** 1879–1957, British town planner and architect, best known for *The County of London Plan* (1943) and *The Greater London Plan* (1944)

Aberdare (ˌæbəˈdɛə) *n* a town in South Wales, in Rhondda Cynon Taff county borough. Pop: 31 705 (2001)

Aberdeen[1] (ˌæbəˈdiːn) *n* **1** a city in NE Scotland, on the North Sea: centre for processing North Sea oil and gas; university (1494). Pop: 184 788 (2001) **2** City of Aberdeen a council area in NE Scotland, established in 1996. Pop: 206 600 (2003 est). Area: 186 sq km (72 sq miles) > ˌAberˈdonian *n, adj*

Aberdeen[2] (ˌæbəˈdiːn) *n* **George Hamilton-Gordon**, 4th Earl of. 1784–1860, British statesman. He was foreign secretary under Wellington (1828) and Peel (1841–46); became prime minister of a coalition ministry in 1852 but was compelled to resign after mismanagement of the Crimean War (1855)

Aberdeen Angus *n* a black hornless breed of beef cattle originating in Scotland

Aberdeenshire (ˌæbəˈdiːnˌʃɪə, -ʃə) *n* a council area and historical county of N Scotland, on the North Sea: became part of Grampian Region in 1975 but reinstated as an independent unitary authority (with adjusted borders) in 1996: rises to the Grampian and Cairngorm Mountains in the SW: chiefly agricultural (esp sheep and stock raising). Administrative centre: Aberdeen. Pop: 229 330 (2003 est). Area 6319 sq km (2439 sq miles)

Aberfan (ˌæbəˈvæn) *n* a former coal-mining village in S Wales, in Merthyr Tydfil county borough: scene of a disaster in 1966 when a slag heap collapsed onto part of the village killing 144 people (including 116 children)

aberrant (æˈbɛrənt) *adj* **1** deviating from the normal or usual type, as certain animals from the group in which they are classified **2** behaving in an abnormal or untypical way **3** deviating from truth, morality, etc [rare before c19: from the present participle of Latin *aberrāre* to wander away] > abˈerrance *or* abˈerrancy *n*

aberration (ˌæbəˈreɪʃən) *n* **1** deviation from what is normal, expected, or usual **2** departure from truth, morality, etc **3** a lapse in control of one's mental faculties **4** *optics* a defect in a lens or mirror that causes the formation of either a distorted image or one with coloured fringes **5** *astronomy* the apparent displacement of a celestial body due to the finite speed of light and the motion of the observer with the earth

Aberystwyth (ˌæbəˈrɪstwɪθ) *n* a resort and university town in Wales, in Ceredigion on Cardigan Bay. Pop: 15 935 (2001)

abet (əˈbɛt) *vb* abets, abetting, abetted (*tr*) to assist or encourage, esp in crime or wrongdoing [c14: from Old French *abeter* to lure on, entice, from *beter* to bait] > aˈbetment *or* aˈbettal *n* > aˈbetter *or esp law* aˈbettor *n*

abeyance (əˈbeɪəns) *n* **1** (usually preceded by *in* or *into*) a state of being suspended or put aside temporarily **2** (usually preceded by *in*) *law* an indeterminate state of ownership, as when the person entitled to an estate has not been ascertained [c16-17: from Anglo-French, from Old French *abeance* expectation, literally a gaping after, a reaching towards]

ABH *abbreviation* actual bodily harm

abhor (əbˈhɔː) *vb* -hors, -horring, -horred (*tr*) to detest vehemently; find repugnant; reject [c15: from Latin *abhorrēre* to shudder at, shrink from, from *ab-* away from + *horrēre* to bristle, shudder] > abˈhorrer *n*

abhorrence (əbˈhɒrəns) *n* **1** a feeling of extreme loathing or aversion **2** a person or thing that is loathsome

abhorrent (əbˈhɒrənt) *adj* **1** repugnant; loathsome **2** (when *postpositive*, foll by *of*) feeling extreme aversion or loathing (for): *abhorrent of vulgarity* **3** (usually *postpositive* and foll by *to*) conflicting (with): *abhorrent to common sense*

Abia (æbˈiːə) *n* a state of SE Nigeria. Capital: Umuahia. Pop: 2 833 999 (2006 est). Area: 6320 sq km (2440 sq miles)

abide (əˈbaɪd) *vb* abides, abiding, abode *or* abided **1** (*tr*) to tolerate; put up with **2** (*tr*) to accept or submit to; suffer: *to abide the court's decision* **3** (*intr*; foll by *by*) **a** to comply (with): *to abide by the decision* **b** to remain faithful (to): *to abide by your promise* **4** (*intr*) to remain or continue **5** (*intr*) *archaic* to dwell **6** (*tr*) *archaic* to await in expectation [Old English *ābīdan*, from *a-* (intensive) + *bīdan* to wait, bide] > aˈbider *n*

abiding (əˈbaɪdɪŋ) *adj* permanent; enduring: *an abiding*

a

belief in the power of faith

Abidjan (ˌæbɪˈdʒɑːn; *French* abidʒɑ̃) *n* a port in Côte d'Ivoire, on the Gulf of Guinea: the legislative capital (Yamoussoukro became the administrative capital in 1983). Pop: 3 516 000 (2005 est)

Abigail (ˈæbɪˌɡeɪl) *n Old Testament* the woman who brought provisions to David and his followers and subsequently became his wife (I Samuel 25:1–42)

ability (əˈbɪlɪtɪ) *n*, *pl* **-ties** **1** possession of the qualities required to do something; necessary skill, competence, or power **2** considerable proficiency; natural capability: *a man of ability* **3** (*plural*) special talents [c14: from Old French from Latin *habilitās* aptitude, handiness, from *habilis* ABLE]

Abingdon (ˈæbɪŋdən) *n* a market town in S England, in Oxfordshire. Pop: 36 010 (2001)

ab initio *Latin* (æb ɪˈnɪʃɪˌəʊ) from the start; from scratch: *ab initio courses*

abiogenesis (ˌeɪbaɪəʊˈdʒɛnɪsɪs) *n* **1** Also called: autogenesis the hypothetical process by which living organisms first arose on earth from nonliving matter **2** another name for **spontaneous generation** [c19: New Latin, from A-¹ + BIO- + GENESIS]

abiotrophy (ˌeɪbaɪəʊˈtrɒfɪ) *n* the progressive degeneration of tissues, cells, etc [c20: from Greek A-¹ + BIO- + TROPHY] > ˌabioˈtrophic *adj*

abject (ˈæbdʒɛkt) *adj* **1** utterly wretched or hopeless **2** miserable; forlorn; dejected **3** indicating humiliation; submissive: *an abject apology* **4** contemptible; despicable; servile: *an abject liar* [c14: (in the sense: rejected, cast out): from Latin *abjectus* thrown or cast away, from *abjicere*, from *ab-* away + *jacere* to throw] > abˈjection *n* > ˈabjectly *adv* > ˈabjectness *n*

abjure (əbˈdʒʊə) *vb* (*tr*) **1** to renounce or retract, esp formally, solemnly, or under oath **2** to abstain from or reject [c15: from Old French *abjurer* or Latin *abjurāre* to deny on oath] > ˌabjuˈration *n* > abˈjurer *n*

Abkhazia (æbˈkɑːzɪə) *n* an administrative division of NW Georgia, between the Black Sea and the Caucasus Mountains: a subtropical region, with mountains rising over 3900 m (13 000 ft); Abkhazian separatists seized control of the region in 1993. Capital: Sukhumi. Pop: 220 600 (2006 est). Area: 8600 sq km (3320 sq miles). Also called: Abkhaz Autonomous Republic

ablation (æbˈleɪʃən) *n* **1** the surgical removal of an organ, structure, or part **2** the melting or wearing away of an expendable part, such as the heat shield of a space re-entry vehicle on passing through the earth's atmosphere **3** the wearing away of a rock or glacier [c15: from Late Latin *ablātiōn-*, from Latin *auferre* to carry away, remove]

ablative (ˈæblətɪv) *grammar* ▷ *adj* **1** (in certain inflected languages such as Latin) denoting a case of nouns, pronouns, and adjectives indicating the agent in passive sentences or the instrument, manner, or place of the action described by the verb ▷ *n* **2 a** the ablative case **b** a word or speech element in the ablative case

ablaut (ˈæblaʊt; *German* ˈaplaut) *n linguistics* vowel gradation, esp in Indo-European languages. See **gradation** (sense 5) [German, coined 1819 by Jakob Grimm from *ab* off + *Laut* sound]

ablaze (əˈbleɪz) *adj*, *adv* (*postpositive*) **1** on fire; burning **2** brightly illuminated **3** emotionally aroused

able (ˈeɪbᵊl) *adj* **1** (*postpositive*) having the necessary power, resources, skill, time, opportunity, etc, to do something **2** capable; competent; talented **3** *law* qualified, competent, or authorized to do some specific act [c14: ultimately from Latin *habilis* easy to hold, manageable, apt, from *habēre* to have, hold + *-ilis* -ILE]

-able *suffix forming adjectives* **1** capable of, suitable for, or deserving of (being acted upon as indicated): *enjoyable; pitiable; readable; separable; washable* **2** inclined to; given to; able to; causing: *comfortable; reasonable; variable* [via Old French from Latin *-ābilis, -ībilis*, forms of *-bilis*, adjectival suffix] > **-ably** *suffix forming adverbs* > **-ability** *suffix forming nouns*

able-bodied *adj* physically strong and healthy; robust

able-bodied seaman *n* an ordinary seaman, esp one in the merchant navy, who has been trained in certain skills. Also called: able seaman Abbreviation: AB

abled (ˈeɪbᵊld) *adj* having a range of physical powers as specified (esp in the phrases **less abled, differently abled**)

ableism (ˈeɪbᵊlˌɪzəm) *n* discrimination against disabled or handicapped people

able rating *n* (esp in the Royal Navy) a rating who is qualified to perform certain duties of seamanship

abloom (əˈbluːm) *adj* (*postpositive*) in flower; blooming

ablution (əˈbluːʃən) *n* **1** the ritual washing of a priest's hands or of sacred vessels **2** (*often plural*) the act of washing (esp in the phrase **perform one's ablutions**) **3** (*plural*) *military informal* a washing place [c14: ultimately from Latin *ablūere* to wash away] > abˈlutionary *adj*

ably (ˈeɪblɪ) *adv* in a competent or skilful manner

ABM *abbreviation* antiballistic missile

abnegate (ˈæbnɪˌɡeɪt) *vb* (*tr*) **1** to deny to oneself; renounce (privileges, pleasure, etc) [c17: from Latin *abnegāre* to deny] > ˌabneˈgation *n* > ˈabneˌgator *n*

abnormal (æbˈnɔːməl) *adj* **1** not normal; deviating from the usual or typical; extraordinary **2** *informal* odd in behaviour or appearance; strange [c19: AB-¹ + NORMAL, replacing earlier *anormal* from Medieval Latin *anormalus*, a blend of Late Latin *anōmalus* ANOMALOUS + Latin *abnormis* departing from a rule] > abˈnormally *adv*

abnormality (ˌæbnɔːˈmælɪtɪ) *n*, *pl* **-ties** **1** an abnormal feature, event, etc **2** a physical malformation; deformity **3** deviation from the typical or usual; irregularity

Abo (ˈæbəʊ) *n*, *pl* **Abos** (*sometimes not capital*) *Austral dated, taboo* **a** short for **Aborigine b** (*as modifier*): *an Abo reserve*

Åbo (ˈoːbuː) *n* the Swedish name for **Turku**

aboard (əˈbɔːd) *adv*, *adj*, *prep* **1** on, in, onto, or into (a ship, train, aircraft, etc) **2** *nautical* alongside (a vessel) **3** all aboard! a warning to passengers to board a vehicle, ship, etc

abode¹ (əˈbəʊd) *n* a place in which one lives; one's home [c17: n formed from ABIDE]

abode² (əˈbəʊd) *vb* a past tense and past participle of **abide**

abolish (əˈbɒlɪʃ) *vb* (*tr*) to do away with (laws, regulations, customs, etc); put an end to [c15: from Old French *aboliss-* (lengthened stem of *abolir*), ultimately from Latin *abolēre* to destroy] > aˈbolishable *adj* > aˈbolisher *n* > aˈbolishment *n*

abolition (ˌæbəˈlɪʃən) *n* **1** the act of abolishing or the state of being abolished; annulment **2** (*often capital*) (in British territories) the ending of the slave trade (1807) or the ending of slavery (1833): accomplished after a long campaign led by William Wilberforce **3** (*often capital*) (in the US) the emancipation of the slaves, accomplished by the Emancipation Proclamation issued in 1863 and ratified in 1865 [c16: from Latin *abolitio*, from *abolēre* to destroy] > ˌaboˈlitionary *adj* > ˌaboˈlitionism *n* > ˌaboˈlitionist *n, adj*

abomasum (ˌæbəˈmeɪsəm) *n* the fourth and last compartment of the stomach of ruminants, which receives and digests food from the psalterium and passes it on to the small intestine [c18: New Latin, from AB-¹ + *omāsum* bullock's tripe]

A-bomb *n* short for **atomic bomb**

abominable (əˈbɒmɪnəbᵊl) *adj* **1** offensive; loathsome; detestable **2** *informal* very bad, unpleasant, or inferior: *abominable weather; abominable workmanship* [c14: from Latin *abōminābilis*, from *abōminārī* to ABOMINATE] > aˈbominably *adv*

abominable snowman *n* a large legendary manlike or apelike creature, alleged to inhabit the Himalayan Mountains. Also called: yeti [a translation of Tibetan *metohkangmi*, from *metoh* foul + *kangmi* snowman]

abominate (əˈbɒmɪˌneɪt) *vb* (*tr*) to dislike intensely; loathe; detest [c17: from the past participle of Latin *abōminārī* to regard as an ill omen, from *ab-* away from + *ōmin-*, from OMEN] > aˈbomiˌnator *n*

abomination (əˌbɒmɪˈneɪʃən) *n* **1** a person or thing that is disgusting **2** an action that is vicious, vile, etc **3** intense loathing

aboriginal (ˌæbəˈrɪdʒɪnᵊl) *adj* existing in a place from the earliest known period; indigenous; autochthonous > ˌaboˈriginally *adv*

Aboriginal (ˌæbəˈrɪdʒɪnəl) *adj* 1 of, relating to, or characteristic of the indigenous peoples of Australia ▷ *n* 2 another word for an Australian **Aborigine** ▷ Abo,rigiˈnality *n*

aborigine (ˌæbəˈrɪdʒɪnɪ) *n* an original inhabitant of a country or region who has been there from the earliest known times [c16: back formation from *aborigines*, from Latin: inhabitants of Latium in pre-Roman times, probably representing some tribal name but associated in folk etymology with *ab origine* from the beginning]

Aborigine (ˌæbəˈrɪdʒɪnɪ) *n* 1 Also called: Aboriginal a member of the indigenous people who were living in Australia when European settlers arrived 2 any of the languages of this people

abort (əˈbɔːt) *vb* 1 to undergo or cause (a woman) to undergo the termination of pregnancy before the fetus is viable 2 (*tr*) to cause (a fetus) to be expelled from the womb before it is viable 3 (*intr*) to fail to come to completion; go wrong 4 (*tr*) to stop the development of; cause to be abandoned 5 (*intr*) to give birth to a dead or nonviable fetus 6 (of a space flight, military operation, etc) to fail or terminate prematurely 7 (*intr*) (of an organism or part of an organism) to fail to develop into the mature form ▷ *n* 8 the premature termination or failure of (a space flight, military operation, etc) [c16: from Latin *abortāre*, from the past participle of *aboriri* to miscarry, from *ab-* wrongly, badly + *oriri* to appear, arise, be born]

abortifacient (əˌbɔːtɪˈfeɪʃənt) *adj* 1 causing abortion ▷ *n* 2 a drug or agent that causes abortion

abortion (əˈbɔːʃən) *n* 1 an operation or other procedure to terminate pregnancy before the fetus is viable 2 the premature termination of pregnancy by spontaneous or induced expulsion of a nonviable fetus from the uterus 3 the products of abortion; an aborted fetus 4 a failure to develop to completion or maturity 5 a person or thing that is deformed

abortionist (əˈbɔːʃənɪst) *n* a person who performs abortions, esp illegally

abortion pill *n* a drug, such as mifepristone, used to terminate a pregnancy in its earliest stage

abortive (əˈbɔːtɪv) *adj* 1 failing to achieve a purpose; fruitless 2 (of organisms) imperfectly developed; rudimentary 3 causing abortion; abortifacient

ABO system *n* a system for classifying human blood on the basis of the presence or absence of two antigens on the red cell membrane: there are four such blood types (A, B, AB, and O)

Aboukir Bay *or* **Abukir Bay** (ˌæbuːˈkɪə) *n* a bay on the N coast of Egypt, where the Nile enters the Mediterranean: site of the Battle of the Nile (1798), in which Nelson defeated the French fleet

aboulia (əˈbuːlɪə, -ˈbjuː-) *n* a variant spelling of **abulia**

abound (əˈbaʊnd) *vb* (*intr*) 1 to exist or occur in abundance; be plentiful 2 (foll by *with* or *in*) to be plentifully supplied (with); teem (with): *the gardens abound with flowers; the fields abound in corn* [c14: via Old French from Latin *abundāre* to overflow, from *undāre* to flow, from *unda* wave]

about (əˈbaʊt) *prep* 1 relating to; concerning; on the subject of 2 near or close to (in space or time) 3 carried on: *I haven't any money about me* 4 on every side of; all the way around 5 active in or engaged in 6 about to **a** on the point of; intending to: *she was about to jump* **b** (with a negative) determined not to: *nobody is about to miss it* ▷ *adv* 7 approximately; near in number, time, degree, etc: *about 50 years old* 8 nearby 9 here and there; from place to place; in no particular direction: *walk about to keep warm* 10 all around; on every side 11 in or to the opposite direction 12 in rotation or revolution: *turn and turn about* 13 used in informal phrases to indicate understatement: *I've had just about enough of your insults; it's about time you stopped* 14 archaic in circumference; around ▷ *adj* 15 (predicative) active; astir after sleep: *up and about* 16 (predicative) in existence, current, or in circulation: *there aren't many about nowadays* [Old English *abūtan, onbūtan* on the outside of, around, from ON + *būtan* outside]

about turn *or US* **about face** *interj* 1 a military command to a formation of men to reverse the direction in which they are facing ▷ *n* about-turn *or* about-face 2 a complete change or reversal, as of opinion, attitude, direction, etc ▷ *vb* about-turn *or* about-face 3 (*intr*) to perform an about-turn

above (əˈbʌv) *prep* 1 on top of or higher than; over 2 greater than in quantity or degree: *above average in weight* 3 superior to or prior to: *to place honour above wealth* 4 too honourable or high-minded for: *above petty gossiping* 5 too respected for; beyond: *above suspicion; above reproach* 6 too difficult to be understood by: *the talk was above me* 7 louder or higher than (other noise) 8 in preference to: *I love you above all others* 9 north of 10 upstream from 11 above all; most of all; especially 12 above and beyond in addition to ▷ *adv* 13 in or to a higher place: *the sky above* 14 **a** in a previous place (in something written) **b** (in combination): *the above-mentioned clause* 15 higher in rank or position 16 in or concerned with heaven ▷ *n* 17 the above something that is above or previously mentioned ▷ *adj* 18 mentioned or appearing in a previous place (in something written) [Old English *abufan*, from *a-* on + *bufan* above]

above board *adj, adv* (**aboveboard** *when prenominal*) in the open; without dishonesty, concealment, or fraud

above-the-line *adj* 1 denoting entries printed above the horizontal line on a company's profit-and-loss account separating the entries that show how the profit (or loss) was made from the entries showing how the profit is to be distributed 2 (of an advertising campaign) employing an advertising agency to use the press, television, radio, cinema, and posters 3 (in national accounts) denoting transactions concerned with revenue shown above a horizontal line that separates them from capital transactions

abracadabra (ˌæbrəkəˈdæbrə) *interj* 1 a spoken formula, used esp by conjurors ▷ *n* 2 a word used in incantations, etc, considered to possess magic powers 3 gibberish; nonsense [c17: from Latin: magical word used in certain Gnostic writings, perhaps related to Greek *Abraxas*; see ABRAXAS]

abrade (əˈbreɪd) *vb* (*tr*) to scrape away or wear down by friction; erode [c17: from Latin *abrādere* to scrape away, from AB-¹ + *rādere* to scrape] ▷ aˈbrader *n*

Abraham (ˈeɪbrəˌhæm, -həm) *n* 1 Old Testament the first of the patriarchs, the father of Isaac and the founder of the Hebrew people (Genesis 11–25) 2 Abraham's bosom the place where the just repose after death (Luke 16:22)

abranchiate (əˈbræŋkɪɪt, -ˌeɪt) *or* **abranchial** *adj* zoology having no gills [c19: A-¹ + BRANCHIATE]

abrasion (əˈbreɪʒən) *n* 1 the process of scraping or wearing down by friction 2 a scraped area or spot; graze 3 geography the effect of mechanical erosion of rock, esp a river bed, by rock fragments scratching and scraping it; wearing down [c17: from Medieval Latin *abrāsiōn-*, from the past participle of Latin *abrādere* to ABRADE]

abrasive (əˈbreɪsɪv) *n* 1 a substance or material such as sandpaper, pumice, or emery, used for cleaning, grinding, smoothing, or polishing ▷ *adj* 2 causing abrasion; grating; rough 3 irritating in manner or personality; causing tension or annoyance

abraxas (əˈbræksəs) *or* **abrasax** (əˈbræsæks) *n* an ancient charm composed of Greek letters: originally believed to have magical powers and inscribed on amulets, etc, but from the second century AD personified by Gnostics as a deity, the source of divine emanations [from Greek: invented word]

abreaction (ˌæbrɪˈækʃən) *n* psychoanal the release and expression of emotional tension associated with repressed ideas by bringing those ideas into consciousness

abreast (əˈbrest) *adj* (postpositive) 1 alongside each other and facing in the same direction 2 (foll by *of* or *with*) up to date (with); fully conversant (with)

abridge (əˈbrɪdʒ) *vb* (*tr*) 1 to reduce the length of (a written work) by condensing or rewriting 2 to curtail; diminish [c14: via Old French *abregier* from Late Latin *abbreviāre* to shorten] ▷ aˈbridgable *or* aˈbridgeable *adj* ▷ aˈbridger *n*

abridgment *or* **abridgement** (əˈbrɪdʒmənt) *n* 1 a

shortened version of a written work **2** the act of abridging or state of being abridged

abroad (ə'brɔːd) *adv* **1** to or in a foreign country or countries ▷ *adj* (*postpositive*) **2** (of news, rumours, etc) in general circulation; current **3** out in the open **4** over a wide area [C13: from A-² + BROAD]

abrogate ('æbrəʊ,ɡeɪt) *vb* (*tr*) to cancel or revoke formally or officially; repeal; annul [C16: from Latin *abrogātus* repealed, from AB-¹ + *rogāre* to propose (a law)]

abrupt (ə'brʌpt) *adj* **1** sudden; unexpected **2** brusque or brief in speech, manner, etc; curt **3** (of a style of writing or speaking) making sharp transitions from one subject to another; disconnected **4** precipitous; steep **5** *botany* shaped as though a part has been cut off; truncate **6** *geology* (of strata) cropping out suddenly [C16: from Latin *abruptus* broken off, from AB-¹ + *rumpere* to break] > **ab'ruptly** *adv* > **ab'ruptness** *n*

Abruzzi (Italian a'bruttsi) *or* **Abruzzo** (Italian a'bruttso) *n* a region of S central Italy, between the Apennines and the Adriatic. Capital: Aquila. Pop: 1 273 284 (2003 est). Area: 10 794 sq km (4210 sq miles)

abs (æbz) *pl n informal* abdominal muscles

Absalom ('æbsələm) *n Old Testament* the third son of David, who rebelled against his father and was eventually killed by Joab (II Samuel 15–18)

ABS brake *n* another name for **antilock brake** [from German *Antiblockiersystem*]

abscess ('æbsɛs, -sɪs) *n* **1** a localized collection of pus formed as the product of inflammation and usually caused by bacteria ▷ *vb* **2** (*intr*) to form such a collection of pus [C16: from Latin *abscessus* a going away, a throwing off of bad humours, hence an abscess, from *abscēdere* to go away] > '**abscessed** *adj*

abscissa (æb'sɪsə) *n, pl* **-scissas** *or* **-scissae** (-'sɪsiː) the horizontal or *x*-coordinate of a point in a two-dimensional system of Cartesian coordinates. It is the distance from the *y*-axis measured parallel to the *x*-axis. See **ordinate** [C17: New Latin, originally *linea abscissa* a cut-off line]

abscission (æb'sɪʒən, -'sɪʃ-) *n* **1** the separation of leaves, branches, flowers, and bark from plants by the formation of an abscission layer **2** the act of cutting off [C17: from Latin *abscissiōn-*, from AB-¹ + *scissiō* a cleaving]

abscond (əb'skɒnd) *vb* (*intr*) to run away secretly, esp from an open institution or to avoid prosecution or punishment [C16: from Latin *abscondere* to hide, put away, from *abs-* AB-¹ + *condere* to stow] > **ab'sconder** *n*

abseil ('æbseɪl) *vb* (*intr*) **1** *mountaineering* to descend a steep slope or vertical drop by a rope secured from above and coiled around one's body or through karabiners attached to one's body in order to control the speed of descent **2** to descend by rope from a helicopter ▷ *n* **3** an instance or the technique of abseiling ▷ Also called: rappel [C20: from German *abseilen* to descend by a rope, from *ab-* down + *Seil* rope]

absence ('æbsəns) *n* **1** the state of being away **2** the time during which a person or thing is away **3** the fact of being without something; lack [C14: via Old French from Latin *absentia*, from *absēns* being away]

absent *adj* ('æbsənt) **1** away or not present **2** lacking; missing **3** inattentive; absent-minded ▷ *vb* (æb'sɛnt) **4** (*tr*) to remove (oneself) or keep away [C14: from Latin *absent-*, stem of *absēns*, present participle of *abesse* to be away] > '**absently** *adv*

absentee (,æbsən'tiː) *n* **a** a person who is absent **b** (*as modifier*)

absenteeism (,æbsən'tiːɪzəm) *n* persistent absence from work, school, etc

absente reo (æb'sɛntɪ 'riːəʊ) *law* in the absence of the defendant [Latin, literally: the defendant being absent]

absent-minded *adj* preoccupied; forgetful; inattentive > ,absent-'mindedly *adv* > ,absent-'mindedness *n*

absinthe *or* **absinth** ('æbsɪnθ) *n* **1** a potent green alcoholic drink, technically a gin, originally having high wormwood content **2** another name for **wormwood** (sense 1) [C15: via French and Latin from Greek *apsinthion* wormwood]

absolute ('æbsə,luːt) *adj* **1** complete; perfect **2** free from limitations, restrictions, or exceptions; unqualified

3 having unlimited authority; despotic: *an absolute ruler* **4** undoubted; certain: *the absolute truth* **5** not dependent on, conditioned by, or relative to anything else; independent: *an absolute term in logic; the absolute value of a quantity in physics* **6** pure; unmixed: *absolute alcohol* **7** (of a grammatical construction) syntactically independent of the main clause, as for example the construction *Joking apart* in the sentence *Joking apart, we'd better leave now* **8** *grammar* (of a transitive verb) used without a direct object, as the verb *intimidate* in the sentence *His intentions are good, but his rough manner tends to intimidate* **9** *grammar* (of an adjective) used as a noun, as for instance *young* and *aged* in the sentence *The young care little for the aged* **10** *law* (of a court order or decree) coming into effect immediately and not liable to be modified; final ▷ *n* **11** something that is absolute [C14: from Latin *absolūtus* unconditional, freed from, from *absolvere*. See ABSOLVE]

Absolute ('æbsə,luːt) *n* (*sometimes not capital*) *philosophy* **a** the ultimate basis of reality **b** that which is totally unconditioned, unrestricted, pure, perfect, or complete

absolutely (,æbsə'luːtlɪ) *adv* **1** in an absolute manner, esp completely or perfectly ▷ *sentence substitute* **2** yes; certainly; unquestionably

absolute magnitude *n* the apparent magnitude a given star would have if it were situated at a distance of 10 parsecs (32.6 light years) from the earth

absolute majority *n* a number of votes totalling over 50 per cent, such as the total number of votes or seats obtained by a party that beats the combined opposition

absolute pitch *n* **1** the ability to identify exactly the pitch of a note without comparing it to another. Also called (not in technical usage): **perfect pitch** **2** the exact pitch of a note determined by its number of vibrations per second

absolute temperature *n* another name for **thermodynamic temperature**

absolute value *n maths* **1** the positive real number equal to a given real but disregarding its sign. Written $|x|$. Where r is positive, $|r| = r = |{-}r|$ **2** Also called: **modulus** a measure of the magnitude of a complex number, represented by the length of a line in the Argand diagram: $|x + iy| = \sqrt{(x^2 + y^2)}$, so $|4 + 3i| = 5$

absolute zero *n* the lowest temperature theoretically attainable, at which the particles constituting matter would be in the lowest energy states available; the zero of thermodynamic temperature; zero on the International Practical Scale of Temperature: equivalent to –273.15°C or –459.67°F

absolution (,æbsə'luːʃən) *n* **1** the act of absolving or the state of being absolved; release from guilt, obligation, or punishment **2** *Christianity* **a** a formal remission of sin pronounced by a priest in the sacrament of penance **b** the prescribed form of words granting such a remission [C12: from Latin *absolūtiōn-* acquittal, forgiveness of sins, from *absolvere* to ABSOLVE]

absolutism ('æbsəluː,tɪzəm) *n* the principle or practice of a political system in which unrestricted power is vested in a monarch, dictator, etc; despotism > '**abso,lutist** *n, adj*

absolve (əb'zɒlv) *vb* (*tr*) **1** (usually foll by *from*) to release from blame, sin, punishment, obligation, or responsibility **2** to pronounce not guilty; acquit; pardon [C15: from Latin *absolvere* to free from, from AB-¹ + *solvere* to make loose]

absorb (əb'sɔːb, -'zɔːb) *vb* (*tr*) **1** to soak or suck up (liquids) **2** to engage or occupy (the interest, attention, or time) of (someone); engross **3** to receive or take in (the energy of an impact) **4** *physics* to take in (all or part of incident radiated energy) and retain the part that is not reflected or transmitted **5** to take in or assimilate; incorporate **6** to pay for as part of a commercial transaction: *the distributor absorbed the cost of transport* **7** *chem* to cause to undergo a process in which one substance, usually a liquid or gas, permeates into or is dissolved by a liquid or solid: *porous solids absorb water; hydrochloric acid absorbs carbon dioxide* [C15: via Old French from Latin *absorbēre* to suck, swallow, from AB-¹ + *sorbēre* to suck] > ab,sorba'bility *n* > ab'sorbable *adj*

absorbed (əb'sɔːbd, -'zɔːbd) *adj* engrossed; deeply

interested > ab'sorbedly *adv*

absorbed dose *n* the amount of energy transferred by nuclear or ionizing radiation to a unit mass of absorbing material

absorbent (əb'sɔːbənt, -'zɔː-) *adj* **1** able to absorb ▷ *n* **2** a substance that absorbs > ab'sorbency *n*

absorbing (əb'sɔːbɪŋ, -'zɔːb-) *adj* occupying one's interest or attention; engrossing; gripping > ab'sorbingly *adv*

absorptance (əb'sɔːptəns, -'zɔːp-) *or* **absorption factor** *n physics* a measure of the ability of an object to absorb radiation, equal to the ratio of the absorbed radiant flux to the incident flux. For a layer of material the ratio of the flux absorbed between the entry and exit surfaces of the layer to the flux leaving the entry surface is the **internal absorptance** [C20: ABSORPTION + -ANCE]

absorption (əb'sɔːpʃən, -'zɔːp-) *n* **1** the process of absorbing or the state of being absorbed **2** *physiol* **a** normal assimilation by the tissues of the products of digestion **b** the passage of a gas, fluid, drug, etc, through the mucous membranes or skin [C16: from Latin *absorptiōn-*, from *absorbēre* to ABSORB] > ab'sorptive *adj*

absorption spectrum *n* the characteristic pattern of dark lines or bands that occurs when electromagnetic radiation is passed through an absorbing medium into a spectroscope. An equivalent pattern occurs as coloured lines or bands in the emission spectrum of that medium

abstain (əb'steɪn) *vb* (*intr*; usually foll by *from*) **1** to choose to refrain **2** to refrain from voting, esp in a committee, legislature, etc [C14: via Old French from Latin *abstinēre*, from *abs-* AB-¹ + *tenēre* to hold, keep] > ab'stainer *n*

abstemious (əb'stiːmɪəs) *adj* moderate or sparing, esp in the consumption of alcohol or food; temperate [C17: from Latin *abstēmius*, from *abs-* AB-¹ + *tēm-*, from *tēmētum* intoxicating drink] > ab'stemiously *adv* > ab'stemiousness *n*

abstention (əb'stɛnʃən) *n* **1** a voluntary decision not to act; the act of refraining or abstaining **2** the act of withholding one's vote [C16: from Late Latin *abstentiōn-*, from Latin *abstinēre*. See ABSTAIN]

abstinence ('æbstɪnəns) *n* the act or practice of refraining from some action or from the use of something, esp alcohol [C13: via Old French from Latin *abstinentia*, from *abstinēre* to ABSTAIN] > 'abstinent *adj*

abstract *adj* ('æbstrækt) **1** having no reference to material objects or specific examples; not concrete **2** not applied or practical; theoretical **3** hard to understand; recondite; abstruse **4** denoting art characterized by geometric, formalized, or otherwise nonrepresentational qualities ▷ *n* ('æbstrækt) **5** a condensed version of a piece of writing, speech, etc; summary **6** an abstract term or idea **7** an abstract painting, sculpture, etc **8** in the abstract without reference to specific circumstances or practical experience ▷ *vb* (æb'strækt) (*tr*) **9** to think of (a quality or concept) generally without reference to a specific example; regard theoretically **10** to form (a general idea) by abstraction **11** ('æbstrækt) (*also intr*) to summarize or epitomize **12** to remove or extract [C14: (in the sense: extracted): from Latin *abstractus* drawn off, removed from (something specific), from *abs-* AB-¹ + *trahere* to draw]

abstracted (æb'stræktɪd) *adj* **1** lost in thought; preoccupied **2** taken out or separated; extracted > ab'stractedly *adv*

abstract expressionism *n* a school of painting in New York in the 1940s that combined the spontaneity of expressionism with abstract forms in unpremeditated, apparently random, compositions

abstraction (æb'strækʃən) *n* **1** absence of mind; preoccupation **2** the process of formulating generalized ideas or concepts by extracting common qualities from specific examples **3** an idea or concept formulated in this way: *good and evil are abstractions* **4** an abstract painting, sculpture, etc **5** the act of withdrawing or removing > ab'stractive *adj*

abstract noun *n* a noun that refers to an abstract

concept, as for example *kindness*

abstruse (əb'struːs) *adj* not easy to understand; recondite; esoteric [C16: from Latin *abstrūsus* thrust away, concealed, from *abs-* AB-¹ + *trūdere* to thrust] > ab'strusely *adv* > ab'struseness *n*

absurd (əb'sɜːd) *adj* **1** at variance with reason; manifestly false **2** ludicrous; ridiculous [C16: via French from Latin *absurdus* dissonant, senseless, from AB-¹ (intensive) + *surdus* dull-sounding, indistinct] > ab'surdity *or* ab'surdness *n* > ab'surdly *adv*

ABTA ('æbtə) *n acronym for* Association of British Travel Agents

Abu-Bekr (ə,buː'bɛkər) *or* **Abu-Bakr** (ə,buː'bækər) *n* 573–634 AD, companion and father-in-law of Mohammed; the first caliph of Islam

Abu Dhabi ('æbuː 'dɑːbɪ) *n* a sheikhdom (emirate) of SE Arabia, on the S coast of the Persian Gulf: the chief sheikhdom and capital of the United Arab Emirates, consisting principally of the port of Abu Dhabi and a desert hinterland; contains major oilfields. Pop: 476 000 (2005 est). Area: 67 350 sq km (25 998 sq miles)

Abu Hanifah ('æbuː hæ'niːfə) *n* 700–67 AD, Muslim theologian and teacher of jurisprudence

Abuja (ə'buːdʒə) *n* the federal capital of Nigeria, in the centre of the country. Pop: 467 000 (2005 est)

Abukir Bay (,æbuː'kɪə) *n* a variant spelling of **Aboukir Bay**

abulia *or* **aboulia** (ə'buːlɪə, -'bjuː-) *n psychiatry* a pathological inability to take decisions [C19: New Latin, from Greek *aboulia* lack of resolution, from A-¹ + *boulē* will]

abundance (ə'bʌndəns) *n* **1** a copious supply; great amount **2** fullness or benevolence: *from the abundance of my heart* **3** degree of plentifulness **4** Also called: *abondance* a call in solo whist undertaking to make nine tricks **5** affluence [C14: via Old French from Latin *abundantia*, from *abundāre* to ABOUND]

abundant (ə'bʌndənt) *adj* **1** existing in plentiful supply **2** (*postpositive*; foll by *in*) having a plentiful supply (of) [C14: from Latin *abundant-*, present participle of *abundāre* to ABOUND] > a'bundantly *adv*

abuse *vb* (ə'bjuːz) (*tr*) **1** to use incorrectly or improperly; misuse **2** to maltreat, esp physically or sexually **3** to speak insultingly or cruelly to; revile ▷ *n* (ə'bjuːs) **4** improper, incorrect, or excessive use; misuse **5** maltreatment of a person; injury **6** insulting, contemptuous, or coarse speech **7** an evil, unjust, or corrupt practice **8** See **child abuse 9** *archaic* a deception [C14 (vb): via Old French from Latin *abūsus*, past participle of *abūtī* to misuse, from AB-¹ + *ūtī* to USE] > a'buser *n*

Abu Simbel (,æbuː 'sɪmbᵊl) *n* a former village in S Egypt: site of two temples of Rameses II, which were moved to higher ground (1966–67) before the area behind the Aswan High Dam was flooded. Also called: Ipsambul

abusive (ə'bjuːsɪv) *adj* **1** characterized by insulting or coarse language **2** characterized by maltreatment **3** incorrectly used; corrupt > a'busively *adv* > a'busiveness *n*

abut (ə'bʌt) *vb* abuts, abutting, abutted (usually foll by *on, upon,* or *against*) to adjoin, touch, or border on (something) at one end [C15: from Old French *abouter* to join at the ends, border on; influenced by *abuter* to touch at an end, buttress]

abutment (ə'bʌtmənt) *or* **abuttal** *n* **1** the state or process of abutting **2 a** something that abuts **b** the thing on which something abuts **c** the point of junction between them **3** *architect, civil engineering* a construction that takes the thrust of an arch or vault or supports the end of a bridge

abutter (ə'bʌtə) *n property law* the owner of adjoining property

abuzz (ə'bʌz) *adj* (*postpositive*) humming, as with conversation, activity, etc; buzzing

Abydos (ə'baɪdəs) *n* **1** an ancient town in central Egypt: site of many temples and tombs **2** an ancient Greek colony on the Asiatic side of the Dardanelles (Hellespont): scene of the legend of Hero and Leander

abysm (ə'bɪzəm) *n* an archaic word for **abyss** [C13: via

a

Old French from Medieval Latin *abysmus* ABYSS]

abysmal (ə'bɪzməl) *adj* **1** immeasurable; very great **2** *informal* extremely bad > a'bysmally *adv*

abyss (ə'bɪs) *n* **1** a very deep or unfathomable gorge or chasm **2** anything that appears to be endless or immeasurably deep, such as time, despair, or shame **3** hell or the infernal regions conceived of as a bottomless pit [c16: via Late Latin from Greek *abussos* bottomless (as in the phrase *abussos limnē* bottomless lake), from A-[1] + *bussos* depth]

abyssal (ə'bɪsəl) *adj* of or belonging to the ocean depths, esp below 2000 metres (6500 feet): *abyssal zone*

Abyssinia (,æbɪ'sɪnɪə) *n* a former name for **Ethiopia**

ac *internet domain name* Ascension Island

Ac *the chemical symbol for* actinium

AC *abbreviation* **1** alternating current. See **DC 2** ante Christum [Latin: before Christ] **3** athletic club **4** Companion of the Order of Australia **5** appellation d'origine contrôlée: the highest French wine classification; indicates that the wine meets strict requirements concerning area of production, strength, etc. See *vin de pays*

a/c *abbreviation* *book-keeping* **1** account **2** account current

acacia (ə'keɪʃə) *n* **1** any shrub or tree of the tropical and subtropical leguminous genus *Acacia*, having compound or reduced leaves and small yellow or white flowers in dense inflorescences **2** gum acacia another name for **gum arabic** [c16: from Latin, from Greek *akakia*, perhaps related to *akē* point]

academe ('ækə,diːm) *n* *literary* any place of learning, such as a college or university [c16: first used by Shakespeare in *Love's Labour's Lost* (1594); see ACADEMY]

academic (,ækə'dɛmɪk) *adj* **1** belonging or relating to a place of learning, esp a college, university, or academy **2** of purely theoretical or speculative interest **3** excessively concerned with intellectual matters and lacking experience of practical affairs **4** (esp of a schoolchild) having an aptitude for study **5** conforming to set rules and traditions; conventional: *an academic painter* **6** relating to studies such as languages, philosophy, and pure science, rather than applied, technical, or professional studies ▷ *n* **7** a member of a college or university > ,aca'demically *adv*

academician (ə,kædə'mɪʃən, ,ækədə-) *n* a member of an academy (sense 1)

academy (ə'kædəmɪ) *n, pl* -mies **1** an institution or society for the advancement of literature, art, or science **2** a school for training in a particular skill or profession: *a military academy* **3** a secondary school: now used only as part of a name, and often denoting a private school [c16: via Latin from Greek *akadēmeia* name of the grove where Plato taught, named after the legendary hero *Akadēmos*]

Academy Award *n* the official name for an **Oscar**

Acadia (ə'keɪdɪə) *n* **1 a** the Atlantic Provinces of Canada **b** the French-speaking areas of these provinces **2** (formerly) a French colony in the present-day Atlantic Provinces: ceded to Britain in 1713 > A'cadian *adj, n*

açaí (*Portuguese* asai) *n* a berry that grows on palm trees in the Brazilian rainforests. Because it is rich in nutrients, it is used to make energy drinks. Also called: palm berry [c21: Portuguese]

acanthus (ə'kænθəs) *n, pl* -thuses *or* -thi (-θaɪ) **1** any shrub or herbaceous plant of the genus *Acanthus*, native to the Mediterranean region but widely cultivated as ornamental plants, having large spiny leaves and spikes of white or purplish flowers: family *Acanthaceae* **2** a carved ornament based on the leaves of the acanthus plant, esp as used on the capital of a Corinthian column [c17: New Latin, from Greek *akanthos*, from *akantha* thorn, spine]

a cappella (ɑː kə'pɛlə) *adj, adv* *music* without instrumental accompaniment [Italian: literally, according to (the style of the) chapel]

Acapulco (,ækə'pʊlkəʊ; *Spanish* aka'pulko) *n* a port and resort in SW Mexico, in Guerrero state. Pop: 761 000 (2005 est)

acariasis (,ækə'raɪəsɪs) *n* infestation of the hair follicles and skin with acarids, esp mites [c19: New Latin. See ACARUS, -IASIS]

acarid ('ækərɪd) *or* **acaridan** (ə'kærɪdᵊn) *n* any of the small arachnids of the order *Acarina* (or *Acari*), which includes the ticks and mites [c19: from ACARUS]

acarpous (eɪ'kɑːpəs) *adj* (of plants) producing no fruit [from Greek *akarpos*, from A-[1] + *karpos* fruit]

acarus ('ækərəs) *n, pl* -ri (-,raɪ) any of the free-living mites of the widely distributed genus *Acarus*, several of which, esp *A. siro*, are serious pests of stored flour, grain, etc [c17: New Latin, from Greek *akari* a small thing, a mite]

ACAS *or* **Acas** ('eɪkæs) *n acronym for* (in Britain) Advisory Conciliation and Arbitration Service

acc. *abbreviation* *grammar* accusative

Accardo (*Italian* ak'kardo) *n* **Salvatore**. born 1941, Italian violinist and conductor

accede (æk'siːd) *vb* (*intr;* usually foll by *to*) **1** to assent or give one's consent; agree **2** to enter upon or attain (to an office, right, etc): *the prince acceded to the throne* **3** *international law* to become a party (to an agreement between nations, etc), as by signing a treaty [c15: from Latin *accēdere* to approach, agree, from *ad*- to + *cēdere* to go, yield] > ac'cedence *n*

accelerando (æk,sɛlə'rændəʊ) *adj, adv* *music* (to be performed) with increasing speed [Italian]

accelerate (æk'sɛlə,reɪt) *vb* **1** to go, occur, or cause to go or occur more quickly; speed up **2** (*tr*) to cause to happen sooner than expected **3** (*tr*) to increase the velocity of (a body, reaction, etc); cause acceleration [c16: from Latin *accelerātus*, from *accelerāre* to go faster, from *ad*- (intensive) + *celerāre* to hasten, from *celer* swift] > ac'celerative *or* ac'celeratory *adj*

acceleration (æk,sɛlə'reɪʃən) *n* **1** the act of accelerating or the state of being accelerated **2** the rate of increase of speed or the rate of change of velocity **3** the power to accelerate

acceleration of free fall *n* the acceleration of a body falling freely in a vacuum near the surface of the earth in the earth's gravitational field: the standard value is 9.806 65 metres per second per second or 32.174 feet per second per second. Symbol: *g* Also called: **acceleration due to gravity, acceleration of gravity**

accelerator (æk'sɛlə,reɪtə) *n* **1** a device for increasing speed, esp a pedal for controlling the fuel intake in a motor vehicle; throttle **2** *physics* a machine for increasing the kinetic energy of subatomic particles or atomic nuclei and focusing them on a target **3** *chem* a substance that increases the speed of a chemical reaction, esp one that increases the rate of vulcanization of rubber, the rate of development in photography, the rate of setting of synthetic resins, or the rate of setting of concrete; catalyst

accelerometer (æk,sɛlə'rɒmɪtə) *n* an instrument for measuring acceleration, esp of an aircraft or rocket

accent *n* ('æksənt) **1** the characteristic mode of pronunciation of a person or group, esp one that betrays social or geographical origin **2** the relative prominence of a spoken or sung syllable, esp with regard to stress or pitch **3** a mark (such as ', ,, ´ or `) used in writing to indicate the stress or prominence of a syllable. Such a mark may also be used to indicate that a written syllable is to be pronounced, esp when such pronunciation is not usual, as in *turnèd* **4** any of various marks or symbols conventionally used in writing certain languages to indicate the quality of a vowel, or for some other purpose, such as differentiation of homographs. See **circumflex 5** rhythmic stress in verse or prose **6** *music* **a** stress placed on certain notes in a piece of music, indicated by a symbol printed over the note concerned **b** the rhythmic pulse of a piece or passage, usually represented as the stress on the first beat of each bar **7** a distinctive characteristic of anything, such as taste, pattern, style, etc **8** particular attention or emphasis: *an accent on learning* **9** a strongly contrasting detail ▷ *vb* (æk'sɛnt) (*tr*) **10** to mark with an accent in writing, speech, music, etc **11** to lay particular emphasis or stress on [c14: via Old French from Latin *accentus*, from *ad*- to + *cantus* chant, song. The Latin is a rendering of Greek *prosōidia* a song sung to music, the tone of a syllable]

accentor (æk'sɛntə) *n* any small sparrow-like songbird

of the genus *Prunella*, family *Prunellidae*, which inhabit mainly mountainous regions of Europe and Asia. See also **hedge sparrow**

accentual (æk'sɛntʃʊəl) *adj* 1 of, relating to, or having accents; rhythmic 2 *prosody* of or relating to verse based on the number of stresses in a line rather than on the number of syllables > ac'centually *adv*

accentuate (æk'sɛntʃʊ‚eɪt) *vb* (*tr*) to stress or emphasize > ac‚centu'ation *n*

accept (ək'sɛpt) *vb* (*mainly tr*) 1 to take or receive (something offered) 2 to give an affirmative reply to 3 to take on the responsibilities, duties, etc, of: *he accepted office* 4 to tolerate or accommodate oneself to 5 to consider as true or believe in (a philosophy, theory, etc) 6 (*may take a clause as object*) to be willing to grant or believe: *you must accept that he lied* 7 to receive with approval or admit, as into a community, group, etc 8 *commerce* to agree to pay (a bill, draft, shipping document, etc), esp by signing 9 to receive as adequate, satisfactory, or valid [c14: from Latin *acceptāre*, from *ad-* + *capere* to take] > ac'cepter *n*

acceptable (ək'sɛptəbᵊl) *adj* 1 satisfactory; adequate 2 pleasing; welcome 3 tolerable > ac‚cepta'bility *or* ac'ceptableness *n* > ac'ceptably *adv*

acceptance (ək'sɛptəns) *n* 1 the act of accepting or the state of being accepted or acceptable 2 favourable reception; approval 3 (*often foll by of*) belief (in) or assent (to) 4 *commerce* a formal agreement by a debtor to pay a draft, bill, etc 5 (*plural*) *Austral & NZ* a list of horses accepted as starters in a race

acceptation (‚æksɛp'teɪʃən) *n* the accepted meaning, as of a word, phrase, etc

accepted (ək'sɛptɪd) *adj* commonly approved or recognized; customary; established

acceptor (ək'sɛptə) *n* 1 *commerce* the person or organization on which a draft or bill of exchange is drawn after liability has been accepted, usually by signature 2 Also called: acceptor impurity *electronics* an impurity, such as gallium, added to a semiconductor material to increase its p-type conductivity by increasing the number of holes in the semiconductor

access ('æksɛs) *n* 1 the act of approaching or entering 2 the condition of allowing entry, esp (of a building or room) allowing entry by wheelchairs, prams, etc 3 the right or privilege to approach, reach, enter, or make use of something 4 a way or means of approach or entry 5 the opportunity or right to see or approach someone: *she fights for divorce and free access to her children* 6 (*modifier*) designating programmes made by the general public as distinguished from those made by professional broadcasters: *access television* 7 a sudden outburst or attack, as of rage or disease ▷ *vb* 8 to gain access to; make accessible or available 9 (*tr*) *computing* **a** to obtain or retrieve (information) from a storage device **b** to place (information) in a storage device [c14: from Old French or from Latin *accessus* an approach, from *accēdere* to ACCEDE]

accessible (ək'sɛsəbᵊl) *adj* 1 easy to approach, enter, or use 2 accessible to likely to be affected by; open to; susceptible to 3 obtainable; available

accession (ək'sɛʃən) *n* 1 the act of entering upon or attaining to an office, right, condition, etc 2 an increase due to an addition 3 an addition, as to a collection 4 *property law* an addition to land or property by natural increase or improvement 5 *international law* the formal acceptance of a convention or treaty 6 agreement; consent ▷ *vb* 7 (*tr*) to make a record of (additions to a collection) > ac'cessional *adj*

access land *n* (in England and Wales) areas of the countryside which are open to the public

accessory (ək'sɛsərɪ) *n, pl* -ries 1 a supplementary part or object, as of a car, appliance, etc 2 (*often plural*) a small accompanying item of dress, esp of women's dress 3 a person who incites someone to commit a crime or assists the perpetrator of a crime, either before or during its commission ▷ *adj* 4 supplementary; additional; subordinate 5 assisting in or having knowledge of an act, esp a crime [c17: from Late Latin *accessōrius*: see ACCESS] > accessorial (‚æksɛ'sɔːrɪəl) *adj*

> ac'cessorily *adv*

access road *n* a road providing a means of entry into a region or of approach to another road, esp a motorway

access time *n computing* the time required to retrieve a piece of stored information

acciaccatura (ɑː‚tʃɑːkə'tʊərə) *n, pl* -ras *or* -re (-reɪ, -riː) a small grace note melodically adjacent to a principal note and played simultaneously with or immediately before it [c18: Italian: literally, a crushing sound]

accidence ('æksɪdəns) *n* inflectional morphology; the part of grammar concerned with changes in the form of words by internal modification or by affixation, for the expression of tense, person, case, number, etc [c15: from Latin *accidentia* accidental matters, hence inflections of words, from *accidere* to happen. See ACCIDENT]

accident ('æksɪdənt) *n* 1 an unforeseen event or one without an apparent cause 2 anything that occurs unintentionally or by chance; chance; fortune: *I met him by accident* 3 a misfortune or mishap, esp one causing injury or death 4 *geology* a surface irregularity in a natural formation, esp in a rock formation or a river system [c14: via Old French from Latin *accident-* chance, happening, from the present participle of *accidere* to befall, happen, from *ad-* to + *cadere* to fall]

accidental (‚æksɪ'dentᵊl) *adj* 1 occurring by chance, unexpectedly, or unintentionally 2 nonessential; incidental 3 *music* denoting sharps, flats, or naturals that are not in the key signature of a piece ▷ *n* 4 an incidental, nonessential, or supplementary circumstance, factor, or attribute 5 *music* a symbol denoting a sharp, flat, or natural that is not a part of the key signature > ‚acci'dentally *adv*

accident-prone *adj* more liable than most people to be involved in accidents

accidie ('æksɪdɪ) *or* **acedia** *n* spiritual sloth; apathy; indifference [in use c13 to c16 and revived c19: via Late Latin from Greek *akēdia*, from A-¹ + *kēdos* care]

accipiter (æk'sɪpɪtə) *n* any hawk of the genus *Accipiter*, typically having short rounded wings and a long tail [c19: New Latin, from Latin: hawk] > accipitrine (æk'sɪpɪ‚traɪn, -trɪn) *adj*

acclaim (ə'kleɪm) *vb* 1 (*tr*) to acknowledge publicly the excellence of (a person, act, etc) 2 to salute with cheering, clapping, etc; applaud 3 (*tr*) to acknowledge publicly that (a person) has (some position, quality, etc): *they acclaimed him king* ▷ *n* 4 an enthusiastic approval, expression of enthusiasm, etc [c17: from Latin *acclāmāre* to shout at, shout applause, from *ad-* to + *clamāre* to shout] > ac'claimer *n*

acclamation (‚æklə'meɪʃən) *n* 1 an enthusiastic reception or exhibition of welcome, approval, etc 2 an expression of approval by a meeting or gathering through shouts or applause 3 *Canadian* an instance of electing or being elected without opposition > acclamatory (ə'klæmətərɪ, -trɪ) *adj*

acclimatize, acclimatise (ə'klaɪmə‚taɪz) *or* **acclimate** (ə'klaɪmeɪt, 'æklɪ‚meɪt) *vb* to adapt or become accustomed to a new climate or environment > ac'clima‚tizable, ac'clima‚tisable *or* ac'climatable *adj* > ac‚climati'zation, ac‚climati'sation *or* ‚accli'mation *n* > ac'clima‚tizer, ac'clima‚tiser *n*

acclivity (ə'klɪvɪtɪ) *n, pl* -ties an upward slope, esp of the ground. See **declivity** [c17: from Latin *acclīvitās*, from *acclīvis* sloping up, steep] > ac'clivitous *or* acclivous (ə'klaɪvəs) *adj*

accolade ('ækə‚leɪd, ‚ækə'leɪd) *n* 1 strong praise or approval; acclaim 2 an award or honour 3 the ceremonial gesture used to confer knighthood, originally an embrace, now a touch on the shoulder with a sword 4 a rare word for **brace** (sense 6) [c17: via French and Italian from Vulgar Latin *accollāre* (unattested) to hug; related to Latin *collum* neck]

accommodate (ə'kɒmə‚deɪt) *vb* 1 (*tr*) to supply or provide, esp with lodging or board and lodging 2 (*tr*) to oblige or do a favour for 3 to adjust or become adjusted; adapt 4 (*tr*) to bring into harmony; reconcile 5 (*tr*) to allow room for; contain 6 (*tr*) to lend money to, esp on a temporary basis until a formal loan has been arranged [c16: from Latin *accommodāre* to make fit, from *ad-* to +

commodus having the proper measure]

accommodating (ə'kɒmə,deɪtɪŋ) *adj* willing to help; kind; obliging

accommodation (ə,kɒmə'deɪʃən) *n* **1** lodging or board and lodging **2** adjustment, as of differences or to new circumstances; adaptation, settlement, or reconciliation **3** something fulfilling a need, want, etc; convenience or facility **4** *physiol* the automatic or voluntary adjustment of the shape of the lens of the eye for far or near vision **5** willingness to help or oblige **6** *commerce* a loan, usually made as an act of favour by a bank before formal credit arrangements are agreed

accommodation address *n* an address on letters, etc, to a person or business that does not wish or is not able to receive post at a permanent or actual address

accommodation ladder *n* *nautical* a flight of stairs or a ladder for lowering over the side of a ship for access to and from a small boat, pier, etc

accompaniment (ə'kʌmpənɪmənt, ə'kʌmpnɪ-) *n* **1** something that accompanies or is served or used with something else **2** *music* a subordinate part for an instrument, voices, or an orchestra

accompanist (ə'kʌmpənɪst, ə'kʌmpnɪst) *or sometimes US* **accompanyist** (ə'kʌmpəni:ɪst) *n* a person who plays a musical accompaniment for another performer, esp a pianist accompanying a singer

accompany (ə'kʌmpənɪ, ə'kʌmpnɪ) *vb* -nies, -nying, -nied **1** (*tr*) to go along with, so as to be in company with or escort **2** (*tr*; foll by *with*) to supplement **3** (*tr*) to occur, coexist, or be associated with **4** to provide a musical accompaniment for (a performer) [c15: from Old French *accompaignier*, from *compaing* COMPANION[1]]

accomplice (ə'kɒmplɪs, ə'kʌm-) *n* a person who helps another in committing a crime [c15: from *a complice*, interpreted as one word. See COMPLICE]

accomplish (ə'kɒmplɪʃ, ə'kʌm-) *vb* (*tr*) **1** to manage to do; achieve **2** to conclude successfully; complete [c14: from Old French *acomplir* to complete, ultimately from Latin *complēre* to fill up. See COMPLETE]

accomplished (ə'kɒmplɪʃt, ə'kʌm-) *adj* **1** successfully completed; achieved **2** expert; proficient

accomplishment (ə'kɒmplɪʃmənt, ə'kʌm-) *n* **1** the act of carrying out or achieving **2** something achieved or successfully completed **3** (*often plural*) skill or talent **4** (*often plural*) social grace, style, and poise

accord (ə'kɔ:d) *n* **1** agreement; conformity; accordance (esp in the phrase **in accord with**) **2** consent or concurrence of opinion **3** with one accord unanimously **4** pleasing relationship between sounds, colours, etc; harmony **5** of one's own accord voluntarily ▷ *vb* **6** to be or cause to be in harmony or agreement **7** (*tr*) to grant; bestow [c12: via Old French from Latin *ad-* to + *cord-*, stem of *cor* heart]

accordance (ə'kɔ:dəns) *n* conformity; agreement; accord (esp in the phrase **in accordance with**)

according (ə'kɔ:dɪŋ) *adj* **1** (foll by *to*) in proportion; in relation **2** (foll by *to*) on the report (of); as stated (by) **3** (foll by *to*) in conformity (with); in accordance (with) **4** (foll by *as*) depending (on whether)

accordingly (ə'kɔ:dɪŋlɪ) *adv* **1** in an appropriate manner; suitably ▷ *sentence connector* **2** consequently

accordion (ə'kɔ:dɪən) *n* **1** a portable box-shaped instrument of the reed organ family, consisting of metallic reeds that are made to vibrate by air from a set of bellows controlled by the player's hands. Notes are produced by means of studlike keys **2** short for **piano accordion** [c19: from German *Akkordion*, from *Akkord* harmony, chord] > **ac'cordionist** *n*

accordion pleats *pl n* tiny knife pleats

accost (ə'kɒst) *vb* (*tr*) to approach, stop, and speak to (a person), as to ask a question, accuse of a crime, solicit sexually, etc [c16: from Late Latin *accostāre* to place side by side, from *costa* side, rib] > **ac'costable** *adj*

accouchement *French* (akuʃmɑ̃; *English* ə'ku:ʃmənt) *n* childbirth or the period of confinement [c19: from *accoucher* to put to bed, to give birth. See COUCH]

account (ə'kaʊnt) *n* **1** a verbal or written report, description, or narration of some occurrence, event, etc **2** an explanation of conduct, esp one made to someone

in authority **3** ground; basis; consideration (often in the phrases **on this** (**that, every, no,** etc) **account, on account of**) **4** importance, consequence, or value: *of little account* **5** assessment; judgment **6** profit or advantage: *to turn an idea to account* **7** part or behalf (only in the phrase **on one's** *or* **someone's account**) **8** *finance* **a** a business relationship between a bank, department store, stockbroker, etc, and a depositor, customer, or client permitting the latter certain banking or credit services **b** the sum of money deposited at a bank **c** the amount of credit available to the holder of an account **d** a record of these **9** a statement of monetary transactions with the resulting balance **10 a** a regular client or customer, esp a firm that purchases commodities on credit **b** an area of business assigned to another: *they transferred their publicity account to a new agent* **11 call to account** or **bring to account** to insist on explanation **b** to rebuke; reprimand **c** to hold responsible **12 give a bad account of oneself** to perform badly: *he gave a bad account of himself in the examination* **13 give a good account of oneself** to perform well **14 on account a** on credit **b** Also called: **to account** as partial payment **15 on account of** (*preposition*) because of; by reason of **16 take account of** *or* **take into account** to take into consideration; allow for **17 settle accounts with** *or* **square accounts with a** to pay or receive a balance due **b** to get revenge on (someone) **18 See bank account, credit account** ▷ *vb* **19** (*tr*) to consider or reckon: *he accounts himself poor* [c13: from Old French *acont*, from *conter, compter* to COUNT[1]]

accountable (ə'kaʊntəb°l) *adj* **1** responsible to someone or for some action; answerable **2** able to be explained > **ac,counta'bility** *n* > **ac'countably** *adv*

accountancy (ə'kaʊntənsɪ) *n* the profession or business of an accountant

accountant (ə'kaʊntənt) *n* a person concerned with the maintenance and audit of business accounts and the preparation of consultant reports in tax and finance

account executive *n* an executive in an advertising agency or public relations firm who manages a client's account

account for *vb* (*intr, preposition*) **1** to give reasons for (an event, act, etc) **2** to make or provide a reckoning of (expenditure, payments, etc) **3** to be responsible for destroying, killing, or putting (people, aircraft, etc) out of action

accounting (ə'kaʊntɪŋ) *n* the skill or practice of maintaining and auditing accounts and preparing reports on the assets, liabilities, etc, of a business

accoutre *or US* **accouter** (ə'ku:tə) *vb* (*tr; usually passive*) to provide with equipment or dress, esp military [c16: from Old French *accoustrer* to equip with clothing, ultimately related to Latin *consuere* to sew together]

accoutrement (ə'ku:trəmənt, ə'ku:tə-) *or US* **accouterment** (ə'ku:tərmənt) *n* **1** equipment worn by soldiers in addition to their clothing and weapons **2** (*usually plural*) clothing, equipment, etc; trappings: *the correct accoutrements for any form of sport*

Accra (ə'krɑ:) *n* the capital of Ghana, a port on the Gulf of Guinea: built on the site of three 17th-century trading fortresses founded by the English, Dutch, and Danish. Pop: 1 970 000 (2005 est)

accredit (ə'krɛdɪt) *vb* (*tr*) **1** to ascribe or attribute **2** to give official recognition to; sanction; authorize **3** to certify or guarantee as meeting required standards **4** (often foll by *at* or *to*) **a** to furnish or send (an envoy, etc) with official credentials **b** to appoint (someone) as an envoy, etc [c17: from French *accréditer*, from the phrase *mettre à crédit* to put to CREDIT] > **ac,credi'tation** *n*

accrete (ə'kri:t) *vb* **1** to grow or cause to grow together; be or become fused **2** to make or become bigger, as by addition [c18: back formation from ACCRETION]

accretion (ə'kri:ʃən) *n* **1** any gradual increase in size, as through growth or external addition **2** something added, esp extraneously, to cause growth or an increase in size **3** the growing together of normally separate plant or animal parts [c17: from Latin *accretiō* increase, from *accrēscere*. See ACCRUE] > **ac'cretive** *or* **ac'cretionary** *adj*

accrual (ə'kru:əl) *n* **1** the act of accruing **2** something that has accrued **3** *accounting* a charge incurred in one accounting period that has not been paid by the end of it

accrue (ə'kru:) *vb* **-crues, -cruing, -crued** (*intr*) **1** to increase by growth or addition, esp (of capital) to increase by periodic addition of interest **2** (often foll by *to*) to fall naturally (to); come into the possession (of); result (for) [C15: from Old French *accreue* growth, ultimately from Latin *accrēscere* to increase, from *ad-* to, in addition + *crēscere* to grow]

acculturate (ə'kʌltʃə,reɪt) *vb* (of a cultural or social group) to assimilate the cultural traits of another group [C20: from AD- + CULTURE + -ATE¹] > ac,cultur'ation *n*

accumulate (ə'kju:mjʊ,leɪt) *vb* to gather or become gathered together in an increasing quantity; amass; collect [C16: from Latin *accumulātus*, past participle of *accumulāre* to heap up, from *cumulus* to heap] > ac'cumulable *adj* > ac'cumulative *adj*

accumulation (ə,kju:mjʊ'leɪʃən) *n* **1** the act or process of collecting together or becoming collected **2** something that has been collected, gathered, heaped, etc **3** *finance* the continuous growth of capital by retention of interest or earnings

accumulator (ə'kju:mjʊ,leɪtə) *n* **1** Also called: **battery, storage battery** a rechargeable device for storing electrical energy in the form of chemical energy, consisting of one or more separate secondary cells **2** *horse racing, Brit* a collective bet, esp on four or more races, in which the stake and winnings on each successive race are carried forward to become the stake on the next, so that both stakes and winnings accumulate progressively so long as the bet continues to be a winning one **3** a register in a computer or calculator used for holding the results of a computation or data transfer

accuracy ('ækjʊrəsɪ) *n, pl* **-cies** faithful measurement or representation of the truth; correctness; precision

accurate ('ækjərɪt) *adj* **1** faithfully representing or describing the truth **2** showing a negligible or permissible deviation from a standard: *an accurate ruler* **3** without error; precise; meticulous **4** *maths* (to *n* significant digits) representing the first *n* digits of the given number starting with the first nonzero digit, but approximating to the nearest digit in the final position [C16: from Latin *accūrātus*, past participle of *accūrāre* to perform with care, from *cūra* care] > 'accurately *adv*

accursed (ə'kɜ:sɪd, ə'kɜ:st) *or* **accurst** (ə'kɜ:st) *adj* **1** under or subject to a curse; doomed **2** (*prenominal*) hateful; detestable; execrable [Old English *ācursod*, past participle of *ācursian* to put under a CURSE] > **accursedly** (ə'kɜ:sɪdlɪ) *adv* > ac'cursedness *n*

accusation (,ækjʊ'zeɪʃən) *n* **1** an allegation that a person is guilty of some fault, offence, or crime; imputation **2** a formal charge brought against a person stating the crime that he is alleged to have committed

accusative (ə'kju:zətɪv) *adj* **1** *grammar* denoting a case of nouns, pronouns, and adjectives in inflected languages that is used to identify the direct object of a finite verb, of certain prepositions, and for certain other purposes **2** another word for **accusatorial** ▷ **3** *grammar* the accusative case [C15: from Latin; in grammar, from the phrase *cāsus accūsātīvus* accusative case, a mistaken translation of Greek *ptōsis aitiatikē* the case indicating causation. See ACCUSE] > **accusatival** (ə,kju:zə'taɪvᵊl) *adj* > ac'cusatively *adv*

accusatorial (ə,kju:zə'tɔ:rɪəl) *or* **accusatory** (ə'kju:zətərɪ, -trɪ, ,ækjʊ'zeɪtərɪ) *adj* **1** containing or implying blame or strong criticism **2** *law* denoting criminal procedure in which the prosecutor is distinct from the judge and the trial is conducted in public. See **inquisitorial** (sense 3)

accuse (ə'kju:z) *vb* to charge (a person or persons) with some fault, offence, crime, etc; impute guilt or blame [C13: via Old French from Latin *accūsāre* to call to account, from *ad-* to + *causa* lawsuit] > ac'cuser *n* > ac'cusing *adj* > ac'cusingly *adv*

accused (ə'kju:zd) *n* **the accused** *law* the defendant or defendants appearing on a criminal charge

accustom (ə'kʌstəm) *vb* (*tr*; usually foll by *to*) to make (oneself) familiar (with) or used (to), as by practice, habit, or experience [C15: from Old French *acostumer*, from *costume* CUSTOM]

accustomed (ə'kʌstəmd) *adj* **1** usual; customary **2** (*postpositive*; foll by *to*) used or inured (to) **3** (*postpositive*; foll by *to*) in the habit (of): *accustomed to walking after meals*

AC/DC *adj informal* (of a person) bisexual [C20: humorous reference to electrical apparatus that is adaptable for ALTERNATING CURRENT and DIRECT CURRENT]

ace (eɪs) *n* **1** any die, domino, or any of four playing cards with one spot **2** a single spot or pip on a playing card, die, etc **3** *tennis* a winning serve that the opponent fails to reach **4** a fighter pilot accredited with destroying several enemy aircraft **5** *informal* an expert or highly skilled person: *an ace at driving* **6** **an ace up one's sleeve** *or* **an ace in the hole** a hidden and powerful advantage ▷ *adj* **7** *informal* superb; excellent [C13: via Old French from Latin *as* a unit, perhaps from a Greek variant of *heis* one]

-acea *suffix forming plural proper nouns* denoting animals belonging to a class or order: *Crustacea* (class); *Cetacea* (order) [New Latin, from Latin, neuter plural of *-āceus* -ACEOUS]

-aceae *suffix forming plural proper nouns* denoting plants belonging to a family: *Liliaceae; Ranunculaceae* [New Latin, from Latin, feminine plural of *-āceus* -ACEOUS]

acedia (ə'si:dɪə) *n* another word for **accidie**

Aceh ('a:tʃeɪ) *n* an autonomous region of N Indonesia, in N Sumatra; mountainous with rain forests; scene of separatist conflict since the later 1990s; coastal areas suffered badly in the Indian Ocean tsunami of December 2004. Capital: Banda Aceh. Pop: 3 930 905 (2000). Area: 55 392 sq km (21 381 sq miles)

ACE inhibitor *n* any one of a class of drugs, including captopril, enalapril, and ramipril, that cause the arteries to widen by preventing the synthesis of angiotensin: used to treat high blood pressure and heart failure [C20: from *a*(*ngiotensin-*)*c*(*onverting*) *e*(*nzyme*) *inhibitor*]

-aceous *suffix forming adjectives* relating to, belonging to, having the nature of, or resembling: *herbaceous; larvaceous* [New Latin, from Latin *-āceus* of a certain kind; related to *-āc, -āx*, adjectival suffix]

acephalous (ə'sefələs) *adj* having no head or one that is reduced and indistinct, as certain insect larvae [C18: via Medieval Latin from Greek *akephalos*. See A-¹, -CEPHALIC]

acer ('eɪsə) *n* any tree or shrub of the genus *Acer*, often cultivated for their brightly coloured foliage. See also **maple**

acerbate ('æsə,beɪt) *vb* (*tr*) **1** to embitter or exasperate **2** to make sour or bitter [C18: from Latin *acerbātus*, past participle of *acerbāre* to make sour]

acerbic (ə'sɜ:bɪk) *adj* harsh, bitter, or astringent; sour [C17: from Latin *acerbus* sour, bitter]

acerbity (ə'sɜ:bɪtɪ) *n, pl* **-ties** **1** vitriolic or embittered speech, temper, etc **2** sourness or bitterness of taste

acerola (,æsɪ'rəʊlə) *n* **1** a small tree or shrub, *Malpighia glabra*, that grows in the rainforests of N South America, Central America, and Jamaica **2** the small, soft, bright red fruit of this tree, which looks like a cherry but has a sharp flavour ▷ Also called: **Amazon cherry** [C21: from Portuguese]

acetabulum (,æsɪ'tæbjʊləm) *n, pl* **-la** (-lə) the deep cuplike cavity on the side of the hipbone that receives the head of the thighbone [Latin: vinegar cup, hence a cuplike cavity, from *acētum* vinegar + *-abulum*, suffix denoting a container]

acetal ('æsɪ,tæl) *n* 1,1-diethoxyethane; a colourless volatile liquid used as a solvent and in perfumes. Formula: $CH_3CH(OC_2H_5)_2$ [C19: from German *Azetal*, from ACETO- + ALCOHOL]

acetaldehyde (,æsɪ'tældɪ,haɪd) *n* a colourless volatile pungent liquid, miscible with water, used in the manufacture of organic compounds and as a solvent and reducing agent. Formula: CH_3CHO. Systematic name: **ethanal**

acetanilide (,æsɪ'tænɪ,laɪd) *or* **acetanilid** (,æsɪ'tænɪlɪd) *n* a white crystalline powder used in the manufacture of dyes and rubber, as an analgesic in medicine, and as a precursor in penicillin manufacture. Formula:

$C_6H_5NHCOCH_3$ [C19: from ACETO- + ANILINE + -IDE]

acetate ('æsɪˌteɪt) *n* **1** any salt or ester of acetic acid, containing the monovalent ion CH_3COO^- or the group CH_3COO- **2** short for **acetate rayon, cellulose acetate** **3** a sound recording disc composed of an acetate lacquer coating on an aluminium or plastic base: used for demonstration or other short-term purposes [C19: from ACETIC + -ATE^1]

acetate rayon *n* a synthetic textile fibre made from cellulose acetate

acetic (ə'si:tɪk, ə'set-) *adj* of, containing, producing, or derived from acetic acid or vinegar [C19: from Latin *acētum* vinegar]

acetic acid *n* a colourless pungent liquid, miscible with water, widely used in the manufacture of acetic anhydride, vinyl acetate, plastics, pharmaceuticals, dyes, etc. Formula: CH_3COOH. Systematic name: ethanoic acid

acetify (ə'setɪˌfaɪ) *vb* -fies, -fying, -fied to become or cause to become acetic acid or vinegar > aˌcetifiˈcation *n*

aceto- or before a vowel **acet-** *combining form* containing an acetyl group or derived from acetic acid: *acetone* [from Latin *acētum* vinegar]

acetone ('æsɪˌtəʊn) *n* a colourless volatile flammable pungent liquid, miscible with water, used in the manufacture of chemicals and as a solvent and thinner for paints, varnishes, and lacquers. Formula: CH_3COCH_3 [C19: from German *Azeton*, from ACETO- + -ONE]

acetous ('æsɪtəs, ə'si:-) or **acetose** ('æsɪˌtəʊs, -ˌtəʊz) *adj* **1** containing, producing, or resembling acetic acid or vinegar **2** tasting like vinegar [C18: from Late Latin *acētōsus* vinegary, from *acētum* vinegar]

acetyl ('æsɪˌtaɪl, ə'si:taɪl) *n* (*modifier*) of, consisting of, or containing the monovalent group CH_3CO- [C19: from ACET(IC) + -YL]

acetylcholine (ˌæsɪtaɪl'kəʊli:n, -lɪn) *n* a chemical substance secreted at the ends of many nerve fibres, esp in the autonomic nervous system, and responsible for the transmission of nervous impulses. Formula: $CH_3CO_2(CH_2)_2N(CH_3)_3^+$

acetylene (ə'setɪˌli:n) *n* **1** a colourless flammable gas used in the manufacture of organic chemicals and in cutting and welding metals. Formula: C_2H_2. Systematic name: ethyne **2** another name for **alkyne**

acetylsalicylic acid (ˌæsɪtaɪlˌsælɪ'sɪlɪk, ə'si:taɪl-) *n* the chemical name for **aspirin**

Achaea (ə'ki:ə) or **Achaia** (ə'kaɪə) *n* **1** a department of Greece, in the N Peloponnese. Capital: Patras. Pop: 318 928 (2001). Area: 3209 sq km (1239 sq miles). Modern Greek name: Akhaïa **2** a province of ancient Greece, in the N Peloponnese on the Gulf of Corinth: enlarged as a Roman province in 27 BC

Achaean (ə'ki:ən) or **Achaian** (ə'kaɪən) *n* **1** a member of a principal Greek tribe in the Mycenaean era ▷ *adj* **2** of or relating to Achaea or the Achaeans

Achates (ə'keɪti:z) *n* **1** *classical myth* Aeneas' faithful companion in Virgil's *Aeneid* **2** a loyal friend

ache (eɪk) *vb* (*intr*) **1** to feel, suffer, or be the source of a continuous dull pain **2** to suffer mental anguish ▷ *n* **3** a continuous dull pain [Old English *ācan* (vb), *æce* (n), Middle English *aken* (vb), *ache* (n). Compare BAKE, BATCH] > 'aching *adj*

Achebe (ə'tʃeɪbɪ) *n* Chinua. born 1930, Nigerian novelist. His works include *Things Fall Apart* (1958), *A Man of the People* (1966), and *Anthills of the Savannah* (1987)

Achelous (ˌækɪ'ləʊəs) *n* *classical myth* a river god who changed into a snake and a bull while fighting Hercules but was defeated when Hercules broke off one of his horns

achene or **akene** (ə'ki:n) *n* a dry one-seeded indehiscent fruit with the seed distinct from the fruit wall. It may be smooth, as in the buttercup, or feathery, as in clematis [C19: from New Latin *achaenium* that which does not yawn or open, from A-^{1} + Greek *khainein* to yawn]

Acheron ('ækəˌrɒn) *n* *Greek myth* **1** one of the rivers in Hades over which the souls of the dead were ferried by Charon. See **Styx** **2** the underworld or Hades

Acheson ('ætʃɪsən) *n* **Dean** (**Gooderham**). 1893–1971, US lawyer and statesman: secretary of state (1949–53) under President Truman

Acheulian or **Acheulean** (ə'ʃu:lɪən, -jən) *archaeol* ▷ *n* **1** (in Europe) the period in the Lower Palaeolithic following the Abbevillian, represented by the use of soft hammerstones in hand axe production made of chipped stone, bone, antler, or wood. The Acheulian dates from the Riss glaciation **2** (in Africa) the period represented by every stage of hand axe development ▷ *adj* **3** of or relating to this period [C20: after St *Acheul*, town in northern France]

achieve (ə'tʃi:v) *vb* (*tr*) **1** to bring to a successful conclusion; accomplish; attain **2** to gain as by hard work or effort: *to achieve success* [C14: from Old French *achever* to bring to an end, from the phrase *a chef* to a head, to a conclusion] > a'chievable *adj* > a'chiever *n*

achievement (ə'tʃi:vmənt) *n* **1** something that has been accomplished, esp by hard work, ability, or heroism **2** successful completion; accomplishment

achillea (ˌækɪ'li:ə) *n* any plant of the N temperate genus *Achillea*, with white, yellow, or purple flowers, some species of which are widely grown as garden plants: family *Asteraceae* (composites) [from ACHILLES, who was credited with discovering medicinal properties in the plant]

Achilles (ə'kɪli:z) *n* *Greek myth* Greek hero, the son of Peleus and the sea goddess Thetis: in the *Iliad* the foremost of the Greek warriors at the siege of Troy. While he was a baby his mother plunged him into the river Styx making his body invulnerable except for the heel by which she held him. After slaying Hector, he was killed by Paris who wounded him in the heel > Achillean (ˌækɪ'li:ən) *adj*

Achilles heel *n* a small but fatal weakness

Achilles tendon *n* the fibrous cord that connects the muscles of the calf to the heelbone

Achill Island ('ækɪl) *n* an island in the Republic of Ireland, off the W coast of Co Mayo. Area: 148 sq km (57 sq miles). Pop: 2620 (2002)

Achitophel (ə'kɪtəˌfɛl) *n* *Bible* the Douay spelling of **Ahithophel**

achromat ('ækrəˌmæt) *n* Also called: **achromatic lens** a lens designed to bring light of two chosen wavelengths to the same focal point, thus reducing chromatic aberration

achromatic (ˌækrə'mætɪk) *adj* **1** without colour **2** capable of reflecting or refracting light without chromatic aberration **3** *music* involving no sharps or flats > ˌachro'matically *adv* > achromatism (ə'krəʊməˌtɪzəm) or achromaticity (əˌkrəʊmə'tɪsɪtɪ) *n*

acid ('æsɪd) *n* **1** any substance that dissociates in water to yield a sour corrosive solution containing hydrogen ions, having a pH of less than 7, and turning litmus red **2** a sour-tasting substance **3** a slang name for **LSD** ▷ *adj* **4** *chem* **a** of, derived from, or containing acid **b** being or having the properties of an acid **5** sharp or sour in taste **6** cutting, sharp, or hurtful in speech, manner, etc; vitriolic; caustic [C17: (first used by Francis Bacon): from French *acide* or Latin *acidus*, from *acēre* to be sour or sharp] > 'acidly *adv* > 'acidness *n*

acid-fast *adj* (of bacteria and tissues) resistant to decolorization by mineral acids after staining

Acid House or **Acid** *n* a type of funk-based electronically edited disco music of the late 1980s, which has hypnotic sound effects and is associated with hippy culture and the use of the drug ecstasy [C20: perhaps from ACID (LSD) + HOUSE (MUSIC)]

acidic (ə'sɪdɪk) *adj* another word for **acid**

acidify (ə'sɪdɪˌfaɪ) *vb* -fies, -fying, -fied to convert into or become acid > a'cidiˌfiable *adj* > aˌcidifi'cation *n*

acidity (ə'sɪdɪtɪ) *n, pl* -ties **1** the quality or state of being acid **2** the amount of acid present in a solution, often expressed in terms of pH

acidosis (ˌæsɪ'dəʊsɪs) *n* a condition characterized by an abnormal increase in the acidity of the blood and extracellular fluids > acidotic (ˌæsɪ'dɒtɪk) *adj*

acid rain *n* rain that contains a high concentration of pollutants, chiefly sulphur dioxide and nitrogen oxide, released into the atmosphere by the burning of fossil fuels such as coal or oil

a

acid reflux *n* the regurgitation of stomach acid into the oesophagus, causing heartburn

acid rock *n* a type of rock music characterized by electronically amplified bizarre instrumental effects [C20: from ACID (sense 3), alluding to its supposed inspiration by drug-induced states of consciousness]

acid test *n* a rigorous and conclusive test to establish worth or value [C19: from the testing of gold with nitric acid]

acidulate (ə'sɪdjʊˌleɪt) *vb* (*tr*) to make slightly acid or sour [C18: ACIDULOUS + -ATE¹] > a,cidu'lation *n*

acidulous (ə'sɪdjʊləs) *or* **acidulent** *adj* **1** rather sour **2** sharp or sour in speech, manner, etc; acid [C18: from Latin *acidulus* sourish, diminutive of *acidus* sour]

acinus ('æsɪnəs) *n*, *pl* -ni (-ˌnaɪ) **1** *anatomy* any of the terminal saclike portions of a compound gland **2** *botany* any of the small drupes that make up the fruit of the blackberry, raspberry, etc **3** *botany* *obsolete* a collection of berries, such as a bunch of grapes [C18: New Latin, from Latin: grape, berry]

Acis ('eɪsɪs) *n* *Greek myth* a Sicilian shepherd and the lover of the nymph Galatea. In jealousy, Polyphemus crushed him with a huge rock, and his blood was turned by Galatea into a river

ack-ack ('æk,æk) *n* *military* **a** anti-aircraft fire **b** (*as modifier*): *ack-ack guns* [C20: British army World War I phonetic alphabet for AA, abbreviation of *anti-aircraft*]

acknowledge (ək'nɒlɪdʒ) *vb* (*tr*) **1** (*may take a clause as object*) to recognize or admit the existence, truth, or reality of **2** to indicate recognition or awareness of, as by a greeting, glance, etc **3** to express appreciation or thanks for **4** to make the receipt of known to the sender: *to acknowledge a letter* **5** to recognize, esp in legal form, the authority, rights, or claims of [C15: probably from earlier *knowledge*, on the model of Old English *oncnāwan*, Middle English *aknowen* to confess, recognize] > ac'knowledgeable *adj*

acknowledgment *or* **acknowledgement** (ək'nɒlɪdʒmənt) *n* **1** the act of acknowledging or state of being acknowledged **2** something done or given as an expression of thanks, as a reply to a message, etc **3** (*plural*) an author's statement acknowledging his use of the works of other authors, usually printed at the front of a book

ACL *abbreviation* anterior cruciate ligament

aclinic line (ə'klɪnɪk) *n* another name for **magnetic equator** [C19: *aclinic*, from Greek *aklinēs* not bending, from A-¹ + *klinein* to bend, lean]

acme ('ækmɪ) *n* the culminating point, as of achievement or excellence; summit; peak [C16: from Greek *akmē*]

acne ('æknɪ) *n* Also called: **acne vulgaris** a chronic skin disease common in adolescence, involving inflammation of the sebaceous glands and characterized by pustules on the face, neck, and upper trunk. See also **rosacea** [C19: New Latin, from a misreading of Greek *akmē* eruption on the face. See ACME]

acolyte ('ækəˌlaɪt) *n* **1** a follower or attendant **2** *Christianity* an officer who attends or assists a priest [C16: via Old French and Medieval Latin from Greek *akolouthos* a follower]

Aconcagua (*Spanish* akoŋ'kaɣwa) *n* a mountain in W Argentina: the highest peak in the Andes and in the W Hemisphere. Height: 6960 m (22 835 ft)

aconite ('ækəˌnaɪt) *n* **1** any of various N temperate plants of the ranunculaceous genus *Aconitum*, such as monkshood and wolfsbane, many of which are poisonous. See **winter aconite** **2** the dried poisonous root of many of these plants, sometimes used as an antipyretic [C16: via Old French or Latin from Greek *akoniton* aconite, monkshood] > aconitic (ˌækə'nɪtɪk) *adj*

Açores (ə'sorəʃ) *n* the Portuguese name for (the) **Azores**

acorn ('eɪkɔːn) *n* the fruit of an oak tree, consisting of a smooth thick-walled nut in a woody scaly cuplike base [C16: a variant (through influence of *corn*) of Old English *æcern* the fruit of a tree, acorn; related to Gothic *akran* fruit, yield]

acoustic (ə'kuːstɪk) *or* **acoustical** *adj* **1** of or related to sound, the sense of hearing, or acoustics **2** designed to respond to, absorb, or control sound: *an acoustic tile* **3** (of a musical instrument or recording) without electronic amplification: *an acoustic bass; an acoustic guitar* [C17: from Greek *akoustikos*, from *akouein* to hear] > a'coustically *adv*

acoustic neuroma *n* a benign brain tumour of the vestibulocochlear nerve, one of the nerves connecting the ear to the brain, which can cause hearing and balance problems

acoustics (ə'kuːstɪks) *n* (*functioning as singular*) the scientific study of sound and sound waves

acoustic shock *n* a condition characterized by dizziness and partial hearing loss suffered by some people exposed to sudden loud noises over telephone or radio headsets; associated esp with workers in call centres

acquaint (ə'kweɪnt) *vb* (*tr*)(foll by *with* or *of*) to make (a person) familiar or conversant (with); inform (of) [C13: via Old French and Medieval Latin from Latin *accognitus*, from *accognōscere* to know perfectly, from *ad-* (intensive) + *cognōscere* to know]

acquaintance (ə'kweɪntəns) *n* **1** a person with whom one has been in contact but who is not a close friend **2** knowledge of a person or thing, esp when slight **3** make the acquaintance of to come into social contact with **4** those persons collectively whom one knows > ac'quaintance,ship *n*

acquaintance violence *n* impulsive aggressive behaviour towards someone with whom the attacker has been in contact

acquainted (ə'kweɪntɪd) *adj* (*postpositive*) **1** (sometimes foll by *with*) on terms of familiarity but not intimacy **2** (foll by *with*) having knowledge or experience (of); familiar (with)

acquiesce (ˌækwɪ'ɛs) *vb* (*intr*; often foll by *in* or *to*) to comply (with); assent (to) without protest [C17: from Latin *acquiēscere* to remain at rest, agree without protest, from *ad-* at + *quiēscere* to rest, from *quiēs* QUIET] > ,acqui'escence *n*

acquire (ə'kwaɪə) *vb* (*tr*) to get or gain (something, such as an object, trait, or ability), esp more or less permanently [C15: via Old French from Latin *acquīrere*, from *ad-* in addition + *quaerere* to get, seek] > ac'quirable *adj* > ac'quirement *n*

acquired behaviour *n* *psychol* the behaviour of an organism resulting from the effects of the environment

acquired characteristic *n* a characteristic of an organism that results from increased use or disuse of an organ or the effects of the environment and cannot be inherited

acquired immune deficiency syndrome *or* **acquired immunodeficiency syndrome** *n* the full name for: AIDS

acquired immunity *n* the immunity produced by exposure of an organism to antigens, which stimulates the production of antibodies

acquired taste *n* **1** a liking for something that is at first considered unpleasant **2** the thing so liked

acquisition (ˌækwɪ'zɪʃən) *n* **1** the act of acquiring or gaining possession **2** something acquired **3** a person or thing of special merit added to a group [C14: from Latin *acquīsitiōn-*, from *acquīrere* to ACQUIRE]

acquisitive (ə'kwɪzɪtɪv) *adj* inclined or eager to acquire things, esp material possessions > ac'quisitively *adv* > ac'quisitiveness *n*

acquit (ə'kwɪt) *vb* -quits, -quitting, -quitted (*tr*) **1** (foll by *of*) **a** to free or release (from a charge of crime) **b** to pronounce not guilty **2** (foll by *of*) to free or relieve (from an obligation, duty, responsibility, etc) **3** to repay or settle (something, such as a debt or obligation) **4** to perform (one's part); conduct (oneself) [C13: from Old French *aquiter*, from *quiter* to release, free from, QUIT] > ac'quitter *n* > ac'quittal *n*

acquittance (ə'kwɪtəns) *n* **1** a release from or settlement of a debt, etc **2** a record of this, such as a receipt

acre ('eɪkə) *n* **1** a unit of area used in certain English-speaking countries, equal to 4840 square yards or 4046.86 square metres **2** (*plural*) **a** land, esp a large area **b** *informal* a large amount **3** *farm* the long acre NZ to graze cows on the verge of a road [Old English *æcer* field, acre; related to Old Norse *akr*, German *Acker*, Latin *ager* field, Sanskrit *ajra* field]

Acre *n* **1** ('ɑ:krə) a state of W Brazil: mostly unexplored tropical forests; acquired from Bolivia in 1903. Capital: Rio Branco. Pop: 586 942 (2002). Area: 152 589 sq km (58 899 sq miles) **2** ('eɪkə, 'ɑ:kə) a city and port in N Israel, strategically situated on the **Bay of Acre** in the E Mediterranean: taken and retaken during the Crusades (1104, 1187, 1191, 1291), taken by the Turks (1517), by Egypt (1832), and by the Turks again (1839). Pop: 45 600 (2001)

acreage ('eɪkərɪdʒ) *n* **1** land area in acres ▷ *adj* **2** *Austral* of or relating to a large allotment of land, esp in a rural area

acrid ('ækrɪd) *adj* **1** unpleasantly pungent or sharp to the smell or taste **2** sharp or caustic, esp in speech or nature [c18: from Latin *ācer* sharp, sour; probably formed on the model of ACID] > acridity (ə'krɪdɪtɪ) *or* 'acridness *n* > 'acridly *adv*

acridine ('ækrɪˌdi:n) *n* a colourless crystalline solid used in the manufacture of dyes. Formula: $C_{13}H_9N$

acriflavine (ˌækrɪ'fleɪvɪn, -vi:n) *n* a brownish or orange-red powder used in medicine as an antiseptic and disinfectant. Formula: $C_{14}H_{14}N_3Cl$ [c20: from ACRIDINE + FLAVIN]

acriflavine hydrochloride *n* a red crystalline water-soluble solid substance obtained from acriflavine and used as an antiseptic

Acrilan ('ækrɪˌlæn) *n trademark* an acrylic fibre or fabric, characterized by strength, softness, and crease-resistance and used for clothing, upholstery, carpets, etc

acrimony ('ækrɪmənɪ) *n, pl* -nies bitterness or sharpness of manner, speech, temper, etc [c16: from Latin *ācrimōnia*, from *ācer* sharp, sour] > acrimonious (ˌækrɪ'məʊnɪəs) *adj* > ˌacri'moniously *adv* > ˌacri'moniousness *n*

acro- *combining form* **1** denoting something at a height, summit, top, tip, beginning, or end: *acropolis; acrogen* **2** denoting an extremity of the human body: *acromegaly* [from Greek *akros* extreme, topmost]

acrobat ('ækrəˌbæt) *n* **1** an entertainer who performs acts that require skill, agility, and coordination, such as tumbling, swinging from a trapeze, or walking a tightrope **2** a person noted for his frequent and rapid changes of position or allegiances: *a political acrobat* [c19: via French from Greek *akrobatēs* acrobat, one who walks on tiptoe, from ACRO- + *bat-*, from *bainein* to walk] > ˌacro'batic *adj* > ˌacro'batically *adv*

acrobatics (ˌækrə'bætɪks) *n* **1** (*functioning as plural*) the skills or feats of an acrobat **2** (*functioning as plural*) any activity requiring agility and skill: *mental acrobatics*

acrogen ('ækrədʒən) *n* any flowerless plant, such as a fern or moss, in which growth occurs from the tip of the main stem [c19: from ACRO- + Greek *genēs* born; see -GEN] > acrogenic (ˌækrə'dʒenɪk) *or* acrogenous (ə'krɒdʒɪnəs) *adj*

acrolein (ə'krəʊlɪɪn) *n* a colourless or yellowish flammable poisonous pungent liquid used in the manufacture of resins and pharmaceuticals. Formula: CH_2:CHCHO [c19: from Latin *ācer* sharp + *olēre* to smell + -IN]

acromegaly (ˌækrəʊ'megəlɪ) *n* a chronic disease characterized by enlargement of the bones of the head, hands, and feet, and swelling and enlargement of soft tissue, esp the tongue. It is caused by excessive secretion of growth hormone by the pituitary gland [c19: from French *acromégalie*, from ACRO- + Greek *megal-*, stem of *megas* big] > acromegalic (ˌækrəʊmɪ'gælɪk) *adj, n*

acronym ('ækrənɪm) *n* a pronounceable name made up of a series of initial letters or parts of words; for example, *UNESCO* for the *United Nations Educational, Scientific, and Cultural Organization* [c20: from ACRO- + -ONYM]

acrophobia (ˌækrə'fəʊbɪə) *n* abnormal fear or dread of being at a great height [c19: from ACRO- + -PHOBIA] > ˌacro'phobic *adj, n*

acropolis (ə'krɒpəlɪs) *n* the citadel of an ancient Greek city [c17: from Greek, from ACRO- + *polis* city]

Acropolis (ə'krɒpəlɪs) *n* the citadel of Athens on which the Parthenon and the Erechtheum stand

acrosome ('ækrəˌsəʊm) *n* a cap-like structure on the tip

of a spermatozoon that releases enzymes on encountering the ovum allowing fusion with the ovum in the sexual reproductive process; this part of the process is known as the acrosome reaction [c19: from ACRO- + -SOME³]

across (ə'krɒs) *prep* **1** from one side to the other side of **2** on or at the other side of **3** so as to transcend boundaries or barriers: *people united across borders by religion and history; the study of linguistics across cultures* ▷ *adv* **4** from one side to the other **5** on or to the other side [c13: on *croice, acros*, from Old French *a croix* crosswise]

across-the-board *adj* (of salary increases, taxation cuts, etc) affecting all levels or classes equally

acrostic (ə'krɒstɪk) *n* a number of lines of writing, such as a poem, certain letters of which form a word, proverb, etc. A **single acrostic** is formed by the initial letters of the lines, a **double acrostic** by the initial and final letters, and a **triple acrostic** by the initial, middle, and final letters [c16: via French from Greek *akrostikhis*, from ACRO- + *stikhos* line of verse, STICH]

acrylic (ə'krɪlɪk) *adj* **1** of, derived from, or concerned with acrylic acid ▷ *n* **2** short for **acrylic fibre, acrylic resin** [c20: from ACROLEIN + -YL + -IC]

acrylic acid *n* a colourless corrosive pungent liquid, miscible with water, used in the manufacture of acrylic resins. Formula: CH_2:CHCOOH

acrylic fibre *n* a textile fibre, such as Orlon or Acrilan, produced from acrylonitrile

acrylic resin *n* any of a group of polymers or copolymers of acrylic acid, its esters, or amides, used as synthetic rubbers, textiles, paints, adhesives, and as plastics such as Perspex

act (ækt) *n* **1** something done or performed; a deed **2** the performance of some physical or mental process; action **3** (*capital when part of a name*) the formally codified result of deliberation by a legislative body; a law, edict, decree, statute, etc **4** (*often plural*) a formal written record of transactions, proceedings, etc, as of a society, committee, or legislative body **5** a major division of a dramatic work **6 a** a short performance of skill, a comic sketch, dance, etc, esp one that is part of a programme of light entertainment **b** those giving such a performance **7** an assumed attitude or pose, esp one intended to impress ▷ *vb* **8** (*intr*) to do something; carry out an action **9** (*intr*) to function in a specified way; operate; react: *his mind acted quickly* **10** to perform (a part or role) in a play, etc **11** (*tr*) to present (a play, etc) on stage **12** (*intr; usually foll by for or as*) to be a substitute (for); function in place (of) **13** (*intr; foll by as*) to serve the function or purpose (of) **14** (*intr*) to conduct oneself or behave (as if one were): *she usually acts like a lady* **15** (*intr*) to behave in an unnatural or affected way **16** (*copula*) to pose as; play the part of: *to act the fool* **17** (*copula*) to behave in a manner appropriate to (esp in the phrase **act one's age**) **18** get in on the act *informal* to become involved in a profitable undertaking or advantageous situation in order to share in the benefits **19** get one's act together *informal* to become organized or prepared ▷ See also **act on, act up** [c14: from Latin *actus* a doing, performance, and *actum* a thing done, from the past participle of *agere* to do] > 'actable *adj* > ˌacta'bility *n*

ACT¹ *abbreviation* **1** Australian Capital Territory **2** (formerly in Britain) advance corporation tax

ACT² (ækt) *n acronym for* (in New Zealand) Association of Consumers and Taxpayers: a small political party of the right

Actaeon (æk'ti:ən, 'æktɪən) *n Greek myth* a hunter of Boeotia who, having accidentally seen Artemis bathing, was turned into a stag and torn apart by his own hounds

ACTH *n* adrenocorticotrophic hormone; a polypeptide hormone, secreted by the anterior lobe of the pituitary gland, that stimulates growth of the adrenal gland and the synthesis and secretion of corticosteroids. It is used in treating rheumatoid arthritis, allergic and skin diseases, and many other disorders. Also called: corticotrophin

acting ('æktɪŋ) *adj* (*prenominal*) **1** taking on duties temporarily, esp as a substitute for another **2** operating or functioning **3** intended for stage performance; provided with directions for actors: *an acting version of "Hedda Gabler"* ▷ *n* **4** the art or profession of an actor

actinia (æk'tɪnɪə) *n, pl* **-tiniae** (-'tɪnɪ,iː) *or* **-tinias** any sea anemone of the genus *Actinia*, which are common in rock pools [c18: New Latin, literally: things having a radial structure. See ACTINO-, -IA]

actinic (æk'tɪnɪk) *adj* (of radiation) producing a photochemical effect [c19: from ACTINO- + -IC] > ac'tinically *adv* > 'actin,ism *n*

actinide ('æktɪ,naɪd) *n* a member of the actinide series. Also called: **actinon** [c19: from ACTINO- + -IDE]

actinide series *n* a series of 15 radioactive elements with increasing atomic numbers from actinium to lawrencium

actinium (æk'tɪnɪəm) *n* a radioactive element of the actinide series, occurring as a decay product of uranium. It is used as an alpha-particle source and in neutron production. Symbol: Ac; atomic no: 89; half-life of most stable isotope,^{227}Ac: 21.6 years; relative density: 10.07; melting pt: 1051°C; boiling pt: 3200 ± 300°C [c19: New Latin, from ACTINO- + -IUM]

actino- *or before a vowel* **actin-** *combining form* **1** indicating a radial structure: *actinomorphic* **2** indicating radioactivity or radiation: *actinometer* [from Greek *aktino-*, from *aktis* beam, ray]

actinoid ('æktɪ,nɔɪd) *adj* having a radiate form, as a sea anemone or starfish

actinometer (,æktɪ'nɒmɪtə) *n* an instrument for measuring the intensity of radiation, esp of the sun's rays

actinomorphic (,æktɪnəʊ'mɔːfɪk) *or* **actinomorphous** *adj botany* (esp of a flower) having radial symmetry, as buttercups

actinomycin (,æktɪnəʊ'maɪsɪn) *n* any of several toxic antibiotics obtained from bacteria of the genus *Streptomyces*, used in treating some cancers; the most commonly used is dactinomycin (actinomycin D)

actinozoan (,æktɪnəʊ'zəʊən) *n, adj* another word for **anthozoan**

action ('ækʃən) *n* **1** the state or process of doing something or being active; operation **2** something done, such as an act or deed **3** movement or posture during some physical activity **4** activity, force, or energy: *a man of action* **5** (*usually plural*) conduct or behaviour **6** *law* a legal proceeding brought by one party against another, seeking redress of a wrong or recovery of what is due; lawsuit **7** the operating mechanism, esp in a piano, gun, watch, etc **8** the force applied to a body **9** the way in which something operates or works **10** out of action not functioning **11** the events that form the plot of a story, film, play, or other composition **12** *military* **a** a minor engagement **b** fighting at sea or on land: *he saw action in the war* **13** *Brit* short for **industrial action** **14** *informal* the profits of an enterprise or transaction (esp in the phrase **a piece of the action**) **15** *slang* the main activity, esp social activity ▷ *vb* (*tr*) **16** to put into effect; take action concerning ▷ *interj* **17** a command given by a film director to indicate that filming is to begin [c14: *accioun*, ultimately from Latin *āctiōn-*, stem of *āctiō*, from *agere* to do, act]

actionable ('ækʃənəbᵊl) *adj law* affording grounds for legal action > 'actionably *adv*

action painting *n* a development of abstract expressionism evolved in the 1940s, characterized by broad vigorous brush strokes and accidental effects of thrown, smeared, dripped, or spattered paint. Also called: **tachisme**

action replay *n* the rerunning of a small section of a television film or tape of a match or other sporting contest, often in slow motion

action stations *pl n* **1** *military* the positions taken up by individuals in preparation for or during a battle ▷ *interj* **2** *military* a command to take up such positions **3** *informal* a warning to get ready for something

Actium ('æktɪəm) *n* a town of ancient Greece that overlooked the naval battle in 31 BC at which Octavian's fleet under Agrippa defeated that of Mark Antony and Cleopatra

activate ('æktɪ,veɪt) *vb* (*tr*) **1** to make active or capable of action **2** *physics* to make radioactive **3** *chem* to increase the rate of (a reaction) **4** to purify (sewage) by aeration **5** *US military* to create, mobilize, or organize (a unit) > ,acti'vation *n* > 'acti,vator *n*

activated carbon *n* a porous highly adsorptive form of carbon used to remove colour or impurities from liquids and gases, in the separation and extraction of chemical compounds, and in the recovery of solvents

activated sludge *n* a mass of aerated precipitated sewage added to untreated sewage to bring about purification by hastening decomposition by microorganisms

active ('æktɪv) *adj* **1** in a state of action; moving, working, or doing something **2** busy or involved: *an active life* **3** physically energetic **4** exerting influence; effective: *an active ingredient* **5** *grammar* denoting a voice of verbs used to indicate that the subject of a sentence is performing the action or causing the event or process described by the verb, as *kicked* in *The boy kicked the football* **6** being fully engaged in military service (esp in the phrase **on active service**) **7** (of a volcano) erupting periodically; not extinct **8** *astronomy* (of the sun) exhibiting a large number of sunspots, solar flares, etc, and a marked variation in intensity and frequency of radio emission ▷ *n* **9** *grammar* **a** the active voice **b** an active verb [c14: from Latin *āctīvus*. See ACT, -IVE] > 'actively *adv* > 'activeness *n*

active list *n military* a list of officers available for full duty

active matrix *n computing* **a** a liquid crystal display in which each pixel is individually controlled to provide a sharp image at a wide viewing angle; it is used in laptop and notebook computers **b** (*as modifier*): *an active-matrix screen*

activism ('æktɪ,vɪzəm) *n* a policy of taking direct and often militant action to achieve an end, esp a political or social one > 'activist *n*

activity (æk'tɪvɪtɪ) *n, pl* **-ties** **1** the state or quality of being active **2** lively action or movement **3** any specific deed, action, pursuit, etc: *recreational activities* **4** the number of disintegrations of a radioactive substance in a given unit of time, usually expressed in curies or disintegrations per second **5** the capacity of a substance to undergo chemical change

act of God *n law* a sudden and inevitable occurrence caused by natural forces and not by the agency of man, such as a flood, earthquake, or a similar catastrophe

Acton ('æktən) *n* **1 John Emerich Edward Dalberg,** 1st Baron. 1834–1902, English historian: a proponent of Christian liberal ethics and adviser of Gladstone **2** his grandfather, Sir **John Francis Edward.** 1736–1811, European naval commander and statesman: admiral of Tuscany (1774–79) and Naples (1779 onwards) and chief minister of Naples (1779–1806)

act on *or* **act upon** *vb* (*intr, preposition*) **1** to regulate one's behaviour in accordance with (advice, information, etc) **2** to have an effect on (illness, a part of the body, etc)

actor ('æktə) *n* a person who acts in a play, film, broadcast, etc

actress ('æktrɪs) *n* **1** a woman who acts in a play, film, broadcast, etc **2** *informal* a woman who puts on a false manner in order to deceive others
  ⊜ USAGE Use of the word *actress* to refer to a female who
  ⊜ acts is old-fashioned. Gender-neutral form: *actor*

actual ('æktʃʊəl) *adj* **1** existing in reality or as a matter of fact **2** real or genuine **3** existing at the present time; current ▷ See also **actuals** [c14: *actuel* existing, from Late Latin *āctuālis* relating to acts, practical, from Latin *āctus* ACT]

actual bodily harm *n criminal law* injury caused by one person to another that interferes with the health or comfort of the victim. Abbreviation: ABH

actuality (,æktʃʊ'ælɪtɪ) *n, pl* **-ties** **1** true existence; reality **2** (*sometimes plural*) a fact or condition that is real

actualize *or* **actualise** ('æktʃʊə,laɪz) *vb* (*tr*) **1** to make actual or real **2** to represent realistically > ,actuali'zation *or* ,actuali'sation *n*

actually ('æktʃʊəlɪ) *adv* **1 a** as an actual fact; really **b** (*as* *sentence modifier*): *actually, I haven't seen him* **2** at present

actuals ('æktʃʊəlz) *pl n* See **physicals**

actuary ('æktʃʊərɪ) *n, pl* **-aries** a person qualified to calculate commercial risks and probabilities involving uncertain future events, esp in such contexts as life assurance [c16: (meaning: registrar): from Latin *āctuārius* one who keeps accounts, from *actum* public business, and *acta* documents, deeds. See ACT, -ARY] > **actuarial** (,æktʃʊ'eərɪəl) *adj*

actuate ('æktʃʊ,eɪt) *vb* (*tr*) **1** to put into action or mechanical motion **2** to motivate or incite into action: *actuated by unworthy desires* [c16: from Medieval Latin *actuātus*, from *actuāre* to incite to action, from Latin *āctus* ACT] > ,actu'ation *n* > 'actu,ator *n*

act up *vb* (*intr, adverb*) *informal* to behave in a troublesome way: *the engine began to act up when we were miles from anywhere*

actus reus ('æktəs 'reɪəs) *n law* a criminal action regarded as a constituent element of a crime, as compared with the state of mind of the perpetrator [Latin, literally: guilty act]

acuity (ə'kju:ɪtɪ) *n* keenness or acuteness, esp in vision or thought [c15: from Old French, from Latin *acūtus* ACUTE]

aculeus (ə'kju:lɪəs) *n* **1** a prickle or spine, such as the thorn of a rose **2** a sting or ovipositor [c19: from Latin, diminutive of *acus* needle]

acumen ('ækjʊ,mɛn, ə'kju:mən) *n* the ability to judge well; keen discernment; insight [c16: from Latin: sharpness, from *acuere* to sharpen, from *acus* needle] > a'cuminous *adj*

acuminate *adj* (ə'kju:mɪnɪt, -,neɪt) **1** narrowing to a sharp point, as some types of leaf ▷ *vb* (ə'kju:mɪ,neɪt) **2** (*tr*) to make pointed or sharp [c17: from Latin *acūmināre* to sharpen; see ACUMEN] > a,cumi'nation *n*

acupoint ('ækjʊ,pɔɪnt) *n* any of the specific points on the body where a needle is inserted in acupuncture or pressure is applied in acupressure [c19: from ACU(PUNCTURE) + POINT]

acupressure ('ækjʊ,prɛʃə) *n* another name for **shiatsu** [c19: from ACU(PUNCTURE) + PRESSURE]

acupuncture ('ækjʊ,pʌŋktʃə) *n* the insertion of the tips of needles into the skin at specific points for the purpose of treating various disorders by stimulating nerve impulses. Originally Chinese, this method of treatment is practised in many parts of the world. Also called: stylostixis [c17: from Latin *acus* needle + PUNCTURE] > 'acu,puncturist *n*

acute (ə'kju:t) *adj* **1** penetrating in perception or insight **2** sensitive to details; keen **3** of extreme importance; crucial **4** sharp or severe; intense **5** having a sharp end or point **6** *maths* (of an angle) less than 90° **7** (of a disease) **a** arising suddenly and manifesting intense severity **b** of relatively short duration **8** *phonetics* of or relating to an accent (´) placed over vowels, denoting that the vowel is pronounced with higher musical pitch (as in ancient Greek), with a certain special quality (as in French), etc **9** (of a hospital, hospital bed, or ward) intended to accommodate short-term patients with acute illnesses ▷ *n* **10** an acute accent [c14: from Latin *acūtus*, past participle of *acuere* to sharpen, from *acus* needle] > a'cutely *adv* > a'cuteness *n*

acute accent *n* the diacritical mark (´), used in the writing system of some languages to indicate that the vowel over which it is placed has a special quality (as in French *été*) or that it receives the strongest stress in the word (as in Spanish *hablé*)

acute dose *n* a total dose of radiation administered over such a short period that biological recovery is impossible

ad (æd) *n* short for **advertisement**

AD *abbreviation* anno Domini (indicating years numbered from the supposed year of the birth of Christ): *70 AD* [(sense 4) Latin: in the year of the Lord]

● USAGE In strict usage, AD is only employed with
● specific years: *he died in 1621 AD*, but *he died in the 17th*
● *century* (and not *the 17th century AD*). Formerly the
● practice was to write AD preceding the date (AD 1621),
● and it is also strictly correct to omit *in* when AD is

● used, since this is already contained in the meaning
● of the Latin *anno Domini* (in the year of Our Lord), but
● this is no longer general practice. BC is used with both
● specific dates and indications of the period: *Heraclitus*
● *was born about 540 BC; the battle took place in the 4th*
● *century* BC

ad- *prefix* **1** to; towards: *adsorb; adverb* **2** near; next to: *adrenal* [from Latin: to, towards. As a prefix in words of Latin origin, *ad-* became *ac-*, *af-*, *ag-*, *al-*, *an-*, *acq-*, *ar-*, *as-*, and *at-* before *c, f, g, l, n, q, r, s*, and *t*, and became *a-* before *gn, sc, sp, st*]

adage ('ædɪdʒ) *n* a traditional saying that is accepted by many as true or partially true; proverb [c16: via Old French from Latin *adagium*; related to *āio* I say]

adagio (ə'dɑ:dʒɪ,əʊ; *Italian* a'dadʒo) *music* ▷ *adj, adv* **1** (to be performed) slowly ▷ *n, pl* **-gios** **2** a movement or piece to be performed slowly [c18: Italian, from *ad* at + *agio* ease]

Adam¹ ('ædəm) *n* **1** *Old Testament* the first man, created by God: the progenitor of the human race (Genesis 2–3) **2** not know someone from Adam to have no knowledge of or acquaintance with someone

Adam² *n* **1** (*French* adɑ̃) **Adolphe**. 1803–56, French composer, best known for his romantic ballet *Giselle* (1841) **2** ('ædəm) **Robert**. 1728–92, Scottish architect and furniture designer. Assisted by his brother, **James,** 1730–94, he emulated the harmony of classical and Italian Renaissance architecture ▷ *adj* **3** in the neoclassical style made popular by Robert Adam

adamant ('ædəmənt) *adj* **1** unshakable in purpose, determination, or opinion; unyielding ▷ *n* **2** any extremely hard or apparently unbreakable substance **3** a legendary stone said to be impenetrable, often identified with the diamond or loadstone [Old English: from Latin *adamant-*, stem of *adamas*, from Greek; literal meaning perhaps: unconquerable, from A-¹ + *daman* to tame, conquer]

Adami (ə'dæmɪ) *n* **Edward Fenech**. born 1934, Maltese politician, president of Malta from 2004

Adamkus (ə'dæmkəs) **Valdas**. born 1926, Lithuanian politician, president of Lithuania from 2004

Adamov (*French* adamɔf) *n* **Arthur**. 1908–70, French dramatist, born in Russia: one of the foremost exponents of the Theatre of the Absurd. His plays include *Le Professeur Taranne* (1953), *Le Ping-Pong* (1955), and *Le Printemps '71* (1960)

Adams¹ ('ædəmz) *n* a mountain in SW Washington, in the Cascade Range. Height: 3751 m (12 307 ft)

Adams² ('ædəmz) *n* **1 Gerry**, full name *Gerrard Adams*. born 1948, Northern Ireland politician; president of Sinn Féin from 1983: negotiated the Irish Republican Army ceasefires in 1994–96 and 1997 **2 Henry** (**Brooks**). 1838–1918, US historian and writer. His works include *Mont Saint Michel et Chartres* (1913) and his autobiography *The Education of Henry Adams* (1918) **3 John**. 1735–1826, second president of the US (1797–1801); US ambassador to Great Britain (1785–88); helped draft the Declaration of Independence (1776) **4 John Coolidge**. born 1947, US composer; works include the operas *Nixon in China* (1987) and *The Death of Klinghoffer* (1991) **5 John Couch**. 1819–92, British astronomer who deduced the existence and position of the planet Neptune **6 John Quincey**. son of John Adams. 1767–1848, sixth president of the US (1825–29); secretary of state (1817–25) **7 Richard**. born 1920, British author; his novels include *Watership Down* (1972), *The Plague Dogs* (1977), and *Traveller* (1988) **8 Samuel**. 1722–1803, US revolutionary leader; one of the organizers of the Boston Tea Party; a signatory of the Declaration of Independence

Adam's apple *n* the visible projection of the thyroid cartilage of the larynx at the front of the neck

Adana ('ædənə) *n* a city in S Turkey, capital of Adana province. Pop: 1 248 000 (2005 est). Also called: Seyhan

adapt (ə'dæpt) *vb* **1** (often foll by *to*) to adjust (someone or something, esp oneself) to different conditions, a new environment, etc **2** (*tr*) to fit, change, or modify to suit a new or different purpose [c17: from Latin *adaptāre*, from *ad-* to + *aptāre* to fit, from *aptus* APT] > a'daptable *adj* > a,dapta'bility *or* a'daptableness *n* > a'daptive *adj*

a

adaptation (ˌædəp'teɪʃən, ˌædæp-) n **1** the act or process of adapting or the state of being adapted; adjustment **2** something that is produced by adapting something else **3** something that is changed or modified to suit new conditions or needs **4** biology an inherited or acquired modification in organisms that makes them better suited to survive and reproduce in a particular environment

adaptogen (ə'dæptədʒən) n any of various natural substances used in herbal medicine to normalize and regulate the systems of the body [c20: from ADAPT + -GEN]

adaptor or **adapter** (ə'dæptə) n **1** a person or thing that adapts **2** any device for connecting two parts, esp ones that are of different sizes or have different mating fitments **3 a** a plug used to connect an electrical device to a mains supply when they have different types of terminals **b** a device used to connect several electrical appliances to a single mains socket

ADC abbreviation **1** aide-de-camp **2** analogue-digital converter

add (æd) vb **1** to combine (two or more numbers or quantities) by addition **2** (tr; foll by to) to increase (a number or quantity) by another number or quantity using addition **3** (tr; often foll by to) to join (something) to something else in order to increase the size, quantity, effect, or scope; unite (with): to add insult to injury **4** (intr; foll by to) to have an extra and increased effect (on) **5** (tr) to say or write further **6** (tr; foll by in) to include ▷ See also **add up** [c14: from Latin addere, literally: to put to, from ad- to + -dere to put]

ADD abbreviation attention deficit disorder

Addams ('ædəmz) n **Jane.** 1860–1935, US social reformer, feminist, and pacifist, who founded Hull House, a social settlement in Chicago: Nobel peace prize 1931

addax ('ædæks) n a large light-coloured antelope, Addax nasomaculatus, having ribbed loosely spiralled horns and inhabiting desert regions in N Africa: family Bovidae, order Artiodactyla [c17: Latin, from an unidentified ancient N African language]

addend ('ædɛnd, ə'dɛnd) n any of a set of numbers that is to be added [c20: short for ADDENDUM]

addendum (ə'dɛndəm) n, pl -da (-də) **1** something added; an addition **2** a supplement or appendix to a book, magazine, etc [c18: from Latin, literally: a thing to be added, neuter gerundive of addere to ADD]

adder ('ædə) n **1** Also called: viper a common viper, Vipera berus, that is widely distributed in Europe, including Britain, and Asia and is typically dark greyish in colour with a black zigzag pattern along the back **2** any of various similar venomous or nonvenomous snakes ▷ See also **death adder, puff adder** [Old English nǣdre snake; in Middle English a naddre was mistaken for an addre; related to Old Norse nathr, Gothic nadrs]

adder's-tongue n any of several terrestrial ferns of the genus Ophioglossum, esp O. vulgatum, that grow in the N hemisphere and have a spore-bearing body that sticks out like a spike from the leaf: family Ophioglossaceae

addict vb (ə'dɪkt) **1** (tr; usually passive; often foll by to) to cause (someone or oneself) to become dependent (on something, esp a narcotic drug) ▷ n ('ædɪkt) **2** a person who is addicted, esp to narcotic drugs **3** informal a person who is devoted to something: a jazz addict [c16 (as adj and as vb; n use c20): from Latin addictus given over, from addīcere to give one's assent to, from ad- to + dīcere to say] > ad'diction n > ad'dictive adj

Addington ('ædɪŋtən) n **Henry,** 1st Viscount Sidmouth. 1757–1844, British statesman; prime minister (1801–04) and Home Secretary (1812–21)

Addis Ababa ('ædɪs 'æbəbə) n the capital of Ethiopia, on a central plateau 2400 m (8000 ft) above sea level: founded in 1887; became capital in 1896. Pop: 2 899 000 (2005 est)

Addison ('ædɪsⁿn) n **Joseph.** 1672–1719, English essayist and poet who, with Richard Steele, founded The Spectator (1711–14) and contributed most of its essays, including the de Coverley Papers

Addison's disease ('ædɪsⁿnz) n a disease characterized by deep bronzing of the skin, anaemia, and extreme weakness, caused by underactivity of the adrenal glands [c19: named after Thomas Addison (1793–1860), British physician who identified it]

addition (ə'dɪʃən) n **1** the act, process, or result of adding **2** a person or thing that is added or acquired **3** a mathematical operation in which the sum of two numbers or quantities is calculated. Usually indicated by the symbol + **4** obsolete a title following a person's name **5** in addition (adverb) also; as well; besides **6** in addition to (preposition) besides; as well as [c15: from Latin additiōn-, from addere to ADD]

additional (ə'dɪʃənᵊl) adj added or supplementary > ad'ditionally adv

additionality (əˌdɪʃə'nælɪtɪ) n **1** (in Britain) the principle that money raised by the National Lottery should only be spent on projects that would not otherwise be funded by government spending **2** (in the European Union) the principle that the EU contributes to the funding of a project in a member country provided that the member country also contributes

Additional Member System n a system of voting in which people vote separately for the candidate and the party of their choice. Parties are allocated extra seats if the number of constituencies they win does not reflect their overall share of the vote. See also **proportional representation**

additive ('ædɪtɪv) adj **1** characterized or produced by addition; cumulative ▷ n **2** any substance added to something to improve it, prevent deterioration, etc **3** short for **food additive** [c17: from Late Latin additīvus, from addere to ADD]

addle ('ædᵊl) vb **1** to make or become confused or muddled **2** to make or become rotten ▷ adj **3** (in combination) indicating a confused or muddled state: addle-brained; addle-pated [c18 (vb), back formation from addled, from c13 addle rotten, from Old English adela filth; related to dialect German Addel liquid manure]

add-on n a feature that can be added to a standard model or package to give increased benefits

address (ə'drɛs) n **1** the conventional form by which the location of a building is described **2** the written form of this, as on a letter or parcel, preceded by the name of the person or organization for whom it is intended **3** the place at which someone lives **4** a speech or written communication, esp one of a formal nature **5** skilfulness or tact **6** archaic manner or style of speaking or conversation **7** computing a number giving the location of a piece of stored information **8** (usually plural) expressions of affection made by a man in courting a woman ▷ vb -dresses, -dressing, -dressed or obsolete or poetic -drest (tr) **9** to mark (a letter, parcel, etc) with an address **10** to speak to, refer to in speaking, or deliver a speech to **11** (used reflexively; foll by to) **a** to speak or write to **b** to apply oneself to: he addressed himself to the task **12** to direct (a message, warning, etc) to the attention of **13** to adopt a position facing (the ball in golf, a partner in a dance, the target in archery, etc) [c14 (in the sense: to make right, adorn) and c15 (in the modern sense: to direct words): via Old French from Vulgar Latin addrictiāre (unattested) to make straight, direct oneself towards, from Latin ad- to + dīrectus DIRECT] > ad'dresser or ad'dressor n

address bar n computing the space provided (on a browser) for showing the addresses of websites

addressee (ˌædrɛ'siː) n a person or organization to whom a letter, parcel, etc, is addressed

adduce (ə'djuːs) vb (tr) to cite (reasons, examples, etc) as evidence or proof [c15: from Latin addūcere to lead or bring to] > ad'ducent adj > ad'ducible or ad'duceable adj > adduction (ə'dʌkʃən) n

adduct (ə'dʌkt) vb (tr) **1** (of a muscle) to draw or pull (a leg, arm, etc) towards the median axis of the body ▷ n **2** chem a compound formed by direct combination of two or more different compounds or elements [c19: from Latin addūcere; see ADDUCE] > ad'duction n

add up vb (adverb) **1** to find the sum (of) **2** (intr) to result in a correct total **3** (intr) informal to make sense **4** (intr; foll by to) to amount to

-ade suffix forming nouns a sweetened drink made of

a

various fruits: *lemonade*; *limeade* [from French, from Latin -*āta* made of, feminine past participle of verbs ending in -*āre*]

Adelaide ('ædɪ,leɪd) *n* the capital of South Australia: **Port Adelaide**, 11 km (7 miles) away on St Vincent Gulf, handles the bulk of exports. Pop: 1 002 127 (2001)

Aden ('eɪdᵊn) *n* **1** the main port and commercial capital of Yemen, on the N coast of the **Gulf of Aden**, an arm of the Indian Ocean at the entrance to the Red Sea: capital of South Yemen until 1990: formerly an important port of call on shipping routes to the East. Pop: 584 000 (2005 est) **2** a former British colony and protectorate on the S coast of the Arabian Peninsula: became part of South Yemen in 1967, now part of Yemen. Area: 195 sq km (75 sq miles)

Adenauer (*German* 'a:dənauər) *n* **Konrad** ('kɔnra:t). 1876–1967, German statesman; chancellor of West Germany (1949–63)

adenine ('ædənɪn, -,ni:n, -,naɪn) *n* a purine base present in tissues of all living organisms as a constituent of the nucleic acids DNA and RNA and of certain coenzymes; 6-aminopurine. Formula: $C_5H_5N_5$; melting pt: 360–365°C

adeno- *or before a vowel* **aden-** *combining form* gland or glandular: *adenoid*; *adenology* [New Latin, from Greek *adēn* gland]

adenoidal (,ædɪ'nɔɪdᵊl) *adj* having the nasal tones or impaired breathing of one with enlarged adenoids

adenoids ('ædɪ,nɔɪdz) *pl n* a mass of lymphoid tissue at the back of the throat behind the uvula: when enlarged it often restricts nasal breathing, esp in young children

adenoma (,ædɪ'nəumə) *n, pl* -**mas** *or* -**mata** (-mətə) **1** a tumour, usually benign, occurring in glandular tissue **2** a tumour having a glandlike structure

adenopathy (,ædɪ'nɒpəθɪ) *n pathol* **1** enlargement of the lymph nodes **2** enlargement of a gland

adenosine (æ'dɛnə,si:n, ,ædɪ'nəusi:n) *n biochem* a nucleoside formed by the condensation of adenine and ribose. It is present in all living cells in a combined form, as in ribonucleic acids. Formula: $C_{10}H_{13}N_5O_4$ [c20: a blend of ADENINE + RIBOSE]

adept *adj* (ə'dɛpt) **1** very proficient in something requiring skill or manual dexterity **2** skilful; expert ▷ *n* ('ædɛpt) **3** a person who is skilled or proficient in something [c17: from Medieval Latin *adeptus*, from Latin *adipiscī* to attain, from *ad-* to + *apiscī* to attain] > **a'deptness** *n*

adequate ('ædɪkwɪt) *adj* able to fulfil a need or requirement without being abundant, outstanding, etc [c17: from Latin *adaequāre* to equalize, from *ad-* to + *aequus* EQUAL] > **adequacy** ('ædɪkwəsɪ) *n* > **'adequately** *adv*

à deux *French* (a dø) *adj, adv* of or for two persons

ADFA *abbreviation* Australian Defence Force Academy

ADH *abbreviation* antidiuretic hormone. See **vasopressin**

ADHD *abbreviation* attention deficit hyperactivity disorder

adhere (əd'hɪə) *vb* (*intr*) **1** (usually foll by *to*) to stick or hold fast **2** (foll by *to*) to be devoted (to a political party, cause, religion, etc); be a follower (of) **3** (foll by *to*) to follow closely or exactly [c16: via Medieval Latin *adhērēre* from Latin *adhaerēre* to stick to]

● USAGE See at **adhesion**

adherent (əd'hɪərənt) *n* **1** (usually foll by *of*) a supporter or follower ▷ *adj* **2** sticking, holding fast, or attached

adhesion (əd'hi:ʒən) *n* **1** the quality or condition of sticking together or holding fast **2** ability to make firm contact without skidding or slipping **3** attachment or fidelity, as to a political party, cause, etc **4** an attraction or repulsion between the molecules of unlike substances in contact: distinguished from *cohesion* **5** *pathol* abnormal union of structures or parts [c17: from Latin *adhaesiōn-* a sticking. See ADHERE]

● USAGE *Adhesion* is the preferred term when talking
● about sticking or holding fast in a physical sense.
● *Adherence* is preferred when talking about attachment
● to a political party, cause, etc

adhesive (əd'hi:sɪv) *adj* **1** able to or designed to adhere; sticky: *adhesive tape* **2** tenacious or clinging ▷ *n* **3** a substance used for sticking objects together, such as glue, cement, or paste > **ad'hesively** *adv*

> **ad'hesiveness** *n*

ad hoc (æd 'hɒk) *adj, adv* for a particular purpose only; lacking generality or justification: *an ad hoc decision*; *an ad hoc committee* [Latin, literally: to this]

ad hominem *Latin* (æd 'hɒmɪ,nɛm) *adj, adv* directed against a person rather than against his arguments [literally: to the man]

adiabatic (,ædɪə'bætɪk, ,eɪ-) *adj* **1** (of a thermodynamic process) taking place without loss or gain of heat ▷ *n* **2** a curve or surface on a graph representing the changes in two or more characteristics (such as pressure and volume) of a system undergoing an adiabatic process [c19: from Greek *adiabatos* not to be crossed, impassable (to heat), from A-¹ + *diabatos* passable, from *dia-* across + *bainein* to go]

Adichie (ə'dɪtʃɪ) *n* **Chimamanda Ngozi**, born 1977, Nigerian novelist; her novels include *Purple Hibiscus* (2003) and *Half of a Yellow Sun* (2006), which won the 2007 Orange Prize for Fiction

Adie ('eɪdɪ) *n* **Kathryn**, known as Kate. born 1945, British television journalist, noted esp for her frontline reporting of revolutions, wars, etc

adieu (ə'dju:; *French* adjø) *sentence substitute, n, pl* **adieus** *or* **adieux** (ə'dju:z; *French* adjø) goodbye; farewell [c14: from Old French, from *a* to + *dieu* God]

Adi Granth (,a:dɪ 'grʌnt) *n* another name for **Guru Granth** [from Punjabi: first book]

ad infinitum (æd ,ɪnfɪ'naɪtəm) *adv* without end; endlessly; to infinity [Latin]

ad interim (æd 'ɪntərɪm) *adj, adv* for the meantime; for the present: *ad interim measures* [Latin]

adipocere (,ædɪpəu'sɪə, 'ædɪpəu,sɪə) *n* a waxlike fatty substance formed during the decomposition of corpses [c19: via French from New Latin *adiposus* fat (see ADIPOSE) + French *cire* wax]

adipose ('ædɪ,pəus, -,pəuz) *adj* **1** of, resembling, or containing fat; fatty ▷ *n* **2** animal fat [c18: from New Latin *adiposus*, from Latin *adeps* fat]

Adirondack Mountains (,ædɪ'rɒndæk) *or* **Adirondacks** *pl n* a mountain range in NE New York State. Highest peak: Mount Marcy, 1629 m (5344 ft)

adit ('ædɪt) *n* an almost horizontal shaft into a mine, for access or drainage [c17: from Latin *aditus* an approach, from *adīre* to go, from *ad-* towards + *īre* to go]

adj. *abbreviation* adjective

adjacent (ə'dʒeɪsᵊnt) *adj* being near or close, esp having a common boundary; adjoining; contiguous [c15: from Latin *adjacēre* to lie next to, from *ad-* near + *jacēre* to lie] > **ad'jacently** *adv*

adjacent angles *pl n* two angles that have the same vertex and a side in common

adjective ('ædʒɪktɪv) *n* **1 a** a word imputing a characteristic to a noun or pronoun **b** (*as modifier*): *an adjective phrase* ▷ *adj* **2** additional or dependent [c14: from Late Latin *adjectīvus* attributive, from *adjicere* to throw to, add, from *ad-* to + *jacere* to throw; in grammatical sense, from the Latin phrase *nōmen adjectīvum* attributive noun] > **adjectival** (,ædʒɪk'taɪvᵊl) *adj*

adjoin (ə'dʒɔɪn) *vb* **1** to be next to (an area of land, etc) **2** (*tr;* foll by *to*) to join; affix or attach [c14: via Old French from Latin *adjungere*, from *ad-* to + *jungere* to join]

adjoining (ə'dʒɔɪnɪŋ) *adj* being in contact; connected or neighbouring

adjourn (ə'dʒɜ:n) *vb* **1** (*intr*) (of a court, etc) to close at the end of a session **2** to postpone or be postponed, esp temporarily or to another place **3** (*tr*) to put off (a problem, discussion, etc) for later consideration; defer **4** (*intr*) *informal* to move elsewhere: *let's adjourn to the kitchen* [c14: from Old French *ajourner* to defer to an arranged day, from *a-* to + *jour* day, from Late Latin *diurnum*, from Latin *diurnus* daily, from *diēs* day] > **adjournment** *n*

adjudge (ə'dʒʌdʒ) *vb* (*tr; usually passive*) **1** to pronounce formally; declare **2 a** to determine judicially; judge **b** to order or pronounce by law; decree: *he was adjudged bankrupt* **c** to award (costs, damages, etc) **3** *archaic* to sentence or condemn [c14: via Old French from Latin *adjūdicāre*. See ADJUDICATE]

adjudicate (ə'dʒu:dɪ,keɪt) *vb* **1** (when *intr*, usually foll by *upon*) to give a decision (on), esp a formal or binding one **2** (*intr*) to serve as a judge or arbiter, as in a competition [c18: from Latin *adjūdicāre* to award something to someone, from *ad-* to + *jūdicāre* to act as a judge, from *jūdex* judge] > ad judi'cation *n* > adjudicative (ə'dʒu:dıkətıv) *adj*

adjunct ('ædʒʌŋkt) *n* **1** something incidental or not essential that is added to something else **2** a person who is subordinate to another **3** *grammar* **a** part of a sentence other than the subject or the predicate **b** part of a sentence that may be omitted without making the sentence ungrammatical; a modifier ▷ *adj* **4** added or connected in a secondary or subordinate position; auxiliary [c16: from Latin *adjunctus*, past participle of *adjungere* to ADJOIN] > adjunctive (ə'dʒʌŋktıv) *adj* > 'adjunctly *adv*

adjure (ə'dʒʊə) *vb* (*tr*) **1** to command, often by exacting an oath; charge **2** to appeal earnestly to [c14: from Latin *adjūrāre* to swear to, from *ad-* to + *jūrāre* to swear, from *jūs* oath] > adjuration (,ædʒʊə'reıʃən) *n* > ad'juratory *adj* > ad'jurer *or* ad'juror *n*

adjust (ə'dʒʌst) *vb* **1** (*tr*) to alter slightly, esp to achieve accuracy; regulate **2** to adapt, as to a new environment, etc **3** (*tr*) to put into order **4** (*tr*) *insurance* to determine the amount payable in settlement of (a claim) [c17: from Old French *adjuster*, from *ad-* to + *juste* right, JUST] > ad'justable *adj* > ad'juster *n*

adjustment (ə'dʒʌstmənt) *n* **1** the act of adjusting or state of being adjusted **2** a control for regulating

adjutant ('ædʒətənt) *n* an officer who acts as administrative assistant to a superior officer [c17: from Latin *adjūtāre* to AID] > 'adjutancy *n*

adjutant bird *or* **adjutant stork** *n* either of two large carrion-eating storks, *Leptoptilos dubius* or *L. javanicus*, which are closely related and similar to the marabou and occur in S and SE Asia [so called for its supposedly military gait]

adjutant general *n, pl* adjutants general **1** *Brit army* a member of the Army Board responsible for personnel and administrative functions **2** *US army* the adjutant of a military unit with general staff

adjuvant ('ædʒəvənt) *adj* **1** aiding or assisting ▷ *n* **2** something that aids or assists; auxiliary [c17: from Latin *adjuvāns*, present participle of *adjuvāre*, from *juvāre* to help]

Adler *n* **1** (*German* 'a:dlər) **Alfred** ('alfre:t). 1870–1937, Austrian psychiatrist, noted for his descriptions of overcompensation and inferiority feelings **2** ('ædlə) **Larry**, full name *Lawrence Cecil Adler*. 1914–2001, US harmonica player

Adlerian (æd'lıərıən) *adj* of or relating to the Austrian psychiatrist Alfred Adler (1870–1937) or his ideas

ad-lib (æd'lıb) *vb* -libs, -libbing, -libbed **1** to improvise and deliver without preparation (a speech, musical performance, etc) ▷ *adj* (**ad lib** *when predicative*) **2** improvised; impromptu ▷ *adv* **ad lib 3** without restraint; freely ▷ *n* **4** an improvised performance, often humorous [c18: short for Latin *ad libitum*, literally: according to pleasure]

ad libitum ('lıbıtʊm, -təm) *adj, adv music* (to be performed) at the performer's discretion [see AD-LIB]

Adm. *abbreviation* Admiral

adman ('æd,mæn, -mən) *n, pl* -men *informal* a person who works in advertising

admeasure (æd'mɛʒə) *vb* to measure out (land, etc) as a share; apportion [c14: *amesuren*, from Old French *amesurer*, from *mesurer* to MEASURE; the modern form derives from AD- + MEASURE]

Admetus (æd'mi:təs) *n Greek myth* a king of Thessaly, one of the Argonauts, who was married to Alcestis

admin ('ædmın) *n informal* short for **administration**

administer (əd'mınıstə) *vb* (*mainly tr*) **1** (*also intr*) to direct or control (the affairs of a business, government, etc) **2** to put into execution; dispense: *administer justice* **3** (when *intr*, foll by *to*) to give or apply (medicine, assistance, etc) as a remedy or relief **4** to apply formally; perform **5** to supervise or impose the taking of (an oath, etc) **6** to manage or distribute (an estate, property, etc) [c14: *amynistre*, via Old French from Latin *administrare*,

from *ad-* to + *ministrāre* to MINISTER]

administrate (əd'mını,streıt) *vb* to manage or direct (the affairs of a business, institution, etc)

administration (əd,mını'streıʃən) *n* **1** management of the affairs of an organization, such as a business or institution **2** the duties of an administrator **3** the body of people who administer an organization **4** the conduct of the affairs of government **5** term of office: often used of presidents, governments, etc **6** the executive branch of government along with the public service; the government as a whole **7** (*often capital*) *chiefly US* the political executive, esp of the US; the government **8** *property law* **a** the conduct or disposal of the estate of a deceased person **b** the management by a trustee of an estate subject to a trust **9** a the administering of something, such as a sacrament, oath, or medical treatment **b** the thing that is administered > ad'ministrative *adj* > ad'ministratively *adv*

administration order *n law* **1** an order by a court appointing a person to manage a company that is in financial difficulty, in an attempt to ensure the survival of the company or achieve the best realization of its assets **2** an order by a court for the administration of the estate of a debtor who has been ordered by the court to pay money that he owes

administrator (əd'mını,streıtə) *n* **1** a person who administers the affairs of an organization, official body, etc **2** *property law* a person authorized to manage an estate, esp when the owner has died intestate or without having appointed executors **3** a person who manages a computer system

admirable ('ædmərəbªl) *adj* deserving or inspiring admiration; excellent > 'admirably *adv*

admiral ('ædmərəl) *n* **1** the supreme commander of a fleet or navy **2** Also called: **admiral of the fleet, fleet admiral** a naval officer of the highest rank, equivalent to general of the army or field marshal **3** a senior naval officer entitled to fly his own flag. See also **rear admiral, vice admiral 4** *chiefly Brit* the master of a fishing fleet **5** any of various nymphalid butterflies, esp the red admiral or white admiral [c13: *amyral*, from Old French *amiral* emir, and from Medieval Latin *admīrālis* (the spelling with *d* probably influenced by *admīrābilis* admirable); both from Arabic *amīr* emir, commander, esp in the phrase *amīr-al* commander of, as in *amīr-al-bahr* commander of the sea] > 'admiral,ship *n*

admiralty ('ædmərəltı) *n, pl* -ties **1** the office or jurisdiction of an admiral **2** jurisdiction over naval affairs

Admiralty Board *n* the Admiralty Board (formerly) a department of the British Ministry of Defence, responsible for the administration and planning of the Royal Navy

Admiralty House *n* the official residence of the Governor General of Australia, in Sydney

Admiralty Islands *pl n* a group of about 40 volcanic and coral islands in the SW Pacific, part of Papua New Guinea, in the Bismarck Archipelago: main island: Manus. Pop (whole province): 43 589 (2000). Area: about 2000 sq km (800 sq miles). Also called: **Admiralties**

Admiralty Range *n* a mountain range in Antarctica, on the coast of Victoria Land, northwest of the Ross Sea

admiration (,ædmə'reıʃən) *n* **1** pleasurable contemplation or surprise **2** a person or thing that is admired

admire (əd'maıə) *vb* (*tr*) **1** to regard with esteem, respect, approval, or pleased surprise **2** *archaic* to wonder at [c16: from Latin *admīrāri* to wonder at, from *ad-* to, at + *mīrāri* to wonder, from *mīrus* wonderful] > ad'mirer *n* > ad'miring *adj* > ad'miringly *adv*

admissible (əd'mısəbªl) *adj* **1** able or deserving to be considered or allowed **2** deserving to be admitted or allowed to enter **3** *law* (esp of evidence) capable of being or bound to be admitted in a court of law > ad,missi'bility *or* ad'missibleness

admission (əd'mıʃən) *n* **1** permission to enter or the right, authority, etc, to enter **2** the price charged for entrance **3** acceptance for a position, office, etc **4** a confession, as of a crime, mistake, etc **5** an

a

acknowledgment of the truth or validity of something [c15: from Latin *admissiōn-*, from *admittere* to ADMIT] > ad'missive *adj*

admit (əd'mɪt) *vb* -mits, -mitting, -mitted (*mainly tr*) 1 (*may take a clause as object*) to confess or acknowledge (a crime, mistake, etc) 2 (*may take a clause as object*) to concede (the truth or validity of something) 3 to allow to enter; let in 4 (foll by *to*) to allow participation (in) or the right to be part (of) 5 (when *intr*, foll by *of*) to allow (of); leave room (for) [c14: from Latin *admittere* to let come or go to, from *ad-* to + *mittere* to send]

admittance (əd'mɪt³ns) *n* 1 the right or authority to enter 2 the act of giving entrance 3 *electrical engineering* the reciprocal of impedance, usually measured in siemens. It can be expressed as a complex quantity, the real part of which is the conductance and the imaginary part the susceptance

admittedly (əd'mɪtɪdlɪ) *adv* (*sentence modifier*) willingly conceded: *admittedly I am afraid*

admix (əd'mɪks) *vb* (*tr*) *rare* to mix or blend [c16: back formation from obsolete *admixt*, from Latin *admīscēre* to mix with]

admixture (əd'mɪkstʃə) *n* 1 a less common word for **mixture** 2 anything added in mixing; ingredient

admonish (əd'mɒnɪʃ) *vb* (*tr*) 1 to reprove firmly but not harshly 2 to advise to do or against doing something; warn; caution [c14: via Old French from Vulgar Latin *admonestāre* (unattested), from Latin *admonēre* to put one in mind of, from *monēre* to advise] > admonition (ˌædmə'nɪʃən) *n* > ad'monitory *adj*

ad nauseam (æd 'nɔːzɪˌæm, -sɪ-) *adv* to a disgusting extent [Latin: to (the point of) nausea]

ado (ə'duː) *n* bustling activity; fuss; bother; delay (esp in the phrases **without more ado, with much ado**) [c14: from the phrase *at do* a to-do, from Old Norse *at* to (marking the infinitive) + DO¹]

ADO *Austral abbreviation* accumulated day off

adobe (ə'dəʊbɪ) *n* 1 a sun-dried brick used for building 2 a building constructed of such bricks 3 the clayey material from which such bricks are made [c19: from Spanish]

adobo (ə'dəʊbəʊ) *n, pl* -bos the national dish of the Philippines, which consists of chunks of meat, fish, or vegetables, marinated in vinegar, soy sauce, garlic, and spices and then stewed in the marinade [c20: from Spanish]

adolescence (ˌædə'lɛsəns) *n* the period in human development that occurs between the beginning of puberty and adulthood [c15: via Old French from Latin *adolēscentia*, from *adolēscere* to grow up, from *alēscere* to grow, from *alēre* to feed, nourish]

adolescent (ˌædə'lɛs³nt) *adj* 1 of or relating to adolescence 2 *informal* behaving in an immature way; puerile ▷ *n* 3 an adolescent person

Adonai (ˌædɒ'naɪ, -'neɪaɪ) *n Judaism* a name for God [c15: from Hebrew: lord; compare ADONIS]

Adonis (ə'dəʊnɪs) *n* 1 *Greek myth* a handsome youth loved by Aphrodite. Killed by a wild boar, he was believed to spend part of the year in the underworld and part on earth, symbolizing the vegetative cycle 2 a handsome young man [c16: from Latin, via Greek *Adōnis* from Phoenician *adōni* my lord, a title of the god Tammuz; related to Hebrew ADONAI]

adopt (ə'dɒpt) *vb* (*tr*) 1 *law* to bring (a person) into a specific relationship, esp to take (another's child) as one's own child 2 to choose and follow (a plan, technique, etc) 3 to take over (an idea, etc) as if it were one's own 4 to take on; assume: *to adopt a title* 5 to accept (a report, etc) [c16: from Latin *adoptāre* to choose for oneself, from *optāre* to choose] > a'doptee *n* > a'doption *n*

adopted (ə'dɒptɪd) *adj* having been adopted

adoptive (ə'dɒptɪv) *adj* 1 acquired or related by adoption: *an adoptive father* 2 of or relating to adoption. See **adopted**

adorable (ə'dɔːrəb³l) *adj* 1 very attractive; charming; lovable 2 *becoming rare* deserving or eliciting adoration > a'dorably *adv* > a'dorableness *n*

adoration (ˌædə'reɪʃən) *n* 1 deep love or esteem 2 the act of worshipping

adore (ə'dɔː) *vb* 1 (*tr*) to love intensely or deeply 2 to worship (a god) with religious rites 3 (*tr*) *informal* to like very much [c15: via French from Latin *adōrāre*, from *ad-* to + *ōrāre* to pray] > a'dorer *n* > a'doring *adj* > a'doringly *adv*

adorn (ə'dɔːn) *vb* (*tr*) 1 to decorate 2 to increase the beauty, distinction, etc, of [c14: via Old French from Latin *adōrnāre*, from *ōrnāre* to furnish, prepare] > a'dornment *n*

Adorno (*German* a'dɔrno) *n* **Theodor Wiesengrund.** 1903–69, German philosopher, sociologist, and music critic. His writings include *The Philosophy of the New Music* (1949) and *Negative Dialectics* (1966)

Adowa (ˈɑːdʊˌwɑː) *n* a variant spelling of **Aduwa**

ADP *n biochem* adenosine diphosphate; a nucleotide derived from ATP with the liberation of energy that is then used in the performance of muscular work

Adrastus (ə'dræstəs) *n Greek myth* a king of Argos and leader of the Seven against Thebes of whom he was the sole survivor

ad rem *Latin* (æd 'rɛm) *adj, adv* to the point; without digression

adrenal (ə'driːn³l) *adj* 1 on or near the kidneys 2 of or relating to the adrenal glands or their secretions ▷ *n* 3 an adrenal gland [c19: from AD- (near) + RENAL]

adrenal gland *n* an endocrine gland at the anterior end of each kidney. Its medulla secretes adrenaline and noradrenaline and its cortex secretes several steroid hormones. Also called: **suprarenal gland**

adrenaline *or* **adrenalin** (ə'drɛnəlɪn) *n* a hormone that is secreted by the adrenal medulla in response to stress and increases heart rate, pulse rate, and blood pressure, and raises the blood levels of glucose and lipids. It is extracted from animals or synthesized for such medical uses as the treatment of asthma. Chemical name: aminohydroxyphenylpropionic acid; formula: $C_9H_{13}NO_3$. US name: **epinephrine**

adrenalized *or* **adrenalised** (ə'driːnəlaɪzd) *adj* tense or highly charged: *adrenalized with excitement*

Adrian (ˈeɪdrɪən) *n* **Edgar Douglas,** Baron Adrian. 1889–1977, English physiologist, noted particularly for his research into the function of neurons: shared with Sherrington the Nobel prize for physiology and medicine 1932

Adrian IV *n* original name *Nicholas Breakspear.* ?1100–59, the only English pope (1154–59)

Adrianople (ˌeɪdrɪə'nəʊp³l) *or* **Adrianopolis** (ˌeɪdrɪə'nɒpəlɪs) *n* former names of **Edirne**

Adriatic (ˌeɪdrɪ'ætɪk) *adj* 1 of or relating to the Adriatic Sea, or to the inhabitants of its coast or islands ▷ *n* 2 the Adriatic short for the **Adriatic Sea**

Adriatic Sea *n* an arm of the Mediterranean between Italy and the Balkan Peninsula

adrift (ə'drɪft) *adj, adv* (*postpositive*) 1 floating without steering or mooring; drifting 2 without purpose; aimless 3 *informal* off course or amiss

adroit (ə'drɔɪt) *adj* 1 skilful or dexterous 2 quick in thought or reaction [c17: from French *à droit* according to right, rightly] > a'droitly *adv* > a'droitness *n*

adsorb (əd'sɔːb, -'zɔːb) *vb* to undergo or cause to undergo a process in which a substance, usually a gas, accumulates on the surface of a solid forming a thin film, often only one molecule thick [c19: AD- + -*sorb* as in ABSORB] > ad'sorbable *adj* > ad'sorption *n*

adsorbate (əd'sɔːbeɪt, -bɪt, -'zɔː-) *n* a substance that has been or is to be adsorbed on a surface

adulate (ˈædjʊˌleɪt) *vb* (*tr*) to flatter or praise obsequiously [c17: back formation from c15 *adulation*, from Latin *adūlāri* to flatter]

adulation (ˌædjʊ'leɪʃən) *n* obsequious flattery or praise; extreme admiration

adulatory (ˌædjʊ'leɪtərɪ, 'ædjʊˌleɪtərɪ) *adj* expressing praise, esp obsequiously; flattering

adult (ˈædʌlt, ə'dʌlt) *adj* 1 having reached maturity; fully developed 2 of or intended for mature people: *adult education* 3 regarded as suitable only for adults, because of being pornographic ▷ *n* 4 a person who has attained maturity; a grownup 5 a mature fully grown animal or plant 6 *law* a person who has attained the age of legal majority (18 years for most purposes) [c16: from Latin *adultus*, from *adolēscere* to grow up, from *alēscere* to grow, from *alere* to feed, nourish] > **'adulthood** *n*

adulterant (ə'dʌltərənt) *n* **1** a substance or ingredient that adulterates ▷ *adj* **2** adulterating

adulterate *vb* (ə'dʌltə,reɪt) **1** (*tr*) to debase by adding inferior material: *to adulterate milk with water* ▷ *adj* (ə'dʌltərɪt, -,reɪt) **2** adulterated; debased or impure [c16: from Latin *adulterāre* to corrupt, commit adultery, probably from *alter* another, hence to approach another, commit adultery] > a,dulter'ation *n* > a'dulter,ator *n*

adulterer (ə'dʌltərə) *n* a person who has committed adultery [c16: originally also *adulter*, from Latin *adulter*, back formation from *adulterāre* to ADULTERATE]

adulterous (ə'dʌltərəs) *adj* of, characterized by, or inclined to adultery > a'dulterously *adv*

adultery (ə'dʌltərɪ) *n, pl* -teries voluntary sexual intercourse between a married man or woman and a partner other than the legal spouse [c15: *adulterie*, altered (as if directly from Latin *adulterium*) from c14 *avoutrie*, via Old French from Latin *adulterium*, from *adulter*, back formation from *adulterāre*. See ADULTERATE]

adumbrate ('ædʌm,breɪt) *vb* (*tr*) **1** to outline; give a faint indication of **2** to foreshadow **3** to overshadow; obscure [c16: from Latin *adumbrātus* represented only in outline, from *adumbrāre* to cast a shadow on, from *umbra* shadow] > ,adum'bration *n* > adumbrative (æd'ʌmbrətɪv) *adj*

Aduwa *or* **Adowa** ('ɑːdu,wɑː) *n* a town in N Ethiopia: Emperor Menelik II defeated the Italians here in 1896. Pop: 46 272 (2005 est)

adv. *abbreviation* **1** adverb **2** adverbial [Latin: against]

ad valorem (æd və'lɔːrəm) *adj, adv* (of taxes) in proportion to the estimated value of the goods taxed. Abbreviation: a.v. [from Latin]

advance (əd'vɑːns) *vb* **1** to go or bring forward in position **2** (foll by *on*) to move (towards) in a threatening manner **3** (*tr*) to present for consideration; suggest **4** to bring or be brought to a further stage of development; improve; further **5** (*tr*) to cause (an event) to occur earlier **6** (*tr*) to supply (money, goods, etc) beforehand, either for a loan or as an initial payment **7** to increase (a price, value, rate of occurrence, etc) or (of a price, etc) to be increased **8** (*intr*) to improve one's position; be promoted ▷ *n* **9** forward movement; progress in time or space **10** improvement; progress in development **11** *commerce* **a** the supplying of commodities or funds before receipt of an agreed consideration **b** the commodities or funds supplied in this manner **12** Also called: advance payment a money payment made before it is legally due: *this is an advance on your salary* **13** a loan of money **14** an increase in price, value, rate of occurrence, etc **15** a less common word for **advancement** (sense 1) **16** in advance **a** beforehand: *payment in advance* **b** (foll by *of*) ahead in time or development: *ideas in advance of the time* **17** (*modifier*) forward in position or time: *advance booking; an advance warning* See also **advances** [c15: *advauncen*, altered (on the model of words beginning with Latin *ad-*) from c13 *avauncen*, via Old French from Latin *abante* from before, from *ab-* away from + *ante* before] > ad'vancer *n*

advanced (əd'vɑːnst) *adj* **1** being ahead in development, knowledge, progress, etc **2** having reached a comparatively late stage: *a man of advanced age* **3** ahead of the times

advanced gas-cooled reactor *n* a nuclear reactor using carbon dioxide as the coolant, graphite as the moderator, and ceramic uranium dioxide cased in stainless steel as the fuel. Abbreviation: AGR

advance directive *n* another name for **living will**

Advanced level *n* (in Britain) the formal name for **A level**

advanced skills teacher *n* Brit *education* a teacher who has achieved high standards of classroom practice and success and who, after passing a national assessment, is paid to share his or her skills and experience with other teachers. Abbreviation: AST

advancement (əd'vɑːnsmənt) *n* **1** promotion in rank, status, etc; preferment **2** a less common word for **advance** (senses 9, 10)

advances (əd'vɑːnsɪz) *pl n* (*sometimes singular*; often foll by *to* or *towards*) personal overtures made in an attempt to become friendly, gain a favour, etc

advantage (əd'vɑːntɪdʒ) *n* **1** (often foll by *over* or *of*) superior or more favourable position or power **2** benefit or profit (esp in the phrase **to one's advantage**) **3** *tennis* the point scored after deuce **4** take advantage of **a** to make good use of **b** to impose upon the weakness, good nature, etc, of; abuse **c** to seduce **5** to advantage to good effect [c14: *avantage* (later altered to *advantage* on the model of words beginning with Latin *ad-*), from Old French *avant* before, from Latin *abante* from before, away. See ADVANCE]

advantageous (,ædvən'teɪdʒəs) *adj* producing advantage > ,advan'tageously *adv*

advection (əd'vɛkʃən) *n* the transference of heat energy in a horizontal stream of gas, esp of air [c20: from Latin *advectiō* conveyance, from *advehere*, from *ad-* to + *vehere* to carry]

advent ('ædvɛnt, -vənt) *n* an arrival or coming, esp one which is awaited [c12: from Latin *adventus*, from *advenīre*, from *ad-* to + *venīre* to come]

Advent ('ædvɛnt, -vənt) *n* Christianity the season including the four Sundays preceding Christmas or (in Eastern Orthodox churches) the forty days preceding Christmas

Advent calendar *n* Brit a large card with a brightly coloured sometimes tinselled design on it that contains small numbered doors for children to open on each of the days of Advent, revealing pictures beneath them

Adventist ('ædvɛntɪst, 'ædvən-) *n* a member of any of the Christian groups, such as the **Seventh-Day Adventists** that hold that the Second Coming of Christ is imminent

adventitious (,ædvɛn'tɪʃəs) *adj* **1** added or appearing accidentally or unexpectedly **2** (of a plant or animal part) developing in an abnormal position, as a root that grows from a stem [c17: from Latin *adventīcius* coming from outside, from *adventus* a coming] > ,adven'titiously *adv*

adventure (əd'vɛntʃə) *n* **1** a risky undertaking of unknown outcome **2** an exciting or unexpected event or course of events **3** a hazardous financial operation; commercial speculation ▷ *vb* **4** to take a risk or put at risk **5** (*intr*; foll by *into, on, upon*) to dare to go or enter (into a place, dangerous activity, etc) **6** to dare to say (something): *he adventured his opinion* [c13: *aventure* (later altered to *adventure* after the Latin spelling), via Old French ultimately from Latin *advenīre* to happen to (someone), arrive]

adventure playground *n* Brit a playground for children that contains building materials, discarded industrial parts, etc, used by the children to build with, hide in, climb on, etc

adventurer (əd'vɛntʃərə) *n* **1** a person who seeks adventure, esp one who seeks success or money through daring exploits **2** a person who seeks money or power by unscrupulous means **3** a speculator

adventure racing *n* a contest in which teams compete in an expedition-length race which involves two or more sporting disciplines, often running, mountain biking, climbing, kayaking, and elements of navigation and orienteering

adventure tourism *n* Austral & NZ tourism involving activities that are physically challenging

adventurism (əd'vɛntʃə,rɪzəm) *n* recklessness, esp in politics and finance > ad'venturist *n*

adventurous (əd'vɛntʃərəs) *adj* **1** Also called: adventuresome daring or enterprising **2** dangerous; involving risk

adverb ('æd,vɜːb) *n* **a** a word or group of words that serves to modify a whole sentence, a verb, another adverb, or an adjective; for example, *probably, easily, very,* and *happily* respectively in the sentence *They could probably easily envy the very happily married couple* **b** (*as modifier*): *an adverb marker* [c15–c16: from Latin *adverbium* adverb, literally: added word, a translation of Greek *epirrhēma* a word spoken afterwards]

adversarial (,ædvɜː'sɛərɪəl) *adj* pertaining to or characterized by antagonism and conflict

a

adversary ('ædvəsərɪ) *n, pl* -saries **1** a person or group that is hostile to someone; enemy **2** an opposing contestant in a game or sport [c14: from Latin *adversārius*, from *adversus* against. See ADVERSE]

adversative (əd'vɜːsətɪv) *grammar* ▷ *adj* **1** (of a word, phrase, or clause) implying opposition or contrast. *But* and *although* are adversative conjunctions introducing adversative clauses ▷ *n* **2** an adversative word or speech element

adverse ('ædvɜːs, æd'vɜːs) *adj* **1** antagonistic or inimical; hostile: *adverse criticism* **2** unfavourable to one's interests: *adverse circumstances* **3** contrary or opposite in direction or position: *adverse winds* [c14: from Latin *adversus* opposed to, hostile, from *advertere* to turn towards, from *ad*- to, towards + *vertere* to turn] ▷ ad'versely *adv*
> ad'verseness *n*

adversity (əd'vɜːsɪtɪ) *n, pl* -ties **1** distress; affliction; hardship **2** an unfortunate event or incident

advert¹ (əd'vɜːt) *vb* (*intr*; foll by *to*) to draw attention (to); refer (to) [c15: from Latin *advertere* to turn one's attention to. See ADVERSE]

advert² ('ædvɜːt) *n* *Brit informal* short for **advertisement**

advertise *or sometimes US* **advertize** ('ædvə,taɪz) *vb* **1** to present or praise (goods, a service, etc) to the public, esp in order to encourage sales **2** to make (something, such as a vacancy, article for sale, etc) publicly known, as to possible applicants, buyers, etc: *to advertise a job* **3** (*intr*; foll by *for*) to make a public request (for), esp in a newspaper, etc: *she advertised for a cook* [c15: from a lengthened stem of Old French *avertir*, ultimately from Latin *advertere* to turn one's attention to. See ADVERSE]
> 'adver,tiser *or sometimes US* 'adver,tizer *n*

advertisement *or sometimes US* **advertizement** (əd'vɜːtɪsmənt, -tɪz-) *n* any public notice, as a printed display in a newspaper, short film on television, announcement on radio, etc, designed to sell goods, publicize an event, etc

advertising *or sometimes US* **advertizing** ('ædvə,taɪzɪŋ) *n* **1** the promotion of goods or services for sale through impersonal media, such as radio or television **2** the business that specializes in creating such publicity **3** advertisements collectively; publicity

Advertising Standards Authority *n* an independent UK body set up by the advertising industry to ensure that all advertisements comply with the British Code of Advertising Practice. Abbreviation: ASA

advertorial (,ædvɜː'tɔːrɪəl) *n* advertising material presented under the guise of editorial material [c20: from ADVERT² + (EDIT)ORIAL]

advice (əd'vaɪs) *n* **1** recommendation as to appropriate choice of action; counsel **2** (*sometimes plural*) formal notification of facts, esp when communicated from a distance [c13: *avis* (later *advise*), via Old French from a Vulgar Latin phrase based on Latin *ad* to, according to + *vīsum* view (hence: according to one's view, opinion)]

advisable (əd'vaɪzəbᵊl) *adj* worthy of recommendation; prudent; sensible > ad'visably *adv* > ad,visa'bility *or* ad'visableness *n*

advise (əd'vaɪz) *vb* (*when tr, may take a clause as object or an infinitive*) **1** to offer advice (to a person or persons); counsel: *he advised the king; to advise caution; he advised her to leave* **2** (*tr*; sometimes foll by *of*) formal to inform or notify **3** (*intr*; foll by *with*) *chiefly US or obsolete* to consult or discuss [c14: via Old French from Vulgar Latin *advīsāre* (unattested), from Latin *ad*- to + *vīsāre* (unattested), from *vīsere* to view, from *vidēre* to see]

advised (əd'vaɪzd) *adj* resulting from deliberation. See also **ill-advised, well-advised** > advisedly (əd'vaɪzɪdlɪ) *adv*

adviser *or* **advisor** (əd'vaɪzə) *n* **1** a person who advises **2** *education* a person responsible for advising students on academic matters, career guidance, etc **3** *Brit education* a subject specialist who advises heads of schools on current teaching methods and facilities

advisory (əd'vaɪzərɪ) *adj* **1** giving advice; empowered to make recommendations: *an advisory body* ▷ *n, pl* -ries **2** a statement issued to give advice, recommendations, or a warning: *a travel advisory* **3** a person or organization with an advisory function: *the Prime Minister's media advisory*

advocaat ('ædvəʊ,kɑː, -,kɑːt, 'ædvə-) *n* a liqueur having a raw egg base [c20: Dutch, from *advocatenborrel*, from *advocaat* ADVOCATE (n) + *borrel* drink]

advocacy ('ædvəkəsɪ) *n, pl* -cies active support, esp of a cause

advocate *vb* ('ædvə,keɪt) **1** (*tr; may take a clause as object*) to support or recommend publicly; plead for or speak in favour of ▷ *n* ('ædvəkɪt, -,keɪt) **2** a person who upholds or defends a cause; supporter **3** a person who intercedes on behalf of another **4** a person who pleads his client's cause in a court of law **5** *Scots law* the usual word for **barrister** [c14: via Old French from Latin *advocātus* legal witness, advocate, from *advocāre* to call as witness, from *vocāre* to call]

advowson (əd'vaʊzᵊn) *n* *English ecclesiastical law* the right of presentation to a vacant benefice [c13: via Anglo-French and Old French from Latin *advocātiōn*- the act of summoning, from *advocāre* to summon]

advt *abbreviation* advertisement

adware ('æd,wɛə) *n* **1** a type of computer software that collects information about a user's browsing patterns in order to display relevant advertisements in his or her Web browser **2** computer software that is given to a user with advertisements already embedded

Adygei Republic *or* **Adygea** (,a:dɪ'geɪə; *Russian* adɪ'gɛja) *n* a constituent republic of SW Russia, bordering on the Caucasus Mountains: chiefly agricultural but with some mineral resources. Capital: Maikop. Pop: 447 000 (2002). Area: 7600 sq km (2934 sq miles)

adze *or US* **adz** (ædz) *n* a heavy hand tool with a steel cutting blade attached at right angles to a wooden handle, used for dressing timber [Old English *adesa*]

Adzhar Autonomous Republic (ə'dʒɑː) *or* **Adzharia** (ə'dʒɑːrɪə) *n* an administrative division of SW Georgia, on the Black Sea: part of Turkey from the 17th century until 1878; mostly mountainous, reaching 2805 m (9350 ft), with a subtropical coastal strip. Capital: Batumi. Pop: 376 016 (2002). Area: 3000 sq km (1160 sq miles)

A.E. *or* **AE** *n* the pen name of (George William): **Russell**

AEA *abbreviation* (in Britain) Atomic Energy Authority

AEC *abbreviation* (in the US) Atomic Energy Commission

aedes (er'iːdiːz) *n* any mosquito of the genus *Aedes* (formerly *Stegomyia*) of tropical and subtropical regions, esp *A. aegypti*, which transmits yellow fever and dengue [c20: New Latin, from Greek *aēdēs* unpleasant, from A-¹ + *ēdos* pleasant]

aedile *or sometimes US* **edile** ('iːdaɪl) *n* a magistrate of ancient Rome in charge of public works, games, buildings, and roads [c16: from Latin *aedīlis* concerned with buildings, from *aedēs* a building]

Aeëtes (iː'iːtiːz) *n* *Greek myth* a king of Colchis, father of Medea and keeper of the Golden Fleece

Aegean (iː'dʒiːən) *adj* of or relating to the Aegean Sea or Islands

Aegean Islands *pl n* the islands of the Aegean Sea, including the Cyclades, Dodecanese, Euboea, and Sporades. The majority are under Greek administration

Aegean Sea *n* an arm of the Mediterranean between Greece and Turkey

Aegeus (iː'dʒiːuːs, 'iːdʒiəs) *n* *Greek myth* an Athenian king and father of Theseus

Aegina (iː'dʒaɪnə) *n* **1** an island in the Aegean Sea, in the Saronic Gulf. Area: 85 sq km (33 sq miles) **2** a town on the coast of this island: a city-state of ancient Greece **3** Gulf of Aegina another name for **Saronic Gulf**

Aegir ('eɪdʒɪə) *n* *Norse myth* the god of the sea

aegis *or sometimes US* **egis** ('iːdʒɪs) *n* **1** sponsorship or protection; auspices (esp in the phrase **under the aegis of**) **2** *Greek myth* the shield of Zeus, often represented in art as a goatskin [c18: from Latin, from Greek *aigis* shield of Zeus, perhaps related to *aig*-, stem of *aix* goat]

Aegisthus (iː'dʒɪsθəs) *n* *Greek myth* a cousin to and the murderer of Agamemnon, whose wife Clytemnestra he had seduced. He usurped the kingship of Mycenae until Orestes, Agamemnon's son, returned home and killed him

Aegospotami (,iːgəs'pɒtə,maɪ) *n* a river of ancient Thrace that flowed into the Hellespont. At its mouth the Spartan fleet under Lysander defeated the Athenians in 405 BC, ending the Peloponnesian War

aegrotat (ˈaɪgrəʊˌtæt, ˈiː-, iːˈɡrəʊtæt) n 1 (in British and certain other universities, and, sometimes, schools) a certificate allowing a candidate to pass an examination although he has missed all or part of it through illness 2 a degree or other qualification obtained in such circumstances [c19: Latin, literally: he is ill]

Ælfric (ˈælfrɪk) n called Grammaticus. ?955–?1020, English abbot, writer, and grammarian

-aemia, -haemia, US **-emia** or **-hemia** n combining form denoting blood, esp a specified condition of the blood in names of diseases: leukaemia [New Latin, from Greek -aimia, from haima blood]

Aeneas (ɪˈniːəs) n classical myth a Trojan prince, the son of Anchises and Aphrodite, who escaped the sack of Troy and sailed to Italy via Carthage and Sicily. After seven years, he and his followers established themselves near the site of the future Rome

Aeneas Silvius or **Aeneas Sylvius** (ˈsɪlvɪəs) n the literary name of **Pius II**

Aeneid (ɪˈniːɪd) n an epic poem in Latin by Virgil relating the experiences of Aeneas after the fall of Troy, written chiefly to provide an illustrious historical background for Rome

aeolian (iːˈəʊlɪən) adj of or relating to the wind; produced or carried by the wind [c18: from AEOLUS, god of the winds]

aeolian harp n a stringed instrument that produces a musical sound when a current of air or wind passes over the strings. Also called: **wind harp**

Aeolian Islands pl n another name for (the) **Lipari Islands**

Aeolis (ˈiːəlɪs) or **Aeolia** (iːˈəʊlɪə) n the ancient name for the coastal region of NW Asia Minor, including the island of Lesbos, settled by the Aeolian Greeks (about 1000 BC)

aeolotropic (ˌiːələʊˈtrɒpɪk) adj a less common word for **anisotropic** [c19: from Greek aiolos fickle + -TROPIC]

Aeolus (ˈiːələs, iːˈəʊləs) n Greek myth the god of the winds 2 the founding king of the Aeolians in Thessaly

aeon or esp US **eon** (ˈiːən, ˈiːɒn) n 1 an immeasurably long period of time; age 2 a period of one thousand million years [c17: from Greek aiōn an infinitely long time]

aerate (ˈɛəreɪt) vb (tr) 1 to charge (a liquid) with a gas, esp carbon dioxide, as in the manufacture of effervescent drink 2 to expose to the action or circulation of the air, so as to purify > aer'ation n > 'aerator n

aeri- combining form a variant of **aero-**

aerial (ˈɛərɪəl) adj 1 of, relating to, or resembling air 2 existing, occurring, moving, or operating in the air: aerial cable car; aerial roots of a plant 3 ethereal; light and delicate 4 imaginary; visionary 5 extending high into the air; lofty 6 of or relating to aircraft: aerial combat ▷ n 7 Also called: **antenna** the part of a radio or television system having any of various shapes, such as a dipole, Yagi, long-wire, or vertical aerial, by means of which radio waves are transmitted or received [c17: via Latin from Greek aērios, from aēr air]

aerialist (ˈɛərɪəlɪst) n chiefly US a trapeze artist or tightrope walker

aerial top dressing n the process of spreading lime, fertilizer, etc over farmland from an aeroplane

aerie (ˈɛərɪ, ˈɪərɪ) n a variant spelling (esp US) of **eyrie**

aeriform (ˈɛərɪˌfɔːm) adj 1 having the form of air; gaseous 2 unsubstantial

aero (ˈɛərəʊ) n (modifier) of or relating to aircraft or aeronautics: an aero engine

aero-, aeri- or before a vowel **aer-** combining form 1 denoting air, atmosphere, or gas: aerodynamics 2 denoting aircraft: aeronautics [ultimately from Greek aēr air]

aerobatics (ˌɛərəʊˈbætɪks) n (functioning as singular or plural) spectacular or dangerous manoeuvres, such as loops or rolls, performed in an aircraft or glider; stunt flying [c20: from AERO- + (ACRO)BATICS]

aerobe (ˈɛərəʊb) or **aerobium** (ɛəˈrəʊbɪəm) n, pl -obes or -obia (-ˈəʊbɪə) an organism that requires oxygen for respiration [c19: from AERO- + Greek bios life. Compare MICROBE]

aerobic (ɛəˈrəʊbɪk) adj 1 (of an organism or process) depending on oxygen 2 of or relating to aerobes 3 designed for or relating to aerobics: aerobic shoes; aerobic dances

aerobics (ɛəˈrəʊbɪks) n (functioning as singular) any system of sustained exercises designed to increase the amount of oxygen in the blood and strengthen the heart and lungs

aerodrome (ˈɛərəˌdrəʊm) n obsolete a landing area, esp for private aircraft, that is usually smaller than an airport

aerodynamic braking n 1 the use of aerodynamic drag to slow spacecraft re-entering the atmosphere 2 the use of airbrakes to retard flying vehicles or objects 3 the use of a parachute or reversed thrust to decelerate an aircraft during landing

aerodynamics (ˌɛərəʊdaɪˈnæmɪks) n (functioning as singular) the study of the dynamics of gases, esp of the forces acting on a body passing through air > ˌaerody'namic adj > ˌaerody'namically adv > ˌaerody'namicist n

aero engine n an engine for powering an aircraft

aerofoil (ˈɛərəʊˌfɔɪl) n a cross section of an aileron, wing, tailplane, or rotor blade

aerogram or **aerogramme** (ˈɛərəˌɡræm) n Also called: **air letter** an airmail letter written on a single sheet of lightweight paper that folds and is sealed to form an envelope

aerolite (ˈɛərəˌlaɪt) n a stony meteorite consisting of silicate minerals

aerology (ɛəˈrɒlədʒɪ) n the study of the atmosphere, particularly its upper layers > aerologic (ˌɛərəˈlɒdʒɪk) or ˌaero'logical adj > aer'ologist n

aeromechanics (ˌɛərəʊmɪˈkænɪks) n (functioning as singular) the mechanics of gases, esp air > ˌaerome'chanical adj

aeronautics (ˌɛərəˈnɔːtɪks) n (functioning as singular) the study or practice of all aspects of flight through the air > aeronautical (ˌɛərəˈnɔːtɪkᵊl, ˌaero'nautical) adj > ˌaero'nautically adv

aeropause (ˈɛərəˌpɔːz) n the region of the upper atmosphere above which aircraft cannot fly

aeroplane (ˈɛərəˌpleɪn) or US and Canadian **airplane** (ˈɛəˌpleɪn) n a heavier-than-air powered flying vehicle with fixed wings [c19: from French aéroplane, from AERO- + Greek -planos wandering, related to PLANET]

aerosol (ˈɛərəˌsɒl) n 1 a colloidal dispersion of solid or liquid particles in a gas; smoke or fog 2 a substance, such as a paint, polish, or insecticide, dispensed from a small metal container by a propellant under pressure 3 Also called: **air spray** such a substance together with its container [c20: from AERO- + SOL(UTION)]

aerospace (ˈɛərəˌspeɪs) n 1 the atmosphere and space beyond 2 (modifier) of or relating to rockets, missiles, space vehicles, etc, that fly or operate in aerospace: the aerospace industry

aerostat (ˈɛərəˌstæt) n a lighter-than-air craft, such as a balloon [c18: from French aérostat, from AERO- + Greek -statos standing] > ˌaero'static or ˌaero'statical adj

aerostatics (ˌɛərəˈstætɪks) n (functioning as singular) 1 the study of gases in equilibrium and bodies held in equilibrium in gases. See **aerodynamics** 2 the study of lighter-than-air craft, such as balloons

aerugo (ɪˈruːɡəʊ) n (esp of old bronze) another name for: **verdigris** [c18: from Latin, from aes copper, bronze] > aeruginous (ɪˈruːdʒɪnəs) adj

aery (ˈɛərɪ, ˈɪərɪ) n, pl aeries a variant spelling of **eyrie**

Aeschines (ˈiːskəˌniːz) n ?389–?314 BC, Athenian orator; the main political opponent of Demosthenes

Aeschylus (ˈiːskələs) n ?525–?456 BC, Greek dramatist, regarded as the father of Greek tragedy. Seven of his plays are extant, including Seven Against Thebes, The Persians, Prometheus Bound, and the trilogy of the Oresteia > Aeschylean (ˌiːskəˈliːən) adj

Aesculapius (ˌiːskjʊˈleɪpɪəs) n the Roman god of medicine or healing. Greek counterpart: **Asclepius** > Aesculapian (ˌiːskjʊˈleɪpɪən) adj

Aesir (ˈeɪsɪə) pl n the chief gods of Norse mythology dwelling in Asgard [Old Norse, literally: gods]

Aesop (ˈiːsɒp) n ?620–564 BC, Greek author of fables in

which animals are given human characters and used to satirize human failings > Ae'sopian or Ae'sopic adj

aesthesia or US **esthesia** (iːsˈθiːzɪə) n the normal ability to experience sensation, perception, or sensitivity [C20: back formation from ANAESTHESIA]

aesthete or US **esthete** ('iːsθiːt) n a person who has or who affects a highly developed appreciation of beauty, esp in poetry and the visual arts [C19: back formation from AESTHETICS]

aesthetic (iːsˈθɛtɪk, ɪs-), **aesthetical** or sometimes US **esthetic, esthetical 1** connected with aesthetics or its principles **2 a** relating to pure beauty rather than to other considerations **b** artistic or relating to good taste: an aesthetic consideration ▷ n **3** a principle of taste or style adopted by a particular person, group, or culture: the Bauhaus aesthetic of functional modernity > aes'thetically or sometimes US es'thetically adv > aestheticism or sometimes US estheticism (iːsˈθɛtɪˌsɪzəm, ɪs-) n

aesthetic labour n workers employed by a company for their appearance or accent, with the aim of promoting the company's image

aesthetics or sometimes US **esthetics** (iːsˈθɛtɪks, ɪs-) n (functioning as singular) **1** the branch of philosophy concerned with the study of such concepts as beauty, taste, etc **2** the study of the rules and principles of art [C18: from Greek aisthētikos perceptible by the senses, from aisthesthai to perceive]

aestival or US **estival** (iːˈstaɪvᵊl, ˈɛstɪ-) adj rare of or occurring in summer [C14: from French, from Late Latin aestīvālis, from Latin aestās summer]

aestivate or US **estivate** ('iːstɪˌveɪt, 'ɛs-) vb (intr) **1** to pass the summer **2** (of animals such as the lungfish) to pass the summer or dry season in a dormant condition [C17: from Latin aestīvātus, from aestīvāre to stay during the summer, from aestās summer] > aestivation or US estivation (ˌiːstɪˈveɪʃən, ˌɛs-) n

aet. or **aetat.** abbreviation aetatis [Latin: at the age of]

Æthelbert ('æθəlˌbɜːt) n a variant spelling of **Ethelbert**

Æthelred ('æθəlˌrɛd) n a variant spelling of **Ethelred**

Æthelwulf ('æθəlˌwʊlf) n a variant spelling of **Ethelwulf**

aether ('iːθə) n a variant spelling of **Ether** (senses 3, 4)

aetiology or **etiology** (ˌiːtɪˈɒlədʒɪ) n, pl -gies **1** the study of the causes of diseases **2** the cause of a disease [C16: from Late Latin aetiologia, from Greek aitiologia, from aitia cause] > ˌaeti'ologist or ˌeti'ologist n > aetiological or etiological (ˌiːtɪəˈlɒdʒɪkᵊl) adj > ˌaetio'logically or ˌetio'logically adv

Aetna ('ɛtnə) n the Latin name for Mount **Etna**

Aetolia (iːˈtəʊlɪə) n a mountainous region forming (with the region of Acarnania) a department of W central Greece, north of the Gulf of Patras: a powerful federal state in the 3rd century BC. Chief city: Missolonghi. Pop (with Acarnania): 219 092 (2001). Area: 5461 sq km (2108 sq miles)

a.f. abbreviation audio frequency

afar (əˈfɑː) adv **1** at, from, or to a great distance ▷ n **2** a great distance (esp in the phrase from afar) [C14: a fer, altered from earlier on fer and of fer; see A-², FAR]

Afars and the Issas ('ɑːfɑːz, 'iːsɑːs) n Territory of the Afars and the Issas a former name (1967–77) of **Djibouti**

AFC abbreviation **1** Air Force Cross **2** Association Football Club **3** automatic frequency control

afeard or **afeared** (əˈfɪəd) adj (postpositive) an archaic or dialect word for **afraid** [Old English āfǣred, from āfǣran to frighten, from fǣran to FEAR]

affable ('æfəbᵊl) adj **1** showing warmth and friendliness; kindly; mild; benign **2** easy to converse with; approachable; amicable [C16: from Latin affābilis easy to talk to, from affārī to talk to, from ad- to + fārī to speak; compare FABLE, FATE] > ˌaffa'bility n > 'affably adv

affair (əˈfɛə) n **1** a thing to be done or attended to; matter; business **2** an event or happening: a strange affair **3** (qualified by an adjective or descriptive phrase) something previously specified, esp a man-made object; thing: our house is a tumbledown affair **4** a sexual relationship between two people who are not married to each other [C13: from Old French, from à faire to do]

affairs (əˈfɛəz) pl n **1** personal or business interests **2** matters of public interest: current affairs

affect¹ vb (əˈfɛkt) (tr) **1** to act upon or influence, esp in an adverse way **2** to move or disturb emotionally or mentally **3** (of pain, disease, etc) to attack ▷ n ('æfɛkt) **4** the emotion associated with an idea or set of ideas [C17: from Latin affectus, p.p. of afficere, from ad- to + facere to do]

affect² (əˈfɛkt) vb (mainly tr) **1** to put on an appearance or show of; make a pretence of: to affect ignorance **2** to imitate or assume, esp pretentiously **3** to have or use by preference **4** to adopt the character, manner, etc, of **5** to incline naturally or habitually towards [C15: from Latin affectāre to strive after, pretend to have; related to afficere to AFFECT¹]

affectation (ˌæfɛkˈteɪʃən) n **1** an assumed manner of speech, dress, or behaviour, esp one that is intended to impress others **2** (often foll by of) deliberate pretence or false display [C16: from Latin affectātiōn- an aiming at, striving after, from affectāre; see AFFECT²]

affected¹ (əˈfɛktɪd) adj (usually postpositive) **1** deeply moved, esp by sorrow or grief **2** changed, esp detrimentally [C17: from AFFECT¹ + -ED²]

affected² (əˈfɛktɪd) adj **1** behaving, speaking, etc, in an artificial or assumed way, esp in order to impress others **2** feigned: affected indifference [C16: from AFFECT² + -ED²] > af'fectedly adv

affecting (əˈfɛktɪŋ) adj evoking feelings of pity, sympathy, or pathos; moving > af'fectingly adv

affection (əˈfɛkʃən) n **1** a feeling of fondness or tenderness for a person or thing; attachment **2** (often plural) emotion, feeling, or sentiment: to play on a person's affections **3** pathol any disease or pathological condition **4** the act of affecting or the state of being affected [C13: from Latin affectiōn- disposition, from afficere to AFFECT¹] > af'fectional adj

affectionate (əˈfɛkʃənɪt) adj having or displaying tender feelings, affection, or warmth > af'fectionately adv

affective (əˈfɛktɪv) adj concerned with or arousing the emotions or affection > affectivity (ˌæfɛkˈtɪvɪtɪ) or af'fectiveness n

affective disorder n any mental disorder, such as depression or mania, that is characterized by abnormal disturbances of mood

affectless (əˈfɛktlɪs) adj **a** showing no emotion or concern for others **b** not giving rise to any emotion or feeling: an affectless novel [C20: from AFFECT¹ (sense 4) + -LESS]

afferent ('æfərənt) adj bringing or directing inwards to a part or an organ of the body, esp towards the brain or spinal cord [C19: from Latin afferre to carry to, from ad- to + ferre to carry]

affiance (əˈfaɪəns) vb (tr) to bind (a person or oneself) in a promise of marriage; betroth [C14: via Old French from Medieval Latin affidāre to trust (oneself) to, from fīdāre to trust, from fīdus faithful]

affidavit (ˌæfɪˈdeɪvɪt) n law a declaration in writing made upon oath before a person authorized to administer oaths, esp for use as evidence in court [C17: from Medieval Latin, literally: he declares on oath, from affidare to trust (oneself) to; see AFFIANCE]

affiliate vb (əˈfɪlɪˌeɪt) **1** (tr; foll by to or with) to receive into close connection or association (with a larger body, group, organization, etc); adopt as a member, branch, etc **2** (foll by with) to associate (oneself) or be associated, esp as a subordinate or subsidiary; bring or come into close connection ▷ n (əˈfɪlɪɪt, -ˌeɪt) **3 a** a person or organization that is affiliated with another **b** (as modifier): an affiliate member [C18: from Medieval Latin affiliātus adopted as a son, from affiliāre, from Latin filius son] > afˌfili'ation n

affiliation order n law (formerly) an order made by a magistrates' court that a man adjudged to be the father of an illegitimate child shall contribute a specified periodic sum towards the child's maintenance

affine ('æfaɪn) adj maths of, characterizing, or involving transformations which preserve collinearity, esp in classical geometry, those of translation, rotation and reflection in an axis [C16: via French from Latin affinis bordering on, related]

affinity (əˈfɪnɪtɪ) n, pl -ties **1** (foll by with or for) a natural liking, taste, or inclination towards a person or thing **2** the person or thing so liked **3** a close similarity in appearance or quality; inherent likeness **4** relationship by marriage or by ties other than of blood, as by adoption **5** similarity in structure, form, etc, between different animals, plants, or languages **6** *chem* the tendency for two substances to combine; chemical attraction **7** *biology* a measure of the degree of interaction between two molecules, such as an antigen and antibody or a hormone and its receptor [C14: via Old French from Latin *affinität-* connected by marriage, from *affinis* bordering on, related] > **affinitive** *adj*

affinity card *n* *Brit* a credit card issued by a bank or credit-card company, which donates a small percentage of the money spent using the card to a specified charity

affirm (əˈfɜːm) *vb* (mainly tr) **1** (may take a clause as object) to declare to be true; assert positively **2** to uphold, confirm, or ratify **3** (intr) *law* to make an affirmation [C14: via Old French from Latin *affirmāre* to present (something) as firm or fixed, assert, from *ad-* to + *firmāre* to make FIRM¹] > **affirmer** *or* **affirmant** *n*

affirmation (ˌæfəˈmeɪʃən) *n* **1** the act of affirming or the state of being affirmed **2** a statement of the existence or truth of something; assertion **3** *law* a solemn declaration permitted on grounds of conscientious objection to taking an oath

affirmative (əˈfɜːmətɪv) *adj* **1** confirming or asserting something as true or valid **2** indicating agreement or assent **3** *logic* (of a categorial proposition) affirming the satisfaction by the subject of the predicate, as in *all birds have feathers; some men are married* > *n* **4** a positive assertion **5** a word or phrase stating agreement or assent, such as *yes* (esp in the phrase **answer in the affirmative**) > *sentence substitute* **6** *military* a signal codeword used to express assent or confirmation > **affirmatively** *adv*

affix *vb* (əˈfɪks) (tr; usually foll by *to* or *on*) **1** to attach, fasten, join, or stick **2** to add or append: *to affix a signature to a document* **3** to attach or attribute (guilt, blame, etc) > *n* (ˈæfɪks) **4** a linguistic element added to a word or root to produce a derived or inflected form: *-ment* in *establishment* is a derivational affix; *-s* in *drowns* is an inflectional affix. See also **prefix, suffix, infix** **5** something fastened or attached; appendage [C15: from Medieval Latin *affixāre*, from *ad-* to + *fixāre* to FIX] > **affixation** (ˌæfɪkˈseɪʃən) *or* **affixture** (əˈfɪkstʃə) *n*

afflatus (əˈfleɪtəs) *n* an impulse of creative power or inspiration, esp in poetry, considered to be of divine origin (esp in the phrase **divine afflatus**) [C17: Latin, from *afflātus*, from *afflāre* to breathe or blow on, from *flāre* to blow]

afflict (əˈflɪkt) *vb* (tr) to cause suffering or unhappiness to; distress greatly [C14: from Latin *afflictus*, past participle of *afflīgere* to knock against, from *flīgere* to knock, to strike] > **afflictive** *adj*

affliction (əˈflɪkʃən) *n* **1** a condition of great distress, pain, or suffering **2** something responsible for physical or mental suffering, such as a disease, grief, etc

affluence (ˈæfluəns) *n* **1** an abundant supply of money, goods, or property; wealth **2** *rare* abundance or profusion

affluent (ˈæfluənt) *adj* **1** rich; wealthy **2** abundant; copious **3** flowing freely > *n* **4** *archaic* a tributary stream [C15: from Latin *affluent-*, present participle of *affluere* to flow towards, from *fluere* to flow]

affluential (ˌæfluˈenʃəl) *n* an affluent person who does not display his or her wealth in the form of material possessions

affluent society *n* a society in which the material benefits of prosperity are widely available

afflux (ˈæflʌks) *n* a flowing towards a point: *an afflux of blood to the head* [C17: from Latin *affluxus*, from *fluxus* FLUX]

afford (əˈfɔːd) *vb* **1** (preceded by *can, could,* etc) to be able to do or spare something, esp without incurring financial difficulties or without risk of undesirable consequences **2** to give, yield, or supply [Old English *geforthian* to further, promote, from *forth* FORTH; the Old English prefix *ge-* was later reduced to *a-*, and the modern spelling (C16) is influenced by words beginning *aff-*] > **affordable** *adj* > **af,forda'bility** *n*

afforest (əˈfɒrɪst) *vb* (tr) to plant trees on; convert into forested land [C15: from Medieval Latin *afforestāre*, from *forestis* FOREST] > **af,forest'ation** *n*

affranchise (əˈfræntʃaɪz) *vb* (tr) to release from servitude or an obligation [C15: from Old French *afranchiss-*, a stem of *afranchir*, from *franchir* to free; see FRANK] > **affranchisement** *n*

affray (əˈfreɪ) *n* *law* a fight, noisy quarrel, or disturbance between two or more persons in a public place [C14: via Old French from Vulgar Latin *exfridāre* (unattested) to break the peace; compare German *Friede* peace]

affricate (ˈæfrɪkɪt) *n* a composite speech sound consisting of a stop and a fricative articulated at the same point, such as the sound written *ch,* as in *chair* [C19: from Latin *affricāre* to rub against, from *fricāre* to rub; compare FRICTION]

affright (əˈfraɪt) *archaic or poetic* > *vb* **1** (tr) to frighten > *n* **2** a sudden terror [Old English *āfyrhtan,* from *a-,* a prefix indicating the beginning or end of an action + *fyrhtan* to FRIGHT]

affront (əˈfrʌnt) *n* **1** a deliberate insult > *vb* (tr) **2** to insult, esp openly **3** to offend the pride or dignity of [C14: from Old French *afronter* to strike in the face, from Vulgar Latin *affrontāre* (unattested), from the Latin phrase *ad frontem* to the face]

Afg. *or* **Afgh.** *abbreviation* Afghanistan

afghan (ˈæfɡæn, -ɡən) *n* **1** a knitted or crocheted wool blanket or shawl, esp one with a geometric pattern **2** a sheepskin coat, often embroidered and having long fur trimming around the edges [from AFGHANISTAN]

Afghan (ˈæfɡæn, -ɡən) *or* **Afghani** (æfˈɡænɪ, -ˈɡɑː-) *n* **1** a native, citizen, or inhabitant of Afghanistan **2** another name for **Pashto** > *adj* **3** denoting or relating to Afghanistan, its people, or their language

Afghan hound *n* a tall graceful breed of hound with a long silky coat

Afghani (æfˈɡɑːnɪ) *n* **Jamal ad-Din al-**. 1839–97, Iranian Muslim religious and political reformer; a proponent of Muslim unity, he resisted European interference in Muslim countries

Afghanistan (æfˈɡænɪˌstɑːn, -ˌstæn) *n* a republic in central Asia: became independent in 1919; occupied by Soviet troops, 1979–89; controlled by mujaheddin forces from 1992 until 1996 when Taliban forces seized power; in the US-led 'war on terror' (2001) the Taliban were overthrown and replaced by an interim administration, although the Taliban insurgency continues; generally arid and mountainous, with the Hindu Kush range rising over 7500 m (25 000 ft) and fertile valleys of the Amu Darya, Helmand, and Kabul Rivers. Official languages: Pashto and Dari (Persian), Tajik also widely spoken. Religion: Muslim. Currency: afghani. Capital: Kabul. Pop: 24 926 000 (2004 est). Area: 657 500 sq km (250 000 sq miles)

aficionado (əˌfɪsjəˈnɑːdəʊ; *Spanish* afiθjoˈnaðo) *n, pl* **-dos** (-dəʊz; *Spanish* -ðos) **1** an ardent supporter or devotee: *a jazz aficionado* **2** a devotee of bullfighting [Spanish, from *aficionar* to arouse affection, from *aficion* AFFECTION]

afield (əˈfiːld) *adv, adj* (postpositive) **1** away from one's usual surroundings or home (esp in the phrase **far afield**) **2** off the subject; away from the point (esp in the phrase **far afield**) **3** in or to the field, esp the battlefield

afire (əˈfaɪə) *adv, adj* (postpositive) **1** on fire; ablaze **2** intensely interested or passionate: *he was afire with enthusiasm for the new plan*

AFIS *n* Automated Fingerprint Identification System: a computer system that scans fingerprints from crime scenes and compares them with millions of others around the world

AFK *text messaging* *abbreviation* away from keyboard

AFL *abbreviation* Australian Football League: the national body for Australian Rules football

aflame (əˈfleɪm) *adv, adj* (postpositive) **1** in flames; ablaze **2** deeply aroused, as with passion: *he was aflame with desire*

aflatoxin (ˌæfləˈtɒksɪn) *n* a toxin produced by the fungus *Aspergillus flavus* growing on peanuts, maize, etc, causing liver disease (esp cancer) in man [C20: from *A(spergillus) fla(vus)* + TOXIN]

afloat (ə'fləʊt) *adj, adv* (*postpositive*) **1** floating **2** aboard ship; at sea **3** covered with water; flooded **4** aimlessly drifting **5** in circulation; afoot: *nasty rumours were afloat* **6** free of debt; solvent

aflutter (ə'flʌtə) *adj, adv* (*postpositive*) in or into a nervous or excited state

AFM *abbreviation* Air Force Medal

afoot (ə'fʊt) *adj, adv* (*postpositive*) **1** in circulation or operation; astir: *mischief was afoot* **2** on or by foot

afore (ə'fɔː) *adv, prep, conj* an archaic or dialect word for **before**

aforementioned (ə'fɔːˌmenʃənd) *adj* (*usually prenominal*) (chiefly in legal documents) stated or mentioned before or already

aforesaid (ə'fɔːˌsɛd) *adj* (*usually prenominal*) (chiefly in legal documents) spoken of or referred to previously

aforethought (ə'fɔːˌθɔːt) *adj* (*immediately postpositive*) premeditated (esp in the phrase **malice aforethought**)

a fortiori (eɪ ˌfɔːtɪˈɔːraɪ, -rɪ, ɑː) *adv* for similar but more convincing reasons [Latin]

afp *abbreviation* alpha-fetoprotein

afraid (ə'freɪd) *adj* (*postpositive*) **1** (often foll by *of*) feeling fear or apprehension; frightened **2** reluctant (to do something), as through fear or timidity **3** (often foll by *that*; used to lessen the effect of an unpleasant statement) regretful: *I'm afraid that I shall have to tell you to go* [c14: *affraied*, past participle of AFFRAY (to frighten)]

afreet *or* **afrit** ('æfriːt, ə'friːt) *n Arabian myth* a powerful evil demon or giant monster [c19: from Arabic *'ifrīt*]

afresh (ə'frɛʃ) *adv* once more; once again; anew

Africa ('æfrɪkə) *n* the second largest of the continents, on the Mediterranean in the north, the Atlantic in the west, and the Red Sea, Gulf of Aden, and Indian Ocean in the east. The Sahara desert divides the continent unequally into North Africa (an early centre of civilization, in close contact with Europe and W Asia, now inhabited chiefly by Arabs) and Africa south of the Sahara (relatively isolated from the rest of the world until the 19th century and inhabited chiefly by Negroid peoples). It was colonized mainly in the 18th and 19th centuries by Europeans and now comprises independent nations. The largest lake is Lake Victoria and the chief rivers are the Nile, Niger, Congo, and Zambezi. Pop: 887 964 000 (2005 est). Area: about 30 300 000 sq km (11 700 000 sq miles)

African ('æfrɪkən) *adj* **1** denoting or relating to Africa or any of its peoples, languages, nations, etc ▷ *n* **2** a native, inhabitant, or citizen of any of the countries of Africa **3** a member or descendant of any of the peoples of Africa, esp a Black person

Africana (ˌæfrɪˈkɑːnə) *pl n* objects of cultural or historical interest of African origin

African-American *n* **1** an American of African descent ▷ *adj* **2** of or relating to Americans of African descent

African-Canadian *n* **1** a Canadian of African descent ▷ *adj* **2** of or relating to Canadians of African descent

African National Congress *n* (in South Africa) a political party, founded in 1912 as an African nationalist movement and banned there from 1960 to 1990 because of its active opposition to apartheid: in 1994 won South Africa's first multiracial elections. Abbreviation: ANC

African violet *n* any of several tropical African plants of the genus *Saintpaulia*, esp *S. ionantha*, cultivated as house plants, with violet, white, or pink flowers and hairy leaves: family *Gesneriaceae*

Afrikaans (ˌæfrɪˈkɑːns, -'kɑːnz) *n* one of the official languages of the Republic of South Africa, closely related to Dutch [c20: from Dutch: African]

Afrikander *or* **Africander** (afrɪˈkandə, ˌæfrɪˈkændə) *n* **1** a breed of humpbacked beef cattle originally raised in southern Africa **2** a southern African breed of fat-tailed sheep **3** a former name for an **Afrikaner** [c19: from South African Dutch, formed on the model of *Hollander*]

Afrikaner (afrɪˈkɑːnə, ˌæfrɪˈkɑːnə) *n* a White native of the Republic of South Africa whose mother tongue is Afrikaans. ▷ See also **Boer**

afrit ('æfriːt, ə'friːt) *n* a variant spelling of **afreet**

Afro ('æfrəʊ) *n, pl* -ros a hairstyle in which the hair is shaped into a wide frizzy bush [c20: independent use of combining form AFRO-]

Afro- *combining form* indicating Africa or African: *Afro-Asiatic*

Afro-American *n, adj* another word for **African-American**

Afro-Caribbean *adj* **1** denoting or relating to Caribbean people of African descent or their culture ▷ *n* **2** a Caribbean of African descent

Afro-pessimism *n* the belief that the provision of aid to African countries is futile

afrormosia (ˌæfrɔːˈməʊzɪə) *n* a hard teaklike wood obtained from tropical African trees of the leguminous genus *Pericopsis* [c20: from AFRO- + *Ormosia* (genus name)]

aft (ɑːft) *adv, adj chiefly nautical* towards or at the stern or rear: *the aft deck; aft of the engines* [c17: perhaps a shortened form of earlier ABAFT]

after ('ɑːftə) *prep* **1** following in time; in succession to: *after dinner; time after time* **2** following; behind **3** in pursuit or search of: *chasing after a thief; he's only after money* **4** concerning: *to inquire after his health* **5** considering: *after what you have done, you shouldn't complain* **6** next in excellence or importance to **7** in imitation of; in the manner of **8** in accordance with or in conformity to: *a man after her own heart* **9** with a name derived from **10** *US* past (the hour of): *twenty after three* **11** after all **a** in spite of everything: *it's only a game, after all* **b** in spite of expectations, efforts, etc **12** after you please go, enter, etc, before me ▷ *adv* **13** at a later time; afterwards **14** coming afterwards; in pursuit **15** *nautical* further aft; sternwards ▷ *conj* **16** (*subordinating*) at a time later than that at which ▷ *adj* **17** *nautical* further aft: *the after cabin* [Old English *æfter*; related to Old Norse *aptr* back, *eptir* after, Old High German *aftar*]

afterbirth ('ɑːftəˌbɜːθ) *n* the placenta and fetal membranes expelled from the uterus after the birth of the offspring

afterburner ('ɑːftəˌbɜːnə) *n* **1** a device in the exhaust system of an internal-combustion engine for removing or rendering harmless potentially dangerous components in the exhaust gases **2** a system of fuel injection and combustion located behind the turbine of an aircraft jet engine to produce additional thrust

afterburning ('ɑːftəˌbɜːnɪŋ) *n* Also called: reheat a process in which additional fuel is ignited in the exhaust gases of a jet engine to produce additional thrust

aftercare ('ɑːftəˌkeə) *n* **1** support services by a welfare agency for a person discharged from an institution, such as hospital, hostel, or prison **2** *med* the care before and after discharge from hospital of a patient recovering from an illness or operation **3** any system of maintenance or upkeep of an appliance or product: *contact lens aftercare*

afterdamp ('ɑːftəˌdæmp) *n* a poisonous mixture of gases containing carbon dioxide, carbon monoxide, and nitrogen formed after the explosion of firedamp in coal mines

aftereffect ('ɑːftərɪˌfɛkt) *n* any result occurring some time after its cause

afterglow ('ɑːftəˌgləʊ) *n* **1** the glow left after a light has disappeared, such as that sometimes seen after sunset **2** the glow of an incandescent metal after the source of heat has been removed

afterimage ('ɑːftərˌɪmɪdʒ) *n* a sustained or renewed sensation, esp visual, after the original stimulus has ceased

afterlife ('ɑːftəˌlaɪf) *n* life after death or at a later time in a person's lifetime

aftermath ('ɑːftəˌmɑːθ, -ˌmæθ) *n* **1** signs or results of an event or occurrence considered collectively, esp of a catastrophe or disaster: *the aftermath of war* **2** *agriculture* a second mowing or crop of grass from land that has already yielded one crop earlier in the same year [c16: AFTER + *math* a mowing, from Old English *mæth*]

aftermost ('ɑːftəˌməʊst) *adj* closer or closest to the rear or (in a vessel) the stern; last

afternoon ('ɑːftəˈnuːn) *n* **1 a** the period of the day between noon and evening **b** (*as modifier*): *afternoon tea* **2 a** middle or later part: *the afternoon of life*

afternoons (ˌɑːftəˈnuːnz) *adv informal* during the afternoon, esp regularly

afterpains (ˈɑːftəˌpeɪnz) *pl n* cramplike pains caused by contraction of the uterus after childbirth

afterparty (ˈɑːftəˌpɑːtɪ) *n* a small party held after a larger event, such as a pop concert or film première, to which only a select group of guests is invited

afters (ˈɑːftəz) *n* (*functioning as singular or plural*) *Brit informal* dessert; sweet

aftershave lotion (ˈɑːftəˌʃeɪv) *n* a lotion, usually styptic and perfumed, for application to the face after shaving

aftertaste (ˈɑːftəˌteɪst) *n* **1** a taste that lingers on after eating or drinking **2** a lingering impression or sensation

afterthought (ˈɑːftəˌθɔːt) *n* **1** a comment, reply, etc, that occurs to one after the opportunity to deliver it has passed **2** an addition to something already completed

afterwards (ˈɑːftəwədz) *or* **afterward** *adv* after an earlier event or time; subsequently [Old English *æfterweard, æfteweard,* from AFT + WARD]

Ag *the chemical symbol for* silver [from Latin *argentum*]

AG *abbreviation* **1** Adjutant General **2** Attorney General

aga *or* **agha** (ˈɑːɡə) *n* (in the Ottoman Empire) a title of respect, often used with the title of a senior position [C17: Turkish, literally: lord]

Agadir (ˌæɡəˈdɪə) *n* a port in SW Morocco, which became the centre of an international crisis (1911), when a gunboat arrived to protect German interests. Britain issued a strong warning to Germany but the French negotiated and war was averted. In 1960 the town was virtually destroyed by an earthquake, about 10 000 people being killed. Pop: 385 000 (2003)

again (əˈɡɛn, əˈɡeɪn) *adv* **1** another or second time; once more; anew: *he had to start again* **2** once more in a previously experienced or imagined place, state, or condition: *he is ill again; he came back again* **3** in addition to the original amount, quantity, etc (esp in the phrases **as much again; half as much again**) **4** (*sentence modifier*) on the other hand **5** besides; also **6** *archaic* in reply; back: *he answered again to the questioning voice* **7** again and again continuously; repeatedly ▷ *sentence connector* **8** moreover; furthermore [Old English *ongegn* opposite to, from A-² + *gegn* straight]

against (əˈɡɛnst, əˈɡeɪnst) *prep* **1** opposed to; in conflict or disagreement with **2** standing or leaning beside or in front of: *a ladder against the wall* **3** coming in contact with **4** in contrast to: *silhouettes are outlines against a light background* **5** having an adverse or unfavourable effect on: *the economic system works against small independent companies* **6** as a protection from or means of defence from the adverse effects of: *a safeguard against contaminated water* **7** in exchange for or in return for **8** *now rare* in preparation for: *he gave them warm clothing against their journey through the night* **9** as against as opposed to or as compared with [C12: *ageines,* from *again, ageyn,* etc, AGAIN + -es genitive ending; the spelling with -t (C16) was probably due to confusion with superlatives ending in -st]

Aga Khan (ˈɑːɡə ˈkɑːn) *n* the hereditary title of the head of the Ismaili sect of Muslims

Aga Khan IV *n* Prince **Karim** (kəˈriːm). born 1936, spiritual leader of the Ismaili sect of Muslims from 1957

Agamemnon (ˌæɡəˈmɛmnɒn) *n Greek myth* a king of Mycenae who led the Greeks at the siege of Troy. On his return home he was murdered by his wife Clytemnestra and her lover Aegisthus. See also **Menelaus**

agamic (əˈɡæmɪk) *adj* asexual; occurring or reproducing without fertilization [C19: from Greek *agamos* unmarried, from A-¹ + *gamos* marriage]

agamogenesis (ˌæɡəməʊˈdʒɛnɪsɪs) *n* asexual reproduction, such as fission or parthenogenesis [C19: AGAMIC + GENESIS]

Agana (əˈɡɑːnjə) *n* the former name for **Hagåtña**

agapanthus (ˌæɡəˈpænθəs) *n* a liliaceous plant, *Agapanthus africanus,* of southern Africa, having rounded clusters of blue or white funnel-shaped flowers [C19: New Latin, from Greek *agapē* love + *anthos* flower]

agape (əˈɡeɪp) *adj* (*postpositive*) **1** (esp of the mouth) wide open **2** very surprised, expectant, or eager, esp as indicated by a wide open mouth [C17: A-² + GAPE]

Agape (ˈæɡəpɪ) *n Christianity* **1** Christian love, esp as contrasted with erotic love; charity **2** a communal meal in the early Church taken in commemoration of the Last Supper; love feast [C17: Greek *agapē* love]

agar (ˈeɪɡə) *n* a complex gelatinous carbohydrate obtained from seaweeds, esp those of the genus *Gelidium,* used as a culture medium for bacteria, a laxative, in food such as ice cream as a thickening agent (**E406**), etc. Also called: agar-agar [C19: Malay]

agaric (ˈæɡərɪk, əˈɡærɪk) *n* any saprotrophic basidiomycetous fungus of the family *Agaricaceae,* having gills on the underside of the cap. The group includes the edible mushrooms and poisonous forms such as the fly agaric [C16: via Latin *agaricum,* from Greek *agarikon,* perhaps named after *Agaria,* a town in Sarmatia]

Agartala (ˌʌɡəˈtlɑː) *n* a city in NE India, capital of the state of Tripura. Pop: 189 327 (2001)

Agassi (ˈæɡəsɪ) *n* **Andre** (ˈɑːndreɪ). born 1970, US tennis player: won the Wimbledon men's singles in 1992 and the US Open in 1994 and 1999

Agassiz (*French* aɡasi) *n* **Jean Louis Rodolphe** (ʒɑ̃ lwi rɔdɔlf). 1807–73, Swiss natural historian and geologist, settled in the US after 1846

agate¹ (ˈæɡɪt) *n* **1** an impure microcrystalline form of quartz consisting of a variegated, usually banded chalcedony, used as a gemstone and in making pestles and mortars, burnishers, and polishers. Formula: SiO_2 **2** a playing marble of this quartz or resembling it [C16: via French from Latin *achātēs,* from Greek *akhatēs*]

agate² (əˈɡeɪt) *adv Northern English dialect* on the way [C16: A-² + GATE]

Agate (ˈæɡeɪt) *n* **James** (**Evershed**). 1877–1947, British theatre critic; drama critic for *The Sunday Times* (1923–47) and author of a nine-volume diary *Ego* (1935–49)

agave (əˈɡeɪvɪ, æˈɡeɪvɪ) *n* any plant of the genus *Agave,* native to tropical America, with tall flower stalks rising from a massive, often armed, rosette of thick fleshy leaves: family *Agavaceae.* Some species are the source of fibres such as sisal or of alcoholic beverages such as pulque and tequila [C18: New Latin, from Greek *agauē,* feminine of *agauos* illustrious, probably alluding to the height of the plant]

age (eɪdʒ) *n* **1** the period of time that a person, animal, or plant has lived or is expected to live **2** the period of existence of an object, material, group, etc: *the age of this table is 200 years* **3** a period or state of human life: *he should know better at his age; she had got beyond the giggly age* **b** (*as modifier*): *age group* **4** the latter part of life **5 a** a period of history marked by some feature or characteristic; era **b** (*capital when part of a name*): *the Middle Ages; the Space Age* **6** generation: *the Edwardian age* **7** *geology, palaeontol* **a** a period of the earth's history distinguished by special characteristics: *the age of reptiles* **b** the period during which a stage of rock strata is formed; a subdivision of an epoch **8** (*often plural*) *informal* a relatively long time: *she was an age washing her hair; I've been waiting ages* **9** *psychol* the level in years that a person has reached in any area of development, such as mental or emotional, compared with the normal level for his chronological age **10** of age adult and legally responsible for one's actions (usually at 18 or, formerly, 21 years) ▷ *vb* **ages, ageing** *or* **aging, aged 11** to grow or make old or apparently old; become or cause to become old or aged **12** to begin to seem older: *to have aged a lot in the past year* **13** *brewing* to mature or cause to mature [C13: via Old French from Vulgar Latin *aetaticum* (unattested), from Latin *aetās,* ultimately from *aevum* lifetime; compare AEON]

-age *suffix forming nouns* **1** indicating a collection, set, or group: *acreage; baggage* **2** indicating a process or action or the result of an action: *haulage; passage; breakage* **3** indicating a state, condition, or relationship: *bondage; parentage* **4** indicating a house or place: *orphanage* **5** indicating a charge or fee: *postage* **6** indicating a rate: *dosage; mileage* [from Old French, from Late Latin *-āticum,* noun suffix, neuter of *-āticus,* adjectival suffix, from *-ātus* -ATE¹ + *-icus* -IC]

aged (ˈeɪdʒɪd) *adj* **1 a** advanced in years; old **b** (*as collective noun; preceded by the*): *the aged* **2** of, connected with, or characteristic of old age **3** (eɪdʒd) (*postpositive*) having the age of: *a woman aged twenty*

Agee ('eɪdʒiː) *n* **James.** 1909–55, US novelist, poet, and film critic. His works include the autobiographical novel *A Death in the Family* (1957)

ageing *or* **aging** ('eɪdʒɪŋ) *n* **1** the process of growing old or developing the appearance and characteristics of old age ▷ *adj* **2** becoming or appearing older or elderly: *an ageing car* **3** giving or creating the appearance of age or elderliness: *that dress is really ageing on her*

ageism *or* **agism** ('eɪdʒɪzəm) *n* discrimination against people on the grounds of age; specifically, discrimination against the elderly > 'ageist *or* 'agist *adj*

ageless ('eɪdʒlɪs) *adj* **1** apparently never growing old **2** timeless; eternal: *an ageless quality*

agency ('eɪdʒənsɪ) *n, pl* -cies **1** a business or other organization providing a specific service: *an employment agency* **2** the place where an agent conducts business **3** the business, duties, or functions of an agent **4** action, power, or operation: *the agency of fate* [C17: from Medieval Latin *agentia*, from Latin *agere* to do]

agenda (ə'dʒɛndə) *n* **1** Also called: **agendum** (*functioning as singular*) a schedule or list of items to be attended to **2** Also called: **agendas, agendums** (*functioning as plural*) matters to be attended to, as at a meeting of a committee [C17: Latin, literally: things to be done, from *agere* to do]

agent ('eɪdʒənt) *n* **1** a person who acts on behalf of another person, group, business, government, etc; representative **2** a person or thing that acts or has the power to act **3** a phenomenon, substance, or organism that exerts some force or effect: *a chemical agent* **4** the means by which something occurs or is achieved; instrument **5** a person representing a business concern, esp a travelling salesman [C15: from Latin *agent-*, noun use of the present participle of *agere* to do] > **agential** (eɪ'dʒɛnʃəl) *adj*

agent-general *n, pl* agents-general a representative in London of a Canadian province or an Australian state

Agent Orange *n* a highly poisonous herbicide used as a spray for defoliation and crop destruction, esp by US forces during the Vietnam War [C20: named after the identifying colour stripe on its container]

agent provocateur French (aʒɑ̃ prɔvɔkatœr) *n, pl* agents provocateurs (aʒɑ̃ prɔvɔkatœr) a secret agent employed to provoke suspected persons to commit illegal acts and so be discredited or liable to punishment

age of consent *n* **1** the age at which a person is considered legally competent to consent to sexual intercourse **2** the age at which a person can enter into a legally binding contract

Age of Reason *n* the Age of Reason the 18th century in W Europe. See also **Enlightenment**

age-old *or* **age-long** *adj* very old or of long duration; ancient

age-proof *adj* **1** not adversely affected by a person's age: *an age-proof career* ▷ *vb* **2** (*tr*) to make (something) age-proof

ageratum (ˌædʒə'reɪtəm) *n* any tropical American plant of the genus *Ageratum*, such as *A. houstonianum* and *A. conyzoides*, which have thick clusters of purplish-blue flowers [C16: New Latin, via Latin from Greek *agēraton* that which does not age, from A-¹ + *gērat-*, stem of *gēras* old age; the flowers of the plant remain vivid for a long time]

agglomerate *vb* (ə'glɒməˌreɪt) **1** to form or be formed into a mass or cluster; collect ▷ *n* (ə'glɒmərɪt, -ˌreɪt) **2** a confused mass **3** a rock consisting of angular fragments of volcanic lava ▷ *adj* (ə'glɒmərɪt, -ˌreɪt) **4** formed into a mass [C17: from Latin *agglomerāre*, from *glomerāre* to wind into a ball, from *glomus* ball, mass] > ag,glomer'ation *n* > ag'glomerative *adj*

agglutinate (ə'gluːtɪˌneɪt) *vb* **1** to adhere or cause to adhere, as with glue **2** *linguistics* to combine or be combined by agglutination **3** (*tr*) to cause (bacteria, red blood cells, etc) to clump together [C16: from Latin *agglūtināre* to glue to, from *gluten* glue] > ag'glutinable *adj* > ag'glutinant *adj*

agglutination (əˌgluːtɪ'neɪʃən) *n* **1** the act or process of

agglutinating **2** a united mass or group of parts **3** *chem* the formation of clumps of particles in a suspension **4** *immunol* the formation of a mass of particles, such as erythrocytes, by the action of antibodies **5** *linguistics* the building up of words from component morphemes in such a way that these undergo little or no change of form or meaning in the process of combination

aggrandize *or* **aggrandise** ('ægrənˌdaɪz, ə'grænˌdaɪz) *vb* (*tr*) **1** to increase the power, wealth, prestige, scope, etc, of **2** to cause (something) to seem greater; magnify; exaggerate [C17: from Old French *aggrandiss-*, long stem of *aggrandir* to make bigger, from Latin *grandis* GRAND; the ending -*ize* is due to the influence of verbs ending in -*ise*, -*ize*] > aggrandizement *or* aggrandisement (ə'grændɪzmənt) *n* > 'aggran,dizer *or* 'aggran,diser *n*

aggravate ('ægrəˌveɪt) *vb* (*tr*) **1** to make (a disease, situation, problem, etc) worse or more severe **2** *informal* to annoy; exasperate, esp by deliberate and persistent goading [C16: from Latin *aggravāre* to make heavier, from *gravis* heavy] > 'aggra,vating *adj* > ,aggra'vation *n*

aggravated ('ægrəˌveɪtɪd) *adj law* (of a criminal offence) made more serious by its circumstances

aggravated trespass *n law* an offence in which a trespasser in the open air attempts to interfere with a lawful activity, such as hunting

aggregate *adj* ('ægrɪgɪt, -ˌgeɪt) **1** formed of separate units collected into a whole; collective; corporate **2** (of fruits and flowers) composed of a dense cluster of carpels or florets ▷ *n* ('ægrɪgɪt, -ˌgeɪt) **3** a sum or assemblage of many separate units; sum total **4** *geology* a rock, such as granite, consisting of a mixture of minerals **5** the sand and stone mixed with cement and water to make concrete **6** in the aggregate taken as a whole ▷ *vb* ('ægrɪˌgeɪt) **7** to combine or be combined into a body, etc **8** (*tr*) to amount to (a number) [C16: from Latin *aggregāre* to add to a flock or herd, attach (oneself) to, from *grex* flock] > aggregative ('ægrɪˌgeɪtɪv) *adj* > ,aggre'gation *n*

aggregator ('ægrɪˌgeɪtə) *n* **1** a business organization that collates the details of an individual's financial affairs so that the information can be presented on a single website **2** a firm that brings together a large group of consumers on whose behalf it negotiates reduced rates for good or services, esp in the energy sector **3** a web application that draws together syndicated content from various online sources and displays it in a single location for the user's convenience

aggress (ə'grɛs) *vb* (*intr*) to attack first or begin a quarrel [C16: from Medieval Latin *aggressāre* to attack, from Latin *aggredī* to attack, approach]

aggression (ə'grɛʃən) *n* **1** an attack or harmful action, esp an unprovoked attack by one country against another **2** any offensive activity, practice, etc **3** *psychol* a hostile or destructive mental attitude or behaviour [C17: from Latin *aggression-*, from *aggrĕdi* to attack] > aggressor (ə'grɛsə) *n*

aggressive (ə'grɛsɪv) *adj* **1** quarrelsome or belligerent **2** assertive; vigorous > ag'gressively *adv* > ag'gressiveness *n*

aggrieve (ə'griːv) *vb* (*tr*) **1** (*often impersonal or passive*) to grieve; distress; afflict **2** to injure unjustly, esp by infringing a person's legal rights [C14: *agreven*, via Old French from Latin *aggravāre* to AGGRAVATE]

aggrieved (ə'griːvd) *adj* feeling resentment at having been treated unjustly > aggrievedly (ə'griːvɪdlɪ) *adv*

aggro ('ægrəʊ) *n Brit slang* aggressive behaviour, esp by youths in a gang [C20: from AGGRAVATION]

aghast (ə'gɑːst) *adj* (*postpositive*) overcome with amazement or horror [C13: *agast*, from Old English *gæstan* to frighten. The spelling with *gh* is on the model of GHASTLY]

agile ('ædʒaɪl) *adj* **1** quick in movement; nimble **2** mentally quick or acute [C15: from Latin *agilis*, from *agere* to do, act] > 'agilely *adv* > agility (ə'dʒɪlɪtɪ) *n*

agin (ə'gɪn) *prep* an informal, facetious, or dialect word for **against** [C19: from obsolete *again* AGAINST]

Agincourt ('ædʒɪnˌkɔːt; *French* aʒɛ̃kur) *n* a battle fought in 1415 near the village of Azincourt, N France: a decisive victory for English longbowmen under Henry V over

French forces vastly superior in number

agio ('ædʒɪəʊ) *n, pl* **-ios a** the difference between the nominal and actual values of a currency **b** the charge payable for conversion of the less valuable currency [C17: from Italian, literally: ease]

agitate ('ædʒɪˌteɪt) *vb* **1** (*tr*) to excite, disturb, or trouble (a person, the mind, or feelings); worry **2** (*tr*) to cause to move vigorously; shake, stir, or disturb **3** (*intr*; often foll by *for* or *against*) to attempt to stir up public opinion for or against something [C16: from Latin *agitātus*, from *agitāre* to move to and fro, set into motion, from *agere* to act, do] > 'agiˌtated *adj* > 'agiˌtatedly *adv* > agitation (ˌædʒɪ'teɪʃən) *n* > ˌagi'tational *adj*

agitato (ˌædʒɪ'tɑːtəʊ) *adj, adv music* (to be performed) in an agitated manner

agitator ('ædʒɪˌteɪtə) *n* **1** a person who agitates for or against a cause, etc **2** a device, machine, or part used for mixing, shaking, or vibrating a material, usually a fluid

agitprop ('ædʒɪtˌprɒp) *n* **a** any promotion, as in the arts, of political propaganda, esp of a Communist nature **b** (*as modifier*): *agitprop theatre* [C20: short for Russian *Agitpropbyuro*, from *agit(atsiya)* agitation + *prop(aganda)* propaganda]

Aglaia (ə'glaɪə) *n Greek myth* one of the three Graces [Greek: splendour, from *aglaos* splendid]

agleam (ə'gliːm) *adj* (*postpositive*) glowing; gleaming

aglet ('æglɪt) *or* **aiglet** *n* **1** a metal sheath or tag at the end of a shoelace, ribbon, etc **2** a variant spelling of **aiguillette** [C15: from Old French *aiguillette* a small needle]

agley (ə'gleɪ, ə'glaɪ, ə'gliː) *or* **aglee** (ə'gliː) *adv, adj Scot* awry; askew [from *gley* squint]

aglitter (ə'glɪtə) *adj* (*postpositive*) sparkling; glittering

aglow (ə'gləʊ) *adj* (*postpositive*) glowing

aglu *or* **agloo** ('æglu:) *n Canadian* a breathing hole made in ice by a seal [C19: from Inuktitut]

AGM *abbreviation* annual general meeting

agnail ('ægˌneɪl) *n* another name for **hangnail**

agnate ('ægneɪt) *adj* **1** related by descent from a common male ancestor **2** related in any way; cognate ▷ *n* **3** a male or female descendant by male links from a common male ancestor [C16: from Latin *agnātus* born in addition, added by birth, from *agnāsci*, from *ad-* in addition + *gnāsci* to be born]

Agnes ('ægnɪs) *n* **Saint**. ?292–?304 AD, Christian child martyr under Diocletian. Feast day: Jan 21

Agnesi (*Italian* a:n'jezi) *n* **Maria Gaetana**. 1718–99, Italian mathematician and philosopher, noted for her work on differential calculus

Agnew ('ægnju:) *n* **Spiro** ('spɪərəʊ) **Theodore**. 1918–96, US Republican politician; vice president (1969–73)

Agni ('ʌgnɪ) *n Hinduism* the god of fire, one of the three chief deities of the Vedas [Sanskrit: fire]

Agnon ('ægnɒn) *n* **Shmuel Yosef**, real name Samuel Josef Czaczkes. 1888–1970, Israeli novelist, born in Austria-Hungary. His works, which treat contemporary Jewish themes, include *The Day Before Yesterday* (1945). Nobel prize for literature 1966

agnostic (æg'nɒstɪk) *n* **1** a person who holds that knowledge of a Supreme Being, ultimate cause, etc, is impossible **2** a person who claims, with respect to any particular question, that the answer cannot be known with certainty ▷ *adj* **3** of or relating to agnostics [C19: coined 1869 by T. H. Huxley from A-[1] + GNOSTIC] > ag'nosticism *n*

Agnus Dei ('ægnʊs 'deɪɪ) *n Christianity* **1** the figure of a lamb bearing a cross or banner, emblematic of Christ **2** a chant beginning with these words or a translation of them, forming part of the Roman Catholic Mass or sung as an anthem in the Anglican liturgy [Latin: Lamb of God]

ago (ə'gəʊ) *adv* in the past: *five years ago; long ago* [C14 *ago*, from Old English *āgān* to pass away]
  ● **USAGE** The use of *ago* with *since* (*it's ten years ago since he wrote the novel*) is redundant and should be avoided: *it is ten years since he wrote the novel*

agog (ə'gɒg) *adj* (*postpositive*) highly impatient, eager, or curious [C15: perhaps from Old French *en gogues* in merriment, origin unknown]

-agogue *or esp US* **-agog** *n combining form* indicating a person or thing that leads or incites to action: *pedagogue; demagogue* [via Late Latin from Greek *agōgos* leading, from *agein* to lead] > **-agogy** *n combining form*

agon ('ægəʊn, -gɒn) *n, pl* **agones** (ə'gəʊni:z) (in ancient Greece) a festival at which competitors contended for prizes. Among the best known were the Olympic, Pythian, Nemean, and Isthmian Games [C17: Greek: contest, from *agein* to lead]

agonic (ə'gɒnɪk, eɪ'gɒnɪk) *adj* forming no angle [C19: from Greek *agōnos*, from A-[1] + *gōnia* angle]

agonic line *n* an imaginary line on the surface of the earth connecting points of zero magnetic declination

agonize *or* **agonise** ('ægəˌnaɪz) *vb* **1** to suffer or cause to suffer agony **2** (*intr*) to make a desperate effort; struggle; strive [C16: via Medieval Latin from Greek *agōnizesthai* to contend for a prize, from *agōn* AGON] > 'agoˌnizingly *or* 'agoˌnisingly *adv*

agony ('ægənɪ) *n, pl* **-nies 1** acute physical or mental pain; anguish **2** the suffering or struggle preceding death [C14: via Late Latin from Greek *agōnia* struggle, from *agōn* contest]

agony aunt *n* (*sometimes capital*) a person who writes the replies to readers' letters in an agony column

agony column *n* **1** a magazine or newspaper feature in which advice is offered to readers who have sent in letters about their personal problems **2** a part of a newspaper containing advertisements for lost relatives, personal messages, etc

agora ('ægərə) *n, pl* **-rae** (-riː, -raɪ) (*often capital*) **a** the marketplace in Athens, used for popular meetings, or any similar place of assembly in ancient Greece **b** the meeting itself [from Greek, from *agorein* to gather]

agoraphobia (ˌægərə'fəʊbɪə) *n* a pathological fear of being in public places, often resulting in the sufferer becoming housebound > ˌagora'phobic *adj, n*

Agostini (*Italian* agos'ti:ni) *n* **Giacomo** ('dʒa:komo). born 1944, Italian racing motorcyclist: world champion (500 cc. class) 1966–72, 1975; (350 cc. class) 1968–74

Agostino di Duccio (*Italian* ago'sti:no dɪ 'duttʃo) *n* 1415–81, Italian sculptor, noted for his carved marble panels in the interior of the Tempio Malatestiano at Rimini

agouti (ə'guːtɪ) *n, pl* **-tis** *or* **-ties** any hystricomorph rodent of the genus *Dasyprocta*, of Central and South America and the Caribbean: family *Dasyproctidae*. Agoutis are agile and long-legged, with hooflike claws, and are valued for their meat [C18: via French and Spanish from Guarani]

AGR *abbreviation* advanced gas-cooled reactor

Agra ('a:grə) *n* a city in N India, in W Uttar Pradesh on the Jumna River: a capital of the Mogul empire until 1658; famous for its Mogul architecture, esp the Taj Mahal. Pop: 1 259 979 (2001)

Agram ('a:gram) *n* the German name for **Zagreb**

agrarian (ə'grɛərɪən) *adj* **1** of or relating to land or its cultivation or to systems of dividing landed property **2** of or relating to rural or agricultural matters ▷ *n* **3** a person who favours the redistribution of landed property [C16: from Latin *agrārius*, from *ager* field, land] > a'grarianism *n*

agree (ə'griː) *vb* **agrees, agreeing, agreed** (*mainly intr*) **1** (often foll by *with*) to be of the same opinion; concur **2** (*also tr*; when *intr*, often foll by *to*; when *tr, takes a clause as object or an infinitive*) to give assent; consent **3** (*also tr*; when *intr*, foll by *on* or *about*; when *tr, may take a clause as object*) to come to terms (about); arrive at a settlement (on) **4** (foll by *with*) to be similar or consistent; harmonize; correspond **5** (foll by *with*) to be agreeable or suitable (to one's health, temperament, etc) **6** (*tr; takes a clause as object*) to concede or grant; admit: *they agreed that the price they were asking was too high* **7** *grammar* to undergo agreement [C14: from Old French *agreer*, from the phrase *a gre* at will or pleasure]

agreeable (ə'griːəbᵊl) *adj* **1** pleasing; pleasant **2** prepared to consent **3** (foll by *to* or *with*) in keeping; consistent **4** (foll by *to*) to one's liking > a'greeableness *n* > a'greeably *adv*

agreed (ə'griːd) *adj* **1** determined by common consent:

the agreed price ▷ *interj* **2** an expression of agreement or consent

agreement (ə'gri:mənt) *n* **1** the act of agreeing **2** a settlement, esp one that is legally enforceable; covenant; treaty **3** a contract or document containing such a settlement **4** the state of being of the same opinion; concord; harmony **5** the state of being similar or consistent; correspondence; conformity **6** Also called: concord *grammar* the determination of the inflectional form of one word by some grammatical feature, such as number or gender, of another word, esp one in the same sentence [c14: from Old French]

agribusiness ('ægrɪ,bɪznɪs) *n* the various businesses collectively that process, distribute, and support farm products [c20: from AGRI(CULTURE) + BUSINESS]

Agricola (ə'grɪkələ) *n* **Gnaeus Julius** ('ni:əs 'dʒu:lɪəs) 40–93 AD, Roman general; governor of Britain who advanced Roman rule north to the Firth of Forth

agriculture ('ægrɪ,kʌltʃə) *n* the science or occupation of cultivating land and rearing crops and livestock; farming; husbandry [c17: from Latin *agricultūra*, from *ager* field, land + *cultūra* CULTURE] > ,agri'cultural *adj* > ,agri'culturist *or* ,agri'culturalist *n*

Agrigento (*Italian* agri'dʒɛnto) *n* a town in Italy, in SW Sicily: site of six Greek temples. Pop: 54 619 (2001). Former name (until 1927): Girgenti (ɡɜː'ɡɛntɪ)

agrimony ('ægrɪmənɪ) *n* **1** any of various N temperate rosaceous plants of the genus *Agrimonia*, which have compound leaves, long spikes of small yellow flowers, and bristly burlike fruits **2** any of several other plants, such as hemp agrimony [c15: altered from *egrimonie* (c14), via Old French from Latin *agrimōnia*, variant of *argemōnia* from Greek *argemōnē* poppy]

Agrippa (ə'grɪpə) *n* **Marcus Vipsanius** ('mɑːkəs vɪp'seɪnɪəs). 63–12 BC, Roman general: chief adviser and later son-in-law of Augustus

Agrippina (,ægrɪ'pi:nə) *n* **1** called *the Elder. c.* 14 BC–33 AD, Roman matron: granddaughter of Augustus, wife of Germanicus, mother of Caligula and Agrippina the Younger **2** called *the Younger.* 15–59 AD, mother of Nero, who put her to death after he became emperor

agritourism ('ægrɪ,tʊərɪzəm) *or* **agrotourism** ('ægrəʊ,tʊərɪzəm) *n* tourism in which customers stay in accommodation on working farms and may have the opportunity to help with farm work > 'agri,tourist *n* [c20: from AGRI(CULTURE) + TOURISM]

agro- *combining form* denoting fields, soil, or agriculture: *agronomy* [from Greek *agros* field]

agrobiology (,ægrəʊbaɪ'ɒlədʒɪ) *n* the science of plant growth and nutrition in relation to agriculture

agrodolce (,ægrəʊ'dɒltʃɪ) *n* an Italian sweet-and-sour sauce, made with onions, garlic, red wine vinegar, sugar, and raisins [c21: from Italian]

agroforestry (,ægrəʊ'fɒrɪstrɪ) *n* a method of farming integrating herbaceous and tree crops

agronomics (,ægrə'nɒmɪks) *n* (*functioning as singular*) the branch of economics dealing with the distribution, management, and productivity of land > ,agro'nomic *or* ,agro'nomical *adj*

agronomy (ə'grɒnəmɪ) *n* the science of cultivation of land, soil management, and crop production > a'gronomist *n*

agrostemma (,ægrəʊ'stɛmə) *n* See **corncockle** [New Latin, from Greek *agros* a field + *stemma* a garland]

aground (ə'graʊnd) *adv, adj* (*postpositive*) on or onto the ground or bottom, as in shallow water

agterskot ('axtə,skɒt) *n* *South African* the final payment to a farmer for crops. See **voorskot** [c20: Afrikaans *agter* after + *skot* shot, payment]

Aguascalientes (*Spanish* aɣwaska'ljentes) *n* **1** a state in central Mexico. Pop: 943 506 (2000). Area: 5471 sq km (2112 sq miles) **2** a city in central Mexico, capital of Aguascalientes state, about 1900 m (6200 ft) above sea level, with hot springs. Pop: 830 000 (2005 est)

ague ('eɪgjuː) *n* **1** a fever with successive stages of fever and chills esp when caused by malaria **2** a fit of shivering [c14: from Old French (*fievre*) *ague* acute fever; see ACUTE] > 'aguish *adj*

ah (ɑː) *interj* an exclamation expressing pleasure, pain, sympathy, etc, according to the intonation of the speaker

AH *abbreviation* (indicating years in the Muslim system of dating, numbered from the Hegira (622 AD)) anno Hegirae [Latin]

aha (ɑː'hɑː) *interj* an exclamation expressing triumph, surprise, etc, according to the intonation of the speaker

Ahab ('eɪhæb) *n* *Old Testament* the king of Israel from approximately 869 to 850 BC and husband of Jezebel: rebuked by Elijah (I Kings 16:29–22:40)

aha moment *n* an instant at which the solution to a problem becomes clear

Ahasuerus (ə,hæzjuː'ɪərəs) *n* *Old Testament* a king of ancient Persia and husband of Esther, generally identified with Xerxes

ahead (ə'hɛd) *adj* **1** (*postpositive*) in front; in advance ▷ *adv* **2** at or in the front; in advance; before **3** onwards; forwards: *go straight ahead* **4** ahead of **a** in front of; at a further advanced position than **b** *stock exchange* in anticipation of: *the share price rose ahead of the annual figures* **5** be ahead *informal* to have an advantage; be winning **6** get ahead to advance or attain success

ahem (ə'hɛm) *interj* a clearing of the throat, used to attract attention, express doubt, etc

Ahern (ə'hɜːn) *n* **Bertie**. born 1951, Irish politician; leader of the Fianna Fáil party from 1994; prime minister of the Republic of Ireland from 1997

ahi ('ɑːhiː) *n* another name for **yellowfin tuna** [Hawaiian]

ahimsa (ɑː'hɪmsɑː) *n* (in Hindu, Buddhist, and Jainist philosophy) the law of reverence for, and nonviolence to, every form of life [Sanskrit, from A-¹ + *himsā* injury]

Ahithophel (ə'hɪθə,fɛl) *or* **Achitophel** *n* *Old Testament* a member of David's council, who became one of Absalom's advisers in his rebellion and hanged himself when his advice was overruled (II Samuel 15:12–17:23)

Ahmedabad *or* **Ahmadabad** ('ɑːmədə,bɑːd) *n* a city in W India, in Gujarat: famous for its mosque. Pop: 3 515 361 (2001)

Ahmednagar *or* **Ahmadnagar** (,ɑːməd'nʌgə) *n* a city in W India, in Maharashtra: formerly one of the kingdoms of Deccan. Pop: 307 455 (2001)

ahoy (ə'hɔɪ) *interj* *nautical* a hail used to call a ship or to attract attention

Ahriman ('ɑːrɪmən) *n* *Zoroastrianism* the supreme evil spirit and diabolical opponent of Ormazd

Ahura Mazda (ə'hʊərə 'mæzdə) *n* *Zoroastrianism* another name for **Ormazd**

Ahvenanmaa ('ɑhvɛnɑmmɑː) *n* the Finnish name for the **Åland Islands**

Ahwaz (ɑː'wɑːz) *or* **Ahvaz** (ɑː'vɑːz) *n* a town in SW Iran, on the Karun River. Pop: 967 000 (2005 est)

ai ('ɑːiː) *n, pl* **ais** the three-toed sloth. See **sloth** (sense 1) [c17: from Portuguese, from Tupi]

AI *abbreviation* **1** artificial insemination **2** artificial intelligence

aid (eɪd) *vb* **1** to give support to (someone to do something); help or assist **2** (*tr*) to assist financially ▷ *n* **3** assistance; help; support **4** a person, device, etc, that helps or assists **5** Also called: artificial aid *mountaineering* any of various devices such as piton or nut when used as a direct help in the ascent **6** (in medieval Europe; in England after 1066) a feudal payment made to the king or any lord by his vassals, usually on certain occasions such as the marriage of a daughter or the knighting of an eldest son [c15: via Old French *aidier* from Latin *adjūtāre* to help, from *juvāre* to help] > 'aider *n*

Aid *or* **-aid** *n combining form* denoting a charitable organization or function that raises money for a cause: *Band Aid*; *Ferryaid*

Aidan ('eɪdⁿn) *n* **Saint**. died 651 AD, Irish missionary in Northumbria, who founded the monastery at Lindisfarne (635). Feast day: Aug 31

aide (eɪd) *n* **1** an assistant **2** short for **aide-de-camp**

aide-de-camp *or* **aid-de-camp** ('eɪd də 'kɒŋ) *n, pl* **aides-de-camp** *or* **aids-de-camp** a military officer serving as personal assistant to a senior. Abbreviation: ADC [c17: from French: camp assistant]

aide-mémoire *French* (ɛdmɛmwar; *English* 'eɪd mɛm'wɑː) *n,*

pl aides-mémoire (ɛdmɛmwar; *English* 'eɪdz mɛm'wɑ:) **1** a note serving as a reminder **2** a summarized diplomatic communication [from *aider* to help + *mémoire* memory]

AIDS *or* **Aids** (eɪdz) *n acronym for* acquired immune (or immuno-)deficiency syndrome: a condition, caused by a virus, in which certain white blood cells (lymphocytes) are destroyed, resulting in loss of the body's ability to protect itself against disease. AIDS is transmitted by sexual intercourse, through infected blood and blood products, and through the placenta

AIDS-related complex *n* See **ARC**

AIF *abbreviation* (formerly) Australian Imperial Force

aiglet ('eɪglɪt) *n* a variant of **aglet**

aigrette *or* **aigret** ('eɪgrɛt, eɪ'grɛt) *n* **1** a long plume worn on hats or as a headdress, esp one of long egret feathers **2** an ornament or piece of jewellery in imitation of a plume of feathers [C19: French]

aiguille (eɪ'gwiːl, 'eɪgwiːl) *n* **1** a rock mass or mountain peak shaped like a needle **2** an instrument for boring holes in rocks or masonry [C19: French, literally: needle]

aiguillette (ˌeɪgwɪ'lɛt) *n* **1** an ornamentation worn by certain military officers, consisting of cords with metal tips **2** a variant of **aglet** [C19: F; see AGLET]

AIH *abbreviation* artificial insemination (by) husband

Aiken ('eɪkən) *n* **1** Conrad (*Potter*). 1889–1973, US poet, short-story writer, and critic. His works include *Collected Poems* (1953) and the novel *Blue Voyage* (1927) **2** Howard Hathaway. 1900–73, US mathematician; pioneered the construction of electronic computers

aikido ('aɪkɪdəʊ) *n* a Japanese system of self-defence employing similar principles to judo, but including blows from the hands and feet [from Japanese, from *ai* to join, receive + *ki* spirit, force + *do* way]

ail (eɪl) *vb* **1** (*tr*) to trouble; afflict **2** (*intr*) to feel unwell [Old English *eglan* to trouble, from *egle* troublesome, painful, related to Gothic *agls* shameful]

ailanthus (eɪ'lænθəs) *n, pl* -thuses an E Asian simaroubaceous deciduous tree, *Ailanthus altissima*, planted in Europe and North America, having pinnate leaves, small greenish flowers, and winged fruits. Also called: tree of heaven [C19: New Latin, from native name (in Amboina) *ai lanto* tree (of) the gods]

aileron ('eɪlərɒn) *n* a flap hinged to the trailing edge of an aircraft wing to provide lateral control, as in a bank or roll [C20: from French, diminutive of *aile* wing]

ailing ('eɪlɪŋ) *adj* unwell or unsuccessful

ailment ('eɪlmənt) *n* a slight but often persistent illness

aim (eɪm) *vb* **1** to point (a weapon, missile, etc) or direct (a blow) at a particular person or object; level **2** (*tr*) to direct (satire, criticism, etc) at a person, object, etc **3** (*intr*; foll by *at* or an infinitive) to propose or intend **4** (*intr*; often foll by *at* or *for*) to direct one's efforts or strive (towards) ▷ *n* **5** the action of directing something at an object **6** the direction in which something is pointed; line of sighting (esp in the phrase **to take aim**) **7** the object at which something is aimed; target **8** intention; purpose [C14: via Old French *aesmer* from Latin *aestimāre* to ESTIMATE]

AIM *abbreviation* (in Britain) Alternative Investment Market

aimless ('eɪmlɪs) *adj* having no goal, purpose, or direction > 'aimlessly *adv* > 'aimlessness *n*

Ain (French ɛ̃) *n* **1** a department in E central France, in Rhône-Alpes region. Capital: Bourg. Pop: 539 006 (2003 est). Area: 5785 sq km (2256 sq miles) **2** a river in E France, rising in the Jura Mountains and flowing south to the Rhône. Length: 190 km (118 miles)

ain't (eɪnt) *not standard contraction of* am not, is not, are not, have not, or has not: *I ain't seen it*

A into G *abbreviation* NZ *slang* arse into gear (esp in the phrase **get your A into G**)

Aintree ('eɪntrɪ) *n* a suburb of Liverpool, in Merseyside: site of the racecourse over which the Grand National steeplechase has been run since 1839

Ainu ('aɪnu:) *n* **1** *pl* -nus, -nu a member of the aboriginal people of Japan, now mostly intermixed with Mongoloid immigrants whose skin colour is more yellowish **2** the language of this people, sometimes tentatively associated with Altaic, still spoken in parts of Hokkaido and elsewhere [Ainu: man]

air (ɛə) *n* **1** the mixture of gases that forms the earth's atmosphere. At sea level dry air has a density of 1.226 kilograms per cubic metre and consists of 78.08 per cent nitrogen, 20.95 per cent oxygen, 0.93 per cent argon, 0.03 per cent carbon dioxide, with smaller quantities of ozone and inert gases; water vapour varies between 0 and 4 per cent and in industrial areas sulphur gases may be present as pollutants **2** the space above and around the earth; sky. Related adj: **aerial 3** breeze; slight wind **4** public expression; utterance **5** a distinctive quality: *an air of mystery* **6** a person's distinctive appearance, manner, or bearing **7** *music* a simple tune for either vocal or instrumental performance **8** transportation in aircraft (esp in the phrase **by air**) **9 in the air a** in circulation; current **b** in the process of being decided; unsettled **10** into thin air leaving no trace behind **11** off the air not in the act of broadcasting or being broadcast on radio or television **12** on the air in the act of broadcasting or being broadcast on radio or television **13** take the air to go out of doors, as for a short walk or ride **14** up in the air a uncertain **b** *informal* agitated or excited **15** (*modifier*) *astrology* of or relating to a group of three signs of the zodiac, Gemini, Libra, and Aquarius ▷ *vb* **16** to expose or be exposed to the air so as to cool or freshen; ventilate **17** to expose or be exposed to warm or heated air so as to dry: *to air linen* **18** (*tr*) to make known publicly; display; publicize: *to air one's opinions* **19** (*intr*) (of a television or radio programme) to be broadcast ▷ See also **airs** [C13: via Old French and Latin from Greek *aēr* the lower atmosphere]

Aïr ('a:ɪə) *n* a mountainous region of N central Niger, in the Sahara, rising to 1500 m (5000 ft): a former native kingdom. Area: about 77 700 sq km (30 000 sq miles). Also called: Azbine, Asben

air bag *n* a safety device in a car, consisting of a bag that inflates automatically in an accident and prevents the passengers from being thrown forwards

air base *n* a centre from which military aircraft operate

air bladder *n* **1** Also called: swim bladder *ichthyol* an air-filled sac, lying above the alimentary canal in bony fishes, that regulates buoyancy at different depths by a variation in the pressure of the air **2** any air-filled sac, such as one of the bladders of seaweeds

airborne ('ɛəˌbɔːn) *adj* **1** conveyed by or through the air **2** (of aircraft) flying; in the air

air brake *n* **1** a brake operated by compressed air, esp in heavy vehicles and trains **2** Also called: dive brake an articulated flap or small parachute for reducing the speed of an aircraft

airbrick ('ɛəˌbrɪk) *n chiefly Brit* a brick with holes in it, put into the wall of a building for ventilation

airbrush ('ɛəˌbrʌʃ) *n* **1** an atomizer for spraying paint or varnish by means of compressed air ▷ *vb* (*tr*) **2** to paint or varnish (something) by using an airbrush **3** to improve the image of (a person or thing) by concealing defects beneath a bland exterior: *an airbrushed version of the government's record*

airbrush out *vb* (*tr, adverb*) to remove evidence of (someone or something from photographs, books, or history)

air chief marshal *n* a senior officer of the Royal Air Force and certain other air forces, of equivalent rank to admiral in the Royal Navy

air cleaner *n* a filter that prevents dust and other particles from entering the air-intake of an internal-combustion engine. Also called: air filter

Air Command *n Canadian* the Canadian air force

air commodore *n* a senior officer of the Royal Air Force and certain other air forces, of equivalent rank to brigadier in the Army

air conditioning *n* a system or process for controlling the temperature and sometimes the humidity and purity of the air in a house, etc > air conditioner *n* > air-condition *vb*

air-cool *vb* (*tr*) to cool (an engine) by a flow of air. See **water-cool**

aircraft ('ɛəˌkrɑːft) *n, pl* -craft any machine capable of flying by means of buoyancy or aerodynamic forces,

a

such as a glider, helicopter, or aeroplane

aircraft carrier n a warship built with an extensive flat deck space for the launch and recovery of aircraft

aircraftman ('ɛə,krɑːftmən) n, pl -men a serviceman of the most junior rank in the RAF > 'aircraft,woman or 'aircrafts,woman fem n

air curtain n an air stream across a doorway to exclude draughts, etc

air cushion n 1 an inflatable cushion, usually made of rubber or plastic 2 the pocket of air that supports a hovercraft

Airdrie ('ɛədrɪ; Scot 'ɛrdrɪ) n a town in W central Scotland, in North Lanarkshire, E of Glasgow: manufacturing and pharmaceutical industries. Pop: 36 326 (2001)

airdrop ('ɛə,drɒp) n 1 a delivery of supplies, troops, etc, from an aircraft by parachute ▷ vb -drops, -dropping, -dropped 2 (tr) to deliver (supplies, etc) by an airdrop

Aire (ɛə) n a river in N England rising in the Pennines and flowing southeast to the Ouse. Length: 112 km (70 miles)

Airedale ('ɛə,deɪl) n a large rough-haired tan-coloured breed of terrier characterized by a black saddle-shaped patch covering most of the back. Also called: Airedale terrier [C19: name of a district in Yorkshire]

air engine n 1 an engine that uses the expansion of heated air to drive a piston 2 a small engine that uses compressed air to drive a piston

airfield ('ɛə,fiːld) n a landing and taking-off area for aircraft, usually with permanent buildings

air filter n another name for **air cleaner**

airfoil ('ɛə,fɔɪl) n US & Canadian a cross section of an aileron, wing, tailplane, or rotor blade. Also called: aerofoil

air force n **a** the branch of a nation's armed services primarily responsible for air warfare **b** (as modifier): an air-force base

airframe ('ɛə,freɪm) n the body of an aircraft, excluding its engines

air guitar n an imaginary guitar played while miming to rock music

air gun n a gun discharged by means of compressed air

airhead ('ɛə,hɛd) n slang a stupid or simple-minded person; idiot [C20: from AIR + HEAD]

air hole n 1 a hole that allows the passage of air, esp for ventilation 2 a section of open water in a frozen surface

air hostess n a stewardess on an airliner

airily ('ɛərɪlɪ) adv 1 in a jaunty or high-spirited manner 2 in a light or delicate manner

airing ('ɛərɪŋ) n 1 a exposure to air or warmth, as for drying or ventilation **b** (as modifier): airing cupboard 2 an excursion in the open air 3 exposure to public debate

air kiss n 1 a kissing gesture, esp one directed towards a person's cheek, made without making physical contact ▷ vb air-kiss 2 to make such a gesture towards a person

airless ('ɛəlɪs) adj 1 lacking fresh air; stuffy or sultry 2 devoid of air > 'airlessness n

air letter n another name for **aerogram**

airlift ('ɛə,lɪft) n 1 the transportation by air of passengers, troops, cargo, etc, esp when other routes are blocked ▷ vb 2 (tr) to transport by an airlift

airline ('ɛə,laɪn) n 1 a a system or organization that provides scheduled flights for passengers or cargo **b** (as modifier): an airline pilot 2 a hose or tube carrying air under pressure

airliner ('ɛə,laɪnə) n a large passenger aircraft

airlock ('ɛə,lɒk) n 1 a bubble in a pipe causing an obstruction or stoppage to the flow 2 an airtight chamber with regulated air pressure used to gain access to a space that has air under pressure

airmail ('ɛə,meɪl) n 1 the system of conveying mail by aircraft 2 mail conveyed by aircraft ▷ adj 3 of, used for, or concerned with airmail

airman ('ɛəmən) n, pl -men an aviator, esp a man who serves in his country's air force > 'air,woman fem n

air marshal n 1 a senior Royal Air Force officer of equivalent rank to a vice admiral in the Royal Navy 2 a Royal Australian Air Force officer of the highest rank 3 a Royal New Zealand Air Force officer of the highest rank

when chief of defence forces

air mass n a large body of air having characteristics of temperature, moisture, and pressure that are approximately uniform horizontally

Air Miles pl n points awarded by certain companies to purchasers of flight tickets and some other products that may be used to pay for other flights

air miss n a situation in which two aircraft pass very close to one another in the air; near miss

airplane ('ɛə,pleɪn) n US & Canadian a heavier-than-air powered flying vehicle with fixed wings. Also called: aeroplane

airplay ('ɛə,pleɪ) n (of recorded music) radio exposure

air pocket n a localized region of low air density or a descending air current, causing an aircraft to suffer an abrupt decrease in height

airport ('ɛə,pɔːt) n a landing and taking-off area for civil aircraft, usually with surfaced runways and aircraft maintenance and passenger facilities

air power n the strength of a nation's air force

air pump n a device for pumping air in or out of something

air rage n aggressive behaviour by an airline passenger that endangers the safety of the crew or other passengers

air raid n **a** an attack by hostile aircraft **b** (as modifier): an air-raid shelter

air-raid warden n a member of a civil defence organization responsible for enforcing regulations, etc, during an air attack

air rifle n a rifle discharged by compressed air

airs (ɛəz) pl n affected manners intended to impress others (esp in the phrases **give oneself airs, put on airs**)

air sac n any of the membranous air-filled extensions of the lungs of birds, which increase the efficiency of gaseous exchange in the lungs

airscrew ('ɛə,skruː) n Brit an aircraft propeller

air-sea rescue n an air rescue at sea

air shaft n a shaft for ventilation, esp in a mine or tunnel

airship ('ɛə,ʃɪp) n a lighter-than-air self-propelled craft. Also called: dirigible, zeppelin

airshow ('ɛə,ʃəu) n an occasion when an air base is open to the public and a flying display and, usually, static exhibitions are held

airsick ('ɛə,sɪk) adj sick or nauseated from travelling in an aircraft

airside ('ɛə,saɪd) n the part of an airport nearest the aircraft, the boundary of which is the security check, customs, passport control, etc. See **landside** (sense 1)

airspace ('ɛə,speɪs) n the atmosphere above the earth or part of the earth, esp the atmosphere above a country deemed to be under its jurisdiction

airspeed ('ɛə,spiːd) n the speed of an aircraft relative to the air in which it moves

airstrip ('ɛə,strɪp) n a cleared area for the landing and taking off of aircraft; runway. Also called: landing strip

air terminal n Brit a building in a city from which air passengers are taken by road or rail to an airport or the terminal building of an airport

airtight ('ɛə,taɪt) adj 1 not permitting the passage of air either in or out 2 having no weak points; rigid or unassailable

air-to-air adj operating between aircraft in flight

air-traffic control n an organization that determines the altitude, speed, and direction at which planes fly in a given area, giving instructions to pilots by radio > air-traffic controller n

airtsy-mairtsy ('ɛətsɪ'mɛətsɪ) adj Midlands English dialect affected; effeminate

air vice-marshal n 1 a senior Royal Air Force officer of equivalent rank to a rear admiral in the Royal Navy 2 a Royal Australian Air Force officer of the second highest rank 3 a Royal New Zealand Air Force officer of the highest rank

airwaves ('ɛə,weɪvz) pl n informal radio waves used in radio and television broadcasting

airway ('ɛə,weɪ) n 1 an air route, esp one that is fully equipped with emergency landing fields, navigational aids, etc **2** a passage for ventilation, esp in a mine **3** a passage down which air travels from the nose or mouth to the lungs **4** *med* a tubelike device inserted via the throat to keep open the airway of an unconscious patient

air waybill *n* a document made out by the consignor of goods by air freight giving details of the goods and the name of the consignee

airworthy ('ɛəˌwɜːðɪ) *adj* (of an aircraft) safe to fly

airy ('ɛərɪ) *adj* airier, airiest **1** abounding in fresh air **2** spacious or uncluttered **3** nonchalant; superficial **4** visionary; fanciful: *airy promises; airy plans* **5** of or relating to air **6** weightless and insubstantial **7** light and graceful in movement **8** high up in the air; lofty

Airy ('ɛərɪ) *n* Sir **George Biddell**. 1801–92, British astronomer, noted for his estimate of the earth's density from gravity measurements in mines; astronomer royal (1835–81)

AIS *abbreviation* Australian Institute of Sport

Aisha *or* **Ayesha** ('ɑːiːʃɑː) *n* ?613–678 AD, the favourite wife of Mohammed; daughter of Abu Bekr

aisle (aɪl) *n* **1** a passageway separating seating areas in a theatre, church, etc; gangway **2** a lateral division in a church flanking the nave or chancel [c14 *ele* (later *aile*, *aisle*, through confusion with *isle* (island)), via Old French from Latin *āla* wing] > **aisled** *adj*

Aisne (eɪn; *French* ɛn) *n* **1** a department of NE France, in Picardy region. Capital: Laon. Pop: 535 326 (2003 est). Area: 7428 sq km (2897 sq miles) **2** a river in N France, rising in the Argonne Forest and flowing northwest and west to the River Oise: scene of a major Allied offensive in 1918 which turned the tide finally against Germany in World War I. Length: 282 km (175 miles)

ait (eɪt) *or* **eyot** *n dialect* an islet, esp in a river [Old English *ȳgett* small island, from *ieg* ISLAND]

aitch (eɪtʃ) *n* the letter *h* or the sound represented by it [c16: a phonetic spelling]

aitchbone ('eɪtʃˌbəʊn) *n* **1** the rump bone or floor of the pelvis in cattle **2** a cut of beef from or including the rump bone [c15 *hach-boon*, altered from earlier *nache-bone*, *nage-bone* (a *nache* mistaken for *an ache*, *an aitch*; compare ADDER¹); *nache* buttock, via Old French from Late Latin *natica*, from Latin *natis* buttock]

Aitken ('eɪtkɪn) *n* **1 Robert Grant**. 1864–1951, US astronomer who discovered over three thousand double stars **2 William Maxwell**. See **Beaverbrook**

Aix-en-Provence (*French* ɛksɑ̃prɔvɑ̃s) *n* a city and spa in SE France: the medieval capital of Provence. Pop: 134 222 (1999). Also called: **Aix**

Aix-la-Chapelle (*French* ɛkslaʃapɛl) *n* the French name for **Aachen**

Aix-les-Bains (*French* ɛkslebɛ̃) *n* a town in E France: a resort with sulphurous springs. Pop: 25 732 (1999)

Aíyina ('ɛɪlə) *n* transliteration of the Modern Greek name for **Aegina**

Ajaccio (əˈdʒætsɪˌəʊ, -ˈdʒeɪ-) *n* the capital of Corsica, a port on the W coast. Pop: 52 880 (1999)

ajar (əˈdʒɑː) *adj, adv* (*postpositive*) (esp of a door or window) slightly open [c18: altered form of obsolete *on char*, literally: on the turn; *char*, from Old English *cierran* to turn]

Ajax ('eɪdʒæks) *n Greek myth* called *Ajax the Lesser*, a Locrian king, a swift-footed Greek hero of the Trojan War

Ajmer (ʌdʒˈmɪə) *n* a city in NW India, in Rajasthan: textile centre. Pop: 485 197 (2001)

AK *abbreviation* **1** Alaska **2** Knight of the Order of Australia

AK-47 *n* a type of Kalashnikov assault rifle [c20: from *A(utomat) K(alashnikov)*]

a.k.a. *or* **AKA** *abbreviation* also known as

akathisia (ˌækəˈθiːzɪə) *n* the inability to sit still because of uncontrollable movement caused by reaction to drugs [c20: from A- + -*kithisia*, ultimately from Greek *cathedra* seat]

Akbar ('ækbɑː) *n* called *Akbar the Great*. 1542–1605, Mogul emperor of India (1556–1605), who extended the Mogul empire to include N India

akene (əˈkiːn) *n* a variant spelling of **achene**

Akhaïa (aˈxaːja) *n* transliteration of the Modern Greek name for **Achaea**

Akhenaten *or* **Akhenaton** (ˌækəˈnɑːtⁿn) *n* original name *Amenhotep IV*. died ?1358 BC, king of Egypt, of the 18th dynasty; he moved his capital from Thebes to Tell El Amarna and introduced the cult of Aten

Akhmatova (*Russian* axˈmatəvə) *n* **Anna** ('annə) pseudonym of *Anna Gorenko*. 1889–1966, Russian poet: noted for her concise and intensely personal lyrics

Akihito (ˌækɪˈhiːtəʊ) *n* born 1933, Emperor of Japan from 1989

akimbo (əˈkɪmbəʊ) *adj, adv* arms akimbo *or* with arms akimbo with hands on hips and elbows projecting outwards [c15 *in kenebowe*, literally: in keen bow, that is, in a sharp curve]

akin (əˈkɪn) *adj* (*postpositive*) **1** related by blood; of the same kin **2** (often foll by *to*) having similar characteristics, properties, etc

Akkad *or* **Accad** ('ækæd) *n* **1** a city on the Euphrates in N Babylonia, the centre of a major empire and civilization (2360–2180 BC) **2** an ancient region lying north of Babylon, from which the Akkadian language and culture is named

Akkadian *or* **Accadian** (əˈkædɪən, əˈkeɪ-) *n* **1** a member of an ancient Semitic people who lived in central Mesopotamia in the third millennium BC **2** the extinct language of this people, belonging to the E Semitic subfamily of the Afro-Asiatic family

Akkerman (*Russian* akɪrˈman) *n* the former name (until 1946) of **Belgorod-Dnestrovski**

Akmola *or* **Aqmola** (ækˈməʊlə; *Kazakh* akmɔˈla) *n* a former name (1994–98) of **Astana**

Aktöbe (aktøˈbe) *n* an industrial city in W Kazakhstan. Pop: 291 000 (2005 est). Kazakh name: **Aqtöbe**. Former name (until 1991): **Aktyubinsk**

Aktyubinsk (*Russian* akˈtjubinsk) *n* the former name (until 1991) of **Aqtöbe**

Akure (əˈkuːre) *n* a city in SW Nigeria, capital of Ondo state: agricultural trade centre. Pop: 434 000 (2005 est)

al *internet domain name* Albania

Al *the chemical symbol for* aluminium

AL *abbreviation* **1** Alabama **2** Anglo-Latin **3** (in the US and Canada) American League (of baseball teams) ▷ *international car registration* **4** Albania

-al¹ *suffix forming adjectives* of; related to; connected with: *functional; sectional; tonal* [from Latin -*ālis*]

-al² *suffix forming nouns* the act or process of doing what is indicated by the verb stem: *rebuttal; recital; renewal* [via Old French -*aille*, -*ail*, from Latin -*ālia*, neuter plural used as substantive, from -*ālis* -AL¹]

-al³ *suffix forming nouns* **1** indicating an aldehyde: *ethanal* **2** indicating a pharmaceutical product: *phenobarbital* [shortened from ALDEHYDE]

ala ('eɪlə) *n, pl* alae ('eɪliː) **1** *zoology* a wing or flat winglike process or structure, such as a part of some bones and cartilages **2** *botany* a winglike part, such as one of the wings of a sycamore seed or one of the flat petals of a sweet pea flower [c18: from Latin *āla* a wing]

à la (ɑː lɑː; æ lə; *French* a la) *prep* **1** in the manner or style of **2** as prepared in (a particular place) or by or for (a particular person) [c17: from French, short for *à la mode de* in the style of]

Ala. *abbreviation* Alabama

Alabama (ˌæləˈbæmə) *n* **1** a state of the southeastern US, on the Gulf of Mexico: consists of coastal and W lowlands crossed by the Tombigbee, Black Warrior, and Alabama Rivers, with parts of the Tennessee Valley and Cumberland Plateau in the north; noted for producing cotton and white marble. Capital: Montgomery. Pop: 4 500 752 (2003 est). Area: 131 333 sq km (50 708 sq miles). Abbreviations: Ala, *or* (with zip code) AL **2** a river in Alabama, flowing southwest to the Mobile and Tensaw Rivers. Length: 507 km (315 miles) > Alabamian *adj, n*

alabaster ('æləˌbɑːstə, -ˌbæstə) *n* **1** a fine-grained usually white, opaque, or translucent variety of gypsum used for statues, vases, etc **2** a variety of hard semitranslucent calcite, often banded like marble ▷ *adj* **3** of or resembling alabaster [c14: from Old French *alabastre*, from Latin *alabaster*, from Greek *alabastros*]

a

> ˌalaˈbastrine *adj*

à la carte (ɑː lɑː ˈkɑːt, æ lə; *French* a la kart) *adj, adv* (of a menu or a section of a menu) having dishes listed separately and individually priced. See **table d'hôte** [C19: from French, literally: according to the card]

alack (əˈlæk) *or* **alackaday** (əˌlækəˌdeɪ) *interj* an archaic or poetic word for: **alas** [C15: from *a* ah! + *lack* loss, LACK]

alacrity (əˈlækrɪtɪ) *n* liveliness or briskness [C15: from Latin *alacritās*, from *alacer* lively]

Ala Dağ *or* **Ala Dagh** (Turkish aˈla dɑː) *n* **1** the E part of the Taurus Mountains, in SE Turkey, rising over 3600 m (12 000 ft) **2** a mountain range in E Turkey, rising over 3300 m (11 000 ft) **3** a mountain range in NE Turkey, rising over 3000 m (10 000 ft)

Alagna (əˈlænja) *n* **Roberto.** born 1963, Italian opera singer, born in France; a lyric tenor, he is married to the soprano Angela Gheorghiu

Alagoas (Portuguese alaˈɡoaʃ) *n* a state in NE Brazil, on the Atlantic coast. Capital: Maceió. Pop: 2 887 535 (2002). Area: 30 776 sq km (11 031 sq miles)

Alai (ɑːˈlaɪ) *n* a mountain range in central Asia, in SW Kyrgyzstan, running from the Tian Shan range in China into Tajikistan. Average height: 4800 m (16 000 ft), rising over 5850 m (19 500 ft)

Alain-Fournier (French alɛ̃furnje) *n* real name *Henri-Alban Fournier.* 1886–1914, French novelist; author of *Le Grand Meaulnes* (1913; translated as *The Lost Domain,* 1959)

Alamein (ˈæləˌmeɪn) *n* See **El Alamein**

Alamo (ˈæləˌməʊ) *n* **the Alamo** a mission in San Antonio, Texas, the site of a siege and massacre in 1836 by Mexican forces under Santa Anna of a handful of American rebels fighting for Texan independence from Mexico

à la mode (ɑː lɑː ˈməʊd, æ lə; *French* a la mɔd) *adj* **1** fashionable in style, design, etc **2** (of meats) braised with vegetables in wine [C17: from French: according to the fashion]

Alanbrooke (ˈælənˌbrʊk) *n* **Alan Francis Brooke,** 1st Viscount. 1883–1963, British field marshal; chief of Imperial General Staff (1941–46)

Åland Islands (ˈɑːlənd, ˈɔːlənd; *Swedish* ˈoːland) *pl n* a group of over 6000 islands under Finnish administration, in the Gulf of Bothnia. Capital: Mariehamn. Pop: 26 347 (2003 est). Finnish name: Ahvenanmaa

Al-Anon (ˈælənˌnɒn) *n* an association for the families and friends of alcoholics to give mutual support

alar (ˈeɪlə) *adj* relating to, resembling, or having wings or alae [C19: from Latin *āla* a wing]

Alar (ˈeɪlɑː) *n* a chemical sprayed on cultivated apple trees in certain countries, to increase fruit set. Also called: **daminozide**

Alarcón (Spanish alarˈkon) *n* **Pedro Antonio de** (ˈpeðro anˈtonjo de). 1833–91, Spanish novelist and short-story writer, noted for his humorous sketches of rural life, esp in *The Three-Cornered Hat* (1874)

Alaric (ˈælərɪk) *n* ?370–410 AD, king of the Visigoths, who served under the Roman emperor Theodosius I but later invaded Greece and Italy, capturing Rome in 410

alarm (əˈlɑːm) *vb* (*tr*) **1** to fill with apprehension, anxiety, or fear **2** to warn about danger; alert **3** to fit or activate a burglar alarm on a house, car, etc ▷ *n* **4** fear or terror aroused by awareness of danger; fright **5** apprehension or uneasiness **6** a noise, signal, etc, warning of danger **7** any device that transmits such a warning: *a burglar alarm* **8 a** the device in an alarm clock that triggers off the bell or buzzer **b** short for **alarm clock 9** archaic a call to arms [C14: from Old French *alarme,* from Old Italian *all'arme* to arms; see ARM²]
> aˈlarming *adj*

alarm clock *n* a clock with a mechanism that sounds at a set time: used esp for waking a person up

alarmist (əˈlɑːmɪst) *n* **1** a person who alarms or attempts to alarm others needlessly or without due grounds **2** a person who is easily alarmed ▷ *adj* **3** characteristic of an alarmist

alarum (əˈlærəm, -ˈlɑːr-, -ˈlɛər-) *n* **1** archaic an alarm, esp a call to arms **2** (used as a stage direction, esp in Elizabethan drama) a loud disturbance or conflict (esp in the phrase **alarums and excursions**) [C15: variant of ALARM]

alas (əˈlæs) *sentence connector* **1** unfortunately; regrettably: *there were, alas, none left* ▷ *interj* **2** an exclamation of grief, compassion, or alarm [C13: from Old French *ha las!* oh wretched!; *las* from Latin *lassus* weary]

Alas. *abbreviation* Alaska

Alaska (əˈlæskə) *n* **1** the largest state of the US, in the extreme northwest of North America: the aboriginal inhabitants are Inuit and Yupik; the earliest White settlements were made by the Russians; it was purchased by the US from Russia in 1867. It is mostly mountainous and volcanic, rising over 6000 m (20 000 ft), with the Yukon basin in the central region; large areas are covered by tundra; it has important mineral resources (chiefly coal, oil, and natural gas). Capital: Juneau. Pop: 648 818 (2003 est). Area: 1 530 694 sq km (591 004 sq miles). Abbreviations: Alas, *or* (with zip code) AK **2 Gulf of Alaska** the N part of the Pacific, between the Alaska Peninsula and the Alexander Archipelago
> Aˈlaskan *adj, n*

Alaska Highway *n* a road extending from Dawson Creek, British Columbia, to Fairbanks, Alaska: built by the US Army (1942). Length: 2452 km (1523 miles). Originally called: Alcan Highway

Alaska Peninsula *n* an extension of the mainland of SW Alaska between the Pacific and the Bering Sea, ending in the Aleutian Islands. Length: about 644 km (400 miles)

Alaska Range *n* a mountain range in S central Alaska. Highest peak: Mount McKinley, 6194 m (20 320 ft)

alate (ˈeɪleɪt) *adj* having wings or winglike extensions [C17: from Latin *ālātus,* from *āla* wing]

alb (ælb) *n* Christianity a long white linen vestment with sleeves worn by priests and others [Old English *albe,* from Medieval Latin *alba (vestis)* white (clothing)]

Alb. *abbreviation* Albania(n)

Alba (Spanish ˈalβa) Duke of Alba *n* See **Alva**

albacore (ˈælbəˌkɔː) *n* a tunny, *Thunnus alalunga,* occurring mainly in warm regions of the Atlantic and Pacific. It has very long pectoral fins and is a valued food fish [C16: from Portuguese *albacor,* from Arabic *al-bakrah,* from *al* the + *bakr* young camel]

Alba Longa (ˈælbə ˈlɒŋɡə) *n* a city of ancient Latium, southeast of modern Rome: the legendary birthplace of Romulus and Remus

Alban (ˈɔːlbən) *n* **Saint.** 3rd century AD, the first English martyr. He was beheaded by the Romans on the site on which St Alban's Abbey now stands, for admitting his conversion to Christianity. Feast day: June 17

Albania (ælˈbeɪnɪə) *n* a republic in SE Europe, on the Balkan Peninsula: became independent in 1912 after more than four centuries of Turkish rule; established as a republic (1946) under Communist rule; multiparty constitution adopted in 1991. It is generally mountainous, rising over 2700 m (9000 ft), with extensive forests. Language: Albanian. Religion: Muslim majority. Currency: lek. Capital: Tirana. Pop: 3 193 000 (2004 est). Area: 28 749 sq km (11 100 sq miles)
> Alˈbanian *n, adj*

Albany (ˈɔːlbənɪ) *n* **1** a city in E New York State, on the Hudson River: the state capital. Pop: 93 919 (2003 est) **2** a river in central Canada, flowing east and northeast to James Bay. Length: 982 km (610 miles) **3** a port in southwest Western Australia: founded as a penal colony. Pop: 22 415 (2001)

albatross (ˈælbəˌtrɒs) *n* **1** any large oceanic bird of the genera *Diomedea* and *Phoebetria,* family *Diomedeidae,* of cool southern oceans: order *Procellariiformes* (petrels). They have long narrow wings and are noted for a powerful gliding flight. See also **wandering albatross 2** a constant and inescapable burden or handicap **3** golf a score of three strokes under par for a hole [C17: from Portuguese *alcatraz* pelican, from Arabic *al-ghattās,* from *al* the + *ghattās* white-tailed sea eagle; influenced by Latin *albus* white: C20 in sense 2, from *The Rime of the Ancient Mariner* (1798) by English poet Samuel Taylor Coleridge (1772–1834)]

albedo (ælˈbiːdəʊ) *n* the ratio of the intensity of light reflected from an object, such as a planet, to that of the light it receives from the sun [C19: from Church Latin: whiteness, from Latin *albus* white]

Albee (ˈɔːlbiː) *n* **Edward.** born 1928, US dramatist. His plays include *Who's Afraid of Virginia Woolf?* (1962), *Seascape* (1975), *Marriage Play* (1986), *Three Tall Women* (1990), and *Goat* (2004)

albeit (ɔːlˈbiːɪt) *conj* even though [C14 *al be it*, that is, although it be (that)]

Albemarle Sound (ˈælbəˌmɑːl) *n* an inlet of the Atlantic in NE North Carolina. Length: about 96 km (60 miles)

Albéniz (*Spanish* alˈβeniθ) *n* **Isaac** (isaˈak). 1860–1909, Spanish composer; noted for piano pieces inspired by folk music, such as the suite *Iberia*

Alberich (*German* ˈalbərɪç) *n* (in medieval German legend) the king of the dwarfs and guardian of the treasures of the Nibelungs

Albers (ˈælbəz) *n* **Josef.** 1888–1976, US painter, designer, and poet, born in Germany. His works include a series of abstract paintings entitled *Homage to the Square*

albert (ˈælbət) *n* a kind of watch chain usually attached to a waistcoat [C19: named after Prince *Albert* (1819–61), Prince Consort of Queen Victoria of Great Britain and Ireland]

Albert¹ (ˈælbət) *n* **Lake Albert** a lake in E Africa, between the Democratic Republic of Congo (formerly Zaïre) and Uganda in the great Rift Valley, 660 m (2200 ft) above sea level: a source of the Nile, fed by the Victoria Nile, which leaves as the Albert Nile. Area: 5345 sqkm (2064 sq miles)

Albert² (ˈælbət) *n* **Prince.** full name *Albert Francis Charles Augustus Emmanuel of Saxe-Coburg-Gotha.* 1819–61, Prince Consort of Queen Victoria of Great Britain and Ireland

Albert I *n* **1** *c.* 1255–1308, king of Germany (1298–1308) **2** 1875–1934, king of the Belgians (1909–34) **3** called *Albert the Bear. c.* 1100–70. German military leader: first margrave of Brandenburg

Albert II *n* full name *Albert Felix Humbert Theodore Christian Eugene Marie.* born 1934, king of Belgium from 1993

Alberta (ælˈbɜːtə) *n* a province of W Canada: mostly prairie, with the Rocky Mountains in the southwest Capital: Edmonton. Pop: 3 201 895 (2004 est). Area: 661 188 sq km (255 285 sq miles). Abbreviation: **AB** > **Al'bertan** *adj*

Alberta clipper *n* *meteorol* (in Canada) an area of low pressure that forms in winter near the Rocky Mountains

Albert Edward *n* a mountain in SE New Guinea, in the Owen Stanley Range. Height: 3993 m (13 100 ft)

Alberti (*Italian* alˈbɛrti) *n* **Leon Battista** (leˈɔn batˈtista). 1404–72, Italian Renaissance architect, painter, writer, and musician: among his architectural designs are the façades of Sta. Maria Novella at Florence and S. Francesco at Rimini

Albertus Magnus (ælˈbɜːtəs ˈmægnəs) *n* **Saint.** original name *Albert, Count von Böllstadt.* ?1193– 1280, German scholastic philosopher; teacher of Thomas Aquinas and commentator on Aristotle. Feast day: Nov 15

albescent (ælˈbɛsᵊnt) *adj* shading into, growing, or becoming white [C19: from Latin *albēscere* to grow white, from *albus* white] > **al'bescence** *n*

Albi (*French* albi) *n* a town in S France: connected with the Albigensian heresy and the crusade against it. Pop: 46 274 (1999)

Albigenses (ˌælbɪˈdʒɛnsiːz) *pl n* members of a Manichean sect that flourished in S France from the 11th to the 13th century [from Medieval Latin: inhabitants of Albi, from *Albiga* **ALBI**] > **Albi'gensian** *adj* > **Albi'gensianism** *n*

albino (ælˈbiːnəʊ) *n*, *pl* **-nos** **1** a person with congenital absence of pigmentation in the skin, eyes, and hair **2** any animal or plant that is deficient in pigment [C18: via Portuguese from Spanish, from *albo* white, from Latin *albus*] > **albinism** (ˈælbɪˌnɪzəm) *n* > **albinotic** (ˌælbɪˈnɒtɪk) *adj*

Albinoni (*Italian* albiˈnoːni) *n* **Tomaso** (toˈmaːzo). 1671–1750, Italian composer and violinist. He wrote concertos and over 50 operas

Albinus (ælˈbiːnəs) *n* another name for **Alcuin**

Albion (ˈælbɪən) *n* *archaic, or poetic* Britain or England [C13: from Latin, of Celtic origin]

albite (ˈælbaɪt) *n* a colourless, milky-white, yellow, pink, green, or black mineral of the feldspar group and plagioclase series, found in igneous sedimentary and metamorphic rocks. It is used in the manufacture of glass and ceramics. Composition: sodium aluminium silicate. Formula: $NaALSi_3O_8$. Crystal structure: triclinic [C19: from Latin *albus* white]

Alboin (ˈælbɔɪn, -bəʊɪn) *n* died 573 AD, king of the Lombards (565–73); conqueror of N Italy

Ålborg (*Danish* ˈɔlbɒr) *n* a variant spelling of **Aalborg**

album (ˈælbəm) *n* **1** a book or binder consisting of blank pages, pockets, or envelopes for keeping photographs, stamps, autographs, drawings, poems, etc **2** one or more CDs, cassettes, or long-playing records released as a single item **3** a booklike holder containing sleeves for gramophone records **4** *chiefly Brit* an anthology, usually large and illustrated [C17: from Latin: blank tablet, from *albus* white]

albumen (ˈælbjʊmɪn, -men) *n* **1** the white of an egg; the nutritive and protective gelatinous substance, mostly an albumin, that surrounds the yolk **2** a variant spelling of **albumin** [C16: from Latin: white of an egg, from *albus* white]

albumin *or* **albumen** (ˈælbjʊmɪn) *n* any of a group of simple water-soluble proteins that are coagulated by heat and are found in blood plasma, egg white, etc [C19: from **ALBUMEN** + **-IN**] > **albuminous** (ælˈbjuːmɪnəs) *adj*

albuminoid (ælˈbjuːmɪˌnɔɪd) *adj* **1** resembling albumin ▷ *n* **2** another name for **scleroprotein**

albuminuria (ælˌbjuːmɪˈnjʊərɪə) *n* *pathol* the presence of albumin in the urine. Also called: **proteinuria**

Albuquerque¹ (ˈælbəˌkɜːkɪ) *n* a city in central New Mexico, on the Rio Grande. Pop: 471 856 (2003 est)

Albuquerque² (ˈælbəˌkɜːkɪ; *Portuguese* ɑlbuˈkɛrkə) *n* **Afonso de** (əˈfõsu dəː). 1453–1515, Portuguese navigator who established Portuguese colonies in the East by conquering Goa, Ceylon, Malacca, and Ormuz

Albury-Wodonga (ˈɔːbərɪ, -brɪ wəˈdɒŋə) *n* a town in SE Australia, in S central New South Wales, on the Murray River: commercial centre of an agricultural region. Pop: 69 880 (2001)

Alcaeus (ælˈsiəs) *n* 7th century BC, Greek lyric poet who wrote hymns, love songs, and political odes

Alcaic (ælˈkeɪɪk) *adj* **1** of or relating to a metre used by the 7th-century BC Greek lyric poet Alcaeus, consisting of a strophe of four lines each with four feet ▷ *n* **2** (*usually plural*) verse written in the Alcaic form [C17: from Late Latin *Alcaicus* of Alcaeus]

alcalde (ælˈkældɪ; *Spanish* alˈkalde) *or* **alcade** (ælˈkeɪd) *n* (in Spain and Spanish America) the mayor or chief magistrate in a town [C17: from Spanish, from Arabic *al-qāḍī* the judge, from *qaḍā* to judge]

Alcan Highway (ˈælkæn) *n* original name of the **Alaska Highway**

Alcatraz (ˈælkəˌtræz) *n* an island in W California, in San Francisco Bay: a federal prison until 1963

alcazar (ˈælkəˌzɑː; *Spanish* alˈkaθar) *n* any of various palaces or fortresses built in Spain by the Moors [C17: from Spanish, from Arabic *al-qasr* the castle]

Alcazar de San Juan (ˈælkəˌzɑː; *Spanish* alˈkaθar) *n* a town in S central Spain: associated with Cervantes and Don Quixote. Pop: 27 229 (2003 est)

Alcestis (ælˈsɛstɪs) *n* *Greek myth* the wife of king Admetus of Thessaly. To save his life, she died in his place, but was rescued from Hades by Hercules

alchemist (ˈælkəmɪst) *n* a person who practises alchemy

alchemize *or* **alchemise** (ˈælkəˌmaɪz) *vb* (*tr*) to alter (an element, metal, etc) by alchemy; transmute

Alchevsk (ælˈtʃɛvsk) *n* a city in E Ukraine. Pop: 117 000 (2005 est). Former name (until 1992): **Kommunarsk**

alchemy (ˈælkəmɪ) *n*, *pl* **-mies** **1** the pseudoscientific predecessor of chemistry that sought a method of transmuting base metals into gold, an elixir to prolong life indefinitely, a panacea or universal remedy, and an alkahest or universal solvent **2** a power like that of alchemy: *her beauty had a potent alchemy* [C14 *alkamye*, via Old French from Medieval Latin *alchimia*, from Arabic *al-kīmiyā'*, from *al* the + *kīmiyā'* transmutation, from Late

Greek *khēmeia* the art of transmutation] > alchemic (ˈælˈkɛmɪk) *or* al'chemical *or* ˌalchemˈistic *adj*

Alcibiades (ˌælsɪˈbaɪəˌdiːz) *n* 450–404 BC, Athenian statesman and general in the Peloponnesian War: brilliant, courageous, and unstable, he defected to the Spartans in 415, but returned and led the Athenian victories at Abydos (411) and Cyzicus (410) > Alciˌbiaˈdean *adj*

Alcman (ˈælkmən) *n* 7th century BC, Greek lyric poet

Alcock (ˈɔːlkɒk) *n* Sir **John William**. 1892–1919, English aviator who with A.W. Brown made the first nonstop flight across the Atlantic (1919)

alcohol (ˈælkəˌhɒl) *n* 1 Also called: ethanol, ethyl alcohol a colourless flammable liquid, the active principle of intoxicating drinks, produced by the fermentation of sugars, esp glucose, and used as a solvent and in the manufacture of organic chemicals. Formula: C_2H_5OH 2 a drink or drinks containing this substance 3 *chem* any one of a class of organic compounds that contain one or more hydroxyl groups bound to carbon atoms. The simplest alcohols have the formula ROH, where R is an alkyl group. See **phenol** (sense 2) ▷ See also **diol, triol** [c16: via New Latin from Medieval Latin, from Arabic *al-kuhl* powdered antimony; see KOHL]

alcohol-free *adj* 1 (of beer or wine) containing only a trace of alcohol. See **low-alcohol** 2 (of a period of time) during which no alcoholic drink is consumed: *there should be one or two alcohol-free days a week*

alcoholic (ˌælkəˈhɒlɪk) *n* 1 a person affected by alcoholism ▷ *adj* 2 of, relating to, containing, or resulting from alcohol

alcoholism (ˈælkəhɒˌlɪzəm) *n* a condition in which dependence on alcohol harms a person's health, social functioning, or family life

alcopop (ˈælkəˌpɒp) *n informal* an alcoholic drink that tastes like a soft drink [c20: from ALCO(HOL) + POP¹ (sense 10)]

Alcott (ˈɔːlkət) *n* **Louisa May**. 1832–88, US novelist, noted for her children's books, esp *Little Women* (1869)

alcove (ˈælkəʊv) *n* 1 a recess or niche in the wall of a room, as for a bed, books, etc 2 any recessed usually vaulted area, as in a garden wall 3 any covered or secluded spot, such as a summerhouse [c17: from French *alcôve*, from Spanish *alcoba*, from Arabic *al-qubbah* the vault, arch]

Alcuin (ˈælkwɪn) *or* **Albinus** *n* 735–804 AD, English scholar and theologian; friend and adviser of Charlemagne

Aldeburgh (ˈɔːlbərə) *n* a small resort in SE England, in Suffolk: site of an annual music festival established in 1948 by Benjamin Britten. Pop: 2654 (2001)

aldehyde (ˈældɪˌhaɪd) *n* 1 any organic compound containing the group -CHO. Aldehydes are oxidized to carboxylic acids and take part in many addition reactions 2 (*modifier*) consisting of, containing, or concerned with the group -CHO: *aldehyde group or radical* [c19: from New Latin al(*cohol*) dehyd(*rogenātum*) dehydrogenated alcohol] > aldehydic (ˌældəˈhɪdɪk) *adj*

al dente Italian (al ˈdɛnte) *adj* (of a pasta dish) cooked so as to be firm when eaten [literally: to the tooth]

alder (ˈɔːldə) *n* 1 any N temperate betulaceous shrub or tree of the genus *Alnus*, having toothed leaves and conelike fruits. The bark is used in dyeing and tanning and the wood for bridges, etc because it resists underwater rot 2 any of several similar trees or shrubs [Old English *alor*; related to Old High German *elira*, Latin *alnus*]

alderman (ˈɔːldəmən) *n*, *pl* -men 1 (in England and Wales until 1974) one of the senior members of a local council, elected by other councillors 2 (in the US, Canada, Australia, etc) a member of the governing body of a municipality 3 *history* a variant spelling of **ealdorman** [Old English *aldormann*, from *ealdor* chief (comparative of *eald* OLD) + *mann* MAN] > aldermanic (ˌɔːldəˈmænɪk) *adj*

Aldermaston (ˈɔːldəˌmɑːstən) *n* a village in S England, in West Berkshire unitary authority, Berkshire, SW of Reading: site of the Atomic Weapons Research Establishment and starting point of the Aldermaston

marches (1958–63), organized by the Campaign for Nuclear Disarmament. Pop: 927 (2001)

Alderney (ˈɔːldənɪ) *n* 1 one of the Channel Islands, in the English Channel: separated from the French coast by a dangerous tidal channel (the **Race of Alderney**). Pop: 2294 (2001). Area: 8 sq km (3 sq miles) 2 an early, but now extinct, breed of dairy cattle originating from the island of Alderney

Aldershot (ˈɔːldəˌʃɒt) *n* a town in S England, in Hampshire: site of a large military camp. Pop: 58 170 (2001)

Aldine (ˈɔːldaɪn, -diːn) *adj* 1 relating to Aldus Manutius or to his editions of the classics ▷ *n* 2 a book printed by the Aldine press 3 any of the several typefaces designed by Aldus Manutius

Aldington (ˈɔːldɪŋtən) *n* **Richard**. 1892–1962, English poet, novelist, and biographer. His novels include *Death of a Hero* (1929) and *The Colonel's Daughter* (1931), which reflect postwar disillusion following World War I

Aldis lamp (ˈɔːldɪs) *n* a portable lamp used to transmit Morse code [c20: originally a trademark, after A. C. W. *Aldis*, its inventor]

Aldiss (ˈɔːldɪs) *n* **Brian W(ilson)**. born 1925, British novelist, best known for his science fiction. His works include *Non-Stop* (1958), *Enemies of the System* (1978), *The Helliconia Trilogy* (1983–86), *Forgotten Life* (1988), and *The Detached Retina* (1995)

Aldridge-Brownhills (ˈɔːldrɪdʒˈbraʊnˌhɪlz) *n* a town in central England, in Walsall unitary authority, West Midlands: formed by the amalgamation of neighbouring towns in 1966. Pop: 35 525 (2001)

aldrin (ˈɔːldrɪn) *n* a brown to white poisonous crystalline solid, more than 95 per cent of which consists of the compound $C_{12}H_8Cl_6$, which is used as an insecticide. Melting pt: 105°C [c20: named after K. *Alder* (1902–58) German chemist]

Aldrin (ˈɔːldrɪn) *n* **Edwin Eugene Jr.**, known as *Buzz*. born 1930, US astronaut; the second man to set foot on the moon on July 20, 1969, during the Apollo 11 flight

Aldus Manutius (ˈɔːldəs məˈnjuːʃɪəs) *n* 1450–1515, Italian printer, noted for his fine editions of the classics. He introduced italic type

ale (eɪl) *n* 1 a beer fermented in an open vessel using yeasts that rise to the top of the brew. See **beer, lager¹** 2 (formerly) an alcoholic drink made by fermenting a cereal, esp barley, but differing from beer by being unflavoured by hops 3 *chiefly Brit* another word for **beer** [Old English *alu, ealu*; related to Old Norse *öl*, Old Saxon *alofat*]

aleatory (ˈeɪlɪətərɪ, -trɪ) *or* **aleatoric** (ˌeɪlɪəˈtɒrɪk) *adj* 1 dependent on chance 2 (esp of a musical composition) involving elements chosen at random by the performer [c17: from Latin *āleātōrius*, from *āleātor* gambler, from *ālea* game of chance, dice, of uncertain origin]

Alecto (əˈlɛktəʊ) *n Greek myth* one of the three Furies; the others are Megaera and Tisiphone

alee (əˈliː) *adv, adj* (*postpositive*) *nautical* on or towards the lee: *with the helm alee*

alehouse (ˈeɪlˌhaʊs) *n* 1 *archaic* a place where ale was sold; tavern 2 *informal* another name for **pub**

Aleichem (ɑːˈleɪçɛm) *n* **Sholom**, real name **Solomon Rabinowitz**. 1859–1916, US Jewish writer, born in Russia. His works include *Tevye the Milkman*, which was adapted for the stage musical *Fiddler on the Roof*

Aleixandre (Spanish aleˈsandre) *n* **Vicente** (Viˈθente). 1898–1984, Spanish poet, whose collections include *La destrucción o el amor* (1935; Destruction or Love): Nobel prize for literature 1977

Alekhine (ˈælɪˌkiːn; *Russian* aˈljɔxin) *n* **Alexander**. 1892–1946, Russian-born chess player who lived in France; world champion (1927–35, 1937–46)

Aleksandropol (*Russian* alɪksanˈdrɔpəlj) *n* the former name (from 1837 until after the Revolution) of **Kumayri**

Aleksandrovsk (*Russian* alɪkˈsandrəfsk) *n* the former name (until 1921) of **Zaporozhye**

Alemán (*Spanish* aleˈman) *n* **Mateo** (maˈteo). 1547–?1614, Spanish novelist, author of the picaresque novel *Guzmán de Alfarache* (1599)

Alembert (*French* alɑ̃bɛr) *n* See **d'Alembert**

alembic (ə'lɛmbɪk) *n* **1** an obsolete type of retort used for distillation **2** anything that distils or purifies [c14: from Medieval Latin *alembicum*, from Arabic *al-anbīq* the still, from Greek *ambix* cup]

Alençon (*French* alɑ̃sɔ̃) *n* a town in NW France: early lace-manufacturing centre. Pop: 28 935 (1999)

aleph ('ɑːlɪf; *Hebrew* 'aːlɛf) *n* the first letter in the Hebrew alphabet (א) articulated as a glottal stop and transliterated with a superior comma (') [Hebrew: ox]

aleph-null *or* **aleph-zero** *n* the smallest infinite cardinal number; the cardinal number of the set of positive integers

Aleppo (ə'lɛpəʊ) *n* an ancient city in NW Syria: industrial and commercial centre. Pop: 2 505 000 (2005 est)

alert (ə'lɜːt) *adj* (*usually postpositive*) **1** vigilantly attentive: *alert to the problems* **2** brisk, nimble, or lively ▷ *n* **3** an alarm or warning, esp a siren warning of an air raid **4** the period during which such a warning remains in effect **5** on the alert **a** on guard against danger, attack, etc **b** watchful; ready: *on the alert for any errors* ▷ *vb* (*tr*) **6** to warn or signal (troops, police, etc) to prepare for action **7** to warn of danger, an attack, etc [c17: from Italian *all'erta* on the watch, from *erta* lookout post, from *ergere* to build up, from Latin *ērigere*; see ERECT] > a'lertly *adv* > a'lertness *n*

Alessandria (*Italian* ales'sandrja) *n* a town in NW Italy, in Piedmont. Pop: 85 438 (2001)

Ålesund *or* **Aalesund** (*Norwegian* 'ɔːləsun) *n* a port and market town in W Norway, on an island between Bergen and Trondheim: fishing and sealing fleets. Pop: 40 001 (2004 est)

aleurone layer (ə'lʊərən, -rəʊn) *or* **aleuron** (ə'lʊərɒn, -rən) *n* the outer protein-rich layer of certain seeds, esp of cereal grains [c19: from Greek *aleuron* flour]

Aleut (æ'luːt, 'æliː͡ʊt) *n* **1** a member of a people inhabiting the Aleutian Islands and SW Alaska, related to the Inuit **2** the language of this people, related to Inuktitut [from Russian *aleút*, probably of Chukchi origin] > Aleutian (ə'luːʃən) *adj, n*

Aleutian Islands *pl n* a chain of over 150 volcanic islands, extending southwestwards from the Alaska Peninsula between the N Pacific and the Bering Sea

A level *n* (in Britain) **1 a** a public examination in a subject taken for the General Certificate of Education (**GCE**), usually at the age of 17–18 **b** the course leading to this examination **c** (*as modifier*): *A-level maths* **2** a pass in a particular subject at A level: *she has three A levels*

A2 level *n* (in British Education) **a** the second part of an A-level course, taken after the AS level examination **b** the examination at the end of this

alewife ('eɪl,waɪf) *n*, *pl* **-wives** a North American fish, *Pomolobus pseudoharengus*, similar to the herring *Clupea harengus*: family *Clupeidae* (herrings) [c19: perhaps an alteration (through influence of *alewife*, that is, a large rotund woman, alluding to the fish's shape) of French *alose* shad]

Alexander (,ælɪg'zɑːndə) *n* **Harold** (**Rupert Leofric George**), Earl Alexander of Tunis. 1891–1969, British field marshal in World War II, who commanded the retreat from Dunkirk and commanded in North Africa (1943) and Sicily and Italy (1944–45); governor general of Canada (1946–52); British minister of defence (1952–54)

Alexander I *n* **1** *c*. 1080–1124, king of Scotland (1107–24), son of Malcolm III **2** 1777–1825, tsar of Russia (1801–25), who helped defeat Napoleon and formed the Holy Alliance (1815)

Alexander II *n* **1** 1198–1249, king of Scotland (1214–49), son of William (the Lion) **2** 1818–81, tsar of Russia (1855–81), son of Nicholas I, who emancipated the serfs (1861). He was assassinated by the Nihilists

Alexander III *n* **1** 1241–86, king of Scotland (1249–86), son of Alexander II **2** original name *Orlando Bandinelli*. died 1181, pope (1159–81), who excommunicated Barbarossa **3** 1845–94, tsar of Russia (1881–94), son of Alexander II

Alexander VI *n* original name *Rodrigo Borgia*. 1431–1503, pope (1492–1503): noted for his extravagance and immorality as well as for his patronage of the arts; father of Cesare and Lucrezia Borgia, with whom he is said to have committed incest

Alexander Archipelago (,ælɪg'zɑːndə) *n* a group of over 1000 islands along the coast of SE Alaska

Alexander I Island *n* an island of Antarctica, west of Palmer Land, in the Bellingshausen Sea. Length: about 378 km (235 miles)

Alexander technique *n* a technique for developing awareness of one's posture and movement in order to improve it [c20: named after Frederick Matthias *Alexander* (died 1955), Australian actor who originated it]

Alexander Nevski ('nɛvskɪ, 'nɛf-; *Russian* 'njɛfskij) *n* **Saint**. ?1220–63, Russian prince and military leader, who defeated the Swedes at the River Neva (1240) and the Teutonic knights at Lake Peipus (1242)

Alexander the Great *n* 356–323 BC, king of Macedon, who conquered Greece (336), Egypt (331), and the Persian Empire (328), and founded Alexandria

Alexandra (,ælɪg'zɑːndrə) *n* **1** 1844–1925, queen consort of Edward VII of Great Britain and Ireland **2** 1872–1918, wife of Nicholas II of Russia; her misrule while Nicholas was supreme commander of the Russian forces during World War I precipitated the Russian Revolution

Alexandretta (,ælɪgzɑːn'drɛtə) *n* the former name of **Iskenderun**

Alexandria (,ælɪg'zændrɪə, -'zɑːn-) *n* the chief port of Egypt, on the Nile Delta: cultural centre of ancient times, founded by Alexander the Great (332 BC). Pop: 3 760 000 (2005 est)

Alexandrian (,ælɪg'zændrɪən, -'zɑːn-) *adj* **1** of or relating to Alexander the Great (356–323 BC), king of Macedon, who conquered Greece (336), Egypt (331), and the Persian Empire (328) **2** of or relating to Alexandria in Egypt **3** relating to the Hellenistic philosophical, literary, and scientific ideas that flourished in Alexandria in the last three centuries BC **4** (of writers, literary works, etc) erudite and imitative rather than original or creative ▷ *n* **5** a native or inhabitant of Alexandria

Alexandrine (,ælɪg'zændraɪn, -drɪn, -'zɑːn-) *prosody* ▷ *n* **1** a line of verse having six iambic feet, usually with a caesura after the third foot ▷ *adj* **2** of, characterized by, or written in Alexandrines [c16: from French *alexandrin*, from *Alexandre*, title of 15th-century poem written in this metre]

alexandrite (,ælɪg'zændraɪt) *n* a green variety of chrysoberyl used as a gemstone [c19: named after *Alexander I* (1777–1825), tsar of Russia (1801–25); see -ITE¹]

Alexandroúpolis (*Greek* alɛksan'ðrupɔlis) *n* a port in NE Greece, in W Thrace. Pop: 52 720 (2001 est). Former name (until the end of World War I): **Dedéagach**

alexia (ə'lɛksɪə) *n* a disorder of the central nervous system characterized by impaired ability to read [c19: from New Latin, from A-¹ + Greek *lexis* speech; influenced in meaning by Latin *legere* to read]

Alexis Mikhailovich (ə'lɛksɪs mɪ'kaɪlə,vɪtʃ) *n* 1629–76, tsar of Russia (1645–76); father of Peter the Great

Alexius I Comnenus (ə'lɛksɪəs, kɒm'niːnəs) *n* 1048–1118, ruler of the Byzantine Empire (1081–1118)

alfalfa (æl'fælfə) *n* a leguminous plant, *Medicago sativa*, of Europe and Asia, having compound leaves with three leaflets and clusters of small purplish flowers. It is widely cultivated for forage and as a nitrogen fixer and used as a commercial source of chlorophyll. Also called: **lucerne** [c19: from Spanish, from Arabic *al-fasfasah*, from *al* the + *fasfasah* the best sort of fodder]

al-Farabi ('ælfə'rɑːbɪ) *n* **Mohammed ibn Tarkhan**. died 950, Muslim philosopher, physician, and mathematician, of central Asian origin

al Fayed (æl 'faɪjəd) *n* **Mohamed**. born 1933, Egyptian-born businessman; owner of the Harrods department store from 1985 and of the Ritz Hotel, Paris, from 1979: his son Dodi Fayed (1956–97) died in the same Paris car crash as Diana, Princess of Wales

Alfieri (*Italian* al'fjɛri) *n* **Count Vittorio** (vit'tɔːrjo). 1749–1803, Italian dramatist and poet, noted for his classical tragedies and political satires

Alfonso VI (*Spanish* al'fonso) *n* died 1109, king of Léon (1065–1109) and of Castile (1072–1109). He appointed his vassal, the Spanish hero El Cid, ruler of Valencia

Alfonso XIII (*Spanish* al'fonso) *n* 1886–1941, king of Spain

(1886–1931), who was forced to abdicate on the establishment of the republic in 1931

Alfred the Great ('ælfrɪd) *n* 849–99, king of Wessex (871–99) and overlord of England, who defeated the Danes and encouraged learning and writing in English

alfresco (æl'frɛskəʊ) *adj, adv* in the open air [c18: from Italian: in the cool]

Alfvén (al'ven) *n* **Hannes Olaf Gösta** ('hannɛs 'uːlaf 'jøsta). 1908–95, Swedish physicist, noted for his research on magnetohydrodynamics; shared the Nobel prize for physics in 1970

Alg. *abbreviation* Algeria(n)

algae ('ældʒiː) *pl n, sing* **alga** ('ælgə) unicellular or multicellular organisms formerly classified as plants, occurring in fresh or salt water or moist ground, that have chlorophyll and other pigments but lack true stems, roots, and leaves. Algae, which are now regarded as protoctists, include the seaweeds, diatoms, and spirogyra [c16: from Latin, plural of *alga* seaweed, of uncertain origin] > algal ('ælgəl) *adj* > algoid ('ælgɔɪd) *adj*

Algarve (æl'gɑːv) *n* **the Algarve** an area in the south of Portugal, on the Atlantic; it approximately corresponds to the administrative district of Faro: fishing and tourism important

algebra ('ældʒɪbrə) *n* a branch of mathematics in which arithmetical operations and relationships are generalized by using alphabetic symbols to represent unknown numbers or members of specified sets of numbers [c14: from Medieval Latin, from Arabic *al-jabr* the bone-setting, reunification, mathematical reduction] > algebraist (,ældʒɪ'breɪɪst) *n* > algebraic (,ældʒɪ'breɪɪk) *or* ,alge'braical *adj* > ,alge'braically *adv*

Algeciras (,ældʒɪ'sɪrəs; *Spanish* alxe'θiras) *n* a port and resort in SW Spain, on the Strait of Gibraltar: scene of a conference of the Great Powers in 1906. Pop: 108 779 (2003 est)

Alger ('ældʒə) *n* **Horatio**. 1834–99, US author of adventure stories for boys, including *Ragged Dick* (1867)

Algeria (æl'dʒɪərɪə) *n* a republic in NW Africa, on the Mediterranean: became independent in 1962, after more than a century of French rule; one-party constitution adopted in 1976; religious extremists led a campaign of violence from 1988 until 2000; consists chiefly of the N Sahara, with the Atlas Mountains in the north, and contains rich deposits of oil and natural gas. Official languages: Arabic and Berber; French also widely spoken. Religion: Muslim. Currency: dinar. Capital: Algiers. Pop: 32 339 000 (2004 est). Area: about 2 382 800 sq km (920 000 sq miles)

Algerian (æl'dʒɪərɪən) *adj* **1** of or relating to Algeria or its inhabitants ▷ *n* **2** a native or inhabitant of Algeria

Algerine (,ældʒə'riːn) *adj* **1** of or relating to Algeria or its inhabitants ▷ *n* **2** a native or inhabitant of Algeria

-algia *n combining form* denoting pain or a painful condition of the part specified: *neuralgia; odontalgia* [from Greek *algos* pain] > -algic *adj combining form*

algid ('ældʒɪd) *adj med* chilly or cold [c17: from Latin *algidus*, from *algēre* to be cold] > al'gidity *n*

Algiers (æl'dʒɪəz) *n* the capital of Algeria, an ancient port on the Mediterranean; until 1830 a centre of piracy. Pop: 3 260 000 (2005 est). French name **Alger** (alʒe)

alginate ('ældʒɪ,neɪt) *n* a salt or ester of alginic acid

alginic acid (æl'dʒɪnɪk) *n* a white or yellowish powdery polysaccharide having marked hydrophilic properties. Extracted from kelp, it is used mainly in the food and textile industries and in cosmetics and pharmaceuticals. Formula: $(C_6H_8O_6)_n$; molecular wt: 32 000–250 000

Algol ('ælgɒl) *n* a computer programming language designed for mathematical and scientific purposes; a high-level language [c20 *alg(orithmic) o(riented) l(anguage)*]

algolagnia (,ælgə'lægnɪə) *n* a perversion in which sexual pleasure is gained from the experience or infliction of pain [from ML, from Greek *algos* pain + *lagneiā* lust]

Algonquian (æl'gɒŋkɪən, -kwɪ-) *or* **Algonkian** *n* **1** a family of North American Indian languages whose speakers ranged over an area stretching from the Atlantic between Newfoundland and Delaware to the Rocky Mountains, including Micmac, Mahican, Ojibwa, Fox, Blackfoot, Cheyenne, and Shawnee. Some linguists relate it to Muskogean in a Macro-Algonquian phylum **2** *pl* -ans *or* -an a member of any of the North American Indian peoples that speak one of these languages ▷ *adj* **3** denoting, belonging to, or relating to this linguistic family or its speakers

Algonquin (æl'gɒŋkɪn, -kwɪn) *or* **Algonkin** (æl'gɒŋkɪn) *n* **1** *pl* -quins, -quin *or* -kins, -kin a member of a North American Indian people formerly living along the St Lawrence and Ottawa Rivers in Canada **2** the language of this people, a dialect of Ojibwa ▷ *n, adj* **3** a variant of **Algonquian** [c17: from Canadian French, earlier written as *Algoumequin*; perhaps related to Micmac *algoomaking* at the fish-spearing place]

algorism ('ælgə,rɪzəm) *n* **1** the Arabic or decimal system of counting **2** the skill of computation using any system of numerals **3** another name for **algorithm** [c13: from Old French *algorisme*, from Medieval Latin *algorismus*, from Arabic *al-khuwārizmi*, from the name of abu-Ja'far Mohammed ibn-Mūsa *al-Khuwārizmi*, ninth-century Persian mathematician]

algorithm ('ælgə,rɪðəm) *n* **1** a logical arithmetical or computational procedure that if correctly applied ensures the solution of a problem **2** *logic, maths* a recursive procedure whereby an infinite sequence of terms can be generated. ▷ Also called: algorism [c17: changed from ALGORISM, through influence of Greek *arithmos* number] > ,algo'rithmic *adj*

Algren ('ɔːlgrən) *n* **Nelson**. 1909–81, US novelist. His novels, mostly set in Chicago, include *Never Come Morning* (1942) and *The Man with the Golden Arm* (1949)

Alhambra (æl'hæmbrə) *n* a citadel and palace in Granada, Spain, built for the Moorish kings during the 13th and 14th centuries: noted for its rich ornamentation > Alhambresque (,ælhæm'brɛsk) *adj*

Al Hijrah *or* **Al Hijra** (æl 'hɪdʒrə) *n* an annual Muslim festival marking the beginning of the Muslim year. It commemorates Mohammed's move from Mecca to Medina and involves the exchange of gifts and the telling of stories about Mohammed. See also **Hegira** [from Arabic, *hijrah* emigration or flight]

Al Hufuf *or* **Al Hofuf** (æl hʊ'fuːf) *n* a town in E Saudi Arabia: a trading centre with nearby oilfields and oases. Pop: 331 000 (2005 est)

Ali ('ɑːliː) *n* **1** ?600–661 AD, fourth caliph of Islam (656–61 AD), considered the first caliph by the Shiites: cousin and son-in-law of Mohammed **2** See **Mehemet Ali 3** See **Muhammad Ali**

alias ('eɪlɪəs) *adv* **1** at another time or place known as or named: *Dylan, alias Zimmerman* ▷ *n, pl* -ases **2** an assumed name [c16: from Latin *aliās* (adv) otherwise, at another time, from *alius* other]

aliasing ('eɪlɪəsɪŋ) *n radio, television* the error in a vision or sound signal arising from limitations in the system that generates or processes the signal

alibi ('ælɪ,baɪ) *n, pl* -bis **1** *law* **a** a defence by an accused person that he was elsewhere at the time the crime in question was committed **b** the evidence given to prove this **2** *informal* an excuse ▷ *vb* **3** (*tr*) to provide with an alibi [c18: from Latin *alibī* elsewhere, from *alius* other + -*bī* as in *ubī* where]

Alicante (,ælɪ'kæntɪ) *n* a port in SE Spain: commercial centre. Pop: 305 911 (2003 est)

Alice ('ælɪs) *or* **the Alice** *n Austral slang* short for **Alice Springs**

Alice band *n* an ornamental band worn across the front of the hair to hold it back from the face

Alice-in-Wonderland *adj* fantastic; irrational [c20: alluding to the absurdities of Wonderland in Lewis Carroll's book]

Alice Springs *n* a town in central Australia, in the Northern Territory, in the Macdonnell Ranges. Pop: 23 640 (2001). Former name (until 1931): Stuart

alicyclic (,ælɪ'saɪklɪk, -'sɪk-) *adj* (of an organic compound) having aliphatic properties, in spite of the presence of a ring of carbon atoms [c19: from German *alicyclisch*, from ALI(PHATIC) + CYCLIC]

a

alidade ('ælɪˌdeɪd) *or* **alidad** ('ælɪˌdæd) *n* **1** a surveying instrument used in plane-tabling for drawing lines of sight on a distant object and taking angular measurements **2** the upper rotatable part of a theodolite, including the telescope and its attachments [C15: from French, from Medieval Latin *allidada*, from Arabic *al-'idāda* the revolving radius of a circle]

alien ('eɪljən, 'eɪlɪən) *n* **1** a person owing allegiance to a country other than that in which he lives; foreigner **2** any being or thing foreign to the environment in which it now exists **3** (in science fiction) a being from another world, sometimes specifically an extraterrestrial ▷ *adj* **4** unnaturalized; foreign **5** having foreign allegiance: *alien territory* **6** unfamiliar; strange: *an alien quality in a work of art* **7** (*postpositive and foll by to*) repugnant or opposed (to): *war is alien to his philosophy* **8** (in science fiction) of or from another world [C14: from Latin *aliēnus* foreign, from *alius* other]

alienable ('eɪljənəb³l, 'eɪlɪə-) *adj law* (of property) transferable to another owner > ˌaliena'bility *n*

alienate ('eɪljəˌneɪt, 'eɪlɪə-) *vb* (*tr*) **1** to cause (a friend, sympathizer, etc) to become indifferent, unfriendly, or hostile; estrange **2** to turn away; divert: *to alienate the affections of a person* **3** *law* to transfer the ownership of (property, title, etc) to another person > 'alienˌator *n* > alienation (ˌeɪljə'neɪʃən, ˌeɪlɪə-) *n*

alienee (ˌeɪljə'niː, ˌeɪlɪə-) *n law* a person to whom a transfer of property is made

alienist ('eɪljənɪst, 'eɪlɪə-) *n US* a psychiatrist who specializes in the legal aspects of mental illness

alienor ('eɪljənə, 'eɪlɪə-) *n law* a person who transfers property to another

aliform ('ælɪˌfɔːm, 'eɪlɪ-) *adj* wing-shaped; alar [C19: from New Latin *āliformis*, from Latin *āla* a wing]

Aligarh (ˌɑːlɪ'gɜː, ˌælɪ-) *n* a city in N India, in W Uttar Pradesh, with a famous Muslim university (1920). Pop: 667 732 (2001)

alight¹ (ə'laɪt) *vb* **alights, alighting, alighted** *or* **alit** (*intr*) **1** (usually foll by *from*) to step out (of) or get down (from): *to alight from a taxi* **2** to come to rest; settle; land: *a thrush alighted on the wall* [Old English *ālīhtan*, from A-² + *līhtan* to make less heavy, from *līht* LIGHT²]

alight² (ə'laɪt) *adj, adv* (*postpositive*) **1** burning; on fire **2** illuminated; lit up [Old English *ālīht* lit up, from *ālīhtan* to light up; see LIGHT¹]

align (ə'laɪn) *vb* **1** to place or become placed in a line **2** to bring (components or parts, such as the wheels of a car) into proper or desirable coordination or relation **3** (*tr*; usually foll by *with*) to bring (a person, country, etc) into agreement or cooperation with the policy, etc of another person or group [C17: from Old French *aligner*, from *à ligne* into line]

alignment (ə'laɪnmənt) *n* **1** arrangement in a straight line **2** the line or lines formed in this manner **3** alliance or union with a party, cause, etc **4** proper or desirable coordination or relation of components **5** a ground plan of a railway, motor road, etc

alike (ə'laɪk) *adj* (*postpositive*) **1** possessing the same or similar characteristics: *they all look alike to me* ▷ *adv* **2** in the same or a similar manner, way, or degree: *they walk alike* [Old English *gelīc*; see LIKE¹]

aliment ('ælɪmənt) *n* something that nourishes or sustains the body or mind [C15: from Latin *alimentum* food, from *alere* to nourish] > ˌali'mental *adj*

alimentary (ˌælɪ'mɛntərɪ, -trɪ) *adj* **1** of or relating to nutrition **2** providing sustenance or nourishment

alimentary canal *or* **alimentary tract** *n* the tubular passage extending from the mouth to the anus, through which food is passed and digested

alimentation (ˌælɪmɛn'teɪʃən) *n* **1** nourishment **2** sustenance; support

alimony ('ælɪmənɪ) *n law* (formerly) an allowance paid under a court order by one spouse to another when they are separated but not divorced. See also **maintenance** [C17: from Latin *alimōnia* sustenance, from *alere* to nourish]

A-line *adj* (of a garment, esp a skirt or dress) flaring slightly from the waist or shoulders

Ali Pasha ('ɑːli 'pɑːʃə) *n* known as *the Lion of Janina*.

1741–1822, Turkish pasha and ruler of Albania (1787–1820), who was deposed and assassinated after intriguing against Turkey

aliphatic (ˌælɪ'fætɪk) *adj* (of an organic compound) not aromatic, esp having an open chain structure, such as alkanes, alkenes, and alkynes [C19: from Greek *aleiphat-, aleiphar* oil]

aliquant ('ælɪkwənt) *adj maths* of, signifying, or relating to a quantity or number that is not an exact divisor of a given quantity or number: *5 is an aliquant part of 12* [C17: from New Latin, from Latin *aliquantus* somewhat, a certain quantity of]

aliquot ('ælɪˌkwɒt) *adj maths* of, signifying, or relating to an exact divisor of a quantity or number: *3 is an aliquot part of 12* [C16: from Latin: several, a few]

A list *n* **a** the most socially desirable category **b** (*as modifier*): *an A-list event* ▷ See **B list**

alit (ə'lɪt) *vb* a rare past tense and past participle of **alight¹**

aliterate (eɪ'lɪtərɪt) *n* **1** a person who is able to read but disinclined to do so ▷ *adj* **2** of or relating to aliterates

alive (ə'laɪv) *adj* (*postpositive*) **1** (of people, animals, plants, etc) living; having life **2** in existence; active: *they kept hope alive; the tradition was still alive* **3** (*immediately postpositive and usually used with a superlative*) of those living; now living: *the happiest woman alive* **4** full of life; lively **5** (usually foll by *with*) animated: *a face alive with emotion* **6** (foll by *to*) aware (of); sensitive (to) **7** (foll by *with*) teeming (with): *the mattress was alive with fleas* **8** *electronics* another word for: **live²** (sense 11) [Old English *on līfe* in LIFE]

alizarin (ə'lɪzərɪn) *n* a brownish-yellow powder or orange-red crystalline solid used as a dye and in the manufacture of other dyes. Formula: $C_6H_4(CO)_2C_6H_4(OH)_2$ [C19: probably from French *alizarine*, probably from Arabic *al-'asārah* the juice, from *'asara* to squeeze]

alkali ('ælkəˌlaɪ) *n, pl* **-lis** *or* **-lies** **1** *chem* a soluble base or a solution of a base **2** a soluble mineral salt that occurs in arid soils and some natural waters [C14: from Medieval Latin, from Arabic *al-qili* the ashes (of the plant saltwort)]

alkali metal *n* any of the monovalent metals lithium, sodium, potassium, rubidium, caesium, and francium, belonging to group 1A of the periodic table. They are all very reactive and electropositive

alkaline ('ælkəˌlaɪn) *adj* having the properties of or containing an alkali > alkalinity (ˌælkə'lɪnɪtɪ) *n*

alkaline earth *n* **1** Also called: **alkaline earth metal, alkaline earth element** any of the divalent electropositive metals beryllium, magnesium, calcium, strontium, barium, and radium, belonging to group 2A of the periodic table **2** an oxide of one of the alkaline earth metals

alkalize *or* **alkalise** ('ælkəˌlaɪz) *vb* (*tr*) to make alkaline > 'alkaˌlizable *or* 'alkaˌlisable *adj*

alkaloid ('ælkəˌlɔɪd) *n* any of a group of nitrogenous basic compounds found in plants, typically insoluble in water and physiologically active. Common examples are morphine, strychnine, quinine, nicotine, and caffeine

alkane ('ælkeɪn) *n* any saturated aliphatic hydrocarbon with the general formula C_nH_{2n+2}. Also called: **paraffin**

alkanet ('ælkəˌnɛt) *n* **1** a European boraginaceous plant, *Alkanna tinctoria*, the roots of which yield a red dye **2** Also called: **anchusin, alkannin** the dye obtained from this plant [C14: from Spanish *alcaneta*, diminutive of *alcana* henna, from Medieval Latin *alchanna*, from Arabic *al* the + *hinnā'* henna]

alkene ('ælkiːn) *n* Also called: **olefine, olefin** any unsaturated aliphatic hydrocarbon with the general formula C_nH_{2n}

Alkmaar (*Dutch* 'ɑlkmaːr) *n* a city in the W Netherlands, in North Holland. Pop: 93 000 (2003 est)

Alkoran *or* **Alcoran** (ˌælkɒ'rɑːn) *n* a less common name for the **Koran**

alky *or* **alkie** ('ælkɪ) *n, pl* **-kies** *slang* a heavy drinker or alcoholic

alkyd resin ('ælkɪd) *n* any synthetic resin made from a dicarboxylic acid, such as phthalic acid, and diols or triols: used in paints and adhesives

alkyl (ˈælkɪl) n (modifier) of, consisting of, or containing the monovalent group C_nH_{2n+1} [C19: from German, from Alk(ohol) ALCOHOL + -YL]

alkylating agent (ˈælkɪˌleɪtɪŋ) n any cytotoxic drug containing alkyl groups, such as chlorambucil, that acts by damaging DNA; widely used in chemotherapy

alkyne (ˈælkaɪn) n any unsaturated aliphatic hydrocarbon that has a formula of the type C_nH_{2n-2}

all (ɔːl) determiner **1 a** the whole quantity or amount of; totality of; every one of a class: all the rice; all men are mortal **b** (as pronoun; functioning as sing or plural): all of it is nice; all are welcome **c** (in combination with a noun used as a modifier): an all-ticket match; an all-amateur tournament; an all-night sitting **2** the greatest possible: in all earnestness **3** any whatever: to lose all hope of recovery; beyond all doubt **4** all along all the time **5** all but almost; nearly: all but dead **6** all of no less or smaller than: she's all of thirteen years **7** all over **a** finished; at an end **b** over the whole area (of something); everywhere (in, on, etc): all over England **c** typically; representatively in the phrase that's me (you, him, us, them, etc) all over) **d** unduly effusive towards **8** See all in **9** all in all **a** everything considered: all in all, it was a great success **b** the object of one's attention or interest: you are my all in all **10** all the (foll by a comparative adjective or adverb) so much (more or less) than otherwise: we must work all the faster now **11** all too definitely but regrettably: it's all too true **12** at all **a** (used with a negative or in a question) in any way whatsoever or to any extent or degree: I didn't know that at all **b** even so; anyway: I'm surprised you came at all **13** be all for informal to be strongly in favour of **14** for all **a** in so far as; to the extent that: for all anyone knows, he was a baron **b** notwithstanding: for all my pushing, I still couldn't move it **15** for all that in spite of that: he was a nice man for all that **16** in all altogether: there were five of them in all ▷ adv **17** (in scores of games) apiece; each: the score at half time was three all **18** completely: all alone ▷ n **19** (preceded by my, your, his, etc) (one's) complete effort or interest: to give your all; you are my all **20** totality or whole [Old English eall; related to Old High German al, Old Norse allr, Gothic alls all]

all- combining form a variant of allo-

alla breve (ˈælə ˈbreɪvɪ; Italian ˈalla ˈbrɛːve) n **1** a musical time signature indicating two or four minims to a bar ▷ adj, adv **2** twice as fast as normal [C19: Italian, literally: (according) to the breve]

Allah (ˈælə) n Islam the Muslim name for God; the one Supreme Being [C16: from Arabic, from al the + Ilāh god; compare Hebrew elōah]

Allahabad (ˌæləhəˈbæd, -ˈbɑːd) n a city in N India, in SE Uttar Pradesh at the confluence of the Ganges and Jumna Rivers: Hindu pilgrimage centre. Pop: 990 298 (2001)

all-American adj US **1** representative of the whole of the United States **2** composed exclusively of American members **3** (of a person) typically American

allantoid (əˈlæntɔɪd) adj **1** relating to or resembling the allantois **2** botany shaped like a sausage ▷ n **3** another name for **allantois** [C17: from Greek allantoeidēs sausage-shaped, from allas sausage + -OID] > allantoidal (ˌælænˈtɔɪdəl) adj

allantoin (ˌælənˈtəʊɪn) n a substance derived from the secretions of snails and contained in some plants, used in skin care products and valued for its soothing properties [C19: from ALLANTOIS]

allantois (ˌælənˈtəʊɪs, əˈlæntɔɪs) n a membranous sac growing out of the ventral surface of the hind gut of embryonic reptiles, birds, and mammals. It combines with the chorion to form the mammalian placenta [C17: New Latin, irregularly from Greek allantoeidēs sausage-shaped, ALLANTOID] > allantoic (ˌælənˈtəʊɪk) adj

allay (əˈleɪ) vb **1** to relieve (pain, grief, etc) or be relieved **2** (tr) to reduce (fear, anger, etc) [Old English ālecgan to put down, from lecgan to LAY¹]

All Blacks pl n the All Blacks the international Rugby Union football team of New Zealand [so named because of the players' black playing strip]

all clear n **1** a signal, usually a siren, indicating that some danger, such as an air raid, is over **2** an indication

that obstacles are no longer present; permission to proceed

all-dayer (ˌɔːlˈdeɪə) n an entertainment, such as a pop concert or film screening, that lasts all day

all-dressed adj Canadian (of a hot dog, hamburger, etc) served with all available garnishes

allegation (ˌælɪˈɡeɪʃən) n **1** the act of alleging **2** an unproved statement or assertion, esp one in an accusation

allege (əˈlɛdʒ) vb (tr; may take a clause as object) **1** to declare in or as if in a court of law; state without or before proof: he alleged malpractice **2** to put forward (an argument or plea) for or against an accusation, claim, etc [C14 aleggen, ultimately from Latin allēgāre to dispatch on a mission, from lēx law]

alleged (əˈlɛdʒd) adj (prenominal) **1** stated or described to be such; presumed: the alleged murderer **2** dubious: an alleged miracle

allegedly (əˈlɛdʒɪdlɪ) adv **1** reportedly; supposedly: payments allegedly made to a former colleague **2** (sentence modifier) it is alleged that ▷ interj **3** an exclamation expressing disbelief or scepticism

- USAGE In recent years it has become common for
- speakers to include allegedly in statements that are
- controversial or possibly even defamatory. The
- implication is that, by saying allegedly, the speaker is
- distancing himself or herself from the controversy
- and even protecting himself or herself from possible
- prosecution. However, the effect created may be
- deliberate. The use of allegedly can be a signal that,
- although the statement may seem outrageous, it is in
- fact true: He was drunk at work. Allegedly. Conversely, it is
- also possible to use allegedly as an expression of ironic
- scepticism: He's a hard worker. Allegedly

Allegheny Mountains (ˌælɪˈɡeɪnɪ) or **Alleghenies** pl n a mountain range in Pennsylvania, Maryland, Virginia, and West Virginia: part of the Appalachian system; rising from 600 m (2000 ft) to over 1440 m (4800 ft)

allegiance (əˈliːdʒəns) n **1** loyalty, as of a subject to his sovereign or of a citizen to his country **2** (in feudal society) the obligations of a vassal to his liege lord [C14: from Old French ligeance, from lige LIEGE]

allegorical (ˌælɪˈɡɒrɪkəl) or **allegoric** adj used in, containing, or characteristic of allegory

allegorize or **allegorise** (ˈælɪɡəˌraɪz) vb **1** to transform (a story, narrative, fable, etc) into or compose in the form of allegory **2** (tr) to interpret allegorically > ˌallegoriˈzation or ˌallegoriˈsation n

allegory (ˈælɪɡərɪ) n, pl -ries **1** a poem, play, picture, etc, in which the apparent meaning of the characters and events is used to symbolize a deeper moral or spiritual meaning **2** use of such symbolism to illustrate truth or a moral **3** anything used as a symbol or emblem [C14: from Old French allegorie, from Latin allēgoria, from Greek, from allēgorein to speak figuratively, from allos other + agoreuein to make a speech in public, from agora a public gathering] > ˈallegorist n

allegretto (ˌælɪˈɡrɛtəʊ) music ▷ adj, adv **1** (to be performed) fairly quickly or briskly ▷ n, pl -tos **2** a piece or passage to be performed in this manner [C19: diminutive of ALLEGRO]

Allegri (Italian alˈleɡri) n **Gregorio.** 1582–1652, Italian composer and singer. His compositions include a Miserere for nine voices

allegro (əˈleɪɡrəʊ, -ˈlɛɡ-) music ▷ adj, adv **1** (to be performed) quickly, in a brisk lively manner ▷ n, pl -gros **2** a piece or passage to be performed in this manner [C17: from Italian, from Latin alacer brisk, lively]

allele (əˈliːl) n any of two or more variants of a gene that have the same relative position on homologous chromosomes and are responsible for alternative characteristics, such as smooth or wrinkled seeds in peas. Also called: allelomorph (əˈliːləˌmɔːf) [C20: from German Allel, shortened from allelomorph, from Greek allēl- one another + morphē form]

alleluia (ˌælɪˈluːjə) interj praise the Lord! Used more commonly in liturgical contexts in place of hallelujah [C14: via Medieval Latin from Hebrew hallelūyāh]

allemande (ˈælɪmænd; French almɑ̃d) n **1** the first

movement of the classical suite, composed in a moderate tempo in a time signature of four-four **2** any of several German dances **3** a figure in country dancing or square dancing by means of which couples change position in the set [c17: from French *danse allemande* German dance]

Allen¹ ('ælən) *n* **1** Bog of Allen a region of peat bogs in central Ireland, west of Dublin. Area: over 10 sq km (3.75 sq miles) **2** Lough Allen a lake in Ireland, in county Leitrim

Allen² ('ælən) *n* **1** Ethan. 1738–89, American soldier during the War of Independence who led the Green Mountain Boys of Vermont **2** Lily (Rose Beatrice). born 1985, English pop singer; one of the first performers to come to prominence through exposure on the networking website MySpace rather than through record release **3** Sir Thomas. born 1944, British operatic baritone **4** Woody. real name *Allen Stewart Konigsberg*. born 1935, US film comedian, screenwriter, and director. His films as an actor and director include *Annie Hall* (1977), *Manhattan* (1979), *Hannah and Her Sisters* (1986), *Bullets over Broadway* (1994), and *Anything Else* (2003)

Allenby ('ælənbɪ) *n* Edmund Henry Hynman, 1st Viscount. 1861–1936, British field marshal who captured Palestine and Syria from the Turks in 1918; high commissioner in Egypt (1919–25)

Allende (*Spanish* a'ʎende) *n* **1** Isabel. born 1942, Chilean writer, born in Peru; her works include *Eva Luna* (1989), *Paula* (1995), and *Daughter of Fortune* (1999) **2** Salvador (salβa'ðor). 1908–73, Chilean Marxist politician; president of Chile from 1970 until 1973, when the army seized power and he was killed

allergen ('ælə,dʒɛn) *n* any substance capable of inducing an allergy > ,aller'genic *adj*

allergic (ə'lɜːdʒɪk) *adj* **1** of, relating to, having, or caused by an allergy **2** (*postpositive*; foll by *to*) *informal* having an aversion (to): *he's allergic to work*

allergist ('ælədʒɪst) *n* a physician skilled in the diagnosis and treatment of diseases or conditions caused by allergy

allergy ('ælədʒɪ) *n, pl* -gies **1** a hypersensitivity to a substance that causes the body to react to any contact with that substance. Hay fever is an allergic reaction to pollen **2** *informal* aversion [c20: from German *Allergie* (indicating a changed reaction), from Greek *allos* other + *ergon* activity]

alleviate (ə'liːvɪ,eɪt) *vb* (*tr*) to make (pain, sorrow, etc) easier to bear; lessen; relieve [c15: from Late Latin *alleviāre* to mitigate, from Latin *levis* light] > al,levi'ation *n* > al'levi,ator *n*

● USAGE See at **ameliorate**

alley¹ ('ælɪ) *n* **1** a narrow lane or passage, esp one between or behind buildings **2** See **bowling alley 3** *tennis chiefly US* the space between the singles and doubles sidelines **4** a walk in a park or garden, esp one lined with trees or bushes [c14: from Old French *alee*, from *aler* to go, ultimately from Latin *ambulāre* to walk]

alley² ('ælɪ) *n* a large playing marble [c18: shortened and changed from ALABASTER]

alleyway ('ælɪ,weɪ) *n* a narrow passage; alley

All Fools' Day *n* April Fools' Day. See **April fool**

all hail *interj* an archaic greeting or salutation [c14, literally: all health (to someone)]

Allhallows (,ɔːl'hæləʊz) *n* a less common term for **All Saints' Day**

alliaceous (,ælɪ'eɪʃəs) *adj* **1** of or relating to *Allium*, a genus of plants that have a strong onion or garlic smell and often have bulbs: family *Alliaceae*. The genus occurs in the N hemisphere and includes onion, garlic, leek, chive, and shallot **2** tasting or smelling like garlic or onions **3** of, relating to, or belonging to the *Alliaceae*, a family of flowering plants that includes the genus *Allium* [c18: from Latin *allium* garlic; see -ACEOUS]

alliance (ə'laɪəns) *n* **1** the act of allying or state of being allied; union; confederation **2** a formal agreement or pact, esp a military one, between two or more countries to achieve a particular aim **3** the countries involved in such an agreement **4** a union between families through marriage **5** affinity or correspondence in qualities or

characteristics **6** *botany* a taxonomic category consisting of a group of related families; subclass [c13: from Old French *aliance*, from *alier* to ALLY]

allied (ə'laɪd, 'ælaɪd) *adj* **1** joined, as by treaty, agreement, or marriage; united **2** of the same type or class; related

Allied ('ælaɪd) *adj* of or relating to the Allies

Allier (*French* alje) *n* **1** a department of central France, in Auvergne region. Capital: Moulins. Pop: 342 307 (2003 est). Area: 7382 sq km (2879 sq miles) **2** a river in S central France, rising in the Cévennes and flowing north to the Loire. Length: over 403 km (250 miles)

Allies ('ælaɪz) *pl n* **1** (in World War I) the powers of the Triple Entente (France, Russia, and Britain) together with the nations allied with them **2** (in World War II) the countries that fought against the Axis. The main Allied powers were Britain and the Commonwealth countries, the US, the Soviet Union, France, China, and Poland

alligator ('ælɪ,geɪtə) *n* **1** a large crocodilian, *Alligator mississipiensis*, of the southern US, having powerful jaws and sharp teeth and differing from the crocodiles in having a shorter and broader snout: family *Alligatoridae* (alligators and caymans) **2** a similar but smaller species, *A. sinensis*, occurring in China near the Yangtse River **3** any of various tools or machines having adjustable toothed jaws, used for gripping, crushing, or compacting [c17: from Spanish *el lagarto* the lizard, from Latin *lacerta*]

alligator pear *n* another name for **avocado**

all-important *adj* crucial; vital

all in *adj* **1** (*postpositive*) *informal* completely exhausted; tired out ▷ *adv, adj* (**all-in** *when prenominal*) **2** with all expenses or costs included in the price: *the flat is one hundred pounds a week all in*

Allingham ('ælɪŋəm) *n* Margery. 1904–66, British author of detective stories, featuring Albert Campion. Her works include *Tiger in the Smoke* (1952) and *The Mind Readers* (1965)

all-in wrestling *n* another name for **freestyle** (sense 2b)

alliterate (ə'lɪtə,reɪt) *vb* **1** to contain or cause to contain alliteration **2** (*intr*) to speak or write using alliteration

alliteration (ə,lɪtə'reɪʃən) *n* the use of the same consonant (**consonantal alliteration**) or of a vowel, not necessarily the same vowel (**vocalic alliteration**), at the beginning of each word or each stressed syllable in a line of verse, as in *around the rock the ragged rascal ran* [c17: from Medieval Latin *alliterātiō* (from Latin *al-* (see AD-) + *litera* letter), on the model of *obliterātiō* OBLITERATION] > al'literative *adj*

allium ('ælɪəm) *n* any plant of the genus *Allium*, such as the onion, garlic, shallot, leek, or chive: family *Alliaceae* [c19: from Latin: garlic]

all-nighter (,ɔːl'naɪtə) *n* an entertainment, such as a pop concert or film screening, that lasts all night

allo- *or before a vowel* **all-** *combining form* indicating difference, variation, or opposition: *allopathy; allomorph; allophone; allonym* [from Greek *allos* other, different]

Alloa ('æləʊə) *n* a town in E central Scotland, the administrative centre of Clackmannanshire. Pop: 18 989 (2001)

allocate ('ælə,keɪt) *vb* (*tr*) **1** to assign or allot for a particular purpose **2** a less common word for **locate** (sense 2) [c17: from Medieval Latin *allocāre*, from Latin *locāre* to place, from *locus* a place] > 'allo,catable *adj* > ,allo'cation *n*

allocution (,ælə'kjuːʃən) *n* *rhetoric* a formal or authoritative speech or address, esp one that advises, informs, or exhorts [c17: from Late Latin *allocūtiō*, from Latin *alloquī* to address, from *loquī* to speak]

allomerism (ə'lɒmə,rɪzəm) *n* similarity of crystalline structure in substances of different chemical composition > allomeric (,ælə'mɛrɪk) *or* al'lomerous *adj*

allomorph ('ælə,mɔːf) *n* **1** *linguistics* any of the phonological representations of a single morpheme. For example, the final (s) and (z) sounds of *bets* and *beds* are allomorphs of the English noun-plural morpheme **2** any of two or more different crystalline forms of a chemical compound, such as a mineral

a

> ˌalloˈmorphic *adj*

allopath (ˈæləˌpæθ) *or* **allopathist** (əˈlɒpəθɪst) *n* a person who practises or is skilled in allopathy

allopathy (əˈlɒpəθɪ) *n* the orthodox medical method of treating disease, by inducing a condition different from or opposed to the cause of the disease. Compare **homeopathy** > allopathic (ˌæləˈpæθɪk) *adj*

allophone (ˈæləˌfəʊn) *n* **1** any of several speech sounds that are regarded as contextual or environmental variants of the same phoneme. In English the aspirated initial (p) in *pot* and the unaspirated (p) in *spot* are allophones of the phoneme /p/ **2** *Canadian* a Canadian whose native language is neither French nor English > allophonic (ˌæləˈfɒnɪk) *adj*

All-Ordinaries Index *n* an index of share prices on the Australian Stock Exchange giving a weighted arithmetic average of 245 ordinary shares

allot (əˈlɒt) *vb* **-lots, -lotting, -lotted** (*tr*) **1** to assign or distribute (shares, etc) **2** to designate for a particular purpose: *money was allotted to cover expenses* [c16: from Old French *aloter*, from *lot* portion, LOT]

allotment (əˈlɒtmənt) *n* **1** the act of allotting; apportionment **2** a portion or amount allotted **3** *Brit* a small piece of usually public land rented by an individual for cultivation

allotrope (ˈæləˌtrəʊp) *n* any of two or more physical forms in which an element can exist

allotropy (əˈlɒtrəpɪ) *or* **allotropism** *n* the existence of an element in two or more physical forms. The most common elements having this property are carbon, sulphur, and phosphorus > allotropic (ˌæləˈtrɒpɪk) *adj*

all-out *informal* ▷ *adj* **1** using one's maximum powers: *an all-out effort* ▷ *adv* **all out 2** to one's maximum effort or capacity: *he went all out on the home stretch*

allow (əˈlaʊ) *vb* **1** (*tr*) to permit (to do something); let **2** (*tr*) to set aside: *five hours were allowed to do the job* **3** (*tr*) to let enter or stay: *they don't allow dogs* **4** (*tr*) to acknowledge or concede (a point, claim, etc) **5** (*tr*) to let have; grant: *he was allowed few visitors* **6** (*intr*; foll by *for*) to take into account **7** (*intr*; often foll by *of*) to permit; admit: *a question that allows of only one reply* **8** (*tr*; may take a clause as object*) *US dialect* to assert; maintain [c14: from Old French *alouer*, from Late Latin *allaudāre* to extol, influenced by Medieval Latin *allocāre* to assign, ALLOCATE] > allowable (əˈlaʊəbəl) *adj* > alˈlowably *adv*

allowance (əˈlaʊəns) *n* **1** an amount of something, esp money or food, given or allotted usually at regular intervals **2** a discount, as in consideration for something given in part exchange or to increase business; rebate **3** (in Britain) an amount of a person's income that is not subject to a particular tax and is therefore deducted before his or her liability to taxation is assessed **4** a portion set aside to compensate for something or to cover special expenses **5** admission; concession **6** the act of allowing; sanction; toleration **7 make allowances** *or* **make allowance** (usually foll by *for*) **a** to take mitigating circumstances into account in consideration (of) **b** to allow (for)

Alloway (ˈæləˌweɪ) *n* a village in Scotland, in South Ayrshire, S of Ayr: birthplace of Robert Burns

allowedly (əˈlaʊɪdlɪ) *adv* (*sentence modifier*) by general admission or agreement; admittedly

alloy *n* (ˈælɔɪ, əˈlɔɪ) **1** a metallic material, such as steel, brass, or bronze, consisting of a mixture of two or more metals or of metallic elements with nonmetallic elements. Alloys often have physical properties markedly different from those of the pure metals **2** something that impairs the quality or reduces the value of the thing to which it is added ▷ *vb* (əˈlɔɪ) (*tr*) **3** to add (one metal or element to another metal or element) to obtain a substance with a desired property **4** to debase (a pure substance) by mixing with an inferior element **5** to diminish or impair [c16: from Old French *aloi* a mixture, from *aloier* to combine, from Latin *alligāre* to bind together; from *ligāre* to bind]

all-points bulletin *n* (in the US) an alert broadcast to all police officers within an area, instructing the arrest of a suspect

all-purpose *adj* useful for many things

all right *adj* (*postpositive except in slang use*) **1** adequate; satisfactory **2** unharmed; safe **3** all-right *US slang* acceptable ▷ *sentence substitute* **4** very well: used to express assent ▷ *adv* **5** satisfactorily; adequately: *the car goes all right* **6** without doubt ▷ Also: alright
● USAGE See at alright

all-round *adj* **1** efficient in all respects, esp in sport; versatile: *an all-round player* **2** comprehensive; many-sided; not narrow: *an all-round education*

all-rounder *n* a versatile person, esp in a sport

All Saints' Day *n* a Christian festival celebrated on Nov 1 to honour all the saints

all-singing all-dancing *adj* having every desirable feature possible: *an all-singing all-dancing computer*

All Souls' Day *n* *RC Church* a day of prayer (Nov 2) for the dead in purgatory

allspice (ˈɔːlˌspaɪs) *n* **1** a tropical American myrtaceous tree, *Pimenta officinalis*, having small white flowers and aromatic berries **2** the whole or powdered seeds of this berry used as a spice, having a flavour said to resemble a mixture of cinnamon, cloves, and nutmeg. ▷ Also called: pimento

all-star *adj* (*prenominal*) consisting of star performers

Allston (ˈɔːlstən) *n* **Washington.** 1779–1843, US painter and author, regarded as the earliest US Romantic painter. His paintings include *Elijah in the Desert* (1818) and *Moonlit Landscape* (1819)

all-time *adj* (*prenominal*) *informal* unsurpassed in some respect at a particular time

all told *adv* (*sentence modifier*) taking every one into account; in all

allude (əˈluːd) *vb* (*intr*; foll by *to*) **1** to refer indirectly, briefly, or implicitly **2** (loosely) to mention [c16: from Latin *allūdere*, from *lūdere* to sport, from *lūdus* a game]
● USAGE See at elude

allure (əˈljʊə, əˈlʊə) *vb* **1** (*tr*) to entice or tempt (someone) to a person or place or to a course of action; attract ▷ *n* **2** attractiveness; appeal [c15: from Old French *alurer*, from *lure* bait, LURE] > al'lurement *n* > alluring (əˈljʊərɪŋ, əˈlʊə-) *adj* > al'luringly *adv*

allusion (əˈluːʒən) *n* **1** the act of alluding **2** a passing reference; oblique or obscure mention [c16: from Late Latin *allūsiō*, from Latin *allūdere* to sport with, ALLUDE]

allusive (əˈluːsɪv) *adj* containing or full of allusions > alˈlusiveness *n*

alluvial (əˈluːvɪəl) *adj* **1** of or relating to alluvium ▷ *n* **2** another name for **alluvium**

alluvion (əˈluːvɪən) *n* **1 a** the wash of the sea or of a river **b** an overflow or flood **c** matter deposited as sediment; alluvium **2** *law* the gradual formation of new land, as by the recession of the sea or deposit of sediment on a riverbed [c16: from Latin *alluviō* an overflowing, from *luere* to wash]

alluvium (əˈluːvɪəm) *n, pl* **-viums** *or* **-via** (-vɪə) a fine-grained fertile soil consisting of mud, silt, and sand deposited by flowing water on flood plains, in river beds, and in estuaries [c17: from Latin; see ALLUVION]

ally *vb* (əˈlaɪ) **-lies, -lying, -lied** (usually foll by *to* or *with*) **1** to unite or be united, esp formally, as by treaty, confederation, or marriage **2** (*tr*; *usually passive*) to connect or be related, as through being similar or compatible ▷ *n* (ˈælaɪ, əˈlaɪ) *pl* **-lies 3** a country, person, or group allied with another **4** a plant, animal, substance, etc, closely related to another in characteristics or form [c14: from Old French *alier* to join, from Latin *alligāre* to bind to, from *ligāre* to bind]

allyl (ˈælaɪl, ˈælɪl) *n* (*modifier*) of, consisting of, or containing the monovalent group CH_2:$CHCH_2$⁻: *allyl group or radical; allyl resin* [c19: from Latin *allium* garlic + -YL; first distinguished in a compound isolated from garlic]

allyl resin *n* any of several thermosetting synthetic resins made by polymerizing esters of allyl alcohol with a dibasic acid. They are used as adhesives

Alma-Ata (*Russian* alˈmaːta) *n* the former name of **Almaty**

Almada (*Portuguese* alˈmɑːdə) *n* a town in S central Portugal, on the S bank of the Tagus estuary opposite Lisbon: statue of Christ 110 m (360 ft) high, erected 1959. Pop: 160 826 (2001)

Al Madinah (ˌæl mæˈdiːnə) n the Arabic name for **Medina**

al-Maliki (ælˈmælɪkɪ) **Nouri.** born 1957, Iraqi politician, prime minister of Iraq from 2006

alma mater (ˈælmə ˈmɑːtə, ˈmeɪtə) n (often capitals) one's school, college, or university [c17: from Latin: bountiful mother]

almanac (ˈɔːlməˌnæk) n a yearly calendar giving statistical information on events and phenomena, such as the phases of the moon, times of sunrise and sunset, tides, anniversaries, etc [c14: from Medieval Latin almanachus, perhaps from Late Greek almenikhiaka]

almandine (ˈælməndɪn, -ˌdaɪn) n a deep violet-red garnet that consists of iron aluminium silicate and is used as a gemstone. Formula: $Fe_3Al_2(SiO_4)_3$ [c17: from French, from Medieval Latin alabandīna, from Alabanda, ancient city of Asia Minor where these stones were cut]

Al Mansûrah (ˌæl mænˈsʊərə) n a variant of **El Mansûra**

Al Marj (æl ˈmɑːdʒ) n an ancient town in N Libya: founded in about 550 BC Pop: 121 000 (2005 est). Italian name: **Barce**

Alma-Tadema (ˈælməˈtædɪmə) n Sir **Lawrence.** 1836–1912, Dutch-English painter of studies of Greek and Roman life

Almaty (ælˈmɑːtɪ) n a city in SE Kazakhstan; capital of Kazakhstan (1991–97): an important trading centre. Pop: 1 103 000 (2005 est). Former name (until 1927): **Verny** Also called: **Alma-Ata**

almighty (ɔːlˈmaɪtɪ) adj 1 all-powerful; omnipotent 2 informal (intensifier): an almighty row ▷ adv 3 informal (intensifier): an almighty loud bang

Almighty (ɔːlˈmaɪtɪ) n the Almighty another name for **God**

Almodóvar (Spanish almɔ'doₐva) n **Pedro.** born 1949, Spanish film director. His provocative black comedies include Women on the Verge of a Nervous Breakdown (1988), The Flower of My Secret (1995), Talk to Her (2002), and Volver (2006)

almond (ˈɑːmənd) n 1 a small widely cultivated rosaceous tree, Prunus amygdalus, that is native to W Asia and has pink flowers and a green fruit containing an edible nutlike seed 2 the oval-shaped nutlike edible seed of this plant, which has a yellowish-brown shell 3 (modifier) made of or containing almonds: almond cake [c13: from Old French almande, from Medieval Latin amandula, from Latin amygdala, from Greek amugdalē]

almond-eyed adj having narrow oval eyes

almoner (ˈɑːmənə) n 1 Brit obsolete a trained hospital social worker responsible for the welfare of patients 2 (formerly) a person who distributes alms or charity on behalf of a household or institution [c13: from Old French almosnier, from almosne alms, from Vulgar Latin alemosina (unattested), from Late Latin eleēmosyna; see ALMS]

almost (ˈɔːlməʊst) adv little short of being; very nearly

alms (ɑːmz) pl n charitable donations of money or goods to the poor or needy [Old English ælmysse, from Late Latin eleēmosyna, from Greek eleēmosunē pity; see ELEEMOSYNARY]

almshouse (ˈɑːmzˌhaʊs) n Brit history a privately supported house offering accommodation to the aged or needy

almucantar or **almacantar** (ˌælməˈkæntə) n 1 a circle on the celestial sphere parallel to the horizontal plane 2 an instrument for measuring altitudes [c14: from French, from Arabic almukantarāt sundial]

almuce (ˈælmjuːs) n a fur-lined hood or cape formerly worn by members of certain religious orders, more recently by canons of France [c15: from Old French aumusse, from Medieval Latin almucia, of unknown origin]

aloe (ˈæləʊ) n, pl -oes 1 any plant of the liliaceous genus Aloe, chiefly native to southern Africa, with fleshy spiny-toothed leaves and red or yellow flowers 2 American aloe [c14: from Latin aloē, from Greek]

aloes (ˈæləʊz) n (functioning as singular) bitter aloes a bitter purgative drug made from the leaves of several species of aloe

aloe vera (ˈæləʊ ˈvɪərə) n a juice obtained from the leaves of a liliaceous plant, Aloe vera, used as an emollient in skin and hair preparations

aloft (əˈlɒft) adv, adj (postpositive) 1 in or into a high or higher place; up above 2 nautical in or into the rigging of a vessel [c12: from Old Norse ā lopt in the air; see LIFT¹, LOFT]

alone (əˈləʊn) adj, adv (postpositive) 1 apart from another or others; solitary 2 without anyone or anything else: one man alone could lift it 3 without equal; unique: he stands alone in the field of microbiology 4 to the exclusion of others; only: she alone believed him 5 leave alone, leave be, let alone or let be to refrain from annoying or interfering with 6 leave well alone, leave well enough alone, let well alone or let well enough alone to refrain from interfering with something that is satisfactory 7 let alone much less; not to mention: he can't afford beer, let alone whisky [Old English al one, literally: all (entirely) one]

along (əˈlɒŋ) prep 1 over or for the length of, esp in a more or less horizontal plane: along the road ▷ adv 2 continuing over the length of some specified thing 3 in accompaniment; together with some specified person or people: he says he'd like to come along 4 forward: the horse trotted along at a steady pace 5 to a more advanced state: he got the work moving along 6 along with accompanying; together with: consider the advantages along with the disadvantages [Old English andlang, from and-against + lang LONG¹; compare Old Frisian andlinga, Old Saxon antlang]

● USAGE See at **plus**

alongshore (əˌlɒŋˈʃɔː) adv, adj (postpositive) close to, by, or along a shore

alongside (əˈlɒŋˌsaɪd) prep 1 (often foll by of) along the side of; along beside: alongside the quay ▷ adv 2 along the side of some specified thing: come alongside

aloof (əˈluːf) adj distant, unsympathetic, or supercilious in manner, attitude, or feeling [c16: from A-¹ + loof, a variant of LUFF] > aˈloofly adv > aˈloofness n

alopecia (ˌæləˈpiːʃɪə) n loss of hair, esp on the head; baldness [c14: from Latin, from Greek alōpekia, originally: mange in foxes, from alōpēx fox]

aloud (əˈlaʊd) adv, adj (postpositive) 1 in a normal voice; not in a whisper 2 in a spoken voice; not silently

Aloysius (ˌæləʊˈɪʃəs) n Saint. full name Aloysius Luigi Gonzaga. 1568–91, Italian Jesuit who died nursing plague victims; the patron saint of youth. Feast day: June 21

alp (ælp) n 1 (in the European Alps) an area of pasture above the valley bottom but below the mountain peaks 2 a high mountain ▷ See also **Alps, Australian Alps** [c14: back formation from Alps, from French Alpes (pl), from Latin Alpēs, from Greek Alpeis]

ALP abbreviation Australian Labor Party

alpaca (ælˈpækə) n 1 a domesticated cud-chewing artiodactyl mammal, Lama pacos, closely related to the llama and native to South America: family Camelidae. Its dark shaggy hair is a source of wool 2 the cloth made from the wool of this animal 3 a glossy fabric simulating this, used for linings, etc [c18: via Spanish from Aymara allpaca]

alpenhorn (ˈælpənˌhɔːn) n another name for **alphorn**

alpenstock (ˈælpənˌstɒk) n an early form of ice axe, consisting of a stout stick with an iron tip and sometimes having a pick and adze at the head, formerly used by mountain climbers [c19: from German, from Alpen ALPS + Stock STICK¹]

Alpes-de-Haute-Provence (French alpdəotprɔvɑ̃s) n a department of SE France in Provence-Alpes-Côte-d'Azur region. Capital: Digne. Pop: 144 508 (2003 est). Area: 6988 sq km (2725 sq miles). Former name: **Basses-Alpes**

Alpes-Maritimes (French alp maritim) n a department of the SE corner of France in Provence-Alpes-Côte-d'Azur region. Capital: Nice. Pop: 1 045 973 (2003 est). Area: 4298 sq km (1676 sq miles)

alpha (ˈælfə) n 1 the first letter in the Greek alphabet (A, α), a vowel transliterated as a 2 Brit the highest grade or mark, as in an examination 3 (modifier) a involving or relating to helium-4 nuclei b relating to one of two or more isomeric forms of a chemical compound, esp one in which a group is attached to the carbon atom to which the principal group is attached **4** (*modifier*) denoting the dominant person or animal in a group [via Latin from Greek, of Phoenician origin; related to Hebrew *āleph*, literally: ox]

alpha and omega *n* the first and last, a phrase used in Revelation 1:8 to signify God's eternity

alphabet ('ælfə,bɛt) *n* **1** a set of letters or other signs used in a writing system, usually arranged in a fixed order, each letter or sign being used to represent one or sometimes more than one phoneme in the language being transcribed **2** any set of symbols or characters, esp one representing sounds of speech **3** basic principles or rudiments, as of a subject [c15: from Late Latin *alphabētum*, from Greek *alphabētos*, from the first two letters of the Greek alphabet; see ALPHA, BETA]

alphabetical (,ælfə'bɛtɪkᵊl) *or* **alphabetic** *adj* **1** in the conventional order of the letters or symbols of an alphabet **2** of, characterized by, or expressed by an alphabet > ,alpha'betically *adv*

alphabetize *or* **alphabetise** ('ælfəbə,taɪz) *vb* (*tr*) **1** to arrange in conventional alphabetical order **2** to express by an alphabet > ,alphabeti'zation *or* ,alphabeti'sation *n*

alpha-blocker *n* any of a class of drugs that prevent the stimulation of alpha adrenoceptors, a type of receptor in the sympathetic nervous system, by adrenaline and noradrenaline and that therefore cause widening of blood vessels: used in the treatment of high blood pressure and prostatic hyperplasia

alpha decay *n* the radioactive decay process resulting in emission of alpha particles

alpha-fetoprotein (,ælfə,fiː'təʊ'prəʊtiːn) *n* a protein that forms in the liver of the human fetus. Excessive quantities in the amniotic fluid and maternal blood may indicate spina bifida in the fetus; low levels may point to Down's syndrome. Abbreviation: afp

alpha-hydroxy acid *n* a type of organic acid, commonly used in skin-care preparations, that has a hydroxyl group attached to the carbon atom next to the carbon atom carrying the carboxyl group

alpha male *n* the dominant male animal or person in a group

alphanumeric (,ælfənjuː'mɛrɪk) *or* **alphameric** (,ælfə'mɛrɪk) *adj* (of a character set, code, or file of data) consisting of alphabetical and numerical symbols

alpha particle *n* a helium-4 nucleus, containing two neutrons and two protons, emitted during some radioactive transformations

alpha ray *n* ionizing radiation consisting of a stream of alpha particles

alpha rhythm *or* **alpha wave** *n physiol* the normal bursts of electrical activity from the cerebral cortex of a drowsy or inactive person, occurring at a frequency of 8 to 12 hertz and detectable with an electroencephalograph. See also **brain wave**

alpha stock *n* any of the most active securities on the Stock Exchange of which there are between 100 and 200; at least ten market makers must continuously display the prices of an alpha stock and all transactions in them must be published immediately

Alpheus (æl'fiːəs) *n Greek myth* a river god, lover of the nymph Arethusa. She changed into a spring to evade him, but he changed into a river and mingled with her

alphorn ('ælp,hɔːn) *or* **alpenhorn** *n music* a wind instrument used in the Swiss Alps, consisting of a very long tube of wood or bark with a cornet-like mouthpiece [c19: from German *Alpenhorn* Alps horn]

alpine ('ælpaɪn) *adj* **1** of or relating to high mountains **2** (of plants) growing on mountains, esp above the limit for tree growth **3** connected with or used in mountaineering in medium-sized glaciated mountain areas such as the Alps **4** *skiing* of or relating to racing events on steep prepared slopes, such as the slalom and downhill. See **nordic** ▷ *n* **5** a plant that is native or suited to alpine conditions

alpinist ('ælpɪnɪst) *n* a mountaineer who climbs in medium-sized glaciated mountain areas such as the Alps

Alps (ælps) *pl n* **1** a mountain range in S central Europe, extending over 1000 km (650 miles) from the

Mediterranean coast of France and NW Italy through Switzerland, N Italy, and Austria to Slovenia. Highest peak: Mont Blanc, 4807 m (15 771 ft) **2** a range of mountains in the NW quadrant of the moon, which is cut in two by a straight fracture, the **Alpine Valley**

al-Qaeda *or* **al-Qaida** (æl'kaɪdə, ælkɑː'iːdə) *n* a loosely-knit militant Islamic organization led and funded by Osama bin Laden, by whom it was established in the late 1980s from Arab volunteers who had fought the Soviet troops previously based in Afghanistan; known or believed to be behind a number of operations against Western, especially US, interests, including bomb attacks on two US embassies in Africa in 1998 and the destruction of the World Trade Center in New York in 2001 [c20: from Arabic *al-qā'ida* the base]

already (ɔːl'rɛdɪ) *adv* **1** by or before a stated or implied time: *he is already here* **2** at a time earlier than expected: *is it ten o'clock already?*

alright (ɔːl'raɪt) *adv, sentence substitute, adj* a variant spelling of **all right**

● USAGE The form *alright*, though very common, is still
● considered by many people to be wrong or less
● acceptable than *all right*

Alsace (æl'sæs; *French* alzas) *n* a region and former province of NE France, between the Vosges mountains and the Rhine: famous for its wines. Area: 8280 sq km (3196 sq miles). Ancient name: Alsatia. German name: Elsass

Alsace-Lorraine *n* an area of NE France, comprising the modern regions of Alsace and Lorraine: under German rule 1871–1919 and 1940–44. Area: 14 522 sq km (5607 sq miles). German name: Elsass-Lothringen

Alsatia (æl'seɪʃə) *n* **1** the ancient name for **Alsace 2** an area around Whitefriars, London, in the 17th century, which was a sanctuary for criminals and debtors

Alsatian (æl'seɪʃən) *n* **1** Also called: German shepherd, German shepherd dog a large wolflike breed of dog often used as a guard or guide dog and by the police **2** a native or inhabitant of Alsace ▷ *adj* **3** of or relating to Alsace or its inhabitants

also ('ɔːlsəʊ) *adv* **1** (*sentence modifier*) in addition; as well; too ▷ *sentence connector* **2** besides; moreover [Old English *alswā*; related to Old High German *alsō*, Old Frisian *alsa*; see ALL, SO¹]

also-ran *n* **1** a contestant, horse, etc, failing to finish among the first three in a race **2** an unsuccessful person; loser or nonentity

alstroemeria (,ælstrə'miːrɪə) *n* any plant of the tuberous perennial liliaceous genus *Alstroemeria*, originally S American, grown for their brightly coloured orchid-like flowers. Also called: Peruvian lily [named by Linnaeus for his friend Baron Klas von *Alstroemer*]

Alta. *abbreviation* Alberta

Altaic (æl'teɪɪk) *n* **1** a postulated family of languages of Asia and SE Europe, consisting of the Turkic, Mongolic, and Tungusic branches, and perhaps also Japanese, Korean, and Ainu. See also **Ural-Altaic** ▷ *adj* **2** denoting, belonging to, or relating to this linguistic family or its speakers

Altai Mountains (ɑː'ltaɪ) *pl n* a mountain system of central Asia, in W Mongolia, N China, and S Russia. Highest peak: Belukha, 4506 m (14 783 ft)

Altai Republic *n* another name for **Gorno-Altai Republic**

Altamira (*Spanish* alta'mira) *n* a cave in N Spain, SW of Santander, noted for Old Stone Age wall drawings

altar ('ɔːltə) *n* **1** a raised place or structure where sacrifices are offered and religious rites performed **2** (in Christian churches) the communion table **3** a step in the wall of a dry dock upon which structures supporting a vessel can stand [Old English, from Latin *altāria* (plural) altar, from *altus* high]

altar boy *n RC Church, Church of England* a boy serving as an acolyte

altarpiece ('ɔːltə,piːs) *n* a work of art set above and behind an altar; a reredos

altazimuth (æl'tæzɪməθ) *n* an instrument for measuring the altitude and azimuth of a celestial body by the horizontal and vertical rotation of a telescope [c19: from ALT(ITUDE) + AZIMUTH]

altazimuth mounting n a telescope mounting that allows motion of the telescope about a vertical axis (in azimuth) and a horizontal axis (in altitude)

Altdorf (German 'altdɔrf) n a town in central Switzerland, capital of Uri canton: setting of the William Tell legend. Pop: 8541 (2000)

Altdorfer (German 'altdɔrfər) n **Albrecht** ('albrɛçt). ?1480–?1538, German painter and engraver: one of the earliest landscape painters

alter ('ɔːltə) vb 1 to make or become different in some respect; change 2 (tr) informal, chiefly US a euphemistic word for **castrate, spay** [c14: from Old French alterer, from Medieval Latin alterāre to change, from Latin alter other] > 'alterable adj

alteration (ˌɔːltə'reɪʃən) n 1 an adjustment, change, or modification 2 the act of altering or state of being altered

alterative ('ɔːltərətɪv) adj 1 likely or able to produce alteration 2 obsolete (of a drug) able to restore normal health ▷ n 3 obsolete a drug that restores normal health

altercate ('ɔːltəˌkeɪt) vb (intr) to argue, esp heatedly; dispute [c16: from Latin altercārī to quarrel with another, from alter other]

altercation (ˌɔːltə'keɪʃən) n an angry or heated discussion or quarrel; argument

alter ego ('æltər 'iːɡəʊ, 'ɛɡəʊ) n 1 a second self 2 a very close and intimate friend [Latin: other self]

alternate vb ('ɔːltəˌneɪt) 1 (often foll by with) to occur or cause to occur successively or by turns: day and night alternate 2 (intr; often foll by between) to swing repeatedly from one condition, action, etc, to another 3 (tr) to interchange regularly or in succession 4 (intr) (of an electric current, voltage, etc) to reverse direction or sign at regular intervals, usually sinusoidally, the instantaneous value varying continuously ▷ adj ('ɔːl'tɜːnɪt) 5 occurring by turns: alternate feelings of love and hate 6 every other or second one of a series: he came to work on alternate days 7 botany (of leaves, flowers, etc) arranged singly at different heights on either side of the stem ▷ n ('ɔːltənɪt, ɔːl'tɜːnɪt) 8 US & Canadian a person who substitutes for another in his absence; stand-in [c16: from Latin alternāre to do one thing and then another, from alternus one after the other, from alter other]

alternate angles pl n two angles at opposite ends and on opposite sides of a transversal cutting two lines

alternately (ɔːl'tɜːnɪtlɪ) adv in an alternating sequence or position

alternating current n a continuous electric current that periodically reverses direction, usually sinusoidally. Abbreviation: AC

alternation of generations n the production within the life cycle of an organism of alternating asexual and sexual reproductive forms. It occurs in many plants and lower animals

alternative (ɔːl'tɜːnətɪv) n 1 a possibility of choice, esp between two things, courses of action, etc 2 either of such choices: we took the alternative of walking ▷ adj 3 presenting a choice, esp between two possibilities only 4 (of two things) mutually exclusive 5 denoting a lifestyle, culture, art form, etc, regarded by its adherents as preferable to that of contemporary society because it is less conventional, materialistic, or institutionalized, and, often, more in harmony with nature > al'ternatively adv > al'ternativeness n

alternative curriculum n Brit education any course of study offered as an alternative to the National Curriculum

alternative energy n a form of energy derived from a natural source, such as the sun, wind, tides, or waves. Also called: renewable energy

Alternative Investment Market n a market on the London Stock Exchange enabling small companies to raise capital and have their shares traded in a market without the expenses of a main-market listing. Abbreviation: AIM

alternative medicine n another name for **complementary medicine**

Alternative Vote n (modifier) of or relating to a system of voting in which voters list the candidates in order of preference. If no candidate obtains more than 50% of first-preference votes, the votes for the bottom candidate are redistributed according to the voters' next preference. See **proportional representation**

alternator ('ɔːltəˌneɪtə) n an electrical machine that generates an alternating current

althaea or US **althea** (æl'θiːə) n any Eurasian plant of the malvaceous genus Althaea, such as the hollyhock, having tall spikes of showy white, yellow, or red flowers [c17: from Latin althaea, from Greek althaia marsh mallow (literally: healing plant), from Greek althein to heal]

althorn ('ælt,hɔːn) n a valved brass musical instrument belonging to the saxhorn or flügelhorn families

Althorp House ('ɔːlθɔːp, -θrʌp) n a mansion in Northamptonshire: seat of the Earls Spencer since 1508; originally a medieval house; altered (1787) to its present neoclassical style by Henry Holland. Diana, Princess of Wales is buried on Round Oval Island in the centre of the ornamental lake in Althorp Park

although (ɔːl'ðəʊ) conj (subordinating) despite the fact that; even though: although she was ill, she worked hard

Althusser (ɑːltuːˈsə; French altusɛr) n **Louis**. 1918–90, French Marxist philosopher, author of For Marx (1965) and Reading Capital (1965): committed to a mental hospital (1981) after killing his wife

altimeter (æl'tɪmɪtə, 'ælti,miːtə) n an instrument that indicates height above sea level, esp one based on an aneroid barometer and fitted to an aircraft

Altiplano (Spanish alti'plano) n a plateau of the Andes, covering two thirds of Bolivia and extending into S Peru: contains Lake Titicaca. Height: 3000 m (10 000 ft) to 3900 m (13 000 ft)

altitude ('ælti,tjuːd) n 1 the vertical height of an object above some chosen level, esp above sea level; elevation 2 geometry the perpendicular distance from the vertex to the base of a geometrical figure or solid 3 Also called: elevation astronomy, navigation the angular distance of a celestial body from the horizon measured along the vertical circle passing through the body 4 surveying the angle of elevation of a point above the horizontal plane of the observer 5 (often plural) a high place or region [c14: from Latin altitūdō, from altus high, deep]

Altman ('ɔːltmən) n **Robert**. US film director, 1925–2006; his films include M*A*S*H (1970), Nashville (1975), Short Cuts (1994), and Gosford Park (2001)

alto ('æltəʊ) n, pl -tos 1 the highest adult male voice; countertenor 2 (in choral singing) a shortened form of **contralto** 3 a singer with such a voice 4 a flute, saxophone, etc, that is the third or fourth highest instrument in its group ▷ adj 5 denoting a flute, saxophone, etc, that is the third or fourth highest instrument in its group [c18: from Italian: high, from Latin altus]

alto clef n the clef that establishes middle C as being on the third line of the staff. Also called: viola clef ▷ See also **C clef**

altocumulus (ˌæltəʊ'kjuːmjʊləs) n, pl -li (-laɪ) a globular cloud at an intermediate height of about 2400 to 6000 metres (8000 to 20 000 feet)

altogether (ˌɔːltə'ɡeðə, 'ɔːltə,ɡeðə) adv 1 with everything included: altogether he owed me sixty pounds 2 completely; utterly; totally: he was altogether mad 3 on the whole: altogether it was a very good party ▷ n 4 in the altogether informal naked

altoist ('æltəʊɪst) n a person who plays the alto saxophone

altostratus (ˌæltəʊ'streɪtəs, -'strɑː-) n, pl -ti (-taɪ) a layer cloud at an intermediate height of about 2400 to 6000 metres (8000 to 20 000 feet)

altricial (æl'trɪʃəl) adj 1 (of the young of some species of birds after hatching) naked, blind, and dependent on the parents for food ▷ n 2 an altricial bird, such as a pigeon ▷ See **precocial** [c19: from New Latin altriciālis, from Latin altrix a nurse, from alere to nourish]

Altrincham ('ɔːltrɪŋəm) n a residential town in NW England, in Trafford unitary authority, Greater Manchester. Pop: 40 695 (2001)

altruism ('æltruː,ɪzəm) n the principle or practice of

unselfish concern for the welfare of others [C19: from French *altruisme*, from Italian *altrui* others, from Latin *alterī*, plural of *alter* other] > 'altruist *n* ˌaltru'istic *adj* > ˌaltru'istically *adv*

ALU *computing abbreviation* arithmetic and logic unit

alum ('æləm) *n* **1** Also called: **potash alum** a colourless soluble hydrated double sulphate of aluminium and potassium used in the manufacture of mordants and pigments, in dressing leather and sizing paper, and in medicine as a styptic and astringent. Formula: $K_2SO_4.Al_2(SO_4)_3.24H_2O$ **2** any of a group of isomorphic double sulphates of a monovalent metal or group and a trivalent metal. Formula: $X_2SO_4.Y_2(SO_4)_3.24H_2O$, where X is monovalent and Y is trivalent [C14: from Old French, from Latin *alūmen*]

alumina (ə'lu:mɪnə) *n* another name for **aluminium oxide** [C18: from New Latin, plural of Latin *alūmen* ALUM]

aluminium (ˌæljʊ'mɪnɪəm) *or US and Canadian* **aluminum** (ə'lu:mɪnəm) *n* a light malleable ductile silvery-white metallic element that resists corrosion; the third most abundant element in the earth's crust (8.1 per cent), occurring only as a compound, principally in bauxite. It is used, esp in the form of its alloys, in aircraft parts, kitchen utensils, etc. Symbol: Al; atomic no: 13; atomic wt: 26.9815; valency: 3; relative density: 2.699; melting pt: 660.45°C; boiling pt: 2520°C

aluminium oxide *n* a white or colourless insoluble powder occurring naturally as corundum and used in the production of aluminium and its compounds, abrasives, glass, and ceramics. Formula: Al_2O_3. Also called: **alumina**

aluminize *or* **aluminise** (ə'lu:mɪˌnaɪz) *vb* (*tr*) to cover with aluminium or aluminium paint

aluminous (ə'lu:mɪnəs) *adj* resembling aluminium

alumnus (ə'lʌmnəs) *n*, *pl* **-ni** (-naɪ) *chiefly US & Canadian* a graduate of a school, college, etc [C17: from Latin: nursling, pupil, foster son, from *alere* to nourish]

Alva *or* **Alba** ('ælvə; *Spanish* 'alβa) *n* **Duke of,** title of *Fernando Alvarez de Toledo.* 1508–82, Spanish general and statesman who suppressed the Protestant revolt in the Netherlands (1567–72) and conquered Portugal (1580)

Alvarez ('ælvərez) *n* **Luis Walter.** 1911–88, US physicist. He made (with Felix Bloch) the first measurement of the neutron's magnetic moment (1939). Nobel prize for physics 1968

alveolar (æl'vɪələ, ˌælvɪ'əʊlə) *adj* **1** *anatomy* of, relating to, or resembling an alveolus **2** denoting the part of the jawbone containing the roots of the teeth **3** (of a consonant) articulated with the tongue in contact with the projecting part of the jawbone immediately behind the upper teeth ▷ *n* **4** an alveolar consonant, such as the speech sounds written *t*, *d*, and *s* in English

alveolate (æl'vɪəlɪt, -ˌleɪt) *adj* having many alveoli [C19: from Late Latin *alveolātus* forming a channel, hollowed, from Latin: ALVEOLUS] > ˌalveo'lation *n*

alveolus (æl'vɪələs) *n*, *pl* **-li** (-ˌlaɪ) any small pit, cavity, or saclike dilation, such as a honeycomb cell [C18: from Latin: a little hollow, diminutive of *alveus*]

always ('ɔ:lweɪz, -wɪz) *adv* **1** without exception; on every occasion; every time: *he always arrives on time* **2** continually; repeatedly **3** in any case: *you could always take a day off work* [C13 *alles weiss*, from Old English *ealne weg*, literally: all the way; see ALL, WAY]

Alwyn ('ɔ:lwɪn) *n* **William.** 1905–85, British composer. His works include the oratorio *The Marriage of Heaven and Hell* (1936) and the *Suite of Scottish Dances* (1946)

alyssum ('ælɪsəm) *n* any widely cultivated herbaceous garden plant of the genus *Alyssum*, having clusters of small yellow or white flowers: family *Brassicaceae* (crucifers) [C16: from New Latin, from Greek *alusson*, from *alussos* (adj) curing rabies, referring to the ancient belief in the plant's healing properties]

Alzheimer's disease ('ælts,haɪməz) *n* a disorder of the brain resulting in a progressive decline in intellectual and physical abilities and eventual dementia. Often shortened to **Alzheimer's** [C20: named after A. *Alzheimer* (1864–1915), German physician who first identified it]

am (æm; *unstressed* əm) *vb* (used with I) a form of the present tense (indicative mood) of **be**[1] [Old English *eam*;

related to Old Norse *em*, Gothic *im*, Old High German *bim*, Latin *sum*, Greek *eimi*, Sanskrit *asmi*]

Am *the chemical symbol for* americium

AM *abbreviation* **1** Assembly Member (of the National Assembly of Wales) **2** *US* Master of Arts **3** Also called: **am** amplitude modulation **4** Member of the Order of Australia

Am. *abbreviation* America(n)

a.m., A.M., am *or* **AM** *abbreviation* (indicating the time period from midnight to midday) ante meridiem [Latin: before noon]

Amabokoboko (ama'bɒkɒbɒkɒ) *pl n South African* the official name for the Springbok rugby team [C20: from Nguni *ama*, a plural prefix + *bokoboko*, from *bok* a diminutive of SPRINGBOK]

amadoda (ama'dəʊda) *pl n South African* grown men [from Nguni *ama*, a plural prefix + *doda* men]

amadou ('æmə,du:) *n* a spongy substance made from certain fungi, such as *Polyporus* (or *Fomes*) *fomentarius* and related species, used as tinder to light fires, in medicine to stop bleeding, and, esp formerly, by anglers to dry off dry flies between casts [C18: from French, from Provençal: lover, from Latin *amātor*, from *amāre* to love; so called because it readily ignites]

amah ('ɑ:mə, 'æmə) *n* (in the East, esp formerly) a nurse or maidservant, esp one of Chinese origin [C19: from Portuguese *ama* nurse, wet nurse]

amain (ə'meɪn) *adv* *archaic or poetic* with great strength, speed, or haste [C16: from A-[2] + MAIN[1]]

amakwerekwere (ˌama'kwerɪ'kwerɪ) *pl n South African informal, highly offensive* a term used by Black people to refer to foreign Africans [C20: from Xhosa *ama*, a plural prefix, + *kwerekwere* imitatitive of unintelligible sound]

Amalfi (ə'mælfɪ) *n* a town in Italy: a major Mediterranean port from the 10th to the 18th century, now a resort

amalgam (ə'mælgəm) *n* **1** an alloy of mercury with another metal, esp with silver: *dental amalgam* **2** a blend or combination [C15: from Medieval Latin *amalgama*, of obscure origin]

amalgamate (ə'mælgə,meɪt) *vb* **1** to combine or cause to combine; unite **2** to alloy (a metal) with mercury

amalgamation (ə,mælgə'meɪʃən) *n* **1** the action or process of amalgamating **2** the state of being amalgamated **3** a method of extracting precious metals from their ores by treatment with mercury to form an amalgam **4** *commerce* another word for **merger** (sense 1)

amandla (a'mɑ:ndla) *n South African* a political slogan calling for power to the Black population [C20: Nguni, literally: power]

amantadine (ə'mæntə,di:n) *n* an antiviral drug used in the treatment of some types of influenza and to reduce some of the symptoms of Parkinson's disease [C20: a blend of AMINE + *adamantane* the chemical compound from which it is derived]

amanuensis (ə,mænjʊ'ensɪs) *n*, *pl* **-ses** (-si:z) a person employed to take dictation or to copy manuscripts [C17: from Latin *āmanuensis*, from the phrase *servus ā manū* slave at hand (that is, handwriting)]

Amanullah Khan (ˌæmə'nʊlə kɑ:n) *n* 1892–1960, emir (1919–26) and king (1926–29) of Afghanistan; he obtained Afghan independence from Britain (1919)

Amapá (*Portuguese* ˌamə'pa:) *n* a state of N Brazil, on the Amazon delta. Capital: Macapá. Pop: 516 511 (2002). Area: 143 716 sq km (55 489 sq miles)

amaranth ('æmə,rænθ) *n* **1** *poetic* an imaginary flower that never fades **2** any of numerous tropical and temperate plants of the genus *Amaranthus*, having tassel-like heads of small green, red, or purple flowers: family *Amaranthaceae* **3** a synthetic red food colouring (E123), used in packet soups, cake mixes, etc [C17: from Latin *amarantus*, from Greek *amarantos* unfading, from A-[1] + *marainein* to fade]

amaretti (æmə'retɪ) *pl n* Italian almond biscuits [C20: from Italian *amaro* bitter]

amaretto (æmə'retəʊ) *n* an Italian liqueur with a flavour of almonds [C20: from Italian *amaro* bitter]

amaryllis (ˌæmə'rɪlɪs) *n* **1** Also called: **belladonna lily** an amaryllidaceous plant, *Amaryllis belladonna*, native to southern Africa and having large lily-like reddish or white flowers **2** any of several related plants, esp hippeastrum [C18: from New Latin, from Latin: named after AMARYLLIS]

Amaryllis (ˌæməˈrɪlɪs) n (in pastoral poetry) a name for a shepherdess or country girl

amass (əˈmæs) vb **1** (tr) to accumulate or collect (esp riches, etc) **2** to gather in a heap; bring together [C15: from Old French amasser, from masse MASS] > aˈmasser n

amateur (ˈæmətə, -tʃə, -ˌtjʊə, ˌæməˈtɜː) n **1** a person who engages in an activity, esp a sport, as a pastime rather than professionally or for gain **2** a person unskilled in or having only a superficial knowledge of a subject or activity **3** a person who is fond of or admires something **4** (modifier) consisting of or for amateurs: an amateur event ▷ adj **5** amateurish; not professional or expert: an amateur approach [C18: from French, from Latin amātor lover, from amāre to love] > ˈamateurism n

amateurish (ˈæmətərɪʃ, -tʃər-, -ˌtʃʊər-, ˌæməˈtɜːrɪʃ) adj lacking professional skill or expertise > ˈamateurishly adv

Amati n **1** (Italian aˈmɑːti) a family of Italian violin makers, active in Cremona in the 16th and 17th centuries, esp **Nicolò** (niˈkɔlɔ), 1596–1684, who taught Guarneri and Stradivari **2** (əˈmɑːti) pl Amatis a violin or other stringed instrument made by any member of this family

amative (ˈæmətɪv) adj a rare word for **amorous** [C17: from Medieval Latin amātīvus, from Latin amāre to love]

amatory (ˈæmətərɪ) or **amatorial** (ˌæməˈtɔːrɪəl) adj of, relating to, or inciting sexual love or desire [C16: from Latin amātōrius, from amāre to love]

amaurosis (ˌæmɔːˈrəʊsɪs) n pathol blindness, esp when occurring without observable damage to the eye [C17: via New Latin from Greek: darkening, from amauroun to dim, darken] > amaurotic (ˌæmɔːˈrɒtɪk) adj

amaze (əˈmeɪz) vb (tr) **1** to fill with incredulity or surprise; astonish ▷ n **2** an archaic word for **amazement** [Old English āmasian]

amazement (əˈmeɪzmənt) n incredulity or great astonishment; complete wonder or surprise

amazing (əˈmeɪzɪŋ) adj causing wonder or astonishment: amazing feats > aˈmazingly adv

Amazon[1] (ˈæməzˀn) n **1** Greek myth one of a race of women warriors of Scythia near the Black Sea **2** (often not capital) any tall, strong, or aggressive woman [C14: via Latin from Greek Amazōn, of uncertain origin] > Amazonian (ˌæməˈzəʊnɪən) adj

Amazon[2] (ˈæməzˀn) n a river in South America, rising in the Peruvian Andes and flowing east through N Brazil to the Atlantic: in volume, the largest river in the world; navigable for 3700 km (2300 miles). Length: over 6440 km (4000 miles). Area of basin: over 5 827 500 sq km (2 250 000 sq miles)

Amazonas (ˌæməˈzəʊnəs) n a state of W Brazil, consisting of the central Amazon basin: vast areas of unexplored tropical rainforest. Capital: Manaus. Pop: 2 961 801 (2002). Area: 1 542 277 sq km (595 474 sq miles)

Amazonia (ˌæməˈzəʊnɪə) n the land around the Amazon river

Ambala (əmˈbɑːlə) n a city in N India, in Haryana: site of archaeological remains of a prehistoric Indian civilization: grain, cotton, food processing. Pop: 139 222 (2001)

Ambartsumian (Russian amˌbartsʊmˈjan) n **Viktor A(mazaspovich)**. 1908–96, Armenian astrophysicist, renowned for his description of radio sources as explosions in the core of galaxies

ambassador (æmˈbæsədə) n **1** short for **ambassador extraordinary and plenipotentiary**; a diplomatic minister of the highest rank, accredited as permanent representative to another country or sovereign **2** ambassador extraordinary a diplomatic minister of the highest rank sent on a special mission **3** ambassador plenipotentiary a diplomatic minister of the first rank with treaty-signing powers **4** ambassador-at-large US an ambassador with special duties who may be sent to more than one government **5** an authorized representative or messenger [C14: from

Old French ambassadeur, from Italian ambasciator, from Old Provençal ambaisador, from ambaisa (unattested) mission, errand; see EMBASSY] > amˈbassadress fem n > ambassadorial (æmˌbæsəˈdɔːrɪəl) adj > amˈbassadorˌship n

amber (ˈæmbə) n **1 a** a yellow or yellowish-brown hard translucent fossil resin derived from extinct coniferous trees that occurs in Tertiary deposits and often contains trapped insects. It is used for jewellery, ornaments, etc **2 a** a medium to dark brownish-yellow colour, often somewhat orange, similar to that of the resin **b** (as adjective): an amber dress **3** an amber traffic light used as a warning between red and green [C14: from Medieval Latin ambar, from Arabic 'anbar ambergris]

Amber alert n US & Canadian a notification to the general public, such as by commercial radio or electronic traffic-condition signs, regarding an abduction of a child [C20: named after Amber Hagerman, a child who was abducted and murdered in 1996 in Arlington, Texas]

amber gambler n Brit informal a driver who races through traffic lights when they are at amber

ambergris (ˈæmbəˌgriːs, -ˌgrɪs) n a waxy substance consisting mainly of cholesterol secreted by the intestinal tract of the sperm whale and often found floating in the sea: used in the manufacture of perfumes [C15: from Old French ambre gris grey amber]

amberjack (ˈæmbəˌdʒæk) n any of several large carangid fishes of the genus Seriola, esp S. dumerili, with golden markings when young, occurring in tropical and subtropical Atlantic waters [C19: from AMBER + JACK[1]]

ambi- combining form indicating both: ambidextrous; ambivalence; ambiversion [from Latin: round, on both sides, both, from ambo both; compare AMPHI-]

ambidextrous (ˌæmbɪˈdekstrəs) adj **1** equally expert with each hand **2** informal highly skilled or adept **3** underhanded; deceitful > ambidexterity (ˌæmbɪdekˈsterɪtɪ) or ˌambiˈdextrousness n > ˌambiˈdextrously adv

ambience or **ambiance** (ˈæmbɪəns; French ɑ̃bjɑ̃s) n the atmosphere of a place [C19: from French ambiance, from ambiant surrounding; see AMBIENT]

ambient (ˈæmbɪənt) adj **1** of or relating to the immediate surroundings **2** creating a relaxing atmosphere: ambient music [C16: from Latin ambiēns going round, from ambīre, from AMBI- + īre to go]

ambiguity (ˌæmbɪˈɡjuːɪtɪ) n, pl -ties **1** the possibility of interpreting an expression in two or more distinct ways **2** an instance of this, as in the sentence they are cooking apples **3** vagueness or uncertainty of meaning

ambiguous (æmˈbɪɡjʊəs) adj **1** having more than one possible interpretation or meaning **2** difficult to understand or classify; obscure [C16: from Latin ambiguus going here and there, uncertain, from ambigere to go around, from AMBI- + agere to lead, act] > amˈbiguously adv > amˈbiguousness n

ambisexual (ˌæmbɪˈseksjʊəl) adj **1** biology relating to or affecting both the male and female sexes **2** Also called: ambosexual bisexual

ambit (ˈæmbɪt) n **1** scope or extent **2** limits, boundary, or circumference [C16: from Latin ambitus a going round, from ambīre to go round, from AMBI- + īre to go]

ambition (æmˈbɪʃən) n **1** strong desire for success, achievement, or distinction **2** something so desired; goal; aim [C14: from Old French, from Latin ambitiō a going round (of candidates), a striving to please, from ambīre to go round; see AMBIT]

ambitious (æmˈbɪʃəs) adj **1** having a strong desire for success or achievement; wanting power, money, etc **2** necessitating extraordinary effort or ability: an ambitious project **3** (often foll by of) having a great desire (for something or to do something) > amˈbitiously adv > amˈbitiousness n

ambivalence (æmˈbɪvələns) or **ambivalency** n the simultaneous existence of two opposed and conflicting attitudes, emotions, etc > amˈbivalent adj

amble (ˈæmbˀl) vb (intr) **1** to walk at a leisurely relaxed pace **2** (of a horse) to move slowly, lifting both legs on one side together **3** to ride a horse at an amble or

a

leisurely pace ▷ *n* **4** a leisurely motion in walking **5** a leisurely walk **6** the ambling gait of a horse [c14: from Old French *ambler*, from Latin *ambulāre* to walk]

Ambler ('æmblə) *n* **Eric.** 1909–1998, English novelist]. His thrillers include *The Mask of Dimitrios* (1939), *Journey into Fear* (1940), *A Kind of Anger* (1964), and *Doctor Frigo* (1974)

Ambleside ('æmbªl,saɪd) *n* a town in NW England, in Cumbria: a tourist centre for the Lake District. Pop: 3064 (2001)

amblyopia (,æmblɪ'əʊpɪə) *n* impaired vision with no discernible damage to the eye or optic nerve [c18: New Latin, from Greek *ambluōpia*, from *amblus* dull, dim + *ōps* eye] > **amblyopic** (,æmblɪ'ɒpɪk) *adj*

ambo ('æmbəʊ) *n, pl* **ambos** *Austral informal* **1** an ambulance driver **2** an ambulance

Amboise (*French* ābwaz) *n* a town in NW central France, on the River Loire: famous castle, a former royal residence. Pop: 11 457 (1999)

Ambon ('ɑːmbɒːn) *n* **1** Also called: **Amboina** an island in Indonesia, in the Moluccas. Capital: Amboina. Area: 1000 sq km (386 sq miles) **2** Also called: **Amboina** (æm'bɔɪnə) a port in the Moluccas, the capital of Ambon (Amboina) island

amboyna or **amboina** (æm'bɔɪnə) *n* the mottled curly-grained wood of an Indonesian leguminous tree, *Pterocarpus indicus*, used in making furniture [c19: from the island of AMBOINA]

Ambrose ('æmbrəʊz) *n* **1 Saint.** ?340–397 AD, bishop of Milan; built up the secular power of the early Christian Church; also wrote music and Latin hymns. Feast day: Dec 7 or April 4 > **Am'brosian** *adj* **2 Curtly** ('kɜːtlɪ). born 1963, Antiguan cricketer; played for the West Indies 1987–2000

ambrosia (æm'brəʊzɪə) *n* **1** *classical myth* the food of the gods, said to bestow immortality. See **nectar** (sense 2) **2** anything particularly delightful to taste or smell **3** another name for **beebread** [c16: via Latin from Greek: immortality, from *ambrotos*, from A-¹ + *brotos* mortal] > **am'brosial** or **am'brosian** *adj*

ambry ('æmbrɪ) or **aumbry** ('ɔːmbrɪ) *n, pl* -**bries 1** a recessed cupboard in the wall of a church near the altar, used to store sacred vessels, etc **2** *obsolete* a small cupboard or other storage space [c14: from Old French *almarie*, from Medieval Latin *almārium*, from Latin *armārium* chest for storage, from *arma* arms]

ambulance ('æmbjʊləns) *n* a motor vehicle designed to carry sick or injured people [c19: from French, based on (*hôpital*) *ambulant* mobile or field (hospital), from Latin *ambulāre* to walk]

ambulance chaser *n* *US slang* a lawyer who seeks to encourage and profit from the lawsuits of accident victims > **ambulance chasing** *n*

ambulance stocks *pl n* high performance stocks and shares recommended by a broker to a dissatisfied client to improve their relationship

ambulant ('æmbjʊlənt) *adj* **1** moving about from place to place **2** *med* another word for **ambulatory** (sense 3)

ambulate ('æmbjʊ,leɪt) *vb* (*intr*) to wander about or move from one place to another [c17: from Latin *ambulāre* to walk, AMBLE] > ,ambu'lation *n*

ambulatory ('æmbjʊlətərɪ) *adj* **1** of, relating to, or designed for walking **2** changing position; not fixed **3** Also called: **ambulant** able to walk ▷ *n, pl* -**ries 4** *architect* a place for walking, such as an aisle or a cloister

ambulatory care *n* care given at a hospital to non-resident patients, including minor surgery and outpatient treatment

ambuscade (,æmbə'skeɪd) *n* **1** an ambush ▷ *vb* **2** to ambush or lie in ambush [c16: from French *embuscade*, from Old Italian *imboscata*, probably of Germanic origin; compare AMBUSH]

ambush ('æmbʊʃ) *n* **1** the act of waiting in a concealed position in order to launch a surprise attack **2** a surprise attack from such a position **3** the concealed position from which such an attack is launched **4** the person or persons waiting to launch such an attack ▷ *vb* **5** to lie in wait (for) **6** (*tr*) to attack suddenly from a concealed position [c14: from Old French *embuschier* to position in

ambush, from *em-* IM- + *-buschier*, from *busche* piece of firewood, probably of Germanic origin; see BUSH¹] > 'ambusher *n*

ameba (ə'miːbə) *n, pl* -**bae** (-biː) *or* -**bas** the usual US spelling of **amoeba** > a'mebic *adj*

ameer (ə'mɪə) *n* a variant spelling of **emir**

ameliorate (ə'miːljə,reɪt) *vb* to make or become better; improve [c18: from MELIORATE, influenced by French *améliorer* to improve, from Old French *ameillorer* to make better, from *meillor* better, from Latin *melior*] > a,melio'ration *n* > a'meliorative *adj* > a'melio,rator *n*
● USAGE *Ameliorate* is often wrongly used where *alleviate*
● is meant. *Ameliorate* is properly used to mean
● 'improve', not 'make easier to bear', so one should talk
● about *alleviating* pain or hardship, not *ameliorating* it

amen (,eɪ'mɛn, ,ɑː'mɛn) *interj* **1** so be it!: a term used at the end of a prayer or religious statement ▷ *n* **2** the use of the word *amen*, as at the end of a prayer [c13: via Late Latin via Greek from Hebrew *āmēn* certainly]

Amen, Amon *or* **Amūn** ('ɑːmən) *n* **Egyptian** *myth* a local Theban god, having a ram's head and symbolizing life and fertility, identified by the Egyptians with the national deity Amen-Ra

amenable (ə'miːnəbªl) *adj* **1** open or susceptible to suggestion; likely to listen, cooperate, etc **2** accountable for behaviour to some authority; answerable **3** capable of being or liable to be tested, judged, etc [c16: from Anglo-French, from Old French *amener* to lead up, from Latin *mināre* to drive (cattle), from *minārī* to threaten] > a,mena'bility *or* a'menableness *n* > a'menably *adv*

amend (ə'mɛnd) *vb* (*tr*) **1** to improve; change for the better **2** to remove faults from; correct **3** to alter or revise (legislation, a constitution, etc) by formal procedure [c13: from Old French *amender*, from Latin *ēmendāre* to EMEND] > a'mendable *adj* > a'mender *n*

amendment (ə'mɛndmənt) *n* **1** the act of amending; correction **2** an addition, alteration, or improvement to a motion, document, etc

amends (ə'mɛndz) *n* (*functioning as singular*) recompense or compensation given or gained for some injury, insult, etc: *to make amends* [c13: from Old French *amendes* fines, from *amende* compensation, from *amender* to EMEND]

Amenhotep III (,æmɛn'həʊtɛp) *or* **Amenhotpe III** (,æmɛn'hɒtpɪ) *n* Greek name *Amenophis*. ?1411–?1375 BC, Egyptian pharaoh who expanded Egypt's influence by peaceful diplomacy and erected many famous buildings

Amenhotep IV *or* **Amenhotpe IV** *n* the original name of Akhenaten

amenity (ə'miːnɪtɪ) *n, pl* -**ties 1** (*often plural*) a useful or pleasant facility or service: *a swimming pool was just one of the amenities* **2** the fact or condition of being pleasant or agreeable **3** (*usually plural*) a social courtesy or pleasantry [c14: from Latin *amoenitās* pleasantness, from *amoenus* agreeable]

amenorrhoea *or* *esp US* **amenorrhea** (æ,mɛnə'rɪə, eɪ-) *n* abnormal absence of menstruation [c19: from A-¹ + MENO-¹ + -RHOEA]

Amen-Ra (,ɑːmən'rɑː) *n* *Egyptian myth* the sun-god; the principal deity during the period of Theban hegemony

ament ('æmənt, 'eɪmənt) *n* another name for **catkin**. Also called: **amentum** (ə'mɛntəm) [c18: from Latin *āmentum* strap, thong] > ,amen'taceous *adj*

amentia (ə'mɛnʃə) *n* severe mental deficiency, usually congenital [c14: from Latin: insanity, from *āmēns* mad, from *mēns* mind]

Amer. *abbreviation* America(n)

Amerasian (,æmɛr'eɪʃən, ,æmɛr'eɪʒən) *n* **1** a person of mixed American and Asian parentage; used especially to refer to someone with an American father and an Asian mother ▷ *adj* **2** of or relating to Amerasians

amerce (ə'mɜːs) *vb* (*tr*) *obsolete* **1** *law* to punish by a fine **2** to punish with any arbitrary penalty [c14: from Anglo-French *amercier*, from Old French *à merci* at the mercy (because the fine was arbitrarily fixed); see MERCY] > a'mercement *n*

America (ə'mɛrɪkə) *n* **1** short for the **United States of America 2** Also called: **the Americas** the American continent, including North, South, and Central America [c16: from *Americus*, Latin form of *Amerigo*; after Amerigo

Vespucci (?1454–1512), Florentine navigator in the New World]

American (ə'mɛrɪkən) *adj* 1 of or relating to the United States of America, its inhabitants, or their form of English 2 of or relating to the American continent ▷ *n* 3 a native or citizen of the US 4 a native or inhabitant of any country of North, Central, or South America 5 the English language as spoken or written in the United States

Americana (ə,mɛrɪ'kɑ:nə) *pl n* 1 objects, such as books, documents, relics, etc, relating to America, esp in the form of a collection 2 all forms of traditional music indigenous to America, and their modern variants

American aloe *n* another name for **century plant**

American Dream *n* the American Dream the notion that the American social, economic, and political system makes success possible for every individual

American football *n* 1 a team game similar to rugby, with 11 players on each side. Forward passing is allowed and planned strategies and formations for play are decided during the course of the game 2 the oval-shaped inflated ball used in this game

American Indian *n* 1 Also called: Native American a member of any of the indigenous peoples of North, Central, or South America, esp those of North America ▷ *adj* 2 Also called: Amerindian of or relating to any of these peoples, their languages, or their cultures

Americanism (ə'mɛrɪkə,nɪzəm) *n* 1 a custom, linguistic usage, or other feature peculiar to or characteristic of the United States, its people, or their culture 2 loyalty to the United States, its people, customs, etc

Americanize or **Americanise** (ə'mɛrɪkə,naɪz) *vb* to make or become American in outlook, attitudes, etc > A,meri'cani'zation or A,meri'cani'sation *n*

American Revolution *n* the usual US term for **War of American Independence**

American Samoa *n* the part of Samoa administered by the US. Capital: Pago Pago. Pop: 67 000 (2003 est). Area: 197 sq km (76 sq miles)

americium (,æmə'rɪsɪəm) *n* a white metallic transuranic element artificially produced from plutonium. It is used as an alpha-particle source. Symbol: Am; atomic no: 95; half-life of most stable isotope, ^{243}Am: 7.4×10^3 years; valency: 2,3,4,5, or 6; relative density: 13.67; melting pt: 1176°C; boiling pt: 2607°C (est) [C20: from AMERICA (because it was discovered at Berkeley, California) + -IUM]

Amerigo Vespucci (*Italian* ame'ri:go ves'puttʃi) *n* See **Vespucci**

Amerindian (,æmə'rɪndɪən) Also called: Amerind ('æmərɪnd) *n, adj* a specialist word, esp in linguistics and anthropology, for **American Indian** > Amer'indic *adj*

amethyst ('æmɪθɪst) *n* 1 a purple or violet transparent variety of quartz used as a gemstone. Formula: SiO$_2$ 2 a purple variety of sapphire; oriental amethyst 3 the purple colour of amethyst [C13: from Old French *amatiste*, from Latin *amethystus*, from Greek *amethustos*, literally: not drunken, from A-^{1} + *methuein* to make drunk; referring to the belief that the stone could prevent intoxication] > amethystine (,æmɪ'θɪstaɪn) *adj*

Amex ('æmɛks) *n acronym for* 1 *trademark* American Express 2 American Stock Exchange

AMF *abbreviation* Australian Military Forces

Amhara (æm'hɑ:rə) *n* 1 a region in NW Ethiopia: formerly a kingdom 2 an inhabitant of the former kingdom of Amhara

Amharic (æm'hærɪk) *n* 1 the official language of Ethiopia, belonging to the SE Semitic subfamily of the Afro-Asiatic family ▷ *adj* 2 denoting or relating to this language

Amherst ('æmhɜːst) *n* **Jeffrey**, 1st Baron Amherst. 1717–97, British general who defeated the French in Canada (1758–60): governor general of British North America (1761–63)

amiable ('eɪmɪəb^{ə}l) *adj* having or displaying a pleasant or agreeable nature; friendly [C14: from Old French, from Late Latin *amīcābilis* AMICABLE] > ,amia'bility or 'amiableness *n* > 'amiably *adv*

amianthus (,æmɪ'ænθəs) *n* any of the fine silky varieties of asbestos [C17: from Latin *amiantus*, from Greek *amiantos* unsullied, from A-^{1} + *miainein* to pollute]

amicable ('æmɪkəb^{ə}l) *adj* characterized by friendliness: *an amicable agreement* [C15: from Late Latin *amīcābilis*, from Latin *amīcus* friend; related to *amāre* to love] > ,amica'bility or 'amicableness *n* > 'amicably *adv*

amice ('æmɪs) *n Christianity* a rectangular piece of white linen worn by priests around the neck and shoulders under the alb or, formerly, on the head [C15: from Old French *amis*, plural of *amit*, or from Medieval Latin *amicia*, both from Latin *amictus* cloak, from *amicīre* to clothe, from am- AMBI- + *iacere* to throw]

amicus curiae (æ'mi:kʊs 'kjʊərɪ,i:) *n, pl* amici curiae (æ'mi:kaɪ) *law* a person not directly engaged in a case who advises the court [Latin, literally: friend of the court]

amid (ə'mɪd) or **amidst** *prep* in the middle of; among [Old English *on middan* in the middle; see MID^1]

amide ('æmaɪd) *n* 1 any organic compound containing the functional group -CONH$_2$ 2 (*modifier*) consisting of, containing, or concerned with the group -CONH$_2$: *amide group or radical* 3 an inorganic compound having the general formula M(NH$_2$)$_x$, where M is a metal atom [C19: from AM(MONIA) + -IDE]

amido- *combining form* (in chemistry) indicating the presence of an amide group [from AMIDE]

amidships (ə'mɪdʃɪps) *adv, adj* (*postpositive*) *nautical* at, near, or towards the centre of a vessel

Amiens ('æmɪənz; *French* amjɛ̃) *n* a city in N France: its Gothic cathedral is the largest church in France. Pop: 135 501 (1999)

amigo (æ'mi:gəʊ, ə-) *n, pl* -gos a friend; comrade [Spanish, from Latin *amicus*]

Amin^1 (æ'mi:n, ɑ:-) *n* Lake Amin or Lake Idi Amin a former official name for (Lake) **Edward**

Amin^2 (æ'mi:n, ɑ:-) *n* **Idi** ('i:di:) 1925–2003, Ugandan soldier; dictator and head of state (1971–79). Notorious for his brutality, he was overthrown and exiled

amine (ə'mi:n, 'æmɪn) *n* an organic base formed by replacing one or more of the hydrogen atoms of ammonia by organic groups [C19: from AM(MONIUM) + -INE^2]

-amine *n combining form* indicating an amine: *histamine; methylamine*

amino (ə'maɪnəʊ, -'mi:-) *n* (*modifier*) of, consisting of, or containing the group of atoms -NH$_2$: *amino group or radical; amino acid*

amino acid *n* any of a group of organic compounds containing one or more amino groups, -NH$_2$, and one or more carboxyl groups, -COOH. The alpha-amino acids RCH(NH$_2$)COOH (where R is either hydrogen or an organic group) are the component molecules of proteins; some can be synthesized in the body (**nonessential amino acids**) and others cannot and are thus essential components of the diet (**essential amino acids**)

amino resin *n* any thermosetting synthetic resin formed by copolymerization of amines or amides with aldehydes. Amino resins are used as adhesives and as coatings for paper and textiles

amir (ə'mɪə) *n* a variant spelling of **emir** [C19: from Arabic, variant of EMIR] > a'mirate *n*

Amis ('eɪmɪs) *n* 1 Sir **Kingsley**. 1922–95, British novelist and poet, noted for his novels *Lucky Jim* (1954), *Jake's Thing* (1978), *Stanley and the Women* (1984), *The Old Devils* (1986), and *The Folks that Live on the Hill* (1990) 2 his son, **Martin**. born 1949, British novelist. His works include *The Rachel Papers* (1974), *Money* (1984), *London Fields* (1989), *The Information* (1994), and *Yellow Dog* (2003)

Amish ('ɑ:mɪʃ, 'æ-) *adj* of or relating to a US and Canadian Mennonite sect that traces its origin to Jakob Amman [C19: from German *Amisch*, after Jakob *Amman*, 17th-century Swiss Mennonite bishop]

amiss (ə'mɪs) *adv* 1 in an incorrect, inappropriate, or defective manner 2 take something amiss to be annoyed or offended by something ▷ *adj* 3 (*postpositive*) wrong, incorrect, or faulty [C13 *a mis*, from *mis* wrong; see MISS^1]

amitosis (,æmɪ'təʊsɪs) *n* an unusual form of cell

division in which the nucleus and cytoplasm divide by constriction without the formation of chromosomes; direct cell division [C19: A-¹ + MITOSIS] > amitotic (ˌæmɪˈtɒtɪk) adj

amity (ˈæmɪtɪ) n, pl -ties friendship; cordiality [C15: from Old French amité, from Medieval Latin amīcitās friendship, from Latin amīcus friend]

Amman (əˈmɑːn) n the capital of Jordan, northeast of the Dead Sea: ancient capital of the Ammonites, rebuilt by Ptolemy in the 3rd century BC. Pop: 1 292 000 (2005 est). Ancient names: Rabbath Ammon, Philadelphia

ammeter (ˈæmˌmiːtə) n an instrument for measuring an electric current in amperes [C19: AM(PERE) + -METER]

ammo (ˈæməʊ) n informal short for **ammunition**

Ammon¹ (ˈæmən) n Old Testament the ancestor of the Ammonites

Ammon² (ˈæmən) n myth the classical name of the Egyptian god Amen, identified by the Greeks with Zeus and by the Romans with Jupiter

ammonia (əˈməʊnɪə, -njə) n 1 a colourless pungent highly soluble gas mainly used in the manufacture of fertilizers, nitric acid, and other nitrogenous compounds, and as a refrigerant and solvent. Formula: NH_3 2 a solution of ammonia in water, containing the compound ammonium hydroxide [C18: from New Latin, from Latin (sal) ammōniacus (sal) AMMONIAC]

ammoniac (əˈməʊnɪˌæk) n a strong-smelling gum resin obtained from the stems of the N Asian umbelliferous plant Dorema ammoniacum and formerly used as an expectorant, stimulant, perfume, and in porcelain cement. Also called: gum ammoniac [C14: from Latin ammōniacum, from Greek ammōniakos belonging to Ammon (apparently the gum resin was extracted from plants found in Libya near the temple of Ammon)]

ammoniacal (ˌæməˈnaɪəkʲl) adj of, containing, using, or resembling ammonia

ammoniate (əˈməʊnɪˌeɪt) vb to unite or treat with ammonia > amˌmoniˈation n

ammonify (əˈmɒnɪˌfaɪ, əˈməʊnɪ-) vb -fies, -fying, -fied to treat or impregnate with ammonia or a compound of ammonia > amˌmonifiˈcation n

ammonite (ˈæməˌnaɪt) n 1 any extinct marine cephalopod mollusc of the order Ammonoidea, which were common in Mesozoic times and generally had a coiled partitioned shell. Their closest modern relative is the pearly nautilus 2 the shell of any of these animals, commonly occurring as a fossil [C18: from New Latin Ammōnītēs, from Medieval Latin cornū Ammōnis, literally: horn of Ammon]

ammonium (əˈməʊnɪəm, -njəm) n (modifier) of, consisting of, or containing the monovalent group NH_4- or the ion NH_4+: ammonium compounds

ammonium chloride n a white soluble crystalline solid used chiefly as an electrolyte in dry batteries and as a mordant and soldering flux. Formula: NH_4Cl. Also called: sal ammoniac

ammonium hydroxide n a compound existing only in aqueous solution, formed when ammonia dissolves in water to form ammonium ions and hydroxide ions. Formula: NH_4OH

ammonium sulphate n a white soluble crystalline solid used mainly as a fertilizer and in water purification. Formula: $(NH_4)_2SO_4$

ammunition (ˌæmjʊˈnɪʃən) n 1 any projectiles, such as bullets, rockets, etc, that can be discharged from a weapon 2 bombs, missiles, chemicals, biological agents, nuclear materials, etc, capable of use as weapons 3 any means of defence or attack, as in an argument [C17: from obsolete French amunition, by mistaken division from earlier la munition; see MUNITION]

amnesia (æmˈniːzjə, -ʒə, -zɪə) n a defect in memory, esp one resulting from pathological cause, such as brain damage or hysteria [C19: via New Latin from Greek: forgetfulness, probably from amnēstia oblivion; see AMNESTY] > amnesiac (æmˈniːzɪˌæk) or amnesic (æmˈniːsɪk, -zɪk) adj, n

amnesty (ˈæmnɪstɪ) n, pl -ties 1 a general pardon, esp for offences against a government 2 a period during which a law is suspended to allow people to admit

their crime without fear of prosecution ▷ vb -ties, -tying, -tied 3 (tr) to overlook or forget (an offence) [C16: from Latin amnēstia, from Greek: oblivion, from amnēstos forgetting, from A-¹ + -mnēstos, from mnasthai to remember]

Amnesty International n an international organization founded in Britain in 1961 that works to secure the release of people imprisoned for their beliefs, to ban the use of torture, and to abolish the death penalty. Abbreviation: AI

amnio (ˈæmnɪəʊ) n short for amniocentesis

amniocentesis (ˌæmnɪəʊsɛnˈtiːsɪs) n, pl -ses (-siːz) removal of some amniotic fluid by the insertion into the womb of a hollow needle, for therapeutic or diagnostic purposes [C20: from AMNION + centesis, from Greek kentēsis a puncture, from kentein to prick]

amnion (ˈæmnɪən) n, pl -nions or -nia (-nɪə) the innermost of two membranes enclosing an embryonic reptile, bird, or mammal [C17: via New Latin from Greek: a little lamb, from amnos a lamb]

amniotic fluid n the fluid surrounding the fetus in the womb

amoeba or US **ameba** (əˈmiːbə) n, pl -bae (-biː) or -bas any protozoan of the phylum Rhizopoda, esp any of the genus Amoeba, able to change shape because of the movements of cell processes (pseudopodia). They live in fresh water or soil or as parasites in man and animals [C19: from New Latin, from Greek amoibē change, from ameibein to change, exchange] > aˈmoebic or US aˈmebic adj

amok (əˈmʌk, əˈmɒk) or **amuck** (əˈmʌk) n 1 a state of murderous frenzy, originally observed among Malays ▷ adv 2 run amok to run about with or as if with a frenzied desire to kill [C17: from Malay amoq furious assault]

among (əˈmʌŋ) or **amongst** prep 1 in the midst of: he lived among the Indians 2 to each of: divide the reward among yourselves 3 in the group, class, or number of: ranked among the greatest writers 4 taken out of (a group): he is only one among many 5 with one another within a group; by the joint action of: a lot of gossip among the women employees; decide it among yourselves [Old English amang, contracted from on gemang in the group of, from ON + gemang crowd; see MINGLE, MONGREL]
● USAGE See at **between**

amontillado (əˌmɒntɪˈlɑːdəʊ) n a medium dry Spanish sherry, not as pale in colour as a fino [C19: from Spanish vino amontillado wine of Montilla, town in Spain]

amoral (eɪˈmɒrəl) adj 1 having no moral quality; nonmoral 2 without moral standards or principles > amorality (ˌeɪmɒˈrælɪtɪ) n
● USAGE Amoral is often wrongly used where immoral is
● meant. Immoral is properly used to talk about the
● breaking of moral rules, amoral about people who have
● no moral code or about places or situations where
● moral considerations do not apply

amorist (ˈæmərɪst) n a lover or a writer about love

amoroso (ˌæməˈrəʊsəʊ) adj, adv 1 music (to be played) lovingly ▷ n 2 a rich sweetened sherry of a dark colour [from Italian and Spanish: AMOROUS]

amorous (ˈæmərəs) adj 1 inclined towards or displaying love or desire 2 in love 3 of or relating to love [C14: from Old French, from Medieval Latin amōrōsus, from Latin amor love] > ˈamorously adv > ˈamorousness n

amorphous (əˈmɔːfəs) adj 1 lacking a definite shape; formless 2 of no recognizable character or type 3 (of chemicals, rocks, etc) not having a crystalline structure [C18: from New Latin, from Greek amorphos shapeless, from A-¹ + morphē shape] > aˈmorphism n > aˈmorphousness n

amortize or **amortise** (əˈmɔːtaɪz) vb (tr) 1 finance to liquidate (a debt, mortgage, etc) by instalment payments or by periodic transfers to a sinking fund 2 to write off (a wasting asset) by annual transfers to a sinking fund 3 property law (formerly) to transfer (lands, etc) in mortmain [C14: from Medieval Latin admortizāre, from Old French amortir to reduce to the point of death, ultimately from Latin ad to + mors death]

Amos (ˈeɪmɒs) n Old Testament 1 a Hebrew prophet of the

a

8th century BC **2** the book containing his oracles

amount (ə'maʊnt) n **1** extent; quantity; supply **2** the total of two or more quantities; sum **3** the full value, effect, or significance of something **4** a principal sum plus the interest on it, as in a loan ▷ vb **5** (intr; usually foll by to) to be equal or add up in effect, meaning, or quantity [c13: from Old French amonter to go up, from amont upwards, from a to + mont mountain (from Latin mōns)]

● USAGE The use of a plural noun after amount of (an
● amount of bananas; the amount of refugees) should be
● avoided: a quantity of bananas; the number of refugees

amount of substance n a measure of the number of entities (atoms, molecules, ions, electrons, etc) present in a substance, expressed in moles

amour (French amur) n a love affair, esp a secret or illicit one [c13: from Old French, from Latin amor love]

amour-propre (French amurprɔprə) n self-respect

Amoy (ə'mɔɪ) n **1** a port in SE China, in Fujian province on **Amoy Island**, at the mouth of the Jiulong River opposite Taiwan: one of the first treaty ports opened to European trade (1842). Pop: 746 000 (2005 est). Modern Chinese name: Xiamen **2** the dialect of Chinese spoken in Amoy, Taiwan, and elsewhere: a Min dialect

amp (æmp) n **1** an ampere **2** informal an amplifier

AMP abbreviation adenosine monophosphate

ampelopsis (ˌæmpɪ'lɒpsɪs) n any woody vine of the vitaceous genus Ampelopsis, of tropical and subtropical Asia and America [c19: from New Latin, from Greek ampelos grapevine]

amperage ('æmpərɪdʒ) n the magnitude of an electric current measured in amperes, esp the rated current of an electrical component or device

ampere ('æmpeə) n **1** the basic SI unit of electric current; the constant current that, when maintained in two parallel conductors of infinite length and negligible cross section placed 1 metre apart in free space, produces a force of 2×10^{-7} newton per metre between them. 1 ampere is equivalent to 1 coulomb per second **2** a former unit of electric current (**international ampere**); the current that, when passed through a solution of silver nitrate, deposits silver at the rate of 0.001118 gram per second. 1 international ampere equals 0.999835 ampere Abbreviation: amp Symbol: A [c19: named after André Marie Ampère (1775–1836), French physicist and mathematician]

Ampère ('æmpeə; French ɑ̃pɛr) n André Marie (ɑ̃dre mari). 1775–1836, French physicist and mathematician, who made major discoveries in the fields of magnetism and electricity

ampere-turn n a unit of magnetomotive force; the magnetomotive force produced by a current of 1 ampere passing through one complete turn of a coil. 1 ampere-turn is equivalent to $4\pi/10$ or 1.257 gilberts

ampersand ('æmpə,sænd) n the character (&), meaning and: John Brown & Co [c19: shortened from and per se and, that is, the symbol & by itself (represents) and]

amphetamine (æm'fɛtə,miːn, -mɪn) n a synthetic colourless volatile liquid used medicinally as the white crystalline sulphate, mainly for its stimulant action on the central nervous system, although it also stimulates the sympathetic nervous system. It can have unpleasant or dangerous side effects and drug dependence can occur; 1-phenyl-2-aminopropane. Formula: $C_6H_5CH_2CH(NH_2)CH_3$ [c20: from A(LPHA) + M(ETHYL) + PH(ENYL) + ET(HYL) + -AMINE]

amphi- prefix **1** on both sides; at both ends; of both kinds: amphibian; amphitrichous; amphibious **2** around: amphibole [from Greek]

amphibian (æm'fɪbɪən) n **1** any cold-blooded vertebrate of the class Amphibia, typically living on land but breeding in water. Their aquatic larvae (tadpoles) undergo metamorphosis into the adult form. The class includes the newts and salamanders, frogs and toads, and caecilians **2** a type of aircraft able to land and take off from both water and land **3** any vehicle able to travel on both water and land ▷ adj **4** another word for **amphibious 5** of, relating to, or belonging to the class Amphibia

amphibious (æm'fɪbɪəs) adj **1** able to live both on land and in the water, as frogs, toads, etc **2** designed for operation on or from both water and land **3** relating to military forces and equipment organized for operations launched from the sea against an enemy shore **4** having a dual or mixed nature [c17: from Greek amphibios, literally: having a double life, from AMPHI- + bios life] > am'phibiousness n

amphibole ('æmfɪ,bəʊl) n any of a large group of minerals consisting of the silicates of calcium, iron, magnesium, sodium, and aluminium, usually in the form of long slender dark-coloured crystals. Members of the group, including hornblende, actinolite, and tremolite, are common constituents of igneous rocks [c17: from French, from Greek amphibolos uncertain; so called from the large number of varieties in the group]

amphibology (ˌæmfɪ'bɒlədʒɪ) or **amphiboly** (æm'fɪbəlɪ) n, pl -gies or -lies ambiguity of expression, esp when due to a grammatical construction, as in save rags and waste paper [c14: from Late Latin amphibologia, ultimately from Greek amphibolos ambiguous; see AMPHIBOLE, -LOGY]

amphimixis (ˌæmfɪ'mɪksɪs) n, pl -mixes (-'mɪksiːz) true sexual reproduction by the fusion of gametes from two organisms [c19: from AMPHI- + Greek mixis a blending, from mignunai to mingle] > ,amphi'mictic adj

amphioxus (ˌæmfɪ'ɒksəs) n, pl -oxi (-'ɒksaɪ) or -oxuses another name for the **lancelet** [c19: from New Latin: both ends being sharp, from AMPHI- + Greek oxus sharp]

amphipod ('æmfɪ,pɒd) n **1** any marine or freshwater crustacean of the order Amphipoda, such as the sand hoppers, in which the body is laterally compressed: subclass Malacostraca ▷ adj **2** of, relating to, or belonging to the Amphipoda

amphiprostyle (æm'fɪprə,staɪl, ,æmfɪ'prəʊstaɪl) adj **1** (esp of a classical temple) having a set of columns at both ends but not at the sides ▷ n **2** a temple of this kind

amphisbaena (,æmfɪs'biːnə) n, pl -nae (-niː) or -nas **1** any worm lizard of the genus Amphisbaena **2** classical myth a poisonous serpent having a head at each end and able to move forwards or backwards [c16: via Latin from Greek amphisbaina, from amphis both ways + bainein to go]

amphitheatre or US **amphitheater** ('æmfɪ,θɪətə) n **1** a building, usually circular or oval, in which tiers of seats rise from a central open arena, as in those of ancient Rome **2** a place where contests are held; arena **3** any level circular area of ground surrounded by higher ground **4 a** the first tier of seats in the gallery of a theatre **b** any similarly designated seating area in a theatre **5** a lecture room in which seats are tiered away from a central area

Amphitrite (,æmfɪ'traɪtɪ) n Greek myth a sea goddess, wife of Poseidon and mother of Triton

amphora ('æmfərə) n, pl -phorae (-fə,riː) or -phoras an ancient Greek or Roman two-handled narrow-necked jar for oil, wine, etc [c17: from Latin, from Greek amphoreus, from AMPHI- + phoreus bearer, from pherein to bear]

amphoteric (,æmfə'tɛrɪk) adj chem able to function as either a base or an acid [c19: from Greek amphoteros each of two (from amphō both) + -IC]

ampicillin (,æmpɪ'sɪlɪn) n a semisynthetic penicillin used to treat various infections

ample ('æmpᵊl) adj **1** more than sufficient; abundant: an ample helping **2** large in size, extent, or amount: of ample proportions [c15: from Old French, from Latin amplus spacious] > 'ampleness n

amplification (,æmplɪfɪ'keɪʃən) n **1** the act or result of amplifying **2** material added to a statement, story, etc, in order to expand or clarify it **3** a statement, story, etc, with such additional material **4** electronics the increase in strength of an electrical signal by means of an amplifier

amplifier ('æmplɪ,faɪə) n **1** an electronic device used to increase the strength of the signal fed into it **2** photog an additional lens for altering the focal length of a camera lens **3** a person or thing that amplifies

amplify ('æmplɪ,faɪ) vb -fies, -fying, -fied **1** (tr) to increase in size, extent, effect, etc, as by the addition of extra material; augment; enlarge; expand **2** electronics to produce amplification of (electrical signals); increase the amplitude of (signals) **3** (*intr*) to expand or enlarge a speech, narrative, etc [c15: from Old French *amplifier*, ultimately from Latin *amplificāre* to enlarge, from *amplus* spacious + *facere* to make]

amplitude ('æmplɪˌtjuːd) *n* **1** greatness of extent; magnitude **2** abundance or copiousness **3** breadth or scope, as of the mind **4** *astronomy* the angular distance along the horizon measured from true east or west to the point of intersection of the vertical circle passing through a celestial body **5** *physics* the maximum variation from the zero or mean value of a periodically varying quantity [c16: from Latin *amplitūdō* breadth, from *amplus* spacious]

amplitude modulation *n* one of the principal methods of transmitting audio, visual, or other types of information using radio waves, the relevant signal being superimposed onto a radio-frequency carrier wave. The frequency of the carrier wave remains unchanged but its amplitude is varied in accordance with the amplitude of the input signal. See **frequency modulation**

amply ('æmplɪ) *adv* more than sufficiently; fully; generously

ampoule ('æmpuːl, -pjuːl) *or esp US* **ampule** *n med* a small glass vessel in which liquids for injection are hermetically sealed

ampulla (æm'pʊlə) *n*, *pl* -pullae (-'pʊliː) **1** *anatomy* the dilated end part of certain ducts or canals, such as the end of a uterine tube **2** *Christianity* **a** a vessel for containing the wine and water used at the Eucharist **b** a small flask for containing consecrated oil **3** a Roman two-handled bottle for oil, wine, or perfume [c16: from Latin, diminutive of AMPHORA]

amputate ('æmpjʊˌteɪt) *vb surgery* to remove (all or part of a limb, esp an arm or leg) [c17: from Latin *amputāre*, from *am-* around + *putāre* to trim, prune] > ˌampu'tation *n*

amputee (ˌæmpjʊ'tiː) *n* a person who has had a limb amputated

Amritsar (æm'rɪtsə) *n* a city in India, in NW Punjab: centre of the Sikh religion; site of a massacre in 1919 of unarmed supporters of Indian self-government by British troops; in 1984 the Golden Temple, fortified by Sikhs, was attacked by Indian troops with the loss of many Sikh lives. Pop: 975 695 (2001)

Amsterdam (ˌæmstə'dæm; *Dutch* ɑmstər'dɑm) *n* the commercial capital of the Netherlands, a major industrial centre and port on the IJsselmeer, connected with the North Sea by canal: built on about 100 islands within a network of canals. Pop: 737 000 (2003 est)

amu *abbreviation* atomic mass unit

amuck (ə'mʌk) *n*, *adv* a variant of **amok**

Amu Darya (*Russian* ɑ'mu dar'ja) *n* a river in central Asia, rising in the Pamirs and flowing northwest through the Hindu Kush and across Turkmenistan and Uzbekistan to its delta in the Aral Sea: forms much of the N border of Afghanistan and is important for irrigation. Length: 2400 km (1500 miles). Ancient name: Oxus

amulet ('æmjʊlɪt) *n* a trinket or piece of jewellery worn as a protection against evil; charm [c17: from Latin *amulētum*, of unknown origin]

Amundsen (*Norwegian* 'ɑːmunsən) *n* **Roald** ('rɔːld). 1872–1928, Norwegian explorer and navigator, who was the first man to reach the South Pole (1911)

Amundsen Sea ('ɑːmʊndsən) *n* a part of the South Pacific Ocean, in Antarctica off Byrd Land

Amur (ə'mʊə) *n* a river in NE Asia, rising in N Mongolia as the Argun and flowing southeast, then northeast to the Sea of Okhotsk: forms the boundary between Manchuria and Russia. Length: about 4350 km (2700 miles). Modern Chinese name: Heilong Jiang

amuse (ə'mjuːz) *vb* (*tr*) **1** to keep pleasantly occupied; entertain; divert **2** to cause to laugh or smile [c15: from Old French *amuser* to cause to be idle, from *muser* to MUSE¹]

amusement (ə'mjuːzmənt) *n* **1** something that amuses, such as a game or other pastime **2** a mechanical device used for entertainment, as at a fair **3** the act of amusing

or the state or quality of being amused

amusement arcade *n Brit* a covered area having coin-operated game machines

amusing (ə'mjuːzɪŋ) *adj* mildly entertaining; pleasantly diverting; causing a smile or laugh > a'musingly *adv*

amygdalin (ə'mɪgdəlɪn) *n* a white soluble bitter-tasting crystalline glycoside extracted from bitter almonds and stone fruits such as peaches and apricots. Formula: $C_6H_5CHCNOC_{12}H_{21}O_{10}$

amyl ('æmɪl) *n* (*modifier, no longer in technical usage*) of, consisting of, or containing any of eight isomeric forms of the monovalent group C_5H_{11}-: amyl group or radical [c19: from Latin: AMYLUM]

amylaceous (ˌæmɪ'leɪʃəs) *adj* of or resembling starch

amyl alcohol *n* a colourless flammable liquid existing in eight isomeric forms that is used as a solvent and in the manufacture of organic compounds and pharmaceuticals. Formula: $C_5H_{11}OH$

amylase ('æmɪˌleɪz) *n* any of several enzymes that hydrolyse starch and glycogen to simple sugars, such as glucose. They are present in saliva

amyl nitrite *n* a yellowish unstable volatile fragrant liquid used in medicine as a vasodilator and in perfumes. Formula: $(CH_3)_2CHCH_2CH_2NO_2$

amyloid ('æmɪˌlɔɪd) *n* **1** any substance resembling starch ▷ *adj* **2** starchlike

amylolysis (ˌæmɪ'lɒlɪsɪs) *n* the conversion of starch into sugar > amylolytic (əˌmaɪləʊ'lɪtɪk) *adj*

amylopsin (ˌæmɪ'lɒpsɪn) *n* an enzyme of the pancreatic juice that converts starch into sugar; pancreatic amylase [c19: from AMYLO(LYSIS) + (PE)PSIN]

amylum ('æmɪləm) *n* another name for **starch** (sense 2) [Latin, from Greek *amulon* fine meal, starch, from *amulos* not ground at the mill, from A-¹ + *mulē* mill]

amyotrophic lateral sclerosis (ˌæmɪəʊ'trəʊfɪk) *n* a form of motor neurone disease in which degeneration of motor tracts in the spinal cord causes progressive muscular paralysis starting in the limbs. Also called: Lou Gehrig's disease

Amytal ('æmɪˌtæl) *n trademark* a barbiturate, a brand of amobarbital, used as a sedative and hypnotic

an¹ (æn; *unstressed* ən) *determiner* a form of the indefinite article used before an initial vowel sound: *an old car; an elf; an honour* [Old English *ān* ONE]

● USAGE *An* was formerly often used before words that
● begin with *h* and are unstressed on the first syllable:
● *an hotel; an historic meeting*. Sometimes the initial *h* was
● not pronounced. This usage is now becoming obsolete

an² *or* **an'** (æn; *unstressed* ən) *conj* (*subordinating*) an obsolete or dialect word for **if**. See **and** (sense 8)

An (ɑːn) *n myth* the Sumerian sky god. Babylonian counterpart: Anu

AN *abbreviation* Anglo-Norman

an- *or before a consonant* **a-** *prefix* not; without: *anaphrodisiac* [from Greek]

-an, -ean *or* **-ian** *suffix* **1** (*forming adjectives and nouns*) belonging to or relating to; a person belonging to or coming from: *European* **2** (*forming adjectives and nouns*) typical of or resembling; a person typical of: *Elizabethan* **3** (*forming adjectives and nouns*) adhering to or following; an adherent of: *Christian* **4** (*forming nouns*) a person who specializes or is expert in: *dietitian; phonetician* [from Latin *-ānus*, suffix of adjectives]

ana- *or before a vowel* **an-** *prefix* **1** up; upwards: *anadromous* **2** again: *anagram* **3** back; backwards: *anatropous* [from Greek *ana*]

-ana *or* **-iana** *suffix forming nouns* denoting a collection of objects or information relating to a particular individual, subject, or place: *Shakespeareana; Victoriana; Americana* [New Latin, from Latin *-āna*, literally: matters relating to, neuter plural of *-ānus*; see -AN]

anabaena (ˌænə'biːnə) *n*, *pl* -nas any freshwater alga of the genus *Anabaena*, sometimes occurring in drinking water, giving it a fishy taste and smell [New Latin, from Greek *anabainein* to shoot up, go up, from ANA- + *bainein* to go; so called because they rise to the surface at intervals]

Anabaptist (ˌænə'bæptɪst) *n* **1** a member of any of various 16th-century Protestant movements that rejected infant baptism, insisted that adults be rebaptized, and sought to establish Christian communism ▷ *adj* **2** of or relating to these movements or sects or their doctrines [c16: from Ecclesiastical Latin *anabaptista*, from *anabaptizāre* to baptize again, from Late Greek *anabaptizein*; see ANA-, BAPTIZE] > Ana'baptism *n*

anabas ('ænə,bæs) *n* any of several labyrinth fishes of the genus Anabas, esp the **climbing fish** [c19: from New Latin, from Greek *anabainein* to go up; see ANABAENA]

anabasis (ə'næbəsɪs) *n, pl* -ses (-,si:z) **1** the march of Cyrus the Younger and his Greek mercenaries from Sardis to Cunaxa in Babylonia in 401 BC, described by Xenophon in his *Anabasis* **2** any military expedition, esp one from the coast to the interior [c18: from Greek: a going up, ascent, from *anabainein* to go up; see ANABAENA]

anabatic (,ænə'bætɪk) *adj meteorol* (of air currents) rising upwards, esp up slopes [c19: from Greek *anabatikos* relating to ascents, from *anabainein* to go up; see ANABASIS]

anabiosis (,ænəbaɪ'əʊsɪs) *n* the ability to return to life after apparent death; suspended animation [c19: via New Latin from Greek, from *anabioein* to come back to life, from ANA- + *bios* life] > anabiotic (,ænəbaɪ'ɒtɪk) *adj*

anabolic steroid *n* any of a group of synthetic steroid hormones (androgens) used to stimulate muscle and bone growth for therapeutic or athletic purposes

anabolism (ə'næbə,lɪzəm) *n* a metabolic process in which complex molecules are synthesized from simpler ones with the storage of energy; constructive metabolism [c19: from ANA- + (META)BOLISM]

anachronism (ə'nækrə,nɪzəm) *n* **1** the representation of an event, person, or thing in a historical context in which it could not have occurred or existed **2** a person or thing that belongs or seems to belong to another time [c17: from Latin *anachronismus*, from Greek *anakhronismos* a mistake in chronology, from *anakhronizein* to err in a time reference, from ANA- + *khronos* time] > a,nachro'nistic *adj* > a,nachro'nistically *adv*

anacoluthon (,ænəkə'lu:θɒn) *n, pl* -tha (-θə) *rhetoric* a construction that involves the change from one grammatical sequence to another within a single sentence; an example of anacoluthia [c18: from Late Latin, from Greek *anakolouthon*, from *anakolouthos* not consistent, from AN- + *akolouthos* following]

anaconda (,ænə'kɒndə) *n* a very large nonvenomous arboreal and semiaquatic snake, *Eunectes murinus*, of tropical South America, which kills its prey by constriction: family Boidae (boas) [c18: probably changed from Sinhalese *henakandayā* whip snake, from *hena* lightning + *kanda* stem; originally referring to a snake of Sri Lanka]

Anacreon (ə'nækrɪ,ɒn, -ən) *n* ?572–?488 BC, Greek lyric poet, noted for his short songs celebrating love and wine

anacrusis (,ænə'kru:sɪs) *n, pl* -ses (-si:z) **1** *prosody* one or more unstressed syllables at the beginning of a line of verse **2** *music* an unstressed note or group of notes immediately preceding the strong first beat of the first bar [c19: from Greek *anakrousis* prelude, from *anakrouein* to strike up, from ANA- + *krouein* to strike]

anadromous (ə'nædrəməs) *adj* (of fishes such as the salmon) migrating up rivers from the sea in order to breed [c18: from Greek *anadromos* running upwards, from ANA- + *dromos* a running]

Anadyr (*Russian* a'nadirj) *n* **1** a town in Russia, in NE Siberia at the mouth of the Anadyr River; the capital of Chukot Autonomous Okrug. Pop: 11 038 (2002) **2** a mountain range in Russia, in NE Siberia, rising over 1500 m (5000 ft) **3** a river in Russia, rising in mountains on the Arctic Circle, south of the Anadyr Range, and flowing east to the Gulf of Anadyr. Length: 725 km (450 miles) **4** Gulf of Anadyr an inlet of the Bering Sea, off the coast of NE Russia

anaemia *or US* **anemia** (ə'ni:mɪə) *n* a deficiency in the number of red blood cells or in their haemoglobin content, resulting in pallor, shortness of breath, and lack of energy [c19: from New Latin, from Greek *anaimia* lack of blood, from AN- + *haima* blood]

anaemic *or US* **anemic** (ə'ni:mɪk) *adj* **1** relating to or suffering from anaemia **2** pale and sickly looking; lacking vitality

anaerobe (æ'nɛərəʊb, 'ænərəʊb) *or* **anaerobium** (,ænɛə'rəʊbɪəm) *n, pl* -obes *or* -obia (-'əʊbɪə) an organism that does not require oxygen for respiration

anaerobic (,ænɛə'rəʊbɪk) *adj* **1** (of an organism or process) requiring the absence of or not dependent on the presence of oxygen **2** of or relating to anaerobes > ,anaer'obically *adv*

anaesthesia *or US* **anesthesia** (,ænɪs'θi:zɪə) *n* **1** local or general loss of bodily sensation, esp of touch, as the result of nerve damage or other abnormality **2** loss of sensation, esp of pain, induced by drugs: called **general anaesthesia** when consciousness is lost and **local anaesthesia** when only a specific area of the body is involved [c19: from New Latin, from Greek *anaisthēsia* absence of sensation, from AN- + *aisthēsis* feeling]

anaesthetic *or US* **anesthetic** (,ænɪs'θɛtɪk) *n* **1** a substance that causes anaesthesia ▷ *adj* **2** causing or characterized by anaesthesia

anaesthetics (,ænɪs'θɛtɪks) *n* (*functioning as singular*) the science, study, and practice of anaesthesia and its application. US name: anesthesiology

anaesthetist (ə'ni:sθətɪst) *n Brit* a qualified doctor specializing in the administration of anaesthetics. US name: anesthesiologist

anaesthetize, anaesthetise *or US* **anesthetize** (ə'ni:sθə,taɪz) *vb* (*tr*) to render insensible to pain by administering an anaesthetic > a,naestheti'zation, a,naestheti'sation *or* US a,nestheti'zation *n*

anaglyph ('ænə,glɪf) *n* **1** *photog* a stereoscopic picture consisting of two images of the same object, taken from slightly different angles, in two complementary colours, usually red and cyan (green-blue). When viewed through spectacles having one red and one cyan lens, the images merge to produce a stereoscopic sensation **2** anything cut to stand in low relief, such as a cameo [c17: from Greek *anagluphē* carved in low relief, from ANA- + *gluphē* carving, from *gluphein* to carve] > ,ana'glyphic, ,ana'glyphical *or* anaglyptic (,ænə'glɪptɪk), ,ana'glyptical *adj*

Anaglypta (,ænə'glɪptə) *n trademark* a type of thick embossed wallpaper [c19: from Greek *anagluptos*; see ANAGLYPH]

anagram ('ænə,græm) *n* a word or phrase the letters of which can be rearranged into another word or phrase [c16: from New Latin *anagramma*, shortened from Greek *anagrammatismos*, from *anagrammatizein* to transpose letters, from ANA- + *gramma* a letter] > anagrammatic (,ænəgrə'mætɪk) *or* ,anagram'matical *adj*

anagrammatize *or* **anagrammatise** (,ænə'græmə,taɪz) *vb* to arrange into an anagram

anal ('eɪnᵊl) *adj* **1** of, relating to, or near the anus **2** *psychoanal* relating to a stage of psychosexual development during which the child's interest is concentrated on the anal region and excremental functions [c18: from New Latin *ānālis*; see ANUS] > 'anally *adv*

analects ('ænə,lɛkts) *or* **analecta** (,ænə'lɛktə) *pl n* selected literary passages from one or more works [c17: via Latin from Greek *analekta*, from *analegein* to collect up, from *legein* to gather]

analemma (,ænə'lɛmə) *n, pl* -mas *or* -mata (-mətə) a graduated scale shaped like a figure eight that indicates the daily declination of the sun [c17: from Latin: sundial, pedestal of sundial, from Greek *analēmma* pedestal, from *analambanein* to support] > analemmatic (,ænəlɛ'mætɪk) *adj*

analeptic (,ænᵊ'lɛptɪk) *adj* **1** (of a drug, etc) stimulating the central nervous system ▷ *n* **2** any drug, such as doxapram, that stimulates the central nervous system **3** (formerly) a restorative remedy or drug [c17: from New Latin *analēpticus*, from Greek *analēptikos* stimulating, from *analambanein* to take up; see ANALEMMA]

anal fin *n* a median ventral unpaired fin, situated between the anus and the tail fin in fishes, that helps to maintain stable equilibrium

analgesia (,ænᵊl'dʒi:zɪə, -sɪə) *or* **analgia** (æn'ældʒɪə) *n* **1** inability to feel pain **2** the relief of pain [c18: via New Latin from Greek: insensibility, from AN- + *algēsis* sense of pain]

a

analgesic (ˌænəlˈdʒiːzɪk, -sɪk) *adj* 1 of or causing analgesia ▷ *n* 2 a substance that produces analgesia

analog (ˈænəˌlɒg) *n* a variant spelling of **analogue**
 ● USAGE The spelling *analog* is a US variant of *analogue* in all its senses, and is also the generally preferred spelling in the computer industry

analog computer *n* a mechanical, electrical, or electronic computer that performs arithmetical operations by using some variable physical quantity, such as mechanical movement or voltage, to represent numbers

analogize *or* **analogise** (əˈnæləˌdʒaɪz) *vb* 1 (*intr*) to make use of analogy, as in argument; draw comparisons 2 (*tr*) to make analogous or reveal analogy in

analogous (əˈnæləgəs) *adj* 1 similar or corresponding in some respect 2 *biology* (of organs and parts) having the same function but different evolutionary origin 3 *linguistics* formed by analogy: *an analogous plural* [c17: from Latin *analogus*, from Greek *analogos* proportionate, from ANA- + *logos* speech, ratio]
 ● USAGE The use of *with* after *analogous* should be avoided: *swimming has no event that is analogous to* (not *with*) *the 100 metres in athletics*

analogue *or sometimes US* **analog** (ˈænəˌlɒg) *n* 1 a a physical object or quantity, such as a pointer on a dial or a voltage, used to measure or represent another quantity b (*as modifier*): *analogue watch; analogue recording* 2 something analogous to something else 3 *biology* an analogous part or organ
 ● USAGE See at **analog**

analogue recording *n* a sound recording process in which an audio input is converted into an analogous electrical waveform

analogy (əˈnælədʒɪ) *n, pl* -gies 1 agreement or similarity, esp in a certain limited number of features or details 2 a comparison made to show such a similarity: *to draw an analogy between an atom and the solar system* 3 *biology* the relationship between analogous organs or parts 4 *logic, maths* a form of reasoning in which a similarity between two or more things is inferred from a known similarity between them in other respects 5 *linguistics* imitation of existing models or regular patterns in the formation of words, inflections, etc: *a child may use "sheeps" as the plural of "sheep" by analogy with "dog", "dogs", "cat", "cats", etc* [c16: from Greek *analogia* ratio, correspondence, from *analogos* ANALOGOUS] > analogical (ˌænəˈlɒdʒɪk³l) *or* ˌanaˈlogic *adj*

anal retentive *psychoanal* ▷ *n* 1 a person who exhibits anal personality traits ▷ *adj* anal-retentive 2 exhibiting anal personality traits

analysand (əˈnælɪˌsænd) *n* any person who is undergoing psychoanalysis [c20: from ANALYSE + -*and*, on the model of *multiplicand*]

analyse *or US* **analyze** (ˈænəˌlaɪz) *vb* (*tr*) 1 to examine in detail in order to discover meaning, essential features, etc 2 to break down into components or essential features 3 to make a mathematical, chemical, grammatical, etc, analysis of 4 another word for **psychoanalyse** [c17: back formation from ANALYSIS] > ˈanaˌlyser *or US* ˈanaˌlyzer *n*

analysis (əˈnælɪsɪs) *n, pl* -ses (-ˌsiːz) 1 the division of a physical or abstract whole into its constituent parts to examine or determine their relationship or value 2 a statement of the results of this 3 short for **psychoanalysis** 4 *chem* a the decomposition of a substance into its elements, radicals, or other constituents in order to determine the kinds of constituents present (**qualitative analysis**) or the amount of each constituent (**quantitative analysis**) b the result obtained by such a determination 5 *linguistics* the use of word order together with word function to express syntactic relations in a language, as opposed to the use of inflections 6 *maths* the branch of mathematics principally concerned with the properties of functions, largely arising out of calculus 7 in the last analysis, in the final analysis *or* in the ultimate analysis after everything has been given due consideration [c16: from New Latin, from Greek *analusis*, literally: a dissolving, from *analuein*, from ANA- + *luein* to loosen]

analysis of variance *n statistics* any of a number of techniques for resolving the observed variance between sets of data into components, esp to determine whether the difference between two samples is explicable as random sampling variation with the same underlying population

analyst (ˈænəlɪst) *n* 1 a person who analyses or is skilled in analysis 2 short for **psychoanalyst**

analytic (ˌænəˈlɪtɪk) *or* **analytical** (ˌænəˈlɪtɪk³l) *adj* 1 relating to analysis 2 capable of or given to analysing: *an analytic mind* 3 Also called: isolating *linguistics* denoting languages, such as Chinese, whose morphology is characterized by analysis 4 *logic* (of a proposition) true by virtue of the meanings of the words alone without reference to the facts, as *all spinsters are unmarried* [c16: via Late Latin from Greek *analutikos* from *analuein* to dissolve, break down; see ANALYSIS] > ˌanaˈlytically *adv*

analytical geometry *n* the branch of geometry that uses algebraic notation and analysis to locate a geometric point in terms of a coordinate system; coordinate geometry

analytical philosophy *n* a school of philosophy which flourished in the first half of the 20th century and which sought to resolve philosophical problems by analysing the language in which they are expressed, esp in terms of formal logic as in Russell's theory of descriptions

analytic phonics *n* (*functioning as singular*) same as **phonics** (sense 2). See **synthetic phonics**

Anambra (əˈnæmbrə) *n* a state of S Nigeria. Capital: Awka. Pop: 4 182 031 (2006). Area: 4844 sq km (1870 sq miles)

Ananda (əˈnændə) *n* 5th century BC, the first cousin, favourite disciple, and personal attendant of the Buddha

anandamide (əˈnændəˌmaɪd) *n* a naturally occurring endogenous cannabinoid neurotransmitter found in the brains of mammals and in small quantities in the cocoa bean [c20: from Sanskrit *ananda* bliss]

anandrous (ænˈændrəs) *adj* (of flowers) having no stamens [c19: from Greek *anandros* lacking males, from AN- + *anēr* man]

Ananias (ˌænəˈnaɪəs) *n* 1 New Testament a Jewish Christian of Jerusalem who was struck dead for lying (Acts 5) 2 a liar

anapaest *or* **anapest** (ˈænəpɛst, -piːst) *n prosody* a metrical foot of three syllables, the first two short, the last long (--‒) [c17: via Latin from Greek *anapaistos* reversed (that is, a dactyl reversed), from *anapaiein*, from *ana*- back + *paiein* to strike] > ˌanaˈpaestic *or* ˌanaˈpestic *adj*

anaphora (əˈnæfərə) *n* 1 grammar the use of a word such as a pronoun that has the same reference as a word previously used in the same discourse. In the sentence *John wrote the essay in the library but Peter did it at home*, both *did* and *it* are examples of anaphora 2 *rhetoric* the repetition of a word or phrase at the beginning of successive clauses [c16: via Latin from Greek: repetition, from *anapherein*, from ANA- + *pherein* to bear]

anaphrodisiac (ˌænæfrəˈdɪzɪˌæk) *adj* 1 tending to lessen sexual desire ▷ *n* 2 an anaphrodisiac drug

anaphylactic shock *n* a severe, sometimes fatal, reaction to a substance to which a person has an extreme sensitivity, often involving respiratory difficulty and circulation failure

anaphylaxis (ˌænəfɪˈlæksɪs) *n* extreme sensitivity to an injected antigen, esp a protein, following a previous injection [c20: from ANA- + (PRO)PHYLAXIS]

anaplasmosis (ˌænəplæzˈməʊsɪs) *n* another name for **gallsickness**

anaptyxis (ˌænæpˈtɪksɪs) *n, pl* -tyxes (-ˈtɪksiːz) the insertion of a short vowel between consonants in order to make a word more easily pronounceable [c19: via New Latin from Greek *anaptuxis*, from *anaptussein* to unfold, from ANA- + *ptussein* to fold]

Anapurna (ˌænəˈpʊənə) *n* a variant spelling of **Annapurna**

anarchism (ˈænəˌkɪzəm) *n* 1 political theory a doctrine advocating the abolition of government 2 the principles or practice of anarchists

anarchist ('ænəkɪst) n 1 a person who advocates the abolition of government and a social system based on voluntary cooperation 2 a person who causes disorder or upheaval

anarchy ('ænəkɪ) n 1 general lawlessness and disorder, esp when thought to result from an absence or failure of government 2 the absence or lack of government 3 the absence of any guiding or uniting principle; disorder; chaos 4 the theory or practice of political anarchism [c16: from Medieval Latin anarchia, from Greek anarkhia, from anarkhos without a ruler, from AN- + arkh- leader, from arkhein to rule] > anarchic (æn'ɑːkɪk) or an'archical adj

Anastasia (,ænə'stɑːzɪə, -'steɪ-) n Grand Duchess. 1901–?18, daughter of Tsar Nicholas II, believed to have been executed by the Bolsheviks in 1918, although several women subsequently claimed to be her

anastigmat (æ'næstɪɡ,mæt, ,ænə'stɪɡmæt) n a lens or system of lenses designed to be free of astigmatism [c19 from AN- + ASTIGMATIC] > anastigmatic (,ænəstɪɡ'mætɪk) or stig'matic adj

anastomose (ə'næstə,məʊz) vb to join (two parts of a blood vessel, etc) by anastomosis

anastomosis (ə,næstə'məʊsɪs) n, pl -ses (-siːz) 1 a natural connection between two tubular structures, such as blood vessels 2 the surgical union of two hollow organs or parts that are normally separate [c16: via New Latin from Greek: opening, from anastomoun to equip with a mouth, from stoma mouth]

anastrophe (ə'næstrəfɪ) n rhetoric another term for **inversion** (sense 3) [c16: from Greek, from anastrephein to invert]

anastrozole (ə'næstrə,zəʊl) n an anti-oestrogen drug used in the treatment of breast cancer in post-menopausal women. Also called: Arimidex

anathema (ə'næθəmə) n, pl -mas 1 a detested person or thing: he is anathema to me 2 a formal ecclesiastical curse of excommunication or a formal denunciation of a doctrine 3 the person or thing so cursed 4 a strong curse; imprecation [c16: via Church Latin from Greek: something accursed, dedicated (to evil), from anatithenai to dedicate, from ANA- + tithenai to set]

anathematize or **anathematise** (ə'næθɪmə,taɪz) vb to pronounce an anathema (upon a person, etc); curse > ,anathemati'zation or a,nathemati'sation n

Anatolia (,ænə'təʊlɪə) n the Asian part of Turkey, occupying the peninsula between the Black Sea, the Mediterranean, and the Aegean: consists of a plateau, largely mountainous, with salt lakes in the interior. Historical name: Asia Minor > ,Ana'tolian adj, n

anatomical (,ænə'tɒmɪkᵊl) adj of or relating to anatomy

anatomist (ə'nætəmɪst) n an expert in anatomy

anatomize or **anatomise** (ə'nætə,maɪz) vb (tr) 1 to dissect (an animal or plant) 2 to examine in minute detail

anatomy (ə'nætəmɪ) n, pl -mies 1 the science concerned with the physical structure of animals and plants 2 the physical structure of an animal or plant or any of its parts 3 a book or treatise on this subject 4 dissection of an animal or plant 5 any detailed analysis: the anatomy of a crime 6 informal the human body [c14: from Latin anatomia, from Greek anatomē, from anatemnein to cut up, from ANA- + temnein to cut]

anatto (ə'nætəʊ) n, pl -tos a variant spelling of **annatto**

Anaxagoras (,ænæk'sæɡərəs) n ?500–428 BC, Greek philosopher who maintained that all things were composed of minute particles arranged by an eternal intelligence

Anaximander (ə,næksɪ'mændə) n 611–547 BC, Greek philosopher, astronomer, and mathematician who believed the first principle of the world to be the Infinite

Anaximenes (,ænæk'sɪmə,niːz) n 6th century BC, Greek philosopher who believed air to be the primary substance

ANC abbreviation African National Congress

-ance or **-ancy** suffix forming nouns indicating an action, state or condition, or quality: hindrance; tenancy; resemblance [via Old French from Latin -antia; see -ANCY]

ancestor ('ænsɛstə) n 1 (often plural) a person from whom another is directly descended, esp someone more distant than a grandparent; forefather 2 an early type of animal or plant from which a later, usually dissimilar, type has evolved 3 a person or thing regarded as a forerunner of a later person or thing: the ancestor of the modern camera [c13: from Old French ancestre, from Late Latin antecessor one who goes before, from Latin antecēdere; see ANTECEDE] > 'ancestress fem n

ancestral (æn'sɛstrəl) adj of, inherited from, or derived from ancestors

ancestry ('ænsɛstrɪ) n, pl -tries 1 lineage or descent, esp when ancient, noble, or distinguished 2 ancestors collectively

Anchises (æn'kaɪsiːz) n classical myth a Trojan prince and father of Aeneas. In the Aeneid, he is rescued by his son at the fall of Troy and dies in Sicily

anchor ('æŋkə) n 1 any of several devices, usually of steel, attached to a vessel by a cable and dropped overboard so as to grip the bottom and restrict the vessel's movement 2 an object used to hold something else firmly in place: the rock provided an anchor for the rope 3 a source of stability or security 4 short for **anchorman, anchorwoman** 5 cast anchor, come to anchor or drop anchor to anchor a vessel 6 ride at anchor to be anchored ▷ vb 7 to use an anchor to hold (a vessel) in one place 8 to fasten or be fastened securely; fix or become fixed firmly ▷ See also **anchors** [Old English ancor, from Latin ancora, from Greek ankura; related to Greek ankos bend; compare Latin uncus bent, hooked]

anchorage ('æŋkərɪdʒ) n 1 the act of anchoring 2 any place where a vessel is anchored 3 a place designated for vessels to anchor 4 a fee imposed for anchoring 5 anything used as an anchor 6 a source of security or strength

Anchorage ('æŋkərɪdʒ) n the largest city in Alaska, a port in the south, at the head of Cook Inlet. Pop: 270 951 (2003 est)

anchor ice n Canadian ice that forms at the bottom of a lake or river

anchorite ('æŋkə,raɪt) n a person who lives in seclusion, esp a religious recluse; hermit [c15: from Medieval Latin anchorīta, from Late Latin anachōrēta, from Greek anakhōrētēs, from anakhōrein to retire, withdraw, from khōra a space] > 'anchoress fem n

anchorman ('æŋkə,mæn) n, pl -men 1 sport the last person in a team to compete, esp in a relay race 2 Also called: anchor, presenter (in broadcasting) a person in a central studio who links up and maintains contact with various outside camera units, reporters, etc

anchors ('æŋkəz) pl n slang the brakes of a motor vehicle: he rammed on the anchors

anchorwoman ('æŋkə,wʊmən) n, pl -women 1 sport the last woman in a team to compete, esp in a relay race 2 Also called: anchor, presenter (in broadcasting) a woman in a central studio who links up and maintains contact with various outside camera units, reporters, etc

anchovy ('æntʃəvɪ) n, pl -vies or -vy any of various small marine food fishes of the genus Engraulis and related genera, esp E. encrasicolus of S Europe: family Clupeidae (herrings). They have a salty taste and are often tinned or made into a paste or essence [c16: from Spanish anchova, perhaps ultimately from Greek aphuē small fish]

anchusa (æn'kjuːsə) n any Eurasian plant of the boraginaceous genus Anchusa, having rough hairy stems and leaves and blue flowers [c18: from Latin]

anchylose ('æŋkɪ,ləʊz) vb a former spelling of **ankylose**

ancien régime French (ɑ̃sjɛ̃ reʒim) n, pl anciens régimes (ɑ̃sjɛ̃ reʒim) the political and social system of France before the Revolution of 1789 [literally: old regime]

ancient ('eɪnʃənt) adj 1 dating from very long ago: ancient ruins 2 very old; aged 3 of the far past, esp before the collapse of the Western Roman Empire (476 AD) ▷ n 4 (often plural) a member of a civilized nation in the ancient world, esp a Greek, Roman, or Hebrew 5 (often plural) one of the classical authors of Greek or Roman antiquity 6 archaic an old man [c14: from Old French ancien, from Vulgar Latin anteanus (unattested), from

Latin *ante* before] ▷ 'ancientness *n*

ancient lights *n* (*usually functioning as singular*) the legal right to receive, by a particular window or windows, adequate and unobstructed daylight

anciently ('eɪnʃəntlɪ) *adv* in ancient times

Ancient of Days *n* a name for God, originating in the Authorized Version of the Old Testament (Daniel 7:9)

ancillary (æn'sɪlərɪ) *adj* **1** subsidiary **2** auxiliary; supplementary: *ancillary services* ▷ *n, pl* -laries **3** a subsidiary or auxiliary thing or person [C17: from Latin *ancillāris* concerning maidservants, from *ancilla*, diminutive of *ancūla* female servant]

Ancohuma (ˌæŋkəʊ'uːmə) *n* one of the two peaks of Mount Sorata

ancon ('æŋkɒn) *or* **ancone** ('æŋkəʊn) *n, pl* ancones (æŋ'kəʊniːz) *architect* a projecting bracket or console supporting a cornice [C18: from Greek *ankōn* a bend]

Ancona (*Italian* aŋ'koːna) *n* a port in central Italy, on the Adriatic, capital of the Marches: founded by Greeks from Syracuse in about 390 BC. Pop: 100 507 (2001)

-ancy *suffix forming nouns* a variant of -ance, used to indicate condition or quality: *expectancy; poignancy; malignancy*

ancylostomiasis (ˌænsɪˌlɒstə'maɪəsɪs),

ankylostomiasis *or* **anchylostomiasis** *n* infestation of the human intestine with blood-sucking hookworms, causing progressive anaemia. Also called: hookworm disease [from New Latin, from *Ancylostoma* genus of hookworms, from Greek *ankulos* hooked, crooked + *stoma* mouth]

and (ænd; *unstressed* ənd, ən) *conj* (*coordinating*) **1** along with; in addition to: *boys and girls* **2** as a consequence: *he fell down and cut his knee* **3** afterwards: *we pay the man and go through that door* **4** plus: *two and two equals four* **5** used to join identical words or phrases to give emphasis or indicate repetition or continuity: *better and better; we ran and ran; it rained and rained* **6** used to join two identical words or phrases to express a contrast between instances of what is named: *there are jobs and jobs* **7** *informal* used in place of *to* in infinitives after verbs such as *try, go,* and *come*: *try and see it my way* **8** an obsolete word for *if*: *and it please you* [Old English *and*; related to Old Frisian *anda*, Old Saxon *ande*, Old High German *anti*, Sanskrit *atha*]

● USAGE The use of *and* instead of *to* after *try* and *wait* is
● typical of spoken language, but should be avoided in
● any writing which is not informal: *We must try to*
● *prevent* (not *try and prevent*) *this happening*

-and *or* **-end** *suffix forming nouns* indicating a person or thing that is to be dealt with in a specified way: *analysand; dividend; multiplicand* [from Latin gerundives ending in *-andus, -endus*]

AND *international car registration* Andorra

Andalusia (ˌændə'luːzɪə) *n* a region of S Spain, on the Mediterranean and the Atlantic, with the Sierra Morena in the north, the Sierra Nevada in the southeast, and the Guadalquivir River flowing over fertile lands between them; a centre of Moorish civilization; it became an autonomous region in 1981. Area: about 87 268 sq km (33 700 sq miles)

Andaman and Nicobar Islands ('ændəmən, 'nɪkəʊˌbɑː) *pl n* a territory of India, in the E Bay of Bengal, consisting of two groups of over 200 islands; suffered badly in the Indian Ocean tsunami of December 2004. Capital: Port Blair. Pop: 356 265 (2001). Area: 8140 sq km (3143 sq miles)

Andaman Islands *pl n* a group of islands in the E Bay of Bengal, part of the Indian territory of the Andaman and Nicobar Islands. Area: 6408 sq km (2474 sq miles). Pop: 314 804 (2001)

Andaman Sea *n* part of the Bay of Bengal, between the Andaman and Nicobar Islands and the Malay Peninsula

andante (æn'dæntɪ) *music* ▷ *adj, adv* **1** (to be performed) at a moderately slow tempo ▷ *n* **2** a passage or piece to be performed in this manner [C18: Italian: going, from *andare* to go, from Latin *ambulāre* to walk]

andantino (ˌændæn'tiːnəʊ) *music* ▷ *adj, adv* **1** (to be performed) slightly faster, or slightly more slowly, than andante ▷ *n, pl* -nos **2** a passage or piece to be performed

in this manner [C19: diminutive of ANDANTE]

AND circuit *or* **AND gate** (ænd) *n computing* a logic circuit having two or more input wires and one output wire that has a high-voltage output signal if and only if all input signals are at a high voltage simultaneously: used extensively as a basic circuit in computers. See NAND circuit, NOR circuit, OR circuit [C20: so named because the action performed on electrical signals is similar to the operation of the conjunction *and* in logical constructions]

Andersen ('ændəsən) *n* **Hans Christian**. 1805–75, Danish author of fairy tales, including *The Ugly Duckling, The Tin Soldier,* and *The Snow Queen*

Andersen Nexø ('anərsən) *n* See Nexø

Anderson[1] ('ændəsən) *n* a river in N Canada, in the Northwest Territories, rising in lakes north of Great Bear Lake and flowing west and north to the Beaufort Sea. Length: about 580 km (360 miles)

Anderson[2] ('ændəsən) *n* **1 Carl David**. 1905–91, US physicist, who discovered the positron in cosmic rays (1932): Nobel prize for physics 1936 **2 Elizabeth Garrett**. 1836–1917, English physician and feminist: a campaigner for the admission of women to the professions **3 John**. 1893–1962, Australian philosopher, born in Scotland, whose theories are expounded in *Studies in Empirical Philosophy* (1962) **4** Dame **Judith**, real name *Frances Margaret Anderson*. 1898– 1992, Australian stage and film actress **5 Lindsay** (**Gordon**) 1923–94, British film and theatre director: his films include *This Sporting Life* (1963), *If* (1968), *O Lucky Man!* (1973), and *The Whales of August* (1987) **6 Marian**. 1902–93, US contralto, the first Black permanent member of the Metropolitan Opera Company, New York **7 Philip Warren**. born 1923, US physicist, noted for his work on solid-state physics. Nobel prize for physics 1977 **8 Sherwood**. 1874–1941, US novelist and short-story writer, best known for *Winesburg Ohio* (1919), a collection of short stories illustrating small-town life

Anderssen ('ændəsən) *n* **Adolf** ('aːdɔlf). 1818–79, German chess player: noted for the incisiveness of his combination play

Andes ('ændiːz) *pl n* a major mountain system of South America, extending for about 7250 km (4500 miles) along the entire W coast, with several parallel ranges or cordilleras and many volcanic peaks: rich in minerals, including gold, silver, copper, iron ore, and nitrates. Average height: 3900 m (13 000 ft). Highest peak: Aconcagua, 6960 m (22 835 ft)

Andhra Pradesh ('ændrə praː'dɛʃ) *n* a state of SE India, on the Bay of Bengal: formed in 1953 from parts of Tamil Nadu (then called Madras) and Hyderabad states. Capital: Hyderabad. Pop: 75 727 541 (2001). Area: about 275 068 sq km (106 204 sq miles)

andiron ('ændˌaɪən) *n* another name for **firedog** [C14: from Old French *andier*, of unknown origin; influenced by IRON]

and/or *conj* (*coordinating*) used to join terms when either one or the other or both is indicated: *passports and/or other means of identification*

● USAGE Many people think that *and/or* is only
● acceptable in legal and commercial contexts. In other
● contexts, it is better to use *or both: some alcoholics lose*
● *their jobs or their driving licences or both* (not *their jobs and/or*
● *their driving licences*)

Andong ('æn'dʊŋ) *n* another name for **Dandong**. Former spelling: Tan-tung

Andorra (æn'dɔːrə) *n* a mountainous principality in SW Europe, between France and Spain: according to tradition, given independence by Charlemagne in the 9th century for helping to fight the Moors; placed under the joint sovereignty of the Comte de Foix and the Spanish bishop of Urgel in 1278; under the joint overlordship of the French head of state and the bishop of Urgel from the 16th century; adopted a constitution reducing the powers of the overlords in 1993. Languages: Catalan (official), French, and Spanish. Religion: Roman Catholic. Currency: euro. Capital: Andorra la Vella. Pop: 71 000 (2003 est). Area: 464 sq km (179 sq miles) ▷ An'dorran *adj, n*

Andorra la Vella (*Catalan* an'dɔrra la 'veʎa) *n* the capital of Andorra, situated in the west of the principality. Pop: 22 035 (2003 est)

Andrássy (æn'dræsɪ; *Hungarian* 'ɔndra:ʃi) *n* Count **Gyula** ('djulɒ). 1823–90, Hungarian statesman; the first prime minister of Hungary under the Dual Monarchy of Austria-Hungary (1867)

André ('ɑ:ndreɪ, 'ændrɪ) *n* **John**. 1751–80, British major who was hanged as a spy for conspiring with Benedict Arnold during the War of American Independence

Andrea del Sarto (*Italian* an'drea del 'sarto) *n* See **Sarto**

Andreanof Islands (ˌændrɪ'ɑ:nɒf) *pl n* a group of islands in the central Aleutian Islands, Alaska. Area: 3710 sq km (1432 sq miles)

Andretti (æn'drɛtɪ) *n* **Mario**. born 1940, US racing driver: world champion (1978)

Andrew ('ændru:) *n* *New Testament* **Saint**. one of the twelve apostles of Jesus; the brother of Peter; patron saint of Scotland. Feast day: Nov 30

Andrewes ('ændru:z) *n* **Lancelot**. 1555–1626, English bishop and theologian

Andrews ('ændru:z) *n* **Thomas**. 1813–85, Irish physical chemist, noted for his work on the liquefaction of gases

Andrić (*Serbo-Croat* 'andritʃ) *n* **Ivo** ('i:vɔ). 1892–1975, Serbian novelist; author of *The Bridge on the Drina* (1945): Nobel prize for literature 1961

andro- or before a vowel **andr-** *combining form* **1** male; masculine: *androsterone* **2** (in botany) stamen or anther: *androecium* [from Greek *anēr* (genitive *andros*) man]

Androcles ('ændrəˌkli:z) or **Androclus** ('ændrəkləs) *n* (in Roman legend) a slave whose life was spared in the arena by a lion from whose paw he had once extracted a thorn

androecium (æn'dri:sɪəm) *n*, *pl* -cia (-sɪə) the stamens of a flowering plant collectively [c19: from New Latin, from ANDRO- + Greek *oikion* a little house]

androgen ('ændrədʒən) *n* any of several steroids, produced as hormones by the testes or made synthetically, that promote development of male sexual organs and male secondary sexual characteristics > androgenic (ˌændrə'dʒɛnɪk) *adj*

androgyne ('ændrəˌdʒaɪn) *n* another word for **hermaphrodite** [c17: from Old French, via Latin from Greek *androgunos*, from *anēr* man + *gunē* woman]

androgynous (æn'drɒdʒɪnəs) *adj* **1** *botany* having male and female flowers in the same inflorescence, as cuckoo pint **2** having male and female characteristics; hermaphrodite > an'drogyny *n*

android ('ændrɔɪd) *n* **1** (in science fiction) a robot resembling a human being ▷ *adj* **2** resembling a human being [c18: from Late Greek *androeidēs* manlike; see ANDRO-, -OID]

andrology (æn'drɒlədʒɪ) *n* the branch of medicine concerned with diseases in men, esp of the reproductive organs [c20: from ANDRO- + -LOGY] > an'drologist *n*

Andromache (æn'drɒməkɪ) *n* *Greek myth* the wife of Hector

Andromeda (æn'drɒmɪdə) *n* *Greek myth* the daughter of Cassiopeia and wife of Perseus, who saved her from a sea monster

Andropov¹ (æn'drɒpɒv; *Russian* ən'drɔ:pəf) *n* a former name (1984–91) for **Rybinsk**

Andropov² (æn'drɒpɒv; *Russian* ən'drɔ:pəf) *n* **Yuri Vladimirovich**. 1914–84, Soviet statesman; president of the Soviet Union (1983–84)

Andros ('ændrəs) *n* **1** an island in the Aegean Sea, the northernmost of the Cyclades: long famous for wine. Capital: Andros. Pop: 10 009 (2001). Area: about 311 sq km (120 sq miles) **2** an island in the N Caribbean, the largest of the Bahamas. Pop: 7686 (2000). Area: 4144 sq km (1600 sq miles)

androsterone (æn'drɒstəˌrəun) *n* an androgenic steroid hormone produced in the testes. Formula: $C_{19}H_{30}O_2$

-androus *adj combining form* (in botany) indicating number or type of stamens: *diandrous* [from New Latin -*andrus*, from Greek -*andros*, from *anēr* man]

Andvari (æn'dwɑ:rɪ) *n* *Norse myth* a dwarf who possessed a treasure hoard, which was robbed by Loki

ane (eɪn) *determiner, pron, n* a Scottish word for **one**

-ane *suffix forming nouns* indicating an alkane hydrocarbon: *hexane* [coined to replace -*ene*, -*ine*, and -*one*]

anecdotage ('ænɪkˌdəutɪdʒ) *n* *humorous* talkative or garrulous old age [from ANECDOTE + -AGE, with play on *dotage*]

anecdotal (ˌænɛk'dəut²l) *adj* containing or consisting exclusively of anecdotes rather than connected discourse or research conducted under controlled conditions

anecdote ('ænɪkˌdəut) *n* a short usually amusing account of an incident, esp a personal or biographical one [c17: from Medieval Latin *anecdota* unpublished items, from Greek *anekdotos* unpublished, from AN- + *ekdotos* published, from *ekdidonai*, from *ek-* out + *didonai* to give] > ˌanec'dotalist or ˌanec'dotist *n*

anechoic (ˌænɪ'kəuɪk) *adj* having a low degree of reverberation of sound: *an anechoic recording studio*

Aneirin (ə'naɪ²rɪn) *n* 6th century AD, Welsh poet. His Y *Gododdin*, preserved in *The Book of Aneirin* (?1250), is one of the earliest surviving Welsh poems

anemia (ə'ni:mɪə) *n* the usual US spelling of **anaemia** [c19: from New Latin, from Greek *anaimia* lack of blood] > anemic (ə'ni:mɪk) *adj*

anemo- *combining form* indicating wind: *anemometer*; *anemophilous* [from Greek *anemos* wind]

anemograph (ə'nɛməuˌgrɑ:f) *n* a self-recording anemometer

anemometer (ˌænɪ'mɒmɪtə) *n* Also called: **wind gauge** an instrument for recording the speed and often the direction of winds > anemometric (ˌænɪməu'mɛtrɪk) or ˌanemo'metrical *adj* > anemometry (ˌænɪ'mɒmɪtrɪ) *n*

anemone (ə'nɛmənɪ) *n* any ranunculaceous woodland plant of the genus *Anemone* of N temperate regions, such as the white-flowered *A. nemorosa* (**wood anemone** or **windflower**). Some cultivated anemones have lilac, pale blue, pink, purple, or red flowers [c16: via Latin from Greek: windflower, from *anemos* wind]

anemophilous (ˌænɪ'mɒfɪləs) *adj* (of flowering plants such as grasses) pollinated by the wind > ˌane'mophily *n*

anent (ə'nɛnt) *prep Scot* **1** lying against; alongside **2** concerning; about [Old English on *efen*, literally: on even (ground)]

aneroid ('ænəˌrɔɪd) *adj* not containing a liquid [c19: from French, from AN- + Greek *nēros* wet + -OID]

aneroid barometer *n* a device for measuring atmospheric pressure without the use of fluids. It consists of a partially evacuated metal chamber, the thin corrugated lid of which is displaced by variations in the external air pressure. This displacement is magnified by levers and made to operate a pointer

anesthesia (ˌænɪs'θi:zɪə) *n* the usual US spelling of **anaesthesia**

anesthesiologist (ˌænɪsˌθi:zɪ'ɒlədʒɪst) *n* the US name for **anaesthetist**

anesthesiology (ˌænɪsˌθi:zɪ'ɒlədʒɪ) *n* the US name for **anaesthetics**

anesthetic (ˌænɪs'θɛtɪk) *n, adj* the usual US spelling of **anaesthetic**

anesthetist (ə'nɛsθətɪst) *n* (in the US) a person qualified to administer anaesthesia, often a nurse or someone other than a physician

Aneto (*Spanish* a'neto) *n* **Pico de Aneto** ('piko de) a mountain in N Spain, near the French border: the highest in the Pyrenees. Height: 3404 m (11 168 ft)

aneurysm or **aneurism** ('ænjəˌrɪzəm) *n* a sac formed by abnormal dilation of the weakened wall of a blood vessel [c15: from Greek *aneurusma*, from *aneurunein* to dilate, from *eurunein* to widen]

anew (ə'nju:) *adv* **1** over again; once more **2** in a different way; afresh [Old English of *nīwe*; see OF, NEW]

Anfinsen ('ænfɪnsən) *n* **Christian Boehmer**. 1916–95, US biochemist, noted for his research on the structure of enzymes. Nobel prize for chemistry 1972

Angara (*Russian* anga'ra) *n* a river in S Russia, in Siberia, flowing from Lake Baikal north and west to the Yenisei River: important for hydroelectric power. Length: 1840 km (1150 miles)

angary ('æŋgərɪ) *n* *international law* the right of a belligerent state to use the property of a neutral state or to destroy it if necessary, subject to payment of full compensation to the owners [c19: from French *angarie*, from Late Latin *angaria* enforced service, from Greek *angareia* office of a courier, from *angaros* courier, of Persian origin]

angel ('eɪndʒəl) *n* **1** *theol* one of a class of spiritual beings attendant upon God. In medieval angelology they are divided by rank into nine orders: seraphim, cherubim, thrones, dominations (or dominions), virtues, powers, principalities (or princedoms), archangels, and angels **2** a divine messenger from God **3** a guardian spirit **4** a conventional representation of any of these beings, depicted in human form with wings **5** *informal* a person, esp a woman, who is kind, pure, or beautiful **6** *informal* an investor in a venture, esp a backer of a theatrical production **7** Also called: angel-noble a former English gold coin with a representation of the archangel Michael on it, first minted in Edward IV's reign **8** *informal* an unexplained signal on a radar screen [Old English, from Late Latin *angelus*, from Greek *angelos* messenger]

angel cake *or esp US* **angel food cake** *n* a very light sponge cake made without egg yolks

angel dust *n* a slang name for PCP

Angel Falls *n* a waterfall in SE Venezuela, on the Caroní River; regarded as the highest in the world. Height: 979 m (3212 ft)

angelfish ('eɪndʒəl,fɪʃ) *n, pl* -fish *or* -fishes **1** any of various small tropical marine percoid fishes of the genus *Pomacanthus* and related genera, which have a deep flattened brightly coloured body and brushlike teeth: family *Chaetodontidae* **2** Also called: scalare a South American cichlid, *Pterophyllum scalare*, of the Amazon region, having a compressed body and large dorsal and anal fins: a popular aquarium fish

angel hair *or* **angel's hair** *n* a kind of pasta in the shape of very fine long strands

angelic (æn'dʒɛlɪk) *adj* **1** of or relating to angels **2** Also called: angelical resembling an angel in beauty, purity, etc > an'gelically *adv*

angelica (æn'dʒɛlɪkə) *n* **1** Also called: archangel any tall umbelliferous plant of the genus *Angelica*, having compound leaves and clusters of small white or greenish flowers, esp *A. archangelica*, the aromatic seeds, leaves, and stems of which are used in medicine and cookery **2** the candied stems of this plant, used for decorating and flavouring sweet dishes [c16: from Medieval Latin (*herba*) *angelica* angelic (herb)]

Angelic Doctor *n* an epithet of Saint Thomas Aquinas

Angelico (Italian an'dʒɛ:liko) *n* **Fra** (fra), original name *Guido di Pietro;* monastic name *Fra Giovanni da Fiesole.* ?1400–55, Italian fresco painter and Dominican friar

angel investor *n* same as **business angel**

Angell ('eɪndʒəl) *n* Sir **Norman**, real name *Ralph Norman Angell Lane.* 1874–1967, English writer, pacifist, and economist, noted for his work on the economic futility of war, *The Great Illusion* (1910): Nobel peace prize 1933

Angel of the North *n* a steel sculpture of an angel with wide-open arms, created in 1998 by British sculptor Antony Gormley, which stands on a hilltop outside Gateshead, NE England. It stands 20 m (85 ft) high and has a wingspan of 54 m (175 ft)

Angelou ('ændʒəlu:) *n* **Maya**, real name *Marguerite Johnson.* born 1928, US Black novelist, poet, and dramatist. Her works include the autobiographical novel *I Know Why the Caged Bird Sings* (1970) and its sequels

angel shark *or* **angelfish** *n* any of several sharks constituting the family *Squatinidae*, such as *Squatina squatina*, that have very large flattened pectoral fins and occur in the Atlantic and Pacific Oceans. Also called: monkfish

Angelus ('ændʒɪləs) *n* **RC Church 1** a series of prayers recited in the morning, at midday, and in the evening, commemorating the Annunciation and Incarnation **2** the bell (**Angelus bell**) signalling these prayers [c17: Latin, from the phrase *Angelus domini nuntiavit Mariae* the angel of the Lord brought tidings to Mary]

anger ('æŋgə) *n* **1** a feeling of great annoyance or antagonism as the result of some real or supposed grievance; rage; wrath ▷ *vb* **2** (*tr*) to make angry; enrage [c12: from Old Norse *angr* grief; related to Old English *enge*, Old High German *engi* narrow, Latin *angere* to strangle]

Angers (*French* ã3e) *n* a city in W France, on the River Maine. Pop: 151 279 (1999)

Angevin ('ændʒɪvɪn) *n* **1** a native or inhabitant of Anjou **2** *history* a member of the Plantagenet royal line descended from Geoffrey, Count of Anjou, esp one of the kings of England from Henry II to John (1154–1216) ▷ *adj* **3** of or relating to Anjou or its inhabitants **4** of or relating to the Plantagenet kings of England between 1154 and 1216 [from French, from medieval Latin *Andegavinus*, from *Andegavum*, ANGERS capital of ANJOU]

angina (æn'dʒaɪnə) *n* **1** any disease marked by painful attacks of spasmodic choking, such as Vincent's angina and quinsy **2** Also called: angina pectoris ('pɛktərɪs) a sudden intense pain in the chest, often accompanied by feelings of suffocation, caused by momentary lack of adequate blood supply to the heart muscle [c16: from Latin: quinsy, from Greek *ankhonē* a strangling]

angio- *or before a vowel* **angi-** *combining form* indicating a blood or lymph vessel; seed vessel [from Greek *angeion* vessel]

angioma (,ændʒɪ'əumə) *n, pl* -mas *or* -mata (-mətə) a tumour consisting of a mass of blood vessels (**haemangioma**) or a mass of lymphatic vessels (**lymphangioma**)

angioplasty ('ændʒɪə,plæstɪ) *n* a surgical technique for restoring normal blood flow through an artery narrowed or blocked by atherosclerosis, either by inserting a balloon into the narrowed section and inflating it or by using a laser beam

angiosperm ('ændʒɪə,spɜ:m) *n* any seed-bearing plant of the phylum *Angiospermophyta* (division *Angiospermae* in traditional systems), in which the ovules are enclosed in an ovary, which develops into the fruit after fertilization; any flowering plant. See **gymnosperm** > ,angio'spermous *adj*

Angkor ('æŋkɔ:) *n* a large area of ruins in NW Cambodia, containing **Angkor Thom** (tɔ:m), the capital of the former Khmer Empire, and **Angkor Wat** (wɒt), a three-storey temple, which were overgrown with dense jungle from the 14th to 19th centuries

angle¹ ('æŋgəl) *n* **1** the space between two straight lines that diverge from a common point or between two planes that extend from a common line **2** the shape formed by two such lines or planes **3** the extent to which one such line or plane diverges from another, measured in degrees or radians **4** an angular projection or recess; corner **5** standpoint; point of view: *look at the question from another angle; the angle of a newspaper article* **6** See **angle iron** ▷ *vb* **7** to move in or bend into angles or an angle **8** (*tr*) to produce (an article, statement, etc) with a particular point of view **9** (*tr*) to present, direct, or place at an angle **10** (*intr*) to turn or bend in a different direction [c14: from French, from Old Latin *angulus* corner]

angle² ('æŋgəl) *vb* (*intr*) **1** to fish with a hook and line **2** (often foll *by for*) to attempt to get: *he angled for a compliment* ▷ *n* **3** *obsolete* any piece of fishing tackle, esp a hook [Old English *angul* fish-hook; related to Old High German *ango*, Latin *uncus*, Greek *onkos*]

Angle ('æŋgəl) *n* a member of a West Germanic people from N Germany who invaded and settled large parts of E and N England in the 5th and 6th centuries AD [from Latin *Anglus*, from Germanic (compare ENGLISH), an inhabitant of *Angul*, a district in Schleswig (now *Angeln*), a name identical with Old English *angul* hook, ANGLE², referring to its shape] > 'Anglian *adj, n*

angledug ('æŋgəl,dʌg) *n Southwestern English dialect* an earthworm. Also called: angletwitch

angle iron *n* Also called: angle, angle bar an iron or a steel structural bar that has an L-shaped cross section

angle of incidence *n* **1** the angle that a line or beam of radiation makes with the normal to the surface at the point of incidence **2** Also called: rigging angle of incidence the angle between the chord line of an aircraft wing or tailplane and the aircraft's longitudinal axis

angle of reflection *n* the angle that a beam of reflected radiation makes with the normal to a surface at the point of reflection

angle of refraction *n* the angle that a refracted beam of radiation makes with the normal to the surface between two media at the point of refraction

angle of repose *n* the maximum angle to the horizontal at which rocks, soil, etc, will remain without sliding

angler ('æŋglə) *n* **1** a person who fishes with a rod and line **2** Also called: **angler fish** any spiny-finned fish of the order *Pediculati* (or *Lophiiformes*). They live at the bottom of the sea and typically have a long spiny movable dorsal fin with which they lure their prey

Anglesey ('æŋgᵊlsɪ) *n* an island and county of N Wales, formerly part of Gwynedd (1974–96), separated from the mainland by the Menai Strait. Administrative centre: Llangefni. Pop: 59 500 (2003 est). Area: 720 sq km (278 sq miles)

Anglia ('æŋglɪə) *n* a Latin name for **England**

Anglican ('æŋglɪkən) *adj* **1** denoting or relating to the Anglican communion ▷ *n* **2** a member of the Church of England or one of the Churches in full communion with it [C17: from Medieval Latin *Anglicānus,* from *Anglicus* English, from Latin *Anglī* the Angles] > 'Anglica,nism *n*

Anglicism ('æŋglɪ,sɪzəm) *n* **1** a word, phrase, or idiom peculiar to the English language, esp as spoken in England **2** an English attitude, custom, etc **3** the fact or quality of being English

anglicize, anglicise ('æŋglɪ,saɪz) *or* **anglify** ('æŋglɪ,faɪ) *vb* -**cizes**, -**cizing**, -**cized**, -**cises**, -**cising**, -**cised** *or* -**fies**, -**fying**, -**fied** (*sometimes capital*) to make or become English in outlook, attitude, form, etc

angling ('æŋglɪŋ) *n* the art or sport of catching fish with a rod and line and a baited hook or other lure, such as a fly; fishing

Anglo ('æŋgləʊ) *n*, *pl* -**glos 1** *US* a White inhabitant of the United States who is not of Latin extraction **2** *Canad* an English-speaking Canadian, esp one of Anglo-Celtic origin; an Anglo-Canadian

Anglo- ('æŋgləʊ-) *combining form* denoting English or England: *Anglo-Saxon* [from Medieval Latin *Anglī*]

Anglo-American *adj* **1** of or relating to relations between England and the United States or their peoples ▷ *n* **2** *chiefly US* an inhabitant or citizen of the United States who was or whose ancestors were born in England

Anglo-Catholic *adj* **1** of or relating to a group within the Church of England or the Anglican Communion that emphasizes the Catholic elements in its teaching and practice ▷ *n* **2** a member of this group > Anglo-Ca'tholi,cism *n*

Anglo-Egyptian Sudan *n* the former name (1899–1956) of the **Sudan**

Anglo-French *adj* **1** of or relating to England and France **2** of or relating to Anglo-French ▷ *n* **3** the Norman-French language of medieval England

Anglo-Indian *adj* **1** of or relating to England and India **2** denoting or relating to Anglo-Indians **3** (of a word) introduced into English from an Indian language ▷ *n* **4** a person of mixed English and Indian descent **5** an English person who lives or has lived for a long time in India

Anglomania (,æŋgləʊ'meɪnɪə) *n* excessive respect for English customs, etc > Anglo'mani,ac *n*, *adj*

Anglo-Norman *history* ▷ *adj* **1** relating to the Norman conquerors of England, their society, or their language ▷ *n* **2** a Norman inhabitant of England after 1066 **3** the Anglo-French language

Anglophile ('æŋgləʊfɪl, -,faɪl) *or* **Anglophil** *n* a person having admiration for the English or the English

Anglophobe ('æŋgləʊ,fəʊb) *n* **1** a person who hates or fears England or its people **2** *Canadian* a person who hates or fears Canadian Anglophones > Anglo'phobia *n* > Anglo'phobic *adj*

Anglophone ('æŋglə,fəʊn) (*often not capital*) *n* **1** a person who speaks English, esp a native speaker ▷ *adj*

2 speaking English

Anglo-Saxon *n* **1 a** member of any of the West Germanic tribes (Angles, Saxons, and Jutes) that settled in Britain from the 5th century AD and were dominant until the Norman conquest **2** the language of these tribes. See **Old English 3** any White person whose native language is English and whose cultural affiliations are those common to Britain and the US **4** *informal* plain blunt English, esp English containing taboo words ▷ *adj* **5** forming part of the Germanic element in Modern English: *"forget" is an Anglo-Saxon word* **6** of or relating to the Anglo-Saxons or the Old English language **7** of or relating to the White Protestant culture of Britain, Australia, and the US

Anglosphere ('æŋgləʊ,sfɪə) *n* a group of English-speaking countries that share common roots in British culture and history, usually the UK, the US, Australia, New Zealand, and Canada

Angola (æŋ'gəʊlə) *n* a republic in SW Africa, on the Atlantic: includes the enclave of Cabinda, north of the River Congo; a Portuguese possession from 1575 until its independence in 1975; multiparty constitution adopted in 1991; factional violence. It consists of a narrow coastal plain with a large fertile plateau in the east. Currency: kwanza. Religion: Christian majority. Capital: Luanda. Pop: 14 078 000 (2004 est). Area: 1 246 693 sq km (481 351 sq miles) > An'golan *adj*, *n*

angophora (æŋ'gɒfərə) *n* any tree of the genus *Angophora,* related to the eucalyptus and native to E Australia [New Latin, from Greek *angeion* vessel + *phoreus* bearer]

angora (æŋ'gɔːrə) *n* (*sometimes capital*) **a** the long soft hair of the outer coat of the Angora goat or the fur of the Angora rabbit **b** yarn, cloth, or clothing made from this hair **c** (*as modifier*): *an angora sweater*. See also **mohair** [from *angora,* former name of Ankara, in Turkey]

Angora goat *n* a breed of domestic goat with long soft hair

Angora rabbit *n* a breed of rabbit with long usually white silky hair

Angostura (Spanish aŋgos'tura) *n* the former name (1764–1846) for **Ciudad Bolívar**

angostura bark (,æŋgə'stjʊərə) *n* the bitter aromatic bark of certain South American rutaceous trees of the genus *Cusparia* or *Galipea,* formerly used medicinally to reduce fever [C18 from ANGOSTURA]

Angostura bitters (,æŋgə'stjʊərə) *pl n trademark* a bitter aromatic tonic made from gentian and various spices and vegetable colourings, used as a flavouring in alcoholic drinks

angry ('æŋgrɪ) *adj* -**grier**, -**griest 1** feeling or expressing annoyance, animosity, or resentment; enraged **2** suggestive of anger: *angry clouds* **3** severely inflamed: *an angry sore* > 'angrily *adv*
● USAGE It was formerly considered incorrect to talk
● about being *angry at* a person, but this use is now
● acceptable

angst (æŋst; *German* aŋst) *n* an acute but nonspecific sense of anxiety or remorse [German]

angstrom ('æŋstrʌm, -strəm) *n* Also called: **angstrom unit** a unit of length equal to 10^{-10} metre, used principally to express the wavelengths of electromagnetic radiations. It is equivalent to 0.1 nanometre. Symbol: Å or A [C20: named after Anders J. *Ångström* (1814–74), Swedish physicist]

Ångström ('æŋstrəm; *Swedish* 'ɔŋstrœm) *n* **Anders Jonas** ('andərs 'juːnas). 1814–74, Swedish physicist, noted for his work on spectroscopy and solar physics

Anguilla (æŋ'gwɪlə) *n* an island in the Caribbean, in the Leeward Islands: part of the British associated state of St Kitts-Nevis-Anguilla from 1967 until 1980, when it reverted to the status of a British dependency and is now a UK Overseas Territory. Pop: 12 000 (2003 est). Area: 90 sq km (35 sq miles)

anguine ('æŋgwɪn) *adj* of, relating to, or similar to a snake [C17: from Latin *anguīnus,* from *anguis* snake]

anguish ('æŋgwɪʃ) *n* **1** extreme pain or misery; mental or physical torture; agony ▷ *vb* **2** to afflict or be afflicted with anguish [C13: from Old French *angoisse* a strangling,

from Latin *angustia* narrowness, from *angustus* narrow]
> 'anguished *adj*

angular ('æŋgjʊlə) *adj* **1** lean or bony **2** awkward or stiff in manner or movement **3** having an angle or angles **4** placed at an angle **5** measured by an angle or by the rate at which an angle changes [c15: from Latin *angulāris*, from *angulus* ANGLE¹]

angularity (ˌæŋgjʊ'lærɪtɪ) *n, pl* -ties **1** the condition of being angular **2** an angular form or shape

Angus ('æŋgəs) *n* a council area of E Scotland on the North Sea: the historical county of Angus became part of Tayside region in 1975; reinstated as a unitary authority (excluding City of Dundee) in 1996. Administrative centre: Forfar. Pop: 107 520 (2003 est). Area: 2181 sq km (842 sq miles)

Angus Og (əʊg) *n Irish myth* the god of love and beauty

Anhalt (*German* 'anhalt) *n* a former duchy and state of central E Germany, now part of the state of Saxony-Anhalt: part of East Germany until 1990

anhedral (æn'hiːdrəl) *n* the downward inclination of an aircraft wing in relation to the lateral axis

Anhui or **Anhwei** ('æn'weɪ) *n* a province of E China, crossed by the Yangtze River. Capital: Hefei. Pop: 64 100 000 (2003 est). Area: 139 860 sq km (54 000 sq miles)

anhydride (æn'haɪdraɪd, -drɪd) *n* **1** a compound that has been formed from another compound by dehydration **2** a compound that forms an acid or base when added to water [c19: from ANHYDR(OUS) + -IDE]

anhydrous (æn'haɪdrəs) *adj* containing no water, esp no water of crystallization [c19: from Greek *anudros*; see AN-, HYDRO-]

Aniakchak (ˌænɪ'æktʃæk) *n* an active volcanic crater in SW Alaska, on the Alaska Peninsula: the largest explosion crater in the world. Height: 1347 m (4420 ft). Diameter: 9 km (6 miles)

anil ('ænɪl) *n* a leguminous West Indian shrub, *Indigofera suffruticosa*: a source of indigo. Also called: indigo [c16: from Portuguese, from Arabic *an-nīl*, the indigo, from Sanskrit *nīla* dark blue]

aniline ('ænɪlɪn, -ˌliːn) *n* a colourless oily pungent poisonous liquid used in the manufacture of dyes, plastics, pharmaceuticals, and explosives. Formula: $C_6H_5NH_2$

aniline dye *n* any synthetic dye originally made from raw materials, such as aniline, obtained from coal tar

anima ('ænɪmə) *n* (in Jungian psychology) **a** the feminine principle as present in the male unconscious **b** the inner personality, which is in communication with the unconscious [Latin: air, breath, spirit, feminine of ANIMUS]

animadversion (ˌænɪmæd'vɜːʃən) *n* criticism or censure

animadvert (ˌænɪmæd'vɜːt) *vb* (*intr*) **1** (usually foll by *on* or *upon*) to comment with strong criticism (upon); make censorious remarks (about) **2** to make an observation or comment [c16: from Latin *animadvertere* to notice, pay attention, from *animus* mind + *advertere* to turn to, from *vertere* to turn]

animal ('ænɪməl) *n* **1** *zoology* any living organism characterized by voluntary movement, the possession of cells with noncellulose cell walls and specialized sense organs enabling rapid response to stimuli, and the ingestion of complex organic substances such as plants and other animals **2** any mammal, esp any mammal except man **3** a brutish person **4** *facetious* a person or thing (esp in the phrase **no such animal**) ▷ *adj* **5** of, relating to, or derived from animals **6** of or relating to the physical needs or desires; carnal; sensual [c14: from Latin *animal* (n), from *animālis* (adj) living, breathing; see ANIMA]

animalcule (ˌænɪ'mælkjuːl) *n, pl* -cules or -cula (-kjʊlə) a microscopic animal such as an amoeba or rotifer [c16: from New Latin *animalculum* a small ANIMAL] > ˌani'malcular *adj*

animal husbandry *n* the science of breeding, rearing, and caring for farm animals

animalism ('ænɪməˌlɪzəm) *n* **1** satisfaction of or preoccupation with physical matters; sensuality **2** the doctrine or belief that man lacks a spiritual nature **3** a

trait or mode of behaviour typical of animals

animality (ˌænɪ'mælɪtɪ) *n* **1** the animal side of man, as opposed to the intellectual or spiritual **2** the fact of being or having the characteristics of an animal

animalize or **animalise** ('ænɪməˌlaɪz) *vb* (*tr*) to rouse to brutality or sensuality or make brutal or sensual > ˌanimali'zation or ˌanimali'sation *n*

animal magnetism *n* **1** *sometimes facetious* the quality of being attractive, esp to members of the opposite sex **2** *obsolete* hypnotism

animal rights *pl n* **a** the rights of animals to be protected from exploitation and abuse by humans **b** (*as modifier*): *the animal-rights lobby*

animate *vb* ('ænɪˌmeɪt) (*tr*) **1** to give life to or cause to come alive **2** to make lively; enliven **3** to encourage or inspire **4** to impart motion to; move to action or work **5** to record on film or video tape so as to give movement to ▷ *adj* ('ænɪmɪt) **6** being alive or having life **7** gay, spirited, or lively [c16: from Latin *animāre* to fill with breath, make alive, from *anima* breath, spirit]

animated cartoon *n* a film produced by photographing a series of gradually changing drawings, etc, which give the illusion of movement when the series is projected rapidly

animation (ˌænɪ'meɪʃən) *n* **1** liveliness; vivacity **2** the condition of being alive **3** the techniques used in the production of animated cartoons

animato (ˌænɪ'mɑːtəʊ) *adj, adv music* (to be performed) in a lively manner [Italian]

animatronics (ˌænɪmə'trɒnɪks) *n* (*functioning as singular*) a branch of film and theatre technology that combines traditional puppetry techniques with electronics to create lifelike animated effects [c20: from ANIMA(TION) + (ELEC)TRONICS]

animé ('ænɪˌmeɪ, -mɪ) *n* any of various resins, esp that obtained from the tropical American leguminous tree *Hymenaea courbaril* [French: of uncertain origin]

animism ('ænɪˌmɪzəm) *n* **1** the belief that natural objects, phenomena, and the universe itself have desires and intentions **2** (in the philosophies of the Greek philosophers Plato (?427–?347 BC) and Pythagoras (?580–?500 BC)) the hypothesis that there is an immaterial force that animates the universe [c19: from Latin *anima* vital breath, spirit] > 'animist *n* > ani'mistic *adj*

animosity (ˌænɪ'mɒsɪtɪ) *n, pl* -ties a powerful and active dislike or hostility; enmity [c15: from Late Latin *animōsitās*, from Latin *animōsus* spirited, from ANIMUS]

animus ('ænɪməs) *n* **1** intense dislike; hatred; animosity **2** motive, intention, or purpose **3** (in Jungian psychology) the masculine principle present in the female unconscious [c19: from Latin: mind, spirit]

anion ('æn,aɪən) *n* a negatively charged ion; an ion that is attracted to the anode during electrolysis. See **cation** [c19: from ANA- + ION] > anionic (ˌænaɪ'ɒnɪk) *adj*

anise ('ænɪs) *n* a Mediterranean umbelliferous plant, *Pimpinella anisum*, having clusters of small yellowish-white flowers and liquorice-flavoured seeds [c13: from Old French *anis*, via Latin from Greek *anison*]

aniseed ('ænɪˌsiːd) *n* the liquorice-flavoured aromatic seeds of the anise plant, used medicinally for expelling intestinal gas and in cookery as a flavouring, esp in cakes and confections

anisette (ˌænɪ'zɛt, -'sɛt) *n* a liquorice-flavoured liqueur made from aniseed [c19: from French; see ANISE, -ETTE]

anisotropic (æn,aɪsəʊ'trɒpɪk, ˌænaɪ-) *adj* **1** not isotropic; having different physical properties in different directions: *anisotropic crystals* **2** (of a plant) responding unequally to an external stimulus in different parts of the plant > an,iso'tropically *adv* > anisotropy (ˌænaɪ'sɒtrəpɪ) *n*

Anjou (*French* ɑ̃ʒu) *n* a former province of W France, in the Loire valley: a medieval countship from the 10th century, belonging to the English crown from 1154 until 1204; annexed by France in 1480. Related adj: **Angevin**

Ankara ('æŋkərə) *n* the capital of Turkey: an ancient city in the Anatolian highlands: first a capital in the 3rd century BC, in the Celtic kingdom of Galatia. Pop: 3 593 000 (2005 est)

ankh (æŋk) *n* a tau cross with a loop on the top, symbolizing eternal life: often appearing in Egyptian personal names, such as Tutankhamen [from Egyptian *'nh* life, soul]

Anking ('ɑːn'kɪŋ) *n* a variant transliteration of the Chinese name for **Anqing**

ankle ('æŋkəl) *n* **1** the joint connecting the leg and the foot **2** the part of the leg just above the foot [c14: from Old Norse; related to German, Dutch *enkel*, Latin *angulus* ANGLE¹]

ankle biter *n Austral slang* a child

anklebone ('æŋkəlˌbəʊn) *n* the nontechnical name for **talus¹**

anklet ('æŋklɪt) *n* an ornamental chain worn around the ankle

ankylose *or* **anchylose** ('æŋkɪˌləʊs, -ˌləʊz) *vb* (of bones in a joint, etc) to fuse or stiffen by ankylosis

ankylosis *or* **anchylosis** (ˌæŋkɪ'ləʊsɪs) *n* abnormal adhesion or immobility of the bones in a joint, as by a direct joining of the bones, a fibrous growth of tissues within the joint, or surgery [c18: from New Latin, from Greek *ankuloun* to crook] > **ankylotic** *or* **anchylotic** (ˌæŋkɪ'lɒtɪk) *adj*

An Lu Shan (æn luː ʃæn) *n* 703–57 AD, Chinese military governor. He declared himself emperor (756) and seized the capital Chang An; murdered by a eunuch slave

anna ('ænə) *n* a former Indian copper coin, worth one sixteenth of a rupee [c18: from Hindi *ānā*]

Annaba ('ænəbə) *n* a port in NE Algeria: site of the Roman ruins of Hippo Regius. Pop: 382 000 (2005 est). Former name: Bône

annals ('ænəlz) *pl n* **1** yearly records of events, generally in chronological order **2** history or records of history in general **3** regular reports of the work of a society, learned body, etc [c16: from Latin (*librī*) *annālēs* yearly (books), from *annus* year] > **annalist** *n* > **annal'istic** *adj*

Annan ('ænæn) *n* **Kofi** ('kəʊfɪ). born 1938, Ghanaian international civil servant; secretary-general of the United Nations (1997–2007): Nobel peace prize 2001 with the UN

Annapolis (ə'næpəlɪs) *n* the capital of Maryland, near the mouth of the Severn River on Chesapeake Bay: site of the US Naval Academy. Pop: 36 178 (2003 est)

Annapolis Royal *n* a town in SE Canada in W Nova Scotia on an arm of the Bay of Fundy: the first settlement in Canada (1605). Pop: 550 (2001). Former name (until 1710): Port Royal

Annapurna *or* **Anapurna** (ˌænə'pʊənə) *n* a massif in the Himalayas, in Nepal. Highest peak: 8078 m (26 502 ft)

Ann Arbor (æn 'ɑːbə) *n* a city in SE Michigan: seat of the University of Michigan. Pop: 114 498 (2003 est)

annates ('æneɪts, -əts) *pl n* RC Church the first year's revenue of a see, an abbacy, or a minor benefice, paid to the pope [c16: plural of French *annate*, from Medieval Latin *annāta*, from Latin *annus* year]

annatto *or* **anatto** (ə'nætəʊ) *n, pl* -tos **1** a small tropical American tree, *Bixa orellana*, having red or pinkish flowers and pulpy seeds that yield a dye: family Bixaceae **2** the yellowish-red dye obtained from the pulpy outer layer of the coat of the seeds of this tree, used for colouring fabrics, butter, varnish, etc [from Carib]

Anne (æn) *n* **1** *Princess*, the Princess Royal. born 1950, daughter of Elizabeth II of Great Britain and Northern Ireland; a noted horsewoman and president of the Save the Children Fund **2** *Queen*. 1665–1714, queen of Great Britain and Ireland (1702–14), daughter of James II, and the last of the Stuart monarchs **3** *Saint*. (in Christian tradition) the mother of the Virgin Mary. Feast day: July 26 or 25

anneal (ə'niːl) *vb* **1** to temper or toughen (something) by heat treatment **2** (*tr*) to toughen or strengthen (the will, determination, etc) ▷ *n* **3** an act of annealing [Old English *onǣlan*, from ON + *ǣlan* to burn, from *āl* fire] > **an'nealer** *n*

Anne Boleyn *n* See **Boleyn**

Annecy (French ansi) *n* **1** a city and resort in E France, on Lake Annecy. Pop: 50 348 (1999) **2** Lake Annecy a lake in E France, in the Alps

annelid ('ænəlɪd) *n* **1** any worms of the phylum *Annelida*,

in which the body is divided into segments both externally and internally. The group includes the earthworms, lugworm, ragworm, and leeches ▷ *adj* **2** of, relating to, or belonging to the *Annelida* [c19: from New Latin *Annelida*, from French *annelés*, literally: the ringed ones, from Old French *annel* ring, from Latin *ānellus*, from *ānulus* ring] > **annelidan** (ə'nɛlɪdən) *n, adj*

Anne of Austria *n* 1601–66, wife of Louis XIII of France and daughter of Philip III of Spain: regent of France (1643–61) for her son Louis XIV

Anne of Bohemia *n* 1366–94, queen consort of Richard II of England

Anne of Cleves (kliːvz) *n* 1515–57, the fourth wife of Henry VIII of England: their marriage (1540) was annulled after six months

Anne of Denmark *n* 1574–1619, wife (from 1589) of James I of England and VI of Scotland

annex *vb* (ə'nɛks) (*tr*) **1** to join or add, esp to something larger; attach **2** to add (territory) by conquest or occupation **3** to add or append as a condition, warranty, etc **4** to appropriate without permission ▷ *n* ('ænɛks) **5** a variant spelling (esp US) of **annexe** [c14: from Medieval Latin *annexāre*, from Latin *annectere* to attach to, from *nectere* to join] > **an'nexable** *adj* > **annexation** (ˌænɪk'seɪʃən, -ɛk-) *n* > ˌannex'ational *adj* > ˌannex'ationism *n* > ˌannex'ationist *n*

annexe *or esp US* **annex** ('ænɛks) *n* **1 a** an extension to a main building **b** a building used as an addition to a main building nearby **2** something added or annexed, esp a supplement to a document

Annigoni (*Italian* anni'goːni) *n* **Pietro** ('pjɛːtro). 1910–88, Italian painter; noted esp for his portraits of President Kennedy (1961) and Queen Elizabeth II (1955 and 1970)

annihilate (ə'naɪəˌleɪt) *vb* **1** (*tr*) to destroy completely; extinguish **2** (*tr*) *informal* to defeat totally, as in debate or argument [c16: from Late Latin *annihilāre* to bring to nothing, from Latin *nihil* nothing] > **an'nihiˌlator** *n* > **anˌnihi'lation** *n*

anniversary (ˌænɪ'vɜːsərɪ) *n, pl* -ries **1** the date on which an event occurred in some previous year: *a wedding anniversary* **2** the celebration of this ▷ *adj* **3** of or relating to an anniversary [c13: from Latin *anniversārius* returning every year, from *annus* year + *vertere* to turn]

anno Domini ('ænəʊ 'dɒmɪˌnaɪ, -ˌniː) *adv* **1** the full form of AD ▷ *n* **2** *informal* advancing old age [Latin: in the year of our Lord]

annotate ('ænəʊˌteɪt, 'ænə-) *vb* to supply (a written work, such as an ancient text) with critical or explanatory notes [c18: from Latin *annotāre*, from *nota* mark] > 'annoˌtative *adj* > 'annoˌtator *n*

announce (ə'naʊns) *vb* **1** (*tr; may take a clause as object*) to make known publicly; proclaim **2** (*tr*) to declare the arrival of: *to announce a guest* **3** (*tr; may take a clause as object*) to reveal to the mind or senses; presage: *the dark clouds announced rain* **4** (*intr*) to work as an announcer, as on radio or television [c15: from Old French *anoncer*, from Latin *annuntiāre*, from *nuntius* messenger]

announcement (ə'naʊnsmənt) *n* **1** a public statement **2** a brief item or advertisement, as in a newspaper **3** a formal printed or written invitation **4** the act of announcing

announcer (ə'naʊnsə) *n* a person who announces, esp one who reads the news, introduces programmes, etc, on radio or television

annoy (ə'nɔɪ) *vb* **1** to irritate or displease **2** to harass with repeated attacks [c13: from Old French *anoier*, from Late Latin *inodiāre* to make hateful, from Latin *in odiō* (*esse*) (to be) hated, from *odium* hatred] > **an'noyer** *n* > **a'nnoying** *adj* > **ann'oyingly** *adv*

annoyance (ə'nɔɪəns) *n* **1** the feeling of being annoyed **2** the act of annoying **3** a person or thing that annoys

annual ('ænjʊəl) *adj* **1** occurring, done, etc, once a year or every year; yearly: *an annual income* **2** lasting for a year: *an annual subscription* ▷ *n* **3** a plant that completes its life cycle in less than one year **4** a book, magazine, etc, published once every year [c14: from Late Latin *annuālis*, from Latin *annuus* yearly, from *annus* year] > 'annually *adv*

annual general meeting *n Brit* the statutory meeting of the directors and shareholders of a company or of the members of a society, held once every financial year, at which the annual report is presented. Abbreviation: **AGM**

annualize or **annualise** ('ænjʊəˌlaɪz) vb (tr) to convert (a rate of interest) to an annual rate when it is quoted for a period of less than a year: *credit card companies are obliged to quote an annualized percentage rate to borrowers*

annual percentage rate n the annual equivalent of a rate of interest when the rate is quoted more frequently than annually, usually monthly. Abbreviation: **APR**

annual ring n a ring of wood indicating one year's growth, seen in the transverse section of stems and roots of woody plants growing in temperate climates. Also called: **tree ring**

annuitant (ə'njuːɪtənt) n a person in receipt of or entitled to an annuity

annuity (ə'njuːɪtɪ) n, pl -ties a fixed sum payable at specified intervals, esp annually, over a period, such as the recipient's life, or in perpetuity, in return for a premium paid either in instalments or in a single payment [C15: from French *annuité*, from Medieval Latin *annuitās*, from Latin *annuus* ANNUAL]

annul (ə'nʌl) vb -nuls, -nulling, -nulled (tr) to make (something, esp a law or marriage) void; cancel the validity of; abolish [C14: from Old French *annuller*, from Late Latin *annullāre* to bring to nothing, from Latin *nullus* not any; see NULL] > an'nullable adj

annular ('ænjʊlə) adj ring-shaped; of or forming a ring [C16: from Latin *annulāris*, from *annulus*, *ānulus* ring]

annular eclipse n an eclipse of the sun in which the moon does not cover the entire disc of the sun, so that a ring of sunlight surrounds the shadow of the moon

annular ligament n anatomy any of various ligaments that encircle a part, such as the wrist, ankle, or trachea

annulate ('ænjʊlɪt, -ˌleɪt) adj having, composed of, or marked with rings [C19: from Latin *ānulātus*, from *ānulus* a ring] > ˌannu'lation n

annulet ('ænjʊlɪt) n 1 architect a moulding in the form of a ring, as at the top of a column adjoining the capital 2 heraldry a ring-shaped device on a shield; hollow roundel 3 a little ring [C16: from Latin *ānulus* ring + -ET]

annulment (ə'nʌlmənt) n 1 a formal invalidation, as of a marriage, judicial proceeding, etc 2 the act of annulling

annulus ('ænjʊləs) n, pl -li (-ˌlaɪ) or -luses 1 the area between two concentric circles 2 a ring-shaped part, figure, or space [C16: from Latin, variant of *ānulus* ring]

annunciate (ə'nʌnsɪˌeɪt, -ʃɪ-) vb (tr) a less common word for **announce** [C16: from *annunciātus*, Medieval Latin misspelling of *annuntiātus*, past participle of Latin *annuntiāre*; see ANNOUNCE]

Annunciation (əˌnʌnsɪ'eɪʃən) n 1 the Annunciation New Testament the announcement of the Incarnation by the angel Gabriel to the Virgin Mary (Luke 1:26–38) 2 Also called: **Annunciation Day** the festival commemorating this, held on March 25 (Lady Day)

annunciator (ə'nʌnsɪˌeɪtə) n 1 a device that gives a visual indication as to which of a number of electric circuits has operated, such as an indicator in a hotel showing in which room a bell has been rung 2 a device giving an audible signal indicating the position of a train

annus horribilis ('ænʊs hɒ'riːbɪlɪs) n a terrible year [C20: from Latin, modelled on ANNUS MIRABILIS, first used by Elizabeth II of the year 1992]

annus mirabilis Latin ('ænʊs mɪ'ræbɪlɪs) n, pl anni mirabiles ('ænaɪ mɪ'ræbɪliːz) a year of wonders, catastrophes, or other notable events

anoa (ə'nəʊə) n the smallest of the cattle tribe *Anoa depressicornis*, having small straight horns and inhabiting the island of Celebes in Indonesia [from a native name in Celebes]

anode ('ænəʊd) n 1 the positive electrode in an electrolytic cell 2 the negative terminal of a primary cell. ▷ See **cathode** [C19: from Greek *anodos* a way up, from *hodos* a way; alluding to the movement of the current to or from the positive pole] > anodal (eɪ'nəʊdᵊl) or anodic (ə'nɒdɪk) adj

anodize or **anodise** ('ænəˌdaɪz) vb to coat (a metal, such as aluminium) with a protective oxide

film by electrolysis

anodyne ('ænəˌdaɪn) n 1 a drug that relieves pain; analgesic 2 anything that alleviates mental distress ▷ adj 3 capable of relieving pain or distress [C16: from Latin *anōdynus*, from Greek *anōdunos* painless, from AN- + *odunē* pain]

anoint (ə'nɔɪnt) vb (tr) 1 to smear or rub over with oil or an oily liquid 2 to apply oil to as a sign of consecration or sanctification in a sacred rite [C14: from Old French *enoint*, from *enoindre*, from Latin *inunguere*, from *unguere* to smear with oil] > a'nointer n > a'nointment n

anointing of the sick n RC Church a sacrament in which a person who is seriously ill or dying is anointed by a priest with consecrated oil. Former name: **extreme unction**

anomalous (ə'nɒmələs) adj deviating from the normal or usual order, type, etc; irregular, abnormal, or incongruous [C17: from Late Latin *anōmalus*, from Greek *anōmalos* uneven, inconsistent, from AN- + *homalos* even, from *homos* one and the same] > a'nomalously adv > a'nomalousness n

anomaly (ə'nɒmalɪ) n, pl -lies 1 something anomalous 2 deviation from the normal or usual order, type, etc; irregularity 3 astronomy Also called: **true anomaly** the angle between a planet, the sun, and the previous perihelion of the planet

anomie or **anomy** ('ænəʊmɪ) n sociol lack of social or moral standards in an individual or society [from Greek *anomia* lawlessness, from A-¹ + *nomos* law] > anomic (ə'nɒmɪk) adj

anon (ə'nɒn) adv archaic or literary 1 in a short time; soon 2 ever and anon now and then [Old English *on āne*, literally: in one, that is, immediately]

anon. abbreviation anonymous

anonym ('ænənɪm) n 1 a less common word for **pseudonym** 2 an anonymous person or publication

anonymize or **anonymise** (ə'nɒnɪˌmaɪz) vb (tr) to carry out or organize in such a way as to preserve anonymity: *anonymized AIDS screening*

anonymous (ə'nɒnɪməs) adj 1 from or by a person, author, etc, whose name is unknown or withheld 2 having no known name 3 lacking individual characteristics; unexceptional 4 (often capital) denoting an organization which provides help to applicants who remain anonymous: *Alcoholics Anonymous* [C17: via Late Latin from Greek *anōnumos*, from AN- + *onoma* name] > anonymity (ˌænə'nɪmɪtɪ) n > a'nonymously adv > a'nonymousness n

anopheles (ə'nɒfɪˌliːz) n, pl -les any of various mosquitoes constituting the genus *Anopheles*, some species of which transmit the malaria parasite to man [C19: via New Latin from Greek *anōphelēs* useless, from AN- + *ōphelein* to help, from *ophelos* help]

anorak ('ænəˌræk) n 1 a warm waterproof hip-length jacket usually with a hood, originally worn in polar regions, but now worn for any outdoor activity 2 informal, dismissive a socially inept person with a hobby considered by most people to be boring [from Inuktitut *ánorâq*]

anorexia (ˌænɒ'rɛksɪə) n 1 loss of appetite 2 Also called: **anorexia nervosa** (nɜː'vəʊsə) a disorder characterized by fear of becoming fat and refusal of food, leading to debility and even death [C17: via New Latin from Greek, from AN- + *orexis* appetite] > ˌano'rectic or ˌano'rexic adj, n

anosmia (æn'ɒzmɪə, -ɒs-) n pathol loss of the sense of smell, usually as the result of a lesion of the olfactory nerve, disease in another organ or part, or obstruction of the nasal passages [C19: from New Latin, from AN- + Greek *osmē* smell, from *ozein* to smell] > anosmatic (ˌænɒz'mætɪk) or an'osmic adj

another (ə'nʌðə) determiner 1 a one more; an added: *another chance* b (as pronoun): *help yourself to another* 2 a a different; alternative: *another era from ours* b (as pronoun): *to try one path, then another* 3 a a different example of the same sort b (as pronoun): *we got rid of one loafer, but I think this new man's another* [C14: originally *an other*]

A.N. Other n Brit an unnamed person: used in team lists, etc, to indicate a place that remains to be filled

Anouilh (French anuj) n **Jean** (ʒɑ̃). 1910–87, French

dramatist, noted for his reinterpretations of Greek myths: his works include *Eurydice* (1942), *Antigone* (1944), and *Becket* (1959)

anoxia (æn'ɒksɪə) *n* lack or absence of oxygen [C20: from AN- + OX(YGEN) + -IA] > an'oxic *adj*

Anqing ('ɑːn'tʃɪŋ) *or* **Anking** *n* a city in E China, in SW Anhui province on the Yangtze River: famous seven-storeyed pagoda. Pop: 686 000 (2005 est)

Anschluss ('ænʃlʊs) *n* a political or economic union, esp the annexation of Austria by Nazi Germany (1938) [German: from *anschliessen* to join]

Anselm ('ænsɛlm) *n* **Saint**. 1033–1109, Italian Benedictine monk; archbishop of Canterbury (1093–1109): one of the founders of scholasticism; author of *Cur Deus Homo?* (*Why did God become Man?*). Feast day: Aug 21

anserine ('ænsəˌraɪn, -rɪn) *adj* of or resembling a goose [C19: from Latin *anserīnus*, from *anser* goose]

Ansermet (*French* ɑ̃sɛrmɛ) *n* **Ernest** (ɛrnɛst). 1883–1969, Swiss orchestral conductor; principal conductor of Diaghilev's Ballet Russe

answer ('ɑːnsə) *n* **1** a reply, either spoken or written, as to a question, request, letter, or article **2** a reaction or response in the form of an action: *drunkenness was his answer to disappointment* **3** a solution, esp of a mathematical problem ▷ *vb* **4** (when *tr, may take a clause as object*) to reply or respond (to) by word or act: *to answer a question; he answered; to answer the door; he answered that he would come* **5** (*tr*) to reply correctly to; solve or attempt to solve: *I could answer only three questions* **6** (*intr*; usually foll by *to*) to respond or react (to a stimulus, command, etc): *the steering answers to the slightest touch* **7** (when *intr*, often foll by *for*) to meet the requirements (of); be satisfactory (for); serve the purpose (of): *this will answer his needs; this will answer for a chisel* **8** (when *intr*, foll by *to*) to match or correspond (esp in the phrase **answer** (or **answer to**) **the description**) **9** (*tr*) to give a defence or refutation of (a charge) or in (an argument) [Old English *andswaru* an answer; related to Old Frisian *ondser*, Old Norse *andsvar*; see SWEAR]

answerable ('ɑːnsərəbᵊl) *adj* **1** (*postpositive*; foll by *for* or *to*) responsible or accountable: *answerable for someone's safety; answerable to one's boss* **2** able to be answered

answer back *vb* (*adverb*) to reply rudely to (a person, esp someone in authority) when one is expected to remain silent

answering machine *n* a device by means of which a telephone call is answered automatically and the caller enabled to leave a recorded message. Also called: answerphone

ant (ænt) *n* **1** any small social insect of the widely distributed hymenopterous family *Formicidae*, typically living in highly organized colonies of winged males, wingless sterile females (workers), and fertile females (queens), which are winged until after mating. Related adj: **formic 2** white ant another name for a **termite** [Old English *ǣmette*; related to Old High German *āmeiza*, Old Norse *meita*; see EMMET]

-ant *suffix forming adjectives, suffix forming nouns* causing or performing an action or existing in a certain condition; the agent that performs an action: *pleasant; claimant; deodorant; protestant; servant* [from Latin *-ant-*, ending of present participles of the first conjugation]

antacid (ænt'æsɪd) *n* **1** a substance used to neutralize acidity, esp in the stomach ▷ *adj* **2** having the properties of this substance

Antaeus (æn'tiːəs) *n Greek myth* an African giant who was invincible as long as he touched the ground, but was lifted into the air by Hercules and crushed to death

antagonism (æn'tægəˌnɪzəm) *n* **1** openly expressed and usually mutual opposition **2** the inhibiting or nullifying action of one substance or organism on another

antagonist (æn'tægənɪst) *n* **1** an opponent or adversary, as in a contest, drama, sporting event, etc **2** any muscle that opposes the action of another **3** a drug that counteracts the effects of another drug > antagonistic (ænˌtægə'nɪstɪk) *adj* > anˌtago'nistically *adv*

antagonize *or* **antagonise** (æn'tægəˌnaɪz) *vb* (*tr*) **1** to

make hostile; annoy or irritate **2** to act in opposition to or counteract [C17: from Greek *antagōnizesthai*, from ANTI- + *agōnizesthai* to strive, from *agōn* contest] > anˌtagoni'zation *or* anˌtagoni'sation *n*

Antakya (ɑn'tɑkjɑ) *n* the Turkish name for **Antioch**

antalkali (ænt'ælkəˌlaɪ) *n, pl* **-lis** *or* **-lies** a substance that neutralizes alkalis, esp one used to treat alkalosis

Antananarivo (ˌæntəˌnænə'riːvəʊ) *n* the capital of Madagascar, on the central plateau: founded in the 17th century by a Hova chief; university (1961). Pop: 1 808 000 (2005 est). Former name: Tananarive

Antarctic (ænt'ɑːktɪk) *n* **1** the Antarctic Also called: Antarctic Zone Antarctica and the surrounding waters ▷ *adj* **2** of or relating to the south polar regions [C14: via Latin from Greek *antarktikos*; see ANTI-, ARCTIC]

Antarctica (ænt'ɑːktɪkə) *n* a continent around the South Pole: consists of an ice-covered plateau, 1800–3000 m (6000 ft to 10 000 ft) above sea level, and mountain ranges rising to 4500 m (15 000 ft) with some volcanic peaks; average temperatures all below freezing and human settlement is confined to research stations. All political claims to the mainland are suspended under the Antarctic Treaty of 1959

Antarctic Archipelago *n* the former name of the Palmer Archipelago

Antarctic Circle *n* the imaginary circle around the earth, parallel to the equator, at latitude 66° 32′ S; it marks the southernmost point at which the sun appears above the level of the horizon at the winter solstice

Antarctic Ocean *n* the sea surrounding Antarctica, consisting of the most southerly parts of the Pacific, Atlantic, and Indian Oceans. Also called: Southern Ocean

Antarctic Peninsula *n* the largest peninsula of Antarctica, between the Weddell Sea and the Pacific: consists of Graham Land in the north and the Palmer Peninsula in the south. Former name (until 1964): Palmer Peninsula

ant bear *n* another name for **aardvark**

ante ('æntɪ) *n* **1** the gaming stake put up before the deal in poker by the players **2** *informal* a sum of money representing a person's share, as in a syndicate **3** up the ante *informal* to increase the costs, risks, or considerations involved in taking an action or reaching a conclusion ▷ *vb* **-tes**, **-teing**, **-ted** *or* **-teed 4** to place (one's stake) in poker **5** (usually foll by *up*) *informal, chiefly US* to pay

ante- *prefix* before in time or position; previous to; in front of: *antedate; antechamber* [from Latin]

anteater ('æntˌiːtə) *n* any toothless edentate mammal of the family *Myrmecophagidae* of Central and South America, esp *Myrmecophaga tridactyla* (or *jubata*) (**giant anteater**), having a long tubular snout used for eating termites

antebellum (ˌæntɪ'bɛləm) *adj* of or during the period before a war, esp the American Civil War [Latin *ante bellum*, literally: before the war]

antecede (ˌæntɪ'siːd) *vb* (*tr*) to go before, as in time, order, etc; precede [C17: from Latin *antecēdere*, from *cēdere* to go]

antecedent (ˌæntɪ'siːdᵊnt) *n* **1** an event, circumstance, etc, that happens before another **2** *grammar* a word or phrase to which a pronoun refers. In the sentence "People who live in glass houses shouldn't throw stones," *people* is the antecedent of *who* **3** *logic* the hypothetical clause, usually introduced by "if", in a conditional statement: that which implies the other ▷ *adj* **4** preceding in time or order; prior > ante'cedence *n*

antecedents (ˌæntɪ'siːdᵊnts) *pl n* **1** ancestry **2** a person's past history

antechamber ('æntɪˌtʃeɪmbə) *n* another name for **anteroom** [C17: from Old French, from Italian *anticamera*; see ANTE-, CHAMBER]

antedate *vb* (ˌæntɪ'deɪt, ˌæntɪ'deɪt) (*tr*) **1** to be or occur at an earlier date than **2** to affix a date to (a document, etc) that is earlier than the actual date **3** to cause to occur sooner ▷ *n* ('æntɪˌdeɪt) **4** an earlier date

antediluvian (ˌæntɪdɪˈluːvɪən, -daɪ-) *adj* **1** belonging to the ages before the biblical Flood (Genesis 7, 8) **2** old-fashioned or antiquated ▷ *n* **3** an antediluvian person or thing [c17: from ANTE- + Latin *dīluvium* flood]

antelope (ˈæntɪˌləʊp) *n, pl* **-lopes** or **-lope** any bovid mammal of the subfamily *Antilopinae*, of Africa and Asia. They are typically graceful, having long legs and horns, and include the gazelles, springbok, impala, gerenuk, blackbuck, and dik-diks [c15: from Old French *antelop*, from Medieval Latin *antalopus*, from Late Greek *antholops* a legendary beast]

antemeridian (ˌæntɪməˈrɪdɪən) *adj* before noon; in the morning [c17: from Latin *antemerīdiānus*; see ANTE-, MERIDIAN]

ante meridiem (ˈæntɪ məˈrɪdɪəm) the full form of **a.m.** [Latin, from ANTE- + *merīdiēs* midday]

antenatal (ˌæntɪˈneɪtəl) *adj* occurring or present before birth; during pregnancy

antenna (ænˈtɛnə) *n* **1** *pl* **-nae** (-niː) one of a pair of mobile appendages on the heads of insects, crustaceans, etc, that are often whiplike and respond to touch and taste but may be specialized for swimming or attachment **2** *pl* **-nas** another name for **aerial** (sense 7) [c17: from Latin: sail yard, of obscure origin] ▷ anˈtennal or anˈtennary *adj*

antependium (ˌæntɪˈpɛndɪəm) *n, pl* **-dia** (-dɪə) a covering hung over the front of an altar [c17: from Medieval Latin, from Latin ANTE- + *pendēre* to hang]

antepenult (ˌæntɪpɪˈnʌlt) *n* the third last syllable in a word [c16: shortened from Latin (*syllaba*) *antepaenultima*; see ANTE-, PENULT]

antepenultimate (ˌæntɪpɪˈnʌltɪmət) *adj* **1** third from last ▷ *n* **2** anything that is third from last

ante-post *adj Brit* (of a bet) placed before the runners in a race are confirmed

anterior (ænˈtɪərɪə) *adj* **1** situated at or towards the front **2** earlier in time **3** *zoology* of or near the head end **4** *botany* (of part of a flower or leaf) situated farthest away from the main stem [c17: from Latin, comparative of *ante* before]

anteroom (ˈæntɪˌruːm, -ˌrʊm) *n* a room giving entrance to a larger room, often used as a waiting room

Antheil (ˈæntaɪl) *n* **George.** 1900–59, US composer. His best known work is the controversial *Le Ballet Méchanique* (1924) for motor horns, bells, and aeroplane propellers

anthelion (ænˈhiːlɪən, ænˈθiː-) *n, pl* **-lia** (-lɪə) **1** a faint halo sometimes seen in polar or high altitude regions around the shadow of an object cast onto a thick cloud bank or fog **2** a white spot occasionally appearing on the parhelic circle at the same height as and opposite to the sun [c17: from Late Greek, from *anthēlios* opposite the sun, from ANTE- + *hēlios* sun]

anthelmintic (ˌænθɛlˈmɪntɪk) or **anthelminthic** (ˌænθɛlˈmɪnθɪk) or **antihelminthic** (ˌæntɪhɛlˈmɪnθɪk) *n med* another name for **vermifuge**

anthem (ˈænθəm) *n* **1** a song of loyalty or devotion, as to a nation or college: *a national anthem* **2** a musical composition for a choir, usually set to words from the Bible, sung as part of a church service **3** a religious chant sung antiphonally [Old English *antemne*, from Late Latin *antiphōna* ANTIPHON]

anther (ˈænθə) *n* the terminal part of a stamen consisting usually of two lobes each containing two sacs in which the pollen matures [c18: from New Latin *anthēra*, from Latin: a remedy prepared from flowers, from Greek, from *anthēros* flowery, from *anthos* flower]

antheridium (ˌænθəˈrɪdɪəm) *n, pl* **-ia** (-ɪə) the male sex organ of algae, fungi, bryophytes, and spore-bearing vascular plants, such as ferns, which produces antherozoids [c19: from New Latin, diminutive of *anthēra* ANTHER]

ant hill *n* a mound of soil, leaves, etc, near the entrance of an ants' nest, carried and deposited there by the ants while constructing the nest

anthologize or **anthologise** (ænˈθɒləˌdʒaɪz) *vb* to compile or put into an anthology

anthology (ænˈθɒlədʒɪ) *n, pl* **-gies 1** a collection of literary passages or works, esp poems, by various authors **2** any printed collection of literary pieces, songs, works of art, etc [c17: from Medieval Latin *anthologia*, from Greek, literally: a flower gathering, from *anthos* flower + *legein* to collect] ▷ anˈthologist *n*

Anthony (ˈæntənɪ) *n* **Saint.** ?251–?356 AD, Egyptian hermit, commonly regarded as the founder of Christian monasticism. Feast day: Jan 17

Anthony of Padua *n* **Saint.** 1195–1231, Franciscan friar, who preached in France and Italy. Feast day: June 13

anthozoan (ˌænθəˈzəʊən) *n* **1** any of the solitary or colonial sessile marine coelenterates of the class *Anthozoa*, including the corals, sea anemones, and sea pens, in which the body is in the form of a polyp ▷ *adj* **2** Also called: **actinozoan** of or relating to the class *Anthozoa*

anthracene (ˈænθrəˌsiːn) *n* a colourless tricyclic crystalline solid having a slight blue fluorescence, used in the manufacture of chemicals, esp diphenylamine and alizarin, and as crystals in scintillation counters. Formula: $C_6H_4(CH)_2C_6H_4$ [c19: from ANTHRAX + -ENE]

anthracite (ˈænθrəˌsaɪt) *n* a hard jet-black coal that burns slowly with a nonluminous flame giving out intense heat. Fixed carbon content: 86–98 per cent; calorific value: 3.14×10^7–3.63×10^7 J/kg. Also called: **hard coal** [c19: from Latin *anthracītes* type of bloodstone, from Greek *anthrakitēs* coal-like, from *anthrax* coal, ANTHRAX] ▷ anthracitic (ˌænθrəˈsɪtɪk) *adj*

anthracosis (ˌænθrəˈkəʊsɪs) *n* a lung disease due to inhalation of coal dust

anthrax (ˈænθræks) *n, pl* **-thraces** (-θrəˌsiːz) **1** a highly infectious and often fatal disease of herbivores, esp cattle and sheep, characterized by fever, enlarged spleen, and swelling of the throat. Carnivores are relatively resistant. It is caused by the spore-forming bacterium *Bacillus anthracis* and can be transmitted to man **2** a pustule or other lesion caused by this disease [c19: from Late Latin, from Greek: carbuncle]

anthropic principle *n astronomy* the cosmological theory that the presence of life in the universe limits the ways in which the very early universe could have evolved

anthropo- *combining form* indicating man or human: *anthropology; anthropomorphism* [from Greek *anthrōpos*]

anthropocentric (ˌænθrəpəʊˈsɛntrɪk) *adj* regarding man as the most important and central factor in the universe

anthropogenesis (ˌænθrəpəʊˈdʒɛnɪsɪs) or **anthropogeny** (ˌænθrəˈpɒdʒɪnɪ) *n* the study of the origins of man

anthropoid (ˈænθrəˌpɔɪd) *adj* **1** resembling man **2** resembling an ape; apelike ▷ *n* **3** any primate of the suborder *Anthropoidea*, including monkeys, apes, and man

anthropoid ape *n* any primate of the family *Pongidae*, having no tail, elongated arms, and a highly developed brain. The group includes gibbons, orang-utans, chimpanzees, and gorillas

anthropology (ˌænθrəˈpɒlədʒɪ) *n* the study of humans, their origins, physical characteristics, institutions, religious beliefs, social relationships, etc ▷ anthropological (ˌænθrəpəˈlɒdʒɪkəl) *adj* ▷ ˌanthroˈpologist *n*

anthropometry (ˌænθrəˈpɒmɪtrɪ) *n* the comparative study of sizes and proportions of the human body ▷ anthropometric (ˌænθrəpəˈmɛtrɪk) or ˌanthropoˈmetrical *adj*

anthropomorphic (ˌænθrəpəʊˈmɔːfɪk) *adj* **1** of or relating to anthropomorphism **2** resembling the human form ▷ ˈanthropoˌmorph *n* ▷ ˌanthropoˈmorphically *adv*

anthropomorphism (ˌænθrəpəˈmɔːfɪzəm) *n* the attribution of human form or behaviour to a deity, animal, etc ▷ ˌanthropoˈmorphist *n*

anthropomorphous (ˌænθrəpəˈmɔːfəs) *adj* **1** shaped like a human being **2** another word for **anthropomorphic**

anthropophagi (ˌænθrəˈpɒfəˌgaɪ) *pl n, sing* **-gus** (-gəs) cannibals [c16: from Latin, from Greek *anthrōpophagos*; see ANTHROPO-, -PHAGY]

anthroposophy (ˌænθrəˈpɒsəfɪ) *n* the spiritual and mystical teachings of Rudolf Steiner, based on the belief that creative activities such as myth making, which formed a part of life in earlier times, are psychologically valuable, esp for educational and therapeutic purposes > anthroposophic (ˌænθrəpəʊˈsɒfɪk) adj > ˌanthroˈposophist n

anti (ˈæntɪ) informal ▷ adj **1** opposed to a party, policy, attitude, etc ▷ n **2** an opponent of a party, policy, etc

anti- prefix **1** against; opposing: anticlerical; antisocial **2** opposite to: anticlimax; antimere **3** rival; false: antipope **4** counteracting, inhibiting, or neutralizing: antifreeze; antihistamine **5** designating the antiparticle of the particle specified: antineutron [from Greek anti]

anti-aircraft (ˌæntɪˈeəkrɑːft) n (modifier) of or relating to defence against aircraft attack: anti-aircraft batteries

anti-apartheid adj opposed to apartheid

antiar (ˈæntɪˌɑː) n another name for **upas** (senses 1, 2) [from Javanese]

anti-atom n an atom composed of antiparticles, in which the nucleus contains antiprotons with orbiting positrons

antiballistic missile n a missile designed to destroy an incoming ballistic missile before it reaches its target

Antibes (French ɑ̃tib) n a port and resort in SE France, on the Mediterranean: an important Roman town. Pop: 72 412 (1999)

antibiosis (ˌæntɪbaɪˈəʊsɪs) n an association between two organisms, esp microorganisms, that is harmful to one of them

antibiotic (ˌæntɪbaɪˈɒtɪk) n **1** any of various chemical substances, such as penicillin, streptomycin, chloramphenicol, and tetracycline, produced by various microorganisms, esp fungi, or made synthetically and capable of destroying or inhibiting the growth of microorganisms, esp bacteria ▷ adj **2** of or relating to antibiotics

antibody (ˈæntɪˌbɒdɪ) n, pl -bodies any of various proteins produced in the blood in response to the presence of an antigen. By becoming attached to antigens on infectious organisms antibodies can render them harmless or cause them to be destroyed

antic (ˈæntɪk) n **1** archaic an actor in a ludicrous or grotesque part; clown ▷ adj **2** archaic fantastic; grotesque ▷ See also **antics** [c16: from Italian antico something ancient, or grotesque (from its application to fantastic carvings found in ruins of ancient Rome); see ANTIQUE]

anticathode (ˌæntɪˈkæθəʊd) n the target electrode for the stream of electrons in a vacuum tube, esp an X-ray tube

Antichrist (ˈæntɪˌkraɪst) n **1** New Testament the antagonist of Christ, expected by early Christians to appear and reign over the world until overthrown at Christ's Second Coming **2** (sometimes not capital) an enemy of Christ or Christianity

anticipant (ænˈtɪsɪpənt) adj **1** operating in advance; expectant; anticipating ▷ n **2** a person who anticipates; anticipator

anticipate (ænˈtɪsɪˌpeɪt) vb (mainly tr) **1** (may take a clause as object) to foresee and act in advance of: he anticipated the fall in value by selling early **2** to thwart by acting in advance of; forestall: I anticipated his punch by moving out of reach **3** (also intr) to mention (something) before its proper time: don't anticipate the climax of the story **4** (may take a clause as object) to regard as likely; expect; foresee **5** to make use of in advance of possession: he anticipated his salary in buying a house [c16: from Latin anticipāre to take before, realize beforehand, from anti- ANTE- + capere to take] > anˈticiˌpator or anˈticipative adj > anˈticipatory or anˈticipative adj > anˈticipatively adv

anticipation (ænˌtɪsɪˈpeɪʃən) n **1** the act of anticipating; expectation, premonition, or foresight **2** the act of taking or dealing with funds before they are legally available or due **3** music an unstressed, usually short note introduced before a downbeat and harmonically related to the chord immediately following it

anticlerical (ˌæntɪˈklɛrɪkᵊl) adj **1** opposed to the power and influence of the clergy, esp in politics ▷ n **2** a supporter of an anticlerical party > ˌantiˈclericalism n

anticlimax (ˌæntɪˈklaɪmæks) n **1** a disappointing or ineffective conclusion to a series of events, etc **2** a sudden change from a serious subject to one that is disappointing or ludicrous > anticlimactic (ˌæntɪklaɪˈmæktɪk) adj

anticline (ˈæntɪˌklaɪn) n a formation of stratified rock raised up, by folding, into a broad arch so that the strata slope down on both sides from a common crest > ˌantiˈclinal adj

anticlockwise (ˌæntɪˈklɒkˌwaɪz) adv, adj in the opposite direction to the rotation of the hands of a clock. US equivalent: counterclockwise

anticoagulant (ˌæntɪkəʊˈægjʊlənt) adj **1** acting to prevent or impair coagulation, esp of blood ▷ n **2** an agent that prevents or impairs coagulation

anti-Communist n a person who is opposed to Communism

anticonvulsant (ˌæntɪkənˈvʌlsənt) n **1** any of a class of drugs used to prevent or abolish convulsions ▷ adj **2** of or relating to this class of drugs

Anticosti (ˌæntɪˈkɒstɪ) n an island of E Canada, in the Gulf of St Lawrence; part of Quebec. Area: 7881 sq km (3043 sq miles)

antics (ˈæntɪks) pl n absurd or grotesque acts or postures

anticyclone (ˌæntɪˈsaɪkləʊn) n meteorol a body of moving air of higher pressure than the surrounding air, in which the pressure decreases away from the centre. Winds circulate around the centre in a clockwise direction in the N hemisphere and anticlockwise in the S hemisphere. Also called: high > anticyclonic (ˌæntɪsaɪˈklɒnɪk) adj

antidazzle mirror (ˈæntɪˌdæzᵊl) n a rear-view mirror for road vehicles that only partially reflects headlights behind

antidepressant (ˌæntɪdɪˈprɛsᵊnt) n **1** any of a class of drugs used to alleviate depression ▷ adj **2** of or relating to this class of drugs

antidiuretic hormone n another name for **vasopressin**. Abbreviation: ADH

antidote (ˈæntɪˌdəʊt) n **1** med a drug or agent that counteracts or neutralizes the effects of a poison **2** anything that counteracts or relieves a harmful or unwanted condition; remedy [c15: from Latin antidotum, from Greek antidoton something given as a countermeasure, from ANTI- + didonai to give] > ˌantiˈdotal adj

antiemetic (ˌæntɪˈmɛtɪk) adj **1** preventing vomiting ▷ n **2** any antiemetic drug, such as promethazine or metoclopramide

antifreeze (ˈæntɪˌfriːz) n a liquid, usually ethylene glycol (ethanediol), added to cooling water to lower its freezing point, esp for use in an internal-combustion engine

antifungal (ˌæntɪˈfʌŋɡᵊl) adj **1** inhibiting the growth of fungi **2** (of a drug) possessing antifungal properties and therefore used to treat fungal infections. ▷ Also: antimycotic

antigen (ˈæntɪdʒən, -ˌdʒɛn) n a substance that stimulates the production of antibodies [c20: from ANTI(BODY) + -GEN]

anti-globalization or **anti-globalisation** n a political belief opposed to the emergence of a single world market dominated by multinational companies

Antigone (ænˈtɪɡənɪ) n Greek myth daughter of Oedipus and Jocasta, who was condemned to death for cremating the body of her brother Polynices in defiance of an edict of her uncle, King Creon of Thebes

Antigonus I (ænˈtɪɡənəs) n known as Cyclops. 382–301 BC, Macedonian general under Alexander the Great; king of Macedon (306–301)

Antigua (ænˈtiːɡə) n an island in the Caribbean, one of the Leeward Islands: a British colony, with its dependency Barbuda, until 1967, when it became a British associated state; it became independent in 1981 as part of the state of Antigua and Barbuda. Area: 279 sq km (108 sq miles) > Anˈtiguan adj, n

Antigua and Barbuda n a state in the Caribbean, comprising the islands of Antigua, Barbuda, and Redonda: gained independence in 1981: a member of the Commonwealth. Official language: English. Religion: Christian majority. Currency: East Caribbean dollar. Capital: St John's. Pop: 73 000 (2003 est). Area: 442 sq km

(171 sq miles)

antihero ('ænti,hɪərəʊ) *n*, *pl* -roes a central character in a novel, play, etc, who lacks the traditional heroic virtues

antihistamine (,ænti'histə,miːn, -min) *n* any drug that neutralizes the effects of histamine, used esp in the treatment of allergies

antihydrogen ('ænti,haidrədʒən) *n* hydrogen in which the nucleus is an antiproton with an orbiting positron

anti-inflammatory *adj* **1** reducing inflammation ▷ *n* **2** any anti-inflammatory drug, such as cortisone, aspirin, or ibuprofen

anti-inflationary *adj* of or relating to measures to counteract or combat inflation

antiknock (,ænti'nɒk) *n* a compound, such as lead tetraethyl, added to petrol to reduce knocking in the engine

Anti-Lebanon *n* a mountain range running north and south between Syria and Lebanon, east of the Lebanon Mountains. Highest peak: Mount Hermon, 2814 m (9232 ft)

Antilles (æn'tiliːz) *pl n* the Antilles a group of islands in the Caribbean. See also **Greater Antilles, Lesser Antilles**

antilock brake ('ænti,lɒk) *n* a brake fitted to some road vehicles that prevents skidding and improves control by sensing and compensating for overbraking. Also called: ABS brake

antilogy (æn'tilədʒi) *n*, *pl* -gies a contradiction in terms [c17: from Greek *antilogia*]

antimacassar (,æntimə'kæsə) *n* a cloth covering the back and arms of chairs, etc, to prevent soiling or as decoration [c19: from ANTI- + MACASSAR (OIL)]

antimagnetic (,æntimæg'netik) *adj* of or constructed of a material that does not acquire permanent magnetism when exposed to a magnetic field

antimalarial (,æntimə'leəriəl) *adj* **1** effective in the treatment of malaria ▷ *n* **2** an antimalarial drug or agent

antimasque ('ænti,maːsk) *n* a comic or grotesque dance, presented between the acts of a masque

antimatter ('ænti,mætə) *n* a form of matter composed of antiparticles, such as antihydrogen, consisting of antiprotons and positrons

antimetabolite (,ænti'mi'tæbə,lait) *n* any drug that acts by disrupting the normal growth of a cell. Sulfonamide drugs are antimetabolites and some antimetabolites are used in cancer treatment

antimissile (,ænti'misail) *adj* **1** relating to defensive measures against missile attack: *an antimissile system* ▷ *n* **2** Also called: **antimissile missile** a defensive missile used to intercept and destroy attacking missiles

antimony ('æntiməni) *n* a toxic metallic element that exists in two allotropic forms and occurs principally in stibnite. The stable form is a brittle silvery-white crystalline metal that is added to alloys to increase their strength and hardness and is used in semiconductors. Symbol: Sb; atomic no: 51; atomic wt: 121.757; valency: 0, -3, +3, or +5; relative density: 6.691; melting pt: 630.76°C; boiling pt: 1587°C [c15: from Medieval Latin *antimōnium*, of uncertain origin] ▷ **antimonial** (,ænti'məʊniəl) *adj*, *n*

antimony potassium tartrate *n* a colourless odourless poisonous crystalline salt used as a mordant for textiles and leather, as an insecticide, and as an anthelmintic. Formula: $K(SbO)C_4H_4O_6$. Also called: **tartar emetic**

antimuon (,ænti'mjuːɒn) *n* the antiparticle of a muon

antimycotic (,æntimai'kɒtik) *n*, *adj* another word for **antifungal**

anti-Nazi *adj* opposing any individual or group that espouses Nazi ideologies

antinoise ('ænti,nɔiz) *n* sound generated so that it is out of phase with a noise, such as that made by an engine, in order to reduce the noise level by interference

antinomian (,ænti'nəʊmiən) *adj* **1** relating to the doctrine that by faith and the dispensation of grace a Christian is released from the obligation of adhering to any moral law ▷ *n* **2** a member of a Christian sect holding such a doctrine ▷ ,anti'nomianism *n*

antinomy (æn'tinəmi) *n*, *pl* -mies **1** opposition of one law, principle, or rule to another; contradiction within a

law **2** *philosophy* contradiction existing between two apparently indubitable propositions; paradox [c16: from Latin *antinomia*, from Greek: conflict between laws, from ANTI- + *nomos* law] ▷ **antinomic** (,ænti'nɒmik) *adj*

antinovel ('ænti,nɒvəl) *n* a type of prose fiction in which conventional or traditional novelistic elements are rejected

antinuclear (,ænti'njuːkliə) *adj* opposed to nuclear weapons

Antioch ('ænti,ɒk) *n* a city in S Turkey, on the Orantes River: ancient commercial centre and capital of Syria (300–64 BC); early centre of Christianity. Pop: 155 000 (2005 est). Turkish name: **Antakya**

Antiochus III (æn'taiəkəs) *n* known as *Antiochus the Great*. 242–187 BC, king of Syria (223–187), who greatly extended the Seleucid empire but was forced (190) to surrender most of Asia Minor to the Romans

Antiochus IV *n* ?215–164 BC, Seleucid king of Syria (175–164), who attacked the Jews and provoked the revolt of the Maccabees

antioxidant (,ænti'ɒksidənt) *n* **1** any substance that retards deterioration by oxidation, esp of fats, oils, foods, petroleum products, or rubber **2** *biology* a substance, such as vitamin C, vitamin E, or beta carotene, that counteracts the damaging effects of oxidation in a living organism

antiparticle ('ænti,paːtikəl) *n* any of a group of elementary particles that have the same mass and spin as their corresponding particle but have opposite values for all other nonzero quantum numbers. When a particle collides with its antiparticle, mutual annihilation occurs

antipasto (,ænti'paːstəʊ, -'pæs-) *n*, *pl* -tos a course of hors d'oeuvres in an Italian meal [Italian: before food]

Antipater (æn'tipətə) *n* ?398–319 BC, Macedonian general under Alexander the Great: regent of Macedon (334–323)

antipathetic (æn,tipə'θetik, ,æntipə-) or **antipathetical** *adj* (often foll by *to*) having or arousing a strong aversion

antipathy (æn'tipəθi) *n*, *pl* -thies **1** a feeling of intense aversion, dislike, or hostility **2** the object of such a feeling [c17: from Latin *antipathia*, from Greek *antipatheia*, from ANTI- + *patheia* feeling]

antipersonnel (,ænti,pɜːsə'nel) *adj* (of weapons, etc) designed to cause casualties to personnel rather than to destroy equipment or defences

antiperspirant (,ænti'pɜːspərənt) *n* **1** an astringent substance applied to the skin to reduce or prevent perspiration ▷ *adj* **2** reducing or preventing perspiration

antiphlogistic (,æntiflə'dʒistik) *adj* **1** obsolete of or relating to the prevention or alleviation of inflammation ▷ *n* **2** an antiphlogistic agent or drug

antiphon ('æntifən) *n* **1** a short passage, usually from the Bible, recited or sung as a response after certain parts of a liturgical service **2** a psalm, hymn, etc, chanted or sung in alternate parts **3** any response or answer [c15: from Late Latin *antiphōna* sung responses, from Late Greek, plural of *antiphōnon* (something) responsive, from *antiphōnos*, from ANTI- + *phōnē* sound]

antiphonary (æn'tifənəri) *n*, *pl* -naries a bound collection of antiphons, esp for use in the divine office

antiphony (æn'tifəni) *n*, *pl* -nies **1** the antiphonal singing of a musical composition by two choirs **2** any musical or other sound effect that answers or echoes another

antipode ('æntipəʊd) *n* the exact or direct opposite ▷ **antipodal** (æn'tipədəl) *adj*

antipodes (æn'tipə,diːz) *pl n* **1** either or both of two points, places, or regions that are situated diametrically opposite to one another on the earth's surface, esp the country or region opposite one's own **2** the people who live there **3** the antipodes (*often capital*) Australia and New Zealand [c16: via Late Latin from Greek, plural of *antipous* having the feet opposite, from ANTI- + *pous* foot] ▷ **antipodean** (æn,tipə'diːən) *adj*, *n*

Antipodes Islands *pl n* the Antipodes Islands a group of small uninhabited islands in the South Pacific, southeast of and belonging to New Zealand. Area: 62 sq km (24 sq miles)

antipope (ˈæntɪˌpəʊp) n a rival pope elected in opposition to one who has been canonically chosen

antipsychotic (ˌæntɪsaɪˈkɒtɪk) adj 1 preventing or treating psychosis ▷ n 2 any antipsychotic drug, such as chlorpromazine: used to treat such conditions as schizophrenia

antipyretic (ˌæntɪpaɪˈrɛtɪk) adj 1 preventing or alleviating fever ▷ n 2 an antipyretic remedy or drug > antipyresis (ˌæntɪpaɪˈriːsɪs) n

antiquarian (ˌæntɪˈkwɛərɪən) adj 1 concerned with the study of antiquities or antiques ▷ n 2 a less common name for **antiquary** > ˌantiˈquarianism n

antiquark (ˈæntɪkwɑːk) n the antiparticle of a quark

antiquary (ˈæntɪkwərɪ) n, pl -quaries a person who collects, deals in, or studies antiques, ancient works of art, or ancient times. Also called: antiquarian

antiquate (ˈæntɪˌkweɪt) vb (tr) to make obsolete or old-fashioned [c15: from Latin antīquāre to make old, from antīquus ancient]

antiquated (ˈæntɪˌkweɪtɪd) adj 1 outmoded; obsolete 2 aged; ancient > ˈantiˌquatedness n

antique (ænˈtiːk) n 1 a a decorative object, piece of furniture, or other work of art created in an earlier period, that is collected and valued for its beauty, workmanship, and age b (as modifier): an antique shop 2 any object made in an earlier period 3 the antique the style of ancient art, esp Greek or Roman art, or an example of it ▷ adj 4 made in or in the style of an earlier period 5 of or belonging to the distant past, esp of or in the style of ancient Greece or Rome 6 informal old-fashioned; out-of-date 7 archaic aged or venerable ▷ vb 8 (tr) to give an antique appearance to [c16: from Latin antīquus ancient, from ante before]

antiquities (ænˈtɪkwɪtɪz) pl n remains or relics, such as statues, buildings, or coins, that date from ancient times

antiquity (ænˈtɪkwɪtɪ) n, pl -ties 1 the quality of being ancient or very old: a vase of great antiquity 2 the far distant past, esp the time preceding the Middle Ages in Europe 3 the people of ancient times collectively; the ancients

antiracism (ˌæntɪˈreɪsɪzəm) n the policy of challenging racism and promoting racial tolerance > ˌantiˈracist n, adj

antiretroviral (ˈæntɪˈrɛtrəʊˌvaɪrəl) adj 1 inhibiting the process by which a retrovirus replicates ▷ n 2 any retroviral drug: used to treat diseases caused by retroviruses, such as HIV

antiriot (ˌæntɪˈraɪət) adj (of police officers, equipment, measures, etc) designed for or engaged in the control of crowds

anti-roll bar n a crosswise rubber-mounted bar in the suspension of a motor vehicle, which counteracts the movement downward on one side when cornering

antirrhinum (ˌæntɪˈraɪnəm) n any scrophulariaceous plant of the genus Antirrhinum, esp the snapdragon, which have two-lipped flowers of various colours [c16: via Latin from Greek antirrhinon, from ANTI- (imitating) + rhis nose; so called from a fancied likeness to an animal's snout]

Antisana (Spanish antiˈsana) n a volcano in N central Ecuador, in the Andes. Height: 5756 m (18 885 ft)

antiscorbutic (ˌæntɪskɔːˈbjuːtɪk) adj 1 preventing or curing scurvy ▷ n 2 an antiscorbutic remedy or agent

anti-Semite n a person who persecutes or discriminates against Jews > ˌanti-ˈSemitism n > anti-Seˈmitic adj

antisense RNA (ˈæntɪsɛns) n molecules transcribed, not from DNA in the usual way, but from DNA strands complementary to those that produce normal messenger RNA. Antisense RNA occurs in nature and is inhibitory on gene action. It can be produced synthetically and offers such therapeutic possibilities as turning off viral genes

antisepsis (ˌæntɪˈsɛpsɪs) n 1 destruction of undesirable microorganisms, such as those that cause disease or putrefaction 2 the state or condition of being free from such microorganisms

antiseptic (ˌæntɪˈsɛptɪk) adj 1 of, relating to, or effecting antisepsis 2 entirely free from contamination 3 informal

lacking spirit or excitement; clinical ▷ n 4 an antiseptic agent or substance > ˌantiˈseptically adv

antiserum (ˌæntɪˈsɪərəm) n, pl -rums or -ra (-rə) blood serum containing antibodies against a specific antigen, used to treat or provide immunity to a disease

anti-site n a website through which people can express their contempt for a particular person, organization, pop group, etc

antisocial (ˌæntɪˈsəʊʃəl) adj 1 avoiding the company of other people; unsociable 2 contrary or injurious to the interests of society in general

antispasmodic (ˌæntɪspæzˈmɒdɪk) adj 1 preventing or arresting spasms, esp in smooth muscle ▷ n 2 an antispasmodic drug

antistatic (ˌæntɪˈstætɪk) adj (of a substance, textile, etc) retaining sufficient moisture to provide a conducting path, thus avoiding the effects of static electricity

Antisthenes (ænˈtɪsθəˌniːz) n ?445–365 bc, Greek philosopher, founder of the Cynic school, who taught that the only good was virtue, won by self-control and independence from worldly needs

antistrophe (ænˈtɪstrəfɪ) n (in ancient Greek drama) a the second of two movements made by a chorus during the performance of a choral ode b the second part of a choral ode sung during this movement ▷ See also **strophe** [c17: via Late Latin from Greek antistrophē an answering turn, from ANTI- + strophē a turning] > ˌantiˈstrophically adv

antitank (ˌæntɪˈtæŋk) adj designed to immobilize or destroy armoured vehicles

antithesis (ænˈtɪθɪsɪs) n, pl -ses (-ˌsiːz) 1 the exact opposite 2 contrast or opposition 3 rhetoric the juxtaposition of contrasting ideas, phrases, or words so as to produce an effect of balance, such as my words fly up, my thoughts remain below [c15: via Latin from Greek: a setting against, from ANTI- + tithenai to place] > antithetical (ˌæntɪˈθɛtɪkəl) or antiˈthetic adj

antithrombotic (ˌæntɪθrɒmˈbɒtɪk) adj 1 preventing the formation of blood clots ▷ n 2 an antithrombotic drug

antitoxin (ˌæntɪˈtɒksɪn) n 1 an antibody that neutralizes a toxin 2 blood serum that contains a specific antibody > ˌantiˈtoxic adj

antitrades (ˈæntɪˌtreɪdz) pl n winds in the upper atmosphere blowing in the opposite direction from and above the trade winds

antitrust (ˌæntɪˈtrʌst) n (modifier) chiefly US regulating or opposing trusts, monopolies, cartels, or similar organizations, esp in order to prevent unfair competition

antitussive (ˌæntɪˈtʌsɪv) adj 1 alleviating or suppressing coughing ▷ n 2 any antitussive drug [from ANTI- + Latin tussis a cough]

antitype (ˈæntɪˌtaɪp) n 1 a person or thing that is foreshadowed or represented by a type or symbol, esp a character or event in the New Testament prefigured in the Old Testament 2 an opposite type > antitypic (ˌæntɪˈtɪpɪk) or ˌantiˈtypical adj

antivenin (ˌæntɪˈvɛnɪn) or **antivenene** (ˌæntɪvɪˈniːn) n an antitoxin that counteracts a specific venom, esp snake venom [c19: from ANTI- + VEN(OM) + -IN]

antiviral (ˌæntɪˈvaɪrəl) adj 1 inhibiting the growth of viruses ▷ n 2 any antiviral drug: used to treat diseases caused by viruses, such as herpes infections and AIDS

antivirus (ˈæntɪˌvaɪrəs) n 1 a piece of software designed to prevent viruses entering a computer system or network: antivirus software 2 (modifer) of or relating to such a piece of software

antler (ˈæntlə) n one of a pair of bony outgrowths on the heads of male deer and some related species of either sex. The antlers are shed each year and those of some species grow more branches as the animal ages [c14: from Old French antoillier, from Vulgar Latin anteoculare (unattested) (something) in front of the eye]

antlion (ˈæntˌlaɪən) n 1 Also called: antlion fly any of various neuropterous insects of the family Myrmeleontidae, which typically resemble dragonflies and are most common in tropical regions 2 the larva of this insect, which has very large jaws and buries itself in the sand to await its prey

Antoinette (*French* ãtwanɛt) *n* See **Marie Antoinette**

Antonello da Messina (ˌæntəˈnɛləʊ) *n* ?1430–?79, Italian painter, born in Sicily. His paintings include *St Jerome in His Study* and *Portrait of a Man*

Antonescu (ˌæntɒˈnɛskjuː) *n* **Ion.** 1882–1946, Romanian general and statesman; appointed prime minister (1940) by King Carol II. He was executed for war crimes

Antonine Wall (ˈæntənaɪn) *n* a Roman frontier defence work across S Scotland, extending between the River Clyde and the Firth of Forth. It was built in 142 AD on the orders of Antoninus Pius (86–161 AD), emperor of Rome (138–161)

Antoninus (ˌæntəˈnaɪnəs) *n* See **Marcus Aurelius Antoninus**

Antoninus Pius *n* 86–161 AD, emperor of Rome (138–161); adopted son and successor of Hadrian

Antonioni (ˌæntəʊnɪˈəʊnɪ) *n* ▷ **Michelangelo** (mikeˈlandʒelo). 1912–2007, Italian film director; his films include *L'Avventura* (1959), *La Notte* (1961), *Blow-Up* (1966), *Zabriskie Point* (1970), *Beyond the Clouds* (1995), and *Just To Be Together* (2002)

Antonius (ænˈtəʊnɪəs) *n* **Marcus** (ˈmɑːkəs). Latin name of (Mark) **Antony**

antonomasia (ˌæntənəˈmeɪzɪə) *n* *rhetoric* **1** the substitution of a title or epithet for a proper name, such as *his highness* **2** the use of a proper name for an idea: *he is a Daniel come to judgment* [C16: via Latin from Greek, from *antonomazein* to name differently, from *onoma* name]

Antony (ˈæntənɪ) *n* **Mark.** Latin name *Marcus Antonius*. ?83–30 BC, Roman general who served under Julius Caesar in the Gallic wars and became a member of the second triumvirate (43). He defeated Brutus and Cassius at Philippi (42) but having repudiated his wife for Cleopatra, queen of Egypt, he was defeated by his brother-in-law Octavian (Augustus) at Actium (31)

antonym (ˈæntənɪm) *n* a word that means the opposite of another word [C19: from Greek *antōnumia*, from ANTI- + *onoma* name] ▷ **antonymous** (ænˈtɒnɪməs) *adj*

Antrim (ˈæntrɪm) *n* **1** a historical county of NE Northern Ireland, famous for the Giant's Causeway on the N coast: in 1973 it was replaced for administrative purposes by the districts of Antrim, Ballymena, Ballymoney, Carrickfergus, Larne, Moyle, Newtownabbey, and parts of Belfast and Lisburn. Area: 3100 sq km (1200 sq miles) **2** a district of Northern Ireland, in Co Antrim. Pop: 49 260 (2003 est). Area: 415 sq km (160 sq miles)

antrum (ˈæntrəm) *n*, *pl* **-tra** (-trə) *anatomy* a natural cavity, hollow, or sinus, esp in a bone [C14: from Latin: cave, from Greek *antron*] ▷ **'antral** *adj*

Antung (ˈænˈtʊŋ) *n* a variant transliteration of the Chinese name for **Andong**

antwackie (ˈæntwækɪ) *adj* *Northern English dialect* old-fashioned

Antwerp (ˈæntwɜːp) *n* **1** a province of N Belgium. Pop: 1 668 812 (2004 est). Area: 2859 sq km (1104 sq miles) **2** a port in N Belgium, capital of Antwerp province, on the River Scheldt: a major European port. Pop: 455 148 (2004 est) ▷ French name: **Anvers**

Anu (ˈɑːnuː) *n* **Babylonian myth** the sky god

ANU *abbreviation* Australian National University

Anubis (əˈnjuːbɪs) *n* **Egyptian myth** a deity, a son of Osiris, who conducted the dead to judgment. He is represented as having a jackal's head and was identified by the Greeks with Hermes

Anuradhapura (əˈnʊərədəˌpʊərə, ˌʌnʊˈrɑːdə-) *n* a town in Sri Lanka: ancient capital of Ceylon; site of the sacred bo tree and place of pilgrimage for Buddhists. Pop: 53 151 (2001)

anuran (əˈnjʊərən) *n* **1** any of the vertebrates of the order *Anura* (or *Salientia*), characterized by absence of a tail and very long hind legs specialized for hopping: class *Amphibia* (amphibians). The group includes the frogs and toads ▷ *adj* **2** of, relating to, or belonging to the order *Anura*. ▷ Also called: **salientian** [C20: from New Latin *Anura*, from AN- + Greek *oura* tail]

anuresis (ˌænjʊˈriːsɪs) *n* *pathol* inability to urinate even though urine is formed by the kidneys and retained in the urinary bladder [C20: New Latin, from AN- + Greek *ouresis* urination, from *ouron* urine]

anus (ˈeɪnəs) *n* the excretory opening at the end of the alimentary canal [C16: from Latin]

Anvers (ãvɛr) *n* the French name for **Antwerp**

anvil (ˈænvɪl) *n* **1** a heavy iron or steel block on which metals are hammered during forging **2** any part having a similar shape or function, such as the lower part of a telegraph key **3** *anatomy* the nontechnical name for **incus** [Old English *anfealt*; related to Old High German *anafalz*, Middle Dutch *anvilte*; see ON, FELT²]

anxiety (æŋˈzaɪɪtɪ) *n*, *pl* **-ties 1** a state of uneasiness or tension caused by apprehension of possible future misfortune, danger, etc; worry **2** intense desire; eagerness **3** *psychol* a state of intense apprehension or worry often accompanied by physical symptoms such as shaking, intense feelings in the gut, etc, common in mental illness or after a very distressing experience [C16: from Latin *anxietas*; see ANXIOUS]

anxiety disorder *n* any of various mental disorders characterized by extreme anxiety and including panic disorder, post-traumatic stress disorder, and **generalized anxiety disorder**

anxious (ˈæŋkʃəs, ˈæŋʃəs) *adj* **1** worried and tense because of possible misfortune, danger, etc; uneasy **2** fraught with or causing anxiety; worrying; distressing: *an anxious time* **3** intensely desirous; eager: *anxious for promotion* [C17: from Latin *anxius*; related to Latin *angere* to torment; see ANGER, ANGUISH] ▷ **'anxiously** *adv* ▷ **'anxiousness** *n*

any (ˈɛnɪ) *determiner* **1 a** one, some, or several, as specified, no matter how much or many, what kind or quality, etc: *any cheese in the cupboard is yours; you may take any clothes you like* **b** (*as pronoun; functioning as sing or plural*): *take any you like* **2** (*usually used with a negative*) **a** even the smallest amount or even one: *I can't stand any noise* **b** (*as pronoun; functioning as sing or plural*): *don't give her any* **3** whatever or whichever; no matter what or which: *any dictionary will do; any time of day* **4** an indefinite or unlimited amount or number (esp in the phrases **any amount** or **number**): *any number of friends* ▷ *adv* **5** (*usually used with a negative*) (foll by a comparative adjective) to even the smallest extent: *it isn't any worse now* [Old English *ǣnig*; related to Old Frisian *ēnig*, Old High German *einag*, Old Norse *einigr* anyone, Latin *ūnicus* unique; see AN¹, ONE]

Anyang (ˈɑːnˈjɑːŋ) *n* a town in E China, in Henan province: archaeological site and capital of the Shang dynasty. Pop: 808 000 (2005 est)

anybody (ˈɛnɪˌbɒdɪ, -bədɪ) *pron* **1** any person; anyone **2** (*usually used with a negative or a question*) a person of any importance: *he isn't anybody in this town* ▷ *n*, *pl* **-bodies 3** (often preceded by *just*) any person at random; no matter who

anyhow (ˈɛnɪˌhaʊ) *adv* **1** in any case; at any rate **2** in any manner or by any means whatever **3** in a haphazard manner; carelessly

any more *or esp US* **anymore** (ˌɛnɪˈmɔː) *adv* any longer; still; now or from now on; nowadays: *he does not work here any more*

anyone (ˈɛnɪˌwʌn, -wən) *pron* **1** any person; anybody **2** (*used with a negative or a question*) a person of any importance: *is he anyone in this town?* **3** (often preceded by *just*) any person at random; no matter who

anyplace (ˈɛnɪˌpleɪs) *adv* *US & Canadian informal* in, at, or to any unspecified place

anything (ˈɛnɪˌθɪŋ) *pron* **1** any object, event, action, etc, whatever: *anything might happen* ▷ *n* **2** a thing of any kind: *have you anything to declare?* ▷ *adv* **3** in any way: *he wasn't anything like his father* **4** anything but; by no means; not in the least: *she was anything but happy* **5** like anything (intensifier; usually euphemistic): *he ran like anything*

anyway (ˈɛnɪˌweɪ) *adv* **1** in any case; at any rate; nevertheless; anyhow **2** in a careless or haphazard manner **3** Usually **any way** in any manner; by any means

anywhere (ˈɛnɪˌwɛə) *adv* **1** in, at, or to any place **2** get anywhere to be successful

anywise (ˈɛnɪˌwaɪz) *adv* *chiefly US* in any way or manner; at all

ANZ *abbreviation* Australian and New Zealand Banking Group

ANZAAS ('ænzəs, -zæs) *n acronym for* Australian and New Zealand Association for the Advancement of Science

Anzac ('ænzæk) *n* **1** (in World War I) a soldier serving with the Australian and New Zealand Army Corps **2** (now) any Australian or New Zealand soldier **3** the Anzac landing at Gallipoli in 1915

Anzac Day *n* 25 April, a public holiday in Australia and New Zealand commemorating the Anzac landing at Gallipoli in 1915

Anzio ('ænzɪˌəʊ; *Italian* 'antsjo) *n* a port and resort on the W coast of Italy: site of Allied landings in World War II. Pop: 36 952 (2001)

ANZUS ('ænzəs) *n acronym for* Australia, New Zealand, and the United States, with reference to the security alliance between them

AO *abbreviation* Officer of the Order of Australia

A/O or **a/o** *accounting, banking abbreviation* account of

AOB or **a.o.b.** *abbreviation* any other business

AOC *abbreviation* appellation d'origine contrôlée

AONB *abbreviation* (in England, Wales, and Northern Ireland) Area of Outstanding Natural Beauty: an area designated by the appropriate government bodies as requiring protection to conserve and enhance its natural beauty

Aoraki-Mount Cook (ˌeɪəʊˈræki) *n* the official name for Mount **Cook¹**

aorist ('eɪərɪst, 'eərɪst) *n grammar* a tense of the verb in classical Greek and in certain other inflected languages, indicating past action without reference to whether the action involved was momentary or continuous [c16: from Greek *aoristos* not limited, from A-¹ + *horistos* restricted, from *horizein* to define]

aorta (eɪˈɔːtə) *n, pl* **-tas** or **-tae** (-tiː) the main vessel in the arterial network, which conveys oxygen-rich blood from the heart to all parts of the body except the lungs [c16: from New Latin, from Greek *aortē*, literally: something lifted, from *aeirein* to raise] > a'ortic or a'ortal *adj*

Aosta (*Italian* aˈɔsta) *n* a town in NW Italy, capital of Valle d'Aosta region: Roman remains. Pop: 34 062 (2001)

Aotearoa ('æʊˌtɪəˌrɔːə) *n* the Māori name for **New Zealand** [from Māori *ao tea roa* Land of the Long White Cloud]

aoudad ('ɑːʊˌdæd) *n* a wild mountain sheep, *Ammotragus lervia*, of N Africa, having horns curved in a semicircle and long hair covering the neck and forelegs. Also called: **Barbary sheep** [from French, from Berber *audad*]

Aouita (aʊˈiːtə) *n* **Saïd** (saɪˈiːd). born 1960, Moroccan middle-distance runner: set new world records for the 1500 metres (1987–93) and 5000 metres (1987–94)

ap (æp) *prefix* son of: occurring as part of some surnames of Welsh origin: *ap Thomas* [from Welsh *mab* son]

ap- *prefix* a variant of **apo-**: *aphelion*

apace (əˈpeɪs) *adv* quickly; rapidly [c14: probably from Old French *à pas*, at a (good) pace]

apache (əˈpaːʃ, -ˈpæʃ; *French* apaʃ) *n* a Parisian gangster or ruffian [from French: APACHE]

Apache (əˈpætʃɪ) *n* **1** *pl* **Apaches** or **Apache** a member of a North American Indian people, formerly nomadic and warlike, inhabiting the southwestern US and N Mexico **2** the language of this people, belonging to the Athapascan group of the Na-Dene phylum [from Mexican Spanish, probably from Zuñi *Apachu*, literally: enemy]

apanage ('æpənɪdʒ) *n* a variant spelling of **appanage**

apart (əˈpaːt) *adj, adv* (*postpositive*) **1** to pieces or in pieces: *he had the television apart on the floor* **2** placed or kept separately or to one side for a particular purpose, reason, etc; aside (esp in the phrases **set** or **put apart**) **3** separate in time, place, or position; at a distance: *he stood apart from the group; two points three feet apart* **4** not being taken into account; aside: *these difficulties apart, the project ran smoothly* **5** individual; distinct; separate: *a race apart* **6** separately or independently in use, thought, or function: *considered apart, his reasoning was faulty* **7 apart from** (*preposition*) besides; other than ▷ See also **take apart, tell apart** [c14: from Old French *a part* at (the) side]

apartheid (əˈpaːthaɪt, -heɪt) *n* (in South Africa) the official government policy of racial segregation; officially renounced in 1992 [c20: Afrikaans, from *apart* APART + *-heid* -HOOD]

apartment (əˈpaːtmənt) *n* **1** (*often plural*) any room in a building, usually one of several forming a suite, esp one that is spacious and well furnished and used as living accommodation, offices, etc **2 a** another name (esp US and Canadian) for **flat²** (sense 1) **b** (*as modifier*): *apartment building; apartment house* [c17: from French *appartement*, from Italian *appartamento*, from *appartare* to set on one side, separate]

apathetic (ˌæpəˈθɛtɪk) *adj* having or showing little or no emotion; indifferent [c18: from APATHY + PATHETIC] > ˌapa'thetically *adv*

apathy ('æpəθɪ) *n* absence of interest in or enthusiasm for things generally considered interesting or moving [c17: from Latin, from Greek *apatheia*, from *apathēs* without feeling, from A-¹ + *pathos* feeling]

apatite ('æpəˌtaɪt) *n* a pale green to purple mineral, found in igneous rocks and metamorphosed limestones. It is used in the manufacture of phosphorus, phosphates, and fertilizers. Composition: calcium fluorophosphate or calcium chlorophosphate. General formula: $Ca_5(PO_4,CO_3)_3(F,OH,Cl)$. Crystal structure: hexagonal [c19: from German *Apatit*, from Greek *apatē* deceit; from its misleading similarity to other minerals]

APB *abbreviation* (in the US) all-points bulletin

ape (eɪp) *n* **1** any of various primates, esp those of the family *Pongidae*, in which the tail is very short or absent. See **anthropoid ape 2** (*not in technical use*) any monkey **3** an imitator; mimic ▷ *vb* **4** (*tr*) to imitate [Old English *apa*; related to Old Saxon *ape*, Old Norse *api*, Old High German *affo*] > 'ape,like *adj*

APEC ('eɪpɛk) *n acronym for* **1** Asia-Pacific Economic Cooperation **2** (in Canada) Atlantic Provinces Economic Council

Apeldoorn ('æpəlˌdɔːn; *Dutch* 'aːpəldoːrn) *n* a town in the Netherlands, in central Gelderland province: nearby is the summer residence of the Dutch royal family. Pop: 156 000 (2003 est)

Apelles (əˈpɛliːz) *n* 4th century BC, Greek painter of mythological subjects, none of whose work survives, his fame resting on the testimony of Pliny and other writers

apeman ('eɪpˌmæn) *n, pl* **-men** any of various extinct apelike primates thought to have been the forerunners, or closely related to the forerunners, of modern man

Apennines ('æpəˌnaɪnz) *pl n* **1** a mountain range in Italy, extending over 1250 km (800 miles) from the northwest to the southernmost tip of the peninsula. Highest peak: Monte Corno, 2912 m (9554 ft) **2** a mountain range lying in the N quadrants of the moon, extending over 950 km along the SE border of the Mare Imbrium and rising to 6200 m

aperçu (*French* apɛrsy) *n* **1** an outline; summary **2** an insight [from *apercevoir* to PERCEIVE]

aperient (əˈpɪərɪənt) *med* ▷ *adj* **1** laxative ▷ *n* **2** a mild laxative [c17: from Latin *aperīre* to open]

aperiodic (ˌeɪpɪərɪˈɒdɪk) *adj* **1** not periodic; not occurring at regular intervals **2** *physics* **a** (of a system or instrument) being damped sufficiently to reach equilibrium without oscillation **b** (of an oscillation or vibration) not having a regular period **c** (of an electrical circuit) not having a measurable resonant frequency > aperiodicity (ˌeɪpɪərɪəˈdɪsɪtɪ) *n*

apéritif (aːˌpɛrɪˈtiːf, əˌpɛr-) *n* an alcoholic drink, esp a wine, drunk before a meal to whet the appetite [c19: from French, from Medieval Latin *aperitīvus*, from Latin *aperīre* to open]

aperture ('æpətʃə) *n* **1** a hole, gap, crack, slit, or other opening **2** *physics* a usually circular and often variable opening in an optical instrument or device that controls the quantity of radiation entering or leaving it [c15: from Late Latin *apertūra* opening, from Latin *aperīre* to open]

apetalous (eɪˈpɛtələs) *adj* (of flowering plants) having no petals [c18: from New Latin *apetalus*, see A-¹, PETAL]

apex ('eɪpɛks) *n, pl* **apexes** or **apices** ('æpɪˌsiːz, 'eɪ-) **1** the highest point; vertex **2** the pointed end or tip of something **3** a pinnacle or high point, as of a career, etc [c17: from Latin: point]

APEX ('eɪpɛks) *n acronym for* **1** Advance Purchase Excursion: a reduced airline or long-distance rail fare that must be paid a specified number of days in advance **2** (in Britain) Association of Professional, Executive, Clerical, and Computer Staff

Apex Club *n* (in Australia) an association of business and professional men founded to promote community welfare > **Apexian** (eɪ'pɛksɪən) *adj, n*

apgar score *or* **apgar rating** ('æpgɑ:) *n* a system for determining the condition of an infant at birth by allotting a maximum of 2 points to each of the following: heart rate, breathing effort, muscle tone, response to stimulation, and colour [c20: named after V. Apgar (1909–74), US anaesthetist]

aphaeresis (ə'fɪərɪsɪs) *n* a variant spelling of **apheresis** > **aphaeretic** (ˌæfə'rɛtɪk) *adj*

aphasia (ə'feɪzɪə) *n* a disorder of the central nervous system characterized by partial or total loss of the ability to communicate, esp in speech or writing [c19: via New Latin from Greek, from A-¹ + -phasia, from phanai to speak] > a'phasic *or* a'phasiˌac *adj, n*

aphelion (æp'hi:lɪən, ə'fi:-) *n, pl* -lia (-lɪə) the point in its orbit when a planet or comet is at its greatest distance from the sun [c17: from New Latin aphēlium (with pseudo-Greek ending -ion) from AP- + Greek hēlios sun]

apheresis *or* **aphaeresis** (ə'fɪərɪsɪs) *n* **1** the omission of a letter or syllable at the beginning of a word **2** a method of collecting blood from donors that enables its different components, such as the platelets or plasma, to be separated out [c17: via Late Latin from Greek, from aphairein to remove]

aphesis ('æfɪsɪs) *n* the gradual disappearance of an unstressed vowel at the beginning of a word, as in *squire* from *esquire* [c19: from Greek, from aphienai to set free, send away] > **aphetic** (ə'fɛtɪk) *adj*

aphid ('eɪfɪd) *n* any of the small homopterous insects of the family *Aphididae*, which feed by sucking the juices from plants [c19: back formation from aphides, plural of APHIS]

aphis ('eɪfɪs) *n, pl* **aphides** ('eɪfɪˌdi:z) any of various aphids constituting the genus *Aphis*, such as the blackfly [c18: from New Latin (coined by Linnaeus for obscure reasons)]

aphonia (ə'fəʊnɪə) *or* **aphony** ('æfənɪ) *n* loss of the voice caused by damage to the vocal tract [c18: via New Latin from Greek, from A-¹ + phōnē sound, voice]

aphorism ('æfəˌrɪzəm) *n* a short pithy saying expressing a general truth; maxim [c16: from Late Latin aphorismus, from Greek aphorismos definition, from aphorizein to define, set limits to, from horos boundary] > 'aphorist *n* > ˌapho'ristic *adj*

aphrodisiac (ˌæfrə'dɪzɪæk) *n* **1** a drug, food, etc, that excites sexual desire ▷ *adj* **2** exciting or heightening sexual desire [c18: from Greek aphrodisiakos, from aphrodisios belonging to APHRODITE]

Aphrodite (ˌæfrə'daɪtɪ) *n Greek myth* the goddess of love and beauty, daughter of Zeus. Roman counterpart: Venus¹. Also called: **Cytherea**

aphyllous (ə'fɪləs) *adj* (of plants) having no leaves [c19: from New Latin aphyllus, from Greek aphullos, from A-¹ + phullon leaf]

apian ('eɪpɪən) *adj* of, relating to, or resembling bees [c19: from Latin apiānus, from apis bee]

apiarist ('eɪpɪərɪst) *n* a person who studies or keeps bees

apiary ('eɪpɪərɪ) *n, pl* -aries a place where bees are kept, usually in beehives [c17: from Latin apiārium from apis bee]

apical ('æpɪkəl, 'eɪ-) *adj* of, at, or being the apex [c19: from New Latin apicālis, from Latin: APEX] > 'apically *adv*

apices ('æpɪˌsi:z, 'eɪ-) *n* a plural of **apex**

apiculture ('eɪpɪˌkʌltʃə) *n* the breeding and care of bees [c19: from Latin apis bee + CULTURE] > ˌapi'cultural *adj* > ˌapi'culturist *n*

apiece (ə'pi:s) *adv* (postpositive) for, to, or from each one: *they were given two apples apiece*

Apis ('ɑ:pɪs) *n* (in ancient Egypt) a sacred bull worshipped at Memphis

apish ('eɪpɪʃ) *adj* **1** stupid; foolish **2** resembling an ape **3** slavishly imitative > 'apishly *adv* > 'apishness *n*

aplanatic (ˌæplə'nætɪk) *adj* (of a lens or mirror) free from spherical aberration [c18: from Greek aplanētos prevented from wandering, from A-¹ + planētos, from planaein to wander]

aplenty (ə'plɛntɪ) *adj, adv* (postpositive) in plenty

aplomb (ə'plɒm) *n* equanimity, self-confidence, or self-possession [c18: from French: rectitude, uprightness, from à plomb according to the plumb line, vertically]

apnoea *or US* **apnea** (æp'nɪə) *n* a temporary inability to breathe [c18: from New Latin, from Greek apnoia, from A-¹ + pnein to breathe]

Apo ('ɑ:pəʊ) *n* the highest mountain in the Philippines, on SE Mindanao: active volcano with three peaks. Height: 2954 m (9690 ft)

apo- *or* **ap-** *prefix* **1** away from; off: *apogee* **2** indicating separation of: *apocarpous* [from Greek apo away, off]

Apoc. *abbreviation* **1** Apocalypse **2** Apocrypha or Apocryphal

apocalypse (ə'pɒkəlɪps) *n* **1** a prophetic disclosure or revelation **2** an event of great importance, violence, etc, like the events described in the Apocalypse [c13: from Late Latin apocalypsis, from Greek apokalupsis, from apokaluptein to disclose, from APO- + kaluptein to hide] > aˌpoca'lyptic *adj* > aˌpoca'lyptically *adv*

Apocalypse (ə'pɒkəlɪps) *n Bible* (in the Vulgate and Douay versions of the Bible) the Book of Revelation

apocarpous (ˌæpə'kɑ:pəs) *adj* (of the ovaries of flowering plants such as the buttercup) consisting of separate carpels [c19 from NL, from Gk APO- + karpos fruit]

apochromat (ˌæpə'krəʊmæt) *or* **apochromatic lens** *n* a lens, consisting of three or more elements of different types of glass, that is designed to bring light of three colours to the same focal point, thus reducing its chromatic aberration

apocope (ə'pɒkəpɪ) *n* omission of the final sound or sounds of a word [c16: via Late Latin from Greek apokopē, from apokoptein to cut off]

apocrine ('æpəkraɪn, -krɪn) *adj* denoting a type of glandular secretion in which part of the secreting cell is lost with the secretion, as in mammary glands [c20: from APO- + -crine, from Greek krinein to separate]

Apocrypha (ə'pɒkrɪfə) *n* the Apocrypha (functioning as singular or plural) the 14 books included as an appendix to the Old Testament in the Septuagint and the Vulgate but not included in the Hebrew canon. They are not printed in Protestant versions of the Bible [c14: via Late Latin apocrypha (scripta) hidden (writings), from Greek, from apokruptein to hide away]

apocryphal (ə'pɒkrɪfəl) *adj* **1** of questionable authenticity **2** (sometimes capital) of or like the Apocrypha **3** untrue; counterfeit

apodal ('æpəd(ə)l) *or* **apodous** *adj* (of snakes, eels, etc) without feet; having no obvious hind limbs or pelvic fins [c18: from Greek apous from A-¹ + pous foot]

apodosis (ə'pɒdəsɪs) *n, pl* -ses (-ˌsi:z) *logic, grammar* the consequent of a conditional statement, as the game will be cancelled in if it rains the game will be cancelled [c17: via Late Latin from Greek: a returning or answering (clause), from apodidonai to give back]

apogee ('æpəˌdʒi:) *n* **1** the point in its orbit around the earth when the moon or an artificial satellite is at its greatest distance from the earth **2** the highest point [c17: from New Latin apogaeum (influenced by French apogée), from Greek apogaion, from apogaios away from the earth, from APO- + gaia earth] > ˌapo'gean *adj*

apolipoprotein (ˌæpəˌlɪpəʊ'prəʊtiːn, -ˌlaɪ-) *n* any of a group of glycoproteins that form part of the structure of lipoproteins, some of which have been associated with Alzheimer's disease

apolitical (ˌeɪpə'lɪtɪk(ə)l) *adj* politically neutral; without political attitudes, content, or bias

Apollinaire (*French* apɔlinɛr) *n* **Guillaume** (gijom), real name **Wilhelm Apollinaris de Kostrowitzki**. 1880–1918, French poet, novelist, and dramatist, regarded as a precursor of surrealism; author of *Alcoöls* (1913) and *Calligrammes* (1918)

Apollo (ə'pɒləʊ) *n classical myth* the god of light, poetry, music, healing, and prophecy: son of Zeus and Leto

Apollonius of Perga (ˌæpə'ləʊnɪəs, 'pɜːgə) *n* ?261–?190 BC, Greek mathematician, remembered for his treatise on conic sections

Apollonius of Rhodes (ˌæpə'ləʊnɪəs) *n* 3rd century BC, Greek epic poet and head of the Library of Alexandria. His principal work is the four-volume *Argonautica*

Apollyon (ə'pɒljən) *n New Testament* the destroyer, a name given to the Devil (Revelation 9:11) [c14: via Late Latin from Greek, from *apollunai* to destroy totally]

apologetic (əˌpɒlə'dʒɛtɪk) *adj* 1 expressing or anxious to make apology; contrite 2 protecting or defending in speech or writing > aˌpolo'getically *adv*

apologetics (əˌpɒlə'dʒɛtɪks) *n* (*functioning as singular*) 1 the branch of theology concerned with the defence and rational justification of Christianity 2 a defensive method of argument

apologia (ˌæpə'ləʊdʒɪə) *n* a formal written defence of a cause or one's beliefs or conduct

apologist (ə'pɒlədʒɪst) *n* a person who offers a defence by argument

apologize *or* **apologise** (ə'pɒləˌdʒaɪz) *vb* (*intr*) 1 to express or make an apology; acknowledge failings or faults 2 to make a formal defence in speech or writing

apologue ('æpəˌlɒg) *n* an allegory or moral fable [c17: from Latin, from Greek *apologos*]

apology (ə'pɒlədʒɪ) *n*, *pl* -gies 1 an oral or written expression of regret or contrition for a fault or failing 2 a poor substitute or offering 3 another word for **apologia** [c16: from Old French *apologie*, from Late Latin *apologia*, from Greek: a verbal defence, from APO- + *logos* speech]

apophthegm *or* **apothegm** ('æpəˌθɛm) *n* a short cryptic remark containing some general or generally accepted truth; maxim [c16: from Greek *apophthegma*, from *apophthengesthai* to speak one's opinion frankly, from *phthengesthai* to speak]

apophysis (ə'pɒfɪsɪs) *n*, *pl* -ses (-ˌsiːz) 1 a process, outgrowth, or swelling from part of an animal or plant 2 *geology* a tapering offshoot from a larger igneous intrusive mass [c17: via New Latin from Greek *apophusis* a sideshoot, from APO- + *phusis* growth] > apophysate (ə'pɒfɪsɪt, -ˌseɪt) *adj* > apophysial (ˌæpə'fɪzɪəl) *adj*

apoplectic (ˌæpə'plɛktɪk) *adj* 1 of or relating to apoplexy 2 *informal* furious > ˌapo'plectically *adv*

apoplexy ('æpəˌplɛksɪ) *n* sudden loss of consciousness, often followed by paralysis, caused by rupture or occlusion of a blood vessel in the brain [c14: from Old French *apoplexie*, from Late Latin *apoplēxia*, from Greek: from *apoplēssein* to cripple by a stroke, from *plēssein* to strike]

aport (ə'pɔːt) *adv*, *adj* (*postpositive*) *nautical* on or towards the port side: *with the helm aport*

apostasy (ə'pɒstəsɪ) *n*, *pl* -sies abandonment of one's religious faith, party, a cause, etc [c14: from Church Latin *apostasia*, from Greek *apostasis* desertion, from *apostanai* to stand apart from, desert]

apostate (ə'pɒsteɪt, -tɪt) *n* 1 a person who abandons his religion, party, cause, etc ▷ *adj* 2 guilty of apostasy > apostatical (ˌæpə'stætɪkᵊl) *adj*

apostatize *or* **apostatise** (ə'pɒstəˌtaɪz) *vb* (*intr*) to forsake or abandon one's belief, faith, or allegiance

a posteriori (eɪ pɒsˌtɛrɪ'ɔːraɪ, -rɪ, ɑː) *adj logic* 1 relating to or involving inductive reasoning from particular facts or effects to a general principle 2 derived from or requiring evidence for its validation or support; empirical; open to revision [c18: from Latin, literally: from the latter (that is, from effect to cause)]

apostle (ə'pɒsᵊl) *n* 1 (*often capital*) one of the 12 disciples chosen by Christ to preach his gospel 2 any prominent Christian missionary, esp one who first converts a nation or people 3 an ardent early supporter of a cause, reform movement, etc [Old English *apostol*, from Church Latin *apostolus*, from Greek *apostolos* a messenger, from *apostellein* to send forth]

Apostles' Creed *n* a concise statement of Christian beliefs dating from about 500 AD, traditionally ascribed to the Apostles

apostolate (ə'pɒstəlɪt, -ˌleɪt) *n* the office, authority, or mission of an apostle

apostolic (ˌæpə'stɒlɪk) *adj* 1 of, relating to, deriving from, or contemporary with the Apostles 2 of or relating to the teachings or practice of the Apostles 3 of or relating to the pope regarded as chief successor of the Apostles > ˌapos'tolical *adj*

Apostolic See *n RC Church* the see of the pope regarded as the successor to Saint Peter

Apostolic succession *n* the doctrine that the authority of Christian bishops derives from the Apostles through an unbroken line of consecration

apostrophe¹ (ə'pɒstrəfɪ) *n* the punctuation mark ' used to indicate the omission of a letter or number, such as *he's* for *he has* or *he is*, also used in English to form the possessive, as in *John's father* and *twenty pounds' worth* [c17: from Late Latin, from Greek *apostrophos* mark of elision, from *apostrephein* to turn away]

apostrophe² (ə'pɒstrəfɪ) *n rhetoric* a digression from a discourse, esp an address to an imaginary or absent person or a personification [c16: from Latin *apostrophē*, from Greek: a turning away, digression]

apostrophize *or* **apostrophise** (ə'pɒstrəˌfaɪz) *vb* (*tr*) *rhetoric* to address an apostrophe to

apothecaries' measure *n* a system of liquid volume measure used in pharmacy in which 60 minims equal 1 fluid drachm, 8 fluid drachms equal 1 fluid ounce, and 20 fluid ounces equal 1 pint

apothecaries' weight *n* a system of weights, formerly used in pharmacy, based on the Troy ounce, which contains 480 grains. 1 grain is equal to 0.065 gram

apothecary (ə'pɒθɪkərɪ) *n*, *pl* -caries 1 an archaic word for **pharmacist** 2 *law* a chemist licensed by the Society of Apothecaries of London to prescribe, prepare, and sell drugs [c14: from Old French *apotecaire*, from Late Latin *apothēcārius* warehouseman, from *apothēca*, from Greek *apothēkē* storehouse]

apothegm ('æpəˌθɛm) *n* a variant spelling of **apophthegm**

apothem ('æpəˌθɛm) *n* the perpendicular line or distance from the centre of a regular polygon to any of its sides [c20: from APO- + Greek *thema*, from *tithenai* to place]

apotheosis (əˌpɒθɪ'əʊsɪs) *n*, *pl* -ses (-siːz) 1 the elevation of a person to the rank of a god; deification 2 glorification of a person or thing 3 a glorified ideal 4 the best or greatest time or event: *the apotheosis of De Niro's career* [c17: via Late Latin from Greek: deification, from *theos* god]

apotheosize *or* **apotheosise** (ə'pɒθɪəˌsaɪz) *vb* (*tr*) 1 to deify 2 to glorify or idealize

appal *or US* **appall** (ə'pɔːl) *vb* -pals, -palling, -palled *or US* -palls, -palling, -palled (*tr*) to fill with horror; shock or dismay [c14: from Old French *appalir* to turn pale]

Appalachia (ˌæpə'leɪtʃɪə) *n* a highland region of the eastern US, containing the Appalachian Mountains, extending from Pennsylvania to Alabama > Appa'lachian *adj*

Appalachian Mountains *or* **Appalachians** *pl n* a mountain system of E North America, extending from Quebec province in Canada to central Alabama in the US: contains rich deposits of anthracite, bitumen, and iron ore. Highest peak: Mount Mitchell, 2038 m (6684 ft)

appalling (ə'pɔːlɪŋ) *adj* 1 causing extreme dismay, horror, or revulsion 2 very bad > ap'pallingly *adv*

Appaloosa (ˌæpə'luːsə) *n* a breed of horse, originally from America, typically having a spotted rump [c19: perhaps from *Palouse*, river in Idaho]

appanage *or* **apanage** ('æpənɪdʒ) *n* 1 land or other provision granted by a king for the support of a member of the royal family, esp a younger son 2 a natural or customary accompaniment or perquisite, as to a job or position [c17: from Old French, from Medieval Latin *appānāgium*, from *appānāre* to provide for, from Latin *pānis* bread]

apparatchik (ˌæpə'rɑːtʃɪk) *n* 1 a member of a Communist Party organization 2 an official or bureaucrat in any organization [c20 from Russian, from *apparat* apparatus, instrument + -ckik, suffix denoting agent]

apparatus (ˌæpəˈreɪtəs, -ˈrɑːtəs, ˈæpəˌreɪtəs) n, pl -ratus or -ratuses 1 a collection of instruments, machines, tools, parts, or other equipment used for a particular purpose 2 a machine having a specific function: *breathing apparatus* 3 the means by which something operates; organization 4 *anatomy* any group of organs having a specific function [c17: from Latin, from *apparāre* to make ready]

apparel (əˈpærəl) n 1 something that covers or adorns, esp outer garments or clothing 2 *nautical* a vessel's gear and equipment ▷ vb -els, -elling, -elled or US -els, -eling, -eled 3 *archaic* (tr) to clothe, adorn, etc [c13: from Old French *apareillier* to make ready, from Vulgar Latin *appariculáre* (unattested), from Latin *apparāre*, from *parāre* to prepare]

apparent (əˈpærənt, əˈpɛər-) adj 1 readily seen or understood; evident; obvious 2 (*usually prenominal*) seeming, as opposed to real: *his apparent innocence belied his complicity in the crime* 3 *physics* as observed but ignoring such factors as the motion of the observer, changes in the environment, etc [c14: from Latin *apparēns*, from *apparēre* to APPEAR]

apparently (əˈpærəntlɪ, əˈpɛər-) adv (*sentence modifier*) it appears that; as far as one knows; seemingly

apparent magnitude n another name for **magnitude** (sense 4)

apparition (ˌæpəˈrɪʃən) n 1 an appearance, esp of a ghost or ghostlike figure 2 the figure so appearing; phantom; spectre 3 the act of appearing or being visible [c15: from Late Latin *appāritiō*, from Latin: attendance, from *apparēre* to APPEAR]

appassionato (əˌpæsjəˈnɑːtəʊ) adj, adv *music* (to be performed) in an impassioned manner

appeal (əˈpiːl) n 1 a request for relief, aid, etc 2 the power to attract, please, stimulate, or interest 3 an application or resort to another person or authority, esp a higher one, as for a decision or confirmation of a decision 4 *law* a the judicial review by a superior court of the decision of a lower tribunal b a request for such review 5 *cricket* a verbal request to the umpire from one or more members of the fielding side to declare a batsman out ▷ vb 6 (intr) to make an earnest request for relief, support, etc 7 (intr) to attract, please, stimulate, or interest 8 *law* to apply to a superior court to review (a case or particular issue decided by a lower tribunal) 9 (intr) to resort (to), as for a decision or confirmation of a decision 10 (intr) *cricket* to ask the umpire to declare a batsman out 11 (intr) to challenge the umpire's or referee's decision [c14: from Old French *appeler*, from Latin *appellāre* to entreat (literally: to approach), from *pellere* to push, drive] ▷ apˈpealable adj ▷ apˈpealer n ▷ apˈpealing adj ▷ apˈpealingly adv

appear (əˈpɪə) vb (intr) 1 to come into sight or view 2 (*copula; may take an infinitive*) to seem or look: *the evidence appears to support you* 3 to be plain or clear, as after further evidence, etc: *it appears you were correct after all* 4 to develop or come into being; occur: *faults appeared during testing* 5 to become publicly available; be published: *his biography appeared last month* 6 to be present in court before a magistrate or judge: *he appeared on two charges of theft* [c13: from Old French *aparoir*, from Latin *appārēre* to become visible, attend upon, from *pārēre* to appear]

appearance (əˈpɪərəns) n 1 the act or an instance of appearing, as to the eye, before the public, etc 2 the outward or visible aspect of a person or thing: *her appearance was stunning; it has the appearance of powdered graphite* 3 an outward show; pretence: *he gave an appearance of working hard* 4 keep up appearances to maintain the public impression of wellbeing or normality 5 put in an appearance or make an appearance to come or attend briefly, as out of politeness 6 to all appearances to the extent that can easily be judged; apparently

appearance money n money paid by a promoter of an event to a particular celebrity in order to ensure that the celebrity takes part in the event

appease (əˈpiːz) vb (tr) 1 to calm, pacify, or soothe, esp by acceding to the demands of 2 to satisfy or quell (an

appetite or thirst, etc) [c16: from Old French *apaisier*, from *pais* peace, from Latin *pax*] ▷ apˈpeaser n

appeasement (əˈpiːzmənt) n 1 the policy of acceding to the demands of a potentially hostile nation in the hope of maintaining peace 2 the act of appeasing

Appel (*Dutch* ˈɑpəl) n **Karel** (ˈkɑːrəl). 1921–2006, Dutch abstract expressionist painter

appellant (əˈpɛlənt) n 1 a person who appeals 2 *law* the party who appeals to a higher court from the decision of a lower tribunal ▷ adj 3 *law* another word for **appellate** [c14: from Old French; see APPEAL]

appellate (əˈpɛlɪt) adj *law* 1 of or relating to appeals 2 (of a tribunal) having jurisdiction to review cases on appeal and to reverse decisions of inferior courts [c18: from Latin *appellātus* summoned, from *appellāre* to APPEAL]

appellation (ˌæpɪˈleɪʃən) n 1 an identifying name or title 2 the act of naming or giving a title to

appellative (əˈpɛlətɪv) n 1 an identifying name or title; appellation 2 *grammar* another word for **common noun** ▷ adj 3 of or relating to a name or title 4 (of a proper noun) used as a common noun ▷ apˈpellatively adv

append (əˈpɛnd) vb (tr) 1 to add as a supplement: *to append a footnote* 2 to attach; hang on [c15: from Late Latin *appendere* to hang (something) from, from Latin *pendere* to hang]

appendage (əˈpɛndɪdʒ) n 1 an ancillary or secondary part attached to a main part; adjunct 2 *zoology* any organ that projects from the trunk of animals such as arthropods

appendant (əˈpɛndənt) adj 1 attached, affixed, or added 2 attendant or associated as an accompaniment or result ▷ n 3 a person or thing attached or added

appendicectomy (əˌpɛndɪˈsɛktəmɪ) or *esp US and Canadian* **appendectomy** (ˌæpənˈdɛktəmɪ) n, pl -mies surgical removal of any appendage, esp the vermiform appendix

appendicitis (əˌpɛndɪˈsaɪtɪs) n inflammation of the vermiform appendix

appendix (əˈpɛndɪks) n, pl -dices (-dɪˌsiːz) or -dixes 1 a body of separate additional material at the end of a book, magazine, etc, esp one that is documentary or explanatory 2 any part that is dependent or supplementary in nature or function; appendage 3 *anatomy* See **vermiform appendix** [c16: from Latin: an appendage, from *appendere* to APPEND]

Appenzell (*German* apənˈtsɛl, ˈapəntsɛl) n 1 a canton of NE Switzerland, divided in 1597 into the Protestant demicanton of **Appenzell Outer Rhodes** and the Catholic demicanton of **Appenzell Inner Rhodes**. Capitals: Herisau and Appenzell respectively. Pop: 53 200 and 15 000 (2002 est) respectively. Areas: 243 sq km (94 sq miles) and 171 sq km (66 sq miles) respectively 2 a town in NE Switzerland, capital of Appenzell Inner Rhodes demicanton. Pop: 5447 (2000)

apperceive (ˌæpəˈsiːv) vb (tr) 1 to be aware of perceiving 2 *psychol* to comprehend by assimilating (a perception) to ideas already in the mind [c19: from Old French *aperceveir*, from Latin *percipere* to PERCEIVE]

apperception (ˌæpəˈsɛpʃən) n *psychol* 1 the attainment of full awareness of a sensation or idea 2 the act or process of apperceiving ▷ ˌapperˈceptive adj

appertain (ˌæpəˈteɪn) vb (intr; usually foll by to) to belong (to) as a part, function, right, etc; relate (to) or be connected (with) [c14: from Old French *apertenir* to belong, from Late Latin *appertinēre*, from Latin AD- + *pertinēre* to PERTAIN]

appetence (ˈæpɪtəns) or **appetency** n, pl -tences or -tencies 1 a natural craving or desire 2 an attraction or affinity [c17: from Latin *appetentia*, from *appetere* to crave]

appetite (ˈæpɪˌtaɪt) n 1 a desire for food or drink 2 a desire to satisfy a bodily craving, as for sexual pleasure 3 (usually foll by for) a desire, liking, or willingness: *a great appetite for work* [c14: from Old French *apetit*, from Latin *appetītus* a craving, from *appetere* to desire ardently] ▷ appetitive (əˈpɛtɪtɪv, ˈæpɪˌtaɪtɪv) adj

appetizer or **appetiser** (ˈæpɪˌtaɪzə) n 1 a small amount of food or drink taken to stimulate the appetite 2 any stimulating foretaste

appetizing or **appetising** (ˈæpɪˌtaɪzɪŋ) adj pleasing or stimulating to the appetite; delicious; tasty

Appian Way ('æpiən) n a Roman road in Italy, extending from Rome to Brindisi: begun in 312 BC by Appius Claudius Caecus. Length: about 560 km (350 miles)

applaud (ə'plɔːd) vb **1** to indicate approval of (a person, performance, etc) by clapping the hands **2** (usually tr) to offer or express approval or praise of (an action, person, or thing): I applaud your decision [c15: from Latin applaudere to clap, from plaudere to beat, applaud]

applause (ə'plɔːz) n appreciation or praise, esp as shown by clapping the hands

apple ('æpəl) n **1 a** a rosaceous tree, Malus sieversii, native to Central Asia but widely cultivated in temperate regions in many varieties, having pink or white fragrant flowers and firm rounded edible fruits. See also **crab apple 2** the fruit of this tree, having red, yellow, or green skin and crisp whitish flesh **3** the wood of this tree **4** any of several unrelated trees that have fruits similar to the apple, such as the custard apple, sugar apple, and May apple **5 apple of one's eye** a person or thing that is very precious or much loved [Old English æppel; related to Old Saxon appel, Old Norse apall, Old High German apful]

appledrain ('æpəl,dreɪn) n Southwestern English dialect a wasp

apple green n **a** a bright light green or moderate yellowish-green **b** (as adjective): an apple-green carpet

Apple Isle n the Apple Isle Austral informal Tasmania

apple-pie bed n Brit a way of making a bed so as to prevent the person from entering it

apple-pie order n informal perfect order or condition

applet ('æplɪt) n computing a computer program that runs within a page on the World Wide Web [c20: from APP(LICATION PROGRAM) + -LET]

Appleton ('æpəltən) n Sir Edward (Victor). 1892–1965, English physicist, noted particularly for his research on the ionosphere: Nobel prize for physics 1947

appliance (ə'plaɪəns) n **1** a machine or device, esp an electrical one used domestically **2** any piece of equipment having a specific function **3** another name for a **fire engine**

applicable ('æplɪkəbəl, ə'plɪkə-) adj being appropriate or relevant; able to be applied; fitting > ˌapplica'bility or 'applicableness n > 'applicably adv

applicant ('æplɪkənt) n a person who applies, as for a job, grant, support, etc; candidate [c15: from Latin applicāns, from applicāre to APPLY]

application (ˌæplɪ'keɪʃən) n **1** the act of applying to a particular purpose or use **2** relevance or value: the practical applications of space technology **3** the act of asking for something **4** a verbal or written request, as for a job, etc: he filed his application **5** diligent effort or concentration: a job requiring application **6** something, such as a healing agent or lotion, that is applied, esp to the skin

applicator ('æplɪ,keɪtə) n a device, such as a spatula or rod, for applying a medicine, glue, etc

applicatory ('æplɪkətərɪ) adj suitable for application

applied (ə'plaɪd) adj related to or put to practical use: applied mathematics. ▷ See pure (sense 5)

appliqué (æ'pliːkeɪ) n **1** a decoration or trimming of one material sewn or otherwise fixed onto another **2** the practice of decorating in this way ▷ vb -qués, -quéing, -quéd **3** (tr) to sew or fix (a decoration) on as an appliqué [c18: from French, literally: applied]

apply (ə'plaɪ) vb -plies, -plying, -plied **1** (tr) to put to practical use; utilize; employ **2** (intr) to be relevant, useful, or appropriate **3** (tr) to cause to come into contact with; put onto **4** (intr; often foll by for) to put in an application or request **5** (tr; often foll by to) to devote (oneself, one's efforts) with diligence **6** (tr) to bring into operation or use: the police only applied the law to aliens [c14: from Old French aplier, from Latin applicāre to attach to] > ap'plier n

appoggiatura (ə,pɒdʒə'tʊərə) n, pl -ras or -re (-rɛ) music an ornament consisting of a nonharmonic note (short or long) preceding a harmonic one either before or on the stress [c18: from Italian, literally: a propping, from appoggiare to prop, support]

appoint (ə'pɔɪnt) vb (mainly tr) **1** (also intr) to assign officially, as for a position, responsibility, etc **2** to establish by agreement or decree; fix **3** to prescribe or ordain: laws appointed by tribunal **4** property law to nominate (a person), under a power granted in a deed or will, to take an interest in property **5** to equip with necessary or usual features; furnish: a well-appointed hotel [c14: from Old French apointer to put into a good state, from a point in good condition, literally: to a POINT] > ap'pointer n > appointee (əpɔɪn'tiː, ˌæp-) n

appointive (ə'pɔɪntɪv) adj chiefly US relating to or filled by appointment: an appointive position

appointment (ə'pɔɪntmənt) n **1** an arrangement to meet a person or be at a place at a certain time **2** the act of placing in a job or position **3** the person who receives such a job or position **4** the job or position to which such a person is appointed **5** (usually plural) a fixture or fitting

appointment television n televison programmes that people set aside time to watch

apportion (ə'pɔːʃən) vb (tr) to divide, distribute, or assign appropriate shares of; allot proportionally > ap'portionable adj > ap'portionment n

appose (ə'pəʊz) vb (tr) **1** to place side by side or near to each other **2** (usually foll by to) to place (something) near or against another thing [c16: from Old French apposer, from poser to put, from Latin pōnere] > ap'posable adj

apposite ('æpəzɪt) adj well suited for the purpose; appropriate; apt [c17: from Latin appositus placed near, from appōnere, from pōnere to put, place] > 'appositely adv > 'appositeness n

apposition (ˌæpə'zɪʃən) n **1** a putting into juxtaposition **2** a grammatical construction in which a word, esp a noun phrase, is placed after another to modify its meaning > ˌappo'sitional adj

appositive (ə'pɒzɪtɪv) adj **1** of or relating to apposition ▷ n **2** an appositive word or phrase > ap'positively adv

appraisal (ə'preɪzəl) or **appraisement** n **1** an assessment or estimation of the worth, value, or quality of a person or thing **2** a valuation of property or goods

appraise (ə'preɪz) vb (tr) **1** to assess the worth, value, or quality of **2** to make a valuation of, as for taxation purposes [c15: from Old French apriser, from prisier to PRIZE²] > ap'praisable adj > ap'praiser n

● **USAGE** Appraise is sometimes wrongly used where
● apprise is meant: they had been apprised (not appraised) of my
● arrival

appreciable (ə'priːʃəbəl, -ʃəbəl) adj sufficient to be easily seen, measured, or noticed > ap'preciably adv

appreciate (ə'priːʃɪ,eɪt, -sɪ-) vb (mainly tr) **1** to feel thankful or grateful for **2** (may take a clause as object) to take full or sufficient account of: to appreciate a problem **3** to value highly **4** (usually intr) to raise or increase in value [c17: from Medieval Latin appretiāre to value, prize, from Latin pretium PRICE] > ap'preci,ator n

appreciation (ə,priːʃɪ'eɪʃən, -sɪ-) n **1** thanks or gratitude **2** assessment of the true worth or value of persons or things **3** perceptive recognition of qualities, as in art **4** an increase in value, as of goods or property **5** a written review of a book, etc, esp when favourable

appreciative (ə'priːʃɪətɪv, -ʃə-) or **appreciatory** adj feeling, expressing, or capable of appreciation > ap'preciatively or ap'preciatorily adv > ap'preciativeness n

apprehend (ˌæprɪ'hɛnd) vb **1** (tr) to arrest and escort into custody; seize **2** to perceive or grasp mentally; understand **3** (tr) to await with fear or anxiety; dread [c14: from Latin apprehendere to lay hold of]

apprehensible (ˌæprɪ'hɛnsɪbəl) adj capable of being comprehended or grasped mentally > ˌappre,hensi'bility n

apprehension (ˌæprɪ'hɛnʃən) n **1** fear or anxiety over what may happen **2** the act of capturing or arresting **3** the faculty of comprehending; understanding **4** a notion or conception

apprehensive (ˌæprɪ'hɛnsɪv) adj fearful or anxious > ˌappre'hensively adv > ˌappre'hensiveness n

apprentice (ə'prɛntɪs) n **1** someone who works for a

skilled or qualified person in order to learn a trade or profession, esp for a recognized period **2** any beginner or novice ▷ *vb* **3** (*tr*) to take, place, or bind as an apprentice [C14: from Old French *aprentis*, from Old French *aprendre* to learn, from Latin *apprehendere* to APPREHEND]
> ap'prentice.ship *n*

apprise *or* **apprize** (ə'praɪz) *vb* (*tr*; often foll by *of*) to make aware; inform [C17: from French *appris*, from *apprendre* to teach; learn; see APPREHEND]
● USAGE See at **appraise**

appro ('æprəʊ) *n* an informal shortening of **approval** *on appro*

approach (ə'prəʊtʃ) *vb* **1** to come nearer in position, time, quality, character, etc, to (someone or something) **2** (*tr*) to make advances to, as with a proposal, suggestion, etc **3** (*tr*) to begin to deal with ▷ *n* **4** the act of coming towards or drawing close or closer **5** a close approximation **6** the way or means of entering or leaving; access **7** (*often plural*) an advance or overture to a person **8** a means adopted in tackling a problem, job of work, etc **9** Also called: **approach path** the course followed by an aircraft preparing for landing [C14: from Old French *aprochier*, from Late Latin *appropiāre* to draw near, from Latin *prope* near] > ap'proachable *adj*
> ap,proacha'bility *or* ap'proachableness *n*

approbation (,æprə'beɪʃən) *n* **1** commendation; praise **2** official recognition or approval > 'appro,bative *or* 'appro,batory *adj*

appropriate *adj* (ə'prəʊprɪɪt) **1** right or suitable; fitting **2** *rare* particular; own: *they had their appropriate methods* ▷ *vb* (ə'prəʊprɪ,eɪt) (*tr*) **3** to take for one's own use, esp illegally or without permission **4** to put aside (funds, etc) for a particular purpose or person [C15: from Late Latin *appropriāre* to make one's own, from Latin *proprius* one's own; see PROPER] > ap'propriately *adv*
> ap'propriateness *n* > ap'propri,ator *n*

appropriation (ə,prəʊprɪ'eɪʃən) *n* **1** the act of setting apart or taking for one's own use **2** a sum of money set apart for a specific purpose, esp by a legislature

approval (ə'pruːvəl) *n* **1** the act of approving **2** formal agreement; sanction **3** a favourable opinion; commendation **4** on approval (of articles for sale) for examination with an option to buy or return

approve (ə'pruːv) *vb* **1** (when *intr*, often foll by *of*) to consider fair, good, or right; commend (a person or thing) **2** (*tr*) to authorize or sanction [C14: from Old French *aprover*, from Latin *approbāre* to approve, from *probāre* to test, PROVE]

approved school *n* (in Britain) a former name for **community home**

approx. *abbreviation* approximate(ly)

approximal (ə'prɒksɪməl) *adj anatomy* situated side by side; close together: *approximal teeth or fillings*

approximate *adj* (ə'prɒksɪmɪt) **1** almost accurate or exact **2** inexact; rough; loose **3** much alike; almost the same **4** near; close together ▷ *vb* (ə'prɒksɪ,meɪt) **5** (usually foll by *to*) to come or bring near or close; be almost the same (as) **6** *maths* to find an expression for (some quantity) accurate to a specified degree [C15: from Late Latin *approximāre*, from Latin *proximus* nearest, from *prope* near]

approximately (ə'prɒksɪmɪtlɪ) *adv* close to; around; roughly or in the region of

approximation (ə,prɒksɪ'meɪʃən) *n* **1** the process or result of making a rough calculation, estimate, or guess **2** an imprecise or unreliable record or version **3** *maths* an inexact number, relationship, or theory that is sufficiently accurate for a specific purpose

appurtenance (ə'pɜːtɪnəns) *n* **1** a secondary or less significant thing or part **2** (*plural*) accessories or equipment **3** *property law* a minor right, interest, or privilege which passes when the title to the principal property is transferred [C14: from Anglo-French *apurtenance*, from Old French *apartenance*, from *apartenir* to APPERTAIN]

Apr *abbreviation* April

APR *abbreviation* annual percentage rate

APRA (æ'præ) *n acronym* **1** Australian Prudential Regulatory Authority **2** Australasian Performing Right

Association

apraxia (ə'præksɪə) *n* a disorder of the central nervous system caused by brain damage and characterized by impaired ability to carry out purposeful muscular movements [C19: via New Latin from Greek: inactivity, from A-¹ + *praxis* action] > a'praxic *or* a'practic *adj*

après-ski (,æpreɪ'skiː) *n* **a** social activity following a day's skiing **b** (*as modifier*): *an après-ski outfit* [French, literally: after ski]

apricot ('eɪprɪ,kɒt) *n* **1** a rosaceous tree, *Prunus armeniaca*, native to Africa and W Asia, but widely cultivated for its edible fruit **2** the downy yellow juicy edible fruit of this tree, which resembles a small peach [C16: earlier *apricock*, from Portuguese (*albricoque*) or Spanish, from Arabic *al-birqūq* the apricot, from Late Greek *praikokion*, from Latin *praecox* early-ripening; see PRECOCIOUS]

April ('eɪprəl) *n* the fourth month of the year, consisting of 30 days [C14: from Latin *Aprīlis*, probably of Etruscan origin]

April fool *n* an unsuspecting victim of a practical joke or trick traditionally performed on the first of April (**April Fools' Day** *or* **All Fools' Day**)

a priori (eɪ praɪ'ɔːraɪ, ɑː prɪ'ɔːriː) *adj* **1** *logic* relating to or involving deductive reasoning from a general principle to the expected facts or effects **2** *logic* known to be true independently of or in advance of experience of the subject matter; requiring no evidence for its validation or support [C18: from Latin, literally: from the previous (that is, from cause to effect)] > apriority (,eɪpraɪ'ɒrɪtɪ) *n*

apron ('eɪprən) *n* **1** a protective or sometimes decorative or ceremonial garment worn over the front of the body and tied around the waist **2** the part of a stage extending in front of the curtain line; forestage **3** a hard-surfaced area in front of or around an aircraft hangar, terminal building, etc, upon which aircraft can stand **4** a continuous conveyor belt composed usually of slats linked together **5** a protective plate screening the operator of a machine, artillery piece, etc **6** *geology* a sheet of sand, gravel, etc, deposited at the front of a moraine **7** another name for **skirt** (sense 3) **8** tied to someone's apron strings dependent on or dominated by someone, esp a mother or wife ▷ *vb* **9** (*tr*) to protect or provide with an apron [C16: mistaken division (as if *an apron*) of earlier *a napron*, from Old French *naperon* a little cloth, from *nape* cloth, from Latin *mappa* napkin]

apron stage *n* a stage that projects into the auditorium so that the audience sit on three sides of it

apropos (,æprə'pəʊ) *adj* **1** appropriate; pertinent ▷ *adv* **2** appropriately or pertinently **3** by the way; incidentally **4** apropos of (*preposition*) with regard to; in respect of [C17: from French *à propos* to the purpose]

apse (æps) *n* **1** Also called: **apsis** a domed or vaulted semicircular or polygonal recess, esp at the east end of a church **2** *astronomy* another name for **apsis** (sense 1) [C19: from Latin *apsis*, from Greek: a fitting together, arch, from *haptein* to fasten] > apsidal ('æp'saɪd³l, 'æpsɪd³l') *adj*

apsis ('æpsɪs) *n*, *pl* **apsides** (æp'saɪdiːz, 'æpsɪ,diːz) **1** Also called: **apse** either of two points lying at the extremities of an eccentric orbit of a planet, satellite, etc, such as the aphelion and perihelion of a planet or the apogee and perigee of the moon. The **line of apsides** connects two such points and is the principal axis of the orbit **2** another name for **apse** (sense 1) [C17: via Latin from Greek; see APSE] > apsidal (æp'saɪd³l, 'æpsɪd³l') *adj*

apt (æpt) *adj* **1** suitable for the circumstance or purpose; appropriate **2** (*postpositive*; foll by an infinitive) having a tendency (to behave as specified) **3** having the ability to learn and understand easily; clever (esp in the phrase **an apt pupil**) [C14: from Latin *aptus* fitting, suitable, from *apere* to fasten] > 'aptly *adv* > 'aptness *n*

apterous ('æptərəs) *adj* **1** (of insects) without wings, as silverfish and springtails **2** without winglike expansions, as some plant stems, seeds, and fruits [C18: from Greek *apteros* wingless, from A-¹ + *pteron* wing] > 'apter,ism *n*

apteryx ('æptərɪks) *n* another name for **kiwi** (sense 1) [C19: from New Latin: wingless creature; see APTEROUS]

aptitude ('æptɪ,tjuːd) *n* **1** inherent or acquired ability **2** ease in learning or understanding; intelligence **3** the condition or quality of being apt [c15: via Old French from Late Latin *aptitūdō*, from Latin *aptus* APT]

Apuleius (ˌæpjʊˈliːəs) *n* **Lucius** (ˈluːsɪəs). 2nd century AD, Roman writer, noted for his romance *The Golden Ass*

Apulia (əˈpjuːljə) *n* a region of SE Italy, on the Adriatic. Capital: Bari. Pop: 4 023 957 (2003 est). Area: 19 223 sq km (7422 sq miles). Italian name: **Puglia**

Aqaba *or* **Akaba** (ˈækəbə) *n* the only port in Jordan, in the southwest, on the **Gulf of Aqaba**. Pop: 80 790 (2004)

Aqtöbe (ækˈtjuːbɪ; *Kazakh* aktøbe) an industrial city in W Kazakhstan. Pop: 258 900 (1995 est). Former name (until 1991): **Aktyubinsk**

aqua (ˈækwə) *n, pl* **aquae** (ˈækwiː) *or* **aquas 1** water: used in compound names of certain liquid substances (as in **aqua regia**) or solutions of substances in water (as in **aqua ammoniae**), esp in the names of pharmacological solutions ▷ *adj* **2** short for **aquamarine** (sense 2) [Latin: water]

aquaculture (ˈækwəˌkʌltʃə) *or* **aquiculture** *n* the cultivation of freshwater and marine resources, both plant and animal, for human consumption or use

aquaerobics *or* **aquarobics** (ˌækwəˈrəʊbɪks) *n* (*functioning as singular*) same as **aquafitness** [c20: from Latin *aqua* water + AEROBICS]

aquafitness (ˈækwəˌfɪtnɪs) *n* a keep-fit regime in which exercises are performed standing up in a swimming pool

aqua fortis (ˈfɔːtɪs) *n* an obsolete name for **nitric acid** [c17: from Latin, literally: strong water]

aqualung (ˈækwəˌlʌŋ) *n* breathing apparatus used by divers, etc, consisting of a mouthpiece attached to air cylinders strapped to the back

aquamarine (ˌækwəməˈriːn) *n* **1** a pale greenish-blue transparent variety of beryl used as a gemstone **2** a a pale blue to greenish-blue colour **b** (*as adjective*): *an aquamarine dress* [c19: from New Latin *aqua marīna*, from Latin: sea water (referring to the gem's colour)]

aquanaut (ˈækwəˌnɔːt) *n* **1** a person who lives and works underwater **2** a person who swims or dives underwater [c20: from AQUA + *-naut*, as in ASTRONAUT]

aquaplane (ˈækwəˌpleɪn) *n* **1** a single board on which a person stands and is towed by a motorboat at high speed, as in water skiing ▷ *vb* (*intr*) **2** to ride on an aquaplane **3** (of a motor vehicle travelling at high speeds in wet road conditions) to rise up onto a thin film of water between the tyres and road surface so that actual contact with the road is lost

aqua regia (ˈriːdʒɪə) *n* a yellow fuming corrosive mixture of one part nitric acid and three to four parts hydrochloric acid, used in metallurgy for dissolving metals, including gold. Also called: **nitrohydrochloric acid** [c17: from New Latin: royal water; referring to its use in dissolving gold, the royal metal]

aquarist (ˈækwərɪst) *n* **1** the curator of an aquarium **2** a person who studies aquatic life

aquarium (əˈkwɛərɪəm) *n, pl* **-riums** *or* **-ria** (-rɪə) **1** a tank, bowl, or pool in which aquatic animals and plants are kept for pleasure, study, or exhibition **2** a building housing a collection of aquatic life, as for exhibition [c19: from Latin *aquārius* relating to water, on the model of VIVARIUM]

Aquarius (əˈkwɛərɪəs) *n, Latin genitive* **Aquarii** (əˈkwɛərɪˌaɪ) **1** *astronomy* a zodiacal constellation in the S hemisphere lying between Pisces and Capricorn on the ecliptic **2** *astrology* Also called: **the Water Carrier** the eleventh sign of the zodiac, symbol ♒, having a fixed air classification and ruled by the planets Saturn and Uranus. The sun is in this sign between about Jan 20 and Feb 18 [Latin]

aquatic (əˈkwætɪk, əˈkwɒt-) *adj* **1** growing, living, or found in water **2** *sport* performed in or on water ▷ *n* **3** a marine or freshwater animal or plant [c15: from Latin *aquāticus*, from *aqua* water]

aquatics (əˈkwætɪks, əˈkwɒt-) *pl n* sports or pastimes performed in or on the water

aquatint (ˈækwəˌtɪnt) *n* **1** a technique of etching copper with acid to produce an effect resembling the flat tones of a wash or watercolour. The tone or tint is obtained by acid (aqua) biting through the pores of a ground that only partially protects the copper **2** an etching made in this way ▷ *vb* **3** (*tr*) to etch (a block, etc) in aquatint [c18: from Italian *acqua tinta*: dyed water]

aquavit (ˈækwəˌvɪt) *n* a grain- or potato-based spirit from the Scandinavian countries, flavoured with aromatic seeds and spices, esp caraway. Also called: **akvavit** [from Scandinavian; see AQUA VITAE]

aqua vitae (ˈviːtaɪ, ˈvaɪtiː) *n* an archaic name for **brandy** [Medieval Latin: water of life]

aqueduct (ˈækwɪˌdʌkt) *n* **1** a conduit used to convey water over a long distance, either by a tunnel or more usually by a bridge **2** a structure, usually a bridge, that carries such a conduit or a canal across a valley or river **3** a channel in an organ or part of the body, esp one that conveys a natural body fluid [c16: from Latin *aquaeductus*, from *aqua* water + *dūcere* to convey]

aqueous (ˈeɪkwɪəs, ˈækwɪ-) *adj* **1** of, like, or containing water **2** dissolved in water: *aqueous ammonia* **3** (of rocks, deposits, etc) formed from material laid down in water [c17: from Medieval Latin *aqueus*, from Latin *aqua* water]

aqueous humour *n physiol* the watery fluid within the eyeball between the cornea and the lens

aquiculture (ˈeɪkwɪˌkʌltʃə, ˈækwɪ-) *n* **1** another name for **hydroponics 2** a variant of **aquaculture** ▷ **ˈaquiˌcultural** *adj* ▷ **ˈaquiˌculturist** *n*

aquifer (ˈækwɪfə) *n* a porous deposit of rock, such as a sandstone, containing water that can be used to supply wells

Aquila (ˈækwɪlə; *Italian* ˈaːkwila) *or* **L'Aquila** *n* a city in central Italy, capital of Abruzzi region. Pop: 68 503 (2001)

aquilegia (ˌækwɪˈliːdʒɪə) *n* another name for **columbine¹** [c19: from Medieval Latin, of uncertain origin]

aquiline (ˈækwɪˌlaɪn) *adj* **1** (of a nose) having the curved or hooked shape of an eagle's beak **2** of or resembling an eagle [c17: from Latin *aquilīnus*, from *aquila* eagle]

Aquinas (əˈkwaɪnəs) *n* **Saint Thomas**. 1225–74, Italian theologian, scholastic philosopher, and Dominican friar, whose works include *Summa contra Gentiles* (1259–64) and *Summa Theologiae* (1267–73), the first attempt at a comprehensive theological system. Feast day: Jan 28. ▷ See also **Thomism**

Aquino (əˈkiːnəʊ) *n* **Corazón**, known as *Cory*. born 1933, Philippine stateswoman: president (1986–92)

Aquitaine (ˌækwɪˈteɪn; *French* akitɛn) *n* a region of SW France, on the Bay of Biscay: a former Roman province and medieval duchy. It is generally flat in the west, rising to the slopes of the Massif Central in the northeast and the Pyrenees in the south; mainly agricultural

Ar *the chemical symbol for* argon

Ar. *abbreviation* **1** Arabia(n) **2** Also called: **Ar** Arabic

-ar *suffix forming adjectives* of; belonging to; like: *linear; polar; minuscular* [via Old French *-er* from Latin *-āris*, replacing *-ālis* (-AL¹) after stems ending in l]

ARA *abbreviation* (in Britain) Associate of the Royal Academy

Arab *n* **1** a member of a Semitic people originally inhabiting Arabia, who spread throughout the Middle East, N Africa, and Spain during the seventh and eighth centuries AD **2** a lively intelligent breed of horse, mainly used for riding **3** (*modifier*) of or relating to the Arabs: *the Arab nations* [c14: from Latin *Arabs*, from Greek *Araps*, from Arabic *'Arab*]

arabesque (ˌærəˈbɛsk) *n* **1** *ballet* a classical position in which the dancer has one leg raised behind and both arms stretched out in one of several conventional poses **2** *music* a piece or movement with a highly ornamented or decorated melody **3** *arts* a type of curvilinear decoration in painting, metalwork, etc, with intricate intertwining leaf, flower, animal, or geometrical designs [c18: from French, from Italian *arabesco* in the Arabic style]

Arabia (əˈreɪbɪə) *n* a great peninsula of SW Asia, between the Red Sea and the Persian Gulf: consists chiefly of a desert plateau, with mountains rising over 3000 m (10 000 ft) in the west and scattered oases; includes the present-day countries of Saudi Arabia, Yemen, Oman, Bahrain, Qatar, Kuwait, and the United Arab Emirates. Area: about 2 600 000 sq km (1 000 000

a

sq miles)

Arabian (ə'reɪbɪən) *adj* **1** of or relating to Arabia or the Arabs ▷ *n* **2** another word for **Arab**

Arabian camel *n* a domesticated camel, *Camelus dromedarius*, having one hump on its back and used as a beast of burden in the hot deserts of N Africa and SW Asia

Arabian Desert *n* **1** a desert in E Egypt, between the Nile, the Gulf of Suez, and the Red Sea: mountainous parts rise over 1800 m (6000 ft). Area: about 220 000 sq km (85 000 sq miles) **2** a desert, mainly in Saudi Arabia, forming the desert area of the Arabian Peninsula, esp in the north. Area: about 2 330 000 sq km (900 000 sq miles)

Arabian Sea *n* the NW part of the Indian Ocean, between Arabia and India

Arabic ('ærəbɪk) *n* **1** the language of the Arabs, spoken in a variety of dialects; the official language of Algeria, Egypt, Iraq, Jordan, the Lebanon, Libya, Morocco, Saudi Arabia, the Sudan, Syria, Tunisia, and Yemen. It is estimated to be the native language of some 75 million people throughout the world. It belongs to the Semitic subfamily of the Afro-Asiatic family of languages and has its own alphabet, which has been borrowed by certain other languages such as Urdu ▷ *adj* **2** denoting or relating to this language, any of the peoples that speak it, or the countries in which it is spoken

arabica bean (ə'ræbɪkə) *n* a high-quality coffee bean, obtained from the tree *Coffea arabica*

Arabic numeral *n* one of the symbols 0,1,2,3,4,5,6,7,8,9 (opposed to *Roman numerals*)

arabinose (ə'ræbɪˌnəʊz, -ˌnəʊs) *n* a pentose sugar in plant gums, esp of cedars and pines. It is used as a culture medium in bacteriology. Formula: $C_5H_{10}O_5$ [c19: from *arabin* (from (GUM) ARAB(IC) + -IN) + -OSE[2]]

arabis ('ærəbɪs) *n* any plant of the annual or perennial genus *Arabis*, some of which form low-growing mats with downy grey foliage and white flowers: family *Brassicaceae* (crucifers). Also called: rock cress [New Latin, from Greek *arabis* (fem) of Arabia]

Arabist ('ærəbɪst) *n* a student or expert in Arabic culture, language, history, etc

arable ('ærəb°l) *adj* **1** (of land) being or capable of being tilled for the production of crops **2** of, relating to, or using such land [c15: from Latin *arābilis* that can be ploughed, from *arāre* to plough]

Arab street *n* the Arab street *informal* public opinion in the Arab world

Araby ('ærəbɪ) *n* an archaic or poetic name for **Arabia**

Aracajú (Portuguese ərəkə'ʒu) *n* a port in E Brazil, capital of Sergipe state. Pop: 701 000 (2005 est)

Arachne (ə'ræknɪ) *n Greek myth* a maiden changed into a spider for having presumptuously challenged Athena to a weaving contest [from Greek *arakhnē* spider]

arachnid (ə'ræknɪd) *n* any terrestrial chelicerate arthropod of the class *Arachnida*, characterized by simple eyes and four pairs of legs: the class includes the spiders, scorpions, ticks, mites, and harvestmen [c19: from New Latin *Arachnida*, from Greek *arakhnē* spider] ▷ a'rachnidan *adj, n*

arachnoid (ə'ræknɔɪd) *n* **1** the middle of the three membranes that cover the brain and spinal cord. See **meninges** ▷ *adj* **2** of or relating to the middle of the three meninges **3** *botany* consisting of or covered with soft fine hairs or fibres

arachnophobia (əˌræknə'fəʊbɪə) *n* an abnormal fear of spiders [c20: from Greek *arakhnē* spider + -PHOBIA] ▷ aˌrachno'phobic *adj, n*

Arafat *n* **Yasser** ('jæsə) 1929–2004, Palestinian leader; cofounder of Al Fatah (1956), leader from 1968 of the Palestine Liberation Organization, president of the Palestinian National Authority from 1996: signed a peace agreement with Israel (1993); Nobel peace prize 1994 with Shimon Peres and Yitzhak Rabin

Arafura Sea (ˌærə'fʊərə) *n* a part of the W Pacific Ocean, between N Australia and SW New Guinea

Aragats (*Russian* ˌarɑ'gɑts) *n* Mount Aragats a volcanic mountain in NW Armenia. Height: 4090 m (13 419 ft)

Aragon[1] ('ærəgən) *n* an autonomous region of NE Spain:

independent kingdom from the 11th century until 1479, when it was united with Castile to form modern Spain. Pop: 1 059 600 (2003 est). Area: 47 609 sq km (18 382 sq miles)

Aragon[2] (*French* aragɔ̃) *n* **Louis** (lwi). 1897–1982, French poet, essayist, and novelist; an early surrealist, later a committed Communist. His works include the verse collections *Le Crève-Coeur* (1941) and *Les Yeux d'Elsa* (1942) and the series of novels *Le Monde réel* (1933–51)

Araguaia or **Araguaya** (ˌɑːrə'gwaɪə) *n* a river in central Brazil, rising in S central Mato Grosso state and flowing north to the Tocantins River. Length: over 1771 km (1100 miles)

Arakan Yoma (ˌɑːrɑː'kɑːn 'jəʊmɑː) *n* a mountain range in Myanmar, between the Irrawaddy River and the W coast: forms a barrier between Myanmar and India; teak forests

Araks (a'raks) *n* the Russian name for the **Aras**

Araldite ('ærəlˌdaɪt) *n trademark* a strong epoxy resin best known as a glue

Aral Sea ('ærəl) *n* a lake in Kazakhstan and Uzbekistan, east of the Caspian Sea, formerly the fourth largest lake in the world: shallow and saline, now badly polluted; use of its source waters for irrigation led to a loss of over 50% of its area between 1967 and 1997, after which the reduction began to be slowed. Area originally (to 1960) about 68 000 sq km (26 400 sq miles); water area reduced by 2004 to about 17 158 sq km (6625 sq miles) and the lake divided into sections. Also called: **Lake Aral**

Aram ('ɛəræm, -rəm) *n* the biblical name for ancient Syria > **Aramaean** or **Aramean** (ˌærə'miːən) *adj, n*

Aramaic (ˌærə'meɪɪk) *n* **1** an ancient language of the Middle East, still spoken in parts of Syria and the Lebanon, belonging to the NW Semitic subfamily of the Afro-Asiatic family. Originally the speech of Aram, in the 5th century BC it spread to become the lingua franca of the Persian empire ▷ *adj* **2** of, relating to, or using this language

Aran Islands *pl n* a group of three islands in the Atlantic, off the W coast of the Republic of Ireland: Aranmore or Inishmore (the largest), Inishmaan, and Inisheer. Pop: 1280 (2002). Area: 46 sq km (18 sq miles)

Arany (*Hungarian* 'ɔrɒnj) *n* **János** ('jaːnoʃ). 1817–82, Hungarian epic poet, ballad writer, and scholar

Ararat ('ærəˌræt) *n* an extinct volcanic mountain massif in E Turkey: two main peaks: **Great Ararat** 5155 m (16 916 ft), said to be the resting place of Noah's Ark after the Flood (Genesis 8:4), and **Little Ararat** 3914 m (12 843 ft)

Aras (æ'ræs) *n* a river rising in mountains in E Turkey and flowing east to the Caspian Sea: forms part of the E border of Turkey and the N border of Iran. Length: about 1100 km (660 miles). Russian name: **Araks**

Araucania (ˌærɔː'keɪnɪə; *Spanish* arau'kanja) *n* a region of central Chile, inhabited by Araucanian Indians

araucaria (ˌærɔː'kɛərɪə) *n* any tree of the coniferous genus *Araucaria* of South America, Australia, and Polynesia, such as the monkey puzzle and bunya-bunya [c19: from New Latin (*arbor*) *Araucaria* (tree) from *Arauco*, a province in Chile]

arbalest or **arbalist** ('ɑːbəlɪst) *n* a large medieval crossbow, usually cocked by mechanical means [c11: from Old French *arbaleste*, from Late Latin *arcuballista*, from Latin *arcus* bow + BALLISTA]

Arbela (ɑː'biːlə) *n* an ancient city in Assyria, near which the **Battle of Arbela** took place (331 BC), in which Alexander the Great defeated the Persians. Modern name: **Erbil**

Arber ('ɑːbə) *n* **Werner**. born 1929, Swiss microbiologist, noted for his work on restriction enzymes. Nobel prize for physiology or medicine 1978

arbiter ('ɑːbɪtə) *n* **1** a person empowered to judge in a dispute; referee; arbitrator **2** a person having complete control of something [c15: from Latin, of obscure origin]

arbitrament (ɑː'bɪtrəmənt) *n* **1** the decision or award made by an arbitrator upon a disputed matter **2** another word for **arbitration**

arbitrary ('ɑːbɪtrərɪ) *adj* **1** founded on or subject to personal whims, prejudices, etc; capricious **2** having only relative application or relevance; not absolute **3** (of a government, ruler, etc) despotic or dictatorial **4** *law* (esp of a penalty or punishment) not laid down by statute; within the court's discretion [c15: from Latin *arbitrārius* arranged through arbitration, uncertain]

arbitrate ('ɑːbɪˌtreɪt) *vb* **1** to settle or decide (a dispute); achieve a settlement between parties **2** to submit to or settle by arbitration [c16: from Latin *arbitrāri* to give judgment; see ARBITER] > 'arbi.trator *n*

arbitration (ˌɑːbɪˈtreɪʃən) *n law* the hearing and determination of a dispute, esp an industrial dispute, by an impartial referee selected or agreed upon by the parties concerned

Arblay (ɑːbleɪ; *French* arble) *n* See **d'Arblay**

arbor¹ ('ɑːbə) *n* the US spelling of **arbour**

arbor² ('ɑːbə) *n* **1** a rotating shaft in a machine or power tool on which a milling cutter or grinding wheel is fitted **2** a rotating shaft or mandrel on which a workpiece is fitted for machining [c17: from Latin: tree, mast]

arboraceous (ˌɑːbəˈreɪʃəs) *adj literary* **1** resembling a tree **2** wooded

arboreal (ɑːˈbɔːrɪəl) *adj* **1** of, relating to, or resembling a tree **2** living in or among trees

arborescent (ˌɑːbəˈrɛsᵊnt) *adj* having the shape or characteristics of a tree > ˌarbo'rescence *n*

arboretum (ˌɑːbəˈriːtəm) *n, pl* -ta (-tə) *or* -tums a place where trees or shrubs are cultivated for their scientific or educational interest [c19: from Latin, from *arbor* tree]

arboriculture ('ɑːbərɪˌkʌltʃə) *n* the cultivation of trees or shrubs, esp for the production of timber > ˌarbori'culturist *n*

arborio rice (ɑːˈbɔːrɪəʊ) *n* a variety of round-grain rice used for making risotto [c20: after *Arborio*, a town in N Italy]

arbor vitae ('ɑːbɔː 'viːtaɪ, 'vaɪtiː) *n* any of several Asian and North American evergreen coniferous trees of the genera *Thuja* and *Thujopsis*, esp *Thuja occidentalis*, having tiny scalelike leaves and egglike cones [c17: from New Latin, literally: tree of life]

arbour ('ɑːbə) *n* a leafy glade or bower shaded by trees, vines, shrubs, etc, esp when trained about a trellis [c14 *erber*, from Old French *herbier*, from Latin *herba* grass]

Arbroath (ɑːˈbrəʊθ) *n* a port and resort in E Scotland, in Angus: scene of the barons of Scotland's declaration of independence to Pope John XXII in 1320. Pop: 22 785 (2001)

Arbus ('ɑːbəs) *n* **Diane**, original name *Diane Nemerov*. 1923–71, US photographer, noted esp for her portraits of vagrants, dwarfs, transvestites, etc

Arbuthnot (ɑːˈbʌθnɒt) *n* **John**. 1667–1735, Scottish physician and satirist: author of *The History of John Bull* (1712) and, with others, of the *Memoirs of Martinus Scriblerus* (1741)

arbutus (ɑːˈbjuːtəs) *n, pl* -tuses any of several temperate ericaceous shrubs of the genus *Arbutus*, esp the strawberry tree of S Europe. They have clusters of white or pinkish flowers, broad evergreen leaves, and strawberry-like berries [c16: from Latin; related to *arbor* tree]

arc (ɑːk) *n* **1** something curved in shape **2** part of an unbroken curved line **3** a luminous discharge that occurs when an electric current flows between two electrodes or any other two surfaces separated by a small gap and a high potential difference ▷ *vb* arcs, arcing, arced *or* arcs, arcking, arcked **5** (*intr*) to form an arc ▷ *prefix* **6** *maths* specifying an inverse trigonometric function: usually written arcsin, arctan, arcsec, etc, or sometimes $\sin^{-1}$, $\tan^{-1}$, $\sec^{-1}$, etc [c14: from Old French, from Latin *arcus* bow, arch]

ARC *abbreviation* AIDS-related complex: an early condition in which a person infected with the AIDS virus may suffer from such mild symptoms as loss of weight, fever, etc

arcade (ɑːˈkeɪd) *n* **1** a set of arches and their supporting columns **2** a covered and sometimes arched passageway, usually with shops on one or both sides [c18: from French, from Italian *arcata*, from *arco*, from Latin *arcus* bow, arch]

Arcadia (ɑːˈkeɪdɪə) *n* **1** a department of Greece, in the central Peloponnese. Capital: Tripolis. Pop: 91 326 (2001). Area: 4367 sq km (1686 sq miles) **2** the traditional idealized rural setting of Greek and Roman bucolic poetry and later of the literature of the Renaissance

Arcadian (ɑːˈkeɪdɪən) *adj* **1** of or relating to Arcadia or its inhabitants, esp the idealized Arcadia of pastoral poetry **2** rustic or bucolic: *a life of Arcadian simplicity* ▷ *n* **3** a person who leads or prefers a quiet simple rural life > Ar'cadianism *n*

arcane (ɑːˈkeɪn) *adj* requiring secret knowledge to be understood; mysterious; esoteric [c16: from Latin *arcānus* secret, hidden, from *arcēre* to shut up, keep safe]

arcanum (ɑːˈkeɪnəm) *n, pl* -na (-nə) a secret of nature sought by alchemists [c16: from Latin; see ARCANE]

Arc de Triomphe ('ɑːk də 'triːɒmf; *French* ark də trijɔ̃f) *n* the triumphal arch in Paris begun by Napoleon I to commemorate his victories of 1805–6 and completed in 1836

arch¹ (ɑːtʃ) *n* **1** a curved structure, normally in the vertical plane, that spans an opening **2** Also called: archway a structure in the form of an arch that serves as a gateway **3** something curved like an arch **4 a** any of various parts or structures of the body having a curved or archlike outline, such as the transverse portion of the aorta (**arch of the aorta**) or the raised bony vault formed by the tarsal and metatarsal bones (**arch of the foot**) **b** one of the basic patterns of the human fingerprint, formed by several curved ridges one above the other ▷ *vb* **5** (*tr*) to span (an opening) with an arch **6** to form or cause to form an arch or a curve resembling that of an arch **7** (*tr*) to span or extend over [c14: from Old French *arche*, from Vulgar Latin *arca* (unattested), from Latin *arcus* bow, ARC]

arch² (ɑːtʃ) *adj* **1** (*prenominal*) chief; principal; leading: *his arch rival* **2** (*prenominal*) very experienced; expert: *an arch criminal* **3** knowing or superior **4** playfully or affectedly roguish or mischievous [c16: independent use of ARCH-] > 'archly *adv* > 'archness *n*

arch. *abbreviation* **1** archaic **2** archaism

arch- *or* **archi-** *combining form* **1** chief; principal; of highest rank **2** eminent above all others of the same kind; extreme [ultimately from Greek *arkhi-*, from *arkhein* to rule]

-arch *n combining form* leader; ruler; chief: *patriarch; monarch; heresiarch* [from Greek -*arkhēs*, from *arkhein* to rule; compare ARCH-]

archaean (ɑːˈkɪən) *n* any member of the *Archaea*, a domain of prokaryotic microorganisms, distinguished from bacteria on molecular phylogenetic grounds and often found in hostile environments, such as volcanic vents and hot springs

Archaean *or esp US* **Archean** (ɑːˈkiːən) *adj* of or relating to the highly metamorphosed rocks formed in the early Precambrian era

archaeo- *or* **archeo-** *combining form* **1** indicating ancient or primitive time or condition: *archaeology; archaeopteryx* **2** of, involving, or denoting the study of remains from archaeological sites: *archaeozoology* [from Greek *arkhaio-*, from *arkhaios* from *arkhein* to begin]

archaeology *or* **archeology** (ˌɑːkɪˈɒlədʒɪ) *n* the study of man's past by scientific analysis of the material remains of his cultures [c17: from Late Latin *archaeologia*, from Greek *arkhaiologia* study of what is ancient, from *arkhaios* ancient (from *arkhē* beginning)] > archaeological *or* archeological (ˌɑːkɪəˈlɒdʒɪkᵊl) *adj* > ˌarchae'ologist *or* ˌarche'ologist *n*

archaeopteryx (ˌɑːkɪˈɒptərɪks) *n* any of several extinct primitive birds constituting the genus *Archaeopteryx*, esp *A. lithographica*, which occurred in Jurassic times and had teeth, a long tail, well-developed wings, and a body covering of feathers [c19: from ARCHAEO- + Greek *pterux* winged creature]

archaic (ɑːˈkeɪɪk) *adj* **1** belonging to or characteristic of a much earlier period; ancient **2** out of date; antiquated **3** (of idiom, vocabulary, etc) characteristic of an earlier period of a language and not in ordinary use [c19: from French *archaïque*, from Greek *arkhaïkos*, from *arkhaios* ancient, from *arkhē* beginning, from *arkhein* to begin]

> ar'chaically *adv*

archaism ('ɑːkɪˌɪzəm, -keɪ-) *n* **1** the adoption or imitation of something archaic, such as a word or an artistic or literary style **2** an archaic word, expression, style, etc [c17: from New Latin *archaismus*, from Greek *arkhaïsmos*, from *arkhaizein* to model one's style upon that of ancient writers; see ARCHAIC] > 'archaist *n* > ˌarcha'istic *adj*

archangel ('ɑːkˌeɪndʒəl) *n* a principal angel, a member of the order ranking immediately above the angels in medieval angelology

Archangel ('ɑːkˌeɪndʒəl) *n* a port in NW Russia, on the Dvina River: major centre for the timber trade and White Sea fisheries. Pop: 345 000 (2005 est). Russian name: Arkhangelsk

archbishop ('ɑːtʃ'bɪʃəp) *n* a bishop of the highest rank. Abbreviations: abp, Abp, Arch, Archbb

archbishopric ('ɑːtʃ'bɪʃəprɪk) *n* the rank, office, or jurisdiction of an archbishop

archdeacon ('ɑːtʃ'diːkən) *n* **1** an Anglican clergyman ranking just below a bishop and having supervisory duties under the bishop **2** a clergyman of similar rank in other Churches

archdiocese ('ɑːtʃ'daɪəˌsiːs, -sɪs) *n* the diocese of an archbishop > archdiocesan ('ɑːtʃdaɪ'ɒsɪsⁿn) *adj*

archducal ('ɑːtʃ'djuːkⁿl) *adj* of or relating to an archduke, archduchess, or archduchy

archduchess ('ɑːtʃ'dʌtʃɪs) *n* **1** the wife or widow of an archduke **2** (since 1453) a princess of the Austrian imperial family, esp a daughter of the Austrian emperor

archduchy ('ɑːtʃ'dʌtʃɪ) *n*, *pl* -duchies the territory ruled by an archduke or archduchess

archduke ('ɑːtʃ'djuːk) *n* a chief duke, esp (since 1453) a prince of the Austrian imperial dynasty

Archean (ɑː'kiːən) *adj* a variant spelling (esp US) of **Archaean**

archegonium (ˌɑːkɪ'gəʊnɪəm) *n*, *pl* -nia (-nɪə) a female sex organ, occurring in mosses, spore-bearing vascular plants, and gymnosperms, that produces a single egg cell in its swollen base [c19: from New Latin, from Greek *arkhegonos* original parent, from *arkhe*- chief, first + *gonos* seed, race]

archenemy ('ɑːtʃ'ɛnɪmɪ) *n*, *pl* -mies **1** a chief enemy **2** the archenemy (*often capital*) the devil

archeology (ˌɑːkɪ'ɒlədʒɪ) *n* a variant spelling of **archaeology**

archer ('ɑːtʃə) *n* a person skilled in the use of a bow and arrow [c13: from Old French *archier*, from Late Latin *arcārius*, from Latin *arcus* bow]

Archer¹ ('ɑːtʃə) *n* the Archer the constellation Sagittarius, the ninth sign of the zodiac

Archer² ('ɑːtʃə) *n* **1 Frederick Scott.** 1813–57, British inventor and sculptor. He developed (1851) the wet collodion photographic process, enabling multiple copies of pictures to be made **2 Jeffrey (Howard)**, Baron Archer of Weston-Super-Mare. born 1940, British novelist and Conservative politician. He was an MP from 1969 until 1974. His novels include *Kane and Abel* (1979), *Honour Among Thieves* (1993), and *The Fourth Estate* (1996): in 2000 he was imprisoned for perjury and attempting to pervert the course of justice **3 William.** 1856–1924, Scottish critic and dramatist: made the first English translations of Ibsen

archerfish ('ɑːtʃəˌfɪʃ) *n*, *pl* -fish *or* -fishes any freshwater percoid fish of the family *Toxotidae* of S and SE Asia and Australia, esp *Toxotes jaculatrix*, that catch insects by spitting water at them

archery ('ɑːtʃərɪ) *n* **1** the art or sport of shooting with bows and arrows **2** archers or their weapons collectively

archetype ('ɑːkɪˌtaɪp) *n* **1** a perfect or typical specimen **2** an original model or pattern; prototype **3** *psychoanal* one of the inherited mental images postulated by Jung as the content of the collective unconscious **4** a constantly recurring symbol or motif in literature, painting, etc [c17: from Latin *archetypum* an original, from Greek *arkhetupon*, from *arkhetupos* first-moulded; see ARCH-, TYPE] > ˌarche'typal *adj*

archfiend (ˌɑːtʃ'fiːnd) *n* the archfiend (*often capital*) the chief of fiends or devils; Satan

archi- *combining form* a variant of **arch-**

archidiaconal (ˌɑːkɪdaɪ'ækənⁿl) *adj* of or relating to an archdeacon or his office

archiepiscopal (ˌɑːkɪɪ'pɪskəpⁿl) *adj* of or associated with an archbishop

archil ('ɑːtʃɪl) *n* a variant spelling of **orchil**

Archilochus (ɑː'kɪləkəs) *n* 7th century BC, Greek poet of Paros, notable for using his own experience as subject matter

archimandrite (ˌɑːkɪ'mændraɪt) *n Greek Orthodox Church* the head of a monastery or a group of monasteries [c16: from Late Latin *archimandrīta*, from Late Greek *arkhimandrītēs*, from ARCHI- + *mandra* monastery]

Archimedes¹ (ˌɑːkɪ'miːdiːz) *n* ?287–212 BC, Greek mathematician and physicist of Syracuse, noted for his work in geometry, hydrostatics, and mechanics > Archimedean (ˌɑːkɪ'miːdɪən, -mɪ'diːən) *adj*

Archimedes² (ˌɑːkɪ'miːdiːz) *n* a walled plain in the NE quadrant of the moon, about 80 km in diameter

Archimedes' principle *n* a law of physics stating that the apparent upward force (buoyancy) of a body immersed in a fluid is equal to the weight of the displaced fluid

Archimedes' screw *or* **Archimedean screw** *n* an ancient type of water-lifting device making use of a spiral passage in an inclined cylinder. The water is raised when the spiral is rotated

archipelago (ˌɑːkɪ'pɛlɪˌgəʊ) *n*, *pl* -gos *or* -goes **1** a group of islands **2** a sea studded with islands [c16 (meaning: the Aegean Sea): from Italian *arcipelago*, literally: the chief sea (perhaps originally a mistranslation of Greek *Aigaion pelagos* the Aegean Sea), from ARCHI- + *pelago* sea, from Latin *pelagus*, from Greek *pelagos*] > archipelagic (ˌɑːkɪpə'lædʒɪk) *or* archipelagian (ˌɑːkɪpə'leɪdʒɪən) *adj*

Archipenko (*Russian* ar'xipɪnkə) *n* **Aleksandr Porfiryevich** (alık'sandr par'firjɪvitʃ). 1887–1964, Russian sculptor and painter, in the US after 1923, whose work is characterized by economy of form

architect ('ɑːkɪˌtɛkt) *n* **1** a person qualified to design buildings and to superintend their erection **2** a person similarly qualified in another form of construction: *a naval architect* **3** any planner or creator [c16: from French *architecte*, from Latin *architectus*, from Greek *arkhitektōn* director of works, from ARCHI- + *tektōn* workman; related to *tekhnē* art, skill]

architectonic (ˌɑːkɪtɛk'tɒnɪk) *adj* **1** denoting, relating to, or having architectural qualities **2** *metaphysics* of or relating to the systematic classification of knowledge [c16: from Late Latin *architectonicus* concerning architecture; see ARCHITECT]

architectonics (ˌɑːkɪtɛk'tɒnɪks) *n* (*functioning as singular*) **1** the science of architecture **2** *metaphysics* the scientific classification of knowledge

architecture ('ɑːkɪˌtɛktʃə) *n* **1** the art and science of designing and superintending the erection of buildings and similar structures **2** a style of building or structure: *Gothic architecture* **3** buildings or structures collectively **4** the structure or design of anything > ˌarchi'tectural *adj*

architrave ('ɑːkɪˌtreɪv) *n architect* **1** the lowest part of an entablature that bears on the columns **2** a moulding around a doorway, window opening, etc [c16: via French from Italian, from ARCHI- + *trave* beam, from Latin *trabs*]

archive ('ɑːkaɪv) *n* (*often plural*) **1** a collection of records of or about an institution, family, etc **2** a place where such records are kept **3** *computing* data transferred to a tape or disk for long-term storage rather than frequent use ▷ *vb* (*tr*) **4** to store (documents, data, etc) in an archive or other repository [c17: from Late Latin *archīvum*, from Greek *arkheion* repository of official records, from *arkhē* government] > ar'chival *adj*

archivist ('ɑːkɪvɪst) *n* a person in charge of archives, their collection, and cataloguing

archon ('ɑːkɒn, -kən) *n* (in ancient Athens) one of the nine chief magistrates [c17: from Greek *arkhōn* ruler, from *arkhein* to rule] > 'archonˌship *n*

archpriest ('ɑːtʃ'priːst) *n Christianity* **1** (formerly) a chief assistant to a bishop, performing many of his sacerdotal functions during his absence **2** a senior priest

archway ('ɑːtʃˌweɪ) *n* a passageway or entrance under an arch or arches

-archy *n combining form* government; rule: *anarchy; monarchy* [from Greek *-arkhia*; see **-ARCH**]

Arcimboldo (*Italian* artʃim'boldo) *n* **Giuseppe** 1527–93, Italian painter, best remembered for painting grotesque figures composed of fruit, vegetables, and meat

arc light *n* a light source in which an arc between two electrodes, usually carbon, produces intense white illumination. Also called: **arc lamp**

arctic ('ɑːktɪk) *adj* **1** of or relating to the Arctic: *arctic temperatures* **2** *informal* freezing: *the weather at Christmas was arctic* ▷ *n* **3** (*modifier*) designed or suitable for conditions of extreme cold: *arctic clothing* [C14: from Latin *arcticus*, from Greek *arktikos* northern, literally: pertaining to (the constellation of) the Bear, from *arktos* bear]

Arctic ('ɑːktɪk) *n* **1** the Arctic or Arctic Zone the regions north of the Arctic Circle ▷ *adj* **2** of or relating to the regions north of the Arctic Circle

Arctic Circle *n* the imaginary circle round the earth, parallel to the equator, at latitude 66° 32′ N; it marks the northernmost point at which the sun appears above the level of the horizon on the winter solstice

arctic hare *n* a large hare, *Lepus arcticus*, of the Canadian Arctic whose fur is white in winter

Arctic Monkeys *pl n* British rock group (formed 2002): comprising Alex Turner (born 1986; vocals, guitar), Jamie Cook (born 1985, guitar), Matt Helders (born 1986, drums, vocals) and Nick O'Malley (born 1985, bass guitar); the first major band to achieve widespread success through internet exposure

Arctic Ocean *n* the ocean surrounding the North Pole, north of the Arctic Circle. Area: about 14 100 000 sq km (5 440 000 sq miles)

arctic willow *n* a low-growing shrub, *Salix arctica*, of the tundra

Arcturus (ɑːk'tjʊərəs) *n* the brightest star in the constellation Boötes: a red giant. Visual magnitude: −0.4; spectral type: K2III; distance: 37 light years [C14: from Latin, from Greek *Arktouros*, from *arktos* bear + *ouros* guard, keeper]

arcuate ('ɑːkjuːɪt, -ˌeɪt) *adj* shaped or bent like an arc or bow [C17: from Latin *arcuāre*, from *arcus* ARC]

arc welding *n* a technique in which metal is welded by heat generated by an electric arc struck between two electrodes or between one electrode and the metal workpiece ▷ **arc welder** *n*

-ard *or* **-art** *suffix forming nouns* indicating a person who does something, esp to excess, or is characterized by a certain quality: *braggart; drunkard; dullard* [via Old French from Germanic *-hard* (literally: hardy, bold), the final element in many Germanic masculine names, such as *Bernhard* Bernard, *Gerhart* Gerard, etc]

Ardèche (*French* ardɛʃ) *n* a department of S France, in Rhône-Alpes region. Capital: Privas. Pop: 294 933 (2003 est). Area: 5556 sq km (2167 sq miles)

Arden¹ ('ɑːdⁿn) *n* **Forest of Arden** a region of N Warwickshire, part of a former forest: scene of Shakespeare's *As You Like It*

Arden² ('ɑːdⁿn) *n* **John.** born 1930, British dramatist and novelist. His plays include *Serjeant Musgrave's Dance* (1959) and *The Workhouse Donkey* (1963); novels include *Silence Among the Weapons* (1982): he often works in collaboration with his wife Margaretta D'Arcy

Ardennes (ɑː'dɛn; *French* ardɛn) *n* **1** a department of NE France, in Champagne-Ardenne region. Capital: Mézières. Pop: 288 806 (2003 est). Area: 5253 sq km (2049 sq miles) **2 the Ardennes** a wooded plateau in SE Belgium, Luxembourg, and NE France: scene of heavy fighting in both World Wars

ardent ('ɑːdⁿnt) *adj* **1** expressive of or characterized by intense desire or emotion; passionate **2** intensely enthusiastic; eager **3** glowing, flashing, or shining: *ardent eyes* **4** *rare* burning [C14: from Latin *ārdēre* to burn] ▷ **'ardency** *n* ▷ **'ardently** *adv*

ardour *or US* **ardor** ('ɑːdə) *n* **1** feelings of great intensity and warmth; fervour **2** eagerness; zeal [C14: from Old French *ardour*, from Latin *ārdor*, from *ārdēre* to burn]

Ards (ɑːdz) *n* a district of Northern Ireland, in Co Down. Pop: 74 369 (2003 est). Area: 368 sq km (142 sq miles)

arduous ('ɑːdjʊəs) *adj* **1** requiring great physical or mental effort; difficult to accomplish; strenuous **2** hard to endure; harsh **3** hard to overcome or surmount; steep or difficult: *an arduous track* [C16: from Latin *arduus* steep, difficult]

are¹ (ɑː; *unstressed* ə) *vb* the plural form of the present tense (indicative mood) of the verb 'be' and the singular form used with *you* [Old English *aron*, second person plural of *bēon* to BE]

are² (ɑː) *n* a unit of area equal to 100 sq metres or 119.599 sq yards; one hundredth of a hectare [C19: from French, from Latin *ārea* piece of level ground; see AREA]

area ('ɛərɪə) *n* **1** any flat, curved, or irregular expanse of a surface **2 a** the extent of a two-dimensional surface enclosed within a specified boundary or geometric figure: *the area of Ireland; the area of a triangle* **b** the two-dimensional extent of the surface of a solid, or of some part thereof, esp one bounded by a closed curve: *the area of a sphere* **3** a section, portion, or part **4** region; district; locality **5 a** a geographical division of administrative responsibility **b** (*as modifier*): *area manager* **6** a part or section, as of a building, town, etc, having some specified function or characteristic: *reception area; commercial area; slum area* **7** Also called: **areaway** a sunken area, usually enclosed, giving light, air, and sometimes access to a cellar or basement **8** the range, extent, or scope of anything **9** a subject field or field of study [C16: from Latin: level ground, open space, threshing-floor; related to *ārēre* to be dry] ▷ **'areal** *adj*

arena (ə'riːnə) *n* **1** an enclosure or platform, usually surrounded by seats on all sides, in which sports events, contests, entertainments, etc, take place: *a boxing arena* **2** the central area of an ancient Roman amphitheatre, in which gladiatorial contests and other spectacles were held **3** a sphere or scene of conflict or intense activity: *the political arena* [C17: from Latin *harēna* sand, place where sand was strewn for the combats]

arenaceous (ˌærɪ'neɪʃəs) *adj* **1** (of sedimentary rocks and deposits) composed of sand or sandstone **2** (of plants) growing best in a sandy soil [C17: from Latin *harēnāceus* sandy, from *harēna* sand]

Arendt ('ɛərənt) *n* **Hannah.** 1906–75, US political philosopher, born in Germany. Her publications include *The Origins of Totalitarianism* (1951) and *Eichmann in Jerusalem* (1961)

aren't (ɑːnt) *contraction of* **1** are not **2** *informal, chiefly Brit* (used in interrogative sentences) am not

areola (ə'rɪələ) *n, pl* **-lae** (-ˌliː) *or* **-las** *anatomy* any small circular area, such as the pigmented ring around the human nipple or the inflamed area surrounding a pimple [C17: from Latin: diminutive of AREA] ▷ **a'reolar** *or* **areolate** (ə'rɪəlɪt, -ˌleɪt) *adj*

areole ('ærɪəʊl) *n* **1** *biology* a space outlined on a surface, such as an area between veins on a leaf or on an insect's wing **2** a sunken area on a cactus from which spines, hairs, etc, arise ▷ **'areoˌlate** *adj*

Areopagus (ˌærɪ'ɒpəgəs) *n* **1 a** the hill to the northwest of the Acropolis in Athens **b** (in ancient Athens) the judicial council whose members (Areopagites) met on this hill **2** *literary* any high court [via Latin from Greek *Areiopagus*, contracted from *Areios pagos*, hill of Ares]

Arequipa (ˌærɪ'kiːpə; *Spanish* are'kipa) *n* a city in S Peru, at an altitude of 2250 m (7500 ft): founded in 1540 on the site of an Inca city. Pop: 791 000 (2005 est)

Ares ('ɛəriːz) *n Greek myth* the god of war, born of Zeus and Hera. Roman counterpart: **Mars**

arête (ə'reɪt, ə'rɛt) *n* a sharp ridge separating two cirques or glacial valleys in mountainous regions [C19: from French: fishbone, backbone (of a fish), ridge, sharp edge, from Latin *arista* ear of corn, fishbone]

Arethusa (ˌærɪ'θjuːzə) *n Greek myth* a nymph who was changed into a spring on the island of Ortygia to escape the amorous advances of the river god Alpheus

Aretino (*Italian* are'tiːno) *n* **Pietro** ('pjɛːtro). 1492–1556, Italian satirist, poet, and dramatist, noted for his satirical attacks on leading political figures

Arezzo (ə'rɛtsəʊ; *Italian* a'rettso) *n* a city in central Italy, in E Tuscany. Pop: 91 589 (2001). Ancient Latin name: **Arretium**

Arg. *abbreviation* Argentina

a

argal ('ɑːgəl) *n* another name for **argol**

argali ('ɑːgəlɪ) *or* **argal** *n*, *pl* **-gali** *or* **-gals** a wild sheep, *Ovis ammon*, inhabiting semidesert regions in central Asia: family *Bovidae*, order *Artiodactyla*. It is the largest of the sheep, having massive horns in the male, which may almost form a circle [c18: from Mongolian]

argan ('ɑːgæn) *n* a thorny evergreen tree, *Argania spinosa*, native to SW Morocco, the plum-sized fruit of which contains a nut that yields an oil valued for cooking

argan oil ('ɑːgən) *n* a yellow nutty-flavoured oil extracted from the ripe green olive-like fruits of the argan tree, *Argania spinosa* of SW Morocco, and used in cooking, medicines, and cosmetics [c21: probably from *Argana*, a village northeast of Agadir, Morocco, where it is believed to have originated]

argent ('ɑːdʒənt) *n* **a** an archaic or poetic word for **silver** **b** (*as adjective*; *often postpositive, esp in heraldry*): *a bend argent* [c15: from Old French, from Latin]

Argenteuil (*French* arʒɑ̃tœj) *n* a suburb of Paris, France, with a convent (656) that became famous when Héloïse was abbess (12th century). Pop: 93 961 (1999)

argentiferous (ˌɑːdʒən'tɪfərəs) *adj* containing or bearing silver

Argentina (ˌɑːdʒən'tiːnə) *n* a republic in southern South America: colonized by the Spanish from 1516 onwards; gained independence in 1816 and became a republic in 1852; ruled by military dictatorships for much of the 20th century; civilian rule restored in 1983; consists chiefly of subtropical plains and forests (the Chaco) in the north, temperate plains (the pampas) in the central parts, the Andes in the west, and an infertile plain extending to Tierra del Fuego in the south (Patagonia); an important meat producer. Language: Spanish. Religion: Roman Catholic. Currency: peso. Capital: Buenos Aires. Pop: 38 871 000 (2004 est). Area: 2 776 653 sq km (1 072 067 sq miles). Also called: **the Argentine**

argentine ('ɑːdʒənˌtaɪn) *adj* **1** of, relating to, or resembling silver ▷ *n* **2** any of various small marine salmonoid fishes, such as *Argentina sphyraena*, that constitute the family *Argentinidae* and are characterized by a long silvery body

Argentine ('ɑːdʒənˌtiːn, -ˌtaɪn) *n* **1 the Argentine** another name for **Argentina 2** a native or inhabitant of Argentina ▷ *adj* **3** of or relating to Argentina ▷ Also (for senses 2, 3): **Argentinian** (ˌɑːdʒən'tɪnɪən)

Argerich ('ɑːgərɪtʃ) *n* **Martha.** born 1941, Argentinian concert pianist

argillaceous (ˌɑːdʒɪ'leɪʃəs) *adj* (of sedimentary rocks and deposits) composed of very fine-grained material, such as clay, shale, etc

Argive ('ɑːdʒaɪv, -gaɪv) *adj* **1** (in Homer, Virgil, etc) of or relating to the Greeks besieging Troy, esp those from Argos **2** of or relating to Argos or Argolis **3** a literary word for **Greek** ▷ *n* **4** an ancient Greek, esp one from Argos or Argolis

Argo ('ɑːgəʊ) *n Greek myth* the ship in which Jason sailed in search of the Golden Fleece

argol ('ɑːgɒl) *or* **argal** *n* crude potassium hydrogentartrate, deposited as a crust on the sides of wine vats [c14: from Anglo-French *argoil*, of unknown origin]

Argolis ('ɑːgəlɪs) *n* **1** a department and ancient region of Greece, in the NE Peloponnese. Capital: Nauplion. Pop: 102 392 (2001). Area: 2261 sq km (873 sq miles) **2 Gulf of Argolis** an inlet of the Aegean Sea, in the E Peloponnese

argon ('ɑːgɒn) *n* an extremely unreactive colourless odourless element of the rare gas series that forms almost 1 per cent (by volume) of the atmosphere. It is used in electric lights. Symbol: Ar; atomic no: 18; atomic wt: 39.948; density: 1.7837 kg/m³; freezing pt: –189.3°C; boiling pt: –185.9°C [c19: from Greek, from *argos* idle, inactive, from A-¹ + *ergon* work]

Argonaut ('ɑːgəˌnɔːt) *n* **1** *Greek myth* one of the heroes who sailed with Jason in quest of the Golden Fleece **2** a person who took part in the Californian gold rush of 1849 **3** another name for the **paper nautilus** [c16: from Greek *Argonautēs*, from *Argō* the name of Jason's ship + *nautēs* sailor] > Argo'nautic *adj*

Argonne ('ɑːgɒn; *French* argɔn) *n* **the Argonne** a wooded

region of NE France: scene of major battles in both World Wars

Argos ('ɑːgɒs, -gəs) *n* an ancient city in SE Greece, in the NE Peloponnese: one of the oldest Greek cities, it dominated the Peloponnese in the 7th century BC. Pop (municipality): 29 505 (2001)

argosy ('ɑːgəsɪ) *n*, *pl* **-sies** *archaic or poetic* a large abundantly laden merchant ship, or a fleet of such ships [c16: from Italian *Ragusea (nave)* (ship) of Ragusa]

argot ('ɑːgəʊ) *n* slang or jargon peculiar to a particular group, esp (formerly) a group of thieves [c19: from French, of unknown origin]

Argovie (argɔvi) *n* the French name for **Aargau**

arguable ('ɑːgjʊəb³l) *adj* **1** capable of being disputed; doubtful **2** capable of being supported by argument

arguably ('ɑːgjʊəblɪ) *adv* (*sentence modifier*) it can be argued that

argue ('ɑːgjuː) *vb* **-gues**, **-guing**, **-gued 1** (*intr*) to quarrel; wrangle: *they were always arguing until I arrived* **2** (*intr*; *often foll by for or against*) to present supporting or opposing reasons or cases in a dispute; reason **3** (*tr*; *may take a clause as object*) to try to prove by presenting reasons; maintain **4** (*tr*; *often passive*) to debate or discuss **5** (*tr*) to persuade **6** (*tr*) to give evidence of; suggest: *her looks argue despair* [c14: from Old French *arguer* to assert, charge with, from Latin *arguere* to make clear, accuse; related to Latin *argūtus* clear, *argentum* silver] > 'arguer *n*

argufy ('ɑːgjʊˌfaɪ) *vb* **-fies**, **-fying**, **-fied** *facetious or dialect* to argue or quarrel, esp over something trivial

argument ('ɑːgjʊmənt) *n* **1** a quarrel; altercation **2** a discussion in which reasons are put forward in support of and against a proposition, proposal, or case; debate **3** (*sometimes plural*) a point or series of reasons presented to support or oppose a proposition **4** a summary of the plot or subject of a book, etc **5** *logic* a process of deductive or inductive reasoning that purports to show its conclusion to be true **6** *logic* an obsolete name for the middle term of a syllogism **7** *maths* an element to which an operation, function, predicate, etc, applies, esp the independent variable of a function

argumentation (ˌɑːgjʊmɛn'teɪʃən) *n* the process of reasoning methodically

argumentative (ˌɑːgjʊ'mɛntətɪv) *adj* **1** given to arguing; contentious **2** characterized by argument; controversial

Argus ('ɑːgəs) *n* **1** *Greek myth* a giant with a hundred eyes who was made guardian of the heifer Io. After he was killed by Hermes his eyes were transferred to the peacock's tail **2** a vigilant person; guardian

Argus-eyed *adj* keen-sighted; observant; vigilant

argy-bargy *or* **argie-bargie** ('ɑːdʒɪ'bɑːdʒɪ) *n*, *pl* **-bargies** *Brit informal* a wrangling argument or verbal dispute [c19: from Scottish, compound based on dialect *argle*, probably from ARGUE]

Argyll and Bute (ɑː'gaɪl) *n* a council area in W Scotland on the Atlantic Ocean: in 1975 the historical counties of Argyllshire and Bute became part of Strathclyde region; in 1996 they were reinstated as a single unitary authority. Argyll and Bute is mountainous and includes the islands of Bute, Mull, Islay, and Jura. Administrative centre: Lochgilphead. Pop: 91 300 (2003 est). Area: 6930 sq km (2676 sq miles)

Argyllshire (ɑː'gaɪlˌʃɪə, -ʃə) *n* (until 1975) a county of W Scotland, part of Strathclyde region (1975–96), now part of Argyll and Bute

Århus *or* **Aarhus** (*Danish* 'ʌhuːs) *n* a city and port in Denmark, in E Jutland. Pop: 228 547 (2004 est)

aria ('ɑːrɪə) *n* an elaborate accompanied song for solo voice from a cantata, opera, or oratorio [c18: from Italian: tune, AIR]

Ariadne (ˌærɪ'ædnɪ) *n Greek myth* daughter of Minos and Pasiphaë: she gave Theseus the thread with which he found his way out of the Minotaur's labyrinth

Arian ('ɛərɪən) *adj* **1** of, relating to, or characterizing Arius (?250–336 AD), the Greek Christian theologian, or Arianism ▷ *n* **2** an adherent of Arianism

-arian *suffix forming nouns* indicating a person or thing that advocates, believes, or is associated with something: *vegetarian; millenarian; librarian* [from Latin *-ārius* -ARY + -AN]

Arianism ('ɛərɪəˌnɪzəm) *n* the doctrine of the Greek Christian theologian Arius (?250–336 AD), pronounced heretical at the Council of Nicaea, which asserted that Christ was not of one substance with the Father, but a creature raised by the Father to the dignity of Son of God

Arias Sánchez ('ærɪæs 'sæntʃɛz) *n* **Oscar.** born 1940, Costa Rican statesman; president (1986–90) and from 2006; Nobel peace prize 1987

Arica (əˈriːkə; *Spanish* aˈrika) *n* a port in extreme N Chile: awarded to Chile in 1929 after the lengthy Tacna-Arica dispute with Peru; outlet for Bolivian and Peruvian trade. Pop: 180 000 (2005 est). See also **Tacna-Arica**

arid ('ærɪd) *adj* **1** having little or no rain; dry; parched with heat **2** devoid of interest [C17: from Latin *āridus*, from *ārēre* to be dry] > **aridity** (əˈrɪdɪtɪ) *or* **aridness** *n*

arid zone *n* either of the zones of latitude 15–30° N and S characterized by very low rainfall and desert or semidesert terrain

Ariège (*French* arjɛʒ) *n* a department of SW France, in Midi-Pyrénées region. Capital: Foix. Pop: 139 612 (2003 est). Area: 4903 sq km (1912 sq miles)

Aries ('ɛəriːz) *n*, *Latin genitive* **Arietis** (əˈraɪɪtɪs) *astrology* **a** Also called: the Ram the first sign of the zodiac, symbol ♈, having a cardinal fire classification, ruled by the planet Mars. The sun is in this sign between about March 21 and April 19 **b** a person born during the period when the sun is in this sign [C14: from Latin: ram]

aright (əˈraɪt) *adv* correctly; rightly; properly

aril ('ærɪl) *n* an appendage on certain seeds, such as those of the yew and nutmeg, developed from or near the funicle of the ovule and often brightly coloured and fleshy [C18: from New Latin *arillus*, from Medieval Latin *arilli* raisins, pips of grapes] > **ariliate** *adj*

Arimathea *or* **Arimathaea** (ˌærɪməˈθiːə) *n* a town in ancient Palestine: location unknown

Arimidex (ˌærɪˈdɛks) *n* a trade name for **anastrozole**

Ariminum (əˈrɪmɪnəm) *n* the ancient name of **Rimini**

arioso (ˌɑːrɪˈəʊzəʊ, -æ-) *n*, *pl* -sos *or* -si (-siː) *music* a recitative with the lyrical quality of an aria [C18: from Italian, from ARIA]

Ariosto (*Italian* aˈrjɔsto) *n* **Ludovico** (ludoˈviːko). 1474–1533, Italian poet, famous for his romantic epic *Orlando Furioso* (1516)

arise (əˈraɪz) *vb* arises, arising, arose, arisen (*intr*) **1** to come into being; originate **2** (foll by *from*) to spring or proceed as a consequence; result: *guilt arising from my actions* **3** to get or stand up, as from a sitting, kneeling, or lying position **4** to come into notice **5** to move upwards; ascend [Old English *ārīsan*; related to Old Saxon *arīsan*, Old High German *irrīsan*; see RISE]

Aristarchus of Samos *n* 3rd century BC, Greek astronomer who anticipated Copernicus in advancing the theory that the earth revolves around the sun

Aristarchus of Samothrace *n* ?220–?150 BC, Greek scholar: librarian at Alexandria, noted for his edition of Homer

Aristides (ˌærɪˈstaɪdiːz) *n* known as *Aristides the Just*. ?530–?468 BC, Athenian general and statesman, who played a prominent part in the Greek victories over the Persians at Marathon (490), Salamis (480), and Plataea (479)

Aristippus (ˌærɪˈstɪpəs) *n* ?435–?356 BC, Greek philosopher, who believed pleasure to be the highest good and founded the Cyrenaic school

aristo ('ærɪstəʊ, əˈrɪstəʊ) *n*, *pl* -tos *informal* short for **aristocrat**

aristocracy (ˌærɪˈstɒkrəsɪ) *n*, *pl* -cies **1** a privileged class of people usually of high birth; the nobility **2** such a class as the ruling body of a state **3** government by such a class **4** a state governed by such a class **5** a class of people considered to be outstanding in a sphere of activity [C16: from Late Latin *aristocratia*, from Greek *aristokratia* rule by the best-born, from *aristos* best; see -CRACY]

aristocrat ('ærɪstəˌkræt) *n* **1** a member of the aristocracy; a noble **2** a person who has the manners or qualities of a member of a privileged or superior class **3** a person who advocates aristocracy as a form of government

aristocratic (ˌærɪstəˈkrætɪk) *adj* **1** relating to or characteristic of aristocracy or an aristocrat **2** elegant or stylish in appearance and behaviour > **aristoˈcratically** *adv*

Aristophanes (ˌærɪˈstɒfəˌniːz) *n* ?448–?380 BC, Greek comic dramatist, who satirized leading contemporary figures such as Socrates and Euripides. Eleven of his plays are extant, including *The Clouds, The Frogs, The Birds,* and *Lysistrata*

Aristotelian (ˌærɪstəˈtiːlɪən) *adj* **1** of or relating to Aristotle (384–322 BC), the Greek philosopher or his philosophy ▷ *n* **2** a follower of Aristotle

Aristotelian logic (ˌærɪstəˈtiːlɪən) *n* the logical theories of Aristotle as developed in the Middle Ages, concerned mainly with syllogistic reasoning: traditional as opposed to modern or symbolic logic

Aristotle ('ærɪˌstɒtəl) *n* 384–322 BC, Greek philosopher; pupil of Plato, tutor of Alexander the Great, and founder of the Peripatetic school at Athens; author of works on logic, ethics, politics, poetics, rhetoric, biology, zoology, and metaphysics. His works influenced Muslim philosophy and science and medieval scholastic philosophy

arithmetic *n* (əˈrɪθmətɪk) **1** the branch of mathematics concerned with numerical calculations, such as addition, subtraction, multiplication, and division **2** one or more calculations involving numerical operations **3** knowledge of or skill in using arithmetic ▷ *adj* (ˌærɪθˈmɛtɪk) Also: ˌarithˈmetical **4** of, relating to, or using arithmetic [C13: from Latin *arithmētica*, from Greek *arithmētikē*, from *arithmein* to count, from *arithmos* number] > ˌarithˈmetically *adv* > ˌarithmeˈtician *n*

arithmetic mean *n* an average value of a set of integers, terms, or quantities, expressed as their sum divided by their number: *the arithmetic mean of 3, 4, and 8 is 5*. Often shortened to: mean. Also called: average

arithmetic progression *n* a sequence of numbers or quantities, each term of which differs from the succeeding term by a constant amount, such as 3,6,9,12

-arium *suffix forming nouns* indicating a place for or associated with something: *aquarium; planetarium; solarium* [from Latin *-ārium*, neuter of *-ārius* -ARY]

Arius ('ɛərɪəs) *n* ?250–336 AD, Greek Christian theologian, originator of the doctrine of Arianism

Ariz. *abbreviation* Arizona

Arizona (ˌærɪˈzəʊnə) *n* a state of the southwestern US: consists of the Colorado plateau in the northeast, including the Grand Canyon, divided from desert in the southwest by mountains rising over 3750 m (12 500 ft). Capital: Phoenix. Pop: 5 580 811 (2003 est). Area: 293 750 sq km (113 417 sq miles). Abbreviations: Ariz *or* (with zip code) AZ

Arjuna ('ɑːdʒʊnə) *n* *Hindu myth* the most important of the five princes in the *Mahabharata*. Krishna served as his charioteer in the battle with the Kauravas

ark (ɑːk) *n* **1** the vessel that Noah built and in which he saved himself, his family, and a number of animals and birds during the Flood (Genesis 6–9) **2** a place or thing offering shelter or protection **3** *dialect* a chest, box, or coffer **4** out of the ark *informal* very old [Old English *arc*, from Latin *arca* box, chest]

Ark (ɑːk) *n* *Judaism* **1** Also called: Holy Ark the cupboard at the front of a synagogue, usually in the eastern wall, in which the Torah scrolls are kept **2** Also called: Ark of the Covenant the most sacred symbol of God's presence among the Hebrew people, carried in their journey from Sinai to the Promised Land (Canaan) and eventually enshrined in the holy of holies of the Temple in Jerusalem

Ark. *abbreviation* Arkansas

Arkansas *n* **1** ('ɑːkənˌsɔː) a state of the southern US: mountainous in the north and west, with the alluvial plain of the Mississippi in the east; has the only diamond mine in the US; the chief US producer of bauxite. Capital: Little Rock. Pop: 2 725 714 (2003 est). Area: 134 537 sq km (51 945 sq miles). Abbreviations: Ark *or* (with zip code) AR **2** (ɑːˈkænzəs) a river in the S central US, rising in central Colorado and flowing east and southeast to join the Mississippi in Arkansas.

Length: 2335 km (1450 miles)

Arkhangelsk (ar'xangɪljsk) n the Russian name for **Archangel**

Arkwright ('ɑːkraɪt) n Sir **Richard**. 1732–92, English cotton manufacturer: inventor of the spinning frame (1769) which produced cotton thread strong enough to be used as a warp

Arles (ɑːlz; French arl) n **1** a city in SE France, on the Rhône: Roman amphitheatre. Pop: 50 513 (1999) **2** Kingdom of Arles a kingdom in SE France which had dissolved by 1378: known as the Kingdom of Burgundy until about 1200

Arlington ('ɑːlɪŋtən) n a county of N Virginia: site of **Arlington National Cemetery**

Arlon (French arlɔ̃) n a town in SE Belgium, capital of Luxembourg province. Pop: 25 766 (2004 est)

arm¹ (ɑːm) n **1** (in man) either of the upper limbs from the shoulder to the wrist. Related adj: **brachial 2** the part of either of the upper limbs from the elbow to the wrist; forearm **3 a** the corresponding limb of any other vertebrate **b** an armlike appendage of some invertebrates **4** an object that covers or supports the human arm, esp the sleeve of a garment or the side of a chair, sofa, etc **5** anything considered to resemble an arm in appearance, position, or function, esp something that branches out from a central support or larger mass: *an arm of the sea; the arm of a record player* **6** an administrative subdivision of an organization: *an arm of the government* **7** power; authority: *the arm of the law* **8 arm in arm** with arms linked **9 at arm's length** at a distance; away from familiarity with or subjection to another **10 in the arms of Morpheus** sleeping **11 with open arms** with great warmth and hospitality: *to welcome someone with open arms* [Old English; related to German *Arm*, Old Norse *armr* arm, Latin *armus* shoulder, Greek *harmos* joint]

arm² (ɑːm) vb (tr) **1** to equip with weapons as a preparation for war **2** to provide (a person or thing) with something that strengthens, protects, or increases efficiency **3 a** to activate (a fuse) so that it will explode at the required time **b** to prepare (an explosive device) for use by introducing a fuse or detonator ▷ n **4** (usually plural) a weapon, esp a firearm ▷ See also **arms** [c14: (n) back formation from *arms*, from Old French *armes*, from Latin *arma*; (vb) from Old French *armer* to equip with arms, from Latin *armāre*, from *arma* arms, equipment]

ARM abbreviation adjustable rate mortgage

Arm. abbreviation Armenia(n)

armada (ɑːˈmɑːdə) n a large number of ships or aircraft [c16: from Spanish, from Medieval Latin *armāta* fleet, armed forces, from Latin *armāre* to provide with arms]

Armada (ɑːˈmɑːdə) n the Armada See **Spanish Armada**

armadillo (ˌɑːməˈdɪləʊ) n, pl -los any edentate mammal of the family *Dasypodidae* of Central and South America and S North America, such as *Priodontes giganteus* (**giant armadillo**). They are burrowing animals, with peglike rootless teeth and a covering of strong horny plates over most of the body [c16: from Spanish, diminutive of *armado* armed (man), from Latin *armātus* armed; compare ARMADA]

Armageddon (ˌɑːməˈgɛdᵊn) n **1** New Testament the final battle at the end of the world between the forces of good and evil, God against the kings of the earth (Revelation 16:16) **2** a catastrophic and extremely destructive conflict, esp World War I viewed as this [c19: from Late Latin *Armageðōn*, from Greek, from Hebrew *har megiddōn*, mountain district of *Megiddo*, in N Palestine, site of various battles in the Old Testament]

Armagh (ɑːˈmɑː) n **1** a historical county of S Northern Ireland: in 1973 it was replaced for administrative purposes by the districts of Armagh and Craigavon. Area: 1326 sq km (512 sq miles) **2** a district in Northern Ireland, in Co Armagh. Pop: 55 449 (2003 est). Area: 667 sq km (258 sq miles) **3** a town in S Northern Ireland, in Armagh district, Co Armagh: seat of Roman Catholic and Protestant archbishops. Pop: 14 590 (2001)

Armalite ('ɑːməlaɪt) n trademark a lightweight high-velocity rifle of various calibres, capable of automatic and semiautomatic operation [c20: from *Armalite*

Division, Fairchild Engine and Airplane Company, manufacturers]

armament ('ɑːməmənt) n **1** (often plural) the weapon equipment of a military vehicle, ship, or aircraft **2 a** military force raised and armed ready for war **3** preparation for war involving the production of equipment and arms [c17: from Latin *armāmenta* utensils, from *armāre* to equip]

Armani (ɑːˈmɑːnɪ; Italian arˈmaːni) n **Giorgio**. born 1936, Italian fashion designer, noted for his restrained classical style

armature ('ɑːmətjʊə) n **1** a revolving structure in an electric motor or generator, wound with the coils that carry the current **2** any part of an electric machine or device that moves under the influence of a magnetic field or within which an electromotive force is induced **3** Also called: **keeper** a soft iron or steel bar placed across the poles of a permanent magnet to close the magnetic circuit **4** sculpture a framework to support the clay or other material used in modelling **5** archaic armour [c15: from Latin *armātūra* armour, equipment, from *armāre* to furnish with equipment; see ARM²]

armchair ('ɑːmˌtʃɛə) n **1** a chair, esp an upholstered one, that has side supports for the arms or elbows **2** (modifier) taking no active part; lacking practical experience; theoretical: *an armchair strategist*

armed¹ (ɑːmd) adj **1** equipped with or supported by arms, armour, etc **2** prepared for conflict or any difficulty **3** (of an explosive device) prepared for use; having a fuse or detonator installed **4** (of plants) having the protection of thorns, spines, etc

armed² (ɑːmd) adj **a** having an arm or arms **b** (in combination): *long-armed; one-armed*

armed forces pl n the military forces of a nation or nations, including the army, navy, air force, marines, etc

armed response unit n (in Britain) a unit of police officers who are trained to use firearms in situations where unarmed police officers would be in danger

armed response vehicle n (in Britain) a police vehicle carrying armed officers who are trained to respond to incidents involving firearms

Armenia (ɑːˈmiːnɪə) n **1** a republic in NW Asia: originally part of the historic Armenian kingdom; acquired by Russia in 1828; became the Armenian Soviet Socialist Republic in 1936; gained independence in 1991. It is mountainous, rising over 4000 m (13 000 ft). Language: Armenian. Religion: Christian (Armenian Apostolic) majority. Currency: dram. Capital: Yerevan. Pop: 3 052 000 (2004 est). Area: 29 800 sq km (11 490 sq miles) **2** a former kingdom in W Asia, between the Black Sea and the Caspian Sea, south of Georgia **3** a town in central Colombia: centre of a coffee-growing district. Pop: 349 000 (2005 est) > Arˈmenian n, adj

Armentières ('ɑːmənˌtɪəz; French armɑ̃tjɛr) n a town in N France: site of battles in both World Wars. Pop: 25 273 (1999)

armful ('ɑːmfʊl) n, pl -fuls the amount that can be held by one or both arms

armhole ('ɑːmˌhəʊl) n the opening in an article of clothing through which the arm passes and to which a sleeve is often fitted

Armidale ('ɑːmɪˌdeɪl) n a town in Australia, in NE New South Wales: a centre for tourism. Pop: 20 271 (2001)

armillary sphere n a model of the celestial sphere consisting of rings representing the relative positions of the celestial equator, ecliptic, etc, used by early astronomers for determining the positions of stars

Arminian (ɑːˈmɪnɪən) adj denoting, relating to, or believing in the Christian Protestant doctrines of Jacobus Arminius (real name *Jacob Harmensen*.; 1560–1609), the Dutch theologian, published in 1610, which rejected absolute predestination and insisted that the sovereignty of God is compatible with free will in man. These doctrines deeply influenced Wesleyan and Methodist theology > Arˈminianˌism n

Arminius (ɑːˈmɪnɪəs) n **1** Also called: Hermann ?17 BC–?21 AD, Germanic chieftain: organized a revolt against the Romans in 9 AD **2** Jacobus. (dʒəˈkəʊbəs), real name *Jacob Harmensen*. 1560–1609, Dutch Protestant theologian

armistice ('ɑːmɪstɪs) *n* an agreement between opposing armies to suspend hostilities in order to discuss peace terms; truce [c18: from New Latin *armistitium*, from Latin *arma* arms + *sistere* to stop, stand still]

Armistice Day *n* the anniversary of the signing of the armistice that ended World War I, on Nov 11, 1918, now kept on Remembrance Sunday. See also **Remembrance Sunday**

Armitage ('ɑːmɪtɪdʒ) *n* **Simon** (**Robert**). born 1963, British poet and writer, whose collections include *Zoom!* (1989), *Killing Time* (1999), and *Universal Home Doctor* (2002)

armlet ('ɑːmlɪt) *n* **1** a small arm, as of a lake, the sea, etc **2** a band or bracelet worn round the arm for ornament, identification, etc

armoire (ɑːmˈwɑː) *n* a large cabinet, originally used for storing weapons [c16: from French, from Old French *armaire*, from Latin *armārium* chest, closet; see AMBRY]

armorial (ɑːˈmɔːrɪəl) *adj* of or relating to heraldry or heraldic arms

armour *or US* **armor** ('ɑːmə) *n* **1** any defensive covering, esp that of metal, chain mail, etc, worn by medieval warriors to prevent injury to the body in battle **2** the protective metal plates on a tank, warship, etc **3** *military* armoured fighting vehicles in general; military units equipped with these **4** any protective covering, such as the shell of certain animals **5** heraldic insignia; arms ▷ *vb* **6** (*tr*) to equip or cover with armour [c13: from Old French *armure*, from Latin *armātūra* armour, equipment]

armoured *or US* **armored** ('ɑːməd) *adj* **1** having a protective covering, such as armour or bone **2** comprising units making use of armoured vehicles: *an armoured brigade*

armourer *or US* **armorer** ('ɑːmərə) *n* **1** a person who makes or mends arms and armour **2** a person employed in the maintenance of small arms and weapons in a military unit

armour plate *n* a tough heavy steel, usually containing chromium, nickel, and molybdenum and often hardened on the surface, used for protecting warships, tanks, etc

armoury *or US* **armory** ('ɑːmərɪ) *n*, *pl* **-mouries** *or* **-mories 1** a secure place for the storage of weapons **2** armour generally **3** *US* a building in which training in the use of arms and drill takes place; drill hall **4** resources, as of arguments or objections, on which to draw

armpit ('ɑːmˌpɪt) *n* **1** the small depression beneath the arm where it joins the shoulder. Technical name: axilla **2** *slang* an extremely unpleasant place: *the armpit of the Mediterranean*

armrest ('ɑːmˌrɛst) *n* the part of a chair, sofa, etc, that supports the arm. Sometimes shortened to **arm**

arms (ɑːmz) *pl n* **1** weapons collectively. See also **small arms 2** military exploits: *prowess in arms* **3** the official heraldic symbols of a family, state, etc, including a shield with distinctive devices, and often supports, a crest, or other insignia **4 bear arms a** to carry weapons **b** to serve in the armed forces **c** to have a coat of arms **5** in arms *or* under arms armed and prepared for war **6** lay down one's arms to stop fighting; surrender **7** take arms *or* take up arms to prepare to fight **8** up in arms indignant; prepared to protest strongly [c13: from Old French *armes*, from Latin *arma*; see ARM²]

Armstrong ('ɑːmˌstrɒŋ) *n* **1** (**Daniel**) **Louis**, known as *Satchmo*. 1900–71, US jazz trumpeter, bandleader, and singer **2 Edwin Howard** 1890–1954, US electrical engineer; invented the superheterodyne radio receiver and the FM radio **3 Gillian** born 1950, Australian film director; her films include *My Brilliant Career* (1978), *Little Women* (1994), and *Charlotte Gray* (2001) **4 Lance** born 1971, US cyclist, winner of 7 Tour de France titles, 1999–2005 **5 Neil** (**Alden**) born 1930, US astronaut; commanded Apollo 11 on the first manned lunar landing during which he became the first man to set foot on the moon on July 20, 1969

arm wrestling *n* a contest in which two people sit facing each other, each with one elbow resting on a table, clasp hands, and each tries to force the other's arm flat onto the table while keeping his own elbow touching the table

army ('ɑːmɪ) *n*, *pl* **-mies 1** the military land forces of a nation **2** a military unit usually consisting of two or more corps with supporting arms and services **3** (*modifier*) of, relating to, or characteristic of an army **4** any large body of people united for some specific purpose **5** a large number of people, animals, etc; multitude [c14: from Old French *armee*, from Medieval Latin *armāta* armed forces; see ARMADA]

army ant *n* any of various mainly tropical American predatory ants of the subfamily *Dorylinae*, which live in temporary nests and travel in vast hordes preying on other animals. Also called: **legionary ant**

army worm *n* the caterpillar of a widely distributed noctuid moth, *Leucania unipuncta*, which travels in vast hordes and is a serious pest of cereal crops in North America

Arnaud ('ɑːnəʊ; *French* arno) *n* **Yvonne**. 1892–1958, French actress, who was well-known on the London stage and in British films. A theatre in Guildford is named after her

Arne (ɑːn) *n* **Thomas** (**Augustine**). 1710–78, English composer, noted for his setting of Shakespearean songs and for his song *Rule Britannia*

Arnhem ('ɑːnəm) *n* a city in the E Netherlands, capital of Gelderland province, on the Rhine: site of a World War II battle. Pop: 142 000 (2003 est)

Arnhem Land *n* a region of N Australia in the N Northern Territory, large areas of which are reserved for native Australians

arnica ('ɑːnɪkə) *n* **1** any N temperate or arctic plant of the genus *Arnica*, typically having yellow flowers: family *Asteraceae* (composites) **2** the tincture of the dried flower heads of any of these plants, esp *A. montana*, used in treating bruises [c18: from New Latin, of unknown origin]

Arnim (*German* 'arnɪm) *n* **Achim von** ('aːxɪm fɔn). 1781–1831, German romantic poet. He published, with Clemens Brentano, the collection of folk songs, *Des Knaben Wunderhorn* (1805–08)

Arno ('ɑːnəʊ) *n* a river in central Italy, rising in the Apennines and flowing through Florence to the Ligurian Sea. Length: about 240 km (150 miles)

Arnold¹ ('ɑːnəld) *n* a town in N central England, in S Nottinghamshire. Pop: 37 402 (2001)

Arnold² ('ɑːnəld) *n* **1** Sir **Malcolm**. 1921–2006, English composer, esp of orchestral works in a traditional idiom **2 Matthew**. 1822–88, English poet, essayist, and literary critic, noted particularly for his poems *Sohrab and Rustum* (1853) and *Dover Beach* (1867), and for his *Essays in Criticism* (1865) and *Culture and Anarchy* (1869) **3** his father, **Thomas**. 1795–1842, English historian and educationalist, headmaster of Rugby School, noted for his reforms in public-school education

aroha ('ɑːrəhə) *n* NZ love, compassion, or affectionate regard [Māori]

aroid ('ærɔɪd, 'eər-) *adj* Also called: **araceous** of, relating to, or belonging to the *Araceae*, a family of plants having small flowers massed on a spadix surrounded by a large petaloid spathe. The family includes arum, calla, and anthurium [c19: from New Latin *Arum* type genus + -OID; see ARUM]

aroint thee *or* **aroint ye** (əˈrɔɪnt) *sentence substitute archaic* away! begone! [c17: of unknown origin]

aroma (əˈrəʊmə) *n* **1** a distinctive usually pleasant smell, esp of spices, wines, and plants **2** a subtle pervasive quality or atmosphere [c18: via Latin from Greek: spice]

aromatherapy (əˌrəʊməˈθɛrəpɪ) *n* the use of fragrant essential oils extracted from plants as a treatment in complementary medicine to relieve tension and cure certain minor ailments ▷ **aˌroma'therapist** *n*

aromatic (ˌærəˈmætɪk) *adj* **1** having a distinctive, usually fragrant smell **2** (of an organic compound) having an unsaturated ring containing alternating double and single bonds, esp containing a benzene ring; exhibiting aromaticity. See **aliphatic** ▷ *n* **3** something, such as a plant or drug, giving off a fragrant smell ▷ **ˌaro'matically** *adv* ▷ **aˌroma'ticity** *n*

aromatize *or* **aromatise** (əˈrəʊməˌtaɪz) *vb* (*tr*) to make

aromatic > a,romati'zation or a,romati'sation n

arose (ə'rəʊz) vb the past tense of **arise**

around (ə'raʊnd) prep 1 situated at various points in: a lot of shelves around the house 2 from place to place in: driving around Ireland 3 somewhere in or near 4 approximately in: it happened around 1957, I think ▷ adv 5 surrounding, encircling, or enclosing: a band around her head 6 in all directions from a point of reference: he owns the land for ten miles around 7 in the vicinity, esp restlessly but idly: to wait around; stand around 8 here and there; in no particular place or direction: dotted around 9 informal (of people) active and prominent in a particular area or profession 10 informal present in some place (the exact location being inexact) 11 informal in circulation; available: that type of phone has been around for some years now 12 informal to many places, so as to have gained considerable experience, often of a worldly or social nature: he gets around; I've been around [C17 (rare earlier): from A-² + ROUND]

● USAGE In American English, around is usually used
● instead of round in adverbial and prepositional senses,
● except in a few fixed phrases such as all year round. The
● use of around in adverbial senses is less common in
● British English

arouse (ə'raʊz) vb 1 (tr) to evoke or elicit (a reaction, emotion, or response); stimulate 2 to awaken from sleep > a'rousal n

Arp (French arp) n **Jean** (ʒã) or **Hans** (hans). 1887–1966, Alsatian sculptor, painter, and poet, cofounder of the Dada movement in Zürich, noted particularly for his abstract organic sculptures based on natural forms

Árpád ('ɑːpɑːd) n died 907 AD, Magyar chieftain who conquered Hungary in the late 9th century

arpeggio (ɑː'pɛdʒɪəʊ) n, pl -gios a chord whose notes are played in rapid succession rather than simultaneously [C18: from Italian, from arpeggiare to perform on the harp, from arpa HARP]

arquebus ('ɑːkwɪbəs) or **harquebus** n a portable long-barrelled gun dating from the 15th century: fired by a wheel-lock or matchlock [C16: via Old French harquebuse from Middle Dutch hakebusse, literally: hook gun, from the shape of the butt, from hake hook + busse box, gun, from Late Latin busis box]

arr. abbreviation 1 arranged (by) 2 arrival

arraign (ə'reɪn) vb (tr) 1 to bring (a prisoner) before a court to answer an indictment 2 to call to account; complain about; accuse [C14: from Old French araisnier to speak, accuse, from A-² + raisnier, from Vulgar Latin ratiōnāre (unattested) to talk, argue, from Latin ratiō a reasoning] > ar'raignr n > ar'raignment n

Arran ('ærən) n an island off the SW coast of Scotland, in the Firth of Clyde. Pop: 5045 (2001). Area: 427 sq km (165 sq miles)

arrange (ə'reɪndʒ) vb 1 (tr) to put into a proper, systematic, or decorative order 2 (tr; may take a clause as object or an infinitive) to arrive at an agreement or understanding about; settle 3 (intr, often foll by for; when tr, may take a clause as object or an infinitive) to make plans or preparations in advance (for something): we arranged for her to be met 4 (tr) to adapt (a musical composition) for performance in a different way, esp on different instruments 5 (tr) to adapt (a play, etc) for broadcasting 6 (intr; often foll by with) to come to an agreement [C14: from Old French arangier, from A-² + rangier to put in a row, RANGE] > ar'rangeable adj > ar'ranger n

arrangement (ə'reɪndʒmənt) n 1 the act of arranging or being arranged 2 the form in which things are arranged 3 a thing composed of various ordered parts; the result of arranging: a flower arrangement 4 (often plural) a preparatory measure taken or plan made; preparation 5 an agreement or settlement; understanding 6 an adaptation of a piece of music for performance in a different way, esp on different instruments from those for which it was originally composed

arrant ('ærənt) adj utter; out-and-out: an arrant fool [C14: a variant of ERRANT (wandering, vagabond); sense developed from its frequent use in phrases like arrant thief (hence: notorious)] > 'arrantly adv

arras ('ærəs) n a wall hanging, esp of tapestry

Arras ('ærəs; French arɑs) n a town in N France: formerly famous for tapestry; severely damaged in both World Wars. Pop: 40 590 (1999)

Arrau (ə'raʊ) n **Claudio**. 1903–91, Chilean pianist

array (ə'reɪ) n 1 an impressive display or collection 2 an orderly or regular arrangement, esp of troops in battle order 3 poetic rich clothing; apparel 4 maths a set of numbers or symbols arranged in rows and columns, as in a determinant or matrix 5 law a panel of jurors 6 computing a regular data structure in which individual elements may be located by reference to one or more integer index variables, the number of such indices being the number of dimensions in the array ▷ vb (tr) 7 to dress in rich attire; adorn 8 to arrange in order (esp troops for battle); marshal 9 law to draw up (a panel of jurors) [C13: from Old French aroi arrangement, from arayer to arrange, of Germanic origin; compare Old English arǣdan to make ready] > ar'rayal n

arrears (ə'rɪəz) n 1 Also called: **arrearage** (ə'rɪərɪdʒ) (sometimes singular) something outstanding or owed 2 in arrears or in arrear late in paying a debt or meeting an obligation [C18: from obsolete arrear (adv) behindhand, from Old French arere, from Medieval Latin adretrō, from Latin ad + retrō backwards]

arrest (ə'rɛst) vb (tr) 1 to deprive (a person) of liberty by taking him into custody, esp under lawful authority 2 to seize (a ship) under lawful authority 3 to slow or stop the development or progress of (a disease, growth, etc) 4 to catch and hold (one's attention, sight, etc) ▷ n 5 the act of taking a person into custody, esp under lawful authority 6 the act of seizing and holding a ship under lawful authority 7 the state of being held, esp under lawful authority: under arrest 8 Also called: **arrestation** (,ærɛs'teɪʃən) the slowing or stopping of the development or progress of something 9 the stopping or sudden cessation of motion of something: a cardiac arrest [C14: from Old French arester, from Vulgar Latin arrestāre (unattested), from Latin ad at, to + restāre to stand firm, stop]

arresting (ə'rɛstɪŋ) adj attracting attention; striking > ar'restingly adv

Arretium (æ'riːtɪəm, -'rɛt-) n the ancient Latin name of Arezzo > Arretine ('ærɪ,taɪn) adj

Arrhenius (Swedish a'reːnius) n **Svante August** ('svantə 'aʊɡʊst). 1859–1927, Swedish chemist and physicist, noted for his work on the theory of electrolytic dissociation: Nobel prize for chemistry 1903

arrhythmia (ə'rɪðmɪə) n any variation from the normal rhythm in the heartbeat [C19: New Latin, from Greek arrhuthmia, from A-¹ + rhuthmos RHYTHM]

arrière-pensée (French arjɛrpɑ̃se) n an unrevealed thought or intention [C19: literally: behind thought]

Ar Rimal (ɑːr rɪ'mɑːl) n another name for **Rub' al Khali**

arris ('ærɪs) n, pl -ris or -rises a sharp edge at the meeting of two surfaces at an angle with one another, as at two adjacent sides of a stone block [C17: apparently from Old French areste beard of grain, sharp ridge; see ARÊTE]

arrish ('ærɪʃ) n Southwest English dialect corn stubble [Old English ersc]

arrival (ə'raɪvˀl) n 1 the act or time of arriving 2 a person or thing that arrives or has arrived

arrive (ə'raɪv) vb (intr) 1 to come to a certain place during or after a journey; reach a destination 2 (foll by at) to agree upon; reach: to arrive at a decision 3 to occur eventually: the moment arrived when pretence was useless 4 informal (of a baby) to be born 5 informal to attain success or gain recognition [C13: from Old French ariver, from Vulgar Latin arrīpāre (unattested) to land, reach the bank, from Latin ad to + rīpa river bank]

arrivederci (Italian arrive'dertʃi) sentence substitute goodbye

arriviste (,æriː'viːst; French arivist) n a person who is unscrupulously ambitious [French: from ARRIVE, -IST]

arrogant ('ærəɡənt) adj having or showing an exaggerated opinion of one's own importance, merit, ability, etc; conceited; overbearingly proud: an arrogant teacher; an arrogant assumption [C14: from Latin arrogāre to claim as one's own; see ARROGATE] > 'arrogance n > 'arrogantly adv

arrogate ('ærə,geɪt) vb 1 (tr) to claim or appropriate for oneself presumptuously or without justification 2 (tr) to attribute or assign to another without justification [c16: from Latin *arrogāre*, from *rogāre* to ask] > ,arro'gation n > arrogative (ə'rɒgətɪv) adj

arrondissement (French arɔ̃dismɑ̃) n (in France) 1 the largest administrative subdivision of a department 2 a municipal district of certain cities, esp Paris [c19: from *arrondir* to make round, from AB-¹ + -*rondir* from *rond* ROUND]

arrow ('ærəʊ) n 1 a long slender pointed weapon, usually having feathers fastened at the end as a balance, that is shot from a bow 2 any of various things that resemble an arrow in shape, function, or speed, such as a sign indicating direction or position [Old English *arwe*; related to Old Norse *ör*, Gothic *arhvazna*, Latin *arcus* bow, ARCH¹]

arrowhead ('ærəʊ,hɛd) n 1 the pointed tip of an arrow, often removable from the shaft 2 something that resembles the head of an arrow in shape, such as a triangular decoration on garments used to reinforce joins 3 any aquatic herbaceous plant of the genus *Sagittaria*, esp *S. sagittifolia*, having arrow-shaped aerial leaves and linear submerged leaves: family *Alismataceae*

arrowroot ('ærəʊ,ruːt) n 1 a white-flowered West Indian plant, *Maranta arundinacea*, whose rhizomes yield an easily digestible starch: family *Marantaceae* 2 the starch obtained from this plant

arroyo (ə'rɔɪəʊ) n, pl -os chiefly Southwestern US a steep-sided stream bed that is usually dry except after heavy rain [c19: from Spanish]

Arroyo (ə'rɔɪəʊ) n **Gloria Macapagal**. born 1948, Filipino stateswoman; president of the Philippines from 2001; vice-president (1998–2001)

arse (ɑːs) or US and Canadian **ass** n slang 1 the buttocks 2 the anus 3 a stupid person; fool [OE]

arsenal ('ɑːsənᵊl) n 1 a store for arms, ammunition, and other military items 2 a workshop or factory that produces munitions 3 a store of anything regarded as weapons [c16: from Italian *arsenale* dockyard, from the original Venetian *arsenal* dockyard and naval store, from Arabic *dār siñ'ah*, from *dār* house + *siñ'ah* manufacture]

arsenate ('ɑːsə,neɪt, -nɪt) n a salt or ester of arsenic acid, esp a salt containing the ion AsO_4^{3-}

arsenic n ('ɑːsnɪk) 1 a toxic metalloid element, existing in several allotropic forms, that occurs principally in realgar and orpiment and as the free element. It is used in transistors, lead-based alloys, and high-temperature brasses. Symbol: As; atomic no: 33; atomic wt: 74.92159; valency: -3, 0, +3, or +5; relative density: 5.73 (grey); melting pt: 817°C at a pressure of $3MN/m^2$ (grey); sublimes at 613°C (grey) 2 a nontechnical name for **arsenic trioxide** (As_2O_3), used as rat poison and an insecticide ▷ adj (ɑː'sɛnɪk) 3 of or containing arsenic, esp in the pentavalent state [c14: from Latin *arsenicum*, from Greek *arsenikon* yellow orpiment, from Syriac *zarnīg* (influenced in form by Greek *arsenikos* virile)]

arsenic acid n a white poisonous soluble crystalline solid used in the manufacture of arsenates and insecticides. Formula: H_3AsO_4

arsenical (ɑː'sɛnɪkᵊl) adj 1 of or containing arsenic ▷ n 2 a drug or insecticide containing arsenic

arsenious (ɑː'siːnɪəs) or **arsenous** ('ɑːsɪnəs) adj of or containing arsenic in the trivalent state

arsey or **arsy** ('ɑːsɪ) adj arsier, arsiest Brit slang aggressive, irritable, or argumentative

arson ('ɑːsᵊn) n criminal law the act of intentionally or recklessly setting fire to another's property or to one's own property for some improper reason [c17: from Old French, from Medieval Latin *ārsiō*, from Latin *ārdēre* to burn; see ARDENT] > **arsonist** n

art¹ (ɑːt) n 1 a the creation of works of beauty or other special significance b (as modifier): an art movement 2 the exercise of human skill (as distinguished from *nature*) 3 imaginative skill as applied to representations of the natural world or figments of the imagination 4 a the products of man's creative activities; works of art collectively, esp of the visual arts, sometimes also music, drama, dance, and literature b (as modifier): an art

gallery 5 any branch of the visual arts, esp painting 6 a any field using the techniques of art to display artistic qualities b (as modifier): an art film 7 method, facility, or knack: *the art of threading a needle; the art of writing letters* 8 the system of rules or principles governing a particular human activity: *the art of government* 9 artfulness; cunning 10 get something down to a fine art to become highly proficient at something through practice ▷ See also **arts** [c13: from Old French, from Latin *ars* craftsmanship]

art² (ɑːt) vb archaic (used with the pronoun *thou*) a singular form of the present tense (indicative mood) of be¹ [Old English *eart*, part of *bēon* to BE]

-art suffix forming nouns a variant of **-ard**

Artaud (French arto) n **Antonin** (ɑ̃tɔnɛ̃). 1896–1948, French stage director and dramatist, whose concept of the theatre of cruelty is expounded in *Manifeste du théâtre de la cruauté* (1932) and *Le Théâtre et son double* (1938)

Artaxerxes I (,ɑːtə'zɜːksiːz) n died 425 BC, king of Persia (465–425): son of Xerxes I

Artaxerxes II n died ?358 BC, king of Persia (?404–?358). He defeated his brother Cyrus the Younger at Cunaxa (401)

Art Deco ('dɛkəʊ) n a style of interior decoration, jewellery, architecture, etc, at its height in the 1930s and characterized by geometrical shapes, stylized natural forms, and symmetrical utilitarian designs adapted to mass production [c20: shortened from *art décoratif*, after the *Exposition des arts décoratifs* held in Paris in 1925]

art director n a person responsible for the sets and costumes in a film

artefact or **artifact** ('ɑːtɪ,fækt) n 1 something made or given shape by man, such as a tool or a work of art, esp an object of archaeological interest 2 anything man-made, such as a spurious experimental result 3 cytology a structure seen in tissue after death, fixation, staining, etc, that is not normally present in the living tissue [c19: from Latin phrase *arte factum*, from *ars* skill + *facere* to make]

artel (ɑː'tɛl) n (in the former Soviet Union) a cooperative union or organization, esp of producers, such as peasants [from Russian *artel'*, from Italian *artieri* artisans, from *arte* work, from Latin *ars* ART¹]

Artemis ('ɑːtɪmɪs) n Greek myth the virgin goddess of the hunt and the moon: the twin sister of Apollo. Roman counterpart: Diana. Also called: Cynthia

arterial (ɑː'tɪərɪəl) adj 1 of, relating to, or affecting an artery or arteries 2 denoting or relating to the usually bright red reoxygenated blood returning from the lungs or gills that circulates in the arteries 3 being a major route, esp one with many minor branches > **ar'terially** adv

arterialize or **arterialise** (ɑː'tɪərɪə,laɪz) vb (tr) 1 to change (venous blood) into arterial blood by replenishing the depleted oxygen 2 to provide with arteries > ar,teriali'zation or ar,teriali'sation n

arteriole (ɑː'tɪərɪ,əʊl) n anatomy any of the small subdivisions of an artery that form thin-walled vessels ending in capillaries [c19: from New Latin *arteriola*, from Latin *artēria* ARTERY]

arteriosclerosis (ɑː,tɪərɪəʊsklɪə'rəʊsɪs) n, pl -ses (-siːz) a pathological condition of the circulatory system characterized by thickening and loss of elasticity of the arterial walls > **arteriosclerotic** (ɑː,tɪərɪəʊsklɪə'rɒtɪk) adj

artery ('ɑːtərɪ) n, pl -teries 1 any of the tubular thick-walled muscular vessels that convey oxygenated blood from the heart to various parts of the body. See **pulmonary artery**, **vein** 2 a major road or means of communication in any complex system [c14: from Latin *artēria*, related to Greek *aortē* the great artery, AORTA]

artesian well (ɑː'tiːzɪən, -ʒən) n a well sunk through impermeable strata to strata receiving water from an area at a higher altitude than that of the well, so that there is sufficient pressure to force water to flow upwards [c19: from French *artésien*, from Old French *Arteis* Artois, old province, where such wells were common]

Artex ('ɑːtɛks) n trademark a brand of coating for walls and ceilings that gives a textured finish

art form n a conventionally established form of artistic composition, such as the symphony or the sonnet

artful ('ɑːtfʊl) adj 1 cunning or tricky 2 skilful in achieving a desired end > 'artfully adv > 'artfulness n

art house n 1 a cinema which specializes in showing films which are not part of the commercial mainstream ▷ adj 2 of or relating to such films or a cinema which specializes in showing them

arthralgia (ɑːˈθrældʒə) n pathol pain in a joint

arthritis (ɑːˈθraɪtɪs) n inflammation of a joint or joints characterized by pain and stiffness of the affected parts, caused by gout, rheumatic fever, etc [c16: via Latin from Greek: see ARTHRO-, -ITIS] > arthritic (ɑːˈθrɪtɪk) adj, n

arthro- or before a vowel **arthr-** combining form indicating a joint: arthritis; arthropod [from Greek arthron]

arthropod ('ɑːθrəˌpɒd) n any invertebrate of the phylum Arthropoda, having jointed limbs, a segmented body, and an exoskeleton made of chitin. The group includes the crustaceans, insects, arachnids, and centipedes [c19 from NL, from Gk arthron joint + podus footed, from pous foot]

Arthur ('ɑːθə) n 1 a legendary king of the Britons in the sixth century AD, who led Celtic resistance against the Saxons: possibly based on a historical figure; represented as leader of the Knights of the Round Table at Camelot 2 **Chester Alan**. 1830–86, 21st president of the US (1881–85) 3 not know whether one is Arthur or Martha Austral & NZ informal to be in a state of confusion

Arthurian (ɑːˈθjʊərɪən) adj of or relating to King Arthur and his Knights of the Round Table

artic (ɑːˈtɪk) n informal short for **articulated lorry**

artichoke ('ɑːtɪˌtʃəʊk) n 1 Also called: **globe artichoke** a thistle-like Eurasian plant, Cynara scolymus, cultivated for its large edible flower head containing many fleshy scalelike bracts: family Asteraceae (composites) 2 the unopened flower head of this plant, which can be cooked and eaten 3 See **Jerusalem artichoke** [c16: from Italian articiocco, from Old Spanish alcarchofa, from Arabic al-kharshūf]

article ('ɑːtɪkˀl) n 1 one of a class of objects; item 2 an unspecified or previously named thing, esp a small object 3 a written composition on a subject, often being one of several found in a magazine, newspaper, etc 4 grammar a kind of determiner, occurring in many languages including English, that lacks independent meaning but may serve to indicate the specificity of reference of the noun phrase with which it occurs. See also **definite article**, **indefinite article** 5 a clause or section in a written document such as a treaty, contract, statute, etc 6 (often capital) Christianity See **Thirty-nine Articles** ▷ vb (tr) 7 archaic to accuse [c13: from Old French, from Latin articulus small joint, from artus joint]

articled ('ɑːtɪkˀld) adj bound by a written contract, such as one that governs a period of training: an articled clerk

articular (ɑːˈtɪkjʊlə) adj of or relating to joints or to the structural components in a joint [c15: from Latin articulāris concerning the joints, from articulus small joint; see ARTICLE]

articulate adj (ɑːˈtɪkjʊlɪt) 1 able to express oneself fluently and coherently: an articulate lecturer 2 having the power of speech 3 distinct, clear, or definite; well-constructed: an articulate voice; an articulate document 4 zoology (of arthropods and higher vertebrates) possessing joints or jointed segments ▷ vb (ɑːˈtɪkjʊˌleɪt) 5 to speak or enunciate (words, syllables, etc) clearly and distinctly 6 (tr) to express coherently in words [c16: from Latin articulāre to divide into joints; see ARTICLE] > arˈticulately adv > arˈticulateness or arˈticulacy n > arˈticuˌlator n

articulation (ɑːˌtɪkjʊˈleɪʃən) n 1 the act or process of speaking or expressing in words 2 a the process of articulating a speech sound b the sound so produced, esp a consonant 3 the act or state of being jointed together 4 zoology a a joint such as that between bones or arthropod segments b the way in which jointed parts are connected 5 botany the part of a plant at which natural separation occurs, such as the joint between leaf and stem

artifact ('ɑːtɪˌfækt) n a variant spelling of **artefact**

artifice ('ɑːtɪfɪs) n 1 a clever expedient; ingenious stratagem 2 crafty or subtle deception 3 skill; cleverness 4 a skilfully contrived device [c16: from Old French, from Latin artificium skill, from artifex one possessed of a specific skill, from ars skill + -fex, from facere to make]

artificer (ɑːˈtɪfɪsə) n 1 a skilled craftsman 2 a clever or inventive designer 3 a serviceman trained in mechanics

artificial (ˌɑːtɪˈfɪʃəl) adj 1 produced by man; not occurring naturally: artificial materials of great strength 2 made in imitation of a natural product, esp as a substitute; not genuine: artificial cream 3 pretended; assumed; insincere: an artificial manner 4 lacking in spontaneity; affected: an artificial laugh 5 biology relating to superficial characteristics not based on the interrelationships of organisms: an artificial classification [c14: from Latin artificiālis belonging to art, from artificium skill, ARTIFICE] > artificiality (ˌɑːtɪˌfɪʃɪˈælɪtɪ) n > ˌartiˈficially adv

artificial daylight n physics artificial light having approximately the same spectral characteristics as natural daylight

artificial disintegration n physics radioactive transformation of a substance by bombardment with high-energy particles, such as alpha particles or neutrons

artificial insemination n introduction of spermatozoa into the vagina or uterus by means other than sexual union

artificial intelligence n the study of the modelling of human mental functions by computer programs. Abbreviation: AI

artificial respiration n 1 any of various methods of restarting breathing after it has stopped, by manual rhythmic pressure on the chest, mouth-to-mouth breathing, etc 2 any method of maintaining respiration artificially, as by use of an iron lung

Artigas (ɑːˈtiːgɑːs) n José Gervasio. 1764–1850, the national hero of Uruguay. He fought for Uruguayan independence from Argentina, but was driven into exile in 1820

artillery (ɑːˈtɪlərɪ) n 1 guns, cannon, howitzers, mortars, etc, of calibre greater than 20 mm 2 troops or military units specializing in using such guns 3 the science dealing with the use of guns 4 devices for discharging heavy missiles, such as catapults or slings [c14: from Old French artillerie, from artillier to equip with weapons, of uncertain origin]

artiodactyl (ˌɑːtɪəʊˈdæktɪl) n any placental mammal of the order Artiodactyla, having hooves with an even number of toes; an even-toed ungulate. The order includes pigs, hippopotamuses, camels, deer, cattle, and antelopes [c19: from New Latin artiodactylus, from Greek ártios even + daktulos digit] > ˌartioˈdactylous adj

artisan (ˌɑːtɪˈzæn, ˌɑːtɪˈzæn) n a skilled workman; craftsman [c16: from French, from Old Italian artigiano, from arte ART¹] > artisanal (ɑːˈtɪzənˀl, ˌɑːtɪzənˀl) adj

artist ('ɑːtɪst) n 1 a person who practises or is skilled in an art, esp painting, drawing, or sculpture 2 a person who displays in his work qualities required in art, such as sensibility and imagination 3 a person whose profession requires artistic expertise, esp a designer: a commercial artist 4 a person skilled in some task or occupation 5 slang a person devoted to or proficient in something: a booze artist; a con artist > arˈtistic adj > arˈtistically adv

artiste (ɑːˈtiːst; French artist) n 1 an entertainer, such as a singer or dancer 2 a person who is highly skilled in some occupation: a hair artiste

artistry ('ɑːtɪstrɪ) n 1 artistic workmanship, ability, or quality 2 artistic pursuits 3 great skill

artless ('ɑːtlɪs) adj 1 free from deceit, guile, or artfulness; ingenuous: an artless remark 2 natural, without artifice; unpretentious: artless elegance 3 without art or skill > 'artlessly adv

Art Nouveau (ɑː nuːˈvəʊ; French ar nuvo) n a style of art and architecture of the 1890s, characterized by swelling sinuous outlines and stylized natural forms, such as flowers and leaves [French, literally: new art]

art paper n a high-quality type of paper having a smooth coating of china clay or similar substance on it

arts (ɑːts) *pl n* **1 a** the arts imaginative, creative, and nonscientific branches of knowledge considered collectively, esp as studied academically **b** (*as modifier*): *an arts degree* **2** See **fine art 3** cunning or crafty actions or plots; schemes

Arts and Crafts *pl n* decorative handicraft and design, esp that of the **Arts and Crafts movement**, in late nineteenth-century Britain, which sought to revive medieval craftsmanship

art union *n Austral & NZ* a lottery, often with prizes other than cash

arty ('ɑːtɪ) *adj* artier, artiest *informal* having an ostentatious or affected interest in or desire to imitate artists or artistic standards > 'artiness *n*

Aruba (ə'ruːbə; *Dutch* ɑːrỵ'baː) *n* an island in the Caribbean, off the NW coast of Venezuela, a dependency of the Netherlands with special status; part of the Netherlands Antilles until 1986. Chief town: Oranjestad. Pop: 100 000 (2003 est). Area: about 181 sq km (70 sq miles)

arugula (ə'ruːgjʊlə) *n* another name for **rocket²** (sense 2) [c20: from N Italian dialect]

Aru Islands *or* **Arru Islands** ('ɑːruː) *pl n* a group of islands in Indonesia, in the SW Moluccas. Area: about 8500 sq km (3300 sq miles)

arum ('ɛərəm) *n* **1** any plant of the aroid genus *Arum*, of Europe and the Mediterranean region, having arrow-shaped leaves and a typically white spathe **2** arum lily another name for **calla** (sense 1) [c16: from Latin, a variant of *aros* wake-robin, from Greek *aron*]

Arunachal Pradesh (ˌɑːrə'nɑːkᵊl prə'dɛʃ) *n* a state in NE India, formed in 1986 from the former Union Territory. Capital: Itanagar. Pop: 1 091 117 (2001). Area: 83 743 sq km (32 648 sq miles). Former name (until 1972): North East Frontier Agency

Arundel ('ærəndəl) *n* a town in S England, in West Sussex: 11th-century castle. Pop: 3297 (2001)

arvo ('ɑːvəʊ) *n Austral informal* afternoon

-ary *suffix* **1** (*forming adjectives*) of; related to; belonging to: *cautionary; rudimentary* **2** (*forming nouns*) **a** a person connected with or engaged in: *missionary* **b** a thing relating to; a place for: *commentary; aviary* [from Latin *-ārius, -āria, -ārium*]

Aryan *or* **Arian** ('ɛərɪən) *n* **1** (in Nazi ideology) a Caucasian of non-Jewish descent, esp of the Nordic type **2** a member of any of the peoples supposedly descended from the Indo-Europeans, esp a speaker of an Iranian or Indic language in ancient times ▷ *adj* **3** of, relating to, or characteristic of an Aryan or Aryans ▷ *adj, n* **4** *archaic* Indo-European [c19: from Sanskrit *ārya* of noble birth]

as¹ (æz; *unstressed* əz) *conj* (*subordinating*) **1** (often preceded by *just*) while; when; at the time that: *he caught me as I was leaving* **2** in the way that: *dancing as only she can* **3** that which; what: *I did as I was told* **4** (of) which fact, event, etc (referring to the previous statement): *to become wise, as we all know, is not easy* **5** as it were; in a way; so to speak; as if it were really so **6** since; seeing that **7** in the same way that: *he died of cancer, as his father had done* **8** for instance: *capital cities, as London* ▷ *adv, conj* **9 a** used correlatively before an adjective or adverb and before a noun phrase or a clause to indicate identity of extent, amount, etc: *she is as heavy as her sister; she is as heavy now as she used to be* **b** used with this sense after a noun phrase introduced by *the same*: *she is the same height as her sister* ▷ *prep* **10** in the role of; being: *as his friend, I am probably biased* **11** as for *or* as to with reference to: *as for my past, I'm not telling you anything* **12** as if *or* as though as it would be if: *he talked as if he knew all about it* **13** as is *or* as it is in the existing state of affairs **14** as was in a previous state [Old English *alswā* likewise; see ALSO]
● USAGE See at **like¹**

as² (æs) *n* **1** an ancient Roman unit of weight approximately equal to 1 pound troy (373 grams) **2** the standard monetary unit and copper coin of ancient Rome [c17: from Latin *ās* unity, probably of Etruscan origin]

As *symbol for* **1** *chem* arsenic **2** altostratus

AS *abbreviation* **1** Also: A.S. Anglo-Saxon **2** antisubmarine

ASA *abbreviation* **1** (in Britain) Amateur Swimming Association **2** (in Britain) Advertising Standards Authority **3** (in the US) American Standards Association

ASA/BS *abbrev* an obsolete expression of the speed of a photographic film, replaced by the ISO rating [c20: from *American Standards Association/British Standard*]

asafoetida *or* **asafetida** (ˌæsə'fɛtɪdə) *n* a bitter resin with an unpleasant onion-like smell, obtained from the roots of some umbelliferous plants of the genus *Ferula*: formerly used as a carminative, antispasmodic, and expectorant [c14: from Medieval Latin, from *asa* gum (compare Persian *azā* mastic) + Latin *foetidus* evil-smelling, FETID]

Asantehene (æ'fæntɪˌhɛnɪ) *n* the ruler of the Ashanti people of Ghana

a.s.a.p. *abbreviation* as soon as possible

Asben (æs'bɛn) *n* another name for **Aïr**

asbestos (æs'bɛstɒs, -təs) *n* **a** any of the fibrous amphibole and serpentine minerals, esp chrysotile and tremolite, that are incombustible and resistant to chemicals. It was formerly widely used in the form of fabric or board as a heat-resistant structural material **b** (*as modifier*): *asbestos matting* [c14 (originally applied to a mythical stone the heat of which could not be extinguished): via Latin from Greek: from *asbestos* inextinguishable, from A-¹ + *sbennunai* to extinguish]

asbestosis (ˌæsbɛs'təʊsɪs) *n* inflammation of the lungs resulting from chronic inhalation of asbestos particles

ASBO ('æzˌbəʊ) *n acronym for Brit* anti-social behaviour order: a civil order made against a persistently anti-social individual which restricts his or her activities or movements, a breach of which results in criminal charges

Ascanius (æ'skeɪnɪəs) *n Roman myth* the son of Aeneas and Creusa; founder of Alba Longa, mother city of Rome. Also called: **Iulus**

ascarid ('æskərɪd) *n* any parasitic nematode worm of the family *Ascaridae*, such as the common roundworm of man and pigs [c14: from New Latin *ascaridae*, from Greek *askarides*, plural of *askaris*]

ascend (ə'sɛnd) *vb* **1** to go or move up (a ladder, hill, slope, etc); mount; climb **2** (*intr*) to slope or incline upwards **3** (*intr*) to rise to a higher point, level, degree, etc **4** to trace (a genealogy, etc) back in time **5** to sing or play (a scale, arpeggio, etc) from the lower to higher notes **6** ascend the throne to become king or queen [c14: from Latin *ascendere*, from *scandere*]

ascendancy, ascendency (ə'sɛndənsɪ) *or* **ascendance, ascendence** (ə'sɛndəns) *n* the condition of being dominant, esp through superior economic or political power

ascendant *or* **ascendent** (ə'sɛndənt) *adj* **1** proceeding upwards; rising **2** dominant, superior, or influential ▷ *n* **3** a position or condition of dominance, superiority or control **4** *astrology* (*sometimes capital*) **a** a point on the ecliptic that rises on the eastern horizon at a particular moment and changes as the earth rotates on its axis **b** the sign of the zodiac containing this point **5** in the ascendant increasing in influence, prosperity, etc

ascender (ə'sɛndə) *n* **1** *printing* the part of certain lower-case letters, such as *b* or *h*, that extends above the body of the letter **2** a person or thing that ascends

ascension (ə'sɛnfən) *n* the act of ascending > as'censional *adj*

Ascension¹ (ə'sɛnfən) *n New Testament* the passing of Jesus Christ from earth into heaven (Acts 1:9)

Ascension² (ə'sɛnfən) *n* an island in the S Atlantic, northwest of St Helena: uninhabited until claimed by Britain in 1815. Pop: 1122 (2003 est). Area: 88 sq km (34 sq miles)

Ascension Day *n Christianity* the 40th day after Easter, when the Ascension of Christ into heaven is celebrated

ascent (ə'sɛnt) *n* **1** the act of ascending; climb or upward movement **2** an upward slope; incline or gradient **3** movement back through time, as in tracing of earlier generations (esp in the phrase **line of ascent**)

ascertain (ˌæsə'teɪn) *vb* (*tr*) **1** to determine or discover definitely **2** *archaic* to make certain [c15: from Old French *acertener* to make certain] > ˌascer'tainable *adj* > ˌascer'tainment *n*

ascetic (ə'sɛtɪk) *n* **1** a person who practises great self-denial and austerities and abstains from worldly comforts and pleasures, esp for religious reasons ▷ *adj* Also: as'cetical **2** rigidly abstinent or abstemious; austere **3** of or relating to ascetics or asceticism [c17: from Greek *askētikos*, from *askētēs*, from *askein* to exercise] > as'cetically *adv* > as'ceti,cism *n*

Asch (æʃ) *n* **Sholem** ('ʃəʊləm). 1880–1957, US writer, born in Poland, who wrote in Yiddish. His works include biblical novels

Aschaffenburg (*German* a'ʃafənburk) *n* a city in Germany, on the River Main in Bavaria: seat of the Imperial Diet (1447); ceded to Bavaria in 1814. Pop: 68 607 (2003 est)

Ascham ('æskəm) *n* **Roger.** ?1515–68, English humanist writer and classical scholar: tutor to Queen Elizabeth I

ascidian (ə'sɪdɪən) *n* any minute marine invertebrate animal of the class *Ascidiacea*, such as the sea squirt, the adults of which are degenerate and sedentary: subphylum *Tunicata* (tunicates)

ascidium (ə'sɪdɪəm) *n, pl* -cidia (-'sɪdɪə) part of a plant that is shaped like a pitcher, such as the modified leaf of the pitcher plant [c18: from New Latin, from Greek *askidion* a little bag, from *askos* bag]

Asclepius (ə'skliːpɪəs) *n Greek myth* a god of healing; son of Apollo. Roman counterpart: **Aesculapius**

ascomycete (,æskəmaɪ'siːt) *n* any fungus of the phylum *Ascomycota* (formerly class *Ascomycetes*) in which the spores (ascospores) are formed inside a club-shaped cell (ascus). The group includes yeast, penicillium, aspergillus, truffles, and certain mildews > ,ascomy'cetous *adj*

ascorbic acid (ə'skɔːbɪk) *n* a white crystalline vitamin present in plants, esp citrus fruits, tomatoes, and green vegetables. A deficiency in the diet of man leads to scurvy. Formula: $C_6H_8O_6$. Also called: **vitamin C** [c20 *ascorbic* from A-¹ + SCORB(UT)IC]

Ascot ('æskət) *n* a town in S England, in Bracknell Forest unitary authority, Berkshire: noted for its horse-race meetings, esp **Royal Ascot**, a four-day meeting held in June. Pop: 8755 (2001)

ascribe (ə'skraɪb) *vb* (*tr*) **1** to credit or assign, as to a particular origin or period **2** to attribute as a quality; consider as belonging to: *to ascribe beauty to youth* [c15: from Latin *ascrībere* to enrol, from *ad* in addition + *scrībere* to write] > as'cribable *adj*

● USAGE *Ascribe* is sometimes wrongly used where *subscribe* is meant: *I do not subscribe* (not *ascribe*) *to this view*

ascription (ə'skrɪpʃən) *or* **adscription** (əd'skrɪpʃən) *n* **1** the act of ascribing **2** a statement ascribing something to someone, esp praise to God [c16: from Latin *ascrīptiō*, from *ascrībere* to ASCRIBE]

ASD *abbreviation psychiatry* autistic-spectrum disorder

asdic ('æzdɪk) *n* an early form of **sonar** [c20: from A(*nti-*) S(*ubmarine*) D(*etection*) I(*nvestigation*) C(*ommittee*)]

-ase *suffix forming nouns* indicating an enzyme: *oxidase* [abstracted from DIASTASE]

ASEAN ('æsɪ,æn) *n acronym for* Association of Southeast Asian Nations

asepsis (ə'sɛpsɪs, eɪ-) *n* **1** the state of being free from living pathogenic organisms **2** the methods of achieving a germ-free condition > aseptic (ə'sɛptɪk, eɪ-) *adj*

asexual (eɪ'sɛksjʊəl, æ-) *adj* **1** having no apparent sex or sex organs **2** (of reproduction) not involving the fusion of male and female gametes, as in vegetative reproduction, fission, or budding > asexuality (eɪ,sɛksjʊ'ælɪtɪ, ,æ-) *n* > a'sexually *adv*

Asgard ('æsgɑːd) *or* **Asgarth** ('æsgɑːθ) *n Norse myth* the dwelling place of the principal gods, the Aesir

ash¹ (æʃ) *n* **1** the nonvolatile products and residue formed when matter is burnt **2** fine particles of lava thrown out by an erupting volcano **3** a light silvery grey colour, often with a brownish tinge ▷ See also **ashes** [Old English *æsce*; related to Old Norse, Old High German *aska*, Gothic *azgō*, Latin *aridus* dry]

ash² (æʃ) *n* **1** any oleaceous tree of the genus *Fraxinus*, esp *F. excelsior* of Europe and Asia, having compound leaves, clusters of small greenish flowers, and winged seeds

2 the close-grained durable wood of any of these trees, used for tool handles, etc **3** any of several trees resembling the ash, such as the mountain ash **4** *Austral* any of several Australian trees resembling the ash, esp of the eucalyptus genus [Old English *æsc*; related to Old Norse *askr*, Old Saxon, Old High German *ask*, Lithuanian *uosis*]

ash³ (æʃ) *n* the digraph æ, as in Old English, representing a front vowel approximately like that of the *a* in Modern English *hat*. The character is also used to represent this sound in the International Phonetic Alphabet

ASH (æʃ) *n acronym for* (in Britain) Action on Smoking and Health

ashamed (ə'ʃeɪmd) *adj* (*usually postpositive*) **1** overcome with shame, guilt, or remorse **2** (foll by *of*) suffering from feelings of inferiority or shame in relation to (a person, thing, or deed) **3** (foll by *to*) unwilling through fear of humiliation, shame, etc [Old English *āscamod*, past participle of *āscamian* to shame, from *scamu* SHAME] > ashamedly (ə'ʃeɪmɪdlɪ) *adv*

Ashanti (ə'ʃæntɪ) *n* **1** an administrative region of central Ghana: former native kingdom, suppressed by the British in 1900 after four wars. Capital: Kumasi. Pop: 3 187 607 (2000). Area: 24 390 sq km (9417 sq miles) **2** *pl* -ti *or* -tis a native or inhabitant of Ashanti

A shares *pl n Brit* those ordinary shares in a company which carry restricted voting rights or other restrictions

ash can *n* a US word for **dustbin**. Also called: garbage can, ash bin, trash can

Ashcroft ('æʃkrɒft) *n* Dame **Peggy.** 1907–91, English stage and film actress

Ashdod ('æʃdɒd) *n* a town in central Israel, on the Mediterranean coast: an important city in the Philistine Empire, with its artificial harbour (1961) it is now a major port. Pop: 192 000 (2003 est)

Ashdown ('æʃdaʊn) *n* **Paddy**, Baron. real name *Jeremy John Durham Ashdown*. born 1941, British politician; leader of the Liberal Democrats (formerly the Social and Liberal Democrats) (1988–99); UN high representative in Bosnia-Herzegovina from 2002

Ashe (æʃ) *n* **Arthur** (**Robert**). 1943–93, US tennis player: US champion 1968; Wimbledon champion 1975

ashen¹ ('æʃən) *adj* **1** drained of colour; pallid **2** consisting of or resembling ashes **3** of a pale greyish colour

ashen² ('æʃən) *adj* of, relating to, or made from the ash tree or its timber

Asher ('æʃə) *n* the son of Jacob and ancestor of one of the 12 tribes of Israel

ashes ('æʃɪz) *pl n* **1** ruins or remains, as after destruction or burning **2** the remains of a human body after cremation

Ashes ('æʃɪz) *pl n* the Ashes a cremated cricket stump in a pottery urn now preserved at Lord's. Victory or defeat in test matches between England and Australia is referred to as winning, losing, or retaining the Ashes [from the mock obituary of English cricket in *The Times* in 1882 after a great Australian victory at the Oval, in which it was said that the body would be cremated and the ashes taken to Australia]

Ashford ('æʃfəd) *n* a market town in SE England, in central Kent. Pop: 58 936 (2001)

Ashkenazi (,æʃkə'nɑːzɪ) *n, pl* -zim (-zɪm) **1** (*modifier*) of or relating to the Jews of Germany and E Europe **2** a Jew of German or E European descent **3** the pronunciation of Hebrew used by these Jews ▷ See **Sephardi** [c19: Late Hebrew, from Hebrew *Ashkenaz*, the son of Gomer (Genesis 10:3; I Chronicles 1:6), a descendant of Noah through Japheth, and hence taken to be identified with the ancient Ascanians of Phrygia and, in the medieval period, the Germans]

Ashkenazy (,æʃkə'nɑːzɪ) *n* **Vladimir.** born 1937, Soviet-born Icelandic pianist and conductor

Ashkhabad (*Russian* aʃxa'bat) *or* **Ashgabat** ('aːʃɡəbæt; *Turkmen* aʃɡa'bat) *n* the capital of Turkmenistan. Pop: 598 000 (2003 est)

ashlar *or* **ashler** ('æʃlə) *n* **1** a block of hewn stone with straight edges for use in building **2** Also called: ashlar veneer a thin dressed stone with straight edges, used to face a wall **3** masonry made of ashlar [C14: from Old French *aisselier* crossbeam, from *ais* board, from Latin *axis* axletree; see AXIS[1]]

Ashley ('æʃlɪ) n **1 Jack**, Baron. born 1922, British Labour politician and campaigner for deaf and disabled people **2 Laura**. 1925–85, British designer, who built up a successful chain of retail stores selling dresses and fabrics based on traditional English patterns

ashore (əˈʃɔː) adv **1** towards or onto land from the water ▷ adj, adv (postpositive) **2** on land, having come from the water: *a day ashore before sailing*

ashram ('æʃrəm, 'aːʃ-) n a religious retreat or community where a Hindu holy man lives [from Sanskrit *āśrama*, from *ā-* near + *śrama* religious exertion]

Ashton ('æʃtən) n **Sir Frederick**. 1906–88, British ballet dancer and choreographer. His ballets include *Façade* (1931), to music by Walton, *La Fille mal gardée* (1960), *The Dream* (1964), and *A Month in the Country* (1976)

Ashton-under-Lyne (laɪn) n a town in NW England, in Tameside unitary authority, Greater Manchester. Pop: 43 236 (2001)

Ashtoreth ('æʃtəˌrɛθ) n Old Testament an ancient Semitic fertility goddess, identified with Astarte and Ishtar

ashtray ('æʃˌtreɪ) n a receptacle for tobacco ash, cigarette butts, etc

Ashur ('æʃʊə) n a variant spelling of **Assur**

Ashura (æʃʊˌraː) n Islam a Shiah festival observed on the tenth day of Muharram in the Islamic calendar to commemorate the death of the martyr Imam Hussein bin Ali at the Battle of Karbala in 61 AH (680 AD) [C21: from Arabic *'Ashūrā*]

Ashurbanipal (ˌæʃʊəˈbaːnɪˌpæl) or **Assurbanipal** n died ?626 BC, king of Assyria (?668–?626): son of Esarhaddon. He built the magnificent palace and library at Nineveh. Greek name: Sardanapalus

Ash Wednesday n the first day of Lent, named from the practice of Christians of placing ashes on their heads as a sign of penitence

ashy ('æʃɪ) adj ashier, ashiest **1** of a pale greyish colour; ashen **2** consisting of, covered with, or resembling ash

'Asi ('æsɪ) n the Arabic name for the **Orontes**

Asia ('eɪʃə, 'eɪʒə) n the largest of the continents, bordering on the Arctic Ocean, the Pacific Ocean, the Indian Ocean, and the Mediterranean and Red Seas in the west. It includes the large peninsulas of Asia Minor, India, Arabia, and Indochina and the island groups of Japan, Indonesia, the Philippines, and Ceylon (Sri Lanka): contains the mountain ranges of the Hindu Kush, Himalayas, Pamirs, Tian Shan, Urals, and Caucasus, the great plateaus of India, Iran, and Tibet, vast plains and deserts, and the valleys of many large rivers including the Mekong, Irrawaddy, Indus, Ganges, Tigris, and Euphrates. Pop: 3 917 508 000 (2005 est). Area: 44 391 162 sq km (17 139 445 sq miles)

asiago (ˌæzɪˈɑːgəʊ) n either of two varieties (ripened or fresh) of a cow's-milk cheese produced in NE Italy [Italian]

Asia Minor n the historical name for **Anatolia**

Asian ('eɪʃən, 'eɪʒən) adj **1** of or relating to Asia or to any of its peoples or languages **2** Brit of or relating to natives of the Indian subcontinent or any of their descendants, esp when living in Britain ▷ n **3** a native or inhabitant of Asia or a descendant of one **4** Brit a native of the Indian subcontinent or a descendant of one

Asian flu n a type of influenza recurring in worldwide epidemics, caused by a virus (A2 strain or subsequent antigenic variants), which apparently originated in China in 1957

Asian pear n Also called: nashi the fruit of the Japanese pear, which resembles a large yellow apple, has crisp juicy flesh, and is cultivated in Japan, Korea, the US, and New Zealand

Asiatic (ˌeɪʃɪˈætɪk, -zɪ-) n, adj a word formerly used for **Asian**

Asiatic cholera n another name for **cholera**

aside (əˈsaɪd) adv **1** on or to one side **2** out of hearing; in or into seclusion **3** away from oneself: *he threw the book aside* **4** out of mind or consideration: *he put aside all fears* **5** in or into reserve: *to put aside money for old age* ▷ n

6 something spoken by an actor, intended to be heard by the audience, but not by the others on stage **7** any confidential statement spoken in undertones

A-side n the side of a gramophone record regarded as the more important one

Asimov ('æzɪmɒf) n **Isaac**. 1920–92, US writer and biochemist, born in Russia. His science-fiction works include *Foundation Trilogy* (1951–53; sequel 1982) and the collection of stories *I, Robot* (1950)

asinine ('æsɪˌnaɪn) adj **1** obstinate or stupid **2** resembling an ass [C16: from Latin *asinīnus*, from *asinus* ASS[1]] > **'asiˌninely** adv > **asininity** (ˌæsɪˈnɪnɪtɪ) n

ASIO abbreviation Australian Security Intelligence Organization

Asir (æ'sɪə) n a region of SW Saudi Arabia, in the Southern Province on the Red Sea: under Turkish rule until 1933. Area: 81 000 sq km (31 000 sq miles)

ask (aːsk) vb **1** (often foll by about) to put a question (to); request an answer (from): *she asked (him) about God* **2** (tr) to inquire about: *she asked him the time of the train; she asked the way* **3** (tr) to direct or put (a question) **4** (may take a clause as object or an infinitive; often foll by for) to make a request or demand: *she asked (him) for information; they asked for a deposit* **5** (tr) to demand or expect (esp in the phrases **ask a lot of, ask too much of**) **6** Also: **ask out, ask over** (tr) to request (a person) politely to come or go to a place; invite: *he asked her to the party* ▷ n **7** a big ask or a tough ask Brit, Austral & NZ informal a task which is difficult to fulfil [Old English *āscian*; related to Old Frisian *āskia*, Old Saxon *ēscon*, Old High German *eiscōn*] > **'asker** n

Ask (aːsk) n Norse myth the first man, created by the gods from an ash tree

ask after or Scot **ask for** vb (preposition) to make inquiries about the health of (someone): *he asked after her mother*

askance (əˈskæns) or **askant** (əˈskænt) adv **1** with an oblique glance **2** with doubt or mistrust [C16: of unknown origin]

askew (əˈskjuː) adv, adj at an oblique angle; towards one side; awry

Askey ('æskɪ) n **Arthur**. 1900–82, British comedian

ask for vb (preposition) **1** to try to obtain by requesting **2** (intr) informal to behave in a provocative manner that is regarded as inviting (trouble): *she's asking for trouble; you're asking for it* **3** Scot See **ask after**

asking price n the price suggested by a seller but usually considered to be subject to bargaining

Askja ('aːskjə) n a volcano in E central Iceland: active in 1961; largest crater in Iceland. Height: 1510 m (4954 ft). Area of crater: 88 sq km (34 sq miles)

ASL abbreviation American Sign Language

aslant (əˈslɑːnt) adv **1** at a slant ▷ prep **2** at a slant across or athwart

asleep (əˈsliːp) adj (postpositive) **1** in or into a state of sleep **2** in or into a dormant or inactive state **3** (of limbs, esp when the blood supply to them has been restricted) numb; lacking sensation **4** euphemistic dead

ASLEF ('æzlɛf) n acronym for (in Britain) Associated Society of Locomotive Engineers and Firemen

AS level n Brit **1 a** a public examination taken for the General Certificate of Education, with a smaller course content than an A level: since 2000 taken either as the first part of a full A level or as a qualification in its own right **b** the course leading to this examination **c** (as modifier): *AS-level English* **2** a pass in a subject at AS level: *I've got three AS levels*

ASM abbreviation **1** air-to-surface missile **2** theatre assistant stage manager

Asmara (æsˈmɑːrə) n the capital of Eritrea; cathedral (1922); Grand Mosque (1937); university (1958). Pop: 615 000 (2005 est)

Asnières (French anjɛr) n a suburb of Paris, France, on the Seine. Pop: 75 837 (1999)

Aso ('aːsəʊ) n a group of five volcanic cones in Japan on central Kyushu, one of which, Naka-dake, has the largest crater in the world, between 16 km (10 miles) and 24 km (15 miles) in diameter. Highest cone: 1592 m (5223 ft). Also called: Asosan (ˌaːsəʊ'saːn)

asocial (eɪ'səʊʃəl) adj **1** avoiding contact; not gregarious **2** unconcerned about the welfare of others **3** hostile to society or social practices

Asoka (ə'səʊkə, ə'ʃəʊ-) *n* died 232 BC, Indian emperor (?273–232 BC), who elevated Buddhism to the official state religion

asp (æsp) *n* **1** the venomous snake, probably *Naja haje* (Egyptian cobra), that caused the death of Cleopatra and was formerly used by the Pharaohs as a symbol of their power over life and death **2** Also called: **asp viper** a viper, *Vipera aspis*, that occurs in S Europe and is very similar to but smaller than the adder **3** horned asp another name for **horned viper** [C15: from Latin *aspis*, from Greek]

asparagus (ə'spærəgəs) *n* **1** any Eurasian liliaceous plant of the genus *Asparagus*, esp the widely cultivated *A. officinalis*, having small scaly or needle-like leaves **2** the succulent young shoots of *A. officinalis*, which may be cooked and eaten **3 asparagus fern** a fernlike species of asparagus, *A. plumosus*, native to southern Africa [C15: from Latin, from Greek *asparagos*, of obscure origin]

aspartame (ə'spɑːˌteɪm) *n* an artificial sweetener produced from aspartic acid. Formula: $C_{14}H_{18}N_2O_5$ [C20: from ASPART(IC ACID) + (phenyl)a(lanine) m(ethyl) e(ster)]

Aspasia (ə'speɪzɪə) *n* 5th century BC, Greek courtesan; mistress of Pericles

aspect ('æspɛkt) *n* **1** appearance to the eye; visual effect **2** a distinct feature or element in a problem, situation, etc; facet **3** the way in which a problem, idea, etc, may be considered **4** a facial expression; manner of appearing: *a severe aspect* **5** a position facing a particular direction; outlook: *the southern aspect of a house* **6** a view in a certain direction **7** *astrology* any of several specific angular distances between two planets or a planet and the Ascendant or Midheaven measured, from the earth, in degrees along the ecliptic **8** *grammar* a category of verbs or verbal inflections that expresses such features as the continuity, repetition, or completeness of the action described [C14: from Latin *aspectus* a sight, from *aspicere*, from *ad-* to, at + *specere* to look]

aspect ratio *n* **1** the ratio of width to height of the picture on a television or cinema screen **2** *aeronautics* the ratio of the span of a wing to its mean chord

aspen ('æspən) *n* any of several trees of the salicaceous genus *Populus*, such as *P. tremula* of Europe, in which the leaves are attached to the stem by long flattened stalks so that they quiver in the wind [Old English *æspe*]

Asperger's syndrome ('æspɜːgəz) *n* a form of autism in which the person affected has limited but obsessive interests, and has difficulty relating to other people [C20: after Hans *Asperger* (20th century), Austrian physician who first described it]

asperity (æ'spɛrɪtɪ) *n*, *pl* **-ties 1** roughness or sharpness of temper **2** roughness or harshness of a surface, sound, taste, etc **3** *physics* the elastically compressed region of contact between two surfaces caused by the normal force [C16: from Latin *asperitās*, from *asper* rough]

asperse (ə'spɜːs) *vb* (*tr*) to spread false rumours about; defame [C15: from Latin *aspersus*, from *aspergere* to sprinkle] > **as'perser** *n* > **as'persive** *adj*

aspersion (ə'spɜːʃən) *n* **1** a disparaging or malicious remark; slanderous accusation (esp in the phrase **cast aspersions (on)**) **2** the act of defaming

asphalt ('æsfælt, 'æʃ-, -fəːlt) *n* **1** any of several black semisolid substances composed of bitumen and inert mineral matter. They occur naturally in parts of America and as a residue from petroleum distillation: used as a waterproofing material and in paints, dielectrics, and fungicides **2** a mixture of this substance with gravel, used in road-surfacing and roofing materials **3** (*modifier*) containing or surfaced with asphalt ▷ *vb* **4** (*tr*) to cover with asphalt [C14: from Late Latin *aspaltus*, from Greek *asphaltos*, probably from A-¹ + *sphallein* to cause to fall; referring to its use as a binding agent] > **as'phaltic** *adj*

asphodel ('æsfəˌdɛl) *n* **1** any of various S European liliaceous plants of the genera *Asphodelus* and *Asphodeline*, having clusters of white or yellow flowers **2** an unidentified flower of Greek legend, probably a narcissus, said to cover the Elysian fields [C16: from Latin *asphodelus*, from Greek *asphodelos*, of obscure origin]

asphyxia (æs'fɪksɪə) *n* lack of oxygen in the blood due to restricted respiration; suffocation. If severe enough and prolonged, it causes death [C18: from New Latin, from Greek *asphuxia* a stopping of the pulse, from A-¹ + *sphuxis* pulse, from *sphuzein* to throb] > **as'phyxial** *adj*

asphyxiate (æs'fɪksɪˌeɪt) *vb* to cause asphyxia in or undergo asphyxia; smother; suffocate > **as,phyxi'ation** *n* > **as'phyxi,ator** *n*

aspic ('æspɪk) *n* a savoury jelly based on meat or fish stock, used as a relish or as a mould for meat, vegetables, etc [C18: from French: aspic (jelly), ASP; variously explained as referring to its colour or coldness as compared to that of the snake]

aspidistra (ˌæspɪ'dɪstrə) *n* any Asian plant of the liliaceous genus *Aspidistra*, esp *A. lurida*, a popular house plant with long tough evergreen leaves and purplish flowers borne on the ground [C19: from New Latin, from Greek *aspis* shield, on the model of *Tupistra* genus of liliaceous plants]

aspirant ('æspɪrənt, ə'spaɪərənt) *n* **1** a person who aspires, as to a high position ▷ *adj* **2** aspiring or striving

aspirate *vb* ('æspɪˌreɪt) (*tr*) *phonetics* **a** to articulate (a stop) with some force, so that breath escapes with audible friction as the stop is released **b** to pronounce (a word or syllable) with an initial *h* **2** to draw in or remove by inhalation or suction, esp to suck (air or fluid) from a body cavity or to inhale (fluid) into the lungs after vomiting **3** to supply air to (an internal-combustion engine) ▷ *n* ('æspɪrɪt) **4** *phonetics* **a** a stop pronounced with an audible release of breath **b** the glottal fricative represented in English and several other languages as *h* ▷ *adj* ('æspɪrɪt) **5** *phonetics* (of a stop) pronounced with a forceful and audible expulsion of breath

aspiration (ˌæspɪ'reɪʃən) *n* **1** strong desire to achieve something, such as success **2** the aim of such desire **3** the act of breathing **4** *phonetics* **a** the pronunciation of a stop with an audible and forceful release of breath **b** an aspirated consonant **5** removal of air or fluid from a body cavity by suction **6** *med* **a** the sucking of fluid or foreign matter into the air passages of the body **b** the removal of air or fluid from the body by suction > ˌaspi'rational *adj* > aspiratory (ə'spaɪrətərɪ, -trɪ, 'æspɪrətərɪ, -trɪ) *adj*

aspirator ('æspɪˌreɪtə) *n* a device employing suction, such as a jet pump or one for removing fluids from a body cavity

aspire (ə'spaɪə) *vb* (*intr*) **1** (usually foll by *to* or *after*) to yearn (for) or have a powerful or ambitious plan, desire, or hope (to do or be something): *to aspire to be a great leader* **2** to rise to a great height [C15: from Latin *aspīrāre* to breathe upon, from *spīrāre* to breathe] > **as'piring** *adj*

aspirin ('æsprɪn) *n*, *pl* **-rin** or **-rins 1 a** a white crystalline compound widely used in the form of tablets to relieve pain and fever, to reduce inflammation, and to prevent strokes. Formula: $CH_3COOC_6H_4COOH$. Chemical name: acetylsalicylic acid **2** a tablet of aspirin [C19: from German, from *A*(*cetyl*) + *Spir*(*säure*) spiraeic acid (modern salicylic acid) + -IN; see also SPIRAEA]

aspro ('æsprəʊ) *n*, *pl* **-pros** *Austral informal* an associate professor at an academic institution [C20: from AS(SOCIATE) + PRO(FESSOR)]

asquint (ə'skwɪnt) *adv*, *adj* (*postpositive*) with a glance from the corner of the eye, esp a furtive one [C13: perhaps from Dutch *schuinte* slant, of obscure origin]

Asquith ('æskwɪθ) *n* **Herbert Henry**, 1st Earl of Oxford and Asquith. 1852–1928, British statesman; prime minister (1908–16); leader of the Liberal Party (1908–26)

ass¹ (æs) *n* **1** either of two perissodactyl mammals of the horse family (*Equidae*), *Equus asinus* (**African wild ass**) or *E. hemionus* (**Asiatic wild ass**). They are hardy and sure-footed, having longer ears than the horse. Related adj: **asinine 2** (*not in technical use*) the domesticated variety of the African wild ass; donkey **3** a foolish or ridiculously pompous person [Old English *assa*, probably from Old Irish *asan*, from Latin *asinus*; related to Greek *onos* ass]

ass² (æs) *n* **1** *chiefly US & Canadian slang* the buttocks **2** *chiefly US & Canadian slang* the anus [Old English *ærs*; see ARSE]

Assad ('asat) n 1 **Hafiz al** ('hafɪz æl). born 1928, Syrian statesman and general; president of Syria (1971–2000) 2 his son, **Bashar al** (bæʃəæl). born 1965, Syrian statesman; president of Syria from 2000

assagai ('æsə,gaɪ) n, pl -gais a variant spelling of **assegai**

assai (æ'saɪ) adv music (usually preceded by a musical direction) very: allegro assai [Italian: enough]

assail (ə'seɪl) vb (tr) 1 to attack violently; assault 2 to criticize or ridicule vehemently, as in argument 3 to beset or disturb: his mind was assailed by doubts 4 to encounter with the intention of mastering [c13: from Old French asalir, from Vulgar Latin assalīre (unattested) to leap upon, from Latin assilīre, from salīre to leap] > as'sailable adj > as'sailer n

assailant (ə'seɪlənt) n a person who attacks another, either physically or verbally

Assam (æ'sæm) n 1 a state of NE India, situated in the central Brahmaputra valley: tropical forest, with the heaviest rainfall in the world; produces large quantities of tea. Capital: Dispur. Pop: 26 638 407 (2001 est). Area: 78 438 sq km (30 673 sq miles) 2 a high-quality black tea grown in the state of Assam

assassin (ə'sæsɪn) n a murderer, esp one who kills a prominent political figure [c16: from Medieval Latin assassīnus, from Arabic hashshāshīn, plural of hashshāsh one who eats HASHISH]

assassinate (ə'sæsɪ,neɪt) vb (tr) 1 to murder (a person, esp a public or political figure), usually by a surprise attack 2 to ruin or harm (a person's reputation, etc) by slander > as,sassi'nation n

assault (ə'sɔːlt) n 1 a violent attack, either physical or verbal 2 law an intentional or reckless act that causes another person to expect to be subjected to immediate and unlawful violence 3 a the culmination of a military attack, in which fighting takes place at close quarters b (as modifier): assault troops 4 rape or attempted rape ▷ vb (tr) 5 to make an assault upon 6 to rape or attempt to rape [c13: from Old French asaut, from Vulgar Latin assaltus (unattested), from assalīre (unattested) to leap upon; see ASSAIL] > as'saultive adj

assault and battery n criminal law a threat of attack to another person followed by actual attack, which need amount only to touching with hostile intent

assault course n an obstacle course designed to give soldiers practice in negotiating hazards in making an assault

assault rifle or **assault weapon** n chiefly US a semiautomatic firearm with additional features such as a large magazine, a bayonet fitting, etc

assay vb (ə'seɪ) 1 to subject (a substance, such as silver or gold) to chemical analysis, as in the determination of the amount of impurity 2 (tr) to attempt (something or to do something) ▷ n (ə'seɪ, 'æseɪ) 3 a an analysis, esp a determination of the amount of metal in an ore or the amounts of impurities in a precious metal b (as modifier): an assay office 4 a substance undergoing an analysis 5 a written report on the results of an analysis 6 a test [c14: from Old Northern French assai; see ESSAY] > as'sayer n

assegai or **assagai** ('æsə,gaɪ) n, pl -gais 1 a southern African cornaceous tree, Curtisia faginea, the wood of which is used for making spears 2 a sharp light spear, esp one made of this wood [c17: from Portuguese azagaia, from Arabic az zaghāyah, from al the + zaghāyah assegai, from Berber]

assemblage (ə'sɛmblɪdʒ) n 1 a number of things or persons assembled together; collection; assembly 2 the act or process of assembling or the state of being assembled 3 (,æsəm'blɑːʒ) a three-dimensional work of art that combines various objects into an integrated whole

assemble (ə'sɛmbᵊl) vb 1 to come or bring together; collect or congregate 2 to fit or join together (the parts of something, such as a machine) [c13: from Old French assembler, from Vulgar Latin assimulāre (unattested) to bring together, from Latin simul together]

assembler (ə'sɛmblə) n 1 a person or thing that assembles. See **compiler** (sense 2) 2 a type of computer program that converts a program written in assembly language into machine code. See **compiler** (sense 2)

3 another name for **assembly language**

assembly (ə'sɛmblɪ) n, pl -blies 1 a number of people gathered together, esp for a formal meeting held at regular intervals 2 the act of assembling or the state of being assembled 3 the process of putting together a number of parts to make a machine or other product 4 military a signal for personnel to assemble, as by drum, bugle, etc

Assembly (ə'sɛmblɪ) n, pl -blies the lower chamber in various American state legislatures. See also **House of Assembly, legislative assembly**

assembly language n computing a low-level programming language that allows a programmer complete control of the machine code to be generated

assembly line n a sequence of machines, tools, operations, workers, etc, in a factory, arranged so that at each stage a further process is carried out

Assen (Dutch 'asə) n a city in the N Netherlands, capital of Drenthe province. Pop: 62 000 (2003 est)

assent (ə'sɛnt) n 1 agreement, as to a statement, proposal, etc; acceptance 2 hesitant agreement; compliance ▷ vb 3 (intr; usually foll by to) to agree or express agreement [c13: from Old French assenter, from Latin assentīrī, from sentīre to think]

assert (ə'sɜːt) vb (tr) 1 to insist upon (rights, claims, etc) 2 (may take a clause as object) to state to be true; declare categorically 3 to put (oneself) forward in an insistent manner [c17: from Latin asserere to join to oneself, from serere to join] > as'serter or as'sertor n

assertion (ə'sɜːʃən) n 1 a positive statement, usually made without an attempt at furnishing evidence 2 the act of asserting

assertive (ə'sɜːtɪv) adj 1 confident and direct in claiming one's rights or putting forward one's views 2 given to making assertions or bold demands; dogmatic or aggressive > as'sertively adv > as'sertiveness n

assess (ə'sɛs) vb (tr) 1 to judge the worth, importance, etc, of; evaluate 2 (foll by at) to estimate the value of (income, property, etc) for taxation purposes 3 to determine the amount of (a fine, tax, damages, etc) 4 to impose a tax, fine, etc, on (a person or property) [c15: from Old French assesser, from Latin assidēre to sit beside, from sedēre to sit] > as'sessable adj

assessment (ə'sɛsmənt) n 1 the act of assessing, esp (in Britain) the evaluation of a student's achievement on a course 2 an amount determined as payable 3 a valuation set on taxable property, income, etc 4 evaluation; estimation

assessor (ə'sɛsə) n 1 a person who evaluates the merits, importance, etc, of something, esp (in Britain) work prepared as part of a course of study 2 a person who values property for taxation 3 a person who estimates the value of damage to property for insurance purposes 4 a person with technical expertise called in to advise a court on specialist matters > assessorial (,æsɛ'sɔːrɪəl) adj

asset ('æsɛt) n anything valuable or useful [c19: back formation from ASSETS]

assets ('æsɛts) pl n 1 accounting the property and claims against debtors that a business enterprise may apply to discharge its liabilities. Assets may be fixed, current, liquid, or intangible and are shown balanced against liabilities 2 law the property available to an executor or administrator for settlement of the debts and payment of legacies of the estate of a deceased or insolvent person 3 any property owned by a person or firm [c16 (in the sense: enough to discharge one's liabilities): via Anglo-French from Old French asez enough, from Vulgar Latin ad satis (unattested), from Latin ad up to + satis enough]

asset-stripping n commerce the practice of taking over a failing company at a low price and then selling the assets piecemeal before closing the company down > 'asset-,stripper n

asset value n the value of a share in a company calculated by dividing the difference between the total of its assets and its liabilities by the number of ordinary shares issued

asseverate (ə'sɛvə,reɪt) vb (tr) to assert or declare emphatically or solemnly [c18: from Latin assevērāre to do (something) earnestly, from sevērus SEVERE]

▷ as,sever'ation n

Asshur ('æʃuə) n a variant spelling of **Assur**

assibilate (ə'sɪbɪˌleɪt) vb *phonetics* (tr) to pronounce (a speech sound) with or as a sibilant [C19: from Late Latin *assībilāre* to hiss at, from *sībilāre* to hiss; see SIBILANT] ▷ as,sibi'lation n

assiduity (ˌæsɪ'djuːɪtɪ) n, pl -ties 1 constant and close application 2 (*often plural*) devoted attention

assiduous (ə'sɪdjʊəs) adj 1 hard-working; persevering 2 undertaken with perseverance and care [C16: from Latin *assiduus* sitting down to (something), from *assidēre* to sit beside, from *sedēre* to sit] ▷ as'siduousness n

assign (ə'saɪn) vb (*mainly tr*) 1 to select for and appoint to a post, etc 2 to give out or allot (a task, problem, etc) 3 to set apart (a place, person, time, etc) for a particular function or event: *to assign a day for the meeting* 4 to attribute to a specified cause, origin, or source; ascribe 5 to transfer (one's right, interest, or title to property) to someone else ▷ n 6 *law* a person to whom property is assigned; assignee [C14: from Old French *assigner*, from Latin *assignāre*, from *signāre* to mark out] ▷ as'signable adj ▷ as'signer n

assignation (ˌæsɪg'neɪʃən) n 1 a secret or forbidden arrangement to meet, esp one between lovers 2 the act of assigning; assignment [C14: from Old French, from Latin *assignātiō* a marking out; see ASSIGN]

assignee (ˌæsaɪ'niː) n *law* a person to whom some right, interest, or property is transferred

assignment (ə'saɪnmənt) n 1 something that has been assigned, such as a mission or task 2 a position or post to which a person is assigned 3 the act of assigning or state of being assigned 4 *law* a the transfer to another of a right, interest, or title to property, esp personal property b the document effecting such a transfer

assimilate (ə'sɪmɪˌleɪt) vb 1 (tr) to learn (information, a procedure, etc) and understand it thoroughly 2 (tr) to absorb (food) and incorporate it into the body tissues 3 (intr) to become absorbed, incorporated, or learned and understood 4 (*usually foll by* into *or* with) to bring or come into harmony; adjust or become adjusted: *the new immigrants assimilated easily* 5 (*usually foll by* to *or* with) to become or cause to become similar 6 (*usually foll by* to) *phonetics* to change (a consonant) or (of a consonant) to be changed into another under the influence of one adjacent to it [C15: from Latin *assimilāre* to make one thing like another, from *similis* like, SIMILAR] ▷ as'similable adj ▷ as,simi'lation n ▷ as'similative *or* as'similatory adj ▷ as'simiˌlator n ▷ as'similatively adv

Assiniboine (ə'sɪnɪˌbɔɪn) n a river in W Canada, rising in E Saskatchewan and flowing southeast and east to the Red River at Winnipeg. Length: over 860 km (500 miles)

Assisi (Italian as'siːzi) n a town in central Italy, in Umbria: birthplace of St Francis, who founded the Franciscan religious order here in 1208. Pop: 25 304 (2001)

assist (ə'sɪst) vb 1 to give help or support to (a person, cause, etc); aid 2 to work or act as an assistant or subordinate to (another) ▷ n *US & Canadian* the act of helping; aid; assistance [C15: from French *assister* to be present, from Latin *assistere* to stand by, from *sistere* to cause to stand, from *stāre* to stand] ▷ as'sister n

assistance (ə'sɪstəns) n 1 help; support 2 the act of assisting 3 *Brit informal* See **national assistance**

assistance dog n a dog that has been specially trained to live with and accompany a disabled person, carrying out such tasks as prompting them to take medication or assisting them to cross a road

assistant (ə'sɪstənt) n 1 a a person who assists, esp in a subordinate position b (*as modifier*): *assistant manager* 2 See **shop assistant**

assistant referee n *soccer* the official name for **linesman** (sense 1)

assisted dying n the suicide of a person afflicted by an incurable disease, using a lethal dose of drugs provided by a physician for this purpose

assisted living (ə'sɪstɪd) n a a living environment for elderly people, in which personal and medical care are supplied b (*as modifier*): *private assisted-living apartments*

assize (ə'saɪz) n *Scots law* a trial by jury b another name

for **jury¹** [C13: from Old French *assise* session, from *asseoir* to seat, from Latin *assidēre* to sit beside; see ASSESS]

assizes (ə'saɪzɪz) pl n (formerly in England and Wales) the sessions, usually held four times a year, of the principal court in each county, exercising civil and criminal jurisdiction, attended by itinerant judges: replaced in 1971 by crown courts

assoc. *abbreviation* 1 associate(d) 2 association

associate vb (ə'səʊʃɪˌeɪt, -sɪ-) (*usually foll by* with) 1 (tr) to link or connect in the mind or imagination 2 (intr) to keep company; mix socially: *to associate with writers* 3 (intr) to form or join an association, group, etc 4 (*tr; usually passive*) to consider in conjunction; connect: *rainfall is associated with humidity* 5 (tr) to bring (a person, esp oneself) into friendship, partnership, etc 6 (*tr; often passive*) to express agreement or allow oneself to be connected (with): *Bertrand Russell was associated with the peace movement* ▷ n (ə'səʊʃɪɪt, -,eɪt, -sɪ-) 7 a person joined with another or others in an enterprise, business, etc; partner; colleague 8 a companion or friend 9 something that usually accompanies another thing; concomitant 10 a person having a subordinate position in or admitted to only partial membership of an institution, association, etc ▷ adj (ə'səʊʃɪɪt, -,eɪt, -sɪ-) (*prenominal*) 11 joined with another or others in an enterprise, business, etc; having equal or nearly equal status: *an associate director* 12 having partial rights and privileges or subordinate status: *an associate member* 13 accompanying; concomitant [C14: from Latin *associāre* to ally with, from *sociāre* to join, from *socius* an ally] ▷ as'sociable adj ▷ as'sociˌator n ▷ as'sociateˌship n

association (ə,səʊsɪ'eɪʃən, -ʃɪ-) n 1 a group of people having a common purpose or interest; a society or club 2 the act of associating or the state of being associated 3 friendship or companionship: *their association will not last* 4 a mental connection of ideas, feelings, or sensations 5 *chem* the formation of groups of molecules and ions, esp in liquids, held together by weak chemical bonds 6 *ecology* a group of similar plants that grow in a uniform environment and contain one or more dominant species

association football n a more formal name for **soccer**

associative (ə'səʊʃɪətɪv) adj 1 of, relating to, or causing association or union 2 *maths*, *logic* a being independent of the grouping of numbers, symbols, or terms within a given set, as in conjunction or in an expression such as $(2 \times 3) \times 4 = 2 \times (3 \times 4)$ b referring to this property: *the associative laws of arithmetic*

assonance ('æsənəns) n 1 the use of the same vowel sound with different consonants or the same consonant with different vowels in successive words or stressed syllables, as in a line of verse. Examples are *time* and *light* or *mystery* and *mastery* 2 partial correspondence; rough similarity [C18: from French, from Latin *assonāre* to sound, from *sonāre* to sound] ▷ 'assonant adj, n

assort (ə'sɔːt) vb 1 (tr) to arrange or distribute into groups of the same type; classify 2 (*intr; usually foll by* with) to fit or fall into a class or group; match 3 (tr) to supply with an assortment of merchandise 4 (tr) to put in the same category as others; group [C15: from Old French *assorter*, from *sorte* SORT] ▷ as'sortative *or* as'sortive adj

assorted (ə'sɔːtɪd) adj 1 consisting of various kinds mixed together; miscellaneous 2 arranged in sorts; classified: *assorted categories* 3 matched; suited (esp in the combinations **well-assorted**, **ill-assorted**)

assortment (ə'sɔːtmənt) n 1 a collection or group of various things or sorts 2 the act of assorting

ASSR *abbreviation* (formerly) Autonomous Soviet Socialist Republic

asst *abbreviation* assistant

assuage (ə'sweɪdʒ) vb (tr) 1 to soothe, moderate, or relieve (grief, pain, etc) 2 to give relief to (thirst, appetite, etc); satisfy 3 to pacify; calm [C14: from Old French *assouagier*, from Vulgar Latin *assuāviāre* (*unattested*) to sweeten, from Latin *suāvis* pleasant; see SUAVE] ▷ as'suagement n ▷ as'suager n

Assuan *or* **Assouan** (ɑːs'wɑːn) n variant spellings of **Aswan**

assume (ə'sjuːm) *vb* (*tr*) **1** (*may take a clause as object*) to take for granted; accept without proof; suppose **2** to take upon oneself; undertake or take on or over (a position, responsibility, etc): *to assume office* **3** to pretend to; feign: *he assumed indifference, although the news affected him deeply* **4** to take or put on; adopt: *the problem assumed gigantic proportions* **5** to appropriate or usurp (power, control, etc); arrogate [c15: from Latin *assūmere* to take up, from *sūmere* to take up, from SUB- + *emere* to take] > as'sumable *adj* > as'sumer *n*

assumed (ə'sjuːmd) *adj* **1** false; fictitious: *an assumed name* **2** taken for granted **3** usurped; arrogated

assuming (ə'sjuːmɪŋ) *adj* **1** expecting too much; presumptuous; arrogant ▷ *conj* **2** (often foll by *that*) if it is assumed or taken for granted (*that*)

assumption (ə'sʌmpʃən) *n* **1** the act of taking something for granted or something that is taken for granted **2** an assuming of power or possession of something **3** arrogance; presumption **4** *logic* a statement that is used as the premise of a particular argument but may not be otherwise accepted [c13: from Latin *assūmptiō* a taking up, from *assūmere* to ASSUME] > as'sumptive *adj*

Assumption (ə'sʌmpʃən) *n* *Christianity* **1** the taking up of the Virgin Mary (body and soul) into heaven when her earthly life was ended **2** the feast commemorating this, celebrated by Roman Catholics on Aug 15

Assur, Asur ('æsə) *or* **Asshur, Ashur** ('æʃʊə) *n* **1** the supreme national god of the ancient Assyrians, chiefly a war god, whose symbol was an archer within a winged disc **2** one of the chief cities of ancient Assyria, on the River Tigris about 100 km (60 miles) downstream from the present-day city of Mosul

assurance (ə'ʃʊərəns) *n* **1** a statement, assertion, etc, intended to inspire confidence or give encouragement **2** a promise or pledge of support **3** freedom from doubt; certainty: *his assurance about his own superiority infuriated her* **4** forwardness; impudence **5** *chiefly Brit* insurance providing for certainties such as death as contrasted with fire or theft

Assurbanipal (ˌæsʊə'bɑːnɪˌpæl) *n* a variant spelling of **Ashurbanipal**

assure (ə'ʃʊə) *vb* (*tr; may take a clause as object*) **1** to cause to feel sure or certain; convince: *to assure a person of one's love* **2** to promise; guarantee **3** to state positively or with assurance **4** to make (an event) certain; ensure **5** *chiefly Brit* to insure against loss, esp of life [c14: from Old French *aseürer* to assure, from Medieval Latin *assēcūrāre* to secure or make sure, from *sēcūrus* SECURE] > as'surer *n*

assured (ə'ʃʊəd) *adj* **1** made certain; sure; guaranteed **2** self-assured **3** *chiefly Brit* insured, esp by a life assurance policy **4** *chiefly Brit* **a** the beneficiary under a life assurance policy **b** the person whose life is insured > **assuredly** (ə'ʃʊərɪdlɪ) *adv*

Assyria (ə'sɪrɪə) *n* an ancient kingdom of N Mesopotamia: it established an empire that stretched from Egypt to the Persian Gulf, reaching its greatest extent between 721 and 633 BC. Its chief cities were Assur and Nineveh > As'syrian *n, adj*

AST *abbreviation* Atlantic Standard Time

Astaire (ə'stɛə) *n* **Fred,** real name *Frederick Austerlitz.* 1899–1987, US dancer, singer, and actor, whose films include *Top Hat* (1935), *Swing Time* (1936), and *The Band Wagon* (1953)

Astana (æ'stænə) *n* the capital of Kazakhstan, in the N of the country; replaced Almaty as capital in 1997; an important railway junction. Pop: 335 000 (2005 est). Former names: Akmolinsk until (1961), Tselinograd (1961–94), Akmola (1994–98)

Astanga yoga *or* **Ashtanga yoga** (æ'ʃtæŋɡə) *n* a revived ancient form of yoga that involves a fast and powerful series of movements

Astarte (æ'stɑːtɪ) *n* a fertility goddess worshipped by the Phoenicians: identified with Ashtoreth of the Hebrews and Ishtar of the Babylonians and Assyrians

astatic (æ'stætɪk, eɪ-) *adj* **1** not static; unstable **2** *physics* having no tendency to assume any particular position or orientation [c19: from Greek *astatos* unsteady; see A-[1], STATIC] > a'statically *adv*

astatine ('æstəˌtiːn, -tɪn) *n* a radioactive element of the halogen series: a decay product of uranium and thorium that occurs naturally in minute amounts and is artificially produced by bombarding bismuth with alpha particles. Symbol: At; atomic no: 85; half-life of most stable isotope, [210]At: 8.1 hours; probable valency: 1,3,5, or 7; melting pt: 302°C; boiling pt: 337°C (est) [c20: from Greek *astatos* unstable (see ASTATIC) + -INE[2]]

Astbury ('æstbərɪ) *n* **John.** 1688–1743, English potter; earliest of the great Staffordshire potters

aster ('æstə) *n* **1** any plant of the genus *Aster,* having white, blue, purple, or pink daisy-like flowers: family *Asteraceae* (composites) **2** **China aster** a related Chinese plant, *Callistephus chinensis,* widely cultivated for its showy brightly coloured flowers [c18: from New Latin, from Latin *aster* star, from Greek]

-aster *suffix forming nouns* a person or thing that is inferior or bears only a poor resemblance to what is specified [from Latin: suffix indicating imperfect resemblance]

asterisk ('æstərɪsk) *n* **1** a star-shaped character (*) used in printing or writing to indicate a cross-reference to a footnote, an omission, etc ▷ *vb* **2** (*tr*) to mark with an asterisk [c17: from Late Latin *asteriscus* a small star, from Greek *asteriskos,* from *astēr* star]

asterism ('æstəˌrɪzəm) *n* **1** three asterisks arranged in a triangle (⁂ or ⁎⁎⁎), to draw attention to the text that follows **2** a cluster of stars, which may be a subset or a superset of a constellation [c16: from Greek *asterismos* arrangement of constellations, from *astēr* star]

astern (ə'stɜːn) *adv, adj* (*postpositive*) *nautical* **1** at or towards the stern **2** with the stern first: *full speed astern!* **3** aft of the stern of a vessel

asteroid *n* ('æstəˌrɔɪd) **1** Also called: **minor planet, planetoid** any of numerous small celestial bodies that move around the sun mainly between the orbits of Mars and Jupiter. Their diameters range from 930 kilometres (Ceres) to less than one kilometre **2** Also called: **asteroidean** (ˌæstə'rɔɪdɪən) any echinoderm of the class *Asteroidea;* a starfish ▷ *adj* Also: **asteroidal** (ˌæstə'rɔɪdəl) **3** of, relating to, or belonging to the class *Asteroidea* **4** shaped like a star [c19: from Greek *asteroeidēs* starlike, from *astēr* a star]

asthenia (æs'θiːnɪə) *or* **astheny** ('æsθənɪ) *n* *pathol* an abnormal loss of strength; debility [c19: via New Latin from Greek *astheneia* weakness, from A-[1] + *sthenos* strength]

asthenic (æs'θɛnɪk) *adj* **1** of, relating to, or having asthenia; weak **2** (in constitutional psychology) referring to a physique characterized by long limbs and a small trunk: claimed to be associated with a schizoid personality ▷ *n* **3** a person having long limbs and a small trunk

asthma ('æsmə) *n* a respiratory disorder, often of allergic origin, characterized by difficulty in breathing, wheezing, and a sense of constriction in the chest [c14: from Greek: laborious breathing]

asthmatic (æs'mætɪk) *adj* **1** of, relating to, or having asthma ▷ *n* **2** a person who has asthma > asth'matically *adv*

Asti ('æstɪ) *n* a town in NW Italy: famous for its sparkling wine (**Asti spumante** (spuː'mæntɪ)). Pop: 71 276 (2001)

astigmatic (ˌæstɪg'mætɪk) *adj* relating to or affected with astigmatism [c19: from A-[1] + Greek *stigmat-, stigma* spot, focus; see STIGMA] > ˌastig'matically *adv*

astigmatism (ə'stɪgməˌtɪzəm) *or* **astigmia** (ə'stɪgmɪə) *n* **1** a defect of a lens resulting in the formation of distorted images; caused by the curvature of the lens being different in different planes **2** faulty vision resulting from defective curvature of the cornea or lens of the eye

astilbe (ə'stɪlbɪ) *n* any perennial saxifragaceous plant of the genus *Astilbe* of E Asia and North America: cultivated for their ornamental spikes or panicles of pink or white flowers [c19: New Latin, from Greek: not glittering, from A-[1] + *stilbe,* from *stilbein* to glitter; referring to its inconspicuous individual flowers]

astir (ə'stɜː) *adj* (*postpositive*) **1** awake and out of bed **2** in motion; on the move

a

Astolat ('æstəʊ,læt) *n* a town in Arthurian legend: location unknown

Aston ('æstən) *n* **Francis William.** 1877–1945, English physicist and chemist, who developed the first mass spectrograph, using it to investigate the isotopic structures of elements: Nobel prize for chemistry 1922

astonied (ə'stɒnɪd) *adj archaic* stunned; dazed [c14: from *astonyen* to ASTONISH]

astonish (ə'stɒnɪʃ) *vb* (*tr*) to fill with amazement; surprise greatly [c15: from earlier *astonyen* (see ASTONIED), from Old French *estoner*, from Vulgar Latin *extonāre* (unattested) to strike with thunder, from Latin *tonāre* to thunder]

astonishing (ə'stɒnɪʃɪŋ) *adj* causing great surprise or amazement; astounding > a'stonishingly *adv*

astonishment (ə'stɒnɪʃmənt) *n* **1** extreme surprise; amazement **2** a cause of amazement

Astor ('æstə) *n* **1 John Jacob,** 1st Baron Astor of Hever. 1886–1971, British proprietor of *The Times* (1922–66) **2 Nancy (Witcher),** Viscountess, original name *Nancy Langhorne.* 1879–1964, British Conservative politician, born in the US; the first woman to sit in the British House of Commons

astound (ə'staʊnd) *vb* (*tr*) to overwhelm with amazement and wonder; bewilder [c17: from *astoned* amazed, from Old French *estoné*, from *estoner* to ASTONISH]

astounding (ə'staʊndɪŋ) *adj* causing amazement and wonder; bewildering > a'stoundingly *adv*

astraddle (ə'strædəl) *adj* **1** (*postpositive*) with a leg on either side of something ▷ *prep* **2** astride

astragal ('æstrəgəl) *n* **1** *architect* Also called: **bead** a small convex moulding, usually with a semicircular cross section **2** *anatomy* the ankle or anklebone [c17: from Latin *astragalus*, from Greek *astragalos* anklebone, hence, small round moulding]

astragalus (æ'strægələs) *n, pl* -li (-ˌlaɪ) *anatomy* another name for **talus¹** [c16: via New Latin from Latin: ASTRAGAL]

astrakhan (ˌæstrə'kæn, -'kɑːn) *n* **1** a fur, usually black or grey, made of the closely curled wool of lambs from Astrakhan **2** a cloth with curled pile resembling this **3** (*modifier*) made of such fur or cloth

Astrakhan (ˌæstrə'kæn, -'kɑːn; *Russian* 'astrəxanj) *n* a city in SE Russia, on the delta of the Volga River, 21 m (70 ft) below sea level. Pop: 507 000 (2005 est)

astral ('æstrəl) *adj* **1** relating to, proceeding from, consisting of, or resembling the stars **2** *theosophy* denoting or relating to a supposed supersensible substance believed to form the material of a second body for each person, taking the form of an aura discernible to certain gifted individuals [c17: from Late Latin *astrālis*, from Latin *astrum* star, from Greek *astron*]

astray (ə'streɪ) *adj, adv* (*postpositive*) **1** out of the correct path or direction **2** out of the right, good, or expected way; into error [c13: from Old French *estraie* roaming, from *estraier* to STRAY]

astrict (ə'strɪkt) *vb* (*tr*) *archaic* to bind, confine, or constrict [c16: from Latin *astrictus* drawn closely together, from *astringere* to lighten, from *stringere* to bind] > as'triction *n* > as'trictive *adj* > as'trictively *adv*

astride (ə'straɪd) *adj* (*postpositive*) **1** with a leg on either side **2** with the legs far apart ▷ *prep* **3** with a leg on either side of **4** with a part on both sides of

astringent (ə'strɪndʒənt) *adj* **1** severe; harsh **2** sharp or invigorating **3** causing contraction of body tissues, checking blood flow, or restricting secretions of fluids; styptic ▷ *n* **4** an astringent drug or lotion [c16: from Latin *astringēns* drawing together; see ASTRICT] > as'tringency *or* as'tringence *n* > as'tringently *adv*

astro- *combining form* indicating a heavenly body, star, or star-shaped structure: *astrology; astrocyte* [from Greek, from *astron* star]

astrobiology (ˌæstrəʊbaɪ'ɒlədʒɪ) *n* the branch of biology that investigates the possibility of life elsewhere in the universe

astrochemistry (ˌæstrəʊ'kemɪstrɪ) *n* the study of the chemistry of celestial bodies and space, esp by means of spectroscopy

astrodome ('æstrə,dəʊm) *n* Also called: astrohatch a transparent dome on the top of an aircraft, through which observations can be made, esp of the stars

astrol. *abbreviation* **1** astrological **2** astrology

astrolabe ('æstrə,leɪb) *n* an instrument used by early astronomers to measure the altitude of stars and planets and also as a navigational aid. It consists of a graduated circular disc with a movable sighting device [c13: via Old French and Medieval Latin from Greek, from *astrolabos* (adj), literally: star-taking, from *astron* star + *lambanein* to take]

astrology (ə'strɒlədʒɪ) *n* **1** the study of the motions and relative positions of the planets, sun, and moon, interpreted in terms of human characteristics and activities **2** the primitive study of celestial bodies, which formed the basis of astronomy [c14: from Old French *astrologie*, from Latin *astrologia*, from Greek, from *astrologos* (originally: astronomer); see ASTRO-, -LOGY] > as'trologer *or* as'trologist *n* > astrological (ˌæstrə'lɒdʒɪkəl) *adj*

astronaut ('æstrə,nɔːt) *n* a person trained for travelling in space. See also **cosmonaut** [c20: from ASTRO- + -naut from Greek *nautēs* sailor, on the model of *aeronaut*]

astronautics (ˌæstrə'nɔːtɪks) *n* (*functioning as singular*) the science and technology of space flight > ˌastro'nautic *or* ˌastro'nautical *adj*

Astronomer Royal *n* an honorary title awarded to an eminent British astronomer: until 1972, the Astronomer Royal was also director of the Royal Greenwich Observatory

astronomical (ˌæstrə'nɒmɪkəl) *or* **astronomic** *adj* **1** enormously large; immense **2** of or relating to astronomy > ˌastro'nomically *adv*

astronomical clock *n* **1** a complex clock showing astronomical phenomena, such as the phases of the moon **2** any clock showing sidereal time used in observatories

astronomical unit *n* a unit of distance used in astronomy equal to the mean distance between the earth and the sun. 1 astronomical unit is equivalent to 1.495×10^{11} metres or about 9.3×10^7 miles

astronomy (ə'strɒnəmɪ) *n* the scientific study of the individual celestial bodies (excluding the earth) and of the universe as a whole. Its various branches include astrometry, astrodynamics, cosmology, and astrophysics [c13: from Old French *astronomie*, from Latin *astronomia*, from Greek; see ASTRO-, -NOMY] > as'tronomer *n*

astrophysics (ˌæstrəʊ'fɪzɪks) *n* (*functioning as singular*) the branch of physics concerned with the physical and chemical properties, origin, and evolution of the celestial bodies > ˌastro'physicist *n*

astrotourist ('æstrəʊ,tʊərɪst) *n* a person who pays to travel into space as a form of recreation > ˌastro'tourism *n*

Astroturf ('æstrəʊ,tɜːf) *n trademark* a type of grasslike artificial surface used for playing fields and lawns [c20: from *Astro(dome)*, the baseball stadium in Texas where it was first used + TURF]

Asturias¹ (æ'stʊərɪ,æs) *n* a region and former kingdom of NW Spain, consisting of a coastal plain and the Cantabrian Mountains: a Christian stronghold against the Moors (8th to 13th centuries); rich mineral resources

Asturias² (æ'stʊərɪ,æs) *n* **Miguel Ángel.** 1899–1974, Guatemalan novelist and poet. His novels include *El Señor Presidente* (1946). Nobel prize for literature 1967

astute (ə'stjuːt) *adj* having insight or acumen; perceptive; shrewd [c17: from Latin *astūtus* cunning, from *astus* (n) cleverness] > as'tutely *adv* > as'tuteness *n*

Asunción (*Spanish* asun'sjon) *n* the capital and chief port of Paraguay, on the Paraguay River, 1530 km (950 miles) from the Atlantic. Pop: 1 750 000 (2005 est)

asunder (ə'sʌndə) *adv, adj* (*postpositive*) in or into parts or pieces; apart: *to tear asunder* [Old English *on sundran* apart; see SUNDER]

Asur ('æsə) *n* a variant spelling of **Assur**

Aswan, Assuan *or* **Assouan** (ɑːs'wɑːn) *n* an ancient town in SE Egypt, on the Nile, just below the First Cataract. Pop: 249 000 (2005 est). Ancient name: Syene

Aswan High Dam n a dam on the Nile forming a reservoir (Lake Nasser) extending 480 km (300 miles) from the First to the Third Cataracts: opened in 1971, it was built 6 km (4 miles) upstream from the old **Aswan Dam** (built in 1902 and twice raised). Height of dam: 109 m (365 ft)

asylum (ə'saɪləm) n **1** a safe or inviolable place of refuge, esp as formerly offered by the Christian Church to criminals, outlaws, etc; sanctuary (often in the phrase **give asylum to**) **2** shelter; refuge **3** *international law* refuge afforded to a person whose extradition is sought by a foreign government: *political asylum* **4** *obsolescent* an institution for the shelter, treatment, or confinement of individuals, esp a mental institution (formerly termed **lunatic asylum**) [C15: via Latin from Greek *asulon* refuge, from *asulos* that may not be seized, from A-¹ + *sulon* right of seizure]

asymmetric (ˌæsɪ'mɛtrɪk, -eɪ-) or **asymmetrical** adj **1** not symmetrical; lacking symmetry; misproportioned **2** *logic, maths* (of a relation) never holding between a pair of values *x* and *y* when it holds between *y* and *x*, as "...*is the father of*..." > ˌasym'metrically adv

asymmetrical warfare n warfare between a powerful military force and a weak guerilla force

asymmetric bars adv, pl n *gymnastics* **a** (functioning as plural) a pair of wooden or fibreglass bars placed parallel to each other but set at different heights, for various exercises **b** (functioning as singular) an event in a gymnastic competition in which competitors exercise on such bars

asymmetry (æ'sɪmɪtrɪ, eɪ-) n lack or absence of symmetry in spatial arrangements or in mathematical or logical relations

asymptomatic (ˌæˌsɪmptə'mætɪk, eɪ-) adj (of a disease or suspected disease) without symptoms; providing no subjective evidence of existence

asymptote ('æsɪmˌtəʊt) n a straight line that is closely approached by a plane curve so that the perpendicular distance between them decreases to zero as the distance from the origin increases to infinity [C17: from Greek *asumptōtos* not falling together, from A-¹ + SYN- + *ptōtos* inclined to fall, from *piptein* to fall] > asymptotic (ˌæsɪm'tɒtɪk) or ˌasymp'totical adj >ˌasymp'totically adv

asystole (ə'sɪstəlɪ) n *pathol* the absence of heartbeat; cardiac arrest > asystolic (ˌæsɪs'tɒlɪk) adj

at (æt) prep **1** used to indicate location or position: *are they at the table?; staying at a small hotel* **2** towards; in the direction of: *looking at television; throwing stones at windows* **3** used to indicate position in time: *come at three o'clock* **4** engaged in; in a state of (being): *children at play; stand at ease; he is at his most charming today* **5** (in expressions concerned with habitual activity) during the passing of (esp in the phrase **at night**): *he used to work at night* **6** for; in exchange for: *it's selling at four pounds* **7** used to indicate the object of an emotion: *angry at the driver; shocked at his behaviour* **8** where it's at *slang* the real place of action [Old English *æt*; related to Old Norse *at* to, Latin *ad* to]

At *the chemical symbol for* astatine

AT abbreviation attainment target

at. abbreviation **1** Also: atm atmosphere (unit of pressure) **2** atomic

Atacama Desert (Spanish ata'kama) n a desert region along the W coast of South America, mainly in N Chile: a major source of nitrates. Area: about 80 000 sq km (31 000 sq miles)

Atahualpa (ˌætə'wɑːlpə) or **Atabalipa** (ˌætə'bɑːlɪpə) n ?1500–33, the last Inca emperor of Peru (1525–33), who was put to death by the Spanish under Pizarro

Atalanta (ˌætə'læntə) n *Greek myth* a maiden who agreed to marry any man who could defeat her in a running race. She lost to Hippomenes when she paused to pick up three golden apples that he had deliberately dropped

ataman ('ætəmən) n, pl -mans an elected leader of the Cossacks; hetman [from Russian, from Polish *hetman*, from German *Hauptmann* (literally: head man)]

ataractic (ˌætə'ræktɪk) or **ataraxic** (ˌætə'ræksɪk) adj **1** able to calm or tranquillize ▷ n **2** obsolete an ataractic drug

ataraxia (ˌætə'ræksɪə) or **ataraxy** ('ætəˌræksɪ) n

calmness or peace of mind; emotional tranquillity [C17: from Greek: serenity, from *ataraktos* undisturbed, from A-¹ + *tarassein* to trouble]

Atatürk (ˌætə,tɜːk) n **Kemal** (kɛ'mɑːl), real name *Mustafa Kemal*. 1881– 1938, Turkish general and statesman; founder of the Turkish republic and president of Turkey (1923–38), who westernized and secularized the country

atavism ('ætəˌvɪzəm) n **1** the recurrence in a plant or animal of certain primitive characteristics that were present in an ancestor but have not occurred in intermediate generations **2** reversion to a former or more primitive type [C19: from French *atavisme*, from Latin *atavus* strictly: great-grandfather's grandfather, probably from *atta* daddy + *avus* grandfather] >ˌata'vistic adj >ˌata'vistically adv

ataxia (ə'tæksɪə) or **ataxy** (ə'tæksɪ) n *pathol* lack of muscular coordination [C17: via New Latin from Greek: lack of coordination, from A-¹ + -*taxia*, from *tassein* to put in order] > a'taxic or a'tactic adj

ATB abbreviation *text messaging* all the best

Atbara ('ætbərə, æt'bɑ:-) n **1** a town in NE Sudan. Pop: 110 000 (2005 est) **2** a river in NE Africa, rising in N Ethiopia and flowing through E Sudan to the Nile at Atbara. Length: over 800 km (500 miles)

ATC abbreviation **1** air-traffic control **2** (in Britain) Air Training Corps

ate (ɛt, eɪt) vb the past tense of **eat**

Ate ('eɪtɪ, 'ɑːtɪ) n *Greek myth* a goddess who makes men blind so that they will blunder into guilty acts [C16: via Latin from Greek *atē* a rash impulse]

-ate¹ suffix **1** (forming adjectives) possessing; having the appearance or characteristics of: *fortunate; palmate; Latinate* **2** (forming nouns) a chemical compound, esp a salt or ester of an acid: *carbonate; stearate* **3** (forming nouns) the product of a process: *condensate* **4** forming verbs from nouns and adjectives: *hyphenate; rusticate* [from Latin *-ātus*, past participial ending of verbs ending in *-āre*]

-ate² suffix forming nouns denoting office, rank, or a group having a certain function: *episcopate; electorate* [from Latin *-ātus*, suffix (fourth declension) of collective nouns]

atelier ('ætəlˌjeɪ; French atəlje) n an artist's studio or workshop [C17: from Old French *astelier* workshop, from *astele* chip of wood, from Latin *astula* splinter, from *assis* board]

a tempo (ɑː 'tɛmpəʊ) *music* ▷ adj, adv **1** to the original tempo ▷ n **2** a passage thus marked. Also called: tempo primo [Italian: in (the original) time]

Aten or **Aton** ('ɑːtʰn) n (in ancient Egypt) the solar disc worshipped as the sole god in the reign of Akhenaten

Atget (French adʒɛ) n (**Jean**) **Eugène Auguste**. 1856–1927, French photographer, noted for his pictures of Parisian life

Athabaska or **Athabasca** (ˌæθə'bæskə) n **1** Lake Athabaska a lake in W Canada, in NW Saskatchewan and NE Alberta. Area: about 7770 sq km (3000 sq miles) **2** a river in W Canada, rising in the Rocky Mountains and flowing northeast to Lake Athabaska. Length: 1230 km (765 miles)

athame ('ɑːθæmeɪ) n (in Wicca) a witch's ceremonial knife, usually with a black handle, used in rituals rather than for cutting or carving

Athanasian Creed (ˌæθə'neɪʃən) n *Christianity* a profession of faith widely used in the Western Church which, though formerly attributed to Athanasius, probably originated in Gaul between 381 and 428 AD

Athanasius (ˌæθə'neɪʃəs) n **Saint**. ?296–373 AD, patriarch of Alexandria who championed Christian orthodoxy against Arianism. Feast day: May 2 > Atha'nasian adj

Athapascan, Athapaskan (ˌæθə'pæskən) or **Athabascan, Athabaskan** (ˌæθə'bæskən) n a group of North American Indian languages belonging to the Na-Dene phylum, including Apache and Navaho [from Cree *athapaskaaw* scattered grass or reeds]

atheism ('eɪθɪˌɪzəm) n rejection of belief in God or gods [C16: from French *athéisme*, from Greek *atheos* godless, from A-¹ + *theos* god] > 'atheist n, adj > ˌathe'istic or ˌathe'istical adj

Athelstan ('æθəlstən) n ?895–939 AD, king of Wessex and Mercia (924–939 AD), who extended his kingdom to include most of England

athematic (ˌæθɪˈmætɪk) *adj* **1** *music* not based on themes **2** *linguistics* (of verbs) having a suffix attached immediately to the stem, without an intervening vowel

Athena (əˈθiːnə) *or* **Athene** (əˈθiːnɪ) *n Greek myth* a virgin goddess of wisdom, practical skills, and prudent warfare. She was born, fully armed, from the head of Zeus. Also called: Pallas Athena, Pallas. Roman counterpart: Minerva

athenaeum *or US* **atheneum** (ˌæθɪˈniːəm) *n* **1** an institution for the promotion of learning **2** a building containing a reading room or library, esp one used by such an institution [c18: from Late Latin, from Greek *Athēnaion* temple of Athene, frequented by poets and teachers]

Athenian (əˈθiːnɪən) *n* **1** a native or inhabitant of Athens ▷ *adj* **2** of or relating to Athens

Athens (ˈæθɪnz) *n* the capital of Greece, in the southeast near the Saronic Gulf: became capital after independence in 1834; ancient city-state, most powerful in the 5th century BC; contains the hill citadel of the Acropolis. Pop: 3 238 000 (2005 est)

atheroma (ˌæθəˈrəʊmə) *n*, *pl* *-mas or -mata* (-mətə) *pathol* a fatty deposit on or within the inner lining of an artery, often causing an obstruction to the blood flow [c18: via Latin from Greek *athērōma* tumour full of matter resembling gruel, from *athēra* gruel] > atheromatous (ˌæθəˈrɒmətəs, -ˈrəʊ-) *adj*

atherosclerosis (ˌæθərəʊsklɪəˈrəʊsɪs) *n*, *pl* *-ses* (-siːz) a degenerative disease of the arteries characterized by patchy thickening of the inner lining of the arterial walls, caused by deposits of fatty material; a form of arteriosclerosis [c20: from New Latin, from Greek *athēra* gruel (see ATHEROMA) + SCLEROSIS] > atherosclerotic (ˌæθərəʊsklɪəˈrɒtɪk) *adj*

Atherton (ˈæθət³n) *n* **Mike,** full name *Michael Andrew Atherton.* born 1968, English cricketer: played for Lancashire (1987–2001) and England (1989–2001); captain of England (1993–1998)

athirst (əˈθɜːst) *adj* (*postpositive*) **1** (often foll by *for*) having an eager desire; longing **2** *archaic* thirsty

athlete (ˈæθliːt) *n* **1** a person trained to compete in sports or exercises involving physical strength, speed, or endurance **2** a person who has a natural aptitude for physical activities **3** *chiefly Brit* a competitor in track and field events [c18: from Latin via Greek *athlētēs*, from *athlein* to compete for a prize, from *athlos* a contest]

athlete's foot *n* a fungal infection of the skin of the foot, esp between the toes and on the soles

athletic (æθˈlɛtɪk) *adj* **1** physically fit or strong; muscular or active **2** of, relating to, or suitable for an athlete or for athletics **3** of or relating to a person with a muscular and well-proportioned body > ath'letically *adv* > ath'leticism *n*

athletics (æθˈlɛtɪks) *n* (*functioning as plural or singular*) **1 a** track and field events **b** (*as modifier*): *an athletics meeting* **2** sports or exercises engaged in by athletes

athletic support *n* a more formal term for **jockstrap**

at-home *n* **1** another name for **open day 2** a social gathering in a person's home

Athos (ˈæθɒs, ˈeɪ-) *n* **Mount Athos** a mountainous peninsula in NE Greece: location of the Monastic Republic of Mount Athos, an autonomous administrative division of Greece since 1927; inhabited by Eastern Orthodox monks in about 20 monasteries, some founded in the 10th century; prohibited to women and children. Pop: 1942 (2001)

athwart (əˈθwɔːt) *adv* **1** transversely; from one side to another ▷ *prep* **2** across the path or line of (esp a ship) **3** in opposition to; against [c15: from A-² + THWART]

-atic *suffix forming adjectives* of the nature of the thing specified: *problematic* [from French *-atique*, from Greek *-atikos*]

atigi (ˈætəɡɪ, əˈtiːɡɪ) *n* a type of parka worn by the Inuit in Canada

-ation *suffix forming nouns* indicating an action, process, state, condition, or result: *arbitration; cogitation; hibernation; moderation* [from Latin *-ātiōn-*, suffix of abstract nouns, from *-ātus* -ATE¹ + *-iōn* -ION]

-ative *suffix forming adjectives* of, relating to, or tending to: *authoritative; decorative; informative* [from Latin *-ātīvus*, from *ātus* -ATE¹ + *īvus* -IVE]

ATK *abbreviation* **1** antitank **2** email, *text messaging* at the keyboard

Atkins (ˈætkɪnz) *n* **Robert C.** 1930–2003, US physician, cardiologist, and nutritionist. An advocate of complementary medicine, he devised a widely-used diet (the Atkins diet) based on controlled intake of carbohydrates for weight management and disease prevention

Atkinson (ˈætkɪns³n) *n* Sir **Harry Albert.** 1831–92, New Zealand statesman, born in England: prime minister of New Zealand (1876–77; 1883–84; 1887–91)

Atlanta (ætˈlæntə) *n* a city in N Georgia: the state capital. Pop: 423 019 (2003 est)

Atlantean (ˌætlænˈtiːən, ætˈlæntɪən) *adj literary* of, relating to, or like Atlas; extremely strong

Atlantic (ətˈlæntɪk) *n* **1 the Atlantic** short for **Atlantic Ocean** ▷ *adj* **2** of or relating to or bordering the Atlantic Ocean **3** of or relating to Atlas or the Atlas Mountains [c15: from Latin *Atlanticus*, from Greek (*pelagos*) *Atlantikos* (the sea) of Atlas (so called because it lay beyond the Atlas Mountains)]

Atlantic City *n* a resort in SE New Jersey on Absecon Beach, an island on the Atlantic coast. Pop: 40 385 (2003 est)

Atlantic Intracoastal Waterway *n* a system of inland and coastal waterways along the Atlantic coast of the US from Cape Cod to Florida Bay. Length: 2495 km (1550 miles)

Atlanticism (ətˈlæntɪˌsɪzəm) *n* advocacy of close cooperation in military, political, and economic matters between Western Europe, esp the UK, and the US > At'lanticist *n*

Atlantic Ocean *n* the world's second largest ocean, bounded in the north by the Arctic, in the south by the Antarctic, in the west by North and South America, and in the east by Europe and Africa. Greatest depth: 9220 m (30 246 ft). Area: about 81 585 000 sq km (31 500 000 sq miles)

Atlantic Provinces *pl n* **the Atlantic Provinces** certain of the Canadian provinces with coasts facing the Gulf of St Lawrence or the Atlantic: New Brunswick, Nova Scotia, Prince Edward Island, and Newfoundland and Labrador

Atlantis (ətˈlæntɪs) *n* (in ancient legend) a continent said to have sunk beneath the Atlantic Ocean west of the Straits of Gibraltar

atlas (ˈætləs) *n* **1** a collection of maps, usually in book form **2** a book of charts, graphs, etc, illustrating aspects of a subject: *an anatomical atlas* **3** *anatomy* the first cervical vertebra, attached to and supporting the skull in man **4** *pl* **atlantes** *architect* another name for **telamon** [c16: via Latin from Greek; first applied to maps, from depictions of Atlas supporting the heavens in 16th-century collections of maps]

Atlas (ˈætləs) *n* **1** *Greek myth* a Titan compelled to support the sky on his shoulders as punishment for rebelling against Zeus **2** a US intercontinental ballistic missile, also used in launching spacecraft

Atlas Mountains *pl n* a mountain system of N Africa, between the Mediterranean and the Sahara. Highest peak: Mount Toubkal, 4165 m (13 664 ft)

Atli (ˈɑːtlɪ) *n* *Norse myth* a king of the Huns who married Gudrun for her inheritance and was slain by her after he killed her brothers

ATM *abbreviation* **1** automated teller machine **2** *text messaging* at the moment

atm. *abbreviation* atmosphere (unit of pressure)

atman (ˈɑːtmən) *n* *Hinduism* **1** the personal soul or self; the thinking principle as manifested in consciousness **2** Brahman considered as the Universal Soul, the great Self or Person that dwells in the entire created order [from Sanskrit *ātman* breath; compare Old High German *ātum* breath]

atmolysis (ætˈmɒlɪsɪs) *n*, *pl* *-ses* (-ˌsiːz) a method of separating gases that depends on their differential rates of diffusion through a porous substance

atmosphere ('ætməs,fɪə) n 1 the gaseous envelope surrounding the earth or any other celestial body 2 the air or climate in a particular place: *the atmosphere was thick with smoke* 3 a general pervasive feeling or mood 4 the prevailing tone or mood of a novel, symphony, painting, or other work of art 5 any local gaseous environment or medium: *an inert atmosphere* 6 a unit of pressure; the pressure that will support a column of mercury 760 mm high at 0°C at sea level. 1 atmosphere is equivalent to 101 325 newtons per square metre or 14.72 pounds per square inch. Abbreviations: at, atm > ,atmos'pheric *or* ,atmos'pherical *adj* > ,atmos'pherically *adv*

atmospheric pressure n the pressure exerted by the atmosphere at the earth's surface. It has an average value of 1 atmosphere

atmospherics (,ætməs'fɛrɪks) pl n radio interference, heard as crackling or hissing in receivers, caused by electrical disturbance

at. no. *abbreviation* atomic number

ATO *abbreviation* Australian Tax Office

atom ('ætəm) n 1 a the smallest quantity of an element that can take part in a chemical reaction b this entity as a source of nuclear energy: *the power of the atom* 2 any entity regarded as the indivisible building block of a theory 3 the hypothetical indivisible particle of matter postulated by certain ancient philosophers as the fundamental constituent of matter 4 a very small amount or quantity; minute fragment: *to smash something to atoms; there is not an atom of truth in his allegations* [c16: via Old French and Latin, from Greek *atomos* (n), from *atomos* (adj) that cannot be divided, from A-¹ + *temnein* to cut]

atomic (ə'tɒmɪk) adj 1 of, using, or characterized by atomic bombs or atomic energy: *atomic warfare* 2 of, related to, or comprising atoms: *atomic hydrogen* > a'tomically *adv*

atomic bomb *or* **atom bomb** n a type of bomb in which the energy is provided by nuclear fission. Uranium-235 and plutonium-239 are the isotopes most commonly used in atomic bombs. Also called: A-bomb, fission bomb ▷ See **fusion bomb**

atomic clock n an extremely accurate clock in which an electrical oscillator is controlled by the natural vibrations of an atomic or molecular system such as caesium or ammonia

atomic energy n another name for **nuclear energy**

atomicity (,ætə'mɪsɪtɪ) n 1 the state of being made up of atoms 2 the number of atoms in the molecules of an element 3 a less common name for **valency**

atomic mass unit n a unit of mass used to express atomic and molecular weights that is equal to one twelfth of the mass of an atom of carbon-12. It is equivalent to 1.66×10^{-27} kg. Abbreviation: amu

atomic number n the number of protons in the nucleus of an atom of an element

atomic pile n the original name for a **nuclear reactor**

atomic structure n the concept of an atom as a central positively charged nucleus consisting of protons and neutrons surrounded by a number of electrons. The number of electrons is equal to the number of protons: the whole entity is thus electrically neutral

atomic theory n 1 any theory in which matter is regarded as consisting of atoms, esp that proposed by John Dalton postulating that elements are composed of atoms that can combine in definite proportions to form compounds 2 the current concept of the atom as an entity with a definite structure. See **atomic structure**

atomic weight n the former name for **relative atomic mass**. Abbreviation: at wt

atomize *or* **atomise** ('ætə,maɪz) vb 1 to separate or be separated into free atoms 2 to reduce (a liquid or solid) to fine particles or spray or (of a liquid or solid) to be reduced in this way 3 (tr) to destroy by weapons, esp nuclear weapons

atomizer *or* **atomiser** ('ætə,maɪzə) n a device for reducing a liquid to a fine spray, such as the nozzle used to feed oil into a furnace or an enclosed bottle with a fine outlet used to spray perfumes or medicines

atom smasher n *physics* the nontechnical name for **accelerator** (sense 2)

atomy ('ætəmɪ) n, pl -mies *archaic* an atom or minute particle [c16: from Latin *atomī* atoms, but used as if singular; see ATOM]

Aton ('ɑːtᵊn) n a variant spelling of **Aten**

atonal (eɪ'təʊnᵊl, æ-) adj *music* having no established key

atonality (,eɪtəʊ'nælɪtɪ, ,æ-) n 1 absence of or disregard for an established musical key in a composition 2 the principles of composition embodying this and providing a radical alternative to the diatonic system

atone (ə'təʊn) vb (intr; foll by for) to make amends or reparation (for a crime, sin, etc) [c16: back formation from ATONEMENT] > a'toner n

atonement (ə'təʊnmənt) n 1 satisfaction, reparation, or expiation given for an injury or wrong 2 (often capital) *Christian theol* a the reconciliation of man with God through the life, sufferings, and sacrificial death of Christ b the sufferings and death of Christ [c16: from Middle English phrase *at onement* in harmony]

atonic (eɪ'tɒnɪk, æ-) adj 1 (of a syllable, word, etc) carrying no stress; unaccented 2 *pathol* lacking body or muscle tone ▷ n 3 an unaccented or unstressed syllable, word, etc, such as *for* in *food for thought* [c18: from Latin *atonicus*, from Greek *atonos* lacking tone; see ATONY]

atony ('ætənɪ) n 1 *pathol* lack of normal tone or tension, as in muscles; abnormal relaxation of a muscle 2 *phonetics* lack of stress or accent on a syllable or word [c17: from Latin *atonia*, from Greek: tonelessness, from *atonos* slack, from A-¹ + *tonos* TONE]

atop (ə'tɒp) adv 1 on top; at the top ▷ prep 2 on top of; at the top of

-ator *suffix forming nouns* a person or thing that performs a certain action: *agitator; escalator; radiator* [from Latin *-ātor;* see -ATE¹ -OR¹]

-atory *suffix forming adjectives* of, relating to, characterized by, or serving to: *circulatory; exploratory; migratory; explanatory* [from Latin *-ātōrius;* see -ATE¹, -ORY²]

ATP n adenosine triphosphate; a nucleotide found in the mitochondria of all plant and animal cells. It is the major source of energy for cellular reactions, this energy being released during its conversion to ADP. Formula: $C_{10}H_{16}N_5O_{13}P_3$

atrabilious (,ætrə'bɪljəs) *or* **atrabiliar** adj *rare* irritable [c17: from Latin *ātra bīlis* black bile, from *āter* black + *bīlis* BILE¹] > ,atra'biliousness n

atrazine ('ætrəziːn) n a white crystalline compound widely used as a weedkiller. Formula: $C_8H_{14}N_5Cl$ [c20: from A(MINO) TR(I)AZINE]

Atreus ('eɪtrɪˌuːs, 'eɪtrɪəs) n *Greek myth* a king of Mycenae, son of Pelops, father of Agamemnon and Menelaus, and member of the family known as the **Atreids** ('eɪtrɪɪdz)

atrium ('eɪtrɪəm, 'ɑː-) n, pl **atria** ('eɪtrɪə, 'ɑː-) 1 the open main court of a Roman house 2 a central often glass-roofed hall that extends through several storeys in a building, such as a shopping centre or hotel 3 a court in front of an early Christian or medieval church, esp one flanked by colonnades 4 *anatomy* a cavity or chamber in the body, esp the upper chamber of each half of the heart [c17: from Latin; related to *āter* black, perhaps originally referring to the part of the house that was blackened by smoke from the hearth] > 'atrial adj

atrocious (ə'trəʊʃəs) adj 1 extremely cruel or wicked; ruthless: *atrocious deeds* 2 horrifying or shocking 3 *informal* very bad; detestable: *atrocious writing* [c17: from Latin *ātrōx* dreadful, from *āter* black] > a'trociousness n

atrocity (ə'trɒsɪtɪ) n, pl -ties 1 behaviour or an action that is wicked or ruthless 2 the fact or quality of being atrocious 3 (usually plural) acts of extreme cruelty, esp against prisoners or civilians in wartime

atrophy ('ætrəfɪ) n, pl -phies 1 a wasting away of an organ or part, or a failure to grow to normal size as the result of disease, faulty nutrition, etc 2 any degeneration or diminution, esp through lack of use ▷ vb -phies, -phying, -phied 3 to waste away or cause to waste away [c17: from Late Latin *atrophia*, from Greek, from *atrophos* ill-fed, from A-¹ + -*trophos* from *trephein* to feed] > atrophic (ə'trɒfɪk) adj

atropine ('ætrə,piːn, -pɪn) *or* **atropin** ('ætrəpɪn) n a poisonous alkaloid obtained from deadly nightshade, having an inhibitory action on the autonomic nervous system. It is used medicinally in pre-anaesthetic medication, to speed a slow heart rate, and as an emergency first-aid counter to exposure to chemical warfare nerve agents. Formula: $C_{17}H_{23}NO_3$ [C19: from New Latin *atropa* deadly nightshade, from Greek *atropos* unchangeable, inflexible; see ATROPOS]

Atropos ('ætrə,pɒs) *n Greek myth* the one of the three Fates who severs the thread of life [Greek, from *atropos* that may not be turned, from A-¹ + -*tropos* from *trepein* to turn]

attach (ə'tætʃ) *vb (mainly tr)* 1 to join, fasten, or connect 2 *(reflexive or passive)* to become associated with or join, as in a business or other venture: *he attached himself to the expedition* 3 *(intr;* foll by *to)* to be inherent (in) or connected (with): *responsibility attaches to the job* 4 to attribute or ascribe 5 to include or append, esp as a condition: *a proviso is attached to the contract* 6 *(usually passive) military* to place on temporary duty with another unit 7 to appoint officially 8 *law* to arrest or take (a person, property, etc) with lawful authority [C14: from Old French *atachier* to fasten, changed from *estachier* to fasten with a stake, from *estache* STAKE¹] > at'tachable *adj* > at'tacher *n*

attaché (ə'tæʃeɪ; *French* ataʃe) *n* a specialist attached to a diplomatic mission: *military attaché* [C19: from French: someone attached (to a mission), from *attacher* to ATTACH]

attaché case *n* a small flat rectangular briefcase used for carrying documents, papers, etc

attached (ə'tætʃt) *adj* 1 *(foll by to)* fond (of); full of regard (for) 2 married, engaged, or associated in an exclusive sexual relationship

attachment (ə'tætʃmənt) *n* 1 a means of securing; a fastening 2 *(often foll by to)* affection or regard (for); devotion (to) 3 an object to be attached, esp a supplementary part: *an attachment for an electric drill* 4 the act of attaching or the state of being attached 5 a the lawful seizure of property and placing of it under control of a court b a writ authorizing such arrest or seizure

attack (ə'tæk) *vb* 1 to launch a physical assault (against) with or without weapons; begin hostilities (with) 2 *(intr)* to take the initiative in a game, sport, etc 3 *(tr)* to direct hostile words or writings at; criticize or abuse vehemently 4 *(tr)* to turn one's mind or energies vigorously to (a job, problem, etc) 5 *(tr)* to begin to injure or affect adversely; corrode, corrupt, or infect: *rust attacked the metal* ▷ *n* 6 the act or an instance of attacking 7 strong criticism or abuse 8 an offensive move in a game, sport, etc 9 commencement of a task, etc 10 any sudden and usually severe manifestation of a disease or disorder 11 the attack *ball games* the players in a team whose main role is to attack the opponents' goal or territory 12 *music* decisiveness in beginning a passage, movement, or piece 13 *music* the speed with which a note reaches its maximum volume [C16: from French *attaquer*, from Old Italian *attaccare* to attack, attach, from *estaccare* to attach, from *stacca* STAKE¹; compare ATTACH] > at'tacker *n* > at'tacking *adj*

attain (ə'teɪn) *vb* 1 *(tr)* to achieve or accomplish (a task, goal, aim, etc) 2 *(tr)* to reach or arrive at in space or time 3 *(intr;* often foll by *to)* to arrive (at) with effort or exertion [C14: from Old French *ateindre*, from Latin *attingere* to reach, from *tangere* to touch] > at'tainable *adj* > at,taina'bility *or* at'tainableness *n*

attainder (ə'teɪndə) *n* (formerly) the extinction of a person's civil rights resulting from a sentence of death or outlawry on conviction for treason or felony [C15: from Anglo-French *attaindre* to convict, from Old French *ateindre* to ATTAIN]

attainment (ə'teɪnmənt) *n* an achievement or the act of achieving; accomplishment

attainment target *n Brit éducation* a general defined level of ability that a pupil is expected to achieve in every subject at each key stage in the National Curriculum. Abbreviation: AT

attaint (ə'teɪnt) *vb (tr) archaic* 1 to pass judgment of

death or outlawry upon (a person); condemn by bill of attainder 2 (of sickness) to affect or strike (somebody) ▷ *n* 3 a less common word for **attainder** [C14: from Old French *ateint* convicted, from *ateindre* to ATTAIN]

attar ('ætə), **otto** ('ɒtəʊ) *or* **ottar** ('ɒtə) *n* an essential oil from flowers, esp the damask rose, used pure or as a base for perfume: *attar of roses* [C18: from Persian *'atir* perfumed, from *'itr* perfume, from Arabic]

attempt (ə'tɛmpt) *vb (tr)* 1 to make an effort (to do something) or to achieve (something); try 2 to try to surmount (an obstacle) 3 to try to climb ▷ *n* 4 an endeavour to achieve something; effort 5 a result of an attempt or endeavour 6 an attack, esp with the intention to kill [C14: from Old French *attempter*, from Latin *attemptāre* to strive after, from *tentāre* to try] > at'temptable *adj*

Attenborough ('ætənb,brə) *n* 1 Sir **David**. born 1926, British naturalist and broadcaster; noted esp for his TV series *Life on Earth* (1978), *The Living Planet* (1983), and *The Life of Birds* (1998) 2 his brother, **Richard**, Baron Attenborough. born 1923, British film actor, director, and producer; his films include *Gandhi* (1982), *Cry Freedom* (1987), and *Shadowlands* (1993)

attend (ə'tɛnd) *vb* 1 to be present at (an event, meeting, etc) 2 *(when intr,* foll by *to)* to give care; minister 3 *(when intr,* foll by *to)* to pay attention; listen 4 *(tr; often passive)* to accompany or follow: *a high temperature attended by a severe cough* 5 *(intr;* foll by *on or upon)* to follow as a consequence (of) 6 *(intr;* foll by *to)* to devote one's time; apply oneself: *to attend to the garden* 7 *(tr)* to escort or accompany 8 *(intr;* foll by *on or upon)* to wait (on); serve; provide for the needs (of): *to attend on a guest* [C13: from Old French *atendre*, from Latin *attendere* to stretch towards, from *tendere* to extend]

attendance (ə'tɛndəns) *n* 1 the act or state of attending 2 the number of persons present

attendant (ə'tɛndənt) *n* 1 a person who accompanies or waits upon another 2 a person employed to assist, guide, or provide a service for others, esp for the general public 3 a person who is present ▷ *adj* 4 being in attendance 5 associated; accompanying; related: *attendant problems*

attendee (ə,tɛn'di:) *n* a person who is present at a specified event

attention (ə'tɛnʃən) *n* 1 concentrated direction of the mind, esp to a problem or task 2 consideration, notice, or observation 3 detailed care or special treatment: *to pay attention to one's appearance* 4 *(usually plural)* an act of consideration, courtesy, or gallantry indicating affection or love: *attentions given to a lover* 5 the motionless position of formal military alertness, esp in drill when an upright position is assumed with legs and heels together, arms to the sides, head and eyes facing to the front ▷ *sentence substitute* 6 the order to be alert or to adopt a position of formal military alertness [C14: from Latin *attentiō*, from *attendere* to apply the mind to; see ATTEND]

attention deficit disorder *n* a disorder, particularly of children, characterized by excessive activity and inability to concentrate on one task for any length of time. Abbreviation: ADD

attention deficit hyperactivity disorder *n* a form of attention deficit disorder in which hyperactivity is a prominent symptom. Abbreviation: ADHD

attentive (ə'tɛntɪv) *adj* 1 paying attention; listening carefully; observant 2 *(postpositive; often foll by to)* careful to fulfil the needs or wants (of); considerate (about) > at'tentively *adv* > at'tentiveness *n*

attenuate *vb* (ə'tɛnjʊ,eɪt) 1 to weaken or become weak; reduce in size, strength, density, or value 2 to make or become thin or fine; extend ▷ *adj* (ə'tɛnjʊɪt, -,eɪt) 3 diluted, weakened, slender, or reduced 4 *botany* tapering gradually to a point [C16: from Latin *attenuāre* to weaken, from *tenuis* thin] > at,tenu'ation *n*

attercop ('ætəkɒp) *n archaic or dialect* 1 a spider 2 an ill-natured person [Old English *attorcoppa*, from *ātor* poison and possibly *cop* head]

attest (ə'tɛst) *vb* 1 *(tr)* to affirm the correctness or truth of 2 *(when intr,* usually foll by *to)* to witness (an act, event, etc) or bear witness to (an act, event, etc) as by signature or oath **3** (tr) to make evident; demonstrate **4** (tr) to provide evidence for [c16: from Latin *attestārī* to prove, from *testārī* to bear witness, from *testis* a witness] > at'testable adj > at'testant, at'tester or *esp in legal usage* at'testor, at'testator n > attestation (ˌætɛˈsteɪʃən) n

attested (əˈtɛstɪd) adj Brit (of cattle, etc) certified to be free from a disease, esp from tuberculosis

attic ('ætɪk) n **1** a space or room within the roof of a house **2** architect a storey or low wall above the cornice of a classical façade [c18: special use of ATTIC from the use of Attic-style pilasters to adorn the façade of the top storey]

Attic ('ætɪk) adj **1** of or relating to Attica, its inhabitants, or the dialect of Greek spoken there, esp in classical times **2** (often not capital) classically elegant, simple, or pure ▷ n **3** the dialect of Ancient Greek spoken and written in Athens: the chief literary dialect of classical Greek

Attica ('ætɪkə) n a region and department of E central Greece: in ancient times the territory of Athens. Capital: Athens. Pop: 3 336 700 (2001). Area: 14 157 sq km (5466 sq miles)

Atticism ('ætɪˌsɪzəm) n **1** the idiom or character of the Attic dialect of Ancient Greek, esp in the Hellenistic period **2** an elegant, simple, and clear expression

Attic salt or **Attic wit** n refined incisive wit

Attila (əˈtɪlə) n ?406–453 AD, king of the Huns, who devastated much of the Roman Empire, invaded Gaul in 451 AD, but was defeated by the Romans and Visigoths at Châlons-sur-Marne

attire (əˈtaɪə) vb **1** (tr) to dress, esp in fine elegant clothes; array ▷ n **2** clothes or garments, esp if fine or decorative [c13: from Old French *atirier* to put in order, from *tire* row; see TIER¹]

attitude ('ætɪˌtjuːd) n **1** the way a person views something or tends to behave towards it, often in an evaluative way **2** a theatrical pose created for effect (esp in the phrase **strike an attitude**) **3** a position of the body indicating mood or emotion **4** informal a hostile manner: *don't give me attitude, my girl* **5** the orientation of an aircraft's axes in relation to some plane, esp the horizontal **6** the orientation of a spacecraft in relation to its direction of motion [c17: from French, from Italian *attitudine* disposition, from Late Latin *aptitūdō* fitness, from Latin *aptus* APT] > ˌatti'tudinal adj

attitudinize or **attitudinise** (ˌætɪˈtjuːdɪˌnaɪz) vb (intr) to adopt a pose or opinion for effect; strike an attitude

Attlee ('ætlɪ) n **Clement Richard**, 1st Earl Attlee. 1883–1967, British statesman; prime minister (1945–51); leader of the Labour party (1935–55). His government instituted the welfare state, with extensive nationalization

attn abbreviation attention

atto- prefix denoting 10⁻¹⁸: *attotesla*. Symbol: a² [from Norwegian, Danish *atten* eighteen]

attolaser ('ætəʊˌleɪzə) n a high-power laser capable of producing pulses with a duration measured in attoseconds

attorn (əˈtɜːn) vb (intr) **1** law to acknowledge a new owner of land as one's landlord **2** feudal history to transfer allegiance or do homage to a new lord [c15: from Old French *atourner* to direct to, from *tourner* to TURN] > at'tornment n

attorney (əˈtɜːnɪ) n **1** a person legally appointed and empowered to act for another **2** US a lawyer qualified to represent clients in legal proceedings [c14: from Old French *atourné*, from *atourner* to direct to; see ATTORN] > at'torney,ship n

attorney-at-law n, pl attorneys-at-law law now chiefly US a lawyer qualified to represent in court a party to a legal action

attorney general n, pl attorneys general or attorney generals a country's chief law officer and senior legal adviser to its government

attract (əˈtrækt) vb (mainly tr) **1** to draw (notice, a crowd of observers, etc) to oneself by conspicuous behaviour or appearance (esp in the phrase **attract attention**) **2** (also intr) to exert a force on (a body) that tends to cause an approach or oppose a separation: *the gravitational pull of the earth attracts objects to it* **3** to possess some property that pulls or draws (something) towards itself **4** (also intr) to exert a pleasing, alluring, or fascinating influence (upon); be attractive (to) [c15: from Latin *attrahere* to draw towards, from *trahere* to pull] > at'tractable adj > at'tractor or at'tracter n

attraction (əˈtrækʃən) n **1** the act, power, or quality of attracting **2** a person or thing that attracts or is intended to attract **3** a force by which one object attracts another, such as the gravitational or electrostatic force

attractive (əˈtræktɪv) adj **1** appealing to the senses or mind through beauty, form, character, etc **2** arousing interest: *an attractive opportunity* **3** possessing the ability to draw or pull: *an attractive force* > at'tractively adv

attrib. abbreviation **1** attribute **2** attributive

attribute vb (əˈtrɪbjuːt) **1** (tr; usually foll by to) to regard as belonging (to), produced (by), or resulting (from); ascribe (to): *to attribute a painting to Picasso* ▷ n ('ætrɪˌbjuːt) **2** a property, quality, or feature belonging to or representative of a person or thing **3** an object accepted as belonging to a particular office or position **4** grammar **a** an adjective or adjectival phrase **b** an attributive adjective **5** logic the property, quality, or feature that is affirmed or denied concerning the subject of a proposition [c15: from Latin *attribuere* to associate with, from *tribuere* to give] > at'tributable adj > attribution (ˌætrɪˈbjuːʃən) n

attributive (əˈtrɪbjʊtɪv) adj **1** relating to an attribute **2** grammar (of an adjective or adjectival phrase) modifying a noun and constituting part of the same noun phrase, in English normally preceding the noun, as *black* in *Fido is a black dog* (as opposed to *Fido is black*). See **predicative 3** philosophy relative to an understood domain, as *small* in *that elephant is small*

attrition (əˈtrɪʃən) n **1** the act of wearing away or the state of being worn away, as by friction **2** constant wearing down to weaken or destroy (often in the phrase **war of attrition**) **3** geography the grinding down of rock particles by friction during transportation by water, wind, or ice **4** theol sorrow for sin arising from fear of damnation, esp as contrasted with contrition, which arises purely from love of God [c14: from Late Latin *attrītiō* a rubbing against something, from Latin *atterere* to weaken, from *terere* to rub]

Attu ('ætuː) n the westernmost of the Aleutian Islands, off the coast of SW Alaska: largest of the Near Islands

attune (əˈtjuːn) vb (tr) to adjust or accustom (a person or thing); acclimatize

ATV abbreviation all-terrain vehicle: a vehicle with treads or wheels designed to travel on rough uneven ground

Atwood ('ætwʊd) n **Margaret (Eleanor)** born 1939, Canadian poet and novelist. Her novels include *Lady Oracle* (1976), *The Handmaid's Tale* (1986), *Alias Grace* (1996), the Booker Prize-winning *The Blind Assassin* (2000), and *Oryx and Crake* (2003)

at wt abbreviation atomic weight

atypical (eɪˈtɪpɪkəl) adj not typical; deviating from or not conforming to type > a'typically adv

Au the chemical symbol for gold [from New Latin *aurum*]

aubade (French obad) n a song or poem appropriate to or greeting the dawn [c19: from French, from Old Provençal *aubada* (unattested), from *auba* dawn, ultimately from Latin *albus* white]

Aube (French ob) n **1** a department of N central France, in Champagne-Ardenne region. Capital: Troyes. Pop: 293 925 (2003 est). Area: 6026 sq km (2350 sq miles) **2** a river in N central France, flowing northwest to the Seine. Length: about 225 km (140 miles)

Auber (French obɛr) n **Daniel François Esprit** (danjɛl frɑ̃swa ɛspri). 1782–1871, French composer, who was prominent in development of opéra comique. His works include 48 operas

aubergine ('əʊbəˌʒiːn) n **1** a tropical Old World solanaceous plant, *Solanum melongena*, widely cultivated for its egg-shaped typically dark purple fruit. US, Canadian, and Australian name: **eggplant 2** the fruit of this plant, which is cooked and eaten as a vegetable **3 a** a dark purple colour **b** (as adjective): *an aubergine dress*

[c18: from French, from Catalan *alberginia,* from Arabic *al-bādindjān,* ultimately from Sanskrit *vatin-ganah,* of obscure origin]

Aubrey ('ɔːbrɪ) *n* **John.** 1626–97, English antiquary and author, noted for his vivid biographies of his contemporaries, *Brief Lives* (edited 1898)

aubrietia, aubrieta *or* **aubretia** (ɔː'briːʃə) *n* any trailing purple-flowered plant of the genus *Aubrieta,* native to European mountains but widely planted in rock gardens: family *Brassicaceae* (crucifers) [c19: from New Latin, named after Claude *Aubriet,* 18th-century French painter of flowers and animals]

auburn ('ɔːbᵊn) *n* **a** a moderate reddish-brown colour **b** (*as adjective*): *auburn hair* [c15 (originally meaning: blond): from Old French *alborne* blond, from Medieval Latin *alburnus* whitish, from Latin *albus* white]

Aubusson (French obysɔ̃) *n* **1** a town in central France, in the Creuse department: a centre for flat-woven carpets and for tapestries since the 16th century. Pop: 4662 (1999) ▷ *adj* **2** denoting or relating to these carpets or tapestries

Auckland ('ɔːklənd) *n* the chief port of New Zealand, in the northern part of North Island: former capital of New Zealand (1840–65). Pop: 420 700 (2004 est)

Auckland Islands *pl n* a group of six uninhabited islands, south of New Zealand. Area: 611 sq km (234 sq miles)

au courant *French* (o kurã) *adj* up-to-date, esp in knowledge of current affairs [literally: in the current]

auction ('ɔːkʃən) *n* **1** a public sale of goods or property, esp one in which prospective purchasers bid against each other until the highest price is reached **2** the competitive calls made in bridge and other games before play begins, undertaking to win a given number of tricks if a certain suit is trumps ▷ *vb* **3** (*tr;* often foll by *off*) to sell by auction [c16: from Latin *auctiō* an increasing, from *augēre* to increase]

auction bridge *n* a variety of bridge, now generally superseded by contract bridge, in which all the tricks made score towards game

auctioneer (,ɔːkʃə'nɪə) *n* **1** a person who conducts an auction by announcing the lots and controlling the bidding ▷ *vb* **2** (*tr*) to sell by auction

auctorial (ɔːk'tɔːrɪəl) *adj* of or relating to an author [c19: from Latin *auctor* AUTHOR]

audacious (ɔː'deɪʃəs) *adj* **1** recklessly bold or daring; fearless **2** impudent or presumptuous [c16: from Latin *audāx* bold, from *audēre* to dare] > au'daciousness *or* audacity (ɔː'dæsɪtɪ) *n*

Aude (French od) *n* a department of S France on the Gulf of Lions, in Languedoc-Roussillon region. Capital: Carcassonne. Pop: 321 734 (2003 est). Area: 6342 sq km (2473 sq miles)

Auden ('ɔːdᵊn) *n* **W(ystan) H(ugh).** 1907–73, US poet, dramatist, critic, and librettist, born in Britain; noted for his lyric and satirical poems and for plays written in collaboration with Christopher Isherwood

audible ('ɔːdɪbᵊl) *adj* perceptible to the hearing; loud enough to be heard [c16: from Late Latin *audibilis,* from Latin *audīre* to hear] > audi'bility *or* 'audibleness *n* > 'audibly *adv*

audience ('ɔːdɪəns) *n* **1** a group of spectators or listeners, esp at a public event such as a concert or play **2** the people reached by a book, film, or radio or television programme **3** the devotees or followers of a public entertainer, lecturer, etc; regular public **4** an opportunity to put one's point of view, such as a formal interview with a monarch or head of state [c14: from Old French, from Latin *audientia* a hearing, from *audīre* to hear]

audio ('ɔːdɪəʊ) *n* (*modifier*) **1** of or relating to sound or hearing: *audio frequency* **2** relating to or employed in the transmission, reception, or reproduction of sound [c20: independent use of AUDIO-]

audio- *combining form* indicating hearing or sound: *audiometer; audiovisual* [from Latin *audīre* to hear]

audio book *n* a reading of a book recorded on tape

audio frequency *n* a frequency in the range 20 hertz to 20 000 hertz. A sound wave of this frequency would be audible to the human ear

audiology (,ɔːdɪ'ɒlədʒɪ) *n* the scientific study of hearing, often including the treatment of persons with hearing defects > ,audi'ologist *n*

audiometer (,ɔːdɪ'ɒmɪtə) *n* an instrument for testing the intensity and frequency range of sound that is capable of detection by the human ear > ,audi'ometrist *n* > ,audi'ometry *n*

audiophile ('ɔːdɪəʊ,faɪl) *n* a person who has a great interest in high-fidelity sound reproduction

audiotypist ('ɔːdɪəʊ,taɪpɪst) *n* a typist trained to type from a dictating machine > 'audio,typing *n*

audiovisual (,ɔːdɪəʊ'vɪzjʊəl, -ʒʊəl) *adj* (esp of teaching aids) involving or directed at both hearing and sight > ,audio'visually *adv*

audit ('ɔːdɪt) *n* **1** a an inspection, correction, and verification of business accounts, conducted by an independent qualified accountant **b** (*as modifier*): *audit report* **2** US an audited account **3** any thoroughgoing check or examination ▷ *vb* **4** to inspect, correct, and certify (accounts, etc) [c15: from Latin *audītus* a hearing, from *audīre* to hear]

audition (ɔː'dɪʃən) *n* **1** a test at which a performer or musician is asked to demonstrate his ability for a particular role, etc **2** the act, sense, or power of hearing ▷ *vb* **3** to judge by means of or be tested in an audition [c16: from Latin *audītiō* a hearing, from *audīre* to hear]

auditor ('ɔːdɪtə) *n* **1** a person qualified to audit accounts **2** a person who hears or listens [c14: from Old French *auditeur,* from Latin *audītor* a hearer] > ,audi'torial *adj*

Auditor General *n* (in Canada) a federal official responsible for auditing government departments and making an annual report

auditorium (,ɔːdɪ'tɔːrɪəm) *n, pl* -toriums *or* -toria (-'tɔːrɪə) **1** the area of a concert hall, theatre, school, etc, in which the audience sits **2** US *& Canadian* a building for public gatherings or meetings [c17: from Latin: a judicial examination, from *audītōrius* concerning a hearing; see AUDITORY]

auditory ('ɔːdɪtərɪ, -trɪ) *or* **auditive** ('ɔːdɪtɪv) *adj* of or relating to hearing, the sense of hearing, or the organs of hearing [c14: from Latin *audītōrius* relating to hearing, from *audīre* to hear]

Audubon ('ɔːdə,bɒn) *n* **John James.** 1785–1851, US naturalist and artist, noted particularly for his paintings of birds in *Birds of America* (1827–38)

Auer (German 'aʊər) *n* **Karl** (karl), Baron von Welsbach. 1858–1929, Austrian chemist who discovered the cerium-iron alloy used for flints in cigarette lighters and invented the incandescent gas mantle

Auerbach ('aʊə,baːk) *n* **Frank (Helmuth).** born 1931, British painter, born in Germany, noted esp for his use of impasto

au fait *French* (o fɛ; English əʊ 'feɪ) *adj* fully informed; in touch or expert [c18: literally: to the point]

au fond *French* (o fɔ̃) *adv* fundamentally; essentially [literally: at the bottom]

aufWiedersehen *German* (auf 'viːdərzeːən) *sentence substitute* goodbye, until we see each other again

Aug *abbreviation* August

Augean (ɔː'dʒiːən) *adj* extremely dirty or corrupt [c16: after *Augeas;* see AUGEAN STABLES]

augend ('ɔːdʒɛnd, ɔː'dʒɛnd) *n* a number to which another number, the addend, is added [from Latin *augendum* that is to be increased, from *augēre* to increase]

auger ('ɔːgə) *n* **1** a hand tool with a bit shaped like a corkscrew, for boring holes in wood **2** a larger tool of the same kind for boring holes in the ground [c15: *an augur,* resulting from mistaken division of earlier *a nauger,* from Old English *nafugār* nave (of a wheel) spear (that is, tool for boring hubs of wheels), from *nafu* NAVE² + *gār* spear; see GORE²]

aught *or* **ought** (ɔːt) (*used with a negative or in conditional or interrogative sentences or clauses*) archaic or literary ▷ *pron* **1** anything at all; anything whatever (esp in the phrase **for aught I know**) ▷ *adv* **2** *dialect* in any least part; to any degree [Old English *āwiht,* from *ā* ever, AY¹ + *wiht* thing; see WIGHT¹]

augment (ɔːg'mɛnt) *vb* to make or become greater in number, amount, strength, etc; increase [c15: from Late

Latin *augmentāre* to increase, from *augmentum* growth, from Latin *augēre* to increase] ▷ aug'mentable *adj* ▷ aug'mentor *or* aug'menter *n*

augmentation (ˌɔːgmɛn'teɪʃən) *n* **1** the act of augmenting or the state of being augmented **2** the amount by which something is increased

augmentative (ɔːg'mɛntətɪv) *adj* **1** tending or able to augment **2** *grammar* denoting an affix that may be added to a word to convey the meaning *large* or *great*; for example, the suffix *-ote* in Spanish, where *hombre* means man and *hombrote* big man

augmented (ɔːg'mɛntɪd) *adj* **1** *music* (of an interval) increased or expanded from the state of being perfect or major by the raising of the higher note or the dropping of the lower note by one semitone: *C to G is a perfect fifth, but C to G sharp is an augmented fifth* **2** having been increased, esp in number: *an augmented orchestra*

augmented reality *n* an artificial environment created through the combination of real-world and computer-generated data [C20: based on VIRTUAL REALITY]

au gratin (French o gratẽ) *adj* covered and cooked with browned breadcrumbs and sometimes cheese [French, literally: with the grating]

Augsburg (German 'auksburk) *n* a city in S Germany, in Bavaria: founded by the Romans in 14 BC; site of the diet that produced the **Peace of Augsburg** (1555), which ended the struggles between Lutherans and Catholics in the Holy Roman Empire and established the principle that each ruler should determine the form of worship in his lands. Pop: 259 217 (2003 est)

augur ('ɔːgə) *n* **1** Also called: auspex (in ancient Rome) a religious official who observed and interpreted omens and signs to help guide the making of public decisions **2** any prophet or soothsayer ▷ *vb* **3** to predict (some future event), as from signs or omens **4** (*tr; may take a clause as object*) to be an omen (of); presage **5** (*intr*) to foreshadow future events to be as specified; bode: *this augurs well for us* [C14: from Latin: a diviner, perhaps from *augēre* to increase] ▷ augural ('ɔːgjʊrəl) *adj*

augury ('ɔːgjʊrɪ) *n, pl* -ries **1** the art of or a rite conducted by an augur **2** a sign or portent; omen

august (ɔː'gʌst) *adj* **1** dignified or imposing **2** of noble birth or high rank: *an august lineage* [C17: from Latin *augustus*; related to *augēre* to increase] ▷ au'gustness *n*

August ('ɔːgəst) *n* the eighth month of the year, consisting of 31 days [Old English, from Latin, named after Augustus (63 BC–14 AD), Roman emperor)

Augusta (ɔː'gʌstə) *n* **1** a city in the US, in Georgia. Pop: 193 316 (2003 est) (including Richmond) **2** a port in S Italy, in E Sicily. Pop: 33 820 (2001) **3** a town in the US, in Maine: the state capital; founded (1628) as a trading post; timber industry. Pop: 18 618 (2003 est)

Augustan (ɔː'gʌstən) *adj* **1** characteristic of, denoting, or relating to the Roman emperor Augustus Caesar (63 BC–14 AD), his period, or the poets, notably Virgil, Horace, and Ovid, writing during his reign **2** of, relating to, or characteristic of any literary period noted for refinement and classicism, esp the late 17th century in France (the period of the dramatists Corneille, Racine, and Molière) or the 18th century in England (the period of Swift, Pope, and Johnson, much influenced by Dryden) ▷ *n* **3** an author in an Augustan Age

Augustine (ɔː'gʌstɪn) *n* **1** Saint. 354–430 AD, one of the Fathers of the Christian Church; bishop of Hippo in North Africa (396–430), who profoundly influenced both Catholic and Protestant theology. His most famous works are *Confessions*, a spiritual autobiography, and *De Civitate Dei*, a vindication of the Christian Church. Feast day: Aug 28 **2** Saint. died 604 AD, Roman monk, sent to Britain (597 AD) to convert the Anglo-Saxons to Christianity and to establish the authority of the Roman See over the native Celtic Church; became the first archbishop of Canterbury (601–604). Feast day: May 26 or 27 **3** a member of an Augustinian order

Augustinian (ˌɔːgə'stɪnɪən) *adj* **1** of or relating to Saint Augustine of Hippo (354–430 AD), one of the Fathers of the Christian Church, or to his doctrines, or any of the Christian religious orders that were founded on his doctrines ▷ *n* **2** a member of any of several religious

orders, such as the **Augustinian Canons**, **Augustinian Hermits**, and **Austin Friars** which are governed by the rule of Saint Augustine **3** a person who follows the doctrines of Saint Augustine

Augustus (ɔː'gʌstəs) *n* original name *Gaius Octavianus*; after his adoption by Julius Caesar (44 BC) known as *Gaius Julius Caesar Octavianus*. 63 BC–14 AD, Roman statesman, a member of the second triumvirate (43 BC). After defeating Mark Antony at Actium (31 BC), he became first emperor of Rome, adopting the title Augustus (27 BC)

auk (ɔːk) *n* **1** any of various diving birds of the family *Alcidae* of northern oceans having a heavy body, short tail, narrow wings, and a black-and-white plumage: order *Charadriiformes*. See also **great auk, razorbill 2** little auk or dovekie a small short-billed auk, *Plautus alle*, abundant in Arctic regions [C17: from Old Norse *ālka*; related to Swedish *alka*, Danish *alke*]

au lait (əʊ 'leɪ; *French* o le) *adj* prepared or served with milk [French, literally: with milk]

auld (ɔːld) *adj* a Scot word for **old** [Old English *āld*]

auld lang syne (ˌɔːld læŋ 'səɪn, 'saɪn, 'zaɪn) *n* old times; times past, esp those remembered with affection or nostalgia [Scottish, literally: old long since]

Auld Reekie ('riːkɪ) *n* *Scot* a nickname for **Edinburgh**[1] [literally: Old Smoky]

Aulis ('ɔːlɪs) *n* an ancient town in E central Greece, in Boeotia: traditionally the harbour from which the Greeks sailed at the beginning of the Trojan war

aumbry ('ɔːmbrɪ) *n, pl* -bries a variant of **ambry**

au naturel *French* (o natyrɛl) *adj, adv* **1** naked; nude **2** uncooked or plainly cooked [literally: in (a) natural (condition)]

Aung San Suu Kyi ('aʊŋ 'sæn 'suː 'kiː) *n* born 1945, Burmese politician; cofounder (1988) and general secretary (1988–91; 1995–) of the National League for Democracy: Nobel peace prize 1991

aunt (ɑːnt) *n* (*often capital, esp as a term of address*) **1** a sister of one's father or mother **2** the wife of one's uncle **3** a term of address used by children for any woman, esp for a friend of the parents **4** my aunt! *or* my sainted aunt! an exclamation of surprise or amazement [C13: from Old French *ante*, from Latin *amita* a father's sister]

auntie *or* aunty ('ɑːntɪ) *n, pl* -ies a familiar or diminutive word for **aunt**

Auntie ('ɑːntɪ) *n* **1** *Brit* an informal name for the **BBC** **2** *Austral inf* the Australian Broadcasting Association

Aunt Sally ('sælɪ) *n, pl* -lies *Brit* **1** a figure of an old woman's head, typically with a clay pipe, used in fairgrounds and fêtes as a target for balls or other objects **2** any person who is a target for insults or criticism

Aunty ('ɑːntɪ) *n* *Austral* an informal name for the Australian Broadcasting Association

au pair (əʊ 'pɛə; *French* o pɛr) *n* **a** a young foreigner, usually a girl, who undertakes housework in exchange for board and lodging, esp in order to learn the language **b** (*as modifier*): *an au pair girl* [C20: from French: on an equal footing]

aura ('ɔːrə) *n, pl* auras *or* aurae ('ɔːriː) **1** a distinctive air or quality considered to be characteristic of a person or thing **2** any invisible emanation, such as a scent or odour **3** *pathol* strange sensations, such as noises in the ears or flashes of light, that immediately precede an attack, esp of epilepsy [C18: via Latin from Greek: breeze]

aural ('ɔːrəl) *adj* of or relating to the sense or organs of hearing; auricular [C19: from Latin *auris* ear] ▷ 'aurally *adv*

Aurangzeb *or* **Aurungzeb** ('ɔːrəŋˌzeb) *n* 1618–1707, Mogul emperor of Hindustan (1658–1707), whose reign marked both the height of Mogul prosperity and the decline of its power through the revolts of the Marathas

aureate ('ɔːrɪɪt, -ˌeɪt) *adj* **1** covered with gold; gilded **2** (of a style of writing or speaking) excessively elaborate or ornate; florid [C15: from Late Latin *aureātus* gilded, from Latin *aureus* golden, from *aurum* gold]

Aurelian (ɔː'riːlɪən) *n* Latin name *Lucius Domitius Aurelianus*. ?212–275 AD, Roman emperor (270–275), who conquered Palmyra (273) and restored political unity to the Roman Empire

Aurelius (ɔːˈriːlɪəs) *n* See **Marcus Aurelius Antoninus**

aureole (ˈɔːrɪˌəʊl) *or* **aureola** (ɔːˈriːələ) *n* 1 (esp in paintings of Christian saints and the deity) a border of light or radiance enveloping the head or sometimes the whole of a figure represented as holy 2 a less common word for **halo** 3 another name for **corona** (sense 2) [C13: from Old French *auréole*, from Medieval Latin (*corōna*) *aureola* golden (crown), from Latin *aureolus* golden, from *aurum* gold]

au revoir *French* (o rəvwar) *sentence substitute* goodbye [literally: to the seeing again]

auric (ˈɔːrɪk) *adj* of or containing gold in the trivalent state [C19: from Latin *aurum* gold]

Auric (*French* ɔrik) *n* **Georges** (ʒɔrʒ). 1899–1983, French composer; one of *les Six*. His works include ballet and film music

auricle (ˈɔːrɪkᵊl) *n* 1 the upper chamber of the heart; atrium 2 Also called: pinna *anatomy* the external part of the ear 3 Also called: auricula *biology* an ear-shaped part or appendage, such as that occurring at the join of the leaf blade and the leaf sheath in some grasses [C17: from Latin *auricula* the external ear, from *auris* ear]
> ˈauricled *adj*

auricula (ɔːˈrɪkjʊlə) *n*, *pl* -lae (-ˌliː) *or* -las 1 Also called: bear's-ear a widely cultivated alpine primrose, *Primula auricula*, with leaves shaped like a bear's ear 2 another word for **auricle** (sense 3) [C17: from New Latin, from Latin: external ear; see AURICLE]

auricular (ɔːˈrɪkjʊlə) *adj* 1 of, relating to, or received by the sense or organs of hearing; aural 2 shaped like an ear 3 of or relating to an auricle of the heart

auriferous (ɔːˈrɪfərəs) *adj* (of rock) containing gold; gold-bearing [C18: from Latin *aurifer* gold-bearing, from *aurum* gold + *ferre* to bear]

Aurignacian (ˌɔːrɪɡˈneɪʃən) *adj* of, relating to, or produced during a flint culture of the Upper Palaeolithic type characterized by the use of bone and antler tools, pins, awls, etc, and also by cave art and evidence of the beginnings of religion [C20: from French *Aurignacien*, after *Aurignac*, France, in the Pyrenees, near which is the cave where remains were discovered]

Auriol (*French* ɔrjɔl) *n* **Vincent** (vɛ̃sā). 1884–1966, French statesman; president of the Fourth Republic (1947–54)

auriscope (ˈɔːrɪˌskəʊp) *n* a medical instrument for examinig the external ear. Also called: otoscope
> auriscopic (ˌɔːrɪˈskɒpɪk) *adj*

aurochs (ˈɔːrɒks) *n*, *pl* -rochs a recently extinct member of the cattle tribe, *Bos primigenius*, that inhabited forests in N Africa, Europe, and SW Asia. It had long horns and is thought to be one of the ancestors of modern cattle. Also called: urus [C18: from German, from Old High German *ūrohso*, from *ūro* bison + *ohso* ox]

aurora (ɔːˈrɔːrə) *n*, *pl* -ras *or* -rae (-riː) 1 an atmospheric phenomenon consisting of bands, curtains, or streamers of light, usually green, red, or yellow, that move across the sky in polar regions. It is caused by collisions between air molecules and charged particles from the sun that are trapped in the earth's magnetic field 2 *poetic* the dawn [C14: from Latin: dawn; see EAST]
> auˈroral *adj*

Aurora[1] (ɔːˈrɔːrə) *n* 1 the Roman goddess of the dawn. Greek counterpart: Eos 2 the dawn or rise of something

Aurora[2] (ɔːˈrɔːrə) *n* another name for **Maewo**

aurora australis (ɒˈstreɪlɪs) *n* (sometimes capital) the aurora seen around the South Pole. Also called: southern lights [New Latin: southern aurora]

aurora borealis (ˌbɔːrɪˈeɪlɪs) *n* (sometimes capital) the aurora seen around the North Pole. Also called: northern lights [C17: New Latin: northern aurora]

aurous (ˈɔːrəs) *adj* of or containing gold, esp in the monovalent state [C19: apparently from French *aureux*, from Late Latin *aurōsus* gold-coloured, from Latin *aurum* gold]

Aus. *abbreviation* 1 Australia(n) 2 Austria(n)

Auschwitz (*German* ˈaʊʃvɪts) *n* an industrial town in S Poland; site of a Nazi concentration camp during World War II. Pop: 40 686 (2007 est). Polish name: Oświęcim

auscultation (ˌɔːskəlˈteɪʃən) *n* 1 the diagnostic technique in medicine of listening to the various internal sounds made by the body, usually with the aid of a stethoscope 2 the act of listening [C19: from Latin *auscultātiō* a listening, from *auscultāre* to listen attentively; related to Latin *auris* ear] > auscultatory (ɔːˈskʌltətərɪ) auscultative (ɔːˈskʌltətɪv, ˈɔːskəlˌteɪtɪv) *adj* > ˈausculˌtate *vb* > ˈausculˌtator *n*

Ausonius (ɔːˈsəʊnɪəs) *n* **Decimus Magnus** (ˈdɛsɪməs ˈmæɡnəs). ?310–?395 AD, Latin poet, born in Gaul

auspex (ˈɔːspɛks) *n*, *pl* auspices (ˈɔːspɪˌsiːz) *Roman history* another word for: **augur** (sense 1) [C16: from Latin: observer of birds, from *avis* bird + *specere* to look]

auspice (ˈɔːspɪs) *n*, *pl* -pices (-pɪsɪz) 1 (usually plural) patronage or guidance (esp in the phrase **under the auspices of**) 2 (often plural) a sign or omen, esp one that is favourable [C16: from Latin *auspicium* augury from birds; see AUSPEX]

auspicious (ɔːˈspɪʃəs) *adj* 1 favourable or propitious 2 *archaic* prosperous or fortunate > ausˈpiciously *adv* > ausˈpiciousness *n*

Aussie (ˈɒzɪ) *adj, n* an informal word for **Australian**

Aussie battler *n* *Austral informal* an Australian working-class person. Also called: little Aussie battler

Aust. *abbreviation* 1 Australia(n) 2 Austria(n)

Austen (ˈɒstɪn, ˈɔː-) *n* **Jane**. 1775–1817, English novelist, noted particularly for the insight and delicate irony of her portrayal of middle-class families. Her completed novels are *Sense and Sensibility* (1811), *Pride and Prejudice* (1813), *Mansfield Park* (1814), *Emma* (1816), *Northanger Abbey* (1818), and *Persuasion* (1818)

austere (ɒˈstɪə) *adj* 1 stern or severe in attitude or manner 2 grave, sober, or serious 3 self-disciplined, abstemious, or ascetic: *an austere life* 4 severely simple or plain: *an austere design* [C14: from Old French *austère*, from Latin *austērus* sour, from Greek *austēros* astringent; related to Greek *hauein* to dry] > ausˈterely *adv*

austerity (ɒˈstɛrɪtɪ) *n*, *pl* -ties 1 the state or quality of being austere 2 (often plural) an austere habit, practice, or act 3 a reduced availability of luxuries and consumer goods, esp when brought about by government policy b (as modifier): *an austerity budget*

Austerlitz (ˈɔːstəlɪts) *n* a town in the Czech Republic, in Moravia: site of Napoleon's victory over the Russian and Austrian armies in 1805. Pop: 1795 (2007 est). Czech name: Slavkov

Austin[1] (ˈɒstɪn) *n* a city in central Texas, on the Colorado River: state capital since 1845. Pop: 672 011 (2003 est)

Austin[2] (ˈɒstɪn, ˈɔː-) *n* 1 **Herbert**, 1st Baron. 1866–1941, British automobile engineer, who founded the Austin Motor Company 2 **John**. 1790–1859, British jurist, whose book *The Province of Jurisprudence Determined* (1832) greatly influenced legal theory and the English legal system 3 **J(ohn) L(angshaw)** (ˈlæŋʃɔː). 1911–60, English philosopher, whose lectures *Sense and Sensibilia* and *How to do Things with Words* were published posthumously in 1962

austral[1] (ˈɔːstrəl) *adj* of or coming from the south: *austral winds* [C14: from Latin *austrālis*, from *auster* the south wind]

austral[2] (aʊˈstraːl) *n*, *pl* -trales (-traːles) a former monetary unit of Argentina equal to 100 centavos, replaced by the peso [from Spanish; see AUSTRAL[1]]

Austral. *abbreviation* 1 Australasia 2 Australia(n)

Australasia (ˌɒstrəˈleɪzɪə) *n* 1 Australia, New Zealand, and neighbouring islands in the S Pacific Ocean 2 (loosely) the whole of Oceania > ˌAustraˈlasian *n, adj*

Australia (ɒˈstreɪlɪə) *n* a country and the smallest continent, situated between the Indian Ocean and the Pacific: a former British colony, now an independent member of the Commonwealth, constitutional links with Britain formally abolished in 1986; consists chiefly of a low plateau, mostly arid in the west, with the basin of the Murray River and the Great Dividing Range in the east and the Great Barrier Reef off the NE coast. Official language: English. Religion: Christian majority. Currency: dollar. Capital: Canberra. Pop: 19 913 000 (2004 est). Area: 7 682 300 sq km (2 966 150 sq miles) > Ausˈtralian *n, adj*

Australiana (ɒˌstreɪlɪˈɑːnə) *pl n* objects or documents relating to Australia and its history or culture esp in the form of a collection

Australian Alps *pl n* a mountain range in SE Australia, in E Victoria and SE New South Wales. Highest peak: Mount Kosciuszko, 2195 m (7316 ft)

Australian Antarctic Territory *n* the area of Antarctica, other than Adélie Land, that is claimed by Australia (claims are suspended under the Antarctic Treaty), lying south of latitude 60°S and between longitudes 45°E and 160°E

Australian Capital Territory *n* a territory of SE Australia, within New South Wales: consists of two exclaves, one containing Canberra, the capital of Australia, and one at Jervis Bay (the latter sometimes regarded as a separate entity). Pop: 322 579 (2003 est)

Australian cattle dog *n* a compact strongly-built dog of a breed with pricked ears and a smooth bluish-grey coat, often used for controlling and moving cattle

Australian Rules *n* (*functioning as singular*) a game resembling rugby football, played in Australia between teams of 18 men each on an oval pitch, with a ball resembling a large rugby ball. Players attempt to kick the ball between posts (without crossbars) at either end of the pitch, scoring six points for a goal (between the two main posts) and one point for a behind (between either of two outer posts and the main posts). They may punch or kick the ball and run with it provided that they bounce it every ten yards

Australian salute *n Austral informal* a movement of the hand and arm made to brush flies away from one's face

Australian silky terrier *n* a small compact variety of terrier with pricked ears and a long straight silky coat

Austral Islands ('ɔːstrəl) *pl n* another name for the **Tubuai Islands**

Australoid ('ɒstrə‚lɔɪd) *adj* 1 denoting, relating to, or belonging to a supposed racial group that includes the native Australians and certain other peoples of southern Asia and the Pacific islands. ▷ *n* 2 any member of this racial group

australopithecine (‚ɒstrələʊ'pɪθɪ‚siːn) *n* any of various extinct apelike primates of the genus *Australopithecus* and related genera, remains of which have been discovered in southern and E Africa. Some species are estimated to be over 4.5 million years old [C20: from New Latin *Australopithecus*, from Latin *austrālis* southern, AUSTRAL¹ + Greek *pithēkos* ape]

Australorp ('ɒstrə‚lɔːp) *n* a heavy black breed of domestic fowl [shortened from *Austral(ian Black) Orp(ington)*]

Austrasia (ɒ'streɪʒə, -ʃə) *n* the eastern region of the kingdom of the Merovingian Franks that had its capital at Metz and lasted from 511 AD until 814 AD. It covered the area now comprising NE France, Belgium, and western Germany

Austria ('ɒstrɪə) *n* a republic in central Europe: ruled by the Hapsburgs from 1282 to 1918; formed a dual monarchy with Hungary in 1867 and became a republic in 1919; a member of the European Union; contains part of the Alps, the Danube basin in the east, and extensive forests. Official language: German. Religion: Roman Catholic majority. Currency: euro. Capital: Vienna. Pop: 8 120 000 (2004 est). Area: 83 849 sq km (32 374 sq miles). German name: Österreich > 'Austrian *adj, n*

Austrian blind *n* a window blind consisting of rows of vertically gathered fabric that may be drawn up to form a series of ruches

Austro-¹ ('ɒstrəʊ-) *combining form* southern: *Austro-Asiatic* [from Latin *auster* the south wind]

Austro-² ('ɒstrəʊ-) *combining form* Austrian: *Austro-Hungarian*

Austronesia (‚ɒstrəʊ'niːʒə, -ʃə) *n* the islands of the central and S Pacific, including Indonesia, Melanesia, Micronesia, and Polynesia > Austronesian (‚ɒstrəʊ'niːʒən, -ʃən) *adj, n*

AUT *abbreviation* Association of University Teachers

autarchy ('ɔːtɑːkɪ) *n, pl* -chies unlimited rule; autocracy [C17: from Greek *autarkhia*, from *autarkhos* autocratic; see AUTO-, -ARCHY] > au'tarchic *or* au'tarchical *adj*

autarky ('ɔːtɑːkɪ) *n, pl* -kies (esp of a political unit) a system or policy of economic self-sufficiency aimed at

removing the need for imports [C17: from Greek *autarkeia*, from *autarkēs* self-sufficient, from AUTO- + *arkein* to suffice] > au'tarkic *adj* > 'autarkist *n*

auteur (ɔː'tɜː) *n* a director whose creative influence on a film is so great as to be considered its author [French: author] > au'teurism *n* > au'teurist *adj*

authentic (ɔː'θɛntɪk) *adj* 1 of undisputed origin or authorship; genuine 2 accurate in representation of the facts; trustworthy; reliable: *an authentic account* 3 (of a deed or other document) duly executed, any necessary legal formalities having been complied with 4 *music* a using period instruments and historically researched scores and playing techniques in an attempt to perform a piece as it would have been played at the time it was written b (*in combination*): *an authentic-instrument performance* 5 *music* (of a mode as used in Gregorian chant) commencing on the final and ending an octave higher See **plagal** [C14: from Late Latin *authenticus* coming from the author, from Greek *authentikos*, from *authentēs* one who acts independently, from AUTO- + *hentēs* a doer] > au'thentically *adv* > authenticity (‚ɔːθɛn'tɪsɪtɪ) *n*

authenticate (ɔː'θɛntɪ‚keɪt) *vb* (*tr*) 1 to establish as genuine or valid 2 to give authority or legal validity to > au‚thenti'cation *n* > au'thenti‚cator *n*

author ('ɔːθə) *n* 1 a person who composes a book, article, or other written work. Related adj: **auctorial** 2 a person who writes books as a profession; writer 3 an originator or creator: *the author of this plan* ▷ *vb* (*tr*) 4 to write or originate [C14: from Old French *autor*, from Latin *auctor* author, from *augēre* to increase] > auctorial (ɔː'θɔːrɪəl) *adj*

authoring ('ɔːθərɪŋ) *n computing* a the creation of documents, esp multimedia documents b (*as modifier*): *an authoring tool*

authoritarian (ɔː‚θɒrɪ'tɛərɪən) *adj* 1 favouring, denoting, or characterized by strict obedience to authority 2 favouring, denoting, or relating to government by a small elite with wide powers 3 despotic; dictatorial; domineering ▷ *n* 4 a person who favours or practises authoritarian policies

authoritative (ɔː'θɒrɪtətɪv) *adj* 1 recognized or accepted as being true or reliable 2 exercising or asserting authority; commanding: *an authoritative manner* 3 possessing or supported by authority; official > au'thoritatively *adv* > au'thoritativeness *n*

authority (ɔː'θɒrɪtɪ) *n, pl* -ties 1 the power or right to control, judge, or prohibit the actions of others 2 (*often plural*) a person or group of people having this power, such as a government, police force, etc 3 a position that commands such a power or right (often in the phrase **in authority**) 4 such a power or right delegated, esp from one person to another; authorization: *she has his authority* 5 the ability to influence or control others 6 an expert or an authoritative written work in a particular field 7 evidence or testimony 8 confidence resulting from great expertise 9 (*capital when part of a name*) a public board or corporation exercising governmental authority in administering some enterprise: *Independent Broadcasting Authority* [C14: from French *autorité*, from Latin *auctōritas*, from *auctor* AUTHOR]

authorize *or* **authorise** ('ɔːθə‚raɪz) *vb* (*tr*) 1 to confer authority upon (someone to do something); empower 2 to permit (someone to do or be something) with official sanction > ‚authori'zation *or* ‚authori'sation *n*

Authorized Version *n* the Authorized Version an English translation of the Bible published in 1611 under James I. Also called: **King James Version, King James Bible**

authorship ('ɔːθə‚ʃɪp) *n* 1 the origin or originator of a written work, plan, etc 2 the profession of writing books

autism ('ɔːtɪzəm) *n psychiatry* abnormal self-absorption, usually affecting children, characterized by lack of response to people and actions and inability to communicate [C20: from Greek *autos* self + -ISM] > au'tistic *adj, n*

autistic-spectrum disorder *n psychiatry* any disorder within the spectrum of autism, such as Asperger's syndrome, characterized by impairment in communication, social interaction, and flexibility of thinking and behaviour. Abbreviation: ASD

auto (ˈɔːtəʊ) *n*, *pl* -tos *US & Canadian informal* **a** short for **automobile** **b** (*as modifier*): *auto parts*

auto- *or sometimes before a vowel* **aut-** *combining form* **1** self; same; or of by the same one: *autobiography* **2** acting from or occurring within; self-caused: *autohypnosis* **3** self-propelling; automatic: *automobile* [from Greek *autos* self]

autobahn (ˈɔːtəˌbɑːn) *n* a motorway in German-speaking countries [from German, from *Auto* car + *Bahn* road]

autobiographical (ˌɔːtəˌbaɪəˈɡræfɪkᵊl) *adj* **1** of or concerned with a person's own life **2** of or relating to an autobiography > ˌauto.bio'graphically *adv*

autobiography (ˌɔːtəbaɪˈɒɡrəfɪ, ˌɔːtəbaɪ-) *n*, *pl* -phies an account of a person's life written or otherwise recorded by that person > ˌautobi'ographer *n*

autocephalous (ˌɔːtəʊˈsɛfələs) *adj* (of an Eastern Christian Church) governed by its own national synods and appointing its own patriarchs or prelates

autochthon (ɔːˈtɒkθən, -ɒn) *n*, *pl* -thons *or* -thones (-θəˌniːz) **1** (*often plural*) one of the earliest known inhabitants of any country; aboriginal **2** an animal or plant that is native to a particular region [c17: from Greek *autokhthōn* from the earth itself, from AUTO- + *khthōn* the earth] > **autochthonous** (ɔːˈtɒkθənəs), **autochthonic** (ˌɔːtɒkˈθɒnɪk, ˌɔːtɒkˈθɒnəl) *or* **autochthonal** *adj*

autoclave (ˈɔːtəˌkleɪv) *n* **1** a strong sealed vessel used for chemical reactions at high pressure **2** an apparatus for sterilizing objects (esp surgical instruments) or for cooking by means of steam under pressure [c19: from French AUTO- + *-clave*, from Latin *clāvis* key]

autocracy (ɔːˈtɒkrəsɪ) *n*, *pl* -cies **1** government by an individual with unrestricted authority **2** a country, society, etc, ruled by an autocrat

autocrat (ˈɔːtəˌkræt) *n* **1** a ruler who possesses absolute and unrestricted authority **2** a domineering or dictatorial person > ˌauto'cratic *adj* > ˌauto'cratically *adv*

autocross (ˈɔːtəʊˌkrɒs) *n* a form of motor sport in which cars race over a half-mile circuit of rough grass

Autocue (ˈɔːtəʊˌkjuː) *n* *trademark* an electronic television prompting device whereby a prepared script, unseen by the audience, is enlarged line by line for the speaker

auto-da-fé (ˌɔːtəʊdəˈfeɪ) *n*, *pl* autos-da-fé **1** *history* a ceremony of the Spanish Inquisition including the pronouncement and execution of sentences passed on sinners or heretics **2** the burning to death of people condemned as heretics by the Inquisition [c18: from Portuguese, literally: act of the faith]

autoeroticism (ˌɔːtəʊɪˈrɒtɪˌsɪzəm) *or* **autoerotism** (ˌɔːtəʊˈɛrəˌtɪzəm) *n* *psychol* the arousal and use of one's own body as a sexual object, as through masturbation > ˌautoe'rotic *adj*

autoexposure (ˌɔːtəɪkˈspəʊʒə) *n* another name for **automatic exposure**

autofocus (ˈɔːtəʊˌfəʊkəs) *n* another name for **automatic focus**

autogamy (ɔːˈtɒɡəmɪ) *n* self-fertilization in flowering plants

autogenic training (ˌɔːtəʊˈdʒɛnɪk) *n* a technique for reducing stress through mental exercises to produce physical relaxation. Also called: autogenics

autogenous (ɔːˈtɒdʒɪnəs) *adj* **1** originating within the body **2** self-generated; self-produced **3** denoting a weld in which the filler metal and the parent metal are of similar composition > au'togenously *adv*

autogiro *or* **autogyro** (ˌɔːtəʊˈdʒaɪrəʊ) *n*, *pl* -ros a self-propelled aircraft supported in flight mainly by unpowered rotating horizontal blades [c20: originally a trademark]

autograph (ˈɔːtəˌɡrɑːf, -ˌɡræf) *n* **1 a** a handwritten signature, esp that of a famous person **b** (*as modifier*): *an autograph album* **2** a person's handwriting **3 a** a book, document, etc, handwritten by its author; original manuscript; holograph **b** (*as modifier*): *an autograph letter* ▷ *vb* (*tr*) **4** to write one's signature on or in; sign **5** to write with one's own hand [c17: from Late Latin, from Greek *autographos*, from *autos* self + *graphein* to write]

> **autographic** (ˌɔːtəˈɡræfɪk) *or* ˌauto'graphical *adj* > ˌauto'graphically *adv*

autohypnosis (ˌɔːtəʊhɪpˈnəʊsɪs) *n* *psychol* the process or result of self-induced hypnosis

autoimmune (ˌɔːtəʊɪˈmjuːn) *adj* (of a disease) caused by the action of antibodies produced against substances normally present in the body > ˌautoim'munity *n*

autointoxication (ˌɔːtəʊɪnˌtɒksɪˈkeɪʃən) *n* self-poisoning caused by absorption of toxic products originating within the body

autologous (ɔːˈtɒləɡəs) *adj* (of a tissue graft, blood transfusion, etc) originating from the recipient rather than from a donor

Autolycus[1] (ɔːˈtɒlɪkəs) *n* a crater in the NW quadrant of the moon about 38 km in diameter and 3000 m deep

Autolycus[2] (ɔːˈtɒlɪkəs) *n* *Greek myth* a thief who stole cattle from his neighbour Sisyphus and prevented him from recognizing them by making them invisible

autolysis (ɔːˈtɒlɪsɪs) *n* the destruction of cells and tissues of an organism by enzymes produced by the cells themselves [c20: via German from Greek *autos* self + *lusis* loosening, release] > autolytic (ˌɔːtəʊˈlɪtɪk) *adj*

automat (ˈɔːtəˌmæt) *n* Also called: vending machine a machine that automatically dispenses goods, such as cigarettes, when money is inserted

automate (ˈɔːtəˌmeɪt) *vb* to make (a manufacturing process, factory, etc) automatic, or (of a manufacturing process, etc) to be made automatic

automated teller machine *n* a computerized cash dispenser. Abbreviation: ATM

automatic (ˌɔːtəˈmætɪk) *adj* **1** performed from force of habit or without conscious thought; lacking spontaneity; mechanical: *an automatic smile* **2 a** (of a device, mechanism, etc) able to activate, move, or regulate itself **b** (of an act or process) performed by such automatic equipment **3** (of the action of a muscle, gland, etc) involuntary or reflex **4** occurring as a necessary consequence: *promotion is automatic after a year* **5** (of a firearm) utilizing some of the force of or gas from each explosion to eject the empty shell case, replace it with a new one, and fire continuously until release of the trigger ▷ *n* **6** an automatic firearm **7** a motor vehicle having automatic transmission **8** a machine that operates automatically [c18: from Greek *automatos* acting independently] > ˌauto'matically *adv*

automatic door *n* a self-opening door

automatic exposure *n* the automatic adjustment of the lens aperture and shutter speed of a camera by a control mechanism. Also called: autoexposure

automatic focus *n* **a** a system in a camera which automatically adjusts the lens so that the object being photographed is in focus, often one using infrared light to estimate the distance of the object from the camera **b** (*as modifier*): *automatic-focus lens*. Also called: autofocus

automatic gain control *n* control of a radio receiver in which the gain varies inversely with the magnitude of the input, thus maintaining the output at an approximately constant level

automatic pilot *n* **1** Also called: autopilot a device that automatically maintains an aircraft on a preset course **2** on automatic pilot *informal* acting without conscious thought because of tiredness, shock, or familiarity with the task being performed

automatic transmission *n* a transmission system in a motor vehicle, usually incorporating a fluid clutch, in which the gears change automatically

automation (ˌɔːtəˈmeɪʃən) *n* **1** the use of methods for controlling industrial processes automatically, esp by electronically controlled systems, often reducing manpower **2** the extent to which a process is so controlled

automatism (ɔːˈtɒməˌtɪzəm) *n* **1** the state or quality of being automatic; mechanical or involuntary action **2** *psychol* the performance of actions, such as sleepwalking, without conscious knowledge or control > au'tomatist *n*

automatize *or* **automatise** (ɔːˈtɒməˌtaɪz) *vb* to make (a process, etc) automatic or (of a process, etc) to be made automatic > auˌtomati'zation *or* auˌtomati'sation *n*

automaton (ɔː'tɒmə,tɒn, -t°n) *n*, *pl* -tons *or* -ta (-tə) **1** a mechanical device operating under its own hidden power; robot **2** a person who acts mechanically or leads a routine monotonous life [c17: from Latin, from Greek, from *automatos* spontaneous, self-moving]

automobile ('ɔːtəmə,biːl) *n* another word (esp US) for **car** (sense 1) > **automobilist** (,ɔːtəmə'biːlɪst, -'məʊbɪlɪst) *n*

automobilia (,ɔːtəmə'biːlɪə) *pl n* items connected with cars and motoring of interest to the collector

automotive (,ɔːtə'məʊtɪv) *adj* **1** relating to motor vehicles **2** self-propelling

autonomic (,ɔːtə'nɒmɪk) *adj* **1** occurring involuntarily or spontaneously **2** of or relating to the autonomic nervous system **3** Also called: **autonomous** (of plant movements) occurring as a result of internal stimuli > ,auto'nomically *adv*

autonomic nervous system *n* the section of the nervous system of vertebrates that controls the involuntary actions of the smooth muscles, heart, and glands. It has two divisions: the sympathetic and the parasympathetic

autonomics (,ɔːtə'nɒmɪks) *n* (*functioning as singular*) *electronics* the study of self-regulating systems for process control

autonomous (ɔː'tɒnəməs) *adj* **1** (of a community, country, etc) possessing a large degree of self-government **2** of or relating to an autonomous community **3** independent of others **4** *biology* existing as an organism independent of other organisms or parts [c19: from Greek *autonomos* living under one's own laws, from AUTO- + *nomos* law] > au'tonomously *adv*

autonomy (ɔː'tɒnəmɪ) *n*, *pl* -mies **1** the right or state of self-government, esp when limited **2** a state, community, or individual possessing autonomy **3** freedom to determine one's own actions, behaviour, etc **4** *philosophy* the doctrine that the individual human will is or ought to be governed only by its own principles and laws [c17: from Greek *autonomia* freedom to live by one's own laws; see AUTONOMOUS]

autopilot (,ɔːtə'paɪlɒt, -təʊ-) *n* short for **automatic pilot**

autopsy ('ɔːtəpsɪ, ɔː'tɒp-) *n*, *pl* -sies **1** Also called: necropsy, postmortem examination dissection and examination of a dead body to determine the cause of death **2** an eyewitness observation **3** any critical analysis [c17: from New Latin *autopsia*, from Greek: seeing with one's own eyes, from AUTO- + *opsis* sight]

auto-repeat *n* **1** *computing* a feature of computer keys whereby a character is generated repeatedly as long as the user holds down the key in question ▷ *vb* (*intr*) **2** *computing* (of a computer key) to go on automatically regenerating a character

autoroute ('ɔːtəʊ,ruːt) *n* a French motorway [from French, from *auto* car + *route* road]

autostrada ('ɔːtəʊ,strɑːdə) *n* an Italian motorway [from Italian, from *auto* car + *strada* road]

autosuggestion (,ɔːtəʊsə'dʒestʃən) *n* a process of suggestion in which the person unconsciously supplies or consciously attempts to supply the means of influencing his own behaviour or beliefs

autotomy (ɔː'tɒtəmɪ) *n*, *pl* -mies the casting off by an animal of a part of its body, to facilitate escape when attacked > autotomic (,ɔːtə'tɒmɪk) *adj*

autotrophic (,ɔːtə'trɒfɪk) *adj* (of organisms such as green plants) capable of manufacturing complex organic nutritive compounds from simple inorganic sources such as carbon dioxide, water, and nitrates, using energy from the sun > autotroph ('ɔːtətrəʊf) *n*

autumn ('ɔːtəm) *n* **1** (*sometimes capital*) **a** the season of the year between summer and winter, astronomically from the September equinox to the December solstice in the N hemisphere and from the March equinox to the June solstice in the S hemisphere. Also called: (esp US): **fall** **b** (*as modifier*): *autumn leaves* **2** a period of late maturity, esp one followed by a decline [c14: from Latin *autumnus*, perhaps of Etruscan origin] > autumnal (ɔː'tʌmn°l) *adj* > au'tumnally *adv*

autumn crocus *n* a liliaceous plant, *Colchicum autumnale*, of Europe and N Africa having pink or purplish autumn flowers

Auvergne (əʊ'veən, əʊ'vɜːn; *French* overɲ) *n* a region of S central France: largely mountainous, rising over 1800 m (6000 ft)

auxanometer (,ɔːksə'nɒmɪtə) *n* an instrument that measures the linear growth of plant shoots [c19: from Greek *auxanein* to increase + -METER]

Aux Cayes (əʊ 'keɪ; *French* o kaj) *n* the former name of **Les Cayes**

Auxerre (*French* ozɛr) *n* a town in central France, capital of Yonne department; Gothic cathedral. Pop: 37 790 (1999)

auxiliaries (ɔːg'zɪljərɪz, -'zɪlə-) *pl n* foreign or allied troops serving another nation; mercenaries

auxiliary (ɔːg'zɪljərɪ, -'zɪlə-) *adj* **1** secondary or supplementary **2** supporting ▷ *n*, *pl* -ries **3** a person or thing that supports or supplements; subordinate or assistant **4** *nautical* **a** a sailing vessel with an engine **b** the engine of such a vessel [c17: from Latin *auxiliārius* bringing aid, from *auxilium* help, from *augēre* to increase, enlarge, strengthen]

auxiliary rotor *n* the tail rotor of a helicopter, used for directional and rotary control

auxiliary verb *n* a verb used to indicate the tense, voice, mood, etc, of another verb where this is not indicated by inflection, such as English *will* in *he will go*, *was* in *he was eating* and *he was eaten*, *do* in *I do like you*, etc

auxin ('ɔːksɪn) *n* any of various plant hormones, such as indoleacetic acid, that promote growth and control fruit and flower development. Synthetic auxins are widely used in agriculture and horticulture [c20: from Greek *auxein* to grow]

AV *abbreviation* Authorized Version (of the Bible).

av. *abbreviation* average

Av. *or* **av.** *abbreviation* avenue

a.v. *or* **A/V** *abbreviation* ad valorem

avadavat (,ævədə'væt) *or* **amadavat** (,æmədə'væt) *n* either of two Asian weaverbirds of the genus *Estrilda*, esp *E. amandava*, having a red plumage: often kept as cagebirds [c18: from *Ahmadabad*, Indian city from which these birds were brought to Europe]

avail (ə'veɪl) *vb* **1** to be of use, advantage, profit, or assistance (to) **2** avail oneself of to make use of to one's advantage ▷ *n* **3** use or advantage (esp in the phrases **of no avail, to little avail**) [c13 *availen*, from *vailen*, from Old French *valoir*, from Latin *valēre* to be strong, prevail]

available (ə'veɪləb°l) *adj* obtainable or accessible; capable of being made use of; at hand > a,vaila'bility *or* a'vailableness *n* > a'vailably *adv*

avalanche ('ævə,lɑːntʃ) *n* **1 a** a fall of large masses of snow and ice down a mountain **b** a fall of rocks, sand, etc **2** a sudden or overwhelming appearance of a large quantity of things ▷ *vb* **3** to come down overwhelmingly (upon) [c18: from French, by mistaken division from *la valanche*, from *valanche*, from (northwestern Alps) dialect *lavantse*; related to Old Provençal *lavanca*, of obscure origin]

Avalon ('ævə,lɒn) *n* *Celtic myth* an island paradise in the western seas: in Arthurian legend it is where King Arthur was taken after he was mortally wounded [from Medieval Latin *insula avallonis* island of Avalon, from Old Welsh *aballon* apple]

avant- *prefix* of or belonging to the avant-garde of a specified field

avant-garde (,ævɒŋ'gɑːd; *French* avɑ̃gard) *n* **1** those artists, writers, musicians, etc, whose techniques and ideas are markedly experimental or in advance of those generally accepted ▷ *adj* **2** of such artists, etc, their ideas, or techniques [from French: VANGUARD]

avarice ('ævərɪs) *n* extreme greed for riches; cupidity [c13: from Old French, from Latin *avaritia*, from *avārus* covetous, from *avēre* to crave] > ,ava'riciously *adj* > ,ava'riciousness *n*

avast (ə'vɑːst) *sentence substitute nautical* stop! cease! [c17: perhaps from Dutch *hou'vast* hold fast]

avatar ('ævə,tɑː) *n* **1** *Hinduism* the manifestation of a deity, notably Vishnu, in human, superhuman, or animal form **2** a visible manifestation or embodiment of an abstract concept; archetype [c18: from Sanskrit *avatāra* a going down, from *avatarati* he descends, from *ava* down + *tarati* he passes over]

avaunt (ə'vɔ:nt) *sentence substitute archaic* go away! depart! [c15: from Old French *avant!* forward!, from Late Latin *ab ante* forward, from Latin *ab* from + *ante* before]

avdp. *abbreviation* avoirdupois

ave ('ɑːvɪ, 'ɑːveɪ) *sentence substitute* welcome or farewell [Latin]

Ave¹ ('ɑːvɪ) *n RC Church* short for **Ave Maria**. See **Hail Mary** [c13: from Latin: hail!]

Ave² *or* **ave** *abbreviation* avenue

Avebury ('eɪvbərɪ) *n* a village in Wiltshire, site of an extensive Neolithic stone circle

Aveiro (*Portuguese* ə've:iru) *n* a port in N central Portugal, on the **Aveiro lagoon**: ancient Roman town; linked by canal with the Atlantic Ocean. Pop: 73 335 (2001)

Ave Maria (məˈriːə) *n* another name for **Hail Mary** [c14: from Medieval Latin: hail, Mary!]

avenge (ə'vendʒ) *vb* (*usually tr*) to inflict a punishment in retaliation for (harm, injury, etc) done to (a person or persons); take revenge for or on behalf of: *to avenge a crime; to avenge a murdered friend* [c14: from Old French *avengier*, from *vengier*, from Latin *vindicāre*; see VENGEANCE, VINDICATE] > a'venger *n*

● USAGE The use of *avenge* with a reflexive pronoun was
● formerly considered incorrect, but is now acceptable:
● *she avenged herself on the man who killed her daughter*

avens ('ævɪnz) *n, pl* -ens (*functioning as singular*) 1 any of several temperate or arctic rosaceous plants of the genus *Geum*, such as *G. rivale* (**water avens**), which has a purple calyx and orange-pink flowers 2 **mountain avens** either of two trailing evergreen white-flowered rosaceous shrubs of the genus *Dryas* that grow on mountains in N temperate regions and in the Arctic [c15: from Old French *avence*, from Medieval Latin *avencia* variety of clover]

Aventine ('ævɪn,taɪn, -tɪn) *n* one of the seven hills on which Rome was built

aventurine, aventurin (ə'vɛntjʊrɪn) *or* **avanturine** (ə'væntjʊrɪn) *n* 1 a dark-coloured glass, usually green or brown, spangled with fine particles of gold, copper, or some other metal 2 a variety of quartz containing red or greenish particles of iron oxide or mica: a gemstone [c19: from French, from Italian *avventurina*, from *avventura* chance; so named because usually found by accident; see ADVENTURE]

avenue ('ævɪ,njuː) *n* 1 a a broad street, often lined with trees b (*capital as part of a street name*) a road, esp in a built-up area 2 a main approach road, as to a country house 3 a way bordered by two rows of trees 4 a line of approach: *explore every avenue* [c17: from French, from *avenir* to come to, from Latin *advenīre*, from *venīre* to come]

aver (ə'vɜː) *vb* avers, averring, averred (*tr*) 1 to state positively; assert 2 *law* to allege as a fact or prove to be true [c14: from Old French *averer*, from Medieval Latin *advērāre*, from Latin *vērus* true] > a'verment *n*

average ('ævərɪdʒ, 'ævrɪdʒ) *n* 1 the typical or normal amount, quality, degree, etc: *above average in intelligence* 2 Also called: **arithmetic mean** the result obtained by adding the numbers or quantities in a set and dividing the total by the number of members in the set: *the average of 3, 4, and 8 is 5* 3 (of a continuously variable ratio, such as speed) the quotient of the differences between the initial and final values of the two quantities that make up the ratio 4 *maritime law* a a loss incurred or damage suffered by a ship or its cargo at sea b the equitable apportionment of such loss among the interested parties 5 **on average, on the average** *or* **on an average** usually; typically ▷ *adj* 6 usual or typical 7 mediocre or inferior: *his performance was only average* 8 constituting a numerical average: *the average age; an average speed* 9 approximately typical of a range of values: *the average contents of a matchbox* ▷ *vb* 10 (*tr*) to obtain or estimate a numerical average of 11 (*tr*) to assess the general quality of 12 (*tr*) to perform or receive a typical number of: *to average eight hours' work a day* 13 (*tr*) to divide up proportionately 14 (*tr*) to amount to or be on average: *the children averaged 15 years of age* [c15 *averay* loss arising from damage to ships or cargoes (shared equitably among all concerned, hence the modern sense), from

Old Italian *avaria*, ultimately from Arabic *awār* damage, blemish] > 'averagely *adv* > 'averageness *n*

Averno (*Italian* a'vɛrno) *n* a crater lake in Italy, near Naples: in ancient times regarded as an entrance to hell [from Latin, from Greek *aornos* without birds, from A-¹ + *ornis* bird; referring to the legend that the lake's sulphurous exhalations killed birds]

Averroës (ə'vɛrəʊ,iːz) *n* Arabic name *ibn-Rushd*. 1126–88, Arab philosopher and physician in Spain, noted particularly for his attempts to reconcile Aristotelian philosophy with Islamic religion, which profoundly influenced Christian scholasticism

averse (ə'vɜːs) *adj* (*postpositive*; usually foll by *to*) opposed, disinclined, or loath [c16: from Latin *āversus*, from *āvertere* to turn from, from *vertere* to turn] > a'versely *adv* > a'verseness *n*

aversion (ə'vɜːʃən) *n* 1 (usually foll by *to* or *for*) extreme dislike or disinclination; repugnance 2 a person or thing that arouses this: *he is my pet aversion*

aversion therapy *n psychiatry* a method of suppressing an undesirable habit, such as excessive smoking, by causing the subject to associate an unpleasant effect, such as an electric shock or nausea, with the habit

avert (ə'vɜːt) *vb* (*tr*) 1 to turn away or aside: *to avert one's gaze* 2 to ward off; prevent from occurring: *to avert danger* [c15: from Old French *avertir*, from Latin *āvertere*; see AVERSE] > a'vertible *or* a'vertable *adj*

Avesta (ə'vɛstə) *n* a collection of sacred writings of Zoroastrianism, including the Songs of Zoroaster

Avestan (ə'vɛstən) *n* 1 the oldest recorded language of the Iranian branch of the Indo-European family; the language of the Avesta. Formerly called: **Zend** ▷ *adj* 2 of or relating to the Avesta or its language

Aveyron (*French* avɛrɔ̃) *n* a department of S France in Midi-Pyrénées region. Capital: Rodez. Pop: 266 940 (2003 est). Area: 8771 sq km (3421 sq miles)

avian ('eɪvɪən) *adj* of, relating to, or resembling a bird [c19: from Latin *avis* bird]

avian flu ('eɪvɪən) *n* another name for **bird flu**

aviary ('eɪvɪərɪ) *n, pl* aviaries a large enclosure in which birds are kept [c16: from Latin *aviārium*, from *aviārius* concerning birds, from *avis* bird]

aviation (,eɪvɪ'eɪʃən) *n* a the art or science of flying aircraft b the design, production, and maintenance of aircraft [c19: from French, from Latin *avis* bird]

aviator ('eɪvɪ,eɪtə) *n old-fashioned* the pilot of an aeroplane or airship; flyer > 'avi,atrix *or* 'avi,atress *fem n*

Avicenna (,ævɪ'sɛnə) *n* Arabic name *ibn-Sina*. 980–1037, Arab philosopher and physician whose philosophical writings, which combined Aristotelianism with neo-Platonist ideas, greatly influenced scholasticism, and whose medical work *Qanun* was the greatest single influence on medieval medicine

avid ('ævɪd) *adj* 1 very keen; enthusiastic: *an avid reader* 2 (*postpositive*; often foll by *for* or *of*) eager (for); desirous (of); greedy (for): *avid for revenge* [c18: from Latin *avidus*, from *avēre* to long for] > 'avidly *adv* > avidity (ə'vɪdɪtɪ) *n*

Aviemore (,ævɪ'mɔː) *n* a winter sports resort in Scotland, in Moray between the Monadhliath and Cairngorm Mountains. Pop: 2397 (2001)

avifauna (,eɪvɪ'fɔːnə) *n* all the birds in a particular region > ,avi'faunal *adj*

Avignon (*French* aviɲɔ̃) *n* a city in SE France, on the Rhône: seat of the papacy (1309–77); famous 12th-century bridge, now partly destroyed. Pop: 85 935 (1999)

Ávila (*Spanish* 'aβila) *n* a city in central Spain: 11th-century granite walls and Romanesque cathedral. Pop: 52 078 (2003 est)

avionics (,eɪvɪ'ɒnɪks) *n* 1 (*functioning as singular*) the science and technology of electronics applied to aeronautics and astronautics 2 (*functioning as plural*) the electronic circuits and devices of an aerospace vehicle [c20: from *avi(ation electr)onics*]

avitaminosis (æ,vɪtəmɪn'əʊsɪs, ,eɪvɪ,tæmɪ'nəʊsɪs) *n, pl* -ses (-siːz) any disease caused by a vitamin deficiency in the diet

Avlona (æv'ləʊnə) *n* the ancient name for **Vlorë**

avocado (,ævə'kɑːdəʊ) *n, pl* -dos 1 a pear-shaped fruit having a leathery green or blackish skin, a large stony seed, and a greenish-yellow edible pulp **2** the tropical American lauraceous tree, *Persea americana,* that bears this fruit **3 a** a dull greenish colour resembling that of the fruit **b** (as modifier): *an avocado bathroom suite* Also called (for senses 1, 2): **avocado pear, alligator pear** [C17: from Spanish *aguacate,* from Nahuatl *ahuacatl* testicle, alluding to the shape of the fruit]

avocation (ˌævəˈkeɪʃən) *n* **1** *formal* a minor occupation undertaken as a diversion **2** *not standard* a person's regular job or vocation [C17: from Latin *āvocātiō* a calling away, diversion from, from *āvocāre* to distract, from *vocāre* to call]

avocet (ˈævəˌsɛt) *n* any of several long-legged shore birds of the genus *Recurvirostra,* such as the European R. *avosetta,* having black-and-white plumage and a long upward-curving bill: family *Recurvirostridae,* order *Charadriiformes* [C18: from French *avocette,* from Italian *avocetta,* of uncertain origin]

Avogadro (ˌævəˈɡɑːdrəʊ; *Italian* avoˈɡaːdro) *n* **Amedeo** (ameˈdɛːo), *Conte di Quaregna.* 1776–1856, Italian physicist, noted for his work on gases

Avogadro's constant *or* **Avogadro's number** *n* the number of atoms or molecules in a mole of a substance, equal to 6.022×10^{23} [named after Amedeo *Avogadro* (1776–1856), Italian physicist]

Avogadro's law *or* **Avogadro's hypothesis** *n* the principle that equal volumes of all gases contain the same number of molecules at the same temperature and pressure

avoid (əˈvɔɪd) *vb* (*tr*) **1** to keep out of the way of **2** to refrain from doing **3** to prevent from happening: *to avoid damage to machinery* **4** *law* to make (a plea, contract, etc) void; invalidate; quash [C14: from Anglo-French *avoider,* from Old French *esvuidier,* from *vuidier* to empty, VOID] > a'voidable *adj* > a'voidably *adv* > a'voider *n* > a'voidance *n*

avoirdupois *or* **avoirdupois weight** (ˌævədəˈpɔɪz, ˌævwɑːˈdjuːˈpwɑː) *n* a system of weights used in many English-speaking countries. It is based on the pound, which contains 16 ounces or 7000 grains. 100 pounds (US) or 112 pounds (Brit) is equal to 1 hundredweight and 20 hundredweights equals 1 ton [C14: from Old French *aver de peis* goods of weight]

Avon¹ (ˈeɪvᵊn) *n* **1 a** a former county of SW England, created in 1974 from areas of N Somerset and S Gloucestershire: replaced in 1996 by the unitary authorities of Bath and North East Somerset (Somerset), North Somerset (Somerset), South Gloucestershire (Gloucestershire), and Bristol **2** a river in central England, rising in Northamptonshire and flowing southwest through Stratford-on-Avon to the River Severn at Tewkesbury. Length: 154 km (96 miles) **3** a river in SW England, rising in Gloucestershire and flowing south and west through Bristol to the Severn estuary at **Avonmouth.** Length: 120 km (75 miles) **4** a river in S England, rising in Wiltshire and flowing south to the English Channel. Length: about 96 km (60 miles)

Avon² (ˈeɪvᵊn) *n* **Earl of** title of (Anthony) **Eden**

avouch (əˈvaʊtʃ) *vb* (*tr*) *archaic* **1** to vouch for; guarantee **2** to acknowledge **3** to assert [C16: from Old French *avochier* to summon, call on, from Latin *advocāre;* see ADVOCATE] > a'vouchment *n*

avow (əˈvaʊ) *vb* (*tr*) **1** to state or affirm **2** to admit openly [C13: from Old French *avouer* to confess, from Latin *advocāre* to appeal to, call upon; see AVOUCH, ADVOCATE] > a'vowal *n* > avowed (əˈvaʊd) *adj* > avowedly (əˈvaʊɪdlɪ) *adv* > a'vower *n*

avuncular (əˈvʌŋkjʊlə) *adj* **1** of or concerned with an uncle **2** resembling an uncle; friendly; helpful [C19: from Latin *avunculus* (maternal) uncle, diminutive of *avus* grandfather]

AWACS *or* **Awacs** (ˈeɪwæks) *n acronym for* airborne warning and control system

await (əˈweɪt) *vb* **1** (*tr*) to wait for; expect **2** (*tr*) to be in store for **3** (*intr*) to wait, esp with expectation

awake (əˈweɪk) *vb* **awakes, awaking, awoke** *or* **awaked, awoken** *or* **awaked 1** to emerge or rouse from sleep; wake **2** to become or cause to become alert **3** (usually foll by *to*) to become or make aware (of) **4** Also: **awaken** (*tr*) to arouse (feelings, etc) or cause to remember (memories, etc) ▷ *adj* (*postpositive*) **5** not sleeping **6** (sometimes foll by *to*) lively or alert [Old English *awacian, awacan;* see WAKE¹]

● USAGE See at **wake¹**

award (əˈwɔːd) *vb* (*tr*) **1** to give (something due), esp as a reward for merit: *to award prizes* **2** *law* to declare to be entitled, as by decision of a court of law or an arbitrator ▷ *n* **3** something awarded, such as a prize or medal **4** (in Australia and New Zealand) the amount of an award wage (esp in the phrase **above award**) **5** *law* **a** the decision of an arbitrator **b** a grant made by a court of law, esp of damages in a civil action [C14: from Anglo-Norman *awarder,* from Old Northern French *eswarder* to decide after investigation, from *es-* EX-¹ + *warder* to observe; see WARD] > a'warder *n*

award wage *n* (in Australia and New Zealand) statutory minimum pay for a particular group of workers. Sometimes shortened to **award**

aware (əˈwɛə) *adj* **1** (*postpositive;* foll by *of*) having knowledge; cognizant: *aware of his error* **2** informed of current developments: *politically aware* [Old English *gewær;* related to Old Saxon, Old High German *giwar* Latin *verērī* to be fearful; see BEWARE, WARY] > a'wareness *n*

awash (əˈwɒʃ) *adv, adj* (*postpositive*) *nautical* **1** at a level even with the surface of the sea **2** washed over by the waves

away (əˈweɪ) *adv* **1** from a particular place; off: *to swim away* **2** in or to another, usual, or proper place: *to put toys away* **3** apart; at a distance: *to keep away from strangers* **4** out of existence: *the music faded away* **5** indicating motion, displacement, transfer, etc, from a normal or proper place, from a person's own possession, etc: *to turn one's head away; to give away money* **6** indicating activity that is wasteful or designed to get rid of something: *to sleep away the hours* **7** continuously: *laughing away; fire away* **8** away with a command for a person to go or be removed: *away with you; away with him to prison!* ▷ *adj* (*usually postpositive*) **9** not present: *away from school* **10** distant: *he is a good way away* **11** having started; released: *he was away before sunrise; bombs away!* **12** (also *prenominal*) *sport* played on an opponent's ground ▷ *n* **13** *sport* a game played or won at an opponent's ground ▷ *interj* **14** an expression of dismissal [Old English *on weg* on way]

awayday (əˈweɪˌdeɪ) *n* a trip taken for pleasure, relaxation, etc; day excursion [C20: from *awayday ticket,* name applied to some special-rate railway day returns]

away goal *n* a goal scored by a team playing away from its home ground. Away goals count for more than home goals in certain competitions

awe (ɔː) *n* **1** overwhelming wonder, admiration, respect, or dread **2** *archaic* power to inspire fear or reverence ▷ *vb* **3** (*tr*) to inspire with reverence or dread [C13: from Old Norse *agi;* related to Gothic *agis* fear, Greek *akhesthai* to be grieved]

aweigh (əˈweɪ) *adj* (*postpositive*) *nautical* (of an anchor) no longer hooked into the bottom; hanging by its rode

awe-inspiring *adj* causing or worthy of admiration or respect; amazing or magnificent

awesome (ˈɔːsəm) *adj* **1** inspiring or displaying awe **2** *slang* excellent or outstanding > 'awesomely *adv* > 'awesomeness *n*

awful (ˈɔːfʊl) *adj* **1** very bad; unpleasant **2** *archaic* inspiring reverence or dread **3** *archaic* overcome with awe; reverential ▷ *adv* **4** *not standard* (intensifier): *an awful cold day* [C13: see AWE, -FUL] > 'awfulness *n*

awfully (ˈɔːfəlɪ, ˈɔːflɪ) *adv* **1** in an unpleasant, bad, or reprehensible manner **2** *informal* (intensifier): *I'm awfully keen to come* **3** *archaic* so as to express or inspire awe

awhile (əˈwaɪl) *adv* for a brief period

awkward (ˈɔːkwəd) *adj* **1** lacking dexterity, proficiency, or skill; clumsy; inept **2** ungainly or inelegant in movements or posture **3** unwieldy; difficult to use **4** embarrassing: *an awkward moment* **5** embarrassed: *he felt awkward about leaving* **6** difficult to deal with; requiring tact: *an awkward situation; an awkward customer* **7** deliberately uncooperative or unhelpful **8** dangerous or difficult [c14 *awk*, from Old Norse *öfugr* turned the wrong way round + -WARD] > 'awkwardly *adv* > 'awkwardness *n*

awl (ɔːl) *n* a pointed hand tool with a fluted blade used for piercing wood, leather, etc [Old English *æl*; related to Old Norse *alr*, Old High German *āla*, Dutch *aal*, Sanskrit *ārā*]

awn (ɔːn) *n* any of the bristles growing from the spikelets of certain grasses, including cereals [Old English *agen* ear of grain; related to Old Norse *ögn* chaff, Gothic *ahana*, Old High German *agana*, Greek *akōn* javelin] > awned *adj*

awning ('ɔːnɪŋ) *n* a roof of canvas or other material supported by a frame to provide protection from the weather, esp one placed over a doorway or part of a deck of a ship [c17: of uncertain origin]

awoke (ə'wəʊk) *vb* a past tense or (now rare or dialectal) past participle of **awake**

AWOL ('eɪwɒl) or **A.W.O.L.** *adj military* absent without leave; absent from one's post or duty without official permission but without intending to desert

awry (ə'raɪ) *adv, adj* (*postpositive*) **1** with a slant or twist to one side; askew **2** away from the appropriate or right course; amiss [c14 *on wry*; see A-², WRY]

AWS *abbreviation* automatic warning system: a train safety system which gives audible warnings about the signals being passed, and can apply the brakes automatically if necessary

aw-shucks (ˌɔː'ʃʌks) *adj* (*prenominal*) seeming to be modest, self-deprecating, or shy: *don't be fooled by his aw-shucks attitude* [c20: from the US interjection *aw shucks*, an expression of modesty or diffidence]

axe or US **ax** (æks) *n, pl* axes **1** a hand tool with one side of its head forged and sharpened to a cutting edge, used for felling trees, splitting timber, etc **2** an axe to grind **a** an ulterior motive **b** a grievance **c** a pet subject **3** the axe *informal* **a** dismissal, esp from employment; the sack (esp in the phrase **get the axe**) **b** *Brit* severe cutting down of expenditure, esp the removal of unprofitable sections of a public service ▷ *vb* (*tr*) **4** to chop or trim with an axe **5** *informal* to dismiss (employees), restrict (expenditure or services), or terminate (a project) [Old English *æx*; related to Old Frisian *axa*, Old High German *acchus*, Old Norse *öx*, Latin *ascia*, Greek *axinē*]

axel ('æksəl) *n skating* a jump in which the skater takes off from the forward outside edge of one skate, makes one and a half, two and a half, or three and a half turns in the air, and lands on the backward outside edge of the other skate [c20: named after *Axel* Paulsen (died 1938), Norwegian skater]

Axelrod ('æksəlrɒd) *n* **Julius**. 1912–2004, US neuropharmacologist, renowned for his work on catecholamines. Nobel prize for physiology or medicine (with von Euler and Bernard Katz) 1970

axeman or US **axman** ('æksmən) *n, pl* -men **1** a man who wields an axe, esp to cut down trees **2** a person who makes cuts in expenditure or services, esp on behalf of another: *the chancellor's axeman*

axes¹ ('æksiːz) *n* the plural of **axis¹**

axes² ('æksɪz) *n* the plural of **axe**

axial ('æksɪəl) *adj* **1** relating to, forming, or characteristic of an axis **2** situated in, on, or along an axis > ˌaxi'ality *n* > 'axially *adv*

axil ('æksɪl) *n* the angle between the upper surface of a branch or leafstalk and the stem from which it grows [c18: from Latin *axilla* armpit]

axilla (æk'sɪlə) *n, pl* -lae (-liː) **1** the technical name for the **armpit 2** the area on the undersurface of a bird's wing corresponding to the armpit [c17: from Latin: armpit]

axillary (æk'sɪlərɪ) *adj* **1** of, relating to, or near the armpit **2** *botany* growing in or related to the axil ▷ *n, pl* -laries **3** Also called: axillar (æk'sɪlə, 'æksɪlə) (*usually plural*) one of the feathers growing from the axilla of a bird's wing

axiom ('æksɪəm) *n* **1** a generally accepted proposition or principle, sanctioned by experience; maxim **2** a universally established principle or law that is not a necessary truth **3** a self-evident statement **4** *logic, maths*

a statement or formula that is stipulated to be true for the purpose of a chain of reasoning: the foundation of a formal deductive system [c15: from Latin *axiōma* a principle, from Greek, from *axioun* to consider worthy, from *axios* worthy]

axiomatic (ˌæksɪə'mætɪk) *adj* **1** relating to or resembling an axiom; self-evident **2** containing maxims; aphoristic > ˌaxio'matically *adv*

axis¹ ('æksɪs) *n, pl* axes ('æksiːz) **1** a real or imaginary line about which a body, such as an aircraft, can rotate or about which an object, form, composition, or geometrical construction is symmetrical **2** one of two or three reference lines used in coordinate geometry to locate a point in a plane or in space **3** *anatomy* the second cervical vertebra **4** *botany* the main central part of a plant, typically consisting of the stem and root, from which secondary branches and other parts develop **5** an alliance between a number of states to coordinate their foreign policy **6** Also called: principal axis *optics* the line of symmetry of an optical system, such as the line passing through the centre of a lens [c14: from Latin: axletree, earth's axis; related to Greek *axōn* axis]

axis² ('æksɪs) *n, pl* axises any of several S Asian deer of the genus *Axis*, esp *A. axis*. They typically have a reddish-brown white-spotted coat and slender antlers [c18: from Latin: Indian wild animal, of uncertain identity]

Axis ('æksɪs) *n* **a** the Axis the alliance of Nazi Germany, Fascist Italy, and Japan, established in 1936 and lasting until their defeat in World War II **b** (*as modifier*): *the Axis powers*

axle ('æksəl) *n* a bar or shaft on which a wheel, pair of wheels, or other rotating member revolves [c17: from Old Norse *öxull*; related to German *Achse*; see AXIS¹]

axletree ('æksəlˌtriː) *n* a bar fixed across the underpart of a wagon or carriage that has rounded ends on which the wheels revolve

Axminster carpet ('æksˌmɪnstə) *n* a type of patterned carpet with a cut pile [after *Axminster*, in Devon, where such carpets are made]

axolotl ('æksəˌlɒtəl) *n* any of several aquatic salamanders of the North American genus *Ambystoma*, esp *A. mexicanum* (**Mexican axolotl**), in which the larval form (including external gills) is retained throughout life under natural conditions (see **neoteny**): family *Ambystomidae* [c18: from Nahuatl, from *atl* water + *xolotl* servant, doll]

axon ('æksɒn) *n* the long threadlike extension of a nerve cell that conducts nerve impulses from the cell body [c19: via New Latin from Greek: axis, axle, vertebra]

ay¹ (eɪ) *adv archaic, poetic* ever; always [c12 *ai*, from Old Norse *ei*; related to Old English *ā* always, Latin *aevum* an age, Greek *aiōn*]

ay² (aɪ) *sentence substitute, n* a variant spelling of **aye**

Ayacucho (*Spanish* aja'kutʃo) *n* a city in SE Peru: nearby is the site of the battle (1824) that won independence for Peru. Pop: 150 000 (2005 est)

ayah ('aɪə) *n* (in the East, Africa, and other parts of the former British Empire) a maidservant, nursemaid, or governess, esp one of Indian or Malay origin [c18: from Hindi *āyā*, from Portuguese *aia*, from Latin *avia* grandmother]

ayatollah (ˌaɪə'tɒlə) *n* one of a class of Iranian Shiite religious leaders [via Persian from Arabic, from *aya* sign + *Allah* god]

Ayckbourn ('eɪkbɔːn) *n* Sir **Alan**. born 1939, English dramatist. His plays include *Absurd Person Singular* (1973), the trilogy *The Norman Conquests* (1974), *A Chorus of Disapproval* (1985), and *House and Garden* (2000)

Aycliffe ('eɪklɪf) *n* a town in Co Durham: founded as a new town in 1947. Pop (including Newton Aycliffe): 25 655 (2001)

Aydin or **Aidin** ('aɪdɪn) *n* a town in SW Turkey: an ancient city of Lydia. Pop: 160 000 (2005 est)

aye or **ay** (aɪ) *sentence substitute* **1** yes: archaic or dialectal except in voting by voice ▷ *n* **2 a** a person who votes in the affirmative **b** an affirmative vote ▷ See **nay** [c16: probably from pronoun I, expressing assent]

aye-aye ('aɪˌaɪ) *n* a rare nocturnal arboreal prosimian primate of Madagascar, *Daubentonia madagascariensis*, related to the lemurs: family *Daubentoniidae*. It has long bony fingers and rodent-like incisor teeth adapted for feeding on insect larvae and bamboo pith [c18: from French, from Malagasy *aiay*, probably of imitative origin]

Ayer (ɛə) *n* Sir **Alfred Jules**. 1910–89, English positivist philosopher, noted particularly for his antimetaphysical work *Language, Truth, and Logic* (1936)

Ayers Rock (ɛəz) *n* another name for **Uluru**

Ayesha (ɑːˈiːʃɑː) *n* a variant spelling of **Aisha**

Ayia Napa (ˌaɪjə ˈnæpə) *n* a coastal resort in SE Cyprus. Pop: 9500 (2004 est)

Aykroyd (ˈeɪkˌrɔɪd) *n* **Dan**. born 1952, Canadian film actor and screenwriter, best known for the television show *Saturday Night Live* (1975–80) and the films *The Blues Brothers* (1980), *Ghostbusters* (1984), and *Driving Miss Daisy* (1989)

Aylesbury (ˈeɪlzbərɪ, -brɪ) *n* a town in SE central England, administrative centre of Buckinghamshire. Pop: 69 021 (2001)

Aylward (ˈeɪlwəd) *n* **Gladys**. 1903–70, English missionary in China

Aymara (ˌaɪməˈrɑː) *n* **1** *pl* **-ras** *or* **-ra** a member of a South American Indian people of Bolivia and Peru **2** the language of this people, probably related to Quechua [from Spanish *aimará*, of American Indian origin]

Aymé (*French* ɛme) *n* **Marcel** (marsɛl). 1902–67, French writer: noted for his light and witty narratives

Ayodhya (ɑːˈjəʊdjɑː) *n* an ancient town in N India, in Uttar Pradesh state: as the birthplace of Rama it is sacred to Hindus; also a Buddhist centre. Also called: **Awadh** (əˈwɒd), **Oudh** (aʊd)

Ayr (ɛə) *n* a port in SW Scotland, in South Ayrshire. Pop: 46 431 (2001)

Ayrshire (ˈɛəʃɪə, -ʃə) *n* **1** a historical county of SW Scotland, formerly part of Strathclyde region (1975–96), now divided into the council areas of North Ayrshire, South Ayrshire, and East Ayrshire **2** any one of a hardy breed of brown-and-white dairy cattle

Ayub Khan (aɪˈjuːb ˈkɑːn) *n* **Mohammed**. 1907–74, Pakistani field marshal; president of Pakistan (1958–69)

Ayutthaya (ɑːˈjuːtəjə) *n* a city in S Thailand, on the Chao Phraya River: capital of the country until 1767; noted for its canals and ruins. Pop (province): 727 300 (2000). Also called: **Ayudhya** (ɑːˈjuːdjə) *or* **Ayuthia** (ɑːˈjuːθɪə)

AZ *abbreviation* Arizona

aza- *or before a vowel* **az-** *combining form* denoting the presence of nitrogen, esp a nitrogen atom in place of a -CH group or an -NH group in place of a -CH$_2$ group: *azathioprine* [c20: from AZ(O)- + -*a*-]

azalea (əˈzeɪljə) *n* any ericaceous plant of the group *Azalea*, formerly a separate genus but now included in the genus *Rhododendron*: cultivated for their showy pink or purple flowers [c18: via New Latin from Greek, from *azaleos* dry; from its supposed preference for a dry situation]

Azaña (*Spanish* aˈθaɲa) *n* **Manuel** (maˈnwel). 1880–1940, Spanish statesman; president of the Spanish Republic (1936–39) until overthrown by Franco

Azania (əˈzɑːnɪə, əˈzaːnjə) *n* another name for **South Africa** [perhaps from Arabic *Adzan* East Africa]

Azbine (æzˈbiːn) *n* another name for **Aïr**

azeotrope (əˈziːəˌtrəʊp) *n* a mixture of liquids that boils at a constant temperature, at a given pressure, without change of composition [c20: from A-¹ + *zeo-*, from Greek *zein* to boil + -TROPE] > **azeotropic** (ˌeɪzɪəˈtrɒpɪk) *adj*

Azerbaijan (ˌæzəbaɪˈdʒɑːn) *n* **1** a republic in NW Asia: the region was acquired by Russia from Persia in the early 19th century; became the Azerbaijan Soviet Socialist Republic in 1936 and gained independence in 1991; consists of dry subtropical steppes around the Aras and Kura rivers, surrounded by the Caucasus; contains the extensive Baku oilfields. Language: Azerbaijani (or Azeri). Religion: Shiite Muslim. Currency: manat. Capital: Baku. Pop: 8 447 000 (2004 est). Area: 86 600 sq km (33 430 sq miles) **2** a mountainous region of NW Iran, separated from the republic of Azerbaijan by the Aras River: divided administratively into **Eastern Azerbaijan** and **Western Azerbaijan**. Capitals: Tabriz and Orumiyeh. Pop: 2 119 524 (2002 est) > **Azerbaiˈjani** *n*

azerty keyboard *or* **AZERTY keyboard** (əˈzɜːtɪ) *n* a common European version of typewriter keyboard layout with the characters a, z, e, r, t, and y positioned on the top row of alphabetic characters at the left side of the keyboard

azide (ˈeɪzaɪd) *n* (*modifier*) consisting of, containing, or concerned with the group –N$_3$ or the ion N$_3$⁻: *azide group or radical*

Azikiwe (ˌɑːzɪˈkiːweɪ) *n* **Nnamdi** (ⁿnˈnæmdɪ) 1904–96, Nigerian statesman; first president of Nigeria (1963–66)

Azilian (əˈzɪlɪən) *n* **1** a Palaeolithic culture of Spain and SW France that can be dated to the 10th millennium BC, characterized by flat bone harpoons and schematically painted pebbles ▷ *adj* **2** of or relating to this culture [c19: named after Mas d'*Azil*, France, where artefacts were found]

azimuth (ˈæzɪməθ) *n* **1** *astronomy, navigation* the angular distance usually measured clockwise from the north point of the horizon to the intersection with the horizon of the vertical circle passing through a celestial body **2** *surveying* the horizontal angle of a bearing clockwise from a standard direction, such as north [c14: from Old French *azimut*, from Arabic *as-sumūt*, plural of *as-samt* the path, from Latin *semita* path] > **azimuthal** (ˌæzɪˈmʌθəl) *adj*

azine (ˈeɪziːn, -zɪn) *n* any organic compound having a six-membered ring containing at least one nitrogen atom

azo (ˈeɪzəʊ, ˈæ-) *adj* of, consisting of, or containing the divalent group -N:N-: *an azo group or radical*. ▷ See also **diazo** [independent use of AZO-]

azo- *or before a vowel* **az-** *combining form* indicating the presence of an azo group: *azobenzene* [from French *azote* nitrogen, from Greek *azōos* lifeless, from A-¹ + *zōē* life]

azoic (əˈzəʊɪk, eɪ-) *adj* without life; characteristic of the ages that have left no evidence of life in the form of organic remains [c19: from Greek *azōos* lifeless; see AZO-]

Azores (əˈzɔːz) *pl n* **the Azores** three groups of volcanic islands in the N Atlantic, since 1976 an autonomous region of Portugal. Capital: Ponta Delgada (on São Miguel). Pop: 241 762 (2001). Area: 2335 sq km (901 sq miles). Portuguese name: **Açores**

Azorín (*Spanish* aθoˈrin) *n* real name *José Martínez Ruiz*. 1874–1967, Spanish writer: noted for his stories of the Spanish countryside

Azov (ˈɑːzɒv) *n* **Sea of Azov** a shallow arm of the Black Sea, to which it is connected by the Kerch Strait: almost entirely landlocked; fed chiefly by the River Don. Area: about 37 500 sq km (14 500 sq miles)

AZT *abbreviation* azidothymidine. Also called: **zidovudine**

Aztec (ˈæztɛk) *n* **1** a member of a Mexican Indian people who established a great empire, centred on the valley of Mexico, that was overthrown by Cortés and his followers in the early 16th century **2** the language of the Aztecs. See also **Nahuatl** ▷ *adj* Also: **Aztecan 3** of, relating to, or characteristic of the Aztecs, their civilization, or their language [c18: from Spanish *Azteca*, from Nahuatl *Aztecatl*, from *Aztlan*, their traditional place of origin, literally: near the cranes, from *azta* cranes + *tlan* near]

azure (ˈæʒə, -ʒʊə, ˈeɪ-) *n* **1** a deep blue, occasionally somewhat purple, similar to the colour of a clear blue sky **2** *poetic* a clear blue sky ▷ *adj* **3** of the colour azure; serene **4** (*usually postpositive*) *heraldry* of the colour blue [c14: from Old French *azur*, from Old Spanish, from Arabic *lāzaward* lapis lazuli, from Persian *lāzhuward*]

azurite (ˈæʒʊˌraɪt) *n* an azure-blue mineral associated with copper deposits. It is a source of copper. Composition: copper carbonate. Formula: $Cu_3(CO_3)_2(OH)_2$. Crystal structure: monoclinic

azygous (ˈæzɪɡəs) *adj* *biology* developing or occurring singly [c17: via New Latin from Greek *azugos*, from A-¹ + *zugon* YOKE]

Bb

b *or* **B** (biː) *n, pl* **b's, B's** *or* **Bs** **1** the second letter and first consonant of the modern English alphabet **2** a speech sound represented by this letter, usually a voiced bilabial stop, as in *bell* **3** Also called: **beta** the second in a series, esp the second highest grade in an examination

B *symbol for* **1** *music* **a** a note having a frequency of 493.88 hertz (**B above middle C**) or this value multiplied or divided by any power of 2; the seventh note of the scale of C major **b** the major or minor key having this note as its tonic **2** the supporting or less important of two things **3** a human blood type of the ABO group, containing the B antigen **4** (in Britain) a secondary road **5** *chem* boron **6** magnetic flux density **7** *chess* bishop **8** (on Brit pencils, signifying degree of softness of lead) black **9** Also called: **b** *physics* bel **10** *physics* baryon number **11 a** a person whose job is in middle management, or who holds an intermediate administrative or professional position **b** (*as modifier*): *a B worker*. See also **occupation groupings**

b. *abbreviation* **1** born **2** *cricket* bowled

B. *abbreviation* (on maps, etc) bay

B- *abbreviation* (of US military aircraft) bomber

Ba¹ (bɑː) *n Egyptian myth* the soul, represented as a bird with a human head

Ba² *the chemical symbol for* barium

BA *abbreviation* **1** Bachelor of Arts **2** British Academy **3** British Airways **4** British Association (for the Advancement of Science)

baa (bɑː) *vb* **baas, baaing, baaed** **1** (*intr*) to make the cry of a sheep; bleat ▷ *n* **2** the cry made by sheep

BAA *n* the main airports operator in the United Kingdom; until privatization in 1987, an abbreviation for British Airports Authority

Baader-Meinhof Gang (*German* 'baːdər 'mainhoːf) *n* a group of left-wing West German terrorists, active in the 1970s, who were dedicated to the violent overthrow of capitalist society. Also known as: Red Army Faction [c20: named after its leading members, Andreas *Baader* (1943–77) and Ulrike *Meinhof* (1934–76)]

Baal (bɑːl) *n* **1** any of several ancient Semitic fertility gods **2** *Phoenician myth* the sun god and supreme national deity **3** (*sometimes not capital*) any false god or idol [from Hebrew *báʼal* lord, master]

Baalbek ('baːlbɛk) *n* a town in E Lebanon: an important city in Phoenician and Roman times; extensive ruins. Pop: 150 000 (1998 est). Ancient name: Heliopolis

Baal Shem Tov *or* **Baal Shem Tob** (baːl 'ʃɛm tɒv, 'ʃaːm) *n* original name *Israel ben Eliezer* ?1700–60, Jewish religious leader, teacher, and healer in Poland: founder of modern Hasidism

baas (baːs) *n* a South African word for a boss: often used by Black or Coloured people addressing a White manager or overseer [c17: from Afrikaans, from Middle Dutch *baes* master; see BOSS¹]

baaskap *or* **baasskap** ('baːs,kap) *n* (*sometimes capital*) (formerly in South Africa) control by White people of non-White people [from Afrikaans, from BAAS + -*skap* -SHIP]

Bab (baːb) *n* **the.** title of *Mirza Ali Mohammed* 1819–50, Persian religious leader: founded Babism; executed as a heretic of Islam [from Persian *bāb* gate, from Arabic]

baba ('baːbaː; *French* baba) *n* a small cake of leavened dough, sometimes mixed with currants and usually soaked in rum (**rum baba**) [c19: from French, from Polish, literally: old woman]

babalas ('babalas) *or* **babbelas** *adj South African* drunk; hungover [c20: Afrikaans, from Zulu *I-babalazi* drunk]

Babar ('baːbə) *n* a variant spelling of **Baber**

Babbage ('bæbɪdʒ) *n* **Charles** 1792–1871, English mathematician and inventor, who built a calculating machine that anticipated the modern electronic computer

babbitt ('bæbɪt) *vb* (*tr*) to line (a bearing) or face (a surface) with Babbitt metal or a similar soft alloy

Babbitt ('bæbɪt) *n US derogatory* a narrow-minded and complacent member of the middle class [c20: after George *Babbitt*, central character in the novel *Babbitt* (1922) by Sinclair Lewis] > 'Babbittry *n*

Babbitt metal *n* any of a number of alloys originally based on tin, antimony, and copper but now often including lead: used esp in bearings [c19: named after Isaac *Babbitt* (1799–1862), American inventor]

babble ('bæbᵊl) *vb* **1** to utter (words, sounds, etc) in an incoherent or indistinct jumble **2** (*intr*) to talk foolishly, incessantly, or irrelevantly **3** (*tr*) to disclose (secrets, confidences, etc) carelessly or impulsively **4** (*intr*) (of streams, birds, etc) to make a low murmuring or bubbling sound ▷ *n* **5** incoherent or foolish speech; chatter **6** a murmuring or bubbling sound [c13: compare Dutch *babbelen*, Swedish *babbla*, French *babiller* to prattle, Latin *babulus* fool; probably all of imitative origin]

babbler ('bæblə) *n* **1** a person who babbles **2** any of various insect-eating birds of the Old World tropics and subtropics that have a loud incessant song: family *Muscicapidae* (warblers, thrushes, etc)

babbling brook *n Austral slang* a cook [rhyming slang]

babe (beɪb) *n* **1** a baby **2** *informal* a naive, gullible, or unsuspecting person (often in the phrase **a babe in arms**) **3** *informal* a young woman or man perceived as being sexually attractive

Babel[1] ('beɪbəl) *n* **1** *Old Testament* Also called: **Tower of Babel** a tower presumptuously intended to reach from earth to heaven, the building of which was frustrated when Jehovah confused the language of the builders (Genesis 11:1–9) **2** (*often not capital*) **a** a confusion of noises or voices **b** a scene of noise and confusion [from Hebrew *Bābhēl*, from Akkadian *Bāb-ilu*, literally: gate of God]

Babel[2] (*Russian* 'babɪl) *n* **Issak Emmanuilovich** (i'sak imənu'iləvitʃ) 1894–1941, Russian short-story writer, whose works include *Stories from Odessa* (1924) and *Red Cavalry* (1926)

Bab el Mandeb ('bæb ɛl 'mændɛb) *n* a strait between SW Arabia and E Africa, connecting the Red Sea with the Gulf of Aden

Baber, Babar or **Babur** ('baːbə) *n* original name *Zahir ud-Din Mohammed* 1483–1530, founder of the Mogul Empire: conquered India in 1526

Babeuf (*French* babœf) *n* **François Noël** (frãswa nɔɛl) 1760–97, French political agitator: plotted unsuccessfully to destroy the Directory and establish a communistic system

Babinet (*French* babinɛ) *n* **Jacques** (ʒak) 1794–1872, French physicist, noted for his work on the diffraction of light

Babington ('bæbɪŋtən) *n* **Anthony** 1561–86, English conspirator, hanged for organizing an unsuccessful plot (1586) to assassinate Elizabeth I and place Mary, Queen of Scots, on the English throne

babirusa (ˌbaːbɪ'ruːsə) *n* a wild pig, *Babyrousa babyrussa*, inhabiting marshy forests in Indonesia. It has an almost hairless wrinkled skin and enormous curved canine teeth [c17: from Malay, from *bābī* hog + *rūsa* deer]

Babism ('baːbɪzəm) *n* a pantheistic Persian religious sect, founded in 1844 by the Bab, a Persian religious leader (1819–50), who was executed as a heretic of Islam. It forbids polygamy, concubinage, begging, trading in slaves, and indulgence in alcohol and drugs

baboon (bə'buːn) *n* any of several medium-sized omnivorous Old World monkeys of the genus *Papio* (or *Chaeropithecus*) and related genera, inhabiting open rocky ground or wooded regions of Africa. They have an elongated muzzle, large teeth, and a fairly long tail [c14 *babewyn* gargoyle, later, baboon, from Old French *babouin*, from *baboue* grimace; related to Old French *babine* a thick lip]

babu ('baːbuː) *n* (in India) a title or form of address more or less equivalent to *Mr*, placed before a person's full name or after his first name [Hindi, literally: father]

Babur ('baːbə) *n* a variant spelling of **Baber**

babushka (bə'buːʃkə) *n* **1** a headscarf tied under the chin, worn by Russian peasant women **2** (in Russia) an old woman [Russian: grandmother, from *baba* old woman]

baby ('beɪbɪ) *n, pl* **-bies 1 a** a newborn or recently born child; infant **b** (*as modifier*): *baby food* **2** an unborn child; fetus **3** the youngest or smallest of a family or group **4** a newborn or recently born animal **5** *usually derogatory* an immature person **6** *slang* a young woman or sweetheart: often used as a term of address expressing affection **7** a project of personal concern **8 be left holding the baby** to be left with the responsibility ▷ *adj* **9** (*prenominal*) comparatively small of its type: *a baby car* ▷ *vb* **-bies, -bying, -bied** (*tr*) **10** to treat with love and attention **11** to

treat (someone) like a baby; pamper or overprotect [c14: probably childish reduplication; compare MAMA, PAPA] ▷ **'babyhood** *n* ▷ **'babyish** *adj*

baby bond *n Brit* a sum of money invested shortly after the birth of a child, the returns of which may not be collected until the child reaches adulthood

baby bonus *n Canadian informal* family allowance

baby-boomer *n* a person born during a baby boom, esp (in Britain and the US) one born during the years 1945–55

baby broker *n* an adoption service, esp on the internet

Baby Buggy *n* **1** *trademark Brit* a kind of child's light pushchair **2** *US & Canadian informal* a small pram

baby carriage *n* Also called: **baby buggy** *US & Canadian* a cot-like four-wheeled carriage for a baby. British term: **pram**

Babylon ('bæbɪlən) *n* **1** the chief city of ancient Mesopotamia: first settled around 3000 BC. See also **Hanging Gardens of Babylon 2** *offensive* (in Protestant polemic) the Roman Catholic Church, regarded as the seat of luxury and corruption **3** *dismissive* any society or group in a society considered as corrupt or as a place of exile by another society or group, esp White Britain as viewed by some West Indians [via Latin and Greek from Hebrew *Bābhēl*; see BABEL] ▷ **Babylonian** (ˌbæbɪ'ləʊnɪən) *n, adj*

Babylonia (ˌbæbɪ'ləʊnɪə) *n* the southern kingdom of ancient Mesopotamia: a great empire from about 2200–538 BC, when it was conquered by the Persians

baby-sit *vb* **-sits, -sitting, -sat** (*intr*) to act or work as a baby-sitter ▷ **'baby-ˌsitting** *n, adj*

baby-sitter *n* a person who takes care of a child or children while the parents are out

baby snatcher *n informal* a person who steals a baby from its pram

baby wipe *n* a disposable moistened medicated paper towel, usually supplied in a plastic drum or packet, used for cleaning babies

Bacău ('bækaʊ) *n* a city in E Romania on the River Bistrila: oil refining, textiles, paper. Pop: 128 000 (2005 est)

baccalaureate (ˌbækə'lɔːrɪɪt) *n* the university degree of Bachelor of Arts, Bachelor of Science, etc [c17: from Medieval Latin *baccalaureātus*, from *baccalaureus* advanced student, alteration of *baccalārius* BACHELOR; influenced in folk etymology by Latin *bāca* berry + *laureus* laurel]

baccarat ('bækəˌraː, ˌbækə'raː; *French* bakara) *n* a card game in which two or more punters gamble against the banker [c19: from French *baccara*, of unknown origin]

baccate ('bækeɪt) *adj botany* **1** like a berry in form, texture, etc **2** bearing berries [c19: from Latin *bāca* berry]

Bacchae ('bækiː) *pl n* the priestesses or female devotees of Bacchus [Latin, from Greek *Bakkhai*, plural of *Bakkhē* priestess of BACCHUS]

bacchanal ('bækənªl) *n* **1** a follower of Bacchus **2** a drunken and riotous celebration **3** a participant in such a celebration; reveller ▷ *adj* **4** of or relating to Bacchus [c16: from Latin *Bacchānālis*; see BACCHUS]

bacchanalia (ˌbækə'neɪlɪə) *pl n* **1** (*often capital*) orgiastic rites associated with Bacchus **2** any drunken revelry ▷ ˌbaccha'nalian *adj*

bacchant ('bækənt) *n, pl* **bacchants, bacchantes** (bə'kæntɪz) **1** a priest or votary of Bacchus **2** a drunken reveller [c17: from Latin *bacchāns*, from *bacchārī* to celebrate the BACCHANALIA]

Bacchic ('bækɪk) *adj* **1** of or relating to Bacchus **2** (*often not capital*) riotously drunk

Bacchus ('bækəs) *n* (in ancient Greece and Rome) a god of wine and giver of ecstasy, identified with Dionysus [c15: from Latin, from Greek *Bakkhos*; related to Latin *bāca* small round fruit, berry]

baccy ('bækɪ) *n Brit* an informal name for **tobacco**

bach (bætʃ) *Austral & NZ* ▷ *vb* **1** a variant spelling of **batch**[1] ▷ *n* **2** a simple cottage, esp at the seaside

Bach (*German* bax) *n* **1 Johann Christian** (jo'han 'krɪstjan), 11th son of J. S. Bach. 1735–82, German composer, called *the English Bach*, resident in London from 1762 **2 Johann Christoph** ('krɪstɔf). 1642–1703, German composer: wrote oratorios, cantatas, and motets, some of which were falsely attributed to J. S. Bach, of whom he was a distant relative **3 Johann Sebastian** (zeˈbastjan). 1685–1750, German composer: church organist at Arnstadt (1703–07) and Mühlhausen (1707–08); court organist at Weimar (1708–17); musical director for Prince Leopold of Köthen (1717–28); musical director for the city of Leipzig (1728–50). His output was enormous and displays great vigour and invention within the northern European polyphonic tradition. His works include nearly 200 cantatas and oratorios, settings of the *Passion according to St John* (1723) and *St Matthew* (1729), the six *Brandenburg Concertos* (1720–21), the 48 preludes and fugues of the *Well-tempered Clavier* (completed 1744), and the *Mass in B Minor* (1733–38) **4 Karl** (or **Carl**) **Philipp Emanuel** (karl ˈfiːlɪp eˈmaːnuɛl), 3rd son of J. S. Bach. 1714–88, German composer, chiefly of symphonies, keyboard sonatas, and church music **5 Wilhelm Friedemann** (ˈvɪlhɛlm ˈfriːdəman), eldest son of J. S. Bach. 1710–84, German composer: wrote nine symphonies and much keyboard and religious music

Bacharach (ˈbækəræk) *n* Burt born 1928, US composer of popular songs, usually with lyricist Hal David

bachelor (ˈbætʃələ, ˈbætʃlə) *n* **1 a** an unmarried man **b** (*as modifier*): *a bachelor flat* **2 a** a person who holds the degree of Bachelor of Arts, Bachelor of Education, Bachelor of Science, etc **b** the degree itself **3** Also called: **bachelor-at-arms** (in the Middle Ages) a young knight serving a great noble **4 bachelor seal** a young male seal, esp a fur seal, that has not yet mated [c13: from Old French *bacheler* youth, squire, from Vulgar Latin *baccalāris* (unattested) farm worker, of Celtic origin; compare Irish Gaelic *bachlach* peasant] > ˈ**bachelorhood** *n*

bachelor apartment *n* Canadian a flat consisting of one room that is used as a sitting room and bedroom, as well as a kitchenette and a bathroom

bachelor girl *n* a young unmarried woman, esp one who is self-supporting

Bachelor of Arts *n* **1** a degree conferred on a person who has successfully completed his or her undergraduate studies, usually in a branch of the liberal arts or humanities **2** a person who holds this degree

Bachelor of Science *n* **1** a degree conferred on a person who has successfully completed his or her undergraduate studies in a branch of the sciences **2** a person who holds this degree

bachelor's-buttons *n* (*functioning as singular or plural*) any of various plants of the daisy family with button-like flower heads

Bach flower remedy *n* trademark an alternative medicine consisting of a distillation from various flowers, designed to counteract negative states of mind and restore emotional balance [c20: after Dr E. *Bach* (1886–1936), homeopath who developed this system]

bacillary (bəˈsɪlərɪ) or **bacillar** (bəˈsɪlə) *adj* **1** of, relating to, or caused by bacilli **2** Also called: **bacilliform** (bəˈsɪlɪˌfɔːm) shaped like a short rod

bacillus (bəˈsɪləs) *n, pl* **-cilli** (-ˈsɪlaɪ) **1** any rod-shaped bacterium, such as a clostridium bacterium **2** any of various rodlike spore-producing bacteria constituting the family *Bacillaceae*, esp of the genus *Bacillus* [c19: from Latin: a small staff, from *baculum* walking stick]

back (bæk) *n* **1** the posterior part of the human body, extending from the neck to the pelvis **2** the corresponding or upper part of an animal **3** the spinal column **4** the part or side of an object opposite the front **5** the part or side of anything less often seen or used **6** the part or side of anything that is furthest from the front or from a spectator: *the back of the stage* **7** something that supports, covers, or strengthens the rear of an object **8** ball games **a** a mainly defensive player behind a forward **b** the position of such a player **9** the part of a book to which the pages are glued or that joins the covers **10** at the back of one's mind not in one's conscious thoughts **11** behind one's back without one's knowledge; secretly or deceitfully **12** break one's back to overwork or work very hard **13** break the back of to complete the greatest or hardest part of (a task) **14** get off someone's back informal to stop criticizing or pestering someone **15** put one's back into to devote all

one's strength to (a task) **16** put someone's back up or get someone's back up to annoy someone **17** the back of beyond a very remote place **18** turn one's back on **a** to turn away from in anger or contempt **b** to refuse to help; abandon ▷ *vb* (*mainly tr*) **19** (*also intr*) to move or cause to move backwards **20** to provide support, money, or encouragement for (a person, enterprise, etc) **21** to bet on the success of: *to back a horse* **22** to provide with a back, backing, or lining **23** to provide with a music accompaniment **24** to countersign or endorse **25** (*intr*; foll by *on* or *onto*) to have the back facing (towards): *the house backs onto a river* **26** (*intr*) (of the wind) to change direction in an anticlockwise direction in the northern hemisphere and a clockwise direction in the southern. See **veer**[1] (*sense 3a*) ▷ *adj* (*prenominal*) **27** situated behind **28** of the past: *back issues of a magazine* **29** owing from an earlier date: *back rent* **30** chiefly US, Austral & NZ remote: *back country* **31** (of a road) not direct **32** phonetics of, relating to, or denoting a vowel articulated with the tongue retracted towards the soft palate, as for the vowels in English *hard, fall, hot, full, fool* ▷ *adv* **33** at, to, or towards the rear; away from something considered to be the front; backwards; behind **34** in, to, or towards the original starting point, place, or condition: *to go back home; put the book back; my headache has come back* **35** in or into the past: *to look back on one's childhood* **36** in reply, repayment, or retaliation: *to hit someone back; pay back a debt; to answer back* **37** in check: *the dam holds back the water* **38** in concealment; in reserve: *to keep something back; to hold back information* **39** back and forth to and fro **40** back to front **a** in reverse **b** in disorder ▷ See also **back down, back off, back out, back up** [Old English *bæc*; related to Old Norse *bak*, Old Frisian *bek*, Old High German *bah*]

back bacon *n* lean bacon from the back of a pig's loin

backbencher (ˌbækˈbɛntʃə) *n* Brit, Austral & NZ a Member of Parliament who does not hold office in the government or opposition

backbite (ˈbækˌbaɪt) *vb* **-bites, -biting, -bit, -bitten** *or* **-bit** to talk spitefully about (an absent person) > ˈ**back**ˌ**biter** *n*

backboard (ˈbækˌbɔːd) *n* **1** a board that is placed behind something to form or support its back **2** a board worn to straighten or support the back, as after surgery **3** (in basketball) a flat upright surface supported on a high frame, under which the basket is attached

back boiler *n* a tank or series of pipes at the back of a fireplace for heating water

backbone (ˈbækˌbəʊn) *n* **1** a nontechnical name for **spinal column 2** something that resembles the spinal column in function, position, or appearance **3** strength of character; courage

backbreaking (ˈbækˌbreɪkɪŋ) *adj* demanding great effort; exhausting

backburn (ˈbækˌbɜːn) Austral & NZ ▷ *vb* (*tr*) **1** to clear (an area of scrub, bush, etc) by creating a new fire that burns in the opposite direction to the line of advancing fire ▷ *n* **2** the act or result of backburning

back catalogue *n* the recordings that a musician has made in the past, as distinct from his or her current recording

backchat (ˈbækˌtʃæt) *n* informal the act of answering back, esp impudently

backcloth (ˈbækˌklɒθ) *n* a large painted curtain hanging at the back of a stage set. Also called: **backdrop**

backcomb (ˈbækˌkəʊm) *vb* to comb the under layers of (the hair) towards the roots to give more bulk to a hairstyle. Also called: **tease**

back country *n* Austral & NZ land remote from a town or settled area

backdate (ˌbækˈdeɪt) *vb* (*tr*) to make effective from an earlier date

back door *n* **1** a door at the rear or side of a building **2 a** a means of entry to a job, position, etc, that is secret, underhand, or obtained through influence **b** (*as modifier*): *a backdoor way of making firms pay more*

back down *vb* **1** (*intr, adverb*) to withdraw an earlier claim ▷ *n* **backdown 2** abandonment of an earlier claim

backdrop (ˈbækˌdrɒp) *n* the background to any scene or situation

backed (bækt) *adj* **a** having a back or backing **b** (*in* combination): *high-backed; black-backed*

backer ('bækə) *n* **1** a person who gives financial or other support **2** a person who bets on a competitor or contestant

backfield ('bæk,fiːld) *n American football* **1** the backfield (*sometimes functioning as plural*) the quarterback and running backs in a team **2** the area behind the line of scrimmage from which the backfield begin each play

backfill ('bæk,fɪl) *vb* **1** (*tr*) to refill an excavated trench, esp (in archaeology) at the end of an investigation ▷ *n* **2** the soil used to do this

backfire (,bæk'faɪə) *vb* (*intr*) **1** (of an internal-combustion engine) to emit a loud noise as a result of an explosion in the inlet manifold or exhaust system **2** to start a controlled fire in order to halt an advancing forest or prairie fire by creating a barren area ▷ *n* **3** (in an internal-combustion engine) an explosion of unburnt gases in the exhaust system **4** a controlled fire started to create a barren area that will halt an advancing forest or prairie fire

back formation *n* **1** the invention of a new word on the assumption that a familiar word is derived from it. The verbs *edit* and *burgle* were so created from *editor* and *burglar* **2** a word formed by this process

backgammon ('bæk,gæmən, bæk'gæmən) *n* **1** a game for two people played on a board with pieces moved according to throws of the dice **2** the most complete form of win in this game [C17: BACK¹ + *gammon*, variant of GAME¹]

background ('bæk,graʊnd) *n* **1** the part of a scene or view furthest from the viewer **2 a** an inconspicuous or unobtrusive position (esp in the phrase **in the background**) **b** (*as modifier*): *a background influence* **3** *art* the plane or ground in a picture upon which all other planes or forms appear superimposed **4** a person's social class, education, training, or experience **5** the social, historical, or technical circumstances that lead up to or help to explain something **b** (*as modifier*): *background information* **6 a** a low level of sound, lighting, etc, whose purpose is to be an unobtrusive or appropriate accompaniment to something else, such as a social activity, conversation, or the action of a film **b** (*as modifier*): *background music* **7** Also called: background radiation *physics* low-intensity radiation as, for example, from small amounts of radioisotopes in soil, air, building materials, etc **8** *electronics* unwanted effects, such as noise, occurring in a measuring instrument, electronic device, etc

backhand ('bæk,hænd) *n* **1** *sport* a stroke made across the body with the back of the hand facing the direction of the stroke **2** the side on which backhand strokes are made **3** handwriting slanting to the left ▷ *adv* **4** with a backhand stroke

backhanded (,bæk'hændɪd) *adj* **1** (of a blow, shot, stroke, etc) performed with the arm moving across the body **2** double-edged; equivocal: *a backhanded compliment* **3** (of handwriting) slanting to the left ▷ *adv* **4** in a backhanded manner

backhander ('bæk,hændə) *n* **1** a backhanded stroke or blow **2** *informal* an indirect attack **3** *slang* a bribe

backhouse ('bæk,haʊs) *n Canadian* another word for **outhouse**

backie ('bækɪ) *n Brit informal* a ride on the back of someone's bicycle

backing ('bækɪŋ) *n* **1** support given to a person, cause, or enterprise **2** a body of supporters **3** something that forms, protects, supports, or strengthens the back of something **4** *theatre* a scenic cloth or flat placed behind a window, door, etc, in a set to mask the offstage space **5** *Brit* musical accompaniment, esp for a pop singer **6** *meteorol* an anticlockwise change in wind direction

backing dog *n NZ & Austral* a dog that moves a flock of sheep by jumping on their backs

backlash ('bæk,læʃ) *n* **1** a reaction or recoil between interacting worn or badly fitting parts in a mechanism **2** the play between parts

backlog ('bæk,lɒg) *n* an accumulation of uncompleted work, unsold stock, etc, to be dealt with

back marker *n* a competitor who is at the back of a field in a race

back matter *n* the parts of a book, such as the index and appendices, that follow the main text

backmost ('bæk,məʊst) *adj* furthest back

back number *n* **1** an issue of a newspaper, magazine, etc, that appeared on a previous date **2** *informal* a person or thing considered to be old-fashioned

back off *vb* (*adverb*) *informal* **1** (*intr*) to retreat **2** (*tr*) to abandon (an intention, objective, etc)

back office *n* **a** the administrative and support staff of a financial institution or other business **b** (*as modifier*): *back-office operations*

back out *vb* (*intr, adverb*; often foll by *of*) to withdraw (from an agreement, etc)

backpack ('bæk,pæk) *n* **1** a rucksack or knapsack **2** a pack carried on the back of an astronaut, containing oxygen cylinders, essential supplies, etc ▷ *vb* **3** (*intr*) to travel about or go hiking with a backpack

back passage *n* the rectum

back-pedal *vb* -pedals, -pedalling, -pedalled *or US* -pedals, -pedaling, -pedaled (*intr*) **1** to turn the pedals of a bicycle backwards **2** to retract or modify a previous opinion, principle, etc

back projection *n* a method of projecting pictures onto a translucent screen so that they are viewed from the opposite side, used esp in films to create the illusion that the actors in the foreground are moving

Back River *n* a river in N Canada, flowing northeast through Nunavut to the Arctic Ocean. Length: about 966 km (600 miles)

back room *n* **a** a place where research or planning is done, esp secret research in wartime **b** (*as modifier*): *back-room boys*

back row *n* (*functioning as singular or plural*) *rugby Union* **a** the forwards at the rear of a scrum **b** (*as modifier*): *an Australian back-row forward*

Backs (bæks) *pl n* the Backs the grounds between the River Cam and certain Cambridge colleges

back seat *n* **1** a seat at the back, esp of a vehicle **2** *informal* a subordinate or inconspicuous position (esp in the phrase **take a back seat**)

back-seat driver *n informal* **1** a passenger in a car who offers unwanted advice to the driver **2** a person who offers advice on or tries to direct matters that are not his or her concern

backsheesh ('bækʃiːʃ) *n* a variant spelling of **baksheesh**

back shift *n Brit* **1** a group of workers who work a shift from late afternoon to midnight in an industry or occupation where a day shift or a night shift is also worked **2** the period worked ▷ *US and Canadian name:* swing shift

backside (,bæk'saɪd) *n* ('bæk,saɪd) *informal* the buttocks

backslide ('bæk,slaɪd) *vb* -slides, -sliding, -slid, -slid *or* -slidden (*intr*) to lapse into bad habits or vices from a state of virtue, religious faith, etc > 'back,slider *n*

backspace ('bæk,speɪs) *vb* to move a (typewriter carriage) backwards

backspin ('bæk,spɪn) *n sport* a backward spinning motion imparted to a ball to reduce its speed at impact, as by hitting it with a downward or undercutting motion

back-stabbing *n* actions or remarks that are treacherous and likely to cause harm to a person, esp a friend or colleague

backstage (,bæk'steɪdʒ) *adv* **1** behind the part of the theatre in view of the audience; in the dressing rooms, wings, etc **2** towards the rear of the stage ▷ *adj* **3** situated backstage **4** *informal* away from public view

backstairs ('bæk,steəz) *pl n* **1** a secondary staircase in a house, esp one originally for the use of servants ▷ *adj* Also: backstair **2** underhand: *backstairs gossip*

backstay ('bæk,steɪ) *n nautical* a stay leading aft from the upper part of a mast to the deck or stern

back story *n* the events which take place before, and which help to bring about, the events portrayed in a film

backstreet ('bæk,striːt) *n* **1** a street in a town remote from the main roads **2** (*modifier*) denoting illicit activities regarded as likely to take place in such a street: *a backstreet abortion*

backstroke ('bæk,strəuk) *n* Also called: **back crawl** *swimming* a stroke performed on the back, using backward circular strokes of each arm alternately and flipper movements of the feet

back-to-back *adj* (*usually postpositive*) **1** facing in opposite directions, often with the backs touching **2** *chiefly Brit* (of urban houses) built so that their backs are joined or separated only by a narrow alley

backtrack ('bæk,træk) *vb* (*intr*) **1** to return by the same route by which one has come **2** to retract or reverse one's opinion, action, policy, etc

back up *vb* (*adverb*) **1** (*tr*) to support or assist **2** (*intr*) *cricket* (of a nonstriking batsman) to move down the wicket in readiness for a run as a ball is bowled **3** (of water) to accumulate **4** (of traffic) to become jammed behind an accident or other obstruction **5** *computing* to make a copy of (a data file), esp for storage in another place as a security copy **6** *printing* to print the second side of (a sheet) **7** (*intr*, usually foll by *on*) *Austral* to repeat an action immediately ▷ *n* **backup** **8** a support or reinforcement **9 a** a reserve or substitute **b** (*as modifier*): *backup troops* **10** *US & Canadian* a musical accompaniment, esp for a pop singer **b** (*as modifier*): *backup singer* **11** the overflow from a blocked drain or pipe

backward ('bækwəd) *adj* **1** (*usually prenominal*) directed towards the rear: *a backward glance* **2** retarded in physical, material, or intellectual development **3 a** of or relating to the past; conservative or reactionary **b** (*in combination*): *backward-looking* **4** reluctant or bashful: *a backward lover* ▷ *adv* **5** a variant of **backwards** > '**backwardness** *n*

backwardation (,bækwə'deɪʃən) *n commerce* **1** the difference between the spot price for a commodity, including rent and interest, and the forward price **2** (formerly, on the Stock Exchange) postponement of delivery by a seller of securities until the next settlement period

backwards ('bækwədz) *or* **backward** *adv* **1** towards the rear **2** with the back foremost **3** in the reverse of usual order or direction **4** to or towards the past **5** into a worse state **6** towards the point of origin **7** **bend over backwards, lean over backwards** *or* **fall over backwards** *informal* to make a special effort, esp in order to please

backwash ('bæk,wɒʃ) *n* **1** water washed backwards by the motion of oars or other propelling devices **2** the backward flow of air set up by an aircraft's engines **3** a condition resulting from a previous event; repercussion

backwater ('bæk,wɔːtə) *n* **1** a body of stagnant water connected to a river **2** an isolated, backward, or intellectually stagnant place or condition

backwoods ('bæk,wʊdz) *pl n* **1** *chiefly US & Canadian* partially cleared, sparsely populated forests **2** any remote sparsely populated place **3** (*modifier*) of, from, or like the backwoods **4** (*modifier*) uncouth; rustic > '**back,woodsman** *n*

backword ('bæk,wɜːd) *n Brit dialect* the act or an instance of failing to keep a promise or commitment (esp in the phrase **give (someone) backword**)

back yard *n* **1** a yard at the back of a house, etc **2** in one's own back yard **a** close at hand **b** involving or implicating one

baclava ('bɑːklə,vɑː) *n* a variant spelling of **baklava**

Bacolod (bə'kɒləd) *n* a town in the Philippines, on the NW coast of Negros Island. Pop: 468 000 (2005 est)

bacon ('beɪkən) *n* **1** meat from the back and sides of a pig, dried, salted, and usually smoked **2** **bring home the bacon** *informal* **a** to achieve success **b** to provide material support **3** **save someone's bacon** *Brit informal* to help someone to escape from danger [c12: from Old French *bacon*, from Old High German *bahho*; related to Old Saxon *baco*; see BACK¹]

Bacon ('beɪkən) *n* **1 Francis**, Baron Verulam, Viscount St Albans. 1561–1626, English philosopher, statesman, and essayist; described the inductive method of reasoning: his works include *Essays* (1625), *The Advancement of Learning* (1605), and *Novum Organum* (1620) **2 Francis**. 1909–92, British painter, born in Dublin, noted for his distorted, richly coloured human figures, dogs, and carcasses **3 Roger**. ?1214–92, English Franciscan monk, scholar, and

scientist: stressed the importance of experiment, demonstrated that air is required for combustion, and first used lenses to correct vision. His *Opus Majus* (1266) is a compendium of all the sciences of his age

Baconian (beɪ'kəʊnɪən) *adj* **1** of or relating to Francis Bacon, Baron Verulam, Viscount St Albans (1561–1626), the English philosopher, statesman, and essayist, or to his inductive method of reasoning ▷ *n* **2** a follower of Bacon's philosophy **3** one who believes that plays attributed to Shakespeare were written by Bacon

BACS (bæks) *n acronym for* Bankers' Automated Clearing System; a method of making payments direct to a creditor's bank without using a cheque

bacteria (bæk'tɪərɪə) *pl n*, *sing* **-rium** (-rɪəm) a very large group of microorganisms comprising one of the three domains of living organisms. They are prokaryotic, unicellular, and either free-living in soil or water or parasites of plants or animals [c19: plural of New Latin *bacterium*, from Greek *baktērion*, literally: a little stick, from *baktron* rod, staff] > **bac'terial** *adj* > **bac'terially** *adv*

bactericide (bæk'tɪərɪ,saɪd) *n* a substance able to destroy bacteria > **bac,teri'cidal** *adj*

bacterio-, bacteri- *or sometimes before a vowel* **bacter-** *combining form* indicating bacteria or an action or condition relating to or characteristic of bacteria: *bacteriology; bactericide; bacteroid* [New Latin, from BACTERIA]

bacteriology (bæk,tɪərɪ'ɒlədʒɪ) *n* the branch of science concerned with the study of bacteria > **bacteriological** (bæk,tɪərɪə'lɒdʒɪkəl) *adj* > **bac,teri'ologist** *n*

bacteriophage (bæk'tɪərɪə,feɪdʒ) *n* a virus that is parasitic in a bacterium and multiplies within its host, which is destroyed when the new viruses are released. Often shortened to: **phage** > **bacteriophagic** (bæk,tɪərɪə'fædʒɪk) *adj* > **bacteriophagous** (bæk,tɪərɪ'ɒfəgəs) *adj*

bacterium (bæk'tɪərɪəm) *n* the singular of **bacteria**

Bactria ('bæktrɪə) *n* an ancient country of SW Asia, between the Hindu Kush mountains and the Oxus River: forms the present Balkh region in N Afghanistan

Bactrian camel *n* a two-humped camel, *Camelus bactrianus*, used as a beast of burden in the cold deserts of central Asia

bad¹ (bæd) *adj* **worse**, **worst** **1** not good; of poor quality; inadequate; inferior **2** (*often foll by at*) lacking skill or talent; incompetent: *a bad painter* **3** (often foll by *for*) harmful **4** immoral; evil **5** naughty; mischievous; disobedient **6** rotten; decayed; spoiled: *a bad egg* **7** severe; intense: *a bad headache* **8** incorrect; wrong; faulty: *bad pronunciation* **9** ill or in pain (esp in the phrase **feel bad**) **10** regretful, sorry, or upset (esp in the phrase **feel bad about**) **11** unfavourable; distressing: *bad news; a bad business* **12** offensive; unpleasant; disagreeable: *bad language; bad temper* **13** not valid or sound; void: *a bad cheque* **14** not recoverable: *a bad debt* **15 badder, baddest** *slang* good; excellent **16 go from bad to worse** to deteriorate even more **17 go bad** to putrefy; spoil **18 in a bad way** *informal* **a** seriously ill, through sickness or injury **b** in trouble of any kind **19 make the best of a bad job** to manage as well as possible in unfavourable circumstances **20 not bad** *or* **not so bad** *informal* passable; fair; fairly good **21 too bad** *informal* (often used dismissively) regrettable ▷ *n* **22** unfortunate or unpleasant events collectively (often in the phrase **take the bad with the good**) **23** an immoral or degenerate state (often in the phrase **go to the bad**) **24** the debit side of an account: *£200 to the bad* ▷ *adv* **25** *not standard* badly: *to want something bad* [c13: probably from *bæd-*, as the first element of Old English *bæddel* hermaphrodite, *bædling* sodomite] > '**baddish** *adj* > '**badness** *n*

bad² (bæd) *vb* a variant of: **bade**

bada-bing (,bædə'bɪŋ) *or* **bada-bing bada-boom** (,bædə'buːm) *sentence substitute US slang* an expression used to suggest that something can be done with no difficulty or delay [c20: perhaps imitative of the sound of something clicking into place]

Badajoz ('bædə,hɒz; *Spanish* ba'ðaxoθ) *n* a city in SW Spain: strategically positioned near the frontier with

Portugal. Pop: 138 415 (2003 est)

Badalona (*Spanish* baðaˈlona) *n* a port in NE Spain: an industrial suburb of Barcelona. Pop: 214 440 (2003 est)

bad blood *n* a feeling of intense hatred or hostility; enmity

bad cholesterol *n* a nontechnical name for: **low-density lipoprotein**

baddie or **baddy** (ˈbædɪ) *n, pl* **-dies** a bad character in a story, film, etc, esp an opponent of the hero

bade (bæd, beɪd) or **bad** *vb* past tense of: **bid**

Baden (ˈbaːdən) *n* a former state of West Germany, now part of Baden-Württemberg

Baden-Baden *n* a spa in SW Germany, in Baden-Württemberg. Pop: 53 938 (2003 est)

Baden-Powell (ˈbeɪdᵊnˈpəʊəl, -ˈpaʊəl) *n* **Robert Stephenson Smyth** (smɪθ, smaɪθ), 1st Baron Baden-Powell. 1857–1941, British general, noted for his defence of Mafeking (1899–1900) in the Boer War; founder of the Boy Scouts (1908) and (with his sister Agnes) the Girl Guides (1910)

Baden-Württemberg (*German* ˈbaːdənˈvyrtəmberk) *n* a state of SW Germany. Capital: Stuttgart. Pop: 53 938 (2003 est). Area: 35 742 sq km (13 800 sq miles)

Bader (ˈbaːdə) *n* Sir **Douglas**. 1910–82, British fighter pilot. Despite losing both legs after a flying accident (1931), he became a national hero as a pilot in World War II

badge (bædʒ) *n* **1** a distinguishing emblem or mark worn to signify membership, employment, achievement, etc **2** any revealing feature or mark [C14: from Norman French *bage*; related to Anglo-Latin *bagia*]

badger (ˈbædʒə) *n* **1** any of various stocky omnivorous musteline mammals of the subfamily *Melinae*, such as *Meles meles* (**Eurasian badger**), occurring in Europe, Asia, and North America: order *Carnivora* (carnivores). They are typically large burrowing animals, with strong claws and a thick coat striped black and white on the head ▷ *vb* **2** (*tr*) to pester or harass [C16: variant of *badgeard*, probably from BADGE (from the white mark on its forehead) + -ARD]

Bad Godesberg (*German* baːt ˈɡoːdəsberk) *n* the official name for **Godesberg**

bad hair day *n informal* **1** a day on which one's hair is untidy and unmanageable **2** a day of mishaps and general irritation

badinage (ˈbædɪˌnaːʒ) *n* playful or frivolous repartee or banter [C17: from French, from *badiner* to jest, banter, from Old Provençal *badar* to gape]

badlands (ˈbædˌlændz) *pl n* any deeply eroded barren area

Bad Lands *pl n* a deeply eroded barren region of SW South Dakota and NW Nebraska

badly (ˈbædlɪ) *adv* **worse, worst 1** poorly; defectively; inadequately **2** unfavourably; unsuccessfully; unfortunately: *our scheme worked out badly* **3** severely; gravely: *he was badly hurt* **4** incorrectly or inaccurately: *to speak German badly* **5** improperly; naughtily; wickedly: *to behave badly* **6** without humanity; cruelly: *to treat someone badly* **7** very much (esp in the phrases **need badly, badly in need of, want badly**) **8** regrettably: *he felt badly about it* **9** badly off poor; impoverished

badminton (ˈbædmɪntən) *n* **1** a game played with rackets and a shuttlecock, which is hit back and forth across a high net **2** Also called: **badminton cup** a long refreshing drink of claret with soda water and sugar [C19: named after BADMINTON House, where the game was first played]

Badminton (ˈbædmɪntən) *n* a village in SW England, in South Gloucestershire unitary authority, Gloucestershire: site of Badminton House, seat of the Duke of Beaufort; annual horse trials

bad-mouth *vb* (*tr*) *slang* to speak unfavourably about

Badoglio (*Italian* baˈdɔʎʎo) *n* **Pietro** (ˈpjetro). 1871–1956, Italian marshal; premier (1943–44) following Mussolini's downfall: arranged an armistice with the Allies (1943)

bad seed *n US, Canadian & Austral informal* a person who is seen as being congenitally disposed to wrongdoing and likely to be a bad influence on others

bad-tempered *adj* angry, irritable, or ungracious

bad trot *n Austral slang* a period of ill fortune

Baeck (*German* bɛk) *n* **Leo**. 1873–1956, German Jewish theologian: a leader of the German Jews during the Nazi period. His major work is *The Essence of Judaism* (1905)

Baeda (ˈbiːdə) *n* the Latin name for (Saint) **Bede**

Baedeker (ˈbeɪdɪkə) *n* any of a series of travel guidebooks issued by the German publisher Karl Baedeker (1801–59) or his firm

Baeyer (*German* ˈbaɪər) *n* **Johann Friedrich Wilhelm Adolf von** (ˈjohan ˈfriːdrɪç ˈvɪlhɛlm ˈaːdɔlf fɔn). 1835–1917, German chemist, noted for the synthesis of indigo: Nobel prize for chemistry 1905

Baez (ˈbaɪɛz) *n* **Joan**. born 1941, US rock and folk singer and songwriter, noted for the pure quality of her voice and for her committed pacifist and protest songs

BAF *abbreviation* British Athletic Federation

baffies (ˈbæfɪz) *pl n Scot dialect* slippers

Baffin Bay (ˈbæfɪn) *n* part of the Northwest Passage, situated between Baffin Island and Greenland [named after William *Baffin*, 17th-century English navigator]

Baffin Island *n* the largest island of the Canadian Arctic, between Greenland and Hudson Bay. Area: 476 560 sq km (184 000 sq miles)

baffle (ˈbæfᵊl) *vb* (*tr*) **1** to perplex; bewilder; puzzle **2** to frustrate (plans, efforts, etc) **3** to check, restrain, or regulate (the flow of a fluid or the emission of sound or light) ▷ *n* **4** Also called: **baffle board, baffle plate** a plate or mechanical device designed to restrain or regulate the flow of a fluid, the emission of light or sound, or the distribution of sound, esp in a loudspeaker or microphone [C16: perhaps from Scottish dialect *bachlen* to condemn publicly; perhaps related to French *bafouer* to disgrace] ▷ **ˈbafflement** *n* ▷ **ˈbaffler** *n* ▷ **ˈbaffling** *adj* ▷ **ˈbafflingly** *adv*

BAFTA (ˈbæftə) *n acronym for* British Academy of Film and Television Arts

bag (bæɡ) *n* **1** a flexible container with an opening at one end **2** Also called: **bagful** the contents of or amount contained in such a container **3** a piece of portable luggage **4** short for **handbag 5** anything that hangs loosely, sags, or is shaped like a bag, such as a loose fold of skin under the eyes or the bulging part of a sail **6** any pouch or sac forming part of the body of an animal, esp the udder of a cow **7** *hunting* the quantity of quarry taken in a single hunting trip or by a single hunter **8** *derogatory, slang* an ugly or bad-tempered woman (often in the phrase **old bag**) **9 bag and baggage** *informal* **a** with all one's belongings **b** entirely **10** a bag of bones a lean creature **11 in the bag** *slang* almost assured of succeeding or being obtained ▷ *vb* **bags, bagging, bagged 12** (*tr*) to put into a bag **13** to bulge or cause to bulge; swell **14** (*tr*) to capture or kill, as in hunting **15** (*tr*) to catch, seize, or steal **16** (*intr*) to hang loosely; sag **17** (*tr*) *Brit informal* to reserve or secure the right to do or to have something: *he bagged the best chair* ▷ See also **bags** [C13: probably from Old Norse *baggi*; related to Old French *bague* bundle, pack, Medieval Latin *baga* chest, sack, Flemish *bagge*]

bagasse (bəˈɡæs) *n* the pulp remaining after the extraction of juice from sugar cane or similar plants: used as fuel and for making paper, etc [C19: from French, from Spanish *bagazo* dregs, refuse, from *baga* husk, from Latin *bāca* berry]

bagatelle (ˌbæɡəˈtɛl) *n* **1** something of little value or significance; trifle **2** a board game in which balls are struck into holes, with pins as obstacles; pinball **3** a short light piece of music, esp for piano [C17: from French, from Italian *bagattella*, from (dialect) *bagatta* a little possession, from *baga* a possession, probably from Latin *bāca* berry]

Bagdad (bæɡˈdæd) *n* a variant spelling of **Baghdad**

Bagehot (ˈbædʒət) *n* **Walter**. 1826–77, English economist and journalist: editor of *The Economist*; author of *The English Constitution* (1867) *Physics and Politics* (1872), and *Lombard Street* (1873)

bagel or **beigel** (ˈbeɪɡᵊl) *n* a hard ring-shaped bread roll, characteristic of Jewish baking [C20: from Yiddish *beygel*, ultimately from Old High German *boug* ring]

baggage (ˈbæɡɪdʒ) *n* **1** suitcases, bags, etc, packed for a

b

journey; luggage **2** an army's portable equipment **3** *informal, old-fashioned* **a** a pert young woman **b** an immoral woman or prostitute **4** *Irish informal* a cantankerous old woman **5** *informal* previous knowledge and experience that a person may use or be influenced by in new circumstances: *cultural baggage* [c15: from Old French *bagage*, from *bague* a bundle, perhaps of Scandinavian origin; compare Old Norse *baggi* BAG]

baggy ('bægɪ) *adj* -gier, -giest (of clothes) hanging loosely; puffed out > 'baggily *adv* > 'bagginess *n*

baggy green *n* *Austral informal* **1** the Australian Test cricket cap **2** don the baggy green *or* wear the baggy green to represent Australia at Test cricket

bagh (bɑːg) *n* (in India and Pakistan) a garden [Urdu]

Baghdad *or* **Bagdad** (bæg'dæd) *n* the capital of Iraq, on the River Tigris: capital of the Abbasid Caliphate (762–1258). Pop: 5 910 000 (2005 est)

bag lady *n* a woman who is homeless and wanders city streets with all her possessions in shopping bags

bagman ('bægmən) *n, pl* -men **1** *Brit informal* a travelling salesman **2** *slang, chiefly US* a person who collects or distributes money for racketeers **3** *informal, chiefly Canadian* a person who solicits money or subscriptions for a political party **4** *Austral history* a tramp or swagman, esp one on horseback

bagnio ('bɑːnjəʊ) *n, pl* -ios **1** a brothel **2** *obsolete* an oriental prison for slaves **3** *obsolete* an Italian or Turkish bathhouse [c16: from Italian *bagno*, from Latin *balneum* bath, from Greek *balaneion*]

Bagnold ('bægnəʊld) *n* **Enid** (**Algerine**). 1889–1981, British novelist and playwright; her works include the novel *National Velvet* (1935) and the play *The Chalk Garden* (1955)

bagpipes ('bæg.paɪps) *pl n* any of a family of musical wind instruments in which sounds are produced in reed pipes supplied with air from a bag inflated either by the player's mouth, as in the **Irish bagpipes** or **Highland bagpipes** of Scotland, or by arm-operated bellows, as in the **Northumbrian bagpipes**

Bagram ('bægrəm) *n* an air base in NE Afghanistan, near Kabul; now under the control of US forces

bags (bægz) *pl n* **1** *informal* a lot; great deal **2** short for **Oxford bags 3** *Brit informal* any pair of trousers ▷ *interj* **4** Also called: bags I *children's slang, Brit & Austral* an indication of the desire to do, be, or have something

baguette *or* **baguet** (bæ'gɛt) *n* **1** a narrow French stick loaf **2** a small gem cut as a long rectangle **3** *architect* a small moulding having a semicircular cross section [c18: from French, from Italian *bacchetta* a little stick, from *bacchio* rod, from Latin *baculum* walking stick]

Baguio ('bægɪ,əʊ) *n* a city in the N Philippines, on N Luzon: summer capital of the Republic. Pop: 287 000 (2005 est)

bah (bɑː, bæ) *interj* an expression of contempt or disgust

Baha'í (bə'hɑːɪ) *n* **1** an adherent of the Baha'í Faith ▷ *adj* **2** of or relating to the Baha'í Faith [from Persian *bahāʾí*, literally: of glory, from *bahāʾ uʾllāh* glory of God, from Arabic]

Baha'í Faith *or* **Baha'í** *n* a religious system founded in 1863 by Baha'ullah, based on Babism and emphasizing the value of all religions and the spiritual unity of all mankind

Baha'ísm (ba'hɑː,ɪzəm) *n* another name, not in Baha'í use, for the **Baha'í Faith**

Bahamas (bə'hɑːməz) *or* **Bahama Islands** *pl n* the Bahamas a group of over 700 coral islands (about 20 of which are inhabited) in the Caribbean: a British colony from 1783 until 1964; an independent nation within the Commonwealth from 1973. Language: English. Currency: Bahamian dollar. Capital: Nassau. Pop: 317 000 (2004 est). Area: 13 939 sq km (5381 sq miles) > Bahamian (bə'heɪmɪən, -'hɑː-) *adj, n*

Baha'ullah (,bɑːhɑː'ʊlə) *n* title of *Mirza Hosein Ali*. 1817–92, Persian religious leader: originally a Shiite Muslim, later a disciple of the Bab: founder of the Baha'í Faith

Bahawalpur (,bæhɑː'wɒlpə) *n* an industrial city in Pakistan: cotton, soap. Pop: 563 000 (2005 est)

Bahia (ba'hiːə; *Portuguese* bɐ'iːɐ) *n* **1** a state of E Brazil, on the Atlantic coast. Capital: Salvador. Pop: 13 323 212

(2002). Area: about 562 000 sq km (217 000 sq miles) **2** the former name of **San Salvador**

Bahía Blanca (*Spanish* ba'ia 'blanka) *n* a port in E Argentina. Pop: 276 000 (2005 est)

Bahia de los Cochinos (ba'ia de los ko'tʃinos) *n* the Spanish name for the **Bay of Pigs**

Bahrain *or* **Bahrein** (bɑː'reɪn) *n* an independent sheikhdom on the Persian Gulf, consisting of several islands: under British protection until the declaration of independence in 1971. It has large oil reserves. Language: Arabic. Religion: Muslim. Currency: dinar. Capital: Manama. Pop: 739 000 (2004 est). Area: 678 sq km (262 sq miles) > Bahraini *or* Bahreini (bɑː'reɪnɪ) *adj, n*

bahu (bɑː'huː) *n* (in India) a daughter-in-law [Hindi]

Baikal (baɪ'kɑːl, -'kæl) *n* Lake Baikal a lake in Russia, in SE Siberia: the largest freshwater lake in Eurasia and the deepest in the world. Greatest depth: over 1500 m (5000 ft). Area: about 33 670 sq km (13 000 sq miles). Russian name: Ozero Baykal

Baikonur (baɪ'kəʊnə) *n* a launching site for spacecraft in central Kazakhstan; formerly the centre for the Soviet space programme, now leased from Kazakhstan by Russia

bail¹ (beɪl) *law* ▷ *n* **1** a sum of money by which a person is bound to take responsibility for the appearance in court of another person or himself or herself, forfeited if the person fails to appear **2** the person or persons so binding themselves; surety **3** the system permitting release of a person from custody where such security has been taken: *he was released on bail* **4** jump bail *or* formal forfeit bail to fail to appear in court to answer to a charge **5** stand bail *or* go bail to act as surety (for someone) ▷ *vb* (*tr*) **6** (often foll by *out*) to release or obtain the release of (a person) from custody, security having been taken [c14: from Old French: custody, from *baillier* to hand over, from Latin *bāiulāre* to carry burdens, from *bāiulus* carrier, of obscure origin]

bail² *or* **bale** (beɪl) *vb* (often foll by *out*) to remove (water) from (a boat) [c13: from Old French *baille* bucket, from Latin *bāiulus* carrier] > 'bailer *or* 'baler *n*

bail³ (beɪl) *n* **1** *cricket* either of two small wooden bars placed across the tops of the stumps to form the wicket **2** *agriculture* a partition between stalls in a stable or barn, for horses **3** *Austral & NZ* a framework in a cowshed used to secure the head of a cow during milking ▷ *vb* **4** See **bail up** [c18: from Old French *baile* stake, fortification, probably from Latin *baculum* stick]

bail⁴ *or* **bale** (beɪl) *n* the semicircular handle of a kettle, bucket, etc [c15: probably of Scandinavian origin; compare Old Norse *beygja* to bend]

bail bondsman ('bɒndzmən) *n* *law* an individual or firm that lends bail money to defendants awaiting trial

bailey ('beɪlɪ) *n* the outermost wall or court of a castle [c13: from Old French *baille* enclosed court, from *bailler* to enclose; see BAIL³]

Bailey ('beɪlɪ) *n* **1** **David**. born 1938, English photographer **2** **Nathan** *or* **Nathaniel**. died 1742, English lexicographer: compiler of *An Universal Etymological English Dictionary* (1721–27)

Bailey bridge *n* a temporary bridge made of prefabricated steel panels that can be rapidly assembled [c20: named after Sir Donald Coleman *Bailey* (1901–85), its English designer]

bailie ('beɪlɪ) *n* (in Scotland) a municipal magistrate [c13: from Old French *bailli*, from earlier *baillif* BAILIFF]

bailiff ('beɪlɪf) *n* **1** *Brit* the agent or steward of a landlord or landowner **2** a sheriff's officer who serves writs and summonses, makes arrests, and ensures that the sentences of the court are carried out **3** *chiefly Brit* (formerly) a high official having judicial powers **4** *chiefly US* an official having custody of prisoners appearing in court [c13: from Old French *baillif*, from *bail* custody; see BAIL¹]

bailiwick ('beɪlɪwɪk) *n* **1** *law* the area over which a bailiff has jurisdiction **2** a person's special field of interest, authority, or skill [c15: from BAILI(E) + WICK²]

Baillie ('beɪlɪ) *n* Dame **Isobel**. 1895–1983, British soprano

bail out *or* **bale out** *vb* (*adverb*) **1** (*intr*) to make an emergency parachute jump from an aircraft **2** (*tr*) *informal* to help (a person, organization, etc) out of a predicament

bail up *vb* (*adverb*) **1** *Austral & NZ informal* to confine (a cow) or (of a cow) to be confined by the head in a bail. See *bail*³ **2** (*tr*) *Austral history* (of a bushranger) to hold under guard in order to rob **3** (*intr*) *Austral* to submit to robbery without offering resistance **4** (*tr*) *Austral informal* to accost or detain, esp in conversation; buttonhole

Bainbridge ('bein,bridʒ) *n* **Beryl**. born 1934, British novelist and playwright. Novels include *The Dressmaker* (1973), *Injury Time* (1977), *Master Georgie* (1998), and *According to Queeney* (2001)

bain-marie (French bɛ̃mari) *n, pl bains-marie* (bɛ̃mari) a vessel for holding hot water, in which sauces and other dishes are gently cooked or kept warm [c19: from French, from Medieval Latin *balneum Mariae*, literally: bath of Mary, inaccurate translation of Medieval Greek *kaminos Marios*, literally: furnace of Miriam, alleged author of a treatise on alchemy]

Bairam (baɪ'ræm, 'baɪræm) *n* either of two Muslim festivals, one (**Lesser Bairam**) falling at the end of Ramadan, the other (**Greater Bairam**) 70 days later at the end of the Islamic year [from Turkish *bayrām*]

Baird (bɛəd) *n* **John Logie** (ˈləʊgɪ). 1888–1946, Scottish engineer: inventor of a 240-line mechanically scanned system of television, replaced in 1935 by a 405-line electrically scanned system

bairn (bɛən) *n* *Scot* bern) *n* *Scot & Northern English* a child [Old English *bearn*; related to *bearm* lap, Old Norse, Old High German *barn* child]

Bairnsfather ('bɛənz,fɑːðə) *n* **Bruce**. 1888–1959, British cartoonist, born in India: best known for his cartoons of the war in the trenches during World War I

bait¹ (beɪt) *n* **1** something edible, such as soft bread paste, worms, or pieces of meat, fixed to a hook or in a trap to attract fish or animals **2** an enticement; temptation **3** a variant spelling of: *bate*³ **4** *archaic* a short stop for refreshment during a journey ▷ *vb* **5** (*tr*) to put a piece of food on or in (a hook or trap) **6** (*tr*) to persecute or tease **7** (*tr*) to entice; tempt **8** (*tr*) to set dogs upon (a bear, etc) **9** (*intr*) *archaic* to stop for rest and refreshment during a journey [c13: from Old Norse *beita* to hunt, persecute; related to Old English *bǣtan* to restrain, hunt, Old High German *beizen*]

● USAGE The phrase *with bated breath* is sometimes ● wrongly spelled *with baited breath*

bait² (beɪt) *vb* a variant spelling of *bate*²

baize (beɪz) *n* a woollen fabric resembling felt, usually green, used mainly for the tops of billiard tables [c16: from Old French *baies*, plural of *baie* baize, from *bai* reddish brown, BAY⁵, perhaps the original colour of the fabric]

Baja California Norte ('nɔːteɪ) *n* a state of NW Mexico, in the N part of the Lower California peninsula. Capital: Mexicali. Pop: 2 487 700 (2000). Area: about 71 500 sq km (27 600 sq miles)

Baja California Sur *n* a state of NW Mexico, in the S part of the Lower California peninsula. Capital: La Paz. Pop: 423 516 (2000). Area: 73 475 sq km (28 363 sq miles)

bake (beɪk) *vb* **1** (*tr*) to cook by dry heat in or as if in an oven **2** (*intr*) to cook bread, pastry, etc, in an oven **3** to make or become hardened by heat **4** (*intr*) *informal* to be extremely hot, as in the heat of the sun ▷ *n* **5** *US* a party at which the main dish is baked **6** a batch of things baked at one time **7** *Caribbean* a small flat fried cake [Old English *bacan*; related to Old Norse *baka*, Old High German *bahhan* to bake, Greek *phōgein* to parch, roast]

bakeapple ('beɪk,æpᵊl) *n* *Canadian* the fruit of the cloudberry

baked Alaska *n* a dessert consisting of cake and ice cream covered with meringue and cooked very quickly in a hot oven

baked beans *pl n* haricot beans, baked and tinned in tomato sauce

Bakelite ('beɪkə,laɪt) *n* *trademark* any one of a class of thermosetting resins used as electric insulators and for making plastic ware, telephone receivers, etc [c20: named after L. H. Baekeland (1863–1944), Belgian-born US inventor; see -ITE¹]

baker ('beɪkə) *n* a person whose business or employment is to make or sell bread, cakes, etc

Baker ('beɪkə) *n* **1** Sir **Benjamin**. 1840–1907, British engineer who, with Sir John Fowler, designed and constructed much of the London underground railway, the Forth Railway Bridge, and the first Aswan Dam **2 Chet**, full name *Chesney H. Baker*. 1929–88, US jazz trumpeter and singer **3** Dame **Janet**. born 1933, British mezzo-soprano **4** Sir **Samuel White**. 1821–93, British explorer: discovered Lake Albert (1864)

baker's dozen *n* thirteen [c16: from the bakers' former practice of giving thirteen rolls where twelve were requested, to protect themselves against accusations of giving light weight]

bakery ('beɪkərɪ) *n, pl* -eries **1** Also called: bakehouse a room or building equipped for baking **2** a shop in which bread, cakes, etc, are sold

Bakewell ('beɪkwɛl) *n* **Robert**. 1725–95, English agriculturist; radically improved livestock breeding, esp of cattle and sheep

bakgat (bʌk'xʊt) *adj* *South African* fine, excellent, marvellous [c20: from Afrikaans]

Bakhtaran (ˌbæktəˈrɑːn, -ˈræn) *n* the former name (1987–1995) of **Kermanshah**

baking powder *n* any of various powdered mixtures that contain sodium bicarbonate, starch (usually flour), and one or more slightly acidic compounds, such as cream of tartar: used in baking as a substitute for yeast

bakkie ('bʌki:) *n* *South African* a small truck with an open body and low sides [c20: from Afrikaans *bak* container]

baklava *or* **baclava** ('bɑːklə,vɑː) *n* a rich cake of Middle Eastern origin consisting of thin layers of pastry filled with nuts and honey [from Turkish]

baksheesh *or* **backsheesh** ('bækʃiːʃ) (in some Eastern countries, esp formerly) *n* money given as a tip, a present, or alms [c17: from Persian *bakhshīsh*, from *bakhshīdan* to give; related to Sanskrit *bhaksati* he enjoys]

Bakst (Russian bakst) *n* **Leon Nikolayevich** (lɪ'ɒn nika'lajivitʃ). 1866–1924, Russian painter and stage designer, noted particularly for his richly coloured sets for Diaghilev's *Ballet Russe* (1909–21)

Baku (Russian ba'ku) *n* the capital of Azerbaijan, a port on the Caspian Sea: important for its extensive oilfields. Pop: 1 830 000 (2005 est)

Bakunin (Russian ba'kunin) *n* **Mikhail** (mixa'il). 1814–76, Russian anarchist and writer: a prominent member of the First International, expelled from it after conflicts with Marx

Bala ('bælə) *n* **Lake Bala** a narrow lake in Gwynedd: the largest natural lake in Wales. Length: 6 km (4 miles)

Balaam ('beɪlæm) *n* *Old Testament* a Mesopotamian diviner who, when summoned to curse the Israelites, prophesied future glories for them instead, after being reproached by his ass (Numbers 22–23)

Balaclava *or* **Balaclava helmet** (ˌbælə'klɑːvə) *n* (*often not capitals*) a close-fitting woollen hood that covers the ears and neck, as originally worn by soldiers in the Crimean War [c19: named after BALAKLAVA]

Balaguer (ˌbælə'gwɛə) *n* **Joaquin** ('jɔːakin). 1907–2002, Dominican statesman; president of the Dominican Republic (1960–62, 1966–78, 1986–96)

Balakirev (Russian ba'lakiríf) *n* **Mily Alexeyevich** ('milij alɪk'sjejivitʃ). 1837–1910, Russian composer, whose works include two symphonic poems, two symphonies, and many arrangements of Russian folk songs

Balaklava *or* **Balaclava** (ˌbælə'klɑːvə; *Russian* bələ'klavə) *n* a small port in Ukraine, in S Crimea: scene of an inconclusive battle (1854), which included the charge of the Light Brigade, during the Crimean War

balalaika (ˌbælə'laɪkə) *n* a plucked musical instrument, usually having a triangular body and three strings: used chiefly for Russian folk music [c18: from Russian]

balance ('bæləns) *n* **1** a weighing device, generally consisting of a horizontal beam pivoted at its centre, from the ends of which two pans are suspended. The substance to be weighed is placed in one pan and known weights are placed in the other until the beam returns to the horizontal **2** a state of equilibrium **3** something that brings about such a state

4 equilibrium of the body; steadiness: *to lose one's balance* **5** emotional stability; calmness of mind **6** harmony in the parts of a whole **7** the act of weighing factors, quantities, etc, against each other **8** the power to influence or control: *he held the balance of power* **9** something that remains or is left: *let me have the balance of what you owe me* **10** *accounting* **a** equality of debit and credit totals in an account **b** a difference between such totals **11** in the balance in an uncertain or undecided condition **12** on balance after weighing up all the factors **13** strike a balance to make a compromise ▷ *vb* **14** (*tr*) to weigh in or as if in a balance **15** (*intr*) to be or come into equilibrium **16** (*tr*) to bring into or hold in equilibrium **17** (*tr*) to assess or compare the relative weight, importance, etc, of **18** (*tr*) to act so as to equalize; be equal to **19** (*tr*) to compose or arrange so as to create a state of harmony **20** (*tr*) to bring (a chemical or mathematical equation) into balance **21** (*tr*) *accounting* **a** to compute the credit and debit totals of (an account) in order to determine the difference **b** to equalize the credit and debit totals of (an account) by making certain entries **c** to settle or adjust (an account) by paying any money due **22** (*intr*) (of a business account, balance sheet, etc) to have the debit and credit totals equal **23** to match or counter (one's dancing partner or his or her steps) by moving towards and away from him or her [C13: from Old French, from Vulgar Latin *bilancia* (unattested), from Late Latin *bilanx* having two scalepans, from BI-¹ + *lanx* scale] > 'balanceable *adj* > 'balancer *n*

Balance ('bæləns) *n* the Balance the constellation Libra, the seventh sign of the zodiac

balance of payments *n* the difference over a given time between total payments to foreign nations, arising from imports of goods and services and transfers abroad of capital, interest, grants, etc, and total receipts from foreign nations, arising from exports of goods and services and transfers from abroad of capital, interest, grants, etc

balance of power *n* the distribution of power among countries so that no one nation can seriously threaten the fundamental interests of another

balance of trade *n* *economics* the difference in value between total exports and total imports of goods

balance sheet *n* a statement that shows the financial position of a business enterprise at a specified date by listing the asset balances and the claims on such assets

balance wheel *n* a wheel oscillating against the hairspring of a timepiece, thereby regulating its beat

Balanchine ('bælən,tʃiːn, ,bælən'tʃiːn) *n* **George**. 1904–83, US choreographer, born in Russia

balata ('bælətə) *n* **1** a tropical American sapotaceous tree, *Manilkara bidentata*, yielding a latex-like sap **2** a rubber-like gum obtained from this sap: used as a substitute for gutta-percha [from American Spanish, of Carib origin]

Balaton (*Hungarian* 'bɔlɔtɔn) *n* Lake Balaton a large shallow lake in W Hungary. Area: 689 sq km (266 sq miles)

Balbo (*Italian* 'balbo) *n* **Italo** ('italo). 1896–1940, Italian Fascist politician and airman: minister of aviation (1929–33)

Balboa¹ (bæl'bəʊə; *Spanish* bal'βoa) *n* **Vasco Núñez de** ('basko 'nuɲeθ de). ?1475–1519, Spanish explorer, who discovered the Pacific Ocean in 1513

Balboa² (bæl'bəʊə; *Spanish* bal'βoa) *n* a port in Panama at the Pacific end of the Panama Canal: the administrative centre of the former Canal Zone. Pop: 2750 (1990)

Balcon ('bɔːlkən) *n* Sir **Michael**. 1896–1977, British film producer; his films made at Ealing Studios include the comedies *Kind Hearts and Coronets* (1949) and *The Lavender Hill Mob* (1951)

balcony ('bælkənɪ) *n*, *pl* **-nies 1** a platform projecting from the wall of a building with a balustrade or railing along its outer edge, often with access from a door or window **2** a gallery in a theatre or auditorium, above the dress circle **3** *US & Canadian* any circle or gallery in a theatre or auditorium including the dress circle [C17: from Italian *balcone*, probably from Old High German

balko beam; see BALK] > 'balconied *adj*

bald (bɔːld) *adj* **1** having no hair or fur, esp (of a man) having no hair on all or most of the scalp **2** lacking natural growth or covering **3** plain or blunt: *a bald statement* **4** bare or simple; unadorned **5** Also called: **baldfaced** (of certain birds and other animals) having white markings on the head and face **6** (of a tyre) having a worn tread [C14 *ballede* (literally: having a white spot); related to Danish *bældet*, Greek *phalaros* having a white spot] > 'baldish *adj* > 'baldly *adv* > 'baldness *n*

baldachin, baldaquin ('bɔːldəkɪn) *or* **baldachino** (,bɔːldə'kiːnəʊ) *n* **1** a richly ornamented silk and gold brocade **2** a canopy of fabric or stone over an altar, shrine, or throne in a Christian church or carried in Christian religious processions over an object of veneration [Old English *baldekin*, from Italian *baldacchino*, literally: stuff from Baghdad, from *Baldacco* Baghdad, noted for its brocades]

bald eagle *n* a large eagle, *Haliaeetus leucocephalus*, of North America, having a white head and tail, a yellow bill, and dark wings and body. It is the US national bird

Balder ('bɔːldə) *n* *Norse myth* a god, son of Odin and Frigg, noted for his beauty and sweet nature. He was killed by a bough of mistletoe thrown by the blind god Höd, misled by the malicious Loki

balderdash ('bɔːldə,dæʃ) *n* stupid or illogical talk; senseless rubbish [C16: of unknown origin]

balding ('bɔːldɪŋ) *adj* somewhat bald or becoming bald

baldric ('bɔːldrɪk) *n* a wide silk sash or leather belt worn over the right shoulder to the left hip for carrying a sword, etc [C13: from Old French *baudrei*, of Frankish origin]

Baldwin ('bɔːldwɪn) *n* **1 James Arthur**. 1924–87, US Black writer, whose works include the novel *Go Tell it on the Mountain* (1954) **2 Stanley**, 1st Earl Baldwin of Bewdley. 1867–1947, British Conservative statesman: prime minister (1923–24, 1924–29, 1935–37)

Baldwin I *n* 1058–1118, crusader and first king of Jerusalem (1100–18), who captured Acre (1104), Beirut (1109), and Sidon (1110)

bale¹ (beɪl) *n* **1** a large bundle, esp of a raw or partially processed material, bound by ropes, wires, etc, for storage or transportation **2** *US* 500 pounds of cotton ▷ *vb* **3** to make (hay, etc) into a bale or bales [C14: probably from Old French *bale*, from Old High German *balla* BALL¹]

bale² (beɪl) *n* *archaic* **1** evil; injury **2** woe; suffering; pain [Old English *bealu*; related to Old Norse *böl* evil, Gothic *balwa*, Old High German *balo*]

bale³ (beɪl) *vb* a variant spelling of **bail²**

bale⁴ (beɪl) *n* a variant spelling of **bail⁴**

Bâle (bal) *n* the French name for **Basle**

Balearic Islands (,bælɪ'ærɪk) *pl n* a group of islands in the W Mediterranean, consisting of Majorca, Minorca, Ibiza, Formentera, Cabrera, and 11 islets: a province of Spain. Capital: Palma, on Majorca. Pop: 1 071 500 (2003 est). Area: 5012 sq km (1935 sq miles)

baleen (bə'liːn) *n* whalebone [C14: from Latin *bālaena* whale; related to Greek *phalaina* whale]

baleen whale *n* another name for **whalebone whale**

baleful ('beɪlful) *adj* harmful, menacing, or vindictive > 'balefully *adv* > 'balefulness *n*

Balenciaga (*Spanish* balen'θjaɣa) *n* **Cristobal** (kris'toβal). 1895–1972, Spanish couturier

baler ('beɪlə) *n* an agricultural machine for making bales of hay, etc. Also called: baling machine

Balfour ('bælfɔː, -fə, -fʊə) *n* **Arthur James**, 1st Earl of Balfour. 1848–1930, British Conservative statesman: prime minister (1902–05); foreign secretary (1916–19)

Bali ('baːlɪ) *n* an island in Indonesia, east of Java: mountainous, rising over 3000 m (10 000 ft). Capital: Denpasar. Pop: 3 151 162 (2000). Area: 5558 sq km (2146 sq miles) > ,Bali'nese *adj*, *n*

Balikpapan (,baːlɪk'paːpaːn) *n* a city in Indonesia, on the SE coast of Borneo. Pop: 409 023 (2000)

Baliol *or* **Balliol** ('beɪlɪəl) *n* **Edward**. ?1283–1364, king of Scotland (1332, 1333–56) **2** his father, **John**. 1249–1315, king of Scotland (1292–96): defeated and imprisoned by Edward I of England (1296)

balk *or* **baulk** (bɔːk, bɔːlk) *vb* **1** (*intr*; usually foll by *at*) to stop short, esp suddenly or unexpectedly; jib: *the horse balked at the jump* **2** (*intr*; foll by *at*) to turn away abruptly; recoil: *he balked at the idea of murder* **3** (*tr*) to thwart, check, disappoint, or foil: *he was balked in his plans* ▷ *n* **4** a roughly squared heavy timber beam **5** a timber tie beam of a roof **6** an unploughed ridge to prevent soil erosion or mark a division on common land **7** an obstacle; hindrance; disappointment **8** *baseball* an illegal motion by a pitcher towards the plate or towards the base when there are runners on base, esp without delivering the ball ▷ See also **baulk** [Old English *balca*; related to Old Norse *bálkr* partition, Old High German *balco* beam]

Balkan ('bɔːlkən) *adj* of, denoting, or relating to the Balkan States or their inhabitants, the Balkan Peninsula, or the Balkan Mountains

Balkan Mountains *pl n* a mountain range extending across Bulgaria from the Black Sea to the eastern border. Highest peak: Mount Botev, 2376 m (7793 ft)

Balkan Peninsula *n* a large peninsula in SE Europe, between the Adriatic and Aegean Seas

Balkan States *pl n* the countries of the Balkan Peninsula: the former Yugoslavian Republics, Romania, Bulgaria, Albania, Greece, and the European part of Turkey. Also called: **the Balkans**

Balkh (baːlk) *n* a region of N Afghanistan, corresponding to ancient Bactria. Chief town: Mazar-i-Sharif

Balkhash (*Russian* bal'xaʃ) *n* Lake Balkhash a salt lake in SE Kazakhstan: fed by the Ili River. Area: about 18 000 sq km (7000 sq miles)

Balkis ('bælkɪs) *n* the name in the Koran of the queen of **Sheba**[1]

balky *or* **baulky** ('bɔːkɪ, 'bɔːlkɪ) *adj* **balkier, balkiest** *or* **baulkier, baulkiest** inclined to stop abruptly and unexpectedly: *a balky horse*

ball[1] (bɔːl) *n* **1** a spherical or nearly spherical body or mass **2** a round or roundish body, either solid or hollow, of a size and composition suitable for any of various games: football, golf, billiards, etc **3** a ball propelled in a particular way in a sport: *a high ball* **4** any of various rudimentary games with a ball: *to play ball* **5** *cricket* a single delivery of the ball by the bowler to the batsman **6** *baseball* a single delivery of the ball by a pitcher outside certain limits and not swung at by the batter **7** a a solid nonexplosive projectile for a firearm. See **shell** (sense 6) **b** such projectiles collectively **8** any more or less rounded part or protuberance: *the ball of the foot* **9** *slang* a testicle. See **balls** **10** *vet science* another word for **bolus 11** *horticulture* the hard mass of roots and earth removed with the rest of the plant during transplanting **12** ball of muscle *Austral* a very strong, fit, or forceful person **13** have the ball at one's feet to have the chance of doing something **14** keep the ball rolling to maintain the progress of a project, plan, etc **15** on the ball *informal* alert; informed **16** play ball *informal* to cooperate **17** set the ball rolling *or* start the ball rolling to open or initiate (an action, discussion, movement, etc) **18** the ball is in your court you are obliged to make the next move ▷ *vb* **19** (*tr*) to make, form, wind, etc, into a ball or balls: *to ball wool* **20** (*intr*) to gather into a ball or balls **21** *taboo, slang, chiefly US* to copulate (with) [c13: from Old Norse *böllr*; related to Old High German *balla*, Italian *palla* French *balle*]

● USAGE Sense 9 of this word was formerly considered
● to be taboo, and it was labelled as such in previous
● editions of *Collins English Dictionary*. However, it has now
● become acceptable in speech, although some older or
● more conservative people may object to its use

ball[2] (bɔːl) *n* **1** a social function for dancing, esp one that is lavish or formal **2** *informal* a very enjoyable time (esp in the phrase **have a ball**) [c17: from French *bal* (n), from Old French *baller* (vb), from Late Latin *ballāre* to dance, from Greek *ballizein*]

Ball (bɔːl) *n* **John**. died 1381, English priest: executed as one of the leaders of the Peasants' Revolt (1381)

ballad ('bæləd) *n* **1** a narrative song with a recurrent refrain **2** a narrative poem in short stanzas of popular origin, originally sung to a repeated tune **3** a slow sentimental song, esp a pop song [c15: from Old French

balade, from Old Provençal *balada* song accompanying a dance, from *balar* to dance, from Late Latin *ballāre*; see **BALL**[2]]

ballade (bæ'lɑːd; *French* balad) *n* **1** *prosody* a verse form consisting of three stanzas and an envoy, all ending with the same line. The first three stanzas commonly have eight or ten lines each and the same rhyme scheme **2** *music* an instrumental composition, esp for piano, based on or intended to evoke a narrative

balladeer (ˌbælə'dɪə) *n* a singer of ballads

Ballance ('bæləns) *n* **John**. 1839–93, New Zealand statesman, born in Northern Ireland: prime minister of New Zealand (1891–93)

ball-and-socket joint *or* **ball joint** *n* a coupling between two rods, tubes, etc, that consists of a spherical part fitting into a spherical socket, allowing free movement within a specific conical volume

Ballantyne ('bælən,taɪn) *n* **R(obert) M(ichael)**. 1825–94, British author, noted for such adventure stories as *The Coral Island* (1857)

Ballarat ('bælə,ræt, ˌbælə'ræt) *n* a town in SE Australia, in S central Victoria: originally the centre of a gold-mining region. Pop: 72 999 (2001)

Ballard ('bælɑːd) *n* **J(ames) G(raham)**. born 1930, British novelist, born in China; his books include *Crash* (1973), *The Unlimited Dream Company* (1979), *Empire of the Sun* (1984), *Cocaine Nights* (1996), and *Super-Cannes* (2000)

ballast ('bæləst) *n* **1** any dense heavy material, such as lead or iron pigs, used to stabilize a vessel, esp one that is not carrying cargo **2** crushed rock, broken stone, etc, used for the foundation of a road or railway track **3** anything that provides stability or weight **4** *electronics* a device for maintaining the current in a circuit ▷ *vb* (*tr*) **5** to give stability or weight to [c16: probably from Low German; related to Old Danish, Old Swedish *barlast*, literally: bare load (without commercial value), from *bar* bare, mere + *last* load, burden]

ball bearing *n* **1** a bearing consisting of a number of hard steel balls rolling between a metal sleeve fitted over the rotating shaft and an outer sleeve held in the bearing housing, so reducing friction between moving parts while providing support for the shaft **2** a metal ball, esp one used in such a bearing

ball boy *or* **ball girl** *n* (esp in tennis) a person who retrieves balls that go out of play

ballbreaker ('bɔːl,breɪkə) *n* *slang* a person, esp a woman, whose character and behaviour may be regarded as threatening a man's sense of power [c20: from BALL[1] (in the sense: testicle) + BREAKER[1]]

ball cock *n* a device for regulating the flow of a liquid into a tank, cistern, etc, consisting of a floating ball mounted at one end of an arm and a valve on the other end that opens and closes as the ball falls and rises with the water level in the cistern

ballerina (ˌbælə'riːnə) *n* a female ballet dancer [c18: from Italian, feminine of *ballerino* dancing master, from *ballare* to dance, from Late Latin *ballāre*: see **BALL**[2]]

Ballesteros (ˌbælɛ'stɛrɒs; *Spanish* baʎes'teros) *n* **Severiano** (sevɛ'rjano). born 1957, Spanish professional golfer: won the British Open Championship (1979; 1984; 1988)

ballet ('bæleɪ, bæ'leɪ) *n* **1** a classical style of expressive dancing based on precise conventional steps with gestures and movements of grace and fluidity **2** a theatrical representation of a story or theme performed to music by ballet dancers **3** a troupe of ballet dancers **4** a piece of music written for a ballet [c17: from French, from Italian *balletto* literally: a little dance, from *ballare* to dance; see **BALL**[2]] ▷ **balletic** (bæ'lɛtɪk) *adj*

balletomania (ˌbælɪtəʊ'meɪnɪə) *n* passionate enthusiasm for ballet [c20: from BALLET + -O- + -MANIA] ▷ **balletomane** ('bælɪtəʊ,meɪn) *n*

ball game *n* **1** any game played with a ball **2** *US & Canadian* a game of baseball **3** *informal* a situation; state of affairs (esp in the phrase **a whole new ball game**)

ball hockey *n* *Canadian* a game similar to ice hockey, but played on foot on a hard surface without ice, using a hard plastic ball instead of a puck

ballicatter (ˌbælɪ'kætə) *n* (in Newfoundland) ice that

b

forms along a shore from waves and spray

Balliol ('beɪlɪəl) *n* See **Baliol**

ballista (bə'lɪstə) *n, pl* **-tae** (-ti:) an ancient catapult for hurling stones, etc [C16: from Latin, ultimately from Greek *ballein* to throw]

ballistic (bə'lɪstɪk) *adj* 1 of or relating to ballistics 2 denoting or relating to the flight of projectiles after power has been cut off, moving under their own momentum and the external forces of gravity and air resistance 3 (of a measurement or measuring instrument) depending on a brief impulse or current that causes a movement related to the quantity to be measured: *a ballistic pendulum* 4 **go ballistic** *informal* to become enraged or frenziedly violent ▷ **bal'listically** *adv*

ballistic missile *n* a missile that has no wings or fins and that follows a ballistic trajectory when its propulsive power is discontinued

ballistics (bə'lɪstɪks) *n* (*functioning as singular*) the study of the flight dynamics of projectiles, either through the interaction of the forces of propulsion, the aerodynamics of the projectile, atmospheric resistance, and gravity (**exterior ballistics**), or through these forces along with the means of propulsion, and the design of the propelling weapon and projectile (**interior ballistics**)

ball lightning *n meteorol* a luminous electrically charged ball occasionally seen during electrical storms

ballocks ('bɒləks, 'bæl-) *pl n, interj, vb* a variant spelling of **bollocks**

ball of fire *n informal* a very lively person

balloon (bə'lu:n) *n* 1 an inflatable rubber bag of various sizes, shapes, and colours: usually used as a plaything or party decoration 2 a large impermeable bag inflated with a lighter-than-air gas, designed to rise and float in the atmosphere. It may have a basket or gondola for carrying passengers, etc 3 a circular or elliptical figure containing the words or thoughts of a character in a cartoon 4 *Brit* a a kick or stroke that propels a ball high into the air b (*as modifier*): *a balloon shot* 5 *chem* a round-bottomed flask 6 a large rounded brandy glass 7 *commerce* a a large sum paid as an irregular instalment of a loan repayment b (*as modifier*): *a balloon loan* 8 *surgery* a an inflatable plastic tube used for dilating blood vessels or parts of the alimentary canal b (*as modifier*): *balloon angioplasty* 9 **go down like a lead balloon** *informal* to be completely unsuccessful or unpopular 10 **when the balloon goes up** *informal* when the trouble or action begins ▷ *vb* 11 (*intr*) to go up or fly in a balloon 12 (*intr*) to increase or expand significantly and rapidly: *losses ballooned to £278 million* 13 to inflate or be inflated; distend; swell: *the wind ballooned the sails* 14 (*tr*) *Brit* to propel (a ball) high into the air [C16 in the sense: ball, ball game: from Italian dialect *ballone*, from *balla*, of Germanic origin; compare Old High German *balla* BALL[1]] ▷ **bal'looning** *n* ▷ **bal'loonist** *n* ▷ **bal'loon-,like** *adj*

balloon loan *n* a loan in respect of which interest and capital are paid off in instalments at irregular intervals

balloon payment *n* a large payment that concludes a series of smaller payments, for example in order to repay a loan

ballot ('bælət) *n* 1 the democratic practice of selecting a representative, a course of action, or deciding some other choice by submitting the options to a vote of all qualified persons 2 an instance of voting, usually in secret using ballot papers or a voting machine 3 the paper on which a vote is recorded 4 a list of candidates standing for office 5 the number of votes cast in an election 6 a random selection of successful applicants for something in which the demand exceeds the supply, esp for shares in an oversubscribed new issue 7 *NZ* the allocation by ballot of farming land among eligible candidates, such as ex-servicemen 8 *NZ* a low-interest housing loan allocated by building societies by drawing lots among its eligible members ▷ *vb* **-lots, -loting, -loted** 9 to vote or elicit a vote from: *we balloted the members on this issue* 10 (*tr*; usually foll by *for*) to select (officials, etc) by lot or ballot or to select (successful applicants) at random 11 (*tr*; often foll by *for*) to vote or decide (on an issue, etc) [C16: from Italian *ballotta*, literally: a little ball, from *balla* BALL[1]]

ballot box *n* a box into which ballot papers are dropped after voting

ballotini (,bælə'ti:nɪ) *pl n* small glass beads used in reflective paints [C20: from Italian *ballottini* small balls]

ballot paper *n* a paper used for voting in a ballot, esp (in a parliamentary or local government election) one having the names of the candidates printed on it

ballpark ('bɔ:l,pɑ:k) *n* 1 *US & Canadian* a stadium used for baseball games 2 *informal* a approximate range: *in the right ballpark* b (*as modifier*): *a ballpark figure* 3 *informal* a situation; state of affairs: *it's a whole new ballpark for him*

ball-peen hammer *n* a hammer that has one end of its head shaped in a hemisphere for beating metal, etc

ballpoint, ballpoint pen ('bɔ:l,pɔɪnt) or **ball pen** *n* a pen having a small ball bearing as a writing point

ballroom ('bɔ:l,ru:m, -,rʊm) *n* a large hall for dancing

ballroom dancing *n* social dancing, popular since the beginning of the 20th century, to dances in conventional rhythms (**ballroom dances**) such as the foxtrot and the quickstep

balls (bɔ:lz) *slang* ▷ *pl n* 1 the testicles 2 **by the balls** so as to be rendered powerless 3 nonsense; rubbish 4 courage; forcefulness ▷ *interj* 5 an exclamation of strong disagreement, contempt, annoyance, etc

balls-up or *US* **ballup** ('bɔ:lʌp) *slang* ▷ *n* 1 something botched or muddled ▷ *vb* **balls up** or **ball up** 2 (*tr, adverb*) to muddle or botch

ballsy ('bɔ:lzɪ) *adj slang* courageous and spirited [C20: from BALLS meaning courage, forcefulness]

bally ('bælɪ) *adj, adv Brit slang* a euphemism for **bloody** (sense 6)

ballyhoo (,bælɪ'hu:) *n informal* 1 a noisy, confused, or nonsensical situation or uproar 2 sensational or blatant advertising or publicity ▷ *vb* **-hoos, -hooing, -hooed** 3 (*tr*) *chiefly US* to advertise or publicize by sensational or blatant methods [C19: of uncertain origin]

Ballymena (,bælɪ'mi:nə) *n* a district in central Northern Ireland, in Co Antrim. Pop: 59 516 (2003 est). Area: 634 sq km (247 sq miles)

Ballymoney (,bælɪ'mʌnɪ) *n* a district in N Northern Ireland, in Co Antrim. Pop: 27 809 (2003 est). Area: 417 sq km (161 sq miles)

balm (bɑ:m) *n* 1 any of various oily aromatic resinous substances obtained from certain tropical trees and used for healing and soothing. See also **balsam** (sense 1) 2 any plant yielding such a substance, esp the balm of Gilead 3 something comforting or soothing 4 Also called: **lemon balm** an aromatic Eurasian herbaceous plant, *Melissa officinalis*, having clusters of small fragrant white two-lipped flowers: family *Lamiaceae* (labiates) 5 a pleasant odour [C13: from Old French *basme*, from Latin *balsamum* BALSAM]

Balmain (*French* balmɛ̃) *n* **Pierre Alexandre** (pjɛr alɛksɑ̃drə). 1914–82, French couturier

Balmain bug ('bælmeɪn) *n* a flattish edible Australian shellfish, *Ibacus peronii*, similar to the Moreton Bay bug [named after *Balmain*, a suburb of Sydney, Australia]

Balmer (*German* 'balmər) *n* **Johann Jakob**. 1825–98, Swiss mathematician; discovered (1885) a formula giving the wavelengths of a series of lines in the hydrogen spectrum (the **Balmer series**)

balm of Gilead *n* 1 any of several trees of the burseraceous genus *Commiphora*, esp *C. opobalsamum* of Africa and W Asia, that yield a fragrant oily resin 2 the resin exuded by these trees 3 a North American hybrid female poplar tree, *Populus gileadensis* (or *P. candicans*), with broad heart-shaped leaves 4 a fragrant resin obtained from the balsam fir

Balmoral[1] (bæl'mɒrəl) *n* (*sometimes not capital*) 1 a laced walking shoe 2 Also called: **bluebonnet** a Scottish brimless hat traditionally of dark blue wool with a cockade and plume on one side [C19: named after BALMORAL Castle]

Balmoral[2] (bæl'mɒrəl) *n* a castle in NE Scotland, in SW Aberdeenshire: a private residence of the British sovereign

Balmung ('bælmʊŋ) or **Balmunc** ('bælmʊŋk) *n* (in the *Nibelungenlied*) Siegfried's sword

balmy ('bɑ:mɪ) *adj* **balmier, balmiest** 1 (of weather) mild and pleasant 2 having the qualities of balm; fragrant or soothing 3 a variant spelling of **barmy** ▷ 'balmily *adv* ▷ 'balminess *n*

balneology (ˌbælnɪˈɒlədʒɪ) *n* the branch of medical science concerned with the therapeutic value of baths, esp those taken with natural mineral waters [c19: from Latin *balneum* bath] ▷ balneological (ˌbælnɪəˈlɒdʒɪkəl) *adj* ▷ ˌbalneˈologist *n*

baloney *or* **boloney** (bəˈləʊnɪ) *n informal* foolish talk; nonsense [c20: changed from *Bologna* (sausage)]

BALPA ('bælpə) *n acronym for* British Airline Pilots' Association

balsa ('bɔːlsə) *n* 1 a bombacaceous tree, *Ochroma lagopus*, of tropical America 2 Also called: **balsawood** the very light wood of this tree, used for making rafts, etc 3 a light raft [c18: from Spanish: raft]

balsam ('bɔːlsəm) *n* 1 any of various fragrant oleoresins, such as balm or tolu, obtained from any of several trees and shrubs and used as a base for medicines and perfumes 2 any of various similar substances used as medicinal or ceremonial ointments 3 any of certain aromatic resinous turpentines. See also **Canada balsam** 4 any plant yielding balsam 5 Also called: **busy Lizzie** any of several balsaminaceous plants of the genus *Impatiens*, esp *I. balsamina*, cultivated for its brightly coloured flowers 6 anything healing or soothing [c15: from Latin *balsamum*, from Greek *balsamon*, from Hebrew *bāśām* spice] ▷ balsamic (bɔːlˈsæmɪk) *adj*

balsam fir *n* a fir tree, *Abies balsamea*, of NE North America, that yields Canada balsam

Balthazar ('bælθəˌzɑː, bælˈθæzə) *n* (in Christian tradition) one of the Magi, the others being Caspar and Melchior

Balthus (*French* baltys) *n* real name *Balthasar Klossowski de Rola*. 1908–2001, French painter of Polish descent, noted esp for his paintings of adolescent girls

balti ('bɔːltɪ, 'bælti) *n* **a** a spicy Indian dish, stewed until most of the liquid has evaporated, and served in a woklike pot **b** (*as modifier*): *a balti house* [from Urdu *bāltī* pail]

Baltic ('bɔːltɪk) *adj* 1 denoting or relating to the Baltic Sea or the Baltic States 2 of, denoting, or characteristic of Baltic as a group of languages 3 *Brit informal* extremely cold ▷ *n* 4 a branch of the Indo-European family of languages consisting of Lithuanian, Latvian, and Old Prussian 5 short for **Baltic Sea** 6 Also called: **Baltic Exchange** an international market for shipbrokers in the City of London: formerly housed in the Baltic Exchange building which was demolished after terrorist bomb damage in 1992

Baltics ('bɔːltɪks) *pl n* the Baltics another name for the **Baltic States**

Baltic Sea *n* a sea in N Europe, connected with the North Sea by the Skagerrak, Kattegat, and Öresund; shallow, with low salinity and small tides

Baltic Shield *n* Also called: **Scandinavian Shield**. the wide area of ancient rock in Scandinavia. See **shield** (sense 6)

Baltic States *pl n* the republics of Estonia, Latvia, and Lithuania, which became constituent republics of the former Soviet Union in 1940, regaining their independence in 1991

Baltimore[1] ('bɔːltɪˌmɔː) *n* a port in N Maryland, on Chesapeake Bay. Pop: 628 670 (2003 est)

Baltimore[2] ('bɔːltɪˌmɔː) *n* 1 **David**. born 1938, US molecular biologist: shared the Nobel prize for physiology or medicine (1975) for his discovery of reverse transcriptase 2 **Lord**. See **Calvert** (sense 1)

Baluchistan (bəˈluːtʃɪˌstɑːn, -ˌstæn) *or* **Balochistan** (bəˈlɒtʃɪˌstɑːn, -ˌstæn) *n* 1 a mountainous region of SW Asia, in SW Pakistan and SE Iran 2 a province of SW Pakistan: a former territory of British India (until 1947). Capital: Quetta. Pop: Pop: 7 450 000 (2003 est)

baluster ('bæləstə) *n* any of a set of posts supporting a rail or coping [c17: from French *balustre*, from Italian *balaustro* pillar resembling a pomegranate flower, ultimately from Greek *balaustion*]

balustrade ('bæləˌstreɪd) *n* an ornamental rail or coping with its supporting set of balusters [c17: from French,

from *balustre* **BALUSTER**]

Balzac ('bælzæk; *French* balzak) *n* Honoré de (ɔnɔre də). 1799–1850, French novelist: author of a collection of novels under the general title *La Comédie humaine*, including *Eugénie Grandet* (1833), *Le Père Goriot* (1834), and *La Cousine Bette* (1846)

Bamako (ˌbæməˈkəʊ) *n* the capital of Mali, in the south, on the River Niger. Pop: 1 379 000 (2005 est)

Bamberg ('bæmbɜːɡ; *German* 'bambɛrk) *n* a town in S Germany, in N Bavaria: seat of independent prince-bishops of the Holy Roman Empire (1007–1802). Pop: 69 899 (2003 est)

bambino (bæmˈbiːnəʊ) *n, pl* -nos *or* -ni (-niː) *informal* a young child, esp an Italian one [c18: from Italian]

bamboo (bæmˈbuː) *n* 1 any tall treelike tropical or semitropical fast-growing grass of the genus *Bambusa*, having hollow woody-walled stems with ringed joints and edible young shoots (**bamboo shoots**) 2 the stem of any of these plants, used for building, poles, and furniture [c16: probably from Malay *bambu*]

bamboo network *n* a network of close-knit Chinese entrepreneurs with large corporate empires in southeast Asia

bamboozle (bæmˈbuːzəl) *vb* (*tr*) *informal* 1 to cheat; mislead 2 to confuse [c18: of unknown origin] ▷ bamˈboozler *n* ▷ bamˈboozlement *n*

ban (bæn) *vb* bans, banning, banned 1 (*tr*) to prohibit, esp officially, from action, display, entrance, sale, etc; forbid ▷ *n* 2 an official prohibition or interdiction 3 a public proclamation or edict, esp of outlawry 4 *archaic* a curse; imprecation [Old English *bannan* to proclaim; compare Old Norse *banna* to forbid, High German *bannan* to command]

Banaba (bəˈnɑːbə) *n* an island in the SW Pacific, in the Republic of Kiribati. Phosphates were mined by Britain (1900–79). Area: about 5 sq km (2 sq miles). Pop: 301 (2005). Also called: **Ocean Island** ▷ Ba'naban *adj, n*

banal (bəˈnɑːl) *adj* lacking force or originality; trite; commonplace [c18: from Old French: relating to compulsory feudal service, hence common to all, commonplace] ▷ banality (bəˈnælɪtɪ) *n* ▷ ba'nally *adv*

banana (bəˈnɑːnə) *n* 1 any of several tropical and subtropical herbaceous treelike plants of the musaceous genus *Musa*, esp *M. sapientum*, a widely cultivated species propagated from suckers and having hanging clusters of edible fruit 2 the crescent-shaped fruit of any of these plants [c16: from Spanish or Portuguese, of African origin]

banana prawn *n Austral* a prawn of the genus *Penaeus*, fished commercially in tropical waters of N Australia

banana republic *n dismissive* a small country, esp in Central America, that is politically unstable and has an economy dominated by foreign interest, usually dependent on one export, such as bananas

banana skin *n* 1 the soft outer covering of a banana 2 *informal* something unforeseen that causes an obvious and embarrassing mistake [sense 2 from the common slapstick joke of a person slipping after treading on a banana skin]

Banaras (bəˈnɑːrəz) *n* a variant spelling of **Benares**

Banat ('bænæt, 'baːnɪt) *n* a fertile plain extending through Hungary, Romania, and Serbia

Banbridge ('bænbrɪdʒ) *n* a district in S Northern Ireland, in Co Down. Pop: 43 083 (2003 est). Area: 442 sq km (170 sq miles)

Banbury ('bænbərɪ) *n* a town in central England, in N Oxfordshire: telecommunications, financial services. Pop: 43 867 (2001)

bancassurance ('bæŋkəˌʃʊərəns) *n* the selling of insurance products by a bank to its customers [from French *banc* bank + *assurance* assurance]

band[1] (bænd) *n* 1 a company of people having a common purpose; group: *a band of outlaws* 2 a group of musicians playing either brass and percussion instruments only (**brass band**) or brass, woodwind, and percussion instruments (**concert band** or **military band**) 3 a group of musicians who play popular music, jazz, etc, often for dancing 4 a group of instrumentalists generally; orchestra 5 *Canadian* a formally recognized group of

Canadian Indians on a reserve ▷ *vb* **6** (usually foll by *together*) to unite; assemble [C15: from French *bande* probably from Old Provençal *banda* of Germanic origin; compare Gothic *bandwa* sign, BANNER]

band² ('bænd) *n* **1 a** a thin flat strip of some material, used esp to encircle objects and hold them together: *a rubber band* **2 a** a strip of fabric or other material used as an ornament or distinguishing mark, or to reinforce clothing **b** (*in combination*): *waistband; hairband; hatband* **3 a** stripe of contrasting colour or texture **4** a driving belt in machinery **5** a range of values that are close or related in number, degree, or quality **6 a** *physics* a range of frequencies or wavelengths between two limits **b** *radio* such a range allocated to a particular broadcasting station or service **7** short for **energy band 8** *computing* one or more tracks on a magnetic disk or drum **9** *anatomy* any structure resembling a ribbon or cord that connects, encircles, or binds different parts **10** the cords to which the folded sheets of a book are sewn **11** a thin layer or seam of ore **12** *architect* a strip of flat panelling, such as a fascia or plinth, usually attached to a wall **13 a** large white collar, sometimes edged with lace, worn in the 17th century **14** either of a pair of hanging extensions of the collar, forming part of academic, legal, or (formerly) clerical dress **15** a ring for the finger (esp in phrases such as **wedding band**, **band of gold**, etc) ▷ *vb* (*tr*) **16** to fasten or mark with a band **17** *US & Canadian* to ring (a bird). See **ring¹** (sense 21) [C15: from Old French *bende*, of Germanic origin; compare Old High German *binda* fillet]

Banda ('bændə) *n* **Hastings Kamuzu** (kæ'muːzuː). 1906–97, Malawi statesman. As first prime minister of Nyasaland (from 1963), he led his country to independence (1964) as Malawi: president (1966–94)

Banda Aceh ('bændə 'aːtʃeɪ) *n* a city in N Indonesia, in N Sumatra; the capital of Aceh region; suffered badly in the Indian Ocean tsunami of December 2004. Pop: 154 767 (2000)

bandage ('bændɪdʒ) *n* **1** a piece of material used to dress a wound, bind a broken limb, etc ▷ *vb* **2** to cover or bind with a bandage [C16: from French, from *band* strip, BAND²]

bandanna *or* **bandana** (bæn'dænə) *n* a large silk or cotton handkerchief or neckerchief [C18: from Hindi *bāndhnū* tie-dyeing, from *bāndhnā* to tie, from Sanskrit *bandhnāti* he ties]

Bandaranaike (ˌbændərə'naɪɪkə) *n* **1 Chandrika**. See Chandrika **Kumaratunga 2 Sirimavo** (ˌsɪrɪ'mɑːvəʊ). 1916–2000, prime minister of Sri Lanka, formerly Ceylon (1960–65; 1970–77; 1994–2000); the world's first woman prime minister **3** her husband, **Solomon**. 1899–1959, prime minister of Ceylon (1956–59); assassinated

Bandar Seri Begawan ('bɑːndɑː 'sɛrɪ bə'gɑːwən) *n* the capital of Brunei. Pop: 64 000 (2005 est). Former name: **Brunei**

Banda Sea *n* a part of the Pacific in Indonesia, between Sulawesi and New Guinea

B & B *abbreviation* bed and breakfast

bandbox ('bænd,bɒks) *n* a lightweight usually cylindrical box used for holding small articles, esp hats

bandeau ('bændəʊ) *n, pl* **-deaux** (-dəʊz) a narrow band of ribbon, velvet, etc, worn round the head [C18: from French, from Old French *bandel* a little BAND²]

banderole, banderol ('bændə,rəʊl) *or* **bannerol** *n* **1 a** long narrow flag, usually with forked ends, esp one attached to the masthead of a ship; pennant **2** a ribbon-like scroll or sculptured band bearing an inscription, found esp in Renaissance architecture [C16: from Old French, from Italian *banderuola*, literally: a little banner, from *bandiera* BANNER]

bandicoot ('bændɪ,kuːt) *n* **1** any agile terrestrial marsupial of the family *Peramelidae* of Australia and New Guinea. They have a long pointed muzzle and a long tail and feed mainly on small invertebrates **2** bandicoot rat Also called: **mole rat** any of three burrowing rats of the genera *Bandicota* and *Nesokia*, of S and SE Asia: family *Muridae* [C18: from Telugu *pandikokku*, from *pandi* pig + *kokku* bandicoot]

banding ('bændɪŋ) *n* *Brit* the practice of grouping

schoolchildren according to ability to ensure a balanced intake at different levels of ability to secondary school

bandit ('bændɪt) *n, pl* **-dits** *or* **-ditti** (-'dɪtɪ) a robber, esp a member of an armed gang; brigand [C16: from Italian *bandito*, literally: banished man, from *bandire* to proscribe, from *bando* edict, BAN] > **'banditry** *n*

Bandjarmasin *or* **Bandjermasin** (ˌbændʒə'mɑːsɪn) *n* former spellings of **Banjarmasin**

bandmaster ('bænd,mɑːstə) *n* the conductor of a band

Band of Hope *n* a society promoting lifelong abstention from alcohol among young people: founded in Britain in 1847

bandolier *or* **bandoleer** (ˌbændə'lɪə) *n* a soldier's broad shoulder belt having small pockets or loops for cartridges [C16: from Old French *bandouliere*, from Old Spanish *bandolera*, *bandolero* guerrilla, from Catalan *bandoler*, from *bandol* band, from Spanish *bando*; see BAND¹]

bandore (bæn'dɔː, 'bændɔː) *n* a 16th-century plucked musical instrument resembling a lute but larger and fitted with seven pairs of metal strings. Also called: **pandore, pandora** [C16: from Spanish *bandurria*, from Late Latin *pandūra* three-stringed instrument, from Greek *pandoura*]

band-pass filter *n* **1** *electronics* a filter that transmits only those currents having a frequency lying within specified limits **2** an optical device, consisting of absorbing filters, for transmitting electromagnetic waves of predetermined wavelengths

B and S *n* *Austral informal* a dance held for young people in country areas, usually in a field or barn [abbreviation for BACHELOR AND SPINSTER]

band saw *n* a power-operated saw consisting of an endless toothed metal band running over and driven by two wheels

bandsman ('bændzmən) *n, pl* **-men** a player in a musical band, esp a brass or military band

bandstand ('bænd,stænd) *n* a platform for a band, usually out of doors and roofed

band theory *n* *physics* a theory of the electrical properties of metals, semiconductors, and insulators based on energy bands

Bandung ('bændʊŋ) *n* a city in Indonesia, in SW Java. Pop: 2 136 260 (2000)

bandwagon ('bænd,wægən) *n* **1** *US* a wagon, usually high and brightly coloured, for carrying the band in a parade **2** jump on the bandwagon, climb on the bandwagon *or* get on the bandwagon to join or give support to a party or movement that seems to be assured of success

bandwidth ('bænd,wɪdθ) *n* the range of frequencies within a given waveband used for a particular transmission

bandy ('bændɪ) *adj* **-dier, -diest 1** Also called: **bandy-legged** having legs curved outwards at the knees **2** (of legs) curved outwards at the knees ▷ *vb* **-dies, -dying, -died** (*tr*) **3** to exchange (words) in a heated or hostile manner **4** to give and receive (blows) **5** (often foll by *about*) to circulate (a name, rumour, etc) [C16: probably from Old French *bander* to hit the ball back and forth at tennis]

bane (beɪn) *n* **1** a person or thing that causes misery or distress (esp in the phrase **bane of one's life**) **2** something that causes death or destruction **3 a** a fatal poison **b** (*in combination*): *ratsbane* **4** *archaic* ruin or distress [Old English *bana*; related to Old Norse *bani* death, Old High German *bano* destruction, death]

baneberry ('beɪnbərɪ) *n, pl* **-ries 1** Also called: (*Brit*) herb Christopher, (*US*) cohosh any ranunculaceous plant of the genus *Actaea*, esp *A. spicata*, which has small white flowers and red or white poisonous berries **2** a berry of any of these plants

Banff (bæmf) *n* **1** a town in NE Scotland, in Aberdeenshire. Pop: 3991 (2001) **2** a town in Canada, in SW Alberta, in the Rocky Mountains: surrounded by **Banff National Park**. Pop: 7135 (2001)

Banffshire ('bæmf,ʃɪə, -ʃə) *n* (until 1975) a county of NE Scotland: formerly (1975–96) part of Grampian region, now part of Aberdeenshire

bang¹ (bæŋ) *n* **1** a short loud explosive noise, as of the bursting of a balloon or the report of a gun **2** a hard blow or knock, esp a noisy one; thump: *he gave the ball a bang* **3** *informal* a startling or sudden effect: *he realized with a bang that he was late* **4** *slang* an injection of heroin or other narcotic **5** *taboo, slang* an act of sexual intercourse **6** get a bang out of *US & Canadian slang* to experience a thrill or excitement from **7** with a bang successfully: *the party went with a bang* ▷ *vb* **8** to hit or knock, esp with a loud noise; bump: *to bang one's head* **9** to move noisily or clumsily: *to bang about the house* **10** to close (a door, window, etc) or (of a door, etc) be closed noisily; slam **11** (*tr*) to cause to move by hitting vigorously: *he banged the ball over the fence* **12** to make or cause to make a loud noise, as of an explosion **13** (*tr*) *Brit* **a** to cause (stock prices) to fall by rapid selling **b** to sell rapidly in (a stock market), thus causing prices to fall **14** *taboo, slang* to have sexual intercourse with **15** (*intr*) *slang* to inject heroin, etc **16** bang for one's buck *informal* value for money: *this option offers more bang for your buck* **17** bang goes *informal* that is the end of: *bang goes my job in Wapping* **18** bang one's head against a brick wall to try to achieve something impossible ▷ *adv* **19** with a sudden impact or effect: *bang went his hopes of winning; the car drove bang into a lamp-post* **20** precisely: *bang in the middle of the road* **21** bang to rights *slang* caught red-handed **22** go bang to burst, shut, etc, with a loud noise [C16: from Old Norse *bang*, *banga* hammer; related to Low German *bangen* to beat; all of imitative origin]

bang² (bæŋ) *n* **1** a fringe or section of hair cut straight across the forehead ▷ *vb* (*tr*) **2** to cut (the hair) in such a style **3** to dock (the tail of a horse, etc) [C19: probably short for *bangtail* short tail]

Bangalore (ˌbæŋɡəˈlɔː) *n* a city in S India, capital of Karnataka state: printing, textiles, pharmaceuticals. Pop: 4 292 223 (2001). Alternative official name: Bengaluru (ˌbeŋɡəlˈuːru)

banger (ˈbæŋə) *n Brit* **1** *slang* a sausage **2** *informal* an old decrepit car **3** a type of firework that explodes loudly

Bangka *or* **Banka** (ˈbæŋkə) *n* an island in Indonesia, separated from Sumatra by the **Bangka Strait**. Chief town: Pangkalpinang. Area: about 11 914 sq km (4600 sq miles)

Bangkok (ˈbæŋkɒk, bæŋˈkɒk) *n* the capital and chief port of Thailand, on the Chao Phraya River: became a royal city and the capital in 1782. Pop: 6 604 000 (2005 est)

Bangla (ˈbæŋlə) *n* another name for: **Bengali** (sense 2)

Bangladesh (ˌbɑːŋɡləˈdɛʃ, ˌbæŋ-) *n* a republic in S Asia: formerly the Eastern Province of Pakistan; became independent in 1971 after civil war and the defeat of Pakistan by India; consists of the plains and vast deltas of the Ganges and Brahmaputra Rivers; prone to flooding: economy based on jute and jute products (over 70 per cent of world production); a member of the Commonwealth. Language: Bengali. Religion: Muslim. Currency: taka. Capital: Dhaka. Pop: 149 665 000 (2004 est). Area: 142 797 sq km (55 126 sq miles) ▷ **Bangladeshi** (ˌbɑːŋɡləˈdɛʃɪ, ˌbæŋ-) *adj, n*

bangle (ˈbæŋɡ°l) *n* a bracelet, usually without a clasp, often worn high up round the arm or sometimes round the ankle [C19: from Hindi *baṅgrī*]

bang on *adj, adv Brit informal* **1** with absolute accuracy **2** excellent or excellently

Bangor (ˈbæŋɡɔː, -ɡə) *n* **1** a university town in NW Wales, in Gwynedd, on the Menai Strait. Pop: 15 280 (2001) **2** a town in SE Northern Ireland, in North Down district, Co Down, on Belfast Lough. Pop: 58 388 (2001)

bangtail (ˈbæŋˌteɪl) *n* **1** a horse's tail cut straight across but not through the bone **2** a horse with a tail cut in this way [C19: from *bangtail* short tail]

Bangui (*French* bãgi) *n* the capital of the Central African Republic, in the south part, on the Ubangi River. Pop: 732 000 (2005 est)

Bangweulu (ˌbæŋwɪˈuːlʊ) *n* Lake Bangweulu a shallow lake in NE Zambia, discovered by David Livingstone, who died there in 1873. Area: about 9850 sq km (3800 sq miles), including swamps

banian (ˈbæŋjən) *n* a variant spelling of **banyan**

banish (ˈbænɪʃ) *vb* (*tr*) **1** to expel from a place, esp by an official decree as a punishment **2** to drive away: *to banish gloom* [C14: from Old French *banir*, of Germanic origin; compare Old High German *ban* BAN²] ▷ **ˈbanishment** *n*

banisters *or* **bannisters** (ˈbænɪstəz) *pl n* the railing and supporting balusters on a staircase; balustrade [C17: altered from BALUSTER]

Banja Luka (*Bosnian* ˈbaːnja ˌluːka) *n* a city in NW Bosnia-Herzegovina, on the Vrbas River: scene of battles between the Austrians and Turks in 1527, 1688, and 1737; besieged by Serb forces (1992–95). Pop: 182 000 (2005 est)

Banjarmasin *or* **Banjermasin** (ˌbændʒəˈmɑːsɪn) *n* a port in Indonesia, in SW Borneo. Pop: 527 415 (2000). Former spelling: Bandjarmasin

banjo (ˈbændʒəʊ) *n, pl* **-jos** *or* **-joes** a stringed musical instrument with a long neck (usually fretted) and a circular drumlike body overlaid with parchment, plucked with the fingers or a plectrum [C18: variant (US Southern pronunciation) of BANDORE] ▷ **ˈbanjoist** *n*

Banjul (bænˈdʒuːl) *n* the capital of The Gambia, a port at the mouth of the Gambia River. Pop: 392 000 (2005 est). Former name (until 1973): Bathurst

bank¹ (bæŋk) *n* **1** an institution offering certain financial services, such as the safekeeping of money, conversion of domestic into and from foreign currencies, lending of money at interest, and acceptance of bills of exchange **2** the building used by such an institution **3** a small container used at home for keeping money **4** the funds held by a gaming house or a banker or dealer in some gambling games **5** (in various games) **a** the stock, as of money, pieces, tokens, etc, on which players may draw **b** the player holding this stock **6** any supply, store, or reserve, for future use: *a data bank; a blood bank* ▷ *vb* **7** (*tr*) to deposit (cash, cheques, etc) in a bank **8** (*intr*) to transact business with a bank **9** (*intr*) to engage in the business of banking **10** (*intr*) to hold the bank in some gambling games ▷ See also **bank on** [C15: probably from Italian *banca* bench, moneychanger's table, of Germanic origin; compare Old High German *banc* BENCH]

bank² (bæŋk) *n* **1** a long raised mass, esp of earth; mound; ridge **2** a slope, as of a hill **3** the sloping side of any hollow in the ground, esp when bordering a river: *the left bank of a river is on a spectator's left looking downstream* **4 a** an elevated section, rising to near the surface, of the bed of a sea, lake, or river **b** (*in combination*): *sandbank; mudbank* **5 a** the area around the mouth of a mine **b** the face of a body of ore **6** the lateral inclination of an aircraft about its longitudinal axis during a turn **7** Also called: **banking, camber, cant, superelevation** a bend on a road or on a railway, athletics, cycling, or other track having the outside built higher than the inside in order to reduce the effects of centrifugal force on vehicles, runners, etc, rounding it at speed and in some cases to facilitate drainage **8** the cushion of a billiard table ▷ *vb* **9** (when *tr*, often foll by *up*) to form into a bank or mound **10** (*tr*) to border or enclose (a road, etc) with a bank **11** (*tr*, sometimes foll by *up*) to cover (a fire) with ashes, fresh fuel, etc, so that it will burn slowly **12** to cause (an aircraft) to tip laterally about its longitudinal axis or (of an aircraft) to tip in this way, esp while turning **13** to travel round a bank, esp at high speed **14** (*tr*) *billiards* to drive (a ball) into the cushion [C12: of Scandinavian origin; compare Old Icelandic *bakki* hill, Old Danish *banke*, Swedish *backe*]

bank³ (bæŋk) *n* **1** an arrangement of objects, esp similar objects, in a row or in tiers: *a bank of dials* **2** a tier of oars in a galley ▷ *vb* **3** (*tr*) to arrange in a bank [C17: from Old French *banc* bench, of Germanic origin; see BANK¹]

Banka (ˈbæŋkə) *n* a variant spelling of **Bangka**

bankable (ˈbæŋkəb°l) *adj* **1** appropriate for receipt by a bank **2** dependable or reliable: *a bankable promise* **3** (esp of a star) likely to ensure the financial success of a film ▷ ˌbankaˈbility *n*

bank account *n* **1** an account created by the deposit of money at a bank by a customer **2** the amount of moneys credited to or debited to a depositor at a bank

bank bill *n* **1** Also called: **bank draft** a bill of exchange drawn by one bank on another **2** Also called: **banker's**

b

bill *US* a banknote

bankbook ('bæŋk,bʊk) *n* a book held by depositors at certain banks, in which the bank enters a record of deposits, withdrawals, and earned interest. Also called: passbook

bank card *or* **banker's card** *n* any plastic card issued by a bank, such as a cash card or cheque card

bank draft *n* a cheque drawn by a bank on itself, which is bought by a person to pay a supplier unwilling to accept a normal cheque. Also called: banker's cheque

banker[1] ('bæŋkə) *n* **1** a person who owns or is an executive in a bank **2** an official or player in charge of the bank in any of various games, esp gambling games **3** a result that has been forecast identically in a series of entries on a football pool coupon **4** a person or thing that appears certain to win or be successful

banker[2] ('bæŋkə) *n Austral & NZ informal* a stream almost overflowing its banks (esp in the phrase **run a banker**)

banker's order *n* another name for **standing order** (sense 1)

Bankhead ('bæŋk,hɛd) *n* Tallulah (**Brockman**). 1902–68, US stage and film actress; her successes included the plays *The Little Foxes* (1939) and *The Skin of Our Teeth* (1942)

bank holiday *n* (in Britain) any of several weekdays on which banks are closed by law and which are observed as national holidays

banking ('bæŋkɪŋ) *n* the business engaged in by a bank

bank manager *n* a person who directs the business of a local branch of a bank

banknote ('bæŋk,nəʊt) *n* a promissory note issued by a central bank, serving as money

Bank of England *n* the central bank of the United Kingdom, which acts as banker to the government and the commercial banks. It is responsible for managing the government's debt and implementing its policy on other monetary matters: established in 1694, nationalized in 1946; in 1997 the government restored the authority to set interest rates to the Bank

bank on *vb* (*intr, preposition*) to expect or rely with confidence on: *you can bank on him always arriving on time*

bankroll ('bæŋk,rəʊl) *chiefly US & Canadian* ▷ *n* **1** a roll of currency notes **2** the financial resources of a person, organization, etc ▷ *vb* **3** (*tr*) *slang* to provide the capital for; finance

bankrupt ('bæŋkrʌpt, -rəpt) *n* **1** a person adjudged insolvent by a court, his or her property being transferred to a trustee and administered for the benefit of his creditors **2** any person unable to discharge all his or her debts **3** a person whose resources in a certain field are exhausted or nonexistent: *a spiritual bankrupt* ▷ *adj* **4** adjudged insolvent **5** financially ruined **6** depleted in resources or having completely failed: *spiritually bankrupt* **7** (foll by *of*) *Brit* lacking: *bankrupt of intelligence* ▷ *vb* **8** (*tr*) to make bankrupt [c16: from Old French *banqueroute*, from Old Italian *bancarotta*, from *banca* BANK[1] + *rotta* broken, from Latin *ruptus*, from *rumpere* to break] > **bankruptcy** ('bæŋkrʌptsɪ, -rəptsɪ) *n*

Banks (bæŋks) *n* **1** Iain (**Menzies**). born 1954, Scottish novelist and science fiction writer. His novels include *The Wasp Factory* (1984), *The Crow Road* (1992), and *The Steep Approach to Garbadale* (2007); science-fiction (under the name Iain M. Banks) includes *Look to Windward* (2000) **2** Sir **Joseph**. 1743–1820, British botanist and explorer: circumnavigated the world with James Cook (1768–71)

banksia ('bæŋksɪə) *n* any shrub or tree of the Australian genus *Banksia*, having long leathery evergreen leaves and dense cylindrical heads of flowers that are often red or yellow: family *Proteaceae* [c19: New Latin, named after Sir Joseph Banks (1743–1820), British botanist and explorer]

Banks Island *n* **1** an island of N Canada, in the Northwest Territories: the westernmost island of the Arctic Archipelago. Area: about 67 340 sq km (26 000 sq miles) **2** an island of W Canada, off British Columbia. Length: about 72 km (45 miles)

bank statement *n* a statement of transactions in a bank account, esp one of a series sent at regular intervals to the depositor

banner ('bænə) *n* **1** a long strip of flexible material

displaying a slogan, advertisement, etc, esp one suspended between two points **2** a placard or sign carried in a procession or demonstration **3** something that represents a belief or principle **4** the flag of a nation, army, etc, used as a standard or ensign **5** Also called: banner headline a large headline in a newspaper, etc, extending across the page, esp the front page **6** an advertisement, often animated, that extends across the width of a web page [c13: from Old French *baniere*, of Germanic origin; compare Gothic *bandwa* sign; influenced by Medieval Latin *bannum* BAN[1], *bannīre* to BANISH] > 'bannered *adj*

banner ad *n* **1** a banner advertising a product **2** an advert along the top of a page of a website

Bannister ('bænɪstə) *n* Sir **Roger** (**Gilbert**). born 1929, British athlete and doctor: first man to run a mile in under four minutes (1954)

bannisters ('bænɪstəz) *pl n* a variant spelling of **banisters**

bannock ('bænək) *n* a round flat unsweetened cake originating in Scotland, made from oatmeal or barley and baked on a griddle [Old English *bannuc*; of Celtic origin; compare Gaelic *bannach*, Cornish *banna* a drop, bit; perhaps related to Latin *pānicium*, from *pānis* bread]

Bannockburn ('bænək,bɜːn) *n* a village in central Scotland, south of Stirling: nearby is the site of a victory (1314) of the Scots, led by Robert the Bruce, over the English. Pop: 7396 (2001)

banns *or* **bans** (bænz) *pl n* **1** the public declaration of an intended marriage, usually formally announced on three successive Sundays in the parish churches of both the betrothed **2** forbid the banns to raise an objection to a marriage announced in this way [c14: plural of *bann* proclamation; see BAN[1]]

banquet ('bæŋkwɪt) *n* **1** a lavish and sumptuous meal; feast **2** a ceremonial meal for many people, often followed by speeches ▷ *vb* **-quets, -queting, -queted** **3** (*intr*) to hold or take part in a banquet **4** (*tr*) to entertain or honour (a person) with a banquet [c15: from Old French, from Italian *banchetto*, from *banco* a table, of Germanic origin; see BANK[1]] > 'banqueter *n*

banquette (bæŋ'kɛt) *n* **1** an upholstered bench **2** (formerly) a raised part behind a parapet [c17: from French, from Provençal *banqueta*, literally: a little bench, from *banc* bench; see BANK[3]]

banshee ('bænʃiː, bæn'ʃiː) *n* (in Irish folklore) a female spirit whose wailing warns of impending death [c18: from Irish Gaelic *bean sídhe*, literally: woman of the fairy mound]

Banstead ('bæn,stɛd) *n* a town in S England, in NE Surrey. Pop: 19 332 (2001)

bantam ('bæntəm) *n* **1** any of various very small breeds of domestic fowl **2** a small but aggressive person **3** *boxing* short for **bantamweight** **4** *Canadian* an age level of between 13 and 15 in amateur sport, esp ice hockey [c18: after *Bantam* village in Java, said to be the original home of this fowl]

bantamweight ('bæntəm,weɪt) *n* **1 a** a professional boxer weighing 112–118 pounds (51–53.5 kg) **b** an amateur boxer weighing 51–54 kg (112–119 pounds) **2** a wrestler in a similar weight category (usually 115–126 pounds (52–57 kg))

banter ('bæntə) *vb* **1** to speak to or tease lightly or jokingly ▷ *n* **2** light, teasing, or joking language or repartee [c17: of unknown origin] > 'banterer *n*

Banting ('bæntɪŋ) *n* Sir **Frederick Grant**. 1891–1941, Canadian physiologist: discovered the insulin treatment for diabetes with Best and Macleod (1922) and shared the Nobel prize for physiology or medicine with Macleod (1923)

Bantock ('bæntɒk) *n* Sir **Granville**. 1868–1946, British composer. His works include the *Hebridean Symphony* (1915), five ballets, and three operas

Bantu ('baːntuː, 'bæntuː, bæn'tuː) *n* **1** a group of languages of Africa, including most of the principal languages spoken from the equator to the Cape of Good Hope, but excluding the Khoisan family: now generally regarded as part of the Benue-Congo branch of the Niger-Congo family **2** *pl* **-tu** *or* **-tus** *South African taboo* a

b

Black speaker of a Bantu language ▷ *adj* **3** denoting, relating to, or belonging to this group of peoples or to any of their languages [c19: from Bantu *Ba-ntu* people]

● USAGE Use of the term *Bantu* is only acceptable outside
● South African and when talking about this group of
● languages and their speakers. To refer to African
● people or peoples, the terms *Black* and *African* are
● acceptable within South Africa

Bantustan ('bɑːntʊˌstɑːn, ˌbæntʊ'stɑːn) *n* (formerly, in South Africa) an area reserved for occupation by a Black African people, with limited self-government; abolished in 1993. Official name: **homeland**

Banville (*French* bɑ̃vil) *n* **Théodore de** (teɔdɔr də). 1823–91, French poet, who anticipated the Parnassian school in his perfection of form and command of rhythm

banyan *or* **banian** ('bænjən) *n* **1** a moraceous tree, *Ficus benghalensis*, of tropical India and the East Indies, having aerial roots that grow down into the soil forming additional trunks **2** a member of the Hindu merchant caste of N and W India **3** a loose-fitting shirt, jacket, or robe, worn originally in India [c16: from Hindi *baniyā*, from Sanskrit *vāṇija* merchant]

Banyana Banyana (bə'njɑːnə bə'njɑːnə) *pl n* the South Africa women's national soccer team [c20: from Nguni *banyana* the girls]

banzai ('bɑːnzaɪ, bɑː'nzaɪ) *interj* a patriotic cheer, battle cry, or salutation [Japanese: literally, (may you live for) ten thousand years]

baobab ('beɪəʊˌbæb) *n* a bombacaceous tree, *Adansonia digitata*, native to Africa, that has a very thick trunk, large white flowers, and a gourdlike fruit with an edible pulp called monkey bread [c17: probably from a native African word]

Baoding ('baʊ'dɪŋ), **Paoting** *or* **Pao-ting** *n* a city in NE China, in N Hebei province. Pop: 810 000 (2005 est). Former names: **Ch'ing-yüan**, **Tsingyuan**

BAOR *abbreviation* British Army of the Rhine

Baotou ('baʊ'tuː) *or* **Paotow** *n* an industrial city in N China, in the central Inner Mongolia AR on the Yellow River. Pop: 1 367 000 (2005 est)

bap (bæp) *n Brit* a large soft bread roll [c16: of unknown origin]

baptism ('bæptɪzəm) *n* a Christian religious rite consisting of immersion in or sprinkling with water as a sign that the subject is cleansed from sin and constituted as a member of the Church ▷ **bap'tismal** *adj* ▷ **bap'tismally** *adv*

baptism of fire *n* **1** a soldier's first experience of battle **2** any initiating ordeal or experience

Baptist ('bæptɪst) *n* **1** a member of any of various Christian sects that affirm the necessity of baptism (usually of adults and by immersion) following a personal profession of the Christian faith **2 the Baptist** See **John the Baptist** ▷ *adj* **3** denoting, relating to, or characteristic of any Christian sect that affirms the necessity of baptism following a personal profession of the Christian faith

baptistry *or* **baptistery** ('bæptɪstrɪ) *n*, *pl* **-ries** *or* **-eries 1** a part of a Christian church in which baptisms are carried out **2** a tank in a Baptist church in which baptisms are carried out

baptize *or* **baptise** (bæp'taɪz) *vb* **1** *Christianity* to immerse (a person) in water or sprinkle water on (a person) as part of the rite of baptism **2** (*tr*) to give a name to; christen [c13: from Late Latin *baptizāre*, from Greek *baptizein*, from *baptein* to bathe, dip]

bar¹ (bɑː) *n* **1** a rigid usually straight length of metal, wood, etc, that is longer than it is wide or thick, used esp as a barrier or as a structural or mechanical part: *a bar of a gate* **2** a solid usually rectangular block of any material: *a bar of soap* **3** anything that obstructs or prevents **4** an offshore ridge of sand, mud, or shingle lying near the shore and parallel to it, across the mouth of a river, bay, or harbour, or linking an island to the mainland **5** a counter or room where alcoholic drinks are served **6** a counter, room, or establishment where a particular range of goods, food, services, etc, are sold: *a coffee bar; a heel bar* **7** a narrow band or stripe, as of colour or light **8** a heating element in an electric fire **9** (in

England) the area in a court of law separating the part reserved for the bench and Queen's Counsel from the area occupied by junior barristers, solicitors, and the general public. See also **Bar 10** the place in a court of law where the accused stands during his trial **11** a particular court of law **12** *Brit* (in the House of Lords and House of Commons) the boundary where nonmembers wishing to address either House appear and where persons are arraigned **13** a plea showing that a plaintiff has no cause of action, as when the case has already been adjudicated upon or the time allowed for bringing the action has passed **14** anything referred to as an authority or tribunal: *the bar of decency* **15** Also called: **measure** *music* a group of beats that is repeated with a consistent rhythm throughout a piece or passage of music. The number of beats in the bar is indicated by the time signature **16 a** *Brit* insignia added to a decoration indicating a second award **b** *US* a strip of metal worn with uniform, esp to signify rank or as an award for service **17** *sport* See **crossbar 18** *gymnastics* See **horizontal bar 19** *heraldry* an ordinary consisting of a horizontal line across a shield, typically narrower than a fesse, and usually appearing in twos or threes **20 behind bars** in prison **21 won't have a bar of** *or* **wouldn't have a bar of** *Austral & NZ informal* cannot tolerate; dislike ▷ *vb* **bars**, **barring**, **barred** (*tr*) **22** to fasten or secure with a bar: *to bar the door* **23** to shut in or out with or as if with barriers: *to bar the entrances* **24** to obstruct; hinder: *the fallen tree barred the road* **25** (usually foll by *from*) to prohibit; forbid: *to bar a couple from meeting* **26** (usually foll by *from*) to keep out; exclude: *to bar a person from membership* **27** to mark with a bar or bars **28** *law* to prevent or halt (an action) by showing that the claimant has no cause ▷ *prep* **29** except for **30 bar none** without exception [c12: from Old French *barre*, from Vulgar Latin *barra* (unattested) bar, rod, of unknown origin]

bar² (bɑː) *n* a cgs unit of pressure equal to 10^6 dynes per square centimetre. 1 bar is equivalent to 10^5 newtons per square metre [c20: from Greek *baros* weight]

Bar (bɑː) **the Bar** *n* **1** (in England and elsewhere) barristers collectively **2** *US* the legal profession collectively **3 be called to the Bar** *Brit* to become a barrister **4 be called within the Bar** *Brit* to be appointed as a Queen's Counsel

bar. *abbreviation* **1** barometer **2** barometric **3** barrel (container or unit of measure) **4** barrister

Barabbas (bə'ræbəs) *n New Testament* a condemned robber who was released at the Passover instead of Jesus (Matthew 27:16)

barachois (ˌbærə'ʃwɑː) *n* (in the Atlantic Provinces of Canada) a shallow lagoon formed by a sand bar [French]

Barak ('bærək) *n* **Ehud** (ɛ'hʊd). born 1942, Israeli Labour politician, prime minister (1999–2001)

Baranof Island ('bærənəf) *n* an island off SE Alaska, in the western part of the Alexander Archipelago. Area: 4162 sq km (1607 sq miles)

Bárány (*German* 'bɑːranɪ) *n* **Robert**. 1876–1936, Austrian physician; devised the **Bárány test**, which detects diseases of the semicircular canals of the inner ear: Nobel prize for physiology or medicine 1914

barathea (ˌbærə'θɪə) *n* a fabric made of silk and wool or cotton and rayon, used esp for coats [c19: of unknown origin]

barb¹ (bɑːb) *n* **1** a subsidiary point facing in the opposite direction to the main point of a fish-hook, harpoon, arrow, etc, intended to make extraction difficult **2** any of various pointed parts, as on barbed wire **3** a cutting remark; gibe **4** any of the numerous hairlike filaments that form the vane of a feather **5** a beardlike growth in certain animals **6** a hooked hair or projection on certain fruits ▷ *vb* **7** (*tr*) to provide with a barb or barbs [c14: from Old French *barbe* beard, point, from Latin *barba* beard] ▷ **barbed** *adj*

barb² (bɑːb) *n* a breed of horse of North African origin, similar to the Arab but less spirited [c17: from French *barbe*, from Italian *barbero* a Barbary (horse)]

Barbados (bɑː'beɪdəʊs, -dəʊz, -dɒs) *n* an island in the Caribbean, in the E Lesser Antilles: a British colony from

1628 to 1966, now an independent state within the Commonwealth. Language: English. Currency: Barbados dollar. Capital: Bridgetown. Pop: 271 000 (2004 est). Area: 430 sq km (166 sq miles) ▷ Bar'badian *adj, n*

barbarian (ba:'bɛərɪən) *n* **1** a member of a primitive or uncivilized people **2** a coarse, insensitive, or uncultured person **3** a vicious person ▷ *adj* **4** of an uncivilized culture **5** insensitive, uncultured, or brutal [c16: see BARBAROUS]

barbaric (ba:'bærɪk) *adj* **1** of or characteristic of barbarians **2** primitive or unsophisticated; unrestrained **3** brutal [c15: from Latin *barbaricus* foreign, outlandish; see BARBAROUS] ▷ bar'barically *adv*

barbarism ('ba:bə,rɪzəm) *n* **1** a brutal, coarse, or ignorant act **2** the condition of being backward, coarse, or ignorant **3** a substandard or erroneously constructed or derived word or expression; solecism **4** any act or object that offends against accepted taste [c16: from Latin *barbarismus* error of speech, from Greek *barbarismos*, from *barbaros* BARBAROUS]

barbarity (ba:'bærɪtɪ) *n, pl* -ties **1** the state or condition of being barbaric or barbarous **2** a brutal or vicious act

barbarize *or* **barbarise** ('ba:bə,raɪz) *vb* **1** to make or become barbarous **2** to use barbarisms in (language) ▷ ,barbari'zation *or* ,barbari'sation *n*

Barbarossa (,ba:bə'rɒsə) *n* **1** the nickname of the Holy Roman Emperor **Frederick I**. See **Frederick Barbarossa** **2** real name *Khair ed-Din. c.* 1465–1546, Turkish pirate and admiral: conquered Tunis for the Ottomans (1534)

barbarous ('ba:bərəs) *adj* **1** uncivilized; primitive **2** brutal or cruel **3** lacking refinement [c15: via Latin from Greek *barbaros* barbarian, non-Greek, in origin imitative of incomprehensible speech; compare Sanskrit *barbara* stammering, non-Aryan] ▷ 'barbarously *adv* ▷ 'barbarousness *n*

Barbary ('ba:bərɪ) *n* a historic name for a region of N Africa extending from W Egypt to the Atlantic and including the former **Barbary States** of Tripolitania, Tunisia, Algeria, and Morocco

Barbary ape *n* a tailless macaque, *Macaca sylvana*, that inhabits rocky cliffs and forests in NW Africa and Gibraltar: family *Cercopithecidae*, order *Primates*

Barbary Coast *n* the **Barbary Coast** a historic name for the Mediterranean coast of North Africa: a centre of piracy against European shipping from the 16th to the 19th centuries

barbate ('ba:beɪt) *adj chiefly biology* having tufts of long hairs; bearded [c19: from Latin *barba* a beard]

barbecue ('ba:bɪ,kju:) *n* **1** a meal cooked out of doors over an open fire **2** an outdoor party or picnic at which barbecued food is served **3** a grill or fireplace used in barbecuing **4** the food so cooked ▷ *vb* -cues, -cuing, -cued (*tr*) **5** to cook (meat, fish, etc) on a grill, usually over charcoal and often with a highly seasoned sauce **6** to cook (meat, fish, etc) in a highly seasoned sauce [c17: from American Spanish *barbacoa*, probably from Taino: frame made of sticks]

barbecue stopper *n Austral informal* **1** a controversial current-affairs issue **2** a social gaffe [c21: coined by John Howard (born 1939), Australian politician and prime minister since 1996; from the notion that such a discussion is likely to interrupt a barbecue with loud debate]

barbed wire *n* strong wire with sharply pointed barbs at close intervals

barbel ('ba:bəl) *n* **1** any of several slender tactile spines or bristles that hang from the jaws of certain fishes, such as the catfish and carp **2** any of several European cyprinid fishes of the genus *Barbus*, esp *B. barbus*, that resemble the carp but have a longer body and pointed snout [c14: from Old French, from Latin *barbus*, from *barba* beard]

barbell ('ba:,bɛl) *n* a metal rod to which heavy discs are attached at each end for weightlifting exercises

barber ('ba:bə) *n* **1** a person whose business is cutting men's hair and shaving or trimming beards ▷ *vb* (*tr*) **2** to cut the hair of [c13: from Old French *barbeor*, from *barbe* beard, from Latin *barba*]

Barber ('ba:bə) *n* **Samuel**. 1910–81, US composer: his works include an *Adagio for Strings*, adapted from the second movement of his string quartet No. 1 (1936) and the opera *Vanessa* (1958)

Barbera (ba:'beɪrə) *n* **Joseph**. See **Hanna**

barberry ('ba:bərɪ) *n, pl* -ries any spiny berberidaceous shrub of the widely distributed genus *Berberis*, esp *B. vulgaris*, having clusters of yellow flowers and orange or red berries: widely cultivated as hedge plants [c15: from Old French *berberis*, from Arabic *barbārīs*]

barbershop ('ba:bə,ʃɒp) *n* **1** *now chiefly US* the premises of a barber **2** (*modifier*) denoting or characterized by a type of close four-part harmony for male voices, popular in romantic and sentimental songs of the 1920s and 1930s: *a barbershop quartet*

barber's pole *n* a sign outside a barber's shop consisting of a pole painted with red and white spiral stripes

barbican ('ba:bɪkən) *n* **1** a walled outwork or tower to protect a gate or drawbridge of a fortification **2** a watchtower projecting from a fortification [c13: from Old French *barbacane*, from Medieval Latin *barbacana*, of unknown origin]

Barbican ('ba:bɪkən) *n* the **Barbican** a building complex in the City of London: includes residential developments and the Barbican Arts Centre (completed 1982) housing concert and exhibition halls, theatres, cinemas, etc

barbicel ('ba:bɪ,sɛl) *n ornithol* any of the minute hooks on the barbules of feathers that interlock with those of adjacent barbules [c19: from New Latin *barbicella*, literally: a small beard, from Latin *barba* beard]

Barbirolli (,ba:bə'rɒlɪ) *n* Sir **John**. 1899–1970, English conductor of the Hallé Orchestra (1943–68)

barbiturate (ba:'bɪtjʊrɪt, -,reɪt) *n* a derivative of barbituric acid, such as phenobarbital, used in medicine as a sedative, hypnotic, or anticonvulsant

barbituric acid (,ba:bɪ'tjʊərɪk) *n* a white crystalline solid used in the preparation of barbiturate drugs. Formula: $C_4H_4N_2O_3$ [c19: partial translation of German *Barbitursäure*, perhaps from the name *Barbara* + URIC + *Säure* acid]

Barbour ('ba:bə) *n* **John**. *c.* 1320–95, Scottish poet: author of *The Bruce* (1376), a patriotic epic poem

Barbour jacket *or* **Barbour** ('ba:bə) *n trademark* a hard-wearing waterproof waxed jacket

Barbuda (ba:'bu:də) *n* a coral island in the E Caribbean, in the Leeward Islands: part of the independent state of Antigua and Barbuda. Area: 160 sq km (62 sq miles)

barbule ('ba:bju:l) *n ornithol* any of the minute hairs that project from a barb and in some feathers interlock by hooks and grooves, forming a flat vane [c19: from Latin *barbula* a little beard, from *barba* beard]

Barbusse (*French* barbys) *n* **Henri** (ãri). 1873–1935, French novelist and poet. His novels include *L'Enfer* (1908) and *Le Feu* (1916), reflecting the horror of World War I

barcarole *or* **barcarolle** ('ba:kə,rəʊl, -,rɒl, ,ba:kə'rəʊl) *n* **1** a Venetian boat song in a time of six or twelve quaver beats to the bar **2** an instrumental composition resembling this [c18: from French, from Italian *barcarola*, from *barcaruolo* boatman, from *barca* boat; see BARQUE]

Barce ('ba:tʃe) *or* **Barca** ('barka) *n* the Italian name for **Al Marj**

Barcelona (,ba:sɪ'ləʊnə) *n* the chief port of Spain, on the NE Mediterranean coast: seat of the Republican government during the Civil War (1936–39); the commercial capital of Spain. Pop: 1 582 738 (2003 est)

bar chart *n* another name for **bar graph**

Barclay ('ba:klɪ) *n* **Alexander**. *c.* 1475–1552, English poet. His works include *The Ship of Fools* (1509) and *Eclogues* (c. 1513–14)

Barclay de Tolly ('ba:klɪ də 'tɒlɪ; *Russian* bar'klaɪ də 'tɒlɪ) *n* Prince **Mikhail** (mixa'il). 1761–1818, Russian field marshal: commander in chief against Napoleon in 1812

bar code *n commerce* a machine-readable arrangement of numbers and parallel lines of different widths printed on a package, which can be electronically scanned at a checkout to register the price of the goods and to activate computer stock-checking and reordering. Also called: **Universal Product Code, UPC**

Barcoo River (bɑːˈkuː) n a river in E central Australia, in SW Queensland: joins with the Thomson River to form Cooper Creek

bard[1] (bɑːd) n **a** (formerly) one of an ancient Celtic order of poets who recited verses about the exploits, often legendary, of their tribes **b** (in modern times) a poet who wins a verse competition at a Welsh eisteddfod [c14: from Scottish Gaelic; related to Welsh bardd] > 'bardic adj

bard[2] or **barde** (bɑːd) n **1** a piece of larding bacon or pork fat placed on game or lean meat during roasting to prevent drying out ▷ vb (tr) **2** to place a bard on [c15: from Old French barde, from Old Italian barda, from Arabic barda'ah packsaddle]

Bard (bɑːd) n the Bard an epithet of William Shakespeare (1564–1616), the English dramatist and poet

Bardeen (ˌbɑːˈdiːn) n John. 1908–91, US physicist and electrical engineer, noted for his research on electrical conduction in solids; shared Nobel prize for physics 1956 for research on semiconductors leading to the invention of the transistor; shared Nobel prize for physics 1972 for contributions to the theory of superconductivity

bardie (ˈbɑːdiː) n **1** an edible white wood-boring grub of Australia **2** starve the bardies! Austral slang an exclamation of surprise or protest [from a native Australian language]

bardo (ˈbɑːdəʊ) n (often capital) (in Tibetan Buddhism) the state of the soul between its death and its rebirth [Tibetan bardo between two]

Bardot (French bardo) n Brigitte (briˈʒiːt). born 1934, French film actress

bare[1] (bɛə) adj **1** unclothed; exposed: used esp of a part of the body **2** without the natural, conventional, or usual covering or clothing **3** lacking appropriate furnishings, etc **4** unembellished; simple: the bare facts **5** with one's bare hands without a weapon or tool ▷ vb **6** (tr) to make bare; uncover; reveal [Old English bær; compare Old Norse berr, Old High German bar naked, Old Slavonic bosŭ barefoot] > 'bareness n

bare[2] (bɛə) vb archaic a past tense of **bear**[1]

bareback (ˈbɛəˌbæk) or **barebacked** adj, adv (of horse-riding) without a saddle

bare-bones adj basic or simple; no-frills

barefaced (ˈbɛəˌfeɪst) adj unconcealed or shameless: a barefaced lie > barefacedly (ˈbɛəˌfeɪsɪdlɪ) adv > 'bare,facedness n

barefoot (ˈbɛəˌfʊt) or **barefooted** adj, adv with the feet uncovered

barefoot doctor n (esp in developing countries) a worker trained as a medical auxiliary in a rural area who dispenses medicine, gives first aid, assists at childbirth, etc [c20: translation of Chinese chijiao yisheng, officially translated as primary health worker]

bareheaded (ˌbɛəˈhɛdɪd) adj, adv with head uncovered

Bareilly (bəˈreɪlɪ) n a city in N India, in N central Uttar Pradesh. Pop: 699 839 (2001)

bare-knuckle adj **1** without boxing gloves: a bare-knuckle fight **2** aggressive and without reservations: a bare-knuckle confrontation

barely (ˈbɛəlɪ) adv **1** only just; scarcely: barely enough for their needs **2** informal not quite; nearly: barely old enough **3** scantily; poorly: barely furnished **4** archaic openly

Barenboim (ˈbærənˌbɔɪm) n Daniel. born 1942, Israeli concert pianist and conductor, born in Argentina

Barents Sea (ˈbærənts) n a part of the Arctic Ocean, bounded by Norway, Russia, and the islands of Novaya Zemlya, Spitsbergen, and Franz Josef Land [named after Willem Barents (1550–97) Dutch navigator and explorer]

barf (bɑːf) slang vb ▷ (tr) to vomit [c20: probably of imitative origin]

bargain (ˈbɑːgɪn) n **1** an agreement or contract establishing what each party will give, receive, or perform in a transaction between them **2** something acquired or received in such an agreement **3** US **a** something bought or offered at a low price **b** (as modifier): a bargain price **4** into the bargain or US in the bargain in excess of what has been stipulated; besides **5** make a bargain or strike a bargain to agree on terms ▷ vb **6** (intr) to negotiate the terms of an agreement,

transaction, etc **7** (tr) to exchange, as in a bargain **8** to arrive at (an agreement or settlement) [c14: from Old French bargaigne, from bargaignier to trade, of Germanic origin; compare Medieval Latin barcāniāre to trade, Old English borgian to borrow] > 'bargainer n > 'bargaining n, adj

bargain away vb (tr, adverb) to lose or renounce (freedom, rights, etc) in return for something valueless or of little value

bargain bin n a container in a shop from which customers can buy goods that may be old or imperfect at greatly reduced prices

bargain for vb (intr, preposition) to expect; anticipate (a style of behaviour, change in fortune, etc): he got more than he bargained for

bargain on vb (intr, preposition) to rely or depend on (something): he bargained on her support

barge (bɑːdʒ) n **1** a vessel, usually flat-bottomed and with or without its own power, used for transporting freight, esp on canals **2** a vessel, often decorated, used in pageants, for state occasions, etc **3** navy a boat allocated to a flag officer, used esp for ceremonial occasions and often carried on board his flagship ▷ vb **4** (intr; foll by into) informal to bump (into) **5** (tr) informal to push (someone or one's way) violently **6** (intr; foll by into or in) informal to interrupt rudely or clumsily: to barge into a conversation [c13: from Old French, from Medieval Latin barga, probably from Late Latin barca a small boat; see BARQUE]

bargeboard (ˈbɑːdʒˌbɔːd) n a board, often decorated with carved ornaments, placed along the gable end of a roof

bargee (bɑːˈdʒiː) n, pl bargees or bargemen a person employed on or in charge of a barge

bargepole (ˈbɑːdʒˌpəʊl) n **1** a long pole used to propel a barge **2** not touch with a bargepole informal to refuse to have anything to do with

bar graph n a graph consisting of vertical or horizontal bars whose lengths are proportional to amounts or quantities

Bari (ˈbɑːrɪ) n a port in SE Italy, capital of Apulia, on the Adriatic coast. Pop: 316 532 (2001)

bariatric (ˌbærɪˈætrɪk) adj of or relating to the treatment of obesity: bariatric surgery [c20: from BARO + IATRIC] > ˌbari'atrics pl n

Baring (ˈbɛərɪŋ) n Evelyn, 1st Earl of Cromer. 1841–1917, English administrator. As consul general in Egypt with plenipotentiary powers, he controlled the Egyptian government from 1883 to 1907

barite (ˈbɛəraɪt) n US & Canadian a colourless or white mineral consisting of barium sulphate in orthorhombic crystalline form, occurring in sedimentary rocks and with sulphide ores: a source of barium. Formula: $BaSO_4$. Also called: barytes, heavy spar [c18: from BAR(IUM) + -ITE[1]]

baritone (ˈbærɪˌtəʊn) n **1** the second lowest adult male voice, having a range approximately from G an eleventh below middle C to F a fourth above it **2** a singer with such a voice **3** the second lowest instrument in the families of the saxophone, horn, oboe, etc ▷ adj **4** relating to or denoting a baritone [c17: from Italian baritono a deep voice, from Greek barutonos deep-sounding, from barus heavy, low + tonos TONE]

barium (ˈbɛərɪəm) n a soft silvery-white metallic element of the alkaline earth group. It is used in bearing alloys and compounds are used as pigments. Symbol: Ba; atomic no: 56; atomic wt: 137.327; valency: 2; relative density: 3.5; melting pt: 729°C; boiling pt: 1805°C [c19: from BAR(YTA) + -IUM]

barium hydroxide n a white poisonous crystalline solid, used in the manufacture of organic compounds and in the preparation of beet sugar. Formula: $Ba(OH)_2$. Also called: baryta

barium meal n a preparation of barium sulphate, which is opaque to X-rays, swallowed by a patient before X-ray examination of the upper part of the alimentary canal

barium oxide n a white or yellowish-white poisonous heavy powder used esp as a dehydrating agent. Formula: BaO. Also called: baryta

bark¹ (bɑːk) *n* **1** the loud abrupt usually harsh or gruff cry of a dog or any of certain other animals **2** a similar sound, such as one made by a person, gun, etc **3** his bark is worse than his bite he is bad-tempered but harmless ▷ *vb* **4** (*intr*) (of a dog or any of certain other animals) to make its typical loud abrupt cry **5** (*intr*) (of a person, gun, etc) to make a similar loud harsh sound **6** to say or shout in a brusque, peremptory, or angry tone: *he barked an order* **7** bark up the wrong tree *informal* to misdirect one's attention, efforts, etc; be mistaken [Old English *beorcan*; related to Lithuanian *burgěti* to quarrel, growl]

bark² (bɑːk) *n* **1** a protective layer of dead corky cells on the outside of the stems of woody plants **2** any of several varieties of this substance that can be used in tanning, dyeing, or in medicine ▷ *vb* (*tr*) **3** to scrape or rub off skin, as in an injury **4** to remove the bark or a circle of bark from (a tree or log) **5** to cover or enclose with bark **6** to tan (leather), principally by the tannins in barks [c13: from Old Norse *börkr*; related to Swedish, Danish *bark*, German *Borke*; compare Old Norse *björkr* BIRCH]

bark³ (bɑːk) *n* a variant spelling (esp US) of **barque**

barkentine *or* **barkantine** ('bɑːkən,tiːn) *n* *US & Canadian* a sailing ship of three or more masts rigged square on the foremast and fore-and-aft on the others. British spellings: barquentine, barquantine [c17: from BARQUE + (BRIG)ANTINE]

barker ('bɑːkə) *n* **1** an animal or person that barks **2** a person who stands at a show, fair booth, etc, and loudly addresses passers-by to attract customers

Barker ('bɑːkə) *n* **1** George (Granville). 1913–91, British poet: author of *Calamiterror* (1937) and *The True Confession of George Barker* (1950) **2** Howard. born 1946, British playwright: his plays include *Claw* (1975), *The Castle* (1985), *A Hard Heart* (1992), and *13 Objects* (2003) **3** Ronnie, full name *Ronald William George Barker*. 1929–2005, British comedian: known esp for his partnership with Ronnie Corbett (born 1930) in the TV series *The Two Ronnies* (1971–85)

Barkhausen (*German* 'barkhaʊzⁿn) *n* Heinrich Georg. 1881–1956, German physicist: discovered that ferromagnetic material in an increasing magnetic field becomes magnetized in discrete jumps (the **Barkhausen effect**)

barking ('bɑːkɪŋ) *slang* ▷ *adj* **1** mad; crazy ▷ *adv* **2** (*intensifier*): *barking mad*

Barking and Dagenham *n* a borough of E Greater London. Pop: 165 900 (2003 est). Area: 34 sq km (13 sq miles)

Barkla ('bɑːklə) *n* Charles Glover. 1877–1944, British physicist, noted for his work on X-rays: Nobel prize for physics 1917

Bar Kochba, Bar Kokhba *or* **Bar Kosba** (bɑː 'kɒxbə, 'kɒs-) *n* Simeon. died 135 AD, Jewish leader who led an unsuccessful revolt against the Romans in Palestine

Barletta (*Italian* bar'letta) *n* a port in SE Italy, in Apulia. Pop: 92 094 (2001)

barley ('bɑːlɪ) *n* **1** any of various erect annual temperate grasses of the genus *Hordeum*, esp *H. vulgare*, that have short leaves and dense bristly flower spikes and are widely cultivated for grain and forage **2** the grain of any of these grasses, used in making beer and whisky and for soups, puddings, etc [Old English *bærlīc* (adj); related to *bere* barley, Old Norse *barr* barley, Gothic *barizeins* of barley, Latin *farīna* flour]

barleycorn ('bɑːlɪ,kɔːn) *n* **1** a grain of barley, or barley itself **2** an obsolete unit of length equal to one third of an inch

barley sugar *n* a brittle clear amber-coloured sweet made by boiling sugar, originally with a barley extract

barley water *n* a drink made from an infusion of barley, usually flavoured with lemon or orange

barm (bɑːm) *n* **1** the yeasty froth on fermenting malt liquors **2** an archaic or dialect word for **yeast** [Old English *bearm*; related to *beran* to BEAR, Old Norse *barmr* barm, Gothic *barms* see FERMENT]

barmaid ('bɑː,meɪd) *n* a woman who serves in a pub

barman ('bɑːmən) *n*, *pl* -men a man who serves in a pub

Barmecide ('bɑːmɪ,saɪd) *adj* lavish or plentiful in imagination only; illusory; sham: *a Barmecide feast* [c18: from the name of a prince in *The Arabian Nights* who served empty plates to beggars, alleging that they held sumptuous food]

Bar Mitzvah (bɑː 'mɪtsvə) (*sometimes not capitals*) *Judaism* ▷ *adj* **1** (of a Jewish boy) having assumed full religious obligations, being at least thirteen years of age ▷ *n* **2** the occasion, ceremony, or celebration of that event **3** the boy himself on that day [Hebrew: son of the law]

barmy ('bɑːmɪ) *adj* -mier, -miest *slang* eccentric or foolish. Also called: balmy [c16: originally, full of BARM, hence frothing, excited, flighty, etc]

barn¹ (bɑːn) *n* **1** a large farm outbuilding, used chiefly for storing hay, grain, etc, but also for sheltering livestock **2** *US & Canadian* a large shed for sheltering railroad cars, trucks, etc **3** any large building, esp an unattractive one **4** (*modifier*) relating to a system of poultry farming in which birds are allowed to move freely within a barn: *barn eggs* [Old English *beren*, from *bere* barley + *ærn* room; see BARLEY]

barn² (bɑːn) *n* a unit of nuclear cross section equal to 10^{-28} square metre [c20: from BARN¹; so called because of the relatively large cross section]

Barnabas ('bɑːnəbəs) Saint Barnabas *n* New Testament original name *Joseph*. a Cypriot Levite who supported Saint Paul in his apostolic work (Acts 4:36, 37). Feast day: June 11

barnacle ('bɑːnək²l) *n* **1** any of various marine crustaceans of the subclass *Cirripedia* that, as adults, live attached to rocks, ship bottoms, etc They have feathery food-catching cirri protruding from a hard shell **2** a person or thing that is difficult to get rid of [c16: related to Late Latin *bernicla*, of obscure origin] ▷ **barnacled** *adj*

barnacle goose *n* a N European goose, *Branta leucopsis*, that has a black-and-white head and body and grey wings [c13 *bernekke*, related to Late Latin *bernaca*, from the belief that the goose developed from a shellfish; ultimate origin obscure]

Barnard ('bɑːnɑːd) *n* **1** Christiaan (Neethling). 1923–2001, South African surgeon, who performed the first human heart transplant (1967) **2** Edward Emerson. 1857–1923, US astronomer: noted for his discovery of the fifth satellite of Jupiter and his discovery of comets, nebulae, and a red dwarf (1916)

Barnardo (bə'nɑːdəʊ, bɑː-) *n* Dr Thomas John. 1845–1905, British philanthropist, who founded homes for destitute children

Barnaul (*Russian* bərna'ul) *n* a city in S Russia, on the River Ob. Pop: 605 000 (2005 est)

Barnave (*French* barnav) *n* Antoine Pierre. 1761–93, French revolutionary. A prominent member of the National Assembly, he was executed for his royalist sympathies

barn dance *n* **1** *Brit* a progressive round country dance **2** *US & Canadian* a party with hoedown music and square-dancing **3** a disco or party held in a barn

Barnes (bɑːnz) *n* **1** Djuna. 1892–1982, US novelist, noted for *Nightwood* (1936) **2** William. 1801–86, British poet, best known for *Poems of Rural Life in the Dorset Dialect* (1879)

Barnet ('bɑːnɪt) *n* a borough of N Greater London: scene of a Yorkist victory (1471) in the Wars of the Roses. Pop: 324 400 (2003 est). Area: 89 sq km (34 sq miles)

barney ('bɑːnɪ) *informal* ▷ *n* **1** a noisy argument ▷ *vb* (*intr*) **2** *chiefly Austral & NZ* to argue or quarrel [c19: of unknown origin]

barn owl *n* any owl of the genus *Tyto*, esp *T. alba*, having a pale brown and white plumage, long slender legs, and a heart-shaped face: family *Tytonidae*

Barnsley ('bɑːnzlɪ) *n* **1** an industrial town in N England, in Barnsley unitary authority, South Yorkshire. Pop: 71 599 (2001) **2** a unitary authority in N England, in South Yorkshire. Pop: 220 200 (2003 est). Area: 329 sq km (127 sq miles)

Barnstaple ('bɑːnstəp²l) *n* a town in SW England, in Devon, on the estuary of the River Taw: tourism, agriculture. Pop: 30 765 (2001)

barnstorm ('bɑːn,stɔːm) *vb* (*intr*) **1** to tour rural districts putting on shows, esp theatrical, athletic, or acrobatic shows **2** *chiefly US & Canadian* to tour rural districts making speeches in a political campaign [c19: from BARN[1] + STORM (vb); from the performances often being in barns] > 'barn,storming n, adj

Barnum ('bɑːnəm) n P(hineas) T(aylor). 1810–91, US showman, who created The Greatest Show on Earth (1871) and, with J. A. Bailey, founded the Barnum and Bailey Circus (1881)

barnyard ('bɑːn,jɑːd) n 1 a yard adjoining a barn, in which farm animals are kept 2 (modifier) belonging to or characteristic of a barnyard 3 (modifier) crude or earthy

baro- combining form indicating weight or pressure: barometer [from Greek baros weight; related to Latin gravis heavy]

Barocchio (Italian ba'rɔkkjo) n Giacomo ('dʒakomo). See Vignola

Baroda (bə'rəʊdə) n 1 a former state of W India, part of Gujarat since 1960 2 the former name (until 1976) of Vadodara

barogram ('bærə,græm) n meteorol the record of atmospheric pressure traced by a barograph or similar instrument

barograph ('bærə,grɑːf, -,græf) n meteorol a self-recording aneroid barometer > barographic (,bærə'græfɪk) adj

Baroja (Spanish ba'roxa) n Pío ('pío). 1872–1956, Spanish Basque novelist, who wrote nearly 100 novels, including a series of twenty-two under the general title Memorias de un Hombre de Acción (1944–49)

barometer (bə'rɒmɪtə) n 1 an instrument for measuring atmospheric pressure, usually to determine altitude or weather changes 2 anything that shows change or impending change > barometric (,bærə'mɛtrɪk) or ,baro'metrical adj > ba'rometry n

baron ('bærən) n 1 a member of a specific rank of nobility, esp the lowest rank in the British Isles 2 (in Europe from the Middle Ages) originally any tenant-in-chief of a king or other overlord, who held land from his superior by honourable service; a land-holding nobleman 3 a powerful businessman or financier: a press baron [c12: from Old French, of Germanic origin; compare Old High German baro freeman, Old Norse berjask to fight]

baronage ('bærənɪdʒ) n 1 barons collectively 2 the rank or dignity of a baron

Baron-Cohen (,bærən'kəʊən) n Sacha. born 1970, British television and film comedian, best known for his creation of the characters Ali G and Borat

baroness ('bærənɪs) n 1 the wife or widow of a baron 2 a woman holding the rank of baron in her own right

baronet ('bærənɪt, -,nɛt) n (in Britain) a commoner who holds the lowest hereditary title of honour, ranking below a baron. Abbreviation: Bt [c15: order instituted 1611, from BARON + -ET] > 'baronetage n > 'baronetcy n

baronial (bə'rəʊnɪəl) adj of, relating to, or befitting a baron or barons

baron of beef n a cut of beef consisting of a double sirloin joined at the backbone

barony ('bærənɪ) n, pl -nies 1 a the domain of a baron b (in Ireland) a division of a county c (in Scotland) a large estate or manor 2 the rank or dignity of a baron

baroque (bə'rɒk, bə'rəʊk) n (often capital) 1 a style of architecture and decorative art that flourished throughout Europe from the late 16th to the early 18th century, characterized by extensive ornamentation 2 a 17th-century style of music characterized by extensive use of the thorough bass and of ornamentation 3 any ornate or heavily ornamented style ▷ adj 4 denoting, being in, or relating to the baroque 5 (of pearls) irregularly shaped [c18: from French, from Portuguese barroco a rough or imperfectly shaped pearl]

baroreceptor ('bærəʊrɪ,sɛptə) or **baroceptor** n a collection of sensory nerve endings, principally in the carotid sinuses and the aortic arch, that monitor blood pressure changes in the body

baroscope ('bærə,skəʊp) n any instrument for measuring atmospheric pressure, esp a manometer with one side open to the atmosphere > baroscopic (,bærə'skɒpɪk) adj

barouche (bə'ruːʃ) n a four-wheeled horse-drawn

carriage, popular in the 19th century, having a retractable hood over the rear half, seats inside for two couples facing each other, and a driver's seat outside at the front [c19: from German (dialect) Barutsche, from Italian baroccio, from Vulgar Latin birotium (unattested) vehicle with two wheels, from Late Latin birotus two-wheeled, from BI-[1] + rota wheel]

Barozzi (Italian ba'rottsi) n See (Giacomo Barozzi da) Vignola

barperson ('bɑː,pɜːsən) n, pl -persons a person who serves in a pub: used esp in advertisements

barque or esp US **bark** (bɑːk) n 1 a sailing ship of three or more masts having the foremasts rigged square and the aftermast rigged fore-and-aft 2 poetic any boat, esp a small sailing vessel [c15: from Old French, from Old Provençal barca, from Late Latin, of unknown origin]

barquentine or **barquantine** ('bɑːkən,tiːn) n a sailing ship of three or more masts rigged square on the foremast and fore-and-aft on the others [c17: from BARQUE + (BRIG)ANTINE]

Barquisimeto (Spanish barkisi'meto) n a city in NW Venezuela. Pop: 1 009 000 (2005 est)

barra ('bærə) n Austral informal a barramundi

Barra ('bærə) n an island in NW Scotland, in the Outer Hebrides: fishing, crofting, tourism. Pop: 1078 (2001)

barrack[1] ('bærək) vb to house (people, esp soldiers) in barracks

barrack[2] ('bærək) vb Brit, Austral & NZ informal 1 to criticize loudly or shout against (a player, team, speaker, etc); jeer 2 (intr; foll by for) to shout support (for) [c19: from northern Irish: to boast]

barrack-room lawyer n a person who freely offers opinions, esp in legal matters, that he or she is unqualified to give

barracks ('bærəks) pl n (sometimes singular; when plural, sometimes functions as singular) 1 a building or group of buildings used to accommodate military personnel 2 any large building used for housing people, esp temporarily 3 a large and bleak building [c17: from French baraque, from Old Catalan barraca hut, of uncertain origin]

barracouta (,bærə'kuːtə) n a large predatory Pacific fish, Thyrsites atun, with a protruding lower jaw and strong teeth: family Gempylidae [c17: variant of BARRACUDA]

barracuda (,bærə'kjuːdə) n, pl -da or -das any predatory marine teleost fish of the mostly tropical family Sphyraenidae, esp Sphyraena barracuda. They have an elongated body, strong teeth, and a protruding lower jaw [c17: from American Spanish, of unknown origin]

barrage ('bærɑːʒ) n 1 military the firing of artillery to saturate an area, either to protect against an attack or to support an advance 2 an overwhelming and continuous delivery of something, as words, questions, or punches 3 a usually gated construction, similar to a low dam, across a watercourse, esp one to increase the depth of water to assist navigation or irrigation [c19: from French, from barrer to obstruct; see BAR[1]]

barrage balloon n one of a number of tethered balloons with cables or net suspended from them, used to deter low-flying air attack

barramundi (,bærə'mʌndɪ) n, pl -dis, -dies or -di any of several large edible Australian fishes esp the percoid species Lates calcarifer (family Centropomidae) of NE coastal waters or the freshwater species Scleropages leichardti (family Osteoglossidae) of Queensland

Barranquilla (Spanish barran'kiʎa) n a port in N Colombia, on the Magdalena River. Pop: 1 918 000 (2005 est)

Barras (French baras) n Paul François Jean Nicolas, Vicomte de Barras. 1755–1829, French revolutionary: member of the Directory (1795–99)

barratry or **barretry** ('bærətrɪ) n 1 criminal law (formerly) the vexatious stirring up of quarrels or bringing of lawsuits 2 maritime law a fraudulent practice committed by the master or crew of a ship to the prejudice of the owner or charterer 3 the purchase or sale of public or Church offices [c15: from Old French baraterie deception, from barater to BARTER] > 'barratrous, or 'barretrous adj > 'barrator n

Barrault (French baro) n **Jean-Louis** (ʒɑ̃lwi). 1910–94, French actor and director, noted particularly as a mime

barre (French bar) n a rail at hip height used for ballet practice and leg exercises [literally: bar]

barrel ('bærəl) n 1 a cylindrical container usually bulging outwards in the middle and held together by metal hoops; cask 2 Also called: **barrelful** the amount that a barrel can hold 3 a unit of capacity used in the oil and other industries, normally equal to 42 US gallons or 35 Imperial gallons 4 a thing or part shaped like a barrel, esp a tubular part of a machine 5 the tube through which the projectile of a firearm is discharged 6 the trunk of a four-legged animal: *the barrel of a horse* 7 over a barrel *informal* powerless 8 scrape the barrel *informal* to be forced to use one's last and weakest resource ▷ vb -rels, -relling, -relled or US -rels, -reling, -reled 9 (tr) to put into a barrel or barrels 10 (intr; foll by along, in, etc) *informal* (intr) to travel or move very fast [c14: from Old French baril perhaps from barre BAR¹]

barrel-chested adj having a large rounded chest

barrel organ n an instrument consisting of a cylinder turned by a handle and having pins on it that interrupt the air flow to certain pipes, thereby playing any of a number of tunes

barrel roll n a flight manoeuvre in which an aircraft rolls about its longitudinal axis while following a spiral course in line with the direction of flight

barrel vault n *architect* a vault in the form of a half cylinder

barren ('bærən) adj 1 incapable of producing offspring, seed, or fruit; sterile: *a barren tree* 2 unable to support the growth of crops, etc; unproductive; bare: *barren land* 3 lacking in stimulation or ideas; dull 4 not producing worthwhile results; unprofitable: *a barren period in a writer's life* 5 (foll by of) totally lacking (in); devoid (of): *his speech was barren of wit* 6 (of rock strata) having no fossils [c13: from Old French brahain, of uncertain origin] ▷ 'barrenness n

Barren Lands pl n the Barren Lands a region of tundra in N Canada, extending westwards from Hudson Bay: sparsely inhabited, chiefly by Inuit

Barrès (French barɛs) n **Maurice** (mɔris). 1862–1923, French novelist, essayist, and politician: a fervent nationalist and individualist

barricade (,bærɪ'keɪd, 'bærɪ,keɪd) n 1 a barrier for defence, esp one erected hastily, as during street fighting ▷ vb (tr) 2 to erect a barricade across (an entrance, passageway, etc) or at points of access to (a room, district of a town, etc) [c17: from Old French, from barriquer to barricade, from barrique a barrel, from Spanish barrica, from barril BARREL]

Barrie ('bærɪ) n Sir **James Matthew**. 1860–1937, Scottish dramatist and novelist, noted particularly for his popular children's play *Peter Pan* (1904)

barrier ('bærɪə) n 1 anything serving to obstruct passage or to maintain separation, such as a fence or gate 2 anything that prevents or obstructs passage, access, or progress 3 anything that separates or hinders union: *a language barrier* [c14: from Old French barriere, from barre BAR¹]

barrier cream n a cream used to protect the skin, esp the hands, from dirt and from the action of oils or solvents

barrier-nurse vb (tr) to tend (infectious patients) in isolation, to prevent the spread of infection ▷ barrier nursing n

barrier reef n a long narrow coral reef near and lying parallel to the shore, separated from it by deep water

barring ('bɑːrɪŋ) prep unless (something) occurs; except for

Barrington ('bærɪŋtən) n **Jonah**. born 1940, British squash player; winner of the Open Championship 1966–67, 1969–72

barrister ('bærɪstə) n 1 Also called: **barrister-at-law** (in England) a lawyer who has been called to the bar and is qualified to plead in the higher courts. See **solicitor** 2 (in Canada) a lawyer who pleads in court 3 US a less common word for **lawyer** [c16: from BAR¹]

Barros (Portuguese 'bɑːrruʃ) n **João de** (ʒu[~ə]u 'də:). 1496–1570, Portuguese historian: noted for his history of the Portuguese in the East Indies, *Décadas da Ásia* (1552–1615)

barrow¹ ('bærəu) n 1 See **wheelbarrow**, **handbarrow** 2 Also called: **barrowful** the amount contained in or on a barrow 3 chiefly Brit a handcart, typically having two wheels and a canvas roof, used esp by street vendors [Old English bearwe; related to Old Norse barar BIER, Old High German bāra]

barrow² ('bærəu) n a heap of earth placed over one or more prehistoric tombs, often surrounded by ditches. **Long barrows** are elongated Neolithic mounds usually covering stone burial chambers; **round barrows** are Bronze Age, covering burials or cremations [Old English beorg; related to Old Norse bjarg, Gothic bairgahei hill, Old High German berg mountain]

Barrow ('bærəu) n 1 a river in SE Ireland, rising in the Slieve Bloom Mountains and flowing south to Waterford Harbour. Length: about 193 km (120 miles) 2 See **Barrow-in-Furness**, **Barrow Point**

barrow boy n Brit a man who sells his wares from a barrow; street vendor

Barrow-in-Furness n an industrial town in NW England, in S Cumbria. Pop: 47 194 (2001)

Barrow Point n the northernmost tip of Alaska, on the Arctic Ocean

barry or **Barry Crocker** ('bærɪ) n Austral slang a mistake or blunder; a disappointing performance [rhyming slang for SHOCKER]

Barry¹ ('bærɪ) n a port in SE Wales, in Vale of Glamorgan county borough on the Bristol Channel. Pop: 50 661 (2001)

Barry² n 1 ('bærɪ) Sir **Charles**. 1795–1860, English architect: designer of the Houses of Parliament in London 2 (French bari) **Comtesse du**. See **du Barry** 3 **John**, real name *John Barry Prendergast*. born 1933, British composer of film scores, including several for films in the James Bond series

Barrymore ('bærɪ,mɔ:) n a US family of actors, esp **Ethel** (1879–1959), **John** (1882–1942), and **Lionel** (1878–1954)

Barry Mountains pl n a mountain range in SE Australia, in E Victoria: part of the Australian Alps

bar sinister n 1 (not in heraldic usage) another name for **bend sinister** 2 the condition, implication, or stigma of being of illegitimate birth

Bart (bɑːt) n **Lionel**. 1930–99, British composer and playwright. His musicals include *Oliver* (1960)

Bart. abbreviation Baronet

bartender ('bɑː,tendə) n chiefly US & Canadian a man who serves in a bar. Also called: **barman**

barter ('bɑːtə) vb 1 to trade (goods, services, etc) in exchange for other goods, services, etc, rather than for money 2 (intr) to haggle over the terms of such an exchange; bargain ▷ n 3 trade by the exchange of goods [c15: from Old French barater to cheat; perhaps related to Greek prassein to do]

Barth n 1 (German bart) **Heinrich**. 1821–65, German explorer: author of *Travels and Discoveries in North and Central Africa* (1857–58) 2 (bɑːθ) **John** (**Simmons**). born 1930, US novelist; his novels include *The Sot-Weed Factor* (1960), *Giles Goat-Boy* (1966), and *Once Upon a Time* (1994) 3 (German bart) **Karl**. 1886–1968, Swiss Protestant theologian. He stressed man's dependence on divine grace in such works as *Commentary on Romans* (1919)

Barthes (French bart) n **Roland**. 1915–80, French writer and critic, who applied structuralist theory to literature and popular culture: his books include *Mythologies* (1957) and *Elements of Semiology* (1964)

Bartholdi (French bartɔldi) n **Frédéric August**. 1834–1904, French sculptor and architect, who designed (1884) the Statue of Liberty

Bartholomew (bɑː'θɒlə,mju:) n **Saint Bartholomew** n *New Testament* one of the twelve apostles (Matthew 10:3). Feast day: Aug 24 or June 11

bartizan ('bɑːtɪzən, ,bɑːtɪ'zæn) n a small turret projecting from a wall, parapet, or tower [c19: variant of bertisene, erroneously for bretising, from bretasce parapet; see BRATTICE] ▷ **bartizaned** ('bɑːtɪzənd, ,bɑːtɪ'zænd) adj

Bartók ('bɑːtɒk; *Hungarian* 'bɔrtoːk) *n* **Béla** ('beːlɔ). 1881–1945, Hungarian composer, pianist, and collector of folk songs, by which his music was deeply influenced. His works include six string quartets, three piano concertos, several piano pieces including *Mikrokosmos* (1926–37), ballets (including *The Miraculous Mandarin*, 1919), and the opera *Bluebeard's Castle* (produced 1918)

Bartoli (*Italian* baˈtoli) *n* **Cecilia**. born 1966, Italian mezzo-soprano, noted for her performances in Mozart and Rossini operas

Bartolommeo (*Italian* bartolomˈmeo) *n* **Fra**. original name *Baccio della Porta*. 1472–1517, Italian painter of the Florentine school, noted for his austere religious works

Barton ('bɑːtᵊn) *n* **1** Sir **Derek** (**Harold Richard**). 1918–98, British organic chemist: shared the Nobel prize for chemistry (1969) for his work on conformational analysis **2** Sir **Edmund** 1849–1920, Australian statesman; first prime minister of Australia (1901–03) **3** **Elizabeth**, known as the *Maid of Kent*. ?1506–34, English nun, who claimed the gift of prophecy. Her criticism of Henry VIII's attempt to annul his first marriage led to her execution **4** **John** (**Bernard Adie**). born 1928, British theatre director, noted esp for his productions of Shakespeare

Baruch ('bɑːrʊk, 'bɑː-) *n Bible* **a** a disciple of Jeremiah (Jeremiah 32–36) **b** the book of the Apocrypha said to have been written by him

baryon ('bærɪˌɒn) *n* any of a class of elementary particles that have a mass greater than or equal to that of the proton, participate in strong interactions, and have a spin of ½. Baryons are either nucleons or hyperons. The **baryon number** is the number of baryons in a system minus the number of antibaryons [C20: *bary-*, from Greek *barus* heavy + -ON] > ˌbary'onic *adj*

Baryshnikov (bəˈrɪʃnɪkɒf) *n* **Mikhail**. born 1948, Soviet-born ballet dancer, who defected (1974) to the West while on tour with the Kirov Ballet: director (1980–90) of the American Ballet Theatre

baryta (bəˈraɪtə) *n* another name for barium oxide or barium hydroxide [C19: New Latin, from Greek *barutēs* weight, from *barus* heavy]

barytes (bəˈraɪtiːz) *n* a colourless or white mineral consisting of barium sulphate in orthorhombic crystalline form, occurring in sedimentary rocks and with sulphide ores: a source of barium. Formula: BaSO₄ [C18: from Greek *barus* heavy + -*itēs* -ITE¹]

basal ('beɪsᵊl) *adj* **1** at, of, or constituting a base **2** of or constituting a foundation or basis; fundamental; essential > 'basally *adv*

basal metabolism *n* the amount of energy required by an individual in the resting state, for such functions as breathing and circulation of the blood

basalt ('bæsɔːlt) *n* **1** a fine-grained dark basic igneous rock consisting of plagioclase feldspar, a pyroxene, and olivine: the most common volcanic rock and usually extrusive **2** a form of black unglazed pottery resembling basalt [C18: from Late Latin *basaltēs*, variant of *basanītēs*, from Greek *basanītēs* touchstone, from *basanos*, of Egyptian origin] > baˈsaltic *adj*

bascule ('bæskjuːl) *n* **1** Also called: **balance bridge**, **counterpoise bridge** a bridge with a movable section hinged about a horizontal axis and counterbalanced by a weight **2** a movable roadway forming part of such a bridge [C17: from French: seesaw, from *bas* low + *cul* rump; see BASE², CULET]

base¹ (beɪs) *n* **1** the bottom or supporting part of anything **2** the fundamental or underlying principle or part, as of an idea, system, or organization; basis **3 a** a centre of operations, organization, or supply **b** (*as modifier*): *base camp* **4** anything from which a process, as of measurement, action, or thought, is or may be begun; starting point: *the new discovery became the base for further research* **5** the main ingredient of a mixture: *to use rice as a base in cookery* **6** a chemical compound that combines with an acid to form a salt and water. A solution of a base in water turns litmus paper blue, produces hydroxyl ions, and has a pH greater than 7. Bases are metal oxides or hydroxides or amines **7** *biochem* any of the nitrogen-containing constituents of nucleic acids:

adenine, thymine (in DNA), uracil (in RNA), guanine, or cytosine **8** a medium such as oil or water in which the pigment is dispersed in paints, inks, etc; vehicle **9** *biology* **a** the part of an organ nearest to its point of attachment **b** the point of attachment of an organ or part **10** the bottommost layer or part of anything **11** *architect* the lower part of a column or pier **12** the lower side or face of a geometric construction **13** *maths* **a** the number of distinct single-digit numbers in a counting system, and so the number represented as 10 in a place-value system: *the binary system has two digits, 0 and 1, and 10 to base two represents 2* **b** (of a logarithm or exponential) the number whose powers are expressed: *since 1000 = 10³, the logarithm of 1000 to base 10 is 3* **14** *electronics* the region in a transistor between the emitter and collector **15** a starting or finishing point in any of various games > *vb* **16** (*tr* foll by *on* or *upon*) to use as a basis (for); found (on) **17** (often foll by *at* or *in*) to station, post, or place (a person or oneself) [C14: from Old French, from Latin *basis* pedestal; see BASIS]

base² (beɪs) *adj* **1** devoid of honour or morality; ignoble; contemptible **2** of inferior quality or value **3** debased; alloyed; counterfeit: *base currency* **4** *English history* **a** (of land tenure) held by villein or other ignoble service **b** holding land by villein or other ignoble service **5** *archaic* born of humble parents; plebeian **6** *archaic* illegitimate [C14: from Old French *bas*, from Late Latin *bassus* of low height, perhaps from Greek *bassōn* deeper] > 'baseness *n*

baseball ('beɪsˌbɔːl) *n* **1** a team game with nine players on each side, played on a field with four bases connected to form a diamond. The object is to score runs by batting the ball and running round the bases **2** the hard rawhide-covered ball used in this game

baseball cap *n* a close-fitting thin cap with a deep peak

baseborn ('beɪsˌbɔːn) *adj archaic* **1** born of humble parents **2** illegitimate

base hospital *n Austral* a hospital serving a large rural area

Basel ('bɑːzᵊl) *n* a variant spelling of **Basle**

baseless ('beɪslɪs) *adj* not based on fact; unfounded > 'baselessness *n*

baseline ('beɪsˌlaɪn) *n* **1** *surveying* a measured line through a survey area from which triangulations are made **2** a line at each end of a tennis court that marks the limit of play

baseliner ('beɪsˌlaɪnə) *n tennis* a player who plays most of his or her shots from the back of court

basement ('beɪsmənt) *n* **1 a** a partly or wholly underground storey of a building, esp the one immediately below the main floor **b** (*as modifier*): *a basement flat* **2** the foundation or substructure of a wall or building

base metal *n* any of certain common metals such as copper, lead, zinc, and tin, as distinct from the precious metals, gold, silver, and platinum

basenji (bəˈsɛndʒɪ) *n* a small smooth-haired breed of dog of African origin having a tightly curled tail and an inability to bark [C20: from a Bantu language]

base rate *n* **1** *Brit* the rate of interest used by individual commercial banks as a basis for their lending rates **2** *Brit informal* the rate at which the Bank of England lends to the discount houses, which effectively controls the interest rates charged throughout the banking system **3** *statistics* the average number of times an event occurs divided by the average number of times on which it might occur

bases¹ ('beɪsiːz) *n* the plural of **basis**

bases² ('beɪsɪz) *n* the plural of **base¹**

Basescu (bæjsɛsku:) *n* **Traian**. born 1951, Romanian politician, president of Romania from 2007

base unit *n physics* any of the fundamental units in a system of measurement. The base SI units are the metre, kilogram, second, ampere, kelvin, candela, and mole

bash (bæʃ) *informal* > *vb* **1** (*tr*) to strike violently or crushingly **2** (*tr*; often foll by *in*, *down*, etc) to smash, break, etc, with a crashing blow **3** (*intr*; foll by *into*) to crash (into); collide (with): *to bash into a lamppost* **4** to

b

dent or be dented ▷ *n* **5** a heavy blow, as from a fist **6** a party **7** have a bash *informal* to make an attempt [c17: of uncertain origin]

bashful ('bæʃful) *adj* **1** disposed to attempt to avoid notice through shyness or modesty; diffident; timid **2** indicating or characterized by shyness or modesty [c16: from *bash*, short for ABASH + -FUL] > 'bashfully *adv* > 'bashfulness *n*

-bashing *adj combining form, n combining form informal or slang* **a** indicating a malicious attack on members of a particular group: *queer-bashing; union-bashing* **b** indicating any of various other activities: *Bible-bashing; spud-bashing; square-bashing* > -basher *n combining form*

Bashkir Republic *n* a constituent republic of E central Russia, in the S Urals: established as the first Soviet autonomous republic in 1919; rich mineral resources. Capital: Ufa. Pop: 4 012 900 (2002). Area: 143 600 sq km (55 430 sq miles). Also called: **Bashkiria** (bæʃ'kɪərɪə), **Bashkortostan** (bæʃˌkɔːtɔˌstaːn; *Russian* baʃkʌrtɔ'staːn)

Bashkirtseff or **Bashkirtsev** (bəʃˈkjɪrtsəf) *n* **Marie**, original name *Marya Konstantinovna Bashkirtseva*. 1858–84, Russian painter and diarist who wrote in French, noted esp for her *Journal* (1887)

basho ('bæʃəʊ) *n, pl* **basho** a grand tournament in sumo wrestling [c20: from Japanese]

Basho (baːˈʃɔː) *n* full name **Matsuo Basho**, originally *Matsuo Munefusa*. 1644–94, Japanese poet and travel writer, noted esp for his haiku

basic ('beɪsɪk) *adj* **1** of, relating to, or forming a base or basis; fundamental; underlying **2** elementary or simple: *a few basic facts* **3** excluding additions or extras: *basic pay* **4** *chem* **a** of, denoting, or containing a base; alkaline **b** (of a salt) containing hydroxyl or oxide groups not all of which have been replaced by an acid radical: *basic lead carbonate*, $2PbCO_3 \cdot Pb(OH)_2$ **5** *metallurgy* of, concerned with, or made by a process in which the furnace or converter is made of a basic material, such as magnesium oxide **6** (of such igneous rocks as basalt) containing between 52 and 45 per cent silica ▷ *n* **7** (*usually plural*) a fundamental principle, fact, etc

BASIC or **Basic** ('beɪsɪk) *n* a computer programming language that uses common English terms [c20: acronym of *b*(eginner's) *a*(ll-purpose) *s*(ymbolic) *i*(nstruction) *c*(ode)]

basically ('beɪsɪklɪ) *adv* **1** in a fundamental or elementary manner; essentially: *strident and basically unpleasant* **2** (*sentence modifier*) in essence; in summary; put simply: *basically we had underestimated mother nature*

Basic Curriculum *n Brit education* in England and Wales, the National Curriculum plus religious education

basic English *n* a simplified form of English, proposed by C. K. Ogden and I. A. Richards, containing a vocabulary of approximately 850 of the commonest English words, intended as an international language

basic industry *n* an industry which is highly important in a nation's economy

basicity (beɪˈsɪsɪtɪ) *n chem* **a** the state of being a base **b** the extent to which a substance is basic

basic rate *n* the standard or lowest level on a scale of money payable, esp in taxation

basic slag *n* a furnace slag produced in steel-making, containing large amounts of calcium phosphate: used as a fertilizer

basic wage *n* **1** a person's wage excluding overtime, bonuses, etc **2** *Austral* the statutory minimum wage for any worker

basidiomycete (bæˌsɪdɪəʊmaɪˈsiːt) *n* any fungus of the phylum Basidiomycota (formerly class *Basidiomycetes*), in which the spores are produced in basidia. The group includes boletes, puffballs, smuts, and rusts [c19: from BASIDI(UM) + -MYCETE] > ˌbasidiomy'cetous *adj*

basidium (bæˈsɪdɪəm) *n, pl* **-ia** (-ɪə) the structure, produced by basidiomycetous fungi after sexual reproduction, in which spores are formed at the tips of projecting slender stalks [c19: from New Latin, from Greek *basidion*; see BASIS, -IUM] > ba'sidial *adj*

Basie ('beɪsɪ) *n* **William**, known as **Count Basie**. 1904–84, US jazz pianist, bandleader, and composer: associated particularly with the polished phrasing and style of big-band jazz

basil ('bæzəl) *n* Also called: **sweet basil** a Eurasian plant, *Ocimum basilicum*, having spikes of small white flowers and aromatic leaves used as herbs for seasoning: family Lamiaceae (labiates) [c15: from Old French *basile*, from Late Latin *basilicum*, from Greek *basilikon*, from *basilikos* royal, from *basileus* king]

Basil ('bæzəl) *n* **Saint**, called *the Great*, ?329–379 AD, Greek patriarch: an opponent of Arianism and one of the founders of monasticism. Feast day: Jan 2, June 14, or Jan 1

Basil I *n* known as *the Macedonian*. died 886 AD, Byzantine emperor (876–86): founder of the Macedonian dynasty

Basilan (bəˈsiːlaːn, baːˈsiːlæn) *n* **1** a group of islands in the Philippines, SW of Mindanao **2** the main island of this group, separated from Mindanao by the **Basilan Strait**. Area: 1282 sq km (495 sq miles) **3** a city on Basilan Island. Pop: 381 000 (2005 est)

basilar ('bæsɪlə) *adj chiefly anatomy* of or situated at a base: *basilar artery*. Also called: **basilary** ('bæsɪlərɪ, -sɪlrɪ) [c16: from New Latin *basilaris*, from Latin *basis* BASE[1]; compare Medieval Latin *bassile* pelvis]

Basildon ('bæzɪldən) *n* a town in SE England, in S Essex: designated a new town in 1955. Pop: 99 876 (2001)

basilica (bəˈzɪlɪkə) *n* **1** a Roman building, used for public administration, having a large rectangular central nave with an aisle on each side and an apse at the end **2** a rectangular early Christian or medieval church, usually having a nave with clerestories, two or four aisles, one or more vaulted apses, and a timber roof **3** a Roman Catholic church having special ceremonial rights [c16: from Latin, from Greek *basilikē* hall, from *basilikē oikia* the king's house, from *basileus* king; see BASIL] > ba'silican, or ba'silic *adj*

Basilicata (Italian bazili'kata) *n* a region of S Italy, between the Tyrrhenian Sea and the Gulf of Taranto. Capital: Potenza. Pop: 596 821 (2003 est). Area: 9985 sq km (3855 sq miles)

basilisk ('bæzɪˌlɪsk) *n* **1** (in classical legend) a serpent that could kill by its breath or glance **2** any small arboreal semiaquatic lizard of the genus *Basiliscus* of tropical America: family Iguanidae (iguanas). The males have an inflatable head crest, used in display [c14: from Latin *basiliscus*, from Greek *basiliskos* royal child, from *basileus* king]

basin ('beɪsən) *n* **1** a round container open and wide at the top with sides sloping inwards towards the bottom or base, esp one in which liquids are mixed or stored **2** Also called: **basinful** the amount a basin will hold **3** a washbasin or sink **4** any partially enclosed or sheltered area where vessels may be moored or docked **5** the catchment area of a particular river and its tributaries or of a lake or sea **6** a depression in the earth's surface **7** *geology* a part of the earth's surface consisting of rock strata that slope down to a common centre [c13: from Old French *bacin*, from Late Latin *bacchīnon*, from Vulgar Latin *bacca* (unattested) container for water; related to Latin *bāca* berry]

Basingstoke ('beɪzɪŋˌstəʊk) *n* a town in S England, in N Hampshire. Pop: 90 171 (2001)

basis ('beɪsɪs) *n, pl* **-ses** (-siːz) **1** something that underlies, supports, or is essential to something else, esp an abstract idea **2** a principle on which something depends or from which something has issued [c14: via Latin from Greek: step, from *bainein* to step, go]

basis point *n* a measure used for describing interest rates, equal to one hundredth of a percentage point (0.01%)

bask (baːsk) *vb* (*intr; usually foll by in*) **1** to lie in or be exposed to pleasant warmth, esp that of the sun **2** to flourish or feel secure under some benevolent influence or favourable condition [c14: from Old Norse *bathask* to BATHE]

basket ('baːskɪt) *n* **1** a container made of interwoven strips of pliable materials, such as cane, straw, thin wood, or plastic, and often carried by means of a handle or handles **2** Also called: **basketful** the amount a basket will hold **3** something resembling such a container in appearance or function, such as the structure suspended from a balloon **4** *basketball* **a** an open horizontal metal hoop fixed to the backboard, through which a player must throw the ball to score points **b** a point or points scored in this way **5** a group or collection of similar or related things: *a basket of currencies* **6** *informal* a euphemism for **bastard** (senses 1, 2) **7** the list of items an internet shopper chooses to buy at one time from a website: *add these items to your basket* [C13: probably from Old Northern French *baskot* (unattested), from Latin *bascauda* basketwork holder, of Celtic origin]

basketball ('bɑːskɪt,bɔːl) *n* **1** a game played by two opposing teams of five men (or six women) each, usually on an indoor court. Points are scored by throwing the ball through an elevated horizontal metal hoop **2** the inflated ball used in this game

basket case *n slang* **1** a person who is suffering from extreme nervous strain; nervous wreck **2** *chiefly US & Canadian highly offensive* a person who has had both arms and both legs amputated **3 a** someone or something that is incapable of functioning normally **b** (*as modifier*): *a basket-case economy*

basket chair *n* a chair made of wickerwork; a wicker chair

basketry ('bɑːskɪtrɪ) *n* **1** the art or practice of making baskets **2** baskets collectively

basket weave *n* a weave of two or more yarns together, resembling that of a basket, esp in wool or linen fabric

basketweaver ('bɑːskɪt,wiːvə) *n Austral derogatory, slang* a person who advocates simple, natural, and unsophisticated living

basketwork ('bɑːskɪt,wɜːk) *n* another word for **wickerwork**

basking shark *n* a very large plankton-eating shark, *Cetorhinus maximus*, often floating at the sea surface: family *Cetorhinidae*. Also called: **sailfish**

Basle (bɑːl) *or* **Basel** ('bɑːzəl) *n* **1** a canton of NW Switzerland, divided into the demicantons of **Basle-Landschaft** and **Basle-Stadt**. Pops.: 263 200 and 186 900 (2002 est). Areas: 427 sq km (165 sq miles) and 36 sq km (14 sq miles) respectively **2** a city in NW Switzerland, capital of Basle canton, on the Rhine: oldest university in Switzerland. Pop: 165 000 (2002 est) ▷ French name: **Bâle**

basmati rice (bəzˈmætɪ) *n* a variety of long-grain rice with slender aromatic grains, used for savoury dishes [from Hindi, literally: aromatic]

basophil ('beɪsəfɪl) *or* **basophile** Also called: **basophilic** (,beɪsəˈfɪlɪk) *adj* **1** (of cells or cell contents) easily stained by basic dyes *n* **2** a basophil cell, esp a leucocyte [C19: from Greek; see BASE¹ + -PHILE]

Basotho-Qwaqwa (bəˈsuːtuːˈkwɑːkwə, -ˈsəʊtəʊ-) *n* (formerly) a Bantustan in South Africa, in the Orange Free State; the only Bantustan without exclaves: abolished in 1993. Also called: **Qwaqwa**

Basov (*Russian* 'basəf) *n* **Nikolai Gennediyevich** (nikaˈlaj gjiˈnadjejivitʃ). 1922–2001, Russian physicist: shared the Nobel prize for physics (1964) for his pioneering work on the maser

basque (bæsk, bɑːsk) *n* a tight-fitting bodice for women [C19: perhaps from BASQUE]

Basque (bæsk, bɑːsk) *n* **1** a member of a people of unknown origin living around the W Pyrenees in France and Spain **2** the language of this people, of no known relationship with any other language ▷ *adj* **3** relating to, denoting, or characteristic of this people or their language [C19: from French, from Latin *Vascō* a Basque]

Basque Provinces *or* **Basque Country** *n* an autonomous region of N Spain, comprising the provinces of Álava, Guipúzcoa, and Vizcaya: inhabited mainly by Basques, who retained virtual autonomy from the 9th to the 19th century. Pop: 1 840 700 (2003 est). Area: about 7250 sq km (2800 sq miles)

Basra, Basrah ('bæzrə) *or* **Busra, Busrah** ('bʌsrə) *n* a port in SE Iraq, on the Shatt-al-Arab. Pop: 1 187 000 (2005 est)

bas-relief (,bɑːrɪˈliːf, ,bæs-, 'bɑːrɪ,liːf, 'bæs-) *n* sculpture in low relief, in which the forms project slightly from the background but no part is completely detached from it [C17: from French, from Italian *basso rilievo* low relief;

see BASE², RELIEF]

Bas-Rhin (*French* barɛ̃) *n* a department of NE France in Alsace region. Capital: Strasbourg. Pop: 1 052 698 (2003 est). Area: 4793 sq km (1869 sq miles)

bass¹ (beɪs) *n* **1** the lowest adult male voice usually having a range from E a 13th below middle C to D a tone above it **2** a singer with such a voice **3** the bass the lowest part in a piece of harmony. See also **thorough bass 4** *informal* short for **bass guitar, double bass 5 a** the low-frequency component of an electrical audio signal, esp in a record player or tape recorder **b** the knob controlling this on such an instrument ▷ *adj* **6** relating to or denoting the bass **7** denoting the lowest and largest instrument in a family [C15 *bas* BASE¹; modern spelling influenced by BASSO]

bass² (bæs) *n* **1** any of various sea perches, esp *Morone labrax*, a popular game fish with one large spiny dorsal fin separate from a second smaller one **2** the European perch **3** any of various predatory North American freshwater percoid fishes, such as *Micropterus salmoides*, (**largemouth bass**): family *Centrarchidae* (sunfishes, etc) [C15: changed from BASE², influenced by Italian *basso* low]

bass clef (beɪs) *n* the clef that establishes F a fifth below middle C on the fourth line of the staff

bass drum (beɪs) *n* a large shallow drum of low and indefinite pitch

Bassein (bɑːˈseɪn) *n* a city in Myanmar, on the Irrawaddy delta: a port on the **Bassein River** (the westernmost distributary of the Irrawaddy). Pop: 231 000 (2005 est)

Basse-Normandie (*French* basnɔrmɑ̃di) *n* a region of NW France, on the English Channel: consists of the Cherbourg peninsula in the west rising to the Normandy hills in the east; mainly agricultural

Bassenthwaite ('bæsⁿn,θweɪt) *n* a lake in NW England, in Cumbria near Keswick. Length: 6 km (4 miles)

Basses-Alpes (*French* basalp) *n* the former name for **Alpes-de-Haute-Provence**

Basses-Pyrénées (*French* baspirene) *pl n* the former name for **Pyrénées-Atlantiques**

basset ('bæsɪt) *n* a long low smooth-haired breed of hound with short strong legs and long ears. Also called: **basset hound** [C17: from French, from *basset* short, from *bas* low; see BASE²]

Basseterre (bæsˈtɛə; *French* bastɛr) *n* a port in the Caribbean, on St Kitts in the Leeward Islands: the capital of St Kitts-Nevis. Pop: 13 220 (2001)

Basse-Terre ('bæs'tɛə; *French* bastɛr) *n* **1** a mountainous island in the Caribbean, in the Leeward Islands, comprising part of Guadeloupe. Area: 848 sq km (327 sq miles) **2** a port in W Guadeloupe, on Basse-Terre Island: the capital of the French Overseas Department of Guadeloupe. Pop: 12 410 (1999)

basset horn *n* an obsolete woodwind instrument of the clarinet family [C19: probably from German *Bassetthorn*, from Italian *bassetto*, diminutive of BASSO + HORN]

bass guitar (beɪs) *n* a guitar that has the same pitch and tuning as a double bass, usually electrically amplified

bassinet (,bæsɪˈnɛt) *n* a wickerwork or wooden cradle or pram, usually hooded [C19: from French: little basin, from *bassin* BASIN; associated in folk etymology with French *barcelonnette* a little cradle, from *berceau* cradle]

bassist ('beɪsɪst) *n* a player of a double bass, esp in a jazz band

basso ('bæsəʊ) *n, pl* **-sos** *or* **-si** (-sɪ) (esp in operatic or solo singing) a singer with a bass voice [C19: from Italian, from Late Latin *bassus* low; see BASE²]

bassoon (bəˈsuːn) *n* **1** a woodwind instrument, the tenor of the oboe family. Range: about three and a half octaves upwards from the B flat below the bass staff **2** an orchestral musician who plays the bassoon [C18: from French *basson*, from Italian *bassone*, from *basso* deep; see BASE²] **> bas'soonist** *n*

basso rilievo (*Italian* 'basso ri'ljevo) *n, pl* **-vos** Italian name for **bas-relief**

Bass Strait (bæs) *n* a channel between mainland Australia and Tasmania, linking the Indian Ocean and the Tasman Sea

bass viol (beɪs) *n* **1** another name for **viola da gamba** **2** *US* a less common name for **double bass** (sense 1)

bast (bæst) *n* **1** Also called: bass fibrous material obtained from the phloem of jute, hemp, flax, lime, etc, used for making rope, matting, etc **2** *botany* another name for **phloem** [Old English *bæst*; related to Old Norse, Middle High German *bast*]

bastard ('bɑːstəd, 'bæs-) *n* **1** *informal, offensive* an obnoxious or despicable person **2** *informal, often humorous or affectionate* a person, esp a man: *lucky bastard* **3** *informal* something extremely difficult or unpleasant: *that job is a real bastard* **4** *old-fashioned or offensive* a person born of unmarried parents; an illegitimate baby, child, or adult **5** something irregular, abnormal, or inferior **6** a hybrid, esp an accidental or inferior one ▷ *adj* (*prenominal*) **7** old-fashioned, or offensive illegitimate by birth **8** irregular, abnormal, or inferior in shape, size, or appearance **9** resembling a specified thing, but not actually being such: *a bastard cedar* **10** counterfeit; spurious [C13: from Old French *bastart*, perhaps from *bast* in the phrase *fils de bast* son of the packsaddle (that is, of an unlawful and not the marriage bed), from Medieval Latin *bastum* packsaddle, of uncertain origin] ▷ '**bastardly** *adj*

bastardize *or* **bastardise** ('bɑːstə,daɪz, 'bæs-) *vb* (*tr*) **1** to debase; corrupt **2** *archaic* to declare illegitimate

baste¹ (beɪst) *vb* (*tr*) to sew with loose temporary stitches [C14: from Old French *bastir* to build, of Germanic origin; compare Old High German *besten* to sew with BAST]

baste² (beɪst) *vb* to moisten (meat) during cooking with hot fat and the juices produced [C15: of uncertain origin]

baste³ (beɪst) *vb* (*tr*) to beat thoroughly; thrash [C16: probably from Old Norse *beysta*]

Bastia ('bɑːstjə) *n* a port in NE Corsica: the main commercial and industrial town of the island: capital of Haute-Corse department. Pop: 37 884 (1999)

Bastille (bæ'stiːl; *French* bastij) *n* a fortress in Paris, built in the 14th century: a prison until its destruction in 1789, at the beginning of the French Revolution [C14: from Old French *bastile* fortress, from Old Provençal *bastida*, from *bastir* to build, of Germanic origin; see BASTE¹]

bastinado (,bæstɪ'neɪdəʊ) *n*, *pl* -does **1** punishment or torture in which the soles of the feet are beaten with a stick **2** a blow or beating with a stick ▷ *vb* -does, -doing, -doed (*tr*) **3** to beat (a person) on the soles of the feet [C16: from Spanish *bastonada*, from *baston* stick, from Late Latin *bastum* see BATON]

bastion ('bæstɪən) *n* **1** a projecting work in a fortification designed to permit fire to the flanks along the face of the wall **2** any fortified place **3** a thing or person regarded as upholding or defending an attitude, principle, etc: *the last bastion of opposition* [C16: from French, from earlier *bastillon* bastion, from *bastille* BASTILLE]

Bastogne (bæ'stəʊn; *French* bastɔɲ) *n* a town in SE Belgium: of strategic importance to Allied defences during the Battle of the Bulge; besieged by the Germans during the winter of 1944–45. Pop: 14 070 (2004 est)

Basutoland (bə'suːtəʊ,lænd) *n* the former name (until 1966) of **Lesotho**

bat¹ (bæt) *n* **1** any of various types of club with a handle, used to hit the ball in certain sports, such as cricket, baseball, or table tennis **2** a flat round club with a short handle, resembling a table-tennis bat, used by a man on the ground to guide the pilot of an aircraft when taxiing **3** *cricket* short for **batsman** **4** any stout stick, esp a wooden one **5** *informal* a blow from such a stick **6** *US & Canadian slang* a drinking spree; binge **7** *slang* speed; rate; pace: *they went at a fair bat* **8** carry one's bat *cricket* (of an opening batsman) to reach the end of an innings without being dismissed **9** off one's own bat **a** of one's own accord; without being prompted by someone else **b** by one's own unaided efforts ▷ *vb* bats, batting, batted **10** (*tr*) to strike with or as if with a bat **11** (*intr*) *sport* (of a player or a team) to take a turn at batting [Old English *batt* club, probably of Celtic origin; compare Gaelic *bat*, Russian *bat*]

bat² (bæt) *n* **1** any placental mammal of the order *Chiroptera*, being a nocturnal mouselike animal flying with a pair of membranous wings (patagia). The group is divided into the *Megachiroptera* (**fruit bats**) and *Microchiroptera* (**insectivorous bats**) **2** *slang* an irritating or eccentric woman (esp in the phrase **old bat**) **3** blind as a bat having extremely poor eyesight **4** have bats in the belfry *or* have bats in one's belfry *informal* to be mad or eccentric; have strange ideas [C14 *bakke*, probably of Scandinavian origin; compare Old Norse *ledhrblaka* leather-flapper, Swedish dialect *natt-batta* night bat]

bat³ (bæt) *vb* bats, batting, batted (*tr*) **1** to wink or flutter (one's eyelids) **2** not bat an eye *or* not bat an eyelid *informal* to show no surprise or concern [C17: probably a variant of BATE²]

Bataan (bə'tæn, -'tɑːn) *n* a peninsula in the Philippines, in W Luzon: scene of the surrender of US and Philippine forces to the Japanese during World War II, later retaken by American forces

Batangas (bə'tæŋɡəs) *n* a port in the Philippines, in SW Luzon. Pop: 293 000 (2005 est)

Batan Islands (bə'tɑːn) *pl n* a group of islands in the Philippines, north of Luzon. Capital: Basco. Pop: 16 467 (2000). Area: 197 sq km (76 sq miles)

Batavia (bə'teɪvɪə) *n* **1** an ancient district of the Netherlands, on an island at the mouth of the Rhine **2** an archaic or literary name for **Holland¹ 3** a former name for **Jakarta**

batch¹ (bætʃ) *n* **1** a group or set of usually similar objects or people, esp if sent off, handled, or arriving at the same time **2** the bread, cakes, etc, produced at one baking **3** the amount of a material needed for an operation ▷ *vb* (*tr*) **4** to group (items) for efficient processing **5** to handle by batch processing [C15 *bache*; related to Old English *bacan* to BAKE; compare Old English *gebæc* batch, German *Gebäck*]

batch² *or* **bach** (bætʃ) *vb Austral & NZ informal* **1** (*intr*) (of a man) to do his own cooking and housekeeping **2** to live alone

batch processing *n* a system by which the computer programs of a number of individual users are submitted to the computer as a single batch

bate¹ (beɪt) *vb* another word for **abate**

bate² (beɪt) *vb* (*intr*) (of hawks) to jump violently from a perch or the falconer's fist, often hanging from the leash while struggling to escape [C13: from Old French *batre* to beat, from Latin *battuere*; related to BAT¹]

bate³ (beɪt) *n Brit slang* a bad temper or rage [C19: from BAIT¹, alluding to the mood of a person who is being baited]

bateau (bæ'təʊ; *French* bato) *n*, *pl* -teaux (-təʊz; *French* -to) a light flat-bottomed boat used on rivers in Canada and the northern US [C18: from French: boat, from Old French *batel*, from Old English *bāt*; see BOAT]

bateleur eagle ('bætələ:) *n* an African crested bird of prey, *Terathopius ecaudatus*, with a short tail and long wings: subfamily *Circaetinae*, family *Accipitridae* (hawks, etc) [C19: from French *bateleur* juggler]

Bates (beɪts) *n* **1** Sir **Alan** (**Arthur**). 1934–2003, British film and stage actor. His films include *A Kind of Loving* (1962), *Women in Love* (1969), *The Go-Between* (1971), and *The Cherry Orchard* (1999) **2** H(**erbert**) **E**(**rnest**). 1905–74, English writer of short stories and novels, which include *The Darling Buds of May* (1958), *A Moment in Time* (1964), and *The Triple Echo* (1970)

bath (bɑːθ) *n*, *pl* baths (bɑːðz) **1** a large container, esp one made of enamelled iron or plastic, used for washing or medically treating the body **2** the act or an instance of washing in such a container **3** the amount of liquid contained in a bath **4** (*usually plural*) a place that provides baths or a swimming pool for public use **5 a** a vessel in which something is immersed to maintain it at a constant temperature, to process it photographically, electrolytically, etc, or to lubricate it **b** the liquid used in such a vessel ▷ *vb* **6** *Brit* to wash in a bath [Old English *bæth*; compare Old High German *bad*, Old Norse *bath*; related to Swedish *basa* to clean with warm water, Old High German *bāen* to warm]

Bath (bɑːθ) *n* a city in SW England, in Bath and North

East Somerset unitary authority, Somerset, on the River Avon: famous for its hot springs; a fashionable spa in the 18th century; Roman remains, notably the baths; university (1966). Pop: 90 144 (2001)

Bath and North East Somerset ('sʌməsɛt) *n* a unitary authority in SW England, in Somerset; formerly (1974–96) part of the county of Avon. Pop: 170 900 (2003 est). Area: 351 sq km (136 sq miles)

bath bun *n Brit* a sweet bun containing spices and dried fruit [c19: from Bath, where it was originally made]

Bath chair *n* a wheelchair for invalids, often with a hood

bath cube *n* a cube of soluble scented material for use in a bath

bathe (beɪð) *vb* **1** (*intr*) to swim or paddle in a body of open water or a river, esp for pleasure **2** (*tr*) to apply liquid to (skin, a wound, etc) in order to cleanse or soothe **3** to immerse or be immersed in a liquid **4** *chiefly US & Canadian* to wash in a bath **5** (*tr; often passive*) to suffuse ▷ *n* **6** *Brit* a swim or paddle in a body of open water or a river [Old English *bathian*; related to Old Norse *batha*, Old High German *badōn*] > 'bather *n*

bathers ('beɪðəz) *pl n Austral* a swimming costume

bathhouse ('bɑːθˌhaʊs) *n* a building containing baths, esp for bathing

bathing cap ('beɪðɪŋ) *n* a tight rubber cap worn by a swimmer to keep the hair dry

bathing costume ('beɪðɪŋ) *n* another name for **swimming costume**

bathing machine ('beɪðɪŋ) *n* a small hut, on wheels so that it could be pulled to the sea, used in the 18th and 19th centuries for bathers to change their clothes

bathing suit ('beɪðɪŋ) *n* a garment worn for bathing, esp an old-fashioned one that covers much of the body

batho- *combining form* a variant of **bathy-**

batholith ('bæθəlɪθ) *or* **batholite** ('bæθəˌlaɪt) *n* a very large irregular-shaped mass of igneous rock, esp granite, formed from an intrusion of magma at great depth, esp one exposed after erosion of less resistant overlying rocks > ˌbatho'lithic *or* ˌbatho'litic *adj*

Bath Oliver *n Brit* a kind of unsweetened biscuit [c19: named after William Oliver (1695–1764), a physician at Bath]

bathometer (bə'θɒmɪtə) *n* an instrument for measuring the depth of water > bathometric (ˌbæθə'mɛtrɪk) *adj* > bathometry (bə'θɒmɪtrɪ) *n*

bathos ('beɪθɒs) *n* **1** a sudden ludicrous descent from exalted to ordinary matters or style in speech or writing **2** insincere or excessive pathos [c18: from Greek: depth, from *bathus* deep] > ba'thetic *adj*

bathrobe ('bɑːθˌrəʊb) *n* **1** a loose-fitting garment of towelling, for wear before or after a bath or swimming **2** *US & Canadian* a dressing gown

bathroom ('bɑːθˌruːm, -ˌrʊm) *n* **1** a room containing a bath or shower and usually a washbasin and lavatory **2** *US & Canadian* another name for **lavatory**

bath salts *pl n* soluble scented salts for use in a bath

Bathsheba (bæθ'ʃiːbə, 'bæθʃɪbə) *n Old Testament* the wife of Uriah, who committed adultery with David and later married him and became the mother of his son Solomon (II Samuel 11–12)

bathtub ('bɑːθˌtʌb) *n* a bath, esp one not permanently fixed

bathtub race *n Canadian* a sailing race between bathtubs fitted with outboard motors

Bathurst ('bæθəst) *n* **1** a town in SE Australia, in E New South Wales: scene of a gold rush in 1851. Pop: 27 036 (2001) **2** a port in E Canada, in NE New Brunswick: rich mineral resources. Pop: 16 427 (2001) **3** the former name (until 1973) of **Banjul**

bathy- *or* **batho-** *combining form* indicating depth: *bathysphere; bathometer* [from Greek *bathus* deep]

bathyscaph ('bæθɪˌskæf), **bathyscaphe** ('bæθɪˌskeɪf, -ˌskæf) *or* **bathyscape** ('bæθɪˌskeɪp) *n* a submersible vessel having a flotation compartment with an observation capsule underneath, capable of reaching ocean depths of over 10 000 metres (about 5000 fathoms) [c20: from BATHY- + -*scaph*, from Greek *skaphē* light boat]

bathysphere ('bæθɪˌsfɪə) *n* a strong steel deep-sea diving sphere, lowered by cable

batik *or* **battik** ('bætɪk) *n* **a** a process of printing fabric in which parts not to be dyed are covered by wax **b** fabric printed in this way [c19: via Malay from Javanese: painted]

Batista (*Spanish* ba'tista) *n* Fulgencio (ful'xenθjo), full name *Batista y Zaldívar*. 1901–73, Cuban military leader and dictator: president of Cuba (1940–44, 1952–59); overthrown by Fidel Castro

batiste (bæ'tiːst) *n* a fine plain-weave cotton fabric: used esp for shirts and dresses [c17: from French, from Old French *toile de baptiste*, probably after *Baptiste* of Cambrai, 13th-century French weaver, its reputed inventor]

Batley ('bætlɪ) *n* a town in N England, in Kirklees unitary authority, West Yorkshire. Pop: 49 448 (2001)

batman ('bætmən) *n, pl* -men an officer's personal servant in any of the armed forces [c18: from Old French *bat, bast*, from Medieval Latin *bastum* packsaddle]

Batman ('bætmən) *n* John. 1801–39, a pioneer who selected the site of the city of Melbourne

baton ('bætən, -tɒn) *n* **1** a thin stick used by the conductor of an orchestra, choir, etc, to indicate rhythm or expression **2** a short stick carried for use as a weapon, as by a policeman; truncheon **3** *athletics* a short bar carried by a competitor in a relay race and transferred to the next runner at the end of each stage **4** a long stick with a knob on one end, carried, twirled, and thrown up and down by a drum major or drum majorette, esp at the head of a parade **5** a staff or club carried by an official as a symbol of authority [c16: from French *bâton*, from Late Latin *bastum* rod, probably ultimately from Greek *bastazein* to lift up, carry]

Baton Rouge ('bæt*ə*n 'ruːʒ) *n* the capital of Louisiana, in the SE part on the Mississippi River. Pop: 225 090 (2003 est)

baton round *n* the official name for **plastic bullet**

batrachian (bə'treɪkɪən) *n* **1** any amphibian, esp a frog or toad ▷ *adj* **2** of or relating to the frogs and toads [c19: from New Latin *Batrachia*, from Greek *batrakhos* frog]

bats (bæts) *adj informal* crazy; very eccentric [from BATS-IN-THE-BELFRY (sense 2)]

bats-in-the-belfry *n* (*functioning as singular*) **1** a hairy Eurasian campanulaceous plant, *Campanula trachelium*, with bell-shaped blue-purple flowers ▷ *adj* **2** *slang* mad; demented

batsman ('bætsmən) *n, pl* -men **1** *cricket* **a** a person who bats or whose turn it is to bat **b** a player who specializes in batting **2** a person on the ground who uses bats to guide the pilot of an aircraft when taxiing

battalion (bə'tæljən) *n* **1** a military unit comprised of three or more companies or formations of similar size **2** (*usually plural*) any large array [c16: from French *bataillon*, from Old Italian *battaglione*, from *battaglia* company of soldiers, BATTLE]

batten[1] ('bæt*ə*n) *n* **1** a sawn strip of wood used in building to cover joints, provide a fixing for tiles or slates, support lathing, etc **2** a long narrow board used for flooring **3** a lath used for holding a tarpaulin along the side of a raised hatch on a ship **4** *theatre* **a** a row of lights **b** the strip or bar supporting them ▷ *vb* **5** (*tr*) to furnish or strengthen with battens **6** batten down the hatches **a** to use battens in nailing a tarpaulin over a hatch on a ship to make it secure **b** to prepare for action, a crisis, etc [c15: from French *bâton* stick; see BATON]

batten[2] ('bæt*ə*n) *vb* (*intr*; usually foll by *on*) to thrive, esp at the expense of someone else [c16: probably from Old Norse *batna* to improve; related to Old Norse *betr* BETTER[1], Old High German *bazzen* to get better]

Batten ('bæt*ə*n) *n* Jean. 1909–82, New Zealand aviator: the first woman to fly single-handed from Australia to Britain (1935)

batter[1] ('bætə) *vb* **1** to hit (someone or something) repeatedly using heavy blows, as with a club or other heavy instrument; beat heavily **2** (*tr; often passive*) to damage or injure, as by blows, heavy wear, etc **3** (*tr*) *social welfare* to subject (a person, esp a close relative living in the same house) to repeated physical violence [C14 *bateren*, probably from *batten* to BAT¹] > **'batterer** *n* > **'battering** *n*

batter² ('bætə) *n* a mixture of flour, eggs, and milk, used to make cakes, pancakes, etc, and to coat certain foods before frying [C15 *bater*, probably from *bateren* to BATTER¹]

batter³ ('bætə) *n* *sport* a player who bats

batter⁴ ('bætə) *n* **1** the slope of the face of a wall that recedes gradually backwards and upwards > *vb* **2** (*intr*) to have such a slope [C16 (vb: to incline): of uncertain origin]

battered¹ ('bætəd) *adj* subjected to persistent physical violence, esp by a close relative living in the same house: *a battered baby*

battered² ('bætəd) *adj* coated in batter: *battered cod*

battering ram *n* (formerly) a large beam used to break down the walls or doors of fortifications

Battersea ('bætəsɪ) *n* a district in London, in Wandsworth: noted for its dogs' home, power station (now a leisure centre), and park

battery ('bætərɪ) *n, pl* **-teries 1** two or more primary cells connected together, usually in series, to provide a source of electric current **2** another name for **accumulator** (sense 1) **3** a number of similar things occurring together: *a battery of questions* **4** *criminal law* unlawful beating or wounding of a person or mere touching in a hostile or offensive manner **5** a fortified structure on which artillery is mounted **6** a group of guns, missile launchers, searchlights, or torpedo tubes of similar type or size operated as a single entity **7** a small tactical unit of artillery usually consisting of two or more troops, each of two, three or four guns **8** *chiefly Brit* **a** a large group of cages for intensive rearing of poultry **b** (*as modifier*): *battery hens* **9** *baseball* the pitcher and the catcher considered together [C16: from Old French *batterie* beating, from *battre* to beat, from Latin *battuere*]

batting ('bætɪŋ) *n* **1** Also called: **batt** cotton or woollen wadding used in quilts, mattresses, etc **2** the action of a person or team that hits with a bat, esp in cricket or baseball

battle ('bætəl) *n* **1** a fight between large armed forces; military or naval engagement; combat **2** conflict; contention; struggle > *vb* **3** (when *intr*, often foll by *against*, *for*, or *with*) to fight in or as if in military combat; contend (with) **4** to struggle in order to achieve something or arrive somewhere: *he battled through the crowd* **5** (*intr*) *Austral* to scrape a living, esp by doing odd jobs [C13: from Old French *bataile*, from Late Latin *battālia* exercises performed by soldiers, from *battuere* to beat] > **'battler** *n*

Battle¹ ('bætəl) *n* a town in SE England, in East Sussex: site of the Battle of Hastings (1066); medieval abbey. Pop: 5190 (2001)

Battle² ('bætəl) *n* **Kathleen**. born 1948, US opera singer: a coloratura soprano, she made her professional debut in 1972 and sang with New York City's Metropolitan Opera (1977–94)

battle-axe *n* **1** (formerly) a large broad-headed axe **2** *informal* an argumentative domineering woman

battle-axe block *n* *Austral* a block of land behind another, with access from the street through a narrow drive

battle cruiser *n* a warship of battleship size but with lighter armour and fewer guns and capable of high speed

battle cry *n* **1** a shout uttered by soldiers going into battle **2** a slogan used to rally the supporters of a campaign, movement, etc

battledore ('bætəl,dɔː) *n* **1** Also called: **battledore and shuttlecock** an ancient racket game **2** a light racket, smaller than a tennis racket, used for striking the shuttlecock in this game **3** (formerly) a wooden utensil used for beating clothes, in baking, etc [C15 *batyldoure*, perhaps from Old Provençal *batedor* a beater, from Old French *battre* to beat, BATTER¹]

battledress ('bætəl,drɛs) *n* the ordinary uniform of a soldier, consisting of tunic and trousers

battle fatigue *n* *psychol* a type of mental disorder,

characterized by anxiety, depression, and loss of motivation, caused by the stress of active warfare. Also called: **combat fatigue**

battlefield ('bætəl,fiːld) *or* **battleground** ('bætəl,graʊnd) *n* the place where a battle is fought; an area of conflict

battle group *n* a group of warships usu. consisting of at least one aircraft carrier, other surface ships, submarines, landing craft, etc

battlement ('bætəlmənt) *n* a parapet or wall with indentations or embrasures, originally for shooting through [C14: from Old French *batailles*, plural of *bataille* BATTLE] > **'battlemented** *adj*

battle royal *n* **1** a fight, esp with fists or cudgels, involving more than two combatants; melee **2** a long violent argument

battleship ('bætəl,ʃɪp) *n* a heavily armoured warship of the largest type having many large-calibre guns

batty ('bætɪ) *adj* **-tier, -tiest** *slang* **1** insane; crazy **2** odd; eccentric [C20: from BAT²; compare the phrase *have bats in the belfry*]

Batum (bɑːˈtuːm) *or* **Batumi** (bɑːˈtuːmɪ) *n* a city in Georgia: capital of the Adzhar Autonomous Republic; a major Black Sea port. Pop: 118 000 (2005 est)

batwoman ('bætwʊmən) *n, pl* **-women** a female servant in any of the armed forces

bauble ('bɔːbəl) *n* **1** a showy toy or trinket of little value; trifle **2** (formerly) a mock staff of office carried by a court jester [C14: from Old French *baubel* plaything, of obscure origin]

Bauchi ('baʊtʃɪ) *n* **1** a state of N Nigeria; tin mining. Capital: Bauchi. Pop: 4 676 465 (2006). Area: 45 837 sq km (17 698 sq miles) **2** a town in N central Nigeria, capital of Bauchi state. Pop: 76 070 (1991 est)

baud (bɔːd) *n* a unit used to measure the speed of electronic code transmissions, equal to one unit interval per second [C20: named after J. M. E. *Baudot* (1845–1903), French inventor]

Baudelaire (*French* bodlɛr) *n* **Charles Pierre** (ʃarl pjɛr). 1821–67, French poet, noted for his macabre imagery; author of *Les fleurs du mal* (1857)

Baudouin I (*French* bodwɛ̃) *n* 1930–93, king of Belgium (1951–93)

Baudrillard (*French* bodrijar) *n* **Jean**. 1929–2007, French sociologist and theorist of postmodernism; his books include *Séduction* (1979), *America* (1986), and *The Spirit of Terrorism* (2002)

bauera ('baʊərə) *n* any small evergreen Australian shrub of the genus *Bauera*, having pink or purple flowers [C19: named after Franz (1758–1840) and Ferdinand (1760–1826) *Bauer*, Australian botanical artists]

Bauhaus ('baʊ,haʊs) *n* a German school of architecture and applied arts founded in 1919 by Walter Gropius on experimental principles of functionalism and truth to materials. After being closed by the Nazis in 1933, its ideas were widely disseminated by its students and staff, including Kandinsky, Klee, Feininger, Moholy-Nagy, and Mies van der Rohe [C20: German, literally: building house]

bauhinia (bɔːˈhɪnɪə, bəʊ-) *n* any climbing or shrubby leguminous plant of the genus *Bauhinia*, of tropical and warm regions, widely cultivated for ornament [C18: New Latin, named after Jean and Gaspard *Bauhin*, 16th-century French herbalists]

baulk (bɔːk; *usually for sense 1* bɔːlk) *n* **1** *billiards* Also (US): **balk** the space, usually 29 inches deep, between the baulk line and the bottom cushion **2** *archaeol* a strip of earth left between excavation trenches for the study of the complete stratigraphy of a site > *vb*, *n* **3** a variant spelling of **balk**

baulk line *or US* **balk line** *n* *billiards* **1** Also called: **string line** a straight line across a billiard table behind which the cue balls are placed at the start of a game **2** one of four lines parallel to the cushions dividing the table into a central panel and eight smaller ones (the baulks)

Baum (bɔːm, baːm) *n* L(**yman**) **Frank** 1856–1919, US novelist, author of *The Wonderful Wizard of Oz* (1900) and its sequels

Baumgarten (*German* 'baʊmɡartən) *n* **Alexander Gottlieb**. 1714–62, German philosopher, noted for his pioneering work on aesthetics, a term that he originated

Bautzen ('baʊtsən) *n* a town in E Germany, in Saxony: site of an indecisive battle in 1813 between Napoleon's army and an allied army of Russians and Prussians. Pop: 42 160 (2003 est)

bauxite ('bɔːksaɪt) *n* a white, red, yellow, or brown amorphous claylike substance comprising aluminium oxides and hydroxides, often with such impurities as iron oxides. It is the chief ore of aluminium. General formula: $Al_2O_3.nH_2O$ [C19: from French, from (*Les*) *Baux* in southern France, where it was originally found]

Bavaria (bə'vɛərɪə) *n* a state of S Germany: a former duchy and kingdom; mainly wooded highland, with the Alps in the south. Capital: Munich. Pop: 12 155 000 (2000 est). Area: 70 531 sq km (27 232 sq miles) ▷ Ba'varian *adj*, *n*

bawd (bɔːd) *n* *archaic* **1** a person who runs a brothel, esp a woman **2** a prostitute [C14: shortened from Old French *baudetrot*, from *baude* feminine of *baud* merry + *trot* one who runs errands; compare Old High German *bald* BOLD]

bawdy ('bɔːdɪ) *adj* bawdier, bawdiest **1** (of language, plays, etc) containing references to sex, esp to be humorous ▷ *n* **2** obscenity or eroticism, esp in writing or drama ▷ 'bawdily *adv* ▷ 'bawdiness *n*

bawdyhouse ('bɔːdɪˌhaʊs) *n* an archaic word for **brothel**

bawl (bɔːl) *vb* **1** (*intr*) to utter long loud cries, as from pain or frustration; wail **2** to shout loudly, as in anger ▷ *n* **3** a loud shout or cry [C15: probably from Icelandic *baula* to low; related to Medieval Latin *baulāre* to bark, Swedish *böla* to low; all of imitative origin] ▷ 'bawler *n* ▷ 'bawling *n*

bawl out *vb* (*tr, adverb*) *informal* to scold loudly

Bax (bæks) *n* Sir **Arnold (Edward Trevor)**. 1883–1953, English composer of romantic works, often based on Celtic legends, including the tone poem *Tintagel* (1917)

Baxter ('bækstə) *n* **1 James (Keir)**. 1926–72, New Zealand lyric poet. His works include *The Fallen House* (1953) and *In Fires of No Return* (1958) **2 Richard**. 1615–91, English Puritan divine and devotional writer: prominent in church affairs during the Restoration

bay[1] (beɪ) *n* **1** a wide semicircular indentation of a shoreline, esp between two headlands or peninsulas **2** an extension of lowland into hills that partly surround it **3** *US* an extension of prairie into woodland [C14: from Old French *baie*, perhaps from Old French *baer* to gape, from Medieval Latin *batāre* to yawn]

bay[2] (beɪ) *n* **1** an alcove or recess in a wall **2** any partly enclosed compartment, as one in which hay is stored in a barn **3** See **bay window 4** an area off a road in which vehicles may park or unload, esp one adjacent to a shop, factory, etc **5** a compartment in an aircraft, esp one used for a specified purpose: *the bomb bay* **6** *nautical* a compartment in the forward part of a ship between decks, often used as the ship's hospital **7** *Brit* a tracked recess in the platform of a railway station, esp one forming the terminus of a branch line [C14: from Old French *baee* gap or recess in a wall, from *baer* to gape; see BAY[1]]

bay[3] (beɪ) *n* **1** a deep howl or growl, esp of a hound on the scent **2 at bay a** (of a person or animal) forced to turn and face attackers: *the dogs held the deer at bay* **b** at a distance: *to keep a disease at bay* **3 bring to bay** to force into a position from which retreat is impossible ▷ *vb* **4** (*intr*) to howl (at) in deep prolonged tones **5** (*tr*) to utter in a loud prolonged tone **6** (*tr*) to drive to or hold at bay [C13: from Old French *abaiier* to bark, of imitative origin]

bay[4] (beɪ) *n* **1** Also called: **bay laurel, sweet bay** a small evergreen Mediterranean laurel, *Laurus nobilis*, with glossy aromatic leaves, used for flavouring in cooking, and small blackish berries **2** any of various other trees with strongly aromatic leaves used in cooking, esp a member of the genera *Myrica* or *Pimenta* **3** any of several magnolias. See **sweet bay 4** any of certain other trees or shrubs, esp bayberry **5** (*plural*) a wreath of bay leaves. See **laurel** (sense 4) [C14: from Old French *baie* laurel berry, from Latin *bāca* berry]

bay[5] (beɪ) *n* **1 a** a moderate reddish-brown colour **b** (*as adjective*) **2** an animal of this colour, esp a horse [C14: from Old French *bai*, from Latin *badius*]

Bayamón (*Spanish* baja'mon) *n* a city in NE central Puerto Rico, south of San Juan. Pop: 224 915 (2003 est)

Bayard ('beɪəd; *French* bajar) *n* **Chevalier de** (ʃəvalje də), original name *Pierre de Terrail* ?1473–1524, French soldier, known as *le chevalier sans peur et sans reproche* (the fearless and irreproachable knight)

Baybars I (baɪ'bɑːs) *n* 1223–77, sultan of Egypt and Syria (1260–77), of the Mameluke dynasty

bayberry ('beɪbərɪ) *or* **bay** *n*, *pl* -ries **1** any of several North American aromatic shrubs or small trees of the genus *Myrica*, that bear grey waxy berries: family *Myricaceae* **2** Also called: **bay rum tree** a tropical American myrtaceous tree, *Pimenta racemosa*, that yields an oil used in making bay rum **3** the fruit of any of these plants

Bayern ('baɪərn) *n* the German name for **Bavaria**

Bayeux (*French* baijø) *n* a town in NW France, on the River Aure: its museum houses the Bayeux tapestry and there is a 13th-century cathedral: dairy foods, plastic. Pop: 14 961 (1999)

Bayezid II (ˌbaɪjə'ziːd) *n* ?1447–1512, sultan of Turkey; he greatly extended Turkish dominions in Greece and the Balkans

Bayle (*French* bɛl) *n* **Pierre** (pjɛr). 1647–1706, French philosopher and critic, noted for his *Dictionnaire historique et critique* (1697), which profoundly influenced Voltaire and the French Encyclopedists

bay leaf *n* a leaf, usually dried, of the Mediterranean laurel, *Laurus nobilis*, used in cooking to flavour soups and stews

Baylis ('beɪlɪs) *n* **1 Lillian Mary**. 1874–1937, British theatre manager: founded the Old Vic (1912) and the Sadler's Wells company for opera and ballet (1931) **2 Trevor (Graham)**. born 1937, British inventor of the clockwork radio (1992)

Bay of Pigs *n* a bay on the SW coast of Cuba: scene of an unsuccessful invasion of Cuba by US-backed troops (April 17, 1961). Spanish name: Bahía de los Cochinos

bayonet ('beɪənɪt) *n* **1 a** a blade that can be attached to the muzzle of a rifle for stabbing in close combat **2 a** a type of fastening in which a cylindrical member is inserted into a socket against spring pressure and turned so that pins on its side engage in slots in the socket ▷ *vb* -nets, -neting, -neted *or* -nets, -netting, -netted **3** (*tr*) to stab or kill with a bayonet [C17: from French *baïonnette*, from BAYONNE where it originated]

Bayonne (*French* bajɔn) *n* a port in SW France: a commercial centre for the Basque region. Pop: 40 078 (1999)

bayou ('baɪuː) *n* (in the southern US) a sluggish marshy tributary of a lake or river [C18: from Louisiana French, from Choctaw *bayuk*]

Bayreuth (*German* baɪ'rɔyt) *n* a city in E Germany, in NE Bavaria: home and burial place of Richard Wagner; annual festivals of his music. Pop: 74 818 (2003 est)

bay rum *n* an aromatic liquid, used in medicines and cosmetics, originally obtained by distilling the leaves of the bayberry tree (*Pimenta racemosa*) with rum: now also synthesized from alcohol, water, and various oils

bay window *n* a window projecting from the wall of a building and forming an alcove of a room

bazaar *or* **bazar** (bə'zɑː) *n* **1** (esp in the Orient) a market area, esp a street of small stalls **2** a sale in aid of charity, esp of miscellaneous secondhand or handmade articles **3** a shop where a large variety of goods is sold [C16: from Persian *bāzār*, from Old Persian *abēcharish*]

bazooka (bə'zuːkə) *n* a portable tubular rocket-launcher that fires a projectile capable of piercing armour: used by infantrymen as a short-range antitank weapon [C20: named after a pipe instrument invented by Bob Burns (1896–1956), American comedian]

BB *abbreviation* **1** Boys' Brigade ▷ *symbol for* **2** double black: denoting a very soft lead (on Brit pencils)

B2B *abbreviation* business-to-business; denoting trade between commercial organizations rather than between businesses and private customers

BBC *abbreviation* British Broadcasting Corporation

BBL *abbreviation* *text messaging* be back later

BBQ *abbreviation* barbecue

b

BBS *abbreviation text messaging* be back soon

BC *abbreviation* **1** Also called: B.C. (indicating years numbered back from the supposed year of the birth of Christ) before Christ **2** British Columbia

BCE *abbreviation* Before Common Era (used, esp by non-Christians, in numbering years BC)

BCG *abbreviation trademark* bacille Calmette-Guérin (antituberculosis vaccine)

BCNU *text messaging abbreviation* be seeing you

BCNZ *abbreviation* (the former) Broadcasting Corporation of New Zealand

B complex *n* short for **vitamin B complex**

BD *abbreviation* Bachelor of Divinity

bdellium ('dɛlɪəm) *n* **1** any of several African or W Asian trees of the burseraceous genus *Commiphora* that yield a gum resin **2** the aromatic gum resin, similar to myrrh, produced by any of these trees [c16: from Latin, from Greek *bdellion*, perhaps from Hebrew *bĕdhōlāh*]

BDS *abbreviation* Bachelor of Dental Surgery

be (bi:; *unstressed* bɪ) *vb, pres. sing.* 1st pers **am**, 2nd pers **are**, 3rd pers **is**, pres. pl **are**, past sing 1st pers **was**, 2nd pers **were**, 3rd pers **was**, past pl **were**, pres. part **being**, past part **been** (*intr*) **1** to have presence in the realm of perceived reality; exist; live: *I think, therefore I am; not all that is can be understood* **2** (used in the perfect or past perfect tenses only) to pay a visit; go: *have you been to Spain?* **3** to take place; occur: *my birthday was last Thursday* **4** (*copula*) used as a linking verb between the subject of a sentence and its noun or adjective complement or complementing phrase. In this case *be* expresses the relationship of either essential or incidental equivalence or identity (*John is a man; John is a musician*) or specifies an essential or incidental attribute (*honey is sweet; Susan is angry*). It is also used with an adverbial complement to indicate a relationship of location in space or time (*Bill is at the office; the dance is on Saturday*) **5** (takes a present participle) forms the progressive present tense: *the man is running* **6** (takes a past participle) forms the passive voice of all transitive verbs and (archaically) certain intransitive ones: *a good film is being shown on television tonight; I am done* **7** (takes an infinitive) expresses intention, expectation, supposition, or obligation: *the president is to arrive at 9.30; you are not to leave before I say so* [Old English *bēon*; related to Old High German *bim* am, Latin *fui* I have been, Greek *phuein* to bring forth, Sanskrit *bhavati* he is]

Be the chemical symbol for beryllium

BE *abbreviation* **1** bill of exchange **2** Bachelor of Education **3** Bachelor of Engineering

be- *prefix forming transitive verbs* **1** (from nouns) to surround completely; cover on all sides: *befog* **2** (from nouns) to affect completely or excessively: *bedazzle* **3** (from nouns) to consider as or cause to be: *befool; befriend* **4** (from nouns) to provide or cover with: *bejewel* **5** (from verbs) at, for, against, on, or over: *bewail; berate* [Old English *be-*, *bi-*, unstressed variant of *bī* BY]

beach (bi:tʃ) *n* **1** an extensive area of sand or shingle sloping down to a sea or lake, esp the area between the high- and low-water marks on a seacoast ▷ *vb* **2** to run or haul (a boat) onto a beach [c16: perhaps related to Old English *bæce* river, BECK²]

beachcomber ('bi:tʃ,kəʊmə) *n* **1** a person who searches shore debris for anything of worth, esp a vagrant living on a beach **2** Canadian (in British Columbia) a person who is paid for salvaging loose logs and returning them to logging companies **3** a long high wave rolling onto a beach

beachhead ('bi:tʃ,hɛd) *n military* an area on a beach that has been captured from the enemy and on which troops and equipment are landed [c20: modelled on BRIDGEHEAD]

Beachy Head ('bi:tʃɪ) *n* a headland in East Sussex, on the English Channel, consisting of chalk cliffs 171 m (570 ft) high

beacon ('bi:kən) *n* **1** a signal fire or light on a hill, tower, etc, esp one used formerly as a warning of invasion **2** a hill on which such fires were lit **3** a lighthouse, signalling buoy, etc, used to warn or guide ships in dangerous waters **4** short for **radio beacon** **5** a radio or other signal marking a flight course in air navigation **6** short for **Belisha beacon** **7** a person or thing that serves as a guide, inspiration, or warning [Old English *beacen* sign; related to Old Frisian *bāken*, Old Saxon *bōcan*, Old High German *bouhhan*]

beacon school *n Brit* a notably successful school whose methods and practices are brought to the attention of the education service as a whole in order that they may be adopted by other schools

Beaconsfield¹ ('bɛkənz,fi:ld, 'bi:k-) *n* a town in SE England, in Buckinghamshire. Pop: 12 292 (2001)

Beaconsfield² ('bɛkənz,fi:ld, 'bi:k-) *n* **1st Earl of.** title of (Benjamin) **Disraeli**

beacon status *n Brit* a ranking awarded by the government to an organization, rendering it eligible for extra funding, and aimed at encouraging organizations to share good practice with each other

bead (bi:d) *n* **1** a small usually spherical piece of glass, wood, plastic, etc, with a hole through it by means of which it may be strung with others to form a necklace, etc **2** a small drop of moisture **3** a small bubble in or on a liquid **4** a small metallic knob acting as the sight of a firearm **5** draw a bead on to aim a rifle or pistol at **6** Also called: **astragal** *architect, furniture* a small convex moulding having a semicircular cross section **7** count one's beads, say one's beads or tell one's beads to pray with a rosary ▷ *vb* **8** (*tr*) to decorate with beads **9** to form into beads or drops [Old English *bed* prayer; related to Old High German *gibet* prayer] ▷ **'beaded** *adj*

beading ('bi:dɪŋ) *n* **1** another name for **bead** (sense 6) **2** Also called: **beadwork** ('bi:d,wɜ:k) a narrow strip of some material used for edging or ornamentation

beadle ('bi:dᵊl) *n* **1** (formerly, in the Church of England) a minor parish official who acted as an usher and kept order **2** (in Scotland) a church official attending on the minister **3** *Judaism* a synagogue attendant **4** an official in certain British universities and other institutions [Old English *bydel*; related to Old High German *butil* bailiff] ▷ **'beadleship** *n*

Beadle ('bi:dᵊl) *n* **George Wells.** 1903–89, US biologist, who shared the Nobel prize for physiology or medicine in 1958 for his work in genetics

beadsman or **bedesman** ('bi:dzmən) *n, pl* -men **1** a person who prays for another's soul, esp one paid or fed for doing so **2** a person kept in an almshouse

beady ('bi:dɪ) *adj* **beadier, beadiest** **1** small, round, and glittering: used esp of eyes **2** resembling or covered with beads ▷ **'beadiness** *n*

beagle ('bi:gᵊl) *n* **1** a small sturdy breed of hound, having a smooth dense coat usually of white, tan, and black; often used (esp formerly) for hunting hares **2** *archaic* a person who spies on others ▷ *vb* **3** (*intr*) to hunt with beagles, normally on foot [c15: of uncertain origin]

Beaglehole ('bi:gᵊl,həʊl) *n* **John.** 1901–71, New Zealand historian and author. His works include *Exploration of the Pacific* (1934) and *The Journals of James Cook* (1955)

beak¹ (bi:k) *n* **1** the projecting jaws of a bird, covered with a horny sheath; bill **2** any beaklike mouthpart in other animals, such as turtles **3** *slang* a person's nose, esp one that is large, pointed, or hooked **4** any projecting part, such as the pouring lip of a bucket **5** *nautical* another word for **ram** (sense 5) [c13: from Old French *bec*, from Latin *beccus*, of Gaulish origin] ▷ **beaked** (bi:kt) *adj* ▷ **'beaky** *adj*

beak² (bi:k) *n* a Brit slang word for **judge, magistrate, headmaster** or **schoolmaster** [c19: originally thieves' jargon]

beaker ('bi:kə) *n* **1** a cup usually having a wide mouth **2** a cylindrical flat-bottomed container used in laboratories, usually made of glass and having a pouring lip [c14: from Old Norse *bikarr*; related to Old High German *behhāri*, Middle Dutch *bēker* beaker, Greek *bikos* earthenware jug]

Beaker folk *n* a prehistoric people thought to have originated in the Iberian peninsula and spread to central Europe and Britain during the second millennium BC [c20: named after the beakers found among their remains]

Beale (bi:l) *n* **Dorothea.** 1831–1906, British schoolmistress, a champion of women's education and suffrage. As principal of Cheltenham Ladies' College (1858–1906) she introduced important reforms

be-all and end-all *n informal* the ultimate aim or justification

beam (biːm) *n* **1** a long thick straight-sided piece of wood, metal, concrete, etc, esp one used as a horizontal structural member **2** the breadth of a ship or boat taken at its widest part, usually amidships **3** a ray or column of light, as from a beacon **4** a broad smile **5** one of the two cylindrical rollers on a loom, one of which holds the warp threads before weaving, the other the finished work **6** the main stem of a deer's antler from which the smaller branches grow **7** the central shaft of a plough to which all the main parts are attached **8** a narrow unidirectional flow of electromagnetic radiation or particles: *a beam of light; an electron beam* **9** the horizontal centrally pivoted bar in a balance **10** *informal* the width of the hips (esp in the phrase **broad in the beam**) **11** a **beam in one's eye** a fault or grave error greater in oneself than in another person **12** off beam *or* off the beam **a** not following a radio beam to maintain a course **b** *informal* wrong, mistaken, or irrelevant **13** on the beam **a** following a radio beam to maintain a course **b** *informal* correct, relevant, or appropriate ▷ *vb* **14** to send out or radiate (rays of light) **15** (*tr*) to divert or aim (a radio signal or broadcast, light, etc) in a certain direction: *to beam a programme to Tokyo* **16** (*intr*) to smile broadly with pleasure or satisfaction [Old English *beam*; related to Gothic *bagms* tree, Old High German *boum* tree]
▷ **'beaming** *adj, n*

beam-ends *pl n* **1** the ends of a vessel's beams **2** on one's **beam-ends** out of resources; destitute

bean (biːn) *n* **1** any of various leguminous plants of the widely cultivated genus *Phaseolus* producing edible seeds in pods **2** any of various other plants whose seeds are produced in pods or podlike fruits **3** *US & Canadian slang* another word for **head 4** not have a bean *slang* to be without money **5** full of beans *informal* full of energy and vitality [Old English *bēan*; related to Old Norse *baun*, Old Frisian *bāne*, Old High German *bōna* bean]

beanbag ('biːnˌbæg) *n* **1** a small cloth bag filled with dried beans and thrown in games **2** Also called: **sag bag** a very large cushion loosely filled with foam rubber or polystyrene granules so that it moulds into a comfortable shape: used as an informal low seat

beanbag gun *n* a gun that fires a fabric bag containing lead shot, designed to stun or knock the target to the ground

bean-counter *n informal* an accountant

bean curd *n* another name for **tofu**

beanfeast ('biːnˌfiːst) *n Brit informal* **1** an annual dinner given by employers to employees **2** any festive or merry occasion

beanie *or* **beany** ('biːnɪ) *n, pl* **beanies** a round close-fitting hat resembling a skullcap

beano ('biːnəʊ) *n, pl* **beanos** *Brit slang* a celebration, party, or other enjoyable time

beanpole ('biːnˌpəʊl) *n* **1** a tall stick or pole used to support bean plants **2** *slang* a tall thin person

bean sprout *n* the sprout of a newly germinated mung bean, eaten as a vegetable, esp in Chinese dishes

beanstalk ('biːnˌstɔːk) *n* the stem of a bean plant

bear¹ (bɛə) *vb* **bears, bearing, bore, borne** (mainly *tr*) **1** to support or hold up; sustain **2** to bring or convey: *to bear gifts* **3** to take, accept, or assume the responsibility of: *to bear an expense* **4** (*past participle* **born** in passive use except when foll by *by*) to give birth to: *to bear children* **5** (*also intr*) to produce by or as if by natural growth: *to bear fruit* **6** to tolerate or endure: *she couldn't bear him* **7** to admit of; sustain: *his story does not bear scrutiny* **8** to hold in the conscious mind or in one's feelings: *to bear a grudge; I'll bear that idea in mind* **9** to show or be marked with: *he still bears the scars* **10** to render or supply (esp in the phrase **bear witness**) **11** to conduct or manage (oneself, the body, etc): *she bore her head high* **12** to have, be, or stand in (relation or comparison): *his account bears no relation to the facts* **13** (*intr*) to move, be located, or lie in a specified direction **14** bear a hand to give assistance **15** bring to bear to bring into operation or effect ▷ See also **bear**

down, bear up [Old English *beran*; related to Old Norse *bera*, Old High German *beran* to carry, Latin *ferre*, Greek *pherein* to bear, Sanskrit *bharati* he carries]

bear² (bɛə) *n, pl* **bears** *or* **bear 1** any plantigrade mammal of the family *Ursidae*: order *Carnivora* (carnivores). Bears are typically massive omnivorous animals with a large head, a long shaggy coat, and strong claws **2** any of various bearlike animals, such as the koala and the ant bear **3** a clumsy, churlish, or ill-mannered person **4** a teddy bear **5** *stock exchange* **a** a speculator who sells in anticipation of falling prices to make a profit on repurchase **b** (*as modifier*): *a bear market*. See **bull¹** (sense 4) ▷ *vb* **bears, bearing, beared 6** (*tr*) to lower or attempt to lower the price or prices of (a stock market or a security) by speculative selling [Old English *bera*; related to Old Norse *bjorn*, Old High German *bero*]

Bear (bɛə) the Bear *n* **1** the English name for **Ursa Major** *or* **Ursa Minor 2** an informal name for **Russia**

bearable ('bɛərəbᵊl) *adj* endurable; tolerable

bear-baiting *n* (formerly) an entertainment in which dogs attacked and enraged a chained bear

beard (bɪəd) *n* **1** the hair growing on the lower parts of a man's face **2** any similar growth in animals **3** a tuft of long hairs in plants such as barley and wheat; awn **4** a barb, as on an arrow or fish-hook ▷ *vb* (*tr*) **5** to oppose boldly or impertinently [Old English *beard*; related to Old Norse *barth*, Old High German *bart*, Latin *barba*]
▷ **'bearded** *adj*

bearded dragon *n* **1** Also called: **bearded lizard, jew lizard** a large Australian lizard, *Amphibolurus barbatus*, with an erectile frill around the neck **2** another name for **frill-necked lizard**

beardless ('bɪədlɪs) *adj* **1** without a beard **2** too young to grow a beard; immature

bear down *vb* (*intr, adverb*; often foll by *on* or *upon*) **1** to press or weigh down **2** to approach in a determined or threatening manner

Beardsley ('bɪədzlɪ) *n* **Aubrey (Vincent)**. 1872–98, English illustrator: noted for his stylized black-and-white illustrations, esp those for Oscar Wilde's *Salome* and Pope's *Rape of the Lock*

beard-stroking *n* **1** deep thought: *the response involved much beard-stroking* ▷ *adj* **2** boringly intellectual: *a beard-stroking bore*

beardy ('bɪədɪ) *adj* **-dier, -diest 1** wearing a beard ▷ *n, pl* **-dies** a person who has a beard

bearer ('bɛərə) *n* **1** a person or thing that bears, presents, or upholds **2** a person who presents a note or bill for payment **3** (*modifier*) *finance* payable to the person in possession: *bearer bonds*

bear garden *n* **1** (formerly) a place where bears were exhibited and where bear-baiting took place **2** a place or scene of tumult and disorder

bear hug *n* **1** a wrestling hold in which the arms are locked tightly round an opponent's chest and arms **2** any similar tight embrace **3** *commerce* an approach to the board of one company by another to indicate that an offer is to be made for their shares

bearing ('bɛərɪŋ) *n* **1** a support, guide, or locating piece for a rotating or reciprocating mechanical part **2** (foll by *on* or *upon*) relevance (to): *it has no bearing on this problem* **3** a person's general social conduct, esp in manners, dress, and behaviour **4** the act, period, or capability of producing fruit or young **5** anything that carries weight or acts as a support **6** the angular direction of a line, point, or course measured from true north or south (**true bearing**), magnetic north or south (**magnetic bearing**), or one's own position **7** (*usually plural*) the position or direction, as of a ship, fixed with reference to two or more known points **8** (*usually plural*) a sense of one's relative position or situation; orientation (esp in the phrases **lose, get,** *or* **take one's bearings**) **9** *heraldry* **a** a device or emblem on a heraldic shield; charge **b** another name for **coat of arms**

bearing rein *n chiefly Brit* a rein from the bit to the saddle, designed to keep the horse's head in the desired position

bearish ('bɛərɪʃ) *adj* **1** like a bear; rough; clumsy; churlish **2** *stock exchange* causing, expecting, or

characterized by a fall in prices: *a bearish market*
> 'bearishness *n*
bear on *vb* (*intr, preposition*) **1** to be relevant to; relate to
2 to be burdensome to or afflict
bear out *vb* (*tr, adverb*) to show to be true or truthful;
confirm: *the witness will bear me out*
bear paw *n* *Canadian* a type of small round snowshoe
bear raid *n* an attempt to force down the price of a
security or commodity by sustained selling
bearskin ('bɛə,skɪn) *n* **1** the pelt of a bear, esp when used
as a rug **2** a tall helmet of black fur worn by certain
regiments in the British Army
bear up *vb* (*intr, adverb*) to endure cheerfully
bear with *vb* (*intr, preposition*) to be patient with
beast (bi:st) *n* **1** any animal other than man, esp a large
wild quadruped **2** savage nature or characteristics: *the
beast in man* **3** a brutal, uncivilized, or filthy person [c13:
from Old French *beste*, from Latin *bestia*, of obscure
origin]
beastly ('bi:stlɪ) *adj* **-lier, -liest 1** *informal* unpleasant;
disagreeable; nasty: *beastly weather* **2** *obsolete* of or like a
beast; bestial ▷ *adv* **3** *informal* (intensifier): *the weather is so
beastly hot* > 'beastliness *n*
beast of burden *n* an animal, such as a donkey or ox,
used for carrying loads
beast of prey *n* any animal that hunts other animals
for food
beat (bi:t) *vb* **beats, beating, beat, beaten** *or* **beat**
1 (when *intr*, often foll by *against, on*, etc) to strike with or
as if with a series of violent blows; dash or pound
repeatedly (against) **2** (*tr*) to punish by striking; flog **3** to
move or cause to move up and down; flap: *the bird beat its
wings heavily* **4** (*intr*) to throb rhythmically; pulsate **5** (*tr*;
sometimes foll by *up*) *cookery* to stir or whisk (an
ingredient or mixture) vigorously **6** (*tr*; sometimes foll
by *out*) to shape, make thin, or flatten (a piece of metal)
by repeated blows **7** (*tr*) *music* to indicate (time) by the
motion of one's hand, baton, etc, or by the action of a
metronome **8** (when *tr*, sometimes foll by *out*) to
produce (a sound or signal) by or as if by striking a drum
9 to overcome (an opponent) in a contest, battle, etc
10 (*tr*; often foll by *back, down, off* etc) to drive, push, or
thrust **11** (*tr*) to arrive or finish before (someone or
something); anticipate or forestall **12** (*tr*) to form (a path
or track) by repeatedly walking or riding over it **13** to
scour (woodlands, coverts, etc) so as to
rouse game for shooting **14** (*tr*) *slang* to puzzle or baffle:
it beats me how he can do that **15** (*intr*) *nautical* to steer a
sailing vessel as close as possible to the direction from
which the wind is blowing **16 beat a retreat** to
withdraw or depart in haste **17 beat it** *slang* (*often
imperative*) to go away **18 beat the bounds** *Brit* (formerly)
to define the boundaries of a parish by making a
procession around them and hitting the ground with
rods **19 can you beat it?** *or* **can you beat that?** *slang* an
expression of utter amazement or surprise ▷ *n* **20** a
stroke or blow **21** the sound made by a stroke or blow
22 a regular sound or stroke; throb **23 a** an assigned or
habitual round or route, as of a policeman or sentry
b (*as modifier*): *beat police officers* **24** the basic rhythmic unit
in a piece of music, usually grouped in twos, threes, or
fours **25 a** pop or rock music characterized by a heavy
rhythmic beat **b** (*as modifier*): *a beat group* **26** *physics* the
low regular frequency produced by combining two
sounds or electrical signals that have similar
frequencies **27** *prosody* the accent, stress, or ictus in a
metrical foot **28** (*modifier, often capital*) of, characterized
by, or relating to the Beat Generation ▷ *adj*
29 (*postpositive*) *slang* totally exhausted ▷ See also **beat
down, beat up** [Old English *bēatan*; related to Old Norse
bauta, Old High German *bōzan*] > 'beatable *adj*
beatbox ('bi:t,bɒks) *n* *informal* a drum machine
beat down *vb* (*adverb*) **1** (*tr*) *informal* to force or persuade
(a seller) to accept a lower price: *I beat him down three
pounds* **2** (*intr*) (of the sun) to shine intensely; be very hot
beaten ('bi:tᵊn) *adj* **1** defeated or baffled **2** shaped or
made thin by hammering: *a bowl of beaten gold* **3** much
travelled; well trodden (esp in the phrase **the beaten
track**) **4 off the beaten track a** in or into unfamiliar

territory **b** out of the ordinary; unusual **5** (of food)
mixed by beating; whipped **6** tired out; exhausted
beater ('bi:tə) *n* **1** a person who beats or hammers: *a
panel beater* **2** an instrument or device used for beating: *a
carpet beater* **3** a person who rouses wild game from
woodland, undergrowth, etc
Beat Generation *n* (*functioning as singular or plural*)
1 members of the generation that came to maturity in
the 1950s, whose rejection of the social and political
systems of the West was expressed through contempt
for regular work, possessions, traditional dress, etc, and
espousal of anarchism, communal living, drugs, etc **2** a
group of US writers, notably Jack Kerouac, Allen
Ginsberg, and William Burroughs, who emerged in the
1950s
beatific (,biːə'tɪfɪk) *adj* **1** displaying great happiness,
calmness, etc **2** of, conferring, or relating to a state of
celestial happiness [c17: from Late Latin *beātificus*, from
Latin *beātus*, from *beāre* to bless + *facere* to make]
> ,bea'tifically *adv*
beatify (bɪ'ætɪ,faɪ) *vb* **-fies, -fying, -fied 1** (*tr*) *RC Church*
(of the pope) to declare formally that (a deceased person)
showed a heroic degree of holiness in his or her life and
therefore is worthy of public veneration: the first step
towards canonization **2** (*tr*) to make extremely happy
[c16: from Old French *beatifier*, from Late Latin *beātificāre*
to make blessed; see BEATIFIC] > beatification
(bɪ,ætɪfɪ'keɪʃən) *n*
beating ('bi:tɪŋ) *n* **1** a whipping or thrashing, as in
punishment **2** a defeat or setback **3 take some beating**
or **take a lot of beating** to be difficult to improve upon
beatitude (bɪ'ætɪ,tjuːd) *n* **1** supreme blessedness or
happiness **2** an honorific title of the Eastern Christian
Church, applied to those of patriarchal rank [c15: from
Latin *beātitūdo*, from *beātus* blessed; see BEATIFIC]
Beatitude (bɪ'ætɪ,tjuːd) *n* *New Testament* any of eight
distinctive sayings of Jesus in the Sermon on the Mount
(Matthew 5:3–11) in which he declares that the poor, the
meek, those that mourn, the merciful, the
peacemakers, the pure of heart, those that thirst for
justice, and those that are persecuted will, in various
ways, receive the blessings of heaven
beatnik ('bi:tnɪk) *n* **1 a** member of the Beat Generation
(sense 1) **2** *informal* any person with long hair and
shabby clothes [c20: from BEAT (n) + -NIK, by analogy
with SPUTNIK]
Beaton ('bi:tᵊn) *n* Sir **Cecil** (**Walter Hardy**). 1904–80,
British photographer, noted esp for his society portraits
Beatrix ('bi:ətrɪks) *n* full name *Beatrix Wilhelmina Armgard*.
born 1938, queen of the Netherlands from 1980
Beatty ('bi:tɪ) *n* **1 David**, 1st Earl Beatty. 1871–1936, British
admiral of the fleet in World War I **2 Warren**, full name
Henry Warren Beatty. Born 1937, US film actor and director:
his films include *Bonnie and Clyde* (1967), *Heaven Can Wait*
(1978), *Reds* (1981, also directed), *Bugsy* (1991), and *Bulworth*
(1998, also wrote and directed)
beat up ▷ *vb* **1** (*tr, adverb*) to strike or kick (a
person), usually repeatedly, so as to inflict severe
physical damage ▷ *adj* **beat-up 2** worn-out; dilapidated
beau (bəʊ) *n, pl* **beaux** (bəʊ, bəʊz) *or* **beaus** (bəʊz) **1** a
lover, sweetheart, or escort of a girl or woman **2** a man
who is greatly concerned with his clothes and
appearance; dandy [c17: from French, from Old French
biau, from Latin *bellus* handsome, charming]
Beaufort ('bəʊfət) *n* **1 Henry**. ?1374–1447, English
cardinal, half-brother of Henry IV; chancellor (1403–04,
1413–17, 1424–26) **2 Lady Margaret**, Countess of
Richmond and Derby. ?1443–1509, mother of Henry VII.
She helped to found two Cambridge colleges and was a
patron of Caxton
Beaufort scale *n* *meteorol* an international scale of wind
velocities ranging for practical purposes from 0 (calm)
to 12 (hurricane force). In the US an extension of the
scale, from 13 to 17 for winds over 64 knots, is used [c19:
after Sir Francis *Beaufort* (1774–1857), British admiral and
hydrographer who devised it]
Beaufort Sea *n* part of the Arctic Ocean off the N coast
of North America
beau geste (French bo ʒɛst) *n, pl* **beaux gestes** (bo ʒɛst) a

noble or gracious gesture or act, esp one that is meaningless [literally: beautiful gesture]

Beauharnais (French bɔarnɛ) n 1 **Alexandre** (alɛksãdr), Vicomte de. 1760–94, French general, who served in the War of American Independence and the French Revolutionary wars; first husband of Empress Joséphine: guillotined 2 his son, **Eugène de** (øʒɛn də). 1781–1824, viceroy of Italy (1805–14) for his stepfather Napoleon I 3 (**Eugénie**) (øʒeni) **Hortense de** (ɔrtɑ̃s də). 1783–1837, queen of Holland (1806–10) as wife of Louis Bonaparte; daughter of Alexandre Beauharnais and sister of Eugène: mother of Napoleon III 4 **Joséphine de** (ʒozefin də), previous name of the Empress Josephine. See **Josephine**

beaujolais ('bəʊʒə,leɪ) n (sometimes capital) a popular fresh-tasting red or white wine from southern Burgundy in France

Beaulieu ('bjuːlɪ) n a village in S England, in Hampshire: site of Palace House, seat of Lord Montagu and once the gatehouse of the ruined 13th-century abbey; the National Motor Museum is in its grounds. Pop: 809 (2001)

Beaumarchais (French bomarʃɛ) n **Pierre Augustin Caron de** (pjɛr ogystɛ̃ karɔ̃ də). 1732–99, French dramatist, noted for his comedies The Barber of Seville (1775) and The Marriage of Figaro (1784)

Beaumaris (bəʊ'mærɪs) n a resort in N Wales, on the island of Anglesey: 13th-century castle. Pop: 1513 (2001)

beau monde ('bəʊ 'mɒnd; French bo mɔ̃d) n the world of fashion and society [c18: French, literally: fine world]

Beaumont[1] ('bəʊmɒnt) n a city in SE Texas. Pop: 112 434 (2003 est)

Beaumont[2] ('bəʊmɒnt) n **Francis**. 1584–1616, English dramatist, who collaborated with John Fletcher on plays including The Knight of the Burning Pestle (1607) and The Maid's Tragedy (1611)

Beaune (bəʊn) n 1 a town in E France, near Dijon: an important trading centre for Burgundy wines. Pop: 21 923 (1999) 2 a wine produced in this district

beaut (bjuːt) slang, chiefly Austral & NZ ▷ n 1 a person or thing that is outstanding or distinctive ▷ adj 2 good or excellent ▷ interj 3 Also called: **you beaut!** an exclamation of pleasure or pleasure

beauteous ('bjuːtɪəs) adj a poetic word for **beautiful** > '**beauteousness** n

beautician (bjuː'tɪʃən) n a person who works in or manages a beauty salon

beautiful ('bjuːtɪfʊl) adj 1 possessing beauty; aesthetically pleasing 2 highly enjoyable; very pleasant > '**beautifully** adv

beautify ('bjuːtɪ,faɪ) vb -fies, -fying, -fied to make or become beautiful > **beautification** (,bjuːtɪfɪ'keɪʃən) n > '**beauti,fier** n

beauty ('bjuːtɪ) n, pl -ties 1 the combination of all the qualities of a person or thing that delight the senses and please the mind 2 a very attractive and well-formed girl or woman 3 informal an outstanding example of its kind 4 informal an advantageous feature: one beauty of the job is the short hours ▷ interj 5 (NZ 'bjuːdɪ) an expression of approval or agreement [c13: from Old French biauté, from biau beautiful; see BEAU]

beauty queen n an attractive young woman, esp one who has won a beauty contest

beauty salon or **beauty parlour** n an establishment providing women with services to improve their beauty, such as hairdressing, manicuring, facial treatment, and massage

beauty sleep n informal sleep, esp sleep before midnight

beauty spot n 1 a place of outstanding beauty 2 a small dark-coloured patch or spot worn on a lady's face as an adornment or as a foil to her complexion 3 a mole or other similar natural mark on the skin

Beauvais (French bovɛ) n a market town in N France, 64 km (40 miles) northwest of Paris. Pop: 55 392 (1999)

Beauvoir (French bovwar) n See **de Beauvoir**

beaux (bəʊ, bəʊz) n a plural of **beau**

beaux-arts (bəʊ'zɑː) pl n 1 another word for **fine art** 2 (modifier) relating to the classical decorative style, esp that of the École des Beaux-Arts in Paris: beaux-arts

influences [c19: French, literally: fine arts]

beaver[1] ('biːvə) n 1 a large amphibious rodent, Castor fiber, of Europe, Asia, and North America: family Castoridae. It has soft brown fur, a broad flat hairless tail, and webbed hind feet, and constructs complex dams and houses (lodges) in rivers 2 the fur of this animal 3 a tall hat of beaver fur or a fabric resembling it, worn, esp by men, during the 19th century 4 a woollen napped cloth resembling beaver fur, formerly much used for overcoats, etc 5 obsolete a full beard 6 a bearded man 7 (modifier) having the colour of beaver or made of beaver fur or some similar material ▷ vb 8 (intr; usually foll by away) to work industriously or steadily [Old English beofor; compare Old Norse biōrr, Old High German bibar, Latin fiber, Sanskrit babhrú red-brown]

beaver[2] ('biːvə) n a movable piece on a medieval helmet used to protect the lower part of the face [c15: from Old French baviere, from baver to dribble]

Beaverbrook ('biːvə,brʊk) n **1st Baron**, title of William Maxwell Aitken. 1879–1964, British newspaper proprietor and Conservative politician, born in Canada, whose newspapers included the Daily Express; minister of information (1918); minister of aircraft production (1940–41)

beaver fever n Canadian an infectious disease caused by drinking water that has been contaminated with wildlife

Beaver Tail n trademark a flat oval doughnut served fried and sugared

Bebel (German 'beːbəl) n **August** ('aʊɡʊst). 1840–1913, German socialist leader: one of the founders of the Social Democratic Party (1869)

Bebington ('bebɪŋtən) n a town in NW England, in Wirral unitary authority, Merseyside: docks and chemical works. Pop: 57 066 (2001)

bebop ('biːbɒp) n the full name for **bop**[1] (sense 1) [c20: imitative of the rhythm of the music] > '**bebopper** n

becalmed (bɪ'kɑːmd) adj (of a sailing boat or ship) motionless through lack of wind

became (bɪ'keɪm) vb the past tense of **become**

because (bɪ'kɒz, -'kəz) conj 1 (subordinating) on account of the fact that; on account of being; since: because it's so cold we'll go home 2 because of (preposition) on account of: I lost my job because of her [c14 bi cause, from bi BY + CAUSE]
● USAGE See at **reason**

Beccaria (Italian bɛka'ria) n **Cesare Bonesana** ('tʃezare bɔne'zaːna), Marchese de. 1738–94, Italian legal theorist and political economist; author of the influential treatise Crimes and Punishments (1764), which attacked corruption, torture, and capital punishment

béchamel sauce (,beɪʃə'mɛl) n a thick white sauce flavoured with onion and seasonings [c18: named after the Marquis of Béchamel, steward of Louis XIV of France and its creator]

Béchar (French beʃar) n a city in NW Algeria: an oasis. Pop: 149 000 (2005 est). Former name: **Colomb-Béchar**

bêche-de-mer (,beʃdə'mɛə) n, pl bêches-de-mer (,beʃdə'mɛə) another name for **trepang** [c19: quasi-French, from earlier English biche de mer, from Portuguese bicho do mar worm of the sea]

Bechet ('beʃeɪ) n **Sidney** (**Joseph**). 1897–1959, US jazz soprano saxophonist and clarinettist

Bechstein (German 'beçtaɪn) n **Karl**. 1826–1900, German piano maker; founder (1853) of the Bechstein company of piano manufacturers in Berlin

Bechuana (bɛ'tʃwaːnə, ,betʃʊ'aːnə, ,bekjʊ-) n, pl -na or -nas a former name for a member of the Bantu people of Botswana

Bechuanaland (bɛ'tʃwaːnə,lænd, ,betʃʊ'aːnə,lænd, ,bekjʊ-) n the former name (until 1966) of **Botswana**

beck[1] (bɛk) n 1 a nod, wave, or other gesture or signal 2 at someone's beck and call ready to obey someone's orders instantly; subject to someone's slightest whim [c14: short for becnen to BECKON]

beck[2] (bɛk) n (in N England) a stream, esp a swiftly flowing one [Old English becc, from Old Norse bekkr; related to Old English bece, Old Saxon beki, Old High German bah brook, Sanskrit bhanga wave]

Beckenbauer ('bekən,baʊə) n **Franz**. born 1945, German footballer: team captain when West Germany won the

World Cup (1974): manager of West Germany (1984–90), coaching the team to success in the 1990 World Cup

Becker ('bɛkə) n **Boris**. born 1967, German tennis player: Wimbledon champion 1985, 1986, and 1989: the youngest man ever to win Wimbledon

Becket ('bɛkɪt) n **Saint Thomas à**. 1118–70, English prelate; chancellor (1155–62) to Henry II; archbishop of Canterbury (1162–70): murdered following his opposition to Henry's attempts to control the clergy. Feast day: Dec 29 or July 7

Beckett ('bɛkɪt) n **1 Margaret Mary**. born 1943, British Labour politician; leader of the House of Commons (1998–2001); secretary of state for environment, food, and rural affairs (2001–06); foreign secretary (2006–07) **2 Samuel (Barclay)**. 1906–89, Irish dramatist and novelist writing in French and English, whose works portray the human condition as insignificant or absurd in a bleak universe. They include the plays *En attendant Godot* (*Waiting for Godot*, 1952), *Fin de partie* (*Endgame*, 1957), and *Not I* (1973) and the novel *Malone meurt* (*Malone Dies*, 1951): Nobel prize for literature 1969

Beckford ('bɛkfəd) n **William**. 1759–1844, English writer and dilettante; author of the oriental romance *Vathek* (1787)

Beckham ('bɛkəm) n **1 David**. born 1975, British footballer; captain of England (2000–06): married to the pop singer Victoria Beckham **2 Victoria Caroline**, née *Adams*, known as *Posh Spice*. born 1974, English pop singer, member of the Spice Girls, 1994–2001 and from 2007

Beckmann (German 'bɛkman) n **1 Ernst Otto** (ɛrnst 'ɔ:to). 1853–1923, German chemist: devised the Beckmann thermometer, used for measuring small temperature changes in liquids **2 Max** (maks). 1884–1950, German expressionist painter

beckon ('bɛkən) vb **1** to summon with a gesture of the hand or head **2** to entice or lure ▷ n **3** a summoning gesture [Old English *bīecnan*, from *bēacen* sign; related to Old Saxon *bōknian*; see BEACON] > 'beckoner n > 'beckoning adj, n

becloud (bɪ'klaʊd) vb (tr) to cover or obscure with a cloud

become (bɪ'kʌm) vb **-comes, -coming, -came, -come** (mainly intr) **1** (copula) to come to be; develop or grow into: *he became a monster* **2** (foll by *of*; usually used in a question) to fall to or be the lot (of); happen (to): *what became of him?* **3** (tr) (of clothes, etc) to enhance the appearance of (someone); suit: *that dress becomes you* **4** (tr) to be appropriate; befit: *it ill becomes you to complain* [Old English *becuman* to happen; related to Old High German *biqueman* to come to, Gothic *biquiman* to appear suddenly]

becoming (bɪ'kʌmɪŋ) adj suitable; appropriate > be'comingly adv > be'comingness n

becquerel (ˌbɛkə'rɛl) n the derived SI unit of radioactivity equal to one disintegration per second [c20: named after Antoine Henri Becquerel (1852–1908), French physicist]

Becquerel (French bɛkrɛl) n **Antoine Henri** (ãtwan ãri). 1852–1908, French physicist, who discovered the photographic action of the rays emitted by uranium salts and so instigated the study of radioactivity: Nobel prize for physics 1903

BECTU ('bɛktu:) n acronym for (in Britain) Broadcasting, Entertainment, Cinematograph and Theatre Union

bed (bɛd) n **1** a piece of furniture on which to sleep **2** the mattress and bedclothes on such a piece of furniture: *an unmade bed* **3** sleep or rest: *time for bed* **4** any place in which a person or animal sleeps or rests **5** med a unit of potential occupancy in a hospital or residential institution **6** informal sexual intercourse **7** a plot of ground in which plants are grown, esp when considered together with the plants in it **8** the bottom of a river, lake, or sea **9** a part of this used for cultivation of a plant or animal: *oyster beds* **10** a layer of crushed rock, gravel, etc, used as a foundation for a road, railway, etc **11** any underlying structure or part **12** a layer of rock, esp sedimentary rock **13** go to bed **a** (often foll by *with*) to have sexual intercourse (with) **b** journalism, printing (of a newspaper, magazine, etc) to go to press; start printing **14** in bed with informal cooperating closely with (another person, organization, etc) esp covertly

15 put to bed *journalism* to finalize work on (a newspaper, magazine, etc) so that it is ready to go to press **16** take to one's bed to remain in bed, esp because of illness ▷ vb **beds, bedding, bedded 17** (usually foll by *down*) to go to or put into a place to sleep or rest **18** (tr) to have sexual intercourse with **19** (tr) to place, fix, or sink firmly into position; embed **20** geology to form or be arranged in a distinct layer; stratify **21** (tr; often foll by *out*) to plant in a bed of soil [Old English *bedd*; related to Old High German *betti*, Old English *betti*, Gothic *badi*]

BEd abbreviation Bachelor of Education

bed and board n sleeping accommodation and meals

bed and breakfast *chiefly Brit* ▷ n **1** (in a hotel, boarding house, etc) overnight accommodation and breakfast ▷ adj **2** (of a stock-exchange transaction) establishing a loss for tax purposes, shares being sold after hours one evening and bought back the next morning when the market opens

bed bath n another name for **blanket bath**

bed-blocking n *Brit* the use of hospital beds by elderly patients who cannot leave hospital because they have no place in a residential care home > 'bed-ˌblocker n

bedbug ('bɛd,bʌg) n any of several bloodsucking insects of the heteropterous genus *Cimex*, esp *C. lectularius* of temperate regions, having an oval flattened wingless body and infesting dirty houses: family Cimicidae

bedchamber ('bɛd,tʃeɪmbə) n an archaic word for **bedroom**

bedclothes ('bɛd,kləʊðz) pl n sheets, blankets, and other coverings of a bed

beddable ('bɛdəbəl) adj sexually attractive

bedding ('bɛdɪŋ) n **1** bedclothes, sometimes considered together with a mattress **2** litter, such as straw, for animals **3** something acting as a foundation, such as mortar under a brick **4** the arrangement of a mass of rocks into distinct layers; stratification

bedding plant n a plant that may be grown in a garden bed

Beddoes ('bɛdəʊz) n **Thomas Lovell**. 1803–49, British poet, noted for his macabre imagery, esp in *Death's Jest-Book* (1850)

Bede (bi:d) n **Saint**, known as *the Venerable Bede*. ?673–735 AD, English monk, scholar, historian, and theologian, noted for his Latin *Ecclesiastical History of the English People* (731). Feast day: May 27 or 25. Latin name: **Baeda**

bedeck (bɪ'dɛk) vb (tr) to cover with decorations; adorn

bedevil (bɪ'dɛvəl) vb **-ils, -illing, -illed** or US **-ils, -iling, -iled** (tr) **1** to harass or torment **2** to throw into confusion **3** to possess, as with a devil > be'devilment n

bedew (bɪ'dju:) vb (tr) to wet or cover with or as if with drops of dew

bedfellow ('bɛd,fɛləʊ) n **1** a person with whom one shares a bed **2** a temporary ally or associate

Bedford[1] ('bɛdfəd) n **1** a town in SE central England, administrative centre of Bedfordshire, on the River Ouse. Pop: 82 488 (2001) **2** short for **Bedfordshire**

Bedford[2] ('bɛdfəd) n **1 David**. born 1937, British composer, influenced by rock music **2 Duke of**, title of *John of Lancaster*. 1389–1435, son of Henry IV of England: protector of England and regent of France (1422–35)

Bedfordshire ('bɛdfəd,ʃɪə, -ʃə) n a county of S central England: mainly low-lying, with the Chiltern Hills in the south: the geographical county includes Luton, which became a separate unitary authority in 1997. Administrative centre: Bedford. Pop (excluding Luton): 388 600 (2003 est). Area (excluding Luton): 1192 sq km (460 sq miles). Abbreviation: Beds

bedight (bɪ'daɪt) archaic ▷ vb **-dights, -dighting, -dight** or **-dighted 1** (tr) to array or adorn ▷ adj **2** (past participle of the verb) adorned or bedecked [c14: from DIGHT]

bedim (bɪ'dɪm) vb **-dims, -dimming, -dimmed** (tr) to make dim or obscure

Bedivere ('bɛdɪ,vɪə) n **Sir Bedivere** (in Arthurian legend) a knight who took the dying King Arthur to the barge in which he was carried to Avalon

bedizen (bɪ'daɪzən, -'dɪzən) vb (tr) archaic to dress or decorate gaudily or tastelessly [c17: from BE- + obsolete *dizen* to dress up, of uncertain origin] > be'dizenment n

bed jacket n a woman's short upper garment worn over

a nightgown when sitting up in bed

bedlam ('bɛdləm) *n* **1** a noisy confused place or situation; state of uproar **2** *archaic* a lunatic asylum; madhouse [C13 *bedlem, bethlem*, after the Hospital of St Mary of *Bethlehem* in London]

bed linen *n* sheets and pillowcases for a bed

Bedloe's Island ('bɛdləuz) *or* **Bedloe Island** *n* the former name (until 1956) of **Liberty Island**

Bedouin *or* **Beduin** ('bɛduɪn) *n* **1** *pl* **-ins** *or* **-in** a member of any of the nomadic tribes of Arabs inhabiting the deserts of Arabia, Jordan, and Syria, as well as parts of the Sahara **2** a wanderer or rover ▷ *adj* **3** of or relating to the Bedouins **4** wandering or roving [C14: from Old French *beduin*, from Arabic *badāwi*, plural of *badwi*, from *badw* desert]

bedpan ('bɛdˌpæn) *n* a shallow vessel placed under a bedridden patient to collect faeces and urine

bedraggle (bɪ'dræg³l) *vb* (*tr*) to make (hair, clothing, etc) limp, untidy, or dirty, as with rain or mud

bedraggled (bɪ'dræg³ld) *adj* (of hair, clothing, etc) limp, untidy, or dirty, as with rain or mud

bedridden ('bɛdˌrɪd³n) *adj* confined to bed because of illness, esp for a long or indefinite period [Old English *bedreda*, from *bedd* BED + *-rida* rider, from *rīdan* to RIDE]

bedrock ('bɛdˌrɒk) *n* **1** the solid unweathered rock that lies beneath the loose surface deposits of soil, alluvium, etc **2** basic principles or facts (esp in the phrase **get down to bedrock**) **3** the lowest point, level, or layer

bedroll ('bɛdˌrəʊl) *n* a portable roll of bedding, such as a sleeping bag, used esp for sleeping in the open

bedroom ('bɛdˌruːm, -ˌrʊm) *n* **1** a room furnished with beds or used for sleeping **2** (*modifier*) containing references to sex: *a bedroom comedy*

Beds *abbreviation* Bedfordshire

bedside ('bɛdˌsaɪd) *n* **a** the space by the side of a bed, esp of a sick person **b** (*as modifier*): *a bedside lamp; a doctor's bedside manner*

bedsit ('bɛdˌsɪt) *n* a furnished sitting room containing sleeping accommodation and sometimes cooking and washing facilities. Also called: **bedsitter, bedsitting room**

bedsore ('bɛdˌsɔː) *n* the nontechnical name for **decubitus ulcer**

bedspread ('bɛdˌsprɛd) *n* a top cover on a bed over other bedclothes

bedstead ('bɛdˌstɛd) *n* the framework of a bed, usually including a headboard and springs but excluding the mattress and other coverings

bedstraw ('bɛdˌstrɔː) *n* any of numerous rubiaceous plants of the genus *Galium*, which have small white or yellow flowers and prickly or hairy fruits: some species formerly used as straw for beds as they are aromatic when dry

bedtime ('bɛdˌtaɪm) *n* **a** the time when one usually goes to bed **b** (*as modifier*): *a bedtime story*

bed-wetting *n* the act or habit of involuntarily urinating in bed

Bedworth ('bɛdwəθ) *n* a town in central England, in N Warwickshire. Pop: 30 001 (2001)

bee¹ (biː) *n* **1** any hymenopterous insect of the superfamily *Apoidea*, which includes social forms such as the honeybee and solitary forms such as the carpenter bee **2 busy bee** a person who is industrious or has many things to do **3** have a bee in one's bonnet to be preoccupied or obsessed with an idea [Old English *bīo*; related to Old Norse *bȳ*, Old High German *bīa*, Dutch *bij*, Swedish *bi*]

bee² (biː) *n* a social gathering for a specific purpose, as to carry out a communal task or hold competitions: *quilting bee* [C18: perhaps from dialect *bean* neighbourly help, from Old English *bēn* boon]

Beeb (biːb) *n* **the Beeb** an informal name for **BBC**

beebread ('biːˌbrɛd) *n* a mixture of pollen and nectar prepared by worker bees and fed to the larvae. Also called: **ambrosia**

beech (biːtʃ) *n* **1** any N temperate tree of the genus *Fagus*, esp *F. sylvatica* of Europe, having smooth greyish bark: family *Fagaceae* **2** any tree of the related genus *Nothofagus*, of temperate Australasia and South America

3 the hard wood of any of these trees, used in making furniture, etc **4** See **copper beech** [Old English *bēce*; related to Old Norse *bók*, Old High German *buohha*, Middle Dutch *boeke*, Latin *fāgus* beech, Greek *phēgos* edible oak] ▷ **beechen** *or* **beechy** *adj*

Beecham ('biːtʃəm) *n* Sir **Thomas**. 1879–1961, English conductor who did much to promote the works of Delius, Sibelius, and Richard Strauss

Beecher ('biːtʃə) *n* **Henry Ward**. 1813–87, US clergyman: a leader in the movement for the abolition of slavery

Beecher Stowe *n* See (Harriet Elizabeth Beecher) **Stowe**

beechnut ('biːtʃˌnʌt) *n* the small brown triangular edible nut of the beech tree. Collectively, the nuts are often termed **beech mast**, esp when lying on the ground

bee-eater *n* any insectivorous bird of the family *Meropidae* of tropical and subtropical regions of the Old World, having a long downward-curving bill and long pointed wings and tail: order *Coraciiformes* (kingfishers, etc)

beef (biːf) *n* **1** the flesh of various bovine animals, esp the cow, when killed for eating **2** *pl* **beeves** (biːvz) an adult ox, bull, cow, etc, reared for its meat **3** *informal* human flesh, esp when muscular **4** *pl* **beefs** a complaint ▷ *vb* **5** (*intr*) *slang* to complain, esp repeatedly **6** (*tr*; often foll by *up*) *informal* to strengthen; reinforce [C13: from Old French *boef*, from Latin *bōs* ox; see COW¹]

beefburger ('biːfˌbɜːgə) *n* a flat fried cake of minced beef; hamburger

beefcake ('biːfˌkeɪk) *n* *slang* men displayed for their muscular bodies, esp in photographs

beefeater ('biːfˌiːtə) *n* a nickname often applied to the Yeomen of the Guard and the Yeomen Warders at the Tower of London

beef road *n* *Austral* a road used for transporting cattle

beefsteak ('biːfˌsteɪk) *n* a piece of beef that can be grilled, fried, etc, cut from any lean part of the animal

beefsteak plant *n* an Asian plant, *Perilla frutescens crispa*, with aromatic red or green leaves which are used in cooking: family *Lamiaceae*. Also called: **shiso, Japanese basil**

beef stroganoff *n* a dish of thin strips of beef cooked with onions, mushrooms, and seasonings, served in a sour-cream sauce [C19: named after Count Paul *Stroganoff*, 19th-century Russian diplomat]

beef tea *n* a drink made by boiling pieces of lean beef: often given to invalids to stimulate the appetite

beef tomato *n* a very large fleshy variety of tomato. Also called: **beefsteak tomato**

beefy ('biːfɪ) *adj* **beefier, beefiest** *informal* muscular; brawny ▷ **'beefiness** *n*

beehive ('biːˌhaɪv) *n* **1** a man-made receptacle used to house a swarm of bees **2** a dome-shaped hair style in which the hair is piled high on the head **3** a place where busy people are assembled

Beehive ('biːˌhaɪv) *n* **the Beehive** *informal* **1** the dome-shaped building that houses sections of Parliament in Wellington, New Zealand **2** the New Zealand government

beekeeper ('biːˌkiːpə) *n* a person who keeps bees for their honey; apiarist ▷ **'bee,keeping** *n*

beeline ('biːˌlaɪn) *n* the most direct route between two places (esp in the phrase **make a beeline for**)

Beelzebub (bɪ'ɛlzɪˌbʌb) *n* Satan or any devil or demon [Old English *Belzebub*, ultimately from Hebrew *bá'al zebūb*, literally: lord of flies]

bee moth *n* any of various pyralid moths, such as the wax moth, whose larvae live in the nests of bees or wasps, feeding on nest materials and host larvae

been (biːn, bɪn) *vb* the past participle of **be¹**

beep (biːp) *n* **1** a short high-pitched sound, esp one made by the horn of a car, bicycle, etc, or by electronic apparatus ▷ *vb* **2** to make or cause to make such a noise [C20: of imitative origin] ▷ **'beeper** *n*

beer (bɪə) *n* **1** an alcoholic drink brewed from malt, sugar, hops, and water and fermented with yeast **2** a slightly fermented drink made from the roots or leaves of certain plants: *ginger beer; nettle beer* **3** (*modifier*) relating to or used in the drinking of beer: *beer glass; beer mat* **4** (*modifier*) in which beer is drunk, esp (of licensed premises) having a licence to sell beer: *beer house; beer cellar; beer garden* [Old English *beor*; related to Old Norse *bjórr*, Old Frisian *biār*, Old High German *bior*]

beer and skittles *n* (*functioning as singular*) *informal* enjoyment or pleasure

Beerbohm ('bɪəbəʊm) *n* Sir (**Henry**) **Max**(**imilian**). 1872–1956, English critic, wit, and caricaturist, whose works include *Zuleika Dobson* (1911), a satire on Oxford undergraduates

beer parlour or **beer parlor** *n Canadian* a room in a tavern, hotel, etc in which beer is served

Beersheba (bɪəˈʃiːbə) *n* a town in S Israel: commercial centre of the Negev. In biblical times it marked the southern limit of Palestine. Pop: 183 000 (2003 est)

beery ('bɪərɪ) *adj* beerier, beeriest 1 smelling or tasting of beer 2 given to drinking beer > **'beerily** *adv*

bee's knees *n* the bee's knees (*functioning as singular*) *informal* an excellent or ideally suitable person or thing

beestings, biestings or *US* **beestings** ('biːstɪŋz) *n* (*functioning as singular*) the first milk secreted by the mammary glands of a cow or similar animal immediately after giving birth; colostrum [Old English *bȳsting*, from *bēost* beestings; related to Middle Dutch *biest*]

beeswax ('biːzˌwæks) *n* **a** a yellowish or dark brown wax secreted by honeybees for constructing honeycombs **b** this wax after refining, purifying, etc, used in polishes, ointments, and for modelling

beeswing ('biːzˌwɪŋ) *n* a light filmy crust of tartar that forms in port and some other wines after long keeping in the bottle

beet (biːt) *n* 1 any chenopodiaceous plant of the genus *Beta*, esp the Eurasian species *B. vulgaris*, widely cultivated in such varieties as the sugar beet, mangelwurzel, beetroot, and spinach beet 2 the leaves of any of several varieties of this plant, which are cooked and eaten as a vegetable 3 red beet the US name for **beetroot** [Old English *bēte*, from Latin *bēta*]

Beethoven ('beɪtˌhəʊv³n) *n* **Ludwig van** ('luːtvɪç fan). 1770–1827, German composer, who greatly extended the form and scope of symphonic and chamber music, bridging the classical and romantic traditions. His works include nine symphonies, 32 piano sonatas, 16 string quartets, five piano concertos, a violin concerto, two masses, the opera *Fidelio* (1805), and choral music

beetle¹ ('biːt³l) *n* 1 any insect of the order *Coleoptera*, having biting mouthparts and forewings modified to form shell-like protective elytra 2 a game played with dice in which the players draw or assemble a beetle-shaped form ▷ *vb* (*intr*; foll by *along, off*, etc) 3 *informal* to scuttle or scurry; hurry [Old English *bitela*; related to *bitol* teeth, BIT, *bītan* to BITE]

beetle² ('biːt³l) *n* 1 a heavy hand tool, usually made of wood, used for ramming, pounding, or beating 2 a machine used to finish cloth by stamping it with wooden hammers [Old English *bīetel*, from *bēatan* to BEAT; related to Middle Low German *bētel* chisel, Old Norse *beytill* penis]

beetle³ ('biːt³l) *vb* 1 (*intr*) to overhang; jut ▷ *adj* 2 overhanging; prominent [c14: perhaps related to BEETLE¹] > **'beetling** *adj*

beetle-browed *adj* having bushy or overhanging eyebrows

Beeton ('biːt³n) *n* **Isabella Mary**, known as *Mrs Beeton*. 1836–65, British cookery writer, author of *The Book of Household Management* (1861)

beetroot ('biːtˌruːt) *n* a variety of the beet plant, *Beta vulgaris*, that has a bulbous dark red root that may be eaten as a vegetable, in salads, or pickled

beet sugar *n* the sucrose obtained from sugar beet, identical in composition to cane sugar

beeves (biːvz) *n archaic* the plural of **beef** (sense 2)

BEF *abbreviation* British Expeditionary Force, the British armies that served in France and Belgium 1914–18 and in France 1939–40

befall (bɪˈfɔːl) *vb* -falls, -falling, -fell, -fallen *archaic or literary* 1 (*intr*) to take place; come to pass 2 (*tr*) to happen to 3 (*intr*; usually foll by *to*) to be due, as by right [Old English *befeallan*; related to Old High German *bifallan*,

Dutch *bevallen*; see BE-, FALL]

befit (bɪˈfɪt) *vb* -fits, -fitting, -fitted (*tr*) to be appropriate to or suitable for [c15: from BE- + FIT¹] > be'**fitting** *adj* > be'**fittingly** *adv*

befog (bɪˈfɒg) *vb* -fogs, -fogging, -fogged (*tr*) 1 to surround with fog 2 to make confused, vague, or less clear

before (bɪˈfɔː) *conj* (*subordinating*) 1 earlier than the time when 2 rather than: *he'll resign before he agrees to it* ▷ *prep* 3 preceding in space or time; in front of; ahead of: *standing before the altar* 4 in the presence of: *to be brought before a judge* 5 in preference to: *to put friendship before money* ▷ *adv* 6 at an earlier time; previously; beforehand; in front [Old English *beforan*; related to Old Frisian *befara*, Old High German *bifora*]

beforehand (bɪˈfɔːˌhænd) *adj, adv* (*postpositive*) early; in advance; in anticipation

befoul (bɪˈfaʊl) *vb* (*tr*) to make dirty or foul; soil; defile

befriend (bɪˈfrɛnd) *vb* (*tr*) to be a friend to; assist; favour

befuddle (bɪˈfʌd³l) *vb* (*tr*) 1 to confuse, muddle, or perplex 2 to make stupid with drink > be'**fuddlement** *n*

beg (bɛg) *vb* begs, begging, begged 1 (when *intr*, often foll by *for*) to solicit (for money, food, etc), esp in the street 2 to ask (someone) for (something or leave to do something) formally, humbly, or earnestly: *I beg forgiveness; I beg to differ* 3 (*intr*) (of a dog) to sit up with forepaws raised expectantly 4 **beg the question a** to evade the issue **b** to assume the thing under examination as proved **c** to suggest that a question needs to be asked: *the firm's success begs the question: why aren't more companies doing the same?* 5 **go begging** or **go a-begging** to be unwanted or unused ▷ See also **beg off** [c13: probably from Old English *bedecian*; related to Gothic *bidagwa* BEGGAR]

● USAGE The use of *beg the question* to mean that a
● question needs to be asked is considered by some
● people to be incorrect

began (bɪˈgæn) *vb* the past tense of **begin**

beget (bɪˈgɛt) *vb* -gets, -getting, -got or -gat, -gotten or -got (*tr*) 1 to father 2 to cause or create [Old English *begietan*; related to Old Saxon *bigetan*, Old High German *pigezzan*, Gothic *bigitan* to find; see BE-, GET] > be'**getter** *n*

beggar (ˈbɛgə) *n* 1 a person who begs, esp one who lives by begging 2 a person who has no money or resources; pauper 3 *ironic, humorous, chiefly Brit* fellow: *lucky beggar!* ▷ *vb* (*tr*) 4 to be beyond the resources of (esp in the phrase **to beggar description**) 5 to impoverish; reduce to begging > **'beggar,hood** or **'beggardom** *n*

beggarly (ˈbɛgəlɪ) *adj* meanly inadequate; very poor > **'beggarliness** *n*

beggar-my-neighbour *n* a card game in which one player tries to win all the cards of the other player

beggary (ˈbɛgərɪ) *n* extreme poverty or need

begin (bɪˈgɪn) *vb* -gins, -ginning, -gan, -gun 1 to start or cause to start (something or to do something) 2 to bring or come into being for the first time; arise or originate 3 to start to say or speak 4 (*used with a negative*) to have the least capacity (to do something): *he couldn't begin to compete with her* 5 **to begin with** in the first place [Old English *beginnan*; related to Old High German *biginnan*, Gothic *duginnan*]

Begin (ˈbeɪgɪn) *n* **Menachem** (məˈnɑːkɪm). 1913–92, Israeli statesman, born in Poland. In Palestine after 1942, he became a leader of the militant Zionists; prime minister of Israel (1977–83); Nobel peace prize jointly with Sadat 1978. In 1979 he concluded the Camp David treaty with Anwar Sadat of Egypt

beginner (bɪˈgɪnə) *n* a person who has just started to do or learn something; novice

beginning (bɪˈgɪnɪŋ) *n* 1 a start; commencement 2 (*often plural*) a first or early part or stage 3 the place where or time when something starts 4 an origin; source

begird (bɪˈgɜːd) *vb* -girds, -girding, -girt or -girded (*tr*) *poetic* 1 to surround; gird around 2 to bind [Old English *begierdan*; see BE-, GIRD¹]

beg off *vb* (*intr, adverb*) to ask to be released from an engagement, obligation, etc

begone (bɪˈgɒn) *sentence substitute* go away! [c14: from BE (imperative) + GONE]

begonia (bɪˈɡəʊnjə) *n* any plant of the genus *Begonia*, of warm and tropical regions, widely cultivated for their ornamental leaves and waxy flowers: family *Begoniaceae* [c18: New Latin, named after Michel *Bégon* (1638–1710), French patron of science]

begorra (bɪˈɡɒrə) *interj* an emphatic exclamation, regarded as a characteristic utterance of Irish people [c19: euphemistic alteration of *by God!*]

begot (bɪˈɡɒt) *vb* a past tense and past participle of **beget**

begotten (bɪˈɡɒtᵊn) *vb* a past participle of **beget**

begrime (bɪˈɡraɪm) *vb* (*tr*) to make dirty; soil

begrudge (bɪˈɡrʌdʒ) *vb* (*tr*) **1** to give, admit, or allow unwillingly or with a bad grace **2** to envy (someone) the possession of (something) > be'grudgingly *adv*

begrudgery (bɪˈɡrʌdʒərɪ) *n* Irish informal resentment of any person who has achieved success or wealth

beguile (bɪˈɡaɪl) *vb* -guiles, -guiling, -guiled (*tr*) **1** to charm; fascinate **2** to delude; influence by slyness **3** (often foll by *of* or *out of*) to deprive (someone) of something by trickery; cheat (someone) of **4** to pass pleasantly; while away > be'guilement *n* > be'guiler *n* > be'guiling *adj* > be'guilingly *adv*

beguine (bɪˈɡiːn) *n* **1** a dance of South American origin in bolero rhythm **2** a piece of music in the rhythm of this dance [c20: from Louisiana French, from French *béguin* flirtation]

begum (ˈbeɪɡəm) *n* (in Pakistan and certain other Muslim countries) a woman of high rank, esp the widow of a prince [c18: from Urdu *begam*, from Turkish *begim*; see BEY]

begun (bɪˈɡʌn) *vb* the past participle of **begin**

behalf (bɪˈhɑːf) *n* interest, part, benefit, or respect (only in the phrases **on** (**someone's**) **behalf, on** or *US and Canadian* **in behalf of, in this** (*or* that) **behalf**) [Old English *be halfe* from *be* by + *halfe* side; compare Old Norse *af halfu*] ● USAGE *On behalf of* is sometimes wrongly used where ● *on the part of* is intended. The distinction is that *on* ● *behalf of someone* means 'for someone's benefit' or ● 'representing someone', while *on the part of someone* can ● be roughly paraphrased as 'by someone'. So, the ● following example is incorrect: *another act of apparent* ● *negligence, this time not on behalf of the company itself, but on* ● *behalf of its banker*, when what was meant was there ● was negligence by the company and its banker

Behan (ˈbiːən) *n* Brendan. 1923–64, Irish writer, noted esp for his plays *The Quare Fellow* (1954) and *The Hostage* (1958) and for an account of his detention as a member of the Irish Republican Army, *Borstal Boy* (1958)

behave (bɪˈheɪv) *vb* **1** (*intr*) to act or function in a specified or usual way **2** to conduct (oneself) in a specified way: *he behaved badly towards her* **3** to conduct (oneself) properly or as desired [c15: see BE-, HAVE]

behaviour *or US* **behavior** (bɪˈheɪvjə) *n* **1** manner of behaving or conducting oneself **2** on one's best behaviour behaving with careful good manners **3** *psychol* the aggregate of all the responses made by an organism in any situation **4** the action, reaction, or functioning of a system, under normal or specified circumstances [c15: from BEHAVE; influenced in form by Middle English *havior*, from Old French *havoir*, from Latin *habēre* to have] > be'havioural *or US* be'havioral *adj*

behavioural science *n* the application of scientific methods to the study of the behaviour of organisms

behaviourism *or US* **behaviorism** (bɪˈheɪvjəˌrɪzəm) *n* a school of psychology that regards the objective observation of the behaviour of organisms (usually by means of automatic recording devices) as the only proper subject for study and that often refuses to postulate any intervening mechanisms between the stimulus and the response > be'haviourist *or US* be'haviorist *adj, n* > be,haviour'istic *or US* be,havior'istic *adj*

behaviour therapy *n* any of various means of treating psychological disorders, such as desensitization, aversion therapy, and instrumental conditioning, that depend on the patient systematically learning new modes of behaviour

behead (bɪˈhɛd) *vb* (*tr*) to remove the head from;

decapitate [Old English *behēafdian*, from BE- + *heafod* HEAD; related to Middle High German *behoubeten*]

beheld (bɪˈhɛld) *vb* the past tense and past participle of **behold**

behemoth (bɪˈhiːmɒθ) *n* **1** *Old Testament* a gigantic beast, probably a hippopotamus, described in Job 40:15 **2** a huge or monstrous person or thing [c14: from Hebrew *běhēmōth*, plural of *běhēmāh* beast]

behest (bɪˈhɛst) *n* an authoritative order or earnest request [Old English *behǣs*, from *behātan*; see BE-, HEST]

behind (bɪˈhaɪnd) *prep* **1** in or to a position further back than; at the rear of; at the back of **2** in the past in relation to: *I've got the exams behind me now* **3** late according to; not keeping up with: *running behind schedule* **4** concerning the circumstances surrounding: *the reasons behind his departure* ▷ *adv* **5** in or to a position further back; following **6** remaining after someone's departure: *he left it behind* **7** in debt; in arrears: *to fall behind with payments* ▷ *adj* **8** (*postpositive*) in a position further back; retarded: *the man behind prodded me* ▷ *n* **9** *informal* the buttocks **10** *Australian rules football* a score of one point made by kicking the ball over the **behind line** between a goalpost and one of the smaller outer posts (**behind posts**) [Old English *behindan*]

behindhand (bɪˈhaɪndˌhænd) *adj, adv* (*postpositive*) **1** remiss in fulfilling an obligation **2** in debt; in arrears **3** delayed in development; backward **4** late; behind time

Behistun (ˌbeɪhɪˈstuːn), **Bisitun** *or* **Bisutun** *n* a village in W Iran by the ancient road from Ecbatana to Babylon. On a nearby cliff is an inscription by Darius in Old Persian, Elamite, and Babylonian describing his enthronement

Behn (bɛn) *n* Aphra (ˈæfrə). 1640–89, English dramatist and novelist, best known for her play *The Rover* (1678) and her novel *Oroonoko* (1688)

behold (bɪˈhəʊld) *vb* -holds, -holding, -held (often used in the imperative to draw attention to something) *archaic or literary* to look (at); observe [Old English *bihealdan*; related to Old High German *bihaltan*, Dutch *behouden*; see BE-, HOLD] > be'holder *n*

beholden (bɪˈhəʊldᵊn) *adj* indebted; obliged; under a moral obligation [Old English *behealden*, past participle of *behealdan* to BEHOLD]

behoof (bɪˈhuːf) *n, pl* -hooves *rare* advantage or profit [Old English *behōf*; related to Middle High German *behuof* something useful; see BEHOVE]

behove (bɪˈhəʊv) *or US* **behoove** (bɪˈhuːv) *vb* (*tr; impersonal*) *archaic* to be necessary or fitting for: *it behoves me to arrest you* [Old English *behōfian*; related to Middle Low German *behoven*]

Behrens (ˈbeərənz; German ˈbeːrəns) *n* Peter. 1868–1940, German architect

Behring *n* **1** (German ˈbeːrɪŋ) Emil (Adolf) von (ˈeːmiːl fɔn). 1854–1917, German bacteriologist, who discovered diphtheria and tetanus antitoxins: Nobel prize for physiology or medicine 1901 **2** (ˈbɛrɪŋ, ˈbeər-) a variant spelling of **Bering**

Beiderbecke (ˈbaɪdəˌbɛk) *n* Leon Bismarcke, known as Bix. 1903–31, US jazz cornettist, composer, and pianist

beige (beɪʒ) *n* **1** a a very light brown, sometimes with a yellowish tinge, similar to the colour of undyed wool b (*as adjective*): *beige gloves* **2** a fabric made of undyed or unbleached wool [c19: from Old French, of obscure origin]

Beijing (ˈbeɪˈdʒɪŋ) *n* the capital of the People's Republic of China, in the northeast in Beijing municipality (traditionally in Hebei province); the country's second largest city: dates back to the 12th century BC; consists of two central walled cities, the Outer City (containing the commercial quarter) and the Inner City, which contains the Imperial City, within which is the Purple or Forbidden City; many universities. Pop: 10 849 000 (2005 est)

being (ˈbiːɪŋ) *n* **1** the state or fact of existing; existence **2** essential nature; self **3** something that exists or is thought to exist, esp something that cannot be assigned to any category: *a being from outer space* **4** a person; human being

Beira (ˈbaɪərə) *n* a port in E Mozambique: terminus of a transcontinental railway from Lobito, Angola, through the Democratic Republic of Congo (formerly Zaïre), Zambia, and Zimbabwe. Pop: 566 000 (2005 est)

Beirut or **Beyrouth** (ˌbeɪˈruːt) n the capital of Lebanon, a port on the Mediterranean: part of the Ottoman Empire from the 16th century until 1918; many universities (including Lebanese, American, French, and Arab). Pop: 1 875 000 (2005 est)

Béjart (French beʒar) n **Maurice** (mɔrɪs). born 1927, French dancer and choreographer. His choreography is characterized by a combination of classic and modern dance and acrobatics

bejewel (bɪˈdʒuːəl) vb -els, -elling, -elled or US -els, -eling, -eled (tr) to decorate with or as if with jewels

Bekaa or **Beqaa** (bɪˈkɑː) n a broad valley in central Lebanon, between the Lebanon and Anti-Lebanon Mountains

Békésy (Hungarian ˈbeːkeʃɪ) n **Georg von** (ˈgeːɔrk fɔn). 1899–1972, US physicist, born in Hungary; noted for his work on the mechanism of hearing: Nobel prize for physiology or medicine 1961

bel (bɛl) n a unit for comparing two power levels, equal to the logarithm to the base ten of the ratio of the two powers [C20: named after Alexander Graham Bell (1847–1922), Scots-born US scientist]

Bel (beɪl) n (in Babylonian and Assyrian mythology) the god of the earth

belabour or US **belabor** (bɪˈleɪbə) vb (tr) **1** to beat severely; thrash **2** to attack verbally; criticize harshly

Belarus (ˈbɛləˌrʌs, -ˌrʊs), **Byelorussia** or **Belorussia** (ˌbjɛləʊˈrʌʃə, ˌbɛl-) n a republic in E Europe; part of the medieval Lithuanian and Polish empires before occupied by Russia; a Soviet republic (1919–91); in 1997 formed a close political and economic union with Russia: mainly low-lying and forested. Languages: Belarussian; Russian. Religion: believers are mostly Christian. Currency: rouble. Capital: Minsk. Pop: 9 851 000 (2004 est). Area: 207 600 sq km (80 134 sq miles). Also called: Byelorussian Republic, Bielorussia, White Russia

Belarussian, Belarusian, Byelorussian or **Belorussian** (ˌbɛləʊˈrʌʃən, ˌbjɛl-) adj **1** of, relating to, or characteristic of Belarus, its people, or their language ▷ n **2** the official language of Belarus: an East Slavonic language closely related to Russian **3** a native or inhabitant of Belarus ▷ Also called: White Russian

belated (bɪˈleɪtɪd) adj late or too late: belated greetings > beˈlatedly adv > beˈlatedness n

Belau (bəˈlaʊ) n an alternative name for the (Republic of) **Palau**

belay (bɪˈleɪ) vb -lays, -laying, -layed **1** nautical to make fast (a line) by securing to a pin, cleat, or bitt **2** (usually imperative) nautical to stop; cease **3** (ˈbiːˌleɪ) mountaineering to secure (a climber) to a mountain by tying the rope off round a rock spike, piton, nut, etc ▷ n **4** (ˈbiːˌleɪ) mountaineering the attachment (of a climber) to a mountain by tying the rope off round a rock spike, piton, nut, etc, to safeguard the party in the event of a fall [Old English belecgan; related to Old High German bileggan, Dutch beleggen]

belaying pin n nautical a cylindrical, sometimes tapered pin, usually of metal or wood, that fits into a hole in a pin or fife rail: used for belaying

bel canto (bɛl ˈkæntəʊ) n music a style of singing characterized by beauty of tone rather than dramatic power [C19: Italian, literally: beautiful singing]

belch (bɛltʃ) vb **1** (usually intr) to expel wind from the stomach noisily through the mouth; eructate **2** to expel or be expelled forcefully from inside: smoke belching from factory chimneys ▷ n **3** an act of belching; eructation [Old English bialcan; related to Middle Low German belken to shout, Dutch balken to bray]

beldam or **beldame** (ˈbɛldəm) n archaic an old woman, esp an ugly or malicious one; hag [C15: from bel- grand (as in grandmother), from Old French bel beautiful, from Latin bellus + dam mother, variant of DAME]

beleaguer (bɪˈliːgə) vb (tr) **1** to trouble persistently; harass **2** to lay siege to [C16: from BE- + LEAGUER¹]

Belém (Portuguese bəˈlẽɪ) n a port in N Brazil, the capital

of Pará state, on the Pará River: major trading centre for the Amazon basin. Pop: 2 097 000 (2005 est)

belemnite (ˈbɛləmˌnaɪt) n **1** any extinct marine cephalopod mollusc of the order Belemnoidea, related to the cuttlefish **2** the long pointed conical internal shell of any of these animals: a common Mesozoic fossil [C17: from Greek belemnon dart]

Belfast (ˈbɛlfɑːst, bɛlˈfɑːst) n **1** the capital of Northern Ireland, a port on Belfast Lough in Belfast district, Co Antrim and Co Down: became the centre of Irish Protestantism and of the linen industry in the 17th century; seat of the Northern Ireland assembly and executive. Pop: 276 459 (2001) **2** a district of W Northern Ireland, in Co Antrim and Co Down. Pop: 271 596 (2003 est). Area: 115 sq km (44 sq miles)

belfry (ˈbɛlfrɪ) n, pl -fries **1** the part of a tower or steeple in which bells are hung **2** a tower or steeple [C13: from Old French berfrei, of Germanic origin; compare Middle High German bercfrit fortified tower, Medieval Latin berfredus tower]

Belg. or **Bel.** abbreviation **1** Belgian **2** Belgium

Belgaum (bɛlˈgaʊm) n a city in India, in Karnataka: cotton, furniture, leather. Pop: 399 600 (2001)

Belgian (ˈbɛldʒən) n **1** a native, citizen, or inhabitant of Belgium ▷ adj **2** of, relating to, or characteristic of Belgium or the Belgians

Belgian Congo n a former name (1908–60) of **Congo** (sense 1)

Belgian hare n a large red breed of domestic rabbit

Belgium (ˈbɛldʒəm) n a federal kingdom in NW Europe: at various times under the rulers of Burgundy, Spain, Austria, France, and the Netherlands before becoming an independent kingdom in 1830. It formed the Benelux customs union with the Netherlands and Luxembourg in 1948 and and was a founder member of the Common Market, now the European Union. It consists chiefly of a low-lying region of sand, woods, and heath (the Campine) in the north and west, and a fertile undulating central plain rising to the Ardennes Mountains in the southeast. Languages: French, Flemish (Dutch), German. Religion: Roman Catholic majority. Currency: euro. Capital: Brussels. Pop: 10 339 000 (2004 est). Area: 30 513 sq km (11 778 sq miles)

Belgorod-Dnestrovski or **Byelgorod-Dnestrovski** (Russian ˈbjɛlgərət-dnjɪˈstrɔfskij) n a port in SW Ukraine, on the Dniester estuary: belonged to Romania from 1918 until 1940; under Soviet rule (1944–91). Pop: 48 100 (2004 est). Romanian name: Cetatea Albă. Former name (until 1946): Akkerman

Belgrade (bɛlˈgreɪd, ˈbɛlgreɪd) n the capital of Serbia, in the E part at the confluence of the Danube and Sava Rivers: became the capital of Serbia in 1878, of Yugoslavia in 1929, and later of the State Union of Serbia and Montenegro (2003–2006). Pop: 1 280 639 (2002). Serbian name: Beograd

Belgravia (bɛlˈgreɪvɪə) n a fashionable residential district of W central London, around Belgrave Square

Belial (ˈbiːlɪəl) n a demon mentioned frequently in apocalyptic literature: identified in the Christian tradition with the devil or Satan [C13: from Hebrew bəlīyyaʿal, from bəlīy without + yaʿal worth]

belie (bɪˈlaɪ) vb -lies, -lying, -lied (tr) **1** to show to be untrue; contradict **2** to misrepresent; disguise the nature of **3** to fail to justify; disappoint [Old English belēogan; related to Old Frisian biliuga, Old High German biliugan; see BE-, LIE¹]

belief (bɪˈliːf) n **1** a principle, proposition, idea, etc, accepted as true **2** opinion; conviction **3** religious faith **4** trust or confidence, as in a person or a person's abilities, probity, etc

believe (bɪˈliːv) vb **1** (tr; may take a clause as object) to accept (a statement, supposition, or opinion) as true: I believe God exists **2** (tr) to accept the statement or opinion of (a person) as true **3** (intr; foll by in) to be convinced of the truth or existence (of): to believe in fairies **4** (intr) to have religious faith **5** (when tr, takes a clause as object) to think, assume, or suppose **6** (tr; foll by of; used with can, could, would, etc) to think that someone is able to do (a particular action): I wouldn't have believed it of him [Old

English *beliefan*] > be'lievable *adj* > be'liever *n*

belike (bɪ'laɪk) *adv archaic or dialect* perhaps; maybe

Belisarius (ˌbelɪ'sɑːrɪəs) *n* ?505–565 AD, Byzantine general under Justinian I. He recovered North Africa from the Vandals and Italy from the Ostrogoths and led forces against the Persians

Belisha beacon (bə'liːʃə) *n* a flashing light in an orange globe mounted on a post, indicating a pedestrian crossing on a road [c20: named after Leslie Hore-*Belisha* (1893–1957), British politician]

belittle (bɪ'lɪtᵊl) *vb* (*tr*) **1** to consider or speak of (something) as less valuable or important than it really is; disparage **2** to cause to make small; dwarf > be'littlement *n* > be'littler *n*

Belitung (bɪ'liːtʊŋ) *n* another name for **Billiton**

Belize (bə'liːz) *n* a state in Central America, on the Caribbean Sea: site of a Mayan civilization until the 9th century AD; colonized by the British from 1638; granted internal self-government in 1964; became an independent state within the Commonwealth in 1981. Official language: English; Carib and Spanish are also spoken. Currency: Belize dollar. Capital: Belmopan. Pop: 261 000 (2004 est). Area: 22 965 sq km (8867 sq miles). Former name (until 1973): **British Honduras** > Be'lizean *adj, n*

Belize City *n* a port and the largest city in Belize, on the Caribbean coast: capital until 1973, when that function was transferred inland to Belmopan owing to hurricane risk. Pop: 53 000 (2005 est)

bell[1] (bel) *n* **1** a hollow, usually metal, cup-shaped instrument that emits a musical ringing sound when struck, often by a clapper hanging inside it **2** the sound made by such an instrument or device, as for showing the hours or marking the beginning or end of a period of time **3** an electrical device that rings or buzzes as a signal **4** the bowl-shaped termination of the tube of certain musical wind instruments, such as the trumpet or oboe **5** *nautical* a signal rung on a ship's bell to count the number of half-hour intervals during each of six four-hour watches reckoned from midnight. Thus, one bell may signify 12.30, 4.30, or 8.30 a.m. or p.m **6** *Brit slang* a telephone call (esp in the phrase **give someone a bell**) **7** beat seven bells out of *or* knock seven bells out of *Brit informal* to give a severe beating to **8** bell, book, and candle **a** instruments used formerly in excommunications and other ecclesiastical acts **b** *informal* the solemn ritual ratification of such acts **9** ring a bell to sound familiar; recall to the mind something previously experienced, esp indistinctly **10** sound as a bell in perfect condition ▷ *vb* **11** to be or cause to be shaped like a bell **12** (*tr*) to attach a bell or bells to [Old English *belle*; related to Old Norse *bjalla*, Middle Low German *bell*; see BELL[2]]

bell[2] (bel) *n* **1** a bellowing or baying cry, esp that of a hound or a male deer in rut ▷ *vb* **2** to utter (such a cry) [Old English *bellan*; related to Old Norse *belja* to bellow, Old High German *bellan* to roar, Sanskrit *bhāsate* he talks; see BELLOW]

Bell (bel) *n* **1** Acton, Currer ('kʌrə), and Ellis. pen names of the sisters Anne, Charlotte, and Emily Brontë. See **Brontë 2 Alexander Graham.** 1847–1922, US scientist, born in Scotland, who invented the telephone (1876) **3** Sir **Francis Henry Dillon.** 1851–1936, New Zealand statesman; prime minister of New Zealand (1925) **4** Gertrude (Margaret Lowthian). 1868–1926, British traveller, writer, and diplomat; secretary to the British High Commissioner in Baghdad (1917–26) **5** Joshua. born 1967, US violinist **6** (Susan) Jocelyn, married name *Jocelyn* Burnell, born 1943, British radio astronomer, who discovered the first pulsar **7** Vanessa, original name *Vanessa Stephen.* 1879–1961, British painter; a member of the Bloomsbury group, sister of Virginia Woolf and wife of the art critic Clive Bell (1881–1964)

belladonna (ˌbelə'dɒnə) *n* **1** either of two alkaloid drugs, atropine or hyoscyamine, obtained from the leaves and roots of the deadly nightshade **2** another name for **deadly nightshade** [c16: from Italian, literally: beautiful lady; supposed to refer to its use by women as a cosmetic]

Bellamy ('beləmɪ) *n* **David (James).** born 1933, British botanist, writer, and broadcaster

Bellarmine ('belɑːˌmiːn) *n* **Saint Robert.** 1542–1621, Italian Jesuit theologian and cardinal; an important influence during the Counter-Reformation

Bellay (French belɛ) *n* **Joachim du** (ʒɔaʃɛ̃ dy). 1522–60, French poet, a member of the Pléiade

bellbird ('belˌbɜːd) *n* **1** any of several tropical American passerine birds of the genus *Procnias* having a bell-like call: family *Cotingidae* (cotingas) **2** either of two other birds with a bell-like call: an Australian flycatcher, *Oreoica gutturalis* (**crested bellbird**), or a New Zealand honeyeater, *Anthornis melanura*

bell-bottoms *pl n* trousers that flare from the knee and have wide bottoms > 'bell-ˌbottomed *adj*

bellboy ('belˌbɔɪ) *n* a man or boy employed in a hotel, club, etc, to carry luggage and answer calls for service; page; porter. Also called: bellhop

bell buoy *n* a navigational buoy fitted with a bell, the clapper of which strikes when the waves move the buoy

belle (bel) *n* **1** a beautiful girl or woman **2** the most attractive or admired girl or woman at a place, function, etc (esp in the phrase **the belle of the ball**) [c17: from French, feminine of BEAU]

Belleau Wood ('beləʊ; French belo) *n* a forest in N France: site of a battle (1918) in which the US Marines halted a German advance on Paris

belle époque (French bel epɔk) *n* the period of comfortable well-established life in Europe before World War I [literally: fine period]

Belle Isle *n* an island in the Atlantic, at the N entrance to the **Strait of Belle Isle**, between Labrador and Newfoundland. Area: about 39 sq km (15 sq miles)

Bellerophon (bə'lɛrəˌfɒn) *n Greek myth* a hero of Corinth who performed many deeds with the help of the winged horse Pegasus, notably the killing of the monster Chimera

belles-lettres (French bɛllɛtrə) *n* (*functioning as singular*) literary works, esp essays and poetry, valued for their aesthetic rather than their informative or moral content [c17: from French: fine letters] > bel'letrist *n*

bellflower ('belˌflaʊə) *n* another name for **campanula**

bellfounder ('belˌfaʊndə) *n* a foundry worker who casts bells

bellicose ('belɪˌkəʊs, -ˌkəʊz) *adj* warlike; aggressive; ready to fight [c15: from Latin *bellicōsus*, from *bellum* war] > bellicosity (ˌbelɪ'kɒsɪtɪ) *n*

belligerati (bɪˌlɪdʒə'rɑːtɪ) *pl n* intellectuals, such as writers, who advocate war or imperialism [c20: from *bellig*(*erent*) + -*ati* as in LITERATI]

belligerence (bɪ'lɪdʒərəns) *n* the act or quality of being belligerent or warlike; aggressiveness

belligerency (bɪ'lɪdʒərənsɪ) *n* the state of being at war

belligerent (bɪ'lɪdʒərənt) *adj* **1** marked by readiness to fight or argue; aggressive **2** relating to or engaged in a legally recognized war or warfare ▷ *n* **3** a person or country engaged in fighting or war [c16: from Latin *belliger*, from *bellum* war + *gerere* to wage]

Bellingshausen Sea ('belɪŋzˌhaʊzᵊn) *n* an area of the S Pacific Ocean off the coast of Antarctica [named after Fabian Gottlieb *Bellingshausen* (1778–1852), Russian explorer]

Bellini (Italian bel'lini) *n* **1** Giovanni (dʒo'vanni). ?1430–1516, Italian painter of the Venetian school, noted for his altarpieces, landscapes, and Madonnas. His father Jacopo (?1400–70) and his brother **Gentile** (?1429–1507) were also painters **2** Vincenzo (vin'tʃɛntso). 1801–35, Italian composer of operas, esp *La Sonnambula* (1831) and *Norma* (1831)

Bellinzona (Italian bellin'tsona) *n* a town in SE central Switzerland, capital of Ticino canton. Pop: 16 463 (2000)

bell jar *n* a bell-shaped glass cover used to protect flower arrangements or fragile ornaments or to cover apparatus in experiments, esp to prevent gases escaping

bellman ('belmən) *n, pl* -men a man who rings a bell, esp (formerly) a town crier

bell metal *n* an alloy of copper and tin, with some zinc and lead, used in casting bells

Belloc ('belɒk) *n* **Hilaire** ('hɪlɛə, hɪ'lɛə). 1870–1953, British poet, essayist, and historian, born in France, noted particularly for his verse for children in *The Bad Child's Book of Beasts* (1896) and *Cautionary Tales* (1907)

bellow ('bɛləʊ) *vb* **1** (*intr*) to make a loud deep raucous cry like that of a bull; roar **2** to shout (something) unrestrainedly, as in anger or pain; bawl ▷ *n* **3** the characteristic noise of a bull **4** a loud deep sound, as of pain or anger [C14: probably from Old English *bylgan*; related to *bellan* to BELL²]

Bellow ('bɛləʊ) *n* **Saul**. 1915–2005, US novelist, born in Canada. His works include *Dangling Man* (1944), *The Adventures of Angie March* (1954), *Herzog* (1964), *Humboldt's Gift* (1975), *The Dean's December* (1981), and *Ravelstein* (2000): Nobel prize for literature 1976

bellows ('bɛləʊz) *n* (*functioning as singular or plural*) **1** Also called: **pair of bellows** an instrument consisting of an air chamber with flexible sides or end, a means of compressing it, an inlet valve, and a constricted outlet that is used to create a stream of air, as for producing a draught for a fire or for sounding organ pipes **2** a flexible corrugated element used as an expansion joint, pump, or means of transmitting axial motion [C16: from plural of Old English *belig* BELLY]

bell pull *n* a handle, rope, or cord pulled to operate a doorbell or servant's bell

bell push *n* a button pressed to operate an electric bell

bell-ringer *n* a person who rings church bells > 'bell-ˌringing *n*

bells and whistles *pl n* additional features or accessories which are nonessential but very attractive [C20: from the bells and whistles which used to decorate fairground organs]

bell tent *n* a cone-shaped tent having a single central supporting pole

bellwether ('bɛlˌwɛðə) *n* **1** a sheep that leads the herd, often bearing a bell **2** a leader, esp one followed unquestioningly

belly ('bɛlɪ) *n*, *pl* -lies **1** the lower or front part of the body of a vertebrate, containing the intestines and other abdominal organs; abdomen **2** the stomach, esp when regarded as the seat of gluttony **3** a part, line, or structure that bulges deeply: *the belly of a sail* **4** the inside or interior cavity of something **5** the front or inner part or underside of something **6** the surface of a stringed musical instrument over which the strings are stretched **7** *Austral & NZ* the wool from a sheep's belly **8** *archaic* the womb **9** go belly up *informal* to die, fail, or come to an end ▷ *vb* -lies, -lying, -lied **10** to swell out or cause to swell out; bulge [Old English *belig*; related to Old High German *balg*, Old Irish *bolg* sack, Sanskrit *barhi* chaff]

bellyache ('bɛlɪˌeɪk) *n* **1** an informal term for **stomachache** ▷ *vb* **2** (*intr*) *slang* to complain repeatedly > 'belly,acher *n*

bellyband ('bɛlɪˌbænd) *n* a strap around the belly of a draught animal, holding the shafts of a vehicle

bellybutton ('bɛlɪˌbʌtən) *n* an informal name for the navel

belly dance *n* **1** a sensuous and provocative dance of Middle Eastern origin, performed by women, with undulating movements of the hips and abdomen ▷ *vb* belly-dance **2** (*intr*) to perform such a dance > belly dancer *n*

belly flop *n* **1** a dive into water in which the body lands horizontally ▷ *vb* belly-flop -flops, -flopping, -flopped **2** (*intr*) to perform a belly flop

bellyful ('bɛlɪˌfʊl) *n* **1** as much as one wants or can eat **2** *slang* more than one can tolerate

belly landing *n* the landing of an aircraft on its fuselage without use of its landing gear

belly laugh *n* a loud deep hearty laugh

Belmondo (bɛl'mɒndəʊ; *French* bɛlmɔ̃do) *n* **Jean-Paul** (ʒɑ̃pol). born 1933, French film actor

Belmopan (ˌbɛlməʊ'pæn) *n* (since 1973) the capital of Belize, about 50 miles inland: founded in 1970. Pop: 10 000 (2005 est)

Belo Horizonte (*Portuguese* 'bɛːlori'zõːntə) *n* a city in SE Brazil, the capital of Minas Gerais state. Pop: 5 304 000 (2005 est)

belong (bɪ'lɒŋ) *vb* (*intr*) **1** (foll by *to*) to be the property or possession (of) **2** (foll by *to*) to be bound to (a person, place, or club) by ties of affection, dependence, allegiance, or membership **3** (foll by *to*, *under*, *with*, etc) to be classified (with): *this plant belongs to the daisy family* **4** (foll by *to*) to be a part or adjunct (of) **5** to have a proper or usual place **6** *informal* to be suitable or acceptable, esp socially [C14 *belongen*, from BE- (intensive) + *longen*; related to Old High German *bilangēn* to reach; see LONG³]

belonging (bɪ'lɒŋɪŋ) *n* secure relationship; affinity (esp in the phrase **a sense of belonging**)

belongings (bɪ'lɒŋɪŋz) *pl n* (*sometimes singular*) the things that a person owns or has with him; possessions; effects

Belorussia (ˌbjɛləʊ'rʌʃə, ˌbɛl-) *n* a variant spelling of **Belarus** > ˌBelo'russian *adj*, *n*

Belostok (bjɪla'stɔk) *n* transliteration of the Russian name for **Białystok**

beloved (bɪ'lʌvɪd, -'lʌvd) *adj* **1** dearly loved ▷ *n* **2** a person who is dearly loved, such as a wife or husband

Belovo (*Russian* 'bjeləvə) *n* a variant spelling of **Byelovo**

below (bɪ'ləʊ) *prep* **1** at or to a position lower than; under **2** less than in quantity or degree **3** south of **4** downstream of **5** unworthy of; beneath ▷ *adv* **6** at or to a lower position or place **7** at a later place (in something written) **8** *archaic* beneath heaven; on earth or in hell [C14: *bilooghe*, from *bi* BY + *looghe* LOW¹]

below-the-line *adj* **1** denoting the entries printed below the horizontal line on a company's profit-and-loss account that show how any profit is to be distributed **2** (of an advertising campaign) employing sales promotions, direct marketing, in-store exhibitions and displays, trade shows, sponsorship, and merchandising that do not involve an advertising agency **3** (in national accounts) below the horizontal line separating revenue from capital transactions ▷ See **above-the-line**

Bel Paese ('bɛl pɑː'eɪzɪ) *n* a mild creamy Italian cheese [C20: from Italian, literally: beautiful country]

Belsen ('bɛlsən; *German* 'bɛlzən) *n* a village in NE Germany: with Bergen, the site of a Nazi concentration camp (1943–45)

Belshazzar (bɛl'ʃæzə) *n* 6th century BC, the son of Nabonidus, coregent of Babylon with his father for eight years: referred to as king and son of Nebuchadnezzar in the Old Testament (Daniel 5:1, 17; 8:1); described as having received a divine message of doom written on a wall at a banquet (**Belshazzar's Feast**)

belt (bɛlt) *n* **1** a band of cloth, leather, etc, worn, usually around the waist, to support clothing, carry tools, weapons, or ammunition, or as decoration **2** a narrow band, circle, or stripe, as of colour **3** an area, esp an elongated one, where a specific thing or specific conditions are found; zone: *the town belt; a belt of high pressure* **4** a belt worn as a symbol of rank (as by a knight or an earl), or awarded as a prize (as in boxing or wrestling), or to mark particular expertise (as in judo or karate) **5** See **seat belt 6** a band of flexible material between rotating shafts or pulleys to transfer motion or transmit goods: *a fan belt; a conveyer belt* **7** *informal* a sharp blow, as with a bat or the fist **8** below the belt **a** *boxing* below the waist, esp in the groin **b** *informal* in an unscrupulous or cowardly way **9** tighten one's belt to take measures to reduce expenditure **10** under one's belt **a** (of food or drink) in one's stomach **b** as part of one's experience: *he had a linguistics degree under his belt* ▷ *vb* **11** (*tr*) to fasten or attach with or as if with a belt **12** (*tr*) to hit with a belt **13** (*tr*) *slang* to give a sharp blow; punch **14** (*intr*; often foll by *along*) *slang* to move very fast, esp in a car **15** (*tr*) *rare* to encircle; surround [Old English, from Latin *balteus*] > 'belted *n*

belt-and-braces *adj* providing double security, in case one security measure should fail: *a belt-and-braces policy*

Beltane ('bɛlteɪn, -tən) *n* an ancient Celtic festival with a sacrificial bonfire on May Day. It is also celebrated by modern pagans [C15: from Scottish Gaelic *bealltainn*]

belter ('bɛltə) *n* *informal* **1** an event, person, quality, etc, that is admirable, outstanding, or thrilling: *a real belter of a match* **2 a** a rousing or spirited popular song that is sung loudly and enthusiastically **b** a person who sings popular songs in a loud and spirited manner

belting ('bɛltɪŋ) n 1 the material used to make a belt or belts 2 belts collectively 3 informal a beating ▷ adj 4 Brit informal excellent; first-class

belt man n Austral & NZ (formerly) the member of a beach life-saving team who swam out with a line attached to his belt

belt out vb (tr, adverb) informal to sing loudly or emit (sound, esp pop music) loudly

belt up vb (adverb) slang to become or cause to become silent; stop talking: often used in the imperative

beluga (bɪ'luːgə) n 1 a large white sturgeon, Acipenser (or Huso) huso, of the Black and Caspian Seas: a source of caviar and isinglass 2 another name for **white whale** [c18: from Russian byeluga, from byely white]

belvedere ('bɛlvɪ,dɪə, ,bɛlvɪ'dɪə) n a building, such as a summerhouse or roofed gallery, sited to command a fine view [c16: from Italian: beautiful sight]

Belyi or **Bely** ('bjɛlɪ) n **Andrei** (ʌn'dreɪ), real name Boris Nikolayevich Bugaev. 1880–1934, Russian poet, novelist, and critic: a leading exponent of symbolism. His novels include Petersburg (1913)

Bembo (Italian 'bɛmbo) n **Pietro** ('pjɛːtro). 1470–1547, Italian scholar, poet, and cardinal (1539). His treatise Prose della volgar lingua (1525) helped to establish a standard form of literary Italian

bemire (bɪ'maɪə) vb (tr) 1 to soil with or as if with mire 2 (usually passive) to stick fast in mud or mire

bemoan (bɪ'məʊn) vb (tr) to grieve over (a loss, etc); mourn; lament (esp in the phrase **bemoan one's fate**) [Old English bemǣnan; see BE-, MOAN]

bemuse (bɪ'mjuːz) vb (tr) to confuse; bewilder

bemused (bɪ'mjuːzd) adj preoccupied; lost in thought

ben (bɛn) Scot ▷ n 1 an inner room in a house or cottage ▷ prep, adv 2 in; within; inside; into the inner part (of a house) ▷ See **but²** [Old English binnan, from BE- + innan inside]

Benacerraf (,bɛnə'sɛrɑːf) n **Baruj**. born 1920, US immunologist: shared the Nobel prize for physiology or medicine (1980) for his work on histocompatibility antigens

Benares (bɪ'nɑːrɪz) or **Banaras** n the former name of Varanasi

Benavente y Martínez (Spanish bɛnaˈβɛnte i marˈtineθ) n **Jacinto**. 1866–1954, Spanish dramatist and critic, who wrote over 150 plays. Nobel prize for literature 1922

Ben Bella (bɛn ˈbɛlə) n **Mohammed Ahmed** ('aːmɪd). born 1916, Algerian statesman: first prime minister (1962–65) and president (1963–65) of independent Algeria: overthrown and imprisoned (1965–80)

Benbow ('bɛnbəʊ) n **John**. 1653–1702, English admiral, noted esp for his heroic death during the War of the Spanish Succession

bench (bɛntʃ) n 1 a long seat for more than one person, usually lacking a back or arms 2 a plain stout worktable 3 the bench (sometimes capital) a a judge or magistrate sitting in court in a judicial capacity b judges or magistrates collectively 4 a ledge in a mine or quarry from which work is carried out 5 (in a gymnasium) a low table, which may be inclined, used for various exercises 6 a platform on which dogs or other domestic animals are exhibited at shows 7 NZ a hollow on a hillside formed by sheep ▷ vb (tr) 8 to provide with benches 9 to exhibit (a dog, etc) at a show 10 US & Canadian sport to take or keep (a player) out of a game, often for disciplinary reasons [Old English benc; related to Old Norse bekkr, Old High German bank, Danish, Swedish bänk]

bencher ('bɛntʃə) n (often plural) Brit 1 a member of the governing body of one of the Inns of Court, usually a judge or a Queen's Counsel 2 See **backbencher**

benchmark ('bɛntʃ,mɑːk) n 1 a mark on a stone post or other permanent feature, at a point whose exact elevation and position is known: used as a reference point in surveying 2 a criterion by which to measure something; standard; reference point ▷ vb 3 to measure or test against a benchmark: the firm benchmarked its pay against that in industry

bench press n a weight-training exercise in which a

person lies on a bench and pushes a barbell upwards with both hands from chest level until the arms are straight, then lowers it again

bench test n the critical evaluation of a new or repaired component, device, apparatus, etc, prior to installation to ensure that it is in perfect condition

bench warrant n a warrant issued by a judge or court directing that an offender be apprehended

bend¹ (bɛnd) vb **bends, bending, bent** 1 to turn or cause to turn from a particular direction: the road bends left past the church 2 (intr; often foll by down, etc) to incline the body; stoop; bow 3 to submit or cause to submit: to bend before superior force 4 (tr) to turn or direct (one's eyes, steps, attention, etc) 5 (tr) nautical to attach or fasten, as a sail to a boom or a line to a cleat 6 **bend over backwards** informal to make a special effort, esp in order to please ▷ n 7 a curved part, as in a road or river 8 nautical a knot or eye in a line for joining it to another or to an object 9 the act or state of bending 10 **round the bend** Brit slang mad; crazy; eccentric [Old English bendan; related to Old Norse benda, Middle High German benden; see BIND, BAND³] > '**bendable** adj > '**bendy** adj

bend² (bɛnd) n heraldry an ordinary consisting of a diagonal line traversing a shield [Old English bend BAND²; see BEND¹]

Benda (French bɛ̃da) n **Julien** (ʒyljã). 1867–1956, French philosopher and novelist, who defended reason and intellect and attacked the influence of Bergson: author of La Trahison des clercs (1927)

bender ('bɛndə) n 1 informal a drinking bout 2 informal a makeshift shelter constructed by placing tarpaulin or plastic sheeting over bent saplings or woven branches

Bendigo ('bɛndɪ,gəʊ) n a city in SE Australia, in central Victoria: founded in 1851 after the discovery of gold. Pop: 68 715 (2001)

bends (bɛndz) the bends pl n (functioning as singular or plural) a nontechnical name for **decompression sickness**

bend sinister n heraldry a diagonal line bisecting a shield from the top right to the bottom left, typically indicating a bastard line

beneath (bɪ'niːθ) prep 1 below, esp if covered, protected, or obscured by 2 not as great or good as would be demanded by: beneath his dignity ▷ adv 3 below; underneath [Old English beneothan, from BE- + neothan low; see NETHER]

benedicite (,bɛnɪ'daɪsɪtɪ) n (esp in Christian religious orders) a blessing or grace [c13: from Latin, from benedīcere, from bene well + dīcere to speak]

Benedict ('bɛnɪ,dɪkt) n **Saint**. ?480–?547 AD, Italian monk: founded the Benedictine order at Monte Cassino in Italy in about 540 AD. His Regula Monachorum became the basis of the rule of all Western Christian monastic orders. Feast day: July 11 or March 14

Benedict XV n original name Giacomo della Chiesa. 1854–1922, pope (1914–22); noted for his repeated attempts to end World War I and for his organization of war relief

Benedictine n 1 (,bɛnɪ'dɪktɪn, -taɪn) a monk or nun who is a member of a Christian religious community founded by or following the rule of Saint Benedict (?480–?547 AD), the Italian monk 2 (,bɛnɪ'dɪktiːn) a greenish-yellow liqueur made from a secret formula developed at the Benedictine monastery at Fécamp in France in about 1510 ▷ adj 3 (,bɛnɪ'dɪktɪn, -taɪn) of or relating to Saint Benedict, his order, or his rule

benediction (,bɛnɪ'dɪkʃən) n 1 an invocation of divine blessing, esp at the end of a Christian religious ceremony 2 a Roman Catholic service in which the congregation is blessed with the sacrament 3 the state of being blessed [c15: from Latin benedictio, from benedīcere to bless; see BENEDICITE] > **bene'dictory** adj

Benedictus (,bɛnɪ'dɪktəs) n (sometimes not capital) Christianity 1 a short canticle beginning Benedictus qui venit in nomine Domini in Latin and Blessed is he that cometh in the name of the Lord in English 2 a canticle beginning Benedictus Dominus Deus Israel in Latin and Blessed be the Lord God of Israel in English

benefaction (,bɛnɪ'fækʃən) n 1 the act of doing good, esp by giving a donation to charity 2 the donation or help given [c17: from Late Latin benefactiō, from Latin bene well

+ *facere* to do]

benefactor ('bɛnɪˌfæktə, ˌbɛnɪ'fæk-) *n* a person who supports or helps a person, institution, etc, esp by giving money; patron ▷ 'bene,factress *fem n*

benefice ('bɛnɪfɪs) *n* **1** *Christianity* an endowed Church office yielding an income to its holder; a Church living **2** the property or revenue attached to such an office ▷ *vb* **3** (*tr*) to provide with a benefice [C14: from Old French, from Latin *beneficium* benefit, from *beneficus*, from *bene* well + *facere* to do]

beneficent (bɪ'nɛfɪsᵊnt) *adj* charitable; generous [C17: from Latin *beneficent-*, from *beneficus*; see BENEFICE] ▷ be'neficence *n*

beneficial (ˌbɛnɪ'fɪʃəl) *adj* **1** (sometimes foll by *to*) causing a good result; advantageous **2** *law* entitling a person to receive the profits or proceeds of property [C15: from Late Latin *beneficiālis*, from Latin *beneficium* kindness]

beneficiary (ˌbɛnɪ'fɪʃərɪ) *n, pl* -ciaries **1** a person who gains or benefits in some way from something **2** *law* a person entitled to receive funds or other property under a trust, will, or insurance policy **3** the holder of an ecclesiastical or other benefice **4** *NZ* a person who receives government assistance: *social security beneficiary* ▷ *adj* **5** of or relating to a benefice or the holder of a benefice

benefit ('bɛnɪfɪt) *n* **1** something that improves or promotes **2** advantage or sake **3** (*sometimes plural*) a payment or series of payments made by an institution, such as an insurance company or trade union, to a person who is ill, unemployed, etc **4** a theatrical performance, sports event, etc, to raise money for a charity ▷ *vb* -fits, -fiting, -fited *or esp US* -fits, -fitting, -fitted **5** to do or receive good; profit [C14: from Anglo-French *benfet*, from Latin *benefactum*, from *bene facere* to do well]

benefit in kind *n* a nonpecuniary benefit, such as a company car or medical insurance, given to an employee

benefit of clergy *n* *Christianity* **1** sanction by the church: *marriage without benefit of clergy* **2** (in the Middle Ages) a privilege that placed the clergy outside the jurisdiction of secular courts and entitled them to trial in ecclesiastical courts

benefit society *n* a US term for **friendly society**

Benelux ('bɛnɪˌlʌks) *n* **1** the customs union formed by Belgium, the Netherlands, and Luxembourg in 1948; became an economic union in 1960 **2** these countries collectively

Beneš (*Czech* 'bɛnɛʃ) *n* **Eduard** ('ɛ:duart). 1884–1948, Czech statesman; president of Czechoslovakia (1935–38; 1946–48) and of its government in exile (1939–45)

Benét (bə'neɪ) *n* **Stephen Vincent**. 1898–1943, US poet and novelist, best known for his poem on the American Civil War *John Brown's Body* (1928)

Benevento (ˌbɛnə'vɛntəʊ) *n* a city in S Italy, in N Campania: at various times under Samnite, Roman, Lombard, Saracen, Norman, and papal rule. Pop: 61 791 (2001)

benevolence (bɪ'nɛvələns) *n* **1** inclination or tendency to help or do good to others; charity **2** an act of kindness

benevolent (bɪ'nɛvələnt) *adj* **1** intending or showing goodwill; kindly; friendly **2** doing good or giving aid to others, rather than making profit; charitable: *a benevolent organization* [C15: from Latin *benevolēns*, from *bene* well + *velle* to wish]

Benfleet ('bɛnˌfliːt) *n* a town in SE England, in S Essex on an inlet of the Thames estuary. Pop: 48 539 (2001)

BEng *abbreviation* Bachelor of Engineering

Bengal (bɛn'gɔːl, bɛŋ-) *n* **1** a former province of NE India, in the great deltas of the Ganges and Brahmaputra Rivers: in 1947 divided into West Bengal (belonging to India) and East Bengal (Bangladesh) **2 Bay of Bengal** a wide arm of the Indian Ocean, between India and Myanmar **3** a breed of medium-large cat with a spotted or marbled coat

Bengali (bɛn'gɔːlɪ, bɛŋ-) *n* **1** a member of a people living chiefly in Bangladesh and in West Bengal. The West Bengalis are mainly Hindus; the East Bengalis of Bangladesh are mainly Muslims **2** Also called: **Bangla** the language of this people: the official language of Bangladesh and the chief language of West Bengal; it belongs to the Indic branch of the Indo-European family ▷ *adj* **3** of or relating to Bengal, the Bengalis, or their language

Bengal light *n* a firework or flare that burns with a steady bright blue light, formerly used as a signal

Bengaluru (ˌbɛŋgəl'uːru) *n* the alternative official name for **Bangalore**

Bengbu ('bɛŋ'buː), **Pengpu** *or* **Pang-fou** *n* a city in E China, in Anhui province. Pop: 779 000 (2005 est)

Benghazi *or* **Bengasi** (bɛn'gɑːzɪ) *n* a port in N Libya, on the Gulf of Sidra: centre of Italian colonization (1911–42); scene of much fighting in World War II. Pop: 1 080 500 (2002 est). Ancient names: **Hesperides**

Benguela (bɛŋ'gwɛlə) *n* a port in W Angola: founded in 1617; a terminus (with Lobito) of the railway that runs from Beira in Mozambique through the Copper Belt of Zambia and Zimbabwe. Pop: about 200 000 (1990 est)

Ben-Gurion (bɛn'gʊərɪən) *n* **David**, original name *David Gruen*. 1886–1973, Israeli socialist statesman, born in Poland; first prime minister of Israel (1948–53, 1955–63)

Beni (*Spanish* 'beni) *n* a river in N Bolivia, rising in the E Cordillera of the Andes and flowing north to the Marmoré River. Length: over 1600 km (1000 miles)

Benidorm ('bɛnɪdɔːm) *n* a a coastal resort town in W Spain, on the Costa Blanca

benighted (bɪ'naɪtɪd) *adj* **1** lacking cultural, moral, or intellectual enlightenment; ignorant **2** *archaic* overtaken by night ▷ be'nightedness *n*

benign (bɪ'naɪn) *adj* **1** showing kindliness; genial **2** (of soil, climate, etc) mild; gentle **3** favourable; propitious **4** *pathol* (of a tumour, etc) not threatening to life or health; not malignant [C14: from Old French *benigne*, from Latin *benignus*, from *bene* well + *gignere* to produce] ▷ be'nignly *adv*

benignant (bɪ'nɪgnənt) *adj* **1** kind; gracious, as a king to his subjects **2** a less common word for **benign** (senses 3, 4) ▷ be'nignancy *n*

benignity (bɪ'nɪgnɪtɪ) *n, pl* -ties **1** the quality of being benign; favourable attitude **2** a kind or gracious act

Beni Hasan ('bɛnɪ hæ'sɑːn) *n* a village in central Egypt, on the Nile, with cliff-cut tombs dating from 2000 BC

Benin (bɛ'niːn) *n* **1** a republic in W Africa, on the **Bight of Benin**, a section of the Gulf of Guinea: in the early 19th century a powerful kingdom, famed for its women warriors; became a French colony in 1893, gaining independence in 1960. It consists chiefly of coastal lagoons and swamps in the south, a fertile plain and marshes in the centre, and the Atakora Mountains in the northwest. Official language: French. Religion: animist majority. Currency: franc. Capital: Porto Novo (the government is based in Cotonou). Pop: 6 918 000 (2004 est). Area: 112 622 sq km (43 474 sq miles). Former name (until 1975): **Dahomey 2** a former kingdom of W Africa, powerful from the 14th to the 17th centuries: now a province of S Nigeria: noted for its bronzes

Benin City *n* a city in S Nigeria, capital of Edo state: former capital of the kingdom of Benin. Pop: 1 022 000 (2005 est)

benison (bɛnɪzᵊn, -sᵊn) *n* *archaic* a blessing, esp a spoken one [C13: from Old French *beneison*, from Latin *benedictiō* BENEDICTION]

Benjamin¹ ('bɛndʒəmɪn) *n* **1** *Old Testament* **a** the youngest and best-loved son of Jacob and Rachel (Genesis 35:16–18; 42:4) **b** the tribe descended from this patriarch **2** *archaic* a youngest and favourite son

Benjamin² ('bɛndʒəmɪn) *n* **1 Arthur**. 1893–1960, Australian composer. In addition to *Jamaican Rumba* (1938), he wrote five operas and a harmonica concerto (1953) **2** (*German* 'bɛnɪamin) **Walter** ('valtər). 1892–1940, German critic and cultural theorist

Ben Lomond (bɛn 'ləʊmənd) *n* **1** a mountain in W central Scotland, on the E side of Loch Lomond. Height: 973 m (3192 ft) **2** a mountain in NE Tasmania. Height: 1527 m (5010 ft) **3** a mountain in SE Australia, in NE New South Wales. Height: 1520 m (4986 ft)

Benn (bɛn) *n* **Antony (Neil) Wedgwood**, known as *Tony Benn*. born 1925, British Labour politician, a leading figure on the party's left wing. He renounced (1963) the title of Viscount Stansgate

Bennett ('bɛnɪt) n 1 **Alan**. born 1934, British actor and playwright. His plays include *Forty Years On* (1968), *The Old Country* (1977), *The Madness of George III* (1991), *The History Boys* (2004), and the monologues for television *Talking Heads* (1987, 1998) 2 (**Enoch**) **Arnold**. 1867–1931, British novelist, noted for *The Old Wives' Tale* (1908), *Clayhanger* (1910), and other works set in the Staffordshire Potteries 3 **James Gordon**. 1837–1931, US newspaper editor, born in Scotland. He founded (1835) the *New York Herald* and introduced techniques of modern news reporting 4 **Jill**. 1931–90, British actress 5 **Richard Bedford**, 1st Viscount. 1870–1947, Canadian Conservative statesman; prime minister (1930–35) 6 Sir **Richard Rodney**. born 1936, British composer, noted for film music and his operas *The Mines of Sulphur* (1965) and *Victory* (1970)

Ben Nevis (bɛn 'nɛvɪs) n a mountain in W Scotland, in the Grampian mountains: highest peak in Great Britain. Height: 1344 m (4408 ft)

Bennington ('bɛnɪŋtən) n a town in SW Vermont: the site of a British defeat (1777) in the War of American Independence. Pop: 15 637 (2003 est)

Benny ('bɛnɪ) n **Jack**, real name *Benjamin Kubelsky*. 1894–1974, US comedian

Benoît de Sainte-Maure (*French* bənwa də sɛ̃t mɔr) n 12th-century French trouvère: author of the *Roman de Troie*, which contains the episode of Troilus and Cressida

Benoni (bɪ'nəʊnɪ) n a city in NE South Africa: gold mines. Pop: 94 341 (2001)

Benson ('bɛnsən) n **E(dward) F(rederic)**. 1867–1940, British writer, noted esp for a series of comic novels featuring the characters Mapp and Lucia

bent[1] (bɛnt) adj 1 not straight; curved 2 (foll by *on*) fixed (on a course of action); resolved (to); determined (to) 3 *slang* a dishonest; corrupt b (of goods) stolen c crazy; mad ▷ n 4 personal inclination, propensity, or aptitude 5 capacity of endurance (esp in the phrase **to the top of one's bent**)

bent[2] (bɛnt) n 1 short for **bent grass** 2 a stalk of bent grass 3 *archaic* any stiff grass or sedge 4 *Scot & Northern English dialect* heath or moorland [Old English *bionot*; related to Old Saxon *binet*, Old High German *binuz* rush]

bent grass n any perennial grass of the genus *Agrostis*, esp *A. tenuis*, which has a spreading panicle of tiny flowers. Some species are planted for hay or in lawns

Bentham ('bɛnθəm) n **Jeremy**. 1748–1832, British philosopher and jurist: a founder of utilitarianism. His works include *A Fragment on Government* (1776) and *Introduction to the Principles of Morals and Legislation* (1789)

Benthamism ('bɛnθə,mɪzəm) n the philosophy of utilitarianism as first expounded by the British philosopher and jurist Jeremy Bentham (1748–1832) in terms of an action being good that has a greater tendency to augment the happiness of the community than to diminish it > 'Bentha,mite n, adj

benthos ('bɛnθɒs) or **benthon** n the animals and plants living at the bottom of a sea or lake [C19: from Greek: depth; related to *bathus* deep] > 'benthic, 'benthal or ben'thonic adj

Bentinck ('bɛntɪŋk) n Lord **William Cavendish**. 1774–1839, British statesman, governor general of Bengal (1828–35)

Bentley ('bɛntlɪ) n **Edmund Clerihew**. 1875–1956, English journalist, noted for his invention of the clerihew

bento or **bento box** ('bɛntəʊ) n, pl **-tos** a thin box, made of plastic or lacquered wood, divided into compartments which contain small separate dishes comprising a Japanese meal, esp lunch [Japanese *bentō* box lunch]

Benton ('bɛntən) n **Thomas Hart**. 1889–1975, US painter of rural life; a leader of the American Regionalist painters in the 1930s

bentonite ('bɛntə,naɪt) n a valuable clay, formed by the decomposition of volcanic ash, that swells as it absorbs water: used as a filler in the building, paper, and pharmaceutical industries [C19: from Fort *Benton*, Montana, USA, where found, + -ITE[1]]

bentwood ('bɛnt,wʊd) n a wood bent in moulds after being heated by steaming, used mainly for furniture b (*as modifier*): a *bentwood chair*

Benue ('bɛnʊ,eɪ) n a state of SE Nigeria. Capital: Makurdi. Pop: 4 219 244 (2006). Area: 34 059 sq km (13 150 sq miles)

benumb (bɪ'nʌm) vb (tr) 1 to make numb or powerless; deaden physical feeling in, as by cold 2 (*usually passive*) to make inactive; stupefy (the mind, senses, will, etc)

Benxi ('bɛn'ʃi:), **Penchi** or **Penki** n an industrial city in SE China, in S Liaoning province. Pop: 967 000 (2005 est)

Benz (bɛnz; *German* bɛnts) n **Karl** (**Friedrich**) (karl). 1844–1929, German engineer; designed and built the first car to be driven by an internal-combustion engine (1885)

Benzedrine ('bɛnzɪ,dri:n, -drɪn) n a trademark for amphetamine

benzene ('bɛnzi:n, bɛn'zi:n) n a colourless flammable toxic aromatic liquid used in the manufacture of styrene, phenol, etc, as a solvent for fats, resins, etc, and as an insecticide. Formula: C_6H_6

benzene ring n the hexagonal ring of bonded carbon atoms in the benzene molecule or its derivatives. Also called: benzene nucleus

benzine ('bɛnzi:n, bɛn'zi:n) or **benzin** ('bɛnzɪn) n a volatile mixture of the lighter aliphatic hydrocarbon constituents of petroleum

benzo- or *sometimes before a vowel* **benz-** *combining form* 1 indicating a benzene ring fused to another ring in a polycyclic compound 2 indicating derivation from benzene or benzoic acid or the presence of phenyl groups [from BENZOIN]

benzoate ('bɛnzəʊ,eɪt, -ɪt) n any salt or ester of benzoic acid, containing the group C_6H_5COO– or the ion C_6H_5COO–

benzocaine ('bɛnzəʊ,keɪn) n a white crystalline ester used as a local anaesthetic; ethyl *para*-aminobenzoate. Formula: $C_9H_{11}NO_2$

benzodiazepine (,bɛnzəʊdaɪ'eɪzə,pi:n) n any of a group of chemical compounds that are used as minor tranquillizers, such as diazepam (Valium) and chlordiazepoxide (Librium) [C20: from BENZO- + DI-[1] + AZA- + EP- + -INE[2]]

benzoic (bɛn'zəʊɪk) adj of, containing, or derived from benzoic acid or benzoin

benzoic acid n a white crystalline solid occurring in many natural resins, used in the manufacture of benzoates, plasticizers, and dyes and as a food preservative (E210). Formula: C_6H_5COOH

benzoin ('bɛnzəʊɪn, -zəʊɪn, bɛn'zəʊɪn) n 1 Also called: benjamin a gum resin containing benzoic acid, obtained from various trees of the genus *Styrax*, esp *S. benzoin* of Java and Sumatra, and used in ointments, perfume, etc [C16: from French *benjoin*, from Old Catalan *benjui*, from Arabic *lubān jāwī*, literally: frankincense of Java]

benzol or **benzole** ('bɛnzɒl) n 1 a crude form of benzene, containing toluene, xylene, and other hydrocarbons, obtained from coal tar or coal gas and used as a fuel 2 an obsolete name for **benzene**

Ben-Zvi (bɛn'zvi:; *Hebrew* bɛn'tsvi:) n **Itzhak** ('jɪtsxak). 1884–1963, Israeli statesman; president (1952–63)

Beograd (be'ɔgrad) n the Serbian name for **Belgrade**

Beothuk (bɪ'θʊk) n a member of an extinct Native Canadian people formerly living in Newfoundland

bequeath (bɪ'kwi:ð, -'kwi:θ) vb (tr) 1 *law* to dispose of (property, esp personal property) by will 2 to hand down; pass on, as to following generations [Old English *becwethan*; related to Old Norse *kvetha* to speak, Gothic *qithan*, Old High German *quethan*] > be'queathal n

bequest (bɪ'kwɛst) n a the act of bequeathing b something that is bequeathed [C14: BE- + Old English *-cwiss* degree; see BEQUEATH]

Béranger (*French* berɑ̃ʒe) n **Pierre Jean de** (pjɛr ʒɑ̃ də). 1780–1857, French lyric and satirical poet

Berar (bɛ'rɑː) n a region of W central India: part of Maharashtra state since 1956; important for cotton growing

berate (bɪ'reɪt) vb (tr) to scold harshly

Berber ('bɜːbə) n 1 a member of a Caucasoid Muslim people of N Africa 2 the language of this people, forming a subfamily of the Afro-Asiatic family of languages. There are extensive differences between

b

dialects ▷ *adj* **3** of or relating to this people or their language

Berbera ('bɜːbərə) *n* a port in N Somalia, (in the separatist area called Somaliland), on the Gulf of Aden. Pop: about 200 000 (2000 est)

berberis ('bɜːbərɪs) *n* any shrub of the berberidaceous genus *Berberis*. See **barberry** [c19: from Medieval Latin, of unknown origin]

berceuse (*French* bɛrsøz) *n* **1** a cradlesong or lullaby **2** an instrumental piece suggestive of this, in six-eight time [c19: from French: lullaby, from *bercer* to rock]

Berchtesgaden (*German* 'bɛrçtəsgaːdən) *n* a town in Germany, in SE Bavaria: site of the fortified mountain retreat of Adolf Hitler. Pop: 7667 (2003 est)

Berdyayev (*Russian* bɪr'djajɪf) *n* **Nikolai Aleksandrovich** (nikaˈlaj alɪkˈsandrəvɪtʃ). 1874– 1948, Russian philosopher. Although he was a Marxist, his Christian views led him to criticize Soviet communism and he was forced into exile (1922)

bereave (bɪ'riːv) *vb* (*tr*) (usually foll by *of*) to deprive (of) something or someone valued, esp through death [Old English *bereafian*; see REAVE[1]]

bereaved (bɪ'riːvd) *adj* having been deprived of something or someone valued, esp through death

bereavement (bɪ'riːvmənt) *n* **1** the condition of having been deprived of something or someone valued, esp through death **2** a death

bereft (bɪ'rɛft) *adj* (usually foll by *of*) deprived; parted (from): *bereft of hope*

Berenson ('bɛrənsən) *n* **Bernard** 1865–1959, US art historian, born in Lithuania: an authority on art of the Italian Renaissance

Beresford ('bɛrɪsˌfəd) *n* **Bruce**. born 1940, Australian film director. His films include *The Adventures of Barry McKenzie* (1972), *Breaker Morant* (1980), *Driving Miss Daisy* (1989) and *Evelyn* (2002)

beret ('bɛreɪ) *n* a round close-fitting brimless cap of soft wool material or felt [c19: from French *béret*, from Old Provençal *berret*, from Medieval Latin *birrettum* cap; see BIRETTA]

Berezina (*Russian* bɪrɪzi'na) *n* a river in Belarus, rising in the north and flowing south to the River Dnieper: linked with the River Dvina and the Baltic Sea by the **Berezina Canal**. Length: 563 km (350 miles)

Berezniki (*Russian* bɪrɪzni'ki) *n* a city in E Russia: chemical industries. Pop: 169 000 (2005 est)

berg[1] (bɜːg) *n* short for **iceberg**

berg[2] (bɜːg) *n* a South African word for **mountain**

Berg (bɜːg; *German* bɛrk) *n* **1** **Alban** (**Maria Johannes**) ('albaːn). 1885–1935, Austrian composer: a pupil of Schoenberg. His works include the operas *Wozzeck* (1921) and *Lulu* (1935), a violin concerto (1935), chamber works, and songs **2** **Paul**. born 1926, US molecular biologist, the first to identify transfer RNA (1956). Nobel prize for chemistry 1980

Bergamo (*Italian* 'bɛrgamo) *n* a walled city in N Italy, in Lombardy. Pop: 113 143 (2001)

bergamot ('bɜːgəˌmɒt) *n* **1** Also called: **bergamot orange** a small Asian spiny rutaceous tree, *Citrus bergamia*, having sour pear-shaped fruit **2** essence of bergamot a fragrant essential oil from the fruit rind of this plant, used in perfumery and some teas (including Earl Grey) **3** a Mediterranean mint, *Mentha citrata*, that yields an oil similar to essence of bergamot [c17: from French *bergamote*, from Italian *bergamotta*, of Turkic origin; related to Turkish *bey-armudu* prince's pear; see BEY]

Bergen *n* **1** (*Norwegian* 'bærgən) a port in SW Norway: chief city in medieval times. Pop: 237 430 (2004 est) **2** ('bɛrxən) the Flemish name for **Mons**

Bergerac (*French* bɛrʒarak) *n* See **Cyrano de Bergerac**

Bergie ('bɜːgɪ) *n* *South African slang* a vagabond, esp one living on the slopes of Table Mountain in the Western Cape province of South Africa [from Afrikaans *berg* mountain]

Bergius (*German* 'bɛrgjʊs) *n* **Friedrich** (**Karl Rudolph**) ('friːdrɪç). 1884– 1949, German chemist, who invented a process for producing oil by high-pressure hydrogenation of coal: Nobel prize for chemistry 1931

Bergman ('bɜːgmən) *n* **1** (**Ernst**) **Ingmar** ('ɪŋmar).

1918–2007, Swedish film and stage director, whose films include *The Seventh Seal* (1956), *Wild Strawberries* (1957), *Persona* (1966), *Scenes from a Marriage* (1974), *Autumn Sonata* (1978), and *Fanny and Alexander* (1982) **2** **Ingrid**. 1915–82, Swedish film and stage actress, working in Hollywood 1938–48; noted for her leading roles in many films, including *Casablanca* (1942), *For Whom the Bell Tolls* (1943), *Anastasia* (1956), and *The Inn of the Sixth Happiness* (1958)

bergschrund ('bɛrkʃrʊnt, 'bɜːgʃruːnt) *n* a crevasse at the head of a glacier [c19: German: mountain crack]

Bergson ('bɜːgsən; *French* bɛrksɔn) *n* **Henri Louis** (ɑ̃ri lwi). 1859–1941, French philosopher, who sought to bridge the gap between metaphysics and science. His main works are *Memory and Matter* (1896, trans. 1911) and *Creative Evolution* (1907, trans. 1911): Nobel prize for literature 1927 ▷ **Bergsonian** (bɜːgˈsəʊnɪən) *adj, n*

Bergström (*Swedish* 'bærjstrøm) *n* **Sune** ('sʊnə). 1916–2004, Swedish biochemist; shared the Nobel prize for medicine and physiology (1982) for work on prostaglandin

berg wind *n* a hot dry wind in South Africa blowing from the plateau down to the coast

Beria ('bɛrɪə; *Russian* 'bjerijə) *n* **Lavrenti Pavlovich** (laˈvrjentij 'pavləvɪtʃ). 1899–1953, Soviet chief of secret police; killed by his associates shortly after Stalin's death

beriberi (ˌbɛrɪ'bɛrɪ) *n* a disease, endemic in E and S Asia, caused by dietary deficiency of thiamine (vitamin B_1). It affects the nerves to the limbs, producing pain, paralysis, and swelling [c19: from Sinhalese, by reduplication from *beri* weakness]

Bering *or* **Behring** ('bɛrɪŋ, 'bɛər–; *Danish* 'beːreŋ) *n* **Vitus** ('viːtʊs). 1681–1741, Danish navigator, who explored the N Pacific for the Russians and discovered Bering Island and the Bering Strait

Bering Sea *n* a part of the N Pacific Ocean, between NE Siberia and Alaska. Area: about 2 275 000 sq km (878 000 sq miles)

Bering Strait *n* a strait between Alaska and Russia, connecting the Bering Sea and the Arctic Ocean

Berio (*Italian* 'bɛrjo) *n* **Luciano** (luˈtʃano). 1925–2003, Italian composer, living in the US, noted esp for works that exploit instrumental and vocal timbre and technique

Beriosova (bɛrɪ'əʊsəvə) *n* **Svetlana** (svɪt'lanə). 1932–98, British ballet dancer, born in Lithuania

berk *or* **burk** (bɜːk) *n* *Brit slang* a stupid person; fool [c20: shortened from *Berkeley* or *Berkshire Hunt* rhyming slang for *cunt*]

Berkeley[1] ('bɜːklɪ) *n* a city in W California, on San Francisco Bay: seat of the University of California. Pop: 102 049 (2003 est)

Berkeley[2] *n* **1** ('bɜːklɪ) **Busby**. real name *William Berkeley Enos*. 1895–1976, US dance director, noted esp for his elaborate choreography in film musicals **2** ('bɑːklɪ) **George**. 1685–1753, Irish philosopher and Anglican bishop, whose system of subjective idealism was expounded in his works *A Treatise concerning the Principles of Human Knowledge* (1710) and *Three Dialogues between Hylas and Philonous* (1713). He also wrote *Essay towards a New Theory of Vision* (1709) **3** ('bɑːklɪ) **Sir Lennox** (**Randal Francis**). 1903–89, British composer; his works include four symphonies, four operas, and the *Serenade for Strings* (1939)

berkelium (bɜː'kiːlɪəm, 'bɜːklɪəm) *n* a metallic transuranic element produced by bombardment of americium. Symbol: Bk; atomic no: 97; half-life of most stable isotope, ^{247}Bk: 1400 years; valency: 3 or 4; relative density: 14 (est) [c20: named after BERKELEY, where it was discovered]

berko ('bɜːkəʊ) *adj* *Austral slang* berserk

Berks (bɑːks) *abbreviation* Berkshire

Berkshire ('bɑːkʃɪə, -ʃə) *n* **1** a historic county of S England: since reorganization in 1974 the River Thames has marked the N boundary while the **Berkshire Downs** occupy central parts; the county council was replaced by six unitary authorities in 1998. Area: 1259 sq km (486 sq miles). Abbreviation: **Berks 2** a rare breed of pork and bacon pig having a black body and white points

berley or **burley** ('bɜːlɪ) *Austral* ▷ *n* **1** bait scattered on water to attract fish **2** *slang* rubbish; nonsense ▷ *vb* (*tr*) **3** to scatter (bait) on water **4** to hurry (someone); urge on [origin unknown]

Berlichingen (*German* 'bɛrlɪçɪŋən) *n* **Götz von** (gœts fɔn), called *the Iron Hand*. 1480–1562, German warrior knight, who robbed merchants and kidnapped nobles for ransom

berlin (bəˈlɪn, 'bɜːlɪn) *n* **1** Also called: **berlin wool** (*sometimes capital*) a fine wool yarn used for tapestry work, etc **2** a four-wheeled two-seated covered carriage, popular in the 18th century [c18: named after BERLIN]

Berlin[1] (bɜːˈlɪn; *German* bɛrˈliːn) *n* the capital of Germany (1871–1945 and from 1990), formerly divided (1945–90) into the eastern sector, capital of East Germany, and the western sectors, which formed an exclave in East German territory closely affiliated with West Germany: a wall dividing the sectors was built in 1961 by the East German authorities to stop the flow of refugees from east to west; demolition of the wall began in 1989 and the city was formally reunited in 1990: formerly (1618–1871) the capital of Brandenburg and Prussia. Pop: 3 388 477 (2003 est)

Berlin[2] (bɜːˈlɪn) *n* **1 Irving**. original name *Israel Baline*, 1888–1989, US composer and writer of lyrics, born in Russia. His musical comedies include *Annie Get Your Gun* (1946); his most popular song is *White Christmas* **2** Sir **Isaiah**. 1909–97, British philosopher, born in Latvia, historian, and diplomat. His books include *Historical Inevitability* (1954) and *The Magus of the North* (1993)

Berliner (bɜːˈlɪnə) *n* **1** a native or inhabitant of Berlin **2** a newspaper having a format between that of a broadsheet and a tabloid, approximately 18.5 inches by 12.4 inches (47 x 31.5 centimetres) [c20: (for sense 2) this format was first adopted by Berlin newspapers]

Berlioz ('bɛəlɪˌəʊz; *French* bɛrljoz) *n* **Hector** (**Louis**) (ɛktɔr). 1803–69, French composer, regarded as a pioneer of modern orchestration. His works include the cantata *La Damnation de Faust* (1846), the operas *Les Troyens* (1856–59) and *Béatrice et Bénédict* (1860–62), the *Symphonie fantastique* (1830), and the oratorio *L'Enfance du Christ* (1854)

Berlusconi (*Italian* ˌbɛrlusˈkɔnɪ) *n* **Silvio** ('silvjo). born 1936, Italian politician and media tycoon: prime minister of Italy (1994, 2001–06)

berm or **berme** (bɜːm) *n* **1** a narrow path or ledge at the edge of a slope, road, or canal **2** NZ the grass verge of a suburban street, usually kept mown **3** *military* a man-made ridge of sand, designed as an obstacle to tanks, which, in crossing it, have to expose their vulnerable underparts [c18: from French *berme*, from Dutch *berm*, probably from Old Norse *barmr* BRIM]

Bermejo (*Spanish* berˈmexo) *n* a river in Argentina, rising in the northwest and flowing southeast to the Paraguay River. Length: about 1600 km (1000 miles)

Bermuda (bəˈmjuːdə) *n* a UK Overseas Territory consisting of a group of over 150 coral islands (**the Bermudas**) in the NW Atlantic: discovered in about 1503, colonized by the British by 1612, although not acquired by the British crown until 1684. Capital: Hamilton. Pop: 82 000 (2003 est). Area: 53 sq km (20 sq miles) ▷ Berˈmudian *n, adj*

Bermuda shorts *pl n* close-fitting shorts that come down to the knees. Also called: **Bermudas**

Bermuda Triangle *n* an area in the Atlantic Ocean bounded by Bermuda, Puerto Rico, and Florida where ships and aeroplanes are alleged to have disappeared mysteriously

Bern (bɜːn; *German* bɛrn) *n* **1** the capital of Switzerland, in the W part, on the Aar River: entered the Swiss confederation in 1353 and became the capital in 1848. Pop: 122 700 (2002 est) **2** a canton of Switzerland, between the French frontier and the Bernese Alps. Capital: Bern. Pop: 950 200 (2002 est). Area: 6884 sq km (2658 sq miles)

Bernadette of Lourdes (ˌbɜːnəˈdɛt) *n* **Saint**. original name *Marie Bernarde Soubirous*. 1844–79, French peasant girl born in Lourdes, whose visions of the Virgin Mary led to the establishment of Lourdes as a centre of pilgrimage, esp for the sick or crippled. Feast day: Feb 18

Bernadotte *n* **1** (*Swedish* 'bɛrnədɔt) **Folke** ('fɔlke), Count. 1895–1948, Swedish diplomat, noted for his work with the Red Cross during World War II and as United Nations mediator in Palestine (1948). He was assassinated by Jewish terrorists **2** ('bɜːnəˌdɒt; *French* bɛrnadɔt) **Jean Baptiste Jules** (ʒɑ̃ batist ʒyl). 1764–1844, French marshal under Napoleon; king of Norway and Sweden (1818–44) as Charles XIV

Bernanos (*French* bɛrnanos) *n* **Georges** (ʒɔrʒ). 1888–1948, French novelist and Roman Catholic pamphleteer, best known for *The Diary of a Country Priest* (1936)

Bernard *n* **1** (*French* bɛrnar) **Claude** (klod). 1813–78, French physiologist, noted for his research on the action of secretions of the alimentary canal and the glycogenic function of the liver **2** ('bɜːnəd) **Saint**, known as *Bernard of Menthon* and the *Apostle of the Alps*. 923–1008, French monk who founded hospices in the Alpine passes. Feast day: Aug 20

Bernard of Clairvaux *n* **Saint**. ?1090–1153, French abbot and theologian, who founded the stricter branch of the Cistercians in 1115

Berners-Lee ('bɜːnəz 'liː) *n* Sir **Tim**. born 1955, British computer scientist who created the World Wide Web

Bernese Alps or **Bernese Oberland** ('bɜːniːz) *n* a mountain range in SW Switzerland, the N central part of the Alps. Highest peak: Finsteraarhorn, 4274 m (14 022 ft)

Bernhardt ('bɜːnhɑːt; *French* bɛrnar) *n* **Sarah**. original name *Rosine Bernard*. 1844–1923, French actress, regarded as one of the greatest tragic actresses of all time

Bernina (bəˈniːnə; *Italian* berˈnina) *n* **Piz Bernina** a mountain in SE Switzerland, the highest peak of the **Bernina Alps** in the S Rhaetian Alps. Height: 4049 m (13 284 ft)

Bernina Pass *n* a pass in the Alps between SE Switzerland and N Italy, east of Piz Bernina. Height: 2323 m (7622 ft)

Bernini (*Italian* berˈnini) *n* **Gian Lorenzo** (dʒan loˈrɛntso). 1598–1680, Italian painter, architect, and sculptor: the greatest exponent of the Italian baroque

Bernoulli or **Bernouilli** (*French* bɛrnuji; *German* bɛrˈnʊli) *n* **1 Daniel** (danjɛl), son of Jean Bernoulli. 1700–82, Swiss mathematician and physicist, who developed an early form of the kinetic theory of gases and stated the principle of conservation of energy in fluid dynamics **2 Jacques** (ʒak) or **Jakob** ('jaːkɔp). 1654–1705, Swiss mathematician, noted for his work on calculus and the theory of probability **3** his brother, **Jean** (ʒɑ̃) or **Johann** (joˈhan). 1667–1748, Swiss mathematician who developed the calculus of variations

Bernstein ('bɜːnstaɪn, -stiːn) *n* **Leonard**. 1918–90, US conductor and composer, whose works include *The Age of Anxiety* (1949), the score of the musical *West Side Story* (1957), and *Mass* (1971)

berretta (bɪˈrɛtə) *n* a variant spelling of **biretta**

berry ('bɛrɪ) *n, pl* **-ries 1** any of various small edible fruits such as the blackberry and strawberry **2** *botany* an indehiscent fruit with two or more seeds and a fleshy pericarp, such as the grape or gooseberry **3** any of various seeds or dried kernels, such as a coffee bean **4** the egg of a lobster, crayfish, or similar animal ▷ *vb* **-ries, -rying, -ried** (*intr*) **5** to bear or produce berries **6** to gather or look for berries [Old English *berie*; related to Old High German *beri*, Dutch *bezie*]

Berry *n* **1** ('bɛrɪ) **Chuck**, full name *Charles Edward Berry*. born 1926, US rock-and-roll guitarist, singer, and songwriter. His frequently covered songs include "Maybellene" (1955), "Roll Over Beethoven" (1956), "Johnny B. Goode" (1958), "Memphis, Tennessee" (1959), and "Promised Land" (1964) **2** (*French* bɛri) **Jean de France** (ʒɑ̃ də frɑ̃s), Duc de. 1340–1416, French prince, son of King John II; coregent (1380–88) for Charles VI and a famous patron of the arts

Berryman ('bɛrɪmən) *n* **John**. 1914–72, US poet and critic, author of *Homage to Mistress Bradstreet* (1956) and *Dream Songs* (1964–68)

berserk (bəˈzɜːk, -ˈsɜːk) *adj* **1** frenziedly violent or destructive (esp in the phrase **go berserk**) ▷ *n* **2** Also called: **berserker** a member of a class of ancient Norse

b

warriors who worked themselves into a frenzy before battle and fought with insane fury and courage [c19: Icelandic *berserkr*, from *björn* bear + *serkr* shirt]

berth (bɜːθ) *n* **1** a bed or bunk in a vessel or train, usually narrow and fixed to a wall **2** *nautical* a place assigned to a ship at a mooring **3** *nautical* sufficient distance from the shore or from other ships or objects for a ship to manoeuvre **4** **give a wide berth to** to keep clear of; avoid **5** *informal* a job, esp as a member of a ship's crew ▷ *vb* **6** (*tr*) *nautical* to assign a berth to (a vessel) **7** *nautical* to dock (a vessel) **8** (*tr*) to provide with a sleeping place, as on a vessel or train **9** (*intr*) *nautical* to pick up a mooring in an anchorage [c17: probably from BEAR[1] + -TH[1]]

bertha (ˈbɜːθə) *n* a wide deep capelike collar, often of lace, usually to cover up a low neckline [c19: from French *berthe*, from *Berthe*, 8th-century Frankish queen, mother of Charlemagne]

Bertolucci (*Italian* bertoˈluttʃi) *n* **Bernardo** (berˈnardo). born 1940, Italian film director: his films include *The Spider's Stratagem* (1970), *The Conformist* (1970), *1900* (1976), *The Last Emperor* (1987), *The Sheltering Sky* (1990), and *The Dreamers* (2003)

Berwick (ˈbɛrɪk) *n* **James Fitzjames, Duke of Berwick.** 1670–1734, marshal of France and illegitimate son of James II of England. He led French forces during the War of the Spanish Succession (1701–14)

Berwickshire (ˈbɛrɪkʃɪə, -ʃə) *n* (until 1975) a county of SE Scotland: part of the Borders region from 1975 to 1996, now part of Scottish Borders council area

Berwick-upon-Tweed (twiːd) *n* a town in N England, in N Northumberland at the mouth of the Tweed: much involved in border disputes between England and Scotland between the 12th and 16th centuries; neutral territory 1551–1885. Pop: 12 870 (2001). Also called: **Berwick**

beryl (ˈbɛrɪl) *n* a white, blue, yellow, green, or pink mineral, found in coarse granites and igneous rocks. It is a source of beryllium and is sometimes used as a gemstone; the green variety is emerald, the blue is aquamarine. Composition: beryllium aluminium silicate. Formula: $Be_3Al_2Si_6O_{18}$. Crystal structure: hexagonal [c13: from Old French, from Latin *bēryllus*, from Greek *bēryllos* of Indic origin] ▷ **ˈberyline** *adj*

beryllium (bɛˈrɪlɪəm) *n* a corrosion-resistant toxic silvery-white metallic element that occurs chiefly in beryl and is used mainly in X-ray windows and in the manufacture of alloys. Symbol: Be; atomic no: 4; atomic wt: 9.012; valency: 2; relative density: 1.848; melting pt: 1289°C; boiling pt: 2472°C [c19: from Latin *bēryllus*, from Greek *bēryllos*]

Berzelius (bəˈziːlɪəs; *Swedish* bærˈseːlɪʊs) *n* Baron **Jöns Jakob** (ˈjœns ˈjɑːkɔp). 1779–1848, Swedish chemist, who invented the present system of chemical symbols and formulas, discovered several elements, and determined the atomic and molecular weight of many substances

Besançon (*French* bəzɑ̃sɔ̃) *n* a city in E France, on the Doubs River: university (1422). Pop: 117 733 (1999)

Besant (ˈbɛzənt, bɪˈzænt) *n* **Annie,** *née* **Wood.** 1847–1933, British theosophist, writer, and political reformer in England and India

beseech (bɪˈsiːtʃ) *vb* **-seeches, -seeching, -sought** *or* **-seeched** (*tr*) to ask (someone) earnestly (to do something *or* for something); beg [c12: see BE-, SEEK; related to Old Frisian *besēka*]

beseem (bɪˈsiːm) *vb archaic* to be suitable for; befit

beset (bɪˈsɛt) *vb* **-sets, -setting, -set** (*tr*) **1** (esp of dangers, temptations, or difficulties) to trouble or harass constantly **2** to surround or attack from all sides **3** *archaic* to cover with, esp with jewels

besetting (bɪˈsɛtɪŋ) *adj* tempting, harassing, or assailing (esp in the phrase **besetting sin**)

beside (bɪˈsaɪd) *prep* **1** next to; at, by, or to the side of **2** as compared with **3** away from; wide of **4** *archaic* besides **5** **beside oneself** (*postpositive; often foll by with*) overwhelmed; overwrought: *beside oneself with grief* ▷ *adv* **6** at, by, to, or along the side of something or someone [Old English *be sīdan*; see BY, SIDE]

besides (bɪˈsaɪdz) *prep* **1** apart from; even considering ▷ *sentence connector* **2** anyway; moreover ▷ *adv* **3** as well

besiege (bɪˈsiːdʒ) *vb* (*tr*) **1** to surround (a fortified area, esp a city) with military forces to bring about its surrender **2** to crowd round; hem in **3** to overwhelm, as with requests or queries ▷ **beˈsieger** *n*

Beslan (ˈbɛzlɑːn) *n* a town in the North Ossetian Republic in Russia: scene of a massacre in 2004 when Chechen extremists held a school hostage, leading to a siege in which 344 people were killed. Pop: 35 550 (2002)

besmear (bɪˈsmɪə) *vb* (*tr*) **1** to smear over; daub **2** to sully; defile (often in the phrase **besmear (a person's) reputation**)

besmirch (bɪˈsmɜːtʃ) *vb* (*tr*) **1** to make dirty; soil **2** to reduce the brightness or lustre of **3** to sully (often in the phrase **besmirch (a person's) name**)

besom[1] (ˈbiːzəm) *n* a broom, esp one made of a bundle of twigs tied to a handle [Old English *besma*; related to Old High German *besmo* broom]

besom[2] (ˈbɪzəm, ˈbiːzəm) *n Scot & Northern English dialect* a derogatory term for a **woman** [perhaps from Old English *bysen* example; related to Old Norse *bysn* wonder]

besotted (bɪˈsɒtɪd) *adj* **1** stupefied with drink; intoxicated **2** infatuated; doting **3** foolish; muddled

besought (bɪˈsɔːt) *vb* the past tense and past participle of **beseech**

bespangle (bɪˈspæŋɡəl) *vb* (*tr*) to cover or adorn with or as if with spangles

bespatter (bɪˈspætə) *vb* (*tr*) **1** to splash all over, as with dirty water **2** to defile; slander; besmirch

bespeak (bɪˈspiːk) *vb* **-speaks, -speaking, -spoke, -spoken** *or* **-spoke** (*tr*) **1** to engage, request, or ask for in advance **2** to indicate or suggest: *this act bespeaks kindness* **3** *poetic* to speak to; address

bespectacled (bɪˈspɛktəkəld) *adj* wearing spectacles

bespoke (bɪˈspəʊk) *adj chiefly Brit* **1** (esp of clothing or a website, computer program, etc) made to the customer's specifications **2** making or selling such suits, jackets, etc: *a bespoke tailor*

besprinkle (bɪˈsprɪŋkəl) *vb* (*tr*) to sprinkle all over with liquid, powder, etc

Bessarabia (ˌbɛsəˈreɪbɪə) *n* a region in E Europe, mostly in Moldova and Ukraine: long disputed by the Turks and Russians; a province of Romania from 1918 until 1940. Area: about 44 300 sq km (17 100 sq miles)

Bessel (ˈbɛsəl) *n* **Friedrich Wilhelm** (ˈfriːdrɪç ˈvɪlhɛlm). 1784–1846, German astronomer and mathematician. He made the first authenticated measurement of a star's distance (1841) and systematized a series of mathematical functions used in physics

Bessemer process *n* (formerly) a process for producing steel by blowing air through molten pig iron at about 1250°C in a Bessemer converter: silicon, manganese, and phosphorus impurities are removed and the carbon content is controlled [c19: named after Sir Henry *Bessemer* (1813–98), English engineer]

best (bɛst) *adj* **1** the superlative of **good** **2** most excellent of a particular group, category, etc **3** most suitable, advantageous, desirable, attractive, etc **4** the best part of most of ▷ *adv* **5** the superlative of **well[1]** **6** in a manner surpassing all others; most excellently, advantageously, attractively, etc ▷ *n* **7** **the best** the most outstanding or excellent person, thing, or group in a category **8** the most effective effort of which a person or group is capable **9** a winning majority **10** Also called: **all the best best wishes 11** a person's smartest outfit of clothing **12 at best a** in the most favourable interpretation **b** under the most favourable conditions **13 for the best a** for an ultimately good outcome **b** with good intentions **14 get the best of** *or* **have the best of** to surpass, defeat, or outwit; better **15 give someone best** to concede someone's superiority **16 make the best of** to cope as well as possible in the unfavourable circumstances of (often in the phrases **make the best of a bad job, make the best of it**) ▷ *vb* **17** (*tr*) to gain the advantage over or defeat [Old English *betst*; related to Gothic *batista*, Old High German *bezzist*]

Best (bɛst) *n* **1 Charles Herbert.** 1899–1978, Canadian physiologist: associated with Banting and Macleod in their discovery of insulin in 1922 **2 George.** 1946–2005, Northern Ireland footballer

bestial ('bɛstɪəl) *adj* **1** brutal or savage **2** sexually depraved; carnal **3** lacking in refinement; brutish **4** of or relating to a beast [c14: from Late Latin *bestiālis*, from Latin *bestia* BEAST]

bestiality (ˌbɛstɪˈælɪtɪ) *n, pl* **-ties 1** bestial behaviour, character, or action **2** sexual activity between a person and an animal

bestialize *or* **bestialise** ('bɛstɪəˌlaɪz) *vb* (*tr*) to make bestial or brutal

bestiary ('bɛstɪərɪ) *n, pl* **-aries** a moralizing medieval collection of descriptions (and often illustrations) of real and mythical animals

bestir (bɪˈstɜː) *vb* **-stirs, -stirring, -stirred** (*tr*) to cause (oneself, or, rarely, another person) to become active; rouse

best man *n* the (male) attendant of the bridegroom at a wedding

bestow (bɪˈstəʊ) *vb* (*tr*) **1** to present (a gift) or confer (an award or honour) **2** *archaic* to apply (energy, resources, etc) **3** *archaic* to house (a person) or store (goods) ▷ be'stowal *or* be'stowment *n*

best practice *n* the recognized methods of correctly running businesses or providing services

bestrew (bɪˈstruː) *vb* **-strews, -strewing, -strewed, -strewn** *or* **-strewed** (*tr*) to scatter or lie scattered over (a surface)

bestride (bɪˈstraɪd) *vb* **-strides, -striding, -strode** *or archaic* **-strid, -stridden** *or* **-strid** (*tr*) **1** to have or put a leg on either side of **2** to extend across; span **3** to stride over or across

bestseller (ˌbɛstˈsɛlə) *n* **1** a book, record, CD, or other product that has sold in great numbers, esp over a short period **2** the author of one or more such books, etc ▷ ˌbest'selling *adj*

bet (bɛt) *n* **1** an agreement between two parties that a sum of money or other stake will be paid by the loser to the party who correctly predicts the outcome of an event **2** the money or stake risked **3** the predicted result in such an agreement **4** a person, event, etc, considered as likely to succeed or occur **5** a course of action (esp in the phrase **one's best bet**) **6** *informal* an opinion; view: *my bet is that you've been up to no good* ▷ *vb* **bets, betting, bet** *or* **betted 7** (when *intr* foll by *on* or *against*) to make or place a bet with (a person or persons) **8** (*tr*) to stake (money, etc) in a bet **9** (*tr; may take a clause as object*) *informal* to predict (a certain outcome) **10 you bet** *informal* of course; naturally [c16: probably short for ABET]

beta ('biːtə) *n* **1** the second letter in the Greek alphabet (Β, β), a consonant, transliterated as *b* **2** the second highest grade or mark, as in an examination [from Greek *bēta*, from Hebrew; see BETH]

beta-blocker *n* any of a class of drugs, such as propranolol, that inhibit the activity of the nerves that are stimulated by adrenaline; they therefore decrease the contraction and speed of the heart: used in the treatment of high blood pressure and angina pectoris

betacarotene (ˌbiːtəˈkærəˌtiːn) *n* the most important form of the plant pigment carotene, which occurs in milk, vegetables, and other foods and, when eaten by man and animals, is converted in the body to vitamin A

beta coefficient *n stock exchange* a measure of the extent to which a particular security rises or falls in value in response to market movements

beta decay *n* the radioactive transformation of an atomic nucleus accompanying the radioactive decay of an electron. It involves unit change of atomic number but none in mass number

betake (bɪˈteɪk) *vb* **-takes, -taking, -took, -taken** (*tr*) **1** betake oneself to go; move **2** *archaic* to apply (oneself) to

beta particle *n* a high-speed electron or positron emitted by a nucleus during radioactive decay or nuclear fission

beta ray *n* a stream of beta particles

beta rhythm *or* **beta wave** *n physiol* the normal electrical activity of the cerebral cortex, occurring at a frequency of 13 to 30 hertz and detectable with an electroencephalograph

beta stock *n* any of the second rank of active securities

on the Stock Exchange, of which there are about 500. Continuous display of prices by market makers is required but not immediate publication of transactions

betatron ('biːtəˌtrɒn) *n* a type of particle accelerator for producing high-energy beams of electrons, having an alternating magnetic field to keep the electrons in a circular orbit of fixed radius and accelerate them by magnetic induction. It produces energies of up to about 300 MeV

betel ('biːtəl) *n* an Asian piperaceous climbing plant, *Piper betle*, the leaves of which are chewed, with the betel nut, by the peoples of SE Asia [c16: from Portuguese, from Malayalam *vettila*]

betel nut *n* the seed of the betel palm, chewed with betel leaves and lime by people in S and SE Asia as a digestive stimulant and narcotic

betel palm *n* a tropical Asian feather palm, *Areca catechu*, with scarlet or orange fruits

bête noire (*French* bɛt nwar) *n, pl* **bêtes noires** (bɛt nwar) a person or thing that one particularly dislikes or dreads [literally: black beast]

beth (bɛt) *n* the second letter of the Hebrew alphabet (ב) transliterated as *b* [from Hebrew *bēth-, bayith* house]

Bethany ('bɛθənɪ) *n* a village in the West Bank, near Jerusalem at the foot of the Mount of Olives: in the New Testament, the home of Lazarus and the lodging place of Jesus during Holy Week

Bethe ('beɪtə) *n* **Hans Albrecht** (hans 'albrɛçt). 1906–2005, US physicist, born in Germany; noted for his research on astrophysics and nuclear physics: Nobel prize for physics 1967

Bethel ('bɛθəl) *n* **1** an ancient town in the West Bank, near Jerusalem: in the Old Testament, the place where the dream of Jacob occurred (Genesis 28:19) **2** a chapel of any of certain Nonconformist Christian sects **3** a seamen's chapel [c17: from Hebrew *bēth 'Ēl* house of God]

Bethesda (bəˈθɛzdə) *n* **1** *New Testament* a pool in Jerusalem reputed to have healing powers, where a paralysed man was healed by Jesus (John 5:2) **2** a chapel of any of certain Nonconformist Christian sects

bethink (bɪˈθɪŋk) *vb* **-thinks, -thinking, -thought** *archaic or dialect* **1** to cause (oneself) to consider or meditate **2** (*tr; often foll by of*) to remind (oneself)

Bethlehem ('bɛθlɪˌhɛm, -lɪəm) *n* a town in the West Bank, near Jerusalem: birthplace of Jesus and early home of King David

Bethmann Hollweg (*German* 'beːtman 'hɔlveːk) *n* **Theobald von** ('teːɔbalt fɔn). 1856–1921, chancellor of Germany (1909–17)

Bethsaida (bɛθˈseɪdə) *n* a ruined town in N Israel, near the N shore of the Sea of Galilee

betide (bɪˈtaɪd) *vb* to happen or happen to; befall (often in the phrase **woe betide (someone)**) [c13: BE- + *tide* to happen]

betimes (bɪˈtaɪmz) *adv archaic* **1** in good time; early **2** in a short time; soon [c14 *bitimes*; see BY, TIME]

Betjeman ('bɛtʃəmən) *n* **Sir John**. 1906–84, English poet, noted for his nostalgic and humorous verse and essays and for his concern for the preservation of historic buildings, esp of the Victorian era. Poet laureate (1972–84)

betoken (bɪˈtəʊkən) *vb* (*tr*) **1** to indicate; signify **2** to portend; augur

betony ('bɛtənɪ) *n, pl* **-nies 1** a Eurasian plant, *Stachys* (or *Betonica*) *officinalis*, with a spike of reddish-purple flowers, formerly used in medicine and dyeing: family *Lamiaceae* (labiates) **2** any of several related plants of the genus *Stachys* [c14: from Old French *betoine*, from Latin *betonica*, variant of *vettonica*, probably named after the *Vettones*, an ancient Iberian tribe]

betray (bɪˈtreɪ) *vb* (*tr*) **1** to hand over or expose (one's nation, friend, etc) treacherously to an enemy **2** to disclose (a secret, confidence, etc) treacherously **3** to break (a promise) or be disloyal to (a person's trust) **4** to show signs of; indicate **5** to reveal unintentionally: *his grin betrayed his satisfaction* [c13: from BE- + *trayen* from Old French *trair*, from Latin *trādere*] ▷ be'trayal *n* ▷ be'trayer *n*

betroth (bɪˈtrəʊð) *vb* (*tr*) *archaic* to promise to marry or to

b

give in marriage [C14 *betreuthen*, from BE- + *treuthe* TROTH, TRUTH]

betrothal (bɪˈtrəʊðəl) *n* 1 engagement to be married 2 a mutual promise to marry

betrothed (bɪˈtrəʊðd) *adj* 1 engaged to be married ▷ *n* 2 the person to whom one is engaged; fiancé or fiancée

better (ˈbɛtə) *adj* 1 the comparative of **good** 2 more excellent than other members of a particular group, category, etc 3 more suitable, advantageous, attractive, etc 4 improved in health 5 fully recovered in health 6 in more favourable circumstances, esp financially 7 **better off** in more favourable circumstances, esp financially 8 **the better part of** a large part of ▷ *adv* 9 the comparative of **well**[1] 10 in a more excellent manner; more advantageously, attractively, etc 11 in or to a greater degree or extent; more 12 **had better** would be wise, sensible, etc to: *I had better be off* 13 **think better of** a to change one's course of action after reconsideration b to rate (a person) more highly ▷ *n* 14 **the better** something that is the more excellent, useful, etc, of two such things 15 (*usually plural*) a person who is superior, esp in social standing or ability 16 **for the better** by way of improvement 17 **get the better of** to defeat, outwit, or surpass ▷ *vb* 18 to make or become better 19 (*tr*) to improve upon; surpass [Old English *betera*; related to Old Norse *betri*, Gothic *batiza*, Old High German *beziro*]

better half *n humorous* one's spouse

betterment (ˈbɛtəmənt) *n* 1 a change for the better; improvement 2 *property law* an improvement effected on real property that enhances the value of the property

Betti (*Italian* ˈbetti) *n* **Ugo** (ˈuɡo). 1892–1953, Italian writer, noted esp for his plays, including *La Padrona* (1927), *Corruzione al palazzo di giustizia* (1949), and *La Regina e gli insorte* (1951)

betting shop *n* (in Britain) a licensed bookmaker's premises not on a racecourse

between (bɪˈtwiːn) *prep* 1 at a point or in a region intermediate to two other points in space, times, degrees, etc 2 in combination; together: *between them, they saved enough money to buy a car* 3 confined or restricted to: *between you and me* 4 indicating a reciprocal relation or comparison 5 indicating two or more alternatives ▷ *adv* Also: **in between** 6 between one specified thing and another [Old English *betwēonum*; related to Gothic *tweihnai* two together; see TWO, TWAIN]

● USAGE After *distribute* and words with a similar
● meaning, *among* should be used rather than *between*:
● *this enterprise issued shares which were distributed among its*
● *workers*

betweentimes (bɪˈtwiːnˌtaɪmz) *or* **betweenwhiles** (bɪˈtwiːnˌwaɪlz) *adv* between other activities

betwixt (bɪˈtwɪkst) *prep, adv* 1 *archaic* another word for **between** 2 betwixt and between in an intermediate, indecisive, or middle position [Old English *betwix*; related to Old High German *zwiski* two each]

Betws-y-Coed (ˌbɛtsɪˈkɔɪd) *n* a village in N Wales, in Conwy county borough, on the River Conwy: noted for its scenery. Pop: 534 (2001)

Beulah (ˈbjuːlə) *n Old Testament* the land of Israel (Isaiah 62:4) [Hebrew, literally: married woman]

Beuthen (ˈbɔɪtən) *n* the German name for **Bytom**

Beuys (*German* bɔɪs) *n* **Joseph** (ˈjoːzɛf). 1921–86, German artist, a celebrated figure of the avant-garde, noted esp for his sculptures made of felt and animal fat

BeV *abbreviation* (in the US) gigaelectronvolts (GeV) [C20: from b(illion) e(lectron) v(olts)]

Bevan (ˈbɛvən) *n* **Aneurin** (əˈnaɪərɪn) known as **Nye** 1897–1960, British Labour storiesman, born in Wales: noted for his oratory. As minister of health (1945–51) he introduced the National Health Service (1948) ▷ ˈBevanˌite *n, adj*

bevel (ˈbɛvəl) *n* 1 Also called: **cant** a surface that meets another at an angle other than a right angle ▷ *vb* **-els, -elling, -elled** *or US* **-els, -eling, -eled** 2 (*intr*) to be inclined; slope 3 (*tr*) to cut a bevel on (a piece of timber, etc) [C16: from Old French *bevel* (unattested), from *baïf*, from *baer* to gape; see BAY[1]]

bevel gear *n* a gear having teeth cut into a conical

surface known as the pitch zone. Two such gears mesh together to transmit power between two shafts at an angle to each other

bevel square *n* a woodworker's square with an adjustable arm that can be set to mark out an angle or to check the slope of a surface

beverage (ˈbɛvərɪdʒ, ˈbɛvrɪdʒ) *n* any drink, usually other than water [C13: from Old French *bevrage*, from *beivre* to drink, from Latin *bibere*]

beverage room *n Canadian* a room in a tavern, hotel, etc, in which alcoholic drinks are served

Beveridge (ˈbɛvərɪdʒ) *n* **William Henry**, 1st Baron Beveridge. 1879–1963, British economist, whose *Report on Social Insurance and Allied Services* (1942) formed the basis of social-security legislation in Britain

Beverley (ˈbɛvəlɪ) *n* a market town in NE England, the administrative centre of the East Riding of Yorkshire. Pop: 29 110 (2001)

Beverly Hills (ˈbɛvəlɪ) *n* a town in SW California, near Los Angeles: famous as the home of film stars. Pop: 34 941 (2003 est)

Bevin (ˈbɛvɪn) *n* **Ernest**. 1881–1951, British Labour statesman and trade unionist, who was largely responsible for the creation of the Transport and General Workers' Union (1922): minister of labour (1940–45); foreign secretary (1945–51)

bevvy (ˈbɛvɪ) *informal* ▷ *n, pl* **-vies** 1 a drink, esp an alcoholic one 2 a session of drinking [probably from Old French *bevee, buvee* drinking]

bevy (ˈbɛvɪ) *n, pl* **bevies** 1 a flock of quails 2 a group, esp of girls [C15: of uncertain origin]

bewail (bɪˈweɪl) *vb* to express great sorrow over (a person or thing); lament > beˈwailer *n*

beware (bɪˈweə) *vb* (*usually used in the imperative or infinitive, often foll by of*) to be cautious or wary (of); be on one's guard (against) [C13 *be war*, from BE (imperative) + war WARY]

Bewick (ˈbjuːɪk) *n* **Thomas**. 1753–1828, English wood engraver; his best-known works are *Chillingham Bull* (1789), a large woodcut, *Aesop's Fables* (1818), and his *History of British Birds* (1797–1804)

bewilder (bɪˈwɪldə) *vb* (*tr*) to confuse utterly; puzzle [C17: see BE-, WILDER] > beˈwildering *adj* > beˈwilderingly *adv* > beˈwilderment *n*

bewitch (bɪˈwɪtʃ) *vb* (*tr*) 1 to attract and fascinate; enchant 2 to cast a spell over [C13 *bewicchen*; see BE-, WITCH] > beˈwitching *adj*

bewray (bɪˈreɪ) *vb* (*tr*) an obsolete word for **betray** [C13: from BE- + Old English *wrēgan* to accuse; related to Gothic *wrōhjan*]

Bexhill *or* **Bexhill-on-Sea** (ˌbɛksˈhɪl) *n* a resort in S England, in East Sussex on the English Channel. Pop: 39 451 (2001)

Bexley (ˈbɛkslɪ) *n* a borough of SE Greater London. Pop: 219 100 (2003 est). Area: 61 sq km (23 sq miles)

bey (beɪ) *n* 1 (in the Ottoman Empire) a title given to senior officers, provincial governors, certain other officials or nobles, and (sometimes) Europeans 2 (in modern Turkey) a title of address, corresponding to *Mr*. ▷ Also called: **beg** [C16: Turkish: lord]

Beyoğlu (ˈbeɪɔːluː) *n* a district of Istanbul, north of the Golden Horn: the European quarter. Former name: Pera

beyond (bɪˈjɒnd) *prep* 1 at or to a point on the other side of; at or to the further side of: *beyond those hills there is a river* 2 outside the limits or scope of ▷ *adv* 3 at or to the other or far side of something 4 outside the limits of something ▷ *n* 5 **the beyond** the unknown; the world outside the range of human perception, esp life after death in certain religious beliefs [Old English *begeondan*; see BY, YONDER]

Beyrouth (beɪˈruːt, ˈbeɪruːt) *n* a variant spelling of **Beirut**

Beza (*French* bəza) *n* See **de Bèze**

bezel (ˈbɛzəl) *n* 1 the sloping face adjacent to the working edge of a cutting tool 2 the upper oblique faces of a cut gem 3 a grooved ring or part holding a gem, watch crystal, etc 4 a retaining outer rim used in vehicle instruments, e.g. in tachometers and speedometers 5 a small indicator light used in vehicle instrument panels [C17: probably from French *biseau*, perhaps from Latin *bis* twice]

Béziers (*French* bezje) *n* a city in S France: scene of a massacre (1209) during the Albigensian Crusade. It is a centre of the wine trade. Pop: 69 153 (1999)

bezique (bɪˈziːk) *n* **1** a card game for two or more players with tricks similar to whist but with additional points scored for honours and sequences: played with two packs with nothing below a seven **2** (in this game) the queen of spades and jack of diamonds declared together [c19: from French *bésigue*, of unknown origin]

Bezwada (beɪzˌwɑːdə) *n* the former name of Vijayawada

B/F or **b/f** *abbreviation* *book-keeping* brought forward

BFN *abbreviation* *text messaging* bye for now

BFPO *abbreviation* British Forces Post Office

Bhagalpur (ˈbɑːɡəlˌpʊə) *n* a city in India, in Bihar: agriculture, textiles, university (1960). Pop: 340 349 (2001)

bhaji (ˈbɑːdʒɪ) *n, pl* **-ji, -jis, -jia** (ˈbɑːdʒɜə) an Indian savoury made of chopped vegetables mixed in a spiced batter and deep-fried [c19: from Hindi *bhājī* fried vegetables]

bhang or **bang** (bæŋ) *n* a preparation of the leaves and flower tops of Indian hemp, which has psychoactive properties: much used in India [c16: from Hindi *bhāng*]

bhangra (ˈbæŋɡrə) *n* a type of Asian pop music that combines elements of traditional Punjabi music with Western pop [c20: from Hindi]

bharal or **burhel** (ˈbʌrəl) *n* a wild Himalayan sheep, *Pseudois nayaur*, with a bluish-grey coat and round backward-curving horns [Hindi]

Bharat (ˈbʌrʌt) *n* transliteration of the Hindi name for India

Bhaskar (ˈbʌsˌkɑː) *n* **Sanjeev** (ˈsændʒiːv). born 1964, British actor and writer of Asian origin, known for the TV comedy series *Goodness Gracious Me* (1998) and *The Kumars at No. 42* (2001–06)

bhat (bɑːt) *n, pl* **bhat** the standard monetary unit of Thailand

Bhatpara (bɑːtˈpɑːrə) *n* a city in NE India, in West Bengal on the Hooghly River: jute and cotton mills. Pop: 441 956 (2001)

Bhavnagar (ˈbɑːvnəɡə) *n* a port in W India, in S Gujarat. Pop: 510 958 (2001)

bhindi (ˈbɪndɪ) *n* the okra as used in Indian cooking: its green pods are eaten as vegetables [Hindi]

Bhisho (ˈbɪʃəʊ) *n* a town in S S Africa, on the Buffalo River adjacent to King Williams Town; the capital of Eastern Cape, it was formerly the capital of the Ciskei Bantu homeland: it is the centre of a sheep and cattle ranching area with various industries

Bhopal (bəʊˈpɑːl) *n* a city in central India, the capital of Madhya Pradesh state and of the former state of Bhopal: site of a poisonous gas leak from a US-owned factory, which killed over 7000 people in 1984 and was implicated in a further 15 000 deaths afterwards. Pop: 1 433 875 (2001)

bhp *abbreviation* brake horsepower

BHP *abbreviation* (in Australia) Broken Hill Proprietary

Bhubaneswar (ˌbʊbəˈneɪʃwə) *n* an ancient city in E India, the capital of Orissa state: many temples built between the 7th and 16th centuries. Pop: 647 302 (2001)

bhuna (ˈbuːnə) *n* an Indian dish or sauce in which spices are dry-roasted in a pan and then combined with a moistening agent such as yogurt or water [from Urdu]

Bhutan (buːˈtɑːn) *n* a kingdom in central Asia: disputed by Tibet, China, India, and Britain since the 18th century but most closely connected with India; contains inaccessible stretches of the E Himalayas in the north. Official language: Dzongka; Nepali is also spoken. Official religion: Mahayana Buddhist. Currencies: ngultrum and Indian rupee. Capital: Thimbu. Pop: 2 325 000 (2004 est). Area: about 46 600 sq km (18 000 sq miles) > Bhutanˈese *n, adj*

Bhutto (ˈbuːtəʊ) *n* **1 Benazir** (ˈbɛnəzɪə). 1953–2007, Pakistani stateswoman; prime minister of Pakistan (1988–90; 1993–96); deposed and subsequently defeated in elections in 1997; assassinated during the 2007 election campaign **2** her father, **Zulfikar Ali** (ˈzʊlfɪkɑː:

ˈɑːlɪ). 1928–79, Pakistani statesman; president (1971–73) and prime minister (1973–77) of Pakistan: executed for the murder of a political rival

Bi *the chemical symbol for* bismuth

bi-¹ or *sometimes before a vowel* **bin-** *combining form* **1** two; having two: *bifocal* **2** occurring every two; lasting for two: *biennial* **3** on both sides, surfaces, directions, etc: *bilateral* **4** occurring twice during: *biweekly* **5 a** denoting an organic compound containing two identical cyclic hydrocarbon systems: *biphenyl* **b** (rare in technical usage) indicating an acid salt of a dibasic acid: *sodium bicarbonate* **c** (not in technical usage) equivalent of **di-¹** (sense 2a) [from Latin, from *bis* TWICE]

bi-² *combining form* a variant of **bio-**

Biafra (bɪˈæfrə) *n* **1** a region of E Nigeria, formerly a local government region: seceded as an independent republic (1967–70) during the Civil War, but defeated by Nigerian government forces **2 Bight of Biafra** former name (until 1975) of (The Bight of) **Bonny** > Biˈafran *adj, n*

Biak (biːˈjɑːk) *n* an island in Indonesia, north of New Guinea: the largest of the Schouten Islands. Area: 2455 sq km (948 sq miles)

Bialik (ˈbjɑːlɪk) *n* **Hayyim Nahman** (ˈhaɪm ˈnɑxman) or **Chaim Nachman**. 1873–1934, Russian Jewish poet and writer. His long poems *The Talmud Student* (1894) and *In the City of Slaughter* (1903) established him as the major Hebrew poet of modern times

Białystok (*Polish* bjaˈwɪstɔk) *n* a city in E Poland: belonged to Prussia (1795–1807) and to Russia (1807–1919). Pop: 315 000 (2005 est). Russian name: Belostok

biannual (baɪˈænjʊəl) *adj* occurring twice a year. See **biennial** > biˈannually *adv*

Biarritz (ˈbɪərɪts, bɪəˈriːts; *French* bjarits) *n* a town in SW France, on the Bay of Biscay: famous resort, patronized by Napoleon III and by Queen Victoria and Edward VII of Great Britain and Ireland. Pop: 30 055 (1999)

bias (ˈbaɪəs) *n* **1** mental tendency or inclination, esp an irrational preference or prejudice **2** a diagonal line or cut across the weave of a fabric **3** *electronics* the voltage applied to an electronic device or system to establish suitable working conditions **4** *bowls* **a** a bulge or weight inside one side of a bowl **b** the curved course of such a bowl on the green **5** *statistics* an extraneous latent influence on, unrecognized conflated variable in, or selectivity in a sample which influences its distribution and so renders it unable to reflect the desired population parameters ▷ *adv* **6** obliquely; diagonally ▷ *vb* **-ases, -asing, -ased** or **-asses, -assing, -assed** (*tr*) **7** (*usually passive*) to cause to have a bias; prejudice; influence [c16: from Old French *biais*, from Old Provençal, perhaps ultimately from Greek *epikarsios* oblique] > ˈbiased or ˈbiassed *adj*

bias binding *n* a strip of material cut on the bias for extra stretch and often doubled, used for binding hems, interfacings, etc, or for decoration

biathlon (baɪˈæθlən, -lɒn) *n* *sport* a contest in which skiers with rifles shoot at four targets along a 20-kilometre (12.5-mile) cross-country course

biaxial (baɪˈæksɪəl) *adj* (esp of a crystal) having two axes

bib (bɪb) *n* **1** a piece of cloth or plastic worn, esp by babies, to protect their clothes while eating **2** the upper part of some aprons, dungarees, etc, that covers the upper front part of the body **3** Also called: **pout, whiting pout** a light-brown European marine gadoid food fish, *Gadus* (or *Trisopterus*) *luscus*, with a barbel on its lower jaw **4 stick one's bib in** *Austral informal* to interfere ▷ *vb* **bibs, bibbing, bibbed 5** *archaic* to drink (something); tipple [c14 *bibben* to drink, probably from Latin *bibere*]

bib and tucker *n* *informal* an outfit of clothes (esp in the phrase **best bib and tucker**)

bibcock (ˈbɪbˌkɒk) or **bib** *n* a tap having a nozzle bent downwards and supplied from a horizontal pipe

bibelot (ˈbɪbləʊ; *French* biblo) *n* an attractive or curious trinket [c19: from French, from Old French *beubelet*, perhaps from a reduplication of *bel* beautiful]

Bible (ˈbaɪbʰl) *n* **1 a** *the* **Bible** the sacred writings of the Christian religion, comprising the Old and New Testaments and, in the Roman Catholic Church, the

Apocrypha **b** (as modifier): a Bible reading **2** (often not capital) any book containing the sacred writings of a religion **3** (usually not capital) a book regarded as authoritative [C13: from Old French, from Medieval Latin biblia books, from Greek, plural of biblion book, diminutive of biblos papyrus, from Bublos Phoenician port from which Greece obtained Egyptian papyrus]

Bible Belt n the Bible Belt those states of the S US where Protestant fundamentalism is dominant

Bible-thumper n slang an enthusiastic or aggressive exponent of the Bible. Also called: Bible-basher > 'Bible-,thumping n, adj

biblical ('bɪblɪkəl) adj **1** of, occurring in, or referring to the Bible **2** resembling the Bible in written style

Biblicist ('bɪblɪsɪst) or **Biblist** n **1** a biblical scholar **2** a person who takes the Bible literally

biblio- combining form indicating book or books: bibliography; bibliomania [from Greek biblion book]

bibliography (,bɪblɪ'ɒgrəfɪ) n, pl -phies **1** a list of books or other material on a subject **2** a list of sources used in the preparation of a book, thesis, etc **3 a** the study of the history, classification, etc, of literary material **b** a work on this subject > ,bibli'ographer n > bibliographic (,bɪblɪə'græfɪk) or ,biblio'graphical adj

bibliomancy ('bɪblɪəʊ,mænsɪ) n prediction of the future by interpreting a passage chosen at random from a book, esp the Bible

bibliomania (,bɪblɪəʊ'meɪnɪə) n extreme fondness for books > ,biblio'mani,ac n, adj

bibliophile ('bɪblɪə,faɪl) or **bibliophil** ('bɪblɪəfɪl) n a person who collects or is fond of books > bibliophilism (,bɪblɪ'ɒfə,lɪzəm) n

bibliopole ('bɪblɪəʊ,pəʊl) or **bibliopolist** (,bɪblɪ'ɒpəlɪst) n a dealer in books, esp rare or decorative ones [C18: from Latin bibliopōla, from Greek bibliopōlēs bookseller, from BIBLIO- + pōlein to sell] > ,bibli'opoly n

bibulous ('bɪbjʊləs) adj addicted to alcohol [C17: from Latin bibulus, from bibere to drink] > 'bibulously adv > 'bibulousness n

bicameral (baɪ'kæmərəl) adj (of a legislature) consisting of two chambers [C19: from BI-¹ + Latin camera CHAMBER] > bi'cameral,ism n

bicarb ('baɪkɑːb) n short for **bicarbonate of soda**

bicarbonate (baɪ'kɑːbənɪt, -,neɪt) n a salt of carbonic acid containing the ion HCO_3^-; an acid carbonate

bicarbonate of soda n sodium bicarbonate, esp when used as a medicine or as a raising agent in baking

bice (baɪs) n **1** Also called: bice blue a medium blue colour; azurite **2** Also called: bice green a yellowish-green colour; malachite [C14: from Old French bis dark grey, of uncertain origin]

bicentenary (,baɪsɛn'tiːnərɪ) or US **bicentennial** (,baɪsɛn'tɛnɪəl) adj **1** marking a 200th anniversary **2** occurring every 200 years **3** lasting 200 years ▷ n, pl -naries **4** a 200th anniversary

bicephalous (baɪ'sɛfələs) adj **1** biology having two heads **2** crescent-shaped

biceps ('baɪsɛps) n, pl -ceps anatomy any muscle having two heads or origins, esp the muscle that flexes the forearm [C17: from Latin: having two heads, from BI-¹ caput head]

bichloride (baɪ'klɔːraɪd) n another name for **dichloride**

bichloride of mercury n another name for **mercuric chloride**

bichromate (baɪ'krəʊ,meɪt, -mɪt) n another name for **dichromate**

bicker ('bɪkə) vb (intr) **1** to argue over petty matters; squabble **2** poetic **a** (esp of a stream) to run quickly **b** to flicker; glitter ▷ n **3** a petty squabble [C13: of unknown origin] > 'bickerer n

bicolour ('baɪ,kʌlə), **bicoloured** or US **bicolor**, **bicolored** adj two-coloured

biconcave (baɪ'kɒnkeɪv, ,baɪkɒn'keɪv) adj (of a lens) having concave faces on both sides; concavo-concave

biconditional (,baɪkən'dɪʃənəl) n another name for **equivalence** (sense 2)

biconvex (baɪ'kɒnvɛks, ,baɪkɒn'vɛks) adj (of a lens) having convex faces on both sides; convexo-convex

bicuspid (baɪ'kʌspɪd) or **bicuspidate** (baɪ'kʌspɪ,deɪt) adj **1** having or terminating in two cusps or points ▷ n **2** a bicuspid tooth; premolar

bicycle ('baɪsɪkəl) n **1** a vehicle with a tubular metal frame mounted on two spoked wheels, one behind the other. The rider sits on a saddle, propels the vehicle by means of pedals that drive the rear wheel through a chain, and steers with handlebars on the front wheel. Often shortened to: bike (informal) cycle ▷ vb **2** (intr) to ride a bicycle; cycle [C19: from BI-¹ + Late Latin cyclus, from Greek kuklos wheel] > 'bicyclist or 'bicycler n

bicycle clip n one of a pair of clips worn around the ankles by cyclists to keep the trousers tight and out of the chain

bid (bɪd) vb bids, bidding, bad, bade or esp for senses 1, 2, 5, 6 bid, bidden or bid **1** (often foll by for or against) to offer (an amount) in attempting to buy something, esp in competition with others as at an auction **2** commerce to respond to an offer by a seller by stating (the more favourable terms) on which one is willing to make a purchase **3** (tr) to say (a greeting, blessing, etc): to bid farewell **4** to order; command: do as you are bid! **5** (intr; usually foll by for) to attempt to attain power, etc **6** bridge to declare in the auction before play how many tricks one expects to make **7** bid defiance to resist boldly **8** bid fair to seem probable ▷ n **9** a an offer of a specified amount, as at an auction **b** the price offered **10** commerce **a** a statement by a buyer, in response to an offer by a seller, of the more favourable terms that would be acceptable **b** the price or other terms so stated **11** an attempt, esp an attempt to attain power **12** bridge **a** the number of tricks a player undertakes to make **b** a player's turn to make a bid ▷ See also **bid up** [Old English biddan; related to German bitten] > 'bidder n

Bida ('baɪdɑː) or **El Beda** (ɛl 'beɪdɑː) n the former name of Doha

Bidault (French bido) n **Georges** (ʒɔːrʒ). 1899–1983, French statesman; prime minister (1946, 1949–50). His opposition to Algerian independence led him to support the OAS: he was charged with treason (1963) and fled abroad

biddable ('bɪdəbəl) adj **1** having sufficient value to be bid on, as a hand or suit at bridge **2** docile; obedient > 'biddableness n

bidding ('bɪdɪŋ) n **1** an order; command (often in the phrases do or follow the bidding of, at someone's bidding) **2** an invitation; summons **3** the act of making bids, as at an auction or in bridge

Biddle ('bɪdəl) n **John**. 1615–62, English theologian; founder of Unitarianism in England

biddy¹ ('bɪdɪ) n, pl -dies a dialect word for **chicken, hen** [C17: perhaps imitative of calling chickens]

biddy² ('bɪdɪ) n, pl -dies informal, offensive a woman, esp an old gossipy or interfering one [C18: from pet form of Bridget]

biddy-biddy or **biddi-biddi** ('bɪdɪ,bɪdɪ) n, pl -biddies **1** a low-growing rosaceous plant, Acaena viridior of New Zealand, having prickly burs **2** the burs of this plant ▷ Also called: (Austral.) bidgee-widgee ('bɪdʒɪ,wɪdʒɪ) [from Māori piri piri]

bide (baɪd) vb bides, biding, bided or bode, bided **1** (intr) archaic, or dialect to continue in a certain place or state; stay **2** (tr) archaic or dialect to tolerate; endure **3** bide one's time to wait patiently for an opportunity [Old English bīdan; related to Old Norse bītha to wait, Gothic beidan, Old High German bītan]

bidentate (baɪ'dɛn,teɪt) adj having two teeth or toothlike parts or processes

bidet ('biːdeɪ) n a small low basin for washing the genitals and anal area [C17: from French: small horse, probably from Old French bider to trot]

bid up vb (adverb) to increase the market price of (a commodity) by making artificial bids

Biel (biːl) n **1** a town in NW Switzerland, on Lake Biel. Pop: 48 655 (2000). French name: Bienne **2** Lake Biel a lake in NW Switzerland: remains of lake dwellings were discovered here in the 19th century. Area: 39 sq km (15 sq miles)

Bielefeld (German 'biːləfɛlt) n a city in Germany, in NE North Rhine-Westphalia: food, textiles. Pop: 328 452

(2003 est)

Bielsko-Biała (Polish ˈbjɛlskɔˈbjawa) n a town in S Poland: created in 1951 by the union of Bielsko and Biala Krakowska; a leading textile centre since the 16th century. Pop: 356 000 (2005 est)

Bien Hoa (ˈbjɛn ˈhəʊə) n a town in S Vietnam: a former capital of Cambodia. Pop: 520 000 (2005 est)

Bienne (bjɛn) n the French name for **Biel**

biennial (baɪˈɛnɪəl) adj **1** occurring every two years **2** lasting two years. See **biannual** ▷ n **3** a plant, such as the carrot, that completes its life cycle within two years, developing vegetative storage parts during the first year and flowering and fruiting in its second year **4** an event that takes place every two years ▷ biˈennially adv

bier (bɪə) n a platform or stand on which a corpse or a coffin containing a corpse rests before burial [Old English bǣr; related to beran to BEAR[1], Old High German bāra bier, Sanskrit bhārá a burden]

Bierce (bɪəs) n **Ambrose** (**Gwinett**). 1842–?1914, US journalist and author of humorous sketches, horror stories, and tales of the supernatural: he disappeared during a mission in Mexico (1913)

biestings (ˈbiːstɪŋz) n a variant spelling of **beestings**

biff (bɪf) slang ▷ n **1** a blow with the fist ▷ vb **2** (tr) to give (someone) such a blow [c20: probably of imitative origin]

bifid (ˈbaɪfɪd) adj divided into two lobes by a median cleft [c17: from Latin bifidus from BI-[1] + -fidus, from findere to split] ▷ biˈfidity n ▷ ˈbifidly adv

bifocal (baɪˈfəʊkˀl) adj **1** optics having two different focuses **2** relating to a compound lens permitting near and distant vision

bifocals (baɪˈfəʊkˀlz) pl n a pair of spectacles with bifocal lenses

bifurcate vb (ˈbaɪfəˌkeɪt) **1** to fork or divide into two parts or branches ▷ adj (ˈbaɪfəˌkeɪt, -kɪt) **2** forked or divided into two sections or branches [c17: from Medieval Latin bifurcātus, from Latin bifurcus, from BI-[1] + furca fork] ▷ ˌbifurˈcation n

big (bɪg) adj bigger, biggest **1** of great or considerable size, height, weight, number, power, or capacity **2** having great significance; important **3** important through having power, influence, wealth, authority, etc **4** informal considerable in extent or intensity (esp in the phrase **in a big way**) **5 a** elder: my big brother **b** grown-up **6 a** generous; magnanimous: that's very big of you **b** (in combination): big-hearted **7** extravagant; boastful: he's full of big talk **8** too big for one's boots or too big for one's breeches conceited; unduly self-confident **9** in an advanced stage of pregnancy (esp in the phrase **big with child**) ▷ adv informal **10** boastfully; pretentiously (esp in the phrase **talk big**) **11** in an exceptional way; well: his talk went over big with the audience **12** on a grand scale (esp in the phrase **think big**) ▷ See also **big up** [c13: perhaps of Scandinavian origin; compare Norwegian dialect bugge big man] ▷ ˈbigness n

bigamy (ˈbɪɡəmɪ) n, pl -mies the crime of marrying a person while one is still legally married to someone else [c13: via French from Medieval Latin bigamus; see BI-[1], -GAMY] ▷ ˈbigamist n ▷ ˈbigamous adj

Big Apple n the Big Apple informal New York City [c20: probably from US jazzmen's earlier use to mean any big, esp northern, city; of obscure origin]

big band n a large jazz or dance band, popular esp in the 1930s to the 1950s

big bang n (sometimes capitals) the major modernization that took place on the London Stock Exchange on Oct 27 1986, after which the distinction between jobbers and brokers was abolished and operations became fully computerized

big-bang theory n a cosmological theory postulating that approximately 12 billion years ago all the matter of the universe, packed into a small superdense mass, was hurled in all directions by a cataclysmic explosion. As the fragments slowed down, the galaxies and stars evolved but the universe is still expanding. See **steady-state theory**

Big Brother n a person, organization, etc, that exercises total dictatorial control [c20: after a character in the novel 1984 (1949) by English writer George Orwell (1903–1950)]

big business n large commercial organizations collectively, esp when considered as exploitative or socially harmful

big deal interj slang an exclamation of scorn, derision, etc, used esp to belittle a claim or offer

big dipper n (in amusement parks) a narrow railway with open carriages that run swiftly over a route of sharp curves and steep inclines

big end n Brit the larger end of a connecting rod in an internal-combustion engine

big game n large animals that are hunted or fished for sport

big gun n informal an important or influential person

big hair n a hairstyle with volume created by hair products or styling techniques such as backcombing, etc

bighead (ˈbɪgˌhɛd) n informal a conceited person ▷ ˌbigˈheaded adj ▷ ˌbigˈheadedness n

big hitter n **1** a sportsperson who is capable of hitting the ball long or hard **2** informal an influential and important person: one of the government's big hitters

bighorn (ˈbɪgˌhɔːn) n, pl -horns or -horn a large wild sheep, Ovis canadensis, inhabiting mountainous regions in North America and NE Asia: family Bovidae, order Artiodactyla. The male has massive curved horns, and the species is well adapted for climbing and leaping

bight (baɪt) n **1** a wide indentation of a shoreline, or the body of water bounded by such a curve **2** the slack middle part of an extended rope **3** a curve or loop in a rope [Old English byht; see BOW[2]]

Bight n the Bight Austral informal the major indentation of the S coast of Australia, from Cape Pasley in W Australia to the Eyre Peninsula in S Australia

bigmouth (ˈbɪgˌmaʊθ) n slang a noisy, indiscreet, or boastful person ▷ ˈbig-ˌmouthed adj

big name n informal **a** a famous person **b** (as modifier): a big-name performer

big noise n informal an important person

bignonia (bɪgˈnəʊnɪə) n any tropical American bignoniaceous climbing shrub of the genus Bignonia (or Doxantha), cultivated for their trumpet-shaped yellow or reddish flowers [c19: from New Latin, named after the Abbé Jean-Paul Bignon (1662–1743)]

big-note vb Austral informal to boast about (oneself)

bigot (ˈbɪgət) n a person who is intolerant of any ideas other than his or her own, esp on religion, politics, or race [c16: from Old French: name applied contemptuously to the Normans by the French, of obscure origin] ▷ ˈbigoted adj ▷ ˈbigotry n

big shot n informal an important or influential person

Big Smoke n the Big Smoke informal a large city, esp London

big stick n informal force or the threat of using force

big tent n **a** a political approach in which a party claims to be open to a wide spectrum of constituents and groups **b** (as modifier): big-tent politics

big ticket adj (prenominal) (of retail goods) belonging to the most expensive and prestigious class

big time n informal **a** the big time the highest or most profitable level of an occupation or profession, esp the entertainment business **b** (as modifier): a big-time comedian ▷ ˈbig-ˈtimer n

big top n informal **1** the main tent of a circus **2** the circus itself

big tree n a giant Californian coniferous tree, Sequoiadendron giganteum, with a wide tapering trunk and thick spongy bark: family Taxodiaceae. It often reaches a height of 90 metres. Also called: giant sequoia, wellingtonia See also **sequoia**

big up vb bigs, bigging, bigged (tr, adverb) slang to make important, prominent, or famous: we'll do our best to big you up

bigwig (ˈbɪgˌwɪg) n informal an important person

Bihar (bɪˈhɑː) n a state of NE India: consists of part of the Ganges plain; important for rice: lost the S to the new state of Jharkhand in 2000. Capital: Patna. Pop: 82 878 796 (2001). Area: 99 225 sq km (38 301 sq miles)

Biisk (Russian bijsk) n a variant spelling of **Biysk**

b

Bijapur (bɪˈdʒɑːpʊə) n an ancient city in W India, in N Mysore: capital of a former kingdom, which fell at the end of the 17th century: cotton. Pop: 245 946 (2001)

bijou (ˈbiːʒuː) n, pl -joux (-ʒuːz) 1 something small and delicately worked, such as a trinket 2 (modifier) often ironic small but elegant and tasteful: a bijou residence [c19: from French, from Breton bizou finger ring, from biz finger; compare Welsh bys finger, Cornish bis]

bijugate (ˈbaɪdʒʊˌɡeɪt, baɪˈdʒuːɡeɪt) or **bijugous** adj (of compound leaves) having two pairs of leaflets

Bikaner (ˈbiːkəˌnɪə) n a walled city in NW India, in Rajasthan: capital of the former state of Bikaner, on the edge of the Thar Desert. Pop: 529 007 (2001)

bike (baɪk) n, vb informal short for **bicycle, motorcycle** 2 get off one's bike Austral & NZ slang to lose one's self-control ▷ n 3 slang a promiscuous woman

biker (ˈbaɪkə) n informal a member of a motorcyle gang

biker jacket n a short, close-fitting leather jacket with zips and studs, often worn by motorcyclists

Bikila (bɪˈkiːlə) n **Abebe** (əˈbeɪbeɪ). 1932–73, Ethiopian long-distance runner: winner of the Marathon at the Olympic Games in Rome (1960) and Tokyo (1964)

bikini (bɪˈkiːnɪ) n, pl -nis a woman's very brief two-piece swimming costume [c20: after Bikini atoll, from a comparison between the devastating effect of the atomic-bomb test and the effect caused by women wearing bikinis]

Bikini (bɪˈkiːnɪ) n an atoll in the N Pacific; one of the Marshall Islands: site of a US atomic-bomb test in 1946

Biko (ˈbiːkəʊ) n **Steven Bantu**, known as Steve. 1946–77, Black South African civil rights leader: founder of the South African Students Organization. His death in police custody caused worldwide concern

bilabial (baɪˈleɪbɪəl) adj 1 of, relating to, or denoting a speech sound articulated using both lips: (p) is a bilabial stop, (w) a bilabial semivowel ▷ n 2 a bilabial speech sound

bilabiate (baɪˈleɪbɪˌeɪt, -ɪt) adj botany divided into two lips: the snapdragon has a bilabiate corolla

bilateral (baɪˈlætərəl) adj 1 having or involving two sides 2 affecting or undertaken by two parties; mutual 3 having identical sides or parts on each side of an axis; symmetrical

bilateral symmetry n the property of an organism or part of an organism such that, if cut in only one plane, the two cut halves are mirror images of each other. See also **radial symmetry**

Bilbao (bɪlˈbɑːəʊ; Spanish bilˈβau) n a port in N Spain, on the Bay of Biscay: the largest city in the Basque Provinces: famous since medieval times for the production of iron and steel goods: modern buildings include the Guggenheim Art Museum (1997). Pop: 353 567 (2003 est)

bilberry (ˈbɪlbərɪ) n, pl -ries 1 any of several ericaceous shrubs of the genus Vaccinium, having edible blue or blackish berries 2 the fruit of any of these plants [c16: probably of Scandinavian origin; compare Danish bøllebær, from bølle bilberry + bær BERRY]

bilboes (ˈbɪlbəʊz) pl n a long iron bar with two sliding shackles, formerly used to confine the ankles of a prisoner [c16: perhaps changed from BILBAO]

Bildungsroman (German ˈbɪldʊŋsroːmaːn) n a novel concerned with a person's formative years and development [literally: education novel]

bile (baɪl) n 1 a bitter greenish to golden brown alkaline fluid secreted by the liver and stored in the gall bladder. It is discharged during digestion into the duodenum, where it aids the emulsification and absorption of fats 2 irritability or peevishness [c17: from French, from Latin bīlis, probably of Celtic origin; compare Welsh bustl bile]

bilge (bɪldʒ) n 1 nautical the parts of a vessel's hull where the vertical sides curve inwards to form the bottom 2 (often plural) the parts of a vessel between the lowermost floorboards and the bottom 3 Also called: **bilge water** the dirty water that collects in a vessel's bilge 4 informal silly rubbish; nonsense 5 the widest part of the belly of a barrel or cask ▷ vb 6 (intr) nautical (of a vessel) to take in water at the bilge 7 (tr) nautical to damage (a vessel) in the bilge, causing it to leak [c16:

probably a variant of BULGE]

bilharzia (bɪlˈhɑːtsɪə) n 1 another name for a **schistosome** 2 another name for **schistosomiasis** [c19: New Latin, named after Theodor Bilharz (1825–62), German parasitologist who discovered schistosomes]

bilharziasis (ˌbɪlhɑːˈtsaɪəsɪs) or **bilharziosis** (bɪlˌhɑːtsɪˈəʊsɪs) n another name for **schistosomiasis**

biliary (ˈbɪlɪərɪ) adj of or relating to bile, to the ducts that convey bile, or to the gall bladder

bilingual (baɪˈlɪŋɡwəl) adj 1 able to speak two languages, esp with fluency 2 written or expressed in two languages ▷ n 3 a bilingual person > biˈlingualˌism n

bilious (ˈbɪlɪəs) adj 1 of or relating to bile 2 affected with or denoting any disorder related to excess secretion of bile 3 informal bad-tempered; irritable [c16: from Latin bīliōsus full of BILE¹] > ˈbiliousness n

bilk (bɪlk) vb (tr) 1 to balk; thwart 2 (often foll by of) to cheat or deceive, esp to avoid making payment to 3 to escape from; elude ▷ n 4 a swindle or cheat 5 a person who swindles or cheats [c17: perhaps variant of BALK] > ˈbilker n

bill¹ (bɪl) n 1 money owed for goods or services supplied 2 a written or printed account or statement of money owed 3 chiefly Brit such an account for food and drink in a restaurant, hotel, etc 4 any printed or written list of items, events, etc, such as a theatre programme 5 a statute in draft, before it becomes law 6 a printed notice or advertisement; poster 7 US & Canadian a piece of paper money; note 8 an obsolete name for **promissory note** 9 See **bill of exchange** 10 See **bill of fare** ▷ vb (tr) 11 to send or present an account for payment to (a person) 12 to enter (items, goods, etc) on an account or statement 13 to advertise by posters 14 to schedule as a future programme [c14: from Anglo-Latin billa, alteration of Late Latin bulla document, BULL³]

bill² (bɪl) n 1 the mouthpart of a bird, consisting of projecting jaws covered with a horny sheath; beak. It varies in shape and size according to the type of food eaten and may also be used as a weapon 2 any beaklike mouthpart in other animals 3 a narrow promontory ▷ vb (intr) (of birds) to touch bills together (esp in the phrase **bill and coo**) 4 (of birds, esp doves) to touch bills together 5 (of lovers) to kiss and whisper amorously [Old English bile; related to bill BILL³]

bill³ (bɪl) n 1 a pike or halberd with a narrow hooked blade 2 short for **billhook** [Old English bill sword, related to Old Norse bīldr instrument used in blood-letting, Old High German bil pickaxe]

billable (ˈbɪləb°l) adj referring to time worked, esp by a lawyer, on behalf of a particular client and for which that client will be expected to pay: a timesheet of my billable hours

billabong (ˈbɪləˌbɒŋ) n Austral 1 a backwater channel that forms a lagoon or pool 2 a branch of a river running to a dead end [c19: from a native Australian language, from billa river + bong dead]

billboard (ˈbɪlˌbɔːd) n another name for **hoarding** [c19: from BILL¹ + BOARD]

billet¹ (ˈbɪlɪt) n 1 accommodation, esp for a soldier, in civilian lodgings 2 the official requisition for such lodgings 3 a space or berth allocated, esp for slinging a hammock, in a ship 4 informal a job ▷ vb -lets, -leting, -leted 5 (tr) to assign a lodging to (a soldier) 6 to lodge or be lodged [c15: from Old French billette, from bulle a document; see BULL³]

billet² (ˈbɪlɪt) n 1 a chunk of wood, esp for fuel 2 metallurgy a a metal bar of square or circular cross section b an ingot cast into the shape of a prism [c15: from Old French billette a little log, from bille log, probably of Celtic origin]

billet-doux (ˌbɪlɪˈduː, French bijɛdu) n, pl billets-doux (ˌbɪlɪˈduːz, French bijɛdu) old-fashioned or humorous a love letter [c17: from French, literally: a sweet letter, from billet (see BILLET¹) + doux sweet, from Latin dulcis]

billhook (ˈbɪlˌhʊk) n a cutting tool with a wooden handle and a curved blade terminating in a hook at its tip, used for pruning, chopping, etc. Also called: **bill**

billiard (ˈbɪljəd) n (modifier) of or relating to billiards: a billiard table; a billiard cue; a billiard ball

billiards ('bɪljədz) *n* (*functioning as singular*) any of various games in which long cues are used to drive balls now made of composition or plastic. It is played on a rectangular table covered with a smooth tight-fitting cloth and having raised cushioned edges [c16: from Old French *billard* curved stick, from Old French *bille* log; see BILLET²]

billing ('bɪlɪŋ) *n* **1** *theatre* the relative importance of a performer or act as reflected in the prominence given in programmes, advertisements, etc **2** *chiefly US & Canadian* public notice or advertising (esp in the phrase **advance billing**)

billingsgate ('bɪlɪŋz,geɪt) *n* obscene or abusive language [c17: after BILLINGSGATE, which was notorious for such language]

Billingsgate ('bɪlɪŋz,geɪt) *n* the largest fish market in London, on the N bank of the River Thames; moved to new site at Canary Wharf in 1982 and the former building converted into offices

Billings method *n* a natural method of birth control that involves examining the colour and viscosity of the cervical mucus to discover when ovulation is occurring [c20: devised by Drs John and Evelyn *Billings* in the 1960s]

billion ('bɪljən) *n*, *pl* -**lions** *or* -**lion** **1** one thousand million: it is written as 1 000 000 000 or 10^9 **2** (formerly, in Britain) one million million: it is written as 1 000 000 000 000 or 10^{12} **3** (*often plural*) any exceptionally large number ▷ *determiner* **4** (*preceded by a or a cardinal number*) amounting to a billion [c17: from French, from BI-¹ + -*llion* as in *million*] > 'billionth *adj*, *n*

billionaire (,bɪljə'nɛə) *n* a person whose assets are worth over a billion of the monetary units of his country

Billiton ('bɪlɪtɒn, bɪ'li:tɒn) *n* an island of Indonesia, in the Java Sea between Borneo and Sumatra. Chief town: Tanjungpandan. Area: 4833 sq km (1866 sq miles). Also called: Belitung

bill of attainder *n* (formerly) a legislative act finding a person guilty without trial of treason or felony and declaring him attainted

bill of exchange *n* (now chiefly in foreign transactions) a document, usually negotiable, containing an instruction to a third party to pay a stated sum of money at a designated future date or on demand

bill of fare *n* another name for **menu**

bill of health *n* **1** a certificate, issued by a port officer, that attests to the health of a ship's company **2** clean bill of health *informal* **a** a good report of one's physical condition **b** a favourable account of a person's or a company's financial position

bill of lading *n* (in foreign trade) a document containing full particulars of goods shipped or for shipment

bill of quantities *n* a document drawn up by a quantity surveyor providing details of the prices, dimensions, etc, of the materials required to build a large structure, such as a factory

Bill of Rights *n* **1** an English statute of 1689 guaranteeing the rights and liberty of the individual subject **2** the first ten amendments to the US Constitution, added in 1791, which guarantee the liberty of the individual **3** (*usually not capitals*) any charter or summary of basic human rights

bill of sale *n law* a deed transferring personal property, either outright or as security for a loan or debt

billow ('bɪləʊ) *n* **1** a large sea wave **2** a swelling or surging mass, as of smoke or sound **3** a large atmospheric wave, usually in the lee of a hill ▷ *vb* **4** to rise up, swell out, or cause to rise up or swell out [c16: from Old Norse *bylgja*; related to Swedish *bölja*, Danish *bölg*, Middle High German *bulge*; see BELLOW, BELLY] > 'billowing *adj*, *n* > 'billowy *adj* > 'billowiness *n*

billposter ('bɪl,pəʊstə) *or* **billsticker** *n* a person who is employed to stick advertising posters to walls, fences, etc > 'bill,posting *or* 'bill,sticking *n*

billy ('bɪlɪ) *or* **billycan** ('bɪlɪ,kæn) *n*, *pl* -**lies** *or* -**lycans** **1** a metal can or pot for boiling water, etc, over a campfire **2** *Austral & NZ* (*as modifier*): billy-tea **3** *Austral & NZ informal* to make tea [c19: from Scot *billypot* cooking vessel]

billy goat *n* a male goat

Billy No-Mates *n slang* a person with no friends

Billy the Kid *n* nickname of *William H. Bonney*. 1859–81, US outlaw

bilobate (baɪ'ləʊ,beɪt) *or* **bilobed** ('baɪ,ləʊbd) *adj* divided into or having two lobes

biltong ('bɪl,tɒŋ) *n South African* strips of meat dried and cured in the sun [c19: Afrikaans, from Dutch *bil* buttock + *tong* TONGUE]

BIM *abbreviation* British Institute of Management

bimanous ('bɪmənəs, baɪ'meɪ-) *adj* (of man and the higher primates) having two hands distinct in form and function from the feet [c19: from New Latin *bimana* two handed, from BI-¹ + Latin *manus* hand]

bimanual (baɪ'mænjʊəl) *adj* using or requiring both hands

bimbo ('bɪmbəʊ) *n*, *pl* -**bos** *or* -**boes** **1** an attractive but empty-headed young woman **2** a person, esp a foolish one [c20: from Italian: little child, perhaps via Polari]

bimetallic (,baɪmɪ'tælɪk) *adj* **1** consisting of two metals **2** of, relating to, or based on bimetallism

bimetallic strip *n* a strip consisting of two metals of different coefficients of expansion welded together so that it buckles on heating: used in thermostats, etc

bimetallism (baɪ'mɛtə,lɪzəm) *n* the use of two metals, esp gold and silver, in fixed relative values as the standard of value and currency > bi'metallist *n*

bimonthly (baɪ'mʌnθlɪ) *adj*, *adv* **1** every two months **2** (often avoided because of confusion with sense 1) twice a month; semimonthly ▷ *n*, *pl* -**lies** **3** a periodical published every two months

bimorph ('baɪmɔːf) *or* **bimorph cell** *n electronics* an assembly of two piezoelectric crystals cemented together so that an applied voltage causes one to expand and the other to contract, converting electrical signals into mechanical energy. Conversely, bending can generate a voltage: used in loudspeakers, gramophone pick-ups, etc

bin (bɪn) *n* **1** a large container or enclosed space for storing something in bulk, such as coal, grain, or wool **2** Also called: bread bin a small container for bread **3** Also called: dustbin, rubbish bin a container for litter, rubbish, etc ▷ *vb* **bins**, **binning**, **binned 4** (*tr*) to store in a bin **5** (*tr*) to put in a wastepaper bin [Old English *binne* basket, probably of Celtic origin; related to *bindan* to BIND]

bin- *prefix* a variant, esp before a vowel, of: bi-¹ binocular

binary ('baɪnərɪ) *adj* **1** composed of, relating to, or involving two; dual **2** *maths*, *computing* of, relating to, or expressed in binary notation or binary code **3** (of a compound or molecule) containing atoms of two different elements ▷ *n*, *pl* -**ries 4** something composed of two parts or things **5** *astronomy* See **binary star** [c16: from Late Latin *bīnārius*; see BIN-]

binary code *n computing* the representation of each one of a set of numbers, letters, etc, as a unique sequence of bits, as in ASCII

binary notation *or* **binary system** *n* a number system having a base of two, numbers being expressed by sequences of the digits 0 and 1: used in computing, as 0 and 1 can be represented electrically as *off* and *on*

binary number *n* a number expressed in binary notation, as 1101.101 = $1 \times 2^3 + 1 \times 2^2 + 0 \times 2^1 + 1 \times 2^0 + 1 \times 2^{-1} + 0 \times 2^{-2} + 1 \times 2^{-3} = 13\frac{5}{8}$

binary star *n* a double star system comprising two stars orbiting around their common centre of mass. A **visual binary** can be seen through a telescope. A **spectroscopic binary** can only be observed by the spectroscopic Doppler shift as each star moves towards or away from the earth

binary weapon *n* a chemical weapon consisting of a projectile containing two substances separately that mix to produce a lethal agent when the projectile is fired

binate ('baɪneɪt) *adj botany* occurring in two parts or in pairs: binate leaves [c19: from New Latin *bīnātus*, probably from Latin *combīnātus* united] > 'bi,nately *adv*

binaural (baɪ'nɔːrəl, bɪn-) *adj* **1** relating to, having, or hearing with both ears **2** employing two separate channels for recording or transmitting sound; so creating an impression of depth

Binchy ('bɪntʃɪ) *n* **Maeve** (meɪv). born 1940, Irish

novelist and journalist; her bestselling novels include *Circle of Friends* (1990) and *Quentins* (2002)

bind (baɪnd) *vb* **binds, binding, bound 1** to make or become fast or secure with or as if with a tie or band **2** (*tr; often foll by up*) to encircle or enclose with a band: *to bind the hair* **3** (*tr*) to place (someone) under obligation; oblige **4** (*tr*) to impose legal obligations or duties upon (a person or party to an agreement) **5** (*tr*) to make (a bargain, agreement, etc) irrevocable; seal **6** (*tr*) to restrain or confine with or as if with ties, as of responsibility or loyalty **7** (*tr*) to place under certain constraints; govern **8** (*tr; often foll by up*) to bandage or swathe **9** to cohere or stick or cause to cohere or stick: *egg binds fat and flour* **10** to make or become compact, stiff, or hard: *frost binds the earth* **11** (*tr*) to enclose and fasten (the pages of a book) between covers **12** (*tr*) to provide (a garment, hem, etc) with a border or edging, as for decoration or to prevent fraying **13** (*tr; sometimes foll by out or over*) to employ as an apprentice; indenture **14** (*intr*) *slang* to complain ▷ *n* **15** something that binds **16** *informal* a difficult or annoying situation ▷ See also **bind over** [Old English *bindan*; related to Old Norse *binda*, Old High German *bintan*, Latin *offendix* BAND², Sanskrit *badhnāti* he binds]

binder ('baɪndə) *n* **1** a firm cover or folder with rings or clasps for holding loose sheets of paper together **2** a material used to bind separate particles together, give an appropriate consistency, or facilitate adhesion to a surface **3** a person who binds books; bookbinder **4** something used to fasten or tie, such as rope or twine **5** Also called: **reaper binder** *obsolete* a machine for cutting grain and binding it into bundles or sheaves **6** an informal agreement giving insurance coverage pending formal issue of a policy

bindery ('baɪndərɪ) *n*, *pl* **-eries** a place in which books are bound

bindi-eye ('bɪndɪ,aɪ) *n Austral* **1** any of various small weedy Australian herbaceous plants of the genus *Calotis*, with burlike fruits: family *Asteraceae* (composites) **2** any bur or prickle [c20: perhaps from a native Australian language]

binding ('baɪndɪŋ) *n* **1** anything that binds or fastens **2** the covering within which the pages of a book are bound **3** the material or tape used for binding hems, etc ▷ *adj* **4** imposing an obligation or duty **5** causing hindrance; restrictive

bind over *vb* (*tr, adverb*) to place (a person) under a legal obligation, such as one to keep the peace

bindweed ('baɪnd,wiːd) *n* any convolvulaceous plant of the genera *Convolvulus* and *Calystegia* that twines around a support. See also **convolvulus**

bine (baɪn) *n* the climbing or twining stem of any of various plants, such as the woodbine or bindweed [c19: variant of BIND]

Binet-Simon scale ('biːneɪ'saɪmən) *n psychol* a test comprising questions and tasks, used to determine the mental age of subjects, usually children. Also called: **Binet scale, Binet test** [c20: named after Alfred *Binet* (1857–1911) + Théodore *Simon* (1873–1961), French psychologists]

binge (bɪndʒ) *n informal* **1** a bout of excessive eating or drinking **2** excessive indulgence in anything: *a shopping binge* ▷ *vb* **binges, bingeing** *or* **binging, binged** (*intr*) **3** to indulge in a binge (esp of eating or drinking) [c19: probably Lincolnshire dialect *binge* to soak]

binge drinking *n* the practice of drinking excessive amounts of alcohol regularly ▷ **binge drinker** *n*

Bingen ('bɪŋən) *n* a town in W Germany on the Rhine: wine trade and tourist centre. Pop: 24 716 (2003 est)

bingo ('bɪŋɡəʊ) *n*, *pl* **-gos** a gambling game, usually played with several people, in which numbers selected at random are called out and the players cover the numbers on their individual cards. The first to cover a given arrangement of numbers is the winner [c19: perhaps from *bing*, imitative of a bell ringing to mark the win]

bin Laden (,bɪn'lɑːdən) *n* **Osama** (ʊ'saːmə). born 1957, Saudi-born leader of the al-Qaida terrorist network: presumed architect of the terrorist attacks on New York

and Washington of September 11 2001

bin liner *n* a plastic bag used to line the inside of a rubbish bin

binman ('bɪn,mæn, 'bɪnmən) *n*, *pl* **-men** another name for: **dustman**

binnacle ('bɪnəkʰl) *n* a housing for a ship's compass [c17: changed from c15 *bitakle*, from Portuguese *bitácula*, from Late Latin *habitāculum* dwelling-place, from Latin *habitāre* to inhabit; spelling influenced by BIN]

Binnig (German 'bɪnɪg) *n* **Gerd (Karl)**. born 1947, German physicist: shared the Nobel prize for physics (1986) for work on the superconductivity of semiconductors and development of the scanning tunnelling microscope

binocular (bɪ'nɒkjʊlə, baɪ-) *adj* involving, relating to, seeing with or intended for both eyes: *binocular vision* [c18: from BI-¹ + Latin *oculus* eye]

binoculars (bɪ'nɒkjʊləz, baɪ-) *pl n* an optical instrument for use with both eyes, consisting of two small telescopes joined together

binomial (baɪ'nəʊmɪəl) *n* **1** a mathematical expression consisting of two terms, such as $3x + 2y$ **2** a two-part taxonomic name for an animal or plant ▷ *adj* **3** referring to two names or terms [c16: from Medieval Latin *binōmius* from BI-¹ + Latin *nōmen* NAME] ▷ **bi'nomially** *adv*

binomial distribution *n* a statistical distribution giving the probability of obtaining a specified number of successes in a specified number of independent trials of an experiment with a constant probability of success in each. Symbol: $Bi(n, p)$, where n is the number of trials and p the probability of success in each

binomial theorem *n* a mathematical theorem that gives the expansion of any binomial raised to a positive integral power, n. It contains $n + 1$ terms: $(x + a)^n = x^n + nx^{n-1}a + [n(n-1)/2] x^{n-2}a^2 +...+ (^n_k) x^{n-k}a^k + ... + a^n$, where $(^n_k) = n!/(n-k)!k!$, the number of combinations of k items selected from n

bint (bɪnt) *n offensive, slang* a derogatory term for **girl, woman** [c19: from Arabic, literally: daughter]

binturong ('bɪntjʊ,rɒŋ, bɪn'tjʊərɒŋ) *n* an arboreal SE Asian viverrine mammal, *Arctictis binturong*, closely related to the palm civets but larger and having long shaggy black hair [from Malay]

Binyon ('bɪnjən) *n* **(Robert) Laurence**. 1869–1943, British poet and art historian, best known for his elegiac war poems "For the Fallen" (1914) and "The Burning of the Leaves" (1944)

bio- *or before a vowel* **bi-** *combining form* **1** indicating or involving life or living organisms: *biogenesis; biolysis* **2** indicating a human life or career: *biography; biopic* [from Greek *bios* life]

bioactive (,baɪəʊ'æktɪv) *adj* (of a substance) having or producing an effect on living tissue ▷ **bioac'tivity** *n*

bioassay (,baɪəʊə'seɪ, -'æseɪ) *n* **1** a method of determining the concentration, activity, or effect of a change to a substance by testing its effect on a living organism and comparing this with the activity of an agreed standard ▷ *vb* (,baɪəʊə'seɪ) **2** (*tr*) to subject to a bioassay

bioastronautics (,baɪəʊ,æstrə'nɔːtɪks) *n* (*functioning as singular*) the study of the effects of space flight on living organisms

biobank ('baɪəʊ,bæŋk) *n* any large store of human biological samples for research into the genetic and environmental causes of disease [c20: from BIO- + BANK¹]

Bío-Bío (Spanish 'biːo'biːo) *n* a river in central Chile, rising in the Andes and flowing northwest to the Pacific. Length: about 390 km (240 miles)

biochemical oxygen demand *n* a measure of the organic pollution of water: the amount of oxygen, in mg per litre of water, absorbed by a sample kept at 20°C for five days. Abbreviation: BOD

biochemistry (,baɪəʊ'kɛmɪstrɪ) *n* the study of the chemical compounds, reactions, etc, occurring in living organisms ▷ **bio'chemical** *adj* ▷ **bio'chemist** *n*

biochip ('baɪə,tʃɪp) *n* a small glass or silicon plate containing an array of biochemical molecules or structures, used as a biosensor or in gene sequencing

biocide ('baɪə,saɪd) *n* a chemical, such as a pesticide, capable of killing living organisms ▷ **bio'cidal** *adj*

biocoenology or **biocenology** (ˌbaɪəʊsɪˈnɒlədʒɪ) n the branch of ecology concerned with the relationships and interactions between the members of a natural community [c20: from BIO- + ceno-, from Greek koinos common + -LOGY]

biocomputing (ˌbaɪəʊˌkəmˈpjuːtɪŋ) n the application of computing to problems in biology, biochemistry, and genetics

biodata (ˈbaɪəʊˌdeɪtə, -ˌdɑːtə) n information regarding an individual's education and work history, esp in the context of a selection process [c20: from BIO(GRAPHICAL) + DATA]

biodegradable (ˌbaɪəʊdɪˈɡreɪdəbᵊl) adj (of sewage constituents, packaging material, etc) capable of being decomposed by bacteria or other biological means > **biodegradability** (ˌbaɪəʊˌdɛɡreɪdɪˈbɪlɪtɪ) n

biodiesel (ˈbaɪəʊˌdiːzᵊl) n a biofuel intended for use in diesel engines

biodiversity (ˌbaɪəʊdaɪˈvɜːsɪtɪ) n the existence of a wide variety of plant and animal species in their natural environments, which is the aim of conservationists concerned about the indiscriminate destruction of rainforests and other habitats

bioengineering (ˌbaɪəʊˌɛndʒɪˈnɪərɪŋ) n 1 the design and manufacture of aids, such as artificial limbs, to rectify defective body functions 2 the design, manufacture, and maintenance of engineering equipment used in biosynthetic processes, such as fermentation > ˌbioˌengiˈneer n

bioethanol (ˌbaɪəʊˈɛθənɒl) n a biofuel based on alcohol which may be combined with petrol for use in vehicles

bioethics (ˌbaɪəʊˈɛθɪks) n (functioning as singular) the study of ethical problems arising from biological research and its applications in such fields as organ transplantation, genetic engineering, or artificial insemination

biofeedback (ˌbaɪəʊˈfiːdbæk) n physiol, psychol a technique for teaching the control of autonomic functions, such as the rate of heartbeat or breathing, by recording the activity and presenting it (usually visually) so that the person can know the state of the autonomic function he or she is learning to control

biofuel (ˈbaɪəʊˌfjʊəl) n a gaseous, liquid, or solid substance of biological origin that is used as a fuel

biog. abbreviation 1 biographical 2 biography

biogenesis (ˌbaɪəʊˈdʒɛnɪsɪs) n the principle that a living organism must originate from a parent organism similar to itself > ˌbiogeˈnetic or ˌbiogeˈnetical adj

biogenic (ˌbaɪəʊˈdʒɛnɪk) adj produced or originating from a living organism

biography (baɪˈɒɡrəfɪ) n, pl -phies 1 an account of a person's life by another 2 such accounts collectively > biˈographer n > biographical (ˌbaɪəˈɡræfɪkᵊl) or archaic ˌbioˈgraphic adj

bioindustry (ˈbaɪəʊˌɪndəstrɪ) n, pl -tries an industry that makes use of biotechnology and other advanced life science methodologies in the creation or alteration of life forms or processes

bioinformatics (ˌbaɪəʊˌɪnfəˈmætɪks) n (functioning as singular) the branch of information science concerned with large databases of biochemical or pharmaceutical information

Bioko (baɪˈəʊkəʊ) n an island in the Gulf of Guinea, off the coast of Cameroon: part of Equatorial Guinea. Capital: Malabo. Area: 2017 sq km (786 sq miles). Former names: Fernando Po, Macías Nguema

biol. abbreviation 1 biological 2 biology

biological (ˌbaɪəˈlɒdʒɪkᵊl) adj 1 of or relating to biology 2 (of a detergent) containing enzymes said to be capable of removing stains of organic origin from items to be washed ▷ n 3 (usually plural) a drug, such as a vaccine, that is derived from a living organism > ˌbioˈlogically adv

biological clock n 1 an inherent periodicity in the physiological processes of living organisms that is not dependent on the periodicity of external factors 2 the hypothetical mechanism responsible for this periodicity ▷ See also **circadian**

biological control n the control of destructive organisms by the use of other organisms, such as the natural predators of the pests

biological warfare n the use of living organisms or their toxic products to induce death or incapacity in humans and animals and damage to plant crops, etc

biology (baɪˈɒlədʒɪ) n the study of living organisms, including their structure, functioning, evolution, distribution, and interrelationships > biˈologist n

bioluminescence (ˌbaɪəʊˌluːmɪˈnɛsəns) n the production of light by living organisms as a result of the oxidation of a light-producing substance (luciferin) by the enzyme luciferase: occurs in many marine organisms, insects such as the firefly, etc > ˌbioˌlumiˈnescent adj

biomass (ˈbaɪəʊˌmæs) n the total number of living organisms in a given area, expressed in terms of living or dry weight per unit area

biomathematics (ˌbaɪəʊˌmæθəˈmætɪks, -ˌmæθˈmæt-) n (functioning as singular) the study of the application of mathematics to biology

biomechanics (ˌbaɪəʊmɪˈkænɪks) n (functioning as singular) the study of the mechanics of the movement of living organisms

biomedical (ˌbaɪəʊˈmɛdɪkᵊl) adj of or relating to biology and medicine or biomedicine

biomedicine (ˌbaɪəʊˈmɛdɪsɪn, -ˈmɛdsɪn) n 1 the medical study of the effects of unusual environmental stress on human beings, esp in connection with space travel 2 the study of herbal remedies

biometric (ˌbaɪəʊˈmɛtrɪk) adj 1 a relating to the analysis of biological data using statistical and mathematical methods b relating to digital scanning of the physiological or behavioural characteristics of individuals as a means of identification: biometric fingerprinting 2 relating to the statistical calculation of the probable duration of human life

biometry (baɪˈɒmɪtrɪ) or **biometrics** (ˌbaɪəˈmɛtrɪks) n (functioning as singular) the analysis of biological data using mathematical and statistical methods

biomorph (ˈbaɪəʊˌmɔːf) n a set of two-dimensional branching biomorphic images that can be used to illustrate evolutionary concepts

biomorphic (ˌbaɪəʊˈmɔːfɪk) adj having the form of a living organism

bionic (baɪˈɒnɪk) adj 1 of or relating to bionics 2 (in science fiction) having certain physiological functions augmented or replaced by electronic equipment

bionics (baɪˈɒnɪks) n (functioning as singular) 1 the study of certain biological functions, esp those relating to the brain, that are applicable to the development of electronic equipment, such as computer hardware, designed to operate in a similar manner 2 the technique of replacing a limb or body part by an artificial limb or part that is electronically or mechanically powered [c20: from BIO- + (ELECTR)ONICS]

bionomics (ˌbaɪəˈnɒmɪks) n (functioning as singular) a less common name for **ecology** (senses 1, 2) [c19: from BIO- + nomics on pattern of ECONOMICS] > ˌbioˈnomic adj > bionomist (baɪˈɒnəmɪst) n

bio-organism n a dangerous fast-proliferating organism that could be used as the basis of a biological weapon

biophysics (ˌbaɪəʊˈfɪzɪks) n (functioning as singular) the physics of biological processes and the application of methods used in physics to biology > ˌbioˈphysical adj > ˌbioˈphysically adv > biophysicist (ˌbaɪəʊˈfɪzɪsɪst) n

biopic (ˈbaɪəʊˌpɪk) n informal a film based on the life of a famous person, esp one giving a popular treatment [c20: from bio(graphical) + pic(ture)]

bioprospecting (ˌbaɪəʊˈprɒspɛktɪŋ) n searching for plant or animal species for use as a source of commercially exploitable products, such as medicinal drugs

biopsy (ˈbaɪɒpsɪ) n, pl -sies examination, esp under a microscope, of tissue from a living body to determine the cause or extent of a disease [c20: from BIO- + Greek opsis sight]

biorhythm (ˈbaɪəʊˌrɪðəm) n a cyclically recurring pattern of physiological states in an organism or organ, such as alpha rhythm or circadian rhythm; believed by

b

some to affect physical and mental states and behaviour

bioscope ('baɪə,skəʊp) *n* **1** a kind of early film projector **2** a South African word for **cinema**

bioscopy (baɪ'ɒskəpɪ) *n, pl* **-pies** examination of a body to determine whether it is alive

-biosis *n combining form* indicating a specified mode of life [New Latin, from Greek *biōsis*; see BIO-, -OSIS] > **-biotic** *adj combining form*

biosolids ('baɪəʊ,sɒlɪdz) *pl n* semisolid or solid organic material obtained from the recycling of sewage, used esp as a fertilizer

biosphere ('baɪə,sfɪə) *n* the part of the earth's surface and atmosphere inhabited by living things

biosurgery ('baɪəʊ,sɜːdʒərɪ) *n* the use of live sterile maggots to treat patients with infected wounds

biosynthesis (,baɪəʊ'sɪnθɪsɪs) *n* the formation of complex compounds from simple substances by living organisms > biosynthetic (,baɪəʊsɪn'θɛtɪk) *adj* > ,biosyn'thetically *adv*

biotech ('baɪəʊ,tɛk) *n* **a** short for **biotechnology** **b** (*as modifier*): *a biotech company*

biotechnology (,baɪəʊtɛk'nɒlədʒɪ) *n* (in industry) the technique of using microorganisms, such as bacteria, to perform chemical processing, such as waste recycling, or to produce other materials, such as beer and wine, cheese, antibiotics, and (using genetic engineering) hormones, vaccines, etc

biotic (baɪ'ɒtɪk) *adj* of or relating to living organisms [c17: from Greek *biotikos*, from *bios* life]

biotin ('baɪətɪn) *n* a vitamin of the B complex, abundant in egg yolk and liver, deficiency of which causes dermatitis and loss of hair. Formula: $C_{10}H_{16}N_2O_3S$ [c20: *biot-* from Greek *biotē* life, way of life + -IN]

bipartisan (,baɪpɑː'tɪzæn, baɪ'pɑːtɪ,zæn) *adj* consisting of or supported by two political parties > ,biparti'sanship *n*

bipartite (baɪ'pɑːtaɪt) *adj* **1** consisting of or having two parts **2** affecting or made by two parties; bilateral **3** *botany* (esp of some leaves) divided into two parts almost to the base > bi'partitely *adv* > bipartition (,baɪpɑː'tɪʃən) *n*

biped *n* ('baɪpɛd) **1** any animal with two feet ▷ *adj* Also: bipedal (baɪ'piːdəl, -'pɛdəl) **2** having two feet

bipinnate (baɪ'pɪn,eɪt) *adj* (of pinnate leaves) having the leaflets themselves divided into smaller leaflets > bi'pin,nately *adv*

biplane ('baɪ,pleɪn) *n* a type of aeroplane having two sets of wings, one above the other

bipolar (baɪ'pəʊlə) *adj* **1** having two poles: *a bipolar dynamo; a bipolar neuron* **2** relating to or found at the North and South Poles **3** having or characterized by two opposed opinions, natures, etc **4** (of a transistor) utilizing both majority and minority charge carriers > bi'polarity *n*

bipolar disorder, bipolar affective disorder *or* **bipolar syndrome** *n* a mental health problem characterized by an alternation between extreme euphoria and deep depression

biprism ('baɪ,prɪzəm) *n* a prism having a highly obtuse angle to facilitate beam splitting

biquadratic (,baɪkwɒ'drætɪk) *maths* ▷ *adj* Also: quartic **1** of or relating to the fourth power ▷ *n* **2** a biquadratic equation, such as $x^4 + x + 6 = 0$

biracial (baɪ'reɪʃəl) *adj* for, representing, or including members of two races, esp White and Black > bi'racialism *n*

birch (bɜːtʃ) *n* **1** any betulaceous tree or shrub of the genus *Betula*, having thin peeling bark. See also **silver birch 2** the hard close-grained wood of any of these trees **3** the birch a bundle of birch twigs or a birch rod used, esp formerly, for flogging offenders ▷ *adj* **4** of, relating to, or belonging to the birch **5** consisting or made of birch ▷ *vb* **6** (*tr*) to flog with a birch [Old English *bierce*; related to Old High German *birihha*, Sanskrit *bhūrja*] > 'birchen *adj*

birchbark biting ('bɜːtʃ,bɑːk) *n* a Native Canadian craft in which designs are bitten onto bark from birch trees

bird (bɜːd) *n* **1** any warm-blooded egg-laying vertebrate of the class *Aves*, characterized by a body covering of feathers and forelimbs modified as wings. Birds vary in

size between the ostrich and the humming bird **2** *informal* a person (usually preceded by a qualifying adjective, as in the phrases **rare bird, odd bird, clever bird**) **3** *slang, chiefly Brit* a girl or young woman, esp one's girlfriend **4** *slang* prison or a term in prison (esp in the phrase **do bird**; shortened from *birdlime*, rhyming slang for *time*) **5** **a bird in the hand** something definite or certain **6** **birds of a feather** people with the same characteristics, ideas, interests, etc **7** **get the bird** *informal* **a** to be fired or dismissed **b** (esp of a public performer) to be hissed at, booed, or derided **8** **kill two birds with one stone** to accomplish two things with one action **9** **for the birds** *or* **strictly for the birds** *informal* deserving of disdain or contempt; not important [Old English *bridd*, of unknown origin]

Bird (bɜːd) *n* nickname of (Charlie) **Parker**

birdbath ('bɜːd,bɑːθ) *n* a small basin or trough for birds to bathe in, usually in a garden

bird-brained *adj informal* silly; stupid

birdcage ('bɜːd,keɪdʒ) *n* **1** a wire or wicker cage in which captive birds are kept **2** *Austral & NZ* an area on a racecourse where horses parade before a race **3** *NZ inf* a second-hand car dealer's yard

bird call *n* **1** the characteristic call or song of a bird **2** an imitation of this

bird flu *n* a form of influenza occurring in poultry mainly in Japan, China and Southeast Asia, caused by a virus capable of spreading to humans. Also called: avian flu

birdie ('bɜːdɪ) *n* **1** *golf* a score of one stroke under par for a hole **2** *informal* a bird, esp a small bird ▷ *vb* **3** (*tr*) *golf* to play (a hole) in one stroke under par

birding ('bɜːdɪŋ) *n* another name for **birdwatching**

birdlime ('bɜːd,laɪm) *n* a sticky substance, prepared from holly, mistletoe, or other plants, smeared on twigs to catch small birds ▷ *vb* **1** (*tr*) to smear (twigs) with birdlime to catch (small birds)

bird-nesting *or* **birds'-nesting** *n* searching for birds' nests as a hobby, often to steal the eggs

bird of paradise *n* **1** any songbird of the family *Paradisaeidae* of New Guinea and neighbouring regions, the males of which have brilliantly coloured ornate plumage **2** **bird-of-paradise flower** any of various banana-like plants of the genus *Strelitzia*, esp *S. reginae*, that are native to tropical southern Africa and South America and have purple bracts and large orange or yellow flowers resembling birds' heads: family *Strelitziaceae*

bird of passage *n* **1** a bird that migrates seasonally **2** a transient person or one who roams about

bird of prey *n* a bird, such as a hawk, eagle, or owl, that hunts and kills other animals, esp vertebrates, for food. It has strong talons and a sharp hooked bill

birdseed ('bɜːd,siːd) *n* a mixture of various kinds of seeds for feeding cagebirds

bird's-eye *adj* **1 a** seen or photographed from high above **b** summarizing the main points of a topic; summary (esp in the phrase **bird's-eye view**) **2** having markings resembling birds' eyes

bird's-eye chilli *n* a small red hot-tasting chilli

bird's-foot *or* **bird-foot** *n, pl* **-foots** any of various other plants whose flowers, leaves, or pods resemble a bird's foot or claw

birdshot ('bɜːd,ʃɒt) *n* small pellets designed for shooting birds

bird strike *n* a collision of an aircraft with a bird

bird table *n* a table or platform in the open on which food for birds may be placed

bird-watcher *n* a person who studies wild birds in their natural surroundings > 'bird-,watching *n*

birefringence (,baɪrɪ'frɪndʒəns) *n* another name for **double refraction** > ,bire'fringent *adj*

bireme ('baɪriːm) *n* an ancient galley having two banks of oars [c17: from Latin *birēmus*, from BI-[1] + -*rēmus* oar]

Birendra Bir Bikram Shah Dev (bɪ'rɛndrə bɪə 'bɪkræm ʃɑː dɛv) *n* 1945–2001, king of Nepal (1972–2001): he, his queen, and six other members of the royal family were shot dead by his son, Crown Prince Dipendra, who then committed suicide

biretta or **berretta** (bɪ'rɛtə) n RC Church a stiff clerical cap having either three or four upright pieces projecting outwards from the centre to the edge: coloured black for priests, purple for bishops, red for cardinals, and white for certain members of religious orders [c16: from Italian berretta, from Old Provençal berret, from Late Latin birrus hooded cape]

Birgitta (bɪə'gɪtə) n Saint Birgitta See **Bridget** (sense 2)

Birkbeck ('bɜːkbɛk) n George. 1776–1841, British educationalist, who helped to establish vocational training for working men: founder and first president of the London Mechanics Institute (1824), which later became Birkbeck College

Birkenhead[1] (,bɜːkən'hɛd) n a port in NW England, in Wirral unitary authority, Merseyside: former shipbuilding centre. Pop: 83 729 (2001)

Birkenhead[2] ('bɜːkən,hɛd) n Frederick Edwin Smith, 1st Earl of, known as F. E. Smith. 1872–1930, British Conservative statesman, lawyer, and orator

birl (bɜːl; Scot bɪrl) vb 1 Scot to spin; twirl 2 US & Canadian to cause (a floating log) to spin using the feet while standing on it, esp as a sport among lumberjacks ▷ n 3 a variant spelling of **burl**[2] [c18: probably imitative and influenced by WHIRL and HURL]

Birmingham ('bɜːmɪŋəm) n 1 an industrial city in central England, in Birmingham unitary authority, in the West Midlands: the second largest city in Great Britain; two cathedrals; three universities (1900, 1966, 1992). Pop: 970 892 (2001). Related adjective: (informal) **brummie** 2 a unitary authority in central England, in the West Midlands. Pop: 992 100 (2003 est). Area: 283 sq km (109 sq miles) 3 ('bɜːmɪŋ,hæm) an industrial city in N central Alabama: rich local deposits of coal, iron ore, and other minerals. Pop: 236 620 (2003 est)

Biro ('baɪrəʊ) n, pl -ros trademark Brit a kind of ballpoint [c20: named after Laszlo Bíró (1900–85), Hungarian inventor]

Birobidzhan or **Birobijan** (Russian birəbid'ʒan) n 1 a city in SE Russia: capital of the Jewish Autonomous Region. Pop: 77 250 (2002) 2 another name for the **Jewish Autonomous Region**

birth (bɜːθ) n 1 the process of bearing young; parturition; childbirth 2 the act or fact of being born; nativity 3 the coming into existence of something; origin 4 ancestry; lineage: of high birth 5 natural or inherited talent: an artist by birth 6 give birth a to bear (offspring) b to produce, originate, or create (an idea, plan, etc) ▷ vb (tr) rare 7 to bear or bring forth (a child) [c12: from Old Norse byrth; related to Gothic gabaurths, Old Swedish byrdh, Old High German berd child; see BEAR[1], BAIRN]

birth certificate n an official form giving details of the time and place of a person's birth, and his or her name, sex, mother's name and (usually) father's name

birth control n limitation of child-bearing by means of contraception

birthday ('bɜːθ,deɪ) n 1 a an anniversary of the day of one's birth b (as modifier): birthday present 2 the day on which a person was born

birthing ball n a large soft rubber ball used by women during childbirth to give support and to aid pain relief

birthing centre ('bɜːθɪŋ) n NZ a private maternity hospital

birthing pool n a large bath in which a woman can give birth

birthmark ('bɜːθ,mɑːk) n a blemish or new growth on skin formed before birth, usually brown or dark red; naevus

birth mother n the woman who gives birth to a child, regardless of whether she is the genetic mother or subsequently brings up the child

birthplace ('bɜːθ,pleɪs) n the place where someone was born or where something originated

birth rate n the ratio of live births in a specified area, group, etc, to the population of that area, etc, usually expressed per 1000 population per year

birthright ('bɜːθ,raɪt) n 1 privileges or possessions that a person has or is believed to be entitled to as soon as he is born 2 the privileges or possessions of a first-born son

3 inheritance; patrimony

birthstone ('bɜːθ,stəʊn) n a precious or semiprecious stone associated with a month or sign of the zodiac and thought to bring luck if worn by a person born in that month or under that sign

Birtwistle ('bɜːt,wɪsəl) n Sir Harrison. born 1934, English composer, whose works include the operas Punch and Judy (1967), The Mask of Orpheus (1984), Gawain (1991), and Exody (1998)

biryani or **biriani** (,bɪrɪ'ɑːnɪ) n any of a variety of Indian dishes made with rice, highly flavoured and coloured with saffron or turmeric, mixed with meat or fish [from Urdu]

bis (bɪs) adv 1 twice; for a second time (used in musical scores to indicate a part to be repeated) ▷ sentence substitute 2 encore! again! [c19: via Italian from Latin, from Old Latin duis]

Bisayas (bi'sajas) pl n the Spanish name for the **Visayan Islands**

Biscay ('bɪskeɪ, -kɪ) n Bay of Biscay a large bay of the Atlantic Ocean between W France and N Spain: notorious for storms

biscuit ('bɪskɪt) n 1 Brit a small flat dry sweet or plain cake of many varieties, baked from a dough. US and Canadian word **cookie** 2 a pale brown or yellowish-grey colour 3 Also called: **bisque** earthenware or porcelain that has been fired but not glazed 4 take the biscuit slang to be regarded (by the speaker) as the most surprising thing that could have occurred [c14: from Old French, from (pain) bescuit twice-cooked (bread), from bes BIS + cuire to cook, from Latin coquere]

bise (biːz) n a cold dry northerly wind in Switzerland and the neighbouring parts of France and Italy, usually in the spring [c14: from Old French, of Germanic origin; compare Old Swedish bīsa whirlwind]

bisect (baɪ'sɛkt) vb 1 (tr) maths to divide into two equal parts 2 to cut or split into two [c17: BI-[1] + -sect from Latin secāre to cut] ▷ **bisection** (baɪ'sɛkʃən) n

bisector (baɪ'sɛktə) n maths a straight line or plane that bisects an angle

bisexual (baɪ'sɛksjʊəl) adj 1 sexually attracted by both men and women 2 showing characteristics of both sexes 3 of or relating to both sexes ▷ n 4 a bisexual organism; a hermaphrodite 5 a bisexual person ▷ **bisexuality** (baɪ,sɛksjʊ'ælɪtɪ) or esp US bi'sexualism n

Bishkek (bɪʃ'kɛk) n the capital of Kyrgyzstan. Pop: 828 000 (2005 est). Also called: Pishpek. Former name (1926–91): Frunze

bishop ('bɪʃəp) n 1 (in the Roman Catholic, Anglican, and Greek Orthodox Churches) a clergyman having spiritual and administrative powers over a diocese or province of the Church. See also **suffragan**. Related adjective: **episcopal** 2 a chesspiece, capable of moving diagonally over any number of unoccupied squares of the same colour 3 mulled wine, usually port, spiced with oranges, cloves, etc [Old English biscop, from Late Latin epīscopus, from Greek episkopos, from EPI- + skopos watcher]

Bishop ('bɪʃəp) n Elizabeth. 1911–79, US poet, who lived in Brazil. Her poetry reflects her travelling experience, esp in the tropics

Bishop Auckland n a town in N England, in central Durham: seat of the bishops of Durham since the 12th century: light industries. Pop: 24 764 (2001)

bishopric ('bɪʃəprɪk) n the see, diocese, or office of a bishop

Bisitun (,biːsɪ'tuːn) n another name for **Behistun**

Bisk (Russian bijsk) n a variant spelling of **Biysk**

Biskra ('bɪskrɑː) n a town and oasis in NE Algeria, in the Sahara. Pop: 204 000 (2005 est)

Bisley ('bɪzlɪ) n a village in SE England, in Surrey: annual meetings of the National Rifle Association

Bismarck[1] ('bɪzmɑːk) n a city in North Dakota, on the Missouri River: the state capital. Pop: 56 344 (2003 est)

Bismarck[2] (German 'bɪsmark) n Prince Otto (Eduard Leopold) von ('ɔto fɔn), called the Iron Chancellor. 1815–98, German statesman; prime minister of Prussia (1862–90). Under his leadership Prussia defeated Austria and France, and Germany was united. In 1871 he became the first chancellor of the German Reich

b

Bismarck Archipelago *n* a group of over 200 islands in the SW Pacific, northeast of New Guinea: part of Papua New Guinea. Main islands: New Britain, New Ireland, Lavongai, and the Admiralty Islands. Chief town: Rabaul, on New Britain. Pop: 566 610 (2000). Area: 49 658 sq km (19 173 sq miles)

bismuth ('bɪzməθ) *n* a brittle pinkish-white crystalline metallic element having low thermal and electrical conductivity, which expands on cooling. It is widely used in alloys, esp low-melting alloys in fire safety devices; its compounds are used in medicines. Symbol: Bi; atomic no: 83; atomic wt: 208.98037; valency: 3 or 5; relative density: 9.747; melting pt: 271.4°C; boiling pt: 1564±5°C [C17: from New Latin *bisemūtum*, from German *Wismut*, of unknown origin]

bison ('baɪsᵊn) *n, pl* **-son** 1 Also called: American bison, buffalo a member of the cattle tribe, *Bison bison*, formerly widely distributed over the prairies of W North America but now confined to reserves and parks, with a massive head, shaggy forequarters, and a humped back 2 Also called: wisent, European bison a closely related and similar animal, *Bison bonasus*, formerly widespread in Europe [C14: from Latin *bisōn*, of Germanic origin; related to Old English *wesand*, Old Norse *vīsundr*]

bisque¹ (bɪsk) *n* a thick rich soup made from shellfish [C17: from French]

bisque² (bɪsk) *n* 1 a pink to yellowish tan colour b (*as modifier*): *a bisque tablecloth* 2 *ceramics* another name for: **biscuit** (sense 3) [C20: shortened from BISCUIT]

bisque³ (bɪsk) *n tennis, golf, croquet* an extra point, stroke, or turn allowed to an inferior player, usually taken when desired [C17: from French, of obscure origin]

Bissau (bɪ'saʊ) *or* **Bissão** (*Portuguese* bi'sãʊn) *n* a port on the Atlantic, the capital of Guinea-Bissau (until 1974 Portuguese Guinea). Pop: 369 000 (2005 est)

bistable (baɪ'steɪbᵊl) *adj* 1 having two stable states: *bistable circuit* ▷ *n* 2 *computing* another name for **flip-flop** (sense 2)

bistort ('bɪstɔːt) *n* 1 Also called: snakeroot, snakeweed, Easter-ledges a Eurasian polygonaceous plant, *Polygonum bistorta*, having leaf stipules fused to form a tube around the stem and a spike of small pink flowers 2 Also called: snakeroot a related plant, *Polygonum bistortoides*, of W North America, with oval clusters of pink or white flowers 3 any of several other plants of the genus *Polygonum* [C16: from French *bistorte*, from Latin *bis* twice + *tortus* from *torquēre* to twist]

bistoury ('bɪstərɪ) *n, pl* **-ries** a long surgical knife with a narrow blade [C15: from Old French *bistorie* dagger, of unknown origin]

bistre *or US* **bister** ('bɪstə) *n* 1 a transparent water-soluble brownish-yellow pigment made by boiling the soot of wood, used for pen and wash drawings 2 a a yellowish-brown to dark brown colour b (*as modifier*): *bistre paint* [C18: from French, of unknown origin]

bistro ('biːstrəʊ) *n, pl* **-tros** a small restaurant [French: of obscure origin; perhaps from Russian *bistro* fast]

bisulphate (baɪ'sʌlˌfeɪt) *n* a salt or ester of sulphuric acid containing the monovalent group -HSO₄ or the ion HSO_4^-

bisulphide (baɪ'sʌlfaɪd) *n* another name for **disulphide**

Bisutun (ˌbiːsʊ'tuːn) *n* another name for **Behistun**

bit¹ (bɪt) *n* 1 a small piece, portion, or quantity 2 a short time or distance 3 *US & Canadian informal* the value of an eighth of a dollar: spoken of only in units of two: *two bits* 4 any small coin 5 short for **bit part** 6 a bit rather; somewhat: *a bit dreary* 7 a bit of a matter: *a bit of a dope* b a considerable amount: *that must take quite a bit of courage* 8 bit by bit gradually 9 do one's bit to make one's expected contribution [Old English *bite* action of biting]

bit² (bɪt) *n* 1 a metal mouthpiece, for controlling a horse on a bridle 2 anything that restrains or curbs 3 a cutting or drilling tool, part, or head in a brace, etc 4 the part of a key that engages the levers of a lock ▷ *vb* bits, bitting, bitted (*tr*) 5 to put a bit in the mouth of (a horse) 6 to restrain; curb [Old English *bita*; related to Old English *bītan* to BITE]

bit³ (bɪt) *vb* the past tense and (archaic) past participle of **bite**

bit⁴ (bɪt) *n maths, computing* 1 a single digit of binary notation, represented either by 0 or by 1 2 the smallest unit of information, indicating the presence or absence of a single feature [C20: from abbreviation of BINARY DIGIT]

bitch (bɪtʃ) *n* 1 a female dog or other female canine animal, such as a wolf 2 *offensive, slang* a malicious, spiteful, or coarse woman 3 *slang* a difficult situation or problem ▷ *vb informal* 4 (*intr*) to complain; grumble 5 to behave (towards) in a spiteful or malicious manner 6 (*tr, often foll by up*) to botch; bungle [Old English *bicce*]

bitchin' ('bɪtʃɪn) *or* **bitching** ('bɪtʃɪn) *US slang adj* 1 wonderful or excellent ▷ *adv* 2 extremely: *bitchin' good*

bitchy ('bɪtʃɪ) *adj* bitchier, bitchiest *informal* characteristic of or behaving like a bitch; malicious; snide > 'bitchiness *n*

bite (baɪt) *vb* bites, biting, bit, bitten 1 to grip, cut off, or tear with or as if with the teeth or jaws 2 (of animals, insects, etc) to injure by puncturing or tearing (the skin or flesh) with the teeth, fangs, etc, esp as a natural characteristic 3 (*tr*) to cut or penetrate, as with a knife 4 (of corrosive material such as acid) to eat away or into 5 to smart or cause to smart; sting 6 (*intr*) *angling* (of a fish) to take or attempt to take the bait or lure 7 to take firm hold of or act effectively upon 8 (*tr*) *informal* to annoy or worry: *what's biting her?* 9 (*often passive*) *slang* to cheat 10 (*tr; often foll by for*) *Austral & NZ slang* to ask (for); scrounge from 11 bite the dust See **dust** (sense 9) 12 put the bite on someone *Austral slang* to ask someone for money ▷ *n* 13 the act of biting 14 a thing or amount bitten off 15 a wound, bruise, or sting inflicted by biting 16 *angling* an attempt by a fish to take the bait or lure 17 a light meal; snack 18 a cutting, stinging, or smarting sensation 19 *dentistry* the angle or manner of contact between the upper and lower teeth when the mouth is closed naturally [Old English *bītan*; related to Latin *findere* to split, Sanskrit *bhedati* he splits] > 'biter *n*

Bithynia (bɪ'θɪnɪə) *n* an ancient country on the Black Sea in NW Asia Minor

biting ('baɪtɪŋ) *adj* 1 piercing; keen: *a biting wind* 2 sarcastic; incisive > 'bitingly *adv*

bitmap ('bɪtˌmæp) *n computing* 1 a picture created on a visual display unit where each pixel corresponds to one or more bits in memory, the number of bits per pixel determining the number of available colours ▷ *vb* -maps, -mapping, -mapped 2 (*tr*) to create a bitmap of

bitmap font *n computing* a font format in which letters and symbols are stored as a pattern of dots. See **outline font**

Bitolj (*Macedonian* 'bitolj) *or* **Bitola** ('biːtəʊlə) *n* a city in SW Macedonia: under Turkish rule from 1382 until 1913 when it was taken by the Serbs. Pop: 77 000 (2005 est)

bit part *n* a very small acting role with few lines to speak

bitstream ('bɪtˌstriːm) *n computing* a sequence of digital data transmitted electronically

bitt (bɪt) *nautical* ▷ *n* 1 one of a pair of strong posts on the deck of a ship for securing mooring and other lines 2 another word for **bollard** (sense 1) ▷ *vb* 3 (*tr*) to secure (a line) by means of a bitt [C14: probably of Scandinavian origin; compare Old Norse *biti* cross beam, Middle High German *bizze* wooden peg]

bitten ('bɪtᵊn) *vb* the past participle of **bite**

bitter ('bɪtə) *adj* 1 having or denoting an unpalatable harsh taste, as the peel of an orange or coffee dregs. See **sour** (sense 1) 2 showing or caused by strong unrelenting hostility or resentment 3 difficult or unpleasant to accept or admit: *a bitter blow* 4 cutting; sarcastic: *bitter words* 5 bitingly cold: *a bitter night* ▷ *adv* 6 very; extremely (esp in the phrase **bitter cold**) ▷ *n* 7 a thing that is bitter 8 *Brit* beer with a high hop content, with a slightly bitter taste [Old English *biter*; related to *bītan* to BITE] > 'bitterly *adv* > 'bitterness *n*

bitter end *n* 1 *nautical* the end of a line, chain, or cable, esp the end secured in the chain locker of a vessel 2 a to the bitter end until the finish of a task, job, or undertaking, however unpleasant or difficult b until final defeat or death [C19: in both senses perhaps from BITT]

b

Bitter Lakes *pl n* two lakes, the **Great Bitter Lake** and Little Bitter Lake in NE Egypt: part of the Suez Canal

bittern ('bɪtən) *n* any wading bird of the genera *Ixobrychus* and *Botaurus*, related and similar to the herons but with shorter legs and neck, a stouter body, and a booming call: family *Ardeidae*, order Ciconiiformes [c14: from Old French *butor*, perhaps from Latin *būtiō* bittern + *taurus* bull; referring to its cry]

bitters ('bɪtəz) *pl n* **1** bitter-tasting spirits of varying alcoholic content flavoured with plant extracts **2** a similar liquid containing a bitter-tasting substance, used as a tonic to stimulate the appetite or improve digestion

bittersweet ('bɪtə,swiːt) *n* **1** any of several North American woody climbing plants of the genus *Celastrus*, esp *C. scandens*, having orange capsules that open to expose scarlet-coated seeds: family Celastraceae **2** another name for **woody nightshade** ▷ *adj* **3** tasting of or being a mixture of bitterness and sweetness **4** pleasant but tinged with sadness

BitTorrent ('bɪt,tɒrənt) *n trademark* a file transfer protocol which enables users to upload and download large files on the internet in the form of software, games, film, video, music, etc, from other users rather than from a central server [c21: from BIT⁴ (sense 1) + TORRENT, the name used in this system for a file that allows the data to be downloaded]

bitty ('bɪtɪ) *adj* **-tier, -tiest 1** lacking unity; disjointed **2** containing bits, sediment, etc ▷ 'bittiness *n*

bitumen ('bɪtjʊmɪn) *n* **1** any of various viscous or solid impure mixtures of hydrocarbons that occur naturally in asphalt, tar, mineral waxes, etc: used as a road surfacing and roofing material **2** the bitumen *Austral & NZ informal* any road with a bitumen surface [c15: from Latin *bitūmen*, perhaps of Celtic origin] ▷ bituminous (bɪ'tjuːmɪnəs) *adj*

bituminize or **bituminise** (bɪ'tjuːmɪ,naɪz) *vb (tr)* to treat with or convert into bitumen ▷ bi,tumini'zation or bi,tumini'sation *n*

bituminous coal *n* a soft black coal, rich in volatile hydrocarbons, that burns with a smoky yellow flame. Fixed carbon content: 46–86 per cent; calorific value: $1.93 \times 10^7 – 3.63 \times 10^7$ J/kg

bivalent (baɪ'veɪlənt, 'bɪvə-) *adj* **1** *chem* another word for **divalent 2** (of homologous chromosomes) associated together in pairs ▷ bi'valency *n*

bivalve ('baɪ,vælv) *n* **1** Also called: pelecypod, lamellibranch any marine or freshwater mollusc of the class *Pelecypoda* (formerly *Bivalvia* or *Lamellibranchia*), having a laterally compressed body, a shell consisting of two hinged valves, and gills for respiration. The group includes clams, cockles, oysters, and mussels ▷ *adj* **2** Also called: pelecypod, lamellibranch of, relating to, or belonging to the *Pelecypoda*

bivouac ('bɪvʊ,æk, 'bɪvwæk) *n* **1** a temporary encampment with few facilities, as used by soldiers, mountaineers, etc ▷ *vb* **-acs, -acking, -acked 2** (intr) to make such an encampment [c18: from French *bivuac*, probably from Swiss German *Beiwacht*, literally: BY + WATCH]

biweekly (baɪ'wiːklɪ) *adj, adv* **1** every two weeks **2** (often avoided because of confusion with sense 1) twice a week; semiweekly. See bi-¹ ▷ *n, pl* **-lies 3** a periodical published every two weeks

biyearly (baɪ'jɪəlɪ) *adj, adv* **1** every two years; biennial or biennially **2** (often avoided because of confusion with sense 1) twice a year; biannual or biannually. See bi-¹

Biysk, Biisk or **Bisk** (*Russian* bijsk) *n* a city in SW Russia, at the foot of the Altai Mountains. Pop: 216 000 (2005 est)

biz (bɪz) *n informal* short for **business**

bizarre (bɪ'zɑː) *adj* odd or unusual, esp in an interesting or amusing way [c17: from French: from Italian *bizzarro* capricious, of uncertain origin] ▷ bi'zarreness *n*

Bizerte (bɪ'zɜːtə; *French* bizɛrt) or **Bizerta** *n* a port in N Tunisia, on the Mediterranean at the canalized outlet of Lake Bizerte. Pop: 118 000 (2005 est)

Bizet ('biːzeɪ; *French* bizɛ) *n* **Georges** (ʒɔrʒ). 1838–75,

French composer, whose works include the opera *Carmen* (1875) and incidental music to Daudet's *L'Arlésienne* (1872)

bizzo ('bɪzəʊ) *n Austral informal* **1** empty and irrelevant talk or ideas; nonsense: *all that bizzo* **2** a businessman's club

bizzy ('bɪzɪ) *n, pl* **-zies** *Brit slang, chiefly Liverpudlian* a policeman [c20: from BUSY]

Björneborg (bjœrnə'bɔrj) *n* the Swedish name for **Pori**

Bjørnson ('bjɜːnsən; *Norwegian* 'bjœrnsᵊn) or **Bjørnstjerne** ('bjɜːnstjɛənə; *Norwegian* 'bjœrnstjɛrnə). 1832–1910, Norwegian poet, dramatist, novelist, theatre director, and newspaper editor; mainly remembered for social dramas, such as *The Bankrupt* (1875): Nobel prize for literature 1903

bk *abbreviation* **1** bank **2** book

Bk *the chemical symbol for* berkelium

bkg *abbreviation* banking

BL *abbreviation* **1** Bachelor of Law **2** Bachelor of Letters **3** Barrister-at-Law **4** British Library

B/L, b/l or **b.l.** *pl* **Bs/L, bs/l** or **bs.l** *abbreviation* bill of lading

blab (blæb) *vb* **blabs, blabbing, blabbed 1** to divulge (secrets) indiscreetly **2** (intr) to chatter thoughtlessly; prattle ▷ *n* **3** a less common word for **blabber** (senses 1, 2) [c14: of Germanic origin; compare Old High German *blabbizōn*, Icelandic *blabbra*]

blabber ('blæbə) *n* **1** a person who blabs **2** idle chatter ▷ *vb* **3** (intr) to talk without thinking; chatter [c15 *blabberen*, probably of imitative origin]

black (blæk) *adj* **1** of the colour of jet or carbon black, having no hue due to the absorption of all or nearly all incident light. See white (sense 1) **2** without light; completely dark **3** without hope or alleviation; gloomy: *the future looked black* **4** very dirty or soiled: *black factory chimneys* **5** angry or resentful: *she gave him black looks* **6** (of a play or other work) dealing with the unpleasant realities of life, esp in a pessimistic or macabre manner: *black comedy* **7** (of coffee or tea) without milk or cream **8** causing, resulting from, or showing great misfortune: *black areas of unemployment* **9 a** wicked or harmful: *a black lie* **b** (in combination): *black-hearted* **10** causing or deserving dishonour or censure: *a black crime* **11** (of the face) purple, as from suffocation **12** *Brit* (of goods, jobs, works, etc) being subject to boycott by trade unionists, esp in support of industrial action elsewhere ▷ *n* **13** a black colour **14** a dye or pigment of or producing this colour **15** black clothing, worn esp as a sign of mourning **16** *chess, draughts* **a** a black or dark-coloured piece or square **b** (usually capital) the player playing with such pieces **17** complete darkness: *the black of the night* **18** a black ball in snooker, etc **19** (in roulette and other gambling games) one of two colours on which players may place even bets, the other being red **20** in the black in credit or without debt **21** *archery* a black ring on a target, between the outer and the blue, scoring three points ▷ *vb* **22** another word for: **blacken 23** (tr) to polish (shoes, etc) with blacking **24** (tr) to bruise so as to make black: *he blacked her eye* **25** (tr) *Brit, Austral & NZ* (of trade unionists) to organize a boycott of (specified goods, jobs, work, etc) in support of industrial action elsewhere ▷ See also **blackout** [Old English *blæc*; related to Old Saxon *blak* ink, Old High German *blakra* to blink] ▷ 'blackish *adj* ▷ 'blackishly *adv* ▷ 'blackly *adv* ▷ 'blackness *n*

Black¹ (blæk) *n* **1** a member of a human population having dark pigmentation of the skin ▷ *adj* **2** of or relating to a Black person or Black people

Black² (blæk) *n* **1** Sir **James** (**Whyte**). born 1924, British biochemist. He discovered beta-blockers and drugs for peptic ulcers: Nobel prize for physiology or medicine 1988 **2 Joseph**. 1728–99, Scottish physician and chemist, noted for his pioneering work on carbon dioxide and heat

blackamoor ('blækə,mʊə, -,mɔː) *n archaic* a Black African or other person with dark skin [c16: see BLACK, MOOR]

black-and-blue *adj* **1** (of the skin) discoloured, as from a bruise **2** feeling pain or soreness, as from a beating

Black and Tans *pl n* the Black and Tans a specially

recruited armed auxiliary police force sent to Ireland in 1921 by the British Government to combat Sinn Féin [name suggested by the colour of their uniforms and the *Black and Tans* hunt in Munster]

black-and-white *n* **1 a** a photograph, picture, sketch, etc, in black, white, and shades of grey rather than in colour **b** (*as modifier*): *black-and-white film* **2** in black and white **a** in print or writing **b** in extremes: *he always saw things in black and white*

black art *n* the black art another name for **black magic**

black-backed gull *n* either of two common black-and-white European coastal gulls, *Larus fuscus* (**lesser black-backed gull**) and *L. marinus* (**great black-backed gull**)

blackball ('blæk,bɔːl) *n* **1** a negative vote or veto **2** a black wooden ball used to indicate disapproval or to veto in a vote ▷ *vb* (*tr*) **3** to vote against in a ballot **4** to exclude (someone) from a group, profession, etc; ostracize [c18: see sense 2]

black bean *n* an Australian leguminous tree, *Castanospermum australe*, having thin smooth bark and yellow or reddish flowers: used in furniture manufacture. Also called: **Moreton Bay chestnut**

black bear *n* **1** American black bear a bear, *Euarctos* (or *Ursus*) *americanus*, inhabiting forests of North America. It is smaller and less ferocious than the brown bear **2** Asiatic black bear a bear, *Selenarctos thibetanus*, of central and E Asia, whose coat is black with a pale V-shaped mark on the chest

Blackbeard ('blæk,bɪəd) *n* nickname of (Edward) **Teach**. See **Teach**

black belt *n* *martial arts* **a** a black belt worn by an instructor or expert competitor in the dan grades, usually from first to fifth dan **b** a person entitled to wear this

blackberry ('blækbərɪ) *n, pl* -ries **1** Also called: **bramble** any of several woody plants of the rosaceous genus *Rubus*, esp *R. fruticosus*, that have thorny stems and black or purple glossy edible berry-like fruits (drupelets) ▷ *vb* -ries, -rying, -ried **2** (*intr*) to gather blackberries

BlackBerry or **Blackberry** *n* *trademark* a hand-held device for sending and receiving e-mail

blackbird ('blæk,bɜːd) *n* **1** a common European thrush, *Turdus merula*, in which the male has a black plumage and yellow bill and the female is brown **2** any of various American orioles having a black plumage, esp any of the genus *Agelaius* **3** *history* a person, esp a South Sea Islander, who was kidnapped and sold as a slave, esp in Australia ▷ *vb* **4** (*tr*) (formerly) to kidnap and sell into slavery

blackboard ('blæk,bɔːd) *n* a hard or rigid surface made of a smooth usually dark substance, used for writing or drawing on with chalk, esp in teaching

black body *n* *physics* a hypothetical body that would be capable of absorbing all the electromagnetic radiation falling on it. Also called: **full radiator**

black book *n* **1** a book containing the names of people to be punished, blacklisted, etc **2** in someone's black books *informal* out of favour with someone

black box *n* **1** a self-contained unit in an electronic or computer system whose circuitry need not be known to understand its function **2** an informal name for **flight recorder**

black boy or **blackboy** ('blæk,bɔɪ) *n* another name for **grass tree** (sense 1)

black bream *n* a dark-coloured food and game fish, *Acanthopagrus australis*, of E Australian seas

blackbuck ('blæk,bʌk) *n* an Indian antelope, *Antilope cervicapra*, the male of which has spiral horns, a dark back, and a white belly

Blackburn ('blækbɜːn) *n* **1** a city in NW England, in Blackburn with Darwen unitary authority, Lancashire: formerly important for textiles, now has mixed industries. Pop: 105 085 (2001) **2** Mount Blackburn a mountain in SE Alaska, the highest peak in the Wrangell Mountains. Height: 5037 m (16 523 ft)

Blackburn with Darwen ('dɑːwɛn) *n* a unitary authority in NW England, in Lancashire. Pop: 139 800 (2003 est). Area: 137 sq km (53 sq miles)

blackbutt ('blæk,bʌt) *n* any of various Australian

eucalyptus trees having rough fibrous bark and hard wood used as timber

blackcap ('blæk,kæp) *n* a brownish-grey Old World warbler, *Sylvia atricapilla*, the male of which has a black crown

Black Caps *pl n* the Black Caps the international cricket team of New Zealand [c20: so named because of the players' black caps]

blackcock ('blæk,kɒk) *n* the male of the black grouse

black cohosh *n* a plant of the ranunculaceous family, *Cimicifuga racemosa*, which is used as a natural alternative to hormone replacement therapy

Black Country *n* the Black Country the formerly heavily industrialized region of central England, northwest of Birmingham

blackcurrant (,blæk'kʌrənt) *n* **1** a N temperate shrub, *Ribes nigrum*, having red or white flowers and small edible black berries: family *Grossulariaceae* **2** the fruit of this shrub

blackdamp ('blæk,dæmp) *n* air that is low in oxygen content and high in carbon dioxide as a result of an explosion in a mine. Also called: **chokedamp**

Black Death *n* the Black Death a form of bubonic plague pandemic in Europe and Asia during the 14th century, when it killed over 50 million people. See **bubonic plague**

black disc *n* a conventional black vinyl gramophone record as opposed to a compact disc

black earth *n* another name for **chernozem**

black economy *n* that portion of the income of a nation that remains illegally undeclared either as a result of payment in kind or as a means of tax avoidance

blacken ('blækən) *vb* **1** to make or become black or dirty **2** (*tr*) to defame; slander (esp in the phrase **blacken someone's name**)

Blackett ('blækɪt) *n* **Patrick Maynard Stuart**, Baron. 1897–1974, English physicist, noted for his work on cosmic radiation and his discovery of the positron. Nobel prize for physics 1948

black eye *n* bruising round the eye

black-eyed Susan *n* any of several North American plants of the genus *Rudbeckia*, esp *R. hirta*, having flower heads of orange-yellow rays and brown-black centres: family *Asteraceae* (composites)

blackface ('blæk,feɪs) *n* **a** a performer made up to imitate a Black person **b** the make-up used by such a performer, usually consisting of burnt cork

blackfish ('blæk,fɪʃ) *n, pl* -fish or -fishes **1** a minnow-like Alaskan freshwater fish, *Dallia pectoralis*, related to the pikes and thought to be able to survive prolonged freezing **2** a female salmon that has recently spawned. See **redfish** (sense 1)

black flag *n* another name for the **Jolly Roger**

blackfly ('blæk,flaɪ) *n, pl* -flies a black aphid, *Aphis fabae*, that infests beans, sugar beet, and other plants. Also called: **bean aphid**

Black Forest *n* the Black Forest a hilly wooded region of SW Germany, in Baden-Württemberg: a popular resort area

Black Friar *n* a Dominican friar

black grouse *n* **1** Also called: **black game** a large N European grouse, *Lyrurus tetrix*, the male of which has a bluish-black plumage and lyre-shaped tail **2** a related and similar species, *Lyrurus mlokosiewiczi*, of W Asia

blackguard ('blægɑːd, -gəd) *n* **1 a** an unprincipled contemptible person; scoundrel **b** (*as modifier*): *blackguard language* ▷ *vb* **2** (*tr*) to ridicule or denounce with abusive language **3** (*intr*) to behave like a blackguard [c16: originally a collective noun referring to the lowest menials in court, camp followers, vagabonds; see BLACK, GUARD] ▷ **'blackguardism** *n* ▷ **'blackguardly** *adj*

blackhead ('blæk,hɛd) *n* **1** a black-tipped plug of fatty matter clogging a pore of the skin, esp the duct of a sebaceous gland **2** any of various birds, esp gulls or ducks, with black plumage on the head

Blackheath ('blækhiːθ) *n* a residential district in SE London, mainly in the boroughs of Lewisham and Greenwich: a large heath formerly notorious for highwaymen

Black Hills *pl n* a group of mountains in W South Dakota and NE Wyoming: famous for the gigantic sculptures of US presidents on the side of Mount Rushmore. Highest peak: Harney Peak, 2207 m (7242 ft)

black hole *astronomy* ▷ *n* **1** an object in space so dense that its escape velocity exceeds the speed of light **2** any place regarded as resembling a black hole in that items or information entering it cannot be retrieved

black ice *n* a thin transparent layer of new ice on a road or similar surface

blacking ('blækɪŋ) *n* any preparation, esp one containing lampblack, for giving a black finish to shoes, metals, etc

Black Isle *n* the Black Isle a peninsula in NE Scotland, in Highland council area, between the Cromarty and Moray Firths [so called because until the late 18th century much of it was uncultivated black moor]

blackjack¹ ('blæk,dʒæk) *chiefly US & Canadian* ▷ *n* **1** a truncheon of leather-covered lead with a flexible shaft ▷ *vb* **2** (*tr*) to hit with or as if with a blackjack **3** (*tr*) to compel (a person) by threats [C19: from BLACK + JACK¹ (implement)]

blackjack² ('blæk,dʒæk) *n cards* pontoon or any of various similar card games [C20: from BLACK + JACK¹ (the knave)]

black knight *n commerce* a person or firm that makes an unwelcome takeover bid for a company. See **grey knight, white knight**

black lead (lɛd) *n* another name for **graphite**

blackleg ('blæklɛg) *n* **1** Also called: scab *Brit* a person who acts against the interests of a trade union, as by continuing to work during a strike or taking over a striker's job ▷ *vb* **-legs, -legging, -legged 2** *Brit* to act against the interests of a trade union, esp by refusing to join a strike

black light *n* the invisible electromagnetic radiation in the ultraviolet and infrared regions of the spectrum

blacklist ('blæk,lɪst) *n* **1** a list of persons or organizations under suspicion, or considered untrustworthy, disloyal, etc, esp one compiled by a government or an organization ▷ *vb* **2** (*tr*) to put on a blacklist

black magic *n* magic used for evil purposes by invoking the power of the devil

blackmail ('blæk,meɪl) *n* **1** the act of attempting to obtain money by intimidation, as by threats to disclose discreditable information **2** the exertion of pressure or threats, esp unfairly, in an attempt to influence someone's actions ▷ *vb* (*tr*) **3** to exact or attempt to exact (money or anything of value) from (a person) by threats or intimidation; extort **4** to attempt to influence the actions of (a person), esp by unfair pressure or threats [C16: from BLACK + Old English *māl* terms]
> **'blackmailer** *n*

Black Maria (mə'raɪə) *n* a police van for transporting prisoners

black mark *n* an indication of disapproval, failure, etc

black market *n* **1** any system in which goods or currencies are sold and bought illegally, esp in violation of controls or rationing **2** the place where such a system operates ▷ *vb* **black-market 3** to sell (goods) on the black market > **black marketeer** *n*

black mass *n* (*sometimes capitals*) a blasphemous travesty of the Christian Mass, performed by practitioners of black magic

black money *n* **1** that part of a nation's income that relates to its black economy **2** any money that a person or organization acquires illegally, as by a means that involves tax evasion **3** *US* money to fund a government project that is concealed in the cost of some other project

Blackmore ('blæk,mɔː) *n* R(ichard) D(oddridge). 1825–1900, English novelist; author of *Lorna Doone* (1869)

Black Mountain *n* the Black Mountain a mountain range in S Wales, in E Carmarthenshire and W Powys. Highest peak: Carmarthen Van, 802 m (2632 ft)

Black Mountains *pl n* a mountain range running from N Monmouthshire and SE Powys (Wales) to SW Herefordshire (England). Highest peak: Waun Fach, 811 m (2660 ft)

Black Muslims *n* (*esp in the US*) a political and religious movement of Black people who adopt the religious practices of Islam and seek to establish a new Black nation

black nightshade *n* a poisonous solanaceous plant, *Solanum nigrum*, a common weed in cultivated land, having small white flowers with backward-curved petals and black berry-like fruits

blackout ('blæk,aʊt) *n* **1** the extinguishing or hiding of all artificial light, esp in a city visible to an enemy attack from the air **2** a momentary loss of consciousness, vision, or memory **3** a temporary electrical power failure or cut **4** the suspension of radio or television broadcasting, as by a strike or for political reasons ▷ *vb* **black out** (*adverb*) **5** (*tr*) to obliterate or extinguish (lights) **6** (*tr*) to create a blackout in (a city etc) **7** (*intr*) to lose vision, consciousness, or memory temporarily **8** (*tr, adverb*) to stop (news, a television programme) from being released or broadcast

black pepper *n* a pungent condiment made by grinding the dried unripe berries, together with their black husks, of the pepper plant *Piper nigrum*

Blackpool ('blæk,puːl) *n* a town and resort in NW England, in Blackpool unitary authority, Lancashire on the Irish Sea: famous for its tower, 158 m (518 ft) high, and its illuminations. Pop: 142 283 (2001)

Black Power *n* a social, economic, and political movement of Black people, esp in the US, to obtain equality with White people

Black Prince *n* the Black Prince See **Edward²** (sense 1)

black pudding *n* a kind of black sausage made from minced pork fat, pig's blood, and other ingredients. Also called: blood pudding

Black Rod *n* (*in Britain*) an officer of the House of Lords and of the Order of the Garter, whose main duty is summoning the Commons at the opening and proroguing of Parliament

Black Sea *n* an inland sea between SE Europe and Asia: connected to the Aegean Sea by the Bosporus, the Sea of Marmara, and the Dardanelles, and to the Sea of Azov by the Kerch Strait. Area: about 415 000 sq km (160 000 sq miles). Ancient names: **Pontus Euxinus, Euxine Sea**

black section *n* (*in Britain*) an unofficial group within the Labour Party in any constituency that represents the interests of local Black people

black sheep *n* a person who is regarded as a disgrace or failure by his family or peer group

Blackshirt ('blæk,ʃɜːt) *n* (*in Europe*) a member of a fascist organization, esp a member of the Italian Fascist party before and during World War II

blacksmith ('blæk,smɪθ) *n* an artisan who works iron with a furnace, anvil, hammer, etc [C14: see BLACK, SMITH]

blacksnake ('blæk,sneɪk) *n* **1** any of several Old World black venomous elapid snakes, esp *Pseudechis porphyriacus* (**Australian blacksnake**) **2** any of various dark nonvenomous snakes, such as *Coluber constrictor* (black racer)

black spot *n* **1** a place on a road where accidents frequently occur **2** any dangerous or difficult place **3** a disease of roses, *Diplocarpon rosae*, that causes circular black blotches on the leaves

Blackstone ('blæk,stəʊn, -stən) *n* Sir William. 1723–80, English jurist noted particularly for his *Commentaries on the Laws of England* (1765–69), which had a profound influence on jurisprudence in the US

black stump *n* the black stump *Austral* an imaginary marker of the extent of civilization (esp in the phrase **beyond the black stump**)

black taxi *n South African* a minibus used to transport workers from the townships to the city centres

blackthorn ('blæk,θɔːn) *n* Also called: sloe a thorny Eurasian rosaceous shrub, *Prunus spinosa*, with black twigs, white flowers, and small sour plumlike fruits

black tie *n* **1** a black bow tie worn with a dinner jacket **2** (*modifier*) denoting an occasion when a dinner jacket should be worn

blacktop ('blæk,tɒp) *n chiefly US & Canadian* a bituminous mixture used for paving

black tracker n Austral an Aboriginal tracker working for the police

black velvet n a mixture of stout and champagne in equal proportions

Black Volta n a river in W Africa, rising in SW Burkina Faso and flowing northeast, then south into Lake Volta: forms part of the border of Ghana with Burkina-Faso and with Côte d'Ivoire. Length: about 800 km (500 miles)

Black Watch n the Black Watch the Royal Highland Regiment in the British army [so called for their dark tartan]

blackwater fever n med a rare and serious complication of malaria, characterized by massive destruction of red blood cells, producing dark red or blackish urine

blackwater rafting n NZ the sport of riding through underground caves on a large rubber tube. Also called: cave tubing

black wattle n 1 a small Australian acacia tree, A. mearnsii, with yellow flowers 2 a tall Australian shrub, Callicoma serratifolia

black widow n an American spider, Latrodectus mactans, the female of which is black with red markings, highly venomous, and commonly eats its mate

Blackwood¹ ('blæk,wʊd) n bridge a conventional bidding sequence of four and five no-trumps, which are requests to the partner to show aces and kings respectively [c20: named after Easeley F. Blackwood, its American inventor]

Blackwood² ('blæk,wʊd) n Algernon (Henry). 1869–1951, British novelist and short- story writer; noted for his supernatural tales

bladder ('blædə) n 1 anatomy a distensible membranous sac, usually containing liquid or gas, esp the urinary bladder 2 an inflatable part of something 3 a hollow vesicular or saclike part or organ in certain plants, such as the bladderwort or bladderwrack [Old English blǣdre] > 'bladdery adj

bladderwort ('blædə,wɜ:t) n any aquatic plant of the genus Utricularia, some of whose leaves are modified as small bladders to trap minute aquatic animals: family Lentibulariaceae

bladderwrack ('blædə,ræk) n any of several seaweeds of the genera Fucus and Ascophyllum, esp F. vesiculosus, that grow in the intertidal regions of rocky shores and have branched brown fronds with air bladders

blade (bleid) n 1 the part of a sharp weapon, tool, etc, that forms the cutting edge 2 the thin flattish part of various tools, implements, etc, as of a propeller, turbine, etc 3 the flattened expanded part of a leaf, sepal, or petal 4 the long narrow leaf of a grass or related plant 5 the striking surface of a bat, club, stick, or oar 6 the metal runner on an ice skate 7 the upper part of the tongue lying directly behind the tip 8 archaic a dashing or swaggering young man 9 short for **shoulder blade** 10 a poetic word for a **sword** or **swordsman** [Old English blæd; related to Old Norse blath leaf, Old High German blat, Latin folium leaf] > 'bladed adj

blae (ble, bleɪ) adj Scot bluish-grey; slate-coloured [from Old Norse blár]

blaeberry ('bleɪbərɪ) n, pl -ries Brit another name for: bilberry (senses 1, 2) [c15: from BLAE + BERRY]

Blaenau Gwent ('blaɪ,naʊ 'gwent) n a county borough of SE Wales, created in 1996 from NW Gwent. Administrative centre: Ebbw Vale. Pop: 68 900 (2003 est). Area: 109 sq km (42 sq miles)

blag (blæg) slang ▷ n 1 a robbery, esp with violence ▷ vb blags, blagging, blagged (tr) 2 to obtain by wheedling or cadging: she blagged free tickets from her mate 3 to snatch (wages, someone's handbag, etc); steal 4 to rob (esp a bank or post office) [c19: of unknown origin] > 'blagger n

Blagoveshchensk (Russian bləgɐ'vjeʃtʃɪnsk) n a city and port in E Russia, in Siberia on the Amur River. Pop: 222 000 (2005 est)

blah or blah blah (blɑ:) n slang worthless or silly talk; claptrap [c20 imit]

blain (bleɪn) n a blister, blotch, or sore on the skin [Old English blegen; related to Middle Low German bleine]

Blair (blɛə) n Tony, full name Anthony Charles Lynton Blair. born 1953, British politician; leader of the Labour Party

from 1994; prime minister (1997–2007)

Blairite ('blɛəraɪt) adj 1 of or relating to the modernizing policies of Tony Blair (full name Anthony Charles Lynton Blair; born 1953), British Labour politician and prime minister from 1997 ▷ n 2 a supporter of the modernizing policies of Tony Blair

Blake (bleɪk) n 1 Sir Peter. born 1932, British painter, a leading exponent of pop art in the 1960s: co-founder of the Brotherhood of Ruralists (1969) 2 Quentin (Saxby). born 1932, British artist, illustrator, and children's writer; noted esp for his illustrations to books by Roald Dahl 3 Robert. 1599–1657, English admiral, who commanded Cromwell's fleet against the Royalists, the Dutch, and the Spanish 4 William. 1757–1827, English poet, painter, engraver, and mystic. His literary works include Songs of Innocence (1789) and Songs of Experience (1794), The Marriage of Heaven and Hell (1793), and Jerusalem (1820). His chief works in the visual arts include engravings of a visionary nature, such as the illustrations for The Book of Job (1826), for Dante's poems, and for his own Prophetic Books (1783–1804)

Blakey ('bleɪkɪ) n Art, full name Arthur Blakey. (1919–90), US Black jazz drummer and leader of the Jazz Messengers band

blame (bleɪm) n 1 responsibility for something that is wrong or deserving censure; culpability 2 an expression of condemnation; reproof ▷ vb (tr) 3 (usually foll by for) to attribute responsibility to; accuse: I blame him for the failure 4 (usually foll by on) to ascribe responsibility for (something) to: I blame the failure on him 5 to find fault with [c12: from Old French blasmer, ultimately from Late Latin blasphēmāre to BLASPHEME] > 'blamable or 'blameable adj > 'blamably or 'blameably adv

blame culture n the tendency to look for one person or organization that can be held responsible for a bad state of affairs, an accident, etc

blameful ('bleɪmfʊl) adj deserving blame; guilty > 'blamefully adv > 'blamefulness n

blameless ('bleɪmlɪs) adj free from blame; innocent > 'blamelessness n

blameworthy ('bleɪm,wɜ:ðɪ) adj deserving disapproval or censure > 'blame,worthiness n

Blanc¹ (French blɑ̃) n 1 Mont Blanc See Mont Blanc 2 Cape Blanc a headland in N Tunisia: the northernmost point of Africa 3 Cape Blanc Also called: Cape Blanco ('blæŋkəʊ) a peninsula in Mauritania, on the Atlantic coast

Blanc² (French blɑ̃) n (Jean Joseph Charles) Louis (lwi). 1811–82, French socialist: author of L'Organisation du travail (1840), in which he advocated the establishment of cooperative workshops subsidized by the state

blanch (blɑ:ntʃ) vb (mainly tr) 1 (also intr) to remove colour from, or (of colour) to be removed; whiten; fade: the sun blanched the carpet; over the years the painting blanched 2 (usually intr) to become or cause to become pale, as with sickness or fear 3 to plunge tomatoes, nuts, etc, into boiling water to loosen the skin 4 to plunge (meat, green vegetables, etc) in boiling water or bring to the boil in water in order to whiten, preserve the natural colour, or reduce or remove a bitter or salty taste 5 to cause (celery, chicory, etc) to grow free of chlorophyll by the exclusion of sunlight [c14: from Old French blanchir from blanc white; see BLANK]

Blanche of Castile (blɑ:ntʃ) n ?1188–1252, queen consort (1223–26) of Louis VIII of France, born in Spain. The mother of Louis IX, she acted as regent during his minority (1226–36) and his absence on a crusade (1248–52)

Blanchett ('blɑ:ntʃət) n Cate (keɪt), full name Catherine Elise Blanchett. born 1969, Australian actress; her films include Elizabeth (1998), the Lord of the Rings trilogy (2001–03), and Notes on a Scandal (2006)

blancmange (blə'mɒnʒ) n a jelly-like dessert, stiffened usually with cornflour and set in a mould [c14: from Old French blanc manger, literally: white food]

Blanco (French blanko) n Serge (sɛrʒ). born 1958, French Rugby Union footballer

bland (blænd) adj 1 devoid of any distinctive or stimulating characteristics; uninteresting; dull: bland *food* **2** gentle and agreeable; suave **3** (of the weather) mild and soothing [c15: from Latin *blandus* flattering] > '**blandly** *adv* > '**blandness** *n*

blandish ('blændɪʃ) *vb* (*tr*) to seek to persuade or influence by mild flattery; coax [c14: from Old French *blandir* from Latin *blandīrī*]

blandishments ('blændɪʃmənts) *pl n* (*rarely singular*) flattery intended to coax or cajole

blank (blæŋk) *adj* **1** (of a writing surface) bearing no marks; not written on **2** (of a form, etc) with spaces left for details to be filled in **3** without ornament or break; unrelieved **4** not filled in; empty; void **5** exhibiting no interest or expression: *a blank look* **6** lacking understanding; confused: *he looked blank even after the explanations* **7** absolute; complete: *blank rejection* **8** devoid of ideas or inspiration: *his mind went blank in the exam* ▷ *n* **9** an emptiness; void; blank space **10** an empty space for writing in, as on a printed form **11** a printed form containing such empty spaces **12** something characterized by incomprehension or mental confusion: *my mind went a complete blank* **13** a mark, often a dash, in place of a word, esp a taboo word **14** short for **blank cartridge 15** a plate or plug used to seal an aperture **16** a piece of material prepared for stamping, punching, forging, etc **17 draw a blank** to get no results from something ▷ *vb* (*tr*) **18** (usually foll by *out*) to cross out, blot, or obscure [c15: from Old French *blanc* white, of Germanic origin; related to Old English *blanca* a white horse] > '**blankness** *n*

blank cartridge *n* a cartridge containing powder but no bullet: used in battle practice or as a signal

blank cheque *n* **1** a signed cheque on which the amount payable has not been specified **2** complete freedom of action

blanket ('blæŋkɪt) *n* **1** a large piece of thick cloth for use as a bed covering, animal covering, etc, enabling a person or animal to retain natural body heat **2** a concealing cover or layer, as of smoke, leaves, or snow **3** (*modifier*) applying to or covering a wide group or variety of people, conditions, situations, etc: *blanket insurance against loss, injury, and theft* **4 born on the wrong side of the blanket** *informal* illegitimate ▷ *vb* (*tr*) **5** to cover with or as if with a blanket; overlie **6** to cover a very wide area, as in a publicity campaign; give blanket coverage **7** (usually foll by *out*) to obscure or suppress [c13: from Old French *blancquete*, from *blanc*; see BLANK]

blanket bath *n* an all-over wash given to a person confined to bed

blanket bog *n* a very acid peat bog, low in nutrients, extending widely over a flat terrain, found in cold wet climates

blanket stitch *n* a strong reinforcing stitch for the edges of blankets and other thick material

blankety ('blæŋkɪtɪ) *adj, adv* a euphemism for any taboo word [c20: from BLANK]

blank verse *n prosody* unrhymed verse, esp in iambic pentameters

Blanqui (*French* blākɪ) *n* **Louis Auguste** (*French* lwi ogyst). 1805–81, French revolutionary, who organized secret socialist societies and preached violent insurrection; he spent over 30 years in prison

Blantyre-Limbe (blæn'taɪə'lɪmbeɪ) *n* a city in S Malawi: largest city in the country; formed in 1956 from the adjoining towns of Blantyre and Limbe. Pop: 647 000 (2005 est)

blare (bleə) *vb* **1** to sound loudly and harshly **2** to proclaim loudly and sensationally ▷ *n* **3** a loud and usually harsh or grating noise [c14: from Middle Dutch *bleren*; of imitative origin]

blarney ('blɑːnɪ) *n* flattering talk [c19: after the BLARNEY STONE]

Blasco Ibáñez (*Spanish* 'blasko i'βaɲeθ) *n* **Vicente** (bi'θente). 1867–1928, Spanish novelist, whose books include *Blood and Sand* (1909) and *The Four Horsemen of the Apocalypse* (1916)

blasé ('blɑːzeɪ) *adj* **1** indifferent to something because of familiarity or surfeit **2** lacking enthusiasm; bored [c19: from French, past participle of *blaser* to cloy]

blaspheme (blæs'fiːm) *vb* **1** (*tr*) to show contempt or disrespect for (God, a divine being, or sacred things), esp in speech **2** (*intr*) to utter profanities, curses, or impious expressions [c14: from Late Latin *blasphēmāre*, from Greek *blasphēmein* from *blasphēmos* BLASPHEMOUS] > **blas'phemer** *n*

blasphemous ('blæsfɪməs) *adj* expressing or involving impiousness or gross irreverence towards God, a divine being, or something sacred [c15: via Late Latin, from Greek *blasphēmos* evil-speaking, from *blapsis* evil + *phēmē* speech]

blasphemy ('blæsfɪmɪ) *n, pl* -mies **1** blasphemous behaviour or language **2** Also called: **blasphemous libel** *law* the crime committed if a person insults, offends, or vilifies the deity, Christ, or the Christian religion

blast (blɑːst) *n* **1** an explosion, as of dynamite **2 a** the rapid movement of air away from the centre of an explosion, combustion of rocket fuel, etc **b** a wave of overpressure caused by an explosion; shock wave **3** the charge of explosive used in a single explosion **4** a sudden strong gust of wind or air **5** a sudden loud sound, as of a trumpet **6** a violent verbal outburst, as of criticism **7** a forcible jet or stream of air, esp one used to intensify the heating effect of a furnace, increase the draught in a steam engine, or break up coal at a coalface **8** any of several diseases of plants and animals, esp one producing withering in plants **9** *US slang* a very enjoyable or thrilling experience: *the party was a blast* **10 full blast** *or* **at full blast** at maximum speed, volume, etc ▷ *interj* **11** *slang* an exclamation of annoyance (esp in phrases such as **blast it!** and **blast him!**) ▷ *vb* **12** to destroy or blow up with explosives, shells, etc **13** to make or cause to make a loud harsh noise **14** to wither or cause to wither; blight or be blighted **15** to criticize severely [Old English *blǣst*, related to Old Norse *blāstr*]

-blast *n combining form* (in biology) indicating an embryonic cell or formative layer: *mesoblast* [from Greek *blastos* bud]

blasted ('blɑːstɪd) *adj* **1** blighted or withered ▷ *adj, adv* (*prenominal*) **2** *slang* (*intensifier*): *a blasted idiot; don't be so blasted cheeky*

blast furnace *n* a vertical cylindrical furnace for smelting iron, copper, lead, and tin ores. The ore, scrap, solid fuel, and slag-forming materials are fed through the top and a blast of preheated air is forced through the charge from the bottom. Metal and slag are run off from the base

blasto- *combining form* (in biology) indicating an embryo or bud or the process of budding [from Greek *blastos*; see -BLAST]

blastoff ('blɑːst,ɒf) *n* **1** the launching of a rocket under its own power **2** the time at which this occurs ▷ *vb* **blast off 3** (*adverb; when tr, usually passive*) (of a rocket, spacemen, etc) to be launched

blastula ('blæstjʊlə) *n, pl* -las *or* -lae (-liː) an early form of an animal embryo that develops from a morula, consisting of a sphere of cells with a central cavity. Also called: **blastosphere** [c19: New Latin; see BLASTO-] > '**blastular** *adj*

blat (blæt) *vb* **blats, blatting, blatted** *US & Canadian* **1** (*intr*) to cry out or bleat like a sheep **2** (*tr*) to utter indiscreetly in a loud voice [c19: of imitative origin]

blatant ('bleɪt⁹nt) *adj* glaringly conspicuous or obvious: *a blatant lie* **1** offensively noticeable **2** offensively noisy [c16: coined by Edmund Spenser; probably influenced by Latin *blatīre* to babble; compare Middle Low German *pladderen*] > '**blatancy** *n*

blather ('blæðə) *Scot or* **blether** *vb* **1** (*intr*) to speak foolishly ▷ *n* **2** foolish talk; nonsense **3** a person who blathers [c15: from Old Norse *blathra*, from *blathr* nonsense]

blatherskite ('blæðə,skaɪt) *n* **1** a talkative silly person **2** foolish talk; nonsense [c17: see BLATHER]

Blavatsky (blə'vætskɪ) *n* **Elena Petrovna** (jɪ'ljenə pɪ'trɔvnə), called *Madame Blavatsky*. 1831–91, Russian theosophist; author of *Isis Unveiled* (1877)

blaxploitation (,blæksplɔɪ'teɪʃən) *n* a genre of films featuring Black stereotypes [c20: from BLA(CK) + (E)XPLOITATION]

Blaydon ('bleɪd⁹n) *n* an industrial town in NE England, in Gateshead unitary authority, Tyne and Wear. Pop: 14 648 (2001)

blaze[1] (bleɪz) n 1 a strong fire or flame 2 a very bright light or glare 3 an outburst (of passion, acclaim, patriotism, etc) 4 brilliance; brightness ▷ vb (intr) 5 to burn fiercely 6 to shine brightly 7 (often foll by up) to become stirred, as with anger or excitement 8 (usually foll by away) to shoot continuously ▷ See also **blazes** [Old English blæse]

blaze[2] (bleɪz) n 1 a mark, usually indicating a path, made on a tree, esp by chipping off the bark 2 a light-coloured marking on the face of a domestic animal, esp a horse ▷ vb (tr) 3 to indicate or mark (a tree, path, etc) with a blaze 4 blaze a trail to explore new territories, areas of knowledge, etc, in such a way that others can follow [c17: probably from Middle Low German bles white marking; compare BLEMISH]

blaze[3] (bleɪz) vb (tr; often foll by abroad) to make widely known; proclaim [c14: from Middle Dutch blāsen, from Old High German blāsan; related to Old Norse blāsa]

blazer ('bleɪzə) n a fairly lightweight jacket, often striped or in the colours of a sports club, school, etc

blazes ('bleɪzɪz) pl n 1 slang a euphemistic word for **hell** 2 informal (intensifier): to run like blazes; what the blazes are you doing?

blazon ('bleɪz°n) vb (tr) 1 (often foll by abroad) to proclaim loudly and publicly 2 heraldry to describe (heraldic arms) in proper terms 3 to draw and colour (heraldic arms) conventionally ▷ n 4 heraldry a conventional description or depiction of heraldic arms [c13: from Old French blason coat of arms] > 'blazoner n

blazonry ('bleɪzənrɪ) n, pl -ries 1 the art or process of describing heraldic arms in proper form 2 heraldic arms collectively 3 colourful or ostentatious display

bldg abbreviation building

bleach (bliːtʃ) vb 1 to make or become white or colourless, as by exposure to sunlight, by the action of chemical agents, etc ▷ n 2 a bleaching agent 3 the act of bleaching [Old English blǣcan; related to Old Norse bleikja, Old High German bleih pale] > 'bleacher n

bleaching powder n a white powder with the odour of chlorine, consisting of chlorinated calcium hydroxide with an approximate formula $CaCl(OCl).4H_2O$. It is used in solution as a bleaching agent and disinfectant. Also called: chloride of lime, chlorinated lime

bleak[1] (bliːk) adj 1 exposed and barren; desolate 2 cold and raw 3 offering little hope or excitement; dismal: a bleak future [Old English blāc bright, pale; related to Old Norse bleikr white, Old High German bleih pale] > 'bleakness n

bleak[2] (bliːk) n any slender silvery European cyprinid fish of the genus Alburnus, esp A. lucidus, occurring in slow-flowing rivers [c15: probably from Old Norse bleikja white colour; related to Old High German bleiche BLEACH]

blear (blɪə) archaic ▷ vb 1 (tr) to make (eyes or sight) dim with or as if with tears; blur ▷ adj 2 a less common word for **bleary** [c13: blere to make dim; related to Middle High German blerre blurred vision]

bleary ('blɪərɪ) adj blearier, bleariest 1 (of eyes or vision) dimmed or blurred, as by tears or tiredness 2 indistinct or unclear > 'bleariness n

bleary-eyed or **blear-eyed** adj with eyes blurred, as with old age or after waking

Bleasdale ('bliːzdeɪl) n Alan. born 1946, British playwright, best known for his television series The Boys From the Blackstuff (1983) and GBH (1991)

bleat (bliːt) vb 1 (intr) (of a sheep, goat, or calf) to utter its characteristic plaintive cry 2 (intr) to speak with any similar sound 3 to whine; whimper ▷ n 4 the characteristic cry of sheep, goats, and young calves 5 any sound similar to this 6 a weak complaint or whine [Old English blǣtan; related to Old High German blāzen, Dutch blaten, Latin flēre to weep; see BLARE] > 'bleater n > 'bleating n, adj

bleb (blɛb) n 1 a fluid-filled blister on the skin 2 a small air bubble [c17: variant of BLOB]

Bledisloe Cup ('blɛdɪsləʊ) n rugby Union a trophy competed for, usually annually, by New Zealand and Australia since 1932 [c20: after Charles Bathurst, 1st

Viscount Bledisloe (1867–1958), Governor General of New Zealand who donated the trophy]

bleed (bliːd) vb bleeds, bleeding, bled 1 (intr) to lose or emit blood 2 (tr) to remove or draw blood from (a person or animal) 3 (intr) to be injured or die, as for a cause or one's country 4 (of plants) to exude (sap or resin), esp from a cut 5 (tr) informal to obtain relatively large amounts of money, goods, etc, esp by extortion 6 (tr) to draw liquid or gas from (a container or enclosed system): to bleed the hydraulic brakes 7 (intr) (of dye or paint) to run or become mixed, as when wet 8 to print or be printed so that text, illustrations, etc, run off the trimmed page 9 one's heart bleeds used to express sympathetic grief, but often used ironically [Old English blēdan; see BLOOD]

bleeder ('bliːdə) n 1 slang a dismissive a despicable person b any person; fellow 2 pathol a nontechnical name for a **haemophiliac**

bleeding ('bliːdɪŋ) adj, adv Brit slang (intensifier): a bleeding fool; it's bleeding beautiful

bleeding heart n 1 any of several plants of the genus Dicentra, esp the widely cultivated Japanese species D. spectabilis, which has finely divided leaves and heart-shaped nodding pink flowers: family Fumariaceae 2 informal a person who is excessively softhearted

bleep (bliːp) n 1 a short high-pitched signal made by an electronic apparatus; beep 2 another word for **bleeper** ▷ vb 3 (intr) to make such a noise 4 (tr) to call (someone) by triggering the bleeper he or she is wearing [c20: of imitative origin]

bleeper ('bliːpə) n a small portable radio receiver, carried esp by doctors, that sounds a coded bleeping signal to call the carrier. Also called: **bleep**

blemish ('blɛmɪʃ) n 1 a defect; flaw; stain ▷ vb 2 (tr) to flaw the perfection of; spoil; tarnish [c14: from Old French blemir to make pale, probably of Germanic origin]

blench (blɛntʃ) vb (intr) to shy away, as in fear; quail [Old English blencan to deceive]

blend (blɛnd) vb 1 to mix or mingle (components) together thoroughly 2 (tr) to mix (different grades or varieties of tea, whisky, tobacco, etc) to produce a particular flavour, consistency, etc 3 (intr) to look good together; harmonize 4 (intr) (esp of colours) to shade imperceptibly into each other ▷ n 5 a mixture or type produced by blending 6 the act of blending 7 Also called: portmanteau word a word formed by joining together the beginning and the end of two other words: "brunch" is a blend of "breakfast" and "lunch" [Old English blandan; related to blendan to deceive, Old Norse blanda, Old High German blantan]

blende (blɛnd) n 1 another name for **sphalerite** 2 any of several sulphide ores, such as antimony sulphide [c17: German Blende, from blenden to deceive, BLIND; so called because it is easily mistaken for galena]

blended learning n education the use of both classroom teaching and on-line learning in education

blender ('blɛndə) n 1 a person or thing that blends 2 Also called: liquidizer a kitchen appliance with blades used for puréeing vegetables, blending liquids, etc

Blenheim ('blɛnɪm) n a village in SW Germany, site of a victory of Anglo-Austrian forces under the Duke of Marlborough and Prince Eugène of Savoy that saved Vienna from the French and Bavarians (1704) during the War of the Spanish Succession

blenny ('blɛnɪ) n, pl -nies any blennioid fish of the family Blenniidae of coastal waters, esp of the genus Blennius, having a tapering scaleless body, a long dorsal fin, and long raylike pelvic fins [c18: from Latin blennius, from Greek blennos slime]

blent (blɛnt) vb archaic or literary a past participle of **blend**

blepharitis (ˌblɛfəˈraɪtɪs) n inflammation of the eyelids [c19: from Greek blephar(on) eyelid + -ITIS]

Blériot (French blerjo) n Louis (lwi). 1872–1936, French aviator and aeronautical engineer: made the first flight across the English Channel (1909)

blesbok or **blesbuck** ('blɛsˌbʌk) n, pl -boks, -bok or -bucks, -buck an antelope, Damaliscus dorcas (or albifrons), of southern Africa. The coat is a deep reddish-brown with a white blaze between the eyes; the horns are lyre-shaped [c19: Afrikaans, from Dutch *bles* BLAZE[2] + *bok* goat, BUCK[1]]

bless (blɛs) *vb* **blesses, blessing, blessed** *or* **blest** (*tr*) **1** to consecrate or render holy, beneficial, or prosperous by means of a religious rite **2** to give honour or glory to (a person or thing) as divine or holy **3** to call upon God to protect; give a benediction to **4** to worship or adore (God); call or hold holy **5** (*often passive*) to grant happiness, health, or prosperity to **6** (*usually passive*) to endow with a talent, beauty, etc **7** *rare* to protect against evil or harm **8 bless!** (*interjection*) an exclamation of well-wishing **9 bless you!** (*interjection*) **a** a traditional phrase said to a person who has just sneezed **b** an exclamation of well-wishing or surprise **10 bless me!, bless my soul!** *or* **God bless my soul!** (*interjection*) an exclamation of surprise [Old English *blǣdsian* to sprinkle with sacrificial blood; related to *blōd* BLOOD]

blessed ('blɛsɪd, blɛst) *adj* **1** made holy by religious ceremony; consecrated **2** worthy of deep reverence or respect **3** *RC Church* (of a person) beatified by the pope **4** characterized by happiness or good fortune **5** bringing great happiness or good fortune **6** a euphemistic word for **damned**: *I'm blessed if I know* > **'blessedly** *adv* > **'blessedness** *n*

Blessed Sacrament *n* *chiefly RC Church* the consecrated elements of the Eucharist

Blessed Virgin *n* *chiefly RC Church* another name for **Mary** (sense 1a)

blessing ('blɛsɪŋ) *n* **1** the act of invoking divine protection or aid **2** the words or ceremony used for this **3** a short prayer of thanksgiving before or after a meal; grace **4** approval; good wishes **5** the bestowal of a divine gift or favour

blest (blɛst) *vb* a past tense and past participle of **bless**

Bletchley Park ('blɛtʃlɪ) *n* the Buckinghamshire estate which was the centre of British code-breaking operations during World War II

blether ('blɛðə) *vb, n* *Scot* a variant spelling of **blather** [c16: from Old Norse *blathra*, from *blathr* nonsense]

blethered ('blɛðəd) *adj* *Northern English dialect* weary

blew (bluː) *vb* the past tense of **blow[1]**

Blida ('bliːdə) *n* a city in N Algeria, on the edge of the Mitidja Plain. Pop: 269 000 (2005 est)

Bligh (blaɪ) *n* **William**. 1754–1817, British admiral; Governor of New South Wales (1806–9), deposed by the New South Wales Corps: as a captain, commander of *H.M.S. Bounty* when the crew mutinied in 1789

blight (blaɪt) *n* **1** any plant disease characterized by withering and shrivelling without rotting **2** any factor, such as bacterial attack or air pollution, that causes the symptoms of blight in plants **3** a person or thing that mars or prevents growth, improvement, or prosperity **4** an ugly urban district ▷ *vb* **5** to cause or suffer a blight **6** (*tr*) to frustrate or disappoint **7** (*tr*) to spoil; destroy [c17: perhaps related to Old English *blǣce* rash; compare BLEACH]

blighter ('blaɪtə) *n* *Brit informal* **1** a fellow: *where's the blighter gone?* **2** a despicable or irritating person or thing

Blighty ('blaɪtɪ) *n* (*sometimes not capital*) *Brit slang* (used esp by troops serving abroad) **1** England; home **2** (esp in World War I) **a** Also called: **a blighty one** a slight wound that causes the recipient to be sent home to England **b** leave in England [c20: from Hindi *bilāyatī* foreign land, England, from Arabic *wilāyat* country, from *waliya* he rules]

blimey ('blaɪmɪ) *interj* *Brit slang* an exclamation of surprise or annoyance [c19: short for *gorblimey* God blind me]

blimp[1] (blɪmp) *n* **1 a** small nonrigid airship, esp one used for observation or as a barrage balloon **2** *films* a soundproof cover fixed over a camera during shooting [c20: probably from (*type*) *B-limp*]

blimp[2] (blɪmp) *n* (*often capital*) *chiefly Brit* a person, esp a military officer, who is stupidly complacent and reactionary. Also called: **Colonel Blimp** [c20: after a character created by Sir David Low (1891–1963), New Zealand-born British cartoonist]

blimp out *vb* (*intr, adverb*) *slang* to become greatly overweight

blind (blaɪnd) *adj* **1 a** unable to see; sightless **b** (*as collective noun*, preceded by *the*): *the blind* **2** (usually foll by *to*) unable or unwilling to understand or discern **3** not based on evidence or determined by reason: *blind hatred* **4** acting or performed without control or preparation **5** done without being able to see, relying on instruments for information **6** hidden from sight: *a blind corner; a blind stitch* **7** closed at one end: *a blind alley* **8** completely lacking awareness or consciousness: *a blind stupor* **9** *informal* very drunk **10** having no openings or outlets: *a blind wall* **11** (intensifier): *not a blind bit of notice* ▷ *adv* **12** without being able to see ahead or using only instruments: *to drive blind; flying blind* **13** without adequate knowledge or information; carelessly: *to buy a house blind* **14 bake blind** to bake (the empty crust of a pie, pastry, etc) by half filling with dried peas, crusts of bread, etc, to keep it in shape ▷ *vb* (*mainly tr*) **15** to deprive of sight permanently or temporarily **16** to deprive of good sense, reason, or judgment **17** to darken; conceal **18** (foll by *with*) to overwhelm by showing detailed knowledge: *to blind somebody with science* ▷ *n* **19** (*modifier*) for or intended to help blind and partially sighted people: *a blind school* **20** a shade for a window, usually on a roller **21** any obstruction or hindrance to sight, light, or air **22** a person, action, or thing that serves to deceive or conceal the truth **23** Also called: **blinder** *Brit dated, slang* a drunken orgy; binge [Old English *blind*; related to Old Norse *blindr*, Old High German *blint*; Lettish *blendu* to see dimly; see BLUNDER] > **'blindly** *adv* > **'blindness** *n*

● USAGE It is preferable to avoid using phrases such as *the blind*. Instead you should talk about *blind and partially sighted people*

blind alley *n* **1** an alley open at one end only; cul-de-sac **2** *informal* a situation in which no further progress can be made

blind date *n* *informal* a social meeting between two people who have not met before

blinder ('blaɪndə) *n* **1** an outstanding performance in sport **2** *Brit slang* another name for **blind** (sense 23)

blinders ('blaɪndəz) *pl n* *US & Canadian* leather sidepieces attached to a horse's bridle to prevent sideways vision. Also called (in Britain and other countries): **blinkers**

blindfold ('blaɪnd,fəʊld) *vb* (*tr*) **1** to prevent (a person or animal) from seeing by covering the eyes ▷ *n* **2** a piece of cloth, bandage, etc, used to cover the eyes ▷ *adj, adv* **3** having the eyes covered with a cloth or bandage **4** *chess* not seeing the board and pieces **5** rash; inconsiderate [changed (c16) through association with FOLD[1] from Old English *blindfellian* to strike blind; see BLIND, FELL[2]]

blinding ('blaɪndɪŋ) *n* **1** sand or grit spread over a road surface to fill up cracks **2** the process of laying blinding ▷ *adj* **3** making one blind or as if blind **4** most noticeable; brilliant or dazzling > **'blindingly** *adv*

blind man's buff *n* a game in which a blindfolded person tries to catch and identify the other players [c16: *buff*, perhaps from Old French *buffe* a blow; see BUFFET[2]]

blind register *n* (in the United Kingdom) a list of those who are blind and are therefore entitled to financial and other benefits

blind side *n* **1** *rugby* the side of the field between the scrum and the nearer touchline **2** the side on which a person's vision is obscured

blindsight ('blaɪnd,saɪt) *n* the ability to respond to visual stimuli without having any conscious visual experience; it can occur after some forms of brain damage

blind spot *n* **1** a small oval-shaped area of the retina in which vision is not experienced. It marks the nonphotosensitive site of entrance into the eyeball of the optic nerve **2** a place or area, as in an auditorium or part of a road, where vision is completely or partially obscured or hearing is difficult or impossible **3** a subject about which a person is ignorant or prejudiced, or an occupation in which he or she is inefficient

blind trust *n* a trust fund that manages the financial affairs of a person without informing him or her of any investments made, usually so that the beneficiary cannot be accused of using public office for private gain

b

b

blindworm ('blaɪnd,wɜːm) n another name for **slowworm**

bling-bling ('blɪŋ,blɪŋ) or **bling** adj **1** slang flashy; ostentatious; glitzy ▷ n **2** ostentatious jewellery [c20: imitative of jewellery clashing together or of light reflecting off jewellery]

blink (blɪŋk) vb **1** to close and immediately reopen (the eyes or an eye), usually involuntarily **2** (intr) to look with the eyes partially closed, as in strong sunlight **3** to shine intermittently, as in signalling, or unsteadily **4** (tr; foll by away, from, etc) to clear the eyes of (dust, tears, etc) **5** (when tr, usually foll by at) to be surprised or amazed **6** (when intr, foll by at) to pretend not to know or see (a fault, injustice, etc) ▷ n **7** the act or an instance of blinking **8** a glance; glimpse **9** short for **iceblink** (sense 1) **10** on the blink slang not working properly [c14: variant of BLENCH¹; related to Middle Dutch blinken to glitter, Danish blinke to wink, Swedish blinka]

blinker ('blɪŋkə) n **1** a flashing light for sending messages, as a warning device, etc, such as a direction indicator on a road vehicle **2** (often plural) a slang word for **eye¹** ▷ **blinkered** adj

blinkers ('blɪŋkəz) pl n (sometimes singular) chiefly Brit leather sidepieces attached to a horse's bridle to prevent sideways vision

blinking ('blɪŋkɪŋ) adj, adv informal (intensifier): a blinking fool; a blinking good film

blip (blɪp) n **1** a repetitive sound, such as that produced by an electronic device, by dripping water, etc **2** Also called: pip the spot of light or a sharply peaked pulse on a radar screen indicating the position of an object **3** a temporary irregularity recorded in performance of something ▷ vb blips, blipping, blipped **4** (intr) to produce such a noise [c20: of imitative origin]

blipvert ('blɪp,vɜːt) n a very short television advertisement [c20: from BLIP + (AD)VERT]

bliss (blɪs) n **1** perfect happiness; serene joy **2** the ecstatic joy of heaven [Old English blīths; related to blīthe BLITHE, Old Saxon blīdsea bliss]

Bliss (blɪs) n Sir **Arthur**. 1891–1975, British composer; Master of the Queen's Musick (1953–75). His works include the Colour Symphony (1922), film and ballet music, and a cello concerto (1970)

blissful ('blɪsfʊl) adj **1** serenely joyful or glad **2** blissful ignorance unawareness or inexperience of something unpleasant ▷ **blissfully** adv ▷ **blissfulness** n

B list n a a category considered to be slightly below the most socially desirable **b** (as modifier): B-list celebrities

blister ('blɪstə) n **1** a small bubble-like elevation of the skin filled with serum, produced as a reaction to a burn, mechanical irritation, etc **2** NZ slang a rebuke ▷ vb **3** to have or cause to have blisters **4** (tr) to attack verbally with great scorn or sarcasm [c13: from Old French blestre, probably from Middle Dutch bluyster blister; see BLAST] ▷ **blistered** adj

blister pack n a type of packet in which small items are displayed and sold, consisting of a transparent dome of plastic or similar material mounted on a firm backing such as cardboard. Also called: bubble pack

BLit abbreviation Bachelor of Literature

blithe (blaɪð) adj **1** very happy or cheerful **2** heedless; casual and indifferent [Old English blīthe] ▷ **blithely** adv ▷ **blitheness** n

blithering ('blɪðərɪŋ) adj **1** talking foolishly; jabbering **2** informal stupid; foolish: you blithering idiot [c19: variant of BLATHER + -ING²]

blithesome ('blaɪðsəm) adj literary cheery; merry

BLitt abbreviation Bachelor of Letters [Latin Baccalaureus Litterarum]

blitz (blɪts) n **1** a violent and sustained attack, esp with intensive aerial bombardment **2** any sudden intensive attack or concerted effort **3** American football a defensive charge on the quarterback ▷ vb **4** (tr) to attack suddenly and intensively [c20: shortened from German Blitzkrieg lightning war]

Blitz (blɪts) n the Blitz the systematic night-time bombing of Britain in 1940–41 by the German Luftwaffe

blitzkrieg ('blɪts,kriːg) n a swift intensive military

attack, esp using tanks supported by aircraft, designed to defeat the opposition quickly [c20: from German: lightning war]

Blixen ('blɪksən) n **Karen**. See **Dinesen**

blizzard ('blɪzəd) n a strong bitterly cold wind accompanied by a widespread heavy snowfall [c19: of uncertain origin]

bloat (bləʊt) vb **1** to swell or cause to swell, as with a liquid, air, or wind **2** to become or cause to be puffed up, as with conceit **3** (tr) to cure (fish, esp herring) by half-drying in smoke [c17: probably related to Old Norse blautr soaked, Old English blāt pale]

bloater ('bləʊtə) n a herring, or sometimes a mackerel, that has been salted in brine, smoked, and cured

blob (blɒb) n **1** a soft mass or drop, as of some viscous liquid **2** a spot, dab, or blotch of colour, ink, etc **3** a indistinct or shapeless form or object [c15: perhaps of imitative origin; compare BUBBLE]

bloc (blɒk) n a group of people or countries combined by a common interest or aim [c20: from French: BLOCK]

Bloch (blɒk) n **1 Ernest**. 1880–1959, US composer, born in Switzerland, who found inspiration in Jewish liturgical and folk music: his works include the symphonies Israel(1916) and America (1926) **2 Felix**. 1905–83, US physicist, born in Switzerland: Nobel prize for physics (1952) for his work on the magnetic moments of atomic particles **3 Konrad Emil**. 1912–2000, US biochemist, born in Germany: shared the Nobel prize for physiology or medicine in 1964 for his work on fatty-acid metabolism **4** (French blɔk) **Marc**. 1886–1944, French historian and Resistance fighter; author of Feudal Society (1935) and Strange Defeat (1940), an essay on the fall of France: killed by the Nazis

block (blɒk) n **1** a large solid piece of wood, stone, or other material with flat rectangular sides, as for use in building **2** such a piece on which particular tasks may be done, as chopping, cutting, or beheading **3** Also called: building block one of a set of wooden or plastic cubes as a child's toy **4** a form on which things are shaped or displayed: a wig block **5** slang a person's head (esp in the phrase knock someone's block off) **6** do one's block Austral & NZ slang to become angry **7** a dull, unemotional, or hardhearted person **8** a large building of offices, flats, etc **9** a a group of buildings in a city bounded by intersecting streets on each side **b** the area or distance between such intersecting streets **10** Austral & NZ an area of land for a house, farm, etc **11** Austral & NZ a log, usually a willow, fastened to a timber base and used in a wood-chopping competition **12** a piece of wood, metal, or other material having an engraved, cast, or carved design in relief, used either for printing or for stamping book covers, etc **13** a casing housing one or more freely rotating pulleys. See also **block and tackle** **14** an obstruction or hindrance **15** pathol a interference in the normal physiological functioning of an organ or part **b** See **heart block** **c** See **nerve block** **16** psychol a short interruption of perceptual or thought processes **17** obstruction of an opponent in a sport **18 a** a section or quantity, as of tickets or shares, handled or considered as a single unit **b** (as modifier): a block booking; block voting **19** athletics short for **starting block** ▷ vb (mainly tr) **20** to shape by use of a block: to block a hat **21** (often foll by up) to obstruct (a passage, channel, etc) or prevent or impede the motion or flow of (something or someone) by introducing an obstacle: to block the traffic; to block up a pipe **22** to impede, retard, or prevent (an action, procedure, etc) **23** to stamp (a title, design, etc) on (a book cover, etc) by means of a block (see sense 12), esp using gold leaf or other foil **24** (also intr) sport to obstruct or impede movement by (an opponent) **25** to interrupt a physiological function, as by use of an anaesthetic **26** (also intr) cricket to play (a ball) defensively ▷ See also **block in**, **block out** [c14: from Old French bloc, from Dutch blok; related to Old High German bloh] ▷ **blocker** n

blockade (blɒ'keɪd) n **1** military the interdiction of a nation's sea lines of communications, esp of an individual port by the use of sea power **2** something that prevents access or progress **3** med the inhibition of the effect of a hormone or a drug, a transport system, or the action of a nerve by a drug ▷ *vb* (*tr*) **4** to impose a blockade on **5** to obstruct the way to [C17: from BLOCK + -ade, as in AMBUSCADE] > **block'ader** *n*

blockage ('blɒkɪdʒ) *n* **1** the act of blocking or state of being blocked **2** an object causing an obstruction

block and tackle *n* a hoisting device in which a rope or chain is passed around a pair of blocks containing one or more pulleys. The upper block is secured overhead and the lower block supports the load, the effort being applied to the free end of the rope or chain

blockboard ('blɒk,bɔːd) *n* a type of plywood in which soft wood strips are bonded together and sandwiched between two layers of veneer

blockbuster ('blɒk,bʌstə) *n informal* **1** a large bomb used to demolish extensive areas or strengthened targets **2** a very successful, effective, or forceful person, thing, etc **3** a lavish film, show, novel, etc, that proves to be an outstanding popular success

block diagram *n* **1** a diagram showing the interconnections between the parts of an industrial process **2** *computing* a diagram showing the interconnections between electronic components or parts of a program

blockhead ('blɒk,hed) *n derogatory* a stupid person > **'block,headed** *adj*

blockhouse ('blɒk,haʊs) *n* **1** (formerly) a wooden fortification with ports or loopholes for defensive fire, observation, etc **2** a concrete structure strengthened to give protection against enemy fire, with apertures to allow defensive gunfire **3** a building constructed of logs or squared timber **4** a reinforced concrete building close to a rocket-launching site for protecting personnel and equipment during launching

block in *vb* (*tr, adverb*) to sketch in outline, with little detail

blockish ('blɒkɪʃ) *adj* lacking vivacity or imagination; stupid > **'blockishly** *adv*

block letter *n* Also called: **block capital** a plain capital letter

block out *vb* (*tr, adverb*) **1** to plan or describe (something) in a general fashion **2** to prevent the entry or consideration of (something)

block release *n Brit* the release of industrial trainees from work for study at a college for several weeks

block vote *n Brit* (at a conference, esp of trade unionists) the system whereby each delegate's vote has a value in proportion to the number of people he or she represents

Bloemfontein ('bluːmfɒn,teɪn) *n* a city in central South Africa: capital of Free State province and judicial capital of the country. Pop: 111 698 (2001)

blog (blɒg) *n informal* a journal written on-line and accessible to users of the internet > **'blogger** *n*

blogosphere ('blɒgə,sfɪə) *n informal* a collective term for the weblogs on the internet [C21: from BLOG + -O- + -SPHERE]

Blois (*French* blwa) *n* a town in N central France, on the Loire: 13th-century castle. Pop: 49 171 (1999)

Blok (blɒk) *n* **Aleksandr Aleksandrovich** (alɪkˈsandr alɪkˈsandrəvɪtʃ). 1880–1921, Russian poet whose poems, which include *Verses about the Beautiful Lady* (1901–2) and *Rasput'ya* (1902–4), contain a mixture of symbolism, romanticism, tragedy, and irony

bloke (bləʊk) *n Brit & Austral* an informal word for **man** [C19: from Shelta]

blokeish *or* **blokish** ('bləʊkɪʃ) *adj informal, sometimes derogatory* denoting or exhibiting the characteristics believed typical of an ordinary man. Also called: **blokey** ('bləʊkɪ) > **'blokeishness** *or* **'blokishness** *n*

blond (blɒnd) *adj* **1** (of men's hair) of a light colour; fair **2** (of a person, people or a race) having fair hair, a light complexion, and, typically, blue or grey eyes **3** (of soft furnishings, wood, etc) light in colour ▷ *n* **4** a person, esp a man, having light-coloured hair and skin [C15: from Old French *blond*, probably of Germanic origin; related to Late Latin *blundus* yellow, Italian *biondo*, Spanish *blondo*]

blonde (blɒnd) *adj* **1** (of women's hair) of a light colour; fair **2** (of a person, people or a race) having fair hair, a

light complexion, and, typically, blue or grey eyes ▷ *n* **3** a person, esp a woman, having light-coloured hair and skin [C15: from Old French *blond* (fem *blonde*), probably of Germanic origin; related to Late Latin *blundus* yellow, Italian *biondo*, Spanish *blondo*] > **'blondeness** *n*

Blondin (*French* blɔ̃dɛ̃) *n* **Charles**, real name *Jean-François Gravelet*. 1824–97, French acrobat and tightrope walker; best known for walking a tightrope across Niagara Falls (1859)

blood (blʌd) *n* **1** a reddish fluid in vertebrates that is pumped by the heart through the arteries and veins, supplies tissues with nutrients, oxygen, etc, and removes waste products. It consists of a fluid (see **blood plasma**) containing cells (erythrocytes, leucocytes, and platelets) **2** a similar fluid in such invertebrates as annelids and arthropods **3** bloodshed, esp when resulting in murder **4** life itself; lifeblood **5** relationship through being of the same family, race, or kind; kinship **6** flesh and blood **a** near kindred or kinship, esp that between a parent and child **b** human nature (esp in the phrase **it's more than flesh and blood can stand**) **7** in one's blood as a natural or inherited characteristic or talent **8** the blood royal or noble descent: *a prince of the blood* **9** temperament; disposition: temper **10 a** good or pure breeding; pedigree **b** (*as modifier*): *blood horses* **11** people viewed as members of a group, esp as an invigorating force (in the phrases **new blood, young blood**) **12** *chiefly Brit rare* a dashing young man; dandy; rake **13** in cold blood showing no passion; deliberately; ruthlessly **14** make one's blood boil to cause to be angry or indignant **15** make one's blood run cold to fill with horror ▷ *vb* (*tr*) **16** *hunting* to cause (young hounds) to taste the blood of a freshly killed quarry and so become keen to hunt **17** to initiate (a person) to war [Old English *blōd*; related to Old Norse *blōth*, Old High German *bluot*]

Blood (blʌd) *n* **Thomas**, known as *Colonel Blood*. ?1618–80, Irish adventurer, who tried to steal the crown jewels (1671)

blood-and-thunder *adj* denoting or relating to a melodramatic adventure story

blood bank *n* a place where whole blood, blood plasma, or other blood products are stored until required in transfusion

blood bath *n* indiscriminate slaughter; a massacre

blood brother *n* **1** a brother by birth **2** a man or boy who has sworn to treat another as his brother, often in a ceremony in which their blood is mingled

blood count *n* the number of red and white blood corpuscles and platelets in a specific sample of blood

bloodcurdling ('blʌd,kɜːdlɪŋ) *adj* terrifying; horrifying > **'blood,curdlingly** *adv*

blood donor *n* a person who gives his or her blood to be used for transfusion

blood doping *n* the illegal practice of removing a quantity of blood from an athlete long before a race and reinjecting it shortly before a race, so boosting oxygenation of the blood

blooded ('blʌdɪd) *adj* **1** (of horses, cattle, etc) of good breeding **2** (*in combination*) having blood or temperament as specified: *hot-blooded, cold-blooded, warm-blooded, red-blooded, blue-blooded*

blood group *n* any one of the various groups into which human blood is classified on the basis of its agglutinogens. Also called: **blood type**

blood heat *n* the normal temperature of the human body, 98.4°F or 37°C

bloodhound ('blʌd,haʊnd) *n* a large breed of hound having a smooth glossy coat of red, tan, or black and loose wrinkled skin on its head: formerly much used in tracking and police work

bloodless ('blʌdlɪs) *adj* **1** without blood **2** conducted without violence (esp in the phrase **bloodless revolution**) **3** anaemic-looking; pale **4** lacking vitality; lifeless **5** lacking in emotion; cold; unfeeling > **'bloodlessly** *adv* > **'bloodlessness** *n*

blood-letting ('blʌd,letɪŋ) *n* **1** the therapeutic removal of blood, as in relieving congestive heart failure. See also **phlebotomy 2** bloodshed, esp in a blood feud

bloodline ('blʌd,laɪn) *n* all the members of a family

group over generations, esp regarding characteristics common to that group; pedigree

blood money *n* **1** compensation paid to the relatives of a murdered person **2** money paid to a hired murderer **3** a reward for information about a criminal, esp a murderer

blood orange *n* a variety of orange all or part of the pulp of which is dark red when ripe

blood poisoning *n* a nontechnical term for **septicaemia**

blood pressure *n* the pressure exerted by the blood on the inner walls of the arteries, being relative to the elasticity and diameter of the vessels and the force of the heartbeat

blood pudding *n* another name for **black pudding**

blood relation *or* **blood relative** *n* a person related to another by birth, as distinct from one related by marriage

bloodshed ('blʌd,ʃed) *n* slaughter; killing

bloodshot ('blʌd,ʃɒt) *adj* (of an eye) inflamed

blood sport *n* any sport involving the killing of an animal, esp hunting

bloodstain ('blʌd,steɪn) *n* a dark discoloration caused by blood, esp dried blood > 'blood,stained *adj*

bloodstock ('blʌd,stɒk) *n* thoroughbred horses, esp those bred for racing

bloodstone ('blʌd,stəʊn) *n* a dark-green variety of chalcedony with red spots: used as a gemstone. Also called: **heliotrope**

bloodstream ('blʌd,stri:m) *n* the flow of blood through the vessels of a living body

blood substitute *n* a substance such as plasma, albumin, or dextran, used to replace lost blood or increase the blood volume

bloodsucker ('blʌd,sʌkə) *n* **1** an animal that sucks blood, esp a leech or mosquito **2** a person or thing that preys upon another person, esp by extorting money > 'blood,sucking *adj*

blood sugar *n med* the glucose concentration in the blood: the normal fasting value is between 3.9 and 5.6 mmol/l

bloodthirsty ('blʌd,θɜːstɪ) *adj* -thirstier, -thirstiest **1** murderous; cruel **2** taking pleasure in bloodshed or violence **3** describing or depicting killing and violence; gruesome > 'blood,thirstily *adv* > 'blood,thirstiness *n*

blood type *n* another name for **blood group**

blood vessel *n* an artery, capillary, or vein

bloodwood ('blʌd,wʊd) *n* any of several species of Australian eucalyptus that exude a red sap

bloody ('blʌdɪ) *adj* bloodier, bloodiest **1** covered or stained with blood **2** resembling or composed of blood **3** marked by much killing and bloodshed: *a bloody war* **4** cruel or murderous: *a bloody tyrant* **5** of a deep red colour; blood-red ▷ *adv, adj* **6** *slang, chiefly Brit* (intensifier): *a bloody fool; bloody fine food* ▷ *vb* bloodies, bloodying, bloodied **7** (*tr*) to stain with blood > 'bloodily *adv* > 'bloodiness *n*

Bloody Mary *n* a drink consisting of tomato juice and vodka

bloody-minded *adj Brit informal* deliberately obstructive and unhelpful

bloom¹ (blu:m) *n* **1** a blossom on a flowering plant; a flower **2** the state, time, or period when flowers open (esp in the phrases **in bloom, in full bloom**) **3** open flowers collectively **4** a healthy, vigorous, or flourishing condition; prime (esp in the phrase **the bloom of youth**) **5** youthful or healthy rosiness in the cheeks or face; glow **6** a fine whitish coating on the surface of fruits, leaves, etc, consisting of minute grains of a waxy substance **7** any coating similar in appearance, such as that on new coins **8** *ecology* a visible increase in the algal constituent of plankton, which may be seasonal or due to excessive organic pollution **9** Also called: **chill** a dull area formed on the surface of gloss paint, lacquer, or varnish ▷ *vb* (*mainly intr*) **10** (of flowers) to open; come into flower **11** to bear flowers; blossom **12** to flourish or grow **13** to be in a healthy, glowing, or flourishing condition [c13: of Germanic origin; compare Old Norse *blōm* flower, Old High German *bluomo*, Middle Dutch *bloeme*; see **BLOW³**]

bloom² (blu:m) *n* a rectangular mass of metal obtained

by rolling or forging a cast ingot [Old English *blōma* lump of metal]

bloomer¹ ('blu:mə) *n* a plant that flowers, esp in a specified way: *a night bloomer*

bloomer² ('blu:mə) *n Brit informal* a stupid mistake; blunder [c20: from **BLOOMING**]

bloomer³ ('blu:mə) *n Brit* a medium-sized loaf, baked on the sole of the oven, glazed and notched on top [c20: of uncertain origin]

bloomers ('blu:məz) *pl n* **1** *informal* women's or girls' baggy knickers **2** (formerly) loose trousers gathered at the knee worn by women for cycling and athletics [from *bloomer*, a garment introduced in about 1850 and publicized by Mrs A. *Bloomer* (1818–94), US social reformer]

Bloomfield ('blu:m,fi:ld) *n* **Leonard**. 1887–1949, US linguist, influential for his strictly scientific and descriptive approach to comparative linguistics; author of *Language* (1933)

blooming ('blu:mɪŋ) *adv, adj Brit informal* (intensifier): *a blooming genius; blooming painful* [c19: euphemistic for **BLOODY**]

Bloomington ('blu:mɪŋtən) *n* a city in central Indiana: seat of the University of Indiana (1820). Pop: 70 642 (2003 est)

Bloomsbury ('blu:mzbərɪ, -brɪ) *n* **1** a district of central London in the borough of Camden: contains the British Museum, part of the University of London, and many publishers' offices ▷ *adj* **2** relating to or characteristic of the Bloomsbury Group

Bloomsbury Group *n* a group of writers, artists, and intellectuals living and working in and around Bloomsbury in London from about 1907 to 1930. Influenced by the philosophy of G. E. Moore, they included Leonard and Virginia Woolf, Clive and Vanessa Bell, Roger Fry, E. M. Forster, Lytton Strachey, Duncan Grant, and John Maynard Keynes

Bloomsday ('blu:mzdeɪ) *n* an annual celebration in Dublin on June 16th of the life of the Irish author James Joyce (1882–1941) and in particular, his novel *Ulysses*, which is entirely set in Dublin on June 16th, 1904 [c20: Leopold Bloom, the central character in *Ulysses*]

blossom ('blɒsəm) *n* **1** the flower or flowers of a plant, esp conspicuous flowers producing edible fruit **2** the time or period of flowering (esp in the phrases **in blossom, in full blossom**) ▷ *vb* (*intr*) **3** (of plants) to come into flower **4** to develop or come to a promising stage [Old English *blōstm*; related to Middle Low German *blōsem*, Latin *flōs* flower] > 'blossomy *adj*

blot (blɒt) *n* **1** a stain or spot of ink, paint, dirt, etc **2** something that spoils or detracts from the beauty or worth of something **3** a blemish or stain on one's character or reputation ▷ *vb* blots, blotting, blotted **4** (of ink, dye, etc) to form spots or blobs on (a material) or (of a person) to cause such spots or blobs to form on (a material) **5** (*intr*) to stain or become stained or spotted **6** (*tr*) to cause a blemish in or on; disgrace **7** to soak up (excess ink, etc) by using blotting paper or some other absorbent material **8** (of blotting paper or some other absorbent material) to absorb (excess ink, etc) **9** (*tr; often foll by out*) **a** to darken or hide completely; obscure; obliterate **b** to destroy; annihilate [c14: probably of Germanic origin; compare Middle Dutch *bluyster* **BLISTER**]

blotch (blɒtʃ) *n* **1** an irregular spot or discoloration, esp a dark and relatively large one such as an ink stain ▷ *vb* **2** to become or cause to become marked by such discoloration [c17: probably from **BOTCH**, influenced by **BLOT¹**] > 'blotchy *adj* > 'blotchily *adv* > 'blotchiness *n*

blotter ('blɒtə) *n* something used to absorb excess ink or other liquid, esp a sheet of blotting paper with a firm backing

blotting paper *n* a soft absorbent unsized paper, used esp for soaking up surplus ink

blotto ('blɒtəʊ) *adj slang* unconscious, esp through drunkenness [c20: from **BLOT¹** (vb); compare *blot out*]

blouse (blaʊz) *n* **1** a woman's shirtlike garment made of cotton, nylon, etc ▷ *vb* **2** to hang or make so as to hang in full loose folds [c19: from French, of unknown origin]

blouson ('blu:zɒn) *n* a short jacket or top having the shape of a blouse [c20: French]

blow¹ (bləʊ) *vb* **blows, blowing, blew, blown 1** (of a current of air, the wind, etc) to be or cause to be in motion **2** (*intr*) to move or be carried by or as if by wind or air **3** to expel (air, cigarette smoke, etc) through the mouth or nose **4** to force or cause (air, dust, etc) to move (into, in, over, etc) by using an instrument or by expelling breath **5** (*intr*) to breathe hard; pant **6** (sometimes foll by *up*) to inflate with air or the breath **7** (*intr*) (of wind, a storm, etc) to make a roaring or whistling sound **8** to cause (a whistle, siren, etc) to sound by forcing air into it, as a signal, or (of a whistle, etc) to sound thus **9** (*tr*) to force air from the lungs through (the nose) to clear out mucus or obstructing matter **10** (often foll by *up, down, in,* etc) to explode, break, or disintegrate completely **11** *electronics* to burn out (a fuse, valve, etc) because of excessive current or (of a fuse, valve, etc) to burn out **12** (*tr*) to wind (a horse) by making it run excessively **13** to cause (a wind instrument) to sound by forcing one's breath into the mouthpiece, or (of such an instrument) to sound in this way **14** (*intr*) (of flies) to lay eggs (in) **15** to shape (glass, ornaments, etc) by forcing air or gas through the material when molten **16** (*tr*) *slang* to spend (money) freely **17** (*tr*) *slang* to use (an opportunity) ineffectively **18** *slang* to go suddenly away (from) **19** (*tr*) *slang* to expose or betray (a person or thing meant to be kept secret) **20** *past participle* **blowed** *informal* another word for: **damn 21 blow hot and cold** to vacillate **22 blow one's top,** *esp US & Canadian* **blow one's stack** or **blow one's lid** *informal* to lose one's temper ▷ *n* **23** the act or an instance of blowing **24** the sound produced by blowing **25** a blast of air or wind **26 a** *Brit* a slang name for **cannabis** (sense 2) **b** *US* a slang name for **cocaine** ▷ See also **blow away** [Old English *blāwan*, related to Old Norse *blǣr* gust of wind, Old High German *blāen*, Latin *flāre*]

blow² (bləʊ) *n* **1 a** powerful or heavy stroke with the fist, a weapon, etc **2** at one blow or at a blow by or with only one action; all at one time **3** a sudden setback; unfortunate event **4 come to blows a** to fight **b** to result in a fight **5** an attacking action: *a blow for freedom* **6** *Austral & NZ* a stroke of the shears in sheep-shearing [c15: probably of Germanic origin; compare Old High German *bliuwan* to beat]

blow³ (bləʊ) *vb* **blows, blowing, blew, blown 1** (*intr*) (of a plant or flower) to blossom or open out ▷ *n* **2** a mass of blossoms **3** the state or period of blossoming (esp in the phrase **in full blow**) [Old English *blōwan*; related to Old Frisian *blōia* to bloom, Old High German *bluoen*, Latin *flōs* flower; see **BLOOM¹**]

blow away *vb* (*tr, adverb*) *slang, chiefly US* **1** to kill (someone) by shooting **2** to defeat decisively

blow-by-blow *adj* (*prenominal*) explained in great detail: *a blow-by-blow account of the argument*

blow-dry *vb* **-dries, -drying, -dried** (*tr*) **1** to style (hair) while drying it with a hand-held hairdryer ▷ *n* **2** this method of styling the hair

blower ('bləʊə) *n* **1 a** mechanical device, such as a fan, that blows **2** a low-pressure rotary compressor, esp in a furnace or internal-combustion engine **3** an informal name for **telephone**

blowfish ('bləʊˌfɪʃ) *n, pl* **-fish** or **-fishes** a popular name for: **puffer** (sense 2)

blowfly ('bləʊˌflaɪ) *n, pl* **-flies** any of various dipterous flies of the genus *Calliphora* and related genera that lay their eggs in rotting meat, dung, carrion, and open wounds: family *Calliphoridae.* Also called: **bluebottle**

blowgun ('bləʊˌgʌn) *n* the US word for **blowpipe** (sense 1)

blowhard ('bləʊˌhɑːd) *informal* ▷ *n* **1** a boastful person ▷ *adj* **2** blustering or boastful

blowhole ('bləʊˌhəʊl) *n* **1** the nostril, paired or single, of whales, situated far back on the skull **2** a hole in ice through which whales, seals, etc, breathe **3 a** a vent for air or gas, esp to release fumes from a tunnel, passage, etc **b** *NZ* a hole emitting gas or steam in a volcanic region **4** *geology* a hole in a cliff top leading to a sea cave through which air is forced by the action of the sea

blow in *vb* (*intr, adverb*) *informal* to arrive or enter suddenly

blow-in *n Austral informal* an unwelcome newcomer or stranger

blow job *n* a slang term for **fellatio**

blowlamp ('bləʊˌlæmp) *n* another name for **blowtorch**

blown (bləʊn) *vb* the past participle of **blow¹·³**

blow out *vb* (*adverb*) **1** to extinguish (a flame, candle, etc) or (of a flame, candle, etc) to become extinguished **2** (*intr*) (of a tyre) to puncture suddenly, esp at high speed **3** (*intr*) (of a fuse) to melt suddenly **4** (*tr; often reflexive*) to diminish or use up the energy of: *the storm blew itself out* **5** (*intr*) (of an oil or gas well) to lose oil or gas in an uncontrolled manner ▷ *n* **blowout 6** the sudden melting of an electrical fuse **7** a sudden burst in a tyre **8** the uncontrolled escape of oil or gas from an oil or gas well **9** *slang* a large filling meal or lavish entertainment

blow over *vb* (*intr, adverb*) to cease or be finished: *the storm blew over*

blowpipe ('bləʊˌpaɪp) *n* **1** a long tube from which pellets, poisoned darts, etc, are shot by blowing **2** Also called: **blow tube** a tube for blowing air or oxygen into a flame to intensify its heat and direct it onto a small area **3** a long narrow iron pipe used to gather molten glass and blow it into shape

blowsy or **blowzy** ('blaʊzɪ) *adj* **blowsier, blowsiest** or **blowzier, blowziest 1** (esp of a woman) untidy in appearance; slovenly or sluttish **2** (of a woman) ruddy in complexion; red-faced [c18: from dialect *blowze* beggar girl, of unknown origin]

blow through *vb* (*intr, adverb*) *Austral informal* to leave; make off

blowtorch ('bləʊˌtɔːtʃ) *n* a small burner that produces a very hot flame, used to remove old paint, melt soft metal, etc

blow up *vb* (*adverb*) **1** to explode or cause to explode **2** (*tr*) to increase the importance of (something): *they blew the whole affair up* **3** (*intr*) to come into consideration: *we lived well enough before this thing blew up* **4** (*intr*) to come into existence with sudden force: *a storm had blown up* **5** *informal* to lose one's temper (with a person) **6** (*tr*) *informal* to reprimand (someone) **7** (*tr*) *informal* to enlarge the size or detail of (a photograph) ▷ *n* **blow-up 8** an explosion **9** *informal* an enlarged photograph or part of a photograph **10** *informal* a fit of temper or argument

blowy ('bləʊɪ) *adj* **blowier, blowiest** another word for: **windy** (sense 1)

blub (blʌb) *vb* **blubs, blubbing, blubbed** *Brit* a slang word for **blubber** (senses 1–3)

blubber ('blʌbə) *vb* **1** to sob without restraint **2** to utter while sobbing **3** (*tr*) to make (the face) wet and swollen or disfigured by crying ▷ *n* **4** a thick insulating layer of fatty tissue below the skin of aquatic mammals such as the whale: used by man as a source of oil **5** *informal* excessive and flabby body fat **6** the act or an instance of weeping without restraint ▷ *adj* **7** (*often in combination*) swollen or fleshy: *blubber-faced; blubber-lips* [c12: perhaps from Low German *blubbern* to **BUBBLE**, of imitative origin] > 'blubberer > 'blubbery *adj*

Blücher (German 'blycər) *n* **Gebhard Leberecht von** ('gɛphart 'le:bərɛçt fɔn). 1742–1819, Prussian field marshal, who commanded the Prussian army against Napoleon at Waterloo (1815)

bludge (blʌdʒ) *Austral & NZ informal* ▷ *vb* **1** (when *intr,* often foll by *on*) to scrounge from (someone) **2** (*intr*) to evade work ▷ *n* **3** a very easy task; undemanding employment [c19: back formation from slang *bludger* pimp, from **BLUDGEON**]

bludgeon ('blʌdʒən) *n* **1** a stout heavy club, typically thicker at one end **2** a person, line of argument, etc, that is effective but unsubtle ▷ *vb* (*tr*) **3** to hit or knock down with or as with a bludgeon **4** (often foll by *into*) to force; bully; coerce [c18: of uncertain origin]

bludger ('blʌdʒə) *n Austral & NZ informal* **1** a person who scrounges **2** a person who avoids work **3** a person in authority regarded as ineffectual by those working under him

blue (bluː) *n* **1** any of a group of colours, such as that of a clear unclouded sky, that have wavelengths in the range

490–445 nanometres. Blue is the complementary colour of yellow and with red and green forms a set of primary colours **2** a dye or pigment of any of these colours **3** blue cloth or clothing: *dressed in blue* **4** a sportsperson who represents or has represented Oxford or Cambridge University and has the right to wear the university colour (dark blue for Oxford, light blue for Cambridge) **5** *Brit* an informal name for **Tory 6** any of numerous small blue-winged butterflies of the genera *Lampides*, *Polyommatus*, etc: family *Lycaenidae* **7** *archery* a blue ring on a target, between the red and the black, scoring five points **8** *Austral & NZ slang* an argument or fight: *he had a blue with a taxi driver* **9** Also called: **bluey** *Austral & NZ slang* a court summons, esp for a traffic offence **10** *Austral & NZ informal* a mistake; error **11** **out of the blue** apparently from nowhere; unexpectedly ▷ *adj* **bluer, bluest 12** of the colour blue **13** (of the flesh) having a purple tinge, as from cold or contusion **14** depressed, moody, or unhappy **15** indecent, titillating, or pornographic: *blue films* ▷ *vb* **blues, blueing** or **bluing, blued 16** to make, dye, or become blue **17** (*tr*) to treat (laundry) with blueing **18** (*tr*) *slang* to spend extravagantly or wastefully; squander ▷ See also **blues** [c13: from Old French *bleu*, of Germanic origin; compare Old Norse *blār*, Old High German *blāo*, Middle Dutch *blā*; related to Latin *flāvus* yellow] > **'blueness** *n*

Blue (bluː) or **Bluey** *n Austral informal* a nickname for a person with red hair

blue baby *n* a baby born with a bluish tinge to the skin because of lack of oxygen in the blood, esp caused by a congenital defect of the heart

Bluebeard ('bluː,bɪəd) *n* **1** a villain in European folk tales who marries several wives and murders them in turn. In many versions the seventh and last wife escapes the fate of the others **2** a man who has had several wives

bluebell ('bluː,bel) *n* **1** Also called: **wild hyacinth, wood hyacinth** a European liliaceous woodland plant, *Hyacinthoides* (or *Endymion*) *non-scripta*, having a one-sided cluster of blue bell-shaped flowers **2** Also called: **Spanish bluebell** a similar and related plant, *hispanica*, widely grown in gardens and becoming naturalized **3** a Scot name for **harebell 4** any of various other plants with blue bell-shaped flowers

blueberry ('bluː,bərɪ, -brɪ) *n, pl* **-ries 1** Also called: **huckleberry** any of several North American ericaceous shrubs of the genus *Vaccinium*, such as *V. pennsylvanicum*, that have blue-black edible berries with tiny seeds. See also **bilberry 2** the fruit of any of these plants

bluebird ('bluː,bɜːd) *n* **1** any North American songbird of the genus *Sialia*, having a blue or partly blue plumage: subfamily *Turdinae* (thrushes) **2 fairy bluebird** any songbird of the genus *Irena*, of S and SE Asia, having a blue-and-black plumage: family *Irenidae*

blue blood *n* royal or aristocratic descent [c19: translation of Spanish *sangre azul*] > **'blue-'blooded** *adj*

bluebottle ('bluː,bɒtⁱl) *n* **1** another name for the **blowfly 2** any of various blue-flowered plants, esp the cornflower **3** *Brit* an informal word for a **policeman 4** *Austral & NZ* an informal name for **Portuguese man-of-war**

blue box *n Canadian* a blue plastic container for domestic refuse that is to be collected and recycled

bluebush ('bluː,bʊʃ) *n* any of various blue-grey herbaceous Australian shrubs of the genus *Maireana*

blue cattle dog *n* an Australian breed of dog with a bluish coat, developed for herding cattle. Also called: **Australian cattle dog, blue heeler**

blue cheese *n* cheese containing a blue mould, esp Stilton, Roquefort, or Danish blue

blue chip *n* **1** a gambling chip with the highest value **2** *finance* a stock considered reliable with respect to both dividend income and capital value

blue-collar *adj* of, relating to, or designating manual industrial workers. See **white-collar**

blue-eyed boy *n informal, chiefly Brit* the favourite or darling of a person or group

bluefish ('bluː,fɪʃ) *n, pl* **-fish** or **-fishes 1** Also called: **snapper** a predatory bluish marine percoid food and game fish, *Pomatomus saltatrix*, related to the horse

mackerel: family *Pomatomidae* **2** any of various other bluish fishes

Blue Flag *n* an award given to a seaside resort that meets EU standards of cleanliness of beaches and purity of water in bathing areas

blue fox *n* **1** a variety of the arctic fox that has a pale grey winter coat and is bred for its fur **2** the fur of this animal

blue funk *n slang* a state of great terror or loss of nerve

bluegrass ('bluː,grɑːs) *n* **1** any of several North American bluish-green grasses of the genus *Poa*, esp *P. pratensis* (**Kentucky bluegrass**), grown for forage **2** a type of folk music originating in Kentucky, characterized by a simple harmonized accompaniment

blue-green algae *pl n* the former name for **cyanobacteria**

blue ground *n mineralogy* another name for **kimberlite**

blue gum *n* a tall fast-growing widely cultivated Australian myrtaceous tree, *Eucalyptus globulus*, having aromatic leaves containing a medicinal oil, bark that peels off in shreds, and hard timber. The juvenile leaves are bluish in colour

blue heeler *n Austral & NZ* a cattle dog that controls cattle by biting their heels

bluejacket ('bluː,dʒækɪt) *n* a sailor in the Navy

bluejacking ('bluː,dʒækɪŋ) *n* the practice of using one Bluetooth-enabled mobile phone to gain access to another, esp in order to send anonymous text messages [c21: from BLUE(TOOTH) + (HIGH)JACKING]

blue jay *n* a common North American jay, *Cyanocitta cristata*, having bright blue plumage with greyish-white underparts

blue moon *n* **once in a blue moon** *informal* almost never

blue mould *n* Also called: **green mould** any fungus of the genus *Penicillium* that forms a bluish mass on decaying food, leather, etc

Blue Mountains *pl n* **1** a mountain range in the US, in NE Oregon and SE Washington. Highest peak: Rock Creek Butte, 2773 m (9097 ft) **2** a mountain range in the Caribbean, in E Jamaica: Blue Mountain coffee is grown on its slopes. Highest peak: Blue Mountain Peak, 2256 m (7402 ft) **3** a plateau in SE Australia, in E New South Wales: part of the Great Dividing Range. Highest part: about 1134 m (3871 ft)

Blue Nile *n* a river in E Africa, rising in central Ethiopia as the Abbai and flowing southeast, then northwest to join the White Nile. Length: about 1530 km (950 miles)

blue note *n jazz* a flattened third or seventh, used frequently in the blues

blue-on-blue *adj military* of or relating to friendly fire: *blue-on-blue contacts* [c20: from the colour used to mark a country's own troops and allies on a military map]

blue pencil *n* **1** deletion, alteration, or censorship of the contents of a book or other work ▷ *vb* **blue-pencil -cils, -cilling, -cilled** or *US* **-cils, -ciling, -ciled 2** (*tr*) to alter or delete parts of (a book, film, etc), esp to censor

blue peter *n* a signal flag of blue with a white square at the centre, displayed by a vessel about to leave port [c19: from the name *Peter*]

blue pointer *n* a large shark, *Isuropsis mako*, of Australian coastal waters, having a blue back and pointed snout

blueprint ('bluː,prɪnt) *n* **1** Also called: **cyanotype** a photographic print of plans, technical drawings, etc, consisting of white lines on a blue background **2** an original plan or prototype that influences subsequent design or practice ▷ *vb* **3** (*tr*) to make a blueprint of (a plan)

blue ribbon *n* **1** (in Britain) a badge of blue silk worn by members of the Order of the Garter **2** a badge awarded as the first prize in a competition

Blue Ridge Mountains *pl n* a mountain range in the eastern US, extending from West Virginia into Georgia: part of the Appalachian mountains. Highest peak: Mount Mitchell, 2038 m (6684 ft)

blue-ringed octopus *n* a highly venomous octopus, *Octopus maculosus*, of E Australia which exhibits blue bands on its tentacles when disturbed

blues (bluːz) **the blues** *pl n* (*sometimes functioning as singular*) **1** a feeling of depression or deep unhappiness

2 a type of folk song devised by Black Americans at the beginning of the 20th century, usually employing a basic 12-bar chorus, the tonic, subdominant, and dominant chords, frequent minor intervals, and blue notes

blue screen *n* a special effects film technique involving filming actors against a blue screen on which effects such as computerized graphics can be added later and integrated into a single sequence

blue-singlet *adj Austral* working-class

blue-sky *or* **blue-skies** *n* (*modifier*) of or denoting theoretical research without regard to any future application of its result: *a blue-sky project*

blue-sky thinking *n* creative ideas that are not limited by current thinking or beliefs

bluesnarfing ('blu:ˌsnɑːfɪŋ) *n* the practice of using one Bluetooth-enabled mobile phone to steal contact details, ring tones, images, etc from another [c21: from BLUE(TOOTH) + SNARF]

bluestocking ('blu:ˌstɒkɪŋ) *n usually dismissive* a scholarly or intellectual woman [from the blue worsted stockings worn by members of a c18 literary society]

bluestone ('blu:ˌstəʊn) *n* 1 a blue-grey sandstone containing much clay, used for building and paving 2 the blue crystalline form of copper sulphate

blue swimmer *n* 1 an edible bluish Australian swimming crab, *Portunus pelagicus* 2 *Austral informal* an Australian ten-dollar note

bluetit ('blu:ˌtɪt) *n* a common European tit, *Parus caeruleus*, having a blue crown, wings, and tail, yellow underparts, and a black and grey head

Bluetooth ('blu:ˌtu:θ) *n* a short-range radio technology that allows wireless communication between a computer and a keyboard, between mobile phones, etc [c20: after the 10th-century Danish King Harald Blatand (Harold Bluetooth), instrumental in uniting warring factions in Scandinavia]

blue whale *n* the largest mammal: a widely distributed bluish-grey whalebone whale, *Sibbaldus* (or *Balaenoptera*) *musculus*, closely related and similar to the rorquals: family *Balaenopteridae*

bluey ('blu:ɪ) *n Austral informal* 1 a blanket 2 a swagman's bundle 3 hump bluey *or* hump one's bluey to carry one's bundle; tramp 4 *slang* a variant of **blue** (sense 9) 5 a cattle dog [(for senses 1, 2, 4) c19: from BLUE (on account of their colour) + -Y²]

Bluey ('blu:ɪ) *n* a variant of **Blue**

bluff¹ (blʌf) *vb* 1 to pretend to be confident about an uncertain issue or to have undisclosed resources, in order to influence or deter (someone) ▷ *n* 2 deliberate deception intended to create the impression of a stronger position or greater resources than one actually has 3 call someone's bluff to challenge someone to give proof of his claims [c19: originally US poker-playing term, from Dutch *bluffen* to boast] > **bluffer** *n*

bluff² (blʌf) *n* 1 a steep promontory, bank, or cliff, esp one formed by river erosion on the outside bend of a meander 2 *Canadian* a clump of trees on the prairie; copse ▷ *adj* 3 good-naturedly frank and hearty 4 (of a bank, cliff, etc) presenting a steep broad face [c17 (in the sense: nearly perpendicular): perhaps from Middle Dutch *blaf* broad] > **bluffly** *adv* > **bluffness** *n*

bluish *or* **blueish** ('blu:ɪʃ) *adj* somewhat blue

Blum (blu:m) *n* **Léon** (leɔ̃). 1872–1950, French socialist statesman; premier of France (1936–37; 1938; 1946–47)

Blumberg ('blʊmbɜːɡ) *n* **Baruch Samuel**. born 1925, US physician, noted for work on antigens: shared the Nobel prize for physiology or medicine 1976

Blunden ('blʌndən) *n* **Edmund (Charles)**. 1896–1974, British poet and scholar, noted esp for *Undertones of War* (1928), a memoir of World War I in verse and prose

blunder ('blʌndə) *n* 1 a stupid or clumsy mistake 2 a foolish tactless remark ▷ *vb* (*mainly intr*) 3 to make stupid or clumsy mistakes 4 to make foolish tactless remarks 5 (often foll by *about, into,* etc) to act clumsily; stumble 6 (*tr*) to mismanage; botch [c14: of Scandinavian origin; compare Old Norse *blunda* to close one's eyes, Norwegian dialect *blundra*; see BLIND] > **blunderer** *n* > **blundering** *n, adj*

blunderbuss ('blʌndəˌbʌs) *n* an obsolete short musket with large bore and flared muzzle, used to scatter shot at short range [c17: changed (through the influence of BLUNDER) from Dutch *donderbus*; from *donder* THUNDER + obsolete *bus* gun]

blunge (blʌndʒ) *vb* (*tr*) to mix (clay or a similar substance) with water in order to form a suspension for use in ceramics [c19: probably from BLEND + PLUNGE]

Blunkett ('blʌnkɪt) *n* **David**. born 1947, British Labour politician; secretary of state for education and employment (1997–2001); home secretary (2001–04); secretary of state for work and pensions (2005)

blunt (blʌnt) *adj* 1 (esp of a knife or blade) lacking sharpness or keenness; dull 2 not having a sharp edge or point: *a blunt instrument* 3 (of people, manner of speaking, etc) lacking refinement or subtlety; straightforward and uncomplicated ▷ *vb* (*tr*) 4 to make less sharp 5 to diminish the sensitivity or perception of; make dull [c12: probably of Scandinavian origin; compare Old Norse *blundr* dozing, *blunda* to close one's eyes; see BLUNDER, BLIND] > **bluntly** *adv* > **bluntness** *n*

Blunt (blʌnt) *n* 1 **Anthony**. 1907–83, British art historian and Soviet spy 2 **Wilfred Scawen**. 1840–1922, British poet, traveller, and anti-imperialist

blur (blɜː) *vb* **blurs**, **blurring**, **blurred** 1 to make or become vague or less distinct: *heat haze blurs the hills; education blurs class distinctions* 2 to smear or smudge 3 (*tr*) to make (the judgment, memory, or perception) less clear; dim ▷ *n* 4 something vague, hazy, or indistinct 5 a smear or smudge [c16: perhaps variant of BLEAR] > **blurred** *adj* > **blurry** *adj*

Blu-ray *n trademark* an optical disk used to store digital information such as high-definition video, and able to store more information than a standard DVD [c21: from the colour of the laser used to read and write this type of disc]

blurb (blɜːb) *n* a promotional description, as found on the jackets of books [c20: coined by Gelett Burgess (1866–1951), US humorist and illustrator]

blurt (blɜːt) *vb* (*tr; often foll by out*) to utter suddenly and involuntarily [c16: probably of imitative origin]

blush (blʌʃ) *vb* 1 (*intr*) to become suddenly red in the face from embarrassment, shame, modesty, or guilt; redden 2 to make or become reddish or rosy ▷ *n* 3 a sudden reddening of the face from embarrassment, shame, modesty, or guilt 4 a rosy glow 5 a cloudy area on the surface of freshly applied gloss paint 6 at first blush when first seen; as a first impression [Old English *blȳscan*; related to *blȳsian* to burn, Middle Low German *blüsen* to light a fire]

blusher ('blʌʃə) *n* a cosmetic applied to the face to imbue it with a rosy colour

bluster ('blʌstə) *vb* 1 to speak or say loudly or boastfully 2 to act in a bullying way 3 (*tr, foll by into*) to force or attempt to force (a person) into doing something by behaving thus 4 (*intr*) (of the wind) to be noisy or gusty ▷ *n* 5 boisterous talk or action; swagger 6 empty threats or protests 7 a strong wind; gale [c15: probably from Middle Low German *blüsteren* to storm, blow violently] > **blusterer** *n* > **blustery** *or* **blusterous** *adj*

Blu-tack ('blu:ˌtæk) *n* 1 *trademark* a type of blue, malleable, sticky material used to attach paper, card, etc to walls and other surfaces ▷ *vb* 2 (*tr*) to attach (paper, card, etc) to a wall or other surface by means of this material

Blvd *abbreviation* Boulevard

Blyth¹ (blaɪð) *n* a port in N England, in SE Northumberland, on the North Sea. Pop: 35 691 (2001)

Blyth² (blaɪð) *n* **Sir Chay** (tʃeɪ). born 1940, British yachtsman. He sailed round the world alone (1970–71) and won many races

Blyton ('blaɪtᵊn) *n* **Enid (Mary)**. 1897–1968, British writer of children's books; creator of Noddy and the *Famous Five* series of adventure stories

BM *abbreviation* 1 Bachelor of Medicine 2 *surveying* benchmark 3 British Museum

BMA *abbreviation* British Medical Association

BME *abbreviation* Black and Minority Ethnic

b

B-movie *n* a film originally made (esp in Hollywood in the 1940s and 50s) as a supporting film, now often considered as a genre in its own right

BMus *abbreviation* Bachelor of Music

BMX *abbreviation* **1** bicycle motocross; stunt riding on rough ground or over an obstacle course on a bicycle **2** a bicycle designed for bicycle motocross

Bn *abbreviation* **1** Baron **2** *Also called:* **bn** Battalion

B4N *abbreviation* text messaging bye for now

BNFL *abbreviation* British Nuclear Fuels Limited

BNP *abbreviation* British National Party

bo *or* **boh** (bəʊ) *interj* an exclamation uttered to startle or surprise someone, esp a child in a game

BO *abbreviation* **1** *informal* body odour **2** box office

b.o. *abbreviation* **1** back order **2** branch office **3** broker's order **4** buyer's option

boa ('bəʊə) *n* **1** any large nonvenomous snake of the family *Boidae*, most of which occur in Central and South America and the Caribbean. They have vestigial hind limbs and kill their prey by constriction **2** a woman's long thin scarf, usually of feathers or fur [c19: from New Latin, from Latin: a large Italian snake, water snake]

Boabdil (*Spanish* boaβ'ðil) *n* original name *Abu-Abdullah*, called *El Chico*, ruled as *Mohammed XI*. died ?1538, last Moorish king of Granada (1482–83; 1486–92)

boa constrictor *n* a very large snake, *Constrictor constrictor*, of tropical America and the Caribbean, that kills its prey by constriction: family *Boidae* (boas)

Boadicea (ˌbəʊədɪ'siːə) *n* another name for **Boudicca**

boar (bɔː) *n* **1** an uncastrated male pig **2** See **wild boar** [Old English *bār*; related to Old High German *bēr*]

board (bɔːd) *n* **1** a long wide flat relatively thin piece of sawn timber **2 a** a smaller flat piece of rigid material for a specific purpose: *ironing board* **b** (*in combination*): *breadboard; cheeseboard* **3** a person's food or meals, provided regularly for money or sometimes as payment for work done (esp in the phrases **full board, board and lodging**) **4** *archaic* a table, esp one used for eating at, and esp when laden with food **5 a** (*sometimes functioning as plural*) a group of people who officially administer a company, trust, etc **b** (*as modifier*): *a board meeting* **6** any other committee or council: *a board of interviewers* **7** the boards (*plural*) the acting profession; the stage **8** stiff cardboard or similar material covered with paper, cloth, etc, used for the outside covers of a book **9** a flat thin rectangular sheet of composite material, such as plasterboard or chipboard **10** *chiefly US* **a** a list on which stock-exchange securities and their prices are posted **b** *informal* the stock exchange itself **11** *nautical* the side of a ship **12** *Austral & NZ* the part of the floor of a sheep-shearing shed, esp a raised part, where the shearers work **13** any of various portable surfaces specially designed for indoor games such as chess, backgammon, etc **14** go by the board to be in disuse, neglected, or lost: *in these days courtesy goes by the board* **15** on board on or in a ship, boat, aeroplane, or other vehicle ▷ *vb* **16** to go aboard (a vessel, train, aircraft, or other vehicle) **17** to attack (a ship) by forcing one's way aboard **18** (*tr*; often foll by *up*, *in*, etc) to cover or shut with boards **19** (*intr*) to give or receive meals or meals and lodging in return for money or work **20** (*sometimes foll by out*) to receive or arrange for (someone, esp a child) to receive food and lodging away from home, usually in return for payment [Old English *bord*; related to Old Norse *borth* ship's side, table, Old High German *bort* ship's side, Sanskrit *bardhaka* a cutting off]

boarder ('bɔːdə) *n* **1** *Brit* a pupil who lives at school during term time **2** another word for **lodger 3** a person who boards a ship, esp one who forces his way aboard in an attack

boarding ('bɔːdɪŋ) *n* **1** a structure of boards, such as a floor or fence **2** timber boards collectively **3 a** the act of embarking on an aircraft, train, ship, etc **b** (*as modifier*): *a boarding pass*

boarding house *n* a private house in which accommodation and meals are provided for paying guests

boarding school *n* a school providing living accommodation for some or all of its pupils

Board of Trade *n* (in the United Kingdom) a ministry within the Department of Trade: responsible for the supervision of commerce and the promotion of export trade

boardroom ('bɔːdˌruːm, -ˌrʊm) *n* a room where the board of directors of a company meets

board school *n* *Brit* (formerly) a school managed by a board elected by local ratepayers

board shorts *pl n* shorts with longer legs, originally meant to protect a surfer's legs against the surfboard

boardwalk ('bɔːdˌwɔːk) *n* *US & Canadian* a promenade, esp along a beach, usually made of planks

Boas ('bəʊæz; *German* 'boːas) *n* **Franz** (frants). 1858–1942, US anthropologist, born in Germany. He made major contributions to cultural and linguistic anthropology in studies of North American Indians, including *The Mind of Primitive Man* (1911; 1938)

boast (bəʊst) *vb* **1** (*intr*; sometimes foll by *of* or *about*) to speak in exaggerated or excessively proud terms of one's possessions, skills, or superior qualities; brag **2** (*tr*) to possess (something to be proud of): *the city boasts a fine cathedral* ▷ *n* **3** a bragging statement **4** a possession, attribute, attainment, etc, that is or may be bragged about [c13: of uncertain origin] > 'boaster *n* > 'boasting *n*, *adj*

boastful ('bəʊstfʊl) *adj* tending to boast; characterized by boasting > 'boastfully *adv* > 'boastfulness *n*

boat (bəʊt) *n* **1** a small vessel propelled by oars, paddle, sails, or motor for travelling, transporting goods, etc, esp one that can be carried aboard a larger vessel **2** (not in technical use) another word for: **ship 3** a container for gravy, sauce, etc **4** in the same boat sharing the same problems **5** burn one's boats **6** miss the boat to lose an opportunity **7** rock the boat *informal* to cause a disturbance in the existing situation ▷ *vb* **8** (*intr*) to travel or go in a boat, esp as a form of recreation **9** (*tr*) to transport or carry in a boat [Old English *bāt*; related to Old Norse *beit* boat]

boater ('bəʊtə) *n* a stiff straw hat with a straight brim and flat crown

boathook ('bəʊtˌhʊk) *n* a pole with a hook at one end, used aboard a vessel for fending off other vessels or obstacles or for catching a line or mooring buoy

boathouse ('bəʊtˌhaʊs) *n* a shelter by the edge of a river, lake, etc, for housing boats

boatie ('bəʊtɪ) *n* *Austral & NZ informal* a boating enthusiast

boating ('bəʊtɪŋ) *n* the practice of rowing, sailing, or cruising in boats as a form of recreation

boatload ('bəʊtˌləʊd) *n* the amount of cargo or number of people held by a boat or ship

boatman ('bəʊtmən) *n*, *pl* **-men** a man who works on, hires out, repairs, or operates a boat or boats

boatswain, bosun *or* **bo's'n** ('bəʊsən) *n* a petty officer on a merchant ship or a warrant officer on a warship who is responsible for the maintenance of the ship and its equipment [Old English *bātswegen*; see BOAT, SWAIN]

boat train *n* a train scheduled to take passengers to or from a particular ship

Boa Vista (*Portuguese* 'boːə 'viʃtə) *n* a town in N Brazil, capital of the state of Roraima, on the Rio Branco. Pop: 275 000 (2005 est)

Boaz ('bəʊæz) *n* *Old Testament* a kinsman of Naomi, who married her daughter-in-law Ruth (Ruth 2–4); one of David's ancestors

bob¹ (bɒb) *vb* **bobs, bobbing, bobbed 1** to move or cause to move up and down repeatedly, as while floating in water **2** to move or cause to move with a short abrupt movement, as of the head **3** (*intr*; usually foll by *up*) to appear or emerge suddenly **4** (*intr*; usually foll by *for*) to attempt to get hold (of a floating or hanging object, esp an apple) in the teeth as a game ▷ *n* **5** a short abrupt movement, as of the head [c14: of uncertain origin]

bob² (bɒb) *n* **1** a hairstyle for women and children in which the hair is cut short evenly all round the head **2** a dangling or hanging object, such as the weight on a pendulum or on a plumb line **3** short for **bobsleigh** ▷ *vb* **bobs, bobbing, bobbed 4** (*tr*) to cut (the hair) in a bob **5** (*tr*) to cut short (something, esp the tail of an animal);

dock or crop **6** (*intr*) to ride on a bobsled [C14 *bobbe* bunch of flowers, perhaps of Celtic origin]

bob³ (bɒb) *n, pl* **bob** *Brit* (formerly) an informal word for a **shilling** [C19: of unknown origin]

bobbejaan ('bɒbəˌjɑːn) *n South African* **1** a baboon **2** a large black spider **3** a monkey wrench [Afrikaans]

bobbin ('bɒbɪn) *n* a spool or reel on which thread or yarn is wound, being unwound as required; spool; reel [C16: from Old French *bobine*, of unknown origin]

bobble ('bɒbʰl) *n* **1** a short jerky motion, as of a cork floating on disturbed water; bobbing movement **2** a tufted ball, usually for ornament, as on a knitted hat ▷ *vb* **3** (*intr*) *sport* (of a ball) to bounce with a rapid erratic motion due to an uneven playing surface [C19: from BOB¹ (vb)]

bobblehead ('bɒbəlˌhɛd) *n* a collectable doll with a bobbing oversized head representing a celebrity or a cartoon character

bobby ('bɒbɪ) *n, pl* **-bies** *informal* a British policeman [C19: from *Bobby* after Sir *Robert* Peel (1788–1850), British Conservative statesman, who, as Home Secretary, set up the Metropolitan Police Force in 1828]

bobby calf *n* an unweaned calf culled for slaughter

bobby-dazzler *n dialect* anything outstanding, striking, or showy, esp an attractive girl [C19: expanded form of *dazzler* something striking or attractive]

bobby pin *n US, Canadian, Austral & NZ* a metal hairpin bent in order to hold the hair in place

bobby socks *pl n* ankle-length socks worn by teenage girls, esp in the US in the 1940s

bobcat ('bɒbˌkæt) *n* a North American feline mammal, *Lynx rufus*, closely related to but smaller than the lynx, having reddish-brown fur with dark spots or stripes, tufted ears, and a short tail [C19: from BOB² (referring to its short tail) + CAT¹]

Bobo-Dioulasso ('bəʊbəʊdjuːˈlæsəʊ) *n* a city in W Burkina Faso. Pop: 396 000 (2005 est)

bobolink ('bɒbəˌlɪŋk) *n* an American songbird, *Dolichonyx oryzivorus*, the male of which has a white back and black underparts in the breeding season: family *Icteridae* (American orioles) [C18: of imitative origin]

bobotie (bʊˈbʊtɪ) *n* a South African dish consisting of curried mincemeat with a topping of beaten egg baked to a crust [C19: from Afrikaans, probably from Malay]

Bobruisk *or* **Bobruysk** (bɒˈbruːɪsk) *n* a port in Belarus, on the River Berezina: engineering, timber, tyre manufacturing. Pop: 219 000 (2005 est)

bobsleigh ('bɒbˌsleɪ) *n* **1** a racing sledge for two or more people, with a steering mechanism enabling the driver to direct it down a steeply banked ice-covered run ▷ *vb* **2** (*intr*) to ride on a bobsleigh. Also called: **bobsled** [C19: BOB² + SLEIGH]

bobstay ('bɒbˌsteɪ) *n* a strong stay between a bowsprit and the stem of a vessel for holding down the bowsprit [C18: perhaps from BOB¹ + STAY³]

bobsy-die ('bɒbzɪˌdaɪ) *n NZ informal* fuss; confusion; pandemonium (esp in the phrases **kick up bobsy-die**, **play bobsy-die**) [from C19 *bob's a-dying*]

bobtail ('bɒbˌteɪl) *n* **1** a docked or diminutive tail ▷ *adj* Also: **bobtailed 2** having the tail cut short ▷ *vb* (*tr*) **3** to dock the tail of **4** to cut short; curtail [C16: from BOB² + TAIL¹]

Boccaccio (*Italian* bokˈkattʃo) *n* **Giovanni** (dʒoˈvanni). 1313–75, Italian poet and writer, noted particularly for his *Decameron* (1353), a collection of 100 short stories. His other works include *Filostrato* (?1338) and *Teseida* (1341)

Boccherini (*Italian* bokkeˈriːni) *n* **Luigi** (luˈiːdʒi). 1743–1805, Italian composer and cellist

Boccioni (*Italian* botˈtʃoni) *n* **Umberto** (umˈbɛrto). 1882–1916, Italian painter and sculptor: principal theorist of the futurist movement

bocconcini *or* **boconcini** (*Italian* bokontʃini) *pl n* small bite-sized pieces of mozzarella cheese [C21: Italian: mouthful]

Boche (bɒʃ) *n derogatory, slang* (esp in World Wars I and II) **1** a German, esp a German soldier **2** the Boche (*usually functioning as plural*) Germans collectively, esp German soldiers regarded as the enemy [C20: from French, probably shortened from *alboche* German, from *allemand* German + *caboche* pate]

Bochum (*German* ˈbɔːxum) *n* an industrial city in NW Germany, in W North Rhine-Westphalia: university (1965). Pop: 387 283 (2003 est)

bockedy ('bɒkədɪ) *adj Irish* (of a structure, piece of furniture, etc) unsteady [from Irish Gaelic *bacaideach* limping]

bod (bɒd) *n informal* **1** a fellow; chap: *he's a queer bod* **2** another word for: **body** (sense 1) [C18: short for BODY]

BOD *abbreviation* biochemical oxygen demand

bodacious (bəʊˈdeɪʃəs) *adj slang, chiefly US* impressive or remarkable; excellent [C19: from English dialect; blend of BOLD + AUDACIOUS]

bode¹ (bəʊd) *vb* **1** to be an omen of (good or ill, esp of ill); portend; presage **2** (*tr*) *archaic* to predict; foretell [Old English *bodian*; related to Old Norse *botha* to proclaim, Old Frisian *bodia* to invite] > 'bodement *n*

bode² (bəʊd) *vb* the past tense of **bide**

bodega (bəʊˈdiːɡə; *Spanish* boˈðeɣa) *n* a shop selling wine and sometimes groceries, esp in a Spanish-speaking country [C19: from Spanish, ultimately from Greek *apothēkē* storehouse, from *apotithenai* to store, put away]

Bodensee ('boːdənzeː) *n* the German name for (Lake) **Constance**

bodge (bɒdʒ) *vb* **1** *informal* to make a mess of; botch **2** *Austral informal* to make or adjust in a false or clumsy way: *I bodged the figures* [C16: changed from BOTCH]

bodgie ('bɒdʒɪ) *Austral & NZ* ▷ *n* **1** an unruly or uncouth young man, esp in the 1950s; teddy boy ▷ *adj* **2** inferior; worthless [C20: from BODGE]

Bodh Gaya ('bɒd ɡəˈjɑː) *n* a variant spelling of **Buddh Gaya**

Bodhidharma (ˌbəʊdɪˈdɑːmə, ˌbɒd-) *n* 6th century AD, Indian Buddhist monk, who taught in China (from 520): considered the founder of Zen Buddhism

Bodhisattva (ˌbəʊdɪˈsætvə, -wə, ˌbɒd-, ˌbəʊdiːˈsʌtvə) *n* (in Mahayana Buddhism) a divine being worthy of nirvana who remains on the human plane to help men to salvation [Sanskrit, literally: one whose essence is enlightenment, from *bodhi* enlightenment + *sattva* essence]

bodice ('bɒdɪs) *n* **1** the upper part of a woman's dress, from the shoulder to the waist **2** a tight-fitting corset worn laced over a blouse, as in certain national costumes, or (formerly) as a woman's undergarment [C16: originally Scottish *bodies*, plural of BODY]

bodice ripper *n informal* a romantic novel, usually on a historical theme, that involves some sex and violence

-bodied *adj* (*in combination*) having a body or bodies as specified: *able-bodied; long-bodied; many-bodied*

bodiless ('bɒdɪlɪs) *adj* having no body or substance; incorporeal or insubstantial

bodily ('bɒdɪlɪ) *adj* **1** relating to or being a part of the human body ▷ *adv* **2** by taking hold of the body: *he threw him bodily from the platform* **3** in person; in the flesh

bodkin ('bɒdkɪn) *n* **1** a blunt large-eyed needle used esp for drawing tape through openwork **2** *archaic* a dagger **3** *archaic* a long ornamental hairpin [C14: probably of Celtic origin; compare Gaelic *biodag* dagger]

Bodmin ('bɒdmɪn) *n* a market town in SW England, in Cornwall, near **Bodmin Moor**, a granite upland rising to 420 m (1375 ft). Pop: 12 778 (2001)

body ('bɒdɪ) *n, pl* **bodies 1 a** the entire physical structure of an animal or human being **b** (*as modifier*): *body odour* **2** the flesh, as opposed to the spirit **3** the trunk or torso, not including the limbs, head, or tail **4** a dead human or animal; corpse **5** the largest or main part of anything: *the body of a vehicle; the body of a plant* **6** a separate or distinct mass of water or land **7** a number of individuals regarded as a single entity; group: *the student body; they marched in a body* **8** fullness in the appearance of the hair **9** the characteristic full quality of certain wines, determined by the density and the content of alcohol or tannin **10** substance or firmness, esp of cloth **11 a** the pigment contained in or added to paint, dye, etc **b** the opacity of a paint in covering a surface **12** (in watercolour painting) (*as modifier*): *body colour* **13** an informal or dialect word for a **person 14 keep body and soul together** to manage to keep alive; survive ▷ *vb*

b

bodies, bodying, bodied (*tr*) **15** (usually foll by *forth*) to give a body or shape to [Old English *bodig*; related to Old Norse *buthkr* box, Old High German *botah* body]

body blow *n* Also called: **body punch** *boxing* a blow to the body of an opponent

bodyboard ('bɒdɪ,bɔːd) *n* a surfboard that is shorter and blunter than the standard board and on which the surfer lies rather than stands

body building *n* the practice of performing regular exercises designed to make the muscles of the body conspicuous

bodycheck ('bɒdɪ,tʃɛk) *sport* ▷ *n* **1** obstruction of another player ▷ *vb* **2** (*tr*) to deliver a bodycheck to (an opponent)

body combat *n* a type of fitness programme in which individuals perform non-contact martial arts moves to music

body double *n* *films* a person who substitutes for a star for the filming of a scene that involves shots of the body rather than the face

bodyguard ('bɒdɪ,gɑːd) *n* a person or group of people who escort and protect someone, esp a political figure

body horror *n* a horror film genre in which the main feature is the graphically depicted destruction or degeneration of a human body or bodies

body language *n* the nonverbal imparting of information by means of conscious or subconscious bodily gestures, posture, etc

body-line *adj* *cricket* denoting or relating to fast bowling aimed at the batsman's body

body mass index *n* an index used to indicate whether a person is over- or underweight. It is obtained by dividing a person's weight in kilograms by the square of their height in metres. An index of 20–25 is normal

body-packer *n* a person who smuggles illicit drugs in balloons, condoms, or similar plastic bags which have either been swallowed or inserted in the rectum or vagina

body politic *n* the body politic the people of a nation or the nation itself considered as a political entity; the state

body search *n* **1** a form of search by police, customs officials, etc, that involves examination of a prisoner's or suspect's bodily orifices ▷ *vb* **body-search 2** (*tr*) to search (a prisoner or suspect) in this manner

bodyshell ('bɒdɪ,ʃɛl) *n* the external shell of a motor vehicle

body shop *n* a place where the bodywork of motor vehicles is built or repaired

body snatcher *n* (formerly) a person who robbed graves and sold the corpses for dissection

body stocking *n* a one-piece undergarment for women, usually of nylon, covering the torso

bodysuit ('bɒdɪ,suːt, -,sjuːt) *n* a one-piece undergarment for a baby

body swerve **1** *sport* (esp in football games) the act or an instance of swerving past an opponent **2** *Scot* the act or an instance of avoiding (a situation considered unpleasant): *I think I'll give the meeting a body swerve* ▷ *vb* **body-swerve 3** *sport* (esp in football games) to pass (an opponent) using a body swerve **4** *Scot* to avoid (a situation or person considered unpleasant)

body warmer *n* a sleeveless type of jerkin, usually quilted, worn as an outer garment for extra warmth

bodywork ('bɒdɪ,wɜːk) *n* the external shell of a motor vehicle

Boeotia (bɪ'əʊʃɪə) *n* a region of ancient Greece, northwest of Athens. It consisted of ten city-states, which formed the Boeotian League, led by Thebes: at its height in the 4th century BC. Modern Greek name: Voiotia

Boeotian (bɪ'əʊʃɪən) *n* **1** a native or inhabitant of Boeotia, a region of ancient Greece ▷ *adj* **2** of or relating to Boeotia or its inhabitants

Boer (bʊə, 'bəʊə, bɔː) *n, adj* **a** a descendant of any of the Dutch or Huguenot colonists who settled in South Africa, mainly in Cape Colony, the Orange Free State, and the Transvaal **b** (*as modifier*): *a Boer farm* [C19: from Dutch *Boer*; see BOOR]

boerbul ('bʊə,bʊl) *n* *South African* a crossbred mastiff

used esp as a watchdog [from Afrikaans *boerboel* a breed of mastiff]

boeremusiek ('bʊərə,mjuːzɪk) *n* *South African* a special variety of light music associated with the culture of the Afrikaners [Afrikaans]

boet (but) *n* *South African* brother; mate, chum [Afrikaans]

Boethius (bəʊ'iːθɪəs) *n* **Anicius Manlius Severinus** (ə'nɪsɪəs 'mænlɪəs ,sɛvə'raɪnəs). ?480–?524 AD, Roman philosopher and statesman, noted particularly for his work *De Consolatione Philosophiae*. He was accused of treason and executed by Theodoric

boffin ('bɒfɪn) *n* **1** *Brit informal* a scientist, esp one carrying out military research **2** a person who has extensive skill or knowledge in a particular field: *a Treasury boffin* [C20: of uncertain origin]

boffo ('bɒfəʊ) *adj* *slang* very good; highly successful [C20: of uncertain origin]

Bofors gun ('bəʊfəz) *n* an automatic single- or double-barrelled anti-aircraft gun with a 40 millimetre bore [C20: named after *Bofors*, Sweden, where it was first made]

bog (bɒg) *n* **1** wet spongy ground consisting of decomposing vegetation, which ultimately forms peat **2** an area of such ground **3** *slang* a word for **lavatory** (sense 1) [C13: from Gaelic *bogach* swamp, from *bog* soft] ▷ **'boggy** *adj* ▷ **'bogginess** *n*

bogan[1] ('bəʊgən) *n* *Canadian* (esp in the Maritime Provinces) a sluggish side stream. Also called: **logan**, **pokelogan** [of Algonquian origin]

bogan[2] ('bəʊgən) *n* *Austral informal* **1** a fool **2** a hooligan [C20: of unknown origin]

Bogarde ('bəʊgɑːd) *n* **Sir Dirk**, real name *Derek Jules Gaspard Ulric Niven van den Bogaerde*. 1920–99, British film actor and writer: his films include *The Servant* (1963) and *Death in Venice* (1970). His writings include the autobiographical *A Postillion Struck by Lightning* (1977) and the novel *A Period of Adjustment* (1994)

Bogart ('bəʊgɑːt) *n* **Humphrey (DeForest)**. nicknamed *Bogie*. 1899–1957, US film actor: his films include *High Sierra* (1941), *Casablanca* (1942), *The Big Sleep* (1946), *The African Queen* (1951), and *The Caine Mutiny* (1954)

Boğazköy (Turkish bɔː'azkœi) *n* a village in central Asia Minor: site of the ancient Hittite capital

bogbean ('bɒg,biːn) *n* another name for **buckbean**

bog down *vb* **bogs, bogging, bogged** (*adverb*; when *tr*, *often passive*) to impede or be impeded physically or mentally

bogey *or* **bogy** ('bəʊgɪ) *n* **1** an evil or mischievous spirit **2** something that worries or annoys **3** *golf* **a** a score of one stroke over par on a hole. See **par** (sense 5) **b** *obsolete* a standard score for a hole or course, regarded as one that a good player should make **4** *slang* a piece of dried mucus discharged from the nose [C19: probably related to BUG and BOGLE; compare BUGABOO]

bogeyman ('bəʊgɪ,mæn) *n, pl* -men a person, real or imaginary, used as a threat, esp to children

bogger (bɒgə) *n* *Austral slang* a lavatory

boggle ('bɒgəl) *vb* (*intr*; often foll by *at*) **1** to be surprised, confused, or alarmed (esp in the phrase **the mind boggles**) **2** to hesitate or be evasive when confronted with a problem [C16: probably variant of BOGLE]

bogie *or* **bogy** ('bəʊgɪ) *n* **1** an assembly of four or six wheels forming a pivoted support at either end of a railway coach. It provides flexibility on curves **2** *chiefly Brit* a small railway truck of short wheelbase, used for conveying coal, ores, etc [C19: of unknown origin]

bogle ('bəʊgəl, 'bɒg-) *n* a dialect or archaic word for **bogey** (sense 1) [C16: from Scottish *bogill*, perhaps from Gaelic; compare Welsh *bygel*; see BUG]

bog myrtle *n* another name for **sweet gale**

Bognor Regis ('bɒgnə 'riːdʒɪs) *n* a resort in S England, in West Sussex on the English Channel: electronics industries. *Regis* was added to the name after King George V's convalescence there in 1929. Pop: 62 141 (2001)

bog oak *n* oak or other wood found preserved in peat bogs; bogwood

bog off *Brit slang* ▷ *interj* **1** go away! ▷ *vb* **bogs, bogging, bogged 2** (*intr, adverb*) to go away

bogong ('bəʊ,ɡɒŋ) *or* **bugong** ('buː,ɡɒŋ) *n* an edible dark-coloured Australian noctuid moth, *Agrotis infusa*

Bogor ('bəʊɡɔː) *n* a city in Indonesia, in W Java: botanical gardens and research institutions. Pop: 750 819 (2000). Former name: Buitenzorg

Bogotá (,bəʊɡə'taː; *Spanish* boɣo'ta) *n* the capital of Colombia, on a central plateau of the E Andes: originally the centre of Chibcha civilization; founded as a city in 1538 by the Spaniards. Pop: 7 594 000 (2005 est)

bog-standard *adj informal* completely ordinary; run-of-the-mill

bogtrotter ('bɒɡ,trɒtə) *n* a highly offensive term for an Irish person

bogus ('bəʊɡəs) *adj* spurious or counterfeit; not genuine [c19: from *bogus* apparatus for making counterfeit money; perhaps related to BOGEY] > 'bogusly *adv* > 'bogusness *n*

bogy ('bəʊɡɪ) *n, pl* -gies a variant spelling of **bogey** or **bogie**

Bohai ('bɔː'haɪ) *or* **Pohai** *n* a large inlet of the Yellow Sea on the coast of NE China. Also called: Gulf of Chihli

bohea (bəʊ'hiː) *n* a black Chinese tea, once regarded as the choicest, but now as an inferior grade [c18: from Chinese (Fukien dialect) *bu-i*, from Mandarin Chinese *Wu-i Shan* range of hills on which this tea was grown]

Bohemia (bəʊ'hiːmɪə) *n* 1 a former kingdom of central Europe, surrounded by mountains: independent from the 9th to the 13th century; belonged to the Hapsburgs from 1526 until 1918 2 an area of the W Czech Republic, formerly a province of Czechoslovakia (1918–1949). From 1939 until 1945 it formed part of the German protectorate of Bohemia-Moravia. Czech name: Čechy 3 a district frequented by unconventional people, esp artists or writers

Bohemian (bəʊ'hiːmɪən) *n* 1 a native or inhabitant of Bohemia, esp of the old kingdom of Bohemia; a Czech 2 (*often not capital*) a person, esp an artist or writer, who lives an unconventional life 3 the Czech language > *adj* 4 of, relating to, or characteristic of Bohemia, its people, or their language 5 unconventional in appearance, behaviour, etc

Bohemian Forest *n* a mountain range between the SW Czech Republic and SE Germany. Highest peak: Arber, 1457 m (4780 ft)

Bohemianism (bəʊ'hiːmɪə,nɪzəm) *n* unconventional behaviour or appearance, esp of an artist

Bohemond I ('bəʊəmənd) *n* ?1056–?1111, prince of Antioch (1099–1111); a leader of the first crusade, he helped to capture Antioch (1098)

Böhm (*German* bøːm) *n* **Karl** (karl). 1894–1981, Austrian orchestral conductor

Böhme, Boehme (*German* 'bøːmə) *or* **Böhm** *n* **Jakob** ('jaːkɔp). 1575–1624, German mystic

boho ('bəʊhəʊ) *n, pl* -hos *informal* short for **Bohemian** (senses 2, 5)

Bohol (bəʊ'hɔːl) *n* an island of the central Philippines. Chief town: Tagbilaran. Pop: 1 139 130 (2000). Area: about 3900 sq km (1500 sq miles)

Bohr (bɔː; *Danish* boːr) *n* 1 **Aage Niels** ('ɔɡə neːls). born 1922, Danish physicist, noted for his work on nuclear structure. He shared the Nobel prize for physics 1975 2 his father, **Niels** (**Henrik David**). 1885–1962, Danish physicist, who applied the quantum theory to Rutherford's model of the atom to explain spectral lines: Nobel prize for physics 1922

bohrium ('bɔːrɪəm) *n* a transuranic element artificially produced in minute quantities by bombarding ^{204}Bi atoms with ^{54}Cr nuclei. Symbol: Bh; atomic no: 107 [c20: after Niels *Bohr* (1885–1962), Danish physicist]

Boiardo (*Italian* bo'jardo) *n* **Matteo Maria** (mat'tɛːo ma'riːa), conte de Scandiano 1434–94, Italian poet; author of the historical epic *Orlando Innamorato* (1487)

boil¹ (bɔɪl) *vb* 1 to change or cause to change from a liquid to a vapour so rapidly that bubbles of vapour are formed copiously in the liquid 2 to reach or cause to reach boiling point 3 to cook or be cooked by the process of boiling 4 (*intr*) to bubble and be agitated like something boiling; seethe: *the ocean was boiling* 5 (*intr*) to be extremely angry or indignant (esp in the phrase

make one's blood boil) > *n* 6 the state or action of boiling (esp in the phrases **on the boil, off the boil**). > See also **boil away, boil down, boil over** [c13: from Old French *boillir*, from Latin *bullīre* to bubble, from *bulla* a bubble]

boil² (bɔɪl) *n* a red painful swelling with a hard pus-filled core caused by bacterial infection of the skin and subcutaneous tissues, esp at a hair follicle. Technical name: furuncle [Old English *býle*; related to Old Norse *beyla* swelling, Old High German *būlla* bladder, Gothic *ufbauljan* to inflate]

boil away *vb* (*adverb*) to cause (liquid) to evaporate completely by boiling or (of liquid) to evaporate completely

boil down *vb* (*adverb*) 1 to reduce or be reduced in quantity and usually altered in consistency by boiling 2 **boil down to** a (*intr*) to be the essential element in something b (*tr*) to summarize; reduce to essentials

Boileau (*French* bwalo) *n* **Nicolas** (nikɔla). full name *Nicolas Boileau-Despréaux*. 1636–1711, French poet and critic; author of satires, epistles, and *L'Art poétique* (1674), in which he laid down the basic principles of French classical literature

boiled shirt *n informal* a dress shirt with a stiff front

boiler ('bɔɪlə) *n* 1 a closed vessel or arrangement of enclosed tubes in which water is heated to supply steam to drive an engine or turbine or provide heat 2 a domestic device burning solid fuel, gas, or oil, to provide hot water, esp for central heating 3 a large tub for boiling laundry

boilermaker ('bɔɪlə,meɪkə) *n* a person who works with metal in heavy industry; plater or welder

boilerplate ('bɔɪlə,pleɪt) *n* 1 a form of mild-steel plate used in the production of boiler shells 2 a copy made with the intention of making other copies from it 3 a set of instructions incorporated in several places in a computer program or a standard form of words used repeatedly in drafting contracts, guarantees, etc 4 a draft contract that can easily be modified to cover various types of transaction

boiler room *n* 1 any room in a building (often in the basement) that contains a boiler for central heating, etc 2 the part of a steam ship that houses the boilers and furnaces 3 the room or department in which the real work of an organization goes on unseen 4 (*chiefly US*) an office used by a team of telephone salespeople, esp of stocks and shares, operating under high pressure

boiler suit *n Brit* a one-piece work garment consisting of overalls and a shirt top usually worn over ordinary clothes to protect them

boiling point *n* 1 the temperature at which a liquid boils at a given pressure, usually atmospheric pressure at sea level; the temperature at which the vapour pressure of a liquid equals the external pressure 2 *informal* the condition of being angered or highly excited

boiling-water reactor *n* a nuclear reactor using water as coolant and moderator, steam being produced in the reactor itself: enriched uranium oxide cased in zirconium is the fuel

boilover ('bɔɪl,əʊvə) *n Austral* 1 a surprising result in a sporting event, esp in a horse race 2 a sudden conflict

boil over *vb* (*adverb*) 1 to overflow or cause to overflow while boiling 2 (*intr*) to burst out in anger or excitement

Bois de Boulogne (*French* bwa də bulɔn) *n* a large park in W Paris, formerly a forest: includes the racecourses of Auteuil and Longchamp

Boise *or* **Boise City** ('bɔɪzɪ, -sɪ) *n* a city in SW Idaho: the state capital. Pop: 190 117 (2003 est)

Bois-le-Duc (bwa lə dyk) *n* the French name for **'s Hertogenbosch**

boisterous ('bɔɪstərəs, -strəs) *adj* 1 noisy and lively; unrestrained or unruly 2 (of the wind, sea, etc) turbulent or stormy [c13 *boistuous*, of unknown origin] > 'boisterously *adv* > 'boisterousness *n*

Boito (*Italian* 'bɔːito) *n* **Arrigo** (ar'riɡo). 1842–1918, Italian operatic composer and librettist, whose works include the opera *Mefistofele* (1868) and the librettos for Verdi's *Otello* and *Falstaff*

Bokassa I (bə'kæsə) *n* original name *Jean Bedel Bokassa*.

1921–96, president of the Central African Republic (1972–76); emperor of the renamed Central African Empire from 1976 until overthrown in 1979

bok choy ('bɒk 'tʃɔɪ) *n* a Chinese plant, *Brassica chinensis*, that is related to the cabbage and has edible stalks and leaves. Also called: Chinese cabbage, Chinese leaf, pakchoi cabbage [from Chinese dialect, literally: white vegetable]

Bokhara (bʊ'xɑ:rə) *n* a variant spelling of **Bukhara**

Bol. *abbreviation* Bolivia(n)

bola ('bəʊlə) *or* **bolas** ('bəʊləs) *n, pl* -las *or* -lases a missile used by gauchos and Indians of South America, consisting of two or more heavy balls on a cord. It is hurled at a running quarry, such as an ox or rhea, so as to entangle its legs [Spanish: ball, from Latin *bulla* knob]

Boland ('bʊələnt) *n* an area of high altitude in S South Africa

Bolan Pass (bəʊ'lɑ:n) *n* a mountain pass in W central Pakistan through the Brahui Range, between Sibi and Quetta, rising to 1800 m (5900 ft)

bold (bəʊld) *adj* 1 courageous, confident, and fearless; ready to take risks 2 showing or requiring courage: *a bold plan* 3 immodest or impudent: *she gave him a bold look* 4 standing out distinctly; conspicuous: *a figure carved in bold relief* 5 very steep: *the bold face of the cliff* 6 imaginative in thought or expression [Old English *beald*; related to Old Norse *ballr* dangerous, terrible, *baldinn* defiant, Old High German *bald* bold] > 'boldly *adv* > 'boldness *n*

Bolden ('bəʊldən) *n* **Buddy**, real name *Charles Bolden*. 1868–1931, US Black jazz cornet player; a pioneer of the New Orleans style

bold face *n* 1 *printing* a weight of type characterized by thick heavy lines, as the entry words in this dictionary ▷ *adj* boldface 2 (of type) having this weight

Boldrewood ('bəʊldə,wʊd) *n* **Rolf**, real name *Thomas Alexander Browne*. 1826–1915, Australian writer, born in the UK, noted for his novels of the Australian outback, esp *Robbery Under Arms* (1882–3)

bole (bəʊl) *n* the trunk of a tree [c14: from Old Norse *bolr*; related to Middle High German *bole* plank]

bolero (bə'lɛərəʊ) *n, pl* -ros 1 a Spanish dance, often accompanied by the guitar and castanets, usually in triple time 2 a piece of music composed for or in the rhythm of this dance 3 (*also* 'bɒlərəʊ) a kind of short jacket not reaching the waist, with or without sleeves and open at the front: worn by men in Spain and by women elsewhere [c18: from Spanish; perhaps related to *bola* ball]

Boleyn (bʊ'lɪn, 'bʊlɪn) *n* **Anne**. 1507–36, second wife of Henry VIII of England; mother of Elizabeth I. She was executed on a charge of adultery

Bolger ('bəʊldʒə) *n* **James**. born 1935, New Zealand politician; prime minister (1990–97)

Bolingbroke ('bɒlɪŋ,brʊk) *n* 1 the surname of Henry IV of England. See **Henry IV** 2 **Henry St John**, 1st Viscount Bolingbroke. 1678–1751, English politician; fled to France in 1714 and acted as secretary of state to the Old Pretender; returned to England in 1723. His writings include *A Dissertation on Parties* (1733–34) and *Idea of a Patriot King* (1738)

bolívar ('bɒlɪ,vɑ:; *Spanish* bo'liβar) *n, pl* -vars *or* -vares (-βares) the standard monetary unit of Venezuela, equal to 100 céntimos [named after Simon *Bolívar* (1783–1830), South American soldier and liberator]

Bolívar ('bɒlɪ,vɑ:; *Spanish* bo'liβar) *n* **Simon** (si'mon). 1783–1830, South American soldier and liberator. He drove the Spaniards from Venezuela, Colombia, Ecuador, and Peru and hoped to set up a republican confederation, but was prevented by separatist movements in Venezuela and Colombia (1829–30). Upper Peru became a separate state and was called Bolivia in his honour

Bolivia (bə'lɪvɪə) *n* an inland republic in central S America: original Aymará Indian population conquered by the Incas in the 13th century; colonized by Spain from 1538; became a republic in 1825; consists of low plains in the east, with ranges of the Andes rising to over 6400 m (21 000 ft) and the Altiplano, a plateau averaging 3900 m (13 000 ft) in the west; contains some

of the world's highest inhabited regions; important producer of tin and other minerals. Official languages: Spanish, Quechua, and Aymara. Religion: Roman Catholic. Currency: boliviano. Capital: La Paz (administrative); Sucre (judicial). Pop: 8 973 000 (2004 est). Area: 1 098 580 sq km (424 260 sq miles) > Bo'livian *adj, n*

boliviano (bə,lɪvɪ'ɑ:nəʊ; *Spanish* boli'vjano) *n, pl* -nos (-nəʊz; *Spanish* -nos) (until 1963 and from 1987) the standard monetary unit of Bolivia, equal to 100 centavos

boll (bəʊl) *n* the fruit of such plants as flax and cotton, consisting of a rounded capsule containing the seeds [c13: from Dutch *bolle*; related to Old English *bolla* BOWL¹]

Böll (*German* bœl) *n* **Heinrich** ('haɪnrɪç) (**Theodor**). 1917–85, German novelist and short-story writer; his novels include *Group Portrait with Lady* (1971): Nobel prize for literature 1972

bollard ('bɒlɑ:d, 'bɒləd) *n* 1 a strong wooden or metal post mounted on a wharf, quay, etc, used for securing mooring lines 2 *Brit* a small post or marker placed on a kerb or traffic island to make it conspicuous to motorists [c14: perhaps from BOLE¹ + -ARD]

bollocking ('bɒləkɪŋ) *n* *slang* a severe telling-off; dressing-down [from *bollock* (vb) (in the sense: to reprimand)]

bollocks ('bɒləks), **ballocks** *or* US **bollix** ('bɒlɪks) *slang pl n* 1 another word for **testicles** 2 nonsense; rubbish ▷ *interj* 3 an exclamation of annoyance, disbelief, etc [Old English *beallucas*, diminutive (pl) of *beallu* (unattested); see BALL¹]

boll weevil *n* a greyish weevil, *Anthonomus grandis*, of the southern US and Mexico, whose larvae live in and destroy cotton bolls

Bollywood ('bɒlɪ,wʊd) *n* *informal* **a** the Indian film industry **b** (*as modifier*): *a Bollywood star* [c20: from BO(MBAY) + (HO)LLYWOOD]

Bologna¹ (bə'ləʊnjə; *Italian* bo'loɲɲa) *n* a city in N Italy, at the foot of the Apennines: became a free city in the Middle Ages; university (1088). Pop: 371 217 (2001)

Bologna² (bə'ləʊnjə; *Italian* bo'loɲɲa) *n* Giovanni da Bologna See **Giambologna**

bologna sausage *n* *chiefly US & Canadian* a large smoked sausage made of seasoned mixed meats. Also called: baloney, boloney, (*esp Brit*) polony

bolometer (bəʊ'lɒmɪtə) *n* a sensitive instrument for measuring radiant energy by the increase in the resistance of an electrical conductor [c19: from *bol-*, from Greek *bolē* ray of light, stroke, from *ballein* to throw + -METER] > bolometric (,bəʊlə'mɛtrɪk) *adj*

boloney (bə'ləʊnɪ) *n* 1 a variant spelling of **baloney** 2 *chiefly US* another name for **bologna sausage**

Bolshevik ('bɒlʃɪvɪk) *n, pl* -viks *or* -viki (-'vi:kɪ) 1 (formerly) a Russian Communist. See **Menshevik** 2 any Communist 3 (*often not capital*) *humorous, derogatory* any political radical, esp a revolutionary [c20: from Russian *Bol'shevik* majority, from *bol'shoi* great; from the fact that this group formed a majority of the Russian Social Democratic Party in 1903] > 'Bolshe,vism *n* > 'Bolshevist *adj, n* > ,Bolshe'vistic *adj*

bolshie *or* **bolshy** ('bɒlʃɪ) (*sometimes capital*) *Brit informal* ▷ *adj* 1 difficult to manage; rebellious 2 politically radical or left-wing ▷ *n, pl* -shies 3 *dismissive* any political radical [c20: shortened from BOLSHEVIK]

bolster ('bəʊlstə) *vb* (*tr*) 1 (*often foll by up*) to support or reinforce; strengthen: *to bolster morale* 2 to prop up with a pillow or cushion ▷ *n* 3 a long narrow pillow or cushion 4 any pad or padded support 5 a cold chisel having a broad blade splayed towards the cutting edge, used for cutting stone slabs, etc [Old English *bolster*; related to Old Norse *bolstr*, Old High German *bolstar*, Dutch *bulster*]

bolt¹ (bəʊlt) *n* 1 a bar that can be slid into a socket to lock a door, gate, etc 2 a bar or rod that forms part of a locking mechanism and is moved by a key or a knob 3 a metal rod or pin that has a head at one end and a screw thread at the other to take a nut 4 a sliding bar in a breech-loading firearm that ejects the empty cartridge, replaces it with a new one, and closes the breech 5 a flash of lightning 6 a sudden start or movement, esp in order to escape 7 a roll of something, such as cloth, wallpaper, etc **8** an arrow, esp for a crossbow **9** a bolt from the blue a sudden, unexpected, and usually unwelcome event **10** shoot one's bolt to exhaust one's effort ▷ *vb* **11** (*tr*) to secure or lock with or as with a bolt or bolts: *bolt your doors* **12** (*tr*) to eat hurriedly: *don't bolt your food* **13** (*intr*; usually foll by *from* or *out*) to move or jump suddenly: *he bolted from the chair* **14** (*intr*) (esp of a horse) to start hurriedly and run away without warning **15** (*tr*) to roll or make (cloth, wallpaper, etc) into bolts **16** (*intr*) (of cultivated plants) to produce flowers and seeds prematurely ▷ *adv* **17** stiffly, firmly, or rigidly (archaic except in the phrase **bolt upright**) [Old English *bolt* arrow; related to Old High German *bolz* bolt for a crossbow]

bolt² or **boult** (bəʊlt) *vb* (*tr*) **1** to pass (flour, a powder, etc) through a sieve **2** to examine and separate [c13: from Old French *bulter*, probably of Germanic origin; compare Old High German *būtil* bag] > **'bolter** or **'boulter** *n*

Bolt (bəʊlt) *n* **Robert** (**Oxton**). 1924–95, British playwright. His plays include *A Man for All Seasons* (1960) and he also wrote a number of screenplays

bolt hole *n* a place of escape from danger

Bolton ('bəʊltən) *n* **1** a town in NW England, in Bolton unitary authority, Greater Manchester: centre of the woollen trade since the 14th century; later important for cotton. Pop: 139 403 (2001) **2** a unitary authority in NW England, in Greater Manchester. Pop: 263 800 (2003 est). Area: 140 sq km (54 sq miles)

boltrope ('bəʊlt,rəʊp) *n* *nautical* a rope sewn to the foot or luff of a sail to strengthen it [c17: from BOLT¹ + ROPE]

Boltzmann (German 'bɔltsman) *n* **Ludwig** ('luːtvɪç). 1844–1906, Austrian physicist. He established the principle of the equipartition of energy and developed the kinetic theory of gases with J. C. Maxwell

bolus ('bəʊləs) *n*, *pl* **-luses** **1** a small round soft mass, esp of chewed food **2** *obsolete* a large pill or tablet used in veterinary and clinical medicine [c17: from New Latin, from Greek *bōlos* clod, lump]

Bolzano (Italian bol'tsano) *n* a city in NE Italy, in Trentino-Alto Adige: belonged to Austria until 1919. Pop: 94 989 (2001). German name: Bozen

Boma ('bəʊmə) *n* a port in the Democratic Republic of Congo (formerly Zaïre), on the Congo River, capital of the Belgian Congo until 1926: forest products. Pop: 607 000 (2005 est)

bomb (bɒm) *n* **1 a** a hollow projectile containing an explosive, incendiary, or other destructive substance, esp one carried by aircraft **b** (*as modifier*): *bomb disposal; a bomb bay* **c** (*in combination*): *a bombload; bombproof* **2** any container filled with explosive: *a car bomb; a letter bomb* **3** the bomb **a** a hydrogen or atomic bomb considered as the ultimate destructive weapon **b** *slang* something excellent: *it's the bomb* **4** a round or pear-shaped mass of volcanic rock, solidified from molten lava that has been thrown into the air **5** *med* a container for radioactive material, applied therapeutically to all part of the body: *a cobalt bomb* **6** *Brit slang* a large sum of money (esp in the phrase **make a bomb**) **7** *US & Canadian slang* a disastrous failure: *the new play was a total bomb* **8** *Austral & NZ slang* an old or dilapidated motorcar **9** *American football* a very long high pass **10** (in rugby union) another term for **up-and-under** **11** like a bomb *Brit & NZ informal* with great speed or success; very well (esp in the phrase **go like a bomb**) ▷ *vb* **12** to attack with or as if with a bomb or bombs; drop bombs (on) **13** (*intr*; often foll by *off*, *along*, etc) *informal* to move or drive very quickly **14** (*intr*) *slang* to fail disastrously; be a flop [c17: from French *bombe*, from Italian *bomba*, probably from Latin *bombus* a booming sound, from Greek *bombos*, of imitative origin; compare Old Norse *bumba* drum]

bombaceous (,bɒmbə'keɪʃəs) *adj* of, relating to, or belonging to the *Bombacaceae*, a family of tropical trees, including the kapok tree and baobab, that have very thick stems, often with water-storing tissue [c19: from New Latin *Bombācāceae*, from Medieval Latin *bombāx* cotton, from Latin *bombyx* silkworm, silk, from Greek *bombux*]

bombard *vb* (bɒm'bɑːd) (*tr*) **1** to attack with

concentrated artillery fire or bombs **2** to attack with vigour and persistence **3** to attack verbally, esp with questions **4** *physics* to direct high-energy particles or photons against (atoms, nuclei, etc) esp to produce ions or nuclear transformations ▷ *n* ('bɒmbɑːd) **5** an ancient type of cannon that threw stone balls [c15: from Old French *bombarder* to pelt, from *bombarde* stone-throwing cannon, probably from Latin *bombus* booming sound; see BOMB] > **bom'bardment** *n*

bombardier (,bɒmbə'dɪə) *n* **1** the member of a bomber aircrew responsible for aiming and releasing the bombs **2** *Brit* a noncommissioned rank below the rank of sergeant in the Royal Artillery [c16: from Old French: one directing a bombard; see BOMBARD]

Bombardier (,bɒmbə'dɪə) *n* *trademark Canadian* a snow tractor, typically having caterpillar tracks at the rear and skis at the front [c20: named after J. A. *Bombardier*, Canadian inventor and manufacturer]

bombast ('bɒmbæst) *n* pompous and grandiloquent language [c16: from Old French *bombace*, from Medieval Latin *bombāx* cotton; see BOMBACACEOUS] > **bom'bastic** *adj* > **bom'bastically** *adv*

Bombay (bɒm'beɪ) *n* **1** the former English name of **Mumbai 2** a breed of black short-haired medium-sized cat

Bombay duck *n* a teleost fish, *Harpodon nehereus*, that resembles and is related to the lizard fish: family *Harpodontidae*. It is eaten dried with curry dishes as a savoury. Also called: bummalo [c19: changed from *bombil* (see BUMMALO) through association with Bombay (now Mumbai), from which it was exported]

bombazine or **bombasine** (,bɒmbə'ziːn, 'bɒmbə,ziːn) *n* a twilled fabric, esp one with a silk warp and worsted weft, formerly worn dyed black for mourning [c16: from Old French *bombasin*, from Latin *bombӯcinus* silken, from *bombyx* silkworm, silk; see BOMBACACEOUS]

bomb belt *n* a belt carrying explosives which is worn around the waist by a suicide bomber

bomber ('bɒmə) *n* **1** a military aircraft designed to carry out bombing missions **2** a person who plants bombs

Bomberg ('bɒmbɜːg) *n* **David**. 1890–1957, British painter, noted esp for his landscapes

bomber jacket *n* a short jacket finishing at the waist with an elasticated band, usually having a zip front and cuffed sleeves

bomblet ('bɒmlɪt) *n* one of a number of small bombs contained in a larger bomb

bombora (bɒm'bɔːrə) *n* *Austral* **1** a submerged reef **2** a turbulent area of sea over such a reef [from a native Australian language]

bombshell ('bɒm,ʃɛl) *n* **1** (esp formerly) a bomb or artillery shell **2** a shocking or unwelcome surprise

bombsight ('bɒm,saɪt) *n* a mechanical or electronic device in an aircraft for aiming bombs

Bomu ('bəʊmuː) or **Mbomu** (ᵊm'bəʊmuː) *n* a river in central Africa, rising in the SE Central African Republic and flowing west into the Uele River, forming the Ubangi River. Length: about 800 km (500 miles)

Bon (bɒn) *n* **Cape Bon** a peninsula of NE Tunisia

Bona ('bəʊnə) *n* **Mount Bona** a mountain in S Alaska, in the Wrangell Mountains. Height: 5005 m (16 420 ft)

bona fide ('bəʊnə 'faɪdɪ) *adj* **1** real or genuine: *a bona fide manuscript* **2** undertaken in good faith: *a bona fide agreement* [c16: from Latin]

bona fides ('bəʊnə 'faɪdiːz) *n* *law* good faith; honest intention [Latin]

Bonaire (bɒn'eə) *n* an island in the S Caribbean, in the E Netherlands Antilles: one of the Leeward Islands. Chief town: Kralendijk. Pop: 11 537 (2007 est). Area: about 288 sq km (111 sq miles)

bonanza (bə'nænzə) *n* **1** a source, usually sudden and unexpected, of luck or wealth **2** *US & Canadian* a mine or vein rich in ore [c19: from Spanish, literally: calm sea, hence, good luck, from Medieval Latin *bonacia*, from Latin *bonus* good + *malacia* dead calm, from Greek *malakia* softness]

Bonaparte ('bəʊnə,pɑːt; *French* bɔnapart) *n* **1** See **Napoleon I 2 Jérôme** (ʒerom), brother of Napoleon I. 1784–1860, king of Westphalia (1807–13) **3 Joseph** (ʒozɛf), brother of Napoleon I. 1768–1844, king of Naples (1806–08) and of Spain (1808–13) **4 Louis** (lwi), brother of Napoleon I. 1778–1846, king of Holland (1806–10) **5 Lucien** (lysjɛ̃), brother of Napoleon I. 1775–1840, prince of Canino

Bonar Law ('bɒnə lɔː) *n* See **Law** (sense 1)

Bonaventura (,bɒnəven'tjʊərə) *or* **Bonaventure** ('bɒnə,ventʃə) *n* **Saint**, called *the Seraphic Doctor*. 1221–74, Italian Franciscan monk, mystic, theologian, and philosopher; author of a *Life of St Francis* and *Journey of the Soul to God* Feast day: July 14

bonbon ('bɒnbɒn) *n* a sweet [c19: from French, originally a children's word from *bon* good]

bonce (bɒns) *n* Brit slang the head [c19 (originally: a type of large playing marble): of unknown origin]

bond (bɒnd) *n* **1** something that binds, fastens, or holds together, such as a chain or rope **2** (often plural) something that brings or holds people together; tie: *a bond of friendship* **3** (plural) something that restrains or imprisons; captivity or imprisonment **4** a written or spoken agreement, esp a promise **5** finance a certificate of debt issued in order to raise funds. It carries a fixed rate of interest and is repayable with or without security at a specified future date **6** law a written acknowledgment of an obligation to pay a sum or to perform a contract **7** any of various arrangements of bricks or stones in a wall in which they overlap so as to provide strength **8** chemical bond a mutual attraction between two atoms resulting from a redistribution of their outer electrons, determining chemical properties; shown in some formulae by a dot (.) or score (–) **9** See **bond paper 10** in bond *commerce* deposited in a bonded warehouse ▷ *vb* (mainly tr) **11** (also intr) to hold or be held together, as by a rope or an adhesive; bind; connect **12** to put or hold (goods) in bond **13** law to place under bond **14** finance to issue bonds on; mortgage [c13: from Old Norse *band*; see BAND²]

Bond (bɒnd) *n* **Edward**. born 1934, British dramatist: his plays, including *Saved* (1965), *Lear* (1971), *Restoration* (1981), and *In the Company of Men* (1990), are noted for their violent imagery and socialist commitment

bondage ('bɒndɪdʒ) *n* **1** slavery or serfdom; servitude **2** a sexual practice in which one partner is physically bound

bonded ('bɒndɪd) *adj* **1** finance consisting of, secured by, or operating under a bond or bonds **2** commerce deposited in a bonded warehouse; placed or stored in bond

bonded warehouse *n* a warehouse in which dutiable goods are deposited until duty is paid or the goods are cleared for export

bondholder ('bɒnd,həʊldə) *n* an owner of one or more bonds issued by a company or other institution

Bondi ('bɒndɪ) *n* Sir **Hermann**. 1919–2005, British mathematician and cosmologist, born in Austria; joint originator (with Sir Fred Hoyle and Thomas Gold) of the steady-state theory of the universe

Bondi Beach ('bɒndaɪ) *n* a beach in Sydney, Australia, popular with surfers

bonding ('bɒndɪŋ) *n* the process by which individuals become emotionally attached to one another

bondmaid ('bɒnd,meɪd) *n* an unmarried female serf or slave

bond paper *n* a superior quality of strong white paper, used esp for writing and typing

bondservant ('bɒnd,sɜːvənt) *n* a serf or slave

bondsman ('bɒndzmən) *n, pl* -men **1** law a person bound by bond to act as surety for another **2** another word for **bondservant**

bond washing *n* a series of deals in bonds made with the intention of avoiding taxation

bone (bəʊn) *n* **1** any of the various structures that make up the skeleton in most vertebrates **2** the porous rigid tissue of which these parts are made, consisting of a matrix of collagen and inorganic salts, esp calcium phosphate, interspersed with canals and small holes **3** something consisting of bone or a bonelike substance **4** (plural) the human skeleton or body **5** a thin strip of whalebone, light metal, plastic, etc, used to stiffen corsets and brassieres **6** (plural) the essentials (esp in the

phrase **the bare bones**) **7** (plural) dice **8** close to the bone *or* near the bone **a** risqué or indecent **b** in poverty; destitute **9** feel in one's bones to have an intuition of **10** have a bone to pick to have grounds for a quarrel **11** make no bones about **a** to be direct and candid about **b** to have no scruples about **12** point the bone (often foll by *at*) Austral to wish bad luck (on) ▷ *vb* (mainly tr) **13** to remove the bones from (meat for cooking, etc) **14** to stiffen (a corset, etc) by inserting bones **15** Brit a slang word for **steal** ▷ See also **bone up** [Old English *bān*; related to Old Norse *béin*, Old Frisian *bēn*, Old High German *bein*] > 'boneless *adj*

Bône (French bon) *n* a former name of **Annaba**

bone ash *n* the residue obtained when bones are burned in air, consisting mainly of calcium phosphate. It is used as a fertilizer and in the manufacture of bone china

bone china *n* porcelain containing bone ash

bone-dry *adj* informal **a** completely dry: *a bone-dry well* **b** (postpositive): *the well was bone dry*

bonehead ('bəʊn,hed) *n* slang a stupid or obstinate person > ,bone'headed *adj*

bone idle *adj* very idle; extremely lazy

bone marrow *n* See **marrow¹** (sense 1)

bone meal *n* the product of dried and ground animal bones, used as a fertilizer or in stock feeds

boner ('bəʊnə) *n* slang a blunder

bonesetter ('bəʊn,setə) *n* a person who sets broken or dislocated bones, esp one who has no formal medical qualifications

boneshaker ('bəʊn,ʃeɪkə) *n* **1** an early type of bicycle having solid tyres and no springs **2** slang any decrepit or rickety vehicle

bone up *vb* (adverb; when intr, usually foll by *on*) informal to study intensively

bonfire ('bɒn,faɪə) *n* a large outdoor fire [c15: alteration (through influence of French *bon* good) of *bone-fire*; from the use of bones as fuel]

bong (bɒŋ) *n* **1** a deep reverberating sound, as of a large bell ▷ *vb* (intr) **2** to make a deep reverberating sound [c20: of imitative origin]

bongo¹ ('bɒŋgəʊ) *n, pl* -go *or* -gos a rare spiral-horned antelope, *Boocercus* (or *Taurotragus*) *eurycerus*, inhabiting forests of central Africa. The coat is bright red-brown with narrow cream stripes [of African origin]

bongo² ('bɒŋgəʊ) *n, pl* -gos *or* -goes a small bucket-shaped drum, usually one of a pair, played by beating with the fingers [American Spanish, probably of imitative origin]

Bongo ('bɒŋgəʊ) *n* **Omar**. original name *Albert Bernard Bongo*. born 1935, Gabonese statesman; president of Gabon from 1967

Bonheur (French bonœr) *n* **Rosa** (roza). 1822–99, French painter of animals

Bonhoeffer (German 'bo:nhœfər) *n* **Dietrich** ('di:trɪç). 1906–45, German Lutheran theologian: executed by the Nazis

bonhomie ('bɒnəmi:; French bɔnɔmi) *n* exuberant friendliness [c18: from French, from *bonhomme* good-humoured fellow, from *bon* good + *homme* man]

Boniface ('bɒnɪ,feɪs) *n* **Saint**. original name *Wynfrith*. ?680–?755 AD. Anglo-Saxon missionary: archbishop of Mainz (746–755). Feast day: June 5

Boniface VIII *n* original name *Benedict Caetano*. ?1234–1303, pope (1294–1303)

Bonington ('bɒnɪŋtən) *n* **1** Sir **Chris**(tian John Storey). born 1934, British mountaineer and writer; led 1970 Annapurna I and 1975 Everest expeditions; reached Everest summit in 1985 **2 Richard Parkes**. 1801–28, British painter of landscapes and historical scenes

Bonin Islands ('bəʊnɪn) *pl n* a group of 27 volcanic islands in the W Pacific: occupied by the US after World War II; returned to Japan in 1968. Largest island: Chichijima. Area: 103 sq km (40 sq miles). Japanese name: Ogasawara Gunto

bonito (bə'ni:təʊ) *n, pl* -tos **1** any of various small tunny-like marine food fishes of the genus *Sarda*, of warm Atlantic and Pacific waters: family *Scombridae* (tunnies and mackerels) **2** any of various similar fishes

[c16: from Spanish *bonito*, from Latin *bonus* good]

bonk (bɒŋk) *vb informal* **1** (*tr*) to hit **2** to have sexual intercourse (with) [c20: probably of imitative origin] ▷ **'bonking** *n*

bonkbuster ('bɒŋk,bʌstə) *n informal* a novel characterized by graphic descriptions of the heroine's frequent sexual encounters [c20: from BONK (sense 2) + (BLOCK)BUSTER]

bonkers ('bɒŋkəz) *adj slang, chiefly Brit* mad; crazy [C20 (originally in the sense: slightly drunk, tipsy): of unknown origin]

bon mot (French bɔ̃ mo) *n, pl* **bons mots** (bɔ̃ mo) a clever and fitting remark [French, literally: good word]

Bonn (bɒn; German bɔn) *n* a city in W Germany, in North Rhine-Westphalia on the Rhine: the former capital (1949–90) of West Germany; university (1786). Pop: 311 052 (2003 est)

Bonnard (French bɔnar) *n* **Pierre** (pjɛr). 1867–1947, French painter and lithographer, noted for the effects of light and colour in his landscapes and sunlit interiors

bonnet ('bɒnɪt) *n* **1** any of various hats worn, esp formerly, by women and girls, usually framing the face and tied with ribbons under the chin **2** Also called: (*in Scotland*) **bunnet a** a soft cloth cap **b** formerly, a flat brimless cap worn by men **3** the hinged metal part of a motor vehicle body that provides access to the engine, or to the luggage space in a rear-engined vehicle **4** a cowl on a chimney **5** *nautical* a piece of sail laced to the foot of a foresail to give it greater area in light winds **6** (in the US and Canada) a headdress of feathers worn by some tribes of American Indians, esp formerly as a sign of war [c14: from Old French *bonet*, from Medieval Latin *abonnis*, of unknown origin]

Bonnie Prince Charlie ('bɒnɪ) *n* See **Stuart** (sense 2)

bonny ('bɒnɪ) *adj* **-nier**, **-niest 1** *Scot & Northern English dialect* beautiful or handsome: *a bonny lass* **2** (esp of babies) plump [c15: of uncertain origin; perhaps from Old French *bon* good, from Latin *bonus*]

Bonny ('bɒnɪ) *n* **Bight of Bonny** a wide bay at the E end of the Gulf of Guinea off the coasts of Nigeria and Cameroon

Bonporti (Italian bon'pɔrti) *n* **Francesco Antonio**. 1672–1749, Italian composer and violinist, noted esp for his *Invenzioni* (1712), a series of short instrumental suites

bonsai ('bɒnsaɪ) *n, pl* **-sai 1** the art of growing dwarfed ornamental varieties of trees or shrubs in small shallow pots or trays by selective pruning, etc **2** a tree or shrub grown by this method [c20: Japanese: plant grown in a pot, from *bon* basin, bowl + *sai* to plant]

bonsela (bɒn'sɛlə) *n South African informal* a present or gratuity [from Zulu *Ibanselo* a gift]

bontebok ('bɒntɪ,bʌk) *n, pl* **-boks** or **-bok** an antelope, *Damaliscus pygargus* (or *dorcas*), of southern Africa, having a deep reddish-brown coat with a white blaze, tail, and rump patch [c18: Afrikaans, from *bont* pied + *bok* BUCK¹]

Bontempelli (Italian bontem'pɛlli) *n* **Massimo**. 1878–1960, Italian dramatist, poet, novelist, and critic. His works include the play *Nostra Dea* (1925) and the novel *The Faithful Lover* (1953)

bonus ('bəʊnəs) *n* **1** something given, paid, or received above what is due or expected **2** *chiefly Brit* an extra dividend allotted to shareholders out of profits **3** *insurance, Brit* a dividend, esp a percentage of net profits, distributed to policyholders either annually or when the policy matures [c18: from Latin *bonus* (adj) good]

bonus issue *n Brit* an issue of shares made by a company without charge and distributed pro rata among existing shareholders. Also called: **scrip issue**

bon vivant (French bɔ̃ vivɑ̃) *n, pl* **bons vivants** (bɔ̃ vivɑ̃) a person who enjoys luxuries, esp good food and drink [literally: good living (man)]

bon voyage (French bɔ̃ vwajaʒ) *sentence substitute* a phrase used to wish a traveller a pleasant journey [French, literally: good journey]

bony ('bəʊnɪ) *adj* **bonier**, **boniest 1** resembling or consisting of bone or bones **2** having many bones **3** having prominent bones: *bony cheeks* **4** thin or emaciated

bony fish *n, n* any fish of the class *Osteichthyes*, including most of the extant species, having a skeleton of bone rather than cartilage

Bonynge ('bɒnɪŋ) *n* **Richard**. born 1930, Australian conductor, esp of opera; married to the soprano Joan Sutherland

bonze (bɒnz) *n* a Chinese or Japanese Buddhist priest or monk [c16: from French, from Portuguese *bonzo*, from Japanese *bonsō*, from Sanskrit *bon* + *sō* priest or monk]

bonzer ('bɒnzə) *adj Austral & NZ slang, archaic* excellent; very good [c20: of uncertain origin; perhaps from BONANZA]

boo (buː) *interj* **1** an exclamation uttered to startle or surprise someone, esp a child **2** a shout uttered to express disgust, dissatisfaction, or contempt, esp at a theatrical production, political meeting, etc ▷ *vb* **boos**, **booing**, **booed 3** to shout "boo" at (someone or something), esp as an expression of disgust, dissatisfaction, or disapproval: *to boo the actors*

boob (buːb) *slang* ▷ *n* **1** an ignorant or foolish person; booby **2** *Brit* an embarrassing mistake; blunder **3** a female breast ▷ *vb* **4** (*intr*) *Brit* to make a blunder [c20: back formation from BOOBY]

boobialla (,buːbɪ'ælə) *n Austral* **1** another name for **golden wattle** (sense 2) **2** any of various trees or shrubs of the genus *Myoporum*, esp *M. insulare* [from a native Australian language]

boo-boo *n, pl* **-boos** *informal* an embarrassing mistake; blunder [c20: perhaps from nursery talk; compare BOOHOO]

boob tube *n slang* **1** a close-fitting strapless top, worn by women **2** *chiefly US & Canadian* a television receiver

booby ('buːbɪ) *n, pl* **-bies 1** an ignorant or foolish person **2** *Brit* the losing player in a game **3** any of several tropical marine birds of the genus *Sula*: family Sulidae, order Pelecaniformes (pelicans, cormorants, etc). They have a straight stout bill and the plumage is white with darker markings [c17: from Spanish *bobo*, from Latin *balbus* stammering]

booby prize *n* a mock prize given to the person having the lowest score or giving the worst performance in a competition

booby trap *n* **1** a hidden explosive device primed in such a way as to be set off by an unsuspecting victim **2** a trap for an unsuspecting person, esp one intended as a practical joke, such as an object balanced above a door to fall on the person who opens it ▷ *vb* **booby-trap, traps**, **-trapping, -trapped 3** (*tr*) to set a booby trap in or on (a building or object) or for (a person)

boodle ('buːdᵊl) *n slang* money or valuables, esp when stolen, counterfeit, or used as a bribe [c19: from Dutch *boedel* all one's possessions, from Old Frisian *bōdel* movable goods, inheritance; see CABOODLE]

boogie ('buːgɪ) *slang* ▷ *vb* **-gies**, **-gieing**, **-gied** (*intr*) **1** to dance to pop music **2** to make love [c20: originally African-American slang, perhaps from Kongo *mbugi* devilishly good]

boogie board *n* another name for **bodyboard**

boogie-woogie ('bʊgɪ'wʊgɪ, 'buːgɪ'wuːgɪ) *n* a style of piano jazz using a dotted bass pattern, usually with eight notes in a bar and the harmonies of the 12-bar blues

boohai (buː'haɪ) *n* **up the boohai** *NZ informal* thoroughly lost [from the remote township of *Puhoi*]

boohoo (,buː'huː) *vb* **-hoos**, **-hooing**, **-hooed 1** to sob or pretend to sob noisily ▷ *n, pl* **-hoos 2** (*sometimes plural*) distressed or pretended sobbing [c20: nursery talk]

book (bʊk) *n* **1** a number of printed or written pages bound together along one edge and usually protected by thick paper or stiff pasteboard covers **2 a** a written work or composition, such as a novel, technical manual, or dictionary **b** (*as modifier*): *the book trade; book reviews* **c** (*in combination*): *bookseller; bookshop; bookshelf; bookrack* **3** a number of blank or ruled sheets of paper bound together, used to record lessons, keep accounts, etc **4** (*plural*) a record of the transactions of a business or society **5** the script of a play or the libretto of an opera, musical, etc **6** a major division of a written composition, as of a long novel or of the Bible **7** a

b

number of tickets, sheets, stamps, etc, fastened together along one edge **8** *bookmaking* a record of the bets made on a horse race or other event **9** (in card games) the number of tricks that must be taken by a side or player before any trick has a scoring value **10** strict or rigid regulations, rules, or standards (esp in the phrases **according to the book, by the book**) **11** a source of knowledge or authority: *the book of life* **12** an **open book** a person or subject that is thoroughly understood **13** a **closed book** a person or subject that is unknown or beyond comprehension: *chemistry is a closed book to him* **14** **bring to book** to reprimand or require (someone) to give an explanation of his conduct **15** **close the books** *book-keeping* to balance accounts in order to prepare a statement or report **16** **in someone's bad books** regarded by someone with disfavour **17** **in someone's good books** regarded by someone with favour **18** **keep the books** to keep written records of the finances of a business or other enterprise **19** **on the books** enrolled as a member **20** **throw the book at** **a** to charge with every relevant offence **b** to inflict the most severe punishment on ▷ *vb* **21** to reserve (a place, passage, etc) or engage the services of (a performer, driver, etc) in advance **22** (*tr*) to take the name and address of (a person guilty of a minor offence) with a view to bringing a prosecution **23** (*tr*) (of a football referee) to take the name of (a player) who grossly infringes the rules while playing, two such acts resulting in the player's dismissal from the field **24** (*tr*) *archaic* to record in a book ▷ See also **book in** [Old English *bōc*; related to Old Norse *bōk*, Old High German *buoh* book, Gothic *bōka* letter; see BEECH (the bark of which was used as a writing surface)]

bookbinder ('bʊk,baɪndə) *n* a person whose business or craft is binding books > 'book,binding *n*

bookbindery ('bʊk,baɪndərɪ) *n, pl* -eries a place in which books are bound. Often shortened to bindery

bookcase ('bʊk,keɪs) *n* a piece of furniture containing shelves for books, often fitted with glass doors

book club *n* a club that sells books at low prices to members, usually by mail order, esp on condition that they buy a minimum number

bookcrossing ('bʊk,krɒsɪŋ) *n* the practice of deliberately leaving books in places where they will be found and read by other people

book end *n* one of a pair of usually ornamental supports for holding a row of books upright

Booker Prize ('bʊkə) *n* the former name for **Man Booker Prize**

bookie ('bʊkɪ) *n informal* short for **bookmaker**

book in *vb* (*adverb*) **1** to reserve a room for (oneself or someone else) at a hotel **2** *chiefly Brit* to record something in a book or register, esp one's arrival at a hotel

booking ('bʊkɪŋ) *n* **1** *chiefly Brit* a reservation, as of a table or room in a hotel, seat in a theatre, or seat on a train, aircraft, etc **2** *theatre* an engagement for the services of an actor or acting company

bookish ('bʊkɪʃ) *adj* **1** fond of reading; studious **2** consisting of or forming opinions or attitudes through reading rather than direct personal experience; academic **3** of or relating to books > 'bookishness *n*

book-keeping *n* the skill or occupation of maintaining accurate records of business transactions > 'book-,keeper *n*

book-learning *n* knowledge gained from books rather than from direct personal experience

booklet ('bʊklɪt) *n* a thin book, esp one having paper covers; pamphlet

bookmaker ('bʊk,meɪkə) *n* a person who as an occupation accepts bets, esp on horseraces, and pays out to winning betters > 'book,making *n*

bookmark ('bʊk,mɑːk) *n* **1** Also called: bookmarker a strip or band of some material, such as leather or ribbon, put between the pages of a book to mark a place **2** *computing* **a** an address for a website stored on a computer so that the user can easily return to the site **b** an identifier placed in a document so that part of the document can be accessed easily ▷ *vb* **3** (*tr*) *computing* to

identify and store (a website) so that one can return to it easily

Book of Common Prayer *n* the official book of church services of the Church of England, until 1980, when the Alternative Service Book was sanctioned

bookplate ('bʊk,pleɪt) *n* a label bearing the owner's name and an individual design or coat of arms, pasted into a book

book rest *n* a cradle for holding an open book so that it may be read comfortably

bookstall ('bʊk,stɔːl) *n* a stall or stand where periodicals, newspapers, or books are sold

book token *n Brit* a gift token to be exchanged for books

book value *n* **1** the value of an asset of a business according to its books **2** the net capital value of an enterprise as shown by the excess of book assets over book liabilities

bookwork ('bʊk,wɜːk) **1** the keeping of accounts **2** learning through the study of books rather than from practical experience

bookworm ('bʊk,wɜːm) *n* **1** a person excessively devoted to studying or reading **2** any of various small insects that feed on the binding paste of books, esp the book louse

Boole (buːl) *n* **George**. 1815–64, English mathematician. In *Mathematical Analysis of Logic* (1847) and *An Investigation of the Laws of Thought* (1854), he applied mathematical formulae to logic, creating Boolean algebra

boom[1] (buːm) *vb* **1** to make a deep prolonged resonant sound, as of thunder or artillery fire **2** to prosper or cause to prosper vigorously and rapidly: *business boomed* ▷ *n* **3** a deep prolonged resonant sound **4** a period of high economic growth characterized by rising wages, profits, and prices, full employment, and high levels of investment, trade, and other economic activity **5** any similar period of high activity **6** the activity itself: *a baby boom* [c15: perhaps from Dutch *bommen*, of imitative origin]

boom[2] (buːm) *n* **1** *nautical* a spar to which a sail is fastened to control its position relative to the wind **2** a pole, usually extensible, carrying an overhead microphone and projected over a film or television set **3** a barrier across a waterway, usually consisting of a chain of connected floating logs, to confine free-floating logs, protect a harbour from attack, etc [c16: from Dutch *boom* tree, BEAM]

boomer ('buːmə) *n* **1** *Austral* a large male kangaroo **2** *Austral & NZ informal* anything exceptionally large [from English dialect]

boomerang ('buːmə,ræŋ) *n* **1** a curved flat wooden missile of native Australians, which can be made to return to the thrower **2** an action or statement that recoils on its originator ▷ *vb* **3** (*intr*) to recoil or return unexpectedly, causing harm to its originator; backfire [c19: from a native Australian language]

boomerang kid *n* a young adult who, after having lived on his or her own for a time, returns to live in the parental home, usually due to financial problems caused by unemployment or the high cost of living independently

boomslang ('buːm,slæŋ) *n* a large greenish venomous arboreal colubrid snake, *Dispholidus typus*, of southern Africa [c18: from Afrikaans, from *boom* tree + *slang* snake]

boon[1] (buːn) *n* something extremely useful, helpful, or beneficial; a blessing or benefit: *the car was a boon to him* [c12: from Old Norse *bōn* request; related to Old English *bēn* prayer]

boon[2] (buːn) *adj* **1** close, special, or intimate (in the phrase **boon companion**) **2** *archaic* jolly or convivial [c14: from Old French *bon* from Latin *bonus* good]

boondocks ('buːn,dɒks) *pl n US & Canadian slang* **1** wild, desolate, or uninhabitable country **2** a remote rural or provincial area [c20: from Tagalog *bundok* mountain]

Boone (buːn) *n* **Daniel**. 1734–1820, American pioneer, explorer, and guide, esp in Kentucky

boong (buːŋ) *n Austral highly offensive* an Aborigine or Black person [c20: perhaps of native Australian origin]

boongary ('buːŋgærɪ) *n* a tree kangaroo, *Dendrolagus*

b

lumholtzi, of northeastern Queensland [from a native Australian language]

boor (bʊə) *n* an ill-mannered, clumsy, or insensitive person [Old English *gebūr*; related to Old High German *gibūr* farmer, dweller, Albanian *būr* man; see NEIGHBOUR]

boorish ('bʊərɪʃ) *adj* ill-mannered, clumsy, or insensitive; rude > 'boorishly *adv* > 'boorishness *n*

boost (buːst) *n* **1** encouragement, improvement, or help: *a boost to morale* **2** an upward thrust or push **3** an increase or rise **4** the amount by which the induction pressure of a supercharged internal-combustion engine exceeds that of the ambient pressure ▷ *vb* (*tr*) **5** to encourage, assist, or improve: *to boost morale* **6** to lift by giving a push from below or behind **7** to increase or raise: *to boost the voltage in an electrical circuit* **8** to cause to rise; increase: *to boost sales* **9** to advertise on a big scale **10** to increase the induction pressure of (an internal-combustion engine) above that of the ambient pressure; supercharge [C19: of unknown origin]

booster ('buːstə) *n* **1** a person or thing that supports, assists, or increases power or effectiveness **2** Also called: launch vehicle the first stage of a multistage rocket **3** *radio, television* **a** a radio-frequency amplifier connected between an aerial and a receiver to amplify weak incoming signals **b** a radio-frequency amplifier that amplifies incoming signals, retransmitting them at higher power **4** another name for **supercharger** **5** short for **booster dose**

booster dose *n* a supplementary injection of a vaccine given to maintain the immunization provided by an earlier dose

boot¹ (buːt) *n* **1** a strong outer covering for the foot; shoe that extends above the ankle, often to the knee **2** an enclosed compartment of a car for holding luggage, etc, usually at the rear. US and Canadian name: trunk **3** an instrument of torture used to crush the foot and lower leg **4** a kick: *he gave the door a boot* **5** die with one's boots on to die while still active **6** lick the boots of to be servile, obsequious, or flattering towards **7** put the boot in *slang* **a** to kick a person, esp when he or she is already down **b** to harass someone or aggravate a problem **c** to finish off (something) with unnecessary brutality **8** the boot *slang* dismissal from employment; the sack **9** the boot is on the other foot *or* the boot is on the other leg the situation is or has now reversed ▷ *vb* **10** (*tr*) to equip with boots **11** (*tr*) *informal* (often foll by *out*) to eject forcibly **12** Also boot up. to dismiss from employment to start up the operating system of (a computer) or (of a computer) to begin operating [C14 *bote*, from Old French, of uncertain origin]

boot² (buːt) *vb* (*usually impersonal*) **1** *archaic* to be of advantage or use to (a person): *what boots it to complain?* ▷ *n* **2** *obsolete* an advantage **3** to boot as well; in addition [Old English *bōt* compensation; related to Old Norse *bōt* remedy, Gothic *bōta*, Old High German *buoza* improvement]

bootblack ('buːtˌblæk) *n* *chiefly US* another word for shoeblack

boot camp *n* **1** *US slang* a basic training camp for new recruits to the US Navy or Marine Corps **2** a centre for juvenile offenders, with a strict disciplinary regime, hard physical exercise, and community labour programmes

boot-cut *adj* (of trousers) slightly flared at the bottom of the legs

bootee ('buːtiː, buːˈtiː) *n* **1** a soft shoe for a baby, esp a knitted one **2** a boot for women and children, esp an ankle-length one

Boötes (bəʊˈəʊtiːz) *n*, *Latin genitive* Boötis (bəʊˈəʊtɪs) a constellation in the N hemisphere lying near Ursa Major and containing the first magnitude star Arcturus [C17: via Latin from Greek: ploughman, from *boōtein* to plough, from *bous* ox]

booth (buːð, buːθ) *n*, *pl* booths (buːðz) **1** a stall for the display or sale of goods, esp a temporary one at a fair or market **2** a small enclosed or partially enclosed room or cubicle, such as one containing a telephone (**telephone booth**) or one in which a person casts his or her vote at an election (**polling booth**) **3** two long high-backed benches with a long table between, used esp in bars and inexpensive restaurants **4** (*formerly*) a temporary structure for shelter, dwelling, storage, etc [C12: of Scandinavian origin; compare Old Norse *buth*, Swedish, Danish *bod* shop, stall; see BOWER¹]

Booth (buːð) *n* **1 Edwin Thomas**, son of Junius Brutus Booth. 1833–93, US actor **2 John Wilkes**, son of Junius Brutus Booth. 1838–65, US actor; assassin of Abraham Lincoln **3 Junius Brutus** ('dʒuːnɪəs 'bruːtəs). 1796–1852, US actor, born in England **4 William**. 1829–1912, British religious leader; founder and first general of the Salvation Army (1878)

Boothia Peninsula ('buːθɪə) *n* a peninsula of N Canada: the northernmost part of the mainland of North America, lying west of the **Gulf of Boothia**, an arm of the Arctic Ocean

Boothroyd ('buːθrɔɪd) *n* **Betty**. Baroness. born 1929, British politician; speaker of the House of Commons (1992–2000)

bootjack ('buːtˌdʒæk) *n* a device that grips the heel of a boot to enable the foot to be withdrawn easily

Bootle ('buːtᵊl) *n* a port in NW England, in Sefton unitary authority, Merseyside; on the River Mersey adjoining Liverpool. Pop: 59 123 (2001)

bootleg ('buːtˌlɛg) *vb* -legs, -legging, -legged **1** to make, carry, or sell (illicit goods, esp alcohol) ▷ *n* **2** something made or sold illicitly, such as alcohol during Prohibition in the US **3** an illegally made copy of a CD, tape, etc ▷ *adj* **4** produced, distributed, or sold illicitly [C17: see BOOT¹, LEG; from the practice of smugglers of carrying bottles of liquor concealed in their boots] > 'boot,legger *n*

bootless ('buːtlɪs) *adj* of little or no use; vain; fruitless [Old English *bōtlēas*, from *bōt* compensation; Old Norse *bótalauss*]

bootlick ('buːtˌlɪk) *vb* *informal* to seek favour by servile or ingratiating behaviour towards (someone, esp someone in authority); toady > 'boot,licker *n*

bootstrap ('buːtˌstræp) *n* **1** a leather or fabric loop on the back or side of a boot for pulling it on **2** by one's bootstraps *or* by one's own bootstraps by one's own efforts; unaided **3 a** Also called: boot a technique for loading the first few program instructions into a computer main store to enable the rest of the program to be introduced from an input device **b** (*as modifier*): *a bootstrap loader* **4** *commerce* an offer to purchase a controlling interest in a company, esp with the intention of purchasing the remainder of the equity at a lower price

booty¹ ('buːtɪ) *n*, *pl* -ties any valuable article or articles, esp when obtained as plunder [C15: from Old French *butin*, from Middle Low German *buite* exchange; related to Old Norse *býta* to exchange, *býti* barter]

booty² ('buːtɪ) *n* *slang* the buttocks [C20: from BUTT¹ buttocks]

booze (buːz) *informal* ▷ *n* **1** alcoholic drink **2** a drinking bout or party ▷ *vb* **3** (*usually intr*) to drink (alcohol), esp in excess [C13: from Middle Dutch *būsen*]

booze cruise *n* *Brit informal* a day trip to a foreign country, esp from England across the English Channel to France, for the purposes of buying cheap alcohol, cigarettes, etc

boozer ('buːzə) *n* *informal* **1** a person who is fond of drinking **2** *Brit, Austral & NZ* a bar or pub

booze-up *n* *Brit, Austral & NZ slang* a drinking spree

boozy ('buːzɪ) *adj* boozier, booziest *informal* inclined to or involving excessive drinking of alcohol; drunken: *a boozy lecturer; a boozy party*

bop¹ (bɒp) *n* **1** a form of jazz originating in the 1940s, characterized by rhythmic and harmonic complexity and instrumental virtuosity. Originally called: bebop ▷ *vb* bops, bopping, bopped **2** (*intr*) to dance to pop music [C20: shortened from BEBOP] > 'bopper *n*

bop² (bɒp) *informal* ▷ *vb* bops, bopping, bopped **1** (*tr*) to strike; hit ▷ *n* **2** a blow [C19: of imitative origin]

bo-peep (ˌbəʊˈpiːp) *n* a game for very young children, in which one hides (esp hiding one's face in one's hands) and reappears suddenly

Bophuthatswana (ˌbəʊpuːtɑːtˈswɑːnə) *n* (*formerly*) a Bantu homeland in N South Africa: consisted of six separate areas; granted declared independent by South Africa in 1977 although this was not internationally recognized; abolished in 1993. Capital: Mmabatho

bora¹ ('bɔːrə) n (*sometimes capital*) a violent cold north wind blowing from the mountains to the E coast of the Adriatic, usually in winter [c19: from Italian (Venetian dialect), from Latin *boreās* the north wind]

bora² ('bɔːrə) n an initiation ceremony of native Australians, introducing youths to manhood [from a native Australian language]

Bora Bora ('bɔːrə 'bɔːrə) n an island in the S Pacific, in French Polynesia, in the Society Islands: one of the Leeward Islands. Area: 39 sq km (15 sq miles)

boracic (bə'ræsɪk) adj another word for **boric**

borage ('bɒrɪdʒ, 'bʌrɪdʒ) n a European boraginaceous plant, *Borago officinalis*, with star-shaped blue flowers. The young leaves have a cucumber-like flavour and are sometimes used in salads or as seasoning [c13: from Old French *bourage*, perhaps from Arabic *abū 'āraq* literally: father of sweat, from its use as a diaphoretic]

Borås (*Swedish* bu'rɔːs) n a city in SW Sweden, chiefly producing textiles. Pop: 98 831 (2004 est)

borate n ('bɔːreɪt, -ɪt) 1 a salt or ester of boric acid. Salts of boric acid consist of BO_3 and BO_4 units linked together ▷ vb ('bɔːreɪt) 2 (tr) to treat with borax, boric acid, or borate

borax ('bɔːræks) n, pl -raxes, -races (-rə,siːz) Also called: tincal a soluble readily fusible white mineral consisting of impure hydrated disodium tetraborate in monoclinic crystalline form, occurring in alkaline soils and salt deposits. Formula: $Na_2B_4O_7.10H_2O$ [c14: from Old French *boras*, from Medieval Latin *borax*, from Arabic *būraq*, from Persian *būrah*]

borazon ('bɔːrə,zɒn, -zᵊn) n an extremely hard form of boron nitride [c20: from BOR(ON) + AZO- + -ON]

borborygmus (,bɔːbə'rɪgməs) n, pl -mi (-maɪ) rumbling of the stomach [c18: from Greek]

Bordeaux (bɔː'dəʊ; *French* bɔrdo) n 1 a port in SW France, on the River Garonne: a major centre of the wine trade. Pop: 215 363 (1999) 2 any of several red, white, or rosé wines produced around Bordeaux

Bordeaux mixture n horticulture a fungicide consisting of a solution of equal quantities of copper sulphate and quicklime [c19: loose translation of French *bouillie bordelaise*, from *bouillir* to boil + *bordelais* of BORDEAUX]

bordello (bɔː'dɛləʊ) n, pl -los a brothel [c16: from Italian, from Old French *borde* hut, cabin]

border ('bɔːdə) n 1 a band or margin around or along the edge of something 2 the dividing line or frontier between political or geographic regions 3 a region straddling such a boundary 4 a design or ornamental strip around the edge or rim of something, such as a printed page or dinner plate 5 a long narrow strip of ground planted with flowers, shrubs, trees, etc, that skirts a path or wall or surrounds a lawn or other area: *a herbaceous border* ▷ vb 6 (tr) to decorate or provide with a border 7 (when *intr*, foll by *on* or *upon*) a to be adjacent (to); lie along the boundary (of) b to be nearly the same (as); verge (on): *his stupidity borders on madness* [c14: from Old French *bordure*, from *border* to border, from *bort* side of a ship, of Germanic origin; see BOARD]

Border¹ ('bɔːdə) the Border n 1 (*often plural*) the area straddling the border between England and Scotland 2 the area straddling the border between Northern Ireland and the Republic of Ireland 3 the region in S South Africa around East London

Border² ('bɔːdə) n **Allan** (**Robert**). born 1955, Australian cricketer; captain of Australia (1985–94)

borderer ('bɔːdərə) n a person who lives in a border area, esp the border between England and Scotland

borderland ('bɔːdə,lænd) n 1 land located on or near a frontier or boundary 2 an indeterminate region

borderless ('bɔːdə,lɪs) adj 1 without a band or margin around or along the edge: *borderless prints* 2 (of an island) not divided by a national border 3 without limits: *an intellectual curiosity that seems borderless* 4 (of trade, travel, etc) not constrained by the presence of international borders: *a borderless business world*

borderline ('bɔːdə,laɪn) n 1 a border; dividing line; line of

demarcation 2 an indeterminate position between two conditions or qualities: *the borderline between friendship and love* ▷ adj 3 on the edge of one category and verging on another: *a borderline failure in the exam*

borderline personality disorder n psychiatry a mental condition on the dividing line between a psychiatric disorder and normality characterized by impulsiveness, extreme mood swings, and often aggressiveness

Borders Region n a former local government region in S Scotland, formed in 1975 from Berwick, Peebles, Roxburgh, Selkirk, and part of Midlothian; replaced in 1996 by Scottish Borders council area

Bordet (*French* bɔrdɛ) n **Jules** (**Jean Baptiste Vincent**) (ʒyl). 1870–1961, Belgian bacteriologist and immunologist, who discovered complement. Nobel prize for physiology or medicine 1919

bore¹ (bɔː) vb 1 to produce (a hole) in (a material) by use of a drill, auger, or other cutting tool 2 to increase the diameter of (a hole), as by an internal turning operation on a lathe or similar machine 3 (tr) to produce (a hole in the ground, tunnel, mine shaft, etc) by digging, drilling, cutting, etc 4 (intr) informal (of a horse or athlete in a race) to push other competitors, esp in order to try to get them out of the way ▷ n 5 a hole or tunnel in the ground, esp one drilled in search of minerals, oil, etc 6 a the hollow part of a tube or cylinder, esp of a gun barrel b the diameter of such a hollow part; calibre 7 Austral an artesian well [Old English *borian*; related to Old Norse *bora*, Old High German *borōn* to bore, Latin *forāre* to pierce, Greek *pharos* ploughing, *phárunx* PHARYNX]

bore² (bɔː) vb 1 (tr) to tire or make weary by being dull, repetitious, or uninteresting ▷ n 2 a dull, repetitious, or uninteresting person, activity, or state [c18: of unknown origin] > **bored** adj > **'boring** adj > **'boringly** adv

bore³ (bɔː) n a high steep-fronted wave moving up a narrow estuary, caused by the tide [c17: from Old Norse *bāra* wave, billow]

bore⁴ (bɔː) vb the past tense of **bear¹**

boreal ('bɔːrɪəl) adj of or relating to the north or the north wind [c15: from Latin *boreās* the north wind]

Boreal ('bɔːrɪəl) adj of or denoting the coniferous forests in the north of the N hemisphere

Boreas ('bɔːrɪəs) n Greek myth the god personifying the north wind [c14: via Latin from Greek]

boredom ('bɔːdəm) n the state of being bored; tedium

boree (bɔːriː) n Austral another name for **myall** [from a native Australian language]

borer ('bɔːrə) n 1 a machine or hand tool for boring holes 2 any of various insects, insect larvae, molluscs, or crustaceans that bore into rock or plant material, esp wood

Borg (bɔːg; *Swedish* bɔrj) n **Björn** (bjœrn). born 1956, Swedish tennis player: Wimbledon champion 1976–80

Borgerhout (*Flemish* bɔrxər'hɔut) n a town in N Belgium, near Antwerp. Pop: 40 142 (2002 est)

Borges (*Spanish* 'bɔrxes) n **Jorge Luis** ('xorxe lwis). 1899–1986, Argentinian poet, short-story writer, and literary scholar. The short stories collected in *Ficciones* (1944) he described as "games with infinity"

Borghese (*Italian* bor'geze) n a noble Italian family whose members were influential in Italian art and politics from the 16th to the 19th century

Borgia (*Italian* 'bordʒa) n 1 **Cesare** ('tʃezare), son of Rodrigo Borgia (Pope Alexander VI). 1475–1507, Italian cardinal, politician, and military leader; model for Machiavelli's *The Prince* 2 his sister, **Lucrezia** (lu'krɛttsja), daughter of Rodrigo Borgia. 1480–1519, Italian noblewoman. After her third marriage (1501), to the Duke of Ferrara, she became a patron of the arts and science 3 **Rodrigo** (rod'rigo). See **Alexander VI**

Borglum ('bɔːgləm) n (**John**) **Gutzon** ('gatsən). 1867–1941, US sculptor, noted for his monumental busts of US presidents carved in the mountainside of Mount Rushmore

boric ('bɔːrɪk) adj of or containing boron. Also called: boracic

boric acid n Also called: orthoboric acid a white soluble weakly acid crystalline solid used in the manufacture of heat-resistant glass and porcelain enamels, as a fireproofing material, and as a mild antiseptic. Formula: H_3BO_3

Boris I (ˈbɒrɪs) n known as *Boris of Bulgaria.* died 907 AD, khan of Bulgaria. His reign saw the conversion of Bulgaria to Christianity and the birth of a national literature

Borlaug (ˈbɔːlɔːɡ) n **Norman** (**Ernest**). born 1914, US agronomist, who bred new strains of high-yielding cereal crops for use in developing countries. Nobel peace prize 1970

borlotti bean (bɔːˈlɒtɪ) n a variety of kidney bean with a pinkish-brown speckled skin that turns brown when cooked: grown in southern Europe, East Africa, and Taiwan [from Italian, plural of *borlotto* kidney bean]

Bormann (German ˈbɔrman) n **Martin**. 1900–45, German Nazi politician; Hitler's adviser and private secretary (1942–45): committed suicide

born (bɔːn) vb **1 was not born yesterday** is not gullible or foolish ▷ adj **2** possessing or appearing to have possessed certain qualities from birth: *a born musician* **3 a** being at birth in a particular social status or other condition as specified: *ignobly born* **b** (*in combination*): *lowborn* **4 in all one's born days** *informal* so far in one's life

● USAGE Care should be taken not to use *born* where
● *borne* is intended: *he had borne* (not *born*) *his ordeal with*
● *great courage; the following points should be borne in mind*

Born (bɔːn) n **Max**. 1882–1970, British nuclear physicist, born in Germany, noted for his fundamental contribution to quantum mechanics: Nobel prize for physics 1954

born-again (ˈbɔːnəˌɡɛn) adj **1** having experienced conversion, esp to evangelical Christianity **2** showing the enthusiasm of one newly converted to any cause: *a born-again monetarist* ▷ n **3** a person who shows fervent enthusiasm for a new-found cause, belief, etc

borne (bɔːn) vb **1** for all active uses of the verb, the past participle of **bear¹ 2** for all passive uses of the verb except sense 4 unless followed by *by*, the past participle of **bear¹ 3 be borne in on** or **be borne in upon** (of a fact) to be realized by (someone)

Borneo (ˈbɔːnɪˌəʊ) n an island in the W Pacific, between the Sulu and Java Seas, part of the Malay Archipelago: divided into Kalimantan (**Indonesian Borneo**), the Malaysian states of Sarawak and Sabah, and the sultanate of Brunei; mountainous and densely forested. Area: over 750 000 sq km (290 000 sq miles) ▷ **Bornean** (ˈbɔːnɪən) adj, n

Bornholm (Danish bɔrnˈhɔlm) n an island in the Baltic Sea, south of Sweden: administratively part of Denmark. Chief town: Rønne. Pop: 43 956 (2003 est). Area: 588 sq km (227 sq miles)

Borno (ˈbɔːnəʊ) n a state of NE Nigeria, on Lake Chad. Capital: Maiduguri. Pop: 4 151 193 (2006). Area: 70 898 sq km (27 374 sq miles)

Borodin (ˈbɒrədɪn; Russian bərɐˈdin) n **Aleksandr Porfirevich** (alɪkˈsandr pərfiˈrjevɪtʃ). 1834–87, Russian composer, whose works include the unfinished opera *Prince Igor*, symphonies, songs, and chamber music

Borodino (ˌbɒrəˈdiːnəʊ; Russian bərədiˈno) n a village in E central Russia, about 110 km (70 miles) west of Moscow: scene of a battle (1812) in which Napoleon defeated the Russians but irreparably weakened his army

boron (ˈbɔːrɒn) n a very hard almost colourless crystalline metalloid element that in impure form exists as a brown amorphous powder. It occurs principally in borax and is used in hardening steel. The naturally occurring isotope **boron-10** is used in nuclear control rods and neutron detection instruments. Symbol: B; atomic no: 5; atomic wt: 10.81; valency: 3; relative density: 2.34 (crystalline), 2.37 (amorphous); melting pt: 2092°C; boiling pt: 4002°C [c19: from BOR(AX) + (CARB)ON]

boron carbide n a black extremely hard inert substance having a high capture cross section for thermal neutrons. It is used as an abrasive and refractory and in control rods in nuclear reactors. Formula: B_4C

boronia (bəˈrəʊnɪə) n any aromatic rutaceous shrub of the Australian genus *Boronia*

boron nitride n a white inert crystalline solid existing both in a graphite-like form and in an extremely hard diamond-like form (borazon). It is used as a refractory, high temperature lubricant and insulator, and heat shield. Formula: BN

borosilicate glass n any of a range of heat- and chemical-resistant glasses, such as Pyrex, prepared by fusing together boron(III) oxide, silicon dioxide, and, usually, a metal oxide

Borotra (bɔrɔtra) n **Jean** (**Robert**) (ʒɑ̃). 1898–1994, French tennis player: secretary general of physical education under the Vichy government (1940)

borough (ˈbʌrə) n **1** a town, esp (in Britain) one that forms the constituency of an MP or that was originally incorporated by royal charter. See also **burgh 2** any of the 32 constituent divisions that together with the City of London make up Greater London **3** any of the five constituent divisions of New York City **4** (in the US) a self-governing incorporated municipality [Old English *burg*; related to *beorgan* to shelter, Old Norse *borg* wall, Gothic *baurgs* city, Old High German *burg* fortified castle]

Borromini (Italian borro'miːni) n **Francesco**, original name *Francesco Castelli*. 1599–1667, Italian baroque architect, working in Rome: his buildings include the churches of San Carlo (1641) and Sant' Ivo (1660)

borrow (ˈbɒrəʊ) vb **1** to obtain or receive (something, such as money) on loan for temporary use, intending to give it, or something equivalent or identical, back to the lender **2** to adopt (ideas, words, etc) from another source; appropriate **3** *not standard* to lend **4** *golf* to putt the ball uphill of the direct path to the hole [Old English *borgian*; related to Old High German *borgēn* to take heed, give security] ▷ **'borrower** n

Borrow (ˈbɒrəʊ) n **George** (**Henry**). 1803–81, English traveller and writer. His best-known works are the semiautobiographical novels of Gypsy life and language, *Lavengro* (1851) and its sequel *The Romany Rye* (1857)

Bors (bɔːs) n **Sir Bors** (in Arthurian legend) **1** one the knights of the Round Table, nephew of Lancelot **2** an illegitimate son of King Arthur

borscht (bɔːʃt), **borsch** (bɔːʃ) or **borshch** (bɔːʃtʃ) n a Russian and Polish soup based on beetroot [c19: from Russian *borshch*]

borstal (ˈbɔːstəl) n **1** (formerly in Britain) an informal name for an establishment in which offenders aged 15 to 21 could be detained for corrective training. Since the Criminal Justice Act 1982, they have been replaced by **youth custody centres** (now known as **young offender institutions**) **2** (formerly) a similar establishment in Australia and New Zealand [c20: named after *Borstal*, village in Kent where the first institution was founded]

bort, boart (bɔːt) or **bortz** (bɔːts) n an inferior grade of diamond used for cutting and drilling or, in powdered form, as an industrial abrasive [Old English *gebrot* fragment; related to Old Norse *brot* piece, Old High German *broz* bud]

borzoi (ˈbɔːzɔɪ) n, pl **-zois** a tall graceful fast-moving breed of dog with a long silky coat, originally used in Russia for hunting wolves. Also called: **Russian wolfhound** [c19: from Russian *borzoi*, literally: swift; related to Old Slavonic *brŭzŭ* swift]

boscage or **boskage** (ˈbɒskɪdʒ) n *literary* a mass of trees and shrubs; thicket [c14: from Old French *bosc*, probably of Germanic origin; see BUSH¹, -AGE]

Bosch (bɒʃ) n **1 Carl**. 1874–1940, German chemist, who adapted the Haber process to produce ammonia for industrial use. He shared the Nobel prize for chemistry 1931 **2 Hieronymus** (hɪˈrɒnɪməs), original name probably *Jerome van Aken* (or *Aeken*). ?1450–1516, Dutch painter, noted for his macabre allegorical representations of biblical subjects in brilliant transparent colours, esp the triptych *The Garden of Earthly Delights*

Bose (bəʊs) n **1 Sir Jagadis Chandra** (dʒəɡəˈdiːs ˈtʃʌndrə). 1858–1937, Indian physicist and plant physiologist **2 Satyendra Nath** (səˈtjɛndrə ˈnɑːθ). 1894–1974, Indian physicist, who collaborated with Einstein in devising Bose-Einstein statistics **3 Subhas Chandra** (sʊbˈhɑːʃ ˈtʃʌndrə), known as *Netaji*. 1897–1945, Indian nationalist leader; president of the Indian National Congress

(1938–39); organized the Indian National Army, with Japanese support, in Singapore to free India from British Rule

Bose-Einstein statistics *pl n* *(functioning as singular)* *physics* the branch of quantum statistics applied to systems of particles of zero or integral spin that do not obey the exclusion principle

bosh (bɒʃ) *n* *informal* empty or meaningless talk or opinions; nonsense [C19: from Turkish *boş* empty]

bosk (bɒsk) *n* *literary* a small wood of bushes and small trees [C13: variant of *busk* BUSH¹]

bosky ('bɒskɪ) *adj* boskier, boskiest *literary* containing or consisting of bushes or thickets

bo's'n ('bəʊsᵊn) *n* *nautical* a variant spelling of **boatswain**

Bosnia ('bɒznɪə) *n* a region of central Bosnia-Herzegovina: belonged to Turkey (1463–1878), to Austria-Hungary (1879–1918), then to Yugoslavia (1918–91) ⊳ **Bosnian** *adj, n*

Bosnia-Herzegovina *or esp US* **Bosnia and Herzegovina** *n* a country in SW Europe; a constituent republic of Yugoslavia until 1991; in a state of civil war (1992–95); Serbian and Croatian forces were also involved: mostly barren and mountainous, with forests in the east. Languages: Bosnian, Croatian and Serbian (formerly all regarded together as Serbo-Croatian. Religion: Muslim, Serbian Orthodox, and Roman Catholic. Currency: marka (pegged to the euro). Capital: Sarajevo. Pop: 4 186 000 (2004 est). Area: 51 129 sq km (19 737 sq miles)

bosom ('bʊzəm) *n* **1** the chest or breast of a person, esp the female breasts **2** the part of a woman's dress, coat, etc, that covers the chest **3** a protective centre or part: *the bosom of the family* **4** the breast considered as the seat of emotions **5** *(modifier)* very dear; intimate ⊳ *vb* *(tr)* **6** to embrace **7** to conceal or carry in the bosom [Old English *bōsm*; related to Old High German *buosam*]

bosomy ('bʊzəmɪ) *adj* (of a woman) having large breasts

boson ('bəʊzɒn) *n* any of a group of elementary particles, such as a photon or pion, that has zero or integral spin and obeys the rules of Bose-Einstein statistics. See **fermion** [C20: named after Satyendra Nath Bose (1894–1974), Indian physicist; see -ON]

Bosporus ('bɒspərəs) *or* **Bosphorus** ('bɒsfərəs) *n* the Bosporus a strait between European and Asian Turkey, linking the Black Sea and the Sea of Marmara

boss¹ (bɒs) *informal* ⊳ *n* **1** a person in charge of or employing others **2** *chiefly US* a professional politician who controls a party machine or political organization, often using devious or illegal methods ⊳ *vb* **3** to employ, supervise, or be in charge of **4** (usually foll by *around* or *about*) to be domineering or overbearing towards (others) ⊳ *adj* **5** *slang* excellent; fine: *a boss hand at carpentry; that's boss!* [C19: from Dutch *baas* master; probably related to Old High German *basa* aunt, Frisian *baes* master]

boss² (bɒs) *n* **1** a knob, stud, or other circular rounded protuberance, esp an ornamental one on a vault, a ceiling, or a shield **2** an area of increased thickness, usually cylindrical, that strengthens or provides room for a locating device on a shaft, hub of a wheel, etc **3** an exposed rounded mass of igneous or metamorphic rock, esp the uppermost part of an underlying batholith ⊳ *vb* *(tr)* **4** to ornament with bosses; emboss [C13: from Old French *boce*, from Vulgar Latin *bottia* (unattested); related to Italian *bozza* metal knob, swelling]

bossa nova ('bɒsə 'nəʊvə) *n* **1** a dance similar to the samba, originating in Brazil **2** a piece of music composed for or in the rhythm of this dance [C20: from Portuguese, literally: new voice]

bosset ('bɒsɪt) *n* either of the rudimentary antlers found in young deer [C19: from French *bossette* a small protuberance, from *bosse* BOSS²]

boss screen *n* a screen image within a computer game that can be activated instantly, designed to hide the evidence of game-playing, especially at work

Bossuet (French bɔsɥɛ) *n* **Jacques Bénigne** (ʒak beniɲ). 1627–1704, French bishop: noted for his funeral orations

bossy ('bɒsɪ) *adj* bossier, bossiest *informal* domineering, overbearing, or authoritarian ⊳ **bossily** *adv*

⊳ **bossiness** *n*

Boston ('bɒstən) *n* **1** a port in E Massachusetts, the state capital. Pop: 581 616 (2003 est) **2** a port in E England, in SE Lincolnshire. Pop: 35 124 (2001)

Boston bluefish *n* *Canadian* another name for **pollack**

bosun ('bəʊsᵊn) *n* *nautical* a variant spelling of **boatswain**

Boswell ('bɒzwəl) *n* **James.** 1740–95, Scottish author and lawyer, noted particularly for his *Life of Samuel Johnson* (1791) ⊳ **Boswellian** (bɒz'welɪən) *adj*

Bosworth Field ('bɒzwɜːθ, -wəθ) *n* *English history* the site, two miles south of Market Bosworth in Leicestershire, of the battle that ended the Wars of the Roses (August 1485). Richard III was killed and Henry Tudor was crowned king as Henry VII

bot¹ *or* **bott** (bɒt) *n* **1** the larva of a botfly, which typically develops inside the body of a horse, sheep, or man **2** any similar larva [C15: probably from Low German; related to Dutch *bot*, of obscure origin]

bot² (bɒt) *Austral informal* ⊳ *vb* **1** to scrounge or borrow ⊳ *n* **2** a scrounger **3** on the bot wanting to scrounge [C20: perhaps from BOTFLY, alluding to the creature's bite; see BITE (sense 12)]

bot³ (bɒt) *n* *computing* an autonomous computer program that performs time-consuming tasks, esp on the internet [C20: from (RO)BOT]

bot. *abbreviation* **1** botanical **2** botany

botanical (ˌbə'tænɪkᵊl) *or* **botanic** *adj* **1** of or relating to botany or plants ⊳ *n* **2** any drug or pesticide that is made from parts of a plant [C17: from Medieval Latin *botanicus*, from Greek *botanikos* relating to plants, from *botanē* plant, pasture, from *boskein* to feed; perhaps related to Latin *bōs* ox, cow] ⊳ **botanically** *adv*

botanize *or* **botanise** ('bɒtəˌnaɪz) *vb* **1** *(intr)* to collect or study plants **2** *(tr)* to explore and study the plants in (an area or region)

botany ('bɒtənɪ) *n, pl* -nies **1** the study of plants, including their classification, structure, physiology, ecology, and economic importance **2** the plant life of a particular region or time **3** the biological characteristics of a particular group of plants [C17: from BOTANICAL; compare ASTRONOMY, ASTRONOMICAL] ⊳ **botanist** *n*

Botany Bay *n* **1** an inlet of the Tasman Sea, on the SE coast of Australia: surrounded by the suburbs of Sydney **2** (in the 19th century) a British penal settlement that was in fact at Port Jackson, New South Wales

Botany wool *n* a fine wool from the merino sheep [C19: from BOTANY BAY, where the wool came from originally]

botargo (bə'tɑːgəʊ) *n, pl* -gos *or* -goes a relish consisting of the roe of mullet or tunny, salted and pressed into rolls [C15: from obsolete Italian, from Arabic *butarkhah*]

botch (bɒtʃ) *vb* *(tr; often foll by* up*)* to spoil through clumsiness or ineptitude **1** to repair badly or clumsily ⊳ *n* **2** Also called: **botch-up** a badly done piece of work or repair (esp in the phrase **make a botch of** (**something**)) [C14: of unknown origin] ⊳ **botcher** *n*

botfly ('bɒtˌflaɪ) *n, pl* -flies any of various stout-bodied hairy dipterous flies of the families *Oestridae* and *Gasterophilidae*, the larvae of which are parasites of man, sheep, and horses

both (bəʊθ) *determiner* **1 a** the two; two considered together: *both dogs were dirty* **b** *(as pronoun)*: *both are to blame* ⊳ *conj* **2** *(coordinating)* used preceding words, phrases, or clauses joined by *and*, used to emphasize that not just one, but also the other of the joined elements is included: *both Ellen and Keith enjoyed the play; both new and exciting* [C12: from Old Norse *bāthir*; related to Old High German *bēde*, Latin *ambō*, Greek *amphō*]

Botha ('bəʊtə) *n* **1 Louis.** 1862–1919, South African statesman and general; first prime minister of the Union of South Africa (1910–19) **2 P**(ieter) **W**(illem). 1916–2006, South African politician; defence minister (1965–78); prime minister (1978–84); state president (1984–89)

Botham ('bəʊθəm) *n* **Sir Ian** (**Terence**). born 1955, English cricketer: played for Somerset (1973–86), Worcestershire (1987–91), and Durham (1991–93); captained England (1980–81)

Bothe (German 'boːtə) *n* **Walther** (**Wilhelm Georg Franz**) ('valtər). 1891–1957, German physicist, who developed new methods of detecting subatomic particles. He shared the Nobel prize for physics 1954

bother ('bɒðə) *vb* **1** (*tr*) to give annoyance, pain, or trouble to; irritate: *his bad leg is bothering him again* **2** (*tr*) to trouble (a person) by repeatedly disturbing; pester **3** (*intr*) to take the time or trouble; concern oneself: *don't bother to come with me* **4** (*tr*) to make (a person) alarmed or confused ▷ *n* **5** a state of worry, trouble, or confusion **6** a person or thing that causes fuss, trouble, or annoyance **7** *informal* a disturbance or fight; trouble (esp in the phrase **a spot of bother**) ▷ *interj* **8** *chiefly Brit* an exclamation of slight annoyance [c18: perhaps from Irish Gaelic *bodhar* deaf, vexed; compare Irish Gaelic *buairim* I vex]

botheration (ˌbɒðəˈreɪʃən) *n, interj informal* another word for: **bother** (senses 5, 8)

bothersome ('bɒðəsəm) *adj* causing bother; troublesome

Bothnia ('bɒθnɪə) *n* Gulf of Bothnia an arm of the Baltic Sea, extending north between Sweden and Finland

Bothwell ('bɒθwəl, 'bɒð-) *n* **Earl of**, title of *James Hepburn*. 1535–78, Scottish nobleman; third husband of Mary Queen of Scots. He is generally considered to have instigated the murder of Darnley (1567)

bothy ('bɒθɪ) *n, pl* **bothies** *chiefly Scot* **1** a cottage or hut **2** (esp in NE Scotland) a farmworker's summer quarters [c18: perhaps from BOOTH]

botnet ('bɒt,nɛt) *n* (*sometimes with a capital*) a network of computers infected by a program that communicates with its creator in order to send unsolicited emails, attack websites, etc [c20: from (RO)BOT + NET(WORK)]

Botox ('bəʊtɒks) *n trademark* a preparation of botulinum toxin used to treat muscle spasm and to remove wrinkles [c20: from BOT(ULINUM) (T)OX(IN)]

bo tree (bəʊ) *n* another name for the **peepul** [c19: from Sinhalese, from Pali *bodhitaru* tree of wisdom, from Sanskrit *bodhi* wisdom, awakening; see BODHISATTVA]

Botswana (bɒˈtʃwɑːnə, bʊtˈswɑːnə, bɒt-) *n* a republic in southern Africa: established as the British protectorate of Bechuanaland in 1885 as a defence against the Boers; became an independent state within the Commonwealth in 1966; consists mostly of a plateau averaging 1000 m (3300 ft), with the extensive Okavango swamps in the northwest and the Kalahari Desert in the southwest. Languages: English and Tswana. Religion: animist majority. Currency: pula. Capital: Gaborone. Pop: 1 795 000 (2004 est.). Area: about 570 000 sq km (220 000 sq miles)

bott (bɒt) *n* a variant spelling of **bot¹**

Botticelli (Italian bottiˈtʃɛlli) *n* **Sandro** ('sandro), original name *Alessandro di Mariano Filipepi*. 1444–1510, Italian (Florentine) painter, illustrator, and engraver, noted for the graceful outlines and delicate details of his mythological and religious paintings

bottle ('bɒt³l) *n* **1 a** a vessel, often of glass and typically cylindrical with a narrow neck that can be closed with a cap or cork, for containing liquids **b** (*as modifier*): *a bottle rack* **2** Also called: **bottleful** the amount such a vessel will hold **3** *Brit slang* nerve; courage (esp in the phrase **lose one's bottle**) **4** the **bottle** *informal* drinking of alcohol, esp to excess ▷ *vb* (*tr*) **5** to put or place (wine, beer, jam, etc) in a bottle or bottles **6** to store (gas) in a portable container under pressure ▷ See also **bottle out**, **bottle up** [c14: from Old French *botaille*, from Medieval Latin *butticula* literally: a little cask, from Late Latin *buttis* cask, BUTT⁴]

bottle bank *n* a large container into which the public may throw glass bottles for recycling

bottlebrush ('bɒt³l,brʌʃ) *n* **1** a cylindrical brush on a thin shaft, used for cleaning bottles **2** Also called: **callistemon** any of various Australian myrtaceous shrubs or trees of the genera *Callistemon* and *Melaleuca*, having dense spikes of large red flowers with protruding brushlike stamens

bottled gas *or* **bottle gas** *n* butane or propane gas liquefied under pressure in portable containers and used in camping stoves, blowtorches, etc

bottle-feed *vb* **-feeds, -feeding, -fed** to feed (a baby) with milk from a bottle instead of breast-feeding

bottle glass *n* glass used for making bottles, consisting of a silicate of sodium, calcium, and aluminium

bottle green *n, adj* a dark green colour

bottle-jack *n NZ* a large jack used for heavy lifts

bottleneck ('bɒt³l,nɛk) *n* **1 a** a narrow stretch of road or a junction at which traffic is or may be held up **b** the hold up **2** something that holds up progress, esp of a manufacturing process

bottlenose dolphin ('bɒt³l,nəʊz) *n* any dolphin of the genus *Tursiops*, esp *T. truncatus*, some of which have been kept in captivity and trained to perform tricks

bottle out *vb* (*intr, adverb*) *Brit slang* to lose one's nerve

bottle party *n* a party to which guests bring drink

bottler ('bɒt³lə) *n Austral & NZ informal* an excellent or outstanding person or thing

bottle shop *n Austral, NZ & South African* a shop or part of a hotel where alcohol is sold in unopened containers for consumption elsewhere. Also called: **bottle store**

bottle tree *n* **1** any of several Australian sterculiaceous trees of the genus *Sterculia* (or *Brachychiton*) that have a bottle-shaped swollen trunk **2** another name for **baobab**

bottle up *vb* (*tr, adverb*) **1** to restrain (powerful emotion) **2** to keep (an army or other force) contained or trapped

bottom ('bɒtəm) *n* **1** the lowest, deepest, or farthest removed part of a thing: *the bottom of a hill* **2** the least important or successful position: *the bottom of a class* **3** the ground underneath a sea, lake, or river **4** the inner depths of a person's true feelings (esp in the phrase **from the bottom of one's heart**) **5** the underneath part of a thing **6** *nautical* the parts of a vessel's hull that are under water **7** (in literary or commercial contexts) a boat or ship **8** (*often plural*) *US & Canadian* the low land bordering a river **9** (esp of horses) staying power; stamina **10** importance, seriousness, or influence: *his views all have weight and bottom* **11** *informal* the buttocks **12** at bottom in reality; basically or despite appearances to the contrary **13** be at the bottom of to be the ultimate cause of **14** get to the bottom of to discover the real truth about ▷ *adj* (*prenominal*) **15** lowest or last **16** bet one's bottom dollar on *or* put one's bottom dollar on to be absolutely sure of (one's opinion, a person, project, etc) **17** of, relating to, or situated at the bottom or a bottom: *the bottom shelf* **18** fundamental; basic ▷ *vb* **19** (*tr*) to provide (a chair, etc) with a bottom or seat **20** (*tr*) to discover the full facts or truth of; fathom **21** (usually foll by *on* or *upon*) to base or be founded (on an idea, etc) [Old English *botm*; related to Old Norse *botn*, Old High German *bodam*, Latin *fundus*, Greek *puthmēn*]

bottom drawer *n Brit* a young woman's collection of clothes, linen, cutlery, etc, in anticipation of marriage. US & Canadian equivalent: **hope chest**

bottom feeder *n* **1 a** fish that feeds on material at the bottom of a river, lake, sea, etc **2** an objectionable and unimpressive person or thing **3** Also called: **bottom fisher** a speculator who buys shares in companies that are performing poorly in anticipation of improved performance

bottoming ('bɒtəmɪŋ) *n* the lowest level of foundation material for a road or other structure

bottomless ('bɒtəmlɪs) *adj* **1** having no bottom **2** unlimited; inexhaustible **3** very deep

bottom line *n* **1** the last line of a financial statement that shows the net profit or loss of a company or organization **2** the final outcome of a process, discussion, etc

bottom out *vb* (*intr, adverb*) to reach the lowest point and level out

bottomry ('bɒtəmrɪ) *n, pl* **-ries** *maritime law* a contract whereby the owner of a ship borrows money to enable the vessel to complete the voyage and pledges the ship as security for the loan [c16: from Dutch *bodemerij*, from *bodem* BOTTOM (hull of a ship) + *-erij* -RY]

bottom-up *adj* from the lowest level of a hierarchy or process to the top: *a bottom-up approach to corporate decision-making*

bottom-up processing *n* a processing technique, either in the brain or in a computer, in which incoming information is analysed in successive steps and later-

b

stage processing does not affect processing in earlier stages

Bottrop (*German* ˈbɔtrɔp) *n* an industrial city in W Germany, in North Rhine-Westphalia in the Ruhr. Pop: 120 324 (2003 est)

botulism (ˈbɒtjʊˌlɪzəm) *n* severe poisoning from ingestion of botulin, which affects the central nervous system producing difficulty in swallowing, visual disturbances, and respiratory paralysis: often fatal [c19: first formed as German *Botulismus* literally: sausage poisoning, from Latin *botulus* sausage]

Botvinnik (ˈbɒtvɪnɪk) *n* **Mikhail Moiseivich** (mixaˈil məiˈsjejivitʃ). 1911–95, Soviet chess player; world champion (1948–57, 1958–60, 1961–63)

Bouaké (*French* bwake) *n* a market town in S central Côte d'Ivoire. Pop: 521 000 (2005 est)

Boucher (*French* buʃe) *n* **François** (frɑ̃swa). 1703–70, French rococo artist, noted for his delicate ornamental paintings of pastoral scenes and mythological subjects

Bouches-du-Rhône (*French* buʃdyrɔn) *n* a department of S central France, in Provence-Alpes-Côte d'Azur region. Capital: Marseille. Pop: 1 883 645 (2003 est). Area: 5284 sq km (2047 sq miles)

Boucicault (ˈbuːsɪˌkəʊ) *n* **Dion** (ˈdaɪən). real name *Dionysius Lardner Boursiquot* 1822–90, Irish dramatist and actor. His plays include *London Assurance* (1841), *The Octoroon* (1859), and *The Shaughran* (1874)

bouclé (ˈbuːkleɪ) *n* **1** a curled or looped yarn or fabric giving a thick knobbly effect ▷ *adj* **2** of or designating such a yarn or fabric: *a bouclé wool coat* [c19: from French *bouclé* curly, from *boucle* a curl, BUCKLE]

Boudicca (bəʊˈdɪkə) *n* died 62 AD, a queen of the Iceni, who led a revolt against Roman rule in Britain; after being defeated she poisoned herself. Also called: Boadicea

Boudin (*French* budɛ̃) *n* **Eugène** (øʒɛn). 1824–98, French painter: one of the first French landscape painters to paint in the open air; a forerunner of impressionism

boudoir (ˈbuːdwɑː, -dwɔː) *n* a woman's bedroom or private sitting room [c18: from French, literally: room for sulking in, from *bouder* to sulk]

bouffant (ˈbuːfɒŋ) *adj* **1** (of a hair style) having extra height and width through back-combing; puffed out **2** (of sleeves, skirts, etc) puffed out [c20: from French, from *bouffer* to puff up]

Bougainville¹ (ˈbuːgənˌvɪl) *n* an island in the W Pacific, in Papua New Guinea: the largest of the Solomon Islands: unilaterally declared independence in 1990; occupied by government troops in 1992, and granted autonomy in 2001. Chief town: Kieta. Area: 10 049 sq km (3880 sq miles)

Bougainville² (*French* bugɛ̃vil) *n* **Louis Antoine de** (lwi ɑ̃twan də). 1729–1811, French navigator

bougainvillea *or* **bougainvillaea** (ˌbuːgənˈvɪlɪə) *n* any tropical woody nyctaginaceous widely cultivated climbing plant of the genus *Bougainvillea*, having inconspicuous flowers surrounded by showy red or purple bracts [c19: New Latin, named after Louis Antoine de *Bougainville* (1729–1811), French navigator]

bough (baʊ) *n* any of the main branches of a tree [Old English *bōg* arm, twig; related to Old Norse *bōgr* shoulder, ship's bow, Old High German *buog* shoulder, Greek *pēkhus* forearm, Sanskrit *bāhu*; see BOW³, ELBOW]

bought (bɔːt) *vb* the past tense and past participle of **buy**

bougie (ˈbuːʒiː, buːˈʒiː) *n med* a long slender semiflexible cylindrical instrument for inserting into body passages, such as the rectum or urethra, to dilate structures, introduce medication, etc [c18: from French, originally a wax candle from *Bougie* (Bujiya), Algeria]

bouillabaisse (ˌbuːjəˈbɛs) *n* a rich stew or soup of fish and vegetables flavoured with spices, esp saffron [c19: from French, from Provençal *bouiabaisso*, literally: boil down]

bouillon (ˈbuːjɒn) *n* a plain unclarified broth or stock [c18: from French, from *bouillir* to BOIL¹]

Boulanger (*French* bulɑ̃ʒe) *n* **1 Georges** (ʒɔrʒ). 1837–91, French general and minister of war (1886–87). Accused of attempting a coup d'état, he fled to Belgium, where he

committed suicide **2 Nadia** (**Juliette**) (nadja). 1887–1979, French teacher of musical composition: her pupils included Elliott Carter, Aaron Copland, Darius Milhaud, and Virgil Thomson. She is noted also for her work in reviving the works of Monteverdi

boulder (ˈbəʊldə) *n* a smooth rounded mass of rock that has a diameter greater than 25cm and that has been shaped by erosion and transported by ice or water from its original position [c13: probably of Scandinavian origin; compare Swedish dialect *bullersten*, from Old Swedish *bulder* rumbling + *sten* STONE]

boulder clay *n* an unstratified glacial deposit consisting of fine clay, boulders, and pebbles

Boulder Dam *n* the former name (1933–47) of **Hoover Dam**

boule¹ (ˈbuːliː) *n* **1** the parliament in modern Greece **2** the senate of an ancient Greek city-state [c19: from Greek *boulē* senate]

boule² (buːl) *n* a pear-shaped imitation ruby, sapphire, etc, made from synthetic corundum [c19: from French: ball]

boule³ (buːl) *n* a round loaf of white bread [c20: from French: a ball]

boules (*French* buːl) *pl n* (*functioning as singular*) a game, popular in France, in which metal bowls are thrown to land as near as possible to a target ball. It is played on rough surfaces [plural of *boule* BALL¹; see BOWL²]

boulevard (ˈbuːlvɑː, -vɑːd) *n* a wide usually tree-lined road in a city, often used as a promenade [c18: from French, from Middle Dutch *bolwerc* BULWARK; so called because originally often built on the ruins of an old rampart]

Boulez (ˈbuːlɛz; *French* bulɛ) *n* **Pierre** (pjɛr). born 1925, French composer and conductor, whose works employ total serialism

boulle, boule *or* **buhl** (buːl) *adj* **1** denoting or relating to a type of marquetry of patterned inlays of brass and tortoiseshell, occasionally with other metals such as pewter, much used on French furniture from the 17th century ▷ *n* **2** Also called: **boullework** something ornamented with such marquetry [c18: named after André Charles *Boulle* (1642–1732), French cabinet-maker]

Boulogne (bʊˈlɔɪn; *French* bulɔɲ) *n* a port in N France, on the English Channel. Pop: 44 859 (1999)

Boulogne-Billancourt (*French* bulɔɲbijɑ̃kur) *n* an industrial suburb of SW Paris. Pop: 106 367 (1999). Also called: Boulogne-sur-Seine (*French* bulɔɲsyrsɛn)

boult (bəʊlt) *vb* a variant spelling of **bolt²**

Boult (bəʊlt) *n* Sir **Adrian** (**Cedric**). 1889–1983, English conductor

Boulton (ˈbəʊltən) *n* **Matthew**. 1728–1809, British engineer and manufacturer, who financed Watt's steam engine and applied it to various industrial purposes

Boumédienne (buːˌmeɪdɪˈɛn) *n* **Houari** (ˈhaʊərɪ). 1927–78, Algerian statesman and soldier: president of Algeria (1965–78) after overthrowing Ben Bella in a coup

bounce (baʊns) *vb* **1** (*intr*) (of an elastic object, such as a ball) to rebound from an impact **2** (*tr*) to cause (such an object) to hit a solid surface and spring back **3** to rebound or cause to rebound repeatedly **4** to move or cause to move suddenly, excitedly, or violently; spring **5** *slang* (of a bank) to send (a cheque) back or (of a cheque) to be sent back unredeemed because of lack of funds in the drawer's account **6** (*tr*) *slang* to force (a person) to leave (a place or job); throw out; eject ▷ *n* **7** a leap; jump; bound **8** the quality of being able to rebound; springiness **9** *informal* vitality; vigour; resilience **10** *Brit* swagger or impudence [c13: probably of imitative origin; compare Low German *bunsen* to beat, Dutch *bonken* to thump]

bounce back *vb* (*intr, adverb*) to recover one's health, good spirits, confidence, etc, easily after a setback

bouncer (ˈbaʊnsə) *n* *slang* a person employed at a club, pub, disco, etc, to throw out drunks or troublemakers and stop those considered undesirable from entering

bouncing (ˈbaʊnsɪŋ) *adj* (when *postpositive*, foll by *with*) vigorous and robust (esp in the phrase **a bouncing baby**)

bouncy (ˈbaʊnsɪ) *adj* bouncier, bounciest **1** lively, exuberant, or self-confident **2** having the capability or quality of bouncing: *a bouncy ball* **3** responsive to bouncing; springy: *a bouncy bed*

bouncy castle *n* a very large inflatable model, usually of a castle, on which children may bounce at fairs, etc

bound¹ (baʊnd) *vb* **1** the past tense and past participle of **bind** ▷ *adj* **2** in bonds or chains; tied with or as if with a rope **3** (*in combination*) restricted; confined: *housebound; fogbound* **4** (*postpositive*, foll by an infinitive) destined; sure; certain: *it's bound to happen* **5** (*postpositive*, often foll by *by*) compelled or obliged to act, behave, or think in a particular way, as by duty, circumstance, or convention **6** (of a book) secured within a cover or binding **7** *logic* (of a variable) occurring within the scope of a quantifier that indicates the degree of generality of the open sentence in which the variable occurs: in (x) (Fx → bxy), x is bound and y is free. See **free** (sense 19) **8** **bound up with** closely or inextricably linked with

bound² (baʊnd) *vb* **1** to move forwards or make (one's way) by leaps or jumps **2** to bounce; spring away from an impact ▷ *n* **3** a jump upwards or forwards **4** a bounce, as of a ball [c16: from Old French *bond* a leap, from *bondir* to jump, resound, from Vulgar Latin *bombitire* (unattested) to buzz, hum, from Latin *bombus* booming sound]

bound³ (baʊnd) *vb* **1** (*tr*) to place restrictions on; limit **2** (when *intr*, foll by *on*) to form a boundary of (an area of land or sea, political or administrative region, etc) ▷ *n* **3** See **bounds** [c13: from Old French *bonde*, from Medieval Latin *bodina*, of Gaulish origin]

bound⁴ (baʊnd) *adj* **a** (*postpositive*, often foll by *for*) going or intending to go towards; on the way to: *a ship bound for Jamaica; homeward bound* **b** (*in combination*): *northbound traffic* [c13: from Old Norse *buinn*, past participle of *būa* to prepare]

boundary (ˈbaʊndərɪ, -drɪ) *n, pl* **-ries** **1** something that indicates the farthest limit, as of an area; border **2** *cricket* **a** the marked limit of the playing area **b** a stroke that hits the ball beyond this limit **c** the four runs scored with such a stroke, or the six runs if the ball crosses the boundary without touching the ground

boundary rider *n Austral* an employee on a sheep or cattle station whose job is to maintain fences in good repair and to prevent stock from straying

bounden (ˈbaʊndən) *adj* morally obligatory (archaic except in the phrase **bounden duty**)

bounder (ˈbaʊndə) *n old-fashioned, Brit slang* a morally reprehensible person; cad

boundless (ˈbaʊndlɪs) *adj* unlimited; vast: *boundless energy* > **ˈboundlessly** *adv*

bounds (baʊndz) *pl n* **1** (*sometimes singular*) a limit; boundary (esp in the phrase **know no bounds**) **2** something that restrains or confines, esp the standards of a society: *within the bounds of modesty* ▷ See also **out of bounds**

bounteous (ˈbaʊntɪəs) *adj literary* **1** giving freely; generous **2** plentiful; abundant > **ˈbounteously** *adv* > **ˈbounteousness** *n*

bountiful (ˈbaʊntɪfʊl) *adj* **1** plentiful; ample (esp in the phrase **a bountiful supply**) **2** giving freely; generous > **ˈbountifully** *adv*

bounty (ˈbaʊntɪ) *n, pl* **-ties** **1** generosity in giving to others; liberality **2** a generous gift; something freely provided **3** a payment made by a government, as, formerly, to a sailor on enlisting or to a soldier after a campaign **4** any reward or premium [c13 (in the sense: goodness): from Old French *bontet*, from Latin *bonitās* goodness, from *bonus* good]

bouquet (*n* **1** (bəʊˈkeɪ, buː-) a bunch of flowers, esp a large carefully arranged one **2** Also called: **nose** (buːˈkeɪ) the characteristic aroma or fragrance of a wine or liqueur **3** a compliment or expression of praise [c18: from French: thicket, from Old French *bosc* forest, wood, probably of Germanic origin; see **bush¹**]

bouquet garni (ˈbuːkeɪ ɡɑːˈniː) *n, pl* bouquets garnis (ˈbuːkeɪz ɡɑːˈniː) a bunch of herbs tied together and used for flavouring soups, stews, etc [c19: from French, literally: garnished bouquet]

bourbon (ˈbɜːbən) *n* a whiskey distilled, chiefly in the US, from maize, esp one containing at least 51 per cent

maize (the rest being malt and rye) and aged in charred white-oak barrels [c19: named after *Bourbon* county, Kentucky, where it was first made]

Bourbon (ˈbʊəbən; *French* burbɔ̃) *n* **a** a member of the European royal line that ruled in France from 1589 to 1793 (when Louis XVI was executed by the revolutionaries) and was restored in 1815, continuing to rule in its Orleans branch from 1830 until 1848. Bourbon dynasties also ruled in Spain (1700–1808; 1813–1931) and Naples and Sicily (1734–1806; 1815–1860) **b** (*as modifier*): *the Bourbon kings*

bourdon (ˈbʊədⁿn, ˈbɔːdⁿn) *n* **1** a 16-foot organ stop of the stopped diapason type **2** the drone of a bagpipe **3** a drone or pedal point in the bass of a harmonized melody [c14: from Old French: drone (of a musical instrument), of imitative origin]

bourgeois (ˈbʊəʒwɑː, bʊəˈʒwɑː) *often disparaging* ▷ *n, pl* **-geois** **1** a member of the middle class, esp one regarded as being conservative and materialistic or (in Marxist thought) a capitalist exploiting the working class **2** a mediocre, unimaginative, or materialistic person ▷ *adj* **3** characteristic of, relating to, or comprising the middle class **4** conservative or materialistic in outlook: *a bourgeois mentality* **5** (in Marxist thought) dominated by capitalists or capitalist interests [c16: from Old French *borjois, burgeis* burgher, citizen, from *bourg* town; see **burgess**] > **bourgeoise** (ˈbʊəʒwɑːz, bʊəˈʒwɑːz) *fem n*

Bourgeois (*French* burʒwa) *n* **Léon Victor Auguste.** (leɔ̃ viktɔr oɡyst). 1851–1925, French statesman; first chairman of the League of Nations: Nobel peace prize 1920

bourgeoisie (ˌbʊəʒwɑːˈziː) *the bourgeoisie n* **1** the middle classes **2** (in Marxist thought) the ruling class of the two basic classes of capitalist society, consisting of capitalists, manufacturers, bankers, and other employers. The bourgeoisie owns the most important of the means of production, through which it exploits the working class

bourgeon (ˈbɜːdʒən) *n, vb* a variant spelling of **burgeon**

Bourges (*French* burʒ) *n* a city in central France. Pop: 72 480 (1999)

Bourgogne (burɡɔn) *n* the French name for **Burgundy**

Bourguiba (bʊəˈɡiːbə) *n* **Habib ben Ali** (hæˈbɪb ben ˈaːliː). 1903–2000, Tunisian statesman: president of Tunisia (1957–87); a moderate and an advocate of gradual social change. He was deposed in a coup and kept under house arrest for the rest of his life

Bourke-White (ˌbɜːkˈwaɪt) *n* **Margaret.** 1906–71, US photographer, a pioneer of modern photojournalism: noted esp for her coverage of World War II

bourn¹ or **bourne** (bɔːn) *n archaic* **1** a destination; goal **2** a boundary [c16: from Old French *borne*; see **bound³**]

bourn² (bɔːn) *n chiefly Southern Brit* a stream, esp an intermittent one in chalk areas. See **burn²** [c16: from Old French *bodne* limit; see **bound³**]

Bournemouth (ˈbɔːnməθ) *n* **1** a resort in S England, in Bournemouth unitary authority, Dorset, on the English Channel. Pop: 167 527 (2001) **2** a unitary authority in SE Dorset. Pop: 163 700 (2003 est). Area: 46 sq km (17 sq miles)

bourrée (ˈbʊəreɪ) *n* **1** a traditional French dance in fast duple time, resembling a gavotte **2** a piece of music composed in the rhythm of this dance [c18: from French *bourrée* a bundle of faggots (it was originally danced round a fire of faggots)]

Bourse (bʊəs) *n* a stock exchange of continental Europe, esp Paris [c19: from French, literally: purse, from Medieval Latin *bursa*, ultimately from Greek: leather]

boustrophedon (ˌbuːstrəˈfiːdⁿn, ˌbaʊ-) *adj* having alternate lines written from right to left and from left to right [c17: from Greek, literally: turning as in ploughing with oxen, from *bous* ox + *-strophēdon* from *strephein* to turn; see **strophe**]

bout (baʊt) *n* **1 a** a period of time spent doing something, such as drinking **b** a period of illness **2** a contest or fight, esp a boxing or wrestling match [c16: variant of obsolete *bought* turn; related to German *Bucht* **bight**; see **about**]

boutique (buːˈtiːk) *n* **1** a shop, esp a small one selling

b

fashionable clothes and other items **2 a** of or denoting a small specialized producer or business **b** (as modifier): a boutique winery **3** a small specialized stall or shopping area within a supermarket, esp selling fresh meat, seafood, etc [c18: from French, probably from Old Provençal botica, ultimately from Greek apothēkē storehouse; see APOTHECARY]

boutonniere (ˌbuːtɒnɪˈɛə) n another name for **buttonhole** (sense 2) [c19: from French: buttonhole, from bouton BUTTON]

bouzouki (buːˈzuːkɪ) n a Greek long-necked stringed musical instrument related to the mandolin [c20: from Modern Greek mpouzouki, perhaps from Turkish büjük large]

Bovet (French bɔvɛ) n Daniel. 1907–92, Italian pharmacologist, born in Switzerland, noted for his pioneering work on antihistamine drugs. Nobel prize for physiology or medicine 1957

bovine (ˈbəʊvaɪn) adj **1** of, relating to, or belonging to the Bovini (cattle), a bovid tribe including domestic cattle **2** (of people) dull; sluggish; stolid [c19: from Late Latin bovīnus concerning oxen or cows, from Latin bōs ox, cow]

bovine somatotrophin n the full name for BST (sense 1)

bovine spongiform encephalopathy n the full name for BSE

Bovril (ˈbɒvrɪl) n trademark a concentrated beef extract, used for flavouring, as a stock, etc

bovver (ˈbɒvə) n Brit slang **a** rowdiness, esp caused by gangs of teenage youths **b** (as modifier): a bovver boy [c20: slang pronunciation of BOTHER]

bow¹ (baʊ) vb **1** to lower (one's head) or bend (one's knee or body) as a sign of respect, greeting, assent, or shame **2** to bend or cause to bend; incline downwards **3** (intr; usually foll by to or before) to comply or accept: bow to the inevitable **4** (tr; foll by in, out, to etc) to usher (someone) into or out of a place with bows and deference: the manager bowed us to our car **5** (tr; usually foll by down) to bring (a person, nation, etc) to a state of submission **6** bow and scrape to behave in an excessively deferential or obsequious way ▷ n **7** a lowering or inclination of the head or body as a mark of respect, greeting, or assent **8** take a bow to acknowledge or receive applause or praise ▷ See also **bow out** [Old English būgan, related to Old Norse bjūgr bent, Old High German biogan to bend, Dutch buigen]

bow² (bəʊ) n **1** a weapon for shooting arrows, consisting of an arch of flexible wood, plastic, metal, etc bent by a string (**bowstring**) fastened at each end **2 a** a long slightly curved stick across which are stretched strands of horsehair, used for playing the strings of a violin, viola, cello, or related instrument **b** a stroke with such a stick **3 a** a decorative interlacing of ribbon or other fabrics, usually having two loops and two loose ends **b** the knot forming such an interlacing; bowknot **4** something that is curved, bent, or arched ▷ vb **5** to form or cause to form a curve or curves **6** to make strokes of a bow across (violin strings) [Old English boga arch, bow; related to Old Norse bogi a bow, Old High German bogo, Old Irish bocc, and bow¹]

bow³ (baʊ) n chiefly nautical **a** (often plural) the forward end or part of a vessel **b** (as modifier): the bow mooring line [c15: probably from Low German boog; related to Dutch boeg, Danish bov ship's bow, shoulder; see BOUGH]

Bow (bəʊ) n Clara, known as the It Girl. 1905–65, US film actress, noted for her vivacity and sex appeal

bow compass (bəʊ) n a compass for drawing, in which the legs are joined by a flexible metal bow-shaped spring rather than a hinge, the angle being adjusted by a screw

bowdlerize or **bowdlerise** (ˈbaʊdləˌraɪz) vb (tr) to remove passages or words regarded as indecent from (a play, novel, etc); expurgate [c19: after Thomas Bowdler (1754–1825), English editor who published an expurgated edition of Shakespeare] ▷ ˌbowdleriˈzation or ˌbowdleriˈsation n ▷ ˈbowdlerˌizer or ˈbowdlerˌiser n ▷ ˈbowdlerism n

bowel (ˈbaʊəl) n **1** an intestine, esp the large intestine in man **2** (plural) innards; entrails **3** (plural) the deep or

innermost part (esp in the phrase **the bowels of the earth**) **4** (plural) archaic the emotions, esp of pity or sympathy [c13: from Old French bouel, from Latin botellus a little sausage, from botulus sausage]

bowel movement n **1** the discharge of faeces; defecation **2** the waste matter discharged; faeces

Bowen (ˈbəʊən) n Elizabeth (Dorothea Cole). 1899–1973, British novelist and short-story writer, born in Ireland. Her novels include The Death of the Heart (1938) and The Heat of the Day (1949)

bower¹ (ˈbaʊə) n **1 a** a shady leafy shelter or recess, as in a wood or garden; arbour **2** literary a lady's bedroom or apartments, esp in a medieval castle; boudoir [Old English būr dwelling; related to Old Norse būr pantry, Old High German būr dwelling]

bower² (ˈbaʊə) n nautical a vessel's bow anchor [c18: from BOW³ + -ER¹]

bowerbird (ˈbaʊəˌbɜːd) n **1** any of various songbirds of the family Ptilonorhynchidae, of Australia and New Guinea. The males build bower-like display grounds in the breeding season to attract the females **2** informal, chiefly Austral a person who collects miscellaneous objects

Bowery (ˈbaʊərɪ) n the Bowery a street in New York City noted for its cheap hotels and bars, frequented by vagrants and drunks [c17: from Dutch bouwerij, from bouwen to farm + erij -ERY; see BOOR, BOER]

bowfin (ˈbəʊˌfɪn) n a primitive North American freshwater bony fish, Amia calva, with an elongated body and a very long dorsal fin: family Amiidae

bowhead (ˈbəʊˌhɛd) n a large-mouthed arctic whale, Balaena mysticetus, that has become rare through overfishing but is now a protected species

Bowie n **1** (ˈbaʊɪ, ˈbəʊɪ) David, real name David Jones. born 1947, British rock singer, songwriter, and film actor. His recordings include "Space Oddity" (1969), The Rise and Fall of Ziggy Stardust and the Spiders from Mars (1972), Heroes (1977), Let's Dance (1983), and Heathen (2002) **2** (ˈbəʊɪ) James, known as Jim Bowie. 1796–1836, US frontiersman. A hero of the Texas Revolution against Mexico (1835–36), he died at the Battle of the Alamo

bowie knife (ˈbəʊɪ) n a stout hunting knife with a short hilt and a guard for the hand [c19: named after Jim Bowie (1796–1836), US frontiersman, who popularized it]

bowl¹ (bəʊl) n **1** a round container open at the top, used for holding liquid, keeping fruit, serving food, etc **2** Also called: bowlful the amount a bowl will hold **3** the rounded or hollow part of an object, esp of a spoon or tobacco pipe **4** any container shaped like a bowl, such as a sink or lavatory **5** chiefly US a bowl-shaped building or other structure, such as a football stadium or amphitheatre **6** a bowl-shaped depression of the land surface **7** literary a drinking cup [Old English bolla; related to Old Norse bolli, Old Saxon bollo]

bowl² (bəʊl) n **1** a wooden ball used in the game of bowls, having flattened sides, one side usually being flatter than the other in order to make it run on a curved course **2** a large heavy ball with holes for gripping with the fingers and thumb, used in tenpin bowling ▷ vb **3** to roll smoothly or cause to roll smoothly, esp by throwing underarm along the ground **4** (intr; usually foll by along) to move easily and rapidly, as in a car **5** cricket **a** to send (a ball) down the pitch from one's hand towards the batsman, keeping the arm straight while doing so **b** Also called: bowl out to dismiss (a batsman) by delivering a ball that breaks his wicket **6** (intr) to play bowls or tenpin bowling **7** (tr) (in tenpin bowling) to score (a specified amount) ▷ See also **bowl over, bowls** [c15: from French boule, ultimately from Latin bulla bubble]

bow legs (bəʊ) pl n a condition in which the legs curve outwards like a bow between the ankle and the thigh. Also called: bandy legs ▷ bow-legged (bəʊˈlɛgɪd, bəʊˈlɛgd) adj

bowler¹ (ˈbəʊlə) n **1** one who bowls in cricket **2** a player at the game of bowls

bowler² (ˈbəʊlə) n a stiff felt hat with a rounded crown and narrow curved brim. US and Canadian name: derby [c19: after John Bowler, 19th-century London hatter]

Bowles (bəʊlz) *n* **Paul**. 1910–99, US novelist, short-story writer, and composer, living in Tangiers. His novels include *The Sheltering Sky* (1949) and *The Spider's House* (1955)

bowline ('bəʊlɪn) *n* *nautical* **1** a line for controlling the weather leech of a square sail when a vessel is close-hauled **2** a knot used for securing a loop that will not slip at the end of a piece of rope [c14: probably from Middle Low German *bōline*, equivalent to BOW³ + LINE¹]

bowling ('bəʊlɪŋ) *n* **1** any of various games in which a heavy ball is rolled down a special alley, usually made of wood, at a group of wooden pins, esp the games of tenpin bowling (tenpins) and skittles (ninepins) **2** the game of bowls **3** *cricket* the act of delivering the ball to the batsman

bowling alley *n* **1 a** a long narrow wooden lane down which the ball is rolled in tenpin bowling **b** a similar lane or alley, usually with raised sides, for playing skittles (ninepins) **2** a building having several lanes for tenpin bowling

bowling crease *n* *cricket* a line marked at the wicket, over which a bowler must not advance fully before delivering the ball

bowling green *n* an area of closely mown turf on which the game of bowls is played

bowl over *vb* (*tr, adverb*) **1** *informal* to surprise (a person) greatly, esp in a pleasant way; astound; amaze **2** to knock (a person or thing) down; cause to fall over

bowls (bəʊlz) *n* (*functioning as singular*) **1** a game played on a bowling green in which a small bowl (the jack) is pitched from a mark and two opponents or opposing teams take turns to roll biased wooden bowls towards it, the object being to finish as near the jack as possible **2** skittles or tenpin bowling

bowman ('bəʊmən) *n*, *pl* **-men** an archer

bow out (baʊ) *vb* (*adverb; usually tr; often foll by of*) to retire or withdraw gracefully

bowser ('baʊzə) *n* **1** a tanker containing fuel for aircraft, military vehicles, etc **2** *Austral & NZ obsolete* a petrol pump [originally a US proprietary name, from S. F. *Bowser*, US inventor, who made the first one in 1885]

bowshot ('bəʊˌʃɒt) *n* the distance an arrow travels from the bow

bowsprit ('bəʊsprɪt) *n* *nautical* a spar projecting from the bow of a vessel, esp a sailing vessel, used to carry the headstay as far forward as possible [c15: from Middle Low German *bōchsprēt*, from *bōch* BOW³ + *sprēt* pole]

bowstring ('bəʊˌstrɪŋ) *n* the string of an archer's bow, usually consisting of three strands of hemp

bow tie (bəʊ) *n* a man's tie done in a bow, now chiefly in plain black for formal evening wear

bow window (bəʊ) *n* a bay window in the shape of a curve

bow-wow ('baʊˌwaʊ, -'waʊ) *n* **1** a child's word for **dog** **2** an imitation of the bark of a dog ▷ *vb* **3** (*intr*) to bark or imitate a dog's bark

bowyangs ('bəʊjæŋz) *pl n* *Austral & NZ history* a pair of strings or straps secured round each trouser leg below the knee, worn esp by sheep-shearers and other labourers [c19: from English dialect *bowy-yanks* leggings]

box¹ (bɒks) *n* **1 a** a receptacle or container made of wood, cardboard, etc, usually rectangular and having a removable or hinged lid **2** Also called: **boxful** the contents of such a receptacle or the amount it can contain **3** any of various containers for a specific purpose **4** (*often in combination*) any of various small cubicles, kiosks, or shelters: *a telephone box or callbox; a sentry box; a signal box on a railway* **5** a separate compartment in a public place for a small group of people, as in a theatre or certain restaurants **6** an enclosure within a courtroom. See **witness box** **7** a compartment for a horse in a stable or a vehicle **8** *Brit* a small country house occupied by sportsmen when following a field sport, esp shooting **9 a** a protective housing for machinery or mechanical parts **b** (*in combination*): *a gearbox* **10** a shaped device of light tough material worn by sportsmen to protect the genitals, esp in cricket **11** a section of printed matter on a page, enclosed by lines, a border, or white space **12** a central

agency to which mail is addressed and from which it is collected or redistributed: *a post-office box; to reply to a box number in a newspaper advertisement* **13** short for **penalty box** **14** the raised seat on which the driver sits in a horse-drawn coach **15** *NZ* a wheeled container for transporting coal in a mine **16** *Austral & NZ* an accidental mixing of herds or flocks **17** *taboo, slang* the female genitals **18** the **box** *Brit informal* television ▷ *vb* **19** (*tr*) to put into a box **20** (*tr; usually foll by in or up*) to prevent from moving freely; confine **21** (*tr; foll by in*) *printing* to enclose (text) within a ruled frame **22** (*tr*) *Austral & NZ* to mix (flocks or herds) accidentally **23** **box the compass** *nautical* to name the compass points in order [Old English *box*, from Latin *buxus* from Greek *puxos* BOX³] ▷ 'box,like *adj*

box² (bɒks) *vb* **1** (*tr*) to fight (an opponent) in a boxing match **2** (*intr*) to engage in boxing **3** (*tr*) to hit (a person) with the fist; punch or cuff ▷ *n* **4** a punch with the fist, esp on the ear [c14: of uncertain origin; perhaps related to Dutch *boken* to shunt, push into position]

box³ (bɒks) *n* **1** a dense slow-growing evergreen tree or shrub of the genus *Buxus*, esp *B. sempervirens*, which has small shiny leaves and is used for hedges, borders, and garden mazes: family *Buxaceae* **2** the wood of this tree **3** any of several trees the timber or foliage of which resembles this tree, esp various species of *Eucalyptus* with rough bark [Old English, from Latin *buxus*]

box camera *n* a simple box-shaped camera having an elementary lens, shutter, and viewfinder

box chronometer *n* *nautical* a ship's chronometer, supported on gimbals in a wooden box

boxer ('bɒksə) *n* **1** a person who boxes, either professionally or as a hobby; pugilist **2** a medium-sized smooth-haired breed of dog with a short nose and a docked tail

Boxer ('bɒksə) *n* a member of a nationalistic Chinese secret society that led an unsuccessful rebellion in 1900 against foreign interests in China [c18: rough translation of Chinese *I Ho Ch'üan*, literally: virtuous harmonious fist, altered from *I Ho T'uan* virtuous harmonious society]

boxer shorts *pl n* men's underpants shaped like shorts but having a front opening. Also called: **boxers**

box girder *n* a girder that is hollow and square or rectangular in shape

Boxgrove man ('bɒksɡrəʊv) *n* a type of primitive man, probably *Homo heidelbergensis*, and probably dating from the Middle Palaeolithic period some 500 000 years ago; remains were found at Boxgrove in West Sussex in 1993 and 1995

boxing ('bɒksɪŋ) *n* **a** the act, art, or profession of fighting with the fists, esp the modern sport practised under Queensberry rules **b** (*as modifier*): *a boxing enthusiast*

Boxing Day *n* *Brit* the first day (traditionally and strictly, the first weekday) after Christmas, observed as a holiday [c19: from the custom of giving Christmas boxes to tradesmen and staff on this day]

boxing glove *n* one of a pair of thickly padded mittens worn for boxing

box junction *n* (in Britain) a road junction having yellow cross-hatching painted on the road surface. Vehicles may only enter the hatched area when their exit is clear

box kite *n* a kite with a boxlike frame open at both ends

box office *n* **1** an office at a theatre, cinema, etc, where tickets are sold **2 a** the public appeal of an actor or production **b** (*as modifier*): *a box-office success*

box pleat *n* a flat double pleat made by folding under the fabric on either side of it

boxroom ('bɒksˌruːm, -ˌrʊm) *n* a small room or large cupboard in which boxes, cases, etc, may be stored

box seat *n* **1** a seat in a theatre box **2** **in the box seat** *Brit, Austral & NZ* in the best position

box spanner *n* a spanner consisting of a steel cylinder with a hexagonal end that fits over a nut: used esp to turn nuts in positions that are recessed or difficult of access

box spring *n* a coiled spring contained in a boxlike frame, used as a base for mattresses, chairs, etc

boxwood (ˈbɒksˌwʊd) n 1 the hard close-grained yellow wood of the box tree, used to make tool handles, small turned or carved articles, etc 2 the box tree

boxy (ˈbɒksɪ) adj squarish or chunky in style or appearance: a boxy square-cut jacket

boy (bɔɪ) n 1 a male child; lad; youth 2 a man regarded as immature or inexperienced: he's just a boy when it comes to dealing with women 3 See old boy 4 informal a group of men, esp a group of friends 5 usually derogatory (esp in former colonial territories) a Black person or native male servant of any age 6 Austral a jockey or apprentice 7 short for boyfriend 8 boys will be boys youthful indiscretion or exuberance must be expected and tolerated 9 jobs for the boys informal appointment of one's supporters to posts, without reference to their qualifications or ability 10 the boy Irish informal the right tool for a particular task: that's the boy to cut it ▷ interj 11 an exclamation of surprise, pleasure, contempt, etc [C13 (in the sense: male servant; C14: young male): of uncertain origin; perhaps from Anglo-French abuié fettered (unattested), from Latin boia fetter]

Boyce (bɔɪs) n William. ?1710–79, English composer, noted esp for his church music and symphonies

boycott (ˈbɔɪkɒt) vb 1 (tr) to refuse to have dealings with (a person, organization, etc) or refuse to buy (a product) as a protest or means of coercion ▷ n 2 an instance or the use of boycotting [C19: after Captain C. C. Boycott (1832–97), Irish land agent for the Earl of Erne, County Mayo, Ireland, who was a victim of such practices for refusing to reduce rents]

Boycott (ˈbɔɪkɒt) n Geoff(rey). born 1940, English cricketer: captained Yorkshire (1970–78); played for England (1964–74, 1977–82)

Boyd (bɔɪd) n 1 Arthur. 1920–99, Australian painter and sculptor, noted for his large ceramic sculptures and his series of engravings 2 Martin (A'Beckett). 1893–1972, Australian novelist, author of Lucinda Brayford (1946) and of the Langton tetralogy The Cardboard Crown (1952), A Difficult Young Man (1955), Outbreak of Love (1957), and When Blackbirds Sing (1962) 3 Michael. born 1955, British theatre director; artistic director of the Royal Shakespeare Company from 2003

Boyd Orr (ɔː) n John, 1st Baron Boyd Orr of Brechin Mearns. 1880–1971, Scottish biologist; director general of the United Nations Food and Agriculture Organization: Nobel peace prize 1949

Boyer (French bwaje) n Charles. (ʃɑːl), known as the Great Lover. 1899–1978, French film actor

boyfriend (ˈbɔɪˌfrɛnd) n a male friend with whom a person is romantically or sexually involved; sweetheart or lover

boyhood (ˈbɔɪhʊd) n the state or time of being a boy

boyish (ˈbɔɪɪʃ) adj of or like a boy in looks, behaviour, or character, esp when regarded as attractive or endearing: a boyish smile

Boyle (bɔɪl) n Robert. 1627–91, Irish scientist who helped to dissociate chemistry from alchemy. He established that air has weight and studied the behaviour of gases; author of The Sceptical Chymist (1661)

Boyle's law n the principle that the pressure of a gas varies inversely with its volume at constant temperature [C18: named after Robert Boyle (1627–91), Irish scientist]

Boyne (bɔɪn) n a river in the E Republic of Ireland, rising in the Bog of Allen and flowing northeast to the Irish Sea: William III of England defeated the deposed James II in a battle (Battle of the Boyne) on its banks in 1690, completing the overthrow of the Stuart cause in Ireland. Length: about 112 km (70 miles)

boyo (ˈbɔɪəʊ) n Brit informal a boy or young man: often used in direct address [from Irish and Welsh]

Boyoma Falls (bɔɪˈəʊmə) pl n a series of seven cataracts in the NE Democratic Republic of Congo (formerly Zaïre), on the upper River Congo: forms an unnavigable stretch of 90 km (56 miles), which falls 60 m (200 ft). Former name: Stanley Falls

boy racer n informal a a young man who drives his car aggressively and at inappropriately high speeds b (as modifier): the boy-racer market

Boys' Brigade n (in Britain) an organization for boys, founded in 1883, with the aim of promoting discipline and self-respect

boy scout n See Scout

boysenberry (ˈbɔɪzªnbərɪ) n, pl -ries 1 a type of bramble: a hybrid of the loganberry and various blackberries and raspberries 2 the large red edible fruit of this plant [C20: named after Rudolph Boysen, American botanist who developed it]

Boz (bɒz) n pen name of (Charles) Dickens

Bozcaada (ˌbɒzdʒaaˈda) n the Turkish name for Tenedos

Bozen (ˈboːtsən) n the German name for Bolzano

bp abbreviation 1 (of alcoholic density) below proof 2 boiling point 3 bishop

BP abbreviation 1 blood pressure 2 British Pharmacopoeia

BPC abbreviation British Pharmaceutical Codex

B.P.E. abbreviation (in the US and Canada) Bachelor of Physical Education

BPhil abbreviation Bachelor of Philosophy

bpi abbreviation bits per inch (used of a computer tape or disk surface)

BPR abbreviation business process re-engineering

b.pt. abbreviation boiling point

Bq symbol for becquerel(s)

br abbreviation brother

Br abbreviation 1 (in a religious order) Brother ▷ the chemical symbol for 2 bromine

BR abbreviation British Rail (formerly)

Br. abbreviation 1 Britain 2 British

bra (brɑː) n short for brassiere

braai (braɪ) South African ▷ vb 1 to grill or roast (meat) over open coals ▷ n 2 short for braaivleis [Afrikaans]

braaivleis (ˈbraɪˌfleɪs) n South African 1 a picnic at which meat is cooked over an open fire; a barbecue 2 the meat cooked at such a barbecue [from Afrikaans braai roast + vleis meat]

Brabant (brəˈbænt) n 1 a former duchy of W Europe: divided when Belgium became independent (1830), the south forming the Belgian provinces of Antwerp and Brabant and the north forming the province of North Brabant in the Netherlands 2 a former province of central Belgium; replaced in 1995 by the provinces of Flemish Brabant and Walloon Brabant

Brabham (ˈbræbəm) n Sir John Arthur, known as Jack. born 1926, Australian motor-racing driver: world champion 1959, 1960, and 1966

brace (breɪs) n 1 a hand tool for drilling holes, with a socket to hold the drill at one end and a cranked handle by which the tool can be turned. See also brace and bit 2 something that steadies, binds, or holds up another thing 3 a structural member, such as a beam or prop, used to stiffen a framework 4 a pair; two, esp of game birds 5 either of a pair of characters, { }, used for connecting lines of printing or writing or as a third sign of aggregation in complex mathematical or logical expressions that already contain parentheses and square brackets 6 Also called: accolade a line or bracket connecting two or more staves of music 7 (often plural) an appliance of metal bands and wires that can be tightened to maintain steady pressure on the teeth for correcting uneven alignment 8 med any of various appliances for supporting the trunk, a limb, or teeth 9 See braces ▷ vb (mainly tr) 10 to provide, strengthen, or fit with a brace 11 to steady or prepare (oneself or something) as before an impact 12 (also intr) to stimulate; freshen; invigorate: sea air is bracing [C14: from Old French: the two arms, from Latin bracchia arms]

brace and bit n a hand tool for boring holes, consisting of a cranked handle into which a drilling bit is inserted

bracelet (ˈbreɪslɪt) n an ornamental chain worn around the arm or wrist [C15: from Old French, from bracel, literally: a little arm, from Latin bracchium arm; see BRACE]

bracelets (ˈbreɪslɪts) pl n a slang name for handcuffs

bracer (ˈbreɪsə) n a person or thing that braces 1 informal a tonic, esp an alcoholic drink taken as a tonic

braces (ˈbreɪsɪz) pl n Brit a pair of straps worn over the shoulders by men for holding up the trousers

brachial (ˈbreɪkɪəl, ˈbræk-) adj of or relating to the arm or to an armlike part or structure

brachiate *adj* (ˈbreɪkɪɪt, -ˌeɪt, ˈbræk-) 1 *botany* having widely divergent paired branches ▷ *vb* (ˈbreɪkɪˌeɪt, ˈbræk-) 2 (*intr*) (of some arboreal apes and monkeys) to swing by the arms from one hold to the next [c19: from Latin *bracchiātus* with armlike branches] ▷ ˌbrachiˈation *n*

brachio- *or before a vowel* **brachi-** *combining form* indicating a brachium: *brachiopod*

brachiopod (ˈbreɪkɪəˌpɒd, ˈbræk-) *n* any marine invertebrate animal of the phylum *Brachiopoda*, having a ciliated feeding organ (lophophore) and a shell consisting of dorsal and ventral valves [c19: from New Latin *Brachiopoda*; see BRACHIUM, -POD]

brachiosaurus (ˌbreɪkɪəˈsɔːrəs, ˌbræk-) *n* a dinosaur of the genus *Brachiosaurus*, up to 30 metres long: the largest land animal ever known

brachium (ˈbreɪkɪəm, ˈbræk-) *n, pl* -chia (-kɪə) 1 *anatomy* the arm, esp the upper part 2 a corresponding part, such as a wing, in an animal 3 *biology* a branching or armlike part [c18: New Latin, from Latin *bracchium* arm, from Greek *brakhīōn*]

brachy- *combining form* indicating something short: *brachycephalic* [from Greek *brakhus* short]

brachycephalic (ˌbrækɪsɪˈfælɪk) *Also called:* **brachycephalous** (ˌbrækɪˈsɛfələs) *adj* having a head nearly as broad from side to side as from front to back, esp one with a cephalic index over 80 ▷ ˌbrachyˈcephaly *or* ˌbrachyˈcephalism *n*

brachytherapy (ˌbrækɪˈθɛrəpɪ) *n* a form of radiotherapy in which sealed sources of radioactive material are inserted temporarily into body cavities or directly into tumours

bracing (ˈbreɪsɪŋ) *adj* 1 refreshing; stimulating; invigorating ▷ *n* 2 a system of braces used to strengthen or support

bracken (ˈbrækən) *n* 1 *Also called:* **brake** any of various large coarse ferns, esp *Pteridium aquilinum*, having large fronds with spore cases along the undersides and extensive underground stems 2 a clump of any of these ferns [c14: of Scandinavian origin; compare Swedish *bräken*, Danish *bregne*]

bracket (ˈbrækɪt) *n* 1 an L-shaped or other support fixed to a wall to hold a shelf, etc 2 one or more wall shelves carried on brackets 3 *architect* a support projecting from the side of a wall or other structure 4 *Also called:* **square bracket** either of a pair of characters, [ ], used to enclose a section of writing or printing to separate it from the main text 5 a general name for **parenthesis**, **square bracket** *and* **brace** (sense 5) 6 a group or category falling within or between certain defined limits: *the lower income bracket* 7 the distance between two preliminary shots of artillery fire in range-finding ▷ *vb* -kets, -keting, -keted (*tr*) 8 to fix or support by means of a bracket or brackets 9 to put (written or printed matter) in brackets, esp as being irrelevant, spurious, or bearing a separate relationship of some kind to the rest of the text 10 to couple or join (two lines of text, etc) with a brace 11 (often foll by *with*) to group or class together 12 to adjust (artillery fire) until the target is hit [c16: from Old French *braguette* codpiece, diminutive of *bragues* breeches, from Old Provençal *braga*, from Latin *brāca* breeches]

brackish (ˈbrækɪʃ) *adj* (of water) slightly briny or salty [c16: from Middle Dutch *brac* salty; see -ISH] ▷ ˈbrackishness *n*

Bracknell (ˈbræknəl) *n* a town in SE England, in Bracknell Forest unitary authority, Berkshire: designated a new town in 1949. Pop: 70 795 (2001)

Bracknell Forest *n* a unitary authority in SE England, in E Berkshire. Pop: 110 100 (2003 est). Area: 109 sq km (42 sq miles)

bract (brækt) *n* a specialized leaf, usually smaller than the foliage leaves, with a single flower or inflorescence growing in its axil [c18: from New Latin *bractea*, Latin: thin metal plate, gold leaf, variant of *brattea*, of obscure origin] ▷ ˈbracteal *adj* ▷ **bracteate** (ˈbræktɪɪt, -ˌeɪt) *adj, n* [c19: from Latin *bracteātus* gold-plated; see BRACT]

bracteole (ˈbræktɪˌəʊl) *n* a secondary bract subtending a flower in an inflorescence. *Also called:* **bractlet**

[c19: from New Latin *bracteola*, from *bractea* thin metal plate; see BRACT]

brad (bræd) *n* a small tapered nail having a small head that is either symmetrical or formed on one side only [Old English *brord* point, prick; related to Old Norse *broddr* spike, sting, Old High German *brort* edge]

bradawl (ˈbrædˌɔːl) *n* an awl used to pierce wood, leather, or other materials for the insertion of brads, screws, etc

Bradbury (ˈbrædbrɪ) *n* 1 Sir **Malcolm** (**Stanley**). 1932–2000, British novelist and critic. His novels include *The History Man* (1975), *Rates of Exchange* (1983), *Cuts* (1988), and *Doctor Criminale* (1992) 2 **Ray**. born 1920, US science-fiction writer. His novels include *Fahrenheit 451* (1953), *Death is a Lonely Business* (1986), and *A Graveyard for Lunatics* (1990)

Bradford (ˈbrædfəd) *n* 1 an industrial city in N England, in Bradford unitary authority, West Yorkshire: a centre of the woollen industry from the 14th century and of the worsted trade from the 18th century; university (1966). Pop: 293 717 (2001) 2 a unitary authority in West Yorkshire. Pop: 477 800 (2003 est). Area: 370 sq km (143 sq miles)

Bradlaugh (ˈbrædlɔː) *n* **Charles**. 1833–91, British radical and freethinker: barred from taking his seat in parliament (1880–86) for refusing to take the parliamentary oath

Bradley (ˈbrædlɪ) *n* 1 **A**(**ndrew**) **C**(**ecil**). 1851–1935, English critic; author of *Shakespearian Tragedy* (1904) 2 **F**(**rancis**) **H**(**erbert**). 1846–1924, English idealist philosopher and metaphysical thinker; author of *Ethical Studies* (1876), *Principles of Logic* (1883), and *Appearance and Reality* (1893) 3 **Henry**. 1845–1923, English lexicographer; one of the editors of the *Oxford English Dictionary* 4 **James**. 1693–1762, English astronomer, who discovered the aberration of light and the nutation of the earth's axis

Bradman (ˈbrædmən) *n* Sir **Don**(**ald George**). 1908–2001, Australian cricketer: an outstanding batsman

Bradshaw (ˈbrædˌʃɔː) *n* a British railway timetable, published annually from 1839 to 1961 [c19: named after its original publisher, George Bradshaw (1801–53)]

Bradstreet (ˈbrædˌstriːt) *n* **Anne** (**Dudley**). ?1612–72, US poet, born in England: regarded as the first significant US poet

bradycardia (ˌbrædɪˈkɑːdɪə) *n* *pathol* an abnormally low rate of heartbeat

brae (breɪ; *Scot* bre) *n* *Scot* 1 a hill or hillside; slope 2 (*plural*) an upland area [c14 *bra*; related to Old Norse *brā* eyelash, Old High German *brāwa* eyelid, eyebrow; compare BROW]

Braeburn (ˈbreɪˌbɜːn) *n* a variety of eating apple from New Zealand having sweet flesh and green and red skin

Braemar (ˌbreɪˈmɑː) *n* a village in NE Scotland, in Aberdeenshire; Balmoral Castle is nearby: site of the Royal Braemar Gathering, an annual Highland Games meeting

brag (bræg) *vb* brags, bragging, bragged 1 to speak of (one's own achievements, possessions, etc) arrogantly and boastfully ▷ *n* 2 boastful talk or behaviour, or an instance of this 3 something boasted of 4 a braggart; boaster 5 a card game: an old form of poker [c13: of unknown origin] ▷ ˈbragger *n*

Braga (*Portuguese* ˈbraɡə) *n* a city in N Portugal: capital of the Roman province of Lusitania; 12th-century cathedral, seat of the Primate of Portugal. Pop: 164 193 (2001)

Bragg (bræg) *n* 1 **Billy**. born 1957, British rock singer and songwriter, noted for his political protest songs; recordings include *Between the Wars* (1985), *Workers' Playtime* (1988), *Mermaid Avenue* (1998), and *England, Half English* (2002) 2 **Melvyn**, Baron. born 1939, British novelist, broadcaster, and television executive; presenter of *The South Bank Show* since 1978 3 Sir **William Henry**, 1862–1942, British physicist, who shared a Nobel prize for physics (1915) with his son, for their study of crystal structures by means of X-rays 4 his son, Sir (**William**) **Lawrence**, 1890–1971, British physicist

braggadocio (ˌbræɡəˈdəʊtʃɪˌəʊ) *n, pl* -os 1 vain empty boasting 2 a person who boasts; braggart [c16: from

Braggadocchio, name of a boastful character in Spenser's *Faerie Queene*; probably from BRAGGART + Italian *-occhio* (augmentative suffix)]

braggart ('brægət) *n* **1** a person who boasts loudly or exaggeratedly; bragger ▷ *adj* **2** boastful [C16: see BRAG]

Bragg's law *n* the principle that when a beam of X-rays of wavelength λ enters a crystal, the maximum intensity of the reflected ray occurs when sin θ = *n*λ/2*d*, where θ is the complement of the angle of incidence, *n* is a whole number, and *d* is the distance between layers of atoms [C20: named after Sir William Henry *Bragg* (1862–1942), and his son, Sir Lawrence *Bragg* (1890–1971), British physicists]

Bragi ('brɑːɡɪ) *or* **Brage** ('brɑːɡə) *n Norse myth* the god of poetry and music, son of Odin

Brahe (brɑː; *Danish* 'brɑːə) *n* **Tycho** ('ty:ço). 1546–1601, Danish astronomer, who designed and constructed instruments that he used to plot accurately the positions of the planets, sun, moon, and stars

Brahma ('brɑːmə) *n* a Hindu god: in later Hindu tradition, the Creator who, with Vishnu, the Preserver, and Shiva, the Destroyer, constitutes the triad known as the Trimurti [from Sanskrit, from *brahman* praise]

Brahman ('brɑːmən) *n, pl* **-mans 1** (*sometimes not capital*) a member of the highest or priestly caste in the Hindu caste system. Also called (esp formerly): Brahmin **2** another name for **Brahma** [C14: from Sanskrit *brāhmana*, from *brahman* prayer] > Brahmanic (brɑːˈmænɪk) *or* Brah'manical *adj*

Brahmanism ('brɑːməˌnɪzəm) *or* **Brahminism** *n* (*sometimes not capital*) the religious and social system of orthodox Hinduism, characterized by diversified pantheism, the caste system, and the sacrifices and family ceremonies of Hindu tradition > 'Brahmanist *or* 'Brahminist *n*

Brahmaputra (ˌbrɑːməˈpuːtrə) *n* a river in S Asia, rising in SW Tibet as the Tsangpo and flowing through the Himalayas and NE India to join the Ganges at its delta in Bangladesh. Length: about 2900 km (1800 miles)

Brahmin ('brɑːmɪn) *n, pl* **-min** *or* **-mins 1** the older spelling of **Brahman** (sense 1) **2** (in the US) a highly intelligent or socially exclusive person, esp a member of one of the older New England families

Brahms (brɑːmz) *n* **Johannes** (joˈhanəs). 1833–97, German composer, whose music, though classical in form, exhibits a strong lyrical romanticism. His works include four symphonies, four concertos, chamber music, and *A German Requiem* (1868)

braid (breɪd) *vb* (*tr*) **1** to interweave several strands of (hair, thread, etc); plait **2** to decorate with an ornamental trim or border: *to braid a skirt* ▷ *n* **3** a length of hair, fabric, etc, that has been braided; plait **4** narrow ornamental tape of woven silk, wool, etc [Old English *bregdan* to move suddenly, weave together; compare Old Norse *bregtha*, Old High German *brettan* to draw a sword] > 'braider *n* > 'braiding *n*

Brăila (Romanian brəˈila) *n* a port in E Romania: belonged to Turkey (1544–1828). Pop: 192 000 (2005 est)

Braille[1] (breɪl) *n* **1** a system of writing for the blind consisting of raised dots that can be interpreted by touch, each dot or group of dots representing a letter, numeral, or punctuation mark **2** any writing produced by this method ▷ *vb* **3** (*tr*) to print or write using this method

Braille[2] (French braj) *n* **Louis** (lwi). 1809–52, French inventor, musician, and teacher of the blind, who himself was blind from the age of three and who devised the Braille system of raised writing

brain (breɪn) *n* **1** the soft convoluted mass of nervous tissue within the skull of vertebrates that is the controlling and coordinating centre of the nervous system and the seat of thought, memory, and emotion. It includes the cerebrum, brainstem, and cerebellum **2** (*often plural*) *informal* intellectual ability: *he's got brains* **3** *informal* shrewdness or cunning **4** *informal* an intelligent or intelligent person **5** (*usually plural; functioning as singular*) *informal* a person who plans and organizes an undertaking or is in overall control of an organization, etc **6** an electronic device, such as a

computer, that performs apparently similar functions to the human brain **7** on the brain constantly in mind: *I had that song on the brain* ▷ *vb* (*tr*) **8** to smash the skull of **9** *slang* to hit hard on the head [Old English *brægen*; related to Old Frisian *brein*, Middle Low German *bregen*, Greek *brekhmos* forehead]

brain candy *n informal* something that is entertaining or enjoyable but lacks depth or significance

brainchild ('breɪnˌtʃaɪld) *n, pl* **-children** *informal* an idea or plan produced by creative thought; invention

braindead ('breɪnˌdɛd) *adj* **1** having suffered brain death **2** *informal* not using or showing intelligence; stupid

brain death *n* irreversible cessation of respiration due to irreparable brain damage, even though the heart may continue beating with the aid of a mechanical ventilator: widely considered as the criterion of death

brain drain *n informal* the emigration of scientists, technologists, academics, etc, for better pay, equipment, or conditions

Braine (breɪn) *n* **John** (**Gerard**). 1922–86, English novelist, whose works include *Room at the Top* (1957) and *Life at the Top* (1962)

brain fever *n* inflammation of the brain or its covering membranes

brain fingerprinting *n* a technique in which sensors worn on the head are used to measure the involuntary brain activity of someone in response to certain images or pieces of evidence pertaining to a crime

brainfood ('breɪnˌfuːd) *n* any foodstuff containing nutrients thought to promote brain function, such as oily fish which is rich in omega-3 oils

brain gain *n informal* the immigration into a country of scientists, technologists, academics, etc, attracted by better pay, equipment, or conditions

brainiac ('breɪnɪˌæk) *n informal* a highly intelligent person [C20: from a super-intelligent character in an American comic strip]

brainless ('breɪnlɪs) *adj* stupid or foolish

brainpan ('breɪnˌpæn) *n informal* the skull

brainstem ('breɪnˌstɛm) *n* the stalklike part of the brain consisting of the medulla oblongata, the midbrain, and the pons Varolii

brainstorm ('breɪnˌstɔːm) *n* **1** a severe outburst of excitement, often as the result of a transitory disturbance of cerebral activity **2** *Brit informal* a sudden mental aberration **3** *informal* another word for **brainwave**

brainstorming ('breɪnˌstɔːmɪŋ) *n* intensive discussion to solve problems or generate ideas

brains trust *n* a group of knowledgeable people who discuss topics in public or on radio or television

brain-teaser *or* **brain-twister** *n informal* a difficult problem

brain up *vb* (*tr*) to make more intellectually demanding or sophisticated: *we need to brain up the curriculum*

brainwash ('breɪnˌwɒʃ) *vb* (*tr*) to effect a radical change in the ideas and beliefs of (a person), esp by methods based on isolation, sleeplessness, hunger, extreme discomfort, pain, and the alternation of kindness and cruelty > 'brainˌwashing *n*

brainwave ('breɪnˌweɪv) *n informal* a sudden inspiration or idea

brain wave *n* any of the fluctuations of electrical potential in the brain as represented on an electroencephalogram. They vary in frequency from 1 to 30 hertz

brainy ('breɪnɪ) *adj* **brainier, brainiest** *informal* clever; intelligent > 'braininess *n*

braise (breɪz) *vb* to cook (meat, vegetables, etc) by lightly browning in fat and then cooking slowly in a closed pan with a small amount of liquid [C18: from French *braiser*, from Old French *brese* live coals, probably of Germanic origin; compare Old English *brædan*, Old High German *brātan* to roast]

brak[1] (brak) *adj South African* (of water) brackish or salty [C19: Afrikaans]

brak[2] (brak) *n South African* a mongrel dog [C20: from Afrikaans, literally: setter]

brake[1] (breɪk) *n* **1** (*often plural*) a device for slowing or

stopping a vehicle, wheel, shaft, etc, or for keeping it stationary, esp by means of friction **2** a machine or tool for crushing or breaking flax or hemp to separate the fibres **3** *Also called:* brake harrow a heavy harrow for breaking up clods **4** short for **shooting brake** ▷ *vb* **5** to slow down or cause to slow down, by or as if by using a brake **6** (*tr*) to crush or break up using a brake [c18: from Middle Dutch *braeke*; related to *breken* to BREAK]
> 'brakeless *adj*

brake² (breɪk) *n* an area of dense undergrowth, shrubs, brushwood, etc; thicket [Old English *bracu*; related to Middle Low German *brake*, Old French *bracon* branch]

brake³ (breɪk) *n* another name for **bracken** (sense 1)

brake⁴ (breɪk) *vb archaic, chiefly biblical* a past tense of **break**

brake-fade *n* the decrease in efficiency of braking of a motor vehicle due to overheating of the brakes

brake horsepower *n* the rate at which an engine does work, expressed in horsepower. It is measured by the resistance of an applied brake. Abbreviation: bhp

brake light *n* a red light attached to the rear of a motor vehicle that lights up when the brakes are applied, serving as a warning to following drivers

brake lining *n* a curved thin strip of an asbestos composition riveted to a brake shoe to provide it with a renewable surface

brake pad *n* the flat metal casting, together with the bound friction material, in a disc brake

brake shoe *n* **1** the curved metal casting to which the brake lining is riveted in a drum brake **2** the curved metal casting together with the attached brake lining ▷ *Sometimes shortened to:* shoe

brakesman ('breɪksmən) *n, pl* -men a pithead winch operator

brake van *n railways, Brit* the coach or vehicle from which the guard applies the brakes; guard's van

Brakpan ('bræk,pæn) *n* a city in E South Africa: gold-mining centre. Pop: 62 116 (2001)

Bramante (*Italian* bra'mante) *n* **Donato** (do'nato). ?1444–1514, Italian architect and artist of the High Renaissance. He modelled his designs for domed centrally planned churches on classical Roman architecture

bramble ('bræmbᵊl) *n* **1** any of various prickly herbaceous plants or shrubs of the rosaceous genus *Rubus*, esp the blackberry **2** *Scot and N Ireland* a blackberry **3** any of several similar and related shrubs [Old English *brǣmbel*; related to Old Saxon *brāmal*, Old High German *brāmo*] > 'brambly *adj*

brambling ('bræmblɪŋ) *n* a Eurasian finch, *Fringilla montifringilla*, with a speckled head and back and, in the male, a reddish brown breast and darker wings and tail

bran (bræn) *n* **1** husks of cereal grain separated from the flour by sifting **2** food prepared from these husks [c13: from Old French, probably of Gaulish origin]

Branagh ('brænə) *n* **Kenneth**. born 1961, British actor and director, born in Northern Ireland. He founded the Renaissance Theatre Company in 1986. His films include *Henry V* (1989), *Mary Shelley's Frankenstein* (1994), *Hamlet* (1997), and *Harry Potter and the Chamber of Secrets* (2002)

branch (brɑːntʃ) *n* **1** a secondary woody stem arising from the trunk or bough of a tree or the main stem of a shrub **2** an offshoot or secondary part: *a branch of a deer's antlers* **3 a** a subdivision or subsidiary section of something larger or more complex: *branches of learning; branch of the family* **b** (*as modifier*): *a branch office* **4** *US* any small stream ▷ *vb* **5** (*intr*) (of a tree or other plant) to produce or possess branches **6** (*intr*; usually foll by *from*) (of stems, roots, etc) to grow and diverge (from another part) **7** to divide or be divided into subsidiaries or offshoots **8** (*intr*; often foll by *off*) to diverge from the main way, road, topic, etc [c13: from Old French *branche*, from Late Latin *branca* paw, foot] > 'branch,like *adj*

branchia ('bræŋkɪə) *n, pl* -chiae (-kɪ,iː) a gill in aquatic animals > 'branchi,ate *adj* > 'branchial *adj*

branch out *vb* (*intr, adverb*; often foll by *into*) to expand or extend one's interests

branch plant or **branch factory** *n Canadian* a plant or factory in Canada belonging to a company whose headquarters are in another country

Brancusi (bræn'kuːzɪ; *Romanian* brɪŋ'kuʃj) *n* **Constantin** (konstan'tin). 1876–1957, Romanian sculptor, noted for his streamlined abstractions of animal forms

brand (brænd) *n* **1** a particular product or a characteristic that serves to identify a particular product **2** a particular kind or variety **3** an identifying mark made, usually by burning, on the skin of animals or (formerly) slaves or criminals, esp as a proof of ownership **4** an iron heated and used for branding animals, etc **5** a mark of disgrace or infamy; stigma **6** a burning or burnt piece of wood, as in a fire **7** *archaic or poetic* **a** a flaming torch **b** a sword **8** a fungal disease of garden plants characterized by brown spots on the leaves, caused by the rust fungus *Puccinia arenariae* ▷ *vb* (*tr*) **9** to label, burn, or mark with or as with a brand **10** to place indelibly in the memory: *the scene of slaughter was branded in their minds* **11** to denounce; stigmatize: *they branded him a traitor* [Old English *brand-*, related to Old Norse *brandr*, Old High German *brant*; see BURN¹]
> 'branding *n* > 'brander *n*

Brand (brænd) *n* **Russell**, born 1975, English comedian and television presenter

brandade (*French* brɑ̃dad) *n* a Provençal dish of salt cod puréed with olive oil and milk [French, from Modern Provençal *brandado*, literally, something that has been shaken]

brand awareness *n marketing* the extent to which consumers are aware of a particular product or service

Brandenburg ('brændən,bɜːg; *German* 'brandənburk) *n* **1** a state in NE Germany, part of East Germany until 1990. A former electorate, it expanded under the Hohenzollerns to become the kingdom of Prussia (1701). The district east of the Oder River became Polish in 1945. Capital: Potsdam. Pop: 2 575 000 (2003 est). Area: 29 481 sq km (11 219 sq miles) **2** a city in NE Germany: former capital of the Prussian province of Brandenburg. Pop: 75 485 (2003 est)

brandish ('brændɪʃ) *vb* (*tr*) **1** to wave or flourish (a weapon) in a triumphant, threatening, or ostentatious way ▷ *n* **2** a threatening or defiant flourish [c14: from Old French *brandir*, from *brand* sword, of Germanic origin; compare Old High German *brant* weapon] > 'brandisher *n*

brand leader *n marketing* a product with the highest number of total sales within its category

brandling ('brændlɪŋ) *n* a small red earthworm, *Eisenia foetida* (or *Helodrilus foetidus*), found in manure and used as bait by anglers [c17: from BRAND + -LING¹]

brand name *n* another name for **brand** (sense 2)

brand-new *adj* absolutely new [c16: from BRAND (n) + NEW, likened to newly forged iron]

Brando ('brændəʊ) *n* **Marlon**. 1924–2004, US actor; his films include *On the Waterfront* (1954) and *The Godfather* (1972), for both of which he won Oscars, *Last Tango in Paris* (1972), *Apocalypse Now* (1979), *A Dry White Season* (1989), and *Don Juan de Marco* (1995)

Brandt (brænt) *n* **1 Bill**, full name *William Brandt*. 1905–83, British photographer. His photographic books include *The English at Home* (1936) and *Perspectives of Nudes* (1961) **2 Georg** ('geɪɔːg). 1694–1768, Swedish chemist, who isolated cobalt (1742) and exposed fraudulent alchemists **3** (*German* brant) **Willy** ('vɪli). 1913–92, German statesman; socialist chancellor of West Germany (1969–74); chairman of the Social Democratic party (1964–87). His policy of détente and reconciliation with E Europe brought him international acclaim. Nobel peace prize 1971

brandy ('brændɪ) *n, pl* -dies **1** an alcoholic drink consisting of spirit distilled from grape wine **2** a distillation of wines made from other fruits: *plum brandy* [c17: from earlier *brandewine*, from Dutch *brandewijn* burnt wine, from *bernen* to burn or distil + *wijn* WINE; compare German *Branntwein*]

brandy butter *n* butter and sugar creamed together with brandy and served with Christmas pudding, etc. *Also called:* hard sauce

brandy snap *n* a crisp sweet biscuit, rolled into a cylinder after baking and often filled with whipped cream

Branson ('brænsən) *n* Sir **Richard**. born 1950, British entrepreneur. In 1969 he founded the Virgin record company, adding other interests later, including Virgin Atlantic Airways (1984), Virgin Radio (1993), and the Virgin Rail Group (1996): made the fastest crossing of the Atlantic by boat (1986) and the first of the Pacific by hot-air balloon (1991)

brant (brænt) *n, pl* **brants** or **brant** *US & Canadian* a small goose, *Branta bernicla*, that has a dark grey plumage and short neck and occurs in most northern coastal regions. Also called (in Britain and certain other countries): **brent goose**

Brantford ('bræntfəd) *n* a city in central Canada, in SW Ontario. Pop: 86 417 (2001)

Branting (*Swedish* 'brantiŋ) *n* **Karl Hjalmar** (jalmar). 1860–1925, Swedish politician; prime minister (1920; 1921–23; 1924–25). He founded Sweden's welfare state and shared the Nobel peace prize 1921

bran tub *n* (in Britain) a tub containing bran in which small wrapped gifts are hidden, used at parties, fairs, etc

Braque (*French* brak) *n* **Georges** (ʒɔrʒ). 1882–1963, French painter who developed cubism (1908–14) with Picasso

brash¹ (bræʃ) *adj* **1** tastelessly or offensively loud, showy, or bold **2** hasty; rash **3** impudent [C19: perhaps influenced by RASH¹] > **'brashly** *adv* > **'brashness** *n*

brash² (bræʃ) *n* loose rubbish, such as broken rock, hedge clippings, etc; debris [C18: of unknown origin] > **'brashy** *adj* > **'brashiness** *n*

brasier ('breɪzɪə) *n* a less common spelling of **brazier**¹,²

brasil (brə'zɪl) *n* a variant spelling of **brazil**

Brasília (brə'zɪljə; *Portuguese* brɐ'ziliːɐ) *n* the capital of Brazil (since 1960), on the central plateau: the former capital was Rio de Janeiro. Pop: 3 341 000 (2005 est)

Braşov (*Romanian* bra'ʃov) *n* an industrial city in central Romania: formerly a centre for expatriate Germans; ceded by Hungary to Romania in 1920. Pop: 249 000 (2005 est). Former name (1950–61): **Stalin** German name: **Kronstadt** Hungarian name: **Brassó**

brass (brɑːs) *n* **1** an alloy of copper and zinc containing more than 50 per cent of copper. **Alpha brass** (containing less than 35 per cent of zinc) is used for most engineering materials requiring forging, pressing, etc. **Alpha-beta brass** (35–45 per cent zinc) is used for hot working and extrusion. **Beta brass** (45–50 per cent zinc) is used for castings. Small amounts of other metals, such as lead or tin, may be added. See **bronze** (sense 1) **2** an object, ornament, or utensil made of brass **3 a** the large family of wind instruments including the trumpet, trombone, French horn, etc, each consisting of a brass tube blown directly by means of a cup- or funnel-shaped mouthpiece **b** (*sometimes functioning as plural*) instruments of this family forming a section in an orchestra **4** (*functioning as plural*) *informal* important or high-ranking officials, esp military officers: *the top brass*. See also **brass hat** **5** *Northern English dialect* money **6** *Brit* an engraved brass memorial tablet or plaque, set in the wall or floor of a church **7** *informal* bold self-confidence; cheek; nerve **8** (*modifier*) of, consisting of, or relating to brass or brass instruments: *a brass ornament; a brass band* [Old English bræs; related to Old Frisian bres copper, Middle Low German bras metal]

Brassaï (*French* brasai) *n* real name *Gyula Halész*. 1899–1984, French photographer, artist, and writer, born in Hungary: noted for his photographs of Paris by night

brassard ('bræsɑːd) or **brassart** ('bræsət) *n* an identifying armband or badge [C19: from French, from *bras* arm, from Latin BRACHIUM]

brass band *n* See **band**¹ (sense 2)

brasserie ('bræsərɪ) *n* **1** a bar in which drinks and often food are served **2** a small and usually cheap restaurant [C19: from French, from *brasser* to stir, brew]

brass hat *n* *Brit informal* a top-ranking official, esp a military officer [C20: from the gold leaf decoration on the peaks of caps worn by officers of high rank]

brassica ('bræsɪkə) *n* any plant of the genus *Brassica*, such as cabbage, rape, turnip, and mustard: family *Brassicaceae* (crucifers) [C19: from Latin: cabbage]

brassie or **brassy** ('bræsɪ, 'brɑː-) *n, pl* **brassies** *golf* a former name for a club, a No. 2 wood, originally having a brass-plated sole and with a shallower face than a driver to give more loft

brassiere ('bræsɪə, 'bræz-) *n* a woman's undergarment for covering and supporting the breasts. Often shortened to: **bra** [C20: from C17 French: bodice, from Old French *braciere* a protector for the arm, from *braz* arm]

Brassó ('brɒʃoː) *n* the Hungarian name for **Braşov**

brass rubbing *n* **1** the taking of an impression of an engraved brass tablet or plaque by placing a piece of paper over it and rubbing the paper with graphite, heelball, or chalk **2** an impression made in this way

brass tacks *pl n* *informal* basic realities; hard facts (esp in the phrase **get down to brass tacks**)

brassy ('brɑːsɪ) *adj* **1** brassier, brassiest **1** insolent; brazen **2** flashy; showy **3** (of sound) harsh, strident, or resembling the sound of a brass instrument **4** like brass, esp in colour **5** decorated with or made of brass > **'brassily** *adv* > **'brassiness** *n*

brat (bræt) *n* a child, esp one who is ill-mannered or unruly: used contemptuously or playfully [C16: perhaps special use of earlier *brat* rag, from Old English *bratt* cloak, of Celtic origin; related to Old Irish *bratt* cloth]

Bratislava (ˌbrætɪ'slɑːvə) *n* the capital of Slovakia since 1918, a port on the River Danube; capital of Hungary (1541–1784) and seat of the Hungarian parliament until 1848. Pop: 428 672 (2001). German name: **Pressburg** Hungarian name: **Pozsony**

bratpack ('bræt,pæk) *n* **1** a group of precocious and successful young actors, writers, etc **2** a group of ill-mannered young people > **'brat,packer** *n*

Brattain ('brætən) *n* **Walter Houser**. 1902–87, US physicist, who shared the Nobel prize for physics (1956) with W. B. Shockley and John Bardeen for their invention of the transistor

brattice ('brætɪs) *n* **1** a partition of wood or treated cloth used to control ventilation in a mine **2** *medieval fortifications* a fixed wooden tower or parapet [C13: from Old French *bretesche* wooden tower, from Medieval Latin *breteschia*, probably from Latin *Britō* a Briton]

Braun (*German* braun) *n* **1 Eva** ('eːfa). 1910–45, Adolf Hitler's mistress, whom he married shortly before their suicides in 1945 **2 Karl Ferdinand**. 1850–1918, German physicist, who invented crystal diodes (leading to the development of crystal radio) and the oscilloscope. He shared the Nobel prize for physics (1909) with Marconi **3** See (**Wernher**) **von Braun**

Braunschweig ('braunʃvaik) *n* the German name for: **Brunswick**

bravado (brə'vɑːdəʊ) *n, pl* **-does** or **-dos** vaunted display of courage or self-confidence; swagger [C16: from Spanish *bravada* (modern *bravata*), from Old Italian *bravare* to challenge, provoke, from *bravo* wild, BRAVE]

brave (breɪv) *adj* **1 a** having or displaying courage, resolution, or daring; not cowardly or timid **b** (*as collective noun preceded by the*): *the brave* **2** fine; splendid: *a brave sight; a brave attempt* ▷ *n* **3** a warrior of a Native American tribe ▷ *vb* (tr) **4** to dare or defy: *to brave the odds* **5** to confront with resolution or courage: *to brave the storm* [C15: from French, from Italian *bravo* courageous, wild, perhaps ultimately from Latin *barbarus* BARBAROUS] > **'bravely** *adv* > **'braveness** *n* > **'bravery** *n*

bravo *interj* **1** (brɑː'vəʊ) well done! ▷ *n* **2** (brɑː'vəʊ) *pl* **-vos** a cry of "bravo" **3** ('brɑːvəʊ) *pl* **-voes** or **-vos** a hired killer or assassin [C18: from Italian: splendid!; see BRAVE]

bravura (brə'vjʊərə, -'vʊərə) *n* **1** a display of boldness or daring **2** *music* brilliance of execution [C18: from Italian: spirit, courage, from *bravare* to show off, see BRAVADO]

braw (brɔː, brɑː) *adj* *chiefly Scot* fine or excellent, esp in appearance or dress [C16: Scottish variant of BRAVE]

brawl (brɔːl) *n* **1** a loud disagreement or fight **2** *US slang* an uproarious party ▷ *vb* (intr) **3** to quarrel or fight noisily; squabble **4** (esp of water) to flow noisily [C14: probably related to Dutch *brallen* to boast, behave aggressively] > **'brawler** *n*

brawn (brɔːn) *n* **1** strong well-developed muscles **2** physical strength, esp as opposed to intelligence **3** *Brit* a seasoned jellied loaf made from the head and sometimes the feet of a pig or calf [c14: from Old French *braon* slice of meat, of Germanic origin; compare Old High German *brāto*, Old English *brǣd* flesh]

brawny ('brɔːnɪ) *adj* brawnier, brawniest muscular and strong > '**brawniness** *n*

bray (breɪ) *vb* 1 (*intr*) (of a donkey) to utter its characteristic loud harsh sound; heehaw 2 (*intr*) to make a similar sound, as in laughing 3 (*tr*) to utter with a loud harsh sound ▷ *n* 4 the loud harsh sound uttered by a donkey 5 a similar loud cry or uproar [c13: from Old French *braire*, probably of Celtic origin]

Braz. *abbreviation* Brazil(ian)

braze¹ (breɪz) *vb* (*tr*) 1 to decorate with, make like, or make of brass 2 to make like brass, as in hardness [Old English *brǣsen*, from *brǣs* BRASS]

braze² (breɪz) *vb* (*tr*) to make a joint between (two metal surfaces) by fusing a layer of brass or high-melting solder between them [c16: from Old French: to burn, of Germanic origin; see BRAISE] > '**brazer** *n*

brazen ('breɪzᵊn) *adj* 1 shameless and bold 2 made of or resembling brass 3 having a ringing metallic sound like that of a brass trumpet ▷ *vb* (*tr*) 4 (usually foll by *out* or *through*) to face and overcome boldly or shamelessly [Old English *brǣsen*, from *brǣs* BRASS] > '**brazenly** *adv* > '**brazenness** *n*

brazier¹ *or* **brasier** ('breɪzɪə) *n* a person engaged in brass-working or brass-founding [c14: from Old English *brǣsian* to work in brass + -ER¹] > '**braziery** *n*

brazier² *or* **brasier** ('breɪzɪə) *n* a portable metal receptacle for burning charcoal or coal, used for cooking, heating, etc [c17: from French *brasier*, from *braise* live coals; see BRAISE]

brazil *or* **brasil** (brə'zɪl) *n* 1 Also called: **brazil wood** the red wood obtained from various tropical leguminous trees of the genus *Caesalpinia*, such as *C. echinata* of America: used for cabinetwork 2 the red or purple dye extracted from any of these woods 3 short for **brazil nut** [c14: from Old Spanish *brasil*, from *brasa* glowing coals, of Germanic origin; referring to the redness of the wood; see BRAISE]

Brazil (brə'zɪl) *n* a republic in South America, comprising about half the area and half the population of South America: colonized by the Portuguese from 1500 onwards; became independent in 1822 and a republic in 1889; consists chiefly of the tropical Amazon basin in the north, semiarid scrub in the northeast, and a vast central tableland; an important producer of coffee and minerals, esp iron ore. Official language: Portuguese. Religion: Roman Catholic majority. Currency: real. Capital: Brasília. Pop: 180 655 000 (2004 est). Area: 8 511 957 sq km (3 286 470 sq miles) > Bra'**zilian** *adj, n*

brazil nut *n* 1 a tropical South American tree, *Bertholletia excelsa*, producing large globular capsules, each containing several closely packed triangular nuts: family *Lecythidaceae* 2 the nut of this tree, having an edible oily kernel and a woody shell ▷ Often shortened to: **brazil**

Brazzaville (French brazavil) *n* the capital of Congo-Brazzaville, in the south on the River Congo. Pop: 1 153 000 (2005 est) [c19: named after Pierre de *Brazza* (1852–1905), French explorer]

BRB *abbreviation* text messaging be right back

BRCS *abbreviation* British Red Cross Society

breach (briːtʃ) *n* 1 a crack, break, or rupture 2 a breaking, infringement, or violation of a promise, obligation, etc 3 any severance or separation ▷ *vb* 4 (*tr*) to break through or make an opening, hole, or incursion in 5 (*tr*) to break a promise, law, etc [Old English *brǣc*; influenced by Old French *brèche*, from Old High German *brecha*, from *brechan* to BREAK]

breach of promise *n* law (formerly) failure to carry out one's promise to marry

breach of the peace *n* law an offence against public order causing an unnecessary disturbance of the peace

bread (brɛd) *n* 1 a food made from a dough of flour or meal mixed with water or milk, usually raised with yeast or baking powder and then baked 2 necessary food; nourishment 3 a slang word for **money** 4 cast one's bread upon the waters to do good without expectation of advantage or return 5 to know which side one's bread is buttered to know what to do in order to keep one's advantages 6 take the bread out of someone's mouth to deprive someone of a livelihood ▷ *vb* 7 (*tr*) to cover with breadcrumbs before cooking [Old English *brēad*; related to Old Norse *braud*, Old Frisian *brād*, Old High German *brōt*]

bread and butter *informal* ▷ *n* 1 (*modifier*) a means of support or subsistence; livelihood 2 bread-and-butter **a** providing a basic means of subsistence **b** expressing gratitude, as for hospitality (esp in the phrase **bread-and-butter letter**)

breadbasket ('brɛd,bɑːskɪt) *n* 1 a basket for carrying bread or rolls 2 a slang word for **stomach**

breadboard ('brɛd,bɔːd) *n* 1 a wooden board on which dough is kneaded or bread is sliced 2 an experimental arrangement of electronic circuits giving access to components so that modifications can be carried out easily

breadfruit ('brɛd,fruːt) *n*, *pl* -fruits *or* -fruit 1 a moraceous tree, *Artocarpus communis* (or *A. altilis*), of the Pacific Islands, having large round edible starchy usually seedless fruit 2 the fruit of this tree, which is eaten baked or roasted and has a texture like bread

breadline ('brɛd,laɪn) *n* 1 a queue of people waiting for free food given out by a government agency or a charity organization 2 on the breadline impoverished; living at subsistence level

breadsticks ('brɛd,stɪks) *pl n* bread baked in long thin crisp sticks

breadth (brɛdθ, brɛtθ) *n* 1 the linear extent or measurement of something from side to side; width 2 a piece of fabric having a standard or definite width 3 distance, extent, size, or dimension 4 openness and lack of restriction, esp of viewpoint or interest; liberality [c16: from obsolete *brēde* (from Old English *brǣdu*, from *brād* BROAD) + -TH¹; related to Gothic *braidei*, Old High German *breitī*]

breadthways ('brɛdθ,weɪz) *or esp US* **breadthwise** ('brɛdθ,waɪz, 'brɛtθ-) *adv* from side to side

breadwinner ('brɛd,wɪnə) *n* a person supporting a family with his or her earnings

break (breɪk) *vb* breaks, breaking, broke, broken 1 to separate or become separated into two or more pieces 2 to damage or become damaged so as to be inoperative: *my radio is broken* 3 to crack or become cracked without separating 4 to burst or cut the surface of (skin, etc) 5 to discontinue or become discontinued: *they broke for lunch; to break a journey* 6 to disperse or become dispersed: *the clouds broke* 7 (*tr*) to fail to observe (an agreement, promise, law, etc): *to break one's word* 8 (foll by *with*) to discontinue an association (with) 9 to disclose or be disclosed: *he broke the news gently* 10 (*tr*) to fracture (a bone) in (a limb, etc) 11 (*tr*) to divide (something complete or perfect): *to break a set of books* 12 to bring or come to an end: *the summer weather broke at last* 13 (*tr*) to bring to an end by or as if by force: *to break a strike* 14 (when *intr*, often foll by *out*) to escape (from): *he broke jail; he broke out of jail* 15 to weaken or overwhelm or be weakened or overwhelmed, as in spirit 16 (*tr*) to cut through or penetrate: *a cry broke the silence* 17 (*tr*) to improve on or surpass: *to break a record* 18 (*tr*; often foll by *in*) to accustom (a horse) to the bridle and saddle, to being ridden, etc 19 (*tr*; often foll by *of*) to cause (a person) to give up (a habit): *this cure will break you of smoking* 20 (*tr*) to weaken the impact or force of: *this net will break his fall* 21 (*tr*) to decipher: *to break a code* 22 (*tr*) to lose the order of: *to break ranks* 23 (*tr*) to reduce to poverty or the state of bankruptcy 24 (when *intr*, foll by *into*) to obtain, give, or receive smaller units in exchange for; change: *to break a pound note* 25 (*tr*) *chiefly military* to demote to a lower rank 26 (*intr*; often foll by *from* or *out of*) to proceed suddenly 27 (*intr*) to come into being: *light broke over the mountains* 28 (*intr*; foll by *into* or *out into*) **a** to burst into song, laughter, etc **b** to change to a faster pace 29 (*tr*) to open with explosives: *to break a safe* 30 (*intr*) (of waves) **a** (often foll by *against*) to strike violently **b** to collapse into foam or surf 31 (*intr*) (of

b

prices, esp stock exchange quotations) to fall sharply **32** (*intr*) to make a sudden effort, as in running, horse racing, etc **33** (*intr*) *cricket* (of a ball) to change direction on bouncing **34** (*intr*) *billiards, snooker* to scatter the balls at the start of a game **35** (*intr*) *boxing, wrestling* (of two fighters) to separate from a clinch **36** (*intr*) *music* (of the male voice) to undergo a change in register, quality, and range at puberty **37** (*tr*) to open the breech of (certain firearms) by snapping the barrel away from the butt on its hinge **38** (*tr*) to interrupt the flow of current in (an electrical circuit) **39** (*intr*) *informal, chiefly US* to become successful; make a breakthrough **40 break camp** to pack up equipment and leave a camp **41 break the bank** to ruin financially or deplete the resources of a bank (as in gambling) **42 break the mould** to make a change that breaks an established habit, pattern, etc **43 break service** *tennis* to win a game in which an opponent is serving ▷ *n* **44** the act or result of breaking; fracture **45** a crack formed as the result of breaking **46** a brief respite or interval between two actions **47** a sudden rush, esp to escape: *to make a break for freedom* **48** a breach in a relationship **49** any sudden interruption in a continuous action **50** *Brit* a short period between classes at school **51** *informal* a fortunate opportunity, esp to prove oneself **52** *informal* a piece of (good or bad) luck **53** (esp in a stock exchange) a sudden and substantial decline in prices **54** *billiards, snooker* a series of successful shots during one turn **55** *billiards, snooker* the opening shot with the cue ball that scatters the placed balls **56** Also called: **service break, break of serve** *tennis* the act or instance of breaking an opponent's service **57** a *jazz* a short usually improvised solo passage b an instrumental passage in a pop song **58** a discontinuity in an electrical circuit **59** access to a radio channel by a citizens' band operator ▷ *interj* **60** *boxing, wrestling* a command by a referee for two opponents to separate ▷ See also **breakaway, break down** [Old English *brecan*; related to Old Frisian *breka*, Gothic *brikan*, Old High German *brehhan*, Latin *frangere* Sanskrit *bhráj* bursting forth]

breakable ('breɪkəb°l) *adj* **1** capable of being broken ▷ *n* **2** (*usually plural*) a fragile easily broken article

breakage ('breɪkɪdʒ) *n* **1** the act or result of breaking **2** the quantity or amount broken **3** compensation or allowance for goods damaged while in use, transit, etc

breakaway ('breɪkəˌweɪ) *n* **1** a a loss or withdrawal of a group of members from an association, club, etc b (*as modifier*): *a breakaway faction* **2** *Austral* a stampede of cattle, esp at the smell of water ▷ *vb* **break away** (*intr, adverb*) **3** (often foll by *from*) to leave hastily or escape **4** to withdraw or secede

break dance *n* **1** an acrobatic dance style originating in the 1980s ▷ *vb* **break-dance 2** (*intr*) to perform a break dance > **break dancer** *n* > **break dancing** *n*

break down *vb* (*adverb*) **1** (*intr*) to cease to function; become ineffective **2** to yield or cause to yield, esp to strong emotion or tears **3** (*tr*) to crush or destroy **4** (*intr*) to have a nervous breakdown **5** to analyse or be subjected to analysis **6** to separate or cause to separate into simpler chemical elements; decompose **7 break it down** *Austral & NZ informal* a stop it b don't expect me to believe that; come off it ▷ *n* **breakdown 8** an act or instance of breaking down; collapse **9** short for **nervous breakdown 10** an analysis or classification of something into its component parts: *he prepared a breakdown of the report* **11** a lively American country dance

breaker ('breɪkə) *n* **1** a person or thing that breaks something, such as a person or firm that breaks up old cars, etc **2** a large wave with a white crest on the open sea or one that breaks into foam on the shore

break even *vb* **1** (*intr, adverb*) to attain a level of activity, as in commerce, or a point of operation, as in gambling, at which there is neither profit nor loss ▷ *n* **breakeven 2** *accounting* the level of commercial activity at which the total cost and total revenue of a business enterprise are equal

breakfast ('brɛkfəst) *n* **1** the first meal of the day **2** the food at this meal ▷ *vb* **3** to eat or supply with breakfast [C15: from BREAK + FAST²] > **'breakfaster** *n*

breakfast club *n* a service that provides a breakfast for children who arrive early at school

break in *vb* (*adverb*) **1** (sometimes foll by *on*) to interrupt **2** (*intr*) to enter a house, etc, illegally, esp by force **3** (*tr*) to accustom (a person or animal) to normal duties or practice **4** (*tr*) to use or wear (shoes, new equipment, etc) until comfortable or running smoothly **5** (*tr*) *Austral & NZ* to bring (new land) under cultivation ▷ *n* **break-in 6** the illegal entering of a building, esp by thieves

breaking and entering *n* (formerly) the gaining of unauthorized access to a building with intent to commit a crime or, having committed the crime, the breaking out of the building

breaking point *n* the point at which something or someone gives way under strain

breakneck ('breɪkˌnɛk) *adj* (*prenominal*) (of speed, pace, etc) excessive and dangerous

break off *vb* **1** to sever or detach or be severed or detached **2** (*adverb*) to end (a relationship, association, etc) or (of a relationship, etc) to be ended **3** (*intr, adverb*) to stop abruptly; halt: *he broke off in the middle of his speech*

break out *vb* **1** (*intr, adverb*) to begin or arise suddenly **2** (*intr, adverb*) to make an escape, esp from prison or confinement **3** (*intr, adverb*, foll by *in*) (of the skin) to erupt (in a rash, pimples, etc) ▷ *n* **break-out 4** an escape, esp from prison or confinement

break-out group *n* a group of people who detach themselves from a larger group or meeting in order to hold separate discussions

break through *vb* **1** (*intr*) to penetrate **2** (*intr, adverb*) to achieve success, make a discovery, etc, esp after lengthy efforts ▷ *n* **breakthrough 3** a significant development or discovery, esp in science **4** the penetration of an enemy's defensive position or line in depth and strength

break up *vb* (*adverb*) **1** to separate or cause to separate **2** to put an end to (a relationship) or (of a relationship) to come to an end **3** to dissolve or cause to dissolve; disrupt or be disrupted: *the meeting broke up at noon* **4** (*intr*) *Brit* (of a school) to close for the holidays **5** (*intr*) (of a person making a telephone call) to be inaudible at times, owing to variations in the signal: *you're breaking up* **6** *informal* to lose or cause to lose control of the emotions **7** *slang* to be or cause to be overcome with laughter ▷ *n* **break-up 8** a separation or disintegration **9** *Canad* a in the Canadian north, the breaking up of the ice on a body of water that marks the beginning of spring b this season

break-up value *n* *commerce* **1** the value of an organization assuming that it will not continue to trade **2** the value of a share in a company based only on the value of its assets

breakwater ('breɪkˌwɔːtə) *n* **1** Also called: **mole** a massive wall built out into the sea to protect a shore or harbour from the force of waves **2** another name for **groyne**

bream¹ (briːm; *Austral* brɪm) *or Austral* **brim** (brɪm) *n, pl* **bream** *or* **brim 1** any of several Eurasian freshwater cyprinid fishes of the genus *Abramis*, esp *A. brama*, having a deep compressed body covered with silvery scales **2** short for **sea bream 3** *Austral* any of various marine fishes [C14: from Old French *bresme*, of Germanic origin; compare Old High German *brahsema*; perhaps related to *brehan* to glitter]

bream² (briːm) *vb* *nautical* (formerly) to clean debris from (the bottom of a vessel) by heating to soften the pitch [C15: probably from Middle Dutch *bremme* broom; from using burning broom as a source of heat]

Bream (briːm) *n* **Julian** (*Alexander*). born 1933, English guitarist and lutenist

breast (brɛst) *n* **1** the front part of the body from the neck to the abdomen; chest **2** either of the two soft fleshy milk-secreting glands on the chest in sexually mature human females **3** a similar organ in certain other mammals **4** anything that resembles a breast in shape or position: *the breast of the hill* **5** a source of nourishment **6** the source of human emotions **7** the part of a garment that covers the breast **8** a projection from the side of a wall, esp that formed by a chimney

b

9 beat one's breast to display guilt and remorse publicly or ostentatiously **10** make a clean breast of to make a confession of ▷ vb (tr) **11** to confront boldly; face: *breast the storm* **12** to oppose with the breast or meet at breast level: *breasting the waves* **13** to reach the summit of: *breasting the mountain top* [Old English brēost; related to Old Norse brjōst, Old High German brust, Dutch borst, Swedish bräss, Old Irish brū belly, body]

breastbone ('brɛst,bəʊn) n the nontechnical name for **sternum**

breast-feed vb -feeds, -feeding, -fed to feed (a baby) with milk from the breast; suckle

breastpin ('brɛst,pɪn) n a brooch worn on the breast, esp to close a garment

breastplate ('brɛst,pleɪt) n a piece of armour covering the chest

breaststroke ('brɛst,strəʊk) n a swimming stroke in which the arms are extended in front of the head and swept back on either side while the legs are drawn up beneath the body and thrust back together

breastwork ('brɛst,wɜːk) n fortifications a temporary defensive work, usually breast-high

breath (brɛθ) n **1** the intake and expulsion of air during respiration **2** the air inhaled or exhaled during respiration **3** a single respiration or inhalation of air, etc **4** the vapour, heat, or odour of exhaled air **5** a slight gust of air **6** a short pause or rest **7** a brief time **8** a suggestion or slight evidence; suspicion: *a breath of scandal* **9** a whisper or soft sound **10** life, energy, or vitality: *the breath of new industry* **11** phonetics the passage of air through the completely open glottis without vibration of the vocal cords, as in exhaling or pronouncing fricatives such as (f) or (h) or stops such as (p) or (k) **12** catch one's breath to rest until breathing is normal, esp after exertion **13** in the same breath done or said at the same time **14** out of breath gasping for air after exertion **15** save one's breath to refrain from useless talk **16** take one's breath away to overwhelm with surprise, etc **17** under one's breath *or* below one's breath in a quiet voice or whisper [Old English brǣth; related to brǣdan to burn, Old High German brādam heat, breath]

breathable ('briːðəbəl) adj **1** (of air) fit to be breathed **2** (of a material) allowing air to pass through so that perspiration can evaporate

Breathalyser *or* **Breathalyzer** ('brɛθə,laɪzə) n trademark a device for estimating the amount of alcohol in the breath: used in testing people suspected of driving under the influence of alcohol [C20: BREATH + (AN)ALYSER]

breathe (briːð) vb **1** to take in oxygen from (the surrounding medium, esp air) and give out carbon dioxide; respire **2** (intr) to exist; be alive **3** (intr) to rest to regain breath, composure, etc **4** (intr) (esp of air) to blow lightly **5** (intr) machinery to take in air, esp for combustion **6** (tr) phonetics to articulate (a speech sound) without vibration of the vocal cords **7** to exhale or emit: *the dragon breathed fire* **8** (tr) to impart; instil: *to breathe confidence into the actors* **9** (tr) to speak softly; whisper **10** (tr) to permit to rest: *to breathe a horse* **11** (intr) (of a material) to allow air to pass through so that perspiration can evaporate **12** breathe again, breathe freely *or* breathe easily to feel relief **13** breathe one's last to die or be finished or defeated [C13: from BREATH]

breather ('briːðə) n **1** informal a short pause for rest **2** a person who breathes in a specified way: *a deep breather* **3** a vent in a container to equalize internal and external pressure, such as the pipe in the crankcase of an internal-combustion engine

breathing ('briːðɪŋ) n **1** the passage of air into and out of the lungs to supply the body with oxygen **2** a single breath: *a breathing between words* **3** phonetics **a** expulsion of breath (**rough breathing**) or absence of such expulsion (**smooth breathing**) preceding the pronunciation of an initial vowel or rho in ancient Greek **b** either of two symbols indicating this

breathless ('brɛθlɪs) adj **1** out of breath; gasping, etc **2** holding one's breath or having it taken away by excitement, etc **3** (esp of the atmosphere) motionless and stifling **4** rare lifeless; dead > 'breathlessly adv > 'breathlessness n

breathtaking ('brɛθ,teɪkɪŋ) adj causing awe or excitement > 'breath,takingly adv

breath test n Brit a chemical test of a driver's breath to determine the amount of alcohol he has consumed

breathy ('brɛθɪ) adj breathier, breathiest **1** (of the speaking voice) accompanied by an audible emission of breath **2** (of the singing voice) lacking resonance > 'breathily adv > 'breathiness n

breccia ('brɛtʃɪə) n a rock consisting of angular fragments embedded in a finer matrix, formed by erosion, impact, volcanic activity, etc [C18: from Italian, from Old High German brecha a fragment; see BREACH] > 'brecci,ated adj

Brecht (German brɛçt) n **Bertolt** ('bɛrtɔlt). 1898–1956, German dramatist, theatrical producer, and poet, who developed a new style of "epic" theatre and a new theory of theatrical alienation, notable also for his wit and compassion. His early works include *The Threepenny Opera* (1928) and *Rise and Fall of the City of Mahagonny* (1930) (both with music by Kurt Weill). His later plays are concerned with moral and political dilemmas and include *Mother Courage and her Children* (1941), *The Good Woman of Setzuan* (1943), and *The Caucasian Chalk Circle* (1955) > 'Brechtian adj, n

Brecon ('brɛkən) *or* **Brecknock** ('brɛknɒk) n **1** a town in SE Wales, in Powys: textile and leather industries. Pop: 7901 (2001) **2** short for **Breconshire**

Breconshire ('brɛkənʃɪə, -ʃə) *or* **Brecknockshire** ('brɛknɒkʃɪə, -ʃə) n (until 1974) a county of SE Wales, now mainly in Powys: over half its area forms the **Brecon Beacons National Park**

bred (brɛd) vb the past tense and past participle of **breed** [sense 2: diminutive form of *inbred*]

Breda ('briːdə; *Dutch* breːˈdaː) n a city in the S Netherlands, in North Brabant province: residence of Charles II of England during his exile. Pop: 164 000 (2003 est)

bredie ('briːdɪ) n South African a meat and vegetable stew [C19: from Portuguese *bredo* ragout]

breech n (briːtʃ) **1** the lower dorsal part of the human trunk; buttocks; rump **2** the lower part or bottom of something **3** the part of a firearm behind the barrel or bore ▷ vb (briːtʃ, brɪtʃ) (tr) **4** to fit (a gun) with a breech **5** archaic to clothe in breeches or any other clothing [Old English brēc, plural of brōc leg covering; related to Old Norse brōk, Old High German bruoh]

● USAGE *Breech* is sometimes wrongly used as a verb
● where *breach* is meant: *the barrier/agreement was breached*
● (not *breeched*)

breechblock ('briːtʃ,blɒk) n a metal block in breech-loading firearms that is withdrawn to insert the cartridge and replaced to close the breech before firing

breech delivery n birth of a baby with the feet or buttocks appearing first

breeches ('brɪtʃɪz, 'briː-) pl n **1** trousers extending to the knee or just below, worn for riding, mountaineering, etc **2** informal or dialect any trousers

breeches buoy n a ring-shaped life buoy with a support in the form of a pair of short breeches, in which a person is suspended for safe transfer from a ship

breeching ('brɪtʃɪŋ, 'briː-) n the strap of a harness that passes behind a horse's haunches

breech-loader ('briːtʃ,ləʊdə) n a firearm that is loaded at the breech

breed (briːd) vb breeds, breeding, bred **1** to bear (offspring) **2** (tr) to bring up; raise **3** to produce or cause to produce by mating; propagate **4** to produce and maintain new or improved strains of (domestic animals and plants) **5** to produce or be produced; generate: *to breed trouble; violence breeds in densely populated areas* ▷ n **6** a group of organisms within a species, esp a group of domestic animals, originated and maintained by man and having a clearly defined set of characteristics **7** a lineage or race **8** a kind, sort, or group [Old English brēdan, of Germanic origin; related to BROOD]

breeder ('briːdə) n **1** a person who breeds plants or animals **2** something that reproduces, esp to excess

b

3 an animal kept for breeding purposes **4** a source or cause: *a breeder of discontent* **5** short for **breeder reactor**
breeder reactor *n* a type of nuclear reactor that produces more fissionable material than it consumes
breeding ('bri:dɪŋ) *n* **1** the process of bearing offspring; reproduction **2** the process of producing plants or animals by sexual reproduction **3** the result of good training, esp the knowledge of correct social behaviour; refinement
Breed's Hill (bri:dz) *n* a hill in E Massachusetts, adjoining Bunker Hill: the true site of the Battle of Bunker Hill (1775)
breeze¹ (bri:z) *n* **1** a gentle or light wind **2** *meteorol* a wind of force two to six inclusive on the Beaufort scale **3** *informal* an easy task or state of ease **4** *informal, chiefly Brit* a disturbance, esp a lively quarrel ▷ *vb* (*intr*) **5** to move quickly or casually: *he breezed into the room* [c16: probably from Old Spanish *briza* northeast wind]
breeze² (bri:z) *n* ashes of coal, coke, or charcoal used to make breeze blocks [c18: from French *braise* live coals; see BRAISE]
breeze block *n* a light building brick made from the ashes of coal, coke, etc, bonded together by cement and used esp for walls that bear relatively small loads
breezeway ('bri:z,weɪ) *n* a roofed passageway connecting two buildings, sometimes with the sides enclosed
breezy ('bri:zɪ) *adj* breezier, breeziest **1** fresh; windy: *a breezy afternoon* **2** casual or carefree; lively; light-hearted: *her breezy nature* > 'breezily *adv* > 'breeziness *n*
Bregenz (*German* bre'ɡɛnts) *n* a resort in W Austria, the capital of Vorarlberg province. Pop: 26 752 (2001)
Brel (brɛl) *n* **Jacques** (ʒak). 1929–78, Belgian-born composer and singer, based in Paris. His songs include "Ne me quitte pas" ("If You Go Away")
Bremen ('breɪmən) *n* **1** a state of NW Germany, centred on the city of Bremen and its outport Bremerhaven. Pop: 663 000 (2003 est). Area: 404 sq km (156 sq miles) **2** an industrial city and port in NW Germany, on the Weser estuary. Pop: 544 853 (2003 est)
Bremerhaven (*German* breˈmərˈhaːfən) *n* a port in NW Germany: an outport for Bremen. Pop: 118 276 (2003 est). Former name (until 1947): Wesermünde
bremsstrahlung ('brɛmzˌʃtraːlən) *n* the radiation produced when an electrically charged particle, especially an electron, is slowed down by the electric field of an atomic nucleus or an atomic ion [c20: German: braking radiation]
Brendel (*German* 'brɛndəl) *n* **Alfred**. born 1931, Austrian pianist and poet
Bren gun (brɛn) *n* an air-cooled gas-operated light machine gun taking .303 calibre ammunition: used by British and Commonwealth forces in World War II [c20: after Br(no), now in the Czech Republic, where it was first made and En(field), England, where manufacture was continued]
Brennan ('brɛnən) *n* **Christopher John**. 1870–1932, Australian poet and classical scholar, disciple of Mallarmé and exponent of French symbolism in Australian verse
Brenner Pass ('brɛnə) *n* a pass over the E Alps, between Austria and Italy. Highest point: 1372 m (4501 ft)
Brent (brɛnt) *n* a borough of NW Greater London. Pop: 267 800 (2003 est). Area: 44 sq km (17 sq miles)
Brentano (*German* brɛn'taːno) *n* **Clemens** (**Maria**) ('kleːmənz). 1778–1842, German romantic poet and compiler of fairy stories and folk songs esp (with Achim von Arnim) the collection *Des Knaben Wunderhorn* (1805–08)
brent goose (brɛnt) *n* a small goose, *Branta bernicla*, that has a dark grey plumage and short neck and occurs in most northern coastal regions. Also called: brent, (*esp US and Canadian*) brant [c16: perhaps of Scandinavian origin; compare Old Norse *brandgās* sheldrake]
Brenton ('brɛntᵊn) *n* **Howard** born 1942, British dramatist, author of such controversial plays as *The Churchill Play* (1974), *The Romans in Britain* (1980), (with David Hare) *Pravda* (1985), and several topical satires with Tariq Ali

Brentwood ('brɛnt,wʊd) *n* a residential town in SE England, in SW Essex near London. Pop: 47 593 (2001)
Brescia (*Italian* 'brɛʃʃa) *n* a city in N Italy, in Lombardy: at its height in the 16th century. Pop: 187 567 (2001)
Breslau ('brɛzlaʊ) *n* the German name for **Wrocław**
Bresson (*French* brɛsɔ̃) *n* **Robert** (rɔbɛr). 1901–99, French film director: his films include *Le Journal d'un curé de campagne* (1950), *Une Femme douce* (1969), and *L'Argent* (1983)
Brest (brɛst) *n* **1** a port in NW France, in Brittany: chief naval station of the country, planned by Richelieu in 1631 and fortified by Vauban. Pop: 149 634 (1999) **2** a city in SW Belarus: Polish until 1795 and from 1921 to 1945. Pop: 299 000 (2005 est). Polish name: Brześć nad Bugiem
Bretagne (brətaɲ) *n* the French name for **Brittany**
brethren ('brɛðrɪn) *pl n* **1** *archaic* a plural of **brother** **2** fellow members of a religion, sect, society, etc
Breton¹ ('brɛtᵊn; *French* brətɔ̃) *adj* **1** of, relating to, or characteristic of Brittany, its people, or their language ▷ *n* **2** a native or inhabitant of Brittany, esp one who speaks the Breton language **3** the indigenous language of Brittany, belonging to the Brythonic subgroup of the Celtic family of languages
Breton² (*French* brətɔ̃) *n* **André** (ɑ̃dre). 1896–1966, French poet and art critic: founder and chief theorist of surrealism, publishing the first surrealist manifesto in 1924
Breuer ('brɔɪə) *n* **1 Josef** ('joːzɛf). 1842–1925, Austrian physician: treated the mentally ill by hypnosis **2 Marcel Lajos** (mɑːˈsɛl 'lɔjoʃ). 1902–81, US architect and furniture designer, born in Hungary. He developed bent plywood and tubular metal furniture and designed the UNESCO building in Paris (1953–58)
Breughel ('brɔɪɡᵊl) *n* a variant spelling of **Brueghel**
breve (bri:v) *n* **1** an accent, (˘), placed over a vowel to indicate that it is of short duration or is pronounced in a specified way **2** *music* a note, now rarely used, equivalent in time value to two semibreves **3** *RC Church* a less common word for **brief** (sense 7) [c13: from Medieval Latin *breve*, from Latin *brevis* short; see BRIEF]
brevet ('brɛvɪt) *n* **1** a document entitling a commissioned officer to hold temporarily a higher military rank without the appropriate pay and allowances ▷ *vb* -vets, -vetting, -vetted *or* -vets, -veting, -veted **2** (*tr*) to promote by brevet [c14: from Old French *brievet* a little letter, from *brief* letter; see BRIEF] > 'brevetcy *n*
breviary ('bri:vjərɪ) *n, pl* -ries *RC Church* a book of psalms, hymns, prayers, etc, to be recited daily by clerics in major orders and certain members of religious orders as part of the divine office [c16: from Latin *breviārium* an abridged version, from *breviāre* to shorten, from *brevis* short]
brevity ('brɛvɪtɪ) *n, pl* -ties **1** conciseness of expression; lack of verbosity **2** a short duration; brief time [c16: from Latin *brevitās* shortness, from *brevis* BRIEF]
brew (bru:) *vb* **1** to make (beer, ale, etc) from malt and other ingredients by steeping, boiling, and fermentation **2** to prepare (a drink, such as tea) by boiling or infusing **3** (*tr*) to devise or plan: *to brew a plot* **4** (*intr*) to be in the process of being brewed **5** (*intr*) to be impending or forming: *there's a storm brewing* ▷ *n* **6** a beverage produced by brewing, esp tea or beer **7** an instance or time of brewing: *last year's brew* **8** a mixture [Old English *brēowan*; related to Old Norse *brugga*, Old Saxon *breuwan*, Old High German *briuwan*] > 'brewer *n*
brewery ('brʊərɪ) *n, pl* -eries a place where beer, ale, etc, is brewed
brewing ('bru:ɪŋ) *n* a quantity of a beverage brewed at one time
brewis ('bru:ɪs) *or* **brevis** ('brɛvɪs) *n* dialect, chiefly Northern English, Canadian & US **1** bread soaked in broth, gravy, etc **2** thickened broth **3** (bru:z) Canadian a Newfoundland stew of cod or pork, hardtack, and potatoes [c16: from Old French *broez*, from *broet*, diminutive of *breu* BROTH]
Brewster ('bru:stə) *n* **Sir David**. 1781–1868, Scottish physicist, noted for his studies of the polarization of light
Brezhnev ('brɛʒnɛf; *Russian* 'brjɛʒnɪf) *n* **Leonid Ilyich** (lɪɑ'nit 'ilitʃ). 1906–82, Soviet statesman; president of the

Soviet Union (1977–82); general secretary of the Soviet Communist Party (1964–82)

Brian ('braɪən) *n* **Havergal** ('hævəgəl). 1876–1972, English composer, who wrote 32 symphonies, including the large-scale *Gothic Symphony* (1919–27)

Brian Boru (bə'ruː) *n* ?941–1014, king of Ireland (1002–14): killed during the defeat of the Danes at the battle of Clontarf

Briand (*French* briɑ̃) *n* **Aristide** (aristid). 1862–1932, French socialist statesman: prime minister of France 11 times. He was responsible for the separation of Church and State (1905) and he advocated a United States of Europe. Nobel peace prize 1926

briar¹ *or* **brier** ('braɪə) *n* **1** Also called: **tree heath** an ericaceous shrub, *Erica arborea*, of S Europe, having a hard woody root (briarroot) **2** a tobacco pipe made from the root of this plant [C19: from French *bruyère* heath, from Late Latin *brūcus*, of Gaulish origin] ▷ **'briary** *or* **'briery** *adj*

briar² ('braɪə) *n* a variant spelling of **brier¹**

Briareus (braɪ'ɛərɪəs) *n Greek myth* a giant with a hundred arms and fifty heads who aided Zeus and the Olympians against the Titans ▷ **Bri'arean** *adj*

briarroot *or* **brierroot** ('braɪə,ruːt) *n* the hard woody root of the briar, used for making tobacco pipes. Also called: **briarwood, brierwood**

bribe (braɪb) *vb* **1** to promise, offer, or give something, usually money, to (a person) to procure services or gain influence, esp illegally ▷ *n* **2** a reward, such as money or favour, given or offered for this purpose **3** any persuasion or lure [C14: from Old French *briber* to beg, of obscure origin] ▷ **'bribery** *n*

bric-a-brac ('brɪkə,bræk) *n* miscellaneous small objects, esp furniture and curios, kept because they are ornamental or rare [C19: from French; phrase based on *bric* piece]

Brice (braɪs) *n* **Fanny**, real name *Fanny Borach*. 1891–1951, US actress and singer. The film *Funny Girl* was based on her life

brick (brɪk) *n* **1 a** a rectangular block of clay mixed with sand and fired in a kiln or baked by the sun, used in building construction **b** (*as modifier*): *a brick house* **2** the material used to make such blocks **3** any rectangular block: *a brick of ice* **4** bricks collectively **5** *informal* a reliable, trustworthy, or helpful person **6** *Brit* a child's building block **7 drop a brick** *Brit informal* to make a tactless or indiscreet remark **8 like a ton of bricks** *informal* (used esp of the manner of punishing or reprimanding someone) with great force; severely ▷ *vb* (*tr*) **9** (usually foll by *in*, *up* or *over*) to construct, line, pave, fill, or wall up with bricks: *to brick up a window; brick over a patio* [C15: from Old French *brique*, from Middle Dutch *bricke*; related to Middle Low German *brike*, Old English *brecan* to BREAK]

brickbat ('brɪk,bæt) *n* **1** a piece of brick or similar material, esp one used as a weapon **2** blunt criticism

brickie *or* **bricky** ('brɪkɪ) *n Brit informal* a bricklayer

bricklayer ('brɪk,leɪə) *n* a person trained or skilled in laying bricks

brick red *n, adj* a reddish-brown colour

bricks and clicks *n* **1** a combination of traditional business carried out on physical premises and internet trading ▷ *modifier* bricks-and-clicks **2** combining traditional business carried out on physical premises and internet trading: *bricks-and-clicks companies* [C20: from BRICKS AND MORTAR and *click*, meaning an act of pressing and releasing a computer mouse button]

bricks and mortar *n* **1 a** a building or buildings: *he invested in bricks and mortar rather than stocks and shares* **b** (*as modifier*): *a bricks-and-mortar fortune* **2 a** a physical business premises rather than an internet presence **b** (*as modifier*): *bricks-and-mortar firms*

brickwork ('brɪk,wɜːk) *n* **1** a structure, such as a wall, built of bricks **2** construction using bricks

brickyard ('brɪk,jɑːd) *n* a place in which bricks are made, stored, or sold

bricolage ('brɪkə,lɑːʒ; *French* brikɔlaʒ) *n architect* the jumbled effect produced by the close proximity of buildings from different periods and in different architectural styles [F: odd jobs, do-it-yourself]

bridal ('braɪd³l) *adj* of or relating to a bride or a wedding; nuptial [Old English *brȳdealu*, literally: "bride ale", that is, wedding feast]

bride (braɪd) *n* a woman who has just been or is about to be married [Old English *brȳd*; related to Old Norse *brūthr*, Gothic *brūths* daughter-in-law, Old High German *brūt*]

Bride (braɪd) *n* **Saint Bride** See **Bridget** (sense 1)

bridegroom ('braɪd,gruːm, -,grʊm) *n* a man who has just been or is about to be married [C14: changed (through influence of GROOM) from Old English *brȳdguma*, from *brȳd* BRIDE¹ + *guma* man; related to Old Norse *brūthgumi*, Old High German *brūtigomo*]

bride price *or* **bride wealth** *n* (in some societies) money, property, or services given by a bridegroom to the kinsmen of his bride in order to establish his rights over the woman

bridesmaid ('braɪdz,meɪd) *n* a girl or young unmarried woman who attends a bride at her wedding

bridge¹ (brɪdʒ) *n* **1** a structure that spans and provides a passage over a road, railway, river, or some other obstacle **2** something that resembles this in shape or function **3** the hard ridge at the upper part of the nose, formed by the underlying nasal bones **4** the part of a pair of glasses that rests on the nose **5** Also called: **bridgework** a dental plate containing one or more artificial teeth that is secured to the surrounding natural teeth **6** a platform athwartships and above the rail, from which a ship is piloted and navigated **7** a piece of wood, usually fixed, supporting the strings of a violin, guitar, etc, and transmitting their vibrations to the sounding board **8** Also called: **bridge passage** a passage in a musical, literary, or dramatic work linking two or more important sections **9** Also called: **bridge circuit** *electronics* any of several networks, such as a Wheatstone bridge, consisting of two branches across which a measuring device is connected. The resistance, capacitance, etc, of one component can be determined from the known values of the others when the voltage in each branch is balanced **10** *computing* a device that connects networks and sends packets between them **11** *billiards, snooker* a support for a cue made by placing the fingers on the table and raising the thumb **12** *cross a bridge when one comes to it* to deal with a problem only when it arises; not to anticipate difficulties ▷ *vb* (*tr*) **13** to build or provide a bridge over something; span: *to bridge a river* **14** to connect or reduce the distance between: *let us bridge our differences* [Old English *brycg*; related to Old Norse *bryggja* gangway, Old Frisian *bregge*, Old High German *brucka*, Danish, Swedish *bro*] ▷ **'bridgeable** *adj*

bridge² (brɪdʒ) *n* a card game for four players, based on whist, in which one hand (the dummy) is exposed and the trump suit decided by bidding between the players. See also **contract bridge, auction bridge** [C19: of uncertain origin, but compare Turkish *bir-üç* (unattested phrase) one-three (said perhaps to refer to the one exposed hand and the three players' hands)]

Bridge (brɪdʒ) *n* **Frank.** 1879–1941, English composer, esp of chamber music. He taught Benjamin Britten

bridgehead ('brɪdʒ,hɛd) *n military* **1** an area of ground secured or to be taken on the enemy's side of an obstacle, esp a defended river **2** a fortified or defensive position at the end of a bridge nearest to the enemy **3** an advantageous position gained for future expansion

Bridgend (,brɪdʒ'ɛnd) *n* a county borough in S Wales, created in 1996 from S Mid Glamorgan. Administrative centre: Bridgend. Pop: 129 900 (2003 est). Area: 264 sq km (102 sq miles)

Bridge of Sighs *n* a covered 16th-century bridge in Venice, between the Doges' Palace and the prisons, through which prisoners were formerly led to trial or execution

Bridgeport ('brɪdʒ,pɔːt) *n* a port in SW Connecticut, on Long Island Sound. Pop: 139 664 (2003 est)

bridge roll *n Brit* a soft bread roll in a long thin shape [C20: from BRIDGE² or perhaps BRIDGE¹]

Bridges ('brɪdʒɪz) *n* **Robert** (**Seymour**). 1844–1930, English poet: poet laureate (1913–30)

Bridget ('brɪdʒɪt) Saint Bridget *n* 1 Also called: Bride, Brigid 453–523 AD, Irish abbess; a patron saint of Ireland. Feast day: Feb 1 2 Also called: Birgitta ?1303-73, Swedish nun and visionary; patron saint of Sweden. Feast day: July 23

Bridgetown ('brɪdʒ,taʊn) *n* the capital of Barbados, a port on the SW coast. Pop: 144 000 (2005 est)

bridgework ('brɪdʒ,wɜːk) *n* a partial denture attached to the surrounding teeth

bridging loan *n* a loan made to cover the period between two transactions, such as the buying of another house before the sale of the first is completed

Bridgman ('brɪdʒmən) *n* **Percy Williams**. 1882–1961, US physicist: Nobel prize for physics (1946) for his work on high-pressure physics and thermodynamics

Bridgwater ('brɪdʒ,wɔːtə) *n* a town in SW England, in central Somerset. Pop: 36 563 (2001)

Bridie ('braɪdɪ) *n* **James**, real name *Osborne Henry Mavor*. 1888–1951, Scottish physician and dramatist, who founded the Glasgow Citizens' Theatre. His plays include *The Anatomist* (1930)

bridle ('braɪd³l) *n* 1 a headgear for a horse, etc, consisting of a series of buckled straps and a metal mouthpiece (bit) by which the animal is controlled through the reins 2 something that curbs or restrains; check 3 a Y-shaped cable, rope, or chain, used for holding, towing, etc ▷ *vb* 4 (*tr*) to put a bridle on (a horse, mule, etc) 5 (*tr*) to restrain; curb: *he bridled his rage* 6 (*intr*; often foll by *at*) to show anger, scorn, or indignation [Old English *brigdels*; related to *bregdan* to BRAID[1], Old High German *brittil*, Middle Low German *breidel*]

bridle path *or* **bridleway** ('braɪd³l,weɪ) *n* a path suitable for riding or leading horses

Brie (briː) *n* 1 a soft creamy white cheese, similar to Camembert but milder 2 a mainly agricultural area in N France, between the Rivers Marne and Seine: noted esp for its cheese

brief (briːf) *adj* 1 short in duration 2 short in length or extent; scanty: *a brief bikini* 3 abrupt in manner; brusque: *the professor was brief with me this morning* 4 terse or concise; containing few words ▷ *n* 5 a condensed or short statement or written synopsis; abstract 6 *law* a document containing all the facts and points of law of a case by which a solicitor instructs a barrister to represent a client 7 *RC Church* a letter issuing from the Roman court written in modern characters, as contrasted with a papal bull; papal brief 8 short for **briefing** 9 **hold a brief for** to argue for; champion 10 **in brief** in short; to sum up ▷ *vb* 11 to prepare or instruct by giving a summary of relevant facts 12 to make a summary or synopsis of 13 *English law* **a** to instruct (a barrister) by brief **b** to retain (a barrister) as counsel [c14: from Old French *bref*, from Latin *brevis*; related to Greek *brakhus*] > **'briefly** *adv* > **'briefness** *n*

briefcase ('briːf,keɪs) *n* a flat portable case, often of leather, for carrying papers, books, etc

briefing ('briːfɪŋ) *n* 1 a meeting at which detailed information or instructions are given, as for military operations, etc 2 the facts presented during such a meeting

briefless ('briːflɪs) *adj* (said of a barrister) without clients

briefs (briːfs) *pl n* men's underpants or women's pants without legs

brier[1] *or* **briar** ('braɪə) *n* any of various thorny shrubs or other plants, such as the sweetbrier and greenbrier [Old English *brēr, brǣr*, of obscure origin] > **'briery** *or* **'briary** *adj*

brier[2] ('braɪə) *n* a variant spelling of **briar**[1]

brierroot ('braɪə,ruːt) *n* a variant spelling of **briarroot**. Also called: **brierwood**

brig[1] (brɪg) *n* 1 *nautical* a two-masted square-rigger 2 *chiefly US* a prison, esp in a navy ship [c18: shortened from BRIGANTINE]

brig[2] (brɪg) *n* a Scot and northern English word for a **bridge**[1]

Brig. *abbreviation* Brigadier

brigade (brɪ'geɪd) *n* 1 a formation of fighting units, together with support arms and services, smaller than a

division and usually commanded by a brigadier 2 a group of people organized for a certain task: *a rescue brigade* ▷ *vb* (*tr*) 3 to organize into a brigade [c17: from Old French, from Old Italian, from *brigare* to fight, perhaps of Celtic origin; see BRIGAND]

brigadier (,brɪgə'dɪə) *n* 1 an officer of the British Army or Royal Marines who holds a rank junior to a major general but senior to a colonel, usually commanding a brigade 2 an equivalent rank in other armed forces [c17: from French, from BRIGADE]

brigalow ('brɪgələʊ) *n* *Austral* **a** any of various acacia trees **b** (*as modifier*): *brigalow country* [c19: from a native Australian language]

brigand ('brɪgənd) *n* a bandit or plunderer, esp a member of a gang operating in mountainous areas [c14: from Old French, from Old Italian *brigante* fighter, from *brigare* to fight, from *briga* strife, of Celtic origin] > **'brigandage** *or* **'brigandry** *n*

brigantine ('brɪgən,tiːn, -,taɪn) *n* a two-masted sailing ship, rigged square on the foremast and fore-and-aft with square topsails on the mainmast [c16: from Old Italian *brigantino* pirate ship, from *brigante* BRIGAND]

Briggs (brɪgz) *n* **Henry**. 1561–1631, English mathematician: introduced common logarithms

Brighouse[1] ('brɪg,haʊs) *n* a town in N England, in Calderdale unitary authority, West Yorkshire: machine tools, textiles, engineering. Pop: 32 360 (2001)

Brighouse[2] ('brɪg,haʊs) *n* **Harold**. 1882–1958, British novelist and dramatist, best known for his play *Hobson's Choice* (1915)

bright (braɪt) *adj* 1 emitting or reflecting much light; shining 2 (of colours) intense or vivid 3 full of promise: *a bright future* 4 full of animation; cheerful: *a bright face* 5 *informal* quick witted or clever: *a bright child* 6 magnificent; glorious 7 polished; glistening 8 (of a liquid) translucent and clear 9 **bright and early** very early in the morning ▷ *adv* 10 brightly: *the fire was burning bright* [Old English *beorht*; related to Old Norse *bjartr*, Gothic *bairhts* clear, Old High German *beraht*, Norwegian *bjerk*, Swedish *brokig* pied] > **'brightly** *adv* > **'brightness** *n*

Bright (braɪt) *n* **John**. 1811–89, British liberal statesman, economist, and advocate of free trade: with Richard Cobden he led the Anti-Corn-Law League (1838–46)

brighten ('braɪt³n) *vb* 1 to make or become bright or brighter 2 to make or become cheerful

brightening agent *n* a compound applied to a textile to increase its brightness by the conversion of ultraviolet radiation to visible (blue) light, used in detergents

Brighton ('braɪt³n) *n* a coastal resort in S England, in Brighton and Hove unitary authority, East Sussex: patronized by the Prince Regent, who had the Royal Pavilion built (1782); seat of the University of Sussex (1966) and the University of Brighton (1992). Pop: 134 293 (2001)

Brighton and Hove (həʊv) *n* a city and unitary authority in S England, in East Sussex. Pop: 251 500 (2003 est). Area: 72 sq km (28 sq miles)

Bright's disease (braɪts) *n* chronic inflammation of the kidneys; chronic nephritis [c19: named after Richard Bright (1789–1858), British physician]

brightwork ('braɪt,wɜːk) *n* shiny metal trimmings or fittings on ships, cars, etc

Brigid ('brɪdʒɪd) *n* Saint Brigid See **Bridget** (sense 1)

brill[1] (brɪl) *n*, *pl* brill *or* brills a European food fish, *Scophthalmus rhombus*, a flatfish similar to the turbot but lacking tubercles on the body: family *Bothidae* [c15: probably from Cornish *brýthel* mackerel, from Old Cornish *brýth* speckled; related to Welsh *brith* spotted]

brill[2] (brɪl) *adj* *Brit sl* excellent or wonderful [C20 shortened form of BRILLIANT]

Brillat-Savarin (French brijasavarɛ̃) *n* **Anthelme** (ɑ̃tɛlm). 1755–1826, French lawyer and gourmet; author of *Physiologie du Goût* (1825)

brilliance ('brɪljəns) *or* **brilliancy** *n* 1 great brightness; radiance 2 excellence or distinction in physical or mental ability; exceptional talent 3 splendour; magnificence

brilliant ('brɪljənt) *adj* 1 shining with light; sparkling 2 (of a colour) having a high saturation and reflecting a considerable amount of light; vivid **3** outstanding; exceptional: *a brilliant success* **4** splendid; magnificent: *a brilliant show* **5** of outstanding intelligence or intellect: *a brilliant mind; a brilliant idea* ▷ *n* **6** Also called: brilliant cut **a** a popular circular cut for diamonds and other gemstones in the form of two many-faceted pyramids (the top one truncated) joined at their bases **b** a diamond of this cut [c17: from French *brillant* shining, from *briller* to shine, from Italian *brillare*, from *brillo* BERYL] > 'brilliantly *adv*

brilliantine ('brɪljənˌtiːn) *n* a perfumed oil used to make the hair smooth and shiny [c19: from French, from *brillant* shining]

brim (brɪm) *n* **1** the upper rim of a vessel: *the brim of a cup* **2** a projecting rim or edge: *the brim of a hat* **3** the brink or edge of something ▷ *vb* brims, brimming, brimmed **4** to fill or be full to the brim: *eyes brimming with tears* [c13: from Middle High German *brem*, probably from Old Norse *barmr*; see BERM] > 'brimless *adj*

brimful or **brimfull** (ˌbrɪm'fʊl) *adj* (*postpositive*, foll by *of*) filled up to the brim (with)

brimstone ('brɪmˌstəʊn) *n* **1** an obsolete name for: sulphur **2** a common yellow butterfly, *Gonepteryx rhamni*, of N temperate regions of the Old World: family *Pieridae* [Old English *brynstān*; related to Old Norse *brennistein*; see BURN¹, STONE]

Brindisi (Italian 'brindizi) *n* a port in SE Italy, in SE Apulia: important naval base in Roman times and a centre of the Crusades in the Middle Ages. Pop: 89 081 (2001). Ancient name: Brundisium

brindle ('brɪndᵊl) *n* **1** a brindled animal **2** a brindled colouring [c17: back formation from BRINDLED]

brindled ('brɪndᵊld) *adj* brown or grey streaked or patched with a darker colour: *a brindled dog* [c17: changed from c15 *brended*, literally: branded, probably of Scandinavian origin; compare Old Norse *bröndottr*; see BRAND]

Brindley ('brɪndlɪ) *n* **James**. 1716–72, British canal builder, who constructed (1759–61) the Bridgewater Canal, the first in England

brine (braɪn) *n* **1** a strong solution of salt and water, used for salting and pickling meats, etc **2** the sea or its water ▷ *vb* **3** (*tr*) to soak in or treat with brine [Old English *brīne*; related to Middle Dutch *brīne*, Old Slavonic *bridŭ* bitter, Sanskrit *bibhrāya* burnt] > 'brinish *adj*

bring (brɪŋ) *vb* brings, bringing, brought (*tr*) **1** to carry, convey, or take (something or someone) to a designated place or person: *bring that book to me; will you bring Jessica to Tom's party?* **2** to cause to happen or occur to (oneself or another): *to bring disrepect on oneself* **3** to cause to happen as a consequence: *responsibility brings maturity* **4** to cause to come to mind: *it brought back memories* **5** to cause to be in a certain state, position, etc: *the punch brought him to his knees* **6** to force, persuade, or make (oneself): *I couldn't bring myself to do it* **7** to sell for; fetch: *the painting brought 20 pounds* **8** *law* **a** to institute (proceedings, charges, etc) **b** to put (evidence, etc) before a tribunal **9** bring forth to give birth to ▷ See also **bring about, bring down** [Old English *bringan*; related to Gothic *briggan*, Old High German *bringan*] > 'bringer *n*

bring about *vb* (*tr, adverb*) **1** to cause to happen **2** to turn (a ship) around

bring-and-buy sale *n* *Brit & NZ* an informal sale, often conducted for charity, to which people bring items for sale and buy those that others have brought

bring down *vb* (*tr, adverb*) to cause to fall

bring forward *vb* (*tr, adverb*) **1** to present or introduce (a subject) for discussion **2** *book-keeping* to transfer (a figure representing the sum of the figures on a page or in a column) to the top of the next page or column **3** to move to an earlier time or date: *the kickoff has been brought forward to 2 p.m.*

bring in *vb* (*tr, adverb*) **1** to yield (income, profit, or cash) **2** to produce or return (a verdict) **3** to put forward or introduce (a legislative bill, etc)

bring off *vb* (*tr, adverb*) to succeed in achieving (something), esp with difficulty or contrary to expectations

bring out *vb* (*tr, adverb*) **1** to produce or publish or have

published **2** to expose, reveal, or cause to be seen: *she brought out the best in me* **3** (foll by *in*) to cause (a person) to become covered (with spots, a rash, etc) **4** *Brit* to introduce (a girl) formally into society as a debutante

bring over *vb* (*tr, adverb*) to cause (a person) to change allegiances

bring round or **bring around** *vb* (*tr, adverb*) **1** to restore (a person) to consciousness, esp after a faint **2** to convince (another person, usually an opponent) of an opinion or point of view

bring to *vb* (*tr*) **1** (*adverb*) to restore (a person) to consciousness **2** (*adverb*) to cause (a ship) to turn into the wind and reduce her headway

bring up *vb* (*tr, adverb*) **1** to care for and train (a child); rear **2** to raise (a subject) for discussion; mention **3** to vomit (food)

brinjal ('brɪndʒəl) *n* (in India and Africa) another name for the **aubergine** [c17: from Portuguese *berinjela*, from Arabic; see AUBERGINE]

brink (brɪŋk) *n* **1** the edge, border, or verge of a steep place **2** the land at the edge of a body of water **3** the verge of an event or state: *the brink of disaster* [c13: from Middle Dutch *brinc*, of Germanic origin; compare Old Norse *brekka* slope, Middle Low German *brink* edge of a field]

brinkmanship ('brɪŋkmənˌʃɪp) *n* the art or practice of pressing a dangerous situation, esp in international affairs, to the limit of safety and peace in order to win an advantage from a threatening or tenacious foe

briny ('braɪnɪ) *adj* brinier, briniest **1** of or resembling brine; salty ▷ *n* **2** the briny an informal name for the **sea** > 'brininess *n*

brio ('briːəʊ) *n* liveliness or vigour; spirit. See also **con brio** [c19: from Italian, of Celtic origin]

brioche ('briːəʊʃ, -ɒʃ; French briɔʃ) *n* a soft roll or loaf made from a very light yeast dough, sometimes mixed with currants [c19: from Norman dialect, from *brier* to knead, of Germanic origin; compare French *broyer* to pound, BREAK]

briquette or **briquet** (brɪ'kɛt) *n* a small brick made of compressed coal dust, sawdust, charcoal, etc, used for fuel [c19: from French: a little brick, from *brique* BRICK]

Brisbane ('brɪzbən) *n* a port in E Australia, the capital of Queensland: founded in 1824 as a penal settlement; vast agricultural hinterland. Pop: 1 508 161 (2001)

brisk (brɪsk) *adj* **1** lively and quick; vigorous: *a brisk walk; trade was brisk* **2** invigorating or sharp: *brisk weather* ▷ *vb* **3** (often foll by *up*) to enliven; make or become brisk [c16: probably variant of BRUSQUE] > 'briskly *adv* > 'briskness *n*

brisket ('brɪskɪt) *n* **1** the breast of a four-legged animal **2** the meat from this part, esp of beef [c14: probably of Scandinavian origin; related to Old Norse *brjösk* gristle, Norwegian and Danish *brusk*]

brisling ('brɪslɪŋ) *n* another name for a sprat, esp a Norwegian sprat seasoned, smoked, and canned in oil [c20: from Norwegian; related to obsolete Danish *bretling*, German *Breitling*]

Brissot (French briso) *n* **Jacques-Pierre** (ʒakpjɛr). 1754–93, French journalist and revolutionary; leader of the Girondists: executed by the Jacobins

bristle ('brɪsᵊl) *n* **1** any short stiff hair of an animal or plant **2** something resembling these hair: *toothbrush bristle* ▷ *vb* **3** (when *intr*, often foll by *up*) to stand up or cause to stand up like bristles **4** (*intr*; sometimes foll by *up*) to show anger, indignation, etc: *she bristled at the suggestion* **5** (*intr*) to be thickly covered or set: *the target bristled with arrows* [c13 *bristil, brustel*, from earlier *brust*, from Old English *byrst*; related to Old Norse *burst*, Old High German *borst*] > 'bristly *adj*

Bristol ('brɪstᵊl) *n* **1** City of Bristol a port and industrial city in SW England, mainly in Bristol unitary authority, on the River Avon seven miles from its mouth on the Bristol Channel: a major port, trading with America, in the 17th and 18th centuries; the modern port consists chiefly of docks at Avonmouth and Portishead; noted for the **Clifton Suspension Bridge** (designed by I. K. Brunel, 1834) over the Avon gorge; Bristol university (1909) and University of the West of England (1992). Pop: 420 556 (2001) **2** City of Bristol a unitary authority in SW

England, created in 1996 from part of Avon county. Pop: 391 500 (2003 est). Area: 110 sq km (42 sq miles)

Bristol board *n* a heavy smooth cardboard of fine quality, used for printing and drawing

Bristol Channel *n* an inlet of the Atlantic, between S Wales and SW England, merging into the Severn estuary. Length: about 137 km (85 miles)

Bristol fashion *adv, adj (postpositive)* shipshape and Bristol fashion in good order; efficiently arranged

bristols ('brɪstəlz) *pl n Brit slang* a woman's breasts [c20: short for *Bristol Cities*, rhyming slang for *titties*]

Bristow ('brɪstəʊ) *n* Eric. born 1957, British darts player

Brit¹ (brɪt) *n informal* a British person

Brit² *abbreviation* 1 Britain 2 British

Britain ('brɪt°n) *n* another name for **Great Britain, United Kingdom**

Britannia (brɪ'tænɪə) *n* 1 a female warrior carrying a trident and wearing a helmet, personifying Great Britain or the British Empire 2 (in the ancient Roman Empire) the S part of Great Britain 3 short for **Britannia coin**

Britannia coin *n* any of four British gold coins introduced in 1987 for investment purposes; their denominations are £100, £50, £25, and £10

Britannia metal *n* an alloy of low melting point consisting of tin with 5–10 per cent antimony, 1–3 per cent copper, and sometimes small quantities of zinc, lead, or bismuth: used for decorative purposes and for bearings

Britannic (brɪ'tænɪk) *adj* of Britain; British (esp in the phrases *His or Her Britannic Majesty*)

Britart ('brɪt,ɑːt) *n* a movement in modern British art beginning in the late 1980s, often conceptual or using controversial materials, including such artists as Damien Hirst and Rachel Whiteread [c20: *Brit* short for *British*]

britches ('brɪtʃɪz) *pl n* a variant spelling of **breeches**

Briticism ('brɪtɪ,sɪzəm) *n* a custom, linguistic usage, or other feature peculiar to Britain or its people

British ('brɪtɪʃ) *adj* 1 relating to, denoting, or characteristic of Britain or any of the natives, citizens, or inhabitants of the United Kingdom 2 relating to or denoting the English language as spoken and written in Britain, esp the S dialect generally regarded as standard ▷ *n* 3 *(functioning as plural)* the natives or inhabitants of Britain

British Antarctic Territory *n* a UK Overseas Territory in the S Atlantic (claims are suspended under the Antarctic Treaty): created in 1962 and consisting of the South Shetland Islands, the South Orkney Islands, and Graham Land; formerly part of the Falkland Islands Dependencies

British Cameroons *pl n* a former British trust territory of West Africa. See **Cameroon**

British Columbia *n* a province of W Canada, on the Pacific coast: largely mountainous with extensive forests, rich mineral resources, and important fisheries. Capital: Victoria. Pop: 4 196 383 (2004 est). Area: 930 532 sq km (359 279 sq miles). Abbreviation: **BC** ▷ **British Columbian** *adj, n*

British Council *n* an organization founded (1934) to extend the influence of British culture and education throughout the world

British East Africa *n* the former British possessions of Uganda, Kenya, Tanganyika, and Zanzibar, before their independence in the 1960s

British Empire *n* (formerly) the United Kingdom and the territories under its control, which reached its greatest extent at the end of World War I when it embraced over a quarter of the world's population and more than a quarter of the world's land surface

Britisher ('brɪtɪʃə) *n* (not used by the British) 1 a native or inhabitant of Great Britain 2 any British subject

British Guiana *n* the former name (until 1966) of Guyana

British Honduras *n* the former name of **Belize**

British India *n* the 17 provinces of India formerly governed by the British under the British sovereign: ceased to exist in 1947 when the independent states of India and Pakistan were created

British Indian Ocean Territory *n* a UK Overseas Territory in the Indian Ocean: consists of the Chagos Archipelago (formerly a dependency of Mauritius) and formerly included (until 1976) Aldabra, Farquhar, and Des Roches, now administratively part of the Seychelles. Diego Garcia is an important US naval base

British Isles *pl n* a group of islands in W Europe, consisting of Great Britain, Ireland, the Isle of Man, Orkney, Shetland, the Channel Islands belonging to Great Britain, and the islands adjacent to these

Britishism ('brɪtɪ,ʃɪzəm) *n* a variant of **Briticism**

British Legion *n Brit* a shortened form of **Royal British Legion**

Britishness ('brɪtɪʃnəs) *n* the qualities generally associated with British people, often taken to include tolerance and fairness

British North America *n* (formerly) Canada or its constituent regions or provinces that formed part of the British Empire

British Somaliland *n* a former British protectorate (1884–1960) in E Africa, on the Gulf of Aden: united with Italian Somaliland in 1960 to form Somalia (or the Somali Republic); in 1991 the self-styled republic of Somaliland, covering the same area as the former British Somaliland, declared itself independent and continues to function largely as a separate entity, though without international recognition

British thermal unit *n* a unit of heat in the fps system equal to the quantity of heat required to raise the temperature of 1 pound of water by 1°F. 1 British thermal unit is equivalent to 1055.06 joules or 251.997 calories. Abbrevs **btu, BthU**

British Virgin Islands *pl n* a UK Overseas Territory in the Caribbean, consisting of 36 islands in the E Virgin Islands: formerly part of the Federation of the Leeward Islands (1871–1956). Capital: Road Town, on Tortola. Pop: 21 000 (2003 est). Area: 153 sq km (59 sq miles)

British West Africa *n* the former British possessions of Nigeria, The Gambia, Sierra Leone, and the Gold Coast, and the former trust territories of Togoland and Cameroons

British West Indies *pl n* a former name for the states in the Caribbean that are members of the Commonwealth: the Bahamas, Barbados, Jamaica, Trinidad and Tobago, Antigua and Barbuda, Saint Kitts-Nevis, Dominica, Grenada, Saint Lucia, and Saint Vincent and the Grenadines; along with the islands which remain as United Kingdom dependencies: Anguilla, the Cayman Islands, Montserrat, the Turks and Caicos Islands and the British Virgin Islands

Briton ('brɪt°n) *n* 1 a native or inhabitant of Britain 2 *history* any of the early Celtic inhabitants of S Britain who were largely dispossessed by the Anglo-Saxon invaders after the 5th century AD [c13: from Old French *Breton*, from Latin *Britto*, of Celtic origin]

Britpack ('brɪt,pæk) *n* **a** a group of young and successful British actors, directors, artists, etc **b** *(as modifier)*: *Britpack talent* [c20: a play on **BRATPACK**]

Britpop ('brɪt,pɒp) *n* the characteristic pop music performed by some British bands of the mid 1990s

Brittany ('brɪtənɪ) *n* a region of NW France, the peninsula between the English Channel and the Bay of Biscay: settled by Celtic refugees from Wales and Cornwall during the Anglo-Saxon invasions; disputed between England and France until 1364. French name: Bretagne. Related adjective: **Breton**

Britten ('brɪt°n) *n* (**Edward**) **Benjamin**, Baron Britten. 1913–76, English composer, pianist, and conductor. His works include the operas *Peter Grimes* (1945) and *Billy Budd* (1951), the choral works *Hymn to St Cecilia* (1942) and *A War Requiem* (1962), and numerous orchestral pieces

brittle ('brɪt°l) *adj* 1 easily cracked, snapped, or broken; fragile 2 curt or irritable 3 hard or sharp in quality ▷ *n* 4 a crunchy sweet made with treacle and nuts: *peanut brittle* [c14: from Old English *brytel* (unattested); related to *brytsen* fragment, *brēotan* to break] ▷ **'brittleness** *n*

brittle-star *n* any echinoderm of the class *Ophiuroidea*, occurring on the sea bottom and having five long slender arms radiating from a small central disc

Brno ('bɜːnəʊ; *Czech* 'brnɔ) *n* a city in the Czech Republic; formerly the capital of Moravia: the country's second largest city. Pop: 375 000 (2005 est). German name: Brünn

bro (bruː) *n South African informal* a friend, often used in direct address [C20: from Afrikaans *broer* brother]

bro. (brəʊ) *abbreviation* brother

broach (brəʊtʃ) *vb* **1** (*tr*) to initiate (a topic) for discussion **2** (*tr*) to tap or pierce (a container) to draw off (a liquid): *to broach a cask; to broach wine* **3** (*tr*) to open in order to begin to use ▷ *n* **4** a long tapered toothed cutting tool for enlarging holes **5** a spit for roasting meat, etc [C14: from Old French *broche*, from Vulgar Latin *brocca* (unattested), from Latin *brochus* projecting]

broad (brɔːd) *adj* **1** having relatively great breadth or width **2** of vast extent; spacious: *a broad plain* **3** (*postpositive*) from one side to the other: *four miles broad* **4** of great scope or potential: *that invention had broad applications* **5** not detailed; general: *broad plans* **6** clear and open; full (esp in the phrase **broad daylight**) **7** obvious or plain: *broad hints* **8** liberal; tolerant: *a broad political stance* **9** widely spread; extensive: *broad support* **10** vulgar; coarse; indecent: *a broad joke* **11** (of a dialect or pronunciation) consisting of a large number of speech sounds characteristic of a particular geographical area: *a broad Yorkshire accent* **12** *finance* denoting an assessment of liquidity as including notes and coin in circulation with the public, banks' till money and balances, most private-sector bank deposits, and sterling bank-deposit certificates: *broad money*. See **narrow** (sense 7) **13** *phonetics* broad **a** the long vowel in English words such as *father*, *half*, as represented in the received pronunciation of Southern British English ▷ *n* **14** the broad part of something **15** *slang, chiefly US & Canadian* **a** a girl or woman **b** a prostitute **16** *Brit dialect* a river spreading over a lowland. See also **Broads** [Old English *brād*; related to Old Norse *breithr*, Old Frisian *brēd*, Old High German *breit*, Gothic *braiths*] > **broadly** *adv*

B-road *n* (in Britain) a secondary road

broadband ('brɔːd,bænd) *n* a transmission technique using a wide range of frequencies that enables messages to be sent simultaneously, used in fast internet connections

broad bean *n* **1** an erect annual Eurasian bean plant, *Vicia faba*, cultivated for its large edible flattened seeds, used as a vegetable **2** the seed of this plant

broadcast ('brɔːd,kɑːst) *vb* **-casts, -casting, -cast** or **-casted** **1** to transmit (announcements or programmes) on radio or television **2** (*intr*) to take part in a radio or television programme **3** (*tr*) to make widely known throughout an area: *to broadcast news* **4** (*tr*) to scatter (seed, etc) over an area, esp by hand ▷ *n* **5 a** a transmission or programme on radio or television **b** (*as modifier*): *a broadcast signal* **6** the act of scattering seeds ▷ *adj* **7** dispersed over a wide area ▷ *adv* **8** far and wide > '**broad,caster** *n* > '**broad,casting** *n*

Broad Church *n* **1** a party within the Church of England which favours a broad and liberal interpretation of Anglican formularies and rubrics and objects to positive definition in theology **2** (*usually not capitals*) a group or movement which embraces a wide and varied number of views, approaches, and opinions ▷ *adj* **Broad-Church** **3** of or relating to this party in the Church of England

broadcloth ('brɔːd,klɒθ) *n* **1** fabric woven on a wide loom **2** a closely woven fabric of wool, worsted, cotton, or rayon with lustrous finish, used for clothing

broaden ('brɔːdᵊn) *vb* to make or become broad or broader; widen

broad gauge *n* **1** a railway track with a greater distance between the lines than the standard gauge of 56½ inches (about 1.44 metres) used now by most mainline railway systems ▷ *adj* **broad-gauge** **2** of, relating to, or denoting a railway having this track

broad-leaved *adj* denoting trees other than conifers, most of which have broad rather than needle-shaped leaves

broadline ('brɔːd,laɪn) *n chiefly US* **a** a company that deals in high volume at the cheaper end of a product

line **b** (*as modifier*): *broadline distributors*

broadloom ('brɔːd,luːm) *n* (*modifier*) of or designating carpets or carpeting woven on a wide loom to obviate the need for seams

broad-minded *adj* **1** tolerant of opposing viewpoints; not prejudiced; liberal **2** not easily shocked by permissive sexual habits, pornography, etc > ,broad-'mindedly *adv* > ,broad-'mindedness *n*

Broads (brɔːdz) *pl n* the Broads **1** a group of shallow navigable lakes, connected by a network of rivers, in E England, in Norfolk and Suffolk **2** the region around these lakes: a tourist centre; several bird sanctuaries

broadsheet ('brɔːd,ʃiːt) *n* **1** a newspaper having a large format, approximately 15 by 24 inches (38 by 61 centimetres) **2** another word for **broadside** (sense 4)

broadside ('brɔːd,saɪd) *n* **1** *nautical* the entire side of a vessel, from stem to stern and from waterline to rail **2** *naval* **a** all the armament fired from one side of a warship **b** the simultaneous discharge of such armament **3** a strong or abusive verbal or written attack **4** Also called: **broadside ballad** a ballad or popular song printed on one side of a sheet of paper and sold by hawkers, esp in 16th-century England ▷ *adv* **5** with a broader side facing an object; sideways

broad-spectrum *n* (*modifier*) effective against a wide variety of diseases or microorganisms: *a broad-spectrum antibiotic*

broadsword ('brɔːd,sɔːd) *n* a broad-bladed sword used for cutting rather than stabbing

broadtail ('brɔːd,teɪl) *n* **1** the highly valued black wavy fur obtained from the skins of newly born karakul lambs; caracul **2** another name for **karakul**

Broadway ('brɔːd,weɪ) *n* **1** a thoroughfare in New York City, famous for its theatres: the centre of the commercial theatre in the US ▷ *adj* **2** of or relating to or suitable for the commercial theatre, esp on Broadway

Broca (*French* brɔka) *n* Paul (pɔl). 1824–80, French surgeon and anthropologist who discovered the motor speech centre of the brain and did pioneering work in brain surgery

brocade (brəʊ'keɪd) *n* **1** a rich fabric woven with a raised design, often using gold or silver threads ▷ *vb* **2** (*tr*) to weave with such a design [C17: from Spanish *brocado*, from Italian *broccato* embossed fabric, from *brocco* spike, from Latin *brochus* projecting; see BROACH¹]

broccoli ('brɒkəlɪ) *n* **1** a cultivated variety of cabbage, *Brassica oleracea italica*, having branched greenish flower heads **2** the flower head of this plant, eaten as a vegetable before the buds have opened [C17: from Italian, plural of *broccolo* a little sprout, from *brocco* sprout, spike; see BROCADE]

broch (brɒk, brɒx) *n* (in Scotland) a circular dry-stone tower large enough to serve as a fortified home; they date from the Iron Age and are found esp in the north and the islands [C17: from Old Norse *borg*; related to Old English *burh* settlement, burgh]

brochette (brɒ'ʃɛt; *French* brɔʃɛt) *n* a skewer or small spit, used for holding pieces of meat, etc, while roasting or grilling [C19: from Old French *brochete* small pointed tool; see BROACH¹]

brochure ('brəʊʃjʊə, -ʃə) *n* a pamphlet or booklet, esp one containing summarized or introductory information or advertising [C18: from French, from *brocher* to stitch (a book)]

brock (brɒk) *n* a Brit name, used esp as a form of address in stories, for **badger** (sense 1) [Old English *broc*, of Celtic origin; compare Welsh *broch*]

Brocken (*German* 'brɔkən) *n* a mountain in central Germany: the highest peak of the Harz Mountains; important in German folklore. Height: 1142 m (3747 ft). The **Brocken Bow** or **Brocken Spectre** is an atmospheric phenomenon in which an observer, when the sun is low, may see his enlarged shadow against the clouds, often surrounded by coloured lights

brocket ('brɒkɪt) *n* any small deer of the genus *Mazama*, of tropical America, having small unbranched antlers [C15: from Anglo-French *broquet*, from *broque* horn, from Vulgar Latin *brocca* (unattested); see BROACH]

broderie anglaise (,brəʊdərɪ ɑːnˈɡlɛz) *n* open

embroidery on white cotton, fine linen, etc [C19: French: English embroidery]

Brodsky ('brɒdskɪ) n **Joseph**, original name *Iosif Aleksandrovich Brodsky*. 1940–96, US poet, born in the Soviet Union. His collections include *The End of a Beautiful Era* (1977). Nobel prize for literature 1987

Broederbond ('brudə,bɔːnt, 'bruːdə,bɒnt) n (in South Africa) a secret society of Afrikaner Nationalists committed to securing and maintaining Afrikaner control over important areas of government [Afrikaans: band of brothers]

broekies ('bruːkiːz) pl n *South African informal* underpants [C19: Afrikaans]

Broglie (brɔj) n See **de Broglie** (sense 1)

brogue[1] (brəʊg) n a broad gentle-sounding dialectal accent, esp that used by the Irish in speaking English [C18: probably from BROGUE[2], alluding to the footwear of the peasantry]

brogue[2] (brəʊg) n **1** a sturdy walking shoe, often with ornamental perforations **2** an untanned shoe worn formerly in Ireland and Scotland [C16: from Irish Gaelic *bróg* boot, shoe, probably from Old Norse *brók* leg covering]

broider ('brɔɪdə) vb (tr) an archaic word for **embroider** [C15: from Old French *brosder*, of Germanic origin; see EMBROIDER]

broil[1] (brɔɪl) vb **1** *chiefly US & Canadian* to cook (meat, fish, etc) by direct heat, as under a grill or over a hot fire, or (of meat, fish, etc) to be cooked in this way. Usual equivalent (in Britain and other countries): **grill 2** to become or cause to become extremely hot **3** (intr) to be furious [C14: from Old French *bruillir* to burn, of uncertain origin]

broil[2] (brɔɪl) archaic ▷ n **1** a loud quarrel or disturbance; brawl ▷ vb **2** (intr) to brawl; quarrel [C16: from Old French *brouiller* to mix, from *breu* broth; see BREWIS, BROSE]

broiler ('brɔɪlə) n **1** a young tender chicken suitable for roasting **2** *chiefly US* a pan, grate, etc for broiling food **3** a very hot day

broke (brəʊk) vb **1** the past tense of **break** ▷ adj **2** *informal* having no money; bankrupt **3 go for broke** *slang* to risk everything in a gambling or other venture

broken ('brəʊkən) vb **1** the past participle of **break** ▷ adj **2** fractured, smashed, or splintered: *a broken vase* **3** interrupted; disturbed; disconnected: *broken sleep* **4** intermittent or discontinuous: *broken sunshine* **5** not functioning **6** spoilt or ruined by divorce (esp in the phrases **broken home, broken marriage**) **7** (of a trust, promise, contract, etc) violated; infringed **8** (of the speech of a foreigner) imperfect in grammar, vocabulary, and pronunciation: *broken English* **9** Also called: **broken-in** made tame or disciplined by training **10** exhausted or weakened as through ill-health or misfortune **11** irregular or rough; uneven: *broken ground* **12** bankrupt or out of money **13** (of colour) having a multicoloured decorative effect, as by stippling paint onto a surface **14** *South African informal* drunk ▷ 'brokenly adv

broken chord n *music* a chord played as an arpeggio

broken-down adj **1** worn out, as by age or long use; dilapidated **2** not in working order

brokenhearted (,brəʊkən'hɑːtɪd) adj overwhelmed by grief or disappointment ▷ ,broken'heartedly adv

Broken Hill n a town in SE Australia, in W New South Wales: mining centre for lead, silver, and zinc. Pop: 19 834 (2001)

broken wind (wɪnd) n *vet science* another name for **heaves** (sense 1)

broker ('brəʊkə) n **1** an agent who, acting on behalf of a principal, buys or sells goods, securities, etc, in return for a commission: *insurance broker* **2** (formerly) short for **stockbroker 3** a dealer in second-hand goods [C14: from Anglo-French *brocour* broacher (of casks, hence, one who sells, agent), from Old Northern French *broquier* to tap a cask, from *broque* tap of a cask; see BROACH]

brokerage ('brəʊkərɪdʒ) n **1** commission charged by a broker to his principals **2** a broker's business or office

broker-dealer n another name for **stockbroker**

brolga ('brɒlgə) n a large grey Australian crane, *Grus*

rubicunda, having a red-and-green head and a trumpeting call. Also called: **native companion** [C19: from a native Australian language]

brolly ('brɒlɪ) n, pl **-lies** an informal Brit name for **umbrella** (sense 1)

Bromberg ('brɒmbɛrk) n the German name for **Bydgoszcz**

bromeliad (brəʊ'miːlɪ,æd) n any plant of the tropical American family *Bromeliaceae*, typically epiphytes with a rosette of fleshy leaves. The family includes the pineapple and Spanish moss [C19: from New Latin *Bromelia* type genus, after Olaf *Bromelius* (1639–1705), Swedish botanist]

bromide ('brəʊmaɪd) n **1** any salt of hydrobromic acid, containing the monovalent ion Br⁻ (**bromide ion**) **2** any compound containing a bromine atom, such as methyl bromide **3** a dose of sodium or potassium bromide given as a sedative **4 a** a trite saying; platitude **b** a dull or boring person [C19, C20 (cliché): from BROM(INE) + -IDE]

bromide paper n a type of photographic paper coated with an emulsion of silver bromide usually containing a small quantity of silver iodide

bromine ('brəʊmiːn, -mɪn) n a pungent dark red volatile liquid element of the halogen series that occurs in natural brine and is used in the production of chemicals, esp ethylene dibromide. Symbol: Br; atomic no: 35; atomic wt: 79.904; valency: 1, 3, 5, or 7; relative density 3.12; density (gas): 7.59 kg/m³; melting pt: −7.2°C; boiling pt: 58.78°C [C19: from French *brome* bromine, from Greek *brōmos* bad smell + -INE[2], of uncertain origin]

Bromley ('brɒmlɪ) n a borough of SE Greater London. Pop: 298 300 (2003 est). Area: 153 sq km (59 sq miles)

Bromsgrove ('brɒmz,grəʊv) n a town in W central England, in N Worcestershire. Pop: 29 237 (2001)

bronchi ('brɒŋkaɪ) n the plural of **bronchus**

bronchia ('brɒŋkɪə) pl n another name for **bronchial tubes** [C17: from Late Latin, from Greek *bronkhia*, plural of *bronkhion*, diminutive of *bronkhus* windpipe, throat]

bronchial ('brɒŋkɪəl) adj of or relating to the bronchi or the bronchial tubes > 'bronchially adv

bronchial tubes pl n the bronchi or their smaller divisions

bronchiectasis (,brɒŋkɪ'ɛktəsɪs) n chronic dilation of the bronchi or bronchial tubes, which often become infected [C19: from BRONCHO- + Greek *ektasis* a stretching]

bronchiole ('brɒŋkɪ,əʊl) n any of the smallest bronchial tubes, usually ending in alveoli [C19: from New Latin *bronchiolum*, diminutive of Late Latin *bronchium*, singular of BRONCHIA] > bronchiolar (,brɒŋkɪ'əʊlə) adj

bronchitis (brɒŋ'kaɪtɪs) n inflammation of the bronchial tubes, characterized by coughing, difficulty in breathing, etc, caused by infection or irritation of the respiratory tract > bronchitic (brɒŋ'kɪtɪk) adj, n

broncho- or before a vowel **bronch-** combining form indicating or relating to the bronchi: *bronchitis* [from Greek: BRONCHUS]

bronchodilator ('brɒŋkəʊdaɪ,leɪtə) n any drug or other agent that causes dilation of the bronchial tubes by relaxing bronchial muscle: used, esp in the form of aerosol sprays, for the relief of asthma

bronchopneumonia (,brɒŋkəʊnjuː'məʊnɪə) n inflammation of the lungs, originating in the bronchioles

bronchoscope ('brɒŋkə,skəʊp) n an instrument for examining and providing access to the interior of the bronchial tubes

bronchus ('brɒŋkəs) n, pl **-chi** (-kaɪ) either of the two main branches of the trachea, which contain cartilage within their walls [C18: from New Latin, from Greek *bronkhos* windpipe]

bronco or **broncho** ('brɒŋkəʊ) n, pl **-cos** or **-chos** (in the US and Canada) a wild or partially tamed pony or mustang of the western plains [C19: from Mexican Spanish, short for Spanish *potro bronco* unbroken colt, probably from Latin *broccus* projecting (as knots on wood), hence, rough, wild]

Brontë ('brɒntɪ) n **1 Anne**, pen name *Acton Bell*. 1820–49, English novelist; author of *The Tenant of Wildfell Hall* (1847)

b

2 her sister, **Charlotte**, pen name *Currer Bell*. 1816–55, English novelist, author of *Jane Eyre* (1847), *Villette* (1853), and *The Professor* (1857) **3** her sister, **Emily**, (**Jane**), pen name *Ellis Bell*. 1818–48, English novelist and poet; author of *Wuthering Heights* (1847)

brontosaurus (ˌbrɒntəˈsɔːrəs) *or* **brontosaur** (ˈbrɒntəˌsɔː) *n* any very large herbivorous quadrupedal dinosaur of the genus *Apatosaurus*, common in North America during Jurassic times, having a long neck and long tail: suborder *Sauropoda* (sauropods) [c19: from New Latin, from Greek *brontē* thunder + *sauros* lizard]

Bronx (brɒŋks) *n* the Bronx a borough of New York City, on the mainland, separated from Manhattan by the Harlem River. Pop: 1 363 198 (2003 est)

Bronx cheer *n chiefly US* a loud noise, imitating a fart, made with the lips and tongue and expressing derision or contempt; raspberry

bronze (brɒnz) *n* **1** any hard water-resistant alloy consisting of copper and smaller proportions of tin and sometimes zinc and lead **2** a yellowish-brown colour or pigment **3** a statue, medal, or other object made of bronze **4** short for **bronze medal** ▷ *adj* **5** made of or resembling bronze **6** of a yellowish-brown colour ▷ *vb* **7** (esp of the skin) to make or become brown; tan **8** (*tr*) to give the appearance of bronze to [c18: from French, from Italian *bronzo*, perhaps ultimately from Latin *Brundisium* Brindisi, famed for its bronze] > ˈbronzy *adj*

Bronze Age *n archaeol* **a** a technological stage between the Stone and Iron Ages, beginning in the Middle East about 4500 BC and lasting in Britain from about 2000 to 500 BC, during which weapons and tools were made of bronze and there was intensive trading **b** (*as modifier*): *a Bronze-Age tool*

bronze medal *n* a medal of bronze, awarded to a competitor who comes third in a contest or race

bronze whaler *n* a shark, *Carcharhinus brachyurus*, of southern Australian waters, having a bronze-coloured back

bronzing (ˈbrɒnzɪŋ) *n building trades* **1** blue pigment producing a metallic lustre when ground into paint media at fairly high concentrations **2** the application of a mixture of powdered metal or pigments of a metallic lustre, and a binding medium, such as gold size, to a surface

Bronzino (brɒnˈdziːno) *n* **Il**, real name *Agnolo di Cosimo*. 1503–72, Florentine mannerist painter

brooch (brəʊtʃ) *n* an ornament with a hinged pin and catch, worn fastened to clothing [c13: from Old French *broche*; see BROACH]

brood (bruːd) *n* **1** a number of young animals, esp birds, produced at one hatching **2** all the offspring in one family: often used jokingly or contemptuously **3** a group of a particular kind; breed **4** (*as modifier*) kept for breeding: *a brood mare* ▷ *vb* **5** (of a bird) **a** to sit on or hatch (eggs) **b** (*tr*) to cover (young birds) protectively with the wings **6** (when *intr*, often foll by *on*, *over* or *upon*) to ponder morbidly or persistently [Old English *brōd*; related to Middle High German *bruot*, Dutch *broed*; see BREED] > ˈbrooding *n, adj*

brooder (ˈbruːdə) *n* **1** an enclosure or other structure, usually heated, used for rearing young chickens or other fowl **2** a person or thing that broods

broody (ˈbruːdɪ) *adj* broodier, broodiest **1** moody; meditative; introspective **2** (of poultry) wishing to sit on or hatch eggs **3** *informal* (of a woman) wishing to have a baby of her own > ˈbroodiness *n*

brook¹ (brʊk) *n* a natural freshwater stream smaller than a river [Old English *brōc*; related to Old High German *bruoh* swamp, Dutch *broek*]

brook² (brʊk) *vb* (*tr; usually used with a negative*) to bear; tolerate [Old English *brūcan*; related to Gothic *brūkjan* to use, Old High German *brūhhan*, Latin *fruī* to enjoy]

Brook (brʊk) *n* **Peter** (**Paul Stephen**). born 1925, British stage and film director, noted esp for his experimental work in the theatre

Brooke (brʊk) *n* **1** Alan Francis. See Alanbrooke **2** Sir James. 1803–68, British soldier; first rajah of Sarawak (1841–63) **3** Rupert (Chawner). 1887–1915, British lyric poet, noted for his idealistic war poetry, which made

him a national hero

brooklet (ˈbrʊklɪt) *n* a small brook

brooklime (ˈbrʊkˌlaɪm) *n* either of two blue-flowered scrophulariaceous trailing plants, *Veronica americana* of North America or *V. beccabunga* of Europe and Asia, growing in moist places. See also **speedwell** [c16: variant of C15 brokelemk speedwell, from BROOK¹ + *-lemk*, from Old English *hleomoce*; influenced by *lime*]

Brooklyn (ˈbrʊklɪn) *n* a borough of New York City, on the SW end of Long Island. Pop: 2 465 326 (2000)

Brookner (ˈbrʊknə) *n* **Anita**. born 1928, British writer and art historian. Her novels include *Hotel du Lac* (1984), which won the Booker Prize, *Brief Lives* (1990), and *The Next Big Thing* (2002)

Brooks (brʊks) *n* **1** Geraldine. born 1955, Australian writer. Her novels include *March* (2005), which won the Pulitzer prize **2** Mel, real name *Melvyn Kaminsky*. born 1926, US comedy writer, actor, and film director. His films include *The Producers* (1968), *Blazing Saddles* (1974), *High Anxiety* (1977), and *Dracula: Dead and Loving It* (1996) **3** (Troyal) Garth. born 1962, US country singer and songwriter; his bestselling records include *Ropin' the Wind* (1991) and *Scarecrow* (2001)

Brooks Range (brʊks) *n* a mountain range in N Alaska. Highest peak: Mount Isto, 2761 m (9058 ft)

brook trout *n* a North American freshwater trout, *Salvelinus fontinalis*, introduced in Europe and valued as a food and game fish

broom (bruːm, brʊm) *n* **1** an implement for sweeping consisting of a long handle to which is attached either a brush of straw, bristles, or twigs, bound together, or a solid head into which are set tufts of bristles or fibres **2** any of various yellow-flowered Eurasian leguminous shrubs of the genera *Cytisus*, *Genista*, and *Spartium*, esp *C. scoparius* **3** new broom a newly appointed official, etc, eager to make changes ▷ *vb* **4** (*tr*) to sweep with a broom [Old English *brōm*; related to Old High German *brāmo*, Middle Dutch *bremme*]

broomrape (ˈbruːmˌreɪp, ˈbrʊm-) *n* any orobanchaceous plant of the genus *Orobanche*: brownish small-flowered leafless parasites on the roots of other plants, esp on legumes [c16: adaptation and partial translation of Medieval Latin *rāpum genistae* tuber (hence: root nodule) of Genista (a type of broom plant)]

broomstick (ˈbruːmˌstɪk, ˈbrʊm-) *n* the long handle of a broom

Broonzy (ˈbruːnzɪ) *n* **William Lee Conley**, called *Big Bill*. 1893–1958, US blues singer and guitarist

bros. *or* **Bros.** *abbreviation* brothers

brose (brəʊz) *n Scot* oatmeal or pease porridge, sometimes with butter or fat added [C13 broys, from Old French *broez*, from *breu* broth, of Germanic origin]

bro talk *n* **1** NZ Māori English **2** NZ English spoken with a Māori accent [c20: BRO¹ (sense 1) + TALK]

broth (brɒθ) *n* **1** a soup made by boiling meat, fish, vegetables, etc, in water **2** another name for **stock** (sense 19) [Old English *broth*; related to Old Norse *broth*, Old High German *brod*, German *brodeln* to boil; see BREW]

brothel (ˈbrɒθəl) *n* **1** a house or other place where men pay to have sexual intercourse with prostitutes **2** *Austral informal* any untidy or messy place [c16: short for *brothel-house*, from C14 brothel useless person, from Old English *brēothan* to deteriorate; related to *briethel* worthless]

brother (ˈbrʌðə) *n, pl* brothers *or* (*archaic except when referring to fellow members of a religion, sect, society, etc*) brethren **1** a male person having the same parents as another person **2 a** a male person belonging to the same group, profession, nationality, trade union, etc, as another or others; fellow member **b** (*as modifier*): *brother workers* **3** comrade; friend: used as a form of address **4** *Christianity* a member of a male religious order who undertakes work for the order without actually being in holy orders. Related adjective: **fraternal** [Old English *brōthor*; related to Old Norse *brōthir*, Old High German *bruoder*, Greek *phratēr*, Sanskrit *bhrātar*]

brotherhood (ˈbrʌðəˌhʊd) *n* **1** the state of being related as a brother or brothers **2** an association or fellowship, such as a trade union **3** all persons engaged in a particular profession, trade, etc **4** the belief, feeling, or

b

hope that all people should regard and treat one another as equals

brother-in-law *n, pl* **brothers-in-law 1** the brother of one's wife or husband **2** the husband of one's sister **3** the husband of the sister of one's husband or wife

brotherly ('brʌðəlɪ) *adj* of, resembling, or suitable to a brother, esp in showing loyalty and affection; fraternal > '**brotherliness** *n*

brougham ('bruːəm, bruːm) *n* **1** a four-wheeled horse-drawn closed carriage having a raised open driver's seat in front **2** *obsolete* a large car with an open compartment at the front for the driver **3** *obsolete* an early electric car [C19: named after Henry Peter, Lord Brougham (1778–1868)]

brought (brɔːt) *vb* the past tense and past participle of **bring**

brouhaha ('bruːhɑːhɑː) *n* a loud confused noise; commotion; uproar [French, of imitative origin]

brow (braʊ) *n* **1** the part of the face from the eyes to the hairline; forehead **2** short for **eyebrow 3** the expression of the face; countenance: *a troubled brow* **4** the jutting top of a hill, etc [Old English *brū*; related to Old Norse *brūn* eyebrow, Lithuanian *bruvis*, Greek *ophrus*, Sanskrit *bhrūs*]

browbeat ('braʊˌbiːt) *vb* **-beats, -beating, -beat, -beaten** (*tr*) to discourage or frighten with threats or a domineering manner; intimidate

brown (braʊn) *n* **1** any of various colours, such as those of wood or earth, produced by low intensity light in the wavelength range 620–585 nanometres **2** a dye or pigment producing these colours ▷ *adj* **3** of the colour brown **4** (of bread) made from a flour that has not been bleached or bolted, such as wheatmeal or wholemeal flour **5** deeply tanned or sunburnt ▷ *vb* **6** to make (esp food as a result of cooking) brown or (esp of food) to become brown [Old English *brūn*; related to Old Norse *brūnn*, Old High German *brūn*, Greek *phrunos* toad, Sanskrit *babhru* reddish-brown] > '**brownish** or '**browny** *adj* > '**brownness** *n*

Brown (braʊn) *n* **1** Sir Arthur Whitten ('wɪtan) 1886–1948, British aviator who with J.W. Alcock made the first flight across the Atlantic (1919) **2** Ford Madox. 1821–93, British painter, associated with the Pre-Raphaelite Brotherhood. His paintings include *The Last of England* (1865) and *Work* (1865) **3** George (Alfred), Lord George-Brown. 1914–85, British Labour politician; vice-chairman and deputy leader of the Labour party (1960–70); foreign secretary 1966–68 **4** George Mackay. 1921–96, Scottish poet, novelist, and short-story writer. His works, which include the novels *Greenvoe* (1972) and *Magnus* (1973), reflect the history and culture of Orkney **5** (James) Gordon. born 1951, British Labour politician; Chancellor of the Exchequer (1997–2007); prime minister from 2007 **6** Herbert Charles. 1912–2004, US chemist, who worked on the compounds of boron. Nobel prize for chemistry 1979 **7** James. 1933–2006, US soul singer and songwriter, noted for his dynamic stage performances and for his commitment to Black rights **8** John. 1800–59, US abolitionist leader, hanged after leading an unsuccessful rebellion of slaves at Harper's Ferry, Virginia **9** Lancelot, called *Capability Brown*. 1716–83, British landscape gardener **10** Michael (Stuart). born 1941, US physician: shared the Nobel prize for physiology or medicine (1985) for work on cholesterol **11** Robert. 1773–1858, Scottish botanist who was the first to observe the Brownian movement in fluids

brown bear *n* a large ferocious brownish bear, *Ursus arctos*, inhabiting temperate forests of North America, Europe, and Asia

brown coal *n* a low-quality coal intermediate in grade between peat and lignite

brown dwarf *n* a type of celestial body midway in mass between a large planet and a star

Browne (braʊn) *n* **1** Coral (Edith). 1913–91, Australian actress: married to Vincent Price **2** Hablot Knight. See **Phiz 3** Sir Thomas. 1605–82, English physician and author, noted for his magniloquent prose style. His works include *Religio Medici* (1642) and *Hydriotaphia or Urn Burial* (1658)

browned-off *adj informal* thoroughly discouraged or disheartened; fed up

brown fat *n* tissue composed of a type of fat cell that dissipates as heat most of the energy released when food is oxidized; brown adipose tissue. It is present in hibernating animals and human babies and is thought to be important in adult weight control

brownfield ('braʊnˌfiːld) *n* (*modifier*) denoting or located in an urban area that has previously been built on: *Hampshire has many brownfield developments*

Brownian movement ('braʊnɪən) *n* random movement of microscopic particles suspended in a fluid, caused by bombardment of the particles by molecules of the fluid. First observed in 1827, it provided strong evidence in support of the kinetic theory of molecules [C19: named after Robert Brown (1773–1858), Scottish botanist]

brownie ('braʊnɪ) *n* **1** (in folklore) an elf said to do helpful work at night, esp household chores **2** a small square nutty chocolate cake [C16: diminutive of BROWN (that is, a small brown man)]

Brownie Guide or **Brownie** ('braʊnɪ) *n* a member of the Brownie Guides, one of the junior branches (aged 7–10 years) in The Guide Association

Brownie point *n* a notional mark to one's credit earned for being seen to do the right thing [C20: from the mistaken notion that Brownie Guides earn points for good deeds]

browning ('braʊnɪŋ) *n Brit* a substance used to darken soups, gravies, etc

Browning ('braʊnɪŋ) *n* **1** Elizabeth Barrett. 1806–61, English poet and critic; author of the *Sonnets from the Portuguese* (1850) **2** her husband, Robert. 1812–89, English poet, noted for his dramatic monologues and *The Ring and the Book* (1868–69)

brown paper *n* a coarse unbleached paper used for wrapping

brown rice *n* unpolished rice, in which the grains retain the outer yellowish-brown layer (bran)

Brown Shirt *n* **1** (in Nazi Germany) a storm trooper **2** a member of any fascist party or group

brownstone ('braʊnˌstəʊn) *n US* a reddish-brown iron-rich sandstone used for building

brown sugar *n* sugar that is unrefined or only partially refined

brown toast *n Canadian* toasted wholemeal bread

brown trout *n* a common brownish variety of the trout *Salmo trutta* that occurs in the rivers of N Europe and has been successfully introduced in North America

browse (braʊz) *vb* **1** to look through (a book, articles for sale in a shop, etc) in a casual leisurely manner **2** *computing* to search for and read hypertext, esp on the World Wide Web **3** (of deer, goats, etc) to feed upon (vegetation) by continual nibbling ▷ *n* **4** the act or an instance of browsing **5** the young twigs, shoots, leaves, etc, on which certain animals feed [C15: from French *broust, brost* (modern French *brout*) bud, of Germanic origin; compare Old Saxon *brustian* to bud]

browser ('braʊzə) *n* **1** a person or animal that browses **2** *computing* a software package that enables a user to find and read hypertext files, esp on the World Wide Web

browser skin *n computing* a changeable decorative background for a browser

Broz (*Serbo-Croat* brɔːz) *n* Josip ('jɔsip). original name of Marshal Tito. See **Tito**

Brubeck ('bruːbek) *n* Dave. born 1920, US modern jazz pianist and composer; formed his own quartet in 1951

Bruce[1] (bruːs) *n* **1** James. 1730–94, British explorer, who discovered the source of the Blue Nile (1770) **2** Lenny. 1925–66, US comedian, whose satirical sketches, esp of the sexual attitudes of his contemporaries, brought him prosecutions for obscenity, but are now regarded as full of insight as well as wit **3** Robert the Bruce. See **Robert I 4** Stanley Melbourne, 1st Viscount Bruce of Melbourne. 1883–1967, Australian statesman; prime minister, in coalition with Sir Earle Page's Country Party, of Australia (1923–29)

Bruce[2] (bruːs) *n Brit* a jocular name for an Australian man

brucellosis (ˌbruːsɪˈləʊsɪs) *n* an infectious disease of cattle, goats, dogs, and pigs, caused by bacteria of the genus *Brucella* and transmittable to man (e.g. by drinking contaminated milk): symptoms include fever, chills, and severe headache. Also called: **undulant fever** [C20: from New Latin *Brucella*, named after Sir David Bruce (1855–1931), Australian bacteriologist and physician]

Bruch (*German* brʊx) *n* **Max** (maks). 1838–1920, German composer, noted chiefly for his three violin concertos

Bruckner (*German* ˈbrʊknər) *n* **Anton** (ˈantoːn). 1824–96, Austrian composer and organist in the Romantic tradition. His works include nine symphonies, four masses, and a Te Deum

Brudenell (ˈbruːdənəl) *n* **James Thomas**, the 7th Earl of Cardigan. See **Cardigan¹**

Brueghel, Bruegel *or* **Breughel** (ˈbrɔɪɡəl; *Flemish* ˈbrøːxəl) *n* **1 Jan** (jɑn). 1568–1625, Flemish painter, noted for his detailed still lifes and landscapes **2** his father, **Pieter** (ˈpiːtər), called *the Elder.* ?1525–69, Flemish painter, noted for his landscapes, his satirical paintings of peasant life, and his allegorical biblical scenes **3** his son, **Pieter**, called *the Younger.* ?1564–1637, Flemish painter, noted for his gruesome pictures of hell

Bruges (bruːʒ; *French* bryʒ) *n* a city in NW Belgium, capital of West Flanders province: centre of the medieval European wool and cloth trade. Pop: 117 025 (2004 est)

bruin (ˈbruːɪn) *n* a name for a bear, used in children's tales, fables, etc [C17: from Dutch *bruin* brown, the name of the bear in the epic *Reynard the Fox*]

bruise (bruːz) *vb* (*mainly tr*) **1** (*also intr*) to injure (tissues) without breaking the skin, usually with discoloration, or (of tissues) to be injured in this way **2** to offend or injure (someone's feelings) by an insult, unkindness, etc **3** to damage the surface of (something), as by a blow **4** to crush (food, etc) by pounding or pressing ▷ *n* **5** a bodily injury without a break in the skin, usually with discoloration; contusion [Old English *brȳsan*, of Celtic origin; compare Irish *brúigim* I bruise]

bruiser (ˈbruːzə) *n inf* a strong tough person, esp a boxer or a bully

bruit (bruːt) *vb* **1** (*tr; often passive; usually foll by about*) to report; rumour ▷ *n* **2** *archaic* **a** a rumour **b** a loud outcry; clamour [C15: via French from Medieval Latin *brūgītus*, probably from Vulgar Latin *bragere* (unattested) to yell + Latin *rugīre* to roar]

brumby (ˈbrʌmbɪ) *n, pl* **-bies** *Austral* **1** a wild horse, esp one descended from runaway stock **2** *informal* a wild or unruly person [C19: of unknown origin]

brume (bruːm) *n poetic* heavy mist or fog [C19: from French: mist, winter, from Latin *brūma*, contracted from *brevissima diēs* the shortest day] > ˈbrumous *adj*

Brummagem (ˈbrʌmədʒəm) *n* **1** an informal name for Birmingham **2** (*sometimes not capital*) something that is cheap and flashy, esp imitation jewellery ▷ *adj* **3** (*sometimes not capital*) cheap and gaudy; tawdry [C17: from earlier *Bromcham*, local variant of **BIRMINGHAM**]

Brummell (ˈbrʌməl) *n* **George Bryan**, called *Beau Brummell.* 1778–1840, English dandy: leader of fashion in the Regency period

brunch (brʌntʃ) *n* a meal eaten late in the morning, combining breakfast with lunch [C20: from BR(EAKFAST) + (L)UNCH]

Brundisium (brʌnˈdɪzɪəm) *n* the ancient name for Brindisi

Brunei (bruːˈnaɪ, ˈbruːnaɪ) *n* **1** a sultanate in NW Borneo, consisting of two separate areas on the South China Sea, otherwise bounded by Sarawak: controlled all of Borneo and parts of the Philippines and the Sulu Islands in the 16th century; under British protection since 1888; internally self-governing since 1971; became fully independent in 1984 as a member of the Commonwealth. The economy depends chiefly on oil and natural gas. Official language: Malay; English is also widely spoken. Religion: Muslim. Currency: Brunei dollar. Capital: Bandar Seri Begawan. Pop: 366 000 (2004 est). Area: 5765 sq km (2226 sq miles) **2** the former name of Bandar Seri Begawan

Brunel (bruːˈnɛl) *n* **1 Isambard Kingdom** (ˈɪzəmˌbɑːd). 1806–59, English engineer: designer of the Clifton

Suspension Bridge (1828), many railway lines, tunnels, bridges, etc, and the steamships *Great Western* (1838), *Great Britain* (1845), and *Great Eastern* (1858) **2** his father, Sir **Marc Isambard**. 1769–1849, French engineer in England

Brunelleschi (Italian brunelˈleski) *n* **Filippo** (fiˈlippo). 1377–1446, Italian architect, whose works in Florence include the dome of the cathedral, the Pazzi chapel of Santa Croce, and the church of San Lorenzo

brunette (bruːˈnɛt) *n* **1** a girl or woman with dark brown hair ▷ *adj* Also: **brunet 2** dark brown: *brunette hair* [C17: from French, feminine of *brunet* dark, brownish, from *brun* brown, of Germanic origin; see BROWN]

Brunhild (ˈbrʊnhɪld, -hɪlt) *or* **Brünnhilde** (German brynˈhɪldə) *n* (in the *Nibelungenlied*) a legendary queen won for King Gunther by the magic of Siegfried: corresponds to Brynhild in Norse mythology

Brüning (German ˈbryːnɪŋ) *n* **Heinrich**. (ˈhainrɪç). 1885–1970, German statesman; chancellor (1930–32). He was forced to resign in 1932, making way for the Nazis

Brünn (bryn) *n* the German name for Brno

Bruno (ˈbruːnəʊ) *n* **1 Franklin Roy**, known as *Frank.* born 1961, British heavyweight boxer **2** (*Italian* ˈbruno) **Giordano**. (dʒorˈdano). 1548–1600, Italian philosopher, who developed a pantheistic monistic philosophy: he was burnt at the stake for heresy

Brunswick (ˈbrʌnzwɪk) *n* **1** a former duchy (1635–1918) and state (1918–46) of central Germany, now part of the state of Lower Saxony; formerly (1949–90) part of West Germany **2** a city in central Germany: formerly capital of the duchy and state of Brunswick. Pop: 245 076 (2003 est) ▷ German name: **Braunschweig**

brunt (brʌnt) *n* the main force or shock of a blow, attack, etc (esp in the phrase **bear the brunt of**) [C14: of unknown origin]

Brusa (Turkish ˈbruːsaː) *n* the former name of Bursa

brush¹ (brʌʃ) *n* **1** a device made of bristles, hairs, wires, etc, set into a firm back or handle: used to apply paint, clean or polish surfaces, groom the hair, etc **2** the act or an instance of brushing **3** a light stroke made in passing; graze **4** a brief encounter or contact, esp an unfriendly one; skirmish **5** the bushy tail of a fox, often kept as a trophy after a hunt, or of certain breeds of dog **6** an electric conductor, esp one made of carbon, that conveys current between stationary and rotating parts of a generator, motor, etc ▷ *vb* **7** (*tr*) to clean, polish, scrub, paint, etc, with a brush **8** (*tr*) to apply or remove with a brush or brushing movement **9** (*tr*) to touch lightly and briefly **10** (*intr*) to move so as to graze or touch something lightly ▷ See also **brush aside, brush off, brush up** [C14: from Old French *broisse*, perhaps from *broce* BRUSH²] > ˈbrusher *n*

brush² (brʌʃ) *n* **1** a thick growth of shrubs and small trees; scrub **2** land covered with scrub **3** broken or cut branches or twigs; brushwood **4** wooded sparsely populated country; backwoods [C16 (dense undergrowth), C14 (cuttings of trees): from Old French *broce*, from Vulgar Latin *bruscia* (unattested) brushwood] > ˈbrushy *adj*

brush aside *or* **brush away** *vb* (*tr, adverb*) to dismiss without consideration; disregard

brush discharge *n* a slightly luminous electrical discharge between points of high charge density when the charge density is insufficient to cause a spark or around sharp points on a highly charged conductor because of ionization of air molecules in their vicinity

brushed (brʌʃt) *adj textiles* treated with a brushing process to raise the nap and give a softer, warmer finish: *brushed nylon*

brushmark (ˈbrʌʃˌmɑːk) *n* the indented lines sometimes left by the bristles of a brush on a painted surface

brush off *slang* ▷ *vb* (*tr, adverb*) **1** to dismiss and ignore (a person), esp curtly ▷ *n* **brushoff 2** an abrupt dismissal or rejection

brush-tailed possum *or* **brush-tail possum** *n* any of several widely-distributed Australian possums of the genus *Trichosurus*

brush turkey *n* any of several gallinaceous birds, esp *Alectura lathami*, of New Guinea and Australia, having a black plumage: family *Megapodidae* (megapodes)

brush up *vb* (*adverb*) **1** (*tr*; often foll by *on*) to refresh one's knowledge, skill, or memory of (a subject) **2** to make (a person or oneself) tidy, clean, or neat as after a journey ▷ *n* **brush-up** **3** *Brit* the act or an instance of tidying one's appearance (esp in the phrase **wash and brush-up**)

brushwood ('brʌʃ,wʊd) *n* **1** cut or broken-off tree branches, twigs, etc **2** another word for **brush²** (sense 1)

brushwork ('brʌʃ,wɜːk) *n* **1** a characteristic manner of applying paint with a brush: *that is not Rembrandt's brushwork* **2** work done with a brush

brusque (bruːsk, brʊsk) *adj* blunt or curt in manner or speech [c17: from French, from Italian *brusco* sour, rough, from Medieval Latin *bruscus* butcher's broom] > 'brusquely *adv* > 'brusqueness *or* brusquerie ('bruːskərɪ) *n*

Brussels ('brʌsəlz) *n* the capital of Belgium, in the central part: became capital of Belgium in 1830; seat of the European Commission. Pop: 999 899 (2004 est.) Flemish name: **Brussel** ('brʏsəl) French name: **Bruxelles**

Brussels carpet *n* a worsted carpet with a heavy pile formed by loops of wool on a linen warp

Brussels lace *n* a fine lace with a raised or appliqué design

Brussels sprout *n* **1** a variety of cabbage, *Brassica oleracea gemmifera*, having a stout stem studded with budlike heads of tightly folded leaves, resembling tiny cabbages **2** the head of this plant, eaten as a vegetable

brut (bruːt; *French* bryt) *adj* (of champagne) not sweet; dry [c19: from French raw, rough, from Latin *brūtus* heavy; see BRUTE]

brutal ('bruːt³l) *adj* **1** cruel; vicious; savage **2** extremely honest or coarse in speech or manner **3** harsh; severe; extreme: *brutal cold* > bru'tality *n* > 'brutally *adv*

brutalism ('bruːtə,lɪzəm) *n* an austere style of architecture characterized by emphasis on such structural materials as undressed concrete and unconcealed service pipes. Also called: **new brutalism** > 'brutalist *n, adj*

brutalize *or* **brutalise** ('bruːtə,laɪz) *vb* **1** to make or become brutal **2** (*tr*) to treat brutally > ,brutali'zation *or* ,brutali'sation *n*

brute (bruːt) *n* **1 a** any animal except man; beast; lower animal **b** (*as modifier*): *brute nature* **2** a brutal person ▷ *adj* (*prenominal*) **3** wholly instinctive or physical (esp in the phrases **brute strength, brute force**) **4** without reason or intelligence **5** coarse and grossly sensual [c15: from Latin *brūtus* heavy, irrational; related to *gravis* heavy]

brutish ('bruːtɪʃ) *adj* **1** of, relating to, or resembling a brute or brutes; animal **2** coarse; cruel; stupid > 'brutishly *adv* > 'brutishness *n*

Bruton ('bruːt³n) *n* **John Gerard**. born 1947, Irish politician: leader of the Fine Gael party (1990–2001); prime minister of the Republic of Ireland (1994–97)

Brutus ('bruːtəs) *n* **1 Lucius Junius** ('luːʃəs 'dʒuːnɪəs). late 6th century BC, Roman statesman who ousted the tyrant Tarquin (509) and helped found the Roman republic **2 Marcus Junius** ('mɑːkəs 'dʒuːnɪəs) ?85–42 BC, Roman statesman who, with Cassius, led the conspiracy to assassinate Caesar (44): committed suicide after being defeated by Antony and Octavian (Augustus) at Philippi (42)

Bruxelles (brysɛl) *n* the French name for **Brussels**

Bryansk (brɪ'ænsk; *Russian* brjansk) *n* a city in W Russia. Pop: 428 000 (2005 est)

Bryant ('braɪənt) *n* **David**. born 1931, British bowler; many times world champion

Brynhild ('brɪnhɪld) *n Norse myth* a Valkyrie won as the wife of Gunnar by Sigurd who wakes her from an enchanted sleep: corresponds to Brunhild in the *Nibelungenlied*

bryology (braɪ'ɒlədʒɪ) *n* the branch of botany concerned with the study of bryophytes > bryological (,braɪə'lɒdʒɪk³l) *adj* > bry'ologist *n*

bryony *or* **briony** ('braɪənɪ) *n, pl* -nies any of several herbaceous climbing plants of the cucurbitaceous genus *Bryonia*, of Europe and N Africa [Old English *bryōnia*, from Latin, from Greek *bruōnia*]

bryophyte ('braɪə,faɪt) *n* any plant of the phyla *Bryophyta* (mosses), *Hepatophyta* (liverworts), or *Anthocerophyta* (hornworts), having stems and leaves but lacking true vascular tissue and roots and reproducing by spores [c19: New Latin, from Greek *bruon* moss + -PHYTE] > bryophytic (,braɪə'fɪtɪk) *adj*

bryozoan (,braɪə'zəʊən) *n* any aquatic invertebrate animal of the phylum *Bryozoa*, forming colonies of polyps each having a ciliated feeding organ (lophophore) [c19: from Greek *bruon* moss + *zōion* animal]

Brythonic (brɪ'θɒnɪk) *n* **1** the S group of Celtic languages, consisting of Welsh, Cornish, and Breton ▷ *adj* **2** of, relating to, or characteristic of this group of languages ▷ Also called: **Brittonic**

Brześć nad Bugiem (bʒɛʃtʃ nad 'bugjɛm) *n* the Polish name for **Brest** (sense 2)

BS *abbreviation* British Standard(s) (indicating the catalogue or publication number of the British Standards Institution)

B.S. *abbreviation* (in the US and Canada) Bachelor of Science

B-sample *n* a urine or blood sample used in doping tests in professional sports to confirm or invalidate the presence of banned substances in the first sample, the A-sample

BSc *abbreviation* Bachelor of Science

BSC *abbreviation* (in Britain) Broadcasting Standards Commission

BSE *abbreviation* bovine spongiform encephalopathy: a fatal slow-developing disease of cattle, affecting the nervous system. It is caused by a prion protein and is thought to be transmissable to humans, causing a variant form of Creutzfeldt-Jakob disease. Also called: *informal* mad cow disease

BSI *abbreviation* British Standards Institution

B-side *n* the less important side of a gramophone record

BSJA *abbreviation* (in Britain) British Show Jumping Association

BSL *abbreviation* British Sign Language

BST *abbreviation* **1** bovine somatotrophin: a growth hormone that can be used to increase milk production in dairy cattle **2** British Summer Time

Bt *abbreviation* Baronet

BT *abbreviation* British Telecom [c20: shortened from TELECOMMUNICATIONS]

BTEC ('bɪ,tɛk) *n acronym for* (in Britain) **1** Business and Technology Council **2** a certificate or diploma in a vocational subject awarded by this body

btu *or* **BThU** *abbreviation* British thermal unit

bubal ('bjuːb³l) *or* **bubalis** ('bjuːbəlɪs) *n* any of various antelopes, esp an extinct N African variety of hartebeest [c15: from Latin *būbalus* African gazelle, from Greek *boubalos*, from Greek *bous* ox]

bubble ('bʌb³l) *n* **1 a** a thin film of liquid forming a hollow globule around air or a gas: *a soap bubble* **2** a small globule of air or a gas in a liquid or a solid, as in carbonated drinks, glass, etc **3** the sound made by a bubbling liquid **4** something lacking substance, stability, or seriousness **5** an unreliable scheme or enterprise **6** a dome, esp a transparent glass or plastic one ▷ *vb* **7** to form or cause to form bubbles **8** (*intr*) to move or flow with a gurgling sound **9** (*intr*; often foll by *over*) to overflow (with excitement, anger, etc) [c14: probably of Scandinavian origin; compare Swedish *bubbla*, Danish *boble*, Dutch *bobbel*, all of imitative origin]

bubble and squeak *n* (in Britain and Australia) a dish of leftover boiled cabbage, potatoes, and sometimes cooked meat fried together [c18: so called from the sounds of this dish cooking]

bubble bath *n* **1** a powder, liquid, or crystals used to scent, soften, and foam in bath water **2** a bath to which such a substance has been added

bubble car *n* (in Britain, formerly) a small car, often having three wheels, with a transparent bubble-shaped top

bubble chamber *n* a device that enables the tracks of ionizing particles to be photographed as a row of bubbles in a superheated liquid. Immediately before the particles enter the chamber the pressure is reduced so that the ionized particles act as centres for small vapour bubbles

bubble gum *n* a type of chewing gum that can be blown into large bubbles

bubble-jet printer *n computing* an ink-jet printer that heats the ink before printing

bubble memory *n computing* a method of storing high volumes of data by the use of minute pockets of magnetism (bubbles) in a semiconducting material: the bubbles may be caused to migrate past a read head or to a buffer area for storage

bubble point *n chem* the temperature at which bubbles just start to appear in a heated liquid mixture

bubble tea *n* a cold drink, originally from Taiwan, of tea infused with fruit flavouring, shaken to produce bubbles, and served over tapioca pearls in a clear cup. It is usually drunk through a very wide straw

bubble wrap *n* a type of polythene wrapping containing many small air pockets, used as a protective covering when transporting breakable goods

bubbly ('bʌblɪ) *adj* **-blier, -bliest 1** full of or resembling bubbles **2** lively; animated; excited ▷ *n* **3** an informal name for **champagne**

Buber ('buːbə) *n* **Martin**. 1878–1965, Jewish theologian, existentialist philosopher, and scholar of Hasidism, born in Austria, whose works include *I and Thou* (1923), *Between Man and Man* (1946), and *Eclipse of God* (1952)

bubo ('bjuːbəʊ) *n, pl* **-boes** *pathol* inflammation and swelling of a lymph node, often with the formation of pus, esp in the region of the armpit or groin [C14: from Medieval Latin *bubō* swelling, from Greek *boubōn* groin, glandular swelling] > **bubonic** (bjuːˈbɒnɪk) *adj*

bubonic plague *n* an acute infectious febrile disease characterized by chills, prostration, delirium, and formation of buboes: caused by the bite of a rat flea infected with the bacterium *Yersinia pestis*

Bucaramanga (*Spanish* bukara'manga) *n* a city in N central Colombia, in the Cordillera Oriental: centre of a district growing coffee, tobacco, and cotton. Pop: 1 069 000 (2005 est)

buccal ('bʌkəl) *adj* **1** of or relating to the cheek **2** of or relating to the mouth; oral [C19: from Latin *bucca* cheek]

buccaneer (ˌbʌkəˈnɪə) *n* **1** a pirate, esp one who preyed on the Spanish colonies and shipping in America and the Caribbean in the 17th and 18th centuries ▷ *vb* (*intr*) **2** to be or act like a buccaneer [C17: from French *boucanier*, from *boucaner* to smoke meat, from Old French *boucan* frame for smoking meat, of Tupian origin; originally applied to French and English hunters of wild oxen in the Caribbean]

buccinator ('bʌksɪˌneɪtə) *n* a thin muscle that compresses the cheeks and holds them against the teeth during chewing, etc [C17: from Latin, from *buccināre* to sound the trumpet, from *buccina* trumpet]

Buchan ('bʌkən) *n* **John**, 1st Baron Tweedsmuir. 1875–1940, Scottish statesman, historian, and writer of adventure stories, esp *The Thirty-Nine Steps* (1915) and *Greenmantle* (1916); governor general of Canada (1935–40)

Buchanan (bjuːˈkænən) *n* **1 George**. 1506–82, Scottish historian, who was tutor to Mary, Queen of Scots and James VI; author of *History of Scotland* (1582) **2 James**. 1791–1868, 15th president of the US (1857–61)

Bucharest (ˌbuːkəˈrɛst, ˌbjuː-) *n* the capital of Romania, in the southeast. Pop: 1 764 000 (2005 est). Romanian name: **Bucureşti**

Buchenwald (*German* 'buːxənvalt) *n* a village in E central Germany, near Weimar; site of a Nazi concentration camp (1937–45)

Buchner (*German* 'buːxnər) *n* **Eduard** ('eːduart). 1860–1917, German chemist who demonstrated that alcoholic fermentation is due to enzymes in the yeast: Nobel prize for chemistry 1907

Büchner (*German* 'byːçnər) *n* **Georg** ('geːɔrk). 1813–37, German dramatist; regarded as a forerunner of the Expressionists: author of *Danton's Death* (1835) and *Woyzeck* (1837)

buck¹ (bʌk) *n* **1 a** the male of various animals including the goat, hare, kangaroo, rabbit, and reindeer **b** (*as modifier*): *a buck antelope* **2** *South African* an antelope or deer of either sex **3** *archaic* a robust spirited young man **4** the act of bucking ▷ *vb* **5** (*intr*) (of a horse or other animal) to jump vertically, with legs stiff and back arched **6** (*tr*) (of a horse, etc) to throw (its rider) by bucking **7** (when *intr*, often foll by *against*) *informal, chiefly US & Canadian* to resist or oppose obstinately **8** (*tr; usually passive*) *informal* to cheer or encourage: *I was very bucked at passing the exam* ▷ See also **buck up** [Old English *bucca* he-goat; related to Old Norse *bukkr*, Old High German *bock*, Old Irish *bocc*] > **'bucker** *n*

buck² (bʌk) *n* **1** *US, Canadian & Austral informal* a dollar **2** *South African informal* a rand [C19: of obscure origin]

buck³ (bʌk) *n* **1** *poker* a marker in the jackpot to remind the winner of some obligation when his turn comes to deal **2 pass the buck** *informal* to shift blame or responsibility onto another [C19: probably from *buckhorn knife*, placed before a player in poker to indicate that he was the next dealer]

Buck (bʌk) *n* **Pearl S**(ydenstricker). 1892–1973, US novelist, noted particularly for her novel of Chinese life *The Good Earth* (1931): Nobel prize for literature 1938

buckbean ('bʌkˌbiːn) *n* a marsh plant, *Menyanthes trifoliata*, with white or pink flowers: family *Menyanthaceae*. Also called: **bogbean**

buckboard ('bʌkˌbɔːd) *n* *US & Canadian* an open four-wheeled horse-drawn carriage with the seat attached to a flexible board between the front and rear axles

bucket ('bʌkɪt) *n* **1** an open-topped roughly cylindrical container; pail **2** Also called: **bucketful** the amount a bucket will hold **3** any of various bucket-like parts of a machine, such as the scoop on a mechanical shovel **4** *chiefly US* a turbine rotor blade **5** *Austral & NZ* an ice cream container **6 kick the bucket** *slang* to die ▷ *vb* **-kets, -keting, -keted 7** (*tr*) to carry in or put into a bucket **8** (*intr*; often foll by *down*) (of rain) to fall very heavily **9** (*intr*; often foll by *along*) *chiefly Brit* to travel or drive fast **10** (*tr*) *Austral slang* to criticize severely [C13: from Anglo-French *buket*, from Old English *būc*; compare Old High German *būh* belly, German *Bauch* belly]

bucket seat *n* a seat in a car, aircraft, etc, having curved sides that partially enclose and support the body

bucket shop *n* **1** an unregistered firm of stockbrokers that engages in speculation with clients' funds **2** *chiefly Brit* any small business that cannot be relied upon, esp one selling cheap airline tickets

buckeye ('bʌkˌaɪ) *n* any of several North American trees of the genus *Aesculus*, esp *A. glabra* (Ohio buckeye), having erect clusters of white or red flowers and prickly fruits: family *Hippocastanaceae*

buckhorn ('bʌkˌhɔːn) *n* **a** a horn from a buck, used for knife handles, etc **b** (*as modifier*): *a buckhorn knife*

Buckingham¹ ('bʌkɪŋəm) *n* a town in S central England, in Buckinghamshire; university (1975). Pop: 12 512 (2001)

Buckingham² ('bʌkɪŋəm) *n* **1 George Villiers, 1st Duke of**. 1592–1628, English courtier and statesman; favourite of James I and Charles I: his arrogance, military incompetence, and greed increased the tensions between the King and Parliament that eventually led to the Civil War **2** his son, **George Villiers, 2nd Duke of**. 1628–87, English courtier and writer; chief minister of Charles II and member of the Cabal (1667–73)

Buckingham Palace *n* the London residence of the British sovereign: built in 1703, rebuilt by John Nash in 1821–36 and partially redesigned in the early 20th century

Buckinghamshire ('bʌkɪŋəmˌʃɪə, -ʃə) *n* a county in SE central England, containing the Vale of Aylesbury and parts of the Chiltern Hills: the geographic and ceremonial county includes Milton Keynes, which became an independent unitary authority in 1997. Administrative centre: Aylesbury. Pop (excluding Milton Keynes): 478 000 (2003 est). Area (excluding Milton Keynes): 1568 sq km (605 sq miles). Abbreviation: **Bucks**

buckjumper ('bʌkˌdʒʌmpə) *n* *Austral* an untamed horse

Buckland ('bʌklənd) *n* **William**. 1784–1856, English geologist; he became a proponent of the idea of catastrophic ice ages

buckle ('bʌkəl) *n* **1** a clasp for fastening together two loose ends, esp of a belt or strap, usually consisting of a frame with an attached movable prong **2** an ornamental representation of a buckle, as on a shoe **3** a

b

kink, bulge, or other distortion: *a buckle in a railway track* ▷ *vb* **4** to fasten or be fastened with a buckle **5** to bend or cause to bend out of shape, esp as a result of pressure or heat [c14: from Old French *bocle*, from Latin *buccula* a little cheek, hence, cheek strap of a helmet, from *bucca* cheek]

buckle down *vb* (*intr, adverb*) *informal* to apply oneself with determination

buckler ('bʌklə) *n* **1** a small round shield worn on the forearm or held by a short handle **2** a means of protection; defence [c13: from Old French *bocler*, from *bocle* shield boss; see BUCKLE, BOSS²]

Buckley's chance ('bʌklɪz) *n* *Austral & NZ slang* no chance at all [c19: of obscure origin]

buckminsterfullerene (,bʌkmɪnstə'fʊlə,ri:n) *n* a form of carbon that contains molecules having 60 carbon atoms arranged at the vertices of a polyhedron with hexagonal and pentagonal faces. It is produced in carbon arcs and occurs naturally in small amounts in certain minerals. Also called: fullerene [c20: named after (Richard) *Buckminster Fuller* (1895–1983), US architect and engineer]

bucko ('bʌkəʊ) *n*, *pl* -oes *Irish* a lively young fellow: often a term of address

buckram ('bʌkrəm) *n* **a** cotton or linen cloth stiffened with size, etc, used in lining or stiffening clothes, bookbinding, etc **b** (*as modifier*): *a buckram cover* [c14: from Old French *boquerant*, from Old Provençal *bocaran*, ultimately from BUKHARA, once an important source of textiles]

Bucks (bʌks) *abbreviation* Buckinghamshire

buckshee (,bʌk'ʃi:) *adj* *Brit slang* without charge; free [c20: from BAKSHEESH]

buckshot ('bʌkˌʃɒt) *n* lead shot of large size used in shotgun shells, esp for hunting game [c15 (original sense: the distance at which a buck can be shot)]

buckskin ('bʌkˌskɪn) *n* **1** the skin of a male deer **2 a** a strong greyish-yellow suede leather, originally made from deerskin but now usually made from sheepskin **b** (*as modifier*): *buckskin boots* **3** a stiffly starched cotton cloth **4** a strong satin-woven woollen fabric

buckthorn ('bʌkˌθɔːn) *n* any of several thorny small-flowered shrubs of the genus *Rhamnus*, esp the Eurasian species *R. cathartica*, whose berries were formerly used as a purgative: family *Rhamnaceae* [c16: from BUCK¹ (from the spiny branches, imagined as resembling antlers) + THORN]

bucktooth ('bʌkˌtu:θ) *n*, *pl* -teeth *derogatory* a projecting upper front tooth [c18: from BUCK¹ (deer) + TOOTH]

buck up *vb* (*adverb*) *informal* **1** to make or cause to make haste **2** to make or become more cheerful, confident, etc

buckwheat ('bʌkˌwi:t) *n* **1** any of several polygonaceous plants of the genus *Fagopyrum*, esp *F. esculentum*, which has fragrant white flowers and is cultivated, esp in the US, for its seeds **2** the edible seeds of this plant, ground into flour or used as animal fodder **3** the flour obtained from these seeds [c16: from Middle Dutch *boecweite*, from *boeke* BEECH + *weite* WHEAT, from the resemblance of their seeds to beechnuts]

buckyball ('bʌkɪˌbɔ:l) *n* *informal* a ball-like polyhedral carbon molecule of the type found in buckminsterfullerene and other fullerenes

buckytube ('bʌkɪˌtju:b) *n* *informal* a tube of carbon atoms structurally similar to buckminsterfullerene

bucolic (bju:'kɒlɪk) *adj* *Also*: bucolical **1** of or characteristic of the countryside or country life; rustic **2** of or relating to shepherds; pastoral ▷ *n* **3** (*sometimes plural*) a pastoral poem, often in the form of a dialogue [c16: from Latin *būcolicus*, from Greek *boukolikos*, from *boukolos* cowherd, from *bous* ox] ▷ bu'colically *adv*

Bucovina (,bu:kə'vi:nə) *n* a variant spelling of **Bukovina**

Bucureşti (buku'reʃtj) *n* the Romanian name for **Bucharest**

bud (bʌd) *n* **1** a swelling on a plant stem consisting of overlapping immature leaves or petals **2 a** a partially opened flower **b** (*in combination*): *rosebud* **3** any small budlike outgrowth: *taste buds* **4** something small or immature **5** an asexually produced outgrowth in simple organisms, such as yeasts, and the hydra that develops into a new individual **6** nip in the bud to put an end to

(an idea, movement, etc) in its initial stages ▷ *vb* buds, budding, budded **7** (*intr*) (of plants and some animals) to produce buds **8** (*intr*) to begin to develop or grow **9** (*tr*) *horticulture* to graft (a bud) from one plant onto another, usually by insertion under the bark [c14 *budde*, of Germanic origin; compare Icelandic *budda* purse, Dutch *buidel*]

Budapest (,bju:də'pest; *Hungarian* 'budɔpeʃt) *n* the capital of Hungary, on the River Danube: formed in 1873 from the towns of Buda and Pest. Traditionally Buda, the old Magyar capital, was the administrative and Pest the trade centre: suffered severely in the Russian siege of 1945 and in the unsuccessful revolt against the Communist regime (1956). Pop: 1 719 342 (2003 est)

Buddha ('bʊdə) *n* the Buddha ?563–483 BC, a title applied to Gautama Siddhartha, a nobleman and religious teacher of N India, regarded by his followers as the most recent rediscoverer of the path to enlightenment: the founder of Buddhism

Buddh Gaya ('bʊd gə'jɑ:), **Buddha Gaya** *or* **Bodh Gaya** *n* a town in NE India, in Bihar: site of the sacred bo tree under which Gautama Siddhartha attained enlightenment and became the Buddha; pilgrimage centre. Pop: 30 883 (2001)

Buddhism ('bʊdɪzəm) *n* a religious teaching propagated by the Buddha and his followers, which declares that by destroying greed, hatred, and delusion, which are the causes of all suffering, man can attain perfect enlightenment > 'Buddhist *n, adj*

buddleia ('bʌdlɪə) *n* any ornamental shrub of the genus *Buddleia*, esp *B. davidii*, which has long spikes of mauve flowers and is frequently visited by butterflies: family *Buddleiaceae*. Also called: butterfly bush [c19: named after A. *Buddle* (died 1715), British botanist]

buddy ('bʌdɪ) *n*, *pl* -dies **1** *chiefly US & Canadian* Also called (as a term of address): bud, an informal word for **friend** **2** a volunteer who visits and gives help and support to a person suffering from AIDS ▷ *vb* -dying, -died **3** (*intr*) to act as a buddy to a person suffering from AIDS [c19: probably a baby-talk variant (US) of BROTHER]

buddy-buddy *adj* *informal, chiefly US* on friendly or intimate terms

buddy movie *or* **buddy film** *n* a genre of film dealing with the relationship and adventures of two friends

budge (bʌdʒ) *vb* (*usually used with a negative*) **1** to move, however slightly **2** to change or cause to change opinions, etc [c16: from Old French *bouger*, from Vulgar Latin *bullicāre* (unattested) to bubble, from Latin *bullīre* to boil, from *bulla* bubble]

Budge (bʌdʒ) *n* **Don(ald)**. 1915–2000, US tennis player, the first man to win the Grand Slam of singles championships (Australia, France, Wimbledon, and the US) in one year (1938)

budgerigar ('bʌdʒərɪˌgɑ:) *n* a small green Australian parrot, *Melopsittacus undulatus*: a popular cagebird that is bred in many different coloured varieties [c19: from a native Australian language]

budget ('bʌdʒɪt) *n* **1** an itemized summary of expected income and expenditure of a country, company, etc, over a specified period, usually a financial year **2** (*modifier*) economical; inexpensive: *budget meals for a family* **3** the total amount of money allocated for a specific purpose during a specified period ▷ *vb* -gets, -geting, -geted **4** (*tr*) to enter or provide for in a budget **5** to plan the expenditure of (money, time, etc) **6** (*intr*) to make a budget [c15 (meaning: leather pouch, wallet): from Old French *bougette*, diminutive of *bouge*, from Latin *bulga*, of Gaulish origin; compare Old English *bælg* bag] > 'budgetary *adj*

Budget ('bʌdʒɪt) *n* the Budget an estimate of British government expenditures and revenues and the financial plans for the ensuing fiscal year presented annually to the House of Commons by the Chancellor of the Exchequer

budget account *n* **1** an account with a department store, etc, enabling a customer to make monthly payments to cover his past and future purchases **2** a bank account for paying household bills, being credited with regular or equal monthly payments from the customer's current account

budget deficit *n* the amount by which government expenditure exceeds income from taxation, customs duties, etc, in any one fiscal year

budgie ('bʌdʒɪ) *n informal* short for **budgerigar**

Buenaventura (*Spanish* bwenaβen'tura) *n* a major port in W Colombia, on the Pacific coast. Pop: 250 000 (2005 est)

Buena Vista (*Spanish* 'bwena 'vista) *n* a village in NE Mexico, near Saltillo: site of the defeat of the Mexicans by US forces (1847)

Buenos Aires ('bweɪnɒs 'aɪrɪz; *Spanish* 'bwenos 'aires) *n* the capital of Argentina, a major port and industrial city on the Río de la Plata estuary: became capital in 1880; university (1821). Pop: 13 349 000 (2005 est)

buff¹ (bʌf) *n* **1 a** a soft thick flexible undyed leather made chiefly from the skins of buffalo, oxen, and elk **b** (*as modifier*): *a buff coat* **2 a** a dull yellow or yellowish-brown colour **b** (*as adjective*): *buff paint* **3** Also called: **buffer a** a cloth or pad of material used for polishing an object **b** a flexible disc or wheel impregnated with a fine abrasive for polishing metals, etc, with a power tool **4** *informal* one's bare skin (esp in the phrase **in the buff**) ▷ *vb* **5** to clean or polish (a metal, floor, shoes, etc) with a buff **6** to remove the grain surface of (a leather) [c16: from Old French *buffle*, from Old Italian *bufalo*, from Late Latin *būfalus* BUFFALO]

buff² (bʌf) *n archaic* a blow or buffet (now only in the phrase **blind man's buff**) [c15: back formation from BUFFET²]

buff³ (bʌf) *n informal* an expert on or devotee of a given subject [c20: originally US: an enthusiastic fire watcher, from the buff-coloured uniforms worn by volunteer firemen in New York City]

buffalo ('bʌfə,ləʊ) *n, pl* **-loes** or **-lo** **1** Also called: **Cape buffalo** a member of the cattle tribe, *Syncerus caffer*, mostly found in game reserves in southern and eastern Africa and having upward-curving horns **2** short for **water buffalo** [c16: from Italian *bufalo*, from Late Latin *būfalus*, alteration of Latin *būbalus*; see BUBAL]

Buffalo ('bʌfə,ləʊ) *n* a port in W New York State, at the E end of Lake Erie. Pop: 285 018 (2003 est)

Buffalo Bill *n* nickname of William Frederick Cody. 1846–1917, US showman who toured Europe and the US with his famous *Wild West Show*

buffalo grass *n* **1** a short grass, *Buchloë dactyloides*, growing on the dry plains of the central US **2** *Austral* a grass, *Stenotaphrum americanum*, introduced from North America

buffel grass ('bʌfəl) *n Austral* a pasture grass, *Cenchrus ciliaris*, native to Africa and India, introduced in N Australia

buffer¹ ('bʌfə) *n* **1** one of a pair of spring-loaded steel pads attached at both ends of railway vehicles and at the end of a railway track to reduce shock due to contact **2** a person or thing that lessens shock or protects from damaging impact, circumstances, etc **3** *chem* **a** an ionic compound, usually a salt of a weak acid or base, added to a solution to resist changes in its acidity or alkalinity and thus stabilize its pH **b** Also called: **buffer solution** a solution containing such a compound **4** *computing* a memory device for temporarily storing data ▷ *vb* (*tr*) **5** to insulate against or protect from shock; cushion **6** *chem* to add a buffer to (a solution) [c19: from BUFF²]

buffer² ('bʌfə) *n* **1** any device used to shine, polish, etc; buff **2** a person who uses such a device

buffer³ ('bʌfə) *n Brit informal, offensive* a stupid or bumbling man (esp in the phrase **old buffer**) [c18: perhaps from Middle English *buffer* stammerer]

buffer state *n* a small neutral state between two rival powers

buffer stock *n commerce* a stock of a commodity built up by a government or trade organization with the object of using it to stabilize prices

buffet¹ *n* **1** ('bʊfeɪ) **a** a counter where light refreshments are served **2** ('bʊfeɪ) **a** a meal at which guests help themselves from a number of dishes and often eat standing up **b** (*as modifier*): *a buffet lunch* **3** ('bʌfɪt, 'bʊfeɪ) a piece of furniture used from medieval times to the 18th

century for displaying plates, etc and typically comprising one or more cupboards and some open shelves [c18: from French, of unknown origin]

buffet² ('bʌfɪt) *vb* **-fets, -feting, -feted** **1** (*tr*) to knock against or about; batter **2** (*tr*) to hit, esp with the fist; cuff **3** to force (one's way), as through a crowd **4** (*intr*) to struggle; battle ▷ *n* **5** a blow, esp with a fist or hand **6** aerodynamic excitation of an aircraft structure by separated flows [c13: from Old French *buffeter*, from *buffet* a light blow, from *buffe*, of imitative origin]

Buffet (*French* byfɛ) *n* **Bernard** (bɛrnar). 1928–99, French painter and engraver. His works are characterized by sombre tones and thin angular forms

buffet car ('bʊfeɪ) *n Brit* a railway coach where light refreshments are served

buffeting ('bʌfɪtɪŋ) *n* response of an aircraft structure to buffet, esp an irregular oscillation of the tail

bufflehead ('bʌfʰl,hɛd) *n* a small North American diving duck, *Bucephala* (or *Glaucionetta*) *albeola*: the male has black-and-white plumage and a fluffy head [c17 *buffle* from obsolete *buffle* wild ox (see BUFF¹), referring to the duck's head]

buffo ('bʊfəʊ; *Italian* 'buffo) *n, pl* **-fi** (-fɪ) *or* **-fos** **1** (in Italian opera of the 18th century) a comic part, esp one for a bass **2** Also called: **buffo bass, basso buffo** (*Italian* 'basso 'buffo) a bass singer who performs such a part [c18: from Italian (adj): comic, from *buffo* (n) BUFFOON]

Buffon (*French* byfɔ̃) *n* **Georges Louis Leclerc** (ʒɔrʒ lwi ləklɛr), **Comte de**. 1707–88, French encyclopedist of natural history; principal author of *Histoire naturelle* (36 vols., 1749–89), containing the *Époques de la nature* (1777), which foreshadowed later theories of evolution

buffoon (bə'fuːn) *n* **1** a person who amuses others by ridiculous or odd behaviour, jokes, etc **2** a foolish person [c16: from French *bouffon*, from Italian *buffone*, from Medieval Latin *būfō*, from Latin: toad] ▷ **buffoonery** *n*

bufotalin (,buː'fəʊ'tælɪn) *n* the principal poisonous substance in the skin and saliva of the common European toad

bug (bʌg) *n* **1** any insect of the order *Hemiptera*, esp any of the suborder *Heteroptera*, having piercing and sucking mouthparts specialized as a beak (rostrum) **2** *chiefly US & Canadian* any insect, such as the June bug or the Croton bug **3** *informal* **a** a microorganism, esp a bacterium, that produces disease **b** a disease, esp a stomach infection, caused by a microorganism **4** *informal* an obsessive idea, hobby, etc; craze (esp in the phrases **get the bug, be bitten by the bug, the bug bites**, etc) **5** *informal* a person having such a craze; enthusiast **6** (*often plural*) *informal* an error or fault, as in a machine or system, esp in a computer or computer program **7** *informal* a concealed microphone used for recording conversations, as in spying ▷ *vb* **bugs, bugging, bugged** *informal* **8** (*tr*) to irritate; bother **9** (*tr*) to conceal a microphone in (a room, etc) **10** (*intr*) *US* (of eyes) to protrude [c16: of uncertain origin; perhaps related to Old English *budda* beetle]

Bug (*Russian* buk) *n* **1** Also called: **Southern Bug** a river in E Europe, rising in W Ukraine and flowing southeast to the Dnieper estuary and the Black Sea. Length: 853 km (530 miles) **2** Also called: **Western Bug** a river in E Europe, rising in SW Ukraine and flowing northwest to the River Vistula in Poland, forming part of the border between Poland and Ukraine. Length: 724 km (450 miles)

bugaboo ('bʌgə,buː) *n, pl* **-boos** an imaginary source of fear; bugbear; bogey [c18: probably of Celtic origin; compare Cornish *buccaboo* the devil]

Buganda (bʊ'gændə) *n* a region of Uganda: a powerful Bantu kingdom from the 17th century

Bugatti (*Italian* bʊ'gatti) *n* **Ettore** (**Arco Isidoro**) ('ɛttore). 1881–1947, Italian car manufacturer; founder of the Bugatti car factory at Molsheim (1909)

bugbear ('bʌg,bɛə) *n* **1** a thing that causes obsessive fear or anxiety **2** (in English folklore) a goblin said to eat naughty children and thought to be in the form of a bear [c16: from BUG + BEAR²; compare BUGABOO]

bugger ('bʌgə) *n* **1** a person who practises buggery **2** *slang* a person or thing considered to be contemptible, unpleasant, or difficult **3** *slang* a humorous or affectionate term for a man or child: *a silly old bugger; a friendly little bugger* **4** bugger all *slang* nothing ▷ *vb* **5** to practise buggery (with) **6** (*tr*) *slang, chiefly Brit* to ruin, complicate, or frustrate **7** *slang* to tire; weary ▷ *interj* **8** *slang* an exclamation of annoyance or disappointment [c16: from Old French *bougre*, from Medieval Latin *Bulgarus* Bulgarian; from the condemnation of the dualist heresy rife in Bulgaria from the tenth century to the fifteenth]

bugger about *or* **bugger around** *vb* (*adverb*) *Brit slang* **1** (*intr*) to fool about and waste time **2** (*tr*) to create difficulties or complications for (a person)

bugger off *vb* (*intr, adverb*) *Brit slang* to go away; depart

buggery ('bʌɡərɪ) *n* anal intercourse between a man and another man, a woman, or an animal

buggy¹ ('bʌɡɪ) *n, pl* -gies **1** a light horse-drawn carriage having either four wheels (esp in the US and Canada) or two wheels (esp in Britain and India) **2** short for **Baby Buggy** **3** a small motorized vehicle designed for a particular purpose: *golf buggy; moon buggy* [c18: of unknown origin]

buggy² ('bʌɡɪ) *adj* -gier, -giest **1** infested with bugs **2** *informal* (of a system or machine, esp a computer program) containing errors or faults

bugle¹ ('bju:ɡəl) *n* **1** *music* a brass instrument similar to the cornet but usually without valves: used for military fanfares, signal calls, etc ▷ *vb* **2** (*intr*) to play or sound (on) a bugle [c14: short for *bugle horn* ox horn (musical instrument), from Old French *bugle*, from Latin *būculus* young bullock, from *bōs* ox] ▷ '**bugler** *n*

bugle² ('bju:ɡəl) *n* any of several Eurasian plants of the genus *Ajuga*, esp *A. reptans*, having small blue or white flowers: family *Lamiaceae* (labiates) [c13: from Late Latin *bugula*, of uncertain origin]

bugle³ ('bju:ɡəl) *n* a tubular glass or plastic bead sewn onto clothes for decoration [c16: of unknown origin]

bugloss ('bju:ɡlɒs) *n* any of various hairy Eurasian boraginaceous plants of the genera *Anchusa*, *Lycopsis*, and *Echium*, esp *L. arvensis*, having clusters of blue flowers [c15: from Latin *būglōssa*, from Greek *bouglōssos* ox-tongued, from *bōs* ox + *glōssa* tongue]

bugong ('bu:ɡɒŋ) *n* another name for **bogong**

buhl (bu:l) *adj, n* the usual US spelling of **boulle**

build (bɪld) *vb* builds, building, built **1** to make, construct, or form by joining parts or materials: *to build a house* **2** (*tr*) to order the building of: *the government builds most of our hospitals* **3** (foll by *on* or *upon*) to base; found: *his theory was not built on facts* **4** (*tr*) to establish and develop: *it took ten years to build a business* **5** (*tr*) to make in a particular way or for a particular purpose: *the car was not built for speed* **6** (*intr*; often foll by *up*) to increase in intensity ▷ *n* **7** physical form, figure, or proportions: *a man with an athletic build* [Old English *byldan*; related to *bylda* farmer, *bold* building, Old Norse *bōl* farm, dwelling; see BOWER¹]

builder ('bɪldə) *n* a person who builds, esp one who contracts for and supervises the construction or repair of buildings

building ('bɪldɪŋ) *n* **1** something built with a roof and walls, such as a house or factory **2** the act, business, occupation, or art of building houses, boats, etc

building society *n* a cooperative organization that accepts deposits of money from savers and uses them to make loans, secured by mortgages, to house buyers. Since 1986 they have been empowered to offer banking services

build up *vb* (*adverb*) **1** (*tr*) to construct gradually, systematically, or in stages **2** to increase, accumulate, or strengthen, esp by degrees: *the murmur built up to a roar* **3** (*intr*) to prepare for or gradually approach a climax **4** (*tr*) to improve the health or physique of (a person) ▷ *n* **build-up 5** progressive increase in number, size, etc: *the build-up of industry* **6** a gradual approach to a climax or critical point **7** extravagant publicity or praise, esp in the form of a campaign **8** *military* the process of attaining the required strength of forces and equipment, esp prior to an operation

built (bɪlt) *vb* the past tense and past participle of **build**

built-in *adj* **1** made or incorporated as an integral part: *a*

built-in cupboard; a built-in escape clause **2** essential; inherent ▷ *n* **3** *Austral* a built-in cupboard or wardrobe

built-in obsolescence *n* See **planned obsolescence**

built-up *adj* **1** having many buildings (esp in the phrase **built-up area**) **2** increased by the addition of parts: *built-up heels*

Buitenzorg (*Dutch* 'bœitənzɔrx) *n* the former name of **Bogor**

Bujumbura (,bu:dʒəm'buərə) *n* the capital of Burundi, a port at the NE end of Lake Tanganyika. Pop: 419 000 (2005 est). Former name: Usumbura

Bukavu (bu:'ka:vu:) *n* a port in E Democratic Republic of Congo (formerly Zaïre), on Lake Kivu: commercial and industrial centre. Pop: 294 000 (2005 est)

Bukhara *or* **Bokhara** (bʊ'xɑ:rə) *n* **1** a city in S Uzbekistan. Pop: 299 000 (2005 est) **2** a former emirate of central Asia: a powerful kingdom and centre of Islam; became a territory of the Soviet Union (1920) and was divided between the former Uzbek, Tajik, and Turkmen Soviet Socialist Republics

Bukharin (*Russian* bu'xarin) *n* Nikolai Ivanovich (nika'laj i'vanəvitʃ). 1888–1938, Soviet Bolshevik leader: executed in one of Stalin's purges

bukkake (,bu:'kækı) *n* a sexual practice in which several men ejaculate on the face of an individual woman [c21: Japanese *bukkakeru* to dash (water)]

Bukovina *or* **Bucovina** (,bu:kə'vi:nə) *n* a region of E central Europe, part of the NE Carpathians: the north was seized by the Soviet Union (1940) and later became part of Ukraine; the south remained Romanian

Bulawayo (,bʊlə'weɪəʊ) *n* a city in SW Zimbabwe founded (1893) on the site of the kraal of Lobengula, the last Matabele king; the country's main industrial centre. Pop: 693 000 (2005 est)

bulb (bʌlb) *n* **1** a rounded organ of vegetative reproduction in plants such as the tulip and onion: a flattened stem bearing a central shoot surrounded by fleshy nutritive inner leaves and thin brown outer leaves **2** a plant, such as a hyacinth or daffodil, that grows from a bulb **3** See **light bulb** [c16: from Latin *bulbus*, from Greek *bolbos* onion] ▷ '**bulbous** *adj* ▷ '**bulbously** *adv*

bulbil ('bʌlbɪl) *n* **1** a small bulblike organ of vegetative reproduction growing in leaf axils or on flower stalks of plants such as the onion and tiger lily **2** any small bulblike structure in an animal [c19: from New Latin *bulbillus*, from Latin *bulbus* BULB]

bulbul ('bʊlbʊl) *n* any songbird of the family *Pycnonotidae* of tropical Africa and Asia, having brown plumage and, in many species, a distinct crest [c18: via Persian from Arabic]

Bulg. *abbreviation* Bulgaria(n)

Bulgakov (*Russian* bʊl'gakəf) *n* Mikhail Afanaseyev (ʌfʌ'nasjef). 1891–1940, Soviet novelist, dramatist, and short-story writer; his novels include *The Master and Margerita* (1966–67)

Bulganin (*Russian* bul'ganin) *n* Nikolai Aleksandrovich (nika'laj alık'sandrəvitʃ). 1895–1975, Soviet statesman and military leader; chairman of the council of ministers (1955–58)

Bulgaria (bʌl'gɛərıə, bul-) *n* a republic in SE Europe, on the Balkan Peninsula on the Black Sea: under Turkish rule from 1395 until 1878; became an independent kingdom in 1908 and a republic in 1946; joined the EU in 2007; consists chiefly of the Danube valley in the north and the Balkan Mountains in the central part, separated from the Rhodope Mountains of the south by the valley of the Maritsa River. Language: Bulgarian. Religion: Christian (Bulgarian Orthodox) majority. Currency: lev. Capital: Sofia. Pop: 7 829 000 (2004 est). Area: 110 911 sq km (42 823 sq miles) ▷ **Bul'garian** *adj, n*

bulge (bʌldʒ) *n* **1** a swelling or an outward curve **2** a sudden increase in number or volume, esp of population ▷ *vb* **3** to swell outwards [c13: from Old French *bouge*, from Latin *bulga* bag, probably of Gaulish origin] ▷ '**bulging** *adj* ▷ '**bulgy** *adj*

bulgur ('bʌlgə) *n* Also called: **burghul** a kind of dried cracked wheat [c20: from Turkish, from Arabic *burghul*, from Persian]

bulimia (bjuːˈlɪmɪə) n 1 pathologically insatiable hunger, esp when caused by a brain lesion 2 Also called: bulimia nervosa a disorder characterized by compulsive overeating followed by vomiting: sometimes associated with anxiety about gaining weight [c17: from New Latin, from Greek boulimia, from bous ox + limos hunger]

bulk (bʌlk) n 1 volume, size, or magnitude, esp when great 2 the main part: the bulk of the work is repetitious 3 a large body, esp of a person 4 the part of food which passes unabsorbed through the digestive system 5 in bulk a in large quantities b (of a cargo, etc) unpackaged ▷ vb 6 to cohere or cause to cohere in a mass 7 bulk large to be or seem important or prominent [c15: from Old Norse bulki cargo]

● USAGE The use of a plural noun after bulk was
● formerly considered incorrect, but is now acceptable

bulk buying n the purchase at one time, and often at a reduced price, of a large quantity of a particular commodity

bulkhead (ˈbʌlkˌhɛd) n any upright wall-like partition in a ship, aircraft, vehicle, etc [c15: probably from bulk projecting framework, from Old Norse bálkr partition + HEAD]

bulk modulus n a coefficient of elasticity of a substance equal to minus the ratio of the applied stress (p) to the resulting fractional change in volume (dV/V) in a specified reference state (dV/V is the **bulk strain**)

bulky (ˈbʌlkɪ) adj bulkier, bulkiest very large and massive, esp so as to be unwieldy > ˈbulkily adv > ˈbulkiness n

bull¹ (bʊl) n 1 any male bovine animal, esp one that is sexually mature 2 the male of various other animals including the elephant and whale 3 a very large, strong, or aggressive person 4 stock exchange a a speculator who buys in anticipation of rising prices in order to make a profit on resale b (as modifier): a bull market. See bear² (sense 5) 5 chiefly Brit short for bull's-eye (senses 1, 2) 6 slang short for bullshit 7 a bull in a china shop a clumsy person 8 take the bull by the horns to face and tackle a difficulty without shirking ▷ adj 9 male; masculine: a bull elephant 10 large; strong [Old English bula, from Old Norse boli; related to Middle Low German bulle, Middle Dutch bolle]

bull² (bʊl) n a ludicrously self-contradictory or inconsistent statement [c17: of uncertain origin]

bull³ (bʊl) n a formal document issued by the pope, written in antiquated characters and often sealed with a leaden bulla [c13: from Medieval Latin bulla seal attached to a bull, from Latin: round object]

Bull¹ n the Bull the constellation Taurus, the second sign of the zodiac

Bull² (bʊl) n 1 John. 1563–1628, English composer and organist 2 See John Bull

Bullamakanka (ˌbʊləməˈkæŋkə) n Austral slang an imaginary very remote and backward place

bull ant n any large Australian ant of the genus Myrmecia, having a powerful stinging bite: subfamily Ponerinae. Also called: bulldog ant

bull bars pl n a large protective metal grille on the front of some vehicles, esp four-wheel-drive vehicles

bulldog (ˈbʊlˌdɒg) n a sturdy thickset breed of dog with an undershot jaw, short nose, broad head, and a muscular body

bulldog clip n trademark a clip for holding papers together, consisting of two T-shaped metal clamps held in place by a cylindrical spring

bulldoze (ˈbʊlˌdəʊz) vb (tr) 1 to move, demolish, flatten, etc, with a bulldozer 2 informal to force; push 3 informal to intimidate or coerce [c19: probably from BULL¹ + DOSE]

bulldozer (ˈbʊlˌdəʊzə) n 1 a powerful tractor fitted with caterpillar tracks and a blade at the front, used for moving earth, rocks, etc 2 informal a person who bulldozes

bull dust n Austral 1 fine dust 2 slang nonsense

bullet (ˈbʊlɪt) n 1 a a small metallic missile enclosed in a cartridge, used as the projectile of a gun, rifle, etc b the entire cartridge 2 something resembling a bullet, esp in shape or effect 3 stock exchange a fixed interest security with a single maturity date 4 commerce a security that offers a fixed interest and matures on a fixed date 5 commerce a the final repayment of a loan that repays the whole of the sum borrowed, as interim payments have been for interest only b (as modifier): a bullet loan [c16: from French boulette, diminutive of boule ball; see BOWL²]

bulletin (ˈbʊlɪtɪn) n 1 an official statement on a matter of public interest, such as the illness of a public figure 2 a broadcast summary of the news 3 a periodical publication of an association, etc ▷ vb 4 (tr) to make known by bulletin [c17: from French, from Italian bullettino, from bulletta, diminutive of bulla papal edict, BULL³]

bulletin board n 1 US & Canadian a board on which notices, advertisements, bulletins, etc, are displayed. Also called (in Britain and certain other countries): notice board 2 computing a facility on a computer network allowing any user to leave messages that can be read by any other user, and to download software and information to the user's own computer

bullet point n any of a number of items printed in a list, each after a centred dot, usually the most important points in a longer piece of text

bulletproof (ˈbʊlɪtˌpruːf) adj 1 not penetrable by bullets ▷ vb 2 (tr) to make bulletproof

bullet train n a passenger train that travels at very high speed

bulletwood (ˈbʊlɪtˌwʊd) n the wood of a tropical American sapotaceous tree, Manilkara bidentata, widely used for construction due to its durability and toughness

bullfight (ˈbʊlˌfaɪt) n a traditional Spanish, Portuguese, and Latin American spectacle in which a matador, assisted by banderilleros and mounted picadors, baits and usually kills a bull in an arena > ˈbullˌfighter n > ˈbullˌfighting n

bullfinch (ˈbʊlˌfɪntʃ) n 1 a common European finch, Pyrrhula pyrrhula: the male has a bright red throat and breast, black crown, wings, and tail, and a grey-and-white back 2 any of various similar finches [c14: see BULL¹, FINCH; probably so called from its stocky shape and thick neck]

bullfrog (ˈbʊlˌfrɒg) n any of various large frogs, such as Rana catesbeiana (**American bullfrog**), having a loud deep croak

bullhead (ˈbʊlˌhɛd) n any of various small northern mainly marine scorpaenoid fishes of the family Cottidae that have a large head covered with bony plates and spines

bull-headed adj blindly obstinate; stubborn, headstrong, or stupid > bull-ˈheadedly adv > ˌbull-ˈheadedness n

bullhorn (ˈbʊlˌhɔːn) n US & Canadian a portable loudspeaker having a built-in amplifier and microphone. Also called (in Britain and certain other countries): loud-hailer

bullion (ˈbʊljən) n 1 gold or silver in mass 2 gold or silver in the form of bars and ingots, suitable for further processing [c14 (in the sense: melted gold or silver): from Anglo-French: mint, probably from Old French bouillir to boil, from Latin bullīre]

bullish (ˈbʊlɪʃ) adj 1 like a bull 2 stock exchange causing, expecting, or characterized by a rise in prices 3 informal cheerful and optimistic > ˈbullishness n

bull-necked adj having a short thick neck

bullock (ˈbʊlək) n 1 a gelded bull; steer ▷ vb 2 (intr) Austral & NZ informal to work hard and long [Old English bulluc; see BULL¹, -OCK]

bullocky (ˈbʊləkɪ) n, pl -ockies Austral & NZ informal the driver of a team of bullocks

bullring (ˈbʊlˌrɪŋ) n an arena for bullfighting

bullroarer (ˈbʊlˌrɔːrə) n a wooden slat attached to a thong that makes a roaring sound when the thong is whirled: used esp by native Australians in religious rites

bull's-eye n 1 the small central disc of a target, usually the highest valued area 2 a shot hitting this 3 informal something that exactly achieves its aim 4 a small circular or oval window or opening 5 a thick disc of glass set into a ship's deck, etc, to admit light 6 the glass boss at the centre of a sheet of blown glass **7 a** a small thick plano-convex lens used as a condenser **b** a lamp or lantern containing such a lens **8** a peppermint-flavoured, usually striped, boiled sweet

bullshit (ˈbʊlʃɪt) *slang* ▷ *n* **1** exaggerated or foolish talk; nonsense **2** deceitful or pretentious talk **3** (in the British Army) exaggerated zeal, esp for ceremonial drill, cleaning, polishing, etc. Usually shortened to: **bull** ▷ *vb* -**shits**, -**shitting**, -**shitted 4** (*intr*) to talk in an exaggerated or foolish manner **5** to talk bullshit to

bull's wool *n Austral & NZ informal* nonsense

bull terrier *n* a breed of terrier having a muscular body and thick neck, with a short smooth often white coat: developed by crossing the bulldog with various terriers. See also **pit bull terrier, Staffordshire bull terrier**

bully[1] (ˈbʊlɪ) *n, pl* -**lies 1** a person who hurts, persecutes, or intimidates weaker people ▷ *vb* -**lies**, -**lying**, -**lied 2** (when *tr*, often foll by *into*) to hurt, intimidate, or persecute (a weaker or smaller person), esp to make him do something ▷ *adj* **3** dashing; jolly: *my bully boy* **4** *informal* very good; fine ▷ *interj* **5** Also called: **bully for you** *informal* well done! bravo! [C16 (in the sense: sweetheart, hence fine fellow, hence swaggering coward): probably from Middle Dutch *boele* lover, from Middle High German *buole*, perhaps childish variant of *bruoder* BROTHER]

bully[2] (ˈbʊlɪ) *n, pl* -**lies** any of various small freshwater fishes of the genera *Gobiomorphus* and *Philynodon* of New Zealand. Also called (NZ): **toitoi** [C20: short for COCKABULLY]

bully beef *n* tinned corned beef. Often shortened to: **bully** [C19 *bully*, anglicized version of French *bouilli*, from *boeuf bouilli* boiled beef]

bully-off *hockey* ▷ *n* **1** a method by which a game is restarted after a stoppage. Two opposing players stand with the ball between them and alternately strike their sticks together and against the ground three times before trying to hit the ball ▷ *vb* **bully off 2** (*intr, adverb*) to restart play after a stoppage with a bully-off ▷ Often shortened to: **bully** [C19: perhaps from *bully* scrum in Eton football; of unknown origin]

bullyrag (ˈbʊlɪˌræg) *vb* -**rags**, -**ragging**, -**ragged** (*tr*) to bully, esp by means of cruel practical jokes. Also called: **ballyrag** [C18: of unknown origin]

Bülow (*German* ˈbyːlo) *n* **Prince Bernhard von** (ˈbɛrnhart fɔn). 1849–1929, chancellor of Germany (1900–09)

bulrush (ˈbʊlrʌʃ) *n* **1** a grasslike cyperaceous marsh plant, *Scirpus lacustris*, used for making mats, chair seats, etc **2** a popular name for **reed mace** (sense 1) **3** a biblical word for **papyrus** (sense 1) [C15 *bulrish, bul-* perhaps from BULL[1] + *rish* RUSH[2], referring to the largeness of the plant; sense 2 derived from the famous painting by Sir Lawrence *Alma-Tadema* (1836–1912), Dutch-born English painter, of the finding of the infant Moses in the "bulrushes" — actually reed mace]

Bultmann (*German* ˈbʊltman) *n* **Rudolf Karl**. 1884–1976, German theologian, noted for his demythologizing approach to the New Testament

bulwark (ˈbʊlwək) *n* **1** a wall or similar structure used as a fortification; rampart **2** a person or thing acting as a defence against injury, annoyance, etc **3** (*often plural*) *nautical* a solid vertical fencelike structure along the outward sides of a deck **4** a breakwater or mole ▷ *vb* **5** (*tr*) to defend or fortify with or as if with a bulwark [C15: via Dutch from Middle High German *bolwerk*, from *bol* plank, BOLE + *werk* WORK]

Bulwer-Lytton (ˈbʊlwəˈlɪtᵊn) *n* See **Lytton**

bum[1] (bʌm) *n Brit slang* the buttocks or anus [C14: of uncertain origin]

bum[2] (bʌm) *informal* ▷ *n* **1** a disreputable loafer or idler **2** a tramp; hobo ▷ *vb* **bums, bumming, bummed 3** (*tr*) to get by begging; cadge: *to bum a lift* **4** (*intr*; often foll by *around*) to live by begging or as a vagrant or loafer **5** (*intr*; usually foll by *around*) to spend time to no good purpose; loaf; idle **6 bum someone off** *US & Canadian slang* to disappoint, annoy, or upset someone ▷ *adj* **7** (*prenominal*) of poor quality; useless [C19: probably shortened from earlier *bummer* a loafer, probably from German *bummeln* to loaf]

bum bag *n* a small bag worn on a belt, round the waist

bumbailiff (ˌbʌmˈbeɪlɪf) *n Brit dismissive* (formerly) an officer employed to collect debts and arrest debtors for nonpayment [C17: from BUM + bailiff, so called because he follows hard behind debtors]

bumble (ˈbʌmbᵊl) *vb* **1** to speak or do in a clumsy, muddled, or inefficient way **2** (*intr*) to proceed unsteadily; stumble [C16: perhaps a blend of BUNGLE + STUMBLE] > ˈbumbler *n* > ˈbumbling *n, adj*

bumblebee (ˈbʌmbᵊlˌbiː) *or* **humblebee** *n* any large hairy social bee of the genus *Bombus* and related genera, of temperate regions: family *Apidae* [C16: from BUMBLE + BEE[1]]

Bumbry (ˈbʌmbrɪ) *n* **Grace**. born 1937, US soprano and mezzo-soprano

bumf *or* **bumph** (bʌmf) *n Brit* **1** *informal, derogatory* superfluous documents, forms, publicity material, etc **2** *slang* toilet paper [C19: short for earlier *bumfodder*; see BUM[1]]

bummalo (ˈbʌməˌləʊ) *n, pl* -**lo** another name for **Bombay duck** [C17: from Marathi *bombīla*]

bummer (ˈbʌmə) *n slang* an unpleasant or disappointing experience

bump (bʌmp) *vb* **1** (when *intr*, usually foll by *against* or *into*) to knock or strike with a jolt **2** (*intr*; often foll by *along*) to travel or proceed in jerks and jolts **3** (*tr*) to hurt by knocking **4** *cricket* to bowl (a ball) so that it bounces high on pitching or (of a ball) to bounce high when bowled **5** (*tr*) *informal* to exclude a ticket-holding passenger from a flight as a result of overbooking ▷ *n* **6** an impact; knock; jolt; collision **7** a dull thud or other noise from an impact or collision **8** the shock of a blow or collision **9** a lump on the body caused by a blow **10** a protuberance, as on a road surface **11** any of the natural protuberances of the human skull, said by phrenologists to indicate underlying faculties and character See also **bump into, bump off, bump up** [C16: probably of imitative origin]

bumper[1] (ˈbʌmpə) *n* **1** a horizontal metal bar attached to the front or rear end of a car, lorry, etc, to protect against damage from impact **2** *cricket* a ball bowled so that it bounces high on pitching; bouncer

bumper[2] (ˈbʌmpə) *n* **1** a glass, tankard, etc, filled to the brim, esp as a toast **2** an unusually large or fine example of something ▷ *adj* **3** unusually large, fine, or abundant: *a bumper crop* [C17 (in the sense: a brimming glass): probably from *bump* (obsolete vb) to bulge; see BUMP]

bumper car *n* a low-powered electrically propelled vehicle driven and bumped against similar cars in a special rink at a funfair. Also called: **Dodgem**

bumph (bʌmf) *n* a variant spelling of **bumf**

bump into *vb* (*intr, preposition*) *informal* to meet by chance; encounter unexpectedly

bumpkin (ˈbʌmpkɪn) *n* an awkward simple rustic person (esp in the phrase **country bumpkin**) [C16 (perhaps originally applied to Dutchmen): perhaps from Dutch *boomken* small tree, or from Middle Dutch *boomken* small barrel, alluding to a short or squat person]

bump off *vb* (*tr, adverb*) *slang* to murder; kill

bumptious (ˈbʌmpʃəs) *adj* offensively self-assertive or conceited [C19: perhaps a blend of BUMP + FRACTIOUS] > ˈbumptiously *adv* > ˈbumptiousness *n*

bump up *vb* (*tr, adverb*) *informal* to raise or increase

bumpy (ˈbʌmpɪ) *adj* **bumpier, bumpiest 1** having an uneven surface **2** full of jolts; rough > ˈbumpily *adv* > ˈbumpiness *n*

bun (bʌn) *n* **1** a small roll, similar to bread but usually containing sweetening, currants, spices, etc **2** any of various types of small round sweet cakes **3** a hairstyle in which long hair is gathered into a bun shape at the back of the head [C14: of unknown origin]

bunch (bʌntʃ) *n* **1** a number of things growing, fastened, or grouped together: *a bunch of grapes; a bunch of keys* **2** a collection; group: *a bunch of queries* **3** *informal* a group or company: *a bunch of boys* ▷ *vb* **4** (sometimes foll by *up*) to group or be grouped into a bunch [C14: of obscure origin]

bunchberry (ˈbʌntʃˌbɛrɪ) *n, pl* -**ries** a dwarf variety of dogwood native to North America, *Cornus canadensis*, having red berries

Bunche (bʌntʃ) n Ralph Johnson. 1904–71, US diplomat and United Nations official: awarded the Nobel peace prize in 1950 for his work as UN mediator in Palestine (1948–49); UN undersecretary (1954–71)

bunchy ('bʌntʃɪ) adj bunchier, bunchiest 1 composed of or resembling bunches 2 bulging

buncombe ('bʌŋkəm) n a variant spelling (esp US) of **bunkum**

Bundaberg ('bʌndə,bɜːg) n a town in E Australia, near the E coast of Queensland: centre of a sugar-growing area, with a nearby deep-water port. Pop: 44 556 (2001)

Bundelkhand (,bʌndəl'kʌnd, -'xʌnd) n a region of central India: formerly native states, now mainly part of Madhya Pradesh

bundle ('bʌndəl) n 1 a number of things or a quantity of material gathered or loosely bound together: a bundle of sticks. Related adjective: **fascicular** 2 something wrapped or tied for carrying; package 3 slang a large sum of money 4 go a bundle on slang to be extremely fond of 5 biology a collection of strands of specialized tissue such as nerve fibres 6 botany short for **vascular bundle** 7 drop one's bundle a Austral & NZ slang to panic or give up hope b NZ slang to give birth ▷ vb 8 (tr; often foll by up) to make into a bundle 9 (foll by out, off, into etc) to go or cause to go, esp roughly or unceremoniously 10 (tr; usually foll by into) to push or throw, esp quickly and untidily 11 (tr) to give away (a relatively cheap product) when selling an expensive one to attract business: several free CDs are often bundled with music centres 12 (intr) to sleep or lie in one's clothes on the same bed as one's betrothed: formerly a custom in New England, Wales, and elsewhere [C14: probably from Middle Dutch bundel; related to Old English bindele bandage; see BIND, BOND] > 'bundler n

bundle up vb (adverb) 1 to dress (somebody) warmly and snugly 2 (tr) to make (something) into a bundle or bundles, esp by tying

bunfight ('bʌn,faɪt) n Brit slang 1 a tea party 2 ironic an official function

bung¹ (bʌŋ) n 1 a stopper, esp of cork or rubber, for a cask, piece of laboratory glassware, etc 2 short for **bunghole** ▷ vb (tr) 3 (often foll by up) to close or seal with or as with a bung 4 Brit slang to throw; sling 5 Brit slang to throw; sling [C15: from Middle Dutch bonghe, from Late Latin puncta PUNCTURE]

bung² (bʌŋ) vb Brit slang bung it on (tr) to behave in a pretentious manner [C16 (originally in the sense: a purse): perhaps from Old English pung, changed over time through the influence of BUNG¹]

bung³ (bʌŋ) adj Austral & NZ informal 1 useless 2 go bung a to fail or collapse b to die [C19: from a native Australian language]

bungalow ('bʌŋgə,ləʊ) n a one-storey house, sometimes with an attic [C17: from Hindi banglā (house) of the Bengal type]

bungee jumping or **bungy jumping** ('bʌndʒɪ) n a sport in which a participant jumps from a high bridge, building, etc, secured only by a rubber cord attached to the ankles [C20: from bungie, slang for India rubber, of unknown origin]

bunghole ('bʌŋ,həʊl) n a hole in a cask, barrel, etc, through which liquid can be poured or drained

bungle ('bʌŋgəl) vb 1 (tr) to spoil (an operation) through clumsiness, incompetence, etc; botch ▷ n 2 a clumsy or unsuccessful performance or piece of work; mistake; botch [C16: perhaps of Scandinavian origin; compare dialect Swedish bangla to work without results] > 'bungler n > 'bungling adj, n

Bunin (Russian 'bunin) n Ivan Alekseyevich (i'van alɪk'sjejɪvɪtʃ). 1870–1953, Russian novelist and poet; author of The Gentleman from San Francisco (1922)

bunion ('bʌnjən) n swelling of the first joint of the big toe, which is displaced to one side. An inflamed bursa forms over the joint [C18: perhaps from obsolete bunny a swelling, of uncertain origin]

bunk¹ (bʌŋk) n 1 a narrow shelflike bed fixed along a wall 2 short for **bunk bed** 3 informal any place where one sleeps ▷ vb 4 (intr; often foll by down) to prepare to sleep:

he bunked down on the floor 5 (intr) to occupy a bunk or bed [C19: probably short for BUNKER]

bunk² (bʌŋk) n informal short for **bunkum** (sense 1)

bunk³ (bʌŋk) Brit slang ▷ n 1 a hurried departure, usually under suspicious circumstances (esp in the phrase do a bunk) ▷ vb 2 (usually foll by off) to play truant from (school, work, etc) [C19: perhaps from BUNK¹ (in the sense: to occupy a bunk, hence a hurried departure, as on a ship)]

bunk bed n one of a pair of beds constructed one above the other

bunker ('bʌŋkə) n 1 a large storage container or tank, as for coal 2 an obstacle on a golf course, usually a sand-filled hollow bordered by a ridge. Also called (esp US and Canadian): sand trap 3 an underground shelter, often of reinforced concrete and with a bank and embrasures for guns above ground ▷ vb 4 (tr) golf a to drive (the ball) into a bunker b (passive) to have one's ball trapped in a bunker [C16 (in the sense: chest, box): from Scottish bonkar, of unknown origin]

bunkhouse ('bʌŋk,haʊs) n (in the US and Canada) a building containing the sleeping quarters of workers on a ranch

bunkum or **buncombe** ('bʌŋkəm) n 1 empty talk; nonsense 2 chiefly US empty or insincere speechmaking by a politician to please voters or gain publicity [C19: after Buncombe, a county in North Carolina, alluded to in an inane speech by its Congressional representative Felix Walker (about 1820)]

bunny ('bʌnɪ) n, pl -nies 1 Also called: bunny rabbit a child's word for **rabbit** (sense 1) 2 Also called: bunny girl a night-club hostess whose costume includes rabbit-like tail and ears 3 Austral informal a mug; dupe [C17: from Scottish Gaelic bun scut of a rabbit]

bunny hop n 1 a jump executed with the feet held tightly together and the knees bent 2 a jump over an obstacle executed by a person riding a bicycle and standing up on the pedals 3 US a dance performed by a line of people holding onto each other from behind and moving around the room tapping and stepping with each foot separately and then jumping with both feet held together ▷ vb bunny-hop 4 (intr) to jump with the feet held tightly together and the knees bent 5 to jump a bicycle over an obstacle without dismounting

Bunsen ('bʌns°n; German 'bunzən) n Robert Wilhelm ('roːbɛrt 'vɪlhɛlm). 1811–99, German chemist who with Kirchhoff developed spectrum analysis and discovered the elements caesium and rubidium. He invented the Bunsen burner and the ice calorimeter

Bunsen burner ('bʌns°n) n a gas burner, widely used in scientific laboratories, consisting of a metal tube with an adjustable air valve at the base [C19: named after its inventor Robert Wilhelm Bunsen (1811–99), German chemist]

bunt¹ (bʌnt) vb 1 (of an animal) to butt (something) with the head or horns 2 to cause (an aircraft) to fly in part of an inverted loop or (of an aircraft) to fly in such a loop 3 US & Canadian (in baseball) to hit (a pitched ball) very gently ▷ n 4 the act or an instance of bunting [C19: perhaps nasalized variant of BUTT³]

bunt² (bʌnt) n nautical the baggy centre of a fishing net or other piece of fabric, such as a square sail [C16: perhaps from Middle Low German bunt BUNDLE]

bunt³ (bʌnt) n a disease of cereal plants caused by smut fungi (genus Tilletia) [C17: of unknown origin]

bunting¹ ('bʌntɪŋ) n 1 a coarse, loosely woven cotton fabric used for flags, etc 2 decorative flags, pennants, and streamers [C18: of unknown origin]

bunting² ('bʌntɪŋ) n any of numerous seed-eating songbirds of the families Fringillidae (finches, etc) or Emberizidae, esp those of the genera Emberiza of the Old World and Passerina of North America. They all have short stout bills [C13: of unknown origin]

Bunting ('bʌntɪŋ) n Basil. 1900–85, British poet, author of Briggflatts (1966)

buntline ('bʌntlɪn, -,laɪn) n nautical one of several lines fastened to the foot of a square sail for hauling it up to the yard when furling [C17: from BUNT² + LINE¹]

Buñuel (Spanish bu'ɲwel) n Luis (lwis). 1900–83, Spanish film director. He collaborated with Salvador Dali on the first surrealist films, *Un Chien andalou* (1929) and *L'Age d'or* (1930). His later films include *Viridiana* (1961), *Belle de jour* (1966), and *The Discreet Charm of the Bourgeoisie* (1972)

bunya ('bʌnjə) *n* a tall dome-shaped Australian coniferous tree, *Araucaria bidwillii*, having edible cones (**bunya nuts**) and thickish flattened needles. Also called: bunya-bunya [c19: from a native Australian language]

Bunyan ('bʌnjən) *n* **John**. 1628–88, English preacher and writer, noted particularly for his allegory *The Pilgrim's Progress* (1678)

bunyip ('bʌnjɪp) *n Austral* a legendary monster said to inhabit swamps and lagoons of the Australian interior [c19: from a native Australian language]

Buonaparte (bwona'parte) *n* the Italian spelling of **Bonaparte**

Buonarroti (*Italian* bwonar'roti) *n* See **Michelangelo**

buoy (bɔɪ; *US* 'bu:ɪ) *n* **1** a distinctively shaped and coloured float, anchored to the bottom, for designating moorings, navigable channels, or obstructions in a body of water ▷ *vb* **2** (*tr*; usually foll by *up*) to prevent from sinking: *the belt buoyed him up* **3** (*tr*; usually foll by *up*) to raise the spirits of; hearten **4** (*tr*) *nautical* to mark (a channel or obstruction) with a buoy or buoys **5** (*intr*) to rise to the surface [c13: probably of Germanic origin; compare Middle Dutch *boeie, boeye*; see BEACON]

buoyancy ('bɔɪənsɪ) *n* **1** the ability to float in a liquid or to rise in a fluid **2** the property of a fluid to exert an upward force (upthrust) on a body that is wholly or partly submerged in it **3** the ability to recover quickly after setbacks; resilience **4** cheerfulness

buoyant ('bɔɪənt) *adj* **1** able to float in or rise to the surface of a liquid **2** (of a liquid or gas) able to keep a body afloat or cause it to rise **3** cheerful or resilient [c16: probably from Spanish *boyante*, from *boyar* to float, from *boya* buoy, ultimately of Germanic origin]

BUPA ('bu:pə) *n acronym for* The British United Provident Association Limited: a company which provides private medical insurance

bupivacaine (bju:'pɪvəkeɪn) *n* a local anaesthetic of long duration, used for nerve blocks [c20: perhaps from BU(TYL) + *pi(pecoloxylidide)*, the drug's chemical components + *-vacaine*, from (NO)VOCAINE]

bur (bɜ:) *n* **1** a seed vessel or flower head, as of burdock, having hooks or prickles **2** any plant that produces burs **3** a person or thing that clings like a bur **4** a small surgical or dental drill ▷ *vb* **burs, burring, burred** **5** (*tr*) to remove burs from. Also (for senses 1–4): **burr** [c14: probably of Scandinavian origin; compare Danish *burre* bur, Swedish *kardborre* burdock]

Buraydah or **Buraida** (bu'raɪdə) *n* a town and oasis in central Saudi Arabia. Pop: 462 000 (2005 est)

Burbage ('bɜ:bɪdʒ) *n* **1 James**. ?1530–97, English actor and theatre manager, who built (1576) the first theatre in England **2** his son, **Richard**. ?1567–1619, English actor, associated with Shakespeare

burble ('bɜ:bᵊl) *vb* **1** to make or utter with a bubbling sound; gurgle ▷ *n* **2** a bubbling or gurgling sound **3** a flow of excited speech [c14: probably of imitative origin; compare Spanish *borbollar* to bubble, gush, Italian *borbugliare*] > '**burbler** *n*

burbot ('bɜ:bət) *n, pl* -bots or -bot a freshwater gadoid food fish, *Lota lota*, that has barbels around its mouth and occurs in Europe, Asia, and North America [c14: from Old French *bourbotte*, from *bourbeter* to wallow in mud, from *bourbe* mud, probably of Celtic origin]

Burckhardt (*German* 'burkhart) *n* **Jacob Christoph**. 1818–97, Swiss art and cultural historian; author of *The Civilisation of the Renaissance in Italy* (1860)

burden ('bɜ:dᵊn) *n* **1** something that is carried; load **2** something that is exacting, oppressive, or difficult to bear **3** *nautical* **a** the cargo capacity of a ship **b** the weight of a ship's cargo ▷ *vb* (*tr*) **4** (sometimes foll by *up*) to put or impose a burden on; load **5** to weigh down; oppress [Old English *byrthen*; related to *beran* to BEAR¹, Old Frisian *berthene* burden, Old High German *burdin*]

burden of proof *n law* the obligation, in criminal cases resting initially on the prosecution, to provide evidence that will convince the court or jury of the truth of one's contention

burdensome ('bɜ:dᵊnsəm) *adj* hard to bear; onerous

burdock ('bɜ:ˌdɒk) *n* a coarse weedy Eurasian plant of the genus *Arctium*, having large heart-shaped leaves, tiny purple flowers surrounded by hooked bristles, and burlike fruits: family *Asteraceae* (composites) [c16: from BUR + DOCK⁴]

bureau ('bjuərəu) *n, pl* -reaus or -reaux (-rəuz) **1** chiefly *Brit* a writing desk with pigeonholes, drawers, etc, against which the writing surface can be closed when not in use **2** *US* a chest of drawers **3** an office or agency **4** a government department [c17: from French: desk, office, originally: type of cloth used for covering desks and tables, from Old French *burel*, from Late Latin *burra* shaggy cloth]

bureaucracy (bjuə'rɒkrəsɪ) *n, pl* -cies **1** a system of administration based upon organization into bureaus, division of labour, a hierarchy of authority, etc: designed to dispose of a large body of work in a routine manner **2** government by such a system **3** government or other officials collectively **4** any administration in which action is impeded by unnecessary official procedures and red tape

bureaucrat ('bjuərə,kræt) *n* **1** an official in a bureaucracy **2** an official who adheres to bureaucracy, esp rigidly > **bureaucratic** (,bjuərə'krætɪk) *adj* > ,bureau'cratically *adv*

bureaucratize or **bureaucratise** (bjuə'rɒkrə,taɪz) *vb* (*tr*) to administer by or transform into a bureaucracy > bu,reaucrati'zation or bu,reaucrati'sation *n*

bureau de change ('bjuərəu də 'ʃɒnʒ) *n* a place where foreign currencies can be exchanged [c20: from French, literally: office of exchange]

burette or *US* **buret** (bju'rɛt) *n* a graduated glass tube with a stopcock on one end for dispensing and transferring known volumes of fluids, esp liquids [c15: from French: cruet, oil can, from Old French *buire* ewer, of Germanic origin; compare Old English *būc* pitcher, belly]

burg (bɜ:g) *n* **1** *history* a fortified town **2** *US informal* a town or city [c18 (in the sense: fortress): from Old High German *burg* fortified town; see BOROUGH]

burgage ('bɜ:gɪdʒ) *n history* **1** (in England) tenure of land or tenement in a town or city, which originally involved a fixed money rent **2** (in Scotland) the tenure of land direct from the crown in Scottish royal burghs in return for watching and warding [c14: from Medieval Latin *burgāgium*, from *burgus*, from Old English *burg*; see BOROUGH]

Burgas (Bulgarian bur'gas) *n* a port in SE Bulgaria on an inlet of the Black Sea. Pop: 177 000 (2005 est)

Burgenland (*German* 'burgən,lant) *n* a state of E Austria. Capital: Eisenstadt. Pop: 276 419 (2003 est). Area: 3965 sq km (1531 sq miles)

burgeon or **bourgeon** ('bɜ:dʒən) *vb* **1** (often foll by *forth* or *out*) (of a plant) to sprout (buds) **2** (*intr*; often foll by *forth* or *out*) to develop or grow rapidly; flourish [c13: from Old French *burjon*, perhaps ultimately from Late Latin *burra* shaggy cloth; from the downiness of certain buds]

burger ('bɜ:gə) *n informal* **a** short for **hamburger** **b** (*in combination*): *a cheeseburger*

Bürger (*German* 'byrgər) *n* **Gottfried August** ('gɔtfri:t 'augʊst). 1747–94, German lyric poet, noted particularly for his ballad *Lenore* (1773)

burgess ('bɜ:dʒɪs) *n* **1** (in England) **a** a citizen or freeman of a borough **b** any inhabitant of a borough **2** *English history* a Member of Parliament from a borough, corporate town, or university [c13: from Old French *burgeis*, from *borc* town, from Late Latin *burgus*, of Germanic origin; see BOROUGH]

Burgess ('bɜ:dʒɪs) *n* **1 Anthony**, real name *John Burgess Wilson*. 1917–93, English novelist and critic: his novels include *A Clockwork Orange* (1962), *Tremor of Intent* (1966), *Earthly Powers* (1980), and *Any Old Iron* (1989) **2 Guy**. 1911–63, British spy, who fled to the Soviet Union (with Donald Maclean) in 1951

Burgess Shale *n* a bed of Cambrian sedimentary rock in the Rocky Mountains in British Columbia containing many unique invertebrate fossils [named after the

Burgess Pass, where the bed is exposed]

burgh ('bʌrə) *n* **1** (in Scotland) a town, esp one incorporated by charter, that enjoyed a degree of self-government until the local-government reorganization of 1975 **2** an archaic form of **borough** (sense 1) [C14: Scottish form of BOROUGH] > burghal ('bɜːgəl) *adj*

burgher ('bɜːgə) *n* **1** a member of the trading or mercantile class of a medieval city **2** a respectable citizen; bourgeois **3** *archaic* a citizen or inhabitant of a corporate town, esp on the Continent **4** *South African history* a citizen of the Cape Colony or of one of the Transvaal and Free State republics [C16: from German *Bürger*, or Dutch *burger* freeman of a BOROUGH]

Burghley *or* **Burleigh** ('bɜːlɪ) *n* **William Cecil**, 1st Baron Burghley. 1520–98, English statesman: chief adviser to Elizabeth I; secretary of state (1558–72) and Lord High Treasurer (1572–98)

burghul (bɜːˈguːl) *n* another name for **bulgur**

burglar ('bɜːglə) *n* a person who commits burglary; housebreaker [C15: from Anglo-French *burgler*, from Medieval Latin *burglātor*, probably from *burgāre* to thieve, from Latin *burgus* castle, fortress, of Germanic origin]

burglary ('bɜːglərɪ) *n*, *pl* -ries *English criminal law* the crime of either entering a building as a trespasser with the intention of committing theft, rape, grievous bodily harm, or damage, or, having entered as a trespasser, of committing one or more of these offences > burglarious (bɜːˈglɛərɪəs) *adj*

burgle ('bɜːgəl) *vb* to commit burglary upon (a house, etc)

burgomaster ('bɜːgəˌmɑːstə) *n* the chief magistrate of a town in Austria, Belgium, Germany, or the Netherlands; mayor [C16: partial translation of Dutch *burgemeester*; see BOROUGH, MASTER]

Burgos ('bɜːgɒs) *n* a city in N Spain, in Old Castile: cathedral. Pop: 169 317 (2003 est)

Burgoyne (bɜːˈgɔɪn) *n* **John**. 1722–92, British general in the War of American Independence who was forced to surrender at Saratoga (1777)

Burgundy ('bɜːgəndɪ) *n*, *pl* -dies **1** a region of E France famous for its wines, lying west of the Saône: formerly a semi-independent duchy; annexed to France in 1482. French name: Bourgogne **2** Free County of Burgundy another name for **Franche-Comté 3** a monarchy (1384–1477) of medieval Europe, at its height including the Low Countries, the duchy of Burgundy, and Franche-Comté **4** Kingdom of Burgundy a kingdom in E France, established in the early 6th century AD, eventually including the later duchy of Burgundy, Franche-Comté, and the Kingdom of Provence: known as the Kingdom of Arles from the 13th century **5 a** any red or white wine produced in the region of Burgundy, around Dijon **b** any heavy red table wine **6** (*often not capital*) a blackish-purple to purplish-red colour > Burgundian (bɜːˈgʌndɪən) *adj*, *n*

burial ('bɛrɪəl) *n* the act of burying, esp the interment of a dead body [Old English *byrgels* burial place, tomb; see BURY, -AL²]

burial ground *n* a graveyard or cemetery

burin ('bjʊərɪn) *n* **1** a chisel of tempered steel with a sharp lozenge-shaped point, used for engraving furrows in metal, wood, or marble **2** *archaeol* a prehistoric flint tool with a very small transverse edge [C17: from French, perhaps from Italian *burino*, of Germanic origin: compare Old High German *boro* auger; see BORE¹]

burk (bɜːk) *n* *Brit slang* a variant spelling of **berk**

burka ('bɜːkə) *n* a variant spelling of **burqa** [C19: from Arabic]

Burke (bɜːk) *n* **1 Edmund**. 1729–97, British Whig statesman, conservative political theorist, and orator, born in Ireland: defended parliamentary government and campaigned for a more liberal treatment of the American colonies; denounced the French Revolution **2 Robert O'Hara**. 1820–61, Irish explorer, who led the first expedition (1860–61) across Australia from south to north. He was accompanied by W. J. Wills, George Grey, and John King; King alone survived the return journey **3 William**. 1792–1829, Irish murderer and body snatcher; associate of William Hare

Burkina Faso (bɜːˈkiːnəˈfæsəʊ) *or* **Burkina** *n* an inland republic in W Africa: dominated by Mossi kingdoms (10th–19th centuries); French protectorate established in 1896; became an independent republic in 1960; consists mainly of a flat savanna plateau. Official language: French; Mossi and other African languages also widely spoken. Religion: mostly animist, with a large Muslim minority. Currency: franc. Capital: Ouagadougou. Pop: 13 393 000 (2004 est). Area: 273 200 sq km (105 900 sq miles). Former name (until 1984): Upper Volta

burl¹ (bɜːl) *n* **1** a small knot or lump in wool **2** a roundish warty outgrowth from the trunk, roots, or branches of certain trees ▷ *vb* **3** (*tr*) to remove the burls from (cloth) [C15: from Old French *burle* tuft of wool, probably ultimately from Late Latin *burra* shaggy cloth]

burl² *or* **birl** (bɜːl) *n informal* **1** *Scot, Austral & NZ* an attempt; try (esp in the phrase **give it a burl**) **2** *Austral & NZ* a ride in a car [C20: perhaps from BIRL in the Scot sense: a twist or turn]

burlap ('bɜːlæp) *n* a coarse fabric woven from jute, hemp, or the like [C17: from *borel* coarse cloth, from Old French *burel* (see BUREAU) + LAP¹]

Burleigh ('bɜːlɪ) *n* a variant spelling of **Burghley**

burlesque (bɜːˈlɛsk) *n* **1** an artistic work, esp literary or dramatic, satirizing a subject by caricaturing it **2** a ludicrous imitation or caricature **3** Also called: burlesk *US & Canadian theatre* a bawdy comedy show of the late 19th and early 20th centuries: the striptease eventually became one of its chief elements ▷ *adj* **4** of, relating to, or characteristic of a burlesque ▷ *vb* -lesques, -lesquing, -lesqued **5** to represent or imitate (a person or thing) in a ludicrous way; caricature [C17: from French, from Italian *burlesco*, from *burla* a jest, piece of nonsense] > bur'lesquer *n*

burley ('bɜːlɪ) *n* a variant spelling of **berley**

Burlington ('bɜːlɪŋtən) *n* **1** a city in S Canada on Lake Ontario, northeast of Hamilton. Pop: 150 836 (2001) **2** a town in NW Vermont on Lake Champlain: largest in the state; University of Vermont (1791). Pop: 39 148 (2003 est)

burly ('bɜːlɪ) *adj* -lier, -liest large and thick of build; sturdy; stout [C13: of Germanic origin; compare Old High German *burlīh* lofty] > 'burliness *n*

Burma ('bɜːmə) *n* the official name (until 1989, though still widely used) of: **Myanmar**

Burma Road *n* the route extending from Lashio in Burma (now Myanmar) to Chongqing in China, which was used by the Allies during World War II to supply military equipment to Chiang Kai-shek's forces in China

Burmese (bɜːˈmiːz) *adj* Also: Burman **1** of, relating to, or characteristic of Burma (Myanmar), its people, or their language ▷ *n*, *pl* -mese **2** a native or inhabitant of Burma (Myanmar) **3** the official language of Burma (Myanmar), belonging to the Sino-Tibetan family

burn¹ (bɜːn) *vb* burns, burning, burnt *or* burned **1** to undergo or cause to undergo combustion **2** to destroy or be destroyed by fire **3** (*tr*) to damage, injure, or mark by heat: *he burnt his hand; she was burnt by the sun* **4** to die or put to death by fire: *to burn at the stake* **5** (*intr*) to be or feel hot: *my forehead burns* **6** to smart or cause to smart: *brandy burns one's throat* **7** (*intr*) to feel strong emotion, esp anger or passion **8** (*tr*) to use for the purposes of light, heat, or power: *to burn coal* **9** (*tr*) to form by or as if by fire: *to burn a hole* **10** to char or become charred: *the potatoes are burning in the saucepan* **11** (*tr*) to brand or cauterize **12** to produce by or subject to heat as part of a process: *to burn charcoal* **13** burn one's bridges *or* burn one's boats to commit oneself to a particular course of action with no possibility of turning back **14** burn one's fingers to suffer from having meddled or been rash ▷ *n* **15** an injury caused by exposure to heat, electrical, chemical, or radioactive agents. Burns are classified according to the depth of tissue affected: **first-degree burn**: skin surface painful and red; **second-degree burn**: blisters appear on the skin; **third-degree burn**: destruction of both epidermis and dermis **16** a mark, e.g. on wood, caused by burning **17** a controlled use of rocket propellant, esp for a course correction **18** a hot painful sensation in a muscle, experienced during vigorous exercise **19** *slang* tobacco or a cigarette ▷ See also **burn out** [Old English *beornan* (intr), *bærnan* (tr); related to Old Norse *brenna* (tr or intr), Gothic *brinnan* (intr), Latin *fervēre* to boil, seethe]

burn² (bɜːn; *Scot* bʌrn) *n Scot & Northern English* a small stream; brook [Old English *burna*; related to Old Norse *brunnr* spring, Old High German *brunno*, Lithuanian *briáutis* to burst forth]

Burne-Jones (bɜːndʒəʊnz) *n* Sir **Edward**. 1833–98, English Pre-Raphaelite painter and designer of stained-glass windows and tapestries

burner ('bɜːnə) *n* **1** the part of a stove, lamp, etc, that produces flame or heat **2** an apparatus for burning something, as fuel or refuse

burnet ('bɜːnɪt) *n* **1** a plant of the rosaceous genus *Sanguisorba* (or *Poterium*), such as *S. minor* (or *P. sanguisorba*) (**salad burnet**), which has purple-tinged green flowers and leaves that are sometimes used for salads **2** burnet rose Also called: **Scotch rose** a very prickly Eurasian rose, *Rosa pimpinellifolia*, with white flowers and purplish-black fruits **3** a moth of the genus *Zygaena*, having red-spotted dark green wings and antennae with enlarged tips: family *Zygaenidae* [c14: from Old French *burnete*, variant of *brunete* dark brown (see **BRUNETTE**); so called from the colour of the flowers of some of the plants]

Burnet (bə'nɛt, 'bɜːnɪt) *n* **1 Gilbert**. 1643–1715, Scottish bishop and historian, who played a prominent role in the Glorious Revolution (1688–89); author of *The History of My Own Times* (2 vols: 1724 and 1734) **2** Sir (**Frank**) **Macfarlane** (mək'fɑːlən). 1899–1985, Australian physician and virologist, who shared a Nobel prize for physiology or medicine in 1960 with P. B. Medawar for their work in immunology **3 Thomas**. 1635–1715, English theologian who tried to reconcile science and religion in his *Sacred Theory of the Earth* (1680–89)

Burnett (bɜː'nɛt) *n* **Frances Hodgson** ('hɒdʒsən). 1849–1924, US novelist, born in England; author of *Little Lord Fauntleroy* (1886) and *The Secret Garden* (1911)

Burney ('bɜːnɪ) *n* **1 Charles**. 1726–1814, English composer and music historian, whose books include *A General History of Music* (1776–89) **2** his daughter, **Frances**. known as **Fanny**; married name *Madame D'Arblay*. 1752–1840, English novelist and diarist: author of *Evelina* (1778). Her *Diaries and Letters* (1768–1840) are of historical interest

burning ('bɜːnɪŋ) *adj* **1** intense; passionate **2** urgent; crucial: *a burning problem*

burning bush *n* **1** a rutaceous shrub, *Dictamnus fraxinella*, of S Europe and Asia, whose glands release a volatile inflammable oil that can burn without harming the plant: identified as the bush from which God spoke to Moses (Exodus 3:2–4) **2** any of several shrubs or trees, esp the wahoo, that have bright red fruits or seeds **3** any of several plants, esp kochia, with a bright red autumn foliage

burning glass *n* a convex lens for concentrating the sun's rays into a small area to produce heat or fire

burnish ('bɜːnɪʃ) *vb* **1** to make or become shiny or smooth by friction; polish ▷ *n* **2** a shiny finish; lustre [c14 *burnischen*, from Old French *brunir* to make brown, from *brun* **BROWN**] > **burnisher** *n*

Burnley ('bɜːnlɪ) *n* an industrial town in NW England, in E Lancashire. Pop: 73 021 (2001)

burnous, *or* **burnouse** *or* (*US*) **burnoose** (bɜː'nuːs, -'nuːz) *n* a long circular cloak with a hood attached, worn esp by Arabs [c17: via French *burnous* from Arabic *burnus*, from Greek *birros* cloak]

burn out *vb* (*adverb*) **1** to become or cause to become worn out or inoperative as a result of heat or friction: *the clutch burnt out* **2** (intr) (of a rocket, jet engine, etc) to cease functioning as a result of exhaustion of the fuel supply **3** (tr; *usually passive*) to destroy by fire **4** to become or cause to become exhausted through overwork or dissipation

Burns (bɜːnz) *n* **Robert**. 1759–96, Scottish lyric poet. His verse, written mostly in dialect, includes love songs, nature poetry, and satires. *Auld Lang Syne* and *Tam o' Shanter* are among his best known poems

burnsides ('bɜːnˌsaɪdz) *pl n US* thick side whiskers worn with a moustache and clean-shaven chin [c19: named after General A. E. *Burnside* (1824–81), Union general in the US Civil War]

burnt (bɜːnt) *vb* **1** a past tense and past participle of **burn¹** ▷ *adj* **2** affected by or as if by burning; charred

burnt offering *n* a sacrificial offering burnt, usually on an altar, to honour, propitiate, or supplicate a deity

burnt sienna *n* **1** a reddish-brown dye or pigment obtained by roasting raw sienna in a furnace **2** a dark reddish-orange to reddish-brown colour

burnt umber *n* **1** a brown pigment obtained by heating umber **2** a dark brown colour

burp (bɜːp) *n* **1** *informal* a belch ▷ *vb* **2** (intr) *informal* to belch **3** (tr) to cause (a baby) to burp to relieve flatulence after feeding [c20: of imitative origin]

burqa *or* **burka** ('bɜːkə) *n* a long enveloping garment worn by Muslim women in public [c19: from Arabic]

burr¹ (bɜː) *n* **1** a small power-driven hand-operated rotary file, esp for removing burrs or for machining recesses **2** a rough edge left on a workpiece after cutting, drilling, etc **3** a rough or irregular protuberance, such as a burl on a tree ▷ *n, vb* **4** a variant spelling of **bur** (senses 1–4) [c14: variant of **BUR**]

burr² (bɜː) *n* **1** *phonetics* an articulation of (r) characteristic of certain English dialects, esp the uvular fricative trill of Northumberland or the retroflex r of the West of England **2** a whirring sound ▷ *vb* **3** to pronounce (words) with a burr **4** to make a whirring sound [c18: either special use of **BUR** (in the sense: rough sound) or of imitative origin]

Burr (bɜː) *n* **Aaron**. 1756–1836, US vice-president (1800–04), who fled after killing a political rival in a duel and plotted to create an independent empire in the western US; acquitted (1807) of treason

Burra (bʌrə) *n* **Edward** (**John**). 1905–76, British painter, noted esp for his depiction of squalid and grotesque subjects

Burrell ('bʌrəl) *n* **Paul**. born 1958, British butler and confidant to Diana, Princess of Wales. After her death he was charged with but (2003) acquitted of stealing from her estate. His book, *A Royal Duty* (2003), revealed intimate details of her life

Burren ('bʌrən) *n* the Burren a limestone area on the North Clare coast in the Irish Republic, famous for its wild flowers, caves, and dolmens

burrito (bə'riːtəʊ) *n, pl* -tos *Mexican cookery* a tortilla folded over a filling of minced beef, chicken, cheese, or beans [c20: from Mexican Spanish, from Spanish: literally, a young donkey]

burro ('bʊrəʊ) *n, pl* -ros a donkey, esp one used as a pack animal [c19: Spanish, from Portuguese, from *burrico* donkey, ultimately from Latin *burrīcus* small horse]

Burroughs ('bʌrəʊz) *n* **1 Edgar Rice**. 1875–1950, US novelist, author of the *Tarzan* stories **2 William S(eward)**. 1914–97, US novelist, noted for his experimental works exploring themes of drug addiction, violence, and homosexuality. His novels include *Junkie* (1953), *The Naked Lunch* (1959), and *Interzone* (1989)

burrow ('bʌrəʊ) *n* **1** a hole or tunnel dug in the ground by a rabbit, fox, or other small animal, for habitation or shelter **2** a small snug place affording shelter or retreat ▷ *vb* **3** to dig (a burrow) in, through, or under (ground) **4** (intr; often foll by *through*) to move through or as by digging **5** (intr) to hide or live in a burrow **6** (intr) to delve deeply: *he burrowed into his pockets* **7** to hide (oneself) [c13: probably a variant of **BOROUGH**] > **burrower** *n*

burry ('bʌrɪ) *adj* -rier, -riest **1** full of or covered in burs **2** resembling burs; prickly

bursa ('bɜːsə) *n, pl* -sae (-siː) *or* -sas **1** a small fluid-filled sac that reduces friction between movable parts of the body, esp at joints **2** *zoology* any saclike cavity or structure [c19: from Medieval Latin: bag, pouch, from Greek: skin, hide; see **PURSE**] > **bursal** *adj*

Bursa ('bɜːsə) *n* a city in NW Turkey: founded in the 2nd century BC; seat of Bithynian kings. Pop: 1 413 000 (2005 est). Former name: **Brusa**

bursar ('bɜːsə) *n* **1** an official in charge of the financial management of a school, college, or university **2** *chiefly Scot & NZ* a student holding a bursary [c13: from Medieval Latin *bursārius* keeper of the purse, from *bursa* purse]

bursary ('bɜːsərɪ) *n, pl* **-ries 1** Also called: **bursarship** a scholarship or grant awarded esp in Scottish and New Zealand schools, universities etc **2** *Brit* the treasury of a college, etc > **bursarial** (bɜː'sɛərɪəl) *adj*

bursitis (bɜː'saɪtɪs) *n* inflammation of a bursa, esp one in the shoulder joint

burst (bɜːst) *vb* **bursts, bursting, burst 1** to break or cause to break open or apart suddenly and noisily, esp from internal pressure; explode **2** (*intr*) to come, go, etc, suddenly and forcibly: *he burst into the room* **3** (*intr*) to be full to the point of breaking open **4** (*intr*) to give vent (to) suddenly or loudly: *to burst into song* **5** to cause or suffer the rupture of: *to burst a blood vessel* ▷ *n* **6** a sudden breaking open or apart; explosion **7** a break; breach; rupture **8** a sudden display or increase of effort or action; spurt: *a burst of speed* **9** a sudden and violent emission, occurrence, or outbreak: *a burst of heavy rain; a burst of applause* **10** a volley of fire from a weapon or weapons [Old English *berstan*; related to Old Norse *bresta*, Old Frisian *bersta*, Old High German *brestan*; compare **BREAK**]

burthen ('bɜːðən) *n, vb* an archaic word for **burden** > **'burthensome** *adj*

burton ('bɜːtən) *n* **go for a burton** *Brit slang* **a** to be broken, useless, or lost **b** to die [C15: of uncertain origin]

Burton ('bɜːtən) *n* **1** Sir **Richard Francis**. 1821–90, English explorer, Orientalist, and writer who discovered Lake Tanganyika with John Speke (1858); produced the first unabridged translation of *The Thousand Nights and a Night* (1885–88) **2 Richard**, real name *Richard Jenkins*. 1925–84, Welsh stage and film actor: films include *Becket* (1964), *Who's Afraid of Virginia Woolf?* (1966), and *Equus* (1977) **3 Robert**, pen name *Democritus Junior*. 1577–1640, English clergyman, scholar, and writer, noted for his *Anatomy of Melancholy* (1621) **4 Tim**. born 1958, US film director whose work includes *Beetlejuice* (1988), *Batman* (1989), *Ed Wood* (1994), and *Big Fish* (2003)

Burton-upon-Trent *n* a town in W central England, in E Staffordshire: famous for brewing. Pop: 43 784 (2001)

Burundi (bə'rʊndɪ) *n* a republic in E central Africa: inhabited chiefly by the Hutu, Tutsi, and Twa (Pygmy); made part of German East Africa in 1899; part of the Belgian territory of Ruanda-Urundi from 1923 until it became independent in 1962; ethnic violence has erupted at times between Hutu and Tutsi, as in Rwanda; consists mainly of high plateaus along the main Nile-Congo dividing range, dropping rapidly to the Great Rift Valley in the west. Official languages: Kirundi and French. Religion: Christian majority. Currency: Burundi franc. Capital: Bujumbura. Pop: 7 068 000 (2004 est.). Area: 27 731 sq km (10 707 sq miles). Former name (until 1962): Urundi > Bu'rundian *adj, n*

bury ('bɛrɪ) *vb* **buries, burying, buried** (*tr*) **1** to place (a corpse) in a grave, usually with funeral rites; inter **2** to place in the earth and cover with soil **3** to cover from sight; hide **4** to embed; sink: *to bury a nail in plaster* **5** to occupy (oneself) with deep concentration; engross: *to be buried in a book* **6** to dismiss from the mind; abandon: *to bury old hatreds* [Old English *byrgan* to bury, hide; related to Old Norse *bjarga* to save, preserve, Old English *beorgan* to defend]

Bury ('bɛrɪ) *n* **1** a town in NW England, in Bury unitary authority, Greater Manchester: an early textile centre. Pop: 60 178 (2001) **2** a unitary authority in NW England, in Greater Manchester. Pop: 181 900 (2003 est.). Area: 99 sq km (38 sq miles)

Buryat Republic *or* **Buryatia** (bʊə'jɑːtɪə; *Russian* bu'rja:tija) *n* a constituent republic of SE central Russia, on Lake Baikal: mountainous, with forests covering over half the total area. Capital: Ulan-Ude. Pop: 981 000 (2002). Area: 351 300 sq km (135 608 sq miles)

Bury St Edmunds ('bɛrɪ sənt 'ɛdməndz) *n* a market town in E England, in Suffolk. Pop: 36 218 (2001)

bus (bʌs) *n, pl* **buses** *or* **busses 1** a large motor vehicle designed to carry passengers between stopping places along a regular route. More formal name: omnibus **2** (*modifier*) of or relating to a bus or buses: *a bus driver; a bus station* **3** *informal* a car or aircraft, esp one that is old and shaky **4** *electronics, computing* short for **busbar**

5 *astronautics* a platform in a space vehicle used for various experiments and processes **6 miss the bus** to miss an opportunity; be too late ▷ *vb* **buses, busing, bused** *or* **busses, bussing, bussed 7** to travel or transport by bus **8** *chiefly US & Canadian* to transport (children) by bus from one area to a school in another in order to create racially integrated classes [C19: short for **OMNIBUS**]

busbar ('bʌz,bɑː) *n* **1** an electrical conductor, maintained at a specific voltage and capable of carrying a high current, usually used to make a common connection between several circuits in a system **2** a group of such electrical conductors at a low voltage, used for carrying data in binary form between the various parts of a computer or its peripherals

busby ('bʌzbɪ) *n, pl* **-bies 1** a tall fur helmet with a bag hanging from the top to the right side, worn by certain soldiers, usually hussars, as in the British Army **2** (not in official usage) another name for **bearskin** (sense 2) [C18 (in the sense: large bushy wig): perhaps from a proper name]

Busby ('bʌzbɪ) *n* Sir **Matthew**, known as *Matt*. 1909–94, British footballer. He managed Manchester United (1946–69)

bush¹ (bʊʃ) *n* **1** a dense woody plant, smaller than a tree, with many branches arising from the lower part of the stem; shrub **2** a dense cluster of such shrubs; thicket **3** something resembling a bush, esp in density: *a bush of hair* **4 the bush** an uncultivated or sparsely settled area, esp in Africa, Australia, New Zealand, or Canada: usually covered with trees or shrubs, varying from open shrubby country to dense rainforest **5** Also called: **bush lot, woodlot** *Canadian* an area of land on a farm on which timber is grown and cut **6 the bush** *informal* the countryside, as opposed to the city: *out in the bush* **7** *obsolete* a bunch of ivy hung as a vintner's sign in front of a tavern **8 beat about the bush** to avoid the point at issue; prevaricate ▷ *adj* **9** *Austral & NZ informal* rough-and-ready **10** *US & Canadian informal* unprofessional, unpolished, or second-rate **11 go bush** *informal, Austral & NZ* to abandon city amenities and live rough ▷ *vb* **12** (*intr*) to grow thick and bushy **13** (*tr*) to cover, decorate, support, etc, with bushes **14 bush it** (*tr*) *Australia* to camp out in the bush [C13: of Germanic origin; compare Old Norse *buski*, Old High German *busc*, Middle Dutch *bosch*; related to Old French *bosc* wood, Italian *bosco*]

bush² (bʊʃ) *n* **1** a thin metal sleeve or tubular lining serving as a bearing or guide ▷ *vb* **2** to fit a bush to (a casing, bearing, etc) [C15: from Middle Dutch *busse* box, bush; related to German *Büchse* tin, Swedish *hjulbössa* wheel-box, Late Latin *buxis* **BOX¹**]

Bush (bʊʃ) *n* **1 George**. born 1924, US Republican politician; vice president of the US (1981–89): 41st president of the US (1989–93) **2** his son, **George W(alker)**. born 1946, US Republican statesman: 43rd president of the US (from 2001)

bushbaby ('bʊʃ,beɪbɪ) *n, pl* **-babies** any agile nocturnal arboreal prosimian primate of the genera *Galago* and *Euoticus*, occurring in Africa south of the Sahara: family Lorisidae (lorises). They have large eyes and ears and a long tail. Also called: **galago**

bush-bash *vb* *Austral slang* (*intr*) **1** to clear scrubland **2** to drive through thick scrubland ▷ Also called: **scrub-bash**

bushbuck ('bʊʃ,bʌk) *or* **boschbok** *n, pl* **-bucks, -buck** *or* **-boks, -bok** a small nocturnal spiral-horned antelope, *Tragelaphus scriptus*, of the bush and tropical forest of Africa. Its coat is reddish-brown with a few white markings

bush carpenter *n* *Austral & NZ informal* a rough-and-ready unskilled workman

bushed (bʊʃt) *adj* *informal* **1** (*postpositive*) extremely tired; exhausted **2** *Canadian* mentally disturbed from living in isolation, esp in the north **3** *Austral & NZ* lost or bewildered, as in the bush

bushel ('bʊʃəl) *n* **1** a *Brit* unit of dry or liquid measure equal to 8 Imperial gallons. 1 Imperial bushel is equivalent to 0.036 37 cubic metres **2** a US unit of dry measure equal to 64 US pints. 1 US bushel is equivalent to 0.035 24 cubic metres **3** a container with a capacity equal to either of these quantities **4** *US informal* a large amount; great deal **5** hide one's light under a bushel to conceal one's abilities or good qualities [C14: from Old French *boissel*, from *boisse* one sixth of a bushel, of Gaulish origin]

bushfire ('bʊʃ,faɪə) *n* an uncontrolled fire in the bush; a scrub or forest fire

bushfly ('bʊʃ,flaɪ) *n*, *pl* -flies any of various small black dipterous flies of Australia, esp *Musca vetustissima*, that breed in faeces and dung: family *Calliphoridae*

bush house *n* *chiefly Austral* a shed or hut in the bush or a garden

Bushido (,buːʃɪ'dəʊ) *n* (*sometimes not capital*) the feudal code of the Japanese samurai, stressing self-discipline, courage and loyalty [C19: from Japanese *bushi* warrior (from Chinese *wushih*) + *dō* way (from Chinese *tao*)]

bushie ('bʊʃɪ) *n* a variant spelling of **bushy²**

bushing ('bʊʃɪŋ) *n* **1** another word for **bush²** (sense 1) **2** an adaptor having ends of unequal diameters, often with internal screw threads, used to connect pipes of different sizes **3** a layer of electrical insulation enabling a live conductor to pass through an earthed wall, etc

Bushire (bju:'ʃaɪə) *n* a port in SW Iran, on the Persian Gulf. Pop: 166 000 (2005 est)

bush jacket *or* **bush shirt** *n* a casual jacket or shirt having four patch pockets and a belt

bushland ('bʊʃ,lænd) *n* uncultivated land (esp in Australia) that is covered with trees, shrubs, or other natural vegetation

bush lawyer *n* *Austral & NZ* **1** any of several prickly trailing plants of the genus *Rubus* **2** *informal* a person unqualified in the law who claims competence in it

Bushman ('bʊʃmən) *n*, *pl* -man *or* -men **1** a member of a hunting and gathering people of southern Africa, esp the Kalahari region, typically having leathery yellowish skin, short stature, and prominent buttocks **2** any language of this people, belonging to the Khoisan family [C18: from Afrikaans *boschjesman*]

bushmaster ('bʊʃ,mɑːstə) *n* a large greyish-brown highly venomous snake, *Lachesis muta*, inhabiting wooded regions of tropical America: family *Crotalidae* (pit vipers)

bushmeat ('bʊʃ,miːt) *n* meat taken from any animal native to African forests, including species that may be endangered or not usually eaten outside Africa

bushranger ('bʊʃ,reɪndʒə) *n* **1** *Austral history* an escaped convict or robber living in the bush **2** *US* a person who lives away from civilization; backwoodsman

bush singlet *n* *NZ* a black woollen singlet often worn by farm labourers

bush tea *n* **1** a leguminous shrub of the genus *Cyclopia*, of southern Africa **2** a beverage prepared from the dried leaves of any of these plants

bush telegraph *n* a means of spreading rumour, gossip, etc

bush tucker *n* *Austral*. **a** any wild animal, insect, plant or plant extract, etc traditionally used as food by native Australians **b** cooking based around ingredients taken from the Australian wilderness

bushveld ('bʊʃ,fɛlt, -,vɛlt) *n* the bushveld an area of low altitude in N South Africa, having scrub vegetation

bushwhack ('bʊʃ,wæk) *vb* **1** (*tr*) *US, Canadian & Austral* to ambush **2** (*intr*) *US, Canadian & Austral* to cut or beat one's way through thick woods **3** (*intr*) *US, Canadian & Austral* to range or move around in woods or the bush **4** (*intr*) *US & Canadian* to fight as a guerrilla in wild or uncivilized regions **5** (*intr*) *NZ* to work in the bush, esp at timber felling

bushwhacker ('bʊʃ,wækə) *n* **1** *US, Canadian & Austral* a person who travels around or lives in thinly populated woodlands **2** *Austral informal* an unsophisticated person; boor **3** a Confederate guerrilla during the American Civil War **4** *US* any guerrilla **5** *NZ* a person who works in the bush, esp at timber felling

bushy¹ ('bʊʃɪ) *adj* bushier, bushiest **1** covered or overgrown with bushes **2** thick and shaggy: *bushy eyebrows* > 'bushily *adv* > 'bushiness *n*

bushy² *or* **bushie** ('bʊʃɪ) *n*, *pl* bushies *Austral informal* **1** a person who lives in the bush **2** an unsophisticated uncouth person

business ('bɪznɪs) *n* **1** a trade or profession **2** an industrial, commercial, or professional operation; purchase and sale of goods and services **3** a commercial or industrial establishment, such as a firm or factory **4** commercial activity; dealings (esp in the phrase **do business**) **5** volume or quantity of commercial activity: *business is poor today* **6** commercial policy or procedure: *overcharging is bad business* **7** proper or rightful concern or responsibility (often in the phrase **mind one's own business**) **8** a special task; assignment **9** an affair; matter **10** serious work or activity: *get down to business* **11** a complicated affair; rigmarole **12** Also called: stage business *theatre* an incidental action, such as lighting a pipe, performed by an actor for dramatic effect **13** mean business to be in earnest **14** do the business *informal* to achieve what is required: *it tastes vile, but it does the business* [Old English *bisignis* solicitude, attentiveness, from *bisig* BUSY + -*nis* -NESS]

business angel *n* *informal* an investor in a business venture, esp one in its early stages. Also called: angel investor

business casual *n* *informal* a style of casual clothing worn by businesspeople at work instead of more formal attire

business college *n* a college providing courses in secretarial studies, business management, accounting, commerce, etc

businesslike ('bɪznɪs,laɪk) *adj* efficient and methodical

businessman ('bɪznɪs,mæn, -mən) *n*, *pl* -men a person, esp a man, engaged in commercial or industrial business, esp as an owner or executive

business park *n* an area specially designated and landscaped to accommodate business offices, warehouses, light industry, etc

businessperson ('bɪznɪs,pɜrsən) *n*, *pl* -people *or* -persons a person engaged in commercial or industrial business, esp as an owner or executive

business plan *n* a detailed plan setting out the objectives of a business, the strategy and tactics planned to achieve them, and the expected profits, usually over a period of three to ten years

business process re-engineering *n* restructuring an organization by means of a radical reassessment of its core processes and predominant competencies. Abbreviation: BPR

businesswoman ('bɪznɪs,wʊmən) *n*, *pl* -women a woman engaged in commercial or industrial business, esp as an owner or executive

busk (bʌsk) *vb* (*intr*) *Brit* to make money by singing, dancing, acting, etc, in public places, as in front of theatre queues [C20: perhaps from Spanish *buscar* to look for] > 'busker *n* > 'busking *n*

buskin ('bʌskɪn) *n* **1** (*formerly*) a sandal-like covering for the foot and leg, reaching the calf and usually laced **2** Also called: cothurnus a thick-soled laced half boot resembling this, worn esp by actors of ancient Greece **3** the buskin *chiefly literary* tragic drama [C16: perhaps from Spanish *borzeguí*; related to Old French *bouzeguin*, Italian *borzacchino*, of obscure origin]

busman's holiday ('bʌsmənz) *n* *informal* a holiday spent doing the same sort of thing as one does at work [C20: alluding to a bus driver having a driving holiday]

Busra *or* **Busrah** ('bʌsrə) *n* variant spellings of **Basra**

buss (bʌs) *n*, *vb* an archaic or dialect word for **kiss** [C16: probably of imitative origin; compare French *baiser*, German dialect *Bussi* little kiss]

Buss (bʌs) *n* **Frances Mary**. 1827–94, British educationalist; a pioneer of secondary education for girls, who campaigned for women's admission to university

Bussell ('bʌsəl) *n* **Darcey (Andrea)**. born 1969, British ballet dancer, principal ballerina with the Royal Ballet (1989–2006)

bust¹ (bʌst) *n* **1** the chest of a human being, esp a woman's bosom **2** a sculpture of the head, shoulders, and upper chest of a person [C17: from French *buste*, from Italian *busto* a sculpture, of unknown origin]

bust² (bʌst) *informal* ▷ *vb* busts, busting, busted *or* bust **1** to burst or break **2** to make or become bankrupt **3** (*tr*) (of the police) to raid, search, or arrest **4** (*tr*) *US & Canadian* to demote, esp in military rank ▷ *n* **5** a raid, search, or arrest by the police **6** *chiefly US* a punch; hit **7** *US & Canadian* a failure, esp a financial one; bankruptcy **8** a drunken party ▷ *adj* **9** broken **10** bankrupt **11** **go bust** to become bankrupt [C19: from a dialect pronunciation of BURST]

bustard (ˈbʌstəd) *n* any terrestrial bird of the family *Otididae*, inhabiting open regions of the Old World: order *Gruiformes* (cranes, rails, etc). They have long strong legs, a heavy body, a long neck, and speckled plumage [C15: from Old French *bistarde*, influenced by Old French *oustarde*, both from Latin *avis tarda* slow bird]

bustier (ˈbuːstɪeɪ) *n* a type of close-fitting usually strapless top worn by women

bustle¹ (ˈbʌsəl) *vb* **1** (when *intr*, often foll by *about*) to hurry or cause to hurry with a great show of energy or activity ▷ *n* **2** energetic and noisy activity [C16: probably from obsolete *buskle* to make energetic preparation, from dialect *busk* from Old Norse *būask* to prepare] > ˈbustler *n* > ˈbustling *adj*

bustle² (ˈbʌsəl) *n* a cushion or a metal or whalebone framework worn by women in the late 19th century at the back below the waist in order to expand the skirt [C18: of unknown origin]

bust-up *informal* ▷ *n* **1** a quarrel, esp a serious one ending a friendship, etc **2** *Brit* a disturbance or brawl ▷ *vb* **bust up** (*adverb*) **3** (*intr*) to quarrel and part **4** (*tr*) to disrupt (a meeting), esp violently

busy (ˈbɪzɪ) *adj* busier, busiest **1** actively or fully engaged; occupied **2** crowded with or characterized by activity: *a busy day* **3** *chiefly US & Canadian* (of a room, telephone line, etc) in use; engaged **4** overcrowded with detail: *a busy painting* **5** meddlesome; inquisitive; prying ▷ *vb* busies, busying, busied **6** (*tr*) to make or keep (someone, esp oneself) busy; occupy [Old English *bisig*; related to Middle Dutch *besich*, perhaps to Latin *festīnāre* to hurry] > ˈbusily *adv* > ˈbusyness *n*

busybody (ˈbɪzɪˌbɒdɪ) *n*, *pl* **-bodies** a meddlesome, prying, or officious person > ˈbusyˌbodying *n*

busy Lizzie (ˈlɪzɪ) *n* a balsaminaceous plant, *Impatiens balsamina*, that has pink, red, or white flowers and is often grown as a pot plant

but¹ (bʌt; *unstressed* bət) *conj* (*coordinating*) **1** contrary to expectation: *he cut his knee but didn't cry* **2** in contrast; on the contrary: *I like opera but my husband doesn't* **3** (*usually used after a negative*) other than: *we can't do anything but wait* ▷ *conj* (*subordinating*) **4** (*usually used after a negative*) without it happening or being the case that: *we never go out but it rains* **5** (foll by *that*) except that: *nothing is impossible but that we live forever* **6** *archaic* if not; unless ▷ *sentence connector* **7** *informal* used to introduce an exclamation: *my, but you're nice* **8** except; save: *they saved all but one of the pigs* **9** **but for** were it not for: *but for you, we couldn't have managed* ▷ *adv* **10** just; merely; only: *he was but a child; I can but try* **11** *Scot, Austral & NZ informal* though; however: *it's a rainy day: warm, but* **12** **all but** almost; practically: *he was all but dead when we found him* ▷ *n* **13** an objection (esp in the phrase **ifs and buts**) [Old English *būtan* without, outside, except, from *be* BY + *ūtan* OUT; related to Old Saxon *biūtan*, Old High German *biūzan*]

but² (bʌt) *Scot* ▷ *n* **1** the outer room of a two-roomed cottage: usually the kitchen ▷ *prep*, *adv* **2** in or into the outer part (of a house) ▷ See **ben** [C18: from *but* (adv) outside, hence, outer room; see BUT¹]

butadiene (ˌbjuːtəˈdaɪiːn) *n* a colourless easily liquefiable flammable gas that polymerizes readily and is used mainly in the manufacture of synthetic rubbers. Formula: $CH_2:CHCH:CH_2$ [C20: from BUTA(NE) + DI-¹ + -ENE]

butane (ˈbjuːteɪn, bjuːˈteɪn) *n* a colourless flammable gaseous alkane that exists in two isomeric forms, both of which occur in natural gas. The stable isomer, n-butane, is used mainly in the manufacture of rubber and fuels (such as Calor Gas). Formula: C_4H_{10} [C19: from BUT(YL) + -ANE]

butanol (ˈbjuːtəˌnɒl) *n* a colourless substance existing in four isomeric forms. The three liquid isomers are used as solvents for resins, lacquers, etc, and in the manufacture of organic compounds. Formula: C_4H_9OH. Also called: butyl alcohol [C19: from BUTAN(E) + -OL¹]

butanone (ˈbjuːtəˌnəʊn) *n* a colourless soluble flammable liquid used mainly as a solvent for resins, as a paint remover, and in lacquers, cements, and adhesives. Formula: $CH_3COC_2H_5$. Also called: methyl ethyl ketone [C20: from BUTAN(E) + -ONE]

butch (bʊtʃ) *slang* ▷ *adj* **1** (of a woman or man) markedly or aggressively masculine ▷ *n* **2** a lesbian who is noticeably masculine **3** a strong rugged man [C18: back formation from BUTCHER]

butcher (ˈbʊtʃə) *n* **1** a retailer of meat **2** a person who slaughters or dresses meat for market **3** an indiscriminate or brutal murderer ▷ *vb* (*tr*) **4** to slaughter or dress (animals) for meat **5** to kill indiscriminately or brutally **6** to make a mess of; botch; ruin [C13: from Old French *bouchier*, from *bouc* he-goat, probably of Celtic origin; see BUCK¹; compare Welsh *bwch* he-goat]

butcherbird (ˈbʊtʃəˌbɜːd) *n* **1** a shrike, esp one of the genus *Lanius* **2** any of several Australian magpies of the genus *Cracticus* that impale their prey on thorns

butcher's-broom *n* a liliaceous evergreen shrub, *Ruscus aculeatus*, that has stiff prickle-tipped flattened green stems, which resemble and function as true leaves. The plant was formerly used for making brooms

butchery (ˈbʊtʃərɪ) *n*, *pl* **-eries** **1** the business or work of a butcher **2** wanton and indiscriminate slaughter; carnage **3** a less common word for **slaughterhouse**

Bute¹ (bjuːt) *n* an island off the coast of SW Scotland, in Argyll and Bute council area: situated in the Firth of Clyde, separated from the Cowal peninsula by the **Kyles of Bute**. Chief town: Rothesay. Pop: 7228 (2001). Area: 121 sq km (47 sq miles)

Bute² (bjuːt) *n* **John Stuart**, 3rd Earl of Bute. 1713–92, British Tory statesman; prime minister (1762–63)

Butenandt (*German* ˈbuːtənant) *n* **Adolf Frederick Johann.** 1903–95, German organic chemist. He shared the Nobel prize for chemistry (1939) for his pioneering work on sex hormones

Buteshire (ˈbjuːtˌʃɪə, -ʃə) *n* (until 1975) a county of SW Scotland, consisting of islands in the Firth of Clyde and Kilbrannan Sound: formerly part of Strathclyde region (1975–96), now part of Argyll and Bute council area

Buteyko method (ˌbuːˈteɪkəʊ) *n* a breath control technique used to prevent hyperventilation and treat asthma without drugs [C20: named after Konstantin P. *Buteyko* (born 1923), Russian physician]

Buthelezi (ˌbuːtəˈleɪzɪ) *n* **Mangosouthu Gatsha** (ˌmæŋɡəʊˈsuːtuː ˈɡætʃə), known as **Chief Buthelezi**. born 1928, Zulu leader, chief minister of the KwaZulu territory of South Africa from 1970 until its abolition in 1994; founder of the Inkatha movement and advocate of Zulu autonomy; minister of home affairs (1994–2004)

butler (ˈbʌtlə) *n* the male servant of a household in charge of the wines, table, etc: usually the head servant [C13: from Old French *bouteillier*, from *bouteille* BOTTLE]

Butler (ˈbʌtlə) *n* **1 Joseph.** 1692–1752, English bishop and theologian, author of *Analogy of Religion* (1736) **2 Josephine (Elizabeth)**. 1828–1906, British social reformer, noted esp for her campaigns against state regulation of prostitution **3 Reg**, full name *Reginald Cotterell Butler*. 1913–81, British metal sculptor; his works include *The Unknown Political Prisoner* (1953) **4 R(ichard) A(usten)**, Baron Butler of Saffron Walden, known as *Rab Butler*. 1902–82, British Conservative politician: Chancellor of the Exchequer (1951–55); Home Secretary (1957–62); Foreign Secretary (1963–64) **5 Samuel**. 1612–80, English poet and satirist; author of *Hudibras* (1663–78) **6 Samuel**. 1835–1902, British novelist, noted for his satirical work *Erewhon* (1872) and his autobiographical novel *The Way of All Flesh* (1903)

butlery (ˈbʌtlərɪ) *n*, *pl* **-leries** **1** a butler's room **2** another name for **buttery²** (sense 1)

butt¹ (bʌt) *n* **1** the thicker or blunt end of something, such as the end of the stock of a rifle **2** the unused end of something, esp of a cigarette; stub **3** *tanning* the portion of a hide covering the lower backside of the animal **4** *US & Canadian informal* the buttocks **5** *US* a slang word for **cigarette 6** *building trades* short for **butt joint** [C15 (in the sense: thick end of something, buttock): related to Old English *buttuc* end, ridge, Middle Dutch *bot* stumpy]

butt² (bʌt) *n* **1 a** a person or thing that is the target of ridicule, wit, etc **2** *shooting, archery* **a** a mound of earth behind the target on a target range that stops bullets or wide shots **b** the target itself **c** (*plural*) the target range **3** a low barrier, usually of sods or peat, behind which sportsmen shoot game birds, esp grouse **4** *archaic* goal; aim ▷ *vb* **5** (usually foll by *on* or *against*) to lie or be placed end on to; abut: *to butt a beam against a wall* [C14 (in the sense: mark for archery practice): from Old French *but*; related to French *butte* knoll, target]

butt³ (bʌt) *vb* **1** to strike or push (something) with the head or horns **2** (*intr*) to project; jut **3** (*intr*; foll by *in* or *into*) to intrude, esp into a conversation; interfere; meddle **4 butt out** *informal, chiefly US & Canadian* to stop interfering or meddling ▷ *n* **5** a blow with the head or horns [C12: from Old French *boter*, of Germanic origin; compare Middle Dutch *botten* to strike; see BEAT, BUTTON] ▷ 'butter *n*

butt⁴ (bʌt) *n* a large cask, esp one with a capacity of two hogsheads, for storing wine or beer [C14: from Old French *botte*, from Old Provençal *bota*, from Late Latin *buttis* cask, perhaps from Greek *butinē* chamber pot]

Butt (bʌt) *n* Dame **Clara**. 1872–1936, English contralto

butte (bjuːt) *n Western US & Canadian* an isolated steep-sided flat-topped hill [C19: from French, from Old French *bute* mound behind a target, from *but* target; see BUTT²]

butter ('bʌtə) *n* **1 a** an edible fatty whitish-yellow solid made from cream by churning, for cooking and table use **b** (*as modifier*): *butter icing* **2** any substance with a butter-like consistency, such as peanut butter or vegetable butter **3** look as if butter wouldn't melt in one's mouth to look innocent, although probably not so ▷ *vb* (*tr*) **4** to put butter on or in **5** to flatter ▷ See also **butter up** [Old English *butere*, from Latin *būtyrum*, from Greek *bouturon*, from *bous* cow + *turos* cheese]

butter bean *n* a variety of lima bean that has large pale flat edible seeds and is grown in the southern US

butterbur ('bʌtə,bɜː) *n* a plant of the Eurasian genus *Petasites* with fragrant whitish or purple flowers, woolly stems, and leaves formerly used to wrap butter: family *Asteraceae* (composites)

buttercup ('bʌtə,kʌp) *n* any of various yellow-flowered ranunculaceous plants of the genus *Ranunculus*, such as *R. acris* (meadow buttercup), which is native to Europe but common throughout North America

butterfat ('bʌtə,fæt) *n* the fatty substance of milk from which butter is made, consisting of a mixture of glycerides, mainly butyrin, olein, and palmitin

Butterfield ('bʌtə,fiːld) *n* **William**. 1814–1900, British architect of the Gothic Revival; his buildings include Keble College, Oxford (1870) and All Saints, Margaret Street, London (1849–59)

butterfingers ('bʌtə,fɪŋgəz) *n* (*functioning as singular*) *informal* a person who drops things inadvertently or fails to catch things ▷ 'butter,fingered *adj*

butterfish ('bʌtə,fɪʃ) *n, pl* **-fish** or **-fishes** any eel-like blennioid food fish, *Pholis gunnellus*, occurring in North Atlantic coastal regions: family *Pholidae* (gunnels). It has a slippery scaleless golden brown skin with a row of black spots along the base of the long dorsal fin

butterflies ('bʌtə,flaɪz) *pl n* *informal* tremors in the stomach region due to nervousness

butterfly ('bʌtə,flaɪ) *n, pl* **-flies 1** any diurnal insect of the order *Lepidoptera* that has a slender body with clubbed antennae and typically rests with the wings (which are often brightly coloured) closed over the back. See **moth 2** a person who never settles with one group, interest, or occupation for long **3** a swimming stroke in which the arms are plunged forward together in large circular movements **4** *commerce* the simultaneous purchase and sale of traded call options, at different exercise prices or with different expiry dates, on a stock exchange or commodity market [Old English *buttorflēoge*; the name perhaps is based on a belief that butterflies stole milk and butter]

butterfly collar *n* the Irish name for **wing collar**

butterfly effect *n* the idea, used in chaos theory, that a very small difference in the initial state of a physical system can make a significant difference to the state at some later time [C20: from the theory that a butterfly flapping its wings in one part of the world might ultimately cause a hurricane in another part of the world]

butterfly nut *n* another name for **wing nut**

Buttermere ('bʌtə,mɪə) *n* a lake in NW England, in Cumbria, in the Lake District, southwest of Keswick. Length: 2 km (1.25 miles)

buttermilk ('bʌtə,mɪlk) *n* the sourish liquid remaining after the butter has been separated from milk, often used for making scones and soda bread

butter muslin *n* a fine loosely woven cotton material originally used for wrapping butter

butternut ('bʌtə,nʌt) *n* **1** a walnut tree, *Juglans cinerea* of E North America **2** the oily edible egg-shaped nut of this tree **3** NZ short for **butternut pumpkin**

butternut pumpkin *n Austral* a variety of pumpkin, eaten as vegetable. Also called (NZ): **butternut**

butterscotch ('bʌtə,skɒtʃ) *n* **1 a** a kind of hard brittle toffee made with butter, brown sugar, etc **2 a** a flavouring made from these ingredients **b** (*as modifier*): *butterscotch icing* [C19: perhaps first made in Scotland]

butter tart *n Canadian* a kind of tart made with butter, brown sugar, and raisins

butter up *vb* (*tr, adverb*) to flatter

butterwort ('bʌtə,wɜːt) *n* a plant of the genus *Pinguicula*, esp *P. vulgaris*, that grows in wet places and has violet-blue spurred flowers and fleshy greasy glandular leaves on which insects are trapped and digested: family *Lentibulariaceae*

Butterworth ('bʌtəwəθ) *n* **1 George**. 1885–1916, British composer, noted for his interest in folk song and his settings of Housman's poems **2 Nick**. born 1946, English writer and illustrator of children's books

buttery¹ ('bʌtərɪ) *adj* containing, like, or coated with butter ▷ 'butteriness *n*

buttery² ('bʌtərɪ) *n, pl* **-teries 1** a room for storing foods or wines **2** *Brit* (in some universities) a room in which food is supplied or sold to students [C14: from Anglo-French *boterie*, from Anglo-Latin *buteria*, probably from *butta* cask, BUTT⁴]

butt joint *n* a joint between two plates, planks, bars, sections, etc, when the components are butted together and do not overlap or interlock. The joint may be strapped with jointing plates laid across it or welded (**butt weld**). Sometimes shortened to: **butt**

buttock ('bʌtək) *n* **1** either of the two large fleshy masses of thick muscular tissue that form the human rump. See also **gluteus**. Related adjectives: **natal, gluteal 2** the analogous part in some mammals [C13: perhaps from Old English *buttuc* round slope, diminutive of *butt* (unattested) strip of land; see BUTT¹ -OCK]

button ('bʌtⁿn) *n* **1** a disc or knob of plastic, wood, etc, attached to a garment, etc, usually for fastening two surfaces together by passing it through a buttonhole or loop **2** a small round object, such as any of various sweets, decorations, or badges **3** a small disc that completes an electric circuit when pushed, as one that operates a doorbell or machine **4** *biology* any rounded knoblike part or organ, such as an unripe mushroom **5** *fencing* the protective knob fixed to the point of a foil **6** *Brit* an object of no value (esp in the phrase **not worth a button**) ▷ *vb* **7** to fasten with a button or buttons **8** (*tr*) to provide with buttons **9** (*tr*) *fencing* to hit (an opponent) with the button of one's foil ▷ See also **button up** [C14: from Old French *boton*, from *boter* to thrust, butt, of Germanic origin; see BUTT³] ▷ 'buttoner *n* ▷ 'buttonless *adj* ▷ 'buttony *adj*

buttonhole ('bʌtⁿn,həʊl) *n* **1** a slit in a garment, etc, through which a button is passed to fasten two surfaces together **2** a flower or small bunch of flowers worn pinned to the lapel or in the buttonhole, esp at weddings, formal dances, etc. US name: **boutonniere** ▷ *vb* (*tr*) **3** to detain (a person) in conversation **4** to make buttonholes in

buttonhook ('bʌtᵊn,hʊk) n a thin tapering hooked instrument formerly used for pulling buttons through the buttonholes of gloves, shoes, etc

button quail n any small quail-like terrestrial bird of the genus *Turnix*, such as *T. sylvatica* (striped button quail), occurring in tropical and subtropical regions of the Old World: family *Turnicidae*, order *Gruiformes* (cranes, rails, etc). Also called: **hemipode**

button up vb (tr, adverb) 1 to fasten (a garment) with a button or buttons 2 *informal* to conclude (business) satisfactorily

buttress ('bʌtrɪs) n 1 Also called: **pier** a construction, usually of brick or stone, built to support a wall. See also **flying buttress** 2 any support or prop 3 something shaped like a buttress, such as a projection from a mountainside ⊳ vb (tr) 4 to support (a wall) with a buttress 5 to support or sustain [C13: from Old French *bouterez*, short for *ars bouterez* thrusting arch, from *bouter* to thrust, BUTT³]

butty¹ ('bʌtɪ) n, pl -ties *chiefly Northern English dialect* a sandwich: *a jam butty* [C19: from *buttered* (bread)]

butty² ('bʌtɪ) n, pl -ties *English dialect* (esp in mining parlance) a friend or workmate [C19: perhaps from obsolete *booty* sharing, from BOOT², later applied to a middleman in a mine]

Butung ('buːtʊŋ) n an island of Indonesia, southeast of Sulawesi: hilly and forested. Chief town: Baubau. Area: 4555 sq km (1759 sq miles)

butyl ('bjuː,taɪl, -tɪl) n (modifier) of, consisting of, or containing any of four isomeric forms of the group C_4H_9-: *butyl rubber* [C19: from BUT(YRIC ACID) + -YL]

butyl alcohol n another name for **butanol**

butyl rubber n a copolymer of isobutene and isoprene, used in tyres and as a waterproofing material

butyric acid (bjuː'tɪrɪk) n a carboxylic acid existing in two isomeric forms, one of which produces the smell in rancid butter. Its esters are used in flavouring. Formula: $C_3(CH_2)_2COOH$ [C19 *butyric*, from Latin *būtyrum* BUTTER]

buxom ('bʌksəm) adj 1 (esp of a woman) healthily plump, attractive, and vigorous 2 (of a woman) full-bosomed [C12: *buhsum* compliant, pliant, from Old English *būgan* to bend, BOW¹; related to Middle Dutch *būchsam* pliant, German *biegsam*] > **'buxomly** adv > **'buxomness** n

Buxtehude (German bʊkstə'huːdə) n **Dietrich** ('diːtrɪç). 1637–1707, Danish composer and organist, resident in Germany from 1668, who influenced Bach and Handel

Buxton ('bʌkstən) n a town in N England, in NW Derbyshire in the Peak District: thermal springs. Pop: 20 836 (2001)

buy (baɪ) vb **buys, buying, bought** (mainly tr) 1 to acquire by paying or promising to pay a sum of money or the equivalent; purchase 2 to be capable of purchasing: *money can't buy love* 3 to acquire by any exchange or sacrifice: *to buy time by equivocation* 4 (intr) to act as a buyer 5 to bribe or corrupt; hire by or as by bribery 6 *slang* to accept as true, practical, etc 7 (intr; foll by *into*) to purchase shares of (a company): *we bought into General Motors* 8 (tr) *theol* (esp of Christ) to ransom or redeem (a Christian or the soul of a Christian) 9 *have bought it slang* to be killed ⊳ n 10 a purchase (often in the phrases **good** or **bad buy**) ⊳ See also **buy in, buy into, buy off, buy out, buy up** [Old English *bycgan*; related to Old Norse *byggja* to let out, lend, Gothic *bugjan* to buy]

● USAGE The use of *off* after *buy* as in *I bought this off my* ● *neighbour* was formerly considered incorrect, but is ● now acceptable in informal contexts

buy-back ('baɪ,bæk) n *commerce* the repurchase by a company of some or all of its shares from an investor, who acquired them by putting venture capital into the company when it was formed

buyer ('baɪə) n 1 a person who buys; purchaser; customer 2 a person employed to buy merchandise, materials, etc, as for a shop or factory

buy in (adverb) 1 (tr) to buy back for the owner (an item in an auction) at or below the reserve price 2 (intr) to purchase shares in a company 3 Also called: **buy into** (tr) *US informal* to pay money to secure a position or place for (someone, esp oneself) in some organization, esp a

business or club 4 to purchase (goods, etc) in large quantities ⊳ n **buy-in** 5 the purchase of a company by a manager or group who does not work for that company

buy into vb (intr, preposition) 1 to agree with or accept as valid (an argument, theory, etc) 2 *Austral & NZ informal* to get involved in (an argument, fight, etc)

buy off vb (tr, adverb) to pay (a person or group) to drop a charge, end opposition, relinquish a claim, etc

buy out vb (tr, adverb) 1 to purchase the ownership, controlling interest, shares, etc, of (a company, etc) 2 to gain the release of (a person) from the armed forces by payment of money 3 to pay (a person) once and for all to give up (property, interest, etc) ⊳ n **buyout** 4 the purchase of a company, esp by its former management or staff. See also **leveraged buyout, management buyout**

buy-to-let n (modifier) of or relating to the practice of buying a property to let to tenants rather than to live in oneself: *the buy-to-let boom*

buy up vb (tr, adverb) 1 to purchase all, or all that is available, of (something) 2 *commerce* to purchase a controlling interest in (a company, etc), as by the acquisition of shares

buzz (bʌz) n 1 a rapidly vibrating humming sound, as that of a prolonged z or of a bee in flight 2 a low sound, as of many voices in conversation 3 a rumour; report; gossip 4 *informal* a telephone call: *I'll give you a buzz* 5 *slang* a a pleasant sensation, as from a drug such as cannabis b a sense of excitement; kick ⊳ vb 6 (intr) to make a vibrating sound like that of a prolonged z 7 (intr) to talk or gossip with an air of excitement or urgency: *the town buzzed with the news* 8 (tr) to utter or spread (a rumour) 9 (intr; often foll by *about*) to move around quickly and busily; bustle 10 (tr) to signal or summon with a buzzer 11 (tr) *informal* to call by telephone 12 (tr) *informal* a to fly an aircraft very low over (an object): *to buzz a ship* b to fly an aircraft very close to or across the path of (another aircraft), esp to warn or intimidate 13 (tr) (esp of insects) to make a buzzing sound with (wings, etc) [C16: of imitative origin] > **'buzzing** n, adj

buzzard ('bʌzəd) n any diurnal bird of prey of the genus *Buteo*, typically having broad wings and tail and a soaring flight: family *Accipitridae* (hawks, etc) [C13: from Old French *buisard*, variant of *buison* buzzard, from Latin *būteō* hawk, falcon]

buzzer ('bʌzə) n 1 a device that produces a buzzing sound, esp one similar to an electric bell without a hammer or gong 2 NZ a wood planing machine

buzz off vb (intr, adverb; often imperative) *informal, chiefly Brit* to go away; leave; depart

buzz word n *informal* a word, often originating in a particular jargon, that becomes a vogue word in the community as a whole or among a particular group

BVM abbreviation Beata Virgo Maria [Latin: Blessed Virgin Mary]

bwana ('bwɑːnə) n (in E Africa) a master, often used as a respectful form of address corresponding to *sir* [Swahili, from Arabic *abūna* our father]

by (baɪ) prep 1 used to indicate the agent after a passive verb: *seeds eaten by the birds* 2 used to indicate the person responsible for a creative work: *this song is by Schubert* 3 via; through: *enter by the back door* 4 followed by a gerund to indicate a means used: *he frightened her by hiding behind the door* 5 beside; next to; near: *a tree by the house* 6 passing the position of; past: *he drove by the old cottage* 7 not later than; before: *return the books by Tuesday* 8 used to indicate extent, after a comparative: *it is hotter by five degrees than it was yesterday* 9 (esp in oaths) invoking the name of: *I swear by all the gods* 10 multiplied by: *four by three equals twelve* 11 (in habitual sentences) during the passing of (esp in the phrases **by day, by night**) 12 placed between measurements of the various dimensions of something: *a plank fourteen inches by seven* ⊳ adv 13 near: *the house is close by* 14 away; aside: *he put some money by each week for savings* 15 passing a point near something; past: *he drove by* 16 Scot past; over and done with: *that's a' by now* 17 Scot aside; behind one: *you must put that by you* ⊳ n, pl byes 18 a variant spelling of **bye¹** [Old English *bī*; related to Gothic *bi*, Old High German *bī*, Sanskrit *abhi* to, towards]

by- *or* **bye-** *prefix* **1** near: *bystander* **2** secondary or incidental: *by-effect; by-election; by-path; by-product* [from BY]

by and by *adv* presently or eventually

by and large *adv* in general; on the whole [c17: originally nautical (meaning: to the wind and off it)]

Byatt ('baɪət) *n* **Dame A(ntonia) S(usan)**. born 1936, British novelist; her books include *The Virgin in the Garden* (1978), *Possession* (1990), and *A Whistling Woman* (2002)

by-catch *n* unwanted fish and other sea animals caught in a fishing net along with the desired kind of fish

Bydgoszcz (*Polish* 'bɪdɡɔʃtʃ) *n* an industrial city and port in N Poland: under Prussian rule from 1772 to 1919. Pop: 579 000 (2005 est). German name: **Bromberg**

bye¹ *or* **by** (baɪ) *n* **1** *sport* the situation in which a player or team in an eliminatory contest wins a preliminary round by virtue of having no opponent **2** *golf* one or more holes of a stipulated course that are left unplayed after the match has been decided **3** *cricket* a run scored off a ball not struck by the batsman: allotted to the team as an extra and not to the individual batsman **4** something incidental or secondary **5** **by the bye** incidentally; by the way: used as a sentence connector [c16: a variant of BY]

bye² *or* **bye-bye** *sentence substitute Brit informal* goodbye

bye-byes *n* (*functioning as singular*) an informal word, used esp to children, for **sleep**: *go to bye-byes*

by-election *or* **bye-election** *n* (in the United Kingdom and other countries of the Commonwealth) an election held during the life of a parliament to fill a vacant seat in the lower chamber

Byelgorod-Dnestrovski *n* a variant spelling of **Belgorod-Dnestrovski**

Byelorussia *n* a variant spelling of **Belarus**

Byelostok (bjɪla'stɔk) *n* a Russian name for **Białystok**

Byelovo *or* **Belovo** (*Russian* 'bjeləvə) *n* a city in W central Russia. Pop: 65 000 (2005 est)

bygone ('baɪ,ɡɒn) *adj* **1** (*usually prenominal*) past; former ▷ *n* **2** (*often plural*) a past occurrence **3** (*often plural*) an artefact, implement, etc, of former domestic or industrial use, now often collected for interest **4** **let bygones be bygones** to agree to forget past quarrels

bylaw *or* **bye-law** ('baɪ,lɔ:) *n* **1** a rule made by a local authority for the regulation of its affairs or management of the area it governs **2** a regulation of a company, society, etc [c13: probably of Scandinavian origin; compare Old Norse *bӯr* dwelling, town; see BOWER¹, LAW¹]

by-line *n* **1** *journalism* a line under the title of a newspaper or magazine article giving the author's name **2** *soccer* another word for **touchline**

Byng (bɪŋ) *n* **1** **George**, Viscount Torrington. 1663–1733, British admiral: defeated fleet of James Edward Stuart, the Old Pretender, off Scotland (1708); defeated Spanish fleet off Messina (1717) **2** his son **John**. 1704–57, English admiral: executed after failing to relieve Minorca **3** **Julian Hedworth George**, 1st Viscount Byng of Vimy. 1862–1935, British general in World War I; governor general of Canada (1921–26)

BYO *n* *Austral & NZ* an unlicensed restaurant at which diners may drink their own wine, etc [c20: from the phrase *bring your own*]

bypass ('baɪ,pɑ:s) *n* **1** a main road built to avoid a city or other congested area **2** any system of pipes or conduits for redirecting the flow of a liquid **3** a means of redirecting the flow of a substance around an appliance through which it would otherwise pass **4** *surgery* **a** the redirection of blood flow, either to avoid a diseased blood vessel or in order to perform heart surgery. See **coronary bypass** **b** (*as modifier*): *bypass surgery* **5** *electronics* **a** an electrical circuit, esp one containing a capacitor, connected in parallel around one or more components, providing an alternative path for certain frequencies **b** (*as modifier*): *a bypass capacitor* ▷ *vb* **-passes, -passing, -passed** *or* **-past** (*tr*) **6** to go around or avoid (a city, obstruction, problem, etc) **7** to cause (traffic, fluid, etc) to go through a bypass **8** to proceed without reference to (regulations, a superior, etc); get round; avoid

bypass engine *n* a gas turbine in which a part of the compressor delivery bypasses the combustion zone,

flowing directly into or around the main exhaust gas flow to provide additional thrust. See **turbofan**

bypath ('baɪ,pɑ:θ) *n* a little-used path or track, esp in the country

by-play *n* secondary action or talking carried on apart while the main action proceeds, esp in a play

by-product *n* **1** a secondary or incidental product of a manufacturing process **2** a side effect

Byrd (bɜːd) *n* **1** **Richard Evelyn**. 1888–1957, US rear admiral, aviator, and polar explorer **2** **William**. 1543–1623, English composer and organist, noted for his madrigals, masses, and music for virginals

Byrd Land *n* a part of Antarctica, east of the Ross Sea: claimed for the US by Admiral Richard E. Byrd in 1929, though all claims are suspended under the Antarctic Treaty of 1959. Former name: **Marie Byrd Land**

byre (baɪə) *n* *Brit* a shelter for cows [Old English *bӯre*; related to *būr* hut, cottage; see BOWER¹]

byroad ('baɪ,rəʊd) *n* a secondary or side road

Byron ('baɪərən) *n* **George Gordon**, 6th Baron. 1788–1824, British Romantic poet, noted also for his passionate and disastrous love affairs. His major works include *Childe Harold's Pilgrimage* (1812–18), and *Don Juan* (1819–24). He spent much of his life abroad and died while fighting for Greek independence ▷ **Byronic** (baɪ'rɒnɪk) *adj* ▷ **By'ronically** *adv* ▷ **'Byron,ism** *n*

byssinosis (,bɪsɪ'nəʊsɪs) *n* a lung disease caused by prolonged inhalation of fibre dust in textile factories [c19: from New Latin, from Greek *bussinos* of linen (see BYSSUS) + -OSIS]

byssus ('bɪsəs) *n*, *pl* **byssuses** *or* **byssi** ('baɪsaɪ) a mass of strong threads secreted by a sea mussel or similar mollusc that attaches the animal to a hard fixed surface [c17: from Latin, from Greek *bussos* linen, flax, ultimately of Egyptian origin]

bystander ('baɪ,stændə) *n* a person present but not involved; onlooker; spectator

byte (baɪt) *n* *computing* **1** a group of bits, usually eight, processed as a single unit of data **2** the storage space in a memory or other storage device that is allocated to such a group of bits **3** a subdivision of a word [c20: probably a blend of BIT⁴ + BITE]

Bytom (*Polish* 'bitɔm) *n* an industrial city in SW Poland, in Upper Silesia: under Prussian and German rule from 1742 to 1945. Pop: 185 793 (2007 est). German name: **Beuthen**

byway ('baɪ,weɪ) *n* **1** a secondary or side road, esp in the country **2** an area, field of study, etc, that is very obscure or of secondary importance

byword ('baɪ,wɜːd) *n* **1** a person, place, or thing regarded as a perfect or proverbial example of something: *their name is a byword for good service* **2** an object of scorn or derision **3** a common saying; proverb [Old English *bīwyrde*; see BY, WORD; compare Old High German *pīwurti*, from Latin *prōverbium* proverb]

Byzantine (bɪ'zæn,taɪn, -,ti:n, baɪ-, 'bɪzən,ti:n, -,taɪn) *adj* **1** of, characteristic of, or relating to Byzantium or the Byzantine Empire **2** of, relating to, or characterizing the Orthodox Church or its rites and liturgy **3** of or relating to the highly coloured stylized form of religious art developed in the Byzantine Empire **4** of or relating to the style of architecture developed in the Byzantine Empire, characterized by massive domes with square bases, rounded arches, spires and minarets, and the extensive use of mosaics **5** denoting the Medieval Greek spoken in the Byzantine Empire **6** (of attitudes, etc) inflexible or complicated ▷ *n* **7** an inhabitant of Byzantium ▷ **Byzantinism** (bɪ'zæntaɪ,nɪzəm, -tiː, baɪ-, 'bɪzəntɪ,nɪzəm, -taɪ-) *n*

Byzantine Empire *n* the continuation of the Roman Empire in the East, esp after the deposition of the last emperor in Rome (476 AD). It was finally extinguished by the fall of Constantinople, its capital, in 1453

Byzantium (bɪ'zæntɪəm, baɪ-) *n* an ancient Greek city on the Bosporus: founded about 660 BC; rebuilt by Constantine I in 330 AD and called Constantinople; present-day Istanbul

Bz *or* **Bz.** *abbreviation* benzene

Cc

c¹ *or* **C** (si:) *n, pl* **c's** *or* **C's, Cs** 1 the third letter and second consonant of the modern English alphabet 2 a speech sound represented by this letter, in English usually either a voiceless alveolar fricative, as in *cigar*, or a voiceless velar stop, as in *case* 3 the third in a series, esp the third highest grade in an examination 4 something shaped like a C

c² *symbol for* 1 centi- 2 cubic 3 cycle 4 *maths* constant 5 specific heat capacity 6 the speed of light and other types of electromagnetic radiation in a vacuum

C *symbol for* 1 *music* **a** a note having a frequency of 261.63 hertz (**middle C**) or this value multiplied or divided by any power of 2; the first degree of a major scale containing no sharps or flats (**C major**) **b** the major or minor key having this note as its tonic **c** a time signature denoting four crotchet beats to the bar. See also **alla breve** (sense 2), **common time** 2 *chem* carbon 3 *biochem* cytosine 4 capacitance 5 heat capacity 6 cold (water) 7 *physics* compliance 8 Celsius 9 centigrade 10 century: C20 11 coulomb 12 *the Roman numeral for* 100 ▷ *n* 13 a computer programming language combining the advantages of a high-level language with the ability to address the computer at a level comparable with that of an assembly language

c. *abbreviation* 1 carat 2 *cricket* caught 3 cent(s) 4 century or centuries 5 (used esp preceding a date) circa: *c. 1800* [(for sense 5) Latin: about]

C. *abbreviation* 1 (on maps as part of name) Cape 2 Catholic 3 Celtic 4 Conservative 5 Corps

c/- *abbreviation* Austral (in addresses) care of

C1 *n* **a** a person whose job is supervisory or clerical, or who works in junior management **b** (*as adjective*): *C1 worker* ▷ See also **occupation groupings**

C2 *n* **a** a skilled manual worker, or a manual worker with responsibility for other people **b** (*as adjective*): *C2 worker* ▷ See also **occupation groupings**

Ca *the chemical symbol for* calcium

CA *abbreviation* 1 California 2 Central America 3 chartered accountant 4 chief accountant 5 (in Britain) Consumers' Association

CAA *abbreviation* (in Britain) Civil Aviation Authority

Caaba ('kɑːbə) *n* a variant spelling of **Kaaba**

cab (kæb) *n* 1 **a** a taxi **b** (*as modifier*): *a cab rank* 2 the enclosed compartment of a lorry, locomotive, crane, etc, from which it is driven or operated 3 (formerly) a light horse-drawn vehicle used for public hire [C19: shortened from CABRIOLET]

CAB *abbreviation* (in Britain) Citizens' Advice Bureau

cabal (kə'bæl) *n* 1 a small group of intriguers, esp one formed for political purposes 2 a secret plot, esp a political one; conspiracy; intrigue 3 a secret or exclusive set of people; clique ▷ *vb* -bals, -balling, -balled (*intr*) 4 to form a cabal; conspire; plot [C17: from French *cabale*, from Medieval Latin *cabala*; see CABBALA]

cabala (kə'bɑːlə) *n* a variant spelling of **kabbalah**

Caballé (*Spanish* kaβaˈʎe) *n* **Montserrat** (monserˈrat). born 1933, Spanish operatic soprano

caballero (ˌkæbəˈljɛərəʊ; *Spanish* kaβaˈʎero) *n, pl* -ros (-rəʊz; *Spanish* -ros) a Spanish gentleman [C19: from Spanish: gentleman, horseman, from Late Latin *caballārius* rider, groom, from *caballus* horse; compare CAVALIER]

cabana (kə'bɑːnə) *n* chiefly US a tent used as a dressing room by the sea [from Spanish *cabaña*: CABIN]

cabaret ('kæbəˌreɪ) *n* 1 a floor show of dancing, singing, or other light entertainment at a nightclub or restaurant 2 chiefly US a nightclub or restaurant providing such entertainment [C17: from Norman French: tavern, probably from Late Latin *camera* an arched roof, CHAMBER]

cabbage ('kæbɪdʒ) *n* 1 Also called: **cole** any of various cultivated varieties of the plant *Brassica oleracea capitata*, typically having a short thick stalk and a large head of green or reddish edible leaves: family *Brassicaceae* (crucifers). See also **brassica** 2 **a** the head of a cabbage **b** the edible leaf bud of the cabbage palm 3 *informal* **a** dull or unimaginative person 4 *informal, offensive* **a** person who has no mental faculties and is dependent on others for his or her subsistence [C14: from Norman French *caboche* head; perhaps related to Old French *boce* hump, bump, Latin *caput* head]

cabbage palm *or* **cabbage tree** *n* 1 a West Indian palm, *Roystonea* (or *Oreodoxa*) *oleracea*, whose leaf buds are eaten like cabbage 2 a similar Brazilian palm, *Euterpe oleracea*

c

cabbage rose n a rose, *Rosa centifolia*, with a round compact full-petalled head

cabbage tree n 1 Also called: ti a tree, *Cordyline australis*, of New Zealand having a tall branchless trunk and a palmlike top 2 any of several other similar trees of the genus *Cordyline*

cabbage white n any large white butterfly of the genus *Pieris*, esp the Eurasian species *P. brassicae*, the larvae of which feed on the leaves of cabbages and related vegetables: family *Pieridae*

cabbala (kəˈbɑːlə) n a variant spelling of **kabbalah** > **cabbalism** (ˈkæbəˌlɪzəm) n > **cabbalist** n > ˌcabbaˈlistic adj

cabbie or **cabby** (ˈkæbɪ) n, pl -bies informal a cab driver

CABE abbreviation (in Britain) Commission for Architecture and the Built Environment

caber (ˈkeɪbə; Scot ˈkebər) n Scot a heavy section of trimmed tree trunk thrown in competition at Highland games (**tossing the caber**) [c16: from Gaelic *cabar* pole]

Cabernet Sauvignon (ˈkæbəneɪ ˈsəʊvɪnjɒn; French kabɛrnɛ soviɲɔ̃) n (sometimes not capitals) 1 a black grape originally grown in the Bordeaux area of France, and now throughout the wine-producing world 2 any of various red wines made from this grape [French]

cabin (ˈkæbɪn) n 1 a small simple dwelling; hut 2 a simple house providing accommodation for travellers or holiday-makers at a motel or holiday camp 3 a room used as an office or living quarters in a ship 4 a covered compartment used for shelter or living quarters in a small boat 5 (in a warship) the compartment or room reserved for the commanding officer 6 Brit another name for **signal box** 7 a the enclosed part of a light aircraft in which the pilot and passengers sit b the part of an airliner in which the passengers are carried ▷ vb 8 to confine in a small space [c14: from Old French *cabane*, from Old Provençal *cabana*, from Late Latin *capanna* hut]

cabin boy n a boy who waits on the officers and passengers of a ship

cabin cruiser n a power boat fitted with a cabin and comforts for pleasure cruising or racing

Cabinda (kəˈbiːndə) n an exclave of Angola, separated from the rest of the country by part of the Democratic Republic of Congo (formerly Zaïre). Pop: about 300 000 (2002 est). Area: 7270 sq km (2807 sq miles)

cabinet (ˈkæbɪnɪt) n 1 a piece of furniture containing shelves, cupboards, or drawers for storage or display 2 the outer case of a television, radio, etc 3 a (often capital) the executive and policy-making body of a country, consisting of all government ministers or just the senior ministers b (sometimes capital) an advisory council to a president, sovereign, governor, etc c (as modifier): a cabinet reshuffle; a cabinet minister 4 a a standard size of paper, 6 × 4 inches (15 × 10 cm) or 6½ × 4⅝4 inches (16.5 × 10.5 cm), for mounted photographs b (as modifier): a cabinet photograph 5 archaic a private room [c16: from Old French, diminutive of *cabine*, of uncertain origin]

cabinet-maker n a craftsman specializing in the making of fine furniture > **cabinet-ˌmaking** n

cabinetwork (ˈkæbɪnɪtˌwɜːk) n 1 the making of furniture, esp of fine quality 2 an article made by a cabinet-maker

cabin fever n chiefly Canadian acute depression resulting from being isolated or sharing cramped quarters in the wilderness, esp during the long northern winter

cable (ˈkeɪbəl) n 1 a strong thick rope, usually of twisted hemp or steel wire 2 nautical an anchor chain or rope 3 a a unit of distance in navigation, equal to one tenth of a sea mile (about 600 feet) b Also called: cable length, cable's length a unit of length in nautical use that has various values, including 100 fathoms (600 feet) 4 a wire or bundle of wires that conducts electricity: a submarine cable. See also coaxial cable ▷ vb 5 to send (a message) to (someone) by cable 6 (tr) to fasten or provide with a cable or cables 7 (tr) to supply (a place) with or link (a place) to cable television [c13: from Old Norman French, from Late Latin *capulum* halter]

cable car n 1 a cabin suspended from and moved by an overhead cable in a mountain area 2 a passenger car on a cable railway

cable television n a television service in which programmes are distributed to subscribers' televisions by cable rather than by broadcast transmission

cabochon (ˈkæbəʃɒn; French kabɔʃɔ̃) n a smooth domed gem, polished but unfaceted [c16: from Old French, from Old Norman French *caboche* head; see CABBAGE]

caboodle (kəˈbuːdəl) n informal a lot, bunch, or group (esp in the phrases **the whole caboodle, the whole kit and caboodle**) [c19: probably contraction of KIT¹ and BOODLE]

caboose (kəˈbuːs) n 1 US informal short for **calaboose** 2 railways, US & Canadian a guard's van, esp one with sleeping and eating facilities for the train crew 3 nautical a a deckhouse for a galley aboard ship or formerly in Canada, on a lumber raft b chiefly Brit the galley itself 4 Canadian a a mobile bunkhouse used by lumbermen, etc b an insulated cabin on runners, equipped with a stove [c18: from Dutch *cabūse*, of unknown origin]

Cabot (ˈkæbət) n 1 John Italian name *Giovanni Caboto*. 1450–98, Italian explorer, who landed in North America in 1497, under patent from Henry VII of England, and explored the coast from Nova Scotia to Newfoundland 2 his son, Sebastian. ?1476–1557, Italian navigator and cartographer, who served the English and Spanish crowns: explored the La Plata region of Brazil (1526–30)

cabotage (ˈkæbəˌtɑːʒ) n 1 nautical coastal navigation or shipping, esp within the borders of one country 2 reservation to a country's carriers of its internal traffic, esp air traffic [c19: from French, from *caboter* to sail near the coast, apparently from Spanish *cabo* CAPE²]

Cabral (Portuguese kəˈbral) n Pedro Álvarez (ˈpɛːdru ˈalvərəʒ). ?1460–?1526, Portuguese navigator: discovered and took possession of Brazil for Portugal in 1500

cabrio (ˈkæbrɪˌəʊ) n short for **cabriolet**

cabriole (ˈkæbrɪˌəʊl) n Also called: cabriole leg a type of furniture leg, popular in the first half of the 18th century, in which an upper convex curve descends tapering to a concave curve [c18: from French, from *cabrioler* to caper; from its being based on the leg of a capering animal; see CABRIOLET]

cabriolet (ˌkæbrɪəʊˈleɪ) n a small two-wheeled horse-drawn carriage with two seats and a folding hood [c18: from French, literally: a little skip, from *cabriole*, from Latin *capreolus* wild goat, from *caper* goat; referring to the lightness of movement]

cacao (kəˈkɑːəʊ, -ˈkeɪəʊ) n 1 a small tropical American evergreen tree, *Theobroma cacao*, having yellowish flowers and reddish-brown seed pods from which cocoa and chocolate are prepared: family *Sterculiaceae* 2 cacao bean another name for **cocoa bean** 3 cacao butter another name for **cocoa butter** [c16: from Spanish, from Nahuatl *cacuatl* cacao beans]

cachalot (ˈkæʃəˌlɒt) n another name for **sperm whale** [c18: from French, from Portuguese, *cachalote*, of unknown origin]

cache (kæʃ) n 1 a hidden store of provisions, weapons, treasure, etc 2 the place where such a store is hidden 3 computing a small high-speed memory that improves computer performance ▷ vb 4 (tr) to store in a cache [c19: from French, from *cacher* to hide]

cachepot (ˈkæʃˌpɒt, ˌkæʃˈpəʊ) n an ornamental container for a flowerpot [French: pot-hider]

cachet (ˈkæʃeɪ) n 1 an official seal on a document, letter, etc 2 a distinguishing mark; stamp 3 prestige; distinction 4 philately a mark stamped by hand on mail for commemorative purposes 5 a hollow wafer, formerly used for enclosing an unpleasant-tasting medicine [c17: from Old French, from *cacher* to hide]

cachexia (kəˈkɛksɪə) or **cachexy** (kəˈkɛksɪ) n a generally weakened condition of body or mind resulting from any debilitating chronic disease [c16: from Late Latin from Greek *kakhexia*, from *kakos* bad + *hexis* condition, habit]

cachinnate (ˈkækɪˌneɪt) vb (intr) to laugh loudly [c19: from Latin *cacchināre*, probably of imitative origin] > ˌcachinˈnatory adj > ˌcachinˈnation n

cachou (ˈkæʃuː, kæˈʃuː) n 1 a lozenge eaten to sweeten the breath 2 another name for **catechu** [c18: via French from Portuguese, from Malay *kāchu*]

cacique (kəˈsiːk) *or* **cazique** (kəˈziːk) *n* **1** Native American chief in a Spanish-speaking region **2** (esp in Spanish America) a local political boss [c16: from Spanish, of Arawak origin; compare Taino *cacique* chief]

cack-handed (ˌkækˈhændɪd) *adj informal* **1** left-handed **2** clumsy [from dialect *cack* excrement, from the fact that clumsy people usually make a mess; via Middle Low German or Middle Dutch from Latin *cacāre* to defecate]

cackle (ˈkækəl) *vb* **1** (*intr*) (esp of a hen) to squawk with shrill notes **2** (*intr*) to laugh or chatter raucously **3** (*tr*) to utter in a cackling manner ▷ *n* **4** the noise or act of cackling **5** noisy chatter **6** cut the cackle *informal* to stop chattering; be quiet [c13: probably from Middle Low German *kākelen*, of imitative origin]

caco- *combining form* bad, unpleasant, or incorrect: *cacophony* [from Greek *kakos* bad]

cacodyl (ˈkækədaɪl) *n* an oily poisonous liquid with a strong garlic smell; tetramethyldiarsine. Formula: [(CH₃)₂As]₂ [c19: from Greek *kakōdēs* evil-smelling (from *kakos* CACO- + *ozein* to smell) + -YL]

cacoethes (ˌkækəʊˈiːθiːz) *n* an uncontrollable urge or desire, esp for something harmful; mania: *a cacoethes for smoking* [c16: from Latin *cacoēthes* malignant disease, from Greek *kakoēthēs* of an evil disposition, from *kakos* CACO- + *ēthos* character]

cacography (kæˈkɒɡrəfɪ) *n* **1** bad handwriting **2** incorrect spelling ▷ cacographic (ˌkækəˈɡræfɪk) *or* ˌcacoˈgraphical *adj*

cacophony (kəˈkɒfənɪ) *n, pl* -nies harsh discordant sound; dissonance ▷ caˈcophonous *or* cacophonic (ˌkækəˈfɒnɪk) *adj*

cactoblastis (ˌkæktəʊˈblæstɪs) *n* a moth, *Cactoblastis cactorum*, that was introduced into Australia to act as a biological control on the prickly pear

cactus (ˈkæktəs) *n, pl* -tuses *or* -ti (-taɪ) **1** any spiny succulent plant of the family *Cactaceae* of the arid regions of America. Cactuses have swollen tough stems, leaves reduced to spines or scales, and often large brightly coloured flowers **2** cactus dahlia a double-flowered variety of dahlia [c17: from Latin: prickly plant, from Greek *kaktos* cardoon] ▷ cactaceous (kækˈteɪʃəs) *adj*

cacuminal (kæˈkjuːmɪnəl) *phonetics* ▷ *adj* **1** Also called: cerebral relating to or denoting a consonant articulated with the tip of the tongue turned back towards the hard palate ▷ *n* **2** a consonant articulated in this manner [c19: from Latin *cacūmen* point, top]

cad (kæd) *n Brit informal, old-fashioned* a man who does not behave in a gentlemanly manner towards others [c18: shortened from CADDIE] ▷ ˈcaddish *adj*

CAD *n acronym* computer-aided design

cadaver (kəˈdeɪvə, -ˈdɑː-) *n med* a corpse [c16: from Latin, from *cadere* to fall] ▷ caˈdaveric *adj*

cadaverous (kəˈdævərəs) *adj* **1** of or like a corpse, esp in being deathly pale; ghastly **2** thin and haggard; gaunt ▷ caˈdaverousness *n*

Cadbury (ˈkædbərɪ) *n* **George.** 1839–1922, British Quaker industrialist and philanthropist. He established, with his brother **Richard Cadbury** (1835–99), the chocolate-making company Cadbury Brothers and the garden village Bournville, near Birmingham, for their workers

CADCAM (ˈkædˌkæm) *n acronym for* computer-aided design and manufacture

caddie *or* **caddy** (ˈkædɪ) *n, pl* -dies **1** *golf* an attendant who carries clubs, etc, for a player ▷ *vb* -dies, -dying, -died **2** (*intr*) to act as a caddie [c17 (originally: a gentleman learning the military profession by serving in the army without a commission, hence c18 (Scottish): a person looking for employment, an errand-boy): from French CADET]

caddis fly *n* any small mothlike insect of the order *Trichoptera*, having two pairs of hairy wings and aquatic larvae (caddis worms) [c17: of unknown origin]

caddis worm *or* **caddis** *n* the aquatic larva of a caddis fly, which constructs a protective case around itself made of silk, sand, stones, etc. Also called: caseworm, strawworm

caddy¹ (ˈkædɪ) *n, pl* -dies *chiefly Brit* a small container, esp for tea [c18: from Malay *kati*]

caddy² (ˈkædɪ) *n, pl* -dies **1** a variant spelling of **caddie** ▷ *vb* -dies, -dying, -died **2** a variant spelling of **caddie**

Cade (keɪd) *n* **Jack.** died 1450, English leader of the Kentish rebellion against the misgovernment of Henry VI (1450)

cadence (ˈkeɪdəns) *or* **cadency** *n, pl* -dences *or* -dencies **1** the beat or measure of something rhythmic **2** a fall in the pitch of the voice, as at the end of a sentence **3** modulation of the voice; intonation **4** a rhythm or rhythmic construction in verse or prose; measure **5** the close of a musical phrase or section [c14: from Old French, from Old Italian *cadenza*, literally: a falling, from Latin *cadere* to fall]

cadenza (kəˈdɛnzə) *n* **1** a virtuoso solo passage occurring near the end of a piece of music, formerly improvised by the soloist but now usually specially composed **2** *South African informal* a fit or convulsion [c19: from Italian; see CADENCE]

cadet (kəˈdɛt) *n* **1** a young person undergoing preliminary training, usually before full entry to the uniformed services, police, etc, esp for officer status **2** (in England and in France before 1789) a gentleman, usually a younger son, who entered the army to prepare for a commission **3** a younger son or brother **4** cadet branch the family or family branch of a younger son **5** (in New Zealand) a person learning sheep farming on a sheep station [c17: from French, from dialect (Gascon) *capdet* captain, ultimately from Latin *caput* head] ▷ caˈdetship *n*

cadge (kædʒ) *vb* **1** to get (food, money, etc) by sponging or begging ▷ *n* **2** *Brit* a person who cadges [c17: of unknown origin] ▷ **cadger** *n*

cadi *or* **kadi** (ˈkɑːdɪ, ˈkeɪdɪ) *n, pl* -dis a judge in a Muslim community [c16: from Arabic *qāḍī* judge]

Cádiz (kəˈdɪz; *Spanish* ˈkaðiθ) *n* a port in SW Spain, on a narrow peninsula that forms the **Bay of Cádiz**, at the E end of the **Gulf of Cádiz**, founded about 1100 BC as a Phoenician trading colony; centre of trade with America from the 16th to 18th centuries. Pop: 134 989 (2003 est)

Cadmean victory (ˈkædmɪən) *n* another name for **Pyrrhic victory**

cadmium (ˈkædmɪəm) *n* a malleable ductile toxic bluish-white metallic element that occurs in association with zinc ores. It is used in electroplating, alloys, and as a neutron absorber in the control of nuclear fission. Symbol: Cd; atomic no: 48; atomic wt: 112.411; valency: 2; relative density: 8.65; melting pt: 321.1°C; boiling pt: 767°C [c19: from New Latin, from Latin *cadmīa* zinc ore, CALAMINE, referring to the fact that both calamine and cadmium are found in the ore]

Cadmus (ˈkædməs) *n Greek myth* a Phoenician prince who killed a dragon and planted its teeth, from which sprang a multitude of warriors who fought among themselves until only five remained, who joined Cadmus to found Thebes ▷ ˈCadmean *adj*

cadre (ˈkɑːdə) *n* **1** the nucleus of trained professional servicemen forming the basis for the training of new units or other military expansion **2** a basic unit or structure, esp of specialists or experts; nucleus; core **3** a group of revolutionaries or other political activists, esp when taking part in military or terrorist activities **4** a member of a cadre [c19: from French, from Italian *quadro*, from Latin *quadrum* square]

caduceus (kəˈdjuːsɪəs) *n, pl* -cei (-sɪˌaɪ) **1** *classical myth* a staff entwined with two serpents and bearing a pair of wings at the top, carried by Hermes (Mercury) as messenger of the gods **2** an insignia resembling this staff used as an emblem of the medical profession [c16: from Latin, from Doric Greek *karukeion*, from *karux* herald]

caducous (kəˈdjuːkəs) *adj biology* (of parts of a plant or animal) shed during the life of the organism [c17: from Latin *cadūcus* falling, from *cadere* to fall]

Cadwalader (kædˈwɒlədə) *n* 7th century AD, legendary king of the Britons, probably a confusion of several historical figures

caecilian (siːˈsɪlɪən) *n* any tropical limbless cylindrical amphibian of the order *Apoda* (or *Gymnophiona*), resembling earthworms and inhabiting moist soil [c19: from Latin *caecilia* a kind of lizard, from *caecus* blind]

C

caecum or US **cecum** ('siːkəm) n, pl **-ca** (-kə) anatomy any structure or part that ends in a blind sac or pouch, esp the pouch that marks the beginning of the large intestine [c18: short for Latin intestinum caecum blind intestine, translation of Greek tuphlon enteron] > **'caecal** or US **'cecal** adj

Cædmon ('kædmən) n 7th century AD, Anglo-Saxon poet and monk, the earliest English poet whose name survives

Caelian ('siːlɪən) n the southeasternmost of the Seven Hills of Rome

Caen (kɒŋ; French kɑ̃) n an industrial city in NW France. Pop: 113 987 (1999)

Caernarfon, Caernarvon or **Carnarvon** (kɑːˈnɑːvᵊn) n a port and resort in NW Wales, in Gwynedd on the Menai Strait: 13th-century castle. Pop: 9726 (2001)

Caernarvonshire (kɑːˈnɑːvᵊnˌʃɪə, -ʃə) n (until 1974) a county of NW Wales, now part of Gwynedd

Caerphilly (kɛəˈfɪlɪ) n **1** a market town in SE Wales, in Caerphilly county borough: site of the largest castle in Wales (13th–14th centuries). Pop: 31 060 (2001) **2** a county borough in SE Wales, created in 1996 from parts of Mid Glamorgan and Gwent. Pop: 170 200 (2003 est). Area: 275 sq km (106 sq miles) **3** a creamy white mild-flavoured cheese

Caesar ('siːzə) n **1 Gaius Julius** ('gaɪəs 'dʒuːlɪəs). 100–44 BC, Roman general, statesman, and historian. He formed the first triumvirate with Pompey and Crassus (60), conquered Gaul (58–50), invaded Britain (55–54), mastered Italy (49), and defeated Pompey (46). As dictator of the Roman Empire (49–44) he destroyed the power of the corrupt Roman nobility. He also introduced the Julian calendar and planned further reforms, but fear of his sovereign power led to his assassination (44) by conspirators led by Marcus Brutus and Cassius Longinus **2** any Roman emperor **3** (sometimes not capital) any emperor, autocrat, dictator, or other powerful ruler **4** a title of the Roman emperors from Augustus to Hadrian **5** (in the Roman Empire) **a** a title borne by the imperial heir from the reign of Hadrian **b** the heir, deputy, and subordinate ruler to either of the two emperors under Diocletian's system of government **6** short for **Caesar salad**

Caesaraugusta (ˌsiːzərɔːˈɡʌstə) n the Latin name for Zaragoza

Caesarea (ˌsiːzəˈrɪə) n an ancient port in NW Israel, capital of Roman Palestine: founded by Herod the Great

Caesarian, Caesarian or US **Cesarean, Cesarian** (sɪˈzɛərɪən) adj **1** of or relating to any of the Caesars, esp Julius Caesar (100–44 BC), Roman general, statesman, and historian ▷ n **2** (sometimes not capital) surgery **a** short for **Caesarean section b** (as modifier): Caesarean birth; Caesarean operation

Caesarean section n surgical incision through the abdominal and uterine walls in order to deliver a baby [c17: from the belief that Julius Caesar was so delivered, the name allegedly being derived from caesus, past participle of caedere to cut]

Caesar salad n a salad of lettuce, cheese, and croutons with a dressing of olive oil, garlic, and lemon juice [c20: named after Caesar Cardini (1896–1956), Mexican restaurateur who invented it]

caesious or US **cesious** ('siːzɪəs) adj botany having a waxy bluish-grey coating [c19: from Latin caesius bluish grey]

caesium or US **cesium** ('siːzɪəm) n a ductile silvery-white element of the alkali metal group that is the most electropositive metal. It occurs in pollucite and lepidolite and is used in photocells. The radioisotope **caesium-137**, with a half-life of 30.2 years, is used in radiotherapy. Symbol: Cs; atomic no: 55; atomic wt: 132.90543; valency: 1; relative density: 1.873; melting pt: 28.39±0.01°C; boiling pt: 671°C

caesura (sɪˈzjʊərə) n, pl **-ras** or **-rae** (-riː) **1** (in modern prosody) a pause, esp for sense, usually near the middle of a verse line **2** (in classical prosody) a break between words within a metrical foot, usually in the third or fourth foot of the line [c16: from Latin, literally: a cutting, from caedere to cut] > **cae'sural** adj

Caetano (kaɪˈtɑːnəʊ; Portuguese kaɪˈtɐnu) n **Marcello** (marˈsɛlu). 1906–80, prime minister of Portugal from 1968 until he was replaced by an army coup in 1974

café ('kæfeɪ, 'kæfɪ) n **1** a small or inexpensive restaurant or coffee bar, serving light meals and refreshments **2** South African a corner shop or grocer [c19: from French: COFFEE]

café au lait French (kafe o lɛ) n **1** coffee with milk **2 a** a light brown colour **b** (as modifier): café au lait brocade

café noir French (kafe nwar) n black coffee

cafeteria (ˌkæfɪˈtɪərɪə) n a self-service restaurant [c20: from American Spanish: coffee shop]

caff (kæf) n a slang word for **café**

caffeinated ('kæfɪˌneɪtəd) adj **1 a** with no natural caffeine removed **b** with added caffeine **2** highly stimulated by caffeine

caffeine or **caffein** ('kæfiːn, 'kæfɪˌiːn) n a white crystalline bitter alkaloid responsible for the stimulant action of tea, coffee, and cocoa: a constituent of many tonics and analgesics. Formula: $C_8H_{10}N_4O_2$ [c19: from German Kaffein, from Kaffee COFFEE]

caftan ('kæfˌtæn, -ˌtɑːn) n a variant spelling of **kaftan**

cage (keɪdʒ) n **1 a** an enclosure, usually made with bars or wire, for keeping birds, monkeys, mice, etc **b** (as modifier): cagebird **2** a thing or place that confines or imprisons **3** something resembling a cage in function or structure: the rib cage **4** the enclosed platform of a lift, esp as used in a mine ▷ vb **5** (tr) to confine in or as in a cage [c13: from Old French, from Latin cavea enclosure, from cavus hollow]

Cage (keɪdʒ) n **John.** 1912–92, US composer of experimental music for a variety of conventional, modified, or invented instruments. He evolved a type of music apparently undetermined by the composer, such as in Imaginary Landscape (1951) for 12 radio sets. Other works include Reunion (1968), Apartment Building 1776 (1976), and Europeras 3 and 4 (1990)

cagey or **cagy** ('keɪdʒɪ) adj **-ier, -iest** informal not open or frank; cautious; wary [c20: of unknown origin] > **'caginess** n

Cagliari¹ (kælˈjɑːrɪ; Italian kaʎˈʎari) n a port in Italy, the capital of Sardinia, on the S coast. Pop: 164 249 (2001)

Cagliari² (Italian kaʎˈʎari) n **Paolo** ('paːolo). original name of (Paolo) **Veronese**

Cagliostro (Italian kaʎˈʎɔstro) n Count **Alessandro di** (alesˈsandro di), original name Giuseppe Balsamo. 1743–95, Italian adventurer and magician, who was imprisoned for life by the Inquisition for his association with freemasonry

Cagney ('kægnɪ) n **James.** 1899–1986, US film actor, esp in gangster roles; his films include The Public Enemy (1931), Angels with Dirty Faces (1938), The Roaring Twenties (1939), and Yankee Doodle Dandy (1942) for which he won an Oscar

cagoule (kəˈguːl) n a lightweight usually knee-length type of anorak [c20: from French]

Cahokia Mounds (kəˈhəʊkɪə) pl n the largest group of prehistoric Indian earthworks in the US, located northeast of East St Louis

cahoots (kəˈhuːts) pl n (sometimes singular) informal **1** US partnership; league (esp in the phrases **go in cahoots with, go cahoot**) **2 in cahoots** in collusion [c19: of uncertain origin]

Caiaphas ('kaɪəˌfæs) n New Testament the high priest at the beginning of John the Baptist's preaching and during the trial of Jesus (Luke 3:2; Matthew 26)

Caicos Islands ('keɪkəs) pl n a group of islands in the Caribbean: part of the British dependency of the **Turks and Caicos Islands**

caiman ('keɪmən) n, pl **-mans** a variant spelling of **cayman**

Cain (keɪn) n **raise Cain a** to cause a commotion **b** to react or protest heatedly [from Cain, the first son of Adam and Eve, who killed his brother Abel (Genesis 4:1–16), used as a euphemism for hell or the devil]

Caine (keɪn) n Sir **Michael.** real name Maurice Micklewhite. born 1933, British film actor. His films include The Ipcress File (1965), Get Carter (1971), Educating Rita (1983), Hannah and Her Sisters (1986), and The Cider House Rules (1999)

Cainozoic (ˌkaɪnəʊˈzəʊɪk, ˌkeɪ-) *adj* a variant of **Cenozoic**

caïque (kɑːˈiːk) *n* **1** a long narrow light rowing skiff used on the Bosporus **2** a sailing vessel of the E Mediterranean with a sprit mainsail, square topsail, and two or more jibs or other sails [c17: from French, from Italian *caicco*, from Turkish *kayik*]

Caird Coast (kɛəd) *n* a region of Antarctica: a part of Coats Land on the SE coast of the Weddell Sea; now included in the British Antarctic Territory (claim suspended under the Antarctic Treaty of 1959)

Cairene (ˈkaɪriːn) *adj* **1** of or relating to Cairo or its inhabitants ▷ *n* **2** a native or inhabitant of Cairo

cairn (kɛən) *n* **1** a mound of stones erected as a memorial or marker **2** Also called: **cairn terrier** a small rough-haired breed of terrier originally from Scotland [c15: from Gaelic *carn*]

cairngorm (ˈkɛənˌgɔːm, ˌkɛrnˈgɔrm) *n* a smoky yellow, grey, or brown variety of quartz, used as a gemstone. Also called: **smoky quartz** [c18: from *Cairn Gorm* (literally: blue cairn), mountain in Scotland where it is found]

Cairngorm Mountains *pl n* a mountain range of NE Scotland: part of the Grampians. Highest peak: Ben Macdui, 1309 m (4296 ft); designated a national park in 2003. Also called: the **Cairngorms**

Cairns (kænz, kɛənz) *n* a port in NE Australia, in Queensland. Pop: 98 981 (2001)

Cairo (ˈkaɪrəʊ) *n* the capital of Egypt, on the Nile: the largest city in Africa and in the Middle East; industrial centre; site of the university and mosque of Al Azhar (founded in 972). Pop: 11 146 000 (2005 est)

caisson (kəˈsuːn, ˈkeɪsⁿn) *n* **1** a watertight chamber open at the bottom and containing air under pressure, used to carry out construction work under water **2** a watertight float filled with air, used to raise sunken ships **3** a watertight structure placed across the entrance of a basin, dry dock, etc, to exclude water from it **4 a** a box containing explosives, formerly used as a mine **b** an ammunition chest [c18: from French, assimilated to *caisse* CASE²]

caisson disease *n* another name for **decompression sickness**

Caithness (keɪθˈnɛs, ˈkeɪθnɛs) *n* (until 1975) a county of NE Scotland, now part of Highland

caitiff (ˈkeɪtɪf) *archaic or poetic* ▷ *n* **1** a cowardly or base person ▷ *adj* **2** cowardly; base [c13: from Old French *caitif* prisoner, from Latin *captīvus* CAPTIVE]

Caius (ˈkaɪəs) *n* same as **Gaius**

Cajal (*Spanish* kaˈxal) *n* **Santiago Ramon y.** 1852–1934, Spanish histologist, a pioneer of modern neurophysiology: shared the Nobel prize for medicine 1906.

cajole (kəˈdʒəʊl) *vb* to persuade (someone) by flattery or pleasing talk to do what one wants; wheedle; coax [c17: from French *cajoler* to coax, of uncertain origin] ▷ caˈjolement *n* ▷ caˈjoler *n* ▷ caˈjolery *n*

Cajun (ˈkeɪdʒən) *n* **1** a native of Louisiana descended from 18th-century Acadian immigrants **2** the dialect of French spoken by such people **3** the music of this ethnic group, combining blues and European folk music ▷ *adj* **4** denoting, relating to, or characteristic of such people, their language, or their music [c19: alteration of ACADIAN; compare *Injun* for *Indian*]

cake (keɪk) *n* **1** a baked food, usually in loaf or layer form, typically made from a mixture of flour, sugar, and eggs **2** a flat thin mass of bread, esp unleavened bread **3** a shaped mass of dough or other food of similar consistency: *a fish cake* **4** a mass, slab, or crust of a solidified or compressed substance, as of soap or ice **5 have one's cake and eat it** to enjoy both of two desirable but incompatible alternatives **6 go like hot cakes** *or* **sell like hot cakes** *informal* to be sold very quickly or in large quantities **7 piece of cake** *informal* something that is easily achieved or obtained **8 take the cake** *informal* to surpass all others, esp in stupidity, folly, etc **9** *informal* the whole or total of something that is to be shared or divided: *the miners are demanding a larger slice of the cake; that is a fair method of sharing the cake* ▷ *vb* **10** (tr) to cover with a hard layer; encrust: *the hull was caked with salt* **11** to form or be formed into a hardened mass [c13: from

Old Norse *kaka*; related to Danish *kage*, German *Kuchen*]

cakewalk (ˈkeɪkˌwɔːk) *n* **1** a dance based on a march with intricate steps, originally performed by African-Americans with the prize of a cake for the best performers **2** a piece of music composed for this dance **3** *informal* an easily accomplished task

CAL *abbreviation* computer-aided (or -assisted) learning

cal. *abbreviation* **1** calendar **2** calibre **3** calorie (small)

Cal. *abbreviation* Calorie (large)

Calabar (ˈkæləˌbɑː) *n* a port in SE Nigeria, capital of Cross River state. Pop: 418 000 (2005 est)

calabash (ˈkæləˌbæʃ) *n* **1** Also called: **calabash tree** a tropical American evergreen tree, *Crescentia cujete*, that produces large round gourds: family *Bignoniaceae* **2** the gourd of either of these plants **3** the dried hollow shell of a gourd used as the bowl of a tobacco pipe, a bottle, rattle, etc **4 calabash nutmeg** a tropical African shrub, *Monodora myristica*, whose oily aromatic seeds can be used as nutmegs: family *Annonaceae* [c17: from obsolete French *calabasse*, from Spanish *calabaza*, perhaps from Arabic *qar'ah yābisah* dry gourd, from *qar'ah* gourd + *yābisah* dry]

calabogus (ˌkæləˈbəʊgəs) *n* *Canadian* a mixed drink containing rum, spruce beer, and molasses [c18: of unknown origin]

calaboose (ˈkæləˌbuːs) *n* *US informal* a prison; jail [c18: from Creole French, from Spanish *calabozo* dungeon, of unknown origin]

calabrese (ˌkæləˈbreɪzɪ) *n* a variety of green sprouting broccoli [c20: from Italian: Calabrian]

Calabria (kəˈlæbrɪə) *n* **1** a region of SW Italy: mostly mountainous and subject to earthquakes. Chief town: Reggio di Calabria. Pop: 2 007 392 (2003 est). Area: 15 080 sq km (5822 sq miles) **2** an ancient region of extreme SE Italy (3rd century BC to about 668 AD); now part of Apulia

Calabrian (kəˈlæbrɪən) *adj* **1** of or relating to Calabria or its inhabitants ▷ *n* **2** a native or inhabitant of Calabria

Calais (ˈkæleɪ; *French* kalɛ) *n* a port in N France, on the Strait of Dover: the nearest French port to England; belonged to England 1347–1558. Pop: 77 333 (1999)

calamander (ˈkæləˌmændə) *n* the hard black-and-brown striped wood of several trees of the genus *Diospyros*, esp *D. quaesita* of India and Sri Lanka, used in making furniture: family *Ebenaceae*. See also **ebony** (sense 2) [c19: metathetic variant of *coromandel* in COROMANDEL COAST]

calamari (ˌkæləˈmɑːrɪ) *n* squid cooked for eating, esp cut into rings and fried in batter [c20: from Italian, pl of *calamaro* squid, from Latin *calamarium* pen-case, referring to the squid's internal shell, from Greek *kalamos* reed]

calamine (ˈkæləˌmaɪn) *n* a pink powder consisting of zinc oxide and ferric oxide, (iron(III) oxide), used medicinally in the form of soothing lotions or ointments [c17: from Old French, from Medieval Latin *calamīna*, from Latin *cadmīa*; see CADMIUM]

calamint (ˈkæləˌmɪnt) *n* any aromatic Eurasian plant of the genus *Satureja* (or *Calamintha*), having clusters of purple or pink flowers: family *Lamiaceae* (labiates) [c14: from Old French *calament* (but influenced by English MINT¹), from Medieval Latin *calamentum*, from Greek *kalaminthē*]

calamitous (kəˈlæmɪtəs) *adj* causing, involving, or resulting in a calamity; disastrous

calamity (kəˈlæmɪtɪ) *n*, *pl* **-ties 1** a disaster or misfortune, esp one causing extreme havoc, distress, or misery **2** a state or feeling of deep distress or misery [c15: from French *calamité*, from Latin *calamitās*; related to Latin *incolumis* uninjured]

Calamity Jane *n* real name **Martha Canary.** ?1852–1903, US frontierswoman, noted for her skill at shooting and riding

calamus (ˈkæləməs) *n*, *pl* **-mi** (-ˌmaɪ) **1** any tropical Asian palm of the genus *Calamus*, some species of which are a source of rattan and canes **2** another name for **sweet flag 3** *ornithol* the basal hollow shaft of a feather; quill [c14: from Latin, from Greek *kalamos* reed, cane, stem]

calandria (kəˈlændrɪə) *n* a cylindrical vessel through which vertical tubes pass, esp one forming part of an evaporator, heat exchanger, or nuclear reactor [c20:

arbitrarily named, from Spanish, literally: lark]

calash (kə'læʃ) or **calèche** n 1 a horse-drawn carriage with low wheels and a folding top 2 a woman's folding hooped hood worn in the 18th century [c17: from French calèche, from German Kalesche, from Czech kolesa wheels]

calcaneus (kæl'keɪnɪəs) or **calcaneum** (kæl'keɪnɪəm) n, pl -nei (-nɪ,aɪ) or -nea (-nɪə) the largest tarsal bone, forming the heel in man [c19: from Late Latin: heel, from Latin calx heel]

calcareous (kæl'kɛərɪəs) adj of, containing, or resembling calcium carbonate; chalky [c17: from Latin calcārius, from calx lime]

calceolaria (,kælsɪə'lɛərɪə) n any tropical American scrophulariaceous plant of the genus Calceolaria: cultivated for its speckled slipper-shaped flowers. Also called: slipperwort [c18: from Latin calceolus small shoe, from calceus]

calces ('kælsi:z) n a plural of **calx**

calci- or before a vowel **calc-** combining form indicating lime or calcium: calcify [from Latin calx, calc- limestone]

calciferol (kæl'sɪfərɒl) n a fat-soluble steroid, found esp in fish-liver oils, produced by the action of ultraviolet radiation on ergosterol. It increases the absorption of calcium from the intestine and is used in the treatment of rickets. Formula: $C_{28}H_{43}OH$. Also called: vitamin D_2 [c20: from CALCIF(EROUS + ERGOST)EROL]

calciferous (kæl'sɪfərəs) adj forming or producing salts of calcium, esp calcium carbonate

calcify ('kælsɪ,faɪ) vb -fies, -fying, -fied 1 to convert or be converted into lime 2 to harden or become hardened by impregnation with calcium salts > ,calcifi'cation n

calcine ('kælsaɪn, -sɪn) vb 1 (tr) to heat (a substance) so that it is oxidized, reduced, or loses water 2 (intr) to oxidize as a result of heating [c14: from Medieval Latin calcināre to heat, from Latin calx lime] > calcination (,kælsɪ'neɪʃən) n

calcite ('kælsaɪt) n a colourless or white mineral (occasionally tinged with impurities), found in sedimentary and metamorphic rocks, in veins, in limestone, and in stalagmites and stalactites. It is used in the manufacture of cement, plaster, paint, glass, and fertilizer. Composition: calcium carbonate. Formula: $CaCO_3$. Crystal structure: hexagonal (rhombohedral)

calcium ('kælsɪəm) n a malleable silvery-white metallic element of the alkaline earth group, the fifth most abundant element in the earth's crust (3.6 per cent), occurring esp as forms of calcium carbonate. It is an essential constituent of bones and teeth and is used as a deoxidizer in steel. Symbol: Ca; atomic no: 20; atomic wt: 40.078; valency: 2; relative density: 1.55; melting pt: 842±2°C; boiling pt: 1494°C [c19: from New Latin, from Latin calx lime]

calcium antagonist n another name for **calcium channel blocker**

calcium carbide n a grey salt of calcium used in the production of acetylene (by its reaction with water) and calcium cyanamide. Formula: CaC_2

calcium carbonate n a white crystalline salt occurring in limestone, chalk, marble, calcite, coral, and pearl: used in the production of lime and cement. Formula: $CaCO_3$

calcium channel blocker n any drug that prevents the influx of calcium ions into cardiac and smooth muscle: used to treat high blood pressure and angina. Also called: calcium antagonist

calcium chloride n a white deliquescent salt occurring naturally in seawater and used in the de-icing of roads and as a drying agent. Formula: $CaCl_2$

calcium hydroxide n a white crystalline slightly soluble alkali with many uses, esp in cement, water softening, and the neutralization of acid soils. Formula: $Ca(OH)_2$. Also called: lime, slaked lime, caustic lime

calcium oxide n a white crystalline base used in the production of calcium hydroxide and bleaching powder and in the manufacture of glass, paper, and steel. Formula: CaO. Also called: lime, quicklime, calx

calcium phosphate n the insoluble nonacid calcium salt of orthophosphoric acid (phosphoric(V) acid): it occurs in bones and is the main constituent of bone ash.

Formula: $Ca_3(PO_4)_2$

calcspar ('kælk,spa:) n another name for **calcite** [c19: partial translation of Swedish kalkspat, from kalk lime (ultimately from Latin calx) + spat SPAR³]

calculable ('kælkjʊləbəl) adj 1 that may be computed or estimated 2 predictable; dependable > ,calcula'bility n > 'calculably adv

calculate ('kælkjʊ,leɪt) vb 1 to solve (one or more problems) by a mathematical procedure; compute 2 (tr; may take a clause as object) to determine beforehand by judgment, reasoning, etc; estimate 3 (tr, usually passive) to design specifically; aim: the car was calculated to appeal to women 4 (intr; foll by on or upon) to depend; rely 5 (tr; may take a clause as object) US dialect to suppose; think [c16: from Late Latin calculāre, from calculus pebble used as a counter; see CALCULUS] > calculative ('kælkjʊlətɪv) adj

calculated ('kælkjʊ,leɪtɪd) adj (usually prenominal) 1 undertaken after considering the likelihood of success or failure: a calculated risk 2 deliberately planned; premeditated: a calculated insult

calculating ('kælkjʊ,leɪtɪŋ) adj 1 selfishly scheming 2 shrewd; cautious > 'calcu,latingly adv

calculation (,kælkjʊ'leɪʃən) n 1 the act, process, or result of calculating 2 an estimation of probability; forecast 3 careful planning or forethought, esp for selfish motives

calculator ('kælkjʊ,leɪtə) n 1 a device for performing mathematical calculations, esp an electronic device that can be held in the hand 2 a person or thing that calculates 3 a set of tables used as an aid to calculations

calculous ('kælkjʊləs) adj pathol of or suffering from a calculus

calculus ('kælkjʊləs) n, pl -luses 1 a branch of mathematics, developed independently by Newton and Leibniz. Both differential calculus and integral calculus are concerned with the effect on a function of an infinitesimal change in the independent variable as it tends to zero 2 any mathematical system of calculation involving the use of symbols 3 pl -li (-,laɪ) pathol a stonelike concretion of minerals and salts found in ducts or hollow organs of the body [c17: from Latin: pebble, stone used in reckoning, from calx small stone, counter]

Calcutta (kæl'kʌtə) n the former official name (still widely used) of **Kolkata**

Calcutta Cup n rugby union a trophy competed for annually by England and Scotland since 1879 [after the CALCUTTA Rugby and Cricket Club, who donated the trophy to the Rugby Football Union in 1878]

Calder ('kɔ:ldə) n **Alexander**. 1898–1976, US sculptor, who originated mobiles and stabiles (moving or static abstract sculptures, generally suspended from wire)

caldera (kæl'dɛərə, 'kɔ:ldərə) n a large basin-shaped crater at the top of a volcano, formed by the collapse or explosion of the cone [c19: from Spanish Caldera (literally: CAULDRON), name of a crater in the Canary Islands]

Calderdale ('kɔ:ldə,deɪl) n a unitary authority in N England, in West Yorkshire. Pop: 193 200 (2003 est). Area: 364 sq km (140 sq miles)

Calderón de la Barca (Spanish kalde'ron de la 'barka) n **Pedro** ('peðro). 1600–81, Spanish dramatist, whose best-known work is La Vida es Sueño. He also wrote autos sacramentales, outdoor plays for the feast of Corpus Christi, 76 of which survive.

caldron ('kɔ:ldrən) n a variant spelling of **cauldron**

Caldwell ('kɔ:ldwɛl, -wəl) n **Erskine** ('3:skɪn). 1903–87, US novelist whose works include Tobacco Road (1933)

calèche (French kalɛʃ) n a variant of **calash**

Caledonia (,kælɪ'dəʊnɪə) n the Roman name for **Scotland**

● USAGE Calendonia is now used poetically and,
● sometimes, humorously

Caledonian (,kælɪ'dəʊnɪən) adj 1 of or relating to Scotland 2 of or denoting a period of mountain building in NW Europe in the Palaeozoic era ▷ n 3 literary a native or inhabitant of Scotland

Caledonian Canal n a canal in N Scotland, linking the Atlantic with the North Sea through the Great Glen:

built 1803–47; now used mostly for leisure boating

calefacient (ˌkælɪˈfeɪʃənt) *adj* **1** causing warmth ▷ *n* **2** *med obsolete* an agent that warms, such as a mustard plaster [c17: from Latin *calefaciēns*, from *calefacere* to heat]

calendar (ˈkælɪndə) *n* **1** a system for determining the beginning, length, and order of years and their divisions **2** a table showing any such arrangement, esp as applied to one or more successive years **3** a list, register, or schedule of social events, pending court cases, appointments, etc ▷ *vb* **4** (*tr*) to enter in a calendar; schedule; register [c13: via Norman French from Medieval Latin *kalendārium* account book, from *Kalendae* the CALENDS; when interest on debts became due] > **calendrical** (kæˈlɛndrɪk³l) *or* ca'lendric *adj*

calendar month *n* See **month** (sense 1)

calendar year *n* See **year** (sense 1)

calender (ˈkælɪndə) *n* **1** a machine in which paper or cloth is glazed or smoothed by passing between rollers ▷ *vb* **2** (*tr*) to subject (material) to such a process [c17: from French *calandre*, of unknown origin]

calends *or* **kalends** (ˈkælɪndz) *pl n* the first day of each month in the ancient Roman calendar [c14: from Latin *kalendae*; related to Latin *calāre* to proclaim]

calendula (kæˈlɛndjʊlə) *n* any Eurasian plant of the genus *Calendula*, esp the pot marigold, having orange-and-yellow rayed flowers: family *Asteraceae* (composites) [c19: from Medieval Latin, from Latin *kalendae* CALENDS; perhaps from its supposed efficacy in curing menstrual disorders]

calf[1] (kɑːf) *n, pl* **calves 1** the young of cattle, esp domestic cattle **2** the young of certain other mammals, such as the buffalo, elephant, giraffe, and whale **3** a large piece of floating ice detached from an iceberg, etc **4** kill the fatted calf to celebrate lavishly, esp as a welcome [Old English *cealf*; related to Old Norse *kālfr*, Gothic *kalbō*, Old High German *kalba*]

calf[2] (kɑːf) *n, pl* **calves** the thick fleshy part of the back of the leg between the ankle and the knee [c14: from Old Norse *kalfi*]

calf love *n* temporary infatuation or love of an adolescent for a member of the opposite sex

calf's-foot jelly *n* a jelly made from the stock of boiled calves' feet and flavourings, formerly often served to invalids

calfskin (ˈkɑːfˌskɪn) *n* **1** the skin or hide of a calf **2** Also called: calf **a** fine leather made from this skin **b** (*as modifier*): *calfskin boots*

Calgary (ˈkælɡərɪ) *n* a city in Canada, in S Alberta: centre of a large agricultural region; oilfields. Pop: 879 277 (2001)

Calgon (ˈkælɡɒn) *n trademark* a chemical compound, sodium hexametaphosphate, with water-softening properties, used in detergents

calibrate (ˈkælɪˌbreɪt) *vb* (*tr*) **1** to measure the calibre of (a gun, mortar, etc) **2** to mark (the scale of a measuring instrument) so that readings can be made in appropriate units **3** to determine the accuracy of (a measuring instrument, etc) > ˌcali'bration *n* > 'caliˌbrator *or* 'caliˌbrater *n*

calibre *or US* **caliber** (ˈkælɪbə) *n* **1** the diameter of a cylindrical body, esp the internal diameter of a tube or the bore of a firearm **2** the diameter of a shell or bullet **3** ability; distinction **4** personal character: *a man of high calibre* [c16: from French, from Italian *calibro*, from Arabic *qālib* shoemaker's last, mould] > 'calibred *or US* 'calibered *adj*

calices (ˈkælɪˌsiːz) *n* the plural of **calix**

calico (ˈkælɪˌkəʊ) *n, pl* **-coes** *or* **-cos 1** a white or unbleached cotton fabric with no printed design **2** *chiefly US* a coarse printed cotton fabric [c16: based on *Calicut*, town in India]

calif (ˈkeɪlɪf, ˈkæl-) *n* a variant spelling of **caliph**

Calif. *abbreviation* California

California (ˌkælɪˈfɔːnɪə) *n* **1** a state on the W coast of the US: the third largest state in area and the largest in population; consists of a narrow, warm coastal plain rising to the Coast Range, deserts in the south, the fertile central valleys of the Sacramento and San Joaquin Rivers, and the mountains of the Sierra Nevada in the east; major industries include the growing of citrus fruits and grapes, fishing, oil production, electronics, information technology, and films. Capital: Sacramento. Pop: 35 484 453 (2003 est). Area: 411 015 sq km (158 693 sq miles). Abbreviation: **Cal., Calif., CA 2** Gulf of California an arm of the Pacific Ocean, between Sonora and Lower California

Californian (ˌkælɪˈfɔːnɪən) *adj* **1** of or relating to California or its inhabitants ▷ *n* **2** a native or inhabitant of California

California poppy *n* a papaveraceous plant, *Eschscholtzia californica*, of the Pacific coast of North America, having yellow or orange flowers and finely divided bluish-green leaves. Also called: eschscholtzia

californium (ˌkælɪˈfɔːnɪəm) *n* a metallic transuranic element artificially produced from curium. Symbol: Cf; atomic no: 98; half-life of most stable isotope, ^{251}Cf: 800 years (approx.) [c20: New Latin; discovered at the University of *California*]

Caligula (kəˈlɪɡjʊlə) *n* original name *Gaius Caesar*, son of Germanicus. 12–41 AD, Roman emperor (37–41), noted for his cruelty and tyranny; assassinated

calipash *or* **callipash** (ˈkælɪˌpæʃ) *n* the greenish glutinous edible part of the turtle found next to the upper shell, considered a delicacy [c17: perhaps changed from Spanish *carapacho* CARAPACE]

calipee (ˈkælɪˌpiː) *n* the yellow glutinous edible part of the turtle found next to the lower shell, considered a delicacy [c17: perhaps a variant of CALIPASH]

caliper (ˈkælɪpə) *n* the usual US spelling of **calliper**

caliph, calif, kalif *or* **khalif** (ˈkeɪlɪf, ˈkæl-) *n Islam* the title of the successors of Mohammed as rulers of the Islamic world, later assumed by the Sultans of Turkey [c14: from Old French, from Arabic *khalīfa* successor]

caliphate, califate, kalifate, *or* **kharlifate** (ˈkeɪlɪˌfeɪt, -fɪt, ˈkæl-) *n* the office, jurisdiction, or reign of a caliph

calisthenics (ˌkælɪsˈθɛnɪks) *n* a variant spelling (esp *US*) of **callisthenics**

calix (ˈkeɪlɪks, ˈkæ-) *n, pl* **calices** (ˈkælɪˌsiːz) a cup; chalice [c18: from Latin: CHALICE]

calk[1] (kɔːk) *vb* a variant spelling of **caulk**

calk[2] (kɔːk) *or* **calkin** (ˈkɔːkɪn, ˈkæl-) *n* **1** a metal projection on a horse's shoe to prevent slipping ▷ *vb* (*tr*) **2** to provide with calks [c17: from Latin *calx* heel]

call (kɔːl) *vb* **1** (often foll by *out*) to speak or utter (words, sounds, etc) loudly so as to attract attention: *he called out her name* **2** (*tr*) to ask or order to come: *to call a policeman* **3** (*intr*; sometimes foll by *on*) to make a visit (to): *she called on him* **4** (*tr*) to summon to a specific office, profession, etc: *he was called to the ministry* **5** (of animals or birds) to utter (a characteristic sound or cry) **6** (*tr*) to summon (a bird or animal) by imitating its cry **7** (*tr*) to name or style: *they called the dog Rover* **8** (*tr*) to designate: *they called him a coward* **9** (*tr*) to regard in a specific way: *I call it a foolish waste of time* **10** (*tr*) to attract (attention) **11** (*tr*) to read (a list, register, etc) aloud to check for omissions or absentees **12** (when *tr*, usually foll by *for*) to give an order (for): *to call a strike* **13** (*intr*) to try to predict the result of tossing a coin **14** (*tr*) to awaken: *I was called early this morning* **15** (*tr*) to cause to assemble: *to call a meeting* **16** (*tr*) *sport* (of an umpire, referee, etc) to pass judgment upon (a shot, player, etc) with a call **17** (*tr*) *Austral & NZ* to broadcast a commentary on (a horse race or other sporting event) **18** (*tr*) to demand repayment of (a loan, redeemable bond, security, etc) **19** (*tr*) *Brit* to award (a student at an Inn of Court) the degree of barrister (esp in the phrase **call to the bar**) **20** (*tr*) *poker* to demand that (a player) expose his hand, after equalling his bet **21** (*intr*) *bridge* to make a bid **22** (in square-dancing) to call out (instructions) to the dancers **23** *billiards* to ask (a player) to say what kind of shot he will play or (of a player) to name his shot **24** (*intr*; foll by *for*) **a** to require: *this problem calls for study* **b** to come or go (for) in order to fetch: *I will call for my book later* **25** (*intr*; foll by *on* or *upon*) to make an appeal or request (to): *they called upon him to reply* **26** (*tr*) to predict the outcome of an event: *we don't know yet if the plan has succeeded because it's too soon to call* **27** call into being to create **28** call to mind to remember or cause to be remembered ▷ *n* **29** a cry or shout **30** the

c

characteristic cry of a bird or animal **31** a device, such as a whistle, intended to imitate the cry of a bird or animal **32** a summons or invitation **33** a summons or signal sounded on a horn, bugle, etc **34** a short visit: *the doctor made six calls this morning* **35** an inner urge to some task or profession; vocation **36** allure or fascination, esp of a place: *the call of the forest* **37** need, demand, or occasion: *there is no call to shout; we don't get much call for stockings these days* **38** demand or claim (esp in the phrase **the call of duty**) **39** *theatre* a notice to actors informing them of times of rehearsals **40** a conversation or a request for a connection by telephone **41** *commerce* a demand for repayment of a loan **b** (*as modifier*): *call money* **42** *finance* a demand for redeemable bonds or shares to be presented for repayment **43** *poker* a demand for a hand or hands to be exposed **44** *bridge* a bid, or a player's turn to bid **45** a decision or judgment **46** *Austral* a broadcast commentary on a horse race or other sporting event **47** Also called: **call option** *stock exchange* an option to buy a stated amount of securities at a specified price during a specified period **48 on call a** (of a loan, etc) repayable on demand **b** available to be called for work outside normal working hours **49** within call; within range; accessible ▷ See also **call down, call forth, call in, call off, call out, call up** [Old English *ceallian*; related to Old Norse *kalla*, Old High German *kallōn*, Old Slavonic *glasŭ* voice]

calla ('kælə) *n* Also called: **calla lily, arum lily** any southern African plant of the aroid genus *Zantedeschia*, esp *Z. aethiopica*, which has a white funnel-shaped spathe enclosing a yellow spadix [c19: from New Latin, probably from Greek *kalleia* wattles on a cock, probably from *kallos* beauty]

Callaghan ('kælə,hæn) *n* (**Leonard**) **James**, Baron Callaghan of Cardiff. 1912–2005, British Labour statesman; prime minister (1976–79)

Callanetics (,kælə'nɛtɪks) *n* (*functioning as singular*) *trademark* a system of exercise involving frequent repetition of small muscular movements and squeezes, designed to improve muscle tone [c20: named after *Callan Pinckney* (born 1939), its US inventor]

Callas ('kæləs) *n* **Maria**, real name *Maria Anna Cecilia Kalageropoulos*. 1923–77, Greek operatic soprano, born in the US

call box *n* a soundproof enclosure for a public telephone. Also called: **telephone kiosk**

callboy ('kɔːl,bɔɪ) *n* a person who notifies actors when it is time to go on stage

call centre *n* an office where staff carry out an organization's telephone transactions

call down *vb* (*tr, adverb*) to request or invoke: *to call down God's anger*

caller ('kɔːlə) *n* **1** a person or thing that calls, esp a person who makes a brief visit **2** *Australia* a racing commentator

call forth *vb* (*tr, adverb*) to cause (something) to come into action or existence

call girl *n* a prostitute with whom appointments are made by telephone

calli- *combining form* beautiful: *calligraphy* [from Greek *kalli-*, from *kallos* beauty]

Callicrates (kə'lɪkrə,tiːz) *n* 5th century BC, Greek architect: with Ictinus, designed the Parthenon

calligraphy (kə'lɪgrəfɪ) *n* handwriting, esp beautiful handwriting considered as an art ▷ **calligraphic** (,kælɪ'græfɪk) *adj* ▷ **cal'ligrapher** or **cal'ligraphist** *n*

Callimachus (kə'lɪməkəs) *n* **1** late 5th century BC, Greek sculptor, reputed to have invented the Corinthian capital **2** ?305–?240 BC, Greek poet of the Alexandrian School; author of hymns and epigrams

call in *vb* (*adverb*) **1** (*intr*; often foll by **on**) to pay a visit, esp a brief or informal one: *call in if you are in the neighbourhood* **2** (*tr*) to demand payment of: *to call in a loan* **3** (*tr*) to take (something) out of circulation, because it is defective or no longer useful **4** (*tr*) to summon to one's assistance: *they had to call in a specialist*

calling ('kɔːlɪŋ) *n* **1** a strong inner urge to follow an occupation, etc; vocation **2** an occupation, profession, or trade

calling card *n* a small card bearing the name and

usually the address of a person, esp for giving to business or social acquaintances. Also called: **visiting card**

calliope (kə'laɪəpɪ) *n US & Canadian* a steam organ [c19: after CALLIOPE (literally: beautiful-voiced)]

Calliope (kə'laɪəpɪ) *n Greek myth* the Muse of epic poetry

calliper *or US* **caliper** ('kælɪpə) *n* **1** Also called: **calliper compasses** (*often plural*) an instrument for measuring internal or external dimensions, consisting of two steel legs hinged together **2** Also called: **calliper splint** *med* a splint consisting of two metal rods with straps attached, for supporting or exerting tension on the leg ▷ *vb* **3** (*tr*) to measure the dimensions of (an object) with callipers [c16: variant of CALIBRE]

calliper rule *n* a measuring instrument having two parallel jaws, one fixed at right angles to the end of a calibrated scale and the other sliding along it

callistemon (kə'lɪstəmən) *n* another name for **bottlebrush** (sense 2)

callisthenics *or* **calisthenics** (,kælɪs'θɛnɪks) *n* **1** (*functioning as plural*) light exercises designed to promote general fitness, develop muscle tone, etc **2** (*functioning as singular*) the practice of callisthenic exercises [c19: from CALLI- + Greek *sthenos* strength] ▷ **callis'thenic** or **calis'thenic** *adj*

Callisto (kə'lɪstəʊ) *n Greek myth* a nymph who attracted the love of Zeus and was changed into a bear by Hera. Zeus then set her in the sky as the constellation Ursa Major

call loan *n* a loan that is repayable on demand. Also called: **demand loan**.

call off *vb* (*tr, adverb*) **1** to cancel or abandon: *the game was called off because of rain* **2** to order (an animal or person) to desist or summon away: *the man called off his dog* **3** to stop (something) or give the order to stop

callose ('kæləʊz) *n* a carbohydrate, a polymer of glucose, found in plants, esp in the sieve tubes

callosity (kə'lɒsɪtɪ) *n, pl* -ties **1** hardheartedness **2** another name for **callus** (sense 1)

callous ('kæləs) *adj* **1** unfeeling; insensitive **2** (of skin) hardened and thickened ▷ *vb* **3** *pathol* to make or become callous [c16: from Latin *callōsus*; see CALLUS] ▷ **'callously** *adv* ▷ **'callousness** *n*

call out *vb* (*adverb*) **1** to utter aloud, esp loudly **2** (*tr*) to summon **3** (*tr*) to order (workers) to strike **4** (*tr*) to challenge to a duel

callow ('kæləʊ) *adj* lacking experience of life; immature [Old English *calu*; related to Old High German *kalo*, Old Slavonic *golŭ* bare, naked, Lithuanian *galva* head, Latin *calvus* bald] ▷ **'callowness** *n*

Callow ('kæləʊ) *n* **Simon**. born 1949, British actor and theatre director

call sign *n* a group of letters and numbers identifying a radio transmitting station, esp an amateur radio station

call up *vb* (*adverb*) **1** to summon to report for active military service, as in time of war **2** (*tr*) to recall (something); evoke **3** (*tr*) to bring or summon (people, etc) into action **4** to telephone ▷ *n* **call-up 5 a** a general order to report for military service **b** the number of men so summoned

callus ('kæləs) *n, pl* **-luses 1** Also called: **callosity** an area of skin that is hard or thick, esp on the palm of the hand or sole of the foot, as from continual friction or pressure **2** an area of bony tissue formed during the healing of a fractured bone **3** *botany* a mass of hard protective tissue produced in woody plants at the site of an injury **4** *biotechnology* a mass of undifferentiated cells produced as the first stage in tissue culture [c16: from Latin, variant of *callum* hardened skin]

calm (kɑːm) *adj* **1** almost without motion; still: *a calm sea* **2** *meteorol* of force 0 on the Beaufort scale; without wind **3** not disturbed, agitated, or excited; under control **4** tranquil; serene: *a calm voice* ▷ *n* **5** an absence of disturbance or rough motion; stillness **6** absence of wind **7** tranquillity ▷ *vb* **8** (often foll by *down*) to make or become calm [c14: from Old French *calme*, from Old Italian *calma*, from Late Latin *cauma* heat, hence a rest during the heat of the day, from Greek *kauma* heat, from *kaiein* to burn] ▷ **'calmly** *adv* ▷ **'calmness** *n*

calmative ('kælmətɪv, 'kɑːmə-) *adj* (of a remedy or agent) sedative

calomel ('kælə,mɛl, -məl) *n* a colourless tasteless powder consisting chiefly of mercurous chloride, used medicinally, esp as a cathartic. Formula: Hg_2Cl_2 [c17: perhaps from New Latin *calomelas* (unattested), literally: beautiful black (perhaps so named because it was originally sublimed from a black mixture of mercury and mercuric chloride), from Greek *kalos* beautiful + *melas* black]

Calor Gas ('kælə) *n trademark* butane gas liquefied under pressure in portable containers for domestic use

caloric (kə'lɒrɪk, 'kælərɪk) *adj* 1 of or concerned with heat or calories ▷ *n* 2 *obsolete* a hypothetical elastic fluid formerly postulated as the embodiment of heat

calorie or **calory** ('kælərɪ) *n, pl* -ries a unit of heat, equal to 4.1868 joules (**International Table calorie**): formerly defined as the quantity of heat required to raise the temperature of 1 gram of water by 1°C under standard conditions. It has now largely been replaced by the joule for scientific purposes. Abbreviation: cal. Also called: small calorie [c19: from French, from Latin *calor* heat]

Calorie ('kælərɪ) *n* 1 Also called: kilogram calorie, kilocalorie, large calorie a unit of heat, equal to one thousand calories, often used to express the heat output of an organism or the energy value of food. Abbreviation: Cal 2 the amount of a specific food capable of producing one thousand calories of energy

calorific (,kælə'rɪfɪk) *adj* of, concerning, or generating heat > ,calo'rifically *adv*

calorific value *n* the quantity of heat produced by the complete combustion of a given mass of a fuel, usually expressed in joules per kilogram

calorimeter (,kælə'rɪmɪtə) *n* an apparatus for measuring amounts of heat, esp to find specific heat capacities, calorific values, etc > calorimetric (,kælərɪ'mɛtrɪk) or ,calori'metrical *adj* > ,calo'rimetry *n*

calorize ('kælə,raɪz) *vb* (*tr*) to coat (a ferrous metal) by spraying with aluminium powder and then heating

Calpe ('kælpɪ) *n* the ancient name for (the Rock of) **Gibraltar**

calque (kælk) *n* another word for **loan translation** [c20: from French: a tracing, from *calquer*, from Latin *calcāre* to tread]

calumet ('kælju,mɛt) *n* a less common name for **peace pipe** [c18: from Canadian French, from French (Normandy dialect): straw, from Late Latin *calamellus* a little reed, from Latin: CALAMUS]

calumniate (kə'lʌmnɪ,eɪt) *vb* (*tr*) to slander > ca,lumni'ation *n* > ca'lumni,ator *n*

calumny ('kæləmnɪ) *n, pl* -nies 1 the malicious utterance of false charges or misrepresentation; slander; defamation 2 such a false charge or misrepresentation [c15: from Latin *calumnia* deception, slander] > calumnious (kə'lʌmnɪəs) or calumniatory (kə'lʌmnɪətərɪ, -trɪ) *adj*

Calvados ('kælvə,dɒs) *n* 1 a department of N France in the Basse-Normandie region. Capital: Caen. Pop: 659 893 (2003 est). Area: 5693 sq km (2198 sq miles) 2 an apple brandy distilled from cider in this region

calvaria (kæl'vɛərɪə) *n* the top part of the skull of vertebrates. Nontechnical name: skullcap [c14: from Late Latin: (human) skull, from Latin *calvus* bald]

Calvary ('kælvərɪ) *n* the place just outside the walls of Jerusalem where Jesus was crucified. Also called: Golgotha [from Late Latin *Calvāria*, translation of Greek *kranion* skull, translation of Aramaic *gulgulta* Golgotha]

calve (kɑːv) *vb* 1 to give birth to (a calf) 2 (of a glacier or iceberg) to release (masses of ice) in breaking up

Calvert ('kælvət) *n* 1 Sir **George**, 1st Baron Baltimore. ?1580–1632, English statesman; founder of the colony of Maryland 2 his son, **Leonard**. 1606–47, English statesman; first colonial governor of Maryland (1634–47)

calves (kɑːvz) *n* the plural of **calf¹** and **calf²**

Calvin ('kælvɪn) *n* 1 **John**, original name *Jean Cauvin, Caulvin,* or *Chauvin*. 1509–64, French theologian: a leader of the Protestant Reformation in France and Switzerland, establishing the first presbyterian government in Geneva. His theological system is described in his *Institutes of the Christian Religion* (1536) 2 **Melvin**. 1911–97, US chemist, noted particularly for his research on photosynthesis: Nobel prize for chemistry 1961

Calvin cycle *n botany* a series of reactions, occurring during photosynthesis, in which glucose is synthesized from carbon dioxide [c20: named after Melvin Calvin (1911–97), US chemist, who elucidated it]

Calvinism ('kælvɪ,nɪzəm) *n* the theological system of John Calvin (original name *Jean Cauvin, Caulvin,* or *Chauvin*; 1509–64), the French theologian and leader of the Protestant Reformation, and his followers, characterized by emphasis on the doctrines of predestination, the irresistibility of grace, and justification by faith > 'Calvinist *n, adj* > ,Calvin'istic or ,Calvin'istical *adj*

Calvino (kæl'viːnəʊ) *n* **Italo**. 1923–85, Italian novelist and short-story writer. His works include *Our Ancestors* (1960) and *Invisible Cities* (1972)

calx (kælks) *n, pl* **calxes** or **calces** ('kælsiːz) 1 the powdery metallic oxide formed when an ore or mineral is roasted 2 another name for **calcium oxide** 3 *anatomy* the heel [c15: from Latin: lime, from Greek *khalix* pebble]

calypso (kə'lɪpsəʊ) *n, pl* -sos a popular type of satirical, usually topical, West Indian ballad, esp from Trinidad, usually extemporized to a percussive syncopated accompaniment [c20: probably from CALYPSO]

Calypso (kə'lɪpsəʊ) *n Greek myth* (in Homer's *Odyssey*) a sea nymph who detained Odysseus on the island of Ogygia for seven years

calypsonian (,kælɪp'səʊnɪən) *n* a performer or writer of calypsos

calyx ('keɪlɪks, 'kælɪks) *n, pl* **calyxes** or **calyces** ('kælɪ,siːz, 'keɪlɪ-) 1 the sepals of a flower collectively, forming the outer floral envelope that protects the developing flower bud 2 any cup-shaped cavity or structure, esp any of the divisions of the human kidney (**renal calyx**) that form the renal pelvis [c17: from Latin, from Greek *kalux* shell, from *kaluptein* to cover, hide]

Calzaghe (kæl'zægɪ) *n* **Joe**. born 1972, Welsh boxer: world middleweight champion from 1997

calzone (kæl'tsəʊnɪ) *n* a dish of Italian origin consisting of pizza dough folded over a filling of cheese and tomatoes, herbs, ham, etc [c20: Italian, literally: trouser leg, from *calzone* trousers]

cam (kæm) *n* a slider or roller attached to a rotating shaft to give a particular type of reciprocating motion to a part in contact with its profile [c18: from Dutch *kam* comb]

-cam *n combining form* camera: *webcam*

Cam (kæm) *n* a river in E England, in Cambridgeshire, flowing through Cambridge to the River Ouse. Length: about 64 km (40 miles)

CAM *abbreviation* computer-aided manufacture

cama ('kɑːmə) *n* the hybrid offspring of a camel and a llama

Camagüey (,kæmə,gweɪ; *Spanish* kama'ɣwej) *n* a city in E central Cuba. Pop: 320 000 (2005 est)

camaraderie (,kæmə'rɑːdərɪ) *n* a spirit of familiarity and trust existing between friends [c19: from French, from COMRADE]

Camargue (kæ'mɑːg) *n* **la Camargue** (la) a delta region in S France, between the channels of the Grand and Petit Rhône: cattle, esp bulls for the Spanish bullrings, and horses are reared

camarilla (,kæmə'rɪlə; *Spanish* kama'riʎa) *n* a group of confidential advisers, esp formerly, to the Spanish kings; cabal [c19: from Spanish: literally: a little room]

Cambay (kæm'beɪ) *n* **Gulf of Cambay** an inlet of the Arabian Sea on the W coast of India, southeast of the Kathiawar Peninsula

camber ('kæmbə) *n* 1 a slight upward curve to the centre of the surface of a road, ship's deck, etc 2 another name for **bank²** (sense 7) 3 an outward inclination of the front wheels of a road vehicle so that they are slightly closer together at the bottom than at the top 4 aerofoil curvature expressed by the ratio of the maximum height of the aerofoil mean line to its chord ▷ *vb* 5 to form or be formed with a surface that curves upwards to its centre [C17: from Old French (northern dialect) *cambre* curved, from Latin *camurus*; related to *camera* CHAMBER]

Camberwell carrot *n informal* a large, almost conical, marijuana cigarette

cambium ('kæmbɪəm) *n, pl* -biums *or* -bia (-bɪə) *botany* a meristem that increases the girth of stems and roots by producing additional xylem and phloem [C17: from Medieval Latin: exchange, from Late Latin *cambiāre* to exchange, barter] > 'cambial *adj*

Cambodia (kæm'bəʊdɪə) *n* a country in SE Asia: became part of French Indochina in 1887; achieved self-government in 1949 and independence in 1953; civil war (1970–74) ended in victory for the Khmer Rouge, who renamed the country Kampuchea (1975) and carried out extreme-radical political and economic reforms resulting in a considerable reduction of the population; Vietnamese forces ousted the Khmer Rouge in 1979 and set up a pro-Vietnamese government who reverted (1981) to the name Cambodia; after Vietnamese withdrawal in 1989 a peace settlement with exiled factions was followed in 1993 by the adoption of a democratic monarchist constitution restoring Prince Sihanouk to the throne. The country contains the central plains of the Mekong River and the Cardamom Mountains in the SW. Official language: Khmer; French is also widely spoken. Currency: riel. Capital: Phnom Penh. Pop: 14 482 000 (2004 est). Area: 181 000 sq km (69 895 sq miles)

Cambodian (kæm'bəʊdɪən) *adj* 1 of or relating to Cambodia or its inhabitants ▷ *n* 2 a native or inhabitant of Cambodia

Cambrai (*French* kābrɛ) *n* a town in NE France: textile industry: scene of a battle in which massed tanks were first used and broke through the German line (November, 1917). Pop: 33 738 (1999)

Cambria ('kæmbrɪə) *n* the Medieval Latin name for **Wales**

Cambrian ('kæmbrɪən) *adj* 1 of, denoting, or formed in the first 65 million years of the Palaeozoic era, during which marine invertebrates, esp trilobites, flourished 2 of or relating to Wales ▷ *n* 3 the Cambrian the Cambrian period or rock system 4 a Welsh person

Cambrian Mountains *pl n* a mountain range in Wales, extending from Carmarthenshire in the S to Denbighshire in the N. Highest peak: Aran Fawddwy, 891 m (2970 ft)

cambric ('keɪmbrɪk) *n* a fine white linen or cotton fabric [C16: from Flemish *Kamerijk* CAMBRAI]

Cambridge ('keɪmbrɪdʒ) *n* 1 a city in E England, administrative centre of Cambridgeshire, on the River Cam: centred around the university, founded in the 12th century: electronics, biotechnology. Pop: 117 717 (2001) 2 short for **Cambridgeshire** 3 a city in the US, in E Massachusetts: educational centre, with Harvard University (1636) and the Massachusetts Institute of Technology. Pop: 101 587 (2003 est). Related adj: **Cantabrigian**

Cambridgeshire ('keɪmbrɪdʒˌʃɪə, -ʃə) *n* a county of E England, in East Anglia: includes the former counties of the Isle of Ely and Huntingdon and lies largely in the Fens: Peterborough became an independent unitary authority in 1998. Administrative centre: Cambridge. Pop (excluding Peterborough): 571 000 (2003 est). Area (excluding Peterborough): 3068 sq km (184 sq miles)

Cambs *abbreviation* Cambridgeshire

Cambyses (kæm'baɪsiːz) *n* died ?522 BC, king of Persia (529–522 BC), who conquered Egypt (525); son of Cyrus the Great

camcorder ('kæmˌkɔːdə) *n* a video camera and recorder combined in a portable unit

Camden¹ ('kæmdən) *n* a borough of N Greater London. Pop: 210 700 (2003 est). Area: 21 sq km (8 sq miles)

Camden² ('kæmdən) *n* **William.** 1551–1623, English antiquary and historian; author of *Britannia* (1586)

came (keɪm) *vb* the past tense of **come**

camel ('kæməl) *n* 1 either of two cud-chewing artiodactyl mammals of the genus *Camelus*: family *Camelidae*. They are adapted for surviving long periods without food or water in desert regions, esp by using

humps on the back for storing fat. See **Arabian camel**, **Bactrian camel** 2 a float attached to a vessel to increase its buoyancy 3 a a fawn colour b (*as adjective*): *a camel dress* [Old English, from Latin *camēlus*, from Greek *kamēlos*, of Semitic origin; related to Arabic *jamal*]

cameleer (ˌkæmɪ'lɪə) *n* a camel-driver

camel hair *or* **camel's hair** *n* 1 the hair of the camel or dromedary, used in clothing, rugs, etc 2 a soft cloth made of or containing this hair or a substitute, usually tan in colour b (*as modifier*): *a camelhair coat* 3 a the hair of the squirrel's tail, used for paintbrushes b (*as modifier*): *a camelhair brush*

camellia (kə'miːlɪə) *n* any ornamental shrub of the Asian genus *Camellia*, esp *C. japonica*, having glossy evergreen leaves and showy roselike flowers, usually white, pink or red in colour: family *Theaceae*. Also called: japonica [C18: New Latin, named after Georg Josef Kamel (1661–1706), Moravian Jesuit missionary, who introduced it to Europe]

camelopard ('kæmɪləˌpɑːd, kə'mɛl-) *n* an obsolete word for **giraffe** [C14: from Medieval Latin *camēlopardus*, from Greek *kamēlopardalis*, from *kamēlos* CAMEL + *pardalis* LEOPARD, because the giraffe was thought to have a head like a camel's and spots like a leopard's]

Camelot ('kæmɪˌlɒt) *n* (in Arthurian legend) the English town where King Arthur's palace and court were situated

camel toe *n slang* the visual effect created when a woman's trousers cling too tightly to the crotch, emphasizing the shape of the pudenda [C20: from the alleged similarity between this effect and the shape of a camel's toe]

Camembert ('kæməmˌbeə; *French* kamɑ̃bɛr) *n* a rich soft creamy cheese [French, from *Camembert*, a village in Normandy where it originated]

cameo ('kæmɪˌəʊ) *n, pl* cameos 1 a medallion, as on a brooch or ring, with a profile head carved in relief 2 an engraving upon a gem or other stone of at least two differently coloured layers, such as sardonyx, so carved that the background is of a different colour from the raised design 3 a stone with such an engraving 4 a a single and often brief dramatic scene played by a well-known actor or actress in a film or television play b (*as modifier*): *a cameo role* 5 a short literary work or dramatic sketch [C15: from Italian *cammeo*, of uncertain origin]

camera ('kæmərə, 'kæmrə) *n* 1 an optical device consisting of a lens system set in a light-proof construction inside which a light-sensitive film or plate can be positioned 2 *television* the equipment used to convert the optical image of a scene into the corresponding electrical signals 3 See **camera obscura** 4 *pl* -erae (-əˌriː) a judge's private room 5 in camera a *law* relating to a hearing from which members of the public are excluded b in private [C18: from Latin: vault, from Greek *kamara*]

cameraman ('kæmərəˌmæn, 'kæmrə-) *n, pl* -men a person who operates a film or television camera

● USAGE Gender-neutral form: *camera operator*

camera obscura (ɒb'skjʊərə) *n* a darkened chamber or small building in which images of outside objects are projected onto a flat surface by a convex lens in an aperture [New Latin: dark chamber]

camera phone *n* a mobile phone incorporating a camera

Cameron ('kæmərən) *n* 1 **James.** born 1954, Canadian film director and screenwriter; his films include *The Terminator* (1984), *Aliens* (1986) and *Titanic* (1997) 2 **Julia Margaret.** 1815–79, British photographer, born in India, renowned for her portrait photographs. 3 (**Mark**) **James** (**Walter**). 1911–85, British journalist, author, and broadcaster. His books include *Witness in Vietnam* (1966) and *Point of Departure* (1967).

Cameroon (ˌkæmə'ruːn, 'kæməˌruːn) *n* 1 a republic in West Africa, on the Gulf of Guinea: became a German colony in 1884; divided in 1919 into the **Cameroons** (administered by Britain) and **Cameroun** (administered by France); Cameroun and the S part of the Cameroons formed a republic in 1961 (the N part joined Nigeria); became a member of the Commonwealth in 1995.

Official languages: French and English. Religions: Christian, Muslim, and animist. Currency: franc. Capital: Yaoundé. Pop: 16 296 000 (2004 est.). Area: 475 500 sq km (183 591 sq miles) **2** an active volcano in W Cameroon: the highest peak on the West African coast. Height: 4070 m (13 352 ft)

Cameroun (kamrun) *n* the French name for **Cameroon**

camiknickers ('kæmɪˌnɪkəz) *pl n* women's knickers attached to a camisole top

camisole ('kæmɪˌsəʊl) *n* **1** a woman's underbodice with shoulder straps, originally designed as a cover for a corset **2** a woman's dressing jacket or short negligée [C19: from French, from Provençal *camisola*, from *camisa* shirt, from Late Latin *camīsia*]

Camoëns ('kæməʊˌɛns) or **Camões** (*Portuguese* ka'mōɪʃ) *n* **Luis Vaz de** (lwiʃ vaʃ 'daː) 1524–80, Portuguese epic poet; author of *The Lusiads* (1572).

camomile or **chamomile** ('kæməˌmaɪl) *n* **1** any aromatic plant of the Eurasian genus *Anthemis*, esp *A. nobilis*, whose finely dissected leaves and daisy-like flowers are used medicinally: family *Asteraceae* (composites) **2** any plant of the related genus *Matricaria*, esp *M. chamomilla* (**German** or **wild camomile**) **3** camomile tea a medicinal beverage made from the fragrant leaves and flowers of any of these plants [C14: from Old French *camomille*, from Medieval Latin *chamomilla*, from Greek *khamaimēlon*, literally, earth-apple (referring to the apple-like scent of the flowers)]

camouflage ('kæməˌflɑːʒ) *n* **1** the exploitation of natural surroundings or artificial aids to conceal or disguise the presence of military units, equipment, etc **2** (*modifier*) (of fabric or clothing) having a design of irregular patches of dull colours (such as browns and greens), as used in military camouflage **3** the means by which animals escape the notice of predators, usually because of a resemblance to their surroundings: includes cryptic and apatetic coloration **4** a device or expedient designed to conceal or deceive ▷ *vb* **5** (*tr*) to conceal by camouflage [C20: from French, from *camoufler*, from Italian *camuffare* to disguise, deceive, of uncertain origin]

camp¹ (kæmp) *n* **1** a place where tents, cabins, or other temporary structures are erected for the use of military troops, for training soldiers, etc **2** tents, cabins, etc, used as temporary lodgings by a group of travellers, holiday-makers, Scouts, etc **3** the group of people living in such lodgings **4** *South African* a field or paddock fenced off as pasture **5** a group supporting a given doctrine or theory: *the socialist camp* **6** *Austral* a place where sheep or cattle gather to rest ▷ *vb* **7** (*intr; often foll by down*) to establish or set up a camp **8** (*intr; often foll by out*) to live temporarily in or as if in a tent [C16: from Old French, ultimately from Latin *campus* field] > 'camping *n*

camp² (kæmp) *informal* ▷ *adj* **1** effeminate; affected in mannerisms, dress, etc **2** homosexual **3** consciously artificial, exaggerated, vulgar, or mannered; self-parodying, esp when in dubious taste ▷ *vb* **4** (*tr*) to perform or invest with a camp quality **5** camp it up **a** to seek to focus attention on oneself by making an ostentatious display, overacting, etc **b** to flaunt one's homosexuality [C20: of uncertain origin] > 'campy *adj*

Camp (kæmp) *n* **Walter (Chauncey).** 1859–1925, US sportsman and administrator; he introduced new rules to American football, which distinguished it from rugby

Campagna (kæm'paːnjə) *n* a low-lying plain surrounding Rome, Italy: once fertile, it deteriorated to malarial marshes; but has since been reclaimed. Area: about 2000 sq km (800 sq miles). Also called: **Campagna di Roma** (dɪ 'rəʊmə)

campaign (kæm'peɪn) *n* **1** a series of coordinated activities, such as public speaking and demonstrating, designed to achieve a social, political, or commercial goal: *a presidential campaign; an advertising campaign* **2** *military* a number of complementary operations aimed at achieving a single objective, usually constrained by time or geographic area ▷ *vb* **3** (*intr; often foll by for*) to conduct, serve in, or go on a campaign [C17: from French *campagne* open country, from Italian *campagna*, from Late Latin *campānia*, from Latin *campus* field] > cam'paigner *n*

Campanella (*Italian* kampa'nɛlla) *n* **Tommaso.**

1568–1639, Italian philosopher and Dominican friar. During his imprisonment by the Spaniards (1599–1626) he wrote his celebrated utopian fantasy, *La città del sole*

Campania (kæm'peɪnɪə; *Italian* kam'paɲɲa) *n* a region of SW Italy: includes the islands of Capri and Ischia. Chief town: Naples. Pop: 5 725 098 (2003 est.). Area: 13 595 sq km (5248 sq miles)

campanile (ˌkæmpə'niːlɪ) *n* (esp in Italy) a bell tower, not usually attached to another building [C17: from Italian, from *campana* bell]

campanology (ˌkæmpə'nɒlədʒɪ) *n* the art or skill of ringing bells musically [C19: from New Latin *campānologia*, from Late Latin *campāna* bell] > campanological (ˌkæmpənə'lɒdʒɪkᵊl) *adj* > ˌcampa'nologist *or* ˌcampa'nologer *n*

campanula (kæm'pænjʊlə) *n* any N temperate plant of the campanulaceous genus *Campanula*, typically having blue or white bell-shaped flowers. Also called: **bellflower** [C17: from New Latin: a little bell, from Late Latin *campāna* bell; see CAMPANILE]

Campbell ('kæmbᵊl) *n* **1** Sir **Colin**, Baron Clyde. 1792–1863, British field marshal who relieved Lucknow for the second time (1857) and commanded in Oudh, suppressing the Indian Mutiny **2** Donald. 1921–67, English water speed record-holder **3** Sir **Malcolm**, father of Donald Campbell. 1885–1948, English racing driver and land speed record-holder **4** Mrs **Patrick**, original name *Beatrice Stella Tanner*. 1865– 1940, English actress **5** Roy. 1901–57, South African poet. His poetry is often satirical and includes *The Flaming Terrapin* (1924) **6** Thomas. 1777–1844, Scottish poet and critic, noted particularly for his war poems *Hohenlinden* and *Ye Mariners of England*

Campbell-Bannerman ('kæmbᵊl'bænəmən) *n* Sir **Henry.** 1836–1908, British statesman and leader of the Liberal Party (1899–1908); prime minister (1905–08), who granted self-government to the Transvaal and the Orange River Colony

Camp David ('deɪvɪd) *n* the US president's retreat in the Appalachian Mountains, Maryland: scene of the **Camp David Agreement** (Sept, 1978) between Anwar Sadat of Egypt and Menachem Begin of Israel, mediated by Jimmy Carter, which outlined a framework for establishing peace in the Middle East. This agreement was the basis of the peace treaty between Israel and Egypt signed in Washington (March, 1979)

camp-drafting *n* *Austral* a competitive test, esp at an agricultural show, of horsemen's skill in drafting cattle

Campeche (*Spanish* kam'petʃe) *n* **1** a state of SE Mexico, on the SW of the Yucatán peninsula: forestry and fishing. Capital: Campeche. Pop: 205 000 (2005 est.). Area: 56 114 sq km (21 666 sq miles) **2** a port in SE Mexico, capital of Campeche state. Pop: 195 000 (2000 est.) **3** Bay of Campeche Also called: **Gulf of Campeche** the SW part of the Gulf of Mexico

camper ('kæmpə) *n* **1** a person who lives or temporarily stays in a tent, cabin, etc **2** a vehicle equipped for camping out

Campese (kæm'peɪzɪ) *n* **David**. born 1962, Australian rugby union player

camp follower *n* **1** any civilian, esp a prostitute, who unofficially provides services to military personnel **2** a nonmember who is sympathetic to a particular group, theory, etc

camphor ('kæmfə) *n* a whitish crystalline aromatic terpene ketone obtained from the wood of the camphor tree or made from pinene: used in the manufacture of celluloid and in medicine as a liniment and treatment for colds. Formula: $C_{10}H_{16}O$ [C15: from Old French *camphre*, from Medieval Latin *camphora*, from Arabic *kāfūr*, from Malay *kāpūr* chalk; related to Khmer *kāpōr* camphor] > camphoric (kæm'fɒrɪk) *adj*

camphorate ('kæmfəˌreɪt) *vb* (*tr*) to apply, treat with, or impregnate with camphor

camphor ball *n* another name for **mothball** (sense 1)

camphor ice *n* an ointment consisting of camphor, white wax, spermaceti, and castor oil, used to treat skin ailments, esp chapped skin

camphor laurel *n* an Australian name for the camphor

c

tree, now occurring in the wild in parts of Australia

Campin ('kæmpɪn) *n* **Robert.** 1379–1444, Flemish painter, noted esp for his altarpieces: usually identified with the so-called Master of Flémalle

campion ('kæmpɪən) *n* any of various caryophyllaceous plants of the genera *Silene* and *Lychnis*, having red, pink, or white flowers [c16: probably from *campion*, obsolete variant of CHAMPION, perhaps so called because originally applied to *Lychnis coronaria*, the leaves of which were used to crown athletic champions]

Campion ('kæmpɪən) *n* **1 Saint Edmund.** 1540–81, English Jesuit martyr. He joined the Jesuits in 1573 and returned to England (1580) as a missionary. He was charged with treason and hanged **2 Jane.** born 1954, New Zealand film director and screenwriter: her films include *An Angel at My Table* (1990), *The Piano* (1993), *Holy Smoke* (1999), and *In the Cut* (2003) **3 Thomas.** 1567–1620, English poet and musician, noted particularly for his songs for the lute

Campobello (,kæmpə'bɛləʊ) *n* an island in the Bay of Fundy, off the coast of SE Canada: part of New Brunswick province. Pop: 1195 (2001). Area: about 52 sq km (20 sq miles).

Campo Formio (*Italian* 'kampo 'fɔrmjo) *n* a village in NE Italy, in Friuli-Venezia Giulia: scene of the signing of a treaty in 1797 that ended the war between revolutionary France and Austria

Campo Grande (*Portuguese* 'kə:mpu 'grɑ:ndə) *n* a city in SW Brazil, capital of Mato Grosso do Sul state on the São Paulo–Corumbá railway: market centre. Pop: 746 000 (2005 est)

camp oven *n Austral & NZ* a metal pot or box with a heavy lid, used for baking over an open fire

camp pie *n Austral history* tinned meat

camp site *n* an area on which holiday-makers may pitch a tent, etc. Also called: **camping site**

campus ('kæmpəs) *n, pl* **-puses 1** the grounds and buildings of a university **2** *chiefly US* the outside area of a college, university, etc [c18: from Latin: field]

campylobacter (,kæmpɪləʊ'bæktə) *n* a rod-shaped bacterium that causes infections in cattle and man. Unpasteurized milk infected with campylobacter is a common cause of gastroenteritis [from Greek *kampulos* bent + BACTER(IUM)]

Cam Ranh ('kæm 'ræn) *n* a port in SE Vietnam: large natural harbour, used at times as a naval base by French, Japanese, US, and Russian forces successively. Pop: 147 000 (2006 est)

camshaft ('kæm,ʃɑ:ft) *n* a shaft having one or more cams attached to it, esp one used to operate the valves of an internal-combustion engine

Camus (*French* kamy) *n* **Albert** (albɛr). 1913–60, French novelist, dramatist, and essayist, noted for his pessimistic portrayal of man's condition of isolation in an absurd world: author of the novels *L'Étranger* (1942) and *La Peste* (1947), the plays *Le Malentendu* (1945) and *Caligula* (1946), and the essays *Le Mythe de Sisyphe* (1942) and *L'Homme révolté* (1951): Nobel prize for literature 1957.

can[1] (kæn; *unstressed* kən) *vb, past* **could** (takes an infinitive without *to* or an implied infinitive) (*intr*) **1** used as an auxiliary to indicate ability, skill, or fitness to perform a task: *I can run a mile in under four minutes* **2** used as an auxiliary to indicate permission or the right to something: *can I have a drink?* **3** used as an auxiliary to indicate knowledge of how to do something **4** used as an auxiliary to indicate the possibility, opportunity, or likelihood [Old English *cunnan*; related to Old Norse *kunna*, Old High German *kunnan*, Latin *cognōscere* to know, Sanskrit *jānāti* he knows; see KEN, UNCOUTH]

can[2] (kæn) *n* **1** a container, esp for liquids, usually of thin sheet metal: *a petrol can; beer can* **2** another name (esp US) for **tin** (sense 2) **3** Also called: **canful** the contents of a can or the amount a can will hold **4** a slang word for **prison 5** *US & Canadian* a slang word for **toilet 6** a shallow cylindrical metal container of varying size used for storing and handling film **7 can of worms** *informal* a complicated problem **8 in the can a** (of a film, piece of music, etc) having been recorded, processed, edited, etc **b** *informal* arranged or agreed: *the contract is*

almost in the can ▷ *vb* **cans, canning, canned 9** to put (food, etc) into a can or cans; preserve in a can [Old English *canne*; related to Old Norse, Old High German *kanna*, Irish *gann*, Swedish *kana* sled]

Can. *abbreviation* **1** Canada **2** Canadian

Cana ('keɪnə) *n New Testament* the town in Galilee, north of Nazareth, where Jesus performed his first miracle by changing water into wine (John 2:1, 11)

Canaan ('keɪnən) *n* an ancient region between the River Jordan and the Mediterranean, corresponding roughly to Israel: the Promised Land of the Israelites

Canaanite ('keɪnə,naɪt) *n* a member of an ancient Semitic people who occupied the land of Canaan before the Israelite conquest

Canada ('kænədə) *n* a country in North America: the second largest country in the world; first permanent settlements by Europeans were made by the French from 1605; ceded to Britain in 1763 after a series of colonial wars; established as the Dominion of Canada in 1867; a member of the Commonwealth. It consists generally of sparsely inhabited tundra regions, rich in natural resources, in the north, the Rocky Mountains in the west, the Canadian Shield in the east, and vast central prairies; the bulk of the population is concentrated along the US border and the Great Lakes in the south. Languages: English and French. Religion: Christian majority. Currency: Canadian dollar. Capital: Ottawa. Pop: 31 743 000 (2004 est). Area: 9 976 185 sq km (3 851 809 sq miles)

Canada balsam *n* a yellow transparent resin obtained from the balsam fir. Because its refractive index is similar to that of glass, it is used as an adhesive in optical devices and as a mounting medium for microscope specimens

Canada Day *n* (in Canada) July 1, the anniversary of the day in 1867 when Canada became the first British colony to receive dominion status: a bank holiday

Canada goose *n* a large common greyish-brown North American goose, *Branta canadensis*, with a black neck and head and a white throat patch

Canada jay *n* a large common jay of North America, *Perisoreus canadensis*, with a grey body, and a white-and-black crestless head

Canadarm ('kænəd,ɑːm) *n* a type of robotic arm, developed in Canada, used on space vehicles

Canadian (kə'neɪdɪən) *adj* **1** of or relating to Canada or its people ▷ *n* **2** a native, citizen, or inhabitant of Canada

Canadian Alliance *n* a Canadian right-wing federal political party, founded in 2000

Canadian bacon *n* the US name for **back bacon**

Canadian English *n* the English language as spoken in Canada

Canadian football *n* a game resembling American football, played on a grass pitch between two teams of 12 players

Canadian Forces *pl n* the official name for the military forces of Canada

Canadianism (kə'neɪdɪə,nɪzəm) *n* **1** the Canadian national character or spirit **2** a linguistic usage, custom, or other feature peculiar to or characteristic of Canada, its people, or their culture

Canadian River *n* a river in the southern US, rising in NE New Mexico and flowing east to the Arkansas River in E Oklahoma. Length: 1458 km (906 miles)

Canadian Shield *n* Also called: Laurentian Shield, Laurentian Plateau (in Canada) the wide area of Precambrian rock extending west from the Labrador coast to the basin of the Mackenzie and north from the Great Lakes to Hudson Bay and the Arctic: rich in minerals

Canadian whisky *n* a blended whisky made in Canada from rye and other grains

canaille *French* (kanaj) *n* the masses; mob; rabble [c17: from French, from Italian *canaglia* pack of dogs]

canakin ('kænɪkɪn) *n* a variant spelling of **cannikin**

canal (kə'næl) *n* **1** an artificial waterway constructed for navigation, irrigation, water power, etc **2** any of various tubular passages or ducts: *the alimentary canal* **3** any of various elongated intercellular spaces in plants **4** *astronomy* any of the indistinct surface features of Mars originally thought to be a network of channels but not seen on close-range photographs. They are caused by an optical illusion in which faint geological features appear to have a geometric structure ▷ *vb* -nals, -nalling, -nalled *or US* -nals, -naling, -naled (*tr*) **5** to dig a canal through **6** to provide with a canal or canals [c15 (in the sense: pipe, tube): from Latin *canālis* channel, water pipe, from *canna* reed, CANE¹]

canal boat *n* a long narrow boat used on canals, esp for carrying freight

Canaletto (*Italian* kana'lɛtto) *n* original name *Giovanni Antonio Canale*. 1697–1768, Italian painter and etcher, noted particularly for his highly detailed paintings of cities, esp Venice, which are marked by strong contrasts of light and shade

canaliculus (ˌkænə'lɪkjʊləs) *n, pl* -li (-ˌlaɪ) a small channel, furrow, or groove, as in some bones and parts of plants [c16: from Latin: a little channel, from *canālis* CANAL] > ˌcana'licular, canaliculate (ˌkænə'lɪkjʊlɪt, -ˌleɪt) *or* ˌcana'licuˌlated *adj*

canalize *or* **canalise** (ˈkænəˌlaɪz) *vb* (*tr*) **1** to provide with or convert into a canal or canals **2** to give a particular direction to or provide an outlet for; channel > ˌcanaliˈzation *or* ˌcanaliˈsation *n*

canal ray *n physics* a stream of positive ions produced in a discharge tube by allowing them to pass through holes in the cathode

Canal Zone *n* a former administrative region of the US, on the Isthmus of Panama around the Panama Canal: bordered on each side by the Republic of Panama, into which it was incorporated in 1979. Also called: **Panama Canal Zone**

canapé (ˈkænəpɪ, -ˌpeɪ; *French* kanape) *n* a small piece of bread, toast, etc, spread with a savoury topping [c19: from French: sofa]

Canara (kə'nɑːrə) *n* a variant spelling of **Kanara**

canard (kæ'nɑːd; *French* kanar) *n* **1** a false report; rumour or hoax **2** an aircraft in which the tailplane is mounted in front of the wing [c19: from French: a duck, hoax, from Old French *caner* to quack, of imitative origin]

canary (kə'nɛərɪ) *n, pl* -naries **1** a small finch, *Serinus canaria*, of the Canary Islands and Azores: a popular cagebird noted for its singing. Wild canaries are streaked yellow and brown, but most domestic breeds are pure yellow **2** See **canary yellow 3** *archaic* a sweet wine from the Canary Islands similar to Madeira [c16: from Old Spanish *canario* of or from the Canary Islands]

Canary Islands *or* **Canaries** *pl n* a group of mountainous islands in the Atlantic off the NW coast of Africa, forming an Autonomous Community of Spain. Pop: 1 944 700 (2003 est)

canary yellow *n* **a** a moderate yellow colour, sometimes with a greenish tinge **b** (*as adjective*): *a canary-yellow car*. Sometimes shortened to **canary**

canasta (kə'næstə) *n* **1** a card game for two to six players who seek to amass points by declaring sets of cards **2** Also called: **meld** a declared set in this game, containing seven or more like cards, worth 500 points if the canasta is pure or 300 if wild (containing up to three jokers) [c20: from Spanish: basket (because two packs, or a basketful, of cards are required), variant of *canastro*, from Latin *canistrum*; see CANISTER]

canaster (kə'næstə) *n* coarsely broken dried tobacco leaves [c19: (meaning: rush basket in which tobacco was packed): from Spanish *canastro*; see CANISTER]

Canaveral (kə'nævərəl) *n* **Cape Canaveral** a cape on the E coast of Florida: site of the US Air Force Missile Test Centre, from which the majority of US space missions have been launched. Former name (1963–73): **Cape Kennedy**

Canberra (ˈkænbərə, -brə) *n* the capital of Australia, in Australian Capital Territory: founded in 1913 as a planned capital. Pop: 309 799 (2001)

cancan (ˈkænˌkæn) *n* a high-kicking dance performed by a female chorus, originating in the music halls of 19th-century Paris [c19: from French, of uncertain origin]

cancel (ˈkænsᵊl) *vb* -cels, -celling, -celled *or US* -cels, -celing, -celed (*mainly tr*) **1** to order (something already arranged, such as a meeting or event) to be postponed indefinitely; call off **2** to revoke or annul: *the order for the new television set was cancelled* **3** to delete (writing, numbers, etc); cross out **4** to mark (a cheque, postage stamp, ticket, etc) with an official stamp or by a perforation to prevent further use **5** (*also intr*; usually foll by *out*) to counterbalance; make up for (a deficiency, etc): *his generosity cancelled out his past unkindness* **6** *maths* to eliminate (numbers, quantities, or terms) as common factors from both the numerator and denominator of a fraction or as equal terms from opposite sides of an equation ▷ *n* **7** a new leaf or section of a book replacing a defective one, one containing errors, or one that has been omitted **8** *music* a US word for **cancellation 9** *music* a US word for **natural** (sense 16b) [c14: from Old French *canceller*, from Medieval Latin *cancellāre*, from Late Latin: to strike out, make like a lattice, from Latin *cancellī* lattice, grating] > 'canceller *or US* 'canceler *n*

cancellate (ˈkænsɪˌleɪt), **cancellous** (ˈkænsɪləs) *or* **cancellated** *adj* **1** *anatomy* having a spongy or porous internal structure: *cancellate bones* **2** *botany* forming a network; reticulate [c17: from Latin *cancellāre* to make like a lattice; see CANCEL]

cancellation (ˌkænsɪ'leɪʃən) *n* **1** the fact or an instance of cancelling **2** something that has been cancelled, such as a theatre ticket, esp when it is available for another person to take: *we have a cancellation in the stalls* **3** the marks or perforation made by cancelling

cancer (ˈkænsə) *n* **1** any type of malignant growth or tumour, caused by abnormal and uncontrolled cell division: it may spread through the lymphatic system or blood stream to other parts of the body **2** the condition resulting from this **3** an evil influence that spreads dangerously [c14: from Latin: crab, a creeping tumour; related to Greek *karkinos* crab, Sanskrit *karkata*] > 'cancerous *adj*

Cancer (ˈkænsə) *n, Latin genitive* **Cancri** (ˈkæŋkriː) **1** *astronomy* a small faint zodiacal constellation in the N hemisphere, lying between Gemini and Leo on the ecliptic and containing the star cluster Praesepe **2** *astrology* Also called: **the Crab** the fourth sign of the zodiac, symbol ♋, having a cardinal water classification and ruled by the moon. The sun is in this sign between about June 21 and July 22 **3** tropic of Cancer See **tropic** (sense 1)

cancerophobia (ˌkænsərəʊ'fəʊbɪə) *n* a morbid dread of being afflicted by cancer

cancroid (ˈkæŋkrɔɪd) *adj* **1** resembling a cancerous growth **2** resembling a crab ▷ *n* **3** a skin cancer, esp one of only moderate malignancy

Cancún (ka:n'ku:n) *n* a coastal resort in SE Mexico on the Yucatán Peninsula. Pop: 457 000 (2004 est)

candela (kæn'di:lə, -'deɪlə) *n* the basic SI unit of luminous intensity; the luminous intensity in a given direction of a source that emits monochromatic radiation of frequency 540×10^{12} hertz and that has a radiant intensity in that direction of (1/683) watt per steradian. Symbol: cd [c20: from Latin: CANDLE]

Candela (kæn'di:lə) *n* **Felix**. 1910–97, Mexican architect, noted for his naturalistic modern style and thin prestressed concrete roofs

candelabrum (ˌkændɪ'lɑːbrəm) *or* **candelabra** *n, pl* -bra (-brə), -brums *or* -bras a large branched candleholder or holder for overhead lights [c19: from Latin, from *candēla* CANDLE]

candescent (kæn'dɛsᵊnt) *adj rare* glowing or starting to glow with heat [c19: from Latin *candescere*, from *candēre* to be white, shine] > can'descence *n*

c & f *abbreviation* cost and freight

C & G *abbreviation* City and Guilds

Candia (ˈkandja) *n* the Italian name for **Iráklion**

candid (ˈkændɪd) *adj* **1** frank and outspoken **2** without partiality; unbiased **3** unposed or informal: *a candid photograph* **4** *obsolete* white [c17: from Latin *candidus* white, from *candēre* to be white] > 'candidly *adv* > 'candidness *n*

candida (ˈkændɪdə) *n* any yeastlike parasitic fungus of the genus *Candida*, esp *C. albicans*, which causes thrush (**candidiasis**) [New Latin, feminine of *candidus* white]

candidate ('kændɪˌdeɪt, -dɪt) *n* **1** a person seeking or nominated for election to a position of authority or honour or selection for a job, promotion, etc **2** a person taking an examination or test **3** a person or thing regarded as suitable or likely for a particular fate or position: *this wine is a candidate for his cellar* [c17: from Latin *candidātus* clothed in white (because the candidate wore a white toga), from *candidus* white] >**candidacy** ('kændɪdəsɪ) or **candidature** ('kændɪdətʃə) *n*

candid camera *n* **a** a small camera that may be used to take informal photographs of people, usually without their knowledge **b** (*as modifier*): *a candid-camera photograph*

candied ('kændɪd) *adj* impregnated or encrusted with or as if with sugar or syrup: *candied peel*

Candiot ('kændɪˌɒt) or **Candiote** ('kændɪˌəʊt) *adj* **1** of or relating to Candia (Iráklion) or Crete; Cretan ▷ *n* **2** a native or inhabitant of Crete; a Cretan

candle ('kændʰl) *n* **1** a cylindrical piece of wax, tallow, or other fatty substance surrounding a wick, which is burned to produce light **2** *physics* another name for **candela 3** burn the candle at both ends to exhaust oneself, esp by being up late and getting up early to work **4** not hold a candle to *informal* to be inferior or contemptible in comparison with **5** not worth the candle *informal* not worth the price or trouble entailed (esp in the phrase **the game's not worth the candle**) ▷ *vb* **6** (*tr*) to examine (eggs) for freshness or the likelihood of being hatched by viewing them against a bright light [Old English *candel*, from Latin *candēla*, from *candēre* to be white, glitter] >'**candler** *n*

candleberry ('kændʰlˌbɛrɪ) *n, pl* -**ries** another name for **wax myrtle**

candlelight ('kændʰlˌlaɪt) *n* **1** a the light from a candle or candles: *they ate by candlelight* **b** (*as modifier*): *a candlelight dinner* **2** dusk; evening

Candlemas ('kændʰlməs) *n Christianity* Feb 2, the Feast of the Purification of the Virgin Mary and the presentation of Christ in the Temple: the day on which the church candles are blessed. In Scotland it is one of the four quarter days

candlenut ('kændʰlˌnʌt) *n* **1** a euphorbiaceous tree, *Aleurites mollucana*, of tropical Asia and Polynesia **2** the nut of this tree, which yields an oil used in paints and varnishes. In their native regions the nuts are strung together and burned as candles

candlepower ('kændʰlˌpaʊə) *n* the luminous intensity of a source of light in a given direction: now expressed in candelas but formerly in terms of the international candle

candlestick ('kændʰlˌstɪk) or **candleholder** ('kændʰlˌhəʊldə) *n* a holder, usually ornamental, with a spike or socket for a candle

candlewick ('kændʰlˌwɪk) *n* **1** unbleached cotton or muslin into which loops of yarn are hooked and then cut to give a tufted pattern. It is used for bedspreads, dressing gowns, etc **2** the wick of a candle **3** (*modifier*) being or made of candlewick fabric

C & M *abbreviation* care and maintenance

can-do *adj* confident and resourceful in the face of challenges: *a can-do attitude*

Candolle (French kɑ̃dɔl) *n* **Augustin Pyrame de.** 1778–1841, Swiss botanist; his *Théorie élémentaire de la botanique* (1813) introduced a new system of plant classification

candour or US **candor** ('kændə) *n* **1** the quality of being open and honest; frankness **2** fairness; impartiality **3** *obsolete* purity or brightness [c17: from Latin *candor*, from *candēre* to be white, shine]

C & W *abbreviation* country and western

candy ('kændɪ) *n, pl* -**dies** **1** chiefly *US & Canadian* confectionery in general; sweets, chocolate, etc ▷ *vb* -**dies, -dying, -died 2** to cause (sugar, etc) to become crystalline, esp by boiling or (of sugar) to become crystalline through boiling **3** to preserve (fruit peel, ginger, etc) by boiling in sugar **4** to cover with any crystalline substance, such as ice or sugar [c18: from Old French *sucre candi* candied sugar, from Arabic *qandi* candied, from *qand* cane sugar, of Dravidian origin]

candyfloss ('kændɪˌflɒs) *n Brit* a very light fluffy confection made from coloured spun sugar, usually held on a stick. US and Canadian name: **cotton candy**. Austral. name: **fairyfloss**

candy-striped *adj* (esp of clothing fabric) having narrow coloured stripes on a white background >**candy stripe** *n*

candytuft ('kændɪˌtʌft) *n* either of two species of *Iberis* grown as annual garden plants for their umbels ("tufts") of white, red, or purplish flowers. See **iberis** [c17: from *Candy*, obsolete variant of CANDIA (Crete) + TUFT]

cane (keɪn) *n* **1** a the long jointed pithy or hollow flexible stem of the bamboo, rattan, or any similar plant **b** any plant having such a stem **2** a strips of such stems, woven or interlaced to make wickerwork, the seats and backs of chairs, etc **b** (*as modifier*): *a cane chair* **3** the woody stem of a reed, young grapevine, blackberry, raspberry, or loganberry **4** a flexible rod with which to administer a beating as a punishment, as to schoolboys **5** a slender rod, usually wooden and often ornamental, used for support when walking; walking stick **6** See **sugar cane 7** a slender rod or cylinder, as of glass ▷ *vb* **8** to whip or beat with or as if with a cane **9** to make or repair with cane **10** *informal* to defeat: *we got well caned in the match* **11** cane it *slang* to do something with great power, force, or speed or consume something such as alcohol in large quantities: *you can do it in ten minutes if you really cane it* [c14: from Old French, from Latin *canna*, from Greek *kanna*, of Semitic origin; related to Arabic *qanāh* reed] >'**caner** *n*

Canea (kæ'nɪə) or **Chania** ('hɑːnɪə) *n* the chief port of Crete, on the NW coast. Pop: 55 838 (2001). Greek name: Khaniá

canebrake ('keɪnˌbreɪk) *n US* a thicket of canes

Canetti (kə'nɛtɪ) *n* **Elias.** 1905–94, British novelist and writer, born in Bulgaria, who usually wrote in German. His works include the novel *Auto da Fé* (1935). Nobel prize for literature 1981

canikin ('kænɪkɪn) *n* a variant spelling of **cannikin**

canine ('keɪnaɪn, 'kæn-) *adj* **1** of or resembling a dog; doglike **2** of, relating to, or belonging to the *Canidae*, a family of mammals, including dogs, jackals, wolves, and foxes, typically having a bushy tail, erect ears, and a long muzzle: order *Carnivora* (carnivores) **3** of or relating to any of the four teeth, two in each jaw, situated between the incisors and the premolars ▷ *n* Also: **canid** ('kænɪd) **4** any animal of the family *Canidae* **5** a canine tooth [c17: from Latin *canīnus*, from *canis* dog]

caning ('keɪnɪŋ) *n* **1** a beating with a cane as a punishment **2** *informal* a severe defeat

Canis Major ('keɪnɪs) *n, Latin genitive* **Canis Majoris** (mə'dʒɔːrɪs) a constellation in the S hemisphere close to Orion, containing Sirius, the brightest star in the sky. Also called: **the Great Dog** [Latin: the greater dog]

Canis Minor *n, Latin genitive* **Canis Minoris** (maɪ'nɔːrɪs) a small constellation in the N hemisphere close to Orion, containing the first magnitude star Procyon. Also called: **the Little Dog** [Latin: the lesser dog]

canister ('kænɪstə) *n* **1** a container, usually made of metal, in which dry food, such as tea or coffee, is stored **2** (*formerly*) **a** a type of shrapnel shell for firing from a cannon **b** Also called: **canister shot, case shot** the shot or shrapnel packed inside this [c17: from Latin *canistrum* basket woven from reeds, from Greek *kanastron*, from *kanna* reed, CANE¹]

canker ('kæŋkə) *n* **1** an ulceration, esp of the lips or lining of the oral cavity **2** *vet science* **a** a disease of horses in which the horn of the hoofs becomes soft and spongy **b** an inflammation of the lining of the external ear, esp in dogs and cats, resulting in a discharge and sometimes ulceration **c** ulceration or abscess of the mouth, eyelids, ears, or cloaca of birds **3** an open wound in the stem of a tree or shrub, caused by injury or parasites **4** something evil that spreads and corrupts ▷ *vb* **5** to infect or become infected with or as if with canker [Old English *cancer*, from Latin *cancer* crab, cancerous sore]

cankerworm ('kæŋkəˌwɜːm) *n* the larva of either of two

geometrid moths, *Paleacrita vernata* or *Alsophila pometaria*, which feed on and destroy fruit and shade trees in North America

CanLit (ˌkænˈlɪt) *n acronym for* Canadian Literature

canna ('kænə) *n* any of various tropical plants constituting the genus *Canna*, having broad leaves and red or yellow showy flowers for which they are cultivated: family *Cannaceae* [c17: from New Latin CANE¹]

cannabinoid ('kænəbɪˌnɔɪd) *n* any of the narcotic chemical substances found in cannabin

cannabis ('kænəbɪs) *n* **1** the hemp plant, esp Indian hemp (*Cannabis indica*). See **hemp 2** the drug obtained from the dried leaves and flowers of the hemp plant, which is smoked or chewed for its psychoactive properties. It produces euphoria and relaxation; repeated use may lead to psychological dependence ▷ See also **hashish, marijuana, bhang** [c18: from Latin, from Greek *kannabis*; see HEMP] >'cannabic *adj*

Cannae ('kæni:) *n* an ancient city in SE Italy: scene of a victory by Hannibal over the Romans (216 BC)

canned (kænd) *adj* **1** preserved and stored in airtight cans or tins: *canned meat* **2** *informal* prepared or recorded in advance; artificial; not spontaneous: *canned music* **3** a slang word for **drunk** (sense 1)

cannel coal *or* **cannel** ('kænəl) *n* a dull coal having a high volatile content and burning with a smoky luminous flame [c16: from northern English dialect *cannel* candle: so called from its bright flame]

cannellini bean (ˌkænɪˈliːnɪ) *n* a cream-coloured, kidney-shaped bean with a mild flavour [Italian: small tubes]

cannelloni *or* **cannelloni** (ˌkænɪˈləʊnɪ) *pl n* tubular pieces of pasta filled with meat or cheese [Italian, plural of *cannellone*, from *cannello* stalk, from *canna* CANE¹]

canner ('kænə) *n* a person or organization whose job is to can foods

cannery ('kænərɪ) *n, pl* -neries a place where foods are canned

Cannes (kæn, kænz; *French* kan) *n* a port and resort in SE France: developed in the 19th century from a fishing village; annual film festival. Pop: 67 304 (1999)

cannibal ('kænɪbəl) *n* **1 a** a person who eats the flesh of other human beings **b** (*as modifier*): *cannibal tribes* **2** an animal that feeds on the flesh of others of its kind [c16: from Spanish *Canibales*, name used by Columbus to designate the Caribs of Cuba and Haiti, from Arawak *caniba*, variant of CARIB] >'cannibalism *n* >ˌcannibaˈlistic *adj*

cannibalize *or* **cannibalise** ('kænɪbəˌlaɪz) *vb* (*tr*) to use (serviceable parts from one machine or vehicle) to repair another, esp as an alternative to using new parts >ˌcannibaliˈzation *or* ˌcannibaliˈsation *n*

cannikin, canakin *or* **canikin** ('kænɪkɪn) *n* a small can, esp one used as a drinking vessel [c16: from Middle Dutch *kanneken*; see CAN², -KIN]

canning ('kænɪŋ) *n* the process or business of sealing food in cans or tins to preserve it

Canning ('kænɪŋ) *n* **1 Charles John**, 1st Earl Canning. 1812–62, British statesman; governor general of India (1856–58) and first viceroy (1858–62) his father, **George**. 1770–1827, British Tory statesman; foreign secretary (1822–27) and prime minister (1827)

Cannock ('kænək) *n* a town in W central England, in S Staffordshire: **Cannock Chase** (a public area of heathland, once a royal preserve) is just to the east. Pop: 65 022 (2001)

cannon ('kænən) *n, pl* -nons *or* -non **1** an automatic aircraft gun of large calibre **2** *history* a heavy artillery piece consisting of a metal tube mounted on a carriage **3** a heavy tube or drum, esp one that can rotate freely on the shaft by which it is supported **4** See **cannon bone 5** *billiards* **a** a shot in which the cue ball is caused to contact one object ball after another **b** the points scored by this. Usual US and Canadian word: carom ▷ *vb* **6** (*intr*; often foll by *into*) to collide (with) **7** short for **cannonade 8** (*intr*) *billiards* to make a cannon [c16: from Old French *canon*, from Italian *cannone* cannon, large tube, from *canna* tube, CANE¹]

cannonade (ˌkænəˈneɪd) *n* **1** an intense and continuous artillery bombardment ▷ *vb* **2** to attack (a target) with cannon

cannonball ('kænənˌbɔːl) *n* **1** a projectile fired from a cannon: usually a solid round metal shot ▷ *vb* (*intr*) **2** (often foll by *along*, etc) to rush along, like a cannonball ▷ *adj* **3** very fast or powerful

cannon bone *n* a bone in the legs of horses and other hoofed animals consisting of greatly elongated fused metatarsals or metacarpals

cannoneer (ˌkænəˈnɪə) *n* (formerly) a soldier who served and fired a cannon; artilleryman

cannon fodder *n* men regarded as expendable because they are part of a huge army

cannot ('kænɒt, kæˈnɒt) *vb* an auxiliary verb expressing incapacity, inability, withholding permission, etc; can not

cannula *or* **canula** ('kænjʊlə) *n, pl* -las *or* -lae (-ˌliː) *surgery* a narrow tube for insertion into a bodily cavity, as for draining off fluid, introducing medication, etc [c17: from Latin: a small reed, from *canna* a reed]

canny ('kænɪ) *adj* -nier, -niest **1** shrewd, esp in business; astute or wary; knowing **2** *Scot & Northeast English dialect* good or nice; knowing **3** *Scot* as a general term of approval **3** *Scot* lucky or fortunate [c16: from CAN¹ (in the sense: to know how) + -Y¹] >'cannily *adv* >'canniness *n*

canoe (kəˈnuː) *n* **1** a light narrow open boat, propelled by one or more paddles ▷ *vb* -noes, -noeing, -noed **2** to go in a canoe or transport by canoe [c16: from Spanish *canoa*, of Carib origin] >caˈnoeing *n* >caˈnoeist *n*

canola (kəˈnəʊlə) *n* a cooking oil extracted from a variety of rapeseed developed in Canada [c20: from CAN(ADA) + -ola, from OLEUM]

canon¹ ('kænən) *n* **1** *Christianity* a Church decree enacted to regulate morals or religious practices **2** (*often plural*) a general rule or standard, as of judgment, morals, etc **3** (*often plural*) a principle or accepted criterion applied in a branch of learning or art **4** *RC Church* the complete list of the canonized saints **5** *RC Church* the prayer in the Mass in which the Host is consecrated **6** a list of writings, esp sacred writings, officially recognized as genuine **7** a piece of music in which an extended melody in one part is imitated successively in one or more other parts. See also **round** (sense 30), **catch** (sense 30) **8** a list of the works of an author that are accepted as authentic **9** (*formerly*) a size of printer's type equal to 48 point [Old English, from Latin, from Greek *kanōn* rule, rod for measuring, standard; related to *kanna* reed, CANE¹]

canon² ('kænən) *n* **1** one of several priests on the permanent staff of a cathedral, who are responsible for organizing services, maintaining the fabric, etc **2** Also called: **canon regular** *RC Church* a member of either of two religious orders, the Augustinian or Premonstratensian Canons, living communally as monks but performing clerical duties [c13: from Anglo-French *canunie*, from Late Latin *canonicus* one living under a rule, from CANON¹]

canonical (kəˈnɒnɪkəl) *or* **canonic** *adj* **1** belonging to or included in a canon of sacred or other officially recognized writings **2** belonging to or in conformity with canon law **3** according to recognized law; accepted **4** *music* in the form of a canon **5** of or relating to a cathedral chapter **6** of or relating to a canon (clergyman) >caˈnonically *adv*

canonical hour *n* *RC Church* one of the seven prayer times appointed for each day by canon law

canonicals (kəˈnɒnɪkəlz) *pl n* the vestments worn by clergy when officiating

canonicity (ˌkænəˈnɪsɪtɪ) *n* the fact or quality of being canonical

canonist ('kænənɪst) *n* a specialist in canon law

canonize *or* **canonise** ('kænəˌnaɪz) *vb* (*tr*) **1** *RC Church* to declare (a person) to be a saint and thus admit to the canon of saints **2** to regard as holy or as a saint **3** to sanction by canon law; pronounce valid >ˌcanoniˈzation *or* ˌcanoniˈsation *n*

canon law *n* the law governing the affairs of a Christian Church, esp the law created or recognized by papal authority in the Roman Catholic Church

c

canonry ('kænənrɪ) *n, pl* -ries **1** the office, benefice, or status of a canon **2** canons collectively [C15: from CANON² + -RY]

canoodle (kə'nu:dªl) *vb* (*intr; often foll by with*) *slang* to kiss and cuddle; pet; fondle [C19: of unknown origin] > ca'noodler *n*

Canopic jar, Canopic urn *or* **Canopic vase** (kə'nəʊpɪk) *n* (in ancient Egypt) one of four containers with tops in the form of animal heads of the gods, for holding the entrails of a mummy

Canopus (kə'nəʊpəs) *n* a port in ancient Egypt east of Alexandria where granite monuments have been found inscribed with the name of Rameses II and written in languages similar to those of the Rosetta stone > Ca'nopic *adj*

canopy ('kænəpɪ) *n, pl* -pies **1** an ornamental awning above a throne or bed or held over a person of importance on ceremonial occasions **2** a rooflike covering over an altar, niche, etc **3** a roofed structure serving as a sheltered passageway or area **4** a large or wide covering, esp one high above: *the sky was a grey canopy* **5** the nylon or silk hemisphere that forms the supporting surface of a parachute **6** the transparent cover of an aircraft cockpit **7** the highest level of branches and foliage in a forest, formed by the crowns of the trees ▷ *vb* -pies, -pying, -pied **8** (*tr*) to cover with or as if with a canopy [C14: from Medieval Latin *canōpeum* mosquito net, from Latin *cōnōpeum* gauze net, from Greek *kōnōpeion* bed with protective net, from *kōnōps* mosquito]

Canova (*Italian* ka'nɔːva) *n* **Antonio** (an'tɔːnjo). 1757–1822, Italian neoclassical sculptor

canst (kænst) *vb archaic* when used with the pronoun *thou* or its relative form, a form of **can¹**

cant¹ (kænt) *n* **1** insincere talk, esp concerning religion or morals; pious platitudes **2** stock phrases that have become meaningless through repetition **3** specialized vocabulary of a particular group, such as thieves, journalists, or lawyers; jargon **4** singsong whining speech, as used by beggars ▷ *vb* **5** (*intr*) to speak in or use cant [C16: probably via Norman French *canter* to sing, from Latin *cantāre*; used disparagingly, from the 12th century, of chanting in religious services] > 'canter *n* > 'cantingly *adv*

cant² (kænt) *n* **1** inclination from a vertical or horizontal plane; slope; slant **2** a sudden movement that tilts or turns something **3** the angle or tilt thus caused **4** a corner or outer angle, esp of a building **5** an oblique or slanting surface, edge, or line ▷ *vb* (*tr*) **6** to tip, tilt, or overturn, esp with a sudden jerk **7** to set in an oblique position **8** another word for **bevel** (sense 1) ▷ *adj* **9** oblique; slanting **10** having flat surfaces and without curves [C14 (in the sense: edge, corner): perhaps from Latin *canthus* iron hoop round a wheel, of obscure origin] > 'cantic *adj*

Cant. *abbreviation* **1** Canterbury **2** *Bible* Canticles

can't (kɑːnt) *vb contraction of* cannot

Cantab. (kæn'tæb) *abbreviation* Cantabrigiensis [Latin: of Cambridge]

cantabile (kæn'tɑːbɪlɪ) *music* ▷ *adj, adv* **1** (to be performed) in a singing style, i.e. flowingly and melodiously ▷ *n* **2** a piece or passage performed in this way [Italian, from Late Latin *cantābilis*, from Latin *cantāre* to sing]

Cantabrian Mountains (kæn'teɪbrɪən) *pl n* a mountain chain along the N coast of Spain, consisting of a series of high ridges that rise over 2400 m (8000 ft): rich in minerals (esp coal and iron)

Cantabrigian (,kæntə'brɪdʒɪən) *adj* **1** of, relating to, or characteristic of Cambridge or Cambridge University, or of Cambridge, Massachusetts, or Harvard University ▷ *n* **2** a member or graduate of Cambridge University or Harvard University **3** an inhabitant or native of Cambridge [C17: from Medieval Latin *Cantabrigia*]

Cantal (*French* kɑ̃tal) *n* **1** a department of S central France, in the Auvergne region. Capital: Aurillac. Pop: 148 359 (2003 est). Area: 5779 sq km (2254 sq miles) **2** a hard strong cheese made in this area

cantaloupe *or* **cantaloup** ('kæntə,lu:p) *n* **1** a cultivated

variety of muskmelon, *Cucumis melo cantalupensis*, with ribbed warty rind and orange flesh **2** any of several other muskmelons [C18: from French, from *Cantaluppi*, former papal villa near Rome, where it was first cultivated in Europe]

cantankerous (kæn'tæŋkərəs) *adj* quarrelsome; irascible [C18: perhaps from C14 (obsolete) *conteckour* a contentious person, from *conteck* strife, from Anglo-French *contek*, of obscure origin] > can'tankerously *adv* > can'tankerousness *n*

cantata (kæn'tɑːtə) *n* a musical setting of a text, esp a religious text, consisting of arias, duets, and choruses interspersed with recitatives [C18: from Italian, from *cantare* to sing, from Latin]

canteen (kæn'ti:n) *n* **1** a restaurant attached to a factory, school, etc, providing meals for large numbers of people **2 a** a small shop that provides a limited range of items, such as toilet requisites, to a military unit **b** a recreation centre for military personnel **3** a temporary or mobile stand at which food is provided **4 a** a box in which a set of cutlery is laid out **b** the cutlery itself **5 a** a flask or canister for carrying water or other liquids, as used by soldiers or travellers [C18: from French *cantine*, from Italian *cantina* wine cellar, from *canto* corner, from Latin *canthus* iron hoop encircling chariot wheel; see CANT²]

Canteloube ('kæntə,lu:b; *French* kɑ̃tlub) *n* (**Marie**) **Joseph** (*French* ʒɔzɛf). 1879–1957, French composer, best known for his *Chants d'Auvergne* (1923–30)

canter ('kæntə) *n* **1** an easy three-beat gait of horses, etc, between a trot and a gallop in speed **2** at a canter easily; without effort ▷ *vb* **3** to move or cause to move at a canter [C18: short for *Canterbury trot*, the supposed pace at which pilgrims rode to Canterbury]

Canterbury ('kæntəbərɪ, -brɪ) *n* **1** a city in SE England, in E Kent: starting point for St Augustine's mission to England (597 AD); cathedral where St Thomas à Becket was martyred (1170); seat of the archbishop and primate of England; seat of the University of Kent (1965). Pop: 43 552 (2001) **2** a regional council area of New Zealand, on E central South Island on **Canterbury Bight**: mountainous with coastal lowlands; agricultural. Chief town: Christchurch. Pop: 520 500 (2004 est). Area: 43 371 sq km (16 742 sq miles)

Canterbury bell *n* a campanulaceous biennial European plant, *Campanula medium*, widely cultivated for its blue, violet, or white flowers

cantharides (kæn'θærɪ,di:z) *pl n, sing* cantharis ('kænθərɪs) a diuretic and urogenital stimulant or irritant prepared from the dried bodies of Spanish fly (family *Meloidae*, not *Cantharidae*), once thought to be an aphrodisiac. Also called: Spanish fly [C15: from Latin, plural of *cantharis*, from Greek *kantharis* Spanish fly]

cant hook *or* **cant dog** *n forestry* a wooden pole with a blunt steel tip and an adjustable hook at one end, used for handling logs

canthus ('kænθəs) *n, pl* -thi (-,θaɪ) the inner or outer corner or angle of the eye, formed by the natural junction of the eyelids [C17: from New Latin, from Latin: iron tyre] > 'canthal *adj*

canticle ('kæntɪkªl) *n* a nonmetrical hymn, derived from the Bible and used in the liturgy of certain Christian churches [C13: from Latin *canticulum*, diminutive of *canticus* a song, from *cantāre* to sing]

cantilena (,kæntɪ'leɪnə) *n* a smooth flowing style in the writing of vocal music [C18: Italian, from Latin *cantilēna* a song]

cantilever ('kæntɪ,li:və) *n* **1** a beam, girder, or structural framework that is fixed at one end and is free at the other **2** a part of a beam or a structure projecting outwards beyond its support [C17: perhaps from CANT² + LEVER]

cantilever bridge *n* a bridge having spans that are constructed as cantilevers and often a suspended span or spans, each end of which rests on one end of a cantilever span

cantillate ('kæntɪ,leɪt) *vb* **1** to chant (passages of the Hebrew Scriptures) according to the traditional Jewish melody **2** to intone or chant [C19: from Late Latin cantillāre to sing softly, from Latin *cantāre* to sing]

cantle ('kænt³l) *n* **1** the back part of a saddle that slopes upwards **2** a slice; a broken-off piece [c14: from Old Northern French *cantel*, from *cant* corner; see CANT²]

canto ('kæntəʊ) *n, pl* -tos a main division of a long poem [c16: from Italian: song, from Latin *cantus*, from *canere* to sing]

canto fermo ('kæntəʊ 'fɜ:məʊ) *or* **cantus firmus** ('kæntəs 'fɜ:məs) *n* **1** a melody that is the basis to which other parts are added in polyphonic music **2** the traditional plainchant as prescribed by use and regulation in the Christian Church [Italian, from Medieval Latin, literally: fixed song]

canton ('kæntɒn, kæn'tɒn) *n* **1** any of the 23 political divisions of Switzerland **2** ('kæntən) *heraldry* a small square or oblong charge on a shield, usually in the top left corner ▷ *vb* **3** (kæn'tɒn) (*tr*) to divide into cantons **4** (kən'tu:n) (esp formerly) to allocate accommodation to (military personnel) [c16: from Old French: corner, division, from Italian *cantone*, from *canto* corner, from Latin *canthus* iron rim; see CANT²] >'cantonal *adj*

Canton *n* **1** (kæn'tɒn) a port in SE China, capital of Guangdong province, on the Zhu Jiang (Pearl River): the first Chinese port open to European trade. Pop: 3 881 000 (2005 est). Chinese names: Guangzhou, Kwangchow **2** ('kæntən) a city in the US, in NE Ohio. Pop: 80 806 (2000)

Cantonese (,kæntə'ni:z) *n* **1** the Chinese language spoken in the city of Canton, Guangdong and Guanxi provinces, Hong Kong, and elsewhere outside China **2** *pl* -ese a native or inhabitant of the city of Canton or Guangdong province ▷ *adj* **3** of or relating to the city of Canton, Guangdong province, or the Chinese language spoken there

cantonment (kən'tu:nmənt) *n military* (esp formerly) **1** a large training camp **2** living accommodation, esp the winter quarters of a campaigning army **3** *history* a permanent military camp in British India

Canton River (kæn'tɒn) *n* another name for the **Zhu Jiang**

cantor ('kæntɔ:) *n* **1** Also called: chazan *Judaism* a man employed to lead synagogue services, esp to traditional modes and melodies **2** *Christianity* the leader of the singing in a church choir [c16: from Latin: singer, from *canere* to sing]

cantorial (kæn'tɔ:rɪəl) *adj* **1** of or relating to a precentor **2** (of part of a choir) on the same side of a cathedral, etc, as the precentor; on the N side of the choir. Compare **decanal**

cantoris (kæn'tɔ:rɪs) *adj* (in antiphonal music) to be sung by the cantorial side of a choir. Compare **decani** [Latin: genitive of *cantor* precentor]

Cantuar. ('kæntjʊ,ɑ:) *abbreviation* Cantuariensis [Latin: (Archbishop) of Canterbury]

Canuck (kə'nʌk) *n US & Canadian informal* **a** a Canadian **b** (formerly) esp a French Canadian [c19: of uncertain origin]

Canute, Cnut *or* **Knut** (kə'nju:t) *n* died 1035, Danish king of England (1016–35), Denmark (1018–35), and Norway (1028–35). He defeated Edmund II of England (1016), but divided the kingdom with him until Edmund's death. An able ruler, he invaded Scotland (1027) and drove Olaf II from Norway (1028)

canvas ('kænvəs) *n* **1 a** a heavy durable cloth made of cotton, hemp, or jute, used for sails, tents, etc **b** (*as modifier*): *a canvas bag* **2 a** a piece of canvas or a similar material on which a painting is done, usually in oils **b** a painting on this material, esp in oils **3** a tent or tents collectively **4** *nautical* any cloth of which sails are made **5** *nautical* the sails of a vessel collectively **6** any coarse loosely woven cloth on which embroidery, tapestry, etc, is done **7** the canvas the floor of a boxing or wrestling ring **8** *rowing* the tapering covered part at either end of a racing boat, sometimes referred to as a unit of length: *to win by a canvas* **9** under canvas **a** in tents **b** *nautical* with sails unfurled [c14: from Norman French *canevas*, ultimately from Latin *cannabis* hemp]

canvasback ('kænvəs,bæk) *n, pl* -backs *or* -back a North American diving duck, *Aythya valisineria*, the male of which has a white body and reddish-brown head

canvass ('kænvəs) *vb* **1** to solicit votes, orders, advertising, etc, from **2** to determine the feelings and opinions of (voters before an election, etc), esp by conducting a survey **3** to investigate (something) thoroughly, esp by discussion or debate **4** *chiefly US* to inspect (votes) officially to determine their validity ▷ *n* **5** a solicitation of opinions, votes, sales orders, etc **6** close inspection; scrutiny [c16: probably from obsolete sense of CANVAS (to toss someone in a canvas sheet, hence, to harass, criticize); the development of current senses is unexplained] >'canvasser *n* >'canvassing *n*

canyon *or* **cañon** ('kænjən) *n* a gorge or ravine, esp in North America, usually formed by the down-cutting of a river in a dry area where there is insufficient rainfall to erode the sides of the valley [c19: from Spanish *cañon*, from *caña* tube, from Latin *canna* cane]

canyoning ('kænjənɪŋ) *n* the sport of travelling down a river situated in a canyon by a variety of means including scrambling, floating, swimming, and abseiling

canzone (kæn'zəʊnɪ) *n, pl* -ni (-nɪ) **1 a** a Provençal or Italian lyric, often in praise of love or beauty **2 a** a song, usually of a lyrical nature **b** (in 16th-century choral music) a polyphonic song from which the madrigal developed [c16: from Italian: song, from Latin *cantiō*, from *canere* to sing]

canzonetta (,kænzə'nɛtə) *or* **canzonet** (,kænzə'nɛt) *n* a short cheerful or lively song, typically of the 16th to 18th centuries [c16: Italian *canzonetta*, diminutive of CANZONE]

caoutchouc ('kaʊtʃu:k, -tʃʊk, kaʊ'tʃu:k, -tʃʊk) *n* another name for **rubber¹** (sense 1) [c18: from French, from obsolete Spanish *cauchuc*, from Quechua]

cap (kæp) *n* **1** a covering for the head, esp a small close-fitting one made of cloth or knitted **2** such a covering serving to identify the wearer's rank, occupation, etc: *a nurse's cap* **3** something that protects or covers, esp a small lid or cover: *lens cap* **4** an uppermost surface or part: *the cap of a wave* **5 a** See **percussion cap b** a small amount of explosive enclosed in paper and used in a toy gun **6** *sport chiefly Brit* **a** an emblematic hat or beret given to someone chosen for a representative team: *he has won three England caps* **b** a player chosen for such a team **7** *botany* the pileus of a mushroom or toadstool **8** *hunting* money contributed to the funds of a hunt by a follower who is neither a subscriber nor a farmer, in return for a day's hunting **9** *anatomy* **a** the natural enamel covering a tooth **b** an artificial protective covering for a tooth **10** an upper financial limit **11** a mortarboard when worn with a gown at an academic ceremony (esp in the phrase **cap and gown**) **12** *meteorol* **a** the cloud covering the peak of a mountain **b** the transient top of detached clouds above an increasing cumulus **13** cap in hand humbly, as when asking a favour ▷ *vb* **caps, capping, capped** (*tr*) **14** to cover, as with a cap: *snow capped the mountain tops* **15** *informal* to outdo; excel: *your story caps them all; to cap an anecdote* **16** to cap it all to provide the finishing touch **17** *sport, Brit* to select (a player) for a representative team **18** to seal off (an oil or gas well) **19** to impose an upper limit on the level of increase of (a tax, such as the council tax) **20** *chiefly Scot & NZ* to award a degree to [Old English *cæppe*, from Late Latin *cappa* hood, perhaps from Latin *caput* head] >'capper *n*

CAP *abbreviation* Common Agricultural Policy: (in the EU) the system for supporting farm incomes by maintaining agricultural prices at agreed levels

cap. *abbreviation* **1** capital **2** capitalize **3** capital letter [Latin: chapter]

Capa ('kæpə) *n* **Robert**, real name *André Friedmann*. 1913–54, Hungarian photographer, who established his reputation as a photojournalist during the Spanish Civil War.

capability (,keɪpə'bɪlɪtɪ) *n, pl* -ties **1** the quality of being capable; ability **2** the quality of being susceptible to the use or treatment indicated: *the capability of a metal to be fused* **3** (usually plural) a characteristic that may be developed; potential aptitude

Capablanca (Spanish kapa'βlaŋka) *n* **José Raúl** (xo'se ra'ul), called *Capa* or the *Chess Machine*, 1888–1942, Cuban chess player; world champion 1921–27

capable ('keɪpəbəl) *adj* **1** having ability, esp in many different fields; competent **2** (*postpositive; foll by of*) able or having the skill (to do something): *she is capable of hard work* **3** (*postpositive; foll by of*) having the temperament or inclination (to do something): *he seemed capable of murder* [c16: from French, from Late Latin *capābilis* able to take in, from Latin *capere* to take] > '**capableness** *n* > '**capably** *adv*

capacious (kə'peɪʃəs) *adj* capable of holding much; roomy; spacious [c17: from Latin *capāx*, from Latin *capere* to take] > **ca'paciously** *adv* > **ca'paciousness** *n*

capacitance (kə'pæsɪtəns) *n* **1** the property of a system that enables it to store electric charge **2** a measure of this, equal to the charge that must be added to such a system to raise its electrical potential by one unit ▷ Former name: capacity [c20: from CAPACIT(Y) + -ANCE] > **ca'pacitive** *adj* > **ca'pacitively** *adv*

capacitor (kə'pæsɪtə) *n* a device for accumulating electric charge, usually consisting of two conducting surfaces separated by a dielectric. Former name: condenser

capacity (kə'pæsɪtɪ) *n, pl* -ties **1** the ability or power to contain, absorb, or hold **2** the amount that can be contained; volume: *a capacity of six gallons* **3 a** the maximum amount something can contain or absorb (esp in the phrase **filled to capacity**) **b** (*as modifier*): *a capacity crowd* **4** the ability to understand or learn; aptitude; capability: *he has a great capacity for Greek* **5** the ability to do or produce (often in the phrase **at capacity**): *the factory's output was not at capacity* **6** a specified position or function **7** a measure of the electrical output of a piece of apparatus such as a motor, generator, or accumulator **8** *electronics* a former name for **capacitance 9** *computing* **a** the number of words or characters that can be stored in a particular storage device **b** the range of numbers that can be processed in a register **10** *legal* competence: *the capacity to make a will* [c15: from Old French *capacite*, from Latin *capācitās*, from *capāx* spacious, from *capere* to take]

cap and bells *n* the traditional garb of a court jester, including a cap with bells attached to it

cap-and-trade *adj* (*prenominal*) denoting a scheme which allows companies with high greenhouse gas emissions to buy an emission allowance from companies which have fewer emissions, in a bid to reduce the overall impact to the environment

cap-a-pie (,kæpə'piː) *adv* (dressed, armed, etc) from head to foot [c16: from Old French]

caparison (kə'pærɪsən) *n* **1** a decorated covering for a horse or other animal, esp (formerly) for a warhorse **2** rich or elaborate clothing and ornaments ▷ *vb* **3** (*tr*) to put a caparison on [c16: via obsolete French from Old Spanish *caparazón* saddlecloth, probably from *capa* CAPE[1]]

cape[1] (keɪp) *n* a sleeveless garment like a cloak but usually shorter [c16: from French, from Provençal *capa*, from Late Latin *cappa*; see CAP]

cape[2] (keɪp) *n* a headland or promontory [c14: from Old French *cap*, from Old Provençal, from Latin *caput* head]

Cape (keɪp) the Cape *n* **1** the SW region of South Africa, in Western Cape province **2** See **Cape of Good Hope**

Cape Barren goose *n* a greyish Australian goose, *Cereopsis novaehollandiae*, having a black bill with a greenish cere [c19: named after *Cape Barren* Island in the Bass Strait]

Cape Breton Island *n* an island off SE Canada, in NE Nova Scotia, separated from the mainland by the Strait of Canso: its easternmost point is **Cape Breton**. Pop: 132 298 (2006). Area: 10 280 sq km (3970 sq miles)

Cape Cod *n* **1** a long sandy peninsula in SE Massachusetts, between **Cape Cod Bay** and the Atlantic **2** Also called: Cape Cod cottage a one-storey cottage of timber construction with a simple gable roof and a large central chimney: originated on Cape Cod in the 18th century

Cape Colony *n* the name from 1652 until 1910 of the former **Cape Province** of South Africa

Cape Coloured *n* (formerly, in South Africa) racial classification under apartheid for people of mixed ethic origin

Cape doctor *n* *South African informal* a strong fresh SE wind blowing in the vicinity of Cape Town, esp in the summer

Cape Dutch *n* **1** an obsolete name for **Afrikaans 2** (in South Africa) a distinctive style of furniture or architecture

Cape Flats *pl n* the strip of low-lying land in South Africa joining the Cape Peninsula proper to the African mainland

cape gooseberry *n* another name for **strawberry tomato**

Cape Horn *n* a rocky headland on an island at the extreme S tip of South America, belonging to Chile. It is notorious for gales and heavy seas; until the building of the Panama Canal it lay on the only sea route between the Atlantic and the Pacific. Also called: the Horn

Čapek (*Czech* 'tʃapɛk) *n* **Karel** ('karɛl). 1890–1938, Czech dramatist and novelist; author of *R.U.R.* (1921), which introduced the word "robot", and (with his brother **Josef**) *The Insect Play* (1921).

capelin ('kæpəlɪn) *or* **caplin** (,kæplɪn) *n* a small marine food fish, *Mallotus villosus*, occurring in northern and Arctic seas: family *Osmeridae* (smelts) [c17: from French *capelan*, from Old Provençal, literally: CHAPLAIN]

capellmeister *or* **kapellmeister** (kæ'pɛl,maɪstə) *n* a person in charge of an orchestra, esp in an 18th-century princely household [from German, from *Kapelle* chapel + *Meister* MASTER]

Capello (kæ'pɛləʊ) *n* **Fabio**. born 1946, Italian football player and coach; manager of clubs including Real Madrid and AC Milan as well as the Italian national team (1972–76); appointed manager of the England national team 2007

Cape of Good Hope *n* a cape in SW South Africa south of Cape Town

Cape Peninsula *n* (in South Africa) the peninsula and the part of the mainland on which Cape Town and most of its suburbs are located

Cape pigeon *n* a species of seagoing petrel, *Daption capensis*, with characteristic white wing patches: a common winter visitor off the coasts of southern Africa: family *Diomedeidae*. Also called: pintado petrel

Cape Province *n* a former province of S South Africa; replaced in 1994 by the new provinces of Northern Cape, Western Cape, Eastern Cape and part of North-West. Capital: Cape Town. Former name (1652–1910): Cape Colony

caper[1] ('keɪpə) *n* **1** a playful skip or leap **2** a high-spirited escapade **3** cut a caper *or* cut capers to skip or jump playfully ▷ *vb* **4** (*intr*) to leap or dance about in a light-hearted manner [c16: probably from CAPRIOLE] > '**caperer** *n* > '**caperingly** *adv*

caper[2] ('keɪpə) *n* a spiny trailing Mediterranean capparidaceous shrub, *Capparis spinosa*, with edible flower buds [c15: from earlier *capers, capres* (assumed to be plural), from Latin *capparis*, from Greek *kapparis*]

capercaillie (,kæpə'keɪljɪ) *or* **capercailzie** (,kæpə'keɪljɪ, -'keɪlzɪ) *n* a large European woodland grouse, *Tetrao urogallus*, having a black plumage and fan-shaped tail in the male [c16: from Scottish Gaelic *capull coille* horse of the woods]

Capernaum (kə'pɜːnɪəm) *n* a ruined town in N Israel, on the NW shore of the Sea of Galilee: closely associated with Jesus Christ during his ministry

Cape smoke *n* *South African informal* South African brandy

Cape sparrow *n* a sparrow, *Passer melanurus*, very common in southern Africa: family *Ploceidae*. Also called (esp South African): mossie

Capet ('kæpɪt, kæ'pɛt; *French* kapɛ) *n* **Hugh** *or* **Hugues** (yg). ?938–996 AD, king of France (987–96); founder of the Capetian dynasty

Cape Town *n* the legislative capital of South Africa and capital of Western Cape province, situated in the southwest on Table Bay: founded in 1652, the first White settlement in southern Africa; important port. Pop: 827 219 (2001)

Cape Verde (vɜːd) *n* a republic in the Atlantic off the coast of West Africa, consisting of a group of ten islands and five islets: an overseas territory of Portugal until 1975, when the islands became independent. Official language: Portuguese. Religion: Christian (Roman Catholic) majority; animist minority. Currency: Cape Verdean escudo. Capital: Praia. Pop: 472 000 (2004 est). Area: 4033 sq km (1557 sq miles)

Cape Verdean (ˈvɜːdɪən) *adj* **1** of or relating to Cape Verde or its inhabitants ▷ *n* **2** a native or inhabitant of Cape Verde

Cape York *n* the northernmost point of the Australian mainland, in N Queensland on the Torres Strait at the tip of **Cape York Peninsula** (a peninsula between the Coral Sea and the Gulf of Carpentaria)

Cap-Haitien (*French* kapaisjɛ̃, -tjɛ̃) *n* a port in N Haiti: capital during the French colonial period. Pop: 134 000 (2005 est). Also called: **le Cap** (lə kap)

capias (ˈkeɪpɪˌæs, ˈkæp-) *n* *law* (formerly) a writ directing a sheriff or other officer to arrest a named person [C15: from Latin, literally: you must take, from *capere*]

capillarity (ˌkæpɪˈlærɪtɪ) *n* a phenomenon caused by surface tension and resulting in the distortion, elevation, or depression of the surface of a liquid in contact with a solid. Also called: **capillary action**

capillary (kəˈpɪlərɪ) *adj* **1** resembling a hair; slender **2** (of tubes) having a fine bore **3** *anatomy* of or relating to any of the delicate thin-walled blood vessels that form an interconnecting network between the arterioles and the venules **4** *physics* of or relating to capillarity ▷ *n*, *pl* -laries **5** *anatomy* any of the capillary blood vessels **6** a fine hole or narrow passage in any substance [C17: from Latin *capillāris*, from *capillus* hair]

capital¹ (ˈkæpɪtᵊl) *n* **1 a** the seat of government of a country or other political unit **b** (*as modifier*): *a capital city* **2** material wealth owned by an individual or business enterprise **3** wealth available for or capable of use in the production of further wealth, as by industrial investment **4 make capital of** or **make capital out of** to get advantage from **5** (*sometimes capital*) the capitalist class or their interests: *capital versus labour* **6** *accounting* **a** the ownership interests of a business as represented by the excess of assets over liabilities **b** the nominal value of the authorized or issued shares **c** (*as modifier*): *capital issues* **7** any assets or resources, esp when used to gain profit or advantage **8 a** a capital letter. Abbreviation: **cap**, **cap b** (*as modifier*): *capital B* ▷ *adj* **9** (*prenominal*) *law* involving or punishable by death: *a capital offence* **10** very serious; fatal: *a capital error* **11** primary, chief, or principal: *our capital concern is that everyone be fed* **12** of, relating to, or designating the large modern majuscule letter used chiefly as the initial letter in personal names and place names and other uniquely specificatory nouns, and often for abbreviations and acronyms. See **small** (sense 8). See also **upper case 13** *chiefly Brit* excellent; first-rate: *a capital idea* [C13: from Latin *capitālis* (adj) concerning the head, chief, from *caput* head; compare Medieval Latin *capitāle* (n) wealth, from *capitālis* (adj)]

capital² (ˈkæpɪtᵊl) *n* the upper part of a column or pier that supports the entablature. Also called: **chapiter, cap** [C14: from Old French *capitel*, from Late Latin *capitellum*, diminutive of *caput* head]

capital account *n* **1** *economics* that part of a balance of payments composed of movements of capital and international loans and grants **2** *accounting* a financial statement showing the net value of a company at a specified date. It is defined as total assets minus total liabilities and represents ownership interests **3** *US* an account of fixed assets

capital expenditure *n* expenditure on acquisitions of or improvements to fixed assets

capital gain *n* the amount by which the selling price of a financial asset exceeds its cost

capital gains tax *n* a tax on the profit made from the sale of an asset. Abbreviation: **CGT**

capital goods *pl n* *economics* goods that are themselves utilized in the production of other goods rather than being sold to consumers. Also called: **producer goods** See **consumer goods**

capitalism (ˈkæpɪtəˌlɪzəm) *n* Also called: **free enterprise, private enterprise** an economic system based on the private ownership of the means of production, distribution, and exchange, characterized by the freedom of capitalists to operate or manage their property for profit in competitive conditions ▷ Compare **socialism** (sense 1)

capitalist (ˈkæpɪtəlɪst) *n* **1** a person who owns capital, esp capital invested in a business **2** *politics* a supporter of capitalism ▷ *adj* **3** of or relating to capital, capitalists, or capitalism > ˌcapitalˈistic *adj*

capitalization or **capitalisation** (ˌkæpɪtəlaɪˈzeɪʃən) *n* **1 a** the act of capitalizing **b** the sum so derived **2** *accounting* the par value of the total share capital issued by a company, including the loan capital and sometimes reserves **3** the act of estimating the present value of future payments, earnings, etc

capitalize or **capitalise** (ˈkæpɪtəˌlaɪz) *vb* (*mainly tr*) **1** (*intr*; foll by *on*) to take advantage (of); profit (by) **2** to write or print (text) in capital letters or with the first letter of (a word or words) in capital letters **3** to convert (debt or retained earnings) into capital stock **4** to authorize (a business enterprise) to issue a specified amount of capital stock **5** to provide with capital **6** *accounting* to treat (expenditures) as assets **7 a** to estimate the present value of (a periodical income) **b** to compute the present value of (a business) from actual or potential earnings

capitally (ˈkæpɪtəlɪ) *adv* *chiefly Brit* in an excellent manner; admirably

capital punishment *n* the punishment of death for a crime; death penalty

capital ship *n* one of the largest and most heavily armed ships in a naval fleet

capital stock *n* **1** the par value of the total share capital that a company is authorized to issue **2** the total physical capital existing in an economy at any moment of time

capitation (ˌkæpɪˈteɪʃən) *n* **1** a tax levied on the basis of a fixed amount per head **2 capitation grant** a grant of money given to every person who qualifies under certain conditions [C17: from Late Latin *capitātiō*, from Latin *caput* head]

Capitol (ˈkæpɪtᵊl) *n* **1 a** another name for the **Capitoline b** the temple on the Capitoline **2 the Capitol** the main building of the US Congress **3** Also called: **statehouse** (*sometimes not capital*) (in the US) the building housing any state legislature [C14: from Latin *Capitōlium*, from *caput* head]

Capitoline (ˈkæpɪtᵊˌlaɪn, kəˈpɪtəʊ-) *n* **1 the Capitoline** the most important of the Seven Hills of Rome. The temple of Jupiter was on the southern summit and the ancient citadel on the northern summit ▷ *adj* **2** of or relating to the Capitoline or temple of Jupiter

capitulate (kəˈpɪtjʊˌleɪt) *vb* (*intr*) to surrender, esp under agreed conditions [C16 (meaning: to arrange under heads, draw up in order; hence, to make terms of surrender): from Medieval Latin *capitulāre* to draw up under heads, from *capitulum* CHAPTER] > caˈpituˌlator *n*

capitulation (kəˌpɪtjʊˈleɪʃən) *n* **1** the act of capitulating **2** a document containing terms of surrender **3** a statement summarizing the main divisions of a subject > caˈpitulatory *adj*

capitulum (kəˈpɪtjʊləm) *n*, *pl* -la (-lə) a racemose inflorescence in the form of a disc of sessile flowers, the youngest at the centre. It occurs in the daisy and related plants [C18: from Latin, literally: a little head, from *caput* head]

capo (ˈkeɪpəʊ, ˈkæpəʊ) *n*, *pl* -pos a device fitted across all the strings of a guitar, banjo, etc, so as to raise the pitch of each string simultaneously. Also called: **capo tasto** (ˈkæpəʊ ˈtæstəʊ) [from Italian *capo tasto* head stop]

capoeira (ˌkæpʊˈeɪrə) *n* a movement discipline combining martial art and dance, which originated among African slaves in 19th-century Brazil [C20: from Portuguese]

capon (ˈkeɪpən) *n* a castrated cock fowl fattened for eating [Old English *capun*, from Latin *cāpō* capon; related to Greek *koptein* to cut off]

caponata (ˌkæpəˈnɑːtə) *n* (in Sicilian cookery) a dish of fried seasoned aubergine and other vegetables, served as an appetizer [Italian]

Capone (kəˈpəʊn) *n* **Alphonse**, called *Al*. 1899–1947, US gangster in Chicago during Prohibition

Caporetto (kapoˈretto) *n* the Italian name for **Kobarid**

capote (kəˈpəʊt; *French* kapɔt) *n* a long cloak or soldier's coat, usually with a hood [c19: from French: cloak, from *cape*; see CAPE¹]

Capote (kəˈpəʊtɪ) *n* **Truman**. 1924–84, US writer; his novels include *Other Voices, Other Rooms* (1948) and *In Cold Blood* (1964), based on an actual multiple murder

Capp (kæp) *n* **Al**, full name *Alfred Caplin*. 1909–79, US cartoonist, famous for his comic strip *Li'l Abner*

Cappadocia (ˌkæpəˈdəʊsɪə) *n* an ancient region of E Asia Minor famous for its horses

Cappadocian (ˌkæpəˈdəʊsɪən) *adj* **1** of or relating to Cappadocia (an ancient region of E Asia Minor) or its inhabitants ▷ *n* **2** a native or inhabitant of Cappadocia

cappuccino (ˌkæpʊˈtʃiːnəʊ) *n, pl* -nos coffee with steamed milk, sometimes served with whipped cream or sprinkled with powdered chocolate [Italian: CAPUCHIN]

Capra (ˈkæprə) *n* **Frank**. 1896–1992, US film director born in Italy. His films include *It Happened One Night* (1934), *It's a Wonderful Life* (1946), and several propaganda films during World War II

Capri (kəˈpriː; *Italian* ˈkapri) *n* an island off W Italy, in the Bay of Naples: resort since Roman times. Pop: 12 200 (2002 est). Area: about 13 sq km (5 sq miles)

capriccio (kəˈprɪtʃɪˌəʊ) *or* **caprice** *n, pl* -priccios, -pricci (-ˈpriːtʃɪ) *or* -prices music a lively piece composed freely and without adhering to the rules for any specific musical form [c17: from Italian: CAPRICE]

capriccioso (kəˌprɪtʃɪˈəʊzəʊ) *adv music* to be played in a free and lively style [Italian: from *capriccio* CAPRICE]

caprice (kəˈpriːs) *n* **1** a sudden or unpredictable change of attitude, behaviour, etc; whim **2** a tendency to such changes **3** another word for **capriccio** [c17: from French, from Italian *capriccio* a shiver, caprice, from *capo* head + *riccio* hedgehog, suggesting a convulsive shudder in which the hair stood on end like a hedgehog's spines; meaning also influenced by Italian *capra* goat, by folk etymology]

capricious (kəˈprɪʃəs) *adj* characterized by or liable to sudden unpredictable changes in attitude or behaviour; impulsive; fickle ▷ ca'priciously *adv*

Capricorn (ˈkæprɪˌkɔːn) *n* **1** astrology Also called: the **Goat**, **Capricornus** the tenth sign of the zodiac, symbol ♑, having a cardinal earth classification and ruled by the planet Saturn. The sun is in this sign between about Dec 22 and Jan 19 **2** astronomy a S constellation **3** tropic of Capricorn See **tropic** (sense 1) [c14: from Latin *Capricornus* (translating Greek *aigokerōs* goat-horned), from *caper* goat + *cornū* horn]

Capricornia (ˌkæprɪˈkɔːnɪə) *n* the regions of Australia in the tropic of Capricorn

caprine (ˈkæpraɪn) *adj* of or resembling a goat [c17: from Latin *caprīnus*, from *caper* goat]

capriole (ˈkæprɪˌəʊl) *n* **1** dressage a high upward but not forward leap made by a horse with all four feet off the ground ▷ *vb* **2** (intr) to perform a capriole [c16: from French, from Old Italian *capriola*, from *capriolo* roebuck, from Latin *capreolus*, *caper* goat]

caps. *abbreviation* capital letters

capsicum (ˈkæpsɪkəm) *n* **1** any tropical American plant of the solanaceous genus *Capsicum*, such as *C. frutescens*, having mild or pungent seeds enclosed in a pod-shaped or bell-shaped fruit **2** the fruit of any of these plants, used as a vegetable or ground to produce a condiment ▷ See also **pepper** (sense 4) [c18: from New Latin, from Latin *capsa* box, CASE²]

capsid¹ (ˈkæpsɪd) *n* any heteropterous bug of the family *Miridae* (formerly *Capsidae*), most of which feed on plant tissues, causing damage to crops [c19: from New Latin *Capsus* (genus)]

capsid² (ˈkæpsɪd) *n* the outer protein coat of a mature virus [c20: from French *capside*, from Latin *capsa* box]

capsize (kæpˈsaɪz) *vb* to overturn accidentally; upset [c18: of uncertain origin]

capstan (ˈkæpstən) *n* **1** a machine with a drum that rotates round a vertical spindle and is turned by a motor or lever, used for hauling in heavy ropes, etc **2** any similar device, such as the rotating shaft in a tape recorder that pulls the tape past the head [c14: from Old Provençal *cabestan*, from Latin *capistrum* a halter, from *capere* to seize]

capstan lathe *n* a lathe for repetitive work, having a rotatable turret resembling a capstan to hold tools for successive operations. Also called: **turret lathe**

capstone (ˈkæpˌstəʊn) *or* **copestone** (ˈkəʊpˌstəʊn) *n* one of a set of slabs on the top of a wall, building, etc

capsule (ˈkæpsjuːl) *n* **1** a soluble case of gelatine enclosing a dose of medicine **2** a thin metal cap, seal, or cover, such as the foil covering the cork of a wine bottle **3** botany **a** a dry fruit that liberates its seeds by splitting, as in the violet, or through pores, as in the poppy **b** the spore-producing organ of mosses and liverworts **4** anatomy a cartilaginous, fibrous, or membranous envelope surrounding any of certain organs or parts **5** See **space capsule 6** an aeroplane cockpit that can be ejected in a flight emergency, complete with crew, instruments, etc **7** (*modifier*) in a highly concise form: *a capsule summary* [c17: from French, from Latin *capsula*, diminutive of *capsa* box] ▷ capsulate (ˈkæpsjʊˌleɪt, -lɪt) *or* 'capsu,lated *adj* ▷ ,capsu'lation *n*

capsulize *or* **capsulise** (ˈkæpsjʊˌlaɪz) *vb* (tr) **1** to state (information) in a highly condensed form **2** to enclose in a capsule

Capt. *abbreviation* Captain

captain (ˈkæptɪn) *n* **1** the person in charge of and responsible for a vessel **2** an officer of the navy who holds a rank junior to a rear admiral but senior to a commander **3** an officer of the army, certain air forces, and the marine corps who holds a rank junior to a major but senior to a lieutenant **4** the officer in command of a civil aircraft, usually the senior pilot **5** the leader of a team in games **6** a person in command over a group, organization, etc; leader: *a captain of industry* **7** US a police officer in charge of a precinct ▷ *vb* **8** (tr) to be captain of [c14: from Old French *capitaine*, from Late Latin *capitāneus* chief, from Latin *caput* head] ▷ 'captaincy *or* 'captain,ship *n*

Captain Cooker (ˈkʊkə) *n* NZ a wild pig [from Captain James Cook (1728–79), British navigator and explorer, who first released pigs in the New Zealand bush]

caption (ˈkæpʃən) *n* **1** a title, brief explanation, or comment accompanying an illustration; legend **2** a heading, title, or headline of a chapter, article, etc **3** graphic material, usually containing lettering, used in television presentation **4** another name for **subtitle** (sense 2) **5** the formal heading of a legal document stating when, where, and on what authority it was taken or made ▷ *vb* **6** to provide with a caption or captions [c14 (meaning: seizure, an arrest; later, heading of a legal document): from Latin *captiō* a seizing, from *capere* to take]

captious (ˈkæpʃəs) *adj* apt to make trivial criticisms; fault-finding; carping [c14 (meaning: catching in error): from Latin *captiōsus*, from *captiō* a seizing; see CAPTION] ▷ 'captiously *adv* ▷ 'captiousness *n*

captivate (ˈkæptɪˌveɪt) *vb* (tr) to hold the attention of by fascinating; enchant [c16: from Late Latin *captivāre*, from *captīvus* CAPTIVE] ▷ 'capti,vatingly *adv* ▷ ,capti'vation *n*

captive (ˈkæptɪv) *n* **1** a person or animal that is confined or restrained, esp a prisoner of war **2** a person whose behaviour is dominated by some emotion: *a captive of love* ▷ *adj* **3** held as prisoner **4** held under restriction or control; confined: *captive water held behind a dam* **5** captivated; enraptured **6** unable by circumstances to avoid speeches, advertisements, etc (esp in the phrase **captive audience**) [c14: from Latin *captīvus*, from *capere* to take]

captivity (kæpˈtɪvɪtɪ) *n, pl* -ties **1** the condition of being captive; imprisonment **2** the period of imprisonment

captor (ˈkæptə) *n* a person or animal that holds another captive [c17: from Latin, from *capere* to take]

capture ('kæptʃə) vb (tr) **1** to take prisoner or gain control over: *to capture an enemy; to capture a town* **2** (in a game or contest) to win control or possession of: *to capture a pawn in chess* **3** to succeed in representing or describing (something elusive): *the artist captured her likeness* **4** *physics* (of an atom, molecule, ion, or nucleus) to acquire (an additional particle) **5** to insert or transfer (data) into a computer ▷ *n* **6** the act of taking by force; seizure **7** the person or thing captured; booty **8** *physics* a process by which an atom, molecule, ion, or nucleus acquires an additional particle **9** Also called: piracy *geography* the process by which the headwaters of one river are diverted into another through erosion caused by the second river's tributaries **10** the act or process of inserting or transferring data into a computer [c16: from Latin *captūra* a catching, that which is caught, from *capere* to take] > '**capturer** *n*

Capua (*Italian* 'kapua) *n* a town in S Italy, in NW Campania: strategically important in ancient times, situated on the Appian Way. Pop: 19 041 (2001)

Capuana (*Italian* ka'pwa:na) *n* **Luigi.** 1839–1915, Italian realist novelist, dramatist, and critic. His works include the novel *Giacinta* (1879) and the play *Malia* (1895)

capuche *or* **capouch** (kə'pu:ʃ) *n* a large hood or cowl, esp that worn by Capuchin friars [c17: from French, from Italian *cappuccio* hood, from Late Latin *cappa* cloak]

capuchin ('kæpjutʃin, -ʃin) *n* **1** any agile intelligent New World monkey of the genus *Cebus*, inhabiting forests in South America, typically having a cowl of thick hair on the top of the head **2** a woman's hooded cloak **3** (*sometimes capital*) a rare variety of domestic fancy pigeon [c16: from French, from Italian *cappuccino*, from *cappuccio* hood; see CAPUCHE]

Capuchin ('kæpjutʃin, 'kæpjuʃin) *n* a friar belonging to a strict and autonomous branch of the Franciscan order founded in 1525 [c17: from French; see CAPUCHE]

capybara (,kæpɪ'bɑ:rə) *n* the largest rodent: a pig-sized amphibious hystricomorph, *Hydrochoerus hydrochaeris*, resembling a guinea pig and inhabiting river banks in Central and South America: family *Hydrochoeridae* [c18: from Portuguese *capibara*, from Tupi]

Caquetá (*Spanish* kake'ta) *n* the Japurá River from its source in Colombia to the border with Brazil

car (kɑ:) *n* **1 a** Also called: motorcar, automobile a self-propelled road vehicle designed to carry passengers, esp one with four wheels that is powered by an internal-combustion engine **b** (*as modifier*): *car coat* **2** a conveyance for passengers, freight, etc, such as a cable car or the carrier of an airship or balloon **3** *Brit* a railway vehicle for passengers only, such as a sleeping car or buffet car **4** *chiefly US & Canadian* a railway carriage or van **5** *chiefly US* the enclosed platform of a lift **6** a poetic word for **chariot** [c14: from Anglo-French *carre*, ultimately related to Latin *carra, carrum* two-wheeled wagon, probably of Celtic origin; compare Old Irish *carr*]

CAR *abbreviation* compound annual return

carabineer *or* **carabinier** (,kærəbɪ'nɪə) *n* variants of **carabineer**

carabiner (,kærə'bi:nə) *n* a variant spelling of **karabiner**

caracal ('kærə,kæl) *n* **1** Also called: desert lynx a lynxlike feline mammal, *Lynx caracal*, inhabiting deserts of N Africa and S Asia, having long legs, a smooth coat of reddish fur, and black-tufted ears **2** the fur of this animal [c18: from French, from Turkish *kara kūlāk*, literally: black ear]

Caracalla (,kærə'kælə) *n* real name *Marcus Aurelius Antoninus*, original name *Bassianus*. 188–217 AD, Roman emperor (211–17): ruled with cruelty and extravagance; assassinated

caracara (,kɑ:rə'kɑ:rə) *n* any of various large carrion-eating diurnal birds of prey of the genera *Caracara, Polyborus*, etc, of S North, Central, and South America, having long legs and naked faces: family *Falconidae* (falcons) [c19: from Spanish or Portuguese, from Tupi; of imitative origin]

Caracas (kə'rækəs, -'rɑ:-; *Spanish* ka'rakas) *n* the capital of Venezuela, in the north: founded in 1567; major industrial and commercial centre, notably for oil companies. Pop: 3 276 000 (2005 est)

caracole (,kærə,kəul) *or* **caracol** ('kærə,kɒl) *n* **1** *dressage* a half turn to the right or left **2** a spiral staircase ▷ *vb* (*intr*) **3** *dressage* to execute a half turn to the right or left [c17: from French, from Spanish *caracol* snail, spiral staircase, turn]

Caractacus (kə'ræktəkəs) *n* same as **Caratacus**

caracul ('kærə,kʌl) *n* **1** Also called: Persian lamb the black loosely curled fur obtained from the skins of newly born lambs of the karakul sheep **2** a variant spelling of **karakul**

carafe (kə'ræf, -'rɑ:f) *n* an open-topped glass container for serving water or wine at table [c18: from French, from Italian *caraffa*, from Spanish *garrafa*, from Arabic *gharrāfah* vessel]

carageen ('kærə,gi:n) *n* a variant spelling of **carrageen**

carambola (,kærəm'bəulə) *n* **1** a tree, *Averrhoa carambola*, probably native to Brazil but cultivated in the tropics, esp SE Asia, for its edible fruit **2** Also called: star fruit the smooth-skinned yellow fruit of this tree, which is star-shaped on cross section [c18: Spanish *carambola* a sour greenish fruit, from Portuguese, from Marathi *karambal*]

caramel ('kærəməl, -,mɛl) *n* **1** burnt sugar, used for colouring and flavouring food **2** a chewy sweet made from sugar, butter, milk, etc [c18: from French, from Spanish *caramelo*, of uncertain origin]

caramelize *or* **caramelise** ('kærəmə,laɪz) *vb* to convert or be converted into caramel

carapace ('kærə,peɪs) *n* the thick hard shield, made of chitin or bone, that covers part of the body of crabs, lobsters, tortoises, etc [c19: from French, from Spanish *carapacho*, of unknown origin]

carat ('kærət) *n* **1** a measure of the weight of precious stones, esp diamonds. It was formerly defined as 3.17 grains, but the international carat is now standardized as 0.20 grams **2** a measure of the proportion of gold in an alloy, expressed as the number of parts of gold in 24 parts of the alloy ▷ Usual US spelling: karat [c16: from Old French, from Medieval Latin *carratus*, from Arabic *qīrāt* weight of four grains, carat, from Greek *keration* a little horn, from *keras* horn]

Caratacus (kə'rætəkəs), **Caractacus** *or* **Caradoc** (kə'rædək) *n* died 54 AD, British chieftain: led an unsuccessful resistance against the Romans (43–50)

Caravaggio (*Italian* kara'vaddʒo) *n* **Michelangelo Merisi da** (mike'landʒelo me'ri:zi da). 1571–1610, Italian painter, noted for his realistic depiction of religious subjects and for his dramatic use of chiaroscuro.

caravan ('kærə,væn) *n* **1 a** a large enclosed vehicle capable of being pulled by a car or lorry and equipped to be lived in. US and Canadian name: trailer **b** (*as modifier*): *a caravan site* **2** (esp in some parts of Asia and Africa) a company of traders or other travellers journeying together, often with a train of camels, through the desert **3** a large covered vehicle, esp a gaily coloured one used by Romany Gypsies, circuses, etc ▷ *vb* -vans, -vanning, -vanned **4** (*intr*) *Brit* to travel or have a holiday in a caravan [c16: from Italian *caravana*, from Persian *kārwān*] > '**cara,vanning** *n*

caravanserai (,kærə'vænsə,raɪ, -,reɪ) *or* **caravansary** (,kærə'vænsərɪ) *n, pl* -rais *or* -ries (in some Eastern countries esp formerly) a large inn enclosing a courtyard providing accommodation for caravans [c16: from Persian *kārwānsarāī* caravan inn]

caravel ('kærə,vɛl) *or* **carvel** ('kɑ:vəl) *n* a two- or three-masted sailing ship, esp one with a broad beam, high poop deck, and lateen rig that was used by the Spanish and Portuguese in the 15th and 16th centuries [c16: from Portuguese *caravela*, diminutive of *caravo* ship, ultimately from Greek *karabos* crab, horned beetle]

caraway ('kærə,weɪ) *n* **1** an umbelliferous Eurasian plant, *Carum carvi*, having finely divided leaves and clusters of small whitish flowers **2** caraway seed the pungent aromatic one-seeded fruit of this plant, used in cooking and in medicine [c14: probably from Medieval Latin *carvi*, from Arabic *karawyā*, from Greek *karon*]

carb (kɑ:b) *n* **1** short for **carburettor** **2** short for **carbohydrate**

carbamate ('kɑ:bə,meɪt) *n* a salt or ester of carbamic

acid. The salts contain the monovalent ion NH_2COO^-, and the esters contain the group NH_2COO-

carbaryl ('kɑːbərɪl) *n* an organic compound of the carbamate group: used as an insecticide, esp to treat head lice

carbide ('kɑːbaɪd) *n* **1** a binary compound of carbon with a more electropositive element **2** See **calcium carbide**

carbine ('kɑːbaɪn) *n* **1** a light automatic or semiautomatic rifle of limited range **2** Also called: **carabin, carabine** a light short-barrelled shoulder rifle formerly used by cavalry [C17: from French *carabine*, from Old French *carabin* carabineer, perhaps variant of *escarrabin* one who prepares corpses for burial, from *scarabée*, from Latin *scarabaeus* SCARAB]

carbineer (ˌkɑːbɪ'nɪə), **carabineer** or **carabinier** (ˌkærəbɪ'nɪə) *n* (formerly) a soldier equipped with a carbine

carbo- *or before a vowel* **carb-** *combining form* carbon: *carbohydrate; carbonate*

carbocyclic (ˌkɑːbəʊ'saɪklɪk) *adj* (of a chemical compound) containing a closed ring of carbon atoms

carbohydrate (ˌkɑːbəʊ'haɪdreɪt) *n* any of a large group of organic compounds, including sugars, such as sucrose, and polysaccharides, such as cellulose, glycogen, and starch, that contain carbon, hydrogen, and oxygen, with the general formula $C_m(H_2O)_n$: an important source of food and energy for animals

carbolic acid (kɑː'bɒlɪk) *n* another name for phenol, esp when it is used as an antiseptic or disinfectant [C19: *carbolic*, from CARBO- + -OL^1 + -IC]

carbon ('kɑːbən) *n* **1 a** a nonmetallic element existing in the three crystalline forms: graphite, diamond, and buckminsterfullerene: occurring in carbon dioxide, coal, oil, and all organic compounds. The isotope **carbon-12** has been adopted as the standard for atomic wt; **carbon-14**, a radioisotope with a half-life of 5700 years, is used in radiocarbon dating and as a tracer. Symbol: C; atomic no: 6; atomic wt: 12.011; valency: 2, 3, or 4; relative density: 1.8–2.1 (amorphous), 1.9–2.3 (graphite), 3.15–3.53 (diamond); sublimes at 3367±25°C; boiling pt: 4827°C **b** (*as modifier*): *a carbon compound* **2** short for **carbon paper, carbon copy 3** a carbon electrode used in a carbon-arc light or in carbon-arc welding **4** a rod or plate, made of carbon, used in some types of battery [C18: from French *carbone*, from Latin *carbō* charcoal, dead or glowing coal]

carbonaceous (ˌkɑːbə'neɪʃəs) *adj* of, resembling, or containing carbon

carbonade (ˌkɑːbə'neɪd, -'nɑːd) *n* a stew of beef and onions cooked in beer [C20: from French]

carbonado (ˌkɑːbə'neɪdəʊ, -'nɑːdəʊ) *n, pl* **-dos** *or* **-does** an inferior dark massive variety of diamond used in industry for polishing and drilling. Also called: **black diamond** [Portuguese, literally: carbonated]

carbon arc *n* **1** an electric arc produced between two carbon electrodes, formerly used as a light source **2** an electric arc produced between a carbon electrode and material to be welded

carbonate *n* ('kɑːbəˌneɪt, -nɪt) **1** a salt or ester of carbonic acid. Carbonate salts contain the divalent ion CO_3^{2-} ▷ *vb* ('kɑːbəˌneɪt) **2** to form or turn into a carbonate **3** (*tr*) to treat with carbon dioxide or carbonic acid, as in the manufacture of soft drinks [C18: from French, from *carbone* CARBON]

carbon black *n* a black finely divided form of amorphous carbon produced by incomplete combustion of natural gas or petroleum: used to reinforce rubber and in the manufacture of pigments and ink

carbon brush *n* a small block of carbon used to convey current between the stationary and moving parts of an electric generator, motor, etc

carbon capture *n* the capture of atmospheric carbon dioxide, esp as a technique to prevent climate change

carbon copy *n* **1** a duplicate copy of writing, typewriting, or drawing obtained by using carbon paper **2** *informal* a person or thing that is identical or very similar to another

carbon credit *n* a unit that represents part of a country or organization's allowance for the emission of carbon dioxide, and which can be traded if the full allowance is not used

carbon dioxide *n* a colourless odourless incombustible gas present in the atmosphere and formed during respiration, the decomposition and combustion of organic compounds, and in the reaction of acids with carbonates: used in carbonated drinks, fire extinguishers, and as dry ice for refrigeration. Formula: CO_2. Also called: carbonic-acid gas

carbon fibre *n* a black silky thread of pure carbon made by heating and stretching textile fibres and used because of its lightness and strength at high temperatures for reinforcing resins, ceramics, and metals, esp in turbine blades and for fishing rods

carbon footprint *n* a measure of the amount of carbon dioxide released into the atmosphere by a single endeavour or by a company, household, or individual through day-to-day activities over a given period

carbon-14 dating *n* another name for **radiocarbon dating**

carbonic (kɑː'bɒnɪk) *adj* (of a compound) containing carbon, esp tetravalent carbon

carbonic acid *n* a weak acid formed when carbon dioxide combines with water: obtained only in aqueous solutions, never in the pure state. Formula: H_2CO_3

carboniferous (ˌkɑːbə'nɪfərəs) *adj* yielding coal or carbon

Carboniferous (ˌkɑːbə'nɪfərəs) *adj* **1** of, denoting, or formed in the fifth period of the Palaeozoic era, between the Devonian and Permian periods, lasting for nearly 64 million years during which coal measures were formed ▷ *n* **2** the Carboniferous the Carboniferous period or rock system

carbonize *or* **carbonise** ('kɑːbəˌnaɪz) *vb* to turn or be turned into carbon as a result of heating, fossilization, chemical treatment, etc > ˌcarboni'zation *or* ˌcarboni'sation *n*

carbon monoxide *n* a colourless odourless poisonous flammable gas formed when carbon compounds burn in insufficient air and produced by the action of steam on hot carbon: used as a reducing agent in metallurgy and as a fuel. Formula: CO

carbon-neutral *adj* not affecting the total amount of carbon dioxide in the earth's atmosphere

carbon paper *n* a thin sheet of paper coated on one side with a dark waxy pigment, often containing carbon, that is transferred by the pressure of writing or of typewriter keys onto the copying surface below

carbon sink *or* **carbon well** *n* areas of vegetation, especially forests, and the phytoplankton-rich seas that absorb the carbon dioxide produced by the burning of fossil fuels

carbon tax *n* a tax on the emissions caused by the burning of coal, gas, and oil, aimed at reducing the production of greenhouse gases

carbon tetrachloride *n* a colourless volatile nonflammable sparingly soluble liquid made from chlorine and carbon disulphide; tetrachloromethane. It is used as a solvent, cleaning fluid, and insecticide. Formula: CCl_4

car-boot sale *n* a sale of goods from car boots in a site hired for the occasion

Carborundum (ˌkɑːbə'rʌndəm) *n* trademark any of various abrasive materials, esp one consisting of silicon carbide

carboxyl group *or* **carboxyl radical** (kɑː'bɒksaɪl, -sɪl) *n* the monovalent group –COOH, consisting of a carbonyl group bound to a hydroxyl group: the functional group in organic acids [C19 *carboxyl*, from CARBO- + OXY-^{2} + -YL]

carboxylic acid (ˌkɑːbɒk'sɪlɪk) *n* any of a class of organic acids containing the carboxyl group. See also **fatty acid**

carboy ('kɑːˌbɔɪ) *n* a large glass or plastic bottle, usually protected by a basket or box, used for containing corrosive liquids such as acids [C18: from Persian *qarāba*]

carbuncle ('kɑːbʌŋkəl) *n* **1** an extensive skin eruption, similar to but larger than a boil, with several openings: caused by staphylococcal infection **2** a rounded gemstone, esp a garnet cut without facets [C13: from Latin *carbunculus* diminutive of *carbō* coal] > 'car,buncled *adj* > carbuncular (kɑː'bʌŋkjʊlə) *adj*

carburation (ˌkɑːbjʊˈreɪʃən) n the process of mixing a hydrocarbon fuel with a correct amount of air to make an explosive mixture for an internal-combustion engine

carburet ('kɑːbjʊˌrɛt, ˌkɑːbjʊˈrɛt, -bə-) vb -rets, -retting, -retted or US -rets, -reting, -reted (tr) to combine or mix (a gas) with carbon or carbon compounds [c18: from CARB(ON) + -URET]

carburettor, carburetter (ˌkɑːbjʊˈrɛtə, 'kɑːbjʊˌrɛtə, -bə-) or US **carburetor** ('kɑːbjʊˌreɪtə, -bə-) n a device used in petrol engines for atomizing the petrol, controlling its mixture with air, and regulating the intake of the air-petrol mixture into the engine

carcajou ('kɑːkəˌdʒuː, -ˌʒuː) n a North American name for **wolverine** [c18: from Canadian French, from Algonquian karkajou]

carcass or **carcase** ('kɑːkəs) n 1 the dead body of an animal, esp one that has been slaughtered for food, with the head, limbs, and entrails removed 2 informal, usually facetious or derogatory a person's body 3 the skeleton or framework of a structure 4 the remains of anything when its life or vitality is gone; shell [c14: from Old French carcasse, of obscure origin]

Carcassonne (French karkasɔn) n a city in SW France: extensive remains of medieval fortifications. Pop: 43 950 (1999)

carcinogen (kɑːˈsɪnədʒən, 'kɑːsɪnəˌdʒɛn) n pathol any substance that produces cancer [c20: from Greek karkinos CANCER + -GEN] > ˌcarcino'genic adj

carcinogenesis (ˌkɑːsɪnəʊˈdʒɛnɪsɪs) n pathol the development of cancerous cells from normal ones

carcinoma (ˌkɑːsɪˈnəʊmə) n, pl -mas or -mata (-mətə) pathol any malignant tumour derived from epithelial tissue [c18: from Latin, from Greek karkinōma, from karkinos CANCER]

card¹ (kɑːd) n 1 a piece of stiff paper or thin cardboard, usually rectangular, with varied uses, as for filing information in an index, bearing a written notice for display, entering scores in a game, etc 2 such a card used for identification, reference, proof of membership, etc: library card; identity card; visiting card 3 such a card used for sending greetings, messages, or invitations, often bearing an illustration, printed greetings, etc: Christmas card; birthday card 4 one of a set of small pieces of cardboard, variously marked with significant figures, symbols, etc, used for playing games or for fortune-telling 5 a short for **playing card** b (as modifier): a card game 6 informal a witty, entertaining, or eccentric person 7 short for **cheque card, credit card** 8 See **compass card** 9 Also called: race card horse racing a daily programme of all the races at a meeting, listing the runners, riders, weights to be carried, distances to be run, and conditions of each race 10 a thing or action used in order to gain an advantage, esp one that is concealed and kept in reserve until needed (esp in the phrase **a card up one's sleeve**) ▷ See also **cards** [c15: from Old French carte, from Latin charta leaf of papyrus, from Greek khartēs, probably of Egyptian origin]

card² (kɑːd) vb 1 (tr) to comb out or clean fibres of wool or cotton before spinning ▷ n 2 (formerly) a machine or comblike tool for carding fabrics or for raising the nap on cloth [c15: from Old French carde card, teasel, from Latin carduus thistle] > 'carding n > 'carder n

cardamom, cardamum ('kɑːdəməm) or **cardamon** ('kɑːdəmən) n 1 a tropical Asian zingiberaceous plant, Elettaria cardamomum, that has large hairy leaves 2 the seeds of this plant, used esp as a spice or condiment [c15: from Latin cardamōmum, from Greek kardamōmon, from kardamon cress + amōmon an Indian spice]

cardboard ('kɑːdˌbɔːd) n 1 a a thin stiff board made from paper pulp and used esp for making cartons b (as modifier): cardboard boxes ▷ adj 2 (prenominal) without substance

cardboard city n informal an area of a city in which homeless people sleep rough, often in cardboard boxes

card-carrying adj being an official member of a specified organization: a card-carrying union member; a card-carrying Communist

Cardenal (Spanish karðeˈnal) n **Ernesto** ('ɛrnɛstəʊ). born 1925, Nicaraguan poet, revolutionary, and Roman Catholic priest; an influential figure in the Sandinista movement

Cárdenas (Spanish 'karðenas) n **Lázaro** ('laθaro). 1895–1970, Mexican statesman and general; president of Mexico (1934–40)

cardholder ('kɑːdˌhəʊldə) n a person who owns a credit or debit card

cardiac ('kɑːdɪˌæk) adj 1 of or relating to the heart 2 of or relating to the portion of the stomach connected to the oesophagus ▷ n 3 a person with a heart disorder [c17: from Latin cardiacus, from Greek, from kardia heart]

cardiac arrest n failure of the pumping action of the heart, resulting in loss of consciousness and absence of pulse and breathing: a medical emergency requiring immediate resuscitative treatment

cardie or **cardy** ('kɑːdɪ) n informal short for **cardigan**

Cardiff ('kɑːdɪf) n 1 the capital of Wales, situated in the southeast, in Cardiff county borough: formerly an important port; seat of the Welsh assembly (1999); university (1883). Pop: 292 150 (2001) 2 a county borough in SE Wales, created in 1996 from part of South Glamorgan. Pop: 315 100 (2003 est). Area: 139 sq km (54 sq miles)

cardigan ('kɑːdɪgən) n a knitted jacket or sweater with buttons up the front [c19: named after James Thomas Brudenell, 7th Earl of Cardigan (1797–1868), British cavalry officer]

Cardigan ('kɑːdɪgən) n **7th Earl of**, title of James Thomas Brudenell. 1797–1868, British cavalry officer. He led the charge of the Light Brigade at Balaklava (1854) during the Crimean War

Cardigan Bay n an inlet of St George's Channel, on the W coast of Wales

Cardiganshire ('kɑːdɪgənˌʃɪə, -ʃə) n a former county of W Wales: became part of Dyfed in 1974; reinstated as **Ceredigion** in 1996

Cardin (French kardɛ̃) n **Pierre** (pjɛr). born 1922, French couturier, noted esp for his collections for men

cardinal ('kɑːdɪn³l) n 1 RC Church any of the members of the Sacred College, ranking next after the pope, who elect the pope and act as his chief counsellors 2 Also called: cardinal red a deep vivid red colour 3 See **cardinal number** 4 Also called: cardinal grosbeak, (US) redbird a crested North American bunting, Richmondena (or Pyrrhuloxia) cardinalis, the male of which has a bright red plumage and the female a brown one 5 a woman's hooded shoulder cape worn in the 17th and 18th centuries ▷ adj 6 (usually prenominal) fundamentally important; principal: cardinal sin 7 of a deep vivid red colour [c13: from Latin cardinālis, literally: relating to a hinge, hence, that on which something depends, principal, from cardō hinge]

cardinalate ('kɑːdɪn³ˌleɪt) or **cardinalship** n 1 the rank, office, or term of office of a cardinal 2 the cardinals collectively

cardinal flower n a campanulaceous plant, Lobelia cardinalis of E North America, that has brilliant scarlet, pink, or white flowers

cardinal number or **cardinal numeral** n a number denoting quantity but not order in a set. Sometimes shortened to **cardinal**. See **ordinal number**

cardinal points pl n the four main points of the compass: north, south, east, and west

cardinal virtues pl n the most important moral qualities, traditionally justice, prudence, temperance, and fortitude

cardinal vowels pl n a set of theoretical vowel sounds, based on the shape of the mouth needed to articulate them, that can be used to classify the vowel sounds of any speaker in any language

card index or **card file** n 1 an index in which each item is separately listed on systematically arranged cards ▷ vb card-index (tr) 2 to make such an index of (a book)

cardio- or before a vowel **cardi-** combining form heart: cardiogram [from Greek kardia heart]

cardiocentesis (ˌkɑːdɪəʊsɛnˈtiːsɪs) n med surgical puncture of the heart

cardiogram ('kɑːdɪəʊˌgræm) n short for **electrocardiogram**

cardiograph ('kɑːdɪəʊˌgrɑːf, -ˌgræf) n 1 an instrument for recording the mechanical force and form of heart movements 2 short for **electrocardiograph** > cardiographer (ˌkɑːdɪˈɒgrəfə) n > cardiographic (ˌkɑːdɪəʊˈgræfɪk) or ˌcardio'graphical adj > ˌcardio'graphically adv > ˌcardi'ography n

cardiology (ˌkɑːdɪˈɒlədʒɪ) n the branch of medical science concerned with the heart and its diseases > ˌcardi'ologist n

cardioplegia (ˌkɑːdɪəʊˈpliːdʒɪə) n med deliberate arrest of the action of the heart, as by hypothermia or the injection of chemicals, to enable complex heart surgery to be carried out

cardiopulmonary resuscitation n an emergency measure to revive a patient whose heart has stopped beating, in which compressions applied with the hands to the patient's chest are alternated with mouth-to-mouth respiration. Abbreviation: CPR

cardiothoracic (ˌkɑːdɪəʊθɔːˈræsɪk) adj of or relating to the heart and the chest

cardiovascular (ˌkɑːdɪəʊˈvæskjʊlə) adj of or relating to the heart and the blood vessels

cardoon (kɑːˈduːn) n a thistle-like S European plant, Cynara cardunculus, closely related to the artichoke, with spiny leaves, purple flowers, and a leafstalk that may be blanched and eaten: family Asteraceae (composites) [C17: from French cardon, ultimately from Latin carduus thistle, artichoke]

Cardoso (Portuguese kaˈdozo) n **Fernando Henrique**. born 1931, Brazilian statesman; president (1995–2002)

cardphone ('kɑːdfəʊn) n a public telephone operated by the insertion of a phonecard instead of coins

card punch n a device, no longer widely used, controlled by a computer, for transferring information from the central processing unit onto punched cards. See **card reader**

card reader n a device, no longer widely used, for reading information on a punched card and transferring it to a computer

cards (kɑːdz) n 1 (usually functioning as singular) **a** any game or games played with cards, esp playing cards **b** the playing of such a game 2 an employee's national insurance and other documents held by the employer 3 get one's cards to be told to leave one's employment 4 on the cards possible or likely. US equivalent: in the cards 5 play one's cards to carry out one's plans; take action (esp in the phrase play one's cards right) 6 put one's cards on the table, lay one's cards on the table or show one's cards to declare one's intentions, resources, etc

cardsharp ('kɑːdˌʃɑːp) or cardsharper n a professional card player who cheats

Carducci (Italian karˈduttʃi) n **Giosuè** (dʒozuˈɛ). 1835–1907, Italian poet: Nobel prize for literature 1906

Cardus ('kɑːdəs) n **Sir Neville**. 1889–1975, British music critic and cricket writer

card vote n Brit a vote by delegates, esp at a trade-union conference, in which each delegate's vote counts as a vote by all his constituents

care (kɛə) vb 1 (when tr, may take a clause as object) to be troubled or concerned; be affected emotionally: he is dying, and she doesn't care 2 (intr; foll by for or about) to have regard, affection, or consideration (for): he cares more for his hobby than his job 3 (intr; foll by for) to have a desire or taste (for): would you care for some tea? 4 (intr; foll by for) to provide physical needs, help, or comfort (for): the nurse cared for her patients 5 (tr) to agree or like (to do something): would you care to sit down, please? 6 for all I care or I couldn't care less I am completely indifferent ▷ n 7 careful or serious attention: under her care the plant flourished; he does his work with care 8 protective or supervisory control: in the care of a doctor 9 (often plural) trouble; anxiety: worry 10 an object of or cause for concern: the baby's illness was her only care 11 caution: handle with care 12 care of at the address of: written on envelopes. Usual abbreviation: c/o 13 in care or into care social welfare made the legal responsibility of a local authority by order of a court [Old English cearu (n), cearian (vb), of Germanic origin; compare Old High German chara lament, Latin garrīre to gossip] > 'carer n

CARE (kɛə) n acronym for 1 Cooperative for American Relief Everywhere, Inc.; a federation of US charities, giving financial and technical assistance to many regions of the world 2 communicated authenticity, regard, empathy: the three qualities believed to be essential in the therapist practising client-centred therapy

care and maintenance n commerce the state of a building, ship, machinery, etc, that is not in current use although it is kept in good condition to enable it to be quickly brought into service if there is demand for it. Abbreviation: C & M

careen (kəˈriːn) vb 1 to sway or cause to sway dangerously over to one side 2 (tr) nautical to cause (a vessel) to keel over to one side, esp in order to clean or repair its bottom 3 (intr) nautical (of a vessel) to keel over to one side [C17: from French carène keel, from Italian carena, from Latin carīna keel] > ca'reenage n

career (kəˈrɪə) n 1 a path or progress through life or history 2 a profession or occupation chosen as one's life's work 3 (modifier) having or following a career as specified: a career diplomat 4 a course or path, esp a swift or headlong one ▷ vb 5 (intr) to move swiftly along; rush in an uncontrolled way [C16: from French carrière, from Late Latin carrāria carriage road, from Latin carrus two-wheeled wagon, CAR]

career girl or **career woman** n a woman whose main priority in life is achieving success in her career or profession

careerist (kəˈrɪərɪst) n a person who values success in his career above all else and seeks to advance it by any possible means

carefree ('kɛəˌfriː) adj without worry or responsibility > 'care,freeness n

careful ('kɛəfʊl) adj 1 cautious in attitude or action; prudent 2 painstaking in one's work; thorough 3 (usually postpositive; foll by of, in, or about) solicitous; protective 4 Brit mean or miserly > 'carefully adv > 'carefulness n

careless ('kɛəlɪs) adj 1 done with or acting with insufficient attention; negligent 2 (often foll by in, of, or about) unconcerned in attitude or action; heedless; indifferent (to) 3 (usually prenominal) carefree 4 (usually prenominal) unstudied; artless: an impression of careless elegance > 'carelessly adv > 'carelessness n

Carême (karɛm) n **Marie Antonin**. 1784–1833, French chef, regarded as the founder of haute cuisine.

care plan n a plan for the medical care of a particular patient or the welfare of a child in care

caress (kəˈrɛs) n 1 a gentle touch or embrace, esp one given to show affection ▷ vb 2 (tr) to touch or stroke gently with affection or as with affection [C17: from French caresse, from Italian carezza, from Latin cārus dear]

caret ('kærɪt) n a symbol (‸) used to indicate the place in written or printed matter at which something is to be inserted [C17: from Latin, literally: there is missing, from carēre to lack]

caretaker ('kɛəˌteɪkə) n 1 a person who is in charge of a place or thing, esp in the owner's absence 2 (modifier) holding office temporarily; interim: a caretaker government

Carew (kəˈruː) n **Thomas**. ?1595–?1639, English Cavalier poet

careworn ('kɛəˌwɔːn) adj showing signs of care, stress, worry, etc

Carey ('kɛərɪ) n 1 **George (Leonard)**. born 1935, Archbishop of Canterbury (1991–2002) 2 **Peter**. born 1943, Australian novelist and writer; his novels include Illywhacker (1985), Oscar and Lucinda (1988), and True History of the Kelly Gang (2001) 3 **William**. 1761–1834, British orientalist and pioneer Baptist missionary in India

Carey Street ('kɛərɪ) n 1 (formerly) the street in which the London bankruptcy court was situated 2 the state of bankruptcy

cargo ('kɑːgəʊ) n, pl -goes or -gos 1 a goods carried by a ship, aircraft, or other vehicle; freight **b** (as modifier): a cargo vessel 2 any load [C17: from Spanish: from cargar to load, from Late Latin carricāre to load a vehicle, from carrus CAR]

cargo pants or **cargo trousers** pl n loose trousers with a large external pocket on the side of each leg

Carib ('kærɪb) n 1 pl -ibs or -ib a member of a group of American Indian peoples of NE South America and the Lesser Antilles 2 the family of languages spoken by these peoples [c16: from Spanish Caribe, from Arawak]

Caribbean (ˌkærɪˈbiːən; US kəˈrɪbɪən) adj 1 of, or relating to, the Caribbean Sea and its islands 2 of, or relating to, the Carib or any of their languages ▷ n 3 **the Caribbean** the states and islands of the Caribbean Sea, including the West Indies, when considered as a geopolitical region 4 short for the **Caribbean Sea** 5 a member of any of the peoples inhabiting the islands of the Caribbean Sea, such as a West Indian or a Carib

Caribbean Sea n an almost landlocked sea, part of the Atlantic Ocean, bounded by the Caribbean islands, Central America, and the N coast of South America. Area: 2 718 200 sq km (1 049 500 sq miles)

Caribbees ('kærɪˌbiːz) pl n **the Caribbees** a former name for the **Lesser Antilles**

Cariboo ('kærɪˌbuː) n **the Cariboo** Canadian a region in the W foothills of the Cariboo Mountains, scene of a gold rush beginning in 1860

Cariboo Mountains pl n a mountain range in SW Canada, in SE British Columbia. Highest peak: Mount Sir Wilfrid Laurier, 3520 m (11 549 ft)

caribou ('kærɪˌbuː) n, pl -bou or -bous a large deer, Rangifer tarandus, of Arctic regions of North America, having large branched antlers in the male and female: also occurs in Europe and Asia, where it is called a reindeer [c18: from Canadian French, of Algonquian origin; compare Micmac khalibu literally: scratcher]

caricature ('kærɪkəˌtjʊə) n 1 a pictorial, written, or acted representation of a person, which exaggerates his characteristic traits for comic effect 2 a ludicrously inadequate or inaccurate imitation ▷ vb 3 (tr) to represent in caricature or produce a caricature of [c18: from Italian caricatura a distortion, exaggeration, from caricare to load, exaggerate; see CARGO]

CARICOM ('kærɪˌkɒm) n acronym for Caribbean Community and Common Market

caries ('kɛərɪːz) n, pl -ies progressive decay of a bone or a tooth [c17: from Latin: decay; related to Greek kēr death]

carillon (kəˈrɪljən) n music 1 a set of bells usually hung in a tower and played either by keys and pedals or mechanically 2 a tune played on such bells 3 an organ stop giving the effect of a bell [c18: from French: set of bells, from Old French quarregnon, ultimately from Latin quattuor four]

carina (kəˈriːnə, -ˈraɪ-) n, pl -nae (-niː) or -nas a keel-like part or ridge, as in the breastbone of birds or the fused lower petals of a leguminous flower [c18: from Latin: keel]

carinate ('kærɪˌneɪt) or **carinated** adj biology having a keel or ridge; shaped like a keel [c17: from Latin carīnāre to furnish with a keel or shell, from carīna keel]

caring ('kɛərɪŋ) adj 1 feeling or showing care and compassion: a caring attitude 2 of or relating to professional social or medical care: nursing is a caring job ▷ n 3 the practice or profession of providing social or medical care

Carinthia (kəˈrɪnθɪə) n a state of S Austria: an independent duchy from 976 to 1276; mainly mountainous, with many lakes and resorts. Capital: Klagenfurt. Pop: 559 440 (2003 est). Area: 9533 sq km (3681 sq miles). German name: **Kärnten**

carioca (ˌkærɪˈəʊkə) n 1 a Brazilian dance similar to the samba 2 a piece of music composed for this dance [c19: from Brazilian Portuguese]

cariogenic (ˌkɛərɪəʊˈdʒɛnɪk) adj (of a substance) producing caries, esp in the teeth

cariole or **carriole** ('kærɪˌəʊl) n 1 a small open two-wheeled horse-drawn vehicle 2 a covered cart [c19: from French carriole, ultimately from Latin carrus; see CAR]

carious ('kɛərɪəs) or **cariose** ('kɛərɪˌəʊz) adj (of teeth or bone) affected with caries; decayed

carjack ('kɑːˌdʒæk) vb (tr) to attack (a driver in a car) in order to rob the driver or to steal the car for another crime [c20: CAR + (HI)JACK]

cark (kɑːk) vb (intr) Austral slang to break down; die [perhaps from the cry of the crow, as a carrion feeding bird]

carl or **carle** (kɑːl) n archaic another word for churl [Old English, from Old Norse karl]

Carl XVI Gustaf (Swedish kɑːrl ˈɡʊstav) n born 1946, king of Sweden from 1973

Carlisle (kɑːˈlaɪl, ˈkɑːlaɪl) n a city in NW England, administrative centre of Cumbria: railway and industrial centre. Pop: 71 773 (2001)

Carlovingian (ˌkɑːləʊˈvɪndʒɪən) adj, n history a variant of **Carolingian**

Carlow ('kɑːləʊ) n 1 a county of SE Republic of Ireland, in Leinster: mostly flat, with barren mountains in the southeast. County town: Carlow. Pop: 46 014 (2002). Area: 896 sq km (346 sq miles) 2 a town in SE Republic of Ireland, county town of Co Carlow. Pop: 18 487 (2002)

Carling ('kɑːlɪŋ) n **Will(iam).** born 1965, British Rugby Union footballer; captain of England (1988–96)

Carlos ('kɑːlɒs) n **Don.** full name Carlos María Isidro de Borbón. 1788–1855, second son of Charles IV: pretender to the Spanish throne and leader of the Carlists

Carlota (Spanish karˈlota) n original name Marie Charlotte Amélie Augustine Victoire Clémentine Léopoldine. 1840–1927, wife of Maximilian; empress of Mexico (1864–67)

Carlyle (kɑːˈlaɪl) n 1 **Robert.** born 1961, Scottish actor; his work includes the television series Cracker and Hamish Macbeth and the films Trainspotting (1996), The Full Monty (1997), The Beach (2000), and 28 Weeks Later (2007) 2 **Thomas.** 1795–1881, Scottish essayist and historian. His works include Sartor Resartus (1833–34), The French Revolution (1837), lectures On Heroes, Hero-Worship, and the Heroic in History (1841), and the History of Frederick the Great (1858–65)

carmagnole (ˌkɑːmənˈjəʊl; French karmaɲɔl) n 1 a dance and song popular during the French Revolution 2 the costume worn by many French Revolutionaries, consisting of a short jacket with wide lapels, black trousers, a red liberty cap, and a tricoloured sash [c18: from French, probably named after Carmagnola, Italy, taken by French Revolutionaries in 1792]

Carmarthen (kɑːˈmɑːðən) n a market town in S Wales, the administrative centre of Carmarthenshire: Norman castle. Pop: 14 648 (2001)

Carmarthenshire (kɑːˈmɑːðənˌʃɪə, -ʃə) n a county of S Wales, formerly part of Dyfed (1974–96): on Carmarthen Bay, with the Cambrian Mountains in the N: generally agricultural (esp dairying). Administrative centre: Carmarthen. Pop: 176 000 (2003 est). Area: 2398 sq km (926 sq miles)

Carmel ('kɑːməl) n **Mount Carmel** a mountain ridge in NW Israel, extending from the Samarian Hills to the Mediterranean. Highest point: about 540 m (1800 ft)

Carmelite ('kɑːməˌlaɪt) n RC Church 1 a member of an order of mendicant friars founded about 1154; a White Friar 2 a member of a corresponding order of nuns founded in 1452, noted for its austere rule 3 (modifier) of or relating to the Carmelite friars or nuns [c14: from French; named after Mount CARMEL, where the order was founded]

Carmichael (kɑːˈmaɪkəl) n **Hoagland Howard** ('həʊɡlənd), known as **Hoagy.** 1899–1981, US pianist, singer, and composer of such standards as "Star Dust" (1929)

carminative ('kɑːmɪnətɪv) adj 1 able to relieve flatulence ▷ n 2 a carminative drug [c15: from French carminatif, from Latin carmināre to card wool, remove impurities, from cārere to card]

carmine ('kɑːmaɪn) n 1 a a vivid red colour, sometimes with a purplish tinge b (as adjective): carmine paint 2 a pigment of this colour obtained from cochineal [c18: from Medieval Latin carmīnus, from Arabic qirmiz KERMES]

Carnac ('kɑːnæk) n a village in NW France: noted for its many megalithic monuments, including alignments of stone menhirs

carnage ('kɑːnɪdʒ) n extensive slaughter, esp of human beings in battle [c16: from French, from Italian carnaggio, from Medieval Latin carnāticum, from Latin carō flesh]

carnal ('kɑːnəl) adj relating to the appetites and passions of the body; sensual; fleshly [c15: from Late

Latin: relating to flesh, from Latin *carō* flesh] > **car'nality** *n* > **'carnally** *adv*

carnal knowledge *n chiefly law* sexual intercourse

Carnap ('kɑːnæp) *n* **Rudolf.** 1891–1970, US logical positivist philosopher, born in Germany: attempted to construct a formal language for the empirical sciences that would eliminate ambiguity

Carnarvon (kɑːˈnɑːvˀn) *n* a variant spelling of **Caernarfon**

carnation (kɑːˈneɪʃən) *n* **1** Also called: **clove pink** a Eurasian caryophyllaceous plant, *Dianthus caryophyllus*, cultivated in many varieties for its white, pink, or red flowers, which have a fragrant scent of cloves **2** the flower of this plant **3 a** a pink or reddish-pink colour **b** (*as adjective*): *a carnation dress* [c16: from French: flesh colour, from Late Latin *carnātiō* fleshiness, from Latin *carō* flesh]

carnauba (kɑːˈnaʊbə) *n* **1** Also called: **wax palm** a Brazilian fan palm, *Copernicia cerifera* **2** Also called: **carnauba wax** the wax obtained from the young leaves of this tree, used esp as a polish [from Brazilian Portuguese, probably of Tupi origin]

Carné (karne) *n* **Marcel.** 1906–96, French film director. His films include *Le Jour se lève* (1939), *Les Portes de la nuit* (1946), and *La Bible* (1976)

Carnegie (kɑːˈnɛɡɪ, kɑːˈneɪ-) *n* **Andrew.** 1835–1919, US steel manufacturer and philanthropist, born in Scotland: endowed public libraries, education, and research trusts

Carnegie Hall ('kɑːnəɡɪ) *n* a famous concert hall in New York (opened 1891); endowed by Andrew Carnegie (1835–1919), Scots-born US steel manufacturer and philanthropist

carnelian (kɑːˈniːljən) *n* a red or reddish-yellow translucent variety of chalcedony, used as a gemstone [c17: variant of *cornelian*, from Old French *corneline*, of uncertain origin; *car-* spelling influenced by Latin *carneus* flesh-coloured]

carnet ('kɑːneɪ) *n* **a** a customs licence authorizing the temporary importation of a motor vehicle **b** an official document permitting motorists to cross certain frontiers [French: notebook, from Old French *quernet*, ultimately from Latin *quaternī* four at a time; see QUIRE]

Carniola (ˌkɑːnɪˈəʊlə) *n* a region of N Slovenia: a former duchy and crownland of Austria (1335–1919); divided between Yugoslavia and Italy in 1919; part of Yugoslavia (1947–92). Slovene name: **Kranj**

carnival ('kɑːnɪvˀl) *n* **1 a** a festive occasion or period marked by merrymaking, processions, etc: esp in some Roman Catholic countries, the period just before Lent **b** (*as modifier*): *a carnival atmosphere* **2** a travelling fair having merry-go-rounds, etc **3** a show or display arranged as an amusement **4** *Austral* a sports meeting [c16: from Italian *carnevale*, from Old Italian *carnelevare* a removing of meat (referring to the Lenten fast)]

carnivore ('kɑːnɪˌvɔː) *n* **1** any placental mammal of the order *Carnivora*, typically having large pointed canine teeth and sharp molars and premolars, specialized for eating flesh. The order includes cats, dogs, bears, raccoons, hyenas, civets, and weasels **2** any other animal or any plant that feeds on animals **3** *informal* an aggressively ambitious person [c19: probably back formation from CARNIVOROUS]

carnivorous (kɑːˈnɪvərəs) *adj* **1** (esp of animals) feeding on flesh **2** (of plants such as the pitcher plant and sundew) able to trap and digest insects and other small animals **3** of or relating to the *Carnivora* **4** *informal* aggressively ambitious or reactionary [c17: from Latin *carnivorus*, from *carō* flesh + *vorāre* to consume] > **car'nivorousness** *n*

Carnot ('kɑːnəʊ; *French* karno) *n* **1** Lazare (**Nicolas Marguerite**) (lazar), known as the *Organizer of Victory*. 1753–1823, French military engineer and administrator: organized the French Revolutionary army (1793–95) **2** **Nicolas Léonard Sadi** (nikɔla leɔnar sadi). 1796–1832, French physicist, whose work formed the basis for the second law of thermodynamics, enunciated in 1850; author of *Réflexions sur la puissance motrice du feu* (1824)

Caro *n* **1** ('kærəʊ) Sir **Antony.** born 1924, British sculptor,

best known for his abstract steel sculptures **2** ('kɑːrəʊ) **Joseph** (**ben Ephraim**) 1488–1575, Jewish legal scholar and mystic, born in Spain; compiler of the *Shulhan Arukh* (1564–65), the most authoritative Jewish legal code

carob ('kærəb) *n* **1** Also called: **algarroba** an evergreen leguminous Mediterranean tree, *Ceratonia siliqua*, with compound leaves and edible pods **2** Also called: **algarroba, Saint John's bread** the long blackish sugary pod of this tree, used as a substitute for chocolate and for animal fodder [c16: from Old French *carobe*, from Medieval Latin *carrūbium*, from Arabic *al kharrūbah*]

carol ('kærəl) *n* **1** a joyful hymn or religious song, esp one (a **Christmas carol**) celebrating the birth of Christ ▷ *vb* **-ols, -olling, -olled** *or US* **-ols, -oling, -oled 2** (*intr*) to sing carols at Christmas **3** to sing (something) in a joyful manner [c13: from Old French, of uncertain origin]

Carol II ('kærəl) *n* 1893–1953, king of Romania (1930–40), who was deposed by the Iron Guard

Carolina (ˌkærəˈlaɪnə) *n* a former English colony on the E coast of North America, first established in 1663: divided in 1729 into North and South Carolina, which are often referred to as **the Carolinas**

Caroline ('kærəˌlaɪn) *or* **Carolean** (ˌkærəˈliːən) *adj* **1** Also called: **Carolinian** characteristic of or relating to Charles I (1600–49) or Charles II (1630–85), Stuart kings of England, Scotland, and Ireland, the society over which they ruled, or their government **2** of or relating to any other king called Charles

Caroline Islands *pl n* an archipelago of over 500 islands and islets in the W Pacific Ocean east of the Philippines, all of which are now part of the Federated States of Micronesia, except for the Palau group: formerly part of the US Trust Territory of the Pacific Islands; centre of a typhoon zone. Area: (land) 1183 sq km (457 sq miles)

Caroline of Ansbach ('ænzbæk) *n* 1683–1737, wife of George II of Great Britain

Caroline of Brunswick *n* 1768–1821, wife of George IV of the United Kingdom: tried for adultery (1820)

Carolingian (ˌkærəˈlɪndʒɪən) *adj* **1** of or relating to the Frankish dynasty founded by Pepin the Short (died 768 AD), son of Charles Martel (?688–741 AD), which ruled in France from 751–987 AD and in Germany until 911 AD ▷ *n* **2** a member of the dynasty of the Carolingian Franks. ▷ Also called: **Carlovingian** or **Carolinian**

Carolinian[1] (ˌkærəˈlɪnɪən) *adj, n* a variant of **Caroline** or **Carolingian**

Carolinian[2] (ˌkærəˈlɪnɪən) *adj* **1** of or relating to North or South Carolina ▷ *n* **2** a native or inhabitant of North or South Carolina

carom ('kærəm) *n billiards, US & Canadian* a shot in which the cue ball is caused to contact one object ball after another. Also called (in Britain and certain other countries): **cannon** [c18: from earlier *carambole* (taken as *carom ball*), from Spanish CARAMBOLA]

carotene ('kærəˌtiːn) *or* **carotin** ('kærətɪn) *n* any of four orange-red isomers of an unsaturated hydrocarbon present in many plants (β-carotene is the orange pigment of carrots) and converted to vitamin A in the liver. Formula: $C_{40}H_{56}$ [c19 *carotin*, from Latin *carōta* CARROT; see -ENE]

carotenoid *or* **carotinoid** (kəˈrɒtɪˌnɔɪd) *n* any of a group of red or yellow pigments, including carotenes, found in plants and certain animal tissues

carotid (kəˈrɒtɪd) *n* **1** either one of the two principal arteries that supply blood to the head and neck ▷ *adj* **2** of or relating to either of these arteries [c17: from French, from Greek *karōtides*, from *karoun* to stupefy; so named by Galen, because pressure on them produced unconsciousness]

carousal (kəˈraʊzˀl) *n* a merry drinking party

carouse (kəˈraʊz) *vb* **1** (*intr*) to have a merry drinking spree; drink freely ▷ *n* **2** another word for **carousal** [c16: via French *carrousser* from German (*trinken*) *gar aus* (to drink) right out] > **ca'rouser** *n* > **ca'rousing** *n*

carousel (ˌkærəˈsɛl, -ˈzɛl) *n* **1** a circular magazine in which slides for a projector are held: it moves round as each slide is shown **2** a rotating conveyor belt for luggage, as at an airport **3** *US & Canadian* Also called (in

Britain and certain other countries): merry-go-round
4 *history* a tournament in which horsemen took part in
races and various manoeuvres in formation [c17: from
French *carrousel*, from Italian *carosello*, of uncertain
origin]

carp¹ (kɑːp) *n*, *pl* **carp** *or* **carps** **1** a freshwater teleost food
fish, *Cyprinus carpio*, having a body covered with cycloid
scales, a naked head, one long dorsal fin, and two
barbels on each side of the mouth: family *Cyprinidae*
2 any other fish of the family *Cyprinidae*; a cyprinid [c14:
from Old French *carpe*, of Germanic origin; compare Old
High German *karpfo*, Old Norse *karfi*]

carp² (kɑːp) *vb* (*intr*; often foll by *at*) to complain or find
fault; nag pettily [c13: from Old Norse *karpa* to boast;
related to Latin *carpere* to pluck] ▷ **'carper** *n* ▷ **'carping** *adj*
▷ **'carpingly** *adv*

-carp *n combining form* (in botany) fruit or a reproductive
structure that develops into a particular part of the fruit
[from New Latin *-carpium*, from Greek *-karpion*, from *karpos*
fruit]

carpaccio (ˌkɑːˈpætʃɪəʊ; *Italian* karˈpattʃo) *n*, *pl* **-os** an
Italian dish of thin slices of raw meat or fish [possibly
after the Italian painter Vittore Carpaccio (?1460–?1525)]

Carpaccio (ˌkɑːˈpætʃɪəʊ, -tʃəʊ; *Italian* karˈpattʃo) *n* **Vittore**
(vitˈtoːre). ?1460–?1525, Italian painter of the Venetian
school

carpal (ˈkɑːpᵊl) *n* **a** any bone of the wrist **b** (*as modifier*):
carpal bones [c18: from New Latin *carpālis*, from Greek
karpos wrist]

car park *n* an area or building reserved for parking cars.
Usual US and Canadian term: **parking lot**

Carpathian Mountains (kɑːˈpeɪθɪən) *or* **Carpathians** *pl*
n a mountain system of central and E Europe,
extending from Slovakia to central Romania: mainly
forested, with rich iron ore resources. Highest peak:
Gerlachovka, 2663 m (8788 ft)

Carpatho-Ukraine (kɑːˈpeɪθəʊjuːˈkreɪn) *n* another
name for **Ruthenia**

carpe diem Latin (ˈkɑːpɪ ˈdiːɛm) enjoy the pleasures of the
moment, without concern for the future [literally: seize
the day!]

carpel (ˈkɑːpᵊl) *n* the female reproductive organ of
flowering plants, consisting of an ovary, style
(sometimes absent), and stigma. The carpels are
separate or fused to form a single pistil [c19: from New
Latin *carpellum*, from Greek *karpos* fruit] ▷ **'carpellary** *adj*

Carpentaria (ˌkɑːpənˈtɛərɪə) *n* **Gulf of Carpentaria** a
shallow inlet of the Arafura Sea, in N Australia between
Arnhem Land and Cape York Peninsula

carpenter (ˈkɑːpɪntə) *n* **1** a person skilled in woodwork,
esp in buildings, ships, etc ▷ *vb* **2** (*intr*) to do the work of
a carpenter **3** (*tr*) to make or fit together by or as if by
carpentry [c14: from Anglo-French, from Latin
carpentārius wagon-maker, from *carpentum* wagon; of
Celtic origin]

Carpenter (ˈkɑːpɪntə) *n* **John Alden**. 1876–1951, US
composer, who used jazz rhythms in orchestral music:
his works include the ballet *Skyscrapers* (1926) and the
orchestral suite *Adventures in a Perambulator* (1915)

Carpentier (*French* karpɑ̃tje) *n* **Georges** (ʒɔrʒ), known as
Gorgeous Georges. 1894–1975, French boxer: world light-
heavyweight champion (1920–22)

carpentry (ˈkɑːpɪntrɪ) *n* **1** the art or technique of
working wood **2** the work produced by a carpenter;
woodwork

carpet (ˈkɑːpɪt) *n* **1** a heavy fabric for covering floors **2** a
covering like a carpet: *a carpet of leaves* **3** on the carpet
informal **a** before authority to be reproved for misconduct
or error **b** under consideration ▷ *vb* **-pets**, **-peting**,
-peted (*tr*) **4** to cover with or as if with a carpet **5** *informal*
to reprimand [c14: from Old French *carpite*, from Old
Italian *carpeta*, from Late Latin *carpeta*, literally: (wool)
that has been carded, from Latin *carpere* to pluck, card]

carpetbag (ˈkɑːpɪtˌbæg) *n* a travelling bag originally
made of carpeting

carpetbagger (ˈkɑːpɪtˌbægə) *n* **1** a politician who seeks
public office in a locality where he has no real
connections **2** *Brit* a person who makes a short-term
investment in a mutual savings or life-assurance

organization in order to benefit from free shares issued
following the organization's conversion to a public
limited company

carpet beetle *or US* **carpet bug** *n* any of various beetles
of the genus *Anthrenus*, the larvae of which feed on
carpets, furnishing fabrics, etc: family *Dermestidae*

carpet bombing *n* systematic intensive bombing of an
area

carpeting (ˈkɑːpɪtɪŋ) *n* carpet material or carpets in
general

carpet slipper *n* one of a pair of slippers, originally one
made with woollen uppers resembling carpeting

carpet snake *or* **carpet python** *n* a large nonvenomous
Australian snake, *Morelia variegata*, having a carpetlike
pattern on its back

carpet-sweeper *n* a household device with a revolving
brush for sweeping carpets

car phone *n* a telephone that operates by cellular radio
for use in a car

carpo- *combining form* (in botany) indicating fruit or a
reproductive structure that develops into part of the
fruit [from Greek *karpos* fruit]

carpool (ˈkɑːˌpuːl) *vb*, *n* another term for **carshare**
▷ **'car,pooling** *n*

carport (ˈkɑːˌpɔːt) *n* a shelter for a car usually consisting
of a roof built out from the side of a building and
supported by posts

-carpous *or* **-carpic** *adj combining form* (in botany)
indicating a certain kind or number of fruit: *apocarpous*
[from New Latin *-carpus*, from Greek *karpos* fruit]

carpus (ˈkɑːpəs) *n*, *pl* **-pi** (-paɪ) **1** the technical name for
wrist 2 the eight small bones of the human wrist that
form the joint between the arm and the hand [c17: New
Latin, from Greek *karpos*]

carr (kɑː) *n Brit* an area of bog or fen in which scrub, esp
willow, has become established [c15: from Old Norse]

Carracci (kəˈrɑːtʃɪ; *Italian* karˈrattʃi) *n* a family of Italian
painters, born in Bologna: **Agostino** (agosˈtiːno)
(1557–1602); his brother, **Annibale** (anˈniːbale)
(1560–1609), noted for his frescoes, esp in the Palazzo
Farnese, Rome; and their cousin, **Ludovico** (ludoˈviːko)
(1555–1619). They were influential in reviving the
classical tradition of the Renaissance and founded a
teaching academy (1582) in Bologna

carrack (ˈkærək) *n* a galleon sailed in the Mediterranean
as a merchantman in the 15th and 16th centuries [c14:
from Old French *caraque*, from Old Spanish *carraca*, from
Arabic *qarāqīr* merchant ships]

carrageen, carragheen *or* **carageen** (ˈkærəˌgiːn) *n* an
edible red seaweed, *Chondrus crispus*, of North America
and N Europe [c19: from *Carragheen*, near Waterford,
Ireland, where it is plentiful]

carrageenan, carragheenan *or* **carageenan**
(ˌkærəˈgiːnən) *n* a carbohydrate extracted from
carrageen, used to make a beverage, medicine, and jelly,
and as an emulsifying and gelling agent (**E407**) in
various processed desserts and drinks

Carrara (kəˈrɑːrə; *Italian* karˈraːra) *n* a town in NW Italy,
in NW Tuscany: famous for its marble. Pop: 65 034 (2001)

carrel *or* **carrell** (ˈkærəl) *n* a small individual study room
or private desk, often in a library, where a student or
researcher can work undisturbed [c16: a variant of
CAROL]

Carrel (kəˈrɛl, ˈkærəl; *French* karɛl) *n* **Alexis** (əˈlɛksɪs; *French*
aleksi). 1873–1944, French surgeon and biologist, active
in the US (1905–39): developed a method of suturing
blood vessels, making the transplantation of arteries
and organs possible: Nobel prize for physiology or
medicine 1912

Carreras (kəˈrɛərəs) *n* **José** (həʊsˈzeɪ). born 1947, Spanish
tenor

Carrey (ˈkærɪ) *n* **Jim**. born 1962, Canadian-born
Hollywood actor noted for his comedy roles; films
include *Ace Ventura, Pet Detective* (1994), *Liar Liar* (1997), *The
Truman Show* (1998), and *The Majestic* (2001)

carriage (ˈkærɪdʒ) *n* **1** *Brit* a railway coach for passengers
2 the manner in which a person holds and moves his
head and body; bearing **3** a four-wheeled horse-drawn
vehicle for persons **4** the moving part of a machine that

bears another part: *a typewriter carriage; a lathe carriage* **5** ('kærɪdʒ, 'kærɪɪdʒ) **a** the act of conveying; carrying **b** the charge made for conveying (esp in the phrases **carriage forward,** when the charge is to be paid by the receiver, and **carriage paid**) [C14: from Old Northern French *cariage,* from *carier* to CARRY]

carriage clock *n* a portable clock, usually in a rectangular case with a handle on the top, of a type originally used by travellers

carriage trade *n* trade from the wealthy part of society

carriageway ('kærɪdʒ,weɪ) *n Brit* the part of a road along which traffic passes in a single line moving in one direction only: *a dual carriageway*

Carrickfergus (,kærɪk'fɜ:gəs) *n* **1** a town in E Northern Ireland, in Carrickfergus district, Co Antrim; historic settlement of Scottish Protestants on Belfast Lough; Norman castle. Pop: 27 201 (2001) **2** a district of E Northern Ireland, in Co Antrim. Pop: 37 659 (2001). Area: 83 sq km (32 sq miles)

carrier ('kærɪə) *n* **1** a person, thing, or organization employed to carry goods, passengers, etc **2** a mechanism by which something is carried or moved, such as a device for transmitting rotation from the faceplate of a lathe to the workpiece **3** *pathol* another name for **vector** (sense 3) **4** *pathol* a person or animal that, without having any symptoms of a disease, is capable of transmitting it to others **5** Also called: **charge carrier** *physics* an electron, ion, or hole that carries the charge in a conductor or semiconductor **6** short for **carrier wave** **7** *chem* **a** the inert solid on which a dyestuff is adsorbed in forming a lake **b** a substance, such as kieselguhr or asbestos, used to support a catalyst **8** See **aircraft carrier**

Carrier ('kærɪə) *n* a member of an Athapaskan Native North American people of British Columbia

carrier bag *n Brit* a large paper or plastic bag for carrying shopping

carrier pigeon *n* any homing pigeon, esp one used for carrying messages

carrier wave *n radio* a wave of fixed amplitude and frequency that is modulated in amplitude, frequency, or phase in order to carry a signal in radio transmission, etc

Carrington ('kærɪŋtən) *n* **1 Dora,** known as *Carrington.* 1893–1932, British painter, engraver, and letter writer; a member of the Bloomsbury Group **2 Peter (Alexander Rupert),** 6th Baron. born 1919, British Conservative politician: secretary of state for defence (1970–74); foreign secretary (1979–82); secretary general of NATO (1984–88)

carriole ('kærɪ,əʊl) *n* a variant spelling of **cariole**

carrion ('kærɪən) *n* **1** dead and rotting flesh **2** (*modifier*) eating carrion **3** something rotten or repulsive [C13: from Anglo-French *caroine,* ultimately from Latin *carō* flesh]

carrion crow *n* a common predatory and scavenging European crow, *Corvus corone,* similar to the rook but having a pure black bill

Carroll ('kærəl) *n* **Lewis.** real name *the Reverend Charles Lutwidge Dodgson.* 1832–98, English writer; an Oxford mathematics don who wrote *Alice's Adventures in Wonderland* (1865) and *Through the Looking-Glass* (1872) and the nonsense poem *The Hunting of the Snark* (1876)

carrot ('kærət) *n* **1** an umbelliferous plant, *Daucus carota sativa,* with finely divided leaves and flat clusters of small white flowers **2** the long tapering orange root of this plant, eaten as a vegetable **3 a** something offered as a lure or incentive **b** carrot and stick reward and punishment as methods of persuasion [C16: from Old French *carotte,* from Late Latin *carōta,* from Greek *karōton;* perhaps related to Greek *karē* head]

carroty ('kærətɪ) *adj* **1** of a reddish or yellowish-orange colour **2** having red hair

carrousel (,kærə'sɛl, -'zɛl) *n* a variant spelling of **carousel**

carry ('kærɪ) *vb* -ries, -rying, -ried (*mainly tr*) **1** (*also intr*) to take or bear (something) from one place to another **2** to transfer for consideration; take: *he carried his complaints to her superior* **3** to have on one's person: *he always carries a watch* **4** (*also intr*) to be transmitted or serve as a medium

for transmitting: *sound carries best over water* **5** to bear or be able to bear the weight, pressure, or responsibility of: *her efforts carry the whole production* **6** to have as an attribute or result: *this crime carries a heavy penalty* **7** to bring or communicate: *to carry news* **8** (*also intr*) to be pregnant with (young) **9** to bear (the head, body, etc) in a specified manner: *she carried her head high* **10** to conduct or bear (oneself) in a specified manner: *she carried herself well in a difficult situation* **11** to continue or extend: *the war was carried into enemy territory* **12** to cause to move or go: *desire for riches carried him to the city* **13** to influence, esp by emotional appeal: *his words carried the crowd* **14** to secure the passage of (a bill, motion, etc) **15** to win (an election) **16** to obtain victory for (a candidate or measure) in an election **17** *chiefly US* to win a plurality or majority of votes in (a district, legislative body, etc): *the candidate carried 40 states* **18** to capture: *our troops carried the town* **19** (of communications media) to include as the content: *this newspaper carries no book reviews* **20** *book-keeping* to transfer (an item) to another account, esp to transfer to the following year's account instead of writing off against profit and loss. Also (esp US): carry over: *to carry a loss* **21** *maths* to transfer (a number) from one column of figures to the next, as from units to tens in multiplication and addition **22** (of a shop, trader, etc) to keep in stock: *to carry confectionery* **23** to support (a musical part or melody) against the other parts **24** (*intr*) (of a ball, projectile, etc) to travel through the air or reach a specified point: *his first drive carried to the green* **25** *informal* to imbibe (alcoholic drink) without showing ill effects **26** (*intr*) *slang* to have drugs on one's person **27** carry all before one to win unanimous support or approval for oneself **28** carry the can *informal* to take the responsibility for some misdemeanour, etc (on behalf of) **29** carry the day to win a contest or competition; succeed ▷ *n, pl* -ries **30** the act of carrying **31** *US & Canadian* a portion of land over which a boat must be portaged **32** the range of a firearm or its projectile **33** the distance travelled by a ball, etc, esp (in golf) the distance from where the ball is struck to where it first touches the ground ▷ See also **carry away, carry forward,** etc [C14 *carien,* from Old Northern French *carier* to move by vehicle, from *car,* from Latin *carrum* transport wagon; see CAR]

carryall ('kærɪ,ɔːl) *n US & Canadian* a large strong bag with handles. Also called (in Britain and certain other countries): holdall

carry away *vb* (*tr, adverb*) **1** to remove forcefully **2** (*usually passive*) to cause (a person) to lose self-control **3** (*usually passive*) to delight or enrapture: *he was carried away by the music*

carrycot ('kærɪ,kɒt) *n* a light cot with handles, similar to but smaller than the body of a pram and often attachable to an unsprung wheeled frame

carry forward *vb* (*tr, adverb*) **1** *book-keeping* to transfer (a balance) to the next page, column, etc **2** Also called: carry over *tax accounting* to apply (a legally permitted credit, esp an operating loss) to the taxable income of following years to ease the overall tax burden

carrying-on *n, pl* carryings-on *informal* **1** unconventional or questionable behaviour **2** excited or flirtatious behaviour, esp when regarded as foolish

carry off *vb* (*tr, adverb*) **1** to remove forcefully **2** to win **3** to manage or handle (a situation) successfully: *he carried off the introductions well* **4** to cause to die: *he was carried off by pneumonia*

carry on *vb* (*adverb*) **1** (*intr*) to continue or persevere **2** (*tr*) to manage or conduct: *to carry on a business* **3** (*intr;* often foll by *with*) *informal* to have an affair **4** (*intr*) *informal* to cause a fuss or commotion ▷ *n* carry-on **5** *informal, chiefly Brit* a fuss or commotion ▷ *adj* carry-on **6** (of luggage) to be taken inside an aircraft by hand personally by a passenger

carry out *vb* (*tr, adverb*) **1** to perform or cause to be implemented: *I wish he could afford to carry out his plan* **2** to bring to completion; accomplish ▷ *n* carry-out *chiefly Scot* **3** alcohol bought at a pub or off-licence for consumption elsewhere **4 a** hot cooked food bought at a shop or restaurant for consumption elsewhere **b** a shop or restaurant that sells such food **c** (*as modifier*): *a carry-out shop*

carry over *vb* (*tr, adverb*) **1** to postpone or defer **2** *book-keeping, tax accounting* another term for **carry forward** ▷ *n* **carry-over 3** something left over for future use, esp goods to be sold **4** *book-keeping* a sum or balance carried forward

carry through *vb* (*tr, adverb*) **1** to bring to completion **2** to enable to endure (hardship, trouble, etc); support

carse (kɑːs; *Scot* kærs) *n Scot* a riverside area of flat fertile alluvium [c14: of uncertain origin; perhaps from a plural form of CARR]

carshare ('kɑː,ʃeə) *vb* **1** (*intr*) to take turns in driving fellow commuters to and from work or friends' children to school and back, so as to avoid the unnecessary use of several underoccupied vehicles ▷ *n* **2** a group of people who carshare together ▷ '**car,sharing** *n*

carsick ('kɑː,sɪk) *adj* nauseated from riding in a car or other vehicle ▷ '**car,sickness** *n*

Carson ('kɑːs³n) *n* **1 Christopher**, known as *Kit Carson*. 1809–68, US frontiersman, trapper, scout, and Indian agent **2 Edward Henry**, Baron. 1854–1935, Anglo-Irish politician and lawyer; led northern Irish resistance to the British government's plan for home rule for Ireland **3 Rachel** (**Louise**). 1907–64, US marine biologist and science writer; author of *Silent Spring* (1962) **4 Willie**, full name *William Hunter Fisher Carson*. born 1942, Scottish jockey; retired in 1997

Carson City ('kɑːs³n) *n* a city in W Nevada, capital of the state. Pop: 55 311 (2003 est)

Carstensz ('kɑːstənz) *n* **Mount Carstensz** a former name of Mount Jaya

cart (kɑːt) *n* **1** a heavy open vehicle, usually having two wheels and drawn by horses, used in farming and to transport goods **2** a light open horse-drawn vehicle having two wheels and springs, for business or pleasure **3** any small vehicle drawn or pushed by hand, such as a trolley **4 put the cart before the horse** to reverse the usual or natural order of things ▷ *vb* **5** (*usually tr*) to use or draw a cart to convey (goods, etc) **6** (*tr*) to carry with effort; haul: *to cart wood home* [c13: from Old Norse *kartr*; related to Old English *cræt* carriage, Old French *carete*; see CAR] ▷ '**carter** *n*

cartage ('kɑːtɪdʒ) *n* the process or cost of carting

Cartagena (,kɑːtə'dʒiːnə; *Spanish* karta'xena) *n* **1** a port in NW Colombia, on the Caribbean: centre for the Inquisition and the slave trade in the 16th century; chief oil port of Colombia. Pop: 1 002 000 (2005 est) **2** a port in SE Spain, on the Mediterranean: important since Carthaginian and Roman times for its minerals. Pop: 194 203 (2003 est)

Carte (kɑːt) *n* See **D'Oyly Carte**

carte blanche ('kɑːt 'blɑːntʃ; *French* kart blɑ̃ʃ) *n*, *pl* **cartes blanches** ('kɑːts 'blɑːntʃ; *French* kart blɑ̃ʃ) complete discretion or authority: *the government gave their negotiator carte blanche* [c18: from French: blank paper]

cartel (kɑː'tel) *n* **1** Also called: **trust** a collusive international association of independent enterprises formed to monopolize production and distribution of a product or service, control prices, etc **2** *politics* an alliance of parties or interests to further common aims [c20: from German *Kartell*, from French, from Italian *cartello* a written challenge, public notice, diminutive of *carta* CARD¹]

Carter ('kɑːtə) *n* **1 Angela**. 1940–92, British novelist and writer; her novels include *The Magic Toyshop* (1967) and *Nights at the Circus* (1984) **2 Elliot** (**Cook**). born 1908, US composer. His works include the *Piano Sonata* (1945–46), four string quartets, and other orchestral pieces; Pulitzer Prize 1960, 1973 **3 Howard**. 1873–1939, English Egyptologist: excavated the tomb of the Pharaoh Tutankhamen **4 James Earl**, known as *Jimmy*. born 1924, US Democratic statesman; 39th president of the US (1977–81); Nobel peace prize 2002

Carteret ('kɑːtərɪt) *n* **John**, 1st Earl Granville. 1690–1763, British statesman, diplomat, and orator who led the opposition to Walpole (1730–42), after whose fall he became a leading minister as secretary of state (1742–44)

Cartesian (kɑː'tiːzɪən, -ʒən) *adj* **1** of or relating to the

works of René Descartes (1596–1650), the French philosopher and mathematician **2** of, relating to, or used in Descartes' mathematical system ▷ Car'tesian,ism *n*

Cartesian coordinates *pl n* a system of representing points in space in terms of their distance from a given origin measured along a set of mutually perpendicular axes. Written (x,y,z) with reference to three axes

Carthage ('kɑːθɪdʒ) *n* an ancient city state, on the N African coast near present-day Tunis. Founded about 800 BC by Phoenician traders, it grew into an empire dominating N Africa and the Mediterranean. Destroyed and then rebuilt by Rome, it was finally razed by the Arabs in 697 AD

Carthaginian (,kɑːθə'dʒɪnɪən) *adj* **1** of or relating to Carthage (an ancient N African city state) or its inhabitants ▷ *n* **2** a native or inhabitant of Carthage

carthorse ('kɑːt,hɔːs) *n* a large heavily built horse kept for pulling carts or carriages

Carthusian (kɑː'θjuːzɪən) *n RC Church* **a** a member of an austere monastic order founded by Saint Bruno in 1084 near Grenoble, France **b** (*as modifier*): *a Carthusian monastery* [c14: from Medieval Latin *Carthusianus*, from Latin *Carthusia* Chartreuse, near Grenoble]

Cartier (*French* kartje) *n* **Jacques** (ʒak). 1491–1557, French navigator and explorer in Canada, who discovered the St Lawrence River (1535)

Cartier-Bresson (*French* kartjebrɛsɔ̃) *n* **Henri** (ɑ̃ri). 1908–2004, French photographer

cartilage ('kɑːtɪlɪdʒ, 'kɑːtlɪdʒ) *n* a tough elastic tissue composing most of the embryonic skeleton of vertebrates. In the adults of higher vertebrates it is mostly converted into bone, remaining only on the articulating ends of bones, in the thorax, trachea, nose, and ears. Nontechnical name: **gristle** [c16: from Latin *cartilāgō*] ▷ cartilaginous (,kɑːtɪ'lædʒɪnəs) *adj*

cartilaginous fish *n* any fish of the class *Chondrichthyes*, including the sharks, skates, and rays, having a skeleton composed entirely of cartilage

Cartland ('kɑːtlənd) *n* Dame **Barbara** (**Hamilton**). 1901–2000, British novelist, noted for her prolific output of popular romantic fiction

cartload ('kɑːt,ləʊd) *n* the amount a cart can hold

cart off, **cart away** or **cart out** *vb* (*tr, adverb*) *informal* to carry or remove brusquely or by force

cartogram ('kɑːtə,græm) *n* a map showing statistical information in diagrammatic form [c20: from French *cartogramme*, from *carte* map, CHART; see -GRAM]

cartography or **chartography** (kɑː'tɒgrəfɪ) *n* the art, technique, or practice of compiling or drawing maps or charts [c19: from French *cartographie*, from *carte* map, CHART] ▷ car'tographer or char'tographer *n* ▷ cartographic (,kɑːtə'græfɪk), ,carto'graphical, ,charto'graphic or ,charto'graphical *adj*

carton ('kɑːt³n) *n* **1** a cardboard box for containing goods **2** a container of waxed paper or plastic in which liquids, such as milk, are sold [c19: from French, from Italian *cartone* pasteboard, from *carta* CARD¹]

cartoon (kɑː'tuːn) *n* **1** a humorous or satirical drawing, esp one in a newspaper or magazine, concerning a topical event **2** Also called: **comic strip** a sequence of drawings in a newspaper, magazine, etc, relating a comic or adventurous situation **3** See **animated cartoon 4** a full-size preparatory sketch for a fresco, tapestry, mosaic, etc, from which the final work is traced or copied [c17: from Italian *cartone* pasteboard, sketch on stiff paper; see CARTON] ▷ car'toonist *n*

cartouche or **cartouch** (kɑː'tuːʃ) *n* **1** a carved or cast ornamental tablet or panel in the form of a scroll, sometimes having an inscription **2** an oblong figure enclosing characters expressing royal or divine names in Egyptian hieroglyphics [c17: from French: scroll, cartridge, from Italian *cartoccio*, from *carta* paper; see CARD¹]

cartridge ('kɑːtrɪdʒ) *n* **1** a cylindrical, usually metal casing containing an explosive charge and often a bullet, for a rifle or other small arms **2** an electromechanical transducer in the pick-up of a record player, usually either containing a piezoelectric crystal

(**crystal cartridge**) or an electromagnet (**magnetic cartridge**) **3** a container for magnetic tape that is inserted into a tape deck in audio or video systems. It is about four times the size of a cassette **4** *computing* a removable unit in a computer, such as an integrated circuit, containing software [c16: from earlier *cartage*, variant of CARTOUCHE (cartridge)]

cartridge belt *n* a belt with pockets for cartridge clips or loops for cartridges

cartridge clip *n* a metallic container holding cartridges for an automatic firearm

cartridge paper *n* **1** an uncoated type of drawing or printing paper, usually made from bleached sulphate wood pulp with an addition of esparto grass **2** a heavy paper used in making cartridges or as drawing or printing paper

cartwheel ('kɑːt,wiːl) *n* **1** the wheel of a cart, usually having wooden spokes and metal tyres **2** an acrobatic movement in which the body makes a sideways revolution on the hands with arms and legs outstretched

Cartwright ('kɑːt,raɪt) *n* **1 Edmund.** 1743–1823, British clergyman, who invented the power loom **2 Dame Silvia** (née **Poulter**). born 1943, New Zealand lawyer. She became a High Court judge in 1993; governor general of New Zealand (2001–06)

caruncle ('kærəŋkəl, kə'rʌŋ-) *n* **1** a fleshy outgrowth on the heads of certain birds, such as a cock's comb **2** an outgrowth near the hilum on the seeds of some plants [c17: from obsolete French *caruncule*, from Latin *caruncula* a small piece of flesh, from *carō* flesh] > **caruncular** (kə'rʌŋkjulə) *or* **ca'runculous** *adj*

Caruso (*Italian* kaˈruːso) *n* **Enrico** (enˈriːko). 1873–1921, an outstanding Italian operatic tenor; one of the first to make gramophone records

carve (kɑːv) *vb* **1** (*tr*) to cut or chip in order to form something: *to carve wood* **2** to decorate or form (something) by cutting or chipping: *to carve statues* **3** to slice (meat) into pieces ▷ See also **carve out, carve up** [Old English *ceorfan*; related to Old Frisian *kerva*, Middle High German *kerben* to notch]

carvel ('kɑːvəl) *n* another word for **caravel**

carvel-built *adj* (of a vessel) having a hull with planks made flush at the seams. Compare **clinker-built**

carven ('kɑːvən) *vb* an archaic or literary past participle of **carve**

carve out *vb* (*tr, adverb*) to make or create (a career): *he carved out his own future*

carver ('kɑːvə) *n* **1** a carving knife **2** (*plural*) a large matched knife and fork for carving meat **3** *Brit* a chair having arms that forms part of a set of dining chairs

Carver ('kɑːvə) *n* **George Washington.** ?1864–1943, US agricultural chemist and botanist

carvery ('kɑːvəri) *n, pl* -veries an eating establishment at which customers pay a set price and may then have unrestricted helpings of food from a variety of meats, salads, and other vegetables

carve up *vb* (*tr, adverb*) **1** to cut (something) into pieces **2** to divide or dismember (a country, land, etc) ▷ *n* carve-up **3** *informal* an act or instance of dishonestly prearranging the result of a competition **4** *slang* the distribution of something, as of booty

carving ('kɑːvɪŋ) *n* a figure or design produced by carving stone, wood, etc

carving knife *n* a long-bladed knife for carving cooked meat for serving

Cary ('kɛəri, 'kæri) *n* (**Arthur**) **Joyce** (Lunel). 1888–1957, British novelist; author of *Mister Johnson* (1939), *A House of Children* (1941), and *The Horse's Mouth* (1944)

caryatid (,kærɪˈætɪd) *n, pl* -ids *or* -ides (-ˌiːdiːz) a column, used to support an entablature, in the form of a draped female figure [c16: from Latin *Caryātides*, from Greek *Karuatides* priestesses of Artemis at *Karuai* (Caryae), village in Laconia]

CAS *abbreviation* (in Canada) Children's Aid Society

Casablanca (,kæsəˈblæŋkə) *n* a port in NW Morocco, on the Atlantic: largest city in the country; industrial centre. Pop: 3 523 000 (2003)

Casals (*Spanish* kaˈsals) *n* **Pablo** ('paβlo). 1876–1973,

Spanish cellist and composer, noted for his interpretation of J. S. Bach's cello suites

Casanova (,kæsəˈnəʊvə) *n* **1 Giovanni Jacopo** (dʒoˈvanni 'jaːkopo). 1725–98, Italian adventurer noted for his *Mémoires*, a vivid account of his sexual adventures and of contemporary society **2** any man noted for his amorous adventures; a rake

Casaubon (kəˈsɔːbᵊn; *French* kazobɔ̃) *n* **Isaac** (izaak). 1559–1614, French Protestant theologian and classical scholar

casbah ('kæzbɑː) *n* (*sometimes capital*) a variant spelling of **kasbah**

cascade (kæsˈkeɪd) *n* **1** a waterfall or series of waterfalls over rocks **2** something resembling this, such as folds of lace **3** a consecutive sequence of chemical or physical processes **4** a series of stages in the processing chain of an electrical signal where each operates the next in turn ▷ *vb* **5** (*intr*) to flow or fall in or like a cascade [c17: from French, from Italian *cascata*, from *cascare* to fall, ultimately from Latin *cadere* to fall]

Cascade Range *n* a chain of mountains in the US and Canada: a continuation of the Sierra Nevada range from N California through Oregon and Washington to British Columbia. Highest peak: Mount Rainier, 4392 m (14 408 ft)

cascading style sheet *n* *computing* a file recording style details, such as fonts, colours, etc, that is read by browsers so that style is consistent over multiple web pages. Abbreviation: CSS

cascara (kæsˈkɑːrə) *n* **1** See **cascara sagrada** **2** Also called: cascara buckthorn, bearwood a shrub or small tree, *Rhamnus purshiana* of NW North America, whose bark is a source of cascara sagrada: family *Rhamnaceae* [c19: from Spanish: bark, from *cascar* to break, from Vulgar Latin *quassicāre* (unattested) to shake violently, shatter, from Latin *quassāre* to dash to pieces]

cascara sagrada (səˈɡrɑːdə) *n* the dried bark of the cascara buckthorn, used as a stimulant and laxative. Often shortened to cascara [Spanish, literally: sacred bark]

case¹ (keɪs) *n* **1** a single instance, occurrence, or example of something **2** an instance of disease, injury, hardship, etc **3** a question or matter for discussion: *the case before the committee* **4** a specific condition or state of affairs; situation **5** a set of arguments supporting a particular action, cause, etc **6 a** a person attended or served by a doctor, social worker, solicitor, etc; patient or client **b** (*as modifier*): *a case study* **7 a** an action or suit at law or something that forms sufficient grounds for bringing an action: *he has a good case* **b** the evidence offered in court to support a claim **8** *grammar* **a** a set of grammatical categories of nouns, pronouns, and adjectives, marked by inflection in some languages, indicating the relation of the noun, adjective, or pronoun to other words in the sentence **b** any one of these categories: *the nominative case* **9** *informal* an odd person; eccentric **10** in any case (*adverb*) no matter what; anyhow **11** in case (*adverb*) **a** in order to allow for eventualities **b** (*as conjunction*) in order to allow for the possibility that: *take your coat in case it rains* **12** in case of (*preposition*) in the event of **13** in no case (*adverb*) under no circumstances: *in no case should you fight back* [Old English *casus* (grammatical) case, associated also with Old French *cas* a happening; both from Latin *cāsus*, a befalling, occurrence, from *cadere* to fall]

case² (keɪs) *n* **1 a** a container, such as a box or chest **b** (*in combination*): *suitcase; briefcase* **2** an outer cover or sheath, esp for a watch **3** a receptacle and its contents: *a case of ammunition* **4** *architect* another word for **casing** (sense 3) **5** a completed cover ready to be fastened to a book to form its binding **6** *printing* a tray divided into many compartments in which a compositor keeps individual metal types of a particular size and style. Cases were originally used in pairs, one (the upper case) for capitals, the other (the lower case) for small letters. See also **upper case, lower case** ▷ *vb* (*tr*) **7** to put into or cover with a case **8** *slang* to inspect carefully (esp a place to be robbed) [c13: from Old French *casse*, from Latin *capsa*, from *capere* to take, hold]

casebook ('keɪsˌbʊk) n a book in which records of legal or medical cases are kept

case-harden vb (tr) 1 metallurgy to form a hard surface layer of high carbon content on (a steel component) by heating in a carburizing environment with subsequent quenching or heat treatment 2 to harden the spirit or disposition of; make callous: experience had case-hardened the judge

case history n a record of a person's background, medical history, etc, esp one used for determining medical treatment

casein ('keɪsiɪn, -siːn) n a phosphoprotein, precipitated from milk by the action of rennin, forming the basis of cheese: used in the manufacture of plastics and adhesives [c19: from Latin cāseus cheese + -IN]

case law n law established by following judicial decisions given in earlier cases. Compare **statute law**

caseload ('keɪsˌləʊd) n the number of cases constituting the work of a doctor, solicitor, social worker, etc over a specified period

casemate ('keɪsˌmeɪt) n an armoured compartment in a ship or fortification in which guns are mounted [c16: from French, from Italian casamatta, perhaps from Greek khasmata apertures, plural of khasma CHASM]

casement ('keɪsmənt) n 1 a window frame that is hinged on one side 2 a window containing frames hinged at the side or at the top or bottom 3 a poetic word for **window** [c15: probably from Old Northern French encassement frame, from encasser to frame, encase, from casse framework, crate, CASE²]

Casement ('keɪsmənt) n Sir **Roger** (**David**). 1864–1916, British diplomat and Irish nationalist: hanged by the British for treason in attempting to gain German support for Irish independence

caseous ('keɪsɪəs) adj of or like cheese [c17: from Latin cāseus CHEESE]

casern or **caserne** (kə'zɜːn) n (formerly) a billet or accommodation for soldiers in a town [c17: from French caserne, from Old Provençal cazerna group of four men, ultimately from Latin quattuor four]

Caserta (Italian ka'zɛrta) n a town in S Italy, in Campania: centre of Garibaldi's campaigns for the unification of Italy (1860); Allied headquarters in World War II. Pop: 75 208 (2001)

case-sensitive adj distinguishing between upper-case and lower-case letters: users can now perform case-sensitive searches

casework ('keɪsˌwɜːk) n social work based on close study of the personal histories and circumstances of individuals and families > 'case,worker n

cash¹ (kæʃ) n 1 banknotes and coins, esp in hand or readily available; money or ready money 2 immediate payment, in full or part, for goods or services (esp in the phrase **cash down**) 3 (modifier) of, for, or paid by cash: a cash transaction ▷ vb 4 (tr) to obtain or pay ready money for ▷ See also **cash in**, **cash up** [c16: from Old Italian cassa money box, from Latin capsa CASE²] > 'cashable adj

cash² (kæʃ) n, pl **cash** any of various Chinese, Indonesian, or Indian coins of low value [c16: from Portuguese caixa, from Tamil kāsu, from Sanskrit karsa weight of gold or silver]

Cash (kæʃ) n **Johnny**. 1932–2003, US country-and-western singer, guitarist, and songwriter. His recordings include the hits "I Walk the Line" (1956), "Ring of Fire" (1963), "A Boy named Sue" (1969), and the American Recordings series of albums (1994–2003)

cash-and-carry adj, adv 1 sold or operated on a basis of cash payment for merchandise that is not delivered but removed by the purchaser ▷ n 2 a wholesale store, esp for groceries, that operates on this basis 3 an operation on a commodities futures market in which spot goods are purchased and sold at a profit on a futures contract

cashback ('kæʃˌbæk) n 1 a a discount offered in return for immediate payment b (as modifier): cashback price £519.99 — save £30! 2 a service provided by some supermarkets in which customers paying by debit card can draw cash b the cash so drawn

cash-book n book-keeping a journal in which all cash or cheque receipts and disbursements are recorded

cash card n an embossed plastic card bearing the name and account details of a bank or building-society customer, used with a personal identification number to obtain money from a cash dispenser: may also function as a cheque card or debit card or both. Also called: **cash-point card**

cash cow n a product, acquisition, etc, that produces a steady flow of cash, esp one with a well-known brand name commanding a high market share

cash crop n a crop grown for sale rather than for subsistence

cash desk n a counter or till in a shop where purchases are paid for

cash discount n a discount granted to a purchaser who pays before a stipulated date

cash dispenser n a computerized device outside a bank that supplies cash or account information when the user inserts his cash card and keys in his identification number. Also called: **automated teller machine**

cashew ('kæʃuː, kæ'ʃuː) n 1 a tropical American anacardiaceous evergreen tree, Anacardium occidentale, bearing kidney-shaped nuts that protrude from a fleshy receptacle 2 Also called: **cashew nut** the edible nut of this tree [c18: from Portuguese cajú, from Tupi acajú]

cash flow n 1 the movement of money into and out of a business 2 a prediction of such movement over a given period

cashier¹ (kæ'ʃɪə) n 1 a person responsible for receiving payments for goods, services, etc, as in a shop 2 Also called: **teller** an employee of a bank responsible for receiving deposits, cashing cheques, and other financial transactions; bank clerk 3 any person responsible for handling cash or maintaining records of its receipt and disbursement [c16: from Dutch cassier or French caissier, from casse money chest; see CASE²]

cashier² (kæ'ʃɪə) vb (tr) to dismiss with dishonour, esp from the armed forces [c16: from Middle Dutch kasseren, from Old French casser, from Latin quassāre to QUASH]

cash in vb (adverb) 1 (tr) to give (something) in exchange, esp for money 2 (intr; often foll by on) informal a to profit (from) b to take advantage (of)

cashmere or **kashmir** ('kæʃmɪə) n 1 a fine soft wool from goats of the Kashmir area 2 a cloth or knitted material made from this or similar wool b (as modifier): a cashmere sweater

Cashmere (kæʃ'mɪə) n a variant spelling of **Kashmir**

cash on delivery n a service entailing cash payment to the carrier on delivery of merchandise. Abbreviation: **COD**

cashpoint ('kæʃˌpɔɪnt) n a cash dispenser

cash register n a till with a keyboard that operates a mechanism for displaying and adding the amounts of cash received in individual sales

cash-strapped adj short of money; impoverished: cash-strapped local authorities

cash up vb (intr, adverb) Brit (of cashiers, shopkeepers, etc) to add up the money taken, esp at the end of a day

Casimir III ('kæzɪmɪə) n known as the Great. 1310–70, king of Poland (1333–70)

Casimir IV n 1427–92, grand duke of Lithuania (1440–92) and king of Poland (1447–92)

casing ('keɪsɪŋ) n 1 a protective case or cover 2 material for a case or cover 3 Also called: **case** a frame containing a door, window, or staircase

casino (kə'siːnəʊ) n, pl -nos 1 a public building or room in which gaming takes place, esp roulette and card games such as baccarat and chemin de fer 2 a variant spelling of **cassino** [c18: from Italian, diminutive of casa house, from Latin]

cask (kɑːsk) n 1 a strong wooden barrel used mainly to hold alcoholic drink: a wine cask 2 any barrel 3 the quantity contained in a cask 4 Austral a lightweight cardboard container with plastic lining and a small tap, used to hold and serve wine [c15: from Spanish casco helmet, perhaps from cascar to break]

casket ('kɑːskɪt) n 1 a small box or chest for valuables, esp jewels 2 chiefly US another name for **coffin** (sense 1) [c15: probably from Old French cassette little box; see CASE²]

C

Caspar ('kæspə, 'kæspɑː) *or* **Gaspar** *n* (in Christian tradition) one of the Magi, the other two being Melchior and Balthazar

Caspian Sea ('kæspɪən) *n* a salt lake between SE Europe and Asia: the largest inland sea in the world; fed mainly by the River Volga. Area: 394 299 sq km (152 239 sq miles)

casque (kæsk) *n zoology* a helmet or a helmet-like process or structure, as on the bill of most hornbills [C17: from French, from Spanish *casco*; see CASK] ▷ **casqued** *adj*

Cassatt (kə'sæt) *n* **Mary.** 1845–1926, US impressionist painter, who lived in France

cassava (kə'sɑːvə) *n* 1 Also called: **manioc** any tropical euphorbiaceous plant of the genus *Manihot*, esp the widely cultivated American species *M. esculenta* (or *utilissima*) (**bitter cassava**) and *M. dulcis* (**sweet cassava**) 2 a starch derived from the root of this plant: an important food in the tropics and a source of tapioca [C16: from Spanish *cazabe* cassava bread, from Taino *caçábi*]

casserole ('kæsə,rəʊl) *n* 1 a covered dish of earthenware, glass, etc, in which food is cooked and served 2 any food cooked and served in such a dish: *chicken casserole* ▷ *vb* 3 to cook or be cooked in a casserole [C18: from French, from Old French *casse* ladle, pan for dripping, from Old Provençal *cassa*, from Late Latin *cattia* dipper, from Greek *kuathion*, diminutive of *kuathos* cup]

cassette (kæ'sɛt) *n* 1 **a** a plastic container for magnetic tape, as one inserted into a tape deck **b** (*as modifier*): *a cassette recorder* 2 the injection of genes from one species into the fertilized egg of another species [C18: from French: little box; see CASE²]

cassia ('kæsɪə) *n* 1 any plant of the mainly tropical leguminous genus *Cassia*, esp *C. fistula*, whose pods yield **cassia pulp**, a mild laxative. See also **senna** 2 a lauraceous tree, *Cinnamomum cassia*, of tropical Asia 3 **cassia bark** the cinnamon-like bark of this tree, used as a spice [Old English, from Latin *casia*, from Greek *kasia*, of Semitic origin; related to Hebrew *qesī'āh* cassia]

cassimere *or* **cassimere** ('kæsɪ,mɪə) *n* a woollen suiting cloth of plain or twill weave [C18: variant of *cashmere*, from KASHMIR]

Cassini (kæ'siːnɪ) *n* **Giovanni Domenico.** 1625–1712, French astronomer, born in Italy. He discovered (1675) **Cassini's division** and four of Saturn's moons

Cassini's division (kæ'siːnɪz) *n* the gap that divides Saturn's rings into two parts, discovered by Giovanni Domenico Cassini (1625–1712) in 1675

cassino *or* **casino** (kə'siːnəʊ) *n* a card game for two to four players in which players pair cards from their hands with others exposed on the table

Cassiodorus (,kæsɪəʊ'dɔːrəs) *n* **Flavius Magnus Aurelius** ('fleɪvɪəs 'mægnəs ɔː'riːlɪəs). ?490–?585 AD, Roman statesman, writer, and monk; author of *Variae*, a collection of official documents written for the Ostrogoths

Cassiopeia¹ (,kæsɪə'piːə) *n* Greek myth the wife of Cepheus and mother of Andromeda

Cassiopeia² (,kæsɪə'piːə) *n, Latin genitive* Cassiopeiae (,kæsɪə'piːiː) a very conspicuous W-shaped constellation near the Pole Star. **Cassiopeia A** is a very strong radio and X-ray source, identified as the remnant of a supernova thought to have occurred in the late 17th century

Cassirer (German ka'siːrər) *n* **Ernst** (ɛrnst). 1874–1945, German neo-Kantian philosopher. *The Philosophy of Symbolic Forms* (1923–29) analyses the symbols that underlie all manifestations, including myths and language, of human culture

cassis (kɑː'siːs) *n* a blackcurrant cordial [C19: from French]

cassiterite (kə'sɪtə,raɪt) *n* a black or brown mineral, found in igneous rocks and hydrothermal veins. It is a source of tin. Composition: tin oxide. Formula: SnO_2. Crystal structure: tetragonal. Also called: **tinstone** [C19: from Greek *kassiteros* tin]

Cassius Longinus ('kæsɪəs lɒn'dʒaɪnəs) *n* **Gaius** ('gaɪəs). died 42 BC, Roman general: led the conspiracy against Julius Caesar (44); defeated at Philippi by Mark Antony (42)

Cassivelaunus (,kæsɪvə'lɔːnəs) *n* 1st century BC, British chieftain, king of the Catuvellauni tribe, who organized resistance to Caesar's invasion of Britain (54 BC)

cassock ('kæsək) *n Christianity* an ankle-length garment, usually black, worn by priests and choristers [C16: from Old French *casaque*, from Italian *casacca* a long coat, of uncertain origin]

Casson ('kæsⁿn) *n* **Sir Hugh** (**Maxwell**). 1910–99, British architect; president of the Royal Academy of Arts (1976–84)

cassowary ('kæsə,wɛərɪ) *n, pl* **-waries** any large flightless bird of the genus *Casuarius*, inhabiting forests in NE Australia, New Guinea, and adjacent islands, having a horny head crest, black plumage, and brightly coloured neck and wattles: order *Casuariiformes* [C17: from Malay *kĕsuari*]

cast (kɑːst) *vb* **casts, casting, cast** (*mainly tr*) 1 to throw or expel with violence or force 2 to throw off or away: *she cast her clothes to the ground* 3 to reject or dismiss: *he cast the idea from his mind* 4 to shed or drop: *the snake cast its skin; the horse cast a shoe; the ship cast anchor* 5 to cause to appear: *to cast a shadow* 6 to express (doubts, suspicions, etc) or cause (them) to be felt 7 to direct (a glance, attention, etc): *cast your eye over this* 8 to place, esp in a violent manner: *he was cast into prison* 9 (*also intr*) *angling* to throw (a line) into the water 10 to draw or choose (lots) 11 to give or deposit (a vote) 12 to select (actors) to play parts in (a play, film, etc) 13 **a** to shape (molten metal, glass, etc) by pouring or pressing it into a mould **b** to make (an object) by such a process 14 (*also intr; often foll by up*) to compute (figures or a total) 15 *astrology* to draw on (a horoscope) details concerning the positions of the planets in the signs of the zodiac at a particular time for interpretation in terms of human characteristics, behaviour, 16 to contrive (esp in the phrase **cast a spell**) 17 to formulate: *he cast his work in the form of a chart* 18 (*also intr*) to twist or cause to twist 19 (*intr*) (of birds of prey) to eject from the crop and bill a pellet consisting of the indigestible parts of birds or animals previously eaten 20 *printing* to stereotype or electrotype ▷ *n* 21 the act of casting or throwing 22 **a** Also called: **casting** something that is shed, dropped, or egested, such as the coil of earth left by an earthworm **b** another name for **pellet** (sense 4) 23 the distance an object is or may be thrown 24 **a** a throw at dice **b** the resulting number shown 25 *angling* the act or an instance of casting 26 the wide sweep made by a sheepdog to get behind a flock of sheep or by a hunting dog in search of a scent 27 **a** the actors in a play collectively **b** (*as modifier*): *a cast list* 28 **a** an object made of metal, glass, etc, that has been shaped in a molten state by being poured or pressed into a mould **b** the mould used to shape such an object 29 form or appearance 30 sort, kind, or style 31 a fixed twist or defect, esp in the eye 32 a distortion of shape 33 *surgery* a rigid encircling casing, often made of plaster of Paris, for immobilizing broken bones while they heal 34 a slight tinge or trace, as of colour 35 fortune or a stroke of fate ▷ See also **cast about, castaway** [C13: from Old Norse *kasta*]

cast about *or* **cast around** *vb* (*intr, adverb*) to make a mental or visual search

Castalia (kæ'steɪlɪə) *n* a spring on Mount Parnassus: in ancient Greece sacred to Apollo and the Muses and believed to be a source of inspiration

castanets (,kæstə'nɛts) *pl n* curved pieces of hollow wood, usually held between the fingers and thumb and made to click together: used esp by Spanish dancers [C17 *castanet*, from Spanish *castañeta*, diminutive of *castaña* CHESTNUT]

castaway ('kɑːstə,weɪ) *n* 1 a person who has been shipwrecked ▷ *adj* (*prenominal*) 2 shipwrecked or cast adrift 3 thrown away or rejected ▷ *vb* **cast away** 4 (*tr, adverb; often passive*) to cause (a ship, person, etc) to be shipwrecked or abandoned

cast back *vb* (*adverb*) to turn (the mind) to the past

cast down *vb* (*tr, adverb*) to make (a person) discouraged or dejected

caste (kɑːst) *n* 1 **a** any of the four major hereditary classes, namely the Brahman, Kshatriya, Vaisya, and

Sudra into which Hindu society is divided. See also **Brahman, Kshatriya, Vaisya b** Also called: caste system the system or basis of such classes **c** the social position or rank conferred by this system **2** any social class or system based on such distinctions as heredity, rank, wealth, profession, etc **3** the position conferred by such a system **4** *entomol* any of various types of specialized individual, such as the worker, in social insects (hive bees, ants, etc) [c16: from Portuguese *casta* race, breed, ancestry, from *casto* pure, chaste, from Latin *castus*]

Castellammare di Stabia (*Italian* kastɛllam'maːre di 'stabja) *n* a port and resort in SW Italy, in Campania on the Bay of Naples: site of the Roman resort of Stabiae, which was destroyed by the eruption of Vesuvius in 79 AD Pop: 66 929 (2001)

castellan ('kæstɪlən) *n rare* a keeper or governor of a castle. Also called: chatelain [c14: from Latin *castellānus*, from *castellum* CASTLE]

castellated ('kæstɪˌleɪtɪd) *adj* **1** having turrets and battlements, like a castle **2** having indentations similar to battlements: *a castellated nut; a castellated filament* [c17: from Medieval Latin *castellātus*, from *castellāre* to fortify as a CASTLE] > ˌcastel'lation *n*

caster ('kɑːstə) *n* **1** a person or thing that casts **2** Also called: castor a bottle with a perforated top for sprinkling sugar, etc, or a stand containing such bottles **3** Also called: castor a small wheel mounted on a swivel so that the wheel tends to turn into its plane of rotation

caster sugar ('kɑːstə) *n* finely ground white sugar

castigate ('kæstɪˌɡeɪt) *vb* (*tr*) to rebuke or criticize in a severe manner; chastise [c17: from Latin *castīgāre* to correct, punish, from *castum* pure + *agere* to compel (to be)] > ˌcasti'gation *n* > 'castiˌgator *n*

Castiglione (ˌkæstɪl'jəʊnɪ, *Italian* kasti'ʎoːne) *n* Count Baldassare (baldas'saːre). 1478–1529, Italian diplomat and writer, noted particularly for his dialogue on ideal courtly life, *Il Libro del Cortegiano* (*The Courtier*) (1528)

Castile (kæ'stiːl) *or* **Castilla** (*Spanish* kas'tiʎa) *n* a former kingdom comprising most of modern Spain: originally part of León, it became an independent kingdom in the 10th century and united with Aragon (1469), the first step in the formation of the Spanish state

Castile soap *n* a hard soap made from olive oil and sodium hydroxide

Castilian (kæ'stɪljən) *n* **1** the Spanish dialect of Castile; the standard form of European Spanish **2** a native or inhabitant of Castile ▷ *adj* **3** denoting, relating to, or characteristic of Castile, its inhabitants, or the standard form of European Spanish

Castilla la Vieja (kas'tiʎa la 'bjexa) *n* the Spanish name for **Old Castile**

casting ('kɑːstɪŋ) *n* **1** an object or figure that has been cast, esp in metal from a mould **2** the process of transferring molten steel to a mould **3** the choosing of actors for a production **4** *zoology* another word for **cast** (sense 22), **pellet** (sense 4)

casting couch *n informal* a couch on which a casting director is said to seduce women seeking a part in a film or play

casting vote *n* the deciding vote used by the presiding officer of an assembly when votes cast on both sides are equal in number

cast iron *n* **1** iron containing so much carbon (1.7 to 4.5 per cent) that it cannot be wrought and must be cast into shape ▷ *adj* cast-iron **2** made of cast iron **3** rigid, strong, or unyielding: *a cast-iron decision*

castle ('kɑːsəl) *n* **1** a fortified building or set of buildings, usually permanently garrisoned, as in medieval Europe **2** any fortified place or structure **3** a large magnificent house, esp when the present or former home of a nobleman or prince **4** the citadel and strongest part of the fortifications of a medieval town **5** *chess* another name for **rook²** ▷ *vb* **6** *chess* to move (the king) two squares laterally on the first rank and place the nearest rook on the square passed over by the king, either towards the king's side (**castling short**) or the queen's side (**castling long**) [c11: from Latin *castellum*, diminutive of *castrum* fort]

Castlebar (ˌkɑːsəl'bɑː) *n* the county town of Co Mayo,

Republic of Ireland; site of the battle (1798) between the French and British known as Castlebar Races. Pop: 11 371 (2002)

castle in the air *or* **castle in Spain** *n* a hope or desire unlikely to be realized; daydream

Castlereagh¹ ('kɑːsəlˌreɪ) *n* a district of E Northern Ireland, in Co Down. Pop: 66 076 (2003 est). Area: 85 sq km (33 sq miles)

Castlereagh² ('kɑːsəlˌreɪ) *n* **Viscount.** title of *Robert Stewart*, Marquis of Londonderry. 1769–1822, British statesman: as foreign secretary (1812–22) led the Grand Alliance against Napoleon and attended the Congress of Vienna (1815)

Castner ('kæstnə) *n* **Hamilton Young.** 1858–98, US chemist, who devised the **Castner process** for extracting sodium from sodium hydroxide

cast-off *adj* **1** (*prenominal*) thrown away; abandoned: *cast-off shoes* ▷ *n* castoff **2** a person or thing that has been discarded or abandoned **3** *printing* an estimate of the amount of space that a piece of copy will occupy when printed in a particular size and style of type ▷ *vb* cast off (*adverb*) **4** to remove (mooring lines) that hold (a vessel) to a dock **5** to knot (a row of stitches, esp the final row) in finishing off knitted or woven material **6** *printing* to estimate the amount of space that will be taken up by (a book, piece of copy, etc) when it is printed in a particular size and style of type

cast on *vb* (*adverb*) to form (the first row of stitches) in knitting and weaving

castor¹ ('kɑːstə) *n* **1** the brownish aromatic secretion of the anal glands of a beaver, used in perfumery and medicine **2** the fur of the beaver **3** a hat made of beaver or similar fur [c14: from Latin, from Greek *kastōr* beaver]

castor² ('kɑːstə) *n* a variant spelling of **caster** (senses 2, 3)

Castor and Pollux *n classical myth* the twin sons of Leda: Pollux was fathered by Zeus, Castor by the mortal Tyndareus. After Castor's death, Pollux spent half his days with his half-brother in Hades and half with the gods in Olympus

castor oil *n* a colourless or yellow glutinous oil obtained from the seeds of the castor-oil plant and used as a fine lubricant and as a cathartic

castor-oil plant *n* a tall euphorbiaceous Indian plant, *Ricinus communis*, cultivated in tropical regions for ornament and for its poisonous seeds, from which castor oil is extracted

castrate (kæ'streɪt) *vb* (*tr*) **1** to remove the testicles of; emasculate; geld **2** to deprive of vigour, masculinity, etc **3** to remove the ovaries of; spay [c17: from Latin *castrāre* to emasculate, geld] > cas'tration *n*

castrato (kæ'strɑːtəʊ) *n, pl* -ti (-tɪ) *or* -tos (in 17th- and 18th-century opera) a male singer whose testicles were removed before puberty, allowing the retention of a soprano or alto voice [c18: from Italian, from Latin *castrātus* castrated]

Castries (kæs'triːs) *n* the capital and chief port of St Lucia. Pop: 14 000 (2005 est)

Castro ('kæstrəʊ; *Spanish* 'kastro) *n* **Fidel** (fɪ'dɛl; *Spanish* fi'ðɛl). full name *Fidel Castro Ruz*. born 1927, Cuban statesman: prime minister from 1959, when he led the Communist overthrow of Batista and president from 1976

cast steel *n* steel containing varying amounts of carbon, manganese, phosphorus, silicon, and sulphur that is cast into shape rather than wrought

cast stone *n building trades* a building component, such as a block or lintel, made from cast concrete with a facing that resembles natural stone

casual ('kæʒjʊəl) *adj* **1** happening by accident or chance **2** offhand; not premeditated: *a casual remark* **3** shallow or superficial: *a casual affair* **4** being or seeming unconcerned or apathetic: *he assumed a casual attitude* **5** (esp of dress) for informal wear: *a casual coat* **6** occasional or irregular: *casual visits; a casual labourer* ▷ *n* **7** (*usually plural*) an informal article of clothing or footwear **8** an occasional worker **9** (*usually plural*) a young man dressed in expensive casual clothes who goes to football matches in order to start fights [c14:

c

from Late Latin *cāsuālis* happening by chance, from Latin *cāsus* event, from *cadere* to fall; see CASE¹] > 'casually *adv* > 'casualness *n*

casual Friday *n* another name for **dress-down Friday**

casualization *or* **casualisation** (ˌkæʒjʊəlaɪˈzeɪʃən) *n* the altering of working practices so that regular workers are re-employed on a casual or short-term basis

casualty ('kæʒjʊəltɪ) *n, pl* -ties **1** a serviceman who is killed, wounded, captured, or missing as a result of enemy action **2** a person who is injured or killed in an accident **3** a hospital department in which victims of accidents, violence, etc, are treated **4** anything that is lost, damaged, or destroyed as the result of an accident, etc

casuarina (ˌkæsjʊəˈriːnə) *n* any tree of the genus *Casuarina*, of Australia and the East Indies, having jointed leafless branchlets: family *Casuarinaceae* [C19: from New Latin, from Malay *kĕsuari* CASSOWARY, referring to the resemblance of the branches to the feathers of the cassowary]

casuist ('kæzjʊɪst) *n* **1** a person, esp a theologian, who attempts to resolve moral dilemmas by the application of general rules and the careful distinction of special cases **2** a person who is oversubtle in his or her analysis of fine distinctions; sophist [C17: from French *casuiste*, from Spanish *casuista*, from Latin *cāsus* CASE¹] > ˌcasu'istic *or* ˌcasu'istical *adj*

casuistry ('kæzjʊɪstrɪ) *n, pl* -ries **1** *philosophy* the resolution of particular moral dilemmas, esp those arising from conflicting general moral rules, by careful distinction of the cases to which these rules apply **2** reasoning that is specious, misleading, or oversubtle

cat (kæt) *n* **1** Also called: **domestic cat** a small domesticated feline mammal, *Felis catus* (or *domesticus*), having thick soft fur and occurring in many breeds in which the colour of the fur varies greatly: kept as a pet or to catch rats and mice **2** Also called: **big cat** any of the larger felines, such as a lion or tiger **3** Also called: **big cat** any of the larger felines, such as a lion or tiger **4** any wild feline mammal of the genus *Felis*, such as the lynx or serval, resembling the domestic cat **5** *old-fashioned* a woman who gossips maliciously **6** *slang* a man; guy **7** *nautical* a heavy tackle for hoisting an anchor to the cathead **8** short for **catboat** **9** *informal* short for **Caterpillar** **10** short for **cat-o'-nine-tails** **11** a bag of cats *Irish informal* a bad-tempered person: *she's a real bag of cats this morning* **12** fight like Kilkenny cats to fight until both parties are destroyed **13** let the cat out of the bag to disclose a secret, often by mistake **14** like a cat on a hot tin roof *or* like a cat on hot bricks in an uneasy or agitated state ▷ *vb* cats, catting, catted **15** (*tr*) *nautical* to hoist (an anchor) to the cathead **16** (*intr*) a slang word for **vomit** [Old English *catte*, from Latin *cattus*; related to Old Norse *kǫttr*, Old High German *kazza*, Old French *chat*, Russian *kot*] > 'cat,like *adj* > 'cattish *adj*

cat² (kæt) *n informal* short for **catamaran** (sense 1)

cat³ (kæt) *n* **1 a** short for **catalytic converter b** (*as modifier*): *a cat car* ▷ *adj* **2** short for **catalytic** *a cat cracker*

CAT *abbreviation* computer-assisted trading

cat. *abbreviation* **1** catalogue **2** catamaran

cata-, kata-, *before an aspirate* **cath-** *or before a vowel* **cat-** *prefix* **1** down; downwards; lower in position: *catadromous*; *cataphyll* **2** indicating reversal, opposition, degeneration, etc [from Greek *kata-*, from *kata*. In compound words borrowed from Greek, *kata-* means: down (*catabolism*), away, off (*catalectic*), against (*category*), according to (*catholic*), and thoroughly (*catalogue*)]

catabolism *or* **katabolism** (kəˈtæbəˌlɪzəm) *n* a metabolic process in which complex molecules are broken down into simple ones with the release of energy; destructive metabolism [C19: from *katabolism*, from Greek *katabolē* a throwing down, from *kataballein*, from *kata-* down + *ballein* to throw] > catabolic *or* katabolic (ˌkætəˈbɒlɪk) *adj*

catachresis (ˌkætəˈkriːsɪs) *n* the incorrect use of words, as *luxuriant* for *luxurious* [C16: from Latin, from Greek *katakhrēsis* a misusing, from *katakhrēsthai*, from *khrēsthai* to use] > catachrestic (ˌkætəˈkrɛstɪk) *or* ˌcata'chrestical *adj*

cataclysm ('kætəˌklɪzəm) *n* **1** a violent upheaval, esp a

political, military, or social nature **2** a disastrous flood; deluge [C17: via French from Latin, from Greek *kataklusmos* deluge, from *katakluzein* to flood, from *kluzein* to wash] > ˌcata'clysmic *or* ˌcata'clysmal *adj* > ˌcata'clysmically *adv*

catacomb ('kætəˌkəʊm, -ˌkuːm) *n* **1** (*usually plural*) an underground burial place, esp the galleries at Rome, consisting of tunnels with vaults or niches leading off them for tombs **2** a series of interconnected underground tunnels or caves [Old English *catacumbe*, from Late Latin *catacumbas* (singular), name of the cemetery under the Basilica of St Sebastian, near Rome; origin unknown]

catadioptric (ˌkætədaɪˈɒptrɪk) *adj* involving a combination of reflecting and refracting components: *a catadioptric telescope* [C18: from CATA- + DIOPTRIC]

catadromous (kəˈtædrəməs) *adj* (of fishes such as the eel) migrating down rivers to the sea in order to breed. Compare **anadromous** [C19: from Greek *katadromos*, from *kata-* down + *dromos*, from *dremein* to run]

catafalque ('kætəˌfælk) *n* a temporary raised platform on which a body lies in state before or during a funeral [C17: from French, from Italian *catafalco*, of uncertain origin; see SCAFFOLD]

Catalan ('kætəˌlæn, -lən) *n* **1** a language of Catalonia, quite closely related to Spanish and Provençal, belonging to the Romance group of the Indo-European family **2** a native or inhabitant of Catalonia ▷ *adj* **3** denoting, relating to, or characteristic of Catalonia, its inhabitants, or their language

catalepsy ('kætəˌlɛpsɪ) *n* a state of prolonged rigid posture, occurring for example in schizophrenia or in hypnotic trances [C16: from Medieval Latin *catalēpsia*, variant of Late Latin *catalēpsis*, from Greek *katalēpsis*, literally: a seizing, from *katalambanein* to hold down, from *kata-* down + *lambanein* to grasp] > ˌcata'leptic *adj*

catalogue *or US* **catalog** ('kætəˌlɒg) *n* **1** a complete, usually alphabetical list of items, often with notes giving details **2** a book, usually illustrated, containing details of items for sale, esp as used by mail-order companies **3** a list of all the books or resources of a library **4** *US & Canadian* a publication issued by a university, college, etc, listing courses offered, regulations, services, etc ▷ *vb* -logues, -loguing, -logued *or US* -logs, -loging, -loged **5** to compile a catalogue of (a library) **6** to add (books, items, etc) to an existing catalogue [C15: from Late Latin *catalogus*, from Greek *katalogos*, from *katalegein* to list, from *kata-* completely + *legein* to collect] > ˌcata'loguer *or* ˌcata'loguist *n*

Catalonia (ˌkætəˈləʊnɪə) *n* a region of NE Spain, with a strong separatist tradition: became an autonomous region with its own parliament in 1979; an important agricultural and industrial region, with many resorts. Pop: 7 012 600 (2003 est). Area: 31 929 sq km (12 328 sq miles). Catalan name: **Catalunya** (ˌkata'luːnɪə) Spanish name: **Cataluña** (kata'luɲa)

catalpa (kə'tælpə) *n* any bignoniaceous tree of the genus *Catalpa* of North America and Asia, having large leaves, bell-shaped whitish flowers, and long slender pods [C18: New Latin, from Carolina Creek *kutuhlpa*, literally: winged head, referring to the appearance of the flowers]

catalyse *or US* **catalyze** ('kætəˌlaɪz) *vb* (*tr*) to influence (a chemical reaction) by catalysis

catalysis (kə'tælɪsɪs) *n, pl* -ses (-ˌsiːz) acceleration of a chemical reaction by the action of a catalyst [C17: from New Latin, from Greek *katalusis*, from *kataluein* to dissolve]

catalyst ('kætəlɪst) *n* **1** a substance that increases the rate of a chemical reaction without itself suffering any permanent chemical change **2** a person or thing that causes a change

catalytic (ˌkætə'lɪtɪk) *adj* of or relating to catalysis; involving a catalyst > ˌcata'lytically *adv*

catalytic converter *n* a device using three-way catalysts to reduce the obnoxious and poisonous components of the products of combustion (mainly oxides of nitrogen, carbon monoxide, and unburnt hydrocarbons) from the exhausts of motor vehicles

catalytic cracker *n* a unit in an oil refinery in which mineral oils with high boiling points are converted to fuels with lower boiling points by a catalytic process

catamaran (ˌkætəməˈræn) *n* **1** a sailing, or sometimes motored, vessel with twin hulls held parallel by a rigid framework **2** a primitive raft made of logs lashed together **3** *old-fashioned* a quarrelsome woman [c17: from Tamil *kattumaram* tied timber]

catamite (ˈkætəˌmaɪt) *n* a boy kept for homosexual purposes [c16: from Latin *Catamītus*, variant of *Ganymēdēs* GANYMEDE]

catamount (ˈkætəˌmaʊnt) *or* **catamountain** *n* any of various medium-sized felines, such as the puma or lynx [c17: short for *cat of the mountain*]

catananche (ˌkætəˈnæŋkɪ) *n* any of the hardy perennial genus *Catananche*, from S Europe; some, esp *C. caerulea*, are grown for their blue-and-white flowers that can be dried as winter decoration: family *Asteraceae* [from Greek *katanangkē* a spell (from their use in love potions)]

Catania (Italian kaˈtaːnja) *n* a port in E Sicily, near Mount Etna. Pop: 313 110 (2001)

cataplexy (ˈkætəˌplɛksɪ) *n* **1** sudden temporary paralysis, brought on by severe shock **2** a state of complete absence of movement assumed by animals while shamming death [c19: from Greek *kataplēxis* amazement, from *kataplēssein* to strike down (with amazement), confound, from *kata-* down + *plēssein* to strike] > ˌcataˈplectic *adj*

catapult (ˈkætəˌpʌlt) *n* **1** a Y-shaped implement with a loop of elastic fastened to the ends of the two prongs, used mainly by children for shooting small stones, etc. US and Canadian name: **slingshot 2** a heavy war engine used formerly for hurling stones, etc **3** a device installed in warships to launch aircraft ▷ *vb* **4** (*tr*) to shoot forth from or as if from a catapult **5** (*foll by over, into*, etc) to move precipitately [c16: from Latin *catapulta*, from Greek *katapeltēs*, from *kata-* down + *pallein* to hurl]

cataract (ˈkætəˌrækt) *n* **1** a large waterfall or rapids **2** a deluge; downpour **3** *pathol* **a** partial or total opacity of the crystalline lens of the eye **b** the opaque area [c15: from Latin *cataracta*, from Greek *katarrhaktēs*, from *katarassein* to dash down, from *arassein* to strike]

catarrh (kəˈtɑː) *n* **1** inflammation of a mucous membrane with increased production of mucus, esp affecting the nose and throat in the common cold **2** the mucus so formed [c16: via French from Late Latin *catarrhus*, from Greek *katarrous*, from *katarrhein* to flow down, from *kata-* down + *rhein* to flow] > caˈtarrhal *or* caˈtarrhous *adj*

catarrhine (ˈkætəˌraɪn) *adj* **1** (of apes and Old World monkeys) having the nostrils set close together and opening to the front of the face ▷ *n* **2** an animal or person with this characteristic [c19: from New Latin *Catarrhina* (for sense 1), all ultimately from Greek *katarrhin* having a hooked nose, from *kata-* down + *rhis* nose]

catastrophe (kəˈtæstrəfɪ) *n* **1** a sudden, extensive, or notable disaster or misfortune **2** the denouement of a play, esp a classical tragedy **3** a final decisive event, usually causing a disastrous end [c16: from Greek *katastrophē*, from *katastrephein* to overturn, from *strephein* to turn] > catastrophic (ˌkætəˈstrɒfɪk) *adj* > ˌcataˈstrophically *adv*

catastrophism (kəˈtæstrəˌfɪzəm) *n* **1** an old doctrine, now discarded, that the earth was created and has subsequently been shaped by sudden divine acts which have no logical connection with each other rather than by gradual evolutionary processes **2** Also called: neo-catastrophism a modern doctrine that the gradual evolutionary processes shaping the earth have been supplemented in the past by the effects of huge natural catastrophes

catatonia (ˌkætəˈtəʊnɪə) *n* a state of muscular rigidity and stupor, sometimes found in schizophrenia [c20: New Latin, from German *Katatonie*, from CATA- + -*tonia*, from Greek *tonos* tension] > catatonic (ˌkætəˈtɒnɪk) *adj, n*

catbird (ˈkætˌbɜːd) *n* **1** any of several North American songbirds of the family *Mimidae* (mockingbirds), esp *Dumetella carolinensis*, whose call resembles the mewing of a cat **2** any of several Australian bowerbirds of the genera *Ailuroedus* and *Scenopoeetes*, having a catlike call

catboat (ˈkætˌbəʊt) *n* a sailing vessel with a single mast, set well forward and often unstayed, and a large sail, usually rigged with a gaff. Shortened form: **cat¹**

cat burglar *n* a burglar who enters buildings by climbing through upper windows, skylights, etc

catcall (ˈkætˌkɔːl) *n* **1** a shrill whistle or cry expressing disapproval, as at a public meeting, etc ▷ *vb* **2** to utter such a call (at); deride with catcalls

catch (kætʃ) *vb* **catches, catching, caught 1** (*tr*) to take hold of so as to retain or restrain **2** (*tr*) to take, seize, or capture, esp after pursuit **3** (*tr*) to ensnare or deceive, as by trickery **4** (*tr*) to surprise or detect in an act: *he caught the dog rifling the larder* **5** (*tr*) to reach with a blow: *the stone caught him on the side of the head* **6** (*tr*) to overtake or reach in time to board **7** (*tr*) to see or hear; attend **8** (*tr*) to be infected with: *to catch a cold* **9** (*tr*) to hook or entangle or become hooked or entangled **10** to fasten or be fastened with or as if with a latch or other device **11** (*tr*) to attract or arrest: *she tried to catch his eye* **12** (*tr*) to comprehend: *I didn't catch his meaning* **13** (*tr*) to hear accurately: *I didn't catch what you said* **14** (*tr*) to captivate or charm **15** (*tr*) to perceive and reproduce accurately: *the painter managed to catch his model's beauty* **16** (*tr*) to hold back or restrain: *he caught his breath in surprise* **17** (*intr*) to become alight: *the fire won't catch* **18** (*tr*) *cricket* to dismiss (a batsman) by intercepting and holding a ball struck by him before it touches the ground **19** (*intr; often foll by at*) **a** to grasp or attempt to grasp **b** to take advantage (of), esp eagerly: *he caught at the chance* **20 catch it** *informal* to be scolded or reprimanded ▷ *n* **21** the act of catching or grasping **22** a device that catches and fastens, such as a latch **23** anything that is caught, esp something worth catching **24** the amount or number caught **25** *informal* a person regarded as an eligible matrimonial prospect **26** a check or break in the voice **27** a break in a mechanism **28** *informal* **a** a concealed, unexpected, or unforeseen drawback or handicap **b** (*as modifier*): *a catch question* **29** *cricket* the catching of a ball struck by a batsman before it touches the ground, resulting in him being out **30** *music* a type of round popular in the 17th, 18th, and 19th centuries, having a humorous text that is often indecent or bawdy and hard to articulate ▷ See also **catch on, catch out, catch up** [c13 *cacchen* to pursue, from Old Northern French *cachier*, from Latin *captāre* to snatch, from *capere* to seize] > **catchable** *adj*

catch-as-catch-can *n* a style of wrestling in which trips, holds below the waist, etc, are allowed

catchcry (ˈkætʃˌkraɪ) *n, pl* -**cries** *Austral* a well-known, frequently used phrase, esp one associated with a particular group, etc

catchfly (ˈkætʃˌflaɪ) *n, pl* -**flies** any of several caryophyllaceous plants of the genus *Silene* that have sticky calyxes and stems on which insects are sometimes trapped

catching (ˈkætʃɪŋ) *adj* **1** infectious **2** attractive; captivating

catching pen *n* *Austral & NZ* a pen adjacent to a shearer's stand containing the sheep ready for shearing

catchment (ˈkætʃmənt) *n* **1** the act of catching or collecting water **2** a structure in which water is collected **3** the water so collected **4** *Brit* the intake of a school from one catchment area

catchment area *n* **1** Also called: **catchment basin, drainage area, drainage basin** the area of land bounded by watersheds draining into a river, basin, or reservoir **2** the area from which people are allocated to a particular school, hospital, etc

catch on *vb* (*intr, adverb*) *informal* **1** to become popular or fashionable **2** to grasp mentally; understand

catch out *vb* (*tr, adverb*) *informal, chiefly Brit* to trap (a person), esp in an error or doing something reprehensible

catchpenny (ˈkætʃˌpɛnɪ) *adj* (*prenominal*) designed to have instant appeal, as in order to sell quickly and easily without regard for quality: *catchpenny ornaments*

catch phrase *n* a well-known frequently used phrase, esp one associated with a particular group, etc

catch-22 *n* a situation in which a person is frustrated by a paradoxical rule or set of circumstances that preclude any attempt to escape from them [C20: from the title of a novel (1961) by J. Heller]

catch up *vb* (*adverb*) **1** (*tr*) to seize and take up (something) quickly **2** (when *intr*, often foll by *with*) to reach or pass (someone or something), after following: *he soon caught him up* **3** (*intr*; usually foll by *on* or *with*) to make up for lost ground or deal with a backlog (in some specified task or activity) **4** (*tr*; *often passive*) to absorb or involve: *she was caught up in her reading* **5** (*tr*) to raise by or as if by fastening

catchweight ('kætʃ,weɪt) *adj wrestling* of or relating to a contest in which normal weight categories have been waived by agreement

catchword ('kætʃ,wɜːd) *n* **1** a word or phrase made temporarily popular, esp by a political campaign; slogan **2** a word printed as a running head in a reference book **3** *theatre* an actor's cue to speak or enter **4** the first word of a printed or typewritten page repeated at the bottom of the page preceding

catchy ('kætʃɪ) *adj* **catchier, catchiest 1** (of a tune, etc) pleasant and easily remembered or imitated **2** tricky or deceptive: *a catchy question* **3** irregular: *a catchy breeze*

cat cracker *n* an informal name for **catalytic cracker**

catechetical (,kætɪ'kɛtɪkˀl) *or* **catechetic** *adj* of or relating to teaching by question and answer > ,cate'chetically *adv*

catechism ('kætɪ,kɪzəm) *n* instruction by a series of questions and answers, esp a book containing such instruction on the religious doctrine of a Christian Church [C16: from Late Latin *catēchismus*, ultimately from Greek *katēkhizein* to CATECHIZE] > ,cate'chismal *adj*

catechize *or* **catechise** ('kætɪ,kaɪz) *vb* (*tr*) **1** to teach or examine by means of questions and answers **2** to give oral instruction in Christianity, esp by using a catechism **3** to put questions to (someone) [C15: from Late Latin *catēchizāre*, from Greek *katēkhizein*, from *katēkhein* to instruct orally, literally: to shout down, from kata- down + *ēkhein* to sound] > 'catechist, 'cate,chizer *or* 'cate,chiser *n*

catechu ('kætɪ,tʃuː) *or* **cachou** *n* a water-soluble astringent resinous substance obtained from any of certain tropical plants, esp the leguminous tree *Acacia catechu* of S Asia, and used in medicine and dyeing [C17: probably from Malay *kachu*, of Dravidian origin]

catechumen (,kætɪ'kjuːmɛn) *n Christianity* a person, esp in the early Church, undergoing instruction prior to baptism [C15: via Old French, from Late Latin, from Greek *katēkhoumenos* one being instructed verbally, from *katēkhein*; see CATECHIZE]

categorial (,kætɪ'gɔːrɪəl) *adj* **1** of or relating to a category **2** *logic* (of a statement) consisting of a subject, S, and a predicate, P, each of which denotes a class, and having one of the following forms: *all S are P* (universal affirmative); *some S are P* (particular affirmative); *some S are not P* (particular negative); *no S are P* (universal negative)

categorical (,kætɪ'gɒrɪkˀl) *or* **categoric** *adj* **1** unqualified; positive; unconditional: *a categorical statement* **2** relating to or included in a category **3** *logic* another word for **categorial** > ,cate'gorically *adv*

categorize *or* **categorise** ('kætɪgə,raɪz) *vb* (*tr*) to place in a category; classify > ,categori'zation *or* ,categori'sation *n*

category ('kætɪgərɪ) *n, pl* -**ries 1** a class or group of things, people, etc, possessing some quality or qualities in common; a division in a system of classification **2** *metaphysics* any one of the most basic classes into which objects and concepts can be analysed **3 a** (in the philosophy of Aristotle) any one of ten most fundamental modes of being, such as quantity, quality, and substance **b** (in the philosophy of Kant) one of twelve concepts required by human beings to interpret the empirical world [C15: from Late Latin *catēgoria*, from Greek *katēgoria*, from *kategorein* to accuse, assert]

category killer *n* a person, product, or business that dominates a particular market

catena (kə'tiːnə) *n, pl* -**nae** (-niː) a connected series, esp of patristic comments on the Bible [C17: from Latin: chain]

catenaccio *Italian* (kate'nattʃo) *n football* an extremely defensive style of play [C20: from Latin *catena* chain]

catenary (kə'tiːnərɪ) *n, pl* -**ries 1** the curve assumed by a heavy uniform flexible cord hanging freely from two points. When symmetrical about the y-axis and intersecting it at $y = a$, the equation is $y = a \cosh x/a$ **2** the hanging cable between pylons along a railway track, from which the trolley wire is suspended ▷ *adj* Also: catenarian (,kætɪ'nɛərɪən) **3** of, resembling, relating to, or constructed using a catenary or suspended chain [C18: from Latin *catēnārius* relating to a chain]

catenate ('kætɪ,neɪt) *vb biology* to arrange or be arranged in a series of chains or rings [C17: from Latin *catēnāre* to bind with chains] > ,cate'nation *n*

cater ('keɪtə) *vb* **1** (*intr*; foll by *for* or *to*) to provide what is required or desired (for) **2** (when *intr*, foll by *for*) to provide food, services, etc (for): *we cater for parties; to cater a banquet* [C16: from earlier *catour* purchaser, variant of *acatour*, from Anglo-Norman *acater* to buy, ultimately related to Latin *acceptāre* to ACCEPT] > 'caterer *n*

cater-cornered ('kætə,kɔːnəd) *adj, adv US & Canadian informal* diagonally placed; diagonal. Also called: catty-cornered, kitty-cornered [C16 *cater*, from dialect *cater* (adv) diagonally, from obsolete *cater* (n) four-spot of dice, from Old French *quatre* four, from Latin *quattuor*]

caterer ('keɪtərə) *n* a person who caters, esp one who as a profession provides food for large social events, etc

caterpillar ('kætə,pɪlə) *n* the wormlike larva of butterflies and moths, having numerous pairs of legs and powerful biting jaws. It may be brightly coloured, hairy, or spiny [C15 *catyrpel*, probably from Old Northern French *catepelose*, literally: hairy cat]

Caterpillar ('kætə,pɪlə) *n trademark* **1** an endless track, driven by sprockets or wheels, used to propel a heavy vehicle and enable it to cross soft or uneven ground **2** a vehicle, such as a tractor, tank, bulldozer, etc, driven by such tracks

caterwaul ('kætə,wɔːl) *vb* (*intr*) **1** to make a yowling noise, as a cat on heat ▷ *n* **2** a shriek or yell made by or sounding like a cat on heat [C14: of imitative origin]

Catesby ('keɪtsbɪ) *n* **Robert.** 1573–1605, English conspirator, leader of the Gunpowder Plot (1605): killed while resisting arrest

catfight ('kæt,faɪt) *n informal* a fight between two women

catfish ('kæt,fɪʃ) *n, pl* -**fish** or -**fishes 1** any of numerous mainly freshwater teleost fishes having whisker-like barbels around the mouth, esp the silurids of Europe and Asia and the horned pouts of North America **2** another name for **wolffish**

catgut ('kæt,gʌt) *n* a strong cord made from the dried intestines of sheep and other animals that is used for stringing certain musical instruments and sports rackets, and, when sterilized, as surgical ligatures

cath- *prefix* a variant of **cata-** *cathode*

Cathar ('kæθə) *or* **Catharist** ('kæθərɪst) *n, pl* -**ars**, -**ari** (-ərɪ) *or* -**arists** a member of a Christian sect in Provence in the 12th and 13th centuries who believed the material world was evil and only the spiritual was good [from Medieval Latin *Cathari*, from Greek *katharoi* the pure] > 'Cathar,ism *n*

catharsis (kə'θɑːsɪs) *n, pl* -**ses 1** (in Aristotelian literary criticism) the purging or purification of the emotions through the evocation of pity and fear, as in tragedy **2** *psychoanal* the bringing of repressed ideas or experiences into consciousness, thus relieving tensions **3** purgation, esp of the bowels [C19: New Latin, from Greek *katharsis*, from *kathairein* to purge, purify]

cathartic (kə'θɑːtɪk) *adj* **1** purgative **2** effecting catharsis ▷ *n* **3** a purgative drug or agent > ca'thartically *adv*

Cathay (kæ'θeɪ) *n* a literary or archaic name for **China** [C14: from Medieval Latin *Cataya*, of Turkic origin]

cathead ('kæt,hɛd) *n* a fitting at the bow of a vessel for securing the anchor when raised

cathedral (kə'θiːdrəl) *n* **a** the principal church of a diocese, containing the bishop's official throne **b** (*as modifier*): *a cathedral city; cathedral clergy* [C13: from Late Latin (*ecclesia*) *cathedrālis* cathedral (church), from *cathedra* bishop's throne, from Greek *kathedra* seat]

Cather ('kæðə) *n* **Willa (Sibert).** 1873–1947, US novelist, whose works include *O Pioneers!* (1913) and *My Ántonia* (1918)

Catherine ('kæθrɪn) *n* **Saint.** died 307 AD, legendary Christian martyr of Alexandria, who was tortured on a spiked wheel and beheaded

Catherine I *n* ?1684–1727, second wife of Peter the Great, whom she succeeded as empress of Russia (1725–27)

Catherine II *n* known as *Catherine the Great.* 1729–96, empress of Russia (1762–96), during whose reign Russia extended her boundaries at the expense of Turkey, Sweden, and Poland: she was a patron of literature and the arts

Catherine de' Medici *or* **Catherine de Médicis** *n* 1519–89, queen of Henry II of France; mother of Francis II, Charles IX, and Henry III of France; regent of France (1560–74). She was largely responsible for the massacre of Protestants on Saint Bartholomew's Day (1572)

Catherine of Aragon *n* 1485–1536, first wife of Henry VIII of England and mother of Mary I. The annulment of Henry's marriage to her (1533) against papal authority marked an initial stage in the English Reformation

Catherine of Braganza *n* 1638–1705, wife of Charles II of England, daughter of John IV of Portugal

Catherine of Siena *n* **Saint.** 1347–80, Italian mystic and ascetic; patron saint of the Dominican order. Feast day: April 29

Catherine wheel *n* **1** Also called: **pinwheel** a type of firework consisting of a powder-filled spiral tube, mounted with a pin through its centre. When lit it rotates quickly, producing a display of sparks and coloured flame **2** a circular window having ribs radiating from the centre [C16: named after St Catherine of Alexandria (died 307 AD), legendary Christian martyr who was tortured on a spiked wheel and beheaded]

catheter ('kæθɪtə) *n* *med* a long slender flexible tube for inserting into a natural bodily cavity or passage for introducing or withdrawing fluid, such as urine or blood [C17: from Late Latin, from Greek *kathetēr*, from *kathienai* to send down, insert]

catheterize *or* **catheterise** ('kæθɪtə,raɪz) *vb* (*tr*) to insert a catheter into

cathexis (kə'θɛksɪs) *n*, *pl* **-thexes** (-'θɛksi:z) *psychoanal* concentration of psychic energy on a single goal [C20: from New Latin, from Greek *kathexis*, from *katekhein* to hold fast, intended to render German *Besetzung* a taking possession of]

cathode ('kæθəʊd) *n* **1** the negative electrode in an electrolytic cell; the electrode by which electrons enter a device from an external circuit **2** the negatively charged electron source in an electronic valve **3** the positive terminal of a primary cell ▷ Compare **anode** [C19: from Greek *kathodos* a descent, from *kata-* down + *hodos* way] > **cathodal** (kæ'θəʊdᵊl) *or* **cathodic** (kæ'θɒdɪk, -'θəʊ-) *adj*

cathode rays *pl n* a stream of electrons emitted from the surface of a cathode in a valve

cathode-ray tube *n* a valve in which a beam of high-energy electrons is focused onto a fluorescent screen to give a visible spot of light. The device, with appropriate deflection equipment, is used in television receivers, visual display units, oscilloscopes, etc

catholic ('kæθəlɪk, 'kæθlɪk) *adj* **1** universal; relating to all men; all-inclusive **2** comprehensive in interests, tastes, etc; broad-minded; liberal [C14: from Latin *catholicus*, from Greek *katholikos* universal, from *katholou* in general, from *kata-* according to + *holos* whole] > **catholically** or **catholicly** (kə'θɒlɪklɪ) *adv*

Catholic ('kæθəlɪk, 'kæθlɪk) *adj* *Christianity* **1** denoting or relating to the entire body of Christians, esp to the Church before separation into the Greek or Eastern and Latin or Western Churches **2** denoting or relating to the Latin or Western Church after this separation **3** denoting or relating to the Roman Catholic Church ▷ *n* **4** a member of any of the Churches regarded as Catholic, esp the Roman Catholic Church

Catholicism (kə'θɒlɪ,sɪzəm) *n* **1** short for **Roman Catholicism** **2** the beliefs, practices, etc, of any Catholic Church

catholicity (,kæθə'lɪsɪtɪ) *n* **1** a wide range of interests, tastes, etc; liberality **2** universality; comprehensiveness

catholicize *or* **catholicise** (kə'θɒlɪ,saɪz) *vb* **1** to make or become catholic **2** (*often capital*) to convert to or become converted to Catholicism

Catiline ('kætɪ,laɪn) *n* Latin name *Lucius Sergius Catilina.* ?108–62 BC, Roman politician: organized an unsuccessful conspiracy against Cicero (63–62) > **Catilinarian** (,kætɪlɪ'nɛərɪən) *adj*

cation ('kætaɪən) *n* a positively charged ion; an ion that is attracted to the cathode during electrolysis. See **anion** [C19: from CATA- + ION] > **cationic** (,kætaɪ'ɒnɪk) *adj*

catkin ('kætkɪn) *n* an inflorescence consisting of a spike, usually hanging, of much reduced flowers of either sex: occurs in birch, hazel, etc [C16: from obsolete Dutch *katteken* kitten, identical in meaning with French *chaton*, German *Kätzchen*]

cat litter *n* absorbent material, often in a granular form, that is used to line a receptacle in which a domestic cat can urinate and defecate indoors

catmint ('kæt,mɪnt) *n* a Eurasian plant, *Nepeta cataria*, having spikes of purple-spotted white flowers and scented leaves of which cats are fond: family *Lamiaeae* (labiates). Also called: **catnip**

catnap ('kæt,næp) *n* **1** a short sleep or doze ▷ *vb* **-naps, -napping, -napped** **2** (*intr*) to sleep or doze for a short time or intermittently

Cato ('keɪtəʊ) *n* **1** **Marcus Porcius** ('mɑ:kəs'pɔ:ʃɪəs), known as *Cato the Elder* or *the Censor.* 234–149 BC, Roman statesman and writer, noted for his relentless opposition to Carthage **2** his great-grandson, **Marcus Porcius,** known as *Cato the Younger* or *Uticensis.* 95–46 BC, Roman statesman, general, and Stoic philosopher; opponent of Catiline and Caesar

cat-o'-nine-tails *n*, *pl* **-tails** a rope whip consisting of nine knotted thongs, used formerly to flog prisoners. Often shortened to **cat**

CATS (kæts) *n acronym for* credit accumulation transfer scheme: a scheme enabling school-leavers and others to acquire transferable certificates for relevant work experience and study towards a recognized qualification

CAT scanner (kæt) *n* former name for **CT scanner** [C20: (*C*)*omputerized* (*A*)*xial* (*T*)*omography*]

cat's cradle *n* a game played by making intricate patterns with a loop of string between the fingers

Catseye ('kæts,aɪ) *n* *trademark Brit* a glass reflector set into a small fixture, placed at intervals along roads to indicate traffic lanes at night

cat's-eye *n* any of a group of gemstones, esp a greenish-yellow variety of chrysoberyl, that reflect a streak of light when cut in a rounded unfaceted shape

Catskill Mountains ('kætskɪl) *pl n* a mountain range in SE New York State: resort. Highest peak: Slide Mountain, 1261 m (4204 ft). Also called: **Catskills**

cat's-paw *n* **1** a person used by another as a tool; dupe **2** a pattern of ripples on the surface of water caused by a light wind [(sense 1) C18: so called from the tale of the monkey who used a cat's paw to draw chestnuts out of a fire]

catsup ('kætsəp) *n* a variant (esp US) of **ketchup**

cat's whisker *n* a pointed wire used to make contact with the crystal in a crystal radio receiver

cat's whiskers *or* **cat's pyjamas** *n* **the cat's whiskers** *or* **the cat's pyjamas** *slang* a person or thing that is excellent or superior

cat-tail *or* **cattail** *n* *Canadian* another word for **bullrush**

Cattegat ('kætɪ,gæt) *n* a former spelling of **Kattegat**

cattery ('kætərɪ) *n*, *pl* **-teries** a place where cats are bred or looked after

cattle ('kætᵊl) *n* (*functioning as plural*) **1** bovid mammals of the tribe *Bovini* (bovines), esp those of the genus *Bos* **2** Also called: **domestic cattle** any domesticated bovine mammals, esp those of the species *Bos taurus* (domestic ox) [C13: from Old Northern French *catel*, Old French *chatel* CHATTEL]

cattle-cake *n* concentrated food for cattle in the form of cakes

cattle dog *n* *Austral informal* a catalogue [supposedly imitative of CATALOGUE]

C

c

cattle-grid n a grid of metal bars covering a hollow or hole dug in a roadway, intended to prevent the passage of livestock while allowing vehicles, etc, to pass unhindered

cattleman ('kæt^əlmən) n, pl -men **1** a person who breeds, rears, or tends cattle **2** chiefly US & Canadian a person who owns or rears cattle on a large scale, usually for beef, esp the owner of a cattle ranch

cattle market n Brit slang a situation or place, such as a beauty contest or nightclub, in which women are felt to be, or feel themselves to be, on display and judged solely by their appearance

cattle-stop n NZ a grid of metal bars covering a hollow or hole dug in a roadway, intended to prevent the passage of livestock while allowing vehicles, etc, to pass unhindered. Also called (in Britain and other countries): cattle-grid

catty ('kætı) or **cattish** adj -tier, -tiest **1** informal spiteful: a catty remark **2** of or resembling a cat > 'cattily or 'cattishly adv > 'cattiness or 'cattishness n

Catullus (kə'tʌləs) n **Gaius Valerius** ('gaɪəs və'lɪərɪəs). ?84–?54 BC, Roman lyric poet, noted particularly for his love poems > Catullan (kə'tʌlən) adj

CATV abbreviation community antenna television

catwalk ('kæt,wɔːk) n **1** a narrow ramp extending from the stage into the audience in a theatre, nightclub, etc, esp as used by models in a fashion show **2** a narrow pathway over the stage of a theatre, along a bridge, etc

Cauca (Spanish 'kauka) n a river in W Colombia, rising in the northwest and flowing north to the Magdalena River. Length: about 1350 km (840 miles)

Caucasia (kɔː'keɪzɪə, -ʒə) n a region in SW Russia, Georgia, Armenia, and Azerbaijan, between the Caspian Sea and the Black Sea: contains the Caucasus Mountains, dividing it into Ciscaucasia in the north and Transcaucasia in the south; one of the most complex ethnic areas in the world, with over 50 different peoples. Also called: the Caucasus

Caucasian (kɔː'keɪzɪən, -ʒən) adj **1** old-fashioned another word for **Caucasoid 2** of or relating to the Caucasus ▷ n **3** a White person; a Caucasoid **4** a native or inhabitant of Caucasia

Caucasoid ('kɔːkə,zɔɪd) adj **1** denoting, relating to, or belonging to the lighter-complexioned supposed racial group of mankind, which includes the peoples indigenous to Europe, N Africa, SW Asia, and the Indian subcontinent and their descendants in other parts of the world ▷ n **2** a member of this racial group

Caucasus ('kɔːkəsəs) n the Caucasus **1** Also called: Caucasus Mountains a mountain range in SW Russia, running along the N borders of Georgia and Azerbaijan, between the Black Sea and the Caspian Sea: mostly over 2700 m (9000 ft). Highest peak: Mount Elbrus, 5642 m (18 510 ft) **2** another name for **Caucasia**

Cauchy ('kəʊʃɪ; French koʃi) n **Augustin Louis** (ogystɛ̃ lwi), Baron Cauchy. 1789–1857, French mathematician, noted for his work on the theory of functions and the wave theory of light

caucus ('kɔːkəs) n, pl -cuses **1** chiefly US & Canadian a closed meeting of the members of one party in a legislative chamber, etc, to coordinate policy, choose candidates, etc **2** Brit a group or faction within a larger group, esp a political party, who discuss tactics, choose candidates, etc **3** Austral a group of MPs from one party who meet to discuss tactics, etc **4** NZ a formal meeting of all Members of Parliament belonging to one political party ▷ vb **5** (intr) to hold a caucus [C18: probably from Algonquian origin; related to caucuasu adviser]

cauda ('kɔːdə) n **1** zoology the area behind the anus of an animal; tail **2** anatomy **a** any tail-like structure **b** the posterior part of an organ [Latin: tail]

caudal ('kɔːd^əl) adj **1** anatomy of or towards the posterior part of the body **2** zoology relating to, resembling, or in the position of the tail [C17: from New Latin caudālis, from CAUDA] > 'caudally adv

caudal fin n the tail fin of fishes and some other aquatic vertebrates, used for propulsion during locomotion

caudate ('kɔːdeɪt) or **caudated** adj having a tail or a tail-like appendage [C17: from New Latin caudātus, from CAUDA] > cau'dation n

caudillo (kɔː'diːljəʊ; Spanish kau'ðiʎo) n, pl -los (-jəʊz; Spanish -ʎos) (in Spanish-speaking countries) a military or political leader [Spanish, from Late Latin capitellum, diminutive of Latin caput head]

caudle ('kɔːd^əl) n a hot spiced wine drink made with gruel, formerly used medicinally [C13: from Old Northern French caudel, from Medieval Latin caldellum, from Latin calidus warm]

caught (kɔːt) vb the past tense and past participle of **catch**

caul (kɔːl) n anatomy a portion of the amniotic sac sometimes covering a child's head at birth [C13: from Old French cale, back formation from calotte close-fitting cap, of Germanic origin]

cauldron or **caldron** ('kɔːldrən) n a large pot used for boiling, esp one with handles [C13: from earlier cauderon, from Anglo-French, from Latin caldārium hot bath, from calidus warm]

Caulfield ('kɔːlfiːld) n **Patrick** (**Joseph**). 1936–2005, British painter and printmaker

cauliflower ('kɒlɪ,flaʊə) n **1** a variety of cabbage, Brassica oleracea botrytis, having a large edible head of crowded white flowers on a very short thick stem **2** the flower head of this plant, used as a vegetable [C16: from Italian caoli fiori, literally: cabbage flowers, from cavolo cabbage (from Latin caulis) + fiore flower (from Latin flōs)]

cauliflower ear n permanent swelling and distortion of the external ear as the result of ruptures of the blood vessels: usually caused by blows received in boxing

caulk or **calk** (kɔːk) vb **1** to stop up (cracks, crevices, etc) with a filler **2** nautical to pack (the seams) between the planks of the bottom of (a vessel) with waterproof material to prevent leakage [C15: from Old Northern French cauquer to press down, from Latin calcāre to trample, from calx heel]

causal ('kɔːz^əl) adj **1** acting as or being a cause **2** stating, involving, or implying a cause: the causal part of the argument > 'causally adv

causality (kɔː'zælɪtɪ) n, pl -ties **1** the relationship of cause and effect **2** causal agency or quality

causation (kɔː'zeɪʃən) n **1** the act or fact of causing; the production of an effect by a cause **2** the relationship of cause and effect > cau'sational adj

causative ('kɔːzətɪv) adj **1** grammar relating to a form or class of verbs, such as persuade, that express causation **2** (often postpositive and foll by of) producing an effect ▷ n **3** the causative form or class of verbs > 'causatively adv

cause (kɔːz) n **1** a person, thing, event, state, or action that produces an effect **2** grounds for action; motive; justification: she had good cause to shout like that **3** the ideals, etc, of a group or movement: the Communist cause **4** the welfare or interests of a person or group in a dispute: they fought for the miners' cause **5 a** a ground for legal action; matter giving rise to a lawsuit **b** the lawsuit itself **6** make common cause with to join with (a person, group, etc) for a common objective ▷ vb **7** (tr) to be the cause of; bring about; precipitate; be the reason for [C13: from Latin causa cause, reason, motive] > 'causeless adj

cause célèbre ('kɔːz sə'lɛbrə, -'lɛb; French koz selɛbrə) n, pl causes célèbres ('kɔːz sə'lɛbrəz, -'lɛb, 'kɔːzɪz sə'lɛbrə, -'lɛbz; French koz selɛbrə) a famous lawsuit, trial, or controversy [C19: from French: famous case]

causerie ('kəʊzərɪ; French kozri) n an informal talk or conversational piece of writing [C19: from French, from causer to chat]

causeway ('kɔːz,weɪ) n **1** a raised path or road crossing water, marshland, sand, etc **2** a paved footpath [C15 cauciwey (from cauci + WAY); cauci paved road, from Medieval Latin (via) calciāta, calciātus paved with limestone, from Latin calx limestone]

caustic ('kɔːstɪk) adj **1** capable of burning or corroding by chemical action: caustic soda **2** sarcastic; cutting: a caustic reply ▷ n **3** Also called: caustic surface a surface that envelops the light rays reflected or refracted by a curved surface **4** Also called: caustic curve a curve formed by the intersection of a caustic surface with a plane **5** chem a caustic substance, esp an alkali [C14: from Latin *causticus*, from Greek *kaustikos*, from *kaiein* to burn] ⊳ 'caustically *adv* ⊳ causticity (kɔː'stɪsɪtɪ) *n*

caustic potash *n* another name for **potassium hydroxide**

caustic soda *n* another name for **sodium hydroxide**

cauterize or **cauterise** ('kɔːtə,raɪz) *vb* (*tr*) (esp in the treatment of a wound) to burn or sear (body tissue) with a hot iron or caustic agent [C14: from Old French *cauteriser*, from Late Latin *cautērizāre*, from *cautērium* branding iron, from Greek *kautērion*, from *kaiein* to burn] ⊳ ,cauteri'zation or ,cauteri'sation *n*

cautery ('kɔːtərɪ) *n*, *pl* -teries 1 the coagulation of blood or destruction of body tissue by cauterizing 2 Also called: cauterant an instrument or chemical agent for cauterizing [C14: from Old French *cautère*, from Latin *cautērium*; see CAUTERIZE]

caution ('kɔːʃən) *n* 1 care, forethought, or prudence, esp in the face of danger; wariness 2 something intended or serving as a warning; admonition 3 *law chiefly Brit* a formal warning given to a person suspected or accused of an offence that his words will be taken down and may be used in evidence 4 *informal* an amusing or surprising person or thing ⊳ *vb* 5 (*tr*) to urge or warn (a person) to be careful 6 (*tr*) *law chiefly Brit* to give a caution to (a person) 7 (*intr*) to warn, urge, or advise: *he cautioned against optimism* [C13: from Old French, from Latin *cautiō*, from *cavēre* to beware]

cautionary ('kɔːʃənərɪ) *adj* serving as a warning; intended to warn: *a cautionary tale*

cautious ('kɔːʃəs) *adj* showing or having caution; wary; prudent ⊳ 'cautiously *adv* ⊳ 'cautiousness *n*

cava ('kɑːvə) *n* a Spanish sparkling wine produced by a method similar to that used for champagne [from Spanish]

Cavaco Silva ('kavaku 'silvə) *n* Aníbal (a'nibal). born 1939, Portuguese statesman; prime minister (1985–95); president from 2006

Cavafy (kə'vɑːfɪ) *n* Constantine. Greek name *Kavafis*.1863–1933, Greek poet of Alexandria in Egypt

cavalcade (,kævəl'keɪd) *n* 1 a procession of people on horseback, in cars, etc 2 any procession [C16: from French, from Italian *cavalcata*, from *cavalcare* to ride on horseback, from Late Latin *caballicāre*, from *caballus* horse]

Cavalcanti (Italian kaval'kanti) *n* Guido ('gwiːdo). ?1255–1300, Italian poet, noted for his love poems

cavalier (,kævə'lɪə) *adj* 1 showing haughty disregard; offhand ⊳ *n* 2 a gallant or courtly gentleman, esp one acting as a lady's escort 3 *archaic* a horseman, esp one who is armed [C16: from Italian *cavaliere*, from Old Provençal *cavalier*, from Late Latin *caballārius* rider, from *caballus* horse, of obscure origin] ⊳ ,cava'lierly *adv*

Cavalier (,kævə'lɪə) *n* a supporter of Charles I during the English Civil War

cavalla (kə'vælə) or **cavally** *n*, *pl* -la, -las or -lies any of various tropical carangid fishes, such as *Gnathanodon speciosus* (golden cavalla) [C19: from Spanish *caballa*, from Late Latin, feminine of *caballus* horse]

Cavallini (Italian kaval'liːni) *n* Pietro ('pjɛːtro). ?1250–?1330, Italian fresco painter and mosaicist. His works include the mosaics of the *Life of the Virgin* in Santa Maria, Trastevere, Rome

cavalry ('kævəlrɪ) *n*, *pl* -ries 1 (esp formerly) the part of an army composed of mounted troops 2 the armoured element of a modern army 3 (*as modifier*): *a cavalry unit; a cavalry charge* [C16: from French *cavallerie*, from Italian *cavalleria*, from *cavaliere* horseman; see CAVALIER] ⊳ 'cavalryman *n*

Cavan ('kævən) *n* 1 a county of N Republic of Ireland: hilly, with many small lakes and bogs. County town: Cavan. Pop: 56 546 (2002). Area: 1890 sq km (730 sq miles) 2 a market town in N Republic of Ireland, county town of Co Cavan. Pop: 6098 (2002)

cavatina (,kævə'tiːnə) *n*, *pl* -ne (-nɪ) 1 a solo song resembling a simple aria 2 an instrumental composition reminiscent of this [C19: from Italian]

cave[1] (keɪv) *n* 1 an underground hollow with access from the ground surface or from the sea, often found in limestone areas and on rocky coastlines 2 *Brit history* a

secession or a group seceding from a political party on some issue ⊳ *vb* 3 (*tr*) to hollow out ⊳ See also **caving** [C13: from Old French, from Latin *cava*, plural of *cavum* cavity, from *cavus* hollow]

cave[2] ('keɪvɪ) *Brit school slang* ⊳ *n* 1 guard or lookout (esp in the phrase **keep cave**) ⊳ *sentence substitute* 2 watch out! [from Latin *cavē!* beware!]

caveat ('keɪvɪ,æt, 'kæv-) *n* 1 *law* a formal notice requesting the court or officer to refrain from taking some specified action without giving prior notice to the person lodging the caveat 2 a warning; caution [C16: from Latin, literally: let him beware]

caveat emptor ('ɛmptɔː) *n* the principle that the buyer must bear the risk for the quality of goods purchased unless they are covered by the seller's warranty [Latin: let the buyer beware]

cave in *vb* (*intr, adverb*) 1 to collapse; subside 2 *informal* to yield completely, esp under pressure ⊳ *n* cave-in 3 the sudden collapse of a roof, piece of ground, etc, into a hollow beneath it; subsidence 4 the site of such a collapse, as at a mine or tunnel

cavel ('keɪvᵊl) *n* NZ a drawing of lots among miners for an easy and profitable place at the coalface [C19: from English dialect *cavel* to cast lots, apportion]

Cavell ('kævᵊl) *n* Edith Louisa. 1865–1915, English nurse: executed by the Germans in World War I for helping Allied prisoners to escape

caveman ('keɪv,mæn) *n*, *pl* -men 1 a man of the Palaeolithic age; cave dweller 2 *informal, facetious* a man who is primitive or brutal in behaviour, etc

cavendish ('kævəndɪʃ) *n* tobacco that has been sweetened and pressed into moulds to form bars [C19: perhaps from the name of the first maker]

Cavendish ('kævəndɪʃ) *n* Henry. 1731–1810, British physicist and chemist: recognized hydrogen, determined the composition of water, and calculated the density of the earth by an experiment named after him

cavern ('kævᵊn) *n* 1 a cave, esp when large and formed by underground water, or a large chamber in a cave ⊳ *vb* (*tr*) 2 to shut in or as if in a cavern 3 to hollow out [C14: from Old French *caverne*, from Latin *caverna*, from *cavus* hollow; see CAVE[1]]

cavernous ('kævənəs) *adj* 1 suggestive of a cavern in vastness, darkness, etc: *cavernous hungry eyes* 2 filled with small cavities; porous 3 (of rocks) containing caverns or cavities

caviar or **caviare** ('kævɪ,ɑː, ,kævɪ'ɑː) *n* the salted roe of sturgeon, esp the beluga, usually served as an hors d'oeuvre [C16: from earlier *cavery*, from Old Italian *caviari*, plural of *caviaro* caviar, from Turkish *havyār*]

cavil ('kævɪl) *vb* -ils, -illing, -illed or US -ils, -iling, -iled 1 (*intr*; foll by *at* or *about*) to raise annoying petty objections; quibble; carp ⊳ *n* 2 a captious trifling objection [C16: from Old French *caviller*, from Latin *cavillārī* to jeer, from *cavilla* raillery] ⊳ 'caviller *n*

caving ('keɪvɪŋ) *n* the sport of climbing in and exploring caves ⊳ 'caver *n*

cavity ('kævɪtɪ) *n*, *pl* -ties 1 a hollow space; hole 2 *dentistry* a soft decayed area on a tooth 3 any empty or hollow space within the body [C16: from French *cavité*, from Late Latin *cavitās*, from Latin *cavus* hollow]

cavity wall *n* a wall that consists of two separate walls, joined by wall-ties, with an airspace between them

cavort (kə'vɔːt) *vb* (*intr*) to prance; caper [C19: perhaps from CURVET] ⊳ ca'vorter *n*

Cavour (Italian ka'vur) *n* Conte Camillo Benso di (ka'millo 'bɛnzo di).1810–61, Italian statesman and premier of Piedmont-Sardinia (1852–59; 1860–61): a leader of the movement for the unification of Italy

cavy ('keɪvɪ) *n*, *pl* -vies any small South American hystricomorph rodent of the family *Caviidae*, esp any of the genus *Cavia*, having a thickset body and very small tail. See also **guinea pig** [C18: from New Latin *Cavia*, from Galibi *cabiai*]

caw (kɔː) *n* 1 the cry of a crow, rook, or raven ⊳ *vb* 2 (*intr*) to make this cry [C16: of imitative origin]

CAW *abbreviation* Canadian Auto Workers (trade union)

Cawdrey ('kɔːdrɪ) *n* Robert. 16th–17th-century English

schoolmaster and lexicographer: compiled the first English dictionary (*A Table Alphabeticall*) in 1604

Cawley ('kɔːlɪ) *n* **Evonne** (née *Goolagong*). born 1951, Australian tennis player: Wimbledon champion 1971 and 1980; Australian champion 1974–76

Cawnpore (ˌkɔːn'pɔː) *or* **Cawnpur** (ˌkɔːn'pʊə) *n* the former name of **Kanpur**

Caxton ('kækstən) *n* **William**. ?1422–91, English printer and translator: published, in Bruges, the first book printed in English (1475) and established the first printing press in England (1477)

cay (keɪ, kiː) *n* a small low island or bank composed of sand and coral fragments, esp in the Caribbean area [c18: from Spanish *cayo*, probably from Old French *quai* QUAY]

Cayenne (keɪ'ɛn) *n* the capital of French Guiana, on an island at the mouth of the Cayenne River: French penal settlement from 1854 to 1938. Pop: 50 594 (1999)

cayenne pepper (keɪ'ɛn) *n* a very hot condiment, bright red in colour, made from the dried seeds and pods of various capsicums. Also called: red pepper [c18: ultimately from Tupi *quiynha*]

Cayes (keɪ; *French* kaj) *n* short for **Les Cayes**

Cayley ('keɪlɪ) *n* **1 Arthur**. 1821–93, British mathematician, who invented matrices **2 Sir George**. 1773–1857, British engineer and pioneer of aerial navigation. He constructed the first man-carrying glider (1853) and invented the caterpillar tractor

cayman *or* **caiman** ('keɪmən) *n*, *pl* -mans any tropical American crocodilian of the genus *Caiman* and related genera, similar to alligators but with a more heavily armoured belly: family *Alligatoridae* (alligators, etc) [c16: from Spanish *caiman*, from Carib *cayman*, probably of African origin]

Cayman Islands ('keɪmən) *pl n* three coral islands in the Caribbean Sea northwest of Jamaica: a dependency of Jamaica until 1962, now a UK Overseas Territory. Capital: George Town. Pop: 40 000 (2003 est). Area: about 260 sq km (100 sq miles)

CB *abbreviation* **1** Citizens' Band **2** Companion of the (Order of the) Bath (an English title) **3** County Borough

CBC *abbreviation* Canadian Broadcasting Corporation

CBD *or* **cbd** *abbreviation* central business district

CBE *abbreviation* Commander of the (Order of the) British Empire

CBI *abbreviation* Confederation of British Industry

CBRN *abbreviation* (of weapons or warfare) chemical, bacteriological, radiological, or nuclear

CBT *abbreviation* **1** computer-based training **2** Cognitive Behavioural Therapy

CBW *abbreviation* chemical or biological weapon

cc *or* **c.c.** *abbreviation* **1** carbon copy *or* copies **2** cubic centimetre(s)

CC *abbreviation* **1** City Council **2** (in Britain) Competition Commission **3** County Council **4** Cricket Club

cc. *abbreviation* chapters

c.c.c. *abbreviation* cwmni cyfyngedig cyhoeddus; a public limited company in Wales

C clef *n* *music* a symbol (𝄡), placed at the beginning of the staff, establishing middle C as being on its centre line. See **alto clef**, **soprano clef**, **tenor clef**

CCS *abbreviation* carbon capture and storage

CCTA *abbreviation* (in Britain) Central Computer and Telecommunications Agency

CCTV *abbreviation* closed-circuit television

cd *symbol for* candela

Cd *the chemical symbol for* cadmium

CD *abbreviation* **1** compact disc **2** Civil Defence (Corps) **3** Corps Diplomatique (Diplomatic Corps) **4** Conference on Disarmament: a United Nations standing conference, held in Geneva, to negotiate a global ban on chemical weapons

CDC *abbreviation* **1** (in the US) Center for Disease Control **2** Commonwealth Development Corporation

CDE *abbreviation* compact disc erasable: a compact disc that can be used to record and rerecord. Compare **CDR**

CDMA *abbreviation* code-division multiple access: a digital technology used in mobile phones

C difficile (dɪ'fɪsɪlɪ, ˌdɪfɪ'ciːl) *n* See **Clostridium difficile**

Cdn *abbreviation* Canadian

cDNA *abbreviation* complementary DNA; a form of DNA artificially synthesized from a messenger RNA template and used in genetic engineering to produce gene clones

CDO *abbreviation for* collateralized debt obligation

CD player *n* a device for playing compact discs

Cdr *military abbreviation* Commander

CDR *abbreviation* compact disc recordable: a compact disc that can be used to record only once. Compare **CDE**

CD-ROM (-'rɒm) *n* compact disc read-only memory; a compact disc used with a computer system as a read-only optical disk

CDT *abbreviation* **1** *US & Canadian* Central Daylight Time **2** Craft, Design, and Technology: a subject on the GCSE syllabus, related to the National Curriculum

CDV *abbreviation* CD-video

CD-video *n* a compact-disc player that, when connected to a television and hi-fi, produces high-quality stereo sound and synchronized pictures from a disc resembling a large compact audio disc

CD writer *n* *computing* a device on a computer for writing CDs

Ce *the chemical symbol for* cerium

CE *abbreviation* **1** Church of England **2** civil engineer **3** Common Era

Ceará (*Portuguese* sia'ra) *n* **1** a state of NE Brazil: sandy coastal plain, rising to a high plateau. Capital: Fortaleza. Pop: 7 654 535 (2002). Area: 150 630 sq km (58 746 sq miles) **2** another name for **Fortaleza**

cease (siːs) *vb* **1** (when *tr*, may take a gerund or an infinitive as object) to bring or come to an end; desist from; stop ▷ *n* **2** without cease without stopping; incessantly [c14: from Old French *cesser*, from Latin *cessāre*, frequentative of *cēdere* to yield, CEDE]

cease-fire *chiefly military* ▷ *n* **1** a period of truce, esp one that is temporary and a preliminary step to establishing a more permanent peace on agreed terms ▷ *interj*, *n* **2** the order to stop firing

ceaseless ('siːslɪs) *adj* without stop or pause; incessant > 'ceaselessly *adv*

Ceauşescu (tʃaʊ'ʃɛsku:) *n* **Nicolae** (ˌnɪkɒ'laɪ). 1918–89, Romanian statesman; chairman of the state council (1967–89) and president of Romania (1974–89): deposed and executed

Cebu (sɪ'buː) *n* **1** an island in the central Philippines. Pop: 2 091 602 (latest est). Area: 4422 sq km (1707 sq miles) **2** a port in the Philippines, on E Cebu island. Pop: 796 000 (2005 est)

Cechy ('tʃɛxi) *n* the Czech name for **Bohemia**

Cecil ('sɛsəl, 'sɪs-) *n* **1 Lord David**. 1902–86, English literary critic and biographer **2 Robert**. See (3rd Marquess of): **Salisbury¹ 3 William**. See (William Cecil) **Burghley**

Cecilia (sɪ'siːljə) *n* **Saint**. died ?230 AD, Roman martyr; patron saint of music. Feast day: Nov 22

cecum ('siːkəm) *n*, *pl* -ca (-kə) US a variant spelling of **caecum** > 'cecal *adj*

cedar ('siːdə) *n* **1** any Old World coniferous tree of the genus *Cedrus*, having spreading branches, needle-like evergreen leaves, and erect barrel-shaped cones: family *Pinaceae*. See also **cedar of Lebanon**, **deodar 2** any of various other conifers, such as the red cedars and white cedars **3** the wood of any of these trees ▷ *adj* **4** made of the wood of a cedar tree [c13: from Old French *cedre*, from Latin *cedrus*, from Greek *kedros*]

cedar of Lebanon *n* a cedar, *Cedrus libani*, of SW Asia with level spreading branches and fragrant wood

cede (siːd) *vb* **1** (when *intr*, often foll by *to*) to transfer, make over, or surrender (something, esp territory or legal rights) **2** (*tr*) to allow or concede (a point in an argument, etc) [c17: from Latin *cēdere* to yield, give way] > 'ceder *n*

cedilla (sɪ'dɪlə) *n* a character (¸) placed underneath a *c* before *a*, *o*, or *u*, esp in French, Portuguese, or Catalan, denoting that it is to be pronounced (s), not (k). The same character is used in the scripts of other languages, as in Turkish under *s* [c16: from Spanish: little *z*, from *ceda* zed, from Late Latin *zeta*; a small *z* was originally written after *c* in Spanish, to indicate a sibilant]

Ceefax ('si:,fæks) *n* *trademark* the BBC teletext service

CEGB *Brit* *abbreviation* (the former) Central Electricity Generating Board

ceil (si:l) *vb* (*tr*) **1** to line (a ceiling) with plaster, boarding, etc **2** to provide with a ceiling [c15 *celen*, perhaps back formation from CEILING]

ceilidh ('keılı) *n* (esp in Scotland and Ireland) an informal social gathering with folk music, singing, dancing, and storytelling [c19: from Gaelic]

ceiling ('si:lıŋ) *n* **1** the inner upper surface of a room **2** an upper limit, such as one set by regulation on prices or wages **3** the upper altitude to which an aircraft can climb measured under specified conditions **4** *meteorol* the highest level in the atmosphere from which the earth's surface is visible at a particular time, usually the base of a cloud layer [c14: of uncertain origin]

Cela (*Spanish* 'θela) *n* **Camilo José** (ka'milo xo'se). 1916–2002, Spanish novelist and essayist. His works include *The Family of Pascual Duarte* (1942), *La Colmena* (1951), and *La Cruz de San Andres* (1994). Nobel prize for literature 1989

celadon ('sɛlə,dɒn) *n* **1** a type of porcelain having a greyish-green glaze: mainly Chinese **2** a pale greyish-green colour, sometimes somewhat yellow [c18: from French, from the name of the shepherd hero of *L'Astrée* (1610), a romance by Honoré d'Urfé]

Celan ('sɛlæn) *n* **Paul**, real name *Paul Antschel*. 1920–70, Romanian Jewish poet, writing in German, whose work reflects the experience of Nazi persecution

celandine ('sɛlən,daın) *n* either of two unrelated plants, *Chelidonium majus* (greater celandine) or *Ranunculus ficaria* (lesser celandine). See **lesser celandine** [c13: earlier *celydon*, from Latin *chelīdonia* (the plant), from *chelīdonius* of the swallow, from Greek *khelidōn* swallow; the plant's season was believed to parallel the migration of swallows]

-cele *n* *combining form* tumour or hernia: *hydrocele* [from Greek *kēlē* tumour]

celeb (sı'lɛb) *n* *informal* a celebrity

Celebes ('sɛlıbi:z, sɛ'li:bız) *n* the English name for **Sulawesi**

Celebes Sea *n* the part of the Pacific Ocean between Sulawesi, Borneo, and Mindanao

celebrant ('sɛlıbrənt) *n* **1** a person participating in a religious ceremony **2** *Christianity* an officiating priest, esp at the Eucharist

celebrate ('sɛlı,breıt) *vb* **1** to rejoice in or have special festivities to mark (a happy day, event, etc) **2** (*tr*) to observe (a birthday, anniversary, etc) **3** (*tr*) to perform (a solemn or religious ceremony), esp to officiate at (Mass) **4** (*tr*) to praise publicly; proclaim [c15: from Latin *celebrāre*, from *celeber* numerous, thronged, renowned] > ,cele'bration *n* > 'cele,brator *n* > 'cele,bratory *adj*

celebrated ('sɛlı,breıtıd) *adj* (*usually prenominal*) famous: *a celebrated pianist; a celebrated trial*

celebrity (sı'lɛbrıtı) *n*, *pl* -ties **1** a famous person **2** fame or notoriety

celebutante (sı'lɛbjʊ,tɑ:nt, -,tænt) *n* a young woman from a wealthy background who becomes a celebrity [c20: from CELEB(RITY) + (DEB)UTANTE]

celeriac (sı'lɛrı,æk) *n* a variety of celery, *Apium graveolens rapaceum*, with a large turnip-like root, used as a vegetable [c18: from CELERY + -*ac*, of unexplained origin]

celerity (sı'lɛrıtı) *n* rapidity; swiftness; speed [c15: from Old French *celerite*, from Latin *celeritās*, from *celer* swift]

celery ('sɛlərı) *n* **1** an umbelliferous Eurasian plant, *Apium graveolens dulce*, whose blanched leafstalks are used in salads or cooked as a vegetable **2** **wild celery** a related and similar plant, *Apium graveolens* [c17: from French *céleri*, from Italian (Lombardy) dialect *selleri* (plural), from Greek *selinon* parsley]

celesta (sı'lɛstə) or **celeste** (sı'lɛst) *n* *music* a keyboard percussion instrument consisting of a set of steel plates of graduated length that are struck with key-operated hammers. The tone is an ethereal tinkling sound. Range: four octaves upwards from middle C [c19: from French, Latinized variant of *céleste* heavenly]

celestial (sı'lɛstıəl) *adj* **1** heavenly; divine; spiritual: *celestial peace* **2** of or relating to the sky: *celestial bodies* [c14:

from Medieval Latin *cēlestiālis*, from Latin *caelestis*, from *caelum* heaven] > ce'lestially *adv*

Celestial Empire *n* an archaic or literary name for the **Chinese Empire**

celestial equator *n* the great circle lying on the celestial sphere the plane of which is perpendicular to the line joining the north and south celestial poles. Also called: equinoctial, equinoctial circle

celestial mechanics *n* the study of the motion of celestial bodies under the influence of gravitational fields

celestial sphere *n* an imaginary sphere of infinitely large radius enclosing the universe so that all celestial bodies appear to be projected onto its surface

celiac ('si:lı,æk) *adj* *anatomy* the usual US spelling of **coeliac**

celibate ('sɛlıbıt) *n* **1** a person who is unmarried, esp one who has taken a religious vow of chastity ▷ *adj* **2** unmarried, esp by vow **3** abstaining from sexual intercourse [c17: from Latin *caelibātus*, from *caelebs* unmarried, of obscure origin] > 'celibacy *n*

Céline (seı'li:n) *n* **Louis-Ferdinand** (lwiferdinã), real name *Louis-Ferdinand Destouches*. 1894–1961, French novelist and physician; became famous with his controversial first novel *Journey to the End of the Night* (1932)

cell (sɛl) *n* **1** a small simple room, as in a prison, convent, monastery, or asylum; cubicle **2** any small compartment: *the cells of a honeycomb* **3** *biology* the basic structural and functional unit of living organisms. It consists of a nucleus, containing the genetic material, surrounded by the cytoplasm in which are mitochondria, lysosomes, ribosomes, and other organelles. All cells are bounded by a cell membrane; plant cells have an outer cell wall in addition **4** *biology* any small cavity or area, such as the cavity containing pollen in an anther **5** a device for converting chemical energy into electrical energy, usually consisting of a container with two electrodes immersed in an electrolyte. See also **dry cell**, **fuel cell** **6** a small group of persons operating as a nucleus of a larger political, religious, or other organization: *Communist cell* **7** the geographical area served by an individual transmitter in a cellular radio network [c12: from Medieval Latin *cella* monk's cell, from Latin: room, storeroom; related to Latin *cēlāre* to hide]

cella ('sɛlə) *n*, *pl* -lae (-li:) the inner room of a classical temple, esp the room housing the statue of a deity. Also called: naos [c17: from Latin: room, shrine; see CELL¹]

cellar ('sɛlə) *n* **1** an underground room, rooms, or storey of a building, usually used for storage **2** a place where wine is stored **3** a stock of bottled wines ▷ *vb* **4** (*tr*) to store in a cellar [c13: from Anglo-French, from Latin *cellārium* food store, from *cella* CELLA]

cellarage ('sɛlərıdʒ) *n* **1** an area of a cellar **2** a charge for storing goods in a cellar, etc

cellar dwellers *pl n* *Austral slang* the team at the bottom of a sports league

cellarer ('sɛlərə) *n* a monastic official responsible for food, drink, etc

cellaret (,sɛlə'rɛt) *n* a case, cabinet, or sideboard with compartments for holding wine bottles

Cellini (tʃı'li:nı; *Italian* tʃɛl'li:ni) *n* **Benvenuto** (benve'nu:to). 1500–71, Italian sculptor, goldsmith, and engraver, noted also for his autobiography

cell line *n* *biology* a clone of animal or plant cells that can be grown in a suitable nutrient culture medium in the laboratory

cello ('tʃɛləʊ) *n*, *pl* -los *music* a bowed stringed instrument of the violin family. Range: more than four octaves upwards from C below the bass staff. It has four strings, is held between the knees, and has an extendible metal spike at the lower end, which acts as a support. Full name: **violoncello** > 'cellist *n*

Cellophane ('sɛlə,feın) *n* *trademark* a flexible thin transparent sheeting made from wood pulp and used as a moisture-proof wrapping [c20: from CELLULOSE + -PHANE]

cellphone ('sɛl,fəʊn) *n* a portable telephone operated by cellular radio. In full: cellular telephone

cellular ('sɛljʊlə) adj 1 of, relating to, resembling, or composed of a cell or cells 2 having cells or small cavities; porous 3 divided into a network of cells 4 textiles woven with an open texture: a cellular blanket 5 designed for or involving cellular radio

cellular radio n radio communication based on a network of transmitters each serving a small area known as a cell: used in personal communications systems in which the mobile receiver switches frequencies automatically as it passes from one cell to another

cellule ('sɛljuːl) n a very small cell [C17: from Latin cellula, diminutive of cella CELL]

cellulite ('sɛljʊ,laɪt) n a name sometimes given to subcutaneous fat alleged to resist dieting [C20: from French, from cellule cell]

cellulitis (,sɛljʊ'laɪtɪs) n inflammation of any of the tissues of the body, characterized by fever, pain, swelling, and redness of the affected area [C19: from Latin cellula CELLULE + -ITIS]

celluloid ('sɛljʊ,lɔɪd) n 1 a flammable thermoplastic material consisting of cellulose nitrate mixed with a plasticizer, usually camphor: used in sheets, rods, and tubes for making a wide range of articles 2 a a cellulose derivative used for coating film b cinema film

cellulose ('sɛljʊ,ləʊz, -,ləʊs) n a polysaccharide consisting of long unbranched chains of linked glucose units: the main constituent of plant cell walls and used in making paper, rayon, and film [C18: from French cellule cell (see CELLULE) + -OSE²]

cellulose acetate n nonflammable material made by acetylating cellulose: used in the manufacture of film, dopes, lacquers, and artificial fibres

cellulose nitrate n a compound made by treating cellulose with nitric and sulphuric acids, used in plastics, lacquers, and explosives: a nitrogen-containing ester of cellulose. See also guncotton

Celsius ('sɛlsɪəs) adj denoting a measurement on the Celsius scale. Symbol: C [C18: named after Anders Celsius (1701–44), Swedish astronomer who invented it]

Celsius scale n a scale of temperature in which 0° represents the melting point of ice and 100° represents the boiling point of water. See also centigrade, Fahrenheit scale

celt (sɛlt) n archaeol a stone or metal axelike instrument with a bevelled edge [C18: from Late Latin celtes chisel, of obscure origin]

Celt (kɛlt, sɛlt) or **Kelt** n 1 a person who speaks a Celtic language 2 a member of an Indo-European people who in pre-Roman times inhabited Britain, Gaul, Spain, and other parts of W and central Europe

Celtic ('kɛltɪk, 'sɛl-) or **Keltic** n 1 a branch of the Indo-European family of languages that includes Gaelic, Welsh, and Breton, still spoken in parts of Scotland, Ireland, Wales, and Brittany. Modern Celtic is divided into the Brythonic (southern) and Goidelic (northern) groups ▷ adj 2 of, relating to, or characteristic of the Celts or the Celtic languages > Celticism ('kɛltɪ,sɪzəm, 'sɛl-) or 'Kelti,cism n

Celtic cross n a Latin cross with a broad ring surrounding the point of intersection

Celtic Sea n the relatively shallow part of the Atlantic Ocean lying between S Ireland, SW Wales, Cornwall, and W Brittany

cembalo ('tʃɛmbaləʊ) n, pl -li (-lɪ) or -los another word for harpsichord [C19: shortened from CLAVICEMBALO]

cement (sɪ'mɛnt) n 1 a fine grey powder made of a mixture of calcined limestone and clay, used with water and sand to make mortar, or with water, sand, and aggregate, to make concrete 2 a binder, glue, or adhesive 3 something that unites or joins; bond 4 dentistry any of various materials used in filling teeth 5 another word for cementum ▷ vb (tr) 6 to join, bind, or glue together with or as if with cement 7 to coat or cover with cement [C13: from Old French ciment, from Latin caementum stone from the quarry, from caedere to hew]

cementum (sɪ'mɛntəm) n a thin bonelike tissue that covers the dentine in the root of a tooth [C19: New Latin, from Latin: CEMENT]

cemetery ('sɛmɪtrɪ) n, pl -teries a place where the dead are buried, esp one not attached to a church [C14: from Late Latin coemētērium, from Greek koimētērion room for sleeping, from koiman to put to sleep]

-cene adj combining form, n combining form denoting a recent geological period [from Greek kainos new]

Cenis (French sənɪ) n Mont Cenis a pass over the Graian Alps in SE France, between Lanslebourg (France) and Susa (Italy): nearby tunnel, opened in 1871. Highest point: 2082 m (6831 ft)

cenobite ('siːnəʊ,baɪt) n a variant spelling of coenobite

cenotaph ('sɛnə,tɑːf) n a monument honouring a dead person or persons buried elsewhere [C17: from Latin cenotaphium, from Greek kenotaphion, from kenos empty + taphos tomb]

Cenotaph ('sɛnə,tɑːf) n the Cenotaph the monument in Whitehall, London, honouring the dead of both World Wars: designed by Sir Edwin Lutyens: erected in 1920

Cenozoic, Caenozoic (,siːnəʊ'zəʊɪk) or **Cainozoic** adj 1 of, denoting, or relating to the most recent geological era, which began 65 000 000 years ago: characterized by the development and increase of the mammals ▷ n 2 the Cenozoic the Cenozoic era [C19: from Greek kainos new, recent + zōikos, from zōion animal]

censer ('sɛnsə) n a container for burning incense, esp one swung at religious ceremonies. Also called: thurible

censor ('sɛnsə) n 1 a person authorized to examine publications, theatrical presentations, films, letters, etc, in order to suppress in whole or part those considered obscene, politically unacceptable, etc 2 any person who controls or suppresses the behaviour of others, usually on moral grounds 3 (in republican Rome) either of two senior magistrates elected to keep the list of citizens up to date, control aspects of public finance, and supervise public morals 4 psychoanal the postulated factor responsible for regulating the translation of ideas and desires from the unconscious to the conscious mind ▷ vb (tr) 5 to ban or cut portions of (a publication, film, letter, etc) 6 to act as a censor of (behaviour, etc) [C16: from Latin, from cēnsēre to consider, assess] > censorial (sɛn'sɔːrɪəl) adj

censorious (sɛn'sɔːrɪəs) adj harshly critical; fault-finding > cen'soriously adv

censorship ('sɛnsəʃɪp) n 1 a policy or programme of censoring 2 the act or system of censoring

censure ('sɛnʃə) n 1 severe disapproval; harsh criticism ▷ vb 2 to criticize (someone or something) severely; condemn [C14: from Latin cēnsūra, from cēnsēre to consider, assess] > censurable ('sɛnʃərəbəl) adj > 'censurableness or ,censura'bility n > 'censurably adv

census ('sɛnsəs) n, pl -suses 1 an official periodic count of a population including such information as sex, age, occupation, etc 2 any offical count: a traffic census 3 (in ancient Rome) a registration of the population and a property evaluation for purposes of taxation [C17: from Latin, from cēnsēre to assess]

cent (sɛnt) n a monetary unit of American Samoa, Andorra, Antigua and Barbuda, Aruba, Australia, Austria, the Bahamas, Barbados, Belgium, Belize, Bermuda, Bosnia and Hercegovina, Brunei, Canada, the Cayman Islands, Cyprus, Dominica, East Timor, Ecuador, El Salvador, Ethiopia, Fiji, Finland, France, French Guiana, Germany, Greece, Grenada, Guadeloupe, Guam, Guyana, Hong Kong, Ireland, Jamaica, Kenya, Kiribati, Kosovo, Liberia, Luxembourg, Malaysia, Malta, the Marshall Islands, Martinique, Mauritius, Mayotte, Micronesia, Monaco, Montenegro, Namibia, Nauru, the Netherlands, the Netherlands Antilles, New Zealand, the Northern Mariana Islands, Palau, Portugal, Puerto Rico, Réunion, Saint Kitts and Nevis, Saint Lucia, Saint Vincent and the Grenadines, San Marino, the Seychelles, Sierra Leone, Singapore, the Solomon Islands, Somalia, South Africa, Spain, Sri Lanka, Surinam, Swaziland, Taiwan, Tanzania, Trinidad and Tobago, Tuvalu, Uganda, the United States, the Vatican City, the Virgin Islands, and Zimbabwe. It is worth one hundredth of their respective standard units [C16: from Latin centēsimus hundredth, from centum hundred]

centaur ('sɛntɔː) n Greek myth one of a race of creatures with the head, arms, and torso of a man, and the lower body and legs of a horse [C14: from Latin, from Greek kentauros, of unknown origin]

centaurea (ˌsɛntɔː'rɪə, sɛn'tɔːrɪə) n any plant of the genus Centaurea, which includes the cornflower and knapweed [C19: ultimately from Greek Kentauros the Centaur; see CENTAURY]

centaury ('sɛntɔːrɪ) n, pl -ries any Eurasian plant of the genus Centaurium, esp C. erythraea, having purplish-pink flowers and formerly believed to have medicinal properties: family Gentianaceae [C14: ultimately from Greek Kentauros the Centaur; from the legend that Chiron the Centaur divulged its healing properties]

centavo (sɛn'taːvəʊ) n, pl -vos 1 a monetary unit of Argentina, Bolivia, Brazil, Cape Verde, Chile, Colombia, Cuba, the Dominican Republic, Guatemala, Guinea-Bissau, Honduras, Mexico, Mozambique, Nicaragua, and the Philippines. It is worth one hundredth of their respective standard units 2 a former monetary unit of Ecuador, El Salvador, and Portugal, worth one hundredth of their former standard units [Spanish: one hundredth part]

centenarian (ˌsɛntɪ'nɛərɪən) n 1 a person who is at least 100 years old ▷ adj 2 being at least 100 years old 3 of or relating to a centenarian

centenary (sɛn'tiːnərɪ) adj 1 of or relating to a period of 100 years 2 occurring once every 100 years ▷ n, pl -naries 3 a 100th anniversary or its celebration [C17: from Latin centēnārius of a hundred, from centēnī a hundred each, from centum hundred]

centennial (sɛn'tɛnɪəl) adj 1 relating to, lasting for, or completing a period of 100 years 2 occurring every 100 years ▷ n 3 chiefly US & Canadian another name for **centenary** [C18: from Latin centum hundred, on the model of BIENNIAL]

center ('sɛntə) n, vb the US spelling of **centre**

centered ('sɛntəd) adj the US spelling of **centred**

centesimal (sɛn'tɛsɪməl) n 1 hundredth ▷ adj 2 relating to division into hundredths [C17: from Latin centēsimus, from centum hundred] > cen'tesimally adv

centesimo (sɛn'tɛsɪˌməʊ) n, pl -mos, -mi a former monetary unit of Italy, San Marino, and the Vatican City worth one hundredth of a lira [C19: from Italian, from Latin centēsimus hundredth, from centum hundred]

centésimo (sɛn'tɛsɪˌməʊ) n, pl -mos or -mi a monetary unit of Panama and Uruguay. It is worth one hundredth of their respective standard units [C19: from Spanish; see CENTESIMO]

centi- or before a vowel **cent-** prefix 1 denoting one hundredth: centimetre. Symbol: c² 2 rare denoting a hundred: centipede [from French, from Latin centum hundred]

centiare ('sɛntɪˌɛə; French sãtjar) or **centare** ('sɛntɛə; French sãtar) n a unit of area equal to one square metre [French, from CENTI- + are from Latin ārea; see AREA]

centigrade ('sɛntɪˌgreɪd) adj 1 a former name for **Celsius** ▷ n 2 a unit of angle equal to one hundredth of a grade

centigram or **centigramme** ('sɛntɪˌgræm) n one hundredth of a gram

centilitre or US **centiliter** ('sɛntɪˌliːtə) n one hundredth of a litre

centime ('sɒnˌtiːm; French sãtim) n 1 a monetary unit of Algeria, Benin, Burkina Faso, Burundi, Cameroon, the Central African Republic, Chad, Comoros, Democratic Republic of Congo, Congo-Brazzaville, Côte d'Ivoire, Djibouti, Equatorial Guinea, French Polynesia, Gabon, Guinea, Guinea-Bissau, Haiti, Liechtenstein, Madagascar, Mali, Mayotte, Morocco, New Caledonia, Niger, Rwanda, Senegal, Switzerland, and Togo. It is worth one hundredth of their respective standard units 2 a former monetary unit of Andorra, Belgium, France, French Guiana, Guadeloupe, Luxembourg, Martinique, Monaco, and Réunion, worth one hundredth of a franc [C18: from French, from Old French centiesme from Latin centēsimus hundredth, from centum hundred]

centimetre or US **centimeter** ('sɛntɪˌmiːtə) n one hundredth of a metre

centimetre-gram-second n See **cgs units**

cêntimo ('sɛntɪˌməʊ) n, pl -mos 1 a monetary unit of Costa Rica, Paraguay, Peru, and Venezuela. It is worth one hundredth of their respective standard currency units 2 a former monetary unit of Andorra and Spain, worth one hundredth of a peseta [from Spanish; see CENTIME]

cêntimo ('sɛntɪˌməʊ) n, pl -mos a monetary unit of Sao Tomê e Principe, worth one hundredth of a dobra

centipede ('sɛntɪˌpiːd) n any carnivorous arthropod of the genera Lithobius, Scutigera, etc, having a body of between 15 and 190 segments, each bearing one pair of legs: class Chilopoda

cento ('sɛntəʊ) n, pl -tos a piece of writing, esp a poem, composed of quotations from other authors [C17: from Latin, literally: patchwork garment]

CENTO ('sɛntəʊ) n acronym for Central Treaty Organization; an organization for military and economic cooperation formed in 1959 by the UK, Iran, Pakistan, and Turkey as a successor to the Baghdad Pact: disbanded 1979

central ('sɛntrəl) adj 1 in, at, of, from, containing, or forming the centre of something: the central street in a city; the central material of a golf ball 2 main, principal, or chief; most important: the central cause of a problem > 'centrally adv

Central African Federation n another name for the **Federation of Rhodesia and Nyasaland**

Central African Republic n a landlocked country of central Africa: joined with Chad as a territory of French Equatorial Africa in 1910; became an independent republic in 1960; a parliamentary monarchy (1976–79); consists of a huge plateau, mostly savanna, with dense forests in the south; drained chiefly by the Shari and Ubangi Rivers. Official language: French; Sango is the national language. Religion: Christian and animist. Currency: franc. Capital: Bangui. Pop: 3 912 000 (2004 est). Area: 622 577 sq km (240 376 sq miles). Former names: Ubangi-Shari (until 1958), Central African Empire (1976–79). French name: Republique Centrafricaine (repyblik sãtrafrikεn)

Central America n an isthmus joining the continents of North and South America, extending from the S border of Mexico to the NW border of Colombia and consisting of Belize, Guatemala, Honduras, El Salvador, Nicaragua, Costa Rica, and Panama. Area: about 518 000 sq km (200 000 sq miles)

Central American adj 1 of or relating to Central America or its inhabitants ▷ n 2 a native or inhabitant of Central America

central bank n a national bank that does business mainly with a government and with other banks: it regulates the volume and cost of credit

central heating n a system for heating the rooms of a building by means of radiators or air vents connected by pipes or ducts to a central source of heat

Central India Agency n a former group of 89 states in India, under the supervision of a British political agent until 1947: most important were Indore, Bhopal, and Rewa

centralism ('sɛntrəˌlɪzəm) n the principle or act of bringing something under central control; centralization > 'centralist n, adj

centralize or **centralise** ('sɛntrəˌlaɪz) vb 1 to draw or move (something) to or towards a centre 2 to bring or come under central control, esp governmental control > ˌcentrali'zation or ˌcentrali'sation n

Central Karoo (kə'ruː) n an arid plateau of S central South Africa, in Cape Province, separated from the Little Karoo to the southwest by the Swartberg range. Average height: 750 m (2500 ft)

central limit theorem n statistics the fundamental result that the sum (or mean) of independent identically distributed random variables with finite variance approaches a normally distributed random variable as their number increases, whence in particular if enough samples are repeatedly drawn from any population, the sum of the sample values can be thought of, approximately, as an outcome from a normally distributed random variable

C

central locking n a system by which all the doors of a motor vehicle can be locked simultaneously when the driver's door is locked

central nervous system n the mass of nerve tissue that controls and coordinates the activities of an animal. In vertebrates it consists of the brain and spinal cord

central processing unit n the part of a computer that performs logical and arithmetical operations on the data as specified in the instructions. Abbreviation: CPU

Central Provinces pl n the Central Provinces the Canadian provinces of Ontario and Quebec

Central Region n a former local government region in central Scotland, formed in 1975 from Clackmannanshire, most of Stirlingshire, and parts of Perthshire, West Lothian, Fife, and Kinross-shire; in 1996 it was replaced by the council areas of Stirling, Clackmannanshire, and Falkirk

central reserve or **central reservation** n Brit the strip, often covered with grass, that separates the two sides of a motorway or dual carriageway

central tendency n statistics the tendency of the values of a random variable to cluster around the mean, median, and mode

centre or US **center** ('sɛntə) n **1** geometry **a** the midpoint of any line or figure, esp the point within a circle or sphere that is equidistant from any point on the circumference or surface **b** the point within a body through which a specified force may be considered to act, such as the centre of gravity **2** the point, axis, or pivot about which a body rotates **3** a point, area, or part that is approximately in the middle of a larger area or volume **4** a place at which some specified activity is concentrated: a shopping centre **5** a person or thing that is a focus of interest **6** a place of activity or influence: a centre of power **7** a person, group, policy, or thing in the middle **8** (usually capital) politics a political party or group favouring moderation, esp the moderate members of a legislative assembly **9** a bar with a conical point upon which a workpiece or part may be turned or ground **10** sport **a** a player who plays in the middle of the forward line **b** the act or an instance of passing the ball from a wing to the middle of the field, court, etc ⊳ vb **11** to move towards, mark, put, or be at a centre **12** (tr) to focus or bring together: to centre one's thoughts **13** (intr; often foll by on) to have as a main point of view or theme: the novel centred on crime **14** (intr; foll by on or round) to have as a centre **15** (tr) sport to pass (the ball) into the middle of the field or court [c14: from Latin centrum the stationary point of a compass, from Greek kentron needle, from kentein to prick]

Centre n **1** the Centre ('sɛntə) the sparsely inhabited central region of Australia **2** (French sɑ̃trə) a region of central France: generally low-lying; drained chiefly by the Rivers Loire, Loir, and Cher

centre bit n a drilling bit with a central projecting point and two side cutters

centreboard ('sɛntə,bɔːd) n a supplementary keel for a sailing vessel, which may be adjusted by raising and lowering

centred ('sɛntəd) or US **centered** adj mentally and emotionally confident, focused, and well-balanced

centrefold or US **centerfold** ('sɛntə,fəʊld) n **1 a** a large coloured illustration folded so that it forms the central spread of a magazine **2 a a** photograph of a nude or nearly nude woman (or man) in a magazine on such a spread **b** the subject of such a photograph

centre forward n sport the central forward in the attack

centre half or **centre back** n soccer a defender who plays in the middle of the defence

centre of gravity n the point through which the resultant of the gravitational forces on a body always acts

centre pass n hockey a push or hit made in any direction to start the game or to restart the game after a goal has been scored

centrepiece ('sɛntə,piːs) n an object used as the centre of something, esp for decoration

centre spread n **1** the pair of two facing pages in the middle of a magazine, newspaper, etc, often illustrated **2** a photograph of a nude or nearly nude woman (or man) in a magazine on such pages

centri- combining form a variant of **centro-**

centric ('sɛntrɪk) or **centrical** adj **1** being central or having a centre **2** relating to or originating at a nerve centre > **centricity** (sɛn'trɪsɪtɪ) n

-centric suffix forming adjectives having a centre as specified: heliocentric [abstracted from ECCENTRIC, CONCENTRIC, etc]

centrifugal (sɛn'trɪfjʊgəl, ˌsɛntrɪˌfjuːgˌl) adj **1** acting, moving, or tending to move away from a centre. See **centripetal 2** of, concerned with, or operated by centrifugal force: centrifugal pump [c18: from New Latin centrifugus, from CENTRI- + Latin fugere to flee] > **cen'trifugally** adv

centrifugal force n a fictitious force that can be thought of as acting outwards on any body that rotates or moves along a curved path

centrifuge ('sɛntrɪ,fjuːdʒ) n **1** any of various rotating machines that separate liquids from solids or dispersions of one liquid in another, by the action of centrifugal force **2** any of various rotating devices for subjecting human beings or animals to varying accelerations for experimental purposes ⊳ vb **3** (tr) to subject to the action of a centrifuge > **centrifugation** (ˌsɛntrɪfjʊ'geɪʃən) n

centring ('sɛntrɪŋ) or US **centering** n a temporary structure, esp one made of timber, used to support an arch during construction

centripetal (sɛn'trɪpɪtəl, ˌsɛntrɪˌpiːtˌl) adj **1** acting, moving, or tending to move towards a centre. See **centrifugal 2** of, concerned with, or operated by centripetal force [c17: from New Latin centripetus seeking the centre; see CENTRI-, -PETAL] > **cen'tripetally** adv

centripetal force n a force that acts inwards on any body that rotates or moves along a curved path and is directed towards the centre of curvature of the path or the axis of rotation

centrist ('sɛntrɪst) n a person holding moderate political views > **'centrism** n

centro-, centri- or before a vowel **centr-** combining form denoting a centre: centroclinal; centromere; centrosome; centrosphere; centrist [from Greek kentron CENTRE]

centuplicate vb (sɛn'tjuː,plɪˌkeɪt) **1** (tr) to increase 100 times ⊳ adj (sɛn'tjuːplɪkɪt, -ˌkeɪt) **2** increased a hundredfold ⊳ n (sɛn'tjuːplɪkɪt, -ˌkeɪt) **3** one hundredfold ⊳ Also called: **centuple** ('sɛntjʊpˌl) [c17: from Late Latin centuplicāre, from centuplex hundredfold, from centum hundred + -plex -fold]

centurion (sɛn'tjʊərɪən) n the officer commanding a Roman century [c14: from Latin centuriō, from centuria CENTURY]

century ('sɛntʃərɪ) n, pl -ries **1** a period of 100 years **2** one of the successive periods of 100 years dated before or after an epoch or event, esp the birth of Christ **3** a score or grouping of 100: to score a century in cricket **4** (in ancient Rome) a unit of foot soldiers, originally 100 strong, later consisting of 60 to 80 men **5** (in ancient Rome) a division of the people for purposes of voting [c16: from Latin centuria, from centum hundred]

century plant n an agave, Agave americana, native to tropical America but naturalized elsewhere, having very large spiny greyish leaves and greenish flowers on a tall fleshy stalk. It blooms only once in its life, after 10 to 30 years (formerly thought to flower after a century). Also called: American aloe

cep (sɛp) n another name for **porcino** [c19: from French cèpe, from Gascon dialect cep, from Latin cippus stake]

cephalic (sɪ'fælɪk) adj **1** of or relating to the head **2** situated in, on, or near the head

-cephalic or **-cephalous** adj combining form indicating skull or head; -headed: brachycephalic [from Greek -kephalos] > **-cephaly** or **-cephalism** n combining form

cephalic index n the ratio of the greatest width of the human head to its greatest length, multiplied by 100

cephalic version n another name for **version** (sense 5)

cephalo- or before a vowel **cephal-** combining form indicating the head: cephalopod [via Latin from Greek kephalo-, from *kephale* head]

Cephalonia (ˌsɛfəˈləʊnɪə) or **Kefallonia** (ˌkɛfəˈləʊnɪə) *n* a mountainous island in the Ionian Sea, the largest of the Ionian Islands, off the W coast of Greece. Pop: 36 404 (2001). Area: 935 sq km (365 sq miles). Modern Greek name: **Kephallinía**

cephalopod (ˈsɛfələˌpɒd) *n* any marine mollusc of the class *Cephalopoda*, characterized by well-developed head and eyes and a ring of sucker-bearing tentacles. The group also includes the octopuses, squids, cuttlefish, and pearly nautilus > ˌcephaˈlopodan *adj, n*

cephalothorax (ˌsɛfələʊˈθɔːræks) *n, pl* **-raxes** or **-races** (-rəˌsiːz) the anterior part of many crustaceans and some other arthropods consisting of a united head and thorax

-cephalus *n combining form* denoting a cephalic abnormality: *hydrocephalus* [New Latin *-cephalus*; see -CEPHALIC]

Cepheid variable (ˈsiːfɪɪd) *n astronomy* any of a class of variable stars with regular cycles of variations in luminosity (most ranging from three to fifty days). There is a relationship between the periods of variation and the absolute magnitudes, which is used for measuring the distance of such stars

Cepheus (ˈsiːfjuːs) *n Greek myth* a king of Ethiopia, father of Andromeda and husband of Cassiopeia

Ceram (sɪˈræm) *n* a variant spelling of **Seram**

ceramic (sɪˈræmɪk) *n* **1** a hard brittle material made by firing clay and similar substances **2** an object made from such a material ▷ *adj* **3** of, relating to, or made from a ceramic **4** of or relating to ceramics: *ceramic arts and crafts* [C19: from Greek *keramikos*, from *keramos* potter's clay, pottery]

ceramic hob *n* (on an electric cooker) a flat ceramic cooking surface having heating elements fitted on the underside, usually patterned to show the areas where heat is produced

ceramic oxide *n* a compound of oxygen with nonorganic material: recently discovered to act as a high-temperature superconductor

ceramics (sɪˈræmɪks) *n* (*functioning as singular*) the art and techniques of producing articles of clay, porcelain, etc > ceramist (ˈsɛrəmɪst) or ce'ramicist *n*

ceramide (ˈsɛrəˌmaɪd) *n* any of a class of biologically important compounds used as moisturizers in skin-care preparations

Cerberus (ˈsɜːbərəs) *n* **1** *Greek myth* a dog, usually represented as having three heads, that guarded the entrance to Hades **2** a sop to Cerberus a bribe or something given to propitiate a potential source of danger or problems > Cerberean (səˈbɪərɪən) *adj*

cere (sɪə) *n* a soft waxy swelling, containing the nostrils, at the base of the upper beak in such birds as the parrot [C15: from Old French *cire* wax, from Latin *cēra*]

cereal (ˈsɪərɪəl) *n* **1** any grass that produces an edible grain, such as oat, rye, wheat, rice, maize, sorghum, and millet **2** the grain produced by such a plant **3** any food made from this grain, esp breakfast food **4** (*modifier*) of or relating to any of these plants or their products [C19: from Latin *cereālis* concerning agriculture, of CERES]

cerebellum (ˌsɛrɪˈbɛləm) *n, pl* **-lums** or **-la** (-lə) one of the major divisions of the vertebrate brain, situated in man above the medulla oblongata and beneath the cerebrum, whose function is coordination of voluntary movements and maintenance of bodily equilibrium [C16: from Latin, diminutive of CEREBRUM] > ˌcere'bellar *adj*

cerebral (ˈsɛrɪbrəl; US səˈriːbrəl) *adj* **1** of or relating to the cerebrum or to the entire brain **2** involving intelligence rather than emotions or instinct **3** *phonetics* another word for **cacuminal** > 'cerebrally *adv*

cerebral haemorrhage *n* bleeding from an artery in the brain, which in severe cases causes a stroke

cerebral palsy *n* a nonprogressive impairment of muscular function and weakness of the limbs, caused by lack of oxygen to the brain immediately after birth, brain injury during birth, or viral infection

cerebrate (ˈsɛrɪˌbreɪt) *vb* (*intr*) *usually facetious* to use the mind; think; ponder; consider

cerebro- or before a vowel **cerebr-** *combining form* indicating the brain: *cerebrospinal* [from CEREBRUM]

cerebrospinal (ˌsɛrɪbrəʊˈspaɪnᵊl) *adj* of or relating to the brain and spinal cord

cerebrovascular (ˌsɛrɪbrəʊˈvæskjʊlə) *adj* of or relating to the blood vessels and the blood supply of the brain

cerebrum (ˈsɛrɪbrəm) *n, pl* **-brums** or **-bra** (-brə) **1** the anterior portion of the brain of vertebrates, consisting of two lateral hemispheres joined by a thick band of fibres: the dominant part of the brain in man, associated with intellectual function, emotion, and personality **2** the brain considered as a whole [C17: from Latin: the brain] > cerebric (ˈsɛrɪbrɪk) *adj*

cerecloth (ˈsɪəˌklɒθ) *n* waxed waterproof cloth of a kind formerly used as a shroud [C15: from earlier *cered cloth*, from Latin *cērāre* to wax]

Ceredigion (ˌkɛrəˈdɪɡjᵊn) *n* a county of W Wales, on Cardigan Bay: created in 1996 from part of Dyfed; corresponds to the former Cardiganshire (abolished 1974): mainly agricultural, with the Cambrian Mountains in the E and N. Administrative centre: Aberaeron. Pop: 77 200 (2003 est). Area: 1793 sq km (692 sq miles)

cerement (ˈsɪəmənt) *n* **1** another name for **cerecloth 2** any burial clothes [C17: from French *cirement*, from *cirer* to wax]

ceremonial (ˌsɛrɪˈməʊnɪəl) *adj* **1** involving or relating to ceremony or ritual ▷ *n* **2** the observance of formality, esp in etiquette **3** a plan for formal observances on a particular occasion; ritual **4** *Christianity* **a** the prescribed order of rites and ceremonies **b** a book containing this > ˌcere'monialism *n* > ˌcere'monialist *n* > ˌcere'monially *adv*

ceremonious (ˌsɛrɪˈməʊnɪəs) *adj* **1** especially or excessively polite or formal **2** observing ceremony; involving formalities > ˌcere'moniously *adv*

ceremony (ˈsɛrɪmənɪ) *n, pl* **-nies** **1** a formal act or ritual, often set by custom or tradition, performed in observation of an event or anniversary **2** a religious rite or series of rites **3** a courteous gesture or act: *the ceremony of toasting the Queen* **4** ceremonial observances or gestures collectively **5** stand on ceremony to insist on or act with excessive formality [C14: from Medieval Latin *cēremōnia*, from Latin *caerimōnia* what is sacred, a religious rite]

Cerenkov (Russian tʃɪˈrjɛnkəf) *n* See **Cherenkov**

Ceres (ˈsɪəriːz) *n* the Roman goddess of agriculture. Greek counterpart: **Demeter**

cerise (səˈriːz, -riːs) *n* a moderate to dark red colour [C19: from French: CHERRY]

cerium (ˈsɪərɪəm) *n* a malleable ductile steel-grey element of the lanthanide series of metals, used in lighter flints and as a reducing agent in metallurgy. Symbol: Ce; atomic no: 58; atomic wt: 140.115; valency: 3 or 4; relative density: 6.770; melting pt: 798°C; boiling pt: 3443°C [C19: New Latin, from CERES (the asteroid) + -IUM]

CERN (sɜːn) *n acronym for* Conseil Européen pour la Recherche Nucléaire; an organization of European states with a centre in Geneva for research in high-energy particle physics, now called the European Laboratory for Particle Physics

Cernăuţi (tʃernəˈutsj) *n* the Romanian name for **Chernovtsy**

Cernuda (Spanish θerˈnuða) *n* **Luis** (lwiʃ). 1902–63, Spanish poet. His major work is the autobiographical *Reality and Desire* (1936–64)

Ceroc (səˈrɒk) *n trademark* a form of dance combining elements of jive and salsa [C20: from French *C'est le Roc* It's Rock]

cerography (sɪəˈrɒɡrəfɪ) *n* the art of engraving on a waxed plate on which a printing surface is created by electrotyping

ceroplastic (ˌsɪərəʊˈplæstɪk) *adj* **1** relating to wax modelling **2** modelled in wax

Cerro de Pasco (Spanish ˈθɛrrɔ ðe ˈpasko) *n* a town in central Peru, in the Andes: one of the highest towns in the world, 4400 m (14 436 ft) above sea level; mining centre. Pop: 70 000 (latest est)

cert (sɜːt) *n informal* something that is a certainty, esp a horse that is certain to win a race (esp in the phrase **a**

dead cert)

certain ('sɜːt°n) *adj* 1 (*postpositive*) positive and confident about the truth of something; convinced: *I am certain that he wrote a book* 2 (*usually postpositive*) definitely known: *it is certain that they were on the bus* 3 (*usually postpositive*) sure; bound; destined: *he was certain to fail* 4 decided or settled upon; fixed: *the date is already certain for the invasion* 5 unfailing; reliable: *his judgment is certain* 6 moderate or minimum: *to a certain extent* ▷ *adv* 7 for certain definitely; without a doubt ▷ *determiner* 8 a known but not specified or named: *certain people may doubt this* b (*as pronoun; functioning as plural*): *certain of the members have not paid their subscriptions* 9 named but not known: *he had written to a certain Mrs Smith* [C13: from Old French, from Latin *certus* sure, fixed, from *cernere* to discern, decide]

certainly ('sɜːt°nlɪ) *adv* 1 with certainty; without doubt: *he certainly rides very well* ▷ *sentence substitute* 2 by all means; definitely: used in answer to questions

certainty ('sɜːt°ntɪ) *n, pl* -ties 1 the condition of being certain 2 something established as certain or inevitable 3 for a certainty without doubt

CertEd *abbreviation* (in Britain) Certificate in Education

certes ('sɜːtɪz) *adv* archaic with certainty; truly [C13: from Old French, ultimately from Latin *certus* CERTAIN]

certificate *n* (sə'tɪfɪkɪt) 1 an official document attesting the truth of the facts stated, as of birth, marital status, death, health, completion of an academic course, ability to practise a profession, etc ▷ *vb* (sə'tɪfɪˌkeɪt) 2 (*tr*) to authorize by or present with an official document [C15: from Old French *certificat*, from *certifier* CERTIFY] > cer'tificatory *adj*

Certificate of Secondary Education *n* See CSE

certification (ˌsɜːtɪfɪ'keɪʃən) *n* 1 the act of certifying or state of being certified 2 *law* a document attesting the truth of a fact or statement

certified ('sɜːtɪˌfaɪd) *adj* 1 holding or guaranteed by a certificate 2 endorsed or guaranteed: *a certified cheque* 3 (of a person) declared legally insane

certified accountant *n* (in Britain) a member of the Chartered Association of Certified Accountants, who is authorized to audit company accounts. See **chartered accountant**

certify ('sɜːtɪˌfaɪ) *vb* -fies, -fying, -fied 1 to confirm or attest (to), usually in writing 2 (*tr*) to endorse or guarantee (that certain required standards have been met) 3 to give reliable information or assurances: *he certified that it was Walter's handwriting* 4 (*tr*) to declare legally insane [C14: from Old French *certifier*, from Medieval Latin *certificāre* to make certain, from Latin *certus* CERTAIN + *facere* to make] > 'certi,fiable *adj* > 'certi,fiably *adv*

certiorari (ˌsɜːtɪɔː'rɛəraɪ) *n law* an order of a superior court directing that a record of proceedings in a lower court be sent up for review [C15: from legal Latin: to be informed]

certitude ('sɜːtɪˌtjuːd) *n* confidence; certainty [C15: from Church Latin *certitūdō*, from Latin *certus* CERTAIN]

cerulean (sɪ'ruːlɪən) *n* a deep blue colour; azure [C17: from Latin *caeruleus*, probably from *caelum* sky]

cerumen (sɪ'ruːmɛn) *n* the soft brownish-yellow wax secreted by glands in the auditory canal of the external ear. Nontechnical name: earwax [C18: from New Latin, from Latin *cēra* wax + ALBUMEN] > ce'ruminous *adj*

Cervantes (sə'væntiːz; *Spanish* θɛr'βantes) *n* **Miguel de** (mi'ɣɛl ðe), full surname *Cervantes Saavedra*. 1547–1616, Spanish dramatist, poet, and prose writer, most famous for *Don Quixote* (1605), which satirizes the chivalric romances and greatly influenced the development of the novel

cervelat ('sɜːvəˌlæt, -ˌlɑː) *n* a smoked sausage made from pork and beef [C17: via obsolete French from Italian *cervellata*]

Cervena (ˌsɜː'vɛnə) *n trademark NZ* a trademarked set of quality standards for farm-produced venison [C20: from Latin *cer(vidae)* deer + VEN(ISON)]

cervical ('sɜːvɪk°l, sə'vaɪ-) *adj* of or relating to the neck or cervix [C17: from New Latin *cervicālis*, from Latin *cervix* neck]

cervical smear *n med* a smear of cellular material taken

from the neck (cervix) of the uterus for detection of cancer. Also called: Pap test, Pap smear

Cervin (sɛrvɛ̃) *n* **Mont Cervin** the French name for **Matterhorn**

cervine ('sɜːvaɪn) *adj* resembling or relating to a deer [C19: from Latin *cervīnus*, from *cervus* a deer]

cervix ('sɜːvɪks) *n, pl* cervixes *or* cervices (sə'vaɪsiːz) 1 the technical name for **neck** 2 any necklike part of an organ, esp the lower part of the uterus that extends into the vagina [C18: from Latin]

cesium ('siːzɪəm) *n* the usual US spelling of **caesium**

Československo ('tʃɛskoslovɛnskɔ) *n* the Czech name for **Czechoslovakia**

cess¹ (sɛs) *n* **Brit** any of several special taxes, such as a land tax in Scotland [C16: short for ASSESSMENT]

cess² (sɛs) *n* an Irish slang word for **luck** [C19: probably from CESS¹]

cessation (sɛ'seɪʃən) *n* a ceasing or stopping; discontinuance; pause: *temporary cessation of hostilities* [C14: from Latin *cessātiō* a delaying, inactivity, from *cessāre* to be idle, desist from, from *cēdere* to yield, CEDE]

cession ('sɛʃən) *n* 1 the act of ceding, esp of ceding rights, property, or territory 2 something that is ceded, esp land or territory [C14: from Latin *cessiō*, from *cēdere* to yield]

cessionary ('sɛʃənərɪ) *n, pl* -aries *law* a person to whom something is transferred; assignee; grantee

cesspool ('sɛsˌpuːl) *or* **cesspit** ('sɛsˌpɪt) *n* 1 Also called: sink, sump a covered cistern, etc, for collecting and storing sewage or waste water 2 a filthy or corrupt place: *a cesspool of iniquity* [C17: changed (through influence of POOL) from earlier *cesperalle*, from Old French *souspirail* vent, air, from *soupirer* to sigh; see SUSPIRE]

cestoid ('sɛstɔɪd) *adj* (esp of tapeworms and similar animals) ribbon-like in form

cesura (sɪ'zjʊərə) *n, pl* -ras *or* -rae (-riː) *prosody* a variant spelling of **caesura**

cetacean (sɪ'teɪʃən) *adj* Also: cetaceous 1 of, relating to, or belonging to the Cetacea, an order of aquatic placental mammals having no hind limbs and a blowhole for breathing: includes toothed whales (dolphins, porpoises, etc) and whalebone whales (rorquals, right whales, etc) ▷ *n* 2 a whale [C19: from New Latin *Cētācea*, ultimately from Latin *cētus* whale, from Greek *kētos*]

cetane ('siːteɪn) *n* a colourless insoluble liquid alkane hydrocarbon used in the determination of the cetane number of diesel fuel. Formula: $C_{16}H_{34}$. Also called: hexadecane [C19: from Latin *cētus* whale + -ANE, so called because related compounds are found in sperm whale oil]

cetane number *n* a measure of the quality of a diesel fuel expressed as the percentage of cetane in a mixture of cetane and 1-methylnapthalene of the same quality as the given fuel. Also called: cetane rating. Compare **octane number**

Cetatea Albă (tʃe'tatea 'albə) *n* the Romanian name for **Belgorod-Dnestrovski**

Cetinje (*Serbian* 'tsɛtinjɛ) *n* a town in Montenegro, in the SW: former capital of Montenegro (until 1945); palace and fortified monastery, residences of Montenegrin prince-bishops. Pop: 15 137 (2003 est 1991)

cetrimide ('sɛtrɪˌmaɪd) *n* a quaternary ammonium compound used as a detergent and, having powerful antiseptic properties, for sterilizing surgical instruments, cleaning wounds, etc

Cetshwayo *or* **Cetewayo** (*Zulu* kɛ'tʃwaːjʊ) *n* ?1826–84, king of the Zulus (1873–79): defeated the British at Isandhlwana (1879) but was overwhelmed by them at Ulundi (1879); captured, he stated his case in London, and was reinstated as ruler of part of Zululand (1883)

Ceuta (*Spanish* 'θeuta) *n* an enclave in Morocco on the Strait of Gibraltar, consisting of a port and military station: held by Spain since 1580. Pop: 74 931 (2003 est)

Cévennes (*French* sevɛn) *n* a mountain range in S central France, on the SE edge of the Massif Central. Highest peak: 1754 m (5755 ft)

Ceylon (sɪ'lɒn) *n* 1 the former name (until 1972) of **Sri Lanka** 2 an island in the Indian Ocean, off the SE coast of India: consists politically of the republic of Sri Lanka. Area: 64 644 sq km (24 959 sq miles)

Ceylonese (ˌsɛləˈniːz, ˌsiːlə-) *adj* of or relating to Ceylon or its inhabitants

Cézanne (*French* sezan) *n* **Paul** (pɔl). 1839–1906, French postimpressionist painter, who was a major influence on modern art, esp cubism, in stressing the structural elements latent in nature, such as the sphere and the cone

Cf *the chemical symbol for* californium

CF *chiefly Brit abbreviation* Chaplain to the Forces

cf. *abbreviation* compare [Latin: comfer]

CFB *abbreviation* (in Canada) Canadian Forces Base

CFC *abbreviation* chlorofluorocarbon

CFL *abbreviation* Canadian Football League

CFS *abbreviation* chronic fatigue syndrome

cg *symbol for* centigram

CGBR *abbreviation* Central Government Borrowing Requirement

cgs units *pl n* a metric system of units based on the centimetre, gram, and second. For scientific and technical purposes these units have been replaced by SI units

CGT *abbreviation* capital gains tax

CH *abbreviation* **1** Companion of Honour (a Brit title) ▷ *international car registration* **2** Switzerland [from French *Confédération Helvétique*]

ch. *abbreviation* **1** chain (unit of measure) **2** chapter **3** chess check **4** chief **5** church

Chablis (ˈʃæblɪ; *French* ʃabli) *n* (*sometimes not capitals*) a dry white burgundy wine made around Chablis, in central France

Chabrier (ˈʃæbrɪeɪ; *French* ʃabrie) *n* (**Alexis**) **Emmanuel** (emanɥel). 1841–94, French composer; noted esp for the orchestral rhapsody *España* (1883)

Chabrol (*French* ʃabrɔl) *n* **Claude** (klod). born 1930, French film director, whose films, such as *Le Beau Serge* (1958), *Les Biches* (1968), *Le Boucher* (1969), *Au Coeur du mensonge* (1999), and *La Fleur du mal* (2003) explore themes of jealousy, guilt, and murder

cha-cha-cha (ˌtʃɑːtʃɑːˈtʃɑː) *or* **cha-cha** *n* **1 a** Latin-American ballroom dance with small steps and swaying hip movements **2** a piece of music composed for this dance ▷ *vb* (*intr*) **3** to perform this dance [c20: from American (Cuban) Spanish]

Chaco (*Spanish* ˈtʃako) *n* See **Gran Chaco**

chaconne (ʃəˈkɒn; *French* ʃakɔn) *n* **1** a musical form consisting of a set of continuous variations upon a ground bass **2** *archaic* a dance in slow triple time probably originating in Spain [c17: from French, from Spanish *chacona*, probably imitative of the castanet accompaniment]

Chad (tʃæd) *n* **1** a republic in N central Africa: made a territory of French Equatorial Africa in 1910; became independent in 1960; contains much desert and the Tibesti Mountains, with Lake Chad in the west; produces chiefly cotton and livestock; suffered intermittent civil war from 1963 and prolonged drought. Official languages: Arabic; French. Religion: Muslim majority, also Christian and animist. Currency: franc. Capital: Ndjamena. Pop: 8 854 000 (2004 est). Area: 1 284 000 sq km (495 750 sq miles). French name: **Tchad** **2** Lake Chad a lake in N central Africa: fed chiefly by the Shari River, it has no apparent outlet. Area: at fullest extent 10 000 to 26 000 sq km (4000 to 10 000 sq miles), varying seasonally; it has shrunk considerably in recent years

chadri (ˈtʃædriː) *n* a shroud which covers the body from heat to foot, usually worn by females in Islamic countries

Chadwick (ˈtʃædwɪk) *n* **1** Sir **Edwin**. 1800–90, British social reformer, known for his *Report on the Sanitary Condition of the Labouring Population of Great Britain* (1842) **2** Sir **James**. 1891–1974, British physicist: discovered the neutron (1932): Nobel prize for physics 1935 **3** Lynn (**Russell**). 1914–2003, British sculptor in metal

chaeta (ˈkiːtə) *n*, *pl* **-tae** (-tiː) any of the chitinous bristles on the body of such annelids as the earthworm and the lugworm: used in locomotion; a seta [c19: New

Latin, from Greek *khaitē* long hair]

chafe (tʃeɪf) *vb* **1** to make or become sore or worn by rubbing **2** (*tr*) to warm (the hands, etc) by rubbing **3** to irritate or be irritated or impatient **4** (*intr*; often foll by *on*, *against*, etc) to cause friction; rub ▷ *n* **5** a soreness or irritation caused by friction [c14: from Old French *chaufer* to warm, ultimately from Latin *calefacere*, from *calēre* to be warm + *facere* to make]

chafer (ˈtʃeɪfə) *n* any of various scarabaeid beetles, such as the cockchafer and rose chafer [Old English *ceafor*; related to Old Saxon *kevera*, Old High German *chevar*]

chaff¹ (tʃɑːf) *n* **1** the mass of husks, etc, separated from the seeds during threshing **2** finely cut straw and hay used to feed cattle **3** something of little worth; rubbish (esp in the phrase **separate the wheat from the chaff**) **4** thin strips of metallic foil released into the earth's atmosphere to confuse radar signals and prevent detection [Old English *ceaf*; related to Old High German *keva* husk] ▷ **'chaffy** *adj*

chaff² (tʃɑːf) *n* **1** light-hearted teasing or joking; banter ▷ *vb* **2** to tease good-naturedly; banter [c19: probably slang variant of CHAFE, perhaps influenced by CHAFF¹] ▷ **'chaffer** *n*

chaffer (ˈtʃæfə) *vb* **1** (*intr*) to haggle or bargain **2** to chatter, talk, or say idly; bandy ▷ *n* **3** haggling or bargaining [c13 *chaffare*, from *chep* bargain + *fare* journey; see CHEAP, FARE] ▷ **'chafferer** *n*

chaffinch (ˈtʃæfɪntʃ) *n* a common European finch, *Fringilla coelebs*, with black and white wings and, in the male, a reddish body and blue-grey head [Old English *ceaffinc*, from *ceaf* CHAFF¹ + *finc* FINCH]

chafing dish (ˈtʃeɪfɪŋ) *n* a vessel with a heating apparatus beneath it, for cooking or keeping food warm at the table

Chagall (*French* ʃagal) *n* **Marc** (mark). 1887–1985, French painter and illustrator, born in Russia, noted for his richly coloured pictures of men, animals, and objects in fantastic combinations and often suspended in space: his work includes 12 stained glass windows for a synagogue in Jerusalem (1961) and the decorations for the ceiling of the Paris Opera House (1964)

chagrin (ˈʃægrɪn) *n* **1** a feeling of annoyance or mortification ▷ *vb* (*tr*) **2** to embarrass and annoy; mortify [c17: from French *chagrin*, *chagriner*, of unknown origin]

chain (tʃeɪn) *n* **1** a flexible length of metal links, used for confining, connecting, pulling, etc, or in jewellery **2** (*usually plural*) anything that confines, fetters, or restrains: *the chains of poverty* **3** Also called: **snow chains** (*usually plural*) a set of metal links that fit over the tyre of a motor vehicle to increase traction and reduce skidding on an icy surface **4 a** a number of establishments such as hotels, shops, etc, having the same owner or management (**b** *as modifier*): *a chain store* **5** a series of related or connected facts, events, etc **6** a series of deals in which each depends on a purchaser selling before being able to buy **7** Also called: **Gunter's chain** a unit of length equal to 22 yards **8** Also called: **engineer's chain** a unit of length equal to 100 feet **9** *chem* two or more atoms or groups bonded together so that the configuration of the resulting molecule, ion, or radical resembles a chain **10** *geography* a series of natural features, esp approximately parallel mountain ranges **11** off the chain *Austral & NZ informal* free from responsibility **12** jerk someone's chain *or* yank someone's chain *informal* to tease, mislead, or harass someone ▷ *vb* **13** (*tr*; often foll by *up*) to confine, tie, or make fast with or as if with a chain [c13: from Old French *chaine*, ultimately from Latin; see CATENA]

Chain (tʃeɪn) *n* Sir **Ernst Boris**. 1906–79, British biochemist, born in Germany: purified and adapted penicillin for clinical use; with Fleming and Florey shared the Nobel prize for physiology or medicine 1945

chain gang *n* US a group of convicted prisoners chained together, usually while doing hard labour

chain letter *n* a letter, often with a request for and promise of money, that is sent to many people who add to or recopy it and send it on to others: illegal in many countries

chain mail *n* another term for **mail²** (sense 1)

chain printer *n* a line printer in which the type is on a continuous chain, used to print computer output

chain reaction *n* **1** a process in which a neutron colliding with an atomic nucleus causes fission and the ejection of one or more other neutrons, which induce other nuclei to split **2** a chemical reaction in which the product of one step is a reactant in the following step **3** a series of rapidly occurring events, each of which precipitates the next

chain saw *n* a motor-driven saw, usually portable, in which the cutting teeth form links in a continuous chain

chain-smoke *vb* to smoke (cigarettes, etc) continually, esp lighting one from the preceding one ▷ **chain smoker** *n*

chain stitch *n* **1** an ornamental looped embroidery stitch resembling the links of a chain ▷ *vb* **chain-stitch 2** to sew (something) with this stitch

chain wheel *n* *engineering* a toothed wheel that meshes with a roller chain to transmit motion

chair (tʃɛə) *n* **1** a seat with a back on which one person sits, typically having four legs and often having arms **2** an official position of authority **3** the person chairing a debate or meeting: *the speaker adjourned the chair* **4** a professorship **5** *railways* an iron or steel cradle bolted to a sleeper in which the rail sits and is locked in position **6** short for **sedan chair 7** take the chair to preside as chairman for a meeting, etc **8** the chair an informal name for **electric chair** ▷ *vb* (*tr*) **9** to preside over (a meeting) **10** *Brit* to carry aloft in a sitting position after a triumph or great achievement **11** to provide with a chair of office **12** to install in a chair [c13: from Old French *chaiere*, from Latin *cathedra*, from Greek *kathedra*, from *kata-* down + *hedra* seat; compare CATHEDRAL]

chairlift (tʃɛə,lɪft) *n* a series of chairs suspended from a power-driven cable for conveying people, esp skiers, up a mountain

chairman (tʃɛəmən) *n, pl* **-men** Also called: **chairperson**, (*fem*) **chairwoman** a person who presides over a company's board of directors, a committee, a debate, an administrative department, etc

● USAGE *Chairman* can seem inappropriate when applied
● to a woman, while *chairwoman* can be offensive. *Chair*
● and *chairperson* can be applied to either a man or a
● woman; *chair* is generally preferred to *chairperson*

chaise (ʃeɪz) *n* **1** a light open horse-drawn carriage, esp one with two wheels designed for two passengers **2** short for **post chaise, chaise longue** [c18: from French, variant of Old French *chaiere* CHAIR]

chaise longue (ʃeɪz 'lɒŋ; *French* ʃɛz lɔ̃g) *n, pl* **chaise longues** *or* **chaises longues** (ʃeɪz 'lɒŋ; *French* ʃɛz lɔ̃g) a long low chair for reclining, with a back and single armrest [c19: from French: long chair]

Chaka (ʃaka) *n* a variant spelling of **Shaka**

chakalaka (ʃaka'laka) *n* *South African* a relish made from tomatoes, onions, and spices [of unknown origin]

chakra (tʃækrə, 'tʃʌkrə) *n* (in yoga) any of the seven major energy centres in the body [c19: from Sanskrit *cakra* wheel, circle]

chalaza (kə'leɪzə) *n, pl* **-zas** *or* **-zae** (-ziː) one of a pair of spiral threads of albumen holding the yolk of a bird's egg in position [c18: New Latin, from Greek: hailstone]

chalcedony (kæl'sɛdənɪ) *n, pl* **-nies** a microcrystalline often greyish form of quartz with crystals arranged in parallel fibres: a gemstone. Formula: SiO₂ [c15: from Late Latin *chalcēdōnius*, from Greek *khalkēdōn* a precious stone (Revelation 21:19), perhaps named after *Khalkēdōn* Chalcedon, town in Asia Minor] ▷ **chalcedonic** (,kælsɪ'dɒnɪk) *adj*

Chalcidice (kæl'sɪdɪsɪ) *n* a peninsula of N central Greece, in Macedonia Central, ending in the three promontories of Kassandra, Sithonia, and Akti. Area: 2945 sq km (1149 sq miles). Modern Greek name: Khalkidíki

Chalcis (ˈkælsɪs) *n* a city on the island of Euboea in SE Greece, at the narrowest point of the Euripus strait: important since the 7th century BC, founding many colonies in ancient times. Pop (municipality): 55 264

(2001). Modern Greek name: Khalkís. Medieval English name: Negropont

chalcogen ('kælkə,dʒɛn) *n* any of the elements oxygen, sulphur, selenium, tellurium, or polonium, of group 6A of the periodic table [c20: from CHALCO(PYRITE) + -GEN]

chalcolithic (,kælkə'lɪθɪk) *adj* *archaeol* of or relating to a period characterized by the use of both stone and bronze implements

chalcopyrite (,kælkə'paɪraɪt, -'paɪə-) *n* a widely distributed yellow mineral consisting of a sulphide of copper and iron in tetragonal crystalline form: the principal ore of copper. Formula: CuFeS₂. Also called: **copper pyrites**

Chaldea *or* **Chaldaea** (kæl'diːə) *n* **1** an ancient region of Babylonia; the land lying between the Euphrates delta, the Persian Gulf, and the Arabian desert **2** another name for **Babylonia**

chaldron ('tʃɔːldrən) *n* a unit of capacity equal to 36 bushels. Formerly used in the US for the measurement of solids, being equivalent to 1.268 cubic metres. Used in Britain for both solids and liquids, it is equivalent to 1.309 cubic metres [c17: from Old French *chauderon* CAULDRON]

chalet ('ʃæleɪ; *French* ʃalɛ) *n* **1** a type of wooden house of Swiss origin, typically low, with wide projecting eaves **2** a similar house used esp as a ski lodge, garden house, etc [c19: from French (Swiss dialect)]

Chaliapin (*Russian* ʃa'ljapin) *n* **Fyodor Ivanovich** ('fjɔdər i'vanəvitʃ). 1873–1938, Russian operatic bass singer

chalice ('tʃælɪs) *n* **1** *poetic* a drinking cup; goblet **2** *Christianity* a gold or silver cup containing the wine at Mass **3** the calyx of a flower, esp a cup-shaped calyx [c13: from Old French, from Latin *calix* cup; related to Greek *kalux* calyx]

chalk (tʃɔːk) *n* **1** a soft fine-grained white sedimentary rock consisting of nearly pure calcium carbonate, containing minute fossil fragments of marine organisms, usually without a cementing material **2** a piece of chalk or a substance like chalk, often coloured, used for writing and drawing on a blackboard **3** as alike as chalk and cheese *or* as different as chalk and cheese *informal* totally different in essentials **4** by a long chalk *Brit informal* by far **5** not by a long chalk *Brit informal* by no means; not possibly **6** (*modifier*) made of chalk ▷ *vb* **7** to draw or mark (something) with chalk **8** (*tr*) to mark, rub, or whiten with or as if with chalk [Old English *cealc*, from Latin *calx* limestone, from Greek *khalix* pebble] ▷ **'chalk,like** *adj* ▷ **'chalky** *adj* ▷ **'chalkiness** *n*

chalk out *vb* (*tr, adverb*) to outline (a plan, scheme, etc); sketch

chalkpit ('tʃɔːk,pɪt) *n* a quarry for chalk

chalk up *vb* (*tr, adverb*) *informal* **1** to score or register (something) **2** to credit (money) to an account etc (esp in the phrase **chalk it up**)

challenge ('tʃælɪndʒ) *vb* (*mainly tr*) **1** to invite or summon (someone to do something, esp to take part in a contest) **2** (*also intr*) to call (something) into question; dispute **3** to make demands on; stimulate: *the job challenges his ingenuity* **4** to order (a person) to halt and be identified or to give a password **5** *law* to make formal objection to (a juror or jury) **6** to lay claim to (attention, etc) **7** to inject (an experimental animal immunized with a test substance) with disease microorganisms to test for immunity to the disease ▷ *n* **8** a call to engage in a fight, argument, or contest **9** a questioning of a statement or fact; a demand for justification or explanation **10** a demanding or stimulating situation, career, object, etc **11** a demand by a sentry, watchman, etc, for identification or a password **12** *law* a formal objection to a person selected to serve on a jury (**challenge to the polls**) or to the whole body of jurors (**challenge to the array**) [c13: from Old French *chalenge*, from Latin *calumnia* CALUMNY] ▷ **'challengeable** *adj* ▷ **'challenger** *n* ▷ **'challenging** *adj*

challenged ('tʃælɪndʒd) *adj* (*in combination*) disabled or disadvantaged in some way: *physically challenged performers*

challis ('ʃælɪ, -lɪs) *or* **challie** ('ʃælɪ) *n* a lightweight plain-weave fabric of wool, cotton, etc, usually with a printed design [c19: probably from a surname]

Chalon-sur-Saône (*French* ʃalōsyrson) *n* an industrial city in E central France, on the Saône River. Pop: 50 124 (1999)

chalybeate (kə'lıbııt) *adj* containing or impregnated with iron salts [c17: from New Latin *chalybēatus*, ultimately from *khalups* iron]

chamber ('tʃeımbə) *n* **1** a meeting hall, esp one used for a legislative or judicial assembly **2** a reception room or audience room in an official residence, palace, etc **3** *archaic or poetic* a room in a private house, esp a bedroom **4 a** a legislative, deliberative, judicial, or administrative assembly **b** any of the houses of a legislature **5** an enclosed space; compartment; cavity **6** an enclosure for a cartridge in the cylinder of a revolver or for a shell in the breech of a cannon **7** short for **chamber pot** **8** (*modifier*) of, relating to, or suitable for chamber music: *a chamber concert* ▷ See also **chambers** [c13: from Old French *chambre*, from Late Latin *camera* room, Latin: vault, from Greek *kamara*]

chamberlain ('tʃeımbəlın) *n* **1** an officer who manages the household of a king **2** the steward of a nobleman or landowner **3** the treasurer of a municipal corporation [c13: from Old French *chamberlayn*, of Frankish origin; related to Old High German *chamarling* chamberlain, Latin *camera* CHAMBER]

Chamberlain ('tʃeımbəlın) *n* **1** Sir (**Joseph**) **Austen**. 1863–1937, British Conservative statesman; foreign secretary (1924–29); awarded a Nobel peace prize for his negotiation of the Locarno Pact (1925) **2** his father, **Joseph**. 1836–1914, British statesman; originally a Liberal, he resigned in 1886 over Home Rule for Ireland and became leader of the Liberal Unionists; a leading advocate of preferential trading agreements with members of the British Empire **3** his son, (**Arthur**) **Neville**. 1869–1940, British Conservative statesman; prime minister (1937–40): pursued a policy of appeasement towards Germany; following the German invasion of Poland, he declared war on Germany on Sept 3, 1939 **4** Owen. 1920–2006, US physicist, who discovered the antiproton. Nobel prize for physics jointly with Emilio Segré 1959

chambermaid ('tʃeımbə,meıd) *n* a woman or girl employed to clean and tidy bedrooms, now chiefly in hotels

chamber music *n* music for performance by a small group of instrumentalists

chamber of commerce *n* (*sometimes capitals*) an organization composed mainly of local businessmen to promote, regulate, and protect their interests

chamber orchestra *n* a small orchestra consisting of about 25 players, used for the authentic performance of baroque and early classical music as well as modern music written specifically for a small orchestra

chamber pop *n* pop music that incorporates orchestral arrangements

chamber pot *n* a vessel for urine, used in bedrooms

chambers ('tʃeımbəz) *pl n* **1** a judge's room for hearing cases not taken in open court **2** (in England) the set of rooms occupied by barristers where clients are interviewed (in London, mostly in the Inns of Court)

Chambéry (*French* ʃãberi) *n* a city in SE France, in the Alps: skiing centre; former capital of the duchy of Savoy. Pop: 55 786 (1999)

chambray ('ʃæmbreı) *n* a smooth light fabric of cotton, linen, etc, with white weft and a coloured warp [c19: after *Cambrai*; see CAMBRIC]

chameleon (kə'miːlıən) *n* **1** any lizard of the family *Chamaeleontidae* of Africa and Madagascar, having long slender legs, a prehensile tail and tongue, and the ability to change colour **2** a changeable or fickle person [c14: from Latin *chamaeleon*, from Greek *khamaileōn*, from *khamai* on the ground + *leōn* LION] ▷ **chameleonic** (kə,miːlı'ɒnık) *adj*

chamfer ('tʃæmfə) *n* **1** a narrow flat surface at the corner of a beam, post, etc, esp one at an angle of 45° ▷ *vb* (*tr*) **2** to cut such a surface on (a beam, etc) [c16: back formation from *chamfering*, from Old French *chamfrein*, from *chant* edge (see CANT²) + *fraindre* to break, from Latin *frangere*]

chamois ('ʃæmı; *French* ʃamwa) *n, pl* **-ois 1** ('ʃæmwɑː) a sure-footed goat antelope, *Rupicapra rupicapra*, inhabiting mountains of Europe and SW Asia, having vertical horns with backward-pointing tips **2** a soft suede leather formerly made from the hide of this animal, now obtained from the skins of sheep and goats **3** Also called: **chamois leather, shammy, shammy leather, chammy, chammy leather** ('ʃæmı) a piece of such leather or similar material used for polishing, etc **4** ('ʃæmwɑː) **a** a yellow to greyish-yellow colour **b** (as *modifier*): *a chamois stamp* ▷ *vb* (*tr*) **5** to dress (leather or skin) like chamois **6** to polish with a chamois [c16: from Old French, from Late Latin *camox* of uncertain origin]

chamomile ('kæmə,maıl) *n* a variant spelling of **camomile**

Chamonix ('ʃæmənı; *French* ʃamɔni) *n* a town in SE France, in the Alps at the foot of Mont Blanc: skiing and tourist centre. Pop: 9830 (1999)

champ¹ (tʃæmp) *vb* **1** to munch (food) noisily like a horse **2** (when *intr*, often foll by *on, at*, etc) to bite (something) nervously or impatiently; gnaw **3 champ at the bit** *or* **chafe at the bit** *informal* to be impatient to start work, a journey, etc ▷ *n* **4** the act or noise of champing [c16: probably of imitative origin]

champ² (tʃæmp) *n informal* short for **champion** (sense 1)

champagne (ʃæm'peın) *n* **1** (*sometimes capital*) a white sparkling wine produced around Reims and Epernay, France **2** (loosely) any effervescent white wine **3 a** a colour varying from a pale orange-yellow to a greyish-yellow **b** (as *adjective*): *a champagne carpet* **4** (*modifier*) denoting a luxurious lifestyle: *a champagne capitalist*

Champagne-Ardenne (ʃæm'peına:'den; *French* ʃãpaɲardɛn) *n* a region of NE France: a countship and commercial centre in medieval times; it consists of a great plain, with sheep and dairy farms and many vineyards

champagne socialist *n* a professed socialist who enjoys an extravagant lifestyle

Champaigne (ʃæm'peın; *French* ʃãpɛɲ) *n* **Philippe de** (filip də). 1602–74, French painter, born in Brussels: noted particularly for his portraits and historical and religious scenes

champers ('ʃæmpəz) *n* a slang name for **champagne**

champerty ('tʃæmpətı) *n, pl* **-ties** *law* (formerly) an illegal bargain between a party to litigation and an outsider whereby the latter agrees to pay for the action and thereby share in any proceeds recovered [c14: from Anglo-French *champartie*, from Old French *champart* share of produce, from *champ* field + *part* share (a feudal lord's)]

Champigny-sur-Marne (*French* ʃãpiɲisyrmarn) *n* a suburb of Paris, on the River Marne. Pop: 74 237 (1999)

champion ('tʃæmpıən) *n* **1 a** a person who has defeated all others in a competition: *a chess champion* **b** (as *modifier*): *a champion team* **2** (as *modifier*): *a champion marrow* **3** a person who defends a person or cause: *champion of the underprivileged* **4** (formerly) a warrior or knight who did battle for another, esp a king or queen, to defend their rights or honour ▷ *adj* **5** *Northern English dialect* first rate; excellent ▷ *adv* **6** *Northern English dialect* very well; excellently ▷ *vb* (*tr*) **7** to support; defend: *we champion the cause of liberty* [c13: from Old French, from Late Latin *campiō*, from Latin *campus* field, battlefield]

championship ('tʃæmpıən,ʃıp) *n* **1** (*sometimes plural*) any of various contests held to determine a champion **2** the title or status of being a champion **3** support for or defence of a cause, person, etc

Champlain¹ (ʃæm'pleın) *n* **Lake Champlain** a lake in the northeastern US, between the Green Mountains and the Adirondack Mountains: linked by the **Champlain Canal** to the Hudson River and by the Richelieu River to the St Lawrence; a major communications route in colonial times

Champlain² (ʃæm'pleın; *French* ʃãplɛ̃) *n* **Samuel de** (samyɛl də). ?1567–1635, French explorer; founder of Quebec (1608) and governor of New France (1633–35)

champlevé *French* (ʃãlve; *English* ʃæmplə'veı) *adj* **1** of or relating to a process of enamelling by which grooves are cut into a metal base and filled with enamel colours ▷ *n* **2** an object enamelled by this process [c19: from *champ* field (level surface) + *levé* raised]

Champollion (*French* ʃɑ̃pɔljɔ̃) *n* **Jean François** (ʒɑ̃ frɑ̃swa). 1790–1832, French Egyptologist, who deciphered the hieroglyphics on the Rosetta stone

Champs-Elysées (fɒnz eɪˈliːzeɪ; *French* ʃɑ̃z elize) *n* a major boulevard in Paris, leading from the Arc de Triomphe: site of the Elysée Palace and government offices

chance (tʃɑːns) *n* **1 a** the unknown and unpredictable element that causes an event to result in a certain way rather than another, spoken of as a real force **b** (*as modifier*): *a chance meeting*. Related adj: **fortuitous** **2** fortune; luck; fate **3** an opportunity or occasion **4** a risk; gamble **5** the extent to which an event is likely to occur; probability **6** an unpredicted event, esp a fortunate one **7 by chance** accidentally: *he slipped by chance* **8** on the chance acting on the possibility; in case ▷ *vb* **9** (*tr*) to risk; hazard **10** to happen by chance; be the case by chance: *I chanced to catch sight of her as she passed* **11 chance on** *or* **chance upon** to come upon by accident **12 chance one's arm** to attempt to do something although the chance of success may be slight [c13: from Old French *cheance*, from *cheoir* to fall, occur, from Latin *cadere*] ▷ **'chanceful** *adj*

chancel (ˈtʃɑːnsəl) *n* the part of a church containing the altar, sanctuary, and choir, usually separated from the nave and transepts by a screen [c14: from Old French, from Latin *cancellī* (plural) lattice]

chancellery *or* **chancellory** (ˈtʃɑːnsələrɪ, -slərɪ) *n, pl* **-leries** *or* **-lories 1** the building or room occupied by a chancellor's office **2** the position, rank, or office of a chancellor **3** *US* the residence or office of an embassy or legation [c14: from Anglo-French *chancellerie*, from Old French *chancelier* CHANCELLOR]

chancellor (ˈtʃɑːnsələ, -slə) *n* **1** the head of the government in several European countries **2** *US* the president of a university or, in some colleges, the chief administrative officer **3** *Brit & Canadian* the honorary head of a university. See also **vice chancellor** (sense 1) **4** *Christianity* a clergyman acting as the law officer of a bishop [c11: from Anglo-French *chanceler*, from Late Latin *cancellārius* porter, secretary, from Latin *cancellī* lattice; see CHANCEL] ▷ **'chancellor,ship** *n*

Chancellor of the Exchequer *n Brit* the cabinet minister responsible for finance

chance-medley *n law* a sudden quarrel in which one party kills another; unintentional but not blameless killing [c15: from Anglo-French *chance medlee* mixed chance]

chancer (ˈtʃɑːnsə) *n slang* an unscrupulous or dishonest opportunist who is prepared to try any dubious scheme for making money or furthering his or her own ends [c19: from CHANCE + -ER[1]]

chancery (ˈtʃɑːnsərɪ) *n, pl* **-ceries 1** Also called: Chancery Division (in England) the Lord Chancellor's court, now a division of the High Court of Justice **2** Also called: court of chancery (in the US) a court of equity **3** *Brit* the political section or offices of an embassy or legation **4** another name for **chancellery 5** a court of public records; archives **6** *Christianity* a diocesan office under the supervision of a bishop's chancellor, having custody of archives, issuing official enactments, etc **7** in chancery **a** *law* (of a suit) pending in a court of equity **b** in an awkward or helpless situation [c14: shortened from CHANCELLERY]

chancre (ˈʃæŋkə) *n pathol* a small hard nodular growth, which is the first diagnostic sign of acquired syphilis [c16: from French, from Latin: CANCER] ▷ **'chancrous** *adj*

chancroid (ˈʃæŋkrɔɪd) *n* **1** a soft venereal ulcer, esp of the male genitals, caused by infection with the bacillus *Haemophilus ducreyi* ▷ *adj* **2** relating to or resembling a chancroid or chancre

chancy *or* **chancey** (ˈtʃɑːnsɪ) *adj* **chancier, chanciest** *informal* of uncertain outcome or temperament; risky

chandelier (ʃændɪˈlɪə) *n* an ornamental hanging light with branches and holders for several candles or bulbs [c17: from French: candleholder, from Latin CANDELABRUM]

Chandernagore (ˌtʃʌndənəˈgɔː) *n* a port in E India, in S West Bengal on the Hooghly River: a former French settlement (1686–1950). Pop: 162 166 (2001)

Chandigarh (ˌtʃʌndɪˈgɑː) *n* a city and Union Territory of N India, joint capital of the Punjab and Haryana: modern city planned in the 1950s by Le Corbusier. Pop: 808 796 (2001), of city; 900 414 (2001), of union territory. Area (of union territory): 114 sq km (44 sq miles)

chandler (ˈtʃɑːndlə) *n* **1** a dealer in a specified trade or merchandise: *corn chandler; ship's chandler* **2** a person who makes or sells candles [c14: from Old French *chandelier* one who makes or deals in candles, from *chandelle* CANDLE]

Chandler (ˈtʃɑːndlə) *n* **Raymond** (**Thornton**). 1888–1959, US thriller writer: created Philip Marlowe, one of the first detective heroes in fiction

Chandragupta (ˌtʃændrəˈguptə) *n* Greek name *Sandracottus*. died ?297 BC, ruler of N India, who founded the Maurya dynasty (325) and defeated Seleucus (?305)

Chandrasekhar (ˌtʃændrəˈsiːkə) *n* **Subrahmanyan** (ˌsʌbrəˈmænjən). 1910–95, US astronomer born in Lahore, India (now Pakistan). His work on stellar evolution led to an understanding of white dwarfs: shared the Nobel prize for physics 1983

Chandrasekhar limit (ˌtʃændrəˈsiːkə) *n astronomy* the upper limit to the mass of a white dwarf, equal to 1.44 solar masses. A star having a mass above this limit will continue to collapse to form a neutron star [c20: named after Subrahmanyan Chandrasekhar (1910–95), Indian-born US astronomer, who calculated it]

Chanel (*French* ʃanɛl) *n* **Gabrielle** (gabriɛl), known as *Coco Chanel*. 1883– 1971, French couturière and perfumer, who created "the little black dress" and the perfume Chanel No. 5

Chang (tʃæŋ) *n* another name for the **Yangtze**

Changan (ˈtʃæŋˈɑːn) *n* a former name of **Xi'an**

Changchiakow *or* **Changchiak'ou** (ˈtʃæŋˈtʃjɑːˈkəʊ) *n* a variant transliteration of the Chinese name for **Zhangjiakou**

Changchow *or* **Ch'ang-chou** (ˈtʃæŋˈtʃəʊ) *n* **1** a variant transliteration of the Chinese name for **Zhangzhou** **2** former spellings of **Changzhou**

Changchun *or* **Ch'ang Ch'un** (ˈtʃæŋˈtʃʊn) *n* a city in NE China, capital of Jilin province: as Hsinking, capital of the Japanese state of Manchukuo (1932–45). Pop: 3 092 000 (2005 est)

Changde (ˈtʃæŋˈdeɪ), **Changteh** *or* **Ch'ang-te** *n* a port in SE central China, in N Hunan province, near the mouth of the Yuan River: severely damaged by the Japanese in World War II. Pop: 1 483 000 (2005 est)

change (tʃeɪndʒ) *vb* **1** to make or become different; alter **2** (*tr*) to replace with or exchange for another: *to change one's name* **3** (sometimes foll by *to* or *into*) to transform or convert or be transformed or converted **4** to give and receive (something) in return; interchange: *to change places with someone* **5** (*tr*) to give or receive (money) in exchange for the equivalent sum in a smaller denomination or different currency **6** (*tr*) to remove or replace the coverings of: *to change a baby* **7** (when *intr*, may be foll by *into* or *out of*) to put on other clothes **8** to operate (the gear lever of a motor vehicle) in order to change the gear ratio: *to change gear* **9** to alight from (one bus, train, etc) and board another ▷ *n* **10** the act or fact of changing or being changed **11** a variation, deviation, or modification **12** the substitution of one thing for another; exchange **13** anything that is or may be substituted for something else **14** variety or novelty (esp in the phrase **for a change**) **15** a different or fresh set, esp of clothes **16** money given or received in return for its equivalent in a larger denomination or in a different currency **17** the balance of money given or received when the amount tendered is larger than the amount due **18** coins of a small denomination regarded collectively **19** (*often capital*) *archaic* a place where merchants meet to transact business; an exchange **20** the act of passing from one state or phase to another **21** the transition from one phase of the moon to the next **22** the order in which a peal of bells may be rung **23 change of heart** a profound change of outlook, opinion, etc **24 get no change out of someone** *slang* not to be successful in attempts to exploit or extract information from someone **25** ring the changes to vary the manner or performance of an action that is often repeated ▷ See also **change down, changeover, change up** [C13: from Old French *changier*, from Latin *cambīre* to exchange, barter] > **'changeless** *adj* > **'changer** *n* > **'changeful** *adj* > **'changefully** *adv*

changeable ('tʃeɪndʒəbəl) *adj* **1** able to change or be changed; fickle: *changeable weather* **2** varying in colour when viewed from different angles or in different lights > ,**change'ability** or **'changeableness** *n* > **'changeably** *adv*

change down *vb* (*intr, adverb*) to select a lower gear when driving

changeling ('tʃeɪndʒlɪŋ) *n* a child believed to have been exchanged by fairies for the parents' true child

change of life *n* a nontechnical name for **menopause**

changeover ('tʃeɪndʒ,əʊvə) *n* **1** an alteration or complete reversal from one method, system, or product to another **2** a reversal of a situation, attitude, etc **3** *sport* the act of transferring to or being relieved by a team-mate in a relay race, as by handing over a baton, etc ▷ *vb* change over (*adverb*) **4** to adopt (a completely different position or attitude): *the driver and navigator changed over after four hours*

change-ringing *n* the art of bell-ringing in which a set of bells is rung in an established order which is then changed

change up *vb* (*intr, adverb*) to select a higher gear when driving

Changsha or **Ch'ang-sha** ('tʃæŋ'ʃɑ:) *n* a port in SE China, capital of Hunan province, on the Xiang River. Pop: 2 051 000 (2005 est)

Changteh or **Ch'ang-te** ('tʃæŋ'teɪ) *n* a variant transliteration of the Chinese name for **Changde**

Changzhou (tʃæŋdʒəʊ) *n* a city in E China, in S Jiangsu province, on the Grand Canal: also known as Wutsin until 1949, when the 7th-century name was officially readopted. Pop: 2 085 500 (2004 est)

Chania or **Hania** ('hɑːniə) *n* the chief port of Crete, on the NW coast. Pop: 82 000 (2005 est). Greek name: Khaniá

channel ('tʃænəl) *n* **1** a broad strait connecting two areas of sea **2** the bed or course of a river, stream, or canal **3** a navigable course through a body of water **4** (*often plural*) a means or agency of access, communication, etc: *to go through official channels* **5** a course into which something can be directed or moved **6** *electronics* **a** a band of radio frequencies assigned for a particular purpose, esp the broadcasting of a television signal **b** a path for an electromagnetic signal: *a stereo set has two channels* **7** a tubular or trough-shaped passage for fluids **8** a groove or flute, as in the shaft of a column **9** *computing* **a** a path along which data can be transmitted between a central processing unit and one or more peripheral devices **b** one of the lines along the length of a paper tape on which information can be stored in the form of punched holes ▷ *vb* **-nels, -nelling, -nelled** or *US* **-nels, -neling, -neled** **10** to provide or be provided with a channel or channels; make or cut channels in (something) **11** (*tr*) to guide into or convey through a channel or channels: *information was channelled through to them* **12** to serve as a medium through whom the spirit of (a person of a former age) allegedly communicates with the living **13** (*tr*) to form a groove or flute in (a column, etc) [C13: from Old French *chanel*, from Latin *canālis* pipe, groove, conduit; see **CANAL**]

Channel ('tʃænəl) *n* the Channel short for **English Channel**

Channel Country *n* the Channel Country an area of E central Australia, in SW Queensland: crossed by intermittent rivers and subject to both flooding and long periods of drought

channel-hop *vb* **-hops, -hopping, -hopped** (*intr*) to change television channels repeatedly using a remote control device

Channel Islands *pl n* a group of islands in the English Channel, off the NW coast of France, consisting of Jersey, Guernsey, Alderney, Brechou or Brecqhou, Sark, Herm, Jethou, and Lihou (all between them

representing the United Kingdom Crown Dependencies of the Bailiwick of Jersey and the Bailiwick of Guernsey) - the only part of the duchy of Normandy remaining to Britain - and the Roches Douvres and the Îles Chausey (which belong to France). Pop: 149 878 (2001). Area: 194 sq km (75 sq miles)

Channel Tunnel *n* the Anglo-French railway tunnel that runs beneath the English Channel, between Folkestone and Coquelles, near Calais; opened in 1994. Also called: **Chunnel, Eurotunnel**

chanson de geste *French* (ʃɑ̃sɔ̃ də ʒɛst) *n* one of a genre of Old French epic poems celebrating heroic deeds, the most famous of which is the *Chanson de Roland* [literally: song of exploits]

chant (tʃɑːnt) *n* **1** a simple song or melody **2** a short simple melody in which several words or syllables are assigned to one note, as in the recitation of psalms **3** a psalm or canticle performed by using such a melody **4** a rhythmic or repetitious slogan, usually spoken or sung, as by sports supporters, etc ▷ *vb* **5** to sing or recite (a psalm, prayer, etc) as a chant **6** to intone (a slogan) rhythmically or repetitiously [C14: from Old French *chanter* to sing, from Latin *cantāre*, frequentative of *canere* to sing] > **'chanting** *n, adj*

chanter ('tʃɑːntə) *n* the pipe on a set of bagpipes that is provided with finger holes and on which the melody is played

chanterelle (,tʃæntə'rɛl) *n* any saprotrophic basidiomycetous fungus of the genus *Cantharellus*, esp *C. cibarius*, having an edible yellow funnel-shaped mushroom: family Cantharellaceae [C18: from French, from New Latin *cantharella*, diminutive of Latin *cantharus* drinking vessel, from Greek *kantharos*]

chanteuse (*French* ʃɑ̃tøz) *n* a female singer, esp in a nightclub or cabaret [French: singer]

chanticleer (,tʃæntɪ'klɪə) or **chantecler** (,tʃæntɪ'klɛə) *n* a name for a cock, used esp in fables [C13: from Old French *Chantecler*, from *chanter cler* to sing clearly]

Chantilly (ʃæn'tɪlɪ; *French* ʃɑ̃tiji) *n* **1** a town in N France, near the **Forest of Chantilly** formerly famous for lace and porcelain. Pop: 10 902 (1999) **2** Also called: **Tiffany** a breed of medium-sized cat with silky semi-long hair ▷ *adj* **3** (of cream) lightly sweetened and whipped

chantry ('tʃɑːntrɪ) *n, pl* **-tries** *Christianity* **1** an endowment for the singing of Masses for the soul of the founder or others designated by him **2** a chapel or altar so endowed [C14: from Old French *chanterie*, from *chanter* to sing; see **CHANT**]

chanty ('ʃæntɪ, 'tʃæn-) *n, pl* **-ties** a variant of **shanty²**

Chanukah ('hɑːnəkə, -nʊ,kɑ:; *Hebrew* xanu'ka) *n* a variant spelling of **Hanukkah**

Chaoan ('tʃaʊ'ɑːn) *n* the former name of **Chaozhou**

Chaochow ('tʃaʊ'tʃəʊ) *n* a former spelling of **Chaozhou**

chaos ('keɪɒs) *n* **1** complete disorder; utter confusion **2** (*usually capital*) the disordered formless matter supposed to have existed before the ordered universe [C15: from Latin, from Greek *khaos*; compare **CHASM, yawn**] > **chaotic** (keɪ'ɒtɪk) *adj* > **cha'otically** *adv*

chaos theory *n* a theory, applied in various branches of science, that apparently random phenomena have underlying order

Chaozhou ('tʃaʊ'tʃəʊ) *n* a city in SE China, in E Guangdong province, on the Han River: river port. Pop: 480 000 (2005 est). Also called: **Chaochow**. Former name: **Chaoan**

chap¹ (tʃæp) *vb* **chaps, chapping, chapped** **1** (of the skin) to make or become raw and cracked, esp by exposure to cold ▷ *n* **2** (*usually plural*) a cracked or sore patch on the skin caused by chapping [C14: probably of Germanic origin; compare Middle Dutch, German *kappen* to chop off]

chap² (tʃæp) *n* *informal* a man or boy; fellow [C16 (in the sense: buyer): shortened from **CHAPMAN**]

chap³ (tʃɒp, tʃæp) *n* a less common word for **chop³**

chaparejos (,ʃæpə'reɪəʊs; *Spanish* tʃapa'rexos) or **chaparajos** (,ʃæpə'reɪəʊs; *Spanish* tʃapa'raxos) *pl n* another name for **chaps** [from Mexican Spanish]

chaparral (,tʃæpə'ræl, ,ʃæp-) *n* (in the southwestern US) a dense growth of shrubs and trees, esp evergreen oaks

[C19: from Spanish, from *chaparra* evergreen oak]

chapati or**chapatti** (tʃəˈpætɪ, -ˈpʌtɪ, pl-ti, -tis or-ties (in Indian cookery) a flat coarse unleavened bread resembling a pancake [from Hindi]

chapeau (ˈʃæpəʊ; *French* ʃapo; pl-peaux (-pəʊ, -pəʊz; *French* -po) or-peaus a hat [C16: from French, from Late Latin *cappellus* hood, from *cappa* CAP]

chapel (ˈtʃæpəl) n **1** a place of Christian worship in a larger building, esp a place set apart, with a separate altar, in a church or cathedral **2** a similar place of worship in or attached to a large house or institution, such as a college, hospital or prison **3** a church subordinate to a parish church **4** (in Britain) **a** a Nonconformist place of worship **b** Nonconformist religious practices or doctrine **5** the members of a trade union in a particular newspaper office, printing house, etc [C13: from Old French *chapele*, from Late Latin *cappella*, diminutive of *cappa* cloak (see CAP); originally denoting the sanctuary where the cloak of St Martin of Tours was kept as a relic]

chaperon or**chaperone** (ˈʃæpəˌrəʊn) n **1** (esp formerly) an older or married woman who accompanies or supervises a young unmarried woman on social occasions ▷ vb **2** to act as a chaperon to [C14: from Old French, from *chape* hood, protective covering; see CAP] >chaperonage (ˈʃæpərənɪdʒ) n

chapfallen (ˈtʃæpˌfɔːlən) or**chopfallen** adj dejected; downhearted; crestfallen [C16: from CHOPS + FALLEN]

chaplain (ˈtʃæplɪn) n a Christian clergyman attached to a private chapel of a prominent person or institution or ministering to a military body, professional group, etc [C12: from Old French *chapelain*, from Late Latin *cappellānus*, from *cappella* CHAPEL] >ˈchaplaincy or ˈchaplainˌship n

chaplet (ˈtʃæplɪt) n **1** an ornamental wreath of flowers, beads, etc, worn on the head **2** a string of beads or something similar **3** RC Church **a** a string of prayer beads constituting one third of the rosary **b** the prayers counted on this string **4** a narrow convex moulding in the form of a string of beads; astragal [C14: from Old French *chapelet* garland of roses, from *chapel* hat; see CHAPEAU] >ˈchapleted adj

Chaplin (ˈtʃæplɪn) n Sir **Charles Spencer**, known as *Charlie Chaplin*. 1889–1977, English comedian, film actor, and director. He is renowned for his portrayal of a downtrodden little man with baggy trousers, bowler hat, and cane. His films, most of which were made in Hollywood, include *The Gold Rush* (1924), *Modern Times* (1936), and *The Great Dictator* (1940) >ˌChaplinˈesque adj

chapman (ˈtʃæpmən) n, pl-men archaic a trader, esp an itinerant pedlar [Old English *cēapman*, from *cēap* buying and selling (see CHEAP)]

Chapman (ˈtʃæpmən) n **George** 1559–1634, English dramatist and poet, noted for his translation of Homer

Chappell (ˈtʃæpəl) n **Greg(ory Stephen)**. born 1948, Australian cricketer: first Australian to score over 7000 test runs

chappie (ˈtʃæpɪ) n informal another word for **chap²**

chaps (tʃæps, ʃæps) pl n leather overalls without a seat, worn by cowboys. Also called: chaparejos, chaparajos [C19: shortened from CHAPAREJOS]

chapter (ˈtʃæptə) n **1** a division of a written work, esp a narrative, usually titled or numbered **2** a sequence of events having a common attribute: *a chapter of disasters* **3** an episode or period in a life, history, etc **4** a numbered reference to that part of a Parliamentary session which relates to a specified Act of Parliament **5** a branch of some societies, clubs, etc, esp of a secret society **6** the collective body or a meeting of the canons of a cathedral or collegiate church or of the members of a monastic or knightly order **7** chapter and verse exact authority for an action or statement ▷ vb **8** (tr) to divide into chapters [C13: from Old French *chapitre*, from Latin *capitulum*, literally: little head, hence, section of writing, from *caput* head; in Medieval Latin: chapter of scripture or of a religious rule, a gathering for the reading of this, hence, assemblage of clergy]

chapterhouse (ˈtʃæptəˌhaʊs) n **1** the building attached to a cathedral, collegiate church, or religious house in

which the chapter meets **2** US the meeting place of a college fraternity or sorority

char¹ (tʃɑː) vb chars, charring, charred **1** to burn or be burned partially, esp so as to blacken the surface; scorch **2** (tr) to reduce (wood) to charcoal by partial combustion [C17: short for CHARCOAL]

char² or**charr** (tʃɑː) n, pl char, chars or charr, charrs any of various troutlike fishes of the genus *Salvelinus*, esp *S. alpinus*, occurring in cold lakes and northern seas: family Salmonidae (salmon) [C17: of unknown origin]

char³ (tʃɑː) n **1** informal short for **charwoman** ▷ vb chars, charring, charred **2** Brit informal to do housework, cleaning, etc, as a job [C18: from Old English *cerr*]

char⁴ (tʃɑː) n Brit a slang word for **tea** [from Chinese *ch'a*]

charabanc (ˈʃærəˌbæŋ; *French* ʃarabɑ̃) n Brit obsolete a motor coach, esp one used for sightseeing tours [C19: from French *char-à-bancs*, wagon with seats]

character (ˈkærɪktə) n **1** the combination of traits and qualities distinguishing the individual nature of a person or thing **2** one such distinguishing quality; characteristic **3** moral force; integrity: *a man of character* **4** a reputation, esp a good reputation **b** (as modifier): *character assassination* **5** a person represented in a play, film, story, etc; role **6** an outstanding person: *one of the great characters of the century* **7** informal an odd, eccentric, or unusual person: *he's quite a character* **8** an informal word for **person** *a shady character* **9** a symbol used in a writing system, such as a letter of the alphabet **10** Also called: sort *printing* any single letter, numeral, punctuation mark, or symbol cast as a type **11** *computing* any letter, numeral, etc, which is a unit of information and can be represented uniquely by a binary pattern **12** a style of writing or printing **13** *genetics* any structure, function, attribute, etc, in an organism, which may or may not be determined by a gene or group of genes **14** a short prose sketch of a distinctive type of person, usually representing a vice or virtue **15** in character typical of the apparent character of a person or thing **16** out of character not typical of the apparent character of a person or thing [C14: from Latin: distinguishing mark, from Greek *kharaktēr* engraver's tool, from *kharassein* to engrave, stamp] >ˈcharacterful adj >ˈcharacterless adj

character actor n an actor who specializes in playing odd or eccentric characters

character assassination n the act of deliberately attempting to destroy a person's reputation by defamatory remarks

characteristic (ˌkærɪktəˈrɪstɪk) n **1** a distinguishing quality, attribute, or trait **2** maths **a** the integral part of a common logarithm, indicating the order of magnitude of the associated number: *the characteristic of 2.4771 is 2* **b** another name for exponent, used esp in number representation in computing ▷ adj **3** indicative of a distinctive quality, etc; typical >ˌcharacterˈistically adv

characterize or**characterise** (ˈkærɪktəˌraɪz) vb (tr) **1** to be a characteristic of **2** to distinguish or mark as a characteristic **3** to describe or portray the character of >ˌcharacterˈization or ˌcharacterˈisation n

charade (ʃəˈrɑːd) n **1** an episode or act in the game of charades **2** chiefly Brit an absurd act; travesty

charades (ʃəˈrɑːdz) n (functioning as singular) a parlour game in which one team acts out each syllable of a word, the other team having to guess the word [C18: from French *charade* entertainment, from Provençal *charrado* chat, from *charra* chatter, of imitative origin]

charcoal (ˈtʃɑːˌkəʊl) n **1** a black amorphous form of carbon made by heating wood or other organic matter in the absence of air: used as a fuel, in smelting metal ores, in explosives, and as an absorbent **2** a stick or pencil of this for drawing **3** a drawing done in charcoal **4** short for **charcoal grey** ▷ vb **5** (tr) to write, draw, or blacken with charcoal [C14: from *char* (origin obscure) + COAL]

charcoal grey n **a** a very dark grey colour **b** (as adjective): *charcoal-grey trousers*

Charcot (*French* ʃarko) n **Jean Martin** (ʒɑ̃ martɛ̃). 1825–93, French neurologist, noted for his attempt using hypnotism to find an organic cause for hysteria, which influenced Freud

charcuterie (ʃɑːˈkuːtəriː) n 1 cooked cold meats 2 a shop selling cooked cold meats [French]

chard (tʃɑːd) n a variety of beet, *Beta vulgaris cicla*, with large succulent leaves and thick stalks, used as a vegetable. Also called: **Swiss chard** [C17: probably from French *carde* edible leafstalk of the artichoke, but associated also with French *chardon* thistle, both ultimately from Latin *carduus* thistle; see CARDOON]

Chardin (French ʃardɛ̃) n **Jean-Baptiste Siméon** (ʒɑ̃batist simeɔ̃). 1699–1779, French still-life and genre painter, noted for his subtle use of scumbled colour

Chardonnay (ˈʃɑːdəˌneɪ) n (*sometimes not capital*) 1 a white grape originally grown in the Burgundy region of France, and now throughout the wine-producing world 2 any of various white wines made from this grape [French]

Chardonnet (French ʃardɔnɛ) n (**Louis Marie**) **Hilaire Bernigaud** (ilɛr bɛrnigo), Comte de. 1839–1924, French chemist and industrialist who produced rayon, the first artificial fibre

Charente (French ʃarɑ̃t) n 1 a department of W central France, in Poitou-Charentes region. Capital: Angoulême. Pop: 341 275 (2003 est). Area: 5972 sq km (2329 sq miles) 2 a river in W France, rising in the Massif Central and flowing west to the Bay of Biscay. Length: 362 km (225 miles)

Charente-Maritime (French ʃarɑ̃tmaritim) n a department of W France, in Poitou-Charentes region. Capital: La Rochelle. Pop: 576 855 (2003 est). Area: 7232 sq km (2820 sq miles)

Chargaff (ˈʃɑːgæf) n **Erwin**. 1905–2002, US biochemist, born in Austria, noted esp for his work on DNA

charge (tʃɑːdʒ) vb 1 to set or demand (a price) 2 (*tr*) to enter or record as an obligation against a person or his account 3 (*tr*) to accuse or impute a fault to (a person, etc), as formally in a court of law 4 (*tr*) to command; place a burden upon or assign responsibility to: *I was charged to take the message to headquarters* 5 to make a rush at or sudden attack upon (a person or thing) 6 (*tr*) to fill (a receptacle) with the proper or appropriate quantity 7 (often foll by *up*) to cause (an accumulator, capacitor, etc) to take or store electricity or (of an accumulator) to have electricity fed into it 8 to fill or suffuse or to be filled or suffused with matter by dispersion, solution, or absorption: *to charge water with carbon dioxide* 9 (*tr*) to fill or suffuse with feeling, emotion, etc: *the atmosphere was charged with excitement* 10 (*tr*) *law* (of a judge) to address (a jury) authoritatively 11 (*tr*) to load (a firearm) 12 (*tr*) *heraldry* to paint (a shield, banner, etc) with a charge ▷ n 13 a price charged for some article or service; cost 14 a financial liability, such as a tax 15 a debt or a book entry recording it 16 an accusation or allegation, such as a formal accusation of a crime in law 17 a an onrush, attack, or assault b the call to such an attack in battle 18 custody or guardianship 19 a person or thing committed to someone's care 20 a a cartridge or shell b the explosive required to discharge a firearm or other weapon c an amount of explosive material to be detonated at any one time 21 the quantity of anything that a receptacle is intended to hold 22 *physics* a the attribute of matter by which it responds to electromagnetic forces responsible for all electrical phenomena, existing in two forms to which the signs negative and positive are arbitrarily assigned b a similar property of a body or system determined by the extent to which it contains an excess or deficiency of electrons c a quantity of electricity determined by the product of an electric current and the time for which it flows, measured in coulombs d the total amount of electricity stored in a capacitor 23 a load or burden 24 a duty or responsibility; control 25 a command, injunction, or order 26 *heraldry* a design, device, or image depicted on heraldic arms 27 **in charge** in command 28 **in charge of** a having responsibility for b *US* under the care of [C13: from Old French *chargier* to load, from Late Latin *carricāre*; see CARRY]

chargeable (ˈtʃɑːdʒəbᵊl) adj 1 charged or liable to be charged 2 liable to result in a legal charge

chargeable asset n any asset that can give rise to

assessment for capital gains tax on its disposal. Exempt assets include principal private residences, cars, investments held in a personal equity plan, and government securities

charge account n another term for **credit account**

chargeback (ˈtʃɑːdʒˌbæk) n the return of funds by a seller to a buyer's debit or credit card account

charge card n a card issued by a chain store, shop, or organization, that enables customers to obtain goods and services for which they pay at a later date

charge carrier n an electron, hole, or ion that transports the electric charge in an electric current

chargé d'affaires (ˈʃɑːʒeɪ dæˈfɛə; French ʃarʒe dafɛr) n, pl **chargés d'affaires** (ˈʃɑːʒeɪ, -ʒeɪz; French ʃarʒe) 1 the temporary head of a diplomatic mission in the absence of the ambassador or minister 2 the head of a diplomatic mission of the lowest level [C18: from French: (one) charged with affairs]

charge hand n *Brit* a workman whose grade of responsibility is just below that of a foreman

charge nurse n *Brit* a nurse in charge of a ward in a hospital. Female equivalent: **sister**

charger¹ (ˈtʃɑːdʒə) n 1 a person or thing that charges 2 a large strong horse formerly ridden into battle 3 a device for charging or recharging an accumulator or rechargeable battery

charger² (ˈtʃɑːdʒə) n *antiques* a large dish for serving at table or for display [C14 *chargeour* something to bear a load, from *chargen* to CHARGE]

charge sheet n *Brit* a document on which a police officer enters details of the charge against a prisoner and the court in which he will appear

char-grilled adj (of food) grilled over charcoal

Chari (ˈtʃɑːrɪ) or **Shari** n a river in N central Africa, rising in the N Central African Republic and flowing north to Lake Chad. Length: about 2250 km (1400 miles)

charily (ˈtʃɛərɪlɪ) adv 1 cautiously; carefully 2 sparingly

chariness (ˈtʃɛərɪnɪs) n the state of being chary

Charing Cross (ˈtʃærɪŋ) n a district of London, in the city of Westminster: the modern cross (1863) in front of Charing Cross railway station replaces the one erected by Edward I (1290), the last of twelve marking the route of the funeral procession of his queen, Eleanor

chariot (ˈtʃærɪət) n 1 a two-wheeled horse-drawn vehicle used in ancient Egypt, Greece, Rome, etc, in war, races, and processions 2 a light four-wheeled horse-drawn ceremonial carriage 3 *poetic* any stately vehicle [C14: from Old French, augmentative of *char* CAR]

charioteer (ˌtʃærɪəˈtɪə) n the driver of a chariot

charisma (kəˈrɪzmə) or **charism** (ˈkærɪzəm) n 1 a special personal quality or power of an individual making him capable of influencing or inspiring large numbers of people 2 a quality inherent in a thing which inspires great enthusiasm and devotion 3 *Christianity* a divinely bestowed power or talent [C17: from Church Latin, from Greek *kharisma*, from *kharis* grace, favour] > **charismatic** (ˌkærɪzˈmætɪk) adj

charismatic movement n *Christianity* any of various groups, within existing denominations, that emphasize communal prayer and the charismatic gifts of speaking in tongues, healing, etc

charitable (ˈtʃærɪtəbᵊl) adj 1 generous in giving to the needy 2 kind or lenient in one's attitude towards others 3 concerned with or involving charity > **charitableness** n > **charitably** adv

charitable trust n a trust set up for the benefit of a charity that complies with the regulations of the Charity Commissioners to enable it to be exempt from paying income tax

charity (ˈtʃærɪtɪ) n, pl **-ties** 1 a the giving of help, money, food, etc, to those in need b (*as modifier*): *a charity show* 2 an institution or organization set up to provide help, money, etc, to those in need 3 the help, money, etc, given to the needy; alms 4 a kindly and lenient attitude towards people 5 love of one's fellow men [C13: from Old French *charite*, from Latin *cāritās* affection, love, from *cārus* dear]

charivari (ˌʃɑːrɪˈvɑːrɪ), **shivaree** or *esp US* **chivaree** (ʃɪvəˈriː) n 1 a discordant mock serenade to newlyweds, made with pans, kettles, etc **2** a confused noise; din [C17: from French, from Late Latin *caribaria* headache, from Greek *karēbaria*, from *karē* head + *barus* heavy]

charlady ('tʃɑːˌleɪdɪ) *n*, *pl-dies* another name for **charwoman**

charlatan ('ʃɑːlətᵊn) *n* someone who professes knowledge or expertise, esp in medicine, that he or she does not have; quack [C17: from French, from Italian *ciarlatano*, from *ciarlare* to chatter] > 'charlatan,ism or 'charlatanry *n*

Charlemagne ('ʃɑːləˌmeɪn) *n* ?742–814 AD, king of the Franks (768–814) and, as Charles I, Holy Roman Emperor (800–814). He conquered the Lombards (774), the Saxons (772–804), and the Avars (791–799). He instituted many judicial and ecclesiastical reforms, and promoted commerce and agriculture throughout his empire, which extended from the Ebro to the Elbe. Under Alcuin his court at Aachen became the centre of a revival of learning

Charles (tʃɑːlz) *n* **1** *Prince of Wales.* born 1948, son of Elizabeth II; heir apparent to the throne of Great Britain and Northern Ireland. He married (1981) Lady Diana Spencer; they separated in 1992 and were divorced in 1996; their son, Prince William of Wales, was born in 1982 and their second son, Prince Henry, in 1984; married (2005) Camilla Parker Bowles **2** *Ray* real name *Ray Charles Robinson.* 1930–2004, US singer, pianist, and songwriter, whose work spans jazz, blues, gospel, pop, and country music

Charles I *n* **1** title as Holy Roman Emperor of Charlemagne. See **Charlemagne 2** title as king of France of Charles II (Holy Roman Emperor). See **Charles II** (sense 1) **3** title as king of Spain of Charles V (Holy Roman Emperor). See **Charles V** (sense 2) **4** title of **Charles Stuart** 1600–49, king of England, Scotland, and Ireland (1625–49); son of James I. He ruled for 11 years (1629–40) without parliament, advised by his minister Strafford, until rebellion broke out in Scotland. Conflict with the Long Parliament led to the Civil War and after his defeat at Naseby (1645) he sought refuge with the Scots (1646). He was handed over to the English army under Cromwell and executed **5** 1887–1922, emperor of Austria, and, as Charles IV, king of Hungary (1916–18). The last ruler of the Austro-Hungarian monarchy, he was forced to abdicate at the end of World War I

Charles II *n* **1** known as *Charles the Bald.* 823–877 AD, Holy Roman Emperor (875–877) and, as Charles I, king of France (843–877) **2** the title as king of France of Charles III (Holy Roman Emperor). See **Charles III** (sense 1) **3** 1630–85, king of England, Scotland, and Ireland (1660–85) following the Restoration (1660); son of Charles I. He did much to promote commerce, science, and the Navy, but his Roman Catholic sympathies caused widespread distrust **4** 1661–1700, the last Hapsburg king of Spain: his reign saw the end of Spanish power in Europe

Charles III *n* **1** known as *Charles the Fat.* 839–888 AD, Holy Roman Emperor (881–887) and, as Charles II, king of France (884–887). He briefly reunited the empire of Charlemagne **2** 1716–88, king of Spain (1759–88), who curbed the power of the Church and tried to modernize his country

Charles IV *n* **1** known as *Charles the Fair.* 1294–1328, king of France (1322–28): brother of Isabella of France, with whom he intrigued against her husband, Edward II of England **2** 1316–78, king of Bohemia (1346–78) and Holy Roman Emperor (1355–78) **3** 1748–1819, king of Spain (1788–1808), whose reign saw the domination of Spain by Napoleonic France: abdicated **4** title as king of Hungary of Charles I. See **Charles I** (sense 5)

Charles V *n* **1** known as *Charles the Wise.* 1337–80, king of France (1364–80) during the Hundred Years' War **2** 1500–58, Holy Roman Emperor (1519–56), king of Burgundy and the Netherlands (1506–55), and, as Charles I, king of Spain (1516–56): his reign saw the empire threatened by Francis I of France, the Turks, and the spread of Protestantism; abdicated

Charles VI *n* **1** known as *Charles the Mad* or *Charles the Well-Beloved.* 1368–1422, king of France (1380–1422): defeated by

Henry V of England at Agincourt (1415), he was forced by the Treaty of Troyes (1420) to recognize Henry as his successor **2** 1685–1740, Holy Roman Emperor (1711–40). His claim to the Spanish throne (1700) led to the War of the Spanish Succession

Charles VII *n* **1** 1403–61, king of France (1422–61), son of Charles VI. He was excluded from the French throne by the Treaty of Troyes, but following Joan of Arc's victory over the English at Orléans (1429), was crowned **2** 1697–1745, Holy Roman Emperor (1742–45) during the War of the Austrian Succession

Charles IX *n* 1550–74, king of France (1560–74), son of Catherine de' Medici and Henry II: his reign was marked by war between Huguenots and Catholics

Charles X *n* **1** title of *Charles Gustavus.* 1622–60, king of Sweden, who warred with Poland and Denmark in an attempt to create a unified Baltic state **2** 1757–1836, king of France (1824–30): his attempt to restore absolutism led to his enforced exile

Charles XI *n* 1655–97, king of Sweden (1660–97), who established an absolute monarchy and defeated Denmark (1678)

Charles XII *n* 1682–1718, king of Sweden (1697–1718), who inflicted defeats on Denmark, Russia, and Poland during the Great Northern War (1700–21)

Charles XIV *n* the title as king of Sweden and Norway of Jean Baptiste Jules Bernadotte. See **Bernadotte**

Charles Albert *n* 1798–1849, king of Sardinia-Piedmont (1831–49) during the Risorgimento: abdicated after the failure of his revolt against Austria

Charles Edward Stuart *n* See **Stuart** (sense 2)

Charles Martel (mɑːˈtɛl) *n* grandfather of Charlemagne. ?688–741 AD, Frankish ruler of Austrasia (715–41), who checked the Muslim invasion of Europe by defeating the Moors at Poitiers (732)

Charles's Wain (weɪn) *n* another name for the **Plough** [Old English *Carles wægn*, from Carl *Charlemagne* (?742–814 AD), king of the Franks and Holy Roman Emperor + *wægn* WAIN]

Charles the Great *n* another name for **Charlemagne**

charleston ('tʃɑːlstən) *n* a fast rhythmic dance of the 1920s, characterized by kicking and by twisting of the legs from the knee down [C20: named after CHARLESTON, South Carolina]

Charleston ('tʃɑːlstən) *n* **1** a city in central West Virginia: the state capital. Pop: 51 394 (2003 est) **2** a port in SE South Carolina, on the Atlantic: scene of the first action in the Civil War. Pop: 101 024 (2003 est)

Charleville-Mézières (French ʃarləvilmezjɛr) *n* twin towns on opposite sides of the River Meuse in NE France. Pop: 55 490 (1999). See **Mézières**

charley horse ('tʃɑːlɪ) *n* US & Canadian informal muscle stiffness or cramp following strenuous athletic exercise [C19: of uncertain origin]

charlie ('tʃɑːlɪ) *n* Brit informal a silly person; fool [C20: shortened from *Charlie Hunt*, rhyming slang for CUNT]

charlock ('tʃɑːlɒk) *n* Also called: wild mustard a weedy Eurasian plant, *Sinapis arvensis* (or *Brassica kaber*), with hairy stems and foliage and yellow flowers: family: *Brassicaceae* (crucifers) [Old English *cerlic*, of obscure origin]

charlotte ('ʃɑːlət) *n* **1** a baked dessert served hot or cold, commonly made with fruit and layers or a casing of bread or cake crumbs, sponge cake, etc: apple charlotte **2** short for **charlotte russe** [C19: from French, from the name *Charlotte*]

Charlotte ('ʃɑːlət) *n* a city in S North Carolina: the largest city in the state. Pop: 584 658 (2003 est)

Charlotte Amalie ('ʃɑːlət əˈmɑːlɪə) *n* the capital of the Virgin Islands of the United States, a port on St Thomas Island. Pop: 18 914 (2000). Former name (1921–37): **Saint Thomas**

Charlottenburg (German ʃarˈlɒtənburk) *n* a district of Berlin (of West Berlin until 1990), formerly an independent city. Pop: 315 473 (2005 est)

charlotte russe (ruːs) *n* a cold dessert made in a mould with sponge fingers enclosing a mixture of whipped cream, custard, etc [French: Russian charlotte]

Charlottetown ('ʃɑːlətˌtaʊn) *n* a port in SE Canada,

capital of the province of Prince Edward Island. Pop: 38 114 (2001)

Charlton ('tʃɑːltᵊn) n **1 Bobby,** full name *Sir Robert Charlton.* born 1937, English footballer; played for England over 100 times **2** his brother, **Jack,** full name *John Charlton.* born 1935, English footballer; played for Leeds United (1952–73) and England; manager of the Republic of Ireland soccer team (1986–95)

charm (tʃɑːm) n **1** the quality of pleasing, fascinating, or attracting people **2** a pleasing or attractive feature **3** a small object worn or kept for supposed magical powers of protection; amulet; talisman **4** a trinket worn on a bracelet **5** a magic spell; enchantment **6** a formula or action used in casting such a spell **7** *physics* an internal quantum number of certain elementary particles, used to explain some scattering experiments **8** like a charm perfectly; successfully ▷ *vb* **9** to attract or fascinate; delight greatly **10** to cast a magic spell on **11** to protect, influence, or heal, supposedly by magic **12** (*tr*) to influence or obtain by personal charm [c13: from Old French *charme,* from Latin *carmen* song, incantation, from *canere* to sing] > 'charmer n

charming ('tʃɑːmɪŋ) adj delightful; pleasant; attractive > 'charmingly adv

charm offensive n a concentrated attempt to gain favour or respectability by conspicuously cooperative or obliging behaviour

charnel ('tʃɑːnᵊl) n **1** short for **charnel house** ▷ adj **2** ghastly; sepulchral; deathly [c14: from Old French: burial place, from Latin *carnālis* fleshly, CARNAL]

charnel house n (esp formerly) a building or vault where corpses or bones are deposited

Charnley ('tʃɑːnlɪ) n *Sir John.* 1911–82, British surgeon noted for his invention of an artificial hip joint and his development of hip-replacement surgery

Charon ('kɛərən) n *Greek myth* the ferryman who brought the dead across the rivers Styx or Acheron to Hades

Charpentier (*French* ʃarpɑ̃tje) n **1 Gustave** (gystav). 1860–1956, French composer, whose best-known work is the opera *Louise* (1900) **2 Marc-Antoine.** ?1645–1704, French composer, best known for his sacred music, particularly the *Te Deum*

char siu (ˌtʃɑː ˈsjuː) or **char sui** (ˈsuːɪ) n barbecued marinated pork [c20: from Cantonese]

chart (tʃɑːt) n **1** a map designed to aid navigation by sea or air **2** an outline map, esp one on which weather information is plotted **3** a sheet giving graphical, tabular, or diagrammatical information **4** the charts *informal* the lists produced weekly from various sources of the bestselling pop singles and albums or the most popular videos ▷ *vb* **5** (*tr*) to make a chart of **6** (*tr*) to plot or outline the course of **7** (*intr*) (of a record or video) to appear in the charts (sense 6) [c16: from Latin, from Greek *khartēs* papyrus, literally: something on which to make marks; related to Greek *kharattein* to engrave]

charter ('tʃɑːtə) n **1** a formal document from the sovereign or state incorporating a city, bank, college, etc, and specifying its purposes and rights **2** (*sometimes capital*) a formal document granting or demanding from the sovereign power of a state certain rights or liberties **3** a document issued by a society or an organization authorizing the establishment of a local branch or chapter **4** a special privilege or exemption **5** (*often capital*) the fundamental principles of an organization; constitution **6 a** the hire or lease of transportation **b** (*as modifier*): *a charter flight* **7** a law, policy, or decision containing a loophole which allows a specified group to engage more easily in an activity considered undesirable: *a beggars' charter* ▷ *vb* **8** to lease or hire by charterparty **9** to hire (a vehicle, etc) **10** to grant a charter of incorporation or liberties to (a group or person) [c13: from Old French *chartre,* from Latin *chartula* a little paper, from *charta* leaf of papyrus; see CHART] > 'charterer n

chartered accountant n (in Britain) an accountant who has passed the professional examinations of the Institute of Chartered Accountants in England and Wales, the Institute of Chartered Accountants of

Scotland, or the Institute of Chartered Accountants in Ireland

chartered bank n *Canad* a privately owned bank that has been incorporated by Parliament to operate in the commercial banking system

chartered librarian n (in Britain) a librarian who has obtained a qualification from the Library Association in addition to a degree or diploma in librarianship

chartered surveyor n (in Britain) a surveyor who is registered with the Royal Institution of Chartered Surveyors as having the qualifications, training, and experience to satisfy their professional requirements

Charteris ('tʃɑːtərɪs) n **Leslie,** original name *Leslie Charles Bowyer Yin.* 1907–93, British novelist, born in Singapore: created the character Simon Templar, known as The Saint, the central character in many adventure novels

Chartism ('tʃɑːˌtɪzəm) n *British history* the principles of the reform movement in Britain from 1838 to 1848, which included manhood suffrage, payment of Members of Parliament, equal electoral districts, annual parliaments, voting by ballot, and the abolition of property qualifications for MPs [named after the *People's Charter,* a document which stated their aims] > 'Chartist n, adj

Chartres (ʃɑːtrə, ʃɑːt; *French* ʃartrə) n a city in NW France: Gothic cathedral; market town. Pop: 40 361 (1999)

chartreuse (ʃɑːˈtrɜːz; *French* ʃartrøz) n **1** either of two liqueurs, green or yellow, made from herbs and flowers **2 a** a colour varying from a clear yellowish-green to a strong greenish-yellow **b** (*as adjective*): *a chartreuse dress* [c19: from French, after *La Grande Chartreuse,* monastery near Grenoble, where the liqueur is produced]

charwoman ('tʃɑːˌwʊmən) n, pl -women *Brit* a woman who is hired to clean, tidy, etc, in a house or office

chary ('tʃɛərɪ) adj charier, chariest **1** wary; careful **2** choosy; finicky **3** shy **4** sparing; mean [Old English *cearig;* related to *caru* CARE, Old High German *charag* sorrowful]

Charybdis (kəˈrɪbdɪs) n a ship-devouring monster in classical mythology, identified with a whirlpool off the north coast of Sicily, lying opposite Scylla on the Italian coast. Compare **Scylla**

chase[1] (tʃeɪs) vb **1** to follow or run after (a person, animal, or goal) persistently or quickly **2** (*tr;* often foll by *out, away,* or *off*) to force to run (away); drive (out) **3** (*tr*) *informal* to court (a member of the opposite sex) in an unsubtle manner **4** (*tr;* often foll by *up*) *informal* to pursue persistently and energetically in order to obtain results, information, etc **5** (*intr*) *informal* to hurry; rush ▷ n **6** the act of chasing; pursuit **7** any quarry that is pursued **8** *Brit* an unenclosed area of land where wild animals are preserved to be hunted **9** *Brit* the right to hunt a particular quarry over the land of others **10** the chase the act or sport of hunting **11** short for **steeplechase 12** give chase to pursue (a person, animal, or thing) actively [c13: from Old French *chacier,* from Vulgar Latin *captiāre* (unattested), from Latin *captāre* to pursue eagerly, from *capere* to take; see CATCH]

chase[2] (tʃeɪs) n **1** *printing* a rectangular steel or cast-iron frame into which metal type and blocks making up pages are locked for printing or plate-making **2** the part of a gun barrel from the front of the trunnions to the muzzle **3** a groove or channel, esp one that is cut in a wall to take a pipe, cable, etc ▷ vb **4** *Also called:* **chamfer** to cut a groove, furrow, or flute in (a surface, column, etc) [c17 (in the sense: frame for letterpress matter): probably from French *châsse* frame (in the sense: bore of a cannon, etc): from Old French *chas* enclosure, from Late Latin *capsus* pen for animals; both from Latin *capsa* CASE[2]]

chase[3] (tʃeɪs) vb (*tr*) *Also called:* **enchase** to ornament (metal) by engraving or embossing [c14: from Old French *enchasser* ENCHASE]

chaser ('tʃeɪsə) n **1** a person or thing that chases **2** a drink drunk after another of a different kind, as beer after spirits

chasm ('kæzəm) n **1** a deep cleft in the ground; abyss **2** a break in continuity; gap **3** a wide difference in interests, feelings, etc [c17: from Latin *chasma*, from Greek *khasma*; related to Greek *khainein* to gape] > **chasmal** (ˈkæzməl) *or* 'chasmic *adj*

chasseur (ʃæˈsɜː; *French* ʃascer) *n* **1** *French army* a member of a unit specially trained and equipped for swift deployment **2** (in some parts of Europe, esp formerly) a uniformed attendant, esp one in the livery of a huntsman ▷ *adj* **3** (*often postpositive*) designating or cooked in a sauce consisting of white wine and mushrooms [c18: from French: huntsman]

Chassid, Chasid, Hassid *or* **Hasid** (ˈhæsɪd; *Hebrew* xəˈsid) *n*, *pl* **Chassidim, Chasidim, Hassidim** *or* **Hasidim** (ˈhæsɪˌdiːm, -dɪm; *Hebrew* xasɪˈdim) **1** a sect of Jewish mystics founded in Poland about 1750, characterized by religious zeal and a spirit of prayer, joy, and charity **2** a Jewish sect of the 2nd century BC, formed to combat Hellenistic influences > **Chassidic, Chasidic, Hassidic** *or* **Hasidic** (həˈsɪdɪk) *adj*

chassis (ˈʃæsɪ) *n*, *pl* **-sis** (-sɪz) **1** the steel frame, wheels, engine, and mechanical parts of a motor vehicle, to which the body is attached **2** *electronics* a mounting for the circuit components of an electrical or electronic device, such as a radio or television **3** the landing gear of an aircraft **4** the frame on which a cannon carriage moves backwards and forwards [c17 (meaning: window frame): from French *châssis* frame, from Vulgar Latin *capsicum* (unattested), ultimately from Latin *capsa* CASE²]

chaste (ʃeɪst) *adj* **1** not having experienced sexual intercourse; virginal **2** abstaining from sexual intercourse, esp that which is unlawful or immoral **3** (of conduct, speech, etc) pure; decent; modest **4** (of style or taste) free from embellishment; simple; restrained [c13: from Old French, from Latin *castus* pure; compare CASTE] > 'chastely *adv* > 'chasteness *n*

chasten (ˈtʃeɪsᵊn) *vb* (*tr*) **1** to bring to a state of submission; subdue; tame **2** to discipline or correct by punishment **3** to moderate; restrain; temper [c16: from Old French *chastier*, from Latin *castigāre*; see CASTIGATE] > 'chastener *n* > 'chastening *adj* > 'chasteningly *adv*

chastise (tʃæsˈtaɪz) *vb* (*tr*) **1** to discipline or punish, esp by beating **2** to scold severely [c14 *chastisen*, irregularly from *chastien* to CHASTEN] > **chastisement** (ˈtʃæstɪzmənt, tʃæsˈtaɪz-) *n* > chas'tiser *n*

chastity (ˈtʃæstɪtɪ) *n* **1** the state of being chaste; purity **2** abstention from sexual intercourse; virginity or celibacy [c13: from Old French *chasteté*, from Latin *castitās*, from *castus* CHASTE]

chasuble (ˈtʃæzjʊbᵊl) *n Christianity* a long sleeveless outer vestment worn by a priest when celebrating Mass [c13: from French, from Late Latin *casubla* garment with a hood, apparently from *casula* cloak, literally: little house, from Latin *casa* cottage]

chat (tʃæt) *n* **1** informal conversation or talk conducted in an easy familiar manner **2** the exchange of messages in an internet or other network chatroom **3** any Old World songbird of the subfamily *Turdinae* (thrushes, etc) having a harsh chattering cry **4** any of various North American warblers, such as *Icteria virens* (**yellow-breasted chat**) **5** any of various Australian wrens (family *Muscicapidae*) of the genus *Ephthianura* and other genera ▷ *vb* **chats, chatting, chatted** (*intr*) **6** to talk in an easy familiar way **7** (*tr*) to exchange messages in a chatroom ▷ See also **chat up** [c16: short for CHATTER]

chatbot (ˈtʃætˌbɒt) *n* a computer program in the form of a virtual e-mail correspondent that can reply to messages from computer users [c20: from CHAT + (RO)BOT]

chateau *or* **château** (ˈʃætəʊ; *French* ʃato) *n*, *pl* **-teaux** (-təʊ, -təʊz; *French* -to) *or* **-teaus 1** a country house, castle, or manor house, esp in France **2** (in the name of a wine) estate or vineyard [c18: from French, from Old French *chastel*, from Latin *castellum* fortress, CASTLE]

Chateaubriand¹ (*French* ʃatobrijɑ̃) *n* **François René** (frɑ̃swa rəne), Vicomte de Chateaubriand. 1768–1848, French writer and statesman: a precursor of the romantic movement in France; his works include *Le Génie du Christianisme* (1802) and *Mémoires d'outre-tombe* (1849–50)

Chateaubriand² (*French* ʃatobrijɑ̃) *n* a thick steak cut

from the fillet of beef [c19: named after François René, Vicomte de Chateaubriand (1768–1848), French writer and statesman]

chateau cardboard *n NZ informal* wine sold in a winebox

Châteauroux (*French* ʃatoru) *n* a town in central France: 10th-century castle (**Château-Raoul**). Pop: 49 632 (1999)

Château-Thierry (ˈʃætəʊˈtɪərɪ; *French* ʃatotjeri) *n* a town in N central France, on the River Marne: scene of the second battle of the Marne (1918) during World War I. Pop: 14 967 (1999)

chatelain (ˈʃætᵊˌleɪn; *French* ʃatlɛ̃) *n* the keeper or governor of a castle [c16: from French, from Latin *castellānus* occupant of a CASTLE]

chatelaine (ˈʃætəˌleɪn; *French* ʃatlɛn) *n* **1** (esp formerly) the mistress of a castle or fashionable household **2** a chain or clasp worn at the waist by women in the 16th to the 19th centuries, with handkerchief, keys, etc, attached

Chatham¹ (ˈtʃætəm) *n* **1** a town in SE England, in N Kent on the River Medway: formerly royal naval dockyard. Pop: 73 468 (2001) **2** a town in SE Canada, in SE Ontario on the Thames River. Pop: 44 156 (2001)

Chatham² (ˈtʃætəm) *n* **1st Earl of** title of the elder (William) Pitt ▷ See **Pitt** (sense 1)

Chatham Island *n* a former name for **San Cristóbal** (sense 1)

Chatham Islands *pl n* a group of islands in the S Pacific Ocean, forming a county of South Island, New Zealand: consists of the main islands of Chatham, Pitt, and several rocky islets. Chief settlement: Waitangi. Pop: 750 (2004 est). Area: 963 sq km (372 sq miles)

chatline (ˈtʃætˌlaɪn) *n* a telephone service enabling callers to join in general conversation with each other

chatroom (ˈtʃætˌruːm, -ˌrʊm) *n* a site on the internet, or another computer network, where users have group discussions by electronic mail, typically about one subject

chat show *n Brit* a television or radio show in which guests, esp celebrities, are interviewed informally. US name: **talk show**

Chattanooga (ˌtʃætᵊˈnuːgə) *n* a city in SE Tennessee, on the Tennessee River: scene of two battles during the Civil War, in which the North defeated the Confederates, cleared Tennessee, and opened the way to Georgia (1863). Pop: 154 887 (2003 est)

chattel (ˈtʃætᵊl) *n* **1** (*often plural*) *property law* **a** chattel personal an item of movable personal property, such as furniture, domestic animals, etc **b** chattel real an interest in land less than a freehold, such as a lease **2** goods and chattels personal property [c13: from Old French *chatel* personal property, from Medieval Latin *capitāle* wealth; see CAPITAL¹]

chatter (ˈtʃætə) *vb* **1** to speak (about unimportant matters) rapidly and incessantly; prattle **2** (*intr*) (of birds, monkeys, etc) to make rapid repetitive high-pitched noises resembling human speech **3** (*intr*) (of the teeth) to click together rapidly through cold or fear **4** (*intr*) to make rapid intermittent contact with a component, as in machining, causing irregular cutting ▷ *n* **5** idle or foolish talk; gossip **6** the high-pitched repetitive noise made by a bird, monkey, etc **7** the rattling of objects, such as parts of a machine [c13: of imitative origin]

chatterati (ˌtʃætəˈrɑːtɪ) *n informal* another word for **chattering classes** [c20: from CHATTER + -*ati* as in LITERATI]

chatterbox (ˈtʃætəˌbɒks) *n informal* a person who talks constantly, esp about trivial matters

chattering classes *pl n* the chattering classes *informal, often derogatory* the educated sections of society, considered as enjoying discussion of political, social, and cultural issues

Chatterton (ˈtʃætətən) *n* **Thomas.** 1752–70, British poet; author of spurious medieval verse and prose: he committed suicide at the age of 17

chatty (ˈtʃætɪ) *adj* **-tier, -tiest 1** full of trivial conversation; talkative **2** informal and friendly; gossip > 'chattily *adv* > 'chattiness *n*

chat up vb (tr, adverb) Brit informal **1** to talk flirtatiously to (a person), esp with the intention of seducing him or her **2** to talk persuasively to (a person), esp with an ulterior motive

Chaucer ('tʃɔːsə) n **Geoffrey.** ?1340–1400, English poet, noted for his narrative skill, humour, and insight, particularly in his most famous work, *The Canterbury Tales.* He was influenced by the continental tradition of rhyming verse. His other works include *Troilus and Criseyde, The Legende of Good Women,* and *The Parlement of Foules*

chauffeur ('ʃəʊfə, ʃəʊ'fɜː) n **1** a person employed to drive a car ▷ vb **2** to act as driver for (a person): *he chauffeured me to the stadium; he chauffeurs for the Duke* [c20: from French, literally: stoker, from *chauffer* to heat] > **chauffeuse** (ʃəʊ'fɜːz) fem n

chaunt (tʃɔːnt) n, vb a less common variant of **chant**

chauvinism ('ʃəʊvɪˌnɪzəm) n **1** aggressive or fanatical patriotism; jingoism **2** enthusiastic devotion to a cause **3** smug irrational belief in the superiority of one's own race, party, sex, etc: *male chauvinism* [c19: from French *chauvinisme,* after Nicolas Chauvin, legendary French soldier under Napoleon, noted for his vociferous and unthinking patriotism] > **'chauvinist** n > ˌchauvin'istic adj > ˌchauvin'istically adv

chav (tʃæv) n Southern English informal, dismissive a young working-class person whose tastes, although sometimes expensive, are considered vulgar by some [perhaps from Romany *chavi* a child] > **'chavish** adj

Chavannes (French ʃavan) n See **Puvis de Chavannes**

cheap (tʃiːp) adj **1** costing relatively little; inexpensive; good value **2** charging low prices: *a cheap hairdresser* **3** of poor quality; shoddy: *cheap furniture; cheap and nasty* **4** worth relatively little: *promises are cheap* **5** not worthy of respect; vulgar **6** ashamed; embarrassed: *to feel cheap* **7** stingy; miserly **8** informal mean; despicable: *a cheap liar* ▷ n **9 on the cheap** Brit informal at a low cost ▷ adv **10** at very little cost [Old English *ceap* barter, bargain, price, property; related to Old Norse *kaup* bargain, Old High German *kouf* trade, Latin *caupō* innkeeper] > **'cheaply** adv > 'cheapness n

cheapen ('tʃiːpən) vb **1** to make or become lower in reputation, quality, etc; degrade or be degraded **2** to make or become cheap or cheaper > **'cheapener** n

cheap-jack informal ▷ n **1** a person who sells cheap and shoddy goods ▷ adj **2** shoddy or inferior [c19: from CHEAP + *Jack* (name used to typify a person)]

cheapo ('tʃiːpəʊ) adj informal very cheap and possibly shoddy

cheap out vb (intr, adverb) US & Canadian informal to take the cheapest option; try to do something as cheaply as possible

cheapskate ('tʃiːpˌskeɪt) n informal a miserly person

cheat (tʃiːt) vb **1** to deceive or practise deceit, esp for one's own gain; trick or swindle (someone) **2** (intr) to obtain unfair advantage by trickery, as in a game of cards **3** (tr) to escape or avoid (something unpleasant) by luck or cunning: *to cheat death* **4** (when intr, usually foll by on) informal to be sexually unfaithful to (one's wife, husband, or lover) ▷ n **5** a person who cheats **6** a deliberately dishonest transaction, esp for gain; fraud **7** informal sham **8** law the obtaining of another's property by fraudulent means [c14: short for ESCHEAT] > **'cheater** n

Cheb (Czech xɛp) n a town in the W Czech Republic, in W Bohemia on the Ohře River: 12th-century castle where Wallenstein was murdered (1634); a centre of the Sudeten-German movement after World War I. Pop: 34 036 (2007 est). German name: **Eger**

Cheboksary (Russian tʃibak'sari) n a port in W central Russia on the River Volga: capital of the Chuvash Republic. Pop: 446 000 (2005 est)

check (tʃɛk) vb **1** to pause or cause to pause, esp abruptly **2** (tr) to restrain or control: *to check one's tears* **3** (tr) to slow the growth or progress of; retard **4** (tr) to rebuke or rebuff **5** (when intr, often foll by on or up on) to examine, investigate, or make an inquiry into (facts, a product, etc) for accuracy, quality, or progress, esp rapidly or informally **6** (tr) chiefly US & Canadian to mark off so as to indicate approval, correctness, or preference **7** (intr; often foll by with) chiefly US & Canadian to correspond to or agree: *this report checks with the other* **8** (tr) chiefly US, Canadian & NZ to leave in or accept (clothing or property) for temporary custody **9** chess to place (an opponent's king) in check **10** (tr) to mark with a pattern of squares or crossed lines **11** to crack or cause to crack **12** (tr) ice hockey to impede (an opponent) **13** (intr) hunting (of hounds) to pause in the pursuit of quarry while relocating a lost scent ▷ n **14** a break in progress; stoppage **15** a restraint or rebuff **16** a person or thing that restrains, halts, etc **17** a control, esp a rapid or informal one, designed to ensure accuracy, progress, etc **18** a means or standard to ensure against fraud or error **19** the US word for **tick**¹ **20** the US spelling of **cheque** **21** chiefly US the bill in a restaurant **22** chiefly US & Canadian a ticket or tag used to identify clothing or property deposited for custody **23** a pattern of squares or crossed lines **24** a single square in such a pattern **25** fabric with a pattern of squares or crossed lines **26** chess the state or position of a king under direct attack, from which it must be moved or protected by another piece **27** a small crack, as one in veneer or one that occurs in timber during seasoning **28** a chip or counter used in some card and gambling games **29** hunting a pause by the hounds in the pursuit of their quarry owing to loss of its scent **30** ice hockey the act of impeding an opponent with one's body or stick **31** in check under control or restraint ▷ interj **32** chess a call made to an opponent indicating that his king is in check **33** chiefly US & Canadian an expression of agreement ▷ See also **check in, check out, checkup** [c14: from Old French *eschec* a check at chess, hence, a pause (to verify something), via Arabic from Persian *shāh* king! (in chess)] > **'checkable** adj > **'checker** n

checked (tʃɛkt) adj having a pattern of small squares

checker¹ ('tʃɛkə) n, vb **1** the usual US spelling of **chequer** ▷ n **2** textiles a variant spelling of **chequer** (sense 2) **3** US & Canadian Also called (in Britain and certain other countries): **draughtsman**

checker² ('tʃɛkə) n chiefly US & Canadian **1** a cashier, esp in a supermarket **2** an attendant in a cloakroom, left-luggage office, etc

checkerboard ('tʃɛkəˌbɔːd) n US & Canadian a square board divided into 64 squares of alternating colours, used for playing checkers or chess. Also called (in Britain and certain other countries): **draughtboard**

checkers ('tʃɛkəz) n (functioning as singular) US & Canadian a game for two players using a checkerboard and 12 checkers each. The object is to jump over and capture the opponent's pieces

check in vb (adverb) **1** (intr) to record one's arrival, as at a hotel or for work; sign in or report **2** (tr) to register the arrival of (passengers, etc) ▷ n **check-in 3** the formal registration of arrival, as at an airport or a hotel **4** the place where one registers arrival at an airport, etc

check list n a list of items, facts, names, etc, to be checked or referred to for comparison, identification, or verification

checkmate ('tʃɛkˌmeɪt) n **1** chess **a** the winning position in which an opponent's king is under attack and unable to escape **b** the move by which this position is achieved **2** utter defeat ▷ vb (tr) **3** chess to place (an opponent's king) in checkmate **4** to thwart or render powerless ▷ interj **5** chess a call made when placing an opponent's king in checkmate [c14: from Old French *eschec mat,* from Arabic *shāh māt,* the king is dead; see CHECK]

check out vb (adverb) **1** (intr) to pay the bill and depart, esp from a hotel **2** (intr) to depart from a place; record one's departure from work **3** to investigate or prove to be in order after investigation: *the police checked out all the statements; their credentials checked out* **4** (tr) informal to have a look at; inspect ▷ n **checkout 5** the latest time for vacating a room in a hotel, etc **6** a counter, esp in a supermarket, where customers pay

checkpoint ('tʃɛkˌpɔɪnt) n a place, as at a frontier or in a motor rally, where vehicles or travellers are stopped for official identification, inspection, etc

checkup ('tʃɛkˌʌp) n **1** an examination to see if

something is in order **2** *med* a medical examination, esp one taken at regular intervals to verify a normal state of health or discover a disease in its early stages ▷ *vb* check up **3** (*intr, adverb*; sometimes foll by *on*) to investigate or make an inquiry into (a person's character, evidence, etc), esp when suspicions have been aroused

Cheddar ('tʃɛdə) *n* **1** (*sometimes not capital*) any of several types of smooth hard yellow or whitish cheese **2** a village in SW England, in N Somerset: situated near **Cheddar Gorge**, a pass through the Mendip Hills renowned for its stalactitic caverns and rare limestone flora. Pop: 4796 (2001)

cheek (tʃiːk) *n* **1** either side of the face, esp that part below the eye **2** *informal* impudence; effrontery **3** (*often plural*) *informal* either side of the buttocks **4** (*often plural*) a side of a door jamb **5** one of the jaws of a vice **6** cheek by jowl close together; intimately linked **7** turn the other cheek to be submissive and refuse to retaliate even when provoked or treated badly ▷ *vb* **8** (*tr*) *informal* to speak or behave disrespectfully to; act impudently towards [Old English *ceace*; related to Middle Low German *kāke*, Dutch *kaak*]

cheekbone ('tʃiːkˌbəʊn) *n* the nontechnical name for **zygomatic bone**

cheeky ('tʃiːkɪ) *adj* cheekier, cheekiest disrespectful in speech or behaviour; impudent > 'cheekily *adv* > 'cheekiness *n*

cheep (tʃiːp) *n* **1** the short weak high-pitched cry of a young bird; chirp ▷ *vb* **2** (*intr*) (of young birds) to utter characteristic shrill sounds > 'cheeper *n*

cheer (tʃɪə) *vb* **1** (usually foll by *up*) to make or become happy or hopeful; comfort or be comforted **2** to applaud with shouts **3** (when *tr*, sometimes foll by *on*) to encourage (a team, person, etc) with shouts, esp in contests ▷ *n* **4** a shout or cry of approval, encouragement, etc, often using such words as **hurrah!** or **rah! rah! rah! 5** three cheers three shouts of hurrah given in unison by a group to honour someone or celebrate something **6** happiness; good spirits **7** state of mind; spirits (archaic, except in the phrases **be of good cheer, with good cheer**) **8** *archaic* provisions for a feast; fare [C13 (in the sense: face, welcoming aspect): from Old French *chere*, from Late Latin *cara* face, from Greek *kara* head]

cheerful ('tʃɪəfʊl) *adj* **1** having a happy disposition; in good spirits **2** pleasantly bright; gladdening: *a cheerful room* **3** hearty; ungrudging; enthusiastic: *cheerful help* > 'cheerfully *adv* > 'cheerfulness *n*

cheerio (ˌtʃɪərɪˈəʊ) *sentence substitute informal, chiefly Brit* **1** a farewell greeting **2** a drinking toast ▷ *n* **3** NZ a type of small sausage

cheerleader ('tʃɪəˌliːdə) *n* a person who leads a crowd in formal cheers, esp at sports events

cheerless ('tʃɪəlɪs) *adj* dreary, gloomy, or pessimistic > 'cheerlessly *adv* > 'cheerlessness *n*

cheers (tʃɪəz) *sentence substitute informal, chiefly Brit* **1** a drinking toast **2** goodbye! cheerio! **3** thanks!

cheery ('tʃɪərɪ) *adj* cheerier, cheeriest showing or inspiring cheerfulness > 'cheerily *adv* > 'cheeriness *n*

cheese (tʃiːz) *n* **1** the curd of milk separated from the whey and variously prepared as a food **2** a mass or complete cake of this substance **3** any of various substances of similar consistency, etc: *lemon cheese* **4** big cheese *slang* an important person [Old English *cēse*, from Latin *cāseus* cheese; related to Old Saxon *kāsi*]

cheeseburger ('tʃiːzˌbɜːgə) *n* a hamburger cooked with a slice of cheese on top of it

cheesecake ('tʃiːzˌkeɪk) *n* **1** a rich tart with a biscuit base, filled with a mixture of cream cheese, cream, sugar, and often sultanas, sometimes having a fruit topping **2** *slang* women displayed for their sex appeal, as in photographs in magazines, newspapers, or films

cheesecloth ('tʃiːzˌklɒθ) *n* a loosely woven cotton cloth formerly used only for wrapping cheese

cheesed off *adj* (*usually postpositive*) *Brit slang* bored, disgusted, or angry

cheeseparing ('tʃiːzˌpɛərɪŋ) *adj* **1** penny-pinching; stingy ▷ *n* **2 a** a paring of cheese rind **b** anything similarly worthless **3** stinginess

cheesy ('tʃiːzɪ) *adj* cheesier, cheesiest **1** like cheese in flavour, smell, or consistency **2** *informal* (of a smile) broad but possibly insincere: *a big cheesy grin* **3** *informal* banal or trite; in poor taste > 'cheesiness *n* > 'cheesily *adv*

cheetah *or* **chetah** ('tʃiːtə) *n* a large feline mammal, *Acinonyx jubatus*, of Africa and SW Asia: the swiftest mammal, having very long legs, nonretractile claws, and a black-spotted light-brown coat [C18: from Hindi *cītā*, from Sanskrit *citrakāya* tiger, from *citra* bright, speckled + *kāya* body]

Cheever ('tʃiːvə) *n* **John.** 1912–82, US novelist and short-story writer. His novels include *The Wapshot Chronicle* (1957) and *Bullet Park* (1969)

chef (ʃɛf) *n* a cook, esp the principal cook in a restaurant [C19: from French, from Old French *chief* head, CHIEF]

chef-d'oeuvre *French* (ʃɛdœvrə) *n, pl* chefs-d'oeuvre (ʃɛdœvrə) a masterpiece

Chefoo ('tʃiːˈfuː) *n* another name for **Yantai**

Che Guevara (tʃeɪ gəˈvɑːrə; *Spanish* tʃe geˈβara) *n* See **Guevara**

Cheiron ('kaɪrɒn, -rən) *n* a variant spelling of **Chiron**

Cheju ('tʃeˈdʒuː) *n* a volcanic island in the N East China Sea, constitutes part of Korea: constitutes a province (Cheju-do) of South Korea. Capital: Cheju. Pop: 302 000 (2005 est). Area: 1792 sq km (692 sq miles). Formerly called: **Quelpart**

Chekhov *or* **Chekov** ('tʃɛkɒf; *Russian* 'tʃɛxəf) *n* **Anton Pavlovich** (an'tɔn 'pavləvitʃ). 1860–1904, Russian dramatist and short-story writer. His plays include *The Seagull* (1896), *Uncle Vanya* (1900), *The Three Sisters* (1901), and *The Cherry Orchard* (1904) > Chekhovian or Chekovian (tʃɛˈkəʊvɪən) *adj*

Chekiang ('tʃɛˈkjæŋ, -kaɪˈæŋ) *n* a variant transliteration of the Chinese name for **Zhejiang**

chela¹ ('kiːlə) *n, pl* lae (-liː) a large pincer-like claw of such arthropods as the crab and scorpion [C17: New Latin, from Greek *khēlē* claw]

chela² ('tʃeɪlə) *n Hinduism* a disciple of a religious teacher [C19: from Hindi *celā*, from Sanskrit *ceta* servant, slave]

chelate ('kiːleɪt) *n* **1** *chem* a coordination compound in which a metal atom or ion is bound to a ligand at two or more points on the ligand, so as to form a heterocyclic ring containing a metal atom ▷ *adj* **2** *zoology* of or possessing chelae **3** *chem* of or denoting a chelate ▷ *vb* **4** (*intr*) *chem* to form a chelate [C20: from CHELA¹]

chelation ('kiːleɪʃən) *n* **1** *chem* the process by which a chelate is formed **2** *animal husbandry* the process by which trace elements in an animal's feed are bonded to amino acids, ensuring their absorption into the animal's body **3** *geol* the chemical removal of metallic ions from a mineral or rock by weathering

chelicera (kɪˈlɪsərə) *n, pl* -erae (-əˌriː) one of a pair of appendages on the head of spiders and other arachnids: often modified as food-catching claws [C19: from New Latin, from French *chélicère*, from *chél*- see CHELA¹ + *-cère* from Greek *keras* horn]

Chelmsford ('tʃɛlmzfəd) *n* a city in SE England, administrative centre of Essex: electronics, retail; university (1992). Pop: 99 962 (2001)

cheloid ('kiːlɔɪd) *n pathol* a variant spelling of **keloid** > che'loidal *adj*

chelonian (kɪˈləʊnɪən) *n* **1** any reptile of the order *Chelonia*, including the tortoises and turtles, in which most of the body is enclosed in a protective bony capsule ▷ *adj* **2** of, relating to, belonging to, or characteristic of the *Chelonia* [C19: from New Latin *Chelonia*, from Greek *khelōnē* tortoise]

Chelsea ('tʃɛlsɪ) *n* a residential district of SW London, in the Royal Borough of Kensington and Chelsea: site of the Chelsea Royal Hospital for old and invalid soldiers (**Chelsea Pensioners**)

Chelsea tractor *n Brit informal* a four-by-four [C21: from the idea of vehicles designed for rough terrain being popular among urban dwellers]

Cheltenham ('tʃɛltᵊnəm) *n* **1** a town in W England, in central Gloucestershire: famous for its schools, racecourse, and saline springs (discovered in 1716). Pop: 98 875 (2001) **2** a style of type

Chelyabinsk (*Russian* tʃɪˈljabinsk) *n* an industrial city in SW Russia. Pop: 1 067 000 (2005 est)

Chelyuskin (*Russian* tʃɪˈljuskin) *n* Cape Chelyuskin a cape in N central Russia, in N Siberia at the end of the Taimyr Peninsula: the northernmost point of Asia

chem. *abbreviation* **1** chemical **2** chemist **3** chemistry

chem- *combining form* variant of **chemo-**

chemical (ˈkɛmɪkᵊl) *n* **1** any substance used in or resulting from a reaction involving changes to atoms or molecules, especially one derived artificially for practical use ▷ *adj* **2** of or used in chemistry **3** of, made from, or using chemicals: *chemical fertilizer*
> ˈchemically *adv*

chemical engineering *n* the branch of engineering concerned with the design, operation, maintenance, and manufacture of the plant and machinery used in industrial chemical processes > chemical engineer *n*

chemical equation *n* a representation of a chemical reaction using symbols of the elements to indicate the amount of substance, usually in moles, of each reactant and product

chemical reaction *n* a process that involves changes in the structure and energy content of atoms, molecules, or ions but not their nuclei. See **nuclear reaction**

chemical warfare *n* warfare in which chemicals other than explosives are used as weapons, esp warfare using asphyxiating or nerve gases, poisons, defoliants, etc

chemiluminescence (ˌkɛmɪˌluːmɪˈnɛsəns) *n* the phenomenon in which a chemical reaction leads to the emission of light without incandescence
> ˌchemiˌlumiˈnescent *adj*

chemin de fer (ʃəˈmæn də ˈfɛə; *French* ʃəmɛ̃dfɛr) *n* a gambling game, a variation of baccarat [French: railway, referring to the fast tempo of the game]

chemise (ʃəˈmiːz) *n* **1** an unwaisted loose-fitting dress hanging straight from the shoulders **2** a loose shirtlike undergarment ▷ Also called: **shift** [C14: from Old French: shirt, from Late Latin *camisa*, perhaps of Celtic origin]

chemist (ˈkɛmɪst) *n* **1** *Brit* a shop selling medicines, cosmetics, etc **2** *Brit* a qualified dispenser of prescribed medicines **3** a person studying, trained in, or engaged in chemistry [C16: from earlier *chimist*, from New Latin *chimista*, shortened from Medieval Latin *alchimista* ALCHEMIST]

chemistry (ˈkɛmɪstrɪ) *n*, *pl* -tries **1** the branch of physical science concerned with the composition, properties, and reactions of substances **2** the composition, properties, and reactions of a particular substance **3** the nature and effects of any complex phenomenon: *the chemistry of humour* [C17: from earlier *chimistrie*, from *chimist* CHEMIST]

Chemnitz (*German* ˈkɛmnɪts) *n* a city in E Germany, in Saxony, at the foot of the Erzgebirge: textiles, engineering. Pop: 249 922 (2003 est). Also called (1953–90): Karl-Marx-Stadt

chemo (ˈkiːməʊ) *n* *informal* short for **chemotherapy**

chemo-, chemi- *or before a vowel* **chem-** *combining form* indicating that chemicals or chemical reactions are involved: *chemotherapy* [New Latin, from Late Greek *khēmeia*; see ALCHEMY]

chemoreceptor (ˌkɛməʊrɪˈsɛptə) *or* **chemoceptor** *n* a sensory receptor in a biological cell membrane to which an external molecule binds to generate a smell or taste sensation

chemosynthesis (ˌkɛməʊˈsɪnθɪsɪs) *n* the formation of organic material by certain bacteria using energy derived from simple chemical reactions

chemotherapy (ˌkiːməʊˈθɛrəpɪ, kiːmə-) *n* treatment of disease, esp cancer, by means of chemical agents. See **radiotherapy** > ˌchemoˈtherapist *n*

Chemulpo (ˌtʃɛmʊlˈpəʊ) *n* a former name of **Inchon**

chemurgy (ˈkɛmɜːdʒɪ) *n* the branch of chemistry concerned with the industrial use of organic raw materials, esp materials of agricultural origin
> chemˈurgic *or* chemˈurgical *adj*

Chenab (tʃɪˈnæb) *n* a river rising in the Himalayas and flowing southwest to the Sutlej River in Pakistan. Length: 1087 km (675 miles)

Cheney (ˈtʃeɪnɪ) *n* **Richard B(ruce)**, known as *Dick*. born

1941, US Republican politician; vice-president from 2001

Chen-chiang (ˈtʃɛnˈtʃæŋ) *n* a variant transliteration of the Chinese name for **Zhenjiang**

Chengchow *or* **Cheng-chou** (ˈtʃɛŋˈtʃəʊ) *n* a variant transliteration of the Chinese name for: **Zhengzhou**

Chengde, Chengteh *or* **Ch'eng-te** (ˈtʃɛŋˈteɪ) *n* a city in NE China, in Hebei on the Luan River: summer residence of the Manchu emperors. Pop: 470 000 (2005 est)

Chengdu, Chengtu *or* **Ch'eng-tu** (ˈtʃɛŋˈtuː) *n* a city in S central China, capital of Sichuan province. Pop: 3 478 000 (2005 est)

Chénier (*French* ʃenje) *n* **1** André (Marie de) (ɑ̃dre). 1762–94, French poet; his work was influenced by the ancient Greek elegiac poets. He was guillotined during the French Revolution **2** his brother, **Marie-Joseph (Blaise de)**. 1764–1811, French dramatist and politician. He wrote patriotic songs and historical plays, such as *Charles IX* (1789)

chenille (ʃəˈniːl) *n* **1** a thick soft tufty silk or worsted velvet cord or yarn used in embroidery and for trimmings, etc **2** a fabric of such yarn **3** a rich and hard-wearing carpet of such fabric [C18: from French, literally: hairy caterpillar, from Latin *canicula*, diminutive of *canis* dog]

Chenin Blanc (ʃəˌnɛ̃ ˈblɒŋk) *n* **1** a white grape grown in the Loire region of France and in South Africa, California, New Zealand, and elsewhere, used for making wine **2** any of various light dry white wines made from this grape

Chennai (tʃɪˈnaɪ) *n* a port in SE India, capital of Tamil Nadu, on the Bay of Bengal: founded in 1639 by the English East India Company as **Fort St George**; traditional burial place of St Thomas; university (1857). Pop: 4 216 268 (2001). Former name: Madras

cheongsam (ˈtʃɒŋˈsæm) *n* a straight dress, usually of silk or cotton, with a stand-up collar and a slit in one side of the skirt, worn by Chinese women [from Chinese (Cantonese), variant of Mandarin *ch'ang shan* long jacket]

Cheops (ˈkiːɒps) *n* original name *Khufu*. Egyptian king of the fourth dynasty (?2613–?2494 BC), who built the largest pyramid at El Gîza

Chephren (ˈkɛfrən) *n* See **Khafre**

Chepstow (ˈtʃɛpstəʊ) *n* a town in S Wales, in Monmouthshire on the River Wye: tourism, light industry. Pop: 10 821 (2001)

cheque *or US* **check** (tʃɛk) *n* **1** a bill of exchange drawn on a bank by the holder of a current account; payable into a bank account, if crossed, or on demand, if uncrossed **2** *Austral & NZ* the total sum of money received for contract work or a crop **3** *Austral & NZ* wages [C18: from CHECK, in the sense: a means of verification]

cheque account *n* an account at a bank or a building society upon which cheques can be drawn

chequebook *or US* **checkbook** (ˈtʃɛkˌbʊk) *n* a book containing detachable blank cheques and issued by a bank or building society to holders of cheque accounts

chequebook journalism *n* the practice of securing exclusive rights to material for newspaper stories by paying a high price for it, regardless of any moral implications such as paying people to boast of criminal or morally reprehensible activities

cheque card *n* a card issued by a bank or building society, guaranteeing payment of a customer's cheques up to a stated value: may also function as a cash card or debit card or both

chequer *or US* **checker** (ˈtʃɛkə) *n* **1** any of the marbles, pegs, or other pieces used in the game of Chinese chequers **2 a** a pattern consisting of squares of different colours, textures, or materials **b** one of the squares in such a pattern ▷ *vb* (*tr*) **3** to make irregular in colour or character; variegate **4** to mark off with alternating squares of colour ▷ See also **chequers** [C13: chessboard, from Anglo-French *escheker*, from *eschec* CHECK]

chequered *or esp US* **checkered** (ˈtʃɛkəd) *adj* marked by fluctuations of fortune (esp in the phrase **a chequered career**)

chequers (ˈtʃɛkəz) *n* (*functioning as singular*) another name for **draughts**

Chequers ('tʃekəz) *n* an estate and country house in S England, in central Buckinghamshire: the official country residence of the British prime minister

Cher (*French* ʃɛr) *n* **1** a department of central France, in E Centre region. Capital: Bourges. Pop: 312 277 (2003 est). Area: 7304 sq km (2849 sq miles) **2** a river in central France, rising in the Massif Central and flowing northwest to the Loire. Length: 354 km (220 miles)

Cherbourg ('ʃɛəbʊəg; *French* ʃɛrbur) *n* a port in NW France, on the English Channel. Pop: 25 370 (1999)

Cherenkov *or* **Cerenkov** (tʃɪ'rɛŋkɒf; *Russian* tʃɪ'rjenkəf) *n* **Pavel Alekseyevich** ('pavıl alık'sjejıvitʃ). 1904–90, Soviet physicist: noted for work on the effects produced by high-energy particles: shared Nobel prize for physics 1958

cherish ('tʃɛrıʃ) *vb* (*tr*) **1** to show great tenderness for; treasure **2** to cling fondly to (a hope, idea, etc); nurse: *to cherish ambitions* [c14: from Old French *cherir*, from *cher* dear, from Latin *cārus*]

Chernenko (tʃɜː'nɛŋkəʊ) *n* **Konstantin** (**Ustinovich**) (kənstan'tin). 1911–85, Soviet statesman; general secretary of the Soviet Communist Party (1984–85)

Chernobyl (tʃɛː'nɒʊbəl, -'nɒbəl) *n* a town in N Ukraine; site of a nuclear power station accident in 1986

Chernovtsy (*Russian* tʃırnaf'tsi) *n* a city in Ukraine on the Prut River: formerly under Polish, Austro-Hungarian, and Romanian rule; part of the Soviet Union (1947–91). Pop: 237 000 (2005 est). German name: Czernowitz. Romanian name: Cernăuţi

chernozem *or* **tschernosem** ('tʃɜː'nəʊˌzɛm) *n* a black soil, rich in humus and carbonates, in cool or temperate semiarid regions, as the grasslands of Russia [from Russian, contraction of *chernaya zemlya* black earth]

Cherokee ('tʃɛrəˌkiː, ˌtʃɛrə'kiː) *n* **1** *pl* -kees *or* -kee a member of a Native American people formerly living in and around the Appalachian Mountains, now chiefly in Oklahoma; one of the Iroquois peoples **2** the language of this people, belonging to the Iroquoian family

cheroot (ʃə'ruːt) *n* a cigar with both ends cut off squarely [c17: from Tamil *curuttu* curl, roll]

cherry ('tʃɛrı) *n*, *pl* -ries **1** any of several trees of the rosaceous genus *Prunus*, such as *P. avium* (**sweet cherry**), having a small fleshy rounded fruit containing a hard stone **2** the fruit or wood of any of these trees **3** any of various unrelated plants, such as the ground cherry and Jerusalem cherry **4 a** a bright red colour; cerise **b** (*as adjective*): *a cherry coat* **5** *slang* virginity or the hymen as its symbol [c14: back formation from Old English *ciris* (mistakenly thought to be plural), ultimately from Late Latin *ceresia*, perhaps from Latin *cerasus* cherry tree, from Greek *kerasios*]

cherry tomato *n* a miniature tomato not much bigger than a cherry

chert (tʃɜːt) *n* a microcrystalline form of silica usually occurring as bands or layers of pebbles in sedimentary rock. Formula: SiO_2. Varieties include flint, lyddite (Lydian stone) [c17: of obscure origin] > 'cherty *adj*

Chertsey ('tʃɜːtsı) *n* a town in S England, in N Surrey on the River Thames. Pop: 10 323 (2001)

cherub ('tʃɛrəb) *n*, *pl* cherubs *or* cherubim ('tʃɛrəbɪm, -ʊbɪm) **1** *theol* a member of the second order of angels, whose distinctive gift is knowledge, often represented as a winged child or winged head of a child **2** an innocent or sweet child [Old English, from Hebrew *kĕrūbh*] > cherubic (tʃə'ruːbɪk) *or* che'rubical *adj* > che'rubically *adv*

Cherubini (ˌkɛrʊ'biːnı) *n* (**Maria**) **Luigi** (**Carlo Zenobio Salvatore**) (luː'iːdʒi). 1760–1842, Italian composer, noted particularly for his church music and his operas

chervil ('tʃɜːvıl) *n* an aromatic umbelliferous Eurasian plant, *Anthriscus cerefolium*, with small white flowers and aniseed-flavoured leaves used as herbs in soups and salads [Old English *cerfelle*, from Latin *caerephylla*, plural of *caerephyllum* chervil, from Greek *khairephullon*, from *khairein* to enjoy + *phullon* leaf]

Cherwell ('tʃɑːwəl) *n* **1st Viscount** title of *Frederick Alexander Lindemann* ('lındəmən). 1886–1957, British physicist, born in Germany, noted for his research on heat capacity, aeronautics, and atomic physics. He was

scientific adviser to Winston Churchill during World War II

Ches. *abbreviation* Cheshire

Chesapeake Bay ('tʃɛsəˌpiːk) *n* the largest inlet of the Atlantic in the coast of the US: bordered by Maryland and Virginia

Cheshire[1] ('tʃɛʃə, 'tʃɛʃıə) *n* a county of NW England: low-lying and undulating, bordering on the Pennines in the east; mainly agricultural: the geographic and ceremonial county includes Warrington and Halton, which became independent unitary authorities in 1998. Administrative centre: Chester. Pop (excluding unitary authorities): 678 700 (2003 est). Area (excluding unitary authorites): 2077 sq km (802 sq miles)

Cheshire[2] ('tʃɛʃə) *n* Group Captain (**Geoffrey**) **Leonard**. 1917–92, British philanthropist: awarded the Victoria Cross in World War II; founded the Leonard Cheshire Foundation Homes for the Disabled: married Sue, Baroness Ryder

Cheshire cheese *n* a mild-flavoured cheese with a crumbly texture, originally made in Cheshire

chess (tʃɛs) *n* a game of skill for two players using a chessboard on which chessmen are moved. Initially each player has one king, one queen, two rooks, two bishops, two knights, and eight pawns, which have different types of moves according to kind. The object is to checkmate the opponent's king [c13: from Old French *esches*, plural of *eschec* check (at chess); see CHECK]

chessboard ('tʃɛsˌbɔːd) *n* a square board divided into 64 squares of two alternating colours, used for playing chess or draughts

chessman ('tʃɛsˌmæn, -mən) *n*, *pl* -men any of the eight pieces and eight pawns used by each player in a game of chess [c17: back formation from *chessmen*, from Middle English *chessemeyne* chess company, from *meynie*, *menye* company, body of men, from Old French *meyné*]

chest (tʃɛst) *n* **1 a** the front part of the trunk from the neck to the belly. Related adj: **pectoral b** (*as modifier*): *a chest cold* **2 get something off one's chest** *informal* to unburden oneself of troubles, worries, etc, by talking about them **3** a box, usually large and sturdy, used for storage or shipping: *a tea chest* [Old English *cest*, from Latin *cista* wooden box, basket, from Greek *kistē* box] > 'chested *adj*

Chester ('tʃɛstə) *n* a city in NW England, administrative centre of Cheshire, on the River Dee: intact surrounding walls; 16th- and 17th-century double-tier shops. Pop: 80 121 (2001)

chesterfield ('tʃɛstəˌfiːld) *n* **1** a man's knee-length overcoat, usually with a fly front to conceal the buttons and having a velvet collar **2** a large tightly stuffed sofa, often upholstered in leather, with straight upholstered arms of the same height as the back [c19: named after a 19th-century Earl of *Chesterfield*]

Chesterfield[1] ('tʃɛstəˌfiːld) *n* an industrial town in N central England, in Derbyshire: famous 14th-century church with twisted spire. Pop: 70 260 (2001)

Chesterfield[2] ('tʃɛstəˌfiːld) *n* **Philip Dormer Stanhope**, 4th Earl of Chesterfield. 1694–1773, English statesman and writer, noted for his elegance, suavity, and wit; author of *Letters to His Son* (1774)

Chesterton ('tʃɛstətⁿn) *n* **G**(**ilbert**) **K**(**eith**). 1874–1936, English essayist, novelist, poet, and critic

chestnut ('tʃɛsˌnʌt) *n* **1** any N temperate fagaceous tree of the genus *Castanea*, such as *C. sativa* (**sweet** or **Spanish chestnut**), which produce flowers in long catkins and nuts in a prickly bur. See **horse chestnut 2** the edible nut of any of these trees **3** the hard wood of any of these trees, used in making furniture, etc **4 a** a reddish-brown to brown colour **b** (*as adjective*): *chestnut hair* **5** a horse of a yellow-brown or golden-brown colour **6** *informal* an old or stale joke [c16: from earlier *chesten nut*: *chesten*, from Old French *chastaigne*, from Latin *castanea*, from Greek *kastanea*]

chest of drawers *n* a piece of furniture consisting of a frame, often on short legs, containing a set of drawers

chesty ('tʃɛstı) *adj* chestier, chestiest *informal* **1** *Brit* suffering from or symptomatic of chest disease: *a chesty cough* **2** having a large well-developed chest or bosom

> 'chestiness *n*

cheval glass (ʃəˈvæl) *n* a full-length mirror mounted so as to swivel within a frame [c19: from French *cheval* support (literally: horse)]

chevalier (ˌʃɛvæˈliə) *n* 1 a member of certain orders of merit, such as the French Legion of Honour 2 *French history* the lowest title of rank in the old French nobility 3 an archaic word for **knight** 4 a chivalrous man; gallant [c14: from Old French, from Medieval Latin *caballārius* horseman, CAVALIER]

Chevalier *n* 1 (ˌʃevəˈliə) **Albert**. 1861–1923, British music hall entertainer, remembered for his cockney songs 2 (ʃɛˈvælie; French ʃəvalje) **Maurice** (mɔris). 1888–1972, French singer and film actor

Cheviot (ˈtʃiːviət, ˈtʃɛv-) *n* 1 a large British breed of sheep reared for its wool 2 (*often not capital*) a rough twill-weave woollen suiting fabric

Cheviot Hills *pl n* a range of hills on the border between England and Scotland, mainly in Northumberland

chèvre (ˈʃɛvrə) *n* any cheese made from goats' milk [c20: from French, literally: goat]

chevron (ˈʃɛvrən) *n* 1 *military* a badge or insignia consisting of one or more V-shaped stripes to indicate a noncommissioned rank or length of service 2 *heraldry* an inverted V-shaped charge on a shield, one of the earliest ordinaries found in English arms 3 (*usually plural*) a pattern of horizontal black and white V-shapes on a road sign indicating a sharp bend 4 any V-shaped pattern or device [c14: from Old French, ultimately from Latin *caper* goat; compare Latin *capreoli* two pieces of wood forming rafters (literally: little goats)]

chevrotain (ˈʃɛvrəˌteɪn, -tɪn) *n* any small timid ruminant artiodactyl mammal of the genera *Tragulus* and *Hyemoschus*, of S and SE Asia: family *Tragulidae*. They resemble rodents, and the males have long tusklike upper canines. Also called: mouse deer [c18: from French, from Old French *chevrot* kid, from *chèvre* goat, from Latin *capra*, feminine of *caper* goat]

chevy (ˈtʃɛvɪ) *n, vb* a variant of **chivy**

chew (tʃuː) *vb* 1 to work the jaws and teeth in order to grind (food); masticate 2 to bite repeatedly: *she chewed her nails anxiously* 3 (*intr*) to use chewing tobacco 4 **chew the fat** *or* **chew the rag** *slang* **a** to argue over a point **b** to talk idly; gossip ▷ *n* 5 the act of chewing 6 something that is chewed [Old English *ceowan*; related to Old High German *kiuwan*, Dutch *kauwen*, Latin *gingīva* a gum]
> 'chewable *adj* > 'chewer *n*

chewing gum *n* a preparation for chewing, usually made of flavoured and sweetened chicle or such substitutes as polyvinyl acetate

chew over *vb* (*tr, adverb*) to consider carefully; ruminate

chewy (ˈtʃuːɪ) *adj* chewier, chewiest of a consistency requiring chewing; somewhat firm and sticky

Cheyenne (ʃaɪˈæn, -ˈɛn) *n* a city in SE Wyoming, capital of the state. Pop: 54 374 (2003 est)

chez French (ʃe) *prep* 1 at the home of 2 with, among, or in the manner of

Chhattisgarh (ˌtʃʌtɪsˈɡɑː) *n* a state of E central India, created from the SE part of Madhya Pradesh in 2000: consists of a hilly plateau, with extensive forests; agricultural. Capital: Raipur. Pop: 20 795 956 (2001). Area: 135 194 sq km (52 199 sq miles)

chi[1] (kaɪ) *n* the 22nd letter of the Greek alphabet (Χ, χ), a consonant, transliterated as *ch* or rarely *kh*

chi[2], **ch'i** *or* **qi** (tʃiː) *n* (*sometimes capital*) (in Oriental medicine, martial arts, etc) vital energy believed to circulate round the body in currents [Chinese, literally: energy]

chiack *or* **chyack** (ˈtʃaɪæk) *Austral informal* ▷ *vb* (*tr*) 1 to tease or banter ▷ *n* 2 good-humoured banter [c19: from *chi-hike*, a shout or greeting]

Chian (ˈkaɪən) *adj* 1 of or relating to Chios ▷ *n* 2 a native or inhabitant of Chios

Chiang Ch'ing (ˈtʃæŋ ˈtʃɪŋ) *n* a variant transliteration of the Chinese name for **Jiang Qing**

Chiang Ching-kuo (ˈtʃæŋ ˈtʃɪŋˈkwəʊ) *or* **Jiang Jing Guo** *n* 1910–88, Chinese statesman; the son of Chiang Kai-shek. He was prime minister of Taiwan (1971–78); president (1978–88)

Chiang Kai-shek (ˈtʃæŋ kaɪˈʃɛk) *or* **Jiang Jie Shi** *n* original name *Chiang Chung-cheng*, 1887–1975, Chinese general: president of China (1928–31; 1943–49) and of the Republic of China (Taiwan) (1950–75). As chairman of the Kuomintang, he allied with the Communists against the Japanese (1937–45), but in the Civil War that followed was forced to withdraw to Taiwan after his defeat by the Communists (1949)

chianti (kɪˈæntɪ) *n* (*sometimes capital*) a dry red wine produced in the Chianti region of Italy

Chiantishire (kɪˈæntɪˌʃɪə) *n Brit informal* a nickname for Tuscany [c20: from CHIANTI + SHIRE[1], alluding to the large numbers of British people living or holidaying in Tuscany]

Chiapas (Spanish ˈtʃjapas) *n* a state of S Mexico: mountainous and forested; Maya ruins in the northeast; rich mineral resources. Capital: Tuxtla Gutiérrez. Pop: 3 920 515 (2000). Area: 73 887 sq km (28 816 sq miles)

chiaroscuro (kɪˌɑːrəˈskʊərəʊ) *n, pl* -ros 1 the artistic distribution of light and dark masses in a picture 2 monochrome painting using light and dark only, as in grisaille [c17: from Italian, from *chiaro* CLEAR + *oscuro* OBSCURE]

chiasma (kaɪˈæzmə) *n, pl* -mas, -mata (-mətə) *or* -asms 1 *cytology* the cross-shaped connection produced by the crossing over of pairing chromosomes during meiosis 2 *anatomy* the crossing over of two parts or structures, such as the fibres of the optic nerves in the brain [c19: from Greek *khiasma* wooden crosspiece, from *khiazein* to mark with an X, from *khi* CHI[1]]

chiasmus (kaɪˈæzməs) *n, pl* -mi (-maɪ) *rhetoric* reversal of the order of words in the second of two parallel phrases: *he came in triumph and in defeat departs* [c19: from New Latin, from Greek *khiasmos* crisscross arrangement; see CHIASMA] > chiastic (kaɪˈæstɪk) *adj*

chib (tʃɪb) *Scot slang* ▷ *vb* chibs, chibbing, chibbed 1 (*tr*) to stab or slash with a sharp weapon ▷ *n* 2 a sharp weapon, such as a knife or razor [perhaps related to CHIV]

Chiba (ˈtʃiːba) *n* an industrial city in central Japan, in SE Honshu on Tokyo Bay. Pop: 880 164 (2002 est)

chic (ʃiːk, ʃɪk) *adj* 1 (esp of fashionable clothes, women, etc) stylish or elegant ▷ *n* 2 stylishness, esp in dress; modishness; fashionable good taste [c19: from French, of uncertain origin] > 'chicly *adv*

Chicago (ʃɪˈkɑːɡəʊ) *n* a port in NE Illinois, on Lake Michigan: the third largest city in the US; it is a major railway and air traffic centre. Pop: 2 869 121 (2003 est)

chicane (ʃɪˈkeɪn) *n* 1 a bridge or whist hand without trumps 2 *motor racing* a short section of sharp narrow bends formed by barriers placed on a motor-racing circuit to provide an additional test of driving skill 3 a less common word for **chicanery** ▷ *vb* 4 (*tr*) to deceive or trick by chicanery 5 (*intr*) to use tricks or chicanery [c17: from French *chicaner* to quibble, of obscure origin] > chi'caner *n*

chicanery (ʃɪˈkeɪnərɪ) *n, pl* -eries 1 verbal deception or trickery, esp in legal quibbling; dishonest or sharp practice 2 a trick, deception, or quibble

chicano (tʃɪˈkɑːnəʊ) *n, pl* -nos an American citizen of Mexican origin [c20: from Spanish *mejicano* Mexican]

Chichagof Island (ˈtʃɪtʃəˌɡɒf) *n* an island of Alaska, in the Alexander Archipelago. Area: 5439 sq km (2100 sq miles)

Chichen Itzá (Spanish tʃiˈtʃen itˈsa) *n* a village in Yucatán state in Mexico: site of important Mayan ruins

Chichester[1] (ˈtʃɪtʃɪstə) *n* a city in S England, administrative centre of West Sussex: Roman ruins; 11th-century cathedral; Festival Theatre. Pop: 27 477 (2001)

Chichester[2] (ˈtʃɪtʃɪstə) *n* Sir **Francis** 1901–72, British yachtsman, who sailed alone round the world in *Gipsy Moth IV* (1966–67)

chichi (ˈʃiːʃiː) *adj* 1 affectedly pretty or stylish ▷ *n* 2 the quality of being affectedly pretty or stylish [c20: from French]

Chichihaerh *or* **Ch'i-ch'i-haerh** (ˈtʃiːˌtʃiːˈhɑː) *n* a variant transliteration of the Chinese name for **Qiqihar**

chick (tʃɪk) *n* 1 the young of a bird, esp of a domestic fowl **2** *slang* a girl or young woman, esp an attractive one **3** a young child: used as a term of endearment [C14: short for CHICKEN]

chickadee ('tʃɪkəˌdiː) *n* any of various small North American songbirds of the genus *Parus*, such as *P. atricapillus* (**black-capped chickadee**), typically having grey-and-black plumage: family *Paridae* (titmice) [C19: imitative of its note]

chicken ('tʃɪkɪn) *n* **1 a** a domestic fowl bred for its flesh or eggs, esp a young one **2** the flesh of such a bird used for food **3** any of various similar birds, such as a prairie chicken **4** *slang* a cowardly person **5** *slang* a young inexperienced person **6** *informal* any of various, often dangerous, games or challenges in which the object is to make one's opponent lose his nerve **7 count one's chickens** before they are hatched to be overoptimistic in acting on expectations which are not yet fulfilled ▷ *adj* **8** *slang* easily scared; cowardly; timid [Old English *ciecen*; related to Old Norse *kjūklingr* gosling, Middle Low German *kūken* chicken]

chicken feed *n slang* a trifling amount of money

chicken fillet *n* **1** a fillet cut from a chicken **2** *informal* a gel-filled pad inserted under clothing to enlarge the appearance of a woman's breast

chicken-hearted or **chicken-livered** *adj* easily frightened; cowardly

chicken out *vb* (*intr, adverb*) *informal* to fail to do something through fear or lack of conviction

chickenpox ('tʃɪkɪnˌpɒks) *n* a highly communicable viral disease most commonly affecting children, characterized by slight fever and the eruption of a rash

chicken run *n South African informal* the departure of white residents from South Africa

chicken wire *n* wire netting with a hexagonal mesh

chickpea ('tʃɪkˌpiː) *n* **1** a bushy leguminous plant, *Cicer arietinum*, cultivated for its edible pealike seeds in the Mediterranean region, central Asia, and Africa **2** Also called: garbanzo the seed of this plant [C16 *ciche peasen*, from *ciche* (from French *chiche*, from Latin *cicer* chickpea) + *peasen*; see PEA]

chickweed ('tʃɪkˌwiːd) *n* any of various caryophyllaceous plants of the genus *Stellaria*, esp *S. media*, a common garden weed with small white flowers

Chiclayo (*Spanish* tʃiˈklajo) *n* a city in NW Peru. Pop: 434 000 (2005 est)

chicle ('tʃɪkəl) *n* a gumlike substance obtained from the sapodilla; the main ingredient of chewing gum [from Spanish, from Nahuatl *chictli*]

chicory ('tʃɪkərɪ) *n, pl* **-ries 1** Also called: succory a blue-flowered plant, *Cichorium intybus*, cultivated for its leaves, which are used in salads, and for its roots: family *Asteraceae* (composites) **2** the root of this plant, roasted, dried, and used as a coffee substitute ▷ See endive [C15: from Old French *chicorée*, from Latin *cichorium*, from Greek *kikhōrion*]

chide (tʃaɪd) *vb* chides, chiding, chided or chid; chided, chid or chidden **1** to rebuke or scold **2** (*tr*) to goad into action [Old English *cīdan*] ▷ 'chider *n* ▷ 'chidingly *adv*

chief (tʃiːf) *n* **1** the head, leader, or most important individual in a group or body of people **2** *heraldry* the upper third of a shield **3 in chief** primarily; especially ▷ *adj* **4** (*prenominal*) **a** most important; principal **b** highest in rank or authority ▷ *adv* **5** *archaic* principally [C13: from Old French, from Latin *caput* head]

chief executive *n* the person with overall responsibility for the efficient running of a company, organization, etc

chief justice *n* **1** (in any of several Commonwealth countries) the judge presiding over a supreme court **2** (in the US) the presiding judge of a court composed of a number of members ▷ See also **Lord Chief Justice**

chiefly ('tʃiːflɪ) *adv* **1** especially or essentially; above all **2** in general; mainly; mostly ▷ *adj* **3** of or relating to a chief or chieftain

Chief of Staff *n* **1** the senior staff officer under the commander of a major military formation or organization **2** the senior officer of each service of the armed forces

chief petty officer *n* the senior naval rank for personnel without commissioned or warrant rank

chieftain ('tʃiːftən, -tɪn) *n* the head or leader of a tribe or clan [C14: from Old French *chevetaine*, from Late Latin *capitāneus* commander; see CAPTAIN] ▷ 'chieftaincy or 'chieftain,ship *n*

chief technician *n* a noncommissioned officer in the Royal Air Force junior to a flight sergeant

Ch'ien-lung (tʃɪ'æn'lʊŋ) *n* a variant transliteration of the Chinese name for **Qian Long**

chiffchaff ('tʃɪf,tʃæf) *n* a common European warbler, *Phylloscopus collybita*, with a yellowish-brown plumage [C18: imitative of its call]

chiffon (ʃɪ'fɒn, 'ʃɪfɒn) *n* **1** a fine transparent or almost transparent plain-weave fabric of silk, nylon, etc **2** (*often plural*) *now rare* feminine finery ▷ *adj* **3** made of chiffon **4** (of soufflés, pies, cakes, etc) having a very light fluffy texture [C18: from French, from *chiffe* rag; probably related to CHIP]

chiffonier or **chiffonnier** (ˌʃɪfə'nɪə) *n* **1** a tall, elegant chest of drawers, originally intended for holding needlework **2** a wide low open-fronted cabinet, sometimes fitted with two grille doors and shelves [C19: from French, from *chiffon* rag; see CHIFFON]

Chifley ('tʃɪflɪ) *n* **Joseph Benedict.** 1885–1951, Australian statesman; prime minister of Australia (1945–49)

chigetai (ˌtʃɪgɪ'taɪ) *n* a variety of the Asiatic wild ass, *Equus hemionus*, of Mongolia [from Mongolian *tchikhitei* long-eared, from *tchikhi* ear]

chigger ('tʃɪgə) *n* **1** Also called: chigoe, redbug *US & Canadian* the parasitic larva of any of various free-living mites of the family *Trombidiidae*, which causes intense itching of human skin **2** another name for the **chigoe** (sense 1)

chignon ('ʃiːnjɒn; *French* ʃiɲɔ̃) *n* an arrangement of long hair in a roll or knot at the back of the head [C18: from French, from Old French *chaignon* link, from *chaine* CHAIN; influenced also by Old French *tignon* coil of hair, from *tigne*, moth, from Latin *tinea* moth]

chigoe ('tʃɪgəʊ) *n* **1** Also called: chigger, jigger, sand flea a tropical flea, *Tunga penetrans*, the female of which lives on or burrows into the skin of its host, which includes man **2** another name for **chigger** (sense 1) [C17: from Carib *chigo*]

Chigwell ('tʃɪgwəl) *n* a town in S England, in W Essex. Pop: 10 128 (2001)

Chihli ('tʃiːliː) *n* Gulf of Chihli another name for **Bohai**

Chihuahua (tʃɪ'wɑːwɑː, -wə) *n* **1** a state of N Mexico: mostly high plateau; important mineral resources, with many silver mines. Capital: Chihuahua. Pop: 728 000 (2005 est). Area: 247 087 sq km (153 194 sq miles) **2** a city in N Mexico, capital of Chihuahua state. Pop: 650 000 (2000 est) **3** a breed of tiny dog originally from Mexico, having short smooth hair, large erect ears, and protruding eyes

chilblain ('tʃɪl,bleɪn) *n pathol* (*usually plural*) an inflammation of the fingers, toes, or ears, caused by prolonged exposure to moisture and cold [C16: from CHILL (*n*) + BLAIN] ▷ 'chil,blained *adj*

child (tʃaɪld) *n, pl* children **1 a** a boy or girl between birth and puberty **b** (*as modifier*): *child labour* **2** a baby or infant **3** an unborn baby **4** with child another term for **pregnant 5** a human offspring; a son or daughter. Related adj: **filial 6** a childish or immature person **7** a member of a family or tribe; descendant: *a child of Israel* **8** a person or thing regarded as the product of an influence or environment: *a child of nature* [Old English *cild*; related to Gothic *kilthei* womb, Sanskrit *jathara* belly, *jartu* womb] ▷ 'childless *adj* ▷ 'childlessness *n*

child abuse *n* physical, sexual, or emotional ill-treatment or neglect of a child, esp by those responsible for its welfare

child-bearing *n* **a** the act or process of carrying and giving birth to a child **b** (*as modifier*): *of child-bearing age*

childbed ('tʃaɪld,bɛd) *n* (often preceded by *in*) the condition of giving birth to a child

child benefit *n* (in Britain and New Zealand) a regular government payment to the parents of children up to a certain age

childbirth ('tʃaɪld,bɜːθ) *n* the act of giving birth to a child

childcare ('tʃaɪld,kɛə) *n Brit* **1** care provided for children without homes (or with a seriously disturbed home life) by a local authority **2** care and supervision of children whose parents are working, provided by a childminder or local authority

child endowment *n Austral* a social security payment for dependent children

Childers ('tʃɪldəz) *n* (**Robert**) **Erskine.** 1870–1922, Irish politician, executed by the Irish Free State for his IRA activities: author of the spy story *The Riddle of the Sands* (1903)

childhood ('tʃaɪldhʊd) *n* the condition of being a child; the period of life before puberty

childish ('tʃaɪldɪʃ) *adj* **1** in the manner of, belonging to, or suitable to a child **2** foolish or petty; puerile: *childish fears* ⊳ '**childishly** *adv* ⊳ '**childishness** *n*

childlike ('tʃaɪld,laɪk) *adj* like or befitting a child, as in being innocent, trustful, etc

child minder *n* a person who looks after children, esp those whose parents are working

children ('tʃɪldrən) *n* the plural of **child**

child's play *n informal* something that is easy to do

chile ('tʃɪlɪ) *n* a variant spelling of **chilli**

Chile ('tʃɪlɪ) *n* a republic in South America, on the Pacific, with a total length of about 4090 km (2650 miles) and an average width of only 177 km (110 miles): gained independence from Spain in 1818; the government of President Allende (elected 1970) attempted the implementation of Marxist policies within a democratic system until overthrown by a military coup (1973); democracy restored 1988. Chile consists chiefly of the Andes in the east, the Atacama Desert in the north, a central fertile region, and a huge S region of almost uninhabitable mountains, glaciers, fjords, and islands; an important producer of copper, iron ore, nitrates, etc. Language: Spanish. Religion: Roman Catholic majority. Currency: peso. Capital: Santiago. Pop: 15 997 000 (2004 est). Area: 756 945 sq km (292 256 sq miles)

Chilean ('tʃɪlɪən) *adj* **1** of or relating to Chile or its inhabitants ⊳ *n* **2** a native or inhabitant of Chile

Chilean sea bass *n* another name for **Patagonian toothfish**

Chile pine *n* another name for the **monkey puzzle**

Chile saltpetre or **Chile nitre** *n* a naturally occurring form of sodium nitrate: a soluble white or colourless mineral occurring in arid regions, esp in Chile and Peru

chiliad ('kɪlɪ,æd) *n* **1** a group of one thousand **2** one thousand years [c16: from Greek *khilias*, from *khilioi* a thousand]

chill (tʃɪl) *n* **1** a moderate coldness **2** a sensation of coldness resulting from a cold or damp environment, or from a sudden emotional reaction **3** a feverish cold **4** a check on enthusiasm or joy ⊳ *adj* **5** another word for **chilly** ⊳ *vb* **6** to make or become cold **7** (*tr*) to cool or freeze (food, drinks, etc) **8** (*tr*) **a** to depress (enthusiasm, etc) **b** to discourage **9** (*intr*) *slang, chiefly US* to relax; calm oneself ⊳ See also **chill out** [Old English *ciele*; related to *calan* to **cool**, Latin *gelidus* icy] ⊳ '**chilling** *adj* ⊳ '**chillingly** *adv* ⊳ '**chillness** *n*

chilled (tʃɪld) *adj* **1** (of a person) feeling cold **2** (of food or drink) kept cool **3** Also: **chilled-out** *informal* relaxed or easy-going in character or behaviour

chiller ('tʃɪlə) *n* **1** *informal* short for **spine-chiller 2** *NZ* a refrigerated storage area for meat

chilli or **chili** ('tʃɪlɪ) *n, pl* **chillies** or **chilies** the small red hot-tasting pod of a type of capsicum used for flavouring sauces, pickles, etc [c17: from Spanish *chile*, from Nahuatl *chilli*]

chilli con carne (kɒn 'kɑːnɪ) *n* a highly seasoned Mexican dish of meat, onions, beans, and chilli powder [from Spanish *chile con carne* chilli with meat]

chilli powder *n* ground chilli blended with other spices

chilli sauce *n* a highly seasoned sauce made of tomatoes cooked with chilli and other spices and seasonings

chill out *informal* ⊳ *vb* **1** (*intr, adverb*) to relax, esp after energetic dancing or a spell of hard work ⊳ *adj* chill-out **2** suitable for relaxation after energetic dancing or hard work: *a chill-out area; chill-out music*

chilly ('tʃɪlɪ) *adj* **-lier, -liest 1** causing or feeling cool or moderately cold **2** without warmth; unfriendly **3** (of people) sensitive to cold ⊳ '**chilliness** *n*

chilly bin *n NZ informal* a portable insulated container with provision for packing food and drink in ice

Chiloé Island (,tʃɪləʊ'eɪ) *n* an island administered by Chile, off the W coast of South America in the Pacific Ocean: timber. Pop: 154 775 (2002, Chiloé province). Area: 8394 sq km (3240 sq miles)

Chilpancingo (*Spanish* tʃilpan'θiŋo) *n* a town in S Mexico, capital of Guerrero state, in the Sierra Madre del Sur. Pop: 166 000 (2005 est)

Chiltern Hills ('tʃɪltən) *pl n* a range of low chalk hills in SE England extending northwards from the Thames valley. Highest point: 260 m (852 ft)

Chiltern Hundreds *pl n* (in Britain) short for **Stewardship of the Chiltern Hundreds**; a nominal office that an MP applies for in order to resign his seat

Chilung or **Chi-lung** (tʃiː'lʊŋ) *n* a port in N Taiwan: fishing and industrial centre. Pop: 406 000 (2005 est). Also called: Keelung, Kilung

Chimborazo (,tʃɪmbə'rɑːzəʊ, -'reɪ-; *Spanish* tʃimbo'raθo) *n* an extinct volcano in central Ecuador, in the Andes: the highest peak in Ecuador. Height: 6267 m (20 561 ft)

Chimbote (*Spanish* tʃim'bote) *n* a port in N central Peru: contains Peru's first steelworks (1958), using hydroelectric power from the Santa River. Pop: 328 000 (2005 est)

chime¹ (tʃaɪm) *n* **1** an individual bell or the sound it makes when struck **2** (*often plural*) the machinery employed to sound a bell in this way **3** Also called: **bell** a percussion instrument consisting of a set of vertical metal tubes of graduated length, suspended in a frame and struck with a hammer **4** agreement; concord ⊳ *vb* **5 a** to sound (a bell) or (of a bell) to be sounded by a clapper or hammer **b** to produce (music or sounds) by chiming **6** (*tr*) to indicate or show (time or the hours) by chiming **7** (*intr; foll by with*) to agree or harmonize [c13: probably shortened from earlier *chymbe bell*, ultimately from Latin *cymbalum* **cymbal**] ⊳ '**chimer** *n*

chime², **chimb** (tʃaɪm) or **chine** *n* the projecting edge or rim of a cask or barrel [Old English *cimb-*; related to Middle Low German *kimme* outer edge, Swedish *kimb*]

chime in *vb* (*intr, adverb*) *informal* **1** to join in or interrupt (a conversation), esp repeatedly and unwelcomely **2** to voice agreement

chimera or **chimaera** (kaɪ'mɪərə, kɪ-) *n* **1** (*often capital*) *Greek myth* a fire-breathing monster with the head of a lion, body of a goat, and tail of a serpent **2** a fabulous beast made up of parts taken from various animals **3** a wild and unrealistic dream or notion **4** *biology* an organism, esp a cultivated plant, consisting of at least two genetically different kinds of tissue as a result of mutation, grafting, etc [c16: from Latin *chimaera*, from Greek *khimaira* she-goat, from *khimaros* he-goat]

chimerical (kaɪ'mɛrɪkᵊl, kɪ-) or **chimeric** (kaɪ'mɛrɪk, kɪ-) *adj* **1** wildly fanciful; imaginary **2** given to or indulging in fantasies ⊳ chi'**merically** *adv*

Chimkent (tʃɪm'kɛnt) *n* the Russian name for **Shymkent**

chimney ('tʃɪmnɪ) *n* **1** a vertical structure of brick, masonry, or steel that carries smoke or steam away from a fire, engine, etc **2** another name for **flue¹** (sense 1) **3** short for **chimney stack 4** an open-ended glass tube fitting around the flame of an oil or gas lamp in order to exclude draughts **5** *Brit* a fireplace, esp an old and large one **6** *geology* the vent of a volcano **7** *mountaineering* a vertical fissure large enough for a person's body to enter [c14: from Old French *cheminée*, from Late Latin *camīnāta*, from Latin *camīnus* furnace, from Greek *kaminos* fireplace, oven]

chimneypot ('tʃɪmnɪ,pɒt) *n* a short pipe on the top of a chimney, which increases the draught and directs the smoke upwards

chimney stack *n* the part of a chimney that rises above the roof of a building

chimney sweep or **chimney sweeper** *n* a person whose job is the cleaning out of soot from chimneys

chimp (tʃɪmp) *n informal* short for **chimpanzee**

chimpanzee (,tʃɪmpæn'ziː) *n* a gregarious and

intelligent anthropoid ape, *Pan troglodytes*, inhabiting forests in central W Africa [C18: from Kongo dialect]

chin (tʃɪn) *n* **1** the protruding part of the lower jaw **2** the front part of the face below the lips **3** keep one's chin up to keep cheerful under difficult circumstances **4** take it on the chin *informal* to face squarely up to a defeat, adversity, etc ▷ *vb* chins, chinning, chinned **5** *gymnastics* to raise one's chin to (a horizontal bar, etc) when hanging by the arms [Old English *cinn*; related to Old Norse *kinn*, Old High German *kinni*, Latin *gena* cheek, Old Irish *gin* mouth, Sanskrit *hanu*]

Chin. *abbreviation* **1** China **2** Chinese

china[1] (ˈtʃaɪnə) *n* **1** ceramic ware of a type originally from China **2** any porcelain or similar ware **3** cups, saucers, etc, collectively **4** (*modifier*) made of china [C16 *chiny*, from Persian *chīnī*]

china[2] (ˈtʃaɪnə) *n* *Brit & South African informal* a friend or companion [C19: originally Cockney rhyming slang: *china plate*, *mate*]

China (ˈtʃaɪnə) *n* **1** People's Republic of China *Also called*: Communist China, Red China a republic in E Asia: the third largest and the most populous country in the world; the oldest continuing civilization (beginning over 2000 years BC); republic established in 1911 after the overthrow of the Manchu dynasty by Sun Yat-sen; People's Republic formed in 1949; the 1980s and 1990s saw economic liberalization but a rejection of political reform; contains vast deserts, steppes, great mountain ranges (Himalayas, Kunlun, Tian Shan, and Nan Shan), a central rugged plateau, and intensively cultivated E plains. Language: Chinese in various dialects, the chief of which is Mandarin. Religion: nonreligious majority; Buddhist and Taoist minorities. Currency: yuan. Capital: Beijing. Pop: 1 300 000 000 (2005 est). Area: 9 560 990 sq km (3 691 502 sq miles) **2** Republic of China *Also called*: Nationalist China, Taiwan a republic (recognized as independent by only 24 nations) in E Asia occupying the island of Taiwan, 13 nearby islands, and 64 islands of the Penghu (Pescadores) group: established in 1949 by the Nationalist government of China under Chiang Kai-shek after its expulsion by the Communists from the mainland; its territory claimed by the People's Republic of China since the political separation from the mainland; under US protection 1954–79; lost its seat at the UN to the People's Republic of China in 1971; state of war with the People's Republic of China formally ended in 1991, though tensions continue owing to the unresolved territorial claim. Language: Mandarin Chinese. Religion: nonreligious majority; Buddhist and Taoist minorities. Currency: New Taiwan dollar. Capital: Taipei. Pop: 22 610 000 (2003 est). Area: 35 981 sq km (13 892 sq miles). Former name: Formosa. Related adj: Sinitic

china clay *or* **china stone** *n* another name for **kaolin**

Chinagraph (ˈtʃaɪnəˌɡrɑːf, -ˌɡræf) *n* *trademark* a coloured pencil used for writing on china, glass, etc

Chinaman (ˈtʃaɪnəmən) *n*, *pl* **-men 1** *archaic or derogatory* a native or inhabitant of China **2** (*often not capital*) *cricket* a ball bowled by a left-handed bowler to a right-handed batsman that spins from off to leg

Chinan *or* **Chi-nan** (ˈtʃiːˈnæn) *n* a variant transliteration of the Chinese name for **Jinan**

China Sea *n* part of the Pacific Ocean off the coast of China: divided by Taiwan into the East China Sea in the north and the South China Sea in the south

china stone *n* **1** a type of kaolinized granitic rock containing unaltered plagioclase **2** any of certain limestones having a very fine grain and smooth texture

Chinatown (ˈtʃaɪnəˌtaʊn) *n* a quarter of any city or town outside China with a predominantly Chinese population

chinaware (ˈtʃaɪnəˌwɛə) *n* articles made of china, esp those made for domestic use

chincherinchee (ˌtʃɪntʃərɪnˈtʃiː, -ˈrɪntʃɪ) *n* a bulbous South African liliaceous plant, *Ornithogalum thyrsoides*, having long spikes of white or yellow long-lasting flowers [of unknown origin]

chinchilla (tʃɪnˈtʃɪlə) *n* **1** a small gregarious hystricomorph rodent, *Chinchilla laniger*, inhabiting

mountainous regions of South America: family Chinchillidae. It has a stocky body and is bred in captivity for its soft silvery grey fur **2** the highly valued fur of this animal **3** a thick napped woollen cloth used for coats [C17: from Spanish, perhaps from Aymara]

chin-chin *sentence substitute informal* a greeting, farewell, or toast [C18: from Chinese (Peking) *ch'ing-ch'ing* please-please]

Chin-Chou *or* **Chin-chow** (ˈtʃɪnˈtʃaʊ) *n* a variant transliteration of the Chinese name for **Jinzhou**

Chindit (ˈtʃɪndɪt) *n* a member of the Allied forces commanded by Orde Wingate fighting behind the Japanese lines in Burma (1943–45) [C20: from Burmese *chinthé* a fabulous lion a symbol of which was their badge; adoption of title perhaps influenced by CHINDWIN]

Chindwin (ˈtʃɪnˈdwɪn) *n* a river in N Myanmar, rising in the Kumôn Range and flowing northwest then south to the Irrawaddy, of which it is the main tributary. Length: about 966 km (600 miles)

chine[1] (tʃaɪn) *n* **1** the backbone **2** the backbone of an animal with adjoining meat, cut for cooking **3** a ridge or crest of land ▷ *vb* **4** (*tr*) to cut (meat) along or across the backbone [C14: from Old French *eschine*, of Germanic origin; compare Old High German *scina* needle, shinbone; see SHIN[1]]

chine[2] (tʃaɪn) *n* *Southern English dialect* a deep fissure in the wall of a cliff [Old English *cīnan* to crack]

Chinese (tʃaɪˈniːz) *adj* **1** of, relating to, or characteristic of China, its people, or their languages ▷ *n* **2** *pl* -nese a native or inhabitant of China or a descendant of one **3** any of the languages of China belonging to the Sino-Tibetan family, sometimes regarded as dialects of one language. They share a single writing system that is not phonetic but ideographic. A phonetic system using the Roman alphabet was officially adopted by the Chinese government in 1966

Chinese cabbage *n* **1** *Also called*: pe-tsai cabbage a Chinese plant, *Brassica pekinensis*, that is related to the cabbage and has crisp edible leaves growing in a loose cylindrical head **2** another name for **bok choy**

Chinese chequers *n* (*functioning as singular*) a board game played with marbles or pegs

Chinese Empire *n* China as ruled by the emperors until the establishment of the republic in 1911–12

Chinese gooseberry *n* another name for **kiwi fruit**

Chinese lantern *n* **1** a collapsible lantern made of thin coloured paper **2** an Asian solanaceous plant, *Physalis franchetii*, cultivated for its attractive orange-red inflated calyx

Chinese leaf *pl n* the edible leaves of a Chinese cabbage

Chinese puzzle *n* **1** an intricate puzzle, esp one consisting of boxes within boxes **2** a complicated problem

Chinese Turkestan *n* the E part of the central Asian region of Turkestan: corresponds generally to the present-day Xinjiang Uygur Autonomous Region of China

Chinese wall *n* **1** a notional barrier between the parts of a business, esp between the market makers and brokers of a stock-exchange business, across which no information should pass to the detriment of clients **2** an insurmountable obstacle

Chinghai *or* **Ch'ing-hai** (ˈtʃɪŋˈhaɪ) *n* a variant transliteration of the Chinese name for **Qinghai**

Chingtao *or* **Ch'ing-tao** (ˈtʃɪŋˈtaʊ) *n* a variant transliteration of the Chinese name for **Qingdao**

Ch'ing-yüan (ˈtʃɪŋˈjuːɑːn) *n* a former name of **Baoding**

Chin-Hsien (ˈtʃɪnˈʃɛn) *n* the former name (1913–47) of **Jinzhou**

chink[1] (tʃɪŋk) *n* **1** a small narrow opening, such as a fissure or crack **2** chink in one's armour a small but fatal weakness [C16: perhaps variant of earlier *chine*, from Old English *cine* crack; related to Middle Dutch *kene*, Danish *kin*] ▷ ˈchinky *adj*

chink[2] (tʃɪŋk) *vb* **1** to make or cause to make a light ringing sound, as by the striking of glasses or coins ▷ *n* **2** such a sound [C16: of imitative origin]

chinless wonder *n* *Brit informal* a person, esp an upper-class one, lacking strength of character

chino ('tʃiːnəʊ) *n*, *pl* **-nos** *US* a durable cotton twill cloth [C20: from American Spanish, of obscure origin]

chinoiserie (ʃiːnˌwɑːzəˈriː, -ˈwɑːzərɪ) *n* **1** a style of decorative or fine art based on imitations of Chinese motifs **2** an object or objects in this style [French, from *chinois* CHINESE; see -ERY]

chinook (tʃɪˈnuːk, -ˈnʊk) *n* Also called: **snow eater** a warm dry southwesterly wind blowing down the eastern slopes of the Rocky Mountains **2** Also called: **wet chinook** a warm moist wind blowing onto the Washington and Oregon coasts from the sea [C19: from Salish *c'inuk*]

Chinook (tʃɪˈnuːk, -ˈnʊk) *n* **1** *pl* **-nook** or **-nooks** a Native American people of the Pacific coast near the Columbia River **2** the language of this people, probably forming a separate branch of the Penutian phylum

Chinook Jargon *n* a pidgin language containing elements of Native American languages, English, and French: formerly used among fur traders and Indians on the NW coast of North America

Chinook salmon *n* a Pacific salmon, *Oncorhynchus tschawytscha*, valued as a food fish

chinos ('tʃiːnəʊz) *pl n* trousers made of chino

chintz (tʃɪnts) *n* a printed, patterned cotton fabric, with glazed finish [C17: from Hindi *chīnt*, from Sanskrit *citra* gaily-coloured]

chintzy ('tʃɪntsɪ) *adj* **chintzier, chintziest 1** of, resembling, or covered with chintz **2** *Brit informal* typical of the decor associated with the use of chintz soft furnishings, as in a country cottage

chinwag ('tʃɪnˌwæɡ) *n Brit informal* a chat or gossipy conversation

Chios ('kiːɒs, -əʊs) *n* **1** an island in the Aegean Sea, off the coast of Turkey: belongs to Greece. Capital: Chios. Pop: 51 936 (2001). Area: 904 sq km (353 sq miles) **2** a port on the island of Chios: in ancient times, one of the 12 Ionian city-states. Pop (municipality): 25 671 (2001). Modern Greek name: **Khíos**

chip (tʃɪp) *n* **1 a** a small piece removed by chopping, cutting, or breaking **2 a** mark left after a small piece has been chopped, cut, or broken off something **3** (in some games) a counter used to represent money **4** a thin strip of potato fried in deep fat **5** *sport* a shot, kick, etc, lofted into the air, esp over an obstacle or an opposing player's head, and travelling only a short distance **6** *electronics* a tiny wafer of semiconductor material, such as silicon, processed to form a type of integrated circuit or component such as a transistor **7** a thin strip of wood or straw used for making woven hats, baskets, etc **8** *NZ* a container for soft fruit, made of thin sheets of wood; punnet **9** cheap as chips *Brit informal* inexpensive; good value **10** chip off the old block *informal* a person who resembles one of his or her parents in behaviour **11** have a chip on one's shoulder *informal* to be aggressively sensitive about a particular thing or bear a grudge **12** have had one's chips *Brit informal* to be defeated, condemned to die, killed, etc **13** when the chips are down *informal* at a time of crisis or testing ▷ *vb* **chips, chipping, chipped 14** to break small pieces from or become broken off in small pieces: *will the paint chip?* **15** (*tr*) to break or cut into small pieces: *to chip ice* **16** (*tr*) to shape by chipping **17** *sport* to strike or kick (a ball) in a high arc **18** *to dig or weed (a crop)* with a hoe [Old English *cipp* (n), *cippian* (vb), of obscure origin] > 'chipper *n*

chip and PIN *n* **a** a system for processing credit cards requiring the customer to enter a unique identification number instead of a signature to authorize a payment **b** (*as modifier*): *chip and PIN transactions* [C21: CHIP (sense 8) + PIN]

chip-based ('tʃɪpˌbeɪst) *adj* (of electronic equipment or components) using or incorporating microchips

chipboard ('tʃɪpˌbɔːd) *n* a thin rigid sheet made of compressed wood chips bound with a synthetic resin

chip heater *n Austral & NZ* a domestic water heater that burns chips of wood

chip in *vb* (*adverb*) *informal* **1** to contribute (money, time, etc) to a cause or fund **2** (*intr*) to interpose a remark or interrupt with a remark

chipmunk ('tʃɪpˌmʌŋk) *n* any burrowing sciurine rodent of the genera *Tamias* of E North America and *Eutamias* of W North America and Asia, typically having black-striped yellowish fur and cheek pouches for storing food [C19: of Algonquian origin; compare Ojibwa *atchitamon* squirrel, literally: headfirst, referring to its method of descent from trees]

chipolata (ˌtʃɪpəˈlɑːtə) *n chiefly Brit* a small sausage in a narrow casing [via French from Italian *cipollata* an onion-flavoured dish, from *cipolla* onion]

Chippendale ('tʃɪpˀnˌdeɪl) *n* **1 Thomas.** ?1718–79, English cabinet-maker and furniture designer ▷ *adj* **2** (of furniture) designed by, made by, or in the style of Thomas Chippendale, characterized by the use of Chinese and Gothic motifs, cabriole legs, and massive carving

chipper ('tʃɪpə) *adj informal* **1** cheerful; lively **2** smartly dressed

chippy[1] ('tʃɪpɪ) *n, pl* **-pies 1** *Brit informal* a fish-and-chip shop **2** *Brit & NZ* a slang word for **carpenter 3** *NZ* a potato crisp [C19: from CHIP (n)]

chippy[2] ('tʃɪpɪ) *adj* **-pier, -piest** *informal* resentful or oversensitive about being perceived as inferior: *a chippy miner's son* [C20: from CHIP (sense 12)] > 'chippiness *n*

chipset ('tʃɪpset) *n* **1 a** highly integrated circuit on the motherboard of a computer that controls many of its data transfer functions **2** *computing* the main processing circuitry on many video cards

chip shot *n golf* a short approach shot to the green, esp one that is lofted

chip wagon *n Canadian* a small van in which chips are cooked and sold

Chirac (French ʃirak) *n* **Jacques (René)** (ʒak). born 1932, French Gaullist politician: president of France (1995–2007); prime minister (1974–76 and 1986–88); mayor of Paris (1977–95)

chirality (kaɪˈrælɪtɪ) *n* the configuration or handedness (left or right) of an asymmetric, optically active chemical compound. Also called: **dissymmetry** [C19: from Greek *kheir* hand + -AL[1] + -ITY] > **chiral** *adj*

Chirico (Italian ˈkiːriko) *n* **Giorgio de** (ˈdʒɔrdʒo de). 1888–1978, Italian artist born in Greece: profoundly influenced the surrealist movement

chiro- or **cheiro-** *combining form* indicating the hand; of or by means of the hand: *chiromancy* [via Latin from Greek *kheir* hand]

chirography (kaɪˈrɒɡrəfɪ) *n* another name for **calligraphy** > **chi'rographer** *n* > **chirographic** (ˌkaɪrəˈɡræfɪk) or **chiro'graphical** *adj*

chiromancy ('kaɪrəˌmænsɪ) *n* another word for **palmistry** > **chiro,mancer** *n*

Chiron or **Cheiron** ('kaɪrɒn, -rən) *n* **1** *Greek myth* a wise and kind centaur who taught many great heroes in their youth, including Achilles, Actaeon, and Jason **2** a minor planet, discovered by Charles Kowal in 1977, revolving round the sun between the orbits of Saturn and Uranus

chiropody (kɪˈrɒpədɪ) *n* the treatment of the feet, esp the treatment of corns, verrucas, etc > **chi'ropodist** *n* > **chiropodial** (ˌkaɪrəʊˈpəʊdɪəl) *adj*

chiropractic (ˌkaɪrəˈpræktɪk) *n* a system of treating bodily disorders by manipulation of the spine and other parts, based on the belief that the cause is the abnormal functioning of a nerve [C20: from CHIRO- + -practic, from Greek *praktikos* effective, PRACTICAL] > **chiro,practor** *n*

chirp (tʃɜːp) *vb* (*intr*) **1** (esp of some birds and insects) to make a short high-pitched sound **2** to speak in a lively fashion ▷ *n* **3** a chirping sound, esp that made by a bird [C15 (as *chirpinge*, gerund): of imitative origin] > 'chirper *n*

chirpy ('tʃɜːpɪ) *adj* **chirpier, chirpiest** *informal* cheerful; lively > 'chirpily *adv* > 'chirpiness *n*

chirr, chirre or **churr** (tʃɜː) *vb* **1** (*intr*) (esp of certain insects, such as crickets) to make a shrill trilled sound ▷ *n* **2** the sound of chirring [C17: of imitative origin]

chirrup ('tʃɪrəp) *vb* (*intr*) **1** (esp of some birds) to chirp repeatedly **2** to make clucking sounds with the lips ▷ *n* **3** such a sound [C16: variant of CHIRP] > 'chirruper *n* > 'chirrupy *adj*

chisel ('tʃɪzˀl) *n* **1 a** a hand tool for working wood, consisting of a flat steel blade with a cutting edge attached to a handle of wood, plastic, etc. It is either struck with a mallet or used by hand **b** a similar tool without a handle for working stone or metal ▷ vb **-els, -elling, -eled** or US **-els, -eling, -eled 2** to carve (wood, stone, metal, etc) or form (an engraving, statue, etc) with or as with a chisel **3** slang to cheat or obtain by cheating [c14: via Old French, from Vulgar Latin cīsellus (unattested), from Latin caesus cut, from caedere to cut]

chiseller ('tʃɪzələ) n **1** a person who uses a chisel **2** informal a cheat **3** Dublin slang a child

Chishima (,tʃiːʃiːˈma) n the Japanese name for the **Kuril Islands**

Chisimaio (,kiːzɪˈmaːjəʊ) n a port in S Somalia, on the Indian Ocean. Pop: reliable recent estimates are not available. Also called: **Kismayu**

Chişinău (kiʃiˈnaʊ) n the capital of Moldova on the Bîk River: manufacturing centre of a rich agricultural region; university (1945). Pop: 662 000 (2005 est). Russian name: **Kishinev**

chi-square distribution ('kaɪ,skweə) n statistics a continuous single-parameter distribution derived as a special case of the gamma distribution and used esp to measure goodness of fit and to test hypotheses and obtain confidence intervals for the variance of a normally distributed variable

chi-square test n statistics a test derived from the chi-square distribution to compare the goodness of fit of theoretical and observed frequency distributions or to compare nominal data derived from unmatched groups of subjects

chit[1] (tʃɪt) n **1** a voucher for a sum of money owed, esp for food or drink **2** Also called: **chitty** ('tʃɪtɪ) chiefly Brit **a** a note or memorandum **b** a requisition or receipt [c18: from earlier chitty, from Hindi cittha note, from Sanskrit citra brightly-coloured]

chit[2] (tʃɪt) n facetious or derogatory a pert, impudent, or self-confident girl or child: a young chit of a thing [c14 (in the sense: young of an animal, kitten): of obscure origin]

Chita (Russian tʃiˈta) n an industrial city in SE Russia, on the Trans-Siberian railway. Pop: 309 000 (2005 est)

chital ('tʃiːt[ə]l) n another name for **axis**[2] [from Hindi]

chitchat ('tʃɪt,tʃæt) n **1** talk of a gossipy nature ▷ vb **-chats, -chatting, -chatted 2** (intr) to gossip

chitin ('kaɪtɪn) n a polysaccharide that is the principal component of the exoskeletons of arthropods and of the bodies of fungi [c19: from French chitine, from Greek khitōn CHITON + -IN] > **'chitinous** adj > **'chitin,oid** adj

chiton ('kaɪt[ə]n, -tɒn) n **1** (in ancient Greece and Rome) a loose woollen tunic worn knee length by men and full length by women **2** Also called: **coat-of-mail shell** any small primitive marine mollusc of the genus Chiton and related genera, having an elongated body covered with eight overlapping shell plates: class Amphineura [c19: from Greek khitōn coat of mail, of Semitic origin; related to Hebrew kethōnet]

Chittagong ('tʃɪtə,gɒŋ) n a port in E Bangladesh, on the Bay of Bengal: industrial centre. Pop: 4 171 000 (2005 est)

chitterlings ('tʃɪtəlɪŋz), **chitlins** ('tʃɪtlɪnz) or **chitlings** ('tʃɪtlɪŋz) pl n (sometimes singular) the intestines of a pig or other animal prepared as a dish [c13: of uncertain origin; perhaps related to Middle High German kutel]

chiv (tʃɪv, ʃɪv) or **shiv** (ʃɪv) slang n **1** a knife ▷ vb **chivs, chivving, chivved** or **shivs, shivving, shivved 2** to stab (someone) [c17: perhaps from Romany chiv blade]

chivalrous ('ʃɪvəlrəs) adj **1** gallant; courteous **2** involving chivalry [c14: from Old French chevalier, from CHEVALIER] > **'chivalrously** adv > **'chivalrousness** n

chivalry ('ʃɪvəlrɪ) n, pl -ries **1** the combination of qualities expected of an ideal knight, esp courage, honour, justice, and a readiness to help the weak **2** courteous behaviour, esp towards women **3** the medieval system and principles of knighthood **4** knights, noblemen, etc, collectively [c13: from Old French chevalerie, from CHEVALIER] > **'chivalric** adj

chive (tʃaɪv) n a small Eurasian purple-flowered alliaceous plant, Allium schoenoprasum, whose long slender hollow leaves are used in cooking to flavour soups,

stews, etc. Also called: **chives** [c14: from Old French cive, ultimately from Latin caepa onion]

chivy, chivvy ('tʃɪvɪ) or **chevy** Brit vb chivies, chivying, chivied; chivvies, chivvying, chivvied; or chevies, chevying, chevied **1** (tr) to harass or nag **2** (tr) to hunt **3** (intr) to run about ▷ n, pl chivies, chivvies or chevies **4** a hunt **5** obsolete a hunting cry [c19: variant of chevy, probably from Chevy Chase, title of a Scottish border ballad]

Chkalov (Russian 'tʃkaləf) n the former name (1938–57) of **Orenburg**

chlamydia (kləˈmɪdɪə) n any Gram-negative bacteria of the genus Chlamydia, which are obligate intracellular parasites and are responsible for such diseases as trachoma, psittacosis, and some sexually transmitted diseases [c20: New Latin, from Greek khlamus mantle + -IA]

Chlodwig ('kloːtvɪç) n the German name for **Clovis I**

chloral ('klɔːrəl) n **1** a colourless oily liquid with a pungent odour, made from chlorine and acetaldehyde and used in preparing chloral hydrate and DDT; trichloroacetaldehyde **2** short for **chloral hydrate**

chloral hydrate n a colourless crystalline soluble solid produced by the reaction of chloral with water and used as a sedative and hypnotic; 2,2,2-trichloro-1,1-ethanediol. Formula: $CCl_3CH(OH)_2$

chloramphenicol (,klɔːræmˈfɛnɪ,kɒl) n a broad-spectrum antibiotic used esp in treating typhoid fever and rickettsial infections: obtained from the bacterium Streptomyces venezuelae or synthesized. Formula: $C_{11}H_{12}N_2O_5Cl_2$ [c20: from CHLORO- + AM(IDO)- + PHE(NO)- + NI(TRO)- + (GLY)COL]

chlorate ('klɔː,reɪt, -rɪt) n any salt of chloric acid, containing the monovalent ion ClO_3^-

chlordane ('klɔː,deɪn) or **chlordan** ('klɔː,dæn) n a white insoluble toxic solid existing in several isomeric forms and usually used, as an insecticide, in the form of a brown impure liquid. Formula: $C_{10}H_6Cl_8$ [c20: from CHLORO- + (IN)D(ENE) + -ANE]

chlorhexidine (klɔːˈhɛksɪdiːn) n an antiseptic compound used in skin cleansers, mouthwashes, etc [c20: from CHLOR(O)- + HEX(ANE) + -I(DE) + (AM)INE]

chloric ('klɔːrɪk) adj of or containing chlorine in the pentavalent state

chloric acid n a strong acid with a pungent smell, known only in solution and in the form of chlorate salts. Formula: $HClO_3$

chloride ('klɔːraɪd) n **1** any salt of hydrochloric acid, containing the chloride ion Cl^- **2** any compound containing a chlorine atom, such as methyl chloride (chloromethane), CH_3Cl > **chloridic** (kləˈrɪdɪk) adj

chloride of lime or **chlorinated lime** n another name for **bleaching powder**

chlorinate ('klɔːrɪ,neɪt) vb (tr) **1** to combine or treat (a substance) with chlorine **2** to disinfect (water) with chlorine > **,chlorin'ation** n > **'chlorin,ator** n

chlorine ('klɔːriːn) or **chlorin** ('klɔːrɪn) n a toxic pungent greenish-yellow gas of the halogen group; the 15th most abundant element in the earth's crust, occurring only in the combined state, mainly in common salt: used in the manufacture of many organic chemicals, in water purification, and as a disinfectant and bleaching agent. Symbol: Cl; atomic no: 17; atomic wt: 35.4527; valency: 1, 3, 5, or 7; density: 3.214 kg/m³; relative density: 1.56; melting pt: –101.03°C; boiling pt: –33.9°C [c19 (coined by Sir Humphrey Davy): from CHLORO- + -INE²], referring to its colour]

chlorite[1] ('klɔːraɪt) n any of a group of green soft secondary minerals consisting of the hydrated silicates of aluminium, iron, and magnesium in monoclinic crystalline form: common in metamorphic rocks [c18: from Latin chlōrītis precious stone of a green colour, from Greek khlōritis, from khlōros greenish yellow] > **chloritic** (klɔːˈrɪtɪk) adj

chlorite[2] ('klɔːraɪt) n any salt of chlorous acid, containing the monovalent ion ClO_2^-

chloro- or before a vowel **chlor-** combining form **1** indicating the colour green: chlorophyll **2** chlorine: chloroform

chlorofluorocarbon (,klɔːrə,flʊərəʊˈkɑːb[ə]n) n chem any of various gaseous compounds of carbon, hydrogen, chlorine, and fluorine, used as refrigerants, aerosol propellants, solvents, and in foam: some cause a breakdown of ozone in the earth's atmosphere. Abbreviation: CFC

chloroform (ˈklɔːrəˌfɔːm) *n* a heavy volatile liquid with a sweet taste and odour, used as a solvent and cleansing agent and in refrigerants: formerly used as an inhalation anaesthetic. Formula: $CHCl_3$ [c19: from CHLORO- + FORM(YL) (in an obsolete sense that applied to a CH radical)]

Chloromycetin (ˌklɔːrəʊmaɪˈsiːtɪn) *n trademark* a brand of **chloramphenicol**

chlorophyll *or US* **chlorophyl** (ˈklɔːrəfɪl) *n* the green pigment of plants and photosynthetic algae and bacteria that traps the energy of sunlight for photosynthesis and exists in several forms, the most abundant being **chlorophyll a** ($C_{55}H_{72}O_5N_4Mg$): used as a colouring agent in medicines or food (**E140**)
> ˈchloroˌphylloid *adj* > ˌchloroˈphyllous *adj*

chloroplast (ˈklɔːrəʊˌplæst) *n* a plastid containing chlorophyll and other pigments, occurring in plants and algae that carry out photosynthesis

chlorosis (klɔːˈrəʊsɪs) *n* **1** Also called: **greensickness** *pathol* a disorder, formerly common in adolescent girls, characterized by pale greenish-yellow skin, weakness, and palpitation and caused by insufficient iron in the body **2** *botany* a deficiency of chlorophyll in green plants caused by mineral deficiency, lack of light, disease, etc, the leaves appearing uncharacteristically pale [c17: from CHLORO- + -OSIS] > chlorotic (klɔːˈrɒtɪk) *adj*

chlorous (ˈklɔːrəs) *adj* **1** of or containing chlorine in the trivalent state **2** of or containing chlorous acid

chlorous acid *n* an unstable acid that is a strong oxidizing agent. Formula: $HClO_2$

chlorpromazine (klɔːˈprɒməˌziːn) *n* a drug derived from phenothiazine, used as a tranquillizer and sedative, esp in psychotic disorders. Formula: $C_{17}H_{19}ClN_2S$ [c20: from CHLORO- + PRO(PYL + A)M(INE) + AZINE]

chlortetracycline (klɔːˌtɛtrəˈsaɪkliːn) *n* an antibiotic used in treating many bacterial and rickettsial infections: obtained from the bacterium *Streptomyces aureofaciens*. Formula: $C_{22}H_{23}ClN_2O_8$

chock (tʃɒk) *n* **1** a block or wedge of wood used to prevent the sliding or rolling of a heavy object **2** *nautical* **a** a fairlead consisting of a ringlike device with an opening at the top through which a rope is placed **b** a cradle-like support for a boat, barrel, etc ▷ *vb* (*tr*) **3** (usually foll by *up*) *Brit* to cram full: *chocked up with newspapers* **4** to fit with or secure by a chock **5** to support (a boat, barrel, etc) on chocks ▷ *adv* **6** as closely or tightly as possible: *chock against the wall* [c17: of uncertain origin; perhaps related to Old French *çoche* log; compare Provençal *soca* tree stump]

chock-a-block *adj, adv* **1** filled to capacity; in a crammed state **2** *nautical* with the blocks brought close together, as when a tackle is pulled as tight as possible

chocker (ˈtʃɒkə) *adj* **1** *informal* full up; packed **2** *Brit slang* irritated; fed up [c20: from CHOCK-A-BLOCK]

chock-full, choke-full *or* **chuck-full** *adj* (*postpositive*) completely full [c17 *choke-full*; see CHOKE, FULL]

choco *or* **chocko** (ˈtʃɒkəʊ) *n, pl* **chocos, chockos** *Austral slang* (in World War II) **a** a member of the citizen army; militiaman **b** a conscript [c20: shortened from *chocolate soldier*]

chocolate (ˈtʃɒkəlɪt, ˈtʃɒklɪt, -lət) *n* **1** a food preparation made from roasted ground cacao seeds, usually sweetened and flavoured **2** a drink or sweetmeat made from this **3 a** a moderate to deep brown colour **b** (*as adjective*): *a chocolate carpet* [c17: from Spanish, from Aztec *xocolatl*, from *xococ* sour, bitter + *atl* water]
> ˈchocolaty *adj*

chocolate-box *n* (*modifier*) *informal* sentimentally pretty or appealing

Choctaw (ˈtʃɒktɔː) *n* **1** *pl* **-taws** *or* **-taw** a member of a Native American people of Alabama **2** the language of this people, belonging to the Muskogean family [c18: from Choctaw *Chahta*]

choice (tʃɔɪs) *n* **1** the act or an instance of choosing or

selecting **2** the opportunity or power of choosing **3** a person or thing chosen or that may be chosen: *he was a possible choice* **4** an alternative action or possibility: *what choice did I have?* **5** a supply from which to select: *a poor choice of shoes* **6** of choice preferred; favourite **7** of superior quality; excellent: *choice wine* **8** carefully chosen, appropriate: *a few choice words will do the trick* **9** vulgar or rude: *choice language* [c13: from Old French *chois*, from *choisir* to CHOOSE] > ˈchoicely *adv*
> ˈchoiceness *n*

choir (kwaɪə) *n* **1** an organized group of singers, esp for singing in church services **2** the part of a cathedral, abbey, or church in front of the altar, lined on both sides with benches, and used by the choir and clergy **3** a number of instruments of the same family playing together: *a brass choir* **4** Also called: **choir organ** one of the manuals on an organ controlling a set of soft sweet-toned pipes [c13 *quer*, from Old French *cuer*, from Latin CHORUS]

choirboy (ˈkwaɪəˌbɔɪ) *n* one of a number of young boys who sing the treble part in a church choir

choir school *n* (in Britain) a school, esp a preparatory school attached to a cathedral, college, etc, offering general education to boys whose singing ability is good

Choiseul[1] (French ʃwazœl) *n* an island in the SW Pacific Ocean, in the Solomon Islands: hilly and densely forested. Area: 3885 sq km (1500 sq miles)

Choiseul[2] (French ʃwazœl) *n* **Étienne François** (etjɛn frɑːswa), Duc de. 1719–85, French statesman; foreign minister (1758–70)

choke (tʃəʊk) *vb* **1** (*tr*) to hinder or stop the breathing of (a person or animal), esp by constricting the windpipe or by asphyxiation **2** (*intr*) to have trouble or fail in breathing, swallowing, or speaking **3** (*tr*) to block or clog up (a passage, pipe, street, etc) **4** (*tr*) to retard the growth or action of: *the weeds are choking my plants* **5** (*intr*) *slang* to die **6** (*tr*) to enrich the petrol-air mixture by reducing the air supply to (a carburettor, petrol engine, etc) ▷ *n* **7** the act or sound of choking **8** a device in the carburettor of a petrol engine that enriches the petrol-air mixture by reducing the air supply **9** any constriction or mechanism for reducing the flow of a fluid in a pipe, tube, etc **10** Also called: **choke coil** *electronics* an inductor having a relatively high impedance, used to prevent the passage of high frequencies or to smooth the output of a rectifier **11** the inedible centre of the head of an artichoke ▷ See also **choke back, choke up** [Old English *ācēocian*, of Germanic origin; related to CHEEK] > ˈchokeable *adj*

choke back *or* **choke down** *vb* (*tr, adverb*) to suppress (anger, tears, etc)

choke chain *n* a collar and lead for a dog so designed that if the dog drags on the lead the collar tightens round its neck

choked (tʃəʊkt) *adj Brit informal* annoyed or disappointed

chokehold (ˈtʃəʊkˌhəʊld) *n* **1** the act of holding a person's neck across the windpipe, esp from behind using one arm **2** complete power or control: *the chokehold the mob has had on the town*

choker (ˈtʃəʊkə) *n* **1** a woman's high collar, popular esp in the late 19th century **2** any neckband or necklace worn tightly around the throat **3** a high clerical collar; stock **4** a person who chokes **5** something that causes a person to choke

choke up *vb* (*tr, adverb*) **1** to block (a drain, pipe, etc) completely **2** *informal* (*usually passive*) to overcome (a person) with emotion, esp without due cause

chokey *or* **choky** (ˈtʃəʊkɪ) *n Brit* a slang word for **prison** [c17: from Anglo-Indian, from Hindi *caukī* a shed or lockup]

choko (ˈtʃəʊkəʊ) *n, pl* **-kos** the cucumber-like fruit of a tropical American cucurbitaceous vine, *Sechium edule*: eaten as a vegetable in the Caribbean, Australia, and New Zealand [c18: from a Brazilian Indian name]

cholangiography (kəˌlændʒɪˈɒɡrəfɪ) *n* radiographic examination of the bile ducts after the introduction into them of a contrast medium

chole- *or before a vowel* **chol-** *combining form* indicating bile or gall: *cholesterol* [from Greek *kholē*]

choler ('kɒlə) n 1 anger or ill humour 2 archaic one of the four bodily humours; yellow bile. See **humour** (sense 8) 3 obsolete biliousness [c14: from Old French colère, from Medieval Latin cholera, from Latin: jaundice, CHOLERA]

cholera ('kɒlərə) n an acute intestinal infection characterized by severe diarrhoea, cramp, etc: caused by ingestion of water or food contaminated with the bacterium Vibrio comma. Also called: Asiatic cholera, epidemic cholera, Indian cholera [c14: from Latin, from Greek kholera jaundice, from kholē bile] > 'chole,roid adj

choleric ('kɒlərɪk) adj 1 bad-tempered 2 bilious or causing biliousness > 'cholerically or 'cholericly adv

cholesterol (kə'lɛstə,rɒl) n a sterol found in all animal tissues, blood, bile, and animal fats: a precursor of other body steroids. A high level of cholesterol in the blood is implicated in some cases of atherosclerosis, leading to heart disease. Formula: $C_{27}H_{45}OH$ [c19: from CHOLE- + Greek stereos hard, solid, so called because first observed in gallstones]

choline ('kəʊliːn, -ɪn, 'kɒl-) n a colourless viscous soluble alkaline substance present in animal tissues, esp as a constituent of lecithin: used as a supplement to the diet of poultry and in medicine for preventing the accumulation of fat in the liver. Formula:$[(CH_3)_3NCH_2CH_2OH]^+OH^-$ [c19: from CHOLE- + -INE², so called because of its action in the liver]

Cholula (Spanish tʃo'lula) n a town in S Mexico, in Puebla state: ancient ruins, notably a pyramid, 53 m (177 ft) high. Pop: 82 964 (2005)

chomp (tʃɒmp) or **chump** vb 1 to chew (food) noisily; champ ▷ n 2 the act or sound of chewing in this manner [variant of CHAMP¹]

Chomsky ('tʃɒmskɪ) n (Avram) Noam ('nəʊəm). born 1928, US linguist and political critic. His theory of language structure, transformational generative grammar, superseded the behaviourist view of Bloomfield > 'Chomskyan or 'Chomsky,ite n, adj

chondrite ('kɒndraɪt) n a stony meteorite consisting mainly of silicate minerals in the form of chondrules > chondritic (kɒn'drɪtɪk) adj

Chongqing ('tʃʊŋ'tʃɪŋ), **Chungking** or **Ch'ung-ch'ing** n a river port in SW China, capital of Chongqing municipality (traditionally in Sichuan province) at the confluence of the Yangtze and Jialing rivers: site of a city since the 11th millennium BC; wartime capital of China (1938–45); major trade centre for W China. Pop: 4 975 000 (2005 est). Former name: Pahsien

choof off (tʃuf) vb (intr, adverb) Austral slang to go away; make off

chook (tʃʊk) n Also called: chookie Austral informal a hen or chicken

choose (tʃuːz) vb chooses, choosing, chose, chosen 1 to select (a person, thing, course of action, etc) from a number of alternatives 2 (tr; takes a clause as object or an infinitive) to consider it desirable or proper: I don't choose to read that book 3 (intr) to like; please: you may stand if you choose 4 cannot choose but to be obliged to: we cannot choose but vote for him 5 nothing to choose between or little to choose between (of two people or objects) almost equal [Old English ceosan; related to Old Norse kjōsa, Old High German kiosan] > 'chooser n

choosy ('tʃuːzɪ) adj choosier, choosiest informal particular in making a choice; difficult to please

chop¹ (tʃɒp) vb chops, chopping, chopped 1 (often foll by down or off) to cut (something) with a blow from an axe or other sharp tool 2 (tr) to produce or make in this manner: to chop firewood 3 (tr; often foll by up) to cut into pieces 4 (tr) Brit informal to dispense with or reduce 5 (intr) to move quickly or violently 6 sport to hit (a ball) sharply downwards 7 boxing, martial arts to punch or strike (an opponent) with a short sharp blow 8 West African an informal word for eat ▷ n 9 a cutting blow 10 the act or an instance of chopping 11 a piece chopped off 12 a slice of mutton, lamb, or pork, generally including a rib 13 Austral & NZ slang a share (esp in the phrase get or hop in for one's chop) 14 West African an informal word for food 15 Austral & NZ a competition of skill and speed in chopping logs 16 sport a sharp downward blow or stroke 17 not much chop Austral & NZ

informal not much good; poor 18 the chop slang dismissal from employment [c16: variant of CHAP¹]

chop² (tʃɒp) vb chops, chopping, chopped 1 (intr) to change direction suddenly; vacillate (esp in the phrase **chop and change**) 2 obsolete to barter 3 chop logic to use excessively subtle or involved logic or argument [Old English ceapian to barter; see CHEAP, CHAPMAN]

chop³ (tʃɒp) n a design stamped on goods as a trademark, esp in the Far East [c17: from Hindi chhāp]

chop chop adv pidgin English for **quickly** [c19: from Chinese dialect; related to Cantonese kap kap]

chophouse ('tʃɒp,haʊs) n a restaurant specializing in steaks, grills, chops, etc

Chopin ('ʃɒpæŋ; French ʃɔpɛ̃) n Frédéric (François) (frederik). 1810–49, Polish composer and pianist active in France, who wrote chiefly for the piano: noted for his harmonic imagination and his lyrical and melancholy qualities

chopper ('tʃɒpə) n 1 chiefly Brit a small hand axe 2 a butcher's cleaver 3 a person or thing that cuts or chops 4 an informal name for a **helicopter** 5 chiefly Brit a slang name for **penis** 6 a device for periodically interrupting an electric current or beam of radiation to produce a pulsed current or beam 7 a type of bicycle or motorcycle with very high handlebars and an elongated saddle 8 NZ a child's bicycle 9 obsolete, slang, chiefly US a sub-machine-gun

choppy ('tʃɒpɪ) adj -pier, -piest (of the sea, weather, etc) fairly rough > 'choppily adv > 'choppiness n

chops (tʃɒps) pl n 1 the jaws or cheeks; jowls 2 the mouth 3 slang a music embouchure b jazz skill 4 lick one's chops informal to anticipate with pleasure [c16: of uncertain origin]

chopsticks ('tʃɒpstɪks) pl n a pair of thin sticks, of ivory, wood, etc, used as eating utensils by the Chinese, Japanese, and other people of East Asia [c17: from pidgin English, from chop quick, of Chinese dialect origin + STICK¹]

chop suey ('suːɪ) n a Chinese-style dish originating in the US, consisting of meat or chicken, bean sprouts, etc, stewed and served with rice [c19: from Chinese (Cantonese) tsap sui odds and ends]

choral adj ('kɔːrəl) 1 relating to, sung by, or designed for a chorus or choir ▷ n (kɒ'rɑːl) 2 a variant spelling of **chorale** > 'chorally adv

chorale or **choral** (kɒ'rɑːl) n 1 a slow stately hymn tune, esp of the Lutheran Church 2 chiefly US a choir or chorus [c19: from German Choralgesang, translation of Latin cantus chorālis choral song]

chord¹ (kɔːd) n 1 maths a a straight line connecting two points on a curve or curved surface b the line segment lying between two points of intersection of a straight line and a curve or curved surface 2 engineering one of the principal members of a truss, esp one that lies along the top or the bottom 3 anatomy a variant spelling of **cord** 4 an emotional response, esp one of sympathy: the story struck the right chord 5 an imaginary straight line joining the leading edge and the trailing edge of an aerofoil 6 archaic the string of a musical instrument [c16: from Latin chorda, from Greek khordē gut, string; see CORD] > 'chorded adj

chord² (kɔːd) n 1 the simultaneous sounding of a group of musical notes, usually three or more in number. See concord (sense 4), discord (sense 3) ▷ vb 2 (tr) to provide (a melodic line) with chords [c15: short for ACCORD; spelling influenced by CHORD¹] > 'chordal adj

chordate ('kɔː,deɪt) n 1 any animal of the phylum Chordata, including the vertebrates and protochordates, characterized by a notochord, dorsal tubular nerve cord, and pharyngeal gill slits ▷ adj 2 of, relating to, or belonging to the Chordata [c19: from Medieval Latin chordata; see CHORD¹ + -ATE¹]

chore (tʃɔː) n 1 a small routine task, esp a domestic one 2 an unpleasant task [c19: variant of Middle English chare; related to CHAR³]

-chore n combining form (in botany) indicating a plant distributed by a certain means: anemochore [from Greek khōrein to move] > -chorous or -choric adj combining form

chorea (kɒ'rɪə) n a disorder of the central nervous

system characterized by uncontrollable irregular brief jerky movements ▷ See **Huntington's disease**, **Sydenham's chorea** [c19: from New Latin, from Latin: dance, from Greek *khoreia*, from *khoros* dance; see CHORUS] > cho'real *or* cho'reic *adj*

choreograph ('kɒrɪə,græf) *vb* (*tr*) to compose the steps and dances for (a piece of music or ballet)

choreography (,kɒrɪ'ɒgrəfɪ) *or* **choregraphy** (kɒ'rɛgrəfɪ) *n* **1** the composition of dance steps and sequences for ballet and stage dancing **2** the steps and sequences of a ballet or dance **3** the notation representing such steps **4** the art of dancing [c18: from Greek *khoreia* dance + -GRAPHY] > ,choreˈographer *or* choˈregrapher *n* > choreographic (,kɒrɪə'græfɪk) *or* choregraphic (,kɒrə'græfɪk) *adj* > ,choreoˈgraphically *or* ,choreˈgraphically *adv*

choric ('kɒrɪk) *adj* of, like, for, or in the manner of a chorus, esp of singing, dancing, or the speaking of verse

chorion ('kɔːrɪən) *n* the outer of two membranes that form a sac around the embryonic reptile, bird, or mammal: contributes to the placenta in mammals. See also **amnion** [c16: from Greek *khorion* afterbirth] > ,choriˈonic *or* ˈchorial *adj*

chorionic gonadotrophin *n* a hormone secreted by the chorionic villi of the placenta in mammals, esp **human chorionic gonadotrophin**. It promotes the secretion of progesterone by the corpus luteum and its presence in the urine is an indication of pregnancy

chorionic villus sampling *n* a method of diagnosing genetic disorders early in pregnancy by the removal by catheter through the cervix or abdomen of a tiny sample of tissue from the chorionic villi. Abbreviation: CVS

chorister ('kɒrɪstə) *n* a singer in a choir, esp a choirboy [c14: from Medieval Latin *chorista*]

Chorley ('tʃɔːlɪ) *n* a town in NW England, in S Lancashire: cotton textiles. Pop: 33 424 (2001)

choroid ('kɔːrɔɪd) *or* **chorioid** ('kɔːrɪ,ɔɪd) *adj* **1** resembling the chorion, esp in being vascular ▷ *n* **2** the brownish vascular membrane of the eyeball between the sclera and the retina [c18: from Greek *khoroeidēs*, erroneously for *khorioeidēs*, from CHORION]

choropleth ('kɔːrə,plɛθ) *n* **a** a symbol or marked and bounded area on a map denoting the distribution of some property **b** (*as modifier*): *a choropleth map* [c20: from Gk *khōra* place + *plēthos* multitude]

chorrie ('tʃɒrɪ) *n* South African informal a dilapidated old car [c20: from Afrikaans *tjor* a crock]

chortle ('tʃɔːt³l) *vb* **1** (*intr*) to chuckle gleefully ▷ *n* **2** a gleeful chuckle [c19: coined (1871) by Lewis Carroll in *Through the Looking-glass*; probably a blend of CHUCKLE + SNORT] > 'chortler *n*

chorus ('kɔːrəs) *n*, *pl* -ruses **1** a large choir of singers or a piece of music composed for such a choir **2** a body of singers or dancers who perform together, in contrast to principals or soloists **3** a section of a song in which a soloist is joined by a group of singers, esp in a recurring refrain **4** an intermediate section of a pop song, blues, etc, as distinct from the verse **5** *jazz* any of a series of variations on a theme **6** (in ancient Greece) **a** a lyric poem sung by a group of dancers, originally as a religious rite **b** an ode or series of odes sung by a group of actors **7 a** (in classical Greek drama) the actors who sang the chorus and commented on the action of the play **b** actors playing a similar role in any drama **8 a** (esp in Elizabethan drama) the actor who spoke the prologue, etc **b** the part of the play spoken by this actor **9** a group of people or animals producing words or sounds simultaneously **10** any speech, song, or other utterance produced by a group of people or animals simultaneously: *a chorus of sighs; the dawn chorus* **11** in chorus in unison ▷ *vb* **12** to speak, sing, or utter (words, etc) in unison [c16: from Latin, from Greek *khoros*]

chorus girl *n* a girl who dances or sings in the chorus of a musical comedy, revue, etc

Chorzów (Polish 'xɔʒuf) *n* an industrial city in SW Poland: under German administration from 1794 to 1921. Pop: 113 739 (2007 est). German name: **Königshütte**

chose (tʃəʊz) *vb* the past tense of **choose**

chosen ('tʃəʊz³n) *vb* **1** the past participle of **choose** ▷ *adj*

2 selected or picked out, esp for some special quality

Chosen ('tʃəʊ'sɛn) *n* the official name for Korea when it was a Japanese province (1910–45)

Chosŏn ('tʃəʊ'sɒn) *n* the Korean name for **North Korea**

Chota Nagpur ('tʃəʊtə 'nɑːɡpʊə) *n* a plateau in E India, mainly in Jharkhand state since 2000: forested, with rich mineral resources and much heavy industry; produces chiefly lac (world's leading supplier), coal (half India's total output), and mica

Chou (tʃəʊ) *n* the imperial dynasty of China from about 1126 to 255 BC

Chou En-lai (tʃəʊɛn'laɪ) *or* **Zhou En Lai** *n* 1898–1976, Chinese Communist statesman; foreign minister of the People's Republic of China (1949–58) and premier (1949–76)

chough (tʃʌf) *n* **1** a large black passerine bird, *Pyrrhocorax pyrrhocorax*, of parts of Europe, Asia, and Africa, with a long downward-curving red bill: family *Corvidae* (crows) **2** alpine chough a smaller related bird, *Pyrrhocorax graculus*, with a shorter yellow bill [c14: of uncertain origin; probably related to Old French *cauwe*, Old English *cēo*]

choux pastry (ʃuː) *n* a very light pastry made with eggs, used for eclairs, etc [partial translation of French *pâte choux* cabbage dough (from its round shape)]

chow (tʃaʊ) *n* **1** *informal* food **2** short for **chow-chow** (sense 1)

chow-chow *n* **1** a thick-coated breed of the spitz type of dog with a curled tail and a characteristic blue-black tongue; it came originally from China. Often shortened to **chow 2** a Chinese preserve of ginger, orange peel, etc in syrup **3** a mixed vegetable pickle [c19: from pidgin English, probably based on Mandarin Chinese *cha* miscellaneous]

chowder ('tʃaʊdə) *n* a thick soup or stew containing clams or fish [c18: from French *chaudière* kettle, from Late Latin *caldāria*; see CAULDRON]

chow mein (meɪn) *n* a Chinese-American dish, consisting of mushrooms, meat, shrimps, etc, served with fried noodles [from Chinese (Cantonese), variant of Mandarin *ch'ao mien* fried noodles]

Chrétien (French kretjɛ̃) *n* (**Joseph Jacques**) **Jean**. born 1934, Canadian Liberal politician; prime minister of Canada (1993–2003)

Chrétien de Troyes (French kretjɛ̃ də trwa) *n* 12th century, French poet, who wrote the five Arthurian romances *Erec; Cligès; Lancelot, le chevalier de la charette; Yvain, le chevalier au lion;* and *Perceval, le conte del Graal*, the first courtly romances

chrism *or* **chrisom** ('krɪzəm) *n* a mixture of olive oil and balsam used for sacramental anointing in the Greek Orthodox and Roman Catholic Churches [Old English *crisma*, from Medieval Latin, from Greek *khrisma* unction, from *khriein* to anoint] > chrismal ('krɪzməl) *adj*

Christ (kraɪst) *n* **1** Jesus of Nazareth (Jesus Christ), regarded by Christians as fulfilling Old Testament prophecies of the Messiah **2** the Messiah or anointed one of God as the subject of Old Testament prophecies **3** an image or picture of Christ ▷ *interj* **4** *taboo, slang* an oath expressing annoyance, surprise, etc ▷ See also **Jesus** [Old English *Crīst*, from Latin *Chrīstus*, from Greek *khristos* anointed one (from *khriein* to anoint), translating Hebrew *māshīah* MESSIAH]

Christadelphian (,krɪstə'dɛlfɪən) *n* **1** a member of a Christian millenarian sect founded in the US about 1848, holding that only the just will enter eternal life, that the wicked will be annihilated, and that the ignorant, the unconverted, and infants will not be raised from the dead ▷ *adj* **2** of or relating to this body or its beliefs and practices [c19: from Late Greek *khristadelphos*, from *khristos* CHRIST + *adelphos* brother]

Christchurch (kraɪst,tʃ3ːtʃ) *n* **1** a city in New Zealand, on E South Island: manufacturing centre of a rich agricultural region. Pop: 344 100 (2004 est) **2** a town and resort in S England, in SE Dorset. Pop: 40 208 (2001)

christen ('krɪs³n) *vb* (*tr*) **1** to give a Christian name to in baptism as a sign of incorporation into a Christian Church **2** another word for **baptize 3** to give a name to (anything), esp with some ceremony **4** *informal* to use for the first time [Old English *cristnian*, from *Crīst* CHRIST] > 'christener *n* > 'christening *n*

Christendom ('krisᵊndəm) *n* the collective body of Christians throughout the world or throughout history

Christian¹ ('kristʃən) *n* **1 a** a person who believes in and follows Jesus Christ **b** a member of a Christian Church or denomination **2** *informal* a person who possesses Christian virtues, esp practical ones ▷ *adj* **3** of, relating to, or derived from Jesus Christ, his teachings, example, or his followers **4** (*sometimes not capital*) exhibiting kindness or goodness > 'Christianly *adj, adv*

Christian² ('kristʃən) *n* **Charlie.** 1919–42, US jazz guitarist

Christian IV ('kristʃən; *Danish* 'kresdjan) *n* 1577–1648, king of Denmark and Norway (1588–1648): defeated in the Thirty Years' War (1629) and by Sweden (1645)

Christian X *n* 1890–1947, king of Denmark (1912–47) and Iceland (1918–44)

Christian Democrat *n* **1** a member or supporter of a Christian Democratic party ▷ *adj* **2** of or relating to a Christian Democratic party

Christian Era *n* the period beginning with the year of Christ's birth. Dates in this era are labelled AD, those previous to it BC. Also called: Common Era

Christiania (,kristi'ɑ:niə) *n* a former name (1624–1877) of Oslo

Christianity (,kristi'æniti) *n* **1** the Christian religion **2** Christian beliefs, practices or attitudes **3** a less common word for **Christendom** (sense 1)

Christianize *or* **Christianise** ('kristʃə,naiz) *vb* (*tr*) **1** to make Christian or convert to Christianity **2** to imbue with Christian principles, spirit, or outlook > ,Christiani'zation *or* ,Christiani'sation *n* > 'Christian,izer *or* 'Christian,iser *n*

Christian name *n* a personal name formally given to Christians at christening

● USAGE This word was often loosely used to mean any
● person's first name as distinct from his or her
● surname. Nowadays, especially in official documents,
● alternatives which do not refer to a particular faith,
● and are therefore more inclusive, are often used: *first*
● *name*, *forename* and *given name*

Christiansand ('kristʃən,sænd; *Norwegian* kristian'san) *n* a variant spelling of **Kristiansand**

Christian Science *n* the religious system and teaching of the Church of Christ, Scientist. It was founded by Mary Baker Eddy (1866) and emphasizes spiritual healing and the unreality of matter > Christian Scientist *n*

Christie ('kristi) *n* **1** Dame Agatha (**Mary Clarissa**). 1890–1976, British author of detective stories, many featuring Hercule Poirot, and several plays, including *The Mousetrap* (1952) **2** John (**Reginald Halliday**). 1898–1953, British murderer. His trial influenced legislation regarding the death penalty after he was found guilty of a murder for which Timothy Evans had been hanged **3** Linford ('linfəd). born 1960, British athlete: Commonwealth (1990), Olympic (1992), World (1993), and European (1994) 100 metres gold medallist **4** William (**Lincoln**). born 1944, French harpsichord player, organist, and conductor, born in the US; founder (1979) and director of the early-music group Les Arts Florissants

Christina (kri'sti:nə) *n* 1626–89, queen of Sweden (1632–54), daughter of Gustavus Adolphus, noted particularly for her patronage of literature

Christine de Pisan (*French* kristin də pizã) *n* ?1364–?1430, French poet and prose writer, born in Venice. Her works include ballads, rondeaux, lays, and a biography of Charles V of France

Christingle (,kris'tiŋgᵊl) *n* (in Britain) a Christian service for children held shortly before Christmas, in which each child is given a decorated fruit with a lighted candle in it [C20: from CHRISTMAS + INGLE]

Christlike ('kraist,laik) *adj* resembling or showing the spirit of Jesus Christ > 'Christ,likeness *n*

Christmas ('krisməs) *n* **1 a** the annual commemoration by Christians of the birth of Jesus Christ on Dec 25 **b** Also called: Christmas Day Dec 25, observed as a day of secular celebrations when gifts and greetings are exchanged **c** (*as modifier*): *Christmas celebrations* **2** Also called: Christmas Day (in England, Wales and Ireland) Dec 25, one of the four quarter days. See **Lady Day, Midsummer's Day, Michaelmas 3** Also called: Christmastide the season of Christmas extending from Dec 24 (Christmas Eve) to Jan 6 (the festival of the Epiphany or Twelfth Night) [Old English *Crīstes mæsse* MASS of CHRIST]

Christmas box *n* a tip or present given at Christmas, esp to postmen, tradesmen, etc

Christmas Eve *n* the evening or the whole day before Christmas Day

Christmas Island *n* **1** the former name (until 1981) of **Kiritimati 2** an island in the Indian Ocean, south of Java: administered by Singapore (1900–58), now by Australia; phosphate mining. Pop: 1500 (2004 est). Area: 135 sq km (52 sq miles)

Christmas pudding *n* *Brit* a rich steamed pudding containing suet, dried fruit, spices, brandy, etc, served at Christmas. Also called: plum pudding

Christmas rose *n* an evergreen ranunculaceous plant, *Helleborus niger*, of S Europe and W Asia, with white or pinkish winter-blooming flowers. Also called: hellebore, winter rose

Christmastide ('krisməs,taid) *n* another name for **Christmas** (sense 3)

Christmas tree *n* **1** an evergreen tree or an imitation of one, decorated as part of Christmas celebrations **2** Also called: Christmas bush *Austral* any of various trees or shrubs flowering at Christmas and used for decoration **3** another name for **pohutukawa**

Christo ('kristəʊ) *n* full name Christo Jaracheff. born 1935, US artist, born in Bulgaria; best known for works in which he wraps buildings, monuments, or natural features in canvas or plastic

Christoff ('kristɒf) *n* **Boris.** 1919–93, Bulgarian bass-baritone, noted esp for his performance in the title role of Mussorgsky's *Boris Godunov*

Christophe (*French* kristɔf) *n* **Henri** (ãri). 1767–1820, Haitian revolutionary leader; king of Haiti (1811–20)

Christopher ('kristəfə) *n* **Saint.** 3rd century AD, Christian martyr; patron saint of travellers

Christy *or* **Christie** ('kristi) *n, pl* -ties (*sometimes not capital*) *skiing* a turn in which the body is swung sharply round with the skis parallel, originating in Norway and used for stopping, slowing down, or changing direction quickly [C20: shortened from CHRISTIANIA]

chroma ('krəʊmə) *n* **1** the attribute of a colour that enables an observer to judge how much chromatic colour it contains irrespective of achromatic colour present. See also **saturation** (sense 4) **2** (in colour television) the colour component in a composite coded signal [C19: from Greek *khrōma* colour]

chromate ('krəʊ,meit) *n* any salt or ester of chromic acid. Simple chromate salts contain the divalent ion, CrO_4^{2-}, and are orange

chromatic (krə'mætik) *adj* **1** of, relating to, or characterized by a colour or colours **2** *music* **a** involving the sharpening or flattening of notes or the use of such notes in chords and harmonic progressions **b** of or relating to the chromatic scale or an instrument capable of producing it: *a chromatic harmonica* **c** of or relating to chromaticism ▷ See **diatonic** [C17: from Greek *khrōmatikos*, from *khrōma* colour] > chro'matically *adv* > chro'maticism *n*

chromatic aberration *n* a defect in a lens system in which different wavelengths of light are focused at different distances because they are refracted through different angles. It produces a blurred image with coloured fringes

chromatics (krəʊ'mætiks) *or* **chromatology** (,krəʊmə'tɒlədʒi) *n* (*functioning as singular*) the science of colour > chromatist ('krəʊmətist) *or* ,chroma'tologist *n*

chromatic scale *n* a twelve-note scale including all the semitones of the octave

chromatin ('krəʊmətin) *n* *cytology* the part of the nucleus that consists of DNA and proteins, forms the chromosomes, and stains with basic dyes

chromato- *or before a vowel* **chromat-** *combining form*

1 indicating colour or coloured: *chromatophore*
2 indicating chromatin: *chromatolysis* [from Greek *khrōma*, *khrōmat-* colour]

chromatography (ˌkrəʊməˈtɒɡrəfɪ) *n* the technique of separating and analysing the components of a mixture of liquids or gases by selective adsorption in, for example, a column of powder (**column chromatography**) or on a strip of paper (**paper chromatography**). See also **gas chromatography** > ˌchromaˈtographer *n* > chromatographic (ˌkrəʊmətəˈɡræfɪk) *adj* > ˌchromatoˈgraphically *adv*

chrome (krəʊm) *n* **1 a** another word for chromium, esp when present in a pigment or dye **b** (*as modifier*): *a chrome dye* **2** anything plated with chromium, such as fittings on a car body **3** a pigment or dye that contains chromium ▷ *vb* **4** to plate or be plated with chromium, usually by electroplating **5** to treat or be treated with a chromium compound, as in dyeing or tanning [C19: via French from Greek *khrōma* colour]

-chrome *adj combining form, n combining form* colour, coloured, or pigment: *monochrome* [from Greek *khrōma* colour]

chrome dioxide *n* another name for **chromium dioxide**

chromel (ˈkrəʊmɛl) *n* a nickel-based alloy containing about 10 per cent chromium, used in heating elements [C20: from CHRO(MIUM) + ME(TA)L]

chrome steel *n* any of various hard rust-resistant steels containing chromium. Also called: **chromium steel**

chrome yellow *n* any yellow pigment consisting of lead chromate mixed with lead sulphate

chromic (ˈkrəʊmɪk) *adj* **1** of or containing chromium in the trivalent state **2** of or derived from chromic acid

chromic acid *n* an unstable dibasic oxidizing acid known only in solution and in the form of chromate salts. Formula: H_2CrO_4

chromite (ˈkrəʊmaɪt) *n* **1** a brownish-black mineral consisting of a ferrous chromic oxide in cubic crystalline form, occurring principally in basic igneous rocks: the only commercial source of chromium and its compounds. Formula: $FeCr_2O_4$ **2** a salt of chromous acid

chromium (ˈkrəʊmɪəm) *n* a hard grey metallic element that takes a high polish, occurring principally in chromite: used in steel alloys and electroplating to increase hardness and corrosion-resistance. Symbol: Cr; atomic no: 24; atomic wt: 51.9961; valency: 2, 3, or 6; relative density: 7.18–7.20; melting pt: 1863±20°C; boiling pt: 2672°C [C19: from New Latin, from French: CHROME]

chromium dioxide *n* a chemical compound used as a magnetic coating on cassette tapes; chromium(IV) oxide. Formula: CrO_2. Also called (not in technical usage): chrome dioxide

chromium steel *n* another name for **chrome steel**

chromo (ˈkrəʊməʊ) *n, pl* -mos short for chromolithograph

chromo- *or before a vowel* **chrom-** *combining form* **1** indicating colour, coloured, or pigment: *chromogen* **2** indicating chromium: *chromyl* [from Greek *khrōma* colour]

chromolithograph (ˌkrəʊməʊˈlɪθəˌɡrɑːf, -ˌɡræf) *n* a picture produced by chromolithography

chromolithography (ˌkrəʊməʊlɪˈθɒɡrəfɪ) *n* the process of making coloured prints by lithography > ˌchromoliˈthographer *n* > chromolithographic (ˌkrəʊməʊlɪθəˈɡræfɪk) *adj*

chromosome (ˈkrəʊməˌsəʊm) *n* any of the microscopic rod-shaped structures that appear in a cell nucleus during cell division, consisting of nucleoprotein arranged into units (genes) that are responsible for the transmission of hereditary characteristics > ˌchromoˈsomal *adj* > ˌchromoˈsomally *adv*

chromosome map *n* a graphic representation of the positions of genes on chromosomes, obtained by observation of chromosome bands or by determining the degree of linkage between genes. See also **genetic map** > chromosome mapping *n*

chromosphere (ˈkrəʊməˌsfɪə) *n* a gaseous layer of the sun's atmosphere extending from the photosphere to the corona and visible during a total eclipse of the sun > chromospheric (ˌkrəʊməˈsfɛrɪk) *adj*

chromous (ˈkrəʊməs) *adj* of or containing chromium in the divalent state

Chron. *Bible abbreviation* Chronicles

chronic (ˈkrɒnɪk) *adj* **1** continuing for a long time; constantly recurring **2** (of a disease) developing slowly, or of long duration. See **acute** (sense 7) **3** inveterate; habitual: *a chronic smoker* **4** *informal* **a** very bad: *the play was chronic* **b** very serious: *he left her in a chronic condition* [C15: from Latin *chronicus* relating to time, from Greek *khronikos*, from *khronos* time] > 'chronically *adv* > chronicity (krɒˈnɪsɪtɪ) *n*

chronic fatigue syndrome *n* another name for **myalgic encephalopathy**. Abbreviation: CFS

chronicle (ˈkrɒnɪkəl) *n* **1** a record or register of events in chronological order ▷ *vb* **2** (*tr*) to record in or as if in a chronicle [C14: from Anglo-French *cronicle*, via Latin *chronica* (pl), from Greek *khronika* annals, from *khronikos* relating to time; see CHRONIC] > 'chronicler *n*

chrono- *or before a vowel* **chron-** *combining form* indicating time: *chronology; chronometer* [from Greek *khronos* time]

chronograph (ˈkrɒnəˌɡrɑːf, -ˌɡræf, ˈkrəʊnə-) *n* **1** an accurate instrument for recording small intervals of time **2** any timepiece, esp a wristwatch designed for maximum accuracy > chronographer (krəˈnɒɡrəfə) *n* > chronographic (ˌkrɒnəˈɡræfɪk) *adj* > ˌchronoˈgraphically *adv*

chronological (ˌkrɒnəˈlɒdʒɪkəl, ˌkrəʊ-) *or* **chronologic** (ˌkrɒnəˈlɒdʒɪk, ˌkrəʊ-) *adj* **1** (esp of a sequence of events) arranged in order of occurrence **2** relating to or in accordance with chronology > ˌchronoˈlogically *adv*

chronology (krəˈnɒlədʒɪ) *n, pl* -gies **1** the determination of the proper sequence of past events **2** the arrangement of dates, events, etc, in order of occurrence **3** a table or list of events arranged in order of occurrence > chroˈnologist *n*

chronometer (krəˈnɒmɪtə) *n* a timepiece designed to be accurate in all conditions of temperature, pressure, etc, used esp at sea > chronometric (ˌkrɒnəˈmɛtrɪk) *or* ˌchronoˈmetrical *adj* > ˌchronoˈmetrically *adv*

chronometry (krəˈnɒmɪtrɪ) *n* the science or technique of measuring time with extreme accuracy

chronon (ˈkrəʊnɒn) *n* a unit of time equal to the time that a photon would take to traverse the diameter of an electron: about 10^{-24} seconds

chrysalid (ˈkrɪsəlɪd) *n* **1** another name for **chrysalis** ▷ *adj* Also: chrysalidal (krɪˈsælɪdəl) **2** of or relating to a chrysalis

chrysalis (ˈkrɪsəlɪs) *n, pl* chrysalises *or* chrysalides (krɪˈsælɪˌdiːz) **1** the obtect pupa of a moth or butterfly **2** anything in the process of developing [C17: from Latin *chrȳsallis*, from Greek *khrusallis*, from *khrusos* gold, of Semitic origin; compare Hebrew *harūz* gold]

chrysanthemum (krɪˈsænθəməm) *n* **1** any widely cultivated plant of the genus *Chrysanthemum*, esp *C. morifolium* of China, having brightly coloured showy flower heads: family *Asteraceae* (composites) **2** any other plant of the genus *Chrysanthemum*, such as oxeye daisy [C16: from Latin: marigold, from Greek *khrusanthemon*, from *khrusos* gold + *anthemon* flower]

chryselephantine (ˌkrɪsɛlɪˈfæntɪn) *adj* (of ancient Greek statues) made of or overlaid with gold and ivory [C19: from Greek *khruselephantinos*, from *khrusos* gold + *elephas* ivory; see ELEPHANT]

chryso- *or before a vowel* **chrys-** *combining form* indicating gold or the colour of gold: *chryselephantine; chrysolite* [from Greek *khrusos* gold]

chrysoberyl (ˈkrɪsəˌbɛrɪl) *n* a rare very hard greenish-yellow mineral consisting of beryllium aluminate in orthorhombic crystalline form and occurring in coarse granite: used as a gemstone in the form of cat's eye and alexandrite. Formula: $BeAl_2O_4$

chrysolite (ˈkrɪsəˌlaɪt) *n* another name for **olivine** > chrysolitic (ˌkrɪsəˈlɪtɪk) *adj*

chrysoprase (ˈkrɪsəˌpreɪz) *n* an apple-green variety of chalcedony: a gemstone [C13 *crisopace*, from Old French, from Latin *chrȳsoprasus*, from Greek *khrusoprasos*, from CHRYSO- + *prason* leek]

Chrysostom (ˈkrɪsəstəm) *n* Saint John. ?345–407 AD, Greek patriarch; archbishop of Constantinople

(398–404). Feast day: Sept 13 or Nov 13

chthonian ('θəʊnɪən) *or* **chthonic** ('θɒnɪk) *adj* of or relating to the underworld [c19: from Greek *khthonios* in or under the earth, from *khthōn* earth]

Chuang-tzu ('tʃwæŋ 'tsu:) *n* a variant transliteration of the Chinese name for **Zhuangzi**

chub (tʃʌb) *n, pl* **chub** *or* **chubs** 1 a common European freshwater cyprinid game fish, *Leuciscus* (or *Squalius*) *cephalus*, having a cylindrical dark greenish body 2 any of various North American fishes, esp certain whitefishes and minnows [c15: of unknown origin]

chubby ('tʃʌbɪ) *adj* -bier, -biest (esp of the human form) plump and round [c17: perhaps from CHUB, with reference to the plump shape of the fish]
> **'chubbiness** *n*

Chu Chiang ('tʃu: 'kjæŋ, kaɪ'æŋ) *n* a variant transliteration of the Chinese name for the **Zhu Jiang**

Ch'ü Ch'iu-pai ('tʃu: 'tʃju:'beɪ) *n* a variant transliteration of the Chinese name for **Qu Qiu Bai**

chuck¹ (tʃʌk) *vb* (*mainly tr*) 1 *informal* to throw 2 to pat affectionately, esp under the chin (sometimes foll by *in* or *up*) *informal* to give up; reject: *he chucked up his job; she chucked her boyfriend* 4 (*intr; usually foll by up*) *slang, chiefly US* to vomit 5 **chuck off at** *Austral & NZ informal* to abuse or make fun of ⊳ *n* 6 a throw or toss 7 a playful pat under the chin 8 **the chuck** *informal* dismissal ⊳ See also **chuck in, chuck out** [c16: of unknown origin]

chuck² (tʃʌk) *n* 1 Also called: **chuck steak** a cut of beef extending from the neck to the shoulder blade 2 Also called: **three jaw chuck** a device that holds a workpiece in a lathe or tool in a drill, having a number of adjustable jaws geared to move in unison to centralize the workpiece or tool [c17: variant of CHOCK]

chuck³ (tʃʌk) *n* Canadian W *coast* a large body of water [c19: from Chinook Jargon, from Nootka *chauk*]

chuck in *vb* (*adverb*) *informal* 1 (*tr*) *Brit* to abandon or give up: *chuck in a hopeless attempt* 2 (*intr*) *Austral* to contribute to the cost of something

chuckle ('tʃʌkəl) *vb* (*intr*) 1 to laugh softly or to oneself 2 (of animals, esp hens) to make a clucking sound ⊳ *n* 3 a partly suppressed laugh [c16: probably from imitative] > **'chuckler** *n* > **'chucklingly** *adv*

chucklehead ('tʃʌkəl,hɛd) *n* *informal* a stupid person; blockhead; dolt > **'chuckle,headed** *adj*
> **'chuckle,headedness** *n*

chuck off *vb* (*tr, adverb*; *often foll by at*) *Austral & NZ informal* to abuse or make fun of

chuck out *vb* (*tr, adverb*; *often foll by of*) *informal* to eject forcibly (from); throw out (of): *he was chucked out of the lobby*

chuddar, chudder, chuddah *or* **chador** ('tʃʌdə) *n* a large shawl or veil worn by Muslim or Hindu women that covers them from head to foot [from Hindi *caddar*, from Persian *chaddar*]

chuddies ('tʃʌdɪz) *pl n* *Indian informal* underpants [c20: possibly from CHUDDAR]

chuddy *n* *Austral & NZ* an informal name for **chewing gum**

Chudskoye Ozero (*Russian* 'tʃutskəjɪ 'ɒzɪrə) *n* the Russian name for Lake **Peipus**

chuff¹ (tʃʌf) *n* 1 a puffing sound or as if of a steam engine ⊳ *vb* 2 (*intr*) to move while emitting such sounds: *the train chuffed on its way* [c20: of imitative origin]

chuff² (tʃʌf) *vb* (*tr; usually passive*) *Brit slang* to please or delight: *he was chuffed by his pay rise* [probably from *chuff* (adj) pleased, happy (earlier: chubby), from c16 *chuff* (obsolete *n*) a fat cheek, of unknown origin]

chug (tʃʌg) *n* 1 a short dull sound, one that is rapidly repeated, such as that made by an engine ⊳ *vb* **chugs, chugging, chugged** 2 (*intr*) (of an engine, etc) to operate while making such sounds [c19: of imitative origin]

chugger ('tʃʌgə) *n* *informal* a charity worker who approaches people in the street to ask for financial support for the charity, esp regular support by direct debit [c21: CH(ARITY) + (M)UGGER]

chukar (tʃʌ'kɑ:) *n* a common Indian partridge, *Alectoris chukar* (or *graeca*), having red legs and bill and a black-barred sandy plumage [from Hindi *cakor*, from Sanskrit *cakora*, probably of imitative origin]

Chu Kiang ('tʃu: 'kjæŋ, kaɪ'æŋ) *n* a variant transliteration of the Chinese name for the **Zhu Jiang**

chukka *or US* **chukker** ('tʃʌkə) *n* *polo* a period of continuous play, generally lasting 7½ minutes [c20: from Hindi *cakkar*, from Sanskrit *cakra* wheel, circle]

chukka boot *or* **chukka** *n* an ankle-high boot made of suede or rubber and worn for playing polo [c19 CHUKKA]

chum¹ (tʃʌm) *n* 1 *informal* a close friend ⊳ *vb* **chums, chumming, chummed** 2 (*intr; usually foll by up with*) to be or become an intimate friend (of) 3 (*tr*) *Scot* to accompany: *I'll chum you home* [c17 (meaning: a person sharing rooms with another): probably shortened from *chamber fellow*, originally student slang (Oxford); compare CRONY]

chummy ('tʃʌmɪ) *adj* -mier, -miest *informal* friendly
> **'chummily** *adv* > **'chumminess** *n*

chump (tʃʌmp) *n* 1 *informal* a stupid person 2 a thick heavy block of wood 3 **a** the thick blunt end of anything, esp of a piece of meat **b** (*as modifier*): *a chump chop* 4 *Brit slang* the head (esp in the phrase **off one's chump**) [c18: perhaps a blend of CHUNK and LUMP¹]

chunder ('tʃʌndə) *slang, chiefly Austral* ⊳ *vb* 1 to vomit ⊳ *n* 2 vomit [c20: of uncertain origin]

Chungking ('tʃʊŋ'kɪŋ, 'tʃʌŋ-) *or* **Ch'ung-ch'ing** ('tʃʊŋ'tʃɪŋ, 'tʃʌŋ-) *n* a variant transliteration of the Chinese name for **Chongqing**

chunk (tʃʌŋk) *n* 1 a thick solid piece, as of meat, wood, etc 2 a considerable amount [c17: variant of CHUCK²]

chunky ('tʃʌŋkɪ) *adj* **chunkier, chunkiest** 1 thick and short 2 consisting of or containing thick pieces: *chunky dog food* 3 *chiefly Brit* (of clothes, esp knitwear) made of thick bulky material > **'chunkily** *adv* > **'chunkiness** *n*

Chunnel ('tʃʌnəl) *n* *informal* a rail tunnel beneath the English Channel, linking England and France, opened in 1994 [c20: from CH(ANNEL) + (T)UNNEL]

chunter ('tʃʌntə) *or* **chunner** ('tʃʌnə) *vb* (*intr; often foll by on*) *Brit informal* to mutter or grumble incessantly in a meaningless fashion [c16: probably of imitative origin]

Chuquisaca (*Spanish* tʃuki'saka) *n* the former name (until 1839) of **Sucre**¹

chur (tʃɜ:) *interj* *NZ* an informal expression of agreement

Chur (*German* ku:r) *n* a city in E Switzerland, capital of Graubünden canton. Pop: 32 989 (2000). French name: **Coire**

church (tʃɜ:tʃ) *n* 1 a building designed for public forms of worship, esp Christian worship 2 an occasion of public worship 3 the clergy as distinguished from the laity 4 (*usually capital*) institutionalized forms of religion as a political or social force: *conflict between Church and State* 5 (*usually capital*) the collective body of all Christians 6 (*often capital*) a particular Christian denomination or group of Christian believers 7 (*often capital*) the Christian religion 8 (in Britain) the practices or doctrines of the Church of England and similar denominations. See **chapel** (sense 4b). Related adj: **ecclesiastical** ⊳ *vb* (*tr*) 9 *Church of England* to bring (someone, esp a woman after childbirth) to church for special ceremonies 10 *US* to impose church discipline upon [Old English *cirice*, from Late Greek *kurikon*, from Greek *kuriakon* (*dōma*) the Lord's (house), from *kuriakos* of the master, from *kurios* master, from *kuros* power]

Church (tʃɜ:tʃ) *n* **Charlotte.** born 1986, Welsh soprano, who made her name with the album *Voice of an Angel* (1998) when she was 12

Church Army *n* a voluntary Anglican organization founded in 1882 to assist the parish clergy

Church Commissioners *pl n* *Brit* a group of representatives of Church and State that administers the endowments and property of the Church of England

churchgoer ('tʃɜ:tʃ,gəʊə) *n* a person who attends church regularly > **'church,going** *n, adj*

Churchill¹ ('tʃɜ:tʃɪl) *n* 1 a river in E Canada, rising in SE Labrador and flowing north and southeast over Churchill Falls, then east to the Atlantic. Length: about 1000 km (600 miles) 2 a river in central Canada, rising in NW Saskatchewan and flowing east through several lakes to Hudson Bay. Length: about 1600 km (1000 miles)

Churchill² ('tʃɜ:tʃɪl) *n* 1 **Caryl.** born 1938, British playwright; her plays include *Cloud Nine* (1978), *Top Girls* (1982), *Serious Money* (1987), and *Far Away* (2000) **2 Charles.** 1731–64, British poet, noted for his polemical satires. His works include *The Rosciad* (1761) and *The Prophecy of Famine* (1763) **3 John.** See (1st Duke of) **Marlborough¹ 4** Lord **Randolph.** 1849–95, British Conservative politician: secretary of state for India (1885–86) and chancellor of the Exchequer and leader of the House of Commons (1886) **5** his son, Sir Winston (**Leonard Spencer**). 1874–1965, British Conservative statesman, orator, and writer, noted for his leadership during World War II. He held various posts under both Conservative and Liberal governments, including 1st Lord of the Admiralty (1911–15), before becoming prime minister (1940–45; 1951–55). His writings include *The World Crisis* (1923–29), *Marlborough* (1933–38), *The Second World War* (1948–54), and *History of the English-Speaking Peoples* (1956–58): Nobel prize for literature 1953

Churchill Falls *pl n* a waterfall in E Canada, in SW Labrador on the Churchill River: site of one of the largest hydroelectric power projects in the world. Height: 75 m (245 ft). Former name (until 1965): Grand Falls

churchly ('tʃɜːtʃlɪ) *adj* appropriate to, associated with, or suggestive of church life and customs > 'churchliness *n*

churchman ('tʃɜːtʃmən) *n, pl* -men **1** a clergyman **2** a male practising member of a church

Church of Christ, Scientist *n* the official name for the **Christian Scientists**

Church of England *n* the reformed established state Church in England, Catholic in order and basic doctrine, with the Sovereign as its temporal head

Church of Jesus Christ of Latter-Day Saints *n* the official name for the Mormon Church

churchwarden (,tʃɜːtʃ'wɔːdᵊn) *n* **1** *Church of England, Episcopal Church* one of two assistants of a parish priest who administer the secular affairs of the church **2** a long-stemmed tobacco pipe made of clay

churchwoman ('tʃɜːtʃ,wʊmən) *n, pl* -women a female practising member of a church

churchyard ('tʃɜːtʃ,jɑːd) *n* the grounds surrounding a church, usually used as a graveyard

churinga (tʃə'rɪŋgə) *n, pl* -ga or -gas a sacred amulet of the native Australians [from a native Australian language]

churl (tʃɜːl) *n* **1** a surly ill-bred person **2** *archaic* a farm labourer [Old English *ceorl*; related to Old Norse *karl*, Middle Low German *kerle*,Greek *gerōn* old man]

churlish ('tʃɜːlɪʃ) *adj* **1** rude or surly **2** of or relating to peasants **3** miserly > 'churlishly *adv* > 'churlishness *n*

churn (tʃɜːn) *n* **1** *Brit* a large container for milk **2** a vessel or machine in which cream or whole milk is vigorously agitated to produce butter **3** any similar device **4** the number of customers who switch from one supplier to another ▷ *vb* **5 a** to stir or agitate (milk or cream) in order to make butter **b** to make (butter) by this process **6** (sometimes foll by *up*) to move or cause to move with agitation: *ideas churned in his head* **7** (of a bank, broker, etc) to encourage an investor or policyholder to change investments, endowment policies, etc, to increase commissions at the client's expense **8** (of a government) to pay benefits to a wide category of people and claw it back by taxation from the well off **9** to promote the turnover of existing subscribers leasing, and new subscribers joining, a cable television system or mobile phone company [Old English *ciern*; related to Old Norse *kjarni*, Middle Low German *kerne* churn, German dialect *Kern* cream] > 'churner *n*

churn out *vb* (*tr, adverb*) *informal* **1** to produce (something) at a rapid rate: *to churn out ideas* **2** to perform (something) mechanically: *to churn out a song*

churr (tʃɜː) *vb, n* a variant spelling of **chirr**

chute¹ (ʃuːt) *n* **1** an inclined channel or vertical passage down which water, parcels, coal, etc, may be dropped **2** a steep slope, used as a slide as for toboggans **3** a slide into a swimming pool **4** a rapid or waterfall [c19: from Old French *cheoite*, feminine past participle of *cheoir* to fall, from Latin *cadere*; in some senses, a variant spelling of SHOOT]

chute² (ʃuːt) *n, vb informal* short for **parachute** > 'chutist *n*

Chu Teh ('tʃuː 'teɪ) or **Zhu De** *n* 1886–1976, Chinese military leader and politician; he became commander in chief of the Red Army (1931) and was chairman of the Standing Committee of the National People's Congress of the People's Republic of China (1959–76)

chutney ('tʃʌtnɪ) *n* a pickle of Indian origin, made from fruit, vinegar, spices, sugar, etc: *mango chutney* [c19: from Hindi *catni*, of uncertain origin]

chutzpah or **hutzpah** ('xʊtspə) *n informal* shameless audacity; impudence [c20: from Yiddish]

Chuvash Republic *n* a constituent republic of W central Russia, in the middle Volga valley: generally low-lying with undulating plains and large areas of forest. Capital: Cheboksary. Pop: 1 313 900 (2002). Area: 18 300 sq km (7064 sq miles). Also called: Chuvashia (tʃuː'vɑːʃɪə)

Chu Xi or **Chu Hsi** ('tʃuː 'siː) *n* 1130–1200, Chinese philosopher, known for his neo-Confucian commentaries, the *Ssu shu* or *Four Books*

chyack ('tʃaɪæk) *vb* a variant spelling of **chiack**

chyle (kaɪl) *n* a milky fluid composed of lymph and emulsified fat globules, formed in the small intestine during digestion [c17: from Late Latin *chȳlus*, from Greek *khulos* juice pressed from a plant; related to Greek *khein* to pour] > chylaceous (kaɪ'leɪʃəs) or 'chylous *adj*

chyme (kaɪm) *n* the thick fluid mass of partially digested food that leaves the stomach [c17: from Late Latin *chȳmus*, from Greek *khumos* juice; compare CHYLE] > 'chymous *adj*

chypre *French* (ʃiprə) *n* a perfume made from sandalwood [literally: Cyprus, where it perhaps originated]

chytrid ('kaɪtrɪd) *n* any aquatic fungus of the phylum Chytridiomycora. Some species, esp *Batrachochytrium dendrobatidis*, are fatal to amphibians [c20: from Greek *khutridion* little pot]

Ci *symbol for* curie

CIA *abbreviation* Central Intelligence Agency; a federal US bureau created in 1947 to coordinate and conduct espionage and intelligence activities

ciabatta (tʃə'bætə) *n* a type of open-textured bread made with olive oil [c20: from Italian, literally: slipper]

Ciano ('tʃɑːnəʊ) *n* **Galeazzo**, full name *Conte Galeazzo Ciano di Cortellazzo*. 1903–44, Italian fascist politician; minister of foreign affairs (1936–43) and son-in-law of Mussolini, whose supporters shot him

CIB *abbreviation* (in New Zealand) Criminal Investigation Branch (of New Zealand police)

Cibber ('sɪbə) *n* **Colley** ('kɒlɪ). 1671–1757, English actor and dramatist; poet laureate (1730–57)

ciborium (sɪ'bɔːrɪəm) *n, pl* -ria (-rɪə) *Christianity* **1** a goblet-shaped lidded vessel used to hold consecrated wafers in Holy Communion **2** a freestanding canopy fixed over an altar and supported by four pillars [c17: from Medieval Latin, from Latin: drinking cup, from Greek *kibōrion* cup-shaped seed vessel of the Egyptian lotus, hence, a cup]

CICA *abbreviation* (in Britain) Criminal Injuries Compensation Authority

cicada (sɪ'kɑːdə) or **cicala** *n, pl* -das, -dae (-diː) or -las, -le (-leɪ) any large broad insect of the homopterous family Cicadidae, most common in warm regions. Cicadas have membranous wings and the males produce a high-pitched drone by vibration of a pair of drumlike abdominal organs [c19: from Latin]

cicala (sɪ'kɑːlə; *Italian* tʃi'kala) *n, pl* -las or -le (-leɪ; *Italian* -le) another name for **cicada** [c19: from Italian, from Latin: CICADA]

cicatrix ('sɪkətrɪks) *n, pl* cicatrices (,sɪkə'traɪsiːz) **1** the tissue that forms in a wound during healing; scar **2** a scar on a plant indicating the former point of attachment of a part, esp a leaf [c17: from Latin: scar, of obscure origin] > cicatricial (,sɪkə'trɪʃəl) *adj* > cicatricose (sɪ'kætrɪ,kəʊs, 'sɪkə-) *adj*

cicatrize or **cicatrise** ('sɪkə,traɪz) *vb* (of a wound or defect in tissue) to close or be closed by scar formation; heal > ,cica'trizant or ,cica'trisant *adj* > ,cicatri'zation or ,cicatri'sation *n* > 'cica,trizer or 'cica,triser *n*

cicely ('sɪsəlɪ) *n, pl* -lies short for **sweet cicely** [c16: from

Latin *seselis,* from Greek, of obscure origin; influenced in spelling by the English proper name *Cicely*]

cicero ('sɪsəˌrəʊ) *n, pl* -ros a measure for type that is somewhat larger than the pica [c19: from its first being used in a 15th-century edition of the writings of Marcus Tullius *Cicero* (106–43 BC), the Roman consul, orator, and writer]

Cicero ('sɪsəˌrəʊ) *n* **Marcus Tullius** ('mɑːkəs 'tʌlɪəs). 106–43 BC, Roman consul, orator, and writer. He foiled Catiline's conspiracy (63) and was killed by Mark Antony's agents after he denounced Antony in the *Philippics.* His writings are regarded as a model of Latin prose Formerly known in English as: Tully

cicerone (ˌsɪsəˈrəʊnɪ, ˌtʃɪtʃ-) *n, pl* -nes or -ni (-nɪ) a person who conducts and informs sightseers; a tour guide [c18: from Italian: antiquarian scholar, guide, after Marcus Tullius *Cicero* (106–43 BC), Roman consul, orator, and writer, alluding to the eloquence and erudition of these men]

ciclosporin or **cyclosporin** (ˌsaɪkləʊˈspɔːrɪn) *n* a drug extracted from a fungus and used after organ transplantation to suppress the body's immune mechanisms, and so prevent rejection of an organ

Cid (sɪd; *Spanish* θið) *n* **El** or **the.** original name *Rodrigo Diaz de Vivar.* ?1043–99, Spanish soldier and hero of the wars against the Moors

CID *abbreviation* (in Britain) Criminal Investigation Department; the detective division of a police force

-cide *n combining form* 1 indicating a person or thing that kills: *insecticide* 2 indicating a killing; murder: *homicide* [from Latin *-cīda* (agent), *-cīdium* (act), from *caedere* to kill] > -cidal *adj combining form*

cider or **cyder** ('saɪdə) *n* 1 an alcoholic drink made from the fermented juice of apples 2 Also called: sweet cider *US & Canadian* an unfermented drink made from apple juice [c14: from Old French *cisdre,* via Medieval Latin, from Late Greek *sikera* strong drink, from Hebrew *shēkhār*]

c.i.f. or **CIF** *abbreviation* cost, insurance, and freight (included in the price quoted)

c.i.f.c.i. *abbreviation* cost, insurance, freight, commission, and interest (included in the price quoted)

cig (sɪg) or **ciggy** ('sɪgɪ) *n, pl* cigs or ciggies *informal* a cigarette

cigar (sɪˈgɑː) *n* a cylindrical roll of cured tobacco leaves, for smoking [c18: from Spanish *cigarro,* perhaps from Mayan *sicar* to smoke]

cigarette or *sometimes US* **cigaret** (ˌsɪgəˈrɛt) *n* a short tightly rolled cylinder of tobacco, wrapped in thin paper and often having a filter tip, for smoking. Shortened forms: cig, ciggy [c19: from French, literally: a little CIGAR]

cigarette card *n* a small picture card, formerly given away with cigarettes, now collected as a hobby

cigarette end *n* the part of a cigarette that is held in the mouth and that remains unsmoked after it is finished

cigarillo (ˌsɪgəˈrɪləʊ) *n, pl* -los a small cigar often only slightly larger than a cigarette

cilantro (sɪˈlæntrəʊ) *n* the US and Canadian name for **coriander** [c20: Spanish]

ciliary ('sɪlɪərɪ) *adj* of or relating to cilia. See **cilium**

ciliary body *n* the part of the vascular tunic of the eye that connects the choroid with the iris

Cilician (sɪˈlɪʃɪən) *adj* 1 of or relating to Cilicia (an ancient region of SE Asia Minor) or its inhabitants ▷ *n* 2 a native or inhabitant of Cilicia

Cilician Gates *pl n* a pass in S Turkey, over the Taurus Mountains. Turkish name: Gülek Bogaz

cilium ('sɪlɪəm) *n, pl* **cilia** ('sɪlɪə) 1 any of the short thread-like projections on the surface of a cell, organism, etc, whose rhythmic beating causes movement of the organism or of the surrounding fluid 2 the technical name for **eyelash** [c18: New Latin, from Latin: (lower) eyelid, eyelash] > **ciliate** ('sɪlɪɪt, -eɪt) or 'cili,ated *adj* > ,cili'ation *n*

Çiller ('ʃɪlə) *n* **Tansu** ('tænzuː). born 1945, Turkish politician; prime minister (1993–96)

Cimabue (*Italian* tʃimaˈbuːe) *n* **Giovanni** (dʒoˈvanni).

?1240–?1302, Italian painter of the Florentine school, who anticipated the movement, led by Giotto, away from the Byzantine tradition in art towards a greater naturalism

Cimarosa (ˌtʃiːˈməˈrəʊzə) *n* **Domenico.** 1749–1801, Italian composer, chiefly remembered for his opera buffa *The Secret Marriage* (1792)

Cimon ('saɪmən) *n* died 449 BC, Athenian military and naval commander: defeated the Persians at Eurymedon (?466)

C in C or **C.-in-C.** *military abbreviation* Commander in Chief

cinch (sɪntʃ) *n* 1 *slang* an easy task 2 *slang* a certainty 3 *US & Canadian* a band around a horse's belly to keep the saddle in position. Also called (in Britain and certain other countries): girth 4 *informal* a firm grip ▷ *vb* 5 (often foll by *up*) *US & Canadian* to fasten a girth around (a horse) 6 (*tr*) *informal* to make sure of 7 (*tr*) *informal* to get a firm grip on [c19: from Spanish *cincha* saddle girth, from Latin *cingula* girdle, from *cingere* to encircle]

cinchona (sɪŋˈkəʊnə) *n* 1 any tree or shrub of the South American rubiaceous genus *Cinchona,* esp *C. calisaya,* having medicinal bark 2 Also called: cinchona bark, Peruvian bark, calisaya, china bark the dried bark of any of these trees, which yields quinine and other medicinal alkaloids 3 any of the drugs derived from cinchona bark [c18: New Latin, named after the Countess of Chinchón (1576–1639), vicereine of Peru] > cinchonic (sɪŋˈkɒnɪk) *adj*

Cincinnati (ˌsɪnsɪˈnætɪ) *n* a city in SW Ohio, on the Ohio River. Pop: 317 361 (2003 est)

Cincinnatus (ˌsɪnsɪˈnɑːtəs) *n* **Lucius Quinctius** ('luːsɪəs 'kwɪŋktɪəs). ?519–438 BC, Roman general and statesman, regarded as a model of simple virtue; dictator of Rome during two crises (458; 439), retiring to his farm after each one

cincture ('sɪŋktʃə) *n* something that encircles or surrounds, esp a belt, girdle, or border [c16: from Latin *cinctūra,* from *cingere* to gird]

cinder ('sɪndə) *n* 1 a piece of incombustible material left after the combustion of coal, coke, etc; clinker 2 a piece of charred material that burns without flames; ember 3 Also called: sinter any solid waste from smelting or refining 4 (*plural*) fragments of volcanic lava; scoriae [Old English *sinder;* related to Old Norse *sindr,* Old High German *sintar,* Old Slavonic *sedra* stalactite] > 'cindery *adj*

Cinderella (ˌsɪndəˈrɛlə) *n* 1 a girl who achieves fame after being obscure 2 a poor, neglected, or unsuccessful person or thing [c19: after *Cinderella,* the heroine of a fairy tale who is aided by a fairy godmother]

cine- *combining form* indicating motion picture or cinema: *cine camera; cinephotography*

cineaste ('sɪnɪˌæst) *n* an enthusiast for films [c20: French, from CINEMA + -*aste,* as -*ast* in *enthusiast*]

cinema ('sɪnɪmə) *n* 1 *chiefly Brit* a place designed for the exhibition of films 2 the cinema **a** the art or business of making films **b** films collectively [c19 (earlier spelling *kinema*): shortened from CINEMATOGRAPH] > cinematic (ˌsɪnɪˈmætɪk) *adj* > ,cine'matically *adv*

cinematograph (ˌsɪnɪˈmætəˌgrɑːf, -ˌgræf) *chiefly Brit* ▷ *n* 1 a combined camera, printer, and projector ▷ *vb* 2 to take pictures (of) with a film camera [c19 (earlier spelling *kinematograph*): from Greek *kinēmat-, kinēma* motion + -GRAPH]

cinematography (ˌsɪnɪməˈtɒgrəfɪ) *n* the art or science of film (motion-picture) photography > cinematographer (ˌsɪnɪməˈtɒgrəfə) *n* > cinematographic (ˌsɪnɪˌmætəˈgræfɪk) *adj* > ,cine,mato'graphically *adv*

cinéma vérité (*French* sinema verite) *n* films characterized by subjects, actions, etc, that have the appearance of real life [French, literally: cinema truth]

cinephile ('sɪnɪˌfaɪl) *n* a person who loves films and cinema

cineraria (ˌsɪnəˈrɛərɪə) *n* a plant, *Senecio cruentus,* of the Canary Islands, widely cultivated for its blue, purple, red, or variegated daisy-like flowers: family *Asteraceae* (composites) [c16: from New Latin, from Latin *cinerārius* of ashes, from *cinis* ashes; from its downy leaves]

cinerarium (ˌsɪnəˈrɛərɪəm) *n, pl* -raria (-ˈrɛərɪə) a place for keeping the ashes of the dead after cremation [C19: from Latin, from *cinerārius* relating to ashes; see CINERARIA] > **cinerary** ('sɪnərərɪ) *adj*

cinerator ('sɪnəˌreɪtə) *n* another name (esp US) for **cremator** (sense 1) > ˌcine'ration *n*

Cinna ('sɪnə) *n* **Lucius Cornelius** ('luːsɪəs kɔː'niːlɪəs). died 84 BC, Roman patrician; an opponent of Sulla

cinnabar ('sɪnəˌbɑː) *n* **1** a bright red or brownish-red mineral form of mercuric sulphide (mercury(II) sulphide), found close to areas of volcanic activity and hot springs. It is the main commercial source of mercury. Formula: HgS. Crystal structure: hexagonal **2** the red form of mercuric sulphide (mercury(II) sulphide), esp when used as a pigment **3** a bright red to reddish-orange; vermilion **4** a large red-and-black European moth, *Callimorpha jacobaeae*: family *Arctiidae* (tiger moths, etc) [C15: from Old French *cenobre*, from Latin *cinnābaris*, from Greek *kinnabari*, of Oriental origin]

cinnamon ('sɪnəmən) *n* **1** a tropical Asian lauraceous tree, *Cinnamomum zeylanicum*, having aromatic yellowish-brown bark **2** the spice obtained from the bark of this tree, used for flavouring food and drink **3 a** a light yellowish brown **b** (as modifier): *a cinnamon coat* [C15: from Old French *cinnamome*, via Latin and Greek, from Hebrew *qinnamown*]

cinque (sɪŋk) *n* the number five in cards, dice, etc [C14: from Old French *cinq* five]

cinquecento (ˌtʃɪŋkwɪ'tʃɛntəʊ) *n* the 16th century, esp in reference to Italian art, architecture, or literature [C18: Italian, shortened from *milcinquecento* 1500]

cinquefoil ('sɪŋkˌfɔɪl) *n* **1** any plant of the N temperate rosaceous genus *Potentilla*, typically having five-lobed compound leaves **2** an ornamental carving in the form of five arcs arranged in a circle and separated by cusps [C13 *sink foil*, from Old French *cincfoille*, from Latin *quinquefolium* plant with five leaves, translating Greek *pentaphullon* from *pente* five + *phullon* leaf]

Cinque Ports (sɪŋk) *pl n* an association of ports on the SE coast of England, originally consisting of Hastings, Romney, Hythe, Dover, and Sandwich, which from late Anglo-Saxon times provided ships for the king's service in return for the profits of justice in their courts. The Cinque Ports declined with the growth of other ports and surrendered their charters in 1685

Cintra ('sɪntrə) *n* the former name for **Sintra**

cipher *or* **cypher** ('saɪfə) *n* **1** a method of secret writing using substitution or transposition of letters according to a key **2** a secret message **3** the key to a secret message **4** an obsolete name for **zero** (sense 1) **5** any of the Arabic numerals (0, 1, 2, 3, etc, to 9) or the Arabic system of numbering as a whole **6** a person or thing of no importance; nonentity **7** a design consisting of interwoven letters; monogram ▷ *vb* **8** to put (a message) into secret writing **9** *rare* to perform (a calculation) arithmetically [C14: from Old French *cifre* zero, from Medieval Latin *cifra*, from Arabic *sifr* zero, empty]

circa ('sɜːkə) *prep* (used with a date) at the approximate time of: *circa* 1182 BC. Abbreviation: *c*. [Latin: about; related to Latin *circus* circle, CIRCUS]

circadian (sɜː'keɪdɪən) *adj* of or relating to biological processes that occur regularly at about 24-hour intervals, even in the absence of periodicity in the environment. See also **biological clock** [C20: from Latin *circa* about + *diēs* day]

Circassia (sɜː'kæsɪə) *n* a region of S Russia, on the Black Sea north of the Caucasus Mountains

Circassian (sɜː'kæsɪən) *n* **1** a native of Circassia **2** a language or languages spoken in Circassia, belonging to the North-West Caucasian family ▷ *adj* Also: Circassic **3** relating to Circassia, its people, or language

Circe ('sɜːsɪ) *n* Greek myth an enchantress who detained Odysseus on her island and turned his men into swine > Circean (sɜː'sɪən) *adj*

circle ('sɜːk²l) *n* **1** *maths* a closed plane curve every point of which is equidistant from a given fixed point, the centre. Equation: $(x - h)^2 + (y - k)^2 = r^2$ where r is the radius and (h, k) are the coordinates of the centre; area πr^2; circumference: $2\pi r$ **2** the figure enclosed by such a curve **3** *theatre* the section of seats above the main level of the

auditorium, usually comprising the dress circle and the upper circle **4** something formed or arranged in the shape of a circle **5** a group of people sharing an interest, activity, upbringing, etc; set: *golf circles; a family circle* **6** a domain or area of activity, interest, or influence **7** a circuit **8** a process or chain of events or parts that forms a connected whole; cycle **9** a parallel of latitude. See also **great circle, small circle** **10** one of a number of Neolithic or Bronze Age rings of standing stones, such as Stonehenge, found in Europe and thought to be associated with some form of ritual or astronomical measurement **11** come full circle to arrive back at one's starting point. See also **vicious circle** **12** go round in circles *or* run round in circles to engage in energetic but fruitless activity ▷ *vb* **13** to move in a circle (around) **14** (*tr*) to enclose in a circle; encircle [C14: from Latin *circulus* a circular figure, from *circus* ring, circle] > 'circler *n*

circlet ('sɜːklɪt) *n* a small circle or ring, esp a circular ornament worn on the head [C15: from Old French *cerclet* a little CIRCLE]

circle time *n* a time in which pre-school or primary school children sit in a circle and take turns to speak, usually with possession of a circulated object being the sign of whose turn it is

circuit ('sɜːkɪt) *n* **1 a** a complete route or course, esp one that is curved or circular or that lies around an object **b** the area enclosed within such a route **2** the act of following such a route: *we made three circuits of the course* **3 a** a complete path through which an electric current can flow **b** (as modifier): *a circuit diagram* **4 a** a periodical journey around an area, as made by judges, salesmen, etc **b** the persons making such a journey **5** an administrative division of the Methodist Church comprising a number of neighbouring churches **6** a number of theatres, cinemas, etc, under one management or in which the same film is shown or in which a company of performers plays in turn **7** *sport* a series of tournaments in which the same players regularly take part: *the international tennis circuit* **8** chiefly Brit a motor racing track, usually of irregular shape ▷ *vb* **9** to make or travel in a circuit around (something) [C14: from Latin *circuitus* a going around, from *circumīre*, from *circum* around + *īre* to go] > 'circuital *adj*

circuit breaker *n* a device that under abnormal conditions, such as a short circuit, interrupts the flow of current in an electrical circuit

circuitous (sə'kjuːɪtəs) *adj* indirect and lengthy; roundabout: *a circuitous route* > cir'cuitously *adv* > cir'cuitousness *n*

circuitry ('sɜːkɪtrɪ) *n* **1** the design of an electrical circuit **2** the system of circuits used in an electronic device

circuity (sə'kjuːɪtɪ) *n, pl* -ties (of speech, reasoning, etc) a roundabout or devious quality

circular ('sɜːkjʊlə) *adj* **1** of, involving, resembling, or shaped like a circle **2** circuitous **3** (of arguments) futile because the truth of the premises cannot be established independently of the conclusion **4** travelling or occurring in a cycle **5** (of letters, announcements, etc) intended for general distribution ▷ *n* **6** a printed or duplicated advertisement or notice for mass distribution > circularity (ˌsɜːkjʊ'lærɪtɪ) *or* 'circularness *n* > 'circularly *adv*

circular breathing *n* a technique for sustaining a phrase on a wind instrument, using the cheeks to force air out of the mouth while breathing in through the nose

circularize *or* **circularise** ('sɜːkjʊləˌraɪz) *vb* (*tr*) **1** to distribute circulars to **2** to canvass or petition (people), as for support, votes, etc, by distributing letters, etc **3** to make circular > ˌcirculari'zation *or* ˌcirculari'sation *n*

circular saw *n* a power-driven saw in which a circular disc with a toothed edge is rotated at high speed

circulate ('sɜːkjʊˌleɪt) *vb* **1** to send, go, or pass from place to place or person to person: *don't circulate the news* **2** to distribute or be distributed over a wide area **3** to move or cause to move through a circuit, system, etc, returning to the starting point: *blood circulates through the body* **4** to move in a circle [C15: from Latin *circulārī* to assemble in a circle, from *circulus* CIRCLE] > 'circu,lative *adj* > 'circu,lator *n* > 'circulatory *adj*

circulating library *n* **1** another name (esp US) for **lending library** **2** a small library circulated in turn to a group of schools or other institutions

circulation (,s3:kjʊ'leɪʃən) *n* **1** the transport of oxygenated blood through the arteries to the capillaries, where it nourishes the tissues, and the return of oxygen-depleted blood through the veins to the heart, where the cycle is renewed **2** the flow of sap through a plant **3** any movement through a closed circuit **4** the spreading or transmission of something to a wider group of people or area **5** (of air and water) free movement within an area or volume **6 a** the distribution of newspapers, magazines, etc **b** the number of copies of an issue of such a publication that are distributed **7** in circulation **a** (of currency) serving as a medium of exchange **b** (of people) active in a social or business context

circulatory system *n anatomy, zoology* the system concerned with the transport of blood and lymph, consisting of the heart, blood vessels, lymph vessels, etc

circum- *prefix* around; surrounding; on all sides: *circumlocution; circumrotate* [from Latin *circum* around, from *circus* circle]

circumambient (,s3:kəm'æmbɪənt) *adj* surrounding [c17: from Late Latin *circumambīre*, from CIRCUM- + *ambīre* to go round] > ,circum'ambience or ,circum'ambiency *n*

circumambulate (,s3:kəm'æmbjʊ,leɪt) *vb* **1** to walk around (something) **2** (*intr*) to avoid the point [c17: from Late Latin CIRCUM- + *ambulāre* to walk] > ,circum,ambu'lation *n*

circumcise ('s3:kəm,saɪz) *vb* (*tr*) **1** to remove the foreskin of (a male) **2** to incise surgically the skin over the clitoris of (a female) **3** to remove the clitoris of (a female) **4** to perform the religious rite of circumcision on (someone) [c13: from Latin *circumcīdere*, from CIRCUM- + *caedere* to cut] > 'circum,ciser *n* > ,circum'cision *n*

circumference (sə'kʌmfərəns) *n* **1** the boundary of a specific area or geometric figure, esp of a circle **2** the length of a closed geometric curve, esp of a circle. The circumference of a circle is equal to the diameter multiplied by π [c14: from Old French *circonference*, from Latin *circumferre* to carry around, from CIRCUM- + *ferre* to bear] > circumferential (sə,kʌmfə'rɛnʃəl) *adj* > cir,cumfer'entially *adv*

circumflex ('s3:kəm,flɛks) *n* **1** a mark (^) placed over a vowel to show that it is pronounced with rising and falling pitch, as in ancient Greek, as a long vowel rather than a short one, as in French, or with some other different quality ▷ *adj* **2** (of certain nerves, arteries, or veins) bending or curving around [c16: from Latin *circumflexus*, from *circumflectere* to bend around, from CIRCUM- + *flectere* to bend] > ,circum'flexion *n*

circumfuse (,s3:kəm'fju:z) *vb* (*tr*) **1** to pour or spread (a liquid, powder, etc) around **2** to surround with a substance, such as a liquid [c16: from Latin *circumfūsus*, from *circumfundere* to pour around, from CIRCUM- + *fundere* to pour] > circumfusion (,s3:kəm'fju:ʒən) *n*

circumlocution (,s3:kəmlə'kju:ʃən) *n* **1** an indirect way of expressing something **2** an indirect expression > circumlocutory (,s3:kəm'lɒkjʊtərɪ, -trɪ) *adj*

circumnavigate (,s3:kəm'nævɪ,geɪt) *vb* (*tr*) to sail or fly completely around > ,circum,navi'gation *n* > ,circum'navi,gator *n*

circumscribe (,s3:kəm'skraɪb, 's3:kəm,skraɪb) *vb* (*tr*) **1** to restrict within limits **2** to mark or set the bounds of **3** to draw a geometric construction around (another construction) so that the two are in contact but do not intersect **4** to draw a line round [c15: from Latin *circumscrībere*, from CIRCUM- + *scrībere* to write] > ,circum'scribable *adj* > ,circum'scriber *n* > circumscription (,s3:kəm'skrɪpʃən) *n*

circumspect ('s3:kəm,spɛkt) *adj* cautious, prudent, or discreet [c15: from Latin *circumspectus*, from CIRCUM- + *specere* to look] > ,circum'spection *n* > 'circum,spectly *adv*

circumstance ('s3:kəmstəns) *n* **1** (*usually plural*) a condition of time, place, etc, that accompanies or influences an event or condition **2** an incident or

occurrence, esp a chance one **3** accessory information or detail **4** formal display or ceremony (archaic except in the phrase **pomp and circumstance**) **5** under no circumstances *or* in no circumstances in no case; never **6** under the circumstances because of conditions; this being the case ▷ *vb* (*tr*) **7** to place in a particular condition or situation [c13: from Old French *circonstance*, from Latin *circumstantia*, from *circumstāre* to stand around, from CIRCUM- + *stāre* to stand]

circumstantial (,s3:kəm'stænʃəl) *adj* **1** of or dependent on circumstances **2** fully detailed **3** incidental > ,circum'stanti'ality *n* > ,circum'stantially *adv*

circumstantial evidence *n* indirect evidence that tends to establish a conclusion by inference

circumstantiate (,s3:kəm'stænʃɪ,eɪt) *vb* (*tr*) to support by giving particulars > ,circum,stanti'ation *n*

circumvallate (,s3:kəm'væleɪt) *vb* (*tr*) to surround with a defensive fortification [c19: from Latin *circumvallāre*, from CIRCUM- + *vallum* rampart] > ,circumval'lation *n*

circumvent (,s3:kəm'vɛnt) *vb* (*tr*) **1** to evade or go around **2** to outwit **3** to encircle (an enemy) so as to intercept or capture [c15: from Latin *circumvenīre*, from CIRCUM- + *venīre* to come] > ,circum'vention *n*

circus ('s3:kəs) *n, pl* -cuses **1** a travelling company of entertainers such as acrobats, clowns, trapeze artistes, and trained animals **2** a public performance given by such a company **3** an oval or circular arena, usually tented and surrounded by tiers of seats, in which such a performance is held **4** a travelling group of professional sportsmen: *a cricket circus* **5** (in ancient Rome) **a** an open-air stadium, usually oval or oblong, for chariot races or public games **b** the games themselves **6** Brit **a** an open place, usually circular, in a town, where several streets converge **b** (*capital when part of a name*): *Piccadilly Circus* **7** *informal* noisy or rowdy behaviour **8** *informal* a person or group of people whose behaviour is wild, disorganized, or (esp unintentionally) comic [c16: from Latin, from Greek *kirkos* ring]

ciré ('sɪəreɪ) *adj* **1** (of fabric) treated with a heat or wax process to make it smooth ▷ *n* **2** such a surface on a fabric **3** a fabric having such a surface [c20: French, from *cirer* to wax, from *cire*, from Latin *cēra* wax]

Cirebon ('tʃɪərə,bɒn) *n* a port in S central Indonesia, on N Java on the Java Sea: scene of the signing of the **Tjirebon Agreement** of Indonesian independence (1946) by the Netherlands. Pop: 272 263 (2000). Former spelling: **Tjirebon**

Cirencester ('saɪrən,sɛstə) *n* a market town in S England, in Gloucestershire: Roman amphitheatre. Pop: 15 861 (2001)

cirque (s3:k) *n* Also called: **corrie**, **cwm** a semicircular or crescent-shaped basin with steep sides and a gently sloping floor formed in mountainous regions by the erosive action of a glacier [c17: from French, from Latin *circus* ring, circle, CIRCUS]

cirrhosis (sɪ'rəʊsɪs) *n* any of various progressive diseases of the liver, characterized by death of liver cells, irreversible fibrosis, etc: caused by inadequate diet, excessive alcohol, chronic infection, etc. Also called: **cirrhosis of the liver** [c19: New Latin, from Greek *kirrhos* orange-coloured + -OSIS; referring to the appearance of the diseased liver] > **cirrhotic** (sɪ'rɒtɪk) *adj*

cirripede ('sɪrɪ,pi:d) *or* **cirriped** ('sɪrɪ,pɛd) *n* **1** any marine crustacean of the subclass *Cirripedia*, including the barnacles, the adults of which are sessile or parasitic ▷ *adj* **2** of, relating to, or belonging to the *Cirripedia*

cirrocumulus (,sɪrəʊ'kju:mjʊləs) *n, pl* -li (-,laɪ) *meteorol* a high cloud of ice crystals grouped into small separate globular masses, usually occurring above 6000 metres (20 000 feet)

cirrostratus (,sɪrəʊ'strɑ:təs) *n, pl* -ti (-taɪ) a uniform layer of cloud above about 6000 metres (20 000 feet)

cirrus ('sɪrəs) *n, pl* -ri (-raɪ) **1** *meteorol* a thin wispy fibrous cloud at high altitudes, composed of ice particles **2** a plant tendril or similar part **3** *zoology* **a** a slender tentacle or filament in barnacles and other marine invertebrates **b** a hairlike structure in other animals, such as a filament on the appendage of an insect or a barbel of a fish [c18: from Latin: curl, tuft, fringe]

CIS *abbreviation* Commonwealth of Independent States

cis- *prefix* on this or the near side of [from Latin]

cisalpine ('sıs'ælpaın) *adj* on this (the southern) side of the Alps, as viewed from Rome

Cisalpine Gaul *n* (in the ancient world) that part of Gaul between the Alps and the Apennines

Ciscaucasia (,sıskɔ:'keızıə, -ʒə) *n* the part of Caucasia north of the Caucasus Mountains

cisco ('sıskəʊ) *n, pl* **-coes** *or* **-cos** any of various whitefish, esp *Coregonus artedi*, of cold deep lakes of North America [c19: short for Canadian French *ciscoette*, from Ojibwa *pemitewiskawet* fish with oily flesh]

Ciskei ('sıskaı) *n* (formerly) a Bantu homeland in SE South Africa; declared independent in 1981 but this was not recognized outside South Africa; abolished in 1993. Capital: Bisho (now Bhisho)

cislunar (sıs'lu:nə) *adj* of or relating to the space between the earth and the moon

cisplatin (sıs'plætın) *n* a cytotoxic drug that acts by preventing DNA replication and hence cell division, used in the treatment of tumours, esp of the ovary and testis [c20: from CIS- + PLATIN(UM)]

cissing ('sısıŋ) *n* building trades the appearance of pinholes, craters, etc, in paintwork due to poor adhesion of the paint to the surface

cissy ('sısı) *n* a variant spelling of **sissy**

cist¹ (sıst) *n* a wooden box for holding ritual objects used in ancient Rome and Greece [c19: from Latin *cista* box, chest, basket, from Greek *kistē*]

cist² (sıst) *or* **kist** *n archaeol* a box-shaped burial chamber made from stone slabs or a hollowed tree trunk [c19: from Welsh: chest, from Latin *cista* box; see CIST¹]

Cistercian (sı'stɜ:ʃən) *n* Also called: **White Monk** a member of a Christian order of monks and nuns founded in 1098, which follows an especially strict form of the Benedictine rule [c17: from French *Cistercien*, from Medieval Latin *Cisterciānus*, from *Cistercium* (modern *Cîteaux*), original home of the order]

cistern ('sıstən) *n* **1** a tank for the storage of water, esp on or within the roof of a house or connected to a WC **2** an underground reservoir for the storage of a liquid, esp rainwater **3** *anatomy* Also called: **cisterna** a sac or partially enclosed space containing body fluid [c13: from Old French *cisterne*, from Latin *cisterna* underground tank, from *cista* box]

cistus ('sıstəs) *n* any plant of the genus *Cistus*. See **rockrose** [c16: New Latin, from Greek *kistos*]

citadel ('sıtəd³l, -,dɛl) *n* **1** a stronghold within or close to a city **2** any strongly fortified building or place of safety; refuge [c16: from Old French *citadelle*, from Old Italian *cittadella* a little city, from *cittade* city, from Latin *cīvitās*]

citation (saı'teıʃən) *n* **1** the quoting of a book or author in support of a fact **2** a passage or source cited for this purpose **3** an official commendation or award, esp for bravery or outstanding service, work, etc, usually in the form of a formal statement made in public **4** *law* **a** an official summons to appear in court **b** the document containing such a summons **5** *law* the quoting of decided cases to serve as guidance to a court ▷ **citatory** ('saıtətərı, -trı) *adj*

cite (saıt) *vb* (*tr*) **1** to quote or refer to (a passage, book, or author) in substantiation as an authority, proof, or example **2** to mention or commend (a soldier, etc) for outstanding bravery or meritorious action **3** to summon to appear before a court of law **4** to enumerate: *he cited the king's virtues* [c15: from Old French *citer* to summon, from Latin *citāre* to rouse, from *citus* quick, from *cière* to excite] ▷ **citable** *or* **citeable** *adj*

cithara ('sıθərə) *or* **kithara** *n* a stringed musical instrument of ancient Greece and elsewhere, similar to the lyre and played with a plectrum [c18: from Greek *kithara*]

cither ('sıθə) *or* **cithern** ('sıθən) *n* variants of **cittern** [c17: from Latin *cithara*, from Greek *kithara* lyre]

citified *or* **cityfied** ('sıtı,faıd) *adj often derogatory* having the customs, manners, or dress of city people

citizen ('sıtız³n) *n* **1** a native registered or naturalized member of a state, nation, or other political community **2** an inhabitant of a city or town **3** a civilian, as opposed to a soldier, public official, etc [c14: from Anglo-French *citesein*, from Old French *citeien*, from *cité*, CITY]

citizen journalism *n* the involvement of non-professionals in reporting news, especially in blogs and other websites

citizenry ('sıtızənrı) *n, pl* **-ries** citizens collectively

citizen's arrest *n* an arrest carried out by an ordinary member of the public rather than an officer of the law

Citizens' Band *n* a range of radio frequencies assigned officially for use by the public for private communication. Abbreviation: **CB**

citizenship ('sıtızən,ʃıp) *n* **1** the condition or status of a citizen, with its rights and duties **2** a person's conduct as a citizen

Citlaltépetl (,si:tlɑ:l'teıpet³l) *n* a volcano in SE Mexico, in central Veracruz state: the highest peak in the country. Height: 5636 m (18 492 ft), though this is disputed between different sources

citrate ('sıtreıt, -rıt, 'saıtreıt) *n* any salt or ester of citric acid. Salts of citric acid are used in beverages and pharmaceuticals [c18: from CITR(US) + -ATE¹]

citric ('sıtrık) *adj* of or derived from citrus fruits or citric acid

citric acid *n* a water-soluble weak tribasic acid found in many fruits, esp citrus fruits, and used in pharmaceuticals and as a flavouring (**E330**). It is extracted from citrus fruits or made by fermenting molasses and is an intermediate in carbohydrate metabolism. Formula: $CH_2(COOH)C(OH)(COOH)CH_2COOH$

citrine ('sıtrın) *n* **1** a brownish-yellow variety of quartz: a gemstone; false topaz **2 a** the yellow colour of a lemon **b** (as modifier): *citrine hair*

citron ('sıtrən) *n* **1** a small Asian rutaceous tree, *Citrus medica*, having lemon-like fruit with a thick aromatic rind **2** the fruit of this tree **3** the rind of either of these fruits, candied and used for decoration and flavouring of foods [c16: from Old French, from Old Provençal, from Latin *citrus* citrus tree]

citronella (,sıtrə'nɛlə) *n* **1** Also called: **citronella grass** a tropical Asian grass, *Cymbopogon* (or *Andropogon*) *nardus*, with bluish-green lemon-scented leaves **2** Also called: **citronella oil** the yellow aromatic oil obtained from this grass, used in insect repellents, soaps, perfumes, etc [c19: New Latin, from French *citronnelle* lemon balm, from *citron* lemon]

citrus ('sıtrəs) *n, pl* **-ruses** **1** any tree or shrub of the tropical and subtropical rutaceous genus *Citrus*, which includes the orange, lemon, lime, grapefruit, citron, and calamondin ▷ *adj* Also: **citrous 2** of, relating to, or belonging to these plants *Citrus* or to the fruits of plants of this genus [c19: from Latin: citrus tree, sandarac tree; related to Greek *kedros* cedar]

Città del Vaticano (tʃit'ta del vati'ka:no) *n* the Italian name for **Vatican City**

cittern ('sıtɜ:n), **cither** *or* **cithern** *n* a medieval stringed instrument resembling a lute but having wire strings and a flat back [c16: perhaps a blend of CITHER + GITTERN]

city ('sıtı) *n, pl* **cities** **1** any large town or populous place **2** (in Britain) a large town that has received this title from the Crown: usually the seat of a bishop **3** (in the US) an incorporated urban centre with its own government and administration established by state charter **4** (in Canada) a similar urban municipality incorporated by the provincial government **5** the people of a city collectively **6** (*modifier*) in or characteristic of a city: *a city girl; city habits*. Related adjectives: **civic, urban, municipal** [c13: from Old French *cité*, from Latin *cīvitās* citizenship, state, from *cīvis* citizen]

City ('sıtı) the City *n* **1** short for **City of London**: the original settlement of London on the N bank of the Thames; a municipality governed by the Lord Mayor and Corporation. Resident pop: 7186 (2001) **2** the area in central London in which the United Kingdom's major financial business is transacted **3** the various financial institutions located in this area

City and Guilds of London Institute *n* (in Britain) an examining body for technical and craft skills, many of the examinations being at a lower standard than for a degree

city chambers *n* (*functioning as singular*) (in Scotland) the municipal building of a city; town hall

City Code *n* (in Britain) short for **City Code on Takeovers and Mergers**: a code laid down in 1968 (later modified) to control takeover bids and mergers

city desk *n* **1** *Brit* the department of a newspaper office dealing with financial and commercial news **2** *US & Canadian* the department of a newspaper office dealing with local news

city editor *n* (on a newspaper) **1** *Brit* the editor in charge of financial and commercial news **2** *US & Canadian* the editor in charge of local news

city father *n* a person who is active or prominent in the public affairs of a city, such as an alderman

cityscape ('sɪtɪskeɪp) *n* an urban landscape; view of a city

city-state *n* a state consisting of a sovereign city and its dependencies. Among the most famous are the great independent cities of the ancient world, such as Athens, Sparta, Carthage, Thebes, Corinth, and Rome

city technology college *n* (in Britain) a type of senior secondary school specializing in technological subjects, set up in inner-city areas with funding from industry as well as the government

Ciudad Bolívar (*Spanish* θiu'ðað bo'liβar) *n* a port in E Venezuela, on the Orinoco River: accessible to ocean-going vessels. Pop: 344 000 (2005 est). Former name (1764–1846): Angostura

Ciudad Guayana (*Spanish* θiu'ðað gwa'jana) *n* an industrial conurbation in E Venezuela, on the River Orinoco: iron and steel processing, gold mining. Pop: 807 000 (2005 est)

Ciudad Juárez (*Spanish* θiu'ðað 'xwareθ) *n* a city in N Mexico, in Chihuahua state on the Río Grande, opposite El Paso, Texas. Pop: 1 469 000 (2005 est)

Ciudad Trujillo (*Spanish* θiu'ðað tru'xiʎo) *n* the former name (1936–61) of **Santo Domingo**

Ciudad Victoria (*Spanish* θiu'ðað bik'torja) *n* a city in E central Mexico, capital of Tamaulipas state. Pop: 285 000 (2005 est)

civet ('sɪvɪt) *n* **1** any catlike viverrine mammal of the genus *Viverra* and related genera, of Africa and S Asia, typically having blotched or spotted fur and secreting a powerfully smelling fluid from anal glands **2** the yellowish fatty secretion of such an animal, used as a fixative in the manufacture of perfumes **3** the fur of such an animal [c16: from Old French *civette*, from Italian *zibetto*, from Arabic *zabād* civet perfume]

civic ('sɪvɪk) *adj* of or relating to a city, citizens, or citizenship: *civic duties* [c16: from Latin *cīvicus*, from *cīvis* citizen] > '**civically** *adv*

civic centre *n* *Brit* the public buildings of a town, including recreational facilities and offices of local administration

civics ('sɪvɪks) *n* (*functioning as singular*) the study of the rights and responsibilities of citizenship

civies ('sɪvɪz) *pl n* *informal* a variant spelling of **civvies**

civil ('sɪvᵊl) *adj* **1** of the ordinary life of citizens as distinguished from military, legal, or ecclesiastical affairs **2** of or relating to the citizen as an individual: *civil rights* **3** of or occurring within the state or between citizens: *civil strife* **4** polite or courteous **5** of or in accordance with Roman law [c14: from Old French, from Latin *cīvīlis*, from *cīvis* citizen] > '**civilly** *adv*

civil defence *n* the organizing of civilians to deal with enemy attacks

civil disobedience *n* a refusal to obey laws, pay taxes, etc: a nonviolent means of protesting or of attempting to achieve political goals

civil engineer *n* a person qualified to design, construct, and maintain public works, such as roads, bridges, harbours, etc > **civil engineering** *n*

civilian (sɪ'vɪljən) *n* **a** a person whose primary occupation is civil or nonmilitary **b** (*as modifier*): *civilian life* [c14 (originally: a practitioner of civil law): from *civile* (from the Latin phrase *jūs cīvīle* civil law) + -IAN]

civility (sɪ'vɪlɪtɪ) *n*, *pl* -ties **1** politeness or courtesy, esp

when formal **2** (*often plural*) an act of politeness

civilization *or* **civilisation** (ˌsɪvɪlaɪ'zeɪʃən) *n* **1** a human society that has highly developed material and spiritual resources and a complex cultural, political, and legal organization; an advanced state in social development **2** the peoples or nations collectively who have achieved such a state **3** the total culture and way of life of a particular people, nation, region, or period **4** the process of bringing or achieving civilization **5** intellectual, cultural, and moral refinement **6** cities or populated areas, as contrasted with sparsely inhabited areas, deserts, etc

civilize *or* **civilise** ('sɪvɪˌlaɪz) *vb* (*tr*) **1** to bring out of savagery or barbarism into a state characteristic of civilization **2** to refine, educate, or enlighten

civilized *or* **civilised** ('sɪvɪˌlaɪzd) *adj* **1** having a high state of culture and social development **2** cultured; polite: *a civilized discussion*

civil law *n* **1** the law of a state relating to private and civilian affairs **2** the body of law in force in ancient Rome, esp the law applicable to private citizens **3** any system of law based on the Roman system as distinguished from the common law and canon law

civil liberty *n* the right of an individual to certain freedoms of speech and action

civil list *n* (in Britain) the annuities voted by Parliament for the support of the royal household and the royal family

civil marriage *n* *law* a marriage performed by some official other than a clergyman

civil rights *pl n* **1** the personal rights of the individual citizen, in most countries upheld by law, as in the US **2** (*modifier*) of, relating to, or promoting equality in social, economic, and political rights

civil servant *n* a member of the civil service

civil service *n* **1** the service responsible for the public administration of the government of a country. It excludes the legislative, judicial, and military branches. Members of the civil service have no official political allegiance and are not generally affected by changes of governments **2** the members of the civil service collectively

civil society *n* the elements such as freedom of speech, an independent judiciary, etc, that make up a democratic society

civil war *n* war between parties, factions, or inhabitants of different regions within the same nation

Civil War *n* **1** *English history* the conflict between Charles I and the Parliamentarians resulting from disputes over their respective prerogatives. Parliament gained decisive victories at Marston Moor in 1644 and Naseby in 1645, and Charles was executed in 1649 **2** *US history* the war fought from 1861 to 1865 between the North and the South, sparked off by Lincoln's election as president but with deep-rooted political and economic causes, exacerbated by the slavery issue. The advantages of the North in terms of population, finance, and communications brought about the South's eventual surrender at Appomattox

civvy ('sɪvɪ) *n*, *pl* **civvies** *slang* **1** a civilian **2** (*plural*) civilian dress as opposed to uniform **3** **civvy street** civilian life

CJ *abbreviation* Chief Justice

CJA *abbreviation* (in Britain) Criminal Justice Act

CJD *abbreviation* Creutzfeldt-Jakob disease

Cl the chemical symbol for chlorine

clachan (*Gaelic* 'klaxən; *English* 'klæ-) *n* *Scot & Irish dialect* a small village; hamlet [c15: from Scottish Gaelic: probably from *clach* stone]

clack (klæk) *vb* **1** to make or cause to make a sound like that of two pieces of wood hitting each other **2** (*intr*) to jabber ▷ *n* **3** a short sharp sound **4** chatter **5** Also called: **clack valve** a simple nonreturn valve using either a hinged flap or a ball [c13: probably from Old Norse *klaka* to twitter, of imitative origin]

Clackmannanshire (klæk'mænənʃɪə, -ʃə) *n* a council area and historical county of central Scotland; became part of the Central region in 1975 but reinstated as an independent unitary authority in 1996; mainly agricultural. Administrative centre: Alloa. Pop: 47 680 (2003 est). Area: 142 sq km (55 sq miles)

Clacton or **Clacton-on-Sea** ('klæktən) n a town and resort in SE England, in E Essex. Pop: 51 284 (2001)

clad¹ (klæd) vb a past participle of **clothe** [Old English *clāthode* clothed, from *clāthian* to CLOTHE]

clad² (klæd) vb clads, cladding, clad (tr) to bond a metal to (another metal), esp to form a protective coating [C14 (in the obsolete sense: to clothe): special use of CLAD¹]

cladding ('klædɪŋ) n 1 the process of protecting one metal by bonding a second metal to its surface 2 the protective coating so bonded to metal 3 the material used for the outside facing of a building, etc

clade (kleɪd) n biology a group of organisms considered as having evolved from a common ancestor [C20: from Greek *klados* branch, shoot]

cladistics (klə'dɪstɪks) n (functioning as singular) biology a method of grouping animals that makes use of lines of descent rather than structural similarities [C20: New Latin, from Greek *klādos* branch, shoot] > cladism ('klædɪzəm) n > cladist ('klædɪst) n

claim (kleɪm) vb (mainly tr) 1 to demand as being due or as one's property; assert one's title or right to: *he claimed the record* 2 (takes a clause as object or an infinitive) to assert as a fact; maintain against denial: *he claimed to be telling the truth* 3 to call for or need; deserve: *this problem claims our attention* 4 to take: *the accident claimed four lives* ▷ n 5 an assertion of a right; a demand for something as due 6 an assertion of something as true, real, or factual: *he made claims for his innocence* 7 a right or just title to something; basis for demand: *a claim to fame* 8 anything that is claimed, esp in a formal or legal manner, such as a piece of land staked out by a miner 9 a demand for payment in connection with an insurance policy, etc b the sum of money demanded [C13: from Old French *claimer* to call, appeal, from Latin *clāmāre* to shout] > 'claimable adj > 'claimer n > 'claimant n

Clair (French klɛr) n **René** (rəne), real name *René Chomette*. 1898–1981, French film director; noted for his comedies including *An Italian Straw Hat* (1928) and pioneering sound films such as *Sous les toits de Paris* (1930); later films include *Les Belles de nuit* (1952)

clairvoyance (klɛə'vɔɪəns) n 1 the alleged power of perceiving things beyond the natural range of the senses 2 keen intuitive understanding [C19: from French: clear-seeing, from *clair* clear, from Latin *clārus* + *voyance*, from *voir* to see, from Latin *vidēre*]

clairvoyant (klɛə'vɔɪənt) adj 1 of, possessing, or relating to clairvoyance 2 having great insight or second sight ▷ n 3 a person claiming to have the power to foretell future events > clair'voyantly adv

clam (klæm) n 1 any of various burrowing bivalve molluscs of the genera *Mya*, *Venus*, etc. Many species, such as the quahog and soft-shell clam, are edible and *Tridacna gigas* is the largest known bivalve, nearly 1.5 metres long 2 the edible flesh of such a mollusc 3 informal a reticent person ▷ vb clams, clamming, clammed 4 (intr) chiefly US to gather clams ▷ See also **clam up** [C16: from earlier *clamshell*, that is, shell that clamps; related to Old English *clamm* fetter, Old High German *klamma* constriction; see CLAMP¹]

clamant ('kleɪmənt) adj 1 noisy 2 calling urgently [C17: from Latin *clāmāns*, from *clāmāre* to shout!]

clambake ('klæm,beɪk) n US & Canadian a picnic, often by the sea, at which clams, etc, are baked

clamber ('klæmbə) vb 1 (usually foll by up, over, etc) to climb (something) awkwardly, esp by using both hands and feet ▷ n 2 a climb performed in this manner [C15: probably a variant of CLIMB] > 'clamberer n

clam-diggers pl n calf-length trousers

clammy ('klæmɪ) adj -mier, -miest 1 unpleasantly sticky; moist 2 (of the weather, atmosphere, etc) close; humid [C14: from Old English *clæman* to smear; related to Old Norse *kleima*, Old High German *kleimen*] > 'clammily adv > 'clamminess n

clamour or US **clamor** ('klæmə) n 1 a loud persistent outcry, as from a large number of people 2 a vehement expression of collective feeling or outrage: *a clamour against higher prices* 3 a loud and persistent noise: *the clamour of traffic* ▷ vb 4 (intr; often foll by for or against) to make a loud noise or outcry; make a public demand 5 (tr) to move, influence, or force by outcry [C14: from Old French *clamour*, from Latin *clāmor*, from *clāmāre* to cry out] > 'clamorous adj > 'clamorously adv > 'clamorousness n

clamp¹ (klæmp) n 1 a mechanical device with movable jaws with which an object can be secured to a bench or with which two objects may be secured together 2 See also **wheel clamp** ▷ vb (tr) 3 to fix or fasten with or as if with a clamp 4 to immobilize (a car) by means of a wheel clamp 5 to inflict or impose forcefully: *they clamped a curfew on the town* [C14: from Dutch or Low German *klamp*; related to Old English *clamm* bond, fetter, Old Norse *kleppr* lump]

clamp² (klæmp) Brit agriculture ▷ n 1 a mound formed out of a harvested root crop, covered with straw and earth to protect it from winter weather 2 a pile of bricks ready for processing in a furnace ▷ vb 3 (tr) to enclose (a harvested root crop) in a mound [C16: from Middle Dutch *klamp* heap; related to CLUMP]

clamp down vb (intr, adverb; often foll by on) 1 to behave repressively; attempt to repress something regarded as undesirable ▷ n **clampdown** 2 a sudden restrictive measure

clam up vb (intr, adverb) informal to keep or become silent or withhold information

clan (klæn) n 1 a group of people interrelated by ancestry or marriage 2 a group of families with a common surname and a common ancestor, acknowledging the same leader, esp among the Scots and the Irish 3 a group of people united by common characteristics, aims, or interests [C14: from Scottish Gaelic *clann* family, descendants, from Latin *planta* sprout, PLANT¹]

Clancy ('klænsɪ) n **Tom.** born 1947, US novelist; his thrillers, many of which have been filmed, include *The Hunt for Red October* (1984), *Clear and Present Danger* (1989), *Debt of Honour* (1994) and *Red Rabbit* (2002)

clandestine (klæn'dɛstɪn) adj secret and concealed, often for illicit reasons; furtive [C16: from Latin *clandestīnus*, from *clam* secretly; related to Latin *celāre* to hide] > clan'destinely adv

clang (klæŋ) vb 1 to make or cause to make a loud resounding noise, as metal when struck 2 (intr) to move or operate making such a sound ▷ n 3 a resounding metallic noise 4 the harsh cry of certain birds [C16: from Latin *clangere*]

clanger ('klæŋə) n 1 informal a conspicuous mistake (esp in the phrase **drop a clanger**) 2 something that clangs or causes a clang [C20: from CLANG, referring to a mistake whose effects seem to clang]

clangour or US **clangor** ('klæŋgə, 'klæŋə) n 1 a loud resonant often-repeated noise 2 an uproar ▷ vb 3 (intr) to make or produce a loud resonant noise [C16: from Latin *clangor* a noise, from *clangere* to CLANG] > 'clangorous adj > 'clangorously adv

clank (klæŋk) n 1 an abrupt harsh metallic sound ▷ vb 2 to make or cause to make such a sound 3 (intr) to move or operate making such a sound [C17: of imitative origin] > 'clankingly adv

clannish ('klænɪʃ) adj 1 of or characteristic of a clan 2 tending to associate closely within a limited group to the exclusion of outsiders; cliquish > 'clannishly adv > 'clannishness n

clansman ('klænzmən) n, pl -men a man belonging to a clan

clap¹ (klæp) vb claps, clapping, clapped 1 to make or cause to make a sharp abrupt sound, as of two nonmetallic objects struck together 2 to applaud (someone or something) by striking the palms of the hands together sharply 3 (tr) to strike (a person) lightly with an open hand, in greeting, encouragement, etc 4 (tr) to place or put quickly or forcibly: *they clapped him into jail* 5 (of certain birds) to flap (the wings) noisily 6 (tr; foll by up or together) to contrive or put together hastily 7 **clap eyes on** informal to catch sight of 8 **clap hold of** informal to grasp suddenly or forcibly ▷ n 9 the sharp abrupt sound produced by striking the hands together 10 the act of clapping, esp in applause 11 a sudden sharp sound, esp of thunder **12** a light blow **13** *archaic* a sudden action or mishap [Old English *clæppan*; related to Old High German *klepfen*, Middle Dutch *klape* rattle, Dutch *klepel* clapper; all of imitative origin]

clap² (klæp) *n* **the clap** a slang word for **gonorrhoea** [c16: from Old French *clapoir* venereal sore, from *clapier* brothel, from Old Provençal, from *clap* heap of stones, of obscure origin]

clapboard ('klæp,bɔːd, 'klæbəd) *n* **1 a** a long thin timber board with one edge thicker than the other, used esp in the US and Canada in wood-frame construction by lapping each board over the one below **b** (*as modifier*): *a clapboard house* ▷ *vb* **2** (*tr*) to cover with such boards [c16: partial translation of Low German *klappholt*, from *klappen* to crack + *holt* wood; related to Dutch *claphout*; see BOARD]

clapped out *adj* **1** (**clapped-out** *when prenominal*) *Brit, Austral & NZ* (esp of machinery) worn out; dilapidated **2** *Austral & NZ* extremely tired; exhausted

clapper ('klæpə) *n* **1** a person or thing that claps **2** Also called: **tongue** a small piece of metal suspended within a bell that causes it to sound when made to strike against its side **3** a slang word for **tongue** (sense 1) **4** **go like the clappers, run like the clappers** *or* **move like the clappers** *Brit informal* to move extremely fast

clapperboard ('klæpə,bɔːd) *n* a pair of boards clapped together during film shooting in order to aid sound synchronization

Clapton ('klæptən) *n* Eric. born 1945, British rock guitarist, noted for his virtuoso style, his work with the Yardbirds (1963–65), Cream (1966–68), and, with Derek and the Dominos, the album *Layla* (1970); later solo work includes *Unplugged* (1992)

claptrap ('klæp,træp) *n informal* **1** contrived but foolish talk **2** insincere and pretentious talk: *politicians' claptrap* [c18 (in the sense: something contrived to elicit applause): from CLAP¹ and TRAP¹]

claque (klæk) *n* **1 a** a group of people hired to applaud **2** a group of fawning admirers [c19: from French, from *claquer* to clap, of imitative origin]

Clare¹ (kleə) *n* a county of W Republic of Ireland, in Munster between Galway Bay and the Shannon estuary. County town: Ennis. Pop: 103 277 (2002). Area: 3188 sq km (1231 sq miles)

Clare² (kleə) *n* **1** Anthony (Ward). (1942–2007), Irish psychiatrist and broadcaster; presenter of the radio series *In the Psychiatrist's Chair* from 1982 **2** John. 1793–1864, English poet, noted for his descriptions of country life, particularly in *The Shepherd's Calendar* (1827) and *The Rural Muse* (1835). He was confined in a lunatic asylum from 1837

Clarendon¹ ('klærəndən) *n* a village near Salisbury in S England: site of a council held by Henry II in 1164 that produced a code of laws (the **Constitutions of Clarendon**) defining relations between church and state

Clarendon² ('klærəndən) *n* **1st Earl of**, title of *Edward Hyde*. 1609–74, English statesman and historian; chief adviser to Charles II (1660–67); author of *History of the Rebellion and Civil Wars in England* (1704–07)

Clare of Assisi *n* Saint. 1194–1253, Italian nun; founder of the Franciscan Order of Poor Clares. Feast day: Aug 11

claret ('klærət) *n* **1** *chiefly Brit* a red wine, esp one from the Bordeaux district of France **2 a** a purplish-red colour **b** (*as adjective*): *a claret carpet* [c14: from Old French (*vin*) *claret* (wine), from Medieval Latin *clārātum*, from *clārāre* to make clear, from Latin *clārus* CLEAR]

clarify ('klærɪ,faɪ) *vb* **-fies, -fying, -fied 1** to make or become clear or easy to understand **2** to make or become free of impurities **3** to make (fat, butter, etc) clear by heating, etc, or (of fat, etc) to become clear as a result of such a process [c14: from Old French *clarifier*, from Late Latin *clārificāre*, from Latin *clārus* clear + *facere* to make] > ˌclarifiˈcation *n* > ˈclariˌfier *n*

clarinet (ˌklærɪˈnɛt) *n music* **1** a keyed woodwind instrument with a cylindrical bore and a single reed. It is a transposing instrument, most commonly pitched in A or B flat **2** an orchestral musician who plays the clarinet [c18: from French *clarinette*, probably from Italian *clarinetto*, from *clarino* trumpet] > ˌclariˈnettist *or*

ˌclariˈnetist *n*

clarion ('klærɪən) *n* **1** a four-foot reed stop of trumpet quality on an organ **2** an obsolete, high-pitched, small-bore trumpet **3** the sound of such an instrument or any similar sound ▷ *adj* **4** (*prenominal*) clear and ringing; inspiring: *a clarion call to action* ▷ *vb* **5** to proclaim loudly [c14: from Medieval Latin *clāriō* trumpet, from Latin *clārus* clear]

clarity ('klærɪtɪ) *n* **1** clearness, as of expression **2** clearness, as of water [c16: from Latin *clāritās*, from *clārus* CLEAR]

Clark (klɑːk) *n* **1** Helen. born 1950, New Zealand politician; Labour prime minister from 1999 **2** James, known as *Jim*. 1936–68, Scottish racing driver; World Champion (1963, 1965) **3** Kenneth, Baron Clark of Saltwood. 1903–83, English art historian: his books include *Civilization* (1969), which he first presented as a television series **4** William. 1770–1838, US explorer and frontiersman: best known for his expedition to the Pacific Northwest (1804–06) with Meriwether Lewis

Clarke (klɑːk) *n* **1** Sir Arthur C(harles). (1917–2008), British science-fiction writer, who helped to develop the first communications satellites. He scripted the film *2001, A Space Odyssey* (1968) **2** Austin. 1896–1974, Irish poet and verse dramatist. His volumes include *The Vengeance of Fionn* (1917), *Night and Morning* (1938), and *Ancient Lights* (1955) **3** Jeremiah. ?1673–1707, English composer and organist, best known for his *Trumpet Voluntary*, formerly attributed to Purcell **4** Kenneth Harry. born 1940, British Conservative politician: secretary of state for health (1988–1990); secretary of state for education (1990–1992); home secretary (1992–93); chancellor of the exchequer (1993–97) **5** Marcus (Andrew Hislop). 1846–81, Australian novelist born in England, noted for his novel *For the Term of His Natural Life*, published in serial form (1870–72); other works include *Twixt Shadow and Shine* (1875)

clarkia ('klɑːkɪə) *n* any North American onagraceous plant of the genus *Clarkia*: cultivated for their red, purple, or pink flowers [c19: New Latin, named after William Clark (1770–1838), US explorer and frontiersman, who discovered it]

Clarkson ('klɑːksən) *n* Thomas. 1760–1846, British campaigner for the abolition of slavery

clary ('kleərɪ) *n, pl* **claries** any of several European plants of the genus *Salvia*, having aromatic leaves and blue flowers: family *Lamiaceae* (labiates) [c14: from earlier *sclarreye*, from Medieval Latin *sclareia*, of obscure origin]

-clase *n combining form* (in mineralogy) indicating a particular type of cleavage: *plagioclase* [via French from Greek *klasis* a breaking, from *klan* to break]

clash (klæʃ) *vb* **1** to make or cause to make a loud harsh sound, esp by striking together **2** (*intr*) to be incompatible; conflict **3** (*intr*) to engage together in conflict or contest **4** (*intr*) (of dates or events) to coincide **5** (*intr*) (of colours) to look ugly or inharmonious together ▷ *n* **6** a loud harsh noise **7** a collision or conflict [c16: of imitative origin] > ˈclasher *n*

clasp (klɑːsp) *n* **1 a** fastening, such as a catch or hook, used for holding things together **2** a firm grasp, hold, or embrace **3** *military* a bar or insignia on a medal ribbon, to indicate either a second award or the battle, campaign, or reason for its award ▷ *vb* (*tr*) **4** to hold in a firm grasp **5** to grasp firmly with the hand **6** to fasten together with or as if with a clasp [c14: of uncertain origin; compare Old English *clyppan* to embrace] > ˈclasper *n*

claspers ('klɑːspəz) *pl n zoology* **1** a paired organ of male insects, used to clasp the female during copulation **2** a paired organ of male sharks and related fish, used to assist the transfer of spermatozoa into the body of the female during copulation

clasp knife *n* a large knife with one or more blades or other devices folding into the handle

class (klɑːs) *n* **1** a collection or division of people or things sharing a common characteristic, attribute, quality, or property **2** a group of persons sharing a similar social position and certain economic, political, and cultural characteristics **3 a** the pattern of divisions that exist within a society on the basis of rank, economic status, etc **b** (*as modifier*): *the class struggle; class distinctions* **4 a** a group of pupils or students who are taught and study together **b** a meeting of a group of students for tuition **5** *chiefly US* a group of students who graduated in a specified year: *the class of '53* **6** (*in combination and as modifier*) *Brit* a grade of attainment in a university honours degree: *second-class honours* **7** one of several standards of accommodation in public transport **8** *informal* excellence or elegance, esp in dress, design, or behaviour **9** *maths, logic* **a** another name for **set²** (sense 3) **b** proper class a class which cannot itself be a member of other classes **10** in a class of its own *or* in a class by oneself unequalled; unparalleled ▷ *vb* **11** to have or assign a place within a group, grade, or class [C17: from Latin *classis* class, rank, fleet; related to Latin *calāre* to summon]

class A drug *n law* (in Britain) any of the most dangerous group of controlled drugs, including heroin, cocaine, and MDMA. Compare **class B drug, class C drug**

class B drug *n law* (in Britain) any of the second most dangerous group of controlled drugs, including amphetamine. Compare **class A drug, class C drug**

class C drug *n law* (in Britain) any of the least dangerous group of controlled drugs, including temazepam and cannabis. Compare **class A drug, class B drug**

class-conscious *adj* aware of belonging to a particular social rank or grade, esp in being hostile or proud because of class distinctions > class-'consciousness *n*

classic ('klæsɪk) *adj* **1** of the highest class, esp in art or literature **2** serving as a standard or model of its kind; definitive **3** adhering to an established set of rules or principles in the arts or sciences: *a classic proof* **4** characterized by simplicity, balance, regularity, and purity of form; classical **5** of lasting interest or significance **6** continuously in fashion because of its simple and basic style: *a classic day dress* ▷ *n* **7** an author, artist, or work of art of the highest excellence **8** a creation or work considered as definitive **9** *horse racing* any of the five principal races for three-year-old horses in Britain, namely the One Thousand Guineas, Two Thousand Guineas, Derby, Oaks, and Saint Leger [C17: from Latin *classicus* of the first rank, from *classis* division, rank, CLASS]

classical ('klæsɪk°l) *adj* **1** of, relating to, or characteristic of the ancient Greeks and Romans or their civilization, esp in the period of their ascendancy **2** designating, following, or influenced by the art or culture of ancient Greece or Rome: *classical architecture* **3** *music* **a** of, relating to, or denoting any music or its period of composition marked by stability of form, intellectualism, and restraint. See **romantic** (sense 5) **b** accepted as a standard: *the classical suite* **c** denoting serious art music in general. See **pop¹** (sense 2) **4** denoting or relating to a style in any of the arts characterized by emotional restraint and conservatism: *a classical style of painting* **5** (of an education) based on the humanities and the study of Latin and Greek **6** *physics* not involving the quantum theory or the theory of relativity: *classical mechanics* > classi'cality *or* 'classicalness *n* > 'classically *adv*

Classical school *n* economic theory based on the works of Adam Smith and David Ricardo, which explains the creation of wealth and advocates free trade

classic car *n chiefly Brit* a car that is more than twenty-five years old. Compare **veteran car, vintage car**

classicism ('klæsɪ,sɪzəm) *or* **classicalism** ('klæsɪkə,lɪzəm) *n* **1** a style based on the study of Greek and Roman models, characterized by emotional restraint and regularity of form, associated esp with the 18th century in Europe; the antithesis of romanticism. See **neoclassicism 2** knowledge or study of the culture of ancient Greece and Rome **3 a** a Greek or Latin form or expression **b** an expression in a modern language, such as English, that is modelled on a Greek or Latin form > classicist ('klæsɪsɪst) *or* classicalist ('klæsɪkəlɪst) *n* > classi'cistic *adj*

classicize *or* **classicise** ('klæsɪ,saɪz) *vb* **1** (*tr*) to make classic **2** (*intr*) to imitate classical style

classics ('klæsɪks) *pl n* **1** the classics a body of literature regarded as great or lasting, esp that of ancient Greece or Rome **2** the classics the ancient Greek and Latin languages **3** (*functioning as singular*) ancient Greek and Roman culture considered as a subject for academic study

classification (,klæsɪfɪ'keɪʃən) *n* **1** systematic placement in categories **2** one of the divisions in a system of classifying **3** *biology* **a** the placing of animals and plants in a series of increasingly specialized groups because of similarities in structure, origin, molecular composition, etc, that indicate a common relationship. The major groups are domain or superkingdom, kingdom, phylum (in animals) or division (in plants), class, order, family, genus, and species **b** the study of the principles and practice of this process; taxonomy [C18: from French; see CLASS, -IFY, -ATION] > ,classifi'catory *adj*

classified ('klæsɪ,faɪd) *adj* **1** arranged according to some system of classification **2** *government* (of information) not available to people outside a restricted group, esp for reasons of national security **3** (of information) closely concealed or secret **4** (of advertisements in newspapers, etc) arranged according to type **5** *Brit* (of newspapers) containing sports results, esp football results **6** (of British roads) having a number in the national road system. If the number is preceded by an M the road is a motorway, if by an A it is a first-class road, and if by a B it is a secondary road

classify ('klæsɪ,faɪ) *vb* -fies, -fying, -fied (*tr*) **1** to arrange or order by classes; categorize **2** *government* to declare (information, documents, etc) of possible aid to an enemy and therefore not available to people outside a restricted group [C18: back formation from CLASSIFICATION] > 'classi,fiable *adj* > 'classi,fier *n*

class interval *n statistics* one of the intervals into which the range of a variable of a distribution is divided, esp one of the divisions of the base line of a bar chart or histogram

classless ('klɑːslɪs) *adj* **1** not belonging to or forming a class **2** characterized by the absence of economic and social distinctions > 'classlessness *n*

class list *n* (in Britain) a list categorizing students according to the class of honours they have obtained in their degree examination

classmate ('klɑːs,meɪt) *n* a friend or contemporary of the same class in a school, college, etc

classroom ('klɑːs,ruːm, -,rʊm) *n* a room in which classes are conducted, esp in a school or college

classroom assistant *n* a person whose job is to help a schoolteacher in the classroom. Also called: **learning support assistant**

class struggle *n* the class struggle *Marxism* the continual conflict between the capitalist and working classes for economic and political power

classy ('klɑːsɪ) *adj* classier, classiest *informal* elegant; stylish > 'classiness *n*

clatter ('klætə) *vb* **1** to make or cause to make a rattling noise, esp as a result of movement **2** (*intr*) to chatter ▷ *n* **3** a rattling sound or noise **4** a noisy commotion, such as one caused by loud chatter [Old English *clatrung* clattering (gerund); related to Dutch *klateren* to rattle, German *klatschen* to smack, Norwegian *klattra* to knock] > 'clatterer *n* > 'clatteringly *adv*

Claude (klɔːd; *French* klod) *n* **Albert.** 1898–1983, US cell biologist, born in Belgium: shared the Nobel prize for physiology or medicine (1974) for work on microsomes and mitochondria

Claudel (*French* klodɛl) *n* **Paul** (**Louis Charles Marie**) (pɔl). 1868–1955, French dramatist, poet, and diplomat, whose works testify to his commitment to the Roman Catholic faith. His plays include *L'Annonce faite à Marie* (1912) and *Le Soulier de satin* (1919–24)

Claude Lorrain (*French* klod lɔrɛ̃) *n* real name *Claude Gelée*. 1600–82, French painter, esp of idealized landscapes, noted for his subtle depiction of light

Claudius ('klɔːdɪəs) *n* full name *Tiberius Claudius Drusus Nero Germanicus*. 10 BC–54 AD, Roman emperor (41–54); invaded Britain (43); poisoned by his fourth wife, Agrippina

Claudius II *n* full name *Marcus Aurelius Claudius*, called

Gothicus. 214–270 AD, Roman emperor (268–270)

clause (klɔːz) *n* **1** *grammar* a group of words, consisting of a subject and a predicate including a finite verb, that does not necessarily constitute a sentence. See also **main clause, subordinate clause, coordinate clause 2** a section of a legal document such as a contract, will, or draft statute [c13: from Old French, from Medieval Latin *clausa* a closing (of a rhetorical period), back formation from Latin *clausula,* from *claudere* to close] > 'clausal *adj*

Clausewitz (German 'klauzəvɪts) *n* **Karl von** (karl fɔn). 1780–1831, Prussian general, noted for his works on military strategy, esp *Vom Kriege* (1833)

Clausius (German 'klauzɪus) *n* **Rudolf Julius** ('ruːdɔlf 'juːlius). 1822–88, German physicist and mathematician. He enunciated the second law of thermodynamics (1850) and developed the kinetic theory of gases

claustrophobia (ˌklɔːstrəˈfəʊbɪə, ˌklɒs-) *n* an abnormal fear of being in a confined space [c19: from New Latin from Latin *claustrum* CLOISTER + – PHOBIA] > ˌclaustro'phobe *n*

claustrophobic (ˌklɔːstrəˈfəʊbɪk, ˌklɒs-) *adj* **1** suffering from claustrophobia **2** unpleasantly cramped, confined, or closed in: *narrow claustrophobic spaces* > ˌclaustro'phobically *adv*

clavate ('kleɪveɪt, -vɪt) or **claviform** ('klævɪˌfɔːm) *adj* shaped like a club with the thicker end uppermost [c19: from Latin *clāva* club] > 'clavately *adv*

clave[1] (kleɪv, klɑːv) *n* *music* one of a pair of hardwood sticks struck together to make a hollow sound, esp to mark the beat of Latin-American dance music [c20: from American Spanish, from Latin *clavis* key]

clave[2] (kleɪv) *vb* *archaic* a past tense of **cleave**[1]

clavicembalo (ˌklævɪˈtʃɛmbələʊ) *n, pl* -los another name for **harpsichord** [c18: from Italian, from Medieval Latin *clāvis* key + *cymbalum* CYMBAL]

clavichord ('klævɪˌkɔːd) *n* a keyboard instrument consisting of a number of thin wire strings struck from below by brass tangents. The instrument is noted for its delicate tones, since the tangents do not rebound from the string until the key is released [c15: from Medieval Latin *clāvichordium,* from Latin *clāvis* key + *chorda* string, CHORD[1]]

clavicle ('klævɪkᵊl) *n* **1** either of the two bones connecting the shoulder blades with the upper part of the breastbone. Nontechnical name: **collarbone 2** the corresponding structure in other vertebrates [c17: from Medieval Latin *clāvicula,* from Latin *clāvis* key] > clavicular (kləˈvɪkjʊlə) *adj*

clavier (kləˈvɪə, 'klævɪə) *n* **a** any keyboard instrument **b** the keyboard itself [c18: from French: keyboard, from Old French (in the sense: key bearer), from Latin *clāvis* key]

claw (klɔː) *n* **1** a curved pointed horny process on the end of each digit in birds, some reptiles, and certain mammals **2** a corresponding structure in some invertebrates, such as the pincer of a crab **3** a part or member like a claw in function or appearance ▷ *vb* **4** to scrape, tear, or dig (something or someone) with claws, etc **5** (*tr*) to create by scratching as with claws: *to claw an opening* [Old English *clawu;* related to Old High German *kluwi,* Sanskrit *glau-* ball, sphere] > 'clawer *n*

claw back *vb* (*tr, adverb*) **1** to get back (something) with difficulty **2** to recover (a sum of money), esp by taxation or a penalty ▷ *n* **clawback 3** the recovery of a sum of money, esp by taxation or a penalty **4** the sum so recovered

claw hammer *n* a hammer with a cleft at one end of the head for extracting nails

clay (kleɪ) *n* **1** a very fine-grained material that consists of hydrated aluminium silicate, quartz, and organic fragments and occurs as sedimentary rocks, soils, and other deposits. It becomes plastic when moist but hardens on heating and is used in the manufacture of bricks, cement, ceramics, etc **2** earth or mud in general **3** *poetic* the material of the human body [Old English *clǣg;* related to Old High German *klīa,* Norwegian *kli,* Latin *glūs* glue, Greek *gloios* sticky oil] > 'clayey, 'clayish or 'clayˌlike *adj*

Clay (kleɪ) *n* **1 Cassius.** See **Muhammad Ali 2 Henry.**

1777–1852, US statesman and orator; secretary of state (1825–29)

claymation (ˌkleɪˈmeɪʃən) *n* the techniques of animation applied to clay models [c20: from CLAY + (ANI)MATION]

claymore ('kleɪˌmɔː; *Scot* ˌkleˈmor) *n* a large two-edged broadsword used formerly by Scottish Highlanders [c18: from Gaelic *claidheamh mōr* great sword]

clay pigeon *n* a disc of baked clay hurled into the air from a machine as a target to be shot at

CLC *abbreviation* Canadian Labour Congress

-cle *suffix forming nouns* indicating smallness: *cubicle; particle* [via Old French from Latin -*culus.* See -CULE]

clean (kliːn) *adj* **1** without dirt or other impurities; unsoiled **2** without anything in it or on it: *a clean page* **3** recently washed; fresh **4** without extraneous or foreign materials **5** without defect, difficulties, or problems **6** (of a nuclear weapon) producing little or no radioactive fallout or contamination **7** (of a wound, etc) having no pus or other sign of infection **8** pure; morally sound **9** without objectionable language or obscenity **10** thorough or complete: *a clean break* **11** dexterous or adroit: *a clean throw* **12** *sport* played fairly and without fouls **13** simple in design: *a ship's clean lines* **14** *aeronautics* causing little turbulence; streamlined **15** honourable or respectable **16** habitually neat **17** (esp of a driving licence) showing or having no record of offences **18** *slang* **a** innocent; not guilty **b** not carrying illegal drugs, weapons, etc ▷ *vb* **19** to make or become free of dirt, filth, etc: *the stove cleans easily* **20** (*tr*) to remove in making clean: *to clean marks off the wall* **21** (*tr*) to prepare (fish, poultry, etc) for cooking: *to clean a chicken* ▷ *adv* **22** in a clean way; cleanly **23** *not standard* (intensifier): *clean forgotten; clean dead* **24** clean bowled *cricket* bowled by a ball that breaks the wicket without hitting the batsman or his bat **25** come clean *informal* to make a revelation or confession ▷ *n* **26** the act or an instance of cleaning: *he gave his shoes a clean* ▷ See also **clean up, clean out** [Old English *clǣne;* related to Old Frisian *klēne* small, neat, Old High German *kleini*] > 'cleanable *adj* > 'cleanness *n*

clean-cut *adj* **1** clearly outlined; neat: *clean-cut lines of a ship* **2** definite

cleaner ('kliːnə) *n* **1** a person, device, chemical agent, etc, that removes dirt, as from clothes or carpets **2** (*usually plural*) a shop, etc that provides a dry-cleaning service **3** take a person to the cleaners *informal* to rob or defraud a person of all of his money

cleanly *adv* ('kliːnlɪ) **1** in a fair manner **2** easily or smoothly: *the screw went into the wood cleanly* ▷ *adj* ('klɛnlɪ) -lier, -liest **3** habitually clean or neat > cleanlily ('klɛnlɪlɪ) *adv* > cleanliness ('klɛnlɪnɪs) *n*

clean out *vb* (*tr, adverb*) **1** (foll by *of* or *from*) to remove (something) (from or away from) **2** *slang* to leave (someone) with no money **3** *informal* to exhaust (stocks, goods, etc) completely

cleanse (klɛnz) *vb* (*tr*) **1** to remove dirt, filth, etc, from **2** to remove guilt from **3** to remove a group of people from (an area) by means of ethnic cleansing [Old English *clǣnsian;* related to Middle Low German *klēnsen;* see CLEAN]

cleanser ('klɛnzə) *n* a cleansing agent, such as a detergent

clean-shaven *adj* (of men) having the facial hair shaved off

clean sheet *n* *sport* an instance of conceding no goals or points in a match or competition (esp in the phrase **keep a clean sheet**)

Cleanthes (klɪˈænθiːz) *n* ?300–?232 BC, Greek philosopher: succeeded Zeno as head of the Stoic school

clean up *vb* (*adverb*) **1** to rid (something) of dirt, filth, or other impurities **2** to make (someone or something) orderly or presentable **3** (*tr*) to rid (a place) of undesirable people or conditions **4** (*intr*) *informal* to make a great profit ▷ *n* **cleanup 5** the process of cleaning up or eliminating something **6** *informal, chiefly US* a great profit

clear (klɪə) *adj* **1** free from darkness or obscurity; bright **2** (of weather) free from dullness or clouds **3** transparent **4** even and pure in tone or colour **5** without discoloration, blemish, or defect: *a clear skin* **6** easy to see or hear; distinct **7** free from doubt or confusion **8** (*postpositive*) certain in the mind; sure: *are you clear?* **9** (*in combination*) perceptive, alert: *clear-headed* **10** evident or obvious: *it is clear that he won't come now* **11** (of sounds or the voice) not harsh or hoarse **12** serene; calm **13** without qualification or limitation; complete: *a clear victory* **14** free of suspicion, guilt, or blame: *a clear conscience* **15** free of obstruction; open: *a clear passage* **16** free from debt or obligation **17** (of money, profits, etc) without deduction; net **18** emptied of freight or cargo **19** *showjumping* (of a round) ridden without any fences being knocked down or any points being lost ▷ *adv* **20** in a clear or distinct manner **21** completely or utterly **22** (*postpositive*; often foll by *of*) not in contact (with); free: *stand clear of the gates* ▷ *n* **23** a clear space **24** in the clear **a** free of suspicion, guilt, or blame **b** *sport* able to receive a pass without being tackled ▷ *vb* **25** to make or become free from darkness, obscurity, etc **26** (*intr*) **a** (of the weather) to become free from dullness, fog, rain, etc **b** (of mist, fog, etc) to disappear **27** (*tr*) to free from impurity or blemish **28** (*tr*) to free from doubt or confusion **29** (*tr*) to rid of objects, obstructions, etc **30** (*tr*) to make or form (a path, way, etc) by removing obstructions **31** (*tr*) to free or remove (a person or thing) from something, such as suspicion, blame, or guilt **32** (*tr*) to move or pass by or over without contact or involvement: *he cleared the wall easily* **33** (*tr*) to rid (the throat) of phlegm or obstruction **34** (*tr*) to make or gain (money) as profit **35** (*tr*; often foll by *off*) to discharge or settle (a debt) **36** (*tr*) to free (a debtor) from obligation **37** (*intr*) (of a cheque) to pass through one's bank and be charged against one's account **38** *banking* to settle accounts by exchanging (commercial documents) in a clearing house **39** to permit (ships, aircraft, cargo, passengers, etc) to unload, disembark, depart, etc, after fulfilling the customs and other requirements, or (of ships, etc) to be permitted to unload, etc **40** to obtain or give (clearance) **41** (*tr*) to obtain clearance from **42** (*tr*) *military* to decode (a message, etc) **43** (*tr*) *computing* to remove data from a storage device and replace it with particular characters that usually indicate zero ▷ See also **clear away, clear off,** etc. [c13 *clere,* from Old French *cler,* from Latin *clārus* clear, bright, brilliant, illustrious] > 'clearer *n* > 'clearness *n*

clearance ('klɪərəns) *n* **1** a the process or an instance of clearing: *slum clearance* **b** (*as modifier*): *a clearance order* **2** space between two parts in motion or in relative motion **3** permission for an aircraft, ship, passengers, etc, to proceed **4** official permission to have access to secret information, projects, areas, etc **5** *banking* the exchange of commercial documents drawn on the members of a clearing house **6** a the disposal of merchandise at reduced prices **b** (*as modifier*): *a clearance sale* **7** the act of clearing an area of land of its inhabitants by mass eviction

clear away *vb* (*adverb*) to remove (objects) from (the table) after a meal

clear-cut *adj* (**clear cut** *when postpositive*) **1** definite; not vague: *a clear-cut proposal* **2** clearly outlined

clearing ('klɪərɪŋ) *n* an area with few or no trees or shrubs in wooded or overgrown land

clearing bank *n* (in Britain) any bank that makes use of the central clearing house in London for the transfer of credits and cheques between banks

clearing house *n* **1** *banking* an institution where cheques and other commercial papers drawn on member banks are cancelled against each other so that only net balances are payable **2** a central agency for the collection and distribution of information or materials

clearly ('klɪəlɪ) *adv* **1** in a clear, distinct, or obvious manner: *I could see everything quite clearly* **2** (*sentence modifier*) it is obvious that; evidently: *clearly the social services must be flexible*

clear off *vb* (*intr, adverb*) *informal* to go away: often used imperatively

clear out *vb* (*adverb*) **1** (*intr*) *informal* to go away: often used imperatively **2** (*tr*) to remove and sort the contents of (a room, container, etc) **3** (*tr*) *slang* to leave (someone)

with no money **4** (*tr*) *slang* to exhaust (stocks, goods, etc) completely

clearstory ('klɪə,stɔːrɪ) *n* a variant spelling of **clerestory**

clear up *vb* (*adverb*) **1** (*tr*) to explain or solve (a mystery, etc) **2** to put (a place or thing that is disordered) in order **3** (*intr*) (of the weather) to become brighter

clearway ('klɪə,weɪ) *n* **1** *Brit* a stretch of road on which motorists may stop only in an emergency **2** an area at the end of a runway over which an aircraft taking off makes its initial climb: it is under the control of the airport

cleat (kliːt) *n* **1** a wedge-shaped block, usually of wood, attached to a structure to act as a support **2** a device consisting of two hornlike prongs projecting horizontally in opposite directions from a central base, used for securing lines on vessels, wharves, etc ▷ *vb* (*tr*) **3** to supply or support with a cleat or cleats **4** to secure (a line) on a cleat [c14: of Germanic origin, compare Old High German *chlōz* clod, lump, Dutch *kloot* ball]

cleavage ('kliːvɪdʒ) *n* **1** *informal* the separation between a woman's breasts, esp as revealed by a low-cut dress **2** a division or split **3** (of crystals) the act of splitting or the tendency to split along definite planes so as to yield smooth surfaces **4** Also called: **segmentation** *embryol* (in animals) the repeated division of a fertilized ovum into a solid ball of cells (a morula), which later becomes hollow (a blastula) **5** the breaking of a chemical bond in a molecule to give smaller molecules or radicals **6** *geology* the natural splitting of certain rocks, or minerals such as slates, or micas along the planes of weakness

cleave¹ (kliːv) *vb* cleaves, cleaving; cleft, cleaved or clove; cleft, cleaved or cloven **1** to split or cause to split, esp along a natural weakness **2** (*tr*) to make by or as if by cutting: *to cleave a path* **3** (when *intr,* foll by *through*) to penetrate or traverse [Old English *clēofan;* related to Old Norse *kljūfa,* Old High German *klioban,* Latin *glūbere* to peel] > 'cleavable *adj*

cleave² (kliːv) *vb* (*intr;* foll by *to*) to cling or adhere [Old English *cleofian;* related to Old High German *klebēn* to stick]

cleaver ('kliːvə) *n* a heavy knife or long-bladed hatchet, esp one used by butchers

cleavers ('kliːvəz) *n* (*functioning as singular*) a Eurasian rubiaceous plant, *Galium aparine,* having small white flowers and prickly stems and fruits. Also called: goosegrass, hairif [Old English *clīfe;* related to *clīfan* to **CLEAVE²**]

Cleese (kliːz) *n* John (**Marwood**). born 1939, British comedy writer and actor, noted for the TV series *Monty Python's Flying Circus* (1969–74) and *Fawlty Towers* (1975, 1978). His films include *A Fish Called Wanda* (1988) and *Fierce Creatures* (1997)

Cleethorpes ('kliːθɔːps) *n* a resort in E England, in North East Lincolnshire unitary authority, Lincolnshire. Pop: 31 853 (2001)

clef (klɛf) *n* one of several symbols placed on the left-hand side beginning of each stave indicating the pitch of the music written after it [c16: from French: key, clef, from Latin *clāvis;* related to Latin *claudere* to close]

cleft (klɛft) *vb* **1** the past tense and a past participle of **cleave¹** ▷ *n* **2** a fissure or crevice **3** an indentation or split in something, such as the chin, palate, etc ▷ *adj* **4** split; divided [Old English *geclyft* (n); related to Old High German *kluft* tongs, German *Kluft* gap, fissure; see **CLEAVE¹**]

cleft palate *n* a congenital crack or fissure in the midline of the hard palate, often associated with a harelip

cleg (klɛg) *n* another name for a horsefly, esp one of the genus *Haematopota* [c15: from Old Norse *kleggi*]

Cleisthenes ('klaɪsθə,niːz) *n* 6th century BC, Athenian statesman: democratized the political structure of Athens

Cleland ('klɛlənd) *n* John. 1709–89, British writer, best known for his bawdy novel *Fanny Hill* (1748–49)

clematis ('klɛmətɪs, klə'meɪtɪs) *n* any N temperate ranunculaceous climbing plant or erect shrub of the genus *Clematis,* having plumelike fruits. Many species are cultivated for their large colourful flowers. See also **traveller's joy** [C16: from Latin, from Greek *klēmatis* climbing plant, brushwood, from *klēma* twig]

Clemenceau (*French* klemãso) *n* **Georges Eugène Benjamin** (ʒɔrʒ œʒɛn bɛʒamɛ̃). 1841–1929, French statesman; prime minister of France (1906–09; 1917–20); negotiated the Treaty of Versailles (1919)

clemency ('klɛmənsɪ) *n, pl* -cies **1** mercy or leniency **2** mildness, esp of the weather [C15: from Latin *clēmentia*, from *clēmēns* gentle]

Clemens ('klɛmənz) *n* **Samuel Langhorne** ('læŋ,hɔːn). See **Twain**

clement ('klɛmənt) *adj* **1** merciful **2** (of the weather) mild [C15: from Latin *clēmēns* mild; probably related to Greek *klinein* to lean]

Clement I ('klɛmənt) *n* **Saint**, called *Clement of Rome*. pope (?88–?97 AD). Feast day: Nov 23

Clement V *n* original name *Bertrand de Got*. ?1264–1314, pope (1305–14): removed the papal seat from Rome to Avignon in France (1309)

Clement VII *n* original name *Giulio de' Medici*. 1478–1534, pope (1523–34): refused to authorize the annulment of the marriage of Henry VIII of England to Catherine of Aragon (1533)

clementine ('klɛmən,tiːn, -,taɪn) *n* a citrus fruit thought to be either a variety of tangerine or a hybrid between a tangerine and sweet orange [C20: from French *clémentine*, perhaps from the female Christian name]

Clement of Alexandria *n* **Saint**. original name *Titus Flavius Clemens*. ?150–?215 AD, Greek Christian theologian: head of the catechetical school at Alexandria; teacher of Origen. Feast day: Dec 5

clench (klɛntʃ) *vb* (*tr*) **1** to close or squeeze together (the teeth, a fist, etc) tightly **2** to grasp or grip firmly ▷ *n* **3** a firm grasp or grip **4** a device that grasps or grips, such as a clamp ▷ *n, vb* **5** another word for **clinch** [Old English *beclencan*, related to Old High German *klenken* to tie, Middle High German *klank* noose, Dutch *klinken* rivet]

Clendinnen (,klɛn'dɪnən) *n* **Inga**. born 1934. Australian historian and writer. Her books include *Reading the Holocaust* (1998) and *Tiger's Eye – a Memoir* (2000)

Cleon ('kliːɒn) *n* died 422 BC, Athenian demagogue and military leader

Cleopatra (,kliːə'pætrə, -'pɑː-) *n* ?69–30 BC, queen of Egypt (51–30), renowned for her beauty: the mistress of Julius Caesar and later of Mark Antony. She killed herself with an asp to avoid capture by Octavian (Augustus)

Cleopatra's Needle (,kliːə'pætrəz, -'pɑː-) *n* either of two Egyptian obelisks, originally set up at Heliopolis about 1500 BC: one was moved to the Thames Embankment, London, in 1878, the other to Central Park, New York, in 1880

clepsydra ('klɛpsɪdrə) *n, pl* -dras *or* -drae (-,driː) an ancient device for measuring time by the flow of water or mercury through a small aperture. Also called: **water clock** [C17: from Latin, from Greek *klepsudra*, from *kleptein* to steal + *hudōr* water]

cleptomania (,klɛptəʊ'meɪnɪə, -'meɪnjə) *n* a variant spelling of **kleptomania**

clerestory *or* **clearstory** ('klɪə,stɔːrɪ) *n, pl* -ries **1** a row of windows in the upper part of the wall of a church that divides the nave from the aisle, set above the aisle roof **2** the part of the wall in which these windows are set [C15: from CLEAR + STOREY] > 'clere,storied *or* 'clear,storied *adj*

clergy ('klɜːdʒɪ) *n, pl* -gies the collective body of men and women ordained as religious ministers, esp of the Christian Church [C13: from Old French *clergie*, from *clerc* ecclesiastic, CLERK]

clergyman ('klɜːdʒɪmən) *n, pl* -men a member of the clergy

cleric ('klɛrɪk) *n* a member of the clergy [C17: from Church Latin *clēricus* priest, CLERK]

clerical ('klɛrɪkᵊl) *adj* **1** relating to or associated with the clergy: *clerical dress* **2** of or relating to office clerks or their work: *a clerical error* **3** supporting or advocating clericalism > 'clerically *adv*

clerical collar *n* a stiff white collar with no opening at the front that buttons at the back of the neck; the distinctive mark of the clergy in certain Churches. Also called: *informal* **dog collar**

clericalism ('klɛrɪkᵊ,lɪzəm) *n* **1** a policy of upholding the power of the clergy **2** the power of the clergy esp when excessively strong > 'clericalist *n*

clericals ('klɛrɪkᵊlz) *pl n* the distinctive dress of a member of the clergy

clerihew ('klɛrɪ,hjuː) *n* a form of comic or satiric verse, consisting of two couplets of metrically irregular lines, containing the name of a well-known person [C20: named after Edmund *Clerihew* Bentley (1875–1956), English writer who invented it]

clerk (klɑːk; *US & Canadian* klɜːrk) *n* **1** a worker, esp in an office, who keeps records, files, etc **2** clerk to the justices (in England) a legally qualified person who sits in court with lay justices to advise them on points of law **3** an employee of a court, legislature, board, corporation, etc, who keeps records and accounts, etc: *a town clerk* **4** Also called: **clerk in holy orders** a cleric **5** *US & Canadian* short for **salesclerk** **6** Also called: **desk clerk** *US & Canadian* a hotel receptionist **7** *archaic* a scholar ▷ *vb* **8** (*intr*) to serve as a clerk [Old English *clerc*, from Church Latin *clēricus*, from Greek *klērikos* cleric, relating to the heritage (alluding to the Biblical Levites, whose inheritance was the Lord), from *klēros* heritage] > 'clerkish *adj* > 'clerkship *n*

clerkess (klɑː'kɛs) *n* a female office clerk

clerk of works *n* an employee who supervises building work in progress or the upkeep of existing buildings

Clermont-Ferrand (*French* klɛrmɔ̃fɛrɑ̃) *n* a city in S central France: capital of Puy-de-Dôme department; industrial centre. Pop: 137 140 (1999)

Cleveland¹ ('kliːvlənd) *n* **1** a former county of NE England formed in 1974 from parts of E Durham and N Yorkshire; replaced in 1996 by the unitary authorities of Hartlepool (Durham), Stockton-on-Tees (Durham), Middlesbrough (North Yorkshire) and Redcar and Cleveland (North Yorkshire) **2** a port in NE Ohio, on Lake Erie: major heavy industries. Pop: 461 324 (2003 est) **3** a hilly region of NE England, extending from the **Cleveland Hills** to the River Tees

Cleveland² ('kliːvlənd) *n* **Stephen Grover**. 1837–1908, US Democratic politician: the 22nd and 24th president of the US (1885–89; 1893–97)

clever ('klɛvə) *adj* **1** displaying sharp intelligence or mental alertness **2** adroit or dexterous, esp with the hands **3** smart in a superficial way **4** *Brit informal* sly; cunning [C13 *cliver* (in the sense: quick to seize, adroit), of uncertain origin] > 'cleverly *adv* > 'cleverness *n*

clevis ('klɛvɪs) *n* the U-shaped component of a shackle for attaching a drawbar to a plough or similar implement [C16: related to CLEAVE¹]

clew (kluː) *n* **1** a ball of thread, yarn, or twine **2** *nautical* either of the lower corners of a square sail or the after lower corner of a fore-and-aft sail ▷ *vb* **3** (*tr*) to coil or roll into a ball [Old English *cliewen* (vb); related to Old High German *kliu* ball]

clianthus (klɪ'ænθəs) *n* any Australian or New Zealand plant of the leguminous genus *Clianthus*, with ornamental clusters of slender scarlet flowers. See also **desert pea** [C19: New Latin, probably from Greek *klei-*, *kleos* glory + *anthos* flower]

cliché ('kliːʃeɪ) *n* **1** a word or expression that has lost much of its force through overexposure **2** an idea, action, or habit that has become trite from overuse **3** *printing chiefly Brit* a stereotype or electrotype plate [C19: from French, from *clicher* to stereotype; imitative of the sound made by the matrix when it is dropped into molten metal] > 'clichéd *or* 'cliché'd *adj*

click (klɪk) *n* **1** a short light often metallic sound **2** the locking member of a ratchet mechanism, such as a pawl or detent **3** *phonetics* any of various stop consonants, found in Khoisan and as borrowings in southern Bantu languages, that are produced by the suction of air into the mouth ▷ *vb* **4** to make or cause to make a clicking sound: *to click one's heels* **5** (usually foll by *on*) *computing* to press and release (a button on a mouse) or to select (a particular function) by pressing and releasing a button on a mouse **6** (*intr*) *slang* to be a great success: *that idea really clicked* **7** (*intr*) *informal* to become suddenly clear: *it finally clicked when her name was mentioned* **8** (*intr*) *slang* to go or fit together with ease: *they clicked from their first meeting* [c17: of imitative origin] > **'clicker** *n*

clicks and mortar *adj* making use of traditional trading methods in conjunction with internet trading. Abbreviation: **C & M** [c20: pun on *bricks and mortar*, with CLICK referring to the computing sense]

click through *vb* (*tr, adverb*) **1** to navigate around (a website) using the links provided to move onto different pages ▷ *adj* **click-through 2** (of a website) able to be navigated by means of links between different pages

client ('klaɪənt) *n* **1** a person, company, etc, that seeks the advice of a professional man or woman **2** a customer **3** a person who is registered with or receiving services or financial aid from a welfare agency **4** *computing* a program or work station that requests data or information from a server [c14: from Latin *cliēns* retainer, dependant; related to Latin *clīnāre* to lean] > **cliental** (klaɪˈɛntˀl) *adj*

clientele (ˌkliːɒnˈtɛl) *or* **clientage** ('klaɪəntɪdʒ) *n* customers or clients collectively [c16: from Latin *clientēla*, from *cliēns* CLIENT]

cliff (klɪf) *n* a steep high rock face, esp one that runs along the seashore and has the strata exposed [Old English *clif*; related to Old Norse *kleif*, Middle Low German *klēf*, Dutch *klif*; see CLEAVE²] > **'cliffy** *adj*

cliffhanger ('klɪfˌhæŋə) *n* **1 a** a situation of imminent disaster usually occurring at the end of each episode of a serialized film **b** the serialized film itself **2** a situation that is dramatic or uncertain > **'cliff,hanging** *adj*

climacteric (klaɪˈmæktərɪk, ˌklaɪmækˈtɛrɪk) *n* **1** a critical event or period **2** another name for **menopause 3** the period in the life of a man corresponding to the menopause, chiefly characterized by diminished sexual activity ▷ *adj* Also: **climacterical** (ˌklaɪmækˈtɛrɪkˀl) **4** involving a crucial event or period [c16: from Latin *clīmactēricus*, from Greek *klimaktērikos*, from *klimakter* rung of a ladder, from *klimax* ladder; see CLIMAX]

climactic (klaɪˈmæktɪk) *or* **climactical** (klaɪˈmæktɪkəl) *adj* consisting of, involving, or causing a climax > **cli'mactically** *adv*

● USAGE See at **climate**

climate ('klaɪmɪt) *n* **1** the long-term prevalent weather conditions of an area, determined by latitude, position relative to oceans or continents, altitude, etc **2** an area having a particular kind of climate **3** a prevailing trend or current of feeling: *the political climate* [c14: from Late Latin *clima*, from Greek *klima* inclination, region; related to Greek *klinein* to lean] > **climatic** (klaɪˈmætɪk), **cli'matical** *or* **'climatal** *adj* > **cli'matically** *adv*

● USAGE *Climatic* is sometimes wrongly used where
● *climactic* is meant. *Climatic* is properly used to talk
● about things relating to climate; *climactic* is used to
● describe something which forms a climax

climatic zone *n* any of the eight principal zones, roughly demarcated by lines of latitude, into which the earth can be divided on the basis of climate

climatology (ˌklaɪməˈtɒlədʒɪ) *n* the study of climate > **climatologic** (ˌklaɪmətəˈlɒdʒɪk) *or* ˌclimato'logical *adj* > ˌclima'tologist *n*

climax ('klaɪmæks) *n* **1** the most intense or highest point of an experience or of a series of events: *the party was the climax of the week* **2** a decisive moment in a dramatic or other work **3** a rhetorical device by which a series of sentences, clauses, or phrases are arranged in order of increasing intensity **4** *ecology* the stage in the development of a community during which it remains stable under the prevailing environmental conditions **5** Also called: **sexual climax** (esp in referring to women) another word for **orgasm** ▷ *vb* **6** to reach or bring to a climax [c16: from Late Latin, from Greek *klimax* ladder]

climb (klaɪm) *vb* (*mainly intr*) **1** (*also tr*; often foll by *up*) to go up or ascend (stairs, a mountain, etc) **2** (often foll by *along*) to progress with difficulty: *to climb along a ledge* **3** to rise to a higher point or intensity: *the temperature climbed* **4** to incline or slope upwards: *the road began to climb* **5** to ascend in social position .**6** (of plants) to grow upwards

by twining, using tendrils or suckers, etc **7** *informal* (foll by *into*) to put (on) or get (into) **8** to be a climber or mountaineer ▷ *n* **9** the act or an instance of climbing **10** a place or thing to be climbed, esp a route in mountaineering [Old English *climban*; related to Old Norse *klembra* to squeeze, Old High German *climban* to clamber] > **'climbable** *adj*

climb down *vb* (*intr, adverb*) **1** to descend **2** (often foll by *from*) to retreat (from an opinion, position, etc) ▷ *n* **climb-down 3** a retreat from an opinion, etc

climber ('klaɪmə) *n* **1** a person or thing that climbs **2** a plant that lacks rigidity and grows upwards by twining, scrambling, or clinging with tendrils and suckers **3** *chiefly Brit* short for **social climber**

clime (klaɪm) *n* *poetic* a region or its climate [c16: from Late Latin *clima*; see CLIMATE]

clinch (klɪntʃ) *vb* **1** (*tr*) to secure (a driven nail) by bending the protruding point over **2** (*tr*) to hold together in such a manner **3** (*tr*) to settle (something, such as an argument, bargain, etc) in a definite way **4** (*tr*) *nautical* to fasten by means of a clinch **5** (*intr*) to engage in a clinch, as in boxing or wrestling ▷ *n* **6** the act of clinching **7 a** a nail with its point bent over **b** the part of such a nail, etc, that has been bent over **8** *boxing, wrestling* an act or an instance in which one or both competitors hold on to the other to avoid punches, regain wind, etc **9** *slang* a lovers' embrace **10** *nautical* a loop or eye formed in a line by seizing the end to the standing part. Also (for senses 1, 2, 4, 7, 8, 10): **clench** [c16: variant of CLENCH]

clincher ('klɪntʃə) *n* **1** *informal* something decisive, such as a fact, score, etc **2** a person or thing that clinches

cline (klaɪn) *n* a continuous variation in form between members of a species having a wide variable geographical or ecological range [c20: from Greek *klinein* to lean] > **'clinal** *adj*

-cline *n combining form* indicating a slope: *anticline* [back formation from INCLINE] > **-clinal** *adj combining form*

Cline (klaɪn) *n Patsy*, original name *Virginia Patterson Hensley*. 1932–63, US country singer; her bestselling records include "Walking After Midnight", "I Fall to Pieces", and "Leavin' On Your Mind"

cling (klɪŋ) *vb* **clings**, **clinging**, **clung** (*intr*) **1** (often foll by *to*) to hold fast or adhere closely (to something), as by gripping or sticking **2** (foll by *together*) to remain in contact (with each other) **3** to be or remain physically or emotionally close ▷ *n* **4** short for **clingstone** [Old English *clingan*; related to CLENCH] > **'clinging** *adj* > **'clingingly** *adv* > **'clingy** *adj* > **'clinginess** *or* **'clingingness** *n*

clingfilm ('klɪŋˌfɪlm) *n* a thin polythene material that clings closely to any surface around which it is placed: used for wrapping food

clingstone ('klɪŋˌstəʊn) *n* **a** a fruit, such as certain peaches, in which the flesh tends to adhere to the stone **b** (*as modifier*): *a clingstone peach*

clinic ('klɪnɪk) *n* **1** a place in which outpatients are given medical treatment or advice, often connected to a hospital **2** a similar place staffed by physicians or surgeons specializing in one or more specific areas: *eye clinic* **3** *Brit* a private hospital or nursing home **4** *obsolete* the teaching of medicine to students at the bedside **5** *chiefly US & Canadian* a group or centre that offers advice or instruction [c17: from Latin *clīnicus* one on a sickbed, from Greek, from *klinē* bed]

clinical ('klɪnɪkˀl) *adj* **1** of or relating to a clinic **2** of or relating to the bedside of a patient, the course of his disease, the observation and treatment of patients directly: *a clinical lecture*; *clinical medicine* **3** scientifically detached; strictly objective: *a clinical attitude to life* **4** plain, simple, and usually unattractive > **'clinically** *adv*

clinical governance *n* a systematic approach to raising standards of health care and tackling poor performance in hospitals

clinically dead *adj* having no respiration, no heartbeat, and with no contraction of the pupils when exposed to a strong light

clinically obese *adj* the state at which being overweight causes medical complications

clinical psychology *n* the branch of psychology that

studies and treats mental illness and mental retardation

clinical thermometer *n* a finely calibrated thermometer for determining the temperature of the body, usually placed under the tongue, in the armpit, or in the rectum

clinician (klɪˈnɪʃən) *n* a physician, psychiatrist, etc, who specializes in clinical work as opposed to one engaged in laboratory or experimental studies

clink¹ (klɪŋk) *vb* **1** to make or cause to make a light and sharply ringing sound ▷ *n* **2** a light and sharply ringing sound [c14: perhaps from Middle Dutch *klinken*; related to Old Low German *chlanch*, German *Klang* sound]

clink² (klɪŋk) *n* a slang word for **prison** [c16: after *Clink*, name of a prison in Southwark, London]

clinker (ˈklɪŋkə) *n* **1** the ash and partially fused residues from a coal-fired furnace or fire **2** a partially vitrified brick or mass of brick **3** *slang, chiefly US* something of poor quality, such as a film ▷ *vb* **4** (*intr*) to form clinker during burning [c17: from Dutch *klinker* a type of brick, from obsolete *klinckaerd*, literally: something that clinks (referring to the sound produced when one was struck), from *klinken* to CLINK¹]

clinker-built *or* **clincher-built** *adj* (of a boat or ship) having a hull constructed with each plank overlapping that below [c18 *clinker* a nailing together, probably from CLINCH]

Clinton (ˈklɪntən) *n* **1** **Bill**, full name *William Jefferson*. born 1946, US Democrat politician; 42nd president of the US (1993–2001) **2** his wife, **Hillary Rodham** born 1947, US politician and lawyer; first lady (1993–2001); senator from 2001

Clio (ˈklaɪəʊ) *n* *Greek myth* the Muse of history [c19: from Latin, from Greek *Kleiō*, from *kleein* to celebrate]

clip¹ (klɪp) *vb* clips, clipping, clipped (*mainly tr*) **1** (*also intr*) to cut, snip, or trim with or as if with scissors or shears, esp in order to shorten or remove a part **2** *Brit* to punch (a hole) in something, esp a ticket **3** to curtail or cut short **4** to move a short section from (a film, etc) **5** to shorten (a word) **6** *informal* to strike with a sharp, often slanting, blow **7** *slang* to obtain (money) by deception or cheating **8** *US slang* to murder; execute ▷ *n* **9** the act or process of clipping **10** something clipped off **11** *informal* a sharp, often slanting, blow **12** *informal* speed: *a rapid clip* **13** *Austral & NZ* the total quantity of wool shorn, as in one place, season, etc **14** another word for **clipped form** [c12: from Old Norse *klippa* to cut; related to Low German *klippen*]

clip² (klɪp) *n* **1** any of various small implements used to hold loose articles together or to attach one article to another **2** short for **paperclip, cartridge clip** ▷ *vb* clips, clipping, clipped (*tr*) **3** to hold together tightly, as with a clip [Old English *clyppan* to embrace); related to Old Frisian *kleppa*, Lithuanian *glebiu*]

clipboard (ˈklɪpˌbɔːd) *n* **1** a portable writing board with a spring clip at the top for holding paper **2** a temporary storage area in desktop publishing where text or graphics are held after the cut command or the copy command

clip joint *n* *slang* a place, such as a nightclub or restaurant, in which customers are overcharged

clipped (klɪpt) *adj* (of speech or voice) abrupt and distinct

clipped form *n* a shortened form of a word, as for example *doc* for *doctor*

clipper (ˈklɪpə) *n* **1** any fast sailing ship **2** a person or thing that cuts or clips

clippers (ˈklɪpəz) *or* **clips** (klɪps) *pl n* **1** a hand tool with two cutting blades for clipping fingernails, hedges, etc **2** a hairdresser's tool, operated either by hand or electrically, with one fixed and one reciprocating set of teeth for cutting short hair

clipping (ˈklɪpɪŋ) *n* **1** something cut out or trimmed off, esp an article from a newspaper; cutting **2** the distortion of an audio or visual signal in which the tops of peaks with a high amplitude are cut off, caused by, for example, overloading of amplifier circuits

clique (kliːk, klɪk) *n* a small, exclusive group of friends or associates [c18: from French, perhaps from Old

French: latch, from *cliquer* to click; suggestive of the necessity to exclude nonmembers] > 'cliquish *adj* > 'cliquishly *adv* > 'cliquishness *n* > cliquey *or* cliquy (ˈkliːkɪ, ˈklɪkɪ) *adj* -ier, -iest

Clisthenes (ˈklaɪsθəˌniːz) *n* a variant spelling of **Cleisthenes**

clit (klɪt) *n* *informal* short for **clitoris**

clitoridectomy (ˌklɪtərɪˈdɛktəmɪ) *n*, *pl* -mies surgical removal of the clitoris: a form of female circumcision, esp practised as a religious or ethnic rite

clitoris (ˈklɪtərɪs, ˈklaɪ-) *n* a part of the female genitalia consisting of a small elongated highly sensitive erectile organ at the front of the vulva: homologous with the penis [c17: from New Latin, from Greek *kleitoris*; related to Greek *kleiein* to close] > 'clitoral *adj*

Clive (klaɪv) *n* **Robert**, Baron Clive of Plassey. 1725–74, British general and statesman, whose victory at Plassey (1757) strengthened British control in India

Cllr *abbreviation* Councillor

cloaca (kləʊˈeɪkə) *n*, *pl* -cae (-kiː) **1** a cavity in the pelvic region of most vertebrates, except higher mammals, and certain invertebrates, into which the alimentary canal and the genital and urinary ducts open **2** a sewer [c18: from Latin: sewer; related to Greek *kluzein* to wash out] > clo'acal *adj*

cloak (kləʊk) *n* **1** a wraplike outer garment fastened at the throat and falling straight from the shoulders **2** something that covers or conceals ▷ *vb* (*tr*) **3** to cover with or as if with a cloak **4** to hide or disguise [c13: from Old French *cloque*, from Medieval Latin *clocca* cloak, bell; referring to the bell-like shape]

cloak-and-dagger *n* (*modifier*) characteristic of or concerned with intrigue and espionage

cloakroom (ˈkləʊkˌruːm, -ˌrʊm) *n* **1** a room in which hats, coats, luggage, etc, may be temporarily deposited **2** *Brit* a euphemistic word for **lavatory**

clobber¹ (ˈklɒbə) *vb* (*tr*) *slang* **1** to beat or batter **2** to defeat utterly **3** to criticize severely [c20: of unknown origin]

clobber² (ˈklɒbə) *n* *Brit slang* personal belongings, such as clothes and accessories [c19: of unknown origin]

clobbering machine *n* *NZ informal* pressure to conform with accepted standards

cloche (klɒʃ) *n* **1** a bell-shaped cover used to protect young plants **2** a woman's almost brimless close-fitting hat, typical of the 1920s and 1930s [c19: from French: bell, from Medieval Latin *clocca*]

clock¹ (klɒk) *n* **1** a timepiece, usually free-standing, hanging, or built into a tower, having mechanically or electrically driven pointers that move constantly over a dial showing the numbers of the hours **2** any clocklike device for recording or measuring, such as a taximeter or pressure gauge **3** the downy head of a dandelion that has gone to seed **4** short for **time clock 5** around the clock *or* round the clock all day and all night **6** the clock an informal word for **speedometer, mileometer 7** *Brit* a slang word for **face** ▷ *vb* **8** (*tr*) *Brit, Austral & NZ slang* to strike, esp on the face or head **9** (*tr*) to record time as with a stopwatch, esp in the calculation of speed [c14: from Middle Dutch *clocke* clock, from Medieval Latin *clocca* bell, ultimately of Celtic origin]

clock² (klɒk) *n* an ornamental design either woven in or embroidered on the side of a stocking [c16: from Middle Dutch *clocke*, from Medieval Latin *clocca* bell]

clock off *or* **clock out** *vb* (*intr, adverb*) to depart from work, esp when it involves registering the time of departure on a card

clock on *or* **clock in** *vb* (*intr, adverb*) to arrive at work, esp when it involves registering the time of arrival on a card

clock up *vb* (*tr, adverb*) to record or register: *this car has clocked up 80 000 miles*

clock-watcher *n* an employee who checks the time in anticipation of a break or of the end of the working day

clockwise (ˈklɒkˌwaɪz) *adv, adj* in the direction that the hands of a clock rotate; from top to bottom towards the right when seen from the front

clockwork (ˈklɒkˌwɜːk) *n* **1** the mechanism of a clock **2** any similar mechanism, as in a wind-up toy **3** like clockwork with complete regularity and precision

clod (klɒd) *n* **1** a lump of earth or clay **2** earth, esp when heavy or in hard lumps **3** Also called: **clodpole, clod poll, clodpate** a dull or stupid person [Old English *clod-* (occurring in compound words) lump; related to CLOUD] > 'cloddy *adj* > 'cloddish *adj* > 'cloddishly *adv* > 'cloddishness *n*

clodhopper ('klɒd,hɒpə) *n informal* **1** a clumsy person; lout **2** (*usually plural*) a large heavy shoe or boot

clog (klɒg) *vb* **clogs, clogging, clogged 1** to obstruct or become obstructed with thick or sticky matter **2** (*tr*) to encumber; hinder; impede **3** (*intr*) to adhere or stick in a mass ▷ *n* **4 a** any of various wooden or wooden-soled shoes **b** (*as modifier*): *clog dance* **5** a heavy block, esp of wood, fastened to the leg of a person or animal to impede motion **6** something that impedes motion or action; hindrance [c14 (in the sense: block of wood): of unknown origin]

cloisonné (klwɑː'zɒneɪ; *French* klwazɔne) *n* **1 a** a design made by filling in with coloured enamel an outline of flattened wire put on edge **b** the method of doing this ▷ *adj* **2** of, relating to, or made by cloisonné [c19: from French, from *cloisonner* to divide into compartments, from *cloison* partition, ultimately from Latin *claudere* to CLOSE²]

cloister ('klɔɪstə) *n* **1** a covered walk, usually around a quadrangle in a religious institution, having an open arcade or colonnade on the inside and a wall on the outside **2** (*sometimes plural*) a place of religious seclusion, such as a monastery **3** life in a monastery or convent ▷ *vb* **4** (*tr*) to confine or seclude in or as if in a monastery [c13: from Old French *cloistre*, from Medieval Latin *claustrum* monastic cell, from Latin: bolt, barrier, from *claudere* to close; influenced in form by Old French *cloison* partition] > 'cloistered *adj*

clomb (kləʊm) *vb archaic* a past tense and past participle of **climb**

clomp (klɒmp) *n, vb* a less common word for **clump** (senses 2, 7)

clone (kləʊn) *n* **1** a group of organisms or cells of the same genetic constitution that are descended from a common ancestor by asexual reproduction, as by cuttings, grafting, etc, in plants **2** Also called: **gene clone** a segment of DNA that has been isolated and replicated by laboratory manipulation: used to analyse genes and manufacture their products (proteins) **3** *informal* a person or thing bearing a very close resemblance to another person or thing **4** *slang* **a** a mobile phone that has been given the electronic identity of an existing mobile phone, so that calls made on the second phone are charged to the owner of the first phone **b** any similar object or device, such as a credit card, that has been given the electronic identity of another device usually in order to commit theft ▷ *vb* **5** to produce or cause to produce a clone **6** *informal* to produce near copies (of a person or thing) **7** (*tr*) *slang* to give (a mobile phone, etc) the electronic identity of an existing mobile phone (or other device), so that calls, purchases, etc made with the second device are charged to the owner of the first device [c20: from Greek *klōn* twig, shoot; related to *klan* to break]

clonk (klɒŋk) *vb* **1** (*intr*) to make a loud dull thud **2** (*tr*) *informal* to hit ▷ *n* **3** a loud thudding sound [c20: of imitative origin]

Clonmel (klɒn'mɛl) *n* the county town of Co Tipperary, Republic of Ireland; birthplace of Laurence Sterne; meat processing and enamelware. Pop: 16 910 (2002)

clonus ('kləʊnəs) *n* a type of convulsion characterized by rapid contraction and relaxation of a muscle [c19: from New Latin, from Greek *klonos* turmoil] > **clonic** ('klɒnɪk) *adj* > clonicity (klɒ'nɪsɪtɪ) *n*

Clooney ('kluːnɪ) *n* **George.** born 1961, US film actor; he starred in the television series *ER* (1994–99) and the films *The Perfect Storm* (2000), *Ocean's Eleven* (2001), *Confessions of a Dangerous Mind* (2002, also directed), and *Syriana* (2005, also directed)

clop (klɒp) *vb* **clops, clopping, clopped 1** (*intr*) to make or move along with a sound as of a horse's hooves striking the ground ▷ *n* **2** a sound of this nature [c20: of imitative origin]

close¹ (kləʊs) *adj* **1** near in space or time; in proximity **2** having the parts near together; dense: *a close formation* **3** down or near to the surface; short: *a close haircut* **4** near in relationship: *a close relative* **5** intimate or confidential: *a close friend* **6** almost equal or even: *a close contest* **7** not deviating or varying greatly from a model or standard: *a close resemblance; a close translation* **8** careful, strict, or searching: *a close study* **9** confined or enclosed **10** shut or shut tight **11** oppressive, heavy, or airless: *a close atmosphere* **12** strictly guarded: *a close prisoner* **13** neat or tight in fit **14** secretive or reticent **15** miserly; not generous, esp with money **16** (of money or credit) hard to obtain; scarce **17** restricted as to public admission or membership **18** hidden or secluded **19** Also called: **closed** restricted or prohibited as to the type of game or fish able to be taken **20** Also called: **closed, narrow** *phonetics* denoting a vowel pronounced with the lips relatively close together ▷ *adv* **21** closely; tightly **22** near or in proximity **23** close to the wind *nautical* sailing as nearly as possible towards the direction from which the wind is blowing. See also **wind¹** (sense 25) [c13: from Old French *clos* close, enclosed, from Latin *clausus* shut up, from *claudere* to close] > 'closely *adv* > 'closeness *n*

close² (kləʊz) *vb* **1** to put or be put in such a position as to cover an opening; shut: *the door closed behind him* **2** (*tr*) to bar, obstruct, or fill up (an entrance, a hole, etc): *to close a road* **3** to bring the parts or edges of (a wound, etc) together or (of a wound, etc) to be brought together **4** (*intr*; foll by *on, over*, etc) to take hold: *his hand closed over the money* **5** to bring or be brought to an end; terminate **6** to complete (an agreement, a deal, etc) successfully or (of an agreement, deal, etc) to be completed successfully **7** to cease or cause to cease to render service: *the shop closed at six* **8** (*intr*) *stock exchange* to have a value at the end of a day's trading, as specified: *steels closed two points down* **9** (*tr*) *archaic* to enclose or shut in ▷ *n* **10** the act of closing **11** the end or conclusion: *the close of the day* **12** (kləʊs) *Brit* a courtyard or quadrangle enclosed by buildings or an entry leading to such a courtyard **13** (kləʊs) *Brit* (*capital when part of a street name*) a small quiet residential road: *Hillside Close* **14** (kləʊs) the precincts of a cathedral or similar building **15** (kləʊs) *Scot* the entry from the street to a tenement building ▷ See also **close down, close in**, etc. > 'closer *n*

close company (kləʊs) *n Brit* a company under the control of its directors or fewer than five independent participants

close corporation (kləʊs) *n South African* a small private limited company

closed (kləʊzd) *adj* **1** blocked against entry; shut **2** restricted; exclusive **3** not open to question or debate **4** (of a hunting season, etc) close **5** *maths* **a** (of a curve or surface) completely enclosing an area or volume **b** (of a set) having members that can be produced by a specific operation on other members of the same set **6** Also called: **checked** *phonetics* denoting a syllable that ends in a consonant **7** not open to public entry or membership: *the closed society of publishing*

closed chain *n chem* another name for **ring¹** (sense 17)

closed circuit *n* a complete electrical circuit through which current can flow when a voltage is applied

closed-circuit television *n* a television system in which signals are transmitted from a television camera to the receivers by cables or telephone links forming a closed circuit, as used in security systems, etc

close down (kləʊz) *vb* (*adverb*) **1** to cease or cause to cease operations **2** (*tr*) *sport* to mark or move towards (an opposing player) in order to prevent him or her running with the ball or making or receiving a pass ▷ *n* **close-down** ('kləʊz,daʊn) **3** a closure or stoppage of operations, esp in a factory **4** *Brit radio, television* the end of a period of broadcasting, esp late at night

closed shop *n* (formerly) an industrial establishment in which there exists a contract between a trade union and the employer permitting the employment of the union's members only

close-fisted (,kləʊs'fɪstɪd) *adj* very careful with money; mean > ,close-'fistedness *n*

close harmony (kləʊs) *n* a type of singing in which all the parts except the bass lie close together and are confined to the compass of a tenth

close-hauled (ˌkləʊsˈhɔːld) *adj nautical* with the sails flat, so as to sail as close to the wind as possible

close in (kləʊz) *vb* (*intr, adverb*) **1** (of days) to become shorter with the approach of winter **2** (foll by *on* or *upon*) to advance (on) so as to encircle or surround

close out (kləʊz) *vb* (*adverb*) to terminate (a client's or other account) on which the margin is inadequate or exhausted, usually by sale of securities to realize cash

close punctuation (kləʊs) *n* punctuation in which many commas, full stops, etc, are used. See **open punctuation**

close quarters (kləʊs) *pl n* **1** a narrow cramped space or position **2** at close quarters **a** engaged in hand-to-hand combat **b** in close proximity; very near together

close season (kləʊs) *or* **closed season** *n* **1** the period of the year when it is prohibited to kill certain game or fish **2** *sport* the period of the year when there is no domestic competition

close shave (kləʊs) *n informal* a narrow escape

closet ('klɒzɪt) *n* **1** a small cupboard or recess **2** a small private room **3** short for **water closet 4** (*modifier*) private or secret **5** (*modifier*) suited or appropriate for use in private: *closet meditations* ▷ *vb* -ets, -eting, -eted **6** (*tr*) to shut up or confine in a small private room, esp for conference or meditation [c14: from Old French, from *clos* enclosure; see CLOSE¹]

close-up ('kləʊs,ʌp) *n* **1** a photograph or film or television shot taken at close range **2** a detailed or intimate view or examination ▷ *vb* **close up** (kləʊz) (*adverb*) **3** to shut entirely **4** (*intr*) to draw together: *the ranks closed up* **5** (*intr*) (of wounds) to heal completely

close with (kləʊz) *vb* (*intr, preposition*) to engage in battle with (an enemy)

Clostridium difficile (dɪ'fɪsɪli, ˌdɪfɪ'ciːl) *n* a faecal organism endemic in hospitals and responsible for the majority of hospital-acquired cases of diarrhoea in elderly patients. Sometimes shortened to: **C difficile**

closure ('kləʊʒə) *n* **1** the act of closing or the state of being closed **2** an end or conclusion **3** something that closes or shuts, such as a cap or seal for a container **4** (in a deliberative body) a procedure by which debate may be halted and an immediate vote taken **5** *chiefly US* **a** the resolution of a significant event or relationship in a person's life **b** a sense of contentment experienced after such a resolution ▷ *vb* **6** (*tr*) (in a deliberative body) to end (debate) by closure [c14: from Old French, from Late Latin *clausūra* bar, from Latin *claudere* to close]

clot (klɒt) *n* **1 a** soft thick lump or mass **2** *Brit informal* a stupid person; fool ▷ *vb* **clots, clotting, clotted 3** to form or cause to form into a soft thick lump or lumps [Old English *clott*, of Germanic origin; compare Middle Dutch *klotte* block, lump]

cloth (klɒθ) *n, pl* **cloths** (klɒθs, klɒðz) **1 a** a fabric formed by weaving, felting or knitting wool, cotton, etc **b** (*as modifier*): *a cloth bag* **2** a piece of such fabric used for a particular purpose, as for a dishcloth **3** the cloth the clergy [Old English *clāth*; related to Old Frisian *klêth*, Middle High German *kleit* cloth, clothing]

clothe (kləʊð) *vb* **clothes, clothing, clothed** *or* **clad** (*tr*) **1** to dress or attire (a person) **2** to provide with clothing or covering **3** to conceal or disguise **4** to endow or invest [Old English *clāthian*, from *clāth* CLOTH; related to Old Norse *klætha*]

clothes (kləʊðz) *pl n* **1** articles of dress **2** *chiefly Brit* short for **bedclothes** [Old English *clāthas*, plural of *clāth* CLOTH]

clotheshorse ('kləʊðz,hɔːs) *n* **1** a frame on which to hang laundry for drying or airing **2** *informal* a dandy

clothesline ('kləʊðz,laɪn) *n* a piece of rope, cord, or wire on which clean washing is hung to dry or air

clothes peg *n* a small wooden or plastic clip for attaching washing to a clothesline

clothes pole *n* Also called **clothes post** a post to which a clothesline is attached

clothes-press *n* a piece of furniture for storing clothes, usually containing wide drawers and a cabinet

clothes prop *n* a long wooden pole with a forked end, used to raise a line of washing

clothier ('kləʊðɪə) *n* a person who makes, sells, or deals in clothes or cloth

clothing ('kləʊðɪŋ) *n* **1** garments collectively **2** something that covers or clothes

Clotho ('kləʊθəʊ) *n Greek myth* one of the three Fates, spinner of the thread of life [Latin, from Greek *Klōtho*, one who spins, from *klōthein* to spin]

cloth of gold *n* cloth woven from silk threads interspersed with gold

Clotilda (klə'tɪldə) *n* ?475–?545 AD, wife of Clovis I of the Franks, whom she converted (496) to Christianity

clotted cream *n Brit* a thick cream made from scalded milk, esp in SW England

clotting factor *n* any one of a group of substances, including factor VIII, the presence of which in the blood is essential for blood clotting to occur. Also called: **coagulation factor**

cloture ('kləʊtʃə) *n* **1** closure in the US Senate ▷ *vb* **2** (*tr*) to end (debate) in the US Senate by cloture [c19: from French *clôture*, from Old French CLOSURE]

cloud (klaʊd) *n* **1** a mass of water or ice particles visible in the sky, usually white or grey, from which rain or snow falls when the particles coagulate **2** any collection of particles visible in the air, esp of smoke or dust **3** something that darkens, threatens, or carries gloom **4** *jewellery* a cloudlike blemish in a transparent stone **5** in the clouds not in contact with reality **6** under a cloud **a** under reproach or suspicion **b** in a state of gloom or bad temper **7** on cloud nine *informal* elated; very happy ▷ *vb* **8** (when *intr*, often foll by *over* or *up*) to make or become cloudy, overcast, or indistinct **9** (*tr*) to make obscure; darken **10** to make or become gloomy or depressed **11** (*tr*) to place under or render liable to suspicion or disgrace **12** to render (liquids) milky or dull or (of liquids) to become milky or dull [c13 (in the sense: a mass of vapour): from Old English *clūd* rock, hill; probably related to CLOD] ▷ **'cloudless** *adj* ▷ **'cloudlessly** *adv* ▷ **'cloudlessness** *n*

cloudberry ('klaʊdbərɪ, -brɪ) *n, pl* -ries a creeping Eurasian herbaceous rosaceous plant, *Rubus chamaemorus*, with white flowers and orange berry-like fruits (drupelets)

cloudburst ('klaʊd,bɜːst) *n* a heavy downpour

cloud chamber *n physics* an apparatus for detecting high-energy particles by observing their tracks through a chamber containing a supersaturated vapour. Each particle ionizes molecules along its path and small droplets condense on them to produce a visible track

cloud-cuckoo-land *or* **cloudland** ('klaʊd,lænd) *n* a realm of fantasy, dreams, or impractical notions

cloudy ('klaʊdɪ) *adj* **cloudier, cloudiest 1** covered with cloud or clouds **2** of or like a cloud or clouds **3** streaked or mottled like a cloud **4** opaque or muddy **5** obscure or unclear **6** troubled by gloom or depression ▷ **'cloudily** *adv* ▷ **'cloudiness** *n*

Clouet (*French* klue) *n* **François** (frɑ̃swa), ?1515–72, and his father, **Jean** (ʒɑ̃), ?1485–?1540, French portrait painters

clough (klʌf) *n dialect* a gorge or narrow ravine [Old English *clōh*]

Clough (klʌf) *n* **1 Arthur Hugh** 1819–61, British poet, author of *Amours de Voyage* (1858) and *Dipsychus* (1865) **2 Brian** 1935–2004, English footballer and manager, noted for his outspoken comments

clout (klaʊt) *n* **1** *informal* a blow with the hand or a hard object **2** power or influence, esp in politics **3** Also called: **clout nail** a short, flat-headed nail used esp for attaching sheet metal to wood **4** *Brit dialect* **a** a piece of cloth: *a dish clout* **b** a garment ▷ *vb* (*tr*) **5** *informal* to give a hard blow to, esp with the hand **6** to patch with a piece of cloth or leather [Old English *clūt* piece of metal or cloth, *clūtian* to patch (c14: to strike with the hand); related to Dutch *kluit* a lump, and to CLOD]

clove¹ (kləʊv) *n* **1** a tropical evergreen myrtaceous tree, *Syzygium aromaticum*, native to the East Indies but cultivated elsewhere, esp Zanzibar **2** the dried unopened flower buds of this tree, used as a pungent fragrant spice [c14: from Old French *clou de girofle*, literally: nail of clove, *clou* from Latin *clāvus* nail + *girofle* clove tree]

clove² (kləʊv) *n* any of the segments of a compound bulb that arise from the axils of the scales of a large bulb [Old English *clufu* bulb; related to Old High German *klovolouh* garlic; see CLEAVE¹]

clove³ (kləʊv) *vb* a past tense of **cleave¹**

clove hitch *n* a knot or hitch used for securing a rope to a spar, post, or larger rope

Clovelly (klə'vɛlɪ) *n* a village in SW England, in Devon on the Bristol Channel: famous for its steep cobbled streets: tourism, fishing. Pop: 472 (2001)

cloven ('kləʊvᵊn) *vb* **1** a past participle of **cleave¹** ▷ *adj* **2** split; cleft; divided

cloven hoof *or* **cloven foot** *n* **1** the divided hoof of a pig, goat, cow, deer, or related animal, which consists of the two middle digits of the foot **2** the mark or symbol of Satan > ˌcloven-'hoofed *or* ˌcloven-'footed *adj*

clove oil *n* a volatile pale-yellow aromatic oil obtained from clove flowers, formerly much used in confectionery, dentistry, and microscopy. Also called: oil of cloves

clover ('kləʊvə) *n* **1** any plant of the leguminous genus *Trifolium*, having trifoliate leaves and dense flower heads. Many species, such as red clover, white clover, and alsike, are grown as forage plants **2** any of various similar or related plants **3** in clover *informal* in a state of ease or luxury [Old English *clāfre*; related to Old High German *klēo*, Middle Low German *klēver*, Dutch *klāver*]

cloverleaf ('kləʊvəˌliːf) *n, pl* -leaves **1** an arrangement of connecting roads, resembling a four-leaf clover in form, that joins two intersecting main roads **2** (*modifier*) in the shape or pattern of a leaf of clover

Clovis I ('kləʊvɪs) *n* German name *Chlodwig*. ?466–511 AD, king of the Franks (481–511), who extended the Merovingian kingdom to include most of Gaul and SW Germany

clown (klaʊn) *n* **1** a comic entertainer, usually grotesquely costumed and made up, appearing in the circus **2** a person who acts in a comic or buffoon-like manner **3** a coarse clumsy rude person; boor **4** *archaic* a countryman or rustic ▷ *vb* (*intr*) **5** to perform as a clown **6** to play jokes or tricks **7** to act foolishly [C16: perhaps of Low German origin; compare Frisian *klönne*, Icelandic *klunni* clumsy fellow] > 'clownery *n* > 'clownish *adj* > 'clownishly *adv* > 'clownishness *n*

cloy (klɔɪ) *vb* to make weary or cause weariness through an excess of something initially pleasurable or sweet [C14 (originally: to nail, hence, to obstruct): from earlier *acloyen*, from Old French *encloer*, from Medieval Latin *inclavāre*, from Latin *clāvāre* to nail, from *clāvus* a nail]

cloying ('klɔɪɪŋ) *adj* initially pleasurable or sweet but wearing in excess > 'cloyingly *adv*

cloze test (kləʊz) *n* a test of the ability to comprehend text in which the reader has to supply the missing words that have been removed from the text at regular intervals [altered from *close* to complete a pattern (in Gestalt theory)]

club (klʌb) *n* **1** a stout stick, usually with one end thicker than the other, esp one used as a weapon **2** a stick or bat used to strike the ball in various sports, esp golf **3** short for **Indian club 4** a group or association of people with common aims or interests **5** the room, building, or facilities used by such a group **6** a building in which elected, fee-paying members go to meet, dine, read, etc **7** a commercial establishment in which people can drink and dance; disco. See also **nightclub 8** *chiefly Brit* an organization, esp in a shop, set up as a means of saving **9** *Brit* an informal word for **friendly society 10 a** the black trefoil symbol on a playing card **b** a card with one or more of these symbols or (*when pl*) the suit of cards so marked **11** in the club *Brit slang* pregnant ▷ *vb* clubs, clubbing, clubbed **12** (*tr*) to beat with or as if with a club **13** (often foll by *together*) to gather or become gathered into a group **14** (often foll by *together*) to unite or combine (resources, efforts, etc) for a common purpose [C13: from Old Norse *klubba*, related to Middle High German *klumpe* group of trees, CLUMP, Old English *clympre* lump of metal]

clubbed (klʌbd) *adj* having a thickened end, like a club

clubber ('klʌbə) *n* a person who regularly frequents nightclubs and similar establishments

clubbing ('klʌbɪŋ) *n* the activity of frequenting nightclubs and similar establishments

club class *n* **1** a class of air travel which is less luxurious than first class but more luxurious than economy class ▷ *adj* club-class **2** of or relating to this class of travel

club foot *n* **1** a congenital deformity of the foot, esp one in which the foot is twisted so that most of the weight rests on the heel. Technical name: **talipes 2** a foot so deformed > ˌclub-'footed *adj*

clubhouse ('klʌbˌhaʊs) *n* the premises of a sports or other club, esp a golf club

clubman ('klʌbmən) *n, pl* -men a man who is an enthusiastic member of a club or clubs

club root *n* a disease of cabbages and related plants, caused by the fungus *Plasmodiophora brassicae*, in which the roots become thickened and distorted

cluck (klʌk) *n* **1** the low clicking sound made by a hen or any similar sound ▷ *vb* **2** (*intr*) (of a hen) to make a clicking sound **3** (*tr*) to call or express (a feeling) by making a similar sound [C17: of imitative origin]

clucky ('klʌkɪ) *adj Austral informal* (of a woman) **1** wishing to have a baby **2** excessively protective towards her children

clue (kluː) *n* **1** something that helps to solve a problem or unravel a mystery **2** not to have a clue **a** to be completely baffled **b** to be completely ignorant or incompetent ▷ *vb* clues, cluing, clued **3** (*tr*; usually foll by *in* or *up*) to provide with helpful information [C15: variant of CLEW]

clued-up *adj informal* shrewd; well-informed

clueless ('kluːlɪs) *adj slang* helpless; stupid

Cluj (kluːʒ, kluːʒ) *n* an industrial city in NW Romania, on the Someșul-Mic River: former capital of Transylvania. Pop: 297 000 (2005 est)

clump (klʌmp) *n* **1** a cluster, as of trees or plants **2** a dull heavy tread or any similar sound **3** an irregular mass **4** an inactive mass of microorganisms, esp a mass of bacteria produced as a result of agglutination **5** an extra sole on a shoe **6** *slang* a blow ▷ *vb* **7** (*intr*) to walk or tread heavily **8** to gather or be gathered into clumps, clusters, clots, etc **9** to cause (bacteria, blood cells, etc) to collect together or (of bacteria, etc) to collect together **10** (*tr*) *slang* to punch (someone) [Old English *clympe*; related to Middle Dutch *klampe* heap of hay, Middle Low German *klampe* CLAMP², Swedish *klimp* small lump] > 'clumpy *adj*

clumsy ('klʌmzɪ) *adj* -sier, -siest **1** lacking in skill or physical coordination **2** awkwardly constructed or contrived [C16 (in obsolete sense: benumbed with cold; hence, awkward): perhaps from C13 dialect *clumse* to benumb, probably from Scandinavian; compare Swedish dialect *klumsig* numb] > 'clumsily *adv* > 'clumsiness *n*

clung (klʌŋ) *vb* the past tense and past participle of **cling**

Cluniac ('kluːnɪˌæk) *adj* of or relating to a reformed Benedictine order founded at the French town of Cluny in 910

clunk (klʌŋk) *n* **1** a blow or the sound of a blow **2** a dull metallic sound ▷ *vb* **3** to make or cause to make such a sound [C19: of imitative origin]

clunker ('klʌŋkə) *n informal* **1** *chiefly US* a dilapidated old car or other machine **2** something that fails: *the novel's last line is a clunker*

clunky ('klʌŋkɪ) *adj* clunkier, clunkiest **1** making a clunking noise **2** *informal* ponderously ungraceful or unsophisticated: *clunky boots* **3** awkward or unsophisticated: *then you guffaw at clunky dialogue*

Cluny ('kluːnɪ; *French* klyni) *n* a town in E central France: reformed Benedictine order founded here in 910; important religious and cultural centre in the Middle Ages. Pop: 4376 (1999)

cluster ('klʌstə) *n* **1** a number of things growing, fastened, or occurring close together **2** a number of persons or things grouped together ▷ *vb* **3** to gather or be gathered in clusters [Old English *clyster*; related to Low German *Kluster*; see CLOD, CLOT] > 'clustered *adj* > 'clustery *adj*

clutch¹ (klʌtʃ) *vb* **1** (*tr*) to seize with or as if with hands or claws **2** (*tr*) to grasp or hold firmly **3** (*intr*; usually foll by *at*) to attempt to get hold or possession (of) ▷ *n* **4** a device that enables two revolving shafts to be joined or disconnected as required, esp one that transmits the drive from the engine to the gearbox in a vehicle **5** a device for holding fast **6** a firm grasp **7** a hand, claw, or talon in the act of clutching: *in the clutches of a bear* **8** (*often plural*) power or control: *in the clutches of the Mafia* [Old English *clyccan*; related to Old Frisian *kletsie* spear, Swedish *klyka* clasp, fork]

clutch² (klʌtʃ) *n* **1** a hatch of eggs laid by a particular bird or laid in a single nest **2** a brood of chickens **3** *informal* a group, bunch, or cluster ▷ *vb* **4** (*tr*) to hatch (chickens) [c17 (Northern English dialect) *cletch*, from Old Norse *klekja* to hatch]

Clutha ('kluːθə) *n* a river in New Zealand, the longest river in South Island; rising in the Southern Alps it flows southeast to the Pacific. Length: 338 km (210 miles)

clutter ('klʌtə) *vb* **1** (*usually tr*; often foll by *up*) to strew or amass (objects) in a disorderly manner **2** (*intr*) to move about in a bustling manner ▷ *n* **3** a disordered heap or mass of objects **4** a state of disorder **5** unwanted echoes that confuse the observation of signals on a radar screen [c15 *clotter*, from *clotteren* to CLOT]

Clwyd ('kluːɪd) *n* a former county in NE Wales, formed in 1974 from Flintshire, most of Denbighshire, and part of Merionethshire; replaced in 1996 by Flintshire, Denbighshire, Wrexham county borough, and part of Conwy county borough

Clyde (klaɪd) *n* **1** Firth of Clyde an inlet of the Atlantic in SW Scotland. Length: 103 km (64 miles) **2** a river in S Scotland, rising in South Lanarkshire and flowing northwest to the Firth of Clyde: formerly extensive shipyards. Length: 170 km (106 miles)

Clydebank (ˌklaɪd'bæŋk, 'klaɪdˌbæŋk) *n* a town in W Scotland, in West Dunbartonshire on the north bank of the River Clyde. Pop: 29 858 (2001)

Clydesdale ('klaɪdzˌdeɪl) *n* a heavy powerful breed of carthorse, originally from Scotland

clypeus ('klɪpɪəs) *n*, *pl* clypei ('klɪpɪˌaɪ) a cuticular plate on the head of some insects between the labrum and the frons [c19: from New Latin, from Latin *clipeus* round shield] > 'clypeal *adj* > clypeate ('klɪpɪˌeɪt) *adj*

Clytemnestra or **Clytaemnestra** (ˌklaɪtɪm'nɛstrə) *n* Greek myth the wife of Agamemnon, whom she killed on his return from the Trojan War

cm *symbol for* centimetre

Cm the chemical symbol for curium

CM *abbreviation* Member of the Order of Canada

Cmdr *military abbreviation* Commander

CMEA *abbreviation* Council for Mutual Economic Assistance. See **Comecon**

CMG *abbreviation* Companion of St Michael and St George (a British title)

CMOS ('siːmɒs) *adj acronym computing* complementary metal oxide silicon: *CMOS memory*

CMV *abbreviation* cytomegalovirus

CNAA *abbreviation* (in Britain) the Council for National Academic Awards: a former degree-awarding body separate from the universities

CNAR *abbreviation* compound net annual rate

CND *abbreviation* (in Britain) Campaign for Nuclear Disarmament

CNG *abbreviation* compressed natural gas

CNN *abbreviation* Cable Network News

Cnossus ('nɒsəs, 'knɒs-) *n* a variant spelling of **Knossos**

CNR *abbreviation* Canadian National Railways

Cnut (kə'njuːt) *n* a variant spelling of **Canute**

Co¹ the chemical symbol for cobalt

Co² *abbreviation* County

Co³ or **co** *abbreviation* **1** (*esp in names of business organizations*) Company **2** and co (kəʊ) *informal* and the rest of them: *Harold and co*

CO *abbreviation* **1** Commanding Officer **2** conscientious objector

co- *prefix* **1** together; joint or jointly; mutual or mutually: *coproduction* **2** indicating partnership or equality: *cofounder; copilot* **3** to the same or a similar degree: *coextend* **4** (in mathematics and astronomy) of the complement of an angle: *cosecant; codeclination* [from Latin, reduced form of COM-]

c/o *abbreviation* **1** care of **2** book-keeping carried over

coach (kəʊtʃ) *n* **1** a vehicle for several passengers, used for transport over long distances, sightseeing, etc **2** a large four-wheeled enclosed carriage, usually horse-drawn **3** a railway carriage carrying passengers **4** a trainer or instructor: *a drama coach* **5** a tutor who prepares students for examinations ▷ *vb* **6** to give tuition or instruction to (a pupil) **7** (*tr*) to transport in a bus or coach [c16: from French *coche*, from Hungarian *kocsi szekér* wagon of Kocs, village in Hungary where coaches were first made; in the sense: to teach, probably from the idea that the instructor carried his pupils] > 'coacher *n*

coach-built *adj* (of a vehicle) having specially built bodywork > 'coach-ˌbuilder *n*

coach class *n* the US and Canadian name for **economy class**. See **economy** (sense 6)

coachman ('kəʊtʃmən) *n*, *pl* -men the driver of a coach or carriage

coachwork ('kəʊtʃˌwɜːk) *n* **1** the design and manufacture of car bodies **2** the body of a car

coadjutor (kəʊ'ædʒʊtə) *n* **1** a bishop appointed as assistant to a diocesan bishop **2** *rare* an assistant [c15: via Old French from Latin *co-* together + *adjūtor* helper, from *adjūtāre* to assist, from *juvāre* to help]

coagulate *vb* (kəʊ'ægjʊˌleɪt) **1** to cause (a fluid, such as blood) to change into a soft semisolid mass or (of such a fluid) to change into such a mass; clot; curdle ▷ *n* (kəʊ'ægjʊlɪt, -ˌleɪt) **2** the solid or semisolid substance produced by coagulation [c16: from Latin *coāgulāre* to make (a liquid) curdle, from *coāgulum* rennet, from *cōgere* to drive together] > coˌaguˈlation *n* > coagulative (kəʊ'ægjʊlətɪv) *adj*

coagulation factor *n med* another name for **clotting factor**

Coahuila (*Spanish* koa'wila) *n* a state of N Mexico: mainly plateau, crossed by several mountain ranges that contain rich mineral resources. Capital: Saltillo. Pop: 2 295 808 (2000). Area: 151 571 sq km (59 112 sq miles)

coal (kəʊl) *n* **1** a combustible compact black or dark-brown rock formed from compaction of layers of partially decomposed vegetation: a fuel and a source of coke, coal gas, and coal tar **b** (*as modifier*): *coal cellar; coal merchant; coal mine; coal dust* **2** one or more lumps of coal **3** short for **charcoal** **4** coals to Newcastle something supplied where it is already plentiful ▷ *vb* **5** to take in, provide with, or turn into coal [Old English *col*; related to Old Norse *kol*, Old High German *kolo*, Old Irish *gūal*] > 'coaly *adj*

coaler ('kəʊlə) *n* a ship, train, etc, used to carry or supply coal

coalesce (ˌkəʊə'lɛs) *vb* (*intr*) to unite or come together in one body or mass; merge; fuse; blend [c16: from Latin *coalēscere* from *co-* + *alēscere* to increase, from *alere* to nourish] > ˌcoa'lescence *n* > ˌcoa'lescent *adj*

coalface ('kəʊlˌfeɪs) *n* the exposed seam of coal in a mine

coalfield ('kəʊlˌfiːld) *n* an area rich in deposits of coal

coalfish ('kəʊlˌfɪʃ) *n*, *pl* -fish or -fishes a dark-coloured gadoid food fish, *Pollachius virens*, occurring in northern seas. Also called (*Brit*): saithe, coley

coal gas *n* a mixture of gases produced by the distillation of bituminous coal and used for heating and lighting: consists mainly of hydrogen, methane, and carbon monoxide

coalition (ˌkəʊə'lɪʃən) *n* **1 a** an alliance or union between groups, factions, or parties, esp for some temporary and specific reason **b** (*as modifier*): *a coalition government* **2** a fusion or merging into one body or mass [c17: from Medieval Latin *coalitiō*, from Latin *coalēscere* to COALESCE] > ˌcoa'litionist or ˌcoa'litioner *n*

Coal Measures *pl n* the Coal Measures a series of coal-bearing rocks formed in the upper Carboniferous period; the uppermost series of the Carboniferous system

coal miner's lung *n* an informal name for **anthracosis**

coal scuttle *n* a domestic metal container for coal

coal tar *n* a black tar, produced by the distillation of bituminous coal, that can be further distilled to yield benzene, toluene, xylene, anthracene, phenol, etc

coal tit *n* a small European songbird, *Parus ater*, having a black head with a white patch on the nape: family *Paridae* (tits)

coaming ('kəʊmɪŋ) *n* a raised frame around the cockpit or hatchway of a vessel for keeping out water [c17: of unknown origin]

coarse (kɔːs) *adj* **1** rough in texture, structure, etc; not fine: *coarse sand* **2** lacking refinement or taste; indelicate; vulgar: *coarse jokes* **3** of inferior quality; not pure or choice **4** (of a metal) not refined **5** (of a screw) having widely spaced threads [c14: of unknown origin] > **'coarsely** *adv* > **'coarseness** *n*

coarse fish *n* a freshwater fish that is not a member of the salmon family > **coarse fishing** *n*

coarsen ('kɔːsᵊn) *vb* to make or become coarse

coast (kəʊst) *n* **1** the line or zone where the land meets the sea or some other large expanse of water. Related adj: **littoral 2** *Brit* the seaside **3** *US* **a** a slope down which a sledge may slide **b** the act or an instance of sliding down a slope **4** the coast is clear *informal* the obstacles or dangers are gone ▷ *vb* **5** to move or cause to move by momentum or force of gravity **6** (*intr*) to proceed without great effort: *to coast to victory* **7** to sail along (a coast) [c13: from Old French *coste* coast, slope, from Latin *costa* side, rib] > **'coastal** *adj*

coaster ('kəʊstə) *n* **1** *Brit* a vessel or trader engaged in coastal commerce **2** a small tray, sometimes on wheels, for holding a decanter, wine bottle, etc **3** a person or thing that coasts **4** a protective disc or mat for glasses or bottles **5** *US* short for **roller coaster**

Coaster ('kəʊstə) *n* a person from the West Coast of the South Island, New Zealand

coastguard ('kəʊst,gɑːd) *n* **1** a maritime force which aids shipping, saves lives at sea, prevents smuggling, etc **2** Also called: **coastguardsman** a member of such a force

coastline ('kəʊst,laɪn) *n* the outline of a coast, esp when seen from the sea, or the land adjacent to it

Coast Mountains *pl n* a mountain range in Canada, on the Pacific coast of British Columbia. Highest peak: Mount Waddington, 4043 m (13 266 ft)

coat (kəʊt) *n* **1** an outdoor garment with sleeves, covering the body from the shoulder to waist, knee, or foot **2** any similar garment, esp one forming the top to a suit **3** a layer that covers or conceals a surface: *a coat of dust* **4** the hair, wool, or fur of an animal ▷ *vb* **5** (*tr*; often foll by *with*) to cover (with) a layer or covering **6** (*tr*) to provide with a coat [c16: from Old French *cote* of Germanic origin; compare Old Saxon *kotta*, Old High German *kozzo*]

Coates (kəʊts) *n* **Joseph Gordon**. 1878–1943, New Zealand statesman; prime minister of New Zealand (1925–28)

coat hanger *n* a curved piece of wood, wire, plastic, etc, fitted with a hook and used to hang up clothes

coati (kəʊ'ɑːtɪ), **coati-mondi** *or* **coati-mundi** (kəʊ,ɑːtɪ'mʌndɪ) *n, pl* **-tis** *or* **-dis** any omnivorous mammal of the genera *Nasua* and *Nasuella*, of Central and South America: family *Procyonidae*, order *Carnivora* (carnivores). They are related to but larger than the raccoons, having a long flexible snout and a brindled coat [c17: from Portuguese *coati*, from Tupi, literally: belt-nosed, from *cua* belt + *tim* nose]

coating ('kəʊtɪŋ) *n* **1** a layer or film spread over a surface for protection or decoration **2** a heavy fabric suitable for coats

coat of arms *n* the heraldic bearings of a person, family, or corporation

coat of mail *n* a protective garment made of linked metal rings (mail) or of overlapping metal plates; hauberk

coat-tail *n* the long tapering tails at the back of a man's tailed coat

coauthor (kəʊ'ɔːθə) *n* **1** a person who shares the writing of a book, article, etc, with another ▷ *vb* **2** (*tr*) to be the joint author of (a book, article, etc)

coax (kəʊks) *vb* **1** to seek to manipulate or persuade (someone) by tenderness, flattery, pleading, etc **2** (*tr*) to obtain by persistent coaxing **3** (*tr*) to work on or tend (something) carefully and patiently so as to make it

function as one desires: *he coaxed the engine into starting* [c16: verb formed from obsolete noun *cokes* fool, of unknown origin] > **'coaxer** *n* > **'coaxingly** *adv*

coaxial (kəʊ'æksɪəl) *or* **coaxal** (kəʊ'æksᵊl) *adj* **1** having or being mounted on a common axis **2** *geometry* (of a set of circles) having all the centres on a straight line **3** *electronics* formed from, using, or connected to a coaxial cable

coaxial cable *n* a cable consisting of an inner insulated core of stranded or solid wire surrounded by an outer insulated flexible wire braid, used esp as a transmission line for radio-frequency signals. Often shortened to: **coax** (kəʊ'æks)

cob (kɒb) *n* **1** a male swan **2** a thickset short-legged type of riding and draught horse **3** short for **corncob**, **corncob pipe**, **cobnut 4** *Brit* another name for **hazel** (sense 1) **5** a small rounded lump or heap of coal, ore, etc **6** *Brit* & *NZ* a building material consisting of a mixture of clay and chopped straw **7** Also called: **cob loaf** *Brit* a round loaf of bread [c15: of uncertain origin; probably related to Icelandic *kobbi* seal; see **CUB**]

cobalt ('kəʊbɔːlt) *n* a brittle hard silvery-white element that is a ferromagnetic metal: occurs principally in cobaltite and smaltite and is widely used in alloys. The radioisotope **cobalt-60**, with a half-life of 5.3 years, is used in radiotherapy and as a tracer. Symbol: Co; atomic no: 27; atomic wt: 58.93320; valency: 2 or 3; relative density: 8.9; melting pt: 1495°C; boiling pt: 2928°C [c17: German *Kobalt*, from Middle High German *kobolt* goblin; from the miners' belief that malicious goblins placed it in the silver ore]

cobalt blue *n* **1** Also called: **Thénard's blue** any greenish-blue pigment containing cobalt aluminate, usually made by heating cobaltous sulphate, aluminium oxide, and phosphoric acid together **2 a** a deep blue to greenish-blue colour **b** (*as adjective*): *a cobalt-blue car*

cobalt bomb *n* **1** a cobalt-60 device used in radiotherapy **2** a nuclear weapon consisting of a hydrogen bomb encased in cobalt, which releases large quantities of radioactive cobalt-60 into the atmosphere

cobber ('kɒbə) *n Austral* & *NZ informal* a friend; mate: used as a term of address to males [c19: from dialect *cob* to take a liking to someone]

Cobbett ('kɒbɪt) *n* **William**. 1763–1835, English journalist and social reformer; founded *The Political Register* (1802); author of *Rural Rides* (1830)

cobble[1] ('kɒbᵊl) *n* **1** short for **cobblestone** ▷ *vb* **2** (*tr*) to pave (a road) with cobblestones [c15 (in *cobblestone*): from **COB**]

cobble[2] ('kɒbᵊl) *vb* (*tr*) **1** to make or mend (shoes) **2** to put together clumsily [c15: back formation from **COBBLER**[1]]

cobbler[1] ('kɒblə) *n* a person who makes or mends shoes [c13 (as surname): of unknown origin]

cobbler[2] ('kɒblə) *n* **1** a sweetened iced drink, usually made from fruit and wine or liqueur **2** *chiefly US* a hot dessert made of fruit covered with a rich cakelike crust [c19: (for sense 1) perhaps shortened from *cobbler's punch*; (for both senses) compare *cobble* (vb)]

cobblers ('kɒbləz) *Brit slang pl n* rubbish; nonsense [c20: from rhyming slang *cobblers' awls* balls]

cobblestone ('kɒbᵊl,stəʊn) *n* a rounded stone used for paving. Sometimes shortened to: **cobble**

Cobden ('kɒbdən) *n* **Richard**. 1804–65, British economist and statesman: with John Bright a leader of the successful campaign to abolish the Corn Laws (1846)

cobelligerent (,kəʊbɪ'lɪdʒərənt) *n* a country fighting in a war on the side of another country

Cobham ('kɒbəm) *n* **Lord Cobham** title of Sir John Oldcastle. See **Oldcastle**

Coblenz (*German* 'koːblɛnts) *n* a variant spelling of **Koblenz**

cobnut ('kɒb,nʌt) *or* **cob** (cɒb) *n* another name for a **hazelnut** [c16: from earlier *cobylle nut*; see **COBBLE**[1], **NUT**]

COBOL *or* **Cobol** ('kəʊ,bɒl) *n* a high-level computer programming language designed for general commercial use [c20: *co(mmon) b(usiness) o(riented) l(anguage)*]

cobra ('kəʊbrə) *n* any highly venomous elapid snake of

the genus *Naja*, such as *N. naja* (**Indian cobra**), of tropical Africa and Asia. When alarmed they spread the skin of the neck region into a hood [c16: from Portuguese *cobra (de capello)* snake (with a hood), from Latin *colubra* snake]

COBRA ('kəʊbrə) *n acronym for* (in the UK) Cabinet Office Briefing Room A: the civil contingencies committee that leads the UK's responses to crises such as terrorist attacks and epidemics

Coburg ('kəʊbɜːg; *German* 'koːbʊrk) *n* a city in E Germany, in N Bavaria. Pop: 42 257 (2003 est)

cobweb ('kɒb,wɛb) *n* **1** a web spun by certain spiders, esp those of the family *Theridiidae*, often found in the corners of disused rooms **2** a single thread of such a web **3** something like a cobweb, as in its flimsiness or ability to trap [c14 *cob*, from *coppe*, from Old English *(ātor)coppe* spider; related to Middle Dutch *koppe* spider, Swedish (dialect) *etterkoppa*] > 'cob,webbed *adj* > 'cob,webby *adj*

cobwebs ('kɒb,wɛbz) *pl n* **1** mustiness, confusion, or obscurity **2** *informal* stickiness of the eyelids experienced upon first awakening

coca ('kəʊkə) *n* **1** either of two shrubs, *Erythroxylon coca* or *E. truxiuense*, native to the Andes: family *Erythroxylaceae* **2** the dried leaves of these shrubs and related plants, which contain cocaine and are chewed by the peoples of the Andes for their stimulating effects [c17: from Spanish, from Quechuan *kúka*]

Coca-Cola (,kəʊkə'kəʊlə) *n* **1** *trademark* a carbonated soft drink flavoured with coca leaves, cola nuts, caramel, etc **2** (*modifier*) denoting the spread of American culture and values to other parts of the world: *Coca-Cola generation*

cocaine *or* **cocain** (kə'keɪn) *n* an addictive narcotic drug derived from coca leaves or synthesized, used medicinally as a topical anaesthetic. Formula: $C_{17}H_{21}NO_4$ [c19: from COCA + -INE¹]

coccus ('kɒkəs) *n*, *pl* **-ci** (-saɪ) any spherical or nearly spherical bacterium, such as a staphylococcus [c18: from New Latin, from Greek *kokkos* berry, grain] > 'coccoid, 'coccal *or* coccic ('kɒksɪk) *adj*

coccyx ('kɒksɪks) *n*, *pl* **coccyges** (kɒk'saɪdʒiːz) a small triangular bone at the end of the spinal column in man and some apes, representing a vestigial tail [c17: from New Latin, from Greek *kokkux* cuckoo, of imitative origin; from the likeness of the bone to a cuckoo's beak] > coccygeal (kɒk'sɪdʒɪəl) *adj*

Cochin ('kəʊtʃɪn, 'kɒtʃ-) *n* **1** a region and former state of SW India: part of Kerala state since 1956 **2** a port in SW India, on the Malabar Coast: the first European settlement in India, founded by Vasco da Gama in 1502: shipbuilding, engineering. Pop: 596 473 (2001). Local official name: **Kochi** **3** a large breed of domestic fowl, with dense plumage and feathered legs, that originated in Cochin China

Cochin China *n* a former French colony of Indochina (1862–1948): now the part of Vietnam that lies south of Phan Thiet

cochineal (,kɒtʃɪ'niːl, 'kɒtʃɪ,niːl) *n* **1** Also called: **cochineal insect** a Mexican homopterous insect, *Dactylopius coccus*, that feeds on cacti **2** a crimson substance obtained from the crushed bodies of these insects, used for colouring food and for dyeing **3** the colour of this dye [c16: from Old Spanish *cochinilla*, from Latin *coccineus* scarlet-coloured, from *coccum* cochineal *kermes*, from Greek *kokkos* kermes berry]

Cochise (kəʊ'tʃiːs, -'tʃiːz) *n* died 1874, Apache Indian chief

cochlea ('kɒklɪə) *n*, *pl* **-leae** (-lɪ,iː) the spiral tube, shaped like a snail's shell, that forms part of the internal ear, converting sound vibrations into nerve impulses [c16: from Latin: snail, spiral, from Greek *kokhlias*; probably related to Greek *konkhē* CONCH] > 'cochlear *adj*

cochlear implant ('kɒklɪə) *n* a device that stimulates the acoustic nerve in the inner ear in order to produce some form of hearing in people who are deaf from inner ear disease

cochleate ('kɒklɪ,eɪt, -lɪɪt) *or* **cochleated** ('kɒklɪ,eɪtɪd, adj *biology* shaped like a snail's shell; spirally twisted

cock¹ (kɒk) *n* **1** the male of the domestic fowl **2 a** any other male bird **b** the male of certain other animals,

such as the lobster **c** (*as modifier*): *a cock sparrow* **3** short for **stopcock, weathercock** **4** a taboo slang word for **penis** **5 a** the hammer of a firearm **b** its position when the firearm is ready to be discharged **6** *Brit informal* a friend, mate, or fellow **7** a jaunty or significant tilting or turning upwards: *a cock of the head* ▷ *vb* **8** (*tr*) to set the firing pin, hammer, or breech block of (a firearm) so that a pull on the trigger will release it and thus fire the weapon **9** (*tr*; sometimes foll by *up*) to raise in an alert or jaunty manner **10** (*intr*) to stick or stand up conspicuously ▷ See also **cockup** [Old English *cocc* (referring to the male fowl); the development of c15 sense spout, tap, and other transferred senses is not clear), ultimately of imitative origin; related to Old Norse *kokkr*, French *coq*, Late Latin *coccus*]

cock² (kɒk) *n* **1** a small, cone-shaped heap of hay, straw, etc ▷ *vb* **2** (*tr*) to stack (hay, straw, etc) in such heaps [c14 (in Old English, *cocc* is attested in place names): perhaps of Scandinavian origin; compare Norwegian *kok*, Danish dialect *kok*]

cockabully (,kɒkə'bʊlɪ) *n*, *pl* **-lies** any of several small freshwater fish of New Zealand [from Māori *kokopu*]

cockade (kɒ'keɪd) *n* a feather or ribbon worn on military headwear [c18: changed from earlier *cockard*, from French *cocarde*, feminine of *cocard* arrogant, strutting, from *coq* COCK¹] > cock'aded *adj*

cock-a-doodle-doo (,kɒkə,duːdəl'duː) *interj* an imitation or representation of a cock crowing

cock-a-hoop *adj* (*usually postpositive*) **1** in very high spirits **2** boastful **3** askew; confused [c16: perhaps from the phrase *to set the cock a hoop* to live prodigally, literally: to put a cock on a *hoop*, a full measure of ale]

cockalorum (,kɒkə'lɔːrəm) *n* **1** a self-important little man **2** bragging talk; crowing [c18: from COCK¹ + *-alorum*, a variant of Latin genitive plural ending *-orum*; perhaps intended to suggest: the cock of all cocks]

cockamamie (,kɒkə'meɪmɪ) *adj slang, chiefly US* ridiculous or nonsensical: *a cockamamie story* [c20: in an earlier sense: a paper transfer, prob. a variant of DECALCOMANIA]

cock-and-bull story *n informal* an obviously improbable story, esp a boastful one or one used as an excuse

cockatoo (,kɒkə'tuː, 'kɒkə,tuː) *n*, *pl* **-toos** **1** any of various parrots of the genus *Kakatoe* and related genera, such as *K. galerita* (**sulphur-crested cockatoo**), of Australia and New Guinea. They have an erectile crest and most of them are light-coloured **2** *Austral & NZ* a small farmer or settler **3** *Austral informal* a lookout during some illegal activity [c17: from Dutch *kaketoe*, from Malay *kakatua*]

cockatrice ('kɒkətrɪs, -,traɪs) *n* **1** a legendary monster, part snake and part cock, that could kill with a glance **2** another name for **basilisk** (sense 1) [c14: from Old French *cocatris*, from Medieval Latin *cocatrix*, from Late Latin *calcātrix* trampler, tracker (translating Greek *ikhneumon* ICHNEUMON), from Latin *calcāre* to tread, from *calx* heel]

cockboat ('kɒk,bəʊt) *or* **cockleboat** ('kɒkəl,bəʊt) *n* any small boat [c15 *cokbote*, perhaps ultimately from Late Latin *caudica* dug-out canoe, from Latin *caudex* tree trunk]

cockchafer ('kɒk,tʃeɪfə) *n* any of various Old World scarabaeid beetles, esp *Melolontha melolontha* of Europe, whose larvae feed on crops and grasses. Also called: May beetle, May bug [c18: from COCK¹ + CHAFER]

Cockcroft ('kɒk,krɒft) *n* Sir **John Douglas**. 1897–1967, English nuclear physicist. With E. T. S. Walton, he produced the first artificial transmutation of an atomic nucleus (1932) and shared the Nobel prize for physics 1951

cockcrow ('kɒk,krəʊ) *n* daybreak

cocked hat *n* **1** a hat with opposing brims turned up and caught together in order to give two points (bicorn) or three points (tricorn) **2 knock into a cocked hat** *slang* to outdo or defeat

Cocker ('kɒkə) *n* **1 Edward**. 1631–75, English arithmetician **2 according to cocker** reliable or reliably; correct or correctly

cockerel ('kɒkərəl, 'kɒkrəl) *n* a young domestic cock, usually less than a year old [c15: diminutive of COCK¹]

Cockerell ('kɒkərəl) *n* Sir **Christopher Sydney**. 1910–99,

British engineer, who invented the hovercraft

cocker spaniel n a small compact breed of spaniel having sleek silky fur, a domed head, and long fringed ears [c19 *cocker*, from *cocking* hunting woodcocks]

cockeyed ('kɒk,aɪd) *adj informal* **1** afflicted with cross-eye, squint, or any other visible abnormality of the eyes **2** appearing to be physically or logically abnormal, absurd, etc; crooked; askew: *cockeyed ideas* **3** drunk

cockfight ('kɒk,faɪt) n a fight between two gamecocks fitted with sharp metal spurs > 'cock,fighting n

cockhorse (,kɒk'hɔːs) n another name for **rocking horse, hobbyhorse**

cockieleekie, cockyleeky or **cock-a-leekie** ('kɒkə'liːkɪ) n *Scot* a soup made from a fowl boiled with leeks

cockle¹ ('kɒkəl) n **1** any sand-burrowing bivalve mollusc of the family *Cardiidae*, esp *Cardium edule* (**edible cockle**) of Europe, typically having a rounded shell with radiating ribs **2** any of certain similar or related molluscs **3** short for **cockleshell** (sense 1) **4** a wrinkle or puckering, as in cloth or paper **5** cockles of one's heart one's deepest feelings (esp in the phrase **warm the cockles of one's heart**) ▷ vb **6** to contract or cause to contract into wrinkles [c14: from Old French *coquille* shell, from Latin *conchȳlium* shellfish, from Greek *konkhulion*, diminutive of *konkhule* mussel; see CONCH]

cockle² ('kɒkəl) n any of several plants, esp the corn cockle, that grow as weeds in cornfields

cockleshell ('kɒkəl,ʃɛl) n **1** the shell of the cockle **2** any of the valves of the shells of certain other bivalve molluscs, such as the scallop **3** any small light boat

cockney ('kɒknɪ) n **1** (*often capital*) a native of London, esp of the working class born in the East End, speaking a characteristic dialect of English. Traditionally defined as someone born within the sound of the bells of St Mary-le-Bow church **2** the urban dialect of London or its East End ▷ *adj* **3** characteristic of cockneys or their dialect of English [c14: from *cokeney*, literally: cock's egg, later applied contemptuously to townsmen, from *cokene*, genitive plural of *cok* COCK¹ + *ey* EGG¹] > 'cockneyish *adj* > 'cockney,ism n

cock of the walk n *informal* a person who asserts himself in a strutting pompous way

cockpit ('kɒk,pɪt) n **1** the compartment in a small aircraft in which the pilot, crew, and sometimes the passengers sit. See **flight deck** (sense 1) **2** the driver's compartment in a racing car **3** *nautical* an enclosed or recessed area towards the stern of a small vessel from which it is steered **4** the site of numerous battles or campaigns **5** an enclosure used for cockfights

cockroach ('kɒk,rəʊtʃ) n any insect of the suborder *Blattodea* (or *Blattaria*), such as *Blatta orientalis* (**oriental cockroach** or **black beetle**): order *Dictyoptera*. They have an oval flattened body with long antennae and biting mouthparts and are common household pests [c17: from Spanish *cucaracha*, of obscure origin]

cockscomb or **coxcomb** ('kɒks,kəʊm) n **1** the comb of a domestic cock **2** an amaranthaceous garden or pot plant, *Celosia cristata*, with yellow, crimson, or purple feathery plumelike flowers in a broad spike resembling the comb of a cock **3** *informal* a conceited dandy

cockshy ('kɒk,ʃaɪ) n, *pl* -shies *Brit* **1** a target aimed at in throwing games **2** the throw itself. Often shortened to **shy** [c18: from *shying* (throwing objects at) a cock, which was given as a prize to the person who hit it]

cocksure (,kɒk'ʃʊə, -'ʃɔː) *adj* overconfident; arrogant [c16: of uncertain origin] > ,cock'sureness n

cocktail ('kɒk,teɪl) n **1 a** any mixed drink with a spirit base, usually drunk before meals **b** (*as modifier*): *the cocktail hour* **2** an appetizer of seafood, mixed fruits, etc **3** any combination of diverse elements, esp one considered potent **4** (*modifier*) appropriate for formal occasions: *a cocktail dress* [c19: of unknown origin]

cockup ('kɒk,ʌp) n **1** *Brit slang* something done badly ▷ vb **cock up** (*tr, adverb*) **2** (of an animal) to raise (its ears), esp in an alert manner **3** *Brit slang* to botch

cocky¹ ('kɒkɪ) *adj* **cockier, cockiest** excessively proud of oneself > 'cockily *adv* > 'cockiness n

cocky² ('kɒkɪ) n, *pl* **cockies** *Austral informal* **1** short for **cockatoo** (sense 2) **2** a farmer whose farm is regarded as

small or of little account

coco ('kəʊkəʊ) n, *pl* -cos short for **coconut, coconut palm** [c16: from Portuguese *coco* grimace; from the likeness of the three holes of the nut to a face]

cocoa ('kəʊkəʊ) or **cacao** n **1 a** powder made from cocoa beans after they have been roasted, ground, and freed from most of their fatty oil **2 a** hot or cold drink made from cocoa and milk or water **3 a** a light to moderate brown colour **b** (*as adjective*): *cocoa paint* [c18: altered from CACAO]

cocoa bean n the seed of the cacao

cocoa butter n a yellowish-white waxy solid that is obtained from cocoa beans and used for confectionery, soap, etc

coconut or **cocoanut** ('kəʊkə,nʌt) n **1** the fruit of the coconut palm, consisting of a thick fibrous oval husk inside which is a thin hard shell enclosing edible white meat. The hollow centre is filled with a milky fluid (**coconut milk**) **2** the meat of the coconut, often shredded and used in cakes, curries, etc [c18: see COCO]

coconut matting n a form of coarse matting made from the fibrous husk of the coconut

coconut oil n the fatty oil obtained from the meat of the coconut and used for making soap, cosmetics, etc

coconut palm n a tall palm tree, *Cocos nucifera*, widely planted throughout the tropics, having coconuts as fruits. Also called: **coco palm, coconut tree**

cocoon (kə'kuːn) n **1 a** silky protective envelope secreted by silkworms and certain other insect larvae, in which the pupae develop **2** a protective spray covering used as a seal on machinery **3** a cosy warm covering ▷ vb **4** (tr) to wrap in a cocoon [c17: from French *cocon*, from Provençal *coucoun* eggshell, from *coco* shell, from Latin *coccum* kermes berry, from Greek *kokkos* grain, seed, berry; compare COCCUS]

cocopan ('kəʊkəʊ,pæn) n (in South Africa) a small wagon running on narrow-gauge railway lines used in mines. Also called: **hopper** [c20: from Zulu *'ngkumbana* short truck]

Cocos Islands ('kəʊkɒs, 'kəʊkəs) *pl* n a group of 27 coral islands in the Indian Ocean, southwest of Java: a Territory of Australia since 1955. Pop: 621 (2001). Area: 13 sq km (5 sq miles). Also called: **Keeling Islands**

cocotte (kəʊ'kɒt, kə-; *French* kɔkɔt) n **1** a small fireproof dish in which individual portions of food are cooked and served **2** a prostitute or promiscuous woman [c19: from French, from nursery word for a hen, feminine of *coq* COCK¹]

Cocteau (*French* kɔkto) n **Jean** (ʒã). 1889–1963, French dramatist, novelist, poet, critic, designer, and film director. His works include the novel *Les Enfants terribles* (1929) and the play *La Machine infernale* (1934)

cod¹ (kɒd) n, *pl* **cod** or **cods** **1** any of the gadoid food fishes of the genus *Gadus*, esp *G. morhua* (or *G. callarias*), which occurs in the North Atlantic and has a long body with three rounded dorsal fins: family *Gadidae* **2** *Austral* any of various unrelated Australian fish, such as the Murray cod [c13: probably of Germanic origin; compare Old High German *cutte*]

cod² (kɒd) n **1** *Brit & US dialect* a pod or husk **2** an obsolete word for **scrotum** [Old English *codd* husk, bag; related to Old Norse *koddi*, Danish *kodde*]

cod³ (kɒd) vb **cods, codding, codded** (tr) **1** *Brit & Irish slang* to make fun of; tease **2** *Brit & Irish slang* to play a trick on; fool ▷ n **3** *Brit & Irish slang* a hoax or trick [c19: perhaps from earlier *cod* a fool, perhaps shortened from CODGER]

Cod n **Cape Cod** See **Cape Cod**

COD *abbreviation* **1** cash on delivery **2** (in the US) collect on delivery

coda ('kəʊdə) n **1** *music* the final, sometimes inessential, part of a musical structure **2** a concluding part of a literary work, esp a summary at the end of a novel of further developments in the lives of the characters [c18: from Italian: tail, from Latin *cauda*]

cod-act vb (intr) *Irish informal* to play tricks; fool [from COD³ + ACT]

coddle ('kɒdəl) vb (tr) **1** to treat with indulgence **2** to cook (something, esp eggs) in water just below the boiling point [c16: of obscure origin; perhaps related to

CAUDLE] > 'coddler n

code (kəʊd) n **1** a system of letters or symbols, and rules for their association by means of which information can be represented or communicated for reasons of secrecy, brevity, etc: *binary code; Morse code.* See also **genetic code** **2** a message in code **3** a symbol used in a code **4** a conventionalized set of principles, rules, or expectations: *a code of behaviour* **5** a system of letters or digits used for identification or selection purposes > vb (tr) **6** to translate, transmit, or arrange into a code [C14: from French, from Latin *cōdex* book, CODEX]

codeine ('kəʊdiːn) n a white crystalline alkaloid prepared mainly from morphine and having a similar but milder action. It is used as an analgesic, an antidiarrhoeal, and to relieve coughing. Formula: $C_{18}H_{21}NO_3$ [C19: from Greek *kōdeia* head of a poppy, from *kōos* hollow place + -INE²]

co-dependency (,kəʊdɪ'pɛndənsɪ) n *psychol* a state of mutual dependence between two people, esp when one partner relies emotionally on supporting and caring for the other partner > ,co-de'pendent *adj, n*

Co Derry *abbreviation* County Londonderry

codex ('kəʊdɛks) n, pl codices (,kəʊdɪ,siːz, 'kɒdɪ-) **1** a volume, in book form, of manuscripts of an ancient text **2** *obsolete* a legal code [C16: from Latin: tree trunk, wooden block, book]

codfish ('kɒd,fɪʃ) n, pl -fish or -fishes a cod, esp *Gadus morhua*

codger ('kɒdʒə) n *informal* a man, esp an old or eccentric one: a term of affection or mild derision (often in the phrase **old codger**) [C18: probably variant of CADGER]

codicil ('kɒdɪsɪl) n **1** *law* a supplement modifying a will or revoking some provision of it **2** an additional provision; appendix [C15: from Late Latin *cōdicillus*, literally: a little book, diminutive of CODEX] > codicillary (,kɒdɪ'sɪlərɪ) *adj*

codify ('kəʊdɪ,faɪ, 'kɒ-) vb -fies, -fying, -fied (tr) to organize or collect together (laws, rules, procedures, etc) into a system or code > 'codi,fier n > codification (,kəʊdɪfɪ'keɪʃən, ,kɒ-) n

codling¹ ('kɒdlɪŋ) or **codlin** ('kɒdlɪn) n **1** any of several varieties of long tapering apples used for cooking **2** any unripe apple [C15 *querdlyng*, of uncertain origin]

codling² ('kɒdlɪŋ) n a codfish, esp a young one

cod-liver oil n an oil extracted from the livers of cod and related fish, rich in vitamins A and D and used to treat deficiency of these vitamins

codology (kɒd'ɒlədʒɪ) n *Irish informal* the art or practice of bluffing or deception

codpiece ('kɒd,piːs) n a bag covering the male genitals, attached to hose or breeches by laces, etc, worn in the 15th and 16th centuries [C15: from COD² + PIECE]

codswallop ('kɒdz,wɒləp) n *Brit slang* nonsense [C20: of unknown origin]

Co Durham *abbreviation* County Durham

Cody ('kəʊdɪ) n **William Frederick.** the real name of **Buffalo Bill**

Coe (kəʊ) n **Sebastian,** Baron. born 1956, English middle-distance runner and Conservative politician: winner of the 1500 metres in the 1980 and 1984 Olympic Games; holds 1000 m record; held records at 800 m, 1500 m, and a mile: member of parliament (1992–97)

co-ed (,kəʊ'ɛd) adj **1** coeducational ▷ n **2** *US* a female student in a coeducational college or university **3** *Brit* a school or college providing coeducation

coeducation (,kəʊedjʊ'keɪʃən) n instruction in schools, colleges, etc, attended by both sexes > ,coedu'cational *adj* > ,coedu'cationally *adv*

coefficient (,kəʊɪ'fɪʃənt) n **1** *maths* a numerical or constant factor in an algebraic term: *the coefficient of the term 3xyz is 3* **2** *physics* a value that relates one physical quantity to another [C17: from New Latin *coefficiēns*, from Latin co- together + *efficere* to EFFECT]

coefficient of expansion n the amount of expansion (or contraction) per unit length of a material resulting from one degree change in temperature. Also called: **expansivity**

coefficient of variation n *statistics* a measure of the relative variation of distribution independent of the units of measurement; the standard deviation divided by the mean, sometimes expressed as a percentage

coel- *prefix* indicating a cavity within a body or a hollow organ or part: *coelacanth; coelenterate; coelenteron* [New Latin, from Greek *koilos* hollow]

coelacanth ('siːlə,kænθ) n a primitive marine bony fish of the genus *Latimeria* (subclass *Crossopterygii*), having fleshy limblike pectoral fins and occurring off the coast of E Africa: thought to be extinct until a living specimen was discovered in 1938 [C19: from New Latin *coelacanthus*, literally: hollow spine, from COEL- + Greek *akanthos* spine]

coelenterate (sɪ'lɛntə,reɪt, -rɪt) n any invertebrate of the phylum *Cnidaria* (formerly *Coelenterata*), having a saclike body with a single opening (mouth), which occurs in polyp and medusa forms. Coelenterates include the hydra, jellyfishes, sea anemones, and corals [C19: from New Latin *Coelenterata*, hollow-intestined (creatures); see COEL-, ENTERON]

coeliac or *US* **celiac** ('siːlɪ,æk) adj of or relating to the abdomen [C17: from Latin *coeliacus*, from Greek *koiliakos*, from *koilia* belly]

coeliac disease n a chronic intestinal disorder of young children caused by sensitivity to the protein gliadin contained in the gluten of cereals, characterized by distention of the abdomen and frothy and pale foul-smelling stools

coelom or *esp US* **celom** ('siːləʊm, -ləm) n the body cavity of many multicellular animals, situated in the mesoderm and containing the digestive tract and other visceral organs [C19: from Greek *koilōma* cavity, from *koilos* hollow; see COEL-] > coelomic or *esp US* celomic (sɪ'lɒmɪk) *adj*

Coen (kuːn) n **Jan Pieterszoon.** 1587–1629, Dutch colonial administrator; governor general of the Dutch East Indies (1618–23, 1627–29)

coeno- or before a vowel **coen-** *combining form* common: *coenocyte* [New Latin, from Greek *koinos* common]

coenobite or **cenobite** ('siːnəʊ,baɪt) n a member of a religious order following a communal rule of life [C17: from Old French or ecclesiastical Latin, from Greek *koinobion* convent, from *koinos* common + *bios* life] > coenobitic (,siːnəʊ'bɪtɪk), ,coeno'bitical, ,ceno'bitic or ,ceno'bitical *adj*

coenzyme (kəʊ'ɛnzaɪm) n *biochem* a nonprotein organic molecule that forms a complex with certain enzymes and is essential for their activity

coequal (kəʊ'iːkwəl) adj **1** of the same size, rank, etc ▷ n **2** a person or thing equal with another > coequality (,kəʊiː'kwɒlɪtɪ) or co'equalness n

coerce (kəʊ'ɜːs) vb (tr) to compel or restrain by force or authority without regard to individual wishes or desires [C17: from Latin *coercēre* to confine, restrain, from co- together + *arcēre* to enclose] > co'ercer n > co'ercible *adj*

coercion (kəʊ'ɜːʃən) n **1** the act or power of coercing **2** government by force > coercive (kəʊ'ɜːsɪv) *adj* > co'ercively *adv*

Coetzee ('kɜːtzɪ) n J(ohn) M(ichael). born 1940, South African novelist: his works include *Life and Times of Michael K* (1983), *Age of Iron* (1990), *Disgrace* (1999), and *Elizabeth Costello* (2003); Nobel prize for literature (2003)

Coeur (kɜː; French kœr) n **Jacques.** ?1395–1456, French merchant; councillor and court banker to Charles VII of France

coeval (kəʊ'iːvˀl) adj **1** of or belonging to the same age or generation ▷ n **2** a contemporary [C17: from Late Latin *coaevus* from Latin co- + *aevum* age] > coevality (,kəʊiː'vælɪtɪ) n > co'evally *adv*

coexecutor (,kəʊɪg'zɛkjʊtə) n *law* a person acting jointly with another or others as executor

coexist (,kəʊɪg'zɪst) vb (intr) **1** to exist together at the same time or in the same place **2** to exist together in peace > ,coex'istence n > ,coex'istent *adj*

coextend (,kəʊɪk'stɛnd) vb to extend or cause to extend equally in space or time > ,coex'tension n

coextensive (,kəʊɪk'stɛnsɪv) adj of the same limits or extent > ,coex'tensively *adv*

C of E *abbreviation* Church of England

coffee ('kɒfɪ) n **1 a** a drink consisting of an infusion of the roasted and ground or crushed seeds of the coffee tree **b** (*as modifier*): *coffee grounds* **2** Also called: coffee beans the beanlike seeds of the coffee tree, used to make this beverage **3 a** a medium to dark brown colour **b** (*as adjective*): *a coffee carpet* [c16: from Italian *caffè*, from Turkish *kahve*, from Arabic *qahwah* coffee]

coffee bar *n* a café; snack bar

coffee cup *n* a cup from which coffee may be drunk, usually smaller than a teacup

coffee house *n* a place where coffee is served, esp one that was a fashionable meeting place in 18th-century London

coffee mill *n* a machine for grinding roasted coffee beans

coffeepot ('kɒfɪˌpɒt) *n* a pot in which coffee is brewed or served

coffee shop *n* a shop where coffee is sold or drunk

coffee table *n* a low table, on which newspapers, etc, may be placed and coffee served

coffee-table book *n* a book designed to be looked at rather than read

coffee tree *n* any of several rubiaceous trees of the genus *Coffea*, esp *C. arabica*, the seeds of which are used in the preparation of the beverage coffee

coffer ('kɒfə) *n* **1 a** a chest, esp for storing valuables **2** (*usually plural*) a store of money **3** Also called: caisson, lacuna an ornamental sunken panel in a ceiling, dome, etc **4** a watertight box or chamber **5** short for **cofferdam** ▷ *vb* (*tr*) **6** to store, as in a coffer **7** to decorate (a ceiling, dome, etc) with coffers [c13: from Old French *coffre*, from Latin *cophinus* basket, from Greek *kophinos*]

cofferdam ('kɒfəˌdæm) *n* **1** a watertight structure, usually of sheet piling, that encloses an area under water, pumped dry to enable construction work to be carried out. Below a certain depth a caisson is required **2** (on a ship) a compartment separating two bulkheads or floors, as for insulation or to serve as a barrier against the escape of gas or oil ▷ Often shortened to **coffer**

coffin ('kɒfɪn) *n* **1 a** a box in which a corpse is buried or cremated **2** the part of a horse's foot that contains the coffin bone ▷ *vb* **3** (*tr*) to place in or as in a coffin [c14: from Old French *cofin*, from Latin *cophinus* basket; see COFFER]

coffin nail *n* a slang term for **cigarette**

coffle ('kɒfˀl) *n* (esp formerly) a line of slaves, beasts, etc, fastened together [c18: from Arabic *qāfilah* caravan]

C of S *abbreviation* Church of Scotland

cog¹ (kɒg) *n* **1** any of the teeth or projections on the rim of a gearwheel or sprocket **2** a gearwheel, esp a small one **3** a person or thing playing a small part in a large organization or process [c13: of Scandinavian origin; compare Danish *kogge*, Swedish *kugge*, Norwegian *kug*]

cog² (kɒg) *n* **1** a tenon that projects from the end of a timber beam for fitting into a mortise ▷ *vb* cogs, cogging, cogged **2** (*tr*) to join (pieces of wood) with cogs [c19: of uncertain origin]

cogent ('kəʊdʒənt) *adj* compelling belief or assent; forcefully convincing [c17: from Latin *cōgent-*, *cōgēns*, driving together, from *cōgere*, from *co-* together + *agere* to drive] > 'cogency *n* > 'cogently *adv*

cogitate ('kɒdʒɪˌteɪt) *vb* to think deeply about (a problem, possibility, etc); ponder [c16: from Latin *cōgitāre*, from *co-* (intensive) + *agitāre* to turn over, AGITATE] > ˌcogi'tation *n* > 'cogiˌtator *n* > 'cogitative *adj* > 'cogitatively *adv* > 'cogitativeness *n*

Cognac ('kɒnjæk; *French* kɔɲak) *n* **1** a town in SW France: centre of the district famed for its brandy. Pop: 19 534 (1999) **2** (*sometimes not capital*) a high-quality grape brandy

cognate ('kɒgneɪt) *adj* **1** akin; related: *cognate languages* **2** related by blood or descended from a common maternal ancestor ▷ *n* **3** something that is cognate with something else [c17: from Latin *cognātus*, from *co-* same + *gnātus* born, variant of *nātus*, past participle of *nāscī* to be born] > 'cognately *adv* > 'cognateness *n* > cog'nation *n*

cognition (kɒg'nɪʃən) *n* **1** the mental act or process by which knowledge is acquired, including perception, intuition, and reasoning **2** the knowledge that results from such an act or process [c15: from Latin *cognitiō*, from *cognōscere* from *co-* (intensive) + *nōscere* to learn; see KNOW] > cog'nitional *adj* > 'cognitive *adj*

Cognitive Behavioural Therapy *n* a form of therapy in which, having learnt to understand their anxiety, patients attempt to overcome their usual behavioural responses to it

cognitive therapy *n psychol* a form of psychotherapy in which the patient is encouraged to change the way he sees the world and himself: used particularly to treat depression

cognizable *or* **cognisable** ('kɒgnɪzəbˀl, 'kɒnɪ-) *adj* **1** perceptible **2** *law* susceptible to the jurisdiction of a court

cognizance *or* **cognisance** ('kɒgnɪzəns, 'kɒnɪ-) *n* **1** knowledge; acknowledgment **2** take cognizance of to take notice of; acknowledge, esp officially **3** the range or scope of knowledge or perception **4** *law* the right of a court to hear and determine a cause or matter **5** *heraldry* a distinguishing badge or bearing [c14: from Old French *conoissance*, from *conoistre* to know, from Latin *cognōscere* to learn; see COGNITION]

cognizant *or* **cognisant** ('kɒgnɪzənt, 'kɒnɪ-) *adj* (usually foll by *of*) aware; having knowledge

cognomen (kɒg'nəʊmɛn) *n, pl* -nomens *or* -nomina (-'nɒmɪnə, -'nəʊ-) (originally) an ancient Roman's third name or nickname, which later became his family name [c19: from Latin: additional name, from *co-* together + *nōmen* name; influenced in form by *cognōscere* to learn] > cognominal (kɒg'nɒmɪnˀl, -'nəʊ-) *adj*

cognoscenti (ˌkɒnjəʊ'ʃɛntɪ, ˌkɒgnəʊ-) *pl n, sing* -te (-'tiː) (*sometimes singular*) people with informed appreciation of a particular field, esp in the fine arts; connoisseurs [c18: from obsolete Italian (modern *conoscente*), from Latin *cognōscere* to know, learn about]

cogwheel ('kɒgˌwiːl) *n* another name for **gearwheel**

cohabit (kəʊ'hæbɪt) *vb* (*intr*) to live together as husband and wife, esp without being married [c16: via Late Latin, from Latin *co-* together + *habitāre* to live] > ˌcohabi'tee, co'habitant *or* co'habiter *n*

cohabitation (kəʊˌhæbɪ'teɪʃən) *n* **1** the state or condition of living together as husband and wife without being married **2** (of political parties) the state or condition of cooperating for specific purposes without forming a coalition

coheir (kəʊ'ɛə) *n* a person who inherits jointly with others > co'heiress *fem n*

Cohen ('kəʊən) *n* **1 Leonard.** born 1934, Canadian singer, songwriter, and poet; recordings include *Songs of Leonard Cohen* (1968), *Songs of Love and Hate* (1971), *I'm Your Man* (1988), and *Ten New Songs* (2001) **2 Stanley.** born 1922, US biochemist: shared the Nobel prize for physiology or medicine 1986

cohere (kəʊ'hɪə) *vb* (*intr*) **1** to hold or stick firmly together **2** to be connected logically; be consistent **3** *physics* to be held together by the action of molecular forces [c16: from Latin *cohaerēre* from *co-* together + *haerēre* to cling, adhere]

coherence (kəʊ'hɪərəns) *or* **coherency** (kəʊ'hɪərənsɪ) *n* **1** logical or natural connection or consistency **2** another word for **cohesion** (sense 1)

coherent (kəʊ'hɪərənt) *adj* **1** capable of logical and consistent speech, thought, etc **2** logical; consistent and orderly **3** cohering or sticking together **4** *physics* (of two or more waves) having the same phase or a fixed phase difference: *coherent light* > co'herently *adv*

cohesion (kəʊ'hiːʒən) *n* **1** the act or state of cohering; tendency to unite **2** *physics* the force that holds together the atoms or molecules in a solid or liquid, as distinguished from adhesion **3** *botany* the fusion in some plants of flower parts, such as petals, that are usually separate [c17: from Latin *cohaesus* stuck together, past participle of *cohaerēre* to COHERE] > co'hesive *adj* > co'hesively *adv* > co'hesiveness *n*

coho ('kəʊhəʊ) *n, pl* -ho *or* -hos a Pacific salmon, *Oncorhynchus kisutch*. Also called: silver salmon [origin unknown; probably from an American Indian language]

cohort ('kəʊhɔːt) *n* **1** one of the ten units of between 300 and 600 men in an ancient Roman Legion **2** any band of warriors or associates: *the cohorts of Satan* **3** *chiefly US* an associate or follower [C15: from Latin *cohors* yard, company of soldiers; related to *hortus* garden]

COI *abbreviation* (in Britain) Central Office of Information

coif (kɔɪf) *n* **1** a close-fitting cap worn under a veil, worn in the Middle Ages by many women but now only by nuns **2** any similar cap, such as a leather cap worn under a chain-mail hood **3** (kwɑːf) a less common word for **coiffure** (sense 1) ▷ *vb* **coifs, coiffing, coiffed** (*tr*) **4** (kwɑːf) to cover with or as if with a coif **5** (kwɑːf) to arrange (the hair) [C14: from Old French *coiffe*, from Late Latin *cofea* helmet, cap, of obscure origin]

coiffeur (kwɑːˈfɜː; *French* kwafœr) *n* a hairdresser ▷ **coiffeuse** (kwɑːˈfɜːz; *French* kwaføz) *fem n*

coiffure (kwɑːˈfjʊə; *French* kwafyr) *n* **1** a hairstyle **2** an obsolete word for **headdress** ▷ *vb* **3** (*tr*) to dress or arrange (the hair)

coign of vantage *n* an advantageous position or stance for observation or action

coil¹ (kɔɪl) *vb* **1** to wind or gather (ropes, hair, etc) into loops or (of rope, hair, etc) to be formed in such loops **2** (*intr*) to move in a winding course ▷ *n* **3** something wound in a connected series of loops **4** a single loop of such a series **5** an arrangement of pipes in a spiral or loop, as in a condenser **6** an electrical conductor wound into the form of a spiral, sometimes with a soft iron core, to provide inductance or a magnetic field **7** an intrauterine contraceptive device in the shape of a coil **8** the transformer in a petrol engine that supplies the high voltage to the sparking plugs [C16: from Old French *coillir* to collect together; see CULL]

coil² (kɔɪl) *n* the troubles and activities of the world (in the Shakespearean phrase **this mortal coil**) [C16: of unknown origin]

Coimbra (*Portuguese* 'kuimbrə) *n* a city in central Portugal: capital of Portugal from 1190 to 1260; seat of the country's oldest university. Pop: 148 474 (2001)

coin (kɔɪn) *n* **1** a metal disc or piece used as money **2** metal currency, as opposed to securities, paper currency, etc **3** *architect* a variant spelling of **quoin 4** pay a person back in his own coin to treat a person in the way that he has treated others ▷ *vb* **5** (*tr*) to make or stamp (coins) **6** (*tr*) to make into a coin **7** (*tr*) to fabricate or invent (words, etc) **8** (*tr*) *informal* to make (money) rapidly (esp in the phrase **coin it in**) [C14: from Old French: stamping die, from Latin *cuneus* wedge]

coinage ('kɔɪnɪdʒ) *n* **1** coins collectively **2** the act of striking coins **3** the currency of a country **4** the act of inventing something, esp a word or phrase **5** a newly invented word, phrase, usage, etc

coincide (ˌkəʊɪnˈsaɪd) *vb* (*intr*) **1** to occur or exist simultaneously **2** to be identical in nature, character, etc **3** to agree [C18: from Medieval Latin *coincidere*, from Latin *co-* together + *incidere* to occur, befall, from *cadere* to fall]

coincidence (kəʊˈɪnsɪdəns) *n* **1** a chance occurrence of events remarkable either for being simultaneous or for apparently being connected **2** the fact, condition, or state of coinciding **3** (*modifier*) *electronics* of or relating to a circuit that produces an output pulse only when both its input terminals receive pulses within a specified interval: *coincidence gate*

coincident (kəʊˈɪnsɪdənt) *adj* **1** having the same position in space or time **2** (usually *postpositive* and foll by *with*) in exact agreement; consonant

coincidental (kəʊˌɪnsɪˈdɛntəl) *adj* of or happening by a coincidence; fortuitous ▷ **co,inci'dentally** *adv*

coin-op ('kɔɪnˌɒp) *n* a launderette or other service installation in which the machines are operated by the insertion of coins

Cointreau ('kwɑːntrəʊ) *n* *trademark* a colourless liqueur with orange flavouring

coir (kɔɪə) *n* the fibre prepared from the husk of the coconut, used in making rope and matting [C16: from Malayalam *kāyar* rope, from *kāyaru* to be twisted]

Coire (kwar) *n* the French name for **Chur**

coitus ('kɔʊɪtəs) *or* **coition** (kəʊˈɪʃən) *n* technical terms for **sexual intercourse** [C18 *coitus*: from Latin: a uniting, from *coīre* to meet, from *īre* to go] ▷ **'coital** *adj*

coitus interruptus (ˌɪntəˈrʌptəs) *n* the deliberate withdrawal of the penis from the vagina before ejaculation

coke¹ (kəʊk) *n* **1** a solid-fuel product containing about 80 per cent of carbon produced by distillation of coal to drive off its volatile constituents: used as a fuel and in metallurgy as a reducing agent for converting metal oxides into metals **2** any similar material, such as the layer formed in the cylinders of a car engine by incomplete combustion of the fuel ▷ *vb* **3** to become or convert into coke [C17: probably a variant of C14 northern English dialect *colk* core, of obscure origin]

coke² (kəʊk) *n* *slang* short for **cocaine**

Coke¹ (kəʊk) *n* *trademark* short for **Coca-Cola**

Coke² (kʊk, kəʊk) *n* **1** Sir **Edward**. 1552–1634, English jurist, noted for his defence of the common law against encroachment from the Crown: the Petition of Right (1628) was largely his work **2** (kʊk) **Thomas William**, 1st Earl of Leicester, known as **Coke of Holkham**. 1752–1842, English agriculturist: pioneered agricultural improvement and considerably improved productivity at his Holkham estate in Norfolk

coked-up ('kəʊkdʌp) *adj* *slang* showing the effects of having taken cocaine

col (kɒl; *French* kɔl) *n* **1** the lowest point of a ridge connecting two mountain peaks, often constituting a pass **2** *meteorol* a pressure region between two anticyclones and two depressions, associated with variable weather [C19: from French: neck, col, from Latin *collum* neck]

Col. *abbreviation* **1** Colombia(n) **2** Colonel **3** *Bible* Colossians

col- *prefix* a variant of **com-**: *collateral*

cola *or* **kola** ('kəʊlə) *n* **1** either of two tropical sterculiaceous trees, *Cola nitida* or *C. acuminata*, widely cultivated in tropical regions for their seeds. See **cola nut 2** a sweet carbonated drink flavoured with cola nuts [C18: from *kola*, probably variant of Mandingo *kolo* nut]

colander ('kɒləndə, 'kʌl-) *n* a pan with a perforated bottom for straining or rinsing foods [C14 *colyndore*, probably from Old Provençal *colador*, via Medieval Latin, from Late Latin *cōlāre* to filter, from *cōlum* sieve]

cola nut *n* any of the seeds of the cola tree, which contain caffeine and theobromine and are used medicinally and in the manufacture of soft drinks

Colbert (*French* kɔlbɛr) *n* **1 Claudette**, real name **Claudette Lily Chauchoin**. 1905–96, French-born Hollywood actress, noted for her sophisticated comedy roles; her films include *It Happened One Night* (1934) and *The Palm Beach Story* (1942) **2 Jean Baptiste** (ʒɑ̃ batist). 1619–83, French statesman; chief minister to Louis XIV: reformed the taille and pursued a mercantilist policy, creating a powerful navy and merchant fleet and building roads and canals

Colby ('kɒlbɪ) *n* (*sometimes not capital*) NZ a type of mild-tasting hard cheese

Colchester ('kəʊltʃɪstə) *n* a town in E England, in NE Essex; university (1964). Pop: 104 390 (2001)

colchicine ('kɒltʃɪˌsiːn, -sɪn, 'kɒlkɪ-) *n* a pale-yellow crystalline alkaloid extracted from seeds or corms of the autumn crocus. It is used in the treatment of gout and to create polyploid plants by inhibiting chromosome separation during meiosis. Formula: $C_{22}H_{25}NO_6$ [C19: from COLCHICUM + -INE²]

colchicum ('kɒltʃɪkəm, 'kɒlkɪ-) *n* **1** any Eurasian liliaceous plant of the genus *Colchicum*, such as the autumn crocus **2** the dried seeds or corms of the autumn crocus: a source of colchicine [C16: from Latin, from Greek *kolkhikon*, from *kolkhikos* of COLCHIS]

Colchis ('kɒlkɪs) *n* an ancient country on the Black Sea south of the Caucasus: the land of Medea and the Golden Fleece in Greek mythology

cold (kəʊld) *adj* **1** having relatively little warmth; of a rather low temperature: *cold weather; cold hands* **2** without sufficient or proper warmth: *this meal is cold* **3** lacking in affection, enthusiasm, or warmth of feeling: *a cold manner* **4** not affected by emotion; objective: *cold logic* **5** dead **6** sexually unresponsive or frigid **7** lacking in freshness: *a cold scent; cold news* **8** chilling to the spirit; depressing **9** (of a colour) having violet, blue, or green predominating; giving no sensation of warmth **10** *informal* (of a seeker) far from the object of a search **11** denoting the contacting of potential customers, voters, etc, without previously approaching them in order to establish their interest: *cold mailing* **12** cold comfort little or no comfort **13** leave someone cold *informal* to fail to excite someone: *the performance left me cold* **14** throw cold water on or pour cold water on *informal* to be unenthusiastic about or discourage ▷ *n* **15** the absence of heat regarded as a positive force: *the cold took away our breath* **16** the sensation caused by loss or lack of heat **17** in the cold or out in the cold *informal* neglected; ignored **18** an acute viral infection of the upper respiratory passages characterized by discharge of watery mucus from the nose, sneezing, etc **19** catch a cold *slang* to make a loss; lose one's investment ▷ *adv* **20** *informal* without preparation: *he played his part cold* [Old English *ceald*; related to Old Norse *kaldr*, Gothic *kalds*, Old High German *kalt*; see COOL] ▷ 'coldish *adj* ▷ 'coldly *adv* ▷ 'coldness *n*

cold-blooded *adj* **1** having or showing a lack of feeling or pity **2** *informal* particularly sensitive to cold **3** (of all animals except birds and mammals) having a body temperature that varies with that of the surroundings. Technical name: poikilothermic ▷ ,cold-'bloodedly *adv* ▷ ,cold-'bloodedness *n*

cold cathode *n electronics* a cathode from which electrons are emitted at ambient temperature, due to a high potential gradient at the surface

cold chisel *n* a toughened steel chisel

cold cream *n* an emulsion of water and fat used cosmetically for softening and cleansing the skin

cold cuts *pl n* cooked meats sliced and served cold

cold feet *pl n informal* loss or lack of courage or confidence

cold frame *n* an unheated wooden frame with a glass top, used to protect young plants from the cold

cold front *n meteorol* the boundary line between a warm air mass and the cold air pushing it from beneath and behind as it moves

cold-hearted *adj* lacking in feeling or warmth; unkind ▷ ,cold-'heartedly *adv* ▷ ,cold-'heartedness *n*

Colditz ('kəʊldɪts) *n* a town in E Germany, on the River Mulde: during World War II its castle was used as a top-security camp for Allied prisoners of war; many daring escape attempts, some successful, were made

cold-rolled *adj* (of metal sheets, etc) having been rolled without heating, producing a smooth surface finish

cold shoulder *informal* ▷ *n* **1** the cold shoulder a show of indifference; a slight ▷ *vb* cold-shoulder (*tr*) **2** to treat with indifference

cold sore *n* a cluster of blisters at the margin of the lips that sometimes accompanies the common cold, caused by a viral infection

cold start *n computing* the reloading of a program or operating system

cold storage *n* **1** the storage of things in an artificially cooled place for preservation **2** *informal* a state of temporary suspension: *to put an idea into cold storage*

Coldstream ('kəʊld,striːm) *n* a town in SE Scotland, in Scottish Borders on the English border: the Coldstream Guards were formed here (1660). Pop: 1813 (2001)

cold sweat *n informal* a bodily reaction to fear or nervousness, characterized by chill and moist skin

cold turkey *n* **1** *slang* a method of curing drug addiction by abrupt withdrawal of all doses **2** the withdrawal symptoms, esp nausea and shivering, brought on by this method

cold war *n* a state of political hostility and military tension between two countries or power blocs, involving propaganda, subversion, threats, economic sanctions, and other measures short of open warfare, esp that between the American and Soviet blocs after World War II (the **Cold War**)

cold wave *n* **1** *meteorol* a sudden spell of low temperatures over a wide area, often following the passage of a cold front **2** *hairdressing* a permanent wave made by chemical agents applied at normal temperatures

cole (kəʊl) *n* any of various plants of the genus *Brassica*, such as the cabbage and rape. Also called: colewort [Old English *cāl*, from Latin *caulis* plant stalk, cabbage]

Cole (kəʊl) *n* **Nat 'King'**, real name *Nathaniel Adams Cole*. 1917–65, US popular singer and jazz pianist

Coleman ('kəʊlmən) *n* **Ornette** (ɔːˈnɛt). born 1930, US avant-garde jazz alto saxophonist and multi-instrumentalist

Colenso (kəˈlɛnzəʊ) *n* **John William**. 1814–83, British churchman; Anglican bishop of Natal from 1853: charged with heresy for questioning the accuracy of the Pentateuch

coleopter (ˌkɒlɪˈɒptə) *n aeronautics obsolete* an aircraft that has an annular wing with the fuselage and engine on the centre line

coleopteran (ˌkɒlɪˈɒptərən) *n* Also: coleopteron **1** any of the insects of the cosmopolitan order *Coleoptera*, in which the forewings are modified to form shell-like protective elytra. The order includes the beetles and weevils ▷ *adj* Also: coleopterous **2** of, relating to, or belonging to the order *Coleoptera* [c18: from New Latin *Coleoptera*, from Greek *koleoptera*, from *koleopteros* sheath-winged, from *koleon* sheath + *pteron* wing]

Coleraine ('kəʊlˌreɪn) *n* **1** a town in N Northern Ireland, in Coleraine district, Co Antrim, on the River Bann; light industries; university (1965). Pop: 24 089 (2001) **2** a district in N Northern Ireland, in Co Antrim and Co Londonderry. Pop: 56 024 (2003 est). Area: 485 sq km (187 sq miles)

Coleridge ('kəʊlərɪdʒ) *n* **Samuel Taylor**. 1772–1834, English Romantic poet and critic, noted for poems such as *The Rime of the Ancient Mariner* (1798), *Kubla Khan* (1816), and *Christabel* (1816), and for his critical work *Biographia Literaria* (1817)

Coleridge-Taylor (ˌkəʊlərɪdʒˈteɪlə) *n* **Samuel**. 1875–1912, British composer, best known for his trilogy of oratorios *Song of Hiawatha* (1898–1900)

coleslaw ('kəʊlˌslɔː) *n* a salad of shredded cabbage, mayonnaise, carrots, onions, etc [c18: from Dutch *koolsla*, from *koolsalade*, literally: cabbage salad]

colestipol (kəˈlɛstɪˌpɒl) *n* a drug that reduces the concentration of cholesterol in the blood: used, together with dietary restriction of cholesterol, to treat selected patients with hypercholesterolaemia and so prevent atherosclerosis

Colet ('kɒlɪt) *n* **John**. ?1467–1519, English humanist and theologian; founder of St Paul's School, London (1509)

coletit ('kəʊlˌtɪt) *n* another name for coal tit

Colette (kɒˈlɛt) *n* full name *Sidonie Gabrielle Claudine Colette*. 1873–1954, French novelist; her works include *Chéri* (1920), *Gigi* (1944), and the series of *Claudine* books

coleus ('kəʊlɪəs) *n, pl* -uses any plant of the Old World genus *Coleus*: cultivated for their variegated leaves, typically marked with red, yellow, or white: family Lamiaceae (labiates) [c19: from New Latin, from Greek *koleos*, variant of *koleon* sheath; from the way in which the stamens are joined]

colewort ('kəʊlˌwɜːt) *n* another name for cole

coley ('kəʊlɪ, 'kɒlɪ) *n Brit* any of various edible fishes, esp the coalfish

colic ('kɒlɪk) *n* a condition characterized by acute spasmodic abdominal pain, esp that caused by inflammation, distention, etc, of the gastrointestinal tract [c15: from Old French *colique*, from Late Latin *cōlicus* ill with colic, from Greek *kōlon*, variant of *kolon* COLON²] ▷ 'colicky *adj*

coliform bacteria ('kɒlɪfɔːm) *pl n* a large group of bacteria inhabiting the intestinal tract of humans and animals that may cause disease and whose presence in water is an indicator of faecal pollution

Coligny or **Coligni** (French kɔliɲi) *n* **Gaspard de** (gaspar də), Seigneur de Châtillon. 1519–72, French Huguenot leader

Colima (Spanish koˈlima) *n* **1** a state of SW Mexico, on the Pacific coast: mainly a coastal plain, rising to the foothills of the Sierra Madre, with important mineral resources. Capital: Colima. Pop: 238 000 (2005 est). Area: 5455 sq km (2106 sq miles) **2** a city in SW Mexico, capital of Colima state, on the Colima River. Pop: 106 967 (1990)

3 Nevado de Colima a volcano in SW Mexico, in Jalisco state. Height: 4339 m (14 235 ft)

coliseum (ˌkɒlɪˈsɪəm) or **colosseum** (ˌkɒləˈsɪəm) n a large building, such as a stadium or theatre, used for entertainments, sports, etc [c18: from Medieval Latin *Coliseum*, variant of COLOSSEUM]

colitis (kɒˈlaɪtɪs, kə-) n inflammation of the colon

collaborate (kəˈlæbəˌreɪt) vb (intr) **1** (often foll by on, with, etc) to work with another or others on a joint project **2** to cooperate as a traitor, esp with an enemy occupying one's own country [c19: from Late Latin *collabōrāre*, from Latin *com-* together + *labōrāre* to work] > col'laborative adj > col'labo,rator n > col,labo'ration n > col,labo'rationist n

collage (kəˈlɑːʒ, kɒ-; French kɔlaʒ) n **1** an art form in which compositions are made out of pieces of paper, cloth, photographs, and other miscellaneous objects, juxtaposed and pasted on a dry ground **2** a composition made in this way **3** any work, such as a piece of music, created by combining unrelated styles [c20: French, from *coller* to stick, from *colle* glue, from Greek *kolla*] > col'lagist n

collagen (ˈkɒlədʒən) n a fibrous scleroprotein of connective tissue and bones that is rich in glycine and proline and yields gelatine on boiling [c19: from Greek *kolla* glue + -GEN]

collapsar (kɒˈlæpsɑː) n astronomy a collapsed star, either a white dwarf, neutron star, or black hole

collapse (kəˈlæps) vb **1** (intr) to fall down or cave in suddenly: *the whole building collapsed* **2** (intr) to fail completely **3** (intr) to break down or fall down from lack of strength **4** to fold (furniture, etc) compactly or (of furniture, etc) to be designed to fold compactly ▷ n **5** the act or instance of suddenly falling down, caving in, or crumbling **6** a sudden failure or breakdown [c18: from Latin *collāpsus*, from *collābī* to fall in ruins, from *lābī* to fall] > col'lapsible or col'lapsable adj > col,lapsi'bility or col,lapsability n

collar (ˈkɒlə) n **1** the part of a garment around the neck and shoulders, often detachable or folded over **2** any band, necklace, garland, etc, encircling the neck **3** a band or chain of leather, rope, or metal placed around an animal's neck to restrain, harness, or identify it **4** biology a marking or structure resembling a collar, such as that found around the necks of some birds or at the junction of a stem and a root **5** a section of a shaft or rod having a locally increased diameter to provide a bearing seat or a locating ring **6** a cut of meat, esp bacon, taken from around the neck of an animal ▷ vb (tr) **7** to put a collar on; furnish with a collar **8** to seize by the collar **9** informal to seize; arrest; detain [c13: from Latin *collāre* neckband, neck chain, collar, from *collum* neck]

collarbone (ˈkɒləˌbəʊn) n the nontechnical name for **clavicle**

collard (ˈkɒləd) n a variety of the cabbage, *Brassica oleracea acephala*, having a crown of edible leaves. See also **kale** [c18: variant of COLEWORT]

collate (kɒˈleɪt, kə-) vb (tr) **1** to examine and compare (texts, statements, etc) in order to note points of agreement and disagreement **2** (in library work) to check the number and order of (the pages of a book) **3** bookbinding **a** to check the sequence of (the sections of a book) after gathering **b** a nontechnical word for **gather** (sense 9) **4** (often foll by to) Christianity to appoint (an incumbent) to a benefice [c16: from Latin *collātus* brought together (past participle of *conferre* to gather), from *com-* together + *lātus*, past participle of *ferre* to bring] > collator (kɒˈleɪtə, kəʊ-, ˈkɒleɪtə, ˈkəʊ-) n

collateral (kɒˈlætərəl, kə-) n **1 a** a security pledged for the repayment of a loan **b** (as modifier): *a collateral loan* **2** a person, animal, or plant descended from the same ancestor as another but through a different line ▷ adj **3** situated or running side by side **4** descended from a common ancestor but through different lines **5** serving to support or corroborate [c14: from Medieval Latin *collaterālis*, from Latin *com-* together + *laterālis* of the side, from *latus* side] > col'laterally adv

collateral damage n military unintentional damage to civil property and civilian casualties, caused as a by-product of military operations

collateralized debt obligation n a debt security collateralized by a number of debt obligations including loans and bonds of different credit quality and maturity. Abbreviation: CDO

collation (kɒˈleɪʃən, kə-) n **1** the act or process of collating **2** a description of the technical features of a book **3** RC Church a light meal permitted on fast days **4** any light informal meal

colleague (ˈkɒliːg) n a fellow worker or member of a staff, department, profession, etc [c16: from French *collègue*, from Latin *collēga* one selected at the same time as another, from *com-* together + *lēgāre* to choose]

collect¹ (kəˈlɛkt) vb **1** to gather together or be gathered together **2** to accumulate (stamps, books, etc) as a hobby or for study **3** (tr) to call for or receive payment of (taxes, dues, etc) **4** (tr) to regain control of (oneself, one's emotions, etc) as after a shock or surprise: *he collected his wits* **5** (tr) to fetch; pick up: *collect your own post; he collected the children after school* **6** (intr; sometimes foll by on) slang to receive large sums of money, as from an investment **7** (tr) Austral & NZ informal to collide with; be hit by ▷ adv, adj **8** US (of telephone calls) on a reverse-charge basis [c16: from Latin *collēctus* collected, from *colligere* to gather together, from *com-* together + *legere* to gather]

collect² (ˈkɒlɛkt) n Christianity a short Church prayer generally preceding the lesson or epistle in Communion and other services [c13: from Medieval Latin *collecta* (from the phrase *ōrātiō ad collēctam* prayer at the (people's) assembly), from Latin *colligere* to COLLECT¹]

collectable or **collectible** (kəˈlɛktəb³l) adj **1** (of antiques, objets d'art, etc) of interest to a collector ▷ n **2** any object regarded as being of interest to a collector

collected (kəˈlɛktɪd) adj **1** in full control of one's faculties; composed **2** assembled in totality or brought together into one volume or a set of volumes: *the collected works of Dickens* > col'lectedly adv > col'lectedness n

collection (kəˈlɛkʃən) n **1** the act or process of collecting **2** a number of things collected or assembled together **3** something gathered into a mass or pile; accumulation: *a collection of rubbish* **4** a sum of money collected or solicited, as in church **5** removal, esp regular removal of letters from a postbox **6** (often plural) (at Oxford University) a college examination or an oral report by a tutor

collective (kəˈlɛktɪv) adj **1** formed or assembled by collection **2** forming a whole or aggregate **3** of, done by, or characteristic of individuals acting in cooperation ▷ n **4 a** a cooperative enterprise or unit, such as a collective farm **b** the members of such a cooperative **5** short for **collective noun** > col'lectively adv > col'lectiveness n > collectivity (ˌkɒlɛkˈtɪvɪtɪ) n

collective bargaining n negotiation between one or more trade unions and one or more employers or an employers' organization on the incomes and working conditions of the employees

collective noun n a noun that is singular in form but that refers to a group of people or things

- ● USAGE Collective nouns are usually used with
- ● singular verbs: *the family is on holiday; General Motors is*
- ● *mounting a big sales campaign*. In British usage, however,
- ● plural verbs are sometimes employed in this context,
- ● esp when reference is being made to a collection of
- ● individual objects or people rather than to the group
- ● as a unit: *the family are all on holiday*. Care should be
- ● taken that the same collective noun is not treated as
- ● both singular and plural in the same sentence: *the*
- ● *family is well and sends its best wishes* or *the family are all well*
- ● *and send their best wishes*, but not *the family is well and send*
- ● *their best wishes*

collective ownership n ownership by a group for the benefit of members of that group

collective unconscious n psychol (in Jungian psychological theory) a part of the unconscious mind incorporating patterns of memories, instincts, and experiences common to all mankind. These patterns are inherited, may be arranged into archetypes, and are observable through their effects on dreams, behaviour, etc

collectivism (kəˈlɛktɪˌvɪzəm) n the principle of ownership of the means of production, by the state or the people > col'lectivist n > colˌlecti'vistic adj

collectivize or **collectivise** (kəˈlɛktɪˌvaɪz) vb (tr) to organize according to the principles of collectivism > colˌlectivi'zation or colˌlectivi'sation n

collector (kəˈlɛktə) n 1 a person or thing that collects 2 a person employed to collect debts, rents, etc 3 the head of a district administration in India 4 a person who collects or amasses objects as a hobby 5 electronics the region in a transistor into which charge carriers flow from the base

colleen ('kɒliːn, kɒˈliːn) n an Irish word for girl [C19: from Irish Gaelic cailín a girl, a young unmarried woman]

college ('kɒlɪdʒ) n 1 an institution of higher education; part of a university 2 a school or an institution providing specialized courses or teaching: a college of music 3 the building or buildings in which a college is housed 4 the staff and students of a college 5 an organized body of persons with specific rights and duties: an electoral college [C14: from Latin collēgium company, society, band of associates, from collēga; see COLLEAGUE]

College of Cardinals n RC Church the collective body of cardinals having the function of electing and advising the pope

college of education n Brit a professional training college for teachers

collegian (kəˈliːdʒɪən) n a current member of a college; student

collegiate (kəˈliːdʒɪɪt) adj 1 Also called: collegial of or relating to a college or college students 2 (of a university) composed of various colleges of equal standing

collegiate church n 1 RC Church, Church of England a church that has an endowed chapter of canons and prebendaries attached to it but that is not a cathedral 2 US Protestantism one of a group of churches presided over by a body of pastors 3 Scot Protestantism a church served by two or more ministers

collegiate institute n Canadian (in certain provinces) a large secondary school with an academic, rather than vocational, emphasis

col legno ('kɒl 'lɛgnəʊ, 'leɪnjəʊ) adv music to be played (on a stringed instrument) by striking the strings with the back of the bow [Italian: with the wood]

Colles' fracture ('kɒlɪs) n a fracture of the radius just above the wrist, with backward and outward displacement of the hand [C19: named after Abraham Colles (died 1843), Irish surgeon]

collet ('kɒlɪt) n 1 (in a jewellery setting) a band or coronet-shaped claw that holds an individual stone 2 mechanical engineering an externally tapered sleeve made in two or more segments and used to grip a shaft passed through its centre when the sleeve is compressed by being inserted in a tapered hole 3 horology a small collar that supports the inner end of the hairspring [C16: from Old French: a little collar, from col neckband, neck, from Latin collum neck]

Collette (kɒˈlɛt) n Toni, full name Antonia Collette. born 1972, Australian film actress. Her films include Muriel's Wedding (1994), The Sixth Sense (1999) and Little Miss Sunshine (2006)

collide (kəˈlaɪd) vb (intr) 1 to crash together with a violent impact 2 to conflict in attitude, opinion, or desire; clash; disagree [C17: from Latin collīdere to clash together, from com- together + laedere to strike, wound]

collider (kəˈlaɪdə) n physics a particle accelerator in which beams of particles are made to collide

collie ('kɒlɪ) n any of several silky-coated breeds of dog developed for herding sheep and cattle [C17: Scottish, probably from earlier colie black with coal dust, from cole COAL]

collier ('kɒlɪə) n chiefly Brit 1 a coal miner 2 a a ship designed to transport coal b a member of its crew [C14: from COAL + -IER]

colliery ('kɒljərɪ) n, pl -lieries chiefly Brit a coal mine

collimate ('kɒlɪˌmeɪt) vb (tr) 1 to adjust the line of sight of (an optical instrument) 2 to use a collimator on (a beam of radiation or particles) 3 to make parallel or bring into line [C17: from New Latin collimāre, erroneously for Latin collīneāre to aim, from com- (intensive) + līneāre, from līnea line] > ˌcolli'mation n

collimator ('kɒlɪˌmeɪtə) n 1 a small telescope attached to a larger optical instrument as an aid in fixing its line of sight 2 an optical system of lenses and slits producing a nondivergent beam of light, usually for use in spectroscopes 3 any device for limiting the size and angle of spread of a beam of radiation or particles

collinear (kɒˈlɪnɪə) adj lying on the same straight line > collinearity (ˌkɒlɪnɪˈærɪtɪ) n

collins ('kɒlɪnz) n a tall fizzy iced drink made with gin, vodka, rum, etc, mixed with fruit juice, soda water, and sugar [C20: probably after the proper name Collins]

Collins ('kɒlɪnz) n 1 Michael. 1890–1922, Irish republican revolutionary: a leader of Sinn Féin; member of the Irish delegation that negotiated the treaty with Great Britain (1921) that established the Irish Free State 2 (William) Wilkie. 1824–89, British author, noted particularly for his suspense novel The Moonstone (1868) 3 William. 1721–59, British poet, noted for his odes; regarded as a precursor of romanticism

collision (kəˈlɪʒən) n 1 a violent impact of moving objects; crash 2 the conflict of opposed ideas, wishes, attitudes, etc [C15: from Late Latin collīsiō from Latin collīdere to COLLIDE]

collocate ('kɒləˌkeɪt) vb (tr) to group or place together in some system or order [C16: from Latin collocāre, from com- together + locāre to place, from locus place] > ˌcollo'cation n

collocutor ('kɒləˌkjuːtə) n a person who talks or engages in conversation with another

collodion (kəˈləʊdɪən) or **collodium** (kəˈləʊdɪəm) n a colourless or yellow syrupy liquid that consists of a solution of pyroxylin in ether and alcohol: used in medicine and in the manufacture of photographic plates, lacquers, etc [C19: from New Latin collōdium, from Greek kollōdēs glutinous, from kolla glue]

collogue (kɒˈləʊg) vb collogues, colloguing, collogued (intr; usually foll by with) to confer confidentially; intrigue or conspire [C16: perhaps from obsolete colleague (vb) to be or act as a colleague, conspire, influenced by Latin colloquī to talk with; see COLLEAGUE]

colloid ('kɒlɔɪd) n 1 Also called: colloidal solution, colloidal suspension a mixture having particles of one component, with diameters between 10^{-7} and 10^{-9} metres, suspended in a continuous phase of another component. The mixture has properties between those of a solution and a fine suspension 2 physiol a gelatinous substance of the thyroid follicles that holds the hormonal secretions of the thyroid gland [C19: from Greek kolla glue + -OID] > colˈloidal adj > colloidality (ˌkɒlɔɪˈdælɪtɪ) n

collop ('kɒləp) n dialect 1 a slice of meat 2 a small piece of anything [C14: of Scandinavian origin; compare Swedish kalops meat stew]

colloq. abbreviation colloquial(ly)

colloquial (kəˈləʊkwɪəl) adj 1 of or relating to conversation 2 denoting or characterized by informal or conversational idiom or vocabulary > colˈloquially adv > colˈloquialness n

colloquialism (kəˈləʊkwɪəˌlɪzəm) n 1 a word or phrase appropriate to conversation and other informal situations 2 the use of colloquial words and phrases

colloquium (kəˈləʊkwɪəm) n, pl -quiums or -quia (-kwɪə) 1 an informal gathering for discussion 2 an academic seminar [C17: from Latin: conversation, conference, COLLOQUY]

colloquy ('kɒləkwɪ) n, pl -quies 1 a formal conversation or conference 2 an informal conference on religious or theological matters [C16: from Latin colloquium from colloquī to talk with, from com- together + loquī to speak] > 'colloquist n

collotype ('kɒləʊˌtaɪp) n 1 Also called: photogelatine process a method of lithographic printing from a flat surface of hardened gelatine: used mainly for fine-detail reproduction in monochrome or colour 2 a print made using this process [C19: from Greek *kolla* glue + TYPE]

collude (kə'luːd) *vb* (*intr*) to conspire together, esp in planning a fraud; connive [C16: from Latin *collūdere*, literally: to play together, hence, conspire together, from *com-* together + *lūdere* to play] > **col'luder** *n*

collusion (kə'luːʒən) *n* **1** secret agreement for a fraudulent purpose; connivance; conspiracy **2** a secret agreement between opponents at law in order to obtain a judicial decision for some wrongful or improper purpose [C14: from Latin *collūsiō*, from *collūdere* to COLLUDE] > **col'lusive** *adj*

collywobbles ('kɒlɪ,wɒbᵊlz) *pl n* slang the collywobbles **1** an upset stomach **2** an intense feeling of nervousness [C19: probably from New Latin *cholera morbus* the disease cholera, influenced through folk etymology by COLIC and WOBBLE]

Colmar (*French* kɔlmar) *n* a city in NE France: annexed to Germany 1871–1919 and 1940–45; textile industry. Pop: 65 136 (1999). German name: **Kolmar**

Colo. *abbreviation* Colorado

colobus ('kɒləbəs) *n* any leaf-eating arboreal Old World monkey of the genus *Colobus*, of W and central Africa, having a slender body, long silky fur, long tail, and reduced or absent thumbs [C19: New Latin, from Greek *kolobos* cut short; referring to its thumb]

cologarithm (kəʊ'lɒgə,rɪðəm) *n* the logarithm of the reciprocal of a number; the negative value of the logarithm: *the cologarithm of 4 is log ¼*. Abbreviation: colog

cologne (kə'ləʊn) *n* a perfumed liquid or solid made of fragrant essential oils and alcohol. Also called: **Cologne water, eau de Cologne** [C18: *Cologne water*, from COLOGNE, where it was first manufactured (1709)]

Cologne (kə'ləʊn) *n* an industrial city and river port in W Germany, in North Rhine-Westphalia on the Rhine: important commercially since ancient times; university (1388). Pop: 965 954 (2003 est). German name: **Köln**

Colombard ('kɒləm,bɑːd) *n* **1** a white grape grown in France, California, and Australia, used for making wine **2** any of various moderately dry, spicy white wines made from this grape

Colomb-Béchar (*French* kɔlɔ̃beʃar) *n* the former name of: **Béchar**

Colombes (*French* kɔlɔ̃b) *n* an industrial and residential suburb of NW Paris. Pop: 76 757 (1999)

Colombia (kə'lɒmbɪə) *n* a republic in NW South America: inhabited by Chibchas and other Indians before Spanish colonization in the 16th century; independence won by Bolívar in 1819; became the Republic of Colombia in 1886; violence and unrest have been endemic since the 1970s. It consists chiefly of a hot swampy coastal plain, separated by ranges of the Andes from the pampas and the equatorial forests of the Amazon basin in the east. Language: Spanish. Religion: Roman Catholic majority. Currency: peso. Capital: Bogotá. Pop: 44 914 000 (2004 est). Area: 1 138 908 sq km (439 735 sq miles)

Colombian (kə'lɒmbɪən) *adj* **1** of or relating to Colombia or its inhabitants ▷ *n* **2** a native or inhabitant of Colombia

Colombo (kə'lʌmbəʊ) *n* the capital and chief port of Sri Lanka, on the W coast, with one of the largest artificial harbours in the world. Pop: 653 000 (2005 est)

colon¹ ('kəʊlən) *n pl* **-lons 1** the punctuation mark :, usually preceding an explanation or an example of what has gone before, a list, or an extended quotation **2** this mark used for certain other purposes, such as expressions of time, as in 2:45 *p.m.*, or when a ratio is given in figures, as in 5:3 [C16: from Latin, from Greek *kōlon* limb, hence part of a strophe, clause of a sentence]

colon² ('kəʊlən) *n, pl* **-lons** or **-la** (-lə) the part of the large intestine between the caecum and the rectum [C16: from Latin: large intestine, from Greek *kolon*] > **colonic** (kə'lɒnɪk) *adj*

colón (kəʊ'ləʊn; *Spanish* ko'lon) *n, pl* **-lons** or **-lones** (*Spanish* -'lones) **1** the standard monetary unit of Costa Rica, divided into 100 céntimos **2** the former standard monetary unit of El Salvador, divided into 100 centavos; replaced by the US dollar in 2001 [C19: American

Spanish, from Spanish, after Cristóbal *Colón* Christopher Columbus]

Colón (kɒ'lɒn; *Spanish* ko'lon) *n* **1** a port in Panama, at the Caribbean entrance to the Panama Canal. Chief Caribbean port. Pop: 157 000 (2005 est) **2** Archipiélago de Colón (,artʃi'pjelaɣo ðe) the official name of the **Galápagos Islands**

colonel ('kɜːnᵊl) *n* an officer of land or air forces junior to a brigadier but senior to a lieutenant colonel [C16: via Old French, from Old Italian *colonnello* column of soldiers, from *colonna* COLUMN] > **'colonelcy** or **'colonel,ship** *n*

colonial (kə'ləʊnɪəl) *adj* **1** of, characteristic of, relating to, possessing, or inhabiting a colony or colonies **2** (*often capital*) characteristic of or relating to the 13 British colonies that became the United States of America (1776) **3** (*often capital*) of or relating to the colonies of the British Empire **4** denoting, relating to, or having the style of Neoclassical architecture used in the British colonies in America in the 17th and 18th centuries **5** of or relating to the period of Australian history before Federation (1901) **6** (of animals and plants) having become established in a community in a new environment ▷ *n* **7** a native of a colony > **co'lonially** *adv*

colonial goose *n* NZ an old-fashioned name for stuffed roast mutton

colonialism (kə'ləʊnɪə,lɪzəm) *n* the policy and practice of a power in extending control over weaker peoples or areas. Also called: **imperialism** > **co'lonialist** *n, adj*

Colonies ('kɒlənɪz) *pl n* the Colonies **1** Brit the subject territories formerly in the British Empire **2** US history the 13 states forming the original United States of America when they declared their independence (1776). These were Connecticut, North and South Carolina, Delaware, Georgia, New Hampshire, New York, Maryland, Massachusetts, Pennsylvania, Rhode Island, Virginia, and New Jersey

colonist ('kɒlənɪst) *n* **1** a person who settles or colonizes an area **2** an inhabitant or member of a colony

colonize or **colonise** ('kɒlə,naɪz) *vb* **1** to send colonists to, or establish a colony in (an area) **2** to settle in (an area) as colonists **3** (*tr*) to transform (a community) into a colony **4** (of plants and animals) to become established in (a new environment) > **,coloni'zation** or **,coloni'sation** *n* > **'colo,nizer** or **'colo,niser** *n*

colonnade (,kɒlə'neɪd) *n* **1** a set of evenly-spaced columns **2** a row of regularly spaced trees [C18: from French, from *colonne* COLUMN; on the model of Italian *colonnato*, from *colonna* column] > **,colon'naded** *adj*

Colonsay ('kɒlənseɪ, -zeɪ) *n* an island in W Scotland, in the Inner Hebrides. Area: about 41 sq km (16 sq miles)

colony ('kɒlənɪ) *n, pl* **-nies 1** a body of people who settle in a country distant from their homeland but maintain ties with it **2** the community formed by such settlers **3** a subject territory occupied by a settlement from the ruling state **4 a** a community of people who form a national, racial, or cultural minority: *an artists' colony; the American colony in London* **b** the area inhabited by a colony of the same type of animal or plant living or growing together, esp in large numbers **5** zoology a group of the same type of animal or plant living or growing together, esp in large numbers **6** bacteriol a group of bacteria, fungi, etc, derived from one or a few spores, esp when grown on a culture medium [C16: from Latin *colōnia*, from *colere* to cultivate, inhabit]

colony-stimulating factor *n* immunol any of a number of substances, secreted by the bone marrow, that cause stem cells to proliferate and differentiate, forming colonies of specific blood cells. Synthetic forms are being tested for their ability to reduce the toxic effects of chemotherapy. Abbreviation: CSF

colophon ('kɒlə,fɒn, -fən) *n* **1** a publisher's emblem on a book **2** (formerly) an inscription at the end of a book showing the title, printer, date, etc [C17: via Late Latin, from Greek *kolophōn* a finishing stroke]

colophony (kɒ'lɒfənɪ) *n* another name for **rosin** (sense 1) [C14: from Latin *Colophōnia rēsina* resin from Colophon]

color ('kʌlə) *n, vb* the US spelling of **colour**

Colorado (,kɒlə'rɑːdəʊ) *n* **1** a state of the central US: consists of the Great Plains in the east and the Rockies in the west; drained chiefly by the Colorado, Arkansas,

South Platte, and Rio Grande Rivers. Capital: Denver. Pop: 4 550 688 (2003 est). Area: 269 998 sq km (104 247 sq miles). Abbreviation: **Colo., CO** **2** a river in SW North America, rising in the Rocky Mountains and flowing southwest to the Gulf of California: famous for the 1600 km (1000 miles) of canyons along its course. Length: about 2320 km (1440 miles) **3** a river in central Texas, flowing southeast to the Gulf of Mexico. Length: about 1450 km (900 miles) **4** a river in central Argentina, flowing southeast to the Atlantic. Length: about 850 km (530 miles) [Spanish, literally: red, from Latin *colōrātus* coloured, tinted red; see COLOUR]

Colorado beetle *n* a black-and-yellow beetle, *Leptinotarsa decemlineata*, that is a serious pest of potatoes, feeding on the leaves: family Chrysomelidae

Colorado Desert *n* an arid region of SE California and NW Mexico, west of the Colorado River. Area: over 5000 sq km (2000 sq miles)

Colorado Springs *n* a city and resort in central Colorado. Pop: 370 448 (2003 est)

colorant ('kʌlərənt) *n* any substance that imparts colour, such as a pigment, dye, or ink; colouring matter

coloration *or* **colouration** (ˌkʌləˈreɪʃən) *n* **1** arrangement of colour and tones; colouring **2** the colouring or markings of insects, birds, etc

coloratura (ˌkɒlərəˈtʊərə) *or* **colorature** (ˈkɒlərəˌtjʊə) *n music* **1 a** (in 18th- and 19th-century arias) a florid virtuoso passage **b** (*as modifier*): *a coloratura aria* **2** Also called: coloratura soprano a lyric soprano who specializes in such music [c19: from obsolete Italian, literally: colouring, from Latin *colōrāre* to COLOUR]

colorific (ˌkʌləˈrɪfɪk) *adj* producing, imparting, or relating to colour

colorimeter (ˌkʌləˈrɪmɪtə) *n* any apparatus for measuring the quality of a colour by comparison with standard colours or combinations of colours > **colorimetric** (ˌkʌlərɪˈmɛtrɪk) *or* ˌcoloriˈmetrical *adj* > ˌcolorˈimetry *n*

colossal (kəˈlɒsᵊl) *adj* **1** of immense size; huge; gigantic **2** (in figure sculpture) approximately twice life-size **3** Also called: giant *architect* of or relating to the order of columns and pilasters that extend more than one storey in a façade > coˈlossally *adv*

Colosseum (ˌkɒləˈsɪəm) *n* an amphitheatre in Rome built about 75–80 AD

colossus (kəˈlɒsəs) *n, pl* **-si** (-saɪ) *or* **-suses** something very large, esp a statue [c14: from Latin, from Greek *kolossos*]

Colossus of Rhodes *n* a giant bronze statue of Apollo built on Rhodes in about 292–280 BC; destroyed by an earthquake in 225 BC; one of the Seven Wonders of the World

colostomy (kəˈlɒstəmɪ) *n, pl* **-mies** the surgical formation of an opening from the colon onto the surface of the body, which functions as an anus

colostrum (kəˈlɒstrəm) *n* the thin milky secretion from the nipples that precedes and follows true lactation. It consists largely of serum and white blood cells [c16: from Latin, of obscure origin]

colotomy (kəˈlɒtəmɪ) *n, pl* **-mies** a colonic incision [c20 COLON² + -TOMY]

colour *or US* **color** ('kʌlə) *n* **1 a** an attribute of things that results from the light they reflect, transmit, or emit in so far as this light causes a visual sensation that depends on its wavelengths **b** the aspect of visual perception by which an observer recognizes this attribute **c** the quality of the light producing this aspect of visual perception **2** Also called: chromatic colour **a** a colour, such as red or green, that possesses hue, as opposed to achromatic colours such as white or black **b** (*as modifier*): *a colour television; a colour film* **3** a substance, such as a dye, pigment, or paint, that imparts colour to something **4 a** the skin complexion of a person, esp as determined by his race (*as modifier*): *colour prejudice; colour problem* **5** the use of all the hues in painting as distinct from composition, form, and light and shade **6** the quantity and quality of ink used in a printing process **7** the distinctive tone of a musical sound; timbre **8** vividness, authenticity, or individuality: *period colour*

9 semblance or pretext (esp in the phrases **take on a different colour, under colour of**) **10** *physics* one of three characteristics of quarks, designated red, blue, or green, but having no relationship with the physical sensation ⊳ *vb* **11** to give or apply colour to (something) **12** (*tr*) to give a convincing or plausible appearance to (something, esp to that which is spoken or recounted): *to colour an alibi* **13** (*tr*) to influence or distort (something, esp a report or opinion): *anger coloured her judgment* **14** (*intr; often foll by up*) to become red in the face, esp when embarrassed or annoyed ⊳ See also **colours** [c13: from Old French *colour* from Latin *color* tint, hue]

colourable ('kʌlərəbᵊl) *adj* **1** capable of being coloured **2** appearing to be true; plausible **3** pretended; feigned

colour bar *n* discrimination against people of a different race, esp as practised by White people against Black people

colour-blind *adj* of or relating to any defect in the normal ability to distinguish certain colours > **colour blindness** *n*

colour code *n* a system of easily distinguishable colours, as for the identification of electrical wires or resistors

colour commentator *n* a sports celebrity who works as part of a commentary team

coloured ('kʌləd) *adj* **1** possessing colour **2** having a strong element of fiction or fantasy; distorted (esp in the phrase **highly coloured**)

Coloured ('kʌləd) *n, pl* **Coloureds** *or* **Coloured** **1** *dated, offensive* an individual who is not a White person, esp a Black person **2** *South Africa* a person of mixed ethnic parentage or descent ⊳ *adj* **3** *dated, offensive* designating or relating to a Coloured person or Coloured people
 ● **USAGE** The use of *Coloured* to refer to a person of mixed
 ● ethnic origin is likely to cause offence and should be
 ● avoided

colourfast ('kʌləˌfɑːst) *adj* (of a fabric) having a colour that does not run or change when washed or worn > 'colourˌfastness *n*

colourful ('kʌləfʊl) *adj* **1** having intense colour or richly varied colours **2** vivid, rich, or distinctive in character > 'colourfully *adv*

colour guard *n* a military guard in a parade, ceremony, etc, that carries and escorts the flag or regimental colours

colouring ('kʌlərɪŋ) *n* **1** the process or art of applying colour **2** anything used to give colour, such as dye, paint, etc **3** appearance with regard to shade and colour **4** arrangements of colours and tones, as in the markings of birds and animals **5** the colour of a person's features or complexion **6** a false or misleading appearance

colourist ('kʌlərɪst) *n* a person who uses colour, esp an artist

colourize, colourise *or US* **colorize** ('kʌləˌraɪz) *vb* (*tr*) to add colour electronically to (an old black-and-white film) > ˌcolouriˈzation, ˌcolouriˈsation *or US* ˌcoloriˈzation *n*

colourless ('kʌləlɪs) *adj* **1** without colour **2** lacking in interest; drab **3** grey or pallid in tone or hue **4** without prejudice; neutral > 'colourlessly *adv*

colours ('kʌləz) *pl n* **1 a** the flag that indicates nationality **b** *military* the ceremony of hoisting or lowering the colours **2 a** pair of silk flags borne by a military unit, esp British, comprising the **Queen's Colour** showing the unit's crest, and the **Regimental Colour** showing the crest and battle honours **3** true nature or character (esp in the phrase **show one's colours**) **4** a distinguishing badge or flag, as of an academic institution **5** *sport, Brit* a badge or other symbol denoting membership of a team, esp at a school or college **6** nail one's colours to the mast to refuse to admit defeat

colour sergeant *n* a sergeant who carries the regimental, battalion, or national colours, as in a colour guard

colour supplement *n Brit* an illustrated magazine accompanying a newspaper, esp a Sunday newspaper

colourway ('kʌləˌweɪ) *n* one of several different combinations of colours in which a given pattern is printed on fabrics, wallpapers, etc

colpo- *or before a vowel* **colp-** *combining form* indicating the vagina: *colpitis; colpotomy* [from Greek *kolpos* womb]

colposcope ('kɒlpə,skəʊp) *n* an instrument for examining the uterine cervix, esp for early signs of cancer [C20: from COLPO- + -SCOPE] > **colposcopy** (kɒlpə'skəʊpɪ) *n*

colt (kəʊlt) *n* **1** a male horse or pony under the age of four **2** *sport* **a** a young and inexperienced player **b** a member of a junior team [Old English *colt* young ass, of obscure origin; compare Swedish dialect *kult* young animal, boy]

colter ('kəʊltə) *n* a variant spelling (esp US) of **coulter**

coltish ('kəʊltɪʃ) *adj* **1** inexperienced; unruly **2** playful and lively > **'coltishness** *n*

Coltrane (kɒl'treɪn) *n* **John** (**William**). 1926–67, US jazz tenor and soprano saxophonist and composer

coltsfoot ('kəʊlts,fʊt) *n*, *pl* -**foots** a European plant, *Tussilago farfara*, with yellow daisy-like flowers and heart-shaped leaves: a common weed: family *Asteraceae* (composites)

colubrine ('kɒljʊ,braɪn, -brɪn) *adj* **1** of or resembling a snake **2** of, relating to, or belonging to the *Colubrinae*, a subfamily of harmless colubrid snakes [C16: from Latin *colubrīnus*, from *coluber* snake]

Colum ('kɒləm) *n* **Padraic** ('pɑːdrɪk). 1881–1972, Irish lyric poet, resident in the US (1914–72)

Columba (kə'lʌmbə) *n* **Saint**. ?521–597 AD, Irish missionary: founded the monastery at Iona (563) from which the Picts were converted to Christianity. Feast day: June 9

Columbia (kə'lʌmbɪə) *n* **1** a river in NW North America, rising in the Rocky Mountains and flowing through British Columbia, then west to the Pacific. Length: about 1930 km (1200 miles) **2** a city in central South Carolina, on the Congaree River: the state capital. Pop: 117 357 (2003 est)

Columbian (kə'lʌmbɪən) *adj* **1** of or relating to the United States **2** relating to Christopher Columbus, Italian navigator and explorer in the service of Spain, who discovered the New World (1492) ▷ *n* **3** a size of printer's type, approximately equal to 16 point; two-line Brevier

columbine ('kɒləm,baɪn) *n* any plant of the ranunculaceous genus *Aquilegia*, having purple, blue, yellow, or red flowers with five spurred petals. Also called: aquilegia [C13: from Medieval Latin *columbīna herba* dovelike plant, from Latin *columbīnus* dovelike, from the resemblance of the flower to a group of doves]

Columbine ('kɒləm,baɪn) *n* (later) the sweetheart of Harlequin in English pantomime

Columbus¹ (kə'lʌmbəs) *n* **1** a city in central Ohio: the state capital. Pop: 728 432 (2003 est) **2** a city in W Georgia, on the Chattahoochee River. Pop: 185 702 (2003 est)

Columbus² (kə'lʌmbəs) *n* **Christopher**. Spanish name *Cristóbal Colón*, Italian name *Cristoforo Colombo*. 1451–1506, Italian navigator and explorer in the service of Spain, who discovered the New World (1492)

column ('kɒləm) *n* **1** an upright post or pillar usually having a cylindrical shaft, a base, and a capital **2 a** a form or structure in the shape of a column: *a column of air* **b** a monument **3** a row, line, or file, as of people in a queue **4** *military* a narrow formation in which individuals or units follow one behind the other **5** *journalism* **a** any of two or more vertical sections of type on a printed page, esp on a newspaper page **b** a regular article or feature in a paper: *the fashion column* **6** a vertical array of numbers or mathematical terms [C15: from Latin *columna*, from *columen* top, peak; related to Latin *collis* hill] > **columnar** (kə'lʌmnə) *adj* > **'columned** *adj*

column inch *n* a unit of measurement for advertising space, one inch deep and one column wide

columnist ('kɒləmɪst, -əmnɪst) *n* a journalist who writes a regular feature in a newspaper

colure (kə'lʊə, 'kəʊlʊə) *n* either of two great circles on the celestial sphere, one of which passes through the celestial poles and the equinoxes and the other through the poles and the solstices [C16: from Late Latin *colūrī*

(plural), from Greek *kolourai* cut short, dock-tailed, from *kolos* docked + *oura* tail; so called because the view of the lower part is curtailed]

Colwyn Bay ('kɒlwɪn) *n* a town and resort in N Wales, in Conwy county borough. Pop: 30 269 (2001)

colza ('kɒlzə) *n* another name for **rape²** [C18: via French (Walloon) *kolzat* from Dutch *koolzaad*, from *kool* cabbage, COLE + *zaad* SEED]

com *an internet domain name for* a commercial company

COM (kɒm) *n* a process in which a computer output is converted direct to microfiche or film, esp 35 or 16 millimetre film [(C)omputer (O)utput on (M)icrofilm]

Com. *abbreviation* **1** Commander **2** committee **3** Commodore

com- *or* **con-** *prefix* together; with; jointly: *commingle* [from Latin *com-*; related to *cum* with. In compound words of Latin origin, *com-* becomes *col-* and *cor-* before *l* and *r*, *co-* before *gn*, *h*, and most vowels, and *con-* before consonants other than *b*, *p*, and *m*. Although its sense in compounds of Latin derivation is often obscured, it means: together, with, etc (*combine, compile*); similar (*conform*); extremely, completely (*consecrate*)]

coma¹ ('kəʊmə) *n*, *pl* -**mas** a state of unconsciousness from which a person cannot be aroused, caused by injury to the head, rupture of cerebral blood vessels, narcotics, poisons, etc [C17: from medical Latin, from Greek *kōma* heavy sleep; related to Greek *koitē* bed, perhaps to Middle Irish *cuma* grief]

coma² ('kəʊmə) *n*, *pl* -**mae** (-miː) **1** *astronomy* the luminous cloud surrounding the frozen solid nucleus in the head of a comet, formed by vaporization of part of the nucleus when the comet is close to the sun **2** *botany* **a** a tuft of hairs attached to the seed coat of some seeds **b** the terminal crown of leaves of palms and moss stems [C17: from Latin: hair of the head, from Greek *komē*]

Comanche (kə'mæntʃɪ) *n* **1** *pl* -**ches** *or* -**che** a member of a Native American people, formerly ranging from the River Platte to the Mexican border, now living in Oklahoma **2** the language of this people, belonging to the Shoshonean subfamily of the Uto-Aztecan family

Comaneci (,kɒmə'netʃɪ) *n* **Nadia**. born 1961, Romanian gymnast; gold medal winner in the 1976 Olympic Games: defected to the US in 1989

comate ('kəʊmeɪt) *adj* *botany* **1** having tufts of hair **2** having or relating to a coma [C17: from Latin *comātus*, from *coma* hair]

comatose ('kəʊmə,təʊs, -,təʊz) *adj* **1** in a state of coma **2** torpid; lethargic

comb (kəʊm) *n* **1** a toothed device of metal, plastic, wood, etc, used for disentangling or arranging hair **2** a tool or machine that separates, cleans, and straightens wool, cotton, etc **3** *Austral & NZ* the fixed cutter on a sheep-shearing machine **4** anything resembling a toothed comb in form or function **5** the fleshy deeply serrated outgrowth on the top of the heads of certain birds, esp the domestic fowl ▷ a honeycomb ▷ *vb* **7** (*tr*) to use a comb on **8** (when *tr*, often foll by *through*) to search or inspect with great care: *the police combed the woods* ▷ See also **comb out** [Old English *camb*; related to Old Norse *kambr*, Old High German *kamb*]

combat *n* ('kɒmbæt, -bət, 'kʌm-) **1** a fight, conflict, or struggle **2 a** an action fought between two military forces **b** (*as modifier*): *a combat jacket* **3** single combat a fight between two individuals; duel ▷ *vb* (kəm'bæt, 'kɒmbæt, 'kʌm-) -**bats**, -**bating**, -**bated** **4** (*tr*) to fight or defy **5** (*intr*; often foll by *with* or *against*) to struggle or strive (against); be in conflict (with): *to combat against disease* [C16: from French, from Old French *combattre*, from Vulgar Latin *combattere* (unattested), from Latin *com-* with + *battuere* to beat, hit]

combatant ('kɒmbət°nt, 'kʌm-) *n* **1** a person or group engaged in or prepared for a fight, struggle, or dispute ▷ *adj* **2** engaged in or ready for combat

combat boot *n* a heavy army boot

combat fatigue *n* another term for **battle fatigue**

combative ('kɒmbətɪv, 'kʌm-) *adj* eager or ready to fight, argue, etc; aggressive > **'combativeness** *n*

combat trousers *or* **combats** ('kɒmbæts, -bəts, 'kʌm-) *pl n* loose casual trousers with large pockets on the legs

combe or **comb** (ku:m) n variant spellings of **coomb**

comber ('kəʊmə) n 1 a person, tool, or machine that combs wool, flax, etc 2 a long curling wave; roller

combination (ˌkɒmbɪ'neɪʃən) n 1 the act of combining or state of being combined 2 a union of separate parts, qualities, etc 3 an alliance of people or parties; group having a common purpose 4 the set of numbers that opens a combination lock 5 Brit a motorcycle with a sidecar attached 6 maths an arrangement of the numbers, terms, etc, of a set into specified groups without regard to order in the group 7 the chemical reaction of two or more compounds, usually to form one other compound 8 chess a tactical manoeuvre involving a sequence of moves and more than one piece > ˌcombi'national adj

combination lock n a type of lock that can only be opened when a set of dials releasing the tumblers of the lock are turned to show a specific sequence of numbers

combinations (ˌkɒmbɪ'neɪʃənz) pl n Brit a one-piece woollen undergarment with long sleeves and legs

combine vb (kəm'baɪn) 1 to integrate or cause to be integrated; join together 2 to unite or cause to unite to form a chemical compound ▷ n ('kɒmbaɪn) 3 agriculture short for **combine harvester** 4 an association of enterprises, esp in order to gain a monopoly of a market 5 an association of business corporations, political parties, sporting clubs, etc, for a common purpose [c15: from Late Latin combīnāre, from Latin com- together + bīnī two by two] > com'binable adj > comˌbina'bility n > combinative ('kɒmbɪˌneɪtɪv, -nətɪv), or combinatorial (ˌkɒmbɪnə'tɔːrɪəl) combinatory ('kɒmbɪnətərɪ, -trɪ) adj

combine harvester ('kɒmbaɪn) n a machine that simultaneously cuts, threshes, and cleans a standing crop of grain

combings ('kəʊmɪŋz) pl n 1 the loose hair, wool, etc, removed by combing 2 the unwanted loose short fibres removed in combing cotton, etc

combining form n a linguistic element that occurs only as part of a compound word, such as anthropo- in anthropology

combo ('kɒmbəʊ) n, pl -bos 1 a small group of musicians, esp of jazz musicians 2 informal any combination

comb out vb (tr, adverb) 1 to remove (tangles or knots) from (the hair) with a comb 2 to isolate and remove for a purpose 3 to survey carefully; examine systematically

combustible (kəm'bʌstəb²l) adj 1 capable of igniting and burning 2 easily annoyed; excitable ▷ n 3 a combustible substance > comˌbusti'bility or com'bustibleness n

combustion (kəm'bʌstʃən) n 1 the process of burning 2 any process in which a substance reacts with oxygen to produce a significant rise in temperature and the emission of light 3 a chemical process in which two compounds, such as sodium and chlorine, react together to produce heat and light [c15: from Old French, from Latin combūrere to burn up, from com- (intensive) + ūrere to burn] > com'bustive n, adj

combustion chamber n an enclosed space in which combustion takes place, such as the space above the piston in the cylinder head of an internal-combustion engine or the chambers in a gas turbine or rocket engine in which fuel and oxidant burn

combustor (kəm'bʌstə) n the combustion system of a jet engine or ramjet, comprising the combustion chamber, the fuel injection apparatus, and the igniter

Comdr military abbreviation Commander

Comdt military abbreviation Commandant

come (kʌm) vb comes, coming, came, come (mainly intr) 1 to move towards a specified person or place 2 to arrive by movement or by making progress 3 to become perceptible: light came into the sky 4 to occur in the course of time: Christmas comes but once a year 5 to happen as a result: no good will come of this 6 to originate or be derived: good may come of evil 7 to occur to the mind: the truth suddenly came to me 8 to extend or reach: she comes up to my shoulder 9 to be produced or offered: that dress comes in red only 10 to arrive at or be brought into a particular state or condition: you will soon come to grief; the new timetable comes into effect on Monday 11 (foll by from) to be or have

been a resident or native (of): I come from London 12 to become: your wishes will come true 13 (tr; takes an infinitive) to be given awareness: I came to realize its enormous value 14 slang to have an orgasm 15 (tr) Brit informal to play the part of: don't come the fine gentleman with me 16 (tr) Brit informal to cause or produce: don't come that nonsense again 17 as...as they come the most characteristic example of a class or type 18 come good informal to recover and perform well after a bad start or setback 19 come to light to be revealed 20 come to light with Austral & NZ informal to find or produce ▷ interj 21 an exclamation expressing annoyance, irritation, etc: come now!; come come! ▷ See also **come about, come across**, etc [Old English cuman; related to Old Norse koma, Gothic qiman, Old High German queman to come, Sanskrit gámati he goes]

come about vb (intr, adverb) 1 to take place; happen 2 nautical to change tacks

come across vb (intr) 1 (preposition) to meet or find by accident 2 (adverb) (of a person or his or her words) to communicate the intended meaning or impression 3 (often foll by with) to provide what is expected

come at vb (intr, preposition) 1 to discover or reach (facts, the truth, etc) 2 to attack (a person): he came at me with an axe 3 Austral slang to agree to do (something)

comeback ('kʌmˌbæk) n informal 1 a return to a former position, status, etc 2 a return or response, esp recriminatory 3 a quick reply; retort ▷ vb **come back** (intr, adverb) 4 to return 5 to become fashionable again 6 come back to someone (of something forgotten) to return to someone's memory

come between vb (intr, preposition) to cause the estrangement or separation of (two people)

come by vb (intr, preposition) to find or obtain (a thing), esp accidentally: do you ever come by any old books?

Comecon ('kɒmɪˌkɒn) n (formerly) an association of Soviet-oriented Communist nations, founded in 1949 to coordinate economic development, etc; it was disbanded in 1991 when free-market policies were adopted by its members [c20 Co(uncil for) M(utual) Econ(omic Assistance)]

comedian (kə'miːdɪən) n 1 an entertainer who specializes in jokes, comic skits, etc 2 an actor in comedy 3 an amusing or entertaining person: sometimes used ironically

comedienne (kəˌmiːdɪ'ɛn) n a female comedian

comedo ('kɒmɪˌdəʊ) n, pl comedos or comedones (ˌkɒmɪ'dəʊniːz) pathol the technical name for **blackhead** [c19: from New Latin, from Latin: glutton, from comedere to eat up, from com- (intensive) + edere to eat]

comedown ('kʌmˌdaʊn) n 1 a decline in position, status, or prosperity 2 informal a disappointment ▷ vb **come down** (intr, adverb) 3 to come to a place regarded as lower 4 to lose status, wealth, etc (esp in the phrase **to come down in the world**) 5 to reach a decision: the report came down in favour of a pay increase 6 (often foll by to) to be handed down or acquired by tradition or inheritance 7 Brit to leave college or university 8 (foll by with) to succumb (to illness or disease) 9 (foll by on) to rebuke or criticize harshly 10 (foll by to) to amount in essence (to): it comes down to two choices

comedy ('kɒmɪdɪ) n, pl -dies 1 a dramatic or other work of light and amusing character 2 the genre of drama represented by works of this type 3 (in classical literature) a play in which the main characters and motive triumph over adversity 4 the humorous aspect of life or of events 5 an amusing event or sequence of events 6 humour or comic style: the comedy of Chaplin [c14: from Old French comédie, from Latin cōmoedia, from Greek kōmōidia, from kōmos village festival + aeidein to sing] > co'medic adj

comedy of manners n a comedy dealing with the way of life and foibles of a social group

come forward vb (intr, adverb) 1 to offer one's services; volunteer 2 to present oneself

come-hither adj (usually prenominal) informal alluring; seductive: a come-hither look

come in vb (intr, mainly adverb) 1 to enter, used in the imperative when admitting a person 2 to prove to be: it came in useful 3 to become fashionable or seasonable

c

4 *cricket* to begin an innings **5** *sport* to finish a race (in a certain position) **6** *radio, television* to be received: *news is coming in of a big fire in Glasgow* **7** (of money) to be received as income **8** to play a role; advance one's interests: *where do I come in?* **9** (foll by *for*) to be the object of: *the Chancellor came in for a lot of criticism in the Commons*

come into *vb* (*intr, preposition*) **1** to enter **2** to inherit

comely ('kʌmlɪ) *adj* **-lier, -liest** good-looking; attractive [Old English *cȳmlīc* beautiful; related to Old High German *cūmi* frail, Middle High German *komlīche* suitably] > **'comeliness** *n*

Comenius (kə'meɪnɪəs) *n* **John Amos**, Czech name *Jan Amos Komensky*. 1592–1670, Czech educational reformer

come of *vb* (*intr, preposition*) **1** to be descended from **2** to result from: *nothing came of his experiments*

come off *vb* (*intr, mainly adverb*) **1** (*also preposition*) to fall (from), losing one's balance **2** to become detached or be capable of being detached **3** (*preposition*) to be removed from (a price, tax, etc): *will anything come off income tax in the budget?* **4** (*copula*) to emerge from or as if from a trial or contest: *he came off the winner* **5** *informal* to take place or happen **6** *informal* to have the intended effect; succeed: *his jokes did not come off* **7** *slang* to have an orgasm

come on *vb* (*intr, mainly adverb*) **1** (of power, a water supply, etc) to become available; start running or functioning **2** to make or show progress; develop: *my plants are coming on nicely* **3** to advance, esp in battle **4** to begin: *she felt a cold coming on; a new bowler has come on* **5** *theatre* to make an entrance on stage **6** **come on!** **a** hurry up! **b** cheer up! pull yourself together! **c** make an effort! **d** don't exaggerate! stick to the facts! **7** to attempt to give a specified impression: *he came on like a hard man* **8** **come on strong** to make a forceful or exaggerated impression **9** **come on to** *informal* to make sexual advances to ▷ *n* **come-on** **10** *informal* anything that serves as a lure or enticement

come out *vb* (*intr, adverb*) **1** to be made public or revealed: *the news of her death came out last week* **2** to make a debut in society or on stage **3 a** Also called: **come out of the closet** to declare openly that one is a homosexual **b** to reveal or declare any habit or practice formerly concealed **4** *chiefly Brit* to go on strike **5** to declare oneself: *the government came out in favour of scrapping the project* **6** to be shown visibly or clearly: *you came out very well in the photos* **7** to yield a satisfactory solution: *these sums just won't come out* **8** to be published: *the paper comes out on Fridays* **9** (foll by *in*) to become covered with **10** (foll by *with*) to speak or declare openly: *you can rely on him to come out with the facts*

come over *vb* (*intr*) **1** (*adverb*) (of a person or his words) to communicate the intended meaning or impression: *he came over very well* **2** (*adverb*) to change allegiances **3** *informal* to undergo or feel a particular sensation: *I came over funny*

comer ('kʌmə) *n* **1** (*in combination*) a person who comes: *all-comers; newcomers* **2** *informal* a potential success

come round *or* **come around** *vb* (*intr, adverb*) **1** to be restored to life or consciousness **2** to change or modify one's mind or opinion

comestible (kə'mɛstɪbəl) *n* (*usually plural*) food [c15: from Late Latin *comestibilis*, from *comedere* to eat up; see COMEDO]

comet ('kɒmɪt) *n* a celestial body that travels around the sun, usually in a highly elliptical orbit: thought to consist of a solid frozen nucleus part of which vaporizes on approaching the sun to form a gaseous luminous coma and a long luminous tail [c13: from Old French *comète*, from Latin *comēta*, from Greek *komētēs* long-haired, from *komē* hair] > **cometary** *or* **cometic** (kɒ'mɛtɪk) *adj*

come through *vb* (*intr*) **1** (*adverb*) to emerge successfully **2** (*preposition*) to survive (an illness, setback, etc)

come to *vb* (*intr*) **1** (*adverb or preposition and reflexive*) to regain consciousness or return to one's normal state **2** (*adverb*) *nautical* to slow a vessel or bring her to a stop **3** (*preposition*) to amount to (a sum of money) **4** (*preposition*) to arrive at (a certain state): *what is the world coming to?*

come up *vb* (*intr, adverb*) **1** to come to a place regarded as

higher **2** (of the sun) to rise **3** to present itself or be discussed: *that question will come up again* **4** *Brit* to begin a term, esp one's first term, at a college or university **5** to appear from out of the ground: *my beans have come up early this year* **6** *informal* to win: *have your premium bonds ever come up?* **7** **come up against** to be faced with; come into conflict or competition with **8** **come up to** to equal or meet a standard **9** **come up with** to produce or find

come upon *vb* (*intr, preposition*) to meet or encounter unexpectedly

comeuppance (,kʌm'ʌpəns) *n* *informal* just retribution [c19: from *come up* (in the sense: to appear before a judge or court for judgment)]

comfit ('kʌmfɪt, 'kɒm-) *n* a sugar-coated sweet containing a nut or seed [c15: from Old French, from Latin *confectum* something prepared, from *conficere* to produce; see CONFECT]

comfort ('kʌmfət) *n* **1** a state of ease or well-being **2** relief from affliction, grief, etc **3** a person, thing, or event that brings solace or ease **4** (*usually plural*) something that affords physical ease and relaxation ▷ *vb* (*tr*) **5** to ease the pain of; soothe; cheer **6** to bring physical ease to [c13: from Old French *confort*, from Late Latin *confortāre* to strengthen very much, from Latin *con-* (intensive) + *fortis* strong] > **'comforting** *adj* > **'comfortless** *adj*

comfortable ('kʌmftəbəl, 'kʌmfətəbəl) *adj* **1** giving comfort or physical relief **2** at ease **3** free from affliction or pain **4** (of a person or situation) relaxing **5** *informal* having adequate income **6** *informal* (of income) adequate to provide comfort > **'comfortably** *adv*

comforter ('kʌmfətə) *n* **1** a person or thing that comforts **2** *chiefly Brit* a woollen scarf **3** a baby's dummy **4** *US* a quilted bed covering

Comforter ('kʌmfətə) *n* *Christianity* an epithet of the Holy Spirit [c14: translation of Latin *consōlātor*, representing Greek *paraklētos*; see PARACLETE]

comfort food *n* food that is enjoyable to eat and makes the eater feel better emotionally

comfrey ('kʌmfrɪ) *n* any hairy Eurasian boraginaceous plant of the genus *Symphytum*, having blue, purplish-pink, or white flowers [c15: from Old French *cunfirie*, from Latin *conferva* water plant; see CONFERVA]

comfy ('kʌmfɪ) *adj* **-fier, -fiest** *informal* short for **comfortable**

comic ('kɒmɪk) *adj* **1** of, relating to, characterized by, or characteristic of comedy **2** (*prenominal*) acting in, writing, or composing comedy: *a comic writer* **3** humorous; funny ▷ *n* **4** a person who is comic, esp a comic actor; comedian **5** a book or magazine containing comic strips [c16: from Latin *cōmicus*, from Greek *kōmikos* relating to COMEDY]

comical ('kɒmɪkəl) *adj* **1** causing laughter **2** ludicrous; laughable > **'comically** *adv*

comic opera *n* a play largely set to music, employing comic effects or situations

comic strip *n* a sequence of drawings in a newspaper, magazine, etc, relating a humorous story or an adventure. Also called: **strip cartoon**

Comines *or* **Commines** (French kɔmin) *n* **Philippe de** (filip də). ?1447–?1511, French diplomat and historian, noted for his *Mémoires* (1489–98)

coming ('kʌmɪŋ) *adj* **1** (*prenominal*) (of time, events, etc) approaching or next **2** promising (esp in the phrase **up and coming**) **3** of future importance: *this is the coming thing* **4** **have it coming to one** *informal* to deserve what one is about to suffer ▷ *n* **5** arrival or approach

Comintern *or* **Komintern** ('kɒmɪn,tɜːn) *n* short for **Communist International**: an international Communist organization founded by Lenin in Moscow in 1919 and dissolved in 1943; it degenerated under Stalin into an instrument of Soviet politics. Also called: **Third International**

comity ('kɒmɪtɪ) *n, pl* **-ties 1** mutual civility; courtesy **2** short for **comity of nations** [c16: from Latin *cōmitās*, from *cōmis* affable, obliging, of uncertain origin]

comity of nations *n* the friendly recognition accorded by one nation to the laws and usages of another

comma ('kɒmə) *n* **1** the punctuation mark (,) indicating a slight pause in the spoken sentence and used where there is a listing of items or to separate a nonrestrictive clause or phrase from a main clause **2** *music* a minute interval [c16: from Latin, from Greek *komma* clause, from *kopteinto* cut]

comma bacillus *n* a comma-shaped bacterium, *Vibrio comma*, that causes cholera in man: family *Spirillaceae*

command (kə'mɑːnd) *vb* **1** (when *tr*, may take a clause as *object or an infinitive*) to order, require, or compel **2** to have or be in control or authority over (a person, situation, etc) **3** (*tr*) to receive as due or because of merit: *his nature commands respect* **4** to dominate (a view, etc) as from a height ▷ *n* **5** an order; mandate **6** the act of commanding **7** the power or right to command **8** the exercise of the power to command **9** ability or knowledge; control: *a command of French* **10** chiefly *military* the jurisdiction of a commander **11** a military unit or units commanding a specific area or function, as in the RAF **12** *Brit* **a** an invitation from the monarch **b** (*as modifier*): *a command performance* **13** *computing* a word or phrase that can be selected from a menu or typed after a prompt in order to carry out an action [c13: from Old French *commander*, from Latin *com-* (intensive) + *mandāre* to entrust, enjoin, command]

Command (kə'mɑːnd) *n* any of the three main branches of the Canadian military forces

commandant ('kɒmən,dænt, -,dɑːnt) *n* an officer commanding a place, group, or establishment

command economy *n* an economy in which business activities and the allocation of resources are determined by government order rather than market forces. Also called: **planned economy**

commandeer (,kɒmən'dɪə) *vb* (*tr*) **1** to seize for public or military use **2** to seize arbitrarily [c19: from Afrikaans *kommandeer*, from French *commander* to COMMAND]

commander (kə'mɑːndə) *n* **1** an officer in command of a military formation or operation **2** a naval commissioned rank junior to captain but senior to lieutenant commander **3** the second in command of larger British warships **4** someone who holds authority **5** a high-ranking member of some knightly or fraternal orders **6** an officer responsible for a district of the Metropolitan Police in London ▷ com'mander,ship *n*

commander in chief *n, pl* commanders in chief the officer holding supreme command of the forces in an area or operation

commanding (kə'mɑːndɪŋ) *adj* (*usually prenominal*) **1** being in command **2** having the air of authority: *a commanding voice* **3** (of a position, situation, etc) exerting control **4** (of a height, viewpoint, etc) overlooking; advantageous ▷ com'mandingly *adv*

commanding officer *n* an officer in command of a military unit

command language *n* *computing* the language used to access a computer system

commandment (kə'mɑːndmənt) *n* **1** a divine command, esp one of the Ten Commandments of the Old Testament **2** *literary* any command

command module *n* the cone-shaped module used as the living quarters in an Apollo spacecraft and functioning as the splashdown vehicle

commando (kə'mɑːndəʊ) *n, pl* -dos or -does **1 a** an amphibious military unit trained for raiding **b** a member of such a unit **2** the basic unit of the Royal Marine Corps **3** (originally) an armed force raised by Boers during the Boer War **4** (*modifier*) denoting or relating to a commando or force of commandos: *a commando raid; a commando unit* [c19: from Afrikaans *kommando*, from Dutch *commando* command, from French *commander* to COMMAND]

command paper *n* (in Britain) a government document that is presented to Parliament, in theory by royal command

command post *n* *military* the position from which a unit commander and his staff exercise command

commedia dell'arte (*Italian* kɔm'meːdia del'larte) *n* a form of popular comedy developed in Italy during the 16th to 18th centuries, with stock characters such as Punchinello, Harlequin, and Columbine, in situations

improvised from a plot outline [Italian, literally: comedy of art]

comme il faut *French* (kɔm il fo) correct or correctly

commemorate (kə'mɛmə,reɪt) *vb* (*tr*) to honour or keep alive the memory of [c16: from Latin *commemorāre* be mindful of, from *com-* (intensive) + *memorāre* to remind, from *memor* mindful] ▷ com'memorative or com'memoratory *adj* ▷ com'memo,rator *n* ▷ co,mmemo'ration *n* ▷ com,memo'rational *adj*

commence (kə'mɛns) *vb* to start or begin; come or cause to come into being, operation, etc [c14: from Old French *comencer*, from Vulgar Latin *cominitiāre* (unattested), from Latin *com-* (intensive) + *initiāre* to begin, from *initium* a beginning]

commencement (kə'mɛnsmənt) *n* **1** the beginning; start **2 a** *US & Canadian* a ceremony for the presentation of awards at secondary schools **b** *US* a ceremony for the conferment of academic degrees

commend (kə'mɛnd) *vb* (*tr*) **1** to present or represent as being worthy of regard, confidence, kindness, etc; recommend **2** to give in charge; entrust **3** to express a good opinion of; praise **4** to give the regards of: *commend me to your aunt* [c14: from Latin *commendāre* to commit to someone's care, from *com-* (intensive) + *mandāre* to entrust] ▷ com'mendable *adj* ▷ com'mendably *adv* ▷ com'mendatory *adj*

commendation (,kɒmɛn'deɪʃən) *n* **1** the act or an instance of commending; praise **2** an award

commensal (kə'mɛnsəl) *adj* **1** (of two different species of plant or animal) living in close association, such that one species benefits without harming the other **2** *rare* of or relating to eating together, esp at the same table ▷ *n* **3** a commensal plant or animal **4** *rare* a companion at table [c14: from Medieval Latin *commensālis*, from Latin *com-* together + *mensa* table] ▷ com'mensalism *n* ▷ commensality (,kɒmɛn'sælɪtɪ) *n*

commensurable (kə'mɛnsərəbəl, -ʃə-) *adj* **1** *maths* **a** having a common factor **b** having units of the same dimensions and being related by whole numbers **2** well-proportioned; proportionate ▷ com,mensura'bility *n* ▷ com'mensurably *adv*

commensurate (kə'mɛnsərɪt, -ʃə-) *adj* **1** having the same extent or duration **2** corresponding in degree, amount, or size; proportionate **3** able to be measured by a common standard; commensurable [c17: from Late Latin *commēnsūrātus*, from Latin *com-* same + *mēnsurāre* to MEASURE] ▷ com'mensurately *adv*

comment ('kɒmɛnt) *n* **1** a remark, criticism, or observation **2** talk or gossip **3** a note explaining or criticizing a passage in a text **4** explanatory or critical matter added to a text ▷ *vb* **5** (when *intr*, often foll by *on*; when *tr*, takes a clause as object) to remark or express an opinion **6** (*intr*) to write notes explaining or criticizing a text [c15: from Latin *commentum* invention, from *comminisci* to contrive, related to *mens* mind] ▷ 'commenter *n*

commentariat (,kɒmən'tɛərɪæt) *n* the journalists and broadcasters who analyse and comment on current affairs [c20: from COMMENTATOR + PROLETARIAT]

commentary ('kɒməntərɪ, -trɪ) *n, pl* -taries **1** an explanatory series of notes or comments **2** a spoken accompaniment to a broadcast, film, etc, esp of a sporting event **3** an explanatory essay or treatise on a text **4** (*usually plural*) a personal record of events or facts: *the commentaries of Caesar*

commentate ('kɒmən,teɪt) *vb* **1** (*intr*) to serve as a commentator **2** (*tr*) *US* to make a commentary on (a text, event, etc)

commentator ('kɒmən,teɪtə) *n* **1** a person who provides a spoken commentary for a broadcast, film, etc, esp of a sporting event **2** a person who writes notes on a text, event, etc

commerce ('kɒmɜːs) *n* **1** the activity embracing all forms of the purchase and sale of goods and services **2** social relations and exchange, esp of opinions, attitudes, etc [c16: from Latin *commercium* trade, from *commercāri*, from *mercāri* to trade, from *merx* merchandise]

commercial (kə'mɜːʃəl) *adj* **1** of, connected with, or engaged in commerce; mercantile **2** sponsored or paid

c

for by an advertiser: *commercial television* **3** having profit as the main aim: *commercial music* **4** (of goods, chemicals, etc) of unrefined quality or presentation and produced in bulk for use in industry ▷ *n* **5** a commercially sponsored advertisement on radio or television > **commerciality** (kə,mɜːʃɪˈælɪtɪ) *n* > com'mercially *adv*

commercial art *n* graphic art for commercial uses such as advertising, packaging, etc

commercial bank *n* a bank primarily engaged in making short-term loans from funds deposited in current accounts

commercial break *n* an interruption in a radio or television programme for the broadcasting of advertisements

commercialism (kəˈmɜːʃəˌlɪzəm) *n* **1** the spirit, principles, or procedure of commerce **2** exclusive or inappropriate emphasis on profit

commercialize *or* **commercialise** (kəˈmɜːʃəˌlaɪz) *vb* (*tr*) **1** to make commercial in aim, methods, or character **2** to exploit for profit, esp at the expense of quality > com,merciali'zation *or* com,merciali'sation *n*

commercial paper *n* a short-term negotiable document, such as a bill of exchange, promissory note, etc, calling for the transference of a specified sum of money at a designated date

commercial traveller *n* another name for **travelling salesman**

commercial vehicle *n* a vehicle for carrying goods or (less commonly) passengers

commie *or* **commy** (ˈkɒmɪ) *informal and derogatory* ▷ *n, pl* -mies **1** short for **communist** ▷ *adj* **2** short for **communist**

commination (ˌkɒmɪˈneɪʃən) *n* **1** the act or an instance of threatening punishment or vengeance **2** *Church of England* a recital of prayers, including a list of God's judgments against sinners, in the office for Ash Wednesday [C15: from Latin *comminātiō*, from *comminārī* to menace, from *com-* (intensive) + *minārī* to threaten] > **comminatory** (ˈkɒmɪnətərɪ, -trɪ) *adj*

Commines (French kɔmin) *n* a variant spelling of (Philippe de) **Comines**

commingle (kɒˈmɪŋᵊl) *vb* to mix or be mixed; blend

comminute (ˈkɒmɪˌnjuːt) *vb* **1** to break (a bone) into several small fragments **2** to divide (property) into small lots [C17: from Latin *comminuere*, from *com-* (intensive) + *minuere* to reduce; related to MINOR] > ,commi'nution *n*

commis (ˈkɒmɪs, ˈkɒmɪ) *n, pl* -mis **1** an agent or deputy ▷ *adj* **2** (of a waiter or chef) apprentice [C16: meaning: deputy: from French, from *commettre* to employ, COMMIT]

commiserate (kəˈmɪzəˌreɪt) *vb* (when *intr*, usually foll by *with*) to feel or express sympathy or compassion (for) [C17: from Latin *commiserārī*, from *com-* together + *miserārī* to bewail, pity, from *miser* wretched] > com,mise'ration *n* > com'miser,ator *n*

commissar (ˈkɒmɪˌsɑː, ˌkɒmɪˈsɑː) *n* (in the former Soviet Union) **1** Also called: political commissar an official of the Communist Party responsible for political education, esp in a military unit **2** Also called: People's Commissar (before 1946) the head of a government department [C20: from Russian *kommissar*, from German, from Medieval Latin *commissārius* COMMISSARY]

commissariat (ˌkɒmɪˈsɛərɪət) *n* **1** (in the former Soviet Union) a government department before 1946 **2** a military department in charge of food supplies, equipment, etc [C17: from New Latin *commissāriātus*, from Medieval Latin *commissārius* COMMISSARY]

commissary (ˈkɒmɪsərɪ) *n, pl* -saries **1** *US* a shop supplying food or equipment, as in a military camp **2** *US army* an officer responsible for supplies and food **3** *US* a snack bar or restaurant in a film studio **4** a representative or deputy, esp an official representative of a bishop [C14: from Medieval Latin *commissārius* official in charge, from *committere* to entrust, COMMIT] > commissarial (ˌkɒmɪˈsɛərɪəl) *adj*

commission (kəˈmɪʃən) *n* **1** a duty or task committed to a person or group to perform **2** authority to undertake or perform certain duties or functions **3** a document granting such authority **4** *military* **a** a document conferring a rank on an officer **b** the rank or authority thereby granted **5** a group of people charged with

certain duties: *a commission of inquiry* **6** a government agency or board empowered to exercise administrative, judicial, or legislative authority. See also **Royal Commission 7 a** the authority given to a person or organization to act as an agent to a principal in commercial transactions **b** the fee allotted to an agent for services rendered **8** the state of being charged with specific duties or responsibilities **9** the act of committing a sin, crime, etc **10** good working condition or (esp of a ship) active service (esp in the phrases **in** *or* **into commission, out of commission**) ▷ *vb* **11** (*tr*) to grant authority to; charge with a duty or task **12** (*tr*) *military* to confer a rank on or authorize an action by **13** (*tr*) to equip and test (a ship) for active service **14** to make or become operative or operable: *the plant is due to commission next year* **15** (*tr*) to place an order for (something): *to commission a portrait* [C14: from Old French, from Latin *commissiō* a bringing together, from *committere* to COMMIT]

commissionaire (kəˌmɪʃəˈnɛə) *n chiefly Brit* a uniformed doorman at a hotel, theatre, etc [C18: from French, from COMMISSION]

commissioned officer *n* a military officer holding a commission, such as Second Lieutenant in the British Army, Acting Sub-Lieutenant in the Royal Navy, Pilot Officer in the Royal Air Force, and officers of all ranks senior to these

commissioner (kəˈmɪʃənə) *n* **1** a person authorized to perform certain tasks or endowed with certain powers **2** *government* any of several types of civil servant **3** a member of a commission > com'missioner,ship *n*

commissioner for oaths *n* a solicitor authorized to authenticate oaths on sworn statements

commit (kəˈmɪt) *vb* -mits, -mitting, -mitted (*tr*) **1** to hand over, as for safekeeping; charge; entrust **2** commit to memory to learn by heart; memorize **3** to confine officially or take into custody: *to commit someone to prison* **4** (*usually passive*) to pledge or align (oneself), as to a particular cause, action, or attitude: *a committed radical* **5** to order (forces) into action **6** to perform (a crime, error, etc); do; perpetrate **7** to surrender, esp for destruction: *she committed the letter to the fire* **8** to refer (a bill, etc) to a committee of a legislature [C14: from Latin *committere* to join, from *com-* together + *mittere* to put, send] > com'mittable *adj* > com'mitter *n*

commitment (kəˈmɪtmənt) *n* **1** the act of committing or pledging **2** the state of being committed or pledged **3** an obligation, promise, etc that restricts one's freedom of action **4** *law* a written order of a court directing that a person be imprisoned. Also called (esp formerly): **mittimus 5** a future financial obligation or contingent liability

committee *n* **1** (kəˈmɪtɪ) a group of people chosen or appointed to perform a specified service or function **2** (ˌkɒmɪˈtiː) (formerly) a person to whom the care of a mentally incompetent person or his property was entrusted by a court [C15: from *committen* to entrust + -EE]

committeeman (kəˈmɪtɪmən, -ˌmæn) *n, pl* -men *chiefly US* a member of one or more committees > com'mittee,woman *fem n*

Committee of the Whole House *n* (in Britain) an informal sitting of the House of Commons to discuss and amend a bill

commode (kəˈməʊd) *n* **1** a piece of furniture, usually highly ornamented, containing drawers or shelves **2** a bedside table with a cabinet below for a chamber pot or washbasin **3** a movable piece of furniture, sometimes in the form of a chair, with a hinged flap concealing a chamber pot [C17: from French, from Latin *commodus* COMMODIOUS]

commodify (kəˈmɒdɪˌfaɪ) *vb* -fies, -fying, -fied (*tr*) to treat (something) inappropriately as if it can be acquired or marketed like other commodities: *you can't commodify art* > com,modifi'cation *n*

commodious (kəˈməʊdɪəs) *adj* **1** (of buildings, rooms, etc) large and roomy; spacious **2** *archaic* suitable; convenient [C15: from Medieval Latin *commodiōsus*, from Latin *commodus* convenient, from *com-* with + *modus* measure] > com'modiousness *n*

commoditize *or* **commoditise** (kəˈmɒdɪˌtaɪz) *vb* (*tr*) another term for **commodify**

commodity (kə'mɒdɪtɪ) *n, pl* **-ties** **1** an article of commerce **2** something of use, advantage, or profit **3** *economics* an exchangeable unit of economic wealth, esp a primary product or raw material [c14: from Old French *commodité*, from Latin *commoditās* suitability, benefit; see COMMODIOUS]

commodore ('kɒmə,dɔː) *n* **1** *Brit* a naval rank junior to rear admiral and senior to captain **2** the senior captain of a shipping line **3** the officer in command of a convoy of merchant ships **4** the senior flag office of a yacht or boat club [c17: probably from Dutch *commandeur*, from French, from Old French *commander* to COMMAND]

Commodus (kə'məʊdəs, 'kɒmədəs) *n* **Lucius Aelius Aurelius** ('luːsɪəs 'iːlɪəs ɔː'riːlɪəs), son of Marcus Aurelius. 161–192 AD, Roman emperor (180–192), noted for his tyrannical reign

common ('kɒmən) *adj* **1** belonging to or shared by two or more people: *common property* **2** belonging to or shared by members of one or more nations or communities; public: *a common culture* **3** of ordinary standard; average **4** prevailing; widespread: *common opinion* **5** widely known or frequently encountered; ordinary: *a common brand of soap* **6** widely known and notorious: *a common nuisance* **7** *derogatory* considered by the speaker to be low-class, vulgar, or coarse **8** (*prenominal*) having no special distinction, rank, or status: *the common man* **9** *maths* **a** having a specified relationship with a group of numbers or quantities: *common denominator* **b** (of a tangent) tangential to two or more circles **10** *grammar* (in certain languages) denoting or belonging to a gender of nouns, esp one that includes both masculine and feminine referents **11** *common or garden informal* ordinary; unexceptional ▷ *n* **12** (*sometimes plural*) a tract of open public land, esp one now used as a recreation area **13** *law* the right to go onto someone else's property and remove natural products, as by pasturing cattle or fishing (esp in the phrase **right of common**) **14** *Christianity* **a** a form of the proper of the Mass used on festivals that have no special proper of their own **b** the ordinary of the Mass **15 in common** mutually held or used with another or others ▷ See also **commons** [c13: from Old French *commun*, from Latin *commūnis* general, universal] > 'commonness *n* > commonly ('kɒmənlɪ) *adv*

commonage ('kɒmənɪdʒ) *n* **1** *chiefly law* **a** the use of something, esp a pasture, in common with others **b** the right to such use **2** the state of being held in common **3** another word for **commonalty** (sense 1)

Common Agricultural Policy *n* the full name for **CAP**

commonality (,kɒmə'nælɪtɪ) *n, pl* **-ties** **1** the fact of being common to more than one individual; commonness **2** another word for **commonalty** (sense 1)

commonalty ('kɒmənəltɪ) *n, pl* **-ties** **1** the ordinary people as distinct from those with authority, rank, or title, esp when considered as a political and social unit or estate of the realm **2** the members of an incorporated society [c13: from Old French *comunalte*, from *comunal* communal]

common carrier *n* a person or firm engaged in the business of transporting goods or passengers

common chord *n* *music* a chord consisting of the keynote, a major or minor third, and a perfect fifth

common cold *n* a mild viral infection of the upper respiratory tract, characterized by sneezing, coughing, watery eyes, nasal congestion, sore throat, etc

commoner ('kɒmənə) *n* **1** a person who does not belong to the nobility **2** a person who has a right in or over common land jointly with another or others **3** *Brit* a student at a university or other institution who is not on a scholarship

common fraction *n* another name for **simple fraction**

common ground *n* an agreed basis, accepted by both or all parties, for identifying issues in an argument

common knowledge *n* something widely or generally known

common law *n* **1** the body of law based on judicial decisions and custom, as distinct from statute law **2** *common-law* (*modifier*) denoting a marriage deemed to exist after a couple have cohabited for several years:

common-law marriage; common-law wife

Common Market *n* the Common Market *formerly* an informal name for **European Economic Community**

common noun *n* *grammar* a noun that refers to each member of a whole class sharing the features connoted by the noun, as for example *planet, orange,* and *drum.* See **proper noun**

commonplace ('kɒmən,pleɪs) *adj* **1** ordinary; everyday **2** dull and obvious; trite: *commonplace prose* ▷ *n* **3** something dull and trite, esp a remark; platitude; truism **4** a passage in a book marked for inclusion in a commonplace book, etc **5** an ordinary or common thing [c16: translation of Latin *locus commūnis* argument of wide application, translation of Greek *koinos topos*] > 'common,placeness *n*

commonplace book *n* a notebook in which quotations, poems, remarks, etc, that catch the owner's attention are entered

common room *n* *chiefly Brit* a sitting room in schools, colleges, etc, for the relaxation of students or staff

commons ('kɒmənz) *n* **1** (*functioning as plural*) the lower classes as contrasted with the ruling classes of society; the commonalty **2** (*functioning as singular*) *Brit* a building or hall for dining, recreation, etc, usually attached to a college **3** (*usually functioning as plural*) *Brit* food or rations (esp in the phrase **short commons**)

Commons ('kɒmənz) *n* the Commons See **House of Commons**

common sense *n* **1** plain ordinary good judgment; sound practical sense ▷ *adj* common-sense *or* common-sensical **2** inspired by or displaying sound practical sense

common time *n* *music* a time signature indicating four crotchet beats to the bar; four-four time. Symbol: C

commonweal ('kɒmən,wiːl) *n* *archaic* **1** the good of the community **2** another name for **commonwealth**

commonwealth ('kɒmən,wɛlθ) *n* **1** the people of a state or nation viewed politically; body politic **2** a state or nation in which the people possess sovereignty; republic **3** a group of persons united by some common interest

Commonwealth ('kɒmən,wɛlθ) *n* the Commonwealth **1** official name: the Commonwealth of Nations an association of sovereign states, almost all of which were at some time dependencies of the UK. All member states recognize the reigning British sovereign as **Head of the Commonwealth 2** the republic that existed in Britain from 1649 to 1660 **3** the official designation of Australia, four states of the US (Kentucky, Massachusetts, Pennsylvania, and Virginia), and Puerto Rico

Commonwealth Day *n* the anniversary of Queen Victoria's birth, May 24, celebrated (now on the second Monday in March) as a holiday in many parts of the Commonwealth. Former name: **Empire Day**

Commonwealth of Independent States *n* a loose organization of former Soviet republics, excluding the Baltic States, formed in 1991. Abbreviation: **CIS**

commotion (kə'məʊʃən) *n* **1** violent disturbance; upheaval **2** political insurrection; disorder **3** a confused noise; din [c15: from Latin *commōtiō*, from *commovēre* to throw into disorder, from *com-* (intensive) + *movēre* to MOVE]

communal ('kɒmjʊnᵊl) *adj* **1** belonging or relating to a community as a whole **2** of or relating to a commune or a religious community > **communality** (,kɒmjʊ'nælɪtɪ) *n* > 'communally *adv*

communalism ('kɒmjʊnə,lɪzəm) *n* **1** a system or theory of government in which the state is seen as a loose federation of self-governing communities **2** the practice or advocacy of communal living or ownership > 'communalist *n* > ,communa'listic *adj*

communalize *or* **communalise** ('kɒmjʊnə,laɪz) *vb* (*tr*) to render (something) the property of a commune or community > ,communali'zation *or* ,communali'sation *n*

communautaire *French* (kɔmynoter) *adj* supporting the principles of the European Community (now the European Union) [literally: community (as modifier)]

commune¹ *vb* (kə'mjuːn) (*intr*; usually foll by *with*) **1** to talk or converse intimately **2** to experience strong emotion or spiritual feelings (for): *to commune with nature*

▷ *n* ('kɒmjuːn) **3** intimate conversation; exchange of thoughts; communion [c13: from Old French *comuner* to hold in common, from *comun* COMMON]

commune² ('kɒmjuːn) *n* **1** a group of families or individuals living together and sharing possessions and responsibilities **2** any small group of people having common interests or responsibilities **3** the smallest administrative unit in Belgium, France, Italy, and Switzerland, governed by a mayor and council **4** a medieval town enjoying a large degree of autonomy [c18: from French, from Medieval Latin *commūnia*, from Latin: things held in common, from *commūnis* COMMON]

Commune ('kɒmjuːn) *n French history* **1** See **Paris Commune 2** a committee that governed Paris during the French Revolution and played a leading role in the Reign of Terror: suppressed 1794

communicable (kə'mjuːnɪkəb³l) *adj* **1** capable of being communicated **2** (of a disease or its causative agent) capable of being passed on readily ▷ com,munica'bility *n* ▷ com'municably *adv*

communicant (kə'mjuːnɪkənt) *n* **1** *Christianity* a person who receives Communion **2** a person who communicates or informs

communicate (kə'mjuːnɪˌkeɪt) *vb* **1** to impart (knowledge) or exchange (thoughts, feelings, or ideas) by speech, writing, gestures, etc **2** (*tr*; usually foll by *to*) to allow (a feeling, emotion, etc) to be sensed (by), willingly or unwillingly; transmit (to): *the dog communicated his fear to the other animals* **3** (*intr*) to have a sympathetic mutual understanding **4** (*intr*; usually foll by *with*) to make or have a connecting passage or route; connect **5** (*tr*) to transmit (a disease); infect **6** (*intr*) *Christianity* to receive or administer Communion [c16: from Latin *commūnicāre* to share, from *commūnis* COMMON] ▷ com'muni,cator *n* ▷ com'municatory *adj*

communication (kə,mjuːnɪ'keɪʃən) *n* **1** the act or an instance of communicating; the imparting or exchange of information, ideas, or feelings **2** something communicated, such as a message, letter, or telephone call **3** (usually plural; sometimes functioning as singular) the study of ways in which human beings communicate, including speech, gesture, telecommunication systems, publishing and broadcasting media, etc **4** a connecting route, passage, or link **5** (plural) *military* the system of routes and facilities by which forces, supplies, etc, are moved up to or within an area of operations

communication cord *n Brit* a cord or chain in a train which may be pulled by a passenger to stop the train in an emergency

communications satellite *n* an artificial satellite used to relay radio, television, and telephone signals around the earth, usually in geostationary orbit

communicative (kə'mjuːnɪkətɪv) *adj* **1** inclined or able to communicate readily; talkative **2** of or relating to communication

communion (kə'mjuːnjən) *n* **1** an exchange of thoughts, emotions, etc **2** possession or sharing in common; participation **3** (foll by *with*) strong feeling or spiritual feelings (for): *communion with nature* **4** a religious group or denomination having a common body of beliefs, doctrines, and practices **5** the spiritual union held by Christians to exist between individual Christians and Christ, their Church, or their fellow Christians [c14: from Latin *commūniō* general participation, from *commūnis* COMMON]

Communion (kə'mjuːnjən) *n Christianity* **1** the act of participating in the Eucharist **2** the celebration of the Eucharist, esp the part of the service during which the consecrated elements are received ▷ Also called: **Holy Communion**

communiqué (kə'mjuːnɪˌkeɪ) *n* an official communication or announcement, esp to the press or public [c19: from French, from *communiquer* to COMMUNICATE]

communism ('kɒmjuˌnɪzəm) *n* **1** advocacy of a classless society in which private ownership has been abolished and the means of production and subsistence belong to the community **2** any social, economic, or political movement or doctrine aimed at achieving such a society

3 (usually capital) a political movement based upon the writings of Karl Marx, the German political philosopher (1818–83), that considers history in terms of class conflict and revolutionary struggle, resulting eventually in the victory of the proletariat and the establishment of a socialist order based on public ownership of the means of production **4** (usually capital) a social order or system of government established by a ruling Communist Party, esp in the former Soviet Union **5** communal living; communalism [c19: from French *communisme*, from *commun* COMMON]

Communism Peak *n* a former name for **Ismoil Somoni**

communist ('kɒmjunɪst) *n* **1** a supporter of any form of communism **2** (often capital) a supporter of Communism or a Communist movement or state **3** (often capital) a member of a Communist party **4** (often capital) US any person holding left-wing views, esp when considered subversive **5** a person who practises communal living; communalist ▷ *adj* **6** of, characterized by, favouring, or relating to communism; communistic ▷ ,commu'nistic *adj* ▷ ,commu'nistically *adv*

Communist China *n* another name for (the People's Republic of) **China**

community (kə'mjuːnɪtɪ) *n, pl* -ties **1 a** the people living in one locality **b** the locality in which they live **c** (as modifier): *community spirit* **2** a group of people having cultural, religious, ethnic, or other characteristics in common: *the Protestant community* **3** a group of nations having certain interests in common **4** the public in general; society **5** common ownership or participation **6** similarity or agreement: *community of interests* **7** (in Wales since 1974 and Scotland since 1975) the smallest unit of local government; a subdivision of a district **8** *ecology* a group of interdependent plants and animals inhabiting the same region and interacting with each other through food and other relationships [c14: from Latin *commūnitās*, from *commūnis* COMMON]

community centre *n* a building used by members of a community for social gatherings, educational activities, etc

community charge *n* (formerly in Britain) a flat-rate charge paid by each adult in a community to his or her local authority in place of rates. Also called: **poll tax**

community chest *n US* a fund raised by voluntary contribution for local welfare activities

community council *n* (in Scotland and Wales) an independent voluntary local body set up to attend to local interests and organize community activities

community education *n* the provision of a wide range of educational and special interest courses and activities by a local authority

community home *n* (in Britain) **1** a home provided by a local authority for children who cannot remain with parents or relatives, or be placed with foster parents **2** a boarding school for young offenders

community policing *n* the assigning of the same one or two policemen to a particular area so that they become familiar with the residents and the residents with them, as a way of reducing crime

community service *n* voluntary work, intended to be for the common good, usually done as part of an organized scheme

community support officer *n Brit* a uniformed officer who is not a member of the police force but who has certain powers to be exercised in supplementing the role of the police, esp crowd control, tackling anti-social behaviour, etc. Abbreviation: **CSO**

communize *or* **communise** ('kɒmjuˌnaɪz) *vb* (*tr*; sometimes capital) **1** to make (property) public; nationalize **2** to make (a person or country) communist ▷ ,communi'zation *or* ,communi'sation *n*

commutate ('kɒmjuˌteɪt) *vb* (*tr*) **1** to reverse the direction of (an electric current) **2** to convert (an alternating current) into a direct current

commutation (,kɒmju'teɪʃən) *n* **1** a substitution or exchange **2** the replacement of one method of payment by another **3** the reduction in severity of a penalty imposed by law **4** the process of commutating an electric current

commutative (kəˈmjuːtətɪv, ˈkɒmjʊˌteɪtɪv) *adj* **1** relating to or involving substitution **2** *maths, logic* **a** (of an operator) giving the same result irrespective of the order of the arguments; thus disjunction and addition are commutative but implication and subtraction are not **b** relating to this property: *the commutative law of addition*

commutator (ˈkɒmjʊˌteɪtə) *n* **1** a device used to reverse the direction of flow of an electric current **2** the segmented metal cylinder or disc mounted on the armature shaft of an electric motor, generator, etc, used to make electrical contact with the rotating coils and ensure unidirectional current flow

commute (kəˈmjuːt) *vb* **1** (*intr*) to travel some distance regularly between one's home and one's place of work **2** (*tr*) to substitute; exchange **3** (*tr*) *law* to reduce (a sentence) to one less severe **4** to pay (an annuity) at one time, esp with a discount, instead of in instalments **5** (*tr*) to transform; change: *to commute base metal into gold* [C17: from Latin *commutāre* to replace, from *com-* mutually + *mutāre* to change] > com'mutable *adj* > ˌcomˌmuta'bility *n*

commuter (kəˈmjuːtə) *n* a person who travels to work over an appreciable distance, usually from the suburbs to the centre of a city

Como (ˈkəʊməʊ; Italian ˈkɔːmo) *n* a city in N Italy, in Lombardy at the SW end of **Lake Como**: tourist centre. Pop: 78 680 (2001)

comodo or **commodo** (kəˈməʊdəʊ) *adj, adv music* (to be performed) at a convenient relaxed speed [Italian: comfortable, from Latin *commodus*, convenient; see COMMODIOUS]

Comoros (ˈkɒməˌrəʊz, kəˈmɔːrəʊz) *pl n* a republic consisting of three volcanic islands in the Indian Ocean, off the NW coast of Madagascar; a French territory from 1947; became independent in 1976 except for Mayotte, the fourth island in the group, which chose to remain French. Official languages: Comorian, French, and Arabic; Swahili is used commercially. Religion: Muslim. Currency: franc. Capital: Moroni. Pop: 790 000 (2004 est). Area: 1862 sq km (719 sq miles)

comose (ˈkəʊməʊs, kəʊˈməʊs) *adj botany* another word for **comate** [C18: from Latin *comōsus* hairy, from *coma* long hair; see COMA²]

Comox (ˈkəʊmɒks) *n* a member of a Salishan Native Canadian people living on Vancouver Island

comp (kɒmp) *informal* ▷ *n* **1** a compositor **2** an accompaniment **3** a competition ▷ *vb* **4** (*intr*) to work as a compositor in the printing industry **5** to play an accompaniment (to)

compact¹ *adj* (kəmˈpækt, ˈkɒmpækt) **1** closely packed together; dense **2** neatly fitted into a restricted space **3** concise; brief **4** well constructed; solid; firm **5** (foll by *of*) composed or made up (of) ▷ *vb* (kəmˈpækt) (*tr*) **6** to pack or join closely together; compress; condense **7** (foll by *of*) to create or form by pressing together: *sediment compacted of three types of clay* **8** *metallurgy* to compress (a metal powder) to form a stable product suitable for sintering ▷ *n* (ˈkɒmpækt) **9** a small flat case containing a mirror, face powder, etc, designed to be carried in a woman's handbag **10** *US & Canadian* a comparatively small and economical car [C16: from Latin *compactus*, from *compingere* to put together, from *com-* together + *pangere* to fasten] > com'pactly *adv* > com'pactness *n*

compact² (ˈkɒmpækt) *n* an official contract or agreement [C16: from Latin *compactum*, from *compaciscī* to agree, from *com-* together + *pacscī* to contract; see PACT]

compact disc (ˈkɒmpækt) *n* a small digital audio disc on which sound is recorded as a series of metallic pits enclosed in PVC; the disc is spun by the compact disc player and read by an optical laser system. Also called: compact audio disc. Abbreviation CD, CAD

compact disc erasable *n* the full name for **CDE**

compact disc recordable *n* the full name for **CDR**

compact video disc *n* a compact laser disc that plays both pictures and sound

compadre (kɒmˈpɑːdreɪ, kəm-) *n Southwestern US* a male friend [from Spanish: godfather, from Medieval Latin *compater*, from Latin *com-* with + *pater* father]

compages (kəmˈpeɪdʒiːz) *n* (*functioning as singular*) a structure or framework [C17: from Latin, from *com-* together + *pag-*, from *pangēre* to fasten]

companion¹ (kəmˈpænjən) *n* **1 a** a person who is an associate of another or others; comrade **2** (esp formerly) an employee, usually a woman, who provides company for an employer, esp an elderly woman **3 a** one of a pair; match **b** (as modifier): *a companion volume* **4** a guidebook or handbook **5** a member of the lowest rank of any of certain orders of knighthood **6** *astronomy* the fainter of the two components of a double star ▷ *vb* **7** (*tr*) to accompany or be a companion to [C13: from Late Latin *compāniō*, literally: one who eats bread with another, from Latin *com-* with + *pānis* bread] > com'panionˌship *n*

companion² (kəmˈpænjən) *n nautical* a raised frame on an upper deck with windows to give light to the deck below [C18: from Dutch *kompanje* quarterdeck, from Old French *compagne*, from Old Italian *compagna* pantry, perhaps ultimately from Latin *pānis* bread]

companionable (kəmˈpænjənəbəl) *adj* suited to be a companion; sociable > com'panionableness or comˌpaniona'bility *n* > com'panionably *adv*

companion animal *n* an animal kept as a pet

companionate (kəmˈpænjənɪt) *adj* **1** resembling, appropriate to, or acting as a companion **2** harmoniously suited

companionway (kəmˈpænjənˌweɪ) *n* a stairway or ladder leading from one deck to another in a boat or ship

company (ˈkʌmpənɪ) *n, pl* **-nies** **1** a number of people gathered together; assembly **2** the fact of being with someone; companionship: *I enjoy her company* **3** a social visitor or visitors; guest or guests **4** a business enterprise **5** the members of an enterprise not specifically mentioned in the enterprise's title. Abbreviation: **Co** **6** a group of actors, usually including business and technical personnel **7** a unit of around 100 troops, usually comprising two or more platoons **8** the officers and crew of a ship **9** a unit of Girl Guides **10** *English history* a medieval guild **11 keep company** or **bear company a** to accompany (someone) **b** (esp of lovers) to associate with each other; spend time together ▷ *vb* **-nies**, **-nying**, **-nied 12** *archaic* to keep company or associate (with someone) [C13: from Old French *compaignie*, from *compain* companion, fellow, from Late Latin *compāniō*; see COMPANION¹]

company doctor *n* **1** a businessperson or accountant who specializes in turning ailing companies into profitable enterprises **2** a physician employed by a company to look after its staff and to advise on health matters

company sergeant major *n military* the senior Warrant Officer II in a British or Commonwealth regiment or battalion, responsible under the company second in command for all aspects of duty and discipline of the NCOs and men in that subunit

company town *n US & Canadian* a town built by a company for its employees

comparable (ˈkɒmpərəbəl) *adj* **1** worthy of comparison **2** able to be compared (with) > ˌcompara'bleness or 'comparability *n*

comparative (kəmˈpærətɪv) *adj* **1** denoting or involving comparison: *comparative literature* **2** judged by comparison; relative: *a comparative loss of prestige* **3** *grammar* denoting the form of an adjective that indicates that the quality denoted is possessed to a greater extent. In English the comparative form of an adjective is usually marked by the suffix *-er* or the word *more* ▷ *n* **4** the comparative form of an adjective > com'paratively *adv* > com'parativeness *n*

comparative advertising *n* a form of advertising in which a product is compared favourably with similar products on the market

compare (kəmˈpɛə) *vb* **1** (*tr*; usually foll by *to*) to regard or represent as analogous or similar; liken: *the general has been compared to Napoleon* **2** (*tr*; usually foll by *with*) to examine in order to observe resemblances or differences: *to compare rum with gin* **3** (*intr*; usually foll by *with*) to be of the same or similar quality or value: *gin compares with rum in alcoholic content* **4** (*intr*) to bear a specified relation of quality or value when examined: *this car compares badly with the other* **5** *(tr)* grammar to give the positive, comparative, and superlative forms of (an adjective) **6 compare notes** to exchange opinions ▷ *n* **7** comparison or analogy (esp in the phrase **beyond compare**) [c15: from Old French *comparer*, from Latin *comparāre* to couple together, match, from *compar* equal to one another, from *com-* together + *par* equal; see PAR]

comparison (kəmˈpærɪsᵊn) *n* **1** the act or process of comparing **2** the state of being compared **3** comparable quality or qualities; likeness: *there was no comparison between them* **4** a rhetorical device involving comparison, such as a simile **5** Also called: **degrees of comparison** *grammar* the listing of the positive, comparative, and superlative forms of an adjective or adverb **6 bear comparison** *or* **stand comparison** to be sufficiently similar in class or range to be compared with (something else), esp favourably

compartment (kəmˈpɑːtmənt) *n* **1** one of the sections into which an area, esp an enclosed space, is divided or partitioned **2** any separate part or section: *a compartment of the mind* **3** a small storage space; locker [c16: from French *compartiment*, ultimately from Late Latin *compartīrī* to share, from Latin *com-* with + *partīrī* to apportion, from *pars* PART] > compartmental (ˌkɒmpɑːˈtmɛntᵊl) *adj* > ˌcompartˈmentally *adv*

compartmentalize *or* **compartmentalise** (ˌkɒmpɑːˈtmɛntᵊˌlaɪz) *vb* *(usually tr)* to put or divide into (compartments, categories, etc), esp to an excessive degree > ˌcompartˌmentaliˈzation *or* ˌcompartˌmentaliˈsation *n*

compass (ˈkʌmpəs) *n* **1** an instrument for finding direction, usually having a magnetized needle which points to magnetic north swinging freely on a pivot **2** Also called: **pair of compasses** *(often plural)* an instrument used for drawing circles, measuring distances, etc, that consists of two arms, joined at one end, one arm of which serves as a pivot or stationary reference point, while the other is extended or describes a circle **3** limits or range: *within the compass of education* **4** *music* the interval between the lowest and highest note attainable by a voice or musical instrument ▷ *vb* *(tr)* **5** to encircle or surround; hem in **6** to comprehend or grasp mentally **7** to achieve; attain; accomplish **8** *obsolete* to plot [c13: from Old French *compas*, from *compasser* to measure, from Vulgar Latin *compassāre* (unattested) to pace out, ultimately from Latin *passus* step] > ˈcompassable *adj*

compass card *n* a compass in the form of a card that rotates so that "0°" or "North" points to magnetic north

compassion (kəmˈpæʃən) *n* a feeling of distress and pity for the suffering or misfortune of another, often including the desire to alleviate it [c14: from Old French, from Late Latin *compassiō* fellow feeling, from *compatī* to suffer with, from Latin *com-* with + *patī* to bear, suffer]

compassionate (kəmˈpæʃənət) *adj* **1** showing or having compassion **2 compassionate leave** leave granted on the grounds of bereavement, family illness, etc > comˈpassionately *adv* > comˈpassionateness *n*

Compassion Club *n* the Compassion Club (in Canada) a nonprofit organization that provides uncontaminated cannabis for medical purposes and natural therapies in a safe environment

compassion fatigue *n* the inability to react sympathetically to a crisis, disaster, etc, because of overexposure to previous crises, disasters, etc

compass rose *n* a circle or decorative device printed on a map or chart showing the points of the compass measured from true north and usually magnetic north

compass saw *n* a hand saw with a narrow tapered blade for making a curved cut

compatible (kəmˈpætəbᵊl) *adj* **1** (usually foll by *with*) able to exist together harmoniously **2** (usually foll by *with*) consistent or congruous: *her deeds were not compatible with her ideology* **3** (of pieces of machinery, computer equipment, etc) capable of being used together without special modification or adaptation [c15: from Medieval Latin *compatibilis*, from Late Latin *compatī* to be in sympathy with; see COMPASSION] > comˌpatiˈbility *or*

com'patibleness *n* > com'patibly *adv*

compatriot (kəmˈpætrɪət) *n* a fellow countryman [c17: from French *compatriote*, from Late Latin *compatriōta*; see PATRIOT] > comˌpatriˈotic *adj*

compeer (ˈkɒmpɪə) *n* **1** a person of equal rank, status, or ability; peer **2** a companion or comrade [c13: from Old French *comper*, from Medieval Latin *compater* godfather; see COMPADRE]

compel (kəmˈpɛl) *vb* -pels, -pelling, -pelled *(tr)* **1** to cause (someone) by force (to be or do something) **2** to obtain by force; exact: *to compel obedience* [c14: from Latin *compellere* to drive together, from *com-* together + *pellere* to drive] > comˈpellable *adj*

compelling (kəmˈpɛlɪŋ) *adj* **1** arousing or denoting strong interest, esp admiring interest **2** (of an argument, evidence, etc) convincing

compendious (kəmˈpɛndɪəs) *adj* containing or stating the essentials of a subject in a concise form; succinct > comˈpendiously *adv* > comˈpendiousness *n*

compendium (kəmˈpɛndɪəm) *n*, *pl* -diums *or* -dia (-dɪə) **1** *Brit* a book containing a collection of useful hints **2** *Brit* a selection, esp of different games or other objects in one container **3** a concise but comprehensive summary of a larger work [c16: from Latin: a saving, literally: something weighed, from *pendere* to weigh]

compensate (ˈkɒmpɛnˌseɪt) *vb* **1** to make amends to (someone), esp for loss or injury **2** *(tr)* to serve as compensation for (injury, loss, etc) **3** to offset or counterbalance the effects of (a force, weight, movement, etc) so as to nullify the effects of an undesirable influence and produce equilibrium **4** *(intr)* to attempt to conceal or offset one's shortcomings by the exaggerated exhibition of qualities regarded as desirable [c17: from Latin *compēnsāre*, from *pēnsāre*, from *pendere* to weigh] > compensatory (ˈkɒmpɛnˌseɪtərɪ, kəmˈpɛnsətəri, -trɪ) *or* compensative (ˈkɒmpɛnˌseɪtɪv, kəmˈpɛnsə-) *adj*

compensation (ˌkɒmpɛnˈseɪʃən) *n* **1** the act or process of making amends for something **2** something given as reparation for loss, injury, etc; indemnity **3** the attempt to conceal or offset one's shortcomings by the exaggerated exhibition of qualities regarded as desirable > ˌcompenˈsational *adj*

compensation culture *n* a culture in which people are very ready to go to law over even relatively minor incidents in the hope of gaining compensation

comper (ˈkɒmpə) *n* *informal* a person who regularly enters competitions in newspapers, magazines, etc, esp competitions offering consumer goods as prizes [c20: COMP(ETITION) + -ER¹] > ˈcomping *n*

compere (ˈkɒmpeə) *Brit* ▷ *n* **1** a master of ceremonies who introduces cabaret, television acts, etc ▷ *vb* **2** to act as a compere (for) [c20: from French, literally: godfather; see COMPEER, COMPADRE]

compete (kəmˈpiːt) *vb* *(intr; often foll by with)* to contend (against) for profit, an award, athletic supremacy, etc; engage in a contest (with) [c17: from Late Latin *competere* to strive together, from Latin: to meet, come together, agree, from *com-* together + *petere* to seek]

competence (ˈkɒmpɪtəns) *n* **1** the condition of being capable; ability **2** a sufficient income to live on **3** the state of being legally competent or qualified

competency (ˈkɒmpɪtənsɪ) *n*, *pl* -cies **1** *law* capacity to testify in a court of law; eligibility to be sworn **2** a less common word for **competence** (senses 1, 2)

competent (ˈkɒmpɪtənt) *adj* **1** having sufficient skill, knowledge, etc; capable **2** suitable or sufficient for the purpose: *a competent answer* **3** *law* (of a witness) having legal capacity; qualified to testify, etc [c14: from Latin *competēns*, from *competere* to be competent; see COMPETE] > ˈcompetently *adv*

competition (ˌkɒmpɪˈtɪʃən) *n* **1** the act of competing; rivalry **2** a contest in which a winner is selected from among two or more entrants **3** a series of games, sports events, etc **4** the opposition offered by a competitor or competitors **5** a competitor or competitors offering opposition

competitive (kəmˈpɛtɪtɪv) *adj* **1** involving or determined by rivalry: *competitive sports* **2** sufficiently low in price or high in quality to be successful against commercial rivals **3** relating to or characterized by an urge to compete: *a competitive personality* > com'petitiveness *n*

competitor (kəm'pɛtɪtə) *n* a person, group, team, firm, etc, that vies or competes; rival

Compiègne (French kɔ̃pjɛn) *n* a city in N France, on the Oise River: scene of the armistice at the end of World War I (1918) and of the Franco-German armistice of 1940. Pop: 41 254 (1999)

compile (kəm'paɪl) *vb* (*tr*) **1** to make or compose from other materials or sources: *to compile a list of names* **2** to collect or gather for a book, hobby, etc **3** *computing* to create (a set of machine instructions) from a high-level programming language, using a compiler [C14: from Latin *compilāre* to pile together, plunder, from *com-* together + *pīlāre* to thrust down, pack] > compilation (ˌkɒmpɪ'leɪʃən) *n*

compiler (kəm'paɪlə) *n* **1** a person who collects or compiles something **2** a computer program by which a high-level programming language, such as COBOL or FORTRAN, is converted into machine language that can be acted upon by a computer. See **assembler**

complacency (kəm'pleɪsənsɪ) *or* **complacence** *n, pl* **-cencies** *or* **-cences** a feeling of satisfaction, esp extreme self-satisfaction; smugness

complacent (kəm'pleɪsᵊnt) *adj* pleased or satisfied, esp extremely self-satisfied [C17: from Latin *complacēns* very pleasing, from *complacēre* to be most agreeable to, from *com-* (intensive) + *placēre* to please] > com'placently *adv*

complain (kəm'pleɪn) *vb* (*intr*) **1** to express resentment, displeasure, etc, esp habitually; grumble **2** (foll by *of*) to state the presence of pain, illness, etc, esp in the hope of sympathy: *she complained of a headache* [C14: from Old French *complaindre*, from Vulgar Latin *complangere* (unattested), from Latin *com-* (intensive) + *plangere* to bewail] > com'plainer *n* > com'plainingly *adv*

complainant (kəm'pleɪnənt) *n law* a person who makes a complaint, usually before justices; plaintiff

complaint (kəm'pleɪnt) *n* **1** the act of complaining; an expression of grievance **2** a cause for complaining; grievance **3** a mild ailment

complaisant (kəm'pleɪzᵊnt) *adj* showing a desire to comply or oblige; polite [C17: from French *complaire*, from Latin *complacēre* to please greatly; compare COMPLACENT] > com'plaisance *n*

complement *n* ('kɒmplɪmənt) **1** a person or thing that completes something **2** a complete amount, number, etc (often in the phrase **full complement**) **3** the officers and crew needed to man a ship **4** *grammar* a noun phrase that follows a copula or similar verb, as for example *an idiot* in the sentence *He is an idiot* **5** *maths* the angle that when added to a specified angle produces a right angle **6** *logic, maths* the class of all things, or of all members of a given universe of discourse, that are not members of a given set **7** *immunol* a group of proteins in the blood serum that, when activated by antibodies, causes destruction of alien cells, such as bacteria ▷ *vb* ('kɒmplɪˌmɛnt) **8** (*tr*) to add to, make complete, or form a complement to [C14: from Latin *complēmentum*, from *complēre* to fill up, from *com-* (intensive) + *plēre* to fill] > ˌcomplemen'tation *n*

complementary (ˌkɒmplɪ'mɛntərɪ, -trɪ) *adj* **1** acting as or forming a complement; completing **2** forming a satisfactory or balanced whole **3** involving or using the treatments and techniques of complementary medicine > ˌcomple'mentarily *or* ˌcomple'mentally *adv* > ˌcomple'mentariness *n*

complementary angle *n* either of two angles whose sum is 90°. See **supplementary angle**

complementary colour *n* one of any pair of colours, such as yellow and blue, that give white or grey when mixed in the correct proportions

complementary DNA *n* a form of DNA artificially synthesized from a messenger RNA template and used in genetic engineering to produce gene clones. Abbreviation: cDNA

complementary medicine *n* the treatment, alleviation, or prevention of disease by such techniques as osteopathy, homeopathy, aromatherapy, and

acupuncture, allied with attention to such factors as diet and emotional stability, which can affect a person's wellbeing. Also called: alternative medicine

complete (kəm'pliːt) *adj* **1** having every necessary part or element; entire **2** ended; finished **3** (*prenominal*) thorough; absolute: *he is a complete rogue* **4** perfect in quality or kind: *he is a complete scholar* **5** (of a logical system) constituted such that a contradiction arises on the addition of any proposition that cannot be deduced from the axioms of the system **6** *archaic* expert or skilled; accomplished ▷ *vb* (*tr*) **7** to make whole or perfect **8** to end; finish **9** (in land law) to pay any outstanding balance on a contract for the conveyance of land in exchange for the title deeds, so that the ownership of the land changes hands **10** *American football* (of a quarterback) to make a forward pass successfully [C14: from Latin *complētus*, past participle of *complēre* to fill up; see COMPLEMENT] > com'pletely *adv* > com'pleteness *n* > com'pletion *n*

completist (kəm'pliːtɪst) *n* a person who collects objects or memorabilia obsessively

complex ('kɒmplɛks) *adj* **1** made up of various interconnected parts; composite **2** (of thoughts, writing, etc) intricate or involved **3** *maths* of or involving one or more complex numbers ▷ *n* **4** a whole made up of interconnected or related parts: *a building complex* **5** *psychoanal* a group of emotional ideas or impulses that have been banished from the conscious mind but that continue to influence a person's behaviour **6** *informal* an obsession or excessive fear: *he's got a complex about cats* **7** any chemical compound in which one molecule is linked to another by a coordinate bond [C17: from Latin *complexus*, from *complectī* to entwine, from *com-* together + *plectere* to braid] > 'complexness *n*

● **USAGE** *Complex* is sometimes wrongly used where
● *complicated* is meant. *Complex* is properly used to say
● only that something consists of several parts. It
● should not be used to say that, because something
● consists of many parts, it is difficult to understand or
● analyse

complex fraction *n maths* a fraction in which the numerator or denominator or both contain fractions. Also called: compound fraction

complexion (kəm'plɛkʃən) *n* **1** the colour and general appearance of a person's skin, esp of the face **2** aspect, character, or nature: *the general complexion of a nation's finances* **3** obsolete **a** the temperament of a person **b** the temperature and general appearance of the body [C14: from medical Latin *complexiō* one's bodily characteristics, from Latin: a combination, from *complectī* to embrace; see COMPLEX] > com'plexional *adj*

complexioned (kəm'plɛkʃənd) *adj* (*in combination*) of a specified complexion: *light-complexioned*

complexity (kəm'plɛksɪtɪ) *n, pl* **-ties 1** the state or quality of being intricate or complex **2** something intricate or complex; complication

complexity theory *n* **1** *mathematics* the study of complex systems, including subjects such as chaos theory and genetic algorithms **2** *computing* a field in theoretical computer science dealing with the resources required during computation to solve a given problem

complex number *n* any number of the form $a + ib$, where a and b are real numbers and $i = \sqrt{-1}$

complex sentence *n grammar* a sentence containing at least one main clause and one subordinate clause

compliance (kəm'plaɪəns) *or* **compliancy** *n* **1** the act of complying; acquiescence **2** a disposition to yield to or comply with others **3** a measure of the ability of a mechanical system to respond to an applied vibrating force, expressed as the reciprocal of the system's stiffness

compliance officer *n* a specialist, usually a lawyer, employed by a financial group operating in a variety of fields and for multiple clients to ensure that no conflict of interest arises and that all obligations and regulations are complied with

compliant (kəm'plaɪənt) *or* **compliable** (kəm'plaɪəbᵊl) *adj* complying, obliging, or yielding > com'pliantly *or* com'pliably *adv*

complicate vb ('kɒmplɪ,keɪt) **1** to make or become complex ▷ adj ('kɒmplɪkɪt) **2** biology folded on itself: a complicate leaf [c17: from Latin complicāre to fold together, from plicāre to fold]

complicated ('kɒmplɪ,keɪtɪd) adj made up of intricate parts or aspects that are difficult to understand or analyse > 'compli,catedly adv

complication (,kɒmplɪ'keɪʃən) n **1** a condition, event, etc, that is complex or confused **2** the act or process of complicating **3** a situation, event, or condition that complicates or frustrates: her coming was a serious complication **4** a disease or disorder arising as a consequence of another disease

complice ('kɒmplɪs, 'kʌm-) n obsolete an associate or accomplice [c15: from Old French, from Late Latin complex partner, associate, from Latin complicāre to fold together; see COMPLICATE]

complicit (,kɒm'plɪsɪt) adj involved with others in reprehensible or illegal activity [c20: back formation from COMPLICITY]

complicity (kəm'plɪsɪtɪ) n, pl -ties **1** the fact or condition of being an accomplice, esp in a criminal act **2** a less common word for **complexity**

compliment n ('kɒmplɪmənt) **1** a remark or act expressing respect, admiration, etc **2** (usually plural) a greeting of respect or regard ▷ vb ('kɒmplɪ,ment) (tr) **3** to express admiration for; congratulate or commend **4** to express or show respect or regard for, esp by a gift [c17: from French, from Italian complimento, from Spanish cumplimiento, from cumplir to complete, do what is fitting, be polite]

● USAGE Avoid confusion with **complement**

complimentary (,kɒmplɪ'mentərɪ, -trɪ) adj **1** conveying, containing, or resembling a compliment **2** expressing praise; flattering **3** given free, esp as a courtesy or for publicity purposes > ,compli'mentarily adv

compline ('kɒmplɪn, -plaɪn) or **complin** ('kɒmplɪn) n RC Church the last of the seven canonical hours of the divine office [c13: from Old French complie, from Medieval Latin hōra complēta, literally: the completed hour, from Latin complēre to fill up, COMPLETE]

complot archaic n ('kɒmplɒt) **1** a plot or conspiracy ▷ vb (kəm'plɒt) -plots, -plotting, -plotted **2** to plot together; conspire [c16: from Old French, of unknown origin] > com'plotter n

comply (kəm'plaɪ) vb -plies, -plying, -plied (intr; usually foll by with) to act in accordance with rules, wishes, etc; be obedient (to) [c17: from Italian complire, from Spanish cumplir to complete; see COMPLIMENT]

compo ('kɒmpəʊ) n, pl -pos **1** a mixture of materials, such as mortar, plaster, etc **2** Austral & NZ informal compensation, esp for injury or loss of work ▷ adj **3** military intended to last for several days: compo rations; a compo pack [short for composition, compensation, composite]

component (kəm'pəʊnənt) n **1** a constituent part or aspect of something more complex **2** Also called: **element** any electrical device, such as a resistor, that has distinct electrical characteristics and that may be connected to other electrical devices to form a circuit **3** maths one of a set of two or more vectors whose resultant is a given vector **4** one of the minimum number of chemically distinct constituents necessary to describe fully the composition of each phase in a system. See **phase rule** ▷ adj **5** forming or functioning as a part or aspect; constituent [c17: from Latin compōnere to put together, from pōnere to place, put] > componential (,kɒmpəʊ'nenʃəl) adj

comport (kəm'pɔːt) vb **1** (tr) to conduct or bear (oneself) in a specified way **2** (intr; foll by with) to agree (with); correspond (to) [c16: from Latin comportāre to bear, collect, from com- together + portāre to carry]

compose (kəm'pəʊz) vb (mainly tr) **1** to put together or make up by combining; put in proper order **2** to be the component elements of **3** to produce or create (a musical or literary work) **4** (intr) to write music **5** to calm (someone, esp oneself); make quiet **6** to adjust or settle (a quarrel, etc) **7** to order the elements of (a painting, sculpture, etc); design **8** printing to set up (type) [c15: from Old French composer, from Latin compōnere to put in place; see COMPONENT]

composed (kəm'pəʊzd) adj (of people) calm; tranquil; serene > composedly (kəm'pəʊzɪdlɪ) adv

composer (kəm'pəʊzə) n **1** a person who composes music **2** a person or machine that composes anything, esp type for printing

composite adj ('kɒmpəzɪt) **1** composed of separate parts; compound **2** of, relating to, or belonging to the plant family Asteraceae **3** maths capable of being factorized or decomposed: a composite function **4** (sometimes capital) denoting or relating to one of the five classical orders of architecture: characterized by a combination of the Ionic and Corinthian styles ▷ n **5** something composed of separate parts; compound **6** any plant of the family Asteraceae (formerly Compositae), typically having flower heads composed of ray flowers (e.g. dandelion), disc flowers (e.g. thistle), or both (e.g. daisy) **7** a material, such as reinforced concrete, made of two or more distinct materials **8** a proposal that has been composited ▷ vb ('kɒmpəˌzaɪt) **9** (tr) to merge related motions from local branches of (a political party, trade union, etc) so as to produce a manageable number of proposals for discussion at national level [c16: from Latin compositus well arranged, from compōnere to collect, arrange; see COMPONENT] > 'compositely adv > 'compositeness n

composite school n Eastern Canadian a secondary school offering both academic and nonacademic courses

composition (,kɒmpə'zɪʃən) n **1** the act of putting together or making up by combining parts or ingredients **2** something formed in this manner or the resulting state or quality; a mixture **3** the parts of which something is composed or made up; constitution **4** a work of music, art, or literature **5** the harmonious arrangement of the parts of a work of art in relation to each other and to the whole **6** a piece of writing undertaken as an academic exercise in grammatically acceptable writing; an essay **7** printing the act or technique of setting up type **8** a settlement by mutual consent, esp a legal agreement whereby the creditors agree to accept partial payment of a debt in full settlement [c14: from Old French, from Latin compositus; see COMPOSITE, -ION]

compositor (kəm'pɒzɪtə) n printing a person who sets and corrects type and generally assembles text and illustrations for printing

compos mentis Latin ('kɒmpəs 'mentɪs) adj (postpositive) of sound mind; sane

compost ('kɒmpɒst) n **1** a mixture of organic residues such as decomposed vegetation, manure, etc, used as a fertilizer **2** a mixture, normally of plant remains, peat, charcoal, etc, in which plants are grown, esp in pots **3** rare a compound or mixture ▷ vb (tr) **4** to make (vegetable matter) into compost **5** to fertilize with compost [c14: from Old French compost, from Latin compositus put together; see COMPOSITE]

Compostela (Spanish kɒmpɒs'tela) n See **Santiago de Compostela**

composure (kəm'pəʊʒə) n calmness, esp of the mind; tranquillity; serenity

compound[1] n ('kɒmpaʊnd) **1** a substance that contains atoms of two or more chemical elements held together by chemical bonds **2** any combination of two or more parts, aspects, etc **3** a word formed from two existing words or combining forms ▷ vb (kəm'paʊnd) (mainly tr) **4** to mix or combine so as to create a compound or other product **5** to make by combining parts, elements, aspects, etc: to compound a new plastic **6** to intensify by an added element: his anxiety was compounded by her crying **7** (also intr) to come to an agreement in (a quarrel, dispute, etc) **8** (also intr) to settle (a debt, promise, etc) for less than what is owed; compromise **9** law to agree not to prosecute in return for a consideration: to compound a crime ▷ adj ('kɒmpaʊnd) **10** composed of or created by the combination of two or more parts, elements, etc **11** (of a word) consisting of elements that are also words or productive combining forms **12** (of a verb or the tense, mood, etc, of a verb) formed by using an auxiliary verb in addition to the main verb **13** music **a** denoting a time in which the number of beats per bar is a multiple of three: *six-four is an example of compound time* **b** (of an interval) greater than an octave **14** (of a steam engine, turbine, etc) having multiple stages in which the steam or working fluid from one stage is used in a subsequent stage **15** (of a piston engine) having a turbocharger powered by a turbine in the exhaust stream [c14: from earlier *compounen*, from Old French *compondre* to collect, set in order, from Latin *compōnere*] > com'poundable *adj*

compound² ('kɒmpaʊnd) *n* **1** (esp formerly in South Africa) an enclosure, esp on the mines, containing the living quarters for Black workers **2** any similar enclosure, such as a camp for prisoners of war [c17: by folk etymology (influenced by COMPOUND¹) from Malay *kampong* village]

compound eye *n* the convex eye of insects and some crustaceans, consisting of numerous separate light-sensitive units (ommatidia)

compound fraction *n* another name for **complex fraction**

compound fracture *n* a fracture in which the broken bone either pierces the skin or communicates with an open wound

compound interest *n* interest calculated on both the principal and its accrued interest

compound leaf *n* a leaf consisting of two or more leaflets borne on the same leafstalk

compound number *n* a quantity expressed in two or more different but related units: *3 hours 10 seconds is a compound number*

compound sentence *n* a sentence containing at least two coordinate clauses

compound time *n* See **compound¹** (sense 13)

comprehend (,kɒmprɪ'hɛnd) *vb* **1** to perceive or understand **2** (*tr*) to comprise or embrace; include [c14: from Latin *comprehendere*, from *prehendere* to seize]

comprehensible (,kɒmprɪ'hɛnsəb³l) *adj* capable of being comprehended > ,compre,hensi'bility *or* ,compre'hensibleness *n* > ,compre'hensibly *adv*

comprehension (,kɒmprɪ'hɛnʃən) *n* **1** the act or capacity of understanding **2** the state of including or comprising something; comprehensiveness

comprehensive (,kɒmprɪ'hɛnsɪv) *adj* **1** of broad scope or content; including all or much **2** (of a car insurance policy) providing protection against most risks, including third-party liability, fire, theft, and damage **3** of, relating to, or being a comprehensive school ▷ *n* **4** short for **comprehensive school** > ,compre'hensively *adv* > ,compre'hensiveness *n*

comprehensive school *n chiefly Brit* a secondary school for children of all abilities from the same district

compress *vb* (kəm'prɛs) **1** (*tr*) to squeeze together or compact into less space; condense **2** *computing* to apply a compression program to (electronic data) so that it takes up less space ▷ *n* ('kɒmprɛs) **3** a wet or dry cloth or gauze pad with or without medication, applied firmly to some part of the body to relieve discomfort, reduce fever, drain a wound, etc [c14: from Late Latin *compressāre*, from Latin *comprimere*, from *premere* to press] > com'pressible *adj* > com'pressive *adj* > com'pressively *adv*

compressed air *n* air at a higher pressure than atmospheric pressure: used esp as a source of power for machines

compressibility (kəm,prɛsɪ'bɪlɪtɪ) *n* **1** the ability to be compressed **2** *physics* the reciprocal of the bulk modulus; the ratio of volume strain to stress at constant temperature. Symbol: k^2

compression (kəm'prɛʃən) *n* **1** Also called: compressure (kəm'prɛʃə) the act of compressing or the condition of being compressed **2** an increase in pressure of the charge in an engine or compressor obtained by reducing its volume

compressor (kəm'prɛsə) *n* **1** any reciprocating or rotating device that compresses a gas **2** the part of a gas turbine that compresses the air before it enters the combustion chambers **3** any muscle that causes compression of any part or structure **4** an electronic device for reducing the variation in signal amplitude in a transmission system

comprise (kəm'praɪz) *vb* (*tr*) **1** to include; contain **2** to constitute the whole of; consist of: *her singing comprised the entertainment* [c15: from French *compris* included, understood, from *comprendre* to COMPREHEND] > com'prisable *adj*

⊛ **USAGE** The use of *of* after *comprise* should be avoided: ⊛ *the library comprises* (not *comprises of*) *500 000 books and* ⊛ *manuscripts*

compromise ('kɒmprə,maɪz) *n* **1** settlement of a dispute by concessions on both or all sides **2** the terms of such a settlement **3** something midway between two or more different things ▷ *vb* **4** to settle (a dispute) by making concessions **5** (*tr*) to expose (a person or persons) to disrepute [c15: from Old French *compromis*, from Latin *comprōmissum* mutual agreement to accept the decision of an arbiter, from *comprōmittere*, from *prōmittere* to promise] > 'compro,miser *n* > 'compro,misingly *adv*

compte rendu French (kɔ̃t rɑ̃dy) *n*, *pl* **comptes rendus** (kɔ̃t rɑ̃dy) a short review or notice, esp of a book [literally: account rendered]

Compton *n* **1** ('kɒmptən) **Arthur Holly.** 1892–1962, US physicist, noted for his research on X-rays, gamma rays, and nuclear energy: Nobel prize for physics 1927 **2** ('kʌmptən) **Denis.** 1918–97, English cricketer, who played for Middlesex and England (1937–57); broke two records in 1947 scoring 3816 runs and 18 centuries in one season

Compton-Burnett ('kɒmptənbɜː'nɛt, -'bɜːnɪt) *n* Dame **Ivy.** 1884–1969, English novelist. Her novels include *Men and Wives* (1931) and *Mother and Son* (1955)

comptroller (kən'trəʊlə) *n* a variant spelling of **controller**, used esp as a title of any of various financial executives

compulsion (kəm'pʌlʃən) *n* **1** the act of compelling or the state of being compelled **2** something that compels **3** *psychiatry* an inner drive that causes a person to perform actions, often of a trivial and repetitive nature, against his or her will. See also **obsession** [c15: from Old French, from Latin *compellere* to COMPEL]

compulsive (kəm'pʌlsɪv) *adj* relating to or involving compulsion > com'pulsively *adv*

compulsory (kəm'pʌlsərɪ) *adj* **1** required by regulations or laws; obligatory **2** involving or employing compulsion; compelling; necessary; essential > com'pulsorily *adv* > com'pulsoriness *n*

compulsory purchase *n* purchase of a house or other property by a local authority or government department for public use or to make way for development, regardless of whether or not the owner wishes to sell

compunction (kəm'pʌŋkʃən) *n* a feeling of remorse, guilt, or regret [c14: from Church Latin *compunctiō*, from Latin *compungere* to sting, from *com-* (intensive) + *pungere* to puncture; see POINT] > com'punctious *adj* > com'punctiously *adv*

computation (,kɒmpjʊ'teɪʃən) *n* a calculation involving numbers or quantities > ,compu'tational *adj*

compute (kəm'pjuːt) *vb* to calculate (an answer, result, etc), often with the aid of a computer [c17: from Latin *computāre*, from *putāre* to think] > com'putable *adj* > com,puta'bility *n*

computed tomography *n med* another name (esp US) for **computerized tomography**

computer (kəm'pjuːtə) *n* **1 a** a device, usually electronic, that processes data according to a set of instructions. The digital computer stores data in discrete units and performs arithmetical and logical operations at very high speed. The analog computer has no memory and is slower than the digital computer but has a continuous rather than a discrete input. The hybrid computer combines some of the advantages of digital and analog computers. See also **digital computer, analog computer b** (*as modifier*): *computer technology* **2** a person who computes or calculates

computer-aided design *n* the use of computer techniques in designing products, esp involving the use of computer graphics. Abbreviation: CAD

computer-aided engineering *n* the use of computers to automate manufacturing processes

computer architecture *n* the structure, behaviour, and

design of computers

computerate (kəm'pju:tərɪt) *adj* able to use computers [C20: COMPUTER + -ATE¹, by analogy with *literate*]

computer dating *n* the use of computers by dating agencies to match their clients

computer game *n* any of various games, recorded on cassette or disc for use in a home computer, that are played by manipulating a mouse, joystick, or the keys on the keyboard of a computer in response to the graphics on the screen

computer graphics *n* (*functioning as singular*) the use of a computer to produce and manipulate pictorial images on a video screen, as in animation techniques or the production of audiovisual aids

computerize or **computerise** (kəm'pju:tə,raɪz) *vb* **1** (*tr*) to cause (certain operations) to be performed by a computer, esp as a replacement for human labour **2** (*intr*) to install a computer **3** (*tr*) to control or perform (operations within a system) by means of a computer **4** (*tr*) to process or store (information) by means of or in a computer > com,puteri'zation or com,puteri'sation *n*

computerized tomography *n med* a radiological technique that produces images of cross sections through a patient's body using low levels of radiation. Also called (esp US): **computed tomography**, **CT scanner**

computer language *n* another term for **programming language**

computer science *n* the study of computers and their application

comrade ('kɒmreɪd, -rɪd) *n* **1** an associate or companion **2** a fellow member of a political party, esp a fellow Communist or socialist [C16: from French *camarade*, from Spanish *camarada* group of soldiers sharing a billet, from *cámara* room, from Latin; see CAMERA, CHAMBER] > 'comradely *adj* > 'comrade,ship *n*

Comsat ('kɒmsæt) *n trademark* short for **communications satellite**

Comte (*French* kɔ̃t) *n* (**Isidore**) **Auguste** (**Marie François**) (ogyst). 1798–1857, French mathematician and philosopher; the founder of positivism > **Comtism** ('kɔ:n,tɪzəm) *n* > 'Comtist or 'Comtian *adj*, *n*

Comus ('kəʊməs) *n* (in late Roman mythology) a god of revelry [C17: from Latin, from Greek *kōmos* a revel]

con¹ (kɒn) *informal n* **1 a** short for **confidence trick b** (*as modifier*): *con man* ▷ *vb* **cons**, **conning**, **conned 2** (*tr*) to swindle or defraud [C19: from CONFIDENCE]

con² (kɒn) *n* (*usually plural*) an argument or vote against a proposal, motion, etc. Compare **pro¹**. See also **pros and cons** [from Latin *contrā* against, opposed to]

con³ or *esp US* **conn** (kɒn) *nautical vb* **cons** or **conns**, **conning**, **conned** (*tr*) to direct the steering of (a vessel) [C17 *cun*, from earlier *condien* to guide, from Old French *conduire*, from Latin *condūcere*; see CONDUCT]

con⁴ (kɒn) *vb* **cons**, **conning**, **conned** (*tr*) *archaic* to study attentively or learn (esp in the phrase **con by rote**) [C15: variant of CAN¹ in the sense: to come to know]

con⁵ (kɒn) *prep music* with [Italian]

con- *prefix* a variant of **com-**

Conakry or **Konakri** (*French* kɔnakri) *n* the capital of Guinea, a port on the island of Tombo. Pop: 1 465 000 (2005 est)

con amore (kɒn æ'mɔ:rɪ) *adj*, *adv music* (to be performed) lovingly [C19: from Italian: with love]

Conan Doyle ('kəʊnən 'dɔɪl, 'kɒnən) *n* Sir **Arthur**. 1859–1930, British author of detective stories and historical romances and the creator of *Sherlock Holmes*

con brio (kɒn 'bri:əʊ) *adj*, *adv music* (to be performed) with liveliness or spirit, as in the phrase **allegro con brio** [Italian: with energy]

concatenate (kɒn'kætɪ,neɪt) *vb* (*tr*) to link or join together, esp in a chain or series [C16: from Late Latin *concatēnāre* from Latin *com-* together + *catēna* CHAIN] > con,cate'nation *n*

concave ('kɒnkeɪv, kɒn'keɪv) *adj* **1** curving inwards **2** *physics* having one or two surfaces curved or ground in the shape of a section of the interior of a sphere, paraboloid, etc: *a concave lens* ▷ *vb* **3** (*tr*) to make concave [C15: from Latin *concavus* arched, from *cavus* hollow] > 'concavely *adv* > 'concaveness *n*

concavity (kɒn'kævɪtɪ) *n*, *pl* **-ties 1** the state or quality of being concave **2** a concave surface or thing; cavity

concavo-concave (kɒn,keɪvəʊkɒn'keɪv) *adj* (esp of a lens) having both sides concave; biconcave

concavo-convex *adj* **1** having one side concave and the other side convex **2** (of a lens) having a concave face with greater curvature than the convex face

conceal (kən'si:l) *vb* (*tr*) **1** to keep from discovery; hide **2** to keep secret [C14: from Old French *conceler*, from Latin *concēlāre*, from *com-* (intensive) + *cēlāre* to hide] > con'cealer *n* > con'cealment *n*

concede (kən'si:d) *vb* **1** (when *tr*, *may take a clause as object*) to admit or acknowledge (something) as true or correct **2** to yield or allow (something, such as a right) **3** (*tr*) to admit as certain in outcome: *to concede an election* [C17: from Latin *concēdere*, from *cēdere* to give way, CEDE] > con'ceder *n*

conceit (kən'si:t) *n* **1** a high, often exaggerated, opinion of oneself or one's accomplishments; vanity **2** *literary* an elaborate image or far-fetched comparison, esp as used by the English Metaphysical poets **3** *archaic* **a** a witty expression **b** fancy; imagination **c** an idea ▷ *vb* (*tr*) **4** *obsolete* to think or imagine [C14: from CONCEIVE]

conceited (kən'si:tɪd) *adj* having a high or exaggerated opinion of oneself or one's accomplishments > con'ceitedly *adv* > con'ceitedness *n*

conceivable (kən'si:vəb°l) *adj* capable of being understood, believed, or imagined; possible > con,ceiva'bility or con'ceivableness *n* > con'ceivably *adv*

conceive (kən'si:v) *vb* **1** (when *intr*, foll by *of*; when *tr*, often takes a clause as object) to have an idea (of); imagine; think **2** (*tr*; takes a clause as object or an infinitive) to hold as an opinion; believe **3** (*tr*) to develop or form, esp in the mind: *she conceived a passion for music* **4** to become pregnant with (young) **5** (*tr*) *rare* to express in words [C13: from Old French *conceivre*, from Latin *concipere* to take in, from *capere* to take]

concelebrate (kən'sɛlɪ,breɪt) *vb Christianity* to celebrate (the Eucharist or Mass) jointly with one or more other priests [C16: from Latin *concelebrāre*] > con,cele'bration *n*

concentrate ('kɒnsən,treɪt) *vb* **1** to come or cause to come to a single purpose or aim: *to concentrate one's hopes on winning* **2** to make or become denser or purer by the removal of certain elements, esp the solvent of a solution **3** (*intr*; often foll by *on*) to bring one's faculties to bear (on); think intensely (about) ▷ *n* **4** a concentrated material or solution [C17: back formation from CONCENTRATION, ultimately from Latin *com-* same + *centrum* CENTRE] > 'concen,trator *n* > 'concen,trative *adj* > 'concen,tratively *adv* > 'concen,trativeness *n*

concentration (,kɒnsən'treɪʃən) *n* **1** intense mental application; complete attention **2** the act or process of concentrating **3** something that is concentrated **4** the strength of a solution, esp the amount of dissolved substance in a given volume of solvent, usually expressed in moles per cubic metre or cubic decimetre (litre) **5** *military* **a** the act of bringing together military forces **b** the application of fire from a number of weapons against a target

concentration camp *n* a guarded prison camp in which nonmilitary prisoners are held, esp one of those in Nazi Germany in which nonmilitary prisoners were exterminated

concentre (kɒn'sɛntə) or *US* **concenter** *vb* to converge or cause to converge on a common centre; concentrate [C16: from French *concentrer*; see CONCENTRATE]

concentric (kən'sɛntrɪk) *adj* having a common centre: *concentric circles* [C14: from Medieval Latin *concentricus*, from Latin *com-* same + *centrum* CENTRE] > con'centrically *adv*

Concepción (*Spanish* konθep'θjon) *n* an industrial city in S central Chile. Pop: 378 000 (2005 est)

concept ('kɒnsɛpt) *n* **1** an idea, esp an abstract idea: *the concepts of biology* **2** *philosophy* a general idea or notion that corresponds to some class of entities and that consists of the characteristic or essential features of the class **3** (*modifier*) (of a product, esp a car) created as an exercise to demonstrate the technical skills and imagination of the designers, and not intended for mass production or sale [C16: from Latin *conceptum* something received or conceived, from *concipere* to take in, CONCEIVE]

conception (kənˈsɛpʃən) *n* **1** something conceived; notion, idea, design, or plan **2** the description under which someone considers something: *her conception of freedom is wrong* **3** the fertilization of an ovum by a sperm in the Fallopian tube followed by implantation in the womb **4** origin or beginning [c13: from Latin *conceptiō*, from *concipere* to CONCEIVE] > con'ceptional *or* con'ceptive *adj*

conceptual (kənˈsɛptjʊəl) *adj* relating to or concerned with concepts; abstract > con'ceptually *adv*

conceptualize *or* **conceptualise** (kənˈsɛptjʊəˌlaɪz) *vb* to form (a concept or concepts) out of observations, experience, data, etc > con,ceptuali'zation *or* con,ceptuali'sation *n*

concern (kənˈsɜːn) *vb* (*tr*) **1** to relate to; be of importance or interest to; affect **2** (usually foll by *with* or *in*) to involve or interest (oneself): *he concerns himself with other people's affairs* ▷ *n* **3** something that affects or is of importance to a person; affair; business **4** regard for or interest in a person or a thing: *he felt a strong concern for her* **5** anxiety, worry, or solicitude **6** important bearing or relation: *his news has great concern for us* **7** a commercial company or enterprise **8** *informal* a material thing, esp one of which one has a low opinion [c15: from Late Latin *concernere* to mingle together, from Latin *com-* together + *cernere* to sift, distinguish]

concerned (kənˈsɜːnd) *adj* **1** (*postpositive*) interested, guilty, involved, or appropriate: *I shall find the boy concerned and punish him* **2** worried, troubled, or solicitous > concernedly (kənˈsɜːnɪdlɪ) *adv*

concerning (kənˈsɜːnɪŋ) *prep* **1** about; regarding; on the subject of ▷ *adj* **2** worrying or troublesome

concernment (kənˈsɜːnmənt) *n rare* affair or business; concern

concert *n* (ˈkɒnsɜːt, -sət) **1 a** a performance of music by players or singers that does not involve theatrical staging **b** (*as modifier*): *a concert version of an opera* **2** agreement in design, plan, or action **3** in concert **a** acting in a co-ordinated fashion with a common purpose **b** (of musicians, esp rock musicians) performing live ▷ *vb* (kənˈsɜːt) **4** to arrange or contrive (a plan) by mutual agreement [c16: from French *concerter* to bring into agreement, from Italian *concertare*, from Late Latin *concertāre* to work together, from Latin: to dispute, debate, from *certāre* to contend]

concertante (ˌkɒntʃəˈtæntɪ) *adj music* characterized by contrasting alternating tutti and solo passages [c18: from Italian, from *concertare* to perform a concert, from *concerto* CONCERT]

concerted (kənˈsɜːtɪd) *adj* **1** mutually contrived, planned, or arranged; combined (esp in the phrases **concerted action, concerted effort**) **2** *music* arranged in parts for a group of singers or players

Concertgebouw (*Dutch* kɔnˈsɛrtxəbɔu) *n* a concert hall in Amsterdam, inaugurated in 1888: the **Concertgebouw Orchestra** established in 1888, has been independent of the hall since World War II

concert grand *n* a full-size grand piano, usually around 7 feet in length

concertina (ˌkɒnsəˈtiːnə) *n* **1** a small hexagonal musical instrument of the reed organ family in which metallic reeds are vibrated by air from a set of bellows operated by the player's hands. Notes are produced by pressing buttons ▷ *vb* **-nas, -naing, -naed** **2** (*intr*) to collapse or fold up like a concertina [c19: CONCERT + *-ina*] > ,concer'tinist *n*

concertino (ˌkɒntʃəˈtiːnəʊ) *n*, *pl* **-ni** (-nɪ) **1** the small group of soloists in a concerto grosso **2** a short concerto [c19: from Italian: a little CONCERTO]

concertmaster (ˈkɒnsətˌmɑːstə) *n* a US and Canadian word for **leader** (sense 2a)

concerto (kənˈtʃɛətəʊ) *n*, *pl* **-tos** *or* **-ti** (-tɪ) a composition for an orchestra and one or more soloists. The classical concerto usually consisted of several movements, and often a cadenza [c18: from Italian: CONCERT]

concerto grosso (ˈɡrɒsəʊ) *n*, *pl* **concerti grossi** (ˈɡrɒsɪ) *or* **concerto grossos** a composition for an orchestra and a group of soloists, chiefly of the baroque period [Italian,

literally: big concerto]

concert party *n* **1** a musical entertainment popular in the early 20th century, esp one at a British seaside resort **2** *stock exchange informal* a group of individuals or companies who secretly agree to purchase shares separately in a particular company, which they plan to amalgamate later into a single holding: a malpractice that is illegal in some countries

concert pitch *n* the frequency of 440 hertz assigned to the A above middle C

concession (kənˈsɛʃən) *n* **1** the act of yielding or conceding, as to a demand or argument **2** something conceded **3** *Brit* a reduction in the usual price of a ticket granted to a special group of customers: *a student concession* **4** any grant of rights, land, or property by a government, local authority, corporation, or individual **5** the right, esp an exclusive right, to market a particular product in a given area **6** *Canadian* (chiefly in Ontario and Quebec) **a** a land subdivision in a township survey **b** another name for **concession road** [c16: from Latin *concessiō* an allowing, from *concēdere* to CONCEDE] > con'cessible *adj* > con'cessive *adj* [c18: from Late Latin *concessīvus*, from Latin *concēdere* to CONCEDE]

concessionaire (kənˌsɛʃəˈnɛə), **concessioner** (kənˈsɛʃənə) *or* **concessionary** *n* someone who holds or operates a concession

concessionary (kənˈsɛʃənərɪ) *adj* **1** of, granted, or obtained by a concession ▷ *n*, *pl* **-aries** **2** another word for **concessionaire**

concession road *n Canadian* (esp in Ontario) one of a series of roads separating concessions in a township

conch (kɒŋk, kɒntʃ) *n*, *pl* **conchs** (kɒŋks) *or* **conches** (ˈkɒntʃɪz) **1** any of various tropical marine gastropod molluscs of the genus *Strombus* and related genera, esp *S. gigas* (giant conch), characterized by a large brightly coloured spiral shell **2** the shell of such a mollusc, used as a trumpet [c16: from Latin *concha*, from Greek *konkhē* shellfish]

conchie *or* **conchy** (ˈkɒntʃɪ) *n*, *pl* **-chies** *informal* short for **conscientious objector**

Conchobar (ˈkɒŋkəʊwə, ˈkɒnʊə) *n* (in Irish legend) a king of Ulster at about the beginning of the Christian era. See also **Deirdre**

conchology (kɒŋˈkɒlədʒɪ) *n* the study and collection of mollusc shells > con'chologist *n*

concierge (ˌkɒnsɪˈɛəʒ; *French* kɔ̃sjɛrʒ) *n* (esp in France) a caretaker of a block of flats, hotel, etc, esp one who lives on the premises [c17: from French, ultimately from Latin *conservus*, from *servus* slave]

conciliar (kənˈsɪlɪə) *adj* of, from, or by means of a council, esp an ecclesiastical one

conciliate (kənˈsɪlɪˌeɪt) *vb* (*tr*) **1** to overcome the hostility of; placate; win over **2** to win or gain (favour, regard, etc), esp by making friendly overtures [c16: from Latin *conciliāre* to bring together, from *concilium* COUNCIL] > con'ciliable *adj* > con'cili,ator *n*

conciliation (kənˌsɪlɪˈeɪʃən) *n* **1** the act or process of conciliating **2** a method of helping the parties in a dispute to reach agreement, esp divorcing or separating couples to part amicably

conciliatory (kənˈsɪljətərɪ, -trɪ) *or* **conciliative** (kənˈsɪlɪətɪv) *adj* intended to placate or reconcile > con'ciliatorily *adv*

concise (kənˈsaɪs) *adj* expressing much in few words; brief and to the point [c16: from Latin *concīsus* cut up, cut short, from *concīdere* to cut to pieces, from *caedere* to cut, strike down] > con'cisely *adv* > con'ciseness *n* > concision (kənˈsɪʒən) *n*

conclave (ˈkɒŋkleɪv, ˈkɒn-) *n* **1** a confidential or secret meeting **2** *RC Church* **a** the closed apartments where the college of cardinals elects a new pope **b** a meeting of the college of cardinals for this purpose [c14: from Medieval Latin *conclāve*, from Latin: cage, place that may be locked, from *clāvis* key]

conclude (kənˈkluːd) *vb* (mainly *tr*) **1** (*also intr*) to come or cause to come to an end or conclusion **2** (*takes a clause as object*) to decide by reasoning; deduce: *the judge concluded that the witness had told the truth* **3** to arrange finally; settle: *to conclude a treaty; it was concluded that he should go* **4** *obsolete* to confine [c14: from Latin *conclūdere* to enclose, end, from *claudere* to close]

conclusion (kən'kluːʒən) *n* **1** end or termination **2** the last main division of a speech, lecture, essay, etc **3** the outcome or result of an act, process, event, etc (esp in the phrase **a foregone conclusion**) **4** a final decision or judgment; resolution (esp in the phrase **come to a conclusion**) **5** *logic* **a** a statement that purports to follow from another or others (the **premises**) by means of an argument **b** a statement that does validly follow from given premises **6** *law* **a** an admission or statement binding on the party making it; estoppel **b** the close of a pleading or of a conveyance **7** in conclusion lastly; to sum up **8** jump to conclusions to come to a conclusion prematurely, without sufficient thought or on incomplete evidence [c14: via Old French from Latin; see CONCLUDE, -ION]

conclusive (kən'kluːsɪv) *adj* **1** putting an end to doubt; decisive; final **2** approaching or involving an end or conclusion > con'clusively *adv*

concoct (kən'kɒkt) *vb* (*tr*) **1** to make by combining different ingredients **2** to invent; make up; contrive [c16: from Latin *concoctus* cooked together, from *concoquere*, from *coquere* to cook] > con'cocter *or* con'coctor *n* > con'coction *n*

concomitance (kən'kɒmɪtəns) *n* **1** existence or occurrence together or in connection with another **2** *Christian theol* the doctrine that the body and blood of Christ are present in the Eucharist

concomitant (kən'kɒmɪtənt) *adj* **1** existing or occurring together; associative ▷ *n* **2** a concomitant act, person, etc [c17: from Late Latin *concomitārī* to accompany, from *com-* with + *comes* companion, fellow]

concord ('kɒnkɔːd, 'kɒŋ-) *n* **1** agreement or harmony between people or nations; amity **2** a treaty establishing peaceful relations between nations **3** agreement or harmony between things, ideas, etc **4** *music* a combination of musical notes, esp one containing a series of consonant intervals **5** *grammar* another word for **agreement** (sense 6) [c13: from Old French *concorde*, from Latin *concordia*, from *concors* of the same mind, harmonious, from *com-* same + *cor* heart]

Concord ('kɒŋkəd) *n* **1** a town in NE Massachusetts: scene of one of the opening military actions (1775) of the War of American Independence. Pop: 16 937 (2003 est) **2** a city in New Hampshire, the state capital: printing, publishing. Pop: 41 823 (2003 est)

concordance (kən'kɔːdᵊns) *n* **1** a state or condition of agreement or harmony **2** a book that indexes the principal words in a literary work, often with the immediate context and an account of the meaning **3** an index produced by computer or machine, alphabetically listing every word in a text

concordant (kən'kɔːdᵊnt) *adj* being in agreement: harmonious > con'cordantly *adv*

concordat (kɒn'kɔːdæt) *n* a pact or treaty, esp one between the Vatican and another state concerning the interests of religion in that state [c17: via French, from Medieval Latin *concordātum*, from Latin: something agreed, from *concordāre* to be of one mind; see CONCORD]

concourse ('kɒnkɔːs, 'kɒŋ-) *n* **1** a crowd; throng **2** a coming together; confluence: *a concourse of events* **3** a large open space for the gathering of people in a public place [c14: from Old French *concours*, ultimately from Latin *concurrere* to run together, from *currere* to run]

concrescence (kən'krɛsəns) *n* *biology* a growing together of initially separate parts or organs [c17: from Latin *concrēscentia*, from *concrēscere* to grow together, from *crēscere* to grow; see CRESCENT] > con'crescent *adj*

concrete ('kɒnkriːt) *n* **1** a construction material made of a mixture of cement, sand, stone, and water that hardens to a stonelike mass ▷ *adj* **2** relating to a particular instance or object; specific as opposed to general **3** relating to or characteristic of things capable of being perceived by the senses, as opposed to abstractions **4** formed by the coalescence of particles; condensed; solid ▷ *vb* **5** (*tr*) to construct in or cover with concrete **6** (kən'kriːt) to become or cause to become solid; coalesce [c14: from Latin *concrētus* grown together,

hardened, from *concrēscere*; see CONCRESCENCE] > 'concretely *adv* > 'concreteness *n*

concrete music *n* music consisting of an electronically modified montage of tape-recorded sounds

concrete noun *n* a noun that refers to a material object, as for example *horse*

concrete poetry *n* poetry in which the visual form of the poem is used to convey meaning

concretion (kən'kriːʃən) *n* **1** the act or process of coming or growing together; coalescence **2** a solid or solidified mass **3** something made real, tangible, or specific **4** any of various rounded or irregular mineral masses formed by chemical precipitation around a nucleus, such as a bone or shell, that is different in composition from the sedimentary rock that surrounds it **5** *pathol* another word for **calculus** > con'cretionary *adj*

concretize *or* **concretise** ('kɒnkrɪˌtaɪz, 'kɒn-) *vb* (*tr*) to render concrete; make real or specific; give tangible form to

concubine ('kɒŋkjʊˌbaɪn, 'kɒn-) *n* **1** (in polygamous societies) a secondary wife, usually of lower social rank **2** a woman who cohabits with a man [c13: from Old French, from Latin *concubīna*, from *concumbere* to lie together, from *cubare* to lie] > concubinary (kɒn'kjʊbɪnərɪ) *n, adj* > con'cubinage *n*

concupiscence (kən'kjuːpɪsəns) *n* strong desire, esp sexual desire [c14: from Church Latin *concupiscentia*, from Latin *concupiscere* to covet ardently, from *cupere* to wish, desire] > con'cupiscent *adj*

concur (kən'kɜː) *vb* -curs, -curring, -curred (*intr*) **1** to agree; be of the same mind; be in accord **2** to combine, act together, or cooperate **3** to occur simultaneously; coincide [c15: from Latin *concurrere* to run together, from *currere* to run]

concurrence (kən'kʌrəns) *n* **1** the act of concurring **2** agreement in opinion; accord; assent **3** cooperation or combination **4** simultaneous occurrence; coincidence

concurrent (kən'kʌrənt) *adj* **1** taking place at the same time or in the same location **2** cooperating **3** meeting at, approaching, or having a common point: *concurrent lines* **4** in accordance or agreement; harmonious > con'currently *adv*

concurrent engineering *n* a method of designing and marketing new products in which development stages are run in parallel rather than in series, to reduce lead times and costs. Also called: **interactive engineering**

concurrent versions system *n* *computing* a system that allows more than one person to work on the same file at the same time, merging their changes but keeping records of the different versions

concuss (kən'kʌs) *vb* (*tr*) **1** to injure (the brain) by a violent blow, fall, etc **2** to shake violently; agitate; disturb [c16: from Latin *concussus* violently shaken, from *concutere* to disturb greatly, from *quatere* to shake]

concussion (kən'kʌʃən) *n* **1** a jarring of the brain, caused by a blow or a fall, usually resulting in loss of consciousness **2** any violent shaking; jarring

Condé (French kɔ̃de) *n* **Prince de** (prɛs də), title of *Louis II de Bourbon, Duc d'Enghien*, called *the Great Condé*. 1621–86, French general, who led Louis XIV's armies against the Fronde (1649) but joined the Fronde in a new revolt (1650–52). He later fought for both France and Spain

condemn (kən'dɛm) *vb* (*tr*) **1** to express strong disapproval of; censure **2** to pronounce judicial sentence on **3** to demonstrate the guilt of: *his secretive behaviour condemned him* **4** to judge or pronounce unfit for use: *that food has been condemned* **5** to compel or force into a particular state or activity: *his disposition condemned him to boredom* [c13: from Old French *condempner*, from Latin *condemnāre*, from *damnāre* to condemn; see DAMN] > condemnable (kən'dɛməbᵊl) *adj* > ˌcondem'nation *n* > condemnatory (ˌkɒndɛm'neɪtərɪ, kən'dɛmnətərɪ, -trɪ) *adj*

condensate (kən'dɛnseɪt) *n* a substance formed by condensation, such as a liquid from a vapour

condensation (ˌkɒndɛn'seɪʃən) *n* **1** the act or process of condensing, or the state of being condensed **2** anything that has condensed from a vapour, esp on a window **3** *chem* a type of reaction in which two organic molecules combine to form a larger molecule as well as a simple molecule such as water, methanol, etc **4** anything that has been shortened, esp an abridged version of a book > ˌconden'sational *adj*

condensation trail *n* another name for **vapour trail**

condense (kən'dɛns) *vb* **1** (*tr*) to increase the density of; compress **2** to reduce or be reduced in volume or size; make or become more compact **3** to change or cause to change from a gaseous to a liquid or solid state **4** *chem* to undergo or cause to undergo condensation [c15: from Latin *condēnsāre*, from *dēnsāre* to make thick, from *dēnsus* DENSE] > con'densable *or* con'densible *adj*

condensed matter *n physics* **a** crystalline and amorphous solids and liquids, including liquid crystals, glasses, polymers, and gels **b** (*as modifier*): *condensed-matter physics*

condensed milk *n* milk reduced by evaporation to a thick concentration, with sugar added. See **evaporated milk**

condenser (kən'dɛnsə) *n* **1 a** an apparatus for reducing gases to their liquid or solid form by the abstraction of heat **b** a device for abstracting heat, as in a refrigeration unit **2** a lens that concentrates light into a small area **3** another name for **capacitor 4** a person or device that condenses

condescend (ˌkɒndɪ'sɛnd) *vb* (*intr*) **1** to act graciously towards another or others regarded as being on a lower level; behave patronizingly **2** to do something that one regards as below one's dignity [c14: from Church Latin *condēscendere* to stoop, condescend, from Latin *dēscendere* to DESCEND] > ˌconde'scending *adj* > ˌconde'scendingly *adv* > ˌconde'scension *n*

condign (kən'daɪn) *adj* (esp of a punishment) fitting; deserved [c15: from Old French *condigne*, from Latin *condignus*, from *dignus* worthy] > con'dignly *adv*

Condillac (French kɔ̃dijak) *n* **Étienne Bonnot de** (etjɛn bɔnɔ də). 1715–80, French philosopher. He developed Locke's view that all knowledge derives from the senses in his *Traité des sensations* (1754)

condiment ('kɒndɪmənt) *n* any spice or sauce such as salt, pepper, mustard, etc [c15: from Latin *condīmentum* seasoning, from *condīre* to pickle]

condition (kən'dɪʃən) *n* **1** a particular state of being or existence; situation with respect to circumstances: *the human condition* **2** something that limits or restricts something else; a qualification **3** (*plural*) external or existing circumstances: *conditions were right for a takeover* **4** state of health or physical fitness, esp good health (esp in the phrases **in condition, out of condition**) **5** an ailment or physical disability: *a heart condition* **6** something indispensable to the existence of something else: *your happiness is a condition of mine* **7** something required as part of an agreement or pact; terms: *the conditions of the lease are set out* **8** *law* **a** a declaration or provision in a will, contract, etc, that makes some right or liability contingent upon the happening of some event **b** the event itself **9** *logic* a statement whose truth is either required for the truth of a given statement (a **necessary condition**) or sufficient to guarantee the truth of the given statement (a **sufficient condition**) **10** rank, status, or position in life **11** **on condition that** *or* **upon condition that** (*conjunction*) provided that > *vb* (*mainly tr*) **12** *psychol* **a** to alter the response of (a person or animal) to a particular stimulus or situation **b** to establish a conditioned response in (a person or animal) **13** to put into a fit condition or state **14** to improve the condition of (one's hair) by use of special cosmetics **15** to accustom or inure **16** to subject to a condition [c14: from Latin *conditiō*, from *condīcere* to discuss, agree together, from *con-* together + *dīcere* to say] > con'ditioner *n* > con'ditioning *n, adj*

conditional (kən'dɪʃənᵊl) *adj* **1** depending on other factors; not certain **2** *grammar* (of a clause, conjunction, form of a verb, or whole sentence) expressing a condition on which something else is contingent: "*If he comes*" *is a conditional clause in the sentence* "*If he comes I shall go*" **3** Also called: **hypothetical** *logic* (of a proposition) consisting of two component propositions associated by the words *if...then* so that the proposition is false only

when the antecedent is true and the consequent false. Usually written: *p→q* or *p⊃q*, where *p* is the antecedent, *q* the consequent, and → or ⊃ symbolizes *implies* ▷ *n* **4** *grammar* a conditional form of a verb > con'ditionally *adv*

conditional access *n* the encryption of television programme transmissions so that only authorized subscribers with suitable decoding apparatus may have access to them

conditioned response *n psychol* a response that is transferred from the second to the first of a pair of stimuli. A well-known Pavlovian example is salivation by a dog when it hears a bell ring, because food has always been presented when the bell has been rung previously

condo ('kɒndəʊ) *n, pl* -**dos** *informal* a condominium building or apartment

condole (kən'dəʊl) *vb* (*intr*; foll by *with*) to express sympathy with someone in grief, pain, etc [c16: from Church Latin *condolēre* to suffer pain (with another), from Latin *com-* together + *dolēre* to grieve, feel pain]

condolence (kən'dəʊləns) *or* **condolement** (kən'dəʊlmənt) *n* (*often plural*) an expression of sympathy with someone in grief, etc

condom ('kɒndɒm, 'kɒndəm) *n* a sheathlike covering of thin rubber worn on the penis or in the vagina during sexual intercourse to prevent conception or infection [c18: of unknown origin]

condominium (ˌkɒndə'mɪnɪəm) *n, pl* -**ums 1** joint rule or sovereignty **2** a country ruled by two or more foreign powers **3** *US & Canadian* an apartment building in which each apartment is individually wholly owned and the common areas are jointly owned Sometimes shortened to: **condo** [c18: from New Latin, from Latin *com-* together + *dominium* ownership; see DOMINION]

condone (kən'dəʊn) *vb* (*tr*) **1** to overlook or forgive an offence **2** *law* (esp of a spouse) to pardon or overlook (an offence, usually adultery) [c19: from Latin *condōnāre* to remit a debt, from *com-* (intensive) + *dōnāre* to DONATE] > condonation (ˌkɒndəʊ'neɪʃən) *n* > con'doner *n*

condor ('kɒndɔː) *n* either of two very large rare New World vultures, *Vultur gryphus* (**Andean condor**), which has black plumage with white around the neck, and *Gymnogyps californianus* (**California condor**), which is similar but nearly extinct [c17: from Spanish *cóndor*, from Quechuan *kuntur*]

Condorcet (French kɔ̃dɔrsɛ) *n* **Marie Jean Antoine Nicolas de Caritat, Marquis de.** 1743–94, French philosopher and politician. His works include *Sketch for a Historical Picture of the Progress of the Human Mind* (1795)

condottiere (ˌkɒndɒ'tjɛərɪ) *n, pl* -**ri** (-riː) a commander or soldier in a professional mercenary company in Europe from the 13th to the 16th centuries [c18: from Italian, from *condotto* leadership, from *condurre* to lead, from Latin *condūcere*; see CONDUCT]

conduce (kən'djuːs) *vb* (*intr*; foll by *to*) to lead or contribute (to a result) [c15: from Latin *condūcere* to lead together, from *com-* together + *dūcere* to lead]

conducive (kən'djuːsɪv) *adj* (when *postpositive*, foll by *to*) contributing, leading, or tending

conduct *n* ('kɒndʌkt) **1** the manner in which a person behaves; behaviour **2** the way of managing a business, affair; etc; handling **3** *rare* the act of guiding or leading ▷ *vb* (kən'dʌkt) **4** (*tr*) to accompany and guide (people, a party, etc) (esp in the phrase **conducted tour**) **5** (*tr*) to lead or direct (affairs, business, etc); control **6** (*tr*) to do or carry out: *conduct a survey* **7** (*tr*) to behave or manage (oneself) **8** to control or guide (an orchestra, choir, etc) by the movements of the hands or a baton **9** to transmit (heat, electricity, etc) [c15: from Medieval Latin *conductus* escorted, from Latin: drawn together, from *condūcere* to CONDUCE] > con'ductible *adj* > conˌducti'bility *n*

conductance (kən'dʌktəns) *n* the ability of a system to conduct electricity, measured by the ratio of the current flowing through the system to the potential difference across it; the reciprocal of resistance. It is measured in reciprocal ohms, mhos, or siemens. Symbol: G

conducting tissue *n botany* another name for **vascular tissue**

conduction (kən'dʌkʃən) n 1 the transfer of energy by a medium without bulk movement of the medium itself. See **convection** (sense 1) 2 the transmission of an electrical or chemical impulse along a nerve fibre 3 the act of conveying or conducting, as through a pipe 4 *physics* another name for **conductivity** (sense 1) > con'ductional *adj*

conductive (kən'dʌktɪv) *adj* of, denoting, or having the property of conduction

conductive education n an educational system, developed in Hungary by András Petö, in which teachers (**conductors**) teach children and adults with motor disorders to function independently, by guiding them to attain their own goals in their own way

conductivity (ˌkɒndʌk'tɪvɪtɪ) n, pl -ties 1 Also called: conduction the property of transmitting heat, electricity, or sound 2 a measure of the ability of a substance to conduct electricity; the reciprocal of resistivity. Symbol: K

conductivity water n water that has a conductivity of less than 0.043×10^{-6} S cm^{-1}

conductor (kən'dʌktə) n 1 an official on a bus who collects fares, checks tickets, etc 2 a person who conducts an orchestra, choir, etc 3 a person who leads or guides 4 *US & Canadian* a railway official in charge of a train 5 a substance, body, or system that conducts electricity, heat, etc 6 See **lightning conductor** > con'ductor,ship n > conductress (kən'dʌktrɪs) *fem* n

conduit ('kɒndɪt, -djuɪt) n 1 a pipe or channel for carrying a fluid 2 a rigid tube or duct for carrying and protecting electrical wires or cables 3 an agency or means of access, communication, etc [c14: from Old French, from Medieval Latin *conductus* channel, aqueduct, from Latin *condūcere* to lead, CONDUCE]

condyle ('kɒndɪl) n the rounded projection on the articulating end of a bone, such as the ball portion of a ball-and-socket joint [c17: from Latin *condylus* knuckle, joint, from Greek *kondulos*] > 'condylar *adj*

cone (kəʊn) n 1 a geometric solid consisting of a plane base bounded by a closed curve, often a circle or an ellipse, every point of which is joined to a fixed point, the vertex, lying outside the plane of the base. A **right circular cone** has a vertex perpendicularly above or below the centre of a circular base. Volume of a cone: $1\frac{1}{3}\pi r^2 h$, where r is the radius of the base and h is the height of the cone 2 anything that tapers from a circular section to a point, such as a wafer shell used to contain ice cream 3 a the reproductive body of conifers and related plants, made up of overlapping scales, esp the mature **female cone**, whose scales each bear a seed b a similar structure in horsetails, club mosses, etc 4 a small cone-shaped bollard used as a temporary traffic marker on roads 5 Also called: retinal cone any one of the cone-shaped cells in the retina of the eye, sensitive to colour and bright light ▷ vb 6 (tr) to shape like a cone or part of a cone [c16: from Latin *cōnus*, from Greek *kōnus* pine cone, geometrical cone]

cone off vb (tr, adverb) Brit to close (one carriageway of a motorway) by placing warning cones across it

coney ('kəʊnɪ) n a variant spelling of **cony**

Coney Island ('kəʊnɪ) n an island off the S shore of Long Island, New York: site of a large amusement park

confab ('kɒnfæb) *informal* ▷ n 1 a conversation or chat ▷ vb -fabs, -fabbing, -fabbed 2 (intr) to converse

confabulate (kən'fæbjʊˌleɪt) vb (intr) 1 to talk together; converse; chat 2 *psychiatry* to replace the gaps left by a disorder of the memory with imaginary remembered experiences consistently believed to be true [c17: from Latin *confābulārī*, from *fābulārī* to talk, from *fābula* a story; see FABLE] > con,fabu'lation n

confect (kən'fɛkt) vb (tr) 1 to prepare by combining ingredients 2 to make; construct [c16: from Latin *confectus* prepared, from *conficere* to accomplish, from *com-* (intensive) + *facere* to make]

confection (kən'fɛkʃən) n 1 the act or process of compounding or mixing 2 any sweet preparation of fruit, nuts, etc, such as a preserve or a sweet 3 *old-fashioned* an elaborate article of clothing, esp for women [c14: from Old French, from Latin *confectiō* a preparing,

from *conficere* to produce; see CONFECT]

confectioner (kən'fɛkʃənə) n a person who makes or sells sweets or confections

confectionery (kən'fɛkʃənərɪ) n, pl -eries 1 sweets and other confections collectively 2 the art or business of a confectioner

confederacy (kən'fɛdərəsɪ, -'fɛdrəsɪ) n, pl -cies 1 a union or combination of peoples, states, etc; alliance; league 2 a combination of groups or individuals for unlawful purposes [c14: from Anglo-French *confederacie*, from Late Latin *confoederātiō* agreement, CONFEDERATION] > con'federal *adj*

Confederacy (kən'fɛdərəsɪ, -'fɛdrəsɪ) n the Confederacy another name for **Confederate States of America**

confederate n (kən'fɛdərɪt, -'fɛdrɪt) 1 a nation, state, or individual that is part of a confederacy 2 someone who is part of a conspiracy; accomplice ▷ *adj* (kən'fɛdərɪt, -'fɛdrɪt) 3 united in a confederacy; allied ▷ vb (kən'fɛdəˌreɪt) 4 to form into or become part of a confederacy [c14: from Late Latin *confoederātus*, from *confoederāre* to unite by a league, from Latin *com-* together + *foedus* treaty]

Confederate (kən'fɛdərɪt, -'fɛdrɪt) *adj* 1 of, supporting, or relating to the Confederate States of America ▷ n 2 a supporter of the Confederate States of America

Confederate States of America pl n *US history* the 11 Southern states (Alabama, Arkansas, Florida, Georgia, North Carolina, South Carolina, Texas, Virginia, Tennessee, Louisiana, and Mississippi) that seceded from the Union in 1861, precipitating a civil war with the North. The Confederacy was defeated in 1865 and the South reincorporated into the US

confederation (kənˌfɛdə'reɪʃən) n 1 the act or process of confederating or the state of being confederated 2 a loose alliance of political units. The union of the Swiss cantons is the oldest surviving confederation 3 (esp in Canada) another name for **federation** > con,feder'ationist n

Confederation (kənˌfɛdə'reɪʃən) n 1 the Confederation *US history* the original 13 states of the United States of America constituted under the Articles of Confederation and superseded by the more formal union established in 1789 2 the federation of Canada, formed with four original provinces in 1867 and since joined by eight more

confer (kən'fɜː) vb -fers, -ferring, -ferred 1 (tr; foll by on or upon) to grant or bestow (an honour, gift, etc) 2 (intr) to hold or take part in a conference or consult together [c16: from Latin *conferre* to gather together, compare, from *com-* together + *ferre* to bring] > con'ferment or con'ferral n > con'ferrable *adj*

conferee or **conferree** (ˌkɒnfɜː'riː) n 1 a person who takes part in a conference 2 a person on whom an honour or gift is conferred

conference ('kɒnfərəns, -frəns) n 1 a meeting for consultation, exchange of information, or discussion, esp one with a formal agenda 2 an assembly of the clergy or of clergy and laity of any of certain Protestant Christian Churches acting as representatives of their denomination 3 *sport* a league or division of clubs or teams [c16: from Medieval Latin *conferentia*, from Latin *conferre* to bring together; see CONFER] > conferential (ˌkɒnfə'rɛnʃəl) *adj*

conference call n a special telephone facility by which three or more people using conventional or cellular phones can be linked up to speak to one another

conferva (kɒn'fɜːvə) n, pl -vae (-viː) or -vas any of various threadlike green algae, esp any of the genus *Tribonema*, typically occurring in fresh water [c18: from Latin: a water plant, from *confervēre* to grow together, heal, literally: to seethe, from *fervēre* to boil; named with reference to its reputed healing properties] > con'ferval *adj* > con'fervoid n, *adj*

confess (kən'fɛs) vb (when tr, may take a clause as object) 1 (when intr, often foll by to) to make an acknowledgement or admission of (faults, misdeeds, crimes, etc) 2 (tr) to admit or grant to be true; concede 3 *Christianity chiefly RC Church* to declare (one's sins) to God or to a priest as his representative, so as to obtain pardon and absolution [c14: from Old French *confesser*, from Late Latin *confessāre*, from Latin *confessus* confessed, from *confitērī* to admit, from *fatērī* to acknowledge; related to Latin *fārī* to speak]

confessedly (kən'fɛsɪdlɪ) *adv* (*sentence modifier*) by admission or confession; avowedly

confession (kən'fɛʃən) *n* **1** the act of confessing **2** something confessed **3** an acknowledgment or declaration, esp of one's faults, misdeeds, or crimes **4** *Christianity chiefly RC Church* the act of a penitent accusing himself or herself of his or her sins **5** confession of faith a formal public avowal of religious beliefs **6** a religious denomination or sect united by a common system of beliefs > con'fessionary *adj*

confessional (kən'fɛʃənᵊl) *adj* **1** of, like, or suited to a confession ▷ *n* **2** *Christianity chiefly RC Church* a small stall, usually enclosed and divided by a screen or curtain, where a priest hears confessions

confessor (kən'fɛsə) *n* **1** *Christianity chiefly RC Church* a priest who hears confessions and sometimes acts as a spiritual counsellor **2** *history* a person who bears witness to his Christian religious faith by the holiness of his life, esp in resisting threats or danger, but does not suffer martyrdom **3** a person who makes a confession

confetti (kən'fɛtɪ) *n* small pieces of coloured paper thrown on festive occasions, esp at the bride and groom at weddings [c19: from Italian, plural of *confetto*, originally, a bonbon; see COMFIT]

confidant (ˌkɒnfɪ'dænt, 'kɒnfɪˌdænt) *n* a person, esp a man, to whom private matters are confided [c17: from French *confident*, from Italian *confidente*, n use of adj: trustworthy, from Latin *confidens* CONFIDENT]

confidante (ˌkɒnfɪ'dænt, 'kɒnfɪˌdænt) *n* a person, esp a woman, to whom private matters are confided

confide (kən'faɪd) *vb* **1** (usually foll by *in*; when *tr*, may take a clause as object) to disclose (secret or personal matters) in confidence (to); reveal in private (to) **2** (*intr*; foll by *in*) to have complete trust **3** (*tr*) to entrust into another's keeping [c15: from Latin *confidere*, from *fidere* to trust; related to Latin *foedus* treaty] > con'fider *n*

confidence ('kɒnfɪdəns) *n* **1** a feeling of trust in a person or thing **2** belief in one's own abilities; self-assurance **3** trust or a trustful relationship: *take me into your confidence* **4** something confided or entrusted; secret **5** in confidence as a secret

confidence trick *or US and Canadian* **confidence game** *n* a swindle involving money in which the victim's trust is won by the swindler

confident ('kɒnfɪdənt) *adj* **1** (*postpositive*; foll by *of*) having or showing confidence or certainty; sure: *confident of success* **2** sure of oneself; bold **3** presumptuous; excessively bold [c16: from Latin *confidens* trusting, having self-confidence, from *confidere* to have complete trust in; see CONFIDE] > 'confidently *adv*

confidential (ˌkɒnfɪ'dɛnʃəl) *adj* **1** spoken, written, or given in confidence; secret; private **2** entrusted with another's confidence or secret affairs: *a confidential secretary* **3** suggestive of or denoting intimacy: *a confidential approach* > ˌconfiˌdenti'ality *or* ˌconfi'dentialness *n* > ˌconfi'dentially *adv*

confiding (kən'faɪdɪŋ) *adj* unsuspicious; trustful > con'fidingly *adv* > con'fidingness *n*

configuration (kənˌfɪɡjʊ'reɪʃən) *n* **1** the arrangement of the parts of something **2** the external form or outline achieved by such an arrangement **3** *psychol* the unit or pattern in perception studied by Gestalt psychologists [c16: from Late Latin *configūrātiō* a similar formation, from *configūrāre* to model on something, from *figūrāre* to shape, fashion] > conˌfigu'rational *or* con'figurative *adj*

configure (ˌkən'fɪɡə) *vb* (*tr*) **1** to arrange or organize **2** *computing* to set up (a piece of hardware or software) as required

confine *vb* (kən'faɪn) (*tr*) **1** to keep or close within bounds; limit; restrict **2** to keep shut in; restrict the free movement of: *arthritis confined him to bed* ▷ *n* ('kɒnfaɪn) **3** (*often plural*) a limit; boundary [c16: from Medieval Latin *confināre* from Latin *confinis* adjacent, from *finis* end, boundary] > con'finer *n*

confined (kən'faɪnd) *adj* **1** enclosed or restricted; limited

2 in childbed; undergoing childbirth

confinement (kən'faɪnmənt) *n* **1** the act of confining or the state of being confined **2** the period from the onset of labour to the birth of a child

confirm (kən'fɜːm) *vb* (*tr*) **1** (*may take a clause as object*) to prove to be true or valid; corroborate; verify **2** (*may take a clause as object*) to assert for a second or further time, so as to make more definite: *he confirmed that he would appear in court* **3** to strengthen or make more firm: *his story confirmed my doubts* **4** to make valid by a formal act or agreement; ratify **5** to administer the rite of confirmation to [c13: from Old French *confermer*, from Latin *confirmāre*, from *firmus* FIRM¹] > con'firmatory *or* con'firmative *adj*

confirmation (ˌkɒnfə'meɪʃən) *n* **1** the act of confirming **2** a rite in several Christian churches that confirms a baptized person in his or her faith and admits him or her to full participation in the church

confirmed (kən'fɜːmd) *adj* **1** (*prenominal*) long-established in a habit, way of life, etc **2** having received the rite of confirmation

confiscate ('kɒnfɪˌskeɪt) *vb* (*tr*) **1** to seize (property), esp for public use and esp by way of a penalty ▷ *adj* **2** seized or confiscated; forfeit [c16: from Latin *confiscāre* to seize for the public treasury, from *fiscus* basket, treasury] > ˌconfis'cation *n* > 'confisˌcator *n* > confiscatory (kən'fɪskətərɪ, -trɪ) *adj*

Confiteor (kən'fɪtɪˌɔː) *n* *RC Church* a prayer consisting of a general confession of sinfulness and an entreaty for forgiveness [c13: from Latin: I confess; from the beginning of the Latin prayer of confession]

conflagration (ˌkɒnflə'ɡreɪʃən) *n* a large destructive fire [c16: from Latin *conflagrātiō*, from *conflagrāre* to be burnt up, from *com-* (intensive) + *flagrāre* to burn; related to Latin *fulgur* lightning]

conflate (kən'fleɪt) *vb* (*tr*) to combine or blend (two things, esp two versions of a text) so as to form a whole [c16: from Latin *conflāre* to blow together, from *flāre* to blow] > con'flation *n*

conflict *n* ('kɒnflɪkt) **1** a struggle or clash between opposing forces; battle **2** a state of opposition between ideas, interests, etc; disagreement or controversy **3** *psychol* opposition between two simultaneous but incompatible wishes or drives, sometimes leading to a state of emotional tension and thought to be responsible for neuroses ▷ *vb* (kən'flɪkt) (*intr*) **4** to come into opposition; clash **5** to fight [c15: from Latin *conflictus*, from *conflīgere* to combat, from *flīgere* to strike] > con'fliction *n*

conflicting (kən'flɪktɪŋ) *adj* clashing; contradictory: *conflicting rumours* > con'flictingly *adv*

confluence ('kɒnfluəns) *or* **conflux** ('kɒnflʌks) *n* **1** a merging or flowing together, esp of rivers **2** a gathering together, esp of people [c17: from Latin *confluēns*, from *confluere* to flow together, from *fluere* to flow] > 'confluent *adj, n*

conform (kən'fɔːm) *vb* **1** (*intr*; usually foll by *to*) to comply in actions, behaviour, etc, with accepted standards or norms **2** (*intr*; usually foll by *with*) to be in accordance; fit in: *he conforms with my idea of a teacher* **3** to make or become similar in character or form **4** (*intr*) to comply with the practices of an established church, esp the Church of England **5** (*tr*) to bring (oneself, ideas, etc) into harmony or agreement [c14: from Old French *conformer*, from Latin *confirmāre* to establish, strengthen, from *firmāre* to make firm, from *firmus* FIRM¹] > con'former *n* > con'formist *n, adj*

conformable (kən'fɔːməbᵊl) *adj* **1** corresponding in character; similar **2** obedient; submissive **3** (foll by *to*) in agreement or harmony (with); consistent (with) **4** (of rock strata) lying in a parallel arrangement so that their original relative positions have remained undisturbed > conˌforma'bility *or* con'formableness *n* > con'formably *adv*

conformal (kən'fɔːməl) *adj* (of a map projection) maintaining true shape over a small area and scale in every direction [c17: from Late Latin *conformālis* having the same shape, from Latin *com-* same + *forma* shape]

conformation (ˌkɒnfɔː'meɪʃən) *n* **1** the general shape or outline of an object; configuration **2** the arrangement of the parts of an object

conformity (kən'fɔːmɪtɪ) or **conformance** n, pl -ities or -ances **1** compliance in actions, behaviour, etc, with certain accepted standards or norms **2** correspondence or likeness in form or appearance; congruity; agreement **3** compliance with the practices of an established church

confound (kən'faʊnd) vb (tr) **1** to astound or perplex; bewilder **2** to mix up; confuse **3** to treat mistakenly as similar to or identical with (one or more other things) **4** (kɒn'faʊnd) to curse or damn (usually as an expletive in the phrase **confound it!**) **5** to contradict or refute (an argument, etc) **6** to rout or defeat (an enemy) [c13: from Old French confondre, from Latin confundere to mingle, pour together, from fundere to pour] > con'founder n

confounded (kən'faʊndɪd) adj **1** bewildered; confused **2** (prenominal) informal execrable; damned > con'foundedly adv

confraternity (ˌkɒnfrə'tɜːnɪtɪ) n, pl -ties a group of men united for some particular purpose, esp Christian laymen organized for religious or charitable service; brotherhood [c15: from Medieval Latin confrāternitās; see CONFRÈRE, FRATERNITY]

confrère ('kɒnfreə) n a fellow member of a profession, fraternity, etc [c15: from Old French, from Medieval Latin confrāter fellow member, from Latin frāter brother]

confront (kən'frʌnt) vb (tr) **1** (usually foll by with) to present or face (with something), esp in order to accuse or criticize **2** to face boldly; oppose in hostility **3** to be face to face with; be in front of [c16: from Medieval Latin confrontārī to stand face to face with, from frons forehead] > confrontation (ˌkɒnfrʌn'teɪʃən) or archaic confrontment (kɒn'frʌntmənt) n > ˌconfron'tational adj

Confucian (kən'fjuːʃən) adj **1** of or relating to the doctrines of Confucius (Chinese name Kong Zi or K'ung Fu-tse.; 551–479 BC), the Chinese philosopher and teacher of ethics ▷ n **2** a follower of Confucius

Confucianism (kən'fjuːʃəˌnɪzəm) n the ethical system of Confucius, the Chinese philosopher and teacher of ethics (551–479 BC), emphasizing moral order, the humanity and virtue of China's ancient rulers, and gentlemanly education > Con'fucianist n

Confucius (kən'fjuːʃəs) n Chinese name Kong Zi or K'ung Fu-tse. 551–479 BC, Chinese philosopher and teacher of ethics (see **Confucianism**). His doctrines were compiled after his death under the title The Analects of Confucius

confuse (kən'fjuːz) vb (tr) **1** to bewilder; perplex **2** to mix up (things, ideas, etc); jumble **3** to make unclear: he confused his talk with irrelevant details **4** to fail to recognize the difference between; mistake (one thing) for another **5** to disconcert; embarrass **6** to cause to become disordered: the enemy ranks were confused by gas [c18: back formation from confused, from Latin confūsus mingled together, from confundere to pour together; see CONFOUND] > con'fusable adj > con'fused adj > confusedly (kən'fjuːzɪdlɪ, -'fjuːzd-) adv > con'fusedness n > con'fusing adj > con'fusingly adv

confusion (kən'fjuːʒən) n **1** the act of confusing or the state of being confused **2** disorder; jumble **3** bewilderment; perplexity **4** lack of clarity; indistinctness **5** embarrassment; abashment

confute (kən'fjuːt) vb (tr) to prove (a person or thing) wrong, invalid, or mistaken; disprove [c16: from Latin confūtāre to check, silence] > con'futable adj > confutation (ˌkɒnfjuː'teɪʃən) n

conga ('kɒŋɡə) n **1** a Latin American dance of three steps and a kick to each bar, usually performed by a number of people in single file **2** Also called: conga drum a large tubular bass drum, used chiefly in Latin American and funk music and played with the hands ▷ vb -gas, -gaing, -gaed **3** (intr) to dance the conga [c20: from American Spanish, feminine of congo belonging to the CONGO]

congé ('kɒnʒeɪ) n **1** permission to depart or dismissal, esp when formal **2** a farewell [c16: from Old French congié, from Latin commeātus leave of absence, from meātus movement, from meāre to go, pass]

congeal (kən'dʒiːl) vb **1** to change or cause to change from a soft or fluid state to a firm or solid state **2** to

form or cause to form into a coagulated mass; curdle; jell [c14: from Old French congeler, from Latin congelāre, from com- together + gelāre to freeze] > con'gealable adj > con'gealment n

congelation (ˌkɒndʒɪ'leɪʃən) n **1** the process of congealing **2** something formed by this process

congener (kən'dʒiːnə, 'kɒndʒɪnə) n a member of a class, group, or other category, esp any animal of a specified genus [c18: from Latin, from com- same + genus kind]

congenial (kən'dʒiːnjəl, -nɪəl) adj **1** friendly, pleasant, or agreeable: a congenial atmosphere to work in **2** having a similar disposition, tastes, etc; compatible; sympathetic [c17: from CON- (same) + GENIAL¹] > congeniality (kənˌdʒiːnɪ'ælɪtɪ) or con'genialness n

congenital (kən'dʒenɪtəl) adj **1** denoting or relating to any nonhereditary condition, esp an abnormal condition, existing at birth: congenital blindness **2** informal complete, as if from birth: a congenital idiot [c18: from Latin congenitus born together with, from genitus born, from gignere to bear, beget] > con'genitally adv

conger ('kɒŋɡə) n any large marine eel of the family Congridae, esp Conger conger, occurring in temperate and tropical coastal waters [c14: from Old French congre, from Latin conger, from Greek gongros sea eel]

congeries (kɒn'dʒɪəriːz) n (functioning as singular or plural) a collection of objects or ideas; mass; heap [c17: from Latin, from congerere to pile up, from gerere to carry]

congest (kən'dʒest) vb **1** to crowd or become crowded to excess; overfill **2** to overload or clog (an organ or part) with blood or (of an organ or part) to become overloaded or clogged with blood **3** (tr; usually passive) to block (the nose) with mucus [c16: from Latin congestus pressed together, from congerere to assemble; see CONGERIES]

congestion (kən'dʒestʃən) n **1** the state of being overcrowded, esp with with traffic or people **2** the state of being overloaded or clogged with blood **3** the state of being blocked with mucus

congestion charging n the practice of charging motorists for the right to drive on busy roads, esp at busy times > congestion charge n

conglomerate n (kən'ɡlɒmərɪt) **1** a thing composed of heterogeneous elements; mass **2** any coarse-grained sedimentary rock consisting of rounded fragments of rock embedded in a finer matrix **3** a large corporation consisting of a group of companies dealing in widely diversified goods, services, etc ▷ vb (kən'ɡlɒməˌreɪt) **4** to form into a cluster or mass ▷ adj (kən'ɡlɒmərɪt) **5** made up of heterogeneous elements; massed **6** (of sedimentary rocks) consisting of rounded fragments within a finer matrix [c16: from Latin conglomerāre to roll up, from glomerāre to wind into a ball, from glomus ball of thread] > conˌglome'ration n

Congo ('kɒŋɡəʊ) n **1** Democratic Republic of Congo a republic in S central Africa, with a narrow strip of land along the Congo estuary leading to the Atlantic in the west: Congo Free State established in 1885, with Leopold II of Belgium as absolute monarch; became the Belgian Congo colony in 1908; gained independence in 1960, followed by civil war and the secession of Katanga (until 1963); President Mobutu Sese Seko seized power in 1965; declared a one-party state in 1978, and was overthrown by rebels in 1997. The country consists chiefly of the Congo basin, with large areas of dense tropical forest and marshes, and the Mitumba highlands reaching over 5000 m (16 000 ft) in the east. Official language: French. Religion: Christian majority, animist minority. Currency: Congolese franc. Capital: Kinshasa. Pop: 54 417 000 (2004 est). Area: 2 344 116 sq km (905 063 sq miles). Former names: Congo Free State, Belgian Congo, Zaïre **2** Republic of Congo another name for **Congo-Brazzaville 3** the second longest river in Africa, rising as the Lualaba on the Katanga plateau in the Democratic Republic of Congo and flowing in a wide northerly curve to the Atlantic: forms the border between Congo-Brazzaville and the Democratic Republic of Congo. Length: about 4800 km (3000 miles). Area of basin: about 3 000 000 sq km (1 425 000 sq miles). Former Zaïrese name (1971–97): Zaïre

Congo-Brazzaville, Congo or **Republic of Congo** n a

republic in W Central Africa: formerly the French colony of Middle Congo, part of French Equatorial Africa, it became independent in 1960; consists mostly of equatorial forest, with savanna and extensive swamps; drained chiefly by the Rivers Congo and Ubangi. Official language: French. Religion: Christian majority. Currency: franc. Capital: Brazzaville. Pop: 3 818 000 (2004 est). Area: 342 000 sq km (132 018 sq miles). Former name: **Middle Congo**

Congo Free State *n* a former name (1885–1908) of (**Democratic Republic of**) **Congo**(sense 2)

Congolese (ˌkɒŋɡəˈliːz) *adj* **1** of or relating to the Republic of the Congo or the Democratic Republic of the Congo or their inhabitants ▷ *n* **2** a native or inhabitant of the Republic of the Congo or the Democratic Republic of the Congo

congrats (kənˈɡræts) *or chiefly Brit* **congratters** (kənˈɡrætəz) *pl n, sentence substitute* informal shortened forms of **congratulations**

congratulate (kənˈɡrætjʊˌleɪt) *vb* (*tr*) **1** (usually foll by *on*) to communicate pleasure, approval, or praise to (a person or persons); compliment **2** (often foll by *on*) to consider (oneself) clever or fortunate (as a result of): *she congratulated herself on her tact* **3** *obsolete* to greet [C16: from Latin *congrātulārī*, from *grātulārī* to rejoice, from *grātus* pleasing] > con,gratu'lation *n* > con'gratulatory *or* con'gratulative *adj*

congratulations (kənˌɡrætjʊˈleɪʃənz) *pl n, sentence substitute* expressions of pleasure or joy; felicitations

congregate (ˈkɒŋɡrɪˌɡeɪt) *vb* to collect together in a body or crowd; assemble [C15: from Latin *congregāre* to collect into a flock, from *grex* flock]

congregation (ˌkɒŋɡrɪˈɡeɪʃən) *n* **1** a group of persons gathered for worship, prayer, etc, esp in a church or chapel **2** the act of congregating or collecting together **3** a group of people, objects, etc, collected together; assemblage **4** the group of persons habitually attending a given church, chapel, etc **5** *RC Church* **a** a society of persons who follow a common rule of life but who are bound only by simple vows **b** an administrative subdivision of the papal curia **6** *chiefly Brit* an assembly of senior members of a university

congregational (ˌkɒŋɡrɪˈɡeɪʃənᵊl) *adj* **1** of or relating to a congregation **2** (*usually cap*) of, relating to, or denoting the Congregational Church, its members, or its beliefs

Congregational Church *n* any evangelical Protestant Christian Church that is governed according to the principles of Congregationalism

Congregationalism (ˌkɒŋɡrɪˈɡeɪʃənəˌlɪzəm) *n* a system of Christian doctrines and ecclesiastical government in which each congregation is self-governing and maintains bonds of faith with other similar local congregations > ˌCongre'gationalist *adj, n*

congress (ˈkɒŋɡrɛs) *n* **1** a meeting or conference, esp of representatives of a number of sovereign states **2** a national legislative assembly **3** a society or association [C16: from Latin *congressus* from *congredī* to meet with, from *com-* together + *gradī* to walk, step]

Congress (ˈkɒŋɡrɛs) *n* **1** the bicameral federal legislature of the US, consisting of the House of Representatives and the Senate **2** Also called: **Congress Party** (in India) a major political party, which controlled the Union government from 1947 to 1977 > Con'gressional *adj*

congressional (kənˈɡrɛʃənᵊl) *adj* of or relating to a congress > con'gressionalist *n*

Congressman (ˈkɒŋɡrɛsmən) *n, pl* -men (in the US) a male member of Congress, esp of the House of Representatives

Congresswoman (ˈkɒŋɡrɛswʊmən) *n, pl* -women (in the US) a female member of Congress, esp of the House of Representatives

Congreve (ˈkɒŋɡriːv) *n* **William.** 1670–1729, English dramatist, a major exponent of Restoration comedy; author of *Love for Love* (1695) and *The Way of the World* (1700)

congruence (ˈkɒŋɡrʊəns) *or* **congruency** (ˈkɒŋɡrʊənsɪ) *n* **1** the quality or state of corresponding, agreeing, or being congruent **2** *maths* the relationship between two integers, *x* and *y*, such that their difference, with respect to another positive integer called the modulus, *n*, is a

multiple of the modulus. Usually written $x \equiv y \pmod{n}$, as in $25 \equiv 11 \pmod 7$)

congruent (ˈkɒŋɡrʊənt) *adj* **1** agreeing; corresponding; congruous **2** having identical shapes so that all parts correspond: *congruent triangles* **3** of or concerning two integers related by a congruence [C15: from Latin *congruere* to meet together, agree]

congruous (ˈkɒŋɡrʊəs) *adj* **1** corresponding or agreeing **2** suitable; appropriate [C16: from Latin *congruus* suitable, harmonious; see **CONGRUENT**] > congruity (kənˈɡruːɪtɪ) *or* 'congruousness *n*

conic (ˈkɒnɪk) *adj* **1** Also: **conical a** having the shape of a cone **b** of or relating to a cone ▷ *n* **2** another name for **conic section** [C16: from New Latin, from Greek *kōnikos*, from *kōnos* **CONE**] > 'conically *adv*

conics (ˈkɒnɪks) *n* (*functioning as singular*) the branch of geometry concerned with the parabola, ellipse, and hyperbola

conic section *n* one of a group of curves formed by the intersection of a plane and a right circular cone. It is either a circle, ellipse, parabola, or hyperbola, depending on the eccentricity, *e*, which is constant for a particular curve: $e = 0$ for a circle; $e < 1$ for an ellipse; $e = 1$ for a parabola; $e > 1$ for a hyperbola

conidium (kəʊˈnɪdɪəm) *n, pl* -nidia (-ˈnɪdɪə) an asexual spore formed at the tip of a specialized hypha (conidiophore) in fungi such as *Penicillium* [C19: from New Latin, from Greek *konis* dust + -**IUM**]

conifer (ˈkəʊnɪfə, ˈkɒn-) *n* any gymnosperm tree or shrub of the phylum *Coniferophyta*, typically bearing cones and evergreen leaves. The group includes the pines, spruces, firs, larches, yews, junipers, cedars, cypresses, and sequoias [C19: from Latin, from *cōnus* **CONE** + *ferre* to bear] > coniferous (kəˈnɪfərəs, kɒ-) *adj*

Coniston Water (ˈkɒnɪstən) *n* a lake in NW England, in Cumbria: scene of the establishment of world water speed records by Sir Malcolm Campbell (1939) and his son Donald Campbell (1959). Length: 8 km (5 miles)

conj. *abbreviation grammar* conjugation, conjunction, *or* conjunctive

conjectural (kənˈdʒɛktʃərəl) *adj* involving or inclined to conjecture > con'jecturally *adv*

conjecture (kənˈdʒɛktʃə) *n* **1** the formation of conclusions from incomplete evidence; guess **2** the inference or conclusion so formed **3** *obsolete* interpretation of occult signs ▷ *vb* **4** to infer or arrive at (an opinion, conclusion, etc) from incomplete evidence [C14: from Latin *conjectūra* an assembling of facts, from *conjicere* to throw together, from *jacere* to throw] > con'jecturable *adj* > con'jecturably *adv* > con'jecturer *n*

conjoin (kənˈdʒɔɪn) *vb* to join or become joined [C14: from Old French *conjoindre*, from Latin *conjungere*, from *jungere* to **JOIN**] > con'joiner *n*

conjoined twins *pl n* twin babies born joined together at some point, such as at the hips. Some have lived for many years without being surgically separated. Non-technical name: **Siamese twins**

conjoint (kənˈdʒɔɪnt) *adj* united, joint, or associated > con'jointly *adv*

conjugal (ˈkɒndʒʊɡᵊl) *adj* of or relating to marriage or the relationship between husband and wife: *conjugal rights* [C16: from Latin *conjugālis*, from *conjunx* wife or husband, from *conjungere* to unite; see **CONJOIN**] > conjugality (ˌkɒndʒʊˈɡælɪtɪ) *n* > 'conjugally *adv*

conjugate *vb* (ˈkɒndʒʊˌɡeɪt) **1** (*tr*) *grammar* to inflect (a verb) systematically; state or set out the conjugation of (a verb) **2** (*intr*) (of a verb) to undergo inflection according to a specific set of rules **3** (*tr*) to join (two or more substances) together, esp in such a way that the resulting substance may easily be turned back into its original components **4** (*intr*) *biology* to undergo conjugation **5** (*tr*) *obsolete* to join together, esp in marriage ▷ *adj* (ˈkɒndʒʊɡɪt, -ˌɡeɪt) **6** joined together in pairs; coupled **7** (*Maths*) **a** (of two angles) having a sum of 360° **b** (of two complex numbers) differing only in the sign of the imaginary part as in $4 + 3i$ and $4 - 3i$ **8** *chem* of, denoting, or concerning the state of equilibrium in which two liquids can exist as two separate phases that are both solutions. The liquid that is the solute in one phase is the solvent in the other **9** *chem* (of acids and bases) related by loss or gain of a proton **10** (of a compound leaf) having one pair of leaflets **11** (of words) cognate; related in origin ▷ *n* ('kɒndʒʊgɪt) **12** one of a pair or set of conjugate substances, values, quantities, words, etc [c15: from Latin *conjugāre* to join together, from *com-* together + *jugāre* to marry, connect, from *jugum* a yoke] > 'conju,gative *adj* > 'conju,gator *n*

conjugation (,kɒndʒʊ'geɪʃən) *n* **1** *grammar* **a** inflection of a verb for person, number, tense, voice, mood, etc **b** the complete set of the inflections of a given verb **2** a joining, union, or conjunction **3** a type of sexual reproduction in ciliate protozoans involving the temporary union of two individuals and the subsequent migration and fusion of the gametic nuclei **4** (in bacteria) the direct transfer of DNA between two cells that are temporarily joined **5** the union of gametes, esp isogametes, as in some algae and fungi **6** the pairing of chromosomes in the early phase of a meiotic division **7** *chem* the existence of alternating double or triple bonds in a chemical compound, with consequent electron delocalization over part of the molecule > ,conju'gational *adj*

conjunct (kən'dʒʌŋkt, 'kɒndʒʌŋkt) *n* *logic* one of the propositions or formulas in a conjunction [c15: from Latin *conjunctus*, from *conjungere* to unite; see CONJOIN]

conjunction (kən'dʒʌŋkʃən) *n* **1** the act of joining together; combination; union **2** simultaneous occurrence of events; coincidence **3** any word or group of words, other than a relative pronoun, that connects words, phrases, or clauses; for example *and* and *while* **4** *astronomy* the position of any two bodies that appear to meet, such as two celestial bodies on the celestial sphere **5** *logic* **a** the operator that forms a compound sentence from two given sentences, and corresponds to the English *and* **b** a sentence so formed. Usually written *p•q*, *p∧q*, or *p.q.*, where *p,q* are the component sentences, it is true only when both these are true **c** the relation between such sentences > con'junctional *adj*

conjunctiva (,kɒndʒʌŋk'taɪvə) *n*, *pl* **-vas** *or* **-vae** (-viː) the delicate mucous membrane that covers the eyeball and the under surface of the eyelid [c16: from New Latin *membrāna conjunctīva* the conjunctive membrane, from Late Latin *conjunctīvus* CONJUNCTIVE] > ,conjunc'tival *adj*

conjunctive (kən'dʒʌŋktɪv) *adj* **1** joining; connective **2** joined **3** of or relating to conjunctions or their use ▷ *n* **4** a less common word for **conjunction** (sense 3) [c15: from Late Latin *conjunctīvus*, from Latin *conjungere* to CONJOIN]

conjunctivitis (kən,dʒʌŋktɪ'vaɪtɪs) *n* inflammation of the conjunctiva

conjuncture (kən'dʒʌŋktʃə) *n* a combination of events, esp a critical one

conjuration (,kɒndʒʊ'reɪʃən) *n* **1** a magic spell; incantation **2** a less common word for **conjuring** **3** *archaic* supplication; entreaty

conjure ('kʌndʒə) *vb* **1** (*intr*) to practise conjuring or be a conjuror **2** (*intr*) to call upon supposed supernatural forces by spells and incantations **3** (kən'dʒʊə) (*tr*) to appeal earnestly or strongly to: *I conjure you to help me* **4** a name to conjure with **a** a person thought to have great power or influence **b** any name that excites the imagination [c13: from Old French *conjurer* to plot, from Latin *conjūrāre* to swear together, form a conspiracy, from *jūrāre* to swear]

conjure up *vb* (*tr, adverb*) **1** to present to the mind; evoke or imagine: *he conjured up a picture of his childhood* **2** to call up or command (a spirit or devil) by an incantation

conjuring ('kʌndʒərɪŋ) *n* **1** the performance of tricks that appear to defy natural laws ▷ *adj* **2** denoting or relating to such tricks or entertainment

conjuror *or* **conjurer** ('kʌndʒərə) *n* **1** a person who practises conjuring, esp for people's entertainment **2** a person who practises magic; sorcerer

conk (kɒŋk) ▷ *vb* **1** to strike (someone) a blow, esp on the head or nose ▷ *n* **2** a punch or blow, esp on the head or nose **3** the head or (esp Brit and NZ) the nose [c19: probably changed from CONCH]

conker ('kɒŋkə) *n* an informal name for **horse chestnut**

(sense 2)

conkers ('kɒŋkəz) *n* (*functioning as singular*) Brit a game in which a player swings a horse chestnut (conker), threaded onto a string, against that of another player to try to break it [c19: from dialect *conker* snail shell, originally used in the game]

conk out *vb* (*intr, adverb*) *informal* **1** (of machines, cars, etc) to fail suddenly **2** to tire suddenly or collapse, as from exhaustion [c20: of uncertain origin]

con man *n* *informal* a person who swindles another by means of a confidence trick

con moto (kɒn 'məʊtəʊ) *adj, adv* *music* (to be performed) in a brisk or lively manner [Italian, literally: with movement]

conn (kɒn) *vb, n* a variant spelling (esp US) of **con³**

Conn (kɒn) *n* 2nd century AD, king of Leinster and high king of Ireland

Conn. *abbreviation* Connecticut

Connacht ('kɒnət) *or* **Connaught** *n* a province and ancient kingdom of NW Republic of Ireland: consists of the counties of Galway, Leitrim, Mayo, Roscommon, and Sligo. Pop: 464 296 (2002). Area: 17 122 sq km (6611 sq miles)

connate ('kɒneɪt) *adj* **1** existing in a person or thing from birth; congenital or innate **2** allied or associated in nature or origin; cognate: *connate qualities* **3** Also called: **coadunate** *biology* (of similar parts or organs) closely joined or united together by growth **4** *geology* (of fluids) produced or originating at the same time as the rocks surrounding them: *connate water* [c17: from Late Latin *connātus* born at the same time, from Latin *nātus*, from *nāscī* to be born]

connect (kə'nɛkt) *vb* **1** to link or be linked together; join; fasten **2** (*tr*) to relate or associate: *I connect him with my childhood* **3** (*tr*) to establish telephone communications with or between **4** (*intr*) to be meaningful or meaningfully related **5** (*intr*) (of two public vehicles, such as trains or buses) to have the arrival of one timed to occur just before the departure of the other, for the convenient transfer of passengers **6** (*intr*) *informal* to hit, punch, kick, etc, solidly [c17: from Latin *connectere* to bind together, from *nectere* to bind, tie] > con'nectible *or* con'nectable *adj* > con'nector *or* con'necter *n*

Connecticut (kə'nɛtɪkət) *n* **1** a state of the northeastern US, in New England. Capital: Hartford. Pop: 3 483 372 (2003 est). Area: 12 973 sq km (5009 sq miles). Abbreviations: Conn., CT **2** a river in the northeastern US, rising in N New Hampshire and flowing south to Long Island Sound. Length: 651 km (407 miles)

connecting rod *n* **1** a rod or bar for transmitting motion, esp one that connects a rotating part to a reciprocating part **2** such a rod that connects the piston to the crankshaft in an internal-combustion engine or reciprocating pump

connection *or* **connexion** (kə'nɛkʃən) *n* **1** the act or state of connecting; union **2** something that connects, joins, or relates; link or bond **3** a relationship or association **4** logical sequence in thought or expression; coherence **5** the relation of a word or phrase to its context: *in this connection the word has no political significance* **6** (*often plural*) an acquaintance, esp one who is influential or has prestige **7** a relative, esp if distant and related by marriage **8** **a** an opportunity to transfer from one train, bus, aircraft, ship, etc, to another **b** the vehicle, aircraft, etc, scheduled to provide such an opportunity **9** a link, usually a wire or metallic strip, between two components in an electric circuit or system **10** a communications link between two points, esp by telephone **11** *slang* a supplier of illegal drugs, such as heroin **12** *rare* sexual intercourse > con'nectional *or* con'nexional *adj*

connective (kə'nɛktɪv) *adj* **1** serving to connect or capable of connecting ▷ *n* **2** a thing that connects **3** *grammar, logic* **a** any word that connects phrases, clauses, or individual words **b** a symbol used in a formal language in the construction of compound sentences from simpler sentences, corresponding to terms such as *or, and, not*, etc, in ordinary speech **4** *botany* the tissue of a stamen that connects the two lobes of the anther

connective tissue *n* an animal tissue developed from the embryonic mesoderm that consists of collagen or elastic fibres, fibroblasts, fatty cells, etc, within a jelly-like matrix. It supports organs, fills the spaces between them, and forms tendons and ligaments

connectivity (ˌkɒnɛkˈtɪvɪtɪ) *n* **1** the state of being or being able to be connected **2** *computing* the state of being connected to the internet **3** *computing* the capacity of a machine or appliance to be connected to other machines, appliances, or facilities

Connell (ˈkɒnəl) *n* **Desmond**. born 1926, Irish cardinal; Archbishop of Dublin and primate of Ireland (1988–2004)

Connemara (ˌkɒnɪˈmɑːrə) *n* a barren coastal region of W Republic of Ireland, in Co Galway: consists of quartzite mountains, peat bogs, and many lakes; noted for its breed of pony originating from the hilly regions

Connery (ˈkɒnərɪ) *n* **Sir Sean**, real name *Thomas Connery*. born 1929, Scottish film actor, who played James Bond in such films as *Goldfinger* (1964). His later films include *The Name of the Rose* (1986), *Indiana Jones and the Last Crusade* (1989), and *Finding Forrester* (2000)

conning tower (ˈkɒnɪŋ) *n* **1** Also called: **sail** a superstructure of a submarine, used as the bridge when the vessel is on the surface **2** the armoured pilot house of a warship [C19: see CON⁴]

connivance (kəˈnaɪvəns) *n* **1** the act or fact of conniving **2** *law* the tacit encouragement of or assent to another's wrongdoing, esp (formerly) of the petitioner in a divorce suit to the respondent's adultery

connive (kəˈnaɪv) *vb* (*intr*) **1** to plot together, esp secretly; conspire **2** (foll by *at*) *law* to give assent or encouragement (to the commission of a wrong) [C17: from French *conniver*, from Latin *connīvēre* to blink, hence, leave uncensured; *-nīvēre* related to *nictāre* to wink] > con'niver *n*

connoisseur (ˌkɒnɪˈsɜː) *n* a person with special knowledge or appreciation of a field, esp in the arts [C18: from French, from Old French *conoiseor*, from *connoistre* to know, from Latin *cognōscere*] > ˌconnois'seurship *n*

Connolly (ˈkɒnəlɪ) *n* **1 Billy**. born 1942, Scottish comedian **2 Cyril (Vernon)**. 1903–74, British critic and writer, founder and editor of *Horizon* (1939–50): his books include *Enemies of Promise* (1938) **3 James**. 1868–1916, Irish labour leader: executed by the British for his part in the Easter Rising (1916)

Connors (ˈkɒnəz) *n* **Jimmy**. born 1952, US tennis player: Wimbledon champion 1974 and 1982; US champion 1974, 1976, 1978, 1982, and 1983

connotation (ˌkɒnəˈteɪʃən) *n* **1** an association or idea suggested by a word or phrase; implication **2** the act or fact of connoting **3** *logic* another name for **intension** (sense 1) > connotative (ˈkɒnəˌteɪtɪv, kəˈnəʊtə-) *or* con'notive *adj*

connote (kɒˈnəʊt) *vb* (*tr; often takes a clause as object*) **1** (of a word, phrase, etc) to imply or suggest (associations or ideas) other than the literal meaning: *the word "maiden" connotes modesty* **2** to involve as a consequence or condition [C17: from Medieval Latin *connotāre*, from *notāre* to mark, make a note, from *nota* mark, sign, note]

connubial (kəˈnjuːbɪəl) *adj* of or relating to marriage; conjugal: *connubial bliss* [C17: from Latin *cōnūbiālis* from *cōnūbium* marriage, from *com-* together + *nūbere* to marry] > conˌnubi'ality *n*

conoid (ˈkəʊnɔɪd) *n* **1** a geometric surface formed by rotating a parabola, ellipse, or hyperbola about one axis ▷ *adj* **2** Also: **conoidal** (kəʊˈnɔɪdᵊl) conical, cone-shaped [C17: from Greek *kōnoeidēs*, from *kōnos* CONE] > co'noidally *adv*

conquer (ˈkɒŋkə) *vb* **1** to overcome (an enemy, army, etc); defeat **2** to overcome (an obstacle, feeling, desire, etc); surmount **3** (*tr*) to gain possession or control of by or as if by force or war; win [C13: from Old French *conquerre*, from Vulgar Latin *conquērere* (unattested) to obtain, from Latin *conquīrere* to search for, collect, from *quaerere* to seek] > 'conquerable *adj* > 'conquering *adj* > 'conqueror *n*

Conqueror (ˈkɒŋkərə) *n* **William the Conqueror** See **William I**

conquest (ˈkɒnkwɛst, ˈkɒŋ-) *n* **1** the act or an instance of conquering or the state of having been conquered;

victory **2** a person, thing, etc, that has been conquered or won **3** the act or art of gaining a person's compliance, love, etc, by seduction or force of personality **4** a person, whose compliance, love, etc, has been won over by seduction or force of personality [C13: from Old French *conqueste,* from Vulgar Latin *conquēsta* (unattested), from Latin *conquīsīta,* feminine past participle of *conquīrere* to seek out, procure; see CONQUER]

Conquest (ˈkɒnkwɛst, ˈkɒŋ-) *n* **the Conquest** See **Norman Conquest**

conquistador (kɒnˈkwɪstəˌdɔː; *Spanish* konkistaˈðɔr) *n, pl* **-dors** *or* **-dores** (*Spanish* -ˈðɔres) an adventurer or conqueror, esp one of the Spanish conquerors of the New World in the 16th century [C19: from Spanish, from *conquistar* to conquer; see CONQUEST]

Conrad (ˈkɒnræd) *n* **Joseph**. real name *Teodor Josef Konrad Korzeniowski*. 1857–1924, British novelist born in Poland, noted for sea stories such as *The Nigger of the Narcissus* (1897) and *Lord Jim* (1900) and novels of politics and revolution such as *Nostromo* (1904) and *Under Western Eyes* (1911)

Cons. *or* **cons.** *abbreviation* Conservative

consanguinity (ˌkɒnsæŋˈgwɪnɪtɪ) *n* **1** relationship by blood; kinship **2** close affinity or connection [C14: see CON-, SANGUINE] > ˌconsan'guineous *or* con'sanguine *adj* > ˌconsan'guineously *adv*

conscience (ˈkɒnʃəns) *n* **1** the sense of right and wrong that governs a person's thoughts and actions **2** conscientiousness; diligence **3** a feeling of guilt or anxiety: *he has a conscience about his unkind action* **4** *obsolete* consciousness **5** in conscience *or* in all conscience **a** with regard to truth and justice **b** certainly **6** on one's conscience causing feelings of guilt or remorse [C13: from Old French, from Latin *conscientia* knowledge, consciousness, from *conscīre* to know; see CONSCIOUS]

conscience clause *n* a clause in a law or contract exempting persons with moral scruples

conscience money *n* money paid voluntarily to compensate for dishonesty, esp money paid voluntarily for taxes formerly evaded

conscience-stricken *adj* feeling anxious or guilty. Also called: **conscience-smitten**

conscientious (ˌkɒnʃɪˈɛnʃəs) *adj* **1** involving or taking great care; painstaking; diligent **2** governed by or done according to conscience > ˌconsci'entiously *adv* > ˌconsci'entiousness *n*

conscientious objector *n* a person who refuses to serve in the armed forces on the grounds of conscience

conscious (ˈkɒnʃəs) *adj* **1 a** alert and awake; not sleeping or comatose **b** aware of one's surroundings, one's own thoughts and motivations, etc **2 a** aware of and giving value or emphasis to a particular fact or phenomenon: *I am conscious of your great kindness to me* **b** (*in combination*): *clothes-conscious* **3** done with full awareness; deliberate: *a conscious effort; conscious rudeness* **4 a** denoting or relating to a part of the human mind that is aware of a person's self, environment, and mental activity and that to a certain extent determines his choices of action **b** (*as noun*): *the conscious is only a small part of the mind* [C17: from Latin *conscius* sharing knowledge, from *com-* with + *scīre* to know] > 'consciously *adv* > 'consciousness *n*

consciousness raising *n* **a** the process of developing awareness in a person or group of a situation regarded as wrong or unjust, with the aim of producing active participation in changing it **b** (*as modifier*): *a consciousness-raising group*

conscript (ˈkɒnskrɪpt) **1 a** a person who is enrolled for compulsory military service **b** (*as modifier*): *a conscript army* ▷ *vb* (kənˈskrɪpt) **2** (*tr*) to enrol (youths, civilians, etc) for compulsory military service [C15: from Latin *conscrīptus,* past participle of *conscrībere* to write together in a list, enrol, from *scrībere* to write]

conscription (kənˈskrɪpʃən) *n* compulsory military service

consecrate (ˈkɒnsɪˌkreɪt) *vb* (*tr*) **1** to make or declare sacred or holy; sanctify **2** to dedicate (one's life, time, etc) to a specific purpose **3** *Christianity* to sanctify (bread and wine) for the Eucharist to be received as the body and blood of Christ **4** to cause to be respected or revered;

venerate: *time has consecrated this custom* [C15: from Latin *consecrāre*, from *com-* (intensive) + *sacrāre* to devote, from *sacer* sacred] > ˌconseˈcration *n* > ˈconseˌcrator *n* > consecratory (ˌkɒnsɪˈkreɪtərɪ) *or* ˈconseˌcrative *adj*

Consecration (ˌkɒnsɪˈkreɪʃən) *n RC Church* the part of the Mass after the sermon during which the bread and wine are believed to change into the Body and Blood of Christ

consecutive (kənˈsɛkjʊtɪv) *adj* 1 (of a narrative, account, etc) following chronological sequence 2 following one another without interruption; successive 3 characterized by logical sequence 4 *music* another word for **parallel** (sense 3) 5 *grammar* expressing consequence or result: *consecutive clauses* [C17: from French *consécutif*, from Latin *consecūtus* having followed, from *consequī* to pursue] > conˈsecutively *adv* > conˈsecutiveness *n*

consensual (kənˈsɛnsjʊəl) *adj* 1 *law* (of a contract, agreement, etc) existing by consent 2 (of certain reflex actions of a part of the body) responding to stimulation of another part > conˈsensually *adv* [from CONSENSUS + -AL¹]

consensus (kənˈsɛnsəs) *n* general or widespread agreement (esp in the phrase **consensus of opinion**) [C19: from Latin, from *consentīre* to feel together, agree; see CONSENT]

● USAGE Since *consensus* refers to a collective opinion,
● the words *of opinion* in the phrase *consensus of opinion* are
● redundant and should therefore be avoided

consent (kənˈsɛnt) *vb* 1 to give assent or permission (to do something); agree; accede ▷ *n* 2 acquiescence to or acceptance of something done or planned by another; permission 3 accordance or harmony in opinion; agreement (esp in the phrase **with one consent**) [C13: from Old French *consentir*, from Latin *consentīre* to feel together, agree, from *sentīre* to feel] > conˈsenting *adj*

consequence (ˈkɒnsɪkwəns) *n* 1 a result or effect of some previous occurrence 2 an unpleasant result (esp in the phrase **take the consequences**) 3 significance or importance: *it's of no consequence; a man of consequence* 4 *logic* a conclusion reached by reasoning 5 in consequence as a result

consequent (ˈkɒnsɪkwənt) *adj* 1 following as an effect or result 2 following as a logical conclusion or by rational argument 3 (of a river) flowing in the direction of the original slope of the land or dip of the strata ▷ *n* 4 something that follows something else, esp as a result 5 *logic* the resultant clause in a conditional sentence [C15: from Latin *consequēns* following closely, from *consequī* to pursue]

consequential (ˌkɒnsɪˈkwɛnʃəl) *adj* 1 important or significant 2 self-important; conceited 3 following as a consequence; resultant, esp indirectly: *consequential loss* > ˌconseˌquentiˈality *or* ˌconseˈquentialness *n* > ˌconseˈquentially *adv*

consequently (ˈkɒnsɪkwəntlɪ) *adv, sentence connector* as a result or effect; therefore; hence

conservancy (kənˈsɜːvənsɪ) *n, pl* -cies 1 (in Britain) a court or commission with jurisdiction over a river, port, area of countryside, etc 2 another word for **conservation** (sense 2)

conservation (ˌkɒnsəˈveɪʃən) *n* 1 the act or an instance of conserving or keeping from change, loss, injury, etc 2 a protection, preservation, and careful management of natural resources and of the environment b (*as modifier*): *a conservation area* > ˌconserˈvational *adj* > ˌconserˈvationist *n*

conservation grade *adj* relating to food produced using traditional methods where possible, and following strict specifications regarding animal feeds and welfare, the use of chemical fertilizers, wildlife conservation, and land management

conservation of energy *n* the principle that the total energy of any isolated system is constant and independent of any changes occurring within the system

conservation of mass *n* the principle that the total mass of any isolated system is constant and is independent of any chemical and physical changes

taking place within the system

conservatism (kənˈsɜːvəˌtɪzəm) *n* 1 opposition to change and innovation 2 a political philosophy advocating the preservation of the best of the established order in society and opposing radical change

conservative (kənˈsɜːvətɪv) *adj* 1 favouring the preservation of established customs, values, etc, and opposing innovation 2 of, characteristic of, or relating to conservatism 3 tending to be moderate or cautious: *a conservative estimate* 4 conventional in style or type: *a conservative suit* 5 *med* (of treatment) designed to alleviate symptoms. See **radical** (sense 4) ▷ *n* 6 a person who is reluctant to change or consider new ideas; conformist 7 a supporter or advocate of conservatism > conˈservatively *adv* > conˈservativeness *n*

Conservative (kənˈsɜːvətɪv) *adj* 1 (in Britain, Canada, and elsewhere) 1 of, supporting, or relating to a Conservative Party 2 of, relating to, or characterizing Conservative Judaism ▷ *n* 3 a supporter or member of a Conservative Party

Conservative Judaism *n* a movement reacting against the radicalism of Reform Judaism, rejecting extreme change and advocating moderate relaxations of traditional Jewish law, by an extension of the process by which its adherents claim traditional Orthodox Judaism evolved

Conservative Party *n* 1 (in Britain) the major right-wing party, which developed from the Tories in the 1830s. It advocates a mixed economy, and encourages property owning and free enterprise 2 (in other countries) any of various political parties generally opposing change

conservatoire (kənˈsɜːvəˌtwɑː) *n* an institution or school for instruction in music. Also called: conservatory [C18: from French: CONSERVATORY]

conservator (ˈkɒnsəˌveɪtə, kənˈsɜːvə-) *n* a person who conserves or keeps safe; custodian, guardian, or protector

conservatorium (kənˌsɜːvəˈtɔːrɪəm) *n Austral* the usual term for **conservatoire**

conservatory (kənˈsɜːvətrɪ) *n, pl* -tories 1 a greenhouse, esp one attached to a house 2 another word for **conservatoire**

conserve *vb* (kənˈsɜːv) (*tr*) 1 to keep or protect from harm, decay, loss, etc 2 to preserve (a foodstuff, esp fruit) with sugar ▷ *n* (ˈkɒnsɜːv, kənˈsɜːv) 3 a preparation of fruit in sugar, similar to jam but usually containing whole pieces of fruit [(vb) C14: from Latin *conservāre* to keep safe, from *servāre* to save, protect; (n) C14: from Medieval Latin *conserva*, from Latin *conservāre*]

consider (kənˈsɪdə) *vb* (*mainly tr*) 1 (*also intr*) to think carefully about or ponder on (a problem, decision, etc); contemplate 2 (*may take a clause as object*) to judge, deem, or have as an opinion: *I consider him a fool* 3 to have regard for; respect: *consider your mother's feelings* 4 to look at; regard: *he considered her face* 5 (*may take a clause as object*) to bear in mind as possible or acceptable: *when buying a car consider this make* 6 to describe or discuss [C14: from Latin *considerāre* to inspect closely, literally: to observe the stars, from *sīdus* star]

considerable (kənˈsɪdərəb²l) *adj* 1 large enough to reckon with: *a considerable quantity* 2 a lot of; much: *he had considerable courage* 3 worthy of respect: *a considerable man in the scientific world* > conˈsiderably *adv*

considerate (kənˈsɪdərɪt) *adj* 1 thoughtful towards other people; kind 2 *rare* carefully thought out; considered > conˈsiderately *adv*

consideration (kənˌsɪdəˈreɪʃən) *n* 1 the act or an instance of considering; deliberation; contemplation 2 take into consideration to bear in mind; consider 3 under consideration being currently discussed or deliberated 4 a fact or circumstance to be taken into account when making a judgment or decision 5 thoughtfulness for other people; kindness 6 payment for a service; recompense; fee 7 thought resulting from deliberation; opinion 8 *law* the promise, object, etc, given by one party to persuade another to enter into a contract 9 estimation; esteem 10 in consideration of a because of b in return for

considered (kən'sɪdəd) *adj* **1** presented or thought out with care: *a considered opinion* **2** (qualified by a preceding adverb) esteemed: *highly considered*

considering (kən'sɪdərɪŋ) *prep* **1** in view of ▷ *adv* **2** *informal* all in all; taking into account the circumstances: *it's not bad considering* ▷ *conj* **3** (subordinating) in view of the fact that

consign (kən'saɪn) *vb* (*mainly tr*) **1** to hand over or give into the care or charge of another; entrust **2** to commit irrevocably: *he consigned the papers to the flames* **3** to commit for admittance: *to consign someone to jail* **4** to address or deliver (goods) for sale, disposal, etc: *it was consigned to his London address* [C15: from Old French *consigner*, from Latin *consignāre* to put one's seal to, sign, from *signum* mark, SIGN] > con'signable *adj*

consignment (kən'saɪnmənt) *n* **1** the act of consigning; commitment **2** a shipment of goods consigned **3** on consignment for payment by the consignee after sale

consist (kən'sɪst) *vb* (*intr*) **1** (foll by *of*) to be composed (of); be formed (of) **2** (foll by *in* or *of*) to have its existence (in); lie (in); be expressed (by): *his religion consists only in going to church* **3** to be compatible or consistent; accord [C16: from Latin *consistere* to halt, stand firm, from *sistere* to stand, cause to stand; related to *stāre* to STAND]

consistency (kən'sɪstənsɪ) *or* **consistence** *n*, *pl* -encies *or* -ences **1** agreement or accordance with facts, form, or characteristics previously shown or stated **2** degree of viscosity or firmness **3** the state or quality of holding or sticking together and retaining shape **4** conformity with previous attitudes, behaviour, practice, etc

consistent (kən'sɪstənt) *adj* **1** showing consistency; not self-contradictory **2** (*postpositive; foll by with*) in agreement or harmony; accordant **3** steady; even: *consistent growth* **4** *logic* (of a set of statements) capable of all being true at the same time or under the same interpretation > con'sistently *adv*

consistory (kən'sɪstərɪ) *n*, *pl* -ries **1** *Church of England* the court of a diocese (other than Canterbury) administering ecclesiastical law **2** *RC Church* an assembly of the cardinals and the pope **3** (in certain Reformed Churches) the governing body of a local congregation or church **4** *archaic* a council or assembly [C14: from Old French *consistorie*, from Medieval Latin *consistōrium* ecclesiastical tribunal, ultimately from Latin *consistere* to stand still] > consistorial (ˌkɒnsɪ'stɔːrɪəl) *or* ˌconsis'torian *adj*

consolation (ˌkɒnsə'leɪʃən) *n* **1** the act of consoling or state of being consoled; solace **2** a person or thing that is a source of comfort in a time of suffering, grief, disappointment, etc > consolatory (kən'sɒlətərɪ, -trɪ) *adj*

consolation prize *n* a prize given to console a loser of a game

console¹ (kən'səʊl) *vb* to serve as a source of comfort to (someone) in disappointment, loss, etc [C17: from Latin *consōlārī*, from *sōlārī* to comfort; see SOLACE] > con'solable *adj* > con'soler *n* > con'solingly *adv*

console² ('kɒnsəʊl) *n* **1** an ornamental bracket, esp one used to support a wall fixture, bust, etc **2** the part of an organ comprising the manuals, pedals, stops, etc **3** a unit on which the controls of an electronic system are mounted **4** a cabinet for a television, gramophone, etc, designed to stand on the floor **5** See **console table** [C18: from French, shortened from Old French *consolateur* one that provides support, hence, supporting bracket, from Latin *consōlātor* a comforter; see CONSOLE¹]

console table ('kɒnsəʊl) *n* a table with one or more curved legs of bracket-like construction, designed to stand against a wall

consolidate (kən'sɒlɪˌdeɪt) *vb* **1** to form or cause to form into a solid mass or whole; unite or be united **2** to make or become stronger or more stable **3** *military* to strengthen or improve one's control over (a situation, force, newly captured area, etc) [C16: from Latin *consolidāre* to make firm, from *solidus* strong, SOLID]

Consolidated Fund *n* *Brit* a fund into which tax revenue is paid in order to meet standing charges, esp interest payments on the national debt

consols ('kɒnsɒlz, kən'sɒlz) *pl n* irredeemable British government securities carrying annual interest rates of

two and a half or four per cent [short for *consolidated stock*]

consommé (kən'sɒmeɪ, ˈkɒnsɒˌmeɪ; *French* kɔ̃sɔme) *n* a clear soup made from meat or chicken stock [C19: from French, from *consommer* to finish, use up, from Latin *consummāre*; so called because all the goodness of the meat goes into the liquid]

consonance ('kɒnsənəns) *or* **consonancy** ('kɒnsəˌnənsɪ) *n*, *pl* -nances *or* -nancies **1** agreement, harmony, or accord **2** *prosody* similarity between consonants, but not between vowels, as between the *s* and *t* sounds in *sweet silent thought* **3** *music* an aesthetically pleasing sensation or perception associated with the interval of the octave, the perfect fourth and fifth, the major and minor third and sixth, and chords based on these intervals

consonant ('kɒnsənənt) *n* **1** a speech sound or letter of the alphabet other than a vowel; a stop, fricative, or continuant ▷ *adj* **2** (*postpositive; foll by with* or *to*) consistent; in agreement **3** harmonious in tone or sound **4** *music* characterized by the presence of a consonance **5** being or relating to a consonant [C14: from Latin *consonāns*, from *consonāre* to sound at the same time, be in harmony, from *sonāre* to sound] > 'consonantly *adv*

consonantal (ˌkɒnsə'næntəl) *adj* relating to, functioning as, or constituting a consonant, such as the semivowel *w* in English *work*

consort *vb* (kən'sɔːt) **1** (*intr; usually foll by with*) to keep company (with undesirable people); associate **2** (*intr*) to agree or harmonize ▷ *n* ('kɒnsɔːt) **3** (esp formerly) a small group of instruments, either of the same type, such as viols, (a **whole consort**) or of different types (a **broken consort**) **4** the husband or wife of a reigning monarch **5** a partner or companion, esp a husband or wife **6** a ship that escorts another [C15: from Old French, from Latin *consors* sharer, partner, from *sors* lot, fate, portion]

consortium (kən'sɔːtɪəm) *n*, *pl* -tia (-tɪə) **1** an association of financiers, companies, etc, esp one formed for a particular purpose **2** *law* the right of husband or wife to the company, assistance, and affection of the other [C19: from Latin: community of goods, partnership; see CONSORT]

conspectus (kən'spɛktəs) *n* **1** an overall view; survey **2** a summary; résumé [C19: from Latin: a viewing, from *conspicere* to observe, from *specere* to look]

conspicuous (kən'spɪkjʊəs) *adj* **1** clearly visible; obvious or showy **2** attracting attention because of a striking quality or feature: *conspicuous stupidity* [C16: from Latin *conspicuus*, from *conspicere* to perceive; see CONSPECTUS] > con'spicuously *adv* > con'spicuousness *n*

conspiracy (kən'spɪrəsɪ) *n*, *pl* -cies **1** a secret plan or agreement to carry out an illegal or harmful act, esp with political motivation; plot **2** the act of making such plans in secret > con'spirator *n* > conspiratorial (kənˌspɪrə'tɔːrɪəl) *or* con'spiratory *adj*

conspiracy theory *n* the belief that the government or a covert organization is responsible for an event that is unusual or unexplained, esp when any such involvement is denied

conspire (kən'spaɪə) *vb* (when *intr*, sometimes foll by *against*) **1** to plan or agree on (a crime or harmful act) together in secret **2** (*intr*) to act together towards some end as if by design: *the elements conspired to spoil our picnic* [C14: from Old French *conspirer*, from Latin *conspīrāre* to plot together, literally: to breathe together, from *spīrāre* to breathe]

con spirito (kɒn 'spɪrɪtəʊ) *adj*, *adv* *music* (to be performed) in a spirited or lively manner (also in the phrases **allegro con spirito, presto con spirito**) [Italian: with spirit]

constable ('kʌnstəbəl, ˌkɒn-) *n* **1** (in Britain, Australia, Canada, New Zealand, etc) a police officer of the lowest rank **2** any of various officers of the peace, esp one who arrests offenders, serves writs, etc **3** the keeper or governor of a royal castle or fortress **4** (in medieval Europe) the chief military officer and functionary of a royal household, esp in France and England **5** an officer of a hundred in medieval England, originally responsible for raising the military levy but later assigned other administrative duties [C13: from Old French, from Late Latin *comes stabulī* officer in charge of the stable, from Latin *comes* comrade + *stabulum* dwelling, stable; see also COUNT²] ▷ 'constable,ship *n*

Constable ('kʌnstəb³l) *n* **John.** 1776–1837, English landscape painter, noted particularly for his skill in rendering atmospheric effects of changing light

constabulary (kən'stæbjʊlərɪ) *chiefly Brit* ▷ *n*, *pl* -laries **1** the police force of a town or district ▷ *adj* **2** of or relating to constables, constabularies, or their duties

Constance ('kɒnstəns) *n* **1** a city in S Germany, in Baden-Württemberg on Lake Constance: tourist centre. Pop: 80 716 (2003 est). German name: Konstanz **2** Lake Constance a lake in W Europe, bounded by S Germany, W Austria, and N Switzerland, through which the Rhine flows. Area: 536 sq km. (207 sq miles). German name: Bodensee

constant ('kɒnstənt) *adj* **1** fixed and invariable; unchanging **2** continual or continuous; incessant: *constant interruptions* **3** resolute in mind, purpose, or affection; loyal ▷ *n* **4** something that is permanent or unchanging **5** a specific quantity that is always invariable: *the velocity of light is a constant* **6** a *maths* a symbol representing an unspecified number that remains invariable throughout a particular series of operations **b** *physics* a theoretical or experimental quantity or property that is considered invariable throughout a particular series of calculations or experiments [C14: from Old French, from Latin *constāns* standing firm, from *constāre* to be steadfast, from *stāre* to stand] ▷ 'constancy *n* ▷ 'constantly *adv*

Constant (*French* kõstã) *n* **Benjamin** (bɛ̃ʒamɛ̃). real name *Henri Benjamin Constant de Rebecque.* 1767–1830, French writer and politician: author of the psychological novel *Adolphe* (1816)

Constanţa (*Romanian* kon'stantsa) *n* a port and resort in SE Romania, on the Black Sea: founded by the Greeks in the 6th century BC and rebuilt by Constantine the Great (4th century); exports petroleum. Pop: 265 000 (2005 est)

Constantia (kən'stænʃə) *n* **1** a region of the Cape Peninsula **2** any of several red or white wines produced around Constantia

Constantine ('kɒnstən,taɪn; *French* kõstãtin) *n* a walled city in NE Algeria: built on an isolated rock; military and trading centre. Pop: 482 000 (2005 est)

Constantine I ('kɒnstən,taɪn, -,tiːn) *n* **1** known as *Constantine the Great.* Latin name *Flavius Valerius Aurelius Constantinus.* ?280–337 AD, first Christian Roman emperor (306–337): moved his capital to Byzantium, which he renamed Constantinople (330) **2** 1868–1923, king of Greece (1913–17; 1920–22): deposed (1917), recalled by a plebiscite (1920), but forced to abdicate again (1922) after defeat by the Turks

Constantine II *n* official title *Constantine XIII.* born 1940, king of Greece (1964–73): went into exile when the army seized power in 1967. He was officially deposed in 1973 and Greece became a republic

Constantine VII *n* known as *Porphyrogenitus.* 905–59 AD, Byzantine emperor (913–59) and scholar: his writings are an important source for Byzantine history

Constantine XI *n* 1404–53, last Byzantine emperor (1448–53): killed when Constantinople was captured by the Turks

Constantinople (,kɒnstæntɪ'nəʊp³l) *n* the former name (330–1926) of Istanbul

constellate ('kɒnstɪ,leɪt) *vb* to form into clusters in or as if in constellations

constellation (,kɒnstɪ'leɪʃən) *n* **1 a** any of the 88 groups of stars as seen from the earth and the solar system, many of which were named by the ancient Greeks after animals, objects, or mythological persons **b** an area on the celestial sphere containing such a group **2 a** gathering of brilliant or famous people or things **3** *psychoanal* a group of ideas felt to be related [C14: from Late Latin *constellātiō*, from Latin *com-* together + *stella* star] ▷ constellatory (kən'stɛlətərɪ, -trɪ) *adj*

consternate ('kɒnstə,neɪt) *vb* (*tr; usually passive*) to fill with anxiety, dismay, dread, or confusion [C17: from Latin *consternāre*, from *sternere* to lay low, spread out]

consternation (,kɒnstə'neɪʃən) *n* a feeling of anxiety, dismay, dread, or confusion

constipate ('kɒnstɪ,peɪt) *vb* (*tr*) to cause constipation in [C16: from Latin *constīpāre* to press closely together, from *stīpāre* to crowd together]

constipated ('kɒnstɪ,peɪtɪd) *adj* **1** suffering from constipation **2** subject to restriction or blockage in a flow of productive activity or creativity

constipation (,kɒnstɪ'peɪʃən) *n* infrequent or difficult evacuation of the bowels, with hard faeces, caused by functional or organic disorders or improper diet

constituency (kən'stɪtjʊənsɪ) *n*, *pl* -cies **1** the whole body of voters who elect one representative to a legislature or all the residents represented by one deputy **2** a district that sends one representative to a legislature

constituent (kən'stɪtjʊənt) *adj* (*prenominal*) **1** forming part of a whole; component **2** having the power to frame a constitution or to constitute a government (esp in the phrases **constituent assembly, constituent power**) ▷ *n* **3** a component part; ingredient **4** a resident of a constituency, esp one entitled to vote **5** *chiefly law* a person who appoints another to act for him, as by power of attorney [C17: from Latin *constituēns* setting up, from *constituere* to establish, CONSTITUTE] ▷ con'stituently *adv*

constitute ('kɒnstɪ,tjuːt) *vb* (*tr*) **1** to make up; form; compose: *the people who constitute a jury* **2** to appoint to an office or function: *a legally constituted officer* **3** to set up (a school or other institution) formally; found **4** *law* to give legal form to (a court, assembly, etc) [C15: from Latin *constituere*, from *com-* (intensive) + *statuere* to place] ▷ 'consti,tuter or 'consti,tutor *n*

constitution (,kɒnstɪ'tjuːʃən) *n* **1** the act of constituting or state of being constituted **2** the fundamental political principles on which a state is governed, esp when considered as embodying the rights of the subjects of that state **3** (*often capital*) (in certain countries, esp Australia and the US) a statute embodying such principles **4** a person's state of health **5** a person's disposition of mind; temperament

constitutional (,kɒnstɪ'tjuːʃən³l) *adj* **1** denoting, characteristic of, or relating to a constitution **2** authorized by or subject to a constitution **3** of or inherent in the physical make-up or basic nature of a person or thing: *a constitutional weakness* **4** beneficial to one's general physical wellbeing ▷ *n* **5** a regular walk taken for the benefit of one's health ▷ ,consti'tutionally *adv*

constitutionalism (,kɒnstɪ'tjuːʃənə,lɪzəm) *n* **1** the principles, spirit, or system of government in accord with a constitution, esp a written constitution **2** adherence to or advocacy of such a system or such principles ▷ ,consti'tutionalist *n*

constitutive ('kɒnstɪ,tjuːtɪv) *adj* **1** having power to enact, appoint, or establish **2** another word for **constituent** (sense 1) ▷ 'consti,tutively *adv*

constrain (kən'streɪn) *vb* (*tr*) **1** to compel or force, esp by persuasion, circumstances, etc; oblige **2** to restrain by or as if by force; confine [C14: from Old French *constreindre*, from Latin *constringere* to bind together, from *stringere* to bind] ▷ con'strainer *n*

constrained (kən'streɪnd) *adj* embarrassed, unnatural, or forced: *a constrained smile*

constraint (kən'streɪnt) *n* **1** compulsion, force, or restraint **2** repression or control of natural feelings or impulses **3** a forced unnatural manner; inhibition **4** something that serves to constrain; restrictive condition: *social constraints kept him silent* **5** *linguistics* any very general restriction on a sentence formation rule

constrict (kən'strɪkt) *vb* (*tr*) **1** to make smaller or narrower, esp by contracting at one place **2** to hold in or inhibit; limit [C18: from Latin *constrictus* compressed, from *constringere* to tie up together; see CONSTRAIN]

constriction (kən'strɪkʃən) *n* **1** a feeling of tightness in some part of the body, such as the chest **2** the act of constricting or condition of being constricted **3** something that is constricted **4** *genetics* a localized narrow region of a chromosome, esp at the centromere ▷ con'strictive *adj*

constrictor (kən'strɪktə) n 1 any of various nonvenomous snakes, such as the pythons, boas, and anaconda, that coil around and squeeze their prey to kill it 2 any muscle that constricts or narrows a canal or passage; sphincter 3 a person or thing that constricts

construct vb (kən'strʌkt) (tr) 1 to put together substances or parts, esp systematically, in order to make or build (a building, bridge, etc); assemble 2 to compose or frame mentally (an argument, sentence, etc) 3 geometry to draw (a line, angle, or figure) so that certain requirements are satisfied ▷ n ('kɒnstrʌkt) 4 something formulated or built systematically 5 a complex idea resulting from a synthesis of simpler ideas 6 psychol a model devised on the basis of observation, designed to relate what is observed to some theoretical framework [c17: from Latin constructus piled up, from construere to heap together, build, from struere to arrange, erect] > con'structible adj > con'structor or con'structer n

construction (kən'strʌkʃən) n 1 the process or act of constructing or manner in which a thing is constructed 2 the thing constructed; a structure 3 a the business or work of building dwellings, offices, etc b (as modifier): a construction site 4 an interpretation or explanation of a law, text, action, etc: they put a sympathetic construction on her behaviour 5 grammar a group of words that together make up one of the constituents into which a sentence may be analysed; a phrase or clause 6 an abstract work of art in three dimensions or relief > con'structional adj > con'structionally adv

constructive (kən'strʌktɪv) adj 1 serving to build or improve; positive: constructive criticism 2 law deduced by inference or construction; not expressed but inferred 3 another word for **structural** > con'structively adv

constructivism (kən'strʌktɪ,vɪzəm) n a movement in abstract art evolved in Russia after World War I, primarily by Naum Gabo, the Russian-born US sculptor (1890–1977), which explored the use of movement and machine-age materials in sculpture and had considerable influence on modern art and architecture > con'structivist adj, n

construe (kən'stru:) vb -strues, -struing, -strued (mainly tr) 1 to interpret the meaning of (something): you can construe that in different ways 2 (may take a clause as object) to discover by inference; deduce 3 to analyse the grammatical structure of; parse (esp a Latin or Greek text as a preliminary to translation) 4 to combine (words) syntactically 5 (also intr) old-fashioned to translate literally, esp aloud as an academic exercise [c14: from Latin construere to pile up; see CONSTRUCT] > con'struable adj

consubstantial (,kɒnsəb'stænʃəl) adj Christian theol (esp of the three persons of the Trinity) regarded as identical in substance or essence though different in aspect [c15: from Church Latin consubstantiālis, from Latin COM- + substantia SUBSTANCE] > ,consub,stanti'ality n > ,consub'stantially adv

consubstantiation (,kɒnsəb,stænʃɪ'eɪʃən) n Christian theol (in the belief of High-Church Anglicans) the doctrine that after the consecration of the Eucharist the substance of the body and blood of Christ coexists within the substance of the consecrated bread and wine. See **transubstantiation**

consuetude ('kɒnswɪ,tjuːd) n an established custom or usage, esp one having legal force [c14: from Latin consuētūdō, from consuēscere to accustom, from CON- + suēscere to be wont]

consul ('kɒnsəl) n 1 an official appointed by a sovereign state to protect its commercial interests and aid its citizens in a foreign city 2 (in ancient Rome) either of two annually elected magistrates who jointly exercised the highest authority in the republic 3 (in France from 1799 to 1804) any of the three chief magistrates of the First Republic [c14: from Latin, from consulere to CONSULT] > consular ('kɒnsjʊlə) adj > 'consul,ship n

consulate ('kɒnsjʊlɪt) n 1 the business premises or residence of a consul 2 government by consuls 3 the office or period of office of a consul or consuls 4 (often capital) a the government of France by the three consuls from 1799 to 1804 b this period of French history 5 (often

capital) the consular government of the Roman republic

consul general n, pl consuls general a consul of the highest grade, usually stationed in a city of considerable commercial importance

consult (kən'sʌlt) vb 1 (when intr, often foll by with) to ask advice from (someone); confer with (someone) 2 (tr) to refer to for information: to consult a map 3 (tr) to have regard for (a person's feelings, interests, etc) in making decisions or plans; consider 4 (intr) to make oneself available to give professional advice, esp at scheduled times and for a fee [c17: from French consulter, from Latin consultāre to reflect, take counsel, from consulere to consult]

consultant (kən'sʌltᵊnt) n 1 a a senior physician, esp a specialist, who is asked to confirm a diagnosis or treatment or to provide an opinion b a physician or surgeon holding the highest appointment in a particular branch of medicine or surgery in a hospital 2 a specialist who gives expert advice or information 3 a person who asks advice in a consultation > con'sultancy n

consultant nurse n (in Britain) another name for **supernurse**

consultation (,kɒnsəl'teɪʃən) n 1 the act or procedure of consulting 2 a conference for discussion or the seeking of advice, esp from doctors or lawyers

consulting (kən'sʌltɪŋ) adj (prenominal) acting in an advisory capacity on professional matters: a consulting engineer

consulting room n a room in which a doctor, esp a general practitioner, sees his patients

consume (kən'sjuːm) vb 1 (tr) to eat or drink 2 (tr; often passive) to engross or obsess 3 (tr) to use up; expend 4 to destroy or be destroyed by burning, decomposition, etc: fire consumed the forest 5 (tr) to waste or squander 6 (passive) to waste away [c14: from Latin consūmere to devour, from com- (intensive) + sūmere to take up, from emere to take, purchase] > con'suming adj

consumedly (kən'sjuːmɪdlɪ) adv old-fashioned (intensifier): a consumedly fascinating performance

consumer (kən'sjuːmə) n 1 a person who acquires goods and services for his or her own personal needs. See **producer** (sense 6) 2 a person or thing that consumes

consumer durable n a manufactured product that has a relatively long useful life, such as a car or a television

consumer goods pl n goods that satisfy personal needs rather than those required for the production of other goods or services

consumerism (kən'sjuːmə,rɪzəm) n 1 protection of the interests of consumers 2 advocacy of a high rate of consumption and spending as a basis for a sound economy > con'sumerist n, adj

consumer terrorism n the practice of introducing dangerous substances to foodstuffs or other consumer products, esp to extort money from the manufacturers

consummate vb ('kɒnsə,meɪt) (tr) 1 to bring to completion or perfection; fulfil 2 to complete (a marriage) legally by sexual intercourse ▷ adj (kən'sʌmɪt, 'kɒnsəmɪt) 3 accomplished or supremely skilled: a consummate artist 4 (prenominal) (intensifier): a consummate fool [c15: from Latin consummāre to complete, from summus highest, utmost] > con'summately adv > ,consum'mation n

consumption (kən'sʌmpʃən) n 1 the act of consuming or the state of being consumed, esp by eating, burning, etc 2 economics expenditure on goods and services for final personal use 3 the quantity consumed 4 pathol a condition characterized by a wasting away of the tissues of the body, esp as seen in tuberculosis of the lungs [c14: from Latin consumptiō a wasting, from consūmere to CONSUME]

consumptive (kən'sʌmptɪv) adj 1 causing consumption; wasteful; destructive 2 pathol relating to or affected with consumption, esp tuberculosis of the lungs ▷ n 3 pathol a person who suffers from consumption > con'sumptively adv > con'sumptiveness n

contact n ('kɒntækt) 1 the act or state of touching physically 2 the state or fact of close association or communication (esp in the phrases **in contact, make**

contact) **3 a** a junction of two or more electrical conductors **b** the part of the conductors that makes the junction **c** the part of an electrical device to which such connections are made **4** an acquaintance, esp one who might be useful in business, as a means of introduction, etc **5** any person who has been exposed to a contagious disease **6** *photog* See **contact print** **7** (*usually plural*) an informal name for **contact lens** **8** (*modifier*) of or relating to irritation or inflammation of the skin caused by touching the causative agent: *contact dermatitis* **9** (*modifier*) denoting an insecticide or herbicide that kills on contact, rather than after ingestion or absorption **10** (*modifier*) of or maintaining contact **11** (*modifier*) requiring or involving (physical) contact: *the contact sport of boxing* ▷ *vb* ('kɒntækt, kən'tækt) **12** (when *intr*, often foll by *with*) to put, come, or be in association, touch, or communication [c17: from Latin *contactus*, from *contingere* to touch on all sides, pollute, from *tangere* to touch] > contactual (kɒn'tæktjʊəl) *adj*

contact centre *n* another name for **call centre**

contact lens *n* a thin convex lens, usually of plastic, which floats on the layer of tears in front of the cornea to correct defects of vision

contactless ('kɒntæktlɪs) *adj* **1** without contacts **2** referring to payment systems which use RFID technology and do not require the customer's signature or pin number

contact print *n* a photographic print made by exposing the printing paper through a negative placed directly onto it

contagion (kən'teɪdʒən) *n* **1** the transmission of disease from one person to another by direct or indirect contact **2** a contagious disease **3** a corrupting or harmful influence that tends to spread; pollutant **4** the spreading of an emotional or mental state among a number of people: *the contagion of mirth* [c14: from Latin *contāgiō* a touching, infection, from *contingere*; see CONTACT]

contagious (kən'teɪdʒəs) *adj* **1** (of a disease) capable of being passed on by direct contact with a diseased individual or by handling clothing, etc, contaminated with the causative agent **2** (of an organism) harbouring or spreading the causative agent of a transmissible disease **3** causing or likely to cause the same reaction or emotion in several people; catching; infectious: *her laughter was contagious*

contain (kən'teɪn) *vb* (*tr*) **1** to hold or be capable of holding or including within a fixed limit or area: *this contains five pints* **2** to keep (one's feelings, behaviour, etc) within bounds; restrain **3** to consist of; comprise: *the book contains three different sections* **4** *military* to prevent (enemy forces) from operating beyond a certain level or area **5** *maths* **a** to be a multiple of, leaving no remainder: *6 contains 2 and 3* **b** to have as a subset [c13: from Old French *contenir*, from Latin *continēre*, from *com-* together + *tenēre* to hold] > con'tainable *adj*

container (kən'teɪnə) *n* **1** an object used for or capable of holding, esp for transport or storage, such as a carton, box, etc **2 a** a large cargo-carrying standard-sized container that can be loaded from one mode of transport to another **b** (*as modifier*): *a container port; a container ship*

container garden *n* a collection of pots or other receptacles containing soil for growing plants out of doors > container gardening *n*

containerize or **containerise** (kən'teɪnə,raɪz) *vb* (*tr*) **1** to convey (cargo) in standard-sized containers **2** to adapt (a port or transportation system) to the use of standard-sized containers > con,taineri'zation or con,taineri'sation *n*

containment (kən'teɪnmənt) *n* the act or condition of containing, esp of restraining the ideological or political power of a hostile country or the operations of a hostile military force

contaminate *vb* (kən'tæmɪ,neɪt) (*tr*) **1** to make impure, esp by touching or mixing; pollute **2** to make radioactive by the addition of radioactive material ▷ *adj* (kən'tæmɪnɪt, -,neɪt) **3** *archaic* contaminated [c15: from Latin *contamināre* to defile; related to Latin *contingere* to touch] > con'taminable *adj* > con'taminant *n*

> con'taminative *adj* > con'tami,nator *n*

contango (kən'tæŋɡəʊ) *n*, *pl* -gos **1** (formerly, on the London Stock Exchange) postponement of payment for and delivery of stock from one account day to the next **2** Also called: carry-over, continuation the fee paid for such a postponement ▷ Compare **backwardation** [c19: apparently an arbitrary coinage based on CONTINUE]

conte French (kɔt) *n* a tale or short story, esp of adventure

contemn (kən'tɛm) *vb* (*tr*) *formal* to treat or regard with contempt; scorn [c15: from Latin *contemnere*, from *temnere* to slight] > contemner (kən'tɛmnə, -'tɛmə) *n*

contemplate ('kɒntɛm,pleɪt, -təm-) *vb* (*mainly tr*) **1** to think about intently and at length; consider calmly **2** (*intr*) to think intently and at length, esp for spiritual reasons; meditate **3** to look at thoughtfully; observe pensively **4** to have in mind as a possibility [c16: from Latin *contemplāre*, from *templum* TEMPLE[1]] > 'contem,plator *n* > contemplation (,kɒntɛm'pleɪʃən, -təm-) *n*

contemplative ('kɒntɛm,pleɪtɪv, -təm-, kən'tɛmplə-) *adj* **1** denoting, concerned with, or inclined to contemplation; meditative ▷ *n* **2** a person dedicated to religious contemplation or to a way of life conducive to this

contemporaneous (kən,tɛmpə'reɪnɪəs) *adj* existing, beginning, or occurring in the same period of time > contemporaneity (kən,tɛmpərə'niːɪtɪ) or con,tempo'raneousness *n*

contemporary (kən'tɛmprərɪ) *adj* **1** belonging to the same age; living or occurring in the same period of time **2** existing or occurring at the present time **3** conforming to modern or current ideas in style, fashion, design, etc **4** having approximately the same age as one another ▷ *n*, *pl* -raries **5** a person living at the same time or of approximately the same age as another **6** something that is contemporary **7** *journalism* a rival newspaper [c17: from Medieval Latin *contemporārius*, from Latin *com-* together + *temporārius* relating to time, from *tempus* time] > con'temporarily *adv* > con'temporariness *n*

● USAGE Since *contemporary* can mean either of the same
● period or of the present period, it is best to avoid this
● word where ambiguity might arise, as in *a production of*
● *Othello in contemporary dress. Modern dress* or *Elizabethan*
● *dress* should be used in this example to avoid
● ambiguity

contemporize or **contemporise** (kən'tɛmpə,raɪz) *vb* to be or make contemporary; synchronize

contempt (kən'tɛmpt) *n* **1** the attitude or feeling of a person towards a person or thing that he considers worthless or despicable; scorn **2** the state of being scorned; disgrace (esp in the phrase **hold in contempt**) **3** wilful disregard of or disrespect for the authority of a court of law or legislative body: *contempt of court* [c14: from Latin *contemptus* a despising, from *contemnere* to CONTEMN]

contemptible (kən'tɛmptəbᵊl) *adj* deserving or worthy of contempt; despicable > con,tempti'bility or con'temptibleness *n* > con'temptibly *adv*

contemptuous (kən'tɛmptjʊəs) *adj* (when *predicative*, often foll by *of*) showing or feeling contempt; disdainful > con'temptuously *adv*

contend (kən'tɛnd) *vb* **1** (*intr*; often foll by *with*) to struggle in rivalry, battle, etc; vie **2** to argue earnestly; debate **3** (*tr*; *may take a clause as object*) to assert or maintain [c15: from Latin *contendere* to strive, from *com-* with + *tendere* to stretch, aim] > con'tender *n*

content[1] ('kɒntɛnt) *n* **1** (*often plural*) everything that is inside a container: *the contents of a box* **2** (*usually plural*) **a** the chapters or divisions of a book **b** a list, printed at the front of a book, of chapters or divisions together with the number of the first page of each **3** the meaning or significance of a poem, painting, or other work of art, as distinguished from its style or form **4** all that is contained or dealt with in a discussion, piece of writing, etc; substance **5** the capacity or size of a thing **6** the proportion of a substance contained in an alloy, mixture, etc: *the lead content of petrol* [c15: from Latin *contentus* contained, from *continēre* to CONTAIN]

content[2] (kən'tɛnt) *adj* (*postpositive*) **1** mentally or emotionally satisfied with things as they are

2 assenting to or willing to accept circumstances, a proposed course of action, etc ▷ *vb* **3** (*tr*) to make (oneself or another person) content or satisfied: *to content oneself with property* ▷ *n* **4** peace of mind; mental or emotional satisfaction [C14: from Old French, from Latin *contentus* contented, that is, having restrained desires, from *continēre* to restrain] > con'tentment *n*

contented (kən'tɛntɪd) *adj* accepting one's situation or life with equanimity and satisfaction

contention (kən'tɛnʃən) *n* **1** a struggling between opponents; competition **2** dispute in an argument (esp in the phrase **bone of contention**) **3** a point asserted in argument [C14: from Latin *contentiō* exertion, from *contendere* to CONTEND]

contentious (kən'tɛnʃəs) *adj* **1** tending to argue or quarrel **2** causing or characterized by dispute; controversial > con'tentiousness *n*

conterminous (kən'tɜːmɪnəs), **conterminal** (kən'tɜːmɪn³l) *or* **coterminous** (kəʊ'tɜːmɪnəs) *adj* **1** enclosed within a common boundary **2** meeting at the ends; without a break or interruption [C17: from Latin *conterminus*, from CON- + *terminus* end, boundary]

contest *n* ('kɒntɛst) **1** a formal game or match in which two or more people, teams, etc, compete and attempt to win **2** a struggle for victory between opposing forces or interests ▷ *vb* (kən'tɛst) **3** (*tr*) to try to disprove; call in question **4** (when *intr*, foll by *with* or *against*) to fight, dispute, or contend (with): *contest an election* [C16: from Latin *contestārī* to introduce a lawsuit, from *testis* witness] > con'testable *adj* > con'tester *n*

contestant (kən'tɛstənt) *n* a person who takes part in a contest; competitor

context ('kɒntɛkst) *n* **1** the parts of a piece of writing, speech, etc, that precede and follow a word or passage and contribute to its full meaning: *it is unfair to quote out of context* **2** the conditions and circumstances that are relevant to an event, fact, etc [C15: from Latin *contextus* a putting together, from *contexere* to interweave, from *com-* together + *texere* to weave, braid]

contiguous (kən'tɪɡjʊəs) *adj* **1** touching along the side or boundary; in contact **2** physically adjacent; neighbouring **3** preceding or following in time [C17: from Latin *contiguus*, from *contingere* to touch; see CONTACT] > con'tiguously *adv*

continent¹ ('kɒntɪnənt) *n* **1** one of the earth's large land masses (Asia, Australia, Africa, Europe, North and South America, and Antarctica) **2** that part of the earth's crust that rises above the oceans and is composed of sialic rocks. Including the continental shelves, the continents occupy 30 per cent of the earth's surface **3** *obsolete* **a** mainland as opposed to islands **b** a continuous extent of land [C16: from the Latin phrase *terra continens* continuous land, from *continēre*; see CONTAIN] > continental (ˌkɒntɪ'nɛnt³l) *adj* > ˌconti'nentally *adv*

continent² ('kɒntɪnənt) *adj* **1** able to control urination and defecation **2** exercising self-restraint, esp from sexual activity; chaste [C14: from Latin *continent-*, present participle of *continēre*; see CONTAIN] > 'continence *or* 'continency *n*

Continent ('kɒntɪnənt) *n* the Continent the mainland of Europe as distinguished from the British Isles

Continental (ˌkɒntɪ'nɛnt³l) *adj* **1** of or characteristic of Europe, excluding the British Isles **2** of or relating to the 13 original British North American colonies during and immediately after the War of American Independence ▷ *n* **3** (*sometimes not capital*) an inhabitant of Europe, excluding the British Isles **4** a regular soldier of the rebel army during the War of American Independence

continental breakfast *n* a light breakfast of coffee and rolls

continental climate *n* a climate characterized by hot summers, cold winters, and little rainfall, typical of the interior of a continent

continental drift *n geology* the theory that the earth's continents move gradually over the surface of the planet on a substratum of magma. The present-day configuration of the continents is thought to be the result of the fragmentation of a single landmass, Pangaea, that existed 200 million years ago

continental quilt *n Brit* a quilt, stuffed with down or a synthetic material and containing pockets of air, used as a bed cover in place of the top sheet and blankets. Also called: duvet, (*Austral*) doona

continental shelf *n* the sea bed surrounding a continent at depths of up to about 200 metres (100 fathoms), at the edge of which the **continental slope** drops steeply to the ocean floor

contingency (kən'tɪndʒənsɪ) *n, pl* -cies **1 a** a possible but not very likely future event or condition; eventuality **b** (*as modifier*): *a contingency plan* **2** something dependent on a possible future event **3** a fact, event, etc, incidental to or dependent on something else **4 a** modification of the measuring of a main clause by use of a bound clause introduced by a binder such as *if, when, though,* or *since.* (in systemic grammar) **b** (*as modifier*): *a contingency clause* **5** *logic* **a** the state of being contingent **b** a contingent statement **6** dependence on chance; uncertainty **7** *statistics* **a** the degree of association between theoretical and observed common frequencies of two graded or classified variables. It is measured by the chi-square test **b** (*as modifier*): *a contingency table; the contingency coefficient*

contingent (kən'tɪndʒənt) *adj* **1** (when *postpositive*, often foll by *on* or *upon*) dependent on events, conditions, etc, not yet known; conditional **2** *logic* (of a proposition) true under certain conditions, false under others; not necessary **3** (in systemic grammar) denoting contingency (sense 4) **4** *metaphysics* (of some being) existing only as a matter of fact; not necessarily existing **5** happening by chance or without known cause; accidental **6** that may or may not happen; uncertain ▷ *n* **7** a part of a military force, parade, etc **8** a representative group distinguished by common origin, interests, etc, that is part of a larger group or gathering **9** a possible or chance occurrence [C14: from Latin *contingere* to touch, fall to one's lot, befall; see also CONTACT] > con'tingently *adv*

continual (kən'tɪnjʊəl) *adj* **1** recurring frequently, esp at regular intervals **2** occurring without interruption; continuous in time [C14: from Old French *continuel*, from Latin *continuus* uninterrupted, from *continēre* to hold together, CONTAIN] > con'tinually *adv*

continuance (kən'tɪnjʊəns) *n* **1** the act or state of continuing **2** the duration of an action, condition, etc **3** *US* the postponement or adjournment of a legal proceeding

continuant (kən'tɪnjʊənt) *phonetics n* **1** a speech sound, such as (l), (r), (f), or (s), in which the closure of the vocal tract is incomplete, allowing the continuous passage of the breath ▷ *adj* **2** relating to or denoting a continuant

continuation (kənˌtɪnjʊ'eɪʃən) *n* **1** a part or thing added, esp to a book or play, that serves to continue or extend; sequel **2** a renewal of an interrupted action, process, etc; resumption **3** the act or fact of continuing without interruption; prolongation **4** another word for **contango** (senses 1, 2)

continue (kən'tɪnjuː) *vb* -ues, -uing, -ued **1** (when *tr*, may take an *infinitive*) to remain or cause to remain in a particular condition, capacity, or place **2** (when *tr*, may take an *infinitive*) to carry on uninterruptedly (a course of action); persist in (something): *he continued running* **3** (when *tr*, may take an *infinitive*) to resume after an interruption: *we'll continue after lunch* **4** to draw out or be drawn out; prolong or be prolonged: *continue the chord until it meets the tangent* **5** (*tr*) *law* chiefly Scots to postpone or adjourn (legal proceedings) [C14: from Old French *continuer*, from Latin *continuāre* to join together, from *continuus* CONTINUOUS]

continuity (ˌkɒntɪ'njuːɪtɪ) *n, pl* -ties **1** logical sequence, cohesion, or connection **2** a continuous or connected whole **3** the comprehensive script or scenario of detail and movement in a film or broadcast **4** the continuous projection of a film, using automatic rewind

continuity girl *or* **continuity man** *n* a girl or man whose job is to ensure continuity and consistency, esp in matters of dress, make-up, etc, in successive shots of a film, esp when these shots are filmed on different

C

days or at different times

continuo (kənˈtɪnjʊˌəʊ) n, pl **-os** 1 music **a** a shortened form of basso continuo. See **thorough bass b** (as modifier): a continuo accompaniment **2** the thorough-bass part as played on a keyboard instrument, often supported by a cello, bassoon, etc [Italian, literally: continuous]

continuous (kənˈtɪnjʊəs) adj **1** prolonged without interruption; unceasing: a continuous noise **2** in an unbroken series or pattern **3** maths (of a function or curve) changing gradually in value as the variable changes in value. A function f is continuous if at every value a of the independent variable the difference between f(x) and f(a) approaches zero as x approaches a. See also **limit** (sense 5) **4** statistics (of a variable) having a continuum of possible values so that its distribution requires integration rather than summation to determine its cumulative probability **5** grammar another word for **progressive** (sense 7) [c17: from Latin continuus, from continēre to hold together, CONTAIN] > con'tinuously adv

continuous assessment n the assessment of a pupil's progress throughout a course of study rather than exclusively by examination at the end of it

continuous creation n **1** the theory that matter is being created continuously in the universe. See **steady-state theory 2** the theory that animate matter is being continuously created from inanimate matter

continuum (kənˈtɪnjʊəm) n, pl **-tinua** (-ˈtɪnjʊə) or **-tinuums** a continuous series or whole, no part of which is perceptibly different from the adjacent parts [c17: from Latin, neuter of continuus CONTINUOUS]

contort (kənˈtɔːt) vb to twist or bend severely out of place or shape, esp in a strained manner [c15: from Latin contortus intricate, obscure, from contorquēre to whirl around, from torquēre to twist, wrench] > con'tortive adj

contortionist (kənˈtɔːʃənɪst) n **1** a performer who contorts his body for the entertainment of others **2** a person who twists or warps meaning or thoughts

contour (ˈkɒntʊə) n **1** the outline of a mass of land, figure, or body; a defining line **2 a** See **contour line b** (as modifier): a contour map **3** (often plural) the shape or surface, esp of a curving form: the contours of her body were full and round ▷ vb (tr) **4** to shape so as to form the contour of something **5** to mark contour lines on **6** to construct (a road, railway, etc) to follow the outline of the land [c17: from French, from Italian contorno, from contornare to sketch, from tornare to TURN]

contour line n a line on a map or chart joining points of equal height or depth. Often shortened to: **contour**

contour ploughing n ploughing following the contours of the land, to minimize the effects of erosion

contra- prefix **1** against; contrary; opposing; contrasting: contraceptive; contradistinction **2** (in music) pitched below: contrabass [from Latin, from contrā against]

contraband (ˈkɒntrəˌbænd) n **1 a** goods that are prohibited by law from being exported or imported **b** illegally imported or exported goods **2** illegal traffic in such goods; smuggling **3** Also called: contraband of war international law in the event that a neutral country may not supply to a belligerent **4** (during the American Civil War) a Black slave captured by the Union forces or one who escaped to the Union lines ▷ adj **5** (of goods) **a** forbidden by law from being imported or exported **b** illegally imported or exported [c16: from Spanish contrabanda, from Italian contrabando (modern contrabbando), from Medieval Latin contrabannum, from CONTRA- + bannum ban, of Germanic origin] > 'contra,bandist n

contrabass (ˌkɒntrəˈbeɪs) n **1** a member of any of various families of musical instruments that is lower in pitch than the bass **2** another name for **double bass** ▷ adj **3** of or denoting the instrument of a family that is lower than the bass > contrabassist (ˌkɒntrəˈbeɪsɪst, -ˈbæs-) n

contrabassoon (ˌkɒntrəbəˈsuːn) n the largest instrument in the oboe family, pitched an octave below the bassoon; double bassoon

contraception (ˌkɒntrəˈsɛpʃən) n the intentional prevention of conception by artificial or natural means. Artificial methods in common use include preventing

the sperm from reaching the ovum (using condoms, diaphragms, etc), inhibiting ovulation (using oral contraceptive pills), preventing implantation (using intrauterine devices), killing the sperm (using spermicides), and preventing the sperm from entering the seminal fluid (by vasectomy). Natural methods include the rhythm method and coitus interruptus [c19: from CONTRA- + CONCEPTION] > ,contra'ceptive adj, n

contract vb (kənˈtrækt) **1** to make or become smaller, narrower, shorter, etc: metals contract as the temperature is reduced **2** (ˈkɒntrækt) (when intr, sometimes foll by for; when tr, may take an infinitive) to enter into an agreement with (a person, company, etc) to deliver (goods or services) or to do (something) on mutually agreed and binding terms, often in writing **3** to draw or be drawn together; coalesce or cause to coalesce **4** (tr) to acquire, incur, or become affected by (a disease, liability, debt, etc) **5** (tr) to shorten (a word or phrase) by the omission of letters or syllables, usually indicated in writing by an apostrophe **6** phonetics to unite (two vowels) or (of two vowels) to be united within a word or at a word boundary so that a new long vowel or diphthong is formed **7** (tr) to wrinkle or draw together (the brow or a muscle) **8** (tr) to arrange (a marriage) for; betroth ▷ n (ˈkɒntrækt) **9** a formal agreement between two or more parties **10** a document that states the terms of such an agreement **11** the branch of law treating of contracts **12** marriage considered as a formal agreement **13** See **contract bridge 14** bridge **a** (in the bidding sequence before play) the highest bid, which determines trumps and the number of tricks one side must try to make **b** the number and suit of these tricks **15** slang **a** a criminal agreement to kill a particular person in return for an agreed sum of money **b** (as modifier): a contract killing [c16: from Latin contractus agreement, something drawn up, from contrahere to draw together, from trahere to draw] > con'tractible adj

contract bridge (ˈkɒntrækt) n the most common variety of bridge, in which the declarer receives points counting towards game and rubber only for tricks he bids as well as makes, any overtricks receiving bonus points. See **auction bridge**

contractile (kənˈtræktaɪl) adj having the power to contract or to cause contraction > contractility (ˌkɒntrækˈtɪlɪtɪ) n

contraction (kənˈtrækʃən) n **1** an instance of contracting or the state of being contracted **2** physiol any normal shortening or tensing of an organ or part, esp of a muscle, e.g. during childbirth **3** pathol any abnormal tightening or shrinking of an organ or part **4** a shortening of a word or group of words, often marked in written English by an apostrophe: I've come for I have come > con'tractive adj

contractor (ˈkɒntræktə, kənˈtræk-) n **1** a person or firm that contracts to supply materials or labour, esp for building **2** something that contracts, esp a muscle

contract out vb (intr, adverb) Brit to agree not to participate in something, esp the state pension scheme

contractual (kənˈtræktjʊəl) adj of the nature of or assured by a contract

contradict (ˌkɒntrəˈdɪkt) vb **1** (tr) to affirm the opposite of (a proposition, statement, etc) **2** (tr) to declare (a proposition, statement, etc) to be false or incorrect; deny **3** (intr) to be argumentative or contrary **4** (tr) to be inconsistent with (a proposition, theory, etc): the facts contradicted his theory **5** (intr) (of two or more facts, principles, etc) to be at variance; be in contradiction [c16: from Latin contrādīcere, from CONTRA- + dīcere to speak, say] > ,contra'dictable adj > ,contra'dicter or ,contra'dictor n

contradiction (ˌkɒntrəˈdɪkʃən) n **1** the act of going against; opposition; denial **2** a declaration of the opposite or contrary **3** a statement that is at variance with itself (often in the phrase **a contradiction in terms**) **4** conflict or inconsistency, as between events, qualities, etc **5** a person or thing containing conflicting qualities **6** logic a statement that is false under all circumstances; necessary falsehood

contradictory (ˌkɒntrəˈdɪktərɪ) adj **1** inconsistent;

incompatible **2** given to argument and contention: *a contradictory person* **3** *logic* (of a pair of statements) unable both to be true or both to be false under the same circumstances >,contra'dictorily *adv* >,contra'dictoriness *n*

contradistinction (ˌkɒntrədɪ'stɪŋkʃən) *n* a distinction made by contrasting different qualities >,contradis'tinctive *adj*

contraflow ('kɒntrəˌfləʊ) *n Brit* two-way traffic on one carriageway of a motorway, esp to allow maintenance work to be carried out or an accident to be cleared

contrail ('kɒntreɪl) *n* another name for **vapour trail** [c20: from CON(DENSATION) + TRAIL]

contralto (kən'træltəʊ, -'trɑːl-) *n, pl* **-tos** *or* **-ti** (-tɪ) **1** the lowest female voice, usually having a range of approximately from F a fifth below middle C to D a ninth above it. In the context of a choir often shortened to: alto **2** a singer with such a voice ▷ *adj* **3** of or denoting a contralto: *the contralto part* [c18: from Italian; see CONTRA-, ALTO]

contraposition (ˌkɒntrəpə'zɪʃən) *n* **1** the act of placing opposite or against, esp in contrast or antithesis **2** *logic* the derivation of the contrapositive of a given categorical proposition

contraption (kən'træpʃən) *n informal, often facetious or derogatory* a device or contrivance, esp one considered strange, unnecessarily intricate, or improvised [c19: perhaps from CON(TRIVANCE) + TRAP¹ + (INVEN)TION]

contrapuntal (ˌkɒntrə'pʌntᵊl) *adj music* characterized by counterpoint [c19: from Italian *contrappunto* COUNTERPOINT + AL¹] >,contra'puntally *adv*

contrariety (ˌkɒntrə'raɪətɪ) *n, pl* **-ties** **1** opposition between one thing and another; disagreement **2** an instance of such opposition; inconsistency; discrepancy

contrariwise ('kɒntrərɪˌwaɪz) *adv* **1** from a contrasting point of view; on the other hand **2** in the reverse way or direction **3** (kən'trɛərɪˌwaɪz) in a contrary manner

contrary ('kɒntrərɪ) *adj* **1** opposed in nature, position, etc: *contrary ideas* **2** (kən'trɛərɪ) perverse; obstinate **3** (esp of wind) adverse; unfavourable **4** (of plant parts) situated at right angles to each other **5** *logic* (of a pair of propositions) related so that they cannot both be true at once, although they may both be false together ▷ *n, pl* **-ries** **6** the exact opposite (esp in the phrase **to the contrary**) **7** on the contrary quite the reverse; not at all **8** either of two exactly opposite objects, facts, or qualities ▷ *adv* (usually foll by *to*) **9** in an opposite or unexpected way: *contrary to usual belief* **10** in conflict (with) or contravention (of): *contrary to nature* [c14: from Latin *contrārius* opposite, from *contrā* against] >con'trariness *n* >con'trarily *adv*

contrasexual (ˌkɒntrə'sɛksjʊəl) *adj* **1** (of a woman) appearing to defy the female sexual stereotype by being content to be single and childless while being sexually active and financially independent ▷ *n* **2** a contrasexual woman

contrast *vb* (kən'trɑːst) **1** (often foll by *with*) to distinguish or be distinguished by comparison of unlike or opposite qualities ▷ *n* ('kɒntrɑːst) **2** distinction or emphasis of difference by comparison of opposite or dissimilar things, qualities, etc (esp in the phrases **by contrast, in contrast to** *or* **with**) **3** a person or thing showing notable differences when compared with another **4** (in painting) the effect of the juxtaposition of different colours, tones, etc **5 a** (of a photographic emulsion) the degree of density measured against exposure used **b** the extent to which adjacent areas of an optical image, esp on a television screen or in a photographic negative or print, differ in brightness **6** *psychol* the phenomenon that when two different but related stimuli are presented close together in space and/or time they are perceived as being more different than they really are [c16: (n): via French from Italian, from *contrastare* (vb), from Latin *contra-* against + *stare* to stand] >con'trasting *adj* >con'trastive *adj* >con'trastively *adv*

contrast medium *n med* a radiopaque substance, such as barium sulphate, used to increase the contrast of an image in radiography

contravene (ˌkɒntrə'viːn) *vb* (*tr*) **1** to come into conflict with or infringe (rules, laws, etc) **2** to dispute or contradict (a statement, proposition, etc) [c16: from Late Latin *contrāvenīre*, from Latin CONTRA- + *venīre* to come]

contretemps ('kɒntrəˌtɑːn; French kɔ̃trətɑ̃) *n, pl* **-temps** **1** an awkward or difficult situation or mishap **2** *fencing* a feint made with the purpose of producing a counterthrust from one's opponent **3** a small disagreement that is rather embarrassing [c17: from French, from *contre* against + *temps* time, from Latin *tempus*]

contribute (kən'trɪbjuːt) *vb* (often foll by *to*) **1** to give (support, money, etc) for a common purpose or fund **2** to supply (ideas, opinions, etc) as part of a debate or discussion **3** (*intr*) to be partly instrumental (in) or responsible (for): *drink contributed to the accident* **4** to write (articles) for a publication [c16: from Latin *contribuere* to collect, from *tribuere* to grant, bestow] >con'tributable *adj* >con'tributive *adj* >con'tributor *n*

contribution (ˌkɒntrɪ'bjuːʃən) *n* **1** the act of contributing **2** something contributed, such as money or ideas **3** an article, story, etc, contributed to a newspaper or other publication **4** *archaic* a levy, esp towards the cost of a war

contributory (kən'trɪbjʊtərɪ, -trɪ) *adj* **1** (often foll by *to*) sharing in or being partly responsible (for the cause of something): *a contributory factor* **2** giving or donating to a common purpose or fund **3** of, relating to, or designating an insurance or pension scheme in which the premiums are paid partly by the employer and partly by the employees who benefit from it **4** liable or subject to a tax or levy ▷ *n, pl* **-ries** **5** a person or thing that contributes **6** *company law* a member or former member of a company liable to contribute to the assets on the winding-up of the company

contrite (kən'traɪt, 'kɒntraɪt) *adj* **1** full of guilt or regret; remorseful **2** arising from a sense of shame or guilt: *contrite promises* **3** *theol* remorseful for past sin and resolved to avoid future sin [c14: from Latin *contrītus* worn out, from *conterere* to bruise, from *terere* to grind]

contrivance (kən'traɪvəns) *n* **1** something contrived, esp an ingenious device; contraption **2** the act or faculty of devising or adapting; inventive skill or ability **3** an artificial rather than natural selection or arrangement of details, parts, etc **4** an elaborate or deceitful plan or expedient; stratagem

contrive (kən'traɪv) *vb* **1** (*tr*) to manage (something or to do something), esp by means of a trick; engineer: *he contrived to make them meet* **2** (*tr*) to think up or adapt ingeniously or elaborately: *he contrived a new mast for the boat* **3** to plot or scheme (treachery, evil, etc) [c14: from Old French *controver*, from Late Latin *contropāre* to represent by figures of speech, compare, from Latin *com-* together + *tropus* figure of speech, TROPE] >con'triver *n*

contrived (kən'traɪvd) *adj* obviously planned, artificial, or lacking in spontaneity; forced; unnatural

control (kən'trəʊl) *vb* **-trols, -trolling, -trolled** (*tr*) **1** to command, direct, or rule **2** to check, limit, curb, or regulate; restrain: *to control one's emotions; to control a fire* **3** to regulate or operate (a machine) **4** to verify (a scientific experiment) by conducting a parallel experiment in which the variable being investigated is held constant or is compared with a standard **5 a** to regulate (financial affairs) **b** to examine and verify (financial accounts) **6** to restrict or regulate the authorized supply of (certain substances, such as drugs) ▷ *n* **7** power to direct or determine: *under control; out of control* **8** a means of regulation or restraint; curb; check: *a frontier control* **9** (*often plural*) a device or mechanism for operating a car, aircraft, etc **10** a standard of comparison used in a statistical analysis or scientific experiment **11 a** a device that regulates the operation of a machine. A **dynamic control** is one that incorporates a governor so that it responds to the output of the machine it regulates **b** (*as modifier*): *control panel; control room* **12** *spiritualism* an agency believed to assist the medium in a séance **13** Also called: control mark a letter, or letter and number, printed on a sheet of postage stamps, indicating authenticity, date, and series of issue **14** one of a number of checkpoints on a car rally, orienteering course, etc, where competitors check in and their time, performance, etc, is recorded [c15: from Old French *conteroller* to regulate, from *contrerolle* duplicate register, system of checking, from *contre*-COUNTER- + *rolle* ROLL] > con'trollable *adj* > con,trolla'bility *or* con'trollableness *n* > con'trollably *adv*

control experiment *n* an experiment designed to check or correct the results of another experiment by removing the variable or variables operating in that other experiment. The comparison obtained is an indication or measurement of the effect of the variables concerned

control freak *n* a person with an obsessive need to be in control of what is happening

controlled explosion *n* the deliberate detonation of an explosive device under strictly controlled circumstances

controller (kən'trəʊlə) *n* **1** a person who directs, regulates, or restrains **2** Also called: **comptroller** a business executive or government officer who is responsible for financial planning, control, etc **3** the equipment concerned with controlling the operation of an electrical device > con'troller,ship *n*

controlling interest *n* a quantity of shares in a business that is sufficient to ensure control over its direction

control tower *n* a tower at an airport from which air traffic is controlled

controversy ('kɒntrə,vɜːsɪ, kən'trɒvəsɪ) *n, pl* -sies dispute, argument, or debate, esp one concerning a matter about which there is strong disagreement and esp one carried on in public or in the press [c14: from Latin *contrōversia*, from *contrōversus* turned in an opposite direction, from CONTRA- + *vertere* to turn] > controversial (,kɒntrə'vɜːʃəl) *adj* > ,contro'versial,ism *n* > ,contro'versialist *n*

controvert ('kɒntrə,vɜːt, ,kɒntrə'vɜːt) *vb* (*tr*) **1** to deny, refute, or oppose (some argument or opinion) **2** to argue or wrangle about [c17: from Latin *contrōversus*; see CONTROVERSY] > ,contro'vertible *adj*

contumacious (,kɒntjʊ'meɪʃəs) *adj* stubbornly resistant to authority; wilfully obstinate > ,contu'maciously *adv*

contumacy ('kɒntjʊməsɪ) *n, pl* -cies **1** obstinate and wilful rebelliousness or resistance to authority; insubordination; disobedience **2** the wilful refusal of a person to appear before a court or to comply with a court order [c14: from Latin *contumācia*, from *contumāx* obstinate; related to *tumēre* to swell, be proud]

contumely ('kɒntjʊmɪlɪ) *n, pl* -lies **1** scornful or insulting language or behaviour **2** a humiliating or scornful insult [c14: from Latin *contumēlia* invective, from *tumēre* to swell, as with wrath] > contumelious (,kɒntjʊ'miːlɪəs) *adj* > ,contu'meliously *adv*

contuse (kən'tjuːz) *vb* (*tr*) to injure (the body) without breaking the skin; bruise [c15: from Latin *contūsus* bruised, from *contundere* to grind, from *tundere* to beat, batter] > con'tusive *adj*

contusion (kən'tjuːʒən) *n* an injury in which the skin is not broken; bruise > con'tusioned *adj*

conundrum (kə'nʌndrəm) *n* **1** a riddle, esp one whose answer makes a play on words **2** a puzzling question or problem [c16: of unknown origin]

conurbation (,kɒnɜː'beɪʃən) *n* a large densely populated urban sprawl formed by the growth and coalescence of individual towns or cities [c20: from CON- + -*urbation*, from Latin *urbs* city; see URBAN]

convalesce (,kɒnvə'lɛs) *vb* (*intr*) to recover from illness, injury, or the aftereffects of a surgical operation, esp by resting [c15: from Latin *convalēscere*, from *com*- (intensive) + *valēscere* to grow strong, from *valēre* to be strong]

convalescence (,kɒnvə'lɛsəns) *n* **1** gradual return to health after illness, injury, or an operation, esp through rest **2** the period during which such recovery occurs > ,conva'lescent *n, adj*

convection (kən'vɛkʃən) *n* **1** a process of heat transfer through a gas or liquid by bulk motion of hotter material into a cooler region. See **conduction** (sense 1) **2** *meteorol* the process by which masses of relatively warm air are raised into the atmosphere, often cooling

and forming clouds, with compensatory downward movements of cooler air [c19: from Late Latin *convectiō* a bringing together, from Latin *convehere* to bring together, gather, from *vehere* to bear, carry] > con'vectional *adj* > con'vective *adj*

convector (kən'vɛktə) *n* a space-heating device from which heat is transferred to the surrounding air by convection

convene (kən'viːn) *vb* **1** to gather, call together, or summon, esp for a formal meeting **2** (*tr*) to order to appear before a court of law, judge, tribunal, etc [c15: from Latin *convenīre* to assemble, from *venīre* to come]

convener *or* **convenor** (kən'viːnə) *n* **1** a person who convenes or chairs a meeting, committee, etc, esp one who is specifically elected to do so: *a convener of shop stewards* **2** the chairman and civic head of certain Scottish councils. See **provost** (sense 2) > con'venership *or* con'venorship *n*

convenience (kən'viːnɪəns) *n* **1** the state or quality of being suitable or opportune **2** a convenient time or situation **3** at your convenience at a time suitable to you **4** usefulness, comfort, or facility **5** an object that is particularly useful, esp a labour-saving device **6** *euphemistic, chiefly Brit* a lavatory, esp a public one **7** make a convenience of to take advantage of; impose upon

convenience food *n* food that needs little preparation, especially food that has been pre-prepared and preserved for long-term storage

convenience store *n* a shop that has long opening hours, caters to local tastes, and is conveniently situated

convenient (kən'viːnɪənt) *adj* **1** suitable for one's purpose or needs; opportune **2** easy to use **3** close by or easily accessible; handy [c14: from Latin *conveniēns* appropriate, fitting, from *convenīre* to come together, be in accord with, from *venīre* to come] > con'veniently *adv*

convent ('kɒnvənt) *n* **1** a building inhabited by a religious community, usually of nuns **2** the religious community inhabiting such a building **3** Also called: **convent school** a school in which the teachers are nuns [c13: from Old French *covent*, from Latin *conventus* meeting, from *convenīre* to come together; see CONVENE]

conventicle (kən'vɛntɪkəl) *n* **1** a secret or unauthorized assembly for worship **2** a small meeting house or chapel for a religious assembly, esp of Nonconformists or Dissenters [c14: from Latin *conventiculum* a meeting, from *conventus*; see CONVENT]

convention (kən'vɛnʃən) *n* **1 a** a large formal assembly of a group with common interests, such as a political party or trade union **b** the persons attending such an assembly **2** *US politics* an assembly of delegates of one party to select candidates for office **3** *diplomacy* an international agreement second only to a treaty in formality: *a telecommunications convention* **4** any agreement, compact, or contract **5** the most widely accepted or established view of what is thought to be proper behaviour, good taste, etc **6** an accepted rule, usage, etc: *a convention used by printers* **7** Also called: **conventional bridge** a bid or play not to be taken at its face value, which one's partner can interpret according to a prearranged bidding system [c15: from Latin *conventiō* an assembling, agreeing]

conventional (kən'vɛnʃənəl) *adj* **1** following the accepted customs and proprieties, esp in a way that lacks originality **2** established by accepted usage or general agreement **3** of or relating to a convention or assembly **4** *arts* represented in a simplified or generalized way; conventionalized **5** (of weapons, warfare, etc) not nuclear > con'ventionally *adv* > con'ventionalism *n* (kən'vɛnʃənə,lɪzəm)

conventionality (kən,vɛnʃə'nælɪtɪ) *n, pl* -ties **1** the quality or characteristic of being conventional, esp in behaviour, thinking, etc **2** (*often plural*) something conventional, esp a normal or accepted rule of behaviour; propriety

conventionalize *or* **conventionalise** (kən'vɛnʃənə,laɪz) *vb* (*tr*) **1** to make conventional **2** to simplify or stylize (a design, decorative device, etc) > con,ventionali'zation *or* con,ventionali'sation *n*

conventual (kənˈvɛntjʊəl) *adj* **1** of, belonging to, or characteristic of a convent ▷ *n* **2** a member of a convent >con'ventually *adv*

converge (kənˈvɜːdʒ) *vb* **1** to move or cause to move towards the same point **2** to meet or cause to meet; join **3** (*intr*) (of opinions, effects, etc) to tend towards a common conclusion or result **4** (*intr*) *maths* (of an infinite series or sequence) to approach a finite limit as the number of terms increases **5** (*intr*) (of animals and plants during evolutionary development) to undergo convergence [c17: from Late Latin *convergere*, from Latin *com-* together + *vergere* to incline] >convergent (kənˈvɜːdʒənt) *adj*

convergence (kənˈvɜːdʒəns) *n* **1** Also called: convergency the act, degree, or a point of converging **2** concurrence of opinions, results, etc **3** *maths* the property or manner of approaching a finite limit, esp of an infinite series: *conditional convergence* **4** the combining of different forms of electronic technology, such as data processing and word processing converging into information processing **5** Also called: convergent evolution the evolutionary development of a superficial resemblance between unrelated animals that occupy a similar environment, as in the evolution of wings in birds and bats

convergent thinking *n psychol* analytical, usually deductive, thinking in which ideas are examined for their logical validity or in which a set of rules is followed, e.g. in arithmetic

conversable (kənˈvɜːsəbʰl) *adj* **1** easy or pleasant to talk to **2** able or inclined to talk

conversant (kənˈvɜːsᵊnt) *adj* (*usually postpositive* and foll by *with*) experienced (in), familiar (with), or acquainted (with) >con'versance *or*con'versancy *n* >con'versantly *adv*

conversation (ˌkɒnvəˈseɪʃən) *n* the interchange through speech of information, ideas, etc; spoken communication

conversational (ˌkɒnvəˈseɪʃənᵊl) *adj* **1** of, using, or in the manner of conversation **2** inclined to or skilled in conversation; conversable >ˌconver'sationally *adv* >ˌconver'sationalist *or*ˌconver'sationist *n*

conversation piece *n* **1** something, esp an unusual object, that provokes conversation **2** (esp in 18th-century Britain) a group portrait in a landscape or domestic setting

converse¹ *vb* (kənˈvɜːs) (*intr*; often foll by *with*) **1** to engage in conversation (with) **2** to commune spiritually (with) ▷ *n* (ˈkɒnvɜːs) **3** conversation (often in the phrase hold converse with) [c16: from Old French *converser*, from Latin *conversārī* to keep company with, from *conversāre* to turn constantly, from *vertere* to turn] >con'verser *n*

converse² (ˈkɒnvɜːs) *adj* **1** (*prenominal*) reversed; opposite; contrary ▷ *n* **2** something that is opposite or contrary **3** *logic* a categorical proposition obtained from another by the transposition of subject and predicate, as *no bad man is bald* from *no bald man is bad* [c16: from Latin *conversus* turned around; see CONVERSE¹]

conversion (kənˈvɜːʃən) *n* **1 a** a change or adaptation in form, character, or function **b** something changed in one of these respects **2** a change to another attitude or belief, as in a change of religion **3** *maths* a change in the units or form of a number or expression: *the conversion of miles to kilometres involves multiplying by 1.61* **4** *logic* a form of inference by which one proposition is obtained as the converse of another proposition **5** *law* **a** unauthorized dealing with or the assumption of rights of ownership to another's personal property **b** the changing of real property into personalty or personalty into realty **6** *rugby* a score made after a try by kicking the ball over the crossbar from a place kick **7** *physics* a change of fertile material to fissile material in a reactor **8** an alteration to a car engine to improve its performance [c14: from Latin *conversiō* a turning around; see CONVERT]

conversion disorder *n* a psychological disorder in which severe physical symptoms like blindness or paralysis appear with no apparent physical cause

convert *vb* (kənˈvɜːt) (*mainly tr*) **1** to change or adapt the form, character, or function of; transform **2** to cause

(someone) to change in opinion, belief, etc **3** to change (a person or his way of life, etc) for the better **4** (*intr*) to admit of being changed (into): *the table converts into a tray* **5** (*also intr*) to change or be changed into another chemical compound or physical state: *to convert water into ice* **6** *law* **a** to assume unlawful proprietary rights over (personal property) **b** to change (property) from realty into personalty or vice versa **7** (*also intr*) *rugby* to make a conversion after (a try) **8** *logic* to transpose the subject and predicate of (a proposition) by conversion **9** to change (a value or measurement) from one system of units to another **10** to exchange (a security or bond) for something of equivalent value ▷ *n* (ˈkɒnvɜːt) **11** a person who has been converted to another belief, religion, etc [c13: from Old French *convertir*, from Latin *convertere* to turn around, alter, transform, from *vertere* to turn] >con'vertive *adj*

converter *or***convertor** (kənˈvɜːtə) *n* **1** a person or thing that converts **2** *physics* **a** a device for converting alternating current to direct current or vice versa **b** a device for converting a signal from one frequency to another or from analogue to digital forms **3** a vessel in which molten metal is refined, using a blast of air or oxygen **4** *computing* a device for converting one form of coded information to another, such as an analogue-to-digital converter

converter reactor *n* a nuclear reactor for converting one fuel into another, esp one that transforms fertile material into fissionable material

convertible (kənˈvɜːtəbʰl) *adj* **1** capable of being converted **2** (of a car) having a folding or removable roof **3** *finance* **a** a bond or debenture that can be converted to ordinary or preference shares on a fixed date at a fixed price **b** (of a paper currency) exchangeable on demand for precious metal to an equivalent value ▷ *n* **4** a car with a folding or removable roof >con,verti'bility *or* con'vertibleness *n* >con'vertibly *adv*

convex (ˈkɒnvɛks, kɒnˈvɛks) *adj* **1** curving or bulging outwards **2** *physics* having one or two surfaces curved or ground in the shape of a section of the exterior of a sphere, paraboloid, ellipsoid, etc: *a convex lens* [c16: from Latin *convexus* vaulted, rounded] >'convexly *adv* >con'vexity *n*,

convexo-concave (kənˌvɛksəʊkɒnˈkeɪv) *adj* **1** having one side convex and the other side concave **2** (of a lens) having a convex face with greater curvature than the concave face. See **concavo-convex** (sense 2)

convexo-convex *adj* (esp of a lens) having both sides convex; biconvex

convey (kənˈveɪ) *vb* (*tr*) **1** to take, carry, or transport from one place to another **2** to communicate (a message, information, etc) **3** (of a channel, path, etc) to conduct, transmit, or transfer **4** *law* to transmit or transfer (the title to property) **5** *archaic* to steal [c13: from Old French *conveier*, from Medieval Latin *conviāre* to escort, from Latin *com-* with + *via* way] >con'veyable *adj*

conveyance (kənˈveɪəns) *n* **1** the act of conveying **2** a means of transport **3** *law* **a** a transfer of the legal title to property **b** the document effecting such a transfer >con'veyancer *n* >con'veyancing *n*

conveyor *or***conveyer** (kənˈveɪə) *n* **1** a person or thing that conveys **2** short for **conveyor belt**

conveyor belt *n* a flexible endless strip of fabric or linked plates driven by rollers and used to transport objects, esp in a factory

convict *vb* (kənˈvɪkt) (*tr*) **1** to pronounce (someone) guilty of an offence ▷ *n* (ˈkɒnvɪkt) **2** a person found guilty of an offence against the law, esp one who is sentenced to imprisonment **3** a person serving a prison sentence ▷ *adj* (ˈkɒnvɪkt) **4** *obsolete* convicted [c14: from Latin *convictus* convicted of crime, from *convincere* to prove guilty, CONVINCE]

conviction (kənˈvɪkʃən) *n* **1** the state or appearance of being convinced **2** a fixed or firmly held belief, opinion, etc **3** the act of convincing **4** the act or an instance of convicting or the state of being convicted **5** carry conviction to be convincing >con'victional *adj*

convince (kənˈvɪns) *vb* (*tr*; *may take a clause as object*) to make (someone) agree, understand, or realize the truth

or validity of something; persuade [c16: from Latin *convincere* to demonstrate incontrovertibly, from *com-* (intensive) + *vincere* to overcome, conquer] ▷ con'vincer *n* ▷ con'vincible *adj* ▷ con'vincing *adj* ▷ con'vincingly *adv*
◉ USAGE The use of *convince* to talk about persuading
◉ someone to do something is considered by many
◉ British speakers to be wrong or unacceptable

convivial (kənˈvɪvɪəl) *adj* sociable; jovial or festive: *a convivial atmosphere* [c17: from Late Latin *convīviālis* pertaining to a feast, from Latin *convīvium*, a living together, banquet, from *vīvere* to live] ▷ con,vivi'ality *n*

convocation (ˌkɒnvəˈkeɪʃən) *n* 1 a large formal assembly, esp one specifically convened 2 the act of convoking or state of being convoked 3 *Church of England* either of the synods of the provinces of Canterbury or York 4 *Episcopal Church* a an assembly of the clergy and part of the laity of a diocese b a district represented at such an assembly 5 (*sometimes capital*) (in some British universities) a legislative assembly composed mainly of graduates 6 (in India) a degree-awarding ceremony 7 (in Australia and New Zealand) the graduate membership of a university ▷ ,convo'cational *adj*

convoke (kənˈvəʊk) *vb* (*tr*) to call (a meeting, assembly, etc) together; summon [c16: from Latin *convocāre*, from *vocāre* to call] ▷ con'voker *n*

convolute (ˈkɒnvəˌluːt) *vb* (*tr*) 1 to form into a twisted, coiled, or rolled shape ▷ *adj* 2 *botany* rolled longitudinally upon itself: *a convolute petal* [c18: from Latin *convolūtus* rolled up, from *convolvere* to roll together, from *volvere* to roll]

convoluted (ˈkɒnvəˌluːtɪd) *adj* 1 (esp of meaning, style, etc) difficult to comprehend; involved 2 wound together; coiled ▷ 'convo,lutedly *adv*

convolution (ˌkɒnvəˈluːʃən) *n* 1 a twisting together; a turn, twist, or coil 2 an intricate, involved, or confused matter or condition 3 Also called: gyrus any of the numerous convex folds or ridges of the surface of the brain ▷ ,convo'lutional *or* ,convo'lutionary *adj*

convolve (kənˈvɒlv) *vb* to wind or roll together; coil; twist [c16: from Latin *convolvere*; see CONVOLUTE]

convolvulus (kənˈvɒlvjʊləs) *n, pl* -luses *or* -li (-ˌlaɪ) any typically twining herbaceous convolvulaceous plant of the genus *Convolvulus*, having funnel-shaped flowers and triangular leaves. See also **bindweed** [c16: from Latin: bindweed; see CONVOLUTE]

convoy (ˈkɒnvɔɪ) *n* 1 a group of merchant ships with an escort of warships 2 a group of land vehicles assembled to travel together 3 the act of travelling or escorting by convoy (esp in the phrase **in convoy**) ▷ *vb* 4 (*tr*) to escort while in transit [c14: from Old French *convoier* to CONVEY]

convulse (kənˈvʌls) *vb* 1 (*tr*) to shake or agitate violently 2 (*tr*) to cause (muscles) to undergo violent spasms or contractions 3 (*intr*; often foll by *with*) *informal* to shake or be overcome (with violent emotion, esp laughter) 4 (*tr*) to disrupt the normal running of (a country, etc): *student riots have convulsed India* [c17: from Latin *convulsus*, from *convellere* to tear up, from *vellere* to pluck, pull] ▷ con'vulsive *adj* ▷ con'vulsively *adv*

convulsion (kənˈvʌlʃən) *n* 1 a violent involuntary contraction of a muscle or muscles 2 a violent upheaval, disturbance, or agitation, esp a social one 3 (*usually plural*) *informal* uncontrollable laughter: *I was in convulsions*

Conwy (ˈkɒnwɪ) *n* 1 a market town and resort in N Wales, in Conwy county borough on the estuary of the River Conwy: medieval town walls, 13th-century castle. Pop: 3847 (2001) 2 a county borough in N Wales, created in 1996 from parts of Gwynedd and Clwyd. Pop: 110 900 (2003 est). Area: 1130 sq km (436 sq miles)

cony *or* **coney** (ˈkəʊnɪ) *n, pl* -nies *or* -neys 1 a rabbit or fur made from the skin of a rabbit 2 (in the Bible) another name for the hyrax, esp the Syrian rock hyrax 3 another name for **pika** 4 *archaic* a fool or dupe [c13: back formation from *conies*, from Old French *conis*, plural of *conil*, from Latin *cunīculus* rabbit]

Conybeare (ˈkɒnɪˌbɪə, ˈkʌn-) *n* **William Daniel.** 1787–1857, British geologist. He summarized all that was known about rocks at the time in *Outlines of the Geology of England and Wales* (1822)

coo (kuː) *vb* coos, cooing, cooed 1 (*intr*) (of doves,

pigeons, etc) to make a characteristic soft throaty call 2 (*tr*) to speak in a soft murmur 3 (*intr*) to murmur lovingly (esp in the phrase **bill and coo**) ▷ *n* 4 the sound of cooing ▷ *interj* 5 *Brit slang* an exclamation of surprise, awe, etc ▷ 'cooingly *adv*

COO *abbreviation* chief operating officer

Cooch Behar *or* **Kuch Bihar** (kuːtʃ bɪˈhɑː) *n* 1 a former state of NE India: part of West Bengal since 1950 2 a city in India, in NE West Bengal: capital of the former state of Cooch Behar. Pop: 76 812 (2001)

cooee *or* **cooey** (ˈkuːiː) *interj* 1 a call used to attract attention, esp (originally) a long loud high-pitched call on two notes used in the Australian bush ▷ *vb* cooees, cooeeing, cooeed *or* cooeys, cooeying, cooeyed 2 (*intr*) to utter this call ▷ *n* 3 *Austral & NZ informal* calling distance (esp in the phrase **within (a) cooee (of)**) [c19: from a native Australian language]

cook (kʊk) *vb* 1 to prepare (food) by the action of heat, as by boiling, baking, etc, or (of food) to become ready for eating through such a process. Related adj: **culinary** 2 to subject or be subjected to the action of intense heat: *the town cooked in the sun* 3 (*tr*) *slang* to alter or falsify (something, esp figures, accounts, etc): *to cook the books* 4 (*tr*) *slang* to spoil or ruin (something) 5 (*intr*) *slang* to happen (esp in the phrase **what's cooking?**) 6 (*tr*) *slang* to prepare (any of several drugs) by heating 7 (*intr*) *music slang* to play vigorously: *the band was cooking* 8 **cook someone's goose** *informal* a to spoil a person's plans b to bring about a person's ruin, downfall, etc ▷ *n* 9 a person who prepares food for eating, esp as an occupation ▷ See also **cook up** [Old English *cōc* (n), from Latin *coquus* a cook, from *coquere* to cook] ▷ 'cookable *adj*

Cook[1] (kʊk) Mount Cook *n* 1 a mountain in New Zealand, in the South Island, in the Southern Alps: the highest peak in New Zealand. Height: reduced in 1991 by a rockfall from 3764 m (12 349 ft) to 3754 m (12 316 ft). Official name: Aoraki-Mount Cook 2 a mountain in SE Alaska, in the St Elias Mountains. Height: 4194 m (13 760 ft)

Cook[2] (kʊk) *n* 1 Captain **James.** 1728–79, British navigator and explorer: claimed the E coast of Australia for Britain, circumnavigated New Zealand, and discovered several Pacific and Atlantic islands (1768–79) 2 Sir **Joseph.** 1860–1947, Australian statesman, born in England: prime minister of Australia (1913–14) 3 Peter (**Edward**). 1937–95, British comedy actor and writer, noted esp for his partnership (1960–73) with Dudley Moore 4 **Robin**, full name *Robert Finlayson Cook*. 1946–2005, British Labour politician; foreign secretary (1997–2001), Leader of the House (2001-2003) 5 **Thomas.** 1808–92, British travel agent; innovator of conducted excursions and founder of the travel agents Thomas Cook and Son

cook-chill *n* a method of food preparation used by caterers, in which cooked dishes are chilled rapidly and reheated as required

Cooke *n* **Norman**, real name *Quentin Cooke*, also known as *Fatboy Slim*. born 1963, British disc jockey, pop musician, and record producer; hit records include *You've Come a Long Way, Baby* (1998) and "Praise You" (2001)

cooker (ˈkʊkə) *n* 1 an apparatus, usually of metal and heated by gas, electricity, oil, or solid fuel, for cooking food; stove 2 *Brit* any large sour apple used in cooking

cookery (ˈkʊkərɪ) *n* 1 the art, study, or practice of cooking 2 *US* a place for cooking 3 *Canadian* a cookhouse at a mining or lumber camp

cookery book *or* **cookbook** (ˈkʊkˌbʊk) *n* a book containing recipes and instructions for cooking

cook-general *n, pl* cooks-general *Brit* (formerly, esp in the 1920s and '30s) a domestic servant who did cooking and housework

cookie *or* **cooky** (ˈkʊkɪ) *n, pl* -ies 1 *US & Canadian* a small flat dry sweet or plain cake of many varieties, baked from a dough. Also called (in Britain and certain other countries): biscuit 2 a Scot word for **bun** 3 *informal* a person: *smart cookie* 4 *computing* a piece of data downloaded to a computer by a website, containing details of the preferences of that computer's user which identify the user when revisiting that website 5 that's the way the cookie crumbles *informal* matters are inevitably or unalterably so [c18: from Dutch *koekje*, diminutive of *koek* cake]

cookie-cutter *n* **1** a shape with a sharp edge for cutting individual biscuits from a sheet of dough ▷ *adj* **2** resembling many others of the same kind: *a row of cookie-cutter houses*

Cook Islands *pl n* a group of islands in the SW Pacific, an overseas territory of New Zealand: consists of the **Lower Cooks** and the **Northern Cooks** Capital: Avarua, on Rarotonga. Pop: 18 000 (2003 est). Area: 234 sq km (90 sq miles)

cookout ('kʊk,aʊt) *n US & Canadian* a party where a meal is cooked and eaten out of doors

cook shop *n* **1** *Brit* a shop that sells cookery equipment **2** *US* a restaurant

Cookson ('kʊksən) *n* Dame **Catherine**. 1906-98, British novelist, known for her popular novels set in northeast England

Cook's tour *n informal* a rapid but extensive tour or survey of anything [c19: after Thomas Cook (1808–92), British travel agent]

Cookstown ('kʊkstaʊn) *n* a district of central Northern Ireland, in Co Tyrone. Pop: 33 387 (2003 est). Area: 622 sq km (240 sq miles)

Cook Strait *n* the strait between North and South Islands, New Zealand. Width: 26 km (16 miles)

Cooktown orchid ('kʊktaʊn) *n* a purple Australian orchid, *Dendrobium bigibbum*, found in Queensland, of which it is the floral emblem [named after *Cooktown*, a coastal town in NE Queensland]

cook up *vb* (*tr, adverb*) **1** *informal* to concoct or invent (a story, alibi, etc) **2** to prepare (a meal), esp quickly **3** *slang* to prepare (a drug) for use by heating, as by dissolving heroin in a spoon

cool (kuːl) *adj* **1** moderately cold: *a cool day* **2** comfortably free of heat: *a cool room* **3** producing a pleasant feeling of coldness: *a cool shirt* **4** able to conceal emotion; calm: *a cool head* **5** lacking in enthusiasm, affection, cordiality, etc: *a cool welcome* **6** calmly audacious or impudent **7** *informal* (esp of numbers, sums of money, etc) without exaggeration; actual: *a cool ten thousand* **8** (of a colour) having violet, blue, or green predominating; cold **9** (of jazz) characteristic of the late 1940s and early 1950s, economical and rhythmically relaxed **10** *informal* sophisticated or elegant, esp in an unruffled way **11** *informal* excellent; marvellous ▷ *adv* **12** *not standard* in a cool manner; coolly ▷ *n* **13** coolness: *the cool of the evening* **14** *slang* calmness; composure (esp in the phrases **keep** or **lose one's cool**) **15** *slang* unruffled elegance or sophistication ▷ *vb* **16** (usually foll by *down* or *off*) to make or become cooler **17** (usually foll by *down* or *off*) to lessen the intensity of (anger or excitement) or (of anger or excitement) to become less intense; calm down **18 cool it** (*usually imperative*) *slang* to calm down; take it easy **19 cool one's heels** to wait or be kept waiting [Old English *cōl*; related to Old Norse *kōlna*, Old High German *kuoli*; see COLD, CHILL] ▷ '**coolly** *adv* ▷ '**coolness** *n*

coolabah or **coolibah** ('kuːlə,baː) *n* an Australian myrtaceous tree, *Eucalyptus microtheca*, that grows along rivers and has smooth bark and long narrow leaves [from a native Australian language]

coolant ('kuːlənt) *n* **1** a fluid used to cool a system or to transfer heat from one part of it to another **2** a liquid, such as an emulsion of oil, water, and soft soap, used to lubricate and cool the workpiece and cutting tool during machining

cool bag or **cool box** *n* an insulated container used to keep food cool on picnics, to carry frozen food, etc

cool drink *n South African* any soft drink

cooler ('kuːlə) *n* **1** a container, vessel, or apparatus for cooling, such as a heat exchanger **2** a drink consisting of wine, fruit juice, and carbonated water

cool hunter *n informal* a person who is employed to identify future trends, esp in fashion or the media

Coolidge ('kuːlɪdʒ) *n* (**John**) **Calvin**. 1872–1933, 30th president of the US (1923–29)

coolie or **cooly** ('kuːlɪ) *n, pl* **-ies** a cheaply hired unskilled Oriental labourer [c17: from Hindi *kulī*, probably of

Dravidian origin; related to Tamil *kūli* hire, hireling]

cooling-off period *n* **1** a period during which the contending sides to a dispute reconsider their options before taking further action **2** a statutory period, often 14 days, that begins when a sale contract or life-assurance policy is received by a member of the public, during which the contract or policy can be cancelled without loss

cooling tower *n* a tall hollow structure in which steam is condensed or water that is used as a coolant in some industrial process is allowed to cool for reuse by trickling down a surface

cool school *n NZ* a school where the students resolve conflict without the involvement of teachers

Coomaraswamy (kuː,maːrə'swaːmɪ) *n* **Ananda** (**Kentish**). 1877–1947, Ceylonese art historian and interpreter of Indian culture to the West

coomb, combe, coombe or **comb** (kuːm) *n* **1** *chiefly Southern English* a short valley or deep hollow, esp in chalk areas **2** *chiefly Northern English* another name for **cirque** [Old English *cumb* (in place names), probably of Celtic origin; compare Old French *combe* small valley and Welsh *cwm* valley]

coon (kuːn) *n* **1** *informal* short for **raccoon 2** *offensive, slang* a Black person or a native Australian **3** *South African offensive* a person of mixed race

coonskin ('kuːn,skɪn) *n* **1** the pelt of a raccoon **2** a raccoon cap with the tail hanging at the back **3** *US* an overcoat made of raccoon

coop[1] (kuːp) *n* **1** a cage or small enclosure for poultry or small animals **2** a small narrow place of confinement, esp a prison cell **3** a wicker basket for catching fish ▷ *vb* **4** (*tr; often foll by up or in*) to confine in a restricted area [c15: probably from Middle Low German *kūpe* basket, tub; related to Latin *cūpa* cask, vat]

coop[2] or **co-op** ('kəʊ,ɒp) *n* a cooperative, cooperative society, or shop run by a cooperative society

cooper ('kuːpə) *n* **1** Also called: **hooper** a person skilled in making and repairing barrels, casks, etc ▷ *vb* **2** (*tr*) to make or mend (barrels, casks, etc) [c13: from Middle Dutch *cūper* or Middle Low German *kūper*; see COOP[1]]

Cooper ('kuːpə) *n* **1** **Anthony Ashley**. See (Earl of) **Shaftesbury 2** **Cary** (**Lynn**). born 1940, British psychologist, noted for his studies of behaviour at work and the causes and treatment of stress **3** **Gary**, real name *Frank James Cooper*. 1901–61, US film actor; his many films include *Sergeant York* (1941) and *High Noon* (1952), for both of which he won Oscars **4** **Sir Henry**. born 1934, British boxer; European heavyweight champion (1964; 1968–71) **5** **James Fenimore** 1789–1851, US novelist, noted for his stories of American Indians, esp *The Last of the Mohicans* (1826) **6** **Leon Neil**. born 1930, US physicist, noted for his work on the theory of superconductivity. He shared the Nobel prize for physics 1972 **7** **Samuel** 1609–72, English miniaturist

cooperage ('kuːpərɪdʒ) *n* **1** Also called: **coopery** the craft, place of work, or products of a cooper **2** the labour fee charged by a cooper

cooperate or **co-operate** (kəʊ'ɒpə,reɪt) *vb* (*intr*) **1** to work or act together **2** to be of assistance or be willing to assist **3** *economics* (of firms, workers, consumers, etc) to engage in economic cooperation [c17: from Late Latin *cooperārī* to work with, combine, from Latin *operārī* to work] ▷ **co'oper,ator** or **co-'oper,ator** *n*

cooperation or **co-operation** (kəʊ,ɒpə'reɪʃən) *n* **1** joint operation or action **2** assistance or willingness to assist **3** *economics* the combination of consumers, workers, farmers, etc, in activities usually embracing production, distribution, or trade **4** *ecology* beneficial but inessential interaction between two species in a community ▷ **co,oper'ationist** or **co-,oper'ationist** *n*

cooperative or **co-operative** (kəʊ'ɒpərətɪv, -'ɒprə-) *adj* **1** willing to cooperate; helpful **2** acting in conjunction with others; cooperating **3 a** (of an enterprise, farm, etc) owned collectively and managed for joint economic benefit **b** (of an economy or economic activity) based on collective ownership and cooperative use of the means of production and distribution ▷ *n* **4** a cooperative organization

cooperative society *n* a commercial enterprise owned and managed by and for the benefit of customers or workers

Cooper Creek ('ku:pə) *n* an intermittent river in E central Australia, in the Channel Country: rises in central Queensland and flows generally southwest, reaching Lake Eyre only during wet-year floods; scene of the death of the explorers Burke and Wills in 1861; the surrounding basin provides cattle pastures after the floods subside. Total length: 1420 km (880 miles)

coopt *or* **co-opt** (kəʊ'ɒpt) *vb* (*tr*) to add (someone) to a committee, board, etc, by the agreement of the existing members [c17: from Latin *cooptāre* to elect, from *optāre* to choose] >co'option, co-'option ,coop'tation *or* ,co-op'tation *n*

coordinate *or* **co-ordinate** *vb* (kəʊ'ɔ:dɪˌneɪt) **1** (*tr*) to organize or integrate (diverse elements) in a harmonious operation **2** to place (things) in the same class or order, or (of things) to be placed in the same class or order **3** (*intr*) to work together, esp harmoniously **4** (*intr*) to take or be in the form of a harmonious order ▷ *n* (kəʊ'ɔ:dɪnɪt, -ˌneɪt) **5** *maths* any of a set of numbers that defines the location of a point in space **6** a person or thing equal in rank, type, etc ▷ *adj* (kəʊ'ɔ:dɪnɪt, -ˌneɪt) **7** of, concerned with, or involving coordination **8** of the same rank, type, etc **9** of or involving the use of coordinates: *coordinate geometry* >co'ordiˌnator *or* co-'ordiˌnator *n*

coordinate clause *n* one of two or more clauses in a sentence having the same status and introduced by coordinating conjunctions

coordinates (kəʊ'ɔ:dɪnɪts, -ˌneɪts) *pl n* clothes of matching or harmonious colours and design, suitable for wearing together

coordinating conjunction *n* a conjunction that introduces coordinate clauses, such as *and*, *but*, and *or*

coordination *or* **co-ordination** (kəʊˌɔ:dɪ'neɪʃən) *n* balanced and effective interaction of movement, actions, etc [c17: from Late Latin *coordinātiō*, from Latin *ordinātiō* an arranging; see ORDINATE]

coot (ku:t) *n* **1** any aquatic bird of the genus *Fulica*, esp *F. atra* of Europe and Asia, having lobed toes, dark plumage, and a white bill with a frontal shield: family *Rallidae* (rails, crakes, etc) **2** a foolish person, esp an old man (often in the phrase **old coot**) [c14: probably from Low German; compare Dutch *koet*]

cootie ('ku:tɪ) *n US & NZ* a slang name for **body louse**. See **louse** (sense 1). Also called (NZ): **kutu**, **kutu** (NZ): **kutu** [c20: perhaps from Malay or Māori *kutu* louse]

cop¹ (kɒp) *slang* ▷ *n* **1** another name for **policeman 2** *Brit* an arrest (esp in the phrase **a fair cop**) ▷ *vb* **cops**, **copping**, **copped** (*tr*) **3** to seize or catch **4** to steal **5** Also called: **cop it** to suffer (a punishment): *you'll cop a clout if you do that!* **6 cop it sweet** *Austral slang* **a** to accept a penalty without complaint **b** to have good fortune ▷ See also **cop off**, **cop out** [c18: (vb) perhaps from obsolete *cap* to arrest, from Old French *caper* to seize; sense 1, back formation from COPPER²]

cop² (kɒp) *n* **1** a conical roll of thread wound on a spindle **2** *now chiefly dialect* the top or crest, as of a hill [Old English *cop, copp* top, summit, of uncertain origin; perhaps related to Old English *copp* CUP]

cop³ (kɒp) *n Brit slang* (*usually used with a negative*) worth or value: *that work is not much cop* [c19: n use of COP¹ (in the sense: to catch, hence something caught, something of value)]

copal ('kəʊpəl, -pæl) *n* a hard aromatic resin, yellow, orange, or red in colour, obtained from various tropical trees and used in making varnishes and lacquers [c16: from Spanish, from Nahuatl *copalli* resin]

copartner (kəʊ'pɑ:tnə) *n* a partner or associate, esp an equal partner in business >co'partnership *n*

cope¹ (kəʊp) *vb* **1** (*intr; foll by with*) to contend (against) **2** (*intr*) to deal successfully with or handle a situation; manage: *she coped well with the problem* [c14: from Old French *coper* to strike, cut, from *coup* blow; see COUP¹]

cope² (kəʊp) *n* **1** a large ceremonial cloak worn at solemn liturgical functions by priests of certain Christian sects **2** any covering shaped like a cope ▷ *vb*

3 (*tr*) to dress (someone) in a cope [Old English *cāp*, from Medieval Latin *cāpa*, from Late Latin *cappa* hooded cloak; see CAP]

cope³ (kəʊp) *vb* (*tr*) **1** to provide (a wall) with a coping ▷ **2** another name for **coping** [c17: probably from French *couper* to cut; see COPE¹]

copeck ('kəʊpɛk) *n* a variant spelling of **kopeck**

Copenhagen (ˌkəʊpən'heɪgən, -ˈhɑ:-, 'kəʊpənˌheɪ-, -ˌhɑ:-) *n* the capital of Denmark, a port on Zealand and the Amager Islands on a site inhabited for some 6000 years: exports chiefly agricultural products; iron and steel works; university (1479). Pop: 501 664 (2004 est). Danish name: København

Copenhagen interpretation *n* an interpretation of quantum mechanics developed by Niels Bohr and his colleagues at the University of Copenhagen, based on the concept of wave-particle duality and the idea that the observation influences the result of an experiment

copepod ('kəʊpɪˌpɒd) *n* any minute free-living or parasitic crustacean of the subclass *Copepoda* of marine and fresh waters: an important constituent of plankton [c19: from New Latin *Copepoda*, from Greek *kōpē* oar + *pous* foot]

coper ('kəʊpə) *n* a horse-dealer [c17 (a dealer, chapman): from dialect *cope* to buy, barter, from Low German; related to Dutch *koopen* to buy]

Copernican system *n* the theory published in 1543 by Copernicus (1473–1543) which stated that the earth and the planets rotated around the sun and which opposed the Ptolemaic system

Copernicus¹ (kə'pɜ:nɪkəs) *n* **Nicolaus** (ˌnɪkə'leɪəs). Polish name *Mikolaj Kopernik*. 1473–1543, Polish astronomer, whose theory of the solar system (the **Copernican system**) was published in 1543 >Co'pernican *adj*

Copernicus² (kə'pɜ:nɪkəs) *n* a conspicuous crater on the moon, over 4000 metres deep and 90 kilometres in diameter, from which a system of rays emanates

copestone ('kəʊpˌstəʊn) *n* **1** Also called: **coping stone** a stone used to form a coping **2** Also called: **capstone** the stone at the top of a building, wall, etc

copier ('kɒpɪə) *n* a person or device that copies

copilot ('kəʊˌpaɪlət) *n* a second or relief pilot of an aircraft

coping ('kəʊpɪŋ) *n* the sloping top course of a wall, usually made of masonry or brick

coping saw *n* a handsaw with a U-shaped frame used for cutting curves in a material too thick for a fret saw

copious ('kəʊpɪəs) *adj* **1** abundant; extensive in quantity **2** having or providing an abundant supply **3** full of words, ideas, etc; profuse [c14: from Latin *cōpiōsus* well supplied, from *cōpia* abundance, from *ops* wealth] >'copiousness *n*

coplanar (kəʊ'pleɪnə) *adj* lying in the same plane: *coplanar lines* >ˌcopla'narity *n*

Copland ('kəʊplənd) *n* **Aaron**. 1900–90, US composer of orchestral and chamber music, ballets, and film music

Copley ('kɒplɪ) *n* **John Singleton**. 1738–1815, US painter

cop off *vb* (*intr, adverb*) **cop off with** *Brit informal* to establish an amorous or sexual relationship with

copolymer (kəʊ'pɒlɪmə) *n* a chemical compound of high molecular weight formed by uniting the molecules of two or more different compounds (monomers)

cop out *slang* ▷ *vb* **1** (*intr, adverb*) to fail to assume responsibility or to commit oneself ▷ *n* **cop-out 2** an instance of avoiding responsibility or commitment [c20: probably from COP¹]

copper¹ ('kɒpə) *n* **1** a malleable ductile reddish metallic element occurring as the free metal, copper glance, and copper pyrites: used as an electrical and thermal conductor and in such alloys as brass and bronze. Symbol: Cu; atomic no: 29; atomic wt: 63.546; valency: 1 or 2; relative density: 8.96; melting pt: 1084.87±0.2°C; boiling pt: 2563°C. Related adjs: **cupric, cuprous 2 a** the reddish-brown colour of copper **b** (*as adjective*): *copper hair* **3** *informal* any copper or bronze coin **4** *chiefly Brit* a large vessel, formerly of copper, used for boiling or washing **5** any of various small widely distributed butterflies of the genera *Lycaena, Heodes*, etc, typically having reddish-brown wings: family *Lycaenidae* ▷ *vb* **6** (*tr*) to coat or cover with copper [Old English *coper*, from Latin *Cyprium aes* Cyprian metal, from Greek *Kupris* Cyprus]

copper² ('kɒpə) *n* a slang word for **policeman** Often shortened to: cop [c19: from COP¹ (vb) + -ER¹]

copperas ('kɒpərəs) *n* a less common name for **ferrous sulphate** [c14: *coperose*, via Old French from Medieval Latin *cuperosa*, perhaps originally in the phrase *aqua cuprosa* copper water]

copper beech *n* a cultivated variety of European beech that has dark purple leaves

Copper Belt *n* a region of Central Africa, along the border between Zambia and the Democratic Republic of Congo: rich deposits of copper

copper-bottomed *adj* reliable, esp financially reliable [from the former practice of coating the bottoms of ships with copper to prevent the timbers rotting]

copper-fasten *vb* (*tr*) *Irish* to make (a bargain or agreement) binding

copperhead ('kɒpə,hɛd) *n* 1 a venomous reddish-brown snake, *Agkistrodon contortrix*, of the eastern US: family *Crotalidae* (pit vipers) 2 a venomous reddish-brown Australian elapid snake, *Denisonia superba*

copperplate ('kɒpə,pleɪt) *n* 1 a polished copper plate on which a design has been etched or engraved 2 a print taken from such a plate 3 a fine handwriting based upon that used on copperplate engravings

copper pyrites *n* (*functioning as singular*) another name for **chalcopyrite**

coppersmith ('kɒpə,smɪθ) *n* a person who works copper or copper alloys

copper sulphate *n* a copper salt found naturally as chalcanthite and made by the action of sulphuric acid on copper oxide. It usually exists as blue crystals of the pentahydrate that form a white anhydrous powder when heated: used as a mordant, in electroplating, and in plant sprays. Formula: $CuSO_4$

coppice ('kɒpɪs) *n* 1 a thicket or dense growth of small trees or bushes, esp one regularly trimmed back to stumps so that a continual supply of small poles and firewood is obtained ▷ *vb* 2 (*tr*) to trim back (trees or bushes) to form a coppice [c14: from Old French *copeiz*, from *couper* to cut] > 'coppiced *adj*

Coppola ('kɒpələ) *n* **Francis Ford**. born 1939, US film director. His films include *The Godfather* (1972), *Apocalypse Now* (1979), *Tucker* (1988), and *The Rainmaker* (1999)

copra ('kɒprə) *n* the dried, oil-yielding kernel of the coconut [c16: from Portuguese, from Malayalam *koppara*, probably from Hindi *khoprā* coconut]

copro- *or before a vowel* **copr-** *combining form* indicating dung or obscenity [from Greek *kopros* dung]

copse (kɒps) *n* another word for **coppice** (sense 1) [c16: by shortening from COPPICE]

Copt (kɒpt) *n* 1 a member of the Coptic Church 2 an Egyptian descended from the ancient Egyptians [c17: from Arabic *qubt* Copts, from Coptic *kyptios* Egyptian, from Greek *Aiguptios*, from *Aiguptos* Egypt]

Coptic ('kɒptɪk) *n* 1 an Afro-Asiatic language, written in the Greek alphabet but descended from ancient Egyptian. It was extinct as a spoken language by about 1600 AD but survives in the Coptic Church ▷ *adj* 2 of or relating to this language 3 of or relating to the Copts

Coptic Church *n* the ancient Christian Church of Egypt

copula ('kɒpjʊlə) *n*, *pl* -las *or* -lae (-,liː) 1 a verb, such as *be*, *seem*, *or taste*, that is used merely to identify or link the subject with the complement of a sentence. Copulas may serve to link nouns (or pronouns), as in *he became king*, nouns (or pronouns) and adjectival complements, as in *sugar tastes sweet*, or nouns (or pronouns) and adverbial complements, as in *John is in jail* 2 anything that serves as a link [c17: from Latin: bond, connection, from *co*- together + *apere* to fasten] > 'copular *adj*

copulate ('kɒpjʊ,leɪt) *vb* (*intr*) to perform sexual intercourse [c17: from Latin *copulāre* to join together; see COPULA] > ,copu'lation *n* > 'copulatory *adj*

copulative ('kɒpjʊlətɪv) *adj* 1 serving to join or unite 2 of or characteristic of copulation 3 *grammar* (of a verb) having the nature of a copula

copy ('kɒpɪ) *n*, *pl* copies 1 an imitation or reproduction of an original 2 a single specimen of something that

occurs in a multiple edition, such as a book, article, etc 3 **a** matter to be reproduced in print **b** written matter or text as distinct from graphic material in books, newspapers, etc 4 the words used to present a promotional message in an advertisement 5 *journalism informal* suitable material for an article or story: *disasters are always good copy* 6 *archaic* a model to be copied, esp an example of penmanship ▷ *vb* copies, copying, copied 7 (when *tr*, often foll by *out*) to make a copy or reproduction of (an original) 8 (*tr*) to imitate as a model [c14: from Medieval Latin *cōpia* an imitation, something copied, from Latin: abundance, riches; see COPIOUS]

copybook ('kɒpɪ,bʊk) *n* 1 a book of specimens, esp of penmanship, for imitation 2 *chiefly US* a book for or containing documents 3 blot one's copybook *informal* to spoil one's reputation by making a mistake, offending against social customs, etc 4 (*modifier*) trite or unoriginal

copycat ('kɒpɪ,kæt) *n informal* **a** a person, esp a child, who imitates or copies another **b** (*as modifier*): *copycat murders*

copyhold ('kɒpɪ,həʊld) *n law* (formerly) a tenure less than freehold of land in England evidenced by a copy of the Court roll

copyist ('kɒpɪɪst) *n* 1 a person who makes written copies; transcriber 2 a person who imitates or copies

copyreader ('kɒpɪ,riːdə) *n US* a person who edits and prepares newspaper copy for publication; subeditor

copyright ('kɒpɪ,raɪt) *n* 1 the exclusive right to produce copies and to control an original literary, musical, or artistic work, granted by law for a specified number of years (in Britain, usually 70 years from the death of the author, composer, etc, or from the date of publication if later) ▷ *adj* 2 (of a work, etc) subject to or controlled by copyright ▷ *vb* 3 (*tr*) to take out a copyright on

copy typist *n* a typist whose job is to type from written or typed drafts rather than dictation

copywriter ('kɒpɪ,raɪtə) *n* a person employed to write advertising copy > 'copy,writing *n*

coquet (kəʊ'kɛt, kɒ-) *vb* -quets, -quetting, -quetted (*intr*) 1 to behave flirtatiously 2 to dally or trifle [c17: from French: a gallant, literally: a little cock, from *coq* cock] > coquetry ('kəʊkɪtrɪ, 'kɒk-) *n*

coquette (kəʊ'kɛt, kɒ'kɛt) *n* 1 a woman who flirts 2 any hummingbird of the genus *Lophornis*, esp the crested Brazilian species *L. magnifica* [c17: from French, feminine of COQUET] > co'quettish *adj* > co'quettishness *n*

Cor. *Bible abbreviation* Corinthians

coracle ('kɒrəkəl) *n* a small roundish boat made of waterproofed hides stretched over a wicker frame [c16: from Welsh *corwgl*; related to Irish *curach* boat]

coracoid ('kɒrə,kɔɪd) *n* a paired ventral bone of the pectoral girdle in vertebrates. In mammals it is reduced to a peg (the **coracoid process**) on the scapula [c18: from New Latin *coracoīdēs*, from Greek *korakoeidēs* like a raven, curved like a raven's beak, from *korax* raven]

coral ('kɒrəl) *n* 1 any marine mostly colonial coelenterate of the class *Anthozoa* having a calcareous, horny, or soft skeleton 2 **a** the calcareous or horny material forming the skeleton of certain of these animals **b** (*as modifier*): *a coral reef* 3 a rocklike aggregation of certain of these animals or their skeletons, forming an island or reef 4 **a** an object made of coral, esp a piece of jewellery **b** (*as modifier*): *a coral necklace* 5 **a** a deep-pink to yellowish-pink colour **b** (*as adjective*): *coral lipstick* 6 the roe of a lobster or crab, which becomes pink when cooked [c14: from Old French, from Latin *corāllium*, from Greek *korallion*, probably of Semitic origin]

coral reef *n* a marine ridge or reef consisting of coral and other organic material consolidated into limestone

coralroot ('kɒrəl,ruːt) *n* any N temperate leafless orchid of the genus *Corallorhiza*, with small yellow-green or purple flowers and branched roots resembling coral

Coral Sea *n* the SW arm of the Pacific, between Australia, New Guinea, and Vanuatu

coral snake *n* 1 any venomous elapid snake of the genus *Micrurus* and related genera, of tropical and subtropical America, marked with red, black, yellow, and white transverse bands 2 any of various other brightly coloured elapid snakes of Africa and SE Asia

coral tree *n* any of various thorny, tropical trees of the leguminous genus *Erythrina*, having bright red flowers and reddish shiny seeds

coral trout *n* an Australian fish, *Plectropomus maculatus*, of the Great Barrier Reef which is an important food fish

cor anglais (ˈkɔːr ˈɑːŋgleɪ) *n*, *pl* **cors anglais** (ˈkɔːz ˈɑːŋgleɪ) *music* a woodwind instrument, the alto of the oboe family. It is a transposing instrument in F. Range: two and a half octaves upwards from E on the third space of the bass staff [C19: from French: English horn]

corbel (ˈkɔːbəl) *architect* ▷ *n* **1** Also called: **truss** a bracket, usually of stone or brick ▷ *vb* **-bels, -belling, -belled** *or US* **-bels, -beling, -beled 2** (*tr*) to lay (a stone or brick) so that it forms a corbel [C15: from Old French, literally: a little raven, from Medieval Latin *corvellus*, from Latin *corvus* raven]

corbie (ˈkɔːbɪ; *Scot* ˈkɔːrbɪ) *n* a Scot name for: **raven¹**, **crow¹** [C15: from Old French *corbin*, from Latin *corvīnus* CORVINE]

corbie-step *or* **corbel step** *n architect* any of a set of steps on the top of a gable. Also called: **crow step**

Corbusier (French kɔrbyzje) *n* **Le.** See **Le Corbusier**

Corcovado *n* **1** (*Spanish* korkoˈβaðo) a volcano in S Chile, in the Andes. Height: 2300 m (7546 ft) **2** (*Portuguese* korkuˈvadu) a mountain in SE Brazil, in SW Rio de Janeiro city, famous for a massive statue of Christ the Redeemer. Height of mountain: 704 m (2310 ft)

Corcyra (kɔːˈsaɪərə) *n* the ancient name for **Corfu**

cord (kɔːd) *n* **1** string or thin rope made of several twisted strands **2** a length of woven or twisted strands of silk, etc, sewn on clothing or used as a belt **3** a ribbed fabric, esp corduroy **4** *US & Canadian* a flexible insulated electric cable, used esp to connect appliances to mains. Also called (in Britain and certain other countries): **flex 5** *anatomy* any part resembling a string or rope: *the spinal cord* **6** a unit of volume for measuring cut wood, equal to 128 cubic feet ▷ *vb* (*tr*) **7** to bind or furnish with a cord or cords [C13: from Old French *corde*, from Latin *chorda* cord, from Greek *khordē*; see CHORD¹] >'cord,like *adj*

cordage (ˈkɔːdɪdʒ) *n* **1** *nautical* the lines and rigging of a vessel **2** an amount of wood measured in cords

cordate (ˈkɔːdeɪt) *adj* heart-shaped

Corday (French kɔrdɛ) *n* **Charlotte** (ʃarlɔt), full name *Marie Anne Charlotte Corday d'Armont*. 1768–93, French Girondist revolutionary, who assassinated Marat

corded (ˈkɔːdɪd) *adj* **1** bound or fastened with cord **2** (of a fabric) ribbed **3** (of muscles) standing out like cords

cordial (ˈkɔːdɪəl) *adj* **1** warm and friendly: *a cordial greeting* **2** giving heart; stimulating ▷ *n* **3** a drink with a fruit base, usually sold in concentrated form and diluted with water before being drunk: *lime cordial* **4** another word for **liqueur** [C14: from Medieval Latin *cordiālis*, from Latin *cor* heart] >'cordially *adv*

cordiality (ˌkɔːdɪˈælɪtɪ) *n*, *pl* **-ties** warmth of feeling

cordillera (ˌkɔːdɪlˈjeərə) *n* a series of parallel ranges of mountains, esp in the northwestern US [C18: from Spanish, from *cordilla*, literally: a little cord, from *cuerda* mountain range, CORD]

Cordilleras (ˌkɔːdɪlˈjeərəz; *Spanish* korðiˈʎeras) *pl n* the Cordilleras the complex of mountain ranges on the W side of the Americas, extending from Alaska to Cape Horn and including the Andes and the Rocky Mountains

cordite (ˈkɔːdaɪt) *n* any of various explosive materials used for propelling bullets, shells, etc, containing cellulose nitrate, sometimes mixed with nitroglycerine, plasticizers, and stabilizers [C19: from CORD + -ITE¹, referring to its stringy appearance]

cordless (ˈkɔːdlɪs) *adj* (of an electrical device) operated by an internal battery so that no connection to mains supply or other apparatus is needed

cordless telephone *n* a portable battery-powered telephone with a short-range radio link to a fixed base unit

Córdoba¹ (*Spanish* ˈkɔrðoβa) *n* **1** a city in central Argentina: university (1613). Pop: 1 592 000 (2005 est) **2** a city in S Spain, on the Guadalquivir River: centre of Moorish Spain (711–1236). Pop: 318 628 (2003 est). English name: **Cordova**

Córdoba² *or* **Córdova** (*Spanish* ˈkɔrðoβa) *n* **Francisco Fernández de** (franˈθisko ferˈnandeθ de). died 1518, Spanish soldier and explorer, who discovered Yucatán

cordon (ˈkɔːdən) *n* **1** a chain of police, soldiers, ships, etc, stationed around an area **2** a ribbon worn as insignia of honour or rank **3** a cord or ribbon worn as an ornament or fastening **4** Also called: **string course, belt course, table** *architect* an ornamental projecting band or continuous moulding along a wall **5** *horticulture* a form of fruit tree consisting of a single stem bearing fruiting spurs, produced by cutting back all lateral branches ▷ *vb* **6** (*tr*; often foll by *off*) to put or form a cordon (around); close (off) [C16: from Old French, literally: a little cord, from *corde* string, CORD]

cordon bleu (French kɔrdɔ̃ blø) *n* **1** *French history* the sky-blue ribbon worn by members of the highest order of knighthood under the Bourbon monarchy **2** any very high distinction ▷ *adj* **3** of or denoting food prepared to a very high standard [French, literally: blue ribbon]

cordon sanitaire *French* (kɔrdɔ̃ saniter) *n* **1** a guarded line serving to cut off an infected area **2** a line of buffer states, esp when protecting a nation from infiltration or attack [C19: literally: sanitary line]

Cordova (ˈkɔːdəvə) *n* the English name for **Córdoba¹** (sense 2)

cordovan (ˈkɔːdəvən) *n* a fine leather now made principally from horsehide, isolated from the skin layers above and below it and tanned [C16: from Spanish *cordobán* (n), from *cordobán* (adj) of CÓRDOBA]

Cordovan (ˈkɔːdəvən) *n* **1** a native or inhabitant of Córdoba, Spain ▷ *adj* **2** of or relating to Córdoba, Spain

cords (kɔːdz) *pl n* trousers, esp jeans, made of corduroy

corduroy (ˈkɔːdəˌrɔɪ, ˌkɔːdəˈrɔɪ) *n* a heavy cotton pile fabric with lengthways ribs [C18: perhaps from the proper name *Corderoy*]

cordwainer (ˈkɔːdˌweɪnə) *n archaic* a shoemaker or worker in cordovan leather

cordwood (ˈkɔːdˌwʊd) *n* wood that has been cut into lengths of four feet so that it can be stacked in cords

core (kɔː) *n* **1** the central part of certain fleshy fruits, such as the apple or pear, consisting of the seeds and supporting parts **2** the central, innermost, or most essential part of something: *the core of the argument* **3** a piece of magnetic material, such as soft iron, placed inside the windings of an electromagnet or transformer to intensify and direct the magnetic field **4** *geology* the central part of the earth, beneath the mantle, consisting mainly of iron and nickel, which has an inner solid part surrounded by an outer liquid part **5** a cylindrical sample of rock, soil, etc, obtained by the use of a hollow drill **6** shaped body of material (in metal casting usually of sand) supported inside a mould to form a cavity of predetermined shape in the finished casting **7** *physics* the region of a nuclear reactor in which the reaction takes place **8** *computing* **a** a ferrite ring formerly used in a computer memory to store one bit of information **b** (*as modifier*): *core memory* **9** *archaeol* a lump of stone or flint from which flakes or blades have been removed **10** *physics* the nucleus together with all complete electron shells of an atom ▷ *vb* **11** (*tr*) to remove the core from (fruit) [C14: of uncertain origin]

coreligionist (ˌkəʊrɪˈlɪdʒənɪst) *n* an adherent of the same religion as another

Corelli (kɒˈrɛlɪ) *n* **1** (*Italian* koˈrɛlli) **Arcangelo** (arˈkandʒelo). 1653–1713, Italian violinist and composer of sonatas and concerti grossi **2 Marie**, real name *Mary Mackay*. 1854–1924, British novelist. Her melodramatic works include *The Sorrows of Satan* (1895) and *The Murder of Delicia* (1896)

coreopsis (ˌkɒrɪˈɒpsɪs) *n* any plant of the genus *Coreopsis*, of America and tropical Africa, cultivated for their yellow, brown, or yellow-and-red daisy-like flowers: family *Asteraceae* (composites) [C18: from New Latin, from Greek *koris* bedbug + -OPSIS; so called from the appearance of the seed]

co-respondent (ˌkəʊrɪˈspɒndənt) *n law* a person cited in divorce proceedings, who is alleged to have committed adultery with the respondent

core strength *n* the strength of the underlying muscles of the torso, which help determine posture

core subjects *pl n Brit education* three foundation subjects (English, mathematics, and science) that are compulsory throughout each key stage in the National Curriculum

core time *n* See **flexitime**

corf (kɔːf), *pl* **corves** *Brit* a wagon or basket used formerly in mines [c14: from Middle Dutch *corf* or Middle Low German *korf*, probably from Latin *corbis* basket]

Corfu (kɔːˈfuː) *n* **1** an island in the Ionian Sea, in the Ionian Islands: forms, with neighbouring islands, a department of Greece. Pop: 107 879 (2001). Area: 641 sq km (247 sq miles) **2** a port on E Corfu island. Pop (municipality): 41 532 (2001) Modern Greek name: **Kérkyra**. Ancient name: **Corcyra**

corgi (ˈkɔːgɪ) *n* either of two long-bodied short-legged sturdy breeds of dog, the Cardigan and the Pembroke [c20: from Welsh, from *cor* dwarf + *ci* dog]

Cori (ˈkɔːrɪ) *n* **Carl Ferdinand**. 1896–1984, US biochemist, born in Bohemia; shared a Nobel prize for physiology or medicine (1947) with his wife **Gerty Theresa Radnitz Cori** (1896–1957) and Bernardo Houssay, for elucidating the stages of glycolysis

coriander (ˌkɒrɪˈændə) *n* a European umbelliferous plant, *Coriandrum sativum*, widely cultivated for its aromatic seeds and leaves, used in flavouring food, etc. US and Canadian name: **cilantro** [c14: from Old French *coriandre*, from Latin *coriandrum*, from Greek *koriannon*, of uncertain origin]

Corinth (ˈkɒrɪnθ) *n* **1** a port in S Greece, in the NE Peloponnese: the modern town is near the site of the ancient city, the largest and richest of the city-states after Athens. Pop (municipality): 36 991 (2001) **2** a region of ancient Greece, occupying most of the Isthmus of Corinth and part of the NE Peloponnese **3 Gulf of Corinth** Also called: **Gulf of Lepanto** an inlet of the Ionian Sea between the Peloponnese and central Greece **4 Isthmus of Corinth** a narrow strip of land between the Gulf of Corinth and the Saronic Gulf: crossed by the **Corinth Canal** making navigation possible between the gulfs

Corinthian (kəˈrɪnθɪən) *adj* **1** of, characteristic of, or relating to Corinth **2** of, denoting, or relating to one of the five classical orders of architecture: characterized by a bell-shaped capital having carved ornaments based on acanthus leaves **3** given to luxury; dissolute ▷ *n* **4** a native or inhabitant of Corinth

Coriolanus (ˌkɒrɪəˈleɪnəs) *n* **Gaius Marcius** (ˈgaɪəs ˈmɑːsɪəs). 5th century BC, a legendary Roman general, who allegedly led an army against Rome but was dissuaded from conquering it by his mother and wife

Coriolis force (ˌkɒrɪˈəʊlɪs) *n* a fictitious force used to explain a deflection in the path of a body moving in latitude relative to the earth when observed from the earth. The deflection (**Coriolis effect**) is due to the earth's rotation and is to the east when the motion is towards a pole [c19: named after Gaspard G. *Coriolis* (1792–1843), French civil engineer]

corium (ˈkɔːrɪəm) *n, pl* **-ria** (-rɪə) Also called: **derma, dermis** the deep inner layer of the skin, beneath the epidermis, containing connective tissue, blood vessels, and fat [c19: from Latin: rind, skin, leather]

cork (kɔːk) *n* **1** the thick light porous outer bark of the cork oak, used widely as an insulator and for stoppers for bottles, casks, etc. Related adj: **suberose 2** a piece of cork or other material used as a stopper **3** an angling float **4** Also called: **phellem** *botany* a protective layer of dead impermeable cells on the outside of the stems and roots of woody plants, produced by the outer layer of the cork cambium ▷ *adj* **5** made of cork. ▷ *vb* (*tr*) **6** to stop up (a bottle, cask, etc) with or as if with a cork; fit with a cork **7** (often foll by *up*) to restrain **8** to black (the face, hands, etc) with burnt cork [c14: probably from Arabic *qurq*, from Latin *cortex* bark, especially of the cork oak] ▷ **ˈcork,like** *adj*

Cork (kɔːk) *n* **1** a county of SW Republic of Ireland, in

Munster province: crossed by ridges of low mountains; scenic coastline. County town: Cork. Pop: 447 829 (2002). Area: 7459 sq km (2880 sq miles) **2** a city and port in S Republic of Ireland, county town of Co Cork, at the mouth of the River Lee: seat of the University College of Cork (1849). Pop: 186 239 (2002)

corkage (ˈkɔːkɪdʒ) *n* a charge made at a restaurant for serving wine, etc, bought off the premises

corked (kɔːkt) *adj* Also called: **corky** (of a wine) tainted through having a cork containing excess tannin

corker (ˈkɔːkə) *n slang* **a** something or somebody striking or outstanding **b** an irrefutable remark that puts an end to discussion

cork oak *n* an evergreen Mediterranean oak tree, *Quercus suber*, with a porous outer bark from which cork is obtained

corkscrew (ˈkɔːkˌskruː) *n* **1** a device for drawing corks from bottles, typically consisting of a pointed metal spiral attached to a handle or screw mechanism **2** (*modifier*) resembling a corkscrew in shape ▷ *vb* **3** to move or cause to move in a spiral or zigzag course

corm (kɔːm) *n* an organ of vegetative reproduction in plants such as the crocus, consisting of a globular stem base swollen with food and surrounded by papery scale leaves [c19: from New Latin *cormus*, from Greek *kormos* tree trunk from which the branches have been lopped]

cormorant (ˈkɔːmərənt) *n* any aquatic bird of the family *Phalacrocoracidae*, of coastal and inland waters, having a dark plumage, a long neck and body, and a slender hooked beak: order *Pelecaniformes* (pelicans, etc) [c13: from Old French *cormareng*, from *corp* raven, from Latin *corvus* + -*mareng* of the sea, from Latin *mare* sea]

corn¹ (kɔːn) *n* **1** *Brit* **a** any of various cereal plants, esp the predominant crop of a region, such as wheat in England and oats in Scotland and Ireland **b** the seeds of such plants, esp after harvesting **c** a single seed of such plants; a grain **2** Also called: **Indian corn** US and Canadian equivalent: **maize a** a tall annual grass, *Zea mays* cultivated for its yellow edible grains, which develop on a spike **b** the grain of this plant, used for food, fodder, and as a source of oil **3** *slang* an idea, song, etc, regarded as banal or sentimental ▷ *vb* (*tr*) **4** to feed (animals) with corn, esp oats **5 a** to preserve in brine **b** to salt [Old English *corn*; related to Old Norse, Old High German *corn*, Gothic *kaúrn*, Latin *grānum*, Sanskrit *jīrná* fragile]

corn² (kɔːn) *n* **1** a hardening or thickening of the skin around a central point in the foot, caused by pressure or friction **2 tread on someone's corns** *Brit informal* to offend or hurt someone by touching on a sensitive subject or encroaching on his privileges [c15: from Old French *corne* horn, from Latin *cornū*]

corn borer *n* the larva of the pyralid moth *Pyrausta nubilalis*, native to S and Central Europe: in E North America a serious pest of maize

corn bread *n* a kind of bread made from maize meal. Also called: **Indian bread**

corn bunting *n* a heavily built European songbird, *Emberiza calandra*, with a streaked brown plumage: family *Emberizidae* (buntings)

corncob (ˈkɔːnˌkɒb) *n* the core of an ear of maize, to which kernels are attached

corncob pipe *n* a pipe made from a dried corncob

corncockle (ˈkɔːnˌkɒkᵊl) *n* a European caryophyllaceous plant, *Agrostemma githago*, that has reddish-purple flowers and grows in cornfields and by roadsides

corncrake (ˈkɔːnˌkreɪk) *n* a common Eurasian rail, *Crex crex*, of fields and meadows, with a buff speckled plumage and reddish wings

corn dolly *n* a decorative figure made by plaiting straw

cornea (ˈkɔːnɪə) *n, pl* **-neas** (-nɪəz) or **-neae** (-nɪˌiː) the convex transparent membrane that forms the anterior covering of the eyeball and is continuous with the sclera [c14: from Medieval Latin *cornea tēla* horny web, from Latin *cornū* HORN] ▷ **ˈcorneal** *adj*

corned (kɔːnd) *adj* (esp of beef) cooked and then preserved or pickled in salt or brine, now often canned

Corneille (French kɔrnɛj) *n* **Pierre** (pjɛr). 1606–84, French tragic dramatist often regarded as the founder of French classical drama. His plays include *Médée* (1635), *Le Cid*

(1636), Horace (1640), and *Polyeucte* (1642)

cornel ('kɔ:n^əl) *n* any cornaceous plant of the genus *Cornus*, such as the dogwood and dwarf cornel [c16: probably from Middle Low German *kornelle*, from Old French *cornelle*, from Vulgar Latin *cornicula* (unattested), from Latin *cornum* cornel cherry, from *cornus* cornel tree]

cornelian (kɔ:'ni:lɪən) *n* a variant spelling of **carnelian**

corner ('kɔ:nə) *n* **1** the place, position, or angle formed by the meeting of two converging lines or surfaces **2** a projecting angle of a solid object or figure **3** the place where two streets meet **4** any small, secluded, secret, or private place **5** a dangerous or awkward position, esp from which escape is difficult: *a tight corner* **6** any part, region or place, esp a remote place **7** something used to protect or mark a corner, as of the hard cover of a book **8** *commerce* a monopoly over the supply of a commodity so that its market price can be controlled **9** *soccer, hockey* a free kick or shot from the corner of the field, taken against a defending team when the ball goes out of play over their goal line after last touching one team's players **10** either of two opposite angles of a boxing ring in which the opponents take their rests **11** cut corners to do something in the easiest and shortest way, esp at the expense of high standards **12** turn the corner to pass the critical point (in an illness, etc) **13** (*modifier*) located on a corner: *a corner shop* ▷ *vb* **14** (*tr*) to manoeuvre (a person or animal) into a position from which escape is difficult or impossible **15** (*tr*) **a** to acquire enough of (a commodity) to attain control of the market **b** Also called: engross to attain control of (a market) in such a manner **16** (*intr*) (in soccer, etc) to take a corner [c13: from Old French *corniere*, from Latin *cornū* point, extremity, HORN]

Corner *n* **the Corner** *informal* an area in central Australia, at the junction of the borders of Queensland and South Australia

cornerback ('kɔ:nə,bæk) *n* *American football* a defensive back

cornerstone ('kɔ:nə,stəun) *n* **1** a stone at the corner of a wall, uniting two intersecting walls; quoin **2** a stone placed at the corner of a building during a ceremony to mark the start of construction **3** a person or thing of prime importance; basis: *the cornerstone of the whole argument*

cornerwise ('kɔ:nə,waɪz) *or* **cornerways** ('kɔ:nə,weɪz) *adv, adj* with a corner in front; diagonally

cornet ('kɔ:nɪt) *n* **1** Also called: cornet à pistons ('kɔ:nɪt ə 'pɪstənz; *French* kɔrnɛ a pistɔ̃) a three-valved brass instrument of the trumpet family. Written range: about two and a half octaves upwards from E below middle C. It is a transposing instrument in B flat or A **2** a person who plays the cornet **3** a cone-shaped paper container for sweets, etc **4** *Brit* a cone-shaped wafer container for ice cream **5** (formerly) the lowest rank of commissioned cavalry officer in the British army **6** the large white headdress of some nuns [c14: from Old French, from *corn*, from Latin *cornū* HORN] > cornetist *or* cornettist (kɔ:'nɛtɪst) *n*

corn exchange *n* a building where corn is bought and sold

cornfield ('kɔ:n,fi:ld) *n* a field planted with cereal crops

cornflakes ('kɔ:n,fleɪks) *pl n* a breakfast cereal made from toasted maize, eaten with milk, sugar, etc

cornflour ('kɔ:n,flauə) *n* a fine starchy maize flour, used esp for thickening sauces. US and Canadian name: cornstarch

cornflower ('kɔ:n,flauə) *n* a Eurasian herbaceous plant, *Centaurea cyanus*, with blue, purple, pink, or white flowers, formerly a common weed in cornfields: family *Asteraceae* (composites). See also **bachelor's-buttons**

Cornforth ('kɔ:n,fɔ:θ) *n* Sir **John Warcup**. born 1917, Australian chemist, who shared the 1975 Nobel prize for chemistry with Vladimir Prelog for their work on stereochemistry

cornice ('kɔ:nɪs) *n* **1** *architect* **a** the top projecting mouldings of an entablature **b** a continuous horizontal projecting course or moulding at the top of a wall, building, etc **2** an overhanging ledge of snow formed by the wind on the edge of a mountain ridge, cliff, or corrie

[c16: from Old French, from Italian, perhaps from Latin *cornix* crow, but influenced also by Latin *corōnis* decorative flourish used by scribes, from Greek *korōnis*, from *korōnē* curved object, CROWN]

corniche ('kɔ:nɪʃ) *n* a coastal road, esp one built into the face of a cliff [c19: from *corniche road*, originally the coastal road between Nice and Monte Carlo; see CORNICE]

Cornish ('kɔ:nɪʃ) *adj* **1** of, relating to, or characteristic of Cornwall, its inhabitants, their former language, or their present-day dialect of English ▷ *n* **2** a former language of Cornwall, belonging to the S Celtic branch of the Indo-European family and closely related to Breton: extinct by 1800 **3** the Cornish (*functioning as plural*) the natives or inhabitants of Cornwall > 'Cornishman *n* > 'Cornishwoman *fem n*

Cornish pasty ('pæstɪ) *n* *cookery* a pastry case with a filling of meat and vegetables

corn meal *n* meal made from maize. Also called: Indian meal

Corno (*Italian* 'kɔrno) *n* **Monte Corno** ('monte) a mountain in central Italy: the highest peak in the Apennines. Height: 2912 m (9554 ft)

corn salad *n* any valerianaceous plant of the genus *Valerianella*, esp the European species *V. locusta*, which often grows in cornfields and whose leaves are sometimes used in salads. Also called: lamb's lettuce

cornstarch ('kɔ:n,stɑ:tʃ) *n* *US & Canadian* a fine starchy maize flour, used esp for thickening sauces. Also called (in Britain and certain other countries): cornflour

cornucopia (,kɔ:nju'kəupɪə) *n* **1** a representation of such a horn in painting, sculpture, etc, overflowing with fruit, vegetables, etc; horn of plenty **2** a great abundance; overflowing supply **3** a horn-shaped container [c16: from Late Latin, from Latin *cornūcōpiae* horn of plenty] > ,cornu'copian *adj*

Cornwall ('kɔ:n,wɔ:l, -wəl) *n* a county of SW England: hilly, with a deeply indented coastline. Administrative centre: Truro. Pop: 513 500 (2003 est). Area: 3564 sq km (1376 sq miles)

Cornwallis (kɔ:n'wɒlɪs) *n* **Charles**, 1st Marquis Cornwallis. 1738–1805, British general in the War of American Independence: commanded forces defeated at Yorktown (1781): defeated Tipu Sahib (1791): governor general of Bengal (1786–93, 1805): negotiated the Treaty of Amiens (1801)

Cornwell ('kɔ:n,wɛl) *n* **Patricia D(aniels)**. born 1956, US crime novelist; her novels, many of which feature the pathologist Dr Kay Scarpetta, include *Postmortem* (1990), *The Last Precinct* (2000), and *Isle of Dogs* (2002)

corn whisky *n* whisky made from maize

corny ('kɔ:nɪ) *adj* cornier, corniest *slang* **1** trite or banal **2** sentimental or mawkish **3** abounding in corn [c16 (c20 in the sense rustic, banal): from CORN¹ + -Y¹]

corolla (kə'rɒlə) *n* the petals of a flower collectively, forming an inner floral envelope [c17 dim. of L *corōna* crown]

corollary (kə'rɒlərɪ) *n*, *pl* -laries **1** a proposition that follows directly from the proof of another proposition **2** an obvious deduction **3** a natural consequence or result [c14: from Latin *corollārium* money paid for a garland, from Latin *corolla* garland, from *corōna* CROWN]

Coromandel Coast (,kɒrə'mændəl) *n* the SE coast of India, along the Bay of Bengal, extending from Point Calimere to the mouth of the Krishna River

corona (kə'rəunə) *n*, *pl* -nas *or* -nae (-ni:) **1** a circle of light around a luminous body, usually the moon **2** Also called: aureole the outermost region of the sun's atmosphere, visible as a faint halo during a solar eclipse **3** *architect* the flat vertical face of a cornice just above the soffit **4** a circular chandelier suspended from the roof of a church **5** *botany* **a** the trumpet-shaped part of the corolla of daffodils and similar plants; the crown **b** a crown of leafy outgrowths from inside the petals of some flowers **6** *anatomy* a crownlike structure, such as the top of the head **7** a long cigar with blunt ends **8** *physics* short for **corona discharge** [c16: from Latin: crown, from Greek *korōnē* anything curved; related to Greek *korōnis* wreath, *korax* crow, Latin *curvus* curved]

coronach ('kɒrənəx, -nək) n Scot or Irish a dirge or lamentation for the dead [c16: from Scottish Gaelic corranach; related to Irish rānadh a crying]

corona discharge n an electrical discharge appearing on and around the surface of a charged conductor, caused by ionization of the surrounding gas. Also called: corona See also **Saint Elmo's fire**

coronary ('kɒrənərı) adj 1 anatomy designating blood vessels, nerves, ligaments, etc, that encircle a part or structure ▷ n, pl -naries 2 short for **coronary thrombosis** [c17: from Latin corōnārius belonging to a wreath or crown; see CORONA]

coronary artery n either of two arteries branching from the aorta and supplying blood to the heart

coronary bypass n the surgical bypass of a narrowed or blocked coronary artery by grafting a section of a healthy blood vessel taken from another part of the patient's body

coronary heart disease n any heart disorder caused by disease of the coronary arteries

coronary thrombosis n a condition of interrupted blood flow to the heart due to a blood clot in a coronary artery, usually as a consequence of atherosclerosis: characterized by intense pain

coronation (,kɒrə'neɪʃən) n the act or ceremony of crowning a monarch [c14: from Old French, from coroner to crown, from Latin corōnāre]

coronation chicken n (sometimes capitals) a dish of cold cooked chicken in a mild creamy curry sauce [c20: so-called because it was served at the coronation lunch of Elizabeth II (born 1926), queen of Great Britain and Northern Ireland from 1952]

coronavirus (kə'rəʊnə,vaɪrəs) n a type of airborne virus accounting for 10-30% of all colds [c20: so-called because of their corona-like appearance in electron micrographs]

coroner ('kɒrənə) n a public official responsible for the investigation of violent, sudden, or suspicious deaths and inquiries into treasure trove. The investigation (**coroner's inquest**) is held in the presence of a jury (**coroner's jury**) [c14: from Anglo-French corouner officer in charge of the pleas of the Crown, from Old French corone CROWN] >'coroner,ship n

coronet ('kɒrənɪt) n 1 any small crown, esp one worn by princes or peers as a mark of rank 2 a woman's jewelled circlet for the head 3 the margin between the skin of a horse's pastern and the horn of the hoof 4 the knob at the base of a deer's antler [c15: from Old French coronete a little crown, from corone CROWN]

Corot (French kɔro) n **Jean Baptiste Camille** (ʒã batist kamij). 1796– 1875, French landscape and portrait painter

co-routine ('kəʊruː,tiːn) n computing a section of a computer program similar to but differing from a subroutine in that it can be left and re-entered at any point

corp. abbreviation 1 corporation 2 corporal

corporal¹ ('kɔːpərəl, -prəl) adj of or relating to the body; bodily [c14: from Latin corporālis of the body, from corpus body] >,corpo'rality n >'corporally adv

corporal² ('kɔːpərəl, -prəl) n 1 a noncommissioned officer junior to a sergeant in the army, air force, or marines 2 (in the Royal Navy) a petty officer who assists the master-at-arms [c16: from Old French, via Italian, from Latin caput head; perhaps also influenced in Old French by corps body (of men)]

corporal³ ('kɔːpərəl, -prəl) orcorporale (,kɔːpə'reɪlı) n a white linen cloth on which the bread and wine are placed during the Eucharist [c14: from Medieval Latin corporāle pallium eucharistic altar cloth, from Latin corporālis belonging to the body, from corpus body (of Christ)]

Corporal of Horse n a noncommissioned rank in the British Household Cavalry above that of sergeant and below that of staff sergeant

corporal punishment n punishment of a physical nature, such as caning, flogging, or beating

corporate ('kɔːpərɪt, -prɪt) adj 1 forming a corporation; incorporated 2 of or belonging to a corporation or corporations: corporate finance 3 of or belonging to a united group; joint [c15: from Latin corporātus made into a body, from corporāre, from corpus body] >corporatism ('kɔːpərɪtɪzəm, -prɪtɪzəm) n >'corporatist n, adj

corporate anorexia n a malaise of a business organization resulting from making too many creative people redundant in efforts to cut costs

corporate culture n the distinctive ethos of an organization that influences the level of formality, loyalty, and general behaviour of its employees

corporate governance n the balance of control between the stakeholders, managers, and directors of an organization

corporate identity orcorporate image n the way an organization is presented to or perceived by its members and the public

corporate manslaughter n law the death of someone caused by an act of corporate negligence

corporate raider n finance a person or organization that acquires a substantial holding of the shares of a company in order to take it over or to force its management to act in a desired way

corporate venturing n finance the provision of venture capital by one company for another in order to obtain information about the company requiring capital or as a step towards acquiring it

corporation (,kɔːpə'reɪʃən) n 1 a group of people authorized by law to act as a legal personality and having its own powers, duties, and liabilities 2 Also called: municipal corporation the municipal authorities of a city or town 3 a group of people acting as one body 4 See public corporation 5 informal a large paunch or belly >corporative ('kɔːpərətɪv, -prətɪv) adj

corporation tax n a British tax on the profits of a company or other incorporated body

corporatize orcorporatise ('kɔːpərətaɪz, -prə-) vb 1 (tr) to convert (a government-controlled industry or enterprise) into an independent company 2 (intr) to be influenced by or take on the features of a large commercial business, esp in being bureaucratic and uncaring

corporeal (kɔː'pɔːrɪəl) adj 1 of the nature of the physical body; not spiritual 2 of a material nature; physical [c17: from Latin corporeus, from corpus body] >cor,pore'ality or cor'porealness n >cor'poreally adv

corps (kɔː) n, plcorps (kɔːz) 1 a military formation that comprises two or more divisions and additional support arms 2 a military body with a specific function: intelligence corps; medical corps 3 a body of people associated together: the diplomatic corps [c18: from French, from Latin corpus body]

corps de ballet ('kɔː də 'bæleɪ; French kɔr də balɛ) n the members of a ballet company who dance together in a group

corps diplomatique (,dɪpləʊmæ'tiːk) n another name for diplomatic corps

corpse (kɔːps) n a dead body, esp of a human being; cadaver [c14: from Old French corps body, from Latin corpus body]

corpulent ('kɔːpjʊlənt) adj physically bulky; fat [c14: from Latin corpulentus fleshy] >'corpulence or 'corpulency n

cor pulmonale (kɔː pʌlmə'nɑːlɪ) n pulmonary heart disease: a serious heart condition in which there is enlargement and failure of the right ventricle resulting from lung disease [New Latin]

corpus ('kɔːpəs) n, pl -pora (-pərə) 1 a collection or body of writings, esp by a single author or on a specific topic: the corpus of Dickens' works 2 the main body, section, or substance of something 3 anatomy a any distinct mass or body b the main part of an organ or structure [c14: from Latin: body]

Corpus Christi¹ ('krɪstɪ) n chiefly RC Church a festival in honour of the Eucharist, observed on the Thursday after Trinity Sunday [c14: from Latin: body of Christ]

Corpus Christi² ('krɪstɪ) n a port in S Texas, on **Corpus Christi Bay**, an inlet of the Gulf of Mexico. Pop: 279 208 (2003 est)

corpuscle ('kɔːpʌsəl) n 1 any cell or similar minute body that is suspended in a fluid, esp any of the red blood corpuscles (erythrocytes) or white blood corpuscles (see leucocytes). See also **erythrocyte, leucocyte 2** Also called: **corpuscule** (kɔː'pʌskjuːl) any minute particle [c17: from Latin *corpusculum* a little body, from *corpus* body] > **corpuscular** (kɔː'pʌskjʊlə) *adj*

corpuscular theory *n* the theory, originally proposed by Newton, and revived with the development of the quantum theory, that light consists of a stream of particles. See **wave theory**

corpus delicti (dɪ'lɪktaɪ) *n law* the body of facts that constitute an offence [New Latin, literally: the body of the crime]

corpus juris ('dʒʊərɪs) *n* a body of law, esp the laws of a nation or state [from Late Latin, literally: a body of law]

corpus luteum ('luːtɪəm) *n*, *pl* **corpora lutea** ('luːtɪə) a yellow glandular mass of tissue that forms in a Graafian follicle following release of an ovum. It secretes progesterone, a hormone necessary to maintain pregnancy [New Latin, literally: yellow body]

corral (kɒ'rɑːl) *n* **1** *chiefly US & Canadian* an enclosure for confining cattle or horses **2** *chiefly US* (formerly) a defensive enclosure formed by a ring of covered wagons ▷ *vb* **-rals, -ralling, -ralled** (*tr*) *US & Canadian* **3** to drive into and confine in or as in a corral **4** *informal* to capture [c16: from Spanish, from Vulgar Latin *currāle* (unattested) area for vehicles, from Latin *currus* wagon, from *currere* to run]

corrasion (kə'reɪʒən) *n* erosion of a rock surface by rock fragments transported over it by water, wind, or ice

correa ('kɒrɪə, kə'riːə) *n* an Australian evergreen shrub of the genus *Correa*, with large showy tubular flowers [c19: after Jose Francesco *Correa* da Serra (1750–1823), Portuguese botanist]

correct (kə'rɛkt) *vb* (*tr*) **1** to make free from errors **2** to indicate the errors in **3** to rebuke or punish in order to set right or improve: *to correct a child; to stand corrected* **4** to counteract or rectify (a malfunction, ailment, etc) **5** to adjust or make conform, esp to a standard ▷ *adj* **6** free from error; true; accurate: *the correct version* **7** in conformity with accepted standards: *correct behaviour* [c14: from Latin *corrigere* to make straight, put in order, from *com-* (intensive) + *regere* to rule] > **cor'rectly** *adv* > **cor'rectness** *n*

correction (kə'rɛkʃən) *n* **1** the act or process of correcting **2** something offered or substituted for an error; an improvement **3** the act or process of punishing; reproof **4** a number or quantity added to or subtracted from a scientific or mathematical calculation or observation to increase its accuracy

corrective (kə'rɛktɪv) *adj* **1** tending or intended to correct ▷ *n* **2** something that tends or is intended to correct

Correggio (*Italian* kor'reddʒo) *n* **Antonio Allegri da** (an'tɔːnjo al'leːɡri da). 1494–1534, Italian painter, noted for his striking use of perspective and foreshortening

Corregidor (kə'rɛɡɪˌdɔː) *n* an island at the entrance to Manila Bay, in the Philippines: site of the defeat of American forces by the Japanese (1942) in World War II

correlate ('kɒrɪˌleɪt) *vb* **1** to place or be placed in a mutual, complementary, or reciprocal relationship **2** (*tr*) to establish or show a correlation ▷ *n* **3** either of two things mutually or reciprocally related

correlation (ˌkɒrɪ'leɪʃən) *n* **1** a mutual or reciprocal relationship between two or more things **2** the act or process of correlating or the state of being correlated **3** *statistics* the extent of correspondence between the ordering of two variables. Correlation is positive or direct when two variables move in the same direction and negative or inverse when they move in opposite directions [c16: from Medieval Latin *correlātiō*, from *com-* together + *relātiō*, RELATION] > **corre'lational** *adj*

correlation coefficient *n statistics* a statistic measuring the degree of correlation between two variables as by dividing their covariance by the square root of the product of their variances. The closer the correlation coefficient is to 1 or –1 the greater the correlation; if it is random, the coefficient is zero

correlative (kɒ'rɛlətɪv) *adj* **1** in mutual, complementary, or reciprocal relationship; corresponding **2** denoting words, usually conjunctions, occurring together though

not adjacently in certain grammatical constructions, as for example *neither* and *nor* in such sentences as *he neither ate nor drank* ▷ *n* **3** either of two things that are correlative **4** a correlative word > **cor'relatively** *adv* > **cor'relativeness** or **cor,rela'tivity** *n*

correspond (ˌkɒrɪ'spɒnd) *vb* (*intr*) **1** (usually foll by *with* or *to*) to conform, be in agreement, or be consistent or compatible (with); tally (with) **2** (usually foll by *to*) to be similar or analogous in character or function **3** (usually foll by *with*) to communicate by letter [c16: from Medieval Latin *correspondēre*, from Latin *respondēre* to RESPOND] > **corre'spondingly** *adv*

correspondence (ˌkɒrɪ'spɒndəns) *n* **1** the act or condition of agreeing or corresponding **2** similarity or analogy **3** agreement or conformity **4** **a** communication by the exchange of letters **b** the letters so exchanged

correspondence school *n* an educational institution that offers tuition (**correspondence courses**) by post

correspondent (ˌkɒrɪ'spɒndənt) *n* **1** a person who communicates by letter or by letters **2** a person employed by a newspaper, etc, to report on a special subject or to send reports from a foreign country **3** a person or firm that has regular business relations with another, esp one in a different part of the country or abroad ▷ *adj* **4** similar or analogous

corrida (ko'rriða) *n* the Spanish word for **bullfight** [Spanish, from the phrase *corrida de toros*, literally: a running of bulls, from *correr* to run, from Latin *currere*]

corridor ('kɒrɪˌdɔː) *n* **1** a hallway or passage connecting parts of a building **2** a strip of land or airspace along the route of a road or river **3** a strip of land or airspace that affords access, either from a landlocked country to the sea (such as the **Polish corridor**, 1919-39, which divided Germany) or from a state to an exclave (such as the **Berlin corridor**, 1945-90, which passed through the former East Germany) **4** a passageway connecting the compartments of a railway coach **5** **corridors of power** the higher echelons of government, the Civil Service, etc, considered as the location of power and influence **6** a flight path that affords safe access for intruding aircraft **7** the path that a spacecraft must follow when re-entering the atmosphere, above which lift is insufficient and below which heating effects are excessive [c16: from Old French, from Old Italian *corridore*, literally: place for running, from *correre* to run, from Latin *currere*]

corrie ('kɒrɪ) *n geology* another name for **cirque** (sense 1) [c18: from Gaelic *coire* cauldron, kettle]

corrigendum (ˌkɒrɪ'dʒɛndəm) *n*, *pl* **-da** (**-də**) **1** an error to be corrected **2** Also called: **erratum** (*sometimes plural*) a slip of paper inserted into a book after printing, listing errors and corrections [c19: from Latin: that which is to be corrected, from *corrigere* to CORRECT]

corrigible ('kɒrɪdʒɪbəl) *adj* **1** capable of being corrected **2** submissive or submitting to correction [c15: from Old French, from Medieval Latin *corrigibilis*, from Latin *corrigere* to set right, CORRECT]

corroborate (kə'rɒbəˌreɪt) *vb* (*tr*) to confirm or support (facts, opinions, etc), esp by providing fresh evidence [c16: from Latin *corrōborāre* to invigorate, from *rōborāre* to make strong, from *rōbur* strength, literally: oak] > **cor,robo'ration** *n* > **corroborative** (kə'rɒbərətɪv) *or* **cor'robo,ratory** *adj* > **cor'roboratively** *adv* > **cor'robo,rator** *n*

corroboree (kə'rɒbərɪ) *n Austral* **1** a native assembly of sacred, festive, or warlike character **2** *informal* any noisy gathering [c19: from a native Australian language]

corrode (kə'rəʊd) *vb* **1** to eat away or be eaten away, esp by chemical action as in the oxidation or rusting of a metal **2** (*tr*) to destroy gradually; consume: *his jealousy corroded his happiness* [c14: from Latin *corrōdere* to gnaw to pieces, from *rōdere* to gnaw; see RODENT, RAT] > **cor'rodible** *adj*

corrosion (kə'rəʊʒən) *n* **1** a process in which a solid, esp a metal, is eaten away and changed by a chemical action, as in the oxidation of iron in the presence of water by an electrolytic process **2** slow deterioration by being eaten or worn away **3** the condition produced by or the product of corrosion

corrosive (kəˈrəʊsɪv) *adj* **1** (esp of acids or alkalis) capable of destroying solid materials **2** tending to eat away or consume ▷ *n* **3** a corrosive substance, such as a strong acid or alkali > cor'rosively *adv* > cor'rosiveness *n*

corrosive sublimate *n* another name for **mercuric chloride**

corrugate (ˈkɒrʊˌɡeɪt) *vb* (*usually tr*) to fold or be folded into alternate furrows and ridges [c18: from Latin *corrūgāre*, from *rūga* a wrinkle] > ˌcorru'gation *n*

corrugated iron *n* a thin structural sheet made of iron or steel, formed with alternating ridges and troughs

corrugated paper *n* a packaging material made from layers of heavy paper, the top layer of which is grooved and ridged

corrupt (kəˈrʌpt) *adj* **1** lacking in integrity; open to or involving bribery or other dishonest practices: *a corrupt official; corrupt practices in an election* **2** morally depraved **3** putrid or rotten **4** (of a text or manuscript) made meaningless or different in meaning from the original by scribal errors or alterations **5** (of computer programs or data) containing errors ▷ *vb* **6** to become or cause to become dishonest or disloyal **7** to debase or become debased morally; deprave **8** (*tr*) to infect or contaminate; taint **9** (*tr*) to cause to become rotten **10** (*tr*) to alter (a text, manuscript, etc) from the original **11** (*tr*) *computing* to introduce errors into (data or a program) [c14: from Latin *corruptus* spoiled, from *corrumpere* to break, literally: break to pieces, from *rumpere* to break] > cor'rupter *or* cor'ruptor *n* > cor'ruptly *adv* > cor'ruptness *n*

corruptible (kəˈrʌptəbəl) *adj* susceptible to corruption; capable of being corrupted > cor'ruptibly *adv*

corruption (kəˈrʌpʃən) *n* **1** the act of corrupting or state of being corrupt **2** moral perversion; depravity **3** dishonesty, esp bribery **4** putrefaction or decay **5** alteration, as of a manuscript **6** an altered form of a word

corsage (kɔːˈsɑːʒ) *n* **1** a flower or small bunch of flowers worn pinned to the lapel, bosom, etc, or sometimes carried by women **2** the bodice of a dress [c15: from Old French, from *cors* body, from Latin *corpus*]

corsair (ˈkɔːsɛə) *n* **1** a pirate **2** a privateer, esp of the Barbary Coast [c15: from Old French *corsaire* pirate, from Medieval Latin *cursārius*, from Latin *cursus* a running, COURSE]

corse (kɔːs) *n* an archaic word for **corpse**

corselet (ˈkɔːslɪt) *n* **1** a piece of armour for the top part of the body **2** a one-piece foundation garment, usually combining a brassiere and a corset [c15: from Old French, from *cors* bodice of a garment, from Latin *corpus* body]

corset (ˈkɔːsɪt) *n* **1 a** a stiffened, elasticated, or laced foundation garment, worn esp by women, that usually extends from below the chest to the hips, providing support for the spine and stomach and shaping the figure **b** a similar garment worn because of injury, weakness, etc, by either sex **2** *informal* a restriction or limitation, esp government control of bank lending ▷ *vb* **3** (*tr*) to dress or enclose in, or as in, a corset [c14: from Old French, literally: a little bodice; see CORSELET] > ˌcorse'tier *n* > 'corsetry *n*

Corsica (ˈkɔːsɪkə) *n* an island in the Mediterranean, west of N Italy: forms, with 43 islets, a region of France; mountainous; settled by Greeks in about 560 BC; sold by Genoa to France in 1768. Capital: Ajaccio. Pop: 265 999 (2003 est). Area: 8682 sq km (3367 sq miles)

Corsican (ˈkɔːsɪkən) *adj* **1** of or relating to Corsica or its inhabitants ▷ *n* **2** a native or inhabitant of Corsica

cortege *or* **cortège** (kɔːˈteɪʒ) *n* **1** a formal procession, esp a funeral procession **2** a train of attendants; retinue [c17: from French, from Italian *corteggio*, from *corteggiare* to attend, from *corte* COURT]

Cortés (kɔːˈtɛz; *Spanish* korˈtes) *or* **Cortez** (kɔːˈtɛz) *n* **Hernando** (ɛrˈnando) *or* **Hernán** (ɛrˈnan). 1485–1547, Spanish conquistador: defeated the Aztecs and conquered Mexico (1523)

cortex (ˈkɔːtɛks) *n*, *pl* **-tices** (-tɪˌsiːz) **1** *anatomy* the outer layer of any organ or part, such as the grey matter in the brain that covers the cerebrum (**cerebral cortex**) or the outer part of the kidney (**renal cortex**) **2** *botany* **a** the

unspecialized tissue in plant stems and roots between the vascular bundles and the epidermis **b** the outer layer of a part such as the bark of a stem [c17: from Latin: bark, outer layer] > cortical (ˈkɔːtɪkəl) *adj*

corticate (ˈkɔːtɪkɪt, -ˌkeɪt) *or* **corticated** (ˈkɔːtɪˌkeɪtɪd) *adj* (of plants, seeds, etc) having a bark, husk, or rind [c19: from Latin *corticātus* covered with bark]

corticosterone (ˌkɔːtɪˈkɒstəˌrəʊn) *n* a glucocorticoid hormone secreted by the adrenal cortex. Formula: $C_{21}H_{30}O_4$ [c20: from *cortico*- combining form indicating the cortex + STER(OL) + -ONE]

cortisone (ˈkɔːtɪˌsəʊn, -ˌzəʊn) *n* a glucocorticoid hormone, the synthetic form of which has been used in treating rheumatoid arthritis, allergic and skin diseases, leukaemia, etc; 17-hydroxy-11-dehydrocorticosterone. Formula: $C_{21}H_{28}O_5$ [c20: shortened from CORTICOSTERONE]

Cortona (kɔːˈtəʊnə; *Italian* kɔrˈtona) *n* a town in central Italy, in Tuscany: Roman and Etruscan remains, 15th-century cathedral. Pop: 22 048 (2001)

Cortot (*French* kɔrto) *n* **Alfred** (alfrɛd). 1877–1962, French pianist, born in Switzerland

corundum (kəˈrʌndəm) *n* a white, grey, blue, green, red, yellow, or brown mineral, found in metamorphosed shales and limestones, in veins, and in some igneous rocks. It is used as an abrasive and as gemstone; the red variety is ruby, the blue is sapphire. Composition: aluminium oxide. Formula: Al_2O_3. Crystal structure: hexagonal (rhombohedral) [c18: from Tamil *kuruntam*; related to Sanskrit *kuruvinda* ruby]

Corunna (kəˈrʌnə) *n* the English name for **La Coruña**

coruscate (ˈkɒrəˌskeɪt) *vb* (*intr*) to emit flashes of light; sparkle [c18: from Latin *coruscāre* to flash, vibrate] > ˌcoru'scation *n*

corvée (ˈkɔːveɪ) *n* **1** *European history* a day's unpaid labour owed by a feudal vassal to his lord **2** the practice or an instance of forced labour [c14: from Old French, from Late Latin *corrogāta* contribution, from Latin *corrogāre* to collect, from *rogāre* to ask]

corvette (kɔːˈvɛt) *n* a lightly armed escort warship [c17: from Old French, perhaps from Middle Dutch *corf* basket, small ship, from Latin *corbis* basket]

corvina (kɔːˈviːnə) *n* **1** a marine food fish, *Menticirrhus undulatus*, found in Pacific waters off Mexico and California **2** any of several related marine fishes of the family *Sciaenidae* [from Spanish *corbina, corvina*, from feminine of *corvino* ravenlike, from Latin *corvus* raven]

corvine (ˈkɔːvaɪn) *adj* **1** of, relating to, or resembling a crow **2** of, relating to, or belonging to the passerine bird family *Corvidae*, which includes the crows, raven, rook, jackdaw, magpies, and jays [c17: from Latin *corvīnus* raven-like, from *corvus* a raven]

Corvo (ˈkɔːvəʊ) *n* **Baron**. See (Frederick William) **Rolfe**

Corybant (ˈkɒrɪˌbænt) *n*, *pl* **Corybants** *or* **Corybantes** (ˌkɒrɪˈbæntiːz) *classical myth* a wild attendant of the goddess Cybele [c14: from Latin *Corybās*, from Greek *Korubas*, probably of Phrygian origin] > ˌCory'bantian, ˌCory'bantic *or* ˌCory'bantine *adj*

corymb (ˈkɒrɪmb, -rɪm) *n* an inflorescence in the form of a flat-topped flower cluster with the oldest flowers at the periphery. This type of raceme occurs in the candytuft [c18: from Latin *corymbus*, from Greek *korumbos* cluster]

coryza (kəˈraɪzə) *n* acute inflammation of the mucous membrane of the nose, with discharge of mucus; a head cold [c17: from Late Latin: catarrh, from Greek *koruza*]

cos[1] *or* **cos lettuce** (kɒs) *n* a variety of lettuce with a long slender head and crisp leaves. Usual US and Canadian name: **romaine** [c17: named after *Kos*, the Aegean island of its origin]

cos[2] (kɒz) *abbreviation* cosine

Cos (kɒs) *n* a variant spelling of **Kos**

Cosa Nostra (ˈkəʊsə ˈnɒstrə) *n* the branch of the Mafia that operates in the US [Italian, literally: our thing]

COSATU (ˌkəʊˈzɑːtuː) *n acronym for* Congress of South Africa Trade Unions

cosec (ˈkəʊsɛk) *abbreviation* cosecant

cosecant (kəʊˈsiːkənt) *n* (of an angle) a trigonometric function that in a right-angled triangle is the ratio of the length of the hypotenuse to that of the opposite side; the reciprocal of sine

Cosgrave ('kɒzgreɪv) n **1 Liam** ('liːəm). born 1920, Irish statesman; prime minister of the Republic of Ireland (1973–77) **2** his father, **W** (**illiam**) **T** (**homas**). 1880–1965, Irish statesman; first prime minister (president of the executive council) of the Irish Free State (1922–32)

cosh[1] (kɒʃ) Brit ▷ n **1** a blunt weapon, often made of hard rubber; bludgeon **2** an attack with such a weapon ▷ vb (tr) **3** to hit with such a weapon, esp on the head [c19: from Romany *kosh*, from *koshter* skewer, stick]

cosh[2] (kɒʃ, 'kɒs'eɪtʃ) n hyperbolic cosine; a hyperbolic function, cosh z = ½(e^z + e^{-z}), related to cosine by the expression cosh iz = cos z, where i = √–1 [c19: from COS(INE) + H(YPERBOLIC)]

cosignatory (kəʊ'sɪgnətərɪ, -trɪ) n, pl -ries **1** a person, country, etc, that signs a document jointly with others ▷ adj **2** signing jointly with another or others

Cosimo I (Italian 'kɔːzimo) n See **Medici** (sense 3)

cosine ('kəʊˌsaɪn) n (of an angle) a trigonometric function that in a right-angled triangle is the ratio of the length of the adjacent side to that of the hypotenuse; the sine of the complement [c17: from New Latin *cosinus*; see CO-, SINE[1]]

cosmetic (kɒz'mɛtɪk) n **1** any preparation applied to the body, esp the face, with the intention of beautifying it ▷ adj **2** serving or designed to beautify the body, esp the face **3** having no other function than to beautify: *cosmetic illustrations in a book* [c17: from Greek *kosmētikos*, from *kosmein* to arrange, from *kosmos* order] >cos'metically adv

cosmetologist (ˌkɒzmɪ'tɒlədʒɪst) n a person skilled or trained in the use of cosmetics and beauty treatments [c20: a blend of COSMETICS + -OLOGIST]

cosmetology (ˌkɒzmɛ'tɒlədʒɪ) n the work of beauty therapists, including hairdressing, facials, manicures, etc

cosmic ('kɒzmɪk) adj **1** of or relating to the whole universe: *cosmic laws* **2** occurring or originating in outer space, esp as opposed to the vicinity of the earth, the solar system, or the local galaxy: *cosmic rays* **3** immeasurably extended in space or time; vast >'cosmically adv

cosmic dust n fine particles of solid matter occurring throughout interstellar space and often collecting into clouds of extremely low density

cosmic rays pl n radiation consisting of particles, esp protons, of very high energy that reach the earth from outer space. Also called: cosmic radiation

cosmic string n a one-dimensional defect in space-time postulated in certain theories of cosmology to exist in the universe as a consequence of the big bang

cosmo- or before a vowel **cosm-** combining form indicating the world or universe: *cosmology; cosmonaut; cosmography* [from Greek: COSMOS]

cosmogony (kɒz'mɒgənɪ) n, pl -nies the study of the origin and development of the universe or of a particular system in the universe, such as the solar system [c17: from Greek *kosmogonia*, from COSMO- + *gonos* creation] >cosmogonic (ˌkɒzmə'gɒnɪk) or cosmo'gonical adj >cos'mogonist n

cosmography (kɒz'mɒgrəfɪ) n **1** a representation of the world or the universe **2** the science dealing with the whole order of nature >cos'mographer or cos'mographist n >cosmographic (ˌkɒzmə'græfɪk) or cosmo'graphical adj

cosmological principle n astronomy the theory that the universe is uniform, homogenous, and isotropic, and therefore appears the same from any position

cosmology (kɒz'mɒlədʒɪ) n **1** the philosophical study of the origin and nature of the universe **2** a particular account of the origin or structure of the universe >cosmological (ˌkɒzmə'lɒdʒɪkəl) or cosmo'logic adj >cos'mologist n

cosmonaut ('kɒzməˌnɔːt) n an astronaut, esp in the former Soviet Union [c20: from Russian *kosmonavt*, from COSMO- + Greek *nautēs* sailor; compare ARGONAUT]

cosmopolitan (ˌkɒzmə'pɒlɪt³n) n **1** a person who has lived and travelled in many countries, esp one who is free of national prejudices ▷ adj **2** having interest in or familiar with many parts of the world **3** sophisticated or urbane **4** composed of people or elements from all parts of the world or from many different spheres [c17: from French, ultimately from Greek *kosmopolitēs*, from *kosmo-* COSMO- + *politēs* citizen] >ˌcosmo'politanism n

cosmopolite (kɒz'mɒpəˌlaɪt) n **1** a less common word for **cosmopolitan** (sense 1) **2** an animal or plant that occurs in most parts of the world >cos'mopoli,tism n

cosmos ('kɒzmɒs) n **1** the world or universe considered as an ordered system **2** any ordered system **3** harmony; order **4** pl -mos or -moses any tropical American plant of the genus *Cosmos*, cultivated as garden plants for their brightly coloured flowers: family *Asteraceae* (composites) [c17: from Greek *kosmos* order, world, universe]

Cosmos ('kɒzmɒs) n astronautics any of various types of Soviet satellite, including Cosmos 1 (launched 1962) and nearly 2000 subsequent satellites

Cossack ('kɒsæk) n **1** (formerly) any of the free warrior-peasants of chiefly East Slavonic descent who lived in communes, esp in Ukraine, and served as cavalry under the tsars ▷ adj **2** of, relating to, or characteristic of the Cossacks: *a Cossack dance* [c16: from Russian *kazak* vagabond, of Turkic origin]

cosset ('kɒsɪt) vb -sets, -seting, -seted (tr) **1** to pamper; coddle; pet ▷ n **2** any pet animal, esp a lamb [c16: of unknown origin]

cost (kɒst) n **1** the price paid or required for acquiring, producing, or maintaining something, usually measured in money, time, or energy; expense or expenditure; outlay **2** suffering or sacrifice; loss; penalty: *count the cost to your health; I know to my cost* **3 a** the amount paid for a commodity by its seller: *to sell at cost* **b** (as modifier): *the cost price* **4** (plural) law the expenses of judicial proceedings **5** at any cost or at all costs regardless of cost or sacrifice involved **6** at the cost of at the expense of losing ▷ vb costs, costing, cost **7** (tr) to be obtained or obtainable in exchange for (money or something equivalent); be priced at: *the ride cost one pound* **8** to cause or require the expenditure, loss, or sacrifice (of): *the accident cost him dearly* **9** to estimate the cost of (a product, process, etc) for the purposes of pricing, budgeting, control, etc [c13: from Old French (n), from *coster* to cost, from Latin *constāre* to stand at, cost, from *stāre* to stand]

costa ('kɒstə) n, pl -tae (-tiː) **1** the technical name for rib[1] (sense 1) **2** a riblike part, such as the midrib of a plant leaf [c19: from Latin: rib, side, wall] >'costal adj

Costa Brava ('kɒstə 'brɑːvə) n a coastal region of NE Spain along the Mediterranean, extending from Barcelona to the French border: many resorts

cost accounting n the recording and controlling of all the expenditures of an enterprise in order to facilitate control of separate activities. Also called: management accounting >cost accountant n

costard ('kʌstəd) n **1** an English variety of apple tree **2** the large ribbed apple of this tree **3** archaic, humorous a slang word for **head** [c14: from Anglo-Norman, from Old French *coste* rib]

Costa Rica ('kɒstə 'riːkə) n a republic in Central America: gained independence from Spain in 1821; mostly mountainous and volcanic, with extensive forests. Official language: Spanish. Official religion: Roman Catholic. Currency: colón. Capital: San José. Pop: 4 250 000 (2004 est). Area: 50 900 sq km (19 652 sq miles)

Costa Rican ('kɒstə 'riːkən) adj **1** of or relating to Costa Rica or its inhabitants ▷ n **2** a native or inhabitant of Costa Rica

cost-benefit adj denoting or relating to a method of assessing a project that takes into account its costs and its benefits to society as well as the revenue it generates: *a cost-benefit analysis; the project was assessed on a cost-benefit basis*

cost-effective adj providing adequate financial return in relation to outlay >cost-effectiveness n

Costello (kɒ'stɛləʊ) n **Elvis**, real name *Declan McManus*. born 1954, British rock singer and songwriter. His recordings include *This Year's Model* (1978), "Oliver's Army" (1979), *Spike* (1989), *Brutal Youth* (1994), and *When I*

Was Cruel (2003)

costermonger ('kɒstə,mʌŋgə) *or* **coster** *n Brit rare* a person who sells fruit, vegetables, etc, from a barrow [c16: *coster-*, from COSTARD + MONGER]

costive ('kɒstɪv) *adj* **1** having constipation; constipated **2** niggardly [c14: from Old French *costivé*, from Latin *constipātus*; see CONSTIPATE] > 'costiveness *n*

costly ('kɒstlɪ) *adj* **-lier, -liest 1** of great price or value; expensive **2** entailing great loss or sacrifice: *a costly victory* **3** splendid; lavish > 'costliness *n*

Costner ('kɒstnə) *n* **Kevin.** born 1955, US film actor: his films include *Robin Hood: Prince of Thieves* (1990), *Dances with Wolves* (1990; also directed), *JFK* (1991), *Waterworld* (1995), and *Open Range* (2003)

cost of living *n* **a** the basic cost of the food, clothing, shelter, and fuel necessary to maintain life, esp at a standard regarded as basic or minimal **b** (*as modifier*): *the cost-of-living index*

cost-plus *n* a method of establishing a selling price in which an agreed percentage is added to the cost price to cover profit

costume ('kɒstjuːm) *n* **1** a complete style of dressing, including all the clothes, accessories, etc, worn at one time, as in a particular country or period; dress **2** *old-fashioned* a woman's suit **3** a set of clothes, esp unusual or period clothes, worn in a play by an actor or at a fancy dress ball: *a jester's costume* **4** short for **swimming costume** ▷ *vb* (*tr*) **5** to furnish the costumes for (a show, film, etc) **6** to dress (someone) in a costume [c18: from French, from Italian: dress, habit, CUSTOM]

costumier (kɒ'stjuːmɪə) *or* **costumer** (kɒ'stjuːmə) *n* a person or firm that makes or supplies theatrical or fancy costumes

cosy *or US* **cozy** ('kəʊzɪ) *adj* **-sier, -siest** *or US* **-zier, -ziest 1** warm and snug **2** intimate; friendly ▷ *n, pl* **-sies** *or* **-zies 3** a cover for keeping things warm: *egg cosy* [c18: from Scots, of unknown origin] > 'cosily *or US* 'cozily *adv* > 'cosiness *or US* 'coziness *n*

cot¹ (kɒt) *n* **1** a child's boxlike bed, usually incorporating vertical bars **2** a collapsible or portable bed **3** a light bedstead **4** *nautical* a hammock-like bed with a stiff frame [c17: from Hindi *khāt* bedstead, from Sanskrit *khátvā*, of Dravidian origin; related to Tamil *kattil* bedstead]

cot² (kɒt) *n* **1** *literary or archaic* a small cottage **2** *Also called*: **cote a** a small shelter, esp one for pigeons, sheep, etc **b** (*in combination*): *dovecot* [Old English *cot*; related to Old Norse *kot* little hut, Middle Low German *cot*]

cot³ (kɒt) *abbreviation* cotangent

cotangent (kəʊ'tændʒənt) *n* (of an angle) a trigonometric function that in a right-angled triangle is the ratio of the length of the adjacent side to that of the opposite side; the reciprocal of tangent

cot death *n* the unexplained sudden death of an infant during sleep. Technical name: **sudden infant death syndrome**

COTC *abbreviation* Canadian Officers Training Corps

cote (kəʊt) *or* **cot** *n* **a** a small shelter for pigeons, sheep, etc **b** (*in combination*): *dovecote* [Old English *cote*; related to Low German *Kote*; see COT²]

Côte d'Azur (*French* kot dazyr) *n* the Mediterranean coast of France, including the French Riviera: forms an administrative region with Provence

Côte d'Ivoire (*French* kot divwar) *n* a republic in West Africa, on the Gulf of Guinea: Portuguese trading for ivory and slaves began in the 16th century; made a French protectorate in 1842 and became independent in 1960; major producer of coffee and cocoa. Official language: French. Religion: Muslim majority, with animist, atheist, and Roman Catholic minorities. Currency: franc. Capital: Yamoussoukro (administrative); Abidjan (legislative). Pop: 16 897 000 (2004 est). Area: 319 820 sq km (123 483 sq miles). Former name (until 1986): the Ivory Coast

Côte-d'Or (*French* kotdɔr) *n* a department of E central France, in NE Burgundy. Capital: Dijon. Pop: 510 334 (2003 est). Area: 8787 sq km (3427 sq miles)

coterie ('kəʊtərɪ) *n* a small exclusive group of friends or people with common interests; clique [c18: from French, from Old French: association of tenants, from *cotier* (unattested) cottager, from Medieval Latin *cotārius* COTTER²; see COT²]

coterminous (kəʊ'tɜːmɪnəs) *or* **conterminous** (kɒn'tɜːmɪnəs) *adj* **1** having a common boundary; bordering; contiguous **2** coextensive or coincident in range, time, scope, etc

Côtes-d'Armor (*French* kotdarmɔr) *n* a department of W France, on the N coast of Brittany. Capital: St Brieuc. Pop: 553 969 (2003 est). Area: 6878 sq km (2656 sq miles)

coth (kɒθ) *n* hyperbolic cotangent; a hyperbolic function that is the ratio of cosh to sinh, being the reciprocal of tanh [c20: from COT(ANGENT) + H(YPERBOLIC)]

cotillion *or* **cotillon** (kə'tɪljən, kəʊ-) *n* **1** a French formation dance of the 18th century **2** *US* a quadrille **3** *US & Canadian* a formal ball, esp one at which debutantes are presented [c18: from French *cotillon* dance, from Old French: petticoat, from *cote* COAT]

cotinga (kə'tɪŋgə) *n* any tropical American passerine bird of the family *Cotingidae*, such as the umbrella bird and the cock-of-the-rock, having a broad slightly hooked bill

Cotman ('kɒtmən) *n* **John Sell.** 1782–1842, English landscape watercolourist and etcher

cotoneaster (kə,təʊnɪ'æstə) *n* any Old World shrub of the rosaceous genus *Cotoneaster*: cultivated for their small ornamental white or pinkish flowers and red or black berries [c18: from New Latin, from Latin *cotōneum* QUINCE]

Cotonou (,kəʊtə'nuː) *n* the chief port and official capital of Benin, on the Bight of Benin. Pop: 891 000 (2005 est)

Cotopaxi (*Spanish* koto'paksi) *n* a volcano in central Ecuador, in the Andes: the world's highest active volcano Height: 5896 m (19 344 ft)

Cotswolds ('kɒts,wəʊldz, -wəldz) *pl n* a range of low hills in SW England, mainly in Gloucestershire: formerly a centre of the wool industry

cotta ('kɒtə) *n RC Church* a short form of surplice [c19: from Italian: tunic, from Medieval Latin; see COAT]

cottage ('kɒtɪdʒ) *n* a small simple house, esp in a rural area [c14: from COT²]

cottage cheese *n* a mild loose soft white cheese made from skimmed milk curds

cottage country *n Canadian* any lakeside region where many country cottages are located

cottage hospital *n Brit* a small rural hospital

cottage industry *n* an industry in which employees work in their own homes, often using their own equipment

cottage pie *n Brit* another term for **shepherd's pie**

cottager ('kɒtɪdʒə) *n* **1** a person who lives in a cottage **2** a rural labourer

cottaging ('kɒtɪdʒɪŋ) *n Brit* homosexual activity between men in a public lavatory [c20: from COTTAGE (sense 4)]

cotter¹ ('kɒtə) *machinery n* **1** any part, such as a pin, wedge, key, etc, that is used to secure two other parts so that relative motion between them is prevented **2** short for **cotter pin** [c14: shortened from *cotterel*, of unknown origin]

cotter² ('kɒtə) *n* **1** *Also called*: cottier *English history* a villein in late Anglo-Saxon and early Norman times occupying a cottage and land in return for labour **2** *Also called*: cottar a peasant occupying a cottage and land in the Scottish Highlands under the same tenure as an Irish cottier [c14: from Medieval Latin *cotārius*, from Middle English *cote* COT²]

cotter pin *n machinery* a split pin secured, after passing through holes in the parts to be attached, by spreading the ends

Cottian Alps ('kɒtɪən) *pl n* a mountain range in SW Europe, between NW Italy and SE France: part of the Alps. Highest peak: Monte Viso, 3841 m (12 600 ft)

cotton ('kɒtⁿn) *n* **1** any of various herbaceous plants and shrubs of the malvaceous genus *Gossypium*, such as sea-island cotton, cultivated in warm climates for the fibre surrounding the seeds and the oil within the seeds

2 the soft white downy fibre of these plants: used to manufacture textiles **3** cotton plants collectively, as a cultivated crop **4** a cloth or thread made from cotton fibres [c14: from Old French *coton*, from Arabic dialect *qutun*, from Arabic *qutn*] ▷ '**cottony** *adj*

Cotton ('kɒtən) *n* **Henry.** 1907–87, British golfer: three times winner of the British Open

cotton bud *n* a small stick with a cotton-wool tip used for cleaning the ears, applying make-up, etc

cotton grass *n* any of various N temperate and arctic grasslike bog plants of the cyperaceous genus *Eriophorum*, whose clusters of long silky hairs resemble cotton tufts

cotton on *vb* (*intr, adverb; often foll by to*) *informal* to perceive the meaning (of)

cotton-picking *adj US & Canadian slang* (intensifier qualifying something undesirable): *you cotton-picking layabout!*

cottonseed ('kɒtən,siːd) *n, pl* **-seeds** *or* **-seed** the seed of the cotton plant: a source of oil and fodder

cotton wool *n* **1** Also called: **purified cotton** *chiefly Brit* bleached and sterilized cotton from which the gross impurities, such as the seeds and waxy matter, have been removed: used for surgical dressings, tampons, etc **2** cotton in the natural state **3** *Brit informal* a state of pampered comfort and protection

cotyledon (,kɒtɪ'liːdən) *n* a simple embryonic leaf in seed-bearing plants, which, in some species, forms the first green leaf after germination [c16: from Latin: a plant, navelwort, from Greek *kotulēdōn*, from *kotulē* cup, hollow] ▷ ,**coty'ledonous** *or* ,**coty'ledo,noid** *adj* ▷ ,**coty'ledonal** *adj*

coucal ('kuːkæl, -kəl) *n* any ground-living bird of the genus *Centropus*, of Africa, S Asia, and Australia, having long strong legs: family *Cuculidae* (cuckoos) [c19: from French, perhaps from *couc(ou)* cuckoo + al(*ouette*) lark]

couch (kautʃ) *n* **1 a** a piece of upholstered furniture, usually having a back and armrests, for seating more than one person **2** a bed, esp one used in the daytime by the patients of a doctor or a psychoanalyst ▷ *vb* **3** (*tr*) to express in a particular style of language: *couched in an archaic style* **4** (when *tr*, *usually reflexive or passive*) to lie down or cause to lie down for or as for sleep **5** (*intr*) *archaic* to lie in ambush; lurk **6** (*tr*) *surgery* to remove (a cataract) by downward displacement of the lens of the eye **7** (*tr*) *archaic* to lower (a lance) into a horizontal position [c14: from Old French *couche* a bed, lair, from *coucher* to lay down, from Latin *collocāre* to arrange, from *locāre* to place; see LOCATE]

couchant ('kautʃənt) *adj* (*usually postpositive*) *heraldry* in a lying position: *a lion couchant* [c15: from French: lying, from Old French *coucher* to lay down; see COUCH]

couchette (kuː'ʃɛt) *n* a bed in a railway carriage, esp one converted from seats [c20: from French, diminutive of *couche* bed]

couch grass (kautʃ, kuːtʃ) *n* a grass, *Agropyron repens*, with a yellowish-white creeping underground stem by which it spreads quickly: a troublesome weed. Also called: **twitch grass**, **quitch grass**

couch potato *n slang* a lazy person whose recreation consists chiefly of watching television and videos

Coué (*French* kue) *n* **Émile** (emil). 1857–1926, French psychologist and pharmacist: advocated psychotherapy by autosuggestion ▷ **Cou'éism** ('kuːeɪ,ɪzəm) *n*

cougar ('kuːgə) *n* **1** another name for **puma 2** *US & Canad slang* a woman in her 30s or 40s who actively pursues casual sexual relationships with young men [c18: from French *couguar*, from Portuguese *cuguardo*, from Tupi *suasuarana*, literally: deerlike, from *suasú* deer + *rana* similar to]

cough (kɒf) *vb* **1** (*intr*) to expel air or solid matter from the lungs abruptly and explosively through the partially closed vocal chords **2** (*intr*) to make a sound similar to this **3** (*tr*) to utter or express with a cough or coughs ▷ *n* **4** an act, instance, or sound of coughing **5** a condition of the lungs or throat that causes frequent coughing [Old English *cohhetten*; related to Middle Dutch *kochen*, Middle High German *kūchen* to wheeze; probably of imitative origin] ▷ '**cougher** *n*

cough drop *n* a lozenge to relieve a cough

cough mixture *n* any medicine that relieves coughing

cough up *vb* (*adverb*) **1** *informal* to surrender (money, information, etc), esp reluctantly **2** (*tr*) to bring into the mouth or eject (phlegm, food, etc) by coughing

could (kʊd) *vb* (takes an infinitive without *to* or an implied infinitive) **1** used as an auxiliary to make the past tense of **can¹ 2** used as an auxiliary, esp in polite requests or in conditional sentences, to make the subjunctive mood of **can¹**: *could I see you tonight?; she'd telephone if she could* **3** used as an auxiliary to indicate suggestion of a course of action: *you could take the car tomorrow if it's raining* **4** (*often foll by well*) used as an auxiliary to indicate a possibility: *he could well be a spy* [Old English *cūthe*; influenced by WOULD, should; see CAN¹]

couldn't ('kʊdənt) *contraction of* could not

couldst (kʊdst) *vb archaic* used with the pronoun *thou* or its relative form, the form of **could**

coulee ('kuːleɪ, -lɪ) *n* **1 a** a flow of molten lava **b** such lava when solidified **2** *Western US & Canadian* a dry stream valley, especially a long steep-sided gorge or ravine that once carried melt water from a glacier [c19: from Canadian French *coulée* a flow, from French, from *couler* to flow, from Latin *cōlāre* to sift, purify; see COLANDER]

coulis ('kuːliː) *n* a thin purée of vegetables, fruit, etc, usually served as a sauce surrounding a dish [c20: French, literally: purée]

coulomb ('kuːlɒm) *n* the derived SI unit of electric charge; the quantity of electricity transported in one second by a current of 1 ampere. Symbol: **C** [c19: named after Charles Augustin de Coulomb (1736–1806), French physicist]

Coulomb ('kuːlɒm; *French* kulɔ̃) *n* **Charles Augustin de** (ʃarl ogystɛ̃ də). 1736–1806, French physicist: made many discoveries in the field of electricity and magnetism

coulometer (kuː'lɒmɪtə) *or* **coulombmeter** ('kuːlɒm,miːtə) *n* an electrolytic cell for measuring the magnitude of an electric charge by determining the total amount of decomposition resulting from the passage of the charge through the cell. Also called: **voltameter** [c19: from COULOMB + METER³]

coulter ('kəultə) *n* a blade or sharp-edged disc attached to a plough so that it cuts through the soil vertically in advance of the ploughshare. Also (esp US): **colter** [Old English *culter*, from Latin: ploughshare, knife]

coumarin *or* **cumarin** ('kuːmərɪn) *n* a white vanilla-scented crystalline ester, used in perfumes and flavourings and as an anticoagulant. Formula: $C_9H_6O_2$ [c19: from French *coumarine*, from *coumarou* tonka-bean tree, from Spanish *cumarú*, from Tupi]

council ('kaunsəl) *n* **1** an assembly of people meeting for discussion, consultation, etc **2** a body of people elected or appointed to serve in an administrative, legislative, or advisory capacity: *a student council* **3** the council (*sometimes capital*) *Brit* the local governing authority of a town, county, etc **4** (*modifier*) of, relating to, provided for, or used by a local council: *a council chamber; council offices* **5** (*modifier*) *Brit* provided by a local council, esp (of housing) at a subsidized rent: *a council house; a council estate* **6** *Austral* an administrative or legislative assembly, esp the upper house of a state parliament in Australia **7** *Christianity* an assembly of bishops, theologians, and other representatives of several churches or dioceses, convened for regulating matters of doctrine or discipline [c12: from Old French *concile*, from Latin *concilium* assembly, from *com-* together + *calāre* to call; influenced also by Latin *consilium* advice, COUNSEL]

● **USAGE** Avoid confusion with **counsel**

council area *n* any of the 32 unitary authorities into which Scotland has been divided for administrative purposes since April 1996

councillor *or US* **councilor** ('kaunsələ) *n* a member of a council

● **USAGE** Avoid confusion with **counsellor**

councilman ('kaunsəlmən) *n, pl* **-men** *chiefly US* a member of a council, esp of a town or city; councillor

council tax *n* (in Britain) a tax, based on the relative value of property, levied to fund local council services

counsel ('kaʊnsəl) *n* **1** advice or guidance on conduct, behaviour, etc **2** discussion, esp on future procedure; consultation: *to take counsel with a friend* **3** a person whose advice or guidance has or has been sought **4** a barrister or group of barristers engaged in conducting cases in court and advising on legal matters **5** *Christianity* any of the **counsels of perfection** or **evangelical counsels**, namely poverty, chastity, and obedience **6 counsel of perfection** excellent but unrealizable advice **7** private opinions or plans (esp in the phrase **keep one's own counsel**) **8** *archaic* wisdom; prudence ▷ *vb* **-sels, -selling, -selled** *or US* **-sels, -seling, -seled 9** (*tr*) to give advice or guidance to **10** (*tr; often takes a clause as object*) to recommend the acceptance of (a plan, idea, etc); urge **11** (*intr*) *archaic* to take counsel; consult [c13: from Old French *counseil*, from Latin *consilium* deliberating body; related to CONSUL, CONSULT]
● USAGE Avoid confusion with **council**

counselling *or US* **counseling** ('kaʊnsəlɪŋ) *n* guidance offered by social workers, doctors, etc, to help a person resolve social or personal problems

counsellor *or US* **counselor** ('kaʊnsələ) *n* **1** a person who gives counsel; adviser **2** Also called: **counselor-at-law** *US* a lawyer, esp one who conducts cases in court; attorney **3** a senior British diplomatic officer
● USAGE Avoid confusion with **councillor**

count¹ (kaʊnt) *vb* **1** to add up or check (each unit in a collection) in order to ascertain the sum; enumerate: *count your change* **2** (*tr*) to recite numbers in ascending order up to and including **3** (*tr; often foll by in*) to take into account or include: *we must count him in* **4** not counting excluding **5** (*tr*) to believe to be; consider; think; deem: *count yourself lucky* **6** (*intr*) to have value, importance, or influence: *this picture counts as a rarity* **7** (*intr*) *music* to keep time by counting beats ▷ *n* **8** the act of counting or reckoning **9** the number reached by counting; sum **10** *law* a paragraph in an indictment containing a distinct and separate charge **11 keep count** to keep a record of items, events, etc **12 lose count** to fail to keep an accurate record of items, events, etc **13** *boxing, wrestling* the act of telling off a number of seconds by the referee, as when a boxer has been knocked down or is pinned by his opponent **14 out for the count** *boxing* knocked out and unable to continue after a count of ten by the referee ▷ See also **count against, countdown**, etc [c14: from Anglo-French *counter*, from Old French *conter*, from Latin *computāre* to calculate, COMPUTE] > '**countable** *adj*

count² (kaʊnt) *n* **1** a nobleman in any of various European countries having a rank corresponding to that of a British earl **2** any of various officials in the late Roman Empire and under various Germanic kings in the early Middle Ages [c16: from Old French *conte*, from Late Latin *comes* occupant of a state office, from Latin: overseer, associate, literally: one who goes with, from COM- with + *īre* to go]

count against *vb* (*intr, preposition*) to have influence to the disadvantage of

countdown ('kaʊnt,daʊn) *n* **1** the act of counting backwards to time a critical operation exactly, such as the launching of a rocket or the detonation of explosives ▷ *vb* **count down** (*intr, adverb*) **2** to count numbers backwards towards zero, esp in timing such a critical operation

countenance ('kaʊntɪnəns) *n* **1** the face, esp when considered as expressing a person's character or mood **2** support or encouragement; sanction **3** composure; self-control (esp in the phrases **keep** or **lose one's countenance; out of countenance**) ▷ *vb* (*tr*) **4** to support or encourage; sanction **5** to tolerate; endure [c13: from Old French *contenance* mien, behaviour, from Latin *continentia* restraint, control; see CONTAIN]
> '**countenancer** *n*

counter¹ ('kaʊntə) *n* **1** a horizontal surface, as in a shop or bank, over which business is transacted **2** (in some cafeterias) a long table on which food is served to customers **3 a** a small flat disc of wood, metal, or plastic, used in various board games **b** a similar disc or token used as an imitation coin **4** a person or thing that

may be used or manipulated **5** a skating figure consisting of three circles **6 under the counter** (**under-the-counter** *when prenominal*) (of the sale of goods, esp goods in short supply) clandestine, surreptitious, or illegal; not in an open manner **7 over the counter** (**over-the-counter** *when prenominal*) (of security transactions) through a broker rather than on a stock exchange [c14: from Old French *comptouer*, ultimately from Latin *computāre* to COMPUTE]

counter² ('kaʊntə) *n* **1** a person who counts **2** an apparatus that records the number of occurrences of events [c14: from Old French *conteor*, from Latin *computātor*; see COUNT¹]

counter³ ('kaʊntə) *adv* **1** in a contrary direction or manner **2** in a wrong or reverse direction **3 run counter to** to have a contrary effect or action to ▷ *adj* **4** opposing; opposite; contrary ▷ *n* **5** something that is contrary or opposite to some other thing **6** an act, effect, or force that opposes another **7** a return attack, such as a blow in boxing **8** *fencing* a parry in which the foils move in a circular fashion **9** the portion of the stern of a boat or ship that overhangs the water aft of the rudder **10** a piece of leather forming the back of a shoe ▷ *vb* **11** to say or do (something) in retaliation or response **12** (*tr*) to move, act, or perform in a manner or direction opposite to (a person or thing) **13** to return the attack of (an opponent) [c15: from Old French *contre*, from Latin *contrā* against]

counter- *prefix* **1** against; opposite; contrary: *counterattack* **2** complementary; corresponding: *counterfoil* [via Norman French from Latin *contrā* against, opposite; see CONTRA-]

counteract (,kaʊntər'ækt) *vb* (*tr*) to oppose, neutralize, or mitigate the effects of by contrary action; check > ,counter'action *n* > ,counter'active *adj*

counterattack ('kaʊntərə,tæk) *n* **1** an attack in response to an attack ▷ *vb* **2** to make a counterattack (against)

counterbalance *n* ('kaʊntə,bæləns) a weight or force that balances or offsets another ▷ *vb* (,kaʊntə'bæləns) (*tr*) **2** to act as a counterbalance ▷ Also called: **counterpoise**

counterblast ('kaʊntə,blɑːst) *n* an aggressive response to a verbal attack

countercheck *n* ('kaʊntə,tʃɛk) **1** a check or restraint, esp one that acts in opposition to another **2** a double check, as for accuracy ▷ *vb* (,kaʊntə'tʃɛk) (*tr*) **3** to oppose by counteraction **4** to double-check

counterclaim ('kaʊntə,kleɪm) *chiefly law* ▷ *n* **1** a claim set up in opposition to another, esp by the defendant in a civil action against the plaintiff ▷ *vb* **2** to set up (a claim) in opposition to another claim > ,counter'claimant *n*

counterclockwise (,kaʊntə'klɒk,waɪz) *adv, adj US & Canadian* in the opposite direction to the rotation of the hands of a clock. Also called (in Britain and certain other countries): **anticlockwise**

counterculture ('kaʊntə,kʌltʃə) *n* an alternative culture, deliberately at variance with the social norm

counterespionage (,kaʊntər'ɛspɪə,nɑːʒ) *n* activities designed to detect and counteract enemy espionage

counterfeit ('kaʊntəfɪt) *adj* **1** made in imitation of something genuine with the intent to deceive or defraud; forged **2** simulated; sham: *counterfeit affection* ▷ *n* **3** an imitation designed to deceive or defraud **4** *archaic* an impostor; cheat ▷ *vb* **5** (*tr*) to make a fraudulent imitation of **6** (*intr*) to make counterfeits **7** to feign; simulate **8** to imitate; copy [c13: from Old French *contrefait*, from *contrefaire* to copy, from *contre*- COUNTER- + *faire* to make, from Latin *facere*] > '**counterfeiter** *n*

counterfoil ('kaʊntə,fɔɪl) *n Brit* the part of a cheque, postal order, receipt, etc, detached and retained as a record of the transaction. Also called (esp US and Canadian): **stub**

counterinsurgency (,kaʊntərɪn'sɜːdʒənsɪ) *n* action taken by a government to counter the activities of rebels, guerrillas, etc

counterintelligence (,kaʊntərɪn'tɛlɪdʒəns) *n* **1** activities designed to frustrate enemy espionage **2** intelligence collected about enemy espionage

counterintuitive (,kaʊntərɪn'tuːɪtɪv) *adj* (of an idea, proposal, etc) seemingly contrary to common sense

counterirritant (ˌkaʊntərˈɪrɪtᵊnt) n 1 an agent that causes a superficial irritation of the skin and thereby relieves inflammation of deep structures ▷ adj 2 producing a counterirritation > ˌcounterˌirriˈtation n

countermand vb (ˌkaʊntəˈmɑːnd) (tr) 1 to revoke or cancel (a command, order, etc) 2 to order (forces, etc) to return or retreat; recall ▷ n (ˈkaʊntəˌmɑːnd) 3 a command revoking another [c15: from Old French contremander, from contre- COUNTER- + mander to command, from Latin mandāre; see MANDATE]

countermarch (ˈkaʊntəˌmɑːtʃ) chiefly military vb 1 to march or cause to march back along the same route ▷ n 2 the act or instance of countermarching

countermeasure (ˈkaʊntəˌmɛʒə) n action taken to oppose, neutralize, or retaliate against some other action

countermove (ˈkaʊntəˌmuːv) n 1 an opposing move ▷ vb 2 to make or do (something) as an opposing move > ˈcounterˌmovement n

counteroffensive (ˈkaʊntərəˌfɛnsɪv) n a series of attacks by a defending force against an attacking enemy

counteroffer (ˈkaʊntərˌɒfə) n a response to a bid in which a seller amends his original offer, making it more favourable to the buyer

counterpane (ˈkaʊntəˌpeɪn) n another word for **bedspread** [c17: from obsolete counterpoint (influenced by pane coverlet), changed from Old French coutepointe quilt, from Medieval Latin culcita puncta quilted mattress]

counterpart (ˈkaʊntəˌpɑːt) n 1 a person or thing identical to or closely resembling another 2 one of two parts that complement or correspond to each other 3 a duplicate, esp of a legal document; copy

counterparty (ˈkaʊntəˌpɑːtɪ) n, pl -parties a person who is a party to a contract

counterplot (ˈkaʊntəˌplɒt) n 1 a plot designed to frustrate another plot ▷ vb -plots, -plotting, -plotted 2 (tr) to oppose with a counterplot

counterpoint (ˈkaʊntəˌpɔɪnt) n 1 the technique involving the simultaneous sounding of two or more parts or melodies 2 a melody or part combined with another melody or part 3 the musical texture resulting from the simultaneous sounding of two or more melodies or parts ▷ vb 4 (tr) to set in contrast ▷ Related adjective: **contrapuntal** [c15: from Old French contrepoint, from contre- COUNTER- + point dot, note in musical notation, that is, an accompaniment set against the notes of a melody]

counterpoise (ˈkaʊntəˌpɔɪz) n 1 a force, influence, etc, that counterbalances another 2 a state of balance; equilibrium 3 a weight that balances another 4 a radial array of metallic wires, rods, or tubes arranged horizontally around the base of a vertical aerial to increase its transmitting efficiency ▷ vb (tr) 5 to oppose with something of equal effect, weight, or force; offset 6 to bring into equilibrium 7 archaic to consider (one thing) carefully in relation to another

counterproductive (ˌkaʊntəprəˈdʌktɪv) adj tending to hinder or act against the achievement of an aim

counterproposal (ˈkaʊntəprəˌpəʊzᵊl) n a proposal offered as an alternative to a previous proposal

Counter-Reformation n the reform movement of the Roman Catholic Church in the 16th and early 17th centuries considered as a reaction to the Protestant Reformation

counter-revolution n a revolution opposed to a previous revolution and aimed at reversing its effects > ˌcounter-ˌrevoˈlutionist n

countershaft (ˈkaʊntəˌʃɑːft) n an intermediate shaft that is driven by, but rotates in the opposite direction to, a main shaft, esp in a gear train

countersign vb (ˈkaʊntəˌsaɪn, ˌkaʊntəˈsaɪn) 1 (tr) to sign (a document already signed by another) ▷ n (ˈkaʊntəˌsaɪn) 2 Also called: countersignature the signature so written 3 a secret sign given in response to another sign 4 chiefly military a password

countersink (ˈkaʊntəˌsɪŋk) vb -sinks, -sinking, -sank, -sunk (tr) 1 to enlarge the upper part of (a hole) in timber, metal, etc, so that the head of a bolt or screw can be sunk below the surface 2 to drive (a screw) or

sink (a bolt) into such an enlarged hole ▷ n 3 Also called: countersink bit a tool for countersinking 4 a countersunk depression or hole

countersuit (ˈkaʊntəˌsuːt) n law a legal claim made as a reaction to a claim made against one

countertenor (ˌkaʊntəˈtɛnə) n 1 an adult male voice with an alto range 2 a singer with such a voice

counterterrorism (ˌkaʊntəˈtɛrəˌrɪzəm) n activities that are intended to prevent terrorist acts or to eradicate terrorist groups > ˌcounterˈterrorist adj

countervail (ˌkaʊntəˈveɪl, ˈkaʊntəˌveɪl) vb 1 (when intr, usually foll by against) to act or act against with equal power or force 2 (tr) to make up for; compensate; offset [c14: from Old French contrevaloir, from Latin contrā valēre, from contrā against + valēre to be strong]

countervailing duty n an extra import duty imposed by a country on certain imports, esp to prevent dumping or to counteract subsidies in the exporting country

counterweigh (ˌkaʊntəˈweɪ) vb another word for **counterbalance**

counterweight (ˈkaʊntəˌweɪt) n a counterbalancing weight, influence, or force > ˈcounterˌweighted adj

countess (ˈkaʊntɪs) n 1 the wife or widow of a count or earl 2 a woman of the rank of count or earl

counting house n rare, chiefly Brit a room or building used by the accountants of a business

countless (ˈkaʊntlɪs) adj innumerable; myriad

count noun n linguistics, logic a noun that can be qualified by the indefinite article, and may be used in the plural, as telephone and thing but not airs and graces or bravery. See **mass noun**

count on vb (intr, preposition) to rely or depend on

count out vb (tr, adverb) 1 informal to leave out; exclude 2 (of a boxing referee) to judge (a floored boxer) to have failed to recover within the specified time

count palatine n, pl counts palatine history 1 (in the Holy Roman Empire) a originally an official who administered the king's domains or his justice b later, a count who exercised royal authority in his own domains 2 (in England and Ireland) an earl or other lord of a county palatine

countrified or **countryfied** (ˈkʌntrɪˌfaɪd) adj in the style, manners, etc, of the country; rural

country (ˈkʌntrɪ) n, pl -tries 1 a territory distinguished by its people, culture, language, geography, etc 2 an area of land distinguished by its political autonomy; state 3 the people of a territory or state 4 a the part of the land that is away from cities or industrial areas; rural districts b (as modifier): country cottage Related adj: pastoral, rural 5 short for **country music** 6 up country away from the coast or the capital 7 one's native land or nation of citizenship 8 across country not keeping to roads, etc 9 go to the country or appeal to the country chiefly Brit to dissolve Parliament and hold an election [c13: from Old French contrée, from Medieval Latin contrāta, literally: that which lies opposite, from Latin contrā opposite]

country and western n another name for **country music**

country club n a club in the country, having sporting and social facilities

country dance n a type of folk dance in which couples are arranged in sets and perform a series of movements, esp facing one another in a line > country dancing n

country house n a large house in the country, esp a mansion belonging to a wealthy family

countryman (ˈkʌntrɪmən) n, pl -men 1 a person who lives in the country 2 a person from a particular country or from one's own country (esp in the phrase **fellow countryman**) > ˈcountryˌwoman fem n

country music n a type of 20th-century popular music based on White folk music of the southeastern US

country park n Brit an area of countryside, usually not less than 10 hectares, set aside for public recreation: often funded by a Countryside Commission grant

country seat n a large estate or property in the country

countryside (ˈkʌntrɪˌsaɪd) n a rural area or its population

county (ˈkaʊntɪ) n, pl -ties 1 a any of the administrative or geographic subdivisions of certain states, esp any of the major units into which England and Wales are or have been divided for purposes of local government **b** (*as modifier*): *county cricket* **2** *NZ* an electoral division in a rural area **3** *obsolete* the lands under the jurisdiction of a count or earl ▷ *adj* **4** *Brit informal* having the characteristics and habits of the inhabitants of country houses and estates, esp an upper-class accent and an interest in horses, dogs, etc [c14: from Old French *conté* land belonging to a count, from Late Latin *comitātus* office of a count, from *comes* COUNT²]

county borough *n* **1** (in England and Wales from 1888 to 1974 and in Wales from 1996) a borough administered independently of any higher tier of local government **2** (in the Republic of Ireland) any of the four largest boroughs, governed independently of the administrative county around it by an elected council that constitutes an all-purpose authority

county palatine *n*, *pl* **counties palatine** **1** the lands of a count palatine **2** (in England and Ireland) a county in which the earl or other lord exercised many royal powers, esp judicial authority

county town *n* the town in which a county's affairs are or were administered

coup (kuː) *n* **1** a brilliant and successful stroke or action **2** short for **coup d'état** [c18: from French: blow, from Latin *colaphus* blow with the fist, from Greek *kolaphos*]

coup de grâce *French* (ku də grɑs) *n*, *pl* **coups de grâce** (ku də grɑs) **1** a mortal or finishing blow, esp one delivered as an act of mercy to a sufferer **2** a final or decisive stroke [literally: blow of mercy]

coup d'état ('kuː deɪ'tɑː; *French* ku deta) *n*, *pl* **coups d'état** ('kuː deɪ'tɑː; *French* ku deta) a sudden violent or illegal seizure of government [French, literally: stroke of state]

coupe (kuːp) *n* **1** a dessert of fruit and ice cream, usually served in a glass goblet **2** a dish or stemmed glass bowl designed for this dessert [c19: from French: goblet, CUP]

coupé ('kuːpeɪ) *n* **1** Also called: **fixed-head coupé** a four-seater car with a fixed roof, a sloping back, and usually two doors **2** a four-wheeled horse-drawn carriage with two seats inside and one outside for the driver [c19: from French, short for *carosse coupé*, literally: cut-off carriage, from *couper* to cut, from *coup* blow, stroke]

Couperin (*French* kuprɛ̃) *n* **François** (frɑ̃swa). 1668–1733, French composer, noted for his harpsichord suites and organ music

Coupland ('kəʊplənd) *n* **Douglas**. born 1961, Canadian novelist and journalist; novels include *Generation X* (1991), *Girlfriend in a Coma* (1998), and *City of Glass* (2000)

couple ('kʌpəl) *n* **1** two people who regularly associate with each other or live together: *an engaged couple* **2** (*functioning as singular or plural*) two people considered as a pair, for or as if for dancing, games, etc **3** a pair of equal and opposite parallel forces that have a tendency to produce rotation with a torque or turning moment equal to the product of either force and the perpendicular distance between them **4** a connector or link between two members, such as a tie connecting a pair of rafters in a roof **5** **a couple of** (*functioning as singular or plural*) **a** a combination of two; a pair of: *a couple of men* **b** *informal* a small number of; a few: *a couple of days* ▷ *pron* **6** (usually preceded by *a*; functioning as singular or plural) two; a pair: *give him a couple* ▷ *vb* **7** (*tr*) to connect (two things) together or to connect (one thing) to (another): *to couple railway carriages* **8** to form or be formed into a pair or pairs **9** to associate, put, or connect together **10** (*intr*) to have sexual intercourse [c13: from Old French: a pair, from Latin *cōpula* a bond; see COPULA]

coupledom ('kʌpəldəm) *n* the state of living as a couple, esp when regarded as being interested in each other to the exclusion of the outside world

coupler ('kʌplə) *n* *music* a device on an organ or harpsichord connecting two keys, two manuals, etc, so that both may be played at once

couplet ('kʌplɪt) *n* two successive lines of verse, usually rhymed and of the same metre [c16: from French, literally: a little pair; see COUPLE]

coupling ('kʌplɪŋ) *n* **1** a mechanical device that connects two things **2** a device for connecting railway cars or trucks together

coupon ('kuːpɒn) *n* **1 a** a detachable part of a ticket or advertisement entitling the holder to a discount, free gift, etc **b** a detachable slip usable as a commercial order form **c** a voucher given away with certain goods, a certain number of which are exchangeable for goods offered by the manufacturers **2** one of a number of detachable certificates attached to a bond, esp a bearer bond, the surrender of which entitles the bearer to receive interest payments **3** one of several detachable cards used for making hire-purchase payments **4** *Brit* a detachable entry form for any of certain competitions, esp football pools [c19: from French, from Old French *colpon* piece cut off, from *colper* to cut, variant of *couper*; see COPE¹]

courage ('kʌrɪdʒ) *n* **1** the power or quality of dealing with or facing danger, fear, pain, etc **2** the courage of one's convictions the confidence to act in accordance with one's beliefs **3** take one's courage in both hands to nerve oneself to perform an action **4** *obsolete* mind; disposition; spirit [c13: from Old French *corage*, from *cuer* heart, from Latin *cor*]

courageous (kə'reɪdʒəs) *adj* possessing or expressing courage ▷ **cou'rageously** *adv* ▷ **cou'rageousness** *n*

courante (kʊ'rɑːnt) *n* *music* **1** an old dance in quick triple time **2** a movement of a (mostly) 16th- to 18th-century suite based on this [c16: from French, literally: running, feminine of *courant*, present participle of *courir* to run, from Latin *currere*]

Courantyne ('kɜːrən,taɪn) *n* a river in N South America, rising in S Guyana and flowing north to the Atlantic, forming the boundary between Guyana and Surinam. Length: 765 km (475 miles)

courbaril ('kʊəbərɪl) *n* a tropical American leguminous tree, *Hymenaea courbaril*. Its wood is a useful timber and its gum is a source of copal. Also called: **West Indian locust** [c18: from a native American name]

Courbet (*French* kurbɛ) *n* **Gustave** (gystav). 1819–77, French painter, a leader of the realist movement; noted for his depiction of contemporary life

coureur de bois (*French* kurœr də bwa) *n*, *pl* **coureurs de bois** (kurœr də bwa) *Canadian history* a French Canadian woodsman or Métis who traded with Indians for furs [Canadian French: trapper (literally: wood-runner)]

courgette (kʊə'ʒɛt) *n* *chiefly Brit* a small variety of vegetable marrow, cooked and eaten as a vegetable. Also called: **zucchini** [from French, diminutive of *courge* marrow, gourd]

courier ('kʊərɪə) *n* **1** a special messenger, esp one carrying diplomatic correspondence **2** a person who makes arrangements for or accompanies a group of travellers on a journey or tour ▷ *vb* **3** (*tr*) to send (a parcel, letter, etc) by courier [c16: from Old French *courier*, from Old Latin *corriere*, from *correre* to run, from Latin *currere*]

Cournand ('kʊənənd, -nænd; *French* kurnɑ̃) *n* **André (Frederic)**. 1895–1988, US physician, born in France: shared the 1956 Nobel prize for physiology or medicine for his work on heart catheterization

Courrèges (*French* kurɛʒ) *n* **André** (ɑ̃dre). born 1923, French couturier: helped to launch unisex fashion in the mid-1960s

course (kɔːs) *n* **1** a continuous progression from one point to the next in time or space; onward movement **2** a route or direction followed **3** the path or channel along which something moves: *the course of a river* **4** an area or stretch of land or water on which a sport is played or a race is run: *a golf course* **5** a period of time; duration: *in the course of the next hour* **6** the usual order of and time required for a sequence of events; regular procedure: *the illness ran its course* **7** a mode of conduct or action: *if you follow that course, you will certainly fail* **8** a connected series of events, actions, etc **9 a** a prescribed number of lessons, lectures, etc, in an educational curriculum **b** the material covered in such a curriculum **10** a prescribed regimen to be followed for a specific period of time: *a course of treatment* **11** a part of a meal served at one time **12** a continuous, usually horizontal,

c

layer of building material, such as a row of bricks, tiles, etc **13** as a matter of course as a natural or normal consequence, mode of action, or event **14** the course of nature the ordinary course of events **15** in course of in the process of **16** in due course at some future time, esp the natural or appropriate time **17** of course a (*adverb*) as expected; naturally **b** (*sentence substitute*) certainly; definitely ▷ *vb* **18** (*intr*) to run, race, or flow, esp swiftly and without interruption **19** to cause (hounds) to hunt by sight rather than scent or (of hounds) to hunt (a quarry) thus [c13: from Old French *cours*, from Latin *cursus* a running, from *currere* to run]

courser¹ ('kɔːsə) *n* **1** a person who courses hounds or dogs, esp greyhounds **2** a hound or dog trained for coursing

courser² ('kɔːsə) *n literary* a swift horse; steed [c13: from Old French *coursier*, from *cours* COURSE]

coursework ('kɔːs,wɜːk) *n* written or oral work completed by a student within a given period, which is assessed as an integral part of an educational course

coursing ('kɔːsɪŋ) *n* **1** hunting with hounds or dogs that follow their quarry by sight **2** a sport in which hounds are matched against one another in pairs for the hunting of hares by sight

court (kɔːt) *n* **1** an area of ground wholly or partly surrounded by walls or buildings **2** *Brit* (*capital when part of a name*) **a** a block of flats: *Selwyn Court* **b** a mansion or country house **c** a short street, sometimes closed at one end **3** a space inside a building, sometimes surrounded with galleries **4** a the residence, retinues, or household of a sovereign or nobleman **b** (*as modifier*): *a court ball* **5** a sovereign or prince and his retinue, advisers, etc **6** any formal assembly, reception, etc, held by a sovereign or nobleman with his courtiers **7** homage, flattering attention, or amorous approaches (esp in the phrase **pay court to someone**) **8** *law* **a** an authority having power to adjudicate in civil, criminal, military, or ecclesiastical matters **b** the regular sitting of such a judicial authority **c** the room or building in which such a tribunal sits **9** a a marked outdoor or enclosed area used for any of various ball games, such as tennis, squash, etc **b** a marked section of such an area: *the service court* **10** a the board of directors or council of a corporation, company, etc **b** *chiefly Brit* the supreme council of some universities **11** a branch of any of several friendly societies **12** go to court to take legal action **13** hold court to preside over admirers, attendants, etc **14** out of court a without a trial or legal case: *the case was settled out of court* **b** too unimportant for consideration **c** *Brit* so as to ridicule completely (in the phrase **laugh out of court**) **15** the ball is in your court you are obliged to make the next move ▷ *vb* **16** to attempt to gain the love of (someone); woo **17** (*tr*) to pay attention to (someone) in order to gain favour **18** (*tr*) to try to obtain (fame, honour, etc) **19** (*tr*) to invite, usually foolishly, as by taking risks: *to court disaster* **20** *old-fashioned* to be conducting a serious emotional relationship usually leading to marriage [c12: from Old French, from Latin *cohors* COHORT]

Court (kɔːt) *n* **Margaret** (née *Smith*). born 1942, Australian tennis player: Australian champion 1960–66, 1969–71, and 1973; US champion 1962, 1965, 1969–70, and 1973; Wimbledon champion 1963, 1965, and 1970

court-bouillon ('kʊət'buːjɒn; *French* kurbujɔ̃) *n* a stock made from root vegetables, water, and wine or vinegar, used primarily for poaching fish [from French, from *court* short, from Latin *curtus* + *bouillon* broth, from *bouillir* to BOIL¹]

court card *n* (in a pack of playing cards) a king, queen, or jack of any suit [c17: altered from earlier *coat-card*, from the decorative coats worn by the figures depicted]

court circular *n* (in countries having a monarchy) a daily report of the activities, engagements, etc, of the sovereign, published in a national newspaper

Courtelle (kɔː'tɛl) *n trademark* a synthetic acrylic fibre resembling wool

courteous ('kɜːtɪəs) *adj* polite and considerate in manner [c13 *corteis*, literally: with courtly manners, from Old French; see COURT] > 'courteously *adv*

> 'courteousness *n*

courtesan *or* **courtezan** (,kɔːtɪ'zæn) *n* (esp formerly) a prostitute, or the mistress of a man of rank [c16: from Old French *courtisane*, from Italian *cortigiana* female courtier, from *cortigiano* courtier, from *corte* COURT]

courtesy ('kɜːtɪsɪ) *n*, *pl* **-sies** **1** politeness; good manners **2** a courteous gesture or remark **3** favour or consent (esp in the phrase **by courtesy of**) **4** common consent as opposed to right (esp in the phrase **by courtesy**) [c13 *curteisie*, from Old French, from *corteis* COURTEOUS]

courtesy light *n* the interior light in a motor vehicle

courtesy title *n* any of several titles having no legal significance, such as those borne by the children of peers

courthouse ('kɔːt,haʊs) *n* a public building in which courts of law are held

courtier ('kɔːtɪə) *n* **1** an attendant at a court **2** a person who seeks favour in an ingratiating manner [c13: from Anglo-French *courteour* (unattested), from Old French *corteier* to attend at court]

courtly ('kɔːtlɪ) *adj* **-lier**, **-liest** **1** of or suitable for a royal court **2** refined in manner **3** ingratiating > 'courtliness *n*

court martial *n*, *pl* **court martials** *or* **courts martial** **1** a military court that tries persons subject to military law ▷ *vb* **court-martial**, **-tials**, **-tialling**, **-tialled** *or US* **-tials**, **-tialing**, **-tialed** **2** (*tr*) to try by court martial

Court of Appeal *n* a branch of the Supreme Court of Judicature that hears appeals from the High Court in both criminal and civil matters and from the county and crown courts

Court of St James's *n* the official name of the royal court of Britain

court plaster *n* a plaster, composed of isinglass on silk, formerly used to cover superficial wounds [c18: so called because formerly used by court ladies for beauty spots]

courtroom ('kɔːt,ruːm, -,rʊm) *n* a room in which the sittings of a law court are held

courtship ('kɔːtʃɪp) *n* **1** the act, period, or art of seeking the love of someone with intent to marry **2** the seeking or soliciting of favours **3** *obsolete* courtly behaviour

court shoe *n* a low-cut shoe for women, having no laces or straps

courtyard ('kɔːt,jɑːd) *n* an open area of ground surrounded by walls or buildings; court

couscous ('kuːskuːs) *n* **1** a type of semolina originating from North Africa, consisting of granules of crushed durum wheat **2** a spicy North African dish consisting of steamed semolina with meat, vegetables, or fruit c17: via French from Arabic *kouskous*, from *kaskasa* to pound until fine

cousin ('kʌzⁿn) *n* **1** Also called: **first cousin**, **cousin-german**, **full cousin** the child of one's aunt or uncle **2** a relative who has descended from one of one's common ancestors. A person's **second cousin** is the child of one of his parents' first cousins. A person's **third cousin** is the child of one of his parents' second cousins. A **first cousin once removed** (or loosely **second cousin**) is the child of one's first cousin **3** a member of a group related by race, ancestry, interests, etc: *our Australian cousins* **4** a title used by a sovereign when addressing another sovereign or a nobleman [c13: from Old French *cosin*, from Latin *consōbrīnus* cousin, from *sōbrīnus* cousin on the mother's side; related to *soror* sister] > 'cousin,hood *or* 'cousin,ship *n* > 'cousinly *adj*, *adv*

Cousin (*French* kuzɛ̃) *n* **Victor** (viktɔr). 1792–1867, French philosopher and educational reformer

Cousteau (*French* kusto) *n* **Jacques Yves** (ʒɑk iv). 1910–97, French underwater explorer

couta ('kuːtə) *n Austral* a type of traditional wooden sailing boat, originally used for fishing. Also called: **couta boat** [c20: from BARRACOUTA]

couture (kuː'tʊə; *French* kutyr) *n* **a** high-fashion designing and dressmaking **b** (*as modifier*): *couture clothes* [from French: sewing, dressmaking, from Old French *cousture* seam, from Latin *consuere* to stitch together, from *suere* to sew]

couturier (kuː'tʊərɪ,eɪ; *French* kutyrje) *n* a person who designs, makes, and sells fashion clothes for women [from French: dressmaker; see COUTURE] > **couturière** (kuːˌtuːrɪˈɛə; *French* kutyrjɛr) *fem n*

couvade (kuːˈvɑːd; *French* kuvad) *n anthropol* a custom in certain cultures of treating the husband of a woman giving birth as if he were bearing the child [C19: from French, from *couver* to hatch, from Latin *cubāre* to lie down]

covalency (kəʊˈveɪlənsɪ) *or US* **covalence** *n* **1** the formation and nature of covalent bonds **2** the number of covalent bonds that a particular atom can make with other atoms in forming a molecule > co'valent *adj* > co'valently *adv*

cove¹ (kəʊv) *n* **1** a small bay or inlet, usually between rocky headlands **2** a narrow cavern formed in the sides of cliffs, mountains, etc, usually by erosion **3** a sheltered place **4** *Also called:* coving *architect* a concave curved surface between the wall and ceiling of a room ▷ *vb* **5** (*tr*) to form an architectural cove in [Old English *cofa*; related to Old Norse *kofi*, Old High German *kubisi* tent]

cove² (kəʊv) *n* **1** *old-fashioned, slang, Brit & Austral* a fellow; chap **2** *Austral history* an overseer of convict labourers [C16: probably from Romany *kova* thing, person]

coven (ˈkʌvən) *n* **1** a meeting of witches **2** a company of 13 witches [C16: probably from Old French *covin* group, ultimately from Latin *convenīre* to come together; compare CONVENT]

covenant (ˈkʌvənənt) *n* **1** a binding agreement; contract **2** *law* **a** an agreement in writing under seal, as to pay a stated annual sum to a charity **b** a particular clause in such an agreement, esp in a lease **3** (in early English law) an action in which damages were sought for breach of a sealed agreement **4** *Bible* God's promise to the Israelites and their commitment to worship him alone ▷ *vb* **5** to agree to a covenant (concerning) [C13: from Old French, from *covenir* to agree, from Latin *convenīre* to come together, make an agreement; see CONVENE] > covenantal (ˌkʌvəˈnæntəl) *adj* > ˌcove'nantally *adv*

Covenanter (ˈkʌvənəntə, ˌkʌvəˈnæntə) *n* a person upholding the National Covenant of 1638 or the Solemn League and Covenant of 1643 between Scotland and England to establish and defend Presbyterianism

Covent Garden (ˈkʌvənt, ˈkɒv-) *n* **1** a district of central London: famous for its former fruit, vegetable, and flower market, now a shopping precinct **2** the Royal Opera House (built 1858) in Covent Garden

Coventry (ˈkɒvəntrɪ) *n* **1** a city in central England, in Coventry unitary authority, West Midlands: devastated in World War II; modern cathedral (1954–62); industrial centre, esp for motor vehicles; two universities (1965, 1992). Pop: 303 475 (2001) **2** a unitary authority in central England, in West Midlands. Pop: 305 000 (2003 est). Area: 97 sq km (37 sq miles) **3** send to Coventry to ostracize or ignore

cover (ˈkʌvə) *vb* (*mainly tr*) **1** to place or spread something over so as to protect or conceal **2** to provide with a covering; clothe **3** to put a garment, esp a hat, on (the body or head) **4** to extend over or lie thickly on the surface of; spread: *snow covered the fields* **5** to bring upon (oneself); invest (oneself) as if with a covering: *covered with shame* **6** (sometimes foll by *up*) to act as a screen or concealment for; hide from view **7** *military* to protect (an individual, formation, or place) by taking up a position from which fire may be returned if those being protected are fired upon **8** (*also intr*, often foll by *for*) to assume responsibility for (a person or thing) **9** (*intr*; foll by *for* or *up for*) to provide an alibi (for) **10** to have as one's territory **11** to travel over **12** (*tr*) to have or place in the aim and within the range of (a firearm) **13** to include or deal with **14** (of an asset or income) to be sufficient to meet (a liability or expense) **15 a** to insure against loss, risk, etc **b** to provide for (loss, risk, etc) by insurance **16** to deposit (an equivalent stake) in a bet or wager **17** to act as reporter or photographer on (a news event, etc) for a newspaper or magazine: *to cover sports events* **18** *sport* to guard or protect (an opponent, team-mate, or area) **19** *music* to record a cover version of **20** (of a male animal, esp a horse) to copulate with (a female animal)

▷ *n* **21** anything that covers, spreads over, protects, or conceals **22 a** a blanket used on a bed for warmth **b** another word for **bedspread 23** a pretext, disguise, or false identity: *the thief sold brushes as a cover* **24** an envelope or package for sending through the post: *under plain cover* **25** *philately* an entire envelope that has been postmarked **26** an individual table setting, esp in a restaurant **27** *Also called:* **cover version** a version by a different artist of a previously recorded musical item **28** *cricket* **a** (*often plural*) the area more or less at right angles to the pitch on the off side and usually about halfway to the boundary **b** (*as modifier*): *a cover drive by a batsman* **29** break cover (esp of game animals) to come out from a shelter or hiding place **30** take cover to make for a place of safety or shelter **31** under cover protected, concealed, or in secret ▷ *See also* cover-up [C13: from Old French *covrir*, from Latin *cooperīre* to cover completely, from *operīre* to cover over]

coverage (ˈkʌvərɪdʒ) *n* **1** the amount or extent to which something is covered **2** *journalism* the amount and quality of reporting or analysis given to a particular subject or event **3** the extent of the protection provided by insurance

cover crop *n* a crop planted between main crops to prevent leaching or soil erosion or to provide green manure

Coverdale (ˈkʌvəˌdeɪl) *n* **Miles.** 1488–1568, the first translator of the complete Bible into English (1535)

covered wagon *n US & Canadian* a large wagon with an arched canvas top, used formerly for prairie travel

cover girl *n* a girl, esp a glamorous one, whose picture appears on the cover of a newspaper or magazine

covering letter *n* an accompanying letter sent as an explanation, introduction, or record

coverlet (ˈkʌvəlɪt) *n* another word for **bedspread**

cover note *n Brit* a certificate issued by an insurance company stating that a policy is operative: used as a temporary measure between the commencement of cover and the issue of the policy

cover point *n cricket* **a** a fielding position in the covers **b** a fielder in this position

cover slip *n* a very thin piece of glass placed over a specimen on a glass slide that is to be examined under a microscope

covert (ˈkʌvət) *adj* **1** concealed or secret ▷ *n* **2** a shelter or disguise **3** a thicket or woodland providing shelter for game **4** short for **covert cloth 5** *ornithol* any of the small feathers on the wings and tail of a bird that surround the bases of the larger feathers [C14: from Old French: covered, from *covrir* to COVER] > 'covertly *adv*

covert cloth *n* a twill-weave cotton or worsted suiting fabric

coverture (ˈkʌvətʃə) *n rare* shelter, concealment, or disguise [C13: from Old French, from *covert* covered; see COVERT]

cover-up *n* **1** concealment or attempted concealment of a mistake, crime, etc ▷ *vb* cover up (*adverb*) **2** (*tr*) to cover completely **3** (when *intr*, often foll by *for*) to attempt to conceal (a mistake or crime)

cover version *n* another name for **cover** (sense 27)

covet (ˈkʌvɪt) *vb* -vets, -veting, -veted (*tr*) to wish, long, or crave for (something, esp the property of another person) [C13: from Old French *coveitier*, from *coveitié* eager desire, ultimately from Latin *cupiditas* CUPIDITY] > 'covetable *adj* > 'coveter *n*

covetous (ˈkʌvɪtəs) *adj* (*usually postpositive* and foll by *of*) jealously eager for the possession of something (esp the property of another person) > 'covetously *adv* > 'covetousness *n*

covey (ˈkʌvɪ) *n* **1** a small flock of grouse or partridge **2** a small group, as of people [C14: from Old French *covee*, from *cover* to sit on, hatch; see COUVADE]

Covilhã (*Portuguese* kuviˈʎɐ̃) *n* **Pero da** (ˈpeːrəʊ da). ?1460–?1526, Portuguese explorer, who established relations between Portugal and Ethiopia

cow¹ (kaʊ) *n* **1** the mature female of any species of cattle, esp domesticated cattle **2** the mature female of various other mammals, such as the elephant, whale, and seal **3** (*not in technical use*) any domestic species of cattle

4 *informal* a disagreeable woman **5** *Austral & NZ slang* something objectionable (esp in the phrase **a fair cow**) [Old English *cū*; related to Old Norse *kȳr*, Old High German *kuo*, Latin *bōs*, Greek *boûs*, Sanskrit *gāus*]

cow² (kaʊ) *vb* (*tr*) to frighten or overawe, as with threats [C17: from Old Norse *kūga* to oppress, related to Norwegian *kue*, Swedish *kuva*]

coward (ˈkaʊəd) *n* a person who shrinks from or avoids danger, pain, or difficulty [C13: from Old French *cuard*, from *coue* tail, from Latin *cauda*; perhaps suggestive of a frightened animal with its tail between its legs]

Coward (ˈkaʊəd) *n* Sir **Noël** (**Pierce**). 1899–1973, English dramatist, actor, and composer, noted for his sophisticated comedies, which include *Private Lives* (1930) and *Blithe Spirit* (1941)

cowardice (ˈkaʊədɪs) *n* lack of courage in facing danger, pain, or difficulty

cowardly (ˈkaʊədlɪ) *adj* of or characteristic of a coward; lacking courage ▷ **ˈcowardliness** *n*

cowbell (ˈkaʊˌbɛl) *n* a bell hung around a cow's neck so that the cow can be easily located

cowberry (ˈkaʊbərɪ, -brɪ) *n*, *pl* -ries **1** a creeping ericaceous evergreen shrub, *Vaccinium vitis-idaea*, of N temperate and arctic regions, with pink or red flowers and edible slightly acid berries **2** the berry of this plant ▷ Also called: **red whortleberry**

cowbird (ˈkaʊˌbɜːd) *n* any of various American orioles of the genera *Molothrus*, *Tangavius*, etc, esp *M. ater* (common or brown-headed cowbird). They have a dark plumage and short bill

cowboy (ˈkaʊˌbɔɪ) *n* **1** Also called: **cowhand** a hired man who herds and tends cattle, usually on horseback, esp in the western US **2** a conventional character of Wild West folklore, films, etc, esp one involved in fighting Indians **3** *informal* a person who is an irresponsible or unscrupulous operator in business ▷ **ˈcowˌgirl** *fem n*

cowcatcher (ˈkaʊˌkætʃə) *n* *US & Canadian* a metal frame on the front of a locomotive to clear the track of animals or other obstructions

cow cocky *n*, *pl* **cow cockies** *Austral & NZ* a one-man dairy farmer

Cowdrey (ˈkaʊdrɪ) *n* (**Michael**) **Colin**, Baron. 1932–2000, English cricketer. He played for Kent and in 114 Test matches (captaining England 27 times)

Cowell (ˈkaʊəl) *n* **Simon**. born 1959, British manager of pop groups and TV personality, best known as an outspoken judge on the TV talent contests *Pop Idol* and *The X Factor*

cower (ˈkaʊə) *vb* (*intr*) to crouch or cringe, as in fear [C13: from Middle Low German *kūren* to lie in wait; related to Swedish *kura* to lie in wait, Danish *kure* to squat]

Cowes (kaʊz) *n* a town in S England, on the Isle of Wight: famous for its annual regatta. Pop: 19 110 (2001)

cowherd (ˈkaʊˌhɜːd) *n* a person employed to tend cattle

cowhide (ˈkaʊˌhaɪd) *n* **1** the hide of a cow **2** the leather made from such a hide ▷ Also called: **cowskin**

cowl (kaʊl) *n* **1** a hood, esp a loose one **2** the hooded habit of a monk **3** a cover fitted to a chimney to increase ventilation and prevent draughts **4** the part of a car body that supports the windscreen and the bonnet ▷ *vb* (*tr*) **5** to cover or provide with a cowl [Old English *cugele*, from Late Latin *cuculla* cowl, from Latin *cucullus* covering, cap, hood]

Cowley (ˈkaʊlɪ) *n* **Abraham**. 1618–67, English poet and essayist, who introduced the Pindaric ode to English literature

cowlick (ˈkaʊˌlɪk) *n* a tuft of hair over the forehead

cowling (ˈkaʊlɪŋ) *n* a streamlined metal covering, esp one fitted around an aircraft engine

cowman (ˈkaʊmən) *n*, *pl* -men **1** *Brit* another name for **cowherd 2** *US & Canadian* a man who owns cattle; rancher

co-worker *n* a fellow worker; associate

cow parsley *n* a common Eurasian umbelliferous hedgerow plant, *Anthriscus sylvestris*, having umbrella-shaped clusters of white flowers. Also called: **keck**, **Queen Anne's lace**

cowpat (ˈkaʊˌpæt) *n* a single dropping of cow dung

cowpea (ˈkaʊˌpiː) *n* **1** a leguminous tropical climbing plant, *Vigna sinensis*, producing long pods containing edible pealike seeds: grown for animal fodder and sometimes as human food **2** Also called: **black-eyed pea** the seed of this plant

Cowper (ˈkuːpə, ˈkaʊ-) *n* **William**. 1731–1800, English poet, noted for his nature poetry, such as in *The Task* (1785), and his hymns

cowpox (ˈkaʊˌpɒks) *n* a contagious viral disease of cows characterized by vesicles on the skin, esp on the teats and udder. Inoculation of humans with this virus provides temporary immunity to smallpox. It can be transmitted to other species, esp cats

cowpuncher (ˈkaʊˌpʌntʃə) or **cowpoke** (ˈkaʊˌpəʊk) *n* *US & Canadian* informal words for **cowboy**

cowrie or **cowry** (ˈkaʊrɪ) *n*, *pl* -ries **1** any marine gastropod mollusc of the mostly tropical family *Cypraeidae*, having a glossy brightly marked shell with an elongated opening **2** the shell of any of these molluscs, esp the shell of *Cypraea moneta* (**money cowry**), used as money in parts of Africa and S Asia [C17: from Hindi *kaurī*, from Sanskrit *kaparda*, of Dravidian origin; related to Tamil *kōtu* shell]

cowslip (ˈkaʊˌslɪp) *n* **1** Also called: **paigle** a primrose, *Primula veris*, native to temperate regions of the Old World, having fragrant yellow flowers **2** *US & Canadian* another name for **marsh marigold** [Old English *cūslyppe*; see COW¹, SLIP³]

cox (kɒks) *n* **1** a coxswain, esp of a racing eight or four ▷ *vb* **2** to act as coxswain of (a boat) ▷ **ˈcoxless** *adj*

Cox (kɒks) *n* **David**. 1783–1859, English landscape painter

coxa (ˈkɒksə) *n*, *pl* **coxae** (ˈkɒksiː) **1** a technical name for the hipbone or hip joint **2** the basal segment of the leg of an insect [C18: from Latin: hip] ▷ **ˈcoxal** *adj*

coxalgia (kɒkˈsældʒɪə) *n* **1** pain in the hip joint **2** disease of the hip joint causing pain [C19: from COXA + -ALGIA] ▷ **coxˈalgic** *adj*

coxcomb (ˈkɒksˌkəʊm) *n* **1** a variant spelling of **cockscomb 2** *obsolete* the cap, resembling a cock's comb, worn by a jester

coxswain (ˈkɒksən, -ˌsweɪn) *n* the helmsman of a lifeboat, racing shell, etc. Also called: **cockswain** [C15: from *cock* a ship's boat + SWAIN]

coy (kɔɪ) *adj* **1** (usually of a woman) affectedly demure, esp in a playful or provocative manner **2** shy; modest **3** evasive, esp in an annoying way [C14: from Old French *coi* reserved, from Latin *quiētus* QUIET] ▷ **ˈcoyish** *adj* ▷ **ˈcoyly** *adv* ▷ **ˈcoyness** *n*

Coy. *military abbreviation* company

coyote (ˈkɔɪəʊt, kɔɪˈəʊt, kɔɪˈəʊtɪ) *n*, *pl* -otes or -ote Also called: **prairie wolf** a predatory canine mammal, *Canis latrans*, related to but smaller than the wolf, roaming the deserts and prairies of North America [C19: from Mexican Spanish, from Nahuatl *coyotl*]

Coypel (*French* kwapɛl) *n* **Antoine**. 1661–1722, French baroque painter, noted esp for his large biblical compositions

coypu (ˈkɔɪpuː) *n*, *pl* -pus or -pu **1** an aquatic South American hystricomorph rodent, *Myocastor coypus*, introduced into Europe: family *Capromyidae*. It resembles a small beaver with a ratlike tail and is bred in captivity for its soft grey underfur **2** the fur of this animal ▷ Also called: **nutria** [C18: from American Spanish *coipú*, from Araucanian *kóypu*]

coz (kʌz) *n* an archaic word and form of address for cousin

cozen (ˈkʌzᵊn) *vb* to cheat or trick (someone) [C16: cant term perhaps related to COUSIN] ▷ **ˈcozenage** *n* ▷ **ˈcozener** *n*

cozy (ˈkəʊzɪ) *adj* -zier, -ziest the usual US spelling of **cosy**

CP *abbreviation* **1** Canadian Press **2** Common Prayer **3** Communist Party

cp. *abbreviation* compare

CPAG *abbreviation* (in Britain) Child Poverty Action Group

cpd *zoology*, *botany*, *chem abbreviation* compound

cpi *abbreviation* characters per inch

Cpl *abbreviation* Corporal

CPO *abbreviation* Chief Petty Officer

CPR *abbreviation* cardiopulmonary resuscitation

cps *abbreviation* **1** *physics* cycles per second **2** *computing* characters per second

CPS *abbreviation* (in England and Wales) Crown Prosecution Service

CPSA *abbreviation* (in Britain) Civil and Public Services Association

CPVE *abbreviation* (in Britain) Certificate of Pre-vocational Education: a certificate awarded for completion of a broad-based course of study offered as a less advanced alternative to traditional school-leaving qualifications

CQ *n telegraphy, telephony* a symbol transmitted by an amateur radio operator requesting two-way communication with any other amateur radio operator listening

Cr *abbreviation* **1** Councillor ▷ *the chemical symbol for* **2** chromium

crab¹ (kræb) *n* **1** any chiefly marine decapod crustacean of the genus *Cancer* and related genera (section *Brachyura*), having a broad flattened carapace covering the cephalothorax, beneath which is folded the abdomen. The first pair of limbs are modified as pincers **2** any of various similar or related arthropods, such as the hermit crab and horseshoe crab **3** short for **crab louse 4** a manoeuvre in which an aircraft flies slightly into the crosswind to compensate for drift **5** a mechanical lifting device, esp the travelling hoist of a gantry crane **6** *wrestling* **7 catch a crab** *rowing* to make a stroke in which the oar either misses the water or digs too deeply, causing the rower to fall backwards ▷ *vb* **crabs, crabbing, crabbed 8** (*intr*) to hunt or catch crabs **9** (*tr*) to fly (an aircraft) slightly into a crosswind to compensate for drift **10** (*intr*) *nautical* to move forwards with a slight sideways motion, as to overcome an offsetting current **11** (*intr*) to move sideways [Old English *crabba*; related to Old Norse *krabbi*, Old High German *krebiz* crab, Dutch *krabben* to scratch]

crab² (kræb) *informal* ▷ *vb* **crabs, crabbing, crabbed 1** (*intr*) to find fault; grumble **2** (*tr*) *chiefly US* to spoil (esp in the phrase **crab someone's act**) ▷ *n* **3** an irritable person **4 draw the crabs** *Austral* to attract unwelcome attention [c16: probably back formation from CRABBED]

crab³ (kræb) *n* short for **crab apple** [c15: perhaps of Scandinavian origin; compare Swedish *skrabbe* crab apple]

Crab (kræb) *n* **the Crab** the constellation Cancer, the fourth sign of the zodiac

crab apple *n* **1** any of several rosaceous trees of the genus *Malus* that have white, pink, or red flowers and small sour apple-like fruits **2** the fruit of any of these trees, used to make jam

Crabbe (kræb) *n* George. 1754–1832, English narrative poet, noted for his depiction of impoverished rural life in *The Village* (1783) and *The Borough* (1810)

crabbed ('kræbɪd) *adj* **1** surly; irritable; perverse **2** (esp of handwriting) cramped and hard to decipher [c13: probably from CRAB¹ (from its wayward gait), influenced by CRAB(APPLE) (from its tartness)] > 'crabbedly *adv* > 'crabbedness *n*

crabby ('kræbɪ) *adj* -bier, -biest bad-tempered

crab louse *n* a parasitic louse, *Pthirus* (or *Phthirus*) *pubis*, that infests the pubic region in man

crabwise ('kræb,waɪz) *adj, adv* (of motion) sideways; like a crab

crack (kræk) *vb* **1** to break or cause to break without complete separation of the parts: *the vase was cracked but unbroken* **2** to break or cause to break with a sudden sharp sound; snap: *to crack a nut* **3** to make or cause to make a sudden sharp sound: *to crack a whip* **4** to cause (the voice) to change tone or become harsh or (of the voice) to change tone, esp to a higher register; break **5** *informal* to fail or cause to fail **6** to yield or cause to yield: *to crack under torture* **7** (*tr*) to hit with a forceful or resounding blow **8** (*tr*) to break into or force open: *to crack a safe* **9** (*tr*) to solve or decipher (a code, problem, etc) **10** (*tr*) *informal* to tell (a joke, etc) **11** to break (a molecule) into smaller molecules or radicals by the action of heat, as in the distillation of petroleum **12** (*tr*) to open (esp a bottle) for drinking: *let's crack another bottle* **13** (*intr*) *Scot & Northern English dialect* to chat; gossip **14** (*tr*)

informal to achieve (esp in the phrase **crack it**) **15** (*tr*) *Austral* to find or catch: *to crack a wave in surfing* **16 crack a smile** *informal* to break into a smile **17 crack hardy** or **crack hearty** *Austral & NZ informal* to disguise one's discomfort, etc; put on a bold front **18 crack the whip** *informal* to assert one's authority, esp to put people under pressure to work harder ▷ *n* **19** a sudden sharp noise **20** a break or fracture without complete separation of the two parts: *a crack in the window* **21** a narrow opening or fissure **22** *informal* a resounding blow **23** a physical or mental defect; flaw **24** a moment or specific instant: *the crack of day* **25** a broken or cracked tone of voice, as a boy's during puberty **26** (often foll by *at*) *informal* an attempt; opportunity to try: *he had a crack at the problem* **27** *slang* a gibe; wisecrack; joke **28** *slang* a person that excels **29** *Scot & Northern English dialect* a talk; chat **30** *slang* a processed form of cocaine hydrochloride used as a stimulant. It is highly addictive **31** Also called: **craic** *informal, chiefly Irish* fun; *informal* entertainment: *the crack was great in here last night* **32** *obsolete, slang* a burglar or burglary **33 crack of dawn a** the very instant that the sun rises **b** very early in the morning **34** a fair **crack of the whip** *informal* a fair chance or opportunity **35 crack of doom** doomsday; the end of the world; the Day of Judgment ▷ *adj* **36** (*prenominal*) *slang* first-class; excellent: *a crack shot* ▷ See also **crack down, crack on, crack up** [Old English *cracian*; related to Old High German *krahhōn*, Dutch *kraken*, Sanskrit *gárjati* he roars]

crackberry ('kræk,bərɪ) *n, pl* -ries *informal* nickname for a BlackBerry handheld device that functions as a telephone, PDA, and e-mailer and appears to have an addictive hold on its users [c21: from CRACK (sense 30) + BLACKBERRY]

crackbrained ('kræk,breɪnd) *adj* insane, idiotic, or crazy

crack down *vb* (*intr, adverb*; often foll by *on*) **1** to take severe measures (against); become stricter (with) ▷ *n* **crackdown 2** severe or repressive measures

cracked (krækt) *adj* **1** damaged by cracking **2** *informal* crazy

cracked wheat *n* whole wheat cracked between rollers so that it will cook more quickly

cracker ('krækə) *n* **1** a decorated cardboard tube that emits a bang when pulled apart, releasing a toy, a joke, or a paper hat **2** short for **firecracker 3** a thin crisp biscuit, usually unsweetened **4** a person or thing that cracks **5** *US* another word for **poor White 6** *Brit slang* a thing or person of notable qualities or abilities **7 not worth a cracker** *Austral & NZ informal* worthless; useless

crackerjack ('krækə,dʒæk) *informal* ▷ *adj* **1** excellent ▷ *n* **2** a person or thing of exceptional quality or ability [c20: changed from CRACK (first-class) + JACK¹ (man)]

crackers ('krækəz) *adj* (*postpositive*) *Brit* a slang word for **insane**

crackhead ('kræk,hed) *n* *slang* a person addicted to the drug crack

cracking ('krækɪŋ) *adj* **1** (*prenominal*) *informal* fast; vigorous (esp in the phrase **a cracking pace**) **2 get cracking** *informal* to start doing something quickly or do something with increased speed ▷ *adv, adj* **3** *Brit informal* first-class; excellent: *a cracking good match* ▷ *n* **4** the process in which molecules are cracked, esp the oil-refining process in which heavy oils are broken down into hydrocarbons of lower molecular weight by heat or catalysis. See also **catalytic cracker**

crackjaw ('kræk,dʒɔː) *informal* ▷ *adj* **1** difficult to pronounce ▷ *n* **2** a word or phrase that is difficult to pronounce

crackle ('kræk³l) *vb* **1** to make or cause to make a series of slight sharp noises, as of paper being crushed or of a wood fire burning **2** (*tr*) to decorate (porcelain or pottery) by causing a fine network of cracks to appear in the glaze **3** (*intr*) to abound in vivacity or energy ▷ *n* **4** the act or sound of crackling **5** intentional crazing in the glaze of a piece of porcelain or pottery **6** Also called: **crackleware** porcelain or pottery so decorated

crackling ('kræklɪŋ) *n* the crisp browned skin of roast pork

crack on *vb* (*intr*; often foll by *with*) *informal* to continue to do something as quickly as possible

crackpot ('kræk,pɒt) *informal* ▷ *n* **1** an eccentric person; crank ▷ *adj* **2** (*usually prenominal*) eccentric; crazy

crack up *vb* (*adverb*) **1** (*intr*) to break into pieces **2** (*intr*) *informal* to undergo a physical or mental breakdown **3** (*tr*) *informal* to present or report, esp in glowing terms: *it's not all it's cracked up to be* **4** *informal, chiefly US & Canadian* to laugh or cause to laugh uproariously or uncontrollably ▷ *n* **crackup 5** *informal* a physical or mental breakdown

Cracow ('krækaʊ, -əʊ, -ɒf) *n* an industrial city in S Poland, on the River Vistula: former capital of the country (1320–1609); university (1364). Pop: 822 000 (2005 est). Polish name: Kraków. German name: Krakau

-cracy *n combining form* indicating a type of government or rule: *plutocracy; mobocracy*. See also **-crat** [from Greek -*kratia*, from *kratos* power]

cradle ('kreɪdªl) *n* **1** a baby's bed with enclosed sides, often with a hood and rockers **2** a place where something originates or is nurtured during its early life: *the cradle of civilization* **3** a frame, rest, or trolley made to support or transport a piece of equipment, aircraft, ship, etc **4** a platform, cage, or trolley, in which workmen are suspended on the side of a building or ship **5** the part of a telephone on which the handset rests when not in use **6** a holder connected to a computer allowing data to be transferred from a PDA, digital camera, etc **7** *agriculture* **a** a framework of several wooden fingers attached to a scythe to gather the grain into bunches as it is cut **b** a scythe equipped with such a cradle; cradle scythe **c** a collar of wooden fingers that prevents a horse or cow from turning its head and biting itself **8** Also called: **rocker** a boxlike apparatus for washing rocks, sand, etc, containing gold or gem stones **9** *engraving* a tool that produces the pitted surface of a copper mezzotint plate before the design is engraved upon it **10** a framework used to prevent the bedclothes from touching a sensitive part of an injured person **11** from the cradle to the grave throughout life ▷ *vb* **12** (*tr*) to rock or place in or as if in a cradle; hold tenderly **13** (*tr*) to nurture in or bring up from infancy **14** (*tr*) to replace (the handset of a telephone) on the cradle **15** to reap (grain) with a cradle scythe **16** (*tr*) to wash (soil bearing gold, etc) in a cradle **17** *lacrosse* to keep (the ball) in the net of the stick, esp while running with it [Old English *cradol*; related to Old High German *kratto* basket] ▷ **'cradler** *n*

cradle snatcher *n informal* someone who marries or has an affair with a much younger person

cradlesong ('kreɪdªl,sɒŋ) *n* another word for **lullaby**

craft (krɑːft) *n* **1** skill or ability, esp in handiwork **2** skill in deception and trickery; guile; cunning **3** an occupation or trade requiring special skill, esp manual dexterity **4 a** the members of such a trade, regarded collectively **b** (*as modifier*): *a craft guild* **5** a single vessel, aircraft, or spacecraft **6** (*functioning as plural*) ships, boats, aircraft, or spacecraft collectively ▷ *vb* **7** (*tr*) to make or fashion with skill, esp by hand [Old English *cræft* skill, strength; related to Old Norse *kraptr* power, skill, Old High German *kraft*]

craftsman ('krɑːftsmən) *n, pl* **-men 1** a member of a skilled trade; someone who practises a craft; artisan **2** Also called: (*fem*) **craftswoman** an artist skilled in the techniques of an art or craft ▷ **'craftsman,like** *adj* ▷ **'craftsmanly** *adj* ▷ **'craftsman,ship** *n*

crafty ('krɑːftɪ) *adj* **craftier, craftiest 1** skilled in deception; shrewd; cunning **2** *archaic* skilful ▷ **'craftily** *adv* ▷ **'craftiness** *n*

crag (kræg) *n* a steep rugged rock or peak [c13: of Celtic origin; related to Old Welsh *creik* rock]

craggy ('krægɪ) *or US* **cragged** ('krægɪd) *adj* **-gier, -giest 1** having many crags **2** (of the face) rugged; rocklike ▷ **'craggily** *adv* ▷ **'cragginess** *n*

craic (kræk) *n* an Irish spelling of **crack** (sense 31)

Craig (kreɪg) *n* **Edward Gordon**. 1872–1966, English theatrical designer, actor, and director. His nonrealistic scenic design greatly influenced theatre in Europe and the US

Craigavon (,kreɪg'ævªn) *n* a district in central Northern Ireland, in Co Armagh. Pop: 57 685 (2001). Area: 279 sq km (108 sq miles)

Craigie ('kreɪgɪ) *n* Sir **William A(lexander)**. 1867–1957, Scottish lexicographer; joint editor of the *Oxford English Dictionary* (1901–33), and of *A Dictionary of American English on Historical Principles* (1938–44)

crake (kreɪk) *n zoology* any of several rails that occur in the Old World, such as the corncrake and the spotted crake [c14: from Old Norse *krāka* crow or *krākr* raven, of imitative origin]

cram (kræm) *vb* **crams, cramming, crammed 1** (*tr*) to force (people, material, etc) into (a room, container, etc) with more than it can hold; stuff **2** to eat or cause to eat more than necessary **3** *informal* to study or cause to study (facts, etc), esp for an examination, by hastily memorizing ▷ *n* **4** the act or condition of cramming **5** a crush [Old English *crammian*; related to Old Norse *kremja* to press]

Cram (kræm) *n* **Steve**. born 1960, English middle-distance runner: European 1500 m champion (1981, 1986); world 1500 m champion (1983)

crambo ('kræmbəʊ) *n* a word game in which one team says a rhyme or rhyming line for a word or line given by the other team [c17: from earlier *crambe*, probably from Latin *crambē repetīta* cabbage repeated, hence an old story, a rhyming game, from Greek *krambē*]

crammer ('kræmə) *n* a person or school that prepares pupils for an examination, esp pupils who have already failed that examination

cramp¹ (kræmp) *n* **1** a painful involuntary contraction of a muscle, typically caused by overexertion, heat, or chill **2** temporary partial paralysis of a muscle group: *writer's cramp* **3** (*usually plural in the US and Canada*) severe abdominal pain ▷ *vb* **4** (*tr*) to affect with or as if with a cramp [c14: from Old French *crampe*, of Germanic origin; compare Old High German *krampho*]

cramp² (kræmp) *n* **1** Also called: **cramp iron** a strip of metal with its ends bent at right angles, used to bind masonry **2** a device for holding pieces of wood while they are glued; clamp **3** something that confines or restricts **4** a confined state or position ▷ *vb* **5** to secure or hold with a cramp **6** to confine, hamper, or restrict **7** cramp someone's style *informal* to prevent a person from using his abilities or acting freely and confidently [c15: from Middle Dutch *crampe* cramp, hook, of Germanic origin; compare Old High German *khramph* bent; see CRAMP¹]

cramped (kræmpt) *adj* **1** closed in; restricted **2** (esp of handwriting) small and irregular; difficult to read

crampon ('kræmpən) *n* **1** one of a pair of pivoted steel levers used to lift heavy objects; grappling iron **2** (*often plural*) one of a pair of frames each with 10 or 12 metal spikes, strapped to boots for climbing or walking on ice or snow ▷ *vb* **3** to climb using crampons [c15: from French, from Middle Dutch *crampe* hook; see CRAMP²]

cran (kræn) *n* a unit of capacity used for measuring fresh herring, equal to 37.5 gallons [c18: of uncertain origin]

Cranach (*German* 'kra:nax) *n* **Lucas** ('lu:kas), known as *the Elder*, real name *Lucas Müller*. 1472–1553, German painter, etcher, and designer of woodcuts

cranberry ('krænbərɪ, -brɪ) *n, pl* **-ries 1** any of several trailing ericaceous shrubs of the genus *Vaccinium*, such as the European *V. oxycoccus*, that bear sour edible red berries **2** the berry of this plant, used to make sauce or jelly [c17: from Low German *kraanbere*, from *kraan* CRANE + *bere* BERRY]

crane (kreɪn) *n* **1** any large long-necked long-legged wading bird of the family *Gruidae*, inhabiting marshes and plains in most parts of the world except South America, New Zealand, and Indonesia: order *Gruiformes*. See also **demoiselle** (sense 1) **2** (*not in ornithological use*) any similar bird, such as a heron **3** a device for lifting and moving heavy objects, typically consisting of a moving boom, beam, or gantry from which lifting gear is suspended. See also **gantry 4** *films* a large trolley carrying a boom, on the end of which is mounted a camera ▷ *vb* **5** (*tr*) to lift or move (an object) by or as if by a crane **6** to stretch out (esp the neck), as to see over other people's heads **7** (*intr*) (of a horse) to pull up short before a jump [Old English *cran*; related to Middle High

German *krane*, Latin *grūs*, Greek *géranos*]

Crane (kreɪn) *n* 1 (**Harold**) **Hart.** 1899–1932, US poet; author of *The Bridge* (1930) 2 **Stephen.** 1871–1900, US novelist and short-story writer, noted particularly for his novel *The Red Badge of Courage* (1895) 3 **Walter.** 1845–1915, British painter, illustrator of children's books, and designer of textiles and wallpaper

crane fly *n* any dipterous fly of the family *Tipulidae*, having long legs, slender wings, and a narrow body. Also called (Brit): **daddy-longlegs**

cranesbill ('kreɪnz,bɪl) *n* any of various plants of the genus *Geranium*, having pink or purple flowers and long slender beaked fruits: family *Geraniaceae*. See also **herb Robert, storksbill**

cranial ('kreɪnɪəl) *adj* of or relating to the skull
> 'cranially *adv*

cranial index *n* the ratio of the greatest length to the greatest width of the cranium, multiplied by 100: used in comparative anthropology. See **cephalic index**

cranial nerve *n* any of the 12 paired nerves that have their origin in the brain and reach the periphery through natural openings in the skull

craniate ('kreɪnɪɪt, -,eɪt) *adj* 1 having a skull or cranium ▷ *adj, n* 2 another word for **vertebrate**

cranio- *or before a vowel* **crani-** *combining form* indicating the cranium or cranial: *craniotomy*

craniology (,kreɪnɪ'ɒlədʒɪ) *n* the branch of science concerned with the shape and size of the human skull, esp with reference to variations between different races
> craniological (,kreɪnɪə'lɒdʒɪkəl) *adj* > ,cranio'logically *adv* > ,crani'ologist *n*

craniometry (,kreɪnɪ'ɒmɪtrɪ) *n* the study and measurement of skulls > craniometric (,kreɪnɪə'mɛtrɪk) *or* ,cranio'metrical *adj* > ,cranio'metrically *adv* > ,crani'ometrist *n*

craniosacral therapy (,kreɪnɪə'seɪkrəl) *n* a form of therapy for various disorders in which the therapist manipulates the bones of the skull

cranium ('kreɪnɪəm) *n, pl* -niums *or* -nia (-nɪə) 1 the skull of a vertebrate 2 the part of the skull that encloses the brain. Nontechnical name: **brainpan** [C16: from Medieval Latin *crānium* skull, from Greek *kranion*]

crank (kræŋk) *n* 1 a device for communicating motion or for converting reciprocating motion into rotary motion or vice versa. It consists of an arm projecting from a shaft, often with a second member attached to it parallel to the shaft 2 Also called: **crank handle, starting handle** a handle incorporating a crank, used to start an engine or motor 3 *informal* **a** an eccentric or odd person, esp someone who stubbornly maintains unusual views **b** *US & Canadian* a bad-tempered person ▷ *vb* 4 (*tr*) to rotate (a shaft) by means of a crank 5 (*tr*) to start (an engine, motor, etc) by means of a crank handle 6 (*tr*) to bend, twist, or make into the shape of a crank 7 (*intr*) *obsolete* to twist or wind ▷ See also **crank up** [Old English *cranc*; related to Middle Low German *krunke* wrinkle, Dutch *krinkel* CRINKLE]

crankcase ('kræŋk,keɪs) *n* the metal housing that encloses the crankshaft, connecting rods, etc, in an internal-combustion engine, reciprocating pump, etc

Cranko ('kræŋkəʊ) *n* **John.** 1927–73, British choreographer, born in South Africa: director of the Stuttgart Ballet (1961–73)

crankpin ('kræŋk,pɪn) *n* a short cylindrical bearing surface fitted between two arms of a crank and set parallel to the main shaft of the crankshaft

crankshaft ('kræŋk,ʃɑːft) *n* a shaft having one or more cranks, esp the main shaft of an internal-combustion engine to which the connecting rods are attached

crank up *vb* (*tr*) *slang* 1 to increase (loudness, output, etc): *he cranked up his pace* 2 to set in motion or invigorate: *news editors have to crank up tired reporters* 3 (*intr, adverb*) to inject a narcotic drug

cranky ('kræŋkɪ) *adj* crankier, crankiest 1 *informal* eccentric 2 *chiefly US, Canadian & Irish informal* fussy and bad-tempered 3 shaky; out of order 4 full of bends and turns 5 *dialect* unwell > 'crankily *adv* > 'crankiness *n*

Cranmer ('krænmə) *n* **Thomas.** 1489–1556, the first Protestant archbishop of Canterbury (1533–56) and principal author of the Book of Common Prayer. He was burnt as a heretic by Mary I

crannog ('krænɒg) *or* **crannoge** ('krænədʒ) *n* an ancient Celtic lake or bog dwelling dating from the late Bronze Age to the 16th century AD, often fortified and used as a refuge [C19: from Irish Gaelic *crannóg*, from Old Irish *crann* tree]

cranny ('krænɪ) *n, pl* -nies a narrow opening, as in a wall or rock face; chink; crevice (esp in the phrase **every nook and cranny**) [C15: from Old French *cran* notch, fissure; compare CRENEL] > 'crannied *adj*

Cranwell ('krænwəl) *n* a village in E England, in Lincolnshire: Royal Air Force College (1920)

crap¹ (kræp) *n* 1 a losing throw in the game of craps 2 another name for **craps** [C20: back formation from CRAPS]

crap² (kræp) *slang* ▷ *n* 1 nonsense 2 rubbish 3 another word for **faeces** ▷ *vb* craps, crapping, crapped 4 (*intr*) another word for **defecate** [C15 *crappe* chaff, from Middle Dutch, probably from *crappen* to break off]

crape (kreɪp) *n* 1 a variant spelling of **crepe** 2 crepe, esp when used for mourning clothes 3 a band of black crepe worn in mourning > 'crapy *adj*

crap out *vb* *slang* 1 US to make a losing throw in craps 2 US to fail; withdraw 3 US to rest 4 to fail to do or attempt something through fear

craps (kræps) *n* (*usually functioning as singular*) 1 a gambling game using two dice, in which a player wins the bet if 7 or 11 is thrown first, and loses if 2, 3, or 12 is thrown 2 **shoot craps** to play this game [C19: probably from *crabs* lowest throw at dice, plural of CRAB¹]

crapulent ('kræpjʊlənt) *or* **crapulous** ('kræpjʊləs) *adj* 1 given to or resulting from intemperance 2 suffering from intemperance; drunken [C18: from Late Latin *crāpulentus* drunk, from Latin *crāpula*, from Greek *kraipalē* drunkenness, headache resulting therefrom]
> 'crapulence *n* > 'crapulently *or* 'crapulously *adv*
> 'crapulousness *n*

crash¹ (kræʃ) *vb* 1 to make or cause to make a loud noise as of solid objects smashing or clattering 2 to fall or cause to fall with force, breaking in pieces with a loud noise as of solid objects smashing 3 (*intr*) to break or smash in pieces with a loud noise 4 (*intr*) to collapse or fail suddenly: *this business is sure to crash* 5 to cause (an aircraft) to hit land or water violently resulting in severe damage or (of an aircraft) to hit land or water in this way 6 to cause (a car, etc) to collide with another car or other object or (of two or more cars) to be involved in a collision 7 to move or cause to move violently or noisily: *to crash through a barrier* 8 (*intr*) (of a computer system or program) to fail suddenly and completely because of a malfunction 9 **crash and burn** *informal* to fail; be unsuccessful ▷ *n* 10 an act or instance of breaking and falling to pieces 11 a sudden loud noise: *the crash of thunder* 12 a collision, as between vehicles 13 a sudden descent of an aircraft as a result of which it hits land or water 14 the sudden collapse of a business, stock exchange, etc, esp one causing further financial failure 15 (*modifier*) **a** requiring or using intensive effort and all possible resources in order to accomplish something quickly: *a crash programme* **b** sudden or vigorous: *a crash halt; a crash tackle* 16 **crash-and-burn** *informal* a complete failure [C14: probably from *crasen* to smash, shatter + *dasshen* to strike violently, DASH¹; see CRAZE] > 'crasher *n*

crash² (kræʃ) *n* a coarse cotton or linen cloth used for towelling, curtains, etc [C19: from Russian *krashenina* coloured linen]

Crashaw ('kræʃɔː) *n* **Richard.** 1613–49, English religious poet, noted esp for the *Steps to the Temple* (1646)

crash barrier *n* a barrier erected along the centre of a motorway, around a racetrack, etc, for safety purposes

crash dive *n* 1 a sudden steep dive from the surface by a submarine ▷ *vb* crash-dive 2 (*usually of an aircraft*) to descend steeply and rapidly, before hitting the ground 3 to perform or cause to perform a crash dive

crash helmet *n* a padded helmet worn for motorcycling, flying, bobsleighing, etc, to protect the head in a crash

crashing ('kræʃɪŋ) *adj* (*prenominal*) *informal* (intensifier) (esp in the phrase **a crashing bore**)

crash-land *vb* to land (an aircraft) in an emergency causing damage or (of an aircraft) to land in this way ▷ 'crash-₁landing *n*

crash team *n* a medical team with special equipment able to be mobilized quickly to treat cardiac arrest

crass (kræs) *adj* stupid; gross [c16: from Latin *crassus* thick, dense, gross] ▷ 'crassly *adv* ▷ 'crassness *or* 'crassi₁tude *n*

Crassus ('kræsəs) *n* **Marcus Licinius** ('mɑːkəs lɪ'sɪnɪəs). ?115–53 BC, Roman general; member of the first triumvirate with Caesar and Pompey

-crat *n combining form* indicating a person who takes part in or is a member of a form of government or class: *democrat; technocrat.* See also **-cracy** [from Greek *-kratēs*, from *-kratia* -CRACY] ▷ **-cratic** *or* **-cratical** *adj combining form*

crate (kreɪt) *n* **1** a fairly large container, usually made of wooden slats or wickerwork, used for packing, storing, or transporting goods **2** *slang* an old car, aeroplane, etc ▷ *vb* **3** (*tr*) to pack or place in a crate [c16: from Latin *crātis* wickerwork, hurdle] ▷ 'crater *n* ▷ 'crateful *n*

crater ('kreɪtə) *n* **1** the bowl-shaped opening at the top or side of a volcano or top of a geyser through which lava and gases are emitted **2** a similarly shaped depression formed by the impact of a meteorite or exploding bomb **3** any of the circular or polygonal walled formations covering the surface of the moon and some other planets, formed probably either by volcanic action or by the impact of meteorites. They can have a diameter of up to 240 kilometres (150 miles) and a depth of 8900 metres (29 000 feet) **4** a large open bowl with two handles, used for mixing wines, esp in ancient Greece ▷ *vb* **5** to make or form craters in (a surface, such as the ground) **6** *slang* to fail; collapse; crash [c17: from Latin: mixing bowl, crater, from Greek *kratēr*, from *kerannunai* to mix] ▷ 'cratered *adj* ▷ 'craterless *adj* ▷ 'crater-₁like *adj*

cravat (krə'væt) *n* a scarf of silk or fine wool, worn round the neck, esp by men [c17: from French *cravate*, from Serbo-Croat *Hrvat* Croat; so called because worn by Croats in the French army during the Thirty Years' War]

crave (kreɪv) *vb* **1** (when *intr*, foll by *for* or *after*) to desire intensely; long (for) **2** (*tr*) to need greatly or urgently **3** (*tr*) to beg or plead for [Old English *crafian*; related to Old Norse *krefja* to demand, *kræfr* strong; see CRAFT] ▷ 'craver *n* ▷ 'craving *n*

craven ('kreɪvªn) *adj* **1** cowardly; mean-spirited ▷ *n* **2** a coward [c13 *cravant*, probably from Old French *crevant* bursting, from *crever* to burst, die, from Latin *crepāre* to burst, crack] ▷ 'cravenly *adv* ▷ 'cravenness *n*

craw (krɔː) *n* **1** a less common word for **crop** (sense 6) **2** the stomach of an animal **3** stick in one's craw *or* stick in one's throat *informal* to be difficult, or against one's conscience, for one to accept, utter, or believe [c14: related to Middle High German *krage*, Middle Dutch *crāghe* neck, Icelandic *kragi* collar]

crawfish ('krɔː₁fɪʃ) *n, pl* **-fish** *or* **-fishes** a variant (esp US) of **crayfish** (sense 2)

Crawford ('krɔːfəd) *n* **1 Joan**, real name *Lucille le Sueur.* 1908–77, US film actress, who portrayed ambitious women in such films as *Mildred Pierce* (1945) **2 Michael**, real name *Michael Dumbell Smith.* born 1942, British actor

crawl¹ (krɔːl) *vb* (*intr*) **1** to move slowly, either by dragging the body along the ground or on the hands and knees **2** to proceed or move along very slowly or laboriously: *the traffic crawled along the road* **3** to act or behave in a servile manner; fawn; cringe **4** to be or feel as if overrun by something unpleasant, esp crawling creatures: *the pile of refuse crawled with insects* **5** (of insects, worms, snakes, etc) to move with the body close to the ground **6** to swim the crawl ▷ *n* **7** a slow creeping pace or motion **8** Also called: **Australian crawl, front crawl** *swimming* a stroke in which the feet are kicked like paddles while the arms reach forward and pull back through the water [c14: probably from Old Norse *krafla* to creep; compare Swedish *kravla*, Middle Low German *krabbelen* to crawl, Old Norse *krabbi* CRAB¹] ▷ 'crawlingly *adv*

crawl² (krɔːl) *n* an enclosure in shallow, coastal water for fish, lobsters, etc [c17: from Dutch *kraal* KRAAL]

crawler ('krɔːlə) *n* **1** *slang* a servile flatterer **2** a person or

animal that crawls **3** *US* an informal name for **earthworm 4** a computer program that is capable of performing recursive searches on the World Wide Web **5** (*plural*) a baby's overalls; rompers

crawler lane *n* a lane on an uphill section of a motorway reserved for slow vehicles

Crawley ('krɔːlɪ) *n* a town in S England, in NE West Sussex: designated a new town in 1956. Pop: 100 547 (2001)

crawling ('krɔːlɪŋ) *n* a defect in freshly applied paint or varnish characterized by bare patches and ridging

crawly ('krɔːlɪ) *adj* **crawlier, crawliest** *informal* feeling or causing a sensation like creatures crawling on one's skin

Craxi ('kræksɪ) *n* **Bettino** (be'tiːno). 1934–2000, Italian socialist statesman; prime minister (1983–87)

crayfish ('kreɪ₁fɪʃ) *or esp US* **crawfish** *n, pl* **-fish** *or* **-fishes 1** any freshwater decapod crustacean of the genera *Astacus* and *Cambarus*, resembling a small lobster **2** any of various similar crustaceans, esp the spiny lobster [c14: *cray*, by folk etymology, from Old French *crevice* crab, from Old High German *krebiz* + FISH]

crayon ('kreɪən, -ɒn) *n* **1 a** a small stick or pencil of charcoal, wax, clay, or chalk mixed with coloured pigment **2** a drawing made with crayons ▷ *vb* **3** to draw or colour with crayons [c17: from French, from *craie*, from Latin *crēta* chalk] ▷ 'crayonist *n*

craze (kreɪz) *n* **1** a short-lived current fashion **2** a wild or exaggerated enthusiasm: *a craze for chestnuts* **3** mental disturbance; insanity ▷ *vb* **4** to make or become mad **5** *ceramics, metallurgy* to develop or cause to develop a fine network of cracks **6** (*tr*) *Brit archaic* or *dialect* to break **7** (*tr*) *archaic* to weaken [C14 (in the sense: to break, shatter): probably of Scandinavian origin; compare Swedish *krasa* to shatter, ultimately of imitative origin]

crazy ('kreɪzɪ) *adj* **-zier, -ziest 1** *informal* insane **2** fantastic, strange; ridiculous: *a crazy dream* **3** (*postpositive; foll by about* or *over*) *informal* extremely fond (of) **4** *slang* very good or excellent ▷ *n, pl* **crazies 5** *informal* a crazy person ▷ 'crazily *adv* ▷ 'craziness *n*

Crazy Horse *n* Indian name *Ta-Sunko-Witko.* ?1849–77, Sioux Indian chief, remembered for his attempts to resist White settlement in Sioux territory

crazy paving *n* *Brit* a form of paving, as for a path, made of slabs of stone of irregular shape fitted together

creak (kriːk) *vb* **1** to make or cause to make a harsh squeaking sound **2** (*intr*) to make such sounds while moving: *the old car creaked along* ▷ *n* **3** a harsh squeaking sound [c14: variant of CROAK, of imitative origin] ▷ 'creaky *adj* ▷ 'creakily *adv* ▷ 'creakiness *n* ▷ 'creakingly *adv*

cream (kriːm) *n* **1 a** the fatty part of milk, which rises to the top if the milk is allowed to stand **b** (*as modifier*): *cream buns* **2** anything resembling cream in consistency: *shoe cream; beauty cream* **3** the best one or most essential part of something; pick: *the cream of the bunch; the cream of the joke* **4** a soup containing cream or milk: *cream of chicken soup* **5** any of various dishes, cakes, biscuits, etc, resembling or containing cream **6** a confection made of fondant or soft fudge, often covered in chocolate **7** cream sherry a full-bodied sweet sherry **8 a** a yellowish-white colour **b** (*as adjective*): *cream wallpaper* ▷ *vb* **9** (*tr*) to skim or otherwise separate the cream from (milk) **10** (*tr*) to beat (foodstuffs, esp butter and sugar) to a light creamy consistency **11** (*intr*) to form cream **12** (*tr*) to add or apply cream or any creamlike substance to: *to cream one's face; to cream coffee* **13** (*tr; sometimes foll by off*) to take away the best part of **14** (*tr*) to prepare or cook (vegetables, chicken, etc) with cream or milk **15** to allow (milk) to form a layer of cream on its surface or (of milk) to form such a layer **16** (*tr*) *slang, chiefly US, Canadian & Austral* to beat thoroughly **17** (*intr*) *slang* (of a man) to ejaculate during orgasm [c14: from Old French *cresme*, from Late Latin *crāmum* cream, of Celtic origin; influenced by Church Latin *chrisma* unction, CHRISM] ▷ 'cream₁like *adj*

cream cheese *n* a smooth soft white cheese made from soured cream or milk

cream cracker *n* *Brit* a crisp unsweetened biscuit, often eaten with cheese

creamer ('kri:mə) n 1 a vessel or device for separating cream from milk 2 a powdered substitute for cream, used in coffee 3 *chiefly US & Canadian* a small jug or pitcher for serving cream

creamery ('kri:məri) n, pl -eries 1 an establishment where milk and cream are made into butter and cheese 2 a place where dairy products are sold 3 a place where milk is left to stand until the cream rises to the top

cream of tartar n another name for potassium hydrogen tartrate, esp when used in baking powders

cream puff n a shell of light pastry with a custard or cream filling

cream soda n a carbonated soft drink flavoured with vanilla

cream tea n afternoon tea including bread or scones served with clotted cream and jam

creamy ('kri:mɪ) adj creamier, creamiest 1 resembling cream in colour, taste, or consistency 2 containing cream > 'creamily adv > 'creaminess n

crease (kri:s) n 1 a line or mark produced by folding, pressing, or wrinkling 2 a wrinkle or furrow, esp on the face 3 *cricket* any three lines near each wicket marking positions for the bowler or batsman. See also **bowling crease, popping crease, return crease** 4 *ice hockey* the small rectangular area in front of each goal cage 5 Also called: **goal crease** *lacrosse* the circular area surrounding the goal ▷ vb 6 to make or become wrinkled or furrowed 7 (tr) to graze with a bullet, causing superficial injury 8 (often foll by *up*) *slang* to be or cause to be greatly amused [C15: from earlier *crest*; probably related to Old French *cresté* wrinkled] > 'creaseless adj > 'creaser n > 'creasy adj

create (kri:'eɪt) vb 1 (tr) to cause to come into existence 2 (tr) to invest with a new honour, office, or title; appoint 3 (tr) to be the cause of: *these circumstances created the revolution* 4 (tr) to act (a role) in the first production of a play 5 (intr) to be engaged in creative work 6 (intr) *Brit slang* to make a fuss or uproar [C14 *creat* created, from Latin *creātus*, from *creāre* to produce, make] > cre'atable adj

creatine ('kri:əˌti:n, -tɪn) or **creatin** ('kri:ətɪn) n an important metabolite involved in many biochemical reactions and present in many types of living cells [C19: *creat*- from Greek *kreas* flesh + -INE²]

creation (kri:'eɪʃən) n 1 the act or process of creating 2 the fact of being created or produced 3 something that has been brought into existence or created, esp a product of human intelligence or imagination 4 the whole universe, including the world and all the things in it 5 an unusual or striking garment or hat > cre'ational adj

Creation (kri:'eɪʃən) n *theol* 1 the Creation God's act of bringing the universe into being 2 the universe as thus brought into being by God

creative (kri:'eɪtɪv) adj 1 having the ability to create 2 characterized by originality of thought; having or showing imagination: *a creative mind* 3 designed to or tending to stimulate the imagination: *creative toys* 4 characterized by sophisticated bending of the rules or conventions: *creative accounting* ▷ n 5 a creative person, esp one who devises advertising campaigns > cre'atively adv > cre'ativeness n > ˌcrea'tivity n

creator (kri:'eɪtə) n a person or thing that creates; originator > cre'ator ship n > cre'atress or cre'atrix fem n

Creator (kri:'eɪtə) n the Creator an epithet of God

creature ('kri:tʃə) n 1 a living being, esp an animal 2 something that has been created, whether animate or inanimate: *a creature of the imagination* 3 a human being; person: used as a term of scorn, pity, or endearment 4 a person who is dependent upon another; tool or puppet [C13: from Church Latin *creātūra*, from Latin *creāre* to create] > 'creatural or 'creaturely adj > 'creatureliness n

creature feature n a horror film featuring a monster

CREB n cyclic amp-response element binding protein; a protein involved in the long-term memory process

crèche (krɛʃ, kreɪʃ; French krɛʃ) n 1 *chiefly Brit* **a** a day nursery for very young children **b** a supervised play area provided for young children for short periods 2 a

tableau of Christ's Nativity 3 a foundling home or hospital [C19: from Old French: manger, crib, ultimately of Germanic origin; compare Old High German *kripja* crib]

Crécy ('krɛsɪ; French kresi) n a village in N France: scene of the first decisive battle of the Hundred Years' War when the English defeated the French (1346). Former English name: **Cressy**

cred (krɛd) n *slang* short for **credibility** (esp in the phrase **street cred**)

credence ('kri:dᵊns) n 1 acceptance or belief, esp with regard to the truth of the evidence of others: *I cannot give credence to his account* 2 something supporting a claim to belief; recommendation; credential (esp in the phrase **letters of credence**) 3 short for **credence table** [C14: from Medieval Latin *crēdentia* trust, credit, from Latin *crēdere* to believe]

credence table n *Christianity* a small table or ledge on which the bread, wine, etc, are placed before being consecrated in the Eucharist

credential (krɪ'dɛnʃəl) n 1 something that entitles a person to confidence, authority, etc 2 (*plural*) a letter or certificate giving evidence of the bearer's identity or competence ▷ adj 3 entitling one to confidence, authority, etc [C16: from Medieval Latin *crēdentia* credit, trust; see CREDENCE] > cre'dentialed adj

credenza (krɪ'dɛnzə) n another name for **credence table** [Italian: see CREDENCE]

credibility (ˌkrɛdɪ'bɪlɪtɪ) n the quality of being believed or trusted

credibility gap n a disparity between claims or statements made and the evident facts of the situation or circumstances to which they relate

credible ('krɛdɪbᵊl) adj 1 capable of being believed 2 trustworthy or reliable: *the latest claim is the only one to involve a credible witness* [C14: from Latin *crēdibilis*, from Latin *crēdere* to believe] > 'credibleness n > 'credibly adv

credit ('krɛdɪt) n 1 commendation or approval, as for an act or quality: *she was given credit for her work* 2 a person or thing serving as a source of good influence, repute, ability, etc: *a credit to the team* 3 influence or reputation coming from the approval or good opinion of others: *he acquired credit within the community* 4 belief in the truth, reliability, quality, etc, of someone or something: *I would give credit to that philosophy* 5 a sum of money or equivalent purchasing power, as at a shop, available for a person's use 6 a the positive balance in a person's bank account b the sum of money that a bank makes available to a client in excess of any deposit 7 a the practice of permitting a buyer to receive goods or services before payment b the time permitted for paying for such goods or services 8 reputation for solvency and commercial or financial probity, inducing confidence among creditors 9 *accounting* a acknowledgment of an income, liability, or capital item by entry on the right-hand side of an account b the right-hand side of an account c an entry on this side b the total of such entries d (*as modifier*): *credit entries* 10 short for **tax credit** 11 *education* a a distinction awarded to an examination candidate obtaining good marks b a section of an examination syllabus satisfactorily completed, as in higher and professional education 12 **letter of credit** an order authorizing a named person to draw money from correspondents of the issuer 13 **on credit** with payment to be made at a future date ▷ vb -its, -iting, -ited (tr) 14 (foll by *with*) to ascribe (to); give credit (for): *they credited him with the discovery* 15 to accept as true; believe 16 to do credit to 17 *accounting* a to enter (an item) as a credit in an account b to acknowledge (a payer) by making such an entry. See **debit** (sense 2) 18 to award a credit to (a student) ▷ See also **credits** [C16: from Old French *crédit*, from Italian *credito*, from Latin *crēditum* loan, from *crēdere* to believe] > 'creditless adj

creditable ('krɛdɪtəbᵊl) adj 1 deserving credit, honour, etc; praiseworthy 2 *obsolete* credible > 'creditableness or ˌcredita'bility n > 'creditably adv

credit account n *Brit* a credit system by means of which customers may obtain goods and services before payment. Also called: **charge account**

credit card *n* a card issued by banks, businesses, etc, enabling the holder to obtain goods and services on credit

credit crunch *n informal* a period during which there is a sudden reduction in the availability of credit from banks and other lenders

creditor ('krɛdɪtə) *n* a person or commercial enterprise to whom money is owed

credit rating *n* an evaluation of the creditworthiness of an individual or business enterprise

credits ('krɛdɪts) *pl n* a list of those responsible for the production of a film or television programme

credit transfer *n* a method of settling a debt by transferring money through a bank or post office, esp for those who do not have cheque accounts

creditworthy ('krɛdɪt,wɜːðɪ) *adj* (of an individual or business enterprise) adjudged as meriting credit on the basis of such factors as earning power, previous record of debt repayment, etc > 'credit,worthiness *n*

credo ('kriːdəʊ, 'kreɪ-) *n, pl* -dos any formal or authorized statement of beliefs, principles, or opinions

Credo ('kriːdəʊ, 'kreɪ-) *n, pl* -dos 1 the Apostles' Creed or the Nicene Creed 2 a musical setting of the Creed [c12: from Latin, literally: I believe; first word of the Apostles' and Nicene Creeds]

credulity (krɪ'djuːlɪtɪ) *n* disposition to believe something on little evidence; gullibility

credulous ('krɛdjʊləs) *adj* 1 tending to believe something on little evidence 2 arising from or characterized by credulity: *credulous beliefs* [c16: from Latin *crēdulus*, from *crēdere* to believe] > 'credulously *adv* > 'credulousness *n*

Cree (kriː) *n* 1 *pl* Cree *or* Crees a member of a Native American people living in Ontario, Saskatchewan, and Manitoba 2 the language of this people, belonging to the Algonquian family [from first syllable of Canadian French *Christianaux*, probably based on Ojibwa *Kenistenoag* (tribal name)]

creed (kriːd) *n* 1 a concise, formal statement of the essential articles of Christian belief, such as the Apostles' Creed or the Nicene Creed 2 any statement or system of beliefs or principles [Old English *crēda*, from Latin *crēdo* I believe] > 'creedal *or* 'credal *adj*

Creed (kriːd) *n* Frederick. 1871–1957, Canadian inventor, resident in Scotland from 1897, noted for his invention of the teleprinter, first used in 1912

creek (kriːk) *n* 1 *chiefly Brit* a narrow inlet or bay, esp of the sea 2 *US, Canadian, Austral & NZ* a small stream or tributary 3 *up the creek slang* in a difficult position [c13: from Old Norse *kriki* nook; related to Middle Dutch *krēke* creek, inlet]

Creek (kriːk) *n* 1 *pl* Creek *or* Creeks a member of a confederacy of Native American peoples formerly living in Georgia and Alabama, now chiefly in Oklahoma 2 any of the languages of these peoples, belonging to the Muskhogean family

creel (kriːl) *n* 1 a wickerwork basket, esp one used to hold fish 2 a wickerwork trap for catching lobsters, etc [c15: from Scottish, of obscure origin]

creep (kriːp) *vb* creeps, creeping, crept (*intr*) 1 to crawl with the body near to or touching the ground 2 to move slowly, quietly, or cautiously 3 to act in a servile way; fawn; cringe 4 to move or slip out of place, as from pressure or wear 5 (of plants) to grow along the ground or over rocks, producing roots, suckers, or tendrils at intervals 6 to develop gradually: *creeping unrest* 7 to have the sensation of something crawling over the skin > *n* 8 the act of creeping or a creeping movement 9 *slang* a person considered to be obnoxious or servile 10 *geology* the gradual downwards movement of loose rock material, soil, etc, on a slope [Old English *crēopan*; related to Old Frisian *kriāpa*, Old Norse *krjūpa*, Middle Low German *krūpen*]

creeper ('kriːpə) *n* 1 a person or animal that creeps 2 a plant, such as the ivy or periwinkle, that grows by creeping 3 *Also called*: tree creeper *US & Canadian* any small songbird of the family *Certhiidae* of the N hemisphere, having a brown-and-white plumage and slender downward-curving bill. They creep up trees to feed on insects 4 a hooked instrument for dragging deep water 5 *informal* a shoe with a soft sole

creeps (kriːps) *pl n* the creeps *informal* a feeling of fear, repulsion, disgust, etc

creepy ('kriːpɪ) *adj* creepier, creepiest 1 *informal* having or causing a sensation of repulsion, horror, or fear, as of creatures crawling on the skin 2 creeping; slow-moving > 'creepily *adv* > 'creepiness *n*

creepy-crawly *Brit informal* ⊳ *n, pl* -crawlies 1 a small crawling creature ⊳ *adj* 2 feeling or causing a sensation as of creatures crawling on one's skin

cremate (krɪ'meɪt) *vb* (*tr*) to burn up (something, esp a corpse) and reduce to ash [c19: from Latin *cremāre*] > cre'mation *n* > cre'mator *n* > crematory ('krɛmətərɪ, -trɪ) *adj, n*

crematorium (,krɛmə'tɔːrɪəm) *n, pl* -riums *or* -ria (-rɪə) *Brit* a building in which corpses are cremated

crème (krɛm, kriːm, kreɪm) *n* 1 cream 2 any of various sweet liqueurs: *crème de moka* ⊳ *adj* 3 (of a liqueur) rich and sweet

crème de la crème *French* (krɛm də la krɛm) *n* the very best [literally: cream of the cream]

crème de menthe ('krɛm də 'mɛnθ, 'mɒt, 'kriːm, 'kreɪm) *n* a liqueur flavoured with peppermint, usually bright green in colour [French, literally: cream of mint]

crème fraîche ('krɛm 'frɛʃ) *n* thickened and slightly fermented cream [French, literally: fresh cream]

Cremona (*Italian* krɛ'moːna) *n* a city in N Italy, in Lombardy on the River Po: noted for the manufacture of fine violins in the 16th–18th centuries. Pop: 70 887 (2001)

crenate ('kriːneɪt) *or* **crenated** ('kriːneɪtɪd) *adj* having a scalloped margin, as certain leaves [c18: from New Latin *crēnātus*, from Medieval Latin, probably from Late Latin *crēna* a notch] > 'crenately *adv*

crenel ('krɛnᵊl) *or* **crenelle** (krɪ'nɛl) *n* any of a set of openings formed in the top of a wall or parapet and having slanting sides, as in a battlement [c15: from Old French, literally: a little notch, from *cren* notch, from Late Latin *crēna*]

crenellate *or US* **crenelate** ('krɛnɪ,leɪt) *vb* (*tr*) to supply with battlements [c19: from Old French *creneler*, from CRENEL] > ,crenel'lation *or US* ,crenel'ation *n*

crenellated *or US* **crenelated** ('krɛnɪ,leɪtɪd) *adj* 1 having battlements 2 (of a moulding, etc) having square indentations

creole ('kriːəʊl) *n* 1 a language that has its origin in extended contact between two language communities, one of which is generally European. It incorporates features from each and constitutes the mother tongue of a community ⊳ *adj* 2 denoting, relating to, or characteristic of creole 3 (of a sauce or dish) containing or cooked with tomatoes, green peppers, onions, etc [c17: via French and Spanish probably from Portuguese *crioulo* slave born in one's household, person of European ancestry born in the colonies, probably from *criar* to bring up, from Latin *creāre* to CREATE]

Creole ('kriːəʊl) *n* 1 (*sometimes not capital*) (in the Caribbean and Latin America) **a** a native-born person of European, esp Spanish, ancestry **b** a native-born person of mixed European and African ancestry who speaks a French or Spanish creole 2 (in Louisiana and other Gulf States of the US) a native-born person of French ancestry 3 the creolized French spoken in Louisiana, esp in New Orleans ⊳ *adj* 4 of, relating to, or characteristic of any of these peoples

Creon ('kriːɒn) *n Greek myth* the successor to Oedipus as king of Thebes; the brother of Jocasta. See also **Antigone**

creosol ('kriːə,sɒl) *n* a colourless or pale yellow insoluble oily liquid with a smoky odour and a burning taste; 2-methoxy-4-methylphenol: an active principle of creosote. Formula: $CH_3O(CH_3)C_6H_3OH$ [c19: from CREOS(OTE) + -OL¹]

creosote ('krɪə,səʊt) *n* 1 a colourless or pale yellow liquid mixture with a burning taste and penetrating odour distilled from wood tar, esp from beechwood, contains creosol and other phenols, and is used as an antiseptic 2 *Also called*: coal-tar creosote a thick dark liquid mixture prepared from coal tar, containing phenols: used as a preservative for wood ⊳ *vb* 3 to treat (wood) with creosote [c19: from Greek *kreas* flesh + *sōtēr* preserver, from *sōzein* to keep safe] > **creosotic** (ˌkrɪəˈsɒtɪk) *adj*

crepe *or* **crape** (kreɪp) *n* **1 a** a light cotton, silk, or other fabric with a fine ridged or crinkled surface **b** (*as modifier*): *a crepe dress* **2** a black armband originally made of this, worn as a sign of mourning **3** a very thin pancake, often rolled or folded around a filling **4** short for **crepe paper, crepe rubber** [c19: from French *crêpe*, from Latin *crispus* curled, uneven, wrinkled]

crepe de Chine (kreɪp də ˈʃiːn) *n* a very thin crepe of silk or a similar light fabric [c19: from French: Chinese crepe]

crepe paper *n* thin crinkled coloured paper, resembling crepe and used for decorations

creperie (ˈkrɛpərɪ, ˈkreɪp-) *n* an eating establishment that specializes in pancakes; pancake house

crepe rubber *n* a type of crude natural rubber in the form of colourless or pale yellow crinkled sheets, prepared by pressing bleached coagulated latex through corrugated rollers: used for the soles of shoes and in making certain surgical and medical goods

crêpe suzette (kreɪp suːˈzɛt) *n, pl* **crêpes suzettes** (*sometimes plural*) an orange-flavoured pancake flambéed in a liqueur or brandy

crepitate (ˈkrɛpɪˌteɪt) *vb* (*intr*) to make a rattling or crackling sound; rattle or crackle [c17: from Latin *crepitāre*] > **ˈcrepitant** *adj* > ˌcrepiˈtation *n*

crepitus (ˈkrɛpɪtəs) *n* **1** a crackling chest sound heard in pneumonia and other lung diseases **2** the grating sound of two ends of a broken bone rubbing together ▷ Also called: **crepitation** [c19: from Latin, from *crepāre* to crack, creak]

crept (krɛpt) *vb* the past tense and past participle of **creep**

crepuscular (krɪˈpʌskjʊlə) *adj* **1** of or like twilight; dim **2** (of certain insects, birds, and other animals) active at twilight or just before dawn [c17: from Latin *crepusculum* dusk, from *creper* dark]

crepy *or* **crepey** (ˈkreɪpɪ) *adj* **-ier, -iest** (*esp of the skin*) having a dry wrinkled appearance like crepe

Cres. *abbreviation* Crescent

crescendo (krɪˈʃɛndəʊ) *n, pl* **-dos** *or* **-di** (-dɪ) **1** *music* **a** a gradual increase in loudness or the musical direction or symbol indicating this. Abbreviation: **cresc.** Symbol: < (written over the music affected) **b** (*as modifier*): *a crescendo passage* **2** a gradual increase in loudness or intensity **3** a peak of noise or intensity: *the cheers reached a crescendo* ▷ *vb* **-does, -doing, -doed 4** (*intr*) to increase in loudness or force ▷ *adv* **5** with a crescendo [c18: from Italian, literally: increasing, from *crescere* to grow, from Latin]

crescent (ˈkrɛsənt, -zənt) *n* **1** the biconcave shape of the moon in its first or last quarters **2** any shape or object resembling this **3** *chiefly Brit* a crescent-shaped street, often lined with houses of the same style **4** the crescent (*often capital*) **a** the emblem of Islam or Turkey **b** Islamic or Turkish power ▷ *adj* **5** *archaic or poetic* increasing or growing [c14: from Latin *crescēns* increasing, from *crescere* to grow]

cresol (ˈkriːsɒl) *n* an aromatic compound derived from phenol, existing in three isomeric forms: found in coal tar and creosote and used in making synthetic resins and as an antiseptic and disinfectant; hydroxytoluene. Formula: $C_6H_4(CH_3)OH$

cress (krɛs) *n* any of various plants of the genera *Lepidium, Cardamine, Arabis*, etc, having pungent-tasting leaves often used in salads and as a garnish: family *Brassicaceae* (crucifers) [Old English *cressa*; related to Old High German *cresso* cress, *kresan* to crawl]

Cressent (French krɛsɑ̃) *n* **Charles.** 1685-1768, French cabinetmaker, noted esp for his marquetry using coloured woods

cresset (ˈkrɛsɪt) *n* *history* a metal basket mounted on a pole in which oil or pitch was burned for illumination [c14: from Old French *craisset*, from *craisse* GREASE]

Cressida (ˈkrɛsɪdə), **Criseyde** *or* **Cressid** *n* (in medieval adaptations of the story of Troy) a lady who deserts her Trojan lover Troilus for the Greek Diomedes

Cressy (ˈkrɛsɪ) *n* *rare* the former English name for **Crécy**

crest (krɛst) *n* **1** a tuft or growth of feathers, fur, or skin along the top of the heads of some birds, reptiles, and other animals **2** something resembling or suggesting this **3** the top, highest point, or highest stage of something **4** an ornamental piece, such as a plume, on top of a helmet **5** *heraldry* a symbol of a family or office, usually representing a beast or bird, borne in addition to a coat of arms and used in medieval times to decorate the helmet ▷ *vb* **6** (*intr*) to come or rise to a high point **7** (*tr*) to lie at the top of; cap **8** (*tr*) to go to or reach the top of (a hill, wave, etc) [c14: from Old French *creste*, from Latin *crista*] > **ˈcrested** *adj* > **ˈcrestless** *adj*

crestfallen (ˈkrɛstˌfɔːlən) *adj* dejected, depressed, or disheartened > **ˈcrestˌfallenly** *adv*

cretaceous (krɪˈteɪʃəs) *adj* consisting of or resembling chalk [c17: from Latin *crētāceus*, from *crēta*, literally: Cretan earth, that is, chalk]

Cretaceous (krɪˈteɪʃəs) *adj* **1** of, denoting, or formed in the last period of the Mesozoic era, between the Jurassic and Tertiary periods, lasting 80 million years during which chalk deposits were formed and flowering plants first appeared ▷ *n* **2** the Cretaceous the Cretaceous period or rock system

Cretan (ˈkriːtən) *adj* **1** of or relating to Crete or its inhabitants ▷ *n* **2** a native or inhabitant of Crete

Crete (kriːt) *n* a mountainous island in the E Mediterranean, the largest island of Greece: of archaeological importance for the ruins of Minoan civilization. Pop: 601 131 (2001). Area: 8331 sq km (3216 sq miles). Modern Greek name: **Kríti**

cretin (ˈkrɛtɪn) *n* **1** *old-fashioned* a person afflicted with cretinism **2** *offensive* a person considered to be extremely stupid [c18: from French *crétin*, from Swiss French *crestin*, from Latin *Chrīstiānus* CHRISTIAN, alluding to the humanity of such people, despite their handicaps] > **ˈcretinous** *adj*

cretinism (ˈkrɛtɪˌnɪzəm) *n* *old-fashioned* a condition arising from a deficiency of thyroid hormone, present from birth, characterized by dwarfism and mental retardation. See also **myxoedema**

cretonne (krɛˈtɒn, ˈkrɛtɒn) *n* a heavy cotton or linen fabric with a printed design, used for furnishing [c19: from French, from *Creton* Norman village where it originated]

Creutzfeldt-Jakob disease (ˈkrɔɪtsfɛlt ˈjaːkɒp) *n* *pathol* a fatal slow-developing disease that affects the central nervous system, characterized by mental deterioration and loss of coordination of the limbs. It is thought to be caused by an abnormal prion protein in the brain [c20: named after Hans G. *Creutzfeldt* (1885-1964) and Alfons *Jakob* (1884-1931), German physicians]

crevasse (krɪˈvæs) *n* **1** a deep crack or fissure, esp in the ice of a glacier **2** *US* a break in a river embankment ▷ *vb* **3** (*tr*) *US* to make a break or fissure in (a dyke, wall, etc) [c19: from French: CREVICE]

crevice (ˈkrɛvɪs) *n* a narrow fissure or crack; split; cleft [c14: from Old French *crevace*, from *crever* to burst, from Latin *crepāre* to crack]

crew[1] (kruː) *n* (*sometimes functioning as plural*) **1** the men who man a ship, boat, aircraft, etc **2** *nautical* a group of people assigned to a particular job or type of work **3** *informal* a gang, company, or crowd ▷ *vb* **4** to serve on (a ship) as a member of the crew [c15 *crue* (military) reinforcement, from Old French *creue* augmentation, from Old French *creistre* to increase, from Latin *crescere*]

crew[2] (kruː) *vb* a past tense of **crow**[2]

crew cut *n* a closely cropped haircut for men, originating in the US [c20: from the style of haircut worn by the boat crews at Harvard and Yale Universities]

Crewe (kruː) *n* a town in NW England, in Cheshire: major railway junction. Pop: 67 683 (2001)

crewel (ˈkruːɪl) *n* a loosely twisted worsted yarn, used in fancy work and embroidery [c15: of unknown origin] > **ˈcrewelist** *n* > **ˈcrewelˌwork** *n*

crew neck *n* a plain round neckline in sweaters > **ˈcrewˌneck** *or* **ˈcrew-ˌnecked** *adj*

crib (krɪb) *n* **1** a child's bed with slatted wooden sides; cot **2** a cattle stall or pen **3** a fodder rack or manger **4** a small crude cottage or room **5** *NZ* a weekend cottage:

c

term is South Island usage only **6** any small confined space **7** a representation of the manger in which the infant Jesus was laid at birth **8** *informal* a theft, esp of another's writing or thoughts **9** *informal, chiefly Brit* a translation of a foreign text or a list of answers used by students, often illicitly, as an aid in lessons, examinations, etc **10** short for **cribbage 11** *cribbage* the discard pile **12** Also called: **cribwork** a framework of heavy timbers laid in layers at right angles to one another, used in the construction of foundations, mines, etc ▷ *vb* **cribs, cribbing, cribbed 13** (*tr*) to put or enclose in or as if in a crib; furnish with a crib **14** (*tr*) *informal* to steal (another's writings or thoughts) **15** (*intr*) *informal* to copy either from a crib or from someone else during a lesson or examination **16** (*intr*) *informal* to grumble [Old English *cribb*; related to Old Saxon *kribbia*, Old High German *krippa*; compare Middle High German *krêbe* basket] > **'cribber**n

cribbage ('krɪbɪdʒ) *n* a game of cards for two to four, in which players try to win a set number of points before their opponents [c17: of uncertain origin]

cribbage board *n* a board, with pegs and holes, used for scoring at cribbage

crib-biting *n* a harmful habit of horses in which the animal leans on the manger or seizes it with the teeth and swallows a gulp of air

crib-wall *n* NZ a supporting wall constructed by laying cribs at right angles to each other, as in cribwork

Crichton ('kraɪtªn) *n* **1 James.** 1560–82, Scottish scholar and writer, called *the Admirable Crichton* because of his talents **2** (**John**) **Michael.** born 1942, US novelist, screenwriter, and film director; his thrillers, many of which have been filmed, include *The Andromeda Strain* (1969), *Jurassic Park* (1990), and *Disclosure* (1994)

crick (krɪk) *informal* ▷ *n* **1** a painful muscle spasm or cramp, esp in the neck or back ▷ *vb* **2** (*tr*) to cause a crick in (the neck, back, etc) [c15: of uncertain origin]

Crick (krɪk) *n* **Francis Harry Compton.** 1916–2004, English molecular biologist: helped to discover the helical structure of DNA; Nobel prize for physiology or medicine shared with James Watson and Maurice Wilkins 1962

cricket[1] ('krɪkɪt) *n* any insect of the orthopterous family *Gryllidae*, having long antennae and, in the males, the ability to produce a chirping sound (stridulation) by rubbing together the leathery forewings [c14: from Old French *criquet*, from *criquer* to creak, of imitative origin]

cricket[2] ('krɪkɪt) *n* **1 a** a game played by two teams of eleven players on a field with a wicket at either end of a 22-yard pitch, the object being for one side to score runs by hitting a hard leather-covered ball with a bat while the other side tries to dismiss them by bowling, catching, running them out, etc **b** (*as modifier*): *a cricket bat* **2** *not cricket informal* not fair play ▷ *vb* (*intr*) **3** to play cricket [c16: from Old French *criquet* goalpost, wicket, of uncertain origin] > **'cricketer**n

cricoid ('kraɪkɔɪd) *adj* **1** of or relating to the ring-shaped lowermost cartilage of the larynx ▷ *n* **2** this cartilage [c18: from New Latin *cricoīdēs*, from Greek *krikoeidēs* ring-shaped, from *krikos* ring]

cri de coeur (ˌkri də 'kɜː) *n*, *pl* **cris de coeur** a cry from the heart; heartfelt or sincere appeal [c20: altered from French *cri du coeur*]

crier ('kraɪə) *n* **1** a person or animal that cries **2** (formerly) an official who made public announcements, esp in a town or court

crikey ('kraɪkɪ) *interj slang* an expression of surprise [c19: euphemistic for Christ!]

crime (kraɪm) *n* **1** an act or omission prohibited and punished by law **2** unlawful acts in general **3** an evil act **4** *informal* something to be regretted [c14: from Old French, from Latin *crīmen* verdict, accusation, crime]

Crimea (kraɪ'mɪə) *n* a peninsula and autonomous region in Ukraine between the Black Sea and the Sea of Azov: a former autonomous republic of the Soviet Union (1921–45), part of the Ukrainian SSR from 1945 until 1991. Russian name: Кrym

Crimean (kraɪ'mɪən) *adj* **1** of or relating to the Crimea or its inhabitants ▷ *n* **2** an inhabitant of the Crimea

crimen injuria ('kraɪmən ɪn'dʒʊərɪə) *n South African law* an action that injures the dignity of another person, esp use of racially offensive language [L, lit.: crime or insult]

crimewave ('kraɪmˌweɪv) *n* a period of increased criminal activity

criminal ('krɪmɪnªl) *n* **1** a person charged with and convicted of crime **2** a person who commits crimes for a living ▷ *adj* **3** of, involving, or guilty of crime **4** (*prenominal*) of or relating to crime or its punishment **5** *informal* senseless or deplorable [c15: from Late Latin *crīminālis*; see CRIME, -AL[1]] > **'criminally**adv > **ˌcrimi'nality**n

criminal conversation *n* another term for **adultery**

criminalize *or* **criminalise** ('krɪmɪnəˌlaɪz) *vb* (*tr*) **1** to make (an activity or action) criminal **2** to treat (a person) as a criminal > **ˌcriminali'zation** *or* **ˌcriminali'sation**n

criminal law *n* the body of law dealing with the constitution of offences and the punishment of offenders

Criminal Records Bureau *n* (in England and Wales) a service offering employers and voluntary organizations access to police, health, and education records

criminology (ˌkrɪmɪ'nɒlədʒɪ) *n* the scientific study of crime, criminal behaviour, law enforcement, etc [c19: from Latin *crimin-* CRIME, -LOGY]

crimp (krɪmp) *vb* (*tr*) **1** to fold or press into ridges **2** to fold and pinch together (something, such as the edges of two pieces of metal) **3** to curl or wave (the hair) tightly, esp with curling tongs **4** *informal, chiefly US* to hinder ▷ *n* **5** the act or result of folding or pressing together or into ridges **6** a tight wave or curl in the hair [Old English *crympan*; related to *crump* bent, Old Norse *kreppa* to contract, Old High German *crumpf*, Old Swedish *crumb* crooked; see CRAMP[1]] > **'crimper**n > **'crimpy**adj

Crimplene ('krɪmpliːn) *n trademark* a synthetic material similar to Terylene, characterized by its crease-resistance

crimson ('krɪmzən) *n* **1 a** a deep or vivid red colour **b** (*as adjective*): *a crimson rose* ▷ *vb* **2** to make or become crimson **3** (*intr*) to blush [c14: from Old Spanish *cremesin*, from Arabic *qirmizi* red of the kermes, from *qirmiz* KERMES] > **'crimsonness**n

cringe (krɪndʒ) *vb* (*intr*) **1** to shrink or flinch, esp in fear or servility **2** to behave in a servile or timid way **3** *informal* to experience a sudden feeling of embarrassment or distaste ▷ *n* **4** the act of cringing **5** the cultural cringe *Austral* subservience to overseas cultural standards [Old English *cringan* to yield in battle; related to Old Norse *krangr* weak, Middle High German *krenken* to weaken] > **'cringer**n

cringle ('krɪŋgªl) *n* an eye at the edge of a sail, usually formed from a thimble or grommet [c17: from Low German *Kringel* small RING[1]; see CRANK, CRINKLE]

crinkle ('krɪŋkªl) *vb* **1** to form or cause to form wrinkles, twists, or folds **2** to fold or cause to make a rustling noise ▷ *n* **3** a wrinkle, twist, or fold **4** a rustling noise [Old English *crincan* to bend, give way; related to Middle Dutch *krinkelen* to crinkle, Middle High German *krank* weak, ill, *krenken* to weaken] > **'crinkly**adj

crinkly ('krɪŋklɪ) *adj* **1** wrinkled; crinkled ▷ *n*, *pl* **-lies 2** *slang* an old person

crinoid ('kraɪnɔɪd, 'krɪn-) *n* **1** any primitive echinoderm of the class *Crinoidea*, having delicate feathery arms radiating from a central disc. The group includes the free-swimming feather stars, the sessile sea lilies, and many stemmed fossil forms ▷ *adj* **2** of, relating to, or belonging to the *Crinoidea* **3** shaped like a lily [c19: from Greek *krinoeidēs* lily-like] > **cri'noidal**adj

crinoline ('krɪnªlɪn) *n* **1** a stiff fabric, originally of horsehair and linen used in lining garments **2** a petticoat stiffened with this, worn to distend skirts, esp in the mid-19th century **3** a framework of steel hoops worn for the same purpose [c19: from French, from Italian *crinolino*, from *crino* horsehair, from Latin *crīnis* hair + *lino* flax, from Latin *līnum*]

Crippen ('krɪpªn) *n* **Hawley Harvey,** known as *Doctor Crippen.* 1862–1910, US doctor living in England: executed for poisoning his wife; the first criminal to be apprehended by the use of radiotelegraphy

cripple ('krɪpᵊl) n 1 *offensive* a person who is lame 2 *offensive* a person who is or seems disabled or deficient in some way: *a mental cripple* ▷ *vb* 3 (*tr*) to make a cripple of; disable [Old English *crypel*; related to *crēopan* to CREEP, Old Frisian *kreppel* a cripple, Middle Low German *kröpel*] > 'crippler n

Cripple Creek n a village in central Colorado: gold-mining centre since 1891, once the richest in the world

Cripps (krɪps) n Sir (**Richard**) **Stafford**. 1889–1952, British Labour statesman; Chancellor of the Exchequer (1947–50)

Criseyde (krɪˈseɪdə) n a variant of **Cressida**

crisis ('kraɪsɪs) n, pl -ses (-siːz) 1 a crucial stage or turning point in the course of something, esp in a sequence of events or a disease 2 an unstable period, esp one of extreme trouble or danger in politics, economics, etc [c15: from Latin: decision, from Greek *krisis*, from *krinein* to decide]

crisp (krɪsp) adj 1 dry and brittle 2 fresh and firm 3 invigorating or bracing: *a crisp breeze* 4 clear; sharp: *crisp reasoning* 5 lively or stimulating 6 clean and orderly; neat 7 concise and pithy; terse 8 wrinkled or curly: *crisp hair* ▷ *vb* 9 to make or become crisp ▷ *n* 10 *Brit* a very thin slice of potato fried and eaten cold as a snack 11 something that is crisp [Old English, from Latin *crispus* curled, uneven, wrinkled] > 'crisply adv > 'crispness n

crispbread ('krɪsp,brɛd) n a thin dry biscuit made of wheat or rye

crisper ('krɪspə) n a compartment in a refrigerator for storing salads, vegetables, etc, in order to keep them fresh

Crispi (Italian 'krispi) n **Francesco** (fran'tʃesko). 1819–1901, Italian statesman; premier (1887–91; 1893–96)

Crispin ('krɪspɪn) n **Saint**, 3rd century AD, legendary Roman Christian martyr, with his brother **Crispinian** (krɪ'spɪnɪən): they are the patron saints of shoemakers. Feast day: Oct 25

crispy ('krɪspɪ) adj crispier, crispiest 1 crisp 2 having waves or curls > 'crispiness n

crisscross ('krɪs,krɒs) vb 1 to move or cause to move in a crosswise pattern 2 to mark with or consist of a pattern of crossing lines ▷ adj 3 (esp of a number of lines) crossing one another in different directions ▷ n 4 a pattern made of crossing lines ▷ adv 5 in a crosswise manner or pattern

crit. *abbreviation* 1 critic 2 criticism

criterion (kraɪ'tɪərɪən) n, pl -ria (-rɪə) or -rions a standard by which something can be judged or decided [c17: from Greek *kritērion* from *kritēs* judge, from *krinein* to decide]

● USAGE *Criteria*, the plural of *criterion*, is not acceptable as a singular noun: *this criterion is not valid*; *these criteria are not valid*

critic ('krɪtɪk) n 1 a person who judges something 2 a professional judge of art, music, literature, etc 3 a person who often finds fault and criticizes [c16: from Latin *criticus*, from Greek *kritikos* capable of judging, from *kritēs* judge; see CRITERION]

critical ('krɪtɪkᵊl) adj 1 containing or making severe or negative judgments 2 containing careful or analytical evaluations 3 of or involving a critic or criticism 4 of or forming a crisis; crucial; decisive 5 urgently needed 6 *informal* so seriously injured or ill as to be in danger of dying 7 *physics* of, denoting, or concerned with a state in which the properties of a system undergo an abrupt change 8 go critical (of a nuclear power station or reactor) to reach a state in which a nuclear-fission chain reaction becomes self-sustaining > ,criti'cality adv > 'critically adv > 'criticalness n

critical density n the density of matter that would be required to halt the expansion of the universe

critical mass n the minimum mass of fissionable material that can sustain a nuclear chain reaction

critical path analysis n a technique for planning complex projects by analysing alternative systems with reference to the critical path, which is the sequence of stages requiring the longest time

critical temperature n the temperature of a substance in its critical state. A gas can only be liquefied by pressure alone at temperatures below its critical temperature

criticism ('krɪtɪ,sɪzəm) n 1 the act or an instance of making an unfavourable or severe judgment, comment, etc 2 the analysis or evaluation of a work of art, literature, etc 3 the occupation of a critic 4 a work that sets out to evaluate or analyse

criticize or **criticise** ('krɪtɪ,saɪz) vb 1 to judge (something) with disapproval; censure 2 to evaluate or analyse (something) > 'criti,cizable or 'criti,cisable adj > 'criti,cizer or 'criti,ciser n

critique (krɪ'tiːk) n 1 a critical essay or commentary, esp on artistic work 2 the act or art of criticizing [c17: from French, from Greek *kritikē*, from *kritikos* able to discern]

croak (krəʊk) vb 1 (*intr*) (of frogs, crows, etc) to make a low, hoarse cry 2 to utter (something) in this manner 3 (*intr*) to grumble or be pessimistic 4 *slang* a (*intr*) to die b (*tr*) to kill ▷ n 5 a low hoarse utterance or sound [Old English *crācettan*; related to Old Norse *krāka* a crow; see CREAK] > 'croaky adj > 'croakiness n

croaker ('krəʊkə) n 1 an animal, bird, etc, that croaks 2 a grumbling person

Croat ('krəʊæt) n 1 a a native or inhabitant of Croatia b a speaker of Croatian ▷ n, adj 2 another word for **Croatian**

Croatia (krəʊ'eɪʃə) n a republic in SE Europe: settled by Croats in the 7th century; belonged successively to Hungary, Turkey, and Austria; formed part of Yugoslavia (1918–91); became independent in 1991 but was invaded by Serbia and fighting continued until 1995; involved in the civil war in Bosnia-Herzegovina (1991–95). Language: Croatian. Religion: Roman Catholic majority. Currency: kuna. Capital: Zagreb. Pop: 4 416 000 (2004 est). Area: 55 322 sq km (21 359 sq miles). Croatian name: **Hrvatska**

Croatian (krəʊ'eɪʃən) adj 1 of, relating to, or characteristic of Croatia, its people, or their language ▷ n 2 the language that is spoken in Croatia, formerly regarded as a dialect of Serbo-Croat (Croato-Serb) 3 a a native or inhabitant of Croatia b a speaker of Croatian

croc (krɒk) n short for **crocodile**

Croce (Italian 'kroːtʃe) n **Benedetto** (bene'detto). 1866–1952, Italian philosopher, critic, and statesman: an opponent of Fascism, he helped re-establish liberalism in postwar Italy

crochet ('krəʊʃeɪ, -ʃɪ) vb -chets (-ʃeɪz, -ʃɪz), -cheting (-ʃeɪɪŋ, -ʃɪɪŋ), -cheted (-ʃeɪd, -ʃɪd) 1 to make (a piece of needlework, a garment, etc) by looping and intertwining thread with a hooked needle (**crochet hook**) ▷ n 2 work made by crocheting [c19: from French *crochet*, diminutive of *croc* hook, probably of Scandinavian origin] > 'crocheter n

crock¹ (krɒk) n 1 an earthen pot, jar, etc 2 a piece of broken earthenware [Old English *crocc* pot; related to Old Norse *krukka* jar, Middle Low German *krūke* pot]

crock² (krɒk) n 1 *slang, chiefly Brit* a person or thing, such as a car, that is old or decrepit (esp in the phrase **old crock**) ▷ vb 2 *slang, chiefly Brit* to become or cause to become weak or disabled [c15: originally Scottish; related to Norwegian *krake* unhealthy animal, Dutch *kraak* decrepit person or animal]

crockery ('krɒkərɪ) n china dishes, earthen vessels, etc, collectively

crocket ('krɒkɪt) n a carved ornament in the form of a curled leaf or cusp, used in Gothic architecture [c17: from Anglo-French *croket* a little hook, from *croc* hook, of Scandinavian origin]

Crockett ('krɒkɪt) n **David**, known as *Davy Crockett*. 1786–1836, US frontiersman, politician, and soldier

crocodile ('krɒkə,daɪl) n 1 any large tropical reptile, such as C. *niloticus* (**African crocodile**), of the family Crocodylidae: order Crocodilia (crocodilians). They have a broad head, tapering snout, massive jaws, and a thick outer covering of bony plates 2 a leather made from the skin of any of these animals b (*as modifier*): *crocodile shoes* 3 *Brit informal* a line of people, esp schoolchildren, walking two by two [c13: via Old French, from Latin *crocodīlus*, from Greek *krokodeilos* lizard, ultimately from *krokē* pebble + *drilos* worm; referring to its fondness for basking on shingle]

crocodile clip *n* a clasp with serrated interlocking edges used for making electrical connections

Crocodile River *n* **1** a river in N South Africa, rising north of Johannesburg and flowing north-westerly into the Marico River on the Botswanan border; a tributary of the Limpopo **2** a river that rises in NE South Africa, in the Kruger National Park, and flows south-easterly into Mozambique

crocodile tears *pl n* an insincere show of grief; false tears [from the belief that crocodiles wept over their prey to lure further victims]

crocodilian (ˌkrɒkəˈdɪlɪən) *n* **1** any large predatory reptile of the order *Crocodilia*, which includes the crocodiles, alligators, and caymans. They live in or near water and have a long broad snout, powerful jaws, and a four-chambered heart, and socketed teeth ▷ *adj* **2** of, relating to, or belonging to the *Crocodilia* **3** of, relating to, or resembling a crocodile

crocus (ˈkrəʊkəs) *n, pl* -cuses any plant of the iridaceous genus *Crocus*, widely cultivated in gardens, having white, yellow, or purple flowers [c17: from New Latin, from Latin *crocus*, from Greek *krokos* saffron, of Semitic origin]

Croesus (ˈkriːsəs) *n* **1** died ?546 BC, the last king of Lydia (560–546), noted for his great wealth **2** any very rich man

croft (krɒft) *n Brit* a small enclosed plot of land, adjoining a house, worked by the occupier and his family, esp in Scotland [Old English *croft*; related to Middle Dutch *krocht* hill, field, Old English *creopan* to CREEP] ▷ 'crofter *n* ▷ 'crofting *n, adj*

Crohn's disease (krəʊnz) *n* inflammation, thickening, and ulceration of any of various parts of the intestine, esp the ileum. Also called: regional enteritis [c20: named after B. B. *Crohn* (1884–1983), US physician]

croissant (ˈkrwʌsɒŋ; *French* krwasã) *n* a flaky crescent-shaped bread roll made of a yeast dough similar to puff pastry [French, literally: crescent]

Croix de Guerre *French* (krwa də gɛr) *n* a French military decoration awarded for gallantry in battle: established 1915 [literally: cross of war]

Cro-Magnon man (ˈkrəʊˈmænjɒn, -ˈmægnɒn) *n* an early type of modern man, *Homo sapiens*, who lived in Europe during late Palaeolithic times, having tall stature, long head, and a relatively large cranial capacity [c19: named after the cave (Cro-Magnon), Dordogne, France, where the remains were first found]

Crome (krəʊm) *n* **John,** known as *Old Crome*. 1768–1821, English landscape painter and etcher

Cromer (ˈkrəʊmə) *n* **1st Earl of,** title of (Evelyn) **Baring**

cromlech (ˈkrɒmlɛk) *n* **1** a circle of prehistoric standing stones **2** (no longer in technical usage) a megalithic chamber tomb or dolmen [c17: from Welsh, from *crom*, feminine of *crwm* bent, arched + *llech* flat stone]

Crompton (ˈkrɒmptən) *n* **1 Richmal,** full name *Richmal Crompton Lamburn*. 1890–1969, British children's author, best known for her *Just William* stories **2 Samuel.** 1753–1827, British inventor of the spinning mule (1779)

Cromwell (ˈkrɒmwəl, -wɛl) *n* **1 Oliver.** 1599–1658, English general and statesman. A convinced Puritan, he was an effective leader of the parliamentary army in the Civil War. After the execution of Charles I he quelled the Royalists in Scotland and Ireland, and became Lord Protector of the Commonwealth (1653–58) **2** his son, **Richard.** 1626–1712, Lord Protector of the Commonwealth (1658–59) **3 Thomas,** Earl of Essex. ?1485–1540, English statesman. He was secretary to Cardinal Wolsey (1514), after whose fall he became chief adviser to Henry VIII. He drafted most of the Reformation legislation, securing its passage through parliament, the power of which he thereby greatly enhanced. He was executed after losing Henry's favour ▷ Cromwellian (krɒmˈwɛlɪən) *adj, n*

crone (krəʊn) *n* a witchlike old woman [c14: from Old Northern French *carogne* carrion, ultimately from Latin *caro* flesh]

Cronin (ˈkrəʊnɪn) *n* **1 A(rchibald) J(oseph).** 1896–1981, British novelist and physician. His works include *Hatter's Castle* (1931), *The Judas Tree* (1961), and *Dr Finlay's Casebook*, a TV series based on his medical experiences **2 James Watson.** born 1931, US physicist; shared the Nobel prize for physics (1980) for his work on parity conservation in weak interactions

Cronje (ˈkrɒnjə) *n* **Hansie,** full name *Wessel Johannes Cronje* (1969–2002); South African cricketer. He captained South Africa (1994–2000); banned for life from cricket for match-fixing in 2001

cronk (krɒŋk) *adj Austral* unfit; unsound [c19]

Cronus (ˈkrəʊnəs), **Cronos** or **Kronos** (ˈkrəʊnɒs) *n Greek myth* a Titan, son of Uranus (sky) and Gaea (earth), who ruled the world until his son Zeus dethroned him. Roman counterpart: Saturn

crony (ˈkrəʊnɪ) *n, pl* -nies a friend or companion [c17: student slang (Cambridge), from Greek *khronios* of long duration, from *khronos* time]

cronyism (ˈkrəʊnɪˌɪzəm) *n* the practice of appointing friends to high-level, esp political, posts regardless of their suitability

crook (krʊk) *n* **1** a curved or hooked thing **2** a staff with a hooked end, such as a bishop's crosier or shepherd's staff **3** a turn or curve; bend **4** *informal* a dishonest person, esp a swindler or thief ▷ *vb* **5** to bend or curve or cause to bend or curve ▷ *adj* **6** *Austral & NZ informal* **a** ill **b** of poor quality **c** unpleasant; bad **7** go crook or go off crook *Austral & NZ informal* to lose one's temper **8** go crook at or go crook on *Austral & NZ informal* to rebuke or upbraid [c12: from Old Norse *krokr* hook; related to Swedish *krok*, Danish *krog* hook, Old High German *krācho* hooked tool]

crooked (ˈkrʊkɪd) *adj* **1** bent, angled or winding **2** set at an angle; not straight **3** deformed or contorted **4** *informal* dishonest or illegal **5** crooked on (*also* krʊkt) *Austral informal* hostile or averse to ▷ 'crookedly *adv* ▷ 'crookedness *n*

Crookes (krʊks) *n* **Sir William.** 1832–1919, English chemist and physicist: he investigated the properties of cathode rays and invented a type of radiometer and the lens named after him

crool (kruːl) *vb Austral slang* **1** (*tr*) to spoil: *don't crool your chances* **2** crool someone's pitch to spoil an opportunity for someone

croon (kruːn) *vb* **1** to sing or speak in a soft low tone ▷ *n* **2** a soft low singing or humming [c14: via Middle Dutch *crōnen* to groan; compare Old High German *chrōnan* to chatter, Latin *gingrīre* to cackle (of geese)] ▷ 'crooner *n*

crop (krɒp) *n* **1** the produce of cultivated plants, esp cereals, vegetables, and fruit **2 a** the amount of such produce in any particular season **b** the yield of some other farm produce: *the lamb crop* **3** a group of products, thoughts, people, etc, appearing at one time or in one season **4** the stock of a thonged whip **5** short for riding crop **6** a pouchlike expanded part of the oesophagus of birds, in which food is stored or partially digested before passing on to the gizzard **7** a short cropped hairstyle **8** a notch in or a piece cut out of the ear of an animal **9** the act of cropping ▷ *vb* crops, cropping, cropped (*mainly tr*) **10** to cut (hair, grass, etc) very short **11** to cut and collect (mature produce) from the land or plant on which it has been grown **12** to clip part of (the ear or ears) of (an animal), esp as a means of identification **13** (of herbivorous animals) to graze on (grass or similar vegetation) ▷ See also **crop out, crop up** [Old English *cropp*; related to Old Norse *kroppr* rump, body, Old High German *kropf* goitre, Norwegian *krōypa* to bend]

crop-dusting *n* the spreading of fungicide, etc on crops in the form of dust, often from an aircraft

crop-eared *adj* having the ears or hair cut short

crop out *vb* (*intr, adverb*) (of a formation of rock strata) to appear or be exposed at the surface of the ground; outcrop

cropper (ˈkrɒpə) *n* **1** a person who cultivates or harvests a crop **2** come a cropper *informal* **a** to fall heavily **b** to fail completely

crop rotation *n* the system of growing a sequence of different crops on the same ground so as to maintain or increase its fertility

crop top *n* a short T-shirt or vest that reveals the wearer's midriff

crop up *vb* (*intr, adverb*) *informal* to occur or appear, esp unexpectedly

croquet ('krəʊkeɪ, -kɪ) *n* a game for two to four players who hit a wooden ball through iron hoops with mallets in order to hit a peg [c19: perhaps from French dialect, variant of CROCHET (little hook)]

croquette (krəʊ'kɛt, krɒ-) *n* a savoury cake of minced meat, fish, etc, fried in breadcrumbs [c18: from French, from *croquer* to crunch, of imitative origin]

Crosby ('krɒzbɪ) *n* **Bing**, real name *Harry Lillis Crosby*. 1904–77, US singer and film actor; famous for his style of crooning: best known for the song "White Christmas" from the film *Holiday Inn* (1942)

crosier or **crozier** ('krəʊʒə) *n* a staff surmounted by a crook or cross, carried by bishops as a symbol of pastoral office [c14: from Old French *crossier* staff bearer, from *crosse* pastoral staff, literally: hooked stick, of Germanic origin]

Crosland ('krɒslənd) *n* **Anthony**. 1918–77, British Labour politician and socialist theorist, author of *The Future of Socialism* (1957)

cross (krɒs) *n* **1** a structure or symbol consisting essentially of two intersecting lines or pieces at right angles to one another **2** a wooden structure used as a means of execution, consisting of an upright post with a transverse piece to which people were nailed or tied **3** a representation of the Cross used as an emblem of Christianity or as a reminder of Christ's death **4** any mark or shape consisting of two intersecting lines, esp such a symbol (×) used as a signature, point of intersection, error mark, etc **5** a sign representing the Cross made either by tracing a figure in the air or by touching the forehead, breast, and either shoulder in turn **6** any conventional variation of the Christian symbol, used emblematically, decoratively, or heraldically, such as a Maltese, tau, or Greek cross **7** a cruciform emblem awarded to indicate membership of an order or as a decoration for distinguished service **8** (*sometimes capital*) Christianity or Christendom, esp as contrasted with non-Christian religions **9** the place in a town or village where a cross has been set up **10** *biology* **a** the process of crossing; hybridization **b** an individual produced as a result of this process **11** a mixture of two qualities or types **12** an opposition, hindrance, or misfortune; affliction (esp in the phrase **bear one's cross**) **13** *boxing* a straight punch delivered from the side, esp with the right hand **14** *football* the act or an instance of kicking or passing the ball from a wing to the middle of the field ▷ *vb* **15** (sometimes foll by *over*) to move or go across (something); traverse or intersect **16 a** to meet and pass **b** (of each of two letters in the post) to be dispatched before receipt of the other **17** (*tr*; usually foll by *out, off,* or *through*) to cancel with a cross or with lines; delete **18** (*tr*) to place or put in a form resembling a cross: *to cross one's legs* **19** (*tr*) to mark with a cross or crosses **20** (*tr*) *Brit* to draw two parallel lines across the face of (a cheque) and so make it payable only into a bank account **21** (*tr*) **a** to trace the form of the Cross, usually with the thumb or index finger upon (someone or something) in token of blessing **b** to make the sign of the Cross upon (oneself) **22** (*intr*) (of telephone lines) to interfere with each other so that three or perhaps four callers are connected together at one time **23** to cause fertilization between (plants or animals of different breeds, races, varieties, etc) **24** (*tr*) to oppose the wishes or plans of; thwart **25** *football* to kick or pass (the ball) from a wing to the middle of the field **26** **cross one's fingers** to fold one finger across another in the hope of bringing good luck **27** **cross one's heart** to promise or pledge, esp by making the sign of a cross over one's heart **28** **cross one's mind** to occur to one briefly or suddenly **29** **cross someone's path** to meet or thwart someone **30** **cross swords** to argue or fight ▷ *adj* **31** angry; ill-humoured; vexed **32** lying or placed across; transverse: *a cross timber* **33** involving interchange; reciprocal **34** contrary or unfavourable **35** another word for **crossbred** (sense 1) [Old English *cros,* from Old Irish *cross* (unattested), from

Latin *crux;* see CRUX] > 'cross**ly** *adv* > 'cross**ness** *n*

Cross[1] (krɒs) *n* **the Cross** **1** the cross on which Jesus Christ was crucified **2** the Crucifixion of Jesus

Cross[2] (krɒs) *n* **Richard Assheton, 1st Viscount**. 1823–1914, British Conservative statesman, home secretary (1874–80); noted for reforms affecting housing, public health, and the employment of women and children in factories

cross- *combining form* **1** indicating action from one individual, group, etc, to another: *cross-cultural; cross-fertilize; cross-refer* **2** indicating movement, position, etc, across something (sometimes implying interference, opposition, or contrary action): *crosscurrent; crosstalk* **3** indicating a crosslike figure or intersection: *crossbones* [from CROSS (in various senses)]

crossbar ('krɒs,bɑː) *n* **1** a horizontal bar, line, stripe, etc **2** a horizontal beam across a pair of goalposts **3** the horizontal bar on a man's bicycle that joins the handlebar and saddle supports

crossbeam ('krɒs,biːm) *n* a beam that spans from one support to another

cross-bench *n* (*usually plural*) *Brit* a seat in Parliament occupied by a neutral or independent member > 'cross-,bench**er** *n*

crossbill ('krɒs,bɪl) *n* any of various widely distributed finches of the genus *Loxia,* such as *L. curvirostra,* that occur in coniferous woods and have a bill with crossed mandible tips for feeding on conifer seeds

crossbones ('krɒs,bəʊnz) *pl n* See **skull and crossbones**

crossbow ('krɒs,bəʊ) *n* a type of medieval bow fixed transversely on a wooden stock grooved to direct a square-headed arrow (quarrel) > 'cross,bow**man** *n*

crossbred ('krɒs,brɛd) *adj* **1** (of plants or animals) produced as a result of crossbreeding ▷ *n* **2** a crossbred plant or animal, esp an animal resulting from a cross between two pure breeds

crossbreed ('krɒs,briːd) *vb* **-breeds, -breeding, -bred** **1** Also called: **interbreed** to breed (animals or plants) using parents of different races, varieties, breeds, etc ▷ *n* **2** the offspring produced by such a breeding

crosscheck (,krɒs'tʃɛk) *vb* **1** to verify (a fact, report, etc) by considering conflicting opinions or consulting other sources ▷ *n* **2** the act or an instance of crosschecking

cross-country *adj, adv* **1** by way of fields, woods, etc, as opposed to roads **2** across a country ▷ *n* **3** a long race held over open ground

crosscurrent ('krɒs,kʌrənt) *n* **1** a current in a river or sea flowing across another current **2** a conflicting tendency moving counter to the usual trend

cross-curricular *adj* *Brit education* denoting or relating to an approach to a topic that includes contributions from several different disciplines and viewpoints

crosscut ('krɒs,kʌt) *adj* **1** cut at right angles or obliquely to the major axis ▷ *n* **2** a transverse cut or course **3** *mining* a tunnel through a vein of ore or from the shaft to a vein ▷ *vb* **-cuts, -cutting, -cut** **4** to cut across

crosscut saw *n* a saw for cutting timber across the grain

crosse (krɒs) *n* a light staff with a triangular frame to which a network is attached, used in playing lacrosse [French, from Old French *croce* CROSIER]

cross-examine *vb* (*tr*) **1** *law* to examine (a witness for the opposing side), as in attempting to discredit his testimony **2** to examine closely or relentlessly > 'cross-ex,ami'nation *n* > ,cross-ex'amin**er** *n*

cross-eye *n* a turning inwards towards the nose of one or both eyes, caused by abnormal alignment > 'cross-,eyed *adj*

cross-fertilization *n* fertilization by the fusion of male and female gametes from different individuals of the same species > ,cross-'fertile *adj*

cross-fertilize *vb* to subject or be subjected to cross-fertilization

crossfire ('krɒs,faɪə) *n* **1** *military* converging fire from one or more positions **2** a lively exchange of opinions, etc

cross-grained *adj* **1** (of timber) having the fibres arranged irregularly or in a direction that deviates from the axis of the piece **2** perverse, cantankerous, or stubborn

cross hairs *pl n* two fine mutually perpendicular lines or wires that cross in the focal plane of a theodolite, gunsight, or other optical instrument and are used to define the line of sight. Also called: **cross wires**

crosshatch ('krɒs,hætʃ) *vb drawing* to shade or hatch (forms, figures, etc) with two or more sets of parallel lines that cross one another

crossing ('krɒsɪŋ) *n* **1** the place where one thing crosses another **2** a place, often shown by markings, lights, or poles, where a street, railway, etc, may be crossed **3** the intersection of the nave and transept in a church **4** the act or process of crossbreeding

crossing over *n biology* the interchange of sections between pairing homologous chromosomes during the diplotene stage of meiosis. It results in the rearrangement of genes and produces variation in the inherited characteristics of the offspring

cross-legged ('krɒs'legɪd, -'legd) *adj* standing or sitting with one leg crossed over the other

Crossman ('krɒsmən) *n* **Richard (Howard Stafford).** 1907–74, British Labour politician. His diaries, published posthumously as the *Crossman Papers* (1975), revealed details of cabinet discussions

cross-match *vb immunol* to test the compatibility of (a donor's and recipient's blood) by checking that the red cells of each do not agglutinate in the other's serum

crossover ('krɒs,əʊvə) *n* **1** a place at which a crossing is made **2** *railways* a point of transfer between two main lines **3** short for **crossover network 4** a recording, book, or other product that becomes popular in a genre other than its own ▷ *adj* **5** (of music, fashion, art, etc) combining two distinct styles **6** (of a performer, writer, recording, book, etc) having become popular in more than one genre

crossover network *n* an electronic network in a loudspeaker system that separates the signal into two or more frequency bands, the lower frequencies being fed to a woofer, the higher frequencies to a tweeter

cross-party *adj* denoting interaction between two or more political parties: *a cross-party group*

crosspatch ('krɒs,pætʃ) *n informal* a peevish bad-tempered person [c18: from CROSS + obsolete *patch* fool]

crosspiece ('krɒs,pi:s) *n* a transverse beam, joist, etc

cross-ply *adj* (of a motor tyre) having the fabric cords in the outer casing running diagonally to stiffen the sidewalls

cross-pollinate *vb* to subject or be subjected to cross-pollination

cross-pollination *n* the transfer of pollen from the anthers of one flower to the stigma of another flower by the action of wind, insects, etc. See **self-pollination**

cross-purpose *n* **1** a contrary aim or purpose **2** at cross-purposes conflicting; opposed; disagreeing

cross-question *vb* **1** (*tr*) to cross-examine ▷ *n* **2** a question asked in cross-examination

cross-refer *vb* to refer from one part of something, esp a book, to another

cross-reference *n* **1** a reference within a text to another part of the text ▷ *vb* **2** to cross-refer

crossroad ('krɒs,rəʊd) *n* **1** *US & Canadian* a road that crosses another road **2** Also called: **crossway** a road that crosses from one main road to another

crossroads ('krɒs,rəʊdz) *n* (*functioning as singular*) **1** an area or the point at which two or more roads cross each other **2** the point at which an important choice has to be made (esp in the phrase **at the crossroads**)

crossruff ('krɒs,rʌf) *bridge, whist* ▷ *n* **1** the alternate trumping of each other's leads by two partners, or by declarer and dummy ▷ *vb* **2** (*intr*) to trump alternately in two hands of a partnership

cross section *n* **1** *maths* a plane surface formed by cutting across a solid, esp perpendicular to its longest axis **2** a section cut off in this way **3** the act of cutting anything in this way **4** a random selection or sample, esp one regarded as representative ▷ ,cross-'sectional *adj*

cross-stitch *n* **1** an embroidery stitch made by two stitches forming a cross **2** embroidery worked with this stitch ▷ *vb* **3** to embroider (a piece of needlework) with cross-stitch

crosstalk ('krɒs,tɔ:k) *n* **1** unwanted signals in one channel of a communications system as a result of a transfer of energy from one or more other channels **2** *Brit* rapid or witty talk or conversation

cross training *n* training in two or more sports to improve performance, esp on one's main sport

crosstree ('krɒs,tri:) *n nautical* either of a pair of wooden or metal braces on the head of a mast to support the topmast, etc

crosswise ('krɒs,waɪz) or **crossways** ('krɒs,weɪz) *adj, adv* **1** across; transversely **2** in the shape of a cross

crossword puzzle ('krɒs,wɜːd) *n* a puzzle in which the solver deduces words suggested by numbered clues and writes them into corresponding boxes in a grid to form a vertical and horizontal pattern. Often shortened to: **crossword**

crotch (krɒtʃ) *n* **1** Also called (Brit): **crutch a** the angle formed by the inner sides of the legs where they join the human trunk **b** the human external genitals or the genital area **c** the corresponding part of a pair of trousers, pants, etc **2** a forked region formed by the junction of two members **3** a forked pole or stick [c16: probably variant of CRUTCH] > **crotched** *adj*

crotchet ('krɒtʃɪt) *n* **1** *music* a note having the time value of a quarter of a semibreve. Usual US and Canadian name: **quarter note 2** a perverse notion [c14: from Old French *crochet*, literally: little hook, from *croche* hook; see CROCKET]

crotchety ('krɒtʃɪtɪ) *adj* **1** *informal* cross; irritable; contrary **2** full of crotchets > 'crotchetiness *n*

croton ('krəʊtᵊn) *n* **1** any shrub or tree of the chiefly tropical euphorbiaceous genus *Croton*, esp *C. tiglium*, the seeds of which yield croton oil **2** any of various tropical plants of the related genus *Codiaeum*, esp *C. variegatum pictum*, a house plant with variegated foliage [c18: from New Latin, from Greek *krotōn* tick, castor-oil plant (whose berries resemble ticks)]

crouch (kraʊtʃ) *vb* **1** (*intr*) to bend low with the limbs pulled up close together, esp (of an animal) in readiness to pounce **2** (*intr*) to cringe, as in humility or fear ▷ *n* **3** the act of stooping or bending [c14: perhaps from Old French *crochir* to become bent like a hook, from *croche* hook]

croup¹ (kru:p) *n* a throat condition, occurring usually in children, characterized by a hoarse cough and laboured breathing, resulting from inflammation and partial obstruction of the larynx [c16 *croup* to cry hoarsely, probably of imitative origin] > 'croupous or 'croupy *adj*

croup² or **croupe** (kru:p) *n* the hindquarters of a quadruped, esp a horse [c13: from Old French *croupe*; related to German *Kruppe*]

croupier ('kru:pɪə; French krupje) *n* a person who deals cards, collects bets, etc, at a gaming table [c18: literally: one who rides behind another, from French *croupe* CROUP²]

crouton ('kru:tɒn) *n* a small piece of fried or toasted bread, usually served in soup [French: diminutive of *croûte* CRUST]

crow¹ (krəʊ) *n* **1** any large gregarious songbird of the genus *Corvus*, esp *C. corone* (the carrion crow) of Europe and Asia: family *Corvidae*. Other species are the raven, rook, and jackdaw and all have a heavy bill, glossy black plumage, and rounded wings **2** any of various similar birds of other families **3** *offensive* an old or ugly woman **4** as the crow flies as directly as possible **5** eat crow *US & Canadian informal* to be forced to do something humiliating **6** stone the crows (*interjection*) *Brit & Austral slang* an expression of surprise, dismay, etc [Old English *crāwa*; related to Old Norse *krāka*, Old High German *krāia*, Dutch *kraai*]

crow² (krəʊ) *vb* (*intr*) **1** (past tense **crowed** or **crew**) to utter a shrill squawking sound, as a cock **2** (often foll by *over*) to boast one's superiority **3** (esp of babies) to utter cries of pleasure ▷ *n* **4** the act or an instance of crowing [Old English *crāwan*; related to Old High German *krāen*, Dutch *kraaien*] > 'crowingly *adv*

crowbar ('krəʊ,bɑ:) *n* a heavy iron lever with one pointed end, and one forged into a wedge shape

crowd (kraʊd) *n* **1** a large number of things or people gathered or considered together **2** a particular group of people, esp considered as a social or business set: *the crowd from the office* **3** **the crowd** the common people; the masses ▷ *vb* **4** (*intr*) to gather together in large numbers; throng **5** (*tr*) to press together into a confined space **6** (*tr*) to fill to excess; fill by pushing into **7** (*tr*) *informal* to urge or harass by urging [Old English *crūdan*; related to Middle Low German *krūden* to molest, Middle Dutch *crūden* to push, Norwegian *kryda* to swarm] ▷ '**crowded** *adj* ▷ '**crowdedness** *n*

crowdsource ('kraʊd,sɔːs) *vb* to outsource work to an unspecified group of people, typically by making an appeal to the general public on the internet [C21: from CROWD + (OUT)SOURCE] ▷ '**crowdsourcing** *n*

crowd surfing *n* the practice of being passed over the top of a crowd of people such as an audience at a pop concert

Crowe (krəʊ) *n* **Russell.** born 1964, Australian film actor, born in New Zealand. His films include *LA Confidential* (1997), *Gladiator* (2000), for which he won an Oscar, *A Beautiful Mind* (2001), and *Master and Commander* (2003)

crowfoot ('krəʊ,fʊt) *n*, *pl* -**foots** any of several plants of the genus *Ranunculus*, such as *R. sceleratus* and *R. aquatilis* (**water crowfoot**) that have yellow or white flowers and divided leaves resembling the foot of a crow

crown (kraʊn) *n* **1** an ornamental headdress denoting sovereignty, usually made of gold embedded with precious stones **2** a wreath or garland for the head, awarded as a sign of victory, success, honour, etc **3** (*sometimes capital*) monarchy or kingship **4** an award, distinction, or title, given as an honour to reward merit, victory, etc **5** anything resembling or symbolizing a crown, such as a sergeant major's badge or a heraldic bearing **6** a *history* a coin worth 25 pence (five shillings) **b** any of several continental coins, such as the krona or krone, with a name meaning *crown* **7** the top or summit of something, esp of a rounded object: *crown of a hill; crown of the head* **8** the centre part of a road, esp when it is cambered **9** the outstanding quality, achievement, state, etc: *the crown of his achievements* **10** a the enamel-covered part of a tooth above the gum **b** artificial crown a substitute crown, usually of gold, porcelain, or acrylic resin, fitted over a decayed or broken tooth **11** the part of an anchor where the arms are joined to the shank ▷ *vb* (*tr*) **12** to put a crown on the head of, symbolically vesting with royal title, powers, etc **13** to place a crown, wreath, garland, etc, on the head of **14** to place something on or over the head or top of **15** to confer a title, dignity, or reward upon **16** to form the summit or topmost part of **17** to cap or put the finishing touch to a series of events: *to crown it all it rained, too* **18** *draughts* to promote (a draught) to a king by placing another draught on top of it, as after reaching the end of the board **19** to attach a crown to (a tooth) **20** *slang* to hit over the head [C12: from Old French *corone*, from Latin *corōna* wreath, crown, from Greek *korōnē* crown, something curved]

Crown (kraʊn) **the Crown** *n* (*sometimes not capital*) **1** the sovereignty or realm of a monarch **2** a the government of a constitutional monarchy **b** (*as modifier*): *Crown property*

crown colony *n* a British colony whose administration and legislature is controlled by the Crown

crown court *n* *English law* a court of criminal jurisdiction holding sessions in towns throughout England and Wales at which circuit judges hear and determine cases

Crown Derby *n* a type of porcelain manufactured at Derby from 1784–1848

crown glass *n* **1** another name for **optical crown 2** an old form of window glass made by blowing a globe and spinning it until it formed a flat disc

crown green *n* a type of bowling green in which the sides are lower than the middle

crowning ('kraʊnɪŋ) *n* *obstetrics* the stage of labour when the infant's head is passing through the vaginal opening

crown jewels *pl n* the jewellery, including the regalia, used by a sovereign on a state occasion

Crown Office *n* (in England) an office of the Queen's Bench Division of the High Court that is responsible for administration and where actions are entered for trial

crown prince *n* the male heir to a sovereign throne

crown princess *n* **1** the wife of a crown prince **2** the female heir to a sovereign throne

Crown Prosecution Service *n* (in England and Wales) an independent prosecuting body, established in 1986, that decides whether cases brought by the police should go to the courts: headed by the Director of Public Prosecutions. See **procurator fiscal** Abbreviation: CPS

crown wheel *n* **1** *horology* the wheel next to the winding knob that has one set of teeth at right angles to the other **2** the larger of the two gears in a bevel gear

crow's-foot *n*, *pl* -**feet** (*often plural*) a wrinkle at the outer corner of the eye

crow's-nest *n* a lookout platform high up on a ship's mast

crow step *n* another term for **corbie-step**

Croydon ('krɔɪdˀn) *n* a borough in S Greater London (since 1965): formerly important for its airport (1915–59). Pop: 336 700 (2003 est.). Area: 87 sq km (33 sq miles)

crozier ('krəʊʒə) *n* a variant spelling of **crosier**

CRP *abbreviation* C-reactive protein; a chemical in the blood that can be measured to indicate inflammation in the body and a person's risk of suffering a heart attack

CRT *abbreviation* **1** cathode-ray tube **2** (in Britain) composite rate tax: a system of paying interest to savers by which a rate of tax for a period, such as one financial year, is determined in advance, and interest is paid net of tax which is deducted at source

CRTC *abbreviation for* Canadian Radio-Television and Telecommunications Commission

crucial ('kruːʃəl) *adj* **1** involving a final or supremely important decision or event; decisive; critical **2** *informal* very important **3** *slang* very good [C18: from French, from Latin *crux* CROSS] ▷ '**crucially** *adv*

cruciate ('kruːʃɪɪt, -,eɪt) *adj* **1** shaped or arranged like a cross: *cruciate petals* ▷ *n* **2** *informal* a short for **cruciate ligament b** (*as modifier*): *cruciate problems* [C17: from New Latin *cruciātus*, from Latin *crux* cross]

cruciate ligament *n* *anatomy* either of a pair of ligaments that cross each other in the knee, connecting the tibia and the femur

crucible ('kruːsɪbˀl) *n* **1** a vessel in which substances are heated to high temperatures **2** the hearth at the bottom of a metallurgical furnace in which the metal collects **3** a severe trial or test [C15 *corusible*, from Medieval Latin *crūcibulum* night lamp, crucible, of uncertain origin]

crucifix ('kruːsɪfɪks) *n* a cross or image of a cross with a figure of Christ upon it [C13: from Church Latin *crucifixus* the crucified Christ, from *crucifigere* to CRUCIFY]

crucifixion (,kruːsɪ'fɪkʃən) *n* a method of putting to death by nailing or binding to a cross, normally by the hands and feet, which was widespread in the ancient world

Crucifixion (,kruːsɪ'fɪkʃən) *n* **1** the Crucifixion the crucifying of Christ at Calvary, regarded by Christians as the culminating redemptive act of his ministry **2** a picture or representation of this

cruciform ('kruːsɪ,fɔːm) *adj* shaped like a cross [C17: from Latin *crux* cross + -FORM] ▷ '**cruci,formly** *adv*

crucify ('kruːsɪ,faɪ) *vb* -**fies**, -**fying**, -**fied** (*tr*) **1** to put to death by crucifixion **2** *slang* to defeat, ridicule, etc, totally **3** to treat very cruelly; torment [C13: from Old French *crucifier*, from Late Latin *crucifigere* to crucify, to fasten to a cross, from Latin *crux* cross + *figere* to fasten] ▷ '**cruci,fier** *n*

crud (krʌd) *n* *slang* **1** a sticky substance, esp when dirty and encrusted **2** an undesirable residue from a process, esp one inside a nuclear reactor **3** something or someone that is worthless, disgusting, or contemptible **4 the crud** a disease; rot [C14: earlier form of CURD]

crude (kruːd) *adj* **1** lacking taste, tact, or refinement; vulgar: *a crude joke* **2** in a natural or unrefined state **3** lacking care, knowledge, or skill: *a crude sketch* **4** (*prenominal*) stark; blunt ▷ *n* **5** short for **crude oil** [C14: from Latin *crūdus* bloody, raw; related to Latin *cruor* blood] ▷ '**crudely** *adv* ▷ '**crudity** *or* '**crudeness** *n*

Cruden ('kruːdˀn) *n* **Alexander.** 1701–70, Scottish

bookseller and compiler of a well-known biblical concordance (1737)

crude oil n petroleum before it has been refined

crudités (ˌkruːdɪˈteɪ) pl n a selection of raw vegetables, usually cut into strips or small chunks and served, with a dip, as an hors d'oeuvre [c20: from French, plural of *crudité*, literally: rawness]

cruel (ˈkruːəl) adj 1 causing or inflicting pain without pity 2 causing pain or suffering [c13: from Old French, from Latin *crūdēlis*, from *crūdus* raw, bloody] > ˈcruelly adv > ˈcruelness n

cruelty (ˈkruːəltɪ) n, pl -ties 1 deliberate infliction of pain or suffering 2 the quality or characteristic of being cruel 3 law conduct that causes danger to life or limb or a threat to bodily or mental health, on proof of which a decree of divorce may be granted

cruelty-free adj (of a cosmetic or other product) developed without being tested on animals

cruet (ˈkruːɪt) n 1 a small container for holding pepper, salt, vinegar, oil, etc, at table 2 a set of such containers, esp on a stand [c13: from Anglo-French, diminutive of Old French *crue* flask, of Germanic origin; compare Old Saxon *krūka*, Old English *crūce* pot]

Cruft (krʌft) n Charles. 1852–1938, British dog breeder, who organized the first (1886) of the annual dog shows known as Cruft's

Cruikshank (ˈkrʊkʃæŋk) n George. 1792–1878, English illustrator and caricaturist

cruise (kruːz) vb 1 (intr) to make a trip by sea in a liner for pleasure, usually calling at a number of ports 2 to sail or travel over (a body of water) for pleasure in a yacht, cruiser, etc 3 (intr) to search for enemy vessels in a warship 4 (intr) (of a vehicle, aircraft, or vessel) to travel at a moderate and efficient speed ▷ n 5 an act or instance of cruising, esp a trip by sea [c17: from Dutch *kruisen* to cross, from *cruis* CROSS; related to French *croiser* to cross, cruise, Spanish *cruzar*, German *kreuzen*]

Cruise (kruːz) n Tom. original name *Thomas Cruise Mapother*. born 1962, US film actor; his films include *Risky Business* (1983), *Top Gun* (1986), *Jerry Maguire* (1989), *Eyes Wide Shut* (1999) and *War of the Worlds* (2005)

cruise control n a system in a road vehicle that automatically maintains a selected speed until cancelled

cruise missile n an air-breathing low-flying subsonic missile that is continuously powered and guided throughout its flight and carries a warhead

cruiser (ˈkruːzə) n 1 a high-speed, long-range warship of medium displacement, armed with medium calibre weapons or missiles 2 Also called: cabin cruiser a pleasure boat, esp one that is power-driven and has a cabin 3 any person or thing that cruises

cruiserweight (ˈkruːzəˌweɪt) n boxing another term (esp Brit) for **light heavyweight**

crumb (krʌm) n 1 a small fragment of bread, cake, or other baked foods 2 a small piece or bit 3 the soft inner part of bread 4 slang a contemptible person ▷ vb 5 (tr) to prepare or cover (food) with breadcrumbs 6 to break into small fragments [Old English *cruma*; related to Middle Dutch *krome*, Middle High German *krume*, Latin *grūmus* heap of earth]

crumble (ˈkrʌmbəl) vb 1 to break or be broken into crumbs or fragments 2 (intr) to fall apart or away ▷ n 3 Brit a baked pudding consisting of a crumbly mixture of flour, fat, and sugar over stewed fruit: *apple crumble* [c16: variant of *crimble*, of Germanic origin; compare Low German *krömeln*, Dutch *kruimelen*]

crumbly (ˈkrʌmblɪ) adj -blier, -bliest 1 easily crumbled or crumbling ▷ n, pl -blies 2 Brit slang an older person > ˈcrumbliness n

crumby (ˈkrʌmɪ) adj crumbier, crumbiest 1 full of or littered with crumbs 2 soft, like the inside of bread 3 a variant spelling of **crummy¹**

crumhorn or **krummhorn** (ˈkrʌmˌhɔːn) n a medieval woodwind instrument of bass pitch, consisting of an almost cylindrical tube curving upwards and blown through a double reed covered by a pierced cap [c17 *cromorne*, *krumhorn*, from German *Krummhorn* curved horn]

crummy (ˈkrʌmɪ) adj -mier, -miest slang 1 of little value;

inferior; contemptible 2 unwell or depressed [c19: variant spelling of CRUMBY]

crumpet (ˈkrʌmpɪt) n chiefly Brit 1 a light soft yeast cake full of small holes on the top side, eaten toasted and buttered 2 slang women collectively [c17: of uncertain origin]

crumple (ˈkrʌmpəl) vb 1 (when intr, often foll by up) to collapse or cause to collapse 2 (when tr, often foll by up) to crush or cause to be crushed so as to form wrinkles or creases ▷ n 3 a loose crease or wrinkle [c16: from obsolete *crump* to bend; related to Old High German *krimpfan* to wrinkle, Old Norse *kreppa* to contract]

crumple zones pl n parts of a motor vehicle, at the front and the rear, that are designed to crumple in a collision, thereby absorbing the impact

crunch (krʌntʃ) vb 1 to bite or chew (crisp foods) with a crushing or crackling sound 2 to make or cause to make a crisp or brittle sound ▷ n 3 the sound or act of crunching 4 the crunch informal the critical moment or situation ▷ adj 5 informal critical; decisive: *crunch time* [c19: changed (through influence of MUNCH) from earlier *craunch*, of imitative origin] > ˈcrunchy adj > ˈcrunchily adv > ˈcrunchiness n

crunk (krʌŋk) n a form of hip-hop music originating in the southern states of the US [c20: from CR(AZY) + (DR)UNK]

crupper (ˈkrʌpə) n 1 a strap from the back of a saddle that passes under the horse's tail to prevent the saddle from slipping forwards 2 the part of the horse's rump behind the saddle [c13: from Old French *crupiere*, from *crupe* CROUP²]

crusade (kruːˈseɪd) n 1 (often capital) any of the military expeditions undertaken in the 11th, 12th, and 13th centuries by the Christian powers of Europe to recapture the Holy Land from the Muslims 2 (formerly) any holy war undertaken on behalf of a religious cause 3 a vigorous and dedicated action or movement in favour of a cause ▷ vb (intr) 4 to campaign vigorously for something 5 to go on a crusade [c16: from earlier *croisade*, from Old French *crois* cross, from Latin *crux*; influenced also by Spanish *cruzada*, from *cruzar* to take up the cross] > cruˈsader n

cruse (kruːz) n a small earthenware container used, esp formerly, for liquids [Old English *crūse*; related to Middle High German *krūse*, Dutch *kroes* jug]

crush (krʌʃ) vb (mainly tr) 1 to press, mash, or squeeze so as to injure, break, crease, etc 2 to break or grind (rock, ore, etc) into small particles 3 to put down or subdue, esp by force 4 to extract (juice, water, etc) by pressing 5 to oppress harshly 6 to hug or clasp tightly 7 to defeat or humiliate utterly, as in argument or by a cruel remark 8 (intr) to crowd; throng 9 (intr) to become injured, broken, or distorted by pressure ▷ n 10 a dense crowd, esp at a social occasion 11 the act of crushing; pressure 12 a drink or pulp prepared by or as if by crushing fruit: *orange crush* 13 informal a an infatuation: *she had a crush on him* b the person with whom one is infatuated [c14: from Old French *croissir*, of Germanic origin; compare Gothic *kriustan* to gnash; see CRUNCH] > ˈcrushable adj > ˈcrusher n

crush barrier n a barrier erected to separate sections of large crowds in order to prevent crushing

crust (krʌst) n 1 a the hard outer part of bread b a piece of bread consisting mainly of this 2 the baked shell of a pie, tart, etc 3 any hard or stiff outer covering or surface: *a crust of ice* 4 the solid outer shell of the earth, with an average thickness of 30–35 km in continental regions and 5 km beneath the oceans, forming the upper part of the lithosphere and lying immediately above the mantle, from which it is separated by the Mohorovičić discontinuity 5 the dry covering of a skin sore or lesion; scab 6 slang impertinence 7 Brit, Austral & NZ slang a living (esp in the phrase **earn a crust**) ▷ vb 8 to cover with or acquire a crust 9 to form or be formed into a crust [c14: from Latin *crūsta* hard surface, rind, shell]

crustacean (krʌˈsteɪʃən) n 1 any arthropod of the mainly aquatic class *Crustacea*, typically having a carapace hardened with lime and including the lobsters, crabs, shrimps, woodlice, barnacles, copepods, and water fleas ▷ adj 2 Also: crustacean of, relating to, or belonging to the Crustacea [c19: from New Latin crūstāceus hard-shelled, from Latin crūsta shell, CRUST]

crustal ('krʌstəl) adj of or relating to the earth's crust

crusty ('krʌstɪ) adj crustier, crustiest 1 having or characterized by a crust, esp having a thick crust 2 having a rude or harsh character or exterior; surly; curt ▷ 'crustily adv ▷ 'crustiness n

crutch (krʌtʃ) n 1 a long staff of wood or metal having a rest for the armpit, for supporting the weight of the body 2 something that supports or sustains 3 Brit another word for **crutch** (sense 1) ▷ vb 4 (tr) to support or sustain (a person or thing) as with a crutch 5 Austral & NZ slang to clip (wool) from the hindquarters of a sheep [Old English crycc; related to Old High German krucka, Old Norse krykkja; see CROSIER, CROOK]

crutchings ('krʌtʃɪŋz) pl n Austral & NZ the wool clipped from a sheep's hindquarters

crux (krʌks) n, pl cruxes or cruces ('kru:si:z) 1 a vital or decisive stage, point, etc (often in the phrase **the crux of the matter**) 2 a baffling problem or difficulty [c18: from Latin: cross]

Cruyff (krɔɪf; Dutch krœjf) n Johan (joː'han). born 1947, Dutch footballer: one of the world's leading strikers; played for Ajax of Amsterdam (1965–73) and Barcelona (1973–78); captained the Dutch team in the 1974 World Cup

cruzado (kru:'zeɪdəʊ; Portuguese kru'za:du) n, pl -does or -dos (-dəʊz; Portuguese -duʃ) a former standard monetary unit of Brazil, replaced by the cruzeiro [c16: literally marked with a cross, from cruzar to bear a cross; see CRUSADE]

cruzeiro (kru:'zɛərəʊ; Portuguese kru'zeiru) n, pl -ros (-rəʊz; Portuguese -ruʃ) a former monetary unit of Brazil, replaced by the cruzeiro real [Portuguese: from cruz CROSS]

cry (kraɪ) vb cries, crying, cried 1 (intr) to utter inarticulate sounds, esp when weeping; sob 2 (intr) to shed tears; weep 3 (intr; usually foll by out) to scream or shout in pain, terror, etc 4 (tr; often foll by out) to utter or shout (words of appeal, exclamation, fear, etc) 5 (intr; often foll by out) (of animals, birds, etc) to utter loud characteristic sounds 6 (tr) to hawk or sell by public announcement: to cry newspapers 7 to announce (something) publicly or in the streets 8 (intr; foll by for) to clamour or beg 9 cry for the moon to desire the unattainable 10 cry one's eyes out or cry one's heart out to weep bitterly ▷ n, pl cries 11 the act or sound of crying; a shout, exclamation, scream, or wail 12 the characteristic utterance of an animal or bird 13 a fit of weeping 14 hunting the baying of a pack of hounds hunting their quarry by scent 15 a far cry a a long way b something very different 16 in full cry (esp of a pack of hounds) in hot pursuit of a quarry ▷ See also **cry down, cry off, etc** [c13: from Old French crier, from Latin quirītāre to call for help]

crybaby ('kraɪˌbeɪbɪ) n, pl -bies a person, esp a child, given to frequent crying or complaint

cry down vb (tr, adverb) to belittle; disparage

crying ('kraɪɪŋ) adj (prenominal) notorious; lamentable (esp in the phrase **crying shame**)

cryo- combining form indicating low temperature; frost, cold, or freezing: cryogenics; cryosurgery [from Greek kruos icy cold, frost]

cryobiology (ˌkraɪəʊbaɪˈɒlədʒɪ) n the branch of biology concerned with the study of the effects of very low temperatures on organisms ▷ ˌcryobiˈologist n

cry off vb (intr) informal to withdraw from or cancel (an agreement or arrangement)

cryogen ('kraɪədʒən) n a substance used to produce low temperatures; a freezing mixture

cryogenics (ˌkraɪəˈdʒɛnɪks) n (functioning as singular) the branch of physics concerned with the study of very low temperatures and the phenomena occurring at these temperatures ▷ ˌcryoˈgenic adj

cryolite ('kraɪəˌlaɪt) n a white or colourless mineral consisting of a fluoride of sodium and aluminium in monoclinic crystalline form: used in the production of

aluminium, glass, and enamel. Formula: Na_3AlF_6

cryonics (kraɪ'ɒnɪks) n (functioning as singular) the practice of freezing a human corpse in the hope of restoring it to life in the future

cryoprecipitate (ˌkraɪəʊprɪ'sɪpɪteɪt) n a precipitate obtained by controlled thawing of a previously frozen substance. Factor VIII, for treating haemophilia, is often obtained as a cryoprecipitate from frozen blood

cryostat ('kraɪəˌstæt) n an apparatus for maintaining a constant low temperature or a vessel in which a substance is stored at a low temperature

cryosurgery (ˌkraɪəʊ'sɜːdʒərɪ) n surgery involving the local destruction of tissues by quick freezing for therapeutic benefit

cry out vb (intr, adverb) 1 to scream or shout aloud, esp in pain, terror, etc 2 (often foll by for) informal to demand in an obvious manner

crypt (krɪpt) n a cellar, vault, or underground chamber, esp beneath a church, where it is often used as a chapel, burial place, etc [c18: from Latin crypta, from Greek kruptē vault, secret place, from kruptos hidden, from kruptein to hide]

cryptanalysis (ˌkrɪptə'nælɪsɪs) n the study of codes and ciphers; cryptography [CRYPTOGRAPH + ANALYSIS] ▷ cryptanalytic (ˌkrɪptænə'lɪtɪk) adj ▷ crypt'analyst n

cryptic ('krɪptɪk) adj 1 hidden; secret; occult 2 (esp of comments, sayings, etc) obscure in meaning 3 (of the coloration of animals) tending to conceal by disguising or camouflaging the shape [c17: from Late Latin crypticus, from Greek kruptikos, from kruptos concealed; see CRYPT] ▷ 'cryptically adv

crypto- or before a vowel **crypt-** combining form secret, hidden, or concealed [New Latin, from Greek kruptos hidden, from kruptein to hide]

cryptocrystalline (ˌkrɪptəʊ'krɪstəlaɪn) adj (of rocks) composed of crystals that can be distinguished individually only by the use of a polarizing microscope

cryptogam ('krɪptəʊˌgæm) n (in former plant classification schemes) any organism that does not produce seeds, including algae, fungi, mosses, and ferns [c19: from New Latin Cryptogamia, from CRYPTO- + Greek gamos marriage] ▷ ˌcrypto'gamic or cryptogamous (krɪp'tɒgəməs) adj

cryptograph ('krɪptəʊˌgræf, -ˌgrɑːf) n 1 something written in code or cipher 2 a code using secret symbols (**cryptograms**)

cryptography (krɪp'tɒgrəfɪ) n the science or study of analysing and deciphering codes, ciphers, etc; cryptanalysis ▷ cryp'tographer, cryp'tographist or cryp'tologist n ▷ cryptographic (ˌkrɪptə'græfɪk) or ˌcrypto'graphical adj ▷ ˌcrypto'graphically adv

crystal ('krɪstəl) n 1 a piece of solid substance, such as quartz, with a regular shape in which plane faces intersect at definite angles, due to the regular internal structure of its atoms, ions, or molecules 2 a single grain of a crystalline substance 3 anything resembling a crystal, such as a piece of cut glass 4 a a highly transparent and brilliant type of glass, often used in cut-glass tableware, ornaments, etc b (as modifier): a crystal chandelier 5 something made of or resembling crystal 6 crystal glass articles collectively 7 electronics a a crystalline element used in certain electronic devices as a detector, oscillator, transducer, etc b (as modifier): crystal pick-up; crystal detector 8 a transparent cover for the face of a watch, usually of glass or plastic 9 (modifier) of or relating to a crystal or the regular atomic arrangement of crystals: crystal structure; crystal lattice ▷ adj 10 resembling crystal; transparent: crystal water [Old English cristalla, from Latin crystallum, from Greek krustallos ice, crystal, from krustainein to freeze]

crystal ball n the glass globe used in crystal gazing

crystal class n crystallog any of 32 possible types of crystals, classified according to their rotational symmetry about axes through a point. Also called: point group

crystal detector n electronics a demodulator, used esp in microwave circuits and in early radio receivers, consisting of a thin metal wire in point contact with a semiconductor crystal

crystal gazing n 1 the act of staring into a crystal globe (crystal ball) supposedly in order to arouse visual perceptions of the future, etc 2 the act of trying to predict something > **crystal gazer**n

crystal healing n (in alternative therapy) the use of the supposed power of crystals to affect the human energy field

crystal lattice n the regular array of points about which the atoms, ions, or molecules composing a crystal are centred

crystalline ('krɪstəˌlaɪn) adj 1 having the characteristics or structure of crystals 2 consisting of or containing crystals 3 made of or like crystal; transparent; clear

crystalline lens n a biconvex transparent elastic structure in the eye situated behind the iris, serving to focus images on the retina

crystallize, crystalize, crystallise or **crystalise** ('krɪstəˌlaɪz) vb 1 to form or cause to form crystals; assume or cause to assume a crystalline form or structure 2 to coat or become coated with sugar 3 to give a definite form or expression to (an idea, argument, etc) or (of an idea, argument, etc) to assume a recognizable or definite form > **'crystal,lizable, 'crystal,izable, 'crystal,lisable** or **'crystal,isable**adj > **,crystalli'zation, ,crystali'zation, ,crystalli'sation** or **,crystali'sation**n

crystallo- or before a vowel **crystall-** combining form crystal: crystallography

crystallography (ˌkrɪstə'lɒɡrəfɪ) n the science concerned with the formation, properties, and structure of crystals > **,crystal'lographer**n > **crystallographic** (ˌkrɪstələʊ'ɡræfɪk) adj

crystalloid ('krɪstəˌlɔɪd) adj 1 resembling or having the appearance or properties of a crystal or crystalloid ▷ n 2 a substance that in solution can pass through a semipermeable membrane

crystal meth (mɛθ) n informal crystal methamphetamine, a concentrated and highly potent form of methamphetamine with dangerous side effects. Also called: **ice**

Crystal Palace n a building of glass and iron designed by Joseph Paxton to house the Great Exhibition of 1851. Erected in Hyde Park, London, it was moved to Sydenham (1852–53): destroyed by fire in 1936

crystal set n an early form of radio receiver having a crystal detector to demodulate the radio signals but no amplifier, therefore requiring earphones

cry up vb (tr, adverb) to praise highly; extol

Cs the chemical symbol for caesium

CS abbreviation 1 Also called: **cs** capital stock 2 chartered surveyor 3 Christian Science 4 Civil Service 5 Also called: **cs** Court of Session

CSA abbreviation (in Britain) Child Support Agency

csc abbreviation cosecant

CSC abbreviation Civil Service Commission

CSE abbreviation (in Britain, formerly) Certificate of Secondary Education

CSF abbreviation 1 physiol cerebrospinal fluid 2 immunol colony-stimulating factor

CS gas n a gas causing tears, salivation, and painful breathing, used in civil disturbances; ortho-chlorobenzal malononitrile. Formula: $C_6H_4ClCH:C(CN)_2$ [c20: from the surname initials of its US inventors, Ben Carson and Roger Staughton]

CSIRO abbreviation (in Australia) Commonwealth Scientific and Industrial Research Organization

CSM abbreviation (in Britain) company sergeant-major

CSO abbreviation (in Britain) community support officer

C-spanner n a sickle-shaped spanner having a projection at the end of the curve, used for turning large narrow nuts that have an indentation into which the projection on the spanner fits

CSS abbreviation computing cascading style sheet

CST abbreviation Central Standard Time

ct abbreviation 1 carat 2 cent 3 court

CTC abbreviation (in Britain) city technology college

ctenophore ('tɛnəˌfɔ:, 'ti:nə-) n any marine invertebrate of the phylum Ctenophora, including the sea gooseberry

and Venus's-girdle, whose body bears eight rows of fused cilia, for locomotion [c19: from New Latin ctenophorus, from Greek kteno-, kteis comb + -PHORE]

ctn abbreviation cotangent

CT scanner n computerized tomography scanner: an X-ray machine that can produce stereographic images. Former name: CAT scanner

CTU abbreviation (in New Zealand) Conference of Trade Unions

CTV abbreviation Canadian Television Network Limited

Cu the chemical symbol for copper [from Late Latin cuprum]

CU text messaging abbreviation see you

cu. abbreviation cubic

cub (kʌb) n 1 the young of certain animals, such as the lion, bear, etc 2 a young or inexperienced person ▷ vb cubs, cubbing, cubbed 3 to give birth to (cubs) [c16: perhaps from Old Norse kubbi young seal; see COB¹] > **'cubbish**adj

Cub (kʌb) n short for Cub Scout

Cuba ('kju:bə) n a republic and the largest island in the Caribbean, at the entrance to the Gulf of Mexico: became a Spanish colony after its discovery by Columbus in 1492; gained independence after the Spanish-American War of 1898 but remained subject to US influence until declared a people's republic under Castro in 1960; subject of an international crisis in 1962, when the US blockaded the island in order to compel the Soviet Union to dismantle its nuclear missile base. Sugar comprises about 80 per cent of total exports; the economy was badly affected by loss of trade following the collapse of the Soviet Union and by the continuing US trade embargo. Language: Spanish. Religion: nonreligious majority. Currency: peso. Capital: Havana. Pop: 11 328 000 (2004 est). Area: 110 922 sq km (42 827 sq miles)

Cuban ('kju:bən) adj 1 of or relating to Cuba or its inhabitants ▷ n 2 a native or inhabitant of Cuba

cubby ('kʌbɪ) n, pl -bies Austral a small room or enclosed area, esp one used as a child's play area

cubbyhole ('kʌbɪˌhəʊl) n a small enclosed space or room [c19: from dialect cub cattle pen; see COVE¹]

cube (kju:b) n 1 a solid having six plane square faces in which the angle between two adjacent sides is a right angle 2 the product of three equal factors: the cube of 2 is 2 × 2 × 2 (usually written 2³) 3 something in the form of a cube ▷ vb 4 to raise (a number or quantity) to the third power 5 (tr) to make, shape, or cut (something, esp food) into cubes [c16: from Latin cubus die, cube, from Greek kubos] > **'cuber**n

cubeb ('kju:bɛb) n 1 a SE Asian treelike piperaceous woody climbing plant, Piper cubeba, with brownish berries 2 the unripe spicy fruit of this plant, dried and used as a stimulant and diuretic and sometimes smoked in cigarettes [c14: from Old French cubebe, from Medieval Latin cubēba, from Arabic kubābah]

cube root n the number or quantity whose cube is a given number or quantity: 2 is the cube root of 8 (usually written $\sqrt[3]{8}$ or $8^{\frac{1}{3}}$)

cube van n Canadian a van with a cube-shaped storage compartment that is wider and taller than the front of the vehicle

cubic ('kju:bɪk) adj 1 having the shape of a cube 2 a having three dimensions b denoting or relating to a linear measure that is raised to the third power: a cubic metre 3 maths of, relating to, or containing a variable to the third power or a term in which the sum of the exponents of the variables is three

cubicle ('kju:bɪkºl) n a partially or totally enclosed section of a room, as in a dormitory [c15: from Latin cubiculum, from cubāre to lie down, lie asleep]

cubic measure n a system of units for the measurement of volumes, based on the cubic inch, the cubic centimetre, etc

cubiform ('kju:bɪˌfɔ:m) adj having the shape of a cube

cubism ('kju:bɪzəm) n (often capital) a French school of painting, collage, relief, and sculpture initiated in 1907 by Pablo Picasso, the Spanish painter and sculptor (1881–1973) and Georges Braque, the French painter (1882–1963), which amalgamated viewpoints of natural

forms into a multifaceted surface of geometrical planes
> 'cubist *adj*, *n* > cu'bistic *adj*

cubit ('kju:bɪt) *n* an ancient measure of length based on the length of the forearm [c14: from Latin *cubitum* elbow, cubit]

cuboid ('kju:bɔɪd) *adj* Also: **cuboidal** (kju:'bɔɪdᵊl) 1 shaped like a cube; cubic 2 of or denoting the cuboid bone ▷ *n* 3 the cubelike bone of the foot; the outer distal bone of the tarsus 4 *maths* a geometric solid whose six faces are rectangles; rectangular parallelepiped

Cub Scout *or* **Cub** *n* a member of a junior branch (for those aged 8–11 years) of the Scout Association

Cuchulain, Cuchulainn *or* **Cuchullain** (ku:'kʌlɪn, kʊ'xʊlɪn) *n Celtic myth* a legendary hero of Ulster

cucking stool ('kʌkɪŋ) *n history* a stool to which suspected witches, scolds, etc, were tied and pelted or ducked into water as a punishment [c13 *cucking stol*, literally: defecating chair, from *cukken* to defecate; compare Old Norse *kúkr* excrement]

cuckold ('kʌkəld) *n* 1 a man whose wife has committed adultery, often regarded as an object of scorn ▷ *vb* 2 (*tr*) to make a cuckold of [c13 *cukeweld*, from Old French *cucuault*, from *cucu* cuckoo; perhaps an allusion to the parasitic cuckoos that lay their eggs in the nests of other birds] > 'cuckoldry *n*

cuckoo ('kʊku:) *n*, *pl* -oos 1 any bird of the family *Cuculidae*, having pointed wings, a long tail, and zygodactyl feet: order *Cuculiformes*. Many species, including the **European cuckoo** (*Cuculus canorus*), lay their eggs in the nests of other birds and have a two-note call 2 *informal* an insane or foolish person ▷ *adj* 3 *informal* insane or foolish ▷ *interj* 4 an imitation or representation of the call of a cuckoo ▷ *vb* -oos, -ooing, -ooed 5 (*intr*) to make the sound imitated by the word *cuckoo* [c13: from Old French *cucu*, of imitative origin; related to German *kuckuck*, Latin *cuculus*, Greek *kokkux*]

cuckoo clock *n* a clock in which a mechanical cuckoo pops out with a sound like a cuckoo's call when the clock strikes

cuckoopint ('kʊku:ˌpaɪnt) *n* a European aroid plant, *Arum maculatum*, with arrow-shaped leaves, a spathe marked with purple, a pale purple spadix, and scarlet berries. Also called: **lords-and-ladies**

cuckoo spit *n* a white frothy mass on the stems and leaves of many plants, produced by froghopper larvae (**cuckoo spit insects**) which feed on the plant juices

cucumber ('kju:ˌkʌmbə) *n* 1 a creeping cucurbitaceous plant, *Cucumis sativus*, cultivated in many forms for its edible fruit 2 the cylindrical fruit of this plant, which has hard thin green rind and white crisp flesh [c14: from Latin *cucumis*, of unknown origin]

cucurbit (kju:'kɜːbɪt) *n* any creeping flowering plant of the mainly tropical and subtropical family *Cucurbitaceae*, which includes the pumpkin, cucumber, squashes, and gourds [c14: from Old French, from Latin *cucurbita* gourd, cup] > cu‚curbi'taceous *adj*

cud (kʌd) *n* 1 partially digested food regurgitated from the first stomach of cattle and other ruminants to the mouth for a second chewing 2 **chew the cud** to reflect or think over something [Old English *cudu*, from *cwidu* what has been chewed; related to Old Norse *kvātha* resin (for chewing), Old High German *quiti* glue, Sanskrit *jatu* rubber]

cuddle ('kʌdᵊl) *vb* 1 to hold (another person or thing) close or (of two people, etc) to hold each other close, as for affection, comfort, or warmth; embrace; hug 2 (*intr*; foll by *up*) to curl or snuggle up into a comfortable or warm position ▷ *n* 3 a close embrace, esp when prolonged [c18: of uncertain origin] > 'cuddlesome *adj* > 'cuddly *adj*

cuddy ('kʌdɪ) *n*, *pl* -dies a small cabin in a boat [c17: perhaps from Dutch *kajute*; compare Old French *cahute*]

cudgel ('kʌdʒᵊl) *n* 1 a short stout stick used as a weapon 2 **take up the cudgels** (often foll by *for* or *on behalf of*) to join in a dispute, esp to defend oneself or another ▷ *vb* -els, -elling, -elled *or US* -els, -eling, -eled 3 (*tr*) to strike with a cudgel or similar weapon 4 **cudgel one's brains** to think hard about a problem [Old English *cycgel*; related to Middle Dutch *koghele* stick with knob]

cudgerie ('kʌdʒərɪ) *n Austral* a large tropical rutaceous tree, *Flindersia schottina*, having light-coloured wood [from Abor.]

Cudlipp ('kʌdlɪp) *n* **Hugh, Baron**. 1913–98, British newspaper editor, a pioneer of tabloid journalism: editorial director of the *Daily Mirror* (1952–63)

cudweed ('kʌdˌwiːd) *n* any of various temperate woolly plants of the genus *Gnaphalium*, having clusters of whitish or yellow button-like flowers: family *Asteraceae* (composites)

Cudworth ('kʌdwəθ) *n* **Ralph**. 1617–88, English philosopher and theologian. His works include *True Intellectual System of the Universe* (1678) and *A Treatise concerning Eternal and Immutable Morality* (1731)

cue¹ (kju:) *n* 1 a (in the theatre, films, music, etc) anything spoken or done that serves as a signal to an actor, musician, etc, to follow with specific lines or action b **on cue** at the right moment 2 a signal or reminder to do something ▷ *vb* cues, cueing, cued 3 (*tr*) to give a cue or cues to (an actor) 4 (usually foll by *in* or *into*) to signal (to something or somebody) at a specific moment in a musical or dramatic performance [c16: probably from name of the letter *q*, used in an actor's script to represent Latin *quando* when]

cue² (kju:) *n* 1 *billiards, snooker* a long tapered shaft with a leather tip, used to drive the balls 2 hair caught at the back forming a tail or braid ▷ *vb* cues, cueing, cued 3 to drive (a ball) with a cue [c18: variant of QUEUE]

cue ball *n billiards, snooker* the ball struck by the cue, as distinguished from the object balls

Cuernavaca (*Spanish* kwɛrnaˈβaka) *n* a city in S central Mexico, capital of Morelos state: resort with nearby Cacahuamilpa Caverns. Pop: 723 000 (2005 est)

cuesta ('kwɛstə) *n* a long low ridge with a steep scarp slope and a gentle back slope, formed by the differential erosion of strata of differing hardness [Spanish: shoulder, from Latin *costa* side, rib]

cuff¹ (kʌf) *n* 1 the part of a sleeve nearest the hand, sometimes turned back and decorative 2 the part of a gauntlet or glove that extends past the wrist 3 *US, Canadian & Austral* the turned-up fold at the bottom of some trouser legs 4 **off the cuff** *informal* improvised; extemporary [c14 *cuffe* glove, of obscure origin]

cuff² (kʌf) *vb* 1 (*tr*) to strike with an open hand ▷ *n* 2 a blow of this kind [c16: of obscure origin]

cuff link *n* one of a pair of linked buttons, used to join the buttonholes on the cuffs of a shirt

Cuiabá *or* **Cuyabá** (*Portuguese* kuiaˈba) *n* 1 a port in W Brazil, capital of Mato Grosso state, on the Cuiabá River. Pop: 777 000 (2005 est) 2 a river in SW Brazil, rising on the Mato Grosso plateau and flowing southwest into the São Lourenço River. Length: 483 km (300 miles)

cui bono *Latin* (kwi: ˈbəʊnəʊ) for whose benefit? for what purpose?

cuirass (kwɪˈræs) *n* 1 a piece of armour, of leather or metal covering the chest and back ▷ *vb* 2 (*tr*) to equip with a cuirass [c15: from French *cuirasse*, from Late Latin *coriacea*, from *coriaceus* made of leather, from Latin *corium* leather]

cuirassier (ˌkwɪərəˈsɪə) *n* a mounted soldier, esp of the 16th century, who wore a cuirass

Cuisenaire rod (ˌkwiːzəˈneə) *n trademark* one of a set of rods of various colours and lengths representing different numbers, used to teach arithmetic to young children [c20: named after Emil-Georges *Cuisenaire* (?1891–1976), Belgian educationalist]

cuisine (kwɪˈziːn) *n* 1 a style or manner of cooking: *French cuisine* 2 the food prepared by a restaurant, household, etc [c18: from French, literally: kitchen, from Late Latin *coquīna*, from Latin *coquere* to cook]

cuisse (kwɪs) *or* **cuish** (kwɪʃ) *n* a piece of armour for the thigh [c15: back formation from *cuisses* (plural), from Old French *cuisseaux* thigh guards, from *cuisse* thigh, from Latin *coxa* hipbone]

Culbertson ('kʌlbətsᵊn) *n* **Ely** ('iːlaɪ). 1891–1955, US authority on contract bridge

cul-de-sac ('kʌldəˌsæk, 'kʊl-) *n*, *pl* **culs-de-sac** *or* **cul-de-sacs** 1 a road with one end blocked off; dead end 2 an inescapable position [c18: from French, literally: bottom of the bag]

-cule *suffix forming nouns* indicating smallness [from Latin *-culus*, diminutive suffix; compare -CLE]

Culebra Cut (kuː'lebrə) *n* the former name of: **Gaillard Cut**

culet ('kjuːlɪt) *n* **1** *jewellery* the flat face at the bottom of a gem **2** either of the plates of armour worn at the small of the back [c17: from obsolete French, diminutive of *cul*, from Latin *cūlus* bottom]

culex ('kjuːleks) *n, pl* **-lices** (-lɪ,siːz) any mosquito of the genus *Culex*, such as *C. pipiens*, the common mosquito [c15: from Latin: midge, gnat; related to Old Irish *cuil* gnat]

Culham ('kʌləm) *n* a village in S central England, in Oxfordshire: site of the UK centre for thermonuclear reactor research and of the Joint European Torus (JET) programme

Culiacán (*Spanish* kulja'kan) *n* a city in NW Mexico, capital of Sinaloa state. Pop: 799 000 (2005 est)

culinary ('kʌlɪnərɪ) *adj* of, relating to, or used in the kitchen or in cookery [c17: from Latin *culīna* kitchen]
> 'culinarily *adv*

cull (kʌl) *vb* (*tr*) **1** to choose or gather the best or required examples **2** to take out (an animal, esp an inferior one) from a herd **3** to reduce the size of (a herd or flock) by killing a proportion of its members **4** to gather (flowers, fruit, etc) ▷ *n* **5** the act or product of culling **6** an inferior animal taken from a herd or group [c15: from Old French *coillir* to pick, from Latin *colligere*; see COLLECT[1]]

Cullen ('kʌlən) *n* **William Douglas**, Baron. born 1935, Scottish judge who conducted public inquiries into the Piper Alpha disaster (1990), the Dunblane school shootings (1996), and the Ladbroke Grove rail disaster (1999)

Culloden (kə'lɒdᵊn) *n* a moor near Inverness in N Scotland: site of a battle in 1746 in which government troops under the Duke of Cumberland defeated the Jacobites under Prince Charles Edward Stuart

culm[1] (kʌlm) *n* *mining* **1** coal-mine waste **2** inferior anthracite [c14: probably related to COAL]

culm[2] (kʌlm) *n* the hollow jointed stem of a grass or sedge [c17: from Latin *culmus* stalk; see HAULM]

culminate ('kʌlmɪ,neɪt) *vb* **1** (when *intr*, usually foll by *in*) to end or cause to end, esp to reach or bring to a final or climactic stage **2** (*intr*) (of a celestial body) to cross the meridian of the observer [c17: from Late Latin *culmināre* to reach the highest point, from Latin *culmen* top]
> 'culminant *adj*

culmination (,kʌlmɪ'neɪʃən) *n* **1** the final, highest, or decisive point **2** the act of culminating **3** *astronomy* the highest or lowest altitude attained by a heavenly body as it crosses the meridian

culottes (kjuː'lɒts) *pl n* women's flared trousers cut to look like a skirt [c20: from French, literally: breeches, from *cul* bottom; see CULET]

culpable ('kʌlpəbᵊl) *adj* deserving censure; blameworthy [c14: from Old French *coupable*, from Latin *culpābilis*, from *culpāre* to blame, from *culpa* fault] > ,culpa'bility *or* 'culpableness *n* > 'culpably *adv*

culpable homicide *n* *Scots law* manslaughter

Culpeper ('kʌlpepə) *n* **Nicholas**. 1616–54, English herbalist and astrologer; his unauthorized translation (1649) of the College of Physicians' *Pharmacopoeia* and his *Herbal* (1653) popularized herbalism

culprit ('kʌlprɪt) *n* **1** *law* a person awaiting trial, esp one who has pleaded not guilty **2** the person responsible for a particular offence, misdeed, etc [c17: from Anglo-French *cul-*, short for *culpable* guilty + *prit* ready, indicating that the prosecution was ready to prove the guilt of the one charged]

CUL8R *text messaging abbreviation* see you later

cult (kʌlt) *n* **1** a specific system of religious worship, esp with reference to its rites and deity **2** a sect devoted to such a system **3** a quasi-religious organization using devious psychological techniques to gain and control adherents **4** intense interest in and devotion to a person, idea, or activity **5** the person, idea, etc, arousing such devotion **6** something regarded as fashionable or

significant by a particular group **7** (*modifier*) of, relating to, or characteristic of a cult or cults: *a cult figure* [c17: from Latin *cultus* cultivation, refinement, from *colere* to till] > 'cultism *n* > 'cultist *n*

cultic ('kʌltɪk) *adj* of or relating to a religious cult

cultish ('kʌltɪʃ) *or* **culty** ('kʌltɪ) *adj* intended to appeal to a small group of fashionable people

cultivable ('kʌltɪvəbᵊl) *or* **cultivatable** ('kʌltɪ,veɪtəbᵊl) *adj* (of land) capable of being cultivated [c17: from French, from Old French *cultiver* to CULTIVATE]
> ,cultiva'bility *n*

cultivar ('kʌltɪ,vɑː) *n* a variety of a plant that was produced from a natural species and is maintained by cultivation [c20: from CULTI(VATED) + VAR(IETY)]

cultivate ('kʌltɪ,veɪt) *vb* (*tr*) **1** to till and prepare (land or soil) for the growth of crops **2** to plant, tend, harvest, or improve (plants) by labour and skill **3** to break up (land or soil) with a cultivator or hoe **4** to improve or foster (the mind, body, etc) as by study, education, or labour **5** to give special attention to: *to cultivate a friendship; to cultivate a hobby* [c17: from Medieval Latin *cultivāre* to till, from Old French *cultiver*, from Medieval Latin *cultīvus* cultivable, from Latin *cultus* cultivated, from *colere* to till, toil over]

cultivated ('kʌltɪ,veɪtɪd) *adj* **1** cultured, refined, or educated **2** (of land or soil) **a** subjected to tillage or cultivation **b** tilled and broken up **3** (of plants) specially bred or improved by cultivation

cultivation (,kʌltɪ'veɪʃən) *n* **1** *agriculture* **a** the planting, tending, improving, or harvesting of crops or plants **b** the preparation of ground to promote their growth **2** development, esp through education, training, etc **3** culture or sophistication, esp social refinement

cultivator ('kʌltɪ,veɪtə) *n* **1** a farm implement equipped with shovels, blades, etc, used to break up soil and remove weeds **2** a person or thing that cultivates

cultural ('kʌltʃərəl) *adj* **1** of or relating to artistic or social pursuits or events considered to be valuable or enlightened **2** of or relating to a culture or civilization **3** (of certain varieties of plant) obtained by specialized breeding

cultural cringe *n* the perception that one's own culture is inferior to that of another group or country

culture ('kʌltʃə) *n* **1** the total of the inherited ideas, beliefs, values, and knowledge, which constitute the shared bases of social action **2** the total range of activities and ideas of a group of people with shared traditions, which are transmitted and reinforced by members of the group **3** a particular civilization at a particular period **4** the artistic and social pursuits, expression, and tastes valued by a society or class, as in the arts, manners, dress, etc **5** the enlightenment or refinement resulting from these pursuits **6** the attitudes, feelings, values, and behaviour that characterize and inform society as a whole or any social group within it **7** the cultivation of plants, esp by scientific methods designed to improve stock or to produce new ones **8** *stockbreeding* the rearing and breeding of animals, esp with a view to improving the strain **9** the act or practice of tilling or cultivating the soil **10** *biology* **a** the experimental growth of microorganisms, such as bacteria and fungi, in a nutrient substance (culture medium), usually under controlled conditions **b** a group of microorganisms grown in this way ▷ *vb* (*tr*) **11** to cultivate (plants or animals) **12** to grow (microorganisms) in a culture medium [c15: from Old French, from Latin *cultūra* a cultivating, from *colere* to till; see CULT] > 'culturist *n*

cultured ('kʌltʃəd) *adj* **1** showing or having good taste, manners, upbringing, and education **2** artificially grown or synthesized: *cultured pearls*

cultured pearl *n* a pearl induced to grow in the shell of an oyster or clam, by the insertion of a small object around which layers of nacre are deposited

culture jamming *n* a form of political and social activism which, by means of fake adverts, hoax news stories, pastiches of company logos and product labels, computer hacking, etc, draws attention to and at the same time subverts the power of the media, governments, and large corporations to control and distort the information that they give to the public in order to promote consumerism, militarism, etc

culture shock *n sociol* the feelings of isolation, rejection, etc, experienced when one culture is brought into sudden contact with another, as when a primitive tribe is confronted by modern civilization

culture vulture *n informal* a person considered to be excessively, and often pretentiously, interested in the arts

cultus ('kʌltəs) *n, pl* **-tuses** or **-ti** (-taɪ) *chiefly RC Church* another word for **cult** (sense 1) [c17: from Latin: a toiling over something, refinement, CULT]

culverin ('kʌlvərɪn) *n* **1** a long-range medium to heavy cannon used during the 15th, 16th, and 17th centuries **2** a medieval musket [c15: from Old French *coulevrine*, from *couleuvre*, from Latin *coluber* serpent]

culvert ('kʌlvət) *n* **1** a drain or covered channel that crosses under a road, railway, etc **2** a channel for an electric cable [c18: of unknown origin]

cum (kʌm) *prep* used between two nouns to designate an object of a combined nature: *a kitchen-cum-dining room* [Latin: with, together with, along with]

Cumae ('kjuːmiː) *n* the oldest Greek colony in Italy, founded about 750 BC near Naples > **Cuˈmaean** *adj*

cumber ('kʌmbə) *vb* (*tr*) **1** to obstruct or hinder **2** *obsolete* to inconvenience [c13: probably from Old French *combrer* to impede, prevent, from *combre* barrier; see ENCUMBER]

Cumberland[1] ('kʌmbələnd) *n* (until 1974) a county of NW England, now part of Cumbria

Cumberland[2] ('kʌmbələnd) *n* **1** Richard. 1631–1718, English theologian and moral philosopher; bishop of Peterborough (1691–1718) **2** William Augustus, Duke of Cumberland, known as *Butcher Cumberland*. 1721–65, English soldier, younger son of George II, noted for his defeat of Prince Charles Edward Stuart at Culloden (1746) and his subsequent ruthless destruction of Jacobite rebels

cumbersome ('kʌmbəsəm) or **cumbrous** ('kʌmbrəs) *adj* **1** awkward because of size, weight, or shape **2** difficult because of extent or complexity: *cumbersome accounts* [c14: *cumber*, short for ENCUMBER + -SOME[1]]

> **ˈcumbersomeness** or **ˈcumbrousness** *n*

Cumbria ('kʌmbrɪə) *n* (since 1974) a county of NW England comprising the former counties of Westmorland and Cumberland together with N Lancashire: includes the Lake District mountain area and surrounding coastal lowlands with the Pennine uplands in the extreme east. Administrative centre: Carlisle. Pop: 489 800 (2003 est). Area: 6810 sq km (2629 sq miles)

Cumbrian ('kʌmbrɪən) *adj* **1** of or relating to Cumbria or its inhabitants ▷ *n* **2** a native or inhabitant of Cumbria

Cumbrian Mountains ('kʌmbrɪən) *pl n* a mountain range in NW England, in Cumbria. Highest peak: Scafell Pike, 977 m (3206 ft)

cumin or **cummin** ('kʌmɪn) *n* **1** an umbelliferous Mediterranean plant, *Cuminum cyminum*, with finely divided leaves and small white or pink flowers **2** the aromatic seeds (collectively) of this plant, used as a condiment and a flavouring [c12: from Old French, from Latin *cumīnum*, from Greek *kuminon*, of Semitic origin; compare Hebrew *kammōn*]

cummerbund or **kummerbund** ('kʌmə,bʌnd) *n* a wide sash, worn with a dinner jacket [c17: from Hindi *kamarband*, from Persian, from *kamar* loins, waist + *band* band]

Cummings ('kʌmɪŋz) *n* Edward Estlin ('estlɪn), (preferred typographical representation of name e. e. cummings). 1894–1962, US poet

cum new *adv, adj* (of shares, etc) with rights to take up any scrip or rights issue. See **ex new**

cumquat ('kʌmkwɒt) *n* a variant spelling of **kumquat**

cumulate *vb* ('kjuːmjʊ,leɪt) **1** to accumulate **2** (*tr*) to combine (two or more sequences) into one ▷ *adj* ('kjuːmjʊlɪt, -,leɪt) **3** heaped up [c16: from Latin *cumulāre* from *cumulus* heap] > **ˈcumuˈlation** *n*

cumulative ('kjuːmjʊlətɪv) *adj* **1** growing in quantity, strength, or effect by successive additions or gradual steps **2** *statistics* **a** (of a frequency) including all values of

a variable either below or above a specified value **b** (of error) tending to increase as the sample size is increased

> **ˈcumulatively** *adv* > **ˈcumulativeness** *n*

cumulonimbus (,kjuːmjʊləʊ'nɪmbəs) *n, pl* **-bi** (-baɪ) or **-buses** *meteorol* a cumulus cloud of great vertical extent, the top often forming an anvil shape and the bottom being dark coloured, indicating rain or hail: associated with thunderstorms

cumulus ('kjuːmjʊləs) *n, pl* **-li** (-,laɪ) a bulbous or billowing white or dark grey cloud associated with rising air currents [c17: from Latin: mass]

> **ˈcumulous** *adj*

Cunard (kjuː'nɑːd) *n* Sir Samuel (1787–1865). Canadian shipping magnate, founder of the Cunard line

Cunaxa (kjuː'næksə) *n* the site near the lower Euphrates where Artaxerxes II defeated Cyrus the Younger in 401 BC

cuneate ('kjuːnɪɪt, -,eɪt) *adj* wedge-shaped: cuneate leaves are attached at the narrow end [c19: from Latin *cuneāre* to make wedge-shaped, from *cuneus* a wedge]

> **ˈcuneately** *adv* > **ˈcuneal** *adj*

cuneiform ('kjuːnɪ,fɔːm) *adj* **1** Also called: **cuneal** wedge-shaped **2** of, relating to, or denoting the wedge-shaped characters employed in the writing of several ancient languages of Mesopotamia and Persia, esp Sumerian, Babylonian, etc **3** of or relating to a tablet in which this script is employed ▷ *n* **4** cuneiform characters or writing [c17: probably from Old French *cunéiforme*, from Latin *cuneus* wedge]

cunjevoi ('kʌndʒɪ,vɔɪ) *n Austral* **1** an aroid plant, *Alocasia macrorrhiza*, of tropical Asia and Australia, cultivated for its edible rhizome **2** a sea squirt [c19: from a native Australian language]

cunnilingus (,kʌnɪ'lɪŋgəs) or **cunnilinctus** (,kʌnɪ'lɪŋktəs) *n* a sexual activity in which the female genitalia are stimulated by the partner's lips and tongue. Compare **fellatio** [c19: from New Latin, from Latin *cunnus* vulva + *lingere* to lick]

cunning ('kʌnɪŋ) *adj* **1** crafty and shrewd, esp in deception; sly **2** made with or showing skill or cleverness; ingenious ▷ *n* **3** craftiness, esp in deceiving; slyness **4** cleverness, skill, or ingenuity [Old English *cunnende*; related to *cunnan* to know (see CAN[1]), *cunnian* to test, experience, Old Norse *kunna* to know] > **ˈcunningly** *adv* > **ˈcunningness** *n*

Cunningham ('kʌnɪŋəm) *n* Merce (mɜːs). born 1919, US dancer and choreographer. His experimental ballets include *Suit for Five* (1956) and *Travelogue* (1977)

Cunninghame Graham ('kʌnɪŋəm 'greɪəm) *n* R(obert) B(ontine). 1852–1936, Scottish traveller, writer, and politician, noted for his essays and short stories: first president (1928) of the Scottish Nationalist Party

Cunobelinus (kjuː,nɒbə'laɪnəs) *n* also called *Cymbeline*. died ?42 AD, British ruler of the Catuvellauni tribe (?10–?42); founder of Colchester (?10)

cunt (kʌnt) *n taboo* **1** the female genitals **2** *offensive, slang* a woman considered sexually **3** *offensive, slang* a mean or obnoxious person [c13: of Germanic origin; related to Old Norse *kunta*, Middle Low German *kunte*]

cup (kʌp) *n* **1** a small open container, usually having one handle, used for drinking from **2** the contents of such a container: *that cup was too sweet* **3** Also called: **teacup, cupful** a unit of capacity used in cooking equal to approximately half a pint, 8 fluid ounces, or about one quarter of a litre **4** something resembling a cup in shape or function, such as the flower base of some plants of the rose family or a cuplike bodily organ **5** either of two cup-shaped parts of a brassiere, designed to support the breasts **6** a cup-shaped trophy awarded as a prize **7** *Brit* **a** a sporting contest in which a cup is awarded to the winner **b** (*as modifier*): *a cup competition* **8** a mixed drink with one ingredient as a base, usually served from a bowl: *claret cup* **9** *golf* the hole or metal container in the hole on a green **10** the chalice or the consecrated wine used in the Eucharist **11** one's lot in life **12** in one's cups drunk **13** one's cup of tea *informal* one's chosen or preferred thing, task, company, etc ▷ *vb* **cups, cupping, cupped** (*tr*) **14** to form (something, such as the hands) into the shape of a cup **15** to put into or as if into a cup **16** *archaic* to draw blood to the surface of the body of (a person) by using a cupping glass [Old English *cuppe*, from Late Latin *cuppa* cup, alteration of Latin *cūpa* cask]

cupbearer ('kʌp,bɛərə) *n* an attendant who fills and serves wine cups, as in a royal household

cupboard ('kʌbəd) *n* a piece of furniture or a recessed area of a room, with a door concealing storage space

cupboard love *n* a show of love inspired only by some selfish or greedy motive

cupcake ('kʌp,keɪk) *n* a small cake baked in a cup-shaped foil or paper case

CUPE ('kju:pɪ) *n acronym for* Canadian Union of Public Employees

cupel ('kju:pəl, kjʊ'pɛl) *n* **1** a refractory pot in which gold or silver is refined **2** a small porous bowl made of bone ash in which gold and silver are recovered from a lead button during assaying ▷ *vb* -pels, -pelling, -pelled *or US* -pels, -peling, -peled **3** (*tr*) to refine (gold or silver) by means of cupellation [c17: from French *coupelle*, diminutive of *coupe* CUP] > ,cupel'lation *n*

Cup Final *n* **1** the Cup Final the annual final of the FA Cup soccer competition, played at Wembley, or the Scottish Cup, played at Hampden Park **2** (*often not capitals*) the final of any cup competition

Cupid ('kju:pɪd) *n* **1** the Roman god of love, represented as a winged boy with a bow and arrow. Greek counterpart: **Eros 2** (*not capital*) any similar figure, esp as represented in Baroque art [c14: from Latin *Cupīdō*, from *cupīdō* desire, from *cupidus* desirous; see CUPIDITY]

cupidity (kju:'pɪdɪtɪ) *n* strong desire, esp for possessions or money; greed [c15: from Latin *cupiditās*, from *cupidus* eagerly desiring, from *cupere* to long for]

cupola ('kju:pələ) *n* **1** a roof or ceiling in the form of a dome **2** a small structure, usually domed, on the top of a roof or dome **3** a protective dome for a gun on a warship **4** a vertical air-blown coke-fired cylindrical furnace in which iron is remelted for casting [c16: from Italian, from Late Latin *cūpula* a small cask, from Latin *cūpa* tub] > cupolated ('kju:pə,leɪtɪd) *adj*

cuppa *or* **cupper** ('kʌpə) *n* Brit informal a cup of tea

cupping ('kʌpɪŋ) *n* med archaic the process of applying a cupping glass to the skin

cupping glass *n* med archaic a glass vessel from which air can be removed by suction or heat to create a partial vacuum; formerly used in drawing blood to the surface of the skin for slow bloodletting. Also called: artificial leech

cupreous ('kju:prɪəs) *adj* **1** of, consisting of, containing, or resembling copper; coppery **2** of the reddish-brown colour of copper [c17: from Late Latin *cupreus*, from *cuprum* COPPER¹]

cupressus (kju:'prɛsəs) *n* any tree of the genus *Cupressus*

cupric ('kju:prɪk) *adj* of or containing copper in the divalent state [c18: from Late Latin *cuprum* copper]

cupriferous (kju:'prɪfərəs) *adj* (of a substance such as an ore) containing or yielding copper

cupro-, cupri- *or before a vowel* **cupr-** combining form indicating copper [from Latin *cuprum*]

cupronickel (,kju:prəʊ'nɪkəl) *n* any ductile corrosion-resistant copper alloy containing up to 40 per cent nickel: used in coins, condenser tubes, turbine blades, etc

cuprous ('kju:prəs) *adj* of or containing copper in the monovalent state

cup tie *n* sport an eliminating match or round between two teams in a cup competition

cupule ('kju:pju:l) *n* biology a cup-shaped part or structure, such as the cup around the base of an acorn [c19: from Late Latin *cūpula*; see CUPOLA]

cur (kɜ:) *n* **1** any vicious dog, esp a mongrel **2** a despicable or cowardly person [c13: shortened from *kurdogge*; probably related to Old Norse *kurra* to growl]

curable ('kjʊərəbəl) *adj* capable of being cured > ,cura'bility *or* 'curableness *n*

Curaçao (,kjʊərə'səʊ) *n* **1** an island in the Caribbean, the largest in the Netherlands Antilles. Capital: Willemstad. Pop: 137 094 (2007 est). Area: 444 sq km (171 sq miles) **2** an orange-flavoured liqueur originally made there

curacy ('kjʊərəsɪ) *n, pl* -cies the office or position of curate

curare *or* **curari** (kjʊ'rɑ:rɪ) *n* **1** black resin obtained from certain tropical South American trees, esp *Chondrodendron tomentosum*, acting on the motor nerves to cause muscular paralysis: used medicinally as a muscle relaxant and by South American Indians as an arrow poison **2** any of various trees of the genera *Chondrodendron* (family *Menispermaceae*) and *Strychnos* (family *Loganiaceae*) from which this resin is obtained [c18: from Portuguese and Spanish, from Carib *kurari*]

curassow ('kjʊərə,səʊ) *n* any gallinaceous ground-nesting bird of the family *Cracidae*, of S North, Central, and South America. Curassows have long legs and tails and, typically, a distinctive crest of curled feathers [c17: anglicized variant of CURAÇAO (island)]

curate ('kjʊərɪt) *n* **1** a clergyman appointed to assist a parish priest **2** Irish an assistant barman [c14: from Medieval Latin *cūrātus*, from *cūra* spiritual oversight, CURE]

curate's egg *n* something that has both good and bad parts [c20: derived from a cartoon in *Punch* (November, 1895) in which a timid curate, who has been served a bad egg while breakfasting with his bishop, says that parts of the egg are excellent]

curative ('kjʊərətɪv) *adj* **1** able to tending to cure ▷ *n* **2** anything able to heal or cure > 'curatively *adv* > 'curativeness *n*

curator (kjʊə'reɪtə) *n* the administrative head of a museum, art gallery, or similar institution [c14: from Latin: one who cares, from *cūrāre* to care for, from *cūra* care] > curatorial (,kjʊərə'tɔ:rɪəl) *adj* > cu'rator,ship *n*

curb (kɜ:b) *n* **1** something that restrains or holds back **2** any enclosing framework, such as a wall of stones around the top of a well **3** Also called: curb bit a horse's bit with an attached chain or strap, which checks the horse ▷ *vb* (*tr*) **4** to control with or as if with a curb; restrain ▷ See also **kerb** [c15: from Old French *courbe* curved piece of wood or metal, from Latin *curvus* curved]

curcuma ('kɜ:kjʊmə) *n* any tropical Asian tuberous plant of the genus *Curcuma*, such as C. *longa*, which is the source of turmeric, and C. *zedoaria*, which is the source of zedoary: family *Zingiberaceae* [c17: from New Latin, from Arabic *kurkum* turmeric]

curcumin ('kɜ:kjʊmɪn) *n* a yellow pigment, derived from the rhizome of *Curcuma longa*, and the main active ingrediant of turmeric. It is an antioxidant and has anti-inflammatory properties [c20: from CURCUMA]

curd (kɜ:d) *n* **1** (*often plural*) a substance formed from the coagulation of milk by acid or rennet, used in making cheese or eaten as a food **2** something similar in consistency ▷ *vb* **3** to turn into or become curd [c15: from earlier *crud*, of unknown origin] > 'curdy *adj*

curdle ('kɜ:dəl) *vb* **1** to turn or cause to turn into curd **2** curdle someone's blood to fill someone with fear [C16 (*crudled*, past participle): from CURD]

cure (kjʊə) *vb* **1** (*tr*) to get rid of (an ailment, fault, or problem); heal **2** (*tr*) to restore to health or good condition **3** (*intr*) to bring about a cure **4** (*tr*) to preserve (meat, fish, etc) by salting, smoking, etc **5** (*tr*) **a** to treat or cure (a substance) by chemical or physical means **b** to vulcanize (rubber) **6** (*tr*) to assist the hardening of (concrete, mortar, etc) by keeping it moist ▷ *n* **7** a return to health, esp after specific treatment **8** any course of medical therapy, esp one proved effective in combating a disease **9** a means of restoring health or improving a condition, situation, etc **10** the spiritual and pastoral charge of a parish **11** a process or method of preserving meat, fish, etc, by salting, pickling, or smoking [(n) C13: from Old French, from Latin *cūra* care; in ecclesiastical sense, from Medieval Latin *cūra* spiritual charge; (vb) C14: from Old French *curer*, from Latin *cūrāre* to attend to, heal, from *cūra* care] > 'cureless *adj* > 'curer *n*

curé ('kjʊəreɪ) *n* a parish priest in France [French, from Medieval Latin *cūrātus*; see CURATE]

cure-all *n* something reputed to cure all ailments

curettage (,kjʊərɪ'tɑ:ʒ, kjʊə'rɛtɪdʒ) *or* **curettement** (kjʊə'rɛtmənt) *n* the process of using a curette. See also **D and C**

curette or **curet** (kjʊəˈrɛt) n 1 a surgical instrument for removing dead tissue, growths, etc, from the walls of certain body cavities ▷ vb -rettes or -rets, -retting, -retted 2 (tr) to scrape or clean with such an instrument [c18: from French, from curer to heal, make clean; see CURE]

curfew (ˈkɜːfjuː) n 1 an official regulation setting restrictions on movement, esp after a specific time at night 2 the time set as a deadline by such a regulation 3 (in medieval Europe) a the ringing of a bell to prompt people to extinguish fires and lights b the time at which the curfew bell was rung c the bell itself [c13: from Old French cuevrefeu, literally: cover the fire]

curia (ˈkjʊərɪə) n, pl -riae (-rɪˌiː) 1 (sometimes capital) the papal court and government of the Roman Catholic Church 2 (in the Middle Ages) a court held in the king's name [c16: from Latin, from Old Latin coviria (unattested), from co- + vir man] ▷ ˈcurial adj

curie (ˈkjʊərɪ, -riː) n a unit of radioactivity that is equal to 3.7 × 10¹⁰ disintegrations per second [c20: named after Pierre Curie (1859–1906), French physicist and chemist]

Curie (ˈkjʊərɪ, -riː; French kyri) n 1 **Marie** (mari). 1867–1934, French physicist and chemist, born in Poland: discovered with her husband Pierre the radioactivity of thorium, and discovered and isolated radium and polonium. She shared a Nobel prize for physics (1903) with her husband and Henri Becquerel, and was awarded a Nobel prize for chemistry (1911) 2 her husband, **Pierre** (pjɛr). 1859–1906, French physicist and chemist

curio (ˈkjʊərɪˌəʊ) n, pl -rios a small article valued as a collector's item, esp something fascinating or unusual [c19: shortened from CURIOSITY]

curiosity (ˌkjʊərɪˈɒsɪtɪ) n, pl -ties 1 an eager desire to know; inquisitiveness 2 the quality of being curious; strangeness 3 something strange or fascinating

curious (ˈkjʊərɪəs) adj 1 eager to learn; inquisitive 2 overinquisitive; prying 3 interesting because of oddness or novelty; strange; unexpected [c14: from Latin cūriōsus taking pains over something, from cūra care] ▷ ˈcuriously adv ▷ ˈcuriousness n

Curitiba (ˌkʊərɪˈtiːbə) n a city in SE Brazil, capital of Paraná state: seat of the University of Paraná (1946). Pop: 2 871 000 (2005 est)

curium (ˈkjʊərɪəm) n a silvery-white metallic transuranic element artificially produced from plutonium. Symbol: Cm; atomic no: 96; half-life of most stable isotope, ²⁴⁷Cm: 1.6 × 10⁷ years; valency: 3 and 4; relative density: 13.51 (calculated); melting pt: 1345±400°C [c20: New Latin, named after Pierre Curie (1859–1906), French physicist and chemist, and his wife Marie Curie (1867–1934), Polish-born French physicist and chemist]

curl (kɜːl) vb 1 (intr) (esp of hair) to grow into curves or ringlets 2 (tr; sometimes foll by up) to twist or roll (something, esp hair) into coils or ringlets 3 (often foll by up) to become or cause to become spiral-shaped or curved; coil 4 (intr) to move in a curving or twisting manner 5 (intr) to play the game of curling 6 curl one's lip to show contempt, as by raising a corner of the lip ▷ n 7 a curve or coil of hair 8 a curved or spiral shape or mark, as in wood 9 the act of curling or state of being curled ▷ See also **curl up** [c14: probably from Middle Dutch crullen to curl; related to Middle High German krol curly, Middle Low German krūs curly]

curler (ˈkɜːlə) n 1 any of various pins, clasps, or rollers used to curl or wave hair 2 a person or thing that curls 3 a person who plays curling

curlew (ˈkɜːljuː) n any large shore bird of the genus Numenius, such as N. arquata of Europe and Asia: family Scolopacidae (sandpipers, etc), order Charadriiformes. They have a long downward-curving bill and occur in northern and arctic regions [c14: from Old French corlieu, perhaps of imitative origin]

curlicue (ˈkɜːlɪˌkjuː) n an intricate ornamental curl or twist [c19: from CURLY + CUE²]

curling (ˈkɜːlɪŋ) n a game played on ice, esp in Scotland and Canada, in which heavy stones with handles (**curling stones**) are slid towards a target (**tee**)

curling tongs pl n a metal scissor-like device that is heated, so that strands of hair may be twined around it in order to form curls. Also called: **curling iron, curling irons, curling pins**

curl up vb (adverb) 1 (intr) to adopt a reclining position with the legs close to the body and the back rounded 2 to become or cause to become spiral-shaped or curved 3 (intr) to retire to a quiet cosy setting: to curl up with a good novel 4 Brit informal to be or cause to be embarrassed or disgusted (esp in the phrase **curl up and die**)

curly (ˈkɜːlɪ) adj curlier, curliest 1 tending to curl; curling 2 having curls 3 (of timber) having irregular curves or waves in the grain ▷ ˈcurliness n

curmudgeon (kɜːˈmʌdʒən) n a surly or miserly person [c16: of unknown origin] ▷ curˈmudgeonly adj

Curnow (kɜːnaʊ) n (**Thomas**) **Allen** (**Monro**). 1911–2001, New Zealand poet and anthologist

currach, curagh or **curragh** Gaelic (ˈkʌrəx, ˈkʌrə) n a Scot or Irish name for **coracle** [c15: from Irish Gaelic currach; compare CORACLE]

currajong (ˈkʌrəˌdʒɒŋ) n a variant spelling of **kurrajong**

currant (ˈkʌrənt) n 1 a small dried seedless grape of the Mediterranean region, used in cooking 2 any of several mainly N temperate shrubs of the genus Ribes, esp R. rubrum (redcurrant) and R. nigrum (blackcurrant): family Grossulariaceae 3 the small acid fruit of any of these plants [c16: shortened from rayson of Corannte raisin of Corinth]

currawong (ˈkʌrəˌwɒŋ) n any Australian crowlike songbird of the genus Strepera, having black, grey, and white plumage: family Cracticidae. Also called: **bell magpie** [from a native Australian name]

currency (ˈkʌrənsɪ) n, pl -cies 1 a metal or paper medium of exchange that is in current use in a particular country 2 general acceptance or circulation; prevalence 3 the period of time during which something is valid, accepted, or in force 4 Austral slang a (formerly) the native-born Australians, as distinct from the British immigrants b (as modifier): a currency lad [c17: from Medieval Latin currentia, literally: a flowing, from Latin currere to run, flow]

current (ˈkʌrənt) adj 1 of the immediate present; in progress 2 most recent; up-to-date 3 commonly known, practised, or accepted; widespread 4 circulating and valid at present: current coins ▷ n 5 (esp of water or air) a steady usually natural flow 6 a mass of air, body of water, etc, that has a steady flow in a particular direction 7 the rate of flow of such a mass 8 Also called: **electric current** physics a a flow of electric charge through a conductor b the rate of flow of this charge. It is measured in amperes 9 a general trend or drift: currents of opinion [c13: from Old French corant, literally: running, from corre to run, from Latin currere] ▷ ˈcurrently adv ▷ ˈcurrentness n

current account n an account at a bank or building society against which cheques may be drawn at any time

current-cost accounting n a method of accounting that values assets at their current replacement cost rather than their original cost. See **historical-cost accounting**

curricle (ˈkʌrɪkəl) n a two-wheeled open carriage drawn by two horses side by side [c18: from Latin curriculum from currus chariot, from currere to run]

curriculum (kəˈrɪkjʊləm) n, pl -la (-lə) or -lums 1 a course of study in one subject at a school or college 2 a list of all the courses of study offered by a school or college 3 any programme or plan of activities [c19: from Latin: course, from currere to run] ▷ curˈricular adj

curriculum vitae (ˈviːtaɪ, ˈvaɪtiː) n, pl curricula vitae an outline of a person's educational and professional history, usually prepared for job applications [Latin, literally: the course of one's life]

currish (ˈkɜːrɪʃ) adj of or like a cur; rude or bad-tempered ▷ ˈcurrishly adv ▷ ˈcurrishness n

curry¹ (ˈkʌrɪ) n, pl -ries 1 a spicy dish of oriental, esp Indian, origin that is made in many ways but usually consists of meat or fish prepared in a hot piquant sauce 2 curry seasoning or sauce 3 give someone curry Austral *slang* to assault (a person) verbally or physically ▷ *vb* -ries, -rying, -ried **4** (*tr*) to prepare (food) with curry powder or sauce [c16: from Tamil *kari* sauce, relish]

curry² ('kʌrɪ) *vb* -ries, -rying, -ried (*tr*) **1** to beat vigorously, as in order to clean **2** to dress and finish (leather) after it has been tanned to make it strong, flexible, and waterproof **3** to groom (a horse) **4** curry favour to ingratiate oneself, esp with superiors [c13: from Old French *correer* to make ready, from Vulgar Latin *conrēdāre* (unattested), from *rēdāre* (unattested) to provide, of Germanic origin]

Curry ('kʌrɪ) *n* John (**Anthony**). 1949–94, British ice skater: won the figure-skating gold medal in the 1976 Olympic Games

currycomb ('kʌrɪˌkəʊm) *n* a square comb consisting of rows of small teeth, used for grooming horses

curry powder *n* a mixture of finely ground pungent spices, such as turmeric, cumin, coriander, ginger, etc, used in making curries

curse (kɜːs) *n* **1** a profane or obscene expression of anger, disgust, surprise, etc; oath **2** an appeal to a supernatural power for harm to come to a specific person, group, etc **3** harm resulting from an appeal to a supernatural power **4** something that brings or causes great trouble or harm **5** the curse *informal* menstruation or a menstrual period ▷ *vb* curses, cursing, cursed *or archaic* curst **6** (*intr*) to utter obscenities or oaths **7** (*tr*) to abuse (someone) with obscenities or oaths **8** (*tr*) to invoke supernatural powers to bring harm to (someone or something) **9** (*tr*) to bring harm upon [Old English *cursian* to curse, from *curs* a curse] > 'curser *n*

cursed ('kɜːsɪd, kɜːst) *or* **curst** *adj* **1** under a curse **2** deserving to be cursed; detestable; hateful > 'cursedly *adv* > 'cursedness *n*

cursive ('kɜːsɪv) *adj* **1** of or relating to handwriting in which letters are formed and joined in a rapid flowing style **2** *printing* of or relating to typefaces that resemble handwriting ▷ *n* **3** a cursive letter or printing type [c18: from Medieval Latin *cursīvus* running, ultimately from Latin *currere* to run] > 'cursively *adv*

cursor ('kɜːsə) *n* **1** the sliding part of a measuring instrument, esp a transparent sliding square on a slide rule **2** any of various means, typically a flashing bar or underline, of identifying a particular position on a computer screen, such as the insertion point for text

cursorial (kɜːˈsɔːrɪəl) *adj zoology* adapted for running: *a cursorial skeleton; cursorial birds*

cursory ('kɜːsərɪ) *adj* hasty and usually superficial; quick [c17: from Late Latin *cursōrius* of running, from Latin *cursus* a course, from *currere* to run] > 'cursorily *adv* > 'cursoriness *n*

curst (kɜːst) *vb* **1** *archaic* a past tense and past participle of **curse** ▷ *adj* **2** a variant of **cursed**

curt (kɜːt) *adj* **1** rudely blunt and brief; abrupt **2** short or concise [c17: from Latin *curtus* cut short, mutilated] > 'curtly *adv* > 'curtness *n*

curtail (kɜːˈteɪl) *vb* (*tr*) to cut short; abridge [c16: changed (through influence of TAIL¹) from obsolete *curtal* to dock; see CURTAL] > cur'tailer *n* > cur'tailment *n*

curtain ('kɜːt³n) *n* **1** a piece of material that can be drawn across an opening or window, to shut out light or to provide privacy **2** a barrier to vision, access, or communication **3** a hanging cloth or similar barrier for concealing all or part of a theatre stage from the audience **4** the curtain the end of a scene of a play, opera, etc, marked by the fall or closing of the curtain **5** the rise or opening of the curtain at the start of a performance ▷ *vb* **6** (*tr*; sometimes foll by *off*) to shut off or conceal with or as if with a curtain **7** (*tr*) to provide (a window, etc) with curtains [c13: from Old French *courtine*, from Late Latin *cortīna* enclosed place, curtain, probably from Latin *cohors* courtyard]

curtain call *n* the appearance of performers at the end of a theatrical performance to acknowledge applause

curtain lecture *n* a scolding or rebuke given in private, esp by a wife to her husband [alluding to the curtained beds where such rebukes were once given]

curtain-raiser *n* **1** *theatre* a short dramatic piece presented before the main play **2** any preliminary event

curtains ('kɜːt³nz) *pl n informal* death or ruin; the end

curtain wall *n* a non-load-bearing external wall attached to a framed structure, often one that is prefabricated

curtal ('kɜːt³l) *obsolete adj* **1** cut short **2** (of friars) wearing a short frock ▷ *n* **3** an animal whose tail has been docked **4** something that is cut short [c16: from Old French *courtault* animal whose tail has been docked, from *court* short, from Latin *curtus*; see CURT]

Curtin ('kɜːtɪn) *n* **John Joseph**. 1885–1945, Australian statesman; prime minister of Australia (1941–45)

curtsy *or* **curtsey** ('kɜːtsɪ) *n, pl* -sies *or* -seys **1** a formal gesture of greeting and respect made by women in which the knees are bent, the head slightly bowed, and the skirt held outwards ▷ *vb* -sies, -sying, -sied *or* -seys, -seying, -seyed **2** (*intr*) to make a curtsy [c16: variant of COURTESY]

curvaceous (kɜːˈveɪʃəs) *adj informal* (esp of a woman) having shapely curves or a well-rounded body

curvature ('kɜːvətʃə) *n* **1** something curved or a curved part of a thing **2** any normal or abnormal curving of a bodily part **3** the act of curving or the state or degree of being curved or bent

curve (kɜːv) *v* **1** a continuously bending line that has no straight parts **2** something that curves or is curved, such as a bend in a road or the contour of a woman's body **3** the act or extent of curving; curvature **4** *maths* a system of points whose coordinates satisfy a given equation; a locus of points **5** a line representing data, esp statistical data, on a graph **6** ahead of the curve ahead of the times; ahead of schedule **7** behind the curve behind the times; behind schedule ▷ *vb* **8** to take or cause to take the shape or path of a curve; bend [c15: from Latin *curvāre* to bend, from *curvus* crooked] > 'curvedness *n* > 'curvy *adj*

curvet (kɜːˈvɛt) *n* **1** *dressage* a low leap with all four feet off the ground ▷ *vb* -vets, -vetting, -vetted *or* -vets, -veting, -veted **2** *dressage* to make or cause to make such a leap **3** (*intr*) to prance or frisk about [c16: from Old Italian *corvetta*, from Old French *courbette*, from *courber* to bend, from Latin *curvāre*]

curvilinear (ˌkɜːvɪˈlɪnɪə) *or* **curvilineal** *adj* consisting of, bounded by, or characterized by a curved line

Curzon ('kɜːz³n) *n* **1** Sir **Clifford**. 1907–82, English pianist **2 George Nathaniel**, 1st Marquis Curzon of Kedleston. 1859–1925, British Conservative statesman; viceroy of India (1898–1905)

Cusack ('kjuːsæk) *n* **Cyril** (**James**). 1910–93, Irish actor

Cusanus (kjuːˈseɪnəs) *n* **Nicholas**. See Nicholas of Cusa

Cusco (Spanish 'kusko) *n* a variant of Cuzco

cuscus ('kʌskʌs) *n, pl* -cuses any of several large nocturnal phalangers of the genus *Phalanger*, of N Australia, New Guinea, and adjacent islands, having dense fur, prehensile tails, large eyes, and a yellow nose [c17: New Latin, probably from a native name in New Guinea]

cusec ('kjuːsɛk) *n* a unit of flow equal to 1 cubic foot per second. 1 cusec is equivalent to 0.028 317 cubic metre per second [c20: from *cu*(bic foot per) *sec*(ond)]

Cush *or* **Kush** (kʌʃ, kuʃ) *n Old Testament* **1** the son of Ham and brother of Canaan (Genesis 10:6) **2** the country of the supposed descendants of Cush (ancient Ethiopia), comprising approximately Nubia and the modern Sudan, and the territory of southern (or Upper) Egypt

cushat ('kʌʃət) *n* another name for **wood pigeon** [Old English *cūscote*; perhaps related to *scēotan* to shoot]

Cushing ('kuʃɪŋ) *n* **Harvey Williams**. 1869–1939, US neurosurgeon: identified a pituitary tumour as a cause of the disease named after him

cushion ('kuʃən) *n* **1** a bag made of cloth, leather, plastic, etc, filled with feathers, air, or other yielding substance, used for sitting on, leaning against, etc **2** something resembling a cushion in function or appearance, esp one to support or pad or to absorb shock **3** the resilient felt-covered rim of a billiard table ▷ *vb* (*tr*) **4** to place on or as on a cushion **5** to provide with cushions **6** to lessen or suppress the effects of **7** to protect, esp against hardship or change **8** to provide with a means of absorbing shock [from Latin *culcita* mattress]

> 'cushiony *adj*

cushion plant *n* a type of low-growing plant having many closely spaced short upright shoots, typical of alpine and arctic habitats

Cushitic (kʊˈʃɪtɪk) *n* **1** a group of languages of Somalia, Ethiopia, NE Kenya, and adjacent regions: a subfamily within the Afro-Asiatic family of languages ▷ *adj* **2** denoting, relating to, or belonging to this group of languages

cushy ('kʊʃɪ) *adj* cushier, cushiest *informal* easy; comfortable [c20: from Hindi *khush* pleasant, from Persian *khōsh*]

cusp (kʌsp) *n* **1** any of the small elevations on the grinding or chewing surface of a tooth **2** any of the triangular flaps of a heart valve **3** a point or pointed end **4** Also called: **spinode** *geometry* a point at which two arcs of a curve intersect and at which the two tangents are coincident **5** *architect* a carving at the meeting place of two arcs **6** *astronomy* either of the points of a crescent moon or of a satellite or inferior planet in a similar phase **7** *astrology* any division between houses or signs of the zodiac [c16: from Latin *cuspis* point, pointed end] > **cuspate** ('kʌspɪt, -peɪt), 'cuspated *or* **cusped** (kʌspt) *adj*

cuspid ('kʌspɪd) *n* a tooth having one point; canine tooth

cuspidate ('kʌspɪˌdeɪt), **cuspidated** *or* **cuspidal** ('kʌspɪdˤl) *adj* **1** having a cusp or cusps **2** (esp of leaves) narrowing to a point [c17: from Latin *cuspidāre* to make pointed, from *cuspis* a point]

cuspidor ('kʌspɪˌdɔː) *n* another word (esp US) for **spittoon** [c18: from Portuguese, from *cuspir* to spit, from Latin *conspuere*, from *spuere* to spit]

cuss (kʌs) *informal* ▷ *n* **1** a curse; oath **2** a person or animal, esp an annoying one ▷ *vb* **3** another word for **curse** (senses 6, 7)

cussed ('kʌsɪd) *adj informal* **1** another word for: **cursed** **2** obstinate **3** annoying: *a cussed nuisance* > 'cussedly *adv* > 'cussedness *n*

custard ('kʌstəd) *n* **1** a baked sweetened mixture of eggs and milk **2** a sauce made of milk and sugar and thickened with cornflour [c15: alteration of Middle English *crustade* kind of pie, probably from Old Provençal *croustado*, from *crosta* CRUST]

custard apple *n* **1** a West Indian tree, *Annona reticulata*: family *Annonaceae* **2** the large heart-shaped fruit of this tree, which has a fleshy edible pulp

custard pie *n* **a** a flat, open pie filled with real or artificial custard, as thrown in slapstick comedy **b** (*as modifier*): *custard-pie humour*

Custer ('kʌstə) *n* **George Armstrong.** 1839–76, US cavalry general: Civil War hero, killed fighting the Sioux Indians at Little Bighorn, Montana

custodian (kʌˈstəʊdɪən) *n* **1** a person who has custody, as of a prisoner, ward, etc **2** a guardian or keeper, as of an art collection, etc > cus'todian,ship *n*

custody ('kʌstədɪ) *n, pl* -dies **1** the act of keeping safe or guarding, esp the right of guardianship of a minor **2** the state of being held by the police; arrest (esp in the phrases **in custody, take into custody**) [c15: from Latin *custōdia*, from *custōs* guard, defender] > **custodial** (kʌˈstəʊdɪəl) *adj*

custom ('kʌstəm) *n* **1** a usual or habitual practice; typical mode of behaviour **2** the long-established habits or traditions of a society collectively; convention **3 a** a practice which by long-established usage has come to have the force of law **b** such practices collectively (esp in the phrase **custom and practice**) **4** habitual patronage, esp of a shop or business **5** the customers of a shop or business collectively ▷ *adj* **6** made to the specifications of an individual customer (often in the combinations **custom-built, custom-made**) ▷ See also **customs** [c12: from Old French *costume*, from Latin *consuētūdō*, from *consuēscere* to grow accustomed to, from *suēscere* to be used to]

customary ('kʌstəmərɪ, -təmrɪ) *adj* **1** in accordance with custom or habitual practice; usual; habitual **2** *law* **a** founded upon long continued practices and usage rather than law **b** (of land, esp a feudal estate) held by

custom ▷ *n, pl* -aries **3** a statement in writing of customary laws and practices > 'customarily *adv* > 'customariness *n*

custom-built *adj* (of cars, houses, etc) made according to the specifications of an individual buyer

customer ('kʌstəmə) *n* **1** a person who buys **2** *informal* a person with whom one has dealings

customer-facing *adj* interacting or communicating directly with customers: *good customer-facing skills*

custom house *or* **customs house** *n* a government office, esp at a port, where customs are collected and ships cleared for entry

customize *or* **customise** ('kʌstəˌmaɪz) *vb* (*tr*) to modify (something) according to a customer's individual requirements

custom-made *adj* (of suits, dresses, etc) made according to the specifications of an individual buyer

customs ('kʌstəmz) *n* (*functioning as singular or plural*) **1** duty on imports or exports **2** the government department responsible for the collection of these duties **3** the part of a port, airport, frontier station, etc, where baggage and freight are examined for dutiable goods and contraband

cut (kʌt) *vb* cuts, cutting, cut **1** to open up or incise (a person or thing) with a sharp edge or instrument; gash **2** (of a sharp instrument) to penetrate or incise (a person or thing) **3** to divide or be divided with or as if with a sharp instrument **4** (*intr*) to use a sharp-edged instrument or an instrument that cuts **5** (*tr*) to trim or prune by or as if by clipping **6** (*tr*) to reap or mow (a crop, grass, etc) **7** (*tr*; sometimes foll by *out*) to make, form, or shape by cutting **8** (*tr*) to hollow or dig out; excavate **9** to strike (an object) sharply **10** *cricket* to hit (the ball) to the off side, usually between cover and third man, with a roughly horizontal bat **11** to hurt or wound the feelings of (a person), esp by malicious speech or action **12** (*tr*) *informal* to refuse to recognize; snub **13** (*tr*) *informal* to absent oneself from (an activity, location, etc), esp without permission or in haste: *to cut class* **14** (*tr*) to abridge, shorten, or edit by excising a part or parts **15** (*tr*; often foll by *down*) to lower, reduce, or curtail **16** (*tr*) to dilute or weaken **17** (*tr*) to dissolve or break up: *to cut fat* **18** (when *intr*, foll by *across* or *through*) to cross or traverse **19** (*intr*) to make a sharp or sudden change in direction; veer **20** to grow (teeth) through the gums or (of teeth) to appear through the gums **21** (*intr*) *films* **a** to call a halt to a shooting sequence **b** (foll by *to*) to move quickly to another scene **22** *films* to edit (film) **23** (*tr*) to switch off (a light, car engine, etc) **24** (*tr*) (of a performer, recording company, etc) to make (a record or tape of a song, concert, performance, etc) **25** *cards* **a** to divide (the pack) at random into two parts after shuffling **b** (*intr*) to pick cards from a spread pack to decide dealer, partners, etc **26** (*tr*) (of a tool) to bite into (an object) **27** cut both ways **a** to have both good and bad effects **b** to affect both sides of something, as two parties in an argument, etc **28** cut a dash to behave or dress showily or strikingly; make a stylish impression **29** cut a person dead *informal* to ignore a person completely **30** cut a good figure to appear or behave well **31** cut a poor figure to appear or behave badly **32** cut and run *informal* to make a rapid escape **33** cut it *slang* be successful in doing something **34** cut it fine *informal* to allow little margin of time, space, etc **35** cut loose **a** to free or become freed from restraint, custody, anchorage, etc **36** cut no ice *informal* to fail to make an impression **37** cut one's teeth on *informal* **a** to use at an early age or stage **b** to practise on **38** detached, divided, or separated by cutting **39** made, shaped, or fashioned by cutting **40** reduced or diminished by or as if by cutting: *cut prices* **41** weakened or diluted **42** *Brit a slang* word for **drunk** **43** cut and dried *informal* settled or arranged in advance ▷ *n* **44** the act of cutting **45** a stroke or incision made by cutting; gash **46** a piece or part cut off, esp a section of food cut from the whole: *a cut of meat* **47** the edge of anything cut or sliced **48** a passage, channel, path, etc, cut or hollowed out **49** an omission or deletion, esp in a text, film, or play **50** a reduction in price, salary, etc **51** a decrease in

c

government finance in a particular department or area, usually leading to a reduction of services, staff numbers, etc **52** informal a portion or share **53** informal a straw, slip of paper, etc, used in drawing lots **54** the manner or style in which a thing, esp a garment, is cut; fashion **55 a** Irish informal a person's general appearance: *I didn't like the cut of him* **b** Irish derogatory a dirty or untidy condition: *look at the cut of your shoes* **56** a direct route; short cut **57** the US name for **block** (sense 12) **58** cricket a stroke made with the bat in a roughly horizontal position **59** films an immediate transition from one shot to the next, brought about by splicing the two shots together **60** words or an action that hurt another person's feelings **61** a refusal to recognize an acquaintance; snub **62** Brit a stretch of water, esp a canal **63** a cut above informal superior (to); better (than) **64** make the cut golf to better or equal the required score after two rounds in a strokeplay tournament, thus avoiding elimination from the final two rounds ▷ See also **cut across, cutback**, etc [c13: probably of Scandinavian origin; compare Norwegian *kutte* to cut, Icelandic *kuti* small knife]

cut across vb (preposition) **1** (intr) to be contrary to ordinary procedure or limitations **2** to cross or traverse, making a shorter route

cut and paste n a technique used in word processing by which a section of text can be moved within a document

cutaneous (kjuː'teɪnɪəs) adj of, relating to, or affecting the skin [c16: from New Latin *cutāneus*, from Latin *cutis* skin; see HIDE²]

cutaway ('kʌtə,weɪ) n **1** a man's coat cut diagonally from the front waist to the back of the knees **2 a** a drawing or model of a machine, engine, etc, in which part of the casing is omitted to reveal the workings **b** (as modifier): *a cutaway model* **3** films, television a shot separate from the main action of a scene, to emphasize something or to show simultaneous events

cutback ('kʌt,bæk) n **1** a decrease or reduction ▷ vb cut back (adverb) **2** (tr) to shorten by cutting off the end; prune **3** (when intr, foll by on) to reduce or make a reduction (in)

cut down vb (adverb) **1** (tr) to fell **2** (when intr, often foll by on) to reduce or make a reduction (in) **3** (tr) to remake (an old garment) in order to make a smaller one **4** (tr) to kill **5** cut a person down to size to reduce in importance or decrease the conceit of

cute (kjuːt) adj **1** appealing or attractive, esp in a pretty way **2** chiefly US informal sexually attractive **3** informal affecting cleverness or prettiness **4** clever; shrewd [C18 (in the sense: clever): shortened from ACUTE] ▷ 'cutely adv ▷ 'cuteness n

cut glass n **1 a** glass, esp bowls, vases, etc, decorated by facet-cutting or grinding **b** (as modifier): *a cut-glass vase* **2** (modifier) (of an accent) upper-class; refined

Cuthbert ('kʌθbət) n Saint. ?635–87 AD, English monk; bishop of Lindisfarne. Feast day: March 20

cuticle ('kjuːtɪk³l) n **1** dead skin, esp that round the base of a fingernail or toenail **2** another name for **epidermis 3** the protective layer, containing cutin, that covers the epidermis of higher plants **4** the hard protective layer covering the epidermis of many invertebrates [c17: from Latin *cutīcula* diminutive of *cutis* skin] ▷ cuticular (kjuːˈtɪkjʊlə) adj

cut in vb (adverb) **1** Also called: cut into (intr; often foll by on) to break in or interrupt **2** (intr) to interrupt a dancing couple to dance with one of them **3** (intr) (of a driver, motor vehicle, etc) to draw in front of another vehicle leaving too little space **4** (tr) informal to allow to have a share **5** (intr) to take the place of a person in a card game

cutis ('kjuːtɪs) n, pl -tes (-tiːz) or -tises zoology a technical name for: skin [c17: from Latin: skin]

cutlass ('kʌtləs) n a curved, one-edged sword formerly used by sailors [c16: from French *coutelas*, from *coutel* knife, from Latin *cultellus* a small knife, from *culter* knife; see COULTER]

cutler ('kʌtlə) n a person who makes or sells cutlery [C14: from French *coutelier*, ultimately from Latin *culter* knife; see CUTLASS]

cutlery ('kʌtlərɪ) n **1** implements used for eating, such as knives, forks, and spoons **2** instruments used for cutting **3** the art or business of a cutler

cutlet ('kʌtlɪt) n **1** a piece of meat taken esp from the best end of neck of lamb, pork, etc **2** a flat croquette of minced chicken, lobster, etc [c18: from Old French *costelette*, literally: a little rib, from *coste* rib, from Latin *costa*]

cutline ('kʌt,laɪn) n US & Canadian **1** a caption accompanying an illustration **2** a line marked on a piece of wood, metal, etc, to show where it is to be cut

cut off vb (tr, adverb) **1** to remove by cutting **2** to intercept or interrupt something, esp a telephone conversation **3** to discontinue the supply of **4** to bring to an end **5** to deprive of rights; disinherit: *she was cut off without a penny* **6** to sever or separate **7** to occupy a position so as to prevent or obstruct (a retreat or escape) ▷ n cutoff **8 a** the act of cutting off; limit or termination **b** (as modifier): *the cutoff point* **9** chiefly US a route or way that is shorter than the usual one; short cut **10** a device to terminate the flow of a fluid in a pipe or duct

cut-offs ('kʌtɒfs) pl n trousers that have been shortened to calf length or to make shorts

cut out vb (adverb) **1** (tr) to delete or remove **2** (tr) to shape or form by cutting **3** (tr; usually passive) to suit or equip for: *you're not cut out for this job* **4** (intr) (of an engine, etc) to cease to operate suddenly **5** (intr) (of an electrical device) to switch off, usually automatically **6** (tr) informal to oust and supplant (a rival) **7** (intr) (of a person) to be excluded from a card game **8** (tr) informal to cease doing something, esp something undesirable (esp in the phrase **cut it out**) **9** (tr) soccer to intercept (a pass) **10** (tr) to separate (cattle) from a herd **11** (intr) Austral & NZ to end or finish: *the road cuts out at the creek* **12** have one's work cut out to have as much work as one can manage ▷ n cutout **13** something that has been or is intended to be cut out from something else **14** a device that switches off or interrupts an electric circuit, esp a switch acting as a safety device **15** Austral slang the end of shearing

cut-price or esp US **cut-rate** adj **1** available at prices or rates below the standard price or rate **2** (prenominal) offering goods or services at prices below the standard price

cutpurse ('kʌt,pɜːs) n an archaic word for **pickpocket**

cutter ('kʌtə) n **1** a person or thing that cuts, esp a person who cuts cloth for clothing **2** a sailing boat with its mast stepped further aft so as to have a larger foretriangle than that of a sloop **3** a ship's boat, powered by oars or sail, for carrying passengers or light cargo **4** a small lightly armed boat, as used in the enforcement of customs regulations

cut-throat n **1** a person who cuts throats; murderer **2** Also called: cut-throat razor Brit a razor with a long blade that usually folds into the handle. US name: straight razor ▷ adj **3** bloodthirsty or murderous; cruel **4** fierce or relentless in competition: *cut-throat prices* **5** (of some games) played by three people: *cut-throat poker*

cutting ('kʌtɪŋ) n **1** a piece cut off from the main part of something **2** horticulture **a** a method of vegetative propagation in which a part of a plant, such as a stem or leaf, is induced to form its own roots **b** a part separated for this purpose **3** an article, photograph, etc, cut from a newspaper or other publication. Also called (esp US and Canadian): clipping **4** the editing process by which a film is cut and made **5** an excavation in a piece of high land for a road, railway, etc, enabling it to remain at approximately the same level **6** Irish informal sharp-wittedness: *there is no cutting in him* **7** (modifier) designed for or adapted to cutting; edged; sharp ▷ adj **8** keen; piercing **9** tending to hurt the feelings: *a cutting remark* ▷ 'cuttingly adv

cutting compound n engineering a mixture, such as oil, water, and soap, used for cooling drills and other cutting tools

cutting edge n **1** the leading position in any field; forefront: *on the cutting edge of space technology* ▷ adj cutting-edge **2** at the forefront of people or things in a field of activity; leading: *cutting-edge technology*

cuttlebone ('kʌt³l,bəʊn) n the internal calcareous shell of the cuttlefish, used as a mineral supplement to the diet of cage-birds and as a polishing agent

cuttlefish ('kʌtᵊl,fɪʃ) *n, pl* **-fish** *or* **-fishes** any cephalopod mollusc of the genus *Sepia* and related genera, which occur near the bottom of inshore waters and have a broad flattened body: order *Decapoda* (decapods)

cut up *vb* (*tr, adverb*) **1** to cut into pieces **2** to inflict injuries on **3** (*usually passive*) *informal* to affect the feelings of deeply **4** *informal* to subject to severe criticism **5** *informal* (of a driver) to overtake or pull in front of (another driver) in a dangerous manner **6** **cut up rough** *Brit informal* to become angry or bad-tempered ▷ *n* cut-up **7** *informal, chiefly US* a joker or prankster

cutwater ('kʌt,wɔ:tə) *n* the forward part of the stem of a vessel, which cuts through the water

cutworm ('kʌt,wɜ:m) *n* the caterpillar of various noctuid moths, esp those of the genus *Argrotis*, which is a pest of young crop plants in North America

cuvée (ku:'veɪ) *n* an individual batch or blend of wine [c19: from French, literally: put in a cask, from *cuve* cask]

Cuvier ('kju:vɪeɪ; *French* kyvje) *n* **Georges** (**Jean-Leopold-Nicolas-Frédéric**) (ʒɔrʒ), Baron. 1769–1832, French zoologist and statesman; founder of the sciences of comparative anatomy and palaeontology

Cuxhaven ('kʊks,ha:vᵊn; *German* kʊks'ha:fən) *n* a port in NW Germany, at the mouth of the River Elbe. Pop: 52 876 (2003 est)

Cuyp *or* **Kuyp** (kaɪp; *Dutch* kœip) *n* **Aelbert** ('a:lbert). 1620–91, Dutch painter of landscapes and animals

cuz (kʌz) *n inf* **1** NZ a term used by a Māori to refer to or address a family member **2** *Austral* a term used by an Aboriginal person to refer to or address a family member [shortened from COUSIN]

Cuzco (*Spanish* 'kuθko) *or* **Cusco** *n* a city in S central Peru: former capital of the Inca Empire, with extensive Inca remains; university (1692). Pop: 307 000 (2005 est)

cuzzie ('kʌzɪ) *or* **cuzzie-bro** ('kʌzɪ,brəʊ) *n* NZ a close friend or family member, often used in direct address [c20: from COUSIN]

CV *abbreviation* curriculum vitae

CVS *abbreviation* **1** chorionic villus sampling **2** *computing* concurrent versions system

Cwlth *abbreviation* Commonwealth

cwm (ku:m) *n* **1** (in Wales) a valley **2** *geology* another name for **cirque** (sense 1)

c.w.o. *or* **CWO** *abbreviation* cash with order

CWS *abbreviation* Cooperative Wholesale Society

cwt *abbreviation* hundredweight [c, from the Latin numeral C one hundred (*centum*)]

CWU *abbreviation* (in Britain) Communications Workers Union

-cy *suffix* **1** (*forming nouns from adjectives ending in -t, -tic, -te, and -nt*) indicating state, quality, or condition: *plutocracy; lunacy; intimacy; infancy* **2** (*forming abstract nouns from other nouns*) rank or office: *captaincy* [via Old French from Latin *-cia, -tia*, Greek *-kia, -tia*, abstract noun suffixes]

CYA *abbreviation* *text messaging* see you: used as a farewell in text messages, emails, etc [C20]

cyan ('saɪæn, 'saɪən) *n* **1** a highly saturated green-blue that is the complementary colour of red and forms, with magenta and yellow, a set of primary colours ▷ *adj* **2** of this colour [c19: from Greek *kuanos* dark blue]

cyanate ('saɪə,neɪt) *n* any salt or ester of cyanic acid, containing the ion ⁻OCN or the group –OCN

cyanic acid (saɪ'ænɪk) *n* a colourless poisonous volatile liquid acid that hydrolyses readily to ammonia and carbon dioxide. Formula: HOCN

cyanide ('saɪə,naɪd) *or* **cyanid** ('saɪənɪd) *n* any salt of hydrocyanic acid. Cyanides contain the ion CN⁻ and are extremely poisonous > ,cyani'dation *n*

cyanite ('saɪə,naɪt) *n* a variant spelling of **kyanite** > ,cya'nitik) *adj*

cyano- *or before a vowel* **cyan-** *combining form* **1** blue or dark blue **2** indicating cyanogen **3** indicating cyanide [from Greek *kuanos* (adj) dark blue, (n) dark blue enamel, lapis lazuli]

cyanoacrylate (,saɪənəʊ'ækrɪleɪt) *n* a substance with an acrylate base, usually sold in the form of a quick-setting highly adhesive glue

cyanobacteria (,saɪənəʊbæk'tɪərɪə) *pl n, sing* **-rium** (-rɪəm) a group of photosynthetic bacteria (phylum *Cyanobacteria*) containing a blue photosynthetic pigment. Former name: **blue-green algae**

cyanocobalamin (,saɪənəʊkəʊ'bæləmɪn) *n* a complex red crystalline compound, containing cyanide and cobalt and occurring in liver: lack of it in the tissues leads to pernicious anaemia. Formula: $C_{63}H_{88}O_{14}N_{14}PCo$. Also called: **vitamin B₁₂** [c20: from CYANO- + COBAL(T) + (VIT)AMIN]

cyanogen (saɪ'ænədʒɪn) *n* an extremely poisonous colourless flammable gas with an almond-like odour: has been used in chemical warfare. Formula: $(CN)_2$ [c19: from French *cyanogène*; see CYANO-, -GEN; so named because it is one of the constituents of Prussian blue]

cyanosis (,saɪə'nəʊsɪs) *n pathol* a bluish-purple discoloration of skin and mucous membranes usually resulting from a deficiency of oxygen in the blood > **cyanotic** (,saɪə'nɒtɪk) *adj*

Cybele ('sɪbɪlɪ) *n classical myth* the Phrygian goddess of nature, mother of all living things and consort of Attis; identified with the Greek Rhea or Demeter

cyber- *combining form* indicating computers: *cyberphobia* [c20: back formation from CYBERNETICS]

cybercafé ('saɪbə,kæfeɪ, -,kæfɪ) *n* a café with computer equipment that gives public access to the internet

cybercrime ('saɪbə,kraɪm) *n* **1** the illegal use of computers and the internet **2** crime committed by means of computers or the internet > ,cyber'criminal *n*

cybernate ('saɪbə,neɪt) *vb* to control (a manufacturing process) with a servomechanism or (of a process) to be controlled by a servomechanism [c20: from CYBER(NETICS) + -ATE¹] > ,cyber'nation *n*

cybernetics (,saɪbə'netɪks) *n* (*functioning as singular*) the branch of science concerned with control systems in electronic and mechanical devices and the extent to which useful comparisons can be made between man-made and biological systems [c20: from Greek *kubernētēs* steersman, from *kubernan* to steer, control] > ,cyber'netic *adj* > ,cyber'neticist *n*

cyberpet ('saɪbə,pet) *n* an electronic toy that simulates the activities of a pet, requiring the owner to feed, discipline, and entertain it

cyberphobia (,saɪbə'fəʊbɪə) *n* an irrational fear of computers > ,cyber'phobic *adj*

cyberpunk ('saɪbə,pʌnk) *n* **1** a genre of science fiction that features rebellious computer hackers and is set in a dystopian society integrated by computer networks **2** a writer of cyberpunk

cybersecurity (,saɪbə,sɪ'kjʊərɪtɪ) *n computing* the state of being safe from electronic crime and the measures taken to achieve this

cybersex ('saɪbə,seks) *n* **1** the exchanging of sexual messages or information via the internet **2** sexual activity performed remotely by means of virtual reality equipment

cyberspace ('saɪbə,speɪs) *n* all of the data stored in a large computer or network represented as a three-dimensional model through which a virtual-reality user can move

cybersquatting ('saɪbə,skwɒtɪŋ) *n* the practice of registering an internet domain name that is likely to be wanted by another person, business, or organization in the hope that it can be sold to them for a profit > 'cyber,squatter *n*

cyberterrorism ('saɪbə,terərɪzəm) *n* the illegal use of computers and the internet to achieve some goal > 'cyber,terrorist *n*

cycad ('saɪkæd) *n* any tropical or subtropical gymnosperm plant of the phylum *Cycadophyta*, having an unbranched stem with fernlike leaves crowded at the top [c19: from New Latin *Cycas* name of genus, from Greek *kukas*, scribe's error for *koîkas*, from *koïx* a kind of palm, probably of Egyptian origin] > ,cyca'daceous *adj*

Cyclades ('sɪklə,di:z) *pl n* a group of over 200 islands in the S Aegean Sea, forming a department of Greece. Capital: Hermoupolis (Ermoupoli, on Syros). Pop: 112 615 (2001). Area: 2572 sq km (993 sq miles). Modern Greek name: Kikládhes

Cycladic (sɪ'klædɪk) *adj* of or relating to the Cyclades or their inhabitants

cyclamate ('saɪklə,meɪt, 'sɪklə,meɪt) *n* a salt or ester of cyclamic acid. Certain of the salts have a very sweet taste and were formerly used as food additives and sugar substitutes [c20: *cycl(ohexyl-sulph)amate*]

cyclamen ('sɪkləmən, -,mɛn) *n* 1 any Old World plant of the primulaceous genus *Cyclamen*, having nodding white, pink, or red flowers, with reflexed petals ▷ *adj* 2 of a dark reddish-purple colour [c16: from Medieval Latin, from Latin *cyclamīnos*, from Greek *kuklaminos*, probably from *kuklos* circle, referring to the bulb-like roots]

cycle ('saɪk³l) *n* 1 a recurring period of time in which certain events or phenomena occur and reach completion or repeat themselves in a regular sequence 2 a completed series of events that follows or is followed by another series of similar events occurring in the same sequence 3 the time taken or needed for one such series 4 a vast period of time; age; aeon 5 a group of poems or prose narratives forming a continuous story about a central figure or event: *the Arthurian cycle* 6 short for **bicycle, motorcycle** 7 a recurrent series of events or processes in plants and animals: *a life cycle; a growth cycle; a metabolic cycle* 8 one of a series of repeated changes in the magnitude of a periodically varying quantity, such as current or voltage ▷ *vb* 9 (*tr*) to process through a cycle or system 10 (*intr*) to move in or pass through cycles 11 to travel by or ride a bicycle or tricycle [c14: from Late Latin *cyclus*, from Greek *kuklos* cycle, circle, ring, wheel; see WHEEL]

cyclic ('saɪklɪk, 'sɪklɪk) *or* **cyclical** ('saɪklɪk³l, 'sɪklɪk³l) *adj* 1 recurring or revolving in cycles 2 (of an organic compound) containing a closed saturated or unsaturated ring of atoms 3 *botany* **a** arranged in whorls: *cyclic petals* **b** having parts arranged in this way: *cyclic flowers* > 'cyclically *adv*

cycling shorts *pl n* tight-fitting shorts reaching partway to the knee for cycling, sport, etc

cyclist ('saɪklɪst) *or US* **cycler** *n* a person who rides or travels by bicycle, motorcycle, etc

cyclo- *or before a vowel* **cycl-** *combining form* 1 indicating a circle or ring: *cyclotron* 2 denoting a cyclic compound [from Greek *kuklos* CYCLE]

cyclogiro ('saɪkləʊ,dʒaɪrəʊ) *n aeronautics obsolete* an aircraft lifted and propelled by pivoted blades rotating parallel to roughly horizontal transverse axes

cyclohexanone (,saɪkləʊ'hɛksə,nəʊn) *n* a colourless liquid used as a solvent for cellulose lacquers. Formula: $C_6H_{10}O$

cycloid ('saɪklɔɪd) *adj* 1 resembling a circle ▷ *n* 2 *geometry* the curve described by a point on the circumference of a circle as the circle rolls along a straight line

cyclometer (saɪ'klɒmɪtə) *n* a device that records the number of revolutions made by a wheel and hence the distance travelled

cyclone ('saɪkləʊn) *n* 1 another name for **depression** (sense 6) 2 a violent tropical storm; hurricane [c19: from Greek *kuklōn* a turning around, from *kukloein* to revolve, from *kuklos* wheel] > **cyclonic** (saɪ'klɒnɪk), **cy'clonical** *or* 'cyclonal *adj* > cy'clonically *adv*

Cyclone ('saɪkləʊn) *adj trademark Austral & NZ* (of fencing) made of interlaced wire and metal

Cyclopean (,saɪkləʊ'piːən, saɪ'kləʊpɪən) *adj* 1 of, relating to, or resembling the Cyclops 2 denoting, relating to, or having the kind of masonry used in preclassical Greek architecture, characterized by large dry undressed blocks of stone

cyclopedia *or* **cyclopaedia** (,saɪkləʊ'piːdɪə) *n* a less common word for **encyclopedia**

cyclopentadiene (,saɪkləʊ,pɛntə'daɪiːn) *n* a colourless liquid unsaturated cyclic hydrocarbon obtained in the cracking of petroleum hydrocarbons and the distillation of coal tar: used in the manufacture of plastics and insecticides. Formula: C_5H_6

cyclophosphamide (,saɪkləʊ'fɒsfə,maɪd) *n* an alkylating agent used in the treatment of leukaemia and lymphomas [c20: from CYCLO- + PHOSPH(ORUS) + AMIDE]

cyclopropane (,saɪkləʊ'prəʊpeɪn, ,sɪk-) *n* a colourless flammable gaseous hydrocarbon, used in medicine as an anaesthetic; trimethylene. It is a cycloalkane with molecules containing rings of three carbon atoms. Formula: C_3H_6; boiling pt: −34°C

Cyclops ('saɪklɒps) *n, pl* **Cyclopes** (saɪ'kləʊpiːz) *or* **Cyclopses** *classical myth* one of a race of giants having a single eye in the middle of the forehead, encountered by Odysseus in the *Odyssey* [c15: from Latin *Cyclōps*, from Greek *Kuklōps*, literally: round eye, from *kuklos* circle + *ōps* eye]

cyclorama (,saɪkləʊ'rɑːmə) *n* 1 Also called: **panorama** a large picture, such as a battle scene, on the interior wall of a cylindrical room, designed to appear in natural perspective to a spectator in the centre 2 *theatre* a curtain or wall curving along the back of a stage, usually painted to represent the sky and serving to enhance certain lighting effects [c19: CYCLO- + Greek *horama* view, sight, on the model of *panorama*] > cycloramic (,saɪkləʊ'ræmɪk) *adj*

cyclostome ('saɪklə,stəʊm, 'sɪk-) *n* any primitive aquatic jawless vertebrate of the class *Cyclostomata*, such as the lamprey and hagfish, having a round sucking mouth and pouchlike gills > cyclostomate (saɪ'klɒstəmɪt, -,meɪt) *or* cyclostomatous (,saɪkləʊ'stɒmətəs, -'stəʊmə-, ,sɪk-) *adj*

cyclostyle ('saɪklə,staɪl) *n* 1 a kind of pen with a small toothed wheel, used for cutting minute holes in a specially prepared stencil. Copies of the design so formed can be printed on a duplicator by forcing ink through the holes 2 an office duplicator using a stencil prepared in this way ▷ *vb* 3 (*tr*) to print on a duplicator using such a stencil > 'cyclo,styled *adj*

cyclothymia (,saɪkləʊ'θaɪmɪə, ,sɪk-) *n psychiatry* a condition characterized by periodical swings of mood between excitement and depression, activity and inactivity > ,cyclo'thymic *or* ,cyclo'thymi,ac *adj, n*

cyclotron ('saɪklə,trɒn) *n* a type of particle accelerator in which the particles spiral inside two D-shaped hollow metal electrodes placed facing each other under the effect of a strong vertical magnetic field, gaining energy by a high-frequency voltage applied between these electrodes

cyder ('saɪdə) *n* a variant spelling (esp Brit) of **cider**

cygnet ('sɪgnɪt) *n* a young swan [c15 *sygnett*, from Old French *cygne* swan, from Latin *cygnus*, from Greek *kuknos*]

cylinder ('sɪlɪndə) *n* 1 a solid consisting of two parallel planes bounded by identical closed curves, usually circles, that are interconnected at every point by a set of parallel lines, usually perpendicular to the planes. Volume *base area × length* 2 a surface formed by a line moving round a closed plane curve at a fixed angle to it 3 any object shaped like a cylinder 4 the chamber in a reciprocating internal-combustion engine, pump, or compressor within which the piston moves 5 the rotating mechanism of a revolver, situated behind the barrel and containing cartridge chambers 6 *printing* any of the rotating drums on a printing press 7 Also called: **cylinder seal** a cylindrical seal of stone, clay, or precious stone decorated with linear designs, found in the Middle East and Balkans: dating from about 6000 BC [c16: from Latin *cylindrus*, from Greek *kulindros* a roller, from *kulindein* to roll] > 'cylinder-,like *adj*

cylindrical (sɪ'lɪndrɪk³l) *or* **cylindric** (sɪ'lɪndrɪk) *adj* of, shaped like, or characteristic of a cylinder > cy,lindri'cality *or* cy'lindricalness *n* > cy'lindrically *adv*

cyma ('saɪmə) *n, pl* -mae (-miː) *or* -mas 1 either of two mouldings having a double curve, part concave and part convex. **Cyma recta** has the convex part nearer the wall and **cyma reversa** has the concave part nearer the wall 2 *botany* a rare variant of **cyme** [c16: from New Latin, from Greek *kuma* something swollen, from *kuein* to be pregnant]

cymbal ('sɪmb³l) *n* a percussion instrument of indefinite pitch consisting of a thin circular piece of brass, which vibrates when clashed together with another cymbal or struck with a stick [Old English *cymbala*, from Medieval Latin, from Latin *cymbalum*, from Greek *kumbalon*, from *kumbē* something hollow]

Cymbeline ('sımbəli:n) n See **Cunobelinus**

cymbidium (sım'bıdıəm) n, pl-diums a genus, *Cymbidium*, of subtropical and tropical orchids native to Australia and Asia, having boat-shaped showy flowers [c19: from Latin *cymba* boat]

cyme (saım) n an inflorescence in which the first flower is the terminal bud of the main stem and subsequent flowers develop as terminal buds of lateral stems [c18: from Latin *cyma* cabbage sprout, from Greek *kuma* anything swollen; see CYMA] >**cymiferous** (saı'mıfərəs) adj >**cymose** ('saıməus, -məuz, saı'məus) adj >'**cymosely** adv

Cymric or **Kymric** ('kımrık) n 1 the Welsh language 2 the Brythonic group of Celtic languages ▷ adj 3 of or relating to the Cymry, any of their languages, Wales, or the Welsh

Cymru (Welsh kum'ri) n the Welsh name for **Wales**

Cymry or **Kymry** ('kımrı) n the Cymry (functioning as plural) 1 the Brythonic branch of the Celtic people, comprising the present-day Welsh, Cornish, and Bretons 2 the Welsh people [Welsh: the Welsh]

Cynewulf, Kynewulf ('kını,wulf) or **Cynwulf** ('kın,wulf) n ?8th century AD, Anglo-Saxon poet; author of *Juliana*, *The Ascension, Elene*, and *The Fates of the Apostles*

cynic ('sınık) n 1 a person who believes the worst about people or the outcome of events ▷ adj 2 a less common word for **cynical** [c16: via Latin from Greek *Kunikos*, from *kuōn* dog]

Cynic ('sınık) n a member of a sect founded by Antisthenes that scorned worldly things and held that self-control was the key to the only good

cynical ('sınık³l) adj 1 distrustful or contemptuous of virtue, esp selflessness in others; believing the worst of others, esp that all acts are selfish 2 sarcastic; mocking 3 showing contempt for accepted standards of behaviour, esp of honesty or morality >'**cynically** adv >'**cynicalness** n

cynicism ('sını,sızəm) n 1 the attitude or beliefs of a cynic 2 a cynical action, remark, idea, etc

Cynicism ('sını,sızəm) n the doctrines of the Cynics

cyno- combining form indicating a dog: *cynopodous*; *cynophobia* [from Greek *kuōn* dog]

cynosure ('sınə,zjuə, -ʃuə) n 1 a person or thing that attracts notice, esp because of its brilliance or beauty 2 something that serves as a guide [c16: from Latin *Cynosūra* the constellation of Ursa Minor, from Greek *Kunosoura*, from CYNO- + *oura* tail]

Cynthia ('sınθıə) n another name for **Artemis**

cypher ('saıfə) n, vb a variant spelling of **cipher**

cypress ('saıprəs) n 1 any coniferous tree of the N temperate genus *Cupressus*, having dark green scalelike leaves and rounded cones: family *Cupressaceae* 2 any of several similar and related trees, such as the widely cultivated *Chamaecyparis lawsoniana* (**Lawson's cypress**), of the western US 3 the wood of any of these trees [Old English *cypresse*, from Latin *cyparissus*, from Greek *kuparissos*; related to Latin *cupressus*]

cypress pine n any coniferous tree of the Australian genus *Callitris*, having leaves in whorls and yielding valuable timber: family *Cupressaceae*

Cyprian[1] ('sıprıən) adj 1 of or relating to Cyprus 2 of or resembling the ancient orgiastic worship of Aphrodite on Cyprus ▷ n 3 (often not capital) obsolete a licentious person, esp a prostitute or dancer ▷ n, adj 4 another word for **Cypriot**

Cyprian[2] ('sıprıən) n Saint. ?200–258 AD, bishop of Carthage and martyr. Feast day: Sept 26 or 16

cyprinid (sı'praınıd, 'sıprınıd) n 1 any teleost fish of the mainly freshwater family *Cyprinidae*, typically having toothless jaws and cycloid scales and including such food and game fishes as the tench, roach, rudd, and dace ▷ adj 2 of, relating to, or belonging to the *Cyprinidae* 3 resembling a carp; cyprinoid [c19: from New Latin *Cyprīnidae*, from Latin *cyprīnus* carp, from Greek *kuprinos*]

cyprinoid ('sıprı,nɔıd, sı'praınɔıd) adj 1 of, relating to, or belonging to the *Cyprinoidea*, a large suborder of teleost fishes including the cyprinids, characins, electric eels, and loaches 2 of, relating to, or resembling the carp ▷ n

3 any fish belonging to the *Cyprinoidea* [c19: from Latin *cyprīnus* carp]

Cypriot ('sıprıət) or **Cypriote** ('sıprı,əut) n 1 a native, citizen, or inhabitant of Cyprus 2 the dialect of Ancient or Modern Greek spoken in Cyprus ▷ adj 3 denoting or relating to Cyprus, its inhabitants, or dialects

cypripedium (,sıprı'pi:dıəm) n any orchid of the genus *Cypripedium*, having large flowers with an inflated pouchlike lip. See also **lady's-slipper** [c18: from New Latin, from Latin *Cypria* the Cyprian, that is, Venus + *pēs* foot (that is, Venus' slipper)]

Cyprus ('saıprəs) n an island in the E Mediterranean: ceded to Britain by Turkey in 1878 and made a colony in 1925; became an independent republic in 1960 as a member of the Commonwealth; invaded by Turkey in 1974 following a Greek-supported military coup, leading to the partition of the island. In 1983 the Turkish-controlled northern sector declared itself to be an independent state as the Turkish Republic of Northern Cyprus but failed to receive international recognition. Attempts by the UN to broker a reunification agreement have failed. Cyprus joined the EU in 2004. The UK maintains two enclaves as military bases (Akrotiri and Dhekelia Sovereign Base Areas), which are not included in Cyprus politically. Languages: Greek and Turkish. Religions: Greek Orthodox and Muslim. Currency: euro and Turkish lira. Capital: Nicosia. Pop (Greek): 675 000 (2001 est); (Turkish): 198 000 (2001 est). Area: 9251 sq km (3571 sq miles)

Cyrano de Bergerac (French sirano də bɛrʒərak) n **Savinien** (savinjẽ). 1619–55, French writer and soldier, famous as a duellist and for his large nose. He became widely known through the verse drama *Cyrano de Bergerac* (1897) by Edmond Rostand

Cyrenaic (,saırə'neıık, ,sırə-) adj 1 (in the ancient world) of or relating to the city of Cyrene or the territory of Cyrenaica 2 of or relating to the philosophical school founded by the Greek philosopher Aristippus (?435–?356 BC) in Cyrene that held pleasure to be the highest good ▷ n 3 a follower of the Cyrenaic school of philosophy

Cyrene (saı'ri:nı) n an ancient Greek city of N Africa, near the coast of Cyrenaica: famous for its medical school

Cyril ('sırəl) n **Saint**. ?827–869 AD, Greek Christian theologian, missionary to the Moravians and inventor of the Cyrillic alphabet; he and his brother Saint Methodius were called *the Apostles of the Slavs*. Feast day: Feb 14 or May 11

Cyrillic (sı'rılık) adj 1 denoting or relating to the alphabet derived from that of the Greeks, supposedly by Saint Cyril, for the writing of Slavonic languages: now used primarily for Russian, Bulgarian, and the Serbian dialect of Serbo-Croat ▷ n 2 this alphabet

Cyril of Alexandria n **Saint**. ?375–444 AD, Christian theologian and patriarch of Alexandria. Feast day: June 27 or June 9

Cyrus ('saırəs) n 1 known as *Cyrus the Great* or *Cyrus the Elder*. died ?529 BC, king of Persia and founder of the Persian empire 2 called *the Younger*. died 401 BC, Persian satrap of Lydia: revolted against his brother Artaxerxes II, but was killed at the battle of Cunaxa. See also **anabasis**

cyst (sıst) n 1 pathol any abnormal membranous sac or blisterlike pouch containing fluid or semisolid material 2 anatomy any normal sac or vesicle in the body 3 a thick-walled protective membrane enclosing a cell, larva, or organism [c18: from New Latin *cystis*, from Greek *kustis* pouch, bag, bladder]

-cyst n combining form indicating a bladder or sac: *otocyst* [from Greek *kustis* bladder]

cystectomy (sı'stɛktəmı) n, pl-mies 1 surgical removal of the gall bladder or of part of the urinary bladder 2 surgical removal of any abnormal cyst

cystic ('sıstık) adj 1 of, relating to, or resembling a cyst 2 having or enclosed within a cyst; encysted 3 relating to the gall bladder or urinary bladder

cysticercus (,sıstı'sɜ:kəs) n, pl-ci (-saı) an encysted larval form of many tapeworms, consisting of a head (scolex) inverted in a fluid-filled bladder [c19: from New

Latin, from Greek *kustis* pouch, bladder + *kerkos* tail]

cystic fibrosis *n* an inheritable disease of the exocrine glands, controlled by a recessive gene: affected children inherit defective alleles from both parents. It is characterized by chronic infection of the respiratory tract and by pancreatic insufficiency

cystitis (sɪˈstaɪtɪs) *n* inflammation of the urinary bladder

cysto- *or before a vowel* **cyst-** *combining form* indicating a cyst or bladder: *cystocarp; cystoscope*

cystoid (ˈsɪstɔɪd) *adj* 1 resembling a cyst or bladder ▷ *n* 2 a tissue mass, such as a tumour, that resembles a cyst but lacks an outer membrane

cystoscope (ˈsɪstəˌskəʊp) *n* a slender tubular medical instrument for examining the interior of the urethra and urinary bladder > cystoscopic (ˌsɪstəˈskɒpɪk) *adj* > cystoscopy (sɪsˈtɒskəpɪ) *n*

-cyte *n combining form* indicating a cell: *spermatocyte* [from New Latin *-cyta*, from Greek *kutos* container, body, hollow vessel]

Cythera (sɪˈθɪərə) *n* 1 a Greek island off the SE coast of the Peloponnese: in ancient times a centre of the worship of Aphrodite. Pop: 3354 (2001). Area: about 285 sq km (110 sq miles) 2 the chief town of this island, on the S coast. Pop: 297 (2001) ▷ Modern Greek name: Kíthira

Cytherea (ˌsɪθəˈriːə) *n* another name for **Aphrodite** > ˌCytherˈean *adj*

cyto- *combining form* indicating a cell: *cytolysis; cytoplasm* [from Greek *kutos* vessel, container; related to *kuein* to contain]

cytogenetics (ˌsaɪtəʊdʒɪˈnɛtɪks) *n* (*functioning as singular*) the branch of genetics that correlates the structure, number, and behaviour of chromosomes with heredity and variation > ˌcytogeˈnetic *adj*

cytokine (ˈsaɪtəʊˌkaɪn) *n* any of various proteins, secreted by cells, that carry signals to neighbouring cells. Cytokines include interferon

cytokinin (ˌsaɪtəʊˈkaɪnɪn) *n* any of a group of plant hormones that promote cell division and retard ageing in plants. Also called: kinin

cytology (saɪˈtɒlədʒɪ) *n* 1 the study of plant and animal cells, including their structure, function, and formation 2 the detailed structure of a tissue, as revealed by microscopic examination > cytological (ˌsaɪtəˈlɒdʒɪkᵊl) *adj* > ˌcytoˈlogically *adv* > cyˈtologist *n*

cytomegalovirus (ˌsaɪtəʊˈmɛɡələʊˌvaɪrəs) *n* a virus of the herpes virus family that may cause serious disease in patients whose immune systems are compromised. Abbreviation: CMV

cytoplasm (ˈsaɪtəʊˌplæzəm) *n* the protoplasm of a cell contained within the cell membrane but excluding the nucleus: contains organelles, vesicles, and other inclusions > ˌcytoˈplasmic *adj*

cytosine (ˈsaɪtəsɪn) *n* a white crystalline pyrimidine occurring in nucleic acids; 6-amino-2-hydroxy pyrimidine. Formula: $C_4H_5N_3O$

cytotoxic (ˌsaɪtəˈtɒksɪk) *adj* poisonous to living cells: denoting certain drugs used in the treatment of leukaemia and other cancers > cytotoxicity (ˌsaɪtəʊtɒkˈsɪsɪtɪ) *n*

cytotoxin (ˌsaɪtəʊˈtɒksɪn) *n* any substance that is poisonous to living cells

Cyzicus (ˈsɪzɪkəs) *n* an ancient Greek colony in NW Asia Minor on the S shore of the Sea of Marmara: site of Alcibiades' naval victory over the Peloponnesians (410 BC)

czar (zɑː) *n* a variant spelling (esp US) of **tsar** > ˈczardom *n*

czardas (ˈtʃɑːdæʃ) *n* 1 a Hungarian national dance of alternating slow and fast sections 2 a piece of music composed for or in the rhythm of this dance [from Hungarian *csárdás*]

Czech (tʃɛk) *adj* 1 **a** of, relating to, or characteristic of the Czech Republic, its people, or its language **b** of, relating to, or characteristic of Bohemia and Moravia, their people, or their language **c** (loosely) of, relating to, or characteristic of the former Czechoslovakia or its people ▷ *n* 2 the official language of the Czech Republic, belonging to the West Slavonic branch of the Indo-European family; also spoken in Slovakia. Czech and Slovak are closely related and mutually intelligible 3 **a** a native or inhabitant of the Czech Republic **b** a native or inhabitant of Bohemia or Moravia **c** (loosely) a native, inhabitant, or citizen of the former Czechoslovakia [C19: from Polish, from Czech *Čech*]

Czechoslovak (ˌtʃɛkəʊˈsləʊvæk) *adj* 1 of, relating to, or characteristic of the former Czechoslovakia, its peoples, or their languages ▷ *n* 2 (loosely) either of the two mutually intelligible languages of the former Czechoslovakia; Czech or Slovak

Czechoslovakia (ˌtʃɛkəʊsləʊˈvækɪə) *n* a former republic in central Europe: formed after the defeat of Austria-Hungary (1918) as a nation of Czechs in Bohemia and Moravia and Slovaks in Slovakia; occupied by Germany from 1939 until its liberation by the Soviet Union in 1945; became a people's republic under the Communists in 1948; invaded by Warsaw Pact troops in 1968, ending Dubček's attempt to liberalize communism; in 1989 popular unrest led to the resignation of the politburo and the formation of a non-Communist government. It consisted of two federal republics, the Czech Republic and Slovakia, which separated in 1993. Czech name: Československo. See also **Czech Republic, Slovakia**

Czechoslovakian (ˌtʃɛkəʊsləʊˈvækɪən) *adj* 1 of, relating to, or characteristic of the former republic of Czechoslovakia, its peoples, or their languages ▷ *n* 2 a native or inhabitant of the former republic of Czechoslovakia

Czech Republic *n* a country in central Europe; formed part of Czechoslovakia until 1993; mostly wooded, with lowlands surrounding the River Morava, rising to the Bohemian plateau in the W and to highlands in the N; joined the EU in 2004. Language: Czech. Religion: Christian majority. Currency: koruna. Capital Prague. Pop: 10 226 000 (2004 est). Area: 78 864 sq km (30 450 sq miles)

Czernowitz (ˈtʃɛrnovɪts) *n* the German name for **Chernovtsy**

Czerny (*German* ˈtʃɛrni) *n* **Karl** (karl). 1791–1857, Austrian pianist, composer, and teacher, noted for his studies

Częstochowa (*Polish* tʃɛ̃stɔˈxɔva) *n* an industrial city in S Poland, on the River Warta: pilgrimage centre. Pop: 293 000 (2005 est)

Dd

d¹ *or* **D** (diː) *n, pl* d's, D's *or* Ds the fourth letter and third consonant of the modern English alphabet

d² *physics symbol for* density *or* relative density

D *symbol for* **1** *music* **a** a note having a frequency of 293.66 hertz (**D above middle C**) or this value multiplied or divided by any power of 2; the second note of the scale of C major **b** a key, string, or pipe producing this note **c** the major or minor key having this note as its tonic **2** *chem* deuterium **3 a** a semiskilled or unskilled manual worker, or a trainee or apprentice to a skilled worker **b** (*as modifier*): D worker. See also **occupation groupings 4** *the Roman numeral for* 500

2,4-D *n* a synthetic auxin widely used as a weedkiller; 2,4-dichlorophenoxyacetic acid

d. *abbreviation* **1** (in animal pedigrees) dam **2** daughter **3** *Brit currency* penny *or* pennies [Latin *denarius*] **4** diameter **5** died **6** dinar(s) **7** dollar(s) **8** drachma(s)

D. *abbreviation* **1** *US politics* Democrat(ic) **2** government Department **3** Duchess

'd *contraction of* would *or* had: I'd; you'd

DA *abbreviation* **1** (in the US) District Attorney **2** Diploma of Art **3** duck's arse (hairstyle)

dab¹ (dæb) *vb* dabs, dabbing, dabbed **1** to touch lightly and quickly **2** (*tr*) to daub with short tapping strokes: *to dab the wall with paint* **3** (*tr*) to apply (paint, cream, etc) with short tapping strokes ▷ *n* **4** a small amount, esp of something soft or moist **5** a small light stroke or tap, as with the hand **6** (*often plural*) *chiefly Brit* a slang word for: **fingerprint** [c14: of imitative origin] >'**dabber** *n*

dab² (dæb) *n* **1** a small common European brown flatfish, *Limanda limanda*, covered with rough toothed scales: family *Pleuronectidae*: a food fish **2** (*often plural*) any of various other small flatfish, esp flounders [c15: from Anglo-French *dabbe*, of uncertain origin]

DAB *abbreviation* digital audio broadcasting

dabba ('dæbə) *n* (in Indian cookery) a round metal box used to transport hot food, either from home or from a restaurant, to a person's place of work [c20: from Hindi: lunchbox]

dabble ('dæb³l) *vb* **1** to dip, move, or splash (the fingers, feet, etc) in a liquid **2** (*intr*; usually foll by *in*, *with*, or *at*) to deal (with) or work (at) frivolously or superficially; play

(at) **3** (*tr*) to daub, mottle, splash, or smear: *his face was dabbled with paint* [c16: probably from Dutch *dabbelen*; see DAB¹] >'**dabbler** *n*

dabchick ('dæb,tʃɪk) *n* any of several small grebes of the genera *Podiceps* and *Podilymbus*, such as *Podiceps ruficollis* of the Old World [c16: probably from Old English *dop* to dive + CHICK; see DEEP, DIP]

dab hand *n Brit informal* a person who is particularly skilled at something; expert: *a dab hand at chess*

da capo (dɑː 'kɑːpəʊ) *adj, adv music* to be repeated (in whole or part) from the beginning [c18: from Italian, literally: from the head]

Dacca ('dækə) *n* the former name (until 1982) of **Dhaka**

dace (deɪs) *n, pl* dace *or* daces **1 a** a European freshwater cyprinid fish, *Leuciscus leuciscus*, with a slender bluish-green body **2** any of various similar fishes [c15: from Old French *dars* DART, probably referring to its swiftness]

dacha *or* **datcha** ('dætʃə) *n* a country house or cottage in Russia [from Russian: a giving, gift]

Dachau (German 'daxau) *n* a town in S Germany, in Bavaria: site of a Nazi concentration camp. Pop: 39 474 (2003 est)

dachshund ('dæks,hʊnd; German 'dakshʊnt) *n* a long-bodied short-legged breed of dog [c19: from German, from *Dachs* badger + *Hund* dog, HOUND¹]

Dacia ('deɪsɪə) *n* an ancient region bounded by the Carpathians, the Tisza, and the Danube, roughly corresponding to modern Romania. United under kings from about 60 BC, it later contained the Roman province of the same name (about 105 to 270 AD) >'**Dacian** *adj, n*

dacks (dæks) *pl n Austral* another word for **daks**

dacoit (də'kɔɪt) *n* (in India and Myanmar) a member of a gang of armed robbers [c19: from Hindi *dakait*, from *dākā* robbery]

Dacron ('deɪkrɒn, 'dæk-) *n* the US name (trademark) for **Terylene**

dactyl ('dæktɪl) *n* Also called: **dactylic** *prosody* a metrical foot of three syllables, one long followed by two short (---) [c14: via Latin from Greek *daktulos* finger, dactyl, comparing the finger's three joints to the three syllables]

dactylic (dæk'tɪlɪk) *adj* **1** of, relating to, or having a dactyl: *dactylic verse* ▷ *n* **2** a variant of **dactyl** (sense 1) > dac'tylically *adv*

dad (dæd) *n* an informal word for **father** [c16: childish word; compare Greek *tata*, Sanskrit *tatas*]

Dada ('dɑːdɑː) *or* **Dadaism** ('dɑːdɑːˌɪzəm) *n* a nihilistic artistic movement of the early 20th century in W Europe and the US, founded on principles of irrationality, incongruity, and irreverence towards accepted aesthetic criteria [c20: from French, from a children's word for hobbyhorse, the name being arbitrarily chosen] > 'Dadaist *n*, *adj* ‚ Dada'istic *adj*

Dadd (dæd) *n* **Richard**. 1817–86, British painter of mythological and fairy scenes. He was committed to an asylum for patricide

daddy ('dædɪ) *n*, *pl* -dies **1** an informal word for **father** **2** the daddy *slang, chiefly US, Canadian & Austral* the supreme or finest example: *the daddy of them all*

daddy-longlegs *n* **1** *Brit* an informal name for a **crane fly** **2** *Austral, US & Canadian* an informal name for **harvestman** (sense 2)

dado ('deɪdəʊ) *n*, *pl* -does *or* -dos **1** the lower part of an interior wall that is decorated differently from the upper part **2** *architect* the part of a pedestal between the base and the cornice ▷ *vb* **3** (*tr*) to provide with a dado [c17: from Italian: die, die-shaped pedestal, perhaps from Arabic *dad* game]

Dadra and Nagar Haveli (dəˈdrɑː ˈnʌɡər əˈvɛlɪ) *n* a union territory of W India, on the Gulf of Cambay: until 1961 administratively part of Portuguese Damão. Capital: Silvassa. Pop: 220 451 (2001). Area: 489 sq km (191 sq miles)

Daedalus ('diːdələs) *n Greek myth* an Athenian architect and inventor who built the labyrinth for Minos on Crete and fashioned wings for himself and his son Icarus to flee the island > Daedalian, Daedalean, (dɪˈdeɪlɪən) *or* Daedalic (dɪˈdælɪk) *adj*

daemon ('diːmən) *or* **daimon** *n* **1** a demigod **2** the guardian spirit of a place or person **3** a variant spelling of **demon** (sense 3) > daemonic (diːˈmɒnɪk) *adj*

daff (dæf) *n informal* short for **daffodil**

daffodil ('dæfədɪl) *n* **1** Also called: Lent lily a widely cultivated Eurasian amaryllidaceous plant, *Narcissus pseudonarcissus*, having spring-blooming yellow flowers **2** any other plant of the genus *Narcissus* **3** a a brilliant yellow colour **b** (*as adjective*): *daffodil paint* **4** a daffodil, or a representation of one, as a national emblem of Wales [c14: from Dutch *de affodil* the asphodel, from Medieval Latin *affodillus*, variant of Latin *asphodelus* ASPHODEL]

daffy ('dæfɪ) *adj* daffier, daffiest *informal* another word for **daft** (senses 1, 2) [c19: from obsolete *daff* fool; see DAFT]

daft (dɑːft) *adj chiefly Brit* **1** *informal* foolish, simple, or stupid **2** a slang word for **insane** **3** *informal* (*postpositive; foll by about*) extremely fond (of) **4** *slang* frivolous; giddy [Old English *gedæfte* gentle, foolish; related to Middle Low German *ondaft* incapable] > 'daftness *n*

Dafydd ap Gruffudd (*Welsh* ˈdævɪθ æp ˈɡrɪfɪθ) *n* died 1283, Welsh leader. Claiming the title Prince of Wales (1282), he led an unsuccessful revolt against Edward I: executed

Dafydd ap Gwilym (*Welsh* ˈdævɪθ æp ˈɡwɪlɪm) *n* ?1320–?1380, Welsh poet

dag¹ (dæɡ) *n* **1** short for **daglock 2** rattle one's dags *NZ informal* to hurry up ▷ *vb* **3** dags, dagging, dagged **3** to cut the daglock away from (a sheep) [c18: of obscure origin] > 'dagger *n*

dag² (dæɡ) *n Austral & NZ informal* **1** a character; eccentric **2** a person who is untidily dressed **3** a person with a good sense of humour [back formation from DAGGY]

Da Gama (də ˈɡɑːmə) *n* See **Gama**

Dagan ('dɑːɡən) *n* an earth god of the Babylonians and Assyrians

Dagenham ('dæɡənəm) *n* part of the Greater London borough of Barking and Dagenham: engineering and chemicals

Dagestan Republic (ˌdɑːɡɪˈstɑːn) *n* a constituent republic of S Russia, on the Caspian Sea: annexed from Persia in 1813; rich mineral resources. Capital: Makhachkala. Pop: 2 584 200 (2002). Area: 50 278 sq km

(19 416 sq miles). Also called: Dagestan, Daghestan

dagga ('dæxə, 'dɑːɡə) *n South African informal* a local name for **marijuana** [c19: from Afrikaans, from Khoikhoi *dagab*]

dagger ('dæɡə) *n* **1** a short stabbing weapon with a pointed blade **2** Also called: obelisk a character (†) used in printing to indicate a cross reference, esp to a footnote **3** at daggers drawn in a state of open hostility **4** look daggers to glare with hostility; scowl [c14: of uncertain origin]

daggy ('dæɡɪ) *Austral & NZ informal adj* daggier, daggiest **1** untidy; dishevelled **2** eccentric [from DAG²]

daglock ('dæɡˌlɒk) *n* a dung-caked lock of wool around the hindquarters of a sheep [c17: see DAG¹, LOCK²]

dago ('deɪɡəʊ) *n*, *pl* -gos *or* -goes *derogatory* a member of a Latin race, esp a Spaniard or Portuguese [c19: alteration of *Diego*, a common Spanish name]

Dagon ('deɪɡɒn) *n Bible* a god worshipped by the Philistines, represented as half man and half fish [c14: via Latin and Greek from Hebrew *Dāgōn*, literally: little fish]

Daguerre (*French* daɡɛr) *n* **Louis Jacques Mandé** (lwi ʒak māde). 1789–1851, French inventor, who devised one of the first practical photographic processes (1838)

daguerreotype (dəˈɡɛrəʊˌtaɪp) *n* **1** one of the earliest photographic processes, in which the image was produced on iodine-sensitized silver and developed in mercury vapour **2** a photograph formed by this process > da'guerreo‚typy *n*

Dahl (dɑːl) *n* **Roald** ('rəʊəld). 1916–90, British writer with Norwegian parents, noted for his short stories and such children's books as *Charlie and the Chocolate Factory* (1964)

dahlia ('deɪljə) *n* **1** any herbaceous perennial plant of the Mexican genus *Dahlia*, having showy flowers and tuberous roots, esp any horticultural variety derived from *D. pinnata*: family *Asteraceae* (composites) **2** the flower or root of any of these plants [c19: named after Anders Dahl, 18th-century Swedish botanist; see -IA]

Dahna ('dɑːxnɑː) *n* a desert area in central Saudi Arabia, to the N of the Rub' al Khali (Empty Quarter)

Dahomey (dəˈhəʊmɪ) *n* the former name (until 1975) of **Benin**

Dáil Éireann ('dɑːl 'eːrɪn) *or* **Dáil** *n* (in the Republic of Ireland) the lower chamber of parliament [from Irish *dáil* assembly (from Old Irish *dāl*) + *Éireann* of Eire]

daily ('deɪlɪ) *adj* **1** of or occurring every day or every weekday ▷ *n*, *pl* -lies **2** a daily publication, esp a newspaper **3** Also called: daily help *Brit* another name for a **charwoman** ▷ *adv* **4** every day **5** constantly; often [Old English *dæglīc*; see DAY, -LY¹]

Daimler ('deɪmlə) *n* **Gottlieb** (**Wilhelm**) (*German* ˈɡɔtliːp ˈvɪlhɛlm). 1834–1900, German engineer and car manufacturer, who collaborated with Nikolaus Otto in inventing the first internal-combustion engine (1876)

daimon ('daɪmɒn) *n* a variant of **daemon** or **demon** (sense 3) > dai'monic *adj*

daimyo bond ('daɪmjəʊ) *n* a bearer bond issued in Japan and the eurobond market by the World Bank [c20: Japanese *daimyo* magnate]

dainty ('deɪntɪ) *adj* -tier, -tiest **1** delicate or elegant: *a dainty teacup* **2** pleasing to the taste; choice; delicious: *a dainty morsel* **3** refined, esp excessively genteel; fastidious ▷ *n*, *pl* -ties **4** a choice piece of food, esp a small cake or sweet; delicacy [c13: from Old French *deintié*, from Latin *dignitās* DIGNITY] > 'daintily *adv*

daiquiri ('daɪkɪrɪ, 'dæk-) *n*, *pl* -ris an iced drink containing rum, lime juice, and syrup or sugar [c20: named after *Daiquiri*, rum-producing town in Cuba]

dairy ('dɛərɪ) *n*, *pl* dairies **1** a company that supplies milk and milk products **2** a a shop that sells provisions, esp milk and milk products **b** *NZ* a shop that remains open outside normal trading hours **3** a room or building where milk and cream are stored or made into butter and cheese **4** a (*modifier*) of or relating to the production of milk and milk products: *dairy cattle* **b** (*in combination*): *a dairymaid; a dairyman* **5** food containing milk or milk products: *she can't eat dairy* [c13 *daierie*, from Old English *dæge* servant girl, one who kneads bread; see DOUGH, LADY]

dairying ('dɛərɪɪŋ) *n* the business of producing, processing, and selling dairy products

dairyman ('dɛərɪmən) *n, pl* **-men** a man who works in a dairy or deals in dairy products

dais ('deɪɪs, deɪs) *n* a raised platform, usually at one end of a hall, used by speakers, etc [c13: from Old French *deis*, from Latin *discus* DISCUS]

daisy ('deɪzɪ) *n, pl* **-sies** 1 a small low-growing European plant, *Bellis perennis*, having a rosette of leaves and flower heads of yellow central disc flowers and pinkish-white outer ray flowers: family *Asteraceae* (composites) 2 any of various other composite plants having conspicuous ray flowers, such as the Michaelmas daisy and Shasta daisy 3 *slang* an excellent person or thing 4 pushing up the daisies dead and buried [Old English *dægesēge* day's eye] > 'daisied *adj*

daisy bush *n* any of various shrubs of the genus *Olearia*, of Australia and New Zealand, with daisy-like flowers: family *Asteraceae* (composites)

daisy chain *n* a garland made, esp by children, by threading daisies together

daisy cutter *n* 1 *soccer* a powerful shot that moves close to the ground 2 *cricket* a ball bowled, kicked, or hit so that it rolls along the ground

daisywheel ('deɪzɪ,wiːl) *n computing* a component of a computer printer in the shape of a wheel with many spokes that prints characters using a disk with characters around the circumference as the print element. Also called: printwheel

Dak. *abbreviation* Dakota

Dakar ('dækə) *n* the capital and chief port of Senegal, on the SE side of Cape Verde peninsula. Pop: 2 313 000 (2005 est)

Dakota (də'kəutə) *n* a former territory of the US: divided into the states of North Dakota and South Dakota in 1889

Dakotan (də'kəutən) *adj* 1 of or relating to Dakota or its inhabitants ▷ *n* 2 a native or inhabitant of Dakota

daks *or* **dacks** (dæks) *pl n Austral* an informal name for trousers [from a brand name]

dal (dɑːl) *n* 1 split grain, a common foodstuff in India; pulse 2 a variant spelling of **dhal**

Daladier (French daladje) *n* **Édouard** (edwar). 1884–1970, French radical socialist statesman; premier of France (1933; 1934; 1938–40) and signatory of the Munich Pact (1938)

Dalai Lama ('dælaɪ 'lɑːmə) *n* 1 (until 1959) the chief lama and ruler of Tibet 2 born 1935, the 14th holder of this office (1940), who fled to India (1959): Nobel peace prize 1989 [from Mongolian *dalai* ocean; see LAMA]

dale (deɪl) *n* an open valley, usually in an area of low hills [Old English *dæl*; related to Old Frisian *del*, Old Norse *dalr*, Old High German *tal* valley]

Dale (deɪl) *n* Sir **Henry Hallet**. 1875–1968, English physiologist: shared a Nobel prize for physiology or medicine in 1936 with Otto Loewi for their work on the chemical transmission of nerve impulses

Dalek ('dɑːlɛk) *n* any of a set of fictional robot-like creations that are aggressive and mobile and produce rasping staccato speech [c20: from a children's television series, *Dr Who*]

d'Alembert (French dalɑ̃bɛr) *n* **Jean Le Rond** (ʒɑ̃ lə rɔ̃). 1717–83, French mathematician, physicist, and rationalist philosopher, noted for his contribution to Newtonian physics in *Traité de dynamique* (1743) and for his collaboration with Diderot in editing the *Encyclopédie*

Dalén (da'leːn) *n* **Nils Gustaf**. 1869–1937, Swedish engineer, inventor of an automatic light-controlled valve known as 'Solventil'. Nobel prize for physics 1912

Dales (deɪlz) *pl n* **the Dales** (*sometimes not capital*) short for the **Yorkshire Dales**

dalesman ('deɪlzmən) *n, pl* **-men** a person living in a dale, esp in the dales of N England

Dalglish (dæl'gliːʃ, dəl-) *n* **Kenny**, born 1951, Scottish footballer: a striker, he played for Celtic (1968–77) and for Liverpool (1977–89): manager of Liverpool (1985–91), of Blackburn Rovers (1991–95), and of Newcastle United (1997–98): Scotland's most-capped footballer

Dalhousie (dæl'hauzɪ) *n* 1 **9th Earl of**, title of George

Ramsay. 1770–1838, British general; governor of the British colonies in Canada (1819–28) 2 his son, **1st Marquis and 10th Earl of**, title of *James Andrew Broun Ramsay*. 1812–60, British statesman: governor general of India (1848– 56)

Dali ('dɑːlɪ; *Spanish* da'li:) *n* **Salvador** ('sælvədɔ:). 1904–89, Spanish surrealist painter

Dalian (dɑː'lɪjɛn) *or* **Talien** (tɑː'lɪjɛn) *n* a city in NE China, at the end of the Liaodong Peninsula: with the adjoining city of Lüshun comprises the port complex of Lüda. Pop: 2 709 000 (2005 est)

Dalit ('dɑːlɪt) *n* a member of the lowest class in India, whom those of the four main castes were formerly forbidden to touch. Formerly called: untouchable [from Hindi, from Sanskrit *dalita*, literally: oppressed]

Dallapiccola (*Italian* dalla'pikkola) *n* **Luigi** (luˈiːdʒi). 1904–75, Italian composer of twelve-tone music. His works include the opera *Il Prigioniero* (1944–48) and the ballet *Marsia* (1948)

Dallas ('dæləs) *n* a city in NE Texas, on the Trinity River: scene of the assassination of President John F. Kennedy (1963). Pop: 1 208 318 (2003 est)

dalles ('dæləs, dælz) *pl n Canadian* a stretch of a river between high rock walls, with rapids and dangerous currents [from Canadian French, from French (Normandy dialect): sink; compare DALE]

dalliance ('dælɪəns) *n* waste of time in frivolous action or in dawdling

dally ('dælɪ) *vb* **-lies, -lying, -lied** (*intr*) 1 to waste time idly; dawdle 2 (usually foll by *with*) to deal frivolously or lightly with; trifle; toy: *to dally with someone's affections* [c14: from Anglo-French *dalier* to gossip, of uncertain origin]

Dalmatia (dæl'meɪʃə) *n* a region of W Croatia along the Adriatic: mountainous, with many offshore islands

Dalmatian (dæl'meɪʃən) *n* 1 a large breed of dog having a short smooth white coat with black or (in liver-spotted dalmatians) brown spots 2 a native or inhabitant of Dalmatia ▷ *adj* 3 of or relating to Dalmatia or its inhabitants

dalmatic (dæl'mætɪk) *n* a wide-sleeved tunic-like vestment open at the sides, worn by deacons and bishops [c15: from Late Latin *dalmatica* (*vestis*) Dalmatian (robe) (originally made of Dalmatian wool)]

dal segno ('dæl 'sɛnjəu) *adj, adv music* (of a piece of music) to be repeated from the point marked with a sign to the word *fine* [Italian, literally: from the sign]

dalton ('dɔːltən) *n* another name for **atomic mass unit** [c20: named after John Dalton (1766–1844), English chemist and physicist]

Dalton ('dɔːltən) *n* **John**. 1766–1844, English chemist and physicist, who formulated the modern form of the atomic theory and the law of partial pressures for gases. He also gave the first accurate description of colour blindness, from which he suffered

daltonism ('dɔːltə,nɪzəm) *n* colour blindness, esp the confusion of red and green [c19: from French *daltonisme*, after John Dalton (1766–1844), English chemist and physicist]

Dalton's atomic theory ('dɔːltənz) *n chem* the theory that matter consists of indivisible particles called atoms and that atoms of a given element are all identical and can neither be created nor destroyed. Compounds are formed by combination of atoms in simple ratios to give compound atoms (molecules). The theory was the basis of modern chemistry [c19: named after John Dalton (1766–1844), English chemist and physicist]

dam¹ (dæm) *n* 1 a barrier of concrete, earth, etc, built across a river to create a body of water for a hydroelectric power station, domestic water supply, etc 2 a reservoir of water created by such a barrier 3 something that resembles or functions as a dam ▷ *vb* dams, damming, dammed 4 (*tr*; often foll by *up*) to obstruct or restrict by or as if by a dam [c12: probably from Middle Low German; compare Old Icelandic *damma* to block up]

dam² (dæm) *n* the female parent of an animal, esp of domestic livestock [c13: variant of DAME]

Dam (*Danish* dam) *n* (**Carl Peter**) **Henrik** ('hɛnrəg). 1895–1976, Danish biochemist who discovered vitamin K

(1934): Nobel prize for physiology or medicine 1943

damage ('dæmɪdʒ) *n* **1** injury or harm impairing the function or condition of a person or thing **2** loss of something desirable **3** *informal* cost; expense (esp in the phrase **what's the damage?**) ▷ *vb* **4** (*tr*) to cause damage to **5** (*intr*) to suffer damage [c14: from Old French, from Latin *damnum* injury, loss, fine] >'**damaging** *adj*

damaged goods *n informal* **1** a person considered to be less than perfect psychologically, as a result of a traumatic experience **2** a person, esp a public figure, whose reputation has been damaged

damages ('dæmɪdʒɪz) *pl n law* money to be paid as compensation to a person for injury, loss, etc

Daman (dɑːˈmɑːn) *n* a coastal town in W India, the chief town of Daman and Diu. Pop: 35 743 (2001)

Daman and Diu (dɑːˈmɑːn ˈdiːuː) *n* a union territory in W India: formerly a district of Portuguese India (1559–1961) then part of the union territory of Goa, Daman, and Diu (1961–87). Area: 112 sq km (43 sq miles). Pop: 158 059 (2001)

damascene ('dæməˌsiːn, ˌdæməˈsiːn) *vb* **1** (*tr*) to ornament (metal, esp steel) by etching or by inlaying, usually with gold or silver ▷ *n* **2** a design or article produced by this process ▷ *adj* **3** of or relating to this process [c14: from Latin *damascēnus* of Damascus]

Damascene ('dæməˌsiːn, ˌdæməˈsiːn) *adj* **1** of or relating to Damascus ▷ *n* **2** a native or inhabitant of Damascus

Damascus (dəˈmɑːskəs, -ˈmæs-) *n* the capital of Syria, in the southwest: reputedly the oldest city in the world, having been inhabited continuously since before 2000 BC Pop: 2 317 000 (2005 est). Arabic name: Dimashq

Damascus steel *or* **damask steel** *n history* a hard flexible steel with wavy markings caused by forging the metal in strips: used for sword blades

damask ('dæməsk) *n* **1 a** a reversible fabric, usually silk or linen, with a pattern woven into it. It is used for table linen, curtains, etc **b** table linen made from this **c** (*as modifier*): *a damask tablecloth* **2** short for **Damascus steel** **3** the wavy markings on such steel **4 a** the greyish-pink colour of the damask rose **b** (*as adjective*): *damask wallpaper* ▷ *vb* **5** (*tr*) another word for **damascene** (sense 1) [c14: from Medieval Latin *damascus*, from Damascus, where this fabric was originally made]

damask rose *n* a rose, *Rosa damascena*, native to Asia and cultivated for its pink or red fragrant flowers, which are used to make the perfume attar [c16: from Medieval Latin *rosa damascēna* rose of Damascus]

dame (deɪm) *n* **1** (formerly) a woman of rank or dignity; lady **2** *archaic, chiefly Brit* a matronly or elderly woman **3** *slang, chiefly US & Canadian* a woman **4** Also called: **pantomime dame** *Brit* the role of a comic old woman in a pantomime, usually played by a man [c13: from Old French, from Latin *domina* lady, mistress of a household]

Dame (deɪm) *n* (in Britain) **1** the title of a woman who has been awarded the Order of the British Empire or any of certain other orders of chivalry **2** the legal title of the wife or widow of a knight or baronet, placed before her name

dame school *n* (formerly) a small school, often in a village, usually run by an elderly woman in her own home to teach young children to read and write

Damien (French damjɛ̃) *n* **Joseph** (ʒozɛf), known as *Father Damien*. 1840–89, Belgian Roman Catholic missionary to the leper colony at Molokai, Hawaii

damn (dæm) *interj* **1** *slang* an exclamation of annoyance (often in exclamatory phrases such as **damn it! damn you!** etc) **2** *informal* an exclamation of surprise or pleasure (esp in the exclamatory phrase **damn me!**) ▷ *adj* **3** (*prenominal*) *slang* deserving damnation; detestable ▷ *adv, adj* (*prenominal*) **4** *slang* (intensifier): *damn fool; a damn good pianist* ▷ *adv* **5** **damn all** *slang* absolutely nothing ▷ *vb* (mainly *tr*) **6** to condemn as bad, worthless, etc **7** to curse **8** to condemn to eternal damnation **9** (*often passive*) to doom to ruin; cause to fail: *the venture was damned from the start* **10** (also *intr*) to prove (someone) guilty: *damning evidence* **11 damn with faint praise** to praise so unenthusiastically that the effect is condemnation ▷ *n* **12** *slang* something of negligible value; jot (esp in the phrase **not worth a damn**) **13 not**

give a damn *informal* to be unconcerned; not care [c13: from Old French *dampner*, from Latin *damnāre* to injure, condemn, from *damnum* loss, injury, penalty]

damnable ('dæmnəbªl) *adj* **1** execrable; detestable **2** liable to or deserving damnation >'**damnableness** *or* ˌdamna'bility *n*

damnably ('dæmnəblɪ) *adv* **1** in a detestable manner **2** (intensifier): *it was damnably unfair*

damnation (dæmˈneɪʃən) *n* **1** the act of damning or state of being damned ▷ *interj* **2** an exclamation of anger, disappointment, etc

damnatory ('dæmnətərɪ, -trɪ) *adj* threatening or occasioning condemnation

damned (dæmd) *adj* **1 a** condemned to hell **b** (*as noun*): *the damned* ▷ *adv, adj slang* **2** (intensifier): *a damned good try; a damned liar; I should damned well think so!* **3** used to indicate amazement, disavowal, or refusal (in such phrases as **I'll be damned** and **damned if I care**)

damnedest ('dæmdɪst) *n informal* utmost; best (esp in the phrases **do** or **try one's damnedest**)

damnify ('dæmnɪˌfaɪ) *vb* **-fies, -fying, -fied** (*tr*) *law* to cause loss or damage to (a person); injure [c16: from Old French *damnifier*, ultimately from Latin *damnum* harm, + *facere* to make] >ˌdamnifi'cation *n*

Damocles ('dæməˌkliːz) *n classical legend* a sycophant forced by Dionysius, tyrant of Syracuse, to sit under a sword suspended by a hair to demonstrate that being a king was not the happy state Damocles had said it was. See also **Sword of Damocles** >ˌDamo'clean *adj*

Damodar ('dæməˌdɑː) *n* a river in NE India, rising in Jharkhand and flowing east through West Bengal to the Hooghly River: the **Damodar Valley** is an important centre of heavy industry

damoiselle, damosel *or* **damozel** (ˌdæməˈzɛl) *n* archaic variants of **damsel**

Damon ('deɪmən) *n* **Matt.** born 1970, US film actor and screenwriter. His films include *Good Will Hunting* (1997, which he co-wrote), *Saving Private Ryan* (1998), *The Talented Mr Ripley* (1999), and the 'Bourne' series (2002–07)

damp (dæmp) *adj* **1** slightly wet, as from dew, steam, etc ▷ *n* **2** slight wetness; moisture; humidity **3** rank air or poisonous gas, esp in a mine **4** a discouragement; damper ▷ *vb* (*tr*) **5** to make slightly wet **6** (often foll by *down*) to stifle or deaden: *to damp one's ardour* **7** (often foll by *down*) to reduce the flow of air to (a fire) to make it burn more slowly or to extinguish it **8** *physics* to reduce the amplitude of (an oscillation or wave) **9** *music* to muffle (the sound of an instrument) [c14: from Middle Low German *damp* steam; related to Old High German *demphen* to cause to steam] >'**dampness** *n*

dampcourse ('dæmpˌkɔːs) *n* a horizontal layer of impervious material in a brick wall, fairly close to the ground, to stop moisture rising. Also called: **damp-proof course**

dampen ('dæmpən) *vb* **1** to make or become damp **2** (*tr*) to stifle; deaden >'**dampener** *n*

damper ('dæmpə) *n* **1** a person, event, or circumstance that depresses or discourages **2 put a damper on** to produce a depressing or inhibiting effect on: *the bad news put a damper on the party* **3** a movable plate to regulate the draught in a stove or furnace flue **4** a device to reduce electronic, mechanical, acoustic, or aerodynamic oscillations in a system **5** *music* the pad in a piano or harpsichord that deadens the vibration of each string as its key is released **6** *chiefly Austral & NZ* any of various unleavened loaves and scones, typically cooked on an open fire

Dampier ('dæmpɪə) *n* **William**. 1652–1715, English navigator, pirate, and writer: sailed round the world twice

damping off *n* any of various diseases of plants, esp the collapse and death of seedlings caused by the parasitic fungus *Pythium debaryanum* and related fungi in conditions of excessive moisture

damp-proof *building trades* ▷ *vb* **1** to protect against the incursion of damp by adding a dampcourse or by coating with a moisture-resistant preparation ▷ *adj* **2** protected against damp or causing protection against damp: *a damp-proof course*

damsel ('dæmzᵊl) n *archaic or poetic* a young unmarried woman; maiden [c13: from Old French *damoisele*, from Vulgar Latin *domnicella* (unattested) young lady, from Latin *domina* mistress; see DAME]

damselfly ('dæmzᵊl,flaɪ) n, *pl* -**flies** any insect of the suborder *Zygoptera* similar to but smaller than dragonflies and usually resting with the wings closed over the back: order *Odonata*

damson ('dæmzən) n **1** a small rosaceous tree, *Prunus domestica instititia* (or *P. instititia*), cultivated for its blue-black edible plumlike fruit and probably derived from the bullace. See also **plum¹** (sense 1) **2** the fruit of this tree [c14: from Latin *prūnum Damascēnum* Damascus plum]

dan (dæn) n *martial arts* **1** any one of the 10 black-belt grades of proficiency **2** a competitor entitled to dan grading [Japanese]

Dan (dæn) n *Old Testament* **1 a** the fourth son of Jacob (Genesis 30:1–6) **b** the tribe descended from him **2** a city in the northern territory of Canaan

Dan. *abbreviation* **1** *Bible* Daniel **2** Danish

Dana ('deɪnə) n **James Dwight** (dwaɪt). 1813–95, American geologist; noted for his work *The System of Mineralogy* (1837)

Danaë ('dæneɪ,iː) n *Greek myth* the mother of Perseus by Zeus, who came to her in prison as a shower of gold

Danaides (də'neɪɪ,diːz) *pl* n, *sing* **Danaid** *Greek myth* the fifty daughters of Danaüs. All but Hypermnestra murdered their bridegrooms and were punished in Hades by having to pour water perpetually into a jar with a hole in the bottom > **Danaidean** (,dænɪ'ɪdɪən, ,dænɪə'diːən) *adj*

Da Nang ('dɑː 'næŋ) n a port in central Vietnam, on the South China Sea. Pop: 448 000 (2005 est). Former name: Tourane

Danaüs ('dænɪəs) n *Greek myth* a king of Argos who told his fifty daughters, the Danaides, to kill their bridegrooms on their wedding night

Danby ('dænbɪ) n **1** Also called: **1st Duke of Leeds 1st Earl of**, title of *Thomas Osborne*. 1631–1712, English politician; Lord Treasurer (1673–78): regarded as the founder of the Tory party **2 Francis**. 1793–1861, Irish painter of romantic landscapes and historical subjects

dance (dɑːns) vb **1** (*intr*) to move the feet and body rhythmically, esp in time to music **2** (*tr*) to perform (a particular dance) **3** (*intr*) to skip or leap, as in joy, etc **4** to move or cause to move in a light rhythmic way **5 dance attendance on someone** to attend someone solicitously or obsequiously ▷ n **6** a series of rhythmic steps and movements, usually in time to music **7** an act of dancing **8 a** a social meeting arranged for dancing; ball **b** (*as modifier*): *a dance hall* **9** a piece of music in the rhythm of a particular dance form, such as a waltz **10** dancelike movements made by some insects and birds, esp as part of a behaviour pattern **11 lead someone a dance** *Brit informal* to cause someone continued worry and exasperation; play up [c13: from Old French *dancier*] > **'danceable** *adj* > **'dancer** n > **'dancing** n, *adj*

dance floor n **a** an area of floor in a disco, etc, where patrons may dance **b** (*as modifier*): *dance-floor music*

dancehall ('dɑːns,hɔːl) n a style of dance-oriented reggae, originating in the late 1980s

dance of death n a pictorial, literary, or musical representation, current esp in the Middle Ages, of a dance in which living people, in order of social precedence, are led off to their graves, by a personification of death

D and C n *med* dilation and curettage; a therapeutic or diagnostic procedure in obstetrics and gynaecology involving dilation of the cervix and curettage of the cavity of the uterus, as for abortion

dandelion ('dændɪ,laɪən) n **1** a plant, *Taraxacum officinale*, native to Europe and Asia and naturalized as a weed in North America, having yellow rayed flowers and deeply notched basal leaves, which are used for salad or wine: family *Asteraceae* (composites) **2** any of several similar related plants [c15: from Old French *dent de lion*, literally: tooth of a lion, referring to its leaves]

dander ('dændə) n **1** small particles or scales of hair or feathers **2 get one's dander up** *or* **get someone's dander**

up *informal* to become or to cause someone to become annoyed or angry [c19: changed from DANDRUFF]

dandify ('dændɪ,faɪ) vb -**fies**, -**fying**, -**fied** (*tr*) to dress like or cause to resemble a dandy

dandle ('dændᵊl) vb (*tr*) **1** to move (a young child, etc) up and down (on the knee or in the arms) **2** to pet; fondle [c16: of uncertain origin] > **'dandler** n

Dandolo (Italian 'dandolo) n **Enrico**. *c*. 1108–1205, Venetian statesman; doge (1192– 1205). During the fourth Crusade he won Greek colonies for Venice

Dandong ('dæn'dʊŋ) n a port in E China, in Liaoning province at the mouth of the Yalu River. Pop: 730 000 (2005 est). Also called: **Andong**. Former spelling: **Tan-tung**

dandruff ('dændrəf) n loose scales of dry dead skin shed from the scalp [c16: *dand*-, of unknown origin + -*ruff*, probably from Middle English *roufe* scab, from Old Norse *hrūfa*]

dandy ('dændɪ) n, *pl* -**dies 1** a man greatly concerned with smartness of dress; beau ▷ *adj* -**dier**, -**diest 3** *informal* very good or fine [c18: perhaps short for *jack-a-dandy*] > **'dandyish** *adj*

dandy-brush n a stiff brush used for grooming a horse

dandy roll *or* **dandy roller** n a light roller used in the manufacture of certain papers to produce watermarks

Dane (deɪn) n **1** a native, citizen, or inhabitant of Denmark **2** any of the Vikings who invaded England from the late 8th to the 11th century AD

Danegeld ('deɪn,gɛld) *or* **Danegelt** ('deɪn,gɛlt) n the tax first levied in the late 9th century in Anglo-Saxon England to provide protection money for or to finance forces to oppose Viking invaders [c11: from *Dan* Dane + *geld* tribute; see YIELD]

Danelaw *or* **Danelagh** ('deɪn,lɔː) n the northern, central and eastern parts of Anglo-Saxon England in which Danish law and custom were observed [Old English *Dena lagu* Danes' law; term revived in the 19th century]

danger ('deɪndʒə) n **1** the state of being vulnerable to injury, loss, or evil; risk **2** a person or thing that may cause injury, pain, etc **3 in danger of** liable to **4 on the danger list** critically ill in hospital [c13: *daunger* power, hence power to inflict injury, from Old French *dongier* (from Latin *dominium* ownership) blended with Old French *dam* injury, from Latin *damnum*] > **'dangerless** *adj*

danger money n extra money paid to compensate for the risks involved in certain dangerous jobs

dangerous ('deɪndʒərəs) *adj* causing danger; perilous > **'dangerously** *adv*

dangerous offender n *US & Canadian* an offender who is deemed by a court of law to be likely to engage in further violent conduct, and who thus becomes eligible for an indefinite prison sentence

dangle ('dæŋgᵊl) vb **1** to hang or cause to hang freely: *his legs dangled over the wall* **2** (*tr*) to display as an enticement: *the hope of a legacy was dangled before her* [c16: perhaps from Danish *dangle*, probably of imitative origin] > **'dangler** n

Daniel¹ ('dænjəl) n **1** *Old Testament* **a** a youth who was taken into the household of Nebuchadnezzar, received guidance and apocalyptic visions from God, and was given divine protection when thrown into the lions' den **b** the book that recounts these experiences and visions (in full **The Book of the Prophet Daniel**) **2** (often preceded by *a*) a wise upright person [sense 2: referring to Daniel in the Apocryphal *Book of Susanna*]

Daniel² ('dænjəl) n **1 Paul** (**Wilson**). born 1958, British conductor; musical director of the English National Opera 1997–2003 **2 Samuel**. ?1562–1619, English poet and writer: author of the sonnet sequence *Delia* (1592)

Danish ('deɪnɪʃ) *adj* **1** of, relating to, or characteristic of Denmark, its people, or their language ▷ n **2** the official language of Denmark, belonging to the North Germanic branch of the Indo-European family

Danish blue n a strong-tasting white cheese with blue veins

Danish pastry n a rich puff pastry filled with apple, almond paste, icing, etc

Danish West Indies *pl* n the former possession of Denmark in the W Lesser Antilles, sold to the US in 1917. Name since 1917: **Virgin Islands of the United States**

dank (dæŋk) *adj* (esp of cellars, caves, etc) unpleasantly damp and chilly [c14: probably of Scandinavian origin; compare Swedish *dank* marshy spot] >'**dankly** *adv* >'**dankness** *n*

Dankworth ('dæŋkwɜːθ) *n* Sir **John** (**Philip William**). born 1927, British jazz composer, bandleader, and saxophonist: married to Cleo Laine

Danmark ('danmarg) *n* the Danish name for **Denmark**

D'Annunzio (*Italian* dan'nuntsjo) *n* **Gabriele** (ɡa'brjeːle). 1863–1938, Italian poet, dramatist, novelist, national hero, and Fascist. His works include the poems in *Alcione* (1904) and the drama *La Figlia di Iorio* (1904)

Dante ('dæntɪ, 'dɑːnteɪ; *Italian* 'dante) *n* full name **Dante Alighieri** (*Italian* ali'ɡjeːri). 1265–1321, Italian poet famous for *La Divina Commedia* (?1309–?1320), an allegorical account of his journey through Hell, Purgatory, and Paradise, guided by Virgil and his idealized love Beatrice. His other works include *La Vita Nuova* (?1292), in which he celebrates his love for Beatrice >**Dantean** ('dæntɪən, dæn'tiːən) *or* **Dantesque** (dæn'tɛsk) *adj*

Danton ('dæntɒn; *French* dɑ̃tɔ̃) *n* **Georges Jacques** (ʒɔrʒ ʒak). 1759–94, French revolutionary leader: a founder member of the Committee of Public Safety (1793) and minister of justice (1792–94). He was overthrown by Robespierre and guillotined

Danube ('dænjuːb) *n* a river in central and SE Europe, rising in the Black Forest in Germany and flowing to the Black Sea. Length: 2859 km (1776 miles). German name: Donau. Czech name: Dunaj. Hungarian name: Duna. Romanian name: Dunărea

Danubian (dæn'juːbɪən) *adj* of or relating to the river Danube

Danzig ('dænsɪɡ; *German* 'dantsɪç) *n* **1** the German name for **Gdańsk 2** a variety of domestic fancy pigeon originating in this area

dap (dæp) *vb* **daps, dapping, dapped 1** *angling* to fish with a natural or artificial fly on a floss silk line so that the wind makes the fly bob on and off the surface of the water **2** (*intr*) (as of a bird) to dip lightly into water **3** to bounce or cause to bounce [c17: of imitative origin]

daphne ('dæfnɪ) *n* any shrub of the Eurasian thymelaeaceous genus *Daphne*, such as the mezereon and spurge laurel: ornamentals with shiny evergreen leaves and clusters of small bell-shaped flowers. See also **laurel** (sense 3) [via Latin from Greek: laurel]

Daphne ('dæfnɪ) *n* Greek myth a nymph who was saved from the amorous attentions of Apollo by being changed into a laurel tree

daphnia ('dæfnɪə) *n* any water flea of the genus *Daphnia*, having a rounded body enclosed in a transparent shell and bearing branched swimming antennae [c19: from New Latin, probably from **Daphne**]

Daphnis ('dæfnɪs) *n* Greek myth a Sicilian shepherd, the son of Hermes and a nymph, who was regarded as the inventor of pastoral poetry

Da Ponte (*Italian* da 'ponte) *n* **Lorenzo** (lo'rentso), real name *Emmanuele Conegliano* 1749–1838, Italian writer; Mozart's librettist for *The Marriage of Figaro* (1786), *Don Giovanni* (1787), and *Cosi fan tutte* (1790)

dapper ('dæpə) *adj* **1** neat and spruce in dress and bearing; trim **2** small and nimble [c15: from Middle Dutch: active, nimble] >'**dapperly** *adv* >'**dapperness** *n*

dapple ('dæpəl) *vb* **1** to mark or become marked with spots or patches of a different colour; mottle ▷ *n* **2** mottled or spotted markings **3** a dappled horse, etc ▷ *adj* **4** marked with dapples or spots [c14: of unknown origin]

dapple-grey *n* a horse with a grey coat having spots of darker colour

Dapsang (dʌp'sʌŋ) *n* another name for **K2**

darbies ('dɑːbɪz) *pl n* Brit a slang term for **handcuffs** [c16: perhaps from the phrase *Father Derby's* or *Father Darby's bonds*, a rigid agreement between a usurer and his client]

d'Arblay ('dɑːbleɪ) *n* See **Burney** (sense 2)

Darby ('dɑːbɪ) *n* **Abraham**. 1677–1717, British iron manufacturer: built the first coke-fired blast furnace (1709)

Darby and Joan *n* **1** an ideal elderly married couple living in domestic harmony **2 Darby and Joan Club** a

club for elderly people [c18: a couple in an 18th-century English ballad]

Darcy ('dɑːsɪ) *n* (**James**) **Les**(**lie**). 1895–1917, Australian boxer and folk hero, who lost only five professional fights and was never knocked out, considered a martyr after his death from septicaemia during a tour of the United States

Dardanelles (ˌdɑːdə'nɛlz) *n* the strait between the Aegean and the Sea of Marmara, separating European from Asian Turkey. Ancient name: **Hellespont**

dare (dɛə) *vb* **1** (*tr*) to challenge (a person to do something) as proof of courage **2** (can take an infinitive with or without *to*) to be courageous enough to try (to do something): *she dares to dress differently from the others; you wouldn't dare!* **3** (*tr*) rare to oppose without fear; defy **4 I dare say** *or* **I daresay a** (it is) quite possible (that) **b** probably: used as sentence substitute ▷ *n* **5** a challenge to do something as proof of courage **6** something done in response to such a challenge [Old English *durran*; related to Old High German *turran* to venture] >'**darer** *n*

daredevil ('dɛəˌdɛvəl) *n* **1** a recklessly bold person ▷ *adj* **2** reckless; daring; bold >'**dare,devilry** *or* 'dare,deviltry *n*

Dar es Salaam ('dɑːr ɛs sə'lɑːm) *n* the chief port of Tanzania, on the Indian Ocean: capital of German East Africa (1891–1916); capital of Tanzania until 1983, when it was officially replaced by Dodoma, though still retaining some functions; university (1963). Pop: 2 683 000 (2005 est)

Darfur (dɑː'fʊə) *n* a region of the W Sudan; an independent kingdom until conquered by Egypt in 1874; since 2003 conflict between the Janjaweed and rebel groups has left thousands dead and homeless

Dari ('dɑːrɪ) *n* the local name for the dialect of the Persian language spoken in Afghanistan

Darien ('dɛərɪən, 'dæ-) *n* **1** the E part of the Isthmus of Panama, between the **Gulf of Darien** on the Caribbean coast and the Gulf of San Miguel on the Pacific coast; chiefly within the republic of Panama but extending also into Colombia: site of a disastrous attempt to establish a Scottish colony in 1698 **2 Isthmus of Darien** the former name of the Isthmus of **Panama**

daring ('dɛərɪŋ) *adj* **1** bold or adventurous; reckless ▷ *n* **2** courage in taking risks; boldness

Dario (*Spanish* da'rio) *n* **Rubén** (ru'βen), real name *Félix Rubén Garcia Sarmiento*. 1867–1916, Nicaraguan poet whose poetry includes *Prosas Profanas* (1896)

Darius I (də'raɪəs) *n* known as *Darius the Great*, surname *Hystaspis*. ?550–486 BC, king of Persia (521–486), who extended the Persian empire and crushed the revolt of the Ionian city states (500). He led two expeditions against Greece but was defeated at Marathon (490)

Darius III *n* died 330 BC, last Achaemenid king of Persia (336–330), who was defeated by Alexander the Great

Darjeeling (dɑː'dʒiːlɪŋ) *n* **1** a town in NE India, in West Bengal in the Himalayas, at an altitude of about 2250 m (7500 ft). Pop: 107 530 (2001) **2** a high-quality black tea grown in the mountains around Darjeeling

dark (dɑːk) *adj* **1** having little or no light **2** (of a colour) reflecting or transmitting little light: *dark brown* **3** (of complexion, hair colour, etc) not fair or blond; swarthy; brunette **4** gloomy or dismal **5** sinister; evil: *a dark purpose* **6** sullen or angry **7** ignorant or unenlightened: *a dark period in our history* **8** secret or mysterious ▷ *n* **9** absence of light; darkness **10** night or nightfall **11** a dark place, patch, or shadow **12** a state of ignorance (esp in the phrase **in the dark**) [Old English *deorc*; related to Old High German *terchennen* to hide] >'**darkly** *adv* >'**darkness** *n*

Dark Ages *pl n* the Dark Ages European history the period from about the late 5th century AD to about 1000 AD, once considered an unenlightened period

Dark Continent *n* the Dark Continent a term for Africa when it was relatively unexplored

darken ('dɑːkən) *vb* **1** to make or become dark or darker **2** to make or become gloomy, angry, or sad: *his mood darkened* **3 darken someone's door** (usually used with a negative) to visit someone: *never darken my door again!* >'**darkener** *n*

dark horse *n* **1** a competitor in a race or contest about whom little is known; an unknown **2** a person who reveals little about himself or his activities, esp one who has unexpected talents or abilities **3** *US politics* a candidate who is unexpectedly nominated or elected

dark lantern *n* a lantern having a sliding shutter or panel to dim or hide the light

darkling ('dɑːklɪŋ) *adv, adj poetic* in the dark or night [C15: from DARK + -LING²]

dark matter *n astronomy* matter known to make up perhaps 90% of the mass of the universe, but not detectable by its absorption or emission of electromagnetic radiation

darkroom ('dɑːˌruːm, -ˌrʊm) *n* a room in which photographs are processed in darkness or safe light

darksome ('dɑːksəm) *adj literary* dark or darkish

dark star *n* an invisible star known to exist only from observation of its radio, infrared, or other spectrum or of its gravitational effect, such as an invisible component of a binary or multiple star

Darlan (*French* darlɑ̃) *n* **Jean Louis Xavier François** (ʒɑ̃ lwi gzavje frɑ̃swa). 1881–1942, French admiral and member of the Vichy government. He cooperated with the Allies after their invasion of North Africa; assassinated

darling ('dɑːlɪŋ) *n* **1** a person very much loved: often used as a term of address **2** a favourite: *the teacher's darling* ▷ *adj* (*prenominal*) **3** beloved **4** much admired; pleasing: *a darling hat* [Old English *dēorling*; see DEAR, -LING¹]

Darling ('dɑːlɪŋ) *n* **Grace.** 1815–42, English national heroine, famous for her rescue (1838) of some shipwrecked sailors with her father, a lighthouse keeper

Darling Downs *pl n* a plateau in NE Australia, in SE Queensland: a vast agricultural and stock-raising area

Darling Range *n* a ridge in SW Western Australia, parallel to the coast. Highest point: about 582 m (1669 ft)

Darling River *n* a river in SE Australia, rising in the Eastern Highlands and flowing southwest to the Murray River. Length: 2740 km (1702 miles)

Darlington ('dɑːlɪŋtən) *n* **1** an industrial town in NE England in Darlington unitary authority, S Durham: developed mainly with the opening of the Stockton-Darlington railway (1825). Pop: 86 082 (2001) **2** a unitary authority in NE England, in Durham. Pop: 98 200 (2003 est). Area: 198 sq km (77 sq miles)

Darmstadt ('dɑːmstæt; *German* 'darmʃtat) *n* an industrial city in central Germany, in Hesse: former capital of the grand duchy of Hesse-Darmstadt (1567–1945). Pop: 139 698 (2003 est)

darn¹ (dɑːn) *vb* **1** to mend (a hole or a garment) with a series of crossing or interwoven stitches ▷ *n* **2** a patch of darned work on a garment [C16: probably from French (Channel Islands dialect) *darner*; compare Welsh, Breton *darn* piece] ▷'darner *n* ▷'darning *n*

darn² (dɑːn) *interj, adj, adv, n* a euphemistic word for **damn** (sense 13)

darnel ('dɑːnᵊl) *n* any of several grasses of the genus *Lolium*, esp *L. temulentum*, that grow as weeds in grain fields in Europe and Asia [C14: probably related to French (Walloon dialect) *darnelle*, of obscure origin]

darning needle *n* a long needle with a large eye used for darning

Darnley ('dɑːnlɪ) *n* **Lord.** title of Henry Stuart (or Stewart). 1545–67, Scottish nobleman; second husband of Mary, Queen of Scots and father of James I of England. After murdering his wife's secretary, Rizzio (1566), he was himself assassinated (1567)

dart (dɑːt) *n* **1** a small narrow pointed missile that is thrown or shot, as in the game of darts **2** a sudden quick movement **3** *zoology* a slender pointed structure, as in snails for aiding copulation or in nematodes for penetrating the host's tissues **4** a tapered tuck made in dressmaking ▷ *vb* **5** to move or throw swiftly and suddenly; shoot [C14: from Old French, of Germanic origin; related to Old English *daroth* spear, Old High German *tart* dart] ▷'darting *adj*

dartboard ('dɑːtˌbɔːd) *n* a circular piece of wood, cork, etc, used as the target in the game of darts. It is divided into numbered sectors with central inner and outer bull's-eyes

darter ('dɑːtə) *n* **1** Also called:**anhinga, snakebird** any aquatic bird of the genus *Anhinga* and family *Anhingidae*, of tropical and subtropical inland waters, having a long slender neck and bill: order *Pelecaniformes* (pelicans, cormorants, etc) **2** any small brightly coloured North American freshwater fish of the genus *Etheostoma* and related genera: family *Percidae* (perches)

Dartford ('dɑːtfəd) *n* a town in SE England, in NW Kent. Pop: 56 818 (2001)

Dartmoor ('dɑːtˌmʊə) *n* **1** a moorland plateau in SW England, in SW Devon: a national park since 1951. Area: 945 sq km (365 sq miles) **2** a prison in SW England, on Dartmoor: England's main prison for long-term convicts **3** a small strong breed of pony, originally from Dartmoor **4** a hardy coarse-woolled breed of sheep originally from Dartmoor

Dartmouth ('dɑːtməθ) *n* a port in SW England, in S Devon: Royal Naval College (1905). Pop: 5512 (2001)

darts (dɑːts) *n* (*functioning as singular*) any of various competitive games in which darts are thrown at a dartboard

Darwin¹ ('dɑːwɪn) *n* a port in N Australia, capital of the Northern Territory: destroyed by a cyclone in 1974 but rebuilt on the same site. Pop: 71 347 (2001). Former name (1869–1911):**Palmerston**

Darwin² ('dɑːwɪn) *n* **1 Charles (Robert).** 1809–82, English naturalist who formulated the theory of evolution by natural selection, expounded in *On the Origin of Species* (1859) and applied to man in *The Descent of Man* (1871) **2** his grandfather, **Erasmus.** 1731–1802, English physician and poet; author of *Zoonomia*, or the *Laws of Organic Life* (1794–96), anticipating Lamarck's views on evolution **3** Sir **George Howard**, son of Charles Darwin. 1845–1912, English astronomer and mathematician noted for his work on tidal friction

Darwinian (dɑːˈwɪnɪən) *adj* **1** of or relating to Charles Darwin or his theory ▷ *n* **2** a person who accepts, supports, or uses this theory

Darwinism ('dɑːwɪˌnɪzəm) *or***Darwinian theory** *n* the theory of the origin of animal and plant species by evolution through a process of natural selection >'Darwinist *or* 'Darwinite *n, adj*

dash¹ (dæʃ) *vb* (*mainly tr*) **1** to hurl; crash: *he dashed the cup to the floor; the waves dashed against the rocks* **2** to mix: *white paint dashed with blue* **3** (*intr*) to move hastily or recklessly; rush **4** (usually foll by *off* or *down*) to write (down) or finish (off) hastily **5** to destroy; frustrate: *his hopes were dashed* **6** to daunt (someone); cast down; discourage ▷ *n* **7** a sudden quick movement; dart **8** a small admixture: *coffee with a dash of cream* **9** a violent stroke or blow **10** the sound of splashing or smashing **11** panache; style: *he rides with dash* **12** the punctuation mark —, used singly in place of a colon, esp to indicate a sudden change of subject or grammatical anacoluthon, or in pairs to enclose a parenthetical remark **13** the symbol (–) used, in combination with the symbol *dot* (•), in the written representation of Morse and other telegraphic codes **14** *athletics* another word (esp US and Canadian) for **sprint** [Middle English *dasche, dasse*]

dash² (dæʃ) *interj informal* a euphemistic word for **damn** (senses 1, 2)

dashboard ('dæʃˌbɔːd) *n* **1** Also called (Brit):**fascia** the instrument panel in a car, boat, or aircraft **2** *obsolete* a board at the side of a carriage or boat to protect against splashing

dasher ('dæʃə) *n* **1** one that dashes **2** *Canad* the ledge along the top of the boards of an ice-hockey rink

dashiki (dɑːˈʃiːkɪ) *n* a large loose-fitting buttonless upper garment worn esp by Black people in the US, Africa, and the Caribbean [C20: of W African origin]

dashing ('dæʃɪŋ) *adj* **1** spirited; lively: *a dashing young man* **2** stylish; showy: *a dashing hat*

Dasht-i-Kavir *or***Dasht-e-Kavir** (ˌdæʃtiːkæˈvɪə) *n* a salt waste on the central plateau of Iran: a treacherous marsh beneath a salt crust. Also called:**Kavir Desert**

Dasht-i-Lut *or***Dasht-e-Lut** (ˌdæʃtiːˈluːt) *n* a desert plateau in central and E central Iran

Dassehra ('dæserɑ) *n* an annual Hindu festival celebrated on the 10th lunar day of Navaratri; images of the goddess Durga are immersed in water

dassie ('dæsɪ) *n* another name for a **hyrax**, esp the rock hyrax [C19: from Afrikaans]

dastardly ('dæstədlɪ) *adj* mean and cowardly
> 'dastardliness *n*

dasyure ('dæsɪ,jʊə) *n* any small carnivorous marsupial, such as *Dasyurus quoll* (**eastern dasyure**), of the subfamily *Dasyurinae*, of Australia, New Guinea, and adjacent islands. See also **Tasmanian devil** [C19: from New Latin *Dasyūrus*, from Greek *dasus* shaggy + *oura* tail; see **DENSE**]

DAT *abbreviation* digital audio tape

dat. *abbreviation* dative

data ('deɪtə, 'dɑːtə) *pl n* **1** a series of observations, measurements, or facts; information **2** Also called: information *computing* the information operated on by a computer program [C17: from Latin, literally: (things) given, from *dare* to give]
● **USAGE** Although now often used as a singular noun,
● *data* is properly a plural

database ('deɪtə,beɪs) *n* **1** a systematized collection of data that can be accessed immediately and manipulated by a data-processing system for a specific purpose **2** *informal* any large store of information: *a database of knowledge*

data capture *n* any process for converting information into a form that can be handled by a computer

datacard ('deɪtə,kɑːd) *n* a credit-card-sized electronic device containing an electronic memory, and sometimes an embedded microchip; smart card

data mining *n* the gathering of information from pre-existing data stored in a database, such as one held by a supermarket about customers' shopping habits

data pen *n* a device for reading or scanning magnetically coded data on labels, packets, etc

data processing *n* **a** a sequence of operations performed on data, esp by a computer, in order to extract information, reorder files, etc **b** (*as modifier*): *a data-processing centre*

data protection *n* (in Britain) safeguards for individuals relating to personal data stored on a computer

data set *n computing* another name for **file¹** (sense 7)

date¹ (deɪt) *n* **1** a specified day of the month: *today's date is October 27* **2** the particular day or year of an event: *the date of the Norman Conquest was 1066* **3** an inscription on a coin, letter, etc, stating when it was made or written **4 a** an appointment for a particular time, esp with a person to whom one is sexually or romantically attached: *she has a dinner date* **b** the person with whom the appointment is made ▷ *vb* **5** (*tr*) to mark (a letter, coin, etc) with the day, month, or year **6** (*tr*) to assign a date of occurrence or creation to **7** (*intr*; foll by *from* or *back to*) to have originated (at a specified time): *his decline dates from last summer* **8** (*tr*) to reveal the age of: *that dress dates her* **9** to make or become old-fashioned: *some good films hardly date at all* **10** *informal, chiefly US & Canadian* **a** to be a boyfriend or girlfriend of (someone) **b** to accompany (someone) on a date [C14: from Old French, from Latin *dare* to give, as in the phrase *epistula data Romae* letter handed over at Rome] > 'datable *or* 'dateable *adj*
● **USAGE** See at **year**

date² (deɪt) *n* **1** the fruit of the date palm, having sweet edible flesh and a single large woody seed **2** short for **date palm** [C13: from Old French, from Latin, from Greek *daktulos* finger]

dated ('deɪtɪd) *adj* **1** unfashionable; outmoded: *dated clothes* **2** (of a security) having a fixed date for redemption

dateless ('deɪtlɪs) *adj* likely to remain fashionable, relevant, or interesting regardless of age; timeless

dateline ('deɪt,laɪn) *n journalism* the date and location of a story, placed at the top of an article

date line *n* (*often capitals*) short for **International Date Line**

date palm *n* a feather palm, *Phoenix dactylifera*, probably native to N Africa and SW Asia and widely grown in other arid warm temperate and subtropical regions for its edible fruit (dates)

date rape *n* **1** the act or an instance of a man raping a woman while they are on a date together **2** an act of sexual intercourse regarded as tantamount to rape, esp if the woman was encouraged to drink excessively or was subjected to undue pressure

date stamp *n* **1** an adjustable rubber stamp for recording the date **2** an inked impression made by this

dating ('deɪtɪŋ) *n* any of several techniques, such as radioactive dating, dendrochronology, or varve dating, for establishing the age of rocks, palaeontological or archaeological specimens, etc

dating agency *n* an agency that provides introductions to people seeking a companion with similar interests

dative ('deɪtɪv) *grammar* ▷ *adj* **1** denoting a case of nouns, pronouns, and adjectives used to express the indirect object, to identify the recipients, and for other purposes ▷ *n* **2 a** the dative case **b** a word or speech element in this case [C15: from Latin *datīvus*, from *dare* to give; translation of Greek *dotikos*] > **datival** (deɪ'taɪvəl) *adj*
> 'datively *adv*

datum ('deɪtəm, 'dɑːtəm) *n, pl* **-ta** (-tə) **1** a single piece of information; fact **2** a proposition taken for granted, often in order to construct some theoretical framework upon it; a given. See also **sense datum** [C17: from Latin: something given; see **DATA**]

datura (də'tjʊərə) *n* any of various chiefly Indian solanaceous plants of the genus *Datura*, such as the moonflower and thorn apple, having large trumpet-shaped flowers, prickly pods, and narcotic properties [C16: from New Latin, from Hindi *dhatūra* jimson weed, from Sanskrit *dhattūra*]

daub (dɔːb) *vb* **1** (*tr*) to smear or spread (paint, mud, etc), esp carelessly **2** (*tr*) to cover or coat (with paint, plaster, etc) carelessly **3** to paint (a picture) clumsily or badly ▷ *n* **4** an unskilful or crude painting **5** something daubed on, esp as a wall covering **6** a smear (of paint, mud, etc) [C14: from Old French *dauber* to paint, whitewash, from Latin *dealbāre*, from *albāre* to whiten, from *albus* white] > 'dauber *n*

Daubigny (*French* dobiɲi) *n* **Charles François** (ʃarl frɑ̃swa). 1817–78, French landscape painter associated with the Barbizon School

Daudet (*French* dodɛ) *n* **Alphonse** (alfɔ̃s). 1840–97, French novelist, short-story writer, and dramatist: noted particularly for his humorous sketches of Provençal life, as in *Lettres de mon moulin* (1866)

Daugava ('daʊɡa,va) *n* the Latvian name for the Western **Dvina**

Daugavpils (*Latvian* 'daʊɡaf,pils) *n* a city in SE Latvia on the Western Dvina River: founded in 1274 by Teutonic Knights; ruled by Poland (1559–1772) and Russia (1772–1915); retaken by the Russians in 1940. Pop: 112 609 (2002 est). German name (until 1893): Dünaburg. Former Russian name (1893–1920): Dvinsk

daughter ('dɔːtə) *n* **1** a female offspring; a girl or woman in relation to her parents **2** a female descendant **3** a female from a certain country, etc, or one closely connected with a certain environment, etc: *a daughter of the church* ▷ *modifier* **4** *biology* denoting a cell or unicellular organism produced by the division of one of its own kind **5** *physics* (of a nuclide) formed from another nuclide by radioactive decay [Old English *dohtor*; related to Old High German *tohter* daughter, Greek *thugatēr*, Sanskrit *duhitá*] > 'daughterhood *n* > 'daughterless *adj* > 'daughterly *adj*

daughter-in-law *n, pl* **daughters-in-law** the wife of one's son

Daumier (*French* domje) *n* **Honoré** (ɔnɔre). 1808–79, French painter and lithographer, noted particularly for his political and social caricatures

daunt (dɔːnt) *vb* (*tr; often passive*) **1** to intimidate **2** to dishearten [C13: from Old French *danter*, changed from *donter* to conquer, from Latin *domitāre* to tame]

daunting ('dɔːntɪŋ) *adj* causing fear or discouragement; intimidating > 'dauntingly *adv*

dauntless ('dɔːntlɪs) *adj* bold; fearless; intrepid > 'dauntlessly *adv* > 'dauntlessness *n*

dauphin ('dɔːfɪn, dɔː'fɪn; *French* dofɛ̃) *n* (1349–1830) the title of the direct heir to the French throne; the eldest son of the king of France [C15: from Old French: originally a family name; adopted as a title by the Counts of Vienne and later by the French crown princes]

dauphine ('dɔ:fi:n, dɔ:'fi:n; French dofin) or **dauphiness** ('dɔ:fɪnɪs) n French history the wife of a dauphin

Davenant ('dævənənt) n Sir **William**. 1606–68, English dramatist and poet: poet laureate (1638–68). His plays include Love and Honour (1634)

davenport ('dævən,pɔ:t) n 1 chiefly Brit a tall narrow desk with a slanted writing surface and drawers at the side 2 US & Canadian a large sofa, esp one convertible into a bed [C19: sense 1 said to be named after Captain Davenport, who commissioned the first ones]

Daventry ('dævəntrɪ) n a town in central England, in Northamptonshire: light industries, site of an important international radio transmitter. Pop: 21 731 (2001)

David ('deɪvɪd) n 1 the second king of the Hebrews (about 1000–962 BC), who united Israel as a kingdom with Jerusalem as its capital 2 **Elizabeth**. 1914–92, British cookery writer. Her books include Mediterranean Food (1950) and An Omelette and a Glass of Wine (1984) 3 (French david) **Jacques Louis** (ʒɑk lwi). 1748–1825, French neoclassical painter of such works as the Oath of the Horatii (1784), Death of Socrates (1787), and The Intervention of the Sabine Women (1799). He actively supported the French Revolution and became court painter to Napoleon Bonaparte in 1804; banished at the Bourbon restoration 4 **Saint**. 6th century AD, Welsh bishop; patron saint of Wales. Feast day: March 1

David I n 1084–1153, king of Scotland (1124–53) who supported his niece Matilda's claim to the English throne and unsuccessfully invaded England on her behalf

David II n 1324–71, king of Scotland (1329–71): he was forced into exile in France (1334–41) by Edward de Baliol; captured following the battle of Neville's Cross (1346), and imprisoned by the English (1346–57)

Davies ('deɪvɪs) n 1 Sir **John**. 1569–1626, English poet, author of Orchestra or a Poem of Dancing (1596) and the philosophical poem Nosce Teipsum (1599) 2 Sir **Peter Maxwell**. born 1934, British composer, whose works include the operas Taverner (1967), The Martyrdom of St Magnus (1977), and Resurrection (1988), six symphonies, and the ten Strathclyde Concertos; appointed Master of the Queen's Music in 2004 3 (**William**) **Robertson**. 1913–95, Canadian novelist and dramatist. His novels include Leaven of Malice (1954), Fifth Business (1970), The Rebel Angels (1981), What's Bred in the Bone (1985), and The Cunning Man (1994) 4 **W(illiam) H(enry)**. 1871–1940, Welsh poet, noted also for his Autobiography of a Super-tramp (1908)

da Vinci (da 'vɪntʃɪ) n See Leonardo da Vinci

Davis ('deɪvɪs) n 1 Sir **Andrew (Frank)**. born 1944, British conductor; chief conductor of the BBC Symphony Orchestra (1989–2000) and of the Chicago Lyric Opera from 2000 2 **Bette** ('betɪ), real name Ruth Elizabeth Davis. 1908–89, US film actress, whose films include Of Human Bondage (1934), Jezebel (1938) for which she won an Oscar, All About Eve (1950), Whatever Happened to Baby Jane? (1962), The Nanny (1965), and The Whales of August (1987) 3 Sir **Colin (Rex)**. born 1927, English conductor, noted for his interpretation of the music of Berlioz 4 **Jefferson**. 1808–89, president of the Confederate States of America during the Civil War (1861–65) 5 **Joe**. 1901–78, English billiards and snooker player: world champion from 1927 to 1946 6 **John**. Also called: **John Davys**. ?1550–1605, English navigator: discovered the Falkland Islands (1592); searched for a Northwest Passage 7 **Miles (Dewey)**. 1926–91, US jazz trumpeter and composer 8 **Steve**. born 1957, English snooker player: world champion 1981, 1983–84, 1987–89

Davisson ('deɪvɪsən) n **Clinton Joseph**. 1881–1958, US physicist, noted for his discovery of electron diffraction; shared the Nobel prize for physics in 1937

Davis Strait ('deɪvɪs) n a strait between Baffin Island, in Canada, and Greenland [named after John Davis (??1550–1605), English navigator]

davit ('dævɪt, 'deɪ-) n a cranelike device, usually one of a pair, fitted with a tackle for suspending or lowering equipment, esp a lifeboat [C14: from Anglo-French daviot, diminutive of Davi David]

Davos ('dævɒs) n a mountain resort in Switzerland: winter sports, site of the Parsenn ski run. Pop: 11 417 (2000). Height: about 1560 m (5118 ft)

Davy ('deɪvɪ) n Sir **Humphry**. 1778–1829, English chemist, who isolated sodium, magnesium, chlorine, and other elements and suggested the electrical nature of chemical combination. He invented the Davy lamp.

Davy Jones ('deɪvɪ) n 1 Also called: **Davy Jones's locker** the ocean's bottom, esp when regarded as the grave of those lost or buried at sea 2 the spirit or devil of the sea [C18: of unknown origin]

Davy lamp n See safety lamp [C19: named after its inventor Sir Humphry Davy (1778–1829), English chemist]

daw (dɔ:) n an archaic, dialect, or poetic name for a jackdaw [C15: related to Old High German taha]

dawdle ('dɔ:dəl) vb 1 (intr) to be slow or lag behind 2 (when tr, often foll by away) to waste (time); trifle [C17: of uncertain origin] > **'dawdler** n

Dawes (dɔ:z) n **Charles Gates**. 1865–1951, US financier, diplomat, and statesman, who devised the Dawes Plan for German reparations payments after World War I; vice president of the US (1925–29); Nobel peace prize 1925

Dawkins ('dɔ:kɪnz) n **Richard**. born 1941, British zoologist, noted for such works as The Selfish Gene (1976), The Blind Watchmaker (1986), River Out of Eden (1995), and The God Delusion (2006)

dawn (dɔ:n) n 1 daybreak; sunrise. Related adj: **auroral** 2 the sky when light first appears in the morning 3 the beginning of something ▷ vb (intr) 4 to begin to grow light after the night 5 to begin to develop, appear, or expand 6 (usually foll by on or upon) to begin to become apparent (to) [Old English dagian to dawn; see DAY] > **'dawn,like** adj

dawn chorus n the singing of large numbers of birds at dawn

dawn raid n stock exchange an unexpected attempt to acquire a substantial proportion of a company's shares at the start of a day's trading as a preliminary to a takeover bid

Dawson Creek ('dɔ:sən) n a town in W Canada, in NE British Columbia: SE terminus of the Alaska Highway. Pop: 10 754 (2001)

day (deɪ) n 1 Also called: **civil day** the period of time, the calendar day, of 24 hours' duration reckoned from one midnight to the next 2 a the period of light between sunrise and sunset, as distinguished from the night b (as modifier): the day shift 3 the part of a day occupied with regular activity, esp work 4 (sometimes plural) a period or point in time: he was a good singer in his day; in days gone by; any day now 5 the period of time, the sidereal day, during which the earth makes one complete revolution on its axis relative to a particular star. The **mean sidereal day** lasts 23 hours 56 minutes 4.1 seconds of the mean solar day 6 the period of time taken by a specified planet to make one complete rotation on its axis: the Martian day 7 (often capital) a day designated for a special observance, esp a holiday: Christmas Day 8 all in a day's work part of one's normal activity; no trouble 9 at the end of the day in the final reckoning 10 day of rest the Sabbath; Sunday 11 in this day and age nowadays 12 that will be the day a I look forward to that b that is most unlikely to happen 13 a time of success, recognition, power, etc: his day will soon come 14 a struggle or issue at hand: the day is lost 15 a the ground surface over a mine b (as modifier): the day level 16 from day to day without thinking of the future 17 call it a day to stop work or other activity 18 day after day without respite; relentlessly 19 day by day gradually or progressively; daily: he weakened day by day 20 day in, day out every day and all day long ▷ Related adjective: **diurnal** See also **days** [Old English dæg; related to Old High German tag, Old Norse dagr]

Day (deɪ) n Sir **Robin**. 1923–2000, British radio and television journalist, noted esp for his political interviews

Dayak ('daɪæk) n, pl -aks or -ak a variant spelling of **Dyak**

Dayan (daɪ'jɑːn) n **Moshe** ('mɒʃe). 1915–81, Israeli soldier and statesman; minister of defence (1967; 1969–74) and foreign minister (1977–79)

day bed *n* a narrow bed, with a head piece and sometimes a foot piece and back, on which to recline during the day

daybook ('deɪ,bʊk) *n* book-keeping a book in which the transactions of each day are recorded as they occur

dayboy ('deɪ,bɔɪ) *n* Brit a boy who attends a boarding school daily, but returns home each evening

daybreak ('deɪ,breɪk) *n* the time in the morning when light first appears; dawn; sunrise

daycare ('deɪ,kɛə) *n* Brit social welfare **1** occupation, treatment, or supervision during the working day for people who might be at risk if left on their own, or whose usual carers need daytime relief **2** welfare services provided by a local authority, health service, or voluntary body during the day

daycentre ('deɪ,sɛntə) *or* **day centre** *n* social welfare (in Britain) **1** a building used for daycare or other welfare services **2** the enterprise itself, including staff, users, and organization

daydream ('deɪ,driːm) *n* **1** a pleasant dreamlike fantasy indulged in while awake; idle reverie **2** a pleasant scheme or wish that is unlikely to be fulfilled; pipe dream ▷ *vb* **3** (*intr*) to have daydreams; indulge in idle fantasy > 'day,dreamer *n* > 'day,dreamy *adj*

daygirl ('deɪ,gɜːl) *n* Brit a girl who attends a boarding school daily, but returns home each evening

Day-Glo *n* trademark **a** a brand of fluorescent colouring materials, as of paint **b** (*as modifier*): Day-Glo colours

day labourer *n* an unskilled worker hired and paid by the day

Day-Lewis ('deɪ'luːɪs) *or* **Day Lewis** *n* C(ecil). 1904–72, British poet, critic, and (under the pen name *Nicholas Blake*) author of detective stories; poet laureate (1968– 72)

daylight ('deɪ,laɪt) *n* **1** light from the sun **2** daybreak **3** see daylight **a** to understand something previously obscure **b** to realize that the end of a difficult task is approaching ▷ See also **daylights**

daylight robbery *n* informal blatant overcharging

daylights ('deɪ,laɪts) *pl n* consciousness or wits (esp in the phrases **scare, knock,** or **beat the (living) daylights out of someone**)

daylight-saving time *n* time set usually one hour ahead of the local standard time, widely adopted in the summer to provide extra daylight in the evening

day lily *n* **1** any widely cultivated Eurasian liliaceous plant of the genus *Hemerocallis*, having large yellow, orange, or red lily-like flowers, which typically last for only one day and are immediately succeeded by others **2** the flower of any of these plants

daylong ('deɪ,lɒŋ) *adj, adv* lasting the entire day; all day

day release *n* Brit a system whereby workers are released for part-time education without loss of pay

day return *n* a reduced fare for a journey (by train, etc) travelling both ways in one day

day room *n* a communal living room in a residential institution such as a hospital

days (deɪz) *adv* informal during the day, esp regularly: he works days

day school *n* **1** a private school taking day students only. See **boarding school 2** a school giving instruction during the daytime. See **night school**

daytime ('deɪ,taɪm) *n* the time between dawn and dusk; the day as distinct from evening or night

day-to-day *adj* routine; everyday: day-to-day chores

day trading *n* the practice of buying and selling shares on the same day, often via the internet, in order to make a quick profit > day trader *n*

day trip *n* a journey made to and from a place within one day > 'day-,tripper *n*

Da Yunhe ('dæ 'juːnhə) *n* the Pinyin transliteration of the Chinese name for the **Grand Canal** (sense 1)

daze (deɪz) *vb* (*tr*) **1** to stun or stupefy, esp by a blow or shock **2** to bewilder, amaze, or dazzle ▷ *n* **3** a state of stunned confusion or shock (esp in the phrase **in a daze**) [c14: from Old Norse *dasa-*, as in *dasask* to grow weary]

dazzle ('dæzᵊl) *vb* **1** (*usually tr*) to blind or be blinded partially and temporarily by sudden excessive light **2** to

amaze, as with brilliance: *she was dazzled by his wit; she dazzles in this film* ▷ *n* **3** bright light that dazzles **4** bewilderment caused by glamour, brilliance, etc: *the dazzle of fame* [c15: from DAZE] > 'dazzler *n* > 'dazzling *adj* > 'dazzlingly *adv*

dB *or* **db** *symbol for* decibel *or* decibels

DBE *abbreviation* Dame (Commander of the Order) of the British Empire (a Brit title)

DBMS *abbreviation* database management system

DBS *abbreviation* **1** direct broadcasting by satellite **2** direct broadcasting satellite

dbx *or* **DBX** *n* trademark electronics a noise-reduction system that works as a compander across the full frequency spectrum

DC *abbreviation* **1** music da capo **2** direct current. See **AC 3** Also: D.C. District of Columbia

DCB *abbreviation* Dame Commander of the Order of the Bath (a Brit title)

DCC *abbreviation* digital compact cassette

DCM *abbreviation* Brit military Distinguished Conduct Medal

DCMS *abbreviation* (in Britain) Department for Culture, Media, and Sport

DD *abbreviation* **1** Also: dd direct debit **2** Doctor of Divinity

D-day *n* the day, June 6, 1944, on which the Allied invasion of Europe began [c20: from *D(ay)-day*; compare H-HOUR]

DDoS *abbreviation* distributed denial of service: a method of attacking a computer system by flooding it with so many messages that it is obliged to shut down

DDR *abbreviation* Deutsche Demokratische Republik (the former East Germany; GDR)

DDS *abbreviation* Doctor of Dental Surgery

DDT *n* dichlorodiphenyltrichloroethane; a colourless odourless substance used as an insecticide. It is toxic to animals and is known to accumulate in the tissues. It is now banned in the UK

de- *prefix forming verbs and verbal derivatives* **1** removal of or from something specified: *deforest; dethrone* **2** reversal of something: *decode; decompose; desegregate* **3** departure from: *decamp* [from Latin, from *dē* (prep) from, away from, out of, etc. In compound words of Latin origin, *de-* also means away, away from (*decease*); down (*degrade*); reversal (*detect*); removal (*defoliate*); and is used intensively (*devote*) and pejoratively (*detest*)]

deacon ('diːkən) *n* Christianity **1** (in the Roman Catholic and other episcopal churches) an ordained minister ranking immediately below a priest **2** (in Protestant churches) a lay official appointed or elected to assist the minister, esp in secular affairs [Old English, ultimately from Greek *diakonos* servant] > 'deacon,ship *n*

deaconess ('diːkənɪs) *n* Christianity (in the early church and in some modern Churches) a female member of the laity with duties similar to those of a deacon

deactivate (diːˈæktɪ,veɪt) *vb* **1** (*tr*) to make (a bomb, etc) harmless or inoperative **2** (*intr*) to become less radioactive > deˈactiˌvator *n*

dead (dɛd) *adj* **1 a** no longer alive **b** (*as noun*): the dead **2** not endowed with life; inanimate **3** no longer in use, valid, effective, or relevant: *a dead issue; a dead language* **4** unresponsive or unaware; insensible: *he is dead to my strongest pleas* **5** lacking in freshness, interest, or vitality: *a dead handshake* **6** devoid of physical sensation; numb: *his gums were dead from the anaesthetic* **7** resembling death; deathlike: *a dead sleep* **8** no longer burning or hot: *dead coals* **9** (of flowers or foliage) withered; faded **10** (*prenominal*) (intensifier): *a dead stop; a dead loss* **11** informal very tired **12** electronics **a** drained of electric charge; fully discharged: *the battery was dead* **b** not connected to a source of potential difference or electric charge **13** lacking acoustic reverberation: *a dead sound; a dead surface* **14** sport (of a ball, etc) out of play **15** unerring; accurate; precise (esp in the phrase **a dead shot**) **16** lacking resilience or bounce: *a dead ball* **17** not yielding a return; idle: *dead capital* **18** (of colours) not glossy or bright; lacklustre **19** stagnant: *dead air* **20** military shielded from view, as by a geographic feature or environmental condition: *a dead zone; dead space* **21** dead from the neck up *informal* stupid or unintelligent **22** **dead to the world** *informal* unaware of one's surroundings, esp fast asleep or very drunk ▷ *n* **23** a period during which coldness, darkness, or some other quality associated with death is at its most intense: *the dead of winter* ▷ *adv* **24** (intensifier): *dead easy; stop dead; dead level* **25** **dead on** exactly right [Old English *dēad*; related to Old High German *tōt*, Old Norse *dauthr*; see DIE¹] ▷ˈdeadness *n*

dead-and-alive *adj Brit* (of a place, activity, or person) dull; uninteresting

dead-ball line *n rugby* a line not more than 22 metres behind the goal line at each end of the field beyond which the ball is out of play

deadbeat (ˈdɛdˌbiːt) *n* **1** *informal* a lazy or socially undesirable person **2** *chiefly US* **a** a person who makes a habit of avoiding or evading his or her responsibilities or debts **b** (*as modifier*): *a deadbeat dad* **3** a high-grade escapement used in pendulum clocks **4** (*modifier*) (of a clock escapement) having a beat without any recoil

dead beat *adj informal* tired out; exhausted

dead-cat bounce *n stock exchange informal* a temporary recovery in prices following a substantial fall as a result of speculators buying stocks they have already sold rather than as a result of a genuine reversal of the downward trend

dead centre *n* **1** the exact top (**top dead centre**) or bottom (**bottom dead centre**) of the piston stroke in a reciprocating engine or pump **2** a pointed rod mounted in the tailstock of a lathe to support a workpiece ▷ Also called: **dead point**

dead data *n computing* data that is no longer relevant

dead duck *n slang* a person or thing doomed to death, failure, etc, esp because of a mistake or misjudgment

deaden (ˈdɛdᵊn) *vb* **1** to make or become less sensitive, intense, lively, etc; damp or be damped down; dull **2** (*tr*) to make acoustically less resonant: *he deadened the room with heavy curtains* ▷ˈdeadening *adj*

dead end *n* **1** another name for **cul-de-sac** **2** a situation in which further progress is impossible

deadeye (ˈdɛdˌaɪ) *n* **1** *nautical* either of a pair of disclike wooden blocks, supported by straps in grooves around them, between which a line is rove so as to draw them together to tighten a shroud **2** *chiefly US informal* an expert marksman

deadfall (ˈdɛdˌfɔːl) *n* a type of trap, used esp for catching large animals, in which a heavy weight falls to crush the prey. Also called: **downfall**

deadhead (ˈdɛdˌhɛd) *n* **1** a dull unenterprising person **2** a person who uses a free ticket, as for a train, the theatre, etc **3** *US & Canadian* a train, etc, travelling empty **4** *US & Canadian* a totally or partially submerged log floating in a lake, etc ▷ *vb* **5** (*tr*) to cut off withered flowers from (a plant) **6** (*intr*) *US & Canadian* to drive an empty bus, train, etc

Dead Heart *n* the **Dead Heart** *Austral* the remote interior of Australia [c20: from the title *The Dead Heart of Australia* (1906) by J. W. Gregory (1864–1932), British geologist]

dead heat *n* **a** a race or contest in which two or more participants tie for first place **b** a tie between two or more contestants in any position

dead leg *n informal* temporary loss of sensation in the leg, caused by a blow to a muscle

dead letter *n* **1** a letter that cannot be delivered or returned because it lacks adequate directions **2** a law or ordinance that is no longer enforced but has not been formally repealed

deadlight (ˈdɛdˌlaɪt) *n* **1** *nautical* **a** a bull's-eye let into the deck or hull of a vessel to admit light to a cabin **b** a shutter of wood or metal for sealing off a porthole or cabin window **2** a skylight designed not to be opened

deadline (ˈdɛdˌlaɪn) *n* a time limit for any activity

dead load *n* the intrinsic invariable weight of a structure, such as a bridge. It may also include any permanent loads attached to the structure. Also called: **dead weight**

deadlock (ˈdɛdˌlɒk) *n* **1** a state of affairs in which further action between two opposing forces is impossible;

stalemate **2** a tie between opposite sides in a contest **3** a lock having a bolt that can be opened only with a key ▷ *vb* **4** to bring or come to a deadlock

dead loss *n* **1** *informal* a person, thing, or situation that is completely useless or unprofitable **2** a complete loss for which no compensation is received

deadly (ˈdɛdlɪ) *adj* **-lier, -liest** **1** likely to cause death: *deadly poison; deadly combat* **2** *informal* extremely boring ▷ *adv, adj* **3** like death in appearance or certainty: *deadly pale; a deadly sleep*

deadly nightshade *n* a poisonous Eurasian solanaceous plant, *Atropa belladonna*, having dull purple bell-shaped flowers and small very poisonous black berries. Also called: **belladonna, dwale**

deadly sins *pl n theol* the sins of pride, covetousness, lust, envy, gluttony, anger, and sloth

dead man's handle *or* **dead man's pedal** *n* a safety switch on a piece of machinery, such as a train, that allows operation only while depressed by the operator

dead march *n* a piece of solemn funeral music played to accompany a procession, esp at military funerals

dead-nettle *n* any Eurasian plant of the genus *Lamium*, such as *L. alba* (white dead-nettle), having leaves resembling nettles but lacking stinging hairs: family Lamiaceae (labiates)

deadpan (ˈdɛdˌpæn) *adj, adv* with a deliberately emotionless face or manner: *deadpan humour*

dead reckoning *n* a method of establishing one's position using the distance and direction travelled rather than astronomical observations

Dead Sea *n* a lake between Israel, Jordan, and the West Bank, now 420 m (1378 ft) below sea level; originally 390 m (1285 ft): the lowest lake in the world, with no outlet and very high salinity; outline, esp at the southern end, reduced considerably in recent years. Area: originally about 950 sq km (365 sq miles); by 2003 about 625 sq km (240 sq miles)

dead set *adv* **1** absolutely: *he is dead set against going to Spain* ▷ *n* **2** the motionless position of a dog when pointing with its muzzle towards game ▷ *adj* **3** (of a hunting dog) in this position

dead soldier *or* **dead marine** *n informal* an empty beer or spirit bottle

dead time *n electronics* the interval of time immediately following a stimulus, during which an electrical device, component, etc, is insensitive to a further stimulus

dead weight *n* **1** a heavy weight or load **2** an oppressive burden; encumbrance **3** the difference between the loaded and the unloaded weights of a ship **4** another name for **dead load**

deadwood (ˈdɛdˌwʊd) *n* **1** dead trees or branches **2** *informal* a useless person; encumbrance

deaf (dɛf) *adj* **1** **a** partially or totally unable to hear **b** (*as collective noun; preceded by the*): *the deaf*. See also **tone-deaf** **2** refusing to heed: *deaf to the cries of the hungry* [Old English *dēaf*; related to Old Norse *daufr*] ▷ˈdeafness *n*
● USAGE

deaf aid *n* a dated and potentially offensive name for **hearing aid**

deaf-and-dumb *offensive* ▷ *adj* **1** unable to hear or speak ▷ *n* **2** a deaf person without speech

deafblind (ˈdɛfˌblaɪnd) *adj* **a** unable to hear or see **b** (*as collective noun; preceded by the*): *the deafblind*
● USAGE See at **elderly**

deafen (ˈdɛfᵊn) *vb* (*tr*) to make deaf, esp momentarily, as by a loud noise

deafening (ˈdɛfᵊnɪŋ) *adj* excessively loud: *deafening music* ▷ˈdeafeningly *adv*

deaf-mute *n* **1** a person who is unable to hear or speak. See also **mute¹** (sense 7) **mutism** (sense 2b) ▷ *adj* **2** unable to hear or speak [c19: translation of French *sourd-muet*]
● USAGE Using this word to refer to people without
● speech is considered outdated and offensive, and
● should be avoided. The phrase *profoundly deaf* is a
● suitable alternative in many contexts

Deak (ˈdɛɑːk) *n* **Ferenc** (ˈferents). 1803–76, Hungarian statesman: minister of justice following the 1848 Hungarian uprising. The Austro-Hungarian dual monarchy was largely his creation

d

d

Deakin ('di:kɪn) n Alfred. 1856–1919, Australian statesman. He was a leader of the movement for Australian federation; prime minister of Australia (1903–04; 1905–08; 1909–10)

deal¹ (di:l) vb **deals, dealing, dealt** (dɛlt) **1** (intr; foll by in) to engage (in) commercially: to deal in upholstery **2** (often foll by out) to apportion (something, such as cards) to a number of people; distribute **3** (tr) to give (a blow) to (someone); inflict **4** (intr) slang to sell any illegal drug ▷ n **5** informal a bargain, transaction, or agreement **6** a particular type of treatment received, esp as the result of an agreement: a fair deal **7** an indefinite amount, extent, or degree (esp in the phrases **good** or **great deal**) **8** cards **a** the process of distributing the cards **b** a player's turn to do this **c** a single round in a card game **9** See **big deal** **10** cut a deal informal, chiefly US to come to an arrangement; make a deal. See also **deal with** **11** the real deal informal a person or thing seen as being authentic and not inferior in any way [Old English dǣlan, from dǣl a part; compare Old High German teil a part, Old Norse deild a share]

deal² (di:l) n **1** a plank of softwood timber, such as fir or pine, or such planks collectively **2** the sawn wood of various coniferous trees, such as that from the Scots pine (**red deal**) or from the Norway Spruce (**white deal**) ▷ adj **3** of fir or pine [c14: from Middle Low German dele plank; see THILL]

Deal (di:l) n a town in SE England, in Kent, on the English Channel: two 16th-century castles: tourism, light industries. Pop: 96 670 (2003 est)

dealer ('di:lə) n **1** a person or firm engaged in commercial purchase and sale; trader: a car dealer **2** cards the person who distributes the cards **3** slang a person who sells illegal drugs

dealings ('di:lɪŋz) pl n (sometimes singular) transactions or business relations

dealt (dɛlt) vb the past tense and past participle of **deal¹**

deal with vb (tr, adverb) **1** to take action on: to deal with each problem in turn **2** to punish: the headmaster will deal with the culprit **3** to be concerned with: the book deals with Dutch art **4** to conduct oneself (towards others), esp with regard to fairness: he can be relied on to deal fairly with everyone **5** to do business with: the firm deals with many overseas suppliers

dean (di:n) n **1** the chief administrative official of a college or university faculty **2** (at Oxford and Cambridge universities) a college fellow with responsibility for undergraduate discipline **3** chiefly Church of England the head of a chapter of canons and administrator of a cathedral or collegiate church **4** RC Church the cardinal bishop senior by consecration and head of the college of cardinals. ▷ Related adjective: **decanal** See also **rural dean** [c14: from Old French deien, from Late Latin decānus one set over ten persons, from Latin decem ten]

Dean¹ (di:n) n **Forest of Dean** a forest in W England, in Gloucestershire, between the Rivers Severn and Wye: formerly a royal hunting ground

Dean² (di:n) n **1 Christopher.** See **Torvill and Dean** **2 James** (Byron). 1931–55, US film actor, who became a cult figure; his films include East of Eden and Rebel Without a Cause (both 1955). He died in a car crash

Deane (di:n) n Sir **William Patrick.** born 1931, Australian lawyer. He became a High Court judge in 1982 and governor-general of Australia (1995–2001)

deanery ('di:nərɪ) n, pl-eries **1** the office or residence of dean **2** the group of parishes presided over by a rural dean

dear (dɪə) adj **1** beloved; precious **2** used in conventional forms of address preceding a title or name, as in Dear Sir or my dear Mr Smith **3** (postpositive; foll by to) important; close: a wish dear to her heart **4 a** highly priced **b** charging high prices **5** appealing or pretty: what a dear little ring! **6** for dear life urgently or with extreme vigour or desperation ▷ interj **7** used in exclamations of surprise or dismay, such as Oh dear! and dear me! ▷ n **8** (often used in direct address) someone regarded with affection and tenderness; darling ▷ adv **9** dearly: his errors have cost him dear [Old English dēore; related to Old Norse dȳrr] ▷ **'dearness** n

dearly ('dɪəlɪ) adv **1** very much: I would dearly like you to go **2** affectionately **3** at a great cost

dearth (dɜːθ) n an inadequate amount, esp of food; scarcity [c13: derthe, from dēr DEAR]

deary or **dearie** ('dɪərɪ) n, pl **dearies** informal a term of affection: now often sarcastic or facetious **2** deary me! or dearie me! an exclamation of surprise or dismay

death (dɛθ) n **1** the permanent end of all functions of life in an organism or some of its cellular components **2** an instance of this: his death ended an era **3** a murder or killing **4** termination or destruction **5** a state of affairs or an experience considered as terrible as death **6** a cause or source of death **7** (usually capital) a personification of death, usually a skeleton or an old man holding a scythe **8** a to death or to the death until dead: bleed to death; a fight to the death **b** to death excessively: bored to death **9** at death's door likely to die soon **10** catch one's death or catch one's death of cold informal to contract a severe cold **11** do to death **a** to kill **b** to overuse (a joke, etc) so that it no longer has any effect **12** in at the death **a** present when an animal that is being hunted is caught and killed **b** present at the finish or climax **13** like death warmed up informal very ill **14** like grim death as if afraid for one's life **15** put to death to kill deliberately or execute ▷ Related adjectives: **fatal, lethal, mortal** [Old English dēath; related to Old High German tōd death, Gothic dauthus]

death adder n a venomous Australian elapid snake, Acanthophis antarcticus, resembling an adder

deathbed ('dɛθ,bɛd) n the bed in which a person is about to die

deathblow ('dɛθ,bləʊ) n a thing or event that destroys life or hope, esp suddenly

death camp n a concentration camp in which the conditions are so brutal that few prisoners survive, or one to which prisoners are sent for execution

death cap or **death angel** n a poisonous woodland saprotrophic basidiomycetous fungus, Amanita phalloides, differing from the edible mushroom (Agaricus) only in its white gills (pinkish-brown in Agaricus) and the presence of a volva

death certificate n a legal document issued by a qualified medical practitioner certifying the death of a person and stating the cause if known

death duty n a tax on property inheritances: in Britain, replaced in 1975 by capital transfer tax and since 1986 by inheritance tax. Also called: **estate duty**

death futures pl n life-insurance policies of terminally ill people that are bought speculatively for a lump sum by a company, enabling it to collect the proceeds of the policies when the sufferers die

death knell or **death bell** n **1** something that heralds death or destruction **2** a bell rung to announce a death

deathless ('dɛθlɪs) adj immortal, esp because of greatness; everlasting > **'deathlessness** n

deathly ('dɛθlɪ) adj **1** deadly **2** resembling death: a deathly quiet

death mask n a cast of a person's face taken shortly after death

death rate n the ratio of deaths in a specified area, group, etc, to the population of that area, group, etc. Also called (esp US): **mortality rate**

death rattle n a low-pitched gurgling sound sometimes made by a dying person, caused by air passing through an accumulation of mucus in the trachea

death's-head n a human skull or a representation of one

death's-head moth n a European hawk moth, Acherontia atropos, having markings resembling a human skull on its upper thorax

death tourist n informal a seriously ill person who seeks to terminate his or her own life by travelling to a country where medically assisted suicide is legal

death trap n a building, vehicle, etc, that is considered very unsafe

Death Valley n a desert valley in E California and W Nevada: the lowest, hottest, and driest area of the US. Lowest point: 86 m (282 ft) below sea level. Area: about 3885 sq km (1500 sq miles)

death warrant n 1 the official authorization for carrying out a sentence of death 2 **sign one's death warrant** or **sign one's own death warrant** to cause one's own destruction

deathwatch ('dɛθˌwɒtʃ) n 1 a vigil held beside a dying or dead person 2 **deathwatch beetle** a beetle, *Xestobium rufovillosum*, whose woodboring larvae are a serious pest The adult produces a rapid tapping sound with its head that was once popularly supposed to presage death

death wish n (in Freudian psychology) the desire for self-annihilation

Deauville ('dəʊviːl; *French* dovil) n a town and resort in NW France: casino Pop: 4364 (1999)

deb (dɛb) n *informal* short for **debutante**

debacle (deɪ'bɑːkəl, dɪ-) n 1 a sudden disastrous collapse or defeat, esp one involving a disorderly retreat; rout 2 the breaking up of ice in a river during spring or summer, often causing flooding 3 a violent rush of water carrying along debris [c19: from French *débâcle*, from Old French *desbacler* to unbolt, ultimately from Latin *baculum* rod, staff]

debag (diː'bæg) vb -bags, -bagging, -bagged (tr) *Brit slang* to remove the trousers from (someone) by force

debar (dɪ'bɑː) vb -bars, -barring, -barred (tr; usually foll by *from*) to exclude from a place, a right, etc; bar > de'barment n

● USAGE See at **disbar**

debark¹ (dɪ'bɑːk) vb a less common word for **disembark** [c17: from French *débarquer*, from dé- DIS¹ + *barque* BARQUE] > debarkation (ˌdiːbɑː'keɪʃən) n

debark² (diː'bɑːk) vb (tr) to remove the bark from (a tree) [c18: from DE- + BARK²]

debase (dɪ'beɪs) vb (tr) to lower in quality, character, or value, as by adding cheaper metal to coins; adulterate [c16: see DE-, BASE²] > de'basement n > de'baser n

debate (dɪ'beɪt) n 1 a formal discussion, as in a legislative body, in which opposing arguments are put forward 2 discussion or dispute 3 the formal presentation and opposition of a specific motion, followed by a vote ▷ vb 4 to discuss (a motion) esp in a formal assembly 5 to deliberate upon (something): *he debated with himself whether to go* [c13: from Old French *debatre* to discuss, argue, from Latin *battuere*] > de'bater n > de'batable or de'bateable adj

debauch (dɪ'bɔːtʃ) vb 1 (when tr, *usually passive*) to lead into a life of depraved self-indulgence 2 (tr) to seduce (a woman) ▷ n 3 an instance or period of extreme dissipation [c16: from Old French *desbaucher* to corrupt, literally: to shape (timber) roughly, from *bauch* beam, of Germanic origin] > de'baucher n > de'bauchery or de'bauchment n

debauchee (ˌdɛbɔː'tʃiː, -ɔː'ʃiː) n a man who leads a life of reckless drinking, promiscuity, and self-indulgence

de Beauvoir (*French* də bovwar) n **Simone** (simɔn). 1908–86, French existentialist novelist and feminist, whose works include *Le sang des autres* (1944), *Le deuxième sexe* (1949), and *Les mandarins* (1954)

debenture (dɪ'bɛntʃə) n 1 Also called: **debenture bond** a long-term bond, bearing fixed interest and usually unsecured, issued by a company or governmental agency 2 a certificate acknowledging the debt of a stated sum of money to a specified person 3 a customs certificate providing for a refund of excise or import duty [c15: from Latin phrase *dēbentur mihi* there are owed to me, from *dēbēre* to owe] > de'bentured adj

de Bèze (*French* də bɛz) n **Théodore** (teodɔr). 1519–1605, French Calvinist theologian and scholar, who lived in Switzerland. He succeeded Calvin as leader of the Swiss Protestants

debilitate (dɪ'bɪlɪˌteɪt) vb (tr) to make feeble; weaken [c16: from Latin *dēbilitāre*, from *dēbilis* weak] > deˌbiliˈtation n

debility (dɪ'bɪlɪtɪ) n, pl -ties weakness or infirmity

debit ('dɛbɪt) *accounting* ▷ n 1 a acknowledgment of a sum owing by entry on the left side of an account b the left side of an account c an entry on this side d the total of such entries e (*as modifier*): *a debit balance* ▷ vb -its, -iting, -ited 2 (tr) a to record (an item) as a debit in an account b to charge (a person or his or her account)

with a debt [c15: from Latin *dēbitum* DEBT]

debit card n an embossed plastic card issued by a bank or building society to enable its customers to pay for goods or services by inserting it into a computer-controlled device at the place of sale, which is connected through the telephone network to the bank or building society. It may also function as a cash card, a cheque card, or both

debonair or **debonaire** (ˌdɛbə'nɛə) adj (esp of a man or his manner) 1 suave and refined 2 carefree; light-hearted 3 courteous and cheerful; affable [c13: from Old French *debonaire*, from *de bon aire* having a good disposition] > ˌdebo'nairly adv > ˌdebo'nairness n

Deborah ('dɛbərə, -brə) n *Old Testament* 1 a prophetess and judge of Israel who fought the Canaanites (Judges 4, 5) 2 Rebecca's nurse (Genesis 35:8)

debouch (dɪ'baʊtʃ) vb (intr) 1 (esp of troops) to move into a more open space, as from a narrow or concealed place 2 (of a river, glacier, etc) to flow from a valley into a larger area or body [c18: from French *déboucher*, from dé- DIS¹ + *bouche* mouth, from Latin *bucca* cheek] > de'bouchment n

Debrett (də'brɛt) n a list of the British aristocracy. In full: **Debrett's Peerage** [c19: after J. Debrett (c. 1750–1822), London publisher who first issued it]

debrief (diː'briːf) vb (of a soldier, astronaut, diplomat, etc) to make or (of his or her superiors) to elicit a report after a mission or event > de'briefing n

debris or **débris** ('deɪbrɪ, 'dɛbrɪ) n 1 fragments or remnants of something destroyed or broken; rubble 2 a collection of loose material derived from rocks, or an accumulation of animal or vegetable matter [c18: from French, from obsolete *debrisier* to break into pieces, from *bruisier* to shatter, of Celtic origin]

de Broglie (*French* də brɔj) n 1 **Prince Louis Victor** (lwi viktɔr). 1892–1987, French physicist, noted for his research in quantum mechanics and his development of wave mechanics: Nobel prize for physics 1929 2 his brother, **Maurice** (mɔris), **Duc de Broglie**. 1875–1960, French physicist, noted for his research into X-ray spectra

Debs (dɛbz) n **Eugene Victor**. 1855–1926, US labour leader; five times Socialist presidential candidate (1900–20)

debt (dɛt) n 1 something that is owed, such as money, goods, or services 2 **bad debt** a debt that has little or no prospect of being paid 3 an obligation to pay or perform something; liability 4 the state of owing something, esp money, or of being under an obligation (esp in the phrases **in debt, in** (**someone's**) **debt**) [c13: from Old French *dette*, from Latin *dēbitum*, from *dēbēre* to owe, from DE- + *habēre* to have; English spelling influenced by the Latin etymon]

debt of honour n a debt that is morally but not legally binding, such as one contracted in gambling

debtor ('dɛtə) n a person or commercial enterprise that owes a financial obligation

debt swap n See **swap** (sense 4)

debud (diː'bʌd) vb -buds, -budding, -budded another word for **disbud**

debug (diː'bʌg) vb -bugs, -bugging, -bugged (tr) *informal* 1 to locate and remove concealed microphones from (a room, etc) 2 to locate and remove defects in (a device, system, plan, etc) 3 to remove insects from [c20: from DE- + BUG¹]

debunk (diː'bʌŋk) vb (tr) *informal* to expose the pretensions or falseness of, esp by ridicule [c20: from DE- + BUNK²] > de'bunker n

debus (diː'bʌs) vb debuses, debusing, debused or debusses, debussing, debussed to unload (goods) or (esp of troops) to alight from a motor vehicle

Debussy (də'bjuːsɪ, 'deɪbjuːsɪ; *French* dəbysi) n (**Achille**) **Claude** (klod). 1862–1918, French composer and critic, the creator of impressionism in music and a profound influence on contemporary composition. His works include *Prélude à l'après- midi d'un faune* (1894) and *La Mer* (1905) for orchestra, the opera *Pelléas et Mélisande* (1902), and many piano pieces and song settings

debut ('deɪbjuː, 'dɛbjuː) n 1 a the first public appearance of an actor, musician, etc, or the first public presentation of a show **b** (*as modifier*): *debut album* **2** the presentation of a debutante [c18: from French *début*, from Old French *desbuter* to play first (hence: make one's first appearance), from *des-* DE- + *but* goal, target; see BUTT²]

debutant (ˈdɛbjʊˌtɑːnt, -ˌtænt) *n* a person who is making a first appearance in a particular capacity, such as a sportsperson playing in a first game for a team

debutante (ˈdɛbjʊˌtɑːnt, -ˌtænt) *n* **1** a young woman of upper-class background who is presented to society, usually at a formal ball **2** a girl or young woman regarded as being upper-class, wealthy, and of a frivolous or snobbish social set [c19: from French, from *débuter* to lead off in a game, make one's first appearance; see DEBUT]

Debye (*Dutch* deˈbɛiə) *n* **Peter Joseph Wilhelm**. 1884–1966, Dutch chemist and physicist, working in the US: Nobel prize for chemistry (1936) for his work on dipole moments

Dec *abbreviation* December

dec. *abbreviation* **1** deceased **2** *music* decrescendo

deca-, deka-, *before a vowel* **dec-** *or before a vowel* **dek-** *prefix* denoting ten: *decagon*. In conjunction with scientific units the symbol **da** is used [from Greek *deka*]

decade (ˈdɛkeɪd, dɪˈkeɪd) *n* **1** a period of ten consecutive years **2** a group or series of ten [c15: from Old French, from Late Latin *decad-, decas*, from Greek *dekas*, from *deka* ten] >de'cadal *adj*

decadence (ˈdɛkədəns) *or* **decadency** *n* **1** deterioration, esp of morality or culture; decay; degeneration **2** the state reached through such a process [c16: from French, from Medieval Latin *dēcadentia*, literally: a falling away; see DECAY]

decadent (ˈdɛkədənt) *adj* **1** characterized by decay or decline, as in being self-indulgent or morally corrupt **2** belonging to a period of decline in artistic standards ▷ *n* **3** a decadent person **4** (*often capital*) one of a group of French and English writers of the late 19th century whose works were characterized by refinement of style and a tendency towards the artificial and abnormal

decaf (ˈdiːkæf) *informal* ▷ *n* **1** decaffeinated coffee ▷ *adj* **2** decaffeinated

decaffeinate (dɪˈkæfɪˌneɪt) *vb* (*tr*) to remove all or part of the caffeine from (coffee, tea, etc)

decagon (ˈdɛkəˌɡɒn) *n* a polygon having ten sides >decagonal (dɪˈkæɡənᵊl) *adj*

decahedron (ˌdɛkəˈhiːdrən) *n* a solid figure having ten plane faces >,deca'hedral *adj*

decal (dɪˈkæl, ˈdiːkæl) *n* **1** short for decalcomania ▷ *vb* decals, decalling, decalled *or US* decals, decaling, decaled **2** to transfer (a design) by decalcomania

decalcify (diːˈkælsɪˌfaɪ) *vb* **-fies, -fying, -fied** (*tr*) to remove calcium or lime from (bones, teeth, etc) >de'calci,fier *n*

decalcomania (dɪˌkælkəˈmeɪnɪə) *n* **1** the art or process of transferring a design from prepared paper onto another surface, such as china, glass or paper **2** a design so transferred [c19: from French *décalcomanie*, from *décalquer* to transfer by tracing, from *dé-* DE- + *calquer* to trace + *-manie* -MANIA]

decalitre *or US* **decaliter** (ˈdɛkəˌliːtə) *n* ten litres. One decalitre is equal to about 2.2 imperial gallons

Decalogue (ˈdɛkəˌlɒɡ) *n* another name for the **Ten Commandments** [c14: from Church Latin *decalogus*, from Greek, from *deka* ten + *logos* word]

decametre *or US* **decameter** (ˈdɛkəˌmiːtə) *n* ten metres

decamp (dɪˈkæmp) *vb* (*intr*) **1** to leave a camp; break camp **2** to depart secretly or suddenly; abscond >de'campment *n*

decanal (dɪˈkeɪnᵊl) *adj* **1** of or relating to a dean or deanery **2** (of part of a choir) on the same side of a cathedral, etc, as the dean; on the S side of the choir [c18: from Medieval Latin *decānālis, decānus* DEAN]

decani (dɪˈkeɪnaɪ) *adj, adv* *music* to be sung by the decanal side of a choir [Latin: genitive of *decānus*]

decant (dɪˈkænt) *vb* **1** to pour (a liquid, such as wine) from one container to another, esp without disturbing any sediment **2** (*tr*) to rehouse (people) while their

homes are being rebuilt or refurbished [c17: from Medieval Latin *dēcanthāre*, from *canthus* spout, rim; see CANTHUS]

decanter (dɪˈkæntə) *n* a stoppered bottle, usually of glass, into which a drink, such as wine, is poured for serving

decapitate (dɪˈkæpɪˌteɪt) *vb* (*tr*) to behead [c17: from Late Latin *dēcapitāre*, from Latin *DE-* + *caput* head] >de,capi'tation *n* >de'capi,tator *n*

decapod (ˈdɛkəˌpɒd) *n* **1** any crustacean of the mostly marine order *Decapoda*, having five pairs of walking limbs: includes the crabs, lobsters, shrimps, prawns, and crayfish **2** any cephalopod mollusc of the order *Decapoda*, having a ring of eight short tentacles and two longer ones: includes the squids and cuttlefish >decapodal (dɪˈkæpədᵊl) *or* de'capodan *or* de'capodous *adj*

decarbonate (diːˈkɑːbəˌneɪt) *vb* (*tr*) to remove carbon dioxide from (a solution, substance, etc) >de,carbon'ation *n* >de'carbon,ator *n*

decarbonize *or* **decarbonise** (diːˈkɑːbəˌnaɪz) *vb* (*tr*) to remove carbon from (the walls of the combustion chamber of an internal-combustion engine). Also called: decoke, decarburize >de,carboni'zation *or* de,carboni'sation *n* >de'carbon,izer *or* de'carbon,iser *n*

decarboxylase (ˌdiːkɑːˈbɒksɪˌleɪs) *n* an enzyme that catalyses the removal of carbon dioxide from a compound

decastyle (ˈdɛkəˌstaɪl) *n* *architect* a portico consisting of ten columns

decasyllable (ˈdɛkəˌsɪləbᵊl) *n* a word or line of verse consisting of ten syllables >decasyllabic (ˌdɛkəsɪˈlæbɪk) *adj*

decathlon (dɪˈkæθlɒn) *n* an athletic contest for men in which each athlete competes in ten different events [c20: from DECA- + Greek *athlon* contest, prize; see ATHLETE] >de'cathlete *n*

Decatur (dəˈkeɪtə) *n* **Stephen**. 1779–1820, US naval officer, noted for his raid on Tripoli harbour (1804) and his role in the War of 1812

decay (dɪˈkeɪ) *vb* **1** to decline or cause to decline gradually in health, prosperity, excellence, etc; deteriorate; waste away **2** to rot or cause to rot as a result of bacterial, fungal, or chemical action; decompose **3** Also: disintegrate (*intr*) *physics* **a** (of an atomic nucleus) to undergo radioactive disintegration **b** (of an elementary particle) to transform into two or more different elementary particles **4** (*intr*) *physics* (of a stored charge, magnetic flux, etc) to decrease gradually when the source of energy has been removed ▷ *n* **5** the process of decline, as in health, mentality, beauty, etc **6** the state brought about by this process **7** decomposition, as of vegetable matter **8** rotten or decayed matter **9** *physics* **a** See radioactive decay **b** a spontaneous transformation of an elementary particle into two or more different particles **10** *physics* a gradual decrease of a stored charge, magnetic flux, current, etc, when the source of energy has been removed [c15: from Old Northern French *decair*, from Late Latin *dēcadere*, literally: to fall away, from Latin *cadere* to fall] >de'cayable *adj*

Deccan (ˈdɛkən) the Deccan *n* **1** a plateau in S India, between the Eastern Ghats, the Western Ghats, and the Narmada River **2** the whole Indian peninsula south of the Narmada River

decease (dɪˈsiːs) *n* **1** a more formal word for **death** ▷ *vb* **2** (*intr*) a more formal word for **die** [c14 (n): from Old French *deces*, from Latin *dēcēdere* to depart]

deceased (dɪˈsiːst) *adj* **a** a more formal word for **dead** (sense 1) **b** (*as noun*): *the deceased*

deceit (dɪˈsiːt) *n* **1** the act or practice of deceiving **2** a statement, act, or device intended to mislead; fraud; trick **3** a tendency to deceive [c13: from Old French *deceite*, from *deceivre* to deceive]

deceitful (dɪˈsiːtfʊl) *adj* full of deceit

deceive (dɪˈsiːv) *vb* (*tr*) **1** to mislead by deliberate misrepresentation or lies **2** to delude (oneself) **3** to be unfaithful to (one's sexual partner) **4** *archaic* to disappoint [c13: from Old French *deceivre*, from Latin

d

dēcipere to ensnare, cheat, from *capere* to take] > de'ceivable *adj* > de'ceiver *n*

decelerate (diːˈsɛləˌreɪt) *vb* to slow down or cause to slow down [C19: from DE- + ACCELERATE] > deˌceler'ation *n* > de'celerˌator *n*

December (dɪˈsɛmbə) *n* the twelfth and last month of the year, consisting of 31 days [C13: from Old French *decembre*, from Latin *december* the tenth month (the Roman year originally began with March), from *decem* ten]

decencies (ˈdiːsᵊnsɪz) *pl n* the decencies those things that are considered necessary for a decent life

decency (ˈdiːsᵊnsɪ) *n, pl* -cies **1** conformity to the prevailing standards of propriety, morality, modesty, etc **2** the quality of being decent

decennial (dɪˈsɛnɪəl) *adj* **1** lasting for ten years **2** occurring every ten years ▷ *n* **3** a tenth anniversary or its celebration > de'cennially *adv*

decent (ˈdiːsᵊnt) *adj* **1** polite or respectable **2** proper and suitable; fitting **3** conforming to conventions of sexual behaviour; not indecent **4** free of oaths, blasphemy, etc **5** good or adequate: *a decent wage* **6** *informal* kind; generous **7** *informal* sufficiently clothed to be seen by other people: *are you decent?* [C16: from Latin *decēns* suitable, from *decēre* to be fitting] > 'decently *adv*

decentralize *or* **decentralise** (diːˈsɛntrəˌlaɪz) *vb* **1** to reorganize (a government, industry, etc) into smaller more autonomous units **2** to disperse (a concentration, as of industry or population) > de'centralist *n, adj* > deˌcentrali'zation *or* deˌcentrali'sation *n*

deception (dɪˈsɛpʃən) *n* **1** the act of deceiving or the state of being deceived **2** something that deceives; trick

deceptive (dɪˈsɛptɪv) *adj* likely or designed to deceive; misleading > de'ceptively *adv* > de'ceptiveness *n*

decern (dɪˈsɜːn) *vb* (*tr*) **1** *Scots law* to decree or adjudge **2** an archaic spelling of **discern** [C15: from Old French *decerner*, from Latin *dēcernere* to judge, from *cernere* to discern]

decertify (diːˈsɜːtɪfaɪ) *vb* -fies, -fying, -fied (*tr*) to withdraw or remove a certificate or certification from (a person, organization, or country) > deˌcertifi'cation *n*

deci- *prefix* denoting one tenth; 10^{-1}: *decimetre* Symbol: d [from French *déci-*, from Latin *decimus* tenth]

decibel (ˈdɛsɪˌbɛl) *n* **1** a unit for comparing two currents, voltages, or power levels, equal to one tenth of a bel **2** a similar unit for measuring the intensity of a sound. It is equal to ten times the logarithm to the base ten of the ratio of the intensity of the sound to be measured to the intensity of some reference sound, usually the lowest audible note of the same frequency ▷ Abbreviation: dB

decide (dɪˈsaɪd) *vb* **1** (*may take a clause or an infinitive as object; when intr, sometimes foll by on or about*) to reach a decision: *decide what you want; he decided to go* **2** (*tr*) to cause (a person) to reach a decision **3** (*tr*) to determine or settle (a contest or question) **4** (*tr*) to influence decisively the outcome of (a contest or question) **5** (*intr*; foll by for or against*) to pronounce a formal verdict [C14: from Old French *decider*, from Latin *dēcīdere*, literally: to cut off, from *caedere* to cut] > de'cidable *adj*

decided (dɪˈsaɪdɪd) *adj* (*prenominal*) **1** unmistakable **2** determined; resolute: *a girl of decided character* > de'cidedly *adv*

decider (dɪˈsaɪdə) *n* the point, goal, game, etc, that determines who wins a match or championship

deciduous (dɪˈsɪdjʊəs) *adj* **1** (of trees and shrubs) shedding all leaves annually at the end of the growing season and then having a dormant period without leaves. See **evergreen** (sense 1) **2** (of antlers, wings, teeth, etc) being shed at the end of a period of growth [C17: from Latin *dēciduus* falling off, from *dēcidere* to fall down, from *cadere* to fall] > de'ciduousness *n*

decilitre *or US* **deciliter** (ˈdɛsɪˌliːtə) *n* one tenth of a litre

decillion (dɪˈsɪljən) *n* **1** (in Britain, France, and Germany) the number represented as one followed by 60 zeros (10^{60}) **2** (in the US and Canada) the number represented as one followed by 33 zeros (10^{33}) [C19: from Latin *decem* ten + -*illion* as in *million*] > de'cillionth *adj*

decimal (ˈdɛsɪməl) *n* **1** Also called: **decimal fraction** a fraction that has a denominator of a power of ten, the power depending on or deciding the decimal place. It is indicated by a decimal point to the left of the numerator, the denominator being omitted. Zeros are inserted between the point and the numerator, if necessary, to obtain the correct decimal place **2** any number used in the decimal system ▷ *adj* **3 a** relating to or using powers of ten **b** of the base ten **4** (*prenominal*) expressed as a decimal [C17: from Medieval Latin *decimālis* of tithes, from Latin *decima* a tenth, from *decem* ten] > 'decimally *adv*

decimal classification *n* another term for **Dewey Decimal System**

decimal currency *n* a system of currency in which the monetary units are parts or powers of ten

decimalize *or* **decimalise** (ˈdɛsɪməˌlaɪz) *vb* to change (a system, number, etc) to the decimal system > ˌdecimali'zation *or* ˌdecimali'sation *n*

decimal place *n* **1** the position of a digit after the decimal point, each successive position to the right having a denominator of an increased power of ten **2** the number of digits to the right of the decimal point

decimal point *n* a full stop or a raised full stop placed between the integral and fractional parts of a number in the decimal system

● USAGE Conventions relating to the use of the decimal
● point are confused. The IX General Conference on
● Weights and Measures resolved in 1948 that the
● decimal point should be a point on the line or a
● comma, but not a centre dot. It also resolved that
● figures could be grouped in threes about the decimal
● point, but that no point or comma should be used for
● this purpose. These conventions are adopted in this
● dictionary. However, the Decimal Currency Board
● recommended that for sums of money the centre dot
● should be used as the decimal point and that the
● comma should be used as the thousand marker.
● Moreover, in some countries the position is reversed,
● the comma being used as the decimal point and the
● dot as the thousand marker

decimal system *n* **1** the number system in general use, having a base of ten, in which numbers are expressed by combinations of the ten digits 0 to 9 **2** a system of measurement, such as the metric system, in which the multiple and submultiple units are related to a basic unit by powers of ten

decimate (ˈdɛsɪˌmeɪt) *vb* (*tr*) **1** to destroy or kill a large proportion of **2** (esp in the ancient Roman army) to kill every tenth man of (a mutinous section) [C17: from Latin *decimāre*, from *decimus* tenth, from *decem* ten] > ˌdeci'mation *n* > 'deciˌmator *n*

● USAGE One talks about the whole of something being
● decimated, not a part: *disease decimated the population*, not
● *disease decimated most of the population*

decimetre *or US* **decimeter** (ˈdɛsɪˌmiːtə) *n* one tenth of a metre. Symbol: dm

decipher (dɪˈsaɪfə) *vb* (*tr*) **1** to determine the meaning of (something obscure or illegible) **2** to convert from code into plain text; decode > de'cipherable *adj* > de'cipherment *n*

decision (dɪˈsɪʒən) *n* **1** a judgment, conclusion, or resolution reached or given; verdict **2** the act of making up one's mind **3** firmness of purpose or character; determination [C15: from Old French, from Latin *dēcīsiō*, literally: a cutting off; see DECIDE]

decision tree *n* a treelike diagram illustrating the choices available to a decision maker, each possible decision and its estimated outcome being shown as a separate branch of the tree

decisive (dɪˈsaɪsɪv) *adj* **1** influential; conclusive **2** characterized by the ability to make decisions, esp quickly; resolute > de'cisively *adv* > de'cisiveness *n*

deck (dɛk) *n* **1** *nautical* any of various platforms built into a vessel **2** a similar floor or platform, as in a bus **3 a** the horizontal platform that supports the turntable and pick-up of a record player **b** See **tape deck 4** *chiefly US* a pack of playing cards **5** Also called: **pack** *obsolete computing* a collection of punched cards relevant to a particular program **6 clear the decks** *informal* to prepare for action, as by removing obstacles from a field of activity or combat **7 hit the deck** *informal* **a** to fall to the floor or ground, esp in order to avoid injury **b** to prepare for action **c** to get out of bed ▷ *vb* (*tr*) **8** (often foll by *out*) to dress or decorate **9** to build a deck on (a vessel) **10** *slang* to knock (a person) to the floor or ground [c15: from Middle Dutch *dec* a covering; related to THATCH]

deck-access *adj* (of a block of flats) having a continuous inset balcony at each level onto which the front door of each flat on that level opens

deckchair ('dɛk,tʃɛə) *n* a folding chair for use out of doors, consisting of a wooden frame suspending a length of canvas

-decker *adj* (*in combination:*) having a certain specified number of levels or layers: *a double-decker bus*

Decker ('dɛkə) *n* a variant spelling of (Thomas) **Dekker**

deck hand *n* **1** a seaman assigned various duties, such as mooring and cargo handling, on the deck of a ship **2** (in Britain) a seaman over 17 years of age who has seen sea duty for at least one year **3** a helper aboard a yacht

decking ('dɛkɪŋ) *n* a wooden deck or platform, esp one in a garden for deckchairs, etc

deckle *or* **deckel** ('dɛkəl) *n* **1** a frame used to contain pulp on the mould in the making of handmade paper **2** Also called: **deckle strap** a strap on each edge of the moving web of paper on a paper-making machine that fixes the width of the paper [c19: from German *Deckel* lid, from *decken* to cover]

deckle edge *n* **1** the rough edge of handmade paper, caused by pulp seeping between the mould and the deckle: often left as ornamentation in fine books and writing papers **2** a trimmed edge imitating this > 'deckle-'edged *adj*

declaim (dɪ'kleɪm) *vb* **1** to make (a speech, statement, etc) loudly and in a rhetorical manner **2** to speak lines from (a play, poem, etc) with studied eloquence; recite **3** (*intr*; foll by *against*) to protest (against) loudly and publicly [c14: from Latin *dēclāmāre*, from *clāmāre* to call out] > de'claimer *n* > declamatory (dɪ'klæmətərɪ, -trɪ) *adj* > de'clamatorily *adv*

declamation (,dɛklə'meɪʃən) *n* **1** a rhetorical or emotional speech, made esp in order to protest or condemn; tirade **2** a speech, verse, etc, that is or can be spoken **3** the act or art of declaiming

declaration (,dɛklə'reɪʃən) *n* **1** an explicit or emphatic statement **2** a formal statement or announcement; proclamation **3** the act of declaring **4** the ruling of a judge or court on a question of law, esp in the chancery division of the High Court **5** *law* an unsworn statement of a witness admissible in evidence under certain conditions **6** *cricket* the voluntary closure of an innings before all ten wickets have fallen **7** *contract bridge* the final contract **8** a statement or inventory of goods, etc, submitted for tax assessment

declarative (dɪ'klærətɪv) *adj* making or having the nature of a declaration > de'claratively *adv*

declare (dɪ'klɛə) *vb* (*mainly tr*) **1** (*may take a clause as object*) to make clearly known or announce officially: *to declare one's interests; war was declared* **2** to state officially that (a person, fact, etc) is as specified: *he declared him fit* **3** (*may take a clause as object*) to state emphatically; assert **4** to show, reveal, or manifest **5** (*intr*; often foll by *for* or *against*) to make known one's choice or opinion **6** to make a complete statement of (dutiable goods, etc) **7** (*also intr*) *cards* **a** to display (a card or series of) on the table so as to add to one's score **b** to decide (the trump suit) by making the final bid **8** (*intr*) *cricket* to close an innings voluntarily before all ten wickets have fallen **9** to authorize the payment of (a dividend) from corporate net profit [c14: from Latin *dēclārāre* to make clear, from *clārus* bright, clear] > de'clarable *adj* > de'clarer *n*

declassify (di:'klæsɪ,faɪ) *vb* -fies, -fying, -fied (*tr*) to release (a document or information) from the security list > de,classifi'cation *n*

declension (dɪ'klɛnʃən) *n* **1** *grammar* **a** inflection of nouns, pronouns, or adjectives for case, number, and gender **b** the complete set of the inflections of such a word **2** a decline or deviation from a standard, belief, etc **3** a downward slope or bend [c15: from Latin *dēclīnātiō*,

literally: a bending aside, hence variation, inflection; see DECLINE] > de'clensional *adj*

declination (,dɛklɪ'neɪʃən) *n* **1** *astronomy* the angular distance, esp in degrees, of a star, planet, etc, from the celestial equator measured north (positive) or south (negative) along the great circle passing through the celestial poles and the body. Symbol: δ **2** a refusal, esp a courteous or formal one > decli'national *adj*

decline (dɪ'klaɪn) *vb* **1** to refuse to do or accept (something), esp politely **2** (*intr*) to grow smaller; diminish **3** to slope or cause to slope downwards **4** (*intr*) to deteriorate gradually, as in quality, health, or character **5** *grammar* to state or list the inflections of (a noun, adjective, or pronoun), or (of a noun, adjective, or pronoun) to be inflected for number, case, or gender ▷ *n* **6** gradual deterioration or loss **7** a movement downward or towards something smaller; diminution **8** a downward slope; declivity **9** *archaic* any slowly progressive disease, such as tuberculosis [c14: from Old French *decliner* to inflect, turn away, sink, from Latin *dēclīnāre* to bend away, inflect grammatically] > de'clinable *adj* > de'cliner *n*

declivity (dɪ'klɪvɪtɪ) *n, pl* -ties a downward slope, esp of the ground [c17: from Latin *dēclīvitās*, from DE- + *clīvus* a slope, hill] > de'clivitous *adj*

declutch (dɪ'klʌtʃ) *vb* (*intr*) to disengage the clutch of a motor vehicle

declutter (di:'klʌtə) *vb* to simplify or get rid of mess, disorder, complications, etc: *declutter your life*

decoct (dɪ'kɒkt) *vb* to extract (the essence or active principle) from (a medicinal or similar substance) by boiling [c15: see DECOCTION]

decoction (dɪ'kɒkʃən) *n* **1** *pharmacol* the extraction of the water-soluble substances of a drug or medicinal plants by boiling **2** the essence or liquor resulting from this [c14: from Old French, from Late Latin *dēcoctiō*, from *dēcoquere* to boil down, from *coquere* to COOK]

decode (di:'kəʊd) *vb* to convert (a message, text, etc) from code into ordinary language > de'coder *n*

decoherence (,di:kəʊ'hɪərəns) *n* *physics* the process in which a system's behaviour changes from that which can be explained by quantum mechanics to that which can be explained by classical mechanics

decoke (di:'kəʊk) *vb* (*tr*) another word for **decarbonize**

décolletage (,deɪkɒl'tɑːʒ; *French* dekɔltaʒ) *n* a low-cut neckline or a woman's garment with a low neck [c19: from French; see DÉCOLLETÉ]

décolleté (deɪ'kɒlteɪ; *French* dekɔlte) *adj* **1** (of a woman's garment) low-cut **2** wearing a low-cut garment ▷ *n* **3** a low-cut neckline [c19: from French *décolleter* to cut out the neck (of a dress), from *collet* collar]

decolonize *or* **decolonise** (di:'kɒlə,naɪz) *vb* (*tr*) to grant independence to (a colony) > de,coloni'zation *or* de,coloni'sation *n*

decolour (di:'kʌlə), **decolorize** *or* **decolorise** *vb* (*tr*) to deprive of colour, as by bleaching > de,color'ation, de,colori'zation *or* de,colori'sation *n*

decommission (,di:kə'mɪʃən) *vb* (*tr*) to dismantle or remove from service (a nuclear reactor, weapon, ship, etc which is no longer required)

decompose (,di:kəm'pəʊz) *vb* **1** to break down (organic matter) or (of organic matter) to be broken down physically and chemically by bacterial or fungal action; rot **2** *chem* to break down or cause to break down into simpler chemical compounds **3** to break up or separate into constituent parts > decomposition (,di:kɒmpə'zɪʃən) *n*

decomposer (,di:kəm'pəʊzə) *n* *ecology* any organism in a community, such as a bacterium or fungus, that breaks down dead tissue enabling the constituents to be recycled to the environment

decompress (,di:kəm'prɛs) *vb* **1** to relieve (a substance) of pressure or (of a substance) to be relieved of pressure **2** to return (a diver, caisson worker, etc) to a condition of normal atmospheric pressure gradually from a condition of increased pressure or (of a diver, etc) to be returned to such a condition > ,decom'pression *n*

decompression chamber *n* a chamber in which the pressure of air can be varied slowly for returning people from abnormal pressures to atmospheric pressure without inducing decompression sickness

decompression sickness or **decompresssion illness** n a disorder characterized by severe pain in muscles and joints, cramp, and difficulty in breathing, caused by a sudden and sustained decrease in air pressure, resulting in the deposition of nitrogen bubbles in the tissues

decongestant (ˌdiːkənˈdʒɛstənt) adj 1 relieving congestion, esp nasal congestion ▷ n 2 a decongestant drug

deconsecrate (diːˈkɒnsɪˌkreɪt) vb (tr) to transfer (a church) to secular use > deˌconseˈcration n

deconstruct (ˌdiːkənˈstrʌkt) vb (tr) 1 to apply the theories of deconstruction to (a text, film, etc) 2 to expose or dismantle the existing structure in (a system, organization, etc)

deconstruction (ˌdiːkənˈstrʌkʃən) n a technique of literary analysis that regards meaning as resulting from the differences between words rather than their reference to the things they stand for. Different meanings are discovered by taking apart the structure of the language used and exposing the assumption that words have a fixed reference point beyond themselves

decontaminate (ˌdiːkənˈtæmɪˌneɪt) vb (tr) to render (an area, building, object, etc) harmless by the removal, distribution, or neutralization of poisons, radioactivity, etc > ˌdeconˌtamiˈnation n

decontrol (ˌdiːkənˈtrəʊl) vb -trols, -trolling, -trolled (tr) to free of restraints or controls, esp government controls: to decontrol prices

décor or **decor** (ˈdeɪkɔː) n 1 a style or scheme of interior decoration, furnishings, etc, as in a room or house 2 stage decoration; scenery [c19: from French, from décorer to DECORATE]

decorate (ˈdɛkəˌreɪt) vb 1 (tr) to make more attractive by adding ornament, colour, etc 2 to paint or wallpaper (a room, house, etc) 3 (tr) to confer a mark of distinction, esp a military medal, upon [c16: from Latin decorāre, from decus adornment; see DECENT] > decorative (ˈdɛkərətɪv, ˈdɛkrətɪv) adj > 'decoratively adv > 'decorativeness n

Decorated style or **Decorated architecture** n a 14th-century style of English architecture characterized by the ogee arch, geometrical tracery, and floral decoration

decoration (ˌdɛkəˈreɪʃən) n 1 an addition that renders something more attractive or ornate; adornment 2 the act, process, or art of decorating 3 a medal, badge, etc, conferred as a mark of honour

decorator (ˈdɛkəˌreɪtə) n 1 Brit a person whose profession is the painting and wallpapering of buildings 2 a person who decorates

decorous (ˈdɛkərəs) adj characterized by propriety in manners, conduct, etc [c17: from Latin decōrus, from decor elegance] > 'decorously adv > 'decorousness n

decorum (dɪˈkɔːrəm) n 1 propriety, esp in behaviour or conduct 2 a requirement of correct behaviour in polite society [c16: from Latin: propriety]

decoupage (ˌdeɪkuːˈpɑːʒ) n the art or process of decorating a surface with shapes or illustrations cut from paper, card, etc [c20: from French, from découper to cut out, from DE- + couper to cut]

decoy n (ˈdiːkɔɪ, dɪˈkɔɪ) 1 a person or thing used to beguile or lead someone into danger; lure 2 military something designed to deceive an enemy or divert his attention 3 a bird or animal, or an image of one, used to lure game into a trap or within shooting range 4 an enclosed space or large trap, often with a wide funnelled entrance, into which game can be lured for capture 5 Canad another word for **deke** (sense 1) ▷ vb (dɪˈkɔɪ) 6 to lure or be lured by or as if by means of a decoy 7 (tr) Canad another word for **deke** (sense 2) [c17: probably from Dutch de kooi, literally: the cage, from Latin cavea CAGE]

decrease vb (dɪˈkriːs) 1 to diminish or cause to diminish in size, number, strength, etc ▷ n (ˈdiːkriːs, dɪˈkriːs) 2 the act or process of diminishing; reduction 3 the amount by which something has been diminished [c14: from Old French descreistre, from Latin dēcrescere to grow less, from DE- + crescere to grow] > de'creasing adj > de'creasingly adv

decree (dɪˈkriː) n 1 an edict, law, etc, made by someone in authority 2 an order or judgment of a court made after hearing a suit, esp in matrimonial proceedings ▷ vb decrees, decreeing, decreed 3 to order, adjudge, or ordain by decree [c14: from Old French decre, from Latin dēcrētum ordinance, from dēcrētus decided, past participle of dēcernere to determine; see DECERN]

decree absolute n the final decree in divorce proceedings, which leaves the parties free to remarry

decree nisi (ˈnaɪsaɪ) n a provisional decree, esp in divorce proceedings, which will later be made absolute unless cause is shown why it should not

decrement (ˈdɛkrɪmənt) n 1 the act of decreasing; diminution 2 maths a negative increment 3 physics a measure of the damping of an oscillator, expressed by the ratio of the amplitude of a cycle to its amplitude after one period [c17: from Latin dēcrēmentum, from dēcrescere to DECREASE]

decrepit (dɪˈkrɛpɪt) adj 1 enfeebled by old age; infirm 2 broken down or worn out by hard or long use; dilapidated [c15: from Latin dēcrepitus, from crepāre to creak] > de'crepi,tude n

decrescendo (ˌdiːkrɪˈʃɛndəʊ) n, adj another word for **diminuendo** [Italian, from decrescere to DECREASE]

decrescent (dɪˈkrɛsənt) adj (esp of the moon) decreasing; waning [c17: from Latin dēcrescēns growing less; see DECREASE] > de'crescence n

decretal (dɪˈkriːtəl) n 1 RC Church a papal edict on doctrine or church law ▷ adj 2 of or relating to a decretal or a decree [c15: from Old French, from Late Latin dēcrētālis; see DECREE]

decriminalize or **decriminalise** (diːˈkrɪmənəˌlaɪz) vb (tr) to remove (an action) from the legal category of criminal offence: to decriminalize the possession of marijuana

decry (dɪˈkraɪ) vb -cries, -crying, -cried (tr) 1 to express open disapproval of; disparage 2 to depreciate by proclamation: to decry obsolete coinage [c17: from Old French descrier, from des- DIS[1] + crier to CRY]

decubitus ulcer (dɪˈkjuːbɪtəs) n a chronic ulcer of the skin and underlying tissues caused by prolonged pressure on the body surface of bedridden patients. Nontechnical name: bedsore

decumbent (dɪˈkʌmbənt) adj 1 lying down or lying flat 2 botany (of certain stems) lying flat with the tip growing upwards [c17: from Latin dēcumbēns, present participle of dēcumbere to lie down] > de'cumbence or de'cumbency n

decury (ˈdɛkjʊərɪ) n, pl -ries (in ancient Rome) a body of ten men [c16: from Latin decuria]

Dedéagach, Dedeagatch or **Dedeağaç** (ˈdɛdeɪɑːˈɡaːtʃ) n a former name (until the end of World War I) of **Alexandroúpolis**

Dedekind (German ˈdeːdəˌkɪnt) n (**Julius Wilhelm**) **Richard** (ˈjuːlɪʊs ˈvɪlhɛlm ˈrɪxaːt). 1831–1916, German mathematician, who devised a way (the **Dedekind cut**) of according irrational and rational numbers the same status

dedicate (ˈdɛdɪˌkeɪt) vb (tr) 1 (often foll by to) to devote (oneself, one's time, etc) wholly to a special purpose or cause; commit wholeheartedly or unreservedly 2 (foll by to) to address or inscribe (a book, artistic performance, etc) to a person, cause, etc as a token of affection or respect 3 (foll by to) to request or play (a record) on radio for another person as a greeting 4 to assign or allocate to a particular project, function, etc 5 to set apart for a deity or for sacred uses; consecrate [c15: from Latin dēdicāre to announce, from dicāre to make known, variant of dīcere to say] > 'dedi,cator n > dedicatory (ˈdɛdɪˌkeɪtərɪ, 'dɛdɪkətərɪ, -trɪ) or 'dedi,cative adj

dedication (ˌdɛdɪˈkeɪʃən) n 1 the act of dedicating or the state of being dedicated 2 an inscription or announcement prefixed to a book, piece of music, etc, dedicating it to a person or thing 3 complete and wholehearted devotion, esp to a career, ideal, etc > ˌdedi'cational adj

deduce (dɪˈdjuːs) vb (tr) 1 (may take a clause as object) to reach (a conclusion about something) by reasoning; conclude (that); infer 2 archaic to trace the origin, course, or derivation of [c15: from Latin dēdūcere to lead away, derive, from DE- + *dūcere* to lead] > de'ducible *adj*

deduct (dɪ'dʌkt) *vb* (*tr*) to take away or subtract (a number, quantity, part, etc) [C15: from Latin *dēductus*, past participle of *dēdūcere* to DEDUCE]

deductible (dɪ'dʌktɪbᵊl) *adj* 1 capable of being deducted 2 *US & Canadian* short for **tax-deductible** ▷ *n* 3 *insurance, US & Canadian* another name for **excess** (sense 6)

deduction (dɪ'dʌkʃən) *n* 1 the act or process of deducting or subtracting 2 something, esp a sum of money, that is or may be deducted 3 **a** the process of reasoning typical of mathematics and logic, whose conclusions follow necessarily from their premises **b** the conclusion of such an argument > de'ductive *adj* > de'ductively *adv*

de Duve (də dy:v) *n Christian.* born 1917, Belgian biochemist, who discovered lysosomes: shared the Nobel prize (1974) for his work in cell biology

Dee¹ (di:) *n* 1 a river in N Wales and NW England, rising in S Gwynedd and flowing east and north to the Irish Sea. Length: about 112 km (70 miles) 2 a river in NE Scotland, rising in the Cairngorms and flowing east to the North Sea. Length: about 140 km (87 miles) 3 a river in S Scotland, flowing south to the Solway Firth. Length: about 80 km (50 miles)

Dee² (di:) *n John.* 1527–1608, English mathematician, astrologer, and magician: best known for his preface (1570) to the first edition of Euclid in English

deed (di:d) *n* 1 something that is done or performed; act 2 a notable achievement; feat; exploit 3 action or performance, as opposed to words 4 *law* a formal legal document signed, witnessed, and delivered to effect a conveyance or transfer of property or to create a legal obligation or contract ▷ *vb* 5 (*tr*) *US & Canadian* to convey or transfer (property) by deed [Old English *dēd*; related to Old High German *tāt*, Gothic *gadeths*; see DO¹]

deed box *n* a lockable metal box for storing documents

deed poll *n law* a deed made by one party only, esp one by which a person changes his name

deejay ('di:,dʒeɪ) *n* an informal name for **disc jockey** [C20: from the initials DJ]

deem (di:m) *vb* (*tr*) to judge or consider [Old English *dēman*; related to Old High German *tuomen* to judge, Gothic *domjan*; see DOOM]

de-emphasize *or* **de-emphasise** (di:'ɛmfə,saɪz) *vb* (*tr*) to remove emphasis from

deemster ('di:mstə) *n* the title of one of the two justices in the Isle of Man. Also called: dempster

de-energize *or* **de-energise** (di:'ɛnədʒaɪz) *vb* (*tr*) *electrical engineering* to disconnect (an electrical circuit) from its source > de-,energi'zation *or* de-,energi'sation *n*

deep (di:p) *adj* 1 extending or situated relatively far down from a surface: *a deep pool* 2 extending or situated relatively far inwards, backwards, or sideways 3 *cricket* relatively far from the pitch: *the deep field; deep third man* 4 (*postpositive*) of a specified dimension downwards, inwards, or backwards: *six feet deep* 5 coming from or penetrating to a great depth 6 difficult to understand or penetrate; abstruse 7 learned or intellectually demanding: *a deep discussion* 8 of great intensity; extreme: *deep happiness; deep trouble* 9 (*postpositive*; foll by *in*) absorbed or enveloped (by); engrossed or immersed (in): *deep in study; deep in debt* 10 very cunning or crafty; devious 11 mysterious or obscure: *a deep secret* 12 (of a colour) having an intense or dark hue 13 low in pitch or tone: *a deep voice* 14 go off the deep end *informal* **a** to lose one's temper; react angrily **b** *chiefly US* to act rashly 15 in deep water in a tricky position or in trouble ▷ *n* 16 any deep place on land or under water, esp below 6000 metres (3000 fathoms) 17 the deep **a** a poetic term for the **ocean b** *cricket* the area of the field relatively far from the pitch 18 the most profound, intense, or central part: *the deep of winter* 19 a vast extent, as of space or time 20 *nautical* one of the intervals on a sounding lead, one fathom apart ▷ *adv* 21 far on in time; late: *they worked deep into the night* 22 profoundly or intensely 23 deep down *informal* in reality, esp as opposed to appearance [Old English *dēop*; related to Old High German *tiof* deep, Old Norse *djupr*] > 'deeply *adv* > 'deepness *n*

deep-discount bond *n* a fixed-interest security that pays little or no interest but is issued at a substantial discount to its redemption value, thus largely substituting capital gain for income

deepen ('di:pᵊn) *vb* to make or become deep, deeper, or more intense > 'deepener *n*

deepfreeze (,di:p'fri:z) *n* 1 a type of refrigerator in which food, etc, is stored for long periods at temperatures below freezing 2 storage in or as if in a deepfreeze 3 *informal* a state of suspended activity ▷ *vb* deep-freeze -freezes, -freezing, -froze, -frozen 4 (*tr*) to freeze or keep in or as if in a deepfreeze

deep-fry *vb* -fries, -frying, -fried to cook (fish, potatoes, etc) in sufficient hot fat to cover the food entirely

deep-laid *adj* (of a plot or plan) carefully worked out and kept secret

deep-rooted *or* **deep-seated** *adj* (of ideas, beliefs, prejudices, etc) firmly fixed, implanted, or held; ingrained

deep-sea *n* (*modifier*) of, found in, or characteristic of the deep parts of the sea

deep-set *adj* (of the eyes) deeply set into the face

Deep South *n* the SE part of the US, esp South Carolina, Georgia, Alabama, Mississippi, and Louisiana

deep space *n* any region of outer space beyond the system of the earth and moon

deep structure *n generative grammar* a representation of a sentence at a level where logical or grammatical relations are made explicit, before transformational rules have been applied. See **surface structure**

deep-vein thrombosis *n, pl* -ses (-si:z) a blood clot in one of the major veins, usually in the legs or pelvis; can be caused by prolonged sitting in the same position, as on long-haul air flights. Abbreviation: DVT

deer (dɪə) *n, pl* deer *or* deers any ruminant artiodactyl mammal of the family *Cervidae*, including reindeer, elk, muntjacs, and roe deer, typically having antlers in the male. Related adj: **cervine** [Old English *dēor* beast; related to Old High German *tior* wild beast, Old Norse *dȳr*]

deer lick *n* a naturally or artificially salty area of ground where deer come to lick the salt

deerskin ('dɪə,skɪn) *n* **a** the hide of a deer **b** (*as modifier*): *a deerskin jacket*

deerstalker ('dɪə,stɔ:kə) *n* 1 Also called: stalker a person who stalks deer, esp in order to shoot them 2 a hat, peaked in front and behind, with earflaps usually turned up and tied together on the top > 'deer,stalking *adj, n*

de-escalate (di:'ɛskə,leɪt) *vb* to reduce the level or intensity of (a crisis, etc) > de-,esca'lation *n*

def (dɛf) *adj slang* very good, esp of hip-hop [C20: perhaps from *definitive*]

def. *abbreviation* definition

deface (dɪ'feɪs) *vb* (*tr*) to spoil or mar the surface, legibility, or appearance of; disfigure > de'faceable *adj* > de'facement *n* > de'facer *n*

de facto (deɪ 'fæktəʊ) *adv* 1 in fact ▷ *adj* 2 existing in fact, whether legally recognized or not: *a de facto regime.* See **de jure** ▷ *n, pl* -tos 3 *Austral & NZ* a de facto husband or wife [C17: Latin]

defalcate ('di:fæl,keɪt) *vb* (*intr*) *law* to misuse or misappropriate property or funds entrusted to one [C15: from Medieval Latin *dēfalcāre* to cut off, from Latin DE- + *falx* sickle] > 'defal,cator *n*

defame (dɪ'feɪm) *vb* (*tr*) to attack the good name or reputation of; slander; libel [C14: from Old French *defamer*, from Latin *dēfāmāre*, from *diffāmāre* to spread by unfavourable report, from *fāma* FAME] > defamation (,dɛfə'meɪʃən) *n* > defamatory (dɪ'fæmətərɪ, -trɪ) *adj* > de'famatorily *adv*

default (dɪ'fɔ:lt) *n* 1 a failure to act, esp a failure to meet a financial obligation or to appear in a court of law at a time specified 2 absence or lack 3 by default in the absence of opposition or a better alternative: *he became prime minister by default* 4 in default of through or in the lack or absence of 5 judgment by default *law* a judgment in the plaintiff's favour when the defendant fails to plead or to appear 6 (*also* 'di:fɔ:lt) *computing* **a** the preset selection of an option offered by a system, which will always be followed except when explicitly altered

b (as modifier): default setting ▷ vb **7** (intr; often foll by on or in) to fail to make payment when due **8** (intr) to fail to fulfil or perform an obligation, engagement, etc: to default in a sporting contest **9** law to lose (a case) by failure to appear in court [C13: from Old French defaute, from defaillir to fail, from Vulgar Latin dēfallīre (unattested) to be lacking]

defaulter (dɪˈfɔːltə) n **1** a person who defaults **2** chiefly Brit a person, esp a soldier, who has broken the disciplinary code of his service

defeat (dɪˈfiːt) vb (tr) **1** to overcome in a contest or competition; win a victory over **2** to thwart or frustrate **3** law to render null and void; annul ▷ n **4** the act of defeating or state of being defeated [C14: from Old French desfait, from desfaire to undo, ruin, from des- DIS-¹ + faire to do, from Latin facere]

defeatism (dɪˈfiːtɪzəm) n a ready acceptance or expectation of defeat > de'featist n, adj

defecate or **defaecate** (ˈdɛfɪˌkeɪt) vb **1** (intr) to discharge waste from the body through the anus **2** (tr) to clarify or remove impurities from (a solution, esp of sugar) [C16: from Latin dēfaecāre to cleanse from dregs, from DE- + faex sediment, dregs] > ˌdefeˈcation or ˌdefaeˈcation n > ˈdefeˌcator or ˈdefaeˌcator n

defect n (dɪˈfɛkt, ˈdiːfɛkt) **1** a lack of something necessary for completeness or perfection; shortcoming; deficiency **2** an imperfection, failing, or blemish ▷ vb (dɪˈfɛkt) **3** (intr) to desert one's country, cause, allegiance, etc, esp in order to join the opposing forces [C15: from Latin dēfectus, from dēficere to forsake, fail; see DEFICIENT] > de'fector n

defection (dɪˈfɛkʃən) n **1** abandonment of duty, allegiance, principles, etc; backsliding **2** another word for **defect** (senses 1, 2)

defective (dɪˈfɛktɪv) adj **1** having a defect or flaw; imperfect; faulty **2** (of a person) below the usual standard or level, esp in intelligence **3** grammar (of a word) lacking the full range of inflections characteristic of its form class, as for example must, which has no past tense > de'fectiveness n

defence or US **defense** (dɪˈfɛns) n **1** resistance against danger, attack, or harm; protection **2** a person or thing that provides such resistance **3** a plea, essay, speech, etc, in support of something; vindication; justification **4** a country's military measures or resources **5** law a defendant's denial of the truth of the allegations or charge against him **6** law the defendant and his legal advisers collectively **7** sport **a** the action of protecting oneself, one's goal, or one's allotted part of the playing area against an opponent's attacks **b** the defence players in a team whose function is to do this **8** American football (usually preceded by the) **a** the team that does not have possession of the ball **b** the members of a team that play in such circumstances **9** (plural) fortifications [C13: from Old French, from Late Latin dēfensum, past participle of dēfendere to DEFEND] > de'fenceless or US de'fenseless adj

defence mechanism n **1** psychoanal a usually unconscious mental process designed to reduce the anxiety, shame, etc, associated with instinctive desires **2** physiol the protective response of the body against disease organisms

defend (dɪˈfɛnd) vb **1** to protect (a person, place, etc) from harm or danger; ward off an attack on **2** (tr) to support in the face of criticism, esp by argument or evidence **3** to represent (a defendant) in court in a civil or criminal action **4** sport to guard or protect (oneself, one's goal, etc) against attack **5** (tr) to protect (a championship or title) against a challenge [C13: from Old French defendre, from Latin dēfendere to ward off, from DE- + -fendere to strike] > de'fender n

defendant (dɪˈfɛndənt) n **1** a person against whom an action or claim is brought in a court of law. See **plaintiff** ▷ adj **2** making a defence; defending

defenestration (diːˌfɛnɪˈstreɪʃən) n the act of throwing someone out of a window [C17: from New Latin dēfenestrātiō, from Latin DE- + fenestra window]

defensible (dɪˈfɛnsɪbəl) adj capable of being defended, as in war, an argument, etc > de,fensi'bility or

de'fensibleness n > de'fensibly adv

defensive (dɪˈfɛnsɪv) adj **1** intended, suitable, or done for defence, as opposed to offence **2** rejecting criticisms of oneself or covering up one's failings ▷ n **3** a position of defence **4** on the defensive in an attitude or position of defence, as in being ready to reject criticism > de'fensively adv

defer¹ (dɪˈfɜː) vb -fers, -ferring, -ferred (tr) to delay or cause to be delayed until a future time; postpone [C14: from Old French differer to be different, postpone; see DIFFER] > de'ferrer n

defer² (dɪˈfɜː) vb -fers, -ferring, -ferred (intr; foll by to) to yield (to) or comply (with) the wishes or judgments of another [C15: from Latin dēferre, literally: to bear down, from DE- + ferre to bear]

deference (ˈdɛfərəns) n **1** submission to or compliance with the will, wishes, etc, of another **2** courteous regard; respect [C17: from French déférence; see DEFER²]

deferent¹ (ˈdɛfərənt) adj another word for **deferential**

deferent² (ˈdɛfərənt) adj (esp of a bodily nerve, vessel, or duct) conveying an impulse, fluid, etc, outwards, down, or away; efferent [C17: from Latin dēferre; see DEFER²]

deferential (ˌdɛfəˈrɛnʃəl) adj marked by or showing deference or respect; respectful > ˌdefer'entially adv

defiance (dɪˈfaɪəns) n **1** open or bold resistance to or disregard for authority, opposition, or power **2** a challenging attitude or behaviour; challenge > de'fiant adj > de'fiantly adv

defibrillation (dɪˌfaɪbrɪˈleɪʃən, -ˌfɪb-) n med the application of an electric current to the heart to restore normal rhythmic contractions after the onset of atrial or ventricular fibrillation

defibrillator (dɪˈfaɪbrɪˌleɪtə, -ˈfɪb-) n med an apparatus for stopping fibrillation of the heart by application of an electric current to the chest wall or directly to the heart

deficiency (dɪˈfɪʃənsɪ) n, pl -cies **1** the state or quality of being deficient **2** a lack or insufficiency; shortage **3** another word for **deficit 4** biology the absence of a gene or a region of a chromosome normally present

deficiency disease n **1** med any condition, such as pellagra, beriberi, or scurvy, produced by a lack of vitamins or other essential substances **2** botany any disease caused by lack of essential minerals

deficient (dɪˈfɪʃənt) adj **1** lacking some essential; incomplete; defective **2** inadequate in quantity or supply; insufficient [C16: from Latin dēficiēns lacking, from dēficere to fall short; see DEFECT] > de'ficiently adv

deficit (ˈdɛfɪsɪt, dɪˈfɪsɪt) n **1** the amount by which an actual sum is lower than that expected or required **2 a** an excess of liabilities over assets **b** an excess of expenditures over revenues during a certain period [C18: from Latin, literally: there is lacking, from dēficere to be lacking]

deficit financing n government spending in excess of revenues so that a budget deficit is incurred, which is financed by borrowing: recommended by Keynesian economists in order to increase economic activity and reduce unemployment

defile¹ (dɪˈfaɪl) vb (tr) **1** to make foul or dirty; pollute **2** to tarnish or sully the brightness of; taint; corrupt **3** to damage or sully (someone's good name, reputation, etc) **4** to make unfit for ceremonial use; desecrate **5** to violate the chastity of [C14: from earlier defoilen (influenced by filen to FILE³), from Old French defouler to trample underfoot, abuse, from DE- + fouler to tread upon; see FULL²] > de'filement n

defile² (ˈdiːfaɪl, dɪˈfaɪl) n **1** a narrow pass or gorge, esp one between two mountains **2** a single file of soldiers, etc ▷ vb **3** chiefly military to march or cause to march in single file [C17: from French défilé, from défiler to file off, from filer to march in a column, from Old French: to spin, from fil thread, from Latin fīlum]

define (dɪˈfaɪn) vb (tr) **1** to state precisely the meaning of (words, terms, etc) **2** to describe the nature, properties, or essential qualities of **3** to determine the boundary or extent of **4** (often passive) to delineate the form or outline of: the shape of the tree was clearly defined by the light behind it **5** to fix with precision; specify [C14: from Old French definer to determine, from Latin dēfinīre to set bounds to, from *finīre* to FINISH > de'finable *adj* > de'finer *n*

defined-benefit *adj* denoting an occupational pension scheme that guarantees a specified payout, usually based on an employee's final salary and years of service. Abbreviation: DB. Also called: final-salary

definite ('dɛfɪnɪt) *adj* **1** clearly defined; exact; explicit **2** having precise limits or boundaries **3** known for certain; sure [C15: from Latin *dēfinītus* limited, distinct; see DEFINE] > 'definiteness *n*

definite article *n* *grammar* a determiner that expresses specificity of reference, such as *the* in English. See **indefinite article**

definite integral *n* *maths* **a** the evaluation of the indefinite integral between two limits, representing the area between the given function and the *x*-axis between these two values of *x* **b** the expression for that function, $\int_a^b f(x)dx$, where $f(x)$ is the given function and $x = a$ and $x = b$ are the limits of integration. Where $F(x) = \int f(x)dx$, the indefinite integral, $\int_a^b f(x)dx = F(b)-F(a)$

definitely ('dɛfɪnɪtlɪ) *adv* **1** in a definite manner **2** (*sentence modifier*) certainly: *he said he was coming, definitely* ▷ *sentence substitute* **3** unquestionably: used to confirm an assumption by a questioner

definition (,dɛfɪ'nɪʃən) *n* **1** a formal and concise statement of the meaning of a word, phrase, etc **2** the act of defining a word, phrase, etc **3** specification of the essential properties of something, or of the criteria which uniquely identify it **4** the act of making clear or definite **5** the state or condition of being clearly defined or definite **6** a measure of the clarity of an optical, photographic, or television image as characterized by its sharpness and contrast

definitive (dɪ'fɪnɪtɪv) *adj* **1** serving to decide or settle finally; conclusive **2** most reliable, complete, or authoritative **3** serving to define or outline **4** *zoology* fully developed; complete **5** (of postage stamps) permanently on sale ▷ *n* **6** *grammar* a word indicating specificity of reference, such as the definite article or a demonstrative adjective or pronoun > de'finitively *adv*

deflate (dɪ'fleɪt) *vb* **1** to collapse or cause to collapse through the release of gas **2** (*tr*) to take away the self-esteem or conceit from **3** *economics* to cause deflation of (an economy, the money supply, etc) [C19: from DE- + (IN)FLATE] > de'flator *n*

deflation (dɪ'fleɪʃən) *n* **1** the act of deflating or state of being deflated **2** *economics* a reduction in the level of total spending and economic activity resulting in lower levels of output, employment, investment, trade, profits, and prices **3** *geology* the removal of loose rock material, sand, and dust by the wind > de'flationary *adj* > de'flationist *n, adj*

deflect (dɪ'flɛkt) *vb* to turn or cause to turn aside from a course; swerve [C17: from Latin *dēflectere*, from *flectere* to bend] > de'flector *n*

deflection *or* **deflexion** (dɪ'flɛkʃən) *n* **1** the act of deflecting or the state of being deflected **2** the amount of deviation **3** the change in direction of a light beam as it crosses a boundary between two media with different refractive indexes **4** a deviation of the indicator of a measuring instrument from its zero position > de'flective *adj*

deflocculate (dɪ'flɒkjʊ,leɪt) *vb* (*tr*) to disperse, forming a colloid or suspension > de,floccu'lation *n* > de'flocculant *n*

deflower (diː'flaʊə) *vb* (*tr*) **1** to deprive of virginity, esp by rupturing the hymen through sexual intercourse **2** to despoil of beauty, innocence, etc; mar; violate **3** to rob or despoil of flowers [C15: from Late Latin *dēflōrātiō*; see DE-, FLOWER] > defloration (,diː'flɔː'reɪʃən) *n*

Defoe (dɪ'fəʊ) *n* Daniel. ?1660–1731, English novelist, journalist, spymaster, and pamphleteer, noted particularly for his novel *Robinson Crusoe* (1719). His other novels include *Moll Flanders* (1722) and *A Journal of the Plague Year* (1722)

defoliant (diː'fəʊlɪənt) *n* a chemical sprayed or dusted onto trees to cause their leaves to fall, esp to remove cover from an enemy in warfare

defoliate (diː'fəʊlɪ,eɪt) *vb* to deprive (a plant) of its leaves, as by the use of a herbicide, or (of a plant) to shed

its leaves [C18: from Medieval Latin *dēfoliāre*, from Latin DE- + *folium* leaf] > de,foli'ation *n*

deforest (diː'fɒrɪst) *vb* (*tr*) to clear of trees. Also: disforest > de,fores'tation *n*

De Forest (də 'fɒrɪst) *n* Lee. 1873–1961, US inventor of telegraphic, telephonic, and radio equipment: patented the first triode valve (1907)

deform (dɪ'fɔːm) *vb* **1** to make or become misshapen or distorted **2** (*tr*) to mar the beauty of; disfigure **3** (*tr*) to subject or be subjected to a stress that causes a change of dimensions [C15: from Latin *dēformāre*, from DE- + *forma* shape, beauty] > de'formable *adj* > deformation (,diː'fɔː'meɪʃən) *n*

deformed (dɪ'fɔːmd) *adj* **1** disfigured or misshapen **2** morally perverted; warped

deformity (dɪ'fɔːmɪtɪ) *n, pl* -ties **1** a deformed condition; disfigurement **2** *pathol* an acquired or congenital distortion of an organ or part **3** a deformed person or thing **4** a defect, esp of the mind or morals; depravity

Defra ('dɛfrə) *n acronym for* (in Britain) Department for Environment, Food and Rural Affairs

defraud (dɪ'frɔːd) *vb* (*tr*) to take away or withhold money, rights, property, etc, from (a person) by fraud; cheat; swindle > de'frauder *n*

defray (dɪ'freɪ) *vb* (*tr*) to furnish or provide money for (costs, expenses, etc); pay [C16: from Old French *deffroier* to pay expenses, from *de-* DIS-¹ + *frai* expenditure, originally: cost incurred through breaking something, from Latin *frangere* to break] > de'frayable *adj* > de'frayal *or* de'frayment *n*

defrock (diː'frɒk) *vb* (*tr*) to deprive (a person in holy orders) of ecclesiastical status; unfrock

defrost (diː'frɒst) *vb* **1** to make or become free of frost or ice **2** to thaw, esp through removal from a refrigerator

defroster (diː'frɒstə) *n* a device by which the de-icing process of a refrigerator is accelerated, usually by circulating the refrigerant without the expansion process

deft (dɛft) *adj* quick and neat in movement; nimble; dexterous [C13 (in the sense: gentle): see DAFT] > 'deftly *adv* > 'deftness *n*

defunct (dɪ'fʌŋkt) *adj* **1** no longer living; dead or extinct **2** no longer operative or valid [C16: from Latin *dēfungī* to discharge (one's obligations), die; see DE-, FUNCTION] > de'functness *n*

defuse *or sometimes US* **defuze** (diː'fjuːz) *vb* (*tr*) **1** to remove the triggering device of (a bomb, etc) **2** to remove the cause of tension from (a crisis, etc)
● USAGE See at diffuse

defy (dɪ'faɪ) *vb* -fies, -fying, -fied (*tr*) **1** to resist (a powerful person, authority, etc) openly and boldly **2** to elude, esp in a baffling way **3** *formal* to challenge or provoke (someone to do something judged to be impossible); dare **4** *archaic* to invite to do battle or combat [C14: from Old French *desfier*, from *des-* DE- + *fier* to trust, from Latin *fidere*] > de'fier *n*

deg. *abbreviation* degree

Degas ('deɪɡɑː; *French* dəɡɑ) *n* Hilaire Germain Edgar (ilɛr ʒɛrmɛ̃ ɛdɡar). 1834– 1917, French impressionist painter and sculptor, noted for his brilliant draughtsmanship and ability to convey movement, esp in his studies of horse racing and ballet dancers

De Gasperi (*Italian* de 'ɡasperi) *n* Alcide (al'tʃiːde). 1881–1954, Italian statesman; prime minister (1945–53). An antifascist, he led the Christian Democratic party during World War II from the Vatican City

de Gaulle (*French* də ɡol) *n* Charles (André Joseph Marie) (ʃarl). 1890–1970, French general and statesman. During World War II, he refused to accept Pétain's armistice with Germany and founded the Free French movement in England (1940). He was head of the provisional governments (1944–46) and, as first president of the Fifth Republic (1959–69), he restored political and economic stability to France

degauss (diː'ɡaʊs, -'ɡɔːs) *vb* (*tr*) to neutralize the magnetic field of a ship's hull (as a protection against magnetic mines) using equipment producing an opposing magnetic field

degeneracy (dɪ'dʒɛnərəsɪ) *n, pl* -cies **1** the act or state of being degenerate **2** the process of becoming degenerate

degenerate vb (dɪ'dʒɛnəˌreɪt) (intr) **1** to become degenerate **2** biology (of organisms or their parts) to become less specialized or functionally useless ▷ adj (dɪ'dʒɛnərɪt) **3** having declined or deteriorated to a lower mental, moral, or physical level; debased; degraded; corrupt ▷ n (dɪ'dʒɛnərɪt) **4** a degenerate person [c15: from Latin dēgenerāre, from dēgener departing from its kind, ignoble, from DE- + genus origin, race]
> de'generately adv > de'generateness n
> de'generative adj

degenerate matter n astronomy the highly compressed state of matter, esp in white dwarfs and neutron stars, supported against gravitational collapse by quantum mechanical effects

degeneration (dɪˌdʒɛnə'reɪʃən) n **1** the process of degenerating **2** the state of being degenerate **3** biology the loss of specialization, function, or structure by organisms and their parts, as in the development of vestigial organs **4** impairment or loss of the function and structure of cells or tissues, as by disease or injury, often leading to death (necrosis) of the involved part **5** electronics negative feedback of a signal

deglaze (di:'gleɪz) vb (tr) to dilute meat sediments in (a pan) in order to make a sauce or gravy

degradable (dɪ'greɪdəbəl) adj **1** (of waste products, packaging materials, etc) capable of being decomposed chemically or biologically **2** capable of being degraded

degradation (ˌdɛgrə'deɪʃən) n **1** the act of degrading or the state of being degraded **2** a state of degeneration, squalor, or poverty **3** some act, constraint, etc, that is degrading **4** the wearing down of the surface of rocks, cliffs, etc, by erosion, weathering, or some other process **5** chem a breakdown of a molecule into atoms or smaller molecules **6** physics an irreversible process in which the energy available to do work is decreased **7** RC Church the permanent unfrocking of a priest

degrade (dɪ'greɪd) vb **1** (tr) to reduce in worth, character, etc; disgrace; dishonour **2** (dɪ'greɪd) (tr) to reduce in rank, status, or degree; remove from office; demote **3** (tr) to reduce in strength, quality, intensity, etc **4** to reduce or be reduced by erosion or down-cutting, as a land surface or bed of a river **5** chem to decompose or be decomposed into atoms or smaller molecules [c14: from Late Latin dēgradāre, from Latin DE- + gradus rank, degree]
> de'grader n

degrading (dɪ'greɪdɪŋ) adj causing humiliation; debasing > de'gradingly adv

degree (dɪ'gri:) n **1** a stage in a scale of relative amount or intensity: a high degree of competence **2** an academic award conferred by a university or college on successful completion of a course or as an honorary distinction (**honorary degree**) **3** any of three categories of seriousness of a burn **4** (in the US) any of the categories into which a crime is divided according to its seriousness **5** genealogy a step in a line of descent, used as a measure of the closeness of a blood relationship **6** grammar any of the forms of an adjective used to indicate relative amount or intensity: in English they are positive, comparative, and superlative **7** music any note of a diatonic scale relative to the other notes in that scale **8** a unit of temperature on a specified scale. Symbol: °. See also **Celsius scale**, **Fahrenheit scale** **9** a measure of angle equal to one three-hundred-and-sixtieth of the angle traced by one complete revolution of a line about one of its ends. Symbol: ° **10** a unit of latitude or longitude, divided into 60 minutes, used to define points on the earth's surface or on the celestial sphere. Symbol: ° **11** a unit on any of several scales of measurement, as for alcohol content or specific gravity. Symbol: ° **12** maths **a** the highest power or the sum of the powers of any term in a polynomial or by itself: $x^4 + x + 3$ and xyz^2 are of the fourth degree **b** the greatest power of the highest order derivative in a differential equation **13** obsolete a step; rung **14** archaic a stage in social status or rank **15** **by degrees** little by little; gradually **16** **to a degree** somewhat; rather [c13: from Old French degre, from Latin DE- + gradus step, GRADE]

degree of difficulty n a rating which reflects the

difficulty of the manoeuvre or action an athlete is attempting to perform in sports such as gymnastics and diving, and which is factored into the final score

degree of freedom n **1** one of the independent components of motion (translation, vibration, and rotation) of an atom or molecule **2** chem one of a number of intensive properties that can be independently varied without changing the number of phases in a system. See also **phase rule**

de Havilland (də 'hævɪlənd) n Sir **Geoffrey**. 1882–1965, British aircraft designer. He produced many military aircraft and the first jet airliners

dehisce (dɪ'hɪs) vb (intr) (of fruits, anthers, etc) to burst open spontaneously, releasing seeds, pollen, etc [c17: from Latin dēhiscere to split open, from DE- + hiscere to yawn, gape] > de'hiscent adj > de'hiscence n

dehorn (di:'hɔ:n) vb (tr) to remove or prevent the growth of the horns of (cattle, sheep, or goats)

dehumanize or **dehumanise** (di:'hju:məˌnaɪz) vb (tr) **1** to deprive of human qualities **2** to render mechanical, artificial, or routine > deˌhumani'zation or deˌhumani'sation n

dehumidifier (ˌdi:hju:'mɪdɪˌfaɪə) n a device for reducing the moisture content of the atmosphere

dehumidify (ˌdi:hju:'mɪdɪˌfaɪ) vb -fies, -fying, -fied (tr) to remove water from (something, esp the air)
> ˌdehuˌmidifi'cation n

dehydrate (di:'haɪdreɪt, ˌdi:haɪ'dreɪt) vb **1** to lose or cause to lose water; make or become anhydrous **2** to lose or cause to lose hydrogen atoms and oxygen atoms in the proportions in which they occur in water, as in a chemical reaction > ˌdehy'dration n > de'hydrator n

dehydroepiandrosterone (di:ˌhaɪdrəʊˌɛpiænˈdrɒstəˌrəʊn) n the most abundant steroid in the human body, that is involved in the manufacture of testosterone, oestrogen, progesterone, and corticosterone

dehydrogenate (di:'haɪdrədʒəˌneɪt), **dehydrogenize** or **dehydrogenise** (di:'haɪdrədʒəˌnaɪz) vb (tr) to remove hydrogen from > deˌhydroge'nation, deˌhydrogeni'zation or deˌhydrogeni'sation n

de-ice (di:'aɪs) vb to free or be freed of ice

de-icer (di:'aɪsə) n **1** a mechanical or thermal device designed to melt or stop the formation of ice on an aircraft, usually fitted to the aerofoil surfaces **2** a chemical or other substance used for this purpose, esp an aerosol that can be sprayed on car windscreens to remove ice or frost

deictic ('daɪktɪk) adj **1** logic proving by direct argument. See **elenctic** ▷ n **2** another word for **indexical** (sense 2) [c17: from Greek deiktikos concerning proof, from deiknunai to show]

deify ('di:ɪˌfaɪ, 'deɪɪ-) vb -fies, -fying, -fied (tr) **1** to exalt to the position of a god or personify as a god **2** to accord divine honour or worship to [c14: from Old French deifier, from Late Latin deificāre, from Latin deus god + facere to make] > 'dei,fier n > ,deifi'cation n

Deighton ('deɪtən) n **Len**. born 1929, British thriller writer. His books include The Ipcress File (1962), Bomber (1970), and the trilogy Berlin Game, Mexico Set, and London Match (1983–85)

deign (deɪn) vb **1** (intr) to think it fit or worthy of oneself (to do something); condescend **2** (tr) archaic to vouchsafe [c13: from Old French deignier, from Latin dignārī to consider worthy, from dignus worthy]

deindividuation (di:ˌɪndɪvɪdjʊ'eɪʃən) n psychol the loss of a person's sense of individuality and personal responsibility

deindustrialization or **deindustrialisation** (ˌdi:ɪnˌdʌstrɪəlaɪ'zeɪʃən) n the decline in importance of manufacturing industry in the economy of a nation or area

de-ionize or **de-ionise** (di:'aɪəˌnaɪz) vb (tr) to remove ions from (water, etc), esp by ion exchange > deˌioni'zation or deˌioni'sation n

Deirdre ('dɪədrɪ) n Irish myth a beautiful girl who was raised by Conchobar to be his wife but eloped with Naoise. When Conchobar treacherously killed Naoise she took her own life: often used to symbolize Ireland.

See also **Naoise**

deism ('di:ɪzəm, 'deɪ-) n belief in the existence of God based solely on natural reason, without reference to revelation. See **theism** [C17: from French *déisme*, from Latin *deus* god] > **deist** n, adj > de'istic or de'istical adj > de'istically adv

deity ('deɪtɪ, 'di:ɪ-) n, pl -ties 1 a god or goddess 2 the state of being divine; godhead 3 the rank, status, or position of a god 4 the nature or character of God [C14: from Old French, from Late Latin *deitās*, from Latin *deus* god]

Deity ('deɪtɪ, 'di:ɪ-) n the Deity the Supreme Being; God

déjà vu ('deɪʒæ 'vu:; French deʒa vy) n the experience of perceiving a new situation as if it had occurred before. It is sometimes associated with exhaustion or certain types of mental disorder [from French, literally: already seen]

deject (dɪ'dʒɛkt) vb (tr) to have a depressing effect on; dispirit; dishearten [C15: from Latin *dēicere* to cast down, from DE- + *iacere* to throw]

dejected (dɪ'dʒɛktɪd) adj miserable; despondent; downhearted > de'jectedly adv

dejection (dɪ'dʒɛkʃən) n 1 lowness of spirits; depression; melancholy 2 a faecal matter evacuated from the bowels; excrement b the act of defecating; defecation

de jure (deɪ 'dʒʊəreɪ) adv according to law; by right; legally. See **de facto** [Latin]

deka- or **dek-** combining form variants of **deca-**

deke (di:k) US & Canadian ▷ n 1 sport (esp in ice hockey) the act or an instance of feinting ▷ vb 2 sport (esp in ice hockey) to deceive (an opponent) by carrying out a feint [C20: shortened from DECOY]

Dekker or **Decker** ('dɛkə) n **Thomas**. ?1572–?1632, English dramatist and pamphleteer, noted particularly for his comedy *The Shoemaker's Holiday* (1600) and his satirical pamphlet *The Gull's Hornbook* (1609)

dekko ('dɛkəʊ) n, pl -kos Brit slang a look; glance; view (esp in the phrase **take a dekko (at)**) [C19: from Hindi *dekho* look! from *dekhnā* to see]

de Klerk (də 'klɜ:k) n **F**(rederik) **W**(illem). born 1936, South African statesman; president (1989–94), second executive deputy president (1994–97). In 1990 he legalized the ANC and released Nelson Mandela from prison, and initiated the abolition of apartheid: Nobel peace prize 1993 jointly with Mandela

de Kooning (də 'ku:nɪŋ) n **Willem**. 1904–97, US abstract expressionist painter, born in Holland

del (del) n maths the differential operator $i(\partial/\partial x) + j(\partial/\partial y) + k(\partial/\partial z)$, where **i**, **j**, and **k** are unit vectors in the x, y, and z directions. Symbol: ∇. Also called: **nabla**

del. abbreviation delegate

Del. abbreviation Delaware

de la Beche (də læ bi:tʃ) n **Henry**. 1796–1855, English geologist. His work led to the founding of the Geological Survey (1835)

Delacroix (French dəlakrwa) n (**Ferdinand Victor**) **Eugène** (øʒɛn). 1798–1863, French romantic painter whose use of colour and free composition influenced impressionism. His paintings of historical and contemporary scenes include *The Massacre at Chios* (1824)

Delagoa Bay (ˌdelə'gəʊə) n an inlet of the Indian Ocean, in S Mozambique

de la Mare (də lɑː mɛə) n **Walter** (**John**). 1873–1956, English poet and novelist, noted esp for his evocative verse for children. His works include the volumes of poetry *The Listeners and Other Poems* (1912) and *Peacock Pie* (1913) and the novel *Memoirs of a Midget* (1921)

Delaroche (French dəlarɔʃ) n (**Hippolyte**) **Paul**. 1797–1859, French painter of portraits and sentimental historical scenes, such as *The Children of Edward IV in the Tower* (1830)

Delaunay (French dəlonɛ) n **Robert** (rɔbɛr). 1885–1941, French painter, whose abstract use of colour characterized Orphism, an attempt to introduce more colour into austere forms of Cubism

Delaware[1] ('delə,wɛə) n pl -wares or -ware a member of a North American Indian people formerly living near the Delaware River

Delaware[2] ('delə,wɛə) n 1 a state of the northeastern US, on the Delmarva Peninsula: mostly flat and low-lying, with hills in the extreme north and cypress swamps in the extreme south. Capital: Dover. Pop: 817 491 (2003 est). Area: 5004 sq km (1932 sq miles). Abbreviations: Del., (with zip code) DE 2 a river in the northeastern US, rising in the Catskill Mountains and flowing south into **Delaware Bay**, an inlet of the Atlantic. Length 660 km (410 miles)

Delawarean (ˌdɛlə'wɛərɪən) adj 1 of or relating to the state of Delaware or its inhabitants 2 of or relating to the Delaware river

De La Warr (ˌdɛlə,wɛə) n **Baron**, title of *Thomas West*, known as *Lord Delaware*. 1577–1618, English administrator in America; first governor of Virginia (1610)

delay (dɪ'leɪ) vb 1 (tr) to put off to a later time; defer 2 (tr) to slow up, hinder, or cause to be late; detain 3 (intr) to be irresolute or put off doing something; procrastinate 4 (intr) to linger; dawdle ▷ n 5 the act or an instance of delaying or being delayed 6 the interval between one event and another; lull; interlude [C13: from Old French *delaier*, from *des-* off + *laier*, variant of *laissier* to leave, from Latin *laxāre* to loosen, from *laxus* slack, LAX] > de'layer n

delayed action or **delay action** n a device for operating a mechanism, such as a camera shutter, a short time after setting

delayed drop n aeronautics a parachute descent with the opening of the parachute delayed, usually for a predetermined period

delayering (di:'leɪərɪŋ) n the process of pruning the administrative structure of a large organization by reducing the number of tiers in its hierarchy

Delbrück (del'bryk) n **Max**. 1906–81, US molecular biologist, born in Germany. Noted for his work on bacteriophages, he shared the Nobel prize for physiology or medicine in 1969

dele ('di:lɪ) n 1 a sign (ẟ) indicating that typeset matter is to be deleted ▷ vb 2 (tr) to mark (matter to be deleted) with a dele [C18: from Latin: delete (imperative), from *dēlēre* to destroy, obliterate; see DELETE]

delectable (dɪ'lɛktəb°l) adj highly enjoyable, esp pleasing to the taste; delightful [C14: from Latin *dēlectābilis*, from *dēlectāre* to DELIGHT] > de'lectableness or de,lecta'bility n

delectation (ˌdi:lɛk'teɪʃən) n pleasure; enjoyment

Deledda (Italian de'ledda) n **Grazia** ('grattsja). 1875–1936, Italian novelist, noted for works, such as *La Madre* (1920), on peasant life in Sardinia: Nobel prize for literature 1926

delegate n ('delɪ,geɪt, -gɪt) 1 a person chosen or elected to act for or represent another or others, esp at a conference or meeting ▷ vb ('delɪ,geɪt) 2 to give or commit (duties, powers, etc) to another as agent or representative; depute 3 (tr) to send, authorize, or elect (a person) as agent or representative [C14: from Latin *dēlēgāre* to send on a mission, from *lēgāre* to send, depute; see LEGATE] > 'delegable adj

delegation (ˌdelɪ'geɪʃən) n 1 a person or group chosen to represent another or others 2 the act of delegating or state of being delegated

de Lesseps (French də lesɛps) n Vicomte **Ferdinand Marie** (fɛrdinɑ̃ mari). 1805–94, French diplomat: directed the construction of the Suez Canal (1859–69) and the unsuccessful first attempt to build the Panama Canal (1881–89)

delete (dɪ'li:t) vb (tr) to remove (something printed or written); erase; cancel; strike out [C17: from Latin *dēlēre* to destroy, obliterate] > de'letion n

deleterious (ˌdelɪ'tɪərɪəs) adj harmful; injurious; hurtful [C17: from New Latin *dēlētērius*, from Greek *dēlētērios* injurious, destructive, from *dēleisthai* to hurt] > ˌdele'teriousness n

Delft (delft) n 1 a town in the SW Netherlands, in South Holland province. Pop: 97 000 (2003 est) 2 Also called: **delftware** tin-glazed earthenware made in Delft since the 17th century, typically having blue decoration on a white ground 3 a similar earthenware made in England

Delhi ('delɪ) n 1 the capital of India, in the N central part, on the Jumna river: consists of **Old Delhi** (a walled city reconstructed in 1639 on the site of former cities of Delhi, which date from the 15th century BC) and **New**

Delhi to the south, chosen as the capital in 1912, replacing Kolkata (then called Calcutta); university (1922). Pop: 9 817 439 (2001) **2** an administrative division (National Capital Territory) of N India, formerly a Union Territory. Capital: Delhi. Area: 1483 sq km (572 sq miles). Pop: 13 782 976 (2001)

deli ('dɛlɪ) *n, pl* **delis** an informal word for **delicatessen**

Delian ('di:lɪən) *n* **1** a native or inhabitant of Delos ▷ *adj* **2** of or relating to Delos **3** of or relating to Delius

deliberate *adj* (dɪ'lɪbərɪt) **1** carefully thought out in advance; planned; studied; intentional **2** careful or unhurried in speech or action: *a deliberate pace* ▷ *vb* (dɪ'lɪbə,reɪt) **2** to consider (something) deeply; ponder; think over [c15: from Latin *dēlīberāre* to consider well, from *lībrāre* to weigh, from *lībra* scales] > de'liberately *adv* > de'liberateness *n* > de'liber,ator *n*

deliberation (dɪ,lɪbə'reɪʃən) *n* **1** thoughtful, careful, or lengthy consideration **2** (*often plural*) formal discussion and debate, as of a committee, jury, etc **3** care, thoughtfulness, or absence of hurry, esp in movement or speech

deliberative (dɪ'lɪbərətɪv) *adj* **1** involved in, organized for, or having the function of deliberating: *a deliberative assembly* **2** characterized by or resulting from deliberation > de'liberatively *adv* > de'liberativeness *n*

Delibes (*French* dəlib) *n* (**Clément Philibert**) **Léo** (leo). 1836–91, French composer, noted particularly for his ballets *Coppélia* (1870) and *Sylvia* (1876), and the opera *Lakmé* (1883)

delicacy ('dɛlɪkəsɪ) *n, pl* -**cies** **1** fine or subtle quality, character, construction, etc **2** fragile, soft, or graceful beauty **3** something that is considered choice to eat, such as caviar **4** fragile construction or constitution; frailty **5** refinement of feeling, manner, or appreciation **6** fussy or squeamish refinement, esp in matters of taste, propriety, etc **7** need for tactful or sensitive handling **8** accuracy or sensitivity of response or operation, as of an instrument

delicate ('dɛlɪkɪt) *adj* **1** exquisite, fine, or subtle in quality, character, construction, etc **2** having a soft or fragile beauty **3** (of colour, tone, taste, etc) pleasantly subtle, soft, or faint **4** easily damaged or injured; lacking robustness, esp in health; fragile **5** precise, skilled, or sensitive in action or operation: *a delicate mechanism* **6** requiring tact and diplomacy **7** excessively refined; squeamish [c14: from Latin *dēlicātus* affording pleasure, from *dēliciae* (pl) delight, pleasure; see DELICIOUS] > 'delicately *adv* > 'delicateness *n*

delicatessen (,dɛlɪkə'tɛsən) *n* **1** a shop selling various foods, esp unusual or imported foods, already cooked or prepared **2** such foods [c19: from German *Delikatessen*, literally: delicacies, pl of *Delikatesse* a delicacy, from French *délicatesse*]

delicious (dɪ'lɪʃəs) *adj* **1** very appealing to the senses, esp to the taste or smell **2** extremely enjoyable or entertaining [c13: from Old French, from Late Latin *dēliciōsus*, from Latin *dēliciae* delights, charms, from *dēlicere* to entice; see DELIGHT] > de'liciously *adv* > de'liciousness *n*

delight (dɪ'laɪt) *vb* **1** (*tr*) to please greatly **2** (*intr; foll by in*) to take great pleasure (in) ▷ *n* **3** extreme pleasure or satisfaction; joy **4** something that causes this [c13: from Old French *delit*, from *deleitier* to please, from Latin *dēlectāre*, from *dēlicere* to allure, from *DE-* + *lacere* to entice; see DELICIOUS; English spelling influenced by *light*]

delighted (dɪ'laɪtɪd) *adj* **1** (*often foll by an infinitive*) extremely pleased (to do something): *I'm delighted to hear it!* ▷ *sentence substitute* **2** I should be delighted to! > de'lightedly *adv*

delightful (dɪ'laɪtfʊl) *adj* giving great delight; very pleasing, beautiful, charming, etc > de'lightfully *adv* > de'lightfulness *n*

Delilah (dɪ'laɪlə) *n* **1** Samson's Philistine mistress, who deprived him of his strength by cutting off his hair (Judges 16:4–22) **2** a voluptuous and treacherous woman; temptress

delimit (di:'lɪmɪt) *or* **delimitate** *vb* (*tr*) to mark or prescribe the limits or boundaries of; demarcate > de,limi'tation *n* > de'limitative *adj*

delineate (dɪ'lɪnɪ,eɪt) *vb* (*tr*) **1** to trace the shape or outline of; sketch **2** to represent pictorially, as by making a chart or diagram; depict **3** to portray in words, esp with detail and precision; describe [c16: from Latin *dēlīneāre* to sketch out, from *līnea* LINE¹] > de,line'ation *n* > de'lineative *adj*

delinquency (dɪ'lɪŋkwənsɪ) *n, pl* -**cies** **1** an offence or misdeed, usually of a minor nature, esp one committed by a young person. See **juvenile delinquency** **2** failure or negligence in duty or obligation; dereliction **3** a delinquent nature or delinquent behaviour [c17: from Late Latin *dēlinquentia* a fault, offence, from Latin *dēlinquere* to transgress, from *DE-* + *linquere* to forsake]

delinquent (dɪ'lɪŋkwənt) *n* **1** someone, esp a young person, guilty of delinquency ▷ *adj* **2** guilty of an offence or misdeed, esp one of a minor nature **3** failing in or neglectful of duty or obligation [c17: from Latin *dēlinquēns* offending; see DELINQUENCY]

deliquesce (,dɛlɪ'kwɛs) *vb* (*intr*) (esp of certain salts) to dissolve gradually in water absorbed from the air [c18: from Latin *dēliquēscere* to melt away, become liquid, from *DE-* + *liquēscere* to melt, from *liquēre* to be liquid] > ,deli'quescence *n* > ,deli'quescent *adj*

delirious (dɪ'lɪrɪəs) *adj* **1** affected with delirium **2** wildly excited, esp with joy or enthusiasm > de'liriously *adv*

delirium (dɪ'lɪrɪəm) *n, pl* -**liriums**, -**liria** (-'lɪrɪə) **1** a state of excitement and mental confusion, often accompanied by hallucinations, caused by high fever, poisoning, brain injury, etc **2** violent excitement or emotion; frenzy [c16: from Latin: madness, from *dēlīrāre*, literally: to swerve from a furrow, hence be crazy, from *DE-* + *līra* ridge, furrow]

delirium tremens ('trɛmɛnz, 'tri:-) *n* a severe psychotic condition occurring in some persons with chronic alcoholism, characterized by delirium, tremor, anxiety, and vivid hallucinations. Abbreviation: **DT's** [c19: New Latin, literally: trembling delirium]

delist (,di:'lɪst) *vb* (*tr*) **1** to remove from a list **2** *stock exchange* to remove (a security) from the register of those that may be traded on the recognized market

Delius ('di:lɪəs) *n* **Frederick.** 1862–1934, English composer, who drew inspiration from folk tunes and the sounds of nature. His works include the opera *A Village Romeo and Juliet* (1901), *A Mass of Life* (1905), and the orchestral variations *Brigg Fair* (1907)

deliver (dɪ'lɪvə) *vb* (*mainly tr*) **1** to carry (goods, etc) to a destination, esp to carry and distribute (goods, mail, etc) to several places: *to deliver letters; our local butcher delivers* **2** (*often foll by over or up*) to hand over, transfer, or surrender **3** (*often foll by from*) to release or rescue (from captivity, harm, corruption, etc) **4** (*also intr*) **a** to aid in the birth of (offspring) **b** to give birth to (offspring) **c** (*usually foll by of*) to aid or assist (a female) in the birth (of offspring) **d** (*passive; foll by of*) to give birth (to offspring) **5** to utter (an exclamation, noise, etc): *to deliver a cry of exultation* **6** to discharge or release (something, such as a blow or shot) suddenly **7** *chiefly US* to cause (voters, constituencies, etc) to support a given candidate, cause, etc **8** **deliver oneself of** to speak with deliberation or at length **9** **deliver the goods** *informal* to produce or perform something promised or expected [c13: from Old French *delivrer*, from Late Latin *dēlīberāre* to set free, from Latin *DE-* + *līberāre* to free] > de'liverable *adj* > de'liverer *n*

deliverance (dɪ'lɪvərəns) *n* **1** a formal pronouncement or expression of opinion **2** rescue from moral corruption or evil; salvation

delivery (dɪ'lɪvərɪ) *n, pl* -**eries** **1 a** the act of delivering or distributing goods, mail, etc **b** something that is delivered **2** the act of giving birth to a child **3** manner or style of utterance, esp in public speaking or recitation: *the chairman had a clear delivery* **4** the act of giving or transferring or the state of being given or transferred **5** the act of rescuing or state of being rescued; liberation **6** *sport* the act or manner of bowling or throwing a ball **7** (in South Africa) the supply of basic services to communities deprived under apartheid

dell (dɛl) *n* a small, esp wooded hollow: *secret gardens and hidden dells* [Old English; related to Middle Low German *delle* valley; compare DALE]

della Robbia (*Italian* ˈdɛlla ˈrobbja) *n* See **Robbia** (sense 2)

Deller (ˈdɛlə) *n* **Alfred** (**George**). 1912–79, British countertenor

Del Mar (dɛl ˈmɑː) *n* **Norman**. 1919–94, British conductor, associated esp with 20th- century British music

Delmarva Peninsula (dɛlˈmɑːvə) *n* a peninsula of the northeast US, between Chesapeake Bay and the Atlantic

Delorme (*French* dəlɔrm) *or* **de l'Orme** *n* **Philibert** (filibɛr). ?1510–70, French Renaissance architect of the Tuileries, Paris

Delors (*French* dəlɔr) *n* **Jacques** (**Lucien Jean**) (ʒak). born 1925, French politician and economist, President of the European Commission (1985–94): originator of the **Delors plan** for closer European union

Delos (ˈdiːlɒs) *n* a Greek island in the SW Aegean Sea, in the Cyclades: a commercial centre in ancient times; the legendary birthplace of Apollo and Artemis. Area: about 5 sq km (2 sq miles). Modern Greek name: Dhílos

de los Angeles (*Spanish* de los ˈaŋxeles) *n* **Victoria** (bikˈtorja). 1923–2005, Spanish soprano

delouse (diːˈlaʊs, -ˈlaʊz) *vb* (*tr*) to rid (a person or animal) of lice as a sanitary measure

Delphi (ˈdɛlfɪ) *n* an ancient Greek city on the S slopes of Mount Parnassus: site of the most famous oracle of Apollo

Delphic (ˈdɛlfɪk) *or* **Delphian** *adj* 1 of or relating to Delphi or its oracle or temple 2 obscure or ambiguous

Delphic oracle *n* the oracle of Apollo at Delphi that gave answers held by the ancient Greeks to be of great authority but also noted for their ambiguity

delphinium (dɛlˈfɪnɪəm) *n*, *pl* -**iums** *or* -**ia** (-ɪə) any ranunculaceous plant of the genus *Delphinium*: many varieties are cultivated as garden plants for their spikes of blue, pink, or white spurred flowers. See also **larkspur** [c17: New Latin, from Greek *delphinion* larkspur, from *delphis* DOLPHIN, referring to the shape of the nectary]

del Sarto (*Italian* dɛl ˈsarto) *n* See **Sarto**

delta (ˈdɛltə) *n* 1 the fourth letter in the Greek alphabet (Δ, δ), a consonant transliterated as *d* 2 (*capital when part of name*) the flat alluvial area at the mouth of some rivers where the mainstream splits up into several distributaries 3 *maths* a finite increment in a variable [c16: via Latin from Greek, of Semitic origin; compare Hebrew *dāleth*] > **deltaic** (dɛlˈteɪɪk) *or* **deltic** *adj*

delta connection *n* a connection used in a three-phase electrical system in which three elements in series form a triangle, the supply being input and output at the three junctions

Delta Force *n* (in the US) an elite army unit involved in counterterrorist operations abroad

delta particle *n* *physics* a very short-lived hyperon

delta ray *n* a particle, esp an electron, ejected from matter by ionizing radiation

delta rhythm *or* **delta wave** *n* *physiol* the normal electrical activity of the cerebral cortex during deep sleep, occurring at a frequency of 1 to 4 hertz and detectable with an electroencephalograph. See also **brain wave**

delta stock *n* any of the fourth rank of active securities on the Stock Exchange. Market makers need not display prices of these securities continuously and any prices displayed are taken only as an indication rather than an offer to buy or sell

delta wing *n* a triangular sweptback aircraft wing

deltiology (ˌdɛltɪˈɒlədʒɪ) *n* the collection and study of picture postcards [c20: from Greek *deltion*, diminutive of *deltos* a writing tablet + -LOGY] > ˌdelti'ologist *n*

deltoid (ˈdɛltɔɪd) *n* the thick muscle forming the rounded contour of the outer edge of the shoulder and acting to raise the arm [c18: from Greek *deltoeidēs* triangular, from DELTA]

delude (dɪˈluːd) *vb* (*tr*) 1 to deceive the mind or judgment of; mislead; beguile 2 *rare* to frustrate (hopes, expectations, etc) [c15: from Latin *dēlūdere* to mock, play false, from DE- + *lūdere* to play] > de'ludable *adj* > de'luder *n*

deluge (ˈdɛljuːdʒ) *n* 1 a great flood of water 2 torrential

rain; downpour ▷ *vb* (*tr*) 3 to flood, as with water; soak, swamp, or drown 4 to overwhelm or overrun; inundate [c14: from Old French, from Latin *dīluvium* a washing away, flood, from *dīluere* to wash away, drench, from *di-* DIS-[1] + *-luere*, from *lavere* to wash]

Deluge (ˈdɛljuːdʒ) *n* the Deluge another name for the **Flood**[1]

delusion (dɪˈluːʒən) *n* 1 a mistaken or misleading opinion, idea, belief, etc 2 *psychiatry* a belief held in the face of evidence to the contrary, that is resistant to all reason 3 the act of deluding or state of being deluded > de'lusional *adj* > de'lusive *adj* > delusory (dɪˈluːsərɪ) *adj*

de luxe (də ˈlʌks, ˈlʊks) *adj* 1 (esp of products, articles for sale, etc) rich, elegant, or sumptuous; superior in quality, number of accessories, etc: *the de luxe model of a car* ▷ *adv* 2 *chiefly US* in a luxurious manner [c19: from French, literally: of luxury]

Delvaux (dɛlvəʊ) *n* **Paul**. 1897–1994, Belgian surrealist painter: his works portray dreamlike figures in mysterious settings

delve (dɛlv) *vb* (*mainly intr; often foll by in or into*) 1 to inquire or research deeply or intensively (for information, etc) 2 to search or rummage (in a drawer, the pockets, etc) 3 (esp of an animal) to dig or burrow deeply (into the ground, etc) 4 (*also tr*) *archaic or dialect* to dig or turn up (earth, a garden, etc), as with a spade [Old English *delfan*; related to Old High German *telban* to dig, Russian *dolbit* to hollow out with a chisel] > 'delver *n*

Dem. *abbreviation US* Democrat(ic)

demagnetize *or* **demagnetise** (diːˈmægnɪˌtaɪz) *vb* to lose magnetic properties or remove magnetic properties from. Also called: degauss > deˌmagneti'zation *or* deˌmagneti'sation *n* > de'magnetˌizer *or* de'magnetˌiser *n*

demagogue *or sometimes US* **demagog** (ˈdɛməˌɡɒɡ) *n* 1 a political agitator who appeals with crude oratory to the prejudice and passions of the mob 2 (esp in the ancient world) any popular political leader or orator [c17: from Greek *dēmagōgos* people's leader, from *dēmos* people + *agein* to lead] > ˌdema'gogic *or* demagogical *adj* > ˌdema'gogically *adv* > demagoguery (ˌdɛməˈɡɒɡərɪ) *or* 'demaˌgoguism *n*

demagogy (ˈdɛməˌɡɒɡɪ) *n*, *pl* -**gogies** 1 demagoguery 2 rule by a demagogue or by demagogues 3 a group of demagogues

demand (dɪˈmɑːnd) *vb* (*tr; may take a clause as object or an infinitive*) 1 to request peremptorily or urgently 2 to require or need as just, urgent, etc: *the situation demands attention* 3 to claim as a right; exact 4 *law* to make a formal legal claim to (property, esp realty) ▷ *n* 5 an urgent or peremptory requirement or request 6 something that requires special effort or sacrifice 7 the act of demanding something or the thing demanded 8 an insistent question or query 9 *economics* a a willingness and ability to purchase goods and services b the amount of a commodity that consumers are willing and able to purchase at a specified price. See **supply**[1] (sense 9) 10 *law* a formal legal claim, esp to real property 11 in demand sought after; popular 12 on demand as soon as requested [c13: from Anglo-French *demaunder*, from Medieval Latin *dēmandāre*, from Latin: to commit to, from DE- + *mandāre* to command, entrust; see MANDATE] > de'mandable *adj* > de'mander *n*

demand feeding *n* the practice of feeding a baby whenever it seems to be hungry, rather than at set intervals

demanding (dɪˈmɑːndɪŋ) *adj* requiring great patience, skill, etc: *a demanding job*

demarcate (ˈdiːmɑːˌkeɪt) *vb* (*tr*) 1 to mark, fix, or draw the boundaries, limits, etc, of 2 to separate or distinguish between (areas with unclear boundaries) > de'marˌcator *n*

demarcation *or* **demarkation** (ˌdiːmɑːˈkeɪʃən) *n* 1 the act of establishing limits or boundaries 2 a limit or boundary 3 a a strict separation of the kinds of work performed by members of different trade unions b (*as modifier*): *demarcation dispute* 4 separation or distinction (often in the phrase **line of demarcation**) [c18: Latinized version of Spanish *demarcación*, from *demarcar* to appoint the boundaries of, from *marcar* to mark, from Italian *marcare*, of Germanic origin; see MARK[1]]

démarche French (demarʃ) *n* a move, step, or manoeuvre, esp in diplomatic affairs [c17: literally: walk, gait, from Old French *demarcher* to tread, trample; see DE-, MARCH[1]]

dematerialize *or* **dematerialise** (ˌdiːməˈtɪərɪəˌlaɪz) *vb* (*intr*) 1 to cease to have material existence, as in science fiction or spiritualism 2 to disappear without trace; vanish >ˌdemaˌterialiˈzation *or* ˌdemaˌterialiˈsation *n*

deme (diːm) *n* 1 (in ancient Attica) a geographical unit of local government 2 *biology* a group of individuals within a species that possess particular characteristics of cytology, genetics, etc [c19: from Greek *dēmos* district in local government, the populace]

demean[1] (dɪˈmiːn) *vb* (*tr*) to lower (oneself) in dignity, status, or character; humble; debase [c17: see DE-, MEAN[2]; on the model of *debase*]

demean[2] (dɪˈmiːn) *vb* (*tr*) *rare* to behave or conduct (oneself) in a specified way [c13: from Old French *demener*, from DE- + *mener* to lead, drive, from Latin *mināre* to drive (animals), from *minārī* to use threats]

demeanour *or US* **demeanor** (dɪˈmiːnə) *n* 1 the way a person behaves towards others; conduct 2 bearing, appearance, or mien [c15: see DEMEAN[2]]

dement (dɪˈment) *vb* 1 (*intr*) to deteriorate mentally, esp because of old age 2 (*tr*) *rare* to drive mad; make insane [c16: from Late Latin *dēmentāre* to drive mad, from Latin DE- + *mēns* mind]

demented (dɪˈmentɪd) *adj* mad; insane >deˈmentedly *adv* >deˈmentedness *n*

dementia (dɪˈmenʃə, -ʃɪə) *n* a state of serious emotional and mental deterioration, of organic or functional origin [c19: from Latin: madness; see DEMENT]

dementia praecox (ˈpriːkɒks) *n* a former name for **schizophrenia** [c19: New Latin, literally: premature dementia]

demerara (ˌdɛməˈrɛərə, -ˈrɑːrə) *n* brown crystallized cane sugar from the Caribbean and nearby countries [c19: named after *Demerara*, a region of Guyana]

Demerara (ˌdɛməˈrɛərə, -ˈrɑːrə) *n* the Demerara a river in Guyana, rising in the central forest area and flowing north to the Atlantic at Georgetown. Length: 346 km (215 miles)

demerit (diːˈmerɪt, ˈdiːˌmerɪt) *n* 1 something, esp conduct, that deserves censure 2 *US & Canadian* a mark given against a person for failure or misconduct, esp in schools or the armed forces 3 a fault or disadvantage [c14 (originally: worth, later specialized to mean: something worthy of blame): from Latin *dēmerērī* to deserve] >deˌmeriˈtorious *adj*

demersal (dɪˈmɜːsəl) *adj* living or occurring on the bottom of a sea or a lake [c19: from Latin *dēmersus* submerged (from *dēmergere* to plunge into, from *mergere* to dip) + -AL[1]]

demesne (dɪˈmeɪn, -ˈmiːn) *n* 1 land, esp surrounding a house or manor, retained by the owner for his own use 2 *property law* the possession and use of one's own property or land 3 a region or district; domain [c14: from Old French *demeine*; see DOMAIN]

Demeter (dɪˈmiːtə) *n* *Greek myth* the goddess of agricultural fertility and protector of marriage and women. Roman counterpart: Ceres

demi- *prefix* 1 half: *demirelief* 2 of less than full size, status, or rank: *demigod* [via French from Medieval Latin *dīmedius*, from *dīmīdius* half, from *dis-* apart + *medius* middle]

demigod (ˈdɛmɪˌgɒd) *n* 1 a a mythological being who is part mortal, part god b a lesser deity 2 a person with outstanding or godlike attributes [c16: translation of Latin *sēmideus*] >ˈdemiˌgoddess *fem n*

demijohn (ˈdɛmɪˌdʒɒn) *n* a large bottle with a short narrow neck, often with small handles at the neck and encased in wickerwork [c18: probably by folk etymology from French *dame-jeanne*, from *dame* lady + *Jeanne* Jane]

demilitarize *or* **demilitarise** (diːˈmɪlɪtəˌraɪz) *vb* (*tr*) 1 to remove any military presence or function in (an area): *demilitarized zone* 2 to free of military character, purpose, etc >deˌmilitariˈzation *or* deˌmilitariˈsation *n*

De Mille (də ˈmɪl) *n* **Cecil B(lount)**. 1881–1959, US film producer and director

demimondaine (ˌdɛmɪˈmɒndeɪn; French dəmimɔ̃dɛn) *n* a woman of the demimonde [c19: from French]

demimonde (ˌdɛmɪˈmɒnd; French dəmimɔ̃d) *n* 1 (esp in the 19th century) those women considered to be outside respectable society, esp on account of sexual promiscuity 2 any social group considered to be not wholly respectable [c19: from French, literally: half-world]

Demirel (Turkish dɛmɪˈrɛl) *n* **Süleyman** (syleɪˈman). born 1924, Turkish statesman; prime minister (1965–71; 1975–77; 1977–78; 1979–80; 1991–93) and president (1993–2000)

demise (dɪˈmaɪz) *n* 1 failure or termination 2 a euphemistic or formal word for **death** 3 *property law* a a transfer of an estate by lease b the passing or transfer of an estate on the death of the owner 4 the immediate transfer of sovereignty to a successor upon the death, abdication, etc, of a ruler (esp in the phrase **demise of the crown**) ▷ *vb* 5 to transfer or be transferred by inheritance, will, or succession 6 (*tr*) *property law* to transfer (an estate, etc) for a limited period; lease 7 (*tr*) to transfer (sovereignty, a title, etc) by or as if by the death, deposition, etc, of a ruler [c16: from Old French, feminine of *demis* dismissed, from *demettre* to send away, from Latin *dīmittere*; see DISMISS] >deˈmisable *adj*

demi-sec (ˌdɛmɪˈsɛk) *adj* (of wine, esp champagne) medium-sweet [c20: from French, from *demi* half + *sec* dry]

demisemiquaver (ˈdɛmɪˌsɛmɪˌkweɪvə) *n* *music* a note having the time value of one thirty-second of a semibreve. Usual US and Canadian name: thirty-second note

demist (diːˈmɪst) *vb* to free or become free of condensation through evaporation produced by a heater and/or blower >deˈmister *n*

demitasse (ˈdɛmɪˌtæs; French dəmitas) *n* 1 a small cup used to serve coffee, esp after a meal 2 the coffee itself [c19: French, literally: half-cup]

demiurge (ˈdɛmɪˌɜːdʒ, ˈdiː-) *n* a (in the philosophy of Plato) the creator of the universe b (in Gnostic and some other philosophies) the creator of the universe, supernatural but subordinate to the Supreme Being [c17: from Church Latin *dēmiūrgus*, from Greek *dēmiourgos* skilled workman, literally: one who works for the people, from *dēmos* people + *ergon* work] >ˌdemiˈurgeous, ˌdemiˈurgic *or* ˌdemiˈurgical *adj*

demiveg (ˈdɛmɪˌvɛdʒ) *informal* ▷ *n* 1 a person who eats poultry and fish, but no red meat ▷ *adj* 2 denoting a person who eats poultry and fish, but no red meat [c20: from DEMI- + VEG(ETARIAN)]

demo (ˈdɛməʊ) *n, pl* -os *informal* 1 short for **demonstration** (sense 4) 2 a demonstration record or tape, used for audition purposes

demo- *or before a vowel* **dem-** *combining form* indicating people or population: *demography* [from Greek *dēmos*]

demob *Brit informal* ▷ *vb* (diːˈmɒb) -mobs, -mobbing, -mobbed ▷ 1 short for **demobilize** ▷ *n* (ˈdiːmɒb) 2 demobilization.

demobilize *or* **demobilise** (diːˈməʊbɪˌlaɪz) *vb* to disband, as troops, etc >deˌmobiliˈzation *or* deˌmobiliˈsation *n*

democracy (dɪˈmɒkrəsɪ) *n, pl* -cies 1 government by the people or their elected representatives 2 a political or social unit governed ultimately by all its members 3 the practice or spirit of social equality 4 a social condition of classlessness and equality [c16: from French *démocratie*, from Late Latin *dēmocratia*, from Greek *dēmokratia* government by the people; see DEMO-, -CRACY]

democrat (ˈdɛməˌkræt) *n* 1 an advocate of democracy; adherent of democratic principles 2 a member or supporter of a democratic party or movement

Democrat (ˈdɛməˌkræt) *n* (in the US) a member or supporter of the Democratic Party >ˌDemoˈcratic *adj*

democratic (ˌdɛməˈkrætɪk) *adj* 1 of, characterized by, derived from, or relating to the principles of democracy 2 upholding or favouring democracy or the interests of the common people 3 popular with or for the benefit of all >ˌdemoˈcratically *adv*

democratic centralism *n* the Leninist principle that policy should be decided centrally by officials, who are nominally democratically elected

Democratic Republic of Congo n the Democratic Republic of Congo See **Congo** (sense 2)

democratize or **democratise** (dɪ'mɒkrə,taɪz) vb (tr) to make democratic ▷ de,mocrati'zation or de,mocrati'sation n

Democritus (dɪ'mɒkrɪtəs) n ?460–?370 BC, Greek philosopher who developed the atomist theory of matter of his teacher, Leucippus

démodé French (demɔde) adj out of fashion; outmoded [French, from dé- out of + mode style, fashion]

demodulate (di:'mɒdjʊ,leɪt) vb to carry out demodulation on (a wave or signal) ▷ de'modu,lator n

demodulation (,di:mɒdjʊ'leɪʃən) n electronics the act or process by which an output wave or signal is obtained having the characteristics of the original modulating wave or signal; the reverse of modulation

demographic (,dɛmə' græfɪk, ,di:mə-) adj 1 of or relating to demography ▷ n 2 a section of the population sharing common characteristics, such as age, sex, class, etc

demographic timebomb n chiefly Brit a predicted shortage of school-leavers and consequently of available workers, caused by an earlier drop in the birth rate, resulting in an older workforce

demography (dɪ'mɒgrəfɪ) n the scientific study of human populations, esp with reference to their size, structure, and distribution [C19: from French démographie, from Greek dēmos the populace; see -GRAPHY] ▷ de'mographer n

demoiselle (dəmwɑː'zɛl) n 1 Also called: demoiselle crane, Numidian crane a small crane, Anthropoides virgo, of central Asia, N Africa, and SE Europe, having grey plumage with long black breast feathers and white ear tufts 2 a less common name for a **damselfly** 3 a literary word for **damsel** [C16: from French: young woman; see DAMSEL]

de Molina (Spanish ðe mo'lina) n Tirso ('tirso). Pen name of Gabriel Téllez. ?1571–1648, Spanish dramatist; author of the first dramatic treatment of the Don Juan legend El Burlador de Sevilla (1630)

demolish (dɪ'mɒlɪʃ) vb (tr) 1 to tear down or break up (buildings, etc) 2 to destroy; put an end to (an argument, etc) 3 facetious to eat up: she demolished the whole cake! [C16: from French démolir, from Latin dēmōlīrī to throw down, destroy, from DE- + mōlīrī to strive, toil, construct, from mōles mass, bulk] ▷ de'molisher n

demolition (,dɛmə'lɪʃən, ,di:-) n 1 the act of demolishing or state of being demolished 2 chiefly military destruction by explosives ▷ ,demo'litionist n, adj

demon ('di:mən) n 1 an evil spirit or devil 2 a person, habit, obsession, etc, thought of as evil, cruel, or persistently tormenting 3 Also called: daemon, daimon an attendant or ministering spirit; genius: the demon of inspiration 4 a a person who is extremely skilful in, energetic at, or devoted to a given activity, esp a sport: a demon at cycling b (as modifier): a demon cyclist 5 a variant spelling of **daemon** (sense 1) 6 Austral & NZ informal, archaic a detective or policeman 7 computing a part of a computer program, such as a help facility, that can run in the background behind the current task or application, and which will only begin to work when certain conditions are met or when it is specifically invoked [C15: from Latin daemōn evil spirit, spirit, from Greek daimōn spirit, deity, fate; see DAEMON] ▷ demonic (dɪ'mɒnɪk) adj

demonetize or **demonetise** (di:'mʌnɪ,taɪz) vb (tr) 1 to deprive (a metal) of its capacity as a monetary standard 2 to withdraw from use as currency ▷ de,moneti'zation or de,moneti'sation n

demoniac (dɪ'məʊnɪ,æk) or **demoniacal** (,di:mə'naɪək²l) adj 1 of, like, or suggestive of a demon; demonic 2 suggesting inner possession or inspiration 3 frantic; frenzied; feverish ▷ n 4 a person possessed by an evil spirit or demon ▷ ,demo'niacally adv

demonism ('di:mə,nɪzəm) n 1 belief in the existence and power of demons 2 another word for **demonology** ▷ 'demonist n

demonize or **demonise** ('di:mə,naɪz) vb (tr) 1 to make into or like a demon 2 to subject to demonic influence 3 to mark out or describe as evil or culpable: the technique of demonizing the enemy in the run-up to war

demonolatry (,di:mə'nɒlətrɪ) n the worship of demons [C17: see DEMON, -LATRY]

demonology (,di:mə'nɒlədʒɪ) n 1 Also called: demonism the study of demons or demonic beliefs 2 a set of people or things that are disliked or held in low esteem: the place occupied by Hitler in contemporary demonology ▷ ,demon'ologist n

demonstrable ('dɛmənstrəb²l, dɪ'mɒn-) adj able to be demonstrated or proved ▷ ,demonstra'bility or 'demonstrableness ▷ demonstrably ('dɛmənstrəblɪ, dɪ'mɒn-) adv

demonstrate ('dɛmən,streɪt) vb 1 (tr) to show, manifest, or prove, esp by reasoning, evidence, etc 2 (tr) to evince; reveal the existence of 3 (tr) to explain or illustrate by experiment, example, etc 4 (tr) to display, operate, and explain the workings of (a machine, product, etc) 5 (intr) to manifest support, protest, etc, by public parades or rallies 6 (intr) to be employed as a demonstrator of machinery, etc 7 (intr) military to make a show of force, esp in order to deceive one's enemy [C16: from Latin dēmōnstrāre to point out, from monstrāre to show]

demonstration (,dɛmən'streɪʃən) n 1 the act of demonstrating 2 proof or evidence leading to proof 3 an explanation, display, illustration, or experiment showing how something works 4 a manifestation of grievances, support, or protest by public rallies, parades, etc 5 a manifestation of emotion 6 a show of military force or preparedness ▷ ,demon'strational adj ▷ ,demon'strationist n

demonstration model n a nearly new product, such as a car or washing machine, that has been used only to demonstrate its performance by a dealer and is offered for sale at a discount

demonstrative (dɪ'mɒnstrətɪv) adj 1 tending to manifest or express one's feelings easily or unreservedly 2 (postpositive; foll by of) serving as proof; indicative 3 involving or characterized by demonstration 4 conclusive; indubitable 5 grammar denoting or belonging to a class of determiners used to point out the individual referent or referents intended, such as this, that, these, and those. See **interrogative, relative** ▷ n 6 grammar a demonstrative word or construction ▷ de'monstratively adv ▷ de'monstrativeness n

demonstrator ('dɛmən,streɪtə) n 1 a person who demonstrates equipment, machines, products, etc 2 a person who takes part in a public demonstration 3 a piece of merchandise, such as a car that one test-drives, used to display merits or performance to prospective buyers

demoralize or **demoralise** (dɪ'mɒrə,laɪz) vb (tr) 1 to undermine the morale of; dishearten: he was demoralized by his defeat 2 to debase morally; corrupt 3 to throw into confusion ▷ de,morali'zation or de,morali'sation n

demos ('di:mɒs) n 1 the people of a nation regarded as a political unit 2 rare the common people; masses [C19: from Greek: the populace; see DEME]

Demosthenes (dɪ'mɒsθə,ni:z) n 384–322 BC, Athenian statesman, orator, and lifelong opponent of the power of Macedonia over Greece

demote (dɪ'məʊt) vb (tr) to lower in rank or position; relegate [C19: from DE- + (PRO)MOTE] ▷ de'motion n

demotic (dɪ'mɒtɪk) adj 1 of or relating to the common people; popular 2 of or relating to a simplified form of hieroglyphics used in ancient Egypt by the ordinary literate class outside the priesthood. See **hieratic** ▷ n 3 the demotic script of ancient Egypt [C19: from Greek dēmotikos of the people, from dēmotēs a man of the people, commoner; see DEMOS] ▷ de'motist n

Dempsey ('dɛmpsɪ) n Jack. real name William Harrison Dempsey. 1895–1983, US boxer; world heavyweight champion (1919–26)

dempster ('dɛmpstə) n a variant spelling of **deemster**

demulcent (dɪ'mʌlsᵊnt) adj 1 soothing; mollifying ▷ n 2 a drug or agent that soothes the irritation of inflamed or injured skin surfaces [C18: from Latin dēmulcēre to caress soothingly, from DE- + mulcēre to stroke]

demur (dɪ'mɜ:) vb -murs, -murring, -murred (intr) 1 to raise objections or show reluctance; object 2 law to raise an objection by entering a demurrer **3** *archaic* to hesitate; delay ▷ *n* Also: **demurral** (dɪ'mʌrəl) **4** the act of demurring **5** an objection raised **6** *archaic* hesitation [C13: from Old French *demorer*, from Latin *dēmorārī* to loiter, linger, from *morārī* to delay, from *mora* a delay] > de'**murrable** *adj*

demure (dɪ'mjʊə) *adj* **1** sedate; decorous; reserved **2** affectedly modest or prim; coy [C14: perhaps from Old French *demorer* to delay, linger; perhaps influenced by *meur* ripe, MATURE] > de'**murely** *adv* > de'**mureness** *n*

demurrage (dɪ'mʌrɪdʒ) *n* **1** the delaying of a ship, railway wagon, etc, caused by the charterer's failure to load, unload, etc, before the time of scheduled departure **2** the extra charge required as compensation for such delay [C17: from Old French *demorage, demourage*; see DEMUR]

demurrer (dɪ'mʌrə) *n* **1** *law* a pleading that admits an opponent's point but denies that it is a relevant or valid argument **2** any objection raised

demutualize or **demutualise** (di:'mju:tʃʊə,laɪz) *vb* to convert (a mutual society, such as a building society) to a public limited company or (of such a society) to be converted > ,demutuali'**zation** or ,demutuali'**sation** *n*

demy (dɪ'maɪ) *n, pl* -**mies** **a** a size of printing paper, 17½ by 22½ inches (444.5 × 571.5 mm) **b** a size of writing paper, 15½ by 20 inches (Brit) (393.5 × 508 mm) or 16 by 21 inches (US) (406.4 × 533.4 mm) [C16: see DEMI-]

demystify (di:'mɪstɪ,faɪ) *vb* -**fies**, -**fying**, -**fied** (*tr*) to remove the mystery from; make clear > de,mystifi'**cation** *n*

demythologize or **demythologise** (,di:mɪ'θɒlə,dʒaɪz) *vb* (*tr*) **1** to eliminate all mythical elements from (a piece of writing, esp the Bible) so as to arrive at an essential meaning **2** to restate (a message, esp a religious one) in rational terms

den (dɛn) *n* **1** the habitat or retreat of a lion or similar wild animal; lair **2** a small or secluded room in a home, often used for carrying on a hobby **3** a squalid or wretched room or retreat **4** a site or haunt: *a den of vice* **5** *Scot* a small wooded valley; dingle ▷ *vb* **dens, denning, denned** **6** (*intr*) to live in or as if in a den [Old English *denn*; related to Old High German *tenni* threshing floor, early Dutch *denne* low ground, den, cave]

Den. *abbreviation* Denmark

Denali (dɪ'nɑːlɪ) *n* another name for Mount **McKinley**

Denali National Park and Preserve (dɪ'nɑːlɪ) *n* a national park in S central Alaska: contains part of the Alaska Range Area: 7847 sq km (3030 sq miles). Former name: Mount McKinley National Park

denar (di:'nɑ:) *n* the standard monetary unit of Macedonia, divided into 100 deni

denarius (dɪ'nɛərɪəs) *n, pl* -**narii** (-'nɛərɪ,aɪ) **1** a silver coin of ancient Rome, often called a penny in translation **2** a gold coin worth 25 silver denarii [C16: from Latin: coin originally equal to ten asses, from *dēnārius* (adj) containing ten, from *dēnī* ten each, from *decem* ten]

denary ('di:nərɪ) *adj* **1** calculated by tens; based on ten; decimal **2** containing ten parts; tenfold [C16: from Latin *dēnārius* containing ten; see DENARIUS]

denationalize or **denationalise** (di:'næʃən²,laɪz) *vb* **1** to return or transfer (an industry, etc) from public to private ownership **2** to deprive (an individual, people, institution, etc) of national character or nationality > de,nationali'**zation** or de,nationali'**sation** *n*

denaturalize or **denaturalise** (di:'nætʃrə,laɪz) *vb* (*tr*) **1** to deprive of nationality **2** to make unnatural > de,naturali'**zation** or de,naturali'**sation** *n*

denature (di:'neɪtʃə), **denaturize** or **denaturise** (di:'neɪtʃə,raɪz) *vb* (*tr*) **1** to change the nature of **2** to change (a protein) by chemical or physical means, such as the action of acid or heat, to cause loss of solubility, biological activity, etc **3** to render (something, such as ethanol) unfit for consumption by adding nauseous substances **4** to render (fissile material) unfit for use in nuclear weapons by addition of an isotope > de'**naturant** *n* > de,natur'**ation** *n*

Denbighshire ('dɛnbɪ,ʃɪə, -ʃə) *n* a county of N Wales: split between Clwyd and Gwynedd in 1974; reinstated with different boundaries in 1996: borders the Irish Sea,

with the Cambrian Mountains in the south: chiefly agricultural. Administrative centre: Ruthin. Pop: 94 900 (2003 est). Area: 844 sq km (327 sq miles).

Den Bosch (dən bɔs) *n* another name for 's **Hertogenbosch**

Dench (dɛntʃ) *n* Dame **Judi** (**Olivia**). born 1934, British actress and theatre director

dendrite ('dɛndraɪt) *n* **1** Also called: **dendron** any of the short branched threadlike extensions of a nerve cell, which conduct impulses towards the cell body **2** a branching mosslike crystalline structure in some rocks and minerals **3** a crystal that has branched during growth and has a treelike form [C18: from Greek *dendrītēs* relating to a tree] > **dendritic** (dɛn'drɪtɪk) or den'**dritical** *adj*

dendro-, dendri- or before a vowel **dendr-** *combining form* tree: *dendrochronology; dendrite* [New Latin, from Greek, from *dendron* tree]

dendrochronology (,dɛndrəʊkrə'nɒlədʒɪ) *n* the study of the annual rings of trees, used esp to date past events

dendrology (dɛn'drɒlədʒɪ) *n* the branch of botany that is concerned with the natural history of trees and shrubs > **dendrological** (,dɛndrə'lɒdʒɪk²l) or dendro'**logic** or den'**drologous** *adj* > den'**drologist** *n*

dene¹ or **dean** (di:n) *n* *Brit* a valley, esp one that is narrow and wooded [Old English *denu* valley; see DEN]

dene² or **dean** (di:n) *n* *dialect, chiefly Southern English* a sandy stretch of land or dune near the sea [C13: probably related to Old English *dūn* hill; see DOWN³]

denervate ('dɛnə,veɪt) *vb* (*tr*) to deprive (a tissue or organ) of its nerve supply > ,dener'**vation** *n*

Deneuve (French dənœv) *n* **Catherine**, original name *Catherine Dorléac*. born 1943, French film actress: her films include *Les Parapluies de Cherbourg* (1964), *Belle de Jour* (1967), *Indochine* (1992), and *Dancing in the Dark* (2000)

dengue ('dɛngɪ) or **dandy** ('dændɪ) *n* an acute viral disease transmitted by mosquitoes, characterized by headache, fever, pains in the joints, and skin rash. Also called: **breakbone fever** [C19: from Spanish, probably of African origin; compare Swahili *kidinga*]

Deng Xiaoping ('dʌŋ 'sjaʊpɪŋ) or **Teng Hsiao-ping** *n* 1904–97, Chinese Communist statesman; deputy prime minister (1973–76; 1977–80) and the dominant figure in the Chinese government from 1977 until his death. He was twice removed from office (1967–73, 1976–77) and rehabilitated. He introduced economic liberalization, but suppressed demands for political reform, most notably in 1989 when over 2500 demonstrators were killed by the military in Tiananmen Square in Beijing

Den Haag (dɛn 'ha:x) *n* a Dutch name for (The) **Hague**

deni (dɪ'nɪ) *n* a monetary unit of the Former Yugoslav Republic of Macedonia, worth one hundredth of a denar

deniable (dɪ'naɪəb²l) *adj* able to be denied; questionable > de'**niably** *adv*

denial (dɪ'naɪəl) *n* **1** a refusal to agree or comply with a statement; contradiction **2** the rejection of the truth of a proposition, doctrine, etc **3** a negative reply; rejection of a request **4** a refusal to acknowledge; renunciation; disavowal **5** a psychological process by which painful truths are not admitted into an individual's consciousness **6** abstinence; self-denial

denier¹ *n* **1** ('dɛnɪ,eɪ, 'dɛnjə) a unit of weight used to measure the fineness of silk and man-made fibres, esp when woven into women's tights, etc. It is equal to 1 gram per 9000 metres **2** (də'njeɪ, -'nɪə) any of several former European coins of various denominations [C15: from Old French: coin, from Latin *dēnārius* DENARIUS]

denier² (dɪ'naɪə) *n* a person who denies

denigrate ('dɛnɪ,greɪt) *vb* (*tr*) to belittle or disparage the character of; defame [C16: from Latin *dēnigrāre* to make very black, defame, from *nigrāre* to blacken, from *niger* black] > ,deni'**gration** *n* > 'deni,**grator** *n*

denim ('dɛnɪm) *n* *textiles* **1** a hard-wearing twill-weave cotton fabric used for trousers, work clothes, etc **2** a similar lighter fabric used in upholstery [C17: from French (*serge*) *de Nîmes* (serge) of NîMES]

denims ('dɛnɪmz) *pl n* jeans or overalls made of denim

De Niro (də 'nɪərəʊ) *n* **Robert**. born 1943, US film actor. His films include *Taxi Driver* (1976), *Raging Bull* (1980),

GoodFellas (1990), *Casino* (1995), and *Analyze This* (1999)

Denis ('dɛnɪs; *French* dəni) *n* **1 Maurice** (mɔris). 1870–1943, French painter and writer on art. One of the leading Nabis, he defined a picture as "essentially a flat surface covered with colours assembled in a certain order" **2** Saint Denis Also: Saint Denys 3rd century AD, first bishop of Paris; patron saint of France. Feast day: Oct 9

denizen ('dɛnɪzən) *n* **1** an inhabitant; occupant; resident **2** *Brit* an individual permanently resident in a foreign country where he enjoys certain rights of citizenship **3** a plant or animal established in a place to which it is not native **4** a naturalized foreign word [c15: from Anglo-French *denisein*, from Old French *denzein*, from *denz* within, from Latin *de intus* from within]

Denmark ('dɛnmɑːk) *n* a kingdom in N Europe, between the Baltic and the North Sea: consists of the mainland of Jutland and about 100 inhabited islands (chiefly Zealand, Lolland, Funen, Falster, Langeland, and Bornholm); extended its territory throughout the Middle Ages, ruling Sweden until 1523 and Norway until 1814, and incorporating Greenland as a province from 1953 to 1979; joined the Common Market (now the EU) in 1973; an important exporter of dairy produce. Language: Danish. Religion: Christian, Lutheran majority. Currency: krone. Capital: Copenhagen. Pop: 5 375 000 (2004 est). Area: 43 031 sq km (16 614 sq miles). Danish name: **Danmark**. Related adj: **Danish**

Denmark Strait *n* a channel between SE Greenland and Iceland, linking the Arctic Ocean with the Atlantic

Denning ('dɛnɪŋ) *n* Baron **Alfred Thompson**. 1899–1999, English judge; Master of the Rolls 1962-82

Dennis ('dɛnɪs) *n* C(**larence**) J(**ames**). 1876–1938, the poet of the Australian larrikin, esp in *The Songs of a Sentimental Bloke* (1915) and *The Moods of Ginger Mick* (1916)

denominate (dɪ'nɒmɪ,neɪt) **1** (*tr*) to give a specific name to; designate ▷ *adj* (dɪ'nɒmɪnɪt, -,neɪt) **2** *maths* (of a number) representing a multiple of a unit of measurement: *4 is the denominate number in 4 miles* [c16: from DE- + Latin *nōmināre* to call by name; see NOMINATE]

denomination (dɪ,nɒmɪ'neɪʃən) *n* **1** a group having a distinctive interpretation of a religious faith and usually its own organization **2** a grade or unit in a series of designations of value, weight, measure, etc: *coins of this denomination are being withdrawn* **3** a name given to a class or group; classification **4** the act of giving a name **5** a name; designation [c15: from Latin *dēnōminātiō* a calling by name; see DENOMINATE] > de,nomi'national *adj*

denominative (dɪ'nɒmɪnətɪv) *adj* **1** giving or constituting a name; naming **2** *grammar* **a** (of a word other than a noun) formed from or having the same form as a noun **b** (*as noun*): *the verb "to mushroom" is a denominative*

denominator (dɪ'nɒmɪ,neɪtə) *n* the divisor of a fraction, as in ⅞. See **numerator** (sense 1)

denotation (,diːnəʊ'teɪʃən) *n* **1** the act or process of denoting; indication **2** a particular meaning, esp one given explicitly rather than by suggestion **3 a** something designated or referred to **b** another name for **extension** (sense 10)

denote (dɪ'nəʊt) *vb* (*tr; may take a clause as object*) **1** to be a sign, symbol, or symptom of; indicate or designate **2** (of words, phrases, expressions, etc) to have as a literal or obvious meaning [c16: from Latin *dēnotāre* to mark, from *notāre* to mark, NOTE] > de'notative *adj* > de'notatively *adv*

denouement (deɪ'nuːmɒn) *or* **dénouement** (*French* denumã) *n* **1 a** the final clarification or resolution of a plot in a play or other work **b** the point at which this occurs **2** final outcome; solution [c18: from French, literally: an untying, from *dénouer* to untie, from Old French *desnoer*, from *des-* DE- + *noer* to tie, knot, from Latin *nōdāre*, from *nōdus* a knot; see NODE]

denounce (dɪ'naʊns) *vb* (*tr*) **1** to deplore or condemn openly or vehemently **2** to give information against; accuse **3** to announce formally the termination of (a treaty, etc) [c13: from Old French *denoncier* to proclaim, from Latin *dēnuntiāre* to make an official proclamation, threaten, from DE- + *nuntiāre* to announce]

de novo (*Latin* diː 'nəʊvəʊ) *adv* from the beginning; anew

dense (dɛns) *adj* **1** thickly crowded or closely set: *a dense crowd* **2** thick; impenetrable **3** *physics* having a high density **4** stupid; dull; obtuse **5** (of a photographic negative) having many dark or exposed areas [c15: from Latin *dēnsus* thick; related to Greek *dasus* thickly covered with hair or leaves]

densimeter (dɛn'sɪmɪtə) *n* *physics* any instrument for measuring density > densimetric (,dɛnsɪ'mɛtrɪk) *adj* > den'simetry *n*

density ('dɛnsɪtɪ) *n, pl* -ties **1** the degree to which something is filled, crowded, or occupied: *high density of building in towns* **2** obtuseness; stupidity **3** a measure of the compactness of a substance, expressed as its mass per unit volume. It is measured in kilograms per cubic metre or pounds per cubic foot. Symbol: ρ. See also **relative density 4** a measure of a physical quantity per unit of length, area, or volume **5** *physics, photog* See **transmission density**, **reflection density**

dent (dɛnt) *n* **1 a** a hollow or dip in a surface, as one made by pressure or a blow **2** an appreciable effect, esp of lessening: *a dent in our resources* ▷ *vb* **3** to impress or be impressed with a dent or dents [c13 (in the sense: a stroke, blow): variant of DINT]

dental ('dɛntəl) *adj* **1** of or relating to the teeth **2** of or relating to dentistry **3** *phonetics* pronounced or articulated with the tip of the tongue touching the backs of the upper teeth, as for *t* in French *tout* ▷ *n* **4** *phonetics* a dental consonant [c16: from Medieval Latin *dentālis*, from Latin *dens* tooth]

dental floss *n* a soft usually flattened often waxed thread for cleaning the teeth and the spaces between them

dental hygiene *n* the maintenance of the teeth and gums in healthy condition, esp by proper brushing, the removal of plaque, etc. Also called: oral hygiene

dental plaque *n* a filmy deposit on the surface of a tooth consisting of a mixture of mucus, bacteria, food, etc. Also called: bacterial plaque

dental surgeon *n* another name for **dentist**

dentate ('dɛnteɪt) *adj* **1** having teeth or toothlike processes **2** (of leaves) having a toothed margin [c19: from Latin *dentātus*] > 'dentately *adv*

denti- *or before a vowel* **dent-** *combining form* indicating a tooth: *dentiform; dentine* [from Latin *dēns, dent-*]

denticulate (dɛn'tɪkjʊlɪt, -,leɪt) *adj* **1** *biology* very finely toothed: *denticulate leaves* **2** *architect* having dentils [c17: from Latin *denticulātus* having small teeth]

dentifrice ('dɛntɪfrɪs) *n* any substance, esp paste or powder, for use in cleaning the teeth [c16: from Latin *dentifricium* tooth powder, from *dent-, dens* tooth + *fricāre* to rub]

dentil ('dɛntɪl) *n* one of a set of small square or rectangular blocks evenly spaced to form an ornamental row, usually under a classical cornice on a building, piece of furniture, etc [c17: from French, from obsolete *dentille* a little tooth, from *dent* tooth]

dentine ('dɛntiːn) *or* **dentin** ('dɛntɪn) *n* the calcified tissue surrounding the pulp cavity of a tooth and comprising the bulk of the tooth [c19: from DENTI- + -IN] > 'dentinal *adj*

dentist ('dɛntɪst) *n* a person qualified to practise dentistry [c18: from French *dentiste*, from *dent* tooth]

dentistry ('dɛntɪstrɪ) *n* the branch of medical science concerned with the diagnosis and treatment of diseases and disorders of the teeth and gums

dentition (dɛn'tɪʃən) *n* **1** the arrangement, type, and number of the teeth in a particular species. Man has a **primary dentition** of deciduous teeth and a **secondary dentition** of permanent teeth **2** teething or the time or process of teething [c17: from Latin *dentītiō* a teething]

D'Entrecasteaux Islands (*French* dãtrəkasto) *pl n* a group of volcanic islands in the Pacific, off the SE coast of New Guinea: part of Papua New Guinea. Pop: 49 167 (1990 est). Area: 3141 sq km (1213 sq miles)

denture ('dɛntʃə) *n* (*usually plural*) **1** Also called: dental plate, false teeth a partial or full set of artificial teeth **2** *rare* a set of natural teeth [c19: from French, from *dent* tooth + -URE]

denuclearize or **denuclearise** (di:'nju:klɪə,raɪz) vb (tr) to deprive (a country, state, etc) of nuclear weapons > de,nucleari'zation or de,nucleari'sation n

denudate ('dɛnjʊ,deɪt, dɪ'nju:deɪt) vb **1** a less common word for **denude** ▷ adj **2** denuded; bare

denude (dɪ'nju:d) vb (tr) **1** to divest of covering; make bare; uncover; strip **2** to expose (rock) by the erosion of the layers above [c16: from Latin dēnūdāre; see NUDE] > denudation (,dɛnjʊ'deɪʃən, ,di:-) n

denumerable (dɪ'nju:mərəb³l) adj maths capable of being put into a one-to-one correspondence with the positive integers; countable > de'numerably adv

denunciate (dɪ'nʌnsɪ,eɪt) vb (tr) to condemn; denounce [c16: from Latin dēnuntiāre; see DENOUNCE] > de'nunci,ator n > de'nunciatory adj

denunciation (dɪ,nʌnsɪ'eɪʃən) n **1** open condemnation; censure; denouncing **2** law obsolete a charge or accusation of crime made by an individual before a public prosecutor or tribunal **3** a formal announcement of the termination of a treaty

Denver ('dɛnvə) n a city in central Colorado: the state capital. Pop: 557 478 (2003 est)

Denver boot n a slang name for **wheel clamp** [c20: from DENVER, Colorado, where it was first used]

deny (dɪ'naɪ) vb -nies, -nying, -nied (tr) **1** to declare (an assertion, statement, etc) to be untrue **2** to reject as false; refuse to accept or believe **3** to withhold; refuse to give **4** to refuse to fulfil the requests or expectations of: it is hard to deny a child **5** to refuse to acknowledge or recognize; disown; disavow: the baron denied his wicked son **6** to refuse (oneself) things desired [c13: from Old French denier, from Latin dēnegāre, from negāre]

Denys ('dɛnɪs; French dəni) n Saint. a variant spelling of (Saint) **Denis**

deodar ('di:əʊ,dɑ:) n **1** a Himalayan cedar, Cedrus deodara, with drooping branches **2** the durable fragrant highly valued wood of this tree [c19: from Hindi deodār, from Sanskrit devadāru, literally: wood of the gods, from deva god + dāru wood]

deodorant (di:'əʊdərənt) n **1** a substance applied to the body to suppress or mask the odour of perspiration or other body odours **2** any substance for destroying or masking odours, such as liquid sprayed into the air

deodorize or **deodorise** (di:'əʊdə,raɪz) vb (tr) to remove, disguise, or absorb the odour of, esp when unpleasant > de,odori'zation or de,odori'sation n > de'odor,izer or de'odor,iser n

deontic (di:'ɒntɪk) adj logic **a** of or relating to such ethical concepts as obligation and permissibility **b** designating the branch of modal logic that deals with the formalization of these concepts [c19: from Greek deon duty, from impersonal dei it behoves, it is binding]

deoxidize or **deoxidise** (di:'ɒksɪ,daɪz) vb **1** (tr) to remove oxygen atoms from (a compound, molecule, etc) **2** another word for **reduce** (sense 12) > de,oxidi'zation or de,oxidi'sation n > de'oxi,dizer or de'oxi,diser n

deoxygenate (di:'ɒksɪdʒɪ,neɪt), **deoxygenize** or **deoxygenise** (di:'ɒksɪdʒɪ,naɪz) vb (tr) to remove oxygen from (water, air, etc) > de,oxygen'ation n

deoxyribonuclease (di:,ɒksɪ,raɪbəʊ'nju:klɪ,eɪz) n the full name for **DNAase**

deoxyribonucleic acid (di:,ɒksɪ,raɪbəʊnju:'kleɪɪk) or **desoxyribonucleic acid** n the full name for **DNA**

dep. abbreviation **1** departs **2** departure **3** deposit **4** depot **5** deputy

dépanneur (,depə'nɜ:) n Canadian (in Quebec) a convenience store [from Canadian French]

Depardieu (French dəpardjø) n **Gérard.** born 1948, French film actor. His films include Jean de Florette (1986), Cyrano de Bergerac (1990), Green Card (1991), The Man in the Iron Mask (1997), and Tais-toi (2003)

depart (dɪ'pɑ:t) vb (mainly intr) **1** to go away; leave **2** to start out; set forth **3** (usually foll by from) to deviate; differ; vary: to depart from normal procedure **4** (tr) to quit (archaic, except in the phrase **depart this life**) [c13: from Old French departir, from DE- + partir to go away, divide, from Latin partīrī to divide, distribute, from pars a part]

departed (dɪ'pɑ:tɪd) adj euphemistic **a** dead; deceased **b** (as sing or collective noun; preceded by the): the departed

department (dɪ'pɑ:tmənt) n **1** a specialized division of a large concern, such as business, store, or university: the geography department **2** a major subdivision or branch of the administration of a government **3** a branch or subdivision of learning: physics is a department of science **4** a territorial and administrative division in several countries, such as France **5** informal a specialized sphere of knowledge, skill, or activity: wine-making is my wife's department [c18: from French département, from départir to divide; see DEPART] > departmental (,di:pɑ:t'mɛnt³l) adj

departmentalize or **departmentalise** (,di:pɑ:t'mɛnt³,laɪz) vb (tr) to organize into departments, esp excessively > depart,mentali'zation or ,depart,mentali'sation n

department store n a large shop divided into departments selling a great many kinds of goods

departure (dɪ'pɑ:tʃə) n **1** the act or an instance of departing **2** a deviation or variation from previous custom; divergence **3** a project, course of action, venture, etc: selling is a new departure for him **4** nautical the net distance travelled due east or west by a vessel **5** a euphemistic word for **death**

depend (dɪ'pɛnd) vb (intr) **1** (foll by on or upon) to put trust (in); rely (on); be sure (of) **2** (usually foll by on or upon; often with it as subject) to be influenced or determined (by); be resultant (from): whether you come or not depends on what father says; it all depends on you **3** (foll by on or upon) to rely (on) for income, support, etc **4** (foll by from) rare to hang down; be suspended **5** to be undecided or pending [c15: from Old French dependre, from Latin dēpendēre to hang from, from DE- + pendēre to hang]

dependable (dɪ'pɛndəb³l) adj able to be depended on; reliable; trustworthy > de,penda'bility or de'pendableness n > de'pendably adv

dependant (dɪ'pɛndənt) n a person who depends on another person, organization, etc, for support, aid, or sustenance, esp financial support

● USAGE Dependant is the generally accepted correct
● spelling in British usage for the noun: if you are single
● and have no dependants ... The adjective should be spelt
● dependent: ... tax allowance for dependent (not dependant)
● children. American usage spells both adjective and
● noun with an e in the last syllable

dependence or sometimes US **dependance** (dɪ'pɛndəns) n **1** the state or fact of being dependent, esp for support or help **2** reliance; trust; confidence

dependency or sometimes US **dependancy** (dɪ'pɛndənsɪ) n, pl -cies **1** a territory subject to a state on which it does not border **2** a dependent or subordinate person or thing **3** psychol overreliance by a person on another person or on a drug, etc **4** another word for **dependence**

dependent or sometimes US **dependant** (dɪ'pɛndənt) adj **1** depending on a person or thing for aid, support, life, etc **2** (postpositive; foll by on or upon) influenced or conditioned (by); contingent (on) **3** subordinate; subject **4** obsolete hanging down ▷ n **5** a variant spelling (esp US) of **dependant** > de'pendently adv

● USAGE See at **dependant**

dependent clause n grammar another term for **subordinate clause**

dependent variable n a variable in a mathematical equation or statement whose value depends on that taken on by the independent variable

depersonalize or **depersonalise** (dɪ'pɜ:sn³,laɪz) vb (tr) **1** to deprive (a person, organization, system, etc) of individual or personal qualities; render impersonal **2** to cause (someone) to lose his or her sense of personal identity [c19: from DE- + PERSONAL + -IZE] > de,personali'zation or de,personali'sation n

depict (dɪ'pɪkt) vb (tr) **1** to represent by or as by drawing, sculpture, painting, etc; delineate; portray **2** to represent in words; describe [c17: from Latin dēpingere, from pingere to paint] > de'picter or de'pictor n > de'piction n > de'pictive adj

depilate ('dɛpɪ,leɪt) vb (tr) to remove the hair from [c16: from Latin dēpilāre, from pilāre to make bald, from pilus hair] > depi'lation n > 'depi,lator n

depilatory (dɪ'pɪlətərɪ, -trɪ) adj **1** able to or serving to remove hair ▷ n, pl -ries **2** a chemical that is used to remove hair from the body

deplane (diːˈpleɪn) vb (intr) chiefly US & Canadian to disembark from an aeroplane [C20: from DE- + PLANE¹]

deplete (dɪˈpliːt) vb (tr) 1 to use up (supplies, money, energy, etc); reduce or exhaust 2 to empty entirely or partially [C19: from Latin dēplēre to empty out, from DE- + plēre to fill] > deˈpletion n

depleted uranium n chem uranium containing a smaller proportion of the isotope uranium–235 than is present in the natural form of uranium; used in anti-tank weapons and other armaments

depletion layer n electronics a region at the interface between dissimilar zones of conductivity in a semiconductor, in which there are few charge carriers

deplorable (dɪˈplɔːrəbəl) adj 1 lamentable 2 worthy of censure or reproach; very bad > deˈplorably adv

deplore (dɪˈplɔː) vb (tr) 1 to express or feel sorrow about; lament; regret 2 to express or feel strong disapproval of; censure [C16: from Old French deplorer, from Latin dēplōrāre to weep bitterly, from plōrāre to weep, lament] > deˈploringly adv

deploy (dɪˈplɔɪ) vb chiefly military 1 to adopt or cause to adopt a battle formation, esp from a narrow front formation 2 (tr) to redistribute (forces) to or within a given area [C18: from French déployer, from Latin displicāre to unfold; see DISPLAY] > deˈployment n

depolarize or **depolarise** (diːˈpəʊləˌraɪz) vb to undergo or cause to undergo a loss of polarity or polarization > deˌpolariˈzation or deˌpolariˈsation n

depone (dɪˈpəʊn) vb chiefly Scots law to declare (something) under oath; testify; depose [C16: from Latin dēpōnere to put down, from DE- + pōnere to put, place]

deponent (dɪˈpəʊnənt) adj 1 grammar (of a verb, esp in Latin) having the inflectional endings of a passive verb but the meaning of an active verb ▷ n 2 grammar a deponent verb 3 law a a person who makes an affidavit b a person, esp a witness, who makes a deposition [C16: from Latin dēpōnēns putting aside, putting down, from dēpōnere to put down, DEPONE]

depopulate (diːˈpɒpjuˌleɪt) vb to be or cause to be reduced in population > deˌpopuˈlation n

deport (dɪˈpɔːt) vb (tr) 1 to remove (an alien) forcibly from a country; expel 2 to conduct, hold, or behave (oneself) in a specified manner [C15: from French déporter, from Latin dēportāre to carry away, banish, from DE- + portāre to carry] > deˈportable adj

deportation (ˌdiːpɔːˈteɪʃən) n the act of expelling an alien from a country; expulsion

deportee (ˌdiːpɔːˈtiː) n a person deported or awaiting deportation

deportment (dɪˈpɔːtmənt) n the manner in which a person behaves, esp in physical bearing: military deportment [C17: from French déportement, from Old French deporter to conduct (oneself); see DEPORT]

depose (dɪˈpəʊz) vb 1 (tr) to remove from an office or position, esp one of power or rank 2 law to testify or give (evidence, etc) on oath, esp when taken down in writing; make a deposition [C13: from Old French deposer to put away, put down, from Late Latin dēpōnere to depose from office, from Latin: to put aside; see DEPONE]

deposit (dɪˈpɒzɪt) vb (tr) 1 to put or set down, esp carefully or in a proper place; place 2 to entrust for safekeeping; consign 3 to place (money) in a bank or similar institution in order to earn interest or for safekeeping 4 to give (money) in part payment or as security 5 to lay down naturally; cause to settle: the river deposits silt ▷ n 6 a an instance of entrusting money or valuables to a bank or similar institution b the money or valuables so entrusted 7 money given in part payment or as security, as when goods are bought on hire-purchase 8 an accumulation of sediments, mineral ores, coal, etc 9 any deposited material, such as a sediment or a precipitate that has settled out of solution 10 a depository or storehouse 11 on deposit in a bank as the first instalment, as when buying on hire-purchase [C17: from Medieval Latin dēpositāre, from Latin dēpositus put down]

deposit account n Brit a bank account that earns interest and usually requires notice of withdrawal

depositary (dɪˈpɒzɪtərɪ, -trɪ) n, pl-taries 1 a person or group to whom something is entrusted for safety or preservation 2 a variant spelling of **depository** (sense 1)

deposition (ˌdɛpəˈzɪʃən, ˌdiːpə-) n 1 law a the giving of testimony on oath b the testimony so given c the sworn statement of a witness used in court in his absence 2 the act or instance of deposing 3 the act or an instance of depositing 4 something that is deposited; deposit [C14: from Late Latin dēpositiō a laying down, disposal, burying, testimony]

depositor (dɪˈpɒzɪtə) n a person who places or has money on deposit in a bank or similar organization

depository (dɪˈpɒzɪtərɪ, -trɪ) n, pl-ries 1 a store, such as a warehouse, for furniture, valuables, etc; repository 2 a variant spelling of **depositary** (sense 1) [C17 (in the sense: place of a deposit): from Medieval Latin dēpositōrium; C18 (in the sense: depositary): see DEPOSIT, -ORY¹]

depot (ˈdɛpəʊ; US & Canadian ˈdiːpəʊ) n 1 a storehouse or warehouse 2 military a a store for supplies b a training and holding centre for recruits and replacements 3 chiefly Brit a building used for the storage and servicing of buses or railway engines 4 US & Canadian a bus or railway station [C18: from French dépôt, from Latin dēpositum a deposit, trust]

Depp (dɛp) n **Johnny**, full name John Christopher, born 1963, US actor; his films include Edward Scissorhands (1990), Sleepy Hollow (1999), and the Pirates of the Caribbean trilogy (2003–07)

deprave (dɪˈpreɪv) vb (tr) 1 to make morally bad; corrupt; vitiate 2 obsolete to defame; slander [C14: from Latin dēprāvāre to distort, corrupt, from DE- + prāvus crooked] > depravation (ˌdɛprəˈveɪʃən) n

depraved (dɪˈpreɪvd) adj morally bad or debased; corrupt; perverted

depravity (dɪˈprævɪtɪ) n, pl-ties the state or an instance of moral corruption

deprecate (ˈdɛprɪˌkeɪt) vb (tr) 1 to express disapproval of; protest against 2 to depreciate (a person, someone's character, etc); belittle [C17: from Latin dēprecārī to avert, ward off by entreaty, from DE- + precārī to PRAY] > ˈdepreˌcating adj > ˈdepreˌcatingly adv > ˌdepreˈcation n > ˈdeprecative adj > ˈdepreˌcator n

deprecatory (ˈdɛprɪkətərɪ) adj 1 expressing disapproval; protesting 2 expressing apology; apologetic > ˈdeprecatorily adv

depreciate (dɪˈpriːʃɪˌeɪt) vb 1 to reduce or decline in value or price 2 (tr) to lessen the value of by derision, criticism, etc; disparage [C15: from Late Latin dēpretiāre to lower the price of, from Latin DE- + pretium PRICE] > deˈpreciˌatingly adv > depreciatory (dɪˈpriːʃɪətərɪ, -trɪ) or deˈpreciative adj

depreciation (dɪˌpriːʃɪˈeɪʃən) n 1 accounting a the reduction in value of a fixed asset due to use, obsolescence, etc b the amount deducted from gross profit to allow for such reduction in value 2 the act or an instance of depreciating or belittling; disparagement 3 a decrease in the exchange value of currency against gold or other currencies brought about by excess supply of that currency under conditions of fluctuating exchange rates

depredation (ˌdɛprɪˈdeɪʃən) n the act or an instance of plundering; robbery; pillage

depress (dɪˈprɛs) vb (tr) 1 to lower in spirits; make gloomy; deject 2 to weaken or lower the force, vigour, or energy of 3 to lower prices of (securities or a security market) 4 to press or push down [C14: from Old French depresser, from Latin dēprimere from DE- + premere to PRESS¹] > deˈpressing adj

depressant (dɪˈprɛsənt) adj 1 med able to diminish or reduce nervous or functional activity 2 causing gloom or dejection; depressing ▷ n 3 a depressant drug

depressed (dɪˈprɛst) adj 1 low in spirits; downcast; despondent 2 lower than the surrounding surface 3 pressed down or flattened 4 Also: distressed characterized by relative economic hardship, such as unemployment: a depressed area 5 lowered in force, intensity, or amount 6 (of plant parts) flattened as though pressed from above 7 zoology flattened from top to bottom: *the depressed bill of the spoonbill*

depression (dɪˈprɛʃən) *n* **1** the act of depressing or state of being depressed **2** a depressed or sunken place or area **3** a mental disorder characterized by extreme gloom, feelings of inadequacy, and inability to concentrate **4** *pathol* an abnormal lowering of the rate of any physiological activity or function, such as respiration **5** an economic condition characterized by substantial and protracted unemployment, low output and investment, etc; slump **6** Also called: *cyclone, low meteorol* a large body of rotating and rising air below normal atmospheric pressure, which often brings rain **7** (esp in surveying and astronomy) the angular distance of an object, celestial body, etc, below the horizontal plane through the point of observation

Depression (dɪˈprɛʃən) *n* **the Depression** the worldwide economic depression of the early 1930s, when there was mass unemployment

depressive (dɪˈprɛsɪv) *adj* **1** tending to depress; causing depression **2** *psychol* tending to be subject to periods of depression > de**ˈpressively** *adv*

depressor (dɪˈprɛsə) *n* **1** a person or thing that depresses **2** any muscle that draws down a part **3** *med* an instrument used to press down or aside an organ or part: *a tongue depressor*

depressurize *or* **depressurise** (dɪˈprɛʃəˌraɪz) *vb* (*tr*) to reduce the pressure of a gas inside (a container or enclosed space), as in an aircraft cabin
> de,pressuri'zation *or* de,pressuri'sation *n*

Depretis (Italian deˈpretis) *n* **Agostino** (agoˈstiːno). 1813–87, Italian statesman; prime minister (1876–78; 1878–79; 1881–87). His policy led to the Triple Alliance (1882) between Italy, Austria-Hungary, and Germany

deprive (dɪˈpraɪv) *vb* (*tr*) **1** (foll by *of*) to prevent from possessing or enjoying; dispossess (of) **2** *archaic* to remove from rank or office; depose; demote [C14: from Old French *depriver*, from Medieval Latin *dēprīvāre*, from Latin DE- + *prīvāre* to deprive of, rob; see PRIVATE]
> de'prival *n* > deprivation (ˌdɛprɪˈveɪʃən) *n*

deprived (dɪˈpraɪvd) *adj* lacking adequate food, shelter, education, etc: *deprived inner-city areas*

deprogramme *or* **deprogram** (diːˈprəʊɡræm) *vb* to free (someone) from the effects of indoctrination, esp by a religious cult or political group

dept *abbreviation* department

depth (dɛpθ) *n* **1** the extent, measurement, or distance downwards, backwards, or inwards **2** the quality of being deep; deepness **3** intensity or profundity of emotion or feeling **4** profundity of moral character; penetration; sagacity; integrity **5** complexity or abstruseness, as of thought or objects of thought **6** intensity, as of silence, colour, etc **7** lowness of pitch **8** (*often plural*) a deep, far, inner, or remote part, such as an inaccessible region of a country **9** (*often plural*) the deepest, most intense, or most severe part: *the depths of winter* **10** (*usually plural*) a low moral state; demoralization **11** (*often plural*) a vast space or abyss **12** beyond one's depth *or* out of one's depth **a** in water deeper than one is tall **b** beyond the range of one's competence or understanding [C14: from *dep* DEEP + -TH¹]

depth charge *or* **depth bomb** *n* a bomb used to attack submarines that explodes at a pre-set depth of water

depth gauge *n* a device attached to a drill bit to prevent the hole from exceeding a predetermined depth

depth of field *n* the range of distance in front of and behind an object focused by an optical instrument, such as a camera or microscope, within which other objects will also appear clear and sharply defined in the resulting image

depth psychology *n* *psychol* the study of unconscious motives and attitudes

deputation (ˌdɛpjʊˈteɪʃən) *n* **1** the act of appointing a person or body of people to represent or act on behalf of others **2** a person or, more often, a body of people so appointed; delegation

depute *vb* (dɪˈpjuːt) (*tr*) **1** to appoint as an agent, substitute, or representative **2** to assign or transfer (authority, duties, etc) to a deputy; delegate ⊳ *n* (ˈdɛpjuːt) **3** *Scot* **a** a deputy **b** (*as modifier; usually postpositive*): *sheriff*

depute [C15: from Old French *deputer*, from Late Latin *dēputāre* to assign, allot, from Latin DE- + *putāre* to think, consider]

deputize *or* **deputise** (ˈdɛpjʊˌtaɪz) *vb* to appoint or act as deputy

deputy (ˈdɛpjʊtɪ) *n, pl* -ties **1 a** a person appointed to act on behalf of or represent another **b** (*as modifier*): *the deputy chairman* **2** a member of the legislative assembly or of the lower chamber of the legislature in various countries, such as France [C16: from Old French *depute*, from *deputer* to appoint; see DEPUTE]

De Quincey (də ˈkwɪnsɪ) *n* **Thomas.** 1785–1859, English critic and essayist, noted particularly for his *Confessions of an English Opium Eater* (1821)

deracinate (dɪˈræsɪˌneɪt) *vb* (*tr*) to pull up by or as if by the roots; uproot; extirpate [C16: from Old French *desraciner*, from *des-* DIS-¹ + *racine* root, from Late Latin *rādīcīna* a little root, from Latin *rādīx* a root]
> de,raci'nation *n*

derail (dɪˈreɪl) *vb* to go or cause to go off the rails, as a train, tram, etc

Derain (French dərɛ̃) *n* **André** (ɑ̃dre). 1880–1954, French painter, noted for his Fauvist pictures (1905–08)

derange (dɪˈreɪndʒ) *vb* (*tr*) **1** to disturb the order or arrangement of; throw into disorder; disarrange **2** to disturb the action or operation of **3** to make insane; drive mad [C18: from Old French *desrengier*, from *des-* DIS-¹ + *reng* row, order] > de'rangement *n*

derby (ˈdɜːrbɪ) *n, pl* -bies *US & Canadian* a stiff felt hat with a rounded crown and narrow curved brim. Also called (in Britain and certain other countries): **bowler**

Derby¹ (ˈdɑːbɪ; *US* ˈdɜːrbɪ) *n* **1 the Derby** an annual horse race run at Epsom Downs, Surrey, since 1780: one of the English flat-racing classics **2** any of various other horse races **3 local Derby** a football match between two teams from the same area [C18: named after the twelfth Earl of Derby (died 1834), who founded the horse race at Epsom Downs in 1780]

Derby² (ˈdɑːbɪ) *n* **1** a city in central England, in Derby unitary authority, Derbyshire: engineering industries (esp aircraft engines and railway rolling stock); university (1991). Pop: 229 407 (2001) **2** a unitary authority in central England, in Derbyshire. Pop: 233 200 (2003 est). Area: 78 sq km (30 sq miles) **3** a firm-textured pale-coloured type of cheese **4 sage Derby** a green-and-white Derby cheese flavoured with sage

Derby³ (ˈdɑːbɪ) *n* **Earl of.** title of *Edward George Geoffrey Smith Stanley.* 1799–1869, British statesman; Conservative prime minister (1852; 1858–59; 1866–68)

Derbyshire (ˈdɑːbɪˌʃɪə, -ʃə) *n* a county of N central England: contains the Peak District and several resorts with mineral springs: the geographical and ceremonial county includes the city of Derby, which became an independent unitary authority in 1997. Administrative centre: Matlock. Pop (excluding Derby city): 743 000 (2003 est). Area (excluding Derby city): 2551 sq km (985 sq miles)

derecognize *or* **derecognise** (diːˈrɛkəɡˌnaɪz) *vb* (*tr*) to cease to recognize a trade union as having special negotiating rights within a company or industry
> ,derecog'nition *n*

deregulate (diːˈrɛɡjʊˌleɪt) *vb* (*tr*) to remove regulations or controls from > de,regu'lation *n*

derelict (ˈdɛrɪlɪkt) *adj* **1** deserted or abandoned, as by an owner, occupant, etc **2** falling into ruins; neglected; dilapidated **3** neglectful of duty or obligation; remiss ⊳ *n* **4** a person abandoned or neglected by society; a social outcast or vagrant **5** property deserted or abandoned by an owner, occupant, etc **6** a vessel abandoned at sea **7** a person who is neglectful of duty or obligation [C17: from Latin *dērelictus* forsaken, from *dērelinquere* to abandon, from DE- + *relinquere* to leave]

dereliction (ˌdɛrɪˈlɪkʃən) *n* **1** deliberate, conscious, or wilful neglect (esp in the phrase **dereliction of duty**) **2** the act of abandoning or deserting or the state of being abandoned or deserted **3** *law* accretion of dry land gained by the gradual receding of the sea or by a river changing its course

derestrict (ˌdiːrɪˈstrɪkt) *vb* (*tr*) to render or leave free from restriction, esp a road from speed limits > ˌdereˈstriction n

deride (dɪˈraɪd) vb (tr) to speak of or treat with contempt, mockery, or ridicule; scoff or jeer at [c16: from Latin dērīdēre to laugh to scorn, from DE- + rīdēre to laugh, smile] > deˈrider n > deˈridingly adv

de rigueur French (də rigœr; English də rɪˈgɜː) adj required by etiquette or fashion [literally: of strictness]

derision (dɪˈrɪʒən) n the act of deriding; mockery; scorn [c15: from Late Latin dērīsiō, from Latin dērīsus; see DERIDE] > deˈrisible adj

derisive (dɪˈraɪsɪv, -zɪv) adj showing or characterized by derision; mocking; scornful > deˈrisively adv > deˈrisiveness n

de-risk (diːˈrɪsk) vb to eliminate risk (from)

derisory (dɪˈraɪsərɪ, -zərɪ) adj 1 ridiculous to or worthy of derision, esp because of being ridiculously small or inadequate 2 another word for **derisive**

derivation (ˌdɛrɪˈveɪʃən) n 1 the act of deriving or state of being derived 2 the source, origin, or descent of something, such as a word 3 something derived; a derivative 4 a the process of deducing a mathematical theorem, formula, etc, as a necessary consequence of a set of accepted statements b this sequence of statements c the operation of finding a derivative > ˌderiˈvational adj

derivative (dɪˈrɪvətɪv) adj 1 resulting from derivation; derived 2 based on or making use of other sources; not original or primary 3 copied from others, esp slavishly; plagiaristic ▷ n 4 a term, idea, etc, that is based on or derived from another in the same class 5 a word derived from another word 6 chem a compound that is formed from, or can be regarded as formed from, a structurally related compound: chloroform is a derivative of methane 7 maths a Also called: differential coefficient, first derivative the change of a function, f(x), with respect to an infinitesimally small change in the independent variable, x; the limit of $[f(a + \Delta x)-f(a)]/\Delta x$, at $x = a$, as the increment, Δx, tends to 0. Symbols: df(x)/dx, f'(x), Df(x): the derivative of x^n is nx^{n-1} b the rate of change of one quantity with respect to another: velocity is the derivative of distance with respect to time 8 finance a financial instrument, such as a futures contract or option, the price of which is largely determined by the commodity, currency, share price, interest rate, etc, to which it is linked

derive (dɪˈraɪv) vb 1 (usually foll by from) to draw or be drawn (from) in source or origin; trace or be traced 2 (tr) to obtain by reasoning; deduce; infer 3 (tr) to trace the source or development of 4 (usually foll by from) to produce or be produced (from) by a chemical reaction [c14: from Old French deriver to spring from, from Latin dērīvāre to draw off, from DE- + rīvus a stream] > deˈrivable adj > deˈriver n

derived unit n a unit of measurement obtained by multiplication or division of the base units of a system without the introduction of numerical factors

-derm n combining form indicating skin: endoderm [via French from Greek derma skin]

derma (ˈdɜːmə) n another name for **corium**. Also called: derm (dɜːm) [c18: New Latin, from Greek: skin, from derein to skin]

dermal (ˈdɜːməl) adj of or relating to the skin

dermatitis (ˌdɜːməˈtaɪtɪs) n inflammation of the skin

dermato-, derma-, before a vowel **dermat-** or before a vowel **derm-** combining form indicating skin: dermatology; dermatome; dermal; dermatitis [from Greek derma skin]

dermatology (ˌdɜːməˈtɒlədʒɪ) n the branch of medicine concerned with the skin and its diseases > dermatological (ˌdɜːmətəˈlɒdʒɪkəl) adj > ˌdermaˈtologist n

dermis (ˈdɜːmɪs) n another name for **corium** [c19: New Latin, from EPIDERMIS] > ˈdermic adj

Dermot MacMurrough (ˈdɜːmət məkˈmʌrə) n ?1110–71, king of Leinster, who, by enlisting the support of the English to win back his kingdom, was responsible for the English conquest of Ireland

dernier cri French (dɛrnje kri) n le dernier cri (lə) the latest fashion; the last word [literally: last cry]

derogate (ˈdɛrəˌgeɪt) vb 1 (intr; foll by from) to cause to seem inferior or be in disrepute; detract 2 (intr; foll by from) to deviate in standard or quality; degenerate 3 (tr) to cause to seem inferior, etc; disparage 4 (tr) to curtail the application of (a law or regulation) [c15: from Latin dērogāre to repeal some part of a law, modify it, from DE- + rogāre to ask, propose a law] > ˌderoˈgation n > derogative (dɪˈrɒgətɪv) adj

derogatory (dɪˈrɒgətərɪ, -trɪ) adj tending or intended to detract, disparage, or belittle; intentionally offensive > deˈrogatorily adv

derrick (ˈdɛrɪk) n 1 a simple crane having lifting tackle slung from a boom 2 the framework erected over an oil well to enable drill tubes to be raised and lowered ▷ vb 3 to raise or lower the jib of (a crane) [c17 (in the sense: gallows): from Derrick, name of a celebrated hangman at Tyburn]

Derrida (French dɛrida) n **Jacques** (ʒak). 1930–2004, French philosopher and literary critic, regarded as the founder of deconstruction: author of L'Ecriture et la différence (1967)

derrière (ˌdɛrɪˈɛə; French dɛrjɛr) n a euphemistic word for **buttocks** [c18: literally: behind (prep), from Old French deriere, from Latin dē retrō from the back]

derring-do (ˈdɛrɪŋˈduː) n archaic or literary a daring spirit or deed; boldness or bold action [c16: from Middle English durring don daring to do, from durren to dare + don to do]

derringer or **deringer** (ˈdɛrɪndʒə) n a short-barrelled pocket pistol of large calibre [c19: named after Henry Deringer, American gunsmith who invented it]

derris (ˈdɛrɪs) n any East Indian leguminous woody climbing plant of the genus Derris, esp D. elliptica, whose roots yield the compound rotenone [c19: New Latin, from Greek: covering, leather, from deros skin, hide, from derein to skin]

derro (ˈdɛrəʊ) n, pl derros Austral slang a vagrant [from DERELICT]

Derry (ˈdɛrɪ) n 1 a district in NW Northern Ireland, in Co Londonderry. Pop: 106 456 (2003 est). Area: 387 sq km (149 sq miles) 2 another name for **Londonderry**

derv (dɜːv) n a Brit name for: diesel oil [c20: from d(iesel) e(ngine) r(oad) v(ehicle)]

dervish (ˈdɜːvɪʃ) n a member of any of various Muslim orders of ascetics, some of which (**whirling dervishes**) are noted for a frenzied, ecstatic, whirling dance [c16: from Turkish: beggar, from Persian darvīsh mendicant monk]

Derwent (ˈdɜːwənt) n 1 a river in S Australia, in S Tasmania, flowing southeast to the Tasman Sea. Length: 172 km (107 miles) 2 a river in N central England, in N Derbyshire, flowing southeast to the River Trent. Length: 96 km (60 miles) 3 a river in N England, in Yorkshire, rising on the North York Moors and flowing south to the River Ouse. Length: 92 km (57 miles) 4 a river in NW England, in Cumbria, rising on the Borrowdale Fells and flowing north and west to the Irish Sea. Length: 54 km (34 miles)

Derwentwater (ˈdɜːwəntˌwɔːtə) n a lake in NW England, in Cumbria in the Lake District. Area: about 8 sq km (3 sq miles)

DES abbreviation (in Britain, formerly) Department of Education and Science

Desai (dɛˈsaɪ) n 1 **Morarji (Ranchhodji)** (məˈrɑːdʒɪ). 1896–1995, Indian statesman, noted for his asceticism. He founded the Janata party in opposition to Indira Gandhi, whom he defeated in the 1977 election; prime minister of India (1977–79) 2 **Kiran**, born 1971, Indian writer; her novel The Inheritance of Loss (2006) won the Man Booker Prize

desalination (diːˌsælɪˈneɪʃən), **desalinization** or **desalinisation** n the process of removing salt, esp from sea water so that it can be used for drinking or irrigation

descale (ˌdiːˈskeɪl) vb (tr) to remove the hard deposit formed by chemicals in water from (a kettle, pipe, etc)

descant n (ˈdɛskænt, ˈdɪs-) 1 Also: discant a decorative counterpoint added above a basic melody 2 a comment, criticism, or discourse ▷ adj (ˈdɛskænt, ˈdɪs-) 3 Also:

discant of or pertaining to the highest member in common use of a family of musical instruments: a *descant recorder* ▷ *vb* (dɛsˈkænt, dɪs-) (*intr*) **4** *Also:* discant (often foll by *on* or *upon*) to compose or perform a descant (for a piece of music) **5** (often foll by *on* or *upon*) to discourse at length or make varied comments [C14: from Old Northern French, from Medieval Latin *discantus*, from Latin DIS-¹ + *cantus* song; see CHANT] ▷ desˈcantern

Descartes (ˈdeɪˌkɑːt; *French* dekart) *n* René (rəne). 1596–1650, French philosopher and mathematician. He provided a mechanistic basis for the philosophical theory of dualism and is regarded as the founder of modern philosophy. He also founded analytical geometry and contributed greatly to the science of optics. His works include *Discours de la méthode* (1637), *Meditationes de Prima Philosophia* (1641), and *Principia Philosophiae* (1644) Related adj: **Cartesian**

descend (dɪˈsɛnd) *vb* (*mainly intr*) **1** (*also tr*) to move, pass, or go down (a hill, slope, staircase, etc) **2** (of a hill, slope, or path) to lead or extend down; slope; incline **3** to move to a lower level, pitch, etc; fall **4** (often foll by *from*) to be connected by a blood relationship (to a dead or extinct individual, race, species, etc) **5** to be passed on by parents or ancestors; be inherited **6** to sink or come down in morals or behaviour; lower oneself **7** (often foll by *on* or *upon*) to arrive or attack in a sudden or overwhelming way **8** (of the sun, moon, etc) to move towards the horizon [C13: from Old French *descendre*, from Latin *dēscendere*, from DE- + *scandere* to climb; see SCAN] ▷ desˈcendableadj

descendant (dɪˈsɛndənt) *n* **1** a person, animal, or plant when described as descended from an individual, race, species, etc **2** something that derives or is descended from an earlier form ▷ *adj* **3** a variant spelling of **descendent**

descendent (dɪˈsɛndənt) *adj* **1** coming or going downwards; descending **2** deriving by descent, as from an ancestor

descender (dɪˈsɛndə) *n* **1** a person or thing that descends **2** *printing* the portion of a letter, such as j, p, or y, below the level of the base of an x or n

descent (dɪˈsɛnt) *n* **1** the act of descending **2** a downward slope or inclination **3** a passage, path, or way leading downwards **4** derivation from an ancestor or ancestral group; lineage **5** (in genealogy) a generation in a particular lineage **6** a decline or degeneration **7** a movement or passage in degree or state from higher to lower **8** (often foll by *on*) a sudden and overwhelming arrival or attack **9** *property law* (formerly) the transmission of real property to the heir on an intestacy

Deschamps (*French* defɑ̃) *n* **1** **Émile** (*French* emil), full name *Émile Deschamps de Saint-Armand*. 1791–1871, French poet, dramatist, and librettist: a leading figure in the French romantic movement **2** **Eustache** (østaʃ). ?1346–?1406, French poet, noted for his *Miroir de mariage*, a satirical attack on women

deschool (ˌdiːˈskuːl) *vb* (*tr*) to separate education from the institution of school and operate through the pupil's life experience as opposed to a set curriculum

describe (dɪˈskraɪb) *vb* (*tr*) **1** to give an account or representation of in words **2** to pronounce or label **3** to draw a line or figure, such as a circle [C15: from Latin *dēscrībere* to copy off, write out, delineate, from DE- + *scrībere* to write] ▷ deˈscribablern

description (dɪˈskrɪpʃən) *n* **1** a statement or account that describes; representation in words **2** the act, process, or technique of describing **3** sort, kind, or variety: *reptiles of every description*

descriptive (dɪˈskrɪptɪv) *adj* **1** characterized by or containing description; serving to describe **2** *grammar* (of an adjective) serving to describe the referent of the noun modified, as for example the adjective *brown* as contrasted with *my* and *former* **3** relating to or based upon description or classification rather than explanation or prescription ▷ deˈscriptivelyadv ▷ deˈscriptivenessn

descry (dɪˈskraɪ) *vb* -scries, -scrying, -scried(*tr*) **1** to discern or make out; catch sight of **2** to discover by looking carefully; detect [C14: from Old French *descrier* to

proclaim, DECRY] ▷ deˈscriern

desecrate (ˈdɛsɪˌkreɪt) *vb* (*tr*) **1** to violate or outrage the sacred character of (an object or place) by destructive, blasphemous, or sacrilegious action **2** to remove the consecration from (a person, object, building, etc); deconsecrate [C17: from DE- + CONSECRATE] ▷ ˈdeseˌcrator or ˈdeseˌcratern ▷ ˌdeseˈcrationn

desegregate (diːˈsɛgrɪˌgeɪt) *vb* to end racial segregation in (a school or other public institution) ▷ ˌdesegreˈgationn

deselect (ˌdiːsɪˈlɛkt) *vb* (*tr*) **1** *Brit politics* (of a constituency organization) to refuse to select (an existing MP) for re-election **2** *computing* to cancel (a highlighted selection of data) on a computer screen **3** *computing* to remove (the check mark) at an option in a dialogue box ▷ ˌdeseˈlectionn

desensitize or **desensitise** (diːˈsɛnsɪˌtaɪz) *vb* (*tr*) to render insensitive or less sensitive: *the patient was desensitized to the allergen; to desensitize photographic film* ▷ deˌsensitiˈzationor deˌsensitiˈsationn ▷ deˈsensiˌtizeror deˈsensiˌtisern

desert¹ (ˈdɛzət) *n* **1** a region that is devoid or almost devoid of vegetation, esp because of low rainfall **2** an uncultivated uninhabited region **3** a place which lacks some desirable feature or quality: *a cultural desert* **4** (*modifier*) of, relating to, or like a desert; infertile or desolate [C13: from Old French, from Church Latin *dēsertum*, from Latin *dēserere* to abandon, literally: to sever one's links with, from DE- + *serere* to bind together]

desert² (dɪˈzɜːt) *vb* **1** (*tr*) to leave or abandon (a person, place, etc) without intending to return, esp in violation of a duty, promise, or obligation **2** *military* to abscond from (a post or duty) with no intention of returning **3** (*tr*) to fail (someone) in time of need [C15: from French *déserter*, from Late Latin *dēsertāre*, from Latin *dēserere* to forsake; see DESERT¹] ▷ deˈsertern ▷ deˈsertedadj

desert³ (dɪˈzɜːt) *n* **1** (*often plural*) something that is deserved or merited; just reward or punishment **2** the state of deserving a reward or punishment [C13: from Old French *deserte*, from *deservir* to DESERVE]

desert boots *pl n* ankle-high suede boots with laces and soft soles, worn informally by men and women

desertification (dɪˌzɜːtɪfɪˈkeɪʃən) *n* a process by which fertile land turns into barren land or desert

desertion (dɪˈzɜːʃən) *n* **1** the act of deserting or abandoning or the state of being deserted or abandoned **2** *law* wilful abandonment, esp of one's spouse or children, without consent and in breach of obligations

desert island *n* a small remote tropical island

desert pea *n* an Australian trailing leguminous plant, *Clianthus formosus*, with scarlet flowers

desert rat *n* **1** a jerboa, *Jaculus orientalis*, inhabiting the deserts of N Africa **2** *Brit informal* a soldier who served in North Africa with the British 7th Armoured Division in 1941–42

deserve (dɪˈzɜːv) *vb* **1** (*tr*) to be entitled to or worthy of; merit **2** (*intr*; foll by *of*) *obsolete* to be worthy [C13: from Old French *deservir*, from Latin *dēservīre* to serve devotedly, from DE- + *servīre* to SERVE] ▷ deˈservedadj ▷ deservedness (dɪˈzɜːvɪdnɪs) *n*

deservedly (dɪˈzɜːvɪdlɪ) *adv* according to merit; justly

deserving (dɪˈzɜːvɪŋ) *adj* **1** (often postpositive and foll by *of*) worthy, esp of praise or reward ▷ *n* **2** *rare* a merit or demerit; desert ▷ deˈservinglyadv ▷ deˈservingnessn

deshabille (ˌdeɪzæˈbiːl) or **dishabille** *n* **1** the state of being partly or carelessly dressed **2** *archaic* clothes worn in such a state [C17: from French *déshabillé* undressed, from *dés-* DIS-¹ + *habiller* to dress; see HABILIMENT]

desi or **deshi** (ˈdeɪsɪ) *adj* *Hinglish* **1** indigenous or local: *a desi buda* **2** authentic: *desi music* [C21: Hindi, from Sanskrit *deśa* a country]

de Sica (*Italian* de ˈsiːka) *n* **Vittorio** (vitˈtɔːrjo). 1902–74, Italian film actor and director. His films, in the neorealist tradition, include *Shoeshine* (1946) and *Bicycle Thieves* (1948)

desiccant (ˈdɛsɪkənt) *adj* **1** desiccating or drying ▷ *n* **2** a substance, such as calcium oxide, that absorbs water and is used to remove moisture; a drying agent [C17: from Latin *dēsiccāns* drying up; see DESICCATE]

desiccate ('dɛsɪˌkeɪt) vb 1 (tr) to remove most of the water from (a substance or material); dehydrate 2 (tr) to preserve (food) by removing moisture; dry 3 (intr) to become dried up [c16: from Latin *dēsiccāre* to dry up, from DE- + *siccāre* to dry, from *siccus* dry] > ˌdesicˈcation n

desiccated ('dɛsɪˌkeɪtɪd) adj 1 dehydrated and powdered: *desiccated coconut* 2 lacking in spirit or animation

desiderate (dɪˈzɪdəˌreɪt) vb (tr) to feel the lack of or need for; long for; miss [c17: from Latin *dēsīderāre*, from DE- + *sīdus* star; see DESIRE] > deˌsiderˈation n

desideratum (dɪˌzɪdəˈrɑːtəm) n, pl -ta (-tə) something lacked and wanted [c17: from Latin; see DESIDERATE]

design (dɪˈzaɪn) vb 1 to work out the structure or form of (something), as by making a sketch, outline, pattern, or plans 2 to plan and make (something) artistically or skilfully 3 (tr) to form or conceive in the mind; invent 4 (tr) to intend, as for a specific purpose; plan ▷ n 5 a plan, sketch, or preliminary drawing 6 the arrangement or pattern of elements or features of an artistic or decorative work: *the design of the desk is Chippendale* 7 a finished artistic or decorative creation 8 the art of designing 9 a plan, scheme, or project 10 an end aimed at or planned for; intention; purpose 11 (often plural; often foll by on or against) a plot or hostile scheme, often to gain possession of (something) by illegitimate means [c16: from Latin *dēsignāre* to mark out, describe, from DE- + *signāre* to mark, from *signum* a mark, SIGN] > deˈsignable adj

designate vb ('dɛzɪgˌneɪt) (tr) 1 to indicate or specify 2 to give a name to; style; entitle 3 to select or name for an office or duty; appoint ▷ adj ('dɛzɪgnɪt, -ˌneɪt) 4 (immediately postpositive) appointed, but not yet in office: *a minister designate* [c15: from Latin *dēsignātus* marked out, defined; see DESIGN] > 'desigˌnator n

designation (ˌdɛzɪgˈneɪʃən) n 1 something that designates, such as a name or distinctive mark 2 the act of designating or the fact of being designated

designedly (dɪˈzaɪnɪdlɪ) adv by intention or design; on purpose; deliberately

designer (dɪˈzaɪnə) n 1 a person who devises and executes designs, as for works of art, clothes, machines, etc 2 (modifier) designed by and bearing the label or signature of a well-known fashion designer: *designer jeans* 3 (modifier) (of things, ideas, etc) having an appearance of fashionable trendiness: *designer pop songs; designer stubble* 4 (modifier) (of cells, chemicals, etc) designed (or produced) to perform a specific function or combat a specific problem: *designer insecticide* 5 (modifier) (of an animal) cross-bred for a specific purpose, such as looks, temperament, or likelihood of causing an allergy: *designer dogs* 6 a person who devises plots or schemes; intriguer

designer baby n informal a baby that is the product of genetic engineering

designer drug n 1 any of various narcotic or hallucinogenic substances manufactured illegally from a range of chemicals 2 med a drug designed to act on a specific molecular target

designing (dɪˈzaɪnɪŋ) adj artful and scheming; conniving; crafty

desirable (dɪˈzaɪərəbᵊl) adj 1 worthy of desire or recommendation: *a desirable residence* 2 arousing desire, esp sexual desire; attractive > deˌsiraˈbility or deˈsirableness n > deˈsirably adv

desire (dɪˈzaɪə) vb (tr) 1 to wish or long for; crave; want 2 to express a wish or make a request for; ask for ▷ n 3 a wish or longing; craving 4 an expressed wish; request 5 sexual appetite; lust 6 a person or thing that is desired [c13: from Old French *desirer*, from Latin *dēsīderāre* to desire earnestly; see DESIDERATE] > deˈsirer n

desirous (dɪˈzaɪərəs) adj (usually postpositive and foll by of) having or expressing desire (for); having a wish or longing (for)

desist (dɪˈzɪst) vb (intr; often foll by from) to cease, as from an action; stop or abstain [c15: from Old French *desister*, from Latin *dēsistere* to leave off, stand apart, from DE- + *sistere* to stand, halt]

desk (dɛsk) n 1 a piece of furniture with a writing surface and usually drawers or other compartments 2 a service counter or table in a public building, such as a hotel: *information desk* 3 a support, lectern, or book rest for the book from which services are read in a church 4 the editorial section of a newspaper, etc, responsible for a particular subject: *the news desk* 5 a music stand shared by two orchestral players [c14: from Medieval Latin *desca* table, from Latin *discus* disc, dish]

desk-bound adj engaged in or involving sedentary work, as at an office desk

deskfast ('dɛskfəst) n breakfast eaten at one's desk at work [c20: from DESK + (BREAK)FAST]

deskill (diːˈskɪl) vb (tr) 1 to mechanize or computerize (a job or process) to such an extent that little human skill is required to do it 2 to cause (skilled persons or a labour force) to work at a job that does not utilize their skills

desktop ('dɛskˌtɒp) n (modifier) denoting a computer system, esp for word processing, that is small enough to use at a desk

desktop publishing n a means of publishing reports, advertising, etc, to typeset quality using a desktop computer. Abbreviation: DTP

desman ('dɛsmən) n, pl -mans either of two molelike amphibious mammals *Desmana moschata* (**Russian desman**) or *Galemys pyrenaicus* (**Pyrenean desman**), having dense fur and webbed feet: family *Talpidae*, order *Insectivora* (insectivores) [c18: from Swedish *desmansråtta*, from *desman* musk (of Germanic origin) + *råtta* rat]

Des Moines (də ˈmɔɪn, ˈmɔɪnz) n 1 a city in S central Iowa: state capital. Pop: 196 093 (2003 est) 2 a river in the N central US, rising in SW Minnesota and flowing southeast to join the Mississippi. Length: 861 km (535 miles)

Desmond ('dɛzmənd) n **15th Earl of,** title of *Gerald Fitzgerald*. died 1583, Anglo-Irish nobleman, who led a Catholic rebellion (1579) against English domination of Ireland

Desmond Tutu (ˌdɛzmənd ˈtuːtuː) n Brit informal a university degree graded 2:2 (second class lower bracket). Often shortened to **Desmond** [c20: from rhyming slang, after Desmond *Tutu* (born 1931), South African clergyman and anti-apartheid campaigner]

Desmoulins (French demulɛ̃) n (**Lucie Simplice**) **Camille** (**Benoît**) (kamij). 1760–94, French revolutionary leader, pamphleteer, and orator

desolate adj ('dɛsəlɪt) 1 uninhabited; deserted 2 made uninhabitable; laid waste; devastated 3 without friends, hope, or encouragement; forlorn, wretched, or abandoned 4 gloomy or dismal; depressing ▷ vb ('dɛsəˌleɪt) (tr) 5 to deprive of inhabitants; depopulate 6 to make barren or lay waste; devastate 7 to make wretched or forlorn 8 to forsake or abandon [c14: from Latin *dēsōlāre* to leave alone, from DE- + *sōlāre* to make lonely, lay waste, from *sōlus* alone] > 'desoˌlater or 'desoˌlator n > 'desolately adv > 'desolateness n

desolation (ˌdɛsəˈleɪʃən) n 1 the act of desolating or the state of being desolated; ruin or devastation 2 solitary misery; wretchedness 3 a desolate region; barren waste

De Soto (də ˈsəʊtəʊ; Spanish de ˈsoto) n **Hernando** (ɛrˈnando). ?1500–42, Spanish explorer, who discovered the Mississippi River (1541). Also called: Fernando De Soto (fɛrˈnando)

despair (dɪˈspɛə) vb 1 (intr; often foll by of) to lose or give up hope: *I despair of his coming* 2 (tr) obsolete to give up hope of; lose hope in ▷ n 3 total loss of hope 4 a person or thing that causes hopelessness or for which there is no hope [c14: from Old French *despoir* hopelessness, from *desperer* to despair, from Latin *dēspērāre*, from DE- + *spērāre* to hope]

despairing (dɪˈspɛərɪŋ) adj marked by or resulting from despair; hopeless or desperate > desˈpairingly adv

despatch (dɪˈspætʃ) vb (tr) n a less common spelling of **dispatch** > desˈpatcher n

Despenser (dɪsˈpɛnsə) n **Hugh le,** Earl of Winchester. 1262–1326, English statesman, a favourite of Edward II. Together with his son **Hugh,** *the Younger* (?1290–1326), he was executed by the king's enemies

desperado (ˌdɛspəˈrɑːdəʊ) n, pl -does or -dos a reckless or desperate person, esp one ready to commit any violent illegal act [c17: probably pseudo-Spanish variant of obsolete *desperate* (n) a reckless character]

desperate ('dɛspərɪt, -prɪt) *adj* **1** careless of danger, as from despair; utterly reckless **2** (of an act) reckless; risky **3** used or undertaken in desperation or as a last resort: *desperate measures* **4** critical; very grave: *in desperate need* **5** (often *postpositive* and foll by *for*) in distress and having a great need or desire **6** moved by or showing despair or hopelessness; despairing [c15: from Latin *dēspērāre* to have no hope; see DESPAIR] > '**desperately** *adv* > '**desperateness** *n*

desperation (,dɛspə'reɪʃən) *n* **1** desperate recklessness **2** the act of despairing or the state of being desperate

despicable (dɪ'spɪkəbəl, 'dɛspɪk-) *adj* worthy of being despised; contemptible; mean [c16: from Late Latin *dēspicābilis*, from *dēspicārī* to disdain; compare DESPISE] > de'**spicably** *adv*

despise (dɪ'spaɪz) *vb* (*tr*) to look down on with contempt; scorn: *he despises flattery* [c13: from Old French *despire*, from Latin *dēspicere* to look down, from DE- + *specere* to look] > de'**spiser** *n*

despite (dɪ'spaɪt) *prep* **1** in spite of; undeterred by ▷ *n* **2** *archaic* contempt; insult **3** in despite of (*preposition*) *rare* in spite of [c13: from Old French *despit*, from Latin *dēspectus* contempt; see DESPISE]

despoil (dɪ'spɔɪl) *vb* (*tr*) to strip or deprive by force; plunder; rob; loot [c13: from Old French *despoillier*, from Latin *dēspoliāre*, from DE- + *spoliāre* to rob (esp of clothing); see SPOIL] > de'**spoiler** *n* > de'**spoilment** *n*

despoliation (dɪ,spəʊlɪ'eɪʃən) *n* **1** the act of despoiling; plunder or pillage **2** the state of being despoiled

despond (dɪ'spɒnd) *vb* **1** (*intr*) to lose heart or hope; become disheartened; despair ▷ *n* **2** ('dɛspɒnd, dɪ'spɒnd) **2** *archaic* despondency [c17: from Latin *dēspondēre* to promise, make over to, yield, lose heart, from DE- + *spondēre* to promise] > de'**spondingly** *adv*

despondent (dɪ'spɒndənt) *adj* downcast or disheartened; lacking hope or courage; dejected > de'**spondence** *or* de'**spondency** *n* > de'**spondently** *adv*

despot ('dɛspɒt) *n* **1** an absolute or tyrannical ruler; autocrat or tyrant **2** any person in power who acts tyrannically [c16: from Medieval Latin *despota*, from Greek *despotēs* lord, master; related to Latin *domus* house] > despotic (dɛs'pɒtɪk) *or* des'**potical** *adj* > des'**potically** *adv*

despotism ('dɛspə,tɪzəm) *n* **1** the rule of a despot; arbitrary, absolute, or tyrannical government **2** arbitrary or tyrannical authority or behaviour

des Prés *or* **Desprez** (French de pre) *n* **Josquin** (ʒɔskɛ̃). ?1450–1521, Flemish Renaissance composer of masses, motets, and chansons

des res (dez rɛz) *n* (in estate agents' jargon) a desirable residence

Dessalines (French desalin) *n* **Jean Jacques** (ʒɑ̃ ʒɑk). ?1758–1806, emperor of Haiti (1804–06) after driving out the French; assassinated

Dessau (German 'dɛsau) *n* an industrial city in E Germany, in Saxony-Anhalt: capital of Anhalt state from 1340 to 1918. Pop: 78 380 (2003 est)

dessert (dɪ'zɜːt) *n* **1** the sweet, usually last course of a meal **2** *chiefly Brit* (esp formerly) fruit, dates, nuts, etc, served at the end of a meal [c17: from French, from *desservir* to clear a table, from *des-* DIS-¹ + *servir* to SERVE]

dessertspoon (dɪ'zɜːt,spuːn) *n* a spoon intermediate in size between a tablespoon and a teaspoon

destination (,dɛstɪ'neɪʃən) *n* **1** the predetermined end of a journey or voyage **2** the ultimate end or purpose for which something is created or a person is destined

destine ('dɛstɪn) *vb* (*tr*) to set apart or appoint (for a certain purpose or person, or to do something); intend; design [c14: from Old French *destiner*, from Latin *dēstināre* to appoint, from DE- + *-stināre*, from *stāre* to stand]

destined ('dɛstɪnd) *adj* (*postpositive*) **1** foreordained or certain; meant: *he is destined to be famous* **2** (usually foll by *for*) heading (towards a specific destination); directed: *a letter destined for Europe*

destiny ('dɛstɪnɪ) *n*, *pl* -nies **1** the future destined for a person or thing; fate; fortune; lot **2** the predetermined or inevitable course of events **3** the ultimate power or agency that predetermines the course of events [c14:

from Old French *destinee*, from *destiner* to DESTINE]

destitute ('dɛstɪ,tjuːt) *adj* **1** lacking the means of subsistence; totally impoverished **2** (*postpositive*; foll by *of*) completely lacking; deprived or bereft (of): *destitute of words* **3** *obsolete* abandoned or deserted [c14: from Latin *dēstitūtus* forsaken, from *dēstituere* to leave alone, from *statuere* to place] > '**desti,tuteness** *n*

destitution (,dɛstɪ'tjuːʃən) *n* the state of being destitute; utter poverty

de-stress *vb* to become or cause to become less stressed or anxious

destrier ('dɛstrɪə) *n* an archaic word for **warhorse** (sense 1) [c13: from Old French, from *destre* right hand, from Latin *dextra*; from the fact that a squire led a knight's horse with his right hand]

destroy (dɪ'strɔɪ) *vb* (*mainly tr*) **1** to ruin; spoil; render useless **2** to tear down or demolish; break up; raze **3** to put an end to; do away with; extinguish **4** to kill or annihilate **5** to crush, subdue, or defeat **6** (*intr*) to be destructive or cause destruction [c13: from Old French *destruire*, from Latin *dēstruere* to pull down, from DE- + *struere* to pile up, build]

destroyer (dɪ'strɔɪə) *n* **1** a small fast lightly armoured but heavily armed warship **2** a person or thing that destroys

destruct (dɪ'strʌkt) *vb* **1** to destroy (one's own missile or rocket) for safety **2** (*intr*) (of a missile or rocket) to be destroyed, for safety, by those controlling it; self-destruct ▷ *n* **3** the act of destructing ▷ *adj* **4** designed to be capable of destroying itself or the object, system, or installation containing it: *destruct mechanism*

destructible (dɪ'strʌktəb³l) *adj* capable of being or liable to be destroyed

destruction (dɪ'strʌkʃən) *n* **1** the act of destroying or state of being destroyed; demolition **2** a cause of ruin or means of destroying [c14: from Latin *dēstructiō* a pulling down; see DESTROY]

destructive (dɪ'strʌktɪv) *adj* **1** (often *postpositive* and foll by *of* or *to*) causing or tending to cause the destruction (of) **2** intended to disprove or discredit, esp without positive suggestions or help; negative: *destructive criticism* > de'**structively** *adv* > de'**structiveness** *or* **destructivity** (,diː:strʌk'tɪvɪtɪ) *n*

destructive distillation *n* the decomposition of a complex substance, such as wood or coal, by heating it in the absence of air and collecting the volatile products

destructor (dɪ'strʌktə) *n* **1** a furnace or incinerator for the disposal of refuse, esp one that uses the resulting heat to generate power **2** a device used to blow up a dangerously defective missile or rocket after launching

desuetude (dɪ'sjuːɪ,tjuːd, 'dɛswɪtjuːd) *n* *formal* the condition of not being in use or practice; disuse: *those ceremonies had fallen into desuetude* [c15: from Latin *dēsuētūdō*, from *dēsuescere* to lay aside a habit, from DE- + *suescere* to grow accustomed]

desulphurize *or* **desulphurise** (diː:'sʌlfjʊ,raɪz) *vb* to free or become free from sulphur

desultory ('dɛsəltərɪ, -trɪ) *adj* **1** passing or jumping from one thing to another, esp in a fitful way; unmethodical; disconnected **2** occurring in a random or incidental way; haphazard: *a desultory thought* [c16: from Latin *dēsultōrius*, relating to one who vaults or jumps, hence superficial, from *dēsilīre* to jump down, from DE- + *salīre* to jump] > '**desultorily** *adv* > '**desultoriness** *n*

detach (dɪ'tætʃ) *vb* (*tr*) **1** to disengage and separate or remove, as by pulling; unfasten; disconnect **2** *military* to separate (a small unit) from a larger, esp for a special assignment [c17: from Old French *destachier*, from *des-* DIS-¹ + *attachier* to ATTACH]

detached (dɪ'tætʃt) *adj* **1** disconnected or standing apart; not attached: *a detached house* **2** having or showing no bias or emotional involvement; disinterested **3** *ophthalmol* (of the retina) separated from the choroid layer of the eyeball to which it is normally attached, resulting in loss of vision in the affected part

detachment (dɪ'tætʃmənt) *n* **1** indifference to other people or to one's surroundings; aloofness **2** freedom from self-interest or bias; disinterest **3** the act of disengaging or separating something **4** the condition of being disengaged or separated; disconnection **5** *military* **a** the separation of a small unit from its main body, esp of ships or troops **b** the unit so detached **6** *Canad* a branch office of a police force

detail ('di:teɪl) *n* **1** an item or smaller part that is considered separately; particular **2** an item or circumstance that is insignificant or unimportant: *passengers' comfort was regarded as a detail* **3** treatment of or attention to items or particulars: *this essay includes too much detail* **4** items collectively; particulars **5** a small or accessory section or element in a painting, building, statue, etc, esp when considered in isolation **6** *military* **a** the act of assigning personnel for a specific duty, esp a fatigue **b** the personnel selected **c** the duty or assignment **7** **go into detail** to include all or most particulars **8** **in detail** including all or most particulars or items thoroughly ▷ *vb* (*tr*) **9** to list or relate fully **10** *military* to select (personnel) for a specific duty [c17: from French *détail*, from Old French *detailler* to cut in pieces, from *de-* DIS-¹ + *tailler* to cut; see TAILOR]

detailed ('di:teɪld) *adj* having many details or giving careful attention to details: *a detailed list of the ingredients required*

detain (dɪ'teɪn) *vb* (*tr*) **1** to delay; hold back; stop **2** to confine or hold in custody; restrain [c15: from Old French *detenir*, from Latin *dētinēre* to hold off, keep back, from *de-* + *tenēre* to hold] > de'tainable *adj* > detainee (,di:teɪ'ni:) *n* > de'tainment *n*

detect (dɪ'tɛkt) *vb* (*tr*) **1** to perceive or notice: *to detect a note of sarcasm* **2** to discover the existence or presence of (esp something likely to elude observation) **3** to extract information from (an electromagnetic wave) **4** *obsolete* to reveal or expose (a crime, criminal, etc) [c15: from Latin *dētectus* uncovered, from *dētegere* to uncover, from *de-* + *tegere* to cover] > de'tectable or de'tectible *adj*

detection (dɪ'tɛkʃən) *n* **1** the act of discovering or the fact of being discovered **2** the act or process of extracting information, esp at audio or video frequencies, from an electromagnetic wave. See also **demodulation**

detective (dɪ'tɛktɪv) *n* **1 a** a police officer who investigates crimes **b** See **private detective c** (*as modifier*): *a detective story* ▷ *adj* **2** used in or serving for detection

detector (dɪ'tɛktə) *n* **1** a person or thing that detects **2** any mechanical sensing device **3** *electronics* a device used in the detection of radio signals

detent (dɪ'tɛnt) *n* the locking piece of a mechanism, often spring-loaded to check the movement of a wheel in one direction only [c17: from Old French *destente*, a loosening, trigger: see DÉTENTE]

détente (deɪ'tã:nt; *French* detɑ̃t) *n* the relaxing or easing of tension, esp between nations [French, literally: a loosening, from Old French *destendre* to release, from *tendre* to stretch]

detention (dɪ'tɛnʃən) *n* **1** the act of detaining or state of being detained **2 a** custody or confinement, esp of a suspect awaiting trial **b** (*as modifier*): *a detention order* **3** a form of punishment in which a pupil is detained after school [c16: from Latin *dētentiō* a keeping back; see DETAIN]

detention centre *n* a place where persons (typically asylum seekers, illegal immigrants, or people awaiting trial) may be detained for short periods by order of a court

deter (dɪ'tɜ:) *vb* **-ters, -terring, -terred** (*tr*) to discourage (from acting) or prevent (from occurring), usually by instilling fear, doubt, or anxiety [c16: from Latin *dēterrēre*, from *de-* + *terrēre* to frighten] > de'terment *n*

deterge (dɪ'tɜ:dʒ) *vb* (*tr*) to wash or wipe away; cleanse: *to deterge a wound* [c17: from Latin *dētergēre* to wipe away, from *de-* + *tergēre* to wipe]

detergent (dɪ'tɜ:dʒənt) *n* **1** a cleansing agent, esp a surface-active chemical such as an alkyl sulphonate, widely used in industry, laundering, shampoos, etc ▷ *adj* Also: **detersive** (dɪ'tɜ:sɪv) **2** having cleansing power [c17: from Latin *dētergēns* wiping off; see DETERGE]

deteriorate (dɪ'tɪərɪə,reɪt) *vb* **1** to make or become worse or lower in quality, value, character, etc; depreciate

2 (*intr*) to wear away or disintegrate [c16: from Late Latin *dēteriōrāre*, from Latin *dēterior* worse] > de,terio'ration *n* > de'teriorative *adj*

determinacy (dɪ'tɜ:mɪnəsɪ) *n* **1** the quality of being defined or fixed **2** the condition of being predicted or deduced

determinant (dɪ'tɜ:mɪnənt) *adj* **1** serving to determine or affect ▷ *n* **2** a factor, circumstance, etc, that influences or determines **3** *maths* a square array of elements that represents the sum of certain products of these elements, used to solve simultaneous equations, in vector studies, etc

determinate (dɪ'tɜ:mɪnɪt) *adj* **1** definitely limited, defined, or fixed; distinct **2** a less common word for **determined 3** able to be predicted or deduced **4** *botany* (of an inflorescence) having the main and branch stems ending in flowers and unable to grow further; cymose > de'terminateness *n*

determination (dɪ,tɜ:mɪ'neɪʃən) *n* **1** the act or an instance of making a decision **2** the condition of being determined; resoluteness **3** the act or an instance of fixing or settling the quality, limit, position, etc, of something **4** a decision or opinion reached, rendered, or settled upon **5** a resolute movement towards some object or end **6** *law* the termination of an estate or interest **7** *law* the decision reached by a court of justice on a disputed matter

determinative (dɪ'tɜ:mɪnətɪv) *adj* **1** able to or serving to settle or determine; deciding ▷ *n* **2** a factor, circumstance, etc, that settles or determines > de'terminatively *adv* > de'terminativeness *n*

determine (dɪ'tɜ:mɪn) *vb* **1** to settle or decide (an argument, question, etc) conclusively, as by referring to an authority **2** (*tr*) to ascertain or conclude, esp after observation or consideration **3** (*tr*) to shape or influence; give direction to **4** (*tr*) to fix in scope, extent, variety, etc: *the river determined the edge of the property* **5** to make or cause to make a decision: *he determined never to marry* **6** (*tr*) *logic* to define or limit (a notion) by adding or requiring certain features or characteristics **7** (*tr*) *geometry* to fix or specify the position, form, or configuration of **8** *chiefly law* to come or bring to an end, as an estate or interest in land [c14: from Old French *determiner*, from Latin *dētermināre* to set boundaries to, from *de-* + *termināre* to limit; see TERMINATE] > de'terminable *adj* > de'terminably *adv*

determined (dɪ'tɜ:mɪnd) *adj* of unwavering mind; resolute; firm > de'terminedly *adv*

determiner (dɪ'tɜ:mɪnə) *n* **1** a word, such as a number, article, possessive adjective, etc, that determines (limits) the meaning of a noun phrase, e.g. *their* in 'their black cat' **2** a person or thing that determines

determinism (dɪ'tɜ:mɪ,nɪzəm) *n* the philosophical doctrine that all events including human actions and choices are fully determined by preceding events and states of affairs, and so that freedom of choice is illusory. Also called: necessitarianism Compare **free will** (sense 1b) > de'terminist *n, adj* > de,termin'istic *adj*

deterrent (dɪ'tɛrənt) *n* **1** something that deters **2** a weapon or combination of weapons, esp nuclear, held by one state, etc, to deter attack by another ▷ *adj* **3** tending or used to deter; restraining [c19: from Latin *dēterrēns* hindering; see DETER] > de'terrence *n*

detest (dɪ'tɛst) *vb* (*tr*) to dislike intensely; loathe [c16: from Latin *dētestārī* to curse (while invoking a god as witness), from *de-* + *testārī* to bear witness, from *testis* a witness] > de'tester *n*

detestable (dɪ'tɛstəbəl) *adj* being or deserving to be abhorred or detested; abominable; odious > de,testa'bility or de'testableness *n* > de'testably *adv*

detestation (,di:tɛs'teɪʃən) *n* **1** intense hatred; abhorrence **2** a person or thing that is detested

dethrone (dɪ'θrəʊn) *vb* (*tr*) to remove from a throne or deprive of any high position or title; depose > de'thronement *n* > de'throner *n*

detonate ('dɛtə,neɪt) *vb* to cause (a bomb, mine, etc) to explode or (of a bomb, mine, etc) to explode; set off or be set off [c18: from Latin *dētonāre* to thunder down, from *de-* + *tonāre* to THUNDER] > ,deto'nation *n*

> 'deto,native *adj*

detonator ('detə,neɪtə) *n* 1 a small amount of explosive, as in a percussion cap, used to initiate a larger explosion 2 a device, such as an electrical generator, used to set off an explosion from a distance 3 a substance or object that explodes or is capable of exploding

detour ('diːtʊə) *n* 1 a deviation from a direct, usually shorter route or course of action ▷ *vb* 2 to deviate or cause to deviate from a direct route or course of action [c18: from French *détour*, from Old French *destorner* to divert, turn away, from *des-* DE- + *torner* to TURN]

detox ('diːtɒks) *informal* ▷ *n* 1 treatment designed to rid the body of poisonous substances, esp alcohol and drugs ▷ *vb* 2 to undergo treatment to rid the body of poisonous substances, esp alcohol and drugs [c20: from (for sense 1) DETOXIFICATION or (for sense 2) DETOXICATE]

detoxicate (diː'tɒksɪ,keɪt) *vb* (*tr*) 1 to rid (a patient) of a poison or its effects 2 to counteract (a poison) [c19: DE- + *-toxicate*, from Latin *toxicum* poison; see TOXIC]
> de'toxicant *adj, n* > de,toxi'cation *n*

detoxification centre *n* a place that specializes in the treatment of alcoholism or drug addiction

detoxify (diː'tɒksɪ,faɪ) *vb* -fies, -fying, -fied (*tr*) 1 to remove poison from; detoxicate 2 to treat (a person) for alcoholism or drug addiction > de,toxifi'cation *n*

DETR *abbreviation* (in Britain) Department of the Environment, Transport, and the Regions

detract (dɪ'trækt) *vb* 1 (when *intr*, usually foll by *from*) to take away a part (of); diminish: *her anger detracts from her beauty* 2 (*tr*) to distract or divert 3 (*tr*) *obsolete* to belittle or disparage [c15: from Latin *dētractus* drawn away, from *dētrahere* to pull away, disparage, from DE- + *trahere* to drag] > de'tractive *or* de'tractory *adj* > de'tractor *n*

● USAGE *Detract* is sometimes wrongly used where
● *distract* is meant: *a noise distracted* (not *detracted*) *my*
● *attention*

detrain (diː'treɪn) *vb* to leave or cause to leave a railway train, as passengers, etc > de'trainment *n*

detriment ('detrɪmənt) *n* 1 disadvantage or damage; harm; loss 2 a cause of damage or damage [c15: from Latin *dētrīmentum*, a rubbing off, hence damage, from *dēterere* to rub away, from DE- + *terere* to rub]

detrimental (,detrɪ'mentəl) *adj* (when *postpositive*, foll by *to*) harmful; injurious; prejudicial: *smoking can be detrimental to health*

detritus (dɪ'traɪtəs) *n* 1 a loose mass of stones, silt, etc, worn away from rocks 2 an accumulation of disintegrated material or debris 3 the organic debris formed from the decay of organisms [c18: from French *détritus*, from Latin *dētrītus* a rubbing away; see DETRIMENT] > de'trital *adj*

Detroit (dɪ'trɔɪt) *n* 1 a city in SE Michigan, on the Detroit River: a major Great Lakes port; largest car-manufacturing centre in the world. Pop: 911 402 (2003 est) 2 a river in central North America, flowing along the US-Canadian border from Lake St Clair to Lake Erie

de trop *French* (də tro) *adj* (*postpositive*) not wanted; in the way; superfluous [literally: of too much]

detumescence (,diːtjʊ'mesəns) *n* the subsidence of a swelling, esp the return of a swollen organ, such as the penis, to the flaccid state [c17: from Latin *dētumescere* to cease swelling, from DE- + *tumescere*, from *tumēre* to swell]

deuce[1] (djuːs) *n* 1 a a playing card or dice with two pips or spots; two b a throw of two in dice 2 *tennis* a tied score (in tennis 40-all) that requires one player to gain two successive points to win the game [c15: from Old French *deus* two, from Latin *duos*, accusative masculine of *duo* two]

deuce[2] (djuːs) *informal* ▷ *interj* 1 an expression of annoyance or frustration ▷ *n* 2 the deuce (intensifier) used in such phrases as what the deuce, where the deuce, etc [c17: probably special use of DEUCE[1] (in the sense: lowest throw at dice)]

deuced ('djuːsɪd, djuːst) *Brit informal* ▷ *adj* 1 (intensifier, usually qualifying something undesirable) damned; confounded: *he's a deuced idiot* ▷ *adv* 2 (intensifier): *deuced good luck*

Deus (Latin 'deɪʊs) *n* God [related to Greek *Zeus*]

deus ex machina (Latin 'deɪʊs ɛks 'mækɪnə) *n* 1 (in ancient Greek and Roman drama) a god introduced into a play to resolve the plot 2 any unlikely or artificial device serving this purpose [literally: god out of a machine, translating Greek *theos ek mēkhanēs*]

Deut. *abbreviation Bible* Deuteronomy

deuteride ('djuːtə,raɪd) *n* a compound of deuterium with some other element. It is analogous to a hydride

deuterium (djuː'tɪərɪəm) *n* a stable isotope of hydrogen, occurring in natural hydrogen (156 parts per million) and in heavy water: used as a tracer in chemistry and biology. Symbol: D or ^{2}H; atomic no: 1; atomic wt: 2.014; boiling pt: −249.7°C [c20: New Latin; see DEUTERO-, -IUM; from the fact that it is the second heaviest hydrogen isotope]

deuterium oxide *n* another name for heavy water

deutero-, deuto- *or before a vowel* **deuter-, deut-** *combining form* second or secondary: *deuterogamy; deuterium* [from Greek *deuteros* second]

deuteron ('djuːtə,rɒn) *n* the nucleus of a deuterium atom, consisting of one proton and one neutron

Deutsch (dɔɪtʃ; German dɔytʃ) *n* **Otto Erich** ('ɔto 'eːrɪç). 1883–1967, Austrian music historian and art critic, noted for his catalogue of Schubert's works (1951)

Deutschland ('dɔytʃlant) *n* the German name for **Germany**

Deutschmark ('dɔɪtʃ,maːk) *or* **Deutsche Mark** ('dɔɪtʃə) *n* the former standard monetary unit of Germany, divided into 100 pfennigs; replaced by the euro in 2002: until 1990 the standard monetary unit of West Germany

deutzia ('djuːtsɪə) *n* any saxifragaceous shrub of the genus *Deutzia*: cultivated for their clusters of white or pink spring-blooming flowers [c19: New Latin, named after Jean *Deutz*, 18th-century Dutch patron of botany]

Deux-Sèvres (French døsɛvrə) *n* a department of W France, in Poitou-Charentes region. Capital: Niort. Pop: 347 652 (2003 est). Area: 6054 sq km (2337 sq miles)

deva ('deɪvə) *n* (in Hinduism and Buddhism) a divine being or god [c19: from Sanskrit: god]

de Valera (də və'lɛərə, -'lɪə-) *n* **Eamon** ('eɪmən). 1882–1975, Irish statesman; president of Sinn Féin (1917–26) and of the Dáil (1918–22); formed the Fianna Fáil party (1927); prime minister (1937–48; 1951–54; 1957–59) and president (1959–73) of the Irish Republic

de Valois (də 'vælwaː) *n* Dame **Ninette** (niː'nɛt). original name *Edris Stannus*. 1898–2001, British ballet dancer and choreographer, born in Ireland: a founder of the Vic-Wells Ballet Company (1931), which under her direction became the Royal Ballet (1956)

devalue (diː'væljuː) *or* **devaluate** (diː'vælju,eɪt) *vb* -values, -valuing, -valued *or* -valuates, -valuating, -valuated 1 to reduce (a currency) or (of a currency) be reduced in exchange value 2 (*tr*) to reduce the value or worth of (something) > de,valu'ation *n*

Devanagari (,deɪvə'naːgərɪ) *n* a syllabic script in which Sanskrit, Hindi, and other modern languages of India are written [c18: from Sanskrit: alphabet of the gods, from *deva* god + *nagari* an Indian alphabet]

devastate ('devə,steɪt) *vb* (*tr*) 1 to lay waste or make desolate; ravage; destroy 2 to confound or overwhelm, as with grief or shock [c17: from Latin *dēvastāre*, from DE- + *vastāre* to ravage; related to *vastus* waste, empty] > ,devas'tation *n* > 'devas,tator *n* > 'devas,tating *adj* > 'devas,tatingly *adv*

develop (dɪ'veləp) *vb* 1 to come or bring to a later or more advanced or expanded stage; grow or cause to grow gradually 2 (*tr*) to elaborate or work out in detail 3 to disclose or unfold (thoughts, a plot, etc) gradually or (of thoughts, etc) to be gradually disclosed or unfolded 4 to come or bring into existence; generate or be generated: *he developed a new faith in God* 5 (*intr*; often foll by *from*) to follow as a result (of); ensue (from): *a row developed following the chairman's remarks* 6 (*tr*) to contract (a disease or illness) 7 (*tr*) to improve the value or change the use of (land), as by building 8 (*tr*) to exploit or make available the natural resources of (a country or region) 9 (*tr*) *photog* to treat (film, plate, or paper previously exposed to light, or the latent image in such material) with chemical solutions in order to produce a visible image 10 *biology* to progress or cause to progress from simple to complex stages in the growth of an individual or the evolution of a species **11** (*tr*) to elaborate upon (a musical theme) by varying the melody, key, etc **12** (*tr*) *maths* to expand (a function or expression) in the form of a series **13** (*tr*) *geometry* to project or roll out (a surface) onto a plane without stretching or shrinking any element **14** *chess* to bring (a piece) into play from its initial position on the back rank [C19: from Old French *desveloper* to unwrap, from *des-* DIS-¹ + *veloper* to wrap; see ENVELOP] > de'velopable*adj*

developer (dɪˈvɛləpə) *n* **1** a person or thing that develops something, esp a person who develops property **2** *photog* a solution of a chemical reducing agent that converts the latent image recorded in the emulsion of a film or paper into a visible image

developing country *n* a nonindustrialized poor country that is seeking to develop its resources by industrialization

development (dɪˈvɛləpmənt) *n* **1** the act or process of growing, progressing, or developing **2** the product or result of developing **3** a fact, event, or happening, esp one that changes a situation **4** an area or tract of land that has been developed **5** Also called: development section the section of a movement, usually in sonata form, in which the basic musical themes are developed **6** *chess* the process of developing pieces > de,velop'mental*adj*

developmental disorder *n* *psychiatry* any condition, such as autism or dyslexia, that appears in childhood and is characterized by delay in the development of one or more psychological functions, such as language skill

development area *n* (in Britain) an area suffering from high unemployment and economic depression, because of the decline of its main industries, that is given government help to establish new industries

Devereux (ˈdɛvərə) *n* **Robert.** See (2nd Earl of) **Essex¹**

devest (dɪˈvɛst) *vb* (*tr*) a rare variant spelling of **divest**

Devi (ˈdeɪviː) *n* a Hindu goddess and embodiment of the female energy of Siva [Sanskrit: goddess; see DEVA]

deviance (ˈdiːvɪəns) *n* **1** Also called: deviancy the act or state of being deviant **2** *statistics* a measure of the degree of fit of a statistical model compared to that of a more complete model

deviant (ˈdiːvɪənt) *adj* **1** deviating, as from what is considered acceptable behaviour ▷ *n* **2** a person whose behaviour, esp sexual behaviour, deviates from what is considered to be acceptable

deviate *vb* (ˈdiːvɪˌeɪt) **1** (*usually intr*) to differ or diverge or cause to differ or diverge, as in belief or thought **2** (*usually intr*) to turn aside or cause to turn aside; diverge or cause to diverge **3** (*intr*) *psychol* to depart from an accepted standard or convention ▷ *n* (ˈdiːvɪɪt) *adj* **4** another word for **deviant** [C17: from Late Latin *dēviāre* to turn aside from the direct road, from DE- + *via* road] > 'devi,ator*n* > 'deviatory*adj*

deviation (ˌdiːvɪˈeɪʃən) *n* **1** an act or result of deviating **2** *statistics* the difference between an observed value in a series of such values and their arithmetic mean **3** the error of a compass due to local magnetic disturbances

device (dɪˈvaɪs) *n* **1** a machine or tool used for a specific task; contrivance **2** *euphemistic* a bomb **3** a plan or plot, esp a clever or evil one; scheme; trick **4** any ornamental pattern or picture, as in embroidery **5** computer hardware that is designed for a specific function **6** a written, printed, or painted design or figure, used as a heraldic sign, emblem, trademark, etc **7** a particular pattern of words, figures of speech, etc, used in literature to produce an effect on the reader **8** leave someone to his own devices to leave someone alone to do as he wishes [C13: from Old French *devis* purpose, contrivance and *devise* difference, intention, from *deviser* to divide, control; see DEVISE]

devil (ˈdɛvəl) *n* **1** *theol* (*often capital*) the chief spirit of evil and enemy of God, often represented as the ruler of hell and often depicted as a human figure with horns, cloven hoofs, and tail **2** *theol* one of the subordinate evil spirits of traditional Jewish and Christian belief **3** a person or animal regarded as cruel, wicked, or ill-natured **4** a person or animal regarded as unfortunate

or wretched **5** a person or animal regarded as clever, daring, mischievous, or energetic **6** *informal* something difficult or annoying **7** *Christian Science* the opposite of truth; an error, lie, or false belief in sin, sickness, and death **8** (in Malaysia) a ghost **9** a portable furnace or brazier, esp one used in road-making or one used by plumbers **10** any of various mechanical devices, usually with teeth, such as a machine for making wooden screws or a rag-tearing machine **11** See **printer's devil** **12** *law* (in England) a junior barrister who does work for another in order to gain experience, usually for a half fee **13** *meteorol* a small whirlwind in arid areas that raises dust or sand in a column **14** between the devil and the deep blue sea between equally undesirable alternatives **15** devil of *informal* (intensifier): *a devil of a fine horse* **16** give the devil his due to acknowledge the talent or the success of an unpleasant or unpleasant person **17** go to the devil **a** to fail or become dissipated **b** (*interjection*) used to express annoyance with the person causing it **18** talk of the devil!*or* speak of the devil! (*interjection*) used when an absent person who has been the subject of conversation appears **19** the devil! (intensifier:) **a** used in such phrases as **what the devil**, **where the devil**, etc **b** an exclamation of anger, surprise, disgust, etc **20** the devil take the hindmost*or* let the devil take the hindmost look after oneself and leave others to their fate **21** the devil to pay problems or trouble to be faced as a consequence of an action ▷ *vb* -ils, -illing, -illed*or US* -ils, -iling, -iled **22** (*tr*) to prepare (esp meat, poultry, or fish) by coating with a highly flavoured spiced paste or mixture of condiments before cooking **23** (*tr*) to tear (rags) with a devil **24** (*intr*) to serve as a printer's devil **25** (*intr*) *chiefly Brit* to do hackwork, esp for a lawyer or author; perform arduous tasks, often without pay or recognition of one's services **26** (*tr*) *US informal* to harass, vex, torment, etc [Old English *dēofol*, from Latin *diabolus*, from Greek *diabolos* enemy, accuser, slanderer, from *diaballein*, literally: to throw across, hence, to slander]

devilfish (ˈdɛvəlˌfɪʃ) *n, pl* -fish*or* -fishes **1** Also called: devil ray*another* name for **manta** (sense 1) **2** another name for **octopus**

devilish (ˈdɛvəlɪʃ, ˈdɛvlɪʃ) *adj* **1** of, resembling, or befitting a devil; diabolic; fiendish ▷ *adv, adj* **2** *informal* (intensifier): *devilish good food; this devilish heat* > 'devilishly*adv* > 'devilishness*n*

devil-may-care *adj* careless or reckless; happy-go-lucky

devilment (ˈdɛvəlmənt) *n* devilish or mischievous conduct

devilry (ˈdɛvəlrɪ) *or* **deviltry** *n, pl* -ries*or* -tries **1** reckless or malicious fun or mischief **2** wickedness or cruelty **3** black magic or other forms of diabolism [C18: from French *diablerie*, from *diable* DEVIL]

devil's advocate *n* **1** a person who advocates an opposing or unpopular view, often for the sake of argument **2** *RC Church* the official appointed to put the case against the beatification or canonization of a candidate [translation of New Latin *advocātus diabolī*]

devil's coach-horse *n* a large black rove beetle, *Ocypus olens*, with large jaws and ferocious habits

devil's food cake *n* *chiefly US & Canadian* a rich chocolate cake

Devil's Island *n* one of the three Safety Islands, off the coast of French Guiana: formerly a leper colony, then a French penal colony from 1895 until 1938. Area: less than 2 sq km (1 sq mile). French name: **Île du Diable**

Devine (dəˈviːn) *n* George (**Alexander Cassady**). 1910–65, British stage director and actor: founded (1956) the English Stage Company in London's Royal Court Theatre

devious (ˈdiːvɪəs) *adj* **1** not sincere or candid; deceitful; underhand **2** (of a route or course of action) rambling; indirect; roundabout **3** going astray from a proper or accepted way; erring [C16: from Latin *dēvius* lying to one side of the road, from DE- + *via* road] > 'deviously*adv* > 'deviousness*n*

devise (dɪˈvaɪz) *vb* **1** to work out, contrive, or plan (something) in one's mind **2** (*tr*) *law* to dispose of (property, esp real property) by will ▷ *n* *law* **3** a disposition of property by will **4** a will or clause in a will disposing of real property [C15: from Old French *deviser* to divide, apportion, intend, from Latin *dīvidere* to DIVIDE] > de'viser *n*

devitalize *or* **devitalise** (diː'vaɪtəˌlaɪz) *vb* (*tr*) to lower or destroy the vitality of; make weak or lifeless > deˌvitali'zation *or* deˌvitali'sation *n*

Devizes (dɪ'vaɪzɪz) *n* a market town in S England, in Wiltshire: agricultural and dairy products. Pop: 14 379 (2001)

devoice (diː'vɔɪs) *vb* (*tr*) *phonetics* to make (a voiced speech sound) voiceless

devoid (dɪ'vɔɪd) *adj* (*postpositive; foll by of*) destitute or void (of); free (from) [C15: originally past participle of *devoid* (*vb*) to remove, from Old French *devoidier*, from *de-* DE- + *voider* to VOID]

devoirs (də'vwɑː; *French* dəvwar) *pl n* (*sometimes singular*) compliments or respects; courteous attentions [C13: from Old French: duty, from *devoir* to be obliged to, owe, from Latin *dēbēre*; see DEBT]

devolution (ˌdiːvə'luːʃən) *n* **1** the act, fact, or result of devolving **2** a passing onwards or downwards from one stage to another **3** a transfer or allocation of authority, esp from a central government to regional governments or particular interests [C16: from Medieval Latin *dēvolūtiō* a rolling down, from Latin *dēvolvere* to roll down, sink into; see DEVOLVE] > ˌdevo'lutionary *adj* > ˌdevo'lutionist *n*, *adj*

devolve (dɪ'vɒlv) *vb* **1** (*foll by on, upon, to*, etc) to pass or cause to pass to a successor or substitute, as duties, power, etc **2** (*intr; foll by on or upon*) *law* (of an estate, etc) to pass to another by operation of law, esp on intestacy or bankruptcy [C15: from Latin *dēvolvere* to roll down, fall into, from DE- + *volvere* to roll] > de'volvement *n*

Devon ('dɛvˀn) *n* **1** Also called: **Devonshire** a county of SW England, between the Bristol Channel and the English Channel, including the island of Lundy: the geographic and ceremonial county includes Plymouth and Torbay, which became independent unitary authorities in 1998; hilly, rising to the uplands of Exmoor and Dartmoor, with wooded river valleys and a rugged coastline. Administrative centre: Exeter. Pop (excluding unitary authorities): 714 900 (2003 est). Area (excluding unitary authorities): 6569 sq km (2536 sq miles) **2** a breed of large red beef cattle originally from Devon

Devonian (də'vəʊnɪən) *adj* **1** of, denoting, or formed in the fourth period of the Palaeozoic era, between the Silurian and Carboniferous periods, lasting 60–70 million years during which amphibians first appeared **2** of or relating to Devon ▷ *n* **3** the Devonian the Devonian period or rock system

Devonshire ('dɛvˀnʃɪə, -ʃə) *n* **8th Duke of,** title of *Spencer Compton Cavendish.* 1833–1908, British politician, also known (1858–91) as Lord Hartington. He led the Liberal Party (1874–80) and left it to found the Liberal Unionist Party (1886)

Devonshire split *n* a kind of yeast bun split open and served with whipped cream or butter and jam

devoré (də'vɔːreɪ) *n* a velvet fabric with a raised pattern created by disintegrating some of the pile with chemicals [from French, past participle of *dévorer* to devour]

devote (dɪ'vəʊt) *vb* (*tr*) to apply or dedicate (oneself, time, money, etc) to some pursuit, cause, etc [C16: from Latin *dēvōtus* devoted, solemnly promised, from *dēvovēre* to vow; see DE-, VOW]

devoted (dɪ'vəʊtɪd) *adj* **1** feeling or demonstrating loyalty or devotion; ardent; devout **2** (*postpositive; foll by to*) set apart, dedicated, or consecrated > de'votedly *adv* > de'votedness *n*

devotee (ˌdɛvə'tiː) *n* **1** a person ardently enthusiastic about or devoted to something, such as a sport or pastime **2** a zealous follower of a religion

devotion (dɪ'vəʊʃən) *n* **1** (often foll by *to*) strong attachment (to) or affection (for a cause, person, etc) marked by dedicated loyalty **2** religious zeal; piety **3** (*often plural*) religious observance or prayers > de'votional *adj, n* > deˌvotion'ality *or* de'votionalness *n* > de'votionally *adv*

devour (dɪ'vaʊə) *vb* (*tr*) **1** to swallow or eat up greedily or voraciously **2** to waste or destroy; consume **3** to consume greedily or avidly with the senses or mind **4** to engulf or absorb [C14: from Old French *devourer*, from Latin *dēvorāre* to gulp down, from DE- + *vorāre* to consume greedily; see VORACIOUS] > de'vourer *n* > de'vouring *adj*

devout (dɪ'vaʊt) *adj* **1** deeply religious; reverent **2** sincere; earnest; heartfelt [C13: from Old French *devot*, from Late Latin *dēvōtus*, from Latin: faithful; see DEVOTE] > de'voutly *adv* > de'voutness *n*

Devoy (də'vɔɪ) *n* Dame **Susan (Elizabeth Anne).** born 1964, New Zealand squash player; winner of the World Open Championship 1985, 1987, 1990, and 1992

De Vries (Dutch də 'vriːs) *n* **Hugo** ('hyːxoː). 1848–1935, Dutch botanist, who rediscovered Mendel's laws and developed the mutation theory of evolution

dew (djuː) *n* **1** drops of water condensed on a cool surface, esp at night, from vapour in the air **2** something like or suggestive of this, esp in freshness: *the dew of youth* **3** small drops of moisture, such as tears ▷ *vb* **4** (*tr*) *poetic* to moisten with or as with dew [Old English *dēaw*; related to Old High German *tou* dew, Old Norse *dögg*]

Dewar ('djuːə) *n* **1 Donald.** 1937–2000, Scottish Labour politician; secretary of state for Scotland (1997–99); first minister of Scotland (1999–2000) **2 Sir James.** 1842–1923, Scottish chemist and physicist. He worked on the liquefaction of gases and the properties of matter at low temperature, invented the vacuum flask, and (with Sir Frederick Abel) was the first to prepare cordite

dewberry ('djuːbərɪ, -brɪ) *n, pl* -ries **1** any trailing bramble, such as *Rubus hispidus* of North America and *R. caesius* of Europe and NW Asia, having blue-black fruits **2** the fruit of any such plant

dewclaw ('djuːˌklɔː) *n* **1** a nonfunctional claw in dogs; the rudimentary first digit **2** an analogous rudimentary hoof in deer, goats, etc > 'dewˌclawed *adj*

dewdrop ('djuːˌdrɒp) *n* a drop of dew

de Wet (də 'vet) *n* **Christian Rudolf.** 1854–1922, Afrikaner military commander and politician, who led the Orange Free State army in the second Boer War (1899–1902). He was imprisoned for treason (1914) after organizing an Afrikaner nationalist rebellion

Dewey ('djuːɪ) *n* **John.** 1859–1952, US pragmatist philosopher and educator: an exponent of progressivism in education, he formulated an instrumentalist theory of learning through experience. His works include *The School and Society* (1899), *Democracy and Education* (1916), and *Logic: the Theory of Inquiry* (1938)

Dewey Decimal System ('djuːɪ) *n* a frequently used system of library book classification and arrangement with ten main subject classes. Also called: **decimal classification** [C19: named after Melvil *Dewey* (1851–1931), US educator who invented the system]

de Wint (də 'wɪnt) *n* **Peter.** 1784–1849, English landscape painter

de Witt (də 'wɪt) *n* **Johan.** 1625–72, Dutch statesman; chief minister of the United Provinces of the Netherlands (1653–72)

dewlap ('djuːˌlæp) *n* **1** a loose fold of skin hanging from beneath the throat in cattle, dogs, etc **2** loose skin on an elderly person's throat [C14 *dewlappe*, from DEW (probably changed by folk etymology from an earlier form of different meaning) + LAP¹ (from Old English *læppa* hanging flap), perhaps of Scandinavian origin; compare Danish *doglæp*]

DEW line (djuː) *n* acronym for distant early warning line, a network of radar stations situated mainly in Arctic regions to give early warning of aircraft or missile attack on North America

dew point *n* the temperature at which water vapour in the air becomes saturated and water droplets begin to form

dew pond *n* a shallow pond, usually man-made, that is kept supplied with water by dew and condensation

dewy ('djuːɪ) *adj* dewier, dewiest **1** moist with or as with dew **2** of or resembling dew **3** *poetic* suggesting, falling, or refreshing like dew: *dewy sleep* > 'dewily *adv* > 'dewiness *n*

dexter ('dɛkstə) adj 1 archaic of or located on the right side 2 (usually postpositive) heraldry of, on, or starting from the right side of a shield from the bearer's point of view and therefore on the spectator's left ▷ Compare **sinister** [c16: from Latin; compare Greek dexios on the right hand]

Dexter ('dɛkstə) n **John.** 1925–90, British actor and theatre director

dexterity (dɛk'stɛrɪtɪ) n 1 physical, esp manual, skill or nimbleness 2 mental skill or adroitness: cleverness [c16: from Latin dexteritās aptness, readiness, prosperity; see DEXTER¹]

dexterous or **dextrous** ('dɛkstrəs) adj possessing or done with dexterity > 'dexterously or 'dextrously adv > 'dexterousness or 'dextrousness n

dextral ('dɛkstrəl) adj 1 of, relating to, or located on the right side, esp of the body; right-hand 2 of or relating to a person who prefers to use his right foot, hand, or eye; right-handed 3 (of the shells of certain gastropod molluscs) coiling in an anticlockwise direction from the apex; dextrorse > **dextrality** (dɛk'strælɪtɪ) n > 'dextrally adv

dextran ('dɛkstrən) n biochem a polysaccharide produced by the action of bacteria on sucrose: used as a substitute for plasma in blood transfusions [c19: from DEXTRO- + -AN]

dextrin ('dɛkstrɪn) or **dextrine** ('dɛkstrɪn, -triːn) n any of a group of sticky substances that are intermediate products in the conversion of starch to maltose: used as thickening agents in foods and as gums [c19: from French dextrine; see DEXTRO-, -IN]

dextro- or before a vowel **dextr-** combining form on or towards the right: dextrorotation [from Latin, from dexter on the right side]

dextrorotation (ˌdɛkstrəʊrəʊ'teɪʃən) n a rotation to the right; clockwise rotation, esp of the plane of polarization of plane-polarized light passing through a crystal, liquid, or solution, as seen by an observer facing the oncoming light. See **laevorotation** > **dextrorotatory** (ˌdɛkstrəʊ'rəʊtətərɪ, -trɪ) or ˌdextro'rotary adj

dextrorse ('dɛkstrɔːs, dɛk'strɔːs) or **dextrorsal** (dɛk'strɔːsəl) adj (of some climbing plants) growing upwards in a helix from left to right or anticlockwise [c19: from Latin dextrorsum towards the right, from DEXTRO- + vorsus turned, variant of versus, from vertere to turn] > 'dextrorsely adv

dextrose ('dɛkstrəʊz, -trəʊs) n a white soluble sweet-tasting crystalline solid that is the dextrorotatory isomer of glucose, occurring widely in fruit, honey, and in the blood and tissue of animals. Formula: $C_6H_{12}O_6$. Also called: grape sugar, dextroglucose

dextrous ('dɛkstrəs) adj a variant spelling of **dexterous** > 'dextrously adv > 'dextrousness n

Dezhnev (Russian dɪʒ'njɔf) n **Cape Dezhnev** a cape in NE Russia at the E end of Chukchi Peninsula: the northeasternmost point of Asia. Former name: East Cape

DF abbreviation Defender of the Faith

D/F or **DF** abbreviation telecomm 1 direction finder 2 direction finding

DFC abbreviation Distinguished Flying Cross

DfEE abbreviation (in Britain) Department for Education and Employment

DFID abbreviation (in Britain) Department for International Development

DFM abbreviation Distinguished Flying Medal

dg or **dg.** abbreviation decigram

Dhahran (dɑː'rɑːn) n a town in E Saudi Arabia: site of the original discovery of oil in the country (1938)

Dhaka or **Dacca** ('dækə) n the capital of Bangladesh, in the E central part: capital of Bengal (1608–39; 1660–1704) and of East Pakistan (1949–71); jute and cotton mills; university (1921). Pop: 12 560 000 (2005 est)

dhal, dal or **dholl** (dɑːl) n 1 a tropical African and Asian leguminous shrub, Cajanus cajan, cultivated in tropical regions for its nutritious pealike seeds 2 Also called: pigeon pea the seed of this shrub 3 a curry made from lentils or other pulses [c17: from Hindi dāl split pulse, from Sanskrit dal to split]

dharma ('dɑːmə) n 1 Hinduism social custom regarded as a religious and moral duty 2 Hinduism a the essential principle of the cosmos; natural law b conduct that conforms with this 3 Buddhism ideal truth as set forth in the teaching of Buddha [Sanskrit: habit, usage, law, from dhārayati he holds]

dharna or **dhurna** ('dʌnə, 'dɑː-) n (in India) a method of obtaining justice, as the payment of a debt, by sitting, fasting, at the door of the person from whom reparation is sought [c18: from Hindi, literally: a placing]

DHB abbreviation (in New Zealand) District Health Board

DHEA abbreviation dehydroisoandrosterone: the major androgen precursor in females, secreted by the adrenal cortex

Dhílos (ðílos) n a transliteration of the Modern Greek name for **Delos**

dhobi ('dəʊbɪ) n, pl -bis (in India, Malaya, East Africa, etc, esp formerly) a washerman [c19: from Hindi, from dhōb washing; related to Sanskrit dhāvaka washerman]

Dhodhekánisos (ðɔðɛ'kanisɔs) n a transliteration of the Modern Greek name for the **Dodecanese**

dhoti ('dəʊtɪ), **dhooti, dhootie** or **dhuti** ('duːtɪ) n, pl -tis a long loincloth worn by men in India [c17: from Hindi]

dhow (daʊ) n a lateen-rigged coastal Arab sailing vessel with one or two masts [c19: from Arabic dāwa]

DHS abbreviation 1 (in Canada) district high school 2 (in the US) Department of Homeland Security

DHSS (formerly, in Britain) abbreviation Department of Health and Social Security

DI abbreviation Donor Insemination

di-¹ prefix 1 twice; two; double: dicotyledon 2 a containing two specified atoms or groups of atoms: dimethyl ether; carbon dioxide b a nontechnical equivalent of **bi-¹** (sense 5c) [via Latin from Greek, from dis twice, double, related to duo two. Compare BI-¹]

di-² combining form variant of **dia-** before a vowel: diopter

dia- or **di-** prefix 1 through, throughout, or during: diachronic 2 across: diactinic 3 apart: diacritic [from Greek dia through, between, across, by]

diabase ('daɪəˌbeɪs) n 1 Brit an altered dolerite 2 US another name for **dolerite** [c19: from French, from Greek diabasis a crossing over, from diabainein to cross over, from DIA- + bainein to go] > ˌdia'basic adj

diabetes (ˌdaɪə'biːtɪs, -tiːz) n any of various disorders, esp diabetes mellitus, characterized by excretion of an abnormally large amount of urine [c16: from Latin: siphon, from Greek, literally: a passing through (referring to the excessive urination), from diabainein to pass through, cross over; see DIABASE]

diabetes mellitus (mə'laɪtəs) n a disorder of carbohydrate metabolism characterized by excessive thirst and excretion of abnormally large quantities of urine containing an excess of sugar, caused by a deficiency of insulin [c18: New Latin, literally: honey-sweet diabetes]

diabetic (ˌdaɪə'bɛtɪk) adj 1 of, relating to, or having diabetes 2 for the use of diabetics ▷ n 3 a person who has diabetes

diablerie (dɪ'ɑːblərɪ; French djablərɪ) n 1 magic or witchcraft connected with devils 2 demonic lore or esoteric knowledge of devils 3 devilry; mischief [c18: from Old French, from diable devil, from Latin diabolus; see DEVIL]

diabolic (ˌdaɪə'bɒlɪk) adj 1 of, relating to, or proceeding from the devil; satanic 2 befitting a devil; extremely cruel or wicked; fiendish 3 very difficult or unpleasant [c14: from Late Latin diabolicus, from Greek diabolikos, from diabolos DEVIL] > ˌdia'bolically adv > ˌdia'bolicalness n

diabolical (ˌdaɪə'bɒlɪkəl) adj informal 1 excruciatingly bad; outrageous 2 (intensifier): a diabolical liberty > ˌdia'bolically adv > ˌdia'bolicalness n

diabolism (daɪ'æbəˌlɪzəm) n 1 activities designed to enlist the aid of devils, esp in witchcraft or sorcery 2 character or conduct that is devilish or fiendish; devilry > di'abolist n

diabolo (dɪ'æbəˌləʊ) n, pl -los 1 a game in which one throws and catches a spinning top on a cord fastened to two sticks held in the hands 2 the top used in this game [c20: from Italian, literally: devil]

diachronic (ˌdaɪə'krɒnɪk) adj of, relating to, or studying the development of a phenomenon through time; historical. Compare **synchronic** [c19: from DIA- + Greek *khronos* time]

diacidic (ˌdaɪəˈsɪdɪk) *adj* (of a base, such as calcium hydroxide Ca(OH)$_2$) capable of neutralizing two protons with one of its molecules. Also: **diacid**

diaconal (daɪˈækənəl) *adj* of or associated with a deacon or the diaconate [c17: from Late Latin *diāconālis*, from *diāconus* DEACON]

diaconate (daɪˈækənɪt, -ˌneɪt) *n* the office, sacramental status, or period of office of a deacon [c17: from Late Latin *diāconātus*; see DEACON]

diacritic (ˌdaɪəˈkrɪtɪk) *n* 1 Also called: **diacritical mark** a sign placed above or below a character or letter to indicate that it has a different phonetic value, is stressed, or for some other reason ▷ *adj* 2 another word for **diacritical** [c17: from Greek *diakritikos* serving to distinguish, from *diakrinein*, from DIA- + *krinein* to separate]

diacritical (ˌdaɪəˈkrɪtɪkəl) *adj* 1 of or relating to a diacritic 2 showing up a distinction

diadem (ˈdaɪəˌdɛm) *n* 1 a royal crown, esp a light jewelled circlet 2 royal dignity or power [c13: from Latin *diadēma*, from Greek: fillet, royal headdress, from *diadein* to bind around, from DIA- + *dein* to bind]

diaeresis or **dieresis** (daɪˈɛrɪsɪs) *n, pl* **-ses** (-ˌsiːz) 1 the mark ¨, in writing placed over the second of two adjacent vowels to indicate that it is to be pronounced separately rather than forming a diphthong with the first, as in some spellings of *coöperate*, *naïve*, etc 2 this mark used for any other purpose, such as to indicate that a special pronunciation is appropriate to a particular vowel 3 a pause in a line of verse occurring when the end of a foot coincides with the end of a word [c17: from Latin *diaerēsis*, from Greek *diairesis* a division, from *diairein*, from DIA- + *hairein* to take; compare HERESY] > **diaeretic** or **dieretic** (ˌdaɪəˈrɛtɪk) *adj*

diag. *abbreviation* diagram

Diaghilev (*Russian* ˈdjaɡɪlif) *n* **Sergei Pavlovich** (sɪrˈgjej ˈpavləvitʃ). 1872–1929, Russian ballet impresario. He founded (1909) and directed (1909–29) the *Ballet Russe* in Paris, introducing Russian ballet to the West

diagnose (ˌdaɪəgˈnəʊz) *vb* 1 to determine or distinguish by diagnosis 2 (*tr*) to examine (a person or thing), as for a disease > **diag'nosable** *adj*

diagnosis (ˌdaɪəgˈnəʊsɪs) *n, pl* **-ses** (-siːz) 1 a the identification of diseases by the examination of symptoms and signs and by other investigations b an opinion or conclusion so reached 2 a thorough analysis of facts or problems in order to gain understanding and aid future planning b an opinion or conclusion reached through such analysis [c17: New Latin, from Greek: a distinguishing, from *diagignōskein* to distinguish, from *gignōskein* to perceive, KNOW] > **diagnostic** (ˌdaɪəgˈnɒstɪk) *adj, n* > ˌdiag'nostically *adv*

diagonal (daɪˈægənəl) *adj* 1 *maths* connecting any two vertices that in a polygon are not adjacent and in a polyhedron are not in the same face 2 slanting; oblique 3 marked with slanting lines or patterns ▷ *n* 4 *maths* a diagonal line or plane 5 something put, set, or drawn obliquely [c16: from Latin *diagōnālis*, from Greek *diagōnios*, from DIA- + *gōnia* angle] > **di'agonally** *adv*

diagram (ˈdaɪəˌgræm) *n* 1 a sketch, outline, or plan demonstrating the form or workings of something 2 *maths* a pictorial representation of a quantity or of a relationship ▷ *vb* **-grams**, **-gramming**, **-grammed** or *US* **-grams**, **-graming**, **-gramed** 3 to show in or as if in a diagram [c17: from Latin *diagramma*, from Greek, from *diagraphein*, from *graphein* to write] > **diagrammatic** (ˌdaɪəgrəˈmætɪk) *adj*

dial (ˈdaɪəl, daɪl) *n* 1 the face of a watch, clock, chronometer, sundial, etc, marked with divisions representing units of time 2 the circular graduated disc of various measuring instruments 3 a the control on a radio or television set used to change the station or channel b the panel on a radio on which the frequency, wavelength, or station is indicated by means of a pointer 4 a numbered disc on a telephone that is rotated a set distance for each digit of a number being called 5 *Brit* a slang word for **face** (sense 1) ▷ *vb* **dials**, **dialling**, **dialled** or *US* **dials**, **dialing**, **dialed** 6 to establish or try to establish a telephone connection with (a subscriber or his number) by operating the dial on a telephone 7 (*tr*) to indicate, measure, or operate with a dial [c14: from Medieval Latin *diālis* daily, from Latin *diēs* day] > 'dialler *n*

dial. *abbreviation* dialect(al)

dial down *vb* (*adverb*) to reduce or become reduced: *to dial down an argument*

dialect (ˈdaɪəˌlɛkt) *n* a a form of a language spoken in a particular geographical area or by members of a particular social class or occupational group, distinguished by its vocabulary, grammar, and pronunciation b a form of a language that is considered inferior [c16: from Latin *dialectus*, from Greek *dialektos* speech, dialect, discourse, from *dialegesthai* to converse, from *legein* to talk, speak]

dialectic (ˌdaɪəˈlɛktɪk) *n* 1 disputation or debate, esp intended to resolve differences between two views rather than to establish one of them as true 2 *philosophy* the conversational Socratic method of argument ▷ *adj* 3 of or relating to logical disputation [c17: from Latin *dialectica*, from Greek *dialektikē* (*tekhnē*) (the art) of argument; see DIALECT] > ˌdialec'tician *n*

dialectical (ˌdaɪəˈlɛktɪkəl) *adj* of or relating to dialectic or dialectics > ˌdia'lectically *adv*

dialectical materialism *n* the economic, political, and philosophical system of Karl Marx (1818–83) and Friedrich Engels (1820–95), the German political philosophers, that combines traditional materialism and Hegelian dialectic

dialectics (ˌdaɪəˈlɛktɪks) *n* (*functioning as plural or* (*sometimes*) *singular*) 1 the study of reasoning or of argumentative methodology 2 a particular methodology or system; a logic 3 the application of the Hegelian dialectic or the rationale of dialectical materialism

dialling code *n* a sequence of numbers which are dialled for connection with another exchange before an individual subscriber's telephone number is dialled

dialling tone or *US and Canadian* **dial tone** *n* a continuous sound, either purring or high-pitched, heard over a telephone indicating that a number can be dialled

dialogue or *often US* **dialog** (ˈdaɪəˌlɒg) *n* 1 conversation between two or more people 2 an exchange of opinions on a particular subject; discussion 3 the lines spoken by characters in drama or fiction 4 a particular passage of conversation in a literary or dramatic work 5 a literary composition in the form of a dialogue 6 a political discussion between representatives of two nations or groups [c13: from Old French *dialoge*, from Latin *dialogus*, from Greek *dialogos*, from *dialegesthai* to converse; see DIALECT]

dialogue box or **dialog box** *n* *computing* a window that may appear on a VDU display to prompt the user to enter further information or select an option

dialyse or *US* **dialyze** (ˈdaɪəˌlaɪz) *vb* (*tr*) to separate by dialysis > ˌdialy'sation or *US* ˌdialy'zation *n*

dialyser or *US* **dialyzer** (ˈdaɪəˌlaɪzə) *n* a machine that performs dialysis, esp one that removes impurities from the blood of patients with malfunctioning kidneys; kidney machine

dialysis (daɪˈælɪsɪs) *n, pl* **-ses** (-ˌsiːz) the separation of small molecules from large molecules and colloids in a solution by the selective diffusion of the small molecules through a semipermeable membrane [c16: from Late Latin: a separation, from Greek *dialusis* a dissolution, from *dialuein* to tear apart, dissolve, from *luein* to loosen] > **dialytic** (ˌdaɪəˈlɪtɪk) *adj*

diam. *abbreviation* diameter

diamagnetic (ˌdaɪəmægˈnɛtɪk) *adj* of, exhibiting, or concerned with diamagnetism

diamagnetism (ˌdaɪəˈmægnɪˌtɪzəm) *n* the phenomenon exhibited by substances that have a relative permeability less than unity and a negative susceptibility. It is caused by the orbital motion of electrons in the atoms of the material and is unaffected by temperature

diamanté (ˌdaɪəˈmæntɪ, ˌdɪə-) *adj* **1** decorated with glittering ornaments, such as artificial jewels or sequins ▷ *n* **2** a fabric so covered [c20: from French, from *diamanter* to adorn with diamonds, from *diamant* DIAMOND]

diameter (daɪˈæmɪtə) *n* **1 a** a straight line connecting the centre of a geometric figure, esp a circle or sphere, with two points on the perimeter or surface **b** the length of such a line **2** the thickness of something, esp with circular cross section [c14: from Medieval Latin *diametrus*, variant of Latin *diametros*, from Greek: diameter, diagonal, from DIA- + *metron* measure]

diametric (ˌdaɪəˈmɛtrɪk) *or* **diametrical** *adj* **1** Also: **diametral** of, related to, or along a diameter **2** completely opposed

diametrically (ˌdaɪəˈmɛtrɪkəlɪ) *adv* completely; utterly (esp in the phrase **diametrically opposed**)

diamond (ˈdaɪəmənd) *n* **1 a** a colourless exceptionally hard mineral (but often tinted yellow, orange, blue, brown, or black by impurities), found in certain igneous rocks (esp the kimberlites of South Africa). It is used as a gemstone, as an abrasive, and on the working edges of cutting tools. Composition: carbon. Formula: C. Crystal structure: cubic **b** (*as modifier*): *a diamond ring* **2** *geometry* a figure having four sides of equal length forming two acute angles and two obtuse angles; rhombus **3 a** a red lozenge-shaped symbol on a playing card **b** a card with one or more of these symbols or (*when plural*) the suit of cards so marked **4** *baseball* **a** the whole playing field **b** the square formed by the four bases ▷ *vb* **5** (*tr*) to decorate with or as with diamonds [c13: from Old French *diamant*, from Medieval Latin *diamas*, modification of Latin *adamas* the hardest iron or steel, diamond; see ADAMANT] > **diamantine** (ˌdaɪəˈmæntaɪn) *adj*

diamond anniversary *n* a 60th, or occasionally 75th, anniversary

diamondback (ˈdaɪəməndˌbæk) *n* **1** Also called: **diamondback terrapin, diamondback turtle** any edible North American terrapin of the genus *Malaclemys*, esp *M. terrapin*, occurring in brackish and tidal waters and having diamond-shaped markings on the shell: family *Emydidae* **2** a large North American rattlesnake, *Crotalus adamanteus*, having cream-and-grey diamond-shaped markings

diamond wedding *n* the 60th, or occasionally the 75th, anniversary of a marriage

diamorphine (ˌdaɪəˈmɔːfiːn) *n* a technical name for **heroin**

Diana (daɪˈænə) *n* **1** the virginal Roman goddess of the hunt and the moon. Greek counterpart: Artemis **2** title *Diana, Princess of Wales*, original name *Lady Diana Frances Spencer*. 1961–97, she married Charles, Prince of Wales, in 1981; they were divorced in 1996: died in a car crash

dianthus (daɪˈænθəs) *n, pl* **-thuses** any Eurasian caryophyllaceous plant of the widely cultivated genus *Dianthus*, such as the carnation, pink, and sweet william [c19: New Latin, from Greek DI-¹ + *anthos* flower]

diapason (ˌdaɪəˈpeɪzᵊn, -ˈpeɪsᵊn) *n music* **1** either of two stops (**open and stopped diapason**) usually found throughout the compass of a pipe organ that give it its characteristic tone colour **2** the compass of an instrument or voice **3** (chiefly in French usage) **a** a standard pitch used for tuning, esp the now largely obsolete one of A above middle C = 435 hertz, known as **diapason normal** (French djapazɔ̃ nɔrmal) **b** a tuning fork or pitch pipe **4** (in classical Greece) an octave [c14: from Latin: the whole octave, from Greek (hē) *dia pasōn* (khordōn sumphōnia*) (concord) through all (the notes), from *dia* through + *pas* all]

diapause (ˈdaɪəˌpɔːz) *n* a period of suspended development and growth accompanied by decreased metabolism in insects and some other animals. It is correlated with seasonal changes [c19: from Greek *diapausis* pause, from *diapauein* to pause, bring to an end, from DIA- + *pauein* to stop]

diaper (ˈdaɪəpə) *n* **1** *US & Canadian* a piece of soft material, esp towelling or a disposable material, wrapped around a baby in order to absorb its excrement.

Also called (in Britain and certain other countries): **nappy 2 a** a woven pattern on fabric consisting of a small repeating design, esp diamonds **b** such a pattern, used as decoration ▷ *vb* **3** (*tr*) to decorate with such a pattern [c14: from Old French *diaspre*, from Medieval Latin *diasprus* made of diaper, from Medieval Greek *diaspros* pure white, from DIA- + *aspros* white, shining]

diaphanous (daɪˈæfənəs) *adj* (usually of fabrics such as silk) fine and translucent [c17: from Medieval Latin *diaphanus*, from Greek *diaphanēs* transparent, from *diaphainein* to show through, from DIA- + *phainein* to show] > di'aphanously *adv*

diaphoresis (ˌdaɪəfəˈriːsɪs) *n* perceptible and excessive sweating; sweat [c17: via Late Latin from Greek, from *diaphorein* to disperse by perspiration, from DIA- + *phorein* to carry, variant of *pherein*]

diaphoretic (ˌdaɪəfəˈrɛtɪk) *adj* **1** relating to or causing sweat ▷ *n* **2** a diaphoretic drug or agent

diaphragm (ˈdaɪəˌfræm) *n* **1** *anatomy* any separating membrane, esp the dome-shaped muscular partition that separates the abdominal and thoracic cavities in mammals **2** a circular rubber or plastic contraceptive membrane placed over the mouth of the uterine cervix before copulation to prevent entrance of sperm **3** any thin dividing membrane **4** Also called: **stop** a disc with a fixed or adjustable aperture to control the amount of light or other radiation entering an optical instrument, such as a camera **5** a thin disc that vibrates when receiving or producing sound waves, used to convert sound signals to electrical signals or vice versa in telephones, etc [c17: from Late Latin *diaphragma*, from Greek, from DIA- + *phragma* fence] > **diaphragmatic** (ˌdaɪəfrægˈmætɪk) *adj*

diapositive (ˌdaɪəˈpɒzɪtɪv) *n* a positive transparency; slide

diarist (ˈdaɪərɪst) *n* a person who keeps or writes a diary, esp one that is subsequently published

diarrhoea *or esp US* **diarrhea** (ˌdaɪəˈrɪə) *n* frequent and copious discharge of abnormally liquid faeces [c16: from Late Latin, from Greek *diarrhoia*, from *diarrhein* to flow through, from DIA- + *rhein* to flow] > ˌdiar'rhoeal, ˌdiar'rhoeic *or esp US* ˌdiar'rheal *or* ˌdiar'rheic *adj*

diary (ˈdaɪərɪ) *n, pl* **-ries 1** a personal record of daily events, appointments, observations, etc **2** a book for keeping such a record [c16: from Latin *diārium* daily allocation of food or money, journal, from *diēs* day]

Dias *or* **Diaz** (ˈdiːəs; *Portuguese* ˈdiəʃ) *n* **Bartholomeu** (ˌbərtuluˈmeu). ?1450–1500, Portuguese navigator who discovered the sea route from Europe to the East via the Cape of Good Hope (1488)

Diaspora (daɪˈæspərə) *n* **1 a** the dispersion of the Jews after the Babylonian and Roman conquests of Palestine **b** the Jewish communities outside Israel **2** (*often not capital*) a dispersion or spreading, as of people originally belonging to one nation or having a common culture **3** *Caribbean* the descendants of Sub-Saharan African peoples living anywhere in the Western hemisphere [c19: from Greek: a scattering, from *diaspeirein* to disperse, from DIA- + *speirein* to scatter, sow; see SPORE]

diastalsis (ˌdaɪəˈstælsɪs) *n, pl* **-ses** (-siːz) *physiol* a downward wave of contraction occurring in the intestine during digestion [c20: New Latin, from DIA- + (PERI)STALSIS] > ˌdia'staltic *adj*

diastase (ˈdaɪəˌsteɪs, -ˌsteɪz) *n* any of a group of enzymes that hydrolyse starch to maltose. They are present in germinated barley and in the pancreas [c19: from French, from Greek *diastasis* a separation; see DIASTASIS] > ˌdia'stasic *adj*

diastasis (daɪˈæstəsɪs) *n, pl* **-ses** (-ˌsiːz) **1** *pathol* **a** the separation of the end part from the long bone to which it is normally attached without fracture of the bone **b** the separation of any two parts normally joined **2** *physiol* the last part of the diastolic phase of the heartbeat [c18: New Latin, from Greek: a separation, from *diistanai* to separate, from DIA- + *histanai* to place, make stand] > **diastatic** (ˌdaɪəˈstætɪk) *adj*

diastole (daɪˈæstəlɪ) *n* the dilatation of the chambers of the heart that follows each contraction, during which they refill with blood. Compare **systole** [c16: via Late

Latin from Greek: an expansion, from *diastellein* to expand, from DIA- + *stellein* to place, bring together, make ready] > diastolic (ˌdaɪəˈstɒlɪk) *adj*

diastrophism (daɪˈæstrəˌfɪzəm) *n* the process of movement and deformation of the earth's crust that gives rise to large-scale features such as continents, ocean basins, and mountains [C19: from Greek *diastrophē* a twisting; see DIA-, STROPHE] > diastrophic (ˌdaɪəˈstrɒfɪk) *adj*

diathermancy (ˌdaɪəˈθɜːmənsɪ) *n, pl* -cies the property of transmitting infrared radiation [C19: from French *diathermansie*, from DIA- + Greek *thermansis* heating, from *thermainein* to heat, from *thermos* hot] > ˌdiaˈthermanous *adj*

diathermy (ˈdaɪəˌθɜːmɪ) *or* **diathermia** (ˌdaɪəˈθɜːmɪə) *n* local heating of the body tissues with an electric current for medical or surgical purposes [C20: from New Latin *diathermia*, from DIA- + Greek *thermē* heat]

diatom (ˈdaɪətəm, -ˌtɒm) *n* any microscopic unicellular alga of the phylum *Bacillariophyta*, occurring in marine or fresh water singly or in colonies, each cell having a cell wall made of two halves and impregnated with silica [C19: from New Latin *Diatoma* (genus name), from Greek *diatomos* cut in two, from *diatemnein* to cut through, from DIA- + *temnein* to cut]

diatomaceous (ˌdaɪətəˈmeɪʃəs) *adj* of, relating to, consisting of, or containing diatoms or their fossil remains

diatomic (ˌdaɪəˈtɒmɪk) *adj* (of a compound or molecule) containing two atoms

diatomite (daɪˈætəˌmaɪt) *n* a soft very fine-grained whitish rock consisting of the siliceous remains of diatoms deposited in the ocean or in ponds or lakes. It is used as an absorbent, filtering medium, insulator, filler, etc

diatonic (ˌdaɪəˈtɒnɪk) *adj* 1 of, relating to, or based upon any scale of five tones and two semitones produced by playing the white keys of a keyboard instrument, esp the natural major or minor scales forming the basis of the key system in Western music 2 not involving the sharpening or flattening of the notes of the major or minor scale nor the use of such notes as modified by accidentals [C16: from Late Latin *diatonicus*, from Greek *diatonikos*, from *diatonos* extending, from *diateinein* to stretch out, from DIA- + *teinein* to stretch]

diatribe (ˈdaɪəˌtraɪb) *n* a bitter or violent criticism or attack; denunciation [C16: from Latin *diatriba* learned debate, from Greek *diatribē* discourse, pastime, from *diatribein* to while away, from DIA- + *tribein* to rub]

Diaz (ˈdiːəs; *Portuguese* ˈdiəʃ) *n* 1 a variant spelling of **Dias** 2 (ˈdiːæz) **Cameron.** born 1972, US film actress; films include *The Mask* (1994), *There's Something About Mary* (1998), and *The Gangs of New York* (2003) 3 (ˈdiːəs; *Spanish* ˈdiaθ) (José de la Cruz) **Porfirio** (pɔrˈfirjo). 1830– 1915, Mexican general and statesman; president of Mexico (1877–80; 1884–1911)

Díaz de Vivar (*Spanish* ˈdiaθ dɛ biˈβar) *n* **Rodrigo** (rɔˈðriɣo). the original name of El Cid. See **Cid**

diazepam (daɪˈæzəˌpæm) *n* a chemical compound used as a minor tranquillizer and muscle relaxant and to treat acute epilepsy. Formula: $C_{16}H_{13}ClN_2O$ [C20: from DI-[1] + AZO- + EP(OXIDE) + -*am*]

diazo (daɪˈeɪzəʊ) *adj* 1 of, consisting of, or containing the divalent group, =N:N, or the divalent group, -N:N- 2 Also called: dyeline of or relating to the reproduction of documents using the bleaching action of ultraviolet radiation on diazonium salts ▷ *n, pl* diazos *or* diazoes 3 a document produced by this method

diazonium (ˌdaɪəˈzəʊnɪəm) *n* (*modifier*) of, consisting of, or containing the group, Ar-N:N-, where Ar is an aryl group [C19: DIAZO + (AMM)ONIUM]

dibasic (daɪˈbeɪsɪk) *adj* 1 (of an acid, such as sulphuric acid, H_2SO_4) containing two acidic hydrogen atoms 2 (of a salt) derived by replacing two acidic hydrogen atoms > dibasicity (ˌdaɪbeɪˈsɪsɪtɪ) *n*

dibble (ˈdɪbᵊl) *n* 1 a small hand tool used to make holes in the ground for planting or transplanting bulbs, seeds, or roots ▷ *vb* 2 to make a hole in (the ground) with a dibble 3 to plant (bulbs, seeds, etc) with a dibble [C15:

of obscure origin] > ˈdibbler *n*

dibs (dɪbz) *pl n* 1 another word for **jacks** 2 a slang word for **money** 3 (foll by *on*) *informal* rights (to) or claims (on): used mainly by children [C18: shortened from *dibstones* children's game played with knucklebones or pebbles, probably from *dib* to tap, dip, variant of DAB[1]]

DiCaprio (dɪˈkæprɪəʊ) *n* **Leonardo.** born 1974, US film actor; his films include *Romeo and Juliet* (1996), *Titanic* (1997), *Gangs of New York* (2003), and *The Departed* (2006)

dice (daɪs) *pl n* 1 cubes of wood, plastic, etc, each of whose sides has a different number of spots (1 to 6), used in games of chance and in gambling to give random numbers 2 Also called: die (*functioning as singular*) one of these cubes 3 small cubes as of vegetables, chopped meat, etc 4 no dice *slang, chiefly US & Canadian* an expression of refusal or rejection ▷ *vb* 5 to cut (food, etc) into small cubes 6 (*intr*) to gamble with or play at a game involving dice 7 (*intr*) to take a chance or risk (esp in the phrase dice with death) 8 (*tr*) *Austral informal* to abandon or reject [C14: plural of DIE[2]] > ˈdicer *n*

dicey (ˈdaɪsɪ) *adj* dicier, diciest *informal, chiefly Brit* difficult or dangerous; risky; tricky

dichloride (daɪˈklɔːraɪd) *n* a compound in which two atoms of chlorine are combined with another atom or group. Also called: bichloride

dichlorodiphenyltrichloroethane (daɪˌklɔːrəʊ daɪˌfiːnaɪltraɪˌklɔːrəʊˈiːθeɪn, -nɪl-, -ˌfɛn-) *n* the full name for DDT

dichloromethane (daɪˌklɔːrəʊˈmiːθeɪn) *n* a noxious colourless liquid widely used as a solvent, e.g. in paint strippers. Formula: CH_2Cl_2. Traditional name: methylene dichloride

dicho- *or before a vowel* **dich-** *combining form* in two parts; in pairs: *dichotomy* [from Greek *dikho-*, from *dikha* in two]

dichotomy (daɪˈkɒtəmɪ) *n, pl* -mies 1 division into two parts or classifications, esp when they are sharply distinguished or opposed 2 *botany* a simple method of branching by repeated division into two equal parts [C17: from Greek *dichotomia*; see DICHO-, -TOMY] > diˈchotomous *or* dichotomic (ˌdaɪkəʊˈtɒmɪk) *adj*

● USAGE *Dichotomy* should always refer to a division of
● some kind into two groups. It is sometimes used to
● refer to a puzzling situation which seems to involve a
● contradiction, but this use is generally thought to be
● incorrect

dichroism (ˈdaɪkrəʊˌɪzəm) *n* a property of a uniaxial crystal, such as tourmaline, of showing a perceptible difference in colour when viewed along two different axes in transmitted white light. Also called: dichromaticism See also **pleochroism**

dichromate (daɪˈkrəʊmeɪt) *n* any salt or ester of dichromic acid. Dichromate salts contain the ion $Cr_2O_7{}^{2-}$. Also called: bichromate

dichromatic (ˌdaɪkrəʊˈmætɪk) *adj* 1 Also: dichroic having or consisting of only two colours 2 (of animal species) having two different colour varieties that are independent of sex and age 3 able to perceive only two (instead of three) primary colours and the mixes of these colours > dichromatism (daɪˈkrəʊməˌtɪzəm) *n*

dichromic (daɪˈkrəʊmɪk) *adj* of or involving only two colours; dichromatic

dick (dɪk) *n slang* 1 *Brit* a fellow or person 2 clever dick *Brit* a person who is obnoxiously opinionated or self-satisfied; know-all 3 a slang word for **penis** [C16 (meaning: fellow): from the name *Dick*, familiar form of *Richard*, applied generally (like *Jack*) to any fellow, lad, etc; hence, C19: penis]

dickens (ˈdɪkɪnz) *n informal* a euphemistic word for **devil**: *what the dickens?* [C16: from the name *Dickens*]

Dickens (ˈdɪkɪnz) *n* **Charles** (**John Huffam**), pen name Boz. 1812–70, English novelist, famous for the humour and sympathy of his characterization and his criticism of social injustice. His major works include *The Pickwick Papers* (1837), *Oliver Twist* (1839), *Nicholas Nickleby* (1839), *Old Curiosity Shop* (1840–41), *Martin Chuzzlewit* (1844), *David Copperfield* (1850), *Bleak House* (1853), *Little Dorrit* (1857), and *Great Expectations* (1861)

Dickensian (dɪˈkɛnzɪən) *adj* 1 of Charles Dickens (1812–70), the English novelist, or his works

d

2 resembling or suggestive of conditions described in Dickens' novels, esp **3** grotesquely comic, as some of the characters of Dickens

dicker ('dɪkə) vb **1** to trade (goods) by bargaining; barter ▷ n **2** a petty bargain or barter [c12: ultimately from Latin *decuria* DECURY; related to Middle Low German *dēker* lot of ten hides]

dickhead ('dɪk,hɛd) n *slang* a stupid or despicable man or boy [c20: from DICK (in the sense: penis) + HEAD]

Dickinson ('dɪkɪnsªn) n **Emily**. 1830–86, US poet, noted for her short mostly unrhymed mystical lyrics

dicky¹ or **dickey** ('dɪkɪ) n, pl **dickies** or **dickeys 1 a** a woman's false blouse front, worn to fill in the neck of a jacket or low-cut dress **2** Also called: **dicky bow** Brit a bow tie **3** Also called: **dickybird, dickeybird** a child's word for a bird, esp a small one **4** a folding outside seat at the rear of some early cars [c18 (in the senses: donkey, shirt front): from *Dickey*, diminutive of *Dick* (name); the relationship of the various senses is obscure]

dicky² or **dickey** ('dɪkɪ) adj **dickier, dickiest** Brit informal in bad condition; shaky, unsteady, or unreliable: *I feel a bit dicky today* [c18: perhaps from the name *Dick* in the phrase *as queer as Dick's hatband* feeling ill]

diclinous ('daɪklɪnəs, daɪ'klaɪ-) adj **1** (of flowering plants) bearing unisexual flowers **2** (of flowers) unisexual. Compare **monoclinous** > **diclinism** n

dicotyledon (,daɪ,kɒtɪ'liːdªn, ,daɪkɒt-) n any flowering plant of the class *Dicotyledonae*, normally having two embryonic seed leaves and leaves with netlike veins. The group includes many herbaceous plants and most families of trees and shrubs > **,dicotyledonous** adj

dicta ('dɪktə) n a plural of **dictum**

Dictaphone ('dɪktə,fəʊn) n *trademark* a tape recorder designed for recording dictation and later reproducing it for typing

dictate vb (dɪk'teɪt) **1** to say (messages, letters, speeches, etc) aloud for mechanical recording or verbatim transcription by another person **2** (tr) to prescribe (commands) authoritatively **3** (intr) to act in a tyrannical manner; seek to impose one's will on others ▷ n ('dɪkteɪt) **4** an authoritative command **5** a guiding principle or rule: *the dictates of reason* [c17: from Latin *dictāre* to say repeatedly, order, from *dīcere* to say]

dictation (dɪk'teɪʃən) n **1** the act of dictating material to be recorded or taken down in writing **2** the material dictated **3** authoritative commands or the act of giving them

dictator (dɪk'teɪtə) n **1 a** a ruler who is not effectively restricted by a constitution, laws, recognized opposition, etc **b** an absolute, esp tyrannical, ruler **2** (in ancient Rome) a person appointed during a crisis to exercise supreme authority **3** a person who makes pronouncements, as on conduct, fashion, etc, which are regarded as authoritative **4** a person who behaves in an authoritarian or tyrannical manner

dictatorial (,dɪktə'tɔːrɪəl) adj **1** of or characteristic of a dictator **2** tending to dictate; tyrannical; overbearing > **,dicta'torially** adv

dictatorship (dɪk'teɪtəʃɪp) n **1** the rank, office, or period of rule of a dictator **2** government by a dictator or dictators **3** a country ruled by a dictator or dictators **4** absolute or supreme power or authority

diction ('dɪkʃən) n **1** the choice and use of words in writing or speech **2** the manner of uttering or enunciating words and sounds; elocution [c15: from Latin *dictiō* a saying, mode of expression, from *dīcere* to speak, say]

dictionary ('dɪkʃənərɪ, -ʃənrɪ) n, pl **-aries 1 a** a reference resource, in printed or electronic form, that consists of an alphabetical list of words with their meanings and parts of speech, and often a guide to accepted pronunciation and syllabification, irregular inflections of words, derived words of different parts of speech, and etymologies **b** a similar reference work giving equivalent words in two or more languages. Such dictionaries often consist of two or more parts, in each of which the alphabetical list is given in a different language **2** a reference publication listing words or terms of a particular subject or activity, giving

information about their meanings and other attributes: *a dictionary of gardening* **3** a collection of information or examples with the entries alphabetically arranged: *a dictionary of quotations* [c16: from Medieval Latin *dictiōnārium* collection of words, from Late Latin *dictiō* word; see DICTION]

dictionary attack n an attempt to hack into a computer or network by submitting every word in a dictionary as a possible password

dictum ('dɪktəm) n, pl **-tums** or **-ta** (-tə) **1** a formal or authoritative statement or assertion; pronouncement **2** a popular saying or maxim **3** law See **obiter dictum** [c16: from Latin, from *dīcere* to say]

did (dɪd) vb the past tense of **do¹**

didactic (dɪ'dæktɪk) adj **1** intended to instruct, esp excessively **2** morally instructive; improving **3** (of works of art or literature) containing a political or moral message to which aesthetic considerations are subordinated [c17: from Greek *didaktikos* skilled in teaching, from *didaskein* to teach] > **di'dactically** adv > **di'dacticism** n

didactics (dɪ'dæktɪks) n (functioning as singular) the art or science of teaching

diddle ('dɪdªl) vb informal (tr) to cheat or swindle [c19: back formation from Jeremy *Diddler*, a scrounger in J. Kenney's farce *Raising the Wind* (1803)] > **'diddler** n

Diderot ('diːdərəʊ; French didro) n **Denis** (dəni). 1713–84, French philosopher, noted particularly for his direction (1745–72) of the great French *Encyclopédie*

didgeridoo (,dɪdʒərɪ'duː) n music a deep-toned native Australian wind instrument made from a long hollowed-out piece of wood [c20: imitative of its sound]

didn't ('dɪdªnt) contraction of did not

dido ('daɪdəʊ) n, pl **-dos** or **-does** (usually plural) informal an antic; prank; trick [c19: originally US: of uncertain origin]

Dido ('daɪdəʊ) n classical myth a princess of Tyre who founded Carthage and became its queen. Virgil tells of her suicide when abandoned by her lover Aeneas

didst (dɪdst) vb archaic (used with the pronoun *thou* or its relative equivalent) a form of the past tense of **do¹**

didymium (daɪ'dɪmɪəm, dɪ-) n a mixture of the metallic rare earths neodymium and praseodymium, once thought to be an element [c19: from New Latin, from Greek *didumos* twin + -IUM]

didymous ('dɪdɪməs) adj biology in pairs or in two parts [c18: from Greek *didumos* twin, from *duo* two]

die¹ (daɪ) vb **dies, dying, died** (mainly intr) **1** (of an organism or its cells, organs, etc) to cease all biological activity permanently **2** (of something inanimate) to cease to exist; come to an end **3** (often foll by away, down, or out) to lose strength, power, or energy, esp by degrees **4** (often foll by away or down) to become calm or quiet; subside **5** to stop functioning: *the engine died* **6** to languish or pine, as with love, longing, etc **7** (usually foll by of) informal to be nearly overcome (with laughter, boredom, etc) **8** theol to lack spiritual life within the soul, thus separating it from God and leading to eternal punishment **9** (tr) to undergo or suffer (a death of a specified kind) (esp in phrases such as **die a violent death**) **10** never say die informal never give up **11** die hard to cease to exist after resistance or a struggle: *old habits die hard* **12** be in harness to die while still working or active, prior to retirement **13** be dying (foll by for or an infinitive) to be eager or desperate (for something or to do something) ▷ See also **die down, die out** [Old English *dīegan*, probably of Scandinavian origin; compare Old Norse *deyja*, Old High German *touwen*]

die² (daɪ) n **1 a** a shaped block of metal or other hard material used to cut or form metal in a drop forge, press, or similar device **b** a tool of metal, silicon carbide, or other hard material with a conical hole through which wires, rods, or tubes are drawn to reduce their diameter **2** an internally-threaded tool for cutting external threads **3** a casting mould giving accurate dimensions and a good surface to the object cast **4** architect the dado of a pedestal, usually cubic **5** another name for **dice** (sense 2) **6** the die is cast the decision that commits a person irrevocably to an action has been taken [c13 *dee*, from Old French *de*, perhaps from Vulgar Latin *datum* (unattested) a piece in games, noun use of past participle of Latin *dare* to play]

die-cast *vb* **-casts, -casting, -cast** (*tr*) to shape or form (a metal or plastic object) by introducing molten metal or plastic into a reusable mould, esp under pressure, by gravity, or by centrifugal force ⊳ 'die-,casting *n*

die down *vb* (*intr, adverb*) 1 (of some perennial plants) to wither and die above ground, leaving only the root alive during the winter 2 to lose strength or power, esp by degrees 3 to become calm or quiet

Diefenbaker ('di:fⁿn,beɪkə) *n* **John George.** 1895–1979, Canadian Conservative statesman; prime minister of Canada (1957–63)

die-hard *n* 1 a person who resists change or who holds onto an untenable position or outdated attitude 2 (*modifier*) obstinately resistant to change

dieldrin ('di:ldrɪn) *n* a crystalline insoluble substance, consisting of a chlorinated derivative of naphthalene: a contact insecticide the use of which is now restricted as it accumulates in the tissues of animals. Formula: $C_{12}H_8OCl_6$ [C20: from DIEL(S-AL)D(E)R (REACTION) + -IN]

dielectric (,daɪɪ'lektrɪk) *n* 1 a substance or medium that can sustain a static electric field within it 2 a substance or body of very low electrical conductivity; insulator ⊳ *adj* 3 of, concerned with, or having the properties of a dielectric [from DIA- + ELECTRIC] ⊳ ,die'lectrically *adv*

Dien Bien Phu (,djen bjen 'fu:) *n* a village in NW Vietnam: French military post during the Indochina War; scene of a major defeat of French forces by the Vietminh (1954)

diene ('daɪi:n) *n* *chem* a hydrocarbon that contains two carbon-to-carbon double bonds in its molecules [from DI-¹ + -ENE]

-diene *n combining form* denoting an organic compound containing two double bonds between carbon atoms: *butadiene* [from DI-¹ + -ENE]

die out or **die off** *vb* (*intr, adverb*) 1 (of a family, race, etc) to die one after another until few or none are left 2 to become extinct, esp after a period of gradual decline

Dieppe (dɪ'ep; *French* djɛp) *n* a port and resort in N France, on the English Channel. Pop: 34 653 (1999)

dieresis (daɪ'erɪsɪs) *n, pl* **-ses** (-,si:z) a variant spelling of **diaeresis**

diesel ('di:z°l) *n* 1 See **diesel engine** 2 a ship, locomotive, lorry, etc, driven by a diesel engine 3 *informal* short for **diesel oil** 4 *South African slang* any cola drink

Diesel ('di:z°l) *n* **Rudolf** ('ru:dɔlf). 1858–1913, German engineer, who invented the diesel engine (1892)

diesel-electric *n* 1 a locomotive fitted with a diesel engine driving an electric generator that feeds electric traction motors ⊳ *adj* 2 of or relating to such a locomotive or system

diesel engine or **diesel motor** *n* a type of internal-combustion engine in which atomized fuel oil is sprayed into the cylinder and ignited by compression alone

diesel oil or **diesel fuel** *n* a fuel obtained from petroleum distillation that is used in diesel engines. It has a relatively low ignition temperature (540°C) and is ignited by the heat of compression. Also called (Brit): **derv**

Dies Irae (*Latin* 'di:eɪz 'ɪəraɪ) *n* 1 *Christianity* a famous Latin hymn of the 13th century, describing the Last Judgment. It is used in the Mass for the dead 2 a musical setting of this hymn, usually part of a setting of the Requiem [literally: day of wrath]

diesis ('daɪɪsɪs) *n, pl* **-ses** (-,si:z) *printing* another name for **double dagger** [C16: via Latin from Greek: a quarter tone, literally: a sending through, from *diienai*; the double dagger was originally used in musical notation]

diestock ('daɪ,stɒk) *n* the device holding the dies used to cut an external screw thread

diet¹ ('daɪət) *n* 1 a specific allowance or selection of food, esp prescribed to control weight or in disorders in which certain foods are contraindicated: *a salt-free diet; a 900-calorie diet* 2 the food and drink that a person or animal regularly consumes 3 regular activities or occupations ⊳ *vb* 4 (*usually intr*) to follow or cause to

follow a dietary regimen [C13: from Old French *diete*, from Latin *diaeta*, from Greek *diaita* mode of living, from *diaitan* to direct one's own life] ⊳ 'dieter *n*

diet² ('daɪət) *n* 1 (*sometimes capital*) a legislative assembly in various countries, such as Japan 2 Also called: Reichstag (*sometimes capital*) the assembly of the estates of the Holy Roman Empire 3 *Scots law* a single session of a court [C15: from Medieval Latin *diēta* public meeting, probably from Latin *diaeta* DIET¹ but associated with Latin *diēs* day]

dietary ('daɪətərɪ, -trɪ) *adj* 1 of or relating to a diet ⊳ *n, pl* **-taries** 2 a regulated diet 3 a system of dieting

dietary fibre *n* fibrous substances in fruits and vegetables, such as the structural polymers of cell walls, consumption of which aids digestion and is believed to help prevent certain diseases. Also called: roughage

dietetic (,daɪɪ'tetɪk) or **dietetical** *adj* 1 denoting or relating to diet or the regulation of food intake 2 prepared for special dietary requirements ⊳ ,die'tetically *adv*

dietetics (,daɪɪ'tetɪks) *n* (*functioning as singular*) the scientific study and regulation of food intake and preparation

diethylene glycol (daɪ'eθɪ,li:n 'glaɪkɒl) *n* a colourless soluble liquid used as an antifreeze and solvent. Formula: $(C_2H_4OH)_2O$

diethylstilbestrol or **diethylstilboestrol** (daɪ,eθɪlstɪl'bestrɒl, -,i:θaɪl-) *n* a synthetic hormone with oestrogenic properties, used to relieve menopausal symptoms. Formula: $OHC_6H_4CH{:}CHC_6H_4OH$. Also called: stilbestrol, stilboestrol

dietician or **dietitian** (,daɪɪ'tɪʃən) *n* a person who specializes in dietetics

Dietrich (*German* 'di:trɪç) *n* **Marlene** (mar'le:nə), real name *Maria Magdalene von Losch*. 1901–92, US film actress and cabaret singer, born in Germany

differ ('dɪfə) *vb* (*intr*) 1 (*often foll by from*) to be dissimilar in quality, nature, or degree (to); vary (from) 2 (*often foll by from* or *with*) to be at variance (with); disagree (with) 3 *dialect* to quarrel or dispute [C14: from Latin *differre*, literally: to bear off in different directions, hence scatter, put off, be different, from *dis-* apart + *ferre* to bear]

difference ('dɪfərəns, 'dɪfrəns) *n* 1 the state or quality of being unlike 2 a specific instance of being unlike 3 a distinguishing mark or feature 4 a significant change in a situation 5 a disagreement or argument 6 a degree of distinctness, as between two people or things 7 the result of the subtraction of one number, quantity, etc, from another 8 *maths* (of two sets) the set of members of the first that are not members of the second 9 *heraldry* an addition to the arms of a family to represent a younger branch 10 make a difference **a** to have an effect **b** to treat differently 11 split the difference **a** to settle a dispute by a compromise **b** to divide a remainder equally 12 with a difference with some peculiarly distinguishing quality, good or bad

different ('dɪfərənt, 'dɪfrənt) *adj* 1 partly or completely unlike 2 not identical or the same; other 3 out of the ordinary; unusual ⊳ 'differently *adv* ⊳ 'differentness *n*

⊛ USAGE The constructions *different from, different to*, and
⊛ *different than* are all found in the works of writers of
⊛ English during the past. Nowadays, however, the
⊛ most widely acceptable preposition to use after
⊛ *different* is *from*. *Different to* is common in British
⊛ English, though it is considered by some people to be
⊛ incorrect, or less acceptable. *Different than* is a standard
⊛ construction in American English, and has
⊛ theadvantage of conciseness when a clause or phrase
⊛ follows, as in *this result is only slightly different than in the*
⊛ *US*. As, however, this idiom is not regarded as totally
⊛ acceptable in British usage, it is preferable either to
⊛ use *different from: this result is only slightly different from that*
⊛ *obtained in the US* or to rephrase the sentence: *this result*
⊛ *differs only slightly from that in the US*

differentia (,dɪfə'renʃɪə) *n, pl* **-tiae** (-ʃɪ,i:) *logic* a feature by which two subclasses of the same class of named objects can be distinguished [C19: from Latin: diversity, DIFFERENCE]

d

differential (ˌdɪfə'rɛnʃəl) *adj* **1** of, relating to, or using a difference **2** constituting a difference; distinguishing **3** *maths* of, containing, or involving one or more derivatives or differentials **4** *physics, engineering* relating to, operating on, or based on the difference between two effects, motions, forces, etc ▷ *n* **5** a factor that differentiates between two comparable things **6** *maths* **a** an increment in a given function, expressed as the product of the derivative of that function and the corresponding increment in the independent variable **b** an increment in a given function of two or more variables, $f(x_1, x_2, ...x_n)$, expressed as the sum of the products of each partial derivative and the increment in the corresponding variable **7** See also **differential gear** **8** *chiefly Brit* the difference between rates of pay for different types of labour, esp when forming a pay structure within an industry **9** (in commerce) a difference in rates, esp between comparable labour services or transportation routes ▷ ˌdiffer'entially *adv*
differential calculus *n* the branch of calculus concerned with the study, evaluation, and use of derivatives and differentials
differential equation *n* an equation containing differentials or derivatives of a function of one independent variable. A **partial differential equation** results from a function of more than one variable
differential gear *n* the epicyclic gear mounted in the driving axle of a road vehicle that permits one driving wheel to rotate faster than the other, as when cornering
differential operator *n* any operator involving differentiation, such as the mathematical operator del ∇, used in vector analysis, where $\nabla = i\partial/\partial x + j\partial/\partial y + k\partial/\partial z$, **i**, **j**, and **k** being unit vectors and $\partial/\partial x, \partial/\partial y$, and $\partial/\partial z$ the partial derivatives of a function in *x*, *y*, and *z*
differentiate (ˌdɪfə'rɛnʃɪˌeɪt) *vb* **1** (*tr*) to serve to distinguish between **2** (when *intr*, often foll by *between*) to perceive, show, or make a difference (in or between); discriminate **3** (*intr*) to become dissimilar or distinct **4** *maths* to perform a differentiation on (a quantity, expression, etc) **5** (*intr*) (of unspecialized cells, etc) to change during development to more specialized forms ▷ ˌdiffer'enti,ator *n*
differentiation (ˌdɪfəˌrɛnʃɪ'eɪʃən) *n* **1** the act, process, or result of differentiating **2** *maths* an operation used in calculus in which the derivative of a function or variable is determined; the inverse of integration
difficult ('dɪfɪkˀlt) *adj* **1** not easy to do; requiring effort **2** not easy to understand or solve; intricate **3** hard to deal with; troublesome: *a difficult child* **4** not easily convinced, pleased, or satisfied **5** full of hardships or trials [C14: back formation from DIFFICULTY] ▷ 'difficultly *adv*
difficulty ('dɪfɪkˀltɪ) *n, pl* -ties **1** the state or quality of being difficult **2** a task, problem, etc, that is hard to deal with **3** (*often plural*) a troublesome or embarrassing situation, esp a financial one **4** a dispute or disagreement **5** (*often plural*) an objection or obstacle **6** a trouble or source of trouble; worry **7** lack of ease; awkwardness [C14: from Latin *difficultās*, from *difficilis* difficult, from *dis-* not + *facilis* easy, FACILE]
diffident ('dɪfɪdənt) *adj* lacking self-confidence; timid; shy [C15: from Latin *diffidere* to distrust, from *dis-* not + *fidere* to trust] ▷ 'diffidence *n* ▷ 'diffidently *adv*
diffract (dɪ'frækt) *vb* to undergo or cause to undergo diffraction ▷ dif'fractive *adj* ▷ dif'fractively *adv* ▷ dif'fractiveness *n*
diffraction (dɪ'frækʃən) *n* **1** *physics* a deviation in the direction of a wave at the edge of an obstacle in its path **2** any phenomenon caused by diffraction and interference of light, such as the formation of light and dark fringes by the passage of light through a small aperture [C17: from New Latin *diffractiō* a breaking to pieces, from Latin *diffringere* to shatter, from *dis-* apart + *frangere* to break]
diffuse *vb* (dɪ'fjuːz) **1** to spread or cause to spread in all directions **2** to undergo or cause to undergo diffusion **3** to scatter or cause to scatter; disseminate; disperse ▷ *adj* (dɪ'fjuːs) **4** spread out over a wide area **5** lacking conciseness **6** characterized by or exhibiting diffusion

[C15: from Latin *diffusus* spread abroad, from *diffundere* to pour forth, from *dis-* away + *fundere* to pour] ▷ diffusely (dɪ'fjuːslɪ) *adv* ▷ diffuseness *n* ▷ diffusible (dɪ'fjuːzəbˀl) *adj*
● **USAGE** This word is quite commonly misused instead of *defuse*, when talking about calming down a situation
diffuser *or* **diffusor** (dɪ'fjuːzə) *n* **1** a person or thing that diffuses **2** a part of a lighting fixture consisting of a translucent or frosted covering or of a rough reflector: used to scatter the light and prevent glare **3** a cone, wedge, or baffle placed in front of the diaphragm of a loudspeaker to diffuse the sound waves **4** a duct, esp in a wind tunnel or jet engine, that widens gradually in the direction of flow to reduce the speed and increase the pressure of the air or fluid **5** *photog* a light-scattering medium, such as a screen of fine fabric, placed in the path of a source of light to reduce the sharpness of shadows and thus soften the lighting **6** a device, attached to a hairdryer, that diffuses the warm air as it comes out
diffusion (dɪ'fjuːʒən) *n* **1** the act or process of diffusing or being diffused; dispersion **2** verbosity **3** *physics* **a** the random thermal motion of atoms, molecules, clusters of atoms, etc, in gases, liquids, and some solids **b** the transfer of atoms or molecules by their random motion from one part of a medium to another **4** *physics* the transmission or reflection of electromagnetic radiation, esp light, in which the radiation is scattered in many directions and not directly reflected or refracted; scattering **5** *anthropol* the transmission of social institutions, skills, and myths from one culture to another
diffusive (dɪ'fjuːsɪv) *adj* characterized by diffusion ▷ diffusively *adv* ▷ diffusiveness *n*
dig (dɪg) *vb* digs, digging, dug **1** (when *tr*, often foll by *up*) to cut into, break up, and turn over or remove (earth, soil, etc), esp with a spade **2** to form or excavate (a hole, tunnel, passage, etc) by digging, usually with an implement or (of animals) with feet, claws, etc **3** (often foll by *through*) to make or force (one's way), esp by removing obstructions: *he dug his way through the crowd* **4** (*tr*, often foll by *out* or *up*) to obtain by digging **5** (*tr*; often foll by *out* or *up*) to find or discover by effort or searching: *to dig out unexpected facts* **6** (*tr*; foll by *in* or *into*) to thrust or jab (a sharp instrument, weapon, etc); poke **7** (*tr*; foll by *in* or *into*) to mix (compost, etc) with soil by digging **8** (*tr*) *informal* to like, understand, or appreciate **9** (*intr*) *US slang* to work hard, esp for an examination ▷ *n* **10** the act of digging **11** a thrust or poke, esp in the ribs **12** a cutting or sarcastic remark **13** *informal* an archaeological excavation ▷ See also **dig in** [C13 *diggen*, of uncertain origin]
Digby chicken *or* **Digby chick** ('dɪgbɪ) *n Canadian informal* dried herring [after *Digby*, a town in Nova Scotia, Canada]
digerati (ˌdɪdʒə'rɑːtɪ) *pl n* the people who earn large amounts of money through internet-related business
digest *vb* (dɪ'dʒɛst, daɪ-) **1** to subject (food) to a process of digestion **2** (*tr*) to assimilate mentally **3** *chem* to soften or disintegrate or be softened or disintegrated by the action of heat, moisture, or chemicals; decompose **4** (*tr*) to arrange in a methodical or systematic order; classify **5** (*tr*) to reduce to a summary ▷ *n* ('daɪdʒɛst) **6** a comprehensive and systematic compilation of information or material, often condensed **7** a magazine, periodical, etc, that summarizes news of current events **8** a compilation of rules of law based on decided cases [C14: from Late Latin *dīgesta* writings grouped under various heads, from Latin *dīgerere* to divide, from *di-* apart + *gerere* to bear]
Digest ('daɪdʒɛst) *n Roman law* an arrangement of excerpts from the writings and opinions of eminent lawyers, contained in 50 books compiled by order of Justinian in the sixth century AD
digestant (dɪ'dʒɛstənt, daɪ-) *n* a substance, such as hydrochloric acid or a bile salt, that promotes or aids digestion
digestible (dɪ'dʒɛstəbˀl, daɪ-) *adj* capable of being

digested or easy to digest > di,gesti'bility or di'gestibleness n

digestion (dɪˈdʒɛstʃən, daɪ-) n 1 the act or process in living organisms of breaking down ingested food material into easily absorbed and assimilated substances by the action of enzymes and other agents 2 mental assimilation, esp of ideas 3 *bacteriol* the decomposition of sewage by the action of bacteria 4 *chem* the treatment of material with heat, solvents, chemicals, etc, to cause softening or decomposition [c14: from Old French, from Latin *digestiō* a dissolving, digestion] > di'gestional *adj*

digestive (dɪˈdʒɛstɪv, daɪ-) or **digestant** (daɪˈdʒɛstənt) *adj* relating to, aiding, or subjecting to digestion > di'gestively *adv*

digestive biscuit n a round semisweet biscuit made from wholemeal flour

digger ('dɪɡə) n 1 a person, animal, or machine that digs 2 a miner, esp one who digs for gold 3 a tool or part of a machine used for excavation, esp a mechanical digger fitted with a head for digging trenches

Digger ('dɪɡə) n (*sometimes not capital*) *archaic, slang* a an Australian or New Zealander, esp a soldier: often used as a term of address b (*as modifier*): *a Digger accent*

diggings ('dɪɡɪŋz) *pl n* 1 (*functioning as plural*) material that has been dug out 2 (*functioning as singular or plural*) a place where mining, esp gold mining, has taken place 3 (*functioning as plural*) *Brit informal* a less common name for **digs**

dight (daɪt) *vb* **dights, dighting, dight** or **dighted** (*tr*) *archaic* to adorn or equip, as for battle [Old English *dihtan* to compose, from Latin *dictāre* to DICTATE]

Digibox ('dɪdʒɪbɒks) n *trademark* a device that converts the signals from a digital television broadcast into a form that can be viewed on a standard television set [c20: from DIGI(TAL) (sense 3) + BOX¹]

digicam ('dɪdʒɪˌkæm) n a digital camera

dig in *vb* (*adverb*) 1 *military* to create (a defensive position) by digging foxholes, trenches, etc 2 *informal* to entrench (oneself) firmly 3 (*intr*) *informal* to defend or maintain a position firmly, as in an argument 4 (*intr*) *informal* to begin vigorously to eat: *don't wait, just dig in* 5 **dig one's heels in** *informal* to refuse stubbornly to move or be persuaded

digit ('dɪdʒɪt) n 1 a finger or toe 2 Also called: **figure** any of the ten Arabic numerals from 0 to 9 [c15: from Latin *digitus* toe, finger]

digital ('dɪdʒɪtˀl) *adj* 1 of, relating to, resembling, or possessing a digit or digits 2 performed with the fingers 3 representing data as a series of numerical values 4 displaying information as numbers rather than by a pointer moving over a dial ▷ n 5 *music* one of the keys on the manuals of an organ or on a piano, harpsichord, etc > 'digitally *adv*

digital audio tape n magnetic tape on which sound is recorded digitally, giving high-fidelity reproduction. Abbreviation: DAT

digital camera n a camera that produces digital images that can be stored in a computer, displayed on a screen and printed

digital clock or **digital watch** n a clock or watch in which the hours, minutes, and sometimes seconds are indicated by digits, rather than by hands on a dial

digital compact cassette n a magnetic tape cassette on which sound can be recorded in a digital format. Abbreviation: DCC

digital computer n an electronic computer in which the input is discrete rather than continuous, consisting of combinations of numbers, letters, and other characters written in an appropriate programming language and represented internally in binary notation

digital divide n *informal* the gap between those people who have internet access and those who do not

digitalin (ˌdɪdʒɪˈteɪlɪn) n a poisonous amorphous crystalline mixture of glycosides extracted from digitalis leaves and formerly used in treating heart disease [c19: from DIGITAL(IS) + -IN]

digitalis (ˌdɪdʒɪˈteɪlɪs) n 1 any Eurasian scrophulariaceous plant of the genus *Digitalis*, such as

the foxglove, having bell-shaped flowers and a basal rosette of leaves 2 a drug prepared from the dried leaves or seeds of the foxglove: a mixture of glycosides used medicinally to treat heart failure and some abnormal heart rhythms [c17: from New Latin, from Latin: relating to a finger (referring to the corollas of the flower); based on German *Fingerhut* foxglove, literally: finger-hat or thimble]

digitalize or **digitalise** ('dɪdʒɪtəˌlaɪz) *vb* (*tr*) another word for **digitize**

digital mapping n a method of preparing maps in which the data is stored in a computer for ease of access and updating > **digital map** n

digital radio n 1 radio in which the audio information is transmitted in digital form and decoded at the radio receiver 2 a radio that can receive and decode digital audio information

digital recording n a sound recording process that converts audio or analogue signals into a series of pulses that correspond to the voltage level. These can be stored on tape or on any other memory system

digital signature n *computing* electronic proof of a person's identity involving the use of encryption; used to authenticate documents

digital television n 1 television in which the picture information is transmitted in digital form and decoded at the television receiver 2 a television set that can decode digital picture information and convert it into visible images

digital versatile disk or **digital video disk** n See DVD

digital video n video output based on digital rather than analogue signals

digitate ('dɪdʒɪˌteɪt) or **digitated** *adj* 1 (of compound leaves) having the leaflets in the form of a spread hand 2 (of animals) having digits or corresponding parts > 'digi,tately *adv* > ,digi'tation n

digitigrade ('dɪdʒɪtɪˌɡreɪd) *adj* 1 (of dogs, cats, horses, etc) walking so that only the toes touch the ground ▷ n 2 a digitigrade animal

digitize or **digitise** ('dɪdʒɪˌtaɪz) *vb* (*tr*) to transcribe (data) into a digital form so that it can be directly processed by a computer > ,digiti'zation or ,digiti'sation n > 'digi,tizer or 'digi,tiser n

digitized or **digitised** ('dɪdʒɪˌtaɪzd) *adj computing* recorded or stored in digital form: *export your digitized colour photos*

dignified ('dɪɡnɪˌfaɪd) *adj* characterized by dignity of manner or appearance; stately > 'digni,fiedly *adv* > 'digni,fiedness n

dignify ('dɪɡnɪˌfaɪ) *vb* **-fies, -fying, -fied** (*tr*) 1 to invest with honour or dignity; ennoble 2 to add distinction to 3 to add a semblance of dignity to, esp by the use of a pretentious name or title [c15: from Old French *dignifier*, from Late Latin *dignificāre*, from Latin *dignus* worthy + *facere* to make]

dignitary ('dɪɡnɪtərɪ, -trɪ) n, *pl* **-taries** a person of high official position or rank, esp in government or the church

dignity ('dɪɡnɪtɪ) n, *pl* **-ties** 1 a formal, stately, or grave bearing 2 the state or quality of being worthy of honour 3 relative importance; rank 4 sense of self-importance (often in the phrases **stand** (or **be**) **on one's dignity, beneath one's dignity**) 5 high rank, esp in government or the church [c13: from Old French *dignite*, from Latin *dignitās* merit, from *dignus* worthy]

digoxin (daɪˈdʒɒksɪn) n a glycoside extracted from the leaves of the woolly foxglove (*Digitalis lanata*) and used in the treatment of heart failure. Formula: $C_{41}H_{64}O_{14}$

digraph ('daɪɡrɑːf, -ɡræf) n a combination of two letters or characters used to represent a single speech sound such as *gh* in English *tough* > **digraphic** (daɪˈɡræfɪk) *adj*

digress (daɪˈɡrɛs) *vb* (*intr*) 1 to depart from the main subject in speech or writing 2 to wander from one's path or main direction [c16: from Latin *dīgressus* turned aside, from *dīgredī*, from *dis-* apart + *gradī* to go] > di'gresser n > di'gression n > di'gressional *adj*

digressive (daɪˈɡrɛsɪv) *adj* characterized by digression or tending to digress > di'gressively *adv* > di'gressiveness n

digs (dɪɡz) *pl n Brit informal* lodgings [c19: shortened from DIGGINGS, perhaps referring to where one *digs* or works, but see also DIG IN]

dihedral (daɪˈhiːdrəl) *adj* **1** having or formed by two intersecting planes; two-sided ▷ *n* **2** Also called: dihedron, dihedral angle the figure formed by two intersecting planes **3** the upward inclination of an aircraft wing in relation to the lateral axis

Dijon (*French* diʒɔ̃) *n* a city in E France: capital of the former duchy of Burgundy. Pop: 149 867 (1999)

dik-dik (ˈdɪkˌdɪk) *n* any small antelope of the genus *Madoqua*, inhabiting semiarid regions of Africa, having an elongated muzzle and, in the male, small stout horns [C19: an East African name, probably of imitative origin]

dike (daɪk) *n*, *vb* a variant spelling of **dyke¹**

diktat (ˈdɪktɑːt) *n* **1** decree or settlement imposed, esp by a ruler or a victorious nation **2** a dogmatic statement [German: dictation, from Latin *dictātum*, from *dictāre* to DICTATE]

dilapidate (dɪˈlæpɪˌdeɪt) *vb* to fall or cause to fall into ruin or decay [C16: from Latin *dīlapidāre* to scatter, waste, from *dis-* apart + *lapidāre* to stone, throw stones, from *lapis* stone]

dilapidated (dɪˈlæpɪˌdeɪtɪd) *adj* falling to pieces or in a state of disrepair; shabby

dilate (daɪˈleɪt, dɪ-) *vb* **1** to expand or cause to expand; make or become wider or larger **2** (*intr*; often foll by *on* or *upon*) to speak or write at length; expand or enlarge [C14: from Latin *dīlātāre* to spread out, amplify, from *dis-* apart + *lātus* wide] ▷ diˈlatable *adj* ▷ diˌlataˈbility or diˈlatableness *n* ▷ diˈlation or dilatation (ˌdaɪləˈteɪʃən, ˌdɪl-) *n* ▷ diˈlative *adj*

dilatory (ˈdɪlətərɪ, -trɪ) *adj* **1** tending or inclined to delay or waste time **2** intended or designed to waste time or defer action [C15: from Late Latin *dīlātōrius* inclined to delay, from *differre* to postpone; see DIFFER] ▷ ˈdilatorily *adv* ▷ ˈdilatoriness *n*

dildo or **dildoe** (ˈdɪldəʊ) *n*, *pl* **-dos** or **-does** an object used as a substitute for an erect penis [C16: of unknown origin]

dilemma (dɪˈlɛmə, daɪ-) *n* **1** a situation necessitating a choice between two equal, esp equally undesirable, alternatives **2** a problem that seems incapable of a solution **3** *logic* a form of argument one of whose premises is the conjunction of two conditional statements and the other of which affirms the disjunction of their antecedents, and whose conclusion is the disjunction of their consequents. Its form is *if p then q and if r then s; either p or r so either q or s* **4** on the horns of a dilemma **a** faced with the choice between two equally unpalatable alternatives **b** in an awkward situation [C16: via Latin from Greek, from DI-¹ + *lēmma* assumption, proposition, from *lambanein* to take, grasp] ▷ dilemmatic (ˌdɪlɪˈmætɪk, ˌdaɪlɪ-) *adj*

● USAGE The use of *dilemma* to refer to a problem that
● seems incapable of a solution is considered by some
● people to be incorrect

dilettante (ˌdɪlɪˈtɑːntɪ) *n*, *pl* **-tantes** or **-tanti** (-ˈtɑːntɪ) **1** a person whose interest in a subject is superficial rather than professional **2** a person who loves the arts ▷ *adj* **3** of or characteristic of a dilettante [C18: from Italian, from *dilettare* to delight, from Latin *dēlectāre*] ▷ ˌdiletˈtantish or ˌdiletˈtanteish *adj* ▷ ˌdiletˈtantism or ˌdiletˈtanteism *n*

diligence¹ (ˈdɪlɪdʒəns) *n* **1** steady and careful application **2** proper attention or care [C14: from Latin *dīligentia* care, attentiveness]

diligence² (ˈdɪlɪdʒəns; *French* diliʒɑ̃s) *n* *history* a stagecoach [C18: from French, shortened from *carosse de diligence*, literally: coach of speed]

diligent (ˈdɪlɪdʒənt) *adj* **1** careful and persevering in carrying out tasks or duties **2** carried out with care and perseverance: *diligent work* [C14: from Old French, from Latin *dīligere* to value, from *dis-* apart + *legere* to read] ▷ ˈdiligently *adv*

dill¹ (dɪl) *n* **1** an umbelliferous aromatic Eurasian plant, *Anethum graveolens*, with finely dissected leaves and umbrella-shaped clusters of yellow flowers **2** the leaves or seedlike fruits of this plant, used for flavouring in pickles, soups, etc, and in medicine [Old English *dile*;

related to Old High German *tilli*]

dill² *n* *informal, chiefly Austral & NZ* a fool; idiot [C20: from DILLY²]

dill pickle *n* a pickled cucumber flavoured with dill

dilly¹ (ˈdɪlɪ) *n*, *pl* **-lies** *slang, chiefly US & Canadian* a person or thing that is remarkable [C20: perhaps from girl's proper name *Dilly*]

dilly² (ˈdɪlɪ) *adj* **-lier, -liest** *Austral & NZ slang* silly [C20: perhaps from SILLY]

dilly bag *n Austral* a small bag, esp one made of plaited grass, etc, often used for carrying food [from native Australian *dilly* small bag or basket]

dilly-dally (ˌdɪlɪˈdælɪ) *vb* **-lies, -lying, -lied** (*intr*) *informal* to loiter or vacillate [C17: by reduplication from DALLY]

dilute (daɪˈluːt) *vb* **1** to make or become less concentrated, esp by adding water or a thinner **2** to make or become weaker in force, effect, etc ▷ *adj* **3** *chem* **a** (of a solution, suspension, mixture, etc) having a low concentration or a concentration that has been reduced by admixture **b** (of a substance) present in solution, esp a weak solution in water: *dilute acetic acid* [C16: from Latin *dīluere*, from *dis-* apart + *-luere*, from *lavāre* to wash] ▷ diˈluter *n*

dilution (daɪˈluːʃən) *n* **1** the act of diluting or state of being diluted **2** a diluted solution

diluvial (daɪˈluːvɪəl, dɪ-) or **diluvian** *adj* of or connected with a deluge, esp with the great Flood described in Genesis [C17: from Late Latin *dīluviālis*; see DILUVIUM]

diluvium (daɪˈluːvɪəm, dɪ-) *n*, *pl* **-via** (-vɪə) *geology* a former name for glacial drift. See drift (sense 12) [C19: from Latin: flood, from *dīluere* to wash away; see DILUTE]

dim (dɪm) *adj* **dimmer, dimmest** **1** badly illuminated **2** not clearly seen; indistinct; faint **3** having weak or indistinct vision **4** lacking in understanding; mentally dull **5** not clear in the mind; obscure: *a dim memory* **6** lacking in brilliance, brightness, or lustre **7** tending to be unfavourable; gloomy or disapproving (esp in the phrase **take a dim view**) ▷ *vb* **dims, dimming, dimmed** **8** to become or cause to become dim **9** (*tr*) to cause to seem less bright, as by comparison **10** (*tr*) *US & Canadian* to switch (car headlights) from the main to the lower beam. [Old English *dimm*; related to Old Norse *dimmr* gloomy, dark] ▷ ˈdimly *adv* ▷ ˈdimness *n*

DiMaggio (dɪˈmædʒɪəʊ) *n* **Joe.** 1914–99, US baseball player

Dimashq (diːˈmæʃk) *n* an Arabic name for **Damascus**

Dimbleby (ˈdɪmbᵊlbɪ) *n* **Richard.** 1913–65, British broadcaster

dime (daɪm) *n* **1** a coin of the US and Canada, worth one tenth of a dollar or ten cents **2 a dime a dozen** very cheap or common [C14: from Old French *disme*, from Latin *decimus* tenth, from *decem* ten]

dimenhydrinate (ˌdaɪmɛnˈhaɪdrɪˌneɪt) *n* a white slightly soluble bitter-tasting crystalline substance: an antihistamine used in the prevention of nausea, esp in travel sickness. Formula: $C_{24}H_{28}ClN_5O_3$ [from *dime(thyl* + AMI)N(E) + (*diphen*)*hydr(am)in(e* + -ATE¹]

dime novel *n US* (formerly) a cheap melodramatic novel, usually in paperback

dimension (dɪˈmɛnʃən) *n* **1** (*often plural*) a measurement of the size of something in a particular direction, such as the length, width, height, or diameter **2** (*often plural*) scope; size; extent **3** aspect: *a new dimension to politics* **4** *maths* the number of coordinates required to locate a point in space ▷ *vb* **5** (*tr*) *chiefly US* to shape or cut to specified dimensions [C14: from Old French, from Latin *dīmensiō* an extent, from *dīmētīrī* to measure out, from *mētīrī*] ▷ diˈmensional *adj* ▷ diˈmensionless *adj*

dimer (ˈdaɪmə) *n chem* a molecule composed of two identical simpler molecules (monomers) [C20: from DI-¹ + -MER]

dimerize or **dimerise** (ˈdaɪməˌraɪz) *vb* to react or cause to react to form a dimer ▷ ˌdimeriˈzation or ˌdimeriˈsation *n*

dimeter (ˈdɪmɪtə) *n prosody* a line of verse consisting of two metrical feet or a verse written in this metre

dimethylformamide (daɪˌmiːθaɪlˈfɔːməˌmaɪd, -ˌmɛθɪl-) *n* a colourless liquid widely used as a solvent and sometimes as a catalyst. Formula: $(CH_3)_2NCHO$. Abbreviation: DMF

dimethylsulphoxide or **dimethylsulfoxide** (dai,miːθailsʌlˈfɒksaid, -,meθil-) n a colourless odourless liquid substance used as a solvent and in medicine as an agent to improve the penetration of drugs applied to the skin. Formula: (CH₃)₂SO

diminish (dɪˈmɪnɪʃ) vb 1 to make or become smaller, fewer, or less 2 (tr) architect to cause (a column, etc) to taper 3 (tr) music to decrease (a minor or perfect interval) by a semitone 4 to belittle or be belittled; reduce in authority, status, etc; depreciate [c15: blend of diminuen to lessen (from Latin dēminuere to make smaller, from minuere to reduce) + archaic minish to lessen]
> diˈminishable adj

diminished (dɪˈmɪnɪʃt) adj 1 reduced or lessened; made smaller 2 music denoting any minor or perfect interval reduced by a semitone

diminished responsibility n law a plea under which proof of an impairing abnormality of mind is submitted as demonstrating lack of premeditation and therefore criminal responsibility

diminishing returns pl n economics progressively smaller rises in output resulting from the increased application of a variable input, such as labour, to a fixed quantity, as of capital or land

diminuendo (dɪ,mɪnjʊˈɛndəʊ) music ▷ n, pl -dos 1 a a gradual decrease in loudness or the musical direction indicating this b a musical passage affected by a diminuendo ▷ adj 2 gradually decreasing in loudness 3 with a diminuendo [c18: from Italian, from diminuire to DIMINISH]

diminution (,dɪmɪˈnjuːʃən) n 1 reduction; decrease 2 music the presentation of the subject of a fugue, etc, in which the note values are reduced in length [c14: from Latin dēminūtiō; see DIMINISH]

diminutive (dɪˈmɪnjʊtɪv) adj 1 very small; tiny 2 grammar a denoting an affix added to a word to convey the meaning small or unimportant or to express affection, as for example the suffix -ette in French b denoting a word formed by the addition of a diminutive affix ▷ n 3 grammar a diminutive word or affix 4 a tiny person or thing > diˈminutively adv > diˈminutiveness n

dimissory (dɪˈmɪsərɪ) adj 1 granting permission to be ordained: a bishop's dimissory letter 2 granting permission to depart

Dimitrovo (Bulgarian di'mitrovo) n the former name (1949–62) of **Pernik**

dimity (ˈdɪmɪtɪ) n, pl -ties a a light strong cotton fabric with woven stripes or squares b (as modifier): a dimity bonnet [c15: from Medieval Latin dimitum, from Greek dimiton, from DI-¹ + mitos thread of the warp]

dimmer (ˈdɪmə) n 1 a device, such as a rheostat, for varying the current through an electric light and thus changing the illumination 2 (often plural) US a a dipped headlight on a road vehicle b a parking light on a car

dimorphism (daɪˈmɔːfɪzəm) n 1 the occurrence within a plant of two distinct forms of any part, such as the leaves of some aquatic plants 2 the occurrence in an animal or plant species of two distinct types of individual 3 a property of certain substances that enables them to exist in two distinct crystalline forms
> diˈmorphic or diˈmorphous adj

dimple (ˈdɪmpəl) n 1 a small natural dent or crease in the flesh, esp on the cheeks or chin 2 any slight depression in a surface ▷ vb 3 to make or become dimpled 4 (intr) to produce dimples by smiling [c13 dympull; compare Old English dyppan to dip, German Tümpel pool] > 'dimply adj

dim sum (ˈdɪm ˈsʌm) n a Chinese appetizer of steamed dumplings containing various fillings [Cantonese]

dimwit (ˈdɪm,wɪt) n informal a stupid or silly person
> ,dim-'witted adj > ,dim-'wittedness n

din (dɪn) n 1 a loud discordant confused noise ▷ vb dins, dinning, dinned 2 (tr; usually foll by into) to instil (into a person) by constant repetition 3 (tr) to subject to a din 4 (intr) to make a din [Old English dynn; compare Old Norse dynr, Old High German tuni]

DIN (dɪn) n 1 a formerly used logarithmic expression of the speed of a photographic film, plate, etc, given as $-10\log_{10}E$, where E is the exposure of a point 0.1 density units above the fog level; high-speed films have high numbers 2 a system of standard plugs, sockets, and cables formerly used for interconnecting domestic audio and video equipment [c20: from German D(eutsche) I(ndustrie) N(orm) German Industry Standard]

dinar (ˈdiːnɑː) n the standard monetary unit of the following countries or territories. Algeria: divided into 100 centimes. Bahrain: divided into 1000 fils. Iraq: divided into 1000 fils. Jordan: divided into 1000 fils. Kuwait: divided into 1000 fils. Libya: divided into 1000 dirhams. Serbia: divided into 100 paras (formerly the standard monetary unit of Yugoslavia). Sudan, Tunisia: divided into 1000 millimes [c17: from Arabic, from Late Greek dēnarion, from Latin dēnārius DENARIUS]

d'Indy (French dɛ̃di) n (**Paul Marie Theodore**) **Vincent** (vɛ̃sɔ̃). 1851–1931, French composer. His works include operas, chamber music, and the Symphony on a French Mountaineer's Song (1866)

dine (daɪn) vb 1 (intr) to eat dinner 2 (intr; often foll by on, off, or upon) to make one's meal (of): the guests dined upon roast beef 3 (tr) informal to entertain to dinner (esp in the phrase **to wine and dine someone**) [c13: from Old French disner, contracted from Vulgar Latin disjējūnāre (unattested) to cease fasting, from dis- not + Late Latin jējūnāre to fast; see JEJUNE]

dine out vb (intr, adverb) 1 to dine away from home, esp in a restaurant 2 (foll by on) to have dinner at the expense of someone else mainly for the sake of one's knowledge or conversation about (a subject or story)

diner (ˈdaɪnə) n 1 a person eating a meal, esp in a restaurant 2 chiefly US & Canadian a small restaurant, often at the roadside 3 a fashionable bar, or a section of one, where food is served

Dinesen (ˈdɪnɪsən) n Isak (ˈaɪzək), pen name of Baroness Karen Blixen. 1885–1962, Danish author of short stories in Danish and English, including Seven Gothic Tales (1934) and Winter's Tales (1942). Her life story was told in the film Out of Africa (1986)

dinette (daɪˈnɛt) n an alcove or small area for use as a dining room

ding (dɪŋ) vb 1 to ring or cause to ring, esp with tedious repetition 2 (tr) another word for din¹ (sense 2) ▷ n 3 an imitation or representation of the sound of a bell [c13: probably of imitative origin, but influenced by DIN¹ + RING²; compare Old Swedish diunga to beat]

Dingaan (ˈdɪŋɡɑːn) n died 1840, Zulu chief (1828–40), who fought the Boer colonists in Natal

dingbat (ˈdɪŋ,bæt) n US slang a crazy or stupid person [c19: of unknown origin]

dingbats (ˈdɪŋ,bæts) pl n the dingbats Austral & NZ slang delirium tremens

ding-dong n 1 the sound of a bell or bells, esp two bells tuned a fourth or fifth apart 2 an imitation or representation of the sound of a bell 3 a a violent exchange of blows or words b (as modifier): a ding-dong battle in the board room ▷ adj 4 sounding or ringing repeatedly [c16: of imitative origin; see DING¹]

dinges (ˈdɪŋəs) n South African informal a jocular word for something whose name is unknown or forgotten; thingumabob [from Afrikaans, from ding thing]

dinghy (ˈdɪŋɪ) n, pl -ghies any small boat, powered by sail, oars, or outboard motor. Also (esp formerly): dingy [c19: from Hindi or Bengali dingi a little boat, from dingā boat]

dingle (ˈdɪŋɡəl) n a small wooded dell [c13: of uncertain origin]

dingo (ˈdɪŋɡəʊ) n, pl -goes a wild dog, Canis dingo, of Australia, having a yellowish-brown coat and resembling a wolf [c18: native Australian name]

dingy (ˈdɪndʒɪ) adj -gier, -giest 1 lacking light or brightness; drab 2 dirty; discoloured [c18: perhaps from an earlier dialect word related to Old English dynge dung] > 'dingily adv > 'dinginess n

dining car n a railway coach in which meals are served at tables. Also called: **restaurant car**

dining room n a room where meals are eaten

dink¹ (dɪŋk) adj 1 Scot & Northern English dialect neat or neatly dressed ▷ vb 2 Austral & NZ chiefly children's slang a (tr) to carry (a second person) on a horse, bicycle, etc b (intr) (of two people) to travel together on a horse, bicycle, etc [c16: of unknown origin]

dink² (dɪŋk) *sport* ▷ *n* 1 a ball struck delicately ▷ *vb* 2 to hit or kick (a ball) delicately [c20: imitative of a delicate strike]

dinkie ('dɪŋkɪ) *n* 1 an affluent married childless person ▷ *adj* 2 designed for or appealing to dinkies [c20: from *d(ouble) i(ncome) n(o) k(ids)* + -IE]

dinkum ('dɪŋkəm) *adj Austral & NZ informal* 1 genuine or right: *a dinkum bloke* 2 **fair dinkum** genuine or true: used to emphasize the truth of something or in asking for the truth of something to be confirmed: *Back to the states? Fair dinkum?* 3 **dinkum oil** *archaic* the truth [c19: from English dialect: work, of unknown origin]

dinky ('dɪŋkɪ) *adj* dinkier, dinkiest *informal* 1 *Brit* small and neat; dainty 2 *US* inconsequential; insignificant [c18 (in the sense: dainty): from DINK¹]

dinky-di ('dɪŋkɪ'daɪ) *adj Austral & NZ informal* another word for **dinkum** (sense 1) [c20: from DINKUM]

dinner ('dɪnə) *n* 1 a meal taken in the evening 2 a meal taken at midday, esp when it is the main meal of the day; lunch 3 a formal evening meal, as of a club, society, etc 4 (*modifier*) of, relating to, or used at dinner: *dinner plate; dinner table; dinner hour* [c13: from Old French *disner*; see DINE]

dinner-dance *n* a formal dinner followed by dancing

dinner jacket *n* a man's semiformal evening jacket without tails, usually black with a silk facing down the collar and lapels. US and Canadian name: tuxedo

dinner service *n* a set of matching plates, dishes, etc, suitable for serving a meal to a certain number of people

dinosaur ('daɪnə,sɔː) *n* 1 any extinct terrestrial reptile of the orders *Saurischia* and *Ornithischia*, many of which were of gigantic size and abundant in the Mesozoic era 2 a person or thing that is considered to be out of date [c19: from New Latin *dinosaurus*, from Greek *deinos* fearful + *sauros* lizard] ▷ ˌdino'saurian *adj*

dint (dɪnt) *n* 1 **by dint of** by means or use of: *by dint of hard work* 2 *archaic* a blow or a mark made by a blow ▷ *vb* 3 (*tr*) to mark with dints [Old English *dynt*; related to Old Norse *dyttr* blow]

D'Inzeo (*Italian* din'tsɛːo) *n* **Piero** ('pjɛːro), born 1923, and his brother **Raimondo** (rai'mondo), born 1925, Italian showjumping riders

Dio Cassius ('daɪəʊ 'kæsɪəs) *n* ?155–?230 AD, Roman historian. His *History of Rome* covers the period of Rome's transition from Republic to Empire

diocesan (daɪ'ɒsɪs²n) *adj* 1 of or relating to a diocese ▷ *n* 2 the bishop of a diocese

diocese ('daɪəsɪs) *n* the district under the jurisdiction of a bishop [c14: from Old French, from Late Latin *diocēsis*, from Greek *dioikēsis* administration, from *dioikein* to manage a household, from *oikos* house]

Dio Chrysostom (*Greek* 'diːo 'krizəstəm) *n* 2nd century AD, Greek orator and philosopher

Diocletian (ˌdaɪə'kliːʃən) *n* full name *Gaius Aurelius Valerius Diocletianus*. 245–313 AD, Roman emperor (284–305), who divided the empire into four administrative units (293) and instigated the last severe persecution of the Christians (303)

diode ('daɪəʊd) *n* 1 a semiconductor device containing one p-n junction, used in circuits for converting alternating current to direct current 2 the earliest and simplest type of electronic valve having two electrodes, an anode and a cathode, between which a current can flow only in one direction. It was formerly widely used as a rectifier and detector but has now been replaced in most electrical circuits by the more efficient and reliable semiconductor diode [c20: from DI-¹ + -ODE²]

Diodorus Siculus (ˌdaɪə'dɔːrəs 'sɪkjʊləs) *n* 1st century BC, Greek historian, noted for his history of the world in 40 books, of which 15 are extant

dioecious *or* **diecious** (daɪ'iːʃəs) *adj* (of some plants) having the male and female reproductive organs in separate flowers on separate plants [c18: from New Latin *Dioecia* name of class, from DI¹ + Greek *oikia* house, dwelling] ▷ di'oeciously *or* di'eciously *adv*

Diogenes (daɪ'ɒdʒɪˌniːz) *n* ?412–?323 BC, Greek Cynic philosopher, who rejected social conventions and advocated self-sufficiency and simplicity of life

Diomede Islands ('daɪəˌmiːd) *pl n* two small islands in the Bering Strait, separated by the international date line and by the boundary line between the US and Russia

Diomedes (ˌdaɪə'miːdiːz), **Diomede** *or* **Diomed** ('daɪəˌmɛd) *n Greek myth* a king of Argos, and suitor of Helen, who fought with the Greeks at Troy

Dion (diːˈɒn) *n* **Céline**. born 1968, Canadian singer. Her worldwide hit singles include 'My Heart Will Go On' (1998)

Dionysian (ˌdaɪə'nɪzɪən) *adj* 1 of or relating to Dionysus 2 (*often not capital*) wild or orgiastic

Dionysius (ˌdaɪə'nɪsɪəs) *n* called *the Elder*. ?430–367 BC, tyrant of Syracuse (405–367), noted for his successful campaigns against Carthage and S Italy

Dionysius Exiguus (ɛg'zɪgjʊəs) *n* died ?556 AD, Scythian monk and scholar, who is believed to have introduced the current method of reckoning dates on the basis of the Christian era

Dionysius of Halicarnassus *n* died ?7 BC, Greek historian and rhetorician; author of a history of Rome

Dionysius the Areopagite (ˌærɪ'ɒpəˌgaɪt) *n* 1st century AD, Greek Christian, thought to have been the first Bishop of Athens: long considered the author of influential theological works actually written *c.* 500. See **Pseudo-Dionysius**

Dionysus *or* **Dionysos** (ˌdaɪə'naɪsəs) *n* the Greek god of wine, fruitfulness, and vegetation, worshipped in orgiastic rites. He was also known as the bestower of ecstasy and god of the drama, and identified with Bacchus

Diophantine equation (ˌdaɪəʊ'fæntaɪn) *n* (in number theory) an equation in more than one variable and with integral coefficients, for which integral solutions are sought [c18: after *Diophantus*, Greek mathematician of the 3rd century AD]

Diophantus (ˌdaɪəʊ'fæntəs) *n* 3rd century AD, Greek mathematician, noted for his treatise on the theory of numbers, *Arithmetica*

dioptre *or US* **diopter** (daɪ'ɒptə) *n* a unit for measuring the refractive power of a lens: the reciprocal of the focal length of the lens expressed in metres [c16: from Latin *dioptra* optical instrument, from Greek, from *dia-* through + *opsesthai* to see] ▷ di'optral *adj*

dioptric (daɪ'ɒptrɪk) *or* **dioptrical** *adj* 1 of or concerned with dioptrics 2 of or denoting refraction or refracted light ▷ di'optrically *adv*

dioptrics (daɪ'ɒptrɪks) *n* (*functioning as singular*) the branch of geometrical optics concerned with the formation of images by lenses [c20: from DIOPTRE + -ICS]

Dior (diːˈɔː; *French* djɔr) *n* **Christian** ('krɪstʃən; *French* kristjã). 1905–57, French couturier, noted for his New Look of narrow waist with a long full skirt (1947); he also created the waistless sack dress

diorama (ˌdaɪə'rɑːmə) *n* 1 a miniature three-dimensional scene, in which models of figures are seen against a background 2 a picture made up of illuminated translucent curtains, viewed through an aperture 3 a museum display, as of an animal, of a specimen in its natural setting [c19: from French, from Greek *dia-* through + Greek *horama* view, from *horan* to see] ▷ dioramic (ˌdaɪə'ræmɪk) *adj*

dioxide (daɪ'ɒksaɪd) *n* any oxide containing two oxygen atoms per molecule, both of which are bonded to an atom of another element

dioxin (daɪ'ɒksɪn) *n* any of a number of mostly poisonous chemical by-products of the manufacture of certain herbicides and bactericides, esp the extremely toxic 2,3,7,8-tetrachlorodibenzo-para-dioxin

dip (dɪp) *vb* dips, dipping, dipped 1 to plunge or be plunged quickly or briefly into a liquid, esp to wet or coat 2 (*intr*) to undergo a slight decline, esp temporarily: *sales dipped in November* 3 (*intr*) to slope downwards 4 (*intr*) to sink or appear to sink quickly 5 (*tr*) to switch (car headlights) from the main to the lower beam. US and Canadian word: dim 6 (*tr*) **a** to immerse (poultry, sheep, etc) briefly in a liquid chemical to rid them of or prevent infestation by insects, etc **b** to immerse (grain, vegetables, or wood) in a preservative liquid 7 (*tr*) to stain or dye by immersing in a liquid **8** (*tr*) to baptize (someone) by immersion **9** (*tr*) to plate or galvanize (a metal, etc) by immersion in an electrolyte or electrolytic cell **10** (*tr*) to scoop up a liquid or something from a liquid in the hands or in a container **11** to lower or be lowered briefly **12** (*tr*) to make (a candle) by plunging the wick into melted wax **13** (*intr*) to plunge a container, the hands, etc, into something, esp to obtain or retrieve an object **14** (*intr*; foll by *in* or *into*) to dabble (in); play (at): *he dipped into black magic* **15** (*intr*) (of an aircraft) to drop suddenly and then regain height ▷ *n* **16** the act of dipping or state of being dipped **17** a brief swim in water **18 a** any liquid chemical preparation in which poultry, sheep, etc are dipped **b** any liquid preservative into which objects, esp of wood, are dipped **19** a preparation of dyeing agents into which fabric is immersed **20** a depression, esp in a landscape **21** something taken up by dipping **22** a container used for dipping; dipper **23** a momentary sinking down **24** the angle of slope of rock strata, fault planes, etc, from the horizontal plane **25** Also called: angle of dip, magnetic dip, inclination the angle between the direction of the earth's magnetic field and the plane of the horizon; the angle that a magnetic needle free to swing in a vertical plane makes with the horizontal **26** a creamy mixture into which pieces of food are dipped before being eaten **27** *surveying* the angular distance of the horizon below the plane of observation **28** a candle made by plunging a wick repeatedly into wax **29** a momentary loss of altitude when flying ▷ See also **dip into** [Old English *dyppan*; related to Old High German *tupfen* to wash, German *taufen* to baptize; see DEEP]

dip. *or* **Dip.** *abbreviation* diploma

DipAD *abbreviation* (in Britain) Diploma in Art and Design

DipEd *abbreviation* (in Britain) Diploma in Education

diphtheria (dɪp'θɪərɪə, dɪf-) *n* an acute contagious disease caused by the bacillus *Corynebacterium diphtheriae*, producing fever, severe prostration, and difficulty in breathing and swallowing as the result of swelling of the throat and formation of a false membrane [C19: New Latin, from French *diphthérie*, from Greek *diphthera* leather; from the nature of the membrane] ▷ **diph'therial, diphtheritic** (,dɪpθə'rɪtɪk, dɪf-) *or* **diphtheric** (dɪp'θɛrɪk, dɪf-) *adj*

diphthong (ˈdɪfθɒŋ, ˈdɪp-) *n* **1** a vowel sound, occupying a single syllable, during the articulation of which the tongue moves from one position to another, causing a continual change in vowel quality, as in the pronunciation of *a* in English *late*, during which the tongue moves from the position of (e) towards (ɪ) **2** a digraph or ligature representing a composite vowel such as this, as *ae* in *Caesar* [C15: from Late Latin *diphthongus*, from Greek *diphthongos*, from DI-¹ + *phthongos* sound] ▷ **diph'thongal** *adj*

diphthongize *or* **diphthongise** (ˈdɪfθɒŋ,aɪz, -,ɡaɪz, ˈdɪp-) *vb* (*often passive*) to make (a simple vowel) into a diphthong ▷ **,diphthongi'zation** *or* **,diphthongi'sation** *n*

dip into *vb* (*intr, preposition*) **1** to draw (upon): *he dipped into his savings* **2** to read (passages) at random or cursorily in (a book, newspaper, etc)

diplo- *or before a vowel* **dipl-** *combining form* double: *diplococcus* [from Greek, from *diploos*, from DI-¹ + -*ploos* -fold]

diplodocus (dɪ'plɒdəkəs, ,dɪpləʊ'dəʊkəs) *n, pl* -**cuses** any herbivorous quadrupedal late Jurassic dinosaur of the genus *Diplodocus*, characterized by a very long neck and tail and a total body length of 27 metres: suborder *Sauropoda* (sauropods) [C19: from New Latin, from DIPLO- + Greek *dokos* beam]

diploid (ˈdɪplɔɪd) *adj* **1** *biology* (of cells or organisms) having pairs of homologous chromosomes so that twice the haploid number is present **2** double or twofold ▷ *n* **3** *biology* a diploid cell or organism ▷ **dip'loidic** *adj*

diploma (dɪ'pləʊmə) *n* **1** a document conferring a qualification, recording success in examinations or successful completion of a course of study **2** an official document that confers an honour or privilege [C17: from Latin: official letter or document, literally: letter folded

double, from Greek; see DIPLO-]

diplomacy (dɪ'pləʊməsɪ) *n, pl* -**cies** **1** the conduct of the relations of one state with another by peaceful means **2** skill in the management of international relations **3** tact, skill, or cunning in dealing with people [C18: from French *diplomatie*, from *diplomatique* DIPLOMATIC]

diplomat (ˈdɪplə,mæt) *n* **1** an official, such as an ambassador or first secretary, engaged in diplomacy **2** a person who deals with people tactfully or skilfully

diplomatic (,dɪplə'mætɪk) *adj* **1** of or relating to diplomacy or diplomats **2** skilled in negotiating, esp between states or people **3** tactful in dealing with people [C18: from French *diplomatique* concerning the documents of diplomacy, from New Latin *diplomaticus*; see DIPLOMA] ▷ **,diplo'matically** *adv*

diplomatic bag *n* a container or bag in which official mail is sent, free from customs inspection, to and from an embassy or consulate

diplomatic corps *or* **diplomatic body** *n* the entire body of diplomats accredited to a given state

diplomatic immunity *n* the immunity from local jurisdiction and exemption from taxation in the country to which they are accredited afforded to diplomats

Diplomatic Service *n* **1** (in Britain) the division of the Civil Service which provides diplomats to represent the U.K. abroad **2** (*not capitals*) the equivalent institution of any other country

diplomatist (dɪ'pləʊmətɪst) *n* a less common word for **diplomat**

dipole (ˈdaɪ,pəʊl) *n* **1** two electric charges or magnetic poles that have equal magnitudes but opposite signs and are separated by a small distance **2** a molecule in which the centre of positive charge does not coincide with the centre of negative charge **3** Also called: dipole aerial a directional radio or television aerial consisting of two equal lengths of metal wire or rods, with a connecting wire fixed between them in the form of a T ▷ **di'polar** *adj*

dipole moment *n chem* a measure of the polarity in a chemical bond or molecule, equal to the product of one charge and the distance between the charges. Symbol: μ

dipper (ˈdɪpə) *n* **1** a ladle used for dipping **2** Also called: water ouzel any aquatic songbird of the genus *Cinclus* and family *Cinclidae*, esp *C. cinclus*. They inhabit fast-flowing streams and resemble large wrens **3** a person or thing that dips, such as the mechanism for directing car headlights downwards **4** *archaic* an Anabaptist ▷ See also **big dipper**

dippy (ˈdɪpɪ) *adj* -**pier**, -**piest** *slang* odd, eccentric, or crazy [C20: of unknown origin]

diprotodon (daɪ'prəʊtəʊ,dɒn) *n* a large extinct marsupial of the Australian genus *Diprotodon* [C19: from Greek from DI-¹ + PROTO- + -ODONT, from its two prominent lower incisors]

dipsomania (,dɪpsəʊ'meɪnɪə) *n* a compulsive desire to drink alcoholic beverages [C19: New Latin, from Greek *dipsa* thirst + -MANIA] ▷ **,dipso'maniac** *n, adj*

dipstick (ˈdɪp,stɪk) *n* **1** a graduated rod or strip dipped into a container to indicate the fluid level **2** *Brit slang* a fool

dip switch *n* a device for dipping car headlights

dipteran (ˈdɪptərən) *or* **dipteron** (ˈdɪptə,rɒn) *n* **1** any dipterous insect ▷ *adj* **2** another word for **dipterous** (sense 1)

dipterous (ˈdɪptərəs) *adj* **1** Also: dipteran of, relating to, or belonging to the *Diptera*, a large order of insects having a single pair of wings and sucking or piercing mouthparts. The group includes flies, mosquitoes, craneflies, and midges **2** *botany* having two winglike parts [C18: from New Latin, from Greek *dipteros*, from *di-* two + *pteros* wing]

diptych (ˈdɪptɪk) *n* **1** a pair of hinged wooden tablets with waxed surfaces for writing **2** a painting or carving on two panels, usually hinged like a book [C17: from Greek *diptukhos* folded together, from DI-¹ + *ptukhos* fold; compare TRIPTYCH]

Dirac (dɪ'ræk) *n* **Paul Adrien Maurice.** 1902-84, English physicist, noted for his work on the application of relativity to quantum mechanics and his prediction of electron spin and the positron: shared the Nobel prize for physics 1933

dire (daɪə) *adj* (*usually prenominal*) **1** Also: **direful** disastrous; fearful **2** desperate; urgent: *a dire need* **3** foreboding disaster; ominous [c16: from Latin *dīrus* ominous, fearful; related to Greek *deos* fear] > 'dire**ly** *adv* > 'dire**ness** *n*

direct (dɪ'rɛkt, daɪ-) *vb* (*mainly tr*) **1** to regulate, conduct, or control the affairs of **2** (*also intr*) to give commands or orders with authority to (a person or group) **3** to tell or show (someone) the way to a place **4** to aim, point, or cause to move towards a goal **5** to address (a letter, parcel, etc) **6** to address (remarks, words, etc) **7** (*also intr*) to provide guidance to (actors, cameramen, etc) in the rehearsal of a play or the filming of a motion picture **8** (*also intr*) to conduct (a piece of music or musicians), usually while performing oneself ▷ *adj* **9** without delay or evasion; straightforward **10** without turning aside; uninterrupted; shortest; straight: *a direct route* **11** without intervening persons or agencies; immediate: *a direct link* **12** honest; frank; candid **13** (*usually prenominal*) precise; exact: *a direct quotation* **14** diametrical: *the direct opposite* **15** in an unbroken line of descent, as from father to son over succeeding generations: *a direct descendant* **16** (of government, decisions, etc) by or from the electorate rather than through representatives **17** *logic, maths* (of a proof) progressing from the premises to the conclusion, rather than eliminating the possibility of the falsehood of the conclusion. Compare **indirect proof 18** *astronomy* moving from west to east on the celestial sphere. Compare **retrograde** (sense 4a) **19** of or relating to direct current **20** *music* (of an interval or chord) in root position; not inverted ▷ *adv* **21** directly; straight [c14: from Latin *dīrigere* to guide, from *dis-* apart + *regere* to rule] > di'**rect**ness *n*

direct access *n* a method of reading data from a computer file without reading through the file from the beginning as on a disk or drum

direct action *n* action such as strikes or civil disobedience, employed by organized labour or other groups to obtain demands from an employer, government, etc

direct current *n* a continuous electric current that flows in one direction only, without substantial variation in magnitude

direct debit *n* an order given to a bank or building society by a holder of an account, instructing it to pay to a specified person or organization any sum demanded by that person or organization. Compare **standing order**

direct-grant school *n* (in Britain, formerly) a school financed by endowment, fees, and a state grant conditional upon admittance of a percentage of nonpaying pupils nominated by the local education authority

direction (dɪ'rɛkʃən, daɪ-) *n* **1** the act of directing or the state of being directed **2** management, control, or guidance **3** the work of a stage or film director **4** the course or line along which a person or thing moves, points, or lies **5** the place towards which a person or thing is directed **6** a line of action; course **7** the name and address on a letter, parcel, etc **8** *music* the process of conducting an orchestra, choir, etc **9** *music* an instruction in the form of a word or symbol heading or occurring in the body of a passage, movement, or piece to indicate tempo, dynamics, mood, etc

directional (dɪ'rɛkʃənªl, daɪ-) *adj* **1** of or relating to a spatial direction **2** *electronics* **a** having or relating to an increased sensitivity to radio waves, sound waves, nuclear particles, etc, coming from a particular direction **b** (of an aerial) transmitting or receiving radio waves more effectively in some directions than in others **3** *physics, electronics* concentrated in, following, or producing motion in a particular direction > di,rection'al**ity** *n*

directional drilling *n* a method of drilling for oil in which the well is not drilled vertically, as when a number of wells are to be drilled from a single platform to reach different areas of an oil field. Also called: deviated drilling

direction finder *n* a highly directional aerial system that can be used to determine the direction of incoming radio signals, used esp as a navigation aid

directions (dɪ'rɛkʃənz, daɪ-) *pl n* (*sometimes singular*) instructions for doing something or for reaching a place

directive (dɪ'rɛktɪv, daɪ-) *n* **1** an instruction; order ▷ *adj* **2** tending to direct; directing **3** indicating direction

directly (dɪ'rɛktlɪ, daɪ-) *adv* **1** in a direct manner **2** at once; without delay **3** (foll by *before* or *after*) immediately; just ▷ *conj* **4** (*subordinating*) as soon as

direct marketing *n* selling goods directly to consumers rather than through retailers, usually by mail order, direct-mail shot, newspaper advertising, door-to-door selling, telephone selling, the internet, or television home-shopping channels. Also called: **direct selling**

direct object *n grammar* a noun, pronoun, or noun phrase whose referent receives the direct action of a verb. For example, *a book* is the direct object in the sentence *They bought Anne a book*

director (dɪ'rɛktə, daɪ-) *n* **1** a person or thing that directs, controls, or regulates **2** a member of the governing board of a business concern who may or may not have an executive function **3** a person who directs the affairs of an institution, trust, educational programme, etc **4** the person responsible for the artistic and technical aspects of making a film or television programme. Compare **producer** (sense 4) **5** *music* another word (esp US) for **conductor** (sense 2) > ,direc'tori**al** *adj* > di'rector,ship *n* > di'rectr**ess** *fem n*

directorate (dɪ'rɛktərɪt, daɪ-) *n* **1** a board of directors **2** Also called: directorship the position of director

director-general *n, pl* directors-general the head of a large organization such as the CBI or BBC

Director of Public Prosecutions *n* (in Britain) an official who, as head of the Crown Prosecution Service, is responsible for conducting all criminal prosecutions initiated by the police. Abbreviation: DPP

director's chair *n* a light wooden folding chair with arm rests and a canvas seat and back

directory (dɪ'rɛktərɪ, -trɪ, daɪ-) *n, pl* -ries **1** a book, arranged alphabetically or classified by trade listing names, addresses, telephone numbers, etc, of individuals or firms **2** a book or manual giving directions **3** a book containing the rules to be observed in the forms of worship used in churches **4** a less common word for **directorate** (sense 2) **5** *computing* an area of a disk, Winchester disk, or floppy disk that contains the names and locations of files currently held on that disk ▷ *adj* **6** directing

Directory (dɪ'rɛktərɪ, -trɪ, daɪ-) *n* the Directory *history* the body of five directors in power in France from 1795 until their overthrow by Napoleon in 1799

direct primary *n US government* a primary in which voters directly select the candidates who will run for office

direct selling *n* another name for **direct marketing**

direct speech *or esp US* **direct discourse** *n* the reporting of what someone has said or written by quoting his exact words

direct tax *n* a tax paid by the person or organization on which it is levied

dirge (dɜːdʒ) *n* **1** a chant of lamentation for the dead **2** the funeral service in its solemn or sung forms **3** any mourning song or melody [c13: changed from Latin *dīrigē* direct (imperative), opening word of the Latin antiphon used in the office of the dead] > 'dirge**ful** *adj*

dirham ('dɪəræm) *n* **1** the standard monetary unit of Morocco, divided into 100 centimes **2 a** a Kuwaiti monetary unit worth one tenth of a dinar and 100 fils **b** a Tunisian monetary unit worth one tenth of a dinar and 100 millimes **c** a Qatari monetary unit worth one hundredth of a riyal **d** a Libyan monetary unit worth one thousandth of a dinar [c18: from Arabic, from Latin: DRACHMA]

Dirichlet (German diri'kleː) *n* Peter Gustav Lejeune ('peːtər 'gʊstaf lə'ʒœn). 1805–59, German mathematician, noted for his work on number theory and calculus

dirigible (dɪ'rɪdʒɪbªl) *adj* **1** able to be steered or directed

▷ *n* **2** another name for **airship** [c16: from Latin *dīrigere* to DIRECT] > ˌdirigi'bility *n*

dirigisme (diːriːˈʒiːzəm) *n* control by the state of economic and social matters [c20: from French] > **dirig'iste** *adj*

dirk (dɜːk) *n* **1** a dagger esp as formerly worn by Scottish Highlanders ▷ *vb* **2** (*tr*) to stab with a dirk [c16: from Scottish *durk*, perhaps from German *Dolch* dagger]

dirndl ('dɜːndəl) *n* **1** a woman's dress with a full gathered skirt and fitted bodice; originating from Tyrolean peasant wear **2** a gathered skirt of this kind [German (Bavarian and Austrian): shortened from *Dirndlkleid*, from *Dirndl* little girl + *Kleid* dress]

dirt (dɜːt) *n* **1** any unclean substance, such as mud, dust, excrement, etc; filth **2** loose earth; soil **3** a packed earth, gravel, cinders, etc, used to make a racetrack **b** (*as modifier*): *a dirt track* **4** *mining* the gravel or soil from which minerals are extracted **5** a person or thing regarded as worthless **6** obscene or indecent speech or writing **7** *slang* gossip; scandalous information **8** moral corruption **9 do someone dirt** *slang* to do something vicious to someone **10 eat dirt** *slang* to accept insult without complaining [c13: from Old Norse *drit* excrement; related to Middle Dutch *drēte*]

dirt bike *n* a type of motorbike designed for use over rough ground

dirt-cheap *adj*, *adv informal* at an extremely low price

dirt road *n* an unsealed country road

dirty ('dɜːtɪ) *adj* **dirtier, dirtiest 1** covered or marked with dirt; filthy **2 a** obscene; salacious: *dirty books* **b** sexually clandestine: *a dirty weekend* **3** causing one to become grimy: *a dirty job* **4** (of a colour) not clear and bright; impure **5** unfair; dishonest; unscrupulous; unsporting **6** mean; nasty: *a dirty cheat* **7** scandalous; unkind **8** revealing dislike or anger **9** (of weather) rainy or squally; stormy **10 dirty linen** *informal* intimate secrets, esp those that might give rise to gossip **11 dirty work** unpleasant or illicit activity **12 do the dirty on** *Brit informal* to behave meanly or unkindly towards ▷ *vb* **dirties, dirtying, dirtied 13** to make or become dirty; stain; soil > 'dirtily *adv* > 'dirtiness *n*

dirty bomb *n informal* a bomb made from nuclear waste combined with conventional explosives that is capable of spreading radioactive material over a very wide area

dis (dɪs) *n* a variant spelling of **diss**

Dis (dɪs) *n* **1** Also called: Orcus, Pluto the Roman god of the underworld **2** the abode of the dead; underworld ▷ Greek equivalent: **Hades**

dis-¹ *prefix* **1** indicating reversal: *disconnect; disembark* **2** indicating negation, lack, or deprivation: *dissimilar; distrust; disgrace* **3** indicating removal or release: *disembowel; disburden* **4** expressing intensive force: *dissever* [from Latin *dis-* apart; in some cases, via Old French *des-*. In compound words of Latin origin, *dis-* becomes *dif-* before *f* and *di-* before some consonants]

dis-² *combining form* variant of **di-¹** before *s*: *dissyllable*

disability (ˌdɪsəˈbɪlɪtɪ) *n*, *pl* **-ties 1** the condition of being unable to perform a task or function because of a physical or mental impairment **2** something that disables; handicap **3** lack of necessary intelligence, strength, etc **4** an incapacity in the eyes of the law to enter into certain transactions

disable (dɪsˈeɪbəl) *vb* (*tr*) **1** to make ineffective, unfit, or incapable, as by crippling **2** to make or pronounce legally incapable **3** to switch off (an electronic device) > dis'ablement *n*

disabled (dɪˈseɪbəld) *adj* **a** lacking one or more physical powers, such as the ability to walk or to coordinate one's movements, as from the effects of a disease or accident, or through mental impairment **b** (*as collective noun; preceded by the*): *the disabled*

● **USAGE** Nowadays it is better to refer to people with
● physical disabilities of various kinds by describing the
● specific difficulty in question rather than talking
● about *the disabled* as a group, which is considered
● somewhat offensive. Some people also object to the
● word *disabled* to refer to facilities for people with
● disabilites, and prefer the word *accessible*.

disabled list *n* the US term for **injury list**

disabuse (ˌdɪsəˈbjuːz) *vb* (*tr; usually foll by of*) to rid (oneself, another person, etc) of a mistaken or misguided idea; set right

disadvantage (ˌdɪsədˈvɑːntɪdʒ) *n* **1** an unfavourable circumstance, state of affairs, thing, person, etc **2** injury, loss, or detriment **3** an unfavourable condition or situation (esp in the phrase **at a disadvantage**) ▷ *vb* **4** (*tr*) to put at a disadvantage; handicap

disadvantaged (ˌdɪsədˈvɑːntɪdʒd) *adj* socially or economically deprived or discriminated against

disadvantageous (dɪsˌædvənˈteɪdʒəs, ˌdɪsæd-) *adj* unfavourable; detrimental > disˌadvan'tageously *adv* > disˌadvan'tageousness *n*

disaffect (ˌdɪsəˈfɛkt) *vb* (*tr; often passive*) to cause to lose loyalty or affection; alienate > ˌdisaf'fectedly *adv*

disaffection (ˌdɪsəˈfɛkʃən) *n* a state of dissatisfaction or alienation: *the growing disaffection between players*

disaffiliate (ˌdɪsəˈfɪlɪˌeɪt) *vb* to sever an affiliation (with); dissociate > ˌdisaf,fili'ation *n*

disafforest (ˌdɪsəˈfɒrɪst) *vb* (*tr*) *English law* to reduce (land) from the status of a forest to the state of ordinary ground > ˌdisaf,fores'tation *or* disaf'forestment *n*

disaggregate (dɪsˈægrɪˌgeɪt) *vb* **1** to separate from a group or mass **2** to divide into parts > ˌdisaggre'gation *n*

disagree (ˌdɪsəˈɡriː) *vb* **-grees, -greeing, -greed** (*intr; often foll by with*) **1** to dissent in opinion (from another person) or dispute (about an idea, fact, etc) **2** to fail to correspond; conflict **3** to be unacceptable (to) or unfavourable (for); be incompatible (with): *curry disagrees with me* **4** to be opposed (to) in principle

disagreeable (ˌdɪsəˈɡriːəbəl) *adj* **1** not likable, esp bad-tempered, offensive, or disobliging **2** not to one's liking; unpleasant > disa'greeableness *or* ˌdisa,greea'bility *n* > disa'greeably *adv*

disagreement (ˌdɪsəˈɡriːmənt) *n* **1** refusal or failure to agree **2** a failure to correspond **3** an argument or dispute

disallow (ˌdɪsəˈlaʊ) *vb* (*tr*) **1** to reject as untrue or invalid **2** to cancel > disal'lowable *adj* > disal'lowance *n*

disappear (ˌdɪsəˈpɪə) *vb* **1** (*intr*) to cease to be visible; vanish **2** (*intr*) to go away or become lost, esp secretly or without explanation **3** (*intr*) to cease to exist, have effect, or be known; become extinct or lost **4** (*tr*) (esp in South and Central America) to arrest secretly and presumably imprison or kill (a member of an opposing political group) > ˌdisap'pearance *n*

disapplication (ˌdɪsæplɪˈkeɪʃən) *n Brit education* a provision for exempting schools or individuals from the requirements of the National Curriculum in special circumstances

disappoint (ˌdɪsəˈpɔɪnt) *vb* (*tr*) **1** to fail to meet the expectations, hopes, desires, or standards of; let down **2** to prevent the fulfilment of (a plan, intention, etc); frustrate; thwart [c15 (originally meaning: to remove from office): from Old French *desapointier*; see DIS-¹, APPOINT]

disappointed (ˌdɪsəˈpɔɪntɪd) *adj* saddened by the failure of an expectation, etc > ˌdisap'pointedly *adv*

disappointing (ˌdɪsəˈpɔɪntɪŋ) *adj* failing to meet one's expectations, hopes, desires, or standards > ˌdisap'pointingly *adv*

disappointment (ˌdɪsəˈpɔɪntmənt) *n* **1** the act of disappointing or the state of being disappointed **2** a person, thing, or state of affairs that disappoints

disapprobation (ˌdɪsæprəʊˈbeɪʃən) *n* moral or social disapproval

disapproval (ˌdɪsəˈpruːvəl) *n* the act or a state or feeling of disapproving; censure; condemnation

disapprove (ˌdɪsəˈpruːv) *vb* **1** (*intr; often foll by of*) to consider wrong, bad, etc **2** (*tr*) to withhold approval from > ˌdisap'proving *adj* > ˌdisap'provingly *adv*

disarm (dɪsˈɑːm) *vb* **1** (*tr*) to remove defensive or offensive capability from (a country, army, etc) **2** (*tr*) to deprive of weapons **3** (*tr*) to win the confidence or affection of **4** (*intr*) (of a nation, etc) to decrease the size and capability of one's armed forces **5** (*intr*) to lay down weapons > dis'armer *n*

disarmament (dɪsˈɑːməmənt) *n* **1** the reduction of offensive or defensive fighting capability, as by a nation

2 the act of disarming or state of being disarmed

disarming (dɪsˈɑːmɪŋ) *adj* tending to neutralize or counteract hostility, suspicion, etc > **disˈarmingly** *adv*

disarrange (ˌdɪsəˈreɪndʒ) *vb* (*tr*) to throw into disorder > ˌdisarˈrangement *n*

disarray (ˌdɪsəˈreɪ) *n* **1** confusion, dismay, and lack of discipline **2** (esp of clothing) disorderliness; untidiness ▷ *vb* (*tr*) **3** to throw into confusion **4** *archaic* to undress

disassemble (ˌdɪsəˈsɛmbᵊl) *vb* (*tr*) to take apart (a piece of machinery, etc); dismantle

disassembler (ˌdɪsəˈsɛmblə) *n* *computing* a computer program that translates machine code into assembly language

disassociate (ˌdɪsəˈsəʊʃɪˌeɪt) *vb* a less common word for **dissociate** > ˌdisasˌsociˈation *n*

disaster (dɪˈzɑːstə) *n* **1** an occurrence that causes great distress or destruction **2** a thing, project, etc, that fails or has been ruined [C16 (originally in the sense: malevolent astral influence): from Italian *disastro*, from *dis-* (pejorative) + *astro* star, from Latin *astrum*, from Greek *astron*] > **disˈastrous** *adj*

disavow (ˌdɪsəˈvaʊ) *vb* (*tr*) to deny knowledge of, connection with, or responsibility for > ˌdisaˈvowal *n* > ˌdisaˈvowedly *adv*

disband (dɪsˈbænd) *vb* to cease to function or cause to stop functioning, as a unit, group, etc > disˈbandment *n*

disbar (dɪsˈbɑː) *vb* -bars, -barring, -barred (*tr*) *law* to deprive of the status of barrister; expel from the Bar > disˈbarment *n*

- ● USAGE *Disbar* is sometimes wrongly used where *debar*
- ● is meant: *he was debarred* (not *disbarred*) *from attending*
- ● *meetings*

disbelief (ˌdɪsbɪˈliːf) *n* refusal or reluctance to believe

disbelieve (ˌdɪsbɪˈliːv) *vb* **1** (*tr*) to reject as false or lying; refuse to accept as true or truthful **2** (*intr*; usually foll by *in*) to have no faith (in) > ˌdisbeˈliever *n* > ˌdisbeˈlieving *adj*

disbud (dɪsˈbʌd) *or* **debud** (diːˈbʌd) *vb* -buds, -budding, -budded **1** to remove superfluous buds, flowers, or shoots from (a plant, esp a fruit tree) **2** *vet science* to remove the horn buds of (calves, lambs, and kids) to prevent horns growing

disburden (dɪsˈbɜːdᵊn) *vb* **1** to remove a load from (a person or animal) **2** (*tr*) to relieve (oneself, one's mind, etc) of a distressing worry or oppressive thought

disburse (dɪsˈbɜːs) *vb* (*tr*) to pay out [C16: from Old French *desborser*, from *des-* DIS-¹ + *borser* to obtain money, from *borse* bag, from Late Latin *bursa*] > disˈbursable *adj* > disˈbursement *n* > disˈburser *n*

- ● USAGE *Disburse* is sometimes wrongly used where
- ● *disperse* is meant: *the police used a water cannon to*
- ● *disperse*(not *disburse*) *the crowd*

disc *or now esp US* **disk** (dɪsk) *n* **1** a flat circular plate **2** something resembling or appearing to resemble this **3** another word for (gramophone) **record 4** *anatomy* any approximately circular flat structure in the body, esp an intervertebral disc **5 a** the flat receptacle of composite flowers, such as the daisy **b** (*as modifier*): *a disc floret* **6 a** Also called: **parking disc** a marker or device for display in a parked vehicle showing the time of arrival or the latest permitted time of departure or both **b** (*as modifier*): *a disc zone; disc parking* **7** *computing* a variant spelling of **disk** (sense 2) [C18: from Latin *discus*, from Greek *diskos* quoit] > **ˈdiscal** *adj*

discard *vb* (dɪsˈkɑːd) **1** (*tr*) to get rid of as useless or undesirable **2** *cards* to throw out (a card or cards) from one's hand **3** *cards* to play (a card not of the suit led nor a trump) when unable to follow suit ▷ *n* (ˈdɪskɑːd) **4** a person or thing that has been cast aside **5** *cards* a discarded card **6** the act of discarding

disc brake *n* a type of brake in which two calliper-operated pads rub against a flat disc attached to the wheel hub when the brake is applied

discern (dɪˈsɜːn) *vb* **1** (*tr*) to recognize or perceive clearly **2** to recognize or perceive (differences) [C14: from Old French *discerner*, from Latin *discernere* to divide, from DIS-¹ (apart) + *cernere* to separate] > disˈcernible *or* (*rarely*) disˈcernable *adj* > disˈcernibly *or* (*rarely*) disˈcernably *adv*

discerning (dɪˈsɜːnɪŋ) *adj* having or showing good taste

or judgment; discriminating

discernment (dɪˈsɜːnmənt) *n* keen perception or judgment

disc floret *or* **disc flower** *n* any of the small tubular flowers at the centre of the flower head of certain composite plants, such as the daisy

discharge *vb* (dɪsˈtʃɑːdʒ) **1** (*tr*) to release or allow to go **2** (*tr*) to dismiss from or relieve of duty, office, employment, etc **3** to fire or be fired, as a gun **4** to pour forth or cause to pour forth: *the boil discharges pus* **5** (*tr*) to remove (the cargo) from (a boat, etc); unload **6** (*tr*) to perform (the duties of) or meet (the demands of an office, obligation, etc) **7** (*tr*) to relieve oneself of (a responsibility, debt, etc) **8** (*intr*) *physics* **a** to lose or remove electric charge **b** to form an arc, spark, or corona in a gas **c** to clear or supply electrical current from a cell or battery **9** (*tr*) *law* to release (a prisoner from custody, etc) ▷ *n* (ˈdɪstʃɑːdʒ, dɪsˈtʃɑːdʒ) **10** a person or thing that is discharged **11 a** dismissal or release from an office, job, institution, etc **b** the document certifying such release **12** the fulfilment of an obligation or release from a responsibility or liability **13** the act of removing a load, as of cargo **14** a pouring forth of a fluid; emission **15 a** the act of firing a projectile **b** the volley, bullet, missile, etc, fired **16** *law* **a** a release, as of a person held under legal restraint **b** an annulment, as of a court order **17** *physics* **a** the act or process of removing or losing charge or of equalizing a potential difference **b** a transient or continuous conduction of electricity through a gas by the formation and movement of electrons and ions in an applied electric field > disˈchargeable *adj* > disˈcharger *n*

discharge tube *n* *electronics* an electrical device in which current flow is by electrons and ions in an ionized gas, as in a fluorescent light or neon tube

disc harrow *n* a harrow with sharp-edged slightly concave discs mounted on horizontal shafts and used to cut clods or debris on the surface of the soil or to cover seed after planting

disciple (dɪˈsaɪpᵊl) *n* **1** a follower of the doctrines of a teacher or a school of thought **2** one of the personal followers of Christ (including his 12 apostles) during his earthly life [Old English *discipul*, from Latin *discipulus* pupil, from *discere* to learn] > disˈcipleˌship *n* > discipular (dɪˈsɪpjʊlə) *adj*

disciplinarian (ˌdɪsɪplɪˈnɛərɪən) *n* a person who imposes or advocates discipline

disciplinary (ˈdɪsɪˌplɪnərɪ) *adj* **1** of, promoting, or used for discipline; corrective **2** relating to a branch of learning

discipline (ˈdɪsɪplɪn) *n* **1** training or conditions imposed for the improvement of physical powers, self-control, etc **2** systematic training in obedience to regulations and authority **3** the state of improved behaviour, etc, resulting from such training or conditions **4** punishment or chastisement **5** a system of rules for behaviour, methods of practice, etc **6** a branch of learning or instruction **7** the laws governing members of a Church ▷ *vb* (*tr*) **8** to improve or attempt to improve the behaviour, orderliness, etc, of by training, conditions, or rules **9** to punish or correct [C13: from Latin *disciplīna* teaching, from *discipulus* DISCIPLE] > ˈdisciˌplinable *adj* > disciplinal (ˌdɪsɪˈplaɪnᵊl, ˈdɪsɪˌplɪnᵊl) *adj* > ˈdisciˌpliner *n*

disc jockey *n* a person who announces and plays recorded music, esp pop music, on a radio programme, etc

disclaim (dɪsˈkleɪm) *vb* **1** (*tr*) to deny or renounce (any claim, connection, etc) **2** (*tr*) to deny the validity or authority of **3** *law* to renounce or repudiate (a legal claim or right)

disclaimer (dɪsˈkleɪmə) *n* a repudiation or denial

disclose (dɪsˈkləʊz) *vb* (*tr*) **1** to make (information) known **2** to allow to be seen; lay bare > disˈcloser *n*

disclosure (dɪsˈkləʊʒə) *n* **1** something that is disclosed **2** the act of disclosing; revelation

Discman (ˈdɪskmən) *n* *trademark* a small portable CD player with light headphones

disco (ˈdɪskəʊ) *n, pl* -cos **1 a** an occasion at which typically young people dance to amplified pop records, usually compered by a disc jockey and featuring special lighting effects **b** (*as modifier*): disco dancing **2** a nightclub or other public place where such dances take place **3** mobile equipment, usually accompanied by a disc jockey who operates it, for providing music for a disco [C20: shortened from DISCOTHEQUE]

discobolus or **discobolos** (dɪsˈkɒbələs) *n*, *pl* -**li** (-ˌlaɪ) (in classical Greece) a discus thrower [C18: from Latin, from Greek *diskobolos*, from *diskos* DISCUS + -*bolos*, from *ballein* to throw]

discography (dɪsˈkɒɡrəfɪ) *n* a classified reference list of gramophone records ▷ dis'cographer *n*

discoid (ˈdɪskɔɪd) *adj* **1** Also: **discoidal** (dɪsˈkɔɪdəl) like a disc ▷ *n* **2** a disclike object

discolour or US **discolor** (dɪsˈkʌlə) *vb* to change or cause to change in colour; fade or stain ▷ dis,color'ation or dis,colour'ation *n*

discombobulate (ˌdɪskəmˈbɒbjʊˌleɪt) *vb* (*tr*) *informal, chiefly US & Canadian* to throw into confusion [C20: probably a whimsical alteration of DISCOMPOSE or DISCOMFIT]

discomfit (dɪsˈkʌmfɪt) *vb* (*tr*) **1** to make uneasy, confused, or embarrassed **2** to frustrate the plans or purpose of **3** *archaic* to defeat in battle [C14: from Old French *desconfire* to destroy, from *des-* (indicating reversal) + *confire* to make, from Latin *conficere* to produce; see CONFECT] ▷ dis'comfiture *n*

discomfort (dɪsˈkʌmfət) *n* **1** an inconvenience, distress, or mild pain **2** something that disturbs or deprives of ease ▷ *vb* **3** (*tr*) to make uncomfortable or uneasy

discommode (ˌdɪskəˈməʊd) *vb* (*tr*) to cause inconvenience or annoyance to; disturb ▷ ,discom'modious *adj*

discompose (ˌdɪskəmˈpəʊz) *vb* (*tr*) **1** to disturb the composure of; disconcert **2** *now rare* to disarrange ▷ ,discom'posure *n*

disconcert (ˌdɪskənˈsɜːt) *vb* (*tr*) **1** to disturb the composure of **2** to frustrate or upset ▷ ,discon'certion or ,discon'certment *n* ▷ ,discon'certed *adj*

disconcerting (ˌdɪskənˈsɜːtɪŋ) *adj* causing a feeling of disturbance, embarrassment, or confusion; perturbing; worrying ▷ ,discon'certingly *adv*

disconformity (ˌdɪskənˈfɔːmɪtɪ) *n*, *pl* -**ties 1** lack of conformity; discrepancy **2** the junction between two parallel series of stratified rocks, representing a considerable period of erosion of the much older underlying rocks before the more recent ones were deposited

disconnect (ˌdɪskəˈnɛkt) *vb* **1** (*tr*) to undo or break the connection of or between (something, such as a plug and a socket) ▷ *n* **2** a lack of a connection; disconnection ▷ ,discon'nection or ,discon'nexion *n*

disconnected (ˌdɪskəˈnɛktɪd) *adj* **1** not rationally connected; confused or incoherent **2** not connected or joined

disconsolate (dɪsˈkɒnsəlɪt) *adj* **1** sad beyond comfort; inconsolable **2** disappointed; dejected [C14: from Medieval Latin *disconsōlātus*, from DIS- + *consōlātus* comforted; see CONSOLE¹] ▷ dis'consolately *adv* ▷ dis'consolateness or dis,conso'lation *n*

discontent (ˌdɪskənˈtɛnt) *n* **1** Also: **discontentment** lack of contentment, as with one's condition or lot in life ▷ *vb* **2** (*tr*) to make dissatisfied ▷ ,discon'tented *adj* ▷ ,discon'tentedness *n*

discontinue (ˌdɪskənˈtɪnjuː) *vb* -**ues**, -**uing**, -**ued 1** to come or bring to an end; interrupt or be interrupted; stop **2** (*tr*) *law* to terminate or abandon (an action, suit, etc) ▷ ,discon'tinuance *n* ▷ ,discon,tinu'ation *n*

discontinuity (dɪsˌkɒntɪˈnjuːɪtɪ) *n*, *pl* -**ties 1** lack of rational connection or cohesion **2** a break or interruption

discontinuous (ˌdɪskənˈtɪnjʊəs) *adj* characterized by interruptions or breaks; intermittent ▷ ,discon'tinuously *adv* ▷ ,discon'tinuousness *n*

discord *n* (ˈdɪskɔːd) **1** lack of agreement or harmony; strife **2** harsh confused mingling of sounds **3** a combination of musical notes containing one or more dissonant intervals ▷ *vb* (dɪsˈkɔːd) **4** (*intr*) to disagree;

clash [C13: from Old French *descort*, from *descorder* to disagree, from Latin *discordāre*, from *discors* at variance, from DIS-¹ + *cor* heart]

discordant (dɪsˈkɔːdᵊnt) *adj* **1** at variance; disagreeing **2** harsh in sound; inharmonious ▷ dis'cordantly *adv* ▷ dis'cordance *n*

discotheque (ˈdɪskəˌtɛk) *n* the full name of **disco** [C20: from French *discothèque*, from Greek *diskos* disc + -*o*- + Greek *thēkē* case]

discount *vb* (dɪsˈkaʊnt, ˈdɪskaʊnt) (*mainly tr*) **1** to leave out of account as being unreliable, prejudiced, or irrelevant **2** to anticipate and make allowance for, often so as to diminish the effect of **3 a** to deduct (a specified amount or percentage) from the usual price, cost, etc **b** to reduce (the regular price, cost, etc) by a stated percentage or amount **4** to sell or offer for sale at a reduced price **5** to buy or sell (a bill of exchange, etc) before maturity, with a deduction for interest determined by the time to maturity and also by risk **6** (*also intr*) to loan money on (a negotiable instrument that is not immediately payable) with a deduction for interest determined by risk and time to maturity ▷ *n* (ˈdɪskaʊnt) **7** a deduction from the full amount of a price or debt, as in return for prompt payment or to a special group of customers. See also **cash discount, trade discount 8** Also called: **discount rate a** the amount of interest deducted in the purchase or sale of or the loan of money on unmatured negotiable instruments **b** the rate of interest deducted **9** (in the issue of shares) a percentage deducted from the par value to give a reduced amount payable by subscribers **10 at a discount a** below the regular price **b** held in low regard; not sought after or valued **11** (*modifier*) offering or selling at reduced prices: *a discount shop* ▷ dis'countable *adj* ▷ 'discounter *n*

discounted cash flow *n* *accounting* a technique for appraising an investment that takes into account the different values of future returns according to when they will be received

discountenance (dɪsˈkaʊntɪnəns) *vb* (*tr*) **1** to make ashamed or confused **2** to disapprove of

discount house *n* **1** *chiefly Brit* a financial organization engaged in discounting bills of exchange, etc on a large scale primarily by borrowing call money from commercial banks **2** *chiefly US* another name for **discount store**

discount market *n* the part of the money market consisting of banks, discount houses, and brokers on which bills are discounted

discount store *n* a shop where goods are sold at a low price

discourage (dɪsˈkʌrɪdʒ) *vb* (*tr*) **1** to deprive of the will to persist in something **2** to inhibit; prevent: *this solution discourages rust* **3** to oppose by expressing disapproval ▷ dis'couragement *n* ▷ dis'couragingly *adv*

discourse *n* (ˈdɪskɔːs, dɪsˈkɔːs) **1** verbal communication; talk; conversation **2** a formal treatment of a subject in speech or writing, such as a sermon or dissertation **3** a unit of text used by linguists for the analysis of linguistic phenomena that range over more than one sentence **4** *archaic* the ability to reason or the reasoning process ▷ *vb* (dɪsˈkɔːs) **5** (*intr*; often foll by *on* or *upon*) to speak or write (about) formally and extensively **6** (*intr*) to hold a discussion **7** (*tr*) *archaic* to give forth (music) [C14: from Medieval Latin *discursus* argument, from Latin: a running to and fro, from *discurrere* to run different ways, from DIS-¹ + *currere* to run]

discourteous (dɪsˈkɜːtɪəs) *adj* showing bad manners; impolite; rude ▷ dis'courteously *adv* ▷ dis'courteousness *n*

discourtesy (dɪsˈkɜːtɪsɪ) *n*, *pl* -**sies 1** bad manners; rudeness **2** a rude remark or act

discover (dɪˈskʌvə) *vb* (*tr*; *may take a clause as object*) **1** to be the first to find or find out about: *Fleming discovered penicillin* **2** to learn about or encounter for the first time; realize **3** to find after study or search **4** to reveal or make known ▷ dis'coverable *adj* ▷ dis'coverer *n*

discovery (dɪˈskʌvərɪ) *n*, *pl* -**eries 1** the act, process, or an instance of discovering **2** a person, place, or thing that has been discovered **3** *law* the compulsory disclosure by a party to an action of relevant documents in his possession

discredit (dɪsˈkrɛdɪt) *vb* (*tr*) **1** to damage the reputation of **2** to cause to be disbelieved or distrusted **3** to reject as untrue or of questionable accuracy ▷ *n* **4** a person, thing, or state of affairs that causes disgrace **5** damage to a reputation **6** lack of belief or confidence

discreditable (dɪsˈkrɛdɪtəbᵊl) *adj* tending to bring discredit; shameful or unworthy

discreet (dɪˈkriːt) *adj* **1** careful to avoid social embarrassment or distress, esp by keeping confidences secret; tactful **2** unobtrusive [C14: from Old French *discret*, from Medieval Latin *discrētus*, from Latin *discernere* to DISCERN] > disˈcreetly *adv* > disˈcreetness *n*
● USAGE See at **discrete**

discrepancy (dɪˈskrɛpənsɪ) *n*, *pl* -cies a conflict or variation, as between facts, figures, or claims [C15: from Latin *discrepāns*, from *discrepāre* to differ in sound, from DIS-¹ + *crepāre* to be noisy] > diˈscrepant *adj*

discrete (dɪˈskriːt) *adj* **1** separate or distinct in form or concept **2** consisting of distinct or separate parts [C14: from Latin *discrētus* separated, set apart; see DISCREET] > disˈcretely *adv* > disˈcreteness *n*
● USAGE This word is quite often used by mistake where
● *discreet* is intended: *reading is a set of discrete skills; she was*
● *discreet* (not *discrete*) *about the affair*

discretion (dɪˈskrɛʃən) *n* **1** the quality of behaving or speaking in such a way as to avoid social embarrassment or distress **2** freedom or authority to make judgments and to act as one sees fit (esp in the phrases **at one's own discretion, at the discretion of**) **3** age of discretion *or* years of discretion the age at which a person is considered to be able to manage his own affairs

discretionary (dɪˈskrɛʃənərɪ, -ənrɪ) *or* **discretional** *adj* having or using the ability to decide at one's own discretion: *discretionary powers*

discretionary trust *n* a trust in which the beneficiaries' shares are not fixed in the trust deed but are left to the discretion of other persons, often the trustees

discriminate *vb* (dɪˈskrɪmɪˌneɪt) **1** (*intr*; usually foll by *in favour of* or *against*) to single out a particular person, group, etc, for special favour or, esp, disfavour, often because of a characteristic such as race, colour, sex, intelligence, etc **2** (when *intr*, foll by *between* or *among*) to recognize or understand the difference (between); distinguish **3** (*intr*) to constitute or mark a difference **4** (*intr*) to be discerning in matters of taste ▷ *adj* (dɪˈskrɪmɪnɪt) **5** showing or marked by discrimination [C17: from Latin *discrīmināre* to divide, from *discrīmen* a separation, from *discernere* to DISCERN] > disˈcriminately *adv*

discriminating (dɪˈskrɪmɪˌneɪtɪŋ) *adj* **1** able to see fine distinctions and differences **2** discerning in matters of taste **3** (of a tariff, import duty, etc) levied at differential rates in order to favour or discourage imports or exports

discrimination (dɪˌskrɪmɪˈneɪʃən) *n* **1** unfair treatment of a person, racial group, minority, etc; action based on prejudice **2** subtle appreciation in matters of taste **3** the ability to see fine distinctions and differences

discriminatory (dɪˈskrɪmɪnətərɪ, -trɪ) *or* **discriminative** (dɪˈskrɪmɪnətɪv) *adj* **1** based on or showing prejudice; biased **2** capable of making fine distinctions

discursive (dɪˈskɜːsɪv) *adj* **1** passing from one topic to another, usually in an unmethodical way; digressive **2** *philosophy* of or relating to knowledge obtained by reason and argument rather than intuition [C16: from Medieval Latin *discursīvus*, from Late Latin *discursus* DISCOURSE] > disˈcursively *adv* > disˈcursiveness *n*

discus (ˈdɪskəs) *n*, *pl* discuses *or* disci (ˈdɪskaɪ) **1** (originally) a circular stone or plate used in throwing competitions by the ancient Greeks **2** *athletics* a similar disc-shaped object with a heavy middle thrown by athletes **3** the discus the event or sport of throwing the discus [C17: from Latin, from Greek *diskos* from *dikein* to throw]

discuss (dɪˈskʌs) *vb* (*tr*) **1** to have a conversation about;

consider by talking over; debate **2** to treat (a subject) in speech or writing [C14: from Late Latin *discussus* examined, from *discutere* to investigate, from Latin: to dash to pieces, from DIS-¹ + *quatere* to shake, strike] > disˈcussant *or* disˈcusser *n* > disˈcussible *or* disˈcussable *adj*

discussion (dɪˈskʌʃən) *n* the examination or consideration of a matter in speech or writing

disdain (dɪsˈdeɪn) *n* **1** a feeling or show of superiority and dislike; contempt; scorn ▷ *vb* **2** (*tr; may take an infinitive*) to refuse or reject with disdain [C13 *dedeyne*, from Old French *desdeign*, from *desdeigner* to reject as unworthy, from Latin *dēdignārī*; see DIS-¹, DEIGN] > disˈdainful *adj* > disˈdainfully *adv*

disease (dɪˈziːz) *n* **1** any impairment of normal physiological function affecting all or part of an organism, esp a specific pathological change caused by infection, stress, etc, producing characteristic symptoms; illness or sickness in general **2** a corresponding condition in plants **3** any situation or condition likened to this [C14: from Old French *desaise*; see DIS-¹, EASE]

diseconomy (ˌdɪsɪˈkɒnəmɪ) *n*, *pl* -mies *economics* disadvantage, such as lower efficiency or higher average costs, resulting from the scale on which an enterprise produces goods or services

disembark (ˌdɪsɪmˈbɑːk) *vb* to land or cause to land from a ship, aircraft, etc > disembarkation (dɪsˌembɑːˈkeɪʃən) *or* ˌdisemˈbarkment *n*

disembarrass (ˌdɪsɪmˈbærəs) *vb* (*tr*) **1** to free from embarrassment, entanglement, etc **2** to relieve or rid of something burdensome

disembodied (ˌdɪsɪmˈbɒdɪd) *adj* **1** lacking a body or freed from the body; incorporeal **2** lacking in substance, solidity, or any firm relation to reality

disembody (ˌdɪsɪmˈbɒdɪ) *vb* -bodies, -bodying, -bodied (*tr*) to free from the body or from physical form > ˌdisemˈbodiment *n*

disembogue (ˌdɪsɪmˈbəʊɡ) *vb* -bogues, -boguing, -bogued **1** (of a river, stream, etc) to discharge (water) at the mouth **2** (*intr*) to flow out [C16: from Spanish *desembocar*, from *des-* DIS-¹ + *embocar* put into the mouth, from *em-* in + *boca* mouth, from Latin *bucca* cheek] > ˌdisemˈboguement *n*

disembowel (ˌdɪsɪmˈbaʊəl) *vb* -els, -elling, -elled *or US* -els, -eling, -eled (*tr*) to remove the entrails of > ˌdisemˈbowelment *n*

disempower (ˌdɪsɪmˈpaʊə) *vb* (*tr*) to deprive (a person) of power or authority > ˌdisemˈpowerment *n*

disenchant (ˌdɪsɪnˈtʃɑːnt) *vb* (*tr; when passive, foll by with* or *by*) to make disappointed or disillusioned

disenchantment (ˌdɪsɪnˈtʃɑːntmənt) *n* a state of disappointment or disillusionment

disencumber (ˌdɪsɪnˈkʌmbə) *vb* (*tr*) to free from encumbrances > ˌdisenˈcumberment *n*

disenfranchise (ˌdɪsɪnˈfræntʃaɪz) *or* **disfranchise** *vb* (*tr*) **1** to deprive (a person) of the right to vote or other rights of citizenship **2** to deprive (a place) of the right to send representatives to an elected body **3** to deprive (a business concern, etc) of some privilege or right **4** to deprive (a person, place, etc) of any franchise or right > disenfranchisement (ˌdɪsɪnˈfræntʃɪzmənt) *or* disˈfranchisement *n*

disengage (ˌdɪsɪnˈɡeɪdʒ) *vb* **1** to release or become released from a connection, obligation, etc **2** *military* to withdraw (forces) from close action **3** *fencing* to move (one's blade) from one side of an opponent's blade to another in a circular motion to bring the blade into an open line of attack > ˌdisenˈgagement *n* > ˌdisenˈgaged *adj*

disentangle (ˌdɪsɪnˈtæŋɡᵊl) *vb* **1** to release or become free from entanglement or confusion **2** (*tr*) to unravel or work out > ˌdisenˈtanglement *n*

disequilibrium (ˌdɪsiːkwɪˈlɪbrɪəm) *n* a loss or absence of equilibrium, esp in an economy

disestablish (ˌdɪsɪˈstæblɪʃ) *vb* (*tr*) to deprive (a church, custom, institution, etc) of established status > ˌdisesˈtablishment *n*

disesteem (ˌdɪsɪˈstiːm) *vb* **1** (*tr*) to think little of ▷ *n*

2 lack of esteem or regard

disfavour or US **disfavor** (dɪsˈfeɪvə) n 1 disapproval or dislike 2 the state of being disapproved of or disliked 3 an unkind act ▷ vb 4 (tr) to regard or treat with disapproval or dislike

disfigure (dɪsˈfɪɡə) vb (tr) 1 to spoil the appearance or shape of; deface 2 to mar the effect or quality of > dis'figurement or disfiguration (ˌdɪsfɪɡəˈreɪʃən) n

disforest (dɪsˈfɒrɪst) vb (tr) 1 another word for **deforest** 2 English law a less common word for **disafforest** > dis,fores'tation n

disfranchise (dɪsˈfræntʃaɪz) vb another word for **disenfranchise**

disgorge (dɪsˈɡɔːdʒ) vb 1 to throw out (swallowed food, etc) from the throat or stomach; vomit 2 to discharge or empty of (contents) 3 (tr) to yield up unwillingly or under pressure > dis'gorgement n

disgrace (dɪsˈɡreɪs) n 1 a condition of shame, loss of reputation, or dishonour 2 a shameful person, thing, or state of affairs 3 exclusion from confidence or trust: he is in disgrace with his father ▷ vb (tr) 4 to bring shame upon; be a discredit to 5 to treat or cause to be treated with disfavour

disgraceful (dɪsˈɡreɪsfʊl) adj shameful; scandalous > dis'gracefully adv

disgruntle (dɪsˈɡrʌntəl) vb (tr; usually passive) to make sulky or discontented [C17: DIS-1 + obsolete gruntle to complain; see GRUNT] > dis'gruntlement n

disgruntled (dɪsˈɡrʌntəld) adj feeling or expressing discontent or anger

disguise (dɪsˈɡaɪz) vb 1 to modify the appearance or manner in order to conceal the identity of (oneself, someone, or something) 2 (tr) to misrepresent in order to obscure the actual nature or meaning ▷ n 3 a mask, costume, or manner that disguises 4 the act of disguising or the state of being disguised [C14: from Old French desguisier, from des- DIS-1 + guise manner; see GUISE] > dis'guised adj

disgust (dɪsˈɡʌst) vb (tr) 1 to sicken or fill with loathing 2 to offend the moral sense, principles, or taste of ▷ n 3 a great loathing or distaste aroused by someone or something 4 in disgust as a result of [C16: from Old French desgouster, from des- DIS-1 + gouster to taste, from goust taste, from Latin gustus] > dis'gustedly adv > dis'gustedness n

dish (dɪʃ) n 1 a container used for holding or serving food, esp an open shallow container of pottery, glass, etc 2 the food that is served or contained in a dish 3 a particular article or preparation of food 4 Also called: **dishful** the amount contained in a dish 5 something resembling a dish, esp in shape 6 a concavity or depression 7 short for **dish aerial** 8 informal an attractive person ▷ vb (tr) 9 to put into a dish 10 to make hollow or concave 11 Brit informal to ruin or spoil ▷ See also **dish out**, **dish up** [Old English disc, from Latin discus quoit, see DISC] > 'dish,like adj

dishabille (ˌdɪsæˈbiːl) n a variant of **deshabille**

dish aerial n a microwave aerial, used esp in radar, radio telescopes, and satellite broadcasting, consisting of a parabolic reflector. Formal name: **parabolic aerial** Also called: **dish antenna**. Often shortened to: **dish**

disharmony (dɪsˈhɑːmənɪ) n, pl -nies 1 lack of accord or harmony 2 a situation, circumstance, etc, that is inharmonious > disharmonious (ˌdɪshɑːˈməʊnɪəs) adj

dishcloth ('dɪʃˌklɒθ) n a cloth or rag for washing or drying dishes

dishdasha ('dɪʃˌdæʃə) n a white long-sleeved collarless garment worn by Muslim men in the Arabian peninsula [Arabic]

dishearten (dɪsˈhɑːtən) vb (tr) to weaken or destroy the hope, courage, enthusiasm, etc, of > dis'hearteningly adv > dis'heartenment n

dished (dɪʃt) adj 1 shaped like a dish; concave 2 (of a pair of road wheels) arranged so that they are closer to one another at the bottom than at the top 3 informal exhausted or defeated

dishevel (dɪˈʃevəl) vb -els, -elling, -elled or US -els, -eling, -eled to disarrange (the hair or clothes) of (someone) [C15: back formation from DISHEVELLED]

> di'shevelment n

dishevelled or US **disheveled** (dɪˈʃevəld) adj 1 (esp of hair) hanging loosely 2 (of general appearance) unkempt; untidy [C15 dischevelee, from Old French deschevelé, from des- DIS-1 + chevel hair, from Latin capillus]

dishonest (dɪsˈɒnɪst) adj not honest or fair; deceiving or fraudulent > dis'honestly adv

dishonesty (dɪsˈɒnɪstɪ) n, pl -ties 1 lack of honesty or fairness; deceit 2 a deceiving act or statement; fraud

dishonour or US **dishonor** (dɪsˈɒnə) vb (tr) 1 to treat with disrespect 2 to fail or refuse to pay (a cheque, bill of exchange, etc) 3 to cause the disgrace of (a woman) by seduction or rape ▷ n 4 lack of honour or respect 5 a state of shame or disgrace 6 a person or thing that causes a loss of honour 7 an insult; affront 8 refusal or failure to accept or pay a commercial paper

dishonourable or US **dishonorable** (dɪsˈɒnərəbəl, -ˈɒnrəbəl) adj 1 characterized by or causing dishonour or discredit 2 having little or no integrity; unprincipled > dis'honourableness or US dis'honorableness n > dis'honourably or US dis'honorably adv

dish out vb informal 1 (tr, adverb) to distribute 2 dish it out to inflict punishment

dishtowel ('dɪʃˌtaʊəl) n chiefly US & Canadian a towel for drying dishes and kitchen utensils. Also called (in Britain and certain other countries): **tea towel**

dish up vb (adverb) 1 to serve (a meal, food, etc) 2 (tr) informal to prepare or present, esp in an attractive manner

dishwasher ('dɪʃˌwɒʃə) n 1 an electrically operated machine for washing, rinsing, and drying dishes, cutlery, etc 2 a person who washes dishes, etc

dishwater ('dɪʃˌwɔːtə) n 1 water in which dishes and kitchen utensils are or have been washed 2 something resembling this

dishy ('dɪʃɪ) adj dishier, dishiest informal, chiefly Brit good-looking or attractive

disillusion (ˌdɪsɪˈluːʒən) vb 1 (tr) to destroy the ideals, illusions, or false ideas of ▷ n 2 Also: **disillusionment** the act of disillusioning or the state of being disillusioned

disincentive (ˌdɪsɪnˈsɛntɪv) n 1 something that acts as a deterrent ▷ adj 2 acting as a deterrent: a disincentive effect on productivity

disincline (ˌdɪsɪnˈklaɪn) vb to make or be unwilling, reluctant, or averse > disinclination (ˌdɪsɪnklɪˈneɪʃən) n

disinfect (ˌdɪsɪnˈfɛkt) vb (tr) to rid of microorganisms potentially harmful to man, esp by chemical means > ,disin'fection n

disinfectant (ˌdɪsɪnˈfɛktənt) n an agent that destroys or inhibits the activity of microorganisms that cause disease

disinfest (ˌdɪsɪnˈfɛst) vb (tr) to rid of vermin > dis,infes'tation n

disinflation (ˌdɪsɪnˈfleɪʃən) n economics a reduction or stabilization of the general price level intended to improve the balance of payments without incurring reductions in output, employment, and investment

disinformation (ˌdɪsɪnfəˈmeɪʃən) n false information intended to deceive or mislead

disingenuous (ˌdɪsɪnˈdʒɛnjʊəs) adj not sincere; lacking candour > ,disin'genuously adv > ,disin'genuousness n

disinherit (ˌdɪsɪnˈhɛrɪt) vb (tr) 1 law to deprive (an heir or next of kin) of inheritance or right to inherit 2 to deprive of a right or heritage > ,disin'heritance n

disintegrate (dɪsˈɪntɪˌɡreɪt) vb 1 to break or be broken into fragments or constituent parts; shatter 2 to lose or cause to lose cohesion or unity 3 (intr) to lose judgment or control; deteriorate 4 physics a to induce or undergo nuclear fission, as by bombardment with fast particles b another word for **decay** (sense 3) > dis,inte'gration n > dis'inte,grator n

disinter (ˌdɪsɪnˈtɜː) vb -ters, -terring, -terred (tr) 1 to remove or dig up; exhume 2 to bring (a secret, hidden facts, etc) to light; expose > ,disin'terment n

disinterest (dɪsˈɪntrɪst, -tərɪst) n 1 freedom from bias or involvement 2 lack of interest; indifference

disinterested (dɪsˈɪntrɪstɪd, -tərɪs-) adj 1 free from bias or partiality; objective 2 not interested > dis'interestedly adv > dis'interestedness n

● USAGE Many people consider that the use of *disinterested* to mean not interested is incorrect and that *uninterested* should be used

disintermediation (ˌdɪsˌɪntəˌmiːdɪˈeɪʃən) *n finance* the elimination of such financial intermediaries as banks and brokers in transactions between principals, often as a result of deregulation and the use of computers

disinvest (dɪsɪnˈvest) *vb economics* **1** (usually foll by *in*) to remove investment (from) **2** (*intr*) to reduce the capital stock of an economy or enterprise, as by not replacing obsolete machinery > disin'vestment *n*

disjoin (dɪsˈdʒɔɪn) *vb* to disconnect or become disconnected; separate > dis'joinable *adj*

disjoint (dɪsˈdʒɔɪnt) *vb* **1** to take apart or come apart at the joints **2** (*tr*) to disunite or disjoin **3** to dislocate or become dislocated **4** (*tr; usually passive*) to end the unity, sequence, or coherence of

disjointed (dɪsˈdʒɔɪntɪd) *adj* **1** having no coherence; disconnected **2** separated at the joint **3** dislocated > dis'jointedly *adv*

disjunct (ˈdɪsdʒʌŋkt) *n logic* one of the propositions or formulas in a disjunction

disjunction (dɪsˈdʒʌŋkʃən) *n* **1** Also called: **disjuncture** the act of disconnecting or the state of being disconnected; separation **2** *logic* **a** the operator that forms a compound sentence from two given sentences and corresponds to the English *or* **b** the relation between such sentences

disjunctive (dɪsˈdʒʌŋktɪv) *adj* **1** serving to disconnect or separate **2** *grammar* denoting a word, esp a conjunction, that serves to express opposition or contrast: *but* in the sentence *She was poor but she was honest* **3** Also called: **alternative** *logic* relating to, characterized by, or containing disjunction ⊳ *n* **4** *grammar* a disjunctive word, esp a conjunction **5** *logic* a disjunctive proposition; disjunction > dis'junctively *adv*

disk (dɪsk) *n* **1** a variant spelling (esp US and Canadian) of **disc 2** Also called: **magnetic disk, hard disk** *computing* a direct-access storage device consisting of a stack of plates coated with a magnetic layer, the whole assembly rotating rapidly as a single unit. Each surface has a read-write head that can move radially to read or write data on concentric tracks

disk drive *n computing* the controller and mechanism for reading and writing data on computer disks

diskette (dɪsˈket) *n computing* another name for **floppy disk**

disk operating system *n* an operating system used on a computer system with one or more disk drives. Often shortened to: **DOS**

dislike (dɪsˈlaɪk) *vb* **1** (*tr*) to consider unpleasant or disagreeable ⊳ *n* **2** a feeling of aversion or antipathy > dis'likable *or* dis'likeable *adj*

dislocate (ˈdɪsləˌkeɪt) *vb* (*tr*) **1** to disrupt or shift out of place or position **2** to displace (an organ or part) from its normal position, esp a bone from its joint

dislocation (ˌdɪsləˈkeɪʃən) *n* **1** the act of displacing or the state of being displaced; disruption **2** (esp of the bones in a joint) the state or condition of being dislocated

dislodge (dɪsˈlɒdʒ) *vb* to remove from or leave a lodging place, hiding place, or previously fixed position > dis'lodgment *or* dis'lodgement *n*

disloyal (dɪsˈlɔɪəl) *adj* not loyal or faithful; deserting one's allegiance or duty > dis'loyally *adv*

disloyalty (dɪsˈlɔɪəltɪ) *n, pl* -ties the condition or an instance of being unfaithful or disloyal

dismal (ˈdɪzməl) *adj* **1** causing gloom or depression **2** causing dismay or terror **3** of poor quality or a low standard; feeble [c13: from *dismal* (noun) list of 24 unlucky days in the year, from Medieval Latin *diēs malī* bad days, from Latin *diēs* day + *malus* bad] > 'dismally *adv* > 'dismalness *n*

dismantle (dɪsˈmænt⁰l) *vb* (*tr*) **1** to take apart **2** to demolish or raze **3** to strip of covering [c17: from Old French *desmanteler* to remove a cloak from; see MANTLE] > dis'mantlement *n*

dismast (dɪsˈmɑːst) *vb* (*tr*) to break off the mast or masts of (a sailing vessel)

dismay (dɪsˈmeɪ) *vb* (*tr*) **1** to fill with apprehension or alarm **2** to fill with depression or discouragement ⊳ *n* **3** consternation or agitation [c13: from Old French *desmaiier* (unattested), from des- DIS-¹ + *esmayer* to frighten, ultimately of Germanic origin; see MAY¹] > dis'maying *adj*

dismember (dɪsˈmembə) *vb* (*tr*) **1** to remove the limbs or members of **2** to cut to pieces **3** to divide or partition (something, such as an empire) > dis'memberment *n*

dismiss (dɪsˈmɪs) *vb* (*tr*) **1** to remove or discharge from employment or service **2** to send away or allow to go or disperse **3** to dispel from one's mind; discard; reject **4** to cease to consider (a subject) **5** to decline further hearing to (a claim or action) **6** *cricket* to bowl out a side for a particular number of runs [c15: from Medieval Latin *dismissus* sent away, variant of Latin *dīmissus*, from *dīmittere*, from *dī-* DIS-¹ + *mittere* to send] > dis'missible *adj* > dis'missive *adj* > dis'missal *n*

dismount (dɪsˈmaʊnt) *vb* **1** to get off a horse, bicycle, etc **2** (*tr*) to disassemble or remove from a mounting ⊳ *n* **3** the act of dismounting

Disney (ˈdɪznɪ) *n* **Walt(er Elias)**. 1901–66, US film producer, who pioneered animated cartoons: noted esp for his creations *Mickey Mouse* and *Donald Duck* and films such as *Fantasia* (1940) > ˌDisney'esque *adj*

Disneyfy (ˈdɪznɪˌfaɪ) *vb* -fies, -fying, -fied (*tr*) to transform (historical places, local customs, etc) into trivial entertainment for tourists [c20: from the DISNEYLAND amusement park] > ˌDisneyfi'cation *n*

Disneyland (ˈdɪznɪˌlænd) *n* an amusement park in Anaheim, California, founded by Walt Disney and opened in 1955. **Walt Disney World**, a second amusement park, opened in 1971 near Orlando, Florida. Further parks operate in Paris, Tokyo, and Hong Kong

disobedience (ˌdɪsəˈbiːdɪəns) *n* lack of obedience

disobedient (ˌdɪsəˈbiːdɪənt) *adj* not obedient; neglecting or refusing to obey > ˌdiso'bediently *adv*

disobey (ˌdɪsəˈbeɪ) *vb* to neglect or refuse to obey (someone, an order, etc) > ˌdiso'beyer *n*

disoblige (ˌdɪsəˈblaɪdʒ) *vb* (*tr*) **1** to disregard the desires of **2** to slight; insult **3** *informal* to cause trouble or inconvenience to > ˌdiso'bliging *adj*

disorder (dɪsˈɔːdə) *n* **1** a lack of order; disarray; confusion **2** a disturbance of public order or peace **3** an upset of health; ailment **4** a deviation from the normal system or order ⊳ *vb* (*tr*) **5** to upset the order of; disarrange; muddle **6** to disturb the health or mind of

disorderly (dɪsˈɔːdəlɪ) *adj* **1** untidy; irregular **2** uncontrolled; unruly **3** *law* violating public peace or order > dis'orderliness *n*

disorderly house *n law* an establishment in which unruly behaviour habitually occurs, esp a brothel or a gaming house

disorganize *or* **disorganise** (dɪsˈɔːgəˌnaɪz) *vb* (*tr*) to disrupt or destroy the arrangement, system, or unity of > disˌorgani'zation *or* disˌorgani'sation *n*

disorientate (dɪsˈɔːrɪenˌteɪt) *or* **disorient** *vb* (*tr*) **1** to cause (someone) to lose his bearings **2** to perplex; confuse > disˌorien'tation *n*

disown (dɪsˈəʊn) *vb* (*tr*) to deny any connection with; refuse to acknowledge > dis'owner *n*

disparage (dɪˈspærɪdʒ) *vb* (*tr*) **1** to speak contemptuously of; belittle **2** to damage the reputation of [c14: from Old French *desparagier*, from *des-* DIS-¹ + *parage* equality, from Latin *par* equal] > dis'paragement *n* > dis'paraging *adj*

disparate (ˈdɪspərɪt) *adj* **1** utterly different or distinct in kind ⊳ *n* **2** (*plural*) unlike things or people [c16: from Latin *disparāre* to divide, from DIS-¹ + *parāre* to prepare; also influenced by Latin *dispar* unequal] > 'disparately *adv* > 'disparateness *n*

disparity (dɪˈspærɪtɪ) *n, pl* -ties **1** inequality or difference, as in age, rank, wages, etc **2** dissimilarity

dispassionate (dɪsˈpæʃənɪt) *adj* devoid of or uninfluenced by emotion or prejudice; objective; impartial > dis'passionately *adv*

dispatch *or* **despatch** (dɪˈspætʃ) *vb* (*tr*) **1** to send off promptly, as to a destination or to perform a task **2** to discharge or complete (a task, duty, etc) promptly **3** *informal* to eat up quickly **4** to murder or execute ⊳ *n* **5** the act of sending off a letter, messenger, etc **6** prompt action or speed (often in the phrase **with dispatch**) **7** an official communication or report, sent in haste **8** *journalism* a report sent to a newspaper, etc, by a correspondent **9** murder or execution [c16: from Italian *dispacciare*, from Provençal *despachar*, from Old French *despeechier* to set free, from *des-* DIS-¹ + *-peechier*, ultimately from Latin *pedica* a fetter] > dis'patcher *n*

dispatch box *n* a case or box used to hold valuables or documents, esp official state documents

dispatch case *n* a case used for carrying papers, documents, books, etc, usually flat and stiff

dispatch rider *n* a horseman or motorcyclist who carries dispatches

dispel (dɪ'spɛl) *vb* **-pels, -pelling, -pelled** (tr) to disperse or drive away [c17: from Latin *dispellere*, from DIS-¹ + *pellere* to drive] > dis'peller *n*

dispensable (dɪ'spɛnsəb³l) *adj* **1** not essential; expendable **2** (of a law, vow, etc) able to be relaxed > dis,pensa'bility *or* dis'pensableness *n*

dispensary (dɪ'spɛnsərɪ, -srɪ) *n, pl* **-ries** a place where medicine and medical supplies are dispensed

dispensation (,dɪspɛn'seɪʃən) *n* **1** the act of distributing or dispensing **2** something distributed or dispensed **3** a system or plan of administering or dispensing **4** *chiefly RC Church* permission to dispense with an obligation of church law **5** any exemption from a rule or obligation **6** *Christianity* **a** the ordering of life and events by God **b** a religious system or code of prescriptions for life and conduct regarded as of divine origin > ,dispen'sational *adj*

dispensatory (dɪ'spɛnsətərɪ, -trɪ) *n, pl* **-ries** a book listing the composition, preparation, and application of various drugs

dispense (dɪ'spɛns) *vb* **1** (tr) to give out or issue in portions **2** (tr) to prepare and distribute (medicine), esp on prescription **3** (tr) to administer (the law, etc) **4** (intr; foll by *with*) to do away (with) or manage (without) **5** to grant a dispensation to (someone) from (some obligation of church law) **6** to exempt or excuse from a rule or obligation [c14: from Medieval Latin *dispensāre* to pardon, from Latin *dispendere* to weigh out, from DIS-¹ + *pendere* to weigh]

dispenser (dɪ'spɛnsə) *n* **1** a device, such as a vending machine, that automatically dispenses a single item or a measured quantity **2** a person or thing that dispenses

dispensing optician *n* See **optician**

dispersal (dɪ'spɜːs³l) *n* **1** the act of dispersing or the condition of being dispersed **2** the spread of animals, plants, or seeds to new areas

disperse (dɪ'spɜːs) *vb* **1** to scatter; distribute over a wide area **2** to dissipate or cause to dissipate **3** to leave or cause to leave a gathering, often in a random manner **4** to separate or be separated by dispersion **5** (tr) to diffuse or spread (news, information, etc) **6** to separate (particles) throughout a solid, liquid, or gas, as in the formation of a suspension or colloid ▷ *adj* **7** of or consisting of the particles in a colloid or suspension: *disperse phase* [c14: from Latin *dispersus* scattered, from *dispergere* to scatter widely, from DI-² + *spargere* to strew] > dis'perser *n*

● USAGE See at **disburse**

dispersion (dɪ'spɜːʃən) *n* **1** another word for **dispersal** **2** *physics* **a** the separation of electromagnetic radiation into constituents of different wavelengths **b** a measure of the ability of a substance to separate by refraction, expressed by the first differential of the refractive index with respect to wavelength at a given value of wavelength **3** *statistics* the degree to which values of a frequency distribution are scattered around some central point, usually the arithmetic mean or median **4** *chem* a system containing particles dispersed in a solid, liquid, or gas **5** *ecology* the distribution pattern of an animal or a plant population

dispirit (dɪ'spɪrɪt) *vb* (tr) to lower the spirit or enthusiasm of; make downhearted or depressed; discourage

dispirited (dɪ'spɪrɪtɪd) *adj* low in spirit or enthusiasm; downhearted or depressed; discouraged > dis'piritedly *adv* > dis'piritedness *n*

dispiriting (dɪ'spɪrɪtɪŋ) *adj* tending to lower the spirit or enthusiasm; depressing; discouraging > dis'piritingly *adv*

displace (dɪs'pleɪs) *vb* (tr) **1** to move from the usual or correct location **2** to remove from office or employment **3** to occupy the place of; replace; supplant

displaced person *n* a person forced from his home or country, esp by war or revolution

displacement (dɪs'pleɪsmənt) *n* **1** the act of displacing or the condition of being displaced **2** the weight or volume displaced by a floating or submerged body in a fluid **3** *psychoanal* the transferring of emotional feelings from their original object to one that disguises their real nature **4** *maths* the distance measured in a particular direction from a reference point. Symbol: *s*

displacement activity *n* *psychol* behaviour that occurs typically when there is a conflict between motives and that has no relevance to either motive: e.g. head scratching

display (dɪ'spleɪ) *vb* **1** (tr) to show or make visible **2** (tr) to disclose or make evident; reveal **3** (tr) to flaunt in an ostentatious way **4** (tr) to spread or open out; unfurl or unfold **5** (tr) to give prominence to (headings, captions, etc) by the use of certain typefaces **6** (intr) *zoology* to engage in a display ▷ *n* **7** the act of exhibiting or displaying; show **8** something exhibited or displayed **9** an ostentatious or pretentious exhibition **10** an arrangement of certain typefaces to give prominence to headings, captions, advertisements, etc **11** *electronics* **a** a device capable of representing information visually, as on a cathode-ray tube screen **b** the information so presented **12** *zoology* a pattern of behaviour in birds, fishes, etc, by which the animal attracts attention while it is courting the female, defending its territory, etc **13** (modifier) relating to or using typefaces that give prominence to the words they are used to set [c14: from Anglo-French *despleier* to unfold, from Late Latin *displicāre* to scatter, from DIS-¹ + *plicāre* to fold] > dis'player *n*

displease (dɪs'pliːz) *vb* to annoy, offend, or cause displeasure to (someone) > dis'pleasing *adj* > dis'pleasingly *adv*

displeasure (dɪs'plɛʒə) *n* **1** the condition of being displeased **2** *archaic* **a** pain **b** an act or cause of offence

disport (dɪ'spɔːt) *vb* **1** (tr) to indulge (oneself) in pleasure **2** (intr) to frolic or gambol ▷ *n* **3** *archaic* amusement [c14: from Anglo-French *desporter*, from *des-* DIS-¹ + *porter* to carry]

disposable (dɪ'spəʊzəb³l) *adj* **1** designed for disposal after use: *disposable cups* **2** available for use if needed: *disposable assets* ▷ *n* **3** something, such as a baby's nappy, that is designed for disposal **4** (plural) short for **disposable goods** > dis,posa'bility *or* dis'posableness *n*

disposable goods *pl n* consumer goods that are used up a short time after purchase, including perishables, newspapers, clothes, etc. Also called: disposables

disposable income *n* **1** the money a person has available to spend after paying taxes, pension contributions, etc **2** the total amount of money that the individuals in a community, country, etc, have available to buy consumer goods

disposal (dɪ'spəʊz³l) *n* **1** the act or means of getting rid of something **2** placement or arrangement in a particular order **3** a specific method of tending to matters, as in business **4** the act or process of transferring something to or providing something for another **5** the power or opportunity to make use of someone or something (esp in the phrase **at one's disposal**)

dispose (dɪ'spəʊz) *vb* **1** (intr; foll by *of*) **a** to deal with or settle **b** to give, sell, or transfer to another **c** to throw out or away **d** to consume, such as food **e** to kill **2** to arrange or settle (matters) by placing into correct or final condition **3** (tr) to make willing or receptive **4** (tr) to adjust or place in a certain order or position **5** (tr; often foll by *to*) to accustom or condition [c14: from Old French *disposer*, from Latin *dispōnere* to set in different places, arrange, from DIS-¹ + *pōnere* to place] > dis'poser *n*

disposed (dɪ'spəʊzd) *adj* **a** having an inclination as specified (towards something) **b** (in combination): *well-*

disposed; *ill-disposed*

disposition (ˌdɪspəˈzɪʃən) *n* 1 a person's usual temperament or frame of mind 2 a natural or acquired tendency, inclination, or habit in a person or thing 3 *archaic* manner of placing or arranging

dispossess (ˌdɪspəˈzɛs) *vb* (*tr*) to take away possession of something, esp property; expel > ˌdisposˈsession *n* > ˌdisposˈsessor *n*

dispraise (dɪsˈpreɪz) *vb* 1 (*tr*) to express disapproval or condemnation of ▷ *n* 2 the disapproval, etc, expressed > disˈpraiser *n*

disproof (dɪsˈpruːf) *n* 1 facts that disprove something 2 the act of disproving

disproportion (ˌdɪsprəˈpɔːʃən) *n* 1 lack of proportion or equality 2 an instance of disparity or inequality ▷ *vb* 3 (*tr*) to cause to become exaggerated or unequal > ˌdisproˈportional *adj*

disproportionate (ˌdɪsprəˈpɔːʃənɪt) *adj* out of proportion; unequal > ˌdisproˈportionately *adv* > ˌdisproˈportionateness *n*

disprove (dɪsˈpruːv) *vb* (*tr*) to show (an assertion, claim, etc) to be incorrect > disˈprovable *adj* > disˈproval *n*

disputable (dɪˈspjuːtəbəl, ˈdɪspjʊtə-) *adj* capable of being argued; debatable > disˌputaˈbility *or* disˈputableness *n* > disˈputably *adv*

disputant (dɪˈspjuːtˁnt, ˈdɪspjʊtənt) *n* 1 a person who argues; contestant ▷ *adj* 2 engaged in argument

disputation (ˌdɪspjʊˈteɪʃən) *n* 1 the act or an instance of arguing 2 a formal academic debate on a thesis 3 an obsolete word for **conversation**

disputatious (ˌdɪspjʊˈteɪʃəs) *or* **disputative** (dɪˈspjuːtətɪv) *adj* inclined to argument > ˌdispuˈtatiousness *or* disˈputativeness *n*

dispute *vb* (dɪˈspjuːt) 1 to argue, debate, or quarrel about (something) 2 (*tr; may take a clause as object*) to doubt the validity, etc, of 3 (*tr*) to seek to win; contest for 4 (*tr*) to struggle against; resist ▷ *n* (dɪˈspjuːt, ˈdɪspjuːt) 5 an argument or quarrel [c13: from Late Latin *disputāre* to contend verbally, from Latin: to discuss, from DIS-¹ + *putāre* to think] > disˈputer *n*

disqualify (dɪsˈkwɒlɪˌfaɪ) *vb* -fies, -fying, -fied (*tr*) 1 to make unfit or unqualified 2 to make ineligible, as for entry to an examination 3 to debar (a player or team) from a sporting contest 4 to divest or deprive of rights, powers, or privileges > disˌqualifiˈcation *n*

disquiet (dɪsˈkwaɪət) *n* 1 a feeling or condition of anxiety or uneasiness ▷ *vb* 2 (*tr*) to make anxious or upset > disˈquieting *adj*

disquietude (dɪsˈkwaɪɪˌtjuːd) *n* a feeling or state of anxiety or uneasiness

disquisition (ˌdɪskwɪˈzɪʃən) *n* a formal written or oral examination of a subject [c17: from Latin *disquīsītiō*, from *disquīrere* to make an investigation, from DIS-¹ + *quaerere* to seek] > ˌdisquiˈsitional *adj*

Disraeli (dɪzˈreɪlɪ) *n* **Benjamin**, 1st Earl of Beaconsfield. 1804–81, British Tory statesman and novelist; prime minister (1868; 1874–80). He gave coherence to the Tory principles of protectionism and imperialism, was responsible for the Reform Bill (1867) and, as prime minister, bought a controlling interest in the Suez Canal. His novels include *Coningsby* (1844) and *Sybil* (1845)

disregard (ˌdɪsrɪˈɡɑːd) *vb* (*tr*) 1 to give little or no attention to; ignore 2 to treat as unworthy of consideration or respect ▷ *n* 3 lack of attention or respect > ˌdisreˈgardful *adj*

disremember (ˌdɪsrɪˈmɛmbə) *vb informal, chiefly US* to fail to recall (someone or something)

disrepair (ˌdɪsrɪˈpɛə) *n* the condition of being worn out or in poor working order; a condition requiring repairs

disreputable (dɪsˈrɛpjʊtəbˀl) *adj* 1 having or causing a lack of repute 2 disordered in appearance > disˈreputably *adv*

disrepute (ˌdɪsrɪˈpjuːt) *n* a loss or lack of credit or repute

disrespect (ˌdɪsrɪˈspɛkt) *n* contempt; rudeness > ˌdisreˈspectful *adj*

disrobe (dɪsˈrəʊb) *vb* 1 to remove the clothing of (a person) or (of a person) to undress 2 (*tr*) to divest of authority, etc > disˈrobement *n*

disrupt (dɪsˈrʌpt) *vb* 1 (*tr*) to throw into turmoil or

disorder 2 (*tr*) to interrupt the progress of (a movement, meeting, etc) 3 to break or split (something) apart [c17: from Latin *disruptus* burst asunder, from *dīrumpere* to dash to pieces, from DIS-¹ + *rumpere* to burst] > disˈrupter *or* disˈruptor *n* > disˈruption *n*

disruptive (dɪsˈrʌptɪv) *adj* involving, causing, or tending to cause disruption

diss *or* **dis** (dɪs) *vb slang, chiefly US* to treat (someone) with contempt [c20: originally Black rap slang, short for DISRESPECT]

dissatisfaction (dɪsˌsætɪsˈfækʃən) *n* the state of being unsatisfied or disappointed

dissatisfy (dɪsˈsætɪsˌfaɪ) *vb* -fies, -fying, -fied (*tr*) to fail to satisfy; disappoint

dissect (dɪˈsɛkt, daɪ-) *vb* 1 to cut open and examine the structure of (a dead animal or plant) 2 (*tr*) to examine critically and minutely [c17: from Latin *dissecāre*, from DIS-¹ + *secāre* to cut] > disˈsection *n* > disˈsector *n*

dissected (dɪˈsɛktɪd, daɪ-) *adj* 1 *botany* in the form of narrow lobes or segments 2 *geology* (of plains) cut by erosion into hills and valleys, esp following tectonic movements

disselboom (ˈdɪsəlˌbʊəm) *n South African* the main haulage shaft of a wagon or cart [from Afrikaans *dissel* shaft + *boom* beam]

dissemble (dɪˈsɛmbəl) *vb* 1 to conceal (one's real motives, emotions, etc) by pretence 2 (*tr*) to pretend; simulate [c15: from earlier *dissimulen*, from Latin *dissimulāre*; probably influenced by obsolete *semble* to resemble] > disˈsemblance *n* > disˈsembler *n*

disseminate (dɪˈsɛmɪˌneɪt) *vb* (*tr*) to distribute or scatter about; diffuse [c17: from Latin *dissēmināre*, from DIS-¹ + *sēmināre* to sow, from *sēmen* seed] > disˌsemiˈnation *n* > disˈsemiˌnator *n*

disseminated sclerosis *n* another name for **multiple sclerosis**

dissension (dɪˈsɛnʃən) *n* disagreement, esp when leading to a quarrel [c13: from Latin *dissēnsiō*, from *dissentīre* to dissent]

dissent (dɪˈsɛnt) *vb* (*intr*) 1 to have a disagreement or withhold assent 2 *Christianity*, to refuse to conform to the doctrines, beliefs, or practices of an established church, and to adhere to a different system of beliefs and practices ▷ *n* 3 a difference of opinion 4 *Christianity* separation from an established church; Nonconformism 5 the voicing of a minority opinion in announcing the decision on a case at law; dissenting judgment [c16: from Latin *dissentīre* to disagree, from DIS-¹ + *sentīre* to perceive, feel] > disˈsenter *n* > disˈsenting *adj*

Dissenter (dɪˈsɛntə) *n Christianity, chiefly Brit* a Nonconformist or a person who refuses to conform to the established church

dissentient (dɪˈsɛnʃənt) *adj* 1 dissenting, esp from the opinion of the majority ▷ *n* 2 a dissenter > disˈsentience *or* disˈsentiency *n*

dissertation (ˌdɪsəˈteɪʃən) *n* 1 a written thesis, often based on original research, usually required for a higher degree 2 a formal discourse > ˌdisserˈtational *adj*

disserve (dɪsˈsɜːv) *vb* (*tr*) *archaic* to do a disservice to

disservice (dɪsˈsɜːvɪs) *n* an ill turn; wrong; injury, esp when trying to help

dissever (dɪˈsɛvə) *vb* 1 to break off or become broken off 2 (*tr*) to divide up into parts [c13: from Old French *dessevrer*, from Late Latin DIS-¹ + *sēparāre* to SEPARATE] > disˈseverance *or* disˈseverment *n*

dissident (ˈdɪsɪdənt) *adj* 1 disagreeing; dissenting ▷ *n* 2 a person who disagrees, esp one who disagrees with the government [c16: from Latin *dissidēre* to be remote from, from DIS-¹ + *sedēre* to sit] > ˈdissidence *n* > ˈdissidently *adv*

dissimilar (dɪˈsɪmɪlə) *adj* not alike; not similar; different > disˈsimilarly *adv* > ˌdissimiˈlarity *n*

dissimilate (dɪˈsɪmɪˌleɪt) *vb* 1 to make or become dissimilar 2 (usually foll by *to*) *phonetics* to change or displace (a consonant) or (of a consonant) to be changed to or displaced by (another consonant) so that its manner of articulation becomes less similar to a speech sound in the same word. Thus (r) in the final syllable of French *marbre* is dissimilated to (l) in its English form *marble* [c19: from DIS-¹ + ASSIMILATE]

dissimilation (ˌdɪsɪmɪˈleɪʃən) n 1 the act or an instance of making dissimilar 2 *phonetics* the alteration or omission of a consonant as a result of being dissimilated

dissimilitude (ˌdɪsɪˈmɪlɪˌtjuːd) n 1 dissimilarity; difference 2 a point of difference

dissimulate (dɪˈsɪmjʊˌleɪt) vb to conceal (one's real feelings) by pretence > disˌsimuˈlation n > disˈsimuˌlator n

dissipate (ˈdɪsɪˌpeɪt) vb 1 to exhaust or be exhausted by dispersion 2 (tr) to scatter or break up 3 (intr) to indulge in the pursuit of pleasure [c15: from Latin *dissipāre* to disperse, from DIS-¹ + *supāre* to throw] > ˈdissiˌpater or ˈdissiˌpator n > ˈdissiˌpative adj

dissipated (ˈdɪsɪˌpeɪtɪd) adj 1 indulging without restraint in the pursuit of pleasure; debauched 2 wasted, scattered, or exhausted > ˈdissiˌpatedly adv > ˈdissiˌpatedness n

dissipation (ˌdɪsɪˈpeɪʃən) n 1 the act of dissipating or condition of being dissipated 2 unrestrained indulgence in physical pleasures, esp alcohol 3 excessive expenditure; wastefulness

dissociate (dɪˈsəʊʃɪˌeɪt, -sɪ-) vb 1 to break or cause to break the association between (people, organizations, etc) 2 (tr) to regard or treat as separate or unconnected 3 to undergo or subject to dissociation > disˈsociative adj

dissociation (dɪˌsəʊsɪˈeɪʃən, -ʃɪ-) n 1 the act of dissociating or the state of being dissociated 2 *chem* a reversible chemical change of the molecules of a single compound into two or more other molecules, atoms, ions, or radicals 3 *psychiatry* the separation of a group of mental processes or ideas from the rest of the personality, so that they lead an independent existence, as in cases of multiple personality

dissoluble (dɪˈsɒljʊbᵊl) adj a less common word for **soluble** [c16: from Latin *dissolūbilis*, from *dissolvere* to DISSOLVE] > disˌsoluˈbility or disˈsolubleness n

dissolute (ˈdɪsəˌluːt) adj given to dissipation; debauched [c14: from Latin *dissolūtus* loose, from *dissolvere* to DISSOLVE] > ˈdissoˌlutely adv > ˈdissoˌluteness n

dissolution (ˌdɪsəˈluːʃən) n 1 the resolution or separation into component parts; disintegration 2 destruction by breaking up and dispersing 3 the termination of a meeting or assembly, such as Parliament 4 the termination of a formal or legal relationship, such as a business enterprise, marriage, etc 5 the act or process of dissolving

dissolve (dɪˈzɒlv) vb 1 to go or cause to go into solution 2 to become or cause to become liquid; melt 3 to disintegrate or disperse 4 to come or bring to an end 5 to dismiss (a meeting, parliament, etc) or (of a meeting, etc) to be dismissed 6 to collapse or cause to collapse emotionally: *to dissolve into tears* 7 to lose or cause to lose distinctness or clarity 8 (tr) to terminate legally, as a marriage, etc 9 (intr) *films, television* to fade out one scene and replace with another to make two scenes merge imperceptibly (**fast dissolve**) or slowly overlap (**slow dissolve**) over a period of about three or four seconds ▷ n 10 *films, television* a scene filmed or televised by dissolving [c14: from Latin *dissolvere* to make loose, from DIS-¹ + *solvere* to release] > disˈsolvable adj

dissonance (ˈdɪsənəns) or **dissonancy** n 1 a discordant combination of sounds 2 lack of agreement or consistency 3 *music* a a sensation commonly associated with all intervals of the second and seventh, all diminished and augmented intervals, and all chords based on these intervals b an interval or chord of this kind

dissonant (ˈdɪsənənt) adj 1 discordant; cacophonous 2 incongruous or discrepant 3 *music* characterized by dissonance [c15: from Latin *dissonāre* to be discordant, from DIS-¹ + *sonāre* to sound]

dissuade (dɪˈsweɪd) vb (tr) 1 (often foll by *from*) to deter (someone) by persuasion from a course of action, policy, etc 2 to advise against (an action, policy, etc) [c15: from Latin *dissuādēre*, from DIS-¹ + *suādēre* to persuade] > disˈsuader n > disˈsuasion n > disˈsuasive adj

dissyllable (dɪˈsɪləbᵊl, ˈdɪsˌsɪl-, ˈdaɪsɪl-) or **disyllable** (ˈdaɪsɪləbᵊl, dɪˈsɪl-) n *grammar* a word of two syllables

> **dissyllabic** (ˌdɪsɪˈlæbɪk, ˌdɪssɪ-, ˌdaɪ-) or **disyllabic** (ˌdaɪsɪˈlæbɪk, ˌdɪ-) adj

dissymmetry (dɪˈsɪmɪtrɪ, dɪsˈsɪm-) n, pl **-tries** 1 lack of symmetry 2 the relationship between two objects when one is the mirror image of the other > **dissymmetric** (ˌdɪsɪˈmɛtrɪk, ˌdɪssɪ-) or ˌdissymˈmetrical adj

distaff (ˈdɪstɑːf) n 1 the rod on which flax is wound preparatory to spinning 2 (*as modifier*) of or concerning women [Old English *distæf*, from *dis-* bunch of flax + *stæf* STAFF¹; see DIZEN]

distaff side n the female side or branch of a family

distal (ˈdɪstᵊl) adj *anatomy* (of a muscle, bone, limb, etc) situated farthest from the centre, median line, or point of attachment or origin [c19: from DISTANT + -AL¹] > ˈdistally adv

distance (ˈdɪstəns) n 1 the intervening space between two points or things 2 the length of this gap 3 the state of being apart in space; remoteness 4 an interval between two points in time 5 the extent of progress; advance 6 a distant place or time 7 a separation or remoteness in relationship; disparity 8 **the distance** the most distant or a faraway part of the visible scene or landscape 9 *horse racing* a *Brit* a point on a racecourse 240 yards from the winning post b *US* the part of a racecourse that a horse must reach in any heat before the winner passes the finishing line in order to qualify for later heats 10 **go the distance** a *boxing* to complete a bout without being knocked out b to be able to complete an assigned task or responsibility 11 **keep one's distance** to maintain a proper or discreet reserve in respect of another person 12 **middle distance** a (in a picture) halfway between the foreground and the horizon b (in a natural situation) halfway between the observer and the horizon ▷ vb (tr) 13 to hold or place at a distance 14 to separate (oneself) mentally or emotionally from something 15 to outdo; outstrip

distance learning n a teaching system consisting of video, audio, and written material designed for a person to use in studying a subject at home

distant (ˈdɪstənt) adj 1 far away or apart in space or time 2 (*postpositive*) separated in space or time by a specified distance 3 apart in relevance, association, or relationship: *a distant cousin* 4 coming from or going to a faraway place 5 remote in manner; aloof 6 abstracted; absent: *a distant look* [c14: from Latin *distāre* to be distant, from DIS-¹ + *stāre* to stand] > ˈdistantly adv > ˈdistantness n

distaste (dɪsˈteɪst) n (often foll by *for*) an absence of pleasure (in); dislike (of); aversion (to)

distasteful (dɪsˈteɪstfʊl) adj unpleasant or offensive > disˈtastefulness n

Di Stéfano (*Spanish* di ˈstefano) n **Alfredo** (alˈfredo). born 1926, Argentinian-born football player, who played for Argentina, Colombia, Spain, and Real Madrid

distemper¹ (dɪsˈtɛmpə) n 1 any of various infectious diseases of animals, esp **canine distemper**, a highly contagious viral disease of dogs, characterized initially by high fever and a discharge from the nose and eyes 2 *archaic* a a disease or disorder b disturbance c discontent [c14: from Late Latin *distemperāre* to derange the health of, from Latin DIS-¹ + *temperāre* to mix in correct proportions]

distemper² (dɪsˈtɛmpə) n 1 a technique of painting in which the pigments are mixed with water, glue, size, etc, used for poster, mural, and scene painting 2 the paint used in this technique or any of various water-based paints, including, in Britain, whitewash ▷ vb 3 to paint (something) with distemper [c14: from Medieval Latin *distemperāre* to soak, from Latin DIS-¹ + *temperāre* to mingle]

distend (dɪˈstɛnd) vb 1 to expand or be expanded by or as if by pressure from within; swell; inflate 2 (tr) to stretch out or extend [c14: from Latin *distendere*, from DIS-¹ + *tendere* to stretch] > disˈtensible adj > disˈtension or disˈtention n

distich (ˈdɪstɪk) n *prosody* a unit of two verse lines, usually a couplet [c16: from Greek *distikhos* having two lines, from DI-¹ + *stikhos* STICH]

distil or *US* **distill** (dɪsˈtɪl) vb **-tils, -tilling, -tilled** or *US*

-tills, -tilling, -tilled **1** to subject to or undergo distillation **2** (sometimes foll by *out* or *off*) to purify, separate, or concentrate, or be purified, separated, or concentrated by distillation **3** to obtain or be obtained by distillation **4** to exude or give off (a substance) in drops or small quantities **5** (*tr*) to extract the essence of as if by distillation [C14: from Latin *dēstillāre* to distil, from DE- + *stillāre* to drip]

distillate ('dɪstɪlɪt, -ˌleɪt) *n* Also called: distillation the product of distillation **2** a concentrated essence

distillation (ˌdɪstɪ'leɪʃən) *n* **1** the act, process, or product of distilling **2** the process of evaporating or boiling a liquid and condensing its vapour **3** purification or separation of mixture by using different evaporation rates or boiling points of their components **4** the process of obtaining the essence or an extract of a substance, usually by heating it in a solvent **5** another name for **distillate** (sense 1) **6** a concentrated essence > dis'tillatory *adj*

distiller (dɪ'stɪlə) *n* a person or organization that distils, esp a company that makes spirits

distillery (dɪ'stɪlərɪ) *n, pl* -eries a place where alcoholic drinks, etc, are made by distillation

distinct (dɪ'stɪŋkt) *adj* **1** easily sensed or understood; clear; precise **2** (when postpositive, foll by *from*) not the same (as); separate (from); distinguished (from) **3** not alike; different **4** sharp; clear **5** recognizable; definite **6** explicit; unequivocal **7** *botany* (of parts of a plant) not joined together; separate [C14: from Latin *distinctus*, from *distinguere* to DISTINGUISH] > dis'tinctly *adv* > dis'tinctness *n*

distinction (dɪ'stɪŋkʃən) *n* **1** the act or an instance of distinguishing or differentiating **2** a distinguishing feature **3** the state of being different or distinguishable **4** special honour, recognition, or fame **5** excellence of character; distinctive qualities **6** distinguished appearance **7** a symbol of honour or rank

distinctive (dɪ'stɪŋktɪv) *adj* serving or tending to distinguish > dis'tinctively *adv* > dis'tinctiveness *n*

distingué French (distɛ̃ge) *adj* distinguished or noble

distinguish (dɪ'stɪŋgwɪʃ) *vb* (*mainly tr*) **1** (when *intr*, foll by *between* or *among*) to make, show, or recognize a difference or differences (between or among); differentiate (between) **2** to be a distinctive feature of; characterize **3** to make out; perceive **4** to mark for a special honour or title **5** to make (oneself) noteworthy **6** to classify; categorize [C16: from Latin *distinguere* to separate, discriminate] > dis'tinguishable *adj* > dis'tinguishing *adj*

distinguished (dɪ'stɪŋgwɪʃt) *adj* **1** noble or dignified in appearance or behaviour **2** eminent; famous; celebrated

distort (dɪ'stɔːt) *vb* (*tr*) **1** (*often passive*) to twist or pull out of shape; make bent or misshapen; contort; deform **2** to alter or misrepresent (facts, motives, etc) **3** *electronics* to reproduce or amplify (a signal) inaccurately, changing the shape of the waveform [C16: from Latin *distortus* misshapen, from *distorquēre* to turn different ways, from DIS-¹ + *torquēre* to twist] > dis'torted *adj*

distortion (dɪ'stɔːʃən) *n* **1** the act or an instance of distorting or the state of being distorted **2** something that is distorted **3** *electronics* an undesired change in the shape of an electromagnetic wave or signal > dis'tortional *adj*

distract (dɪ'strækt) *vb* (*tr*) **1** (*often passive*) to draw the attention of (a person) away from something **2** to divide or confuse the attention of (a person) **3** to amuse or entertain **4** to trouble greatly **5** to make mad [C14: from Latin *distractus* perplexed, from *distrahere* to pull in different directions, from DIS-¹ + *trahere* to drag]

distracted (dɪ'stræktɪd) *adj* **1** bewildered; confused **2** mad > dis'tractedly *adv*

distraction (dɪ'strækʃən) *n* **1** the act or an instance of distracting or the state of being distracted **2** something that serves as a diversion or entertainment **3** an interruption; an obstacle to concentration **4** mental turmoil or madness

distrain (dɪ'streɪn) *vb law* to seize (personal property) by way of distress [C13: from Old French *destreindre*, from Latin *distringere* to impede, from DIS-¹ + *stringere* to draw

tight] > dis'trainment *n* > dis'trainor *or* dis'trainer *n*

distraint (dɪ'streɪnt) *n law* the act or process of distraining; distress

distrait (dɪ'streɪ; *French* distrɛ) *adj* absent-minded; abstracted [C18: from French, from *distraire* to DISTRACT]

distraught (dɪ'strɔːt) *adj* **1** distracted or agitated **2** *rare* mad [C14: changed from obsolete *distract* through influence of obsolete *straught*, past participle of STRETCH]

distress (dɪ'strɛs) *vb* (*tr*) **1** to cause mental pain to; upset badly (*usually passive*) to subject to financial or other trouble **3** to damage (esp furniture), as by scratching or denting it, in order to make it appear older than it is **4** *law* a less common word for **distrain** ▷ *n* **5** mental pain; anguish **6** the act of distressing or the state of being distressed **7** physical or financial trouble **8** in distress (of a ship, aircraft, etc) in dire need of help **9** *law* **a** the seizure and holding of property as security for payment of or in satisfaction of a debt, claim, etc; distraint **b** the property thus seized **c** *US* (*as modifier*): *distress merchandise* [C13: from Old French *destresse* distress, via Vulgar Latin, from Latin *districtus* divided in mind; see DISTRAIN] > dis'tressful *adj* > dis'tressing *adj, n* > dis'tressingly *adv*

distressed (dɪ'strɛst) *adj* **1** much troubled; upset; afflicted **2** in financial straits; poor **3** (of furniture, fabric, etc) having signs of ageing artificially applied **4** *economics* another word for **depressed** (sense 4)

distress signal *n* a signal by radio, Very light, etc from a ship or other vessel in need of immediate assistance

distribute (dɪ'strɪbjuːt) *vb* (*tr*) **1** to give out in shares; dispense **2** to hand out or deliver **3** (*often passive*) to spread throughout a space or area **4** (*often passive*) to divide into classes or categories; classify **5** *printing* to return (used type) to the correct positions in the type case **6** *logic* to incorporate in a distributed term of a categorial proposition **7** *maths, logic* to expand an expression containing two operators in such a way that the precedence of the operators is changed; for example, distributing multiplication over addition in $a(b + c)$ yields $ab + ac$ [C15: from Latin *distribuere* from DIS-¹ + *tribuere* to give] > dis'tributable *adj*

distributed logic *n* a computer system in which remote terminals and electronic devices, distributed throughout the system, supplement the main computer by doing some of the computing or decision making

distributed term *n logic* a term applying equally to every member of the class it designates, as *doctors* in *no doctors are overworked*

distribution (ˌdɪstrɪ'bjuːʃən) *n* **1** the act of distributing or the state or manner of being distributed **2** a thing or portion distributed **3** arrangement or location **4** *commerce* the process of physically satisfying the demand for goods and services **5** *economics* the division of the total income of a community among its members, esp between labour incomes (wages and salaries) and property incomes (rents, interest, and dividends) **6** *statistics* the set of possible values of a random variable, or points in a sample space, considered in terms of new theoretical or observed frequency **7** *law* the apportioning of the estate of a deceased intestate among the persons entitled to share in it **8** *law* the lawful division of the assets of a bankrupt among his creditors **9** *finance* **a** a division of part of a company's profit as a dividend to its shareholders **b** the amount paid by dividend in a particular distribution **10** *engineering* the way in which the fuel-air mixture is supplied to each cylinder of a multicylinder internal-combustion engine > ˌdistri'butional *adj*

distributive (dɪ'strɪbjʊtɪv) *adj* **1** characterized by or relating to distribution **2** *grammar* referring separately to the individual people or items in a group, as the words *each* and *every* ▷ *n* **3** *grammar* a distributive word > dis'tributively *adv* > dis'tributiveness *n*

distributive law *n maths, logic* a theorem asserting that one operator can validly be distributed over another. See **distribute** (sense 7)

distributor *or* **distributer** (dɪ'strɪbjʊtə) *n* **1** a person or thing that distributes **2** a wholesaler or middleman engaged in the distribution of a category of goods, esp to retailers in a specific area **3** the device in a petrol engine that distributes the high-tension voltage to the sparking plugs in the sequence of the firing order

district ('dɪstrɪkt) *n* **1 a** an area of land marked off for administrative or other purposes **b** (*as modifier*): *district nurse* **2** a locality separated by geographical attributes; region **3** any subdivision of any territory, region, etc **4** (in Scotland until 1975) a landward division of a county ▷ *vb* **5** (*tr*) to divide into districts [C17: from Medieval Latin *districtus* area of jurisdiction, from Latin *distringere* to stretch out; see DISTRAIN]

district attorney *n* (in the US) the state prosecuting officer in a specified judicial district

district court *n* **1** (in Scotland) a court of summary jurisdiction held by a stipendiary magistrate or one or more justices of the peace to deal with minor criminal offences **2** (in the US) **a** a federal trial court serving a federal judicial district **b** (in some states) a court having general jurisdiction in a state judicial district **3** (in Australia and New Zealand) a court lower than a high court. Former name: magistrates' court

district high school *n* NZ a school in a rural area that includes primary and post-primary classes

district nurse *n* (in Britain) a nurse employed within the National Health Service to attend patients in a particular area, usually by visiting them in their own homes

District of Columbia *n* a federal district of the eastern US, coextensive with the federal capital, Washington. Pop: 564 326 (2003 est). Area: 178 sq km (69 sq miles). Abbreviations: D.C., (with zip code) DC

distrust (dɪs'trʌst) *vb* **1** to regard as untrustworthy or dishonest ▷ *n* **2** suspicion; doubt > dis'truster *n* > dis'trustful *adj*

disturb (dɪ'stɜːb) *vb* (*tr*) **1** to intrude on; interrupt **2** to destroy or interrupt the quietness or peace of **3** to disarrange; muddle **4** (*often passive*) to upset or agitate; trouble **5** to inconvenience; put out [C13: from Latin *disturbāre*, from DIS-¹ + *turbāre* to confuse] > dis'turber *n* > dis'turbing *adj* > dis'turbingly *adv*

disturbance (dɪ'stɜːbəns) *n* **1** the act of disturbing or the state of being disturbed **2** an interruption or intrusion **3** an unruly outburst or tumult **4** *law* an interference with another's rights **5** *geology* a minor movement of the earth causing a small earthquake **6** *meteorol* a small depression **7** *psychiatry* a mental or emotional disorder

disturbed (dɪ'stɜːbd) *adj psychiatry* emotionally upset, troubled, or maladjusted

disulphide (daɪ'sʌlfaɪd) *n* any chemical compound containing two sulphur atoms per molecule

disunite (ˌdɪsjʊ'naɪt) *vb* **1** to separate or become separate; disrupt **2** (*tr*) to set at variance; estrange > dis'union *n*

disunity (dɪs'juːnɪtɪ) *n, pl* -ties dissension or disagreement

disuse (dɪs'juːs) *n* the condition of being unused; neglect (often in the phrases *in* or *into disuse*)

disutility (ˌdɪsjuː'tɪlɪtɪ) *n, pl* -ties *economics* the shortcomings of a commodity or activity in satisfying human wants. Compare **utility** (sense 4)

disyllable ('daɪsɪləbəl, dɪ'sɪl-) *n* a variant of **dissyllable**

ditch (dɪtʃ) *n* **1** a narrow channel dug in the earth, usually used for drainage, irrigation, or as a boundary marker ▷ *vb* **2** to make a ditch or ditches in (a piece of ground) **3** (*intr*) to edge with a ditch **4** *slang* to crash or be crashed, esp deliberately, as to avoid more unpleasant circumstances: *he had to ditch the car* **5** (*tr*) *slang* to abandon or discard **6** *slang* to land (an aircraft) on water in an emergency **7** (*tr*) *US slang* to evade [Old English *dīc*; related to Old Saxon *dīk*, Old Norse *dīki*, Middle High German *tīch* dyke, pond, Latin *figere* to stick, see DYKE¹] > 'ditcher *n*

Ditch (dɪtʃ) *n* the Ditch NZ an informal name for the **Tasman Sea**

ditchwater ('dɪtʃˌwɔːtə) *n* **1** stagnant water **2** (as) dull as ditchwater extremely uninspiring

dither ('dɪðə) *vb* (*intr*) **1** *chiefly Brit* to be uncertain or indecisive **2** *chiefly US* to be in an agitated state **3** to tremble, as with cold ▷ *n* **4** *chiefly Brit* a state of

indecision **5** a state of agitation [C17: variant of C14 (northern English dialect) *didder*, of uncertain origin] > 'ditherer *n* > 'dithery *adj*

dithionous acid (daɪ'θaɪənəs) *n* an unstable dibasic acid known only in solution and in the form of dithionite salts. It is a powerful reducing agent. Formula: $H_2S_2O_4$. Also called: **hyposulphurous acid** [from DI-¹ + *thion-*, from Greek *theion* sulphur + -OUS]

dithyramb ('dɪθɪˌræm, -ˌræmb) *n* **1** (in ancient Greece) a passionate choral hymn in honour of Dionysus; the forerunner of Greek drama **2** any utterance or a piece of writing that resembles this [C17: from Latin *dīthyrambus*, from Greek *dithurambos*; related to *iambos* IAMB] > ˌdithy'rambic *adj*

dittany ('dɪtənɪ) *n, pl* -nies **1** an aromatic Cretan plant, *Origanum dictamnus*, with pink drooping flowers: formerly credited with great medicinal properties: family *Lamiaceae* (labiates) **2** Also called: **stone mint** a North American labiate plant, *Cunila origanoides*, with clusters of purplish flowers [C14: from Old French *ditan*, from Latin *dictamnus*, from Greek *diktamnon*, perhaps from *Diktē*, mountain in Crete]

ditto ('dɪtəʊ) *n, pl* -tos **1** the aforementioned; the above; the same. Used in accounts, lists, etc, to avoid repetition and symbolized by two small marks (") known as **ditto marks**, placed under the thing repeated **2** *informal* a duplicate ▷ *adv* **3** in the same way ▷ *sentence substitute* **4** *informal* used to avoid repeating or to confirm agreement with an immediately preceding sentence ▷ *vb* -tos, -toing, -toed **5** (*tr*) to copy; repeat [C17: from Italian (Tuscan dialect), variant of *detto* said, from *dicere* to say, from Latin]

ditty ('dɪtɪ) *n, pl* -ties a short simple song or poem [C13: from Old French *ditie* poem, from *ditier* to compose, from Latin *dictāre* DICTATE]

ditty bag *n* a sailor's cloth bag for personal belongings or tools. A box used for these purposes is termed a **ditty box** [C19: perhaps from obsolete *dutty* calico, from Hindi *dhōtī* loincloth, DHOTI]

ditzy *or* **ditsy** ('dɪtzɪ) *adj* -zier, -ziest *or* -sier, -siest *slang* silly and scatterbrained [C20: perhaps from DOTTY + DIZZY]

Diu ('diːuː) *n* a small island off the NW coast of India: together with a mainland area, it formed a district of Portuguese India (1535–1961); formerly part of the Indian Union Territory of Goa, Daman, and Diu (1962–87)

diuretic (ˌdaɪjʊ'rɛtɪk) *adj* **1** acting to increase the flow of urine ▷ *n* **2** a drug or agent that increases the flow of urine [C17: from New Latin, from Greek *diourein* to urinate] > **diuresis** (ˌdaɪjʊ'riːsɪs) *n*

diurnal (daɪ'ɜːnəl) *adj* **1** happening during the day or daily **2** (of flowers) open during the day and closed at night **3** (of animals) active during the day ▷ Compare **nocturnal** [C15: from Late Latin *diurnālis*, from Latin *diurnus*, from *diēs* day] > di'urnally *adv*

div (dɪv) *n* prison slang a stupid or foolish person [C20: probably shortened and changed from DEVIANT]

diva ('diːvə) *n, pl* -vas *or* -ve (-vɪ) a highly distinguished female singer; prima donna [C19: via Italian from Latin: a goddess, from *dīvus* DIVINE]

divagate ('daɪvəˌgeɪt) *vb* (*intr*) *rare* to digress or wander [C16: from Latin DI-² + *vagārī* to wander] > ˌdiva'gation *n*

divalent (daɪ'veɪlənt, 'daɪˌveɪ-) *adj chem* **1** having a valency of two **2** having two valencies ▷ Also: **bivalent** > di'valency *n*

divan (dɪ'væn) *n* **1 a** a backless sofa or couch, designed to be set against a wall **b** a bed resembling such a couch **2** (esp formerly) a room for smoking and drinking, as in a coffee shop **3 a** a Muslim law court, council chamber, or counting house **b** a Muslim council of state [C16: from Turkish *dīvān*, from Persian *dīwān*]

dive (daɪv) *vb* dives, diving, dived *or* US dove, dived (mainly *intr*) **1** to plunge headfirst into water **2** (of a submarine, swimmer, etc) to submerge under water **3** (*also tr*) to fly (an aircraft) in a steep nose-down descending path, or (of an aircraft) to fly in such a path **4** to rush, go, or reach quickly, as in a headlong plunge: *he dived for the ball* **5** (*also tr*; foll by *in* or *into*) to dip or put (one's) hand) quickly or forcefully (into) **6** (usually foll by *in* or *into*) to involve oneself (in something), as in eating food ▷ *n* **7** a headlong plunge into water, esp one of several formalized movements executed as a sport **8** an act or instance of diving **9** a steep nose-down descent of an aircraft **10** *slang* a disreputable or seedy bar or club **11** *boxing slang* the act of a boxer pretending to be knocked down or out [Old English *dŷfan*; related to Old Norse *dŷfa* to dip, Frisian *dīvi*; see DEEP, DIP]

dive bomber *n* a military aircraft designed to release its bombs on a target during a steep dive

diver ('daɪvə) *n* **1** a person or thing that dives **2** a person who works or explores underwater **3** any aquatic bird of the genus *Gavia*, family *Gaviidae*, and order *Gaviiformes* of northern oceans, having a straight pointed bill, small wings, and a long body: noted for swiftness and skill in swimming and diving. US and Canadian name: loon **4** any of various other diving birds

diverge (daɪ'vɜːdʒ) *vb* **1** to separate or cause to separate and go in different directions from a point **2** (*intr*) to be at variance; differ **3** (*intr*) to deviate from a prescribed course **4** (*intr*) *maths* (of a series or sequence) to have no limit [C17: from Medieval Latin *dīvergere*, from Latin DI-² + *vergere* to turn]

divergence (daɪ'vɜːdʒəns) *n* **1** the act or result of diverging or the amount by which something diverges **2** the condition of being divergent

divergent (daɪ'vɜːdʒənt) *adj* **1** diverging or causing divergence **2** *maths* (of a series) having no limit; not convergent > di'vergently *adv*
  ● USAGE The use of *divergent* to mean different as in *they*
  ● *hold widely divergent views* is considered by some people
  ● to be incorrect

divergent thinking *n* *psychol* thinking in an unusual and unstereotyped way, e.g. to generate several possible solutions to a problem

divers ('daɪvəz) *determiner archaic or literary* various; sundry; some [C13: from Old French, from Latin *dīversus* turned in different directions; see DIVERT]

diverse (daɪ'vɜːs, 'daɪvɜːs) *adj* **1** having variety; assorted **2** distinct in kind [C13: from Latin *dīversus*; see DIVERS] > di'versely *adv*

diversify (daɪ'vɜːsɪˌfaɪ) *vb* -fies, -fying, -fied **1** (*tr*) to create different forms of; variegate; vary **2** (of an enterprise) to vary (products, operations, etc) in order to spread risk, expand, etc **3** to distribute (investments) among several securities in order to spread risk [C15: from Old French *diversifier*, from Medieval Latin *dīversificāre*, from Latin *dīversus* DIVERSE + *facere* to make] > di,versifi'cation *n*

diversion (daɪ'vɜːʃən) *n* **1** the act of diverting from a specified course **2** *chiefly Brit* an official detour used by traffic when a main route is closed **3** something that distracts from business, etc; amusement **4** *military* a feint attack designed to draw an enemy away from the main attack > di'versional *or* di'versionary *adj*

diversity (daɪ'vɜːsɪtɪ) *n* **1** the state or quality of being different or varied **2** a point of difference

divert (daɪ'vɜːt) *vb* **1** to turn (a person or thing) aside from a course; deflect **2** (*tr*) to entertain; amuse **3** (*tr*) to distract the attention of [C15: from French *divertir*, from Latin *dīvertere* to turn aside, from DI-² + *vertere* to turn] > di'verting *adj* > di'vertingly *adv*

diverticulitis (ˌdaɪvəˌtɪkjʊ'laɪtɪs) *n* inflammation of one or more diverticula, esp of the colon

diverticulum (ˌdaɪvə'tɪkjʊləm) *n, pl* -la (-lə) any sac or pouch formed by herniation of the wall of a tubular organ or part, esp the intestines [C16: from New Latin, from Latin *dēverticulum* by-path, from *dēvertere* to turn aside, from *vertere* to turn]

divertimento (dɪˌvɜːtɪ'mɛntəʊ) *n, pl* -ti (-tɪ) **1** a piece of entertaining music in several movements, often scored for a mixed ensemble and having no fixed form **2** an episode in a fugue [C18: from Italian]

divertissement (dɪ'vɜːtɪsmənt; *French* divɛrtismɑ̃) *n* a brief entertainment or diversion, usually between the acts of a play [C18: from French: entertainment]

Dives ('daɪviːz) *n* **1** a rich man in the parable in Luke 16:19–31 **2** a very rich man

divest (daɪ'vɛst) *vb* (*tr*; usually foll by *of*) **1** to strip (of

clothes) **2** to deprive or dispossess [C17: changed from earlier DEVEST] > di'vestiture, di'vesture *or* di'vestment *n*

divi ('dɪvɪ) *n* an alternative spelling of **divvy**¹

divide (dɪ'vaɪd) *vb* **1** to separate or be separated into parts or groups; split up; part **2** to share or be shared out in parts; distribute **3** to diverge or cause to diverge in opinion or aim **4** (*tr*) to keep apart or be a boundary between **5** (*intr*) (in Parliament and similar legislatures) to vote by separating into two groups **6** to categorize; classify **7** to calculate the quotient of (one number or quantity) and (another number or quantity) by division **8** (*intr*) to diverge: *the roads divide* **9** (*tr*) to mark increments of (length, angle, etc) as by use of an engraving machine ▷ *n* **10** *chiefly US & Canadian* an area of relatively high ground separating drainage basins; watershed **11** a division; split [C14: from Latin *dīvidere* to force apart, from DI-² + *vid-* separate, from the source of *viduus* bereaved, *vidua* WIDOW]

divided (dɪ'vaɪdɪd) *adj* **1** *botany* another word for **dissected** (sense 1) **2** split; not united

dividend ('dɪvɪˌdɛnd) *n* **1** *finance* **a** a distribution from the net profits of a company to its shareholders **b** a pro-rata portion of this distribution received by a shareholder **2** the share of a cooperative society's surplus allocated at the end of a period to members **3** *insurance* a sum of money distributed from a company's net profits to the holders of certain policies **4** something extra; bonus **5** a number or quantity to be divided by another number or quantity **6** *law* the proportion of an insolvent estate payable to the creditors [C15: from Latin *dīvidendum* what is to be divided; see DIVIDE]

divider (dɪ'vaɪdə) *n* **1** Also called: room divider a screen or piece of furniture placed so as to divide a room into separate areas **2** a person or thing that divides **3** *electronics* an electrical circuit with an output that is a well-defined fraction of the given input: *a voltage divider*

dividers (dɪ'vaɪdəz) *pl n* a type of compass with two pointed arms, used for measuring lines or dividing them

divination (ˌdɪvɪ'neɪʃən) *n* **1** the art, practice, or gift of discerning or discovering future events or unknown things, as though by supernatural powers **2** a prophecy **3** a presentiment or guess > divinatory (dɪ'vɪnətərɪ, -trɪ) *adj*

divine (dɪ'vaɪn) *adj* **1** of, relating to, or characterizing God or a deity **2** godlike **3** of, relating to, or associated with religion or worship **4** of supreme excellence or worth **5** *informal* splendid; perfect ▷ *n* **6** the divine (*often capital*) another term for **God 7** a priest, esp one learned in theology ▷ *vb* **8** to perceive or understand (something) by intuition or insight **9** to conjecture (something); guess **10** to discern (a hidden or future reality) as though by supernatural power **11** (*tr*) to search for (underground supplies of water, metal, etc) using a divining rod [C14: from Latin *dīvīnus*, from *dīvus* a god; related to *deus* a god] > di'vinely *adv* > di'viner *n*

divine office *n* (*sometimes capitals*) the canonical prayers (in the Roman Catholic Church those of the breviary) recited daily by priests, those in religious orders, etc

divine right of kings *n* *history* the concept that the right to rule derives from God and that kings are answerable for their actions to God alone

diving bell *n* an early diving submersible having an open bottom and being supplied with compressed air

diving board *n* a platform or springboard from which swimmers may dive

diving suit *or* **diving dress** *n* a waterproof suit used by divers, having a heavy detachable helmet and an air supply

divining rod *n* a rod, usually a forked hazel twig, said to move or dip when held over ground in which water, metal, etc, is to be found. Also called: dowsing rod

divinity (dɪ'vɪnɪtɪ) *n, pl* -ties **1** the nature of a deity or the state of being divine **2** a god or other divine being **3** the divinity (*often capital*) another term for **God 4** another word for **theology**

divisible (dɪ'vɪzəb³l) *adj* capable of being divided, usually with no remainder: *four is divisible by two* > di,visi'bility *or*

d

di'visibleness *n* >di'visibly *adv*

division (dɪ'vɪʒən) *n* **1** the act of dividing or state of being divided **2** the act of sharing out; distribution **3** something that divides or keeps apart, such as a boundary **4** one of the parts, groups, etc, into which something is divided **5** a part of a government, business, country, etc, that has been made into a unit for administrative, political, or other reasons **6** a formal vote in Parliament or a similar legislative body **7** a difference of opinion, esp one that causes separation **8** (in sports) a section, category, or class organized according to age, weight, skill, etc **9** a mathematical operation, the inverse of multiplication, in which the quotient of two numbers or quantities is calculated. Usually written: $a ÷ b$, $\frac{a}{b}$, a/b **10** *army* a major formation, larger than a regiment or brigade but smaller than a corps, containing the necessary arms to sustain independent combat **11** *biology* (in traditional classification systems) a major category of the plant kingdom that contains one or more related classes. Compare **phylum** (sense 1) [C14: from Latin *dīvīsiō*, from *dīvidere* to DIVIDE] >di'visional *or* di'visionary *adj* >di'visionally *adv*

division sign *n* the symbol ÷, placed between the dividend and the divisor to indicate division, as in $12 ÷ 6 = 2$

divisive (dɪ'vaɪsɪv) *adj* causing or tending to cause disagreement or dissension >di'visively *adv* >di'visiveness *n*

divisor (dɪ'vaɪzə) *n* **1** a number or quantity to be divided into another number or quantity (the dividend) **2** a number that is a factor of another number

divorce (dɪ'vɔːs) *n* **1** the dissolution of a marriage by judgment of a court or by accepted custom **2** a judicial decree declaring a marriage to be dissolved **3** a separation, esp one that is total or complete ▷ *vb* **4** to separate or be separated by divorce; give or obtain a divorce (to a couple or from one's spouse) **5** (*tr*) to remove or separate, esp completely [C14: from Old French, from Latin *dīvortium* from *dīvertere* to separate; see DIVERT] >di'vorceable *adj*

divorcé (dɪ'vɔːseɪ) *n* a man who has been divorced

divot ('dɪvət) *n* a piece of turf dug out of a grass surface, esp by a golf club or by horses' hooves [C16: from Scottish, of obscure origin]

divulge (dɪ'vʌldʒ) *vb* (*tr; may take a clause as object*) to make known (something private or secret); disclose [C15: from Latin *dīvulgāre*, from DI-² + *vulgāre* to spread among the people, from *vulgus* the common people] >di'vulgence *or* di'vulgement *n* >di'vulger *n*

divvy¹ ('dɪvɪ) *informal* ▷ *n*, *pl* -vies **1** *Brit* short for dividend, esp (formerly) one paid by a cooperative society **2** *US & Canadian* a share; portion ▷ *vb* -vies, -vying, -vied **3** (*tr*; usually foll by *up*) to divide and share

divvy² ('dɪvɪ) *n*, *pl* -vies *dialect* a stupid or foolish person [C20: perhaps from DEVIANT]

Diwali (dɪ'wɑːlɪ) *n* a major Hindu religious festival, honouring Lakshmi, the goddess of wealth. Held over the New Year according to the Vikrama calendar, it is marked by feasting, gifts, and the lighting of lamps

dixie ('dɪksɪ) *n* **1** *chiefly military* a large metal pot for cooking, brewing tea, etc **2** a mess tin [C19: from Hindi *degcī*, diminutive of *degcā* pot]

Dixie ('dɪksɪ) *n* **1** Also called: **Dixieland** the southern states of the US; the states that joined the Confederacy during the Civil War ▷ *adj* **2** of, relating to, or characteristic of the southern states of the US [C19: perhaps from the nickname of New Orleans, from *dixie* a ten-dollar bill printed there, from French *dix* ten]

Dixieland ('dɪksɪ,lænd) *n* **1** a form of jazz that originated in New Orleans, becoming popular esp with White musicians in the second decade of the 20th century **2** a revival of this style in the necessary 1950s **3** See **Dixie** (sense 1)

Dixon *n* **Willie**, full name *William James Dixon*. 1915–92, US blues musician, songwriter, and record producer, whose songs have been recorded by many other artists

DIY *or* **d.i.y.** (in Britain and Canada) *abbreviation* do-it-yourself

dizen ('daɪzᵊn) *vb* an archaic word for **bedizen** [C16: from

Middle Dutch *dīsen* to dress a distaff with flax; see DISTAFF] >'dizenment *n*

dizzy ('dɪzɪ) *adj* -zier, -ziest **1** affected with a whirling or reeling sensation; giddy **2** mentally confused or bewildered **3** causing or tending to cause vertigo or bewilderment **4** *informal* foolish or flighty ▷ *vb* -zies, -zying, -zied **5** (*tr*) to make dizzy [Old English *dysig* silly; related to Old High German *tusīg* weak, Old Norse *dos* quiet] >'dizzily *adv* >'dizziness *n*

DJ *or* **dj** *abbreviation* **1** disc jockey **2** dinner jacket

Djailolo *or* **Jilolo** (dʒaɪ'ləʊləʊ) *n* the Dutch name for **Halmahera**

Djakarta (dʒə'kɑːtə) *n* the former spelling of **Jakarta**

djellaba, djellabah, jellaba *or* **jellabah** ('dʒɛləbə) *n* a kind of loose cloak with a hood, worn by men esp in North Africa and the Middle East [from Arabic *jallabah*]

Djibouti *or* **Jibouti** (dʒɪ'buːtɪ) *n* **1** a republic in E Africa, on the Gulf of Aden: a French overseas territory (1946–77); became independent in 1977; mainly desert. Official languages: Arabic and French. Religion: Muslim majority. Currency: Djibouti franc. Capital: Djibouti. Pop: 712 000 (2004 est). Area: 23 200 sq km (8950 sq miles) **2** the capital of Djibouti, a port on the Gulf of Aden: an outlet for Ethiopian goods. Pop: 523 000 (2005 est)

Djilas ('dʒiːlɑːs) *n* **Milovan**. 1911–95, Yugoslav politician and writer; vice president (1953–54): imprisoned (1956–61, 1962–66) for his criticism of the communist system

djinni *or* **djinny** (dʒɪ'niː, 'dʒɪnɪ) *n*, *pl* djinn (dʒɪn) variant spellings of **jinni**

dl *symbol for* decilitre(s)

DLitt *or* **DLit** *abbreviation* **1** Doctor of Letters **2** Doctor of Literature [Latin *Doctor Litterarum*]

dm *symbol for* decimetre

DM *abbreviation* (the former) Deutschmark

DMA *abbreviation computing* direct memory access

D-mark *or* **D-Mark** *n* short for (the former) **Deutschmark**

DMF *abbreviation* dimethylformamide

DMs *abbreviation* Doc Martens

DMus *abbreviation* Doctor of Music

DMV *abbreviation* (in the US and Canada) Department of Motor Vehicles

DNA *n* deoxyribonucleic acid; a nucleic acid that is the main constituent of the chromosomes of all organisms (except some viruses). The DNA molecule consists of two polynucleotide chains in the form of a double helix, containing phosphate and the sugar deoxyribose and linked by hydrogen bonds between the complementary bases adenine and thymine or cytosine and guanine. DNA is self-replicating, plays a central role in protein synthesis, and is responsible for the transmission of hereditary characteristics from parents to offspring

DNAase (,diːɛn'eɪeɪz) *or* **DNase** (,diːɛn'eɪz) *n* deoxyribonuclease; any of a number of enzymes that hydrolyse DNA

DNA fingerprint *or* **DNA profile** *n* another name for **genetic fingerprint**

DNA sequencing *n* the procedure of determining the order of base pairs in a section of DNA

Dneprodzerzhinsk (*Russian* dnɪprədzɜr'ʒinsk) *n* an industrial city in E Ukraine on the Dnieper River. Pop: 250 000 (2005 est)

Dnepropetrovsk (*Russian* dnɪprəpɪ'trofsk) *n* a city in E central Ukraine on the Dnieper River: a major centre of the metallurgical industry. Pop: 1 036 000 (2005 est). Former name (1787–1796, 1802–1926): Yekaterinoslav

DNF *abbreviation motor sport, athletics* did not finish

Dnieper ('dniːpə) *n* a river in NE Europe, rising in Russia, in the Valdai Hills NE of Smolensk and flowing south to the Black Sea: the third longest river in Europe; a major navigable waterway. Length: 2200 km (1370 miles)

Dniester ('dniːstə) *n* a river in E Europe, rising in Ukraine, in the Carpathian Mountains and flowing generally southeast to the Black Sea. Length: 1411 km (877 miles)

D-notice *n* *Brit* an official notice sent to newspapers, prohibiting the publication of certain security information [C20: from their administrative classification letter]

do¹ (duː; *unstressed* dʊ, də) *vb* **does, doing, did, done** **1** to perform or complete (a deed or action): *to do a portrait; the work is done* **2** (often *intr*; foll by *for*) to serve the needs of; be suitable for (a person, situation, etc); suffice **3** (*tr*) to arrange or fix **4** (*tr*) to prepare or provide; serve: *this restaurant doesn't do lunch on Sundays* **5** (*tr*) to make tidy, elegant, ready, etc, as by arranging or adorning: *to do one's hair* **6** (*tr*) to improve (esp in the phrase **do something to** or **for**) **7** (*tr*) to find an answer to (a problem or puzzle) **8** (*tr*) to translate or adapt the form or language of: *the book was done into a play* **9** (*intr*) to conduct oneself: *do as you please* **10** (*intr*) to fare or manage **11** (*tr*) to cause or produce: *complaints do nothing to help* **12** (*tr*) to give or render: *your portrait doesn't do you justice; do me a favour* **13** (*tr*) to work at, esp as a course of study or a profession **14** (*tr*) to perform (a play, etc); act **15** (*tr*) to travel at a specified speed, esp as a maximum **16** (*tr*) to travel or traverse (a distance) **17** (takes an infinitive without *to*) used as an auxiliary before the subject of an interrogative sentence as a way of forming a question: *do you agree?; when did John go out?* **18** (takes an infinitive without *to*) used as an auxiliary to intensify positive statements and commands: *I do like your new house; do hurry!* **19** (takes an infinitive without *to*) used as an auxiliary before a negative adverb to form negative statements or commands: *he does not like cheese; do not leave me here alone!* **20** (takes an infinitive without *to*) used as an auxiliary in inverted constructions: *little did he realize that; only rarely does he come in before ten o'clock* **21** used as an auxiliary to replace an earlier verb or verb phrase to avoid repetition: *he likes you as much as I do* **22** (*tr*) *informal* to visit or explore as a sightseer or tourist **23** (*tr*) to wear out; exhaust **24** (*intr*) to happen (esp in the phrase **nothing doing**) **25** (*tr*) *slang* to serve (a period of time) as a prison sentence **26** (*tr*) *informal* to cheat or swindle **27** (*tr*) *slang* to rob **28** (*tr*) *slang* **a** to arrest **b** to convict of a crime **29** (*tr*) *Austral informal* to lose or spend (money) completely **30** (*tr*) *slang, chiefly Brit* to treat violently; assault **31** (*tr*) *slang* to take or use (a drug) **32** (*tr*) *taboo, slang* (of a male) to have sexual intercourse with **33 do or do a** *informal* to act like; imitate: *he's a good mimic — he can do all his friends well* **34 do or die** to make a final or supreme effort **35 make do** to manage with whatever is available ▷ *n, pl* **dos** or **do's** **36** *slang* an act or instance of cheating or swindling **37** *informal, chiefly Brit & NZ* a formal or festive gathering; party **38 do's and don'ts** *informal* those things that should or should not be done; rules ▷ See also **do away with, do by,** etc [Old English *dōn*; related to Old Frisian *duān*, Old High German *tuon*, Latin *abdere* to put away, Greek *tithenai* to place; see DEED, DOOM]

do² (dəʊ) *n, pl* **dos** a variant spelling of **doh¹**

do. *abbreviation* ditto

DOA *abbreviation* dead on arrival

doable ('duːəbəl) *adj* capable of being done; practical

do away with *vb* (*intr, adverb + preposition*) **1** to kill or destroy **2** to discard or abolish

dobbin ('dɒbɪn) *n* a name for a horse, esp a workhorse, often used in children's tales, etc [C16: from *Robin*, pet form of *Robert*]

Dobbyn ('dɒbɪn) *n* **Dave.** born 1957, New Zealand singer and songwriter; member of Th'Dudes (1976–80) with whom he had the hit singles "Be Mine Tonight" (1979) and "Bliss" (1979); founder of DD Smash (1981–85) with whom he released the album *Cool Bananas* (1982); solo albums include *Loyal* (1986) and *Footrot Flats: The Dog's Tale* (1986)

Dobell (dəʊ'bɛl) *n* **Sir William.** 1899–1970, Australian portrait and landscape painter. Awarded the Archibald prize (1943) for his famous painting of *Joshua Smith*, which resulted in a heated clash between the conservatives and the moderns and led to a lawsuit. His other works include *The Cypriot* (1940), *The Billy Boy* (1943), and *Portrait of a Strapper* (1941)

Doberman pinscher ('dəʊbəmən 'pɪnʃə) or **Doberman** *n* a fairly large slender but muscular breed of dog, originally from Germany, with a glossy black-and-tan

coat, a short tail, and erect ears [C19: probably named after L. *Dobermann*, 19th-century German dog breeder who bred it + *Pinscher*, a type of terrier, perhaps after *Pinzgau*, district in Austria]

dob in *vb* **dobs, dobbing, dobbed** (*adverb*) *Austral & NZ informal* **1** (*tr*) to inform against or report, esp to the police **2** to contribute to a fund for a specific purpose

dobla ('dəʊblaː) *n* a medieval Spanish gold coin [Spanish, from Latin *dupla*, feminine of *duplus* twofold, DOUBLE]

dobra ('dəʊbrə) *n* the standard monetary unit of São Tomé e Principe, divided into 100 cêntimos

Dobruja (*Bulgarian* 'dɔbrudʒa) *n* a region of E Europe, between the River Danube and the Black Sea: the north passed to Romania and the south to Bulgaria after the Berlin Congress (1878). Romanian name: **Dobrogea**

do by *vb* (*intr, preposition*) to treat in the manner specified

Dobzhansky (dɒb'ʒænskɪ) *n* **Theodosius.** 1900–75, US biologist, born in Russia, noted for work on evolution and genetic variation

doc (dɒk) *n informal* short for **doctor**, esp a medical doctor: often used as a term of address

DOC *abbreviation* Denominazione di Origine Controllata: used of wines [Italian, literally: name of origin controlled]

docent ('dəʊsᵊnt) *n* a voluntary worker who acts as a guide in a museum, art gallery, etc [C19: from German *Dozent*, from Latin *docēns* from *docēre* to teach]

DOCG *abbreviation* Denominazione di Origine Controllata Garantita: used of wines [Italian, literally: name of origin guaranteed controlled]

Docherty ('dɒkətɪ) *n* **Pete.** born 1979, English rock musician and songwriter; member of The Libertines (1997–2004) and Babyshambles (from 2005)

docile ('dəʊsaɪl) *adj* **1** easy to manage, control, or discipline; submissive **2** *rare* ready to learn; easy to teach [C15: from Latin *docilis* easily taught, from *docēre* to teach] > **docilely** *adv* > **docility** (dəʊ'sɪlɪtɪ) *n*

dock¹ (dɒk) *n* **1 a** a wharf or pier **2 a** space between two wharves or piers for the mooring of ships **3** an area of water that can accommodate a ship and can be closed off to allow regulation of the water level **4** short for **dry dock 5** *chiefly US & Canadian* a platform from which lorries, goods trains, etc, are loaded and unloaded ▷ *vb* **6** to moor (a vessel) at a dock or (of a vessel) to be moored at a dock **7** to put (a vessel) into a dry dock for repairs or (of a vessel) to come into a dry dock **8** (of two spacecraft) to link together in space or link together (two spacecraft) in space [C14: from Middle Dutch *docke*; perhaps related to Latin *ducere* to lead]

dock² (dɒk) *n* **1** the bony part of the tail of an animal, esp a dog or sheep **2** the part of an animal's tail left after the major part of it has been cut off ▷ *vb* (*tr*) **3** to remove (the tail or part of the tail) of (an animal) by cutting through the bone **4** to deduct (an amount) from (a person's wages, pension, etc) [C14: *dok*, of uncertain origin]

dock³ (dɒk) *n* an enclosed space in a court of law where the accused sits or stands during his trial [C16: from Flemish *dok* sty]

dock⁴ (dɒk) *n* any of various temperate weedy plants of the polygonaceous genus *Rumex*, having greenish or reddish flowers and typically broad leaves [Old English *docce*; related to Middle Dutch, Old Danish *docke*, Gaelic *dogha*]

dockage ('dɒkɪdʒ) *n* **1** a charge levied upon a vessel for using a dock **2** facilities for docking vessels **3** the practice of docking vessels

docker ('dɒkə) *n Brit* a man employed in the loading or unloading of ships. US and Canadian equivalent: longshoreman. See also **stevedore**

docket ('dɒkɪt) *n* **1** *chiefly Brit* a piece of paper accompanying or referring to a package or other delivery, stating contents, delivery instructions, etc, sometimes serving as a receipt **2** *law* **a** an official summary of the proceedings in a court of justice **b** a register containing such a summary **3** *Brit* **a** a customs certificate declaring that duty has been paid **b** a certificate giving particulars of a shipment and allowing its holder to obtain a delivery order **4** a summary of contents, as in a document **5** *US* a list of things to be done **6** *US law* a list of cases awaiting trial ▷ *vb* (*tr*) **7** to fix a docket to (a package, etc) **8** *law* **a** to make a summary of (a document, judgment, etc) **b** to abstract and enter in a book or register **9** to endorse (a document, etc) with a summary [c15: of unknown origin]

docking station *n* a device used to connect one appliance to another, esp a portable computer and a desktop computer, to make use of its external power supply, monitor, and keyboard, esp to enable the transfer of data between the machines

dockland ('dɒk,lænd) *n* the area around the docks

dockyard ('dɒk,jɑːd) *n* a naval establishment with docks, workshops, etc, for the building, fitting out, and repair of vessels

Doc Martens (dɒk 'mɑːtənz) *pl n* *trademark* a brand of lace-up boots with thick lightweight resistant soles. Abbreviation: **DMs**

doctor ('dɒktə) *n* **1** a person licensed to practise medicine **2** a person who has been awarded a higher academic degree in any field of knowledge **3** *chiefly US & Canadian* a person licensed to practise dentistry or veterinary medicine **4** Also called: **Doctor of the Church** (*often capital*) a title given to any of several of the leading Fathers or theologians in the history of the Christian Church down to the late Middle Ages whose teachings have greatly influenced orthodox Christian thought **5** *angling* any of various gaudy artificial flies **6** *informal* a person who mends or repairs things **7** *slang* a cook on a ship or at a camp **8** *archaic* a man, esp a teacher, of learning **9** a cool sea breeze blowing in some countries: *the Cape doctor* **10** **go for the doctor** *Austral slang* to make a great effort or move very fast, esp in a horse race **11** **what the doctor ordered** something needed or desired ▷ *vb* **12** (*tr*) to give medical treatment to **13** (*intr*) *informal* to practise medicine **14** (*tr*) to repair or mend, esp in a makeshift manner **15** (*tr*) to make different in order to deceive, tamper with, falsify, or adulterate **16** (*tr*) to adapt for a desired end, effect, etc **17** (*tr*) to castrate (a cat, dog, etc) [c14: from Latin: teacher, from *docēre* to teach] ▷ '**doctoral** *or* **doctorial** (dɒk'tɔːrɪəl) *adj*

doctorate ('dɒktərɪt, -trɪt) *n* the highest academic degree in any field of knowledge

Doctor of Philosophy *n* a doctorate awarded for original research in any subject except law, medicine, or theology

doctrinaire (,dɒktrɪ'nɛə) *adj* **1** stubbornly insistent on the observation of the niceties of a theory, esp without regard to practicality, suitability, etc **2** theoretical; impractical ▷ *n* **3** a person who stubbornly attempts to apply a theory without regard to practical difficulties ▷ ,doctri'nairism *or* ,doctri'narism *n*

doctrine ('dɒktrɪn) *n* **1** a creed or body of teachings of a religious, political, or philosophical group presented for acceptance or belief; dogma **2** a principle or body of principles that is taught or advocated [c14: from Old French, from Latin *doctrīna* teaching, from *doctor* see DOCTOR] ▷ **doctrinal** (dɒk'traɪnᵊl) *adj* ▷ **doc'trinally** *adv*

docudrama ('dɒkjʊ,drɑːmə) *n* a film or television programme based on true events, presented in a dramatized form

document *n* ('dɒkjʊmənt) **1** a piece of paper, booklet, etc, providing information, esp of an official or legal nature **2** a piece of text or text and graphics stored in a computer as a file for manipulation by document processing software **3** *archaic* evidence; proof ▷ *vb* ('dɒkjʊ,mɛnt) (*tr*) **4** to record or report in detail, as in the press, on television, etc **5** to support (statements in a book) with citations, references, etc **6** to support (a claim, etc) with evidence or proof **7** to furnish (a vessel) with official documents specifying its ownership, registration, weight, dimensions, and function [c15: from Latin *documentum* a lesson, from *docēre* to teach]

documentarian (,dɒkjʊmən'tɛərɪən) *n* *chiefly US* a person who makes documentary films

documentary (,dɒkjʊ'mɛntəri, -trɪ) *adj* **1** Also: **documental** consisting of, derived from, or relating to documents **2** presenting factual material with little or no fictional additions ▷ *n, pl* **-ries** **3** a factual film or television programme about an event, person, etc, presenting the facts with little or no fiction ▷ ,docu'mentarily *adv*

documentation (,dɒkjʊmɛn'teɪʃən) *n* **1** the act of supplying with or using documents or references **2** the documents or references supplied

document reader *n* *computing* a device that reads and inputs into a computer marks and characters on a special form, as by optical or magnetic character recognition

docu-soap ('dɒkjʊ,səʊp) *n* a television documentary series in which the lives of the people filmed are presented as entertainment or drama [c20: from DOCU(MENTARY) + SOAP (OPERA)]

Dodd (dɒd) *n* **C(harles) H(arold)**. 1884–1973, British New Testament scholar. His works include *The Parables of the Kingdom* (1935)

dodder¹ ('dɒdə) *vb* (*intr*) **1** to move unsteadily; totter **2** to shake or tremble, as from age [c17: variant of earlier *dadder*; related to Norwegian *dudra* to tremble] ▷ 'dodderer *n* ▷ 'doddery *adj*

dodder² ('dɒdə) *n* any rootless parasitic plant of the convolvulaceous genus *Cuscuta*, lacking chlorophyll and having slender twining stems with suckers for drawing nourishment from the host plant, scalelike leaves, and whitish flowers [c13: of Germanic origin; related to Middle Dutch, Middle Low German *dodder*, Middle High German *toter*]

doddle ('dɒdᵊl) *n* *Brit informal* something easily accomplished [c20: perhaps from *dodder* (vb) to totter]

dodeca- *combining form* indicating twelve: *dodecagon; dodecahedron; dodecaphonic* [from Greek *dōdeka* twelve]

dodecagon (dəʊ'dɛkə,gɒn) *n* a polygon having twelve sides

dodecahedron (,dəʊdɛkə'hiːdrən) *n* a solid figure having twelve plane faces. A **regular dodecahedron** has regular pentagons as faces ▷ ,dodeca'hedral *adj*

Dodecanese (,dəʊdɪkə'niːz) *pl n* a group of islands in the SE Aegean Sea, forming a department of Greece: part of the Southern Sporades. Capital: Rhodes. Pop: 190 071 (2001). Area: 2663 sq km (1028 sq miles). Modern Greek name: Dhodhekánisos

dodecaphonic (,dəʊdɛkə'fɒnɪk) *adj* of or relating to the twelve-tone system of serial music

dodge (dɒdʒ) *vb* **1** to avoid or attempt to avoid (a blow, discovery, etc), as by moving suddenly **2** to evade (questions, etc) by cleverness or trickery **3** (*intr*) *bell-ringing* to make a bell change places with its neighbour when sounding in successive changes **4** (*tr*) *photog* to lighten or darken (selected areas on a print) by manipulating the light from an enlarger ▷ *n* **5** a plan or expedient contrived to deceive **6** a sudden evasive or hiding movement **7** a clever contrivance **8** *bell-ringing* the act of dodging [c16: of unknown origin]

Dodge City *n* a city in SW Kansas, on the Arkansas River: famous as a frontier town on the Santa Fe Trail. Pop: 25 568 (2003 est)

Dodgem ('dɒdʒəm) *n* *trademark* another name for **bumper car**

dodger ('dɒdʒə) *n* **1** a person who evades or shirks **2** a shifty dishonest person **3** a canvas shelter, mounted on a ship's bridge or over the companionway of a sailing yacht to protect the helmsman from bad weather **4** *archaic, US & Austral* a handbill **5** *Austral informal* food, esp bread

Dodgson ('dɒdʒsən) *n* **Charles Lutwidge** ('lʌtwɪdʒ). the real name of Lewis Carroll. See **Carroll**

dodgy ('dɒdʒi) *adj* **dodgier, dodgiest** *Brit, Austral & NZ informal* **1** risky, difficult, or dangerous **2** uncertain or unreliable; tricky

dodo ('dəʊdəʊ) *n, pl* **dodos** *or* **dodoes** **1** any flightless bird, esp *Raphus cucullatus*, of the recently extinct family *Raphidae* of Mauritius and adjacent islands: order *Columbiformes* (pigeons, etc). They had a hooked bill, short stout legs, and greyish plumage **2** *informal* an intensely conservative or reactionary person who is unaware of changing fashions, ideas, etc **3** **(as) dead as a dodo** (of a person or thing) irretrievably defunct or out of date [c17: from Portuguese *doudo*, from *doudo* stupid]

Dodoma ('dəʊdəmə) *n* a city in central Tanzania, the official capital of the country. Pop: 169 000 (2005 est)

Dodona (dəʊ'dəʊnə) *n* an ancient Greek town in Epirus: seat of an ancient sanctuary and oracle of Zeus and later the religious centre of Pyrrhus' kingdom ⊳ **Dodonaean** or **Dodonean** (ˌdəʊdəʊ'niːən) *adj*

do down *vb* (*tr, adverb*) 1 to belittle or humiliate 2 to deceive or cheat

doe (dəʊ) *n, pl* **does** or **doe** the female of the deer, hare, rabbit, and certain other animals [Old English *dā*; related to Old English *dēon* to suck, Sanskrit *dhēnā* cow]

Doe (dəʊ) *n* 1 *law* (formerly) the plaintiff in a fictitious action, Doe versus Roe, to test a point of law. See also **Roe** 2 John Doe or Jane Doe *US* an unknown or unidentified male or female person

DOE or **DoE** *abbreviation* 1 (in Canada and, formerly, in Britain) Department of the Environment 2 (in the US) Department of Energy

doek (dʊk) *n South African informal* a square of cloth worn mainly by African women to cover the head, esp to indicate married status [c18: from Afrikaans: cloth]

Doenitz (*German* 'dø:nɪts) *n* a variant spelling of **Dönitz**

doer ('duːə) *n* 1 a person or thing that does something or acts in a specified manner: *a doer of good* 2 an active or energetic person 3 a thriving animal, esp a horse

does[1] (dʌz) *vb* (used with a singular noun or the pronouns *he, she,* or *it*) a form of the present tense (indicative mood) of **do**[1]

does[2] (dʊəs) *n South African taboo, slang* a foolish or despicable person [Afrikaans]

doeskin ('dəʊˌskɪn) *n* 1 the skin of a deer, lamb, or sheep 2 a very supple leather made from this skin and used esp for gloves 3 a heavy smooth satin-weave or twill-weave cloth 4 (*modifier*) made of doeskin

doff (dɒf) *vb* (*tr*) 1 to take off or lift (one's hat) in salutation 2 to remove (clothing) [Old English *dōn of*; see **DO**[1], **OFF**; compare **DON**[1]] ⊳ 'doffer *n*

do for *vb* (*preposition*) *informal* 1 (*tr*) to convict of a crime or offence: *they did him for manslaughter* 2 (*intr*) to cause the ruin, death, or defeat of: *the last punch did for him* 3 (*intr*) to do housework for 4 **do well for oneself** to thrive or succeed

dog (dɒg) *n* 1 a domesticated canine mammal, *Canis familiaris*, occurring in many breeds that show a great variety in size and form 2 any other carnivore of the family *Canidae*, such as the dingo and coyote 3 the male of animals of the dog family 4 (*modifier*) spurious, inferior, or useless 5 a mechanical device for gripping or holding, esp one of the axial slots by which gear wheels or shafts are engaged to transmit torque 6 *informal* a fellow; chap 7 *informal* a man or boy regarded as unpleasant, contemptible, or wretched 8 *slang* an unattractive or boring girl or woman 9 *US & Canadian informal* something unsatisfactory or inferior 10 short for **firedog** 11 **a dog's chance** no chance at all 12 **a dog's dinner** or **a dog's breakfast** *informal* something that is messy or bungled 13 **a dog's life** a wretched existence 14 **dog eat dog** ruthless competition or self-interest 15 **like a dog's dinner** *informal* dressed smartly or ostentatiously 16 **put on the dog** *US & Canadian informal* to behave or dress in an ostentatious or showy manner ⊳ *vb* **dogs, dogging, dogged** (*tr*) 17 to pursue or follow after like a dog 18 to trouble; plague 19 to chase with a dog or dogs 20 to grip, hold, or secure by a mechanical device ⊳ *adv* 21 (usually in combination) thoroughly; utterly: *dog-tired* ⊳ See also **dogs** [Old English *docga*, of obscure origin]

dog and bone *n Cockney rhyming slang* a telephone

dog biscuit *n* a hard biscuit for dogs

dog box *n NZ informal* disgrace; disfavour (in the phrase **in the dog box**)

dogcart ('dɒgˌkɑːt) *n* a light horse-drawn two-wheeled vehicle: originally, one containing a box or section for transporting gun dogs

dog-catcher *n Now chiefly US & Canadian* a local official whose job is to catch and impound stray dogs, cats, etc

dog collar *n* 1 a collar for a dog 2 an informal name for a

clerical collar 3 *informal* a tight-fitting necklace

dog days *pl n* 1 the hot period of the summer reckoned in ancient times from the heliacal rising of Sirius (the Dog Star) 2 a period marked by inactivity [c16: translation of Late Latin *diēs caniculārēs*, translation of Greek *hēmerai kunades*]

doge (dəʊdʒ) *n* (formerly) the chief magistrate in the republics of Venice (until 1797) and Genoa (until 1805) [c16: via French from Italian (Venetian dialect), from Latin *dux* leader] ⊳ 'dogeship *n*

dog-ear *vb* 1 (*tr*) to fold down the corner of (a page) ⊳ *n* Also: **dog's-ear** 2 a folded-down corner of a page 3 *computing* a bookmark

dog-eared *adj* 1 having dog-ears 2 shabby or worn

dog-end *n* an informal name for **cigarette end**

dogfight ('dɒgˌfaɪt) *n* 1 close quarters combat between fighter aircraft 2 any rough violent fight

dogfish ('dɒgˌfɪʃ) *n, pl* **-fish** or **-fishes** 1 any of several small spotted European sharks, esp *Scyliorhinus caniculus* (**lesser spotted dogfish**): family Scyliorhinidae 2 a less common name for the **bowfin**

dog fouling *n* the offence of being in charge of a dog and failing to remove the faeces after it defecates in a public place

dogged ('dɒgɪd) *adj* obstinately determined; wilful or tenacious ⊳ 'doggedly *adv* ⊳ 'doggedness *n*

Dogger Bank ('dɒgə) *n* an extensive submerged sandbank in the North Sea between N England and Denmark: fishing ground

doggerel ('dɒgərəl) or **dogrel** ('dɒgrəl) *n* 1 a comic verse, usually irregular in measure b (*as modifier*): *a doggerel rhythm* 2 nonsense; drivel [c14 *dogerel* worthless, perhaps from *dogge* **DOG**]

doggish ('dɒgɪʃ) *adj* 1 of or like a dog 2 surly; snappish ⊳ 'doggishly *adv* ⊳ 'doggishness *n*

doggo ('dɒgəʊ) *adv Brit informal* in hiding and keeping quiet (esp in the phrase **lie doggo**) [c19: probably from **DOG**]

doggone ('dɒgɒn) *US & Canadian informal* ⊳ *interj* 1 an exclamation of annoyance, disappointment, etc ⊳ *adj* (prenominal), *adv* 2 Also called: **doggoned** another word for **damn** (senses 3, 4) [c19: euphemism for *God damn*]

doggy or **doggie** ('dɒgɪ) *n, pl* **-gies** 1 a children's word for a dog ⊳ *adj* 2 of, like, or relating to a dog 3 fond of dogs

doggy bag *n* a bag into which leftovers from a meal may be put and taken away, supposedly for the diner's dog

doggy paddle or **doggie paddle** *n* 1 a swimming stroke in which the swimmer lies on his front, paddles his hands in imitation of a swimming dog, and beats his legs up and down ⊳ *vb* **doggy-paddle** or **doggie-paddle** 2 (*intr*) to swim using the doggy paddle ⊳ Also called: **dog paddle**

doghouse ('dɒgˌhaʊs) *n* 1 *US & Canadian* a hutlike shelter for a dog 2 *informal* disfavour (in the phrase **in the doghouse**)

dogie, dogy or **dogey** ('dəʊgɪ) *n, pl* **-gies** or **-geys** *Western US & Canadian* a motherless calf [c19: from *dough-guts*, because they were fed on flour and water paste]

dog in the manger *n* a a person who prevents others from using something he has no use for b (*as modifier*): *a dog-in-the-manger attitude*

dog Latin *n* spurious or incorrect Latin

dogleg ('dɒgˌleg) *n* 1 a a sharp bend or angle b something with a sharp bend ⊳ *vb* **-legs, -legging, -legged** 2 (*intr*) to go off at an angle ⊳ *adj* 3 of or with the shape of a dogleg ⊳ **doglegged** (ˌdɒg'legɪd, 'dɒgˌlegd) *adj*

dogma ('dɒgmə) *n, pl* **-mas** or **-mata** (-mətə) 1 a religious doctrine or system of doctrines proclaimed by ecclesiastical authority as true 2 a belief, principle, or doctrine or a code of beliefs, principles, or doctrines: *Marxist dogma* [c17: via Latin from Greek: opinion, belief, from *dokein* to seem good]

dogman ('dɒgmən) *n, pl* **-men** *Austral* a person who directs the operation of a crane whilst riding on an object being lifted by it

dogmatic (dɒg'mætɪk) or **dogmatical** *adj* 1 a (of a statement, opinion, etc) forcibly asserted as if authoritative and unchallengeable b (of a person) prone to making such statements **2** of, relating to, or constituting dogma: *dogmatic writings* **3** based on assumption rather than empirical observation > dog'**matically** *adv*

dogmatics (dɒg'mætɪks) *n* (*functioning as singular*) the study of religious dogmas and doctrines. Also called: **dogmatic theology, doctrinal theology**

dogmatize *or* **dogmatise** ('dɒgmə,taɪz) *vb* to say or state (something) in a dogmatic manner > 'dogmatism *n* > 'dogmatist *n* > ,dogmati'zation *or* ,dogmati'sation *n* > 'dogma,tizer *or* 'dogma,tiser *n*

do-gooder *n informal, usually disparaging* a well-intentioned person, esp a naive or impractical one > ,do-'goodery *n* > ,do-'gooding *n, adj*

dog paddle *n* another name for **doggy paddle**

Dogrib ('dɒg,rɪb) *n* **1** a member of a Dene Native Canadian people of northern Canada **2** the Athapascan language of this people [from Dogrib *Thlingchadinne*, dog's flank, referring to the people's belief that they are descended from a dog]

dog-roll *n NZ* a large sausage-shaped roll of processed meat used for dog food

dog rose *n* a prickly wild rose, *Rosa canina*, that is native to Europe and has pink or white delicate scentless flowers [translation of the Latin name, from Greek; from the belief that its root was effective against the bite of a mad dog]

dogs (dɒgz) *pl n* **1** the dogs *Brit informal* greyhound racing **2** *slang* the feet **3** *marketing informal* goods with a low market share, which are unlikely to yield substantial profits **4** go to the dogs *informal* to go to ruin physically or morally **5** let sleeping dogs lie to leave things undisturbed **6** throw someone to the dogs to abandon someone to criticism or attack

Dogs (dɒgz) *n Isle of Dogs* a district in the East End of London, bounded on three sides by the River Thames, and a focus of major office development (Canary Wharf) in recent years

dogsbody ('dɒgz,bɒdɪ) *n, pl* -**bodies 1** *informal* a person who carries out menial tasks for others; drudge ▷ *vb* -**bodies, -bodying, -bodied 2** (*intr*) to act as a dogsbody

dogsled ('dɒg,slɛd) *n chiefly US & Canadian* a sleigh drawn by dogs. Also called (*Brit*): **dog sledge, dog sleigh**

Dog Star *n the Dog Star* another name for **Sirius**

dog-tired *adj* (*usually postpositive*) *informal* exhausted

dogtooth ('dɒg,tuːθ) *n, pl* -**teeth** *architect* a carved ornament in the form of four leaflike projections radiating from a raised centre, used in England in the 13th century

dogtooth violet *n* a name for various plants of the liliaceous genus *Erythronium*, esp the North American *E. americanum*, with yellow nodding flowers, or the European *E. dens-canis*, with purple flowers. Also called: **adders-tongue, fawn lily**

dogtrot ('dɒg,trɒt) *n* a gently paced trot

dog violet *n* a violet, *Viola canina*, that grows in Europe and N Asia and has blue yellow-spurred flowers

dogwatch ('dɒg,wɒtʃ) *n* either of two two-hour watches aboard ship, from four to six p.m. or from six to eight p.m.

dog-whistle *adj* **1** relating to the targeting of potentially controversial messages to specific voters while avoiding offending those voters with whom the message will not be popular: *dog-whistle politics* ▷ *vb* **2** (*intr*) to employ this kind of political strategy [c21: from the fact that a dog whistle operates at frequencies that can be heard only by dogs]

dogwood ('dɒg,wʊd) *n* any of various cornaceous trees or shrubs of the genus *Cornus*, esp *C. sanguinea*, a European shrub with clusters of small white flowers and black berries: the shoots are red in winter

dogy ('dəʊgɪ) *n, pl* -**gies** a variant spelling of **dogie**

doh (dəʊ) *n* **1** *music* (in tonic sol-fa) the first degree of any major scale **2** up to high doh *informal, chiefly Scot* extremely excited or keyed up [c18: from Italian; see GAMUT]

DoH *abbreviation* (in Britain) Department of Health

Doha ('dəʊhɑː, 'dəʊə) *n* the capital and chief port of Qatar, on the E coast of the peninsula. Pop: 370 000

(2002 est). Former name: Bida

Dohnányi (dɒk'nɑːnjɪ, dɒx-; Hungarian 'dohnɑːnji) *n* **Ernö** ('ɛrnøː) *or* **Ernst von** (ɛrnst fɔn). 1877–1960, Hungarian pianist and composer whose works include *Variations on a Nursery Theme* (1913) for piano and orchestra

doily, doiley *or* **doyly** ('dɔɪlɪ) *n, pl* -**lies** *or* -**leys** a decorative mat of lace or lacelike paper, etc, laid on or under plates [c18: named after *Doily*, a London draper]

do in *vb* (*tr, adverb*) *slang* **1** to murder or kill **2** to exhaust

doing ('duːɪŋ) *n, pl* an action or the performance of an action: *whose doing is this?* **2** *informal* a beating or castigation

doings ('duːɪŋz) *pl n* **1** deeds, actions or events **2** *Brit & NZ informal* anything of which the name is not known, or euphemistically left unsaid, etc: *have you got the doings for starting the car?*

Doisy ('dɔɪzɪ) *n* **Edward Adelbert.** 1893–1986, US biochemist. He discovered (1939) the nature of vitamin K and shared a Nobel prize for medicine with Carl Dam (1943)

do-it-yourself *n* **a** the hobby or process of constructing and repairing things oneself **b** (*as modifier*): *a do-it-yourself kit*

dol. *abbreviation* **1** *music* dolce **2** (*pl* dols.) dollar

Dolby ('dɒlbɪ) *n trademark* any of various specialized electronic circuits, esp those used for noise reduction in tape recorders by functioning as companders on high-frequency signals [named after R. *Dolby* (born 1933), its US inventor]

dolce ('dɒltʃɪ; *Italian* 'doltʃe) *adj, adv music* (to be performed) gently and sweetly [Italian: sweet]

Dolcelatte (,dɒltʃɪlɑːtɪ) *n* a soft creamy blue-veined cheese made in Italy [Italian, literally: sweet milk]

dolce vita ('dɒltʃɪ 'viːtə; *Italian* 'doltʃe 'vita) *n* a life of luxury [Italian, literally: sweet life]

doldrums ('dɒldrəmz) *n the doldrums* **1** a depressed or bored state of mind **2** a state of inactivity or stagnation **3 a** a belt of light winds or calms along the equator **b** the weather conditions experienced in this belt, formerly a hazard to sailing vessels [c19: probably from Old English *dol* DULL, influenced by TANTRUM]

dole[1] (dəʊl) *n* **1** a small portion or share, as of money or food, given to a poor person **2** the act of giving or distributing such portions **3** the dole *Brit informal* money received from the state while out of work **4** on the dole *Brit informal* receiving such money **5** *archaic* fate ▷ *vb* **6** (*tr; usually foll by out*) to distribute, esp in small portions [Old English *dāl* share; related to Old Saxon *dēl*, Old Norse *deild*, Gothic *dails*, Old High German *teil*; see DEAL[1]]

dole[2] (dəʊl) *n archaic* grief or mourning [c13: from Old French, from Late Latin *dolus*, from Latin *dolēre* to lament]

dole bludger *n Austral slang, offensive* a person who draws unemployment benefit without making any attempt to find work

doleful ('dəʊlfʊl) *adj* dreary; mournful > 'dolefully *adv* > 'dolefulness *n*

dolerite ('dɒlə,raɪt) *n* **1** a dark basic intrusive igneous rock consisting of plagioclase feldspar and a pyroxene, such as augite; often emplaced in dykes **2** any dark igneous rock whose composition cannot be determined with the naked eye [c19: from French *dolérite*, from Greek *doleros* deceitful; so called because of the difficulty of determining its composition] > doleritic (,dɒlə'rɪtɪk) *adj*

Dolgellau (dɒl'gɛθlaɪ; *Welsh* dɒl'gɛθlaɪ) *n* a market town and tourist centre in NW Wales, in Gwynedd. Pop: 2407 (2001)

dolichocephalic (,dɒlɪkəʊsɪ'fælɪk) *or* **dolichocephalous** (,dɒlɪkəʊ'sɛfələs) *adj* having a head much longer than it is broad, esp one with a cephalic index under 75

Dolin ('dəʊlɪn) *n* Sir **Anton**, real name *Sydney Healey-Kay*. 1904–83, British ballet dancer and choreographer: with Alicia Markova he founded (1949) the London Festival Ballet

D'Oliviera (,dɒlɪ'vɪərə) *n* **Basil** (**Lewis**). born 1931, South African cricketer, who played for Worcestershire and England

doll (dɒl) *n* **1** a small model or dummy of a human

being, used as a toy **2** *slang* a pretty girl or woman of little intelligence: sometimes used as a term of address [c16: probably from *Doll*, pet name for *Dorothy*] ▷'**dollish** *adj* ▷'**dollishly** *adv* ▷'**dollishness** *n*

dollar ('dɒlə) *n* **1** the standard monetary unit of the US and its dependencies, divided into 100 cents **2** the standard monetary unit, comprising 100 cents, of the following countries or territories: Antigua and Barbuda, Australia, the Bahamas, Barbados, Belize, Bermuda, the British Virgin Islands, Brunei, Canada, the Cayman Islands, Dominica, East Timor, Ecuador, El Salvador, Fiji, Grenada, Guatemala, Guyana, Hong Kong, Jamaica, Kiribati, Liberia, Malaysia, the Marshall Islands, Micronesia, Namibia, Nauru, New Zealand, Saint Kitts and Nevis, Saint Lucia, Saint Vincent and the Grenadines, Singapore, Solomon Islands, Taiwan, Trinidad and Tobago, Tuvalu, and Zimbabwe **3** *Brit informal* (formerly) five shillings or a coin of this value **4** **look** *or* **feel (like) a million dollars** *informal* to look or feel extremely well [c16: from Low German *daler*, from German *Taler, Thaler*, short for *Joachimsthaler* coin made from metal mined in *Joachimsthal* Jachymov, town now in the Czech Republic]

dollarbird ('dɒləˌbɜːd) *n* a bird, *Eurystomus orientalis*, of S and SE Asia and Australia, with a round white spot on each wing: family *Coraciidae* (rollers), order *Coraciiformes*

dollar diplomacy *n chiefly US* **1** a foreign policy that encourages and protects capital investment and commercial and financial involvement abroad **2** use of financial power as a diplomatic weapon

Dollfuss (German 'dɔlfuːs) *n* **Engelbert** ('ɛŋəlbɛrt). 1892–1934, Austrian statesman, chancellor (1932–34), who was assassinated by Austrian Nazis

dollop ('dɒləp) *informal* ▷ *n* **1** a semisolid lump **2** a large serving, esp of food ▷ *vb* **3** (*tr*; foll by *out*) to serve out (food) [c16: of unknown origin]

doll up *vb* (*tr, adverb*) *slang* to adorn or dress (oneself or another, esp a child) in a stylish or showy manner

dolly ('dɒlɪ) *n, pl* -**lies 1** a child's word for a **doll 2** *films, television* a wheeled support on which a camera may be mounted **3** a cup-shaped anvil held against the head of a rivet while the other end is being hammered **4** *cricket* a simple catch **5** Also called: **dolly bird** *slang, chiefly Brit* an attractive and intelligent girl, esp one who is considered to be unintelligent ▷ *vb* -**lies**, -**lying**, -**lied 6** *films, television* to wheel (a camera) backwards or forwards on to a dolly

dolly mixture *n* **1** a mixture of small coloured sweets **2** one such sweet

dolma ('dɒlmə, -mɑː) *n, pl* **dolmas** *or* **dolmades** (dɒl'mɑːdiːz) a vine leaf stuffed with a filling of meat and rice [c19: Turkish *dolma* literally something filled]

dolman sleeve ('dɒlmən) *n* a sleeve that is very wide at the armhole and tapers to a tight wrist

dolmen ('dɒlmɛn) *n* **1** (in British archaeology) a Neolithic stone formation, consisting of a horizontal stone supported by several vertical stones, and thought to be a tomb **2** (in French archaeology) any megalithic tomb [c19: from French, probably from Old Breton *tol* table, from Latin *tabula* board + Breton *mēn* stone, of Celtic origin; see TABLE]

Dolmetsch ('dɒlmɛtʃ) *n* **Arnold**. 1858–1940, British musician, born in France. He contributed greatly to the revival of interest in early music and instruments

dolomite ('dɒləˌmaɪt) *n* **1** a white mineral often tinted by impurities, found in sedimentary rocks and veins. It is used in the manufacture of cement and as a building stone (marble). Composition: calcium magnesium carbonate. Formula: $CaMg(CO_3)_2$. Crystal structure: hexagonal (rhombohedral) **2** a sedimentary rock resembling limestone but consisting principally of the mineral dolomite. It is an important source of magnesium and its compounds, and is used as a building material and refractory [c18: named after Déodat de *Dolomieu* (1750–1801), French mineralogist] ▷ **dolomitic** (ˌdɒlə'mɪtɪk) *adj*

Dolomites ('dɒləˌmaɪts) *pl n* a mountain range in NE Italy: part of the Alps; formed of dolomitic limestone. Highest peak: Marmolada, 3342 m (10 965 ft)

doloroso (ˌdɒlə'rəʊsəʊ) *adj, adv music* (to be performed) in a sorrowful manner [Italian: dolorous]

dolorous ('dɒlərəs) *adj* causing or involving pain or sorrow ▷ '**dolorously** *adv* ▷ '**dolorousness** *n*

dolos ('dɒlɒs) *n, pl* -**osse** *South African* a knucklebone of a sheep, buck, etc, used esp by diviners [from Afrikaans, possibly from *dollen* play + *os* ox or from *dobbel* dice + *os* ox]

dolour *or US* **dolor** ('dɒlə) *n poetic* grief or sorrow [c14: from Latin, from *dolēre* to grieve]

dolphin ('dɒlfɪn) *n* **1** any of various marine cetacean mammals of the family *Delphinidae*, esp *Delphinus delphis*, that are typically smaller than whales and larger than porpoises and have a beaklike snout **2** **river dolphin** any freshwater cetacean of the family *Platanistidae*, inhabiting rivers of North and South America and S Asia. They are smaller than marine dolphins and have a longer narrower snout **3** Also called: **dorado** either of two large marine percoid fishes, *Coryphaena hippurus* or *C. equisetis*, that resemble the cetacean dolphins and have an iridescent coloration **4** *nautical* a post or buoy for mooring a vessel [c13: from Old French *dauphin*, via Latin, from Greek *delphin-, delphis*]

dolphinarium (ˌdɒlfɪ'neərɪəm) *n* a pool or aquarium for dolphins, esp one in which they give public displays

dolt (dəʊlt) *n* a slow-witted or stupid person [c16: probably related to Old English *dol* stupid; see DULL] ▷ '**doltish** *adj* ▷ '**doltishly** *adv* ▷ '**doltishness** *n*

-dom *suffix forming nouns* **1** state or condition: *freedom; martyrdom* **2** rank or office: *earldom* **3** domain: *kingdom; Christendom* **4** a collection of persons: *officialdom* [Old English *-dōm*]

Domagk (German 'doːmak) *n* **Gerhard** ('geːrhart). 1895–1964, German biochemist: Nobel prize for medicine (1939) for isolating sulphanilamide for treating bacterial infections

domain (də'meɪn) *n* **1** land governed by a ruler or government **2** land owned by one person or family **3** a field or scope of knowledge or activity **4** a region having specific characteristics or containing certain types of plants or animals **5** *Austral & NZ* a park or recreation reserve maintained by a public authority, often the government **6** *law* the absolute ownership and right to dispose of land **7** *maths* the set of values of the independent variable of a function for which the functional value exists **8** *logic* another term for **universe of discourse 9** *philosophy* range of significance (esp in the phrase **domain of definition**) **10** Also called: **magnetic domain** *physics* one of the regions in a ferromagnetic solid in which all the atoms have their magnetic moments aligned in the same direction **11** *computing* a group of computers, functioning and administered as a unit, that are identified by sharing the same **domain name** on the internet **12** Also called: **superkingdom** *biology* the highest level of classification of living organisms. Three domains are recognized: *Archaea* (see **archaean**), *Bacteria* (see **bacteria**), and *Eukarya* (see **eukaryote**) **13** *biochem* a structurally compact portion of a protein molecule [c17: from French *domaine*, from Latin *dominium* property, from *dominus* lord]

domain name *n computing* a unique name, corresponding to one or more numeric IP addresses, used to identify a particular web page or set of web pages on the internet

dome (dəʊm) *n* **1** a hemispherical roof or vault or a structure of similar form **2** something shaped like this **3** a slang word for the **head** ▷ *vb* (*tr*) **4** to cover with or as if with a dome **5** to shape like a dome [c16: from French, from Italian *duomo* cathedral, from Latin *domus* house] ▷ '**domeˌlike** *adj* ▷ **domical** ('dəʊmɪkᵊl, 'dɒm-) *adj*

Domenichino (Italian domeni'kiːno) *n* full name **Domenico Zampieri** (do'meːniko dzam'pjɛːri). 1581–1641, Italian Baroque painter, noted for his frescoes and the altarpiece *Last Communion of St Jerome* (1614)

Domenico Veneziano (Italian do'meːniko venet'tsjaːno) *n* died 1461, Italian painter, noted for the St Lucy Altarpiece

Dome of the Rock *n* the mosque in Jerusalem, Israel, built in 691 AD by caliph ʿAbd al-Malik: the third most holy place of Islam; stands on the Temple Mount alongside the **al-Aqsa** mosque

Domesday Book *or* **Doomsday Book** *n history* the record of a survey of the land of England carried out by the commissioners of William I in 1086

domestic (dəˈmɛstɪk) *adj* **1** of or involving the home or family **2** enjoying or accustomed to home or family life **3** (of an animal) bred or kept by man as a pet or for purposes such as the supply of food **4** of, produced in, or involving one's own country or a specific country: *domestic and foreign affairs* ▷ *n* **5** a household servant **6** *informal* (esp in police use) an incident of violence in the home, esp between a man and a woman [c16: from Old French *domestique*, from Latin *domesticus* belonging to the house, from *domus* house] > do'mestically *adv*

domesticate (dəˈmɛstɪˌkeɪt) *or sometimes US* **domesticize** (dəˈmɛstɪˌsaɪz) *vb* (*tr*) **1** to bring or keep (wild animals or plants) under control or cultivation **2** to accustom to home life **3** to adapt to an environment: *to domesticate foreign trees* > do'mesticable *adj* > do,mesti'cation *n* > do'mesticative *adj* > do'mesti,cator *n*

domesticity (ˌdəʊmɛˈstɪsɪtɪ) *n, pl* **-ties** **1** home life **2** devotion to or familiarity with home life **3** (*usually plural*) a domestic duty, matter, or condition

domestic science *n* the study of cooking, needlework, and other subjects concerned with household skills

Domett (ˈdɒmɪt) *n* **Alfred.** 1811–87, New Zealand poet, colonial administrator, and statesman, born in England: prime minister of New Zealand (1862–63)

domicile (ˈdɒmɪˌsaɪl) *or* **domicil** (ˈdɒmɪsɪl) *formal* ▷ *n* **1** a dwelling place **2** a permanent legal residence **3** *commerce, Brit* the place where a bill of exchange is to be paid ▷ *vb* Also: **domiciliate** (ˌdɒmɪˈsɪlɪˌeɪt) **4** to establish or be established in a dwelling place [c15: from Latin *domicilium*, from *domus* house]

dominance (ˈdɒmɪnəns) *n* control; ascendancy

dominant (ˈdɒmɪnənt) *adj* **1** having primary control, authority, or influence; governing; ruling **2** predominant or primary: *the dominant topic of the day* **3** occupying a commanding position **4** *genetics* (of an allele) producing the same phenotype in the organism irrespective of whether the allele of the same gene is identical or dissimilar. Compare **recessive** (sense 2) **5** *music* of or relating to the fifth degree of a scale **6** *ecology* (of a plant or animal species within a community) more prevalent than any other species and determining the appearance and composition of the community ▷ *n* **7** *genetics* a dominant allele or character **8** *music* **a** the fifth degree of a scale and the second in importance after the tonic **b** a key or chord based on this **9** *ecology* a dominant plant or animal in a community > 'dominantly *adv*

dominant seventh chord *n* a chord consisting of the dominant and the major third, perfect fifth, and minor seventh above it. Its most natural resolution is to a chord on the tonic

dominate (ˈdɒmɪˌneɪt) *vb* **1** to control, rule, or govern (someone or something) **2** to tower above (surroundings, etc); overlook **3** (*tr; usually passive*) to predominate in (something or someone) [c17: from Latin *dominārī* to be lord over, from *dominus* lord] > 'domi,nating *adj* > 'domi,natingly *adv* > 'dominative *adj* > 'domi,nator *n*

dominatrix (ˌdɒmɪˈneɪtrɪks) *n, pl* **dominatrices** (ˌdɒmɪnəˈtraɪsiːz) **1** a woman who is the dominant sexual partner in a sadomasochistic relationship **2** a dominant woman [c16: from Latin, fem of *dominātor*, from *dominārī* to be lord over]

dominee (ˈduːmɪnɪ, ˈdʊə-) *n* (in South Africa) a minister in any of the Afrikaner Churches. Also called: **predikant** [from Afrikaans, from Dutch; compare DOMINIE]

domineer (ˌdɒmɪˈnɪə) *vb* (*intr; often foll by over*) to act with arrogance or tyranny; behave imperiously [c16: from Dutch *domineren*, from French *dominer* to DOMINATE]

domineering (ˌdɒmɪˈnɪərɪŋ) *adj* acting with or showing arrogance or tyranny; imperious > ,domi'neeringly *adv* > ,domi'neeringness *n*

Domingo (Spanish doˈmiŋɡo) *n* **Placido** (ˈplaθiðo). born 1941, Spanish operatic tenor

Dominic (ˈdɒmɪnɪk) *n* **Saint.** original name Domingo de Guzman. ?1170–1221, Spanish priest; founder of the Dominican order. Feast day: Aug 7

Dominica (ˌdɒmɪˈniːkə, dəˈmɪnɪkə) *n* a republic in the E Caribbean, comprising a volcanic island in the Windward Islands group; a former British colony; became independent as a member of the Commonwealth in 1978. Official language: English. Religion: Roman Catholic majority. Currency: East Caribbean dollar. Capital: Roseau. Pop: 79 000 (2003 est). Area: 751 sq km (290 sq miles)

dominical (dəˈmɪnɪkᵊl) *adj* **1** of, relating to, or emanating from Jesus Christ as Lord **2** of or relating to Sunday as the Lord's Day [c15: from Late Latin *dominicālis*, from Latin *dominus* lord]

Dominican[1] (dəˈmɪnɪkən) *n* **1 a** a member of an order of preaching friars founded by Saint Dominic (original name Domingo de Guzman; ?1170–1221), the Spanish priest, in 1215; a Blackfriar **b** a nun of one of the orders founded under the patronage of Saint Dominic ▷ *adj* **2** of or relating to Saint Dominic or the Dominican order

Dominican[2] (dəˈmɪnɪkən) *adj* **1** of or relating to the Dominican Republic or Dominica ▷ *n* **2** a native or inhabitant of the Dominican Republic or Dominica

Dominican Republic *n* a republic in the Caribbean, occupying the eastern half of the island of Hispaniola: colonized by the Spanish after its discovery by Columbus in 1492; gained independence from Spain in 1821. It is generally mountainous, dominated by the Cordillera Central, which rises over 3000 m (10 000 ft), with fertile lowlands. Language: Spanish. Religion: Roman Catholic majority. Currency: peso. Capital: Santo Domingo. Pop: 8 873 000 (2004 est). Area: 48 441 sq km (18 703 sq miles). Former name (until 1844): Santo Domingo

dominie (ˈdɒmɪnɪ) *n* **1** a Scot word for **schoolmaster 2** a minister or clergyman: also used as a term of address [c17: from Latin *dominē*, vocative case of *dominus* lord]

dominion (dəˈmɪnjən) *n* **1** rule; authority **2** the land governed by one ruler or government **3** sphere of influence; area of control **4** a name formerly applied to self-governing divisions of the British Empire **5** the **Dominion** New Zealand [c15: from Old French, from Latin *dominium* ownership, from *dominus* master]

Dominion Day *n* the former name for **Canada Day**

domino[1] (ˈdɒmɪˌnəʊ) *n, pl* **-noes** a small rectangular block used in dominoes, divided on one side into two equal areas, each of which is either blank or marked with from one to six dots [c19: from French, from Italian, perhaps from *domino!* master, said by the winner]

domino[2] (ˈdɒmɪˌnəʊ) *n, pl* **-noes** *or* **-nos 1** a large hooded cloak worn with an eye mask at a masquerade **2** the eye mask worn with such a cloak [c18: from French or Italian, probably from Latin *dominus* lord, master]

Domino (ˈdɒmɪnəʊ) *n* **Fats.** real name *Antoine Domino* born 1928, US rhythm-and- blues and rock-and-roll pianist, singer, and songwriter. His singles include "Ain't that a Shame" (1955) and "Blueberry Hill" (1956)

domino effect *n* a series of similar or related events occurring as a direct and inevitable result of one initial event [c20: alluding to a row of dominoes, each standing on end, all of which fall when one is pushed: originally used with reference to possible Communist takeovers of countries in SE Asia]

dominoes (ˈdɒmɪˌnəʊz) *n* (*functioning as singular*) any of several games in which matching halves of dominoes are laid together

Dominus Latin (ˈdɒmɪnʊs) *n* God or Christ

Domitian (dəˈmɪʃən) *n* full name *Titus Flavius Domitianus*. 51–96 AD, Roman emperor (81–96): instigated a reign of terror (93); assassinated

Domrémy-la-Pucelle (French dɔremilapysɛl) *or* **Domrémy** *n* a village in NE France, in the Vosges: birthplace of Joan of Arc

don[1] (dɒn) *vb* **dons, donning, donned** (*tr*) to put on (clothing) [c14: from DO¹ + ON; compare DOFF]

don[2] (dɒn) *n* **1** *Brit* a member of the teaching staff at a university or college, esp at Oxford or Cambridge **2** the head of a student dormitory at certain Canadian

d.

universities and colleges **3** a Spanish gentleman or nobleman **4** (in the Mafia) the head of a family [C17: ultimately from Latin *dominus* lord]

Don¹ (dɒn; *Spanish* don) *n* a Spanish title equivalent to *Mr*: placed before a name to indicate respect [C16: via Spanish, from Latin *dominus* lord; see DON²]

Don² (dɒn) *n* **1** a river rising in W Russia, southeast of Tula and flowing generally south, to the Sea of Azov: linked by canal to the River Volga. Length: 1870 km (1162 miles) **2** a river in NE Scotland, rising in the Cairngorm Mountains and flowing east to the North Sea. Length: 100 km (62 miles) **3** a river in N central England, rising in S Yorkshire and flowing northeast to the Humber. Length: about 96 km (60 miles)

Dona (*Portuguese* 'dōːnə) *n* a Portuguese title of address equivalent to *Mrs* or *Madam*: placed before a name to indicate respect [C19: from Latin *domina* lady, feminine of *dominus* master]

Doña ('dɒnjə; *Spanish* 'dɔɲa) *n* a Spanish title of address equivalent to *Mrs* or *Madam*: placed before a name to indicate respect [C17: via Spanish, from Latin *domina*; see DONA]

Donald ('dɒnᵊld) *n* ?1031–1100, king of Scotland (1093–94; 1094–97)

Donar ('dəʊnɑː; *German* 'doːnar) *n* the Germanic god of thunder, corresponding to Thor in Norse mythology

donate (dəʊ'neɪt) *vb* to give (money, time, etc), esp to a charity ▷ do'nator *n*

Donatello (*Italian* dona'tɛllo) *n* real name *Donato di Betto Bardi*. 1386–1466, Florentine sculptor, regarded as the greatest sculptor of the quattrocento, who was greatly influenced by classical sculpture and contemporary humanist theories. His marble relief of *St George Killing the Dragon* (1416–17) shows his innovative use of perspective. Other outstanding works are the classic bronze *David*, and the bronze equestrian monument to Gattamelatta, which became the model of subsequent equestrian sculpture

donation (dəʊ'neɪʃən) *n* **1** the act of giving, esp to a charity **2** a contribution [C15: from Latin *dōnātiō* a presenting, from *dōnāre* to give, from *dōnum* gift]

donative ('dəʊnətɪv) *n* **1** a gift or donation **2** a benefice capable of being conferred as a gift ▷ *adj* **3** of or like a donation **4** being or relating to a benefice [C15: from Latin *dōnātīvum* donation made to soldiers by a Roman emperor, from *dōnāre* to present]

Donatus (dəʊ'nɑːtəs) *n* **1** *Aelius* ('iːlɪəs). 4th century AD, Latin grammarian, who taught Saint Jerome; his textbook *Ars Grammatica* was used throughout the Middle Ages **2** 4th century AD, bishop of Carthage; leader of the Donatists, a heretical Christian sect originating in N Africa in 311 AD

Donau ('doːnau) *n* the German name for the **Danube**

Donbass *or* **Donbas** (dɒn'bɑːs) *n* an industrial region in E Ukraine in the plain of the Rivers Donets and lower Dnieper: the site of a major coalfield. Also called: Donets Basin

Doncaster ('dɒŋkəstə) *n* **1** an industrial town in N England, in Doncaster unitary authority, South Yorkshire, on the River Don. Pop: 67 977 (2001) **2** a unitary authority in N England, in South Yorkshire. Pop: 288 400 (2003 est). Area: 582 sq km (225 sq miles)

donder ('dɒndə) *South African slang* ▷ *vb* (*tr*) **1** to beat (someone) up ▷ *n* **2** a wretch; swine [C19: Afrikaans, from Dutch *donderen* to swear, bully]

done (dʌn) *vb* **1** the past participle of **do¹ 2** be done with *or* have done with to end relations with **3** have done to be completely finished: *have you done?* ▷ *interj* **4** an expression of agreement, as on the settlement of a bargain between two parties ▷ *adj* **5** completed; finished **6** cooked enough: *done to a turn* **7** used up: *they had to surrender when the ammunition was done* **8** socially proper or acceptable: *that isn't done in higher circles* **9** *informal* cheated; tricked **10** done for *informal* **a** dead or almost dead **b** in serious difficulty **11** done in *or* done up *informal* physically exhausted

donee (dəʊ'niː) *n law* a person who receives a gift [C16: from DON(OR) + -EE]

Donegal (ˌdɒnɪ'ɡɔːl, ˌdɒnɪ'ɡɔːl, ˌdʌnɪ'ɡɔːl) *n* a county in NW Republic of Ireland, on the Atlantic: mountainous, with a rugged coastline and many offshore islands. County town: Lifford. Pop: 137 575 (2002). Area: 4830 sq km (1865 sq miles)

doner kebab ('dɒnə) *n* a fast-food dish comprising grilled meat and salad served in pitta bread with chilli sauce [from Turkish *döner* rotating + KEBAB]

Donets (*Russian* da'njets) *n* a river rising in SW Russia, in the Kursk steppe and flowing southeast, through Ukraine, to the Don River. Length: about 1078 km (670 miles)

Donets Basin (də'nɛts) *n* another name for the **Donbass**

Donetsk (*Russian* da'njetsk) *n* a city in E Ukraine: the chief industrial centre of the Donbass; first ironworks founded by a Welshman, John Hughes (1872), after whom the town was named **Yuzovka** (Hughesovka). Pop: 992 000 (2005 est). Former name (from 1924 until 1961): Stalin

dong (dɒŋ) *n* **1** the deep reverberating sound of a large bell **2** *Austral & NZ informal* a heavy blow ▷ *vb* **3** (*intr*) (of a bell) to make a deep reverberating sound **4** (*tr*) *Austral & NZ informal* to strike or punch [C16: of imitative origin]

donga ('dɒŋɡə) *n* *South African, Austral & NZ* a steep-sided gully caused by soil erosion [C19: Afrikaans, from Nguni *donga* washed out gully]

Dongola ('dɒŋɡələ) *n* a small town in the N Sudan, on the Nile: built on the site of Old Dongola, the capital of the Christian Kingdom of Nubia (6th to 14th centuries). Pop: 16 900 (2001 est)

Dongting ('dʊŋ'tɪŋ), **Tungting** *or* **Tung-t'ing** *n* a lake in S China, in NE Hunan province: main outlet flows to the Yangtze; rice-growing in winter. Area: (in winter) 3900 sq km (1500 sq miles)

Dönitz *or* **Doenitz** (*German* 'døːnɪts) *n* **Karl** (karl). 1891–1980, German admiral; commander in chief of the German navy (1943–45); as head of state after Hitler's death he surrendered to the Allies (May 7, 1945)

Donizetti (ˌdɒnɪ'zɛtɪ; *Italian* donid'dzetti) *n* **Gaetano** (gae'taːno). 1797–1848, Italian operatic composer: his works include *Lucia di Lammermoor* (1835), *La Fille du régiment* (1840), and *Don Pasquale* (1843)

donjon ('dʌndʒən, 'dɒn-) *n* the heavily fortified central tower or keep of a medieval castle. Also called: dungeon [C14: archaic variant of *dungeon*]

Don Juan ('dɒn 'dʒuːən; *Spanish* don xwan) *n* **1** a legendary Spanish nobleman and philanderer: hero of many poems, plays, and operas, including treatments by de Molina, Molière, Goldoni, Mozart, Byron, and Shaw **2** a successful seducer of women

donkey ('dɒŋkɪ) *n* **1** Also called: ass a long-eared domesticated member of the horse family (*Equidae*), descended from the African wild ass (*Equus asinus*) **2** a stupid or stubborn person **3** talk the hind leg(s) off a donkey to talk endlessly [C18: perhaps from *dun* dark + -*key*, as in *monkey*]

donkey jacket *n* a hip-length jacket usually made of a thick navy fabric with a waterproof panel across the shoulders

donkey's years *n informal* a long time

donkey vote *n Austral* a vote on a preferential ballot on which the voter's order of preference follows the order in which the candidates are listed

donkey-work *n* **1** groundwork **2** drudgery

Donleavy (dɒn'liːvɪ) *n* **J(ames) P(atrick)**. born 1926, Irish-American novelist. His books include *The Ginger Man* (1956), *The Onion Eaters* (1971), *Are You Listening Rabbi Löw?* (1987), and *The Lady Who Liked Clean Rest Rooms* (1995)

Donna ('dɒnə; *Italian* 'dɔnna) *n* an Italian title of address equivalent to *Madam*, indicating respect [C17: from Italian, from Latin *domina* lady, feminine of *dominus* lord, master]

Donne (dʌn) *n* **John**. 1573–1631, English metaphysical poet and preacher. He wrote love and religious poems, sermons, epigrams, and elegies

donnish ('dɒnɪʃ) *adj* of or resembling a university don ▷ 'donnishness *n*

donnybrook ('dɒnɪˌbrʊk) *n* a rowdy brawl [C19: after *Donnybrook Fair*, an annual event until 1855 near Dublin]

donor ('dəʊnə) *n* **1** a person who makes a donation **2** *med* any person who voluntarily gives blood, skin, a kidney etc, for use in the treatment of another person **3** the atom supplying both electrons in a coordinate bond [C15: from Old French *doneur*, from Latin *dōnātor*, from *dōnāre* to give]

donor card *n* a card carried by a person to show that the bodily organs specified on it may be used for transplants after the person's death

Don Quixote ('dɒn ki:'həʊtɪ, 'kwɪksət; *Spanish* don ki'xote) *n* an impractical idealist [after the hero of Cervantes' *Don Quixote de la Mancha*]

don't (dəʊnt) *contraction of* do not

don't know *n* a person who has not reached a definite opinion on a subject, esp as a response to a questionnaire

doodah ('du:dɑ:) *or US and Canadian* **doodad** ('du:dæd) *n informal* **1** an unnamed thing, esp an object the name of which is unknown or forgotten **2** all of a doodah excited; agitated [C20: of uncertain origin]

doodle ('du:dªl) *informal* ▷ *vb* **1** to scribble or draw aimlessly **2** to play or improvise idly **3** (*intr*; often foll by *away*) *US* to dawdle or waste time ▷ *n* **4** a shape, picture, etc, drawn aimlessly [C20: perhaps from C17 *doodle* a foolish person, but influenced in meaning by DAWDLE; compare Low German *dudeltopf* simpleton] > 'doodler *n*

doodlebug ('du:dªl,bʌg) *n* **1** another name for the V-1 **2** a diviner's rod **3** a US name for **antlion** (sense 2) [C20: probably from DOODLE + BUG[1]]

doo-doo ('du:,du:) *n US & Canadian informal* a child's word for **excrement**

Doohan ('du:ən) *n* **Michael K** (**Mick**). born 1965, Australian racing motorcyclist; 500 cc world champion 1994–98

doohickey ('du:,hɪkɪ) *n US & Canadian informal* another name for **doodah** (sense 1)

Doolittle ('du:lɪtªl) *n* **Hilda**. known as *H.D.* 1886–1961, US imagist poet and novelist, living in Europe

doom (du:m) *n* **1** death or a terrible fate **2** a judgment or decision **3** (*sometimes capital*) another term for the **Last Judgment** ▷ *vb* **4** (*tr*) to destine or condemn to death or a terrible fate [Old English *dōm*; related to Old Norse *dōmr* judgment, Gothic *dōms* sentence, Old High German *tuom* condition, Greek *thomos* crowd, Sanskrit *dhāman* custom; see DO[1], DEEM, DEED, -DOM]

doomsday *or* **domesday** ('du:mz,deɪ) *n* **1** (*sometimes capital*) the day on which the Last Judgment will occur **2** any day of reckoning **3** (*modifier*) characterized by predictions of disaster: *doomsday scenario* [Old English *dōmes dæg* Judgment Day; related to Old Norse *domsdagr*]

doona ('du:nə) *n Austral*. a quilt, stuffed with down or a synthetic material and containing pockets of air, used as a bed cover in place of the top sheet and blankets [from a trademark]

door (dɔ:) *n* **1** a hinged or sliding panel for closing the entrance to a room, cupboard, etc **2** a doorway or entrance to a room or building **3** a means of access or escape: *a door to success* **4** lay at someone's door to lay (the blame or responsibility) on someone **5** out of doors in or into the open air **6** show someone the door to order someone to leave [Old English *duru*; related to Old Frisian *dure*, Old Norse *dyrr*, Old High German *turi*, Latin *forēs*, Greek *thura*]

do-or-die *adj* (*prenominal*) of or involving a determined and sometimes reckless effort to succeed

door furniture *n* locks, handles, etc, designed for use on doors

doorjamb ('dɔ:,dʒæm) *n* one of the two vertical members forming the sides of a doorframe. Also called: **doorpost**

doorkeeper ('dɔ:,ki:pə) *n* a person attending or guarding a door or gateway

doorman ('dɔ:,mæn, -mən) *n*, *pl* -men a man employed to attend the doors of certain buildings

doormat ('dɔ:,mæt) *n* **1** a mat, placed at the entrance to a building, for wiping dirt from shoes **2** *informal* a person who offers little resistance to ill-treatment by others

Doorn (*Dutch* do:rn) *n* a town in the central Netherlands, in Utrecht province: residence of Kaiser Wilhelm II of Germany from his abdication (1919) until his death (1941)

doornail ('dɔ:,neɪl) *n* (**as**) **dead as a doornail** dead beyond any doubt

Doornik ('dɔ:rnɪk) *n* the Flemish name for **Tournai**

Doors (dɔ:z) *pl n* the Doors US rock group (1965–73), originally comprising Jim Morrison, Ray Manzarek (born 1935), Robby Krieger (born 1946), and John Densmore (born 1945). See also **Morrison** (sense 2)

doorsill ('dɔ:,sɪl) *n* a horizontal member of wood, stone, etc, forming the bottom of a doorframe

doorstep ('dɔ:,stɛp) *n* **1** a step in front of a door **2** *informal* a thick slice of bread ▷ *vb* -steps, -stepping, -stepped (*tr*) **3** to canvass (a district) or interview (a member of the public) by or in the course of door-to-door visiting **4** (of a journalist) to wait outside the house of (someone) to obtain an interview, photograph, etc when he or she emerges

doorstop ('dɔ:,stɒp) *n* **1** a heavy object, wedge, or other device which prevents an open door from moving **2** a projecting piece of rubber, etc, fixed to the floor to stop a door from striking a wall

door to door *adj*, *adv* (**door-to-door** *when prenominal*) **1** (of selling, canvassing, etc) from one house to the next **2** (of journeys, deliveries, etc) direct

doorway ('dɔ:,weɪ) *n* **1** an opening into a building, room, etc, esp one that has a door **2** a means of access or escape: *a doorway to freedom*

doosra ('du:zrə) *n cricket* a delivery, bowled by an off-spinner, that turns the opposite way from an off-break [C20: from Urdu, Hindi: second one, other one]

do over *vb* (*tr, adverb*) **1** *informal* to renovate or redecorate **2** *Brit, Austral & NZ slang* to beat up; thrash

doo-wop ('du:,wɒp) *n* rhythm-and-blues harmony vocalizing developed by unaccompanied street-corner groups in the US in the 1950s [C20: of imitative origin]

dop ('dɒp) *South African, informal* ▷ *n* **1** a tot or small drink, usually alcoholic ▷ *vb* dops, dopping, dopped **2** to fail to reach the required standard in (an examination, course, etc) [Afrikaans]

dope (dəʊp) *n* **1** any of a number of preparations made by dissolving cellulose derivatives in a volatile solvent, applied to fabric in order to improve strength, tautness, etc **2** an additive used to improve the properties of something, such as an antiknock compound added to petrol **3** a thick liquid, such as a lubricant, applied to a surface **4** a combustible absorbent material, such as sawdust or wood pulp, used to hold the nitroglycerine in dynamite **5** *slang* any illegal drug, usually cannabis **6** a drug administered to a racehorse or greyhound to affect its performance **7** *informal* a person considered to be stupid or slow-witted **8** *informal* news or facts, esp confidential information ▷ *vb* (*tr*) **9** *electronics* to add impurities to (a semiconductor) in order to produce or modify its properties **10** to apply or add a dopant to **11** to administer a drug to (oneself or another) [C19: from Dutch *doop* sauce, from *doopen* to DIP]

dopey *or* **dopy** ('dəʊpɪ) *adj* dopier, dopiest **1** *slang* silly **2** *informal* half-asleep or in a state of semiconsciousness, as when under the influence of a drug

dopiaza ('dəʊpɪ,ɑ:zə) *n* (in Indian cookery) a dish of meat or fish cooked in an onion sauce: *lamb dopiaza* [C20: from Hindi: *do* two + *pyāz* onion]

doppelgänger ('dɒpªl,gɛnə; *German* 'dɔpəl,gɛŋər) *n* legend a ghostly duplicate of a living person [from German *Doppelgänger*, literally: double-goer]

Doppler effect ('dɒplə) *n* a phenomenon, observed for sound waves and electromagnetic radiation, characterized by a change in the apparent frequency of a wave as a result of relative motion between the observer and the source. Also called: Doppler shift [C19: named after C. J. Doppler (1803–53), Austrian physicist]

Doráti (də'rɑ:tɪ) *n* **Antal** ('æntæl). 1906–88, US conductor and composer

Dorcas ('dɔ:kəs) *n* a charitable woman of Joppa (Acts 9:36–42)

Dorchester ('dɔ:tʃɪstə) *n* a town in S England, administrative centre of Dorset: associated with Thomas Hardy, esp as the inspiration for the Casterbridge of his novels. Pop: 16 171 (2001)

Dordogne (*French* dɔrdɔɲ) *n* 1 a river in SW France, rising in the Auvergne Mountains and flowing southwest and west to join the Garonne river and form the Gironde estuary. Length: 472 km (293 miles) 2 a department of SW France, in Aquitaine region. Capital: Périgueux. Pop: 392 291 (2003 est). Area: 9224 sq km (3597 sq miles)

Dordrecht (*Dutch* 'dɔrdrɛxt) *n* a port in the SW Netherlands, in South Holland province: chief port of the Netherlands until the 17th century. Pop: 120 000 (2003 est). Also called: **Dort**

doré ('dɔreɪ, -riː) *n* another name for **walleye** (senses 5, 6) [c18: from French, gilded; see DORY]

Doré (*French* dɔre) *n* (**Paul**) **Gustave** (gystav). 1832–83, French illustrator, whose style tended towards the grotesque. He illustrated the Bible, Dante's *Inferno*, Cervantes' *Don Quixote*, and works by Rabelais

Dorgon ('dɔːɡɒn) *n* 1612–50, Manchurian prince, who ruled China as regent (1643–50) and helped to establish the Ching dynasty

Doric ('dɒrɪk) *adj* 1 of or relating to the Dorians, esp the Spartans, or their dialect of Ancient Greek 2 of, denoting, or relating to one of the five classical orders of architecture: characterized by a column having no base, a heavy fluted shaft, and a capital consisting of an ovolo moulding beneath a square abacus 3 (*sometimes not capital*) rustic ▷ *n* 4 one of four chief dialects of Ancient Greek, spoken chiefly in the Peloponnese 5 any rural dialect, esp that spoken in the northeast of Scotland

Doris[1] ('dɒrɪs) *n* (in ancient Greece) 1 a small landlocked area north of the Gulf of Corinth. Traditionally regarded as the home of the Dorians, it was perhaps settled by some of them during their southward migration 2 the coastal area of Caria in SW Asia Minor, settled by Dorians

Doris[2] ('dɒrɪs) *n Greek myth* a sea nymph

dork (dɔːk) *n slang* a stupid or incompetent person [c20: of unknown origin]

dorm (dɔːm) *n informal* short for **dormitory**

dormant ('dɔːmənt) *adj* 1 quiet and inactive, as during sleep 2 latent or inoperative 3 (of a volcano) neither extinct nor erupting 4 *biology* alive but in a resting torpid condition with suspended growth and reduced metabolism 5 (*usually postpositive*) *heraldry* (of a beast) in a sleeping position [c14: from Old French *dormant*, from *dormir* to sleep, from Latin *dormīre*] > **dormancy** *n*

dormer ('dɔːmə) *n* a construction with a gable roof and a window at its outer end that projects from a sloping roof. Also called: **dormer window** [c16: from Old French *dormoir*, from Latin *dormītōrium* DORMITORY]

dormie *or* **dormy** ('dɔːmɪ) *adj golf* (of a player or side) as many holes ahead of an opponent as there are still to play: **dormie three** [c19: of unknown origin]

dormitory ('dɔːmɪtərɪ, -trɪ) *n*, *pl* -ries 1 a large room, esp at a school or institution, containing several beds 2 *US* a building, esp at a college or university, providing living and sleeping accommodation 3 (*modifier*) *Brit* denoting or relating to an area from which most of the residents commute to work (esp in the phrase **dormitory suburb**) [c15: from Latin *dormītōrium*, from *dormīre* to sleep]

Dormobile ('dɔːməʊˌbiːl) *n trademark* a vanlike vehicle specially equipped for living in while travelling

dormouse ('dɔːˌmaʊs) *n*, *pl* -mice any small Old World rodent of the family *Gliridae*, esp the Eurasian *Muscardinus avellanarius*, resembling a mouse with a furry tail [c15: *dor-*, perhaps from Old French *dormir* to sleep, from Latin *dormīre* + MOUSE]

dorp (dɔːp) *n archaic or South Africa* a small town or village [c16: from Dutch: village; related to THORP]

Dorpat ('dɔrpat) *n* the German name for **Tartu**

dorsal ('dɔːsəl) *adj anatomy, zoology* relating to the back or spinal part of the body [c15: from Medieval Latin *dorsālis*, from Latin *dorsum* back] > **dorsally** *adv*

dorsal fin *n* any unpaired median fin on the backs of fishes and some other aquatic vertebrates: maintains balance during locomotion

Dorset ('dɔːsɪt) *n* a county in SW England, on the English Channel: mainly hilly but low-lying in the east:

the geographical and ceremonial county includes Bournemouth and Poole, which became independent unitary authorities in 1997. Administrative centre: Dorchester. Pop (excluding unitary authorities): 398 200 (2003 est). Area (excluding unitary authorities): 2544 sq km (982 sq miles)

Dort (*Dutch* dɔrt) *n* another name for **Dordrecht**

Dortmund ('dɔːtmənd; *German* 'dɔrtmʊnt) *n* an industrial city in W Germany, in North Rhine-Westphalia at the head of the **Dortmund–Ems Canal**: university (1966). Pop: 589 661 (2003 est)

dory[1] ('dɔːrɪ) *n*, *pl* -ries any spiny-finned marine teleost food fish of the family *Zeidae*, esp the John Dory, having a deep compressed body [c14: from French *dorée* gilded, from *dorer* to gild, from Late Latin *deaurāre*, ultimately from Latin *aurum* gold]

dory[2] ('dɔːrɪ) *n*, *pl* -ries *US & Canadian* a flat-bottomed rowing boat with a high bow, stern, and sides [c18: from Mosquito (an American Indian language of Honduras and Nicaragua) *dóri* dugout]

DOS (dɒs) *n trademark computing acronym for* disk-operating system, often prefixed, as in MS-DOS and PC-DOS; a computer operating system

dosage ('dəʊsɪdʒ) *n* 1 the administration of a drug or agent in prescribed amounts and at prescribed intervals 2 the optimum therapeutic dose and optimum interval between doses 3 another name for **dose** (sense 3)

dose (dəʊs) *n* 1 *med* a specific quantity of a therapeutic drug or agent taken at any one time or at specified intervals 2 *informal* something unpleasant to experience: *a dose of influenza* 3 Also called: **dosage** the total energy of ionizing radiation absorbed by unit mass of material, esp of living tissue; usually measured in grays (SI unit) or rads 4 Also called: **dosage** a small amount of syrup added to wine, esp sparkling wine, when the sediment is removed and the bottle is corked 5 *slang* a venereal infection, esp gonorrhoea ▷ *vb* 6 to administer a dose or doses to (someone) 7 *med* to give (a therapeutic drug or agent) in appropriate quantities 8 to add syrup to (wine) during bottling [c15: from French, from Late Latin *dosis*, from Greek: a giving, from *didonai* to give]

dosh (dɒʃ) *n Brit* a slang word for **money** [c20: of unknown origin]

dosimeter (dəʊ'sɪmɪtə) *or* **dosemeter** ('dəʊsˌmiːtə) *n* an instrument for measuring the dose of X-rays or other radiation absorbed by matter or the intensity of a source of radiation > **dosimetric** (ˌdəʊsɪ'mɛtrɪk) *adj*

dosing strip *n* (in New Zealand) an area set aside for treating dogs suspected of having hydatid disease

Dos Passos ('dɒs 'pæsɒs) *n* **John** (**Roderigo**). 1896–1970, US novelist of the Lost Generation; author of *Three Soldiers* (1921), *Manhattan Transfer* (1925), and the trilogy *USA* (1930–36)

doss (dɒs) *Brit slang* ▷ *vb* 1 (*intr*; often foll by *down*) to sleep, esp in a dosshouse 2 (*intr*; often foll by *around*) to pass time aimlessly ▷ *n* 3 a bed, esp in a dosshouse 4 a slang word for **sleep** 5 short for **dosshouse** 6 a task or pastime requiring little effort: *making a film is a bit of a doss* [c18: of uncertain origin]

dosser ('dɒsə) *n* 1 *Brit slang* a person who sleeps in dosshouses 2 *Brit slang* another word for **dosshouse** 3 *slang* a lazy person; idler

dosshouse ('dɒsˌhaʊs) *n Brit slang* a cheap lodging house, esp one used by tramps

dossier ('dɒsɪˌeɪ, -sɪə; *French* dosje) *n* a collection of papers containing information on a particular subject or person [c19: from French: a file with a label on the back, from *dos* back, from Latin *dorsum*]

dost (dʌst) *vb archaic or dialect* (used with the pronoun thou or its relative equivalent) a singular form of the present tense (indicative mood) of **do**[1]

Dostoevsky, Dostoyevsky, Dostoevski *or* **Dostoyevski** (ˌdɒstɔɪ'ɛfskɪ; *Russian* dəstʌ'jefskij) *n* **Fyodor Mikhailovich** ('fjɔdər mi'xajləvitʃ). 1821–81, Russian novelist, the psychological perception of whose works has greatly influenced the subsequent development of the novel. His best-known works are *Crime and Punishment* (1866), *The Idiot* (1868), *The Possessed*

(1871), and *The Brothers Karamazov* (1879–80)

dot[1] (dɒt) *n* **1** a small round mark made with or as with a pen, etc; spot; speck; point **2** anything resembling a dot; a small amount: *a dot of paint* **3** the mark (ˈ) that appears above the main stem of the letters *i*, *j* **4** *music* **a** the symbol (•) placed after a note or rest to increase its time value by half **b** this symbol written above or below a note indicating that it must be played or sung staccato **5** *maths, logic* **a** the symbol (.) indicating multiplication or logical conjunction **b** a decimal point **6** the symbol (•) used, in combination with the symbol for *dash* (–), in the written representation of Morse and other telegraphic codes **7** on the dot at exactly the arranged time ▷ *vb* dots, dotting, dotted **8** (*tr*) to mark or form with a dot: *to dot a letter; a dotted crotchet* **9** (*tr*) to scatter or intersperse (with dots or something resembling dots): *bushes dotting the plain* **10** (*intr*) to make a dot or dots **11** dot one's i's and cross one's t's to pay meticulous attention to detail [Old English *dott* head of a boil; related to Old High German *tutta* nipple, Norwegian *dott*, Dutch *dott* lump] > ˈdotter *n*

dot[2] (dɒt) *n civil law* a woman's dowry [C19: from French, from Latin *dōs*; related to *dōtāre* to endow, *dāre* to give]

dotage (ˈdəʊtɪdʒ) *n* **1** feebleness of mind, esp as a result of old age **2** foolish infatuation [C14: from DOTE + -AGE]

dotard (ˈdəʊtəd) *n* a person who is weak-minded, esp through senility [C14: from DOTE + -ARD] > ˈdotardly *adj*

dotcom *or* **dot.com** (ˌdɒtˈkɒm) *n* **a** a company that conducts most of its business on the internet **b** (*as modifier*): *dotcom stocks* [C20: from .com, the domain name suffix of businesses trading on the internet]

dotcommer (ˈdɒtˌkɒmə) *n* a person who carries out business on the internet

dote *or now rarely* **doat** (dəʊt) *vb* (*intr*) (foll by *on* or *upon*) to love to an excessive or foolish degree **2** to be foolish or weak-minded, esp as a result of old age [C13: related to Middle Dutch *doten* to be silly, Norwegian *dudra* to shake] > ˈdoter *or* ˈdoater *n*

doth (dʌθ) *vb archaic or dialect* (used with the pronouns *he*, *she*, or *it* or with a noun) a singular form of the present tense of **do**[1]

dot-matrix printer *n computing* a printer in which each character is produced by an array of dots by a printhead

dotterel *or* **dottrel** (ˈdɒtrəl) *n* **1** a rare Eurasian plover, *Eudromias morinellus*, with reddish-brown underparts and white bands around the head and neck **2** *dialect* a person who is foolish or easily duped [C15 *dotrelle*; see DOTE]

dottle *or* **dottel** (ˈdɒtˀl) *n* the plug of tobacco left in a pipe after smoking [C15: diminutive of *dot* lump; see DOT[1]]

dotty (ˈdɒtɪ) *adj* -tier, -tiest **1** *slang, chiefly Brit* feeble-minded; slightly crazy **2** *Brit slang* (foll by *about*) extremely fond (of) **3** marked with dots [C19: from DOT[1]: sense development of 1 from meaning of "unsteady on one's feet"] > ˈdottily *adv* > ˈdottiness *n*

Dou, Dow *or* **Douw** (daʊ; *Dutch* dɔu) *n* **Gerard** (ˈxeːrɑrt). 1613–75, Dutch portrait and genre painter

Douai (ˈduːeɪ; *French* dwɛ) *n* an industrial city in N France: the political and religious centre of exiled English Roman Catholics in the 16th and 17th centuries. Pop: 42 796 (1999)

Douala *or* **Duala** (duˈɑːlə) *n* the chief port and largest city in W Cameroon, on the Bight of Bonny: capital of the German colony of Kamerun (1901–16). Pop: 1 980 000 (2005 est)

Douay Bible *or* **Douay Version** (ˈduːeɪ) *n* an English translation of the Bible from the Latin Vulgate text completed by Roman Catholic scholars at Douai in 1610

double (ˈdʌbˀl) *adj* (*usually prenominal*) **1** as much again in size, strength, number, etc: *a double portion* **2** composed of two equal or similar parts; in a pair; twofold: *a double egg cup* **3** designed for two users: *a double room* **4** folded in two; composed of two layers: *double paper* **5** stooping; bent over **6** having two aspects or existing in two different ways; ambiguous: *a double meaning* **7** false, deceitful, or hypocritical: *a double life* **8** (of flowers) having more than the normal number of petals **9** *music* **a** (of an instrument) sounding an octave lower than the

pitch indicated by the notation: *a double bass* **b** (of time) duple, usually accompanied by the direction *alla breve* ▷ *adv* **10** twice over; twofold **11** two together; two at a time (esp in the phrase **see double**) ▷ *n* **12** twice the number, amount, size, etc **13** a double measure of spirits, such as whisky or brandy **14** a duplicate or counterpart, esp a person who closely resembles another; understudy **15** a wraith or ghostly apparition that is the exact counterpart of a living person; doppelgänger **16** a sharp turn, esp a return on one's own tracks **17** *bridge* a call that increases certain scoring points if the last preceding bid becomes the contract **18** *billiards, snooker* a strike in which the object ball is struck so as to make it rebound against the cushion to an opposite pocket **19** a bet on two horses in different races in which any winnings from the horse in the first race are placed on the horse in the later race **20 a** the narrow outermost ring on a dartboard **b** a hit on this ring **21** at the double *or* on the double **a** at twice normal marching speed **b** quickly or immediately ▷ *vb* **22** to make or become twice as much **23** to bend or fold (material, a bandage, etc) **24** (*tr*; sometimes foll by *up*) to clench (a fist) **25** (*tr*; often foll by *together* or *up*) to join or couple: *he doubled up the team* **26** (*tr*) to repeat exactly; copy **27** (*intr*) to play two parts or serve two roles **28** *nautical* to sail around (a headland or other point) **29** *music* **a** to duplicate (a voice or instrumental part) either in unison or at the octave above or below it **b** (*intr*; usually foll by *on*) to be capable of performing (upon an instrument additional to one's normal one): *the third trumpeter doubles on cornet* **30** *bridge* to make a call that will double certain scoring points if the preceding bid becomes the contract **31** *billiards, snooker* to cause (a ball) to rebound or (of a ball) to rebound from a cushion across or up or down the table **32** (*intr*; foll by *for*) to act as substitute (for an actor or actress) **33** (*intr*) to go or march at twice the normal speed ▷ See also **double back, doubles, double up** [C13: from Old French, from Latin *duplus* twofold, from *duo* two + *-plus* -FOLD] > ˈdoubler *n*

double agent *n* a spy employed by two mutually antagonistic countries, companies, etc

double back *vb* (*intr, adverb*) to go back in the opposite direction (esp in the phrase **to double back on one's tracks**)

double-bank *vb Austral & NZ informal* to carry a second person on (a horse, bicycle, etc). Also: **dub**

double bar *n music* a symbol, consisting of two ordinary bar lines or a single heavy one, that marks the end of a composition or a section within it

double-barrelled *or US* **double-barreled** *adj* **1** (of a gun) having two barrels **2** extremely forceful or vehement **3** *Brit* (of a surname) having hyphenated parts **4** serving two purposes; ambiguous: *a double-barrelled remark*

double bass (beɪs) *n* **1** Also called (*US*): **bass viol** a stringed instrument, the largest and lowest member of the violin family. Range: almost three octaves upwards from E in the space between the fourth and fifth leger lines below the bass staff. It is normally bowed in classical music, but it is very common in a jazz or dance band, where it is practically always played pizzicato. Informal name: **bass fiddle** ▷ *adj* **double-bass 2** of or relating to an instrument whose pitch lies below that regarded as the bass; contrabass

double bassoon *n music* the lowest and largest instrument in the oboe class; contrabassoon

double-blind *adj* of or relating to an experiment to discover reactions to certain commodities, drugs, etc, in which neither the experimenters nor the subjects know the particulars of the test items during the experiments

double boiler *n US & Canadian* a cooking utensil consisting of two saucepans, one fitting inside the other. The bottom saucepan contains water that, while boiling, gently heats food in the upper pan. Also called (in Britain and certain other countries): **double saucepan**

double-breasted *adj* (of a garment) having overlapping fronts such as to give a double thickness of cloth

double-check *vb* **1** to check twice or again; verify ▷ *n* **double check 2** a second examination or verification

d

3 *chess* a simultaneous check from two pieces brought about by moving one piece to give check and thereby revealing a second check from another piece

double chin *n* a fold of fat under the chin > ˌdouble-ˈchinned *adj*

double concerto *n* a concerto for two solo instruments

double cream *n* thick cream with a high fat-content

double-cross *vb* **1** (*tr*) to cheat or betray ▷ *n* **2** the act or an instance of double-crossing; betrayal > ˈdouble-ˈcrosser *n*

double dagger *n* a character (‡) used in printing to indicate a cross reference, esp to a footnote. Also called: diesis, double obelisk

double day *n* the dual responsibilities borne by working mothers, who when their paid work is over for the day must then work at looking after their family and home

double-dealing *n* **a** action characterized by treachery or deceit **b** (*as modifier*): *double-dealing treachery* > ˈdouble-ˈdealer *n*

double-decker *n* **1** *chiefly Brit* a bus with two passenger decks **2** *informal* **a** a thing or structure having two decks, layers, etc **b** (*as modifier*): *a double-decker sandwich*

double-declutch *vb* (*intr*) *Brit* to change to a lower gear in a motor vehicle by first placing the gear lever into the neutral position before engaging the desired gear, at the same time releasing the clutch pedal and increasing the engine speed. US term: **double-clutch**

double dip *n economics* **a** a recession in which a brief recovery in output is followed by another fall, because demand remains low **b** (*as modifier*): *a double-dip recession*

double-double *n Canadian* a cup of coffee served with two helpings of cream and sugar

double Dutch *n Brit informal* incomprehensible talk; gibberish

double-edged *adj* **1** acting in two ways; having a dual effect: *a double-edged law* **2** (of a remark, argument, etc) having two possible interpretations, esp applicable both for and against or being equally malicious though apparently innocuous **3** (of a sword, knife, etc) having a cutting edge on either side of the blade

double entendre (ˈduːbl ɑːnˈtɑːndrə, -ˈtɑːndrə; *French* dubl ɑ̃tɑ̃drə) *n* **1** a word, phrase, etc, that can be interpreted in two ways, esp one having one meaning that is indelicate **2** the type of humour that depends upon such ambiguity [C17: from obsolete French: double meaning]

double entry *n* **a** a book-keeping system in which any commercial transaction is entered as a debit in one account and as a credit in another **b** (*as modifier*): *double-entry book-keeping*

double exposure *n* **1** the act or process of recording two superimposed images on a photographic medium, usually done intentionally to produce a special effect **2** the photograph resulting from such an act

double-faced *adj* **1** (of textiles) having a finished nap on each side; reversible **2** insincere or deceitful

double feature *n films* a programme showing two full-length films

double first *n Brit* a first-class honours degree in two subjects

double glazing *n* **1** two panes of glass in a window, fitted to reduce the transmission of heat, sound, etc **2** the fitting of glass in such a manner

double-header *n* **1** a train drawn by two locomotives coupled together to provide extra power **2** Also called: twin bill *US & Canadian sport* two games played consecutively by the same teams or by two different teams **3** *Austral & NZ informal* a coin with the impression of a head on each side **4** *Austral informal* a double ice-cream cone

double helix *n biochem* the form of the molecular structure of DNA, consisting of two helical polynucleotide chains linked by hydrogen bonds and coiled around the same axis

double-jointed *adj* having unusually flexible joints permitting an abnormal degree of motion of the parts

double knitting *n* a widely used medium thickness of knitting wool

double negative *n* a syntactic construction, often considered ungrammatical in standard Modern English,

in which two negatives are used where one is needed, as in *I wouldn't never have believed it*

● **USAGE** There are two contexts where double negatives are used. An adjective with negative force is often used with a negative in order to express a nuance of meaning somewhere between the positive and the negative: *he was a not infrequent visitor; it is a not uncommon sight.* Two negatives are also found together where they reinforce each other rather than conflict: *he never went back, not even to collect his belongings.* These two uses of what is technically a double negative are acceptable. A third case, illustrated by *I shouldn't wonder if it didn't rain today,* has the force of a weak positive statement (*I expect it to rain today*) and is common in informal English

double-park *vb* to park (a car or other vehicle) alongside or directly opposite another already parked by the roadside, thereby causing an obstruction

double pneumonia *n* pneumonia affecting both lungs

double-quick *adj* **1** very quick; rapid ▷ *adv* **2** in a very quick or rapid manner

double-reed *adj* relating to or denoting a wind instrument in which the sounds are produced by air passing over two reeds that vibrate against each other

double refraction *n* the splitting of a ray of unpolarized light into two unequally refracted rays polarized in mutually perpendicular planes. Also called: birefringence

doubles (ˈdʌbəlz) *n* (*functioning as plural*) **a** a game between two pairs of players, as in tennis, badminton, etc **b** (*as modifier*): *a doubles player*

double saucepan *n Brit* a cooking utensil consisting of two saucepans, one fitting inside the other. The bottom saucepan contains water that, while boiling, gently heats food in the upper pan. US and Canadian name: double boiler

double-space *vb* to type (copy) with a full space between lines

doublespeak (ˈdʌbəlˌspiːk) *n* the practice of using ambiguous language regarding political, military, or corporate matters in a deliberate attempt to disguise the truth

double spread *n printing* two facing pages of a publication treated as a single unit

double standard *n* a set of principles that allows greater freedom to one person or group than to another

double-stop *vb* -stops, -stopping, -stopped to play (two notes or parts) simultaneously on a violin or related instrument by drawing the bow over two strings

doublet (ˈdʌblɪt) *n* **1** (formerly) a man's close-fitting jacket, with or without sleeves (esp in the phrase **doublet and hose**) **2 a** a pair of similar things, esp two words deriving ultimately from the same source, for example *reason* and *ratio* or *fragile* and *frail* **b** one of such a pair **3** *jewellery* a false gem made by welding a thin layer of a gemstone onto a coloured glass base or by fusing two small stones together to make a larger one **4** *physics* **a** a multiplet that has two members **b** a closely spaced pair of related spectral lines **5** (*plural*) two dice each showing the same number of spots on one throw **6** *physics* two simple lenses designed to be used together, the optical distortion in one being balanced by that in the other [C14: from Old French, from DOUBLE]

double take *n* (esp in comedy) a delayed reaction by a person to a remark, situation, etc

double talk *n* **1** rapid speech with a mixture of nonsense syllables and real words; gibberish **2** empty, deceptive, or ambiguous talk, esp by politicians

doublethink (ˈdʌbəlˌθɪŋk) *n* deliberate, perverse, or unconscious acceptance or promulgation of conflicting facts, principles, etc

double time *n* **1** a doubled wage rate, paid for working on public holidays, etc **2** *music* **a** a time twice as fast as an earlier section **b** two beats per bar **3** a slow running pace, keeping in step **4** *US army* a fast march of 180 paces to the minute

double up *vb* (*adverb*) **1** to bend or cause to bend in two **2** (*intr*) to share a room or bed designed for one person, family, etc **3** (*intr*) *Brit* to use the winnings from one bet

doubloon (dʌ'bluːn) *n* **1** a former Spanish gold coin **2** (*plural*) *slang* money [c17: from Spanish *doblón*, from *dobla*, from Latin *dupla*, feminine of *duplus* twofold]

doubly ('dʌblɪ) *adv* **1** to or in a double degree, quantity, or measure: *doubly careful* **2** in two ways: *doubly wrong*

Doubs (*French* du) *n* **1** a department of E France, in Franche-Comté region. Capital: Besançon. Pop: 505 557 (2003 est). Area: 5258 sq km (2030 sq miles) **2** a river in E France, rising in the Jura Mountains, becoming part of the border between France and Switzerland and flowing generally southwest to the Saône River. Length: 430 km (267 miles)

doubt (daʊt) *n* **1** uncertainty about the truth, fact, or existence of something (esp in the phrases **in doubt, without doubt, beyond a shadow of doubt**, etc) **2** (*often plural*) lack of belief in or conviction about something: *all his doubts about the project disappeared* **3** an unresolved difficulty, point, etc **4** *obsolete* fear **5** give someone the benefit of the doubt to presume someone suspected of guilt to be innocent; judge leniently **6** no doubt almost certainly ▷ *vb* **7** (*tr; may take a clause as object*) to be inclined to disbelieve: *I doubt we are late* **8** (*tr*) to distrust or be suspicious of: *he doubted their motives* **9** (*intr*) to feel uncertainty or be undecided **10** (*tr*) *archaic* to fear [c13: from Old French *douter*, from Latin *dubitāre*] > 'doubtable *adj* > 'doubter *n* > 'doubtingly *adv*
   ● USAGE Where a clause follows *doubt* in a positive
   ● sentence, it was formerly considered correct to use
   ● *whether* (I doubt whether he will come), but now *if* and *that*
   ● are also acceptable. In negative statements, *doubt* is
   ● followed by *that*: I do not doubt that he is telling the truth. In
   ● such sentences, *but* (I do not doubt but that he is telling the
   ● *truth*) is redundant

doubtful ('daʊtfʊl) *adj* **1** unlikely; improbable **2** characterized by or causing doubt; uncertain: *a doubtful answer* **3** unsettled; unresolved **4** of questionable reputation or morality **5** having reservations or misgivings > 'doubtfully *adv* > 'doubtfulness *n*
   ● USAGE It was formerly considered correct to use
   ● *whether* after *doubtful* (it is doubtful whether he will come),
   ● but now *if* and *that* are also acceptable

doubting Thomas *n* a person who insists on proof before he will believe anything; sceptic [after THOMAS (the apostle), who did not believe that Jesus had been resurrected until he had proof]

doubtless ('daʊtlɪs) *adv also* **doubtlessly** (*sentence modifier*), *sentence substitute* **1** certainly **2** probably ▷ *adj* **3** certain; assured > 'doubtlessness *n*

douche (duːʃ) *n* **1** a stream of water or air directed onto the body surface or into a body cavity, for cleansing or medical purposes **2** the application of such a stream of water or air **3** an instrument, such as a special syringe, for applying a douche ▷ *vb* **4** to cleanse or treat or be cleansed or treated by means of a douche [c18: from French, from Italian *doccia*, pipe; related to Latin *ductus* DUCT]

dough (dəʊ) *n* **1** a thick mixture of flour or meal and water or milk, used for making bread, pastry, etc **2** any similar pasty mass **3** a slang word for **money** [Old English *dāg*; related to Old Norse *deig*, Gothic *daigs*, Old High German *teig* dough, Sanskrit *degdhi* he daubs; see DAIRY, DUFF¹, LADY]

doughboy ('dəʊˌbɔɪ) *n* **1** US informal an infantryman, esp in World War I **2** dough that is boiled or steamed as a dumpling

doughnut *or esp US* **donut** ('dəʊnʌt) *n* **1** a small cake of sweetened dough, often ring-shaped or spherical with a jam or cream filling, cooked in hot fat **2** anything shaped like a ring, such as the reaction vessel of a thermonuclear reactor ▷ *vb* -nuts, -nutting, -nutted **3** (*tr*) *informal* (of Members of Parliament) to surround (a speaker) during the televising of Parliament to give the impression that the chamber is crowded or the speaker is well supported

doughnut hole *n* US a funding shortfall in the standard drug benefit offered by many Medicare prescription drug plans

doughty ('daʊtɪ) *adj* -tier, -tiest hardy; resolute [Old

English *dohtig*; related to Old High German *toht* worth, Middle Dutch *duchtich* strong, Greek *tukhē* luck] > 'doughtily *adv* > 'doughtiness *n*

Doughty ('daʊtɪ) *n* **Charles Montagu**. 1843–1926, English writer and traveller; author of *Travels in Arabia Deserta* (1888)

doughy ('dəʊɪ) *adj* doughier, doughiest resembling dough in consistency, colour, etc; soft, pallid, or flabby

Douglas¹ ('dʌgləs) *n* a town and resort on the Isle of Man, capital of the island, on the E coast. Pop: 25 347 (2001)

Douglas² ('dʌgləs) *n* **1** C(lifford) H(ugh). 1879–1952, British economist, who originated the theory of social credit **2** Gavin. ?1474–1522, Scottish poet, the first British translator of the *Aeneid* **3** Keith (Castellain). 1920–44, British poet, noted for his poems of World War II: killed in action **4** Michael (Kirk). born 1944, US film actor; his films include *Romancing the Stone* (1984), *Wall Street* (1987), *Basic Instinct* (1992), and *Wonder Boys* (2000) **5** (George) Norman. 1868–1952, British writer, esp of books on southern Italy such as *South Wind* (1917) **6** Tommy, full name *Thomas Clement Douglas* (1904–86). Canadian statesman: premier of Saskatchewan 1944–61

Douglas fir, Douglas spruce *or* **Douglas hemlock** *n* a North American pyramidal coniferous tree, *Pseudotsuga menziesii*, widely planted for ornament and for timber, having needle-like leaves and hanging cones: family *Pinaceae*. Also called: Oregon fir, Oregon pine [c19: named after David *Douglas* (1798–1834), Scottish botanist]

Douglas-Home ('dʌgləs'hjuːm) *n* Sir **Alexander**. See (Baron Alexander) Home of the Hirsel

Douglas Hurd (ˌdʌgləs 'hɜːd) *n* Brit informal a third-class university degree. Often shortened to: Douglas [c20: from rhyming slang, after Douglas Hurd (born 1930), British Conservative politician]

Doukhobor *or* **Dukhobor** ('duːkəʊˌbɔː) *n* a member of a Russian sect of Christians that originated in the 18th century. In the late 19th century a large minority emigrated to W Canada, where most Doukhobors now live [from Russian *dukhoborcy* spirit wrestler, from *dukh* spirit + *borcy* wrestler]

doula ('duːlə) *n* a woman who is trained to provide support to women and their families during pregnancy, childbirth, and the period of time following the birth [c20: from Greek *doule* female slave]

Dounreay (duːn'reɪ) *n* the site in N Scotland of a nuclear power station, which contained the world's first fast-breeder reactor (1962–77). A prototype fast-breeder operated from 1974 until 1994: a nuclear fuel reprocessing plant has also operated at the site

do up *vb* (*adverb; mainly tr*) **1** to wrap and make into a bundle: *to do up a parcel* **2** to cause the downfall of (a person) **3** to beautify or adorn **4** (*also intr*) to fasten or be fastened: *this skirt does up at the back* **5** *informal* to renovate or redecorate **6** *slang* to assault

dour (dʊə, 'daʊə) *adj* **1** sullen **2** hard or obstinate [c14: probably from Latin *dūrus* hard] > 'dourly *adv* > 'dourness *n*

douroucouli (ˌduːruː'kuːlɪ) *n* a nocturnal omnivorous New World monkey, *Aotus trivirgatus*, of Central and South America, with large eyes, thick fur, and a round head with pale and dark markings [from a South American Indian name]

douse *or* **dowse** (daʊs) *vb* **1** to plunge or be plunged into water or some other liquid; duck **2** (*tr*) to drench with water, esp in order to wash or clean **3** (*tr*) to put out (a light, candle, etc) ▷ *n* **4** an immersion [c16: perhaps related to obsolete *douse* to strike, of obscure origin]

dove (dʌv) *n* **1** any of various birds of the family *Columbidae*, having a heavy body, small head, short legs, and long pointed wings: order *Columbiformes*. They are typically smaller than pigeons **2** politics a person opposed to war **3** a gentle or innocent person: used as a term of endearment **4 a** a greyish-brown colour **b** (*as adjective*): *dove walls* [Old English *dūfe* (unattested except as a feminine proper name); related to Old Saxon *dūbva*, Old High German *tūba*] > 'dove,like *adj*

Dove (dʌv) *n* the Dove *Christianity* a manifestation of the Holy Spirit (John 1:32)

dovecote ('dʌv,kəʊt) *or* **dovecot** ('dʌv,kɒt) *n* a structure for housing pigeons, often raised on a pole or set on a wall, containing compartments for the birds to roost and lay eggs

Dover ('dəʊvə) *n* **1** a port in SE England, in E Kent on the Strait of Dover: the only one of the Cinque Ports that is still important; a stronghold since ancient times and Caesar's first point of attack in the invasion of Britain (55 BC). Pop: 34 087 (2001) **2 Strait of Dover** a strait between SE England and N France, linking the English Channel with the North Sea. Width: about 32 km (20 miles) **3** a city in the US, the capital of Delaware, founded in 1683: 18th-century buildings. Pop: 32 808 (2003 est)

dovetail ('dʌv,teɪl) *n* **1** a wedge-shaped tenon **2** Also called: **dovetail joint** a joint containing such tenons ▷ *vb* **3** (*tr*) to join by means of dovetails **4** to fit or cause to fit together closely or neatly: *he dovetailed his arguments to the desired conclusion*

Dovzhenko (*Russian* dov'ʒenko) *n* **Aleksandr Petrovitch** (alɪk'sandr pe'trɒvɪtʃ). 1894–1956, Soviet film director. His films include *Zemlya* (1930) and *Ivan* (1932)

Dow (daʊ; *Dutch* dɔu) *n* See **Dou**

dowager ('daʊədʒə) *n* **1 a** a widow possessing property or a title obtained from her husband **b** (*as modifier*): *the dowager duchess* **2** a wealthy or dignified elderly woman [c16: from Old French *douagiere*, from *douage* DOWER]

Dowding ('daʊdɪŋ) *n* Baron **Hugh Caswall Tremenheere**, nicknamed *Stuffy*. 1882–1970, British air chief marshal. As commander in chief of Fighter Command (1936–40), he contributed greatly to the British victory in the Battle of Britain (1940)

dowdy ('daʊdɪ) *adj* **-dier, -diest 1** (*esp of a woman's dress*) drab, unflattering, and old-fashioned ▷ *n, pl* **-dies 2** a dowdy woman [c14: *dowd* slut, of unknown origin] > **'dowdily** *adv* > **'dowdiness** *n* > **'dowdyish** *adj*

dowel ('daʊəl) *n* a wooden or metal peg that fits into two corresponding holes to join two adjacent parts. Also called: **dowel pin** [c14: from Middle Low German *dövel* plug, from Old High German *tubili*; related to Greek *thuphos* wedge]

Dowell ('daʊəl) *n* **Anthony.** born 1943, British ballet dancer. He became director of the Royal Ballet in 1986

dower ('daʊə) *n* **1** the life interest in a part of her husband's estate allotted to a widow by law **2** an archaic word for **dowry** (sense 1) **3** a natural gift or talent ▷ *vb* **4** (*tr*) to endow [c14: from Old French *douaire*, from Medieval Latin *dōtārium*, from Latin *dōs* gift]

dower house *n* a house set apart for the use of a widow, often on her deceased husband's estate

do with *vb* **1** could do with *or* can do with to find useful; benefit from: *she could do with a night's sleep* **2** have to do with to be involved in or connected with: *his illness has a lot to do with his failing the exam* **3** to do with concerning; related to **4** what...do with **a** to put or place: *what did you do with my coat?* **b** to handle or treat: *what are we going to do with these hooligans?* **c** to fill one's time usefully: *she didn't know what to do with herself when term ended*

do without *vb* (*intr, preposition*) to forgo; manage without

Dow-Jones average ('daʊ'dʒəʊnz) *n US* a daily index of stock-exchange prices based on the average price of a selected number of securities [c20: named after Charles H. *Dow* (died 1902) and Edward D. *Jones* (died 1920), American financial statisticians]

Dowland ('daʊlənd) *n* **John.** ?1563–1626, English lutenist and composer of songs and lute music

down¹ (daʊn) *prep* **1** used to indicate movement from a higher to a lower position: *they went down the mountain* **2** at a lower or further level or position on, in, or along: *he ran down the street* ▷ *adv* **3** downwards; at or to a lower level or position: *don't fall down* **4** (*particle*) used with many verbs when the result of the verb's action is to lower or destroy its object: *pull down; knock down; bring down* **5** (*particle*) used with several verbs to indicate intensity or completion **6** immediately: *cash down* **7** on paper: *write this down* **8** arranged; scheduled: *the meeting is down for next week* **9** in a helpless position: *they had him down on the ground* **10 a** away from a more important place: *down from London* **b** away from a more northerly

place: *down from Scotland* **c** (of a member of some British universities) away from the university; on vacation **d** in a particular part of a country: *down south* **11** *nautical* (of a helm) having the rudder to windward **12** reduced to a state of lack or want: *down to the last pound* **13** lacking a specified amount: *at the end of the day the cashier was ten pounds down* **14** lower in price: *bacon is down* **15** including all intermediate terms, grades, people, etc: *from managing director down to tea-lady* **16** from an earlier to a later time: *the heirloom was handed down* **17** to a finer or more concentrated state: *to grind down; boil down* **18** *sport* being a specified number of points, goals, etc behind another competitor, team, etc: *six goals down* **19** (of a person) being inactive, owing to illness: *down with flu* **20** (*functioning as imperative*) (to dogs): *down Rover!* **21** down with (*functioning as imperative*) wanting the end of somebody or something: *down with the king!* **22 get down on something** *Austral & NZ* to procure something, esp in advance of needs or in anticipation of someone else ▷ *adj* **23** (*postpositive*) depressed or miserable **24** (*prenominal*) of or relating to a train or trains from a more important place or one regarded as higher: *the down line* **25** (*postpositive*) (of a device, machine, etc, esp a computer) temporarily out of action **26** made in cash: *a down payment* **27** down to the responsibility or fault of: *this defeat was down to me* ▷ *vb* **28** (*tr*) to knock, push or pull down **29** (*tr*) *informal* to drink, esp quickly: *he downed three gins* **30** (*tr*) to bring (someone) down, esp by tackling ▷ *n* **31** *American football* one of a maximum of four consecutive attempts by one team to advance the ball a total of at least ten yards **32** a descent; downward movement **33** a lowering or a poor period (esp in the phrase **ups and downs**) **34 have a down on** *informal* to bear ill will towards (someone or something) [Old English *dūne*, short for *adūne*, variant of *of dūne*, literally: from the hill, from *of*, OFF + *dūn* hill; see DOWN³]

down² (daʊn) *n* **1** the soft fine feathers with free barbs that cover the body of a bird and prevent loss of heat. In the adult they lie beneath and between the contour feathers **2** another name for **eiderdown** (sense 1) **3** *botany* a fine coating of soft hairs, as on certain leaves, fruits, and seeds **4** any growth or coating of soft fine hair, such as that on the human face [c14: of Scandinavian origin; related to Old Norse *dūnn*]

down³ (daʊn) *n archaic* a hill, esp a sand dune. See also **downs** (sense 1) [Old English *dūn*; related to Old Frisian *dūne*, Old Saxon *dūna* hill, Old Irish *dūn* fortress, Greek *this* sandbank; see DUNE, TOWN]

Down (daʊn) *n* **1** a district of SE Northern Ireland, in Co Down. Pop: 65 195 (2003 est). Area: 649 sq km (250 sq miles) **2** a historical county of SE Northern Ireland, on the Irish Sea: generally hilly, rising to the Mountains of Mourne: in 1973 it was replaced for administrative purposes by the districts of Ards, Banbridge, Castlereagh, Down, Newry and Mourne, North Down, and part of Lisburn. Area: 2466 sq km (952 sq miles)

down and dirty *adj* (**down-and-dirty** *when prenominal*) *informal, chiefly US* **1** ruthlessly competitive or underhand: *if Bush gets down and dirty the Governor will give as good as he gets* **2** uninhibited; frank

down-and-out *adj* **1** without any means of livelihood; impoverished and, often, socially outcast ▷ *n* **2** a person who is destitute and, often, homeless; a social outcast or derelict

downbeat ('daʊn,biːt) *n* **1** *music* the first beat of a bar or the downward gesture of a conductor's baton indicating this ▷ *adj* **2** *informal* depressed; gloomy **3** *informal* relaxed; unemphatic

downcast ('daʊn,kɑːst) *adj* **1** dejected **2** (esp of the eyes) directed downwards ▷ *n* **3** *mining* a ventilation shaft

downer ('daʊnə) *n* **1** *slang* Also called: **down** a barbiturate, tranquillizer, or narcotic **2** a depressing experience **3** a state of depression: *he's on a downer today*

downfall ('daʊn,fɔːl) *n* **1** a sudden loss of position, health, or reputation **2** a fall of rain, snow, etc, esp a sudden heavy one

downgrade ('daʊn,greɪd) *vb* (*tr*) **1** to reduce in importance, esteem, or value, esp to demote (a person) to a poorer job **2** to speak of disparagingly ▷ *n* **3** *chiefly US*

& Canadian a downward slope, esp in a road **4** on the **downgrade** waning in importance, popularity, health, etc

downhearted (ˌdaʊnˈhɑːtɪd) *adj* discouraged; dejected > ˌdown'heartedly *adv*

downhill (ˈdaʊnˈhɪl) *adj* **1** going or sloping down ▷ *adv* **2** towards the bottom of a hill; downwards **3** go downhill *informal* to decline; deteriorate ▷ *n* **4** the downward slope of a hill; descent **5** a competitive event in which skiers are timed in a downhill run

downhole (ˈdaʊnˌhəʊl) *adj* (in the oil industry) denoting any piece of equipment that is used in the well itself

down-home *adj slang, chiefly US* of, relating to, or reminiscent of rural life, esp in the southern US; unsophisticated

Downing Street (ˈdaʊnɪŋ) *n* **1** a street in W central London, in Westminster: official residences of the British prime minister and the chancellor of the exchequer **2** *informal* the prime minister or the British Government [named after Sir George *Downing* (1623–84), English statesman]

download (ˈdaʊnˌləʊd) *vb* (*tr*) **1** to copy or transfer (data or a program) into the memory of one computer system from a larger one. Compare **upload** ▷ *n* **2** a file transferred onto a computer from another computer or the internet > ˌdown'loadable *adj*

down-market *adj* relating to commercial products, services, etc, that are cheap, have little prestige, or are poor in quality

Downpatrick (ˌdaʊnˈpætrɪk) *n* a market town in Northern Ireland: reputedly the burial place of Saint Patrick. Pop: 10 316 (2001)

down payment *n* the deposit paid on an item purchased on hire-purchase, mortgage, etc

downpipe (ˈdaʊnˌpaɪp) *n Brit & NZ* a pipe for carrying rainwater from a roof gutter to the ground or to a drain. Also called: **rainwater pipe, drainpipe**

downpour (ˈdaʊnˌpɔː) *n* a heavy continuous fall of rain

downrange (ˈdaʊnˈreɪndʒ) *adj, adv* in the direction of the intended flight path of a rocket or missile

downright (ˈdaʊnˌraɪt) *adj* **1** frank or straightforward; blunt: *downright speech* ▷ *adv, adj* (prenominal) **2** (intensifier): *a downright certainty; downright rude* > ˈdownˌrightly *adv* > ˈdownˌrightness *n*

downs (daʊnz) *pl n* **1** Also called: **downland** rolling upland, esp in the chalk areas of S Britain, characterized by lack of trees and used mainly as pasture **2** *Austral & NZ* a flat grassy area, not necessarily of uplands

Downs (daʊnz) *n* the Downs **1** any of various ranges of low chalk hills in S England, esp the South Downs in Sussex **2** a roadstead off the SE coast of Kent, protected by the Goodwin Sands

downshifting (ˈdaʊnˌʃɪftɪŋ) *n* the practice of simplifying one's lifestyle and becoming less materialistic > ˈdownˌshifter *n*

downside (ˈdaʊnˌsaɪd) *n* the disadvantageous aspect of a situation: *the downside of twentieth-century living*

downsize (ˈdaʊnˌsaɪz) *vb* -sizes, -sizing, -sized (*tr*) **1** to reduce the operating costs of a company by reducing the number of people it employs **2** to upgrade (a computer system) by replacing a mainframe or minicomputer with a network of microcomputers. Compare **rightsize**

Down's syndrome *n* **a** *pathol* a condition caused by the presence of an extra copy of chromosome 21 resulting in learning difficulties and physical differences, such as shorter stature. Former name: **mongolism b** (*as modifier*): *a Down's syndrome baby* [C19: after John *Langdon-Down* (1828–96), English physician]

downstage (ˈdaʊnˈsteɪdʒ) *theatre* ▷ *adv* **1** at or towards the front of the stage ▷ *adj* **2** of or relating to the front of the stage

downstairs (ˈdaʊnˈstɛəz) *adv* **1** down the stairs; to or on a lower floor ▷ *n* **2 a** a lower or ground floor **b** (*as modifier*): *a downstairs room* **3** *Brit informal, old-fashioned* the servants of a household collectively

downstream (ˈdaʊnˈstriːm) *adv, adj* in or towards the lower part of a stream; with the current. Compare **upstream** (sense 2)

downswing (ˈdaʊnˌswɪŋ) *n* a statistical downward trend

in business activity, the death rate, etc

downtime (ˈdaʊnˌtaɪm) *n commerce* time during which a machine or plant is not working because it is incapable of production, as when under repair: the term is sometimes used to include all nonproductive time

down-to-earth *adj* sensible; practical; realistic

downtown (ˈdaʊnˈtaʊn) *US, Canadian & NZ* ▷ *n* **1** the central or lower part of a city, esp the main commercial area ▷ *adv* **2** towards, to, or into this area ▷ *adj* **3** of, relating to, or situated in the downtown area: *downtown Manhattan*

downtrodden (ˈdaʊnˌtrɒdᵊn) *or* **downtrod** *adj* **1** subjugated; oppressed **2** trodden down; trampled

downturn (ˈdaʊnˌtɜːn) *n* a drop or reduction in the success of a business or economy

down under *informal* ▷ *n* **1** Australia or New Zealand ▷ *adv* **2** in or to Australia or New Zealand

downward (ˈdaʊnwəd) *adj* **1** descending from a higher to a lower level, condition, position, etc **2** descending from a beginning ▷ *adv* **3** a variant of **downwards** > ˈdownwardly *adv*

downwards (ˈdaʊnwədz) *or* **downward** *adv* **1** from a higher to a lower place, level, etc **2** from an earlier time or source to a later: *from the Tudors downwards*

downwind (ˈdaʊnˈwɪnd) *adv, adj* in the same direction towards which the wind is blowing; with the wind from behind

downy (ˈdaʊnɪ) *adj* downier, downiest **1** covered with soft fine hair or feathers **2** light, soft, and fluffy **3** made from or filled with down **4** *Brit slang* sharp-witted; knowing > ˈdowniness *n*

dowry (ˈdaʊərɪ) *n, pl* -ries **1** the money or property brought by a woman to her husband at marriage **2** a natural talent or gift [C14: from Anglo-French *douarie*, from Medieval Latin *dōtārium*; see DOWER]

dowse (daʊz) *vb* (*intr*) to search for underground water, minerals, etc, using a divining rod; divine [C17: of unknown origin] > ˈdowser *n*

Dowson (ˈdaʊsᵊn) *n* **Ernest (Christopher)**. 1867–1900, English Decadent poet noted for his lyric *Cynara*

doxology (dɒkˈsɒlədʒɪ) *n, pl* -gies a hymn, verse, or form of words in Christian liturgy glorifying God [C17: from Medieval Latin *doxologia*, from Greek, from *doxologos* uttering praise, from *doxa* praise; see -LOGY] > doxological (ˌdɒksəˈlɒdʒɪkᵊl) *adj*

doxy (ˈdɒksɪ) *n, pl* doxies *archaic, slang* a prostitute or mistress [C16: probably from Middle Flemish *docke* doll; compare Middle Dutch *docke* doll]

doyen (ˈdɔɪən; *French* dwaˈjɛ̃) *n* the senior member of a group, profession, or society [C17: from French, from Late Latin *decānus* leader of a group of ten; see DEAN] > doyenne (dɔɪˈɛn; *French* dwaˈjɛn) *fem n*

Doyle (dɔɪl) *n* See **Conan Doyle**

doyley (ˈdɔɪlɪ) *n* a variant spelling of **doily**

D'Oyly Carte (ˈdɔɪlɪ kɑːt) *n* **Richard**. 1844–1901, British impresario noted for his productions of the operettas of Gilbert and Sullivan

doz. *abbreviation* dozen

doze (dəʊz) *vb* (*intr*) **1** to sleep lightly or intermittently **2** (often foll by *off*) to fall into a light sleep ▷ *n* **3** a short sleep [C17: probably from Old Norse *dūs* lull; related to Danish *döse* to drowse, Swedish dialect *dusa* slumber] > ˈdozer *n*

dozen (ˈdʌzᵊn) *determiner* **1** (preceded by *a* or a numeral) twelve or a group of twelve ▷ *n, pl* dozens *or* dozen **2** by the dozen in large quantities **3** talk nineteen to the dozen to talk without stopping [C13: from Old French *douzaine*, from *douze* twelve, from Latin *duodecim*, from *duo* two + *decem* ten] > ˈdozenth *adj*

dozy (ˈdəʊzɪ) *adj* dozier, doziest **1** drowsy **2** *Brit informal* stupid > ˈdozily *adv* > ˈdoziness *n*

DP *abbreviation* **1** data processing **2** displaced person **3** (in South Africa) Democratic Party

DPB *abbreviation* (in New Zealand) domestic purposes benefit: an allowance paid to solo parents

DPhil *or* **DPh** *abbreviation* Doctor of Philosophy. Also: PhD

dpi *abbreviation* dots per inch: a measure of the resolution of a typesetting machine, computer screen, etc

DPP (in Britain) *abbreviation* Director of Public

Prosecutions

dpt *abbreviation* department

dr *abbreviation* **1** debtor **2** Also: dr. dram

Dr *abbreviation* **1** Doctor **2** (in street names) Drive

DR *abbreviation* dry riser

dr. *abbreviation* **1** debit **2** Also: dr dram **3** (the former) drachma

drab¹ (dræb) *adj* drabber, drabbest **1** dull; dingy; shabby **2** cheerless; dreary: *a drab evening* ⊳ *n* **3** of the colour drab ⊳ *n* **4** a light olive-brown colour [c16: from Old French *drap* cloth, from Late Latin *drappus*, perhaps of Celtic origin] > 'drably *adv* > 'drabness *n*

drab² (dræb) *archaic* ⊳ *n* **1** a slatternly woman **2** a whore ⊳ *vb* drabs, drabbing, drabbed **3** (*intr*) to consort with prostitutes [c16: of Celtic origin; compare Scottish Gaelic *drabag*]

Drabble ('dræbᵊl) *n* Margaret. born 1939, British novelist and editor. Her novels include *The Needle's Eye* (1972), *The Radiant Way* (1987), and *The Seven Sisters* (2002). She edited the 1985 edition of the *Oxford Companion to Literature*

drachm (dræm) *n* **1** Also called: fluid dram *Brit* one eighth of a fluid ounce **2** *US* another name for **dram** (sense 2) **3** another name for **drachma** [c14: learned variant of DRAM]

drachma ('drækmə) *n, pl* -mas *or* -mae (-miː) **1** the former standard monetary unit of Greece, divided into 100 lepta; replaced by the euro in 2002 **2** *US* another name for **dram** (sense 2) **3** a silver coin of ancient Greece [c16: from Latin, from Greek *drakhmē* a handful, from *drassesthai* to seize]

drack *or* **drac** (dræk) *adj Austral slang* (esp of a woman) unattractive [perhaps from *Dracula's* Daughter]

Draco ('dreɪkəʊ) *n* 7th century bc, Athenian statesman and lawmaker, whose code of laws (621) prescribed death for almost every offence

draconian (dreɪ'kəʊnɪən) *or* **draconic** (dreɪ'kɒnɪk) *adj* (*sometimes capital*) **1** of or relating to Draco, 7th-century Athenian statesman and lawmaker, or his code of laws, which prescribed death for almost every offence **2** harsh: *draconian legislation* > dra'conianism *n*

draff (dræf) *n* the residue of husks after fermentation of the grain used in brewing, used as a food for cattle [c13: from Old Norse *draf*; related to Old High German *trebir*, Russian *drob* fragment; see DRIVEL]

draft (drɑːft) *n* **1** a plan, sketch, or drawing of something **2** a preliminary outline of a book, speech, etc **3** another word for **bill of exchange 4** a demand or drain on something **5** *US* selection for compulsory military service **6** detachment of military personnel from one unit to another **7** *Austral & NZ* a group of livestock separated from the rest of the herd or flock ⊳ *vb* (*tr*) **8** to draw up an outline or sketch for something: *to draft a speech* **9** to prepare a plan or design of **10** to detach (military personnel) from one unit to another **11** *chiefly US* to select for compulsory military service **12** to chisel a draft on (stone, etc) **13** *Austral & NZ* **a** to select (cattle or sheep) from a herd or flock **b** to select (farm stock) for sale ⊳ *n, vb* the usual US spelling of **draught** [c16: variant of DRAUGHT] > 'drafter *n*

draftee (drɑːf'tiː) *n US* a conscript

drafty ('drɑːftɪ) *adj* draftier, draftiest the usual US spelling of **draughty**

drag (dræg) *vb* drags, dragging, dragged **1** to pull or be pulled with force, esp along the ground or other surface **2** (*tr*; often foll by *away* or *from*) to persuade to come away (from something attractive or interesting): *he couldn't drag himself away from the shop* **3** to trail or cause to trail on the ground **4** (*tr*) to move (oneself, one's feet, etc) with effort or difficulty: *he drags himself out of bed at dawn* **5** to linger behind **6** (often foll by *on* or *out*) to prolong or be prolonged tediously or unnecessarily: *his talk dragged on for hours* **7** (*tr*; foll by *out* or *from*) to crush (clods) or level (a soil surface) by use of a drag **8** (of hounds) to follow (a fox or its trail) to the place where it has been lying **9** (*intr*) *slang* to draw (on a cigarette, pipe, etc) **10** *computing* to move (data) from one place to another on the screen by manipulating a mouse with its button held down **11 drag anchor** (of a vessel) to move away from its mooring because the anchor has failed to hold

12 drag one's feet *or* **drag one's heels** *informal* to act with deliberate slowness ⊳ *n* **13** the act of dragging or the state of being dragged **14** an implement, such as a dragnet, dredge, etc, used for dragging **15** Also called: drag harrow a type of harrow consisting of heavy beams, often with spikes inserted, used to crush clods, level soil, or prepare seedbeds **16** a sporting coach with seats inside and out, usually drawn by four horses **17** a braking or retarding device, such as a metal piece fitted to the underside of the wheel of a horse-drawn vehicle **18** a person or thing that slows up progress **19** slow progress or movement **20** *aeronautics* the resistance to the motion of a body passing through a fluid, esp through air: applied to an aircraft in flight, it is the component of the resultant aerodynamic force measured parallel to the direction of air flow **21** the trail of scent left by a fox or other animal hunted with hounds **22** an artificial trail of a strong-smelling substance, sometimes including aniseed, drawn over the ground for hounds to follow **23** See **drag hunt 24** *informal* a person or thing that is very tedious; bore: *exams are a drag* **25** *slang* a car **26** short for **drag race 27** *slang* a women's clothes worn by a man, usually by a transvestite (esp in the phrase **in drag**) **b** (*as modifier*): *a drag club; drag show* **c** clothes collectively **28** *informal* a draw on a cigarette, pipe, etc **29** *US slang* influence or persuasive power **30** *chiefly US slang* a street or road ⊳ See also **drag out of, drag up** [Old English *dragan* to DRAW; related to Swedish *dragga*]

dragée (dræ'ʒeɪ) *n* **1** a sweet made of a nut, fruit, etc, coated with a hard sugar icing **2** a tiny beadlike sweet used for decorating cakes, etc **3** a medicinal formulation coated with sugar to disguise the taste [c19: from French; see DREDGE²]

draggle ('drægᵊl) *vb* **1** to make or become wet or dirty by trailing on the ground; bedraggle **2** (*intr*) to lag; dawdle [c16: probably frequentative of DRAG]

draggletailed ('drægᵊl,teɪld) *adj archaic* (esp of a woman) bedraggled; besmirched

draggy ('drægɪ) *adj* -gier, -giest *slang* **1** slow or boring: *a draggy party* **2** dull and listless

draghound ('dræg,haʊnd) *n* a hound used to follow an artificial trail of scent in a drag hunt

drag hunt *n* **1** a hunt in which hounds follow an artificial trail of scent **2** a club that organizes such hunts ⊳ *vb* **drag-hunt 3** to follow draghounds, esp on horseback, or cause (draghounds) to follow an artificial trail of scent

drag king *n* **1** a woman who dresses as a man and impersonates male characteristics for public entertainment **2** *slang* a female transvestite

dragnet ('dræg,nɛt) *n* **1** a heavy or weighted net used to scour the bottom of a pond, river, etc, as when searching for something **2** any system of coordinated efforts by police forces to track down wanted persons

dragoman ('drægəʊmən) *n, pl* -mans *or* -men (in some Middle Eastern countries, esp formerly) a professional interpreter or guide [c14: from French, from Italian *dragomano*, from Medieval Greek *dragoumanos*, from Arabic *targumān* an interpreter, from Aramaic *tūrgemānā*, of Akkadian origin]

dragon ('drægən) *n* **1** a mythical monster usually represented as breathing fire and having a scaly reptilian body, wings, claws, and a long tail **2** *informal* a fierce or intractable person, esp a woman **3** any of various very large lizards, esp the Komodo dragon **4 chase the dragon** *slang* to smoke opium or heroin [c13: from Old French, from Latin *dracō*, from Greek *drakōn*; related to *drakos* eye]

dragonet ('drægənɪt) *n* any small spiny-finned fish of the family *Callionymidae*, having a flat head and a slender tapering brightly coloured body and living at the bottom of shallow seas [c14 (meaning: small dragon): from French; applied to fish c18]

dragonfly ('drægən,flaɪ) *n, pl* -flies any predatory insect of the suborder *Anisoptera*, having a large head and eyes, a long slender body, two pairs of iridescent wings that are outspread at rest, and aquatic larvae: order *Odonata*

dragonnade (,drægə'neɪd) *n* **1** *history* the persecution of

French Huguenots during the reign of Louis XIV by dragoons quartered in their villages and homes **2** subjection by military force ▷ *vb* **3** (*tr*) to subject to persecution by military troops [c18: from French, from *dragon* DRAGOON]

dragoon (drə'guːn) *n* **1** (originally) a mounted infantryman armed with a carbine **2** (*sometimes capital*) a domestic fancy pigeon **3 a** a type of cavalryman **b** (*pl; cap when part of a name*): *the Royal Dragoons* ▷ *vb* (*tr*) **4** to coerce; force: *he was dragooned into admitting it* **5** to persecute by military force [c17: from French *dragon* (special use of DRAGON), soldier armed with a carbine, perhaps suggesting that a carbine, like a dragon, breathed forth fire]

drag out of *vb* (*tr, adverb + preposition*) to obtain or extract (a confession, statement, etc), esp by force: *we dragged the name out of him*. Also: **drag from**

drag queen *n* **1** a man who dresses as a woman and impersonates female characteristics for public entertainment **2** *slang* a male transvestite

drag race *n* a type of motor race in which specially built or modified cars or motorcycles are timed over a measured course > **drag racing** *n*

dragster ('drægstə) *n* a car specially built or modified for drag racing

drag up *vb* (*tr, adverb*) *informal* **1** to rear (a child) poorly and in an undisciplined manner **2** to introduce or revive (an unpleasant fact or story)

drain (dreɪn) *n* **1** a pipe or channel that carries off water, sewage, etc **2** an instance or cause of continuous diminution in resources or energy; depletion **3** *surgery* a device, such as a tube, for insertion into a wound, incision, or bodily cavity to drain off pus, etc **4 down the drain** wasted ▷ *vb* **5** (*tr; often foll by off*) to draw off or remove (liquid) from: *to drain water from vegetables; to drain vegetables* **6** (*intr; often foll by away*) to flow (away) or filter (off) **7** (*intr*) to dry or be emptied as a result of liquid running off or flowing away: *leave the dishes to drain* **8** (*tr*) to drink the entire contents of (a glass, cup, etc) **9** (*tr*) to consume or make constant demands on (resources, energy, etc); exhaust; sap **10** (*intr*) to disappear or leave, esp gradually: *the colour drained from his face* **11** (*tr*) (of a river, etc) to carry off the surface water from (an area) **12** (*intr*) (of an area) to discharge its surface water into rivers, streams, etc [Old English *drēahnian*; related to Old Norse *drangr* dry wood; see DRY] > **'drainer** *n*

drainage ('dreɪnɪdʒ) *n* **1** the process or a method of draining **2** a system of watercourses or drains **3** liquid, sewage, etc, that is drained away

drainage basin or **drainage area** *n* another name for **catchment area**

draining board *n* a sloping grooved surface at the side of a sink, used for draining washed dishes, etc

drainlayer ('dreɪn,leɪə) *n* NZ a person trained to build or repair drains

drainpipe ('dreɪn,paɪp) *n* a pipe for carrying off rainwater, sewage, etc; downpipe

drainpipes ('dreɪn,paɪps) *pl n* trousers with very narrow legs

drake (dreɪk) *n* the male of any duck [c13: perhaps from Low German; compare Middle Dutch *andrake*, Old High German *antrahho*]

Drake (dreɪk) *n* **Sir Francis.** ?1540–96, English navigator and buccaneer, the first Englishman to sail around the world (1577–80). He commanded a fleet against the Spanish Armada (1588) and contributed greatly to its defeat

Drakensberg ('drɑːkənz,bɜːg) *n* a mountain range in southern Africa, extending through Lesotho, E South Africa, and Swaziland. Highest peak: Thabana Ntlenyana, 3482 m (11 425 ft). Sotho name: **Quathlamba**

Dralon ('dreɪlɒn) *n trademark* an acrylic fibre fabric used esp for upholstery

dram (dræm) *n* **1** one sixteenth of an ounce (avoirdupois). 1 dram is equivalent to 0.0018 kilogram **2** Also called: **drachm, drachma** US one eighth of an apothecaries' ounce; 60 grains. 1 dram is equivalent to 0.0039 kilogram **3** a small amount of an alcoholic drink,

esp a spirit; tot **4** the standard monetary unit of Armenia, divided into 100 lumas [c15: from Old French *dragme*, from Late Latin *dragma*, from Greek *drakhmē*; see DRACHMA]

DRAM or **D-RAM** ('diːræm) *n acronym* **1** dynamic random access memory: a widely used type of random access memory. See RAM¹ ▷ *n* **2** a chip containing such a memory

drama ('drɑːmə) *n* **1** a work to be performed by actors on stage, radio, or television; play **2** the genre of literature represented by works intended for the stage **3** the art of the writing and production of plays **4** a situation or sequence of events that is highly emotional, tragic, or turbulent [c17: from Late Latin: a play, from Greek: something performed, from *drān* to do]

drama queen *n informal* a person who tends to react to every situation in an overdramatic or exaggerated manner

dramatic (drə'mætɪk) *adj* **1** of or relating to drama **2** like a drama in suddenness, emotional impact, etc **3** striking; effective **4** acting or performed in a flamboyant way

dramatic irony *n theatre* the irony occurring when the implications of a situation, speech, etc, are understood by the audience but not by the characters in the play

dramatics (drə'mætɪks) *n* **1** (*functioning as singular or plural*) **a** the art of acting or producing plays **b** dramatic productions **2** (*usually functioning as plural*) histrionic behaviour

dramatis personae ('drɑːmətɪs pə'səʊnaɪ) *pl n* (*often functioning as singular*) **1** the characters or a list of characters in a play or story **2** the main personalities in any situation or event [c18: from New Latin]

dramatist ('dræmətɪst) *n* a writer of plays; playwright

dramatize or **dramatise** ('dræmə,taɪz) *vb* **1** (*tr*) to put into dramatic form **2** to express or represent (something) in a dramatic or exaggerated way: *he dramatizes his illness* > **dramatization** or **drama'tisation** *n*

dramaturge ('dræmə,tɜːdʒ) *n* **1** Also called: **dramaturgist** a dramatist, esp one associated with a particular company or theatre **2** Also called: **dramaturg** a literary adviser on the staff of a theatre, film corporation, etc, whose responsibilities may include selection and editing of texts, liaison with authors, preparation of printed programmes, and public relations work [c19: probably from French, from Greek *dramatourgos* playwright, from DRAMA + *ergon* work]

dramaturgy ('dræmə,tɜːdʒɪ) *n* the art and technique of the theatre; dramatics > **drama'turgic** or **drama'turgical** *adj*

dramedy ('drɑːmɪdɪ) *n, pl* **-dies** a television or film drama in which there are important elements of comedy [c20: from DRAM(A) + (COM)EDY]

drank (dræŋk) *vb* the past tense of **drink**

drape (dreɪp) *vb* **1** (*tr*) to hang or cover with flexible material or fabric, usually in folds; adorn **2** to hang or arrange or be hung or arranged, esp in folds **3** (*tr*) to place casually and loosely; hang ▷ *n* **4** (*often plural*) a cloth or hanging that covers something in folds; drapery **5** the way in which fabric hangs [c15: from Old French *draper*, from *drap* piece of cloth; see DRAB¹]

draper ('dreɪpə) *n Brit* a dealer in fabrics and sewing materials

Draper ('dreɪpə) *n* **1 Henry.** 1837–82, US astronomer, who contributed to stellar classification and spectroscopy **2** his father, **John William.** 1811–82, US chemist and historian, born in England, made the first photograph of the moon

drapery ('dreɪpərɪ) *n, pl* **-peries 1** fabric or clothing arranged and draped **2** (*often plural*) curtains or hangings that drape **3** *Brit* the occupation or shop of a draper **4** fabrics and cloth collectively > **'draperied** *adj*

drapes (dreɪps) or **draperies** ('dreɪpərɪz) *pl n chiefly US & Canadian* curtains, esp ones of heavy fabric

drastic ('dræstɪk) *adj* extreme or forceful; severe [c17: from Greek *drastikos*, from *drān* to do, act] > **'drastically** *adv*

drat (dræt) *interj slang* an exclamation of mild annoyance or anger (also in the phrases **drat it! drat**

d

you! etc) [c19: probably alteration of *God rot*]

draught *or US* **draft** (drɑːft) *n* **1** a current of air, esp one intruding into an enclosed space **2 a** the act of pulling a load, as by a vehicle or animal **b** (*as modifier*): *a draught horse* **3** the load or quantity drawn **4** a portion of liquid to be drunk, esp a dose of medicine **5** the act or an instance of drinking; a gulp or swallow **6** the act or process of drawing air, smoke, etc, into the lungs **7** the amount of air, smoke, etc, inhaled in one breath **8 a** beer, wine, etc, stored in bulk, esp in a cask, as opposed to being bottled **b** (*as modifier*): *draught beer* **c** on draught drawn from a cask or keg **9** Also called: draughtsman any one of the 12 flat thick discs used by each player in the game of draughts. US and Canadian equivalent: checker **10** the depth of a loaded vessel in the water, taken from the level of the waterline to the lowest point of the hull **11** feel the draught to be short of money [c14: probably from Old Norse *drahtr*, of Germanic origin; related to DRAW]

draughtboard (ˈdrɑːftˌbɔːd) *n* a square board divided into 64 squares of alternating colours, used for playing draughts or chess

draughts (drɑːfts) *n* (*functioning as singular*) a game for two players using a draughtboard and 12 draughtsmen each. The object is to jump over and capture the opponent's pieces. US and Canadian name: checkers [c14: plural of DRAUGHT (in obsolete sense: a chess move)]

draughtsman *or US* **draftsman** (ˈdrɑːftsmən) *n, pl* -men **1** a person who practises or is qualified in mechanical drawing, employed to prepare detailed scale drawings of machinery, buildings, devices, etc **2** a person skilled in drawing **3** *Brit* any of the 12 flat thick discs used by each player in the game of draughts. US and Canadian equivalent: checker ▷ ˈdraughtsmanˌship *or US* ˈdraftsmanˌship *n*

draughty *or US* **drafty** (ˈdrɑːftɪ) *adj* draughtier, draughtiest *or US* draftier, draftiest characterized by or exposed to draughts of air ▷ ˈdraughtily *or US* ˈdraftily *adv* ▷ ˈdraughtiness *or US* ˈdraftiness *n*

Dravidian (drəˈvɪdɪən) *n* **1** a family of languages spoken in S and central India and Sri Lanka, including Tamil, Malayalam, Telugu, Kannada, and Gondi **2** a member of one of the aboriginal races of India, pushed south by the Indo-Europeans and now mixed with them ▷ *adj* **3** denoting, belonging to, or relating to this family of languages or these peoples

draw (drɔː) *vb* draws, drawing, drew, drawn **1** to cause (a person or thing) to move towards or away by pulling **2** to bring, take, or pull (something) out, as from a drawer, holster, etc **3** (*tr*) to extract or pull or take out: *to draw teeth; to draw a card from a pack* **4** (*tr; often foll by off*) to take (liquid) out of a cask, keg, tank, etc, by means of a tap **5** (*intr*) to move, go, or proceed, esp in a specified direction: *to draw alongside* **6** (*tr*) to attract or elicit: *to draw a crowd; draw attention* **7** (*tr*) to cause to flow: *to draw blood* **8** to depict or sketch (a form, figure, picture, etc) in lines, as with a pencil or pen, esp without the use of colour; delineate **9** (*tr*) to make, formulate, or derive: *to draw conclusions, comparisons, parallels* **10** (*tr*) to write (a legal document) in proper form **11** (*tr; sometimes foll by in*) to suck or take in (air, liquid, etc): *to draw a breath* **12** (*intr*) to induce or allow a draught to carry off air, smoke, etc: *the flue draws well* **13** (*tr*) to take or receive from a source: *draw money from the bank* **14** (*tr*) to earn: *draw interest* **15** (*tr*) *finance* to write out (a bill of exchange or promissory note): *to draw a cheque* **16** (*tr*) to choose at random: *to draw lots* **17** (*tr*) to reduce the diameter of (a wire or metal rod) by pulling it through a die **18** (*tr*) to shape (a sheet of metal or glass) by rolling, by pulling it through a die or by stretching **19** *archery* to bend (a bow) by pulling the string **20** to steep (tea) or (of tea) to steep in boiling water **21** (*tr*) to disembowel: *draw a chicken* **22** (*tr*) to cause (pus, blood, etc) to discharge from an abscess or wound **23** (*intr*) (of two teams, contestants, etc) to finish a game with an equal number of points, goals, etc; tie **24** (*tr*) *bridge, whist* to keep leading a suit in order to force out (all outstanding cards) **25** draw trumps *bridge, whist* to play the trump suit until the opponents have none left

26 (*tr*) *billiards* to cause (the cue ball) to spin back after a direct impact with another ball by applying backspin when making the stroke **27** (*tr*) to search (a place) in order to find wild animals, game, etc, for hunting **28** *golf* to cause (a golf ball) to move with a controlled right-to-left trajectory or (of a golf ball) to veer gradually from right to left **29** (*tr*) *curling* to deliver (the stone) gently **30** (*tr*) *nautical* (of a vessel) to require (a certain depth) in which to float **31** draw a blank to get no results from something **32** draw and quarter to disembowel and dismember (a person) after hanging **33** draw stumps *cricket* to close play, as by pulling out the stumps **34** draw the line See line¹ (sense 42) **35** draw the short straw See short straw **36** draw the bowl *bowls* to deliver the bowl in such a way that it approaches the jack ▷ *n* **37** the act of drawing **38** *US* a sum of money advanced to finance anticipated expenses **39** an event, occasion, act, etc, that attracts a large audience **40** a raffle or lottery **41** something taken or chosen at random, as a ticket in a raffle or lottery **42** a contest or game ending in a tie **43** *US & Canadian* a small natural drainage way or gully ▷ See also **drawback, draw in** [Old English *dragan*; related to Old Norse *draga*; Old Frisian *draga, drega*, Old Saxon *dragan*, Old High German *tragan* to carry]

drawback (ˈdrɔːˌbæk) *n* **1** a disadvantage or hindrance **2** a refund of customs or excise duty paid on goods that are being exported or used in the production of manufactured exports ▷ *vb* **draw back** (*intr, adverb*; often foll by *from*) **3** to retreat; move backwards **4** to turn aside from an undertaking

drawbridge (ˈdrɔːˌbrɪdʒ) *n* a bridge that may be raised to prevent access or to enable vessels to pass

drawdown (ˈdrɔːˌdaʊn) *n* **1** a depletion or reduction, for example of supplies **2** a continuous decline in an investment or fund, usually expressed as a percentage between its highest and lowest levels **3** the intentional draining of a body of water such as a lake or reservoir, to a given depth

drawee (drɔːˈiː) *n* the person or organization on which a cheque or other order for payment is drawn

drawer (ˈdrɔːə) *n* **1** a person or thing that draws, esp a draughtsman **2** a person who draws a cheque. See **draw** (sense 15) **3** a person who draws up a commercial paper **4** *archaic* a person who draws beer, etc, in a bar **5** (drɔː) a boxlike container in a chest, table, etc, made for sliding in and out

drawers (drɔːz) *pl n* a legged undergarment for either sex, worn below the waist

draw in *vb* (*intr, adverb*) (of hours of daylight) to become shorter

drawing (ˈdrɔːɪŋ) *n* **1** a picture or plan made by means of lines on a surface, esp one made with a pencil or pen without the use of colour **2** a sketch, plan, or outline **3** the art of making drawings; draughtsmanship

drawing pin *n Brit* a short tack with a broad smooth head for fastening papers to a drawing board, etc. US and Canadian name: thumbtack

drawing room *n* **1** a room where visitors are received and entertained; living room; sitting room **2** *archaic* a ceremonial or formal reception, esp at court

drawknife (ˈdrɔːˌnaɪf) *or* **drawshave** *n, pl* -knives *or* -shaves a woodcutting tool with two handles at right angles to the blade, used to shave wood. US name: spokeshave

drawl (drɔːl) *vb* **1** to speak or utter (words) slowly, esp prolonging the vowel sounds ▷ *n* **2** the way of speech of someone who drawls [c16: probably frequentative of DRAW] ▷ ˈdrawling *adj*

drawn (drɔːn) *adj* haggard, tired, or tense in appearance

drawn work *n* ornamental needlework done by drawing threads out of the fabric and using the remaining threads to form lacelike patterns. Also called: drawn-thread work

draw off *vb* (*adverb*) **1** (*tr*) to cause (a liquid) to flow from something **2** to withdraw (troops)

draw on *vb* **1** (*intr, preposition*) to use or exploit (a source, fund, etc): *to draw on one's experience* **2** (*intr, adverb*) to come near: *the time for his interview drew on* **3** (*tr, preposition*) to withdraw (money) from (an account) **4** (*tr, adverb*) to put on (clothes) **5** (*tr, adverb*) to lead further; entice or encourage: *the prospect of nearing his goal drew him*

draw out *vb* (*adverb*) **1** to extend or cause to be extended: *he drew out his stay* **2** (*tr*) to cause (a person) to talk freely: *she's been quiet all evening — see if you can draw her out* **3** Also called: **draw from** (*tr*; foll by *of*) to elicit (information) (from) **4** (*tr*) to withdraw (money) as from a bank account or a business **5** (*intr*) (of hours of daylight) to become longer **6** (*intr*) (of a train) to leave a station **7** (*tr*) to extend (troops) in line; lead from camp **8** (*intr*) (of troops) to proceed from camp

drawstring ('drɔːˌstrɪŋ) *n* a cord, ribbon, etc, run through a hem around an opening, as on the bottom of a sleeve or at the mouth of a bag, so that when it is pulled tighter, the opening closes

draw up *vb* (*adverb*) **1** to come or cause to come to a halt **2** (*tr*) a to prepare a draft of (a legal document) **b** to formulate and write out in appropriate form: *to draw up a contract* **3** (*used reflexively*) to straighten oneself **4** to form or arrange (a body of soldiers, etc) in order or formation

dray¹ (dreɪ) *n* **a** a low cart without fixed sides, used for carrying heavy loads **b** (*in combination*): *a drayman* [Old English *dræge* dragnet; related to Old Norse *draga* load of timber carried on horseback and trailing on the ground; see DRAW]

dray² (dreɪ) *n* a variant spelling of **drey**

Drayton ('dreɪt³n) *n* **Michael.** 1563–1631, English poet. His work includes odes and pastorals, and *Poly-Olbion* (1613–22), on the topography of England

dread (drɛd) *vb* (*tr*) **1** to anticipate with apprehension or terror **2** to fear greatly **3** *archaic* to be in awe of ▷ *n* **4** great fear; horror **5** an object of terror **6** *slang* a Rastafarian **7** *archaic* deep reverence ▷ *adj* **8** *literary* awesome; awe-inspiring [Old English *ondrǣdan*; related to Old Saxon *antdrādan*, Old High German *intrātan*]

dreadful ('drɛdfʊl) *adj* **1** extremely disagreeable, shocking, or bad: *what a dreadful play* **2** (*intensifier*): *this is a dreadful waste of time* **3** causing dread; terrifying **4** *archaic* inspiring awe

dreadfully ('drɛdfʊlɪ) *adv* **1** in a shocking, or disagreeable manner **2** (*intensifier*): *you're dreadfully kind*

dreadlocks ('drɛdˌlɒks) *pl n* hair worn in the Rastafarian style of long matted or tightly curled strands

dreadnought or **dreadnaught** ('drɛdˌnɔːt) *n* **1** a battleship armed with heavy guns of uniform calibre **2** an overcoat made of heavy cloth

dream (driːm) *n* **1 a** mental activity, usually in the form of an imagined series of events, occurring during certain phases of sleep **b** (*as modifier*): *a dream sequence* **c** (*in combination*): *dreamland*. Related adj: **oneiric 2 a** a sequence of imaginative thoughts indulged in while awake; daydream; fantasy **b** (*as modifier*): *a dream world* **3** a person or thing seen or occurring in a dream **4** a cherished hope; ambition; aspiration **5** a vain hope **6** a person or thing that is as pleasant, or seemingly unreal as a dream **7 go like a dream** to move, develop, or work very well ▷ *vb* **dreams, dreaming, dreamed** or **dreamt** (drɛmt) **8** (*may take a clause as object*) to undergo or experience (a dream or dreams) **9** (*intr*) to indulge in daydreams **10** (*intr*) to suffer delusions; be unrealistic: *you're dreaming if you think you can win* **11** (*when intr, foll by of* or *about*) to have an image (of) or fantasy (about) in or as if in a dream **12** (*intr; foll by of*) to consider the possibility (of): *I wouldn't dream of troubling you* ▷ *adj* **13** too good to be true; ideal: *dream kitchen* ▷ See also **dream up** [Old English *drēam* song; related to Old High German *troum*, Old Norse *draumr*, Greek *thrulos* noise]

dreamboat ('driːmˌbəʊt) *n old-fashioned, slang* an exceptionally attractive person or thing, esp a person of the opposite sex

dreamt (drɛmt) *vb* a past tense and past participle of **dream**

dream team *n informal* a group of people regarded as having the prefect combination of talents

dream ticket *n* a combination of two people, usu. candidates in an election, that is considered to be ideal

Dreamtime ('driːmˌtaɪm) *n* **1** Also called: **alchera** ('æltʃərə), **alcheringa** (in the mythology of Australian Aboriginal peoples) a mythical Golden Age of the past

2 *Austral informal* any remote period, out of touch with the actualities of the present

dream up *vb* (*tr, adverb*) to invent by ingenuity and imagination: *to dream up an excuse for leaving*

dreamy ('driːmɪ) *adj* **dreamier, dreamiest 1** vague or impractical **2** resembling a dream in quality **3** relaxing; gentle: *dreamy music* **4** *informal* wonderful **5** having dreams, esp daydreams > 'dreamily *adv* > 'dreaminess *n*

dreary ('drɪərɪ) *adj* **drearier, dreariest 1** sad or dull; dismal **2** wearying; boring [Old English *drēorig* gory; related to Old High German *trūrēg* sad] > 'drearily *adv* > 'dreariness *n*

drecksill ('drɛkˌsɪl) *n Southwest English dialect* a doorstep

dredge¹ (drɛdʒ) *n* **1** Also called: **dredger** a machine, in the form of a bucket ladder, grab, or suction device, used to remove material from a riverbed, channel, etc **2** another name for **dredger¹** (sense 1) ▷ *vb* **3** to remove (material) from a riverbed, channel, etc, by means of a dredge **4** (*tr*) to search for (a submerged object) with or as if with a dredge; drag [C16: perhaps ultimately from Old English *dragan* to DRAW; see DRAG]

dredge² (drɛdʒ) *vb* to sprinkle or coat (food) with flour, sugar, etc [C16: from Old French *dragie*, perhaps from Latin *tragēmata* spices, from Greek] > 'dredger *n*

dredger ('drɛdʒə) *n* **1** Also called: **dredge** a vessel used for dredging, often bargelike and sometimes equipped with retractable steel piles that are driven into the bottom for stability **2** another name for **dredge¹** (sense 1)

dredge up *vb* (*tr, adverb*) **1** to bring to notice, esp with considerable effort and from an obscure, remote, or unlikely source: *to dredge up worthless ideas* **2** to raise with or as if with a dredge: *they dredged up the corpse from the lake*

dree (driː) *vb* **drees, dreeing, dreed** (*tr*) *Scot literary* to endure [Old English *drēogan*; related to Old Norse *drȳgja* to perpetrate]

D region or **D layer** *n* the lowest region of the ionosphere, extending from a height of about 60 kilometres to about 90 kilometres: contains a low concentration of free electrons and reflects low-frequency radio waves

dregs (drɛgz) *pl n* **1** solid particles that tend to settle at the bottom of some liquids, such as wine or coffee **2** residue or remains **3** *Brit slang* a despicable person [C14 *dreg*, from Old Norse *dregg*; compare Icelandic *dreggjar* dregs, Latin *fracēs* oil dregs]

dreich or **dreigh** (driːx) *adj Scot dialect* dreary [Middle English *dreig, drih* enduring, from Old English *drēog* (unattested); see DREE]

Dreiser ('draɪsə, -zə) *n* **Theodore (Herman Albert).** 1871–1945, US novelist; his works include *Sister Carrie* (1900) and *An American Tragedy* (1925)

drench (drɛntʃ) *vb* (*tr*) **1** to make completely wet; soak **2** to give liquid medicine to (an animal), esp by force ▷ *n* **3** the act or an instance of drenching **4** a dose of liquid medicine given to an animal [Old English *drencan* to cause to drink; related to Old High German *trenken*] > 'drenching *n, adj*

Drenthe (*Dutch* 'drɛntə) *n* a province of the NE Netherlands: a low plateau, with many raised bogs, partially reclaimed; agricultural, with oil deposits. Capital: Assen. Pop: 481 000 (2003 est). Area: 2647 sq km (1032 sq miles)

Dresden ('drɛzd³n) *n* **1** an industrial city in SE Germany, the capital of Saxony on the River Elbe: it was severely damaged in the Seven Years' War (1760); the baroque city was almost totally destroyed in World War II by Allied bombing (1945). Pop: 483 632 (2003 est) ▷ *adj* **2** relating to, designating, or made of Dresden china

Dresden china *n* porcelain ware, esp delicate and elegantly decorative objects and figures of high quality, made at Meissen, near Dresden, since 1710

dress (drɛs) *vb* **1** to put clothes on (oneself or another); attire **2** (*intr*) **a** to change one's clothes **b** to wear formal or evening clothes **3** (*tr*) to provide (someone) with clothing; clothe **4** (*tr*) to arrange merchandise in (a shop window) for effective display **5** (*tr*) to comb out or arrange (the hair) into position **6** (*tr*) to apply protective or therapeutic covering to (a wound, sore, etc) **7** (*tr*) to prepare (food, esp fowl and fish) for cooking or serving by cleaning, trimming, gutting, etc **8** (*tr*) to put a finish on (the surface of stone, metal, etc) **9** (*tr*) to till and cultivate (land), esp by applying manure, compost, or fertilizer **10** (*tr*) to prune and trim (trees, bushes, etc) **11** (*tr*) to groom (an animal, esp a horse) **12** (*tr*) to convert (tanned hides) into leather **13** *angling* to tie (a fly) **14** *military* to bring (troops) into line or (of troops) to come into line (esp in the phrase **dress ranks**) **15** dress ship *nautical* to decorate a vessel by displaying all signal flags on lines run from the bow to the stern over the mast trucks ▷ *n* **16** a one-piece garment for a woman, consisting of a skirt and bodice **17** complete style of clothing; costume: *formal dress; military dress* **18** (*modifier*) suitable or required for a formal occasion: *a dress shirt* **19** the outer covering or appearance, esp of living things: *trees in their spring dress of leaves* ▷ See also **dress down, dress up** [C14: from Old French *drecier*, ultimately from Latin *dirigere* to DIRECT]

dressage ('drɛsɑːʒ) *n* **1** the method of training a horse to perform manoeuvres in response to the rider's body signals **2** the manoeuvres performed by a horse trained in this method [French: preparation, from Old French *dresser* to prepare; see DRESS]

dress circle *n* a tier of seats in a theatre or other auditorium, usually the first gallery above the ground floor

dress code *n* a set of rules or guidelines regarding the manner of dress acceptable in an office, restaurant, etc

dress down *vb* (*adverb*) **1** (*tr*) *informal* to reprimand severely or scold (a person) **2** (*intr*) to dress in a casual or informal manner, esp at work

dress-down Friday *n* a policy adopted by some business organizations of promoting a relaxed atmosphere by allowing employees to wear informal clothing on a Friday

dresser¹ ('drɛsə) *n* **1** a set of shelves, usually also with cupboards or drawers, for storing or displaying dishes, etc **2** *US* a chest of drawers for storing clothing in a bedroom or dressing room, often having a mirror on the top [C14 *dressour*, from Old French *dreceore*, from *drecier* to arrange; see DRESS]

dresser² ('drɛsə) *n* **1** a person who dresses in a specified way: *a fashionable dresser* **2** *theatre* a person employed to assist actors in putting on and taking off their costumes **3** a tool used for dressing stone or other materials **4** *Brit* a person who assists a surgeon during operations **5** *Brit* See **window-dresser**

dressing ('drɛsɪŋ) *n* **1** a sauce for food, esp for salad **2** Also called (in Britain and certain other countries): **stuffing** *US & Canadian* a mixture of chopped and seasoned ingredients with which poultry, meat, etc, is stuffed before cooking. **3** a covering for a wound, sore, etc **4** manure or artificial fertilizer spread on land **5** size used for stiffening textiles **6** the processes in the conversion of certain rough tanned hides into leather ready for use

dressing-down *n* *informal* a severe scolding or thrashing

dressing gown *n* a full robe worn before dressing or for lounging

dressing room *n* **1** *theatre* a room backstage for an actor to change clothing and to make up **2** any room used for changing clothes, such as one at a sports ground or off a bedroom

dressing station *n* *military* a first-aid post close to a combat area

dressing table *n* a piece of bedroom furniture with a mirror and a set of drawers for clothes, cosmetics, etc

dressmaker ('drɛs,meɪkə) *n* a person whose occupation is making clothes, esp for women > '**dress,making** *n*

dress parade *n* *military* a formal parade of sufficient ceremonial importance for the wearing of dress uniform

dress rehearsal *n* **1** the last complete rehearsal of a play or other work, using costumes, scenery, lighting, etc, as for the first night **2** any full-scale practice

dress shirt *n* a man's shirt, usually white, worn as part of formal evening dress, usually having a stiffened or decorative front

dress suit *n* an ensemble of matching formal evening wear

dress uniform *n* *military* formal ceremonial uniform

dress up *vb* (*adverb*) **1** to attire (oneself or another) in one's best clothes **2** to put fancy dress, disguise, etc, on (oneself or another), as in children's games **3** (*tr*) to improve the appearance or impression of: *it's no good trying to dress up the facts*

dressy ('drɛsɪ) *adj* dressier, dressiest **1** (of clothes) elegant **2** (of persons) dressing stylishly > '**dressiness** *n*

drew (druː) *vb* the past tense of **draw**

drey or **dray** (dreɪ) *n* a squirrel's nest [C17: of unknown origin]

Dreyfus ('dreɪfəs; *French* drɛfys) *n* **Alfred** (alfrɛd). 1859–1935, French army officer, a Jew whose false imprisonment for treason (1894) raised issues of anti-semitism and militarism that dominated French politics until his release (1906)

dribble ('drɪbəl) *vb* **1** (*usually intr*) to flow or allow to flow in a thin stream or drops; trickle **2** (*intr*) to allow saliva to trickle from the mouth **3** (in soccer, basketball, hockey, etc) to propel (the ball) by repeatedly tapping it with the hand, foot, or stick ▷ *n* **4** a small quantity of liquid falling in drops or flowing in a thin stream **5** a small quantity or supply **6** an act or instance of dribbling [C16: frequentative of *drib*, variant of DRIP] > '**dribbler** *n* > '**dribbly** *adj*

driblet or **dribblet** ('drɪblɪt) *n* a small quantity or amount, as of liquid [C17: from obsolete *drib* to fall bit by bit + -LET]

dribs and drabs (drɪbz) *pl n* small sporadic amounts

dried (draɪd) *vb* the past tense and past participle of **dry**

drier¹ ('draɪə) *adj* a comparative of **dry**

drier² ('draɪə) *n* a variant spelling of **dryer¹**

Driesch (*German* driːʃ) *n* **Hans Adolf Eduard** (hans 'aːdɔlf ('ɛdʊaːd). 1867–1941, German zoologist and embryologist

driest ('draɪɪst) *adj* a superlative of **dry**

drift (drɪft) *vb* (*mainly intr*) **1** (*also tr*) to be carried along by or as if by currents of air or water or (of a current) to carry (a vessel, etc) along **2** to move aimlessly from place to place or from one activity to another **3** to wander or move gradually away from a fixed course or point; stray **4** (*also tr*) (of snow, sand, etc) to accumulate in heaps or banks or to drive (snow, sand, etc) into heaps or banks ▷ *n* **5** something piled up by the wind or current, such as a snowdrift **6** tendency, trend, meaning, or purport: *the drift of the argument* **7** a state of indecision or inaction **8** the extent to which a vessel, aircraft, projectile, etc is driven off its course by adverse winds, tide, or current **9** a general tendency of surface ocean water to flow in the direction of the prevailing winds: *North Atlantic Drift* **10** a driving movement, force, or influence; impulse **11** a controlled four-wheel skid, used by racing drivers to take bends at high speed **12** a loose unstratified deposit of sand, gravel, etc, esp one transported and deposited by a glacier or ice sheet **13** a horizontal passage in a mine that follows the mineral vein **14** something, esp a group of animals, driven along by human or natural agencies: *a drift of cattle* **15** Also called: **driftpin** a tapering steel tool driven into holes to enlarge or align them before bolting or riveting **16** an uncontrolled slow change in some operating characteristic of a piece of equipment, esp an electronic circuit or component **17** *South African* a ford [C13: from Old Norse: snowdrift; related to Old High German *trift* pasturage]

driftage ('drɪftɪdʒ) *n* **1** the act of drifting **2** matter carried along or deposited by drifting **3** the amount by which an aircraft or vessel has drifted from its intended course

drifter ('drɪftə) *n* **1** a person or thing that drifts **2** a person who moves aimlessly from place to place, usually without a regular job **3** a boat used for drift-net fishing

drift ice *n* masses of ice floating in the open sea

drift net *n* a large fishing net supported by floats or attached to a drifter that is allowed to drift with the tide or current

driftwood ('drɪft,wʊd) *n* wood floating on or washed ashore by the sea or other body of water

drill¹ (drɪl) *n* **1** a rotating tool that is inserted into a drilling machine or tool for boring cylindrical holes **2** a hand tool, either manually or electrically operated, for drilling holes **3** *military* **a** a training in procedures or movements, as for ceremonial parades and the use of weapons **b** (*as modifier*): drill hall **4** strict and often repetitive training or exercises used as a method of teaching **5** *informal* correct procedure or routine **6** a marine gastropod mollusc, *Urosalpinx cinera*, closely related to the whelk, that preys on oysters ▷ *vb* **7** to pierce, bore, or cut (a hole) in (material) with or as if with a drill: *to drill a hole; to drill metal* **8** to instruct or be instructed in military procedures or movements **9** (*tr*) to teach by rigorous exercises or training **10** (*tr*) *informal* to hit (a ball) in a straight line at great speed **11** (*tr*) *informal* to riddle with bullets [C17: from Middle Dutch *drillen*; related to Old High German *drāen* to turn] > 'driller *n*

drill² (drɪl) *n* **1** a machine for planting seeds in rows or depositing fertilizer **2** a small furrow in which seeds are sown **3** a row of seeds planted using a drill ▷ *vb* **4** to plant (seeds) by means of a drill [C18: of uncertain origin; compare German *Rille* furrow] > 'driller *n*

drill³ (drɪl) *or* **drilling** *n* a hard-wearing twill-weave cotton cloth, used for uniforms, etc [C18: variant of German *Drillich*, from Latin *trilīx*, from TRI- + *licium* thread]

drill⁴ (drɪl) *n* an Old World monkey, *Mandrillus leucophaeus*, of W Africa, related to the mandrill but smaller and less brightly coloured [C17: from a West African word; compare MANDRILL]

drill down *vb* (*intr, adverb*) to look at or examine something in depth: *to drill down through financial data*

drilling platform *n* a structure, either fixed to the sea bed or mobile, which supports the machinery and equipment (the drilling rig), together with the stores, required for digging an offshore oil well

drilling rig *n* **1** the full name for **rig¹** (sense 6) **2** a mobile drilling platform used for exploratory offshore drilling

drillmaster ('drɪl,mɑːstə) *n* **1** Also called: **drill sergeant** *obsolete* a military drill instructor **2** a person who instructs in a strict manner

drill press *n* a machine tool for boring holes, having a stand and work table with facilities for lowering the tool to the workpiece

drily *or* **dryly** ('draɪlɪ) *adv* in a dry manner

drink (drɪŋk) *vb* **drinks, drinking, drank** (dræŋk), **drunk** (drʌŋk) **1** to swallow (a liquid); imbibe **2** (*tr*) to take in or soak up (liquid); absorb **3** (*tr; usually foll by in*) to pay close attention (to); be fascinated (by) **4** (*tr*) to bring (oneself into a certain condition) by consuming alcohol **5** (*tr; often foll by away*) to dispose of or ruin by excessive expenditure on alcohol **6** (*intr*) to consume alcohol, esp to excess **7** (*when intr, foll by to*) to drink (a toast) in celebration, honour, or hope (of) **8 drink someone under the table** to be able to drink more intoxicating beverage than someone **9** drink the health of to salute or celebrate with a toast **10** drink with the flies *Austral informal* to drink alone ▷ *n* **11** liquid suitable for drinking; any beverage **12** alcohol or its habitual or excessive consumption **13** a portion of liquid for drinking; draught **14** the drink *informal* the sea [Old English *drincan*; related to Old Frisian *drinka*, Gothic *drigkan*, Old High German *trinkan*] > 'drinkable *adj* > 'drinker *n*

drink-driving *n* (*modifier*) of or relating to driving a car after drinking alcohol: *drink-driving offences; drink-driving campaign*

drinking fountain *n* a device for providing a flow or jet of drinking water, usually in public places

drinking-up time *n* (in Britain) a short time allowed for finishing drinks before closing time in a public house

drinking water *n* water reserved or suitable for drinking

Drinkwater ('drɪŋk,wɔːtə) *n* **John.** 1882–1937, English dramatist, poet, and critic; author of chronicle plays such as *Abraham Lincoln* (1918) and *Mary Stuart* (1921)

drip (drɪp) *vb* **drips, dripping, dripped 1** to fall or let fall in drops ▷ *n* **2** the formation and falling of drops of liquid **3** the sound made by falling drops **4** *architect* a projection at the front lower edge of a sill or cornice designed to throw water clear of the wall below **5** *informal* an inane, insipid person **6** *med* **a** the usually intravenous drop-by-drop administration of a

therapeutic solution, as of salt or sugar **b** the solution administered **c** the equipment used to administer a solution in this way [Old English *dryppan*, from *dropa* DROP]

drip-dry *adj* **1** designating clothing or a fabric that will dry relatively free of creases if hung up when wet ▷ *vb* **-dries, -drying, -dried 2** to dry or become dry thus

drip-feed *n* **1** another name for **drip** (sense 6) ▷ *vb* **drip feed** (*tr*) **2** to administer a solution (to someone) by means of a drip-feed **3** to supply information constantly but in small amounts **4** *informal* to fund (a new company) in stages rather than by injecting a large sum at its inception ▷ *n* **5** a constant supply of small amounts of information

dripping ('drɪpɪŋ) *n* **1** the fat exuded by roasting meat **2** (*often plural*) liquid that falls in drops ▷ *adv* **3** (*intensifier*): *dripping wet*

drippy ('drɪpɪ) *adj* **-pier, -piest 1** *informal* mawkish, insipid, or inane **2** tending to drip

drive (draɪv) *vb* **drives, driving, drove** (drəʊv), **driven** ('drɪvᵊn) **1** to push, propel, or be pushed or propelled **2** to control and guide the movement of (a vehicle, draught animal, etc): *to drive a car* **3** (*tr*) to compel or urge to work or act, esp excessively **4** (*tr*) to goad or force into a specified attitude or state: *work drove him to despair* **5** (*tr*) to cause (an object) to make or form (a hole, crack, etc) **6** to move or cause to move rapidly by striking or throwing with force **7** *sport* to hit (a ball) very hard and straight, as (in cricket) with the bat swinging more or less vertically **8** *golf* to strike (the ball) with a driver, as in teeing off **9** (*tr*) **a** to chase (game) from cover into more open ground **b** to search (an area) for game **10** to transport or be transported in a driven vehicle **11** (*intr*) to rush or dash violently, esp against an obstacle or solid object **12** (*tr*) to carry through or transact with vigour (esp in the phrase **drive a hard bargain**) **13** (*tr*) to force (a component) into or out of its location by means of blows or a press **14** *mining* to excavate horizontally **15** (*tr*) *NZ* to fell (a tree or trees) by the impact of another felled tree **16 drive home a** to cause to penetrate to the fullest extent **b** to make clear by special emphasis ▷ *n* **17** the act of driving **18** a trip or journey in a driven vehicle **19 a** a road for vehicles, esp a private road leading to a house **b** (*capital when part of a street name*): *Woodland Drive* **20** vigorous or urgent pressure, as in business **21 a** a united effort, esp directed towards a common goal: *a charity drive* **22** *Brit* a large gathering of persons to play cards, etc. See **whist drive 23** energy, ambition, or initiative **24** *psychol* a motive or interest, such as sex, hunger, or ambition, that actuates an organism to attain a goal **25** a sustained and powerful military offensive **26 a** the means by which force, torque, motion, or power is transmitted in a mechanism: *fluid drive* **b** (*as modifier*): *a drive shaft* **27** *sport* a hard straight shot or stroke **28** a search for and chasing of game towards waiting guns **29** *electronics* the signal applied to the input of an amplifier [Old English *drīfan*; related to Old Frisian *drīva*, Old Norse *drīfa*, Gothic *dreiban*, Old High German *trīban*] > 'drivable *or* 'driveable *adj*

drive at *vb* (*intr, preposition*) *informal* to intend or mean: *what are you driving at?*

drive-by shooting *n* an incident in which a person, building, or vehicle is shot at by someone in a moving vehicle. Sometimes shortened to **drive-by**

drive-in *adj* **1** denoting a public facility or service designed to be used by patrons seated in their cars: *a drive-in bank* ▷ *n* **2** *chiefly US & Canadian* a cinema designed to be used in such a manner

drivel ('drɪvᵊl) *vb* **-els, -elling, -elled** *or US* **-els, -eling, -eled 1** to allow (saliva) to flow from the mouth; dribble **2** (*intr*) to speak foolishly or childishly ▷ *n* **3** foolish or senseless talk **4** saliva flowing from the mouth; slaver [Old English *dreflian* to slaver; see DRAFF] > 'driveller *or US* 'driveler *n*

driven ('drɪvᵊn) *vb* the past participle of **drive**

driver ('draɪvə) *n* **1** a person who drives a vehicle **2 in the driver's seat** in a position of control **3** a person who drives animals **4** a mechanical component that exerts a force on another to produce motion **5** *golf* a club, a No. 1

wood, with a large head and deep face for tee shots **6** *electronics* a circuit whose output provides the input of another circuit **7** *computing* a computer program that controls a device **8** something that creates and fuels activity, or gives force or impetus > **'driverless** *adj*

drive-thru *n* **a** a takeaway restaurant, bank, etc designed so that customers can use it without leaving their cars **b** (*as modifier*): *a drive-thru restaurant*

drive-time *n* **a** the time of day when many people are driving to or from work, regarded as a broadcasting slot **b** (*as modifier*): *the daily drive-time show*

driveway ('draɪvˌweɪ) *n* a private road for vehicles, often connecting a house or garage with a public road; drive

driving chain *n* *engineering* a roller chain that transmits power from one toothed wheel to another. Also called: drive chain

driving licence *n* an official document or certificate authorizing a person to drive a motor vehicle

drizzle ('drɪzəl) *n* **1** very light rain, specifically consisting of droplets less than 0.5 mm in diameter ▷ *vb* (*intr*) to rain lightly [Old English *drēosan* to fall; related to Old Saxon *driosan*, Gothic *driusan*, Norwegian *drjōsa*] > **'drizzly** *adj*

Drnovsek (dɜːˈnɒvʃɛk) *n* **Ivan.** born 1950, Slovenian politician, president of Slovenia from 2002

Drobny ('drɒbnɪ; *Czech* 'drɔbni:) *n* **Jaroslav** ('jærəʊˌslɑːvˈ *Czech* 'jarɔslaf). 1921–2001, British tennis and ice-hockey player, born in Czechoslovakia: Wimbledon champion 1954: a member of the Czech ice-hockey team in the 1948 Olympic Games

Drogheda ('drɔɪɪdə) *n* a port in NE Republic of Ireland, in Co Louth near the mouth of the River Boyne: captured by Cromwell in 1649 and its inhabitants massacred. Pop: 31 020 (2002)

drogue (drəʊg) *n* **1** any funnel-like device, esp one of canvas, used as a sea anchor **2 a** a small parachute released behind a jet aircraft to reduce its landing speed **b** a small parachute released before a heavier main parachute during the landing of a spacecraft **3** a device towed behind an aircraft as a target for firing practice **4** a funnel-shaped device on the end of the refuelling hose of a tanker aircraft, to assist stability and the location of the probe of the receiving aircraft **5** another name for **windsock** [c18: probably based ultimately on Old English *dragan* to DRAW]

droll (drəʊl) *adj* amusing in a quaint or odd manner; comical [c17: from French *drôle* scamp, from Middle Dutch: imp] > **'drollness** *n* > **'drolly** *adv*

drollery ('drəʊlərɪ) *n, pl* -eries **1** humour; comedy **2** *rare* a droll act, story, or remark

Drôme (French drom) *n* a department of SE France, in Rhône-Alpes region. Capital: Valence. Pop: 452 652 (2003 est. Area: 6561 sq km (2559 sq miles)

-drome *n combining form* **1** a course, racecourse: *hippodrome* **2** a large place for a special purpose: *aerodrome* [via Latin from Greek *dromos* race, course]

dromedary ('drʌmədərɪ, -drɪ, 'drɒm-) *n, pl* -daries a type of Arabian camel bred for racing and riding, having a single hump and long slender legs [c14: from Late Latin *dromedārius*, from Greek *dromas* running]

-dromous *adj combining form* moving or running: *anadromous; catadromous* [via New Latin from Greek *-dromos*, from *dromos* a running]

drone¹ (drəʊn) *n* **1** a male bee in a colony of social bees, whose sole function is to mate with the queen **2** *Brit* a person who lives off the work of others **3** a pilotless radio-controlled aircraft [Old English *drān*; related to Old High German *treno* drone, Gothic *drunjus* noise, Greek *tenthrēnē* wasp; see DRONE²] > **'dronish** *adj*

drone² (drəʊn) *vb* **1** (*intr*) to make a monotonous low dull sound; buzz or hum **2** (when *intr*, foll by *on*) to utter (words) in a monotonous tone, esp to talk without stopping ▷ *n* **3** a monotonous low dull sound **4** *music* **a** a sustained bass note or chord of unvarying pitch accompanying a melody **b** (*as modifier*): *a drone bass* **5** *music* one of the single-reed pipes in a set of bagpipes, used for accompanying the melody played on the chanter **6** a person who speaks in a low monotonous tone [c16: related to DRONE¹ and Middle Dutch *drōnen*, German

dröhnen] > **'droning** *adj*

drone aircraft *n* a pilotless radio-controlled aircraft used for reconnaissance or bombing

drongo ('drɒŋgəʊ) *n, pl* -gos **1** Also called: drongo shrike any insectivorous songbird of the family *Dicruridae*, of the Old World tropics, having a glossy black plumage, a forked tail, and a stout bill **2** *Austral & NZ slang* a slow-witted person [c19: from Malagasy]

drool (druːl) *vb* **1** (*intr*; often foll by *over*) to show excessive enthusiasm (for) or pleasure (in); gloat (over) ▷ *vb, n* **2** another word for **drivel** (senses 1, 2, 4) [c19: probably alteration of DRIVEL]

droop (druːp) *vb* **1** to sag or allow to sag, as from weakness or exhaustion; hang down; sink **2** (*intr*) to be overcome by weariness; languish; flag **3** (*intr*) to lose courage; become dejected ▷ *n* **4** the act or state of drooping [c13: from Old Norse *drúpa*; see DROP] > **'drooping** *adj* > **'droopy** *adj*

drop (drɒp) *n* **1** a small quantity of liquid that forms or falls in a spherical or pear-shaped mass; globule **2** a very small quantity of liquid **3** a very small quantity of anything **4** something resembling a drop in shape or size, such as a decorative pendant or small sweet **5** the act or an instance of falling; descent **6** a decrease in amount or value; slump: *a drop in prices* **7** the vertical distance that anything may fall **8** a steep or sheer incline or slope **9** short for **fruit drop 10** the act of unloading troops, equipment, or supplies by parachute **11** (in cable television) a short spur from a trunk cable that feeds signals to an individual house **12** *theatre* See **drop curtain 13** another word for **trap door, gallows 14** *chiefly US & Canadian* a slot or aperture through which an object can be dropped to fall into a receptacle **15** *Austral cricket slang* a fall of the wicket: *he came in at first drop* **16** See **drop shot 17** at the drop of a hat without hesitation or delay **18** have the drop on someone *US & NZ* to have the advantage over someone ▷ *vb* drops, dropping, dropped **19** (of liquids) to fall or allow to fall in globules **20** to fall or allow to fall vertically **21** (*tr*) to allow to fall by letting go of **22** to sink or fall or cause to sink or fall to the ground, as from a blow, wound, shot, weariness, etc **23** (*intr*; foll by *back, behind*, etc) to fall, move, or go in a specified manner, direction, etc **24** (*intr*; foll by *in, by*, etc) *informal* to pay a casual visit (to) **25** to decrease or cause to decrease in amount or value **26** to sink or cause to sink to a lower position, as on a scale **27** to make or become less in strength, volume, etc **28** (*intr*) to sink or decline in health or condition **29** (*intr*; sometimes foll by *into*) to pass easily into a state or condition: *to drop a habit* **30** (*intr*) to move along gently as with a current of water or air **31** (*tr*) to allow to pass casually in conversation: *to drop a hint* **32** (*tr*) to leave out (a word or letter) **33** (*tr*) to set down or unload (passengers or goods) **34** (*tr*) to send or post: *drop me a line* **35** (*tr*) to discontinue; terminate: *let's drop the matter* **36** (*tr*) to cease to associate or have to do with **37** (*tr*) *slang, chiefly US* to cease to employ **38** (*tr*; sometimes foll by *in, off*, etc) *informal* to leave or deposit, esp at a specified place **39** (of animals) to give birth to (offspring) **40** *slang, chiefly US & Canadian* to lose (money), esp when gambling **41** (*tr*) to lengthen (a hem, etc) **42** (*tr*) to unload (troops, equipment, or supplies) by parachute **43** (*tr*) *nautical* to leave behind; sail out of sight of **44** (*tr*) *sport* to omit (a player) from a team **45** (*tr*) to lose (a score, game, or contest) **46** (*tr*) *sport* to hit or throw (a ball) into a goal **47** (*tr*) to hit (a ball) with a drop shot ▷ *n, vb* **48** *rugby* short for **drop kick** ▷ See also **drop off, dropout, drops** [Old English *dropian*; related to Old High German *triofan* to DRIP]

drop curtain *n* *theatre* a curtain that is suspended from the flies and can be raised and lowered onto the stage

drop-dead *adv informal* outstandingly or exceptionally: *drop-dead gorgeous*

drop-dead date *n* an absolute deadline that cannot be missed

drop-down menu *n* a menu that appears on a computer screen when its title is selected and remains on display until dismissed

drop forge *n* **1** Also called: drop hammer a device for forging metal between two dies, one of which is fixed, the other acting by gravity or by steam or hydraulic pressure ▷ *vb* drop-forge (*tr*) **2** to forge (metal) into (a component) by the use of a drop forge

drop goal *n rugby* a goal scored with a drop kick during the run of play

drop hammer *n* another name for **drop forge**

drop-in centre *n social welfare* (in Britain) a daycentre run by the social services or a charity that clients may attend on an informal basis

drop kick *n* **1** a kick in certain sports such as rugby, in which the ball is dropped and kicked as it bounces from the ground **2** a wrestling attack, illegal in amateur wrestling, in which a wrestler leaps in the air and kicks his opponent in the face or body with both feet **3** *Austral slang* a stupid or worthless person ▷ *vb* drop-kick **4** to kick (a ball, etc) using a drop kick

drop leaf *n* **a** a hinged flap on a table that can be raised and supported by a bracket or additional pivoted leg to extend the surface **b** (*as modifier*): *a drop-leaf table*

droplet ('drɒplɪt) *n* a tiny drop

drop lock *n finance* a variable-rate bank loan used on international markets that is automatically replaced by a fixed-rate long-term bond if the long-term interest rates fall to a specified level; it thus combines the advantages of a bank loan with those of a bond

drop off *vb* (*adverb*) **1** (*intr*) to grow smaller or less; decline **2** (*tr*) to allow to alight; set down **3** (*intr*) *informal* to fall asleep ▷ *n* drop-off **4** a steep or vertical descent **5** a sharp decrease

dropout ('drɒp,aʊt) *n* **1** a student who fails to complete a school or college course **2** a person who rejects conventional society **3** drop-out *rugby* a drop kick taken by the defending team to restart play, as after a touchdown **4** drop-out *electronics* a momentary loss of signal in a magnetic recording medium as a result of an imperfection in its magnetic coating ▷ *vb* drop out **5** (*intr, adverb*; often foll by *of*) to abandon or withdraw from (a school, social group, job, etc)

dropper ('drɒpə) *n* **1** a small tube having a rubber bulb at one end for drawing up and dispensing drops of liquid **2** a person or thing that drops **3** *angling* a short length of monofilament by which a fly is attached to the main trace or leader above the tail fly **4** *Austral & NZ* a batten attached to the top wire of a fence to keep the wires apart

droppings ('drɒpɪŋz) *pl n* the dung of certain animals, such as rabbits, sheep, and birds

drops (drɒps) *pl n* any liquid medication applied by means of a dropper

drop scone *n* a flat spongy cake made by dropping a spoonful of batter on a griddle

drop shot *n* **a** *tennis* a softly-played return that drops abruptly after clearing the net, intended to give an opponent no chance of reaching the ball and usually achieved by imparting backspin **b** *squash* a similar shot that stops abruptly after hitting the front wall of the court

dropsy ('drɒpsɪ) *n* **1** *pathol* a condition characterized by an accumulation of watery fluid in the tissues or in a body cavity **2** *slang* a tip or bribe [c13: shortened from *ydropise*, from Latin *hydrōpisis*, from Greek *hudrōps*, from *hudōr* water] > dropsical ('drɒpsɪk°l) or 'dropsied *adj*

droshky ('drɒʃkɪ) or **drosky** ('drɒskɪ) *n, pl* -kies an open four-wheeled horse-drawn passenger carriage, formerly used in Russia [c19: from Russian *drozhki*, diminutive of *drogi* a wagon, from *droga* shaft]

drosophila (drɒ'sɒfɪlə) *n, pl* -las or -lae (-,liː) any small dipterous fly of the genus *Drosophila*, esp *D. melanogaster*, a species widely used in laboratory genetics studies: family *Drosophilidae*. They feed on plant sap, decaying fruit, etc. Also called: fruit fly [c19: New Latin, from Greek *drosos* dew, water + *-phila*; see *-PHILE*]

dross (drɒs) *n* **1** the scum formed, usually by oxidation, on the surfaces of molten metals **2** worthless matter; waste [Old English *drōs* dregs; related to Old High German *truosana*] > 'drossy *adj* > 'drossiness *n*

drought (draʊt) *n* **1** a prolonged period of scanty rainfall **2** a prolonged shortage [Old English *drūgoth*; related to

Dutch *droogte*; see DRY] > 'droughty *adj*

drove¹ (drəʊv) *vb* the past tense of **drive**

drove² (drəʊv) *n* **1** a herd of livestock being driven together **2** (*often plural*) a moving crowd of people ▷ *vb* **3** (*tr*) to drive (a group of livestock), usually for a considerable distance [Old English *drāf* herd; related to Middle Low German *drēfwech* cattle pasture; see DRIVE, DRIFT]

drover ('drəʊvə) *n* a person whose occupation is the driving of sheep or cattle, esp to and from market

drown (draʊn) *vb* **1** to die or kill by immersion in liquid **2** (*tr*) to destroy or get rid of as if by submerging: *he drowned his sorrows in drink* **3** (*tr*) to drench thoroughly; inundate; flood **4** (*tr*; sometimes foll by *out*) to render (a sound) inaudible by making a loud noise [c13: probably from Old English *druncnian*; related to Old Norse *drukna* to be drowned]

drowse (draʊz) *vb* **1** to be or cause to be sleepy, dull, or sluggish ▷ *n* **2** the state of being drowsy [c16: probably from Old English *drūsian* to sink; related to *drēosan* to fall]

drowsy ('draʊzɪ) *adj* drowsier, drowsiest **1** heavy with sleepiness; sleepy **2** inducing sleep; soporific **3** sluggish or lethargic; dull > 'drowsily *adv* > 'drowsiness *n*

drub (drʌb) *vb* drubs, drubbing, drubbed (*tr*) **1** to beat as with a stick; cudgel; club **2** to defeat utterly, as in a contest **3** to drum or stamp (the feet) **4** to instil with force or repetition ▷ *n* **5** a blow, as from a stick [c17: probably from Arabic *dáraba* to beat]

drubbing ('drʌbɪŋ) *n* **1** a beating, as with a stick, cudgel, etc **2** a comprehensive or heavy defeat, esp in a sporting competition

drudge (drʌdʒ) *n* **1** a person, such as a servant, who works hard at wearisome menial tasks ▷ *vb* **2** (*intr*) to toil at such tasks [c16: perhaps from *druggen* to toil] > 'drudger *n* > 'drudgingly *adv*

drudgery ('drʌdʒərɪ) *n, pl* -eries hard, menial, and monotonous work

drug (drʌg) *n* **1** any synthetic, semisynthetic, or natural chemical substance used in the treatment, prevention, or diagnosis of disease, or for other medical reasons. Related adj: **pharmaceutical 2** a chemical substance, esp a narcotic, taken for the pleasant effects it produces **3** drug on the market a commodity available in excess of the demands of the market ▷ *vb* drugs, drugging, drugged (*tr*) **4** to mix a drug with (food, drink, etc) **5** to administer a drug to **6** to stupefy or poison with or as if with a drug [c14: from Old French *drogue*, probably of Germanic origin] > 'druggy *adj*

drug addict *n* any person who is abnormally dependent on narcotic drugs

drug-driving *n* (*modifier*) of or relating to driving while under the influence of drugs, esp illegal drugs

drugget ('drʌgɪt) *n* a coarse fabric used as a protective floor-covering, etc [c16: from French *droguet* useless fabric, from *drogue* trash]

druggie ('drʌgɪ) *n informal* a drug addict

druggist ('drʌgɪst) *n US & Canadian* a person qualified to prepare and dispense drugs. Also called: **pharmacist**

druglord ('drʌg,lɔːd) *n* a criminal who controls the distribution and sale of large quantities of illegal drugs

drugstore ('drʌg,stɔː) *n US & Canadian* a shop where medical prescriptions are made up and a wide variety of goods and sometimes light meals are sold

druid ('druːɪd) *n* (*sometimes capital*) **1** a member of an ancient order of priests in Gaul, Britain, and Ireland in the pre-Christian era **2** a member of any of several modern movements attempting to revive druidism [c16: from Latin *druides*, of Gaulish origin; compare Old Irish *druid* wizards] > druidess ('druːɪdɪs) *fem n* > dru'idic or dru'idical *adj* > 'druid,ism *n*

drum (drʌm) *n* **1** *music* a percussion instrument sounded by striking a membrane stretched across the opening of a hollow cylinder or hemisphere **2** beat the drum for *informal* to attempt to arouse interest in **3** the sound produced by a drum or any similar sound **4** an object that resembles a drum in shape, such as a large spool or a cylindrical container **5** *architect* **a** one of a number of cylindrical blocks of stone used to construct the shaft of a column **b** the wall or structure supporting a dome or cupola **6** short for **eardrum 7** Also called: **drumfish** any of various North American marine and freshwater sciaenid fishes, such as *Equetus pulcher* (**striped drum**), that utter a drumming sound **8** a type of hollow rotor for steam turbines or axial compressors **9** *archaic* a drummer **10** the drum *Austral informal* the necessary information (esp in the phrase **give (someone) the drum**) ▷ *vb* **drums, drumming, drummed 11** to play (music) on or as if on a drum **12** to beat or tap (the fingers) rhythmically or regularly **13** (*intr*) (of birds) to produce a rhythmic sound, as by beating the bill against a tree, branch, etc **14** (*tr*; sometimes foll by *up*) to summon or call by drumming **15** (*tr*) to instil by constant repetition ▷ See also **drum up** [c16: probably from Middle Dutch *tromme*, of imitative origin]

drumbeat ('drʌm,biːt) *n* the sound made by beating a drum

drum brake *n* a type of brake used on the wheels of vehicles, consisting of two pivoted shoes that rub against the inside walls of the brake drum when the brake is applied

drumhead ('drʌm,hɛd) *n* **1** *music* the part of a drum that is actually struck with a stick or the hand **2** the head of a capstan, pierced with holes for the capstan bars **3** another name for **eardrum**

drumlin ('drʌmlɪn) *n* a streamlined mound of glacial drift, rounded or elongated in the direction of the original flow of ice [c19: from Irish Gaelic *druim* ridge + -*lin*–LING[1]]

drum machine *n* a synthesizer specially programmed to reproduce the sound of drums and other percussion instruments in variable rhythms and combinations selected by the musician; the resulting beat is produced continually until stopped or changed

drum major *n* the noncommissioned officer, usually of warrant officer's rank, who is appointed to command the corps of drums of a military band and who is in command of both the drums and the band when paraded together

drum majorette *n* a girl who marches at the head of a procession, twirling a baton

drummer ('drʌmə) *n* **1** a person who plays a drum or set of drums **2** *chiefly US* a salesman, esp a travelling salesman

Drummond of Hawthornden ('drʌmənd, 'hɔːθɔːndən) *n* **William.** 1585–1649, Scottish poet, historian, and royalist pamphleteer

drum'n'bass *or* **drum and bass** *n* **a** a type of electronic dance music using mainly bass guitar and drum sounds **b** (*as modifier*): *a drum'n'bass backing*

drumstick ('drʌm,stɪk) *n* **1** a stick used for playing a drum **2** the lower joint of the leg of a cooked fowl

drum up *vb* (*tr, adverb*) to evoke or obtain (support, business, etc) by solicitation or canvassing

drunk (drʌŋk) *adj* **1** intoxicated with alcohol to the extent of losing control over normal physical and mental functions **2** overwhelmed by strong influence or emotion: *drunk with joy* ▷ *n* **3** a person who is drunk or drinks habitually to excess **4** *informal* a drinking bout [Old English *druncen*, past participle of *drincan* to drink; see DRINK]

drunkard ('drʌŋkəd) *n* a person who is frequently or habitually drunk

drunkathon ('drʌŋkə,θɒn) *n* *informal* a session in which excessive quantities of alcohol are consumed

drunken ('drʌŋkən) *adj* **1** intoxicated with or as if with alcohol **2** frequently or habitually drunk **3** (*prenominal*) caused by or relating to alcoholic intoxication: *a drunken brawl* > **drunkenly** *adv* > **drunkenness** *n*

drunk tank *n* *informal* a large police cell used for detaining drunks overnight

drupe (druːp) *n* an indehiscent fruit consisting of outer epicarp, fleshy or fibrous mesocarp, and stony endocarp enclosing a single seed, as in the peach, plum, and cherry [c18: from Latin *druppa* wrinkled overripe olive, from Greek: olive] > **drupaceous** (druː'peɪʃəs) *adj*

drupelet ('druːplɪt) *or* **drupel** ('druːpᵊl) *n* a small drupe, usually one of a number forming a compound fruit

Druse *or* **Druze** (druːz) *n, pl* **Druse** *or* **Druze a** a member of a religious sect, mainly living in Syria, Lebanon, and Israel, having certain characteristics in common with Muslims **b** (*as modifier*): *Druse beliefs* [c18: from Arabic *Durūz* the Druses, after *Ismail al-Darazi* Ismail the tailor, 11th-century Muslim leader who founded the sect]

dry (draɪ) *adj* **drier, driest** *or* **dryer, dryest 1** lacking moisture; not damp or wet **2** having little or no rainfall **3** not in or under water: *dry land* **4** having the water drained away or evaporated: *a dry river* **5** not providing milk: *a dry cow* **6** (of the eyes) free from tears **7 a** *informal* in need of a drink; thirsty **b** causing thirst: *dry work* **8** eaten without butter, jam, etc: *dry toast* **9** (of a wine, cider, etc) not sweet **10** *pathol* not accompanied by or producing a mucous or watery discharge: *a dry cough* **11** consisting of solid as opposed to liquid substances or commodities **12** without adornment; plain: *dry facts* **13** lacking interest or stimulation: *a dry book* **14** lacking warmth or emotion; cold: *a dry greeting* **15** (of wit or humour) shrewd and keen in an impersonal, sarcastic, or laconic way **16** opposed to or prohibiting the sale of alcoholic liquor for human consumption: *a dry area* **17** *electronics* (of a soldered electrical joint) imperfect because the solder has not adhered to the metal, thus reducing conductance ▷ *vb* **dries, drying, dried 18** (when *intr*, often foll by *off*) to make or become dry or free from moisture **19** (*tr*) to preserve (meat, vegetables, fruit, etc) by removing the moisture ▷ *n, pl* **drys** *or* **dries 20** *Brit informal* a Conservative politician who is considered to be a hard-liner **21** the **dry** *Austral informal* the dry season ▷ See also **dry out, dry up** [Old English *drӯge*; related to Old High German *truckan*, Old Norse *draugr* dry wood] > **dryness** *n*

dryad ('draɪəd, -æd) *n, pl* **-ads** *or* **-ades** (-ə,diːz) *Greek myth* a nymph or divinity of the woods [c14: from Latin *Dryas*, from Greek *Druas*, from *drus* tree] > **dryadic** (draɪ'ædɪk) *adj*

dry battery *n* an electric battery consisting of two or more dry cells

dry cell *n* a primary cell in which the electrolyte is in the form of a paste or is treated in some way to prevent it from spilling

dry-clean *vb* (*tr*) to clean (clothing, fabrics, etc) with a solvent other than water, such as trichloroethylene > **dry-cleaner** *n* > **dry-cleaning** *n*

Dryden ('draɪdᵊn) *n* **John.** 1631–1700, English poet, dramatist, and critic of the Augustan period, commonly regarded as the chief exponent of heroic tragedy. His major works include the tragedy *All for Love* (1677), the verse satire *Absalom and Achitophel* (1681), and the *Essay of Dramatick Poesie* (1668)

dry dock *n* a basin-like structure that is large enough to admit a ship and that can be pumped dry for work on the ship's bottom

dry drunk *n* an alcoholic who is not currently drinking alcohol but is still following an irregular undisciplined lifestyle like that of a drunkard

dryer¹ ('draɪə) *n* **1** a person or thing that dries **2** an apparatus for removing moisture by forced draught, heating, or centrifuging **3** any of certain chemicals added to oils such as linseed oil to accelerate their drying when used as bases in paints, etc

dryer² ('draɪə) *adj* a variant spelling of **drier¹**

dry fly *n* *angling* **a** an artificial fly designed and prepared to be floated or skimmed on the surface of the water **b** (*as modifier*): *dry-fly fishing*

dry hole *n* (in the oil industry) a well that is drilled but does not produce oil or gas in commercially worthwhile amounts

dry ice *n* solid carbon dioxide, which sublimes at −78.5°C: used as a refrigerant, and to create billows of smoke in stage shows. Also called: **carbon dioxide snow**

drying ('draɪɪŋ) *n* the processing of timber until it has a moisture content suitable for the purposes for which it is to be used

dryly ('draɪlɪ) *adv* a variant spelling of **drily**

dry measure *n* a unit or a system of units for measuring dry goods, such as fruit, grains, etc

dry out *vb* (*adverb*) **1** to make or become dry **2** to undergo or cause to undergo a course of treatment for alcoholism or drug addiction

dry point *n* **1** a technique of intaglio engraving with a hard steel needle, without acid, on a copper plate **2** the sharp steel needle used in this process **3** an engraving or print produced by this method

dry riser *n* a vertical pipe, not containing water, having connections on different floors of a building for a fireman's hose to be attached. A fire tender can be connected at the lowest level to make water rise under pressure within the pipe. Abbreviation: DR

dry rot *n* **1** crumbling and drying of timber, bulbs, potatoes, or fruit, caused by saprotrophic basidiomycetous fungi **2** any fungus causing this decay, esp of the genus *Merulius* **3** moral degeneration or corrupt practices, esp when previously unsuspected

dry run *n* **1** *military* practice in weapon firing, a drill, or a manoeuvre without using live ammunition **2** *informal* a trial or practice, esp in simulated conditions; rehearsal

drysalter ('draɪˌsɔːltə) *n obsolete* a dealer in certain chemical products, such as dyestuffs and gums, and in dried, tinned, or salted foods and edible oils

Drysdale ('draɪzdeɪl) *n* Sir **George Russell**. 1912–81, Australian painter, esp of landscapes

dry slope *n* an artifical ski slope used for tuition and practice. Also called: dry-ski slope

dry stock *n NZ* cattle that are raised for meat

dry-stone *adj* (of a wall) made without mortar

dry up *vb* (*adverb*) **1** (*intr*) to become barren or unproductive; fail: *in middle age his inspiration dried up* **2** to dry (dishes, cutlery, etc) with a tea towel after they have been washed **3** (*intr*) *informal* to stop talking or speaking

DS *abbreviation* **1** Also: **ds** *music* dal segno **2** Detective Sergeant

DSc *abbreviation* Doctor of Science

DSC *abbreviation military* Distinguished Service Cross

DSM *abbreviation military* Distinguished Service Medal

DSO *abbreviation Brit military* Distinguished Service Order

DSS *abbreviation* (in Britain) **1** Director of Social Services **2** Department of Social Security

DST *abbreviation* Daylight Saving Time

DTI *abbreviation* (in Britain) Department of Trade and Industry

DTP *abbreviation* desktop publishing

DT's *abbreviation informal* delirium tremens

DTT *abbreviation* digital terrestrial television

DU *abbreviation* depleted uranium

Du. *abbreviation* **1** Duke **2** Dutch

dual ('djuːəl) *adj* **1** relating to or denoting two **2** twofold; double **3** (in the grammar of Old English, Ancient Greek, and certain other languages) denoting a form of a word indicating that exactly two referents are being referred to **4** *maths, logic* (of structures or expressions) having the property that the interchange of certain pairs of terms, and usually the distribution of negation, yields equivalent structures or expressions ▷ *n* **5** *grammar* **a** the dual number **b** a dual form of a word [c17: from Latin *duālis* concerning two, from *duo* two] > 'dually *adv*

dual carriageway *n Brit* a road on which traffic travelling in opposite directions is separated by a central strip of turf, etc

dualism ('djuːəˌlɪzəm) *n* **1** the state of being twofold or double **2** *philosophy* the doctrine, as opposed to idealism and materialism, that reality consists of two basic types of substance usually taken to be mind and matter or two basic types of entity, mental and physical. See **monism** **3 a** the theory that the universe has been ruled from its origins by two conflicting powers, one good and one evil, both existing as equally ultimate first causes **b** the theory that there are two personalities, one human and one divine, in Christ > 'dualist *n* > ˌdual'istic *adj*

dub[1] (dʌb) *vb* dubs, dubbing, dubbed **1** (*tr*) to invest (a person) with knighthood by the ritual of tapping on the shoulder with a sword **2** (*tr*) to invest with a title, name, or nickname **3** (*tr*) to dress (leather) by rubbing **4** *angling* to dress (a fly) ▷ *n* **5** the sound of a drum [Old English *dubbian*; related to Old Norse *dubba* to dub a knight, Old High German *tubili* plug, peg]

dub[2] (dʌb) *vb* dubs, dubbing, dubbed *films, television* **1** to alter the soundtrack of (an old recording, film, etc) **2** (*tr*)

to substitute for the soundtrack of (a film) a new soundtrack, esp in a different language **3** (*tr*) to provide (a film or tape) with a soundtrack **4** (*tr*) to alter (a taped soundtrack) by removing some parts and exaggerating others ▷ *n* **5** *films* the new sounds added **6 a** *music* a style of record production associated with reggae, involving the removal or exaggeration of instrumental parts, extensive use of echo, etc **b** (*as modifier*): *a dub mix* [c20: shortened from **DOUBLE**]

dub[3] (dʌb) *vb* dubs, dubbing, dubbed *Austral & NZ informal* short for **double-bank**

Dubai (duːˈbaɪ) *n* a sheikhdom in the NE United Arab Emirates, consisting principally of the port of Dubai, on the Persian Gulf: oilfields. Pop: 1 026 000 (2005 est)

du Barry (dju 'baːrɪ; *French* dy bari) *n* **Comtesse** (kɔ̃tɛs), original name *Marie Jeanne Bécu*. ?1743–93, mistress of Louis XV, guillotined in the French Revolution

dubbin ('dʌbɪn) *or* **dubbing** *n Brit* a greasy mixture of tallow and oil applied to leather to soften it and make it waterproof [c18: from *dub* to dress leather; see **DUB**[1]]

dubbing[1] ('dʌbɪŋ) *n films* **1** the replacement of a soundtrack in one language by one in another language **2** the combination of several soundtracks into a single track **3** the addition of a soundtrack to a film or broadcast

dubbing[2] ('dʌbɪŋ) *n* **1** *angling* hair or fur spun on waxed silk and added to the body of an artificial fly to give it shape **2** a variant of **dubbin**

Dubček (*Czech* 'duptʃɛk) *n* **Alexander** ('aleksandᵊr) 1921–92, Czechoslovak statesman. His reforms as first secretary of the Czechoslovak Communist Party prompted the Russian invasion of 1968

du Bellay (*French* dy bɛlɛ) *n* See **Bellay**

dubiety (djuːˈbaɪɪtɪ) *or* **dubiosity** (ˌdjuːbɪˈbɒsɪtɪ) *n, pl* -ties **1** the state of being doubtful **2** a doubtful matter [c18: from Late Latin *dubietās*, from Latin *dubius* **DUBIOUS**]

dubious ('djuːbɪəs) *adj* **1** marked by or causing doubt: *a dubious reply* **2** unsettled in mind; uncertain; doubtful **3** of doubtful quality; untrustworthy: *a dubious reputation* **4** not certain in outcome [c16: from Latin *dubius* wavering] > 'dubiously *adv* > 'dubiousness *n*

Dublin ('dʌblɪn) *n* **1** the capital of the Republic of Ireland, on **Dublin Bay**: under English rule from 1171 until 1922; commercial and cultural centre; contains one of the world's largest breweries and exports whiskey, stout, and agricultural produce. Pop: 1 004 614 (2002) **2** a county in E Republic of Ireland, in Leinster on the Irish Sea: mountainous in the south but low-lying in the north and centre. County seat: Dublin. Pop: 1 122 821 (2002). Area: 922 sq km (356 sq miles)

Dublin Bay prawn *n* a large prawn usually used in a dish of scampi

Dubna ('dʌbnə) *n* a new town in W Russia, founded in 1956: site of the United Institute of Nuclear Research. Pop: 60 951 (2002)

dubnium ('dʌbnɪəm) *n* a synthetic transactinide element produced in minute quantities by bombarding plutonium with high-energy neon ions. Symbol: Du; atomic no 105 [c20: after *Dubna*, city in Russia where it was first reported]

Dubois (djuːˈbwaː) *n* **W(illiam)** **E(dward)** **B(urghardt)**. 1868–1963, US Black sociologist, writer, and political activist; a founder of the National Association for the Advancement of Colored People (NAACP)

Dubrovnik (duˈbrɒvnɪk) *n* a port in W Croatia, on the Dalmatian coast: an important commercial centre in the Middle Ages; damaged in 1991 when it was shelled by Serbian artillery. Pop: 43 770 (2001). Former Italian name (until 1918): **Ragusa**

Dubuffet (*French* dybyfɛ) *n* **Jean** (ʒɑ̃). 1901–85, French painter, inspired by graffiti and the untrained art of children and psychotics

ducal ('djuːkᵊl) *adj* of or relating to a duke or duchy [c16: from French, from Late Latin *ducālis* of a leader, from *dux* leader]

ducat ('dʌkət) *n* **1** any of various former European gold or silver coins, esp those used in Italy or the Netherlands **2** (*often plural*) any coin or money [c14: from Old French, from Old Italian *ducato* coin stamped with the doge's image, from *duca* doge, from Latin *dux* leader]

Duccio di Buoninsegna (*Italian* 'duttʃo di buonin'seɲɲa) *n* ?1255–?1318, Italian painter; founder of the Sienese school

duce ('duːtʃɪ; *Italian* 'duːtʃe) *n* leader [c20: from Italian, from Latin *dux*]

Duce (*Italian* 'duːtʃe) *n* **Il Duce** (il) the title assumed by Benito Mussolini as leader of Fascist Italy (1922–43)

Duchamp (*French* dyʃã) *n* **Marcel** (marsɛl). 1887–1968, US painter and sculptor, born in France; noted as a leading exponent of Dada. His best-known work is *Nude Descending a Staircase* (1912)

Duchenne dystrophy (duː'ʃɛn) *or* **Duchenne muscular dystrophy** *n* the most common form of muscular dystrophy, usually affecting only boys [named after Guillaume *Duchenne* (1806–75), French neurologist]

duchess ('dʌtʃɪs) *n* **1** the wife or widow of a duke **2** a woman who holds the rank of duke in her own right ▷ *vb* **3** *Austral informal* to overwhelm with flattering attention [c14: from Old French *duchesse*, feminine of *duc* DUKE]

duchesse ('dʌtʃɪs) *n* *Austral & NZ* a dressing table or chest of drawers with a mirror

duchy ('dʌtʃɪ) *n*, *pl* **duchies** the territory of a duke or duchess; dukedom [c14: from Old French *duche*, from *duc* DUKE]

duck¹ (dʌk) *n*, *pl* **ducks** *or* **duck** **1** any of various small aquatic birds of the family *Anatidae*, typically having short legs, webbed feet, and a broad blunt bill: order *Anseriformes* **2** the flesh of this bird, used as food **3** the female of such a bird, as opposed to the male (drake) **4** any other bird of the family *Anatidae*, including geese, and swans **5** Also called: **ducks** *Brit informal* dear or darling: used as a term of endearment or of general address. See also **ducky 6** *informal* a person, esp one regarded as odd or endearing **7** *cricket* a score of nothing by a batsman **8 like water off a duck's back** *informal* without effect **9 take to something like a duck to water** *informal* to become adept at or attracted to something very quickly [Old English *dūce* duck, diver; related to DUCK²]

duck² (dʌk) *vb* **1** to move (the head or body) quickly downwards or away, esp so as to escape observation or evade a blow **2** to submerge or plunge suddenly and often briefly under water **3** (when *intr*, often foll by *out*) *informal* to dodge or escape (a person, duty, etc) **4** (*intr*) *bridge* to play a low card when possessing a higher one rather than try to win a trick ▷ *n* **5** the act or an instance of ducking [c14: related to Old High German *tūhhan* to dive, Middle Dutch *dūken*] > 'ducker *n*

duck³ (dʌk) *n* a heavy cotton fabric of plain weave, used for clothing, tents, etc [c17: from Middle Dutch *doek*; related to Old High German *tuoh* cloth]

duck⁴ (dʌk) *n* an amphibious vehicle used in World War II [c20: from code name DUKW]

duck-billed platypus *n* an amphibious egg-laying mammal, *Ornithorhynchus anatinus*, of E Australia, having dense fur, a broad bill and tail, and webbed feet: family *Ornithorhynchidae*

duckboard ('dʌk,bɔːd) *n* a board or boards laid so as to form a floor or path over wet or muddy ground

duck-egg blue *n* **a** a pale greenish-blue colour **b** (*as adjective*): *duck-egg blue walls*

ducking stool *n* *history* a chair or stool used for the punishment of offenders by plunging them into water

duckling ('dʌklɪŋ) *n* a young duck

ducks and drakes *n* (*functioning as singular*) **1** a game in which a flat stone is bounced across the surface of water **2 make ducks and drakes of** *or* **play (at) ducks and drakes with** to use recklessly; squander or waste

duck's arse *n* a hairstyle in which the hair is swept back to a point at the nape of the neck, resembling a duck's tail. Also called: **DA**

duck soup *n* *US slang* something that is easy to do

duckweed ('dʌk,wiːd) *n* any of various small stemless aquatic plants of the family *Lemnaceae*, esp any of the genus *Lemna*, that have rounded leaves and occur floating on still water in temperate regions

ducky *or* **duckie** ('dʌkɪ) *informal* ▷ *n*, *pl* **duckies 1** *Brit*

darling or dear: used as a term of endearment among women, but now often used in imitation of the supposed usage of homosexual men ▷ *adj* **2** delightful; fine

duct (dʌkt) *n* **1** a tube, pipe, or canal by means of which a substance, esp a fluid or gas, is conveyed **2** any bodily passage, esp one conveying secretions or excretions **3** a narrow tubular cavity in plants, often containing resin or some other substance **4** Also called: **conduit** a channel or pipe carrying electric cable or wires **5** a passage through which air can flow, as in air conditioning **6** the ink reservoir in a printing press [c17: from Latin *ductus* a leading, from Medieval Latin: aqueduct), from *dūcere* to lead] > 'ductless *adj*

ductile ('dʌktaɪl) *adj* **1** (of a metal, such as gold or copper) able to be drawn out into wire **2** able to be moulded; pliant; plastic **3** easily led or influenced; tractable [c14: from Old French, from Latin *ductilis*, from *dūcere* to lead]

ductless gland *n* *anatomy* See **endocrine gland**

dud (dʌd) *informal* ▷ *n* **1** a person or thing that proves ineffectual or a failure **2** a shell, etc, that fails to explode **3** (*plural*) *old-fashioned* clothes or other personal belongings ▷ *adj* **4** failing in its purpose or function: *a dud cheque* [c15 (in the sense: an article of clothing, a thing, used disparagingly): of unknown origin]

dude (duːd, djuːd) *n* *informal* **1** *Western US & Canadian* a city dweller, esp one holidaying on a ranch **2** *US & Canadian* a dandy **3** *US & Canadian* any person: often used to any male in direct address [c19: of unknown origin] > 'dudish *adj* > 'dudishly *adv*

dude ranch *n* *US & Canadian* a ranch used as a holiday resort offering activities such as riding and camping

dudgeon ('dʌdʒən) *n* anger or resentment (archaic except in the phrase **in high dudgeon**) [c16: of unknown origin]

Dudley¹ ('dʌdlɪ) *n* **1** a town in W central England, in Dudley unitary authority, West Midlands: wrought-iron industry. Pop: 194 919 (2001) **2** a unitary authority in W central England, in West Midlands. Pop: 304 800 (2003 est). Area: 98 sq km (38 sq miles)

Dudley² ('dʌdlɪ) *n* **Robert.** See (Earl of) **Leicester¹**

due (djuː) *adj* **1** (*postpositive*) immediately payable **2** (*postpositive*) owed as a debt, irrespective of any date for payment **3** requisite; fitting; proper **4** (*prenominal*) adequate or sufficient; enough **5** (*postpositive*) expected or appointed to be present or arrive **6** due to attributable to or caused by ▷ *n* **7** something that is owed, required, or due **8 give a person his due** to give or allow a person what is deserved or right ▷ *adv* **9** directly or exactly; straight: *a course due west* [c13: from Old French *deu*, from *devoir* to owe, from Latin *debēre*; see DEBT, DEBIT]
  ● USAGE The use of *due to* as a compound preposition
  ● (*the performance was cancelled due to bad weather*) was
  ● formerly considered incorrect, but is now acceptable

duel ('djuːəl) *n* **1** a prearranged combat with deadly weapons between two people following a formal procedure in the presence of seconds and traditionally fought until one party was wounded or killed, usually to settle a quarrel involving a point of honour **2** a contest or conflict between two persons or parties ▷ *vb* **duels, duelling, duelled** *or* *US* **duels, dueling, dueled** (*intr*) **3** to fight in a duel **4** to contest closely [c15: from Medieval Latin *duellum*, from Latin, poetical variant of *bellum* war; associated by folk etymology with Latin *duo* two] > 'dueller *or* 'duellist *n*

duende (duː'ɛndeɪ) *n* inspiration or passion, esp associated with flamenco [c20: Spanish, spirit]

duenna (djuː'ɛnə) *n* (in Spain and Portugal, etc) an elderly woman retained by a family to act as governess and chaperon to young girls [c17: from Spanish *dueña*, from Latin *domina* lady, feminine of *dominus* master]

due process of law *n* the administration of justice in accordance with established rules and principles

dues (djuːz) *pl n* (*sometimes singular*) charges, as for membership of a club or organization; fees

duet (djuː'ɛt) *n* **1** a musical composition for two performers or voices **2** an action or activity performed by a pair of closely connected individuals [c18: from Italian *duetto* a little duet, from *duo* duet, from Latin:

two] > du'ettist n

duff¹ (dʌf) n **1** a thick flour pudding, often flavoured with currants, citron, etc, and boiled in a cloth bag **2** up the duff slang pregnant [C19: Northern English variant of DOUGH]

duff² (dʌf) vb (tr) **1** slang to change the appearance of or give a false appearance to (old or stolen goods); fake **2** Austral slang to steal (cattle), altering the brand **3** Also: sclaff golf informal to bungle (a shot) by hitting the ground behind the ball ▷ adj **4** Brit informal bad or useless, as by not working out or operating correctly; dud ▷ See also **duff up** [C19: probably back formation from DUFFER]

duffel or **duffle** ('dʌfᵊl) n **1** a heavy woollen cloth with a thick nap **2** chiefly US & Canadian equipment or supplies, esp those of a camper [C17: after Duffel, Belgian town]

duffel bag n a cylindrical drawstring canvas bag, originally used esp by sailors for carrying personal articles

duffel coat n a knee-length or short wool coat, usually with a hood and fastened with toggles

duffer ('dʌfə) n **1** informal a dull or incompetent person **2** slang something worthless **3** Austral slang **a** a mine that proves unproductive **b** a person who steals cattle [C19: of uncertain origin]

duff up vb (tr, adverb) Brit slang to beat or thrash (a person) severely

Duffy ('dʌfɪ) n **Carol Ann**. born 1955, British poet and writer; her collections include Standing Female Nude (1985), The World's Wife (1999), and Rapture (2005)

Du Fu ('du: 'fu:) or **Tu Fu** n 712–770 AD, Chinese poet of the Tang dynasty

Dufy (French dyfi) n **Raoul** (raul). 1877–1953, French painter and designer whose style is characterized by swift calligraphic draughtsmanship and bright colouring

dug¹ (dʌg) vb the past tense and past participle of **dig**

dug² (dʌg) n the nipple, teat, udder, or breast of a female mammal [C16: of Scandinavian origin; compare Danish dægge to coddle, Gothic daddjan to give suck]

du Gard (French dy gar) n See **Martin du Gard**

dugong ('du:gɒŋ) n a whalelike sirenian mammal, Dugong dugon, occurring in shallow tropical waters from E Africa to Australia: family Dugongidae [C19: from Malay duyong]

dugout (dʌg,aʊt) n **1** a canoe made by hollowing out a log **2** military a covered excavation dug to provide shelter **3** (at a sports ground) the covered bench where managers, trainers, etc sit and players wait when not on the field **4** (in the Canadian prairies) a reservoir dug on a farm in which water from rain and snow is collected for use in irrigation, watering livestock, etc

Du Guesclin (French dy geklɛ̃) n **Bertrand** (bɛrtrɑ̃). ?1320–80, French military leader; as constable of France (1370–80), he helped to drive the English from France

Duhamel (French dyamɛl) n **Georges** (ʒɔrʒ). 1884–1966, French novelist, poet, and dramatist; author of La Chronique des Pasquier (1933–45)

duiker or **duyker** ('daɪkə) n, pl **-kers** or **-ker 1** Also called: **duikerbok** ('daɪkəbɒk) any small antelope of the genera Cephalophus and Sylvicapra, occurring throughout Africa south of the Sahara, having short straight backward-pointing horns, pointed hooves, and an arched back **2** South African any of several cormorants, esp the long-tailed shag (Phalacrocorax africanus) [C18: via Afrikaans from Dutch duiker diver, from duiken to dive; see DUCK²]

Duisburg (German 'dy:sbʊrk) n an industrial city in NW Germany, in North Rhine-Westphalia at the confluence of the Rivers Rhine and Ruhr: one of the world's largest and busiest inland ports; university (1972). Pop: 506 496 (2003 est)

Duisenberg (Dutch 'dʏs:ʊn,berk) n **Willem Frederik**, known as **Wim**. 1935–2005, Dutch economist; president of the European Central Bank (1998–2003)

du jour (du: 'ʒɔ:; French dy ʒur) adj (postpositive) informal currently very fashionable or popular: the young writer du jour [C20: from French, literally: of the day (as used on restaurant menus of items that change daily)]

Dukas (French dyka) n **Paul** (pɔl). 1865–1935, French composer best known for the orchestral scherzo The Sorcerer's Apprentice (1897)

duke (dju:k) n **1** a nobleman of high rank: in the British Isles standing above the other grades of the nobility **2** the prince or ruler of a small principality or duchy [C12: from Old French duc, from Latin dux leader]

dukes (dju:ks) pl n slang the fists (esp in the phrase **put your dukes up**) [C19: from Duke of Yorks rhyming slang for forks (fingers)]

Dulbecco (dʌl'bɛkəʊ; Italian dʌl'bekko) n **Renato**. born 1914, US physician and molecular biologist, born in Italy: shared the Nobel prize for physiology or medicine (1975) for cancer research

dulcet ('dʌlsɪt) adj (of a sound) soothing or pleasant; sweet [C14: from Latin dulcis sweet]

dulcimer ('dʌlsɪmə) n music **1** a tuned percussion instrument consisting of a set of strings of graduated length stretched over a sounding board and struck with a pair of hammers **2** an instrument used in US folk music, consisting of an elliptical body, a fretted fingerboard, and usually three strings plucked with a goose quill [C15: from Old French doulcemer, from Old Italian dolcimelo, from dolce sweet, from Latin dulcis + -melo, perhaps from Greek melos song]

dull (dʌl) adj **1** slow to think or understand; stupid **2** lacking in interest **3** lacking in perception or the ability to respond; insensitive **4** lacking sharpness; blunt **5** not acute, intense, or piercing **6** not active, busy, or brisk **7** lacking in spirit or animation; listless **8** (of colour) lacking brilliance or brightness; sombre **9** not loud or clear; muffled ▷ vb **10** to make or become dull [Old English dol; related to Old Norse dul conceit, Old High German tol foolish, Greek tholeros confused] > 'dullish adj > 'dullness or 'dulness n > 'dully adv

dullard ('dʌləd) n a dull or stupid person

Dulles ('dʌlɪs) n **John Foster**. 1888–1959, US statesman and lawyer; secretary of state (1953–59)

dulse (dʌls) n any of several seaweeds, esp Rhodymenia palmata, that occur on rocks and have large red edible fronds [C17: from Old Irish duilesc seaweed]

Dulwich ('dʌlɪtʃ) n a residential district in the Greater London borough of Southwark: site of an art gallery and the public school, Dulwich College

duly ('dju:lɪ) adv **1** in a proper or fitting manner **2** at the proper time; punctually [C14: see DUE, -LY²]

duma or **douma** Russian ('du:mə) n Russian history **1** (usually capital) the elective legislative assembly established by Tsar Nicholas II in 1905: overthrown by the Bolsheviks in 1917 **2** (before 1917) any official assembly or council **3** short for **State Duma**, the lower chamber of the Russian parliament [C20: from duma thought, of Germanic origin; related to Gothic dōms judgment]

Dumas (French dyma) n **1 Alexandre**, known as **Dumas père**. 1802–70, French novelist and dramatist, noted for his historical romances The Count of Monte Cristo (1844) and The Three Musketeers (1844) **2** his son, **Alexandre**, known as **Dumas fils**. 1824–95, French novelist and dramatist, noted esp for the play he adapted from an earlier novel, La Dame aux camélias (1852) **3** Jean-Baptiste André (ʒɑ̃batist ɑ̃dre). 1800–84, French chemist, noted for his research on vapour density and atomic weight **4 Marlene**. born 1953, South African painter; especially of expressionist portraits and nudes

Du Maurier (dju: 'mɒrɪ,eɪ) n **1** Dame **Daphne**. 1907–89, English novelist; author of Rebecca (1938) and My Cousin Rachel (1951) **2** her grandfather, **George Louis Palmella Busson** ('pælmɛlə 'bju:sᵊn). 1834–96, British novelist and illustrator; author of Trilby (1894). **3** his son, Sir **Gerald (Hubert Edward)**. 1873–1934, British actor-manager: father of Daphne Du Maurier

dumb (dʌm) adj **1** lacking the power to speak, either because of defects in the vocal organs or because of hereditary deafness **2** lacking the power of human speech: dumb animals **3** temporarily lacking or bereft of the power to speak: struck dumb **4** refraining from speech; uncommunicative **5** producing no sound; silent: a dumb piano **6** made, done, or performed without speech **7** informal **a** slow to understand; dim-witted **b** foolish; stupid ▷ See also **dumb down** [Old English; related to

Old Norse *dumbr*, Gothic *dumbs*, Old High German *tump*] > 'dumbly *adv* > 'dumbness *n*

Dumbarton (dʌmˈbɑːt⁽ə⁾n) *n* a town in W Scotland, in West Dunbartonshire near the confluence of the Rivers Leven and Clyde: centred around the **Rock of Dumbarton**, an important stronghold since ancient times; engineering and distilling. Pop: 20 527 (2001)

Dumbarton Oaks ('dʌmˌbɑːt⁽ə⁾n) *n* an estate in the District of Columbia in the US: scene of conferences in 1944 concerned with creating the United Nations

dumbbell ('dʌm,bel) *n* **1** *gymnastics, weightlifting* an exercising weight consisting of a single bar with a heavy ball or disc at either end **2** a small wooden object shaped like this used in dog training for the dog to retrieve **3** *slang, chiefly US & Canadian* a fool

dumb down *vb* (*tr*) to make or become less intellectually demanding or sophisticated: *attempts to dumb down news coverage*

dumbfound *or* **dumfound** (dʌmˈfaʊnd) *vb* (*tr*) to strike dumb with astonishment; amaze [c17: from DUMB + (CON)FOUND]

dumbledore ('dʌmb⁽ə⁾l,dɔː) *n* *English dialect* a bumblebee [Old English *dumble*, variant of *drumble* to move sluggishly + *dor* humming insect]

dumbo ('dʌmbəʊ) *n, pl* **-bos** *slang* a slow-witted unintelligent person [c20: after the flying elephant in *Dumbo*, the Walt Disney cartoon released in 1941]

dumb show *n* **1** a part of a play acted in pantomime, popular in early English drama **2** meaningful gestures; mime

dumbstruck ('dʌm,strʌk) *or* **dumbstricken** ('dʌm,strɪk⁽ə⁾n) *adj* temporarily deprived of speech through shock or surprise

dumbwaiter ('dʌm,weɪtə) *n* **1** *Brit* **a** a stand placed near a dining table to hold food **b** a revolving circular tray placed on a table to hold food. US and Canadian name: **lazy Susan 2** a lift for carrying food, rubbish, etc, between floors

dumdum ('dʌm,dʌm) *n* a soft-nosed or hollow-nosed small-arms bullet that expands on impact and inflicts extensive laceration. Also called: **dumdum bullet** [c19: named after *Dum-Dum*, town near Kolkata (Calcutta) where these bullets were made]

dumela (duˈmɛla) *sentence substitute South African* hello; good morning [Sotho]

Dumfries (dʌmˈfriːs) *n* a town in S Scotland on the River Nith, administrative centre of Dumfries and Galloway. Pop: 31 146 (2001)

Dumfries and Galloway *n* a council area in SW Scotland: created in 1975 from the counties of Dumfries, Kirkcudbright, and Wigtown; became a unitary authority in 1996; chiefly agricultural. Administrative centre: Dumfries. Pop: 147 210 (2003 est). Area: 6439 sq km (2486 sq miles)

Dumfriesshire (dʌmˈfriːsˌʃɪə, -ʃə) *n* (until 1975) a county in S Scotland, on the Solway Firth, now part of Dumfries and Galloway

dummelhead ('dʌməl,hɛd) *n* *Northern English dialect* a stupid or slow-witted person

dummy ('dʌmɪ) *n, pl* **-mies 1** a figure representing the human form, used for displaying clothes, in a ventriloquist's act, as a target, etc **2** **a** a copy or imitation of an object, often lacking some essential feature of the original **b** (*as modifier*): *a dummy drawer* **3** *slang* a stupid person; fool **4** *derogatory slang* a person without the power of speech; mute **5** *informal* a person who says or does nothing **6** **a** a person who appears to act for himself while acting on behalf of another **b** (*as modifier*): *a dummy buyer* **7** *military* a weighted round without explosives, used in drill and training **8** *bridge* **a** the hand exposed on the table by the declarer's partner and played by the declarer **b** the declarer's partner **9** **a** a prototype of a proposed book, indicating the general appearance and dimensions of the finished product **b** a designer's layout of a page indicating the positions for illustrations, etc **10** a feigned pass or move in a sport such as football or rugby **11** *Brit* a rubber teat for babies to suck or bite on. US and Canadian equivalent: **pacifier 12** (*modifier*) counterfeit; sham

13 (*modifier*) (of a card game) played with one hand exposed or unplayed [c16: see DUMB, -Y³]

dummy run *n* a practice or rehearsal; trial run

Du Mont ('djuː,mɒnt) *n* **Allen Balcom.** 1901–65, US inventor and electronics manufacturer. He developed the cathode-ray tube used in television sets and oscilloscopes

dump (dʌmp) *vb* **1** to drop, fall, or let fall heavily or in a mass **2** (*tr*) to empty (objects or material) out of a container **3** to unload, empty, or make empty (a container), as by tilting or overturning **4** (*tr*) *informal* to dispose of **5** (*tr*) to dispose of (waste, esp radioactive nuclear waste) in the sea or on land **6** *commerce* to market (goods) in bulk and at low prices **7** (*tr*) to store (supplies, arms, etc) temporarily **8** (*intr*) *slang, chiefly US* to defecate **9** (*tr*) *surfing* (of a wave) to hurl a swimmer or surfer down **10** (*tr*) *Austral & NZ* to compact (bales of wool) by hydraulic pressure **11** (*tr*) *computing* to record (the contents of part or all of the memory) on a storage device, such as magnetic tape, at a series of points during a computer run ▷ *n* **12** a place or area where waste materials are dumped **13** a pile or accumulation of rubbish **14** the act of dumping **15** *informal* a dirty or unkempt place **16** *military* a place where weapons, supplies, etc, are stored **17** *slang, chiefly US* an act of defecation [c14: probably of Scandinavian origin; compare Norwegian *dumpa* to fall suddenly, Middle Low German *dumpeln* to duck] > 'dumper *n*

dumpling ('dʌmplɪŋ) *n* **1** a small ball of dough cooked and served with stew **2** a pudding consisting of a round pastry case filled with fruit: *apple dumpling* **3** *informal* a short plump person [c16: dump-, perhaps variant of LUMP¹ + -LING¹]

dumps (dʌmps) *pl n informal* a state of melancholy or depression (esp in the phrase **down in the dumps**) [c16: probably from Middle Dutch *domp* haze, mist; see DAMP]

dump truck *or* **dumper-truck** ('dʌmpə) *n* a small truck used on building sites, having a load-bearing container at the front or back that can be tipped up to unload the contents

dumpy ('dʌmpɪ) *adj* **dumpier, dumpiest** short and plump; squat [c18: perhaps related to DUMPLING] > 'dumpily *adv* > 'dumpiness *n*

dun¹ (dʌn) *vb* **duns, dunning, dunned 1** (*tr*) to press or importune (a debtor) for the payment of a debt ▷ *n* **2** **a** a person, esp a hired agent, who importunes another for the payment of a debt **3** a demand for payment, esp one in writing [c17: of unknown origin]

dun² (dʌn) *n* **1** **a** a brownish-grey colour **2** a horse of this colour **3** *angling* **a** an immature adult mayfly (the subimago), esp one of the genus *Ephemera* **b** an artificial fly imitating this or a similar fly ▷ *adj* **dunner, dunnest 4** of a dun colour **5** dark and gloomy [Old English *dunn*; related to Old Norse *dunna* wild duck, Middle Irish *doun* dark; see DUSK]

Duna ('dunɔ) *n* the Hungarian name for the **Danube**

Dünaburg ('dyːnaʊrk) *n* the German name (until 1893) for **Daugavpils**

Dunaj ('dunaj) *n* the Czech name for the **Danube**

Dunant (*French* dynɑ̃) *n* **Jean Henri** (ʒɑ̃ ɑ̃ri). 1828–1910, Swiss humanitarian, founder of the International Red Cross (1864): shared the Nobel peace prize 1901

Dunărea ('dunərja) *n* the Romanian name for the: **Danube**

Dunbar¹ (dʌnˈbɑː) *n* a port and resort in SE Scotland, in East Lothian: scene of Cromwell's defeat of the Scots (1650). Pop: 6354 (2001)

Dunbar² (dʌnˈbɑː) *n* **William.** ?1460–?1520, Scottish poet, noted for his satirical, allegorical, and elegiac works

Dunbartonshire (dʌnˈbɑːt⁽ə⁾nʃɪə, -ʃə) *n* a historical county of W Scotland: became part of Strathclyde region in 1975; administered since 1996 by the council areas of East Dunbartonshire and West Dunbartonshire

Duncan ('dʌŋkən) *n* **Isadora** (ˌɪzəˈdɔːrə). 1878–1927, US dancer and choreographer, who influenced modern ballet by introducing greater freedom of movement

Duncan I ('dʌŋkən) *n* died 1040, king of Scotland (1034–40); killed by Macbeth

Duncan Smith ('dʌŋkən 'smɪθ) *n* **(George) Iain.** born

1954, British politician; leader of the Conservative Party (2001–03)

dunce (dʌns) *n* a person who is stupid or slow to learn [c16: from *Dunses* or *Dunsmen*, term of ridicule applied to the followers of John *Duns* Scotus (?1265–1308), Scottish scholastic theologian and Franciscan priest, especially by 16th-century humanists]

dunce cap *or* **dunce's cap** *n* a conical paper hat, formerly placed on the head of a dull child at school

Dundalk (dʌn'dɔːk) *n* a town in NE Republic of Ireland, on **Dundalk Bay**: county town of Co Louth. Pop: 32 505 (2002)

Dundee[1] (dʌn'diː) *n* 1 a port in E Scotland, in City of Dundee council area, on the Firth of Tay: centre of the former British jute industry; university (1967). Pop: 154 674 (2001) 2 City of Dundee a council area in E Scotland. Pop: 143 090 (2003 est). Area: 65 sq km (25 sq miles)

Dundee[2] (dʌn'diː) *n* **1st Viscount**, title of *John Graham of Claverhouse*. ?1649– 89, Scottish Jacobite leader, who died from his wounds after winning the Battle of Killiecrankie

Dundee cake *n* *chiefly Brit* a fairly rich fruit cake decorated with almonds

dunderhead ('dʌndə,hɛd) *n* a stupid or slow-witted person; dunce [c17: probably from Dutch *donder* thunder + HEAD; compare BLOCKHEAD] > 'dunder,headed *adj*

Dundonian (dʌn'dəʊnɪən) *n* 1 a native or inhabitant of Dundee ▷ *adj* 2 of or relating to Dundee or its inhabitants

dune (djuːn) *n* a mound or ridge of drifted sand, occurring on the sea coast and in deserts [c18: via Old French from Middle Dutch *dūne*; see DOWN[3]]

Dunedin (dʌn'iːdɪn) *n* a port in New Zealand, on SE South Island: founded (1848) by Scottish settlers. Pop: 121 900 (2004 est)

Dunfermline (dʌn'fɜːmlɪn) *n* a city in E Scotland, in SW Fife: ruined palace, a former residence of Scottish kings. Pop: 39 229 (2001)

dung (dʌŋ) *n* 1 excrement, esp of animals; manure 2 something filthy ▷ *vb* 3 (*tr*) to cover (ground) with manure [Old English: prison; related to Old High German *tunc* cellar roofed with dung, Old Norse *dyngja* manure heap]

Dungannon (dʌn'gænən) *n* a district of S Northern Ireland, in Co Tyrone. Pop: 48 695 (2003 est). Area: 783 sq km (302 sq miles)

dungaree (,dʌŋgə'riː) *n* 1 a coarse cotton fabric used chiefly for work clothes, etc 2 (*plural*) **a** a suit of workman's overalls made of this material consisting of trousers with a bib attached **b** a casual garment resembling this, usually worn by women or children 3 (*plural*) US trousers [c17: from Hindi *dungrī*, after *Dungrī*, district of Mumbai, where this fabric originated]

Dungeness (,dʌndʒə'nɛs) *n* a low shingle headland on the S coast of England, in Kent: two nuclear power stations; automatic lighthouse

dungeon ('dʌndʒən) *n* 1 a close prison cell, often underground 2 a variant of **donjon** [c14: from Old French *donjon*; related to Latin *dominus* master]

dunger ('dʌŋə) *n* *NZ informal* 1 an old decrepit car 2 any old worn-out machine

dunghill ('dʌŋ,hɪl) *n* 1 a heap of dung 2 a foul place, condition, or person

dunk (dʌŋk) *vb* 1 to dip (bread, etc) in tea, soup, etc, before eating 2 to submerge or be submerged in liquid [c20: from Pennsylvania Dutch, from Middle High German *dunken*, from Old High German *dunkōn*; see DUCK[2], TINGE] > 'dunker *n*

Dunkerque (French dœkɛrk) *n* a port in N France, on the Strait of Dover: scene of the evacuation of British and other Allied troops after the fall of France in 1940; industrial centre with an oil refinery and naval shipbuilding yards. Pop: 70 850 (1999). English name: **Dunkirk**

Dún Laoghaire (duːn 'lɪərɪ) *n* a port in E Republic of Ireland, on Dublin Bay. Pop: 24 447 (2002). Former name: Kingstown

dunlin ('dʌnlɪn) *n* a small sandpiper, *Calidris* (or *Erolia*) *alpina*, of northern and arctic regions, having a brown back and black breast in summer [c16: DUN[2] + -LING[1]]

Dunlop ('dʌnlɒp) *n* **John Boyd**. 1840–1921, Scottish veterinary surgeon, who devised the first successful pneumatic tyre, which was manufactured by the company named after him

dunnage ('dʌnɪdʒ) *n* loose material used for packing cargo [c14: of uncertain origin]

dunnakin ('dʌnəkɪn) *n* *dialect* a lavatory. Also called: **dunny** [of obscure origin; but perhaps related to DUNG]

dunnart ('dʌnɑːt) *n* a mouselike insectivorous marsupial of the genus *Sminthopsis* of Australia and New Guinea [c20: from a native Australian language]

dunno (dʌ'nəʊ, dʊ-, də-) *slang* contraction of (I) do not know

dunnock ('dʌnək) *n* another name for **hedge sparrow** [c15: from DUN[2] + -OCK]

dunny ('dʌnɪ) *n, pl* -nies 1 *Scot dialect* a cellar or basement 2 *Austral & NZ informal* **a** an outside lavatory **b** (*as modifier*): *a dunny roll; a dunny seat* [c20: of obscure origin; but see DUNNAKIN]

Dunois (French dynwa) *n* **Jean** (ʒɑ̃), **Comte de Dunois**, known as *the Bastard of Orléans*. ?1403–68, French military commander, who defended Orléans against the English until the siege was raised by Joan of Arc (1429)

Dunsany (dʌn'seɪnɪ) *n* **18th Baron**, title of *Edward John Moreton Drax Plunkett*. 1878–1957, Irish dramatist and short-story writer

Dunsinane (dʌn'sɪnən) *n* a hill in central Scotland, in the Sidlaw Hills: the ruined fort at its summit is regarded as Macbeth's castle. Height: 308 m (1012 ft)
● USAGE The pronunciation ('dʌnsɪ,neɪn) is used in
● Shakespeare's *Macbeth* for the purposes of rhyme

Duns Scotus ('dʌnz 'skɒtəs) *n* **John**. ?1265–1308, Scottish scholastic theologian and Franciscan priest: opposed the theology of St Thomas Aquinas

Dunstable[1] ('dʌnstəbʰl) *n* an industrial town in SE central England, in Bedfordshire. Pop: 50 775 (2001)

Dunstable[2] ('dʌnstəbʰl) *n* **John**. died 1453, English composer, esp of motets and mass settings, noted for his innovations in harmony and rhythm

Dunstan ('dʌnstən) *n* **Saint**. ?909–988 AD, English prelate and statesman; archbishop of Canterbury (959–988). He revived monasticism in England on Benedictine lines and promoted education. Feast day: May 19

duo ('djuːəʊ) *n, pl* **duos** *or* **dui** ('djuːiː) 1 *music* **a** a pair of performers **b** another word for **duet** 2 a pair of actors, entertainers, etc 3 *informal* a pair of closely associated individuals [c16: via Italian from Latin: two]

duo- *combining form* indicating two [from Latin]

duodecimal (,djuːəʊ'dɛsɪməl) *adj* 1 relating to twelve or twelfths ▷ *n* 2 a twelfth 3 one of the numbers used in a duodecimal number system > ,duo'decimally *adv*

duodecimo (,djuːəʊ'dɛsɪ,məʊ) *n, pl* -mos 1 Also called: twelvemo a book size resulting from folding a sheet of paper into twelve leaves 2 a book of this size [c17: from Latin phrase *in duodecimō* in twelfth, from *duodecim* twelve]

duodenum (,djuːəʊ'diːnəm) *n, pl* -na (-nə) *or* -nums the first part of the small intestine, between the stomach and the jejunum [c14: from Medieval Latin, shortened from *intestinum duodenum digitorum* intestine of twelve fingers' length, from Latin *duodēnī* twelve each] > ,duo'denal *adj*

duologue *or sometimes US* **duolog** ('djuːə,lɒg) *n* 1 a part or all of a play in which the speaking roles are limited to two actors 2 a less common word for **dialogue**

duopoly (djuː'ɒpəlɪ) *n, pl* -lies a situation in which control of a commodity or service in a particular market is vested in just two producers or suppliers > duopolistic (djuː,ɒpə'lɪstɪk) *adj*

Duo-Tang ('djuːə,tæŋ) *n* *trademark Canadian* a type of folder with flexible metal fasteners

Duparc (French dypark) *n* **Henri** (ɑ̃rɪ), full name *Marie Eugène Henri Fouques Duparc*. 1848–1933, French composer of songs noted for their sad brooding quality

dupe (djuːp) *n* 1 a person who is easily deceived ▷ *vb* 2 (*tr*) to deceive, esp by trickery; make a dupe or tool of;

cheat; fool [C17: from French, from Old French *duppe*, contraction of *de huppe* of (a) hoopoe (from Latin *upupa*); from the bird's reputation for extreme stupidity] > 'dupable *adj* > 'duper *n* > 'dupery *n*

duple ('dju:p^əl) *adj* **1** a less common word for **double** **2** *music* (of time or music) having two beats in a bar [C16: from Latin *duplus* twofold, double]

Dupleix (*French* dyplɛks) *n* Marquis **Joseph François** (ʒozɛf frãswa). 1697–1763, French governor general in India (1742–54). His plan to establish a French empire in India was frustrated by Clive

Duplessis-Mornay (*French* dyplɛsimɔrnɛ) *n* a variant of (Philippe de) **Mornay**

duplex ('dju:plɛks) *n* **1** *US & Canadian* a duplex apartment or house **2** a double-stranded region in a nucleic acid molecule ▷ *adj* **3** having two parts **4** *machinery* having pairs of components of independent but identical function **5** permitting the transmission of simultaneous signals in both directions in a radio, telecommunications, or computer channel [C19: from Latin: twofold, from *duo* two + *-plex* -FOLD] > du'plexity *n*

duplex apartment *n* *US & Canadian* an apartment on two floors

duplex house *n* *US & Canadian* a house divided into two separate dwellings. Also called: (US): semidetached

duplicate *adj* ('dju:plɪkɪt) **1** copied exactly from an original **2** identical **3** existing as a pair or in pairs; twofold ▷ *n* ('dju:plɪkɪt) **4** an exact copy; double **5** something additional or supplementary of the same kind **6** two exact copies (esp in the phrase **in duplicate**) ▷ *vb* ('dju:plɪ,keɪt) **7** (*tr*) to make a replica of **8** (*tr*) to do or make again **9** (*tr*) to make in a pair; make double [C15: from Latin *duplicāre* to double, from *duo* two + *plicāre* to fold] > 'duplicable *adj*

duplication (,dju:plɪ'keɪʃən) *n* **1** the act of duplicating or the state of being duplicated **2** a copy; duplicate **3** *genetics* a mutation in which there are two or more copies of a gene or of a segment of a chromosome

duplicator ('dju:plɪ,keɪtə) *n* an apparatus for making replicas of an original, such as a machine using a stencil wrapped on an ink-loaded drum

duplicity (dju:'plɪsɪtɪ) *n, pl* **-ties** deception; double-dealing [C15: from Old French *duplicite*, from Late Latin *duplicitās* a being double, from Latin DUPLEX]

du Pré (du: preɪ) *n* **Jacqueline**. 1945–87, English cellist. Multiple sclerosis ended her performing career (1973) after which she became a cello teacher

Dupré (*French* dypre) *n* **Marcel** (marsɛl). 1886–1971, French organist and composer, noted as an improviser

Duque de Caxias (*Portuguese* 'du:ke 'dɑ: kə'ʃiaʃ) *n* a city in SE Brazil, near Rio de Janeiro. Pop: 116 000 (2005 est)

Dur. *abbreviation* Durham

durable ('djʊərəb^əl) *adj* long-lasting; enduring [C14: from Old French, from Latin *dūrābilis*, from *dūrāre* to last; see ENDURE] > ,dura'bility *or* 'durableness *n* > 'durably *adv*

durable goods *pl n* goods, such as most producer goods and some consumer goods, that require infrequent replacement. Also called: **durables**

dural ('djʊərəl) *adj* relating to or affecting the dura mater

Duralumin (djʊ'ræljʊmɪn) *n* *trademark* a light strong aluminium alloy containing 3.5–4.5 per cent of copper with small quantities of silicon, magnesium, and manganese; used in aircraft manufacture

dura mater ('djʊərə 'meɪtə) *n* the outermost and toughest of the three membranes covering the brain and spinal cord [C15: from Medieval Latin, hard mother]

duramen (djʊ'reɪmɛn) *n* another name for **heartwood** [C19: from Latin: hardness, from *dūrāre* to harden]

Durán (djʊ'ræn) *n* **Roberto**. born 1951, Panamanian boxer

durance ('djʊərəns) *n* *archaic or literary* **1** imprisonment **2** duration [C15: from Old French, from *durer* to last, from Latin *dūrāre*]

Durango (djʊ'ræŋgəʊ; *Spanish* du'raŋgo) *n* **1** a state in N central Mexico: high plateau, with the Sierra Madre Occidental in the west; irrigated agriculture (esp cotton) and rich mineral resources. Capital: Durango. Pop: 1 448 661 (2000). Area: 119 648 sq km (46 662 sq miles) **2** a

city in NW central Mexico, capital of Durango state: mining centre. Pop: 520 000 (2005 est)

Durante (də'ræntɪ) *n* **Jimmy**, known as **Schnozzle**. 1893–1980, US comedian

Duras (*French* dyra) *n* **Marguerite**, real name *Marguerite Donnadieu*. 1914–96, French novelist born in Giadinh, Indochina (now in Vietnam). Her works include *The Sea Wall* (1950), *Practicalities* (1990), *Écrire* (1993), and the script for the film *Hiroshima mon amour* (1960)

duration (djʊ'reɪʃən) *n* the length of time that something lasts or continues [C14: from Medieval Latin *dūrātiō*, from Latin *dūrāre* to last] > du'rational *adj*

durative ('djʊərətɪv) *grammar* ▷ *adj* **1** denoting an aspect of verbs that includes the imperfective and the progressive ▷ *n* **2 a** the durative aspect of a verb **b** a verb in this aspect

Durban ('dɜ:b^ən) *n* a port in E South Africa, in E KwaZulu/Natal province on the Indian Ocean: University of Natal (1909); resort and industrial centre, with oil refineries, shipbuilding yards, etc Pop: 536 644 (2001)

Durban poison *n* *South African slang* a particularly potent variety of cannabis grown in Natal

durbar (ˈdɜ:bɑ:, ˌdɜ:'bɑ:) *n* **a** (formerly) the court of a native ruler or a governor in India and British Colonial West Africa **b** a levee at such a court [C17: from Hindi *darbār* court, from Persian, from *dar* door + *bār* entry, audience]

Dürer (*German* 'dy:rər) *n* **Albrecht** ('albreçt). 1471–1528, German painter and engraver, regarded as the greatest artist of the German Renaissance and noted particularly as a draughtsman and for his copper engravings and woodcuts

duress (djʊ'rɛs, djʊə-) *n* **1** compulsion by use of force or threat; constraint; coercion (often in the phrase **under duress**) **2** confinement; imprisonment [C14: from Old French *duresse*, from Latin *dūritia* hardness, from *dūrus* hard]

Durga ('dʊəgæ) *n* *Hinduism* the goddess Parvati portrayed as a warrior: renowned for slaying the buffalo demon, Mahisha [from Sanskrit: the inaccessible one]

Durga Puja (ˌdʊəgæ 'pu:dʒə) *n* another name for **Navaratri** [from Sanskrit DURGA + *puja* worship]

Durham ('dʌrəm) *n* **1** a county of NE England, on the North Sea: rises to the N Pennines in the west: the geographical and ceremonial county includes the unitary authorities of Hartlepool and Stockton-on-Tees (both part of Cleveland until 1996) and Darlington (created in 1997). Administrative centre: Durham. Pop (excluding unitary authorities): 494 200 (2003 est). Area (excluding unitary authorities): 2434 sq km (940 sq miles) **2** a city in NE England, administrative centre of Co Durham, on the River Wear: Norman cathedral; 11th-century castle (founded by William the Conqueror), now occupied by the University of Durham (1832). Pop: 42 939 (2001) **3** a rare variety of shorthorn cattle. See **shorthorn**

during ('djʊərɪŋ) *prep* **1** concurrently with (some other activity) **2** within the limit of (a period of time) [C14: from *duren* to last, ultimately from Latin *dūrāre* to last]

Durkan ('dɜ:kən) *n* (**John**) **Mark**. born 1960, Northern Irish politician; leader of the Social Democratic and Labour Party (SDLP) from 2001

Durkheim ('dɜ:khaɪm; *French* dyrkɛm) *n* **Émile** (emil). 1858–1917, French sociologist, whose pioneering works include *De la Division du travail social* (1893)

durmast *or* **durmast oak** ('dɜ:mɑ:st) *n* a large Eurasian oak tree, *Quercus petraea*, with lobed leaves and sessile acorns. Also called: **sessile oak** [C18: probably alteration of *dun mast*; see DUN², MAST²]

durra ('dʌrə), **doura** *or* **dourah** ('dʊərə) *n* an Old World variety of sorghum, *Sorghum vulgare durra*, with erect hairy flower spikes and round seeds: cultivated for grain and fodder [C18: from Arabic *dhurah* grain]

Durrell ('dʌrəl) *n* **1 Gerald** (**Malcolm**). 1925–95, British zoologist and writer: his books include *The Bafut Beagles* (1954), *My Family and Other Animals* (1956), and *The Aye-aye and I* (1992) **2** his brother, **Lawrence** (**George**). 1912–90, British poet and novelist; author of *The Alexandria Quartet* of novels, consisting of *Justine* (1957), *Balthazar* (1958),

Mountolive (1958), and *Clea* (1960). Later works include *The Avignon Quintet* of novels (1974–85)

Dürrenmatt ('dyrənmat) *n* **Friedrich** (fri:drɪç). 1921–90, Swiss dramatist and writer of detective stories, noted for his grotesque and paradoxical treatment of the modern world: author of *The Visit* (1956) and *The Physicists* (1962)

durrie ('dʌrɪ) *n* a cotton carpet made in India, often in rectangular pieces fringed at the ends: sometimes used as a sofa cover, wall hanging, etc [from Hindi *darī*]

durry ('dʌrɪ) *n*, *pl* **-ries** *Austral slang* a cigarette [from DURRIE a type of Indian carpet]

durst (dɜ:st) *vb* a past tense of **dare**

Duruflé (*French* dyrufle) *n* **Maurice** (mɔris). 1902–86, French composer and organist, best known for his *Requiem* (1947)

durum or **durum wheat** ('djʊərəm) *n* a variety of wheat, *Triticum durum*, with a high gluten content, cultivated mainly in the Mediterranean region, and used chiefly to make pastas [C20: short for New Latin *trīticum dūrum*, literally: hard wheat]

Duse (*Italian* 'du:ze) *n* **Eleonora** (ˌɛliə'nɔ:rə). 1858–1924, Italian actress, noted as a tragedienne

Dushanbe (du:ʃɑ:nbɪ) *n* the capital of Tajikistan; a cultural centre. Pop: 551 000 (2005 est). Former name (1929–61): Stalinabad

dusk (dʌsk) *n* **1** twilight or the darker part of twilight **2** *poetic* gloom; shade ▷ *adj* **3** *poetic* shady; gloomy ▷ *vb* **4** *poetic* to make or become dark [Old English *dox*; related to Old Saxon *dosan* brown, Old High German *tusin* yellow, Norwegian *dusmen* misty, Latin *fuscus* dark brown]

dusky ('dʌskɪ) *adj* **duskier**, **duskiest 1** dark in colour; swarthy or dark-skinned **2** dim ▷ **'duskily** *adv* ▷ **'duskiness** *n*

Düsseldorf ('dʊsəlˌdɔ:f; *German* 'dysəldɔrf) *n* an industrial city in W Germany, capital of North Rhine-Westphalia, on the Rhine: commercial centre of the Rhine-Ruhr industrial area. Pop: 572 511 (2003 est)

dust (dʌst) *n* **1** dry fine powdery material, such as particles of dirt, earth or pollen **2** a cloud of such fine particles **3 a** the mortal body of man **b** the corpse of a dead person **4** the earth; ground **5** *informal* a disturbance; fuss (esp in the phrases **kick up a dust, raise a dust**) **6** something of little or no worth **7** short for **gold dust 8** ashes or household refuse **9 bite the dust a** to fail completely or cease to exist **b** to fall down dead **10 dust and ashes** something that is very disappointing **11 shake the dust off one's feet** to depart angrily or contemptuously **12 throw dust in the eyes of** to confuse or mislead ▷ *vb* **13** (*tr*) to sprinkle or cover (something) with (dust or some other powdery substance) **14** to remove dust by wiping, sweeping, or brushing **15** *archaic* to make or become dirty with dust ▷ See also **dust down, dust-up** [Old English *dūst*; related to Danish *dyst* flour dust, Middle Dutch *dūst* dust, meal dust, Old High German *tunst* storm] ▷ **'dustless** *adj*

dustbin ('dʌstˌbɪn) *n* a large, usually cylindrical container for rubbish, esp one used by a household

dust bowl *n* a semiarid area in which the surface soil is exposed to wind erosion and dust storms occur

Dust Bowl *n* **the Dust Bowl** the area of the south central US that became denuded of topsoil by wind erosion during the droughts of the mid-1930s

dustcart ('dʌstˌkɑ:t) *n* a road vehicle for collecting domestic refuse

dust cover *n* **1** another name for **dustsheet 2** another name for **dust jacket 3** a perspex cover for the turntable of a record player

dust devil *n* a strong miniature whirlwind that whips up dust, litter, leaves, etc into the air

dust down *vb* (*tr, adverb*) **1** to remove dust from by brushing or wiping **2** to reprimand severely ▷ **dusting down** *n*

duster ('dʌstə) *n* **1** a cloth used for dusting furniture, etc **2** a machine for blowing out dust over trees or crops **3** a person or thing that dusts

dusting-powder *n* fine powder (such as talcum powder) used to absorb moisture, etc

dust jacket or **dust cover** *n* a removable paper cover used to protect a bound book

dustman ('dʌstmən) *n*, *pl* **-men** *Brit* a man whose job is to collect domestic refuse

dust mite *n* either of two mites, *Dermatophagoides farinae* or *D. pteronyssinus*, that feed on shed human skill cells. Their excrement is a household allergen associated with respiratory allergies and asthma

dustpan ('dʌstˌpæn) *n* a short-handled hooded shovel into which dust is swept from floors, etc

dustsheet ('dʌstˌʃi:t) *n* *Brit* a large cloth or sheet used for covering furniture to protect it from dust

dust storm *n* a windstorm that whips up clouds of dust

dust-up *informal* ▷ *n* **1** a quarrel, fight, or argument ▷ *vb* **dust up 2** (*tr, adverb*) to attack or assault (someone)

dusty ('dʌstɪ) *adj* **dustier**, **dustiest 1** covered with or involving dust **2** like dust in appearance or colour **3** (of a colour) tinged with grey; pale **4 a dusty answer** an unhelpful or bad-tempered reply ▷ **'dustily** *adv* ▷ **'dustiness** *n*

dusty miller *n* a caryophyllaceous plant, *Cerastium tomentosum*, of SE Europe and Asia, having white flowers and downy stems and leaves: cultivated as a rock plant. Also called: snow-in-summer

Dutch (dʌtʃ) *n* **1** the language of the Netherlands, belonging to the West Germanic branch of the Indo-European family and quite closely related to German and English **2 the Dutch** (*functioning as plural*) the natives, citizens, or inhabitants of the Netherlands **3** See **double Dutch 4 in Dutch** *slang* in trouble ▷ *adj* **5** of, relating to, or characteristic of the Netherlands, its inhabitants, or their language ▷ *adv* **6 go Dutch** *informal* to share expenses equally

Dutch auction *n* an auction in which the price is lowered by stages until a buyer is found

Dutch barn *n* *Brit* a farm building consisting of a steel frame and a curved roof

Dutch courage *n* **1** false courage gained from drinking alcohol **2** alcoholic drink

Dutch door *n* *US & Canadian* a door with an upper and lower leaf that may be opened separately. Also called (in Britain and certain other countries): stable door

Dutch East Indies *n* **the Dutch East Indies** a former name (1798–1945) of **Indonesia**

Dutch elm disease *n* a disease of elm trees caused by the fungus *Ceratocystis ulmi* and characterized by withering of the foliage and stems and eventual death of the parts of the tree above ground

Dutch Guiana or **Netherlands Guiana** *n* the former name of **Surinam**

Dutchman ('dʌtʃmən) *n*, *pl* **-men 1** a native, citizen, or inhabitant of the Netherlands **2** *South African, often derogatory* an Afrikaaner

Dutch New Guinea *n* a former name (until 1963) of Papua

Dutch oven *n* **1** an iron or earthenware container with a cover used for stews, etc **2** a metal box, open in front, for cooking in front of an open fire

Dutch treat *n* *informal* an entertainment, meal, etc, where each person pays for himself

Dutch uncle *n* *informal* a person who criticizes or reproves frankly and severely

Dutch West Indies *pl n* **the Dutch West Indies** a former name of the **Netherlands Antilles**

duteous ('dju:tɪəs) *adj* *formal or archaic* dutiful; obedient ▷ **'duteously** *adv*

dutiable ('dju:tɪəbᵊl) *adj* (of goods) liable to duty ▷ **ˌdutia'bility** *n*

dutiful ('dju:tɪfʊl) *adj* **1** exhibiting or having a sense of duty **2** characterized by or resulting from a sense of duty: *a dutiful answer* ▷ **'dutifully** *adv*

Dutton ('dʌtᵊn) *n* **Clarence Edward**. 1841–1912, American geologist who first developed the theory of isostasy

duty ('dju:tɪ) *n*, *pl* **-ties 1** a task or action that a person is bound to perform for moral or legal reasons **2** respect or obedience due to a superior, older persons, etc **3** the force that binds one morally or legally to one's obligations **4** a government tax, esp on imports **5** *Brit* **a** the quantity or intensity of work for which a machine is designed **b** a measure of the efficiency of a machine **6 a** a job or service allocated **b** (*as modifier*): *duty rota* **7 do**

duty for to act as a substitute for **8** off duty not at work **9** on duty at work [c13: from Anglo-French *dueté*, from Old French *deu* DUE]

duty-bound *adj* morally obliged as a matter of duty

duty-free *adj, adv* **1** with exemption from customs or excise duties ▷ *n* **2** goods sold in a duty-free shop

duty-free shop *n* a shop, esp one at an airport or on board a ship, that sells perfume, tobacco, etc, at duty-free prices

duumvir (djuːˈʌmvə) *n, pl* -virs or -viri (-vɪˌriː) **1** *Roman history* one of two coequal magistrates or officers **2** either of two men who exercise a joint authority [c16: from Latin, from *duo* two + *vir* man] > **duumvirate** (djuːˈʌmvɪrɪt) *n*

Duvalier (*French* dyvalje) *n* **1 François** (frɑ̃swa), known as *Papa Doc.* 1907–71, president of Haiti (1957–71) **2** his son, **Jean-Claude** (ʒɑ̃klod), known as *Baby Doc.* born 1951, Haitian statesman; president of Haiti 1971–86; deposed and exiled

duvet (ˈduːveɪ) *n* **1** another name for **continental quilt 2** Also called: **duvet jacket** a down-filled jacket used esp by mountaineers [c18: from French, from earlier *dumet*, from Old French *dum* DOWN²]

Du Vigneaud (duː ˈviːnjəʊ) *n* **Vincent.** 1901–78, US biochemist: Nobel prize for chemistry (1955) for his synthesis of the hormones oxytocin and vasopressin

dux (dʌks) *n* (in Scottish and certain other schools) the top pupil in a class or school [Latin: leader]

DV *abbreviation* **1** Deo volente [Latin: God willing] **2** Douay Version (of the Bible)

DVD *abbreviation* digital versatile or digital video disk: an optical disk used to store audio, video, or computer data, esp feature films for home viewing

DVD-A *abbreviation* DVD-Audio

DVD writer *n computing* a device on a computer for writing DVDs

Dvina (*Russian* dviˈna) *n* **1 Northern Dvina** a river in NW Russia, formed by the confluence of the Sukhona and Yug Rivers and flowing northwest to *Dvina Bay* in the White Sea. Length: 750 km (466 miles) **2 Western Dvina** a river rising in W Russia, in the Valdai Hills and flowing south and southwest then northwest to the Gulf of Riga. Length: 1021 km (634 miles). Latvian name: Daugava

Dvina Bay or **Dvina Gulf** *n* an inlet of the White Sea, off the coast of NW Russia

Dvinsk (dvinsk) *n* transliteration of the former Russian name for **Daugavpils**

DVLA *abbreviation* (in Britain) Driver and Vehicle Licensing Agency

Dvořák (ˈdvɔːʒæk; *Czech* ˈdvɔrʒaːk) *n* **Antonín** (ˈantɔnjiːn), known as *Anton Dvořák.* 1841–1904, Czech composer, much of whose work reflects the influence of folk music. His best-known work is the *Symphony No. 9 From the New World* (1893)

DVT *abbreviation* deep vein thrombosis

dwaal (dwaːl) *n South African* a state of befuddlement [Afrikaans]

dwale (dweɪl) *n* another name for **deadly nightshade** [c14: perhaps of Scandinavian origin]

dwarf (dwɔːf) *n, pl* **dwarfs** or **dwarves** (dwɔːvz) **1** an abnormally undersized person, esp one with a large head and short arms and legs **2 a** an animal or plant much below the average height for the species **b** (*as modifier*): *a dwarf tree* **3** (in folklore) a small ugly manlike creature, often possessing magical powers **4** *astronomy* short for **dwarf star** ▷ *vb* **5** to become or cause to become comparatively small in size, importance, etc **6** (*tr*) to stunt the growth of [Old English *dweorg*; related to Old Norse *dvergr*, Old High German *twerc*] > **'dwarfish** *adj*

dwarf star *n* any luminosity class V star, such as the sun, lying in the main sequence of the Hertzsprung-Russell diagram. Also called: **main-sequence star** See also **red dwarf**, **white dwarf**

dwell (dwɛl) *vb* **dwells**, **dwelling**, **dwelt** (dwɛlt) or **dwelled** (*intr*) **1** *formal, literary* to live as a permanent resident **2** to live (in a specified state): *to dwell in poverty* ▷ *n* **3** a regular pause in the operation of a machine [Old English *dwellan* to seduce, get lost; related to Old Saxon

bidwellian to prevent, Old Norse *dvelja*, Old High German *twellen* to prevent] > **'dweller** *n*

dwelling (ˈdwɛlɪŋ) *n formal, literary* a place of residence

dwell on or **dwell upon** *vb* (*intr, preposition*) to think, speak, or write at length

dwelt (dwɛlt) *vb* a past tense of **dwell**

dwindle (ˈdwɪndᵊl) *vb* to grow or cause to grow less in size, intensity, or number; diminish or shrink gradually [c16: from Old English *dwīnan* to waste away; related to Old Norse *dvīna* to pine away]

DWP (in Britain) *abbreviation* Department for Work and Pensions

Dy *the chemical symbol for* dysprosium

dyad (ˈdaɪæd) *n* **1** *maths* an operator that is the unspecified product of two vectors. It can operate on a vector to produce either a scalar or vector product **2** an atom or group that has a valency of two **3** a group of two; couple [c17: from Late Latin *dyas*, from Greek *duas* two, a pair] > **dy'adic** *adj*

Dyak or **Dayak** (ˈdaɪæk) *n, pl* -aks or -ak a member of a Malaysian people of the interior of Borneo: noted for their long houses [from Malay *Dayak* upcountry, from *darat* land]

dybbuk (ˈdɪbək; *Hebrew* diˈbuk) *n, pl* -buks or -bukkim (*Hebrew* -buˈkim) *Judaism* (in the folklore of the cabala) the soul of a dead sinner that has transmigrated into the body of a living person [from Yiddish *dibbūk* devil, from Hebrew *dibbūq*; related to *dābhaq* to hang on, cling]

dye (daɪ) *n* **1** a staining or colouring substance, such as a natural or synthetic pigment **2** a liquid that contains a colouring material and can be used to stain fabrics, skins, etc **3** the colour or shade produced by dyeing ▷ *vb* **dyes**, **dyeing**, **dyed** **4** (*tr*) to impart a colour or stain to (something, such as fabric or hair) by or as if by the application of a dye [Old English *dēagian*, from *dēag* a dye; related to Old High German *tugōn* to change, Lettish *dūkans* dark] > **'dyable** or **'dyeable** *adj*

dyed-in-the-wool *adj* **1** extreme or unchanging in attitude, opinion, etc **2** (of a fabric) made of dyed yarn

dyeing (ˈdaɪɪŋ) *n* the process or industry of colouring yarns, fabric, etc

dyestuff (ˈdaɪˌstʌf) *n* a substance that can be used as a dye or from which a dye can be obtained

Dyfed (ˈdʌvɛd) *n* a former county in SW Wales: created in 1974 from Cardiganshire, Pembrokeshire, and Carmarthenshire; in 1996 it was replaced by Pembrokeshire, Carmarthenshire, and Ceredigion

dying (ˈdaɪɪŋ) *vb* **1** the present participle of **die¹** ▷ *adj* **2** relating to or occurring at the moment of death: *a dying wish*

dyke¹ or **dike** (daɪk) *n* **1** an embankment constructed to prevent flooding, keep out the sea, etc **2** a ditch or watercourse **3** a bank made of earth excavated for and placed alongside a ditch **4** *Scot* a wall, esp a dry-stone wall **5** a barrier or obstruction **6** a vertical or near-vertical wall-like body of igneous rock intruded into cracks in older rock **7** *Austral & NZ informal* **a** a lavatory **b** (*as modifier*): *a dyke roll* ▷ *vb* **8** (*tr*) to protect, enclose, or drain (land) with a dyke [c13: modification of Old English *dīc* ditch; compare Old Norse *dīki* ditch]

dyke² or **dike** (daɪk) *n slang* a lesbian [c20: of unknown origin]

Dyke (daɪk) *n* **Greg(ory).** born 1947, British television executive; director-general of the BBC (2000–04)

Dylan (ˈdɪlən) *n* **Bob.** real name *Robert Allen Zimmerman.* born 1941, US rock singer and songwriter, also noted for his acoustic protest songs in the early 1960s. His albums include *The Freewheelin' Bob Dylan* (1963), *Highway 61 Revisited* (1965), *Blonde on Blonde* (1966), *John Wesley Harding* (1968), *Blood on the Tracks* (1974), *Oh Mercy* (1989), *Time Out of Mind* (1997), and *Love and Theft* (2001)

dynamic (daɪˈnæmɪk) *adj* **1** of or concerned with energy or forces that produce motion, as opposed to *static* **2** of or concerned with dynamics **3** Also called: **dynamical** characterized by force of personality, ambition, energy, new ideas, etc **4** *computing* (of a memory) needing its contents refreshed periodically [c19: from French *dynamique*, from Greek *dunamikos* powerful, from *dunamis* power, from *dunasthai* to be able] > **dy'namically** *adv*

dynamic link library *n computing* a set of programs that can be activated and then discarded by other programs. Abbreviation: DLL

dynamic range *n* the range of signal amplitudes over which an electronic communications channel can operate within acceptable limits of distortion. The range is determined by system noise at the lower end and by the onset of overload at the upper end

dynamics (daɪˈnæmɪks) *n* **1** (*functioning as singular*) the branch of mechanics concerned with the forces that change or produce the motions of bodies **2** (*functioning as singular*) the branch of mechanics that includes statics and kinetics **3** (*functioning as singular*) the branch of any science concerned with forces **4** those forces that produce change in any field or system **5** *music* **a** the various degrees of loudness called for in performance **b** Also called: dynamic marks, dynamic markings directions and symbols used to indicate degrees of loudness

dynamism (ˈdaɪnəˌmɪzəm) *n* **1** *philosophy* any of several theories that attempt to explain phenomena in terms of an immanent force or energy **2** the forcefulness of an energetic personality > **ˈdynamist** *n* > ˌdynaˈmistic *adj*

dynamite (ˈdaɪnəˌmaɪt) *n* **1** an explosive consisting of nitroglycerine or ammonium nitrate mixed with kieselguhr, sawdust, or wood pulp **2** *informal* a spectacular or potentially dangerous person or thing ▷ *vb* **3** (*tr*) to mine or blow up with dynamite [C19 (coined by Alfred Nobel): from DYNAMO- + -ITE¹] > ˈdynaˌmiter *n*

dynamo (ˈdaɪnəˌməʊ) *n*, *pl* -mos **1** a device for converting mechanical energy into electrical energy, esp one that produces direct current **2** *informal* an energetic hard-working person [C19: short for *dynamoelectric machine*]

dynamo- *or sometimes before a vowel* **dynam-** *combining form* indicating power: *dynamoelectric; dynamite* [from Greek, from *dunamis* power]

dynamoelectric (ˌdaɪnəməʊɪˈlɛktrɪk) *or* **dynamoelectrical** *adj* of or concerned with the interconversion of mechanical and electrical energy

dynamometer (ˌdaɪnəˈmɒmɪtə) *n* any of a number of instruments for measuring power or force

dynamotor (ˈdaɪnəˌməʊtə) *n* an electrical machine having a single magnetic field and two independent armature windings of which one acts as a motor and the other a generator: used to convert direct current from a battery into alternating current

dynast (ˈdɪnəst, -æst) *n* a ruler, esp a hereditary one [C17: from Latin *dynastēs*, from Greek *dunastēs*, from *dunasthai* to be powerful]

dynasty (ˈdɪnəstɪ) *n*, *pl* -ties **1** a sequence of hereditary rulers **2** any sequence of powerful leaders of the same family [C15: via Late Latin from Greek *dunasteia*, from *dunastēs* DYNAST] > dynastic (dɪˈnæstɪk) *or* dyˈnastical *adj*

dyne (daɪn) *n* the cgs unit of force; the force that imparts an acceleration of 1 centimetre per second per second to a mass of 1 gram. 1 dyne is equivalent to 10^{-5} newton or 7.233×10^{-5} poundal [C19: from French, from Greek *dunamis* power, force]

dys- *prefix* **1** diseased, abnormal, or faulty **2** difficult or painful **3** unfavourable or bad [via Latin from Greek *dus-*]

dysentery (ˈdɪsˌntərɪ, -trɪ) *n* infection of the intestine with bacteria or amoebae, marked chiefly by severe diarrhoea with the passage of mucus and blood [C14: via Latin from Greek *dusenteria*, from *dusentera*, literally: bad bowels, from DYS- + *enteron* intestine] > dysenteric (ˌdɪsənˈtɛrɪk) *adj*

dysfunction (dɪsˈfʌŋkʃən) *n* **1** *med* any disturbance or abnormality in the function of an organ or part **2** (esp of a family) failure to show the characteristics or fulfil the purposes accepted as normal or beneficial

dysfunctional (dɪsˈfʌŋkʃənəl) *adj* **1** *med* (of an organ or part) not functioning normally **2** (esp of a family) characterized by a breakdown of normal or beneficial relationships between members of the group

dysgraphia (dɪsˈɡræfɪə) *n* inability to write correctly, caused by disease of part of the brain

dyslexia (dɪsˈlɛksɪə) *n* a developmental disorder which can cause learning difficulty in one or more of the areas of reading, writing, and numeracy [from DYS- + -lexia from Greek *lexis* word] > dyslectic (dɪsˈlɛktɪk) *adj*, *n*

dysmenorrhoea *or esp US* **dysmenorrhea** (ˌdɪsmɛnəˈrɪə, dɪsˌmɛn-) *n* abnormally difficult or painful menstruation [C19: from DYS- + Greek *mēn* month + *rhoiā* a flowing]

Dyson (ˈdaɪsən) *n* Sir **James**. born 1947, British businessman and industrial designer; inventor of the bagless vacuum cleaner (1979–93)

dyspepsia (dɪsˈpɛpsɪə) *or* **dyspepsy** (dɪsˈpɛpsɪ) *n* indigestion or upset stomach [C18: from Latin, from Greek *duspepsia*, from DYS- + *pepsis* digestion]

dyspeptic (dɪsˈpɛptɪk) *adj also* dyspeptical **1** relating to or suffering from dyspepsia **2** irritable ▷ *n* **3** a person suffering from dyspepsia

dysphasia (dɪsˈfeɪzɪə) *n* a disorder of language caused by a brain lesion [see DYS- + -PHASIA] > dysphasic *adj*, *n*

dysphoria (dɪsˈfɔːrɪə) *n* a feeling of being ill at ease [C20: New Latin, from Greek DYS- + -phoria, from *pherein* to bear]

dyspnoea *or US* **dyspnea** (dɪspˈniːə) *n* difficulty in breathing or in catching the breath [C17: via Latin from Greek *duspnoia*, from DYS- + *pnoē* breath, from *pnein* to breathe] > dyspˈnoeal, dyspˈnoeic *or US* dyspˈneal, dyspˈneic *adj*

dysprosium (dɪsˈprəʊsɪəm) *n* a soft silvery-white metallic element of the lanthanide series: used in laser materials and as a neutron absorber in nuclear control rods. Symbol: Dy; atomic no: 66; atomic wt: 162.50; valency: 3; relative density: 8.551; melting pt: 1412°C; boiling pt: 2567°C [C20: New Latin, from Greek *dusprositos* difficult to get near + -IUM]

dysthymia (dɪsˈθaɪmɪə) *n* *psychiatry* the characteristics of the neurotic and introverted, including anxiety, depression, and compulsive behaviour [C19: New Latin, from Greek *dusthumia*, from DYS- + *thumos* mind] > dysˈthymic *adj*

dysthymic disorder *n* a psychiatric disorder characterized by generalized depression that lasts for at least a year

dystrophy (ˈdɪstrəfɪ) *or* **dystrophia** (dɪˈstrəʊfɪə) *n* any of various bodily disorders, characterized by wasting of tissues. See also **muscular dystrophy** [C19: New Latin *dystrophia*, from DYS- + Greek *trophē* food] > dystrophic (dɪsˈtrɒfɪk) *adj*

Dzaudzhikau (dzəʊdʒɪˈkau) *n* the former name (1944–54) of **Vladikavkaz**

dzo (zəʊ) *n*, *pl* dzos *or* dzo a variant spelling of **zo**

Dzungaria (dzʊŋˈɡɛərɪə, zʊŋ-) *n* another name for **Junggar Pendi**

Ee

e¹ or **E** (iː) n, pl **e's**, **E's** or **Es 1** the fifth letter and second vowel of the modern English alphabet **2** any of several speech sounds represented by this letter, in English as in *he*, *bet*, or *below*

e² *symbol for* **1** *maths* a transcendental number, fundamental to mathematics, that is the limit of $(1 + 1/n)^n$ as n increases to infinity: used as the base of natural logarithms. Approximate value: 2.718 282...; relation to π: $e^{\pi i} = -1$, where $i = \sqrt{-1}$ **2** electron

E *symbol for* **1** earth **2** East **3** English **4** Egypt(ian) **5** exa- **6** *music* **a** a note having a frequency of 329.63 hertz (**E above middle C**) or this value multiplied or divided by any power of 2; the third note of the scale of C major **b** the major or minor key having this note as its tonic **7** *physics* **a** energy **b** electromotive force **8 a** a person without a regular income, or who is dependent on the state on a long-term basis because of unemployment, sickness, old age, etc **b** (*as modifier*): E *worker*. See also **occupation groupings** ▷ *abbreviation* **9** *informal* the drug ecstasy

E. *abbreviation* Earl

e- *prefix* electronic, indicating the involvement of the internet: *e-business; e-money*

E- *prefix* used with numbers indicating a standardized system within the European Union, as of recognized food additives or standard pack sizes. See also **E number**

ea. *abbreviation* each

each (iːtʃ) *determiner* **1 a** every (one) of two or more considered individually: *each day; each person* **b** (*as pronoun*): *each gave according to his ability* ▷ *adv* **2** for, to, or from each one; apiece: *four apples each* [Old English *ǣlc*; related to Old High German *ēogilīh*, Old Frisian *ellik*, Dutch *elk*]

● **USAGE** *Each* is a singular pronoun and should be used
● with a singular form of a verb: *each of the candidates was*
● (not *were*) *interviewed separately*

e-address n an e-mail address

Eadred (ˈɛdrɪd) n died 955 AD, king of England (946–55): regained Northumbria (954) from the Norwegian king Eric Bloodaxe

Eadwig (ˈɛdwɪg) or **Edwy** (ˈɛdwɪ) n died 959 AD, king of England (955–57)

eager (ˈiːgə) *adj* **1** (*postpositive; often foll by* to *or* for) impatiently desirous (of); anxious or avid (for) **2** characterized by or feeling expectancy or great desire **3** *archaic* tart or biting; sharp [C13: from Old French *egre*, from Latin *acer* sharp, keen] > ˈeagerly *adv* > ˈeagerness n

eager beaver n *informal* a person who displays conspicuous diligence, esp one who volunteers for extra work

eagle (ˈiːgəl) n **1** any of various birds of prey of the genera *Aquila, Harpia*, etc, having large broad wings and strong soaring flight: family *Accipitridae* (hawks, etc). Related adj: **aquiline 2** a representation of an eagle used as an emblem, etc, esp representing power: *the Roman eagle* **3** a standard, seal, etc, bearing the figure of an eagle **4** *golf* a score of two strokes under par for a hole **5** a former US gold coin worth ten dollars: withdrawn from circulation in 1934 ▷ *vb* **6** *golf* to score two strokes under par for a hole [C14: from Old French *aigle*, from Old Provençal *aigla*, from Latin *aquila*, perhaps from *aquilus* dark]

eagle-eyed *adj* having keen or piercing eyesight

eagle-hawk n a large aggressive Australian eagle, *Aquila audax*. Also called: **wedge-tailed eagle**

eagle owl n a large owl, *Bubo bubo*, of Europe and Asia. It has brownish speckled plumage and large ear tufts

eaglet (ˈiːglɪt) n a young eagle

Eakins (ˈiːkɪnz) n **Thomas**. 1844–1916, US painter of portraits and sporting life: a noted realist

ealdorman (ˈɔːldəmən) n, pl **-men** an official of Anglo-Saxon England, appointed by the king, who was responsible for law, order, and justice in his shire and for leading his local fyrd in battle [Old English *ealdor* lord + MAN]

Ealing (ˈiːlɪŋ) n a borough of W Greater London, formed in 1965 from Acton, Ealing, and Southall. Pop: 3 050 000 (2003 est). Area: 55 sq km (21 sq miles)

-ean *suffix forming adjectives* a variant of **-an**: *Caesarean*

ear¹ (ɪə) n **1** the organ of hearing and balance in higher vertebrates and of balance only in fishes. In man and other mammals it consists of three parts. See **middle ear** Related adj: **aural 2** the outermost cartilaginous part of the ear (pinna) in mammals, esp man **3** the sense of hearing **4** sensitivity to musical sounds, poetic diction, etc: *he has an ear for music* **5** attention, esp favourable attention; consideration; heed (esp in the phrases **give ear to, lend an ear**) **6** an object resembling the external ear in shape or position, such as a handle on a jug **7** all ears very attentive; listening carefully **8** fall on deaf ears to be ignored or pass unnoticed **9** in one ear and out the other heard but unheeded **10** keep one's ear to the ground *or* have one's ear to the ground to be or try to be well informed about current trends and opinions **11** out on one's ear *informal* dismissed unceremoniously **12** play by ear **a** to act according to the demands of a situation rather than to a plan; improvise **b** to perform a musical piece on an instrument without written music **13** a thick ear *informal* a blow on the ear delivered as punishment, in anger, etc **14** turn a deaf ear to be deliberately unresponsive **15** up to one's ears *informal* deeply involved, as in work or debt [Old English *ēare*; related to Old Norse *eyra*, Old High German *ōra*, Gothic *ausō*, Greek *ous*, Latin *auris*] > **'earless** *adj*

ear² (ɪə) *n* **1** the part of a cereal plant, such as wheat or barley, that contains the seeds, grains, or kernels ▷ *vb* **2** (*intr*) (of cereal plants) to develop such parts [Old English *ēar*; related to Old High German *ahar*, Old Norse *ax*, Gothic *ahs* ear, Latin *acus* chaff, Greek *akros* pointed]

earache ('ɪərˌeɪk) *n* pain in the middle or inner ear

earbash ('ɪəˌbæʃ) *vb* (*intr*) *Austral & NZ slang* to talk incessantly > **'earˌbasher** *n* > **'earˌbashing** *n*

earbud ('ɪəˌbʌd) *n* a small earphone worn in the ear for use with a mobile phone

eardrum ('ɪəˌdrʌm) *n* the nontechnical name for **tympanic membrane**

earful ('ɪəfʊl) *n informal* **1** something heard or overheard **2** a rebuke or scolding, esp a lengthy or severe one

Earhart ('ɛəˌhɑːt) *n* **Amelia**. 1898–1937, US aviator: the first woman to fly the Atlantic (1928). She disappeared on a Pacific flight (1937)

earl (ɜːl) *n* (in the British Isles) a nobleman ranking below a marquess and above a viscount. Female equivalent: **countess** [Old English *eorl*; related to Old Norse *jarl* chieftain, Old Saxon *erl* man] > **'earldom** *n*

Earl Grey *n* a variety of China tea flavoured with oil of bergamot

Earl Marshal *n* an officer of the English peerage who presides over the College of Heralds and organizes royal processions and other important ceremonies

ear lobe *n* the fleshy lower part of the external ear

early ('ɜːlɪ) *adj* **-lier, -liest 1** before the expected or usual time **2** occurring in or characteristic of the first part of a period or sequence **3** occurring in or characteristic of a period far back in time **4** occurring in the near future **5** early days too soon to tell how things will turn out ▷ *adv* **earlier 6** before the expected or usual time [Old English *ǣrlīce*, from *ǣr* ERE + *-līce* -LY²; related to Old Norse *arliga*] > **'earliness** *n*

early closing *n Brit* the shutting of most of the shops in a town one afternoon each week

Early English *n* a style of architecture used in England in the 12th and 13th centuries, characterized by lancet arches, narrow openings, and plate tracery

early music *n* **1** music of the Middle Ages and Renaissance, sometimes also including music of the baroque and early classical periods ▷ *modifier* **early-music 2** of or denoting an approach to musical performance emphasizing the use of period instruments and historically researched scores and playing techniques: *the early-music movement*

early warning *n* advance notice of some impending event or development

earmark ('ɪəˌmɑːk) *vb* (*tr*) **1** to set aside or mark out for a specific purpose **2** to make an identification mark on the ear of (a domestic animal) ▷ *n* **3** a mark of identification on the ear of a domestic animal **4** any distinguishing mark or characteristic

earmuff ('ɪəˌmʌf) *n* one of a pair of pads of fur or cloth, joined by a headband, for keeping the ears warm

earn (ɜːn) *vb* **1** to gain or be paid (money or other payment) in return for work or service **2** (*tr*) to acquire, merit, or deserve through behaviour or action **3** (*tr*) (of securities, investments, etc) to gain (interest, return,

profit, etc) [Old English *earnian*; related to Old High German *arnēn* to reap, Old Saxon *asna* salary, tithe]

earned income *n* income derived from paid employment and comprising mainly wages and salaries

earner ('ɜːnə) *n* **1** a person who earns money **2** *Brit & Austral informal* an activity or thing that produces income, esp illicitly: *a nice little earner*

earnest¹ ('ɜːnɪst) *adj* **1** serious in mind or intention **2** showing or characterized by sincerity of intention **3** demanding or receiving serious attention ▷ *n* **4** seriousness **5** in earnest with serious or sincere intentions [Old English *eornost*; related to Old High German *ernust* seriousness, Old Norse *ern* energetic, efficient, Gothic *arniba* secure] > **'earnestly** *adv* > **'earnestness** *n*

earnest² ('ɜːnɪst) *n* **1** a part or portion of something given in advance as a guarantee of the remainder **2** Also called: **earnest money** *contract law* something given, usually a nominal sum of money, to confirm a contract **3** any token of something to follow; pledge; assurance [C13: from Old French *erres* pledges, plural of *erre* earnest money, from Latin *arrha*, shortened from *arrabō* pledge, from Greek *arrabon*, from Hebrew *'ērābhōn* pledge, from *'ārabh* he pledged]

earnings ('ɜːnɪŋz) *pl n* **1** money or other payment earned **2** the profits of an enterprise

EAROM ('ɪərɒm) *n acronym computing* electrically alterable read-only memory

earphone ('ɪəˌfəʊn) *n* a device for converting electric currents into sound waves, held close to or inserted into the ear

ear piercing *n* **1** the making of a hole in the lobe of an ear, using a sterilized needle, so that an earring may be worn fastened in the hole ▷ *adj* **ear-piercing 2** so loud or shrill as to hurt the ears

earplug ('ɪəˌplʌg) *n* a small piece of soft material, such as wax, placed in the ear to keep out noise or water

earring ('ɪəˌrɪŋ) *n* an ornament for the ear, usually clipped onto the lobe or fastened through a hole pierced in the lobe

earshot ('ɪəˌʃɒt) *n* the range or distance within which sound may be heard (esp in the phrases **within earshot, out of earshot**)

ear-splitting *adj* so loud or shrill as to hurt the ears

earth (ɜːθ) *n* **1** (*sometimes capital*) the third planet from the sun, the only planet on which life is known to exist. It is not quite spherical, being flattened at the poles, and consists of three geological zones, the core, mantle, and thin outer crust. The surface, covered with large areas of water, is enveloped by an atmosphere principally of nitrogen (78 per cent), oxygen (21 per cent), and some water vapour. The age is estimated at over four thousand million years. Distance from sun: 149.6 million km; equatorial diameter: 12 756 km; mass: 5.976×10^{24} kg; sidereal period of axial rotation: 23 hours 56 minutes 4 seconds; sidereal period of revolution about sun: 365.256 days. Related adj: **terrestrial, telluric 2** the inhabitants of this planet: *the whole earth rejoiced* **3** the dry surface of this planet as distinguished from sea or sky; land; ground **4** the loose soft material that makes up a large part of the surface of the ground and consists of disintegrated rock particles, mould, clay, etc; soil **5** worldly or temporal matters as opposed to the concerns of the spirit **6** the hole in which some species of burrowing animals, esp foxes, live **7** *chem* See **rare earth, alkaline earth 8 a** a connection between an electrical circuit or device and the earth, which is at zero potential **b** a terminal to which this connection is made **9** (*modifier*) *astrology* of or relating to a group of three signs of the zodiac, Taurus, Virgo, and Capricorn **10** come back to earth *or* come down to earth to return to reality from a fantasy or daydream **11** on earth used as an intensifier in such phrases as **what on earth, who on earth**, etc **12** run to earth **a** to hunt (an animal, esp a fox) to its earth and trap it there **b** to find (someone) after searching ▷ *vb* **13** (*intr*) (of a hunted fox) to go to ground **14** (*tr*) to connect (a circuit, device, etc) to earth ▷ See also **earth up** [Old English *eorthe*; related to Old Norse *jorth*, Old High German *ertha*, Greek *erā*]

earthbound ('ɜːθ,baʊnd) *adj* **1** confined to the earth **2** moving or heading towards the earth

earth closet *n* a type of lavatory in which earth is used to cover excreta

earthen ('ɜːθən) *adj* (*prenominal*) **1** made of baked clay: *an earthen pot* **2** made of earth

earthenware ('ɜːθən,wɛə) *n* **a** vessels, etc, made of baked clay **b** (*as adjective*): *an earthenware pot*

earth-grazer *n* an asteroid in an orbit that takes it close to the earth. Also called: **near-earth asteroid**

earthling ('ɜːθlɪŋ) *n* (*esp in poetry or science fiction*) an inhabitant of the earth; human being [C16: from EARTH + LING¹]

earthly ('ɜːθlɪ) *adj* **-lier, -liest** **1** of or characteristic of the earth as opposed to heaven; material or materialistic; worldly **2** (*usually used with a negative*) *informal* conceivable or possible; feasible (in such phrases as **not an earthly** (**chance**), etc) > **'earthliness** *n*

earthman ('ɜːθ,mæn) *n, pl* **-men** (*esp in science fiction*) an inhabitant or native of the earth

earthnut ('ɜːθ,nʌt) *n* **1** Also called: **pignut** a perennial umbelliferous plant, *Conopodium majus*, of Europe and Asia, having edible dark brown tubers **2** any of various plants having an edible root, tuber, underground pod, or similar part, such as the peanut or truffle

earthquake ('ɜːθ,kweɪk) *n* a sudden release of energy in the earth's crust or upper mantle, usually caused by movement along a fault plane or by volcanic activity and resulting in the generation of seismic waves which can be destructive. Related adj: **seismic**

earth science *n* any of various sciences, such as geology, geography, and geomorphology, that are concerned with the structure, age, and other aspects of the earth

earth up *vb* (*tr, adverb*) to cover (part of a plant, esp the stem) with soil in order to protect from frost, light, etc

earthward ('ɜːθwəd) *adj* **1** directed towards the earth > *adv* **2** a variant of **earthwards**

earthwards ('ɜːθwədz) *or* **earthward** *adv* towards the earth

earthwork ('ɜːθ,wɜːk) *n* **1** excavation of earth, as in engineering construction **2** a fortification made of earth

earthworm ('ɜːθ,wɜːm) *n* any of numerous oligochaete worms of the genera *Lumbricus, Allolobophora, Eisenia*, etc, which burrow in the soil and help aerate and break up the ground

earthy ('ɜːθɪ) *adj* **earthier, earthiest** **1** of, composed of, or characteristic of earth **2** unrefined, coarse, or crude > **'earthily** *adv* > **'earthiness** *n*

ear trumpet *n* a trumpet-shaped instrument that amplifies sounds and is held to the ear: an old form of hearing aid

earwax ('ɪə,wæks) *n* the nontechnical name for **cerumen**

earwig ('ɪə,wɪɡ) *n* **1** any of various insects of the order *Dermaptera*, esp *Forficula auricularia* (**common European earwig**), which typically have an elongated body with small leathery forewings, semicircular membranous hindwings, and curved forceps at the tip of the abdomen > *vb* **-wigs, -wigging, -wigged** **2** *informal* to eavesdrop **3** (*tr*) *archaic* to attempt to influence (a person) by private insinuation [Old English *ēarwicga*, from *ēare* EAR¹ + *wicga* beetle, insect; probably from a superstition that the insect crept into human ears]

earwigging ('ɪə,wɪɡɪŋ) *n* *informal* a scolding or harangue: *I'll give him an earwigging about that*

earworm ('ɪə,wɜːm) *n* *informal* an irritatingly catchy tune [C20: from German *Ohrwurm* earwig]

ease (iːz) *n* **1** freedom from discomfort, worry, or anxiety **2** lack of difficulty, labour, or awkwardness; facility **3** rest, leisure, or relaxation **4** freedom from poverty or financial embarrassment; affluence: *a life of ease* **5** lack of restraint, embarrassment, or stiffness: *his ease of manner disarmed us* **6** at ease *military* **a** (of a standing soldier, etc) in a relaxed position with the feet apart and hands linked behind the back **b** a command to adopt such a position **c** in a relaxed attitude or frame of mind > *vb* **7** to make or become less burdensome **8** (*tr*) to

relieve (a person) of worry or care; comfort **9** (*tr*) to make comfortable or give rest to **10** (*tr*) to make less difficult; facilitate **11** to move or cause to move into, out of, etc, with careful manipulation **12** (when *intr*, often foll by *off* or *up*) to lessen or cause to lessen in severity, pressure, tension, or strain; slacken, loosen, or abate **13** ease oneself *or* ease nature *archaic, euphemistic* to urinate or defecate [C13: from Old French *aise* ease, opportunity, from Latin *adjacēns* neighbouring (area); see ADJACENT] > **'easeful** *adj*

easel ('iːz°l) *n* a frame, usually in the form of an upright tripod, used for supporting or displaying an artist's canvas, blackboard, etc [C17: from Dutch *ezel* ASS¹; related to Gothic *asilus*, German *Esel*, Latin *asinus* ass]

easement ('iːzmənt) *n* **1** *property law* the right enjoyed by a landowner of making limited use of his neighbour's land, as by crossing it to reach his own property **2** the act of easing or something that brings ease

easily ('iːzɪlɪ) *adv* **1** with ease; without difficulty or exertion **2** by far; beyond question; undoubtedly: *he is easily the best in the contest* **3** probably; almost certainly

easiness ('iːzɪnɪs) *n* **1** the quality or condition of being easy to accomplish, do, obtain, etc **2** ease or relaxation of manner; nonchalance

east (iːst) *n* **1** the direction along a parallel towards the sunrise, at 90° to north; the direction of the earth's rotation **2** the east (*often capital*) any area lying in or towards the east. Related adj: **oriental** **3** *cards* (*usually capital*) the player or position at the table corresponding to east on the compass > *adj* **4** situated in, moving towards, or facing the east **5** (*esp of the wind*) from the east > *adv* **6** in, to, or towards the east > Symbol: E [Old English *ēast*; related to Old High German *ōstar* to the east, Old Norse *austr*, Latin *aurora* dawn, Greek *eōs*, Sanskrit *usās* dawn, morning]

East (iːst) *n* **1** the East *n* **1** the continent of Asia regarded as culturally distinct from Europe and the West; the Orient **2** the countries under Communist rule and formerly under Communist rule, lying mainly in the E hemisphere *adj* **3** of or denoting the eastern part of a specified country, area, etc

East Africa *n* a region of Africa comprising Kenya, Uganda, and Tanzania

East African *adj* **1** of or relating to East Africa or its inhabitants > *n* **2** a native or inhabitant of East Africa

East Anglia *n* **1** a region of E England south of the Wash: consists of Norfolk and Suffolk, and parts of Essex and Cambridgeshire **2** an Anglo-Saxon kingdom that consisted of Norfolk and Suffolk in the 6th century AD; became a dependency of Mercia in the 8th century

East Anglian *adj* **1** of or relating to East Anglia or its inhabitants > *n* **2** a native or inhabitant of East Anglia

East Ayrshire *n* a council area of SW Scotland, comprising the E part of the historical county of Ayrshire: part of Strathclyde region from 1975 to 1996: chiefly agricultural. Administrative centre: Kilmarnock. Pop: 119 530 (2003 est). Area: 1252 sq km (483 sq miles)

East Bengal *n* the part of the former Indian province of Bengal assigned to Pakistan in 1947 (now Bangladesh)

East Bengali *adj* **1** of or relating to East Bengal (now Bangladesh) or its inhabitants > *n* **2** a native or inhabitant of East Bengal

East Berlin *n* (formerly) the part of Berlin under East German control

eastbound ('iːst,baʊnd) *adj* going or leading towards the east

Eastbourne ('iːst,bɔːn) *n* a resort in SE England, in East Sussex on the English Channel. Pop: 106 592 (2001)

east by north *n* one point on the compass north of east, 78° 45′ clockwise from north

east by south *n* one point on the compass south of east, 101° 15′ clockwise from north

East Cape *n* **1** the easternmost point of New Guinea, on Milne Bay **2** the easternmost point of New Zealand, on North Island **3** the former name for Cape **Dezhnev**

East China Sea *n* part of the N Pacific, between the E coast of China and the Ryukyu Islands

East Dunbartonshire *n* a council area of central Scotland to the N of Glasgow: part of Strathclyde region from 1975 until 1996: mainly agricultural and residential. Administrative centre: Kirkintilloch. Pop: 106 970 (2003 est). Area: 172 sq km (66 sq miles)

East End n the East End a densely populated part of E London containing former industrial and dock areas, now extensively redeveloped for offices

Easter ('i:stə) n 1 the most important festival of the Christian Church, commemorating the Resurrection of Christ: falls on the Sunday following the first full moon after the vernal equinox 2 Also called: Easter Sunday, Easter Day the day on which this festival is celebrated 3 the period between Good Friday and Easter Monday Related adj: **Paschal** [Old English ēastre, after a Germanic goddess *Eostre*; related to Old High German *ōstarūn* Easter, Old Norse *austr* to the EAST, Old Slavonic *ustru* like summer]

Easter cactus n a Brazilian cactus, *Rhipsalidopsis gaertneri*, widely cultivated as an ornamental for its showy red flowers

Easter egg n 1 an egg given to children at Easter, usually a chocolate egg or a hen's egg with its shell painted 2 a bonus or extra feature hidden inside a website, computer game, or DVD, that is only revealed after repeated or lengthy viewing or playing

Easter Island n an isolated volcanic island in the Pacific, 3700 km (2300 miles) west of Chile, of which it is a dependency: discovered on Easter Sunday, 1722; annexed by Chile in 1888; noted for the remains of an aboriginal culture, which includes gigantic stone figures. Pop: 3791 (2002). Area: 166 sq km (64 sq miles). Polynesian name: **Rapa Nui**

easterly ('i:stəlɪ) adj 1 of, relating to, or situated in the east ▷ adv, adj 2 towards or in the direction of the east 3 from the east: *an easterly wind* ▷ n, pl -lies 4 a wind from the east

eastern ('i:stən) adj 1 situated in or towards the east 2 facing or moving towards the east

Eastern Cape n a province of S South Africa; formed in 1994 from the E part of the former Cape Province: service industries, agriculture, and mining. Capital: Bhisho (formerly Bisho). Pop: 7 088 547 (2004 est). Area: 169 600 sq km (65 483 sq miles). Also called: **Eastern Province**

Eastern Church n 1 any of the Christian Churches of the former Byzantine Empire 2 any Church owing allegiance to the Orthodox Church and in communion with the Greek patriarchal see of Constantinople 3 any Church, including Uniat Churches, having Eastern forms of liturgy and institutions

Easterner ('i:stənə) n (sometimes not capital) a native or inhabitant of the east of any specified region, esp of the Orient or of the eastern states of the US

Eastern Ghats pl n a mountain range in S India, parallel to the Bay of Bengal: united with the Western Ghats by the Nilgiri Hills; forms the E margin of the Deccan plateau

eastern hemisphere n (often capitals) 1 that half of the globe containing Europe, Asia, Africa, and Australia, lying east of the Greenwich meridian 2 the lands in this, esp Asia

Eastern Orthodox Church n another name for the **Orthodox Church**

Eastern Townships n an area of central Canada, in S Quebec: consists of 11 townships south of the St Lawrence

Eastertide ('i:stə,taɪd) n the Easter season

East Flanders n a province of W Belgium: low-lying, with reclaimed land in the northeast: textile industries. Capital: Ghent. Pop: 1 373 720 (2004 est). Area: 2979 sq km (1150 sq miles)

East German adj 1 of or relating to the former republic of East Germany or its inhabitants ▷ n 2 a native or inhabitant of the former East Germany

East Germany n a former republic in N central Europe: established in 1949 and declared a sovereign state by the Soviet Union in 1954; Communist regime replaced by a multiparty democracy in 1989; reunited with West Germany in 1990. Official name: German Democratic Republic. Abbreviations: **DDR**, **GDR**. See also **Germany**

East Indian n 1 Caribbean an immigrant to the countries of the Caribbean (West Indies) who is of Indian origin; an Asian West Indian ▷ adj 2 US & Canadian of, relating to, or originating in the East Indies

East Indies the East Indies pl n 1 the Malay Archipelago, including or excluding the Philippines 2 SE Asia in general

easting ('i:stɪŋ) n 1 nautical the net distance eastwards made by a vessel moving towards the east 2 cartography the distance eastwards of a point from a given meridian indicated by the first half of a map grid reference

East Kilbride (kɪl'braɪd) n a town in W Scotland, in South Lanarkshire near Glasgow: designated a new town in 1947. Pop: 73 796 (2001)

Eastleigh ('i:st,li:) n a town in S England, in S Hampshire: railway engineering industry. Pop: 52 894 (2001)

East London n a port in S South Africa, in S Eastern Cape province. Pop: 135 560 (2001)

East Lothian n a council area and historical county of E central Scotland, on the Firth of Forth and the North Sea: part of Lothian region from 1975 to 1996: chiefly agricultural. Administrative centre: Haddington. Pop: 91 090 (2003 est). Area: 678 sq km (262 sq miles)

Eastman ('i:stmən) n **George.** 1854–1932, US manufacturer of photographic equipment: noted for the introduction of roll film and developments in colour photography

east-northeast n 1 the point on the compass or the direction midway between northeast and east, 67° 30' clockwise from north ▷ adj, adv 2 in, from, or towards this direction

East Pakistan n the former name (until 1971) of **Bangladesh**

East Pakistani adj 1 of or relating to East Pakistan (now Bangladesh) or its inhabitants ▷ n 2 a native or inhabitant of the former East Pakistan

East Prussia n a former province of NE Germany on the Baltic Sea: separated in 1919 from the rest of Germany by the Polish Corridor and Danzig: in 1945 Poland received the south part, the Soviet Union the north. German name: **Ostpreussen** (ost'prɔysən)

East Prussian adj 1 of or relating to the former German province of East Prussia or its inhabitants ▷ n 2 a native or inhabitant of the former East Prussia

East Renfrewshire n a council area of W central Scotland, comprising part of the historical county of Renfrewshire; part of Strathclyde region from 1975 to 1996: chiefly agricultural and residential. Administrative centre: Giffnock. Pop: 89 680 (2003 est). Area: 173 sq km (67 sq miles)

East Riding of Yorkshire n a county of NE England, a historical division of Yorkshire on the North Sea and the Humber estuary: became part of Humberside in 1974; reinstated as an independent unitary authority in 1996, with a separate authority for Kingston upon Hull: chiefly agricultural and low-lying, with various industries in Hull. Administrative centre: Beverley. Pop (excluding Hull): 321 300 (2003 est). Area (excluding Hull): 748 sq km (675 sq miles)

east-southeast n 1 the point on the compass or the direction midway between east and southeast, 112° 30' clockwise from north ▷ adj, adv 2 in, from, or towards this direction

East Sussex n a county of SE England comprising part of the former county of Sussex: mainly undulating agricultural land, with the South Downs and seaside resorts in the south: Brighton and Hove became an independent unitary authority in 1997 but is part of the geographical and ceremonial county. Administrative centre: Lewes. Pop (excluding Brighton and Hove): 496 100 (2003 est). Area (excluding Brighton and Hove): 1795 sq km (693 sq miles)

East Timor n a small country in SE Asia, comprising part of the island of Timor: colonized by Portugal in the 19th century; declared independence in 1975 but immediately invaded by Indonesia; under UN administration from 1999 and an independent state from 2002. It is mountainous with a monsoon climate; subsistence agriculture is the main occupation.

e

Languages: Portuguese, Tetun (a lingua franca), and Bahasa Indonesia. Religion: Roman Catholic majority. Currency: US dollar. Capital: Dili. Pop: 820 000 (2004 est). Area: 14 874 sq km (5743 sq miles)

East Timorese adj **1** of or relating to East Timor or its inhabitants ▷ n **2** a native or inhabitant of East Timor

eastward ('i:stwəd) adj **1** situated or directed towards the east ▷ adv **2** a variant of **eastwards** ▷ n **3** the eastward part, direction, etc > 'eastwardly adv, adj

eastwards or **eastward** ('i:stwədz) adv towards the east

Eastwood ('i:stwʊd) n **Clint.** born 1930, US film actor and director. His films as an actor include *The Good The Bad and The Ugly* (1966), *Dirty Harry* (1971), and as actor and director *Play Misty for Me* (1971), *Unforgiven* (1993), *Mystic River* (2003), and *Million Dollar Baby* (2004).

easy ('i:zɪ) adj **easier, easiest 1** not requiring much labour or effort; not difficult; simple **2** free from pain, care, or anxiety **3** not harsh or restricting; lenient: *easy laws* **4** tolerant and undemanding; easy-going: *an easy disposition* **5** readily influenced or persuaded; pliant: *she was an easy victim of his wiles* **6** not tight or constricting; loose: *an easy fit* **7** not strained or extreme; moderate; gentle: *an easy pace; an easy ascent* **8** informal ready to fall in with any suggestion made; not predisposed: *he is easy about what to do* **9** slang sexually available ▷ adv **10** informal in an easy or relaxed manner **11** easy does it informal go slowly and carefully; be careful **12** go easy on to use in moderation **13** stand easy military a command to soldiers standing at ease that they may relax further **14** take it easy **a** to avoid stress or undue hurry **b** to remain calm; not become agitated or angry [c12: from Old French aisié, past participle of aisier to relieve, EASE]

easy-care adj (esp of a fabric or garment) hardwearing, practical, and requiring no special treatment during washing, cleaning, etc

easy chair n a comfortable upholstered armchair

easy-going ('i:zɪ'gəʊɪŋ) adj **1** relaxed in manner or attitude; inclined to be excessively tolerant **2** moving at a comfortable pace: *an easy-going horse*

easy meat n informal **1** someone easily seduced or deceived **2** something easy to get or do

easy money n **1** money made with little effort, sometimes dishonestly **2** commerce money that can be borrowed at a low interest rate

Easy Street n (sometimes not capitals) informal a state of financial security

eat (i:t) vb **eats, eating, ate, eaten 1** to take into the mouth and swallow (food, etc), esp after biting and chewing **2** (tr; often foll by *away* or *up*) to destroy as if by eating: *the damp had eaten away the woodwork* **3** (often foll by *into*) to use up or waste: *taxes ate into his inheritance* **4** (often foll by *into* or *through*) to make (a hole, passage, etc) by eating or gnawing: *rats ate through the floor* **5** to take or have (a meal or meals): *we always eat at six* **6** (tr) to include as part of one's diet: *he doesn't eat fish* **7** (tr) informal to cause to worry; make anxious: *what's eating you?* ▷ See also **eat out, eats, eat up** [Old English *etan*; related to Gothic *itan*, Old High German *ezzan*, Latin *edere*, Greek *edein*, Sanskrit *admi*] > 'eater n

eatable ('i:təbəl) adj fit or suitable for eating; edible

eatables ('i:təbəlz) pl n (sometimes singular) food

eating ('i:tɪŋ) n **1** food, esp in relation to its quality or taste: *this fruit makes excellent eating* ▷ adj **2** relating to or suitable for eating, esp uncooked: *eating pears* **3** relating to or for eating: *an eating house*

eat out vb (intr, adverb) to eat away from home, esp in a restaurant

eats (i:ts) pl n informal articles of food; provisions

eat up vb (adverb, mainly tr) **1** (also intr) to eat or consume entirely: often used as an exhortation to children **2** informal to listen to with enthusiasm or appreciation: *the audience ate up the speaker's every word* **3** (often passive) informal to affect grossly: *she was eaten up by jealousy* **4** informal to travel (a distance) quickly: *we just ate up the miles*

eau de Cologne (əʊ də kə'ləʊn) n See **cologne** [French, literally: water of Cologne]

eau de nil (əʊ də ni:l) n, adj a pale yellowish-green colour [French, literally: water of (the) Nile]

eau de vie (əʊ də vi:; *French* od vi) n brandy or other spirits [French, literally: water of life]

eaves (i:vz) pl n the edge of a roof that projects beyond the wall [Old English *efes*; related to Gothic *ubizwa* porch, Greek *hupsos* height]

eavesdrop ('i:vz,drɒp) vb **-drops, -dropping, -dropped** (intr) to listen secretly to the private conversation of others [c17: back formation from earlier *evesdropper*, from Old English *yfesdrype* water dripping from the eaves; see EAVES, DROP; compare Old Norse *upsardropi*] > 'eaves,dropper n

eavestrough ('i:vz,trɒf) n Canadian a gutter at the eaves of a building

ebb (ɛb) vb (intr) **1** (of tide water) to flow back or recede. See **flow** (sense 8) **2** to fall away or decline ▷ n **3** a the flowing back of the tide from high to low water or the period in which this takes place **b** (as modifier): *the ebb tide*. See **flood** (sense 3) **4** at a low ebb in a state or period of weakness, lack of vigour, or decline [Old English *ebba*; related to Old Norse *efja* river bend, Gothic *ibuks* moving backwards, Old High German *ippihōn* to roll backwards, Middle Dutch *ebbe* ebb]

Ebbinghaus ('ɛbɪŋhaʊs) n **Hermann.** ('hɛrman). 1850–1909, German experimental psychologist who undertook the first systematic and large-scale studies of memory and devised tests using nonsense syllables

Ebbw Vale ('ɛbu: veɪl) n a town in S Wales, in Blaenau Gwent county borough: a former coal mining centre. Pop: 18 558 (2001)

EBCDIC ('ɛbsɪ,dɪk) n acronym for extended binary-coded decimal-interchange code: a computer code for representing alphanumeric characters

Eberhard (*German* 'e:bər,hart) n **Johann August** (jo'han 'aʊgʊst). 1739–1809, German philosopher and lexicographer, best known for his German dictionary (1795–1802)

Ebert (*German* 'e:bərt) n **Friedrich.** ('fri:drɪç). 1871–1925, German Social Democratic statesman; first president of the German Republic (1919–25)

ebon ('ɛbən) n, adj a poetic word for **ebony** [c14: from Latin *hebenus*; see EBONY]

ebonics (ɪ'bɒnɪks) n (functioning as singular) US another name for **African-American Vernacular English** [c20: from EBONY + PHONICS]

ebonite ('ɛbə,naɪt) n another name for **vulcanite**

ebonize or **ebonise** ('ɛbə,naɪz) vb (tr) to stain or otherwise finish in imitation of ebony

ebony ('ɛbənɪ) n, pl **-onies 1** any of various tropical and subtropical trees of the genus *Diospyros*, esp *D. ebenum* of S India, that have hard dark wood: family *Ebenaceae* **2** the wood of such a tree, much used for cabinetwork **3** a **a** black colour, sometimes with a dark olive tinge **b** (as adjective): *an ebony skin* [c16 *hebeny*, from Late Latin *ebeninus* from Greek *ebeninos*, from *ebenos* ebony, of Egyptian origin]

e-book n **1** a book in electronic form ▷ vb **2** (tr) to book (hospital appointments, airline tickets, etc) through the internet [c20: electronic book] > 'e-,booking n

Ebor. ('i:bɔ:) abbreviation Eboracensis [Latin: (Archbishop) of York]

Eboracum (i:'bɒrəkəm, ,i:bɔ:'rɑ:kəm) n the Roman name for **York¹** (sense 1)

EBRD abbreviation European Bank for Reconstruction and Development

Ebro ('i:brəʊ; *Spanish* 'eβro) n the second largest river in Spain, rising in the Cantabrian Mountains and flowing southeast to the Mediterranean. Length: 910 km (565 miles)

ebullient (ɪ'bʌljənt, ɪ'bʊl-) adj **1** overflowing with enthusiasm or excitement; exuberant **2** boiling [c16: from Latin *ēbullīre* to bubble forth, be boisterous, from *bullīre* to BOIL¹] > e'bullience or e'bulliency n

ebulliometer (ɪ,bʌlɪ'ɒmɪtə) n physics a device used to determine the boiling point of a solution

ebullition (,ɛbə'lɪʃən) n **1** the process of boiling **2** a sudden outburst, as of intense emotion [c16: from Late Latin *ēbullītiō*; see EBULLIENT]

EC abbreviation **1** European Community (now subsumed within the European Union) **2** (in London postal code)

East Central

ec- combining form out from; away from: ecbolic; eccentric; ecdysis [from Greek ek (before a vowel ex) out of, away from; see EX-¹]

e-card n a pictorial greeting sent by means of the internet [C20: electronic card]

ECB abbreviation European Central Bank

Ecbatana (ɛkˈbætənə) n an ancient city in Iran, on the site of modern Hamadān; capital of Media and royal residence of the Persians and Parthians

eccentric (ɪkˈsɛntrɪk) adj 1 deviating or departing from convention, esp in a bizarre manner; irregular or odd 2 situated away from the centre or the axis 3 not having a common centre: eccentric circles 4 not precisely circular ▷ n 5 a person who deviates from normal forms of behaviour, esp in a bizarre manner 6 a device for converting rotary motion to reciprocating motion [C16: from Medieval Latin eccentricus, from Greek ekkentros out of centre, from ek- EX-¹ + kentron centre] > ec'centrically adv

eccentricity (ˌɛksɛnˈtrɪsɪtɪ) n, pl -ties 1 unconventional or irregular behaviour 2 deviation from a circular path or orbit 3 geometry a number that expresses the shape of a conic section: the ratio of the distance of a point on the curve from a fixed point (the focus) to the distance of the point from a fixed line (the directrix) 4 the degree of displacement of the geometric centre of a rotating part from the true centre, esp of the axis of rotation of a wheel or shaft

eccl. or **eccles.** abbreviation ecclesiastic(al)

Eccles¹ (ˈɛkəlz) n a town in NW England, in Salford unitary authority, Greater Manchester. Pop: 36 610 (2001)

Eccles² (ˈɛkəlz) n Sir John Carew. 1903–97, Australian physiologist: shared the Nobel prize for physiology (1963) with A. L. Hodgkin and A. F. Huxley for their work on conduction of nervous impulses

Eccles. or **Eccl.** abbreviation Bible Ecclesiastes

ecclesiastic (ɪˌkliːzɪˈæstɪk) n 1 a clergyman or other person in holy orders ▷ adj 2 of or associated with the Christian Church or clergy

ecclesiastical (ɪˌkliːzɪˈæstɪkəl) adj of or relating to the Christian Church > ec,clesi'astically adv

ecclesiasticism (ɪˌkliːzɪˈæstɪˌsɪzəm) n exaggerated attachment to the practices or principles of the Christian Church

ecclesiology (ɪˌkliːzɪˈɒlədʒɪ) n 1 the study of the Christian Church 2 the study of Church architecture and decoration > ecclesiological (ɪˌkliːzɪəˈlɒdʒɪkəl) adj

Ecclestone (ˈɛkəlstən) n Bernard, known as Bernie. born 1930, British businessman and sports administrator; head of Formula One motor racing from 1995

eccrine (ˈɛkrɪn) adj of or denoting glands that secrete externally, esp the numerous sweat glands on the human body. See apocrine [from Greek ekkrinein to secrete, from ek- EC- + krinein to separate] > eccrinology (ˌɛkrɪˈnɒlədʒɪ) n

ecdemic (ɛkˈdɛmɪk) adj not indigenous or endemic; foreign: an ecdemic disease

ecdysis (ˈɛkdɪsɪs) n, pl -ses (-ˌsiːz) the periodic shedding of the cuticle in insects and other arthropods or the outer epidermal layer in reptiles [C19: New Latin, from Greek ekdusis, from ekduein to strip, from ek- EX-¹ + duein to put on]

Ecevit (ˈɛʃəvɪt) n Bülent (ˈbuːlənt). 1925–2006, Turkish politician and journalist: prime minister of Turkey (1974, 1977, 1978–79, 1998–2002)

ECG abbreviation 1 electrocardiogram 2 electrocardiograph

Echegaray y Eizaguirre (Spanish etʃeɣaˈrai i eiθaˈɣirre) n José (xoˈse). 1832–1916, Spanish dramatist, statesman, and mathematician. His plays include Madman or Saint (1877); Nobel prize for literature 1904

echelon (ˈɛʃəˌlɒn) n 1 a level of command, responsibility, etc (esp in the phrase the upper echelons) 2 military an arrangement in which units follow one another but are offset sufficiently to allow each unit a line of fire ahead b a group formed in this way ▷ vb 3 to assemble in echelon [C18: from French échelon, literally: rung of a

ladder, from Old French eschiele ladder, from Latin scāla; see SCALE³]

echidna (ɪˈkɪdnə) n, pl -nas or -nae (-niː) any of the spine-covered monotreme mammals of the genera Tachyglossus of Australia and Zaglossus of New Guinea: family Tachyglossidae. They have a long snout and claws for hunting ants and termites. Also called: spiny anteater [C19: from New Latin, from Latin: viper, from Greek ekhidna]

echinoderm (ɪˈkaɪnəˌdɜːm) n any of the marine invertebrate animals constituting the phylum Echinodermata, characterized by tube feet, a calcite body-covering (test), and a five-part symmetrical body. The group includes the starfish, sea urchins, and sea cucumbers

echinus (ɪˈkaɪnəs) n, pl -ni (-naɪ) 1 architect an ovolo moulding between the shaft and the abacus of a Doric column 2 any of the sea urchins of the genus Echinus, such as E. esculentus (edible sea urchin) of the Mediterranean [C14: from Latin, from Greek ekhinos]

echo (ˈɛkəʊ) n, pl -oes 1 a the reflection of sound or other radiation by a reflecting medium, esp a solid object b the sound so reflected 2 a repetition or imitation, esp an unoriginal reproduction of another's opinions 3 something that evokes memories, esp of a particular style or era 4 (sometimes plural) an effect that continues after the original cause has disappeared; repercussion: the echoes of the French Revolution 5 a person who copies another, esp one who obsequiously agrees with another's opinions 6 a the signal reflected by a radar target b the trace produced by such a signal on a radar screen ▷ vb -oes, -oing, -oed 7 to resound or cause to resound with an echo 8 (intr) (of sounds) to repeat or resound by echoes; reverberate 9 (tr) (of persons) to repeat (words, opinions, etc), in imitation, agreement, or flattery 10 (tr) (of things) to resemble or imitate (another style, earlier model, etc) [C14: via Latin from Greek ēkhō; related to Greek ēkhē sound] > 'echoing adj > 'echoless adj > 'echo-ˌlike adj

Echo (ˈɛkəʊ) n Greek myth a nymph who, spurned by Narcissus, pined away until only her voice remained

echocardiogram (ˌɛkəʊˈkɑːdɪəʊˌgræm) n a visual display or record produced using echocardiography

echocardiography (ˌɛkəʊkɑːdɪˈɒgrəfɪ) n examination of the heart using ultrasound techniques

echo chamber n a room with walls that reflect sound. It is used to make acoustic measurements and as a source of reverberant sound to be mixed with direct sound for recording or broadcasting. Also called: reverberation chamber

echography (ɛˈkɒgrəfɪ) n medical examination of the internal structures of the body by means of ultrasound

echoic (ɛˈkəʊɪk) adj 1 characteristic of or resembling an echo 2 onomatopoeic; imitative

echolalia (ˌɛkəʊˈleɪlɪə) n psychiatry the tendency to repeat mechanically words just spoken by another person: can occur in cases of brain damage, mental retardation, and schizophrenia [C19: from New Latin, from ECHO + Greek lalia talk, chatter, from lalein to chatter]

echolocation (ˌɛkəʊləʊˈkeɪʃən) n determination of the position of an object by measuring the time taken for an echo to return from it and its direction

echo sounder n a navigation and position-finding device that determines depth by measuring the time taken for a pulse of high-frequency sound to reach the sea bed or a submerged object and for the echo to return > echo sounding n

echovirus (ˈɛkəʊˌvaɪrəs) or **ECHO virus** n any of a group of viruses that can cause symptoms of mild meningitis, the common cold, or infections of the intestinal and respiratory tracts [C20: from the initials of Enteric Cytopathic Human Orphan ("orphan" because originally believed to be unrelated to any disease) + VIRUS]

Eck (ɛk) n Johann (joˈhan), original name Johann Mayer. 1486–1543, German Roman Catholic theologian; opponent of Luther and the Reformation

Eckert (ˈɛkət) n John Presper. 1919–95, US electronics engineer: built the first electronic computer with John W. Mauchly in 1946

e

Eckhart (*German* 'ɛkhart) *n* **Johannes** (jo'hanəs), called *Meister Eckhart*. ?1260–?1327, German Dominican theologian, mystic, and preacher

éclair (eɪ'klɛə, ɪ'klɛə) *n* a finger-shaped cake of choux pastry, usually filled with cream and covered with chocolate [C19: from French, literally: lightning (probably so called because it does not last long), from *éclairer*, from Latin *clārāre* to make bright, from *clārus* bright]

eclampsia (ɪ'klæmpsɪə) *n* *pathol* a toxic condition of unknown cause that sometimes develops in the last three months of pregnancy, characterized by high blood pressure, abnormal weight gain and convulsions [C19: from New Latin, from Greek *eklampsis* a shining forth, from *eklampein*, from *lampein* to shine]

éclat (eɪ'klɑː; *French* ekla) *n* 1 brilliant or conspicuous success, effect, etc 2 showy display; ostentation 3 social distinction 4 approval; acclaim; applause [C17: from French, from *éclater* to burst; related to Old French *esclater* to splinter, perhaps of Germanic origin; compare SLIT]

eclectic (ɪ'klɛktɪk, ɛ'klɛk-) *adj* 1 (in art, philosophy, etc) selecting what seems best from various styles, doctrines, ideas, methods, etc 2 composed of elements drawn from a variety of sources, styles, etc ▷ *n* 3 a person who favours an eclectic approach, esp in art or philosophy [C17: from Greek *eklektikos*, from *eklegein* to select, from *legein* to gather] > ec'lectically *adv* > e'clecti‚cism *n*

eclipse (ɪ'klɪps) *n* 1 the total or partial obscuring of one celestial body by another. A **solar eclipse** occurs when the moon passes between the sun and the earth; a **lunar eclipse** when the earth passes between the sun and the moon. See also **annular eclipse** 2 the period of time during which such a phenomenon occurs 3 any dimming or obstruction of light 4 a loss of importance, power, fame, etc, esp through overshadowing by another ▷ *vb* (*tr*) 5 to cause an eclipse of 6 to cast a shadow upon; darken; obscure 7 to overshadow or surpass in importance, power, etc [C13: back formation from Old English *eclypsis*, from Latin *eclipsis*, from Greek *ekleipsis* a forsaking, from *ekleipein* to abandon, from *leipein* to leave] > e'clipser *n*

eclipsing binary *or* **eclipsing variable** *n* a binary star whose orbital plane lies in or near the line of sight so that one component is regularly eclipsed by its companion

ecliptic (ɪ'klɪptɪk) *n* 1 *astronomy* a the great circle on the celestial sphere representing the apparent annual path of the sun relative to the stars. It is inclined at 23.45° to the celestial equator. The **poles of the ecliptic** lie on the celestial sphere due north and south of the plane of the ecliptic b (*as modifier*): *the ecliptic plane* 2 an equivalent great circle, opposite points of which pass through the Tropics of Cancer and Capricorn, on the terrestrial globe ▷ *adj* 3 of or relating to an eclipse > e'cliptically *adv*

eclogue ('ɛklɒg) *n* a pastoral or idyllic poem, usually in the form of a conversation or soliloquy [C15: from Latin *ecloga* short poem, collection of extracts, from Greek *eklogē* selection, from *eklegein* to select; see ECLECTIC]

eclosion (ɪ'kləʊʒən) *n* the emergence of an insect larva from the egg or an adult from the pupal case [C19: from French *éclosion*, from *éclore* to hatch, ultimately from Latin *exclūdere* to shut out, EXCLUDE]

ECMO *abbreviation* extracorporeal membrane oxygenation: a method of life support used to oxygenate the blood in newborn babies with lung failure, using a machine incorporating membranes that are impermeable to blood but permeable to oxygen and carbon dioxide

eco- *combining form* denoting ecology or ecological: *ecocide*; *ecosphere*

Eco ('ɛkəʊ) *n* **Umberto**. born 1932, Italian semiologist and writer. His novels include *The Name of the Rose* (1981) and *Foucault's Pendulum* (1988)

ecocentric (‚iːkəʊ'sɛntrɪk) *adj* having a serious concern for environmental issues: *ecocentric management*

Ecofin ('ɛkəʊ‚fɪn) *n* the council of European finance ministers

ecofriendly ('iːkəʊ‚frɛndlɪ) *adj* having a beneficial effect on the environment or at least not causing environmental damage

ecol. *abbreviation* 1 ecological 2 ecology

E. coli (‚iː'kəʊlaɪ) *n* short for *Escherichia coli*, see **Escherichia**

ecological (‚iːkə'lɒdʒɪkᵊl) *adj* 1 of or relating to ecology 2 (of a practice, policy, product, etc) tending to benefit or cause minimal damage to the environment > ‚eco'logically *adv*

ecological footprint *n* the amount of productive land appropriated on average by each person (in the world, a country, etc) for food, water, transport, housing, waste management, and other purposes

ecology (ɪ'kɒlədʒɪ) *n* 1 the study of the relationships between living organisms and their environment 2 the set of relationships of a particular organism with its environment [C19: from German *Ökologie*, from Greek *oikos* house (hence, environment)] > e'cologist *n*

e-commerce *or* **ecommerce** ('iːkɒmɜːs) *n* business transactions conducted on the internet [C20: from E- + COMMERCE]

econ. *abbreviation* 1 economical 2 economics 3 economy

econometrics (ɪ‚kɒnə'mɛtrɪks) *n* (*functioning as singular*) the application of mathematical and statistical techniques to economic problems and theories > e‚cono'metric *or* e‚cono'metrical *adj* > econometrician (ɪ‚kɒnəmə'trɪʃən) *or* econometrist (‚iːkə'nɒmətrɪst) *n*

economic (‚iːkə'nɒmɪk, ‚ɛkə-) *adj* 1 of or relating to an economy, economics, or finance 2 *Brit* capable of being produced, operated, etc, for profit; profitable 3 concerning or affecting material resources or welfare: *economic pests* 4 concerned with or relating to the necessities of life; utilitarian 5 a variant of **economical** 6 *informal* inexpensive; cheap

economical (‚iːkə'nɒmɪkᵊl, ‚ɛkə-) *adj* 1 using the minimum required; not wasteful of time, effort, resources, etc 2 frugal; thrifty 3 a variant of **economic** (senses 1–4) 4 *euphemistic* deliberately withholding information (esp in the phrase **economical with the truth**) > **economically** (‚iːkə'nɒmɪkəlɪ, ‚ɛkə-) *adv*

economic indicator *n* a statistical measure representing an economic variable: *the retail price index is an economic indicator of the actual level of prices*

economic migrant *n* a person who moves from one region, place, or country to another in order to improve his or her standard of living

economic rationalism *n* *Austral & NZ* an economic policy based on the efficiency of market forces, characterized by minimal government intervention, tax cuts, privatization, and deregulation of labour markets

economics (‚iːkə'nɒmɪks, ‚ɛkə-) *n* 1 (*functioning as singular*) the social science concerned with the production and consumption of goods and services and the analysis of the commercial activities of a society 2 (*functioning as plural*) financial aspects

economic sanctions *pl n* any actions taken by one nation or group of nations to harm the economy of another nation or group, often to force a political change

economist (ɪ'kɒnəmɪst) *n* a specialist in economics

economize *or* **economise** (ɪ'kɒnə‚maɪz) *vb* (often foll by *on*) to limit or reduce (expense, waste, etc) > e‚conomi'zation *or* e‚conomi'sation *n*

economy (ɪ'kɒnəmɪ) *n*, *pl* -mies 1 careful management of resources to avoid unnecessary expenditure or waste; thrift 2 a means or instance of this; saving 3 sparing, restrained, or efficient use, esp to achieve the maximum effect for the minimum effort 4 a the complex of human activities concerned with the production, distribution, and consumption of goods and services b a particular type or branch of such production, distribution, and consumption: *a socialist economy; an agricultural economy* 5 the management of the resources, finances, income, and expenditure of a community, business enterprise, etc 6 a a class of travel in aircraft, providing less luxurious accommodation than first class at a lower fare b (*as modifier*): *economy class* 7 (*modifier*) offering or purporting to offer a larger quantity for a lower price: *economy pack* 8 the orderly interplay between the parts of a system or structure [C16: via Latin from

Greek *oikonomia* domestic management, from *oikos* house + -*nomia*, from *nemein* to manage]

economy-class syndrome *n* (not in technical usage) the development of a deep-vein thrombosis in the legs or pelvis of a person travelling for a long period of time in cramped conditions [C20: reference to the restricted legroom of cheaper seats on passenger aircraft]

ecoregion ('i:kəʊˌriːdʒən) *n* an area defined by its environmental conditions, esp climate, landforms, and soil characteristics

ecosphere ('i:kəʊˌsfɪə, 'ɛkəʊ-) *n* the planetary ecosystem, consisting of all living organisms and their environment

écossaise (ˌeɪkɒ'seɪz; *French* ekɔsɛz) *n* **1** a lively dance in two-four time **2** the tune for such a dance [C19: French, literally: Scottish (dance)]

ecosystem ('i:kəʊˌsɪstəm, 'ɛkəʊ-) *n ecology* a system involving the interactions between a community of living organisms in a particular area and its nonliving environment [C20: from ECO(LOGY) + SYSTEM]

ecoterrorist ('i:kəʊˌtɛrərɪst) *n* a person who uses violence in order to achieve environmentalist aims [C20: from ECO- + TERRORIST]

ecotourism ('i:kəʊˌtʊərɪzəm) *n* tourism that is designed to contribute to the protection of the environment or at least minimize damage to it, often involving travel to areas of natural interest in developing countries or participation in environmental projects > 'eco,tourist *n*

eco-warrior *n informal* a person who zealously pursues environmentalist aims [C20: from ECO- + WARRIOR]

e-crime *n* criminal activity that involves the use of computers or networks such as the internet [C20: E- + CRIME]

ecru ('ɛkruː, 'eɪkruː) *n* **1** a greyish-yellow to a light greyish colour; the colour of unbleached linen ▷ *adj* **2** of the colour ecru [C19: from French, from é- (intensive) + *cru* raw, from Latin *crūdus*; see CRUDE]

ecstasy ('ɛkstəsɪ) *n, pl* -sies **1** (*often plural*) a state of exalted delight, joy, etc; rapture **2** intense emotion of any kind: *an ecstasy of rage* **3** *psychol* overpowering emotion characterized by loss of self-control and sometimes a temporary loss of consciousness: often associated with orgasm, religious mysticism, and the use of certain drugs **4** *slang* 3,4-methylenedioxy-methamphetamine; MDMA: a powerful drug that acts as a stimulant and can produce hallucinations [C14: from Old French *extasie*, via Medieval Latin from Greek *ekstasis* displacement, trance, from *existanai* to displace, from *ex-* out + *histanai* to cause to stand]

ecstatic (ɛk'stætɪk) *adj* **1** in a trancelike state of great rapture or delight **2** showing or feeling great enthusiasm ▷ *n* **3** a person who has periods of intense trancelike joy > ec'statically *adv*

ECT *abbreviation* electroconvulsive therapy

ecto- *combining form* indicating outer, outside, external [from Greek *ektos* outside, from *ek, ex* out]

ectoblast ('ɛktəʊˌblæst) *n* another name for **ectoderm** > ˌecto'blastic *adj*

ectoderm ('ɛktəʊˌdɜːm) or **exoderm** *n* the outer germ layer of an animal embryo, which gives rise to epidermis and nervous tissue > ˌecto'dermal or ˌecto'dermic *adj*

ectomorph ('ɛktəʊˌmɔːf) *n* a person with a thin body build: said to be correlated with cerebrotonia > ˌecto'morphic *adj* > 'ecto,morphy *n*

-ectomy *n combining form* indicating surgical excision of a part: *appendectomy* [from New Latin *-ectomia*, from Greek *ek-* out + -TOMY]

ectopic pregnancy *n pathol* the abnormal development of a fertilized egg outside the cavity of the uterus, usually within a Fallopian tube

ectoplasm ('ɛktəʊˌplæzəm) *n* **1** *cytology* the outer layer of cytoplasm in some cells, esp protozoa, which differs from the inner cytoplasm in being a clear gel **2** *spiritualism* the substance supposedly emanating from the body of a medium during trances > ˌecto'plasmic *adj*

ECU ('eɪkjuː; *sometimes* 'iː'siː'juː) *n acronym for* European Currency Unit: a former unit of currency based on the composite value of several different currencies in the

European Union and functioning both as the reserve asset and accounting unit of the European Monetary System; replaced by the euro in 1999

Ecua. *abbreviation* Ecuador

Ecuador ('ɛkwəˌdɔː) *n* a republic in South America, on the Pacific: under the Incas when Spanish colonization began in 1532; gained independence in 1822; declared a republic in 1830. It consists chiefly of a coastal plain in the west, separated from the densely forested upper Amazon basin (Oriente) by ranges and plateaus of the Andes. Official language: Spanish; Quechua is also widely spoken. Religion: Roman Catholic majority. Currency: US dollar. Capital: Quito. Pop: 13 193 000 (2004 est). Area: 283 560 sq km (109 483 sq miles)

Ecuadorean (ˌɛkwə'dɔːrɪən) *adj* **1** of or relating to Ecuador or its inhabitants ▷ *n* **2** a native or inhabitant of Ecuador

ecumenical, oecumenical (ˌiːkjuː'mɛnɪkᵊl, ˌɛk-) or **ecumenic, oecumenic** *adj* **1** of or relating to the Christian Church throughout the world, esp with regard to its unity **2 a** tending to promote unity among Churches **b** of or relating to the international movement initiated among non-Catholic Churches in 1910 aimed at Christian unity: embodied, since 1937, in the World Council of Churches **3** *rare* universal; general; worldwide [C16: via Late Latin from Greek *oikoumenikos*, from *oikein* to inhabit, from *oikos* house] > ˌecu'menically or ˌoecu'menically *adv*

ecumenism (ɪ'kjuːməˌnɪzəm, 'ɛkjʊm-), **ecumenicism** (ˌiːkjuː'mɛnɪˌsɪzəm, ˌɛk-) or **ecumenicalism** *n* the aim of unity among all Christian churches throughout the world

eczema ('ɛksɪmə, ɪg'ziːmə) *n pathol* a skin inflammation with lesions that scale, crust, or ooze a serous fluid, often accompanied by intense itching or burning [C18: from New Latin, from Greek *ekzema*, from *ek-* out + *zein* to boil; see YEAST] > eczematous (ɛk'sɛmətəs) *adj*

ed. *abbreviation* **1** edited **2** *pl* eds edition **3** *pl* eds editor

-ed¹ *suffix* forming the past tense of most English verbs [Old English -*de, -ede, -ode, -ade*]

-ed² *suffix* forming the past participle of most English verbs [Old English -*ed, -od, -ad*]

-ed³ *suffix forming adjectives from nouns* possessing or having the characteristics of: *salaried; red-blooded* [Old English -*ede*]

Edam ('iːdæm; *Dutch* 'eɪdæmɛ) *n* **1** a town in the NW Netherlands, in North Holland province, on the IJsselmeer: cheese, light manufacturing. Pop: 28 000 (2003 est; includes Volendam) **2** a hard round mild-tasting Dutch cheese, yellow in colour with a red outside covering

Edberg ('ɛdbɜːg) *n* **Stefan**. born 1966, Swedish tennis player: Wimbledon champion 1988, 1990

EDC *abbreviation* European Defence Community

Edda ('ɛdə) *n* **1** Also called: Elder Edda, Poetic Edda a collection of mythological Old Norse poems made in the 12th century **2** Also called: Younger Edda, Prose Edda a treatise on versification together with a collection of Scandinavian myths, legends, and poems compiled by Snorri Sturluson (1179–1241), the Icelandic historian and poet [C18: Old Norse] > Eddaic (ɛ'deɪɪk) *adj*

Eddery ('ɛdərɪ) *n* **Patrick**, known as *Pat.* born 1952, Irish jockey

Eddington ('ɛdɪŋtən) *n* Sir **Arthur Stanley**. 1882–1944, English astronomer and physicist, noted for his research on the motion, internal constitution, and luminosity of stars and for his elucidation of the theory of relativity

eddo or **Chinese eddo** ('ɛdəʊ) *n, pl* eddoes other names for **taro**

eddy ('ɛdɪ) *n, pl* -dies **1** a movement in a stream of air, water, or other fluid in which the current doubles back on itself causing a miniature whirlwind or whirlpool **2** a deviation from or disturbance in the main trend of thought, life, etc, esp one that is relatively unimportant ▷ *vb* -dies, -dying, -died **3** to move or cause to move against the main current [C15: probably of Scandinavian origin; compare Old Norse *itha*; related to Old English *ed-* again, back, Old High German *it-*]

Eddy ('ɛdɪ) n **Mary Baker.** 1821–1910, US religious leader; founder of the Christian Science movement (1866)

eddy current n an electric current induced in a massive conductor, such as the core of an electromagnet, transformer, etc, by an alternating magnetic field

Eddystone Rocks ('ɛdɪstən) n a dangerous group of rocks at the W end of the English Channel, southwest of Plymouth: lighthouse

Ede ('eɪdə) n a city in the central Netherlands, in Gelderland province. Pop: 105 000 (2003 est)

Edelman ('ɛdʰlmən) n **Gerald Maurice.** born 1929, US biochemist: he shared the Nobel prize for physiology or medicine (1972) with Rodney Porter for determining the structure of antibodies

edelweiss ('eɪdʰl,vaɪs) n a small alpine flowering plant, *Leontopodium alpinum*, having white woolly oblong leaves and a tuft of attractive floral leaves surrounding the flowers: family *Asteraceae* (composites) [c19: German, literally: noble white]

edema (ɪ'diːmə) n, pl -mata (-mətə) the usual US spelling of **oedema**

Eden[1] ('iːdʰn) n **1** Also called: **Garden of Eden** *Old Testament* the garden in which Adam and Eve were placed at the Creation **2** a delightful place, region, dwelling, etc; paradise **3** a state of great delight, happiness, or contentment; bliss [c14: from Late Latin, from Hebrew *ēdhen* place of pleasure] > **Edenic** (iː'dɛnɪk) adj

Eden[2] ('iːdʰn) n **Sir** (**Robert**) **Anthony, Earl of Avon.** 1897–1977, British Conservative statesman; foreign secretary (1935–38; 1940–45; 1951–55) and prime minister (1955–57). He resigned after the controversy caused by the occupation of the Suez Canal zone by British and French forces (1956)

Eden Project n an environmental compex containing the world's largest greenhouse, built in a disused clay pit near St Austell, Cornwall, to study plant populations in a variety of environments

edentate (iː'dɛnteɪt) n **1** any of the placental mammals that constitute the order *Edentata*, which inhabit tropical regions of Central and South America. The order includes anteaters, sloths, and armadillos ▷ adj **2** of, relating to, or belonging to the order *Edentata* [c19: from Latin *ēdentātus* lacking teeth, from *ēdentāre* to render toothless, from *e-* out + *dēns* tooth]

Edessa (ɪ'dɛsə) n **1** an ancient city on the N edge of the Syrian plateau, founded as a Macedonian colony by Seleucus I: a centre of early Christianity. Modern name: Urfa **2** a market town in Greece: ancient capital of Macedonia. Pop (municipality): 25 729 (2001). Modern Greek name: **Édhessa**

Edgar ('ɛdgə) n **1** 944–975 AD, king of Mercia and Northumbria (957–975) and of England (959–975) **2** ?1074–1107, king of Scotland (1097–1107), fourth son of Malcolm III. He overthrew his uncle Donald to gain the throne **3 David.** born 1948, British dramatist, noted for political plays such as *Destiny* (1976), *Maydays* (1983), and *Albert Speer* (1999): he adapted (1980) *Nicholas Nickleby* and (1991) *Dr Jekyll and Mr Hyde* for the RSC

Edgar Atheling ('æθɪlɪŋ) n ?1050–?1125, grandson of Edmund II; Anglo-Saxon pretender to the English throne in 1066

edge (ɛdʒ) n **1** the border, brim, or margin of a surface, object, etc **2** a brink or verge **3** *maths* a line along which two faces or surfaces of a solid meet **4** the sharp cutting side of a blade **5** keenness, sharpness, or urgency **6** force, effectiveness, or incisiveness: *the performance lacked edge* **7** *dialect* a cliff, ridge, or hillside **8 have the edge on** or **have the edge over** to have a slight advantage or superiority (over) **9 on edge a** nervously irritable; tense **b** nervously excited or eager **10 set someone's teeth on edge** to make someone acutely irritated or uncomfortable ▷ vb **11** (tr) to provide an edge or border for **12** (tr) to shape or trim (the edge or border of something), as with a knife or scissors: *to edge a pie* **13** to push (one's way, someone, something, etc) gradually, esp edgeways **14** (tr) *cricket* to hit (a bowled ball) with the edge of the bat **15** (tr) to sharpen (a knife, etc) [Old English *ecg*; related to Old Norse *egg*, Old High German *ecka* edge, Latin *aciēs* sharpness, Greek *akis* point] > **'edger** n

Edgehill (,ɛdʒ'hɪl) n a ridge in S Warwickshire: site of the indecisive first battle between Charles I and the Parliamentarians (1642) in the Civil War

edgeways ('ɛdʒ,weɪz) or esp US and Canadian **edgewise** ('ɛdʒ,waɪz) adv **1** with the edge forwards or uppermost **2** on, by, with, or towards the edge **3 get a word in edgeways** (usually used with a negative) to succeed in interrupting a conversation in which someone else is talking incessantly

Edgeworth ('ɛdʒwɜːθ) n **Maria.** 1767–1849, Anglo-Irish novelist: her works include *Castle Rackrent* (1800) and *The Absentee* (1812)

edging ('ɛdʒɪŋ) n **1** anything placed along an edge to finish it, esp as an ornament, fringe, or border on clothing or along a path in a garden **2** the act of making an edge ▷ adj **3** relating to or used for making an edge: *edging shears*

edgy ('ɛdʒɪ) adj -ier, -iest (usually postpositive) nervous, irritable, tense, or anxious > **'edgily** adv > **'edginess** n

edh (ɛð) or **eth** n a character of the runic alphabet (ð) used to represent the voiced dental fricative as in *then, mother, bathe*. It is used in modern phonetic transcription for the same purpose

Édhessa (Greek 'ɛðɛsa) n transliteration of the Modern Greek name for **Edessa**

edible ('ɛdɪbʰl) adj fit to be eaten; eatable [c17: from Late Latin *edibilis*, from Latin *edere* to eat] > ,edi'bility or 'edibleness n

edibles ('ɛdɪbʰlz) pl n articles fit to eat; food

edict ('iːdɪkt) n **1** a decree, order, or ordinance issued by a sovereign, state, or any other holder of authority **2** any formal or authoritative command, proclamation, etc [c15: from Latin *ēdictum*, from *ēdīcere* to declare] > **e'dictal** adj

edifice ('ɛdɪfɪs) n **1** a building, esp a large or imposing one **2** a complex or elaborate institution or organization [c14: from Old French, from Latin *aedificium*, from *aedificāre* to build; see EDIFY]

edify ('ɛdɪ,faɪ) vb -fies, -fying, -fied (tr) to improve the morality, intellect, etc, of, esp by instruction [c14: from Old French *edifier*, from Latin *aedificāre* to construct, from *aedēs* a dwelling, temple + *facere* to make] > **'edi,fier** n > **'edi,fying** adj > **'edi,fyingly** adv > ,edifi'cation n

Edinburgh[1] ('ɛdɪnbərə, -brə) n **1** the capital of Scotland and seat of the Scottish Parliament (from 1999), in City of Edinburgh council area on the S side of the Firth of Forth: became the capital in the 15th century; castle; three universities (including University of Edinburgh, 1583); commercial and cultural centre, noted for its annual festival. Pop: 430 082 (2001) **2 City of Edinburgh** a council area in central Scotland, created from part of Lothian region in 1996. Pop: 448 370 (2003 est). Area: 262 sq km (101 sq miles)

Edinburgh[2] ('ɛdɪnbərə, -brə) n **Duke of,** title of Prince Philip Mountbatten. born 1921, husband of Elizabeth II of Great Britain and Northern Ireland

Edirne (ɛ'dirnɛ) n a city in NW Turkey: a Thracian town, rebuilt and renamed by the Roman emperor Hadrian. Pop: 126 000 (2005 est). Former name: **Adrianople**

Edison ('ɛdɪsʰn) n **Thomas Alva.** 1847–1931, US inventor. He patented more than a thousand inventions, including the phonograph, the incandescent electric lamp, the microphone, and the kinetoscope

edit ('ɛdɪt) vb (tr) **1** to prepare (text) for publication by checking and improving its accuracy, clarity, etc **2** to be in charge of (a publication, esp a periodical) **3** to prepare (a film, tape, etc) by rearrangement, selection, or rejection of previously filmed or taped material **4** (tr) to modify (a computer file) by, for example, deleting, inserting, moving, or copying text **5** (often foll by *out*) to remove (incorrect or unwanted matter), as from a manuscript or film [c18: back formation from EDITOR]

edition (ɪ'dɪʃən) n **1** *printing* **a** the entire number of copies of a book, newspaper, or other publication printed at one time from a single setting of type **b** a single copy from this number: *a first edition; the evening edition* **2** one of a number of printings of a book or other publication, issued at separate times with alterations, amendments, etc **3 a** an issue of a work identified by its format: *a leather-bound edition of Shakespeare* **b** an issue of a work identified by its editor or publisher: *the Oxford edition of Shakespeare* **4** a particular instance of a television or radio programme broadcast [C16: from Latin *ēditiō* a bringing forth, publishing, from *ēdere* to give out; see EDITOR]

editor ('ɛdɪtə) *n* **1** a person who edits written material for publication **2** a person in overall charge of the editing and often the policy of a newspaper or periodical **3** a person in charge of one section of a newspaper or periodical: *the sports editor* **4** *films* **a** a person who makes a selection and arrangement of individual shots in order to construct the flowing sequence of images for a film **b** a device for editing film, including a viewer and a splicer **5** *television, radio* a person in overall control of a programme that consists of various items, such as a news or magazine style programme [C17: from Late Latin: producer, exhibitor, from *ēdere* to give out, publish, from *ē-* out + *dāre* to give] > 'editor,ship *n*

editorial (,ɛdɪ'tɔːrɪəl) *adj* **1** of or relating to editing or editors **2** of, relating to, or expressed in an editorial **3** of or relating to the content of a publication rather than its commercial aspects ▷ *n* **4** an article in a newspaper, etc, expressing the opinion of the editor or the publishers > ,edi'torially *adv*

editorialize *or* **editorialise** (,ɛdɪ'tɔːrɪə,laɪz) *vb* (*intr*) to express an opinion in or as in an editorial > ,edi,toriali'zation *or* ,edi,toriali'sation *n*

Edmonton ('ɛdməntən) *n* a city in W Canada, capital of Alberta: oil industry. Pop: 782 101 (2001)

Edmund ('ɛdmənd) *n* **Saint**, also called *Saint Edmund Rich*. 1175–1240, English churchman: archbishop of Canterbury (1234–40). Feast day: Nov 16.

Edmund I *n* ?922–946 AD, king of England (940–946)

Edmund II *n* called *Edmund Ironside*. ?980–1016, king of England in 1016. His succession was contested by Canute and they divided the kingdom between them

EDT *abbreviation* (in the US and Canada) Eastern Daylight Time

educate ('ɛdjʊ,keɪt) *vb* (*mainly tr*) **1** (*also intr*) to impart knowledge by formal instruction to (a pupil); teach **2** to provide schooling for (children) **3** to improve or develop (a person, judgment, taste, skills, etc) **4** to train for some particular purpose or occupation [C15: from Latin *ēducāre* to rear, educate, from *dūcere* to lead] > 'educable *or* 'edu,catable *adj* > ,educa'bility *or* ,edu,cata'bility *n*

educated ('ɛdjʊ,keɪtɪd) *adj* **1** having an education, esp a good one **2** displaying culture, taste, and knowledge; cultivated **3** (*prenominal*) based on experience or information (esp in the phrase **an educated guess**)

education (,ɛdjʊ'keɪʃən) *n* **1** the act or process of acquiring knowledge, esp systematically during childhood and adolescence **2** the knowledge or training acquired by this process **3** the act or process of imparting knowledge, esp at a school, college, or university **4** the theory of teaching and learning **5** a particular kind of instruction or training: *a university education; consumer education* > ,educa'tionalist *or* ,educa'tionist *n*

educational (,ɛdjʊ'keɪʃənᵊl) *adj* **1** providing knowledge; instructive or informative: *an educational toy* **2** of or relating to education > ,edu'cationally *adv*

educator ('ɛdjʊ,keɪtə) *n* **1** a person who educates; teacher **2** a specialist in education; educationalist

educe (ɪ'djuːs) *vb* (*tr*) *rare* **1** to evolve or develop, esp from a latent or potential state **2** to draw out or elicit (information, solutions, etc) [C15: from Latin *ēdūcere* to draw out, from *ē-* out + *dūcere* to lead] > e'ducible *adj* > eductive (ɪ'dʌktɪv) *adj*

Edward¹ ('ɛdwəd) *n* Lake Edward a lake in central Africa, between Uganda and the Democratic Republic of Congo (formerly Zaïre) in the Great Rift Valley: empties through the Semliki River into Lake Albert. Area: about 2150 sq km (830 sq miles)

Edward² ('ɛdwəd) *n* **1** known as *the Black Prince*. 1330–76, Prince of Wales, the son of Edward III of England. He won victories over the French at Crécy (1346) and Poitiers (1356) in the Hundred Years' War **2** Prince. born 1964,

Earl of Wessex, third son of Elizabeth II of Great Britain and Northern Ireland. In 1999 he married Sophie Rhys-Jones (born 1965); their daughter Louise was born in 2003

Edward I *n* 1239–1307, king of England (1272–1307); son of Henry III. He conquered Wales (1284) but failed to subdue Scotland

Edward II *n* 1284–1327, king of England (1307–27); son of Edward I. He invaded Scotland but was defeated by Robert Bruce at Bannockburn (1314). He was deposed by his wife Isabella and Roger Mortimer; died in prison

Edward III *n* 1312–77, king of England (1327–77); son of Edward II. His claim to the French throne in right of his mother Isabella provoked the Hundred Years' War (1337)

Edward IV *n* 1442–83, king of England (1461–70; 1471–83); son of Richard, duke of York. He defeated Henry VI in the Wars of the Roses and became king (1461). In 1470 Henry was restored to the throne, but Edward recovered the crown by his victory at Tewkesbury

Edward V *n* 1470–?83, king of England in 1483; son of Edward IV. He was deposed by his uncle, Richard, Duke of Gloucester (Richard III), and is thought to have been murdered with his brother in the Tower of London

Edward VI *n* 1537–53, king of England (1547–53), son of Henry VIII and Jane Seymour. His uncle the Duke of Somerset was regent until 1552, when he was executed. Edward then came under the control of Dudley, Duke of Northumberland

Edward VII *n* 1841–1910, king of Great Britain and Ireland (1901–10); son of Queen Victoria

Edward VIII *n* 1894–1972, king of Great Britain and Ireland in 1936; son of George V and brother of George VI. He abdicated in order to marry an American divorcée, Mrs Wallis Simpson (1896–1986); created Duke of Windsor (1937)

Edwardian (ɛd'wɔːdɪən) *adj* denoting, relating to, or having the style of life, architecture, dress, etc, current in Britain during the reign (1901–10) of Edward VII (1841–1910) > Ed'wardianism *n*

Edwards ('ɛdwədz) *n* **1 Gareth (Owen)**. born 1947, Welsh Rugby Union footballer: halfback for Wales (1967–78) and the British Lions (1968–74) **2 Jonathan**. 1703–58, American Calvinist theologian and metaphysician; author of *The Freedom of the Will* (1754) **3 Jonathan**. born 1966, British athlete: gold medallist in the Olympic triple jump (2000)

Edward the Confessor *n* **Saint**. ?1002–66, king of England (1042–66); son of Ethelred II; founder of Westminster Abbey. Feast day: Oct 13

Edward the Elder *n* died 924 AD, king of England (899–924), son of Alfred the Great

Edward the Martyr *n* **Saint**. ?963–978 AD, king of England (975–78), son of Edgar: murdered. Feast day: March 18

Edwin ('ɛdwɪn) *n* ?585–633 AD, king of Northumbria (617–633) and overlord of all England except Kent

-ee *suffix forming nouns* **1** indicating a person who is the recipient of an action (as opposed, esp in legal terminology, to the agent, indicated by *-or* or *-er*): *assignee; grantee; lessee* **2** indicating a person in a specified state or condition: *absentee; employee* **3** indicating a diminutive form of something: *bootee* [via Old French *-e*, *-ee*, past participial endings, from Latin *-ātus*, *-āta* -ATE¹]

EEC *abbreviation* European Economic Community (now subsumed within the European Union)

EEG *abbreviation* **1** electroencephalogram **2** electroencephalograph

eel (iːl) *n* **1** any teleost fish of the order *Apodes* (or *Anguilliformes*), such as the European freshwater species *Anguilla anguilla*, having a long snakelike body, a smooth slimy skin, and reduced fins **2** any of various other animals with a long body and smooth skin, such as the mud eel and the electric eel **3** an evasive or untrustworthy person [Old English *ǣl*; related to Old Frisian *ēl*, Old Norse *āll*, Old High German *āl*] > 'eel-,like *adj* > 'eely *adj*

eelgrass ('iːl,ɡrɑːs) *n* any of several perennial submerged marine plants of the genus *Zostera*, esp *Z. marina*, having grasslike leaves: family *Zosteraceae*

eelpout ('i:l‚paʊt) n 1 any marine eel-like blennioid fish of the family Zoarcidae, such as Zoarces viviparus (**viviparous eelpout** or blenny) 2 another name for **burbot** [Old English ǣlepūte; related to Middle Dutch aalpuit]

eelworm ('i:l‚wɜ:m) n any of various nematode worms, esp the wheatworm and the vinegar eel

e'en (i:n) adv, n poetic or archaic a contraction of **even²** or **evening**

e'er (ɛə) adv poetic or archaic a contraction of **ever**

-eer or **-ier** suffix 1 (forming nouns) indicating a person who is concerned with or who does something specified: auctioneer; engineer; profiteer; mutineer 2 (forming verbs) to be concerned with something specified: electioneer [from Old French -ier, from Latin -arius -ARY]

eerie ('ɪərɪ) adj eerier, eeriest (esp of places, an atmosphere, etc) mysteriously or uncannily frightening or disturbing; weird; ghostly [c13: originally Scottish and Northern English, probably from Old English earg cowardly, miserable] > **'eerily** adv > **'eeriness** n

EFA n European Fighter Aircraft

eff (ɛf) vb 1 euphemism for **fuck** eff off 2 eff and blind slang to use obscene language > **'effing** n, adj, adv

efface (ɪ'feɪs) vb (tr) 1 to obliterate or make dim 2 to make (oneself) inconspicuous or humble through modesty, cowardice, or obsequiousness 3 to rub out (a line, drawing, etc); erase [c15: from French effacer, literally: to obliterate the face; see FACE] > **ef'faceable** adj > **ef'facement** n > **ef'facer** n

effect (ɪ'fɛkt) n 1 something that is produced by a cause or agent; result 2 power or ability to influence or produce a result; efficacy 3 the condition of being operative (esp in the phrases in or into effect) 4 take effect to become operative or begin to produce results 5 basic meaning or purpose (esp in the phrase to that effect) 6 an impression, usually one that is artificial or contrived (esp in the phrase for effect) 7 a scientific phenomenon: the Doppler effect 8 in effect a in fact; actually b for all practical purposes 9 the overall impression or result ▷ vb 10 (tr) to cause to occur; bring about; accomplish [c14: from Latin effectus a performing, tendency, from efficere to accomplish, from facere to do] > **ef'fecter** n > **ef'fectible** adj

effective (ɪ'fɛktɪv) adj 1 productive of or capable of producing a result 2 in effect; operative 3 producing a striking impression; impressive: an effective entrance 4 (prenominal) actual rather than theoretical; real 5 (of a military force, etc) equipped and prepared for action ▷ n 6 a serviceman who is equipped and prepared for action > **ef'fectively** adv > **ef'fectiveness** n

effects (ɪ'fɛkts) pl n 1 Also called: **personal effects** personal property or belongings 2 lighting, sounds, etc, to accompany and enhance a stage, film, or broadcast production

effectual (ɪ'fɛktjʊəl) adj 1 capable of or successful in producing an intended result; effective 2 (of documents, agreements, etc) having legal force > **ef‚fectu'ality** or **effectualness** n

effectually (ɪ'fɛktjʊəlɪ) adv 1 with the intended effect; thoroughly 2 to all practical purposes; in effect

effectuate (ɪ'fɛktjʊ‚eɪt) vb (tr) to cause to happen; effect; accomplish > **ef‚fectu'ation** n

effeminate (ɪ'fɛmɪnɪt) adj (of a man or boy) displaying characteristics regarded as typical of a woman; not manly [c14: from Latin effēmināre to make into a woman, from fēmina woman] > **effeminacy** or **ef'feminateness** n

effendi (ɛ'fɛndɪ) n, pl -dis 1 (in the Ottoman Empire) a title of respect used to address men of learning or social standing 2 (in Turkey since 1934) the oral title of address equivalent to Mr [c17: from Turkish efendi master, from Modern Greek aphentēs, from Greek authentēs lord, doer; see AUTHENTIC]

efferent ('ɛfərənt) adj carrying or conducting outwards from a part or an organ of the body, esp from the brain or spinal cord. See **afferent** [c19: from Latin efferre to bear off, from ferre to bear] > **'efference** n

effervesce (‚ɛfə'vɛs) vb (intr) 1 (of a liquid) to give off bubbles of gas 2 (of a gas) to issue in bubbles from a liquid 3 to exhibit great excitement, vivacity, etc [c18: from Latin effervescere to foam up, from fervescere to begin to boil, from fervēre to boil, ferment] > **‚effer'vescingly** adv

effervescent (‚ɛfə'vɛsᵊnt) adj 1 (of a liquid) giving off bubbles of gas; bubbling 2 high-spirited; vivacious > **‚effer'vescence** n

effete (ɪ'fi:t) adj 1 weak, ineffectual, or decadent as a result of overrefinement 2 exhausted of vitality or strength; worn out; spent 3 (of animals or plants) no longer capable of reproduction [c17: from Latin effētus having produced young, hence, exhausted by bearing, from fētus having brought forth; see FETUS] > **effeteness** n

efficacious (‚ɛfɪ'keɪʃəs) adj capable of or successful in producing an intended result; effective as a means, remedy, etc [c16: from Latin efficāx powerful, efficient, from efficere to achieve; see EFFECT] > **‚effi'caciousness** or **efficacy** ('ɛfɪkəsɪ) n

efficiency (ɪ'fɪʃənsɪ) n, pl -cies 1 the quality or state of being efficient; competence; effectiveness 2 the ratio of the useful work done by a machine, engine, device, etc, to the energy supplied to it, often expressed as a percentage

efficient (ɪ'fɪʃənt) adj 1 functioning or producing effectively and with the least waste of effort; competent 2 philosophy producing a direct effect; causative [c14: from Latin efficiēns effecting]

effigy ('ɛfɪdʒɪ) n, pl -gies 1 a portrait of a person, esp as a monument or architectural decoration 2 a crude representation of someone, used as a focus for contempt or ridicule and often hung up or burnt in public (often in the phrases **burn** or **hang in effigy**) [c18: from Latin effigiēs, from effingere to form, portray, from fingere to shape]

effleurage (‚ɛflɜ:'rɑ:ʒ) n a light stroking technique used in massage [c19: from French effleurer to stroke lightly]

effloresce (‚ɛflɔ:'rɛs) vb (intr) 1 to burst forth into or as if into flower; bloom 2 to become powdery by loss of water or crystallization 3 to become encrusted with powder or crystals as a result of chemical change or the evaporation of a solution [c18: from Latin efflōrēscere to blossom, from flōrēscere, from flōs flower]

efflorescence (‚ɛflɔ:'rɛsᵊns) n 1 a bursting forth or flowering 2 chem, geology a the process of efflorescing b the powdery substance formed as a result of this process, esp on the surface of rocks 3 any skin rash or eruption > **‚efflo'rescent** adj

effluence ('ɛflʊəns) or **efflux** ('ɛflʌks) n 1 the act or process of flowing out 2 something that flows out

effluent ('ɛflʊənt) n 1 liquid discharged as waste, as from an industrial plant or sewage works 2 radioactive waste released from a nuclear power station 3 a stream that flows out of another body of water 4 something that flows out or forth ▷ adj 5 flowing out or forth [c18: from Latin effluere to run forth, from fluere to flow]

effluvium (ɛ'flu:vɪəm) n, pl -via (-vɪə) or -viums an unpleasant smell or exhalation, as of gaseous waste or decaying matter [c17: from Latin: a flowing out; see EFFLUENT] > **ef'fluvial** adj

effort ('ɛfət) n 1 physical or mental exertion, usually considerable when unqualified 2 a determined attempt 3 achievement; creation [c15: from Old French esfort, from esforcier to force, ultimately from Latin fortis strong; see FORCE¹] > **'effortful** adj > **'effortless** adj

effrontery (ɪ'frʌntərɪ) n, pl -ies shameless or insolent boldness; impudent presumption; audacity; temerity [c18: from French effronterie, from Old French esfront barefaced, shameless, from Late Latin effrons, literally: putting forth one's forehead; see FRONT]

effulgent (ɪ'fʌldʒənt) adj radiant; brilliant [c18: from Latin effulgēre to shine forth, from fulgēre to shine] > **ef'fulgence** n > **ef'fulgently** adv

effuse (ɪ'fju:z) 1 to pour or flow out 2 to spread out; diffuse ▷ adj (ɪ'fju:s) 3 botany (esp of an inflorescence) spreading out loosely [c16: from Latin effūsus poured out, from effundere to shed, from fundere to pour]

effusion (ɪ'fju:ʒən) n 1 an unrestrained outpouring in speech or words 2 the act or process of being poured out 3 something that is poured out 4 med a the escape of blood or other fluid into a body cavity or tissue b the fluid that has escaped

effusive (ɪˈfjuːsɪv) *adj* **1** extravagantly demonstrative of emotion; gushing **2** (of rock) formed by the solidification of magma ▷ **effusively** *adv* ▷ **effusiveness** *n*

E-FIT (ˈiːfɪt) *n* *trademark* **1** a technique which uses psychological principles and computer technology to generate a likeness of a face: used by the police to trace suspects from witnesses' descriptions **2** an image generated by this technique [C20: from Electronic Facial Identification Technique]

EFL *abbreviation* English as a Foreign Language

eft (ɛft) *n* a dialect or archaic name for a **newt** [Old English *efeta*]

EFTA (ˈɛftə) *n* *acronym for* European Free Trade Association; established in 1960 to eliminate trade tariffs on industrial products; now comprises Norway, Switzerland, Iceland, and Liechtenstein. Free trade was established between EFTA and the EC (now EU) in 1984. In 1994 EFTA (excluding Switzerland) and the EU together created the European Economic Area (EEA)

EFTPOS (ˈɛftpɒs) *n* *acronym* electronic funds transfer at point of sale

EFTS *abbreviation* *computing* electronic funds transfer system

Eg. *abbreviation* **1** Egypt(ian) **2** Egyptology

e.g., eg. *or* **eg** *abbreviation* exempli gratia [Latin: for example]

egad (ɪˈɡæd, iːˈɡæd) *interj* *archaic* a mild oath or expression of surprise [C17: probably variant of *Ah God!*]

egalitarian (ɪˌɡælɪˈtɛərɪən) *adj* **1** of, relating to, or upholding the doctrine of the equality of mankind and the desirability of political, social, and economic equality ▷ *n* **2** an adherent of egalitarian principles [C19: alteration of *equalitarian*, through influence of French *égal* EQUAL] ▷ eˌgaliˈtarianˌism *n*

Egas Moniz (*Portuguese* ˈɛɡas ˈmɔniz) *n* **Antonio Caetanio de Abreu Freire**. 1874–1955, Portuguese neurologist: shared the Nobel prize for physiology or medicine (1949) with Walter Hess for their development of prefrontal leucotomy

Egbert (ˈɛɡbɜːt) *n* ?775–839 AD, king of Wessex (802–839); first overlord of all England (829–830)

Eger *n* **1** (*Hungarian* ˈɛɡɛr) a city in N central Hungary. Pop: 56 696 (2003 est) **2** (ˈeɪɡər) the German name for **Cheb**

egg¹ (ɛɡ) *n* **1** the oval or round reproductive body laid by the females of birds, reptiles, fishes, insects, and some other animals, consisting of a developing embryo, its food store, and sometimes jelly or albumen, all surrounded by an outer shell or membrane **2** Also called: **egg cell** any female gamete; ovum **3** the egg of the domestic hen used as food **4** something resembling an egg, esp in shape or in being in an early stage of development **5 bad egg** *old-fashioned*, *informal* a bad person **6 good egg** *old-fashioned*, *informal* a good person **7 put all one's eggs in one basket** *or* **have all one's eggs in one basket** to stake everything on a single venture **8 teach one's grandmother to suck eggs** to presume to teach someone something that he knows already **9 with egg on one's face** *informal* made to look ridiculous [C14: from Old Norse *egg*; related to Old English *æg*, Old High German *ei*]

egg² (ɛɡ) *vb* (*tr*; usually foll by *on*) to urge or incite, esp to daring or foolish acts [Old English *eggian*, from Old Norse *eggja* to urge; related to Old English *ecg* EDGE, Middle Low German *eggen* to harrow]

egg-and-spoon race *n* a race in which runners carry an egg balanced in a spoon

eggbeater (ˈɛɡˌbiːtə) *n* **1** Also called: **eggwhisk** a kitchen utensil for beating eggs, whipping cream, etc; whisk **2** *chiefly US & Canadian* an informal name for **helicopter**

egger *or* **eggar** (ˈɛɡə) *n* any of various widely distributed moths of the family *Lasiocampidae*, such as *Lasiocampa quercus* (**oak egger**) of Europe, having brown bodies and wings [C18: from EGG¹, from the egg-shaped cocoon]

egghead (ˈɛɡˌhɛd) *n* *informal* an intellectual; highbrow

eggnog (ˌɛɡˈnɒɡ) *n* a drink that can be served either hot or cold, made of eggs, milk, sugar, spice, and brandy, rum, or other spirit. Also called: **egg flip** [C19: from EGG¹ + NOG¹]

eggplant (ˈɛɡˌplɑːnt) *n* **1** a tropical Old World solanaceous plant, *Solanum melongena*, widely cultivated for its egg-shaped typically dark purple fruit **2** the fruit of this plant, which is cooked and eaten as a vegetable. ▷ Also called: **aubergine**

eggshell (ˈɛɡˌʃɛl) *n* **1** the hard porous protective outer layer of a bird's egg, consisting of calcite and protein **2** (*modifier*) (of paint) having a very slight sheen

eggshell porcelain *or* **eggshell china** *n* a type of very thin translucent porcelain originally made in China

egg tooth *n* (in embryo birds and reptiles) a temporary tooth or (in birds) projection of the beak used for piercing the eggshell

Egham (ˈɛɡəm) *n* a town in S England, in N Surrey on the River Thames. Pop: 27 666 (2001)

eglantine (ˈɛɡlənˌtaɪn) *n* another name for **sweetbrier** [C14: from Old French *aiglent*, ultimately from Latin *acus* needle, from *acer* sharp, keen]

EGM *abbreviation* extraordinary general meeting

Egmont¹ (ˈɛɡmɒnt) *n* **Mount Egmont** an extinct volcano in New Zealand, in W central North Island in the **Egmont National Park**: an almost perfect cone. Height: 2518 m (8261 ft)

Egmont² (ˈɛɡmɒnt) *n* **Lamoral** (lamoˈral), Count of Egmont, Prince of Gavre. 1522–68, Flemish statesman and soldier. He attempted to secure limited reforms and religious tolerance in the Spanish government of the Netherlands, refused to join William the Silent's rebellion, but was nevertheless executed for treason by the Duke of Alva

ego (ˈiːɡəʊ, ˈɛɡəʊ) *n*, *pl* **egos 1** the self of an individual person; the conscious subject **2** *psychoanal* the conscious mind, based on perception of the environment from birth onwards: responsible for modifying the antisocial instincts of the id and itself modified by the conscience (superego) **3** one's image of oneself; morale **4** egotism; conceit [C19: from Latin: I]

egocentric (ˌiːɡəʊˈsɛntrɪk, ˌɛɡ-) *adj* **1** regarding everything only in relation to oneself; self-centred; selfish **2** *philosophy* pertaining to a theory in which everything is considered in relation to the self ▷ *n* **3** a self-centred person; egotist ▷ ˌegocenˈtricity *n* ▷ ˌegoˈcentrism *n*

egoism (ˈiːɡəʊˌɪzəm, ˈɛɡ-) *n* **1** concern for one's own interests and welfare **2** *ethics* the theory that the pursuit of one's own welfare is the highest good **3** self-centredness; egotism ▷ **egoist** *n* ▷ ˌegoˈistic *or* ˌegoˈistical *adj*

Egoli (ɛˈɡəʊlɪ) *n* a local name for **Johannesburg** [from Zulu *eGoli* place of gold]

egomania (ˌiːɡəʊˈmeɪnɪə, ˌɛɡ-) *n* *psychiatry* obsessive love for oneself and regard for one's own needs ▷ ˌegoˈmaniˌac *n* ▷ **egomaniacal** (ˌiːɡəʊməˈnaɪkəl, ˌɛɡ-) *adj*

egotism (ˈiːɡəˌtɪzəm, ˈɛɡə-) *n* **1** an inflated sense of self-importance or superiority; self-centredness **2** excessive reference to oneself [C18: from Latin *ego* I + -ISM]

ego trip *n* *informal* something undertaken to boost or draw attention to a person's own image or appraisal of himself

e-government *n* the provision of government information and services by means of the internet and other computer resources [C20: *electronic government*]

egregious (ɪˈɡriːdʒəs, -dʒɪəs) *adj* **1** outstandingly bad; flagrant **2** *archaic* distinguished; eminent [C16: from Latin *ēgregius* outstanding (literally: standing out from the herd), from *ē-* out + *grex* flock, herd] ▷ eˈgregiousness *n*

egress (ˈiːɡrɛs) *n* **1** Also called: **egression** the act of going or coming out; emergence **2** a way out, such as a path; exit **3** right or permission to go out or depart [C16: from Latin *ēgredī* to come forth, depart, from *gradī* to move, step]

egret (ˈiːɡrɪt) *n* any of various wading birds of the genera *Egretta*, *Hydranassa*, etc, that are similar to herons but usually have a white plumage and, in the breeding season, long feathery plumes: family *Ardeidae*, order *Ciconiiformes* [C15: from Old French *aigrette*, from Old Provençal *aigreta*, from *aigron* heron, of Germanic origin;

compare Old High German *heigaro* HERON]

Egypt ('iːdʒɪpt) *n* a republic in NE Africa, on the Mediterranean and Red Sea: its history dates back about 5000 years. Occupied by the British from 1882, it became an independent kingdom in 1922 and a republic in 1953. Over 96 per cent of the total area is desert, with the chief areas of habitation and cultivation in the Nile delta and valley. Cotton is the main export. Official language: Arabic. Official religion: Muslim; Sunni majority. Currency: pound. Capital: Cairo. Pop: 73 389 000 (2004 est). Area: 997 739 sq km (385 229 sq miles). Former official name (1958–71): United Arab Republic

Egyptian (ɪ'dʒɪpʃən) *adj* 1 of, relating to, or characteristic of Egypt, its inhabitants, or their dialect of Arabic 2 of, relating to, or characteristic of the ancient Egyptians, their language, or culture ▷ *n* 3 a native or inhabitant of Egypt 4 a member of an indigenous non-Semitic people who established an advanced civilization in Egypt that flourished from the late fourth millennium BC 5 the extinct language of the ancient Egyptians, belonging to the Afro-Asiatic family of languages. It is recorded in hieroglyphic inscriptions, the earliest of which date from before 3000 BC. It was extinct by the fourth century AD

Egyptology (ˌiːdʒɪp'tɒlədʒɪ) *n* the study of the archaeology and language of ancient Egypt > ˌEgyp'tologist *n*

eh (eɪ) *interj* an exclamation used to express questioning surprise or to seek the repetition or confirmation of a statement or question

EHF *abbreviation* extremely high frequency

Ehrenburg or **Erenburg** ('ɛərənˌbɜːg; *Russian* erɪn'burk) *n* **Ilya Grigorievich** (ilj'ja gri'gɔrjɪvitʃ). 1891–1967, Soviet novelist and journalist. His novel *The Thaw* (1954) was the first published in the Soviet Union to deal with repression under Stalin

Ehrlich (*German* 'eːrlɪç) *n* **Paul** (paul). 1854–1915, German bacteriologist, noted for his pioneering work in immunology and chemotherapy and for his discovery of a remedy for syphilis: Nobel prize for physiology or medicine 1908

EI *abbreviation* 1 East Indian 2 East Indies 3 (in Canada) Employment Insurance

EIB *abbreviation* European Investment Bank

Eichendorff (*German* 'aiçəndɔrf) *n* **Joseph** ('joːzɛf), Freiherr von. 1788–1857, German poet and novelist, regarded as one of the greatest German romantic lyricists

Eichler (*German* 'aiçlər) *n* **August Wilhelm** ('augʊst 'vɪlhɛlm). 1839–87, German botanist: devised the system on which modern plant classification is based

Eichmann (*German* 'aiçman) *n* **Karl Adolf** ('aːdɔlf). 1902–62, Austrian Nazi official, who took a leading role in organizing the extermination of the European Jews. He escaped to Argentina after World War II, but was captured and executed in Israel as a war criminal

eider or **eider duck** ('aidə) *n* any of several sea ducks of the genus *Somateria*, esp *S. mollissima*, and related genera, which occur in the N hemisphere. The male has black and white plumage, and the female is the source of eiderdown [c18: from Old Norse *æthr*; related to Swedish *ejder*, Dutch, German *Eider*]

eiderdown ('aidəˌdaun) *n* 1 the breast down of the female eider duck, with which it lines the nest, used for stuffing pillows, quilts, etc 2 a thick warm cover for a bed, made of two layers of material enclosing a soft filling

eidetic (ai'dɛtɪk) *adj psychol* 1 (of visual, or sometimes auditory, images) exceptionally vivid and allowing detailed recall of something previously perceived: thought to be common in children 2 relating to or subject to such imagery [c20: from Greek *eidētikos*, from *eidos* shape, form] > ei'detically *adv*

Eid-ul-Adha ('iːdʊlˌaːdə) *n* an annual Muslim festival marking the end of the pilgrimage to Mecca. Animals are sacrificed and their meat shared among the poor [from Arabic *id ul adha* festival of sacrifice]

Eid-ul-Fitr ('iːdʊlˌfiːtə) *n* an annual Muslim festival marking the end of Ramadan, involving the exchange of gifts and a festive meal [from Arabic *id ul fitr* festival of fast-breaking]

Eifel ('aifʰl; *German* 'aifəl) *n* a plateau region in W Germany, between the River Moselle and the Belgian frontier: quarrying

Eiffel ('aifʰl; *French* ɛfɛl) *n* **Alexandre Gustave** (alɛksādrə gystav). 1832–1923, French engineer

Eiffel Tower *n* a tower in Paris: designed by A. G. Eiffel; erected for the 1889 Paris Exposition. Height: 300 m (984 ft), raised in 1959 to 321 m (1052 ft)

Eigen (*German* 'aigən) *n* **Manfred**. born 1927, German physical chemist: shared the Nobel prize for chemistry (1967) for developing his relaxation technique for studying fast reactions

Eiger (*German* 'aigər) *n* a mountain in central Switzerland, in the Bernese Alps. Height: 3970 m (13 025 ft)

eight (eɪt) *n* 1 the cardinal number that is the sum of one and seven and the product of two and four 2 a numeral, 8, VIII, etc, representing this number 3 *music* the numeral 8 used as the lower figure in a time signature to indicate that the beat is measured in quavers 4 something representing, represented by, or consisting of eight units, such as a playing card with eight symbols on it 5 *rowing* a a racing shell propelled by eight oarsmen b the crew of such a shell 6 Also called: eight o'clock eight hours after noon or midnight 7 have one over the eight *slang* to be drunk ▷ *determiner* 8 a amounting to eight b (*as pronoun*): *I could only find eight* [Old English *eahta*; related to Old High German *ahto*, Old Norse *ātta*, Old Irish *ocht*, Latin *octō*, Greek *okto*, Sanskrit *astau*]

eighteen ('eɪ'tiːn) *n* 1 the cardinal number that is the sum of ten and eight and the product of two and nine 2 a numeral, 18, XVIII, etc, representing this number 3 the amount or quantity that is eight more than ten 4 something represented by, representing, or consisting of 18 units ▷ *determiner* 5 a amounting to eighteen: *eighteen weeks* b (*as pronoun*): *eighteen of them knew* [Old English *eahtatēne*; related to Old Norse *attjan*, Old High German *ahtozehan*] > 'eigh'teenth *adj, n*

eightfold ('eɪtˌfəʊld) *adj* 1 equal to or having eight times as many or as much 2 composed of eight parts ▷ *adv* 3 by or up to eight times as much

eighth (eɪtθ) *adj* 1 (*usually prenominal*) a coming after the seventh and before the ninth in numbering or counting order, position, time, etc; being the ordinal number of eight: often written 8th b (*as noun*): *the eighth in line* ▷ *n* 2 a one of eight equal or nearly equal parts of an object, quantity, measurement, etc b (*as modifier*): *an eighth part* 3 the fraction equal to one divided by eight (1/8) 4 another word for octave ▷ *adv* 5 Also called: eighthly after the seventh person, position, event, etc

eighth note *n music, US & Canadian* a note having the time value of an eighth of a semibreve. Also called (in Britain and certain other countries): quaver

eightsome reel ('eɪtsəm) *n* a Scottish dance for eight people

eighty ('eɪtɪ) *n, pl* -ies 1 the cardinal number that is the product of ten and eight 2 a numeral, 80, LXXX, etc, representing this number 3 (*plural*) the numbers 80–89, esp a person's age or the year of a particular century 4 the amount or quantity that is eight times as big as ten 5 something represented by, representing, or consisting of 80 units ▷ *determiner* 6 a amounting to eighty: *eighty pages of nonsense* b (*as pronoun*): *eighty are expected* [Old English *eahtatig*, Old High German *ahtozug*] > 'eightieth *adj, n*

Eijkman (*Dutch* 'ɛikman) *n* **Christiaan** ('kriːstiˌaːn). 1858–1930, Dutch physician, who discovered that beriberi is caused by nutritional deficiency: Nobel prize for physiology or medicine 1929

Eilat, Elat or **Elath** (eɪ'laːt) *n* a port in S Israel, on the Gulf of Aqaba: Israel's only outlet to the Red Sea. Pop: 43 500 (2003 est)

eina ('eɪˌnaː) *interj South African* an exclamation of sudden pain [c19: Afrikaans, from Khoi]

Eindhoven (*Dutch* 'aintˌhəʊvʰn) ('einthoːvə) *n* a city in the SE Netherlands, in North Brabant province: radio and electrical industry. Pop: 206 000 (2003 est)

Einstein ('aɪnstaɪn) *n* **Albert**. 1879–1955, US physicist and mathematician, born in Germany. He formulated the special theory of relativity (1905) and the general theory of relativity (1916), and made major contributions to the quantum theory, for which he was awarded the Nobel prize for physics in 1921. He was noted also for his work for world peace ▷ **Ein'steinian** *adj*

einsteinium (aɪn'staɪnɪəm) *n* a metallic transuranic element artificially produced from plutonium. Symbol: Es; atomic no: 99; half-life of most stable isotope, ^{252}Es: 276 days [C20: New Latin, named after Albert *Einstein* (1879–1955), German-born US physicist and mathematician]

Einthoven (*Dutch* 'ɛɪnthoːvə) *n* **Willem**. 1860–1927, Dutch physiologist. A pioneer of electrocardiography, he was awarded the Nobel prize for physiology or medicine in 1924

Eisenach (*German* 'aizənax) *n* a city in central Germany, in Thuringia: birthplace of Johann Sebastian Bach. Pop: 44 081 (2003 est)

Eisenhower ('aɪzən,haʊə) *n* **Dwight David**, known as *Ike*. 1890–1969, US general and Republican statesman; Supreme Commander of the Allied Expeditionary Force (1943–45) and 34th president of the US (1953–61). He commanded Allied forces in Europe and North Africa (1942), directed the invasion of Italy (1943), and was Supreme Commander of the combined land forces of NATO (1950–52)

Eisenstadt (*German* 'aizənʃtat) *n* a town in E Austria, capital of Burgenland province: Hungarian until 1921. Pop: 11 334 (2001)

Eisenstaedt ('aɪzˀn,stæt) *n* **Alfred**. 1898–1995, US photographer, born in Germany

Eisenstein ('aɪzˀn,staɪn; *Russian* ejzin'ʃtjejn) *n* **Sergei Mikhailovich** (sɪr'gjej mi'xajləvitʃ). 1898–1948, Soviet film director. His films include *Battleship Potemkin* (1925), *Alexander Nevsky* (1938), and *Ivan the Terrible* (1944)

Eisk or **Eysk** (*Russian* jejsk) *n* variant transliterations of the Russian name for **Yeisk**

eisteddfod (aɪ'stɛdfəd; *Welsh* aɪ'stɛðvɒd) *n*, *pl* -fods or -fodau (*Welsh* aɪ,stɛð'vɒdaɪ) any of a number of annual festivals in Wales, esp the **Royal National Eisteddfod**, in which competitions are held in music, poetry, drama, and the fine arts [C19: from Welsh, literally: session, from *eistedd* to sit (from *sedd* seat) + *-fod*, from *bod* to be]

either ('aɪðə, 'iːðə) *determiner* **1 a** one or the other (of two): *either coat will do* **b** (*as pronoun*): *either is acceptable* **2** both one and the other: *there were ladies at either end of the table* **3** (*coordinating*) used preceding two or more possibilities joined by "or": *you may have either cheese or a sweet* ▷ *adv* (*sentence modifier*) **4** (*used with a negative*) used to indicate that the clause immediately preceding is a partial reiteration of a previous clause: *John isn't a liar, but he isn't exactly honest either* [Old English *ǣgther*, short for *ǣghwæther* each of two; related to Old Frisian *ēider*, Old High German *ēogihweder*; see EACH, WHETHER]

● USAGE *Either* is followed by a singular verb in good
● usage: *either is good*; *either of these books is useful*. Care
● should be taken to avoid ambiguity when using *either*
● to mean *both* or *each*, as in the following sentence: *a*
● *ship could be moored on either side of the channel*. Agreement
● between the verb and its subject in *either...or...*
● constructions follows the pattern given for
● *neither...nor...*

ejaculate *vb* (ɪ'dʒækjʊ,leɪt) **1** to eject or discharge (semen) in orgasm **2** (*tr*) to utter abruptly; blurt out ▷ *n* (ɪ'dʒækjʊlɪt) **3** another word for **semen** [C16: from Latin *ējaculārī* to hurl out, from *jaculum* javelin, from *jacere* to throw] ▷ **e'jacu,lator** *n* ▷ **e,jacu'lation** *n* ▷ **e'jaculatory** or **e'jaculative** *adj*

eject (ɪ'dʒɛkt) *vb* **1** (*tr*) to drive or force out; expel or emit **2** (*tr*) to compel (a person) to leave; evict; dispossess **3** (*tr*) to dismiss, as from office **4** (*intr*) to leave an aircraft rapidly, using an ejection seat or capsule [C15: from Latin *ejicere*, from *jacere* to throw] ▷ **e'jection** *n*

ejection seat or **ejector seat** *n* a seat, esp as fitted to military aircraft, that is fired by a cartridge or rocket to eject the occupant from the aircraft in an emergency

Ekaterinburg (*Russian* jɪkətɪrin'burk) *n* a variant transliteration of the Russian name for **Yekaterinburg**

Ekaterinodar (*Russian* jɪkətɪrina'dar) *n* the former name (until 1920) of **Krasnodar**

eke (iːk) *sentence connector archaic* also; moreover [Old English *eac*; related to Old Norse, Gothic *auk* also, Old High German *ouh*, Latin *autem* but, *aut* or]

eke out *vb* (*tr, adverb*) **1** to make (a supply) last, esp by frugal use: *they eked out what little food was left* **2** to support (existence) with difficulty and effort **3** to add to (something insufficient), esp with effort: *to eke out an income with evening work*

EKG *abbreviation* (in the US and Canada) **1** electrocardiogram **2** electrocardiograph

Ekman (*Swedish* 'ekman) *n* **Vagn Walfrid** (vaɣˀn waːlfriːd) 1874–1954 Swedish oceanographer: discoverer of the **Ekman Spiral** (a complex interaction on the surface of the sea between wind, rotation of the earth, and friction forces) and the **Ekman Layer** the thin top layer of the sea that flows at 90° to the wind direction

El Aaiún (ɛl aɪ'juːn) *n* a city in Western Sahara, controlled by Morocco: the capital of the former Spanish Sahara; port facilities for rich phosphate deposits nearby. Pop: 197 000 (2005 est)

elaborate *adj* (ɪ'læbərɪt) **1** planned or executed with care and exactness; detailed **2** marked by complexity, ornateness, or detail ▷ *vb* (ɪ'læbə,reɪt) **3** (*intr*; usually foll by *on* or *upon*) to add information or detail (to an account); expand (upon) **4** (*tr*) to work out in detail; develop **5** (*tr*) to make more complicated or ornate **6** (*tr*) to produce by careful labour; create **7** (*tr*) *physiol* to change (food or simple substances) into more complex substances for use in the body [C16: from Latin *ēlabōrāre* to take pains, from *labōrāre* to toil] ▷ **e,labo'ration** *n* ▷ **elaborative** (ɪ'læbərətɪv) *adj* ▷ **e'labo,rator** *n*

Elagabalus (,ɛlə'gæbələs, ,iːlə-) *n* same as **Heliogabalus**

El Alamein or **Alamein** (ɛl 'æləˌmeɪn) *n* a village on the N coast of Egypt, about 112 km (70 miles) west of Alexandria: scene of a decisive Allied victory over the Axis forces (1942)

Elam ('iːləm) *n* an ancient kingdom east of the River Tigris: established before 4000 BC; probably inhabited by a non-Semitic people

Elamite ('iːlə,maɪt) *n* **1** an inhabitant of the ancient kingdom of Elam **2** Also called: **Elamitic, Susian** the extinct language of this people, of no known relationship, recorded in cuneiform inscriptions dating from the 25th to the 4th centuries BC ▷ *adj* **3** of or relating to Elam, its people, or their language

élan (eɪ'lɑːn, eɪ'læn; *French* elɑ̃) *n* a combination of style and vigour: *he performed the concerto with élan* [C19: from French, from *élancer* to throw forth, ultimately from Latin *lancea* LANCE]

eland ('iːlənd) *n* **1** a large spiral-horned antelope, *Taurotragus oryx*, inhabiting bushland in eastern and southern Africa. It has a dewlap and a hump on the shoulders and is light brown with vertical white stripes **2 giant eland** a similar but larger animal, *T. derbianus*, living in wooded areas of central and W Africa [C18: via Afrikaans from Dutch *eland* elk; related to Old Slavonic *jeleni* stag, Greek *ellos* fawn]

elapse (ɪ'læps) *vb* (*intr*) (of time) to pass by [C17: from Latin *ēlābī* to slip away, from *lābī* to slip, glide]

elasmobranch (ɪ'læsmə,bræŋk, ɪ'læz-) *n* **1** any cartilaginous fish of the subclass *Elasmobranchii* (or *Selachii*), which includes the sharks, rays, dogfish, and skates ▷ *adj* **2** of, relating to, or belonging to the *Elasmobranchii* ▷ Also called: **selachian** [C19: from New Latin *elasmobranchii*, from Greek *elasmos* metal plate + *brankhia* gills]

elastane (ɪ'læsteɪn) *n* a synthetic fibre characterized by its ability to revert to its original shape after being stretched

elastic (ɪ'læstɪk) *adj* **1** (of a body or material) capable of returning to its original shape after compression, expansion, stretching, or other deformation **2** capable of adapting to change: *an elastic schedule* **3** quick to recover from fatigue, dejection, etc; buoyant **4** springy or resilient **5** made of elastic ▷ *n* **6** tape, cord, or fabric containing interwoven strands of flexible rubber or similar substance allowing it to stretch and return to its original shape [C17: from New Latin *elasticus* impulsive, from Greek *elastikos*, from *elaunein* to beat, drive] > ela'sticity *n*

elasticate (ɪ'læstɪˌkeɪt) *vb* (*tr*) to insert elastic sections or thread into (a fabric or garment): *an elasticated waistband* > e,lasti'cation *n*

elastic band *n* another name for **rubber band**

elasticize *or* **elasticise** (ɪ'læstɪˌsaɪz) *vb* (*tr*) **1** to make elastic **2** another word for **elasticate**

elastomer (ɪ'læstəmə) *n* any material, such as natural or synthetic rubber, that is able to resume its original shape when a deforming force is removed [C20: from ELASTIC + -MER] > **elastomeric** (ɪˌlæstə'mɛrɪk) *adj*

Elastoplast (ɪ'læstəˌplɑːst) *n trademark* a gauze surgical dressing backed by adhesive tape

Elat *or* **Elath** (eɪ'lɑːt) *n* variant spellings of **Eilat**

elate (ɪ'leɪt) *vb* (*tr*) to fill with high spirits, exhilaration, pride or optimism [C16: from Latin *ēlāt-* stem of past participle of *efferre* to bear away, from *ferre* to carry]

elated (ɪ'leɪtɪd) *adj* full of high spirits, exhilaration, pride or optimism; very happy > e'latedly *adv*

elation (ɪ'leɪʃən) *n* joyfulness or exaltation of spirit, as from success, pleasure, or relief; high spirits

E layer *n* another name for **E region**

Elba ('ɛlbə) *n* a mountainous island off the W coast of Italy, in the Mediterranean: Napoleon Bonaparte's first place of exile (1814–15). Pop: 30 000 (latest est). Area: 223 sq km (86 sq miles)

Elbe (ɛlb; *German* 'ɛlbə) *n* a river in central Europe, rising in the N Czech Republic and flowing generally northwest through Germany to the North Sea at Hamburg. Length: 1165 km (724 miles). Czech name: Labe

Elbert ('ɛlbət) *n* Mount Elbert a mountain in central Colorado, in the Sawatch range. Height: 4399 m (14 431 ft)

Elbląg (*Polish* 'ɛlblɔŋk) *n* a port in N Poland: metallurgical industries. Pop: 129 000 (2005 est)

elbow ('ɛlbəʊ) *n* **1** the joint between the upper arm and the forearm, formed by the junction of the radius and ulna with the humerus **2** the corresponding joint or bone of birds or mammals **3** the part of a garment that covers the elbow **4** something resembling an elbow, such as a sharp bend in a road or river **5** at one's elbow within easy reach **6** out at elbow *or* out at elbows ragged or impoverished **7** up to the elbows with *or* up to the elbows in busily occupied with; deeply immersed in ▷ *vb* **8** (*tr*) to reject; dismiss. Also: give the elbow **9** to make (one's way) by shoving, jostling, etc **10** (*tr*) to knock or shove with or as if with the elbow [Old English *elnboga*; related to Old Norse *olbogi*, Old High German *elinbogo*]

elbow grease *n facetious* vigorous physical labour, esp hard rubbing

elbowroom ('ɛlbəʊˌruːm, -ˌrʊm) *n* sufficient scope to move or function

Elbrus (ɪl'bruːs) *n* a mountain in SW Russia, on the border with Georgia, in the Caucasus Mountains, with two extinct volcanic peaks: the highest mountain in Europe. Height: 5642 m (18 510 ft)

Elburz Mountains (ɛl'bʊəz) *pl n* a mountain range in N Iran, parallel to the SW and S shores of the Caspian Sea. Highest peak: Mount Demavend, 5671 m (18 606 ft)

El Capitan (ɛl ˌkæpɪ'tæn) *n* a mountain in E central California, in the Sierra Nevada: a monolith with a precipice rising over 1100 m (3600 ft) above the floor of the Yosemite Valley. Height: 2306 m (7564 ft)

Elche (*Spanish* 'ɛltʃe) *n* a town in S Spain, in Valencia: noted for Iberian and Roman archaeological finds and the medieval religious drama performed there annually: fruit growing, esp dates, pomegranates, figs. Pop: 207 163 (2003 est)

El Cid Campeador (*Spanish* ɛl θiθ kampea'ðor) *n* See **Cid**

elder[1] ('ɛldə) *adj* **1** born earlier; senior. See **older 2** (in piquet and similar card games) denoting or relating to the nondealer (the **elder hand**), who has certain

advantages in the play **3** *archaic* **a** prior in rank, position, or office **b** of a previous time; former ▷ *n* **4** an older person; one's senior **5** *anthropol* a senior member of a tribe who has influence or authority **6** (in certain Protestant Churches) a lay office having teaching, pastoral, or administrative functions **7** another word for **presbyter** [Old English *eldra*, comparative of *eald* OLD; related to Old Norse *ellri*, Old High German *altiro*, Gothic *althiza*] > 'elder,ship *n*

● USAGE The word *elder* is being increasingly used, as a
● more respectful way of referring to older people: *elder*
● *care, elder abuse*

elder[2] ('ɛldə) *n* Also called: **elderberry** any of various caprifoliaceous shrubs or small trees of the genus *Sambucus*, having clusters of small white flowers and red, purple, or black berry-like fruits [Old English *ellern*; related to Old Norse *elrir*, Old High German *erlīn*, Old Slavonic *jelīcha*, Latin *alnus*]

Elder ('ɛldə) *n* Mark Philip. born 1947, British conductor; musical director of the English National Opera (1979–93) and of the Hallé Orchestra from 2000

elderberry ('ɛldəˌbɛrɪ) *n, pl -ries* **1** the berry-like fruit of the elder, used for making wines, jellies, etc **2** another name for **elder**[2]

elderly ('ɛldəlɪ) *adj* (of people) quite old; past middle age > 'elderliness *n*

eldest ('ɛldɪst) *adj* being the oldest, esp the oldest surviving child of the same parents [Old English *eldesta*, superlative of *eald* OLD]

Eldon ('ɛldən) *n* Earl of, title of John Scott. 1751–1838, British statesman and jurist; Lord Chancellor (1801–06, 1807–27): an inflexible opponent of parliamentary reform, Catholic emancipation, and the abolition of slavery

El Dorado (ɛl dɒ'rɑːdəʊ; *Spanish* ɛl do'raðo) *n* **1** a fabled city in South America, rich in treasure and sought by Spanish explorers in the 16th century **2** Also called: **eldorado** any place of great riches or fabulous opportunity [C16: from Spanish, literally: the gilded (place)]

eldritch *or* **eldrich** ('ɛldrɪtʃ) *adj poetic, Scot* unearthly; weird [C16: perhaps from Old English *ælf* ELF + *rīce* realm; see RICH]

Elea ('iːlɪə) *n* (in ancient Italy) a Greek colony on the Tyrrhenian coast of Lucana

Eleanor of Aquitaine ('ɛlɪnə, -ˌnɔː) *n* ?1122–1204, queen of France (1137–52) by her marriage to Louis VII and queen of England (1154–89) by her marriage to Henry II; mother of the English kings Richard I and John

Eleanor of Castile ('ɛlɪnə, -ˌnɔː) *n* 1246–90, Spanish wife of Edward I of England. **Eleanor Crosses** were erected at each place at which her body rested between Nottingham, where she died, and London, where she is buried

e-learning *n* an internet-based teaching system [C20: electronic *learning*]

elect (ɪ'lɛkt) *vb* **1** (*tr*) to choose (someone) to be (a representative or a public official) by voting: *they elected him Mayor* **2** to select; choose: *to elect to die rather than surrender* **3** (*tr*) (of God) to select or predestine for the grace of salvation ▷ *adj* **4** (*immediately postpositive*) voted into office but not yet installed: *the president elect* **5 a** chosen or choice; selected or elite **b** (*as collective noun;* preceded by *the*): *the elect* **6** *Christianity* **a** selected or predestined by God to receive salvation; chosen **b** (*as collective noun;* preceded by *the*): *the elect* [C15: from Latin *ēligere* to select, from *legere* to choose] > e'lectable *adj*

election (ɪ'lɛkʃən) *n* **1** the selection by vote of a person or persons from among candidates for a position, esp a political office **2** a public vote on an official proposition **3** the act or an instance of choosing **4** *Christianity* **a** the doctrine of Calvin that God chooses certain individuals for salvation without reference to their faith or works **b** the doctrine of Arminius and others that God chooses for salvation those who, by grace, persevere in faith and works

electioneer (ɪˌlɛkʃə'nɪə) *vb* (*intr*) **1** to be active in a political election or campaign ▷ *n* **2** a person who engages in this activity > e,lection'eering *n, adj*

elective (ɪ'lɛktɪv) *adj* 1 of or based on selection by vote: *elective procedure* 2 selected by vote: *an elective official* 3 having the power to elect 4 open to choice; optional: *an elective course of study* ▷ *n* 5 an optional course or hospital placement undertaken by a medical student > e'lectively *adv* > electivity (ˌiːlɛk'tɪvɪtɪ) *or* e'lectiveness *n*

elector (ɪ'lɛktə) *n* 1 someone who is eligible to vote in the election of a government 2 (*often capital*) a member of the US electoral college 3 (*often capital*) (in the Holy Roman Empire) any of the German princes entitled to take part in the election of a new emperor > e'lectorˌship *n*

electoral (ɪ'lɛktərəl) *adj* relating to or consisting of electors

electoral college *n* 1 (*often capitals*) US a body of electors chosen by the voters who formally elect the president and vice president 2 any body of electors with similar functions

electorate (ɪ'lɛktərɪt) *n* 1 the body of all qualified voters 2 the rank, position, or territory of an elector of the Holy Roman Empire 3 *Austral & NZ* the area represented by a Member of Parliament 4 *Austral & NZ* the voters in a constituency

Electra (ɪ'lɛktrə) *n* *Greek myth* the daughter of Agamemnon and Clytemnestra. She persuaded her brother Orestes to avenge their father by killing his murderess Clytemnestra and her lover Aegisthus

electret (ɪ'lɛktrət) *n* a permanently polarized dielectric material; its electric field is similar to the magnetic field of a permanent magnet [c20: from *electr*(*icity* + *magn*)*et*]

electric (ɪ'lɛktrɪk) *adj* 1 of, derived from, produced by, producing, transmitting, or powered by electricity 2 (of a musical instrument) amplified electronically 3 very tense or exciting; emotionally charged ▷ *n* 4 *informal* an electric train, car, etc 5 (*plural*) an electric circuit or electric appliances [c17: from New Latin *electricus* amber-like (because friction causes amber to become charged), from Latin *ēlectrum* amber, from Greek *ēlektron*, of obscure origin]

electrical (ɪ'lɛktrɪkᵊl) *adj* of, relating to, or concerned with electricity > e'lectrically *adv*

electrical engineering *n* the branch of engineering concerned with the practical applications of electricity > electrical engineer *n*

electric blanket *n* a blanket that contains an electric heating element, used to warm a bed

electric chair *n* (in the US) a an electrified chair for executing criminals b the electric chair execution by this method

electric circuit *n* *physics* another name for **circuit** (sense 3a)

electric constant *n* the permittivity of free space, which has the value $8.854\ 187 \times 10^{-12}$ farad per metre

electric discharge *n* *physics* another name for **discharge** (sense 20b)

electric displacement *n* *physics* the electric flux density when an electric field exists in free space into which a dielectric is introduced. Symbol: *D*. Also called: **electric flux density**

electric eel *n* an eel-like freshwater cyprinoid fish, *Electrophorus electricus*, of N South America, having electric organs in the body: family *Electrophoridae*

electric eye *n* another name for **photocell**

electric field *n* a field of force surrounding a charged particle within which another charged particle experiences a force

electric flux *n* the product of the electric displacement and the area across which it is displaced in an electric field. Symbol: Ψ

electric flux density *n* another name for **electric displacement**

electric guitar *n* an electrically amplified guitar, used mainly in pop music

electrician (ɪlɛk'trɪʃən, ˌiːlɛk-) *n* a person whose occupation is the installation, maintenance, and repair of electrical devices

electricity (ɪlɛk'trɪsɪtɪ, ˌiːlɛk-) *n* 1 any phenomenon associated with stationary or moving electrons, ions, or other charged particles 2 the science concerned with electricity 3 an electric current or charge: *a motor powered by electricity* 4 emotional tension or excitement, esp between or among people

electric motor *n* a device that converts electrical energy to mechanical torque

electric organ *n* 1 *music* a a pipe organ operated by electrical means b another name for **electronic organ** 2 *zoology* a small group of modified muscle cells on the body of certain fishes, such as the electric eel, that gives an electric shock to any animal touching them

electric potential *n* a the work required to transfer a unit positive electric charge from an infinite distance to a given point against an electric field b the potential difference between the point and some other reference point. Sometimes shortened to: **potential**

electric ray *n* any ray of the order *Torpediniformes*, of tropical and temperate seas, having a flat rounded body with an electric organ in each of the fins, close to the head

electric shock *n* the physiological reaction, characterized by pain and muscular spasm, to the passage of an electric current through the body. It can affect the respiratory system and heart rhythm. Sometimes shortened to: **shock**

electric susceptibility *n* another name for **susceptibility** (sense 4a)

electrify (ɪ'lɛktrɪˌfaɪ) *vb* **-fies, -fying, -fied** (*tr*) 1 to adapt or equip (a system, device, etc) for operation by electrical power 2 to charge with or subject to electricity 3 to startle or excite intensely; shock or thrill > e'lectriˌfiable *adj* > eˌlectrifi'cation *n* > e'lectriˌfier *n*

electro (ɪ'lɛktrəʊ) *n*, *pl* **-tros** short for **electroplate**, **electrotype**

electro- *or sometimes before a vowel* **electr-** *combining form* 1 electric or electrically: *electrocardiograph*; *electrocute* 2 electrolytic: *electroanalysis* [from New Latin, from Latin *ēlectrum* amber, from Greek *ēlektron*]

electroacoustic (ɪˌlɛktrəʊə'kuːstɪk) *adj* another word for **acoustoelectronic**

electroactive (ɪˌlɛktrəʊ'æktɪv) *adj* (of living tissue) exhibiting electrical activity or responsive to electrical stimuli > eˌlectroac'tivity *n*

electrocardiogram (ɪˌlɛktrəʊ'kɑːdɪəʊˌgræm) *n* a tracing of the electric currents that initiate the heartbeat, used to diagnose possible heart disorders. Abbreviation: ECG

electrocardiograph (ɪˌlɛktrəʊ'kɑːdɪəʊˌgrɑːf, -ˌgræf) *n* an instrument for recording the electrical activity of the heart > eˌlectroˌcardio'graphic *adj* > eˌlectroˌcardio'graphically *adv* > electrocardiography (ɪˌlɛktrəʊˌkɑːdɪ'ɒgrəfɪ) *n*

electrochemistry (ɪˌlɛktrəʊ'kɛmɪstrɪ) *n* the branch of chemistry concerned with the study of electric cells and electrolysis > eˌlectro'chemist *n* > eˌlectro'chemical *adj*

electroconvulsive therapy (ɪˌlɛktrəʊkən'vʌlsɪv) *n* *med* the treatment of certain psychotic conditions by passing an electric current through the brain to induce coma or convulsions. Also called: **electroshock therapy**. See also **shock therapy**

electrocute (ɪ'lɛktrəˌkjuːt) *vb* (*tr*) 1 to kill as a result of an electric shock 2 US to execute in the electric chair [c19: from ELECTRO- + (exe)cute] > eˌlectro'cution *n*

electrode (ɪ'lɛktrəʊd) *n* 1 a conductor through which an electric current enters or leaves an electrolyte, an electric arc, or an electronic valve or tube 2 an element in a semiconducting device that emits, collects, or controls the movement of electrons or holes

electrodeposit (ɪˌlɛktrəʊdɪ'pɒzɪt) *vb* 1 (*tr*) to deposit (a metal) by electrolysis ▷ *n* 2 the deposit so formed > electrodeposition (ɪˌlɛktrəʊˌdɛpə'zɪʃən) *n*

electrodynamics (ɪˌlɛktrəʊdaɪ'næmɪks) *n* (*functioning as singular*) the branch of physics concerned with the interactions between electrical and mechanical forces

electroencephalograph (ɪˌlɛktrəʊɛn'sɛfələˌgrɑːf, -ˌgræf) *n* an instrument for recording the electrical activity of the brain, usually by means of electrodes placed on the scalp: used to diagnose tumours of the brain, to study brain waves, etc. See also **brain wave** > eˌlectroenˌcephalo'graphic *adj*

> electroencephalography (ɪˌlɛktrəʊɛnˌsɛfəˈlɒgrəfɪ) n

electrolyse or US **electrolyze** (ɪˈlɛktrəʊˌlaɪz) vb (tr) **1** to decompose (a chemical compound) by electrolysis **2** to destroy (living tissue, such as hair roots) by electrolysis [C19: back formation from ELECTROLYSIS on pattern of analyse] > e'lectro,lyser or US e'lectro,lyzer n

electrolysis (ɪlɛkˈtrɒlɪsɪs) n **1** the conduction of electricity by a solution or melt, esp the use of this process to induce chemical changes **2** the destruction of living tissue, such as hair roots, by an electric current, usually for cosmetic reasons [C19: from ELECTRO- + -LYSIS]

electrolyte (ɪˈlɛktrəʊˌlaɪt) n **1** a solution or molten substance that conducts electricity **2 a** a chemical compound that dissociates in solution into ions **b** any of the ions themselves

electrolytic (ɪˌlɛktrəʊˈlɪtɪk) adj **1** physics **a** of, concerned with, or produced by electrolysis or electrodeposition **b** of, relating to, or containing an electrolyte ▷ n **2** Also called: **electrolytic capacitor** electronics a small capacitor consisting of two electrodes separated by an electrolyte > e,lectro'lytically adv

electromagnet (ɪˌlɛktrəʊˈmæɡnɪt) n a magnet consisting of an iron or steel core wound with a coil of wire, through which a current is passed

electromagnetic (ɪˌlɛktrəʊmæɡˈnɛtɪk) adj **1** of, containing, or operated by an electromagnet: an electromagnetic pump **2** of, relating to, or consisting of electromagnetism: electromagnetic moment **3** of or relating to electromagnetic radiation: the electromagnetic spectrum > e,lectromag'netically adv

electromagnetic radiation n radiation consisting of self-sustaining oscillating electric and magnetic fields at right angles to each other and to the direction of propagation. It does not require a supporting medium and travels through empty space at the speed of light

electromagnetics (ɪˌlɛktrəʊmæɡˈnɛtɪks) n (functioning as singular) physics another name for **electromagnetism** (sense 2)

electromagnetic spectrum n the complete range of electromagnetic radiation from the longest radio waves (wavelength 10^5 metres) to the shortest gamma radiation (wavelength 10^{-13} metre)

electromagnetic unit n any unit that belongs to a system of electrical cgs units in which the magnetic constant is given the value of unity and is taken as a pure number

electromagnetic wave n a wave of energy propagated in an electromagnetic field

electromagnetism (ɪˌlɛktrəʊˈmæɡnɪˌtɪzəm) n **1** magnetism produced by an electric current **2** Also called: **electromagnetics** the branch of physics concerned with magnetism produced by electric currents and with the interaction of electric and magnetic fields

electrometer (ɪlɛkˈtrɒmɪtə, ˌiːlɛk-) n an instrument for detecting or determining the potential difference or charge by the electrostatic forces between charged bodies > **electrometric** (ɪˌlɛktrəʊˈmɛtrɪk) or e,lectro'metrical adj > elec'trometry n

electromotive (ɪˌlɛktrəʊˈməʊtɪv) adj of, concerned with, producing, or tending to produce an electric current

electromotive force n physics **a** a source of energy that can cause a current to flow in an electrical circuit or device **b** the rate at which energy is drawn from this source when unit current flows through the circuit or device, measured in volts

electromyography (ɪˌlɛktrəʊmaɪˈɒgrəfɪ) n med a technique for recording the electrical activity of muscles: used in the diagnosis of nerve and muscle disorders

electron (ɪˈlɛktrɒn) n a stable elementary particle present in all atoms, orbiting the nucleus in numbers equal to the atomic number of the element in the neutral atom; a lepton with a negative charge of $1.602\ 176\ 462 \times 10^{-19}$ coulomb, a rest mass of $9.109\ 381\ 88 \times 10^{-31}$ kilogram, a radius of $2.817\ 940\ 285 \times 10^{-15}$ metre, and a spin of $\frac{1}{2}$ [C19: from ELECTRO- + -ON]

electronegative (ɪˌlɛktrəʊˈnɛɡətɪv) adj **1** having a negative electric charge **2** (of an atom, group, molecule, etc) tending to gain or attract electrons and form negative ions or polarized bonds

electron gun n a heated cathode with an associated system of electrodes and coils for producing and focusing a beam of electrons, used esp in cathode-ray tubes

electronic (ɪlɛkˈtrɒnɪk, ˌiːlɛk-) adj **1** of, concerned with, using, or operated by devices in which electrons are conducted through a semiconductor, free space, or gas **2** of or concerned with electronics **3** of or concerned with electrons or an electron: an electronic energy level in a molecule **4** involving or concerned with the representation, storage, or transmission of information by electronic systems: electronic mail; electronic shopping > elec'tronically adv

● USAGE Electronic is used to refer to equipment, such as
● television sets, computers, etc, in which the current
● is controlled by transistors, valves, and similar
● components and also to the components themselves.
● Electrical is used in a more general sense, often to refer
● to the use of electricity as a whole as opposed to other
● forms of energy: electrical engineering; an electrical
● appliance. Electric, in many cases used interchangeably
● with electrical, is often restricted to the description of
● particular devices or to concepts relating to the flow
● of current: electric fire; electric charge

electronic flash n photog an electronic device for producing a very bright flash of light by means of an electric discharge in a gas-filled tube

electronic footprint n computing data that identifies a computer that has connected to a particular website

electronic funds transfer at point of sale n a system for debiting a retail sale direct to the customer's bank, building-society, or credit-card account by means of a computer link using the telephone network. Acronym: EFTPOS

electronic ignition n any system that uses an electronic circuit to supply the voltage to the sparking plugs of an internal-combustion engine

electronic ink n a material consisting of microscopic cells that can be turned from white to black and vice versa with the application of a small electric charge allowing electronically stored text to appear on a paper-like substance

electronic keyboard n a typewriter keyboard used to operate an electronic device such as a computer, word processor, etc

electronic mail n the transmission and distribution of messages, information, facsimiles of documents, etc, from one computer terminal to another. Abbreviation: e-mail

electronic music n a form of music consisting of sounds produced by oscillating electric currents either controlled from an instrument panel or keyboard or prerecorded on magnetic tape

electronic organ n music an electrophonic instrument played by means of a keyboard, in which sounds are produced and amplified by any of various electronic or electrical means

electronic organizer n See **personal organizer** (sense 2)

electronic point of sale n a computerized system for recording sales in retail shops, using a laser scanner at the cash till to read bar codes on the packages of the items sold. Acronym: EPOS

electronic publishing n the publication of information on magnetic tape, disks, etc, so that it can be accessed by a computer

electronics (ɪlɛkˈtrɒnɪks, ˌiːlɛk-) n **1** (functioning as singular) the science and technology concerned with the development, behaviour, and applications of electronic devices and circuits **2** (functioning as plural) the circuits and devices of a piece of electronic equipment: the electronics of a television set

electronic signature n computing electronic proof of a person's identity

electronic surveillance n **1** the use of such electronic devices as television monitors, video cameras, etc, to prevent burglary, shop lifting, break-ins, etc **2** monitoring events, conversations, etc, at a distance by electronic means, esp by such covert means as wiretapping or bugging

electronic tag *n* another name for **tag¹** (sense 2)

electronic transfer of funds *n* the transfer of money from one bank or building-society account to another by means of a computer link using the telephone network. Abbreviation: **ETF**

electron lens *n* a system, such as an arrangement of electrodes or magnets, that produces a field for focusing a beam of electrons

electron micrograph *n* a photograph or image of a specimen taken using an electron microscope

electron microscope *n* a powerful type of microscope that uses electrons, rather than light, and electron lenses to produce a magnified image

electron tube *n* an electrical device, such as a valve, in which a flow of electrons between electrodes takes place

electronvolt (ɪˌlɛktrɒn'vəʊlt) *n* a unit of energy equal to the work done on an electron accelerated through a potential difference of 1 volt. 1 electronvolt is equivalent to 1.602 × 10⁻¹⁹ joule

electrophoresis (ɪˌlɛktrəʊfə'riːsɪs) *n* the motion of charged particles in a colloid under the influence of an applied electric field > **electrophoretic** (ɪˌlɛktrəʊfə'rɛtɪk) *adj*

electrophorus (ɪlɛk'trɒfərəs, ˌiːlɛk-) *n* an apparatus for generating static electricity. It consists of an insulating plate charged by friction and used to charge a metal plate by induction [c18: from ELECTRO- + -phorus, from Greek -phoros bearing, from pherein to bear]

electroplate (ɪ'lɛktrəʊˌpleɪt) *vb* **1** (*tr*) to plate (an object) by electrolysis ▷ *n* **2** electroplated articles collectively, esp when plated with silver ▷ *adj* **3** coated with metal by electrolysis; electroplated > e'lectro,plater *n*

electropositive (ɪˌlɛktrəʊ'pɒzɪtɪv) *adj* **1** having a positive electric charge **2** (of an atom, group, molecule, etc) tending to release electrons and form positive ions or polarized bonds

electrorheology (ɪˌlɛktrəʊrɪ'ɒlədʒɪ) *n* **1** the study of the flow of fluids under the influence of electric fields **2** the way in which fluid flow is influenced by an electric field > e,lectrorheo'logical *adj*

electroscope (ɪ'lɛktrəʊˌskəʊp) *n* an apparatus for detecting an electric charge, typically consisting of a rod holding two gold foils that separate when a charge is applied > **electroscopic** (ɪˌlɛktrəʊ'skɒpɪk) *adj*

electroshock therapy (ɪ'lɛktrəʊˌʃɒk) *n* another name for **electroconvulsive therapy**

electrostatic (ɪˌlɛktrəʊ'stætɪk) *adj* **1** of, concerned with, producing, or caused by static electricity **2** concerned with electrostatics > e,lectro'statically *adv*

electrostatics (ɪˌlɛktrəʊ'stætɪks) *n* (*functioning as singular*) the branch of physics concerned with static charges and the electrostatic field

electrostatic unit *n* any unit that belongs to a system of electrical cgs units in which the electric constant is given the value of unity and is taken as a pure number

electrotherapeutics (ɪˌlɛktrəʊˌθɛrə'pjuːtɪks) *n* (*functioning as singular*) the branch of medical science concerned with the use of electrotherapy > e,lectro,thera'peutic *or* e,lectro,thera'peutical *adj*

electrotherapy (ɪˌlɛktrəʊ'θɛrəpɪ) *n* treatment in which electric currents are passed through the tissues to stimulate muscle function in paralysed patients > e,lectro'therapist *n*

electrotype (ɪ'lɛktrəʊˌtaɪp) *n* **1** a duplicate printing plate made by electrolytically depositing a layer of copper or nickel onto a mould of the original ▷ *vb* **2** (*tr*) to make an electrotype of (printed matter, illustrations, etc) > e'lectro,typer *n*

electrovalent bond *n* a type of chemical bond in which one atom loses an electron to form a positive ion and the other atom gains the electron to form a negative ion. The resulting ions are held together by electrostatic attraction > e,lectro'valency *or* e,lectro'valence *n* > e,lectro'valent *adj*

electroweak interaction (ɪˌlɛktrəʊ'wiːk) *n physics* a type of fundamental interaction combining both the electromagnetic interaction and the weak interaction

electrum (ɪ'lɛktrəm) *n* an alloy of gold (55–88 per cent) and silver used for jewellery and ornaments [c14: from Latin, from Greek ēlektron amber]

electuary (ɪ'lɛktjʊərɪ) *n, pl* -**aries** *archaic* a paste taken orally, containing a drug mixed with syrup or honey [c14: from Late Latin ēlēctuārium, probably from Greek ēkleikton electuary, from ekleikhein to lick out, from leikhein to lick]

eleemosynary (ˌɛliːɪ'mɒsɪnərɪ) *adj* **1** of, concerned with, or dependent on charity **2** given as an act of charity [c17: from Church Latin eleēmosyna ALMS]

elegance ('ɛlɪɡəns) *or* **elegancy** *n, pl* -**gances** *or* -**gancies 1** dignified grace in appearance, movement, or behaviour **2** good taste in design, style, arrangement, etc **3** something elegant; a refinement

elegant ('ɛlɪɡənt) *adj* **1** tasteful in dress, style, or design **2** dignified and graceful in appearance, behaviour, etc **3** cleverly simple; ingenious: *an elegant solution to a problem* [c16: from Latin ēlegāns tasteful, related to ēligere to select; see ELECT]

elegiac (ˌɛlɪ'dʒaɪək) *adj* **1** resembling, characteristic of, relating to, or appropriate to an elegy **2** lamenting; mournful; plaintive **3** denoting or written in elegiac couplets or elegiac stanzas ▷ *n* **4** (*often plural*) an elegiac couplet or stanza > ,ele'giacally *adv*

elegize *or* **elegise** ('ɛlɪˌdʒaɪz) *vb* **1** to compose an elegy or elegies (in memory of) **2** (*intr*) to write elegiacally > 'elegist *n*

elegy ('ɛlɪdʒɪ) *n, pl* -**gies 1** a mournful or plaintive poem or song, esp a lament for the dead **2** poetry or a poem written in elegiac couplets or stanzas [c16: via French and Latin from Greek elegeia, from elegos lament sung to flute accompaniment]

element ('ɛlɪmənt) *n* **1** any of the 118 known substances (of which 93 occur naturally) that consist of atoms with the same number of protons in their nuclei **2** one of the fundamental or irreducible components making up a whole **3** a cause that contributes to a result; factor **4** any group that is part of a larger unit, such as a military formation **5** a small amount; hint **6** a distinguishable section of a social group **7** the most favourable environment for an animal or plant **8** the situation in which a person is happiest or most effective (esp in the phrases **in** or **out of one's element**) **9** the resistance wire and its former that constitute the electrical heater in a cooker, heater, etc **10** one of the four substances thought in ancient and medieval cosmology to constitute the universe (earth, air, water, or fire) **11** (*plural*) atmospheric conditions or forces, esp wind, rain, and cold **12** (*plural*) the first principles of a subject **13** *Christianity* the bread or wine consecrated in the Eucharist [c13: from Latin elementum a first principle, alphabet, element, of uncertain origin]

elemental (ˌɛlɪ'mɛnt³l) *adj* **1** fundamental; basic; primal **2** motivated by or symbolic of primitive and powerful natural forces or passions: *elemental rites of worship* **3** of or relating to earth, air, water, and fire considered as elements **4** of or relating to atmospheric forces, esp wind, rain, and cold **5** of, relating to, or denoting a chemical element ▷ *n* **6** *rare* a spirit or force that is said to appear in physical form > ,ele'mental,ism *n*

elementary (ˌɛlɪ'mɛntərɪ, -trɪ) *adj* **1** not difficult; simple; rudimentary **2** of or concerned with the first principles of a subject; introductory or fundamental **3** *chem* another word for **elemental** (sense 5) > ,ele'mentariness *n*

elementary particle *n* any of several entities, such as electrons, neutrons, or protons, that are less complex than atoms and are regarded as the constituents of all matter. Also called: **fundamental particle**

elementary school *n* **1** *Brit* a former name for **primary school 2** *US & Canadian* a state school in which instruction is given for the first six to eight years of a child's education

elenchus (ɪ'lɛŋkəs) *n, pl* -**chi** (-kaɪ) *logic* refutation of an argument by proving the contrary of its conclusion, esp syllogistically [c17: from Latin, from Greek elenkhos

refutation, from *elenkhein* to put to shame, refute]
> e'lenctic *adj*

elephant ('ɛlɪfənt) *n, pl* -**phants** *or* -**phant** **1** either of the two proboscidean mammals of the family *Elephantidae*. The **African elephant** (*Loxodonta africana*) is the larger species, with large flapping ears and a less humped back than the **Indian elephant** (*Elephas maximus*), of S and SE Asia **2 elephant in the room** an obvious truth deliberately ignored by all parties in a situation [c13: from Latin *elephantus*, from Greek *elephas* elephant, ivory, of uncertain origin]

elephant fish *n* a large marine fish, *Callorhinchus milii*, of southwest Pacific waters, having a snout resembling an elephant's trunk. Also called: **reperepe**

elephantiasis (ˌɛlɪfən'taɪəsɪs) *n* *pathol* a complication of chronic filariasis, in which nematode worms block the lymphatic vessels, usually in the legs or scrotum, causing extreme enlargement of the affected area [c16: via Latin from Greek, from *elephas* ELEPHANT + -IASIS]

elephantine (ˌɛlɪ'fæntaɪn) *adj* **1** denoting, relating to, or characteristic of an elephant or elephants **2** huge, clumsy, or ponderous

elephant seal *n* either of two large earless seals, *Mirounga leonina* of southern oceans or *M. angustirostris* of the N Atlantic, the males of which have a long trunklike snout

Eleusinian mysteries *pl n* a mystical religious festival, held in September at Eleusis in classical times, in which initiates celebrated Persephone, Demeter, and Dionysus

Eleusis (ɪ'luːsɪs) *n* a town in Greece, in Attica about 23 km (14 miles) west of Athens, of which it is now an industrial suburb. Modern Greek name: **Elevsís**
> **Eleusinian** (ˌɛljʊ'sɪnɪən) *n, adj*

elevate ('ɛlɪˌveɪt) *vb* (*tr*) **1** to move to a higher place **2** to raise in rank or status; promote **3** to put in a cheerful mood; elate **4** to put on a higher cultural plane; uplift **5** to raise the axis of a gun **6** to raise the intensity or pitch of (the voice) [c15: from Latin *ēlevāre* from *levāre* to raise, from *levis* (adj) light] > ˌele'vatory *adj*

elevated ('ɛlɪˌveɪtɪd) *adj* **1** raised to or being at a higher level **2** inflated or lofty; exalted **3** in a cheerful mood; elated **4** *informal* slightly drunk

elevation (ˌɛlɪ'veɪʃən) *n* **1** the act of elevating or the state of being elevated **2** the height of something above a given or implied place, esp above sea level **3** a raised area; height **4** nobleness or grandeur; loftiness: *elevation of thought* **5** a drawing to scale of the external face of a building or structure **6** a ballet dancer's ability to leap high **7** *astronomy* another name for **altitude** (sense 3) **8** the angle formed between the muzzle of a gun and the horizontal **9** *surveying* the angular distance between the plane through a point of observation and an object above it. See **depression** (sense 7) > ˌele'vational *adj*

elevator ('ɛlɪˌveɪtə) *n* **1** a person or thing that elevates **2** *chiefly US* a mechanical hoist for raising something, esp grain or coal, often consisting of a chain of scoops linked together on a conveyor belt **3** *chiefly US & Canadian* a large granary equipped with an elevator and, usually, facilities for cleaning and grading the grain **4** any muscle that raises a part of the body **5** a control surface on the tailplane of an aircraft, for making it climb or descend

eleven (ɪ'lɛvⁿn) *n* **1** the cardinal number that is the sum of ten and one **2** a numeral 11, XI, etc, representing this number **3** something representing, represented by, or consisting of 11 units **4** (*functioning as singular or plural*) a team of 11 players in football, cricket, hockey, etc **5** Also called: **eleven o'clock** eleven hours after noon or midnight ▷ *determiner* **6 a** amounting to eleven: *eleven chances* **b** (*as pronoun*): *have another eleven today* [Old English *endleofan*; related to Old Norse *ellefo*, Gothic *ainlif*, Old Frisian *andlova*, Old High German *einlif*] > e'leventh *adj, n*

eleven-plus *n* (esp formerly) an examination, taken by children aged 11 or 12, that determines the type of secondary education a child will be given

elevenses (ɪ'lɛvⁿnzɪz) *pl n* (*sometimes functioning as singular*) *Brit informal* a light snack, usually with tea or coffee, taken mid-morning

eleventh hour *n* the latest possible time; last minute

Elevsís (ˌɛlɛf'sɪs) *n* a transliteration of the Modern Greek name for **Eleusis**

elf (ɛlf) *n, pl* **elves** (ɛlvz) **1** (in folklore) one of a kind of legendary beings, usually characterized as small, manlike, and mischievous **2** a mischievous or whimsical child [Old English *ælf*; related to Old Norse *elfr* elf, Middle Low German *alf* incubus, Latin *albus* white]
> 'elfish ('ɛlfɪʃ) *or* 'elvish *adj, n*

El Faiyûm (ɛl faɪ'juːm) *or* **Al Faiyûm** (æl faɪ'juːm) *n* a city in N Egypt: a site of towns going back at least to the 12th dynasty. Pop: 311 000 (2005 est)

El Ferrol (*Spanish* ɛl fɛ'rrɔl) *n* a port in NW Spain, on the Atlantic: fortified naval base, with a deep natural harbour. Pop: 78 764 (2003 est)

elfin ('ɛlfɪn) *adj* **1** of, relating to, or like an elf or elves **2** small, delicate, and charming

elflock ('ɛlfˌlɒk) *n* a lock of hair, fancifully regarded as having been tangled by the elves

Elgar ('ɛlgɑː) *n* Sir **Edward** (**William**). 1857–1934, English composer, whose works include the *Enigma Variations* (1899), the oratorio *The Dream of Gerontius* (1900), two symphonies, a cello concerto, and a violin concerto

Elgin ('ɛlgɪn) *n* a market town in NE Scotland, the administrative centre of Moray, on the River Lossie: ruined 13th-century cathedral; distilling, engineering. Pop: 20 829 (2001)

El Gîza (ɛl 'giːzə) *or* **Giza** *n* a city in NE Egypt, on the W bank of the Nile opposite Cairo: nearby are the Great Pyramid of Cheops (Khufu) and the Sphinx. Pop: 2 221 868 (1996)

Elgon ('ɛlgɒn) *n* **Mount Elgon** an extinct volcano in E Africa, on the Kenya-Uganda border. Height: 4321m (14 178 ft)

El Greco (ɛl 'grɛkəʊ) *n* real name *Domenikos Theotocopoulos*. 1541–1614, Spanish painter, born in Crete; noted for his elongated human forms and dramatic use of colour

Eli ('iːlaɪ) *n* *Old Testament* the highest priest at Shiloh and teacher of Samuel (I Samuel 1–3)

Elia¹ *or* **Eleia** ('iːlɪə) *n* a department of SW Greece, in the W Peloponnese: in ancient times most of the region formed the state of Elis. Pop: 183 521 (2001). Area: 2681 sq km (1035 sq miles). Modern Greek name: **Ilía**

Elia² ('iːlɪə) *n* the pen name of (Charles) **Lamb¹**

Eliade (*Romanian* e'lja:de) *n* **Mircea**. 1907–86, Romanian scholar and writer, noted for his study of religious symbolism. His works include *Patterns of Comparative Religion* (1949)

Elias (ɪ'laɪəs) *n* *Bible* the Douay spelling of **Elijah**

elicit (ɪ'lɪsɪt) *vb* (*tr*) **1** to give rise to; evoke: *to elicit a sharp retort* **2** to bring to light: *to elicit the truth* [c17: from Latin *ēlicere* to lure forth, from *licere* to entice] > e'licitable *adj*
> eˌlici'tation *n* > e'licitor *n*

elide (ɪ'laɪd) *vb* *phonetics* to undergo or cause to undergo elision [c16: from Latin *ēlīdere* to knock, from *laedere* to hit, wound] > e'lidible *adj*

eligible ('ɛlɪdʒəb³l) *adj* **1** fit, worthy, or qualified, as for an office or function **2** desirable and worthy of being chosen, esp as a spouse: *an eligible young man* [c15: from Late Latin *ēligibilis* able to be chosen, from *ēligere* to ELECT] > ˌeligi'bility *n* > 'eligibly *adv*

Elijah (ɪ'laɪdʒə) *n* *Old Testament* a Hebrew prophet of the 9th century BC, who was persecuted for denouncing Ahab and Jezebel. (I Kings 17–21: 21; II Kings 1–2:18)

Elikón (ɛli'kɒn) *n* a transliteration of the Modern Greek name for **Helicon**

eliminate (ɪ'lɪmɪˌneɪt) *vb* (*tr*) **1** to remove or take out; get rid of **2** to reject as trivial or irrelevant; omit from consideration **3** to remove (a competitor, team, etc) from a contest, usually by defeat **4** *slang* to murder in a cold-blooded manner **5** *physiol* to expel (waste matter) from the body **6** *maths* to remove (an unknown variable) from two or more simultaneous equations [c16: from Latin *ēlīmināre* to turn out of the house, from *e-* out + *līmen* threshold] > e'liminable *adj* > eˌlimi'nation *n*
> e'liminative *or* e'liminatory *adj* > e'limiˌnator *n*

Eliot ('ɛlɪət) *n* **1 George**, real name *Mary Ann Evans*. 1819–80, English novelist, noted for her analysis of provincial Victorian society. Her best-known novels include *Adam Bede* (1859), *The Mill on the Floss* (1860), *Silas*

Marner (1861), and *Middlemarch* (1872) **2** Sir **John**. 1592–1632, English statesman, a leader of parliamentary opposition to Charles I **3** T(**homas**) S(**tearns**). 1888–1965, British poet, dramatist, and critic, born in the US His poetry includes *Prufrock and Other Observations* (1917), *The Waste Land* (1922), *Ash Wednesday* (1930), and *Four Quartets* (1943). Among his verse plays are *Murder in the Cathedral* (1935), *The Family Reunion* (1939), *The Cocktail Party* (1950), and *The Confidential Clerk* (1954): Nobel prize for literature 1948

Elis (ˈiːlɪs) *n* an ancient city-state of SW Greece, in the NW Peloponnese: site of the ancient Olympic games

ELISA (ɪˈlaɪzə) *n acronym for* enzyme-linked immunosorbent assay: an immunological technique for accurately measuring the amount of a substance, for example in a blood sample

Elisabeth (ɪˈlɪzəbəθ) *n* a variant spelling of **Elizabeth²** (sense 1)

Élisabethville (ɪˈlɪzəbəθˌvɪl) *n* the former name (until 1966) of **Lubumbashi**

Elisavetgrad (*Russian* jɪlizaˈvjɛtɡrət) *n* a former name (until 1924) of **Kirovograd**

Elisavetpol (*Russian* jɪlizaˈvjɛtpəlj) *n* a former name (until 1920) of **Kirovabad**

Elisha (ɪˈlaɪʃə) *n Old Testament* a Hebrew prophet of the 9th century BC: successor of Elijah (II Kings 3–9)

elision (ɪˈlɪʒən) *n* **1** the omission of a syllable or vowel at the beginning or end of a word, esp when a word ending with a vowel is next to one beginning with a vowel **2** any omission of a part or parts [c16: from Latin *ēlīsiō*, from *ēlīdere* to ELIDE]

elite *or* **élite** (ɪˈliːt, eɪ-) *n* **1** (*sometimes functioning as plural*) the most powerful, rich, gifted, or educated members of a group, community, etc **2** Also called: twelve pitch a typewriter typesize having 12 characters to the inch ▷ *adj* **3** of, relating to, or suitable for an elite; exclusive [c18: from French, from Old French *eslit* chosen, from *eslire* to choose, from Latin *ēligere* to ELECT]

elitism (ɪˈliːtɪzəm, eɪ-) *n* **1 a** the belief that society should be governed by a select group of gifted and highly educated individuals **b** such government **2** pride in or awareness of being one of an elite group ⊳ e'litist *adj, n*

elixir (ɪˈlɪksə) *n* **1** an alchemical preparation supposed to be capable of prolonging life indefinitely (**elixir of life**) or of transmuting base metals into gold **2** anything that purports to be a sovereign remedy; panacea **3** an underlying principle; quintessence **4** a liquid containing a medicinal drug with syrup, glycerine, or alcohol added to mask its unpleasant taste [c14: from Medieval Latin, from Arabic *al iksīr* the elixir, probably from Greek *xērion* powder used for drying wounds, from *xēros* dry]

Elizabeth¹ (ɪˈlɪzəbəθ) *n* **1** a city in NE New Jersey, on Newark Bay. Pop: 123 215 (2003 est) **2** a town in SE South Australia, part of Adelaide. Pop: 26 428 (2006)

Elizabeth² (ɪˈlɪzəbəθ) *n* **1** Saint Elizabeth *Also called:* Saint Elisabeth *New Testament* the wife of Zacharias, mother of John the Baptist, and kinswoman of the Virgin Mary. Feast day: Nov 5 or 8 **2** pen name *Carmen Sylva*. 1843–1916, queen of Romania (1881–1914) and author **3** Russian name *Yelizaveta Petrovna*. 1709–62, empress of Russia (1741–62); daughter of Peter the Great **4** title *the Queen Mother*; original name Lady *Elizabeth Bowes-Lyon*. 1900–2002, queen of Great Britain and Northern Ireland (1936–52) as the wife of George VI; mother of Elizabeth II

Elizabeth I *n* 1533–1603, queen of England (1558–1603); daughter of Henry VIII and Anne Boleyn. She established the Church of England (1559) and put an end to Catholic plots, notably by executing Mary Queen of Scots (1587) and defeating the Spanish Armada (1588). Her reign was notable for commercial growth, maritime expansion, and the flourishing of literature, music, and architecture

Elizabeth II *n* born 1926, queen of Great Britain and Northern Ireland from 1952; daughter of George VI

Elizabethan (ɪˌlɪzəˈbiːθən) *adj* **1** of, characteristic of, or relating to England or its culture in the age of Elizabeth I (1533–1603; reigned 1558–1603) or to the United Kingdom or its culture in the age of Elizabeth II (born

1926; queen from 1952) **2** of, relating to, or designating a style of architecture used in England during the reign of Elizabeth I, characterized by moulded and sculptured ornament based on German and Flemish models ▷ *n* **3** a person who lived in England during the reign of Elizabeth I

Elizabethan sonnet *n* another term for **Shakespearean sonnet**

Elizabeth of Hungary *n* Saint. 1207–31, Hungarian princess who devoted herself to charity and asceticism. Feast day: Nov 17 and 19

elk (ɛlk) *n, pl* **elks** *or* **elk 1** a large deer, *Alces alces*, of N Europe and Asia, having large flattened palmate antlers: also occurs in North America, where it is called a moose **2** American elk another name for **wapiti** [Old English *eolh*; related to Old Norse *elgr*, Old High German *elaho*, Latin *alcēs*, Greek *alkē*, *elaphos* deer]

El Khalil (ɛl xɒˈliːl) *n* transliteration of the Arabic name for **Hebron**

ell (ɛl) *n* an obsolete unit of length equal to approximately 45 inches [Old English *eln* the forearm (the measure originally being from the elbow to the fingertips); related to Old High German *elina*, Latin *ulna*, Greek *ōlenē*]

Ellás (ɛˈlas) *n* transliteration of the Modern Greek name for **Greece**

Ellenborough (ˈɛlənbrə) *n* **Earl of**, title of Edward Law. 1780–1871, British colonial administrator: governor general of India (1742–44)

Ellesmere Island (ˈɛlzmɪə) *n* a Canadian island in the Arctic Ocean: part of Nunavut; mountainous, with many glaciers. Area: 212 688 sq km (82 119 sq miles)

Ellesmere Port *n* a port in NW England, in NW Cheshire on the Mersey estuary and Manchester Ship Canal. Pop: 66 265 (2001)

Ellice Islands (ˈɛlɪs) *pl n* the former name (until 1975) of **Tuvalu**

Ellington (ˈɛlɪŋtən) *n* **Duke**, nickname of *Edward Kennedy Ellington*. 1899–1974, US jazz composer, pianist, and conductor, famous for such works as "Mood Indigo" and "Creole Love Call"

ellipse (ɪˈlɪps) *n* a closed conic section shaped like a flattened circle and formed by an inclined plane that does not cut the base of the cone. Standard equation $x^2/a^2 + y^2/b^2 = 1$, where $2a$ and $2b$ are the lengths of the major and minor axes. Area: πab [c18: back formation from ELLIPSIS]

ellipsis (ɪˈlɪpsɪs) *n, pl* **-ses** (-siːz) **1** Also called: eclipsis omission of parts of a word or sentence **2** *printing* a sequence of three dots (...) indicating an omission in text [c16: from Latin, from Greek *elleipsis* omission, from *elleipein* to leave out, from *leipein* to leave]

ellipsoid (ɪˈlɪpsɔɪd) *n* **a** a geometric surface, symmetrical about the three coordinate axes, whose plane sections are ellipses or circles. Standard equation: $x^2/a^2 + y^2/b^2 + z^2/c^2 = 1$, where $\pm a$, $\pm b$, $\pm c$ are the intercepts on the *x*-, *y*-, and *z*- axes **b** a solid having this shape ⊳ ellipsoidal (ɪˌlɪpˈsɔɪdəl, ˌɛl-) *adj*

ellipsoid of revolution *n* a geometric surface produced by rotating an ellipse about one of its two axes and having circular plane surfaces perpendicular to the axis of revolution

elliptical (ɪˈlɪptɪkəl) *adj* **1** relating to or having the shape of an ellipse **2** relating to or resulting from ellipsis **3** (of speech, literary style, etc) **a** very condensed or concise, often so as to be obscure or ambiguous **b** circumlocutory or long-winded ⊳ el'lipticalness *n*

Ellis (ˈɛlɪs) *n* **1** 1814–90, English philologist: made the first systematic survey of the phonology of British dialects **2** (**Henry**) **Havelock** (ˈhævlɒk). 1859–1939, English essayist: author of works on the psychology of sex

elm (ɛlm) *n* **1** any ulmaceous tree of the genus *Ulmus*, occurring in the N hemisphere, having serrated leaves and winged fruits (samaras): cultivated for shade, ornament, and timber **2** the hard heavy wood of this tree [Old English *elm*; related to Old Norse *almr*, Old High German *elm*, Latin *ulmus*]

El Mansûra (ɛl mænˈsʊərə) *or* Al Mansûrah *n* a city in NE

e

Egypt: scene of a battle (1250) in which the Crusaders were defeated by the Mamelukes and Louis IX of France was captured: cotton-manufacturing centre. Pop: 423 000 (2005 est)

El Minya (εl 'mɪnjə) *n* a river port in central Egypt on the Nile. Pop: 225 000 (2005 est)

El Misti (εl 'miːstiː) *n* a volcano in S Peru, in the Andes. Height: 5852 m (19 199 ft)

El Niño (εl 'niːnjəʊ) *n meteorol* a warming of the eastern tropical Pacific occurring every few years, which alters the weather pattern of the tropics [c20: from Spanish: The Child, i.e. Christ, referring to its original occurrence at Christmas time]

El Obeid (εl əʊ'beɪd) *n* a city in the central Sudan, in Kordofan province: scene of the defeat of a British and Egyptian army by the Mahdi (1883). Pop: 423 000 (2005 est)

elocution (ˌεlə'kjuːʃən) *n* the art of public speaking, esp of voice production, delivery, and gesture [c15: from Latin *ēlocūtiō* a speaking out, from *loquī* to speak] > ˌelo'cutionary *adj* > ˌelo'cutionist *n*

Elohim (ε'ləʊhɪm, ˌεləʊ'hiːm) *n Old Testament* a Hebrew word for God or gods [c17: from Hebrew *'Elōhīm*, plural (used to indicate uniqueness) of *'Elōah* God; probably related to *'El God]*

Elohist (ε'ləʊhɪst) *n Old Testament* the supposed author or authors of one of the four main strands of text of the Pentateuch, identified chiefly by the use of the word *Elohim* for God instead of YHVH (Jehovah)

elongate ('iːlɒŋgeɪt) *vb* **1** to make or become longer; stretch ▷ *adj* **2** long and narrow; slender: *elongate leaves* **3** lengthened or tapered [c16: from Late Latin *ēlongāre* to keep at a distance, from *ē-* away + Latin *longē* (adv) far, but also later: to lengthen, as if from *ē-* + Latin *longus* (adj) long] > ˌelon'gation *n*

elope (ɪ'ləʊp) *vb* (*intr*) to run away secretly with a lover, esp in order to marry [c16: from Anglo-French *aloper*, perhaps from Middle Dutch *lōpen* to run; see LOPE] > e'lopement *n* > e'loper *n*

eloquence ('εləkwəns) *n* **1** ease in using language to best effect **2** powerful and effective language **3** the quality of being persuasive or moving

eloquent ('εləkwənt) *adj* **1** (of speech, writing, etc) characterized by fluency and persuasiveness **2** visibly or vividly expressive, as of an emotion: *an eloquent yawn* [c14: from Latin *ēloquēns*, from *ēloquī* to speak out, from *loquī* to speak]

El Paso (εl 'pæsəʊ) *n* a city in W Texas, on the Rio Grande opposite Ciudad Juárez, Mexico. Pop: 584 113 (2003 est)

Els (εls) *n* **Ernie**, full name *Theodore Ernest Els*. born 1969; South African golfer: won the British Open Championship (2002) and the US Open Championship (1994, 1997)

El Salvador (εl 'sælvəˌdɔː) *n* a republic in Central America, on the Pacific: colonized by the Spanish from 1524; declared independence in 1841, becoming a republic in 1856. It consists of coastal lowlands rising to a central plateau. Coffee constitutes over a third of the total exports. Official language: Spanish. Religion: Roman Catholic majority. Currency: US dollar. Capital: San Salvador. Pop: 6 614 000 (2004 est). Area: 21 393 sq km (8236 sq miles) > ˌSalva'doran, ˌSalva'dorean or ˌSalva'dorian *adj, n*

Elsan ('εlsæn) *n trademark* a type of portable lavatory in which chemicals are used to kill bacteria and deodorize the sludge [c20: from the initials of E. L. Jackson, the manufacturer + SAN(ITATION)]

Elsass ('εlzas) *n* the German name for **Alsace**

Elsass-Lothringen ('εlzas'loːtrɪŋən) *n* the German name for **Alsace-Lorraine**

else (εls) *determiner* (*postpositive; used after an indefinite pronoun or an interrogative*) **1** in addition; more: *there is nobody else here* **2** other; different: *where else could he be?* ▷ *adv* **3** or else **a** if not, then: *go away or else I won't finish my work today* **b** or something terrible will result: used as a threat: *sit down, or else!* [Old English *elles*, genitive of *el-* strange, foreign; related to Old High German *eli-* other, Gothic *alja*, Latin *alius*, Greek *allos*]

elsewhere (ˌεls'wεə) *adv* in or to another place; somewhere else [Old English *elles hwǣr*; see ELSE, WHERE]

Elsinore ('εlsɪˌnɔː, ˌεlsɪ'nɔː) *n* the English name for **Helsingør**

ELT *abbreviation* English Language Teaching: the teaching of English specifically to students whose native language is not English

Elton ('εltən) *n* **1 Ben(jamin) (Charles)**. born 1959, British comedian, scriptwriter, playwright, and novelist; his work includes the *Blackadder* series for television (1987–89), the play *Gasping* (1990), and the novel *High Society* (2002) **2 Charles Sutherland**. 1900–91, British zoologist: initiated the study of animal ecology

Éluard (*French* elɥar) *n* **Paul** (pɔl), real name *Eugène-Émile-Paul Grindel*. 1895–1952, French surrealist poet, noted for his political and love poems

eluate ('εljuːˌeɪt) *n* a solution of adsorbed material in the eluent obtained during the process of elution

elucidate (ɪ'luːsɪˌdeɪt) *vb* to make clear (something obscure or difficult); clarify [c16: from Late Latin *ēlūcidāre* to enlighten; see LUCID] > e'luci'dation *n* > e'luciˌdative or e'luciˌdatory *adj* > e'luciˌdator *n*

elude (ɪ'luːd) *vb* (*tr*) **1** to escape or avoid (capture, one's pursuers, etc), esp by cunning **2** to avoid fulfilment of (a responsibility, obligation, etc); evade **3** to escape discovery, or understanding by; baffle [c16: from Latin *ēlūdere* to deceive, from *lūdere* to play] > e'luder *n* > elusion (ɪ'luːʒən) *n*

● USAGE *Elude* is sometimes wrongly used where *allude* is meant: *he was alluding* (not *eluding*) *to his previous visit to the city*

eluent or **eluant** ('εljuːənt) *n* a solvent used for eluting

elusive (ɪ'luːsɪv) *adj* difficult to catch: *an elusive thief* > e'lusiveness *n*

● USAGE See at **illusory**

elute (iː'luːt, ɪ'luːt) *vb* (*tr*) to wash out (a substance) by the action of a solvent, as in chromatography [c18: from Latin *ēlūtus* rinsed out, from *ēluere* to wash clean, from *luere* to wash, LAVE] > e'lution *n*

elutriate (ɪ'luːtrɪˌeɪt) *vb* (*tr*) to purify or separate (a substance or mixture) by washing and straining or decanting [c18: from Latin *ēlūtriāre* to wash out, from *ēluere*, from *ē-* out + *lavere* to wash] > eˌlutri'ation *n*

elver ('εlvə) *n* a young eel, esp one migrating up a river from the sea [c17: variant of *eelfare* migration of young eels, literally: eel-journey; see EEL, FARE]

elves (εlvz) *n* the plural of **elf**

elvish ('εlvɪʃ) *adj* a variant of **elfish**

Ely ('iːlɪ) *n* **1** a cathedral city in E England, in E Cambridgeshire on the River Ouse. Pop: 13 954 (2001) **2** a former county of E England, part of Cambridgeshire since 1965

Elyot ('εlɪət) *n* **Sir Thomas**. ?1490–1546, English scholar and diplomat; author of *The Boke named the Governour* (1531), a treatise in English on education

Elysée (eˈliˈzeɪ) *n* a palace in Paris, in the Champs Elysées: official residence of the president of France

Elysium (ɪ'lɪzɪəm) *n* **1** Also called: **Elysian fields** *Greek myth* the dwelling place of the blessed after death **2** a state or place of perfect bliss [c16: from Latin, from Greek *Ēlusion pedion* Elysian (that is, blessed) fields]

Elytis (ε'laɪtɪs) *n* **Odysseus**, real name *Odysseus Alepoudelis*. 1912–96, Greek poet, author of the long poems *Axion Est* (1959) and *Maria Nefeli* (1978): Nobel prize for literature 1979

elytron ('εlɪˌtrɒn) or **elytrum** ('εlɪtrəm) *n, pl* **-tra** (-trə) either of the horny front wings of beetles and some other insects, which cover and protect the hind wings [c18: from Greek *elutron* sheath, covering]

em (εm) *n printing* **1** Also called: **mutton, mut** the square of a body of any size of type, used as a unit of measurement **2** Also called: **pica em, pica** a unit of measurement used in printing, equal to one sixth of an inch [c19: from the name of the letter *M*]

em- *prefix* **1** before *b, m,* and *p,* a variant of **en-¹ 2** before *b, m,* and *p,* a variant of **en-²**

'em (əm) *pron* an informal variant of **them**

emaciate (ɪ'meɪsɪˌeɪt) *vb* (*usually tr*) to become or cause to become abnormally thin [c17: from Latin *ēmaciāre* to make lean, from *macer* thin] > e,maci'ation *n*

emaciated (ɪ'meɪsɪ,eɪtɪd) *adj* abnormally thin

e-mail *or* **email** ('i:meɪl) *n* 1 short for **electronic mail** ▷ *vb* (*tr*) 2 to contact (a person) by electronic mail 3 to send (a message, document, etc) by electronic mail

emanate ('emə,neɪt) *vb* 1 (*intr*; often foll by *from*) to issue or proceed from or as from a source 2 (*tr*) to send forth; emit [c18: from Latin *ēmānāre* to flow out, from *mānāre* to flow] > emanative ('emənətɪv) *adj* > 'ema,nator *n* > emanatory ('emə,neɪtərɪ, -trɪ) *adj*

emanation (,emə'neɪʃən) *n* 1 an act or instance of emanating 2 something that emanates or is produced; effusion 3 a gaseous product of radioactive decay, such as radon > ,ema'national *adj*

emancipate (ɪ'mænsɪ,peɪt) *vb* (*tr*) 1 to free from restriction or restraint, esp social or legal restraint 2 (*often passive*) to free from the inhibitions imposed by conventional morality 3 to liberate (a slave) from bondage [c17: from Latin *ēmancipāre* to give independence (to a son), from *mancipāre* to transfer property, from *manceps* a purchaser; see MANCIPLE] > e'manci,pated *adj* > e'manci,pative *adj* > e'manci,pator *n* > emancipatory (ɪ'mænsɪpətərɪ, -trɪ) *adj*

e-marketing *n* the practice of marketing by means of the internet [c20: electronic *marketing*]

emasculate *vb* (ɪ'mæskjʊ,leɪt) (*tr*) 1 to remove the testicles of; castrate; geld 2 to deprive of vigour, effectiveness, etc 3 *botany* to remove the stamens from (a flower) to prevent self-pollination for the purposes of plant breeding ▷ *adj* (ɪ'mæskjʊlɪt, -,leɪt) 4 castrated; gelded 5 deprived of strength, effectiveness, etc [c17: from Latin *ēmasculāre*, from *masculus* male; see MASCULINE] > e,mascu'lation *n* > e'masculative *or* e'masculatory *adj* > e'mascu,lator *n*

embalm (ɪm'bɑ:m) *vb* (*tr*) 1 to treat (a dead body) with preservatives, as by injecting formaldehyde into the blood vessels, to retard putrefaction 2 to preserve or cherish the memory of 3 *poetic* to give a sweet fragrance to [c13: from Old French *embaumer*; see BALM] > em'balmer *n* > em'balmment *n*

embank (ɪm'bæŋk) *vb* (*tr*) to protect, enclose, or confine (a waterway, road, etc) with an embankment

embankment (ɪm'bæŋkmənt) *n* a man-made ridge of earth or stone that carries a road or railway or confines a waterway

embargo (ɛm'bɑ:gəʊ) *n*, *pl* **-goes** 1 a government order prohibiting the departure or arrival of merchant ships in its ports 2 any legal stoppage of commerce 3 a restraint, hindrance, or prohibition ▷ *vb* **-goes, -going, -goed** (*tr*) 4 to lay an embargo upon 5 to seize for use by the state [c16: from Spanish, from *embargar*, from Latin IM- + *barra* BAR¹]

embark (ɛm'bɑ:k) *vb* 1 to board (a ship or aircraft) 2 (*intr*; usually foll by *on* or *upon*) to commence or engage (in) a new project, venture, etc [c16: via French from Old Provençal *embarcar*, from EM- + *barca* boat, BARQUE] > ,embar'kation *n*

embarrass (ɪm'bærəs) *vb* (*mainly tr*) 1 (*also intr*) to feel or cause to feel confusion or self-consciousness; disconcert; fluster 2 (*usually passive*) to involve in financial difficulties 3 *archaic* to make difficult; complicate 4 *archaic* to impede; obstruct; hamper [c17: (in the sense: to impede): via French and Spanish from Italian *imbarrazzare*, from *imbarrare* to confine within bars; see EN-¹, BAR¹] > em'barrassed *adj* > em'barrassing *adj* > em'barrassingly *adv* > em'barrassment *n*

embassy ('embəsɪ) *n*, *pl* **-sies** 1 the residence or place of official business of an ambassador 2 an ambassador and his entourage collectively 3 the position, business, or mission of an ambassador 4 any important or official mission, duty, etc, esp one undertaken by an agent [c16: from Old French *ambassee*, from Old Italian *ambasciata*, from Old Provençal *ambaisada*, ultimately of Germanic origin; see AMBASSADOR]

embattle (ɪm'bætəl) *vb* (*tr*) 1 to deploy (troops) for battle 2 to strengthen or fortify (a position, town, etc) 3 to provide (a building) with battlements [c14: from Old French *embataillier*; see EN-¹, BATTLE]

embay (ɪm'beɪ) *vb* (*tr*; *usually passive*) 1 to form into a bay

2 to enclose in or as if in a bay 3 (esp of the wind) to force (a ship, esp a sailing ship) into a bay

embed *or* **imbed** (ɪm'bɛd) *vb* **-beds, -bedding, -bedded** 1 (usually foll by *in*) to fix or become fixed firmly and deeply in a surrounding solid mass 2 (*tr*) to surround closely 3 (*tr*) to fix or retain (a thought, idea, etc) in the mind 4 (often foll by *with*) to assign a journalist or be assigned as one to accompany an active military unit > em'bedment *n*

embedding (ɪm'bɛdɪŋ) *n* the practice of assigning or being assigned a journalist to accompany an active military unit

embellish (ɪm'bɛlɪʃ) *vb* (*tr*) 1 to improve or beautify by adding detail or ornament; adorn 2 to make (a story) more interesting by adding detail [c14: from Old French *embelir*, from *bel* beautiful, from Latin *bellus*] > em'bellisher *n* > em'bellishment *n*

ember ('embə) *n* 1 a glowing or smouldering piece of coal or wood, as in a dying fire 2 the fading remains of a past emotion: *the embers of his love* [Old English *æmyrge*; related to Old Norse *eimyrja* ember, *eimr* smoke, Old High German *eimuria* ember]

Ember days *pl n* RC, *Anglican Church* any of four groups of three days (always Wednesday, Friday, and Saturday) of prayer and fasting, the groups occurring after Pentecost, after the first Sunday of Lent, after the feast of St Lucy (Dec 13), and after the feast of the Holy Cross (Sept 14) [Old English *ymbrendæg*, from *ymbren*, perhaps from *ymbryne* a (recurring) period, from *ymb* around + *ryne* a course + *dæg* day]

embezzle (ɪm'bɛzəl) *vb* to convert (money or property entrusted to one) fraudulently to one's own use [c15: from Anglo-French *embeseiller* to destroy, from Old French *beseiller* to make away with, of uncertain origin] > em'bezzlement *n* > em'bezzler *n*

embitter (ɪm'bɪtə) *vb* (*tr*) 1 to make (a person) resentful or bitter 2 to aggravate (an already hostile feeling, difficult situation, etc) > em'bittered *adj* > em'bitterment *n*

emblazon (ɪm'bleɪzən) *vb* (*tr*) 1 to portray heraldic arms on (a shield, one's notepaper, etc) 2 to make bright or splendid, as with colours, flowers, etc 3 to glorify, praise, or extol, often so as to attract great publicity > em'blazonment *n*

emblem ('embləm) *n* a visible object or representation that symbolizes a quality, type, group, etc, esp the concrete symbol of an abstract idea [c15: from Latin *emblēma* raised decoration, mosaic, from Greek, literally: something inserted, from *emballein* to insert, from *ballein* to throw] > ,emblem'atic *or* ,emblem'atical *adj* > ,emblem'atically *adv*

embody (ɪm'bɒdɪ) *vb* **-bodies, -bodying, -bodied** (*tr*) 1 to give a tangible, bodily, or concrete form to (an abstract concept) 2 to be an example of or express (an idea, principle, etc), esp in action 3 (often foll by *in*) to collect or unite in a comprehensive whole, system, etc; comprise; include 4 to invest (a spiritual entity) with a body or with bodily form; render incarnate > em'bodiment *n*

embolden (ɪm'bəʊldən) *vb* (*tr*) to encourage; make bold

embolism ('embə,lɪzəm) *n* the occlusion of a blood vessel by an embolus [c14: from Medieval Latin *embolismus*, from Late Greek *embolismos* intercalary; see EMBOLUS] > embolic (ɛm'bɒlɪk) *adj*

embolus ('embələs) *n*, *pl* **-li** (-,laɪ) material, such as part of a blood clot or an air bubble, that is transported by the blood stream until it becomes lodged within a small vessel and impedes the circulation [c17: via Latin from Greek *embolos* stopper, from *emballein* to insert, from *ballein* to throw; see EMBLEM]

embonpoint *French* (ɑ̄bɔ̄pwɛ̃) *n* 1 plumpness or stoutness ▷ *adj* 2 plump; stout [c18: from phrase *en bon point* in good condition]

embosom (ɪm'bʊzəm) *vb* (*tr*) *archaic* 1 to enclose or envelop, esp protectively 2 to clasp to the bosom; hug 3 to cherish

emboss (ɪm'bɒs) *vb* 1 to mould or carve (a decoration or design) on (a surface) so that it is raised above the surface in low relief 2 to cause to bulge; make protrude

[c14: from Old French *embocer*, from EM- + *boce* BOSS²]
> em'bosser *n* > em'bossment *n*

embouchure (ˌɒmbʊˈʃʊə) *n* 1 the mouth of a river or valley 2 *music* a the correct application of the lips and tongue in playing a wind instrument b the mouthpiece of a wind instrument [c18: from French, from Old French *emboucher* to put to one's mouth, from *bouche* mouth, from Latin *bucca* cheek]

embower (ɪmˈbaʊə) *vb* (*tr*) *archaic* to enclose in or as in a bower

embrace (ɪmˈbreɪs) *vb* (*mainly tr*) 1 (*also intr*) (of a person) to take or clasp (another person) in the arms, or (of two people) to clasp each other, as in affection, greeting, etc; hug 2 to accept (an opportunity, challenge, etc) willingly or eagerly 3 to take up (a new idea, faith, etc); adopt: *to embrace Judaism* 4 to comprise or include as an integral part 5 to encircle or enclose ▷ *n* 6 the act of embracing 7 (*often plural*) *euphemistic* sexual intercourse [c14: from Old French *embracier*, from EM- + *brace* a pair of arms, from Latin *bracchia* arms] > em'braceable *adj* > em'bracement *n* > em'bracer *n*

embrasure (ɪmˈbreɪʒə) *n* 1 *fortifications* an opening or indentation, as in a battlement, for shooting through 2 an opening forming a door or window, having splayed sides that increase the width of the opening in the interior [c18: from French, from obsolete *embraser* to widen, of uncertain origin] > em'brasured *adj*

embrocate (ˈɛmbrəʊˌkeɪt) *vb* (*tr*) to apply a liniment or lotion to (a part of the body) [c17: from Medieval Latin *embrocāre*, from *embrocha* poultice, from Greek *embrokhē* lotion, infusion, from *brokhē* a moistening]

embrocation (ˌɛmbrəʊˈkeɪʃən) *n* a drug or agent for rubbing into the skin; liniment

embroider (ɪmˈbrɔɪdə) *vb* 1 to do decorative needlework (upon) 2 to add fictitious or fanciful detail to (a story) 3 to add exaggerated or improbable details to (an account of an event, etc) [c15: from Old French *embroder*; see *em-* EN-¹, BROIDER] > em'broiderer *n*

embroidery (ɪmˈbrɔɪdərɪ) *n*, *pl* -deries 1 decorative needlework done usually on loosely woven cloth or canvas, often being a picture or pattern 2 elaboration or exaggeration, esp in writing or reporting; embellishment

embroil (ɪmˈbrɔɪl) *vb* (*tr*) 1 to involve (a person, oneself, etc) in trouble, conflict, or argument 2 to throw (affairs) into a state of confusion or disorder; complicate; entangle [c17: from French *embrouiller*, from *brouiller* to mingle, confuse] > em'broiler *n* > em'broilment *n*

embryo (ˈɛmbrɪˌəʊ) *n*, *pl* -bryos 1 an animal in the early stages of development following cleavage of the zygote and ending at birth or hatching 2 the human product of conception up to approximately the end of the second month of pregnancy. See **fetus** 3 a plant in the early stages of development: in higher plants, the plumule, cotyledons, and radicle within the seed 4 an undeveloped or rudimentary state (esp in the phrase **in embryo**) 5 something in an early stage of development [c16: from Late Latin, from Greek *embruon*, from *bruein* to swell]

embryology (ˌɛmbrɪˈɒlədʒɪ) *n* 1 the branch of science concerned with the study of embryos 2 the structure and development of the embryo of a particular organism > **embryological** (ˌɛmbrɪəˈlɒdʒɪkəl) *or* ˌembryo'logic *adj* > ˌembry'ologist *n*

embryonic (ˌɛmbrɪˈɒnɪk) *or* **embryonal** (ˈɛmbrɪənəl) *adj* 1 of or relating to an embryo 2 in an early stage; rudimentary; undeveloped > ˌembry'onically *adv*

emcee (ˌɛmˈsiː) *informal* ▷ *n* 1 a master of ceremonies ▷ *vb* -cees, -ceeing, -ceed 2 to act as master of ceremonies (for or at) [c20: from the abbreviation MC]

Emden (*German* ˈɛmdən) *n* a port in NW Germany, in Lower Saxony at the mouth of the River Ems. Pop: 51 445 (2003 est)

-eme *suffix forming nouns linguistics* indicating a minimal distinctive unit of a specified type in a language: *morpheme; phoneme* [c20: via French, abstracted from PHONEME]

emend (ɪˈmɛnd) *vb* (*tr*) to make corrections or improvements in (a text) by critical editing [c15: from Latin *ēmendāre* to correct, from *ē-* out + *mendum* a mistake] > e'mendable *adj*

emendation (ˌiːmɛnˈdeɪʃən) *n* 1 a correction or improvement in a text 2 the act or process of emending > 'emen,dator *n* > emendatory (ɪˈmɛndətərɪ, -trɪ) *adj*

emerald (ˈɛmərəld, ˈɛmrəld) *n* 1 a green transparent variety of beryl: highly valued as a gem 2 a the clear green colour of an emerald b (*as adjective*): *an emerald carpet* [c13: from Old French *esmeraude*, from Latin *smaragdus*, from Greek *smaragdos*; related to Sanskrit *marakata* emerald]

Emerald Isle *n* a poetic name for **Ireland¹**

emerge (ɪˈmɜːdʒ) *vb* (*intr*; often foll by *from*) 1 to come up to the surface of or rise from water or other liquid 2 to come into view, as from concealment or obscurity 3 (foll by *from*) to come out (of) or live (through a difficult experience) 4 to become apparent [c17: from Latin *ēmergere* to rise up from, from *mergere* to dip] > e'merging *adj* > e'mergence *n*

emergency (ɪˈmɜːdʒənsɪ) *n*, *pl* -cies 1 a an unforeseen or sudden occurrence, esp of a danger demanding immediate remedy or action b (*as modifier*): *an emergency exit* 2 a a patient requiring urgent treatment b (*as modifier*): *an emergency ward* 3 state of emergency a condition, declared by a government, in which martial law applies, usually because of civil unrest or natural disaster 4 NZ a player selected to stand by to replace an injured member of a team; reserve

emergency medical technician *n US* a member of the emergency services who is trained to provide basic emergency medical care before a patient is taken to a hospital. Abbreviation: EMT

emergent (ɪˈmɜːdʒənt) *adj* 1 coming into being or notice 2 (of a nation) recently independent > e'mergently *adv*

emeritus (ɪˈmɛrɪtəs) *adj* (*usually postpositive*) retired or honourably discharged from full-time work, but retaining one's title on an honorary basis: *a professor emeritus* [c19: from Latin, from *merēre* to deserve; see MERIT]

emersion (ɪˈmɜːʃən) *n* 1 the act or an instance of emerging 2 Also called: **egress** *astronomy* the reappearance of a celestial body after an eclipse or occultation [c17: from Latin *ēmersus*, from *ēmergere*; see EMERGE]

Emerson (ˈɛməsən) *n* **Ralph Waldo.** (ˈrælf ˈwɔːldəʊ). 1803–82, US poet, essayist, and transcendentalist

emery (ˈɛmərɪ) *n* a a hard greyish-black mineral consisting of corundum with either magnetite or haematite: used as an abrasive and polishing agent, esp as a coating on paper, cloth, etc Formula: Al_2O_3 b (*as modifier*): *emery paper* [c15: from Old French *esmeril*, ultimately from Greek *smuris* powder for rubbing]

emery board *n* a strip of cardboard or wood with a rough surface of crushed emery, for filing one's nails

emetic (ɪˈmɛtɪk) *adj* 1 causing vomiting ▷ *n* 2 an emetic agent or drug [c17: from Late Latin *ēmeticus*, from Greek *emetikos*, from *emein* to vomit]

emf *or* **EMF** *abbreviation* electromotive force

-emia *n combining form* a US variant of **-aemia**

emigrant (ˈɛmɪgrənt) *n* a a person who leaves one place or country, esp a native country, to settle in another b (*as modifier*): *an emigrant worker*

emigrate (ˈɛmɪˌgreɪt) *vb* (*intr*) to leave one place or country, esp one's native country, in order to settle in another [c18: from Latin *ēmigrāre*, from *migrāre* to depart, MIGRATE] > 'emi,gratory *adj* > ˌemi'gration *n*

émigré (ˈɛmɪˌgreɪ; *French* emigre) *n* an emigrant, esp one forced to leave his native country for political reasons [c18: from French, from *émigrer* to EMIGRATE]

Emilia-Romagna (ɪˈmiːlɪərəʊˈmɑːnjə; *Italian* eˈmiːliaroˈmaɲɲa) *n* a region of N central Italy, on the Adriatic: rises from the plains of the Po valley in the north to the Apennines in the south. Capital: Bologna. Pop: 4 030 220 (2003 est). Area: 22 123 sq km (8628 sq miles)

Emin (ˈiːmɪn) *n* **Tracey.** born 1963, British artist, noted for provocative multimedia works such as *Everyone I Have Ever Slept With* (1995) and *My Bed* (1999)

Eminem (ˌɛmɪˈnɛm) *n* real name *Marshall Mathers III*. born

1972, US White rap performer noted for his controversial lyrics; recordings include *The Slim Shady LP* (1999) and *The Eminem Show* (2002); he also starred in the film *8 Mile* (2002)

eminence ('ɛmɪnəns) *n* **1** a position of superiority, distinction, high rank, or fame **2** a high or raised piece of ground **3** *anatomy* a projection of an organ or part [C17: from French, from Latin *ēminentia* a standing out; see EMINENT]

Eminence ('ɛmɪnəns) *or* **Eminency** *n, pl* -nences *or* -nencies (preceded by *Your* or *His*) a title used to address or refer to a cardinal

éminence grise *French* (eminɑ̃s ɡriz) *n, pl* éminences grises (eminɑ̃s ɡriz) a person who wields power and influence unofficially or behind the scenes [C19: literally: grey eminence, originally applied to Père Joseph (François Le Clerc du Tremblay; died 1638), French monk, secretary of Cardinal Richelieu]

eminent ('ɛmɪnənt) *adj* **1** above others in rank, merit, or reputation; distinguished **2** (*prenominal*) noteworthy, conspicuous, or outstanding **3** projecting or protruding; prominent [C15: from Latin *ēminēre* to project, stand out, from *minēre* to stand]

eminent domain *n law* the right of a state to confiscate private property for public use, payment usually being made to the owners in compensation

emir (ɛ'mɪə) *n* (in the Islamic world) **1** an independent ruler or chieftain **2** a military commander or governor **3** a descendant of Mohammed [C17: via French from Spanish *emir*, from Arabic *'amīr* commander] > 'emirate *n*

emissary ('ɛmɪsərɪ, -ɪstɪ) *n, pl* -saries **1 a** an agent or messenger sent on a mission, esp one who represents a government or head of state **b** (*as modifier*): *an emissary delegation* **2** an agent sent on a secret mission, as a spy ▷ *adj* **3** (of veins) draining blood from sinuses in the dura mater to veins outside the skull [C17: from Latin *ēmissārius* emissary, spy, from *ēmittere* to send out; see EMIT]

emission (ɪ'mɪʃən) *n* **1** the act of emitting or sending forth **2** energy, in the form of heat, light, radio waves, etc, emitted from a source **3** a substance, fluid, etc, that is emitted; discharge **4** *physiol* any bodily discharge, esp an involuntary release of semen during sleep [C17: from Latin *ēmissiō*, from *ēmittere* to send forth, EMIT] > e'missive *adj*

emission spectrum *n* the continuous spectrum or pattern of bright lines or bands seen when the electromagnetic radiation emitted by a substance is passed into a spectrometer. The spectrum is characteristic of the emitting substance and the type of excitation to which it is subjected

emissivity (ɪmɪ'sɪvɪtɪ, ˌɛm-) *n* a measure of the ability of a surface to radiate energy; the ratio of the radiant flux emitted per unit area to that emitted by a black body at the same temperature

emit (ɪ'mɪt) *vb* emits, emitting, emitted (*tr*) **1** to give or send forth; discharge **2** to give voice to; utter **3** *physics* to give off (radiation or particles) [C17: from Latin *ēmittere* to send out, from *mittere* to send]

emitter (ɪ'mɪtə) *n* **1** a person or thing that emits **2** a radioactive substance that emits radiation **3** the region in a transistor in which the charge-carrying holes or electrons originate

Emmanuel (ɪ'mænjʊəl) *n* a variant spelling of **Immanuel**

Emmen ('ɛmən; *Dutch* 'ɛmə) *n* a city in the NE Netherlands, in Drenthe province: a new town developed since World War II. Pop: 108 000 (2003 est)

Emmenthal, Emmental ('ɛmənˌtɑːl) *or* **Emmenthaler, Emmentaler** *n* a hard Swiss cheese with holes in it, similar to Gruyère [C20: named after *Emmenthal*, a valley in Switzerland]

emmet ('ɛmɪt) *n* **1** *Brit* an archaic or dialect word for **ant 2** *Cornish dialect* a tourist or holiday-maker [Old English *ǣmette* ANT; related to Old Norse *meita*, Old High German *āmeiza*, Gothic *maitan*]

Emmet ('ɛmɪt) *n* **Robert.** 1778–1803, Irish nationalist, executed for leading an uprising for Irish independence

Emmy ('ɛmɪ) *n, pl* -mys *or* -mies (in the US) one of the gold-plated statuettes awarded annually for outstanding television performances and productions [C20: alteration of *Immy*, short for *image orthicon tube*]

emollient (ɪ'mɒljənt) *adj* **1** softening or soothing, esp to the skin **2** helping to avoid confrontation; calming ▷ *n* **3** any preparation or substance that has a softening or soothing effect, esp when applied to the skin [C17: from Latin *ēmollīre* to soften, from *mollis* soft] > e'mollience *n*

emolument (ɪ'mɒljʊmənt) *n* the profit arising from an office or employment, usually in the form of fees or wages [C15: from Latin *ēmolumentum* benefit; originally, fee paid to a miller, from *ēmolere*, from *molere* to grind]

emote (ɪ'məʊt) *vb* (*intr*) to display exaggerated emotion, as in acting; behave theatrically [C20: back formation from EMOTION]

emoticon (ɪ'məʊtɪˌkɒn) *n* any of several combinations of symbols used in electronic mail and text messaging to indicate the state of mind of the writer, such as :-) to express happiness [C20: from EMOT(ION) + ICON]

emotion (ɪ'məʊʃən) *n* any strong feeling, as of joy, sorrow, or fear [C16: from French, from Old French *esmovoir* to excite, from Latin *ēmovēre* to disturb, from *movēre* to MOVE]

emotional (ɪ'məʊʃənəl) *adj* **1** of, characteristic of, or expressive of emotion **2** readily or excessively affected by emotion **3** appealing to or arousing emotion: *an emotional piece of music* **4** caused, determined, or actuated by emotion rather than reason: *an emotional argument* > eˌmotion'ality *n*

emotional correctness *n* pressure on an individual to be seen to feel the same emotion as others

emotional intelligence *n* awareness of one's own emotions and moods and those of others, esp in managing people

emotionalism (ɪ'məʊʃənəˌlɪzəm) *n* **1** emotional nature, character, or quality **2** a tendency to yield readily to the emotions **3** an appeal to the emotions, esp an excessive appeal, as to an audience > e'motionalist *n* > eˌmotional'istic *adj*

emotionalize *or* **emotionalise** (ɪ'məʊʃənəˌlaɪz) *vb* (*tr*) to make emotional; subject to emotional treatment

emotional labour *n* work that requires good interpersonal skills

emotional literacy *n* the ability to deal with one's emotions and recognize their causes

emotive (ɪ'məʊtɪv) *adj* **1** tending or designed to arouse emotion **2** of or characterized by emotion > e'motively *adv* > e'motiveness *or* ˌemo'tivity *n*

● USAGE *Emotional* is preferred to *emotive* when ● describing a display of emotion: *he was given an* ● *emotional* (not *emotive*) *welcome*

empanel *or* **impanel** (ɪm'pænˀl) *vb* -els, -elling, -elled *or* US -els, -eling, -eled (*tr*) *law* **1** to enter on a list (names of persons to be summoned for jury service) **2** to select (a jury) from the names on such a list > em'panelment *or* im'panelment *n*

empathize *or* **empathise** ('ɛmpəˌθaɪz) *vb* (*intr*) to engage in or feel empathy

empathy ('ɛmpəθɪ) *n* **1** the power of understanding and imaginatively entering into another person's feelings **2** the attribution to an object, such as a work of art, of one's own emotional or intellectual feelings about it [C20: from Greek *empatheia* affection, passion, intended as a rendering of German *Einfühlung*, literally: a feeling in; see EN-², -PATHY] > em'pathic *adj*

Empedocles (ɛm'pɛdəˌkliːz) *n* ?490–430 BC, Greek philosopher and scientist, who held that the world is composed of four elements, air, fire, earth, and water, which are governed by the opposing forces of love and discord

emperor ('ɛmpərə) *n* a monarch who rules or reigns over an empire [C13: from Old French *empereor*, from Latin *imperātor* commander-in-chief, from *imperāre* to command, from IM- + *parāre* to make ready] > 'emperorˌship *n*

emperor penguin *n* an Antarctic penguin, *Aptenodytes forsteri*, with orange-yellow patches on the neck: the largest penguin, reaching a height of 1.3 m (4 ft)

emphasis ('ɛmfəsɪs) *n, pl* -ses (-siːz) **1** special

importance or significance **2** an object, idea, etc, that is given special importance or significance **3** stress made to fall on a particular syllable, word, or phrase in speaking **4** force or intensity of expression **5** sharpness or clarity of form or outline [c16: via Latin from Greek: meaning, (in rhetoric) significant stress; see EMPHATIC]

emphasize or **emphasise** ('ɛmfəˌsaɪz) vb (tr) to give emphasis or prominence to; stress

emphatic (ɪmˈfætɪk) adj **1** expressed, spoken, or done with emphasis **2** forceful and positive; definite; direct **3** sharp or clear in form, contour, or outline [c18: from Greek *emphatikos* expressive, forceful, from *emphainein* to exhibit, display, from *phainein* to show]
> em'phatically adv

emphysema (ˌɛmfɪˈsiːmə) n pathol **1** Also called: pulmonary emphysema a condition in which the air sacs of the lungs are grossly enlarged, causing breathlessness and wheezing **2** the abnormal presence of air in a tissue or part [c17: from New Latin, from Greek *emphusēma*, a swelling up, from *emphusan* to inflate, from *phusan* to blow]

empire ('ɛmpaɪə) n **1** an aggregate of peoples and territories, often of great extent, under the rule of a single person, oligarchy, or sovereign state **2** any monarchy that for reasons of history, prestige, etc, has an emperor rather than a king as head of state **3** the period during which a particular empire exists **4** supreme power; sovereignty **5** a large industrial organization with many ramifications, esp a multinational corporation [c13: from Old French, from Latin *imperium* rule, from *imperāre* to command, from *parāre* to prepare]

Empire ('ɛmpaɪə) the Empire n **1** See British Empire **2** French history **a** the period of imperial rule in France from 1804 to 1815 under Napoleon Bonaparte (1769–1821) **b** Also called: Second Empire the period from 1852 to 1870 when Napoleon III (1808–73) ruled as emperor ▷ adj **3** denoting, characteristic of, or relating to the British Empire **4** denoting, characteristic of, or relating to either French Empire, esp the first: in particular, denoting the neoclassical style of architecture and furniture and the high-waisted style of women's dresses characteristic of the period

empire-builder n informal a person who seeks extra power for its own sake, esp by increasing the number of his subordinates or staff

Empire Day n the former name of **Commonwealth Day**

Empire State n nickname of **New York**

empiric (ɛmˈpɪrɪk) n **1** a person who relies on empirical methods **2** a medical quack; charlatan ▷ adj **3** a variant of **empirical** [c16: from Latin *empīricus*, from Greek *empeirikos* practised, from *peiran* to attempt]

empirical (ɛmˈpɪrɪkᵊl) adj **1** derived from or relating to experiment and observation rather than theory **2** (of medical treatment) based on practical experience rather than scientific proof **3** philosophy (of knowledge) derived from experience rather than by logic from first principles **4** of or relating to medical quackery
> em'piricalness n

empiricism (ɛmˈpɪrɪˌsɪzəm) n **1** philosophy the doctrine that all knowledge of matters of fact derives from experience and that the mind is not furnished with a set of concepts in advance of experience **2** the use of empirical methods **3** medical quackery; charlatanism
> em'piricist n, adj

emplace (ɪmˈpleɪs) vb (tr) to put in place or position

emplacement (ɪmˈpleɪsmənt) n **1** a prepared position for the siting of a gun or other weapon **2** the act of putting or state of being put in place [c19: from French, from obsolete *emplacer* to put in position, from PLACE]

emplane (ɪmˈpleɪn) vb to board or put on board an aeroplane

employ (ɪmˈplɔɪ) vb (tr) **1** to engage or make use of the services of (a person) in return for money; hire **2** to provide work or occupation for; keep busy; occupy: *collecting stamps employs a lot of his time* **3** to use as a means: *to employ secret measures to get one's ends* ▷ n **4** the state of being employed (esp in the phrase **in someone's employ**) [c15: from Old French *emploier*, from Latin *implicāre* to

entangle, engage, from *plicāre* to fold] > em'ployable adj
> em,ploya'bility n

employee (ɛmˈplɔɪːˌ ˌɛmplɔɪˈiː) or sometimes US **employe** n a person who is hired to work for another or for a business, firm, etc, in return for payment

employer (ɪmˈplɔɪə) n **1** a person, business, firm, etc, that employs workers **2** a person who employs; user

employment (ɪmˈplɔɪmənt) n **1** the act of employing or state of being employed **2** the work or occupation in which a person is employed

employment equity n **1** South African a policy or programme designed to reserve jobs for people formerly disadvantaged under apartheid **2** Canadian a policy or programme designed to ensure equal opportunity in employment

employment office n Brit any of a number of government offices established to collect and supply to the unemployed information about job vacancies and to employers information about availability of prospective workers. See also **Jobcentre**

employment tribunal n (in England, Scotland, and Wales) a tribunal that rules on disputes between employers and employees regarding unfair dismissal, redundancy, etc. See also **industrial tribunal**

emporium (ɛmˈpɔːrɪəm) n, pl -riums (-rɪ-) or -ria (-rɪə) a large and often ostentatious retail shop offering for sale a wide variety of merchandise [c16: from Latin, from Greek *emporion*, from *emporos* merchant, from *poros* a journey]

empower (ɪmˈpaʊə) vb (tr) **1** to give or delegate power or authority to; authorize **2** to give ability to; enable or permit

empowerment (ɪmˈpaʊəmənt) n **1** the giving or delegation of power or authority; authorization **2** the giving of an ability; enablement or permission **3** (in South Africa) a policy of providing special opportunities in employment, training, etc for Black people and others disadvantaged under apartheid

empress ('ɛmprɪs) n **1** the wife or widow of an emperor **2** a woman who holds the rank of emperor in her own right [c12: from Old French *empereriz*, from Latin *imperātrix* feminine of *imperātor* EMPEROR]

Empson ('ɛmpsᵊn) n Sir **William**. 1906–84, English poet and critic; author of *Seven Types of Ambiguity* (1930)

empty ('ɛmptɪ) adj -tier, -tiest **1** containing nothing **2** without inhabitants; vacant or unoccupied **3** carrying no load, passengers, etc **4** without purpose, substance, or value: *an empty life* **5** insincere or trivial: *empty words* **6** not expressive or vital; vacant: *she has an empty look* **7** (postpositive, foll by of) devoid; destitute: *a life empty of happiness* **9** informal drained of energy or emotion: *after the violent argument he felt very empty* **10** maths, logic (of a set or class) containing no members ▷ vb -ties, -tying, -tied **11** to make or become empty **12** (when intr, foll by into) to discharge (contents) **13** (tr; often foll by of) to unburden or rid (oneself): *to empty oneself of emotion* ▷ n, pl -ties **14** an empty container, esp a bottle [Old English ǣmtig, from ǣmetta free time, from ǣ- without + -metta, from mōtan to be obliged to; see MUST¹] > 'emptiable adj > 'emptier n > 'emptily adv > 'emptiness n

empty-handed adj **1** carrying nothing in the hands **2** having gained nothing: *they returned from the negotiations empty-handed*

empty-headed adj lacking intelligence or sense; frivolous

empty-nester n informal a married person whose children have grown up and left home

empty-nest syndrome n informal a condition, often involving depression, loneliness, etc, experienced by parents living in a home from which the children have grown up and left

Empty Quarter n another name for **Rub' al Khali**

empyema (ˌɛmpaɪˈiːmə) n, pl -emata (-ˈiːmətə) or -emas a collection of pus in a body cavity, esp in the chest [c17: from Medieval Latin, from Greek *empuēma* abscess, from *empuein* to suppurate, from *puon* pus] > ˌempy'emic adj

empyrean (ˌɛmpaɪˈriːən) n **1** archaic the highest part of the (supposedly spherical) heavens, thought in ancient times to contain the pure element of fire and by early Christians to be the abode of God and the angels **2** *poetic* the heavens or sky ▷ *adj* Also: **empyreal 3** of or relating to the sky, the heavens, or the empyrean **4** heavenly or sublime [c17: from Medieval Latin *empyreus*, from Greek *empuros* fiery, from *pur* fire]

empyreuma (ˌɛmpɪˈruːmə) *n, pl* **-mata** (-mətə) the smell and taste associated with burning vegetable and animal matter [c17: from Greek, from *empureuein* to set on fire]

Ems (ɛmz) *or* **Bad Ems** *n* **1** a town in W Germany, in the Rhineland-Palatinate: famous for the **Ems Telegram** (1870), Bismarck's dispatch that led to the outbreak of the Franco-Prussian War. Pop: 9666 (2003 est) **2** a river in W Germany, rising in the Teutoburger Wald and flowing generally north to the North Sea. Length: about 370 km (230 miles)

EMS *abbreviation* European Monetary System

EMT *abbreviation US* emergency medical technician

emu ('iːmjuː) *n* a large Australian flightless bird, *Dromaius novaehollandiae*, similar to the ostrich but with three-toed feet and grey or brown plumage: order *Casuariiformes* [c17: changed from Portuguese *ema* ostrich, from Arabic *Na-'amah* ostrich]

EMU *abbreviation* **1** European Monetary Union **2** Economic and Monetary Union **3** See **e.m.u.**

e.m.u. *or* **EMU** *abbreviation* electromagnetic unit

emu-bob *Austral informal* ▷ *vb* **-bobs, -bobbing, -bobbed 1** (*intr*) to bend over to collect litter or small pieces of wood ▷ *n* **2** Also called: **emu parade** a parade of soldiers or schoolchildren for litter collection ▷ **'emu-bobbing** *n*

emulate ('ɛmjʊˌleɪt) *vb* (*tr*) **1** to attempt to equal or surpass, esp by imitation **2** to rival or compete with [c16: from Latin *aemulārī*, from *aemulus* competing with; probably related to *imitārī* to IMITATE] ▷ **'emulative** *adj* ▷ **'emuˌlator** *n* ▷ **emuˈlation** *n*

emulous ('ɛmjʊləs) *adj* **1** desiring or aiming to equal or surpass another; competitive **2** characterized by or arising from emulation or imitation [c14: from Latin *aemulus* rivalling; see EMULATE] ▷ **'emulousness** *n*

emulsifier (ɪˈmʌlsɪˌfaɪə) *n* an agent that forms or preserves an emulsion, esp any food additive, such as lecithin, that prevents separation of sauces or other processed foods

emulsify (ɪˈmʌlsɪˌfaɪ) *vb* **-fies, -fying, -fied** to make or form into an emulsion ▷ **eˌmulsiˈfiable** *or* **eˈmulsible** *adj* ▷ **eˌmulsifiˈcation** *n*

emulsion (ɪˈmʌlʃən) *n* **1** *photog* a light-sensitive coating on a base, such as paper or film, consisting of fine grains of silver bromide suspended in gelatine **2** *chem* a colloid in which both phases are liquids: *an oil-in-water emulsion* **3** Also called: **emulsion paint** a type of paint in which the pigment is suspended in a vehicle, usually a synthetic resin, that is dispersed in water as an emulsion. It usually gives a mat finish **4** *pharmacol* a mixture in which an oily medicine is dispersed in another liquid **5** any liquid resembling milk [c17: from New Latin *ēmulsiō*, from Latin *ēmulsus* milked out, from *ēmulgēre* to milk out, drain out, from *mulgēre* to milk] ▷ **eˈmulsive** *adj*

emu oil *n* an oil obtained from the fat of the emu, traditionally used as an emollient by native Australians to relieve pain and speed the healing process

emu-wren *n* any Australian wren of the genus *Stipiturus*, having long plumy tail feathers

en (ɛn) *n* *printing* a unit of measurement, half the width of an em

EN *abbreviation* (in Britain) **1** enrolled nurse **2** English Nature

en-¹ *or* **em-** *prefix forming verbs* **1** (*from nouns*) **a** put in or on: *entomb; enthrone* **b** go on or into: *enplane* **c** surround or cover with: *enmesh* **d** furnish with: *empower* **2** (*from adjectives and nouns*) cause to be in a certain condition: *enable; encourage; enrich; enslave* [via Old French from Latin *in-* IN-²]

en-² *or* **em-** *prefix forming nouns, prefix forming adjectives* in; into; inside: *endemic* [from Greek (often via Latin); compare IN-¹, IN-²]

-en¹ *suffix forming verbs from adjectives and nouns* cause to be;

become; cause to have: *blacken; heighten* [Old English *-n-*, as in *fæst-n-ian* to fasten, of common Germanic origin; compare Icelandic *fastna*]

-en² *suffix forming adjectives from nouns* of; made of; resembling: *ashen; earthen; wooden* [Old English *-en*; related to Gothic *-eins*, Latin *-īnus* -INE¹]

enable (ɪnˈeɪbªl) *vb* (*tr*) **1** to provide (someone) with adequate power, means, opportunity, or authority (to do something) **2** to make possible ▷ **enˈablement** *n* ▷ **enˈabler** *n*

enabling act *n* a legislative act conferring certain specified powers on a person or organization

enact (ɪnˈækt) *vb* (*tr*) **1** to make into an act or statute **2** to establish by law; ordain or decree **3** to represent or perform in or as if in a play; act out ▷ **enˈactable** *adj* ▷ **enˈactive** *or* **enˈactory** *adj* ▷ **enˈactment** *or* **enˈaction** *n* ▷ **enˈactor** *n*

enamel (ɪˈnæməl) *n* **1** a coloured glassy substance, translucent or opaque, fused to the surface of articles made of metal, glass, etc, for ornament or protection **2** an article or articles ornamented with enamel **3** an enamel-like paint or varnish **4** any smooth glossy coating resembling enamel **5** the hard white calcified substance that covers the crown of each tooth **6** (*modifier*) decorated or covered with enamel: *an enamel ring* ▷ *vb* **-els, -elling, -elled** *or US* **-els, -eling, -eled** (*tr*) **7** to ornament with glossy variegated colours, as if with enamel **8** to portray in enamel [c15: from Old French *esmail*, of Germanic origin; compare Old High German *smalz* lard; see SMELT¹] ▷ **eˈnameller** *or* **eˈnamellist** *or US* **eˈnameler** *or* **eˈnamelist** *n* ▷ **eˈnamelˌwork** *n*

enamour *or US* **enamor** (ɪnˈæmə) *vb* (*tr; usually passive and foll by of*) to inspire with love; captivate; charm [c14: from Old French *enamourer*, from *amour* love, from Latin *amor*]

enamoured *or US* **enamored** (ɪnˈæməd) *adj* in love; captivated; charmed

en bloc *French* (ɑ̃ blɔk) *adv* in a lump or block; as a body or whole; all together

en brosse *French* (ɑ̃ brɔs) *adj, adv* (of the hair) cut very short so that the hair stands up stiffly [literally: in the style of a brush]

enc. *abbreviation* **1** enclosed **2** enclosure

encamp (ɪnˈkæmp) *vb* to lodge or cause to lodge in a camp

encampment (ɪnˈkæmpmənt) *n* **1** the act of setting up a camp **2** the place where a camp, esp a military camp, is set up

encapsulate *or* **incapsulate** (ɪnˈkæpsjʊˌleɪt) *vb* (*tr*) **1** to enclose or be enclosed in or as if in a capsule **2** (*tr*) to sum up in a short or concise form; condense; abridge ▷ **enˌcapsuˈlation** *or* **inˌcapsuˈlation** *n*

encase *or* **incase** (ɪnˈkeɪs) *vb* (*tr*) to place or enclose in or as if in a case ▷ **enˈcasement, inˈcasement** *n*

encash (ɪnˈkæʃ) *vb* (*tr*) *Brit formal* to exchange (a cheque) for cash ▷ **enˈcashable** *adj* ▷ **enˈcashment** *n*

encaustic (ɪnˈkɒstɪk) *ceramics* ▷ *adj* **1** decorated by any process involving burning in colours, esp by inlaying coloured clays and baking or by fusing wax colours to the surface ▷ *n* **2** the process of burning in colours **3** a product of such a process [c17: from Latin *encausticus*, from Greek *enkaustikos*, from *enkaiein* to burn in, from *kaiein* to burn] ▷ **enˈcaustically** *adv*

-ence *or* **-ency** *suffix forming nouns* indicating an action, state, condition, or quality: *benevolence; residence; patience* [via Old French from Latin *-entia*, from *-ēns*, present participial ending]

enceinte (ɒnˈsænt; *French* ɑ̃sɛ̃t) *adj* another word for **pregnant** [c17: from French, from Latin *inciēns* pregnant; related to Greek *enkuos*, from *kuein* to be pregnant]

Enceladus (ɛnˈsɛlədəs) *n* *Greek myth* a giant who was punished for his rebellion against the gods by a fatal blow from a stone cast by Athena. He was believed to be buried under Mount Etna in Sicily

encephalic (ˌɛnsɪˈfælɪk, ˌɛnkɪ-) *adj* of or relating to the brain

encephalin (ɛnˈsɛfəlɪn) *n* a variant of **enkephalin**

encephalitis (ˌɛnsɛfəˈlaɪtɪs, ˌɛnkɛf-) *n* inflammation of the brain ▷ **encephalitic** (ˌɛnsɛfəˈlɪtɪk) *adj*

encephalitis lethargica (lɪˈθɑːdʒɪkə) n pathol a technical name for **sleeping sickness** (sense 2)

encephalo- or before a vowel **encephal-** combining form indicating the brain: encephalogram; encephalitis [from New Latin, from Greek enkephalos, from en- in + kephalē head]

encephalogram (ɛnˈsɛfələˌgræm) n an X-ray photograph of the brain, esp one (a **pneumoencephalogram**) taken after replacing some of the cerebrospinal fluid with air or oxygen so that the brain cavities show clearly

encephalon (ɛnˈsɛfəˌlɒn) n, pl -la (-lə) a technical name for **brain** [c18: from New Latin, from Greek enkephalos brain (literally: that which is in the head), from EN-² + kephalē head] > en'cephalous adj

encephalopathy (ɛnˌsɛfəˈlɒpəθɪ) n any degenerative disease of the brain, often associated with toxic conditions. See also **BSE**

enchain (ɪnˈtʃeɪn) vb (tr) 1 to bind with chains 2 to hold fast or captivate (the attention, etc) > en'chainment n

enchant (ɪnˈtʃɑːnt) vb (tr) 1 to cast a spell on; bewitch 2 to delight or captivate utterly; fascinate; charm [c14: from Old French enchanter, from Latin incantāre to chant a spell, from cantāre to chant, from canere to sing] > en'chanter n > en'chantress fem n

enchanted (ɪnˈtʃɑːntɪd) adj 1 under a spell; bewitched; magical 2 utterly delighted or captivated; fascinated; charmed

enchanting (ɪnˈtʃɑːntɪŋ) adj pleasant; delightful > en'chantingly adv

enchantment (ɪnˈtʃɑːntmənt) n 1 the act of enchanting or state of being enchanted 2 a magic spell or act of witchcraft 3 great charm or fascination

enchase (ɪnˈtʃeɪs) vb (tr) a less common word for **chase¹** (sense 3) [c15: from Old French enchasser to enclose, set, from EN-¹ + casse CASE²] > en'chaser n

enchilada (ˌɛntʃɪˈlɑːdə) n a Mexican dish consisting of a tortilla fried in hot fat, filled with meat, and served with a chilli sauce [c19: American Spanish, feminine of enchilado seasoned with chilli, from enchilar to spice with chilli, from chile CHILLI]

-enchyma n combining form denoting cellular tissue: aerenchyma [c20: abstracted from PARENCHYMA]

encipher (ɪnˈsaɪfə) vb (tr) to convert (a message, document, etc) from plain text into code or cipher; encode > en'cipherer n > en'cipherment n

encircle (ɪnˈsɜːkəl) vb (tr) 1 to form a circle around; enclose within a circle; surround > en'circlement n

Encke (German ˈɛŋkə) n **Johann Franz.** 1791–1865, German astronomer, who discovered **Encke's Division** in the outer ring system of Saturn

enclave (ˈɛnkleɪv) n a part of a country entirely surrounded by foreign territory: viewed from the position of the surrounding territories [c19: from French, from Old French enclaver to enclose, from Vulgar Latin inclāvāre (unattested) to lock up, from Latin IN-² + clavis key]

enclitic (ɪnˈklɪtɪk) adj 1 denoting or relating to a monosyllabic word or form that is treated as a suffix of the preceding word, as Latin -que in populusque ▷ n 2 an enclitic word or linguistic form [c17: from Late Latin encliticus, from Greek enklitikos, from enklinein to cause to lean, from EN-² + klinein to lean] > en'clitically adv

enclose or **inclose** (ɪnˈkləʊz) vb (tr) 1 to close; hem in; surround 2 to surround (land) with or as if with a fence 3 to put in an envelope or wrapper, esp together with a letter 4 to contain or hold > en'closable or in'closable adj > en'closer or in'closer n

enclosed order n a Christian religious order that does not permit its members to go into the outside world

enclosure or **inclosure** (ɪnˈkləʊʒə) n 1 the act of enclosing or state of being enclosed 2 a region or area enclosed by or as if by a fence 3 a fence, wall, etc, that serves to enclose 4 something, esp a supporting document, enclosed within an envelope or wrapper, esp together with a letter 5 Brit a section of a sports ground, racecourse, etc, allotted to certain spectators

encode (ɪnˈkəʊd) vb (tr) to convert (a message) from plain text into code > en'codement n > en'coder n

encomiast (ɛnˈkəʊmɪˌæst) n a person who speaks or writes an encomium [c17: from Greek enkōmiastēs, from enkōmiazein to utter an ENCOMIUM] > en,comi'astic or en,comi'astical adj

encomium (ɛnˈkəʊmɪəm) n, pl -miums or -mia (-mɪə) a formal expression of praise; eulogy; panegyric [c16: from Latin, from Greek enkōmion, from EN-² + kōmos festivity]

encompass (ɪnˈkʌmpəs) vb (tr) 1 to enclose within a circle; surround 2 to bring about; cause to happen; contrive: he encompassed the enemy's ruin 3 to include entirely or comprehensively: this book encompasses the whole range of knowledge > en'compassment n

encore (ˈɒŋkɔː) interj 1 again; once more: used by an audience to demand an extra or repeated performance ▷ n 2 an extra or repeated performance given in response to enthusiastic demand ▷ vb 3 (tr) to demand an extra or repeated performance of (a work, piece of music, etc) by (a performer) [c18: from French: still, again, perhaps from Latin in hanc hōram until this hour]

encounter (ɪnˈkaʊntə) vb 1 to come upon or meet casually or unexpectedly 2 to come into conflict with (an enemy, army, etc) in battle or contest 3 (tr) to be faced with; contend with: he encounters many obstacles in his work ▷ n 4 a meeting with a person or thing, esp when casual or unexpected 5 a hostile meeting; contest or conflict [c13: from Old French encontrer, from Vulgar Latin incontrāre (unattested), from Latin IN-² + contrā against, opposite]

encounter group n a group of people who meet in order to develop self-awareness and mutual understanding by openly expressing their feelings, by confrontation, physical contact, etc

encourage (ɪnˈkʌrɪdʒ) vb (tr) 1 to inspire (someone) with the courage or confidence (to do something) 2 to stimulate (something or someone to do something) by approval or help; support > en'couragement n > en'courager n > en'couraging adj > en'couragingly adv

encroach (ɪnˈkrəʊtʃ) vb (intr) 1 (often foll by on or upon) to intrude gradually, stealthily, or insidiously upon the rights, property, etc, of another 2 to advance beyond the usual or proper limits [c14: from Old French encrochier to seize, literally: fasten upon with hooks, from EN-¹ + croc hook, of Germanic origin; see CROOK] > en'croacher n > en'croachment n

encrust or **incrust** (ɪnˈkrʌst) vb 1 (tr) to cover or overlay with or as with a crust or hard coating 2 to form or cause to form a crust or hard coating 3 (tr) to decorate lavishly, as with jewels > ,encrus'tation or ,incrus'tation n

encumber or **incumber** (ɪnˈkʌmbə) vb (tr) 1 to hinder or impede; make difficult; hamper: encumbered with parcels after going shopping at Christmas; his stupidity encumbers his efforts to learn 2 to fill with superfluous or useless matter 3 to burden with debts, obligations, etc [c14: from Old French encombrer, from EN-¹ + combre a barrier, from Late Latin combrus, of uncertain origin]

encumbrance or **incumbrance** (ɪnˈkʌmbrəns) n 1 a thing that impedes or is burdensome; hindrance 2 law a burden or charge upon property, such as a mortgage or lien

-ency suffix forming nouns a variant of **-ence** fluency; permanency

encyclical (ɛnˈsɪklɪkəl) n 1 a letter sent by the pope to all Roman Catholic bishops throughout the world ▷ adj Also: **encyclic** 2 (of letters) intended for general or wide circulation [c17: from Late Latin encyclicus, from Greek enkuklios general, from kuklos circle]

encyclopedia or **encyclopaedia** (ɛnˌsaɪkləʊˈpiːdɪə) n a book, often in many volumes, containing articles on various topics, often arranged in alphabetical order, dealing either with the whole range of human knowledge or with one particular subject: a medical encyclopedia [c16: from New Latin encyclopaedia, erroneously for Greek enkuklios paideia general education, from enkuklios general (see ENCYCLICAL), + paideia education, from pais child] > en,cyclo'pedic or en,cyclo'paedic adj

encyclopedist or **encyclopaedist** (ɛnˌsaɪkləʊˈpiːdɪst) n a person who compiles or contributes to an encyclopedia > en,cyclo'pedism or en,cyclo'paedism n

encyst (ɛn'sɪst) *vb biology* to enclose or become enclosed by a cyst, thick membrane, or shell > en'cystment or ˌencys'tation *n*

end (ɛnd) *n* 1 the extremity of the length of something, such as a road, line, etc 2 the surface at either extremity of a three-dimensional object 3 the extreme extent, limit, or degree of something 4 the most distant place or time that can be imagined: *the ends of the earth* 5 the time at which something is concluded 6 the last section or part 7 a share or part: *his end of the bargain* 8 (*often plural*) a remnant or fragment (esp in the phrase **odds and ends**) 9 a final state, esp death; destruction 10 the purpose of an action or existence 11 *sport* either of the two defended areas of a playing field, rink, etc 12 *bowls, curling* a section of play from one side of the rink to the other 13 **at an end** exhausted or completed 14 **come to an end** to become completed or exhausted 15 **get one's end away** *slang* to have sexual intercourse 16 **in the end** finally 17 **keep one's end up a** to sustain one's part in a joint enterprise **b** to hold one's own in an argument, contest, etc 18 **make ends meet** or **make both ends meet** to spend no more than the money one has 19 **no end** or **no end of** *informal* (intensifier): *I had no end of work* 20 **on end a** upright **b** without pause or interruption 21 **the end** *informal* the worst, esp something that goes beyond the limits of endurance ▷ *vb* 22 to bring or come to a finish; conclude 23 to die or cause to die 24 (*tr*) to surpass; outdo: *a novel to end all novels* 25 **end it all** *informal* to commit suicide ▷ See also **end up** [Old English *ende*; related to Old Norse *endir*, Gothic *andeis*, Old High German *endi*, Latin *antiae* forelocks, Sanskrit *antya* last] > 'ender *n*

end- *combining form* a variant of **endo-**

-end *suffix forming nouns* See **-and**

endamoeba or *US* **endameba** (ˌɛndə'miːbə) *n*, *pl*-bae (-biː) or -bas variants of **entamoeba**

endanger (ɪn'deɪndʒə) *vb* (*tr*) to put in danger or peril; imperil > en'dangerment *n*

endangered (ɪn'deɪndʒəd) *adj* in danger: used esp of animals in danger of extinction: *the giant panda is an endangered species*

endear (ɪn'dɪə) *vb* (*tr*) to cause to be beloved or esteemed > en'dearing *adj*

endearment (ɪn'dɪəmənt) *n* something that endears, such as an affectionate utterance

endeavour or *US* **endeavor** (ɪn'dɛvə) *vb* 1 to try (to do something) ▷ *n* 2 an effort to do or attain something [c14: *endeveren*, from EN-¹ + *-deveren* from *dever* duty, from Old French *deveir*; see DEVOIRS] > en'deavourer or *US* en'deavorer *n*

endemic (ɛn'dɛmɪk) *adj* Also called: **endemial** (ɛn'dɛmɪəl) or **endemical** 1 present within a localized area or peculiar to persons in such an area *n* 2 an endemic disease or plant [c18: from New Latin *endēmicus*, from Greek *endēmos* native, from EN-² + *dēmos* the people] > en'demically *adv* > 'endemism or ˌende'micity *n*

Enderby Land ('ɛndəbɪ) *n* part of the coastal region of Antarctica, between Kemp Land and Queen Maud Land: the westernmost part of the Australian Antarctic Territory (claims are suspended under the Antarctic Treaty); discovered in 1831

endermic (ɛn'dɜːmɪk) *adj* (of a medicine) acting by absorption through the skin [c19: from EN-² + Greek *derma* skin]

Enders ('ɛndəz) *n* **John Franklin**. 1897–1985, US microbiologist: shared the Nobel prize for physiology or medicine (1954) with Frederick Robbins and Thomas Weller for their work on viruses

endgame ('ɛndˌgeɪm) *n* the closing stage of any of certain other games

ending ('ɛndɪŋ) *n* 1 the act of bringing to or reaching an end 2 the last part of something, as a book, film, etc 3 the final part of a word, esp a suffix

endive ('ɛndaɪv) *n* a plant, *Cichorium endivia*, cultivated for its crisp curly leaves, which are used in salads: family *Asteraceae* (composites). See **chicory** [c15: from Old French, from Medieval Latin *endívia*, variant of Latin *intubus, entubus*, of uncertain origin]

endless ('ɛndlɪs) *adj* 1 having or seeming to have no end; eternal or infinite 2 continuing too long or continually recurring 3 formed with the ends joined: *an endless belt* > 'endlessly *adv*

endmost ('ɛndˌməʊst) *adj* nearest the end; most distant

endo- or before a vowel **end-** *combining form* inside; within: *endocrine* [from Greek, from *endon* within]

endoblast ('ɛndəʊˌblæst) *n* 1 *embryol* a less common name for **endoderm** 2 another name for **hypoblast** (sense 1) > ˌendo'blastic *adj*

endocarditis (ˌɛndəʊkɑː'daɪtɪs) *n* inflammation of the endocardium > endocarditic (ˌɛndəʊkɑː'dɪtɪk) *adj*

endocarp ('ɛndəˌkɑːp) *n* the inner, usually woody, layer of the pericarp of a fruit, such as the stone of a peach or cherry > ˌendo'carpal or ˌendo'carpic *adj*

endocrine ('ɛndəʊˌkraɪn, -krɪn) *adj* Also called: **endocrinal** (ˌɛndəʊ'kraɪnᵊl) or **endocrinic** (ˌɛndəʊ'krɪnɪk) or **endocrinous** (ɛn'dɒkrɪnəs) 1 of or denoting endocrine glands or their secretions: *endocrine disorders n* 2 an endocrine gland [c20: from ENDO- + *-crine*, from Greek *krinein* to separate]

endocrine gland *n* any of the glands that secrete hormones directly into the bloodstream, including the pituitary, pineal, thyroid, parathyroid, adrenal, testes, ovaries, and the pancreatic islets of Langerhans. Also called: **ductless gland**

endocrinology (ˌɛndəʊkraɪ'nɒlədʒɪ, -krɪ-) *n* the branch of medical science concerned with the endocrine glands and their secretions > ˌendocri'nologist *n*

endoderm ('ɛndəʊˌdɜːm) or **entoderm** *n* the inner germ layer of an animal embryo, which gives rise to the lining of the digestive and respiratory tracts > ˌendo'dermal or ˌendo'dermic, ˌento'dermal or ˌento'dermic *adj*

end of steel *n Canadian* 1 a point up to which railway tracks have been laid 2 a town located at such a point

endogamy (ɛn'dɒgəmɪ) *n* 1 *anthropol* marriage within one's own tribe or similar unit 2 pollination between two flowers on the same plant > en'dogamous or endogamic (ˌɛndəʊ'gæmɪk) *adj*

endogenous (ɛn'dɒdʒɪnəs) *adj* 1 *biology* developing or originating within an organism or part of an organism: *endogenous rhythms* 2 having no apparent external cause: *endogenous depression* > en'dogeny *n*

endometritis (ˌɛndəʊmɪ'traɪtɪs) *n* inflammation of the endometrium, which is caused by infection, as by bacteria, foreign bodies, etc

endometrium (ˌɛndəʊ'miːtrɪəm) *n*, *pl*-tria (-trɪə) the mucous membrane that lines the uterus [c19: New Latin, from ENDO- + Greek *mētra* uterus] > ˌendo'metrial *adj*

endomorph ('ɛndəʊˌmɔːf) *n* 1 a person with a fat and heavy body build: said to be correlated with viscerotonia 2 a mineral that naturally occurs enclosed within another mineral, as within quartz > ˌendo'morphic *adj* > 'endoˌmorphy *n*

endomorphism (ˌɛndəʊ'mɔːˌfɪzəm) *n geology* changes in a cooling body of igneous rock brought about by assimilation of fragments of, or chemical reaction with, the surrounding country rock

endophyte ('ɛndəʊˌfaɪt) *n* a fungus, or occasionally an alga or other organism, that lives within a plant > endophytic (ˌɛndəʊ'fɪtɪk) *adj*

endoplasm ('ɛndəʊˌplæzəm) *n cytology* the inner cytoplasm in some cells, esp protozoa, which is more granular and fluid than the outer cytoplasm > ˌendo'plasmic *adj*

end organ *n anatomy* the expanded end of a peripheral motor or sensory nerve

endorphin (ɛn'dɔːfɪn) *n* any of a class of polypeptides, including enkephalin, occurring naturally in the brain, that bind to pain receptors and so block pain sensation [c20: from ENDO- + MORPHINE]

endorsation (ˌɛndɔː'seɪʃən) *n Canadian* approval or support

endorse or **indorse** (ɪn'dɔːs) *vb* (*tr*) 1 to give approval or sanction to 2 to sign (one's name) on the back of (a cheque, etc) to specify oneself as payee 3 *commerce* **a** to sign the back of (a negotiable document) to transfer ownership of the rights to a specified payee **b** to specify (a designated sum) as transferable to another as payee **4** to write (a qualifying comment, recommendation, etc) on the back of a document **5** to sign (a document), as when confirming receipt of payment **6** *chiefly Brit* to record (a conviction) on (a driving licence) [c16: from Old French *endosser* to put on the back, from EN-¹ + *dos* back, from Latin *dorsum*] > en'dorsable *or* in'dorsable *adj* > en'dorser *or* en'dorsor, in'dorser *or* in'dorsor *n* > en,dor'see *or* in,dor'see *n*

endorsement *or* **indorsement** (ɪnˈdɔːsmənt) *n* **1** the act or an instance of endorsing **2** something that endorses, such as a signature or qualifying comment **3** approval or support **4** a record of a motoring offence on a driving licence

endoscope (ˈɛndəʊˌskəʊp) *n* a long slender medical instrument used for examining the interior of hollow organs including the lung, stomach, bladder, and bowel > endoscopic (ˌɛndəʊˈskɒpɪk) *adj*

endoskeleton (ˌɛndəʊˈskɛlɪtˀn) *n* the internal skeleton of an animal, esp the bony or cartilaginous skeleton of vertebrates > ,endo'skeletal *adj*

endosperm (ˈɛndəʊˌspɜːm) *n* the tissue within the seed of a flowering plant that surrounds and nourishes the developing embryo > ,endo'spermic *adj*

endothermic (ˌɛndəʊˈθɜːmɪk) *or* **endothermal** *adj* (of a chemical reaction or compound) occurring or formed with the absorption of heat > ,endo'thermically *adv* > ,endo'thermism *n*

endow (ɪnˈdaʊ) *vb* (tr) **1** to provide with or bequeath a source of permanent income **2** (usually foll by *with*) to provide (with qualities, characteristics, etc) **3** *obsolete* to provide with a dower [c14: from Old French *endouer*, from EN-¹ + *douer*, from Latin *dōtāre*, from *dōs* dowry]

endowment (ɪnˈdaʊmənt) *n* **1 a** the source of income with which an institution, etc, is endowed **b** the income itself **2** the act or process of endowing **3** (*usually plural*) natural talents or qualities

endowment assurance *or* **endowment insurance** *n* a form of life insurance that provides for the payment of a specified sum directly to the policyholder at a designated date or to his beneficiary should he die before this date

endpaper (ˈɛndˌpeɪpə) *n* either of two leaves at the front and back of a book pasted to the inside of the board covers and the first leaf of the book to secure the binding

end point *n* **1** *chem* the point at which a titration is complete, usually marked by a change in colour of an indicator **2** the point at which anything is complete

end product *n* the final result or outcome of a process, series, endeavour, etc, esp in manufacturing

endue *or* **indue** (ɪnˈdjuː) *vb* -dues, -duing, -dued (tr)(usually foll by *with*) to invest or provide, as with some quality or trait [c15: from Old French *enduire*, from Latin *indūcere*, from *dūcere* to lead]

end up *vb* (adverb) **1** (copula) to become eventually; turn out to be: *he ended up a thief* **2** (intr) to arrive, esp by a circuitous or lengthy route or process: *he ended up living in New Zealand*

endurance (ɪnˈdjʊərəns) *n* **1** the capacity, state, or an instance of enduring **2** something endured; a hardship, strain, or privation

endure (ɪnˈdjʊə) *vb* **1** to undergo (hardship, strain, privation, etc) without yielding; bear **2** (tr) to permit or tolerate **3** (intr) to last or continue to exist [c14: from Old French *endurer*, from Latin *indūrāre* to harden, from *dūrus* hard] > en'durable *adj*

enduring (ɪnˈdjʊərɪŋ) *adj* **1** permanent; lasting **2** having forbearance; long-suffering > en'duringly *adv* > en'duringness *n*

end user *n* **1** (in international trading) the person, organization, or nation that will be the ultimate recipient of goods, esp such as arms or advanced technology **2** *computing* the ultimate destination, such as a program or operator, of information that is being transferred within a system

endways (ˈɛndˌweɪz) *or esp US and Canadian* **endwise** (ˈɛndˌwaɪz) *adv* **1** having the end forwards or upwards ▷ *adj* **2** vertical or upright **3** lengthways **4** standing or

lying end to end

Endymion (ɛnˈdɪmɪən) *n Greek myth* a handsome youth who was visited every night by the moon goddess Selene, who loved him

end zone *n American football* the area behind the goals at each end of the field that the ball must cross for a touchdown to be awarded

ENE *symbol for* east-northeast

-ene *n combining form* (in chemistry) indicating an unsaturated compound containing double bonds: *benzene; ethylene* [from Greek -*ēnē*, feminine patronymic suffix]

enema (ˈɛnɪmə) *n, pl* -mas *or* -mata (-mətə) *med* **1** the introduction of liquid into the rectum to evacuate the bowels, medicate, or nourish **2** the liquid so introduced [c15: from New Latin, from Greek: injection, from *enienai* to send in, from *hienai* to send]

enemy (ˈɛnəmɪ) *n, pl* -mies **1 a** a person hostile or opposed to a policy, cause, person, or group, esp one who actively tries to do damage; opponent **2 a** an armed adversary; opposing military force **b** (*as modifier*): *enemy aircraft* **3 a** a hostile nation or people **b** (*as modifier*): *an enemy alien* **4** something that harms or opposes; adversary: *courage is the enemy of failure* Related adjective: **inimical** [c13: from Old French *enemi*, from Latin *inimīcus* hostile, from IN-¹ + *amīcus* friend]

energetic (ˌɛnəˈdʒɛtɪk) *adj* having or showing much energy or force; vigorous > ,ener'getically *adv*

energy (ˈɛnədʒɪ) *n, pl* -gies **1** intensity or vitality of action or expression; forcefulness **2** capacity or tendency for intense activity; vigour **3** *physics* **a** the capacity of a body or system to do work **b** a measure of this capacity, expressed as the work that it does in changing to some specified reference state. It is measured in joules (SI units) **4** a source of power [c16: from Late Latin *energīa*, from Greek *energeia* activity, from *energos* effective, from EN-² + *ergon* work]

energy band *n physics* a range of energies associated with the quantum states of electrons in a crystalline solid. In a semiconductor or an insulator there is a **valence band** containing many states, most of which are occupied. Above this is a **forbidden band** with only a few isolated states caused by impurities. Above this is a **conduction band** containing many states most of which are empty. In a metal there is a continuous **valence-conduction band**

energy conversion *n* the process of changing one form of energy into another, such as nuclear energy into heat or solar energy into electrical energy

energy drink *n* a soft drink containing ingredients designed to boost the drinker's energy, esp after exercise

enervate *vb* (ˈɛnəˌveɪt) **1** (tr) to deprive of strength or vitality; weaken physically or mentally; debilitate ▷ *adj* (ɪˈnɜːvɪt) **2** deprived of strength or vitality; weakened [c17: from Latin *ēnervāre* to remove the nerves from, from *nervus* nerve, sinew] > ,ener'vation *n*

enervating (ˈɛnəˌveɪtɪŋ) *adj* tending to deprive of strength or vitality; physically or mentally weakening; debilitating

Enesco (ɛˈnɛskəʊ) *n* **Georges** (ʒɔrʒ), original name *George Enescu.* 1881–1955, Romanian violinist and composer

en famille *French* (ã famij) *adv* **1** with one's family; at home **2** in a casual way; informally

enfant terrible *French* (ãfã tɛriblə) *n, pl* enfants terribles (ãfã tɛriblə) a person given to unconventional conduct or indiscreet remarks [c19: literally: terrible child]

enfeeble (ɪnˈfiːbˀl) *vb* (tr) to make weak; deprive of strength > en'feeblement *n* > en'feebler *n*

en fête *French* (ã fɛt) *adv* dressed for a festivity [c19: literally: in festival]

Enfield (ˈɛnfiːld) *n* a borough of Greater London: a N residential suburb. Pop: 280 300 (2003 est). Area: 55 sq km (31 sq miles)

enfilade (ˌɛnfɪˈleɪd) *military* ▷ *n* **1** a position or formation subject to fire from a flank along the length of its front ▷ *vb* (tr) **2** to subject (a position or formation) to fire from a flank [c18: from French: suite, from *enfiler* to thread on string, from *fil* thread]

enfold *or* **infold** (ɪnˈfəʊld) *vb* (tr) **1** to cover by enclosing

2 to embrace ▷ en'folder *or* in'folder *n* ▷ en'foldment *or* in'foldment *n*

enforce (ɪn'fɔːs) *vb* (*tr*) **1** to ensure observance of or obedience to (a law, decision, etc) **2** to impose (obedience, loyalty, etc) by or as by force **3** to emphasize or reinforce (an argument, demand, etc) ▷ en'forceable *adj* ▷ en,forcea'bility *n* ▷ enforcedly (ɪn'fɔːsɪdlɪ) *adv* ▷ en'forcement *n* ▷ en'forcer *n*

enfranchise (ɪn'fræntʃaɪz) *vb* (*tr*) **1** to grant the power of voting to, esp as a right of citizenship **2** to liberate, as from servitude **3** (in England) to invest (a town, city, etc) with the right to be represented in Parliament ▷ en'franchisement *n* ▷ en'franchiser *n*

ENG *abbreviation* electronic news gathering: TV news obtained at the point of action by means of modern video equipment

Eng. *abbreviation* **1** England **2** English

Engadine ('ɛngə,diːn) *n* the upper part of the valley of the River Inn in Switzerland, in Graubünden canton: tourist and winter sports centre

engage (ɪn'geɪdʒ) *vb* (*mainly tr*) **1** to secure the services of; employ **2** to secure for use; reserve: *engage a room* **3** to involve (a person or his attention) intensely; engross; occupy **4** to attract (the affection of) (a person): *her innocence engaged him* **5** to draw (somebody) into conversation **6** (*intr*) to take part; participate: *he engages in many sports* **7** to promise (to do something) **8** (*also intr*) *military* to begin an action with (an enemy) **9** to bring (a mechanism) into operation: *he engaged the clutch* **10** (*also intr*) to undergo or cause to undergo interlocking, as of the components of a driving mechanism, such as a gear train **11** *machinery* to locate (a locking device) in its operative position or to advance (a tool) into a workpiece to commence cutting [C15: from Old French *engagier*, from EN-¹ + *gage* a pledge, see GAGE¹] ▷ en'gager *n*

engagé French (ɑ̃gaʒe) *adj* (of a writer or artist, esp a man) morally or politically committed to some ideology

engaged (ɪn'geɪdʒd) *adj* **1** pledged to be married; betrothed **2** employed, occupied, or busy **3** *architect* built against or attached to a wall or similar structure: *an engaged column* **4** (of a telephone line) already in use

engaged tone *n* *Brit* a repeated single note heard on a telephone when the number called is already in use

engagement (ɪn'geɪdʒmənt) *n* **1** a pledge of marriage; betrothal **2** an appointment or arrangement, esp for business or social purposes **3** the act of engaging or condition of being engaged **4** a promise, obligation, or other condition that binds **5** a period of employment, esp a limited period **6** an action; battle

engagement ring *n* a ring given by a man to a woman as a token of their betrothal

engaging (ɪn'geɪdʒɪŋ) *adj* pleasing, charming, or winning ▷ en'gagingness *n*

en garde French (ɑ̃ gard) *interj* **1** on guard; a call to a fencer to adopt a defensive stance in readiness for an attack or bout ▷ *adj* **2** (of a fencer) in such a stance

Engels (German 'ɛŋ⁰ls) *n* **Friedrich** ('friːdrɪç). 1820–95, German socialist leader and political philosopher, in England from 1849. He collaborated with Marx on *The Communist Manifesto* (1848) and his own works include *Condition of the Working Classes in England* (1844) and *The Origin of the Family, Private Property and the State* (1884)

engender (ɪn'dʒɛndə) *vb* (*tr*) to bring about or give rise to; produce or cause [C14: from Old French *engendrer*, from Latin *generāre* to beget]

engine ('ɛndʒɪn) *n* **1** any machine designed to convert energy, esp heat energy, into mechanical work: *a steam engine; a petrol engine* **2** a railway locomotive **3** *military* any of various pieces of equipment formerly used in warfare, such as a battering ram or gun **4** *obsolete* any instrument or device: *engines of torture* [C13: from Old French *engin*, from Latin *ingenium* nature, talent, ingenious contrivance, from IN-² + *-genium*, related to *gignere* to beget, produce]

engine driver *n* *chiefly Brit* a person who drives a railway locomotive; train driver

engineer (,ɛndʒɪ'nɪə) *n* **1** a person trained in any branch of the profession of engineering **2** the originator or manager of a situation, system, etc **3** a mechanic;

person who repairs or services machines **4** *US & Canadian* the driver of a railway locomotive **5** an officer responsible for a ship's engines **6** Also called: *informal* **sapper** a member of the armed forces, esp the army, trained in engineering and construction work ▷ *vb* (*tr*) **7** to originate, cause, or plan in a clever or devious manner: *he engineered the minister's downfall* **8** to design, plan, or construct as a professional engineer [C14: *enginer*, from Old French *engineor*, from *enginier* to contrive, ultimately from Latin *ingenium* skill, talent; see ENGINE]

engineering (,ɛndʒɪ'nɪərɪŋ) *n* the profession of applying scientific principles to the design, construction, and maintenance of engines, cars, machines, etc (**mechanical engineering**), buildings, bridges, roads, etc (**civil engineering**), electrical machines and communication systems (**electrical engineering**), chemical plant and machinery (**chemical engineering**), or aircraft (**aeronautical engineering**)

England ('ɪŋglənd) *n* the largest division of Great Britain, bordering on Scotland and Wales: unified in the mid-tenth century and conquered by the Normans in 1066; united with Wales in 1536 and Scotland in 1707; monarchy overthrown in 1649 but restored in 1660. Capital: London. Pop: 49 855 700 (2003 est.). Area: 130 439 sq km (50 352 sq miles). See **United Kingdom, Great Britain**

English ('ɪŋglɪʃ) *n* **1** the official language of Britain, the US, most parts of the Commonwealth, and certain other countries. It is the native language of over 280 million people and is acquired as a second language by many more. It is an Indo-European language belonging to the West Germanic branch **2** the English (*functioning as plural*) the natives or inhabitants of England collectively **3** (*often not capital*) the usual US and Canadian term for **side** (sense 15) ▷ *adj* **4** denoting, using, or relating to the English language **5** relating to or characteristic of England or the English ▷ *vb* (*tr*) **6** *archaic* to translate or adapt into English ▷ 'Englishness *n*

English Channel *n* an arm of the Atlantic Ocean between S England and N France, linked with the North Sea by the Strait of Dover. Length: about 560 km (350 miles). Width: between 32 km (20 miles) and 161 km (100 miles). French name: La Manche

English horn *n* *music* another name for **cor anglais**

Englishman ('ɪŋglɪʃmən) *n*, *pl* -men a male native or inhabitant of England

engorge (ɪn'gɔːdʒ) *vb* (*tr*) **1** *pathol* to congest with blood **2** to eat (food) ravenously or greedily **3** to gorge (oneself); glut; satiate ▷ en'gorgement *n*

engr *abbreviation* **1** engineer **2** engraver

engraft *or* **ingraft** (ɪn'grɑːft) *vb* (*tr*) **1** to graft (a shoot, bud, etc) onto a stock **2** to incorporate in a firm or permanent way; implant: *they engrafted their principles into the document* ▷ ,engraf'tation, ,ingraf'tation *or* en'graftment, in'graftment *n*

engrain (ɪn'greɪn) *vb* a variant spelling of **ingrain**

engrave (ɪn'greɪv) *vb* (*tr*) **1** to inscribe (a design, writing, etc) onto (a block, plate, or other surface used for printing) by carving, etching with acid, or other process **2** to print (designs or characters) from a printing plate so made **3** to fix deeply or permanently in the mind [C16: from EN-¹ + GRAVE³, on the model of French *engraver*] ▷ en'graver *n*

engraving (ɪn'greɪvɪŋ) *n* **1** the art of a person who engraves **2** a block, plate, or other surface that has been engraved **3** a print made from such a surface

engross (ɪn'grəʊs) *vb* (*tr*) **1** to occupy one's attention completely; absorb **2** to write or copy (manuscript) in large legible handwriting **3** *law* to write or type out formally (a deed, agreement, or other document) preparatory to execution [C14 (in the sense: to buy up wholesale): from Old French *en gros* in quantity; C15 (in the sense: to write in large letters): probably from Medieval Latin *ingrossāre*; both from Latin *grossus* thick, GROSS] ▷ en'grossed *adj* ▷ en'grossing *adj* ▷ en'grossment *n*

engulf *or* **ingulf** (ɪn'gʌlf) *vb* (*tr*) **1** to immerse, plunge, bury, or swallow up **2** (*often passive*) to overwhelm: *engulfed by debts* ▷ en'gulfment *n*

enhance (ɪnˈhɑːns) *vb* (*tr*) to intensify or increase in quality, value, power, etc; improve; augment [c14: from Old French *enhaucier*, from EN-¹ + *haucier* to raise, from Vulgar Latin *altiāre* (unattested), from Latin *altus* high] > en'hancement *n* > en'hancer *n*

enharmonic (ˌɛnhɑːˈmɒnɪk) *adj music* **1** denoting or relating to a small difference in pitch between two notes such as A flat and G sharp: not present in instruments of equal temperament such as the piano, but significant in the intonation of stringed and wind instruments **2** denoting or relating to enharmonic modulation [c17: from Latin *enharmonicus*, from Greek *enarmonios*, from EN-² + *harmonia*; see HARMONY] > en'harmonically *adv*

Enid (ˈiːnɪd) *n* (in Arthurian legend) the faithful wife of Geraint

enigma (ɪˈnɪɡmə) *n* a person, thing, or situation that is mysterious, puzzling, or ambiguous [c16: from Latin *aenigma*, from Greek *ainigma*, from *ainissesthai* to speak in riddles, from *ainos* fable, story] > enigmatic (ˌenɪɡˈmætɪk) *or* ˌenig'matical *adj* > ˌenig'matically *adv*

Eniwetok (ˌenəˈwiːtɒk, əˈniːwɪˌtɔːk) *n* an atoll in the W Pacific Ocean, in the NW Marshall Islands: taken by the US from Japan in 1944; became a naval base and later a testing ground for atomic weapons. Pop: 820 (1999 est)

enjambment *or* **enjambement** (ɪnˈdʒæmmənt; *French* ɑ̃ʒɑ̃bmɑ̃) *n prosody* the running over of a sentence from one line of verse into the next [c19: from French, literally: a straddling, from *enjamber* to straddle, from EN-¹ + *jambe* leg; see JAMB] > en'jambed *adj*

enjoin (ɪnˈdʒɔɪn) *vb* (*tr*) **1** to order (someone) to do (something); urge strongly; command **2** to impose or prescribe (a condition, mode of behaviour, etc) **3** *law* to require (a person) to do or refrain from doing (some act), esp by issuing an injunction [c13: from Old French *enjoindre*, from Latin *injungere* to fasten to, from IN-² + *jungere* to JOIN] > en'joiner *n* > en'joinment *n*

enjoy (ɪnˈdʒɔɪ) *vb* (*tr*) **1** to receive pleasure from; take joy in **2** to have the benefit of; use with satisfaction **3** to have as a condition; experience: *the land enjoyed a summer of rain* **4** enjoy oneself to have a good time [c14: from Old French *enjoir*, from EN-¹ + *joir* to find pleasure in, from Latin *gaudēre* to rejoice] > en'joyable *adj* > en'joyableness *n* > en'joyably *adv* > en'joyer *n*

enjoyment (ɪnˈdʒɔɪmənt) *n* **1** the act or condition of receiving pleasure from something **2** the use or possession of something that is satisfying or beneficial **3** something that provides joy or satisfaction

enkephalin (ɛnˈkɛfəlɪn) *or* **encephalin** (ɛnˈsɛfəlɪn) *n* a chemical occurring in the brain, having effects similar to those of morphine

enkindle (ɪnˈkɪndᵊl) *vb* (*tr*) **1** to set on fire; kindle **2** to excite to activity or ardour; arouse

enlace (ɪnˈleɪs) *vb* (*tr*) **1** to bind or encircle with or as with laces **2** to entangle; intertwine > en'lacement *n*

enlarge (ɪnˈlɑːdʒ) *vb* **1** to make or grow larger in size, scope, etc; increase or expand **2** to make (a photographic print) of a larger size than the negative **3** (*intr*; foll by *on* or *upon*) to speak or write (about) in greater detail; expatiate (on) > en'largeable *adj* > en'largement *n* > en'larger *n*

enlighten (ɪnˈlaɪtᵊn) *vb* (*tr*) **1** to give information or understanding to; instruct; edify **2** to free from ignorance, prejudice, or superstition **3** to give spiritual or religious revelation to **4** *poetic* to shed light on > en'lightening *adj*

enlightened (ɪnˈlaɪtᵊnd) *adj* **1** factually well-informed, tolerant of alternative opinions, and guided by rational thought: *an enlightened administration; enlightened self-interest* **2** privy to or claiming a sense of spiritual or religious revelation of truth: *the search for an enlightened spiritual master*

enlightenment (ɪnˈlaɪtᵊnmənt) *n* the act or means of enlightening or the state of being enlightened

Enlightenment (ɪnˈlaɪtᵊnmənt) *n* the Enlightenment an 18th-century philosophical movement stressing the importance of reason and the critical reappraisal of existing ideas and social institutions

enlist (ɪnˈlɪst) *vb* **1** to enter or persuade to enter into an engagement to serve in the armed forces **2** (*tr*) to engage or secure (a person, his services, or his support) for a venture, cause, etc **3** (*intr*; foll by *in*) to enter into or join an enterprise, cause, etc > en'lister *n* > en'listment *n*

enlisted man *n US* a serviceman who holds neither a commission nor a warrant and is not under training for officer rank as a cadet or midshipman

enliven (ɪnˈlaɪvᵊn) *vb* (*tr*) **1** to make active, vivacious, or spirited; invigorate **2** to make cheerful or bright; gladden or brighten > en'livening *adj* > en'livenment *n*

en masse (*French* ɑ̃ mas) *adv* in a group, body, or mass; as a whole; all together [c19: from French]

Ennerdale Water (ˈɛnəˌdeɪl) *n* a lake in NW England, in Cumbria in the Lake District. Length: 4 km (2.5 miles)

Enniskillen (ˌɛnɪsˈkɪlɪn) *or formerly* **Inniskilling** *n* a town in SW Northern Ireland, in Fermanagh, on an island in the River Erne: scene of the defeat of James II's forces in 1689. Pop: 13 599 (2001)

Ennius (ˈɛnɪəs) *n* **Quintus** (ˈkwɪntəs). 239–169 BC, Roman epic poet and dramatist

ennoble (ɪˈnəʊbᵊl) *vb* (*tr*) **1** to make noble, honourable, or excellent; dignify; exalt **2** to raise to a noble rank; confer a title of nobility upon > en'noblement *n* > en'nobler *n* > en'nobling *adj*

ennog (ˈɛnɒɡ) *n Northern English dialect* a back alley

ennui (ˈɒnwiː; *French* ɑ̃nɥi) *n* a feeling of listlessness and general dissatisfaction resulting from lack of activity or excitement [c18: from French: apathy, from Old French *enui* annoyance, vexation; see ANNOY]

Enoch (ˈiːnɒk) *n Old Testament* **1** the eldest son of Cain after whom the first city was named (Genesis 4:17) **2** the father of Methuselah: said to have walked with God and to have been taken by God at the end of his earthly life (Genesis 5:24)

enology (iːˈnɒlədʒɪ) *n* the usual US spelling of **oenology**

enormity (ɪˈnɔːmɪtɪ) *n, pl* **-ties 1** the quality or character of being outrageous; extreme wickedness **2** an act of great wickedness; atrocity **3** *informal* vastness of size or extent [c15: from Old French *enormite*, from Late Latin *ēnormitās* hugeness; see ENORMOUS]

enormous (ɪˈnɔːməs) *adj* **1** unusually large in size, extent, or degree; immense; vast **2** *archaic* extremely wicked; heinous [c16: from Latin *ēnormis*, from ē- out of, away from + *norma* rule, pattern] > e'normously *adv* > e'normousness *n*

Enos (ˈiːnɒs) *n Old Testament* a son of Seth (Genesis 4:26; 5:6)

enosis (ˈɛnəʊsɪs) *n* the union of Greece and Cyprus: the aim of a group of Greek Cypriots [c20: Modern Greek: from Greek *henoun* to unite, from *heis* one]

enough (ɪˈnʌf) *determiner* **1 a** sufficient to answer a need, demand, supposition, or requirement; adequate: *enough cake* **b** (*as pronoun*): *enough is now known* **2** that's enough! that will do: used to put an end to an action, speech, performance, etc ▷ *adv* **3** so as to be adequate or sufficient; as much as necessary: *you have worked hard enough* **4** (*not used with a negative*) very or quite; rather: *she was pleased enough to see me* **5** (intensifier): *oddly enough; surprisingly enough* **6** just adequately; tolerably: *he did it well enough* [Old English *genōh*; related to Old Norse *gnōgr*, Gothic *ganōhs*, Old High German *ginuog*]

en passant (ɒn pæˈsɑːnt; *French* ɑ̃ pasɑ̃) *adv* in passing: in chess, said of capturing a pawn that has made an initial move of two squares to its fourth rank, bypassing the square where an enemy pawn on its own fifth rank could capture it. The capture is made as if the captured pawn had moved one square instead of two [c17: from French]

enprint (ˈɛnprɪnt) *n* a standard photographic print (5 × 3.5 in.) produced from a negative

enquire (ɪnˈkwaɪə) *vb* a variant of **inquire** > en'quirer *n* > en'quiry *n*

enrage (ɪnˈreɪdʒ) *vb* (*tr*) to provoke to fury; put into a rage; anger > en'raged *adj* > en'ragement *n*

en rapport *French* (ɑ̃ rapɔr) *adj, adv* (*postpositive*) in sympathy, harmony, or accord

enrapture (ɪnˈræptʃə) *vb* (*tr*) to fill with delight; enchant

enrich (ɪnˈrɪtʃ) *vb* (*tr*) **1** to increase the wealth of **2** to endow with fine or desirable qualities: *to enrich one's* experience by travelling **3** to make more beautiful; adorn; decorate: *a robe enriched with jewels* **4** to improve in quality, colour, flavour, etc **5** to increase the food value of by adding nutrients: *to enrich dog biscuits with calcium* **6** to make (soil) more productive, esp by adding fertilizer **7** *physics* to increase the concentration or abundance of one component or isotope in (a solution or mixture); concentrate: *to enrich a solution by evaporation; enrich a nuclear fuel* ▷ en'riched *adj* ▷ en'richment *n*

Enright ('ɛnraɪt) *n* D(ennis) J(oseph). 1920–2002, British poet, essayist, and editor

enrol *or US* **enroll** (ɪn'rəʊl) *vb* -rols *or US* -rolls, -rolling, -rolled (*mainly tr*) **1** to record or note in a roll or list **2** (*also intr*) to become or cause to become a member; enlist; register **3** to put on record; record ▷ ,enrol'lee *n* ▷ en'roller *n*

enrolment *or US* **enrollment** (ɪn'rəʊlmənt) *n* **1** the act of enrolling or state of being enrolled **2** a list of people enrolled **3** the total number of people enrolled

en route (ɒn 'ruːt; *French* ã rut) *adv* on or along the way; on the road [c18: from French]

ens (ɛnz) *n, pl* entia ('ɛnʃɪə) *metaphysics* **1** being or existence in the most general abstract sense **2** a real thing, esp as opposed to an attribute; entity [c16: from Late Latin, literally: being, from Latin *esse* to be]

Ens. *abbreviation* Ensign

ENSA ('ɛnsə) *n acronym for* Entertainments National Service Association: a British organization providing entertainment for the armed forces during World War II

Enschede (*Dutch* 'ɛnsxəde:) *n* a city in the E Netherlands, in Overijssel province: a major centre of the Dutch cotton industry. Pop: 152 000 (2003 est)

ensconce (ɪn'skɒns) *vb* (*tr; often passive*) **1** to establish or settle firmly or comfortably: *ensconced in a chair* **2** to place in safety; hide [c16: see EN-¹, SCONCE²]

ensemble (ɒn'sɒmb°l; *French* ãsãblə) *n* **1** all the parts of something considered together and in relation to the whole **2** a person's complete costume; outfit **3** the cast of a play other than the principals; supporting players **4** *music* a group of soloists singing or playing together **5** *music* the degree of precision and unity exhibited by a group of instrumentalists or singers performing together: *the ensemble of the strings is good* **6** the general or total effect of something made up of individual parts ▷ *adv* **7** all together or at once [c15: from French: together, from Latin *insimul*, from IN-² + *simul* at the same time]

enshrine *or* **inshrine** (ɪn'ʃraɪn) *vb* (*tr*) **1** to place or enclose in or as if in a shrine **2** to hold as sacred; cherish; treasure ▷ en'shrinement *n*

enshroud (ɪn'ʃraʊd) *vb* (*tr*) to cover or hide with or as if with a shroud: *the sky was enshrouded in mist*

ensign ('ɛnsaɪn) *n* **1** (*also* 'ɛnsən) a flag flown by a ship, branch of the armed forces, etc, to indicate nationality, allegiance, etc. See also **Red Ensign, White Ensign 2** any flag, standard, or banner **3** a standard-bearer **4** a symbol, token, or emblem; sign **5** (in the US Navy) a commissioned officer of the lowest rank **6** (in the British infantry) a colours bearer **7** (formerly in the British infantry) a commissioned officer of the lowest rank [c14: from Old French *enseigne*, from Latin INSIGNIA] ▷ 'ensign,ship *or* 'ensigncy *n*

ensilage ('ɛnsɪlɪdʒ) *n* **1** the process of ensiling green fodder **2** a less common name for **silage**

ensile (ɛn'saɪl, 'ɛnsaɪl) *vb* (*tr*) **1** to store and preserve (green fodder) in an enclosed pit or silo **2** to turn (green fodder) into silage by causing it to ferment in a closed pit or silo [c19: from French *ensiler*, from Spanish *ensilar*, from EN-¹ + *silo* SILO]

enslave (ɪn'sleɪv) *vb* (*tr*) to make a slave of; reduce to slavery; subjugate ▷ en'slavement *n* ▷ en'slaver *n*

ensnare *or* **insnare** (ɪn'snɛə) *vb* (*tr*) **1** to catch or trap in a snare **2** to trap or gain power over someone by dishonest or underhand means ▷ en'snarement *n* ▷ en'snarer *n*

Ensor ('ɛnsɔ:) *n* James (Sydney). 1860–1949, Belgian expressionist painter, noted for his macabre subjects

ensue (ɪn'sjuː) *vb* -sues, -suing, -sued **1** (*intr*) to follow; come next or afterwards **2** (*intr*) to follow or occur as a consequence; result **3** (*tr*) *obsolete* to pursue [c14: from

Anglo-French *ensuer*, from Old French *ensuivre*, from EN-¹ + *suivre* to follow, from Latin *sequī*] ▷ en'suing *adj*

en suite *French* (ã sɥit) *adv* as part of a set; forming a unit: *a hotel room with bathroom en suite* [c19: literally: in sequence]

ensure (ɛn'ʃʊə, -'ʃɔ:) *or esp US* **insure** *vb* (*tr*) **1** (*may take a clause as object*) to make certain or sure; guarantee: *this victory will ensure his happiness* **2** to make safe or secure; protect ▷ en'surer *n*

ENT *abbreviation med* ear, nose, and throat

-ent *suffix forming adjectives, suffix forming nouns* causing or performing an action or existing in a certain condition; the agent that performs an action: *astringent; dependent* [from Latin *-ent-*, *-ens*, present participial ending]

entablature (ɛn'tæblətʃə) *n architect* **1** the part of a classical temple above the columns, having an architrave, a frieze, and a cornice **2** any construction of similar form [c17: from French, from Italian *intavolatura* something put on a table, hence, something laid flat, from *tavola* table, from Latin *tabula* TABLE]

entablement (ɪn'teɪb°lmənt) *n* the platform of a pedestal, above the dado, that supports a statue [c17: from Old French]

entail (ɪn'teɪl) *vb* (*tr*) **1** to bring about or impose by necessity; have as a necessary consequence: *this task entails careful thought* **2** *property law* to restrict (the descent of an estate) to a designated line of heirs **3** *logic* to have as a necessary consequence ▷ *n* **4** *property law* a the restriction imposed by entailing an estate **b** an estate that has been entailed [c14: *entaillen*, from EN-¹ + *taille* limitation, TAIL²] ▷ en'tailer *n* ▷ en'tailment *n*

entamoeba (,ɛntə'miːbə), **endamoeba,** *US* **entameba** *or* **endameba** *n, pl* -bae (-biː) *or* -bas any parasitic amoeba of the genus *Entamoeba* (or *Endamoeba*), esp *E. histolytica*, which lives in the intestines of man and causes amoebic dysentery

entangle (ɪn'tæŋg°l) *vb* (*tr*) **1** to catch or involve in or as if in a tangle; ensnare or enmesh **2** to make tangled or twisted; snarl **3** to make complicated; confuse **4** to involve in difficulties; entrap ▷ en'tangler *n* ▷ en'tanglement *n*

entasis ('ɛntəsɪs) *n, pl* -ses (-siːz) a slightly convex curve given to the shaft of a column, pier, or similar structure, to correct the illusion of concavity produced by a straight shaft [c18: from Greek, from *enteinein* to stretch tight, from *teinein* to stretch]

Entebbe (ɛn'tɛbɪ) *n* a town in S Uganda, on Lake Victoria: British administrative centre of Uganda (1893–1958); international airport. Pop: 57 518 (2002 est)

entellus (ɛn'tɛləs) *n* an Old World monkey, *Presbytes entellus*, of S Asia. This langur is regarded as sacred in India. Also called: **hanuman** [c19: New Latin, apparently from the name of the aged Sicilian character in Book V of Virgil's *Aeneid*]

entente (*French* ãtãt) *n* **1** short for **entente cordiale 2** the parties to an entente cordiale collectively [c19: French: understanding]

entente cordiale (*French* ãtãt kɔrdjal) *n* **1** a friendly understanding between political powers: less formal than an alliance **2** (*often capitals*) the understanding reached by France and Britain in April 1904, which settled outstanding colonial disputes [c19: French: cordial understanding]

enter ('ɛntə) *vb* **1** to come up or go into (a place, house, etc) **2** to penetrate or pierce **3** (*tr*) to introduce or insert **4** to join (a party, organization, etc) **5** (*when intr, foll by into*) to become involved or take part (in): *to enter a game; to enter into an agreement* **6** (*tr*) to record (an item such as a commercial transaction) in a journal, account, register, etc **7** (*tr*) to record (a name, etc) on a list **8** (*tr*) to present or submit: *to enter a proposal* **9** (*intr*) *theatre* to come on stage: used as a stage direction: *enter Juliet* **10** (*when intr, often foll by into, on,* or *upon*) to begin; start: *to enter upon a new career* **11** (*intr; often foll by upon*) to come into possession (of) **12** (*tr*) to place (evidence, a plea, etc) before a court of law or upon the court records [c13: from Old French *entrer*, from Latin *intrāre* to go in, from *intrā* within] ▷ 'enterable *adj* ▷ 'enterer *n*

enteric (ɛn'tɛrɪk) *or* **enteral** ('ɛntərəl) *adj* intestinal

[C19: from Greek *enterikos*, from *enteron* intestine]

enter into *vb* (*intr, preposition*) **1** to be considered as a necessary part of (one's plans, calculations, etc) **2** to be in sympathy with: *he enters into his patient's problems*

enteritis (,ɛntəˈraɪtɪs) *n* inflammation of the small intestine

entero- *or before a vowel* **enter-** *combining form* indicating an intestine: *enterovirus; enteritis* [from New Latin, from Greek *enteron* intestine]

enteron ('ɛntə,rɒn) *n*, *pl* -tera (-tərə) the alimentary canal, esp of an embryo or a coelenterate [C19: via New Latin from Greek: intestine; related to Latin *inter* between]

enterobiasis (,ɛntərəʊˈbaɪəsɪs) *n* a disease, common in children, caused by infestation of the large intestine with nematodes of the genus *Enterobius*, esp the pinworm (*E. vermicularis*)

enterprise ('ɛntə,praɪz) *n* **1** a project or undertaking, esp one that requires boldness or effort **2** participation in such projects **3** readiness to embark on new ventures; boldness and energy **4 a** initiative in business **b** (*as modifier*): *the enterprise culture* **5** a business unit; a company or firm [C15: from Old French *entreprise* (n), from *entreprendre* from *entre-* between (from Latin: INTER-) + *prendre* to take, from Latin *prehendere* to grasp]
> 'enter,priser *n*

Enterprise Allowance Scheme *n* (in Britain) a scheme to provide a weekly allowance to an unemployed person who wishes to set up a business and is willing to invest a specified amount in it during its first year

enterprise zone *n* a designated zone in a depressed area, esp an inner urban area, where firms are given tax concessions and various planning restrictions are lifted, in order to attract new industry and business to the area: first introduced in Britain in 1981

enterprising ('ɛntə,praɪzɪŋ) *adj* ready to embark on new ventures; full of boldness and initiative
> 'enter,prisingly *adv*

entertain (,ɛntə'teɪn) *vb* **1** to provide amusement for (a person or audience) **2** to show hospitality to (guests) **3** (*tr*) to hold in the mind: *to entertain an idea* [C15: from Old French *entretenir*, from *entre-* mutually + *tenir* to hold, from Latin *tenēre*]

entertainer (,ɛntə'teɪnə) *n* **1** a professional singer, comedian, or other performer who takes part in public entertainments **2** any person who entertains

entertaining (,ɛntə'teɪnɪŋ) *adj* serving to entertain or give pleasure; diverting; amusing

entertainment (,ɛntə'teɪnmənt) *n* **1** the act or art of entertaining or state of being entertained **2** an act, production, etc, that entertains; diversion; amusement

enthalpy ('ɛnθəlpɪ, ɛn'θæl-) *n* a thermodynamic property of a system equal to the sum of its internal energy and the product of its pressure and volume. Symbol: *H* Also called: heat content, total heat [C20: from Greek *enthalpein* to warm in, from EN-² + *thalpein* to warm]

enthral *or US* **enthrall** (ɪn'θrɔːl) *vb* -thrals *or US* -thralls, -thralling, -thralled (*tr*) **1** to hold spellbound; enchant; captivate **2** *obsolete* to hold as thrall; enslave [C16: from EN-¹ + THRALL] > en'thraller *n* > en'thralment *or US* en'thrallment *n*

enthralling (ɪn'θrɔːlɪŋ) *adj* holding the attention completely; fascinating; spellbinding

enthrone (ɛn'θrəʊn) *vb* *tr* **1** to place on a throne **2** to honour or exalt **3** to assign authority to
> en'thronement *n*

enthuse (ɪn'θjuːz) *vb* to feel or show or cause to feel or show enthusiasm

enthusiasm (ɪn'θjuːzɪ,æzəm) *n* **1** ardent and lively interest or eagerness **2** an object of keen interest; passion **3** *archaic* extravagant or unbalanced religious fervour [C17: from Late Latin *enthūsiasmus*, from Greek *enthousiasmos*, from *enthousiazein* to be possessed by a god, from *entheos* inspired, from EN-² + *theos* god]

enthusiast (ɪn'θjuːzɪ,æst) *n* **1** a person filled with or motivated by enthusiasm; fanatic **2** *archaic* a religious visionary, esp one whose zeal for religion is extravagant or unbalanced > en,thusi'astic *adj* > en,thusi'astically *adv*

enthymeme ('ɛnθɪ,miːm) *n* *logic* an incomplete syllogism, in which one or more premises are unexpressed as their truth is considered to be self-evident [C16: via Latin from Greek *enthumēma*, from *enthumeisthai* to infer (literally: to have in the mind), from EN-² + *thumos* mind]

entice (ɪn'taɪs) *vb* (*tr*) to attract or draw towards oneself by exciting hope or desire; tempt; allure [C13: from Old French *enticier*, from Vulgar Latin *intitiāre* (unattested) to incite, from Latin *titiō* firebrand] > en'ticement *n* > en'ticer *n* > en'ticing *adj* > en'ticingly *adv*

entire (ɪn'taɪə) *adj* **1** (*prenominal*) whole; complete: *the entire project is going well* **2** (*prenominal*) without reservation or exception; total: *you have my entire support* **3** not broken or damaged; intact **4** consisting of a single piece or section; undivided; continuous **5** (of leaves, petals, etc) having a smooth margin not broken up into teeth or lobes **6** not castrated: *an entire horse* **7** *obsolete* of one substance or kind; unmixed; pure ▷ *n* **8** an uncastrated horse [C14: from Old French *entier*, from Latin *integer* whole, from IN-¹ + *tangere* to touch] > en'tireness *n*

entirely (ɪn'taɪəlɪ) *adv* **1** without reservation or exception; wholly; completely **2** solely or exclusively; only

entirety (ɪn'taɪərɪtɪ) *n*, *pl* -ties **1** the state of being entire or whole; completeness **2** a thing, sum, amount, etc, that is entire; whole; total

entitle (ɪn'taɪt°l) *vb* (*tr*) **1** to give (a person) the right to do or have something; qualify; allow **2** to give a name or title to **3** to confer a title of rank or honour upon [C14: from Old French *entituler*, from Late Latin *intitulāre*, from Latin *titulus* TITLE] > en'titlement *n*

entity ('ɛntɪtɪ) *n*, *pl* -ties **1** something having real or distinct existence; a thing, esp when considered as independent of other things **2** existence or being [C16: from Medieval Latin *entitās*, from *ēns* being; see ENS] > entitative ('ɛntɪtətɪv) *adj*

ento- *combining form* inside; within: *entoderm* [New Latin, from Greek *entos* within]

entomb (ɪn'tuːm) *vb* (*tr*) **1** to place in or as if in a tomb; bury; inter **2** to serve as a tomb for > en'tombment *n*

entomo- *combining form* indicating an insect: *entomology* [from Greek *entomon* insect (literally: creature cut into sections), from *en-* in + *-tomon*, from *temnein* to cut]

entomol. *or* **entom.** *abbreviation* entomology

entomology (,ɛntə'mɒlədʒɪ) *n* the branch of science concerned with the study of insects > entomological (,ɛntəmə'lɒdʒɪk°l) *or* ,entomo'logic *adj* > ,ento'mologist *n*

entophyte ('ɛntəʊ,faɪt) *n* *botany* a variant of **endophyte** > entophytic (,ɛntəʊ'fɪtɪk) *adj*

entourage ('ɒntʊ,rɑː3; *French* ãturaʒ) *n* **1** a group of attendants or retainers, esp such as surround an important person; retinue **2** surroundings or environment [C19: from French, from *entourer* to surround, from *entour* around, from *tour* circuit; see TOUR, TURN]

entr'acte (ɒn'trækt; *French* ãtrakt) *n* **1** an interval between two acts of a play or opera **2** (esp formerly) an entertainment during an interval, such as dancing between acts of an opera [C19: French, literally: between-act]

entrails ('ɛntreɪlz) *pl n* **1** the internal organs of a person or animal; intestines; guts **2** the innermost parts of anything [C13: from Old French *entrailles*, from Medieval Latin *intrālia*, changed from Latin *interānea* intestines, ultimately from *inter* between]

entrain (ɪn'treɪn) *vb* to board or put aboard a train > en'trainment *n*

entrance¹ ('ɛntrəns) *n* **1** the act or an instance of entering; entry **2** a place for entering, such as a door or gate **3 a** the power, liberty, or right of entering; admission **b** (*as modifier*): *an entrance fee* **4** the coming of an actor or other performer onto a stage [C16: from French, from *entrer* to ENTER]

entrance² (ɪn'trɑːns) *vb* (*tr*) **1** to fill with wonder and delight; enchant **2** to put into a trance; hypnotize > en'trancement *n* > en'trancing *adj*

entrant ('ɛntrənt) *n* a person who enters [C17: from French, literally: entering, from *entrer* to ENTER]

entrap (ɪnˈtræp) *vb* **-traps, -trapping, -trapped** (*tr*) **1** to catch or snare in or as if in a trap **2** to lure or trick into danger, difficulty, or embarrassment > en'trapment *n*

entreat *or* **intreat** (ɪnˈtriːt) *vb* **1** to ask (a person) earnestly; beg or plead with; implore **2** to make an earnest request or petition for (something) **3** an archaic word for **treat** (sense 4) [c15: from Old French *entraiter*, from EN-¹ + *traiter* to TREAT] > en'treatment *or* in'treatment *n*

entreaty (ɪnˈtriːtɪ) *n, pl* **-treaties** an earnest request or petition; supplication; plea

entrechat (*French* ɑ̃trəʃa) *n* a leap in ballet during which the dancer repeatedly crosses his feet or beats them together [c18: from French, from earlier *entrechase*, changed by folk etymology from Italian (*capriola*) *intrecciata*, literally: entwined (caper), from *intrecciare* to interlace, from IN-² + *treccia* TRESS]

entrecôte (*French* ɑ̃trəkot) *n* a beefsteak cut from between the ribs [c19: French *entrecôte*, from *entre-* INTER- + *côte* rib, from Latin *costa*]

entrée (ˈɒntreɪ) *n* **1** a dish served before a main course **2** *chiefly US* the main course of a meal **3** the power or right of entry [c18: from French, from *entrer* to ENTER; in cookery, so called because formerly the course was served after an intermediate course called the *relevé* (remove)]

entremets (*French* ɑ̃trəmɛ) *n, pl* **-mets** (*French* -mɛ) **1** a dessert **2** a light dish, formerly served at formal dinners between the main course and the dessert [c18: from French, from Old French *entremes*, from *entre-* between, INTER- + *mes* dish, MESS]

entrench *or* **intrench** (ɪnˈtrɛntʃ) *vb* **1** (*tr*) to construct (a defensive position) by digging trenches around it **2** (*tr*) to fix or establish firmly, esp so as to prevent removal or change **3** (*intr*; foll by *on* or *upon*) to trespass or encroach; infringe > en'trenched *or* in'trenched *adj* > entrenchmentor en'trenchment *or* in'trenchment *n*

entrepôt (*French* ɑ̃trəpo) *n* **1** a warehouse for commercial goods **2 a** a trading centre or port at a geographically convenient location, at which goods are imported and re-exported without incurring liability for duty **b** (*as modifier*): *an entrepôt trade* [c18: French, from *entreposer* to put in, from *entre-* between, INTER- + *poser* to place (see POSE¹); formed on the model of DEPOT]

entrepreneur (ˌɒntrəprəˈnɜː; *French* ɑ̃trəprənœr) *n* **1** the owner or manager of a business enterprise who, by risk and initiative, attempts to make profits **2** a middleman or commercial intermediary [c19: from French, from *entreprendre* to undertake; see ENTERPRISE] > ˌentrepre'neurial *adj* > ˌentrepre'neurship *n*

entropy (ˈɛntrəpɪ) *n, pl* **-pies** **1** a thermodynamic quantity that changes in a reversible process by an amount equal to the heat absorbed or emitted divided by the thermodynamic temperature. It is measured in joules per kelvin **2** lack of pattern or organization; disorder [c19: from EN-² + -TROPE]

entrust *or* **intrust** (ɪnˈtrʌst) *vb* (*tr*) **1** (usually foll by *with*) to invest or charge (with a duty, responsibility, etc) **2** (often foll by *to*) to put into the care or protection of someone > en'trustment *or* in'trustment *n*

entry (ˈɛntrɪ) *n, pl* **-tries** **1** the act or an instance of entering; entrance **2** a point or place for entering, such as a door, gate, etc **3 a** the right or liberty of entering; admission; access **b** (*as modifier*): *an entry permit* **4** the act of recording an item, such as a commercial transaction, in a journal, account, register, etc **5** an item recorded, as in a diary, dictionary, or account **6** a person, horse, car, etc, entering a competition or contest; competitor **7** the competitors entering a contest considered collectively: *a good entry this year for the speed trials* **8** the action of an actor in going on stage or his manner of doing this **9** *property law* the act of going upon another person's land with the intention of asserting the right to possession **10** any point in a piece of music, esp a fugue, at which a performer commences or resumes playing or singing **11** *cards* a card that enables one to transfer the lead from one's own hand to that of one's partner or to the dummy hand **12** *English dialect* a passage between the

backs of two rows of terraced houses [c13: from Old French *entree*, past participle of *entrer* to ENTER]

entryism (ˈɛntriɪzəm) *n* the policy or practice of members of a particular political group joining an existing political party with the intention of changing its principles and policies, instead of forming a new party > 'entryist *n, adj*

entry-level *adj* **1** (of a job or worker) at the most elementary level in a career structure **2** (of a product) characterized by being at the most appropriate level for use by a beginner: *an entry-level camera*

entwine *or* **intwine** (ɪnˈtwaɪn) *vb* (of two or more things) to twine together or (of one or more things) to twine around (something else) > en'twinement *or* in'twinement *n*

Enugu (ɛˈnuːguː) *n* **1** a state of S Nigeria. Capital: Enugu. Pop: 3 257 298 (2006). Area: 7161 sq km (2765 sq miles) **2** a city in S Nigeria, capital of Enugu state: capital of the former Eastern region and of the breakaway state of Biafra during the Civil War (1967–70): coal-mining. Pop: 549 000 (2005 est)

E number *n* any of a series of numbers with the prefix E indicating a specific food additive recognized by the European Union and used on labels of processed food

enumerate (ɪˈnjuːməˌreɪt) *vb* **1** (*tr*) to mention separately or in order; name one by one; list **2** (*tr*) to determine the number of; count **3** *Canadian* to compile or enter (a name or names) in a voting list for an area [c17: from Latin *ēnumerāre*, from *numerāre* to count, reckon; see NUMBER] > e'numerable *adj* > eˌnumer'ation *n* > e'numerative *adj*

enumerator (ɪˈnjuːməˌreɪtə) *n* **1** a person or thing that enumerates **2** *Brit* a person who issues and retrieves forms during a census of population

enunciable (ɪˈnʌnsɪəbᵊl) *adj* capable of being enunciated

enunciate (ɪˈnʌnsɪˌeɪt) *vb* **1** to articulate or pronounce (words), esp clearly and distinctly **2** (*tr*) to state precisely or formally [c17: from Latin *ēnuntiāre* to declare, from *nuntiāre* to announce, from *nuntius* messenger] > eˌnunci'ation *n* > e'nunciative *or* e'nunciatory *adj* > e'nunciatively *adv* > e'nunciˌator *n*

enuresis (ˌɛnjʊˈriːsɪs) *n* involuntary discharge of urine, esp during sleep [c19: from New Latin, from Greek EN-² + *ourein* to urinate, from *ouron* urine] > enuretic (ˌɛnjʊˈrɛtɪk) *adj, n*

envelop (ɪnˈvɛləp) *vb* **-lops, -loping, -loped** (*tr*) **1** to wrap or enclose in or as if in a covering **2** to conceal or obscure, as from sight or understanding: *a plan enveloped in mystery* **3** to surround or partially surround (an enemy force) [c14: from Old French *envoluper*, from EN-¹ + *voluper*, *voloper*, of obscure origin] > en'velopment *n*

envelope (ˈɛnvəˌləʊp, ˈɒn-) *n* **1** a flat covering of paper, usually rectangular in shape and with a flap that can be folded over and sealed, used to enclose a letter, etc **2** any covering or wrapper **3** *biology* any enclosing structure, such as a membrane, shell, or skin **4** the bag enclosing the gas in a balloon **5** *maths* a curve or surface that is tangent to each one of a group of curves or surfaces **6 push the envelope** *informal* to push the boundaries of what is possible [c18: from French *enveloppe*, from *envelopper* to wrap around; see ENVELOP; sense 8 from aeronautics jargon, referring to graphs of aircraft performance]

envenom (ɪnˈvɛnəm) *vb* (*tr*) **1** to fill or impregnate with venom; make poisonous **2** to fill with bitterness or malice

Enver Pasha (ˈɛnvə ˈpɑːʃə) *n* 1881–1922, Turkish soldier and leader of the Young Turks: minister of war (1914–18)

enviable (ˈɛnvɪəbᵊl) *adj* exciting envy; fortunate or privileged > 'enviableness *n*

envious (ˈɛnvɪəs) *adj* feeling, showing, or resulting from envy [c13: from Anglo-Norman, ultimately from Latin *invidiōsus* full of envy, INVIDIOUS; see ENVY] > 'enviously *adv* > 'enviousness *n*

environ (ɪnˈvaɪrən) *vb* (*tr*) to encircle or surround [c14: from Old French *environner* to surround, from *environ* around, from EN-¹ + *viron* a circle, from *virer* to turn, VEER¹]

environment (ɪnˈvaɪrənmənt) *n* **1** external conditions or surroundings, esp those in which people live or work **2** *ecology* the external surroundings in which a plant or animal lives, which tend to influence its development and behaviour **3** *computing* an operating system, program, or integrated suite of programs that provides all the facilities necessary for a particular application: *a word-processing environment* > en,viron'mental *adj*

environmentalist (ɪn,vaɪrən'mɛntəlɪst) *n* **1** an adherent of environmentalism **2** a person who is concerned with the maintenance of ecological balance and the conservation of the environment

environs (ɪn'vaɪrənz) *pl n* a surrounding area or region, esp the suburbs or outskirts of a town or city; vicinity

envisage (ɪn'vɪzɪdʒ) *vb* (*tr*) **1** to form a mental image of; visualize; contemplate **2** to conceive of as a possibility in the future; foresee [c19: from French *envisager*, from EN-¹ + *visage* face, VISAGE] > en'visagement *n*

envision (ɪn'vɪʒən) *vb* (*tr*) to conceive of as a possibility, esp in the future; foresee

envoy¹ (ˈɛnvɔɪ) *n* **1** Also called: **formal envoy** extraordinary and minister plenipotentiary a diplomat of the second class, ranking between an ambassador and a minister resident **2** an accredited messenger, agent, or representative [c17: from French *envoyé*, literally: sent, from *envoyer* to send, from Vulgar Latin *inviāre* (unattested) to send on a journey, from IN-² + *via* road] > 'envoyship *n*

envoy² or **envoi** (ˈɛnvɔɪ) *n* **1** a brief dedicatory or explanatory stanza concluding certain forms of poetry, notably ballades **2** a postscript in other forms of verse or prose [c14: from Old French *envoye*, from *envoyer* to send; see ENVOY¹]

envy (ˈɛnvɪ) *n, pl* **-vies** **1** a feeling of grudging or somewhat admiring discontent aroused by the possessions, achievements, or qualities of another **2** the desire to have for oneself something possessed by another; covetousness **3** an object of envy ▷ *vb* **-vies, -vying, -vied** **4** to be envious of (a person or thing) [c13: via Old French from Latin *invidia*, from *invidēre* to eye maliciously, from IN-² + *vidēre* to see] > 'envier *n* > 'envyingly *adv*

enwrap or **inwrap** (ɪn'ræp) *vb* **-wraps, -wrapping, -wrapped** (*tr*) **1** to wrap or cover up; envelop **2** (*usually passive*) to engross or absorb: *enwrapped in thought*

enwreath (ɪn'riːð) *vb* (*tr*) to surround or encircle with or as with a wreath or wreaths

Enzed (ˈɛnˈzɛd) *n* *Austral & NZ informal* **1** New Zealand **2** Also called: **Enzedder** a New Zealander

enzootic (,ɛnzəʊ'ɒtɪk) *adj* **1** (of diseases) affecting animals within a limited region ▷ *n* **2** an enzootic disease [c19: from EN-² + Greek *zōion* animal + -OTIC] > ,enzo'otically *adv*

enzyme (ˈɛnzaɪm) *n* any of a group of complex proteins or conjugated proteins that are produced by living cells and act as catalysts in specific biochemical reactions [c19: from Medieval Greek *enzumos* leavened, from Greek EN-² + *zumē* leaven] > enzymatic (,ɛnzaɪ'mætɪk, -zɪ-) or enzymic (ɛn'zaɪmɪk, -'zɪm-) *adj*

enzyme-linked immunosorbent assay (,ɪmjʊnəʊ'sɔːbənt) *n* the full name for **ELISA**

eo- *combining form* early or primeval: *Eocene; eohippus* [from Greek, from *ēōs* dawn]

EOC *abbreviation* Equal Opportunities Commission

Eocene (ˈiːəʊˌsiːn) *adj* **1** of, denoting, or formed in the second epoch of the Tertiary period, which lasted for 20 000 000 years, during which hooved mammals appeared ▷ *n* **2 the Eocene** the Eocene epoch or rock series [c19: from EO- + -CENE]

eohippus (,iːəʊ'hɪpəs) *n, pl* **-puses** the earliest horse: an extinct Eocene dog-sized animal of the genus with four-toed forelegs, three-toed hindlegs, and teeth specialized for browsing [c19: New Latin, from EO- + Greek *hippos* horse]

Eolithic (,iːəʊ'lɪθɪk) *adj* denoting, relating to, or characteristic of the early part of the Stone Age, characterized by the use of crude stone tools

eon (ˈiːən, ˈiːɒn) *n* **1** the usual US spelling of **aeon** **2** *geology* the longest division of geological time, comprising two or more eras

Eos (ˈiːɒs) *n* *Greek myth* the winged goddess of the dawn, the daughter of Hyperion. Roman counterpart: Aurora

eosin (ˈiːəʊsɪn) or **eosine** (ˈiːəʊsɪn, -ˌsiːn) *n* **1** Also called: **bromeosin** a red crystalline water-insoluble derivative of fluorescein. Its soluble salts are used as dyes. Formula: $C_{20}H_8Br_4O_5$ **2** any of several similar dyes [c19: from Greek *ēōs* dawn + -IN; referring to the colour it gives to silk]

Eötvös (ˈɜːtvɒs) *n* Baron **Roland von.** 1848–1919, Hungarian physicist noted for his studies of gravity and surface tension

-eous *suffix of adjectives* relating to or having the nature of: *gaseous* [from Latin *-eus*]

ep- *prefix* variant of epi-: *epexegesis*

EP *n* an extended-play single, one of the formats in which music is sold, usually comprising four or five tracks

EPA *abbreviation* **1** eicosapentaenoic acid: a fatty acid, found in certain fish oils, that can reduce blood cholesterol **2** Environmental Protection Agency

epact (ˈiːpækt) *n* **1** the difference in time, about 11 days, between the solar year and the lunar year **2** the number of days between the beginning of the calendar year and the new moon immediately preceding this [c16: via Late Latin from Greek *epaktē*, from *epagein* to bring in, intercalate, from *agein* to lead]

Epaminondas (ɛ,pæmɪ'nɒndæs) *n* ?418–362 BC, Greek Theban statesman and general: defeated the Spartans at Leuctra (371) and Mantinea (362) and restored power in Greece to Thebes

eparch (ˈɛpɑːk) *n* **1** a bishop or metropolitan in charge of an eparchy (sense 1) **2** a government official in charge of an eparchy (senses 2 or 3) [c17: from Greek *eparkhos*, from *epi-* over, on + -ARCH]

eparchy (ˈɛpɑːkɪ) or **eparchate** (ˈɛpɑːkɪt) *n, pl* **-chies** or **-chates** **1** a diocese of the Eastern Christian Church **2** (in ancient Greece) a province **3** (in modern Greece) a subdivision of a province

epaulette or US **epaulet** (ˈɛpəˌlɛt, -lɪt) *n* a piece of ornamental material on the shoulder of a garment, esp a military uniform [c18: from French *épaulette*, from *épaule* shoulder, from Latin *spatula* shoulder blade; see SPATULA]

e-payment *n* a digital payment for a transaction made on the internet

épée (ˈepeɪ; *French* epe) *n* a sword similar to the foil but with a larger guard and a heavier blade of triangular cross section [c19: from French: sword, from Latin *spatha*, from Greek *spathē* blade; see SPADE¹]

epeirogeny (,ɛpaɪ'rɒdʒɪnɪ) or **epeirogenesis** (ɪ,paɪrəʊ'dʒɛnɪsɪs) *n* the formation and submergence of continents by broad relatively slow displacements of the earth's crust [c19: from Greek *ēpeiros* continent + -GENY] > epeirogenic (ɪ,paɪrəʊ'dʒɛnɪk) or epeirogenetic (ɪ,paɪrəʊdʒɪ'nɛtɪk) *adj*

epergne (ɪ'pɜːn) *n* an ornamental centrepiece for a table: a stand with holders for sweetmeats, fruit, flowers, etc [c18: probably from French *épargne* a saving, from *épargner* to economize, of Germanic origin; compare SPARE]

epexegesis (ɛ,pɛksɪ'dʒiːsɪs) *n, pl* **-ses** (-ˌsiːz) *rhetoric* **1** the addition of a phrase, clause, or sentence to a text to provide further explanation **2** the phrase, clause, or sentence added for this purpose [c17: from Greek; see EPI-, EXEGESIS] > epexegetic (ɛ,pɛksɪ'dʒɛtɪk) or ep,exe'getical *adj*

Eph. or **Ephes.** *abbreviation* Bible Ephesians

ephah or **epha** (ˈiːfə) *n* a Hebrew unit of dry measure equal to approximately one bushel or about 33 litres [c16: from Hebrew *'ephāh*, of Egyptian origin]

ephedra (ɪ'fɛdrə) *n* any gymnosperm shrub of the genus *Ephedra*, of warm regions of America and Eurasia: the source of ephedrine: family Ephedraceae, phylum Gnetophyta [c18: New Latin, from Latin, from Greek *ephedros* a sitting upon, from *epi-* + *hedra* seat]

ephedrine or **ephedrin** (ɪ'fɛdrɪn, 'ɛfɪ,driːn, -drɪn) *n* a white crystalline alkaloid obtained from plants of the genus *Ephedra*: used for the treatment of asthma and hay fever; 1-phenyl-2-methylaminopropanol. Formula:

C₆H₅CH(OH)CH(NHCH₃)CH₃ [c19: from New Latin
EPHEDRA + -INE²]

ephemera (ɪˈfɛmərə) *n*, *pl* **-eras** *or* **-erae** (-əˌriː) **1** a
mayfly, esp one of the genus *Ephemera* **2** something
transitory or short-lived **3** (*functioning as plural*) a class of
collectable items not originally intended to last for more
than a short time, such as tickets, posters, postcards, or
labels **4** a plural of **ephemeron** [c16; see EPHEMERAL]

ephemeral (ɪˈfɛmərəl) *adj* **1** lasting for only a short time;
transitory; short-lived: *ephemeral pleasure* ⊳ *n* **2** a short-
lived organism, such as the mayfly **3** a plant that
completes its life cycle in less than one year, usually less
than six months [c16: from Greek *ephēmeros* lasting only
a day, from *hēmera* day] > eˌphemerˈality *or*
eˈphemeralness *n*

ephemerid (ɪˈfɛmərɪd) *n* any insect of the order
Ephemeroptera (or *Ephemerida*), which comprises the
mayflies. Also called: **ephemeropteran** [c19: from New
Latin *Ephēmerida*, from Greek *ephēmeros* short-lived + -ID²]

ephemeris (ɪˈfɛmərɪs) *n*, *pl* **ephemerides** (ˌɛfɪˈmɛrɪˌdiːz) a
table giving the future positions of a planet, comet, or
satellite [c16: from Latin, from Greek: diary, journal; see
EPHEMERAL]

ephemeron (ɪˈfɛməˌrɒn) *n*, *pl* **-era** (-ərə) *or* **-erons** (*usually
plural*) something transitory or short-lived [c16: see
EPHEMERAL]

Ephesus (ˈɛfɪsəs) *n* (in ancient Greece) a major trading
city on the W coast of Asia Minor: famous for its temple
of Artemis (Diana); sacked by the Goths (262 AD)

ephod (ˈiːfɒd) *n Old Testament* an embroidered vestment
believed to resemble an apron with shoulder straps,
worn by priests in ancient Israel [c14: from Hebrew
ēphōdh]

ephor (ˈɛfɔː) *n*, *pl* **-ors** *or* **-ori** (-əˌraɪ) (in ancient Greece)
one of a board of senior magistrates in any of several
Dorian states, esp the five Spartan ephors, who were
elected by vote of all full citizens and who wielded
effective power [c16: from Greek *ephoros*, from *ephoran* to
supervise, from EPI- + *horan* to look] > ˈephoral *adj*
> ˈephorate *n*

Ephraim (ˈiːfreɪɪm) *n Old Testament* **1 a** the younger son of
Joseph, who received the principal blessing of his
grandfather Jacob (Genesis 48:8–22) **b** the tribe
descended from him **c** the territory of this tribe, west of
the River Jordan **2** the northern kingdom of Israel after
the kingdom of Solomon had been divided into two

Ephraimite (ˈiːfreɪɪˌmaɪt) *n* a member of the tribe of
Ephraim

epi-, eph- *or before a vowel* **ep-** *prefix* **1** on; upon; above;
over: *epidermis; epicentre* **2** in addition to:
epiphenomenon **3** after: *epigenesis; epilogue* **4** near;
close to: *epicalyx* [from Greek, from *epi* (prep)]

epic (ˈɛpɪk) *n* **1 a** a long narrative poem recounting in
elevated style the deeds of a legendary hero, esp one
originating in oral folk tradition **2** the genre of epic
poetry **3** any work of literature, film, etc, having heroic
deeds for its subject matter or having other qualities
associated with the epic **4** an episode in the lives of men
in which heroic deeds are performed or attempted ⊳ *adj*
5 denoting, relating to, or characteristic of an epic or
epics **6** of heroic or impressive proportions [c16: from
Latin *epicus*, from Greek *epikos*, from *epos* speech, word,
song]

epicalyx (ˌɛpɪˈkeɪlɪks, -ˈkæl-) *n*, *pl* **-lyxes** *or* **-lyces** (-lɪˌsiːz)
botany a series of small sepal-like bracts forming an
outer calyx beneath the true calyx in some flowers

epicanthus (ˌɛpɪˈkænθəs) *n*, *pl* **-thi** (-θaɪ) a fold of skin
extending vertically over the inner angle of the eye:
characteristic of Mongolian peoples and a congenital
anomaly among other races [c19: New Latin, from EPI- +
Latin *canthus* corner of the eye, from Greek *kanthos*]
> epiˈcanthic *adj*

epicardium (ˌɛpɪˈkɑːdɪəm) *n*, *pl* **-dia** (-dɪə) *anatomy* the
innermost layer of the pericardium, in direct contact
with the heart [c19: New Latin, from EPI- + Greek *kardia*
heart] > epiˈcardiac *or* epiˈcardial *adj*

epicarp (ˈɛpɪˌkɑːp) *or* **exocarp** *n* the outermost layer of
the pericarp of fruits: forms the skin of a peach or grape
[c19: from French *épicarpe*, from EPI- + Greek *karpos* fruit]

epicene (ˈɛpɪˌsiːn) *adj* **1** having the characteristics of
both sexes; hermaphroditic **2** of neither sex; sexless
3 effeminate **4** *grammar* **a** denoting a noun that may
refer to a male or a female, such as *teacher* as opposed to
businessman or *shepherd* **b** (in Latin, Greek, etc) denoting a
noun that retains the same grammatical gender
regardless of the sex of the referent [c15: from Latin
epicoenus of both genders, from Greek *epikoinos* common to
many, from *koinos* common] > epiˈcenism *n*

epicentre *or US* **epicenter** (ˈɛpɪˌsɛntə) *n* the point on the
earth's surface directly above the focus of an earthquake
or underground nuclear explosion [c19: from New Latin
epicentrum, from Greek *epikentros* over the centre, from EPI-
+ *kentron* needle; see CENTRE] > epiˈcentral *adj*

Epictetus (ˌɛpɪkˈtiːtəs) *n* ?50–?120 AD, Greek Stoic
philosopher, who stressed self-renunciation and the
brotherhood of man

epicure (ˈɛpɪˌkjʊə) *n* **1** a person who cultivates a
discriminating palate for the enjoyment of good food
and drink; gourmet **2** a person devoted to sensual
pleasures [c16: from Medieval Latin *epicūrus*, after
Epicurus; see EPICUREAN] > ˈepicurˌism *n*

epicurean (ˌɛpɪkjʊˈriːən) *adj* **1** devoted to sensual
pleasures, esp food and drink; hedonistic **2** suitable for
an epicure ⊳ *n* **3** an epicure; gourmet > ˌepicuˈreanism *n*

Epicurean (ˌɛpɪkjʊˈriːən) *adj* **1** of or relating to the
philosophy of Epicurus, the Greek philosopher (341–270
BC), who held that the highest good is pleasure ⊳ *n* **2** a
follower of the philosophy of Epicurus
> ˌEpicuˈreanism *n*

Epicurus (ˌɛpɪˈkjʊərəs) *n* 341–270 BC, Greek philosopher,
who held that the highest good is pleasure and that the
world is a series of fortuitous combinations of atoms

epicycle (ˈɛpɪˌsaɪkᵊl) *n* a circle that rolls around the
inside or outside of another circle, so generating an
epicycloid or hypocycloid [c14: from Late Latin *epicyclus*,
from Greek *epikuklos*; see EPI-, CYCLE] > **epicyclic**
(ˌɛpɪˈsaɪklɪk, -ˈsɪklɪk) *or* ˌepiˈcyclical *adj*

epicyclic train *n* a cluster of gears consisting of a
central gearwheel with external teeth (the sun), a
coaxial gearwheel of greater diameter with internal
teeth (the annulus), and one or more planetary gears
engaging with both of them to provide a large gear ratio
in a compact space

epicycloid (ˌɛpɪˈsaɪklɔɪd) *n* the curve described by a
point on the circumference of a circle as this circle rolls
around the outside of another fixed circle, the two
circles being coplanar > ˌepiˈcycloidal *adj*

Epidaurus (ˌɛpɪˈdɔːrəs; *Greek* ɛpiˈðaʊrɔs) *n* an ancient port
in Greece, in the NE Peloponnese, in Argolis on the
Saronic Gulf

epideictic (ˌɛpɪˈdaɪktɪk) *adj* designed to display
something, esp the skill of the speaker in rhetoric. Also
called: **epidictic** (ˌɛpɪˈdɪktɪk) [c18: from Greek *epideiktikos*,
from *epideiknunai* to display, show off, from *deiknunai* to
show]

epidemic (ˌɛpɪˈdɛmɪk) *adj* **1** (esp of a disease) attacking or
affecting many persons simultaneously in a community
or area ⊳ *n* **2** a widespread occurrence of a disease **3** a
rapid development, spread, or growth of something, esp
something unpleasant [c17: from French *épidémique*, via
Late Latin from Greek *epidēmia* literally: among the
people, from EPI- + *dēmos* people] > ˌepiˈdemically *adv*

epidemiology (ˌɛpɪˌdiːmɪˈɒlədʒɪ) *n* the branch of
medical science concerned with the occurrence,
transmission, and control of epidemic diseases
> **epidemiological** (ˌɛpɪˌdiːmɪəˈlɒdʒɪkᵊl) *adj*
> ˌepiˌdemiˈologist *n*

epidermis (ˌɛpɪˈdɜːmɪs) *n* **1** Also called: **cuticle** the thin
protective outer layer of the skin, composed of stratified
epithelial tissue **2** the outer layer of cells of an
invertebrate **3** the outer protective layer of cells of a
plant, which may be thickened by a cuticle [c17: via Late
Latin from Greek, from EPI- + *derma* skin] > epiˈdermal *or*
ˌepiˈdermic *or* ˌepiˈdermoid *adj*

epidiascope (ˌɛpɪˈdaɪəˌskəʊp) *n* an optical device for
projecting a magnified image onto a screen

epididymis (ˌɛpɪˈdɪdɪmɪs) *n*, *pl* **-didymides** (-dɪˈdɪmɪˌdiːz)
anatomy a convoluted tube situated along the posterior

margin of each testis, in which spermatozoa are stored and conveyed to the vas deferens [c17: from Greek *epididumis*, from EPI- + *didumos* twin, testicle; see DIDYMOUS]

epidural (ˌɛpɪˈdjʊərəl) *adj* 1 Also called: **extradural** upon or outside the dura mater ▷ *n* 2 Also called: **epidural anaesthesia a** injection of anaesthetic into the space outside the dura mater enveloping the spinal cord **b** anaesthesia induced by this method [c19: from EPI- + DUR(A MATER) + -AL¹]

epigamic (ˌɛpɪˈɡæmɪk) *adj zoology* attractive to the opposite sex: *epigamic coloration*

epigeal (ˌɛpɪˈdʒiːəl), **epigean** or **epigeous** *adj* 1 of or relating to seed germination in which the cotyledons appear above the ground because of the growth of the hypocotyl 2 living or growing on or close to the surface of the ground [c19: from Greek *epigeios* of the earth, from EPI- + *gē* earth]

epigenetic (ˌɛpɪdʒɪˈnɛtɪk) *adj* 1 of or relating to epigenesis 2 denoting processes by which heritable modifications in gene function occur without a change in the sequence of the DNA > ˌepigeˈnetically *adv*

epigenetics (ˌɛpɪdʒɪˈnɛtɪks) *n* (*functioning as sing*) the study of heritable changes that occur without a change in the DNA sequence

epiglottis (ˌɛpɪˈɡlɒtɪs) *n*, *pl* **-tises** or **-tides** (-tɪˌdiːz) a thin cartilaginous flap that covers the entrance to the larynx during swallowing, preventing food from entering the trachea > ˌepiˈglottal or ˌepiˈglottic *adj*

Epigoni (ɪˈpɪɡəˌnaɪ) *pl n*, *sing* **-onus** (-ənəs) *Greek myth* the descendants of the Seven against Thebes, who undertook a second expedition against the city and eventually captured and destroyed it [c20: from Greek *epigonoi* those born after]

epigram (ˈɛpɪˌɡræm) *n* 1 a witty, often paradoxical remark, concisely expressed 2 a short, pungent, and often satirical poem, esp one having a witty and ingenious ending [c15: from Latin *epigramma*, from Greek: inscription, from *epigraphein* to write upon, from *graphein* to write] > ˌepigramˈmatic *adj* > ˌepigramˈmatically *adv*

epigrammatize or **epigrammatise** (ˌɛpɪˈɡræməˌtaɪz) *vb* to make an epigram or epigrams (about) > ˌepiˈgrammatism *n* > ˌepiˈgrammatist *n*

epigraph (ˈɛpɪˌɡrɑːf, -ˌɡræf) *n* 1 a quotation at the beginning of a book, chapter, etc, suggesting its theme 2 an inscription on a monument or building [c17: from Greek *epigraphē*; see EPIGRAM] > **epigraphic** (ˌɛpɪˈɡræfɪk) or ˌepiˈgraphical *adj*

epigraphy (ɪˈpɪɡrəfɪ) *n* 1 the study of ancient inscriptions 2 epigraphs collectively > eˈpigraphist or eˈpigrapher *n*

epilator (ˈɛpɪˌleɪtə) *n* an electrical appliance consisting of a metal spiral head that rotates at high speed, plucking unwanted hair

epilepsy (ˈɛpɪˌlɛpsɪ) *n* a disorder of the central nervous system characterized by periodic loss of consciousness with or without convulsions. In some cases it is due to brain damage but in others the cause is unknown [c16: from Late Latin *epilēpsia*, from Greek, from *epilambanein* to attack, seize, from *lambanein* to take]

epileptic (ˌɛpɪˈlɛptɪk) *adj* 1 of, relating to, or having epilepsy ▷ *n* 2 a person who has epilepsy > ˌepiˈleptically *adv*

epilogue (ˈɛpɪˌlɒɡ) *n* 1 a a speech, usually in verse, addressed to the audience by an actor at the end of a play **b** the actor speaking this 2 a short postscript to any literary work, such as a brief description of the fates of the characters in a novel [c15: from Latin *epilogus*, from Greek *epilogos*, from *logos* word, speech] > **epilogist** (ɪˈpɪlədʒɪst) *n*

epinephrine (ˌɛpɪˈnɛfrɪn, -riːn) or **epinephrin** *n* a US name for **adrenaline** [c19: from EPI- + *nephro-* + -INE²]

epiphany (ɪˈpɪfənɪ) *n*, *pl* **-nies** 1 the manifestation of a supernatural or divine reality 2 any moment of great or sudden revelation [c17: via Church Latin from Greek *epiphaneia* an appearing, from EPI- + *phainein* to show] > **epiphanic** (ˌɛpɪˈfænɪk) *adj*

Epiphany (ɪˈpɪfənɪ) *n*, *pl* **-nies** a Christian festival held

on Jan 6, commemorating, in the Western Church, the manifestation of Christ to the Magi and, in the Eastern Church, the baptism of Christ

epiphenomenon (ˌɛpɪfɪˈnɒmɪnən) *n*, *pl* **-na** (-nə) 1 a secondary or additional phenomenon; by-product 2 *pathol* an unexpected or atypical symptom or occurrence during the course of a disease > ˌepiphe'nomenal *adj*

epiphyte (ˈɛpɪˌfaɪt) *n* a plant that grows on another plant but is not parasitic on it > **epiphytic** (ˌɛpɪˈfɪtɪk) or ˌepi'phytal or ˌepi'phytical *adj*

Epirus (ɪˈpaɪərəs) *n* 1 a region of NW Greece, part of ancient Epirus ceded to Greece after independence in 1830 2 (in ancient Greece) a region between the Pindus mountains and the Ionian Sea, straddling the modern border with Albania

Epis. *abbreviation* Also called: **Epist** *Bible* Epistle

episcopacy (ɪˈpɪskəpəsɪ) *n*, *pl* **-cies** 1 government of a Church by bishops 2 another word for **episcopate**

episcopal (ɪˈpɪskəpᵊl) *adj* of, denoting, governed by, or relating to a bishop or bishops [c15: from Church Latin *episcopālis*, from *episcopus* BISHOP]

Episcopal (ɪˈpɪskəpᵊl) *adj* belonging to or denoting the Episcopal Church

episcopalian (ɪˌpɪskəˈpeɪlɪən) *adj* Also: episcopal 1 practising or advocating the principle of Church government by bishops ▷ *n* 2 an advocate of such Church government > ˌepisco'palianism *n*

Episcopalian (ɪˌpɪskəˈpeɪlɪən) *adj* 1 belonging to or denoting the Episcopal Church ▷ *n* 2 a member or adherent of this Church

episcopate (ɪˈpɪskəpɪt, -ˌpeɪt) *n* 1 the office, status, or term of office of a bishop 2 bishops collectively

episiotomy (əˌpiːzɪˈɒtəmɪ) *n*, *pl* **-mies** surgical incision into the perineum during the late stages of labour to prevent its laceration during childbirth and to make delivery easier [c20: from *episio-*, from Greek *epision* pubic region + -TOMY]

episode (ˈɛpɪˌsəʊd) *n* 1 an incident, event, or series of events 2 any one of the sections into which a serialized novel or radio or television programme is divided 3 an incident, sequence, or scene that forms part of a narrative but may be a digression from the main story 4 (in ancient Greek tragedy) a section between two choric songs 5 *music* a contrasting section between statements of the subject, as in a fugue or rondo [c17: from Greek *epeisodion* something added, from *epi-* (in addition) + *eisodios* coming in, from *eis-* in + *hodos* road]

episodic (ˌɛpɪˈsɒdɪk) or **episodical** *adj* 1 resembling or relating to an episode 2 divided into or composed of episodes. 3. irregular, occasional, or sporadic > ˌepi'sodically *adv*

epistaxis (ˌɛpɪˈstæksɪs) *n* the technical name for **nosebleed** [c18: from Greek: a dropping, from *epistazein* to drop on, from *stazein* to drip]

epistemology (ɪˌpɪstɪˈmɒlədʒɪ) *n* the theory of knowledge, esp the critical study of its validity, methods, and scope [c19: from Greek *epistēmē* knowledge] > e,piste'mologist *n* > epistemological (ɪˌpɪstɪməˈlɒdʒɪkᵊl) *adj*

epistle (ɪˈpɪsᵊl) *n* 1 a letter, esp one that is long, formal, or didactic 2 a literary work in letter form, esp a dedicatory verse letter of a type originated by Horace [Old English *epistol*, via Latin from Greek *epistolē*, from *epistellein* to send to, from *stellein* to prepare, send]

Epistle (ɪˈpɪsᵊl) *n* 1 *New Testament* any of the apostolic letters of Saints Paul, Peter, James, Jude, or John 2 a reading from one of the Epistles, forming part of the Eucharistic service in many Christian Churches

epistolary (ɪˈpɪstələrɪ) or *archaic* **epistolatory** *adj* 1 relating to, denoting, conducted by, or contained in letters 2 (of a novel or other work) constructed in the form of a series of letters

epistyle (ˈɛpɪˌstaɪl) *n* another name for **architrave** (sense 1) [c17: via Latin *epistȳlium* from Greek *epistulion*, from EPI- + *stulos* column, STYLE]

epitaph (ˈɛpɪˌtɑːf, -ˌtæf) *n* 1 a commemorative inscription on a tombstone or monument 2 a speech or written passage composed in commemoration of a dead person **3** a final judgment on a person or thing [c14: via Latin from Greek *epitaphion*, from *epitaphios* over a tomb, from EPI- + *taphos* tomb] > **epitaphic** (ˌɛpɪˈtæfɪk) *adj* > **ˈepiˌtaphist** *n*

epitaxy (ˈɛpɪˌtæksɪ) *or* **epitaxis** *n* the growth of a thin layer on the surface of a crystal so that the layer has the same structure as the underlying crystal > **epitaxial** (ˌɛpɪˈtæksɪəl) *adj*

epithalamium (ˌɛpɪθəˈleɪmɪəm) *or* **epithalamion** *n, pl* -mia (-mɪə) a poem or song written to celebrate a marriage; nuptial ode [c17: from Latin, from Greek *epithalamion* marriage song, from *thalamos* bridal chamber] > **epithalamic** (ˌɛpɪθəˈlæmɪk) *adj*

epithelium (ˌɛpɪˈθiːlɪəm) *n, pl* -liums *or* -lia (-lɪə) an animal tissue consisting of one or more layers of closely packed cells covering the external and internal surfaces of the body. The cells vary in structure according to their function, which may be protective, secretory, or absorptive [c18: New Latin, from EPI- + Greek *thēlē* nipple] > **ˌepiˈthelial** *adj*

epithet (ˈɛpɪˌθɛt) *n* a descriptive word or phrase added to or substituted for a person's name [c16: from Latin *epitheton*, from Greek, from *epitithenai* to add, from *tithenai* to put] > **ˌepiˈthetic** *or* **ˌepiˈthetical** *adj*

epitome (ɪˈpɪtəmɪ) *n* **1** a typical example of a characteristic or class; embodiment; personification **2** a summary of a written work; abstract [c16: via Latin from Greek *epitomē*, from *epitemnein* to abridge, from EPI- + *temnein* to cut] > **epitomical** (ˌɛpɪˈtɒmɪkəl) *or* **ˌepiˈtomic** *adj*

epitomize *or* **epitomise** (ɪˈpɪtəˌmaɪz) *vb* (*tr*) **1** to be a personification of; typify **2** to make an epitome of

epizootic (ˌɛpɪzəʊˈɒtɪk) *adj* **1** (of a disease) suddenly and temporarily affecting a large number of animals over a large area ▷ *n* **2** an epizootic disease

EPNS *abbreviation* electroplated nickel silver

epoch (ˈiːpɒk) *n* **1** a point in time beginning a new or distinctive period **2** a long period of time marked by some predominant or typical characteristic; era **3** *astronomy* a precise date to which information, such as coordinates, relating to a celestial body is referred **4** *geology* a unit of geological time within a period during which a series of rocks is formed [c17: from New Latin *epocha*, from Greek *epokhē* cessation; related to *ekhein* to hold, have] > **epochal** (ˈɛpˌɒkəl) *adj*

epode (ˈɛpəʊd) *n Greek prosody* **1** the part of a lyric ode that follows the strophe and the antistrophe **2** a type of lyric poem composed of couplets in which a long line is followed by a shorter one, invented by Archilochus [c16: via Latin from Greek *epōidos* a singing after, from *epaidein* to sing after, from *aidein* to sing]

eponym (ˈɛpənɪm) *n* **1** a name, esp a place name, derived from the name of a real or mythical person, as for example *Constantinople* from *Constantine I* **2** the name of the person from which such a name is derived [c19: from Greek *epōnumos* giving a significant name] > **eˈponymy** *n*

eponymous (ɪˈpɒnɪməs) *adj* **1** (of a person) being the person after whom a literary work, film, etc, is named: *the eponymous heroine in the film of Jane Eyre* **2** (of a literary work, film, etc) named after its central character or creator: *the Stooges' eponymous debut album* > **eˈponymously** *adv*

EPOS (ˈiːpɒs) *n acronym* electronic point of sale

epoxide (ɪˈpɒksaɪd) *n* **a** a compound containing an oxygen atom joined to two different groups that are themselves joined to other groups **b** (*as modifier*): *epoxide resin* [c20: from EPI- + OXIDE]

epoxy (ɪˈpɒksɪ) *adj chem* **1** of, consisting of, or containing an oxygen atom joined to two different groups that are themselves joined to other groups: *epoxy group* **2** of, relating to, or consisting of an epoxy resin ▷ *n, pl* epoxies **3** short for **epoxy resin** [c20: from EPI- + OXY-²]

epoxy resin *or* **epoxide resin** *n* any of various tough resistant thermosetting synthetic resins containing epoxy groups: used in surface coatings, laminates, and adhesives

Epping (ˈɛpɪŋ) *n* a town in E England, in Essex, on the edge of Epping Forest: a residential centre for London. Pop: 9889 (2001)

Epping Forest (ˈɛpɪŋ) *n* a forest in E England, northeast of London: formerly a royal hunting ground

eps *abbreviation* earnings per share

epsilon (ˈɛpsɪˌlɒn, ɛpˈsaɪlən) *n* the fifth letter of the Greek alphabet (Ε, ε), a short vowel, transliterated as *e* [Greek *e psilon*, literally: simple *e*]

Epsom (ˈɛpsəm) *n* a town in SE England, in Surrey: famous for its mineral springs and for horse racing. Pop (with Ewell): 64 492 (2001)

Epsom salts *n* (*functioning as singular or plural*) a medicinal preparation of hydrated magnesium sulphate, used as a purgative [c18: named after EPSOM, where they occur naturally in the water]

Epstein (ˈɛpstaɪn) *n* Sir **Jacob**. 1880–1959, British sculptor, born in the US of Russo-Polish parents

EQ *abbreviation* **1** emotional quotient, a (notional) measure of a person's adequacy in such areas as self-awareness, empathy, and dealing sensitively with other people [late C20: by analogy with IQ] **2** equalization, the electronic balancing of sound frequencies on audio recording equipment or hi-fi to reduce distortion or achieve a specific effect

equable (ˈɛkwəbʰl) *adj* **1** even-tempered; placid **2** unvarying; uniform: *an equable climate* [c17: from Latin *aequābilis*, from *aequāre* to make equal] > **ˌequaˈbility** *or* **ˈequableness** *n*

equal (ˈiːkwəl) *adj* **1** (often foll by *to* or *with*) identical in size, quantity, degree, intensity, etc; the same (as) **2** having identical privileges, rights, status, etc **3** having uniform effect or application: *equal opportunities* **4** evenly balanced or proportioned **5** (usually foll by *to*) having the necessary or adequate strength, ability, means, etc (for) ▷ *n* **6** a person or thing equal to another, esp in merit, ability, etc ▷ *vb* equals, equalling, equalled *or US* equals, equaling, equaled **7** (*tr*) to be equal to; correspond to; match **8** (*intr*; usually foll by *out*) to become equal or level **9** (*tr*) to make, perform, or do something equal to [c14: from Latin *aequālis*, from *aequus* level, of obscure origin] > **ˈequally** *adv*

equalitarian (ɪˌkwɒlɪˈtɛərɪən) *adj, n* a less common word for **egalitarian** > **eˌqualiˈtarianism** *n*

equality (ɪˈkwɒlɪtɪ) *n, pl* -ties the state of being equal

equalization payment *or* **equalization grant** *n Canadian* a financial grant made by the federal government to a poorer province in order to facilitate a level of services equal to that of a richer province

equalize *or* **equalise** (ˈiːkwəˌlaɪz) *vb* **1** (*tr*) to make equal or uniform; regularize **2** (*intr*) (in sports) to reach the same score as one's opponent or opponents > **ˌequaliˈzation** *or* **ˌequaliˈsation** *n*

equal opportunity *n* **a** the offering of employment, pay, or promotion equally to all, without discrimination as to sex, race, colour, disability, etc **b** (*as modifier*): *our equal-opportunity policy; an equal-opportunities employer*

equal sign *or* **equals sign** *n* the symbol =, used to indicate a mathematical equality

equanimity (ˌiːkwəˈnɪmɪtɪ, ˌɛkwə-) *n* calmness of mind or temper; composure [c17: from Latin *aequanimitās*, from *aequus* even, EQUAL + *animus* mind, spirit] > **equanimous** (ɪˈkwænɪməs) *adj*

equate (ɪˈkweɪt) *vb* (*mainly tr*) **1** to make or regard as equivalent or similar, esp in order to compare or balance **2** *maths* to indicate the equality of; form an equation from **3** (*intr*) to be equal; correspond [c15: from Latin *aequāre* to make EQUAL] > **eˌquataˈbility** *n*

equation (ɪˈkweɪʒən, -ʃən) *n* **1** a mathematical statement that two expressions are equal: it is either an **identity** in which the variables can assume any value, or a **conditional equation** in which the variables have only certain values (roots) **2** the act of regarding as equal; equating **3** the state of being equal, equivalent, or equally balanced **4** a situation or problem in which a number of factors need to be considered **5** See **chemical equation** > **eˈquational** *adj* > **eˈquationally** *adv*

equator (ɪˈkweɪtə) *n* **1** the great circle of the earth with a latitude of 0°, lying equidistant from the poles; dividing the N and S hemispheres **2** a circle dividing a sphere or other surface into two equal symmetrical parts **3** *astronomy* See **celestial equator** [c14: from Medieval

Latin (*circulus*) *aequātor* (*diei et noctis*) (circle) that equalizes (the day and night), from Latin *aequāre* to make EQUAL]

equatorial (ˌɛkwəˈtɔːrɪəl) *adj* **1** of, like, or existing at or near the equator **2** *astronautics* (of a telescope) mounted on the perpendicular axes, one of which is parallel to the earth's axis: *an equatorial orbit* **3** *astronomy* of or referring to the celestial equator ▷ *n* **4** an equatorial mounting for a telescope

Equatorial Guinea *n* a republic of W Africa, consisting of Río Muni on the mainland and the island of Bioko in the Gulf of Guinea, with four smaller islands: ceded by Portugal to Spain in 1778; gained independence in 1968. Official languages: Spanish and French. Religion: Roman Catholic majority. Currency: franc. Capital: Malabo. Pop: 507 000 (2004 est). Area: 28 049 sq km (10 830 sq miles). Former name (until 1964): Spanish Guinea

equerry (ˈɛkwərɪ; *at the British court* ɪˈkwɛrɪ) *n, pl* -ries **1** an officer attendant upon the British sovereign **2** (formerly) an officer in a royal household responsible for the horses [c16: alteration (through influence of Latin *equus* horse) of earlier *escuirie*, from Old French: stable, group of squires, from *escuyer* SQUIRE]

equestrian (ɪˈkwɛstrɪən) *adj* **1** of or relating to horses and riding **2** on horseback; mounted **3** of, relating to, or composed of knights, esp the imperial free knights of the Holy Roman Empire ▷ *n* **4** a person skilled in riding and horsemanship [c17: from Latin *equestris*, from *eques* horseman, knight, from *equus* horse] > eˈquestrianˌism *n*

equi- *combining form* equal or equally: *equidistant; equilateral*

equiangular (ˌiːkwɪˈæŋɡjʊlə) *adj* having all angles equal

equidistant (ˌiːkwɪˈdɪstənt) *adj* distant by equal amounts from two or more places > ˌequiˈdistance *n* > ˌequiˈdistantly *adv*

equilateral (ˌiːkwɪˈlætərəl) *adj* **1** having all sides of equal length ▷ *n* **2** a geometric figure having all its sides of equal length **3** a side that is equal in length to other sides

equilibrant (ɪˈkwɪlɪbrənt) *n* a force capable of balancing another force and producing equilibrium

equilibrate (ˌiːkwɪˈlaɪbreɪt, ɪˈkwɪlɪˌbreɪt) *vb* to bring to or be in equilibrium; balance [c17: from Late Latin *aequilībrāre*, from *aequilībris* in balance; see EQUILIBRIUM] > equilibration (ˌiːkwɪlaɪˈbreɪʃən, ɪˌkwɪlɪ-) *n*

equilibrist (ɪˈkwɪlɪbrɪst) *n* a person who performs balancing feats, esp on a high wire > eˌquiliˈbristic *adj*

equilibrium (ˌiːkwɪˈlɪbrɪəm) *n, pl* -riums *or* -ria (-rɪə) **1** a stable condition in which forces cancel one another **2** a state or feeling of mental balance; composure **3** any unchanging condition or state of a body, system, etc, resulting from the balance or cancelling out of the influences or processes to which it is subjected. See **thermodynamic equilibrium 4** *physics* a state of rest or uniform motion in which there is no resultant force on a body **5** *physiol* a state of bodily balance, maintained primarily by special receptors in the inner ear [c17: from Latin *aequilibrium*, from *aequi-* EQUI- + *lībra* pound, balance]

equine (ˈɛkwaɪn) *adj* of, relating to, or resembling a horse [c18: from Latin *equīnus*, from *equus* horse]

equinoctial (ˌiːkwɪˈnɒkʃəl) *adj* **1** relating to or occurring at either or both equinoxes **2** *astronomy* of or relating to the celestial equator ▷ *n* **3** a storm or gale at or near an equinox **4** another name for **celestial equator** [c14: from Latin *aequinoctiālis* concerning the EQUINOX]

equinoctial circle *or* **equinoctial line** *n* another name for **celestial equator**

equinoctial point *n* either of the two points at which the celestial equator intersects the ecliptic

equinox (ˈiːkwɪˌnɒks, ˈɛkwɪˌnɒks) *n* **1** either of the two occasions, six months apart, when day and night are of equal length. In the N hemisphere the **vernal equinox** occurs around March 21 (Sept 23 in the S hemisphere). The autumnal equinox occurs around Sept 23 in the N hemisphere (March 21 in the S hemisphere) **2** another name for **equinoctial point** [c14: from Medieval Latin *equinoxium*, changed from Latin *aequinoctium*, from *aequi-* EQUI- + *nox* night]

equip (ɪˈkwɪp) *vb* **equips, equipping, equipped** (*tr*) **1** to furnish with (necessary supplies, etc) **2** (*usually passive*) to

provide with abilities, understanding, etc **3** to dress out; attire [c16: from Old French *eschiper* to embark, fit out (a ship), of Germanic origin; compare Old Norse *skipa* to put in order, *skip* SHIP] > eˈquipper *n*

equipage (ˈɛkwɪpɪdʒ) *n* **1** a horse-drawn carriage, esp one elegantly equipped and attended by liveried footmen **2** (formerly) the stores and equipment of a military unit **3** *archaic* a set of useful articles

equipment (ɪˈkwɪpmənt) *n* **1** an act or instance of equipping **2** the items so provided **3** a set of tools, devices, kit, etc, assembled for a specific purpose, such as a soldier's kit and weapons

equipoise (ˈɛkwɪˌpɔɪz) *n* **1** even balance of weight or other forces; equilibrium **2** a counterbalance; counterpoise ▷ *vb* **3** (*tr*) to offset or balance in weight or force; balance

equipollent (ˌiːkwɪˈpɒlənt) *adj* **1** equal or equivalent in significance, power, or effect ▷ *n* **2** something that is equipollent [c15: from Latin *aequipollēns* of equal importance, from EQUI- + *pollēre* to be able, be strong] > ˌequiˈpollence *or* ˌequiˈpollency *n*

equisetum (ˌɛkwɪˈsiːtəm) *n, pl* -tums *or* -ta (-tə) any tracheophyte plant of the genus *Equisetum*, which comprises the horsetails [c19: New Latin, changed from Latin *equisaetum*, from *equus* horse + *saeta* bristle]

equitable (ˈɛkwɪtəbəl) *adj* **1** impartial or reasonable; fair; just **2** *law* relating to or valid in equity, as distinct from common law or statute law [c17: from French *équitable*, from *équité* EQUITY] > ˈequitableness *n*

equitation (ˌɛkwɪˈteɪʃən) *n* the study and practice of riding and horsemanship [c16: from Latin *equitātiō*, from *equitāre* to ride, from *equus* horse]

equities (ˈɛkwɪtɪz) *pl n* another name for **ordinary shares**

equity (ˈɛkwɪtɪ) *n, pl* -ties **1** the quality of being impartial or reasonable; fairness **2** an impartial or fair act, decision, etc **3** *law* a system of jurisprudence founded on principles of natural justice and fair conduct. It supplements the common law and mitigates its inflexibility, as by providing a remedy where none exists at law **4** *law* an equitable right or claim **5** the interest of ordinary shareholders in a company **6** the market value of a debtor's property in excess of all debts to which it is liable [c14: from Old French *equite*, from Latin *aequitās*, from *aequus* level, EQUAL]

Equity (ˈɛkwɪtɪ) *n* the actors' trade union

equity capital *n* the part of the share capital of a company owned by ordinary shareholders or in certain circumstances by other classes of shareholder

equity-linked policy *n* an insurance or assurance policy in which premiums are invested partially or wholly in ordinary shares for the eventual benefit of the beneficiaries of the policy

equity weighting *n* the practice of assigning different values to currencies according to factors such as geographical location and climate

equivalence (ɪˈkwɪvələns) *or* **equivalency** *n* **1** the state of being equivalent or interchangeable **2** *maths, logic* **a** the relationship between two statements, each of which implies the other **b** Also called: **biconditional** the binary truth-function that takes the value *true* when both component sentences are true or when both are false, corresponding to English *if and only if*. Symbol: ≡ or ↔, as in $-(p \wedge q) \equiv -p \vee -q$

equivalent (ɪˈkwɪvələnt) *adj* **1** equal or interchangeable in value, quantity, significance, etc **2** having the same or a similar effect or meaning **3** *maths, logic* (of two propositions) having an equivalence between them ▷ *n* **4** something that is equivalent [c15: from Late Latin *aequivalēns*, from *aequivalēre* to be equally significant, from Latin *aequi-* EQUI- + *valēre* to be worth] > eˈquivalently *adv*

equivocal (ɪˈkwɪvəkəl) *adj* **1** capable of varying interpretations; ambiguous **2** deliberately misleading or vague; evasive **3** of doubtful character or sincerity; dubious [c17: from Late Latin *aequivocus*, from Latin EQUI- + *vōx* voice] > eˌquivoˈcality *or* eˈquivocalness *n*

equivocate (ɪˈkwɪvəˌkeɪt) *vb* (*intr*) to use vague or ambiguous language, esp in order to avoid speaking directly or honestly; hedge [c15: from Medieval Latin *aequivocāre*, from Late Latin *aequivocus* ambiguous,

EQUIVOCAL] > e'quivo,catingly *adv* > e'quivo,cator *n*
> e'quivocatory *adj* > e,quivo'cation *n*

er (ə, ɜː) *interj* a sound made when hesitating in speech

Er *the chemical symbol for* erbium

ER *abbreviation* **1** (in the US) Emergency Room (in hospitals) **2** Elizabeth Regina [Latin: Queen Elizabeth] **3** Eduardus Rex [Latin: King Edward]

-er¹ *suffix forming nouns* **1** a person or thing that performs a specified action: *reader; decanter; lighter* **2** a person engaged in a profession, occupation, etc: *writer; baker; bootlegger* **3** a native or inhabitant of: *islander; Londoner; villager* **4** a person or thing having a certain characteristic: *newcomer; double-decker; fiver* [Old English *-ere*; related to German *-er*, Latin *-ārius*]

-er² *suffix* forming the comparative degree of adjectives (*deeper, freer, sunnier*, etc) and adverbs (*faster, slower*, etc) [Old English *-rd, -re* (adj), *-or* (adv)]

era ('ɪərə) *n* **1** a period of time considered as being of a distinctive character; epoch **2** an extended period of time the years of which are numbered from a fixed point or event: *the Christian era* **3** a point in time, esp one beginning a new or distinctive period **4** *geology* a major division of geological time, divided into several periods [c17: from Latin *aera* counters, plural of *aes* brass, pieces of brass money]

ERA ('iːrə) *n abbreviation or acronym* **1** (in Britain) Education Reform Act: the 1988 act which established the key elements of the National Curriculum **2** (in the US) Equal Rights Amendment: a proposed amendment to the US Constitution enshrining equality between the sexes

eradicate (ɪ'rædɪ,keɪt) *vb* (*tr*) **1** to obliterate; stamp out **2** to pull or tear up by the roots [c16: from Latin *ērādīcāre* to uproot, from EX-¹ + *rādīx* root] > e'radicable *adj* > e,radi'cation *n* > e'radicative *adj*

erase (ɪ'reɪz) *vb* **1** to obliterate or rub out (something written, typed, etc) **2** (*tr*) to destroy all traces of; remove completely **3** to remove (a recording) from (magnetic tape) [c17: from Latin *ērādere* to scrape off, from EX-¹ + *rādere* to scratch, scrape] > e'rasable *adj*

eraser (ɪ'reɪzə) *n* an object, such as a piece of rubber or felt, used for erasing something written, typed, etc

Erasmus (ɪ'ræzməs) *n* **Desiderius** (,dɛzɪ'dɪərɪəs), real name *Gerhard Gerhards*. ?1466–1536, Dutch humanist, the leading scholar of the Renaissance in northern Europe. He published the first Greek edition of the New Testament in 1516; his other works include the satirical *Encomium Moriae* (1509); *Colloquia* (1519), a series of dialogues; and an attack on the theology of Luther, *De Libero Arbitrio* (1524)

erasure (ɪ'reɪʒə) *n* **1** the act or an instance of erasing **2** the place or mark, as on a piece of paper, where something has been erased

Erato ('ɛrə,təʊ) *n Greek myth* the Muse of love poetry

Eratosthenes (,ɛrə'tɒsθɪ,niːz) *n* ?276–?194 BC, Greek mathematician and astronomer, who calculated the circumference of the earth by observing the angle of the sun's rays at different places

Erbil, Irbil ('ɜːbɪl) *or* **Arbil** *n* a city in N Iraq: important in Assyrian times. Pop: 870 000 (2005 est). Ancient name: Arbela

erbium ('ɜːbɪəm) *n* a soft malleable silvery-white element of the lanthanide series of metals: used in special alloys, room-temperature lasers, and as a pigment. Symbol: Er; atomic no: 68; atomic wt: 167.26; valency: 3; relative density: 9.006; melting pt: 1529°C; boiling pt: 2868°C [c19: from New Latin, from (Ytt)*erb*(y), Sweden, where it was first found + -IUM]

Erciyas Daği (Turkish 'ɛrdʒijas daː'i) *n* an extinct volcano in central Turkey. Height 3916 m (12 848 ft)

ERDF *abbreviation* European Regional Development Fund: a fund to provide money for specific projects for work on the infrastructure in countries of the European Union

ere (ɛə) *conj, prep* a poetic word for **before** [Old English *ǣr*; related to Old Norse *ār* early, Gothic *airis* earlier, Old High German *ēr* earlier, Greek *ēri* early]

Erebus¹ ('ɛrɪbəs) *n Greek myth* **1** the god of darkness, son of Chaos and brother of Night **2** the darkness below the earth, thought to be the abode of the dead or the region they pass through on their way to Hades

Erebus² ('ɛrɪbəs) *n* Mount Erebus a volcano in Antarctica, on Ross Island: discovered by Sir James Ross in 1841 and named after his ship. Height: 3794 m (12 448 ft)

Erechtheum (ɪ'rɛkθɪəm, ,ɛrək'θiːəm) *or* **Erechtheion** (ɪ'rɛkθɪən, ,ɛrək'θiːən) *n* a temple on the Acropolis at Athens, which has a porch of caryatids

Erechtheus (ɛ'rɛkθjuːs, -θɪəs) *n Greek myth* a king of Athens who sacrificed one of his daughters because the oracle at Delphi said this was the only way to win the war against the Eleusinians

erect (ɪ'rɛkt) *adj* **1** upright in posture or position; not bent or leaning **2** *physiol* (of the penis, clitoris, or nipples) firm or rigid after swelling with blood, esp as a result of sexual excitement **3** (of plant parts) growing vertically or at right angles to the parts from which they arise ▷ *vb* (*mainly tr*) **4** to put up; construct; build **5** to raise to an upright position; lift up **6** to found or form; set up **7** (*also intr*) *physiol* to become or cause to become firm or rigid by filling with blood **8** to hold up as an ideal; exalt **9** to draw or construct (a line, figure, etc) on a given line or figure, esp at right angles to it [c14: from Latin *ērigere* to set up, from *regere* to control, govern] > e'rectable *adj* > e'rectness *n* > e'rector *or* e'recter *n*

erectile (ɪ'rɛktaɪl) *adj* **1** *physiol* (of tissues or organs, such as the penis or clitoris) capable of becoming rigid or erect as the result of being filled with blood **2** capable of being erected > erectility (ɪrɛk'tɪlɪtɪ, ,iːrɛk-) *n*

erection (ɪ'rɛkʃən) *n* **1** the act of erecting or the state of being erected **2** something that has been erected; a building or construction **3** *physiol* the enlarged state or condition of erectile tissues or organs, esp the penis, when filled with blood **4** an erect penis

E region *or* **E layer** *n* a region of the ionosphere, extending from a height of 90 to about 150 kilometres. It reflects radio waves of medium wavelength

eremite ('ɛrɪ,maɪt) *n* a Christian hermit or recluse [c13: see HERMIT] > eremitic (,ɛrɪ'mɪtɪk) *or* ,ere'mitical *adj* > eremitism ('ɛrɪmaɪ,tɪzəm) *n*

Erenburg ('ɛrənbɜːg, *Russian* erɪn'burk) *n* a variant spelling of (Ilya Grigorievich) **Ehrenburg**

erepsin (ɪ'rɛpsɪn) *n* a mixture of proteolytic enzymes secreted by the small intestine [c20: *er-*, from Latin *ēripere* to snatch (from *rapere* to seize) + (P)EPSIN]

erethism ('ɛrɪ,θɪzəm) *n* **1** *physiol* an abnormally high degree of irritability or sensitivity in any part of the body **2** *psychiatry* **a** a personality disorder resulting from mercury poisoning **b** an abnormal tendency to become aroused quickly, esp sexually, as the result of a verbal or psychic stimulus [c18: from French *éréthisme*, from Greek *erethismos* irritation, from *erethizein* to excite, irritate]

Eretria (ɪ'rɛtrɪə) *n* an ancient city in Greece, on the S coast of Euboea: founded as an Ionian colony; destroyed by the Persians in 490 BC following which it never regained its former significance

Erevan (*Russian* jɪrɪ'van) *n* a variant spelling of **Yerevan**

erf (ɜːf) *n, pl* **erven** (ɜːvən) *South African* a plot of land, usually urban, marked off for building purposes [Afrikaans]

Erf (ɜːf) *n acronym for* electrorheological fluid: a man-made liquid that thickens or solidifies when an electric current passes through it and returns to a liquid when the current ceases

Erfurt (*German* 'ɛrfurt) *n* an industrial city in central Germany, the capital of Thuringia: university (1392). Pop: 201 645 (2003 est)

erg¹ (ɜːg) *n* the cgs unit of work or energy. 1 erg is equivalent to 10⁻⁷ joule [c19: from Greek *ergon* work]

erg² (ɜːg) *n, pl* **ergs** *or* **areg** an area of shifting sand dunes in a desert, esp the Sahara [c19: from Arabic *'irj*]

ergo ('ɜːgəʊ) *sentence connector* therefore; hence [c14: from Latin: therefore]

ergonomic (,ɜːgə'nɒmɪk) *adj* **1** of or relating to ergonomics **2** designed to minimize physical effort and discomfort, and hence maximize efficiency

ergonomics (,ɜːgə'nɒmɪks) *n* (*functioning as singular*) the study of the relationship between workers and their environment, esp the equipment they use [c20: from Greek *ergon* work + (ECO)NOMICS] > **ergonomist**

(ɜːˈɡɒnəmɪst) *n*

ergosterol (ɜːˈɡɒstəˌrɒl) *n* a plant sterol that is converted into vitamin D by the action of ultraviolet radiation. Formula: $C_{28}H_{43}OH$

ergot (ˈɜːɡət, -ɡɒt) *n* **1** a disease of cereals and other grasses caused by ascomycete fungi of the genus *Claviceps*, esp *C. purpurea*, in which the seeds or grain of the plants are replaced by the spore-containing bodies (sclerotia) of the fungus **2** any fungus causing this disease **3** the dried sclerotia of *C. purpurea*, used as the source of certain alkaloids used to treat haemorrhage, facilitate uterine contraction in childbirth, etc [c17: from French: spur (of a cock), of unknown origin]

ergotism (ˈɜːɡəˌtɪzəm) *n* ergot poisoning, producing either burning pains and eventually gangrene in the limbs or itching skin and convulsions

Erhard (*German* ˈeːrhart) *n* **Ludwig** (ˈluːtvɪç). 1897–1977, German statesman: chief architect of the *Wirtschaftswunder* ("economic miracle") of West Germany's recovery after World War II; chancellor (1963–66)

erica (ˈɛrɪkə) *n* any shrub of the ericaceous genus *Erica*, including the heaths and some heathers [c19: via Latin from Greek *ereikē* heath]

ericaceous (ˌɛrɪˈkeɪʃəs) *adj* of, relating to, or belonging to the Ericaceae, a family of trees and shrubs with typically bell-shaped flowers: includes heather, rhododendron, azalea, and arbutus [c19: from New Latin *Erīcāceae*, from Latin *erīca* heath, from Greek *ereikē*]

Eric XIV (ˈɛrɪk) *n* 1533–77, king of Sweden (1560–68). His attempts to dominate the Baltic led to war with Denmark (1563–70); deposed and imprisoned

Ericson *or* **Ericsson** (ˈɛrɪksᵊn) *n* **Leif** (liːf). 10th–11th centuries AD, Norse navigator, who discovered Vinland (?1000), variously identified as the coast of New England, Labrador, or Newfoundland; son of Eric the Red

Eric the Red (ˈɛrɪk) *n* ?940–?1010 AD, Norse navigator: discovered and colonized Greenland; father of Leif Ericson

Erie (ˈɪərɪ) *n* **1 Lake Erie** a lake between the US and Canada: the southernmost and the shallowest of the Great Lakes; empties by the Niagara River into Lake Ontario. Area: 25 718 sq km (9930 sq miles) **2** a port in NW Pennsylvania, on Lake Erie. Pop: 101 373 (2003 est)

Erie Canal *n* a canal in New York State between Albany and Buffalo, linking the Hudson River with Lake Erie. Length: 579 km (360 miles)

Erigena (ˌɛrɪˈdʒiːnə) *n* **John Scotus**. ?800–?877 AD, Irish Neo-Platonist philosopher

erigeron (ɪˈrɪdʒərən, -ˈrɪɡ-) *n* any plant of the genus *Erigeron*, whose flowers resemble asters but have narrower rays: family *Asteraceae* (composites) [c17: via Latin from Greek, from *ēri* early + *gerōn* old man; from the white down characteristic of some species]

Eriksson (ˈɛrɪksən) *n* **Sven-Goran** (ˈsfɛnˈɡɜːrən). born 1948, Swedish football manager; head coach of the England team (2001–06)

Erin (ˈɪərɪn, ˈɛərɪn) *n* an archaic or poetic name for **Ireland¹** [from Irish Gaelic *Éirinn*, dative of *Ériu* Ireland]

Erinyes (ɪˈrɪnɪˌiːz) *pl n, sing* **Erinys** (ɪˈrɪnɪs, ɪˈraɪ-) *myth* another name for the **Furies**

Eris¹ (ˈɛrɪs) *n* *Greek myth* the goddess of discord, sister of Ares

Eris² (ˈɛrɪs) *n* the largest dwarf planet in the solar system, located beyond the Kuiper belt. It has a diameter of 2400 km

Eritrea (ˌɛrɪˈtreɪə) *n* a small country in NE Africa, on the Red Sea: became an Italian colony in 1890; federated with Ethiopia (1952–93); an independence movement was engaged in war with the Ethiopian government from 1961 until independence was gained in 1993; consists of hot and arid coastal lowlands, rising to the foothills of the Ethiopian highlands. Languages: Tigrinya, Arabic, English, Afar, and others. Religions: Muslim and Christian. Currency: nakfa. Capital: Asmara. Pop: 4 296 000 (2004 est). Area: 117 400 sq km (45 300 sq miles)

Eritrean (ˌɛrɪˈtreɪən) *adj* **1** of or relating to Eritrea or its inhabitants ▷ *n* **2** a native or inhabitant of Eritrea

Erivan (*Russian* jɪrɪˈvan) *n* a variant spelling of **Yerevan**

erk (ɜːk) *n* *Brit slang* an aircraftman or naval rating [c20: perhaps a corruption of *AC* (aircraftman)]

Erlangen (*German* ˈɛrlaŋən) *n* a town in central Germany, in Bavaria: university (1743). Pop: 102 449 (2003 est)

Erlanger (ˈɜːlæŋə) *n* **Joseph**. 1874–1965, US physiologist. He shared a Nobel prize for physiology or medicine (1944) with Gasser for their work on the electrical signs of nervous activity

ERM *abbreviation* Exchange Rate Mechanism

Ermanaric (əˈmænərɪk) *n* died ?375 AD, king of the Ostrogoths: ruled an extensive empire in eastern Europe, which was overrun by the Huns in the 370s

ermine (ˈɜːmɪn) *n, pl* **-mines** *or* **-mine** **1** the stoat in northern regions, where it has a white winter coat with a black-tipped tail **2** the fur of this animal **3** the dignity or office of a judge, noble, or king [c12: from Old French *hermine*, from Medieval Latin *Armenius* (*mūs*) Armenian (mouse)]

Ermoupoli (ɛrˈmupɔli) *n* the modern Greek name for **Hermoupolis**

erne *or* **ern** (ɜːn) *n* another name for the (European) **sea eagle** [Old English *earn;* related to Old Norse *örn* eagle, Old High German *aro* eagle, Greek *ornis* bird]

Erne (ɜːn) *n* a river in N central Republic of Ireland, rising in County Cavan and flowing north across the border, through **Upper Lough Erne** and **Lower Lough Erne** and then west to Donegal Bay. Length: about 96 km (60 miles)

Ernie (ˈɜːnɪ) *n* (in Britain) a machine that randomly selects winning numbers of Premium Bonds [c20: acronym of Electronic Random Number Indicator Equipment]

Ernst (*German* ɛrnst) *n* **Max** (maks). 1891–1976, German painter, resident in France and the US, a prominent exponent of Dada and surrealism: developed the technique of collage

erode (ɪˈrəʊd) *vb* **1** to grind or wear down or away or become ground or worn down or away **2** to deteriorate or cause to deteriorate [c17: from Latin *ērōdere*, from EX-¹ + *rōdere* to gnaw] > e'rodible *adj*

erogenous (ɪˈrɒdʒɪnəs) *or* **erogenic** (ˌɛrəˈdʒɛnɪk) *adj* **1** sensitive to sexual stimulation **2** arousing sexual desire or giving sexual pleasure [c19: from Greek *erōs* love, desire + -GENOUS] > erogeneity (ˌɛrədʒɪˈniːɪtɪ) *n*

Eros (ˈɪərɒs, ˈɛrɒs) *n* *Greek myth* the god of love, son of Aphrodite. Roman counterpart: Cupid [Greek: desire, sexual love]

erosion (ɪˈrəʊʒən) *n* **1** the wearing away of rocks and other deposits on the earth's surface by the action of water, ice, wind, etc **2** the act or process of eroding or the state of being eroded > e'rosive *or* e'rosional *adj*

erotic (ɪˈrɒtɪk) *adj* Also: erotical **1** of, concerning, or arousing sexual desire or giving sexual pleasure **2** marked by strong sexual desire or being especially sensitive to sexual stimulation [c17: from Greek *erōtikos* of love, from *erōs* love] > e'rotically *adv*

erotica (ɪˈrɒtɪkə) *pl n* explicitly sexual literature or art [c19: from Greek *erōtika*, neuter plural of *erōtikos* EROTIC]

eroticism (ɪˈrɒtɪˌsɪzəm) *or* **erotism** (ˈɛrəˌtɪzəm) *n* **1** erotic quality or nature **2** the use of sexually arousing or pleasing symbolism in literature or art **3** sexual excitement or desire

erotogenic (ɪˌrɒtəˈdʒɛnɪk) *adj* originating from or causing sexual stimulation; erogenous

err (ɜː) *vb* (*intr*) **1** to make a mistake; be incorrect **2** to stray from the right course or accepted standards; sin **3** to act with bias, esp favourable bias: *to err on the side of justice* [c14: *erren* to wander, stray, from Old French *errer*, from Latin *errāre*] > 'errancy *n*

errand (ˈɛrənd) *n* **1** a short trip undertaken to perform a necessary task or commission (esp in the phrase **run errands**) **2** the purpose or object of such a trip [Old English *ærende*; related to *ār* messenger, Old Norse *erendi* message, Old High German *ārunti*, Swedish *ärende*]

errant (ˈɛrənt) *adj* (*often postpositive*) **1** archaic or literary wandering in search of adventure **2** erring or straying from the right course or accepted standards [c14: from

Old French: journeying, from Vulgar Latin *iterāre* (unattested), from Latin *iter* journey; influenced by Latin *errāre* to ERR] > **'errantly** *adv* > **'errantry** *n*

erratic (ɪ'rætɪk) *adj* **1** irregular in performance, behaviour, or attitude; inconsistent and unpredictable **2** having no fixed or regular course; wandering ▷ *n* **3** a piece of rock that differs in composition, shape, etc, from the rock surrounding it, having been transported from its place of origin, esp by glacial action [C14: from Latin *errāticus*, from *errāre* to wander, ERR] > **er'ratically** *adv*

erratum (ɪ'rɑːtəm) *n, pl* **-ta** (-tə) **1** an error in writing or printing **2** another name for **corrigendum** [C16: from Latin: mistake, from *errāre* to ERR]

Er Rif (ɛə rɪf) *n* a mountainous region of N Morocco, near the Mediterranean coast

erroneous (ɪ'rəʊnɪəs) *adj* based on or containing error; mistaken; incorrect [C14: (in the sense: deviating from what is right), from Latin *errōneus*, from *errāre* to wander] > **er'roneousness** *n*

error ('ɛrə) *n* **1** a mistake or inaccuracy, as in action or speech **2** an incorrect belief or wrong judgment **3** the condition of deviating from accuracy or correctness, as in belief, action, or speech **4** deviation from a moral standard; wrongdoing **5** *maths, statistics* a measure of the difference between some quantity and an approximation to or estimate of it, often expressed as a percentage [C13: from Latin, from *errāre* to ERR] > **'error-free** *adj*

ersatz ('ɛəzæts, 'ɜː-) *adj* **1** made in imitation of some natural or genuine product; artificial ▷ *n* **2** an ersatz substance or article [C20: German, from *ersetzen* to substitute]

Erse (ɜːs) *n* **1** another name for Irish **Gaelic** ▷ *adj* **2** of or relating to the Irish Gaelic language [C14: from Lowland Scots *Erisch* Irish; Irish being regarded as the literary form of Gaelic]

Ershad ('ɜːʃæd) *n* **Hussain Mohammed.** born 1930, Bangladeshi soldier and statesman. He seized power in a coup in 1982, becoming president in 1983. He was deposed in 1990

Erskine ('ɜːskɪn) *n* **Thomas,** 1st Baron. 1750–1823, Scottish lawyer; noted as a defence advocate, esp in cases involving civil liberties

erst (ɜːst) *adv archaic* **1** long ago; formerly **2** at first [Old English *ǣrest* earliest, superlative of *ǣr* early; see ERE; related to Old High German *ērist*, Dutch *eerst*]

erstwhile ('ɜːst,waɪl) *adj* **1** former; one-time ▷ *adv* **2** *archaic* long ago; formerly

Erté (ɛrte) *n* real name *Romain de Tirtoff.* 1892–1990, French fashion illustrator and designer, born in Russia, noted for his extravagant costumes and tableaux for the Folies-Bergère in Paris

eruct (ɪ'rʌkt) *or* **eructate** *vb* **1** to raise (gas and often a small quantity of acid) from the stomach; belch **2** (of a volcano) to pour out (fumes or volcanic matter) [C17: from Latin *ēructāre*, from *ructāre* to belch] > **eructation** (ɪ,rʌk'teɪʃən, ,iːrʌk-) *n*

erudite ('ɛrʊ,daɪt) *adj* having or showing extensive scholarship; learned [C15: from Latin *ērudītus*, from *ērudīre* to polish, from EX-¹ + *rudis* unpolished, rough] > **erudition** (,ɛrʊ'dɪʃən) *or* **'eru,diteness** *n*

erupt (ɪ'rʌpt) *vb* **1** to eject (steam, water, and volcanic material such as lava and ash) violently or (of volcanic material, etc) to be so ejected **2** (*intr*) (of a skin blemish) to appear on the skin; break out **3** (*intr*) (of a tooth) to emerge through the gum and become visible during the normal process of tooth development **4** (*intr*) to burst forth suddenly and violently, as from restraint [C17: from Latin *ēruptus* having burst forth, from *ērumpere*, from *rumpere* to burst] > **e'ruption** *n*

eruptive (ɪ'rʌptɪv) e'ruptive *adj* **1** erupting or tending to erupt **2** resembling or of the nature of an eruption **3** (of rocks) formed from such products as ash and lava resulting from volcanic eruptions **4** (of a disease) characterized by skin eruptions

-ery *or* **-ry** *suffix forming nouns* **1** indicating a place of business or some other activity: *bakery; brewery; refinery* **2** indicating a class or collection of things: *cutlery; greenery*

3 indicating qualities or actions collectively: *snobbery; trickery* **4** indicating a practice or occupation: *husbandry* **5** indicating a state or condition: *slavery* [from Old French *-erie*; see -ER¹, -Y³]

Erymanthus (,ɛrɪ'mænθəs) *n* Mount Erymanthus a mountain in SW Greece, in the NW Peloponnese. Height: 2224 m (7297 ft)

erysipelas (,ɛrɪ'sɪpɪləs) *n* an acute streptococcal infectious disease of the skin, characterized by fever, headache, vomiting, and purplish raised lesions, esp on the face [C16: from Latin, from Greek *erusipelas*, from Greek *erusi-* red + *-pelas* skin]

erythro- *or* **erythr-** *combining form* red: *erythrocyte* [from Greek *eruthros* red]

erythrocyte (ɪ'rɪθrəʊ,saɪt) *n* a blood cell of vertebrates that transports oxygen and carbon dioxide, combined with the red pigment haemoglobin, to and from the tissues > **erythrocytic** (ɪ,rɪθrəʊ'sɪtɪk) *adj*

erythromycin (ɪ,rɪθrəʊ'maɪsɪn) *n* an antibiotic used in treating certain infections, sometimes used as an alternative to penicillin. It is obtained from the bacterium *Streptomyces erythreus.* Formula: $C_{37}M_{67}NO_{13}$ [C20: from ERYTHRO- + Greek *mukēs* fungus + -IN]

erythropoiesis (ɪ,rɪθrəʊpɔɪ'iːsɪs) *n physiol* the formation of red blood cells [C19: from ERYTHRO- + Greek *poiēsis* a making, from *poiein* to make] > **e,rythropoi'etic** *adj*

Erzgebirge (German 'eːrtsgəbɪrgə) *pl n* a mountain range on the border between Germany and the Czech Republic: formerly rich in mineral resources. Highest peak: Mount Klínovec (Keilberg), 1244 m (4081 ft)

Erzurum ('ɛəzʊrʊm) *n* a city in E Turkey: a strategic centre; scene of two major battles against Russian forces (1877 and 1916); important military base. Pop: 436 000 (2005 est)

Es *the chemical symbol for* einsteinium

-es *suffix* **1** for nouns ending in *ch, s, sh, z,* postconsonantal *y,* for some nouns ending in a vowel, and nouns in *f* with *v* in the plural, a variant of **-s¹** *ashes; heroes; calves* **2** for verbs ending in *ch, s, sh, z,* postconsonantal *y,* or a vowel, a variant of **-s¹** *preaches; steadies; echoes*

Esau ('iːsɔː) *n Bible* son of Isaac and Rebecca and twin brother of Jacob, to whom he sold his birthright (Genesis 25)

Esbjerg (Danish 'ɛsbjɛr) *n* a port in SW Denmark, in Jutland on the North Sea: Denmark's chief fishing port. Pop: 72 550 (2004 est)

escabeche (,ɛskə'bɛtʃɪ) *n* (in Mexican cookery) pickled vegetables such as onions, carrots, jalapeño peppers, and garlic, typically served with fish [Spanish: pickled]

escadrille (,ɛskə'drɪl; *French* ɛskadrij) *n* a French squadron of aircraft, esp in World War I [from French: flotilla, from Spanish *escuadrilla*, from *escuadra* SQUADRON]

escalade (,ɛskə'leɪd) *n* **1** an assault by the use of ladders, esp on a fortification ▷ *vb* **2** to gain access to (a place) by the use of ladders [C16: from French, from Italian *scalata*, from *scalare* to mount, SCALE³]

escalate ('ɛskə,leɪt) *vb* to increase or be increased in extent, intensity, or magnitude [C20: back formation from ESCALATOR] , **,esca'lation** *n*

escalator ('ɛskə,leɪtə) *n* **1** a moving staircase consisting of stair treads fixed to a conveyor belt, for transporting passengers between levels, esp between the floors of a building **2** short for **escalator clause** [C20: originally a trademark]

escalator clause *n* a clause in a contract stipulating an adjustment in wages, prices, etc, in the event of specified changes in conditions, such as a large rise in the cost of living or price of raw materials

escallop (ɛ'skɒləp, ɛ'skæl-) *n, vb* another word for **scallop**

escalope ('ɛskə,lɒp) *n* a thin slice of meat, usually veal, coated with egg and breadcrumbs, fried, and served with a rich sauce [C19: from Old French: shell]

escapade ('ɛskə,peɪd, ,ɛskə'peɪd) *n* **1** a wild or exciting adventure, esp one that is mischievous or unlawful; scrape **2** any lighthearted or carefree episode; prank; romp [C17: from French, from Old Italian *scappata*, from Vulgar Latin *ex-cappāre* (unattested) to ESCAPE]

escape (ɪ'skeɪp) *vb* **1** to get away or break free from (confinements, captors, etc) **2** to manage to avoid (imminent danger, punishment, evil, etc) **3** (*intr*; usually foll by *from*) (of gases, liquids, etc) to issue gradually, as from a crack or fissure; seep; leak **4** (*tr*) to elude; be forgotten by: *the actual figure escapes me* **5** (*tr*) to be articulated inadvertently or involuntarily: *a roar escaped his lips* ▷ *n* **6** the act of escaping or state of having escaped **7** avoidance of injury, harm, etc **8 a** a means or way of escape **b** (*as modifier*): *an escape route* **9** a means of distraction or relief, esp from reality or boredom **10** a gradual outflow; leakage; seepage **11** Also called: escape valve, escape cock a valve that releases air, steam, etc, above a certain pressure; relief valve or safety valve **12** a plant that was originally cultivated but is now growing wild [C14: from Old Northern French *escaper*, from Vulgar Latin *excappāre* (unattested) to escape (literally: to remove one's cloak, hence free oneself), from EX-¹ + Late Latin *cappa* cloak] > es'capable *adj* > es'caper *n*

escapee (ɪˌskeɪ'piː) *n* a person who has escaped, esp an escaped prisoner

escapement (ɪ'skeɪpmənt) *n* **1** *horology* a mechanism consisting of an escape wheel and anchor, used in timepieces to provide periodic impulses to the pendulum or balance **2** any similar mechanism that regulates movement, usually consisting of toothed wheels engaged by rocking levers **3** (in a piano) the mechanism that allows the hammer to clear the string after striking, so that the string can vibrate **4** *rare* an act or means of escaping

escape road *n* a road, usually ending in a pile of sand, provided on a hill for a driver to drive into if his brakes fail or on a bend if he loses control of the turn

escape velocity *n* the minimum velocity that a body must have in order to escape from the gravitational field of the earth or other celestial body

escapism (ɪ'skeɪpɪzəm) *n* an inclination to or habit of retreating from unpleasant or unacceptable reality, as through diversion or fantasy > es'capist *n, adj*

escapologist (ˌeskə'pɒlədʒɪst) *n* an entertainer who specializes in freeing himself or herself from confinement > ˌesca'pology *n*

escargot French (ɛskargo) *n* a variety of edible snail, usually eaten with a sauce made of melted butter and garlic

escarole ('eskərəʊl) *n* US & Canadian a variety of endive with broad leaves, used in salads [C20: French from Italian *scar(i)ola*, from Latin *esca* food]

escarpment (ɪ'skɑːpmənt) *n* **1** the long continuous steep face of a ridge or plateau formed by erosion; scarp **2** a steep artificial slope immediately in front of the rampart of a fortified place

Escaut (ɛsko) *n* the French name for the **Scheldt**

-escent *suffix forming adjectives* beginning to be, do, show, etc: *convalescent; luminescent* [via Old French from Latin *-ēscent-*, stem of present participial suffix of *-ēscere*, ending of inceptive verbs] > -escence *suffix forming nouns*

eschatology (ˌeskə'tɒlədʒɪ) *n* the branch of theology or biblical exegesis concerned with the end of the world [C19: from Greek *eskhatos* last] > eschatological (ˌeskətə'lɒdʒɪk°l) *adj* > ˌescha'tologist *n*

escheat (ɪs'tʃiːt) *law* ▷ *n* **1** (in England before 1926) the reversion of property to the Crown in the absence of legal heirs **2** (in feudal times) the reversion of property to the feudal lord in the absence of legal heirs or upon outlawry of the tenant **3** the property so reverting ▷ *vb* **4** to take (land) by escheat or (of land) to revert by escheat [C14: from Old French *escheter*, from *escheoir* to fall to the lot of, from Late Latin *excadere* (unattested), from Latin *cadere* to fall] > es'cheatable *adj* > es'cheatage *n*

Escherichia (ˌeʃə'rɪkɪə) *n* a genus of Gram-negative rodlike bacteria that are found in the intestines of humans and many animals, esp *E. coli*, which is sometimes pathogenic and is widely used in genetic research [C19: named after Theodor *Escherich* (1857–1911), German paediatrician who first described *E. coli*]

eschew (ɪs'tʃuː) *vb* (*tr*) to keep clear of or abstain from (something disliked, injurious, etc); shun; avoid [C14: from Old French *eschiver*, of Germanic origin; compare Old High German *skiuhan* to frighten away; see SHY¹,

SKEW] > es'chewal *n* > es'chewer *n*

eschscholtzia *or* **eschscholzia** (ɛ'ʃɒltsɪə) *n* See **California poppy** [named after J. F. von *Eschscholtz* (1743–1831), German naturalist]

Escoffier (French ɛskɔfje) *n* (**Georges**) **Auguste** (ogyst). 1846–1935, French chef at the Savoy Hotel, London (1890–99)

Escorial (ˌeskɒrɪ'ɑːl, ɛ'skɔːrɪəl) *or* **Escurial** *n* a village in central Spain, northwest of Madrid: site of an architectural complex containing a monastery, palace, and college, built by Philip II between 1563 and 1584

escort *n* ('eskɔːt) **1** one or more persons, soldiers, vehicles, etc, accompanying another or others for protection, guidance, restraint, or as a mark of honour **2** a man or youth who accompanies a woman or girl ▷ *vb* (ɪs'kɔːt) **3** (*tr*) to accompany or attend as an escort [C16: from French *escorte*, from Italian *scorta*, from *scorgere* to guide, from Latin *corrigere* to straighten; see CORRECT]

escritoire (ˌeskrɪ'twɑː) *n* a writing desk with compartments and drawers, concealed by a hinged flap, on a chest of drawers or plain stand [C18: from French, from Medieval Latin *scriptōrium* writing room in a monastery, from Latin *scrībere* to write]

escrow ('eskrəʊ, ɛ'skrəʊ) *law* ▷ *n* **1** money, goods, or a written document, such as a contract bond, delivered to a third party and held by him pending fulfilment of some condition **2** the state or condition of being an escrow (esp in the phrase **in escrow**) ▷ *vb* (*tr*) **3** to place (money, a document, etc) in escrow [C16: from Old French *escroe*, of Germanic origin; see SCREED, SHRED, SCROLL]

escudo (ɛ'skuːdəʊ; Portuguese ɪʃ'kuðu) *n, pl* **-dos** (-dəʊz; Portuguese -ðuʃ) **1** the standard monetary unit of Cape Verde, divided into 100 centavos **2** the former standard monetary unit of Portugal, divided into 100 centavos; replaced by the euro in 2002 **3** a former monetary unit of Chile, divided into 100 centesimos **4** an old Spanish silver coin worth 10 reals [C19: Spanish, literally: shield, from Latin *scūtum*]

esculent ('eskjʊlənt) *n* **1** any edible substance ▷ *adj* **2** edible [C17: from Latin *ēsculentus* good to eat, from *ēsca* food, from *edere* to eat]

Escurial (ɛ,skjʊərɪ'ɑːl, ɛ'skjʊərɪəl) *n* a variant of **Escorial**

escutcheon (ɪ'skʌtʃən) *n* **1** a shield, esp a heraldic one that displays a coat of arms **2** Also called: escutcheon plate a plate or shield that surrounds a keyhole, door handle, light switch, etc, esp an ornamental one protecting a door or wall surface **3** the place on the stern or transom of a vessel where the name is shown **4** blot on one's escutcheon a stain on one's honour [C15: from Old Northern French *escuchon*, ultimately from Latin *scūtum* shield] > es'cutcheoned *adj*

Esdraelon (ˌesdreɪ'iːlɒn) *n* a plain in N Israel, east of Mount Carmel. Also called: Plain of Jezreel

ESE *symbol for* east-southeast

-ese *suffix forming adjectives, suffix forming nouns* indicating place of origin, language, or style: *Cantonese; Japanese; journalese*

Esenin (jɛ'senɪn) *or* **Yesenin** *n* **Sergey Aleksandrovich**. 1895–1925, Soviet poet, author of *Confessions of a Hooligan* (1924): married to Isadora Duncan

Eşfahān (ˌeʃfə'hɑːn) *n* a variant of **Isfahan**

Esher ('iːʃə) *n* a town in SE England, in NE Surrey near London: racecourse. Pop: 25 172 (2001)

esker ('eskə) *or* **eskar** ('eskɑː, -kə) *n* a long winding ridge of gravel, sand, etc, originally deposited by a meltwater stream running under a glacier [C19: from Old Irish *escir* ridge]

Eskilstuna (Swedish 'eskilstuːna) *n* an industrial city in SE Sweden. Pop: 91 137 (2004 est)

Eskimo ('eskɪˌməʊ) *n* **1** *pl* **-mos** *or* **-mo** a member of a group of peoples inhabiting N Canada, Greenland, Alaska, and E Siberia, having a material culture adapted to an extremely cold climate **2** the language of these peoples **3** a family of languages that includes Eskimo and Aleut ▷ *adj* **4** relating to, denoting, or characteristic of the Eskimos ▷ See also **Inuit, Inuktitut** [C18 from Algonquian *Esquimawes*]

● USAGE *Eskimo* is considered by many to be offensive,

● and in North America the term *Inuit* is usually
● preferred. *Inuit*, however, can be accurately applied
● only to those Aboriginal peoples inhabiting parts of
● Northern Canada, Alaska, and Greenland (as
● distinguished from those in Asia or the Aleutian
● Islands)

Eskimo dog *n* a large powerful breed of sled dog with a long thick coat and curled tail

Eskişehir (*Turkish* ɛsˈkiʃɛˌhir) *n* an industrial city in NW Turkey: founded around hot springs in Byzantine times. Pop: 519 000 (2005 est)

Esky (ˈɛskɪ) *n*, *pl* -kies (*sometimes not capital*) *Austral trademark* a portable insulated container for keeping food and drink cool [C20: from ESKIMO]

ESN *abbreviation* educationally subnormal; formerly used to designate a person of limited intelligence who needs special schooling

esophagus (iːˈsɒfəgəs) *n*, *pl* -gi (-ˌdʒaɪ) *or* -guses the US spelling of **oesophagus**

esoteric (ˌɛsəʊˈtɛrɪk) *adj* **1** restricted to or intended for an enlightened or initiated minority, esp because of abstruseness or obscurity **2** difficult to understand; abstruse **3** not openly admitted; private [C17: from Greek *esōterikos*, from *esōterō* inner] > ˌeso'terically *adv* > ˌeso'tericism *n*

esp *abbreviation* especially

ESP *abbreviation* **1** extrasensory perception **2** electronic stability programme: an electronic system that automatically stabilizes a road vehicle that is being oversteered or is in danger of rolling over by selectively applying individual brakes

espadrille (ˌɛspəˈdrɪl) *n* a light shoe with a canvas upper, esp with a braided cord sole [C19: from French, from Provençal *espardilho*, diminutive of *espart* ESPARTO; so called from the use of esparto for the soles of such shoes]

espalier (ɪˈspæljə) *n* **1** an ornamental shrub or fruit tree that has been trained to grow flat, as against a wall **2** the trellis, framework, or arrangement of stakes on which such plants are trained ▷ *vb* **3** (*tr*) to train (a plant) on an espalier [C17: from French: trellis, from Old Italian: shoulder supports, from *spalla* shoulder, from Late Latin SPATULA]

España (esˈpaɲa) *n* the Spanish name for **Spain**

esparto *or* **esparto grass** (ɛˈspɑːtəʊ) *n*, *pl* -tos any of various grasses, esp *Stipa tenacissima* of S Europe and N Africa, that yield a fibre used to make ropes, mats, etc [C18: from Spanish, via Latin from Greek *sparton* rope made of rushes, from *spartos* a kind of rush]

especial (ɪˈspɛʃəl) *adj* (*prenominal*) **1** unusual; notable; exceptional **2** applying to one person or thing in particular; not general; specific; peculiar: *he had an especial dislike of relatives* [C14: from Old French, from Latin *speciālis* individual; see SPECIAL]

especially (ɪˈspɛʃəlɪ) *adv* **1** in particular; specifically: *for everyone's sake, especially your children's* **2** very much: *especially useful for vegans*

Esperanto (ˌɛspəˈræntəʊ) *n* an international artificial language based on words common to the chief European languages, invented in 1887 [C19: literally: the one who hopes, pseudonym of Dr. L. L. Zamenhof (1859–1917), Polish philologist who invented it] > ˌEspeˈrantist *n*, *adj*

espial (ɪˈspaɪəl) *n* *archaic* **1** the act or fact of being seen or discovered **2** the act of noticing **3** the act of spying upon; secret observation

espionage (ˈɛspɪəˌnɑːʒ, ˌɛspɪəˈnɑːʒ, ˈɛspɪənɪdʒ) *n* **1** the systematic use of spies to obtain secret information, esp by governments to discover military or political secrets **2** the act or practice of spying [C18: from French *espionnage*, from *espionner* to spy, from *espion* spy, from Old Italian *spione*, of Germanic origin; compare German *spähen* to SPY]

Espírito Santo (*Portuguese* iʃˈpiritu ˈsɐntu) *n* a state of E Brazil, on the Atlantic: swampy coastal plain with mountains in the west; heavily forested. Capital: Vitória. Pop: 3 201 722 (2002). Area: 45 597 sq km (17 601 sq miles)

Espíritu Santo (esˈpɪrɪtu: ˈsæntəʊ) *n* an island in the SW

Pacific: the largest and westernmost of the Vanuatu islands. Area: 4856 sq km (1875 sq miles)

esplanade (ˌɛspləˈneɪd, -ˈnɑːd) *n* **1** a long open level stretch of ground for walking along, esp beside the seashore. See **promenade** (sense 1) **2** an open area in front of a fortified place, in which attackers are exposed to the defenders' fire [C17: from French, from Old Italian *spianata*, from *spianare* to make level, from Latin *explānāre*; see EXPLAIN]

Espoo (*Finnish* ˈespo:) *n* a city in S Finland. Pop: 224 231 (2003 est)

espousal (ɪˈspaʊzᵊl) *n* **1** adoption or support: *an espousal of new beliefs* **2** (*sometimes plural*) *archaic* a marriage or betrothal ceremony

espouse (ɪˈspaʊz) *vb* (*tr*) **1** to adopt or give support to (a cause, ideal, etc): *to espouse socialism* **2** *archaic* (esp of a man) to take as spouse; marry [C15: from Old French *espouser*, from Latin *spōnsāre* to affiance, espouse] > es'pouser *n*

espressivo (ˌɛsprɛˈsiːvəʊ) *adj*, *adv* *music* (to be performed) in an expressive manner [Italian]

espresso (ɛˈsprɛsəʊ) *n*, *pl* -sos **1** strong coffee made by forcing steam or boiling water through ground coffee beans **2** an apparatus for making coffee in this way [C20: Italian, short for *caffè espresso*, literally: pressed coffee]

esprit (ɛˈspriː) *n* spirit and liveliness, esp in wit [C16: from French, from Latin *spīritus* a breathing, SPIRIT¹]

esprit de corps (ɛˈspriː də ˈkɔː; *French* ɛspri də kɔr) *n* consciousness of and pride in belonging to a particular group; the sense of shared purpose and fellowship

espy (ɪˈspaɪ) *vb* -pies, -pying, -pied (*tr*) to catch sight of or perceive (something distant or previously unnoticed); detect [C14: from Old French *espier* to SPY, of Germanic origin] > es'pier *n*

Esq. *abbreviation* esquire: used esp in correspondence

-esque *suffix forming adjectives* indicating a specified character, manner, style, or resemblance: *picturesque*; *Romanesque*; *statuesque*; *Chaplinesque* [via French from Italian *-esco*, of Germanic origin; compare -ISH]

Esquiline (ˈɛskwəˌlaɪn) *n* one of the seven hills on which ancient Rome was built

Esquimau (ˈɛskɪˌməʊ) *n*, *pl* -maus *or* -mau **1** a former spelling of **Eskimo** ▷ *adj* **2** a former spelling of **Eskimo**

esquire (ɪˈskwaɪə) *n* **1** *chiefly Brit* a title of respect, usually abbreviated *Esq*, placed after a man's name **2** (in medieval times) the attendant and shield bearer of a knight, subsequently often knighted himself [C15: from Old French *escuier*, from Late Latin *scūtārius* shield bearer, from Latin *scūtum* shield]

ESRC *abbreviation* Economic and Social Research Council

ESRO (ˈɛzrəʊ) *n acronym for* European Space Research Organization

-ess *suffix forming nouns* indicating a female: *waitress; lioness* [via Old French from Late Latin *-issa*, from Greek]

● USAGE The suffix *-ess* in such words as *poetess, authoress*
● is now almost invariably regarded as disparaging or
● extremely old-fashioned; a gender-neutral term *poet*,
● *author* is preferred

Essaouira (ˌɛsəˈwɪərə) *n* a port in SW Morocco on the Atlantic. Pop: 84 000 (2003). Former name (until 1956): Mogador

essay *n* (ˈɛseɪ; *for senses* 2,3 *also* ɛˈseɪ) **1** a short literary composition dealing with a subject analytically or speculatively **2** an attempt or endeavour; effort **3** a test or trial ▷ *vb* (ɛˈseɪ) (*tr*) **4** to attempt or endeavour; try **5** to test or try out [C15: from Old French *essaier* to attempt, from *essai* an attempt, from Late Latin *exagium* a weighing, from Latin *agere* to do, compel, influenced by *exigere* to investigate]

essayist (ˈɛseɪɪst) *n* a person who writes essays

Essen (*German* ˈɛsən) *n* a city in W Germany, in North Rhine-Westphalia: the leading administrative centre of the Ruhr; university. Pop: 589 499 (2003 est)

essence (ˈɛsᵊns) *n* **1** the characteristic or intrinsic feature of a thing, which determines its identity; fundamental nature **2** a perfect or complete form of something, esp a person who typifies an abstract quality **3** *philosophy* the unchanging and unchangeable nature of something which is necessary to its being the thing it is; its necessary properties **4 a** the constituent of a plant, usually an oil, alkaloid, or glycoside, that determines its chemical or pharmacological properties **b** an alcoholic solution of such a substance **5** a substance, usually a liquid, containing the properties of a plant or foodstuff in concentrated form: *vanilla essence* **6** a rare word for **perfume 7 in essence** essentially; fundamentally **8 of the essence** indispensable; vitally important [c14: from Medieval Latin *essentia*, from Latin: the being (of something), from *esse* to be]

Essene (ˈɛsiːn, ɛˈsiːn) *n Judaism* a member of an ascetic sect that flourished in Palestine from the second century BC to the second century AD, living in strictly organized communities > **Essenian** (ɛˈsiːnɪən) *or* **Essenic** (ɛˈsɛnɪk) *adj*

essential (ɪˈsɛnʃəl) *adj* **1** vitally important; absolutely necessary **2** basic; fundamental **3** completely realized; absolute; perfect **4** *biochem* (of an amino acid or a fatty acid) necessary for the normal growth of an organism but not synthesized by the organism and therefore required in the diet **5** derived from or relating to an extract of a plant, drug, etc: *an essential oil* **6** *pathol* (of a disease) having no obvious external cause: *essential hypertension* ▷ *n* **7** something fundamental or indispensable > **essentiality** (ɪˌsɛnʃɪˈælɪtɪ) *or* **es'sentialness** *n*

essential element *n biochem* any chemical element required by an organism for healthy growth. It may be required in large amounts (macronutrient) or in very small amounts (trace element)

essential fatty acid *n biochem* any fatty acid required by the body in manufacturing prostaglandins, found in such foods as oily fish and nuts. Abbreviation: EFA

essentialism (ɪˈsɛnʃəˌlɪzəm) *n philosophy* one of a number of related doctrines which hold that there are necessary properties of things, that these are logically prior to the existence of the individuals which instantiate them, and that their classification depends upon their satisfaction of sets of necessary conditions > **es'sentialist** *n*

essentially (ɪˈsɛnʃəlɪ) *adv* in a fundamental or basic way; in essence

essential oil *n* any of various volatile organic oils present in plants, usually containing terpenes and esters and having the odour or flavour of the plant from which they are extracted: used in flavouring and perfumery

Essequibo (ˌɛsɪˈkwiːbəʊ) *n* a river in Guyana, rising near the Brazilian border and flowing north to the Atlantic: drains over half of Guyana. Length: 1014 km (630 miles)

Essex¹ (ˈɛsɪks) *n* **1** a county of SE England, on the North Sea and the Thames estuary; the geographical and ceremonial county includes Thurrock and Southend-on-Sea, which became independent unitary authorities in 1998. Administrative centre: Chelmsford. Pop (excluding unitary authorities): 1 324 100 (2003 est). Area (excluding unitary authorities): 3446 sq km (1310 sq miles) **2** an Anglo-Saxon kingdom that in the early 7th century AD comprised the modern county of Essex and much of Hertfordshire and Surrey. By the late 8th century, Essex had become a dependency of the kingdom of Mercia

Essex² (ˈɛsɪks) *n* **2nd Earl of,** title of *Robert Devereux.* ?1566–1601, English soldier and favourite of Queen Elizabeth I; executed for treason

Essex girl *n informal, derogatory* a young working-class woman from the Essex area, typically considered as being unintelligent, materialistic, devoid of taste, and sexually promiscuous

Essex Man *n informal, derogatory* a working man, typically a Londoner who has moved out to Essex, who flaunts his new-found success and status

Esslingen (ˈɛsˌlɪŋən) *n* a town in SW Germany, on the River Neckar: Gothic church, medieval buildings: wines, light industry. Pop: 91 980 (2003 est)

Essonne (*French* ɛsɔn) *n* a department of N France, south of Paris in Île-de-France region: formed in 1964. Capital: Évry. Pop: 1 153 434 (2003 est). Area: 1811 sq km (706 sq miles)

est *abbreviation* **1** Also: **estab** established **2** estimate(d)

EST *abbreviation* **1** Eastern Standard Time **2** electric-shock treatment

-est¹ *suffix* forming the superlative degree of adjectives and adverbs: *shortest; fastest* [Old English *-est, -ost*]

-est² *or* **-st** *suffix* forming the archaic second person singular present and past indicative tense of verbs: *thou goest; thou hadst* [Old English *-est, -ast*]

establish (ɪˈstæblɪʃ) *vb* (*usually tr*) **1** to make secure or permanent in a certain place, condition, job, etc **2** to create or set up (an organization, etc) on or as if on a permanent basis **3** to prove correct or free from doubt; validate: *to establish a fact* **4** to cause (a principle, theory, etc) to be widely or permanently accepted: *to establish a precedent* **5** to give (a Church) the status of a national institution **6** (of a person) to become recognized and accepted **7** (in works of imagination) to cause (a character, place, etc) to be credible and recognized [c14: from Old French *establir*, from Latin *stabilīre* to make firm, from *stabilis* STABLE²] > **es'tablisher** *n*

Established Church *n* a Church that is officially recognized as a national institution, esp the Church of England

establishment (ɪˈstæblɪʃmənt) *n* **1** the act of establishing or state of being established **2 a** a business organization or other large institution **b** the place where a business is carried on **3** the staff and equipment of a commercial or other organization **4** any large organization, institution, or system **5** a household or place of residence **6** a body of employees or servants **7** (*modifier*) belonging to or characteristic of the Establishment; orthodox or conservative

Establishment (ɪˈstæblɪʃmənt) *n* **the Establishment** a group or class of people having institutional authority within a society, esp those who control the civil service, the government, the armed forces, and the Church: usually identified with a conservative outlook

estate (ɪˈsteɪt) *n* **1** a large piece of landed property, esp in the country **2** *chiefly Brit* a large area of property development, esp of new houses or (**trading estate**) of factories **3** *property law* **a** a property or possessions **b** the nature of interest that a person has in land or other property, esp in relation to the right of others **c** the total extent of the real and personal property of a deceased person or bankrupt **4** Also called: **estate of the realm** an order or class of persons in a political community, regarded collectively as a part of the body politic: usually regarded as being the lords temporal (peers), lords spiritual, and commons. See also **fourth estate 5** state, period, or position in life, esp with regard to wealth or social standing: *youth's estate; a poor man's estate* [c13: from Old French *estat*, from Latin *status* condition, STATE]

estate agent *n* **1** *Brit* an agent concerned with the valuation, management, lease, and sale of property **2** the administrator of a large landed property, acting on behalf of its owner; estate manager

estate car *n Brit* a car with a comparatively long body containing a large carrying space, reached through a rear door: usually the back seats can be folded forward to increase the carrying space

estate duty *n* another name for **death duty**

Este (ˈɛste) *n* a noble family of Italy founded by Alberto Azzo II (996–1097), who was invested with the town of Este in NE Italy as a fief of the Holy Roman Empire. The family governed Ferrara (13th–16th centuries), Modena, and Reggio (13th–18th centuries)

esteem (ɪˈstiːm) *vb* (*tr*) **1** to have great respect or high regard for: *to esteem a colleague* **2** *formal* to judge or consider; deem: *to esteem an idea improper* ▷ *n* **3** high regard or respect; good opinion **4** *archaic* judgment; opinion [c15: from Old French *estimer*, from Latin *aestimāre* ESTIMATE] > **es'teemed** *adj*

ester (ˈɛstə) *n chem* any of a class of compounds produced by reaction between acids and alcohols with the elimination of water. Esters with low molecular weights, such as ethyl acetate, are usually volatile fragrant liquids; fats are solid esters [c19: from German, probably a contraction of *Essigäther* acetic ether, from *Essig* vinegar (ultimately from Latin *acētum*) + *Äther* ETHER]

Esterházy ('ɛstə,ha:zɪ) *n* a noble Hungarian family that produced many soldiers, diplomats, and patrons of the arts. Prince **Miklós József Esterházy** (1714–90) rebuilt the family castle of Esterháza and employed Haydn as his musical director (1766–90)

Esth. *abbreviation Bible* Esther

Esther ('ɛstə) *n Old Testament* **1** a beautiful Jewish woman who became queen of Persia and saved her people from massacre **2** the book in which this episode is recounted

esthesia (i:s'θi:zɪə) *n* a US spelling of **aesthesia**

esthete ('i:sθi:t) *n* a US spelling of **aesthete**

Esthonia (ɛ'stəʊnɪə, ɛ'sθəʊ-) *n* a former spelling of **Estonia**

Estienne *or* **Étienne** (*French* etjɛn) *n* a family of French printers, scholars, and dealers in books, including **Henri** (āri), ?1460–1520, who founded the printing business in Paris, his son **Robert** (rɔbɛr), 1503–59, and his grandson **Henri**, 1528–98

estimable ('ɛstɪməbəl) *adj* worthy of respect; deserving of admiration: *my estimable companion* > **'estimableness** *n* > **'estimably** *adv*

estimate *vb* ('ɛstɪˌmeɪt) **1** to form an approximate idea of (distance, size, cost, etc); calculate roughly; gauge **2** (*tr; may take a clause as object*) to form an opinion about; judge: *to estimate one's chances* **3** to submit (an approximate price) for (a job) to a prospective client **4** (*tr*) *statistics* to assign a value (a **point estimate**) or range of values (an **interval estimate**) to a parameter of a population on the basis of sampling statistics ▷ *n* ('ɛstɪmɪt) **5** an approximate calculation **6** a statement indicating the likely charge for or cost of certain work **7** a judgment; appraisal; opinion [c16: from Latin *aestimāre* to assess the worth of, of obscure origin] > **'estimative** *adj* > **'estiˌmator** *n*

estimation (ˌɛstɪ'meɪʃən) *n* **1** a considered opinion; judgment: *what is your estimation of the situation?* **2** esteem; respect **3** the act of estimating

estimator ('ɛstɪˌmeɪtə) 'estiˌmator *n* **1** a person or thing that estimates **2** *statistics* a derived random variable that generates estimates of a parameter of a given distribution, such as $\bar{X}$, the mean of a number of identically distributed random variables X_i. If $\bar{X}$ is unbiased, $\bar{x}$, the observed value should be close to $E(X_i)$. See also **sampling statistic**

estival (i:'staɪvəl, 'ɛstɪ-) *adj* the usual US spelling of **aestival**

estivate ('i:stɪˌveɪt, 'ɛs-) *vb* (*intr*) the usual US spelling of **aestivate** > **'estiˌvator** *n*

Estonia (ɛ'stəʊnɪə) *or* **Esthonia** (ɛ'stəʊnɪə, ɛ'sθəʊ-) *n* a republic in NE Europe, on the Gulf of Finland and the Baltic: low-lying with many lakes and forests, it includes numerous islands in the Baltic Sea. It was under Scandinavian and Teutonic rule from the 13th century to 1721, when it passed to Russia: it was an independent republic from 1920 to 1940, when it was annexed by the Soviet Union; became independent in 1991 and joined the EU in 2004. Official language: Estonian. Religion: believers are mostly Christian. Currency: kroon. Capital: Tallinn. Pop: 1 308 000 (2004 est). Area: 45 227 sq km (17 462 sq miles)

Estonian (ɛ'stəʊnɪən) *or* **Esthonian** (ɛ'stəʊnɪən, ɛ'sθəʊ-) *adj* **1** of, relating to, or characteristic of Estonia, its people, or their language ▷ *n* **2** the official language of Estonia: belongs to the Finno-Ugric family **3** a native or inhabitant of Estonia

estop (ɪ'stɒp) *vb* -tops, -topping, -topped (*tr*) **1** *law* to preclude by estoppel **2** *archaic* to stop [c15: from Old French *estoper* to plug, ultimately from Latin *stuppa* tow; see STOP] > **es'toppage** *n*

estoppel (ɪ'stɒpəl) *n law* a rule of evidence whereby a person is precluded from denying the truth of a statement of facts he has previously asserted [c16: from Old French *estoupail* plug, from *estoper* to stop up; see ESTOP]

Estoril ('ɛʃtɒːˌriːl) *n* a resort in W Portugal, near Lisbon, on the Atlantic Ocean: noted esp for a famous avenue of palm trees leading to the seafront. Pop: 23 769 (2001)

estovers (ɛ'stəʊvəz) *pl n law* a right allowed by law to tenants of land to cut timber, esp for fuel and repairs [c15: from Anglo-French, plural of *estover*, n use of Old French *estovoir* to be necessary, from Latin *est opus* there is need]

estradiol (ˌɛstrə'daɪɒl, ˌiːstrə-) *n* the US spelling of **oestradiol**

estrange (ɪ'streɪndʒ) *vb* (*tr*) **1** (*usually passive; often foll by from*) to separate and live apart from (one's spouse): *he is estranged from his wife* **2** (*usually passive; often foll by from*) to antagonize or lose the affection of (someone previously friendly); alienate [c15: from Old French *estranger*, from Late Latin *extrāneāre* to treat as a stranger, from Latin *extrāneus* foreign; see STRANGE] > **es'trangement** *n*

estranged (ɪ'streɪndʒd) *adj* **1** separated and living apart from one's spouse **2** no longer friendly; alienated

estrogen ('ɛstrədʒən, 'iːstrə-) *n* the usual US spelling of **oestrogen** > **estrogenic** (ˌɛstrə'dʒɛnɪk, ˌiːstrə-) *adj* > **ˌestro'genically** *adv*

estrus ('ɛstrəs, 'iːstrəs) *n* the usual US spelling of **oestrus** > **'estrous** *adj*

estuary ('ɛstjʊərɪ) *n*, *pl* -aries **1** the widening channel of a river where it nears the sea, with a mixing of fresh water and (tidal) water **2** an inlet of the sea [c16: from Latin *aestuārium* marsh, channel, from *aestus* tide, billowing movement, related to *aestās* summer] > **estuarial** (ˌɛstjʊ'ɛərɪəl) *adj* > **'estuaˌrine** *adj*

e.s.u. *or* **ESU** *abbreviation* electrostatic unit

E. Sussex *abbreviation* East Sussex

ET *abbreviation* Employment Training: a government scheme offering training in technological and business skills to unemployed people

-et *suffix of nouns* small or lesser: *islet; baronet* [from Old French *-et, -ete*]

eta ('iːtə) *n* the seventh letter in the Greek alphabet (Η, η), a long vowel sound, transliterated as *e* or *ē* [Greek, of Phoenician origin; compare Hebrew HETH]

ETA *abbreviation* estimated time of arrival

e-tail ('iːteɪl) *or* **e-tailing** ('iːteɪlɪŋ) *n* retail conducted via the internet [c20: E- + (RE)TAIL] > **'e-tailer** *n*

et al. *abbreviation* **1** et alibi [Latin: and elsewhere] **2** et alii [Latin: and others]

etalon ('ɛtəˌlɒn) *n physics* a device used in spectroscopy to measure wavelengths by interference effects produced by multiple reflections between parallel half-silvered glass or quartz plates [c20: French *étalon* a fixed standard of weights and measures, from Old French *estalon*; see also STALLION]

etc. *abbreviation* et cetera

et cetera *or* **etcetera** (ɪt'sɛtrə) **1** and the rest; and others; and so forth: used at the end of a list to indicate that other items of the same class or type should be considered or are implied **2** or the like; or something else similar [from Latin, from *et* and + *cetera* the other (things)]

● USAGE It is unnecessary to use *and* before *etc* as *etc* (*et* ● *cetera*) already means *and other things*. The repetition of ● *etc*, as in *he brought paper, ink, notebooks, etc, etc,* is avoided ● except in informal contexts

etceteras (ɪt'sɛtrəz) *pl n* miscellaneous extra things or persons

etch (ɛtʃ) *vb* **1** (*tr*) to wear away the surface of (a metal, glass, etc) by chemical action, esp the action of an acid **2** to cut or corrode (a design, decoration, etc) on (a metal or other plate to be used for printing) by using the action of acid on parts not covered by wax or other acid-resistant coating **3** (*tr*) to cut with or as if with a sharp implement: *he etched his name on the table* **4** (*tr; usually passive*) to imprint vividly: *the event was etched on her memory* [c17: from Dutch *etsen*, from Old High German *azzen* to feed, bite] > **'etcher** *n*

etching ('ɛtʃɪŋ) *n* **1** the art, act, or process of preparing etched surfaces or of printing designs from them **2** an etched plate **3** an impression made from an etched plate

ETD *abbreviation* estimated time of departure

Eteocles (ɪ'tiːəˌkliːz, 'ɛtɪə-) *n Greek myth* a son of Oedipus and Jocasta. He expelled his brother Polynices from Thebes; they killed each other in single combat when Polynices returned as leader of the Seven against Thebes

eternal (ɪˈtɜːnᵊl) *adj* **1 a** without beginning or end; lasting for ever: *eternal life* **b** (*as noun*): *the eternal* **2** (*often capital*) denoting or relating to that which is without beginning and end, regarded as an attribute of God **3** unchanged by time, esp being true or valid for all time; immutable: *eternal truths* **4** seemingly unceasing; occurring again and again: *eternal bickering* [C14: from Late Latin *aeternālis*, from Latin *aeternus*; related to Latin *aevum* age] > ˌeterˈnality *or* eˈternalness *n* > eˈternally *adv*

Eternal City *n* the Eternal City Rome

eternalize, eternalise (ɪˈtɜːnəˌlaɪz) *or* **eternize, eternise** (ɪˈtɜːnaɪz) *vb* (*tr*) **1** to make eternal **2** to make famous for ever; immortalize > ˌeternaliˈzation *or* eˌterniˈzation *or* eˌternaliˈsation *or* eˌterniˈsation *n*

eternal triangle *n* an emotional relationship in which there are conflicts involving a man and two women or a woman and two men

eternity (ɪˈtɜːnɪtɪ) *n, pl* **-ties 1** endless or infinite time **2** the quality, state, or condition of being eternal **3** (*usually plural*) any of the aspects of life and thought that are considered to be timeless, esp timeless and true **4** *theol* the condition of timeless existence, believed by some to characterize the afterlife **5** a seemingly endless period of time: *an eternity of waiting*

eternity ring *n* a ring given as a token of lasting affection, esp one set all around with stones to symbolize continuity

etesian (ɪˈtiːʒɪən) *adj* (of NW winds) recurring annually in the summer in the E Mediterranean [C17: from Latin *etēsius* yearly, from Greek *etēsios*, from *etos* year]

ETF *abbreviation* electronic transfer of funds

Eth. *abbreviation* Ethiopia(n)

-eth¹ *suffix* forming the archaic third person singular present indicative tense of verbs: *goeth; taketh* [Old English *-eth, -th*]

-eth² *or* **-th** *suffix forming ordinal numbers twentieth.* a variant of -th²

ethanal (ˈɛθəˌnæl, ˈiːθə-) *n* the modern name for **acetaldehyde**

ethane (ˈiːθeɪn, ˈɛθ-) *n* a colourless odourless flammable gaseous alkane obtained from natural gas and petroleum: used as a fuel and in the manufacture of organic chemicals. Formula: C_2H_6 [C19: from ETH(YL) + -ANE]

ethanediol (ˈiːθeɪnˌdaɪɒl, ˈɛθ-) *n* a clear colourless syrupy soluble liquid substance, used as an antifreeze and solvent. Formula: CH_2OHCH_2OH [C20: from ETHANE + DI-¹ + -OL¹]

ethanoic acid (ˌɛθəˈnəʊɪk, ˌiːθə-) *n* the modern name for **acetic acid**

ethanol (ˈɛθəˌnɒl, ˈiːθə-) *n* the technical name for **alcohol** (sense 1)

Ethelbert (ˈɛθəlˌbɜːt) *or* **Æthelbert** (ˈæθəlˌbɜːt) *n* **Saint.** ?552–616 AD, king of Kent (560–616): converted to Christianity by St Augustine; issued the earliest known code of English laws. Feast day: Feb 24 or 25

Ethelred I (ˈɛθəlˌrɛd) *or* **Æthelred I** (ˈæθəlˌrɛd) *n* died 871, king of Wessex (866–71). He led resistance to the Danish invasion of England; died following his victory at Ashdown

Ethelred II *or* **Æthelred II** *n* known as *Ethelred the Unready.* ?968–1016 AD, king of England (978–1016). He was temporarily deposed by the Danish king Sweyn (1013) but was recalled on Sweyn's death (1014)

Ethelwulf (ˈɛθəlˌwʊlf) *or* **Æthelwulf** (ˈæθəlˌwʊlf) *n* died 858 AD, king of Wessex (839–858)

ethene (ˈɛθiːn) *n* the technical name for **ethylene**

ether (ˈiːθə) *n* **1** Also called: **diethyl ether, ethyl ether, ethoxyethane** a colourless volatile highly flammable liquid with a characteristic sweetish odour, made by the reaction of sulphuric acid with ethanol: used as a solvent and anaesthetic. Formula: $C_2H_5OC_2H_5$ **2** any of a class of organic compounds with the general formula ROR′ where R and R′ are alkyl groups, as in diethyl ether $C_2H_5OC_2H_5$ **3** the ether the hypothetical medium formerly believed to fill all space and to support the propagation of electromagnetic waves **4** *Greek myth* the upper regions of the atmosphere; clear sky or heaven ▷ Also (for senses 3, 4): **aether** [C17: from Latin *aether*,

from Greek *aithēr*, from *aithein* to burn] > etheric (iːˈθɛrɪk) *adj*

ethereal (ɪˈθɪərɪəl) *adj* **1** extremely delicate or refined; exquisite **2** almost as light as air; impalpable; airy **3** celestial or spiritual **4** of, containing, or dissolved in an ether, esp diethyl ether: *an ethereal solution* **5** of or relating to the ether [C16: from Latin *aethereus*, from Greek *aitherios*, from *aithēr* ETHER] > eˌthereˈality *or* eˈtherealness *n*

etherealize *or* **etherealise** (ɪˈθɪərɪəˌlaɪz) *vb* (*tr*) **1** to make or regard as being ethereal **2** to add ether to or make into ether or something resembling ether > eˌtherealiˈzation *or* eˌtherealiˈsation *n*

Etherege (ˈɛθərɪdʒ) *n* Sir **George.** ?1635–?92, English Restoration dramatist; author of the comedies *The Comical Revenge* (1664), *She would if she could* (1668), and *The Man of Mode* (1676)

etherize *or* **etherise** (ˈiːθəˌraɪz) *vb* (*tr*) *obsolete* to subject (a person) to the anaesthetic influence of ether fumes; anaesthetize > ˌetheriˈzation *or* ˌetheriˈsation *n* > ˈetherˌizer *or* ˈetherˌiser *n*

Ethernet (ˈiːθəˌnɛt) *n trademark computing* a widely used type of local area network

ethic (ˈɛθɪk) *n* **1** a moral principle or set of moral values held by an individual or group: *the Puritan ethic* ▷ *adj* **2** another word for **ethical** [C15: from Latin *ēthicus*, from Greek *ēthikos*, from *ēthos* custom; see ETHOS]

ethical (ˈɛθɪkᵊl) *adj* **1** in accordance with principles of conduct that are considered correct, esp those of a given profession or group **2** of or relating to ethics **3** (of a medicinal agent) available legally only with a doctor's prescription or consent > ˈethically *adv* > ˈethicalness *or* ˌethiˈcality *n*

ethical investment *n* an investment in a company whose activities or products are not considered by the investor to be unethical

ethics (ˈɛθɪks) *n* **1** (*functioning as singular*) the philosophical study of the moral value of human conduct and of the rules and principles that ought to govern it; moral philosophy **2** (*functioning as plural*) a social, religious, or civil code of behaviour considered correct, esp that of a particular group, profession, or individual **3** (*functioning as plural*) the moral fitness of a decision, course of action, etc: *he doubted the ethics of their verdict* > ˈethicist *n*

Ethiopia (ˌiːθɪˈəʊpɪə) *n* a state in NE Africa, on the Red Sea: consolidated as an empire under Menelik II (1889–1913); federated with Eritrea from 1952 until 1993; Emperor Haile Selassie was deposed by the military in 1974 and the monarchy was abolished in 1975; an independence movement in Eritrea was engaged in war with the government from 1961 until 1993. It lies along the Great Rift Valley and consists of deserts in the southeast and northeast and a high central plateau with many rivers (including the Blue Nile) and mountains rising over 4500 m (15 000 ft); the main export is coffee. Language: Amharic. Religion: Christian majority. Currency: birr. Capital: Addis Ababa. Pop: 72 420 000 (2004 est). Area: 1 128 215 sq km (435 614 sq miles). Former name: **Abyssinia**

Ethiopian (ˌiːθɪˈəʊpɪən) *adj* **1** of, relating to, or characteristic of Ethiopia, its people, or any of their languages ▷ *n* **2** a native or inhabitant of Ethiopia **3** any of the languages of Ethiopia, esp Amharic ▷ *n, adj* **4** an archaic word for **Black¹**

Ethiopic (ˌiːθɪˈɒpɪk, -ˈəʊpɪk) *n* **1** the ancient language of Ethiopia, belonging to the Semitic subfamily of the Afro-Asiatic family: a Christian liturgical language **2** the group of languages developed from this language, including Amharic, Tigre, and Tigrinya ▷ *adj* **3** denoting or relating to this language or group of languages **4** a less common word for **Ethiopian**

ethnic (ˈɛθnɪk) *or* **ethnical** *adj* **1** relating to or characteristic of a human group having racial, religious, linguistic, and certain other traits in common **2** relating to the classification of mankind into groups, esp on the basis of racial characteristics **3** denoting or deriving from the cultural traditions of a group of people: *the ethnic dances of Slovakia* **4** characteristic of another culture: *the ethnic look; ethnic food* ▷ *n* **5** *chiefly US &*

Austral a member of an ethnic group, esp a minority group [C14 (in the senses: heathen, Gentile): from Late Latin *ethnicus*, from Greek *ethnikos*, from *ethnos* race] > 'ethnically *adv* > ethnicity (εθ'nɪsɪtɪ) *n*

ethnic cleansing *n euphemistic* the violent removal by one ethnic group of other ethnic groups from the population of a particular area: used esp of the activities of Serbs against Croats and Muslims in the former Yugoslavia

ethno- *combining form* indicating race, people, or culture: *ethnology* [via French from Greek *ethnos* race]

ethnocentrism (,εθnəʊ'sεn,trɪzəm) *n* belief in the intrinsic superiority of the nation, culture, or group to which one belongs, often accompanied by feelings of dislike for other groups > ,ethno'centric *adj* > ,ethno'centrically *adv* > ,ethnocen'tricity *n*

ethnography (εθ'nɒgrəfɪ) *n* the branch of anthropology that deals with the scientific description of individual human societies > eth'nographer *n* > ethnographic (,εθnəʊ'græfɪk) *or* ethno'graphical *adj* > ,ethno'graphically *adv*

ethnology (εθ'nɒlədʒɪ) *n* the branch of anthropology that deals with races and peoples, their relations to one another, their origins, and their distinctive characteristics > ethnologic (,εθnə'lɒdʒɪk) *or* ,ethno'logical *adj* > ,ethno'logically *adv* > eth'nologist *n*

ethnomusicology (,εθnəʊmjuː'zɪ'kɒlədʒɪ) *n* the study of the music of different cultures

ethology (ɪ'θɒlədʒɪ) *n* the study of the behaviour of animals in their normal environment [C17 (in the obsolete sense: mimicry): via Latin from Greek *ēthologia*, from *ēthos* character; current sense, C19] > ethological (,εθə'lɒdʒɪkəl) *adj* > ,etho'logically *adv* > e'thologist *n*

ethos ('iːθɒs) *n* the distinctive character, spirit, and attitudes of a people, culture, era, etc: *the revolutionary ethos* [C19: from Late Latin: habit, from Greek]

ethyl ('iːθaɪl, 'εθɪl) *n* (*modifier*) of, consisting of, or containing the monovalent group C_2H_5-: *ethyl group or radical* [C19: from ETH(ER) + -YL] > ethylic (ɪ'θɪlɪk) *adj*

ethyl acetate *n* a colourless volatile flammable fragrant liquid ester, made from acetic acid and ethanol: used in perfumes and flavourings and as a solvent for plastics, etc Formula: $CH_3COOC_2H_5$

ethyl alcohol *n* another name for **alcohol** (sense 1)

ethylene ('εθɪ,liːn) *n* a colourless flammable gaseous alkene with a sweet odour, obtained from petroleum and natural gas and used in the manufacture of polythene and many other chemicals. Formula: $CH_2{:}CH_2$. Also called: ethene > ethylenic (,εθɪ'liːnɪk) *adj*

ethylene glycol *n* another name for **ethanediol**

ethylene group *or* **ethylene radical** *n chem* the divalent group, -CH_2CH_2-, derived from ethylene

ethylene series *n chem* the homologous series of unsaturated hydrocarbons that contain one double bond and have the general formula, C_nH_{2n}; alkene series

ethyne ('εθaɪn, 'εθaɪn) *n* another name for **acetylene** [C20: from ETHYL + -INE²]

Étienne (French etjɛn) *n* a variant spelling of **Estienne**

etiolate ('iːtɪəʊ,leɪt) *vb* 1 *botany* to whiten (a green plant) through lack of sunlight 2 to become or cause to become pale and weak, as from malnutrition [C18: from French *étioler* to make pale, probably from Old French *estuble* straw, from Latin *stipula*] > ,etio'lation *n*

etiology (,iːtɪ'ɒlədʒɪ) *n, pl* -gies a variant spelling of **aetiology** (,iːtɪ'ɒlədʒɪkəl) *adj* > ,etio'logically *adv* > eti'ologist *n*

etiquette ('εtɪ,kεt, ,εtɪ'kεt) *n* 1 the customs or rules governing behaviour regarded as correct or acceptable in social or official life 2 a conventional but unwritten code of practice followed by members of any of certain professions or groups: *medical etiquette* [C18: from French, from Old French *estiquette* label, from *estiquier* to attach; see STICK²]

Etna ('εtnə) *n* **Mount Etna** an active volcano in E Sicily: the highest volcano in Europe and the highest peak in Italy south of the Alps. Height: 3323 m (10 902 ft)

Eton ('iːtᵊn) *n* 1 a town in S England, in Windsor and Maidenhead unitary authority, Berkshire, near the River Thames: site of **Eton College**, a public school for boys founded in 1440. Pop: 3821 (2001 est) 2 this college

Eton collar *n* a broad stiff white collar worn outside an Eton jacket

Eton crop *n* a short mannish hairstyle worn by women in the 1920s

Eton jacket *n* a waist-length jacket with a V-shaped back, open in front, formerly worn by pupils of Eton College

Etruria (ɪ'trʊərɪə) *n* 1 an ancient country of central Italy, between the Rivers Arno and Tiber, roughly corresponding to present-day Tuscany and part of Umbria 2 a factory established in Staffordshire by Josiah Wedgwood in 1769

Etruscan (ɪ'trʌskən) *or* **Etrurian** (ɪ'trʊərɪən) *n* 1 a member of an ancient people of central Italy whose civilization influenced the Romans, who had suppressed them by about 200 BC 2 the non-Indo-European language of the ancient Etruscans, whose few surviving records have not been fully interpreted ▷ *adj* 3 of, relating to, or characteristic of Etruria, the Etruscans, their culture, or their language

et seq. *abbreviation* 1 et sequens [Latin: and the following] 2 Also called: et seqq et sequentia [Latin: and those that follow]

-ette *suffix of nouns* 1 small: *cigarette; kitchenette* 2 female: *majorette; suffragette* 3 (esp in trade names) imitation: *Leatherette* [from French, feminine of -ET]

étude ('eɪtjuːd; *French* etyd) *n* a short musical composition for a solo instrument, esp one designed as an exercise or exploiting technical virtuosity [C19: from French: STUDY]

étui (ε'twiː) *n, pl* **étuis** a small usually ornamented case for holding needles, cosmetics, or other small articles [C17: from French, from Old French *estuier* to enclose; see TWEEZERS]

etymology (,εtɪ'mɒlədʒɪ) *n, pl* -gies 1 the study of the sources and development of words and morphemes 2 an account of the source and development of a word or morpheme [C14: via Latin from Greek *etumologia*; see ETYMON, -LOGY] > etymological (,εtɪmə'lɒdʒɪkəl) *adj* > ,etymo'logically *adv* > ,ety'mologist *n*

etymon ('εtɪ,mɒn) *n, pl* -mons *or* -ma (-mə) a form of a word or morpheme, usually the earliest recorded form or a reconstructed form, from which another word or morpheme is derived: *the etymon of English "ewe" is Indo-European "*owi"* [C16: via Latin, from Greek *etumon* basic meaning, from *etumos* true, actual]

e-type *n informal* a person who works in or is interested in electronics [C20: electronics]

Etzel ('εtsᵊl) *n German legend* a great king who, according to the *Nibelungenlied*, was the second husband of Kriemhild after the death of Siegfried: identified with Attila the Hun. See **Atli**

Eu *the chemical symbol for* europium

EU *abbreviation* European Union

eu- *combining form* well, pleasant, or good: *eupeptic; euphony* [via Latin from Greek, from *eus* good]

Euboea (juː'bɪə) *n* an island in the W Aegean Sea: the largest island after Crete of the Greek archipelago; linked with the mainland by a bridge across the Euripus channel. Capital: Chalcis. Pop: 198 130 (2001). Area: 3908 sq km (1509 sq miles). Modern Greek name: Éwoia. Former English name: Negropont

Euboean (juː'bɪən) *adj* 1 of or relating to the Greek island of Euboea ▷ *n* 2 a native or inhabitant of Euboea

eucalyptus (,juːkə'lɪptəs) *or* **eucalypt** ('juːkə,lɪpt) *n, pl* -lyptuses *or* -lypti (-'lɪptaɪ) *or* -lypts any myrtaceous tree of the mostly Australian genus *Eucalyptus*, such as the blue gum and ironbark, widely cultivated for the medicinal oil in their leaves (**eucalyptus oil**), timber, and ornament [C19: New Latin, from EU- + Greek *kaluptos* covered, from *kaluptein* to cover, hide]

Eucharist ('juːkərɪst) *n* 1 the Christian sacrament in which Christ's Last Supper is commemorated by the consecration of bread and wine 2 the consecrated elements of bread and wine offered in the sacrament 3 Mass, esp when regarded as the service where the sacrament of the Eucharist is administered [C14: via Church Latin from Greek *eukharistia*, from *eukharistos* thankful, from EU- + *kharizesthai* to show favour, from *kharis* favour] > ˌEucha'ristic *or* ˌEucha'ristical *adj* > ˌEucha'ristically *adv*

euchre ('juːkə) *n* **1** a US and Canadian card game similar to écarté for two to four players, using a poker pack with joker **2** an instance of euchring another player, preventing him from making his contracted tricks ▷ *vb* (*tr*) **3** to prevent (a player) from making his contracted tricks **4** (usually foll by *out*) *US, Canadian, Austral & NZ informal* to outwit or cheat **5** *Austral & NZ informal* to ruin or exhaust [C19: of unknown origin]

Eucken (*German* 'ɔykən) *n* **Rudolph Christoph** ('ruːdɔlf 'krɪstɔf). 1846–1926, German idealist philosopher: Nobel prize for literature 1908

Euclid ('juːklɪd) *n* **1** 3rd century BC, Greek mathematician of Alexandria; author of *Elements*, which sets out the principles of geometry and remained a text until the 19th century at least **2** the works of Euclid, esp his system of geometry > **Euclidean** *or* **Euclidian** (juːˈklɪdɪən) *adj*

eucryphia (juːˈkrɪfɪə) *n* any tree or shrub of the mostly evergreen genus *Eucryphia*, native to Australia and S America, having leaves of a dark lustrous green and white flowers: family *Eucryphiaceae* [from Greek *eu* well + *kryphios* hidden, from *kryptein* to hide, referring to the sepals being joined at the top]

eudemonia *or* **eudaemonia** (ˌjuːdɪˈməʊnɪə) *n* happiness, esp that resulting from a rational active life [C17: from Greek *eudaimōnia*]

eudiometer (ˌjuːdɪˈɒmɪtə) *n* a graduated glass tube used in the study and volumetric analysis of gas reactions [C18: from Greek *eudios*, literally: clear skied (from EU- + *Dios*, genitive of *Zeus* god of the heavens) + -METER] > **eudiometric** (ˌjuːdɪəˈmɛtrɪk) *or* ˌeudio'metrical *adj* > ˌeudio'metrically *adv* > ˌeudi'ometry *n*

Eudoxus of Cnidus (juːˈdɒksəs, 'naɪdəs) *n* ?406–?355 BC, Greek astronomer and mathematician; believed to have calculated the length of the solar year

Eugène (*French* øʒɛn) *n* **Prince**, title of *François Eugène de Savoie-Carignan*. 1663–1736, Austrian general, born in France: with Marlborough defeated the French at Blenheim (1704), Oudenaarde (1708), and Malplaquet (1709)

eugenics (juːˈdʒɛnɪks) *n* (*functioning as singular*) the study of methods of improving the quality of the human race, esp by selective breeding [C19: from Greek *eugenēs* well-born, from EU- + -*genēs* born; see -GEN] > eu'genic *adj* > eu'genically *adv* > eu'genicist *n* > eugenist ('juːdʒənɪst) *n, adj*

Eugénie (*French* øʒeni) *n* original name *Eugénia Maria de Montijo de Guzman, Comtesse de Téba*. 1826–1920, Empress of France (1853–71) as wife of Napoleon III

eukaryote *or* **eucaryote** (juːˈkærɪɒt) *n* any member of the *Eukarya*, a domain of organisms having cells each with a distinct nucleus within which the genetic material is contained. Eukaryotes include protoctists, fungi, plants, and animals. Compare **prokaryote** [from EU- + KARYO- + -*ote* as in *zygote*] > **eukaryotic** *or* **eucaryotic** (ˌjuːkærɪ'ɒtɪk) *adj*

Eula ('juːlə) *n acronym for* end-user licence agreement: the agreement made by a user before being granted permission to use computer software

Euler (*German* 'ɔɪlər) *n* **1 Leonhard** ('leːɔnhart). 1707–83, Swiss mathematician, noted esp for his work on the calculus of variation: considered the founder of modern mathematical analysis **2 Ulf (Svante) von** (ʊlf fɒn). 1905–83, Swedish physiologist: shared the Nobel prize (1970) for physiology or medicine with Julius Axelrod and Bernard Katz for their work on the catecholamines: son of Hans von Euler-Chelpin

Euler-Chelpin (*German* 'ɔɪlər 'kɛlpiːn) *n* **Hans (Karl August) von.** 1873–1964, Swedish biochemist, born in Germany: shared the Nobel prize for chemistry (1929) with Sir Arthur Harden for their work on enzymes: father of Ulf von Euler

eulogize *or* **eulogise** ('juːlədʒaɪz) *vb* to praise (a person or thing) highly in speech or writing > 'eulogist *or* 'eulogizer *or* 'eulogiser *n* > euloˈgistic *or* ˌeuloˈgistical *adj* > ˌeuloˈgistically *adv*

eulogy ('juːlədʒɪ) *n, pl* -gies **1** a formal speech or piece of writing praising a person or thing, esp a person who has recently died **2** high praise or commendation [C16: from Late Latin *eulogia*, from Greek: praise, from EU- + -LOGY; influenced by Latin *ēlogium* short saying, inscription]

Eumenides (juːˈmɛnɪˌdiːz) *pl n* another name for the Furies, used by the Greeks as a euphemism [from Greek, literally: the benevolent ones, from *eumenēs* benevolent, from EU- + *menos* spirit]

eunuch ('juːnək) *n* **1** a man who has been castrated, esp (formerly) for some office such as a guard in a harem **2** *informal* an ineffective man: *a political eunuch* [C15: via Latin from Greek *eunoukhos* attendant of the bedchamber, from *eunē* bed + *ekhein* to have, keep]

euonymus (juːˈɒnɪməs) *or* **evonymus** *n* any tree or shrub of the N temperate genus *Euonymus*, such as the spindle tree, whose seeds are each enclosed in a fleshy, typically red, aril: family *Celastraceae* [C18: from Latin: spindle tree, from Greek *euōnumos* fortunately named, from EU- + *onoma* NAME]

Eupen and Malmédy (*French* øpɛn· malmedi) *n* a region of Belgium in Liège province: ceded by Germany in 1919. Pop: 29 372 (2004 est)

eupepsia (juːˈpɛpsɪə) *or* **eupepsy** (juːˈpɛpsɪ) *n physiol* good digestion [C18: from New Latin, from Greek, from EU- + *pepsis* digestion, from *peptein* to digest] > **eupeptic** (juːˈpɛptɪk) *adj*

euphemism ('juːfɪˌmɪzəm) *n* **1** an inoffensive word or phrase substituted for one considered offensive or hurtful, esp one concerned with religion, sex, death, or excreta. Examples of euphemisms are *sleep with* for *have sexual intercourse with; departed* for *dead; relieve oneself* for *urinate* **2** the use of such inoffensive words or phrases [C17: from Greek *euphēmismos*, from EU- + *phēmē* speech] > ˌeuphe'mistic *adj* > ˌeuphe'mistically *adv*

euphemize *or* **euphemise** ('juːfɪˌmaɪz) *vb* to speak in euphemisms or refer to by means of a euphemism > 'euphe,mizer *or* 'euphe,miser *n*

euphonic (juːˈfɒnɪk) *or* **euphonious** (juːˈfəʊnɪəs) *adj* **1** denoting or relating to euphony; pleasing to the ear **2** (of speech sounds) altered for ease of pronunciation > eu'phonically *or* eu'phoniously *adv* > eu'phoniousness *n*

euphonium (juːˈfəʊnɪəm) *n* a brass musical instrument with four valves; the tenor of the tuba family. It is used mainly in brass bands [C19: New Latin, from EUPH(ONY + HARM)ONIUM]

euphonize *or* **euphonise** ('juːfəˌnaɪz) *vb* **1** to make pleasant to hear; render euphonious **2** to change (speech sounds) so as to facilitate pronunciation

euphony ('juːfənɪ) *n, pl* -nies **1** the alteration of speech sounds, esp by assimilation, so as to make them easier to pronounce **2** a pleasing sound, esp in speech [C17: from Late Latin *euphōnia*, from Greek, from EU- + *phōnē* voice]

euphorbia (juːˈfɔːbɪə) *n* any plant of the genus *Euphorbia*, such as the spurges and poinsettia: family *Euphorbiaceae* [C14 *euforbia*: from Latin *euphorbea* African plant named after *Euphorbus*, first-century AD Greek physician]

euphoria (juːˈfɔːrɪə) *n* a feeling of great elation, esp when exaggerated [C19: from Greek: good ability to endure, from EU- + *pherein* to bear] > **euphoric** (juːˈfɒrɪk) *adj*

euphoriant (juːˈfɔːrɪənt) *adj* **1** relating to or able to produce euphoria ▷ *n* **2** a euphoriant drug or agent

euphotic (juːˈfəʊtɪk, -ˈfɒt-) *adj ecology* denoting or relating to the uppermost part of a sea or lake down to about 100 metres depth, which receives enough light to enable photosynthesis to take place [C20: from EU- + PHOTIC]

euphrasy ('juːfrəsɪ) *n, pl* -sies another name for eyebright [C15 *eufrasie*: from Medieval Latin *eufrasia*, from Greek *euphrasia* gladness, from *euphrainein* to make glad, from EU- + *phrēn* mind]

Euphrates (juːˈfreɪtiːz) *n* a river in SW Asia, rising in E Turkey and flowing south across Syria and Iraq to join the Tigris, forming the Shatt-al-Arab, which flows to the head of the Persian Gulf: important in ancient times for the extensive irrigation of its valley (in Mesopotamia). Length: 3598 km (2235 miles)

Euphrosyne (juːˈfrɒzɪˌniː) n Greek myth one of the three Graces [from Greek: mirth, merriment]

euphuism (ˈjuːfjuːˌɪzəm) n 1 an artificial prose style of the Elizabethan period, marked by extreme use of antithesis, alliteration, and extended similes and allusions 2 any stylish affectation in speech or writing, esp a rhetorical device or expression [c16: after *Euphues*, prose romance by John Lyly] > ˈeuphuist n > ˌeuphuˈistic or ˌeuphuˈistical adj > ˌeuphuˈistically adv

eur- combining form a variant of **euro-**

Eurasia (juəˈreɪʃə, -ʒə) n the continents of Europe and Asia considered as a whole

Eurasian (juəˈreɪʒən, -ʒən) adj 1 of or relating to Eurasia 2 of mixed European and Asian descent ▷ n 3 a person of mixed European and Asian descent

Euratom (juəˈrætəm) n short for **European Atomic Energy Community**; an authority established by the European Economic Community (now the European Union) to develop peaceful uses of nuclear energy

Eure (French œr) n a department of N France, in Haute-Normandie region. Capital: Évreux. Pop: 550 056 (2003 est). Area: 6037 sq km (2354 sq miles)

Eure-et-Loir (French œrelwar) n a department of N central France, in Centre region. Capital: Chartres. Pop: 412 094 (2003 est). Area: 5940 sq km (2317 sq miles)

eureka (juˈriːkə) interj an exclamation of triumph on discovering or solving something [c17: from Greek *heurēka* I have found (it), from *heuriskein* to find; traditionally the exclamation of Archimedes when he realized, during bathing, that the volume of an irregular solid could be calculated by measuring the water displaced when it was immersed]

eureka moment n informal a moment at which a person realizes or solves something

eurhythmic (juːˈrɪðmɪk), **eurhythmical**, esp US **eurythmic** or **eurythmical** adj 1 having a pleasing and harmonious rhythm, order, or structure 2 of or relating to eurhythmics

eurhythmics or esp US **eurythmics** (juːˈrɪðmɪks) n (functioning as singular) 1 a system of training through physical movement to music, originally taught by Émile Jaques-Dalcroze, to develop grace and musical understanding 2 dancing of this style, expressing the rhythm and spirit of the music through body movements

Euripides (juˈrɪpɪˌdiːz) n ?480–406 BC, Greek tragic dramatist. His plays, 18 of which are extant, include *Alcestis, Medea, Hippolytus, Hecuba, Trojan Women, Electra, Iphigeneia in Tauris, Iphigeneia in Aulis*, and *Bacchae*

euro (ˈjuərəu) n, pl -os the official currency unit, divided into 100 cents, of the member countries of the European Union who have adopted European Monetary Union; these are Austria, Belgium, Cyprus, Finland, France, Germany, Greece, Ireland, Italy, Luxembourg, Malta, the Netherlands, Portugal, Slovenia, and Spain; also used by Andorra, Bosnia-Herzegovina, French Guiana, Guadeloupe, Kosovo, Martinique, Mayotte, Monaco, Montenegro, Réunion, San Marino, and the Vatican City

euro- (ˈjuərəu-) or before a vowel **eur-** combining form (sometimes capital) Europe or European: eurodollar

eurobond (ˈjuərəuˌbɒnd) n (sometimes capital) a bond issued in a eurocurrency

Eurocentric (ˌjuərəuˈsɛntrɪk) adj chiefly concerned with or concentrating on Europe and European culture: the Eurocentric curriculum

eurocheque (ˈjuərəuˌtʃɛk) n (sometimes capital) a cheque drawn on a European bank that can be cashed at any bank or bureau de change displaying the EC sign or that can be used to pay for goods or services at any outlet displaying this sign

Eurocommunism (ˌjuərəuˈkɒmjuˌnɪzəm) n the policies, doctrines, and practices of Communist Parties in Western Europe in the 1970s and 1980s, esp those rejecting democratic centralism and favouring nonalignment with the Soviet Union and China > ˌEuroˈcommunist n, adj

eurocrat (ˈjuərəˌkræt) n (sometimes capital) a member, esp a senior member, of the administration of the European Union

eurocreep (ˈjuərəˌkriːp) n the gradual introduction of the euro into use in Britain

eurocurrency (ˈjuərəuˌkʌrənsɪ) n (sometimes capital) a the currency of any country held on deposit in Europe outside its home market: used as a source of short- or medium-term finance, esp in international trade, because of easy convertibility b (as modifier): the eurocurrency market

eurodollar (ˈjuərəuˌdɒlə) n (sometimes capital) a US dollar as part of a European holding. See eurocurrency

Euroland (ˈjuərəuˌlænd) n the geographical area containing the countries that have joined the European single currency

euromarket (ˈjuərəuˌmɑːkɪt) n 1 a market for financing international trade backed by the central banks and commercial banks of the European Union 2 the European Union treated as one large market for the sale of goods and services

Euro MP n informal a member of the European Parliament

euronote (ˈjuərəuˌnəut) n a form of euro-commercial paper consisting of short-term negotiable bearer notes

Europa (juˈrəupə) n Greek myth a Phoenician princess who had three children by Zeus in Crete, where he had taken her after assuming the guise of a white bull. Their offspring were Rhadamanthus, Minos, and Sarpedon

Europe (ˈjuərəp) n 1 the second smallest continent, forming the W extension of Eurasia: the border with Asia runs from the Urals to the Caspian and the Black Sea. The coastline is generally extremely indented and there are several peninsulas (notably Scandinavia, Italy, and Iberia) and offshore islands (including the British Isles and Iceland). It contains a series of great mountain systems in the south (Pyrenees, Alps, Apennines, Carpathians, Caucasus), a large central plain, and a N region of lakes and mountains in Scandinavia. Pop: 724 722 000 (2005 est). Area: about 10 400 000 sq km (4 000 000 sq miles) 2 Brit the continent of Europe except for the British Isles: we're going to Europe for our holiday 3 Brit the European Union: when did Britain go into Europe?

European (ˌjuərəˈpɪən) adj 1 of or relating to Europe or its inhabitants 2 native to or derived from Europe ▷ n 3 a native or inhabitant of Europe 4 a person of European descent 5 a supporter of the European Union or of political union of the countries of Europe or a part of it > ˌEuroˈpeanˌism n

European Central Bank n the central bank of the European Union, established in 1998 to oversee the process of European Monetary Union and subsequently to direct monetary policy within the countries using the euro. Abbreviation: ECB

European Commission n the executive body of the European Union formed in 1967, which initiates action in the EU and mediates between member governments

European Community or **European Communities** n an economic and political association of European States that came into being in 1967, when the legislative and executive bodies of the European Economic Community merged with those of the European Coal and Steel Community and the European Atomic Energy Community: subsumed into the European Union in 1993

European Council n an executive body of the European Union, made up of the President of the European Commission and representatives of the member states, including the foreign and other ministers. The Council acts at the request of the Commission

European Currency Unit n See ECU

European Economic Community n the former W European economic association created by the Treaty of Rome in 1957; in 1967 its executive and legislative bodies merged with those of the European Coal and Steel Community and the European Atomic Energy Community to form the European Community (now part of the European Union). Also called: informal Common Market Abbreviation: EEC

Europeanize or **Europeanise** (ˌjuərəˈpɪəˌnaɪz) vb (tr) 1 to make European in culture, dress, etc 2 to integrate (a country, economy, etc) into the European Union > ,Euro,peani'zation or ,Euro,peani'sation n

European Monetary System n the system used in the European Union for stabilizing exchange rates between the currencies of member states and financing the balance-of-payments support mechanism. The original Exchange Rate Mechanism was formed in 1979 but superseded in 1999 when the euro was adopted as official currency of 11 EU member states. A new exchange rate mechanism (ERM II) based on the euro is used to regulate the currencies of participating states that have not adopted the euro. Abbreviation: EMS

European Monetary Union n the agreement between members of the European Union to establish a common currency. The current participating members are Austria, Belgium, Finland, France, Germany, Greece, Ireland, Italy, Luxembourg, the Netherlands, Portugal, and Spain. Abbreviation: EMU

European Parliament n the assembly of the European Union in Strasbourg. It consists of 626 directly elected members and its role is largely advisory

European Union n an organization created in 1993 with the aim of achieving closer economic and political union between member states of the European Community. The current members are Austria, Belgium, Bulgaria, Cyprus, the Czech Republic, Denmark, Estonia, Finland, France, Germany, Greece, Hungary, Ireland, Italy, Latvia, Lithuania, Luxembourg, Malta, the Netherlands, Poland, Portugal, Romania, Slovakia, Slovenia, Spain, Sweden, and the UK. Abbreviation: EU

European wasp n Austral a large black-and-yellow banded wasp, Vespula germanica, native to Europe, North Africa, and Asia, now established in Australasia and the US

Europhile ('juərəu,faɪl) (sometimes not capital) n **1** a person who admires Europe, Europeans, or the European Union ▷ adj **2** marked by or possessing admiration for Europe, Europeans, or the European Union

europium (ju'rəupɪəm) n a soft ductile reactive silvery-white element of the lanthanide series of metals: used as the red phosphor in colour television and in lasers. Symbol: Eu; atomic no: 63; atomic wt: 151.965; valency: 2 or 3; relative density: 5.244; melting pt: 822°C; boiling pt: 1527°C [C20: named after EUROPE + -IUM]

Europol ('juərəu,pɒl) n acronym European Police Office, an international association devoted to fighting cross-border organized crime within the European Union

Europoort (Dutch 'ø:ro:po:rt) n a port in the Netherlands near Rotterdam: developed in the 1960s; handles chiefly oil

Eurosceptic (,juərəu'skɛptɪk) (in Britain) n **1** a person who is opposed to closer links with the European Union ▷ adj **2** opposing closer links with the European Union

Eurotunnel ('juərəu,tʌnᵊl) n another name for **Channel Tunnel**

Eurozone ('juərəu,zəun) n another name for **Euroland**

Eurus ('juərəs) n Greek myth the east or southeast wind personified [Latin, from Greek euros]

Euryale (ju'raɪəlɪ) n Greek myth one of the three Gorgons

Eurydice (ju'rɪdɪsɪ) n Greek myth a dryad married to Orpheus, who sought her in Hades after she died. She could have left Hades with him had he not broken his pact and looked back at her

Eurystheus (ju'rɪsθju:s, -θɪəs) n Greek myth a grandson of Perseus, who, through the favour of Hera, inherited the kingship of Mycenae, which Zeus had intended for Hercules

eurythmics (ju:'rɪðmɪks) n a variant spelling (esp US) of **eurhythmics** > eu'rythmic or eu'rythmical adj > eu'rythmy n

Eusebio (ju:'seɪbɪəu) n Silva Ferreira da ('sɪlvə fɛr'eɪrə də), born 1942, Portuguese footballer

Eusebius (ju:'si:bɪəs) n ?265–?340 AD, bishop of Caesarea: author of a history of the Christian Church to 324 AD

Eustachian tube (ju:'steɪʃən) n a tube that connects the middle ear with the nasopharynx and equalizes the pressure between the two sides of the eardrum [C18: named after Bartolomeo Eustachio, 16th-century Italian anatomist]

eustatic (ju:'stætɪk) adj denoting or relating to worldwide changes in sea level, caused by the melting of ice sheets, movements of the ocean floor, sedimentation, etc [C20: from Greek, from EU- + STATIC] > eustasy ('ju:stəsɪ) n > eu'statically adv

eutectic (ju:'tɛktɪk) adj **1** (of a mixture of substances, esp an alloy) having the lowest freezing point of all possible mixtures of the substances **2** concerned with or suitable for the formation of eutectic mixtures ▷ n **3** a eutectic mixture **4** the temperature on a phase diagram at which a eutectic mixture forms [C19: from Greek eutēktos melting readily, from EU- + tēkein to melt]

Euterpe (ju:'tɜ:pɪ) n Greek myth the Muse of lyric poetry and music > Eu'terpean adj

euthanasia (,ju:θə'neɪzɪə) n the act of killing someone painlessly, esp to relieve suffering from an incurable illness. Also called: mercy killing [C17: via New Latin from Greek: easy death, from EU- + thanatos death]

euthanize, euthanise ('ju:θə,naɪz) or Austral **euthanaze, euthanase** ('ju:θə,neɪz) vb (tr) to kill (a person or animal) painlessly, esp to relieve suffering from an incurable illness [C20: back formation from EUTHANASIA]

euthenics (ju:'θɛnɪks) n (functioning as singular) the study of the control of the environment, esp with a view to improving the health and living standards of the human race [C20: from Greek euthēnein to thrive] > eu'thenist n

eutrophic (ju:'trɒfɪk, -'trəu-) adj (of lakes and similar habitats) rich in organic and mineral nutrients and supporting an abundant plant life, which in the process of decaying depletes the oxygen supply for animal life [C18: probably from eutrophy, from Greek eutrophia sound nutrition, from eutrophos well-fed, from EU- + trephein to nourish] > 'eutrophy n

Euxine Sea (ju:'ksaɪn) n an ancient name for the **Black Sea**

eV abbreviation electronvolt

EVA abbreviation astronautics extravehicular activity

evacuate (ɪ'vækjʊ,eɪt) vb (mainly tr) **1** (also intr) to withdraw or cause to withdraw from (a place of danger) to a place of greater safety **2** to make empty by removing the contents of **3** (also intr) physiol **a** to eliminate or excrete (faeces); defecate **b** to discharge (any waste product) from (a part of the body) **4** (tr) to create a vacuum in (a bulb, flask, reaction vessel, etc) [C16: from Latin ēvacuāre to void, from vacuus empty] > e,vacu'ation n > e'vacuative adj > e,vacu,ator n > e,vacu'ee n

evade (ɪ'veɪd) vb (mainly tr) **1** to get away from or avoid (imprisonment, captors, etc); escape **2** to get around, shirk, or dodge (the law, a duty, etc) **3** (also intr) to avoid answering (a question) [C16: from French évader, from Latin ēvādere to go forth, from vādere to go] > e'vadable adj > e'vader n

evaginate (ɪ'vædʒɪ,neɪt) vb (tr) med to turn (an organ or part) inside out; turn the outer surface of (an organ or part) back on itself [C17: from Late Latin ēvāgīnāre to unsheathe, from vāgīna sheath] > e,vagi'nation n

evaluate (ɪ'væljʊ,eɪt) vb (tr) **1** to ascertain or set the amount or value of **2** to judge or assess the worth of; appraise **3** maths, logic to determine the unique member of the range of a function corresponding to a given member of its domain [C19: back formation from evaluation, from French, from evaluer to evaluate; see VALUE] > e,valu'ation n > e'valu,ator n > e'valuative adj

evanesce (,ɛvə'nɛs) vb (intr) (of smoke, mist, etc) to fade gradually from sight; vanish [C19: from Latin ēvānēscere to disappear; see VANISH]

evanescent (,ɛvə'nɛsᵊnt) adj **1** passing out of sight; fading away; vanishing **2** ephemeral or transitory > ,eva'nescence n > ,eva'nescently adv

evangel (ɪ'vændʒəl) n **1** archaic the gospel of Christianity **2** (often capital) any of the four Gospels of the New Testament **3** any body of teachings regarded as central or basic **4** US an evangelist [C14: from Church Latin ēvangelium, from Greek evangelion good news, from EU- + angelos messenger; see ANGEL]

evangelical (ˌiːvænˈdʒɛlɪkəl) *Christianity* ▷ *adj* 1 of, based upon, or following from the Gospels 2 denoting or relating to any of certain Protestant sects or parties, which emphasize the importance of personal conversion and faith in atonement through the death of Christ as a means of salvation 3 another word for **evangelistic** ▷ *n* 4 an upholder of evangelical doctrines or a member of an evangelical sect or party, esp the Low-Church party of the Church of England
> ˌevanˈgelicalism *n* > ˌevanˈgelically *adv*

evangelism (ɪˈvændʒɪˌlɪzəm) *n* 1 (in Protestant churches) the practice of spreading the Christian gospel 2 ardent or missionary zeal for a cause

evangelist (ɪˈvændʒɪlɪst) *n* 1 an occasional preacher, sometimes itinerant and often preaching at meetings in the open air 2 a preacher of the Christian gospel 3 any zealous advocate of a cause > eˌvangeˈlistic *adj*

Evangelist (ɪˈvændʒɪlɪst) *n* 1 any of the writers of the New Testament Gospels: Matthew, Mark, Luke, or John 2 a senior official or dignitary of the Mormon Church

evangelize *or* **evangelise** (ɪˈvændʒɪˌlaɪz) *vb* 1 to preach the Christian gospel or a particular interpretation of it (to) 2 (*intr*) to advocate a cause with the object of making converts > eˌvangeliˈzation *or* eˌvangeliˈsation *n*
> eˈvangeˌlizer *or* eˈvangeˌliser *n*

Evans (ˈɛvənz) *n* 1 Sir Arthur (John). 1851–1941, British archaeologist, whose excavations of the palace of Knossos in Crete provided evidence for the existence of the Minoan civilization 2 Dame Edith (Mary Booth). 1888–1976, British actress 3 Sir Geraint (Llewellyn). 1922–92, Welsh operatic baritone 4 Herbert McLean. 1882–1971, US anatomist and embryologist; discoverer of vitamin E (1922) 5 Mary Ann. real name of (George) Eliot 6 Oliver. 1755–1819, US engineer: invented the continuous production line and a high-pressure steam engine 7 Walker. 1903–75, US photographer, noted esp for his studies of rural poverty in the Great Depression

Evanston (ˈɛvənstən) *n* a city in NE Illinois, on Lake Michigan north of Chicago: Northwestern University (1851). Pop: 74 360 (2003 est)

Evansville (ˈɛvənzˌvɪl) *n* a city in SW Indiana, on the Ohio River. Pop: 117 881 (2003 est)

evaporate (ɪˈvæpəˌreɪt) *vb* 1 to change or cause to change from a liquid or solid state to a vapour 2 to lose or cause to lose liquid by vaporization leaving a more concentrated residue 3 to disappear or cause to disappear; fade away or cause to fade away [c16: from Late Latin *ēvapōrāre*, from Latin *vapor* steam; see VAPOUR]
> eˈvaporable *adj* > eˌvapoˈration *n* > eˈvaporative *adj*
> eˈvapoˌrator *n*

evaporated milk *n* thick unsweetened tinned milk from which some of the water has been evaporated

evasion (ɪˈveɪʒən) *n* 1 the act of evading or escaping, esp from a distasteful duty, responsibility, etc, by trickery, cunning, or illegal means: *tax evasion* 2 trickery, cunning, or deception used to dodge a question, duty, etc; means of evading [c15: from Late Latin *ēvāsiō*, from Latin *ēvādere* to go forth; see EVADE]

evasive (ɪˈveɪsɪv) *adj* 1 tending or seeking to evade; avoiding the issue; not straightforward 2 avoiding or seeking to avoid trouble or difficulties: *to take evasive action* 3 hard to catch or obtain; elusive > eˈvasively *adv*
> eˈvasiveness *n*

Evatt (ˈɛvæt) *n* Herbert Vere. 1894–1965, Australian jurist and Labor political leader, president of the General Assembly of the United Nations 1948–49

eve (iːv) *n* 1 the evening or day before some special event or festival 2 the period immediately before an event: *on the eve of civil war* 3 an archaic word for **evening** [c13: variant of EVEN²]

Eve (iːv) *n* *Old Testament* the first woman; mother of the human race, fashioned by God from the rib of Adam (Genesis 2:18-25)

Evelyn (ˈiːvlɪn, ˈɛv-) *n* John. 1620–1706, English author, noted chiefly for his diary (1640–1706)

even¹ (ˈiːvən) *adj* 1 level and regular; flat 2 (*postpositive; foll by with*) on the same level or in the same plane (as) 3 without variation or fluctuation; regular; constant 4 not readily moved or excited; placid; calm: *an even*

temper 5 equally balanced between two sides: *an even game* 6 equal or identical in number, quantity, etc 7 a (of a number) divisible by two b characterized or indicated by such a number: *maps are on the even pages*. See **odd** (sense 4) 8 relating to or denoting two or either of two alternatives, events, etc, that have an equal probability: *an even chance of missing or catching a train* 9 having no balance of debt; neither owing nor being owed 10 just and impartial; fair 11 exact in number, amount, or extent: *an even pound* 12 equal, as in score; level 13 **even money** a a bet in which the winnings are the same as the amount staked b (*as modifier*): *the even-money favourite* 14 **get even** *informal* to exact revenge (on); settle accounts (with) ▷ *adv* 15 (intensifier; used to suggest that the content of a statement is unexpected or paradoxical): *even an idiot can do that* 16 (intensifier; used with comparative forms): *this is even better* 17 notwithstanding; in spite of 18 used to introduce a more precise version of a word, phrase, or statement: *he is base, even depraved* 19 used preceding a clause of supposition or hypothesis to emphasize the implication that whether or not the condition in it is fulfilled, the statement in the main clause remains valid: *even if she died he wouldn't care* 20 *archaic* all the way; fully: *I love thee even unto death* 21 **even as** (*conjunction*) at the very same moment or in the very same way that 22 **even so** in spite of any assertion to the contrary; nevertheless ▷ See also **even out, evens, even up** [Old English *efen*; related to Old Norse *jafn* even, equal, Gothic *ibns*, Old High German *eban*] > **evener** *n* > **evenly** *adv* > **evenness** *n*

even² (ˈiːvən) *n* an archaic word for **eve, evening** [Old English *ǣfen*; related to Old Frisian *ēvend*, Old High German *āband*]

even-handed *adj* dealing fairly with all; impartial
> ˌeven-ˈhandedly *adv* > ˌeven-ˈhandedness *n*

evening (ˈiːvnɪŋ) *n* 1 the latter part of the day, esp from late afternoon until nightfall 2 the latter or concluding period: *the evening of one's life* 3 the early part of the night spent in a specified way: *an evening at the theatre* 4 an entertainment, meeting, or reception held in the early part of the night 5 *Southern US & Brit dialect* the period between noon and sunset 6 (*modifier*) of, used, or occurring in the evening: *the evening papers* [Old English *ǣfnung*; related to Old Frisian *ēvend*, Old High German *āband*]

evening dress *n* attire for wearing at a formal occasion during the evening, esp (for men) a dinner jacket and black tie, or (less commonly, for women) a floor-length gown

evening primrose *n* any onagraceous plant of the genus *Oenothera*, native to North America but widely cultivated and naturalized, typically having yellow flowers that open in the evening

evening primrose oil *n* an oil, obtained from the seeds of the evening primrose, that is claimed to stimulate the production of prostaglandins

evenings (ˈiːvnɪŋz) *adv informal* in the evening, esp regularly

evening star *n* a planet, usually Venus, seen just after sunset during the time that the planet is east of the sun

even out *vb* (*adverb*) to make or become even, as by the removal of bumps, inequalities, etc: *the land evens out beyond that rise*

evens (ˈiːvənz) *adj, adv* 1 (of a bet) winning the same as the amount staked if successful 2 (of a runner) offered at such odds

evensong (ˈiːvənˌsɒŋ) *n* 1 Also called: Evening Prayer, vespers *Church of England* the daily evening service of Bible readings and prayers prescribed in the Book of Common Prayer 2 *archaic* another name for **vespers**

event (ɪˈvɛnt) *n* 1 anything that takes place or happens, esp something important; happening; incident 2 the actual or final outcome; result (esp in the phrases **in the event, after the event**) 3 any one contest in a programme of sporting or other contests: *the high jump is his event* 4 *philosophy* a an occurrence regarded as a bare instant of space-time as contrasted with an object which fills space and has endurance b an occurrence regarded in isolation from, or contrasted with, human agency **5** in any event *or* at all events regardless of circumstances; in any case **6** in the event of in case of; if (such a thing) happens: *in the event of rain the race will be cancelled* **7** in the event that if it should happen that ▷ *vb* **8** to take part or ride (a horse) in eventing [c16: from Latin *ēventus* a happening, from *ēvenīre* to come forth, happen, from *venīre* to come]

even-tempered *adj* not easily angered or excited; calm

eventful (ɪ'vɛntful) *adj* full of events or incidents: *an eventful day* ▶ e'**ventfully** *adv* ▶ e'**ventfulness** *n*

event horizon *n astronomy* the surface around a black hole enclosing the space from which electromagnetic radiation cannot escape due to gravitational attraction. For a non-rotating black hole, the radius is proportional to the mass of the black hole

eventide ('iːvᵊn,taɪd) *n archaic or poetic* another word for **evening**

eventide home ('iːvᵊn,taɪd) *n euphemistic* an old people's home

eventing (ɪ'vɛntɪŋ) *n* the sport of taking part in equestrian competitions (esp **three-day events**), usually consisting of three sections: dressage, cross-country riding, and showjumping ▶ e'**venter** *n*

event television *n* television programmes focusing on events that attract media attention and high ratings

event theatre *n* spectacular and extravagantly-mounted theatrical productions collectively

eventual (ɪ'vɛntʃʊəl) *adj* (prenominal) happening in due course of time; ultimate: *the eventual outcome was his defeat*

eventuality (ɪ,vɛntʃʊ'ælɪtɪ) *n, pl* -ties a possible event, occurrence, or result; contingency

eventually (ɪ'vɛntʃʊəlɪ) *adv* **1** at the very end; finally **2** (as sentence modifier) after a long time or long delay: *eventually, he arrived*

eventuate (ɪ'vɛntʃʊ,eɪt) *vb* (intr) **1** (often foll by *in*) to result ultimately (in) **2** to come about as a result: *famine eventuated from the crop failure* ▶ e,**ventu'ation** *n*

even up *vb* (adverb) to make or become equal, esp in respect of claims or debts; settle or balance

ever ('ɛvə) *adv* **1** at any time: *have you ever seen it?* **2** by any chance; in any case: *how did you ever find out?* **3** at all times; always: *ever busy* **4** in any possible way or manner: *come as fast as ever you can* **5** *informal, chiefly Brit* (intensifier, in the phrases **ever so, ever such,** and **ever such a**): *ever so good; ever such bad luck; ever such a waste* **6** ever and again *or* ever and anon *archaic* now and then; from time to time **7** is he ever! *US & Canadian slang* he displays the quality concerned in abundance ▷ See also **forever** [Old English *ǣfre,* of uncertain origin]

Everest ('ɛvərɪst) *n* **1** Mount Everest a mountain in S Asia on the border between Nepal and Tibet, in the Himalayas: the highest mountain in the world; first climbed by members of a British-led expedition (1953). Height: established as 8848 m (29 028 ft) for many years, but the latest of a series of more recent reassessments (in 1999), not currently accepted by all authorities or by either of the controlling governments, puts it at 8850 m (29 035 ft) **2** any high point of ambition or achievement [c19: named after Sir G. *Everest* (1790–1866), Surveyor-General of India]

Everglades ('ɛvə,ɡleɪdz) *pl n* the Everglades a subtropical marshy region of Florida, south of Lake Okeechobee: contains the **Everglades National Park** established to preserve the flora and fauna of the swamps. Area: over 13 000 sq km (5000 sq miles)

evergreen ('ɛvə,ɡriːn) *adj* **1** (of certain trees and shrubs) bearing foliage throughout the year; continually shedding and replacing leaves. See **deciduous** **2** remaining fresh and vital ▷ *n* **3** an evergreen tree or shrub

evergreen fund *n* a fund that provides capital for new companies and makes regular injections of capital to support their development

everlasting (,ɛvə'lɑːstɪŋ) *adj* **1** never coming to an end; eternal **2** lasting for an indefinitely long period **3** lasting so long or occurring so often as to become tedious; incessant: *I cannot bear her everlasting complaints* ▷ *n* **4** endless duration; eternity **5** Also called: everlasting flower another name for **immortelle** ▶ ,ever'**lastingly** *adv*

▶ ,ever'**lastingness** *n*

Everly Brothers ('ɛvəlɪ) *pl n* the. US pop singing duo comprising Don Everly (born 1937) and Phil Everly (born 1939), noted for their close harmonies

evermore (,ɛvə'mɔː) *adv* (often preceded by *for*) all time to come

evert (ɪ'vɜːt) *vb* (tr) to turn (an eyelid, the intestines, or some other bodily part) outwards or inside out [c16: from Latin *ēvertere* to overthrow, from *vertere* to turn] ▶ e'**versible** *adj* ▶ e'**version** *n*

Evert ('ɛvət) *n* **Chris**(tine). born 1954, US tennis player: Wimbledon champion 1974, 1976, and 1981; US champion 1975–78, 1980, and 1982

every ('ɛvrɪ) *determiner* **1** each one (of the class specified), without exception: *every child knows it* **2** (not used with a negative) the greatest or best possible: *every hope of success* **3** each: used before a noun phrase to indicate the recurrent, intermittent, or serial nature of a thing: *every third day; every now and then; every so often* **4** every bit (used in comparisons with *as*) quite; just; equally: *every bit as funny as the other show* **5** every other each alternate; every second: *every other day* **6** every which way **a** in all directions; everywhere: *I looked every which way for you* **b** *US & Canadian* from all sides: *stones coming at me every which way* [c15 *everich,* from Old English *ǣfre ǣlc,* from *ǣfre* EVER + *ǣlc* EACH]

everybody ('ɛvrɪ,bɒdɪ) *pron* every person; everyone
● **USAGE** See at **everyone**

everyday ('ɛvrɪ,deɪ) *adj* **1** happening each day; daily **2** commonplace or usual; ordinary **3** suitable for or used on ordinary days as distinct from Sundays or special days

Everyman ('ɛvrɪ,mæn) *n* **1** a medieval English morality play in which the central figure represents mankind, whose earthly destiny is dramatized from the Christian viewpoint **2** (often not capital) the ordinary person; common man

everyone ('ɛvrɪ,wʌn, -wən) *pron* every person; everybody
● **USAGE** *Everyone* and *everybody* are interchangeable, as
● are *no one* and *nobody,* and *someone* and *somebody.* Care
● should be taken to distinguish between *everyone* and
● *someone* as single words and *every one* and *some one* as
● two words, the latter form correctly being used to
● refer to each individual person or thing in a particular
● group: *every one of them is wrong*

every one *pron* each person or thing in a group, without exception: *every one of the large cats is a fast runner*

everything ('ɛvrɪθɪŋ) *pron* **1** the entirety of a specified or implied class: *she lost everything in the War* **2** a great deal, esp of something very important: *she means everything to me*

everywhere ('ɛvrɪ,wɛə) *adv* to or in all parts or places

Evesham ('iːvʃəm) *n* a town in W central England, in W Worcestershire, on the River Avon: scene of the Battle of Evesham in 1265 (Lord Edward's defeat of Simon de Montfort and the barons); centre of the **Vale of Evesham,** famous for market gardens and orchards. Pop: 22 179 (2001)

Évian-les-Bains *or* **Évian** (French evjãlɛbɛ̃) *n* a resort and spa town in E France, on Lake Geneva opposite Lausanne; noted for its bottled mineral waters. Pop: 7273 (1999)

evict (ɪ'vɪkt) *vb* (tr) **1** to expel (a tenant) from property by process of law; turn out **2** to recover (property or the title to property) by judicial process or by virtue of a superior title [c15: from Late Latin *ēvincere,* from Latin: to vanquish utterly, from *vincere* to conquer] ▶ e'**viction** *n* ▶ e'**victor** *n* ▶ e'**vic'tee** *n*

evidence ('ɛvɪdəns) *n* **1** ground for belief or disbelief; data on which to base proof or to establish truth or falsehood **2** a mark or sign that makes evident; indication: *his pallor was evidence of ill health* **3** *law* matter produced before a court of law in an attempt to prove or disprove a point in issue, such as the statements of witnesses, documents, material objects, etc **4** in evidence on display; apparent; conspicuous: *her new ring was in evidence* ▷ *vb* (tr) **5** to make evident; show clearly **6** to give proof of or evidence for

evident ('ɛvɪdənt) *adj* easy to see or understand; readily

apparent [c14: from Latin *ēvidēns*, from *vidēre* to see]

evidential (ˌɛvɪˈdɛnʃəl) *adj* relating to, serving as, or based on evidence > **evi'dentially** *adv*

evidently ('ɛvɪdəntlɪ) *adv* **1** without question; clearly; undoubtedly **2** to all appearances; apparently: *they are evidently related*

evil ('i:vəl) *adj* **1** morally wrong or bad; wicked: *an evil ruler* **2** causing harm or injury; harmful: *an evil plan* **3** marked or accompanied by misfortune; unlucky: *an evil fate* **4** (of temper, disposition, etc) characterized by anger or spite **5** not in high esteem; infamous: *an evil reputation* **6** offensive or unpleasant: *an evil smell* **7** *slang* good; excellent ▷ *n* **8** the quality or an instance of being morally wrong; wickedness: *the evils of war* **9** (*sometimes capital*) a force or power that brings about wickedness or harm: *evil is strong in the world* **10** *archaic* an illness or disease, esp scrofula (the **king's evil**) ▷ *adv* **11** (*now usually in combination*) in an evil manner; badly: *evil-smelling* [Old English *yfel*, of Germanic origin; compare Old Frisian *evel*, Old High German *ubil* evil, Old Irish *adbal* excessive] > **'evilly** *adv* > **'evilness** *n*

evildoer ('i:vəlˌdu:ə) *n* a person who does evil > **'evil,doing** *n*

evil eye the evil eye *n* **1** a look or glance superstitiously supposed to have the power of inflicting harm or injury **2** the power to inflict harm, etc, by such a look > ˌevil-'eyed *adj*

evil-minded *adj* inclined to evil thoughts; wicked; malicious or spiteful > ˌevil-'mindedly *adv* > ˌevil-'mindedness *n*

evince (ɪˈvɪns) *vb* (*tr*) to make evident; show (something, such as an emotion) clearly [c17: from Latin *ēvincere* to overcome; see EVICT] > e'vincible *adj* > e'vincive *adj*

● USAGE *Evince* is sometimes wrongly used where *evoke* is meant: *the proposal evoked* (not *evinced*) *a storm of protest*

eviscerate (ɪˈvɪsəˌreɪt) *vb* **1** (*tr*) to remove the internal organs of; disembowel **2** (*tr*) to deprive of meaning or significance **3** (*tr*) *surgery* to remove the contents of (the eyeball or other organ) **4** (*intr*) *surgery* (of the viscera) to protrude through a weakened abdominal incision after an operation ▷ *adj* **5** having been disembowelled [c17: from Latin *ēviscerāre* to disembowel, from *viscera* entrails] > e,viscer'ation *n* > e'viscer,ator *n*

evocation (ˌɛvəˈkeɪʃən) *n* **1** the act or an instance of evoking **2** *French law* the transference of a case from an inferior court for adjudication by a higher tribunal [c17: from Latin *ēvocātiō* a calling forth, from *ēvocāre* to EVOKE] > evocative (ɪˈvɒkətɪv) *adj*

evoke (ɪˈvəʊk) *vb* (*tr*) **1** to call or summon up (a memory, feeling, etc), esp from the past **2** to call forth or provoke; produce; elicit: *his words evoked an angry reply* **3** to cause (spirits) to appear; conjure up [c17: from Latin *ēvocāre* to call forth, from *vocāre* to call] > evocable ('ɛvəkəbəl) *adj* > e'voker *n*

● USAGE See at **evince** and **invoke**

evolute ('ɛvəˌlu:t) *n* **1** a geometric curve that describes the locus of the centres of curvature of another curve (the **involute**). The tangents to the evolute are at right angles to the involute ▷ *adj* **2** *biology* having the margins rolled outwards [c19: from Latin *ēvolūtus* unrolled, from *ēvolvere* to roll out, EVOLVE]

evolution (ˌi:vəˈlu:ʃən) *n* **1** *biology* a gradual change in the characteristics of a population of animals or plants over successive generations: accounts for the origin of existing species from ancestors unlike them **2** a gradual development, esp to a more complex form: *the evolution of modern art* **3** the act of throwing off, as heat, gas, vapour, etc **4** a pattern formed by a series of movements or something similar **5** an algebraic operation in which the root of a number, expression, etc, is extracted **6** *military* an exercise carried out in accordance with a set procedure or plan [c17: from Latin *ēvolūtiō* an unrolling, from *ēvolvere* to EVOLVE] > ˌevo'lutionary or ˌevo'lutional *adj*

evolutionary algorithm *n* *computing* a computer program that is designed to evolve and improve in response to input

evolutionist (ˌi:vəˈlu:ʃənɪst) *n* **1** a person who believes in a theory of evolution, esp Darwin's theory of the

evolution of plant and animal species ▷ *adj* **2** of or relating to a theory of evolution > ˌevo'lutionism *n* > ˌevolution'istic *adj*

evolve (ɪˈvɒlv) *vb* **1** to develop or cause to develop gradually **2** (*intr*) (of animal or plant species) to undergo evolution **3** (*tr*) to yield, emit, or give off (heat, gas, vapour, etc) [c17: from Latin *ēvolvere* to unfold, from *volvere* to roll] > e'volvable *adj* > e'volvement *n* > e'volver *n*

Évora (Portuguese 'ɛvura) *n* a city in S central Portugal: ancient Roman settlement; occupied by the Moors from 712 to 1166; residence of the Portuguese court in 15th and 16th centuries. Pop: 56 525 (2001)

e-voting *n* the application of electronic technology to cast and count votes in an election

Évreux (French evrø) *n* an industrial town in NW France: severely damaged in World War II; cathedral (12th–16th centuries). Pop: 51 198 (1999)

Évros ('ɛvrɒs) *n* a transliteration of the Modern Greek name for the **Maritsa**

Évvoia ('ɛvia) *n* a transliteration of the Modern Greek name for **Euboea**

evzone ('ɛvzəʊn) *n* a soldier in an elite Greek infantry regiment [c19: from Modern Greek, from Greek *euzōnos* literally: well-girt, from EU- + *zōne* girdle]

e-wallet *n* computer software in which digital cash may be stored for use in paying for transactions on the internet

Ewart ('ju:ət) *n* **Gavin (Buchanan)**. 1916–95, British poet, noted for his light satirical verse

ewe (ju:) *n* **a** a female sheep **b** (*as modifier*): *a ewe lamb* [Old English *ēowu*; related to Old Norse *ær* ewe, Old High German *ou*, Latin *ovis* sheep, Sanskrit *avi*]

ewer ('ju:ə) *n* a large jug or pitcher with a wide mouth [c14: from Old French *evier*, from Latin *aquārius* water carrier, from *aqua* water]

Ewing's sarcoma *n* a form of malignant bone tumour most commonly found in children and young people. Also called: **peripheral primitive neuroectodermal tumour** [c20: named after James *Ewing* (1866–1943), US pathologist who first described it]

ex¹ (ɛks) *prep* **1** *finance* not participating in; excluding; without: *ex bonus; ex dividend; ex rights* **2** *commerce* without charge to the buyer until removed from: *ex quay; ex ship; ex works* [c19: from Latin: out of, from]

ex² (ɛks) *n* *informal* (a person's) former wife, husband, etc

Ex. *abbreviation Bible* Exodus

ex-¹ *prefix* **1** out of; outside of; from: *exclosure; exurbia* **2** former: *ex-wife* [from Latin, from *ex* (prep), identical in meaning and origin with Greek *ex, ek*; see EC-]

ex-² *combining form* a variant of **exo-**: *exergonic*

exa- *prefix* denoting 10¹⁸: *exametres* Symbol: E

exabyte ('ɛksəˌbaɪt) *n* *computing* 10¹⁸ or 2⁶⁰ bytes

exacerbate (ɪgˈzæsəˌbeɪt, ɪkˈsæs-) *vb* (*tr*) **1** to make (pain, disease, emotion, etc) more intense; aggravate **2** to exasperate or irritate (a person) [c17: from Latin *exacerbāre* to irritate, from *acerbus* bitter] > ex,acer'bation *n*

exact (ɪgˈzækt) *adj* **1** correct in every detail; strictly accurate: *an exact copy* **2** precise, as opposed to approximate; neither more nor less: *the exact sum* **3** (*prenominal*) specific; particular: *this exact spot* **4** operating with very great precision: *exact instruments* **5** allowing no deviation from a standard; rigorous; strict: *an exact mind* **6** based mainly on measurement and the formulation of laws, as opposed to description and classification: *physics is an exact science* ▷ *vb* (*tr*) **7** to force or compel (payment or performance); extort: *to exact tribute* **8** to demand as a right; insist upon: *to exact respect from one's employees* **9** to call for or require: *this work exacts careful effort* [c16: from Latin *exactus* driven out, from *exigere* to drive forth, from *agere* to drive] > ex'actable *adj* > ex'actness *n* > ex'actor or ex'acter *n*

exacting (ɪgˈzæktɪŋ) *adj* making rigorous or excessive demands: *an exacting job* > ex'actingly *adv* > ex'actingness *n*

exaction (ɪgˈzækʃən) *n* **1** the act or an instance of exacting, esp money **2** an excessive or harsh demand, esp for money; extortion **3** a sum or payment exacted

exactitude (ɪɡˈzæktɪˌtjuːd) *n* the quality of being exact; precision; accuracy

exactly (ɪɡˈzæktlɪ) *adv* **1** in an exact manner; accurately or precisely **2** in every respect; just: *it is exactly what I want* **3** not exactly *ironic* not at all; by no means ▷ *sentence substitute* **4** just so! precisely!

exacum (ˈɛksəkəm) *n* any plant of the annual or perennial tropical genus *Exacum*; some are grown as greenhouse biennials for their bluish-purple platter-shaped flowers: family *Gentianaceae* [Latin, a name for centaury, from *ex* out + *agere* to drive]

exaggerate (ɪɡˈzædʒəˌreɪt) *vb* **1** to regard or represent as larger or greater, more important or more successful, etc, than is true **2** (*tr*) to make greater, more noticeable, etc, than usual: *his new clothes exaggerated his awkwardness* [c16: from Latin *exaggerāre* to magnify, from *aggerāre* to heap, from *agger* heap] > exˈaggerˌatingly *adv* > exˌaggerˈation *n* > exˈaggerative *or* exˈaggeratory *adj* > exˈaggerˌator *n* > exˈaggeˌrated *adj*

ex all *adv finance* without the right to any benefits: *shares quoted ex all*

exalt (ɪɡˈzɔːlt) *vb* (*tr*) **1** to raise or elevate in rank, position, dignity, etc **2** to praise highly; glorify; extol **3** to stimulate the mind or imagination of; excite **4** to increase the intensity of (a colour, etc) **5** to fill with joy or delight; elate **6** *obsolete* to lift up physically [c15: from Latin *exaltāre* to raise, from *altus* high] > exˈalted *adj*

● **USAGE** Exalt is sometimes wrongly used where *exult* is
● meant: *he was exulting (not exalting) in his win earlier*
● *that day*

exaltation (ˌɛɡzɔːlˈteɪʃən) *n* **1** the act of exalting or state of being exalted **2** a feeling of intense well-being or exhilaration; elation; rapture **3** a flock of larks

exam (ɪɡˈzæm) *n* short for **examination**

examen (ɪɡˈzeɪmɛn) *n RC Church* an examination of conscience, usually made daily by Jesuits and others [c17: from Latin: tongue of a balance, from *exigere* to thrust out, from *agere* to thrust]

examination (ɪɡˌzæmɪˈneɪʃən) *n* **1** the act of examining or state of being examined **2** *education* **a** written exercises, oral questions, or practical tasks, set to test a candidate's knowledge and skill **b** (*as modifier*): *an examination paper* **3** *med* **a** a physical inspection of a patient or parts of his body, in order to verify health or diagnose disease **b** laboratory study of secretory or excretory products, tissue samples, etc, esp in order to diagnose disease **4** *law* the formal interrogation of a person on oath, esp of an accused or a witness > exˌamiˈnational *adj*

examination for discovery *n Canadian* a pretrial meeting to disclose evidence that will be presented later

examine (ɪɡˈzæmɪn) *vb* (*tr*) **1** to look at, inspect, or scrutinize carefully or in detail; investigate **2** *education* to test the knowledge or skill of (a candidate) in (a subject or activity) by written or oral questions or by practical tests **3** *law* to interrogate (a witness or accused person) formally on oath **4** *med* to investigate the state of health of (a patient) [c14: from Old French *examiner*, from Latin *exāmināre* to weigh, from *exāmen* means of weighing; see EXAMEN] > exˈaminable *adj* > exˈaminer *n* > exˈamining *adj* > exˌamiˈnee *n*

example (ɪɡˈzɑːmpᵊl) *n* **1** a specimen or instance that is typical of the group or set of which it forms part; sample **2** a person, action, thing, etc, that is worthy of imitation; pattern: *you must set an example to the younger children* **3** a precedent, illustration of a principle, or model: *an example in a maths book* **4** a punishment or the recipient of a punishment serving or intended to serve as a warning: *the headmaster made an example of him* **5** for example as an illustration; for instance ▷ *vb* **6** (*tr; now usually passive*) to present an example of; exemplify [c14: from Old French, from Latin *exemplum* pattern, from *eximere* to take out, from EX-¹ + *emere* to purchase]

exanthema (ˌɛksænˈθiːmə) *or* **exanthem** (ɛkˈsænθəm) *n, pl* **-themata** (-ˈθiːmətə) *or* **-themas, -thems** a skin eruption or rash occurring as a symptom in a disease such as measles or scarlet fever [c17: via Late Latin from Greek, from *exanthein* to burst forth, from *anthein* to blossom, from *anthos* flower] > exanthematous

(ˌɛksænˈθemətəs) *or* exanthematic (ɛkˌsænθɪˈmætɪk) *adj*

exasperate (ɪɡˈzɑːspəˌreɪt) *vb* (*tr*) **1** to cause great irritation or anger to; infuriate **2** to cause (an unpleasant feeling, condition, etc) to worsen; aggravate ▷ *adj* **3** *botany* having a rough prickly surface because of the presence of hard projecting points [c16: from Latin *exasperāre* to make rough, from *asper* rough] > exˈasperˌatedly *adv* > exˈasperˌater *n* > exˈasperˌating *adj* > exˈasperˌatingly *adv* > exˌasperˈation *n*

exbi- *combining form computing* denoting 2 to the power 60 [c20: from EX(A-) + BI(NARY)]

ex cathedra (ɛks kəˈθiːdrə) *adj, adv* **1** with authority **2** *RC Church* (of doctrines of faith or morals) defined by the pope as infallibly true, to be accepted by all Catholics [Latin, literally: from the chair]

excavate (ˈɛkskəˌveɪt) *vb* **1** to remove (soil, earth, etc) by digging; dig out **2** to make (a hole, cavity, or tunnel) in (solid matter) by hollowing or removing the centre or inner part: *to excavate a tooth* **3** to unearth (buried objects) methodically in an attempt to discover information about the past [c16: from Latin *excavāre*, from *cavāre* to make hollow, from *cavus* hollow] > ˌexcaˈvation *n* > ˈexcaˌvator *n*

exceed (ɪkˈsiːd) *vb* **1** to be superior to (a person or thing), esp in size or quality; excel **2** (*tr*) to go beyond the limit or bounds of: *to exceed one's income; exceed a speed limit* **3** to be greater in degree or quantity than (a person or thing) [c14: from Latin *excēdere* to go beyond, from *cēdere* to go] > exˈceedable *adj* > exˈceeder *n*

exceeding (ɪkˈsiːdɪŋ) *adj* **1** very great; exceptional or excessive ▷ *adv* **2** an archaic word for **exceedingly** > exˈceedingly *adv*

excel (ɪkˈsɛl) *vb* **-cels, -celling, -celled** **1** to be superior to (another or others); surpass **2** (*intr; foll by* in *or* at) to be outstandingly good or proficient: *he excels at tennis* [c15: from Latin *excellere* to rise up]

excellence (ˈɛksələns) *n* **1** the state or quality of excelling or being exceptionally good; extreme merit; superiority **2** an action, characteristic, feature, etc, in which a person excels

Excellency (ˈɛksələnsɪ) *or* **Excellence** *n, pl* **-lencies** *or* **-lences** **1** (*usually preceded by* Your, His, *or* Her) a title used to address or refer to a high-ranking official, such as an ambassador or governor **2** *RC Church* a title of bishops and archbishops in many non-English-speaking countries

excellent (ˈɛksələnt) *adj* exceptionally good; extremely meritorious; superior > ˈexcellently *adv*

excelsior (ɪkˈsɛlsɪˌɔː) *interj, adv, n* **1** excellent: used as a motto and as a trademark for various products, esp in the US for fine wood shavings used for packing breakable objects **2** upwards [c19: from Latin: higher]

except (ɪkˈsɛpt) *prep* **1** Also called: **except for** other than; apart from; with the exception of: *he likes everyone except you; except for this mistake, you did very well* **2** **except that** (*conjunction*) but for the fact that; were it not true that ▷ *conj* **3** an archaic word for **unless** **4** *informal* except that; but for the fact that: *I would have arrived earlier, except I lost my way* ▷ *vb* **5** (*tr*) to leave out; omit; exclude **6** (*intr; often foll by* to) *rare* to take exception; object [c14: from Old French *excepter* to leave out, from Latin *exceptāre*, from *excipere* to take out, from *capere* to take]

excepting (ɪkˈsɛptɪŋ) *prep* **1** excluding; except; except for (esp in the phrase **not excepting**) ▷ *conj* **2** an archaic word for **unless**

● **USAGE** The use of *excepting* is considered by many
● people to be acceptable only after *not, only*, or *without*.
● Elsewhere *except* is preferred: *every country agreed to the*
● *proposal except (not excepting) Spain; he was well again except*
● *for (not excepting) a slight pain in his chest*

exception (ɪkˈsɛpʃən) *n* **1** the act of excepting or fact of being excepted; omission **2** anything excluded from or not in conformance with a general rule, principle, class, etc **3** criticism, esp when it is adverse; objection **4** *law* (formerly) a formal objection in the course of legal proceedings **5** *law* a clause or term in a document that restricts the usual legal effect of the document **6** take exception **a** (*usually foll by* to) to make objections (to); demur (at) **b** (*often foll by* at) to be offended (by); be resentful (at)

exceptionable (ɪk'sɛpʃənəbªl) *adj* open to or subject to objection; objectionable > ex'ceptionableness *n*
> ex'ceptionably *adv*

exceptional (ɪk'sɛpʃənªl) *adj* **1** forming an exception; not ordinary **2** having much more than average intelligence, ability, or skill > ex'ceptionally *adv*

excerpt *n* ('ɛksɜːpt) **1 a** part or passage taken from a book, speech, play, etc, and considered on its own; extract ▷ *vb* (ɛk'sɜːpt) **2** (*tr*) to take (a part or passage) from a book, speech, play, etc [c17: from Latin *excerptum*, literally: (something) picked out, from *excerpere* to select, from *carpere* to pluck] > ex'cerptor *n* > ex'cerptible *adj*
> ex'cerption *n*

excess *n* (ɪk'sɛs, 'ɛksɛs) **1** the state or act of going beyond normal, sufficient, or permitted limits **2** an immoderate or abnormal amount, number, extent, or degree too much or too many: *an excess of tolerance* **3** the amount, number, extent, or degree by which one thing exceeds another **4** *chem* a quantity of a reagent that is greater than the quantity required to complete a reaction: *add an excess of acid* **5** overindulgence or intemperance **6** *insurance chiefly Brit* a specified contribution towards the cost of a claim, stipulated on certain insurance policies as being payable by the policyholder **7 in excess of** of more than; over **8 to excess** to an inordinate extent; immoderately: *he drinks to excess* ▷ *adj* ('ɛksɛs, ɪk'sɛs) (*usually prenominal*) **9** more than normal, necessary, or permitted; surplus: *excess weight* **10** payable as a result of previous underpayment: *excess postage; an excess fare for a railway journey* [c14: from Latin *excessus*, from *excēdere* to go beyond; see EXCEED]

excessive (ɪk'sɛsɪv) *adj* exceeding the normal or permitted extents or limits; immoderate; inordinate > ex'cessively *adv* > ex'cessiveness *n*

excess luggage *or* **excess baggage** *n* luggage that is greater in weight or in number of pieces than an airline, etc, will carry free

exchange (ɪks'tʃeɪndʒ) *vb* **1** (*tr*) to give up, part with, or transfer (one thing) for an equivalent: *to exchange gifts; to exchange francs for dollars* **2** (*tr*) to give and receive (information, ideas, etc); interchange **3** (*tr*) to replace (one thing) with another, esp to replace unsatisfactory goods **4** to transfer or hand over (goods) in return for the equivalent value in kind rather than in money; barter; trade **5** (*tr*) *chess* to capture and surrender (pieces, usually of the same value) in a single sequence of moves ▷ *n* **6** the act or process of exchanging **7 a** anything given or received as an equivalent, replacement, or substitute for something else **b** (*as modifier*): *an exchange student* **8** an argument or quarrel; altercation: *the two men had a bitter exchange* **9** Also called: **telephone exchange** a switching centre in which telephone lines are interconnected **10 a** a place where securities or commodities are sold, bought, or traded, esp by brokers or merchants: *a stock exchange; a corn exchange* **b** (*as modifier*): *an exchange broker* **11 a** the system by which commercial debts between parties in different places are settled by commercial documents, esp bills of exchange, instead of by direct payment of money **b** the percentage or fee charged for accepting payment in this manner **12** a transfer or interchange of sums of money of equivalent value, as between different national currencies or different issues of the same currency **13** (*often plural*) the cheques, drafts, bills, etc, exchanged or settled between banks in a clearing house **14** *chess* the capture by both players of pieces of equal value, usually on consecutive moves **15 lose the exchange** *chess* to lose a rook in return for a bishop or knight **16 win the exchange** *chess* to win a rook in return for a bishop or knight **17** *physics* a process in which a particle is transferred between two nucleons, such as the transfer of a meson between two nucleons ▷ See also **bill of exchange, exchange rate, labour exchange** [c14: from Anglo-French *eschaungier*, from Vulgar Latin *excambiāre* (unattested), from Latin *cambīre* to barter]
> ex'changeable *adj* > ex,changea'bility *n*
> ex'changeably *adv* > ex'changer *n*

exchange rate *n* the rate at which the currency unit of

one country may be exchanged for that of another

Exchange Rate Mechanism *n* **1** the mechanism formerly used in the European Monetary System in which participating governments committed themselves to maintain the values of their currencies in relation to the ECU. Abbreviation: **ERM 2** Also called: **Exchange Rate Mechanism II** the mechanism used to stabilize the currencies of European Union states that have not adopted the euro but wish to maintain the value of their currency in relation to it

exchequer (ɪks'tʃɛkə) *n* **1** (*often capital*) government (in Britain and certain other countries) the accounting department of the Treasury, responsible for receiving and issuing funds **2** *informal* personal funds; finances [c13 (in the sense: chessboard, counting table): from Old French *eschequier*, from *eschec* CHECK]

excide (ɪk'saɪd) *vb* (*tr*) *rare* to cut out; excise [c18: from Latin *excīdere* to cut off, from *caedere* to cut]

excisable (ɪk'saɪzəbªl) *adj* **1** liable to an excise tax **2** suitable for deletion

excise[1] ('ɛksaɪz, ɛk'saɪz) *n* **1** Also called: **excise tax** a tax on goods, such as spirits, produced for the home market **2** a tax paid for a licence to carry out various trades, sports, etc **3** *Brit* that section of the government service responsible for the collection of excise, now the Board of Customs and Excise [c15: probably from Middle Dutch *excijs*, probably from Old French *assise* a sitting, assessment, from Latin *assidēre* to sit beside, assist in judging, from *sedēre* to sit] > ex'cisable *adj*

excise[2] (ɪk'saɪz) *vb* (*tr*) **1** to delete (a passage, sentence, etc); expunge **2** to remove (an organ, structure, or part) surgically [c16: from Latin *excīdere* to cut down; see EXCIDE] > excision (ɪk'sɪʒən) *n*

exciseman ('ɛksaɪz,mæn) *n, pl* **-men** *Brit* (formerly) a government agent whose function was to collect excise and prevent smuggling

excitable (ɪk'saɪtəbªl) *adj* **1** easily excited; volatile **2** (esp of a nerve) ready to respond to a stimulus > ex,cita'bility *or* ex'citableness *n* > ex'citably *adv*

excitation (,ɛksɪ'teɪʃən) *n* **1** the act or process of exciting or state of being excited **2** a means of exciting or cause of excitement **3 a** the current in a field coil of a generator, motor, etc, or the magnetizing current in a transformer **b** (*as modifier*): *an excitation current* **4** the action of a stimulus on an animal or plant organ, inducing it to respond

excite (ɪk'saɪt) *vb* (*tr*) **1** to arouse (a person) to strong feeling, esp to pleasurable anticipation or nervous agitation **2** to arouse or elicit (an emotion, response, etc); evoke: *her answers excited curiosity* **3** to cause or bring about; stir up: *to excite a rebellion* **4** to arouse sexually **5** *physiol* to cause a response in or increase the activity of (an organ, tissue, or part); stimulate **6** to raise (an atom, molecule, electron, nucleus, etc) from the ground state to a higher energy level **7** to supply electricity to (the coils of a generator or motor) in order to create a magnetic field **8** to supply a signal to a stage of an active electronic circuit [c14: from Latin *excitāre*, from *exciēre* to stimulate, from *ciēre* to set in motion, rouse]

excited (ɪk'saɪtɪd) *adj* **1** emotionally aroused, esp to pleasure or agitation **2** characterized by excitement: *an excited dance* **3** sexually aroused **4** (of an atom, molecule, etc) occupying an energy level above the ground state
> ex'citedly *adv* > ex'citedness *n*

excitement (ɪk'saɪtmənt) *n* **1** the state of being excited **2** a person or thing that excites; stimulation or thrill

exciting (ɪk'saɪtɪŋ) *adj* causing excitement; stirring; stimulating > ex'citingly *adv*

exclaim (ɪk'skleɪm) *vb* to cry out or speak suddenly or excitedly, as from surprise, delight, horror, etc [c16: from Latin *exclāmāre*, from *clāmāre* to shout]
> ex'claimer *n*

exclamation (,ɛksklə'meɪʃən) *n* **1** an abrupt, emphatic, or excited cry or utterance; interjection; ejaculation **2** the act of exclaiming > ,excla'mational *adj*
> ex'clamatory *adj*

exclamation mark *or US* **exclamation point** *n* **1** the punctuation mark ! used after exclamations and vehement commands **2** this mark used for any other purpose, as to draw attention to an obvious mistake, in road warning signs, (in chess commentaries) beside the notation of a move considered a good one, (in mathematics) as a symbol of the factorial function, or (in logic) occurring with an existential quantifier

exclave ('ɛkskleɪv) n a part of a country entirely surrounded by foreign territory: viewed from the position of the home country [c20: from EX-¹ + -clave, on the model of ENCLAVE]

exclosure (ɪk'skləʊʒə) n an area of land, esp in a forest, fenced round to keep out unwanted animals

exclude (ɪk'skluːd) vb (tr) 1 to keep out; prevent from entering 2 to reject or not consider; leave out 3 to expel forcibly; eject 4 to debar from school, either temporarily or permanently, as a form of punishment [c14: from Latin exclūdere, from claudere to shut] > ex'cludable or ex'cludible adj > ex'cluder n

exclusion (ɪk'skluːʒən) n the act or an instance of excluding or the state of being excluded > ex'clusionary adj

exclusion principle n See **Pauli exclusion principle**

exclusive (ɪk'skluːsɪv) adj 1 excluding all else; rejecting other considerations, possibilities, events, etc: an exclusive preoccupation with money 2 belonging to a particular individual or group and to no other; not shared: exclusive rights; an exclusive story 3 belonging to or catering for a privileged minority, esp a fashionable clique: an exclusive restaurant 4 (postpositive; foll by to) limited (to); found only (in): this model is exclusive to Harrods 5 single; unique; only: the exclusive means of transport on the island was the bicycle 6 separate and incompatible: mutually exclusive principles 7 (immediately postpositive) not including the numbers, dates, letters, etc, mentioned: 1980-84 exclusive 8 (postpositive; foll by of) except (for); not taking account (of): exclusive of bonus payments, you will earn this amount 9 commerce (of a contract, agreement, etc) binding the parties to do business only with each other with respect to a class of goods or services 10 logic (of a disjunction) true if only one rather than both of its component propositions is true ▷ n 11 an exclusive story; a story reported in only one newspaper > ex'clusively adv > exclusivity (ˌɛksklu:'sɪvɪtɪ) or ex'clusiveness n

exclusive OR circuit or **exclusive OR gate** n electronics a computer logic circuit having two or more input wires and one output wire and giving a high-voltage output signal if a low-voltage signal is fed to one or more, but not all, of the input wires. See **OR circuit**

excommunicate RC Church ▷ vb (ˌɛkskə'mju:nɪˌkeɪt) 1 (tr) to sentence (a member of the Church) to exclusion from the communion of believers and from the privileges and public prayers of the Church ▷ adj (ˌɛkskə'mju:nɪkɪt, -ˌkeɪt) 2 having incurred such a sentence ▷ n (ˌɛkskə'mju:nɪkɪt, -ˌkeɪt) 3 an excommunicated person [c15: from Late Latin excommūnicāre, literally: to exclude from the community, from Latin commūnis COMMON] > ˌexcom'municable adj > ˌexcom,muni'cation n > ˌexcom'municative or ˌexcom'municatory adj > ˌexcom'municator n

excoriate (ɪk'skɔːrɪˌeɪt) vb (tr) 1 to strip (the skin) from (a person or animal); flay 2 med to lose (a superficial area of skin), as by scratching, the application of chemicals, etc 3 to denounce vehemently; censure severely [c15: from Late Latin excoriāre to strip, flay, from Latin corium skin, hide] > ex,cori'ation n

excrement ('ɛkskrɪmənt) n waste matter discharged from the body, esp faeces; excreta [c16: from Latin excrēmentum, from excernere to sift, EXCRETE] > excremental (ˌɛkskrɪ'mentᵊl) or excrementitious (ˌɛkskrɪmen'tɪʃəs) adj

excrescence (ɪk'skrɛsᵊns) n a projection or protuberance, esp an outgrowth from an organ or part of the body > excrescential (ˌɛkskrɪ'sɛnʃəl) adj > ex'crescent adj [c17: from Latin excrēscēns, from crēscere to grow]

excreta (ɪk'skriːtə) pl n waste matter, such as urine, faeces, or sweat, discharged from the body; excrement [c19: New Latin, from Latin excernere to EXCRETE] > ex'cretal adj

excrete (ɪk'skriːt) vb 1 to discharge (waste matter, such as urine, sweat, carbon dioxide, or faeces) from the body

through the kidneys, skin, lungs, bowels, etc 2 (of plants) to eliminate (waste matter, such as carbon dioxide and salts) through the leaves, roots, etc [c17: from Latin excernere to separate, discharge, from cernere to sift] > ex'creter n > ex'cretion n > ex'cretive or ex'cretory adj

excruciate (ɪk'skruːʃɪˌeɪt) vb (tr) 1 to inflict mental suffering on; torment 2 obsolete to inflict physical pain on; torture [c16: from Latin excruciāre, from cruciāre to crucify, from crux cross] > ex,cruci'ation n

excruciating (ɪk'skruːʃɪˌeɪtɪŋ) adj 1 unbearably painful; agonizing 2 intense; extreme: he took excruciating pains to do it well 3 informal irritating; trying 4 humorous very bad: an excruciating pun > ex'cruci,atingly adv

exculpate ('ɛkskʌlˌpeɪt, ɪk'skʌlpeɪt) vb (tr) to free from blame or guilt; vindicate or exonerate [c17: from Medieval Latin exculpāre, from Latin EX-¹ + culpāre to blame, from culpa fault, blame] > exculpable (ɪk'skʌlpəbᵊl) adj > ˌexcul'pation n > ex'culpatory adj

excursion (ɪk'skɜːʃən, -ʒən) n 1 a short outward and return journey, esp for relaxation, sightseeing, etc; outing 2 a group of people going on such a journey 3 (modifier) of or relating to special reduced rates offered on certain journeys by rail: an excursion ticket 4 a digression or deviation; diversion: an excursion into politics 5 (formerly) a raid or attack 6 physics a a movement from an equilibrium position, as in an oscillation b the magnitude of this displacement 7 the normal movement of a movable bodily organ or part from its resting position, such as the lateral movement of the lower jaw 8 machinery the locus of a point on a moving part, esp the deflection of a whirling shaft [c16: from Latin excursiō an attack, from excurrere to run out, from currere to run] > ex'cursionist n

excursive (ɪk'skɜːsɪv) adj 1 tending to digress 2 involving detours; rambling [c17: from Latin excursus, from excurrere to run forth] > ex'cursively adv > ex'cursiveness n

excuse vb (ɪk'skjuːz) (tr) 1 to pardon or forgive: he always excuses her unpunctuality 2 to seek pardon or exemption for (a person, esp oneself): to excuse oneself for one's mistakes 3 to make allowances for; judge leniently: to excuse someone's ignorance 4 to serve as an apology or explanation for; vindicate or justify: her age excuses her behaviour 5 to exempt from a task, obligation, etc: you are excused making breakfast 6 to dismiss or allow to leave: he asked them to excuse him 7 to seek permission for (someone, esp oneself) to leave: he excused himself and left 8 be excused euphemistic to go to the lavatory 9 excuse me! an expression used to catch someone's attention or to apologize for an interruption, disagreement, or social indiscretion ▷ n (ɪk'skjuːs) 10 an explanation offered in defence of some fault or offensive behaviour or as a reason for not fulfilling an obligation, etc: he gave no excuse for his rudeness 11 informal an inferior example of something specified; makeshiftsubstitute: she is a poor excuse for a hostess 12 the act of excusing [c13: from Latin excusāre, from EX-¹ + -cūsare, from causa cause, accusation] > ex'cusable adj > ex'cusableness n > ex'cusably adv

excuse-me n a dance in which a person may take another's partner

ex-directory adj chiefly Brit not listed in a telephone directory, by request, and not disclosed to inquirers

ex dividend adv without the right to the current dividend: to quote shares ex dividend

exeat ('ɛksɪæt) n Brit 1 leave of absence from school or some other institution 2 a bishop's permission for a priest to leave his diocese in order to take up an appointment elsewhere [c18: Latin, literally: he may go out, from exīre]

exec. abbreviation 1 executive 2 executor

execrable ('ɛksɪkrəbᵊl) adj 1 deserving to be execrated; abhorrent 2 of very poor quality: an execrable meal [c14: from Latin exsecrābilis, from exsecrārī to EXECRATE] > 'execrableness n > 'execrably adv

execrate ('ɛksɪˌkreɪt) vb 1 (tr) to loathe; detest; abhor 2 (tr) to profess great abhorrence for; denounce; deplore 3 to curse (a person or thing); damn [c16: from Latin exsecrārī to curse, from EX-¹ + -secrārī from sacer SACRED]

> ˌexe'cration *n* > 'exeˌcrative *or* 'exeˌcratory *adj*
> 'exeˌcratively *adv*

executable (ɪgˈzɛkjʊtəbªl) *adj* **1** (of a computer program) able to be run ▷ *n* **2** a file containing a program that will run as soon as it is opened

execute ('ɛksɪˌkjuːt) *vb* (*tr*) **1** to put (a condemned person) to death; inflict capital punishment upon **2** to carry out; complete; perform; do: *to execute an order* **3** to perform; accomplish; effect: *to execute a pirouette* **4** to make or produce: *to execute a drawing* **5** to carry into effect (a judicial sentence, the law, etc); enforce **6** *law* to comply with legal formalities in order to render (a deed, etc) effective, as by signing, sealing, and delivering **7** to sign (a will) in the presence of witnesses and in accordance with other legal formalities **8** to carry out the terms of (a contract, will, etc) [c14: from Old French *executer*, back formation from *executeur* EXECUTOR]
> 'exeˌcuter *n*

execution (ˌɛksɪˈkjuːʃən) *n* **1** the act or process of executing **2** the carrying out or undergoing of a sentence of death **3** the style or manner in which something is accomplished or performed; technique: *as a pianist his execution is poor* **4 a** the enforcement of the judgment of a court of law **b** the writ ordering such enforcement

executioner (ˌɛksɪˈkjuːʃənə) *n* **1** an official charged with carrying out the death sentence passed upon a condemned person **2** an assassin, esp one appointed by a political or criminal organization

executive (ɪgˈzɛkjʊtɪv) *n* **1 a** a person or group responsible for the administration of a project, activity, or business **b** (*as modifier*): *executive duties; an executive position* **2 a** the branch of government responsible for carrying out laws, decrees, etc; administration **b** any administration ▷ *adj* **3** having the function or purpose of carrying plans, orders, laws, etc, into practical effect **4** of, relating to, or designed for an executive: *the executive suite* **5** *informal* of the most expensive or exclusive type: *executive housing; executive class* > ex'ecutively *adv*

Executive Council *n* (in Australia and New Zealand) a body consisting of ministers of the Crown presided over by the Governor or Governor-General that formally approves Cabinet decisions, etc

executive director *n* a member of the board of directors of a company who is also an employee (usually full-time) of that company and who often has a specified area of responsibility, such as finance or production. See **nonexecutive director**

executive officer *n* the second-in-command of any of certain military units

executor (ɪgˈzɛkjʊtə) *n* **1** *law* a person appointed by a testator to carry out the wishes expressed in his will **2** a person who executes [c13: from Anglo-French *executour*, from Latin *executor*, from EX-¹ + *sequi* follow]
> exˌecu'torial *adj* > ex'ecutorˌship *n* > ex'ecutory *adj*

executrix (ɪgˈzɛkjʊtrɪks) *n, pl* **executrices** (ɪgˌzɛkjʊˈtraɪsiːz) *or* **executrixes** *law* a female executor

exegesis (ˌɛksɪˈdʒiːsɪs) *n, pl* **-ses** (-siːz) explanation or critical interpretation of a text, esp of the Bible [c17: from Greek, from *exēgeisthai* to interpret, from EX-¹ + *hēgeisthai* to guide] > exegetic (ˌɛksɪˈdʒɛtɪk) *or* exe'getical *adj*

exegete ('ɛksɪˌdʒiːt) *or* **exegetist** (ˌɛksɪˈdʒiːtɪst, -ˈdʒɛt-) *n* a person who practises exegesis [c18: from Greek *exēgētēs*, from *exēgeisthai* to interpret; see EXEGESIS]

exemplar (ɪgˈzɛmplə, -plɑː) *n* **1** a person or thing to be copied or imitated; model **2** a typical specimen or instance; example **3** a copy of a book or text on which further printings have been based [c14: from Latin *exemplarium* model, from *exemplum* EXAMPLE]

exemplary (ɪgˈzɛmplərɪ) *adj* **1** fit for imitation; model: *an exemplary performance* **2** serving as a warning; admonitory: *an exemplary jail sentence* **3** representative; typical: *an action exemplary of his conduct* > ex'emplarily *adv*
> ex'emplariness *n*

exemplary damages *pl n* *law* damages awarded to a plaintiff above the value of actual loss sustained so that they serve also as a punishment to the defendant and a deterrent to others

exemplify (ɪgˈzɛmplɪˌfaɪ) *vb* **-fies**, **-fying**, **-fied** (*tr*) **1** to show by example **2** to serve as an example of **3** *law* **a** to make an official copy of (a document from public records) under seal **b** to transcribe (a legal document) [c15: via Old French from Medieval Latin *exemplificāre*, from Latin *exemplum* EXAMPLE + *facere* to make]
> ex'empliˌfiable *adj* > exˌemplifiˈcation *n*
> ex'emplifiˌcative *adj* > ex'emplifier *n*

exempt (ɪgˈzɛmpt) *vb* **1** (*tr*) to release from an obligation, liability, tax, etc; excuse: *to exempt a soldier from drill* ▷ *adj* (*sometimes postpositive*) **2** freed from or not subject to an obligation, liability, tax, etc; excused: *exempt gilts; tax-exempt bonus* **3** *obsolete* set apart; remote ▷ *n* **4** a person who is exempt from an obligation, tax, etc [c14: from Latin *exemptus* removed, from *eximere* to take out, from *emere* to buy, obtain] > ex'emption *n*

exequies ('ɛksɪkwɪz) *pl n, sing* **-quy** the rites and ceremonies used at funerals [c14: from Latin *exequiae* (plural) funeral procession, rites, from *exequī* to follow to the end, from *sequī* to follow]

exercise ('ɛksəˌsaɪz) *vb* (*mainly tr*) **1** to put into use; employ: *to exercise tact* **2** (*intr*) to take exercise or perform exercises; exert one's muscles, etc, esp in order to keep fit **3** to practise using in order to develop or train: *to exercise one's voice* **4** to perform or make proper use of: *to exercise one's rights* **5** to bring to bear; exert: *to exercise one's influence* **6** (*often passive*) to occupy the attentions of, esp so as to worry or vex: *to be exercised about a decision* **7** *military* to carry out or cause to carry out, manoeuvres, simulated combat operations, etc ▷ *n* **8** physical exertion, esp for the purpose of development, training, or keeping fit **9** mental or other activity or practice, esp in order to develop a skill **10** a set of movements, questions, tasks, etc, designed to train, improve, or test one's ability in a particular field: *piano exercises* **11** a performance or work of art done as practice or to demonstrate a technique **12** the performance of a function; discharge: *the exercise of one's rights; the object of the exercise is to win* **13** (*sometimes plural*) *military* a manoeuvre or simulated combat operation carried out for training and evaluation **14** (*usually plural*) *US & Canadian* a ceremony or formal routine, esp at a school or college: *opening exercises; graduation exercises* **15** *gymnastics* a particular type of event, such as performing on the horizontal bar [c14: from Old French *exercice*, from Latin *exercitium*, from *exercēre* to drill, from EX-¹ + *arcēre* to ward off] > 'exerˌcisable *adj* > 'exerˌciser *n*

exercise bike *or* **exercise cycle** *n* a stationary exercise machine that is pedalled like a bicycle as a method of increasing cardiovascular fitness

exercise book *n* a notebook used by pupils and students

exercise price *n* *stock exchange* the price at which the holder of a traded option may exercise his right to buy (or sell) a security

exergaming ('ɛksəˌgeɪmɪŋ) *n* the playing of video games that require rigorous physical exercise and are intended as a work-out, such as those in which players race a virtual bicycle on-screen by pedalling a simulator resembling an exercise bike [c21: from EXERCISE + GAMING]

exert (ɪgˈzɜːt) *vb* (*tr*) **1** to use (influence, authority, etc) forcefully or effectively **2** to apply (oneself) diligently; make a strenuous effort [c17 (in the sense: push forth, emit): from Latin *exserere* to stretch out, from EX-¹ + *serere* to bind together, entwine] > ex'ertion *n* > ex'ertive *adj*

exertainment (ˌɛksəˈteɪnmənt) *n* another name for **exergaming**

Exeter ('ɛksɪtə) *n* a city in SW England, administrative centre of Devon; university (1955). Pop: 106 772 (2001)

exeunt *Latin* ('ɛksɪˌʌnt) they go out: used as a stage direction

exeunt omnes *Latin* ('ɛksɪˌʌnt 'ɒmneɪz) they all go out: used as a stage direction

exfoliant (ɛksˈfəʊlɪənt) *n* a gently abrasive cosmetic product designed to remove dead cells from the skin's surface [c20: from EXFOLIATE + -ANT]

exfoliate (ɛksˈfəʊlɪˌeɪt) *vb* **1** (*tr*) to wash (a part of the body) with a granular cosmetic preparation in order to remove dead cells from the skin's surface **2** (of bark, skin, etc) to peel off in (layers, flakes, or scales) **3** (*intr*) (of rocks or minerals) to shed the thin outermost layer because of weathering or heating **4** (of some minerals, esp mica) to split or cause to split into thin flakes: *a factory to exfoliate vermiculite* [C17: from Late Latin *exfoliāre* to strip off leaves, from Latin *folium* leaf] > ex,foli'ation *n* > ex'foliative *adj*

ex gratia (ˈɡreɪʃə) *adj* given as a favour or gratuitously where no legal obligation exists: *an ex gratia payment* [New Latin, literally: out of kindness]

exhale (ɛksˈheɪl, ɪɡˈzeɪl) *vb* **1** to expel (breath, tobacco smoke, etc) from the lungs; breathe out **2** to give off (air, vapour, fumes, etc) or (of air, vapour, etc) to be given off; emanate [C14: from Latin *exhālāre* to breathe out, from *hālāre* to breathe] > ex'halable *adj*, ,exha'lation *n*

exhaust (ɪɡˈzɔːst) *vb* (*mainly tr*) **1** to drain the energy of; tire out **2** to deprive of resources, etc **3** to deplete totally; expend; consume **4** to empty (a container) by drawing off or pumping out (the contents) **5** to develop or discuss thoroughly so that no further interest remains **6** to remove gas from (a vessel, etc) in order to reduce the pressure or create a vacuum; evacuate **7** (*intr*) (of steam or other gases) to be emitted or to escape from an engine after being expanded ▷ *n* **8** gases ejected from an engine as waste products **9** the expulsion of expanded gas or steam from an engine **10** (*as modifier*): *exhaust valve; exhaust pipe* [C16: from Latin *exhaustus* made empty, from *exhaurīre* to draw out, from *haurīre* to draw, drain] > ex'haustible *adj* > ex'hausting *adj*

exhaustion (ɪɡˈzɔːstʃən) *n* **1** extreme tiredness; fatigue **2** the condition of being used up; consumption **3** the act of exhausting or the state of being exhausted

exhaustive (ɪɡˈzɔːstɪv) *adj* **1** comprehensive in scope; thorough **2** tending to exhaust > ex'haustively *adv* > ex'haustiveness *n*

exhibit (ɪɡˈzɪbɪt) *vb* (*mainly tr*) **1** (*also intr*) to display (something) to the public for interest or instruction **2** to manifest; display; show **3** *law* to produce (a document or object) in court to serve as evidence ▷ *n* **4** an object or collection exhibited to the public **5** *law* a document or object produced in court and referred to or identified by a witness in giving evidence [C15: from Latin *exhibēre* to hold forth, from *habēre* to have] > ex'hibitory *adj* > ex'hibitor *n*

exhibition (ˌɛksɪˈbɪʃən) *n* **1** a public display of art, products, skills, activities, etc **2** the act of exhibiting or the state of being exhibited **3** **make an exhibition of oneself** to behave so foolishly in public that one excites notice or ridicule **4** *Brit* an allowance or scholarship awarded to a student at a university or school

exhibitioner (ˌɛksɪˈbɪʃənə) *n* *Brit* a student who has been awarded an exhibition

exhibitionism (ˌɛksɪˈbɪʃəˌnɪzəm) *n* **1** a compulsive desire to attract attention to oneself, esp by absurd or exaggerated behaviour or boasting **2** *psychiatry* a compulsive desire to expose one's genital organs publicly > ,exhi'bitionist *n*, *adj* > ,exhi,bition'istic *adj*

exhibitive (ɪɡˈzɪbɪtɪv) *adj* (*usually postpositive* and foll by *of*) illustrative or demonstrative

exhilarate (ɪɡˈzɪləˌreɪt) *vb* (*tr*) to make lively and cheerful; gladden; elate [C16: from Latin *exhilarāre*, from *hilārāre* to cheer; see HILARIOUS] > ex,hila'ration *n* > ex'hilarative *or* ex'hilaratory *adj*

exhilarating (ɪɡˈzɪləˌreɪtɪŋ) *adj* causing strong feelings of excitement and happiness: *an exhilarating helicopter trip* > ex'hila,ratingly *adv*

exhort (ɪɡˈzɔːt) *vb* to urge or persuade (someone) earnestly; advise strongly [C14: from Latin *exhortārī*, from *hortārī* to urge] > exhortative (ɪɡˈzɔːtətɪv) *or* ex'hortatory *adj* > ex'horter *n* > ,exhor'tation *n*

exhume (ɛksˈhjuːm) *vb* (*tr*) **1** to dig up (something buried, esp a corpse); disinter **2** to reveal; disclose; unearth [C18: from Medieval Latin *exhumāre*, from Latin EX-¹ + *humāre* to bury, from *humus* the ground] > exhumation (ˌɛkshjʊˈmeɪʃən) *n* > ex'humer *n*

ex hypothesi (ɛks haɪˈpɒθəsɪ) *adv* in accordance with or following from the hypothesis stated [C17: New Latin]

exigency (ˈɛksɪdʒənsɪ, ɪɡˈzɪdʒənsɪ) *or* **exigence** (ˈɛksɪdʒəns) *n*, *pl* -gencies *or* -gences **1** the state of being

exigent; urgency **2** (*often plural*) an urgent demand; pressing requirement **3** an emergency

exigent (ˈɛksɪdʒənt) *adj* **1** urgent; pressing **2** exacting; demanding [C15: from Latin *exigere* to drive out, weigh out, from *agere* to drive, compel]

exiguous (ɪɡˈzɪɡjʊəs, ɪkˈsɪɡ-) *adj* scanty or slender; meagre [C17: from Latin *exiguus*, from *exigere* to weigh out; see EXIGENT] > exiguity (ˌɛksɪˈɡjuːɪtɪ) *or* ex'iguousness *n*

exile (ˈɛɡzaɪl, ˈɛksaɪl) *n* **1** a prolonged, usually enforced absence from one's home or country; banishment **2** the expulsion of a person from his native land by official decree **3** a person banished or living away from his home or country; expatriate ▷ *vb* **4** to expel from home or country, esp by official decree as a punishment; banish [C13: from Latin *exsilium* banishment, from *exsul* banished person; perhaps related to Greek *alasthai* to wander] > exilic (ɛɡˈzɪlɪk, ɛkˈsɪlɪk) *or* ex'ilian *adj*

exist (ɪɡˈzɪst) *vb* (*intr*) **1** to have being or reality; to be **2** to eke out a living; stay alive; survive **3** to be living; live **4** to be present under specified conditions or in a specified place [C17: from Latin *exsistere* to step forth, from EX-¹ + *sistere* to stand] > ex'isting *adj* > ex'istent *adj*, *n*

existence (ɪɡˈzɪstəns) *n* **1** the fact or state of existing; being **2** the continuance or maintenance of life; living, esp in adverse circumstances **3** something that exists; a being or entity **4** everything that exists, esp that is living

existential (ˌɛɡzɪˈstɛnʃəl) *adj* **1** of or relating to existence, esp human existence **2** *philosophy* pertaining to what exists, and is thus known by experience rather than reason; empirical as opposed to theoretical **3** *logic* denoting or relating to a formula or proposition asserting the existence of at least one object fulfilling a given condition; containing an existential quantifier **4** of or relating to existentialism

existentialism (ˌɛɡzɪˈstɛnʃəˌlɪzəm) *n* a modern philosophical movement stressing the importance of personal experience and responsibility and the demands that they make on the individual, who is seen as a free agent in a deterministic and seemingly meaningless universe > ,exis'tentialist *adj*, *n*

exit (ˈɛɡzɪt, ˈɛksɪt) *n* **1** a way out; door or gate by which people may leave **2** the act or an instance of going out; departure **3 a** the act of leaving or right to leave a particular place **b** (*as modifier*): *an exit visa* **4** departure from life; death **5** *theatre* the act of going offstage **6** (in Britain) a point at which vehicles may leave or join a motorway ▷ *vb* (*intr*) **7** to go away or out; depart; leave **8** *theatre* to go offstage: used as a stage direction: *exit Hamlet* **9** (*sometimes tr*) *computing* to leave (a computer program or system) [C17: from Latin *exitus* a departure, from *exīre* to go out, from EX-¹ + *īre* to go]

exitance (ˈɛksɪtəns) *n* a measure of the ability of a surface to emit radiation [C20: from EXIT + -ANCE]

exit poll *n* a poll taken by an organization by asking people how they voted in an election as they leave a polling station

exit strategy *n* **1** a method or plan for extricating oneself from an undesirable situation **2** a plan and timetable for withdrawal from a military engagement **3** the method by which an investor intends to cash out of an investment

ex libris (ɛks ˈliːbrɪs) *adj* **1** from the collection or library of: frequently printed on bookplates ▷ *n* ex-libris **2** a bookplate bearing the owner's name, coat of arms, etc [C19: from Latin, literally: from the books (of)]

Exmoor (ˈɛksˌmʊə, -ˌmɔː) *n* **1** a high moorland in SW England, in W Somerset and N Devon: chiefly grazing ground for Exmoor ponies, sheep, and red deer **2** a small stocky breed of pony with a fawn-coloured nose, originally from Exmoor

Exmouth (ˈɛksməθ) *n* a town in SW England, in Devon, at the mouth of the River Exe: tourism, fishing. Pop: 32 972 (2001)

ex new *adv*, *adj* (of shares, etc) without the right to take up any scrip issue or rights issue. See **cum new**

exo- *combining form* external, outside, or beyond: *exobiology; exothermal* [from Greek *exō* outside]

exobiology (ˌɛksəʊbaɪˈɒlədʒɪ) n another name for **astrobiology** > ˌexobiˈologist n

exocarp (ˈɛksəʊˌkɑːp) n another name for **epicarp**

exocrine (ˈɛksəʊˌkraɪn, -krɪn) adj 1 of or relating to exocrine glands or their secretions ▷ n 2 an exocrine gland [C20: EXO- + -crine from Greek krinein to separate]

exocrine gland n any gland, such as a salivary or sweat gland, that secretes its products through a duct onto an epithelial surface

Exod. abbreviation Bible Exodus

exodus (ˈɛksədəs) n the act or an instance of going out [C17: via Latin from Greek exodos from EX-¹ + hodos way]

Exodus (ˈɛksədəs) n 1 the Exodus the departure of the Israelites from Egypt led by Moses 2 the second book of the Old Testament, recounting the events connected with this and the divine visitation of Moses at Mount Sinai

ex officio (ˈɛks əˈfɪʃɪəʊ, əˈfɪsɪəʊ) adv, adj by right of position or office [Latin]

exogamy (ɛkˈsɒɡəmɪ) n sociol anthropol the custom or an act of marrying a person belonging to another tribe, clan, or similar social unit > exogamous (ɛkˈsɒɡəməs) or exogamic (ˌɛksəʊˈɡæmɪk) adj

exogenous (ɛkˈsɒdʒɪnəs) adj 1 having an external origin 2 biology a developing or originating outside an organism or part of an organism b of or relating to external factors, such as light, that influence an organism 3 psychiatry (of a mental illness) caused by external factors

exon (ˈɛksɒn) n Brit one of the four officers who command the Yeomen of the Guard [C17: a pronunciation spelling of French exempt EXEMPT]

exonerate (ɪɡˈzɒnəˌreɪt) vb (tr) 1 to clear or absolve from blame or a criminal charge 2 to relieve from an obligation or task; exempt [C16: from Latin exonerāre to free from a burden, from onus a burden] > exˌonerˈation n > exˈonerative adj > exˈonerˌator n

exophthalmos (ˌɛksɒfˈθælmɒs), **exophthalmus** (ˌɛksɒfˈθælməs) or **exophthalmia** (ˌɛksɒfˈθælmɪə) n abnormal protrusion of the eyeball, as caused by hyperthyroidism [C19: via New Latin from Greek, from EX-¹ + ophthalmos eye] > ˌexophˈthalmic adj

exorbitant (ɪɡˈzɔːbɪtˀnt) adj (of prices, demands, etc) in excess of what is reasonable; excessive; extravagant; immoderate [C15: from Late Latin exorbitāre to deviate, from Latin orbita track] > exˈorbitance n > exˈorbitantly adv

exorcize or **exorcise** (ˈɛksɔːˌsaɪz) vb (tr) to expel or attempt to expel (one or more evil spirits) from (a person or place believed to be possessed or haunted), by prayers, adjurations, and religious rites [C15: from Late Latin exorcizāre, from Greek exorkizein, from EX-¹ + horkizein to adjure] > ˈexorˌcizer or ˈexorˌciser n > ˈexorcism n > ˈexorcist n

exordium (ɛkˈsɔːdɪəm) n, pl -diums, -dia (-dɪə) an introductory part or beginning, esp of an oration or discourse [C16: from Latin, from exōrdīrī to begin, from ōrdīrī to begin] > exˈordial adj

exoskeleton (ˌɛksəʊˈskɛlɪtˀn) n the protective or supporting structure covering the outside of the body of many animals, such as the thick cuticle of arthropods > ˌexoˈskeletal adj

exosphere (ˈɛksəʊˌsfɪə) n the outermost layer of the earth's atmosphere. It extends from about 400 km above the earth's surface

exothermic (ˌɛksəʊˈθɜːmɪk) or **exothermal** adj (of a chemical reaction or compound) occurring or formed with the evolution of heat > ˌexoˈthermically or ˌexoˈthermally adv

exotic (ɪɡˈzɒtɪk) adj 1 originating in a foreign country, esp one in the tropics; not native: an exotic plant 2 having a strange or bizarre allure, beauty, or quality ▷ n 3 an exotic person or thing [C16: from Latin exōticus, from Greek exōtikos foreign, from exō outside] > exˈotically adv > exˈotiˌcism n > exˈoticness n

exotica (ɪɡˈzɒtɪkə) pl n exotic objects, esp when forming a collection [C19: Latin, neuter plural of exōticus; see EXOTIC]

exotic dancer n a striptease dancer or belly dancer

expand (ɪkˈspænd) vb 1 to make or become greater in extent, volume, size, or scope; increase 2 to spread out or be spread out; unfold; stretch out 3 (intr; often foll by on) to enlarge or expatiate on (a story, topic, etc) in detail 4 (intr) to become increasingly relaxed, friendly, or talkative 5 maths to express (a function or expression) as the sum or product of terms [C15: from Latin expandere to spread out, from pandere to spread, extend] > exˈpandable adj

expanded (ɪkˈspændɪd) adj (of a plastic) having been foamed during manufacture by the introduction of a gas in order to make a light packaging material or heat insulator: expanded polystyrene

expanded metal n an open mesh of metal produced by stamping out alternating slots in a metal sheet and stretching it into an open pattern. It is used for reinforcing brittle or friable materials and in fencing

expander (ɪkˈspændə) n 1 a device for exercising and developing the muscles of the body 2 an electronic device for increasing the variations in signal amplitude in a transmission system according to a specified law

expanse (ɪkˈspæns) n 1 an uninterrupted surface of something that spreads or extends, esp over a wide area; stretch 2 expansion or extension [C17: from New Latin expansum the heavens, from Latin expansus spread out, from expandere to EXPAND]

expansible (ɪkˈspænsəbˀl) adj able to expand or be expanded > exˌpansiˈbility n

expansion (ɪkˈspænʃən) n 1 the act of expanding or the state of being expanded 2 something expanded; an expanded surface or part 3 the degree, extent, or amount by which something expands 4 an increase, enlargement, or development, esp in the activities of a company 5 the increase in the dimensions of a body or substance when subjected to an increase in temperature, internal pressure, etc > exˈpansionary adj

expansionism (ɪkˈspænʃəˌnɪzəm) n the doctrine or practice of expanding the economy or territory of a country > exˈpansionist n, adj > exˌpansionˈistic adj

expansive (ɪkˈspænsɪv) adj 1 able or tending to expand or characterized by expansion 2 wide; extensive 3 friendly, open, or talkative 4 grand or extravagant > exˈpansiveness n

expansivity (ˌɛkspænˈsɪvɪtɪ) n 1 the quality of being expansive 2 another name for **coefficient of expansion**

ex parte (ɛks ˈpɑːtɪ) adj law (of an application in a judicial proceeding) on behalf of one side or party only: an ex parte injunction [Latin]

expat (ˌɛksˈpæt) n, adj informal short for **expatriate**

expatiate (ɪkˈspeɪʃɪˌeɪt) vb (intr) 1 (foll by on or upon) to enlarge (on a theme, topic, etc) at length or in detail; elaborate (on) 2 rare to wander about [C16: from Latin exspatiārī to digress, from spatiārī to walk about] > exˌpatiˈation n > exˈpatiˌator n

expatriate adj (ɛksˈpætrɪɪt, -ˌeɪt) 1 resident in a foreign country 2 exiled or banished from one's native country ▷ n (ɛksˈpætrɪɪt, -ˌeɪt) 3 a person who lives in a foreign country 4 an exile; expatriate person ▷ vb (ɛksˈpætrɪˌeɪt) (tr) 5 to exile (oneself) from one's native country or cause (another) to go into exile [C18: from Medieval Latin expatriāre, from Latin EX-¹ + patria native land] > exˌpatriˈation n

expect (ɪkˈspɛkt) vb (tr; may take a clause as object or an infinitive) 1 to regard as probable or likely; anticipate 2 to look forward to or be waiting for 3 to decide that (something) is requisite or necessary; require: the boss expects us to work late today ▷ See also **expecting** [C16: from Latin exspectāre to watch for, from spectāre to look at] > exˈpectable adj

expectant (ɪkˈspɛktənt) adj 1 expecting, anticipating, or hopeful 2 having expectations, esp of possession of something or prosperity 3 pregnant ▷ n 4 a person who expects something > exˈpectantly adv

expectation (ˌɛkspɛkˈteɪʃən) n 1 the act or state of expecting or the state of being expected 2 (usually plural) something looked forward to, whether feared or hoped for 3 an attitude of expectancy or hope; anticipation 4 statistics the numerical probability that an event will occur

expected frequency *n statistics* the number of occasions on which an event may be presumed to occur on average in a given number of trials

expecting (ɪkˈspɛktɪŋ) *adj informal* pregnant

expectorant (ɪkˈspɛktərənt) *med* ▷ *adj* **1** promoting the secretion, liquefaction, or expulsion of sputum from the respiratory passages ▷ *n* **2** an expectorant drug or agent

expectorate (ɪkˈspɛktəˌreɪt) *vb* to cough up and spit out (sputum from the respiratory passages) [C17: from Latin *expectorāre*, literally: to drive from the breast, expel, from *pectus* breast] > exˌpectoˈration *n* > exˈpectoˌrator *n*

expediency (ɪkˈspiːdɪənsɪ) *or* **expedience** *n, pl* -encies *or* -ences **1** appropriateness; suitability **2** the use of or inclination towards methods that are advantageous rather than fair or just **3** another word for **expedient** (sense 3)

expedient (ɪkˈspiːdɪənt) *adj* **1** suitable to the circumstances; appropriate **2** inclined towards methods or means that are advantageous rather than fair or just ▷ *n* Also: expediency **3** something suitable or appropriate, esp something used during an urgent situation [C14: from Latin *expediēns* setting free; see EXPEDITE]

expedite (ˈɛkspɪˌdaɪt) *vb* (*tr*) **1** to hasten the progress of; hasten or assist **2** to do or process (something, such as business matters) with speed and efficiency [C17: from Latin *expedīre*, literally: to free the feet (as from a snare), hence, liberate, from EX-¹ + *pēs* foot] > ˈexpeˌditer *or* ˈexpeˌditor *n*

expedition (ˌɛkspɪˈdɪʃən) *n* **1** an organized journey or voyage for a specific purpose, esp for exploration or for a scientific or military purpose **2** the people and equipment comprising an expedition **3** promptness in acting; dispatch [C15: from Latin *expedītiō*, from *expedīre* to prepare, EXPEDITE] > ˌexpeˈditionary *adj*

expeditious (ˌɛkspɪˈdɪʃəs) *adj* characterized by or done with speed and efficiency; prompt; quick > ˌexpeˈditiously *adv* > ˌexpeˈditiousness *n*

expel (ɪkˈspɛl) *vb* -pels, -pelling, -pelled (*tr*) **1** to eject or drive out with force **2** to deprive of participation in or membership of a school, club, etc [C14: from Latin *expellere* to drive out, from *pellere* to thrust, drive] > exˈpellable *adj* > expellee (ˌɛkspɛˈliː) *n* > exˈpeller *n*

expellant *or* **expellent** (ɪkˈspɛlənt) *adj* **1** forcing out or having the capacity to force out ▷ *n* **2** a medicine used to expel undesirable substances or organisms from the body, esp worms from the digestive tract

expend (ɪkˈspɛnd) *vb* (*tr*) **1** to spend; disburse **2** to consume or use up [C15: from Latin *expendere*, from *pendere* to weigh] > exˈpender *n*

expendable (ɪkˈspɛndəbᵊl) *adj* **1** that may be expended or used up **2** able to be sacrificed to achieve an objective, esp a military one ▷ *n* **3** something that is expendable > exˌpendaˈbility *n*

expenditure (ɪkˈspɛndɪtʃə) *n* **1** something expended, such as time or money **2** the act of expending

expense (ɪkˈspɛns) *n* **1** a particular payment of money; expenditure **2** money needed for individual purchases; cost; charge **3** (*plural*) incidental money spent in the performance of a job, commission, etc, usually reimbursed by an employer or allowable against tax **4** something requiring money for its purchase or upkeep **5** at the expense of to the detriment of [C14: from Late Latin *expēnsa*, from *expēnsus* weighed out; see EXPEND]

expense account *n* **1** an arrangement by which expenses incurred in the course of a person's work are refunded by his employer or deducted from his income for tax purposes **2** a record of such expenses

expensive (ɪkˈspɛnsɪv) *adj* high-priced; costly; dear > exˈpensiveness *n*

experience (ɪkˈspɪərɪəns) *n* **1** direct personal participation or observation; actual knowledge or contact **2** a particular incident, feeling, etc, that a person has undergone **3** accumulated knowledge, esp of practical matters ▷ *vb* (*tr*) **4** to participate in or undergo **5** to be emotionally or aesthetically moved by; feel [C14: from Latin *experientia*, from *experīrī* to prove; related to Latin *perīculum* PERIL] > exˈperienceable *adj*

experienced (ɪkˈspɪərɪənst) *adj* having become skilful or knowledgeable from extensive contact or participation or observation

experiential (ɪkˌspɪərɪˈɛnʃəl) *adj philosophy* relating to or derived from experience; empirical

experiment *n* (ɪkˈspɛrɪmənt) **1** a test or investigation, esp one planned to provide evidence for or against a hypothesis: a *scientific experiment* **2** the act of conducting such an investigation or test; experimentation; research **3** an attempt at something new or different; an effort to be original ▷ *vb* (ɪkˈspɛrɪˌmɛnt) **4** (*intr*) to make an experiment or experiments [C14: from Latin *experīmentum* proof, trial, from *experīrī* to test; see EXPERIENCE] > exˈperiˌmenter *n*

experimental (ɪkˌspɛrɪˈmɛntᵊl) *adj* **1** relating to, based on, or having the nature of experiment **2** based on or derived from experience; empirical **3** tending to experiment **4** tentative or provisional > exˌperiˈmentaˌlism *n*

experimentation (ɪkˌspɛrɪmɛnˈteɪʃən) *n* the act, process, or practice of experimenting

expert (ˈɛkspɜːt) *n* **1** a person who has extensive skill or knowledge in a particular field ▷ *adj* **2** skilful or knowledgeable **3** of, involving, or done by an expert: *an expert job* [C14: from Latin *expertus* known by experience, from *experīrī* to test; see EXPERIENCE] > ˈexpertly *adv* > ˈexpertness *n*

expertise (ˌɛkspɜːˈtiːz) *n* special skill, knowledge, or judgment; expertness [C19: from French: expert skill, from EXPERT]

expiate (ˈɛkspɪˌeɪt) *vb* (*tr*) to atone for or redress (sin or wrongdoing); make amends for [C16: from Latin *expiāre*, from *pius* dutiful; see PIOUS] > ˈexpiˌator *n* > ˈexpiable *adj* > ˌexpiˈation *n*

expiatory (ˈɛkspɪətərɪ, -trɪ) *adj* **1** capable of making expiation **2** given or offered in expiation

expiration (ˌɛkspɪˈreɪʃən) *n* **1** the finish of something; ending; expiry **2** the act, process, or sound of breathing out

expire (ɪkˈspaɪə) *vb* **1** (*intr*) to finish or run out; cease; come to an end **2** to breathe out (air); exhale **3** (*intr*) to die [C15: from Old French *expirer*, from Latin *exspīrāre* to breathe out, from *spīrāre* to breathe] > exˈpirer *n*

expiry (ɪkˈspaɪərɪ) *n, pl* -ries **1 a** a coming to an end, esp of a contract period; termination **b** (*as modifier*): *the expiry date* **2** death

explain (ɪkˈspleɪn) *vb* **1** (when *tr*, may take a clause as object) to make (something) comprehensible, esp by giving a clear and detailed account of the relevant structure, operation, surrounding circumstances, etc **2** (*tr*) to justify or attempt to justify (oneself) by giving reasons for one's actions or words [C15: from Latin *explānāre* to flatten, from *plānus* level] > exˈplainable *adj* > exˈplainer *n*

explain away *vb* (*tr, adverb*) to offer excuses or reasons for (bad conduct, mistakes, etc)

explanation (ˌɛkspləˈneɪʃən) *n* **1** the act or process of explaining **2** a statement or occurrence that explains **3** a clarification of disputed terms or points; reconciliation

explanatory (ɪkˈsplænətərɪ, -trɪ) *or* **explanative** *adj* serving or intended to serve as an explanation > exˈplanatorily *adv*

expletive (ɪkˈspliːtɪv) *n* **1** an exclamation or swearword; an oath or a sound expressing an emotional reaction rather than any particular meaning **2** any syllable, word, or phrase conveying no independent meaning, esp one inserted in a line of verse for the sake of the metre ▷ *adj* Also: expletory (ɪkˈspliːtərɪ) **3** expressing no particular meaning, esp when filling out a line of verse [C17: from Late Latin *explētīvus* for filling out, from *explēre*, from *plēre* to fill]

explicable (ˈɛksplɪkəbᵊl, ɪkˈsplɪk-) *adj* capable of being explained

explicate (ˈɛksplɪˌkeɪt) *vb* (*tr*) *formal* **1** to make clear or explicit; explain **2** to formulate or develop (a theory, hypothesis, etc) [C16: from Latin *explicāre* to unfold, from *plicāre* to fold] > ˌexpliˈcation *n*

explicit (ɪkˈsplɪsɪt) *adj* **1** precisely and clearly expressed, leaving nothing to implication; fully stated

2 graphically detailed, leaving little to the imagination **3** openly expressed without reservations; unreserved [c17: from Latin *explicitus* unfolded, from *explicāre*; see EXPLICATE] > ex'plicitly *adv* > ex'plicitness *n*

explode (ɪkˈspləʊd) *vb* **1** to burst or cause to burst with great violence as a result of internal pressure, esp through the detonation of an explosive; blow up **2** to destroy or be destroyed in this manner **3** (of a gas) to undergo or cause (a gas) to undergo a sudden violent expansion, accompanied by heat, light, a shock wave, and a loud noise, as a result of a fast uncontrolled exothermic chemical or nuclear reaction **4** (*intr*) to react suddenly or violently with emotion, etc **5** (*intr*) (esp of a population) to increase rapidly **6** (*tr*) to show (a theory, etc) to be baseless; refute and make obsolete [c16: from Latin *explōdere* to drive off by clapping, hiss (an actor) off, from EX-¹ + *plaudere* to clap] > ex'ploder *n*

exploded view *n* a drawing or photograph of a complicated mechanism that shows the individual parts separately, usually indicating their relative positions

exploit *n* (ˈɛksplɔɪt) **1** a notable deed or feat, esp one that is noble or heroic ▷ *vb* (ɪkˈsplɔɪt) (*tr*) **2** to take advantage of (a person, situation, etc), esp unethically or unjustly for one's own ends **3** to make the best use of [c14: from Old French: accomplishment, from Latin *explicitum* (something) unfolded, from *explicāre* to EXPLICATE] > ex'ploitable *adj* > ˌexploi'tation *n* > ex'ploitive *or* ex'ploitative *adj*

exploration (ˌɛksplɒˈreɪʃən) *n* **1** the act or process of exploring **2** an organized trip into unfamiliar regions, esp for scientific purposes; expedition > exploratory (ɪkˈsplɒrətərɪ, -trɪ) *or* ex'plorative *adj*

explore (ɪkˈsplɔː) *vb* **1** (*tr*) to examine or investigate, esp systematically **2** to travel to or into (unfamiliar or unknown regions), esp for organized scientific purposes **3** (*tr*) *med* to examine (an organ or part) for diagnostic purposes [c16: from Latin *explōrāre*, from EX-¹ + *plōrāre* to cry aloud; probably from the shouts of hunters sighting prey] > ex'plorer *n*

explosion (ɪkˈspləʊʒən) *n* **1** the act or an instance of exploding **2** a violent release of energy resulting from a rapid chemical or nuclear reaction, esp one that produces a shock wave, loud noise, heat, and light **3** a sudden or violent outburst of activity, noise, emotion, etc **4** a rapid increase, esp in a population [c17: from Latin *explōsiō*, from *explōdere* to EXPLODE]

explosive (ɪkˈspləʊsɪv) *adj* **1** of, involving, or characterized by an explosion or explosions **2** capable of exploding or tending to explode **3** potentially violent or hazardous; dangerous: *an explosive situation* ▷ *n* **4** a substance that decomposes rapidly under certain conditions with the production of gases, which expand by the heat of the reaction. The energy released is used in firearms, blasting, and rocket propulsion > ex'plosiveness *n*

expo (ˈɛkspəʊ) *n, pl* -**pos** short for **exposition** (sense 3)

exponent (ɪkˈspəʊnənt) *n* **1** (usually foll by *of*) a person or thing that acts as an advocate (of an idea, cause, etc) **2** a person or thing that explains or interprets **3** a performer or interpretive artist, esp a musician **4** Also called: **power, index** *maths* a number or variable placed as a superscript to the right of another number or quantity indicating the number of times the number or quantity is to be multiplied by itself ▷ *adj* **5** offering a declaration, explanation, or interpretation [c16: from Latin *expōnere* to set out, expound, from *pōnere* to set, place]

exponential (ˌɛkspəʊˈnɛnʃəl) *adj* **1** *maths* (of a function, curve, series, or equation) of, containing, or involving one or more numbers or quantities raised to an exponent, esp e^x **2** *maths* raised to the power of e, the base of natural logarithms **3** of or involving an exponent or exponents **4** *informal* very rapid ▷ *n* **5** *maths* an exponential function, etc

exponential distribution *n statistics* a continuous single-parameter distribution used esp when making statements about the length of life of certain materials or waiting times between randomly occurring events.

Its density function is $p(x) = \lambda e^{-\lambda x}$ for positive λ and nonnegative x, and it is a special case of the gamma distribution

export *n* (ˈɛkspɔːt) **1** (*often plural*) **a** goods (**visible exports**) or services (**invisible exports**) sold to a foreign country or countries **b** (*as modifier*): *an export licence; export finance* ▷ *vb* (ɪkˈspɔːt, ˈɛkspɔːt) **2** to sell (goods or services) or ship (goods) to a foreign country or countries **3** (*tr*) to transmit or spread (an idea, social institution, etc) abroad [c15: from Latin *exportāre* to carry away, from *portāre* to carry] > ex'portable *adj* > exˌporta'bility *n* > ex'porter *n* > ˌexpor'tation *n*

export reject *n* an article that fails to meet a standard of quality required for export and that is sold on the home market

expose (ɪkˈspəʊz) *vb* (*tr*) **1** to display for viewing; exhibit **2** to bring to public notice; disclose; reveal **3** to divulge the identity of; unmask **4** (foll by *to*) to make subject or susceptible (to attack, criticism, etc) **5** to abandon (a child, animal, etc) in the open to die **6** (foll by *to*) to introduce (to) or acquaint (with) **7** *photog* to subject (a photographic film or plate) to light, X-rays, or some other type of actinic radiation **8** expose oneself to display one's sexual organs in public [c15: from Old French *exposer*, from Latin *expōnere* to set out; see EXPONENT] > ex'posable *adj* > ex'posal *n* > ex'poser *n*

exposé (ɛksˈpəʊzeɪ) *n* the act or an instance of bringing a scandal, crime, etc, to public notice

exposed (ɪkˈspəʊzd) *adj* **1** not concealed; displayed for viewing **2** without shelter from the elements **3** susceptible to attack or criticism; vulnerable

exposition (ˌɛkspəˈzɪʃən) *n* **1** a systematic, usually written statement about, commentary on, or explanation of a specific subject **2** the act of expounding or setting forth information or a viewpoint **3** a large public exhibition, esp of industrial products or arts and crafts **4** the act of exposing or the state of being exposed **5** *music* the first statement of the subjects or themes of a movement in sonata form or a fugue **6** *RC Church* the exhibiting of the consecrated Eucharistic Host or a relic for public veneration [c14: from Latin *expositiō* a setting forth, from *expōnere* to display; see EXPONENT] > ˌexpo'sitional *adj*

expositor (ɪkˈspɒzɪtə) *n* a person who expounds

expository (ɪkˈspɒzɪtərɪ, -trɪ) *or* **expositive** *adj* of, involving, or assisting in exposition; explanatory

ex post facto (ˈɛks pəʊst ˈfæktəʊ) *adj* having retrospective effect [c17: from Latin *ex* from + *post* afterwards + *factus* done, from *facere* to do]

expostulate (ɪkˈspɒstjʊˌleɪt) *vb* (*intr*; usually foll by *with*) to argue or reason (with), esp in order to dissuade from an action or intention [c16: from Latin *expostulāre* to require, from *postulāre* to demand; see POSTULATE] > exˌpostu'lation *n* > ex'postuˌlator *n*

exposure (ɪkˈspəʊʒə) *n* **1** the act of exposing or the condition of being exposed **2** the position or outlook of a house, building, etc; aspect: *the bedroom has a southern exposure* **3** lack of shelter from the weather, esp the cold **4** a surface that is exposed **5** *photog* **a** the act of exposing a photographic film or plate to light, X-rays, etc **b** an area on a film or plate that has been exposed to light, etc **6** *photog* **a** the intensity of light falling on a photographic film or plate multiplied by the time for which it is exposed **b** a combination of lens aperture and shutter speed used in taking a photograph **7** appearance or presentation before the public, as in a theatre, on television, or in films

exposure meter *n photog* an instrument for measuring the intensity of light, usually by means of a photocell, so that the suitable camera settings of shutter speed and f-number (or lens aperture) can be determined. Also called: **light meter**

expound (ɪkˈspaʊnd) *vb* (when *intr*, foll by *on* or *about*) to explain or set forth (an argument, theory, etc) in detail [c13: from Old French *espondre*, from Latin *expōnere* to set forth, from *pōnere* to put] > ex'pounder *n*

express (ɪkˈsprɛs) *vb* (*tr*) **1** to transform (ideas) into words; utter; verbalize **2** to show or reveal; indicate **3** to communicate (emotion, etc) without words, as through music, painting, etc **4** to indicate through a symbol, formula, etc **5** to force or squeeze out: *to express the juice from an orange* **6 express oneself** to communicate one's thoughts or ideas ▷ *adj* (*prenominal*) **7** clearly indicated or shown; explicitly stated **8** done or planned for a definite reason or goal; particular **9** of, concerned with, or designed for rapid transportation of people, merchandise, mail, money, etc: *express delivery; an express depot* ▷ *n* **10 a** a system for sending merchandise, mail, money, etc, rapidly **b** merchandise, mail, etc, conveyed by such a system **c** *chiefly US & Canadian* an enterprise operating such a system **11** *Also called:* **express train a** a fast train stopping at none or only a few of the intermediate stations between its two termini ▷ *adv* **12** by means of a special delivery or express delivery [c14: from Latin *expressus*, literally: squeezed out, hence, prominent, from *exprimere* to force out, from EX-¹ + *premere* to press] > ex'presser *n* > ex'pressible *adj*

expression (ɪkˈsprɛʃən) *n* **1** the act or an instance of transforming ideas into words **2** a manifestation of an emotion, feeling, etc, without words **3** communication of emotion through music, painting, etc **4** a look on the face that indicates mood or emotion **5** the choice of words, phrases, syntax, intonation, etc, in communicating **6** a particular phrase used conventionally to express something **7** the act or process of forcing or squeezing out a liquid **8** *maths* a variable, function, or some combination of constants, variables, or functions > ex'pressional *adj* > ex'pressionless *adj*

expressionism (ɪkˈsprɛʃəˌnɪzəm) *n* (*sometimes capital*) an artistic and literary movement originating in Germany at the beginning of the 20th century, which sought to express emotions rather than to represent external reality: characterized by the use of symbolism and of exaggeration and distortion > ex'pressionist *n, adj* > exˌpression'istic *adj*

expression mark *n* one of a set of musical directions, usually in Italian, indicating how a piece or passage is to be performed

expressive (ɪkˈsprɛsɪv) *adj* **1** of, involving, or full of expression **2** (*postpositive; foll by of*) indicative or suggestive (of) **3** having a particular meaning, feeling, or force; significant > ex'pressiveness *n*

expressly (ɪkˈsprɛslɪ) *adv* **1** for an express purpose; with specific intentions **2** plainly, exactly, or unmistakably

expresso (ɪkˈsprɛsəʊ) *n* a variant of **espresso**

expressway (ɪkˈsprɛsˌweɪ) *n* a motorway

expropriate (ɛksˈprəʊprɪˌeɪt) *vb* (*tr*) **1** to deprive (an owner) of (property), esp by taking it for public use [c17: from Medieval Latin *expropriāre* to deprive of possessions, from *proprius* own] > exˌpropri'ation *n* > ex'propriˌator *n*

expulsion (ɪkˈspʌlʃən) *n* the act of expelling or the fact or condition of being expelled [c14: from Latin *expulsiō* a driving out, from *expellere* to EXPEL] > ex'pulsive *adj*

expunge (ɪkˈspʌndʒ) *vb* (*tr*) to delete or erase; blot out; obliterate [c17: from Latin *expungere* to blot out, from *pungere* to prick] > expunction (ɪkˈspʌŋkʃən) *n* > ex'punger *n*

expurgate (ˈɛkspəˌgeɪt) *vb* (*tr*) to amend (a book, text, etc) by removing (obscene or offensive sections) [c17: from Latin *expurgāre* to clean out, from *purgāre* to purify; see PURGE] > ˌexpur'gation *n* > 'expurˌgator *n*

exquisite (ɪkˈskwɪzɪt, ˈɛkskwɪzɪt) *adj* **1** possessing qualities of unusual delicacy and fine craftsmanship **2** extremely beautiful and pleasing **3** outstanding or excellent **4** sensitive; discriminating **5** fastidious and refined **6** intense or sharp in feeling ▷ *n* **7** *obsolete* a dandy [c15: from Latin *exquīsītus* excellent, from *exquīrere* to search out, from *quaerere* to seek] > ex'quisitely *adv* > ex'quisiteness *n*

ex-serviceman *n, pl* -men a man who has served in the army, navy, or air force

ex-servicewoman *n, pl* -women a woman who has served in the army, navy, or air force

extant (ɛkˈstænt, ˈɛkstənt) *adj* still in existence; surviving [c16: from Latin *exstāns* standing out, from *exstāre*, from *stāre* to stand]

● USAGE *Extant* is sometimes wrongly used simply to say

● that something exists, without any connotation of
● survival: *plutonium is perhaps the deadliest element in*
● *existence* (not *the deadliest element extant*)

extemporaneous (ɪkˌstɛmpəˈreɪnɪəs) or **extemporary** (ɪkˈstɛmpərərɪ, -prərɪ) *adj* **1** spoken, performed, etc, without planning or preparation; impromptu; extempore **2** done in a temporary manner; improvised > exˌtempo'raneously or ex'temporarily *adv* > exˌtempo'raneousness or exˌtemporariness *n*

extempore (ɪkˈstɛmpərɪ) *adv, adj* without planning or preparation; impromptu [c16: from Latin *ex tempore* instantaneously, from EX-¹ out of + *tempus* time]

extemporize or **extemporise** (ɪkˈstɛmpəˌraɪz) *vb* **1** to perform, speak, or compose (an act, speech, piece of music, etc) without planning or preparation **2** to use (a temporary solution) for an immediate need; improvise > exˌtempori'zation or exˌtempori'sation *n* > ex'tempoˌrizer or ex'tempoˌriser *n*

extend (ɪkˈstɛnd) *vb* **1** to draw out or be drawn out; stretch **2** to last for a certain time **3** (*intr*) to reach a certain point in time or distance **4** (*intr*) to exist or occur **5** (*tr*) to increase (a building, etc) in size or area; add to or enlarge **6** (*tr*) to broaden the meaning or scope of: *the law was extended* **7** (*tr*) to put forth, present, or offer **8** to stretch forth (an arm, etc) **9** (*tr*) to lay out (a body) at full length **10** (*tr*) to strain or exert (a person or animal) to the maximum **11** (*tr*) to prolong (the time originally set) for payment of (a debt or loan), completion of (a task), etc [c14: from Latin *extendere* to stretch out, from *tendere* to stretch] > ex'tendible or ex'tendable *adj* > exˌtendi'bility or exˌtenda'bility *n*

extended family *n sociol anthropol* a social unit that contains the nuclear family together with blood relatives, often spanning three or more generations

extended-play *adj* denoting an EP record

extender (ɪkˈstɛndə) *n* **1** a person or thing that extends **2** a substance, such as French chalk or china clay, added to paints to give them body and decrease their rate of settlement **3** a substance added to glues and resins to dilute them or to modify their viscosity

extensible (ɪkˈstɛnsəbᵊl) or **extensile** (ɪkˈstɛnsaɪl) *adj* capable of being extended > exˌtensi'bility or ex'tensibleness *n*

extension (ɪkˈstɛnʃən) *n* **1** the act of extending or the condition of being extended **2** something that can be extended or that extends another object **3** the length, range, etc, over which something is extended; extent **4** an additional telephone set connected to the same telephone line as another set or other sets **5** a room or rooms added to an existing building **6** a delay, esp one agreed by all parties, in the date originally set for payment of a debt or completion of a contract **7** the property of matter by which it occupies space; size **8 a** the act of straightening or extending an arm or leg **b** its position after being straightened or extended **9 a** a service by which some of the facilities of an educational establishment, library, etc, are offered to outsiders **b** (*as modifier*): *a university extension course* **10** *logic* the class of entities to which a given word correctly applies: thus, the extension of *satellite of Mars* is the set containing only Deimos and Phobos [c14: from Late Latin *extensiō* a stretching out; see EXTEND] > ex'tensional *adj* > exˌtensio'nality *n*

extensive (ɪkˈstɛnsɪv) *adj* **1** having a large extent, area, scope, degree, etc; vast **2** widespread **3** *agriculture* involving or farmed with minimum expenditure of capital or labour, esp depending on a large area of land. See **intensive** (sense 3) **4** *logic* of or relating to logical extension > ex'tensiveness *n*

extensor (ɪkˈstɛnsə, -sɔː) *n* any muscle that stretches or extends an arm, leg, or other bodily part. See **flexor** [c18: from New Latin, from Latin *extensus* stretched out]

extent (ɪkˈstɛnt) *n* **1** the range over which something extends; scope **2** an area or volume [c14: from Old French *extente*, from Latin *extentus* extensive, from *extendere* to EXTEND]

extenuate (ɪkˈstɛnjʊˌeɪt) *vb* (*tr*) **1** to represent (an offence, a fault, etc) as being less serious than it appears, as by showing mitigating circumstances **2** to cause to be or appear less serious; mitigate **3** *archaic* **a** to emaciate or weaken **b** to dilute or thin out [c16: from Latin *extenuāre* to make thin, from *tenuis* thin, frail] > ex'tenu,ating *adj* > ex,tenu'ation *n* > ex'tenu,ator *n*

exterior (ık'stıərıə) *n* **1** a part, surface, or region that is on the outside **2** the observable outward behaviour or appearance of a person **3** a film or scene shot outside a studio ▷ *adj* **4** of, situated on, or suitable for the outside **5** coming or acting from without; external [c16: from Latin, comparative of *exterus* on the outside, from *ex* out of] > ex'teriorly *adv*

exterior angle *n* **1** an angle of a polygon contained between one side extended and the adjacent side **2** any of the four angles made by a transversal that are outside the region between the two intersected lines

exteriorize *or* **exteriorise** (ık'stıərıə,raız) *vb* (*tr*) **1** *surgery* to expose (an attached organ or part) outside a body cavity, esp in order to remove it from an operating area **2** another word for **externalize** > ex,teriori'zation *or* ex,teriori'sation *n*

exterminate (ık'stɜ:mı,neıt) *vb* (*tr*) to destroy (living things, esp pests or vermin) completely; annihilate; eliminate [c16: from Latin *extermināre* to drive away, from *terminus* boundary] > ex'terminable *adj* > ex,termi'nation *n* > ex'termi,nator *n*

external (ık'stɜ:n°l) *adj* **1** of, situated on, or suitable for the outside; outer **2** coming or acting from without **3** of or involving foreign nations; foreign **4** of, relating to, or designating a medicine that is applied to the outside of the body **5** *anatomy* situated on or near the outside of the body **6** *Austral & NZ* (of a student) studying a university subject extramurally **7** *philosophy* (of objects, etc) taken to exist independently of a perceiving mind ▷ *n* **8** (*often plural*) an external circumstance or aspect, esp one that is superficial or inessential **9** *Austral & NZ* a student taking an extramural subject [c15: from Latin *externus* outward, from *exterus* on the outside, from *ex* out of] > ex'ternally *adv* > ,exter'nality *n*

External Affairs *pl n Canadian* (formerly) the Canadian federal Foreign Affairs department

externalize (ık'stɜ:nə,laız), **externalise** *vb* (*tr*) **1** to make external; give outward shape to **2** *psychol* to attribute (one's own feelings) to one's surroundings > ex,ternali'zation *or* ex,ternali'sation *n*

extinct (ık'stıŋkt) *adj* **1** (of an animal or plant species) having no living representative; having died out **2** quenched or extinguished **3** (of a volcano) no longer liable to erupt; inactive [c15: from Latin *exstinctus* quenched, from *exstinguere* to EXTINGUISH]

extinction (ık'stıŋkʃən) *n* **1** the act of making extinct or the state of being extinct **2** the act of extinguishing or the state of being extinguished **3** complete destruction; annihilation **4** *physics* reduction of the intensity of radiation as a result of absorption or scattering by matter

extinguish (ık'stıŋgwıʃ) *vb* (*tr*) **1** to put out or quench (a light, flames, etc) **2** to remove or destroy entirely; annihilate **3** *archaic* to eclipse or obscure by or as if by superior brilliance [c16: from Latin *exstinguere*, from *stinguere* to quench] > ex'tinguishable *adj* > ex'tinguisher *n* > ex'tinguishment *n*

extirpate ('ekstə,peıt) *vb* (*tr*) **1** to destroy or root out completely **2** to pull up or out; uproot [c16: from Latin *exstirpāre* to root out, from *stirps* root, stock] > ,extir'pation *n* > 'extir,pator *n*

extol *or US* **extoll** (ık'stəul) *vb* **-tols**, **-tolling**, **-tolled** *or US* **-tolls**, **-tolling**, **-tolled** (*tr*) to praise lavishly; exalt [c15: from Latin *extollere* to elevate, from *tollere* to raise] > ex'toller *n* > ex'tolment *n*

extort (ık'stɔ:t) *vb* (*tr*) **1** to secure (money, favours, etc) by intimidation, violence, or the misuse of influence or authority **2** to obtain by importunate demands [c16: from Latin *extortus* wrenched out, from *extorquēre* to wrest away, from *torquēre* to twist, wrench] > ex'torter *n* > ex'tortive *adj*

extortion (ık'stɔ:ʃən) *n* the act of securing money, favours, etc by intimidation or violence; blackmail > ex'tortioner *or* ex'tortionist *n*

extortionate (ık'stɔ:ʃənıt) *adj* **1** (of prices, etc) excessive; exorbitant **2** (of persons) using extortion > ex'tortionately *adv*

extra ('ekstrə) *adj* **1** being more than what is usual or expected; additional ▷ *n* **2** a person or thing that is additional **3** something for which an additional charge is made **4** an additional edition of a newspaper, esp to report a new development or crisis **5** *films* an actor or person temporarily engaged, usually for crowd scenes **6** *cricket* a run not scored from the bat, such as a wide, no-ball, bye, or leg bye ▷ *adv* **7** unusually; exceptionally: *an extra fast car* [c18: perhaps shortened from EXTRAORDINARY]

extra- *prefix* outside or beyond an area or scope: *extrasensory*; *extraterritorial* [from Latin *extrā* outside, beyond, changed from *extera*, from *exterus* outward]

extra cover *n cricket* a fielding position between cover and mid-off

extract *vb* (ık'strækt) (*tr*) **1** to withdraw, pull out, or uproot by force **2** to remove or separate **3** to derive (pleasure, information, etc) from some source or situation **4** to deduce or develop (a doctrine, policy, etc) **5** *informal* to extort (money, etc) **6** to obtain (a substance) from a mixture or material by a chemical or physical process, such as digestion, distillation, the action of a solvent, or mechanical separation **7** to cut out or copy out (an article, passage, quotation, etc) from a publication **8** to determine the value of (the root of a number) ▷ *n* ('ekstrækt) **9** something extracted, such as a part or passage from a book, speech, etc **10** a preparation containing the active principle or concentrated essence of a material [c15: from Latin *extractus* drawn forth, from *extrahere*, from *trahere* to drag] > ex'tractable *adj* > ex,tracta'bility *n* > ex'tractive *adj*, *n*

● USAGE Extract is sometimes wrongly used where
● *extricate* would be better: *he will find it difficult extricating*
● (*not extracting*) *himself from this situation*

extraction (ık'strækʃən) *n* **1** the act of extracting or the condition of being extracted **2** something extracted; an extract **3** the act or an instance of extracting a tooth or teeth **4** origin, descent, lineage, or ancestry

extractor (ık'stræktə) *n* **1** a person or thing that extracts **2** an instrument for pulling something out or removing tight-fitting components **3** short for **extractor fan**

extractor fan *or* **extraction fan** *n* a fan used in kitchens, bathrooms, workshops, etc, to remove stale air or fumes

extracurricular (,ekstrəkə'rıkjulə) *adj* **1** taking place outside the normal school timetable **2** beyond the regular duties, schedule, etc

extradite ('ekstrə,daıt) *vb* (*tr*) **1** to surrender (an alleged offender) for trial to a foreign state **2** to procure the extradition of [c19: back formation from EXTRADITION] > 'extra,ditable *adj*

extradition (,ekstrə'dıʃən) *n* the surrender of an alleged offender or fugitive to the state in whose territory the alleged offence was committed [c19: from French, from Latin *trāditiō* a handing over; see TRADITION]

extrados (ek'streıdɒs) *n*, *pl* **-dos** (-dəʊz) *or* **-doses** *architect* the outer curve or surface of an arch or vault [c18: from French, from EXTRA- + *dos* back, from Latin *dorsum*]

extradural (,ekstrə'djʊərəl) *adj* another word for **epidural** (sense 1)

extragalactic (,ekstrəgə'læktık) *adj* occurring or existing beyond the Galaxy

extramarital (,ekstrə'mærıt°l) *adj* (esp of sexual relations) occurring outside marriage

extramural (,ekstrə'mjʊərəl) *adj* **1** connected with but outside the normal courses or programme of a university, college, etc **2** located beyond the boundaries or walls of a city, castle, etc

extraneous (ık'streınıəs) *adj* **1** not essential **2** not pertinent or applicable; irrelevant **3** coming from without; of external origin **4** not belonging; unrelated to that to which it is added or in which it is contained [c17: from Latin *extrāneus* external, from *extrā* outside] > ex'traneousness *n*

extranet ('ekstrə,net) *n computing* an intranet that is modified to allow outsiders access to it, esp one

e

belonging to a business that allows access to customers [C20: from EXTRA- + NET[1] (sense 8), modelled on INTRANET]

extraordinary (ık'strɔːdʰnrı, -dʰnərı) adj 1 very unusual, remarkable, or surprising 2 not in an established manner, course, or order 3 employed for particular events or purposes 4 (usually postpositive) (of an official, etc) additional or subordinate to the usual one [C15: from Latin extraordinārius beyond what is usual; see ORDINARY] > ex'traordinarily adv > ex'traordinariness n

extraordinary general meeting n a meeting specially called to discuss a particular item of a company's business, usually one of some importance. The meeting may be called by a group of shareholders or by the directors. Abbreviation: EGM

extraordinary rendition n the process by which a country seizes a person assumed to be involved in terrorist activity and then transports him or her for interrogation to a country where due process of law is unlikely to be respected

extrapolate (ık'stræpə,leıt) vb 1 maths to estimate (a value of a function or measurement) beyond the values already known, by the extension of a curve. See interpolate (sense 4) 2 to infer (something not known) by using but not strictly deducing from the known facts [C19: EXTRA- + -polate, as in INTERPOLATE] > ex,trapo'lation n > ex'trapolative or ex'trapolatory adj > ex'trapo,lator n

extrasensory (,ɛkstrə'sɛnsərı) adj of or relating to extrasensory perception

extrasensory perception n the supposed ability of certain individuals to obtain information about the environment without the use of normal sensory channels

extraterritorial (,ɛkstrə,tɛrı'tɔːrıəl) or **exterritorial** adj 1 beyond the limits of a country's territory 2 of, relating to, or possessing extraterritoriality

extraterritoriality (,ɛkstrə,tɛrı,tɔːrı'ælıtı) n international law 1 the privilege granted to some aliens, esp diplomats, of being exempt from the jurisdiction of the state in which they reside 2 the right or privilege of a state to exercise authority in certain circumstances beyond the limits of its territory

extra time n sport an additional period played at the end of a match, to compensate for time lost through injury or (in certain circumstances) to allow the teams to achieve a conclusive result

extravagance (ık'strævıgəns) n 1 excessive outlay of money; wasteful spending 2 immoderate or absurd speech or behaviour

extravagant (ık'strævıgənt) adj 1 spending money excessively or immoderately 2 going beyond usual bounds; unrestrained 3 ostentatious; showy 4 exorbitant in price; overpriced [C14: from Medieval Latin extravagāns, from EXTRA- + vagārī to wander]

extravaganza (ık,strævə'gænzə) n 1 an elaborately staged and costumed light entertainment 2 any lavish or fanciful display, literary or other composition, etc [C18: from Italian: EXTRAVAGANCE]

extravasate (ık'strævə,seıt) vb pathol to cause (blood or lymph) to escape or (of blood or lymph) to escape into the surrounding tissues from their proper vessels [C17: from Latin EXTRA- + vās vessel] > ex,trava'sation n

extravehicular (,ɛkstrəvı'hıkjʊlə) adj occurring or used outside a spacecraft, either in space or on the surface of the moon or another planet

extraversion (ɛkstrə'vɜːʃən) n a variant spelling of extroversion > 'extra,vert n, adj

extra virgin adj (of olive oil) of the highest quality, extracted by cold pressing rather than chemical treatment

Extremadura (Spanish estrema'ðura) n a region of W Spain: arid and sparsely populated except in the valleys of the Tagus and Guadiana rivers. Area: 41 593 sq km (16 059 sq miles)

extreme (ık'striːm) adj 1 being of a high or of the highest degree or intensity 2 exceeding what is usual or reasonable; immoderate 3 very strict, rigid, or severe; drastic 4 (prenominal) farthest or outermost in direction

▷ n 5 the highest or furthest degree (often in the phrases **in the extreme, go to extremes**) 6 (often plural) either of the two limits or ends of a scale or range of possibilities [C15: from Latin extrēmus outermost, from exterus on the outside; see EXTERIOR] > ex'tremeness n

extremely (ık'striːmlı) adv 1 to the extreme; exceedingly 2 (intensifier): I behaved extremely badly
● USAGE See at very

extreme programming n a discipline of software engineering following a specific structure, designed to simplify and speed up the development process. Abbreviation: XP[1]

extreme sport n a sport that is physically hazardous, such as bungee jumping or snowboarding

extreme unction n RC Church a former name for anointing of the sick

extremist (ık'striːmıst) n 1 a person who favours or resorts to immoderate, uncompromising, or fanatical methods or behaviour, esp in being politically radical ▷ adj 2 of, relating to, or characterized by immoderate or excessive actions, opinions, etc > ex'tremism n

extremity (ık'strɛmıtı) n, pl -ties 1 the farthest or outermost point or section; termination 2 the greatest or most intense degree 3 an extreme condition or state, as of adversity or disease 4 a limb, such as a leg, arm, or wing, or the part of such a limb farthest from the trunk 5 (usually plural) archaic a drastic or severe measure

extremophile (ık'strɛmə,faıl) n a microbe that lives in an environment once thought to be uninhabitable, for example in boiling or frozen water

extricate ('ɛkstrı,keıt) vb (tr) to remove or free from complication, hindrance, or difficulty; disentangle [C17: from Latin extrīcāre to disentangle, from EX-[1] + trīcae trifles, vexations] > 'extricable adj > ,extri'cation n
● USAGE See at extract

extrinsic (ɛk'strınsık) adj 1 not contained or included within; extraneous 2 originating or acting from outside; external [C16: from Late Latin extrīnsecus (adj) outward, from Latin (adv) from without, on the outward side, from exter outward + secus alongside, related to sequī to follow] > ex'trinsically adv

extroversion or **extraversion** (,ɛkstrə'vɜːʃən) n psychol the directing of one's interest outwards, esp towards social contacts [C17: from extro- (variant of EXTRA-, contrasting with INTRO-) + -version, from Latin vertere to turn] > ,extro'versive or ,extra'versive adj

extrovert or **extravert** ('ɛkstrə,vɜːt) psychol ▷ n 1 a person concerned more with external reality than inner feelings ▷ adj 2 of or characterized by extroversion [C20: from extro- (variant of EXTRA-, contrasting with INTRO-) + -vert, from Latin vertere to turn] > 'extro,verted or 'extra,verted adj

extrude (ık'struːd) vb 1 (tr) to squeeze or force out 2 (tr) to produce (moulded sections of plastic, metal, etc) by ejection under pressure through a suitably shaped nozzle or die 3 (tr) to chop up or pulverize (an item of food) and re-form it to look like a whole [C16: from Latin extrūdere to thrust out, from trūdere to push, thrust] > ex'truded adj

extrusion (ık'struːʒən) n 1 the act or process of extruding 2 a the movement of magma onto the surface of the earth through volcano craters and cracks in the earth's crust, forming igneous rock b any igneous rock formed in this way 3 a component or length of material formed by the process of extruding [C16: from Medieval Latin extrūsiō, from extrūdere to EXTRUDE] > ex'trusive adj

exuberant (ıg'zjuːbərənt) adj 1 abounding in vigour and high spirits; full of vitality 2 lavish or effusive; excessively elaborate 3 growing luxuriantly or in profusion [C15: from Latin exūberāns, from ūberāre to be fruitful, from ūber fertile] > ex'uberance n

exuberate (ıg'zjuːbə,reıt) vb (intr) rare 1 to be exuberant 2 to abound or grow in profusion [C15: from Latin exūberāre to be abundant; see EXUBERANT]

exude (ıg'zjuːd) vb 1 to release or be released through pores, incisions, etc, as sweat from the body or sap from trees 2 (tr) to make apparent by mood or behaviour [C16: from Latin exsūdāre, from sūdāre to sweat] > exudation (,ɛksjʊ'deıʃən) n

exult (ɪgˈzʌlt) *vb* (*intr*) **1** to be joyful or jubilant, esp because of triumph or success; rejoice **2** (often foll by *over*) to triumph (over); show or take delight in the defeat or discomfiture (of) [c16: from Latin *exsultāre* to jump or leap for joy, from *saltāre* to leap] > exultation (ˌɛgzʌlˈteɪʃən) *n* > ex'ultingly *adv*

exultant (ɪgˈzʌltənt) *adj* elated or jubilant, esp because of triumph or success > ex'ultantly *adv*

exurbia (ɛksˈɜːbɪə) *n chiefly US* the region outside the suburbs of a city, consisting of residential areas (**exurbs**) that are occupied predominantly by rich commuters (**exurbanites**) [c20: from EX-¹ + Latin *urbs* city, on pattern of *suburbia*] > ex'urban *adj*

exuviate (ɪgˈzjuːvɪˌeɪt) *vb* to shed (a skin or similar outer covering) > ex,uvi'ation *n*

-ey *suffix* a variant of -y¹,²

Eyam (iːm) *n* a village in N central England, in Derbyshire. When plague reached the village in 1665 the inhabitants, led by the Rev. Mompesson, isolated themselves to prevent it spreading further: as a result most of them died, including Mompesson's family

eyas (ˈaɪəs) *n* a nestling hawk or falcon, esp one reared for training in falconry [c15: mistaken division of earlier *a nyas*, from Old French *niais* nestling, from Latin *nīdus* nest]

Eyck (aɪk) *n* See **van Eyck**

eye¹ (aɪ) *n* **1** the organ of sight of animals, containing light-sensitive cells associated with nerve fibres, so that light entering the eye is converted to nervous impulses that reach the brain. In man and other vertebrates the iris controls the amount of light entering the eye and the lens focuses the light onto the retina **2** (*often plural*) the ability to see; sense of vision **3** the visible external part of an eye, often including the area around it **4** a look, glance, expression, or gaze **5** a sexually inviting or provocative look (esp in the phrases **give** (**someone**) **the** (**glad**) **eye, make eyes at**) **6** attention or observation (often in the phrases **catch someone's eye, keep an eye on, cast an eye over**) **7** ability to recognize, judge, or appreciate **8** (*often plural*) opinion, judgment, point of view, or authority: *in the eyes of the law* **9** a structure or marking having the appearance of an eye, such as the bud on a twig or potato tuber or a spot on a butterfly wing **10** a small loop or hole, as at one end of a needle **11** a small area of low pressure and calm in the centre of a tornado or cyclone **12** all eyes *informal* acutely vigilant or observant **13** my eye *or* all my eye *informal* rubbish; nonsense **14** an eye for an eye retributive or vengeful justice; retaliation **15** eyes out *NZ* with every possible effort **16** get one's eye in *chiefly sport* to become accustomed to the conditions, light, etc, with a consequent improvement in one's performance **17** half an eye a modicum of perceptiveness **18** have eyes for to be interested in **19** in one's mind's eye pictured within the mind; imagined or remembered vividly **20** in the public eye exposed to public curiosity or publicity **21** keep an eye open *or* keep an eye out to watch with special attention (for) **22** keep one's eyes peeled *or* keep one's eyes skinned to watch vigilantly (for) **23** look someone in the eye to look at someone openly and without shame or embarrassment **24** make eyes *or* make sheep's eyes *old-fashioned* to ogle amorously **25** more than meets the eye hidden motives, meaning, or facts **26** see eye to eye to agree (with) **27** set eyes on, lay eyes on *or* clap eyes on (*usually used with a negative*) to see **28** turn a blind eye to *or* close one's eyes to to pretend not to notice or ignore deliberately **29** up to one's eyes extremely busy (with) **30** with an eye to *or* having an eye to (*preposition*) **a** regarding; with reference to **b** with the intention or purpose of **31** with one's eyes open in the full knowledge of all relevant facts **32** with one's eyes shut **a** with great ease, esp as a result of thorough familiarity **b** without being aware of all the facts ▷ *vb* **33** eyes, eyeing *or* eying, eyed (*tr*) **33** to look at carefully or warily **34** Also called: eye up to look at in a manner indicating sexual interest; ogle [Old English *ēage*; related to Old Norse *auga*, Old High German *ouga*, Sanskrit *aksi*] > 'eyeless *adj* > 'eye,like *adj*

eye² (aɪ) *n* another word for **nye**

eyeball (ˈaɪˌbɔːl) *n* **1** the entire ball-shaped part of the eye **2** eyeball to eyeball in close confrontation ▷ *vb* **3** (*tr*) *slang* to stare at

eyebank (ˈaɪˌbæŋk) *n* a place in which corneas are stored for use in corneal grafts

eyebath (ˈaɪˌbɑːθ) *n* a small vessel with a rim shaped to fit round the eye, used for applying medicated or cleansing solutions to the eyeball

eyeblack (ˈaɪˌblæk) *n* another name for **mascara**

eyebright (ˈaɪˌbraɪt) *n* any scrophulariaceous annual plant of the genus *Euphrasia*, esp *E. nemorosa*, having small white-and-purple two-lipped flowers: formerly used in the treatment of eye disorders

eyebrow (ˈaɪˌbraʊ) *n* **1** the transverse bony ridge over each eye **2** the arch of hair that covers this ridge

eyebrow pencil *n* a cosmetic in pencil form for applying colour and shape to the eyebrows

eye candy *n informal* **1** a person who is or people considered highly attractive to look at, often implying that they are but lacking in intelligence or depth **2** something intended to be attractive to the eye without being demanding or contributing anything essential

eye-catching *adj* tending to attract attention; striking

eye contact *n* a direct look between two people; meeting of eyes

eyed (aɪd) *adj* **a** having an eye or eyes (as specified) **b** (*in combination*): *one-eyed; brown-eyed*

eye dog *n NZ* a dog trained to control sheep by staring fixedly at them. Also called: **strong-eye dog**

eyeful (ˈaɪfʊl) *n informal* **1** a view, glance, or gaze **2** a very beautiful or attractive sight, esp a woman

eyeglass (ˈaɪˌglɑːs) *n* **1** a lens for aiding or correcting defective vision, esp a monocle **2** another word for **eyepiece**

eyeglasses (ˈaɪˌglɑːsɪz) *pl n Now chiefly US* another word for **spectacles**

eyehole (ˈaɪˌhəʊl) *n* **1** a hole through which something, such as a rope, hook, or bar, is passed **2** the cavity that contains the eyeball; eye socket **3** another word for **peephole**

eyelash (ˈaɪˌlæʃ) *n* **1** any one of the short curved hairs that grow from the edge of the eyelids **2** a row or fringe of these hairs

eyelet (ˈaɪlɪt) *n* **1** a small hole for a lace or cord to be passed through or for a hook to be inserted into **2** a small metal ring or tube with flared ends bent back, reinforcing an eyehole in fabric **3** a chink or small opening, such as a peephole in a wall **4** embroidery a small hole with finely stitched edges, forming part of an ornamental pattern **5** a small eye or eyelike marking ▷ *vb* **6** (*tr*) to supply with an eyelet or eyelets [c14: from Old French *oillet*, literally: a little eye, from *oill* eye, from Latin *oculus* eye; see EYE¹]

eyelevel (ˈaɪˌlɛvəl) *adj* level with a person's eyes when looking straight ahead: *an eyelevel grill*

eyelid (ˈaɪˌlɪd) *n* either of the two muscular folds of skin that can be moved to cover the exposed portion of the eyeball

eyeliner (ˈaɪˌlaɪnə) *n* a cosmetic used to outline the eyes

eye-opener *n informal* **1** something startling or revealing **2** *US & Canadian* an alcoholic drink taken early in the morning

eyepiece (ˈaɪˌpiːs) *n* the lens or combination of lenses in an optical instrument nearest the eye of the observer

eye rhyme *n* a rhyme involving words that are similar in spelling but not in sound, such as *stone* and *none*

eye shadow *n* a coloured cosmetic put around the eyes so as to enhance their colour or shape

eyeshot (ˈaɪˌʃɒt) *n* range of vision; view

eyesight (ˈaɪˌsaɪt) *n* the ability to see; faculty of sight

eyesore (ˈaɪˌsɔː) *n* something very ugly

eyespot (ˈaɪˌspɒt) *n* **1** a small area of light-sensitive pigment in some protozoans, algae, and other simple organisms **2** an eyelike marking, as on the wings of certain butterflies

eyestrain (ˈaɪˌstreɪn) *n* fatigue or irritation of the eyes, resulting from excessive use, as from prolonged reading of small print, or uncorrected defects of vision

Eyetie (ˈaɪtaɪ) *n, adj Brit slang, offensive* Italian [c20: based on a jocular mispronunciation of *Italian*]

eyetooth (ˌaɪˈtuːθ) *n*, *pl* -**teeth** **1** either of the two canine teeth in the upper jaw **2** **give one's eyeteeth for** to go to any lengths to achieve or obtain (something)

eyewash (ˈaɪˌwɒʃ) *n* **1** a mild solution for applying to the eyes for relief of irritation, etc **2** *informal* nonsense; rubbish

eyewitness (ˈaɪˌwɪtnɪs) *n* a person present at an event who can describe what happened

eyot (aɪt) *n* *Brit rare* island [variant of AIT]

Eyre¹ (ɛə) *n* **Lake Eyre** a shallow salt lake or salt flat in NE central South Australia, about 11 m (35 ft) below sea level, divided into two areas (North and South); it usually contains little or no water. Maximum area: 9600 sq km (3700 sq miles) [c19: named after Edward John Eyre (1815–1901), British explorer and colonial administrator]

Eyre² (ɛə) *n* **1** **Edward John.** 1815–1901, British explorer and colonial administrator. He was governor of Jamaica (1864–66) until his authorization of 400 executions to suppress an uprising led to his recall **2** **Sir Richard.** born 1943, British theatre director: director of the Royal National Theatre (1988–97)

Eyre Peninsula *n* a peninsula of South Australia, between the Great Australian Bight and Spencer Gulf

eyrie (ˈɪərɪ, ˈɛərɪ, ˈaɪərɪ) *or* **aerie** *n* **1** the nest of an eagle

or other bird of prey, built in a high inaccessible place **2** any high isolated position or place [c16: from Medieval Latin *airea*, from Latin *ārea* open field, hence nest]

eyrir (ˈeɪrɪə) *n*, *pl* **aurar** (ˈɔːrɑː) an Icelandic monetary unit worth one hundredth of a krona [Old Norse: ounce (of silver), money; related to Latin *aureus* golden]

Eysenck (ˈaɪzɛŋk) *n* **Hans Jürgen** (hænz ˈjɜːgən). 1916–97, British psychologist, born in Germany, who developed a dimensional theory of personality that stressed the influence of heredity

Ez. *or* **Ezr.** *abbreviation Bible* Ezra

Ezek. *abbreviation Bible* Ezekiel

Ezekiel (ɪˈziːkɪəl) *n* *Old Testament* **1** a Hebrew prophet of the 6th century BC, exiled to Babylon in 597 BC **2** the book containing his oracles, which describe the downfall of Judah and Jerusalem and their subsequent restoration

e-zine (ˈiːziːn) *n* a magazine available only in electronic form, for example on the World Wide Web

Ezra (ˈɛzrə) *n* *Old Testament* **1** a Jewish priest of the 5th century BC, who was sent from Babylon by the Persian king Artaxerxes I to reconstitute observance of the Jewish law and worship in Jerusalem after the period of captivity **2** the book recounting his efforts to perform this task

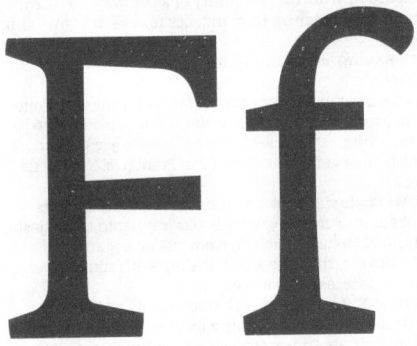

Ff

f *or* **F** (εf) *n, pl* **f's, F's** *or* **Fs** 1 the sixth letter and fourth consonant of the modern English alphabet 2 a speech sound represented by this letter, usually a voiceless labio-dental fricative, as in *fat*

f³ *symbol for* 1 *music* forte: an instruction to play loudly 2 *physics* frequency 3 *maths* function (of) 4 *physics* femto-

f³, f/ *or* **f:** *symbol for* f-number

F *symbol for* 1 *music* **a** a note having a frequency of 349.23 hertz (**F above middle C**) or this value multiplied or divided by any power of 2; the fourth note of the scale of C major **b** the major or minor key having this note as its tonic 2 Fahrenheit 3 *chem* fluorine 4 *physics* force 5 franc(s) 6 farad(s) 7 *genetics* a generation of filial offspring, F_1 being the first generation of offspring, F_2 being the second generation, etc

f. *or* **F.** *abbreviation* 1 fathom(s) 2 female 3 *grammar* feminine 4 *pl* **ff.** *or* **FF.** folio 5 *pl* **ff.** following (page)

F- *abbreviation* fighter

fa (fɑː) *n music* a variant spelling of **fah**

FA *abbreviation* (in Britain) Football Association

f.a. *or* **FA** *abbreviation* fanny adams

F.A.B. *interj Brit* an expression of agreement to, or acknowledgment of, a command [C20: from British television series *Thunderbirds*]

Fabergé ('fæbə,ʒeɪ) *n* **Peter Carl**. 1846–1920, Russian goldsmith and jeweller, known for the golden Easter eggs and other ornate and fanciful objects that he created for the Russian and other royal families

Fabian ('feɪbɪən) *adj* 1 of, relating to, or resembling the delaying tactics of the Roman general Q. Fabius Maximus (died 203 BC) who withstood Hannibal while avoiding a pitched battle; cautious; circumspect ▷ *n* 2 a member of or sympathizer with the Fabian Society [C19: from Latin *Fabiānus* of Fabius] > 'Fabia,nism *n*

Fabian Society *n* an association of British socialists advocating the establishment of democratic socialism by gradual reforms within the law: founded in 1884

Fabius Maximus ('feɪbɪəs 'mæksɪməs) *n* full name *Quintus Fabius Maximus Verrucosus*, called *Cunctator* (the delayer). died 203 BC, Roman general and statesman. As commander of the Roman army during the Second Punic War, he withstood Hannibal by his strategy of harassing the Carthaginians while avoiding a pitched battle

fable ('feɪbəl) *n* 1 **a** a short moral story, esp one with animals as characters 2 a false, fictitious, or improbable account; fiction or lie 3 a story or legend about supernatural or mythical characters or events 4 legends or myths collectively ▷ *vb* 5 to relate or tell (fables) 6 (*intr*) to speak untruthfully; tell lies 7 (*tr*) to talk about or describe in the manner of a fable [C13: from Latin *fābula* story, narrative, from *fārī* to speak, say] > 'fabler *n*

fabled ('feɪbəld) *adj* 1 made famous in fable 2 fictitious

fabliau ('fæblɪ,əʊ; *French* fɑblijo) *n, pl* **fabliaux** ('fæblɪ,əʊz; *French* fɑblijo) a comic usually ribald verse tale, of a kind popular in France in the 12th and 13th centuries [C19: from French: a little tale, from *fable* tale]

Fablon ('fæblɒn, -lɒn) *n trademark* a brand of adhesive-backed plastic material used to cover and decorate shelves, worktops, etc, and for handicraft purposes

Fabre (*French* fɑbrə) *n* **Jean Henri** (ʒɑ̃ ɑ̃ri). 1823–1915, French entomologist; author of many works on insect life, remarkable for their vivid and minute observation, esp *Souvenirs Entomologiques* (1879–1907). Nobel prize for literature 1910

fabric ('fæbrɪk) *n* 1 any cloth made from yarn or fibres by weaving, knitting, felting, etc 2 the texture of a cloth 3 a structure or framework: *the fabric of society* 4 a style or method of construction 5 *rare* a building [C15: from Latin *fabrica* workshop, from *faber* craftsman]

fabricate ('fæbrɪ,keɪt) *vb* (*tr*) 1 to make, build, or construct 2 to devise, invent, or concoct (a story, lie, etc) 3 to fake or forge [C15: from Latin *fabricāre* to build, make, from *fabrica* workshop; see FABRIC] > ,fabri'cation *n* > 'fabri,cator *n*

Fabry (*French* fabri) *n* **Charles** (ʃarl). 1867–1945, French physicist: discovered ozone in the upper atmosphere

fabulist ('fæbjʊlɪst) *n* 1 a person who invents or recounts fables 2 a person who lies or falsifies

fabulous ('fæbjʊləs) *adj* 1 almost unbelievable; astounding; legendary: *fabulous wealth* 2 *informal* extremely good: *a fabulous time at the party* 3 of, relating to, or based upon fable: *a fabulous beast* [C15: from Latin *fābulōsus* celebrated in fable, from *fābula* FABLE]

> **ˈfabulously** adv > **ˈfabulousness** n

façade or **facade** (fə'sɑːd, fæ-) n **1** the face of a building, esp the main front **2** a front or outer appearance, esp a deceptive one [c17: from French, from Italian *facciata*, from *faccia* FACE]

face (feɪs) n **1 a** the front of the head from the forehead to the lower jaw; visage **b** (*as modifier*): *face flannel; face cream* **2 a** the expression of the countenance; look: *a sad face* **b** a distorted expression, esp to indicate disgust; grimace **3** *informal* make-up (esp in the phrase **put one's face on**) **4** outward appearance: *the face of the countryside is changing* **5** appearance or pretence (esp in the phrases **put a bold, good, bad,** etc, **face on**) **6** worth in the eyes of others; dignity (esp in the phrases **lose** or **save face**) **7** *informal* impudence or effrontery **8** the main side of an object, building, etc, or the front: *the face of a palace; a cliff face* **9** the marked surface of an instrument, esp the dial of a timepiece **10** the functional or working side of an object, as of a tool or playing card **11 a** the exposed area of a mine from which coal, ore, etc, may be mined **b** (*as modifier*): *face worker* **12** the uppermost part or surface: *the face of the earth* **13** Also called: **side** any one of the plane surfaces of a crystal or other solid figure **14** *mountaineering* a steep side of a mountain, bounded by ridges **15** *Brit slang* a well-known or important person **16** Also called: **typeface** *printing* **a** the printing surface of any type character **b** the style, the design, or sometimes the size of any type fount **17 in face of** or **in the face of** despite **18 on the face of it** to all appearances **19 set one's face against** to oppose with determination **20 show one's face** to make an appearance **21 to someone's face** in someone's presence; directly and openly: *I told him the truth to his face* ▷ vb **22** (when *intr*, often foll by *to, towards,* or *on*) to look or be situated or placed (in a specified direction): *the house faces on the square* **23** to be opposite: *facing page 9* **24** (*tr*) to meet or be confronted by: *in his work he faces many problems* **25** (*tr*) to provide with a surface of a different material **26** to dress the surface of (stone or other material) **27** (*tr*) to expose (a card) with the face uppermost **28** *military chiefly US* to order (a formation) to turn in a certain direction or (of a formation) to turn as required: *right face!*. ▷ See also **face down, face up to** [c13: from Old French, from Vulgar Latin *facia* (unattested), from Latin *faciēs* form, related to *facere* to make]

Facebook ('feɪs,bʊk) n *trademark* **1** a popular social networking website ▷ vb **2** (*tr; sometimes not cap*) to search for (a person's profile) on the Facebook website

face card n (in a pack of playing cards) a king, queen, or jack of any suit. Also called (in Britain and certain other countries): **court card**

face cloth or **face flannel** n *Brit* a small piece of cloth used to wash the face and hands. US equivalent: **washcloth**

face down vb (*tr, adverb*) to confront and force (someone or something) to back down

faceless ('feɪslɪs) adj **1** without a face **2** without identity; anonymous > **ˈfacelessness** n

face-lift n **1** a cosmetic surgical operation for tightening sagging skin and smoothing unwanted wrinkles on the face **2** any improvement or renovation, as of a building, etc ▷ vb **3** (*tr*) to improve the appearance of, as by a face-lift

facemail ('feɪs,meɪl) n a computer program which uses an electronically generated face to deliver messages on screen

face-off n **1** *ice hockey* the method of starting a game, in which the referee drops the puck, etc between two opposing players **2** a confrontation ▷ vb **face off** (*adverb*) **3** to start play by (a face-off)

face-plant *informal* ▷ vb **1** (*intr*) to fall onto one's face, esp when skiing or snowboarding ▷ n **2** an act or instance of falling onto one's face

face powder n a flesh-tinted cosmetic powder worn to make the face look less shiny, softer, etc

faceprint ('feɪs,prɪnt) n a digitally recorded representation of a person's face that can be used for security purposes because it is as individual as a fingerprint

facer ('feɪsə) n **1** a person or thing that faces **2** *Brit informal* a difficulty or problem

face recognition n the ability of a computer to scan, store, and recognize human faces for use in identifying people

face-saving adj maintaining dignity or prestige > **ˈface-ˌsaver** n

facet ('fæsɪt) n **1** any of the surfaces of a cut gemstone **2** an aspect or phase, as of a subject or personality ▷ vb -ets, -eting, -eted or -ets, -etting, -etted **3** (*tr*) to cut facets in (a gemstone) [c17: from French *facette* a little FACE]

facetiae (fə'siːʃɪˌiː) pl n **1** humorous or witty sayings **2** obscene or coarsely witty books [c17: from Latin: jests, plural of *facētia* witticism, from *facētus* elegant]

face time n the time spent dealing with someone else face to face, esp in a place of work

facetious (fə'siːʃəs) adj **1** characterized by levity of attitude and love of joking **2** jocular or amusing, esp at inappropriate times: *facetious remarks* [c16: from Old French *facetieux*, from *facetie* witty saying; see FACETIAE] > **fa'cetiously** adv > **fa'cetiousness** n

face to face adv, adj (**face-to-face** *as adjective*) **1** opposite one another **2** in confrontation

face up to vb (*intr, adverb + preposition*) to accept (an unpleasant fact, reality, etc)

face value n **1** the value written or stamped on the face of a commercial paper or coin **2** apparent worth or value, as opposed to real worth

facia ('feɪʃɪə) n a variant spelling of **fascia**

facial ('feɪʃəl) adj **1** of or relating to the face ▷ n **2** a beauty treatment for the face, involving cleansing, massage, and cosmetic packs > **ˈfacially** adv

-facient suffix forming adjectives, suffix forming nouns indicating a state or quality: *absorbefacient; rubefacient* [from Latin *facient-, faciēns*, present participle of *facere* to do]

facies ('feɪʃɪˌiːz) n, pl -cies **1** the general form and appearance of an individual or a group of plants or animals **2** the characteristics of a rock or series of rocks reflecting their appearance, composition, and conditions of formation **3** *med* the general facial expression of a patient, esp when typical of a specific disease or disorder [c17: from Latin: appearance, FACE]

facile ('fæsaɪl) adj **1** easy to perform or achieve **2** working or moving easily or smoothly **3** without depth; superficial: *a facile solution* [c15: from Latin *facilis* easy, from *facere* to do] > **ˈfacilely** adv > **ˈfacileness** n

facilitate (fə'sɪlɪˌteɪt) vb (*tr*) to make easier; assist the progress of > **faˌciliˈtation** n

facility (fə'sɪlɪtɪ) n, pl -ties **1** ease of action or performance; freedom from difficulty **2** ready skill or ease deriving from practice or familiarity **3** (*often plural*) the means or equipment facilitating the performance of an action **4** *rare* easy-going disposition **5** (*usually plural*) a euphemistic word for **lavatory** [c15: from Latin *facilitās*, from *facilis* easy; see FACILE]

facing ('feɪsɪŋ) n **1** a piece of material used esp to conceal the seam of a garment and prevent fraying **2** (*usually plural*) a piece of additional cloth, esp in a different colour, on the collar, cuffs, etc, of the jacket of a military uniform, formerly used to denote the regiment **3** an outer layer or coat of material applied to the surface of a wall

facsimile (fæk'sɪmɪlɪ) n **1** an exact copy or reproduction **2** an image produced by facsimile transmission ▷ vb -les, -leing, -led **3** (*tr*) to make an exact copy of [c17: from Latin *fac simile!* make something like it!, from *facere* to make + *similis* similar, like]

facsimile transmission n an international system of transmitting a written, printed, or pictorial document over the telephone system by scanning it photoelectrically and reproducing the image after transmission. Often shortened to: **fax**

fact (fækt) n **1** an event or thing known to have happened or existed **2** a truth verifiable from experience or observation **3** a piece of information: *get me all the facts of this case* **4** *law* (*often plural*) an actual event, happening, etc, as distinguished from its legal consequences.

Questions of fact are decided by the jury, questions of law by the court or judge **5** *philosophy* a proposition that may be either true or false, as contrasted with an evaluative statement **6 after the fact** *criminal law* after the commission of the offence **7 before the fact** *criminal law* before the commission of the offence **8 as a matter of fact, in fact** *or* **in point of fact** in reality or actuality **9 fact of life** an inescapable truth, esp an unpleasant one [c16: from Latin *factum* something done, from *factus* made, from *facere* to make]

faction[1] ('fækʃən) *n* **1** a group of people forming a minority within a larger body, esp a dissentious group **2** strife or dissension within a group [c16: from Latin *factiō* a making, from *facere* to make, do] > **'factional** *adj*

faction[2] ('fækʃən) *n* a television programme, film, or literary work comprising a dramatized presentation of actual events [c20: a blend of FACT and FICTION]

faction fight *n South African* a fight between rival Black groups, usually originating in tribal or clan feuds

factious ('fækʃəs) *adj* given to, producing, or characterized by faction > **'factiously** *adv*

factitious (fæk'tɪʃəs) *adj* **1** artificial rather than natural **2** not genuine; sham: *factitious enthusiasm* [c17: from Latin *factīcius*, from *facere* to make, do] > **fac'titiously** *adv* > **fac'titiousness** *n*

factitive ('fæktɪtɪv) *adj grammar* denoting a verb taking a direct object as well as a noun in apposition, as for example *elect* in *they elected John president*, where *John* is the direct object and *president* is the complement [c19: from New Latin *factitīvus*, from Latin *factitāre* to do frequently, from *facere* to do]

factoid ('fæktɔɪd) *n* a piece of unreliable information believed to be true because of the way it is presented or repeated in print [c20: coined by Norman Mailer (1923–2007), US author, from FACT + -OID]

factor ('fæktə) *n* **1** an element or cause that contributes to a result **2** *maths* one of two or more integers or polynomials whose product is a given integer or polynomial: *2 and 3 are factors of 6* **3** (foll by identifying numeral) *med* any of several substances that participate in the clotting of blood: *factor VIII* **4** a person who acts on another's behalf, esp one who transacts business for another **5** former name for a **gene 6** *commercial law* a person to whom goods are consigned for sale and who is paid a factorage **7** (in Scotland) the manager of an estate ▷ *vb* **8** (*intr*) to engage in the business of a factor [c15: from Latin: one who acts, from *facere* to do] > **'factorable** *adj* > **'factor,ship** *n*

● **USAGE** *Factor* (sense 1) should only be used to refer to
● something which contributes to a result. It should
● not be used to refer to a part of something such as a
● plan or arrangement; instead a word such as
● *component* or *element* should be used

factor VIII *n* a protein that participates in the clotting of blood. It is extracted from donated serum and used in the treatment of the commonest type of haemophilia, in which it is absent

factor of safety *n* the ratio of the breaking stress of a material or structure to the calculated maximum stress when in use. Also called: **safety factor**

factorial (fæk'tɔːrɪəl) *maths* ▷ *n* **1** the product of all the positive integers from one up to and including a given integer. Factorial zero is assigned the value of one: *factorial four is* $1 \times 2 \times 3 \times 4$. Symbol: *n!*, where *n* is the given integer ▷ *adj* **2** of or involving factorials or factors > **fac'torially** *adv*

factorize *or* **factorise** ('fæktə,raɪz) *vb* (*tr*) *maths* to resolve (an integer or polynomial) into factors > ,factori'zation *or* ,factori'sation *n*

factory ('fæktərɪ) *n, pl* **-ries a** a building or group of buildings containing a plant assembly for the manufacture of goods **b** (*as modifier*): *a factory worker* [c16: from Late Latin *factorium*; see FACTOR] > **'factory-,like** *adj*

factory farm *n* a farm in which animals are bred and fattened using modern industrial methods > **factory farming** *n*

factory outlet *or* **factory shop** *n* a usually low-rent site leased by a factory to sell its end-of-line or damaged stock direct to the customer at reduced prices

factory ship *n* a fishing boat that processes the fish that are caught

factotum (fæk'təʊtəm) *n* a person employed to do all kinds of work [c16: from Medieval Latin, from Latin *fac! do!* + *tōtum*, from *tōtus* (adj) all]

facts and figures *pl n* details; precise information

factsheet ('fækt,ʃiːt) *n* a printed sheet containing information relating to items covered in a television or radio programme

facts of life *pl n* **the facts of life** the details of sexual behaviour and reproduction, esp as told to children

factual ('fæktʃʊəl) *adj* **1** of, relating to, or characterized by facts **2** of the nature of fact; real; actual > **'factually** *adv* > **'factualness**, ,factu'ality *n*

facula ('fækjʊlə) *n, pl* **-lae** (-,liː) any of the bright areas on the sun's surface, usually appearing just before a sunspot and subject to the same 11-year cycle [c18: from Latin: little torch, from *fax* torch] > **'facular** *adj*

facultative ('fækəltətɪv) *adj* **1** empowering but not compelling the doing of an act **2** *philosophy* that may or may not occur **3** *biology* able to exist under more than one set of environmental conditions **4** of or relating to a faculty > **'facultatively** *adv*

faculty ('fækltɪ) *n, pl* **-ties 1** one of the inherent powers of the mind or body, such as reason, memory, sight, or hearing **2** any ability or power, whether acquired or inherent **3** a conferred power or right **4 a** a department within a university or college devoted to a particular branch of knowledge **b** the staff of such a department **c** *chiefly US & Canadian* all the teaching staff at a university, college, school, etc **5** all members of a learned profession [c14 (in the sense: department of learning): from Latin *facultās* capability; related to Latin *facilis* easy]

FA Cup *n soccer* (in England) **1** an annual knockout competition for a silver trophy, open to all member teams of the Football Association **2** the trophy itself

fad (fæd) *n informal* **1** an intense but short-lived fashion; craze **2** a personal idiosyncrasy or whim [c19: of uncertain origin] > **'faddish** *adj*

Fadden ('fædⁿn) *n Sir* **Arthur William.** 1895–1973, Australian statesman; prime minister of Australia (1941)

fade (feɪd) *vb* **1** to lose or cause to lose brightness, colour, or clarity **2** (*intr*) to lose freshness, vigour, or youth; wither **3** (*intr*; usually foll by *away* or *out*) to vanish slowly; die out **4 a** to decrease the brightness or volume of (a television or radio programme or film sequence) or (of a television programme, etc) to decrease in this way **b** to decrease the volume of (a sound) in a recording system or (of a sound) to be so reduced in volume **5** (*intr*) (of the brakes of a vehicle) to lose power **6** to cause (a golf ball) to move with a controlled left-to-right trajectory or (of a golf ball) to veer gradually from left to right ▷ *n* **7** the act or an instance of fading [c14: from *fade* (adj) dull, from Old French, from Vulgar Latin *fatidus* (unattested), probably blend of Latin *vapidus* VAPID + Latin *fatuus* FATUOUS] > **'fadedness** *n* > **'fader** *n*

fade-in *n* **1** *films* an optical effect in which a shot appears gradually out of darkness ▷ *vb* **fade in** (*adverb*) **2** Also called: **fade up** to increase or cause to increase gradually, as vision or sound in a film or broadcast

fade-out *n* **1** *films* an optical effect in which a shot slowly disappears into darkness **2** a gradual and temporary loss of a received radio or television signal due to atmospheric disturbances, magnetic storms, etc **3** a slow or gradual disappearance ▷ *vb* **fade out** (*adverb*) **4** to decrease or cause to decrease gradually, as vision or sound in a film or broadcast

fadge (fædʒ) *vb* (*intr*) *archaic, or dialect* **1** to agree **2** to succeed ▷ *n* **3** *NZ* a package of wool in a wool-bale that weighs less than 100 kilograms [c16: of uncertain origin]

faeces *or esp US* **feces** ('fiːsiːz) *pl n* bodily waste matter derived from ingested food and the secretions of the intestines and discharged through the anus [c15: from Latin *faecēs*, plural of *faex* sediment, dregs] > **faecal** *or* (*esp US*) **fecal** ('fiːkᵊl) *adj*

Faenza (Italian fa'ɛntsa) *n* a city in N Italy, in Emilia-Romagna: famous in the 15th and 16th centuries for its majolica earthenware, esp faïence. Pop: 53 641 (2001)

faerie or **faery** ('feɪərɪ, 'feərɪ) n, pl -ries archaic or poetic **1** the land of fairies ▷ adj, n **2** a variant of **fairy**

Faeroes or **Faroes** ('fɛərəʊz) pl n a group of 21 basalt islands in the North Atlantic between Iceland and the Shetland Islands: a self-governing community within the kingdom of Denmark; fishing. Capital: Thorshavn. Pop: 47 000 (2003 est). Area: 1400 sq km (540 sq miles). Also called: Faeroe Islands or Faroe Islands

Faeroese or **Faroese** (,fɛərəʊ'iːz) adj **1** of, relating to, or characteristic of the Faeroes, their inhabitants, or their language ▷ n **2** the chief language of the Faeroes, closely related to Icelandic, although they are not mutually intelligible **3** pl -ese a native or inhabitant of the Faeroes

faff (fæf) vb (intr; often foll by about) Brit informal to dither or fuss [c19: of obscure origin]

Fafnir ('fæfnɪə, 'fæv-) n Norse myth the son of Hreidmar, whom he killed to gain the cursed treasure of Andvari. He became a dragon and was slain by Sigurd while guarding the treasure

fag[1] (fæg) n **1** informal a boring or wearisome task **2** Brit (esp formerly) a young public school boy who performs menial chores for an older boy or prefect ▷ vb fags, fagging, fagged **3** (when tr, often foll by out) informal to become or cause to become exhausted by hard toil or work **4** (usually intr) Brit to do or cause to do menial chores in a public school [c18: of obscure origin]

fag[2] (fæg) n Brit a slang word for **cigarette** [c16 (in the sense: something hanging loose, flap): of obscure origin]

fag[3] (fæg) n slang, chiefly US & Canadian short for **faggot**[2]

fag end n **1** the last and worst part, esp when it is of little use **2** Brit informal the stub of a cigarette [c17: see FAG[2]]

faggot[1] or esp US **fagot** ('fægət) n **1** a bundle of sticks or twigs, esp when bound together and used as fuel **2** a bundle of iron bars, esp a box formed by four pieces of wrought iron and filled with scrap to be forged into wrought iron **3** a ball of chopped meat, usually pork liver, bound with herbs and bread and eaten fried ▷ vb (tr) **4** to collect into a bundle or bundles **5** needlework to do faggoting on (a garment, piece of cloth, etc) [c14: from Old French, perhaps from Greek phakelos bundle]

faggot[2] ('fægət) n slang, chiefly US & Canadian a male homosexual [c20: special use of FAGGOT[1]]

faggoting or esp US **fagoting** ('fægətɪŋ) n **1** decorative needlework done by tying vertical threads together in bundles **2** a decorative way of joining two hems by crisscross stitches

fag hag n slang, usually derogatory a heterosexual woman who prefers the company of homosexual men

fah or **fa** (fɑː) n music (in tonic sol-fa) the fourth degree of any major scale; subdominant [c14: see GAMUT]

Fahd ibn Abdul Aziz (fɑːd 'ɪbʰn 'æbdʊl ə'ziːz) n 1923–2005, king of Saudi Arabia (1982–2005)

Fahrenheit[1] ('færən,haɪt) adj of or measured according to the Fahrenheit scale of temperature. Symbol: F

Fahrenheit[2] (German 'faːrənhaɪt) n **Gabriel Daniel** ('gaːbrieːl 'daːnieːl). 1686–1736, German physicist, who invented the mercury thermometer and devised the temperature scale that bears his name

Fahrenheit scale n a scale of temperatures in which 32° represents the melting point of ice and 212° represents the boiling point of pure water under standard atmospheric pressure. See **Celsius scale**

Fa-hsien ('fɑː'sjen) n a variant transliteration of **Fa Xian**

Faial or **Fayal** (Portuguese fə'ial) n an island in the central Azores archipelago. Chief town: Horta. Area: 171 sq km (66 sq miles)

Faidherbe (French fɛdɛrb) n **Louis Léon César**. 1818–89, French soldier and governor of Senegal (1854–65); founder of Dakar

faïence (faɪ'ɑːns, feɪ-) n tin-glazed earthenware, usually that of French, German, Italian, or Scandinavian origin [c18: from French, strictly: pottery from FAENZA]

fail (feɪl) vb **1** to be unsuccessful in an attempt (at something or to do something) **2** to stop operating or working properly: the steering failed suddenly **3** to judge or be judged as being below the officially accepted

standard required for success in (a course, examination, etc) **4** (tr) to prove disappointing, undependable, or useless to (someone) **5** (tr) to neglect or be unable (to do something) **6** (intr) to prove partly or completely insufficient in quantity, duration, or extent **7** (intr) to weaken; fade away **8** (intr) to go bankrupt or become insolvent ▷ n **9** a failure to attain the required standard, as in an examination **10** without fail definitely; with certainty [c13: from Old French faillir, ultimately from Latin fallere to disappoint; probably related to Greek phēlos deceitful]

failing ('feɪlɪŋ) n **1** a weak point; flaw ▷ prep **2** (used to express a condition) in default of: failing a solution this afternoon, the problem will have to wait until Monday

fail-safe adj **1** designed to return to a safe condition in the event of a failure or malfunction **2** unlikely to fail; foolproof

failure ('feɪljə) n **1** the act or an instance of failing **2** a person or thing that is unsuccessful or disappointing **3** nonperformance of something required or expected: failure to attend will be punished **4** cessation of normal operation; breakdown: a power failure **5** an insufficiency or shortage: a crop failure **6** a decline or loss, as in health or strength **7** the fact of not reaching the required standard in an examination, test, course, etc **8** the act or process of becoming bankrupt or the state of being bankrupt

fain (feɪn) adv **1** (usually with would) archaic willingly; gladly: she would fain be dead ▷ adj **2** obsolete **a** willing or eager **b** compelled [Old English fægen; related to Old Norse fegiun happy, Old High German gifehan to be glad, Gothic fahehs joy; see FAWN[2]]

faint (feɪnt) adj **1** lacking clarity, brightness, volume, etc **2** lacking conviction or force; weak: faint praise **3** feeling dizzy or weak as if about to lose consciousness **4** without boldness or courage; timid (esp in the combination **faint-hearted**) **5** not the faintest, not the faintest idea or not the faintest notion no idea whatsoever: I haven't the faintest ▷ vb (intr) **6** to lose consciousness, esp momentarily, as through weakness **7** archaic or poetic to fail or become weak, esp in hope or courage ▷ n **8** a sudden spontaneous loss of consciousness, usually momentary, caused by an insufficient supply of blood to the brain [c13: from Old French, from faindre to be idle] > 'faintish adj > 'faintly adv > 'faintness n

fair[1] (fɛə) adj **1** free from discrimination, dishonesty, etc; just; impartial **2** in conformity with rules or standards; legitimate: a fair fight **3** (of hair or complexion) light in colour **4** beautiful or lovely to look at **5** moderately or quite good: a fair piece of work **6** unblemished; untainted **7** (of the tide or wind) favourable to the passage of a vessel **8** sunny, fine, or cloudless **9** pleasant or courteous **10** apparently good or valuable, but really false: fair words **11** fair and square in a correct or just way; correctly: act fair, now! **13** absolutely or squarely; quite ▷ vb **14** (intr) dialect (of the weather) to become fine and mild ▷ n **15** archaic a person or thing that is beautiful or valuable, esp a woman [Old English fæger; related to Old Norse fagr, Old Saxon, Old High German fagar, Gothic fagrs suitable] > 'fairness n > 'fairish adj

fair[2] (fɛə) n **1** a travelling entertainment with sideshows, rides, etc, esp one that visits places at the same time each year **2** a gathering of producers of and dealers in a given class of products to facilitate business: a book fair **3** a regular assembly at a specific place for the sale of goods, esp livestock [c13: from Old French feire, from Late Latin fēria holiday, from Latin fēriae days of rest: related to festus FESTAL]

Fairbanks[1] ('fɛə,bæŋks) n a city in central Alaska, at the terminus of the Alaska Highway. Pop: 30 970 (2003 est)

Fairbanks[2] ('fɛə,bæŋks) n **1 Douglas (Elton)**, real name Julius Ullman. 1883–1939, US film actor and producer **2** his son, **Douglas, Jnr.** 1909–2000, US film actor

Fairfax ('fɛəfæks) n **Thomas**, 3rd Baron Fairfax. 1612–71, English general and statesman: commanded the Parliamentary army (1645–50), defeating Charles I at Naseby (1645). He was instrumental in restoring Charles

II to the throne (1660)

fair game n a legitimate object for ridicule or attack

fairground ('fɛə,graʊnd) n an open space used for a fair or exhibition

fairing[1] ('fɛərɪŋ) n an external metal structure fitted around parts of an aircraft, car, vessel, etc, to reduce drag [C20: FAIR[1] + -ING[1]]

fairing[2] ('fɛərɪŋ) n archaic a present, esp from a fair

Fair Isle n an intricate multicoloured pattern knitted with Shetland wool into various garments, such as sweaters [C19: named after one of the Shetland Islands where the pattern originated]

fairly ('fɛəlɪ) adv 1 (not used with a negative) moderately 2 as deserved; justly 3 (not used with a negative) positively; absolutely: the hall fairly rang with applause

fair-minded adj just or impartial > ,fair-'mindedness n

fair play n 1 an established standard of decency, honesty, etc 2 abidance by this standard

fair sex n the fair sex women collectively

fair-spoken adj civil, courteous, or elegant in speech > ,fair-'spokenness n

fair trade n a the practice of directly benefiting producers in the developing world by buying straight from them at a guaranteed price b (as modifier): fair-trade coffee

fairway ('fɛə,weɪ) n 1 (on a golf course) the areas of shorter grass between the tees and greens, esp the avenue approaching a green bordered by rough 2 nautical the navigable part of a river, harbour, etc

fair-weather adj 1 suitable for use in fair weather only 2 not reliable or present in situations of hardship or difficulty (esp in the phrase **fair-weather friend**)

fairy ('fɛərɪ) n, pl fairies 1 an imaginary supernatural being, usually represented in diminutive human form and characterized as clever, playful, and having magical powers 2 slang a male homosexual ▷ adj (prenominal) 3 of or relating to a fairy or fairies 4 resembling a fairy or fairies, esp in being enchanted or delicate [C14: from Old French faerie fairyland, from feie fairy, from Latin Fāta the Fates; see FATE, FAY[1]] > 'fairy-,like adj

fairy cycle n a child's bicycle

fairyfloss ('fɛərɪ,flɒs) n Austral. a very light fluffy confection made from coloured spun sugar, usually held on a stick. Also called: (chiefly Brit) candyfloss, (US and Canadian) cotton candy

fairy godmother n any benefactress, esp an unknown one

fairyland ('fɛərɪ,lænd) n 1 the imaginary domain of the fairies; an enchanted or wonderful place 2 a fantasy world, esp one resulting from a person's wild imaginings

fairy lights pl n small coloured electric bulbs strung together and used for decoration, esp on a Christmas tree

fairy penguin n a small penguin, Eudyptula minor, with a bluish head and back, found on the Australian coast. Also called: little penguin or blue penguin

fairy ring n a ring of dark luxuriant vegetation in grassy ground corresponding to the edge of an underground fungal mycelium: popularly associated with the dancing of fairies: seasonally marked by a ring of mushrooms

fairy tale or **fairy story** n 1 a story about fairies or other mythical or magical beings, esp one of traditional origin told to children 2 a highly improbable account

fairy-tale adj 1 of or relating to a fairy tale 2 resembling a fairy tale, esp in being extremely happy or fortunate: a true story with a fairy-tale ending 3 highly improbable: he came out with a fairy-tale account of his achievements

Faisal I or **Feisal I** ('faɪsəl) n 1885–1933, king of Syria (1920) and first king of Iraq (1921–33): a leader of the Arab revolt against the Turks (1916–18)

Faisal II or **Feisal II** n 1935–58, last king of Iraq (1939–58)

Faisalabad (faɪ'ʒɑːlə,bɑːd) n a city in NE Pakistan: commercial and manufacturing centre of a cotton- and wheat-growing region; university (1961). Pop: 2 533 000 (2005 est). Former name (until 1979): Lyallpur

Faisal Ibn Abdul Aziz ('ɪbⁿ æb'dʊl æ'ziːz) n 1905–75, king of Saudi Arabia (1964–75)

fait accompli French (fɛt akɔ̃pli) n, pl faits accomplis (fɛz akɔ̃pli) something already done and beyond alteration [literally: accomplished fact]

faith (feɪθ) n 1 strong or unshakeable belief in something, esp without proof or evidence 2 a specific system of religious beliefs: the Jewish faith 3 Christianity trust in God and in his actions and promises 4 a conviction of the truth of certain doctrines of religion, esp when this is not based on reason 5 complete confidence or trust in a person, remedy, etc 6 allegiance or loyalty, as to a person or cause (esp in the phrases **keep faith, break faith**) 7 bad faith insincerity or dishonesty 8 good faith honesty or sincerity, as of intention in business (esp in the phrase **in good faith**) ▷ interj 9 archaic indeed; really (also in the phrases **by my faith, in faith**) [C12: from Anglo-French feid, from Latin fidēs trust, confidence]

faithful ('feɪθfʊl) adj 1 having faith; remaining true, constant, or loyal 2 maintaining sexual loyalty to one's lover or spouse 3 consistently reliable: a faithful worker 4 reliable or truthful: a faithful source 5 accurate in detail: a faithful translation ▷ n 6 the faithful a the believers in and loyal adherents of a religious faith, esp Christianity b any group of loyal and steadfast followers > 'faithfully adv > 'faithfulness n

faith healing n treatment of a sick person through the supposed power of religious faith > faith healer n

faithless ('feɪθlɪs) adj 1 unreliable or treacherous 2 dishonest or disloyal 3 lacking faith, esp religious faith > 'faithlessness n

faith school n Brit a school that provides a general education within a framework of a specific religious belief

Faiyûm or **Fayum** (faɪ'juːm) n See El Faiyûm

fajitas (fə'hiːtəz) pl n a Mexican dish of soft tortillas wrapped around fried strips of meat, vegetables, etc [Mexican Spanish]

fake (feɪk) vb 1 (tr) to cause (something inferior or not genuine) to appear more valuable, desirable, or real by fraud or pretence 2 to pretend to have (an illness, emotion, etc) ▷ n 3 an object, person, or act that is not genuine; sham, counterfeit, or forgery ▷ adj 4 not genuine; spurious [originally (C18) thieves' slang to mug or do someone; probably via Polari from Italian facciare to make or do] > 'faker n > 'fakery n

fakir, faqir (fə'kɪə, 'feɪkə) or **fakeer** (fə'kɪə) n 1 a Muslim ascetic who rejects wordly possessions 2 a Hindu ascetic mendicant or holy man [C17: from Arabic faqīr poor]

falafel or **felafel** (fəl'ɑːfəl) n a ball or cake of ground spiced chickpeas, deep-fried and often served with pitta bread [C20: from Arabic felāfil]

Falange ('fælændʒ; Spanish fa'lanxe) n the Fascist movement founded in Spain in 1933; the one legal party in Spain under the regime (1939–75) of Francisco Franco (1892–1975), the Spanish general and statesman [Spanish: PHALANX] > Fa'langist n, adj

falbala ('fælbələ) n a gathered flounce, frill, or ruffle [C18: from French, from (dialect) ferbelà; see FURBELOW]

falcate ('fælkeɪt) or **falciform** ('fælsɪ,fɔːm) adj biology shaped like a sickle [C19: from Latin falcātus, from falx sickle]

falchion ('fɔːltʃən, 'fɔːlʃən) n 1 a short and slightly curved medieval sword broader towards the point 2 an archaic word for **sword** [C14: from Italian falcione, from falce, from Latin falx sickle]

falcon ('fɔːlkən, 'fɒlkən) n 1 any diurnal bird of prey of the family Falconidae, esp any of the genus Falco (gyrfalcon, peregrine falcon, etc), typically having pointed wings and a long tail 2 a any of these or related birds, trained to hunt small game b the female of such a bird. See tercel [C13: from Old French faucon, from Late Latin falcō hawk, probably of Germanic origin; perhaps related to Latin falx sickle]

falconet ('fɔːlkə,nɛt, 'fɒlkə-) n 1 any of various small falcons, esp any of the Asiatic genus Microhierax 2 a small light cannon used from the 15th to 17th centuries

falconry ('fɔːlkənrɪ, 'fɒlkən-) n the art of keeping falcons and training them to return from flight to a lure or to hunt quarry > 'falconer n

falderal ('fældɪˌræl), **falderol** ('fældɪˌrɒl) *or* **folderol** ('fɒldɪˌrɒl) *n* **1** a showy but worthless trifle **2** foolish nonsense **3** a nonsensical refrain in old songs

Faldo ('fældəʊ) *n* **Nick**, born 1957, British golfer: winner of the British Open Championship (1987, 1990, 1992) and the US Masters (1989, 1990, 1996)

faldstool ('fɔːldˌstuːl) *n* a backless seat, sometimes capable of being folded, used by bishops and certain other prelates [C11 *fyldestol*, probably a translation of Medieval Latin *faldistolium* folding stool, of Germanic origin; compare Old High German *faldstuol*]

Falerii (fə'lɪərɪˌaɪ) *n* an ancient city of S Italy, in Latium: important in pre-Roman times

Faliraki (ˌfælɪ'rɑːkɪ) *n* a coastal resort in SE Greece, on Rhodes. Pop: 400 (2000 est)

Falkirk ('fɔːlkɜːk) *n* **1** a town in Scotland, the administrative centre of Falkirk council area: scene of Edward I's defeat of Wallace (1298) and Prince Charles Edward's defeat of General Hawley (1746); formerly a major iron and steel centre; the Falkirk Wheel, an innovative rotating canal boat lift, is nearby. Pop: 32 379 (2001) **2** a council area in central Scotland, on the Firth of Forth: created in 1996 from part of Central Region: largely agricultural, with heavy industry in Falkirk and Grangemouth. Administrative centre: Falkirk. Pop: 145 920 (2003 est). Area: 299 sq km (115 sq miles)

Falkland Islands ('fɔːlklənd) *pl n* a group of over 100 islands in the S Atlantic: a UK Overseas Territory; invaded by Argentina, who had long laid claim to the islands, on 2 April 1982: recaptured by a British expeditionary force on 14 June 1982. Chief town: Stanley. Pop: 3000 (2003 est). Area: about 12 200 sq km (4700 sq miles)

Falkland Islands Dependencies *pl n* the former name (until 1985) for South Georgia and the South Sandwich Islands

Falkner ('fɔːknə) *n* a variant spelling of (William) **Faulkner**

fall (fɔːl) *vb* **falls**, **falling**, **fell** (fɛl), **fallen** ('fɔːlən) (*mainly intr*) **1** to descend by the force of gravity from a higher to a lower place **2** to drop suddenly from an erect position **3** to collapse to the ground, esp in pieces **4** to become less or lower in number, quality, etc: *prices fell in the summer* **5** to become lower in pitch **6** to extend downwards: *her hair fell to her waist* **7** to be badly wounded or killed **8** to slope in a downward direction **9** *Christianity* to yield to temptation or sin **10** to diminish in status, estimation, etc **11** to yield to attack: *the city fell under the assault* **12** to lose power: *the government fell after the riots* **13** to pass into or take on a specified condition: *to fall asleep; fall in love* **14** to adopt a despondent expression: *her face fell* **15** to be averted: *her gaze fell* **16** to come by chance or presumption: *suspicion fell on the butler* **17** to occur; take place: *night fell; Easter falls early this year* **18** (foll by *back, behind,* etc) to move in a specified direction **19** to occur at a specified place: *the accent falls on the last syllable* **20** (foll by *to*) to return (to); be inherited (by): *the estate falls to the eldest son* **21** (often foll by *into, under,* etc) to be classified or included: *the subject falls into two main areas* **22** to issue forth: *a curse fell from her lips* **23** (*tr*) *Austral & NZ dialect* to fell (trees) **24** *cricket* (of a batsman's wicket) to be taken by the bowling side: *the sixth wicket fell for 96* **25** **fall short a** to prove inadequate **b** (often foll by *of*) to fail to reach or measure up to (a standard) ▷ *n* **26** an act or instance of falling **27** something that falls: *a fall of snow* **28** *chiefly US* autumn **29** the distance that something falls: *a hundred-foot fall* **30** a sudden drop from an upright position **31** (*often plural*) **a** a waterfall or cataract **b** (*capital when part of a name*): *Niagara Falls* **32** a downward slope or decline **33** a decrease in value, number, etc **34** a decline in status or importance **35** a capture or overthrow: *the fall of the city* **36** *machinery, nautical* the end of a tackle to which power is applied to hoist it **37** Also called: **pinfall** *wrestling* a scoring move, pinning both shoulders of one's opponent to the floor for a specified period **38 a** the birth of an animal **b** the animals produced at a single birth ▷ See also **fall about**, **fall apart** [Old English *feallan*; related to Old Norse *falla*, Old Saxon, Old High German *fallan* to fall; see FELL²]

Fall (fɔːl) *n* **the Fall** *theol* Adam's sin of disobedience and the state of innate sinfulness ensuing from this for himself and all mankind

Falla (*Spanish* 'faʎa) *n* **Manuel de** (ma'nwɛl de). 1876–1946, Spanish composer and pianist, composer of the opera *La Vida Breve* (1905), the ballet *The Three-Cornered Hat* (1919), guitar and piano music, and songs

fall about *vb* (*intr, adverb*) to laugh in an uncontrolled manner: *we fell about when we saw him*

fallacious (fə'leɪʃəs) *adj* **1** containing or involving a fallacy; illogical; erroneous **2** tending to mislead **3** delusive or disappointing ▷ **fal'laciously** *adv*

fallacy ('fæləsɪ) *n, pl* **-cies 1** an incorrect or misleading notion or opinion based on inaccurate facts or invalid reasoning **2** unsound or invalid reasoning **3** the tendency to mislead **4** *logic* an error in reasoning that renders an argument logically invalid [C15: from Latin *fallācia*, from *fallax* deceitful, from *fallere* to deceive]

fall apart *vb* (*intr, adverb*) **1** to break owing to long use or poor construction: *the chassis is falling apart* **2** to become disorganized and ineffective: *since you resigned, the office has fallen apart*

fall away *vb* (*intr, adverb*) **1** (of friendship) to be withdrawn **2** to slope down

fall back *vb* (*intr, adverb*) **1** to recede or retreat **2** (foll by *on* or *upon*) to have recourse (to) ▷ *n* **fall-back 3** a retreat **4** a reserve, esp money, that can be called upon in need **5 a** anything to which one can have recourse as a second choice **b** (*as modifier*): *a fall-back position*

fall behind *vb* (*intr, adverb*) **1** to drop back; fail to keep up **2** to be in arrears, as with a payment

fall down *vb* (*intr, adverb*) **1** to drop suddenly or collapse **2** (often foll by *on*) *informal* to prove unsuccessful; fail

fallen ('fɔːlən) *vb* **1** the past participle of **fall** ▷ *adj* **2** having sunk in reputation or honour: *a fallen woman* **3** killed in battle with glory

fallen arch *n* collapse of the arch formed by the instep of the foot, resulting in flat feet

fall for *vb* (*intr, preposition*) **1** to become infatuated with (a person) **2** to allow oneself to be deceived by (a lie, trick, etc)

fall guy *n* *informal* **1** a person who is the victim of a confidence trick **2** a scapegoat

fallible ('fælɪbᵊl) *adj* **1** capable of being mistaken; erring **2** liable to mislead [C15: from Medieval Latin *fallibilis*, from Latin *fallere* to deceive] ▷ ˌfalli'bility *or* 'fallibleness *n*

fall in *vb* (*intr, adverb*) **1** to collapse; no longer act as a support **2** to adopt a military formation, esp as a soldier taking his place in a line **3** (of a lease) to expire **4** (often foll by *with*) **a** to meet and join **b** to agree with or support a person, suggestion, etc

falling sickness *or* **falling evil** *n* a former name (nontechnical) for **epilepsy**

falling star *n* an informal name for **meteor**

Fall Line *n* a natural junction, running parallel to the E coast of the US, between the hard rocks of the Appalachians and the softer coastal plain, along which rivers form falls and rapids

fall off *vb* (*intr*) **1** to drop unintentionally to the ground from (a high object, bicycle, etc), esp after losing one's balance **2** (*adverb*) to diminish in size, intensity, etc; decline or weaken ▷ *n* **fall-off** **3** a decline or drop

fall on *vb* (*intr, preposition*) **1** Also: **fall upon** to attack or snatch (an army, booty, etc) **2** **fall on one's feet** to emerge unexpectedly well from a difficult situation

Fallopian tube (fə'ləʊpɪən) *n* either of a pair of slender tubes through which ova pass from the ovaries to the uterus in female mammals [C18: named after Gabriello *Fallopio* (1523–62), Italian anatomist who first described the tubes]

fallout ('fɔːlˌaʊt) *n* **1** the descent of solid material in the atmosphere onto the earth, esp of radioactive material following a nuclear explosion **2** any solid particles that so descend **3** *informal* side-effects; secondary consequences ▷ *vb* **fall out** (*intr, adverb*) **4** *informal* to quarrel or disagree **5** (*intr*) to happen or occur **6** *military* to leave a parade or disciplinary formation

fallow¹ ('fæləʊ) *adj* **1** (of land) left unseeded after being ploughed and harrowed to regain fertility for a crop

2 (of an idea, state of mind, etc) undeveloped or inactive, but potentially useful ▷ *n* **3** land treated in this way ▷ *vb* **4** (*tr*) to leave (land) unseeded after ploughing and harrowing it [Old English *fealga*; related to Greek *polos* ploughed field] > ˈfallowness *n*

fallow² (ˈfæləʊ) *adj* of a light yellowish-brown colour [Old English *fealu*; related to Old Norse *fölr*, Old Saxon, Old High German *falo*, Latin *pallidus* Greek *polios* grey]

fallow deer *n* either of two deer, *Dama dama* or *D. mesopotamica*, native to the Mediterranean region and Persia respectively. The antlers are flattened and the summer coat is reddish with white spots

fall through *vb* (*intr, adverb*) to miscarry or fail

fall to *vb* (*intr*) **1** (*adverb*) to begin some activity, as eating, working, or fighting **2** (*preposition*) to devolve on (a person): *the task fell to me*

Fallujah (fəˈlʊdʒə) a town in central Iraq, about 60 km W of Baghdad; a centre of resistance against the US-led invasion of Iraq, from 2003. Pop: 223 000 (2005 est)

Falmouth (ˈfælməθ) *n* a port and resort in SW England, in S Cornwall. Pop: 21 635 (2001)

false (fɔːls) *adj* **1** not in accordance with the truth or facts **2** irregular or invalid: *a false start* **3** untruthful or lying: *a false account* **4** not genuine, real, or natural; artificial; fake: *false eyelashes* **5** being or intended to be misleading or deceptive: *a false rumour* **6** disloyal or treacherous: *a false friend* **7** based on mistaken or irrelevant ideas or facts: *false pride; a false argument* **8** (*prenominal*) (esp of plants) superficially resembling the species specified: *false hellebore* **9** serving to supplement or replace, often temporarily: *a false keel* **10** *music* (of a note, interval, etc) out of tune ▷ *adv* **11** in a false or dishonest manner (esp in the phrase **play (someone) false**) [Old English *fals*, from Latin *falsus*, from *fallere* to deceive] > ˈfalsely *adv* > ˈfalseness *n*

false colour *n* colour used in a computer or photographic display to help in interpreting the image, as in the use of red to show high temperatures and blue to show low temperatures in an infrared image converter

false dawn *n* zodiacal light appearing just before sunrise

false diamond *n* any of a number of semiprecious stones that resemble diamond, such as zircon and white topaz

falsehood (ˈfɔːlsˌhʊd) *n* **1** the quality of being untrue **2** an untrue statement; lie **3** the act of deceiving or lying

false imprisonment *n law* the restraint of a person's liberty without lawful authority

false pretences *pl n* a similar misrepresentation used to obtain anything, such as trust or affection (esp in the phrase **under false pretences**)

false ribs *pl n* any of the lower five pairs of ribs in man, attached behind to the thoracic vertebrae but in front not attached directly to the breastbone

false step *n* **1** an unwise action **2** a stumble; slip

falsetto (fɔːlˈsɛtəʊ) *n, pl* **-tos** a form of vocal production used by male singers to extend their range upwards beyond its natural compass by limiting the vibration of the vocal cords [c18: from Italian, from *falso* FALSE]

falsies (ˈfɔːlsɪz) *pl n informal* pads of soft material, such as foam rubber, worn to exaggerate the size of or simulate the appearance of a woman's breasts

falsify (ˈfɔːlsɪˌfaɪ) *vb* **-fies, -fying, -fied** (*tr*) **1** to make (a report, evidence, accounts, etc) false or inaccurate by alteration, esp in order to deceive **2** to prove false; disprove [c15: from Old French *falsifier*, from Late Latin *falsificāre*, from Latin *falsus* FALSE + *facere* to make] > ˈfalsiˌfiable *adj* > falsification (ˌfɔːlsɪfɪˈkeɪʃən) *n*

falsity (ˈfɔːlsɪtɪ) *n, pl* **-ties** **1** the state of being false or untrue **2** something false; a lie or deception

Falstaffian (fɔːlˈstɑːfɪən) *adj* jovial, plump, and dissolute [c19: after Sir John *Falstaff*, a character in Shakespeare's *Henry IV, Parts I–II* (1597)]

Falster (ˈfɔːlstə) *n* an island in the Baltic Sea, part of SE Denmark. Chief town: Nykøbing. Pop: 43 537 (2003 est). Area: 513 sq km (198 sq miles)

falter (ˈfɔːltə) *vb* **1** (*intr*) to be hesitant, weak, or unsure; waver **2** (*intr*) to move unsteadily or hesitantly; stumble

3 to utter haltingly or hesitantly; stammer ▷ *n* **4** uncertainty or hesitancy in speech or action **5** a quavering or irregular sound [c14: probably of Scandinavian origin; compare Icelandic *faltrast*] > ˈfalterer *n* > ˈfalteringly *adv*

Falun (ˌfɑːˈlʌn) *n* a city in central Sweden: iron and pyrites mines. Pop: 55 009 (2004 est)

Famagusta (ˌfæməˈɡʊstə) *n* a port in E Cyprus, on Famagusta Bay: became one of the richest cities in Christendom in the 14th century. Pop: 35 453 (2006)

fame (feɪm) *n* **1** the state of being widely known or recognized; renown; celebrity **2** *archaic* rumour or public report ▷ *vb* **3** (*tr; now usually passive*) to make known or famous; celebrate: *he was famed for his ruthlessness* [c13: from Latin *fāma* report; related to *fārī* to say]

familial (fəˈmɪlɪəl) *adj* **1** of or relating to the family **2** occurring in the members of a family: *a familial disease*

familiar (fəˈmɪlɪə) *adj* **1** well-known; easily recognized: *a familiar figure* **2** frequent or customary: *a familiar excuse* **3** (*postpositive; foll by with*) acquainted **4** friendly; informal **5** close; intimate **6** more intimate than is acceptable; presumptuous ▷ *n* **7** Also called: familiar spirit a supernatural spirit often assuming animal form, supposed to attend and aid a witch, wizard, etc **8** a person, attached to the household of the pope or a bishop, who renders service in return for support **9** a friend or frequent companion [c14: from Latin *familiāris* domestic, from *familia* FAMILY] > faˈmiliarly *adv* > faˈmiliarness *n*

familiarity (fəˌmɪlɪˈærɪtɪ) *n, pl* **-ties** **1** reasonable knowledge or acquaintance, as with a subject or place **2** close acquaintanceship or intimacy **3** undue intimacy **4** (*sometimes plural*) an instance of unwarranted intimacy

familiarize *or* **familiarise** (fəˈmɪljəˌraɪz) *vb* (*tr*) **1** to make (oneself or someone else) familiar, as with a particular subject **2** to make (something) generally known or accepted > faˌmiliariˈzation *or* faˌmiliariˈsation *n*

famille *French* (famij) *n* a type of Chinese porcelain characterized either by a design on a background of yellow (**famille jaune**) or black (**famille noire**) or by a design in which the predominant colour is pink (**famille rose**) or green (**famille verte**) [c19: literally: family]

family (ˈfæmɪlɪ, ˈfæmlɪ) *n, pl* **-lies** **1 a** a primary social group consisting of parents and their offspring, the principal function of which is provision for its members **b** (*as modifier*): *family quarrels; a family unit* **2** one's wife or husband and one's children, as distinguished from one's husband or wife **4** a group of persons related by blood; a group descended from a common ancestor **5** all the persons living together in one household **6** any group of related things or beings, esp when scientifically categorized **7** *biology* any of the taxonomic groups into which an order is divided and which contains one or more genera. *Felidae* (cat family) and *Canidae* (dog family) are two families of the order *Carnivora* **8** a group of historically related languages assumed to derive from one original language **9** *maths* a group of curves or surfaces whose equations differ from a given equation only in the values assigned to one or more constants in each curve **10** in the family way *informal* pregnant [c15: from Latin *familia* a household, servants of the house, from *famulus* servant]

family allowance *n* **1** (in Britain) a former name for **child benefit 2** (*capitals*) *Canadian* a regular government payment to the parents of children up to a certain age. Also called (in Britain and certain other countries): child benefit

family balancing *n US* the choosing of the sex of a future child on the basis of how many children of each sex a family already has

family Bible *n* a large Bible used for family worship in which births, marriages, and deaths are recorded

Family Compact *n Canadian* **1** the Family Compact the ruling oligarchy in Upper Canada in the early 19th century **2** (*often not capital*) any influential clique

family man *n* a man who is married and has children, esp one who is devoted to his family

family name *n* a surname, esp when regarded as representing the family honour

family planning *n* the control of the number of children in a family and of the intervals between them, esp by the use of contraceptives

family support *n* NZ a means-tested allowance for families in need

family therapy *n* a form of psychotherapy in which the members of a family participate, with the aim of improving communications between them and the ways in which they relate to each other

family tree *n* a chart showing the genealogical relationships and lines of descent of a family. Also called: genealogical tree

famine ('fæmɪn) *n* **1** a severe shortage of food, as through crop failure or overpopulation **2** acute shortage of anything **3** violent hunger [c14: from Old French, via Vulgar Latin, from Latin *famēs* hunger]

famish ('fæmɪʃ) *vb* (*now usually passive*) to be or make very hungry or weak [c14: from Old French *afamer*, via Vulgar Latin, from Latin *famēs* FAMINE]

famous ('feɪməs) *adj* **1** known to or recognized by many people; renowned **2** *informal* excellent; splendid [c14: from Latin *fāmōsus*; see FAME] > **'famousness** *n* > **'famously** *adv*

fan¹ (fæn) *n* **1** any device for creating a current of air by movement of a surface or number of surfaces, esp a rotating device consisting of a number of blades attached to a central hub **2** any of various hand-agitated devices for cooling onself, esp a collapsible semicircular series of flat segments of paper, ivory, etc **3** something shaped like such a fan, such as the tail of certain birds **4** *agriculture* a kind of basket formerly used for winnowing grain ▷ *vb* **fans, fanning, fanned** (*mainly tr*) **5** to cause a current of air, esp cool air, to blow upon, as by means of a fan: *to fan one's face* **6** to agitate or move (air, smoke, etc) with or as if with a fan **7** to make fiercer, more ardent, etc: *fan one's passion* **8** (*also intr; often foll by* out) to spread out or cause to spread out in the shape of a fan **9** to winnow (grain) by blowing the chaff away from it [Old English *fann*, from Latin *vannus*] > **'fanlike** *adj* > **'fanner** *n*

fan² (fæn) *n* **1** an ardent admirer of a pop star, film actor, football team, etc **2** a devotee of a sport, hobby, etc [c17, re-formed c19: from FAN(ATIC)]

Fanagalo ('fænəgæləʊ) *or* **Fanakalo** *n* (in South Africa) a Zulu-based pidgin with English and Afrikaans components, esp associated with the mines [c20: from Fanagalo *fana ga lo*, literally: to be like this; compare Zulu *fand* to be like, *ka-lo* of this]

fanatic (fə'nætɪk) *n* **1** a person whose enthusiasm or zeal for something is extreme or beyond normal limits **2** *informal* a person devoted to a particular hobby or pastime; fan ▷ *adj* **3** a variant of **fanatical** [c16: from Latin *fānāticus* belonging to a temple, hence, inspired by a god, frenzied, from *fānum* temple]

fanatical (fə'nætɪk*l) *adj* surpassing what is normal or accepted in enthusiasm for or belief in something; excessively or unusually dedicated or devoted > fa'natically *adv*

fanaticism (fə'nætɪ,sɪzəm) *n* wildly excessive or irrational devotion, dedication, or enthusiasm

fan belt *n* any belt that drives a fan, esp the belt that drives a cooling fan together with a dynamo or alternator in a car engine

fancied ('fænsɪd) *adj* **1** imaginary; unreal **2** thought likely to win or succeed: *a fancied runner*

fancier ('fænsɪə) *n* **1** a person with a special interest in something **2** a person who breeds plants or animals, often as a pastime: *a bird fancier*

fanciful ('fænsɪfʊl) *adj* **1** not based on fact; dubious or imaginary: *fanciful notions* **2** made or designed in a curious, intricate, or imaginative way **3** indulging in or influenced by fancy; whimsical > **'fancifully** *adv* > **'fancifulness** *n*

fan club *n* **1** an organized group of admirers of a particular pop singer, film star, etc **2** be a member of someone's fan club *informal* to approve of someone strongly

fancy ('fænsɪ) *adj* **-cier, -ciest 1** not plain; ornamented or decorative: *a fancy cake; fancy clothes* **2** requiring skill to

perform; intricate: *a fancy dance routine* **3** arising in the imagination; capricious or illusory **4** (*often used ironically*) superior in quality or impressive **5** higher than expected: *fancy prices* **6** (of a domestic animal) bred for particular qualities ▷ *n, pl* **-cies 7** a sudden capricious idea; whim **8** a sudden or irrational liking for a person or thing **9** the power to conceive and represent decorative and novel imagery, esp in poetry. Fancy was held by Coleridge to be more casual and superficial than imagination **10** an idea or thing produced by this **11** a mental image **12** Also called: fantasy or fantasia *music* a composition for solo lute, keyboard, etc, current during the 16th and 17th centuries **13** the fancy *archaic* those who follow a particular sport, esp prize fighting ▷ *vb* **-cies, -cying, -cied** (*tr*) **14** to picture in the imagination **15** to suppose; imagine: *I fancy it will rain* **16** (*often used with a negative*) to like: *I don't fancy your chances!* **17** (*reflexive*) to have a high or ill-founded opinion of oneself **18** *informal* to have a wish for; desire: *she fancied some chocolate* **19** *Brit informal* to be physically attracted to (another person) **20** to breed (animals) for particular characteristics ▷ *interj* **21** Also: fancy that! an exclamation of surprise or disbelief [c15 *fantsy*, shortened from *fantasie*; see FANTASY] > **'fancily** *adv* > **'fanciness** *n*

fancy dress *n* **a** a costume worn at masquerades, etc, usually representing a particular role, historical figure, etc **b** (*as modifier*): *a fancy-dress ball*

fancy-free *adj* having no commitments; carefree

fancy goods *pl n* small decorative gifts; knick-knacks

fancy man *n slang* **1** a woman's lover **2** a pimp

fancy woman *n slang* a mistress or prostitute

fancywork ('fænsɪ,wɜːk) *n* any ornamental needlework, such as embroidery or crochet

fan dance *n* a dance in which large fans are manipulated in front of the body, partially revealing or suggesting nakedness

fandangle (fæn'dæŋg*l) *n informal* **1** elaborate ornament **2** nonsense [c19: perhaps from FANDANGO]

fandango (fæn'dæŋgəʊ) *n, pl* **-gos 1** an old Spanish courtship dance in triple time between a couple who dance closely and provocatively **2** a piece of music composed for or in the rhythm of this dance [c18: from Spanish, of uncertain origin]

fane (feɪn) *n archaic or poetic* a temple or shrine [c14: from Latin *fānum*]

fanfare ('fænfɛə) *n* **1** a flourish or short tune played on brass instruments, used as a military signal, at a ceremonial event, etc **2** an ostentatious flourish or display [c17: from French, back formation from *fanfarer* to play a flourish on trumpets; see FANFARONADE]

fanfaronade (,fænfərə'nɑːd) *n rare* boasting or flaunting behaviour; bluster [c17: via French from Spanish *fanfaronada*, from *fanfarron* boaster, from Arabic *farfār* garrulous]

fanfic ('fæn,fɪk) *n* fiction written around previously established characters invented by other authors

fang (fæŋ) *n* **1** the long pointed hollow or grooved tooth of a venomous snake through which venom is injected **2** any pointed tooth, esp the canine or carnassial tooth of a carnivorous mammal **3** the root of a tooth **4** (*usually plural*) *Brit informal* tooth [Old English *fang* what is caught, prey; related to Old Norse *fang* a grip, German *Fang* booty] > **fanged** *adj* > **'fangless** *adj*

Fangio (*Spanish* 'faŋxjo) *n* **Juan Manuel** (xwan ma'nwɛl). 1911–95, Argentinian racing driver who won the World Championship five times between 1951 and 1957

Fang Lizhi (fæŋ 'liː'dʒɪ) *n* born 1936, Chinese astrophysicist and human-rights campaigner, living in the US from 1990

Fa Ngum ('fɑː 'ŋʊm) *n* 1316–74, founder and first king of Lan Xang (1354–73), a kingdom that included the present-day republic of Laos; abdicated

fan heater *n* a space heater consisting of an electrically heated element with an electrically driven fan to disperse the heat by forced convection

fanjet ('fæn,dʒɛt) *n* another name for **turbofan** (sense 1)

fanlight ('fæn,laɪt) *n* **1** a semicircular window over a door or window, often having sash bars like the ribs of a fan **2** a small rectangular window over a door. U.S name: transom

fan mail *n* mail sent to a famous person, such as a pop musician or film star, by admirers

fanny ('fænɪ) *n, pl* **-nies** *slang* **1** *taboo, Brit* the female genitals **2** *chiefly US & Canadian* the buttocks [C20: perhaps from *Fanny*, pet name from *Frances*]

fanny adams *n Brit slang* **1** (usually preceded by *sweet*) absolutely nothing at all **2** *chiefly nautical* (formerly) tinned meat, esp mutton **7** far and plain **7** far and away by fantastic or famous person, such as a pop [c19: from the name of a young murder victim whose body was cut up into small pieces. For sense 1: a euphemism for *fuck all*]

fantail ('fæn,teɪl) *n* **1** a breed of domestic pigeon having a large tail that can be opened like a fan **2** any Old World flycatcher of the genus *Rhipidura*, of Australia, New Zealand, and SE Asia, having a broad fan-shaped tail **3** a tail shaped like an outspread fan **4** an auxiliary sail on the upper portion of a windmill that turns the mill to face the wind **5** *US* a curved part of the deck projecting aft of the sternpost of a ship ▷ **'fan-,tailed** *adj*

fan-tan *n* **1** a Chinese gambling game in which a random number of counters are placed under a bowl and wagers laid on how many will remain after they have been divided by four **2** a card game played in sequence, the winner being the first to use up all his cards [c19: from Chinese (Cantonese) *fan t'an* repeated divisions, from *fan* times + *t'an* division]

fantasia (fæn'teɪzɪə, ,fæntə'zɪə) *n* **1** any musical composition of a free or improvisatory nature **2** a potpourri of popular tunes woven freely into a loosely bound composition [c18: from Italian: fancy; see **FANTASY**]

fantasist ('fæntəsɪst) *n* **1** a person who indulges in fantasies **2** a person who writes musical or literary fantasies

fantasize *or* **fantasise** ('fæntə,saɪz) *vb* **1** (when *tr*, takes a clause as object) to conceive extravagant or whimsical ideas, images, etc **2** (*intr*) to conceive pleasant or satisfying mental images

fantastic (fæn'tæstɪk) *adj* *Also:* **fantastical 1** strange, weird, or fanciful in appearance, conception, etc **2** created in the mind; illusory **3** extravagantly fanciful; unrealistic: *fantastic plans* **4** incredible or preposterous; absurd: *a fantastic verdict* **5** *informal* very large or extreme; great: *a fantastic fortune; he suffered fantastic pain* **6** *informal* very good; excellent **7** of, given to, or characterized by fantasy **8** not constant; capricious; fitful [c14 *fantastik* imaginary, via Late Latin from Greek *phantastikos* capable of imagining, from *phantazein* to make visible] ▷ ,fan'tasticality *or* fan'tasticalness *n* ▷ fan'tastically *adv*

fantasy *or* **phantasy** ('fæntəsɪ) *n, pl* **-sies 1 a** imagination unrestricted by reality **b** (*as modifier*): *a fantasy world* **2** a creation of the imagination, esp a weird or bizarre one **3** *psychol* a series of pleasing mental images, usually serving to fulfil a need not gratified in reality **4** a whimsical or far-fetched notion **5** an illusion, hallucination, or phantom **6** a highly elaborate imaginative design or creation **7** *music* another word for **fantasia¹** (sense 2) **8** *literature* having a large fantasy content **9** (*modifier*) of or relating to a competition, often in a newspaper, in which a participant selects players for an imaginary ideal team, and points are awarded according to the actual performances of the chosen players: *fantasy football* ▷ *vb* **-sies, -sying, -sied 10** a less common word for **fantasize** [c14 *fantasie*, from Latin *phantasia*, from Greek *phantazein* to make visible]

Fantin-Latour (French fātēlatur) *n* (**Ignace**) **Henri** (**Joseph Théodore**) (ãri). 1836–1904, French painter, noted for his still lifes and portrait groups

fan vaulting *n architect* vaulting having ribs that radiate like those of a fan and spring from the top of a capital or corbel. Also called: **palm vaulting**

fanzine ('fæn,ziːn) *n* a small-circulation magazine produced by amateurs for fans of a specific interest, pop group, etc [c20: from FAN² + (MAGA)ZINE]

FAO *abbreviation* **1** Food and Agriculture Organization (of the United Nations) **2** for the attention of

FAQ *abbreviation computing* frequently asked question *or* questions: a text file containing basic information on a particular subject

f.a.q. *abbreviation commerce* fair average quality

far (fɑː) *adv* **farther** *or* **further, farthest** *or* **furthest 1** at, to, or from a great distance **2** at or to a remote time: *far in the future* **3** to a considerable degree; very much: *a far better plan* **4** as far as **a** to the degree or extent that **b** to the distance or place of **c** *informal* with reference to; as for **5** by far by a considerable margin **6** far and away by a very great margin **7** far and wide over great distances; everywhere **8** far be it from me I would not presume; on no account: *far be it from me to tell you what to do* **9** go far **a** to be successful; achieve much: *your son will go far* **b** to be sufficient or last long: *the wine didn't go far* **10** go too far to exceed reasonable limits **11** so far **a** up to the present moment **b** up to a certain point, extent, degree, etc ▷ *adj* (*prenominal*) **12** remote in space or time: *a far country; in the far past* **13** extending a great distance; long **14** more distant: *the far end of the room* **15** far from in a degree, state, etc, remote from: *he is far from happy* [Old English *feorr*; related to Old Frisian *fir*, Old High German *ferro*, Latin *porro* forwards, Greek *pera* further] ▷ **'farness** *n*

farad ('færəd, -æd) *n physics* the derived SI unit of electric capacitance; the capacitance of a capacitor between the plates of which a potential of 1 volt is created by a charge of 1 coulomb. Symbol: F [c19: named after Michael FARADAY]

faraday ('færə,deɪ) *n* a quantity of electricity, used in electrochemical calculations, equivalent to unit amount of substance of electrons. It is equal to the product of the Avogadro number and the charge on the electron and has the value 96 487 coulombs per mole. Symbol: F [c20: named after Michael FARADAY]

Faraday ('færə,deɪ) *n* **Michael.** 1791–1867, English physicist and chemist who discovered electromagnetic induction, leading to the invention of the dynamo. He also carried out research into the principles of electrolysis

faradic (fə'rædɪk) *adj* of or concerned with an intermittent asymmetric alternating current such as that induced in the secondary winding of an induction coil [c19: from French *faradique*, from Michael FARADAY]

farandole ('færən,dəʊl; French farādɔl) *n* **1** a lively dance in six-eight or four-four time from Provence **2** a piece of music composed for or in the rhythm of this dance [c19: from French, from Provençal *farandoulo*, of uncertain origin; compare Spanish *farándula* itinerant group of actors]

faraway ('fɑːrə,weɪ) *adj* (**far away** when postpositive) **1** very distant; remote **2** dreamy or absent-minded

farce (fɑːs) *n* **1** a broadly humorous play based on the exploitation of improbable situations **2** the genre of comedy represented by works of this kind **3** a ludicrous situation or action **4** Also called: **farcemeat** another name for **forcemeat** [c14 (in the sense: stuffing): from Old French, from Latin *farcīre* to stuff, interpolate passages (in the mass, in religious plays, etc)]

farcical ('fɑːsɪkəl) *adj* **1** ludicrous; absurd **2** of or relating to farce ▷ ,farci'cality *or* 'farcicalness *n* ▷ 'farcically *adv*

fardel ('fɑːdəl) *n archaic* a bundle or burden [c13: from Old French *farde*, ultimately from Arabic *fardah*]

fare (fɛə) *n* **1** the sum charged or paid for conveyance in a bus, train, aeroplane, etc **2** a paying passenger, esp when carried by taxi **3** a range of food and drink; diet ▷ *vb* (*intr*) **4** to get on (as specified); manage: *he fared well* **5** (with *it* as a subject) to turn out or happen as specified: *it fared badly with him* **6** *archaic* to eat: *we fared sumptuously* **7** (often foll by *forth*) *archaic* to go or travel [Old English *faran*; related to Old Norse *fara* to travel, Old High German *faran* to go, Greek *poros* ford] ▷ **'farer** *n*

Far East *n* the Far East the countries of E Asia, usually including China, Japan, North and South Korea, Indonesia, Malaysia, and the Philippines: sometimes extended to include all territories east of Afghanistan

Far Eastern *adj* of or relating to the Far East (E Asia) or its inhabitants

fare stage *n* **1** a section of a bus journey for which a set charge is made **2** a bus stop marking the end of such a section

farewell (,fɛə'wɛl) *sentence substitute* **1** goodbye; adieu ▷ *n* **2** a parting salutation **3** an act of departure; leave-taking **4** (modifier) expressing leave-taking: *a farewell speech* ▷ *vb* (tr) **5** *Austral & NZ* to honour (a person) at his departure, retirement, etc

farfalle (faː'fælei, -li) *n* pasta in the shape of bow ties or butterflies [C20: Italian, literally: butterflies]

far-fetched *adj* improbable in nature; unlikely

far-flung *adj* **1** widely distributed **2** far distant; remote

Fargo ('faːgəʊ) *n* **William**. 1818–81, US businessman: founded (1852) with Henry Wells the express mail service Wells, Fargo and Company

Farhi ('faːhɪ) *n* **Nicole**. born 1946, French fashion designer based in Britain: married to Sir David Hare

farina (fə'riːnə) *n* **1** flour or meal made from any kind of cereal grain **2** *chiefly Brit* starch, esp prepared from potato flour [C18: from Latin *fār* spelt, coarse meal]

farinaceous (,færɪ'neɪʃəs) *adj* **1** consisting or made of starch, such as bread, macaroni, and potatoes **2** having a mealy texture or appearance **3** containing starch: *farinaceous seeds*

farm (faːm) *n* **1 a** a tract of land, usually with house and buildings, cultivated as a unit or used to rear livestock **b** (*as modifier*): *farm produce* **c** (*in combination*): *farmland* **2** a unit of land or water devoted to the growing or rearing of some particular type of vegetable, fruit, animal, or fish: *a fish farm* **3** an installation for storage ▷ *vb* **4** (tr) **a** to cultivate (land) **b** to rear (stock, etc) on a farm **5** (intr) to engage in agricultural work, esp as a way of life **6** (tr) to look after a child for a fixed sum **7 a** to collect the moneys due and retain the profits from (a tax district, business, etc) for a specified period on payment of a sum or sums **b** to operate (a franchise) under similar conditions ▷ See also **farm out** [C13: from Old French *ferme* rented land, ultimately from Latin *firmāre* to settle] > 'farmable *adj*

farmed (faːmd) *adj* (of fish and game) reared on a farm rather than caught in the wild

farmer ('faːmə) *n* **1** a person who operates or manages a farm **2** a person who obtains the right to collect and retain a tax, rent, etc, or operate a franchise for a specified period on payment of a fee

Farmer ('faːmə) *n* **John**. ?1565–1605, English madrigal composer and organist

farmer's lung *n* inflammation of the alveoli of the lungs caused by an allergic response to fungal spores in hay

farmers' market *n* a market at which farm produce is sold directly to the public by the producer

farm hand *n* a person who is hired to work on a farm

farmhouse ('faːm,haʊs) *n* a house attached to a farm, esp the dwelling from which the farm is managed

farming ('faːmɪŋ) *n* **a** the business, art, or skill of agriculture **b** (*as modifier*): *farming methods*

farm out *vb* (tr, adverb) **1** to send (work) to be done by another person, firm, etc; subcontract **2** to put (a child, etc) into the care of a private individual; foster **3** to lease to another for a rent or fee the right to operate (a business for profit, land, etc) or the right to collect (taxes)

farmstead ('faːm,stɛd) *n* a farm or the part of a farm comprising its main buildings together with adjacent grounds

farmyard ('faːm,jaːd) *n* an area surrounded by or adjacent to farm buildings

Farnborough ('faːnbərə, -brə) *n* a town in S England, in NE Hampshire: military base, with an aeronautical research centre. Pop: 57 147 (2001)

Farnese (Italian far'neːse) *n* **1** Alesandro (ales'sandro). original name of Pope Paul III. See also **Paul III**

2 Alessandro, duke of Parma and Piacenza. 1545–92, Italian general, statesman, and diplomat in the service of Philip II of Spain. As governor of the Netherlands (1578–92), he successfully suppressed revolts against Spanish rule

Far North *n* the Far North the Arctic and sub-Arctic regions of the world

faro ('fɛərəʊ) *n* a gambling game in which players bet against the dealer on what cards he will turn up [C18: probably spelling variant of *Pharaoh*]

Faroes ('fɛərəʊz) *n* a variant spelling of **Faeroes**

Faroese (,fɛərəʊ'iːz) *adj, n* a variant spelling of **Faeroese**

far-off *adj* (far off *when postpositive*) remote in space or time; distant

farouche French (faruʃ) *adj* sullen or shy [C18: from French, from Old French *faroche*, from Late Latin *forasticus* from without, from Latin *foras* out of doors]

Farouk I or **Faruk I** (fə'ruːk) *n* 1920–65, last king of Egypt (1936–52). He was forced to abdicate (1952)

far-out *slang* ▷ *adj* (far out *when postpositive*) **1** bizarre or avant-garde **2** excellent; wonderful ▷ *interj* far out **3** an expression of amazement or delight

Farquhar ('faːkwə, -kə) *n* **George**. 1678–1707, Irish-born dramatist; author of comedies such as *The Recruiting Officer* (1706) and *The Beaux' Stratagem* (1707)

Farquhar Islands ('faːkwə, -kə) *pl n* an island group in the Indian Ocean: administratively part of the Seychelles

farrago (fə'raːgəʊ) *n, pl* **-gos** *or* **-goes** a hotchpotch [C17: from Latin: mash for cattle (hence, a mixture), from *fār* spelt] > **farraginous** (fə'rædʒɪnəs) *adj*

far-reaching *adj* extensive in influence, effect, or range

Farrell ('færəl) *n* **1 Colin (James)**. born 1976, Irish film actor; he appeared in the TV series *Ballykissangel* before starring in the films *Tigerland* (2000), *Minority Report* (2002), and *Alexander* (2004). **2 J(ames) G(ordon)** 1935–79, British novelist: author of *Troubles* (1970), *The Siege of Krishnapur* (1973), and *The Singapore Grip* (1978) **3 James T(homas)** 1904–79, US writer. His works include the trilogy *Young* (1932), *The Young Manhood of Studs Lonigan* (1934), and *Judgment Day* (1935)

farrier ('færɪə) *n chiefly Brit* **1** a person who shoes horses **2** *archaic* another name for **veterinary surgeon** [C16: from Old French *ferrier*, from Latin *ferrārius* smith, from *ferrum* iron]

farrow ('færəʊ) *n* **1** a litter of piglets ▷ *vb* **2** (of a sow) to give birth to (a litter) [Old English *fearh*; related to Old High German *farah* young pig, Latin *porcus* pig, Greek *porkos*]

far-seeing *adj* having shrewd judgment; far-sighted

Farsi ('faːsiː) *n* another name for **Persian** (sense 3)

far-sighted *adj* **1** possessing prudence and foresight **2** another word for **long-sighted** > ,far-'sightedly *adv* > ,far-'sightedness *n*

fart (faːt) *slang* ▷ *n* **1** an emission of intestinal gas from the anus, esp an audible one **2** a contemptible person ▷ *vb* (intr) **3** to expel intestinal gas from the anus; to break wind **4** fart about *or* fart around **a** to behave foolishly or aimlessly **b** to waste time [Middle English *farten*; related to Old Norse *freta*, Old High German *ferzan* to break wind, Sanskrit *pardatē* he breaks wind]

farther ('faːðə) *adv* **1** to or at a greater distance in space or time **2** in addition ▷ *adj* **3** more distant or remote in space or time **4** additional [C13: see FAR, FURTHER]
  ● USAGE *Farther*, *farthest*, *further*, and *furthest* can all be
  ● used to refer to literal distance, but *further* and *furthest*
  ● are regarded as more correct for figurative senses
  ● denoting greater or additional amount, time, etc:
  ● *further to my letter*. *Further* and *furthest* are also preferred
  ● for figurative distance

farthermost ('faːðə,məʊst) *adj* most distant or remote

farthest ('faːðɪst) *adv* **1** to or at the greatest distance in space or time ▷ *adj* **2** most distant in space or time **3** most extended [C14 *ferthest*, from *ferther* FURTHER]

farthing ('faːðɪŋ) *n* **1** a former British bronze coin, worth a quarter of an old penny, that ceased to be legal tender in 1961 **2** something of negligible value; jot [Old English *fēorthing* from *fēortha* FOURTH + -ING¹]

farthingale ('faːðɪŋ,geɪl) *n* a hoop or framework worn under skirts, esp in the Elizabethan period, to shape and spread them [C16: from French *verdugale*, from Old Spanish *verdugado*, from *verdugo* rod]

Faruk I (fə'ruːk) *n* a variant spelling of **Farouk I**

fasces ('fæsiːz) *pl n, sing* **-cis** (-sɪs) **1** (in ancient Rome) one or more bundles of rods containing an axe with its blade protruding; a symbol of a magistrate's power **2** (in modern Italy) such an object used as the symbol of Fascism [C16: from Latin, plural of *fascis* bundle]

fascia or **facia** ('feɪʃɪə) *n, pl* **-ciae** (-ʃɪ,iː) **1** the flat surface above a shop window **2** *architect* a flat band or surface, esp a part of an architrave or cornice **3** ('fæʃɪə) fibrous connective tissue occurring in sheets beneath the surface of the skin and between muscles and groups of muscles **4** *biology* a distinctive band of colour, as on an insect or plant **5** *Brit* a less common name for **dashboard** (sense 1) [c16: from Latin: band: related to *fascis* bundle; see FASCES] > **'fascial** *or* **'facial** *adj*

fasciate ('fæʃɪˌeɪt) *or* **fasciated** *adj* **1** *botany* (of stems and branches) abnormally flattened due to coalescence **2** (of birds, insects, etc) marked by distinct bands of colour [c17: probably from New Latin *fasciātus* (unattested) having bands; see FASCIA]

fascicle ('fæsɪkᵊl) *n* **1** a bundle or cluster of branches, leaves, etc **2** Also called: **fasciculus** *anatomy* a small bundle of fibres, esp nerve fibres **3** *printing* another name for **fascicule** **4** any small bundle or cluster [c15: from Latin *fasciculus* a small bundle, from *fascis* a bundle] > **'fascicled** *adj* > **fascicular** (fə'sɪkjʊlə) *or* **fasciculate** (fə'sɪkjʊˌleɪt, -lɪt) *adj* > **fas,cicu'lation** *n*

fascicule ('fæsɪˌkjuːl) *n* one part of a printed work that is published in instalments. Also called: **fascicle** *or* **fasciculus**

fascinate ('fæsɪˌneɪt) *vb* (*mainly tr*) **1** to attract and delight by arousing interest or curiosity: *his stories fascinated me for hours* **2** to render motionless, as with a fixed stare or by arousing terror or awe **3** *archaic* to put under a spell [c16: from Latin *fascināre*, from *fascinum* a bewitching] > **,fasci'nation** *n*

fascinating ('fæsɪˌneɪtɪŋ) *adj* **1** arousing great interest **2** enchanting or alluring

fascinator ('fæsɪˌneɪtə) *n* *rare* a lace or crocheted head covering for women

fascism ('fæʃɪzəm) *n* (*sometimes capital*) **1** any ideology or movement inspired by Italian Fascism, such as German National Socialism; any right-wing nationalist ideology or movement with an authoritarian and hierarchical structure that is fundamentally opposed to democracy and liberalism **2** any ideology, movement, programme, tendency, etc, that may be characterized as right-wing, chauvinist, authoritarian, etc **3** prejudice in relation to the subject specified: *body fascism* [c20: from Italian *fascismo*, from *fascio* political group, from Latin *fascis* bundle; see FASCES]

Fascism ('fæʃɪzəm) *n* the political movement, doctrine, system, or regime (1922–43) in Italy of the dictator Benito Mussolini (1883–1945). Fascism encouraged militarism and nationalism, organizing the country along hierarchical authoritarian lines

fascist ('fæʃɪst) (*sometimes capital*) *n* **1** an adherent or practitioner of fascism **2** any person regarded as having right-wing authoritarian views ▷ *adj* Also: **fascistic** (fə'ʃɪstɪk) **3** characteristic of or relating to fascism

Fascist ('fæʃɪst) *n* a supporter or member of the Italian Fascist movement

fashion ('fæʃən) *n* **1 a** a style in clothes, cosmetics, behaviour, etc, esp the latest or most admired style **b** (*as modifier*): *a fashion magazine* **2** (*modifier*) (esp of accessories) designed to be in the current fashion, but not necessarily to last **3 a** a manner of performance; mode; way: *in a striking fashion* **b** (*in combination*): *crab-fashion* **4** a way of life that revolves around the activities, dress, interests, etc, that are most fashionable **5** shape, appearance, or form **6** sort; kind; type **7** after a fashion or in a fashion in some manner, but not very well: *I mended it, after a fashion* **8** of fashion of high social standing ▷ *vb* (*tr*) **9** to give a particular form to **10** to make suitable or fitting **11** *obsolete* to contrive; manage [c13 *facioun* form, manner, from Old French *faceon*, from Latin *factiō* a making, from *facere* to make] > **'fashioner** *n*

fashionable ('fæʃənəbᵊl) *adj* **1** conforming to fashion; in vogue **2** of, characteristic of, or patronized by people of fashion: *a fashionable café* **3** (*usually foll by with*) patronized (by); popular (with) > **,fashiona'bility** *or* **'fashionableness** *n* > **'fashionably** *adv*

fashion-forward *adj* relating to, anticipating, or reflecting the most up-to-date fashion trends

fashionista (,fæʃə'niːstə) *n* *informal* a person who follows trends in the fashion industry obsessively and strives continually to adopt the latest fashions [c20: from FASHION + -ista as in SANDINISTA]

fashion plate *n* **1** an illustration of the latest fashion in dress **2** a fashionably dressed person

fashion victim *n* *informal* a person who slavishly follows fashion

Fassbinder (German 'fasbɪndər) *n* **Rainer Werner** ('raɪnər 'vɛrnər). 1946–82, West German film director. His films include *The Bitter Tears of Petra von Kant* (1972), *Fear Eats the Soul* (1974), and *The Marriage of Maria Braun* (1978)

fast¹ (fɑːst) *adj* **1** acting or moving or capable of acting or moving quickly; swift **2** accomplished in or lasting a short time: *fast work; a fast visit* **3** (*prenominal*) adapted to or facilitating rapid movement: *the fast lane of a motorway* **4** (of a clock, etc) indicating a time in advance of the correct time **5** given to an active dissipated life **6** of or characteristic of such activity: *a fast life* **7** not easily moved; firmly fixed; secure **8** firmly fastened, secured, or shut **9** steadfast; constant (esp in the phrase **fast friends**) **10** *sport* (of a playing surface, running track, etc) conducive to rapid speed, as of a ball used on it or of competitors playing or racing on it **11** that will not fade or change colour readily: *a fast dye* **12** proof against fading **13** *photog* **a** requiring a relatively short time of exposure to produce a given density: *a fast film* **b** permitting a short exposure time: *a fast shutter* **14** *informal* a deceptive or unscrupulous trick (esp in the phrase **pull a fast one**) **15 fast worker** a person who achieves results quickly, esp in seductions ▷ *adv* **16** quickly; rapidly **17** soundly; deeply: *fast asleep* **18** firmly; tightly **19** in quick succession **20** in advance of the correct time: *my watch is running fast* **21** in a reckless or dissipated way **22 fast by** *or* **fast beside** *archaic* close or hard by; very near **23 play fast and loose** *informal* to behave in an insincere or unreliable manner [Old English *fæst* strong, tight; related to Old High German *festi* firm, Old Norse *fastr*]

fast² (fɑːst) *vb* **1** (*intr*) to abstain from eating all or certain foods or meals, esp as a religious observance ▷ *n* **2 a** an act or period of fasting **b** (*as modifier*): *a fast day* [Old English *fæstan*; related to Old High German *fastēn* to fast, Gothic *fastan*] > **'faster** *n*

fastback ('fɑːstˌbæk) *n* a car having a back that forms one continuous slope from roof to rear

fast-breeder reactor *n* a nuclear reactor that uses little or no moderator and produces more fissionable material than it consumes

fast casual *n* a style of fast food involving healthier, fresher, and more varied dishes than traditional fast food, served in more attractive surroundings

fasten ('fɑːsᵊn) *vb* **1** to make or become fast or secure **2** to make or become attached or joined **3** to close or become closed by fixing firmly in place, locking, etc **4** (*tr*; foll by *in* or *up*) to enclose or imprison **5** (*tr*; usually foll by *on*) to cause (blame, a nickname, etc) to be attached (to); place (on) or impute (to) **6** (usually foll by *on* or *upon*) to direct or be directed in a concentrated way; fix **7** (*intr*; usually foll by *on*) take firm hold (of) [Old English *fæstnian*; related to Old Norse *fastna* to pledge, Old High German *fastinōn* to make fast; see FAST¹] > **'fastener** *n*

fastening ('fɑːsᵊnɪŋ) *n* something that fastens, such as a clasp or lock

fast food *n* **1** food that requires little preparation before being served ▷ *adj* **fast-food 2** (of a restaurant, café, etc) serving such food

fast-forward *n* **1** (*sometimes not hyphenated*) the control on a tape deck or video recorder used to wind the tape or video forward at speed **2** *informal* a state of urgency or rapid progress: *my mind went into fast forward* ▷ *vb* **3** (*tr*) to wind (a video or tape) forward using the fast-forward control **4** to deal with speedily: *fast-forward the trials of the new drug* **5** (*intr*) to move forward through a tape or video using the fast-forward control **6** (usually foll by *to*) to direct one's attention towards a particular time or event, ignoring intervening material: *fast-forward to the summer of 2008* [c20: from the fast-forward wind control in a tape deck]

fastidious (fæ'stɪdɪəs) *adj* **1** very critical; hard to please **2** excessively particular about details **3** exceedingly delicate; easily disgusted [c15: from Latin *fastīdiōsus* scornful, from *fastīdium* loathing, from *fastus* pride + *taedium* weariness] > fas'tidiously *adv* > fas'tidiousness *n*

fastie ('fɑːstɪ) *n Austral slang* 1 a deceitful act 2 pull a fastie to play a sly trick

fastigiate (fæ'stɪdʒɪɪt, -ˌeɪt) *or* **fastigiated** *adj biology* 1 (of plants) having erect branches, often appearing to form a single column with the stem 2 (of parts or organs) united in a tapering group [C17: from Medieval Latin *fastīgiātus* lofty, from Latin *fastīgium* height]

fast lane *n* 1 the outside lane on a motorway or dual carriageway for vehicles overtaking or travelling at high speed 2 *informal* the quickest but most competitive route to success

fastness ('fɑːstnɪs) *n* 1 a stronghold; fortress 2 the state or quality of being firm or secure [Old English *fæstnes*; see FAST[1]]

fast-track *adj* 1 denoting the quickest or most direct route or system: *fast-track executives; a fast-track procedure for libel claims* ▷ *vb* 2 (*tr*) to speed up the progress of (a project or person)

fat (fæt) *n* 1 any of a class of naturally occurring soft greasy solids that are esters of glycerol and certain fatty acids. They are present in some plants and in the adipose tissue of animals, forming a reserve energy source, and are used in making soap and paint and in the food industry 2 vegetable or animal tissue containing fat 3 corpulence, obesity, or plumpness 4 the best or richest part of something 5 the fat is in the fire an irrevocable action has been taken, esp one from which dire consequences are expected 6 the fat of the land the best that is obtainable ▷ *adj* fatter, fattest 7 having much or too much flesh or fat 8 consisting of or containing fat; greasy: *fat pork* 9 profitable; lucrative 10 affording great opportunities: *a fat part in the play* 11 fertile or productive: *a fat land* 12 thick, broad, or extended: *a fat log of wood* 13 *slang* very little or none; minimal (in phrases such as **a fat chance, a fat lot of good,** etc) ▷ *vb* fats, fatting, fatted 14 to make or become fat; fatten [Old English *fætt*, past participle of *fætan* to cram; related to Old Norse *feita*, Old High German *feizen* to fatten; compare Gothic *fētjan* to adorn] > 'fatless *adj* > 'fatly *adv* > 'fatness *n* > 'fattish *adj*

fatal ('feɪtəl) *adj* 1 resulting in or capable of causing death: *a fatal accident* 2 bringing ruin; disastrous 3 decisively important; fateful 4 brought on by fate; destined; inevitable [C14: from Old French *fatal* or Latin *fātālis*, from *fātum*, see FATE]

fatalism ('feɪtəˌlɪzəm) *n* 1 the philosophical doctrine that all events are predetermined so that man is powerless to alter his destiny 2 the acceptance of and submission to this doctrine > 'fatalist *n* > ˌfatal'istic *adj*

fatality (fə'tælɪtɪ) *n, pl* -ties 1 an accident or disaster resulting in death 2 a person killed in an accident or disaster 3 the power of causing death or disaster; deadliness 4 the quality or condition of being fated 5 something fixed or dictated by fate

fate (feɪt) *n* 1 the ultimate agency that predetermines the course of events 2 the inevitable fortune that befalls a person or thing; destiny 3 the end or final result 4 a calamitous or unfavourable outcome or result; death, destruction, or downfall ▷ *vb* 5 (*tr; usually passive*) to predetermine; doom: *he was fated to lose the game* [C14: from Latin *fātum* oracular utterance, from *fārī* to speak]

fated ('feɪtɪd) *adj* 1 destined 2 doomed to death or destruction

fateful ('feɪtfʊl) *adj* 1 having important consequences; decisively important 2 bringing death or disaster 3 controlled by or as if by fate 4 prophetic > 'fatefully *adv* > 'fatefulness *n*

Fates (feɪts) *pl n* 1 *Greek myth* the three goddesses who control the destinies of the lives of man, which are likened to skeins of thread that they spin, measure out, and at last cut. See **Atropos, Clotho, Lachesis** 2 *Norse myth* the Norns. See **Norn**[1]

fathead ('fæt,hed) *n informal* a stupid person; fool > 'fat,headed *adj*

father ('fɑːðə) *n* 1 a male parent 2 a person who founds a line or family; forefather 3 any male acting in a paternal capacity 4 (*often capital*) a respectful term of address for an old man 5 a male who originates something: *the father of modern psychology* 6 a leader of an association, council, etc; elder: *a city father* 7 *Brit* the eldest or most senior member in a society, profession, etc 8 (*often plural*) a senator or patrician in ancient Rome ▷ *vb* (*tr*) 9 to procreate or generate (offspring); beget 10 to create, found, originate, etc 11 to act as a father to 12 to acknowledge oneself as father or originator of 13 (foll by *on* or *upon*) to impose or place without a just reason [Old English *fæder*; related to Old Norse *fathir*, Old Frisian *feder*, Old High German *fater*, Latin *pater*, Greek *patēr*, Sanskrit *pitr*] > 'father,hood *n* > 'fatherless *adj*

Father ('fɑːðə) *n* 1 God, esp when considered as the first person of the Christian Trinity 2 Also called: **Church Father** any of the writers on Christian doctrine of the pre-Scholastic period 3 a title used for Christian priests

father confessor *n* 1 *Christianity* a priest who hears confessions and advises on religious or moral matters 2 any person to whom one tells private matters

father-in-law *n, pl* fathers-in-law the father of one's wife or husband

fatherland ('fɑːðəˌlænd) *n* 1 a person's native country 2 the country of a person's ancestors

fatherly ('fɑːðəlɪ) *adj* of, resembling, or suitable to a father > 'fatherliness *n*

Father of the House *n* (in Britain) the longest-serving member of the House of Commons

Father's Day *n* a day observed as a day in honour of fathers; in Britain the third Sunday in June

fathom ('fæðəm) *n* 1 a unit of length equal to six feet (1.829 metres), used to measure depths of water ▷ *vb* (*tr*) 2 to measure the depth of, esp with a sounding line; sound 3 to penetrate (a mystery, problem, etc); discover the meaning of [Old English *fæthm*; related to Old Frisian *fethem* outstretched arms, Old Norse *fathmr* embrace, Old High German *fadum* cubit, Latin *patēre* to gape] > 'fathomable *adj*

Fathometer (fə'ɒmɪtə) *n trademark* a type of echo sounder used for measuring the depth of water

fathomless ('fæðəmlɪs) *adj* another word for **unfathomable** > 'fathomlessness *n*

fatigue (fə'tiːg) *n* 1 physical or mental exhaustion due to exertion 2 a tiring activity or effort 3 *physiol* the temporary inability of an organ or part to respond to a stimulus because of overactivity 4 the progressive cracking of a material subjected to alternating stresses, esp vibrations 5 the temporary inability to respond to a situation or perform a function, because of overexposure or overactivity: *compassion fatigue* 6 any of the mainly domestic duties performed by military personnel, esp as a punishment 7 (*pl*) special clothing worn by military personnel to carry out such duties ▷ *vb* -tigues, -tiguing, -tigued 8 to make or become weary or exhausted [C17: from French, from *fatiguer* to tire, from Latin *fatīgāre*] > 'fatigable ('fætɪgəbəl) *adj*

Fatima ('fætɪmə) *n* ?606–632 AD daughter of Mohammed; wife of Ali

Fátima (*Portuguese* 'fɑtimə) *n* a village in central Portugal: Roman Catholic shrine and pilgrimage centre

Fatshan ('fɑːtʃɑːn) *n* a variant transliteration of the Chinese name for **Foshan**

fatshedera (fæts'hedərə) *n* an evergreen garden shrub with shiny green leaves and umbels of pale green flowers; a bigeneric hybrid between *Fatsia japonica moseri* and *Hedera hibernica*: family *Araliaceae*

fatsia ('fætsɪə) *n* any shrub of the araliaceous genus *Fatsia*, esp *F. japonica*, with large deeply palmate leaves and umbels of white flowers [New Latin, from the Japanese name]

fatso ('fætsəʊ) *n, pl* -sos *or* -soes *slang* a fat person: used as an insulting or disparaging term of address

fat-soluble *adj* soluble in nonpolar substances, such as ether, chloroform, and oils. Fat-soluble compounds are often insoluble in water

fat stock *n* livestock fattened and ready for market

fatten ('fætən) *vb* 1 to grow or cause to grow fat or fatter 2 (*tr*) to cause (an animal or fowl) to become fat by feeding it 3 (*tr*) to make fuller or richer 4 (*tr*) to enrich (soil) by adding fertilizing agents > 'fattening *adj*

fattism ('fætɪzəm) n discrimination on the basis of weight, esp prejudice against those considered to be overweight [C20: from FAT + -ISM, on the model of RACISM] > 'fattist n, adj

fatty ('fætɪ) adj -tier, -tiest 1 containing, consisting of, or derived from fat 2 having the properties of fat; greasy; oily 3 (esp of tissues, organs, etc) characterized by the excessive accumulation of fat ▷ n, pl -ties 4 informal a fat person > 'fattily adv > 'fattiness n

fatty acid n any of a class of aliphatic carboxylic acids, such as palmitic acid, stearic acid, and oleic acid, that form part of a lipid molecule

fatty degeneration n pathol the abnormal formation of tiny globules of fat within the cytoplasm of a cell

fatuity (fə'tjuːɪtɪ) n, pl -ties 1 complacent foolishness; inanity 2 a fatuous remark, act, sentiment, etc > fa'tuitous adj

fatuous ('fætjʊəs) adj complacently or inanely foolish [C17: from Latin fatuus; related to fatiscere to gape] > 'fatuously adv > 'fatuousness n

fatwa or **fatwah** ('fætwɑː) n a non-binding judgement on a point of Islamic law given by a recognized religious authority [Arabic]

fauces ('fɔːsiːz) n, pl -ces anatomy the area between the cavity of the mouth and the pharynx, including the surrounding tissues [C16: from Latin: throat] > faucal ('fɔːkəl) or faucial ('fɔːʃəl) adj

faucet ('fɔːsɪt) n 1 a tap fitted to a barrel 2 US & Canadian a valve by which a fluid flow from a pipe can be controlled by opening and closing an orifice. Also called (in Britain and certain other countries): tap [C14: from Old French fausset, from Provençal falset, from falsar to bore]

Faulkner or **Falkner** ('fɔːknə) n William. 1897–1962, US novelist and short-story writer. Most of his works portray the problems of the southern US, esp the novels set in the imaginary county of Yoknapatawpha in Mississippi. Other novels include The Sound and the Fury (1929) and Light in August (1932): Nobel prize for literature 1949

Faulknerian (fɔːk'nɪərɪən) adj of, relating to, or like William Faulkner (1897–1962), the US novelist and short-story writer, his works, ideas, etc

fault (fɔːlt) n 1 an imperfection; failing or defect; flaw 2 a mistake or error 3 an offence; misdeed 4 responsibility for a mistake or misdeed; culpability 5 electronics a defect in a circuit, component, or line, such as a short circuit 6 geology a fracture in the earth's crust resulting in the relative displacement and loss of continuity of the rocks on either side of it 7 tennis, squash, badminton an invalid serve, such as one that lands outside a prescribed area 8 (in showjumping) a penalty mark given for failing to clear or refusing a fence, exceeding a time limit, etc 9 at fault guilty of error; culpable 10 find fault to seek out minor imperfections or errors (in); carp (at) 11 to a fault excessively ▷ vb 12 geology to undergo or cause to undergo a fault 13 (tr) to find a fault in, criticize, or blame 14 (intr) to commit a fault [C13: from Old French faute, from Vulgar Latin fallita (unattested), ultimately from Latin fallere to fail]

fault-finding n 1 continual and usually trivial criticism ▷ adj 2 given to finding fault > 'fault-,finder n

faultless ('fɔːltlɪs) adj without fault; perfect or blameless > 'faultlessly adv > 'faultlessness n

faulty ('fɔːltɪ) adj faultier, faultiest defective or imperfect > 'faultily adv > 'faultiness n

faun (fɔːn) n (in Roman legend) a rural deity represented as a man with a goat's ears, horns, tail, and hind legs [C14: back formation from Faunes (plural), from Latin FAUNUS] > 'faun,like adj

fauna ('fɔːnə) n, pl -nas or -nae (-niː) 1 all the animal life of a given place or time, esp when distinguished from the plant life (flora) 2 a descriptive list of such animals [C18: from New Latin, from Late Latin Fauna a goddess, sister of FAUNUS] > 'faunal adj

Faunus ('fɔːnəs) n an ancient Italian deity of pastures and forests, later identified with the Greek god Pan

Fauré ('fɔːreɪ; French fore) n Gabriel (Urbain) (gabriɛl). 1845–1924, French composer and teacher, noted particularly for his song settings of French poems, esp those of Verlaine, his piano music, and his Messe de Requiem (1887)

Faust (faʊst) or **Faustus** ('faʊstəs) n German legend a magician and alchemist who sells his soul to the devil in exchange for knowledge and power > 'Faustian adj

Fauve (French fov) n 1 one of a group of French painters prominent from 1905, including Henri Matisse (1869–1954), Maurice de Vlaminck (1876–1958), and André Derain (1880–1954), characterized by the use of bright colours and simplified forms ▷ adj 2 (often not capital) of this group or its style [C20: from French, literally: wild beast, alluding to the violence of colours, etc] > 'Fauvism n > 'Fauvist n, adj

faux pas (,fəʊ 'pɑː; French fo pɑ) n, pl faux pas (,fəʊ 'pɑːz; French fo pɑ) a social blunder or indiscretion [C17: from French: false step]

fava bean ('fɑːvə) n US & Canadian 1 an erect annual Eurasian bean plant, Vicia Faba, cultivated for its large edible flattened seeds, used as a vegetable 2 the seed of this plant. Also called: broad bean [C20: Italian fava from Latin faba bean]

fave (feɪv) adj, n informal short for favourite (senses 1, 2)

favour or US **favor** ('feɪvə) n 1 an approving attitude; good will 2 an act performed out of good will, generosity, or mercy 3 prejudice and partiality; favouritism 4 a condition of being regarded with approval or good will (esp in the phrases in favour, out of favour) 5 a token of love, goodwill, etc 6 a small gift or toy given to a guest at a party 7 history a badge or ribbon worn or given to indicate loyalty, often bestowed on a knight by a lady 8 find favour with to be approved of by someone 9 in favour of a approving b to the benefit of c (of a cheque, etc) made out to d in order to show preference for ▷ vb (tr) 10 to regard with especial kindness or approval 11 to treat with partiality or favouritism 12 to support; advocate 13 to perform a favour for; oblige 14 to help; facilitate 15 informal to resemble: he favours his father 16 to wear habitually: she favours red 17 to treat gingerly or with tenderness; spare: a footballer favouring an injured leg [C14: from Latin favēre to protect] > 'favourer or US 'favorer n

favourable or US **favorable** ('feɪvərəbəl, 'feɪvrə-) adj 1 advantageous, encouraging, or promising 2 giving consent > 'favourably or US 'favorably adv

-favoured adj (in combination) having an appearance (as specified): ill-favoured

favourite or US **favorite** ('feɪvərɪt, 'feɪvrɪt) adj 1 (prenominal) most liked; preferred above all others ▷ n 2 a person or thing regarded with especial preference or liking 3 sport a competitor thought likely to win 4 (pl) computing a place on certain browsers that allows internet users to list the addresses of websites they find and like with a click of the mouse so that they can revisit them merely by opening the list and clicking on the address [C16: from Italian favorito, from favorire to favour, from Latin favēre]

favouritism or US **favoritism** ('feɪvərɪ,tɪzəm, 'feɪvrɪ-) n the practice of giving special treatment to a person or group

Fawcett ('fɔːsɪt) n Dame Millicent Garrett. 1847–1929, British suffragette

Fawkes (fɔːks) n Guy. 1570–1606, English conspirator, executed for his part in the Gunpowder Plot to blow up King James I and the Houses of Parliament (1605). Effigies of him (guys) are burnt in Britain on Guy Fawkes Day (Nov 5)

fawn[1] (fɔːn) n 1 a young deer of either sex aged under one year 2 a a light greyish-brown colour b (as adjective): a fawn raincoat ▷ vb 3 (of deer) to bear (young) [C14: from Old French faon, from Latin fētus offspring; see FETUS] > 'fawn,like adj

fawn[2] (fɔːn) vb (intr; often foll by on or upon) 1 to seek attention and admiration (from) by cringing and flattering 2 (of animals, esp dogs) to try to please by a show of extreme friendliness and fondness (towards) [Old English fægnian to be glad, from fægen glad; see FAIN] > 'fawner n > 'fawning adj

fax (fæks) n 1 Also called: fax machine a machine which

transmits and receives documents in facsimile transmission **2** short for **facsimile transmission** ▷ *vb* **3** (*tr*) to send (a message, document, etc) by fax

Fa Xian ('fɑː 'ʃjɑːn) *or* **Fa-hsien** *n* original name *Sehi*. 5th century AD, Chinese Buddhist monk: his pilgrimage to India (399–414) began relations between China and India

fay (feɪ) *n* a fairy or sprite [c14: from Old French *feie*, ultimately from Latin *fātum* FATE]

Fayal (*Portuguese* fəˈial) *n* a variant spelling of **Faial**

Fayum (faɪˈjuːm) *n* See **El Faiyûm**

faze (feɪz) *vb* (*tr*) to disconcert; worry; disturb [c19: variant of FEEZE]

FB *abbreviation slang* fuck buddy

FBA *abbreviation* Fellow of the British Academy

FBI *abbreviation* (in the US) Federal Bureau of Investigation; an agency of the Justice Department responsible for investigating violations of Federal laws

f-bomb *n* drop an f-bomb *informal* to use the word *fuck* in a situation where it will cause great offence [c20: a play on A-BOMB and H-BOMB, alluding to their explosive impact]

FC *abbreviation* **1** (in Britain) Football Club **2** (in Canada) Federal Court

fcap *abbreviation* foolscap

F clef *n* another name for **bass clef**

FD *abbreviation* Fidei Defensor [Latin: Defender of the Faith]

FDA *abbreviation* (in the US) Food and Drug Administration: a federal agency responsible for monitoring trading and safety standards in the food and drug industries

FDR *abbreviation for* Franklin Delano Roosevelt

Fe *the chemical symbol for* iron [from New Latin *ferrum*]

feal (fiːl) *adj* an archaic word for **faithful** [c16: from Old French *feeil*, from Latin *fidēlis*]

fealty ('fiːəltɪ) *n*, *pl* -ties (in feudal society) the loyalty sworn to one's lord on becoming his vassal [c14: from Old French *fealte*, from Latin *fidēlitās* FIDELITY]

fear (fɪə) *n* **1** a feeling of distress, apprehension, or alarm caused by impending danger, pain, etc **2** a cause of this feeling **3** awe; reverence: *fear of God* **4** concern; anxiety **5** possibility; chance **6** for fear of, for fear that *or* for fear lest to forestall or avoid **7** no fear certainly not ▷ *vb* to be afraid (to do something) or of (a person or thing); dread **9** (*tr*) to revere; respect **10** (*tr; takes a clause as object*) to be sorry: used to lessen the effect of an unpleasant statement: *I fear that you have not won* **11** (*intr; foll by for*) to feel anxiety about something [Old English *fǣr*; related to Old High German *fāra*, Old Norse *fār* hostility, Latin *perīculum* danger] ▷ 'fearless *adj* ▷ 'fearlessly *adv* ▷ 'fearlessness *n*

fearful ('fɪəfʊl) *adj* **1** having fear; afraid **2** causing fear; frightening **3** *informal* very unpleasant or annoying: *a fearful cold* ▷ 'fearfulness *n* ▷ 'fearfully *adv*

fearsome ('fɪəsəm) *adj* **1** frightening **2** timorous; afraid ▷ 'fearsomely *adv*

feasibility study *n* a study designed to determine the practicability of a system or plan

feasible ('fiːzəbᵊl) *adj* **1** able to be done or put into effect; possible **2** likely; probable [c15: from Anglo-French *faisable*, from *faire* to do, from Latin *facere*] ▷ ˌfeasi'bility *or* 'feasibleness *n* ▷ 'feasibly *adv*

feast (fiːst) *n* **1** a large and sumptuous meal, usually given as an entertainment for several people **2** a periodic religious celebration **3** something extremely pleasing or sumptuous: *a feast for the eyes* **4** movable feast a festival or other event of variable date ▷ *vb* **5** (*intr*) **a** to eat a feast **b** (usually foll by *on*) to enjoy the eating (of), as if feasting: *to feast on cakes* **6** (*tr*) to give a feast to **7** (*intr; foll by on*) to take great delight (in): *to feast on beautiful paintings* **8** (*tr*) to regale or delight: *to feast one's mind or one's eyes* [c13: from Old French *feste*, from Latin *festa*, neuter plural (later assumed to be feminine singular) of *festus* joyful; related to Latin *fānum* temple, *fēriae* festivals] ▷ 'feaster *n*

Feast of Dedication *n Judaism* a literal translation of **Chanukah**

Feast of Lights *n Judaism* an English name for **Hanukkah**

Feast of Tabernacles *n Judaism* a literal translation of **Sukkoth**

Feast of Weeks *n Judaism* a literal translation of **Shavuot**

feat (fiːt) *n* a remarkable, skilful, or daring action; exploit; achievement [c14: from Anglo-French *fait*, from Latin *factum* deed; see FACT]

feather ('fɛðə) *n* **1** any of the flat light waterproof epidermal structures forming the plumage of birds, each consisting of a hollow shaft having a vane of barbs on either side. They are essential for flight and help maintain body temperature **2** something resembling a feather, such as a tuft of hair or grass **3** *archery* **a** a bird's feather or artificial substitute fitted to an arrow to direct its flight **b** the feathered end of an arrow, opposite the head **4** *rowing* the position of an oar turned parallel to the water between strokes **5** condition of spirits; fettle: *in fine feather* **6** something of negligible value; jot: *I don't care a feather* **7** feather in one's cap a cause for pleasure at one's achievements ▷ *vb* **8** (*tr*) to fit, cover, or supply with feathers **9** *rowing* to turn (an oar) parallel to the water during recovery between strokes, principally in order to lessen wind resistance **10** to change the pitch of (an aircraft propeller) so that the chord lines of the blades are in line with the airflow **11** (*intr*) (of a bird) to grow feathers **12** feather one's nest to provide oneself with comforts, esp financial [Old English *fether*; related to Old Frisian *fethere*, Old Norse *fjǫthr* feather, Old High German *fedara* wing, Greek *petesthai* to fly, Sanskrit *patati* he flies] ▷ 'feather-ˌlike *adj* ▷ 'feathery *adj* ▷ 'feathering *n*

feather bed *n* **1** a mattress filled with feathers or down ▷ *vb* featherbed -beds, -bedding, -bedded **2** (*tr*) to pamper; spoil

featherbedding ('fɛðəˌbɛdɪŋ) *n* the practice of limiting production, duplicating work, or overmanning, esp in accordance with a union contract, in order to prevent redundancies or create jobs

featherbrain ('fɛðəˌbreɪn) *or* **featherhead** *n* a frivolous or forgetful person ▷ 'feather,brained *or* 'feather,headed *adj*

featheredge ('fɛðərˌɛdʒ) *n* a board or plank that tapers to a thin edge at one side

featherstitch ('fɛðəˌstɪtʃ) *n* **1** a zigzag embroidery stitch ▷ *vb* **2** to decorate (cloth) with featherstitch

featherweight ('fɛðəˌweɪt) *n* **1** a something very light or of little importance **b** (*as modifier*): *featherweight considerations* **2** **a** a professional boxer weighing 118–126 pounds (53.5–57 kg) **b** an amateur boxer weighing 54–57 kg (119–126 pounds)

feature ('fiːtʃə) *n* **1** any one of the parts of the face, such as the nose, chin, or mouth **2** a prominent or distinctive part or aspect, as of a landscape, building, book, etc **3** the principal film in a programme at a cinema **4** an item or article appearing regularly in a newspaper, magazine, etc: *a gardening feature* **5** Also called: feature story a prominent story in a newspaper, etc: *a feature on prison reform* **6** a programme given special prominence on radio or television as indicated by attendant publicity **7** *archaic* general form or make-up ▷ *vb* **8** (*tr*) to have as a feature or make a feature of **9** to give prominence to (an actor, famous event, etc) in a film or (of an actor, etc) to have prominence in a film [c14: from Anglo-French *feture*, from Latin *factūra* a making, from *facere* to make] ▷ 'featureless *adj*

featured *adj* (*in combination*) having features as specified: *heavy-featured*

Feb *abbreviation* February

febri *combining form* indicating fever: *febrifuge* [from Latin *febris* fever]

febrifuge ('fɛbrɪˌfjuːdʒ) *n* **1** any drug or agent for reducing fever ▷ *adj* **2** serving to reduce fever [c17: from Medieval Latin *febrifugia* feverfew; see FEBRI-, -FUGE] ▷ febrifugal (fɪˈbrɪfjʊgᵊl, ˌfɛbrɪˈfjuːgᵊl) *adj*

febrile ('fiːbraɪl) *adj* of or relating to fever; feverish [c17: from medical Latin *febrīlis*, from Latin *febris* fever] ▷ febrility (fɪˈbrɪlɪtɪ) *n*

February ('fɛbrʊərɪ) *n*, *pl* -aries the second month of the year, consisting of 28 or (in a leap year) 29 days [c13: from

Latin *Februārius mēnsis* month of expiation, from *februa* Roman festival of purification held on February 15, from plural of *februum* a purgation]

feces ('fiːsɪz) *pl n* the usual US spelling of **faeces**

Fechner (German 'fɛçnər) *n* **Gustav Theodor** ('gʊstaf 'teːodoːr). 1801–87, German physicist, philosopher, and psychologist, noted particularly for his work on psychophysics, *Elemente der Psychophysik* (1860)

feckless ('fɛklɪs) *adj* feeble; weak; ineffectual; irresponsible [c16: from obsolete *feck* value, effect + -LESS] > 'fecklessly *adv* > 'fecklessness *n*

feculent ('fɛkjʊlənt) *adj* 1 filthy, scummy, muddy, or foul 2 of the nature of or containing waste matter [c15: from Latin *faeculentus*; see FAECES] > 'feculence *n*

fecund ('fiːkənd, 'fɛk-) *adj* 1 greatly productive; fertile 2 intellectually productive; prolific [c14: from Latin *fēcundus*; related to Latin *fētus* offspring] > fecundity (fɪ'kʌndɪtɪ) *n*

fecundate ('fiːkənˌdeɪt, 'fɛk-) *vb* (*tr*) 1 to make fruitful 2 to fertilize; impregnate [c17: from Latin *fēcundāre* to fertilize] > ˌfecun'dation *n*

fed[1] (fɛd) *vb* 1 the past tense and past participle of **feed** 2 fed to death, fed to the teeth, fed up to the teeth, fed to the back teeth or fed up to the back teeth *informal* bored or annoyed

fed[2] (fɛd) *n* US *slang* an agent of the FBI

Fed (fɛd) *n* the Fed US *informal* the Federal Reserve Bank or Federal Reserve Board

Fed. or **fed.** *abbreviation* 1 Federal 2 Federation 3 Federated

fedayee (fəˈdɑːjiː) *n, pl* **-yeen** (-jiːn) (*sometimes capital*) (in Arab states) a commando, esp one fighting against Israel [from Arabic *fidā'i* one who risks his life in a cause, from *fidā'* redemption]

federal ('fɛdərəl) *adj* 1 of or relating to a form of government or a country in which power is divided between one central and several regional governments 2 of or relating to the central government of a federation [c17: from Latin *foedus* league] > 'federally *adv* > 'federaˌlism *n* > 'federalist *n, adj*

Federal ('fɛdərəl) *adj* 1 characteristic of or supporting the Union government during the American Civil War ▷ *n* 2 a supporter of the Union government during the American Civil War

Federal Government *n* the national government of a federated state, such as that of Australia located in Canberra

federalize or **federalise** ('fɛdərəˌlaɪz) *vb* (*tr*) 1 to unite in a federation or federal union; federate 2 to subject to federal control > ˌfederaliˈzation or ˌfederaliˈsation *n*

Federal Republic of Germany *n* the official name of Germany, formerly used to refer to West Germany

Federal Reserve System *n* (in the US) a banking system consisting of twelve **Federal Reserve Districts**, each containing member banks regulated and served by a **Federal Reserve Bank**. It operates under the supervision of the **Federal Reserve Board** and performs functions similar to those of the Bank of England

federate *vb* ('fɛdəˌreɪt) 1 to unite or cause to unite in a federal union ▷ *adj* ('fɛdərɪt) 2 federal; federated > 'federative *adj*

Federated Malay States *pl n* See **Malay States**

federation (ˌfɛdə'reɪʃən) *n* 1 the act of federating 2 the union of several provinces, states, etc, to form a federal union 3 a political unit formed in such a way 4 any league, alliance, or confederacy

Federation of Rhodesia and Nyasaland *n* a federation (1953–63) of Northern Rhodesia, Southern Rhodesia, and Nyasaland

Federer ('fɛdərə) *n* **Roger**. born 1981, Swiss tennis player: won both the Wimbledon men's singles and the US Open each year 2004–07

fedora (fɪ'dɔːrə) *n* a soft felt or velvet medium-brimmed hat, usually with a band [c19: allegedly named after *Fédora* (1882), play by Victorien Sardou (1831–1908)]

fed up *adj* (*usually postpositive*) *informal* annoyed, discontented, or bored: *I'm fed up with your conduct*

fee (fiː) *n* 1 a payment asked by professional people or public servants for their services: *a doctor's fee; school fees*

2 a charge made for a privilege: *an entrance fee* 3 *property law* an interest in land capable of being inherited 4 (in feudal Europe) the land granted by a lord to his vassal 5 in fee *law* (of land) in absolute ownership ▷ *vb* fees, feeing, feed 6 *rare* to give a fee to 7 *chiefly Scot* to hire for a fee [c14: from Old French *fie*, of Germanic origin; see FIEF]

feeble ('fiːbəl) *adj* 1 lacking in physical or mental strength; frail; weak 2 inadequate; unconvincing: *feeble excuses* 3 easily influenced or indecisive [c12: from Old French *feble, fleible*, from Latin *flēbilis* to be lamented, from *flēre* to weep] > 'feebleness *n* > 'feebly *adv*

feeble-minded *adj* 1 lacking in intelligence; stupid 2 mentally defective

feed (fiːd) *vb* feeds, feeding, fed (fɛd) (*mainly tr*) 1 to give food to: *to feed the cat* 2 to give as food: *to feed meat to the cat* 3 (*intr*) to eat food: *the horses feed at noon* 4 to provide food for 5 to gratify; satisfy 6 (*also intr*) to supply (a machine, furnace, etc) with (the necessary materials or fuel) for its operation, or (of such materials) to flow or move forwards into a machine, etc 7 *theatre informal* to cue (an actor, esp a comedian) with lines or actions 8 *sport* to pass a ball to (a team-mate) 9 (*also intr*; foll by *on* or *upon*) to eat or cause to eat ▷ *n* 10 the act or an instance of feeding 11 food, esp that of animals or babies 12 the process of supplying a machine or furnace with a material or fuel 13 the quantity of material or fuel so supplied 14 *theatre informal* a performer, esp a straight man, who provides cues 15 an informal word for **meal**[1] [Old English *fēdan*; related to Old Norse *fœtha* to feed, Old High German *fuotan*, Gothic *fōthjan*; see FOOD, FODDER] > 'feedable *adj*

feedback ('fiːdˌbæk) *n* 1 a the return of part of the output of an electronic circuit, device, or mechanical system to its input, so modifying its characteristics. In **negative feedback** a rise in output energy reduces the input energy; in **positive feedback** an increase in output energy reinforces the input energy b that part of the output signal fed back into the input 2 the return of part of the sound output by a loudspeaker to the microphone or pick-up so that a high-pitched whistle is produced 3 the whistling noise so produced 4 the effect of the product of a biological pathway on the rate of an earlier step in that pathway 5 information in response to an inquiry, experiment, etc

feeder ('fiːdə) *n* 1 a person or thing that feeds or is fed 2 a child's feeding bottle or bib 3 a person or device that feeds the working material into a system or machine 4 a tributary channel, esp one that supplies a reservoir or canal with water 5 a road, service, etc, that links secondary areas to the main traffic network 6 a power line for transmitting electrical power from a generating station to a distribution network

feeding bottle *n* a bottle fitted with a rubber teat from which infants or young animals suck liquids

feel (fiːl) *vb* feels, feeling, felt (fɛlt) 1 to perceive (something) by touching 2 to have a physical or emotional sensation of (something): *to feel heat; to feel anger* 3 (*tr*) to examine (something) by touch 4 (*tr*) to find (one's way) by testing or cautious exploration 5 (*copula*) to seem or appear in respect of the sensation given: *I feel tired; it feels warm* 6 to have an indistinct, esp emotional conviction; sense (esp in the phrase **feel in one's bones**) 7 (*intr*; foll by *for*) to show sympathy or compassion (towards): *I feel for you in your sorrow* 8 to believe, think, or be of the opinion (that) 9 (*tr*; often foll by *up*) *slang* to pass one's hands over the sexual organs of 10 feel like to have an inclination (for something or doing something): *I don't feel like going to the pictures* 11 feel up to (*usually used with a negative or in a question*) to be fit enough for (something or doing something): *I don't feel up to going out tonight* ▷ *n* 12 the act or an instance of feeling, esp by touching 13 the quality of or an impression from something perceived through feeling: *the house has a homely feel about it* 14 the sense of touch 15 an instinctive aptitude; knack: *she's got a feel for this sort of work* [Old English *fēlan*; related to Old High German *fuolen*, Old Norse *fālma* to grope, Latin *palma* PALM[1]]

feeler ('fiːlə) *n* 1 a person or thing that feels 2 an organ in certain animals, such as an antenna or tentacle, that is sensitive to touch **3** a remark designed to probe the reactions or intentions of other people

feeler gauge *n* a thin metal strip of known thickness used to measure a narrow gap or to set a gap between two parts

feel-good *adj* causing or characterized by a feeling of self-satisfaction: *feel-good factor*

feeling ('fiːlɪŋ) *n* **1** the sense of touch **2 a** the ability to experience physical sensations, such as heat, pain, etc **b** the sensation so experienced **3** a state of mind **4** a physical or mental impression: *a feeling of warmth* **5** fondness; sympathy: *to have a great deal of feeling for someone* **6** a sentiment: *a feeling that the project is feasible* **7** an emotional disturbance, esp anger or dislike **8** sensibility in the performance of something **9** (*plural*) emotional or moral sensitivity, as in relation to principles or personal dignity (esp in the phrase **hurt** or **injure the feelings of**) **10** have feelings for to be emotionally or sexually attracted to ▷ *adj* **11** sentient; sensitive **12** expressing or containing emotion > 'feelingly *adv*

feet (fiːt) *n* **1** the plural of **foot** **2** at someone's feet as someone's disciple **3** be run off one's feet *or* be rushed off one's feet to be very busy **4** carry off one's feet *or* sweep off one's feet to fill with enthusiasm **5** feet of clay a weakness that is not widely known **6** have one's feet on the ground *or* keep one's feet on the ground to be practical and reliable **7** on one's feet *or* on its feet **a** standing up **b** in good health **8** stand on one's own feet to be independent

feeze *or* **feaze** (fiːz) *dialect vb* **1** (*tr*) to beat **2** to drive off **3** *chiefly US* to disconcert; worry ▷ *n* **4** a rush **5** *chiefly US* a state of agitation [Old English *fēsian*]

FEI *abbreviation* Fédération Équestre Internationale: the international governing body of equestrian sports [from French]

feign (feɪn) *vb* **1** to put on a show of (a quality or emotion); pretend: *to feign innocence* **2** (*tr*) to make up; invent: *to feign an excuse* **3** (*tr*) to copy; imitate [c13: from Old French *feindre* to pretend, from Latin *fingere* to form, shape, invent] > 'feigningly *adv*

feijoa (fiːˈdʒəʊə) *n* **1** an evergreen myrtaceous shrub, *Feijoa sellowiana*, of South America **2** the fruit of this shrub [c19: from New Latin, named after J. da Silva *Feijo*, 19th-century Spanish botanist]

Feininger ('faɪnɪŋə) *n* **Lyonel.** 1871–1956, US artist, who worked at the Bauhaus, noted for his use of superimposed translucent planes of colour

feint¹ (feɪnt) *n* **1** a mock attack or movement designed to distract an adversary, as in a military manoeuvre or in boxing, fencing, etc **2** a misleading action or appearance ▷ *vb* **3** (*intr*) to make a feint [c17: from French *feinte*, from *feint* pretended, from Old French *feindre* to FEIGN]

feint² (feɪnt) *n printing* the narrowest rule used in the production of ruled paper [c19: variant of FAINT]

Feisal ('faɪsᵊl) *n* a variant spelling of **Faisal**

feisty ('faɪstɪ) *adj* **feistier, feistiest** *informal* lively, resilient, and self-reliant **1** *US & Canadian* frisky **2** *US & Canadian* irritable [c19: from dialect *feist, fist* small dog; related to Old English *fisting* breaking wind]

felafel (fəˈlɑːfəl) *n* a variant spelling of **falafel**

feldspar ('fɛldˌspɑː, 'fɛlˌspɑː) *or* **felspar** *n* any of a group of hard rock-forming minerals consisting of aluminium silicates of potassium, sodium, calcium, or barium: the principal constituents of igneous rocks. The group includes orthoclase, microcline, and the plagioclase minerals [c18: from German *feldspat(h)*, from *feld* field + *spat(h)* SPAR³] > feldspathic ('fɛldˈspæθɪk, fɛlˈspæθ-) *or* fel'spathic *or* 'feldspathˌose *or* 'felspathˌose *adj*

felicitate (fɪˈlɪsɪˌteɪt) *vb* to wish joy to; congratulate > fe'liciˌtator *n* > felicitation (fɪˌlɪsɪˈteɪʃən, fɛˌlɪciˈtation) *n*

felicitous (fɪˈlɪsɪtəs) *adj* **1** well-chosen; apt **2** possessing an agreeable style **3** producing or marked by happiness > fe'licitously *adv*

felicity (fɪˈlɪsɪtɪ) *n, pl* **-ties** **1** happiness; joy **2** a cause of happiness **3** an appropriate expression or style **4** the quality or display of such expressions or style [c14: from

Latin *fēlīcitās* happiness, from *fēlix* happy]

feline ('fiːlaɪn) *adj* **1** of, relating to, or belonging to the *Felidae*, a family of predatory mammals, including cats, lions, leopards, and cheetahs, typically having a round head and retractile claws: order *Carnivora* (carnivores) **2** resembling or suggestive of a cat, esp in stealth or grace ▷ *n* Also: **felid** ('fiːlɪd) **3** any animal belonging to the family *Felidae*; a cat [c17: from Latin *fēlīnus*, from *fēlēs* cat] > 'felinely *adv* > 'felineness *or* felinity (fɪˈlɪnɪtɪ) *n*

Felixstowe ('fiːlɪkˌstəʊ) *n* a port and resort in E England, in Suffolk: ferry connections to Rotterdam and Zeebrugge. Pop: 29 349 (2001)

fell¹ (fɛl) *vb* the past tense of **fall**

fell² (fɛl) *vb* (*tr*) **1** to cut or knock down: *to fell a tree; to fell an opponent* **2** *needlework* to fold under and sew flat (the edges of a seam) ▷ *n* **3** *US & Canadian* the timber felled in one season **4** a seam finished by felling [Old English *fellan*; related to Old Norse *fella*, Old High German *fellen*; see FALL] > 'feller *n*

fell³ (fɛl) *adj* **1** *archaic* cruel or fierce; terrible **2** *archaic* destructive or deadly **3** one fell swoop a single hasty action or occurrence [c13 *fel*, from Old French: cruel, from Medieval Latin *fellō* villain; see FELON¹]

fell⁴ (fɛl) *n* an animal skin or hide [Old English; related to Old High German *fel* skin, Old Norse *berfjall* bearskin, Latin *pellis* skin; see PEEL¹]

fell⁵ (fɛl) *n* (*often plural*) *Northern English & Scot* **a** a mountain, hill, or tract of upland moor **b** (*in combination*): *fell-walking* [c13: from Old Norse *fjall*; related to Old High German *felis* rock]

fellah ('fɛlə) *n, pl* **fellahs, fellahin** *or* **fellaheen** (ˌfɛləˈhiːn) a peasant in Arab countries [c18: from Arabic, dialect variant of *fallāh*, from *falaha* to cultivate]

fellatio (fɪˈleɪʃɪəʊ, fɛ-) *or* **fellation** *n* a sexual activity in which the penis is stimulated by the partner's mouth [c19: New Latin, from Latin *fellāre* to suck]

Felling ('fɛlɪŋ) *n* a town in NE England, in Gateshead unitary authority, Tyne and Wear; formerly noted for coal mining. Pop: 34 196 (2001)

Fellini (Italian fɛlˈliːnɪ) *n* **Federico** (fedeˈriko). 1920–93, Italian film director. His films include *La Dolce Vita* (1959), *8½* (1963), *Satyricon* (1969), and *Intervista* (1987)

Felliniesque (fəˈliːnɪˌɛsk) *adj* referring to or reminiscent of the work of the Italian film-maker Federic FELLINI

felloe ('fɛləʊ) *or* **felly** ('fɛlɪ) *n, pl* **-loes** *or* **-lies** a segment or the whole rim of a wooden wheel to which the spokes are attached and onto which a metal tyre is usually shrunk [Old English *felge*; related to Old High German *felga*, Middle Dutch *velge*, of unknown origin]

fellow ('fɛləʊ) *n* **1** a man or boy **2** an informal word for **boyfriend 3** *informal* one or oneself: *a fellow has to eat* **4** a person considered to be of little importance or worth **5 a** (*often plural*) a companion; comrade; associate **b** (*as modifier*): *fellow travellers* **6** a member of the governing body or established teaching staff at any of various universities or colleges **7 a** a person in the same group, class, or condition: *the surgeon asked his fellows* **b** (*as modifier*): *fellow students; a fellow sufferer* **8** one of a pair; counterpart; mate [Old English *fēolaga*, from Old Norse *fēlagi*, one who lays down money, from *fē* money + *lag* a laying down]

Fellow ('fɛləʊ) *n* a member of any of various learned societies: *Fellow of the British Academy*

fellow feeling *n* **1** mutual sympathy or friendship **2** an opinion held in common

fellowship ('fɛləʊˌʃɪp) *n* **1** the state of sharing mutual interests, experiences, activities, etc **2** a society of people sharing mutual interests, experiences, activities, etc; club **3** companionship; friendship **4** the state or relationship of being a fellow **5** *education* **a** a financed research post providing study facilities, privileges, etc, often in return for teaching services **b** an honorary title carrying certain privileges awarded to a postgraduate student

fellow traveller *n* **1** a companion on a journey **2** a non-Communist who sympathizes with Communism

felon¹ ('fɛlən) *n* **1** *criminal law* (formerly) a person who has committed a felony ▷ *adj* **2** *archaic or poetic* evil; cruel [c13: from Old French: villain, from Medieval Latin *fellō*, of uncertain origin]

felon² ('fɛlən) *n* a purulent inflammation of the end joint of a finger, sometimes affecting the bone [c12: from Medieval Latin *fellō* sore, perhaps from Latin *fel* poison]

felonious (fɪ'ləʊnɪəs) *adj* 1 *criminal law* of, involving, or constituting a felony 2 *obsolete* wicked; base > fe'loniously *adv* > fe'loniousness *n*

felony ('fɛlənɪ) *n, pl* -nies (formerly) a serious crime, such as murder or arson. All distinctions between felony and misdemeanour were abolished in England and Wales in 1967

felspar ('fɛl,spɑː) *n* a variant (esp Brit) of **feldspar** > felspathic (fɛl'spæθɪk) *or* 'felspath,ose *adj*

felt¹ (fɛlt) *vb* the past tense and past participle of **feel**

felt² (fɛlt) *n* 1 a matted fabric of wool, hair, etc, made by working the fibres together under pressure or by heat or chemical action 2 any material, such as asbestos, made by a similar process of matting ▷ *vb* 3 (*tr*) to make into or cover with felt 4 (*intr*) to become matted [Old English; related to Old Saxon *filt*, Old High German *filz* felt, Latin *pellere* to beat, Greek *pelas* close; see ANVIL, FILTER]

felt-tip pen *n* a pen having a writing point made from pressed fibres. Also called: **fibre-tip pen**

felucca (fɛ'lʌkə) *n* a narrow lateen-rigged vessel of the Mediterranean [c17: from Italian *felucca*, probably from obsolete Spanish *faluca*, probably from Arabic *fulūk* ships, from Greek *epholkion* small boat, from *ephelkein* to tow]

fem *abbreviation* 1 female 2 feminine

FEMA *n acronym for* Federal Emergency Management Agency: a US government body intended to coordinate responses to a disaster in the US itself

female ('fiːmeɪl) *adj* 1 of, relating to, or designating the sex producing gametes (ova) that can be fertilized by male gametes (spermatozoa) 2 of, relating to, or characteristic of a woman 3 for or composed of women or girls: *female suffrage; a female choir* 4 (of reproductive organs such as the ovary and carpel) capable of producing female gametes 5 (of flowers) lacking, or having nonfunctional, stamens 6 having an internal cavity into which a projecting male counterpart can be fitted: *a female thread* ▷ *n* 7 a female animal or plant [c14: from earlier *femelle* (influenced by *male*), from Latin *fēmella* a young woman, from *fēmina* a woman] > 'femaleness *n*

female impersonator *n* a male theatrical performer who acts as a woman

feminine ('fɛmɪnɪn) *adj* 1 suitable to or characteristic of a woman 2 possessing qualities or characteristics considered typical of or appropriate to a woman 3 effeminate; womanish 4 *grammar* **a** denoting or belonging to a gender of nouns, occurring in many inflected languages, that includes all kinds of referents as well as some female animate referents **b** (*as noun*): *German Zeit "time" and Ehe "marriage" are feminines* [c14: from Latin *fēminīnus*, from *fēmina* woman] > 'femininely *adv* > 'feminineness *n*

feminism ('fɛmɪ,nɪzəm) *n* a doctrine or movement that advocates equal rights for women > 'feminist *n, adj*

feminize *or* **feminise** ('fɛmɪ,naɪz) *vb* 1 to make or become feminine 2 to cause (a male animal) to develop female characteristics > ,femini'zation *or* ,femini'sation *n*

femme fatale *French* (fam fatal; *English* 'fɛm fə'tæl, -'tɑːl) *n, pl* femmes fatales (fam fatal; *English* 'fɛm fə'tælz, -'tɑːlz) an alluring or seductive woman, esp one who causes men to love her to their own distress [fatal woman]

femto- *prefix* denoting 10^{-15}: *femtometer* Symbol: f^3 [from Danish or Norwegian *femten* fifteen]

femur ('fiːmə) *n, pl* femurs *or* femora ('fɛmərə) 1 the longest thickest bone of the human skeleton, articulating with the pelvis above and the knee below. Nontechnical name: thighbone 2 the corresponding bone in other vertebrates [c18: from Latin: thigh] > femoral ('fɛmərəl) *adj*

fen (fɛn) *n* low-lying flat land that is marshy or artificially drained [Old English *fenn*; related to Old High German *fenna*, Old Norse *fen*, Gothic *fani* clay, Sanskrit *panka* mud] > 'fenny *adj*

fence (fɛns) *n* 1 a structure that serves to enclose an area

such as a garden or field, usually made of posts of timber, concrete, or metal connected by wire, netting, rails, or boards 2 *slang* a dealer in stolen property 3 an obstacle for a horse to jump in steeplechasing or showjumping 4 *machinery* a guard or guide, esp in a circular saw or plane 5 on the fence unable or unwilling to commit oneself ▷ *vb* 6 (*tr*) to construct a fence on or around (a piece of land, etc) 7 (*tr*; foll by *in* or *off*) to close (in) or separate (off) with or as if with a fence: *he fenced in the livestock* 8 (*intr*) to fight using swords or foils 9 (*intr*) to evade a question or argument, esp by quibbling over minor points 10 (*intr*) to engage in skilful or witty debate, repartee, etc [c14 *fens*, shortened from *defens* DEFENCE] > 'fenceless *adj* > 'fencer *n*

fencible ('fɛnsəbᵊl) *n* (formerly) a person who undertook military service in immediate defence of his homeland only

fencing ('fɛnsɪŋ) *n* 1 the practice, art, or sport of fighting with swords, esp the sport of using foils, épées, or sabres under a set of rules to score points 2 **a** wire, stakes, etc, used as fences **b** fences collectively

fend (fɛnd) *vb* 1 (*intr*; foll by *for*) to give support (to someone, esp oneself); provide (for) 2 (*tr*; usually foll by *off*) to ward off or turn aside (blows, questions, attackers, etc) ▷ *n* 3 *Scot & Northern English dialect* a shift or effort [c13 *fenden*, shortened from *defenden* to DEFEND]

fender ('fɛndə) *n* 1 a low metal frame which confines falling coals to the hearth 2 *chiefly US* a metal frame fitted to the front of locomotives to absorb shock, clear the track, etc 3 a cushion-like device, such as a car tyre hung over the side of a vessel to reduce damage resulting from accidental contact or collision 4 *US & Canadian* the part of a car body that surrounds the wheels. Also called (in Britain and certain other countries): wing

Fénelon (*French* fenlɔ̃) *n* François de Salignac de La Mothe (frɑ̃swa də saliɲak də la mɔt). 1651–1715, French theologian and writer; author of *Maximes des saints* (1697), a defence of quietism, and *Les aventures de Télémaque* (1699), which was construed as criticizing the government of Louis XIV

fenestra (fɪ'nɛstrə) *n, pl* -trae (-triː) 1 *biology* a small opening in or between bones, esp one of the openings between the middle and inner ears 2 *zoology* a transparent marking or spot, as on the wings of moths 3 *architect* a window or window-like opening in the outside wall of a building [c19: via New Latin from Latin: wall opening, window]

fenestrated (fɪ'nɛs,treɪtɪd, 'fɛnɪ,streɪtɪd) *or* **fenestrate** *adj* 1 *architect* having windows or window-like openings 2 *biology* perforated or having fenestrae

fenestration (,fɛnɪ'streɪʃən) *n* 1 the arrangement and design of windows in a building 2 a surgical operation to restore hearing by making an artificial opening into the labyrinth of the ear

feng shui ('fʌŋ 'ʃweɪ) *n* the Chinese art of determining the most propitious design and placement of a grave, building, room, etc, so that the maximum harmony is achieved between the flow of chi of the environment and that of the user, believed to bring good fortune [c20: from Chinese *feng* wind + *shui* water]

Fenian ('fiːnɪən) *n* 1 (formerly) a member of an Irish revolutionary organization founded in the US in the 19th century to fight for an independent Ireland ▷ *adj* 2 of or relating to the Fenians [c19: from Irish Gaelic *fēinne*, plural of *fian* band of warriors] > 'Fenianism *n*

fennec ('fɛnɛk) *n* a very small nocturnal fox, *Fennecus zerda*, inhabiting deserts of N Africa and Arabia, having pale fur and enormous ears [c18: from Arabic *fenek* fox]

fennel ('fɛnᵊl) *n* a strong-smelling yellow-flowered umbelliferous plant, *Foeniculum vulgare*, whose seeds and feathery leaves are used to season and flavour food [Old English *fenol*, from Latin *faeniculum* fennel, diminutive of *faenum* hay]

Fenrir ('fɛnrɪə), **Fenris** ('fɛnrɪs) *or* **Fenriswolf** ('fɛnrɪs,wʊlf) *n Norse myth* an enormous wolf, fathered by Loki, which killed Odin

Fens (fɛnz) *pl n* the Fens a flat low-lying area of E England, west and south of the Wash: consisted of marshes until reclaimed in the 17th to 19th centuries

Fenton ('fɛntən) *n* **James** (**Martin**). born 1949, British poet, journalist, and critic. His poetry includes the collections *A German Requiem* (1980) and *Out of Danger* (1993)

fenugreek ('fɛnjʊˌgriːk) *n* an annual heavily scented Mediterranean leguminous plant, *Trigonella foenum-graecum*, with hairy stems and white flowers: cultivated for forage and for its medicinal seeds [Old English *fēnogrēcum*, from Latin *fenum Graecum* literally: Greek hay]

feoff (fiːf) *medieval history* ▷ *n* **1** a variant spelling of **fief** ▷ *vb* **2** (*tr*) to invest with a benefice or fief [C13: from Anglo-French *feoffer*, from *feoff* a FIEF] > 'feoffor *or* 'feoffer *n* > feoffee (fɛˈfiː, fiːˈfiː) *n* > 'feoffment *n*

-fer *n combining form* indicating a person or thing that bears something specified: *crucifer; conifer* [from Latin, from *ferre* to bear]

feral ('fɪərəl, 'fɛr-) *adj* **1** Also called: **ferine** (of animals and plants) existing in a wild or uncultivated state, esp after being domestic or cultivated **2** Also called: **ferine** savage; brutal [C17: from Medieval Latin *ferālis*, from Latin *fera* a wild beast, from *ferus* savage]

fer-de-lance (ˌfɛədəˈlɑːns) *n* a large highly venomous tropical American snake, *Trimeresurus* (or *Bothops*) *atrox*, with a greyish-brown mottled coloration: family *Crotalidae* (pit vipers) [C19: from French, literally: iron (head) of a lance]

Ferdinand ('fɜːdɪˌnænd; *German* 'fɛrdinant) *n* See **Franz Ferdinand**

Ferdinand I ('fɜːdɪˌnænd) *n* **1** known as *Ferdinand the Great*. ?1016–65, king of Castile (1035–65) and León (1037–65): achieved control of the Moorish kings of Saragossa, Seville, and Toledo **2** 1503–64, king of Hungary and Bohemia (1526–64); Holy Roman Emperor (1558–64), bringing years of religious warfare to an end **3** 1751–1825, king of the Two Sicilies (1816–25); king of Naples (1759–1806; 1815–25), as Ferdinand IV, being dispossessed by Napoleon (1806–15) **4** 1793–1875, king of Hungary (1830–48) and emperor of Austria (1835–48); abdicated after the Revolution of 1848 in favour of his nephew, Franz Josef I **5** 1861–1948, ruling prince of Bulgaria (1887–1908) and tsar from 1908 until his abdication in 1918 **6** 1865–1927, king of Romania (1914–27); sided with the Allies in World War I

Ferdinand II *n* **1** 1578–1637, Holy Roman Emperor (1619–37); king of Bohemia (1617–19; 1620–37) and of Hungary (1617–37). His anti-Protestant policies led to the Thirty Years' War **2** title as king of Aragon and Sicily of **Ferdinand V**

Ferdinand III *n* **1** 1608–57, Holy Roman Emperor (1637–57) and king of Hungary (1625–57); son of Ferdinand II **2** title as king of Naples of **Ferdinand V**

Ferdinand V *n* known as *Ferdinand the Catholic*. 1452–1516, king of Castile (1474–1504); as Ferdinand II, king of Aragon (1479–1516) and Sicily (1468–1516); as Ferdinand III, king of Naples (1504–16). His marriage to Isabella I of Castile (1469) led to the union of Aragon and Castile and his reconquest of Granada from the Moors (1492) completed the unification of Spain. He introduced the Inquisition (1478), expelled the Jews from Spain (1492), and financed Columbus' voyage to the New World

Ferdinand VII *n* 1784–1833, king of Spain (1808; 1814–33). He precipitated the Carlist Wars by excluding his brother Don Carlos as his successor

feretory ('fɛrɪtərɪ, -trɪ) *n, pl* -ries *chiefly RC Church* **1** a shrine, usually portable, for a saint's relics **2** the chapel in which a shrine is kept [C14: from Middle French *fiertre*, from Latin *feretrum* a bier, from Greek *pheretron*, from *pherein* to bear]

Fergana *or* **Ferghana** (fəˈgɑːnə) *n* **1** a region of W central Asia, surrounded by high mountains and accessible only from the west: mainly in Uzbekistan and partly in Tajikistan and Kyrgyzstan **2** the chief city of this region, in E Uzbekistan. Pop: 230 000 (2005 est)

Fergus ('fɜːgəs) *n* (in Irish legend) a warrior king of Ulster, who was supplanted by Conchobar

Ferguson ('fɜːgəsən) *n* Sir **Alex**(**ander**) **Chapman**. born 1941, Scottish footballer and manager; manager of Manchester United from 1986

feria ('fɪərɪə) *n, pl* -rias *or* -riae (-rɪˌiː) *RC Church* a weekday, other than Saturday, on which no feast occurs [C19: from Late Latin: day of the week (as in *prīma fēria* Sunday), singular of Latin *fēriae* festivals] > 'ferial *adj*

Ferlinghetti (fɜːlɪŋˈgɛtɪ) *n* **Lawrence**. born 1920, US poet of the Beat Generation. His poetry includes the collections *Pictures of the Gone World* (1955) and *When I Look at Pictures* (1990)

Fermanagh (fəˈmænə) *n* a district and historical county of SW Northern Ireland: contains the Upper and Lower Lough Erne. Pop: 58 705 (2003 est). Area (excluding water): 1700 sq km (656 sq miles)

Fermat (fɜːˈmæt; *French* fɛrma) *n* **Pierre de** (pjɛr də). 1601–65, French mathematician, regarded as the founder of the modern theory of numbers. He studied the properties of whole numbers and, with Pascal, investigated the theory of probability

fermata (fəˈmɑːtə) *n, pl* -tas *or* -te (-tɪ) *music* another word for **pause** (sense 5) [from Italian, from *fermare* to stop, from Latin *firmāre* to establish; see FIRM¹]

ferment *n* ('fɜːmɛnt) **1** any agent or substance, such as a bacterium, mould, yeast, or enzyme, that causes fermentation **2** another word for **fermentation** **3** commotion; unrest ▷ *vb* (fəˈmɛnt) **4** to undergo or cause to undergo fermentation **5** to stir up or seethe with excitement [C15: from Latin *fermentum* yeast, from *fervēre* to seethe] > fer'mentable *adj*

● USAGE See at **foment**

fermentation (ˌfɜːmɛnˈteɪʃən) *n* a chemical reaction in which a ferment causes an organic molecule to split into simpler molecules, esp the anaerobic conversion of sugar to ethyl alcohol by yeast > fer'mentative *adj*

fermentation lock *n* a valve placed on the top of bottles of fermenting wine to allow bubbles to escape

fermi ('fɜːmɪ) *n* a unit of length used in nuclear physics equal to 10^{-15} metre [C20: named after Enrico FERMI]

Fermi ('fɜːmɪ; *Italian* 'fɛrmi) *n* **Enrico** (enˈriːko). 1901–54, Italian nuclear physicist, in the US from 1939. He was awarded a Nobel prize for physics in 1938 for his work on radioactive substances and nuclear bombardment and headed the group that produced the first controlled nuclear reaction (1942)

Fermi-Dirac statistics *pl n physics* the branch of quantum statistics used to calculate the permitted energy arrangements of the particles in a system in terms of the exclusion principle

fermion ('fɜːmɪˌɒn) *n* any of a group of elementary particles, such as a nucleon, that has half-integral spin and obeys Fermi-Dirac statistics. See **boson** [C20: named after Enrico FERMI see -ON]

fermium ('fɜːmɪəm) *n* a transuranic element artificially produced by neutron bombardment of plutonium. Symbol: Fm; atomic no: 100; half-life of most stable isotope, ^{257}Fm: 80 days (approx.) [C20: named after Enrico FERMI]

Fermor ('fɜːmɔː) *n* Sir **Patrick** (**Michael**) **Leigh**. born 1915, British traveller and author, noted esp for the travel books *A Time of Gifts* (1977) and *Between the Woods and the Water* (1986)

fern (fɜːn) *n* **1** any tracheophyte plant of the phylum *Filicinophyta*, having roots, stems, and fronds and reproducing by spores formed in structures (sori) on the fronds **2** any of certain similar but unrelated plants, such as the sweet fern [Old English *fearn*; related to Old High German *farn*, Sanskrit *parná* leaf] > 'ferny *adj*

Fernandel (*French* fɛrnɑ̃dɛl) *n* real name *Fernand Joseph Désiré Contandin*. 1903–71, French comic film actor

Fernando de Noronha (*Portuguese* ferˈnɐndu di noˈrɔɲa) *n* a volcanic island in the S Atlantic northeast of Cape São Roque: constitutes a federal territory of Brazil; a penal colony since the 18th century; inhabited by military personnel. Area: 26 sq km (10 sq miles)

Fernando Po (fəˈnændəʊ pəʊ) *n* a former name (until 1973) of **Bioko**

fernbird ('fɜːnˌbɜːd) *n* a small brown and white New Zealand swamp bird, *Bowdleria punctata*, with a fernlike tail

ferocious (fəˈrəʊʃəs) *adj* savagely fierce or cruel: *a ferocious tiger; a ferocious argument* [C17: from Latin *ferox* fierce, untamable, warlike] > **ferocity** (fəˈrɒsɪtɪ) *or* **feˈrociousness** *n*

-ferous *adj combining form* bearing or producing: *coniferous; crystalliferous* [from -FER + -OUS]

Ferrar (ˈferə) *n* **Nicholas**. 1592–1637, English mystic. He founded (1625) an Anglican religious community at Little Gidding, Huntingdonshire

Ferrara (fəˈrɑːrə; *Italian* ferˈrara) *n* a city in N Italy, in Emilia-Romagna: a centre of the Renaissance under the House of Este; university (1391). Pop: 130 992 (2001)

Ferrari (*Italian* ferˈraːrɪ) *n* **Enzo** (ˈentso). 1898–1988, Italian designer and manufacturer of racing cars

ferrate (ˈfereɪt) *n* a salt containing the divalent ion, FeO₄²⁻. Ferrates are derivatives of the hypothetical acid H₂FeO₄ [C19: from Latin *ferrum* iron]

ferret (ˈferɪt) *n* **1** a domesticated albino variety of the polecat *Mustela putorius*, bred for hunting rats, rabbits, etc **2** an assiduous searcher ▷ *vb* **-rets, -reting, -reted 3** to hunt (rabbits, rats, etc) with ferrets **4** (*tr;* usually foll by *out*) to drive from hiding: *to ferret out snipers* **5** (*tr;* usually foll by *out*) to find by persistent investigation **6** (*intr*) to search around [C14: from Old French *furet*, from Latin *fur* thief] > **ˈferreter** *n* > **ˈferrety** *adj*

ferri- *combining form* indicating the presence of iron, esp in the trivalent state: *ferricyanide; ferriferous*. See **ferro-** [from Latin *ferrum* iron]

ferriage (ˈferɪɪdʒ) *n* **1** transportation by ferry **2** the fee charged for passage on a ferry

ferric (ˈferɪk) *adj* of or containing iron in the trivalent state: *ferric oxide*; designating an iron (III) compound [C18: from Latin *ferrum* iron]

ferric oxide *n* a red crystalline insoluble oxide of iron that occurs as haematite and rust and is made by heating ferrous sulphate: used as a pigment and metal polish (**jeweller's rouge**), and as a sensitive coating on magnetic tape. Formula: Fe₂O₃

Ferrier (ˈferɪə) *n* **Kathleen**. 1912–53, British contralto; noted for her expressive voice

ferrimagnetism (ˌferɪˈmægnɪˌtɪzəm) *n* a phenomenon exhibited by certain substances, such as ferrites, in which the magnetic moments of neighbouring ions are antiparallel and unequal in magnitude. The substances behave like ferromagnetic materials > **ferrimagnetic** (ˌferɪmægˈnetɪk) *adj*

Ferris wheel (ˈferɪs) *n* a fairground wheel having seats freely suspended from its rim; the seats remain horizontal throughout its rotation [C19: named after G.W.G. *Ferris* (1859–96), American engineer]

ferrite (ˈferaɪt) *n* any of a group of ferromagnetic highly resistive ceramic compounds with the formula MFe₂O₄, where M is usually a metal such as cobalt or zinc [C19: from FERRI- + -ITE¹]

ferrite-rod aerial *n* a type of aerial, normally used in radio reception, consisting of a small coil of wire mounted on a ferrite core, the coil serving as a tuning inductance

ferro- *combining form* **1** indicating a property of iron or the presence of iron: *ferromagnetism; ferromanganese* **2** indicating the presence of iron in the divalent state: *ferrocyanide*. See **ferri-** [from Latin *ferrum* iron]

ferrocene (ˈferəʊˌsiːn) *n* a reddish-orange insoluble crystalline compound. Its molecules have an iron atom sandwiched between two cyclopentadiene rings. Formula: Fe(C₅H₅)₂ [C20: from FERRO- + C(YCLOPENTADI)ENE]

ferroconcrete (ˌferəʊˈkɒŋkriːt) *n* another name for **reinforced concrete**

Ferrol (*Spanish* feˈrrɔl) *n* See **El Ferrol**

ferromagnetism (ˌferəʊˈmægnɪˌtɪzəm) *n* the phenomenon exhibited by substances, such as iron, that have relative permeabilities much greater than unity and increasing magnetization with applied magnetizing field. Certain of these substances retain their magnetization in the absence of the applied field. The effect is caused by the alignment of electron spin in regions called domains > **ferromagnetic** (ˌferəʊmægˈnetɪk) *adj*

ferromanganese (ˌferəʊˈmæŋgəˌniːz) *n* an alloy of iron and manganese, used in making additions of

manganese to cast iron and steel

ferrous (ˈferəs) *adj* of or containing iron in the divalent state; designating an iron (II) compound [C19: from FERRI- + -OUS]

ferrous sulphate *n* an iron salt with a saline taste, usually obtained as greenish crystals of the heptahydrate, which are converted to the white monohydrate above 100°C: used in inks, tanning, water purification, and in the treatment of anaemia. Formula: FeSO₄. Also called: **copperas** or **green vitriol**

ferruginous (feˈruːdʒɪnəs) *adj* **1** (of minerals, rocks, etc) containing iron: *a ferruginous clay* **2** rust-coloured [C17: from Latin *ferrūgineus* of a rusty colour, from *ferrūgō* iron rust, from *ferrum* iron]

ferrule *or* **ferule** (ˈferuːl, -rəl) *n* **1** a metal ring, tube, or cap placed over the end of a stick, handle, or post for added strength or stability or to increase wear **2** a bush, gland, small length of tube, etc, esp one used for making a joint [C17: from Middle English *virole*, from Old French *virol*, from Latin *viriola* a little bracelet, from *viria* bracelet; influenced by Latin *ferrum* iron]

ferry (ˈferɪ) *n, pl* **-ries 1** Also called: **ferryboat** a vessel for transporting passengers and usually vehicles across a body of water, esp as a regular service **2 a** such a service **b** (*in combination*): *a ferryman* **3** the act or method of delivering aircraft by flying them to their destination ▷ *vb* **-ries, -rying, -ried 4** to transport or go by ferry **5** to deliver (an aircraft) by flying it to its destination **6** (*tr*) to convey (passengers, goods, etc): *the guests were ferried to the church in taxis* [Old English *ferian* to carry, bring; related to Old Norse *ferja* to transport, Gothic *farjan*; see FARE]

fertigate (ˈfɜːtɪˌgeɪt) *vb* **-ates, -ating, -ated** to fertilize and irrigate at the same time, by adding fertilizers to the water supply [C20: from FERTILIZE + IRRIGATE] > **ˌfertiˈgation** *n*

fertile (ˈfɜːtaɪl) *adj* **1** capable of producing offspring **2 a** (of land) having nutrients capable of sustaining an abundant growth of plants **b** (of farm animals) capable of breeding stock **3** *biology* capable of undergoing growth and development: *fertile seeds; fertile eggs* **4** producing many offspring; prolific **5** highly productive; rich; abundant: *a fertile brain* [C15: from Latin *fertilis*, from *ferre* to bear] > **ˈfertilely** *adv* > **ˈfertileness** *n*

Fertile Crescent *n* an area of fertile land in the Middle East, extending around the Rivers Tigris and Euphrates in a semicircle from Israel to the Persian Gulf, where the Sumerian, Babylonian, Assyrian, Phoenician, and Hebrew civilizations flourished

fertility (fɜːˈtɪlɪtɪ) *n* **1** the ability to produce offspring, esp abundantly **2** the state or quality of being fertile

fertility drug *n* any of a group of preparations used to stimulate ovulation in women hitherto infertile

fertilize *or* **fertilise** (ˈfɜːtɪˌlaɪz) *vb* **1** to provide (an animal, plant, or egg cell) with sperm or pollen to bring about fertilization **2** to supply (soil or water) with mineral and organic nutrients to aid the growth of plants **3** to make fertile or productive > **ˌfertiliˈzation** *or* **ˌfertiliˈsation** *n*

fertilizer *or* **fertiliser** (ˈfɜːtɪˌlaɪzə) *n* **1** any substance, such as manure or a mixture of nitrates, added to soil or water to increase its productivity **2** an object or organism such as an insect that fertilizes an animal or plant

ferula (ˈferʊlə, ˈferjʊ-) *n, pl* **-las** *or* **-lae** (-ˌliː) any large umbelliferous plant of the Mediterranean genus *Ferula*, having thick stems and dissected leaves: cultivated as the source of several strongly scented gum resins, such as galbanum [C14: from Latin: giant fennel]

ferule (ˈferuːl, -rəl) *n* **1** a flat piece of wood, such as a ruler, used in some schools to cane children on the hand ▷ *vb* **2** (*tr*) *rare* to punish with a ferule [C16: from Latin *ferula* giant fennel, whip, rod; the stalk of the plant was used for punishment]

fervent (ˈfɜːvənt) *or* **fervid** (ˈfɜːvɪd) *adj* **1** intensely passionate; ardent: *a fervent desire to change society* **2** *archaic or poetic* boiling, burning, or glowing: *fervent heat* [C14: from Latin *fervēre* to boil, glow] > **ˈfervently** *or* **ˈfervidly** *adv* > **ˈfervency** *n*

fervour *or US* **fervor** (ˈfɜːvə) *n* **1** great intensity of feeling or belief; ardour; zeal **2** *rare* intense heat [C14: from Latin *fervor* heat, from *fervēre* to glow, boil]

Fès (fɛs) *or* **Fez** *n* a city in N central Morocco, traditional capital of the north: became an independent kingdom in the 11th century, at its height in the 14th century; religious centre; university (859). Pop: 664 000 (2003)

fescue ('fɛskjuː) *or* **fescue grass** *n* any grass of the genus *Festuca*: widely cultivated as pasture and lawn grasses, having stiff narrow leaves [C14: from Old French *festu*, ultimately from Latin *festūca* stem, straw]

fess (fɛs) *vb* (*intr*; foll by *up*) *informal, chiefly US* to make a confession [C19: shortened from CONFESS]

fesse *or* **fess** (fɛs) *n heraldry* an ordinary consisting of a horizontal band across a shield, conventionally occupying a third of its length and being wider than a bar [C15: from Anglo-French *fesse*, from Latin *fascia* band, fillet]

fest (fɛst) *n* **a** a meeting or event at which the emphasis is on a particular activity: *a fashion fest* **b** (*in combination*): *schmaltz-fest; lovefest* [C19: from German *Fest* festival]

festal ('fɛstᵊl) *adj* another word for **festive** [C15: from Latin *festum* holiday, banquet; see FEAST] > '**festally** *adv*

fester ('fɛstə) *vb* **1** to form or cause to form pus **2** (*intr*) to become rotten; decay **3** to become or cause to become bitter, irritated, etc, esp over a long period of time; rankle ▷ *n* **4** a small ulcer or sore containing pus [C13: from Old French *festre* suppurating sore, from Latin: FISTULA]

festival ('fɛstɪvᵊl) *n* **1** a day or period set aside for celebration or feasting, esp one of religious significance **2** any occasion for celebration, esp one which commemorates an anniversary or other significant event **3** an organized series of special events and performances, usually in one place: *a festival of drama* **4** *archaic* a time of revelry; merrymaking **5** (*modifier*) relating to or characteristic of a festival [C14: from Church Latin *fēstivālis* of a feast, from Latin *festivus* FESTIVE]

Festival Hall *n* a concert hall in London, on the South Bank of the Thames: constructed for the 1951 Festival of Britain; completed 1964–65

festive ('fɛstɪv) *adj* appropriate to or characteristic of a holiday, etc; merry [C17: from Latin *festivus* joyful, from *festus* of a FEAST] > '**festively** *adv*

festive season *n* the period immediately leading up to Christmas and ending just after New Year

festivity (fɛs'tɪvɪtɪ) *n, pl* -ties **1** merriment characteristic of a festival, party, etc **2** any festival or other celebration **3** (*plural*) festive proceedings; celebrations

festoon (fɛ'stuːn) *n* **1** a decorative chain of flowers, ribbons, etc, suspended in loops; garland **2** a carved or painted representation of this, as in architecture, furniture, or pottery ▷ *vb* (*tr*) **3** to decorate or join together with festoons **4** to form into festoons [C17: from French *feston*, from Italian *festone* ornament for a feast, from *festa* FEAST]

festoon blind *n* a window blind consisting of vertical rows of horizontally gathered fabric that may be drawn up to form a series of ruches

feta ('fɛtə) *n* a white sheep or goat cheese popular in Greece [Modern Greek, from the phrase *turi pheta*, from *turi* cheese + *pheta*, from Italian *fetta* a slice]

fetal *or* **foetal** ('fiːtᵊl) *adj* of, relating to, or resembling a fetus

fetal alcohol syndrome *n* a condition in newborn babies caused by excessive intake of alcohol by the mother during pregnancy: characterized by various defects including mental retardation

fetch¹ (fɛtʃ) *vb* (*mainly tr*) **1** to go after and bring back; get: *to fetch help* **2** to cause to come; bring or draw forth **3** (*also intr*) to cost or sell for (a certain price): *the table fetched six hundred pounds* **4** to utter (a sigh, groan, etc) **5** *informal* to deal (a blow, slap, etc) **6** (used esp as a command to dogs) to retrieve (shot game, an object thrown, etc) **7 fetch and carry** to perform menial tasks or run errands ▷ *n* **8** the reach, stretch, etc, of a mechanism **9** a trick or stratagem [Old English *feccan*; related to Old Norse *feta* to step, Old High German *sih fazzōn* to climb] > '**fetcher** *n*

fetch² (fɛtʃ) *n* the ghost or apparition of a living person [C18: of unknown origin]

fetching ('fɛtʃɪŋ) *adj informal* **1** attractively befitting **2** charming

fetch up *vb* (*adverb*) **1** (*intr*; usually foll by *at* or *in*) *informal* to arrive (at) or end up (in): *to fetch up in New York* **2** *slang* to vomit (food, etc)

fête *or* **fete** (feɪt) *n* **1** a gala, bazaar, or similar entertainment, esp one held outdoors in aid of charity **2** a feast day or holiday, esp one of religious significance ▷ *vb* **3** (*tr*) to honour or entertain with or as if with a fête [C18: from French: FEAST]

fetid *or* **foetid** ('fɛtɪd, 'fiː-) *adj* having a stale nauseating smell, as of decay [C16: from Latin *fētidus*, from *fētēre* to stink; related to *fūmus* smoke] > '**fetidly** *or* '**foetidly** *adv* > '**fetidness** *or* '**foetidness** *n*

fetish *or* **fetich** ('fɛtɪʃ, 'fiːtɪʃ) *n* **1** something, esp an inanimate object, that is believed in certain cultures to be the embodiment or habitation of a spirit or magical powers **2 a** a form of behaviour involving fetishism **b** any object that is involved in fetishism **3** any object, activity, etc, to which one is excessively or irrationally devoted [C17: from French *fétiche*, from Portuguese *feitiço* (n) sorcery, from adj: artificial, from Latin *factīcius* made by art, FACTITIOUS]

fetishism *or* **fetichism** ('fɛtɪˌʃɪzəm, 'fiː-) *n* **1** a condition in which the handling of an inanimate object or a specific part of the body other than the sexual organs is a source of sexual satisfaction **2** belief in or recourse to a fetish for magical purposes > '**fetishist** *or* '**fetichist** *n* > ˌfetish'istic *or* ˌfetich'istic *adj*

fetlock ('fɛtˌlɒk) *or* **fetterlock** *n* **1** a projection behind and above a horse's hoof: the part of the leg between the cannon bone and the pastern **2** Also called: **fetlock joint** the joint at this part of the leg **3** the tuft of hair growing from this part [C14 *fetlak*; related to Middle High German *vizzeloch* fetlock, from *vizzel* pastern + *-och*; see FOOT]

fetor *or* **foetor** ('fiːtə, -tɔː) *n* an offensive stale or putrid odour; stench [C15: from Latin, from *fētēre* to stink]

fettle ('fɛtᵊl) *vb* (*tr*) **1** to line or repair (the walls of a furnace) **2** *Brit dialect* **a** to prepare or arrange (a thing, oneself, etc), esp to put a finishing touch to **b** to repair or mend (something) ▷ *n* **3** state of health, spirits, etc (esp in the phrase **in fine fettle**) [C14 (in the sense: to put in order): back formation from *fetled* girded up, from Old English *fetel* belt]

fettler ('fɛtlə) *n Brit & Austral* a person employed to maintain railway tracks

fetus *or* **foetus** ('fiːtəs) *n, pl* -tuses the embryo of a mammal in the later stages of development, when it shows all the main recognizable features of the mature animal, esp a human embryo from the end of the second month of pregnancy until birth [C14: from Latin: offspring, brood]

feu (fjuː) *n* **1** *Scot legal history* **a** a feudal tenure of land for which rent was paid in money or grain instead of by the performance of military service **b** the land so held **2** *Scots law* a right to the use of land in return for a fixed annual payment (**feu duty**) [C15: from Old French; see FEE]

Feuchtwanger (German 'fɔɪçtvaŋər) *n* **Lion** ('liːɔn). 1884–1958, German novelist and dramatist, lived in the US (1940–58): noted for his historical novels, including *Die hässliche Herzogin* (1923) and *Jud Süss* (1925)

feud¹ (fjuːd) *n* **1** long and bitter hostility between two families, clans, or individuals; vendetta **2** a quarrel or dispute ▷ *vb* **3** (*intr*) to take part in or carry on a feud [C13 *fede*, from Old French *feide*, from Old High German *fēhida*; related to Old English *fæhth* hostility; see FOE]

feud² *or* **feod** (fjuːd) *n feudal law* land held in return for service [C17: from Medieval Latin *feodum*, of Germanic origin; see FEE]

feudal ('fjuːdᵊl) *adj* **1** of, resembling, relating to, or characteristic of feudalism or its institutions **2** of, characteristic of, or relating to a fief **3** *disparaging* old-fashioned, reactionary, etc [C17: from Medieval Latin *feudālis*, from *feudum* FEUD²]

feudalism ('fjuːdəˌlɪzəm) *n* Also called: **feudal system**

the legal and social system that evolved in W Europe in the 8th and 9th centuries, in which vassals were protected and maintained by their lords, usually through the granting of fiefs, and were required to serve under them in war > 'feudalist n ,feudal'istic adj

feudality (fju:'dælɪtɪ) n, pl -ties **1** the state or quality of being feudal **2** a fief or fee

feudalize or **feudalise** ('fju:də,laɪz) vb (tr) to make feudal; create feudal institutions in (a society) > ,feudali'zation or ,feudali'sation n

feudatory ('fju:dətərɪ, -trɪ) (in feudal Europe) n **1** a person holding a fief; vassal ▷ adj **2** relating to or characteristic of the relationship between lord and vassal [c16: from Medieval Latin feudātor]

Feuerbach (German 'fɔɪərbax) n **Ludwig Andreas** ('lu:tvɪç an'dreːas). 1804–72, German materialist philosopher: in The Essence of Christianity (1841), translated into English by George Eliot (1853), he maintained that God is merely an outward projection of man's inner self

feuilleton ('fʊɪ,tɒn; French fœjtɔ̃) n **1** the part of a European newspaper carrying reviews, serialized fiction, etc **2** such a review or article [c19: from French, from feuillet sheet of paper, diminutive of feuille leaf, from Latin folium]

fever ('fi:və) n **1** an abnormally high body temperature, accompanied by a fast pulse rate, dry skin, etc **2** any of various diseases, such as yellow fever or scarlet fever, characterized by a high temperature **3** intense nervous excitement or agitation ▷ vb **4** (tr) to affect with or as if with fever [Old English fēfor, from Latin febris] > 'fevered adj

feverfew ('fi:və,fju:) n a bushy European strong-scented perennial plant, Tanacetum parthenium, with white flower heads, formerly used medicinally: family Asteraceae (composites) [Old English feferfuge, from Late Latin febrifugia, from Latin febris fever + fugāre to put to flight]

feverish ('fi:vərɪʃ) or **feverous** adj **1** suffering from fever, esp a slight fever **2** in a state of restless excitement **3** of, relating to, caused by, or causing fever > 'feverishly or 'feverously adv

fever pitch n a state of intense excitement

fever therapy n a former method of treating disease by raising the body temperature

few (fju:) determiner **1 a** a small number of; hardly any: few men are so cruel **b** (as pronoun; functioning as plural): many are called but few are chosen **2** (preceded by a) **a** a small number of: a few drinks **b** (as pronoun; functioning as plural): a few of you **3** a good few informal several **4** few and far between **a** at great intervals; widely spaced **b** not abundant; scarce **5** not a few or quite a few informal several ▷ n **6** the few a small number of people considered as a class: the few who fell at Thermopylae [Old English fēawa; related to Old High German fao little, Old Norse fār little, silent] > 'fewness n

● USAGE See at less

fey (feɪ) adj **1** interested in or believing in the supernatural **2** attuned to the supernatural; clairvoyant; visionary **3** chiefly Scot fated to die; doomed **4** chiefly Scot in a state of high spirits or unusual excitement, formerly believed to presage death [Old English fǣge marked out for death; related to Old Norse feigr doomed, Old High German feigi] > 'feyness n

Feydeau (French fɛdo) n **Georges** (ʒɔrʒ). 1862–1921, French dramatist, noted for his farces, esp La Dame de chez Maxim (1899) and Occupe-toi d'Amélie (1908)

Feynman ('faɪnmən) n **Richard**. 1918–88, US physicist, noted for his research on quantum electrodynamics; shared the Nobel prize for physics in 1965

fez (fez) n, pl fezzes an originally Turkish brimless felt or wool cap, shaped like a truncated cone, usually red and with a tassel [c19: via French from Turkish, from FEZ]

Fez (fɛz) n a variant of **Fès**

Fezzan (fɛ'zaːn) n a region of SW Libya, in the Sahara: a former province (until 1963)

ff symbol for **1** folios **2** following (pages, lines, etc) **3** music fortissimo: an instruction to play very loudly

Ffestiniog (fɛs'tɪnjɒg) n a town in N Wales, in Gwynedd: tourist attractions include former slate quarries and a narrow-gauge railway at nearby Blaenau Ffestiniog. Pop: 4830 (2001)

FI abbreviation Falkland Islands

fiacre (fɪ'ɑːkrə) n a small four-wheeled horse-drawn carriage, usually with a folding roof [c17: named after the Hotel de St Fiacre, Paris, where these vehicles were first hired out]

fiancé (fɪ'ɒnseɪ) n a man who is engaged to be married [c19: from French, from Old French fiancier to promise, betroth, from fiance a vow, from fier to trust, from Latin fidere]

fiancée (fɪ'ɒnseɪ) n a woman who is engaged to be married

Fianna ('fiːənə) pl n a legendary band of Irish warriors noted for their heroic exploits, attributed to the 2nd and 3rd centuries AD Also called: Fenians

fiasco (fɪ'æskəʊ) n, pl -cos or -coes a complete failure, esp one that is ignominious or humiliating [c19: from Italian, literally: FLASK; sense development obscure]

fiat ('faɪət, -æt) n **1** official sanction; authoritative permission **2** an arbitrary order or decree [c17: from Latin, literally: let it be done, from fierī to become]

fib (fɪb) n **1** a trivial and harmless lie ▷ vb fibs, fibbing, fibbed **2** (intr) to tell such a lie [c17: perhaps from fibble-fable an unlikely story; see FABLE] > 'fibber n

Fibiger (Danish 'fibigər) n **Johannes Andreas Grib** (joˈhanəs anˈdreːas grɪb). 1867–1928, Danish physician: Nobel prize for physiology or medicine (1926) for his work in cancer research

Fibonacci (Italian fiboˈnattʃi) n **Leonardo** (leoˈnardo), also called Leonardo of Pisa. ?1170–?1250, Italian mathematician: popularized the decimal system in Europe

Fibonacci sequence or **Fibonacci series** (,fɪbəˈnɑːtʃɪ) n the infinite sequence of numbers, 0, 1, 1, 2, 3, 5, 8, etc, in which each member (**Fibonacci number**) is the sum of the previous two [named after Leonardo FIBONACCI]

fibre or US **fiber** ('faɪbə) n **1** a natural or synthetic filament that may be spun into yarn, such as cotton or nylon **2** cloth or other material made from such yarn **3** a long fine continuous thread or filament **4** the structure of any material or substance made of or as if of fibres; texture **5** essential substance or nature **6** strength of character (esp in the phrase **moral fibre**) **7** See **dietary fibre 8** botany **a** a narrow elongated thick-walled cell: a constituent of sclerenchyma tissue **b** a very small root or twig [c14: from Latin fibra filament, entrails] > 'fibred or US 'fibered adj

fibreboard or US **fiberboard** ('faɪbə,bɔːd) n a building material made of compressed wood or other plant fibres, esp one in the form of a thin semirigid sheet

fibreglass or US **fiberglass** ('faɪbə,glɑːs) n **1** material consisting of matted fine glass fibres, used as insulation in buildings, in fireproof fabrics, etc **2** a fabric woven from this material or a light strong material made by bonding fibreglass with a synthetic resin; used for car bodies, boat hulls, etc

fibre optics n (functioning as singular) the transmission of information modulated on light carried down very thin flexible fibres of glass. See also **optical fibre** > ,fibre'optic adj

fibrescope or US **fiberscope** ('faɪbə,skəʊp) n an endoscope that transmits images of the interior of a hollow organ by fibre optics

fibril ('faɪbrɪl) or **fibrilla** (faɪ'brɪlə, fɪ-) n, pl -brils or -brillae (-'brɪliː) **1** a small fibre or part of a fibre **2** biology a threadlike structure, such as a root hair or a thread of muscle tissue [c17: from New Latin fibrilla a little FIBRE] > 'fibrilar, fi'brillar or fi'brillose adj

fibrillation (,faɪbrɪˈleɪʃən, ,fɪb-) n **1** a local and uncontrollable twitching of muscle fibres, esp of the heart, not affecting the entire muscle. **Atrial fibrillation** results in rapid and irregular heart and pulse rate. In **ventricular fibrillation**, the heart stops beating **2** irregular twitchings of the muscular wall of the heart, often interfering with the normal rhythmic contractions

fibrin ('fɪbrɪn) n a white insoluble elastic protein formed from fibrinogen when blood clots: forms a network that traps red cells and platelets

fibrinogen (fɪˈbrɪnədʒən) n a soluble protein, a globulin, in blood plasma, converted to fibrin by the action of the enzyme thrombin when blood clots

fibro (ˈfaɪbrəʊ) n Austral informal **a** short for **fibrocement b** (as modifier): a fibro shack

fibro- combining form **1** indicating fibrous tissue: fibroin; fibrosis **2** indicating fibre: fibrocement [from Latin fibra FIBRE]

fibrocement (ˌfaɪbrəʊsɪˈmɛnt) n (formerly) cement combined with asbestos fibre, used esp in sheets for building

fibroid (ˈfaɪbrɔɪd) adj **1** anatomy (of structures or tissues) containing or resembling fibres ▷ n **2** a benign tumour, composed of fibrous and muscular tissue, occurring in the wall of the uterus and often causing heavy menstruation

fibroin (ˈfaɪbrəʊɪn) n a tough elastic protein that is the principal component of spiders' webs and raw silk

fibroma (faɪˈbrəʊmə) n, pl -mata (-mətə) or -mas a benign tumour derived from fibrous connective tissue

fibrosis (faɪˈbrəʊsɪs) n the formation of an abnormal amount of fibrous tissue in an organ or part as the result of inflammation, irritation, or healing

fibrositis (ˌfaɪbrəˈsaɪtɪs) n inflammation of white fibrous tissue, esp that of muscle sheaths

fibrous (ˈfaɪbrəs) adj consisting of, containing, or resembling fibres: fibrous tissue ▷ ˈfibrously adv

fibula (ˈfɪbjʊlə) n, pl -lae (-ˌliː) or -las **1** the outer and thinner of the two bones between the knee and ankle of the human leg. See **tibia 2** the corresponding bone in other vertebrates **3** a metal brooch resembling a safety pin, often highly decorated, common in Europe after 1300 BC [C17: from Latin: clasp, probably from figere to fasten] ▷ ˈfibular adj

-fic suffix forming adjectives causing, making, or producing: honorific [from Latin -ficus, from facere to do, make]

fiche (fiːʃ) n See **microfiche, ultrafiche**

Fichte (German ˈfɪçtə) n **Johann Gottlieb** (joˈhan ˈɡɔtliːp). 1762–1814, German philosopher: expounded ethical idealism

fichu (ˈfiːʃuː) n a woman's shawl or scarf of some light material, worn esp in the 18th century [C19: from French: small shawl, from ficher to fix with a pin, from Latin figere to fasten, FIX]

Ficino (Italian fiˈtʃiːno) n **Marsilio** (marˈsiːljo). 1433–99, Italian Neoplatonist philosopher: attempted to integrate Platonism with Christianity

fickle (ˈfɪkᵊl) adj changeable in purpose, affections, etc; capricious [Old English ficol deceitful; related to fician to wheedle, befician to deceive] ▷ ˈfickleness n

fictile (ˈfɪktaɪl) adj **1** moulded or capable of being moulded from clay; plastic **2** made of clay by a potter [C17: from Latin fictilis that can be moulded, hence, made of clay, from fingere to shape]

fiction (ˈfɪkʃən) n **1** literary works invented by the imagination, such as novels or short stories **2** an invented story or explanation; lie **3** the act of inventing a story or explanation **4** law something assumed to be true for the sake of convenience, though probably false [C14: from Latin fictiō a fashioning, hence something imaginary, from fingere to shape] ▷ ˈfictional adj ▷ ˈfictionally adv ▷ ˈfictive adj

fictionalize or **fictionalise** (ˈfɪkʃənəˌlaɪz) vb (tr) to make into fiction or give a fictional aspect to ▷ ˌfictionaliˈzation or ˌfictionaliˈsation n

fictitious (fɪkˈtɪʃəs) adj **1** not genuine or authentic; assumed; false: to give a fictitious address **2** of, related to, or characteristic of fiction; created by the imagination ▷ ficˈtitiously adv ▷ ficˈtitiousness n

fid (fɪd) n **1** nautical **a** spike for separating strands of rope in splicing **2** a wooden or metal bar for supporting the heel of a topmast [C17: of unknown origin]

-fid adj combining form divided into parts or lobes: bifid; pinnatifid [from Latin -fidus, from findere to split]

fiddle (ˈfɪdᵊl) n **1** informal or sometimes when used of a classical violin disparaging any instrument of the viol or violin family, esp the violin **2** a violin played as a folk instrument **3** nautical a small railing around the top of a table to prevent objects from falling off it in bad weather **4** Brit informal an illegal or fraudulent transaction or arrangement **5** Brit informal a manually delicate or tricky operation **6** at the fiddle or on the fiddle informal engaged in an illegal or fraudulent undertaking **7** fit as a fiddle informal in very good health **8** play second fiddle informal to be subordinate; play a minor part ▷ vb **9** to play (a tune) on the fiddle **10** (intr; often foll by with) to make restless or aimless movements with the hands **11** (when intr, often foll by about or around) informal to spend (time) or act in a careless or inconsequential manner; waste (time) **12** (often foll by with) informal to tamper or interfere (with) **13** informal to contrive to do (something) by illicit means or deception **14** (tr) informal to falsify (accounts, etc); swindle [Old English fithele, probably from Medieval Latin vītula, from vītulārī to celebrate; compare Old High German fidula fiddle; see VIOLA¹]

fiddle-faddle (ˈfɪdᵊlˌfædᵊl) n, interj **1** trivial matter; nonsense ▷ vb **2** (intr) to fuss or waste time, esp over trivial matters [C16: reduplication of FIDDLE] ▷ ˈfiddle-ˌfaddler n

fiddler (ˈfɪdlə) n **1** a person who plays the fiddle, esp in folk music **2** See **fiddler crab 3** informal a cheat or petty rogue

fiddler crab n any of various burrowing crabs of the genus Uca of American coastal regions, the males of which have one of their anterior pincer-like claws very much enlarged [C19: referring to the rapid fiddling movement of the enlarged anterior claw of the males, used to attract females]

fiddlestick (ˈfɪdᵊlˌstɪk) n **1** informal a violin bow **2** any meaningless or inconsequential thing; trifle **3** fiddlesticks! an expression of annoyance or disagreement

fiddling (ˈfɪdlɪŋ) adj **1** trifling or insignificant; petty **2** another word for **fiddly**

fiddly (ˈfɪdlɪ) adj -dlier, -dliest small and awkward to do or handle

Fidei Defensor Latin (ˈfaɪdɪˌaɪ dɪˈfɛnsɔː) n defender of the faith; a title given to Henry VIII by Pope Leo X, and appearing on Brit coins as FID DEF or FD

fidelity (fɪˈdɛlɪtɪ) n, pl -ties **1** devotion to duties, obligations, etc; faithfulness **2** loyalty or devotion, as to a person or cause **3** faithfulness to one's spouse, lover, etc **4** adherence to truth; accuracy in reporting detail **5** electronics the degree to which the output of a system, such as an amplifier or radio, accurately reproduces the characteristics of the input signal [C15: from Latin fidēlitās, from fidēlis faithful, from fidēs faith, loyalty]

fidget (ˈfɪdʒɪt) vb **1** (intr) to move about restlessly **2** (intr; often foll by with) to make restless or uneasy movements (with something); fiddle **3** (tr) to cause to fidget ▷ n **4** (often plural) a state of restlessness or unease, esp as expressed in continual motion: he's got the fidgets **5** a person who fidgets [C17: from earlier fidge, probably from Old Norse fikjast to desire eagerly] ▷ ˈfidgety adj

fiducial (fɪˈdjuːʃɪəl) adj **1** physics used as a standard of reference or measurement: a fiducial point **2** of or based on trust or faith [C17: from Late Latin fidūciālis, from Latin fidūcia confidence, reliance, from fidere to trust]

fiduciary (fɪˈduːʃɪərɪ) law ▷ n, pl -aries **1** a person bound to act for another's benefit, as a trustee in relation to his beneficiary ▷ adj **2 a** having the nature of a trust **b** of or relating to a trust or trustee [C17: from Latin fidūciārius relating to something held in trust, from fidūcia trust; see FIDUCIAL]

fiduciary issue n an issue of banknotes not backed by gold

fie (faɪ) interj obsolete or facetious an exclamation of distaste or mock dismay [C13: from Old French fi, from Latin fī, exclamation of disgust]

fief or **feoff** (fiːf) n (in feudal Europe) the property or fee granted to a vassal for his maintenance by his lord in return for service [C17: from Old French fie, of Germanic origin; compare Old English fēo cattle, money, Latin pecus cattle, pecūnia money, Greek pokos fleece]

fiefdom (ˈfiːfdəm) n **1** (in feudal Europe) the property owned by a lord **2** an area over which a person or organization exerts authority or influence

field (fiːld) n **1** an open tract of uncultivated grassland; meadow **2** a piece of land cleared of trees and undergrowth, usually enclosed with a fence or hedge and used for pasture or growing crops: *a field of barley* **3** a limited or marked off area, usually of mown grass, on which any of various sports, athletic competitions, etc, are held: *a soccer field* **4** an area that is rich in minerals or other natural resources: *a coalfield* **5** short for **battlefield, airfield 6** the mounted followers that hunt with a pack of hounds **7 a** all the runners in a particular race or competitors in a competition **b** the runners in a race or competitors in a competition excluding the favourite **8** *cricket* the fielders collectively, esp with regard to their positions **9** a wide or open expanse: *a field of snow* **10 a** an area of human activity: *the field of human knowledge* **b** a sphere or division of knowledge, interest, etc: *his field is physics* **11** a place away from the laboratory, office, library, etc, usually out of doors, where practical work is done or original material or data collected **12** the surface or background, as of a flag, coin, or heraldic shield, on which a design is displayed **13** Also called: **field of view** the area within which an object may be observed with a telescope, microscope, etc **14** *physics* See **field of force 15** *maths* a set of entities subject to two binary operations, addition and multiplication, such that the set is a commutative group under addition and the set, minus the zero, is a commutative group under multiplication and multiplication is distributive over addition **16** *maths, logic* the set of elements that are either arguments or values of a function; the union of its domain and range **17** *computing* a set of one or more characters comprising a unit of information **18** take the field to begin or carry on activity, esp in sport or military operations **19** play the field *informal* to disperse one's interests or attentions among a number of activities, people, or objects **20** (*modifier*) *military* of or relating to equipment, personnel, etc, specifically designed or trained for operations in the field: *a field gun; a field army* ▷ *vb* **21** (*tr*) *sport* to stop, catch, or return (the ball) as a fielder **22** (*tr*) *sport* to send (a player or team) onto the field to play **23** (*intr*) *sport* (of a player or team) to act or take turn as a fielder or fielders **24** (*tr*) to enter (a person) in a competition: *each party fielded a candidate* **25** (*tr*) *informal* to deal with or handle, esp adequately and by making a reciprocal gesture: *to field a question* [Old English *feld*; related to Old Saxon, Old High German *feld*, Old English *fold* earth, Greek *platus* broad]

Field (fiːld) n **John.** 1782–1837, Irish composer and pianist, lived in Russia from 1803: invented the nocturne

field artillery n artillery capable of deployment in support of front-line troops, due mainly to its mobility

field day n **1 a** day spent in some special outdoor activity, such as nature study or sport **2** *military* a day devoted to manoeuvres or exercises, esp before an audience **3** *informal* a day or time of exciting or successful activity: *the children had a field day with their new toys*

field-effect transistor n a unipolar transistor consisting of three or more electrode regions, the source, one or more gates, and the drain. A current flowing in a channel between the highly doped source and drain is controlled by the electric field arising from a voltage applied between source and gate

fielder ('fiːldə) n *cricket, baseball* **a** a player in the field **b** a member of the fielding rather than the batting side

field event n a competition, such as the discus, high jump, etc, that takes place on a field or similar area as opposed to those on the running track

fieldfare ('fiːld,fɛə) n a large Old World thrush, *Turdus pilaris*, having a pale grey head and rump, brown wings and back, and a blackish tail [Old English *feldefare*; see FIELD, FARE]

field glasses *pl n* another name for **binoculars**

field goal n **1** *basketball* a goal scored while the ball is in normal play rather than from a free throw **2** *American football* a score of three points made by kicking the ball through the opponent's goalposts above the crossbar

field hockey n *US & Canadian* hockey played on a field, as distinguished from ice hockey

field hospital n a temporary hospital set up near a battlefield equipped to provide remedial surgery and post-operative care

Fielding ('fiːldɪŋ) n **Henry.** 1707–54, English novelist and dramatist, noted particularly for his picaresque novel *Tom Jones* (1749) and for *Joseph Andrews* (1742), which starts as a parody of Richardson's *Pamela*: also noted as an enlightened magistrate and a founder of the Bow Street runners (1749)

field magnet n a permanent magnet or an electromagnet that produces the magnetic field in a generator, electric motor, or similar device

field marshal n an officer holding the highest rank in the British and certain other armies

fieldmouse ('fiːld,maʊs) n, *pl* -mice any nocturnal mouse of the genus *Apodemus*, inhabiting woods, fields, and gardens of the Old World: family *Muridae*. They have yellowish-brown fur and feed on fruit, vegetables, seeds, etc

field officer n an officer holding **field rank**, namely that of major, lieutenant colonel, or colonel

field of force n the region of space surrounding a body, such as a charged particle or a magnet, within which it can exert a force on another similar body not in contact with it

Fields (fiːldz) n **1** Dame **Gracie.** real name *Grace Stansfield*. 1898–1979, English popular singer and entertainer **2** **W. C.** real name *William Claude Dukenfield*. 1880–1946, US film actor, noted for his portrayal of comic roles

fieldsman ('fiːldzmən) n, *pl* -men *cricket* another name for **fielder**

field sports *pl n* sports carried on in the open countryside, such as hunting, shooting, or fishing

field tile n *Brit & NZ* an earthenware drain used in farm drainage

field trial n (*often plural*) a test to display performance, efficiency, or durability, as of a vehicle or invention

field trip n an expedition, as by a group of students or research workers, to study something at first hand

field winding ('waɪndɪŋ) n the insulated current-carrying coils on a field magnet that produce the magnetic field intensity required to set up the electrical excitation in a generator or motor

fieldwork ('fiːld,wɜːk) n *military* a temporary structure used in defending or fortifying a place or position

field work n an investigation or search for material, data, etc, made in the field as opposed to the classroom, laboratory, or official headquarters ▷ **field worker** n

fiend (fiːnd) n **1** an evil spirit; demon; devil **2** a person who is extremely wicked, esp in being very cruel or brutal **3** *informal* **a** a person who is intensely interested in or fond of something: *a fresh-air fiend; he is a fiend for cards* **b** an addict: *a drug fiend* [Old English *feond*; related to Old Norse *fjāndi* enemy, Gothic *fijands*, Old High German *fiant*]

fiendish ('fiːndɪʃ) adj **1** of or like a fiend **2** diabolically wicked or cruel **3** *informal* extremely difficult or unpleasant

Fiennes (fiːnz) n **1 Ralph (Nathanial).** born 1962, British actor; his films include *Schindler's List* (1993), *The English Patient* (1997), *The End of the Affair* (2000), and *Spider* (2002) **2** Sir **Ranulph (Twistleton-Wykeham-).** born 1944, British explorer; led the first surface journey around the earth's polar axis (1979–82); unsupported crossing of Antarctica (1992–93)

fierce (fɪəs) adj **1** having a violent and unrestrained nature; savage: *a fierce dog* **2** wild or turbulent in force, action, or intensity: *a fierce storm* **3** vehement, intense, or strong: *fierce competition* **4** *informal* very disagreeable or unpleasant [c13: from Old French *fiers*, from Latin *ferus*] ▷ **'fiercely** adv ▷ **'fierceness** n

fiery ('faɪərɪ) adj fierier, fieriest **1** of, containing, or composed of fire **2** resembling fire in heat, colour, ardour, etc: *a fiery desert wind* **3** easily angered or aroused: *a fiery temper* **4** (of food) producing a burning sensation: *a fiery curry* **5** (of the skin or a sore) inflamed **6** flammable or containing flammable gas ▷ **'fierily** adv ▷ **'fieriness** n

Fiesole[1] (*Italian* 'fiɛːzole) n a town in central Italy, in

Tuscany near Florence: Etruscan and Roman remains. Pop: 14 085 (2001)

Fiesole² (*Italian* 'fjɛːzole) *n* **Giovanni da** (dʒo'vanni da) the monastic name of (Fra) **Angelico**

fiesta (fɪ'ɛstə; *Spanish* 'fjesta) *n* (esp in Spain and Latin America) **1** a religious festival or celebration, esp on a saint's day **2** a holiday or carnival [Spanish, from Latin *festa*, plural of *festum* festival; see FEAST]

FIFA ('fiːfə) *n acronym for* Fédération Internationale de Football Association [from French]

fife (faɪf) *n* **1** a small high-pitched flute similar to the piccolo and usually having no keys, used esp in military bands ▷ *vb* **2** to play (music) on a fife [c16: from Old High German *pfifa*; see PIPE¹] > 'fifer *n*

Fife¹ (faɪf) *n* a council area and historical county of E central Scotland, bordering on the North Sea between the Firths of Tay and Forth: coastal lowlands in the north and east, with several ranges of hills; mainly agricultural. Administrative centre: Glenrothes. Pop: 352 040 (2003 est). Area: 1323 sq km (511 sq miles)

Fife² (faɪf) *n* **Duncan**. See **Phyfe**

FIFO ('faɪfəʊ) *n acronym for* first in, first out (as an accounting principle in costing stock). See **LIFO**

fifteen ('fɪf'tiːn) *n* **1** the cardinal number that is the sum of ten and five **2** a numeral, 15, XV, etc, representing this number **3** something represented by, representing, or consisting of 15 units **4** a rugby football team ▷ *determiner* **5 a** amounting to fifteen: *fifteen jokes* **b** (*as pronoun*): *fifteen of us danced* [Old English *fiftēne*] > 'fifteenth *adj, n*

fifth (fɪfθ) *adj* (*usually prenominal*) **1 a** coming after the fourth in order, position, time, etc Often written: 5th **b** (*as noun*): *he came on the fifth* ▷ *n* **2 a** one of five equal or nearly equal parts of an object, quantity, measurement, etc **b** (*as modifier*): *a fifth part* **3** the fraction equal to one divided by five (1/5) **4** *music* **a** the interval between one note and another five notes away from it counting inclusively along the diatonic scale **b** one of two notes constituting such an interval in relation to the other ▷ *adv* **5** Also: **fifthly** after the fourth person, position, event, etc ▷ *sentence connector* **6** Also called: **fifthly** as the fifth point: linking what follows with the previous statements, as in a speech or argument [Old English *fifta*]

fifth column *n* **1** (originally) a group of Falangist sympathizers in Madrid during the Spanish Civil War who were prepared to join the four columns of insurgents marching on the city **2** any group of hostile or subversive infiltrators; an enemy in one's midst > **fifth columnist** *n*

fifth wheel *n* **1** a spare wheel for a four-wheeled vehicle **2** a superfluous or unnecessary person or thing

fifty ('fɪftɪ) *n, pl* -ties **1** the cardinal number that is the product of ten and five **2** a numeral, 50, L, etc, representing this number **3** something represented by, representing, or consisting of 50 units ▷ *determiner* **4 a** amounting to fifty: *fifty people* **b** (*as pronoun*): *fifty should be sufficient* [Old English *fiftig*] > 'fiftieth *adj, n*

fifty-fifty *adj, adv informal* shared or sharing equally; in equal parts

fig (fɪg) *n* **1** any moraceous tree or shrub of the tropical and subtropical genus *Ficus*, in which the flowers are borne inside a pear-shaped receptacle **2** the fruit of any of these trees, esp of *F. carica*, which develops from the receptacle and has sweet flesh containing numerous seedlike structures **3** (*used with a negative*) something of negligible value; jot: *I don't care a fig for your opinion* [c13: from Old French *figue*, from Old Provençal *figa*, from Latin *ficus* fig tree]

fig. *abbreviation* **1** figurative(ly) **2** figure

fight (faɪt) *vb* **fights, fighting, fought 1** to oppose or struggle against (an enemy) in battle **2** to oppose or struggle against (a person, thing, cause, etc) in any manner **3** (*tr*) to engage in or carry on (a battle, contest, etc) **4** (when *intr* often foll by *for*) to uphold or maintain (a cause, ideal, etc) by fighting or struggling: *to fight for freedom* **5** (*tr*) to make or achieve (a way) by fighting **6** to engage (another or others) in combat **7 fight it out** to contend or struggle until a decisive result is obtained

8 fight shy of to keep aloof from ▷ *n* **9** a battle, struggle, or physical combat **10** a quarrel, dispute, or contest **11** resistance (esp in the phrase **to put up a fight**) **12** a boxing match ▷ See also **fight off** [Old English *feohtan*; related to Old Frisian *fiuchta*, Old Saxon, Old High German *fehtan* to fight]

fighter ('faɪtə) *n* **1** a person who fights, esp a professional boxer **2** a person who has determination **3** *military* an armed aircraft designed for destroying other aircraft

fighter-bomber *n* a high-performance aircraft that combines the roles of fighter and bomber

fighting chance *n* a slight chance of success dependent on a struggle

fighting cock *n* **1** another name for **gamecock 2** a pugnacious person

fighting fish *n* any of various labyrinth fishes of the genus *Betta*, esp the Siamese fighting fish

fighting top *n* one of the gun platforms on the lower masts of sailing men-of-war, used in attacking the crew of an enemy ship with swivel guns and muskets

fight off *vb* (*tr, adverb*) **1** to repulse; repel **2** to struggle to avoid or repress: *to fight off a cold*

fight-or-flight *n* (*modifier*) involving or relating to an involuntary response to stress in which the hormone adrenaline is secreted into the blood in readiness for physical action, such as fighting or running away

figjam ('fɪg,dʒæm) *n Austral slang* a very conceited person [c20: from *f*(uck) *I*(*'m*) *g*(ood) *j*(ust) *a*(sk) *m*(*e*)]

fig leaf *n* **1** a leaf from a fig tree **2** a representation of a leaf, usually a vine leaf rather than an actual fig leaf, used in painting or sculpture to cover the genitals of nude figures **3** a device intended to conceal something regarded as shameful or indecent

figment ('fɪgmənt) *n* a fantastic notion, invention, or fabrication: *a figment of the imagination* [c15: from Late Latin *figmentum* a fiction, from Latin *fingere* to shape]

figurant ('fɪgjʊrənt) *n* a ballet dancer who does group work but no solo roles [c18: from French, from *figurer* to represent, appear, FIGURE] > figurante (,fɪgjʊ'rɒnt) *fem n*

figuration (,fɪgə'reɪʃən) *n* **1** *music* **a** the employment of characteristic patterns of notes, esp in variations on a theme **b** decoration or florid ornamentation in general **2** the act or an instance of representing figuratively, as by means of allegory or emblem **3** a figurative or emblematic representation **4** the act of decorating with a design

figurative ('fɪgərətɪv) *adj* **1** of the nature of, resembling, or involving a figure of speech; not literal; metaphorical **2** using or filled with figures of speech **3** representing by means of an emblem, likeness, figure, etc > 'figuratively *adv* > 'figurativeness *n*

figure ('fɪgə; *US* 'fɪgjər) *n* **1** any written symbol other than a letter, esp a whole number **2** another name for **digit** (sense 2) **3** an amount expressed numerically: *a figure of 1800 was suggested* **4** (*plural*) calculations with numbers: *he's good at figures* **5** visible shape or form; outline **6** the human form, esp as regards size or shape: *a girl with a slender figure* **7** a slim bodily shape (esp in the phrases **keep** or **lose one's figure**) **8** a character or personage, esp a prominent or notable one; personality: *a figure in politics* **9** the impression created by a person through behaviour (esp in the phrase **to cut a fine, bold,** etc, **figure**) **10 a** a person as impressed on the mind: *the figure of Napoleon* **b** (*in combination*): *father-figure* **11** a representation in painting or sculpture, esp of the human form **12** an illustration or explanatory diagram in a text **13** a representative object or symbol; emblem **14** a pattern or design, as on fabric or in wood **15** a predetermined set of movements in dancing or skating **16** *geometry* any combination of points, lines, curves, or planes. A **plane figure**, such as a circle, encloses an area; a **solid figure** such as a sphere, encloses a volume **17** *rhetoric* See **figure of speech 18** *logic* one of the four possible arrangements of the three terms in the premises of a syllogism. See **mood²** (sense 2) **19** *music* **a** a numeral written above or below a note in a part. See **figured bass, thorough bass b** a characteristic short pattern of notes ▷ *vb* **20** (when *tr*, often foll by *up*) to calculate or compute (sums, amounts, etc) **21** (*tr; usually takes a clause as object*) *informal, chiefly US, Canadian & NZ* to think or conclude; consider **22** (*tr*) to represent by a diagram or illustration **23** (*tr*) to pattern or mark with a design **24** (*tr*) to depict or portray in a painting, etc **25** (*tr*) *rhetoric* to express by means of a figure of speech **26** (*tr*) to imagine **27** (*tr*) *music* **a** to decorate (a melody line or part) with ornamentation **b** to provide figures above or below (a bass part) as an indication of the accompanying harmonies required. See **figured bass, thorough bass 28** (*intr; usually foll by in*) to be included: *his name figures in the article* **29** (*intr*) *informal* to accord with expectation; be logical: *it figures that he wouldn't come* **30** go figure *informal* an expression of surprise, astonishment, wonder, etc ▷ See also **figure out** [c13: from Latin *figūra* a shape, from *fingere* to mould] > 'figurer *n*

figured ('fɪgəd) *adj* **1** depicted as a figure in graphic art, painting, or sculpture **2** decorated or patterned with a design **3** having a form **4** *music* **a** ornamental **b** (of a bass part) provided with numerals indicating accompanying harmonies

figured bass (beɪs) *n* a shorthand method of indicating a thorough-bass part in which each bass note is accompanied by figures indicating the intervals to be played in the chord above it in the realization

figurehead ('fɪgə,hɛd) *n* **1** a person nominally having a prominent position, but no real authority **2** a carved bust or full-length figure at the upper end of the stems of some sailing vessels

figure of speech *n* an expression of language, such as simile, metaphor, or personification, by which the usual or literal meaning of a word is not employed

figure out *vb* (*tr, adverb; may take a clause as object*) *informal* **1** to calculate or reckon **2** to understand

figure skating *n* **1** ice skating in which the skater traces outlines of selected patterns **2** the whole art of skating, as distinct from skating at speed > **figure skater** *n*

figurine (,fɪgə'riːn) *n* a small carved or moulded figure; statuette [c19: from French, from Italian *figurina* a little FIGURE]

figwort ('fɪg,wɜːt) *n* any scrophulariaceous plant of the N temperate genus *Scrophularia*, having square stems and small brown or greenish flowers

Fiji ('fiːdʒiː, fiː'dʒiː) *n* **1** an independent republic, consisting of 844 islands (chiefly Viti Levu and Vanua Levu) in the SW Pacific: a British colony (1874–1970); a member of the Commonwealth (1970–87 and from 1997); the large islands are of volcanic origin, surrounded by coral reefs; smaller ones are of coral. Official language: English. Religion: Christian and Hindu. Currency: dollar. Capital: Suva. Pop: 847 000 (2004 est). Area: 18 272 sq km (7055 sq miles) ▷ *n, adj* **2** another word for **Fijian**

Fijian (fiː'dʒiːən) *n* **1** a member of the indigenous people of mixed Melanesian and Polynesian descent inhabiting Fiji **2** the language of this people, belonging to the Malayo-Polynesian family ▷ *adj* **3** of, relating to, or characteristic of Fiji or its inhabitants ▷ Also called: Fiji

filagree ('fɪlə,griː) *n, adj, vb* a less common variant of **filigree**

filament ('fɪləmənt) *n* **1** the thin wire, usually tungsten, inside a light bulb that emits light when heated to incandescence by an electric current **2** *electronics* a high-resistance wire or ribbon, forming the cathode in some valves **3** a single strand of a natural or synthetic fibre; fibril **4** *botany* **a** the stalk of a stamen **b** any of the long slender chains of cells into which some algae and fungi are divided **5** *ornithol* the barb of a down feather **6** *anatomy* any slender structure or part, such as the tail of a spermatozoon; filum **7** *astronomy* **a** a long structure of relatively cool material in the solar corona **b** a long large-scale cluster of galaxies [c16: from New Latin *filamentum*, from Medieval Latin *filāre* to spin, from Latin *filum* thread] > filamentary (,fɪlə'mɛntərɪ, -trɪ) *or* ,fila'mentous *adj*

filaria (fɪ'lɛərɪə) *n, pl* -iae (-ɪ,iː) any parasitic nematode worm of the family *Filariidae*, living in the blood and tissues of vertebrates and transmitted by insects: the cause of filariasis [c19: New Latin (former name of genus), from Latin *filum* thread] > fi'larial *or* fi'larian *adj*

filariasis (,fɪlə'raɪəsɪs, fɪ,lɛərɪ'eɪsɪs) *n* a disease common in tropical and subtropical countries resulting from infestation of the lymphatic system with the nematode worms *Wuchereria bancrofti* or *Brugia malayi*, transmitted by mosquitoes: characterized by inflammation and obstruction of the lymphatic vessels. See also **elephantiasis** [c19: from New Latin; see FILARIA]

filbert ('fɪlbət) *n* **1** any of several N temperate shrubs of the genus *Corylus*, esp *C. maxima*, that have edible rounded brown nuts: family *Corylaceae* **2** Also called: hazelnut, cobnut the nut of any of these shrubs [c14: named after St *Philbert*, 7th-century Frankish abbot, because the nuts are ripe around his feast day, Aug 22]

filch (fɪltʃ) *vb* (*tr*) to steal or take surreptitiously in small amounts; pilfer [c16 *filchen* to steal, attack, perhaps from Old English *gefylce* band of men] > 'filcher *n*

file¹ (faɪl) *n* **1** a folder, box, etc, used to keep documents or other items in order **2** the documents, etc, kept in this way **3** documents or information about a specific subject, person, etc **4** an orderly line or row **5** a line of people in marching formation, one behind another. See **rank¹** (sense 6) **6** any of the eight vertical rows of squares on a chessboard **7** *computing* a named collection of information, in the form of text, programs, graphics, etc, held on a permanent storage device such as a magnetic disk **8** *obsolete* a list or catalogue **9** on file recorded or catalogued for reference, as in a file ▷ *vb* **10** to place (a document, letter, etc) in a file **11** (*tr*) to put on record, esp to place (a legal document) on public or official record; register **12** (*tr*) to bring (a suit, esp a divorce suit) in a court of law **13** (*tr*) to submit (copy) to a newspaper or news agency **14** (*intr*) to march or walk in a file or files: *the ants filed down the hill* [c16 (in the sense: string on which documents are hung): from Old French *filer*, from Medieval Latin *filāre*; see FILAMENT] > 'filer *n*

file² (faɪl) *n* **1** a hand tool consisting essentially of a steel blade with small cutting teeth on some or all of its faces. It is used for shaping or smoothing metal, wood, etc ▷ *vb* **2** (*tr*) to shape or smooth (a surface) with a file [Old English *fīl*; related to Old Saxon *fīla*, Old High German *fīhala* file, Greek *pikros* bitter, sharp] > 'filer *n*

filefish ('faɪl,fɪʃ) *n, pl* -fish *or* -fishes any tropical triggerfish, such as *Alutera scripta*, having a narrow compressed body and a very long dorsal spine [c18: referring to its file-like scales]

filename ('faɪl,neɪm) *n* an arrangement of characters that enables a computer system to permit the user to have access to a particular file

file server *n computing* the central unit of a local area network that controls its operation and provides access to separately stored data files

file sharing *n* the practice of sharing computer data or space on a network

filet ('fɪlɪt, 'fɪleɪ; *French* filɛ) *n* a variant spelling of **fillet** (sense 1–3) [c20: from French: net, from Old Provençal *filat*, from *fil* thread, from Latin *fīlum*]

filet mignon ('fɪleɪ 'miːnjɒn) *n* a small tender boneless cut of beef from the inside of the loin [from French, literally: dainty fillet]

filial ('fɪljəl) *adj* **1** of, resembling, or suitable to a son or daughter: *filial affection* **2** *genetics* designating any of the generations following the parental generation; F_1 indicates the first filial generation, F_2 the second, etc. Abbreviation: F [c15: from Late Latin *fīliālis*, from Latin *fīlius* son] > 'filially *adv*

filibeg, fillibeg *or* **philibeg** ('fɪlɪ,bɛg) *n* the kilt worn by Scottish Highlanders [c18: from Scottish Gaelic *fèileadhbeag*, from *fèileadh* kilt + *beag* small]

filibuster ('fɪlɪ,bʌstə) *n* **1** the process or an instance of obstructing legislation by means of long speeches and other delaying tactics **2** Also called: filibusterer **a** legislator who engages in such obstruction **3** a buccaneer, freebooter, or irregular military adventurer, esp a revolutionary in a foreign country ▷ *vb* **4** to obstruct (legislation) with delaying tactics **5** (*intr*) to engage in unlawful and private military action [c16: from Spanish *filibustero*, from French *flibustier* probably from Dutch *vrijbuiter* pirate, literally: one plundering freely; see FREEBOOTER] > 'fili,busterer *n*

filigree (ˈfɪlɪˌgriː), **filagree** or **fillagree** n **1** delicate ornamental work of twisted gold, silver, or other wire **2** any fanciful delicate ornamentation ▷ adj **3** made of or as if with filigree ▷ vb **-grees, -greeing, -greed 4** (tr) to decorate with or as if with filigree [C17: from earlier *filigreen*, from French *filigrane*, from Latin *fīlum* thread + *grānum* GRAIN] > **ˈfiliˌgreed** adj

filings (ˈfaɪlɪŋz) pl n shavings or particles removed by a file: *iron filings*

Filipino (ˌfɪlɪˈpiːnəʊ) n **1** pl **-nos** a native or inhabitant of the Philippines **2** another name for **Tagalog** ▷ adj **3** of or relating to the Philippines or their inhabitants

fill (fɪl) vb (mainly tr; often foll by up) **1** (also intr) to make or become full: *to fill up a bottle; the bath fills in two minutes* **2** to occupy the whole of: *the party filled two floors of the house* **3** to plug (a gap, crevice, cavity, etc) **4** to meet (a requirement or need) satisfactorily **5** to cover (a page or blank space) with writing, drawing, etc **6** to hold and perform the duties of (an office or position) **7** to appoint or elect an occupant to (an office or position) **8** *building trades* to build up (ground) with fill **9** (also intr) to swell or cause to swell with wind, as in manoeuvring the sails of a sailing vessel **10** to increase the bulk of by adding an inferior substance **11** *poker* to complete (a full house, etc) by drawing the cards needed **12** *chiefly US & Canadian* to put together the necessary materials for (a prescription or order) **13** fill the bill *informal* to serve or perform adequately ▷ n **14** material such as gravel, stones, etc, used to bring an area of ground up to a required level **15** one's fill the quantity needed to satisfy one: *to eat your fill* ▷ See also **fill in, fill out, fill up** [Old English *fyllan*; related to Old Frisian *fella*, Old Norse *fylla*, Gothic *fulljan*, Old High German *fullen*; see FULL[1], FULFIL]

filler (ˈfɪlə) n **1** a person or thing that fills **2** an object or substance used to add weight or size to something or to fill in a gap **3** a paste, used for filling in cracks, holes, etc, in a surface before painting **4** *architect* a small joist inserted between and supported by two beams **5 a** the inner portion of a cigar **b** the cut tobacco for making cigarettes **6** *journalism* articles, photographs, etc, to fill space between more important articles in the layout of a newspaper or magazine **7** *informal* something, such as a musical selection, to fill time in a broadcast or stage presentation **8** a small radio or television transmitter used to fill a gap in coverage

fillet (ˈfɪlɪt) n **1 a** Also called: **fillet steak** a strip of boneless meat, esp the undercut of a sirloin of beef **b** the boned side of a fish **c** the white meat of breast and wing of a chicken **2** a narrow strip of any material **3** a thin strip of ribbon, lace, etc, worn in the hair or around the neck **4** a narrow flat moulding, esp one between other mouldings **5** a narrow band between two adjacent flutings on the shaft of a column **6** Also called: **fillet weld** a narrow strip of welded metal of approximately triangular cross-section used to join steel members at right angles **7** *heraldry* a horizontal division of a shield, one quarter of the depth of the chief **8** Also called: **listel, list** the top member of a cornice **9** *anatomy* a band of sensory nerve fibres in the brain connected to the thalamus **10 a** a narrow decorative line, impressed on the cover of a book **b** a wheel tool used to impress such lines **11** another name for **fairing**[1] ▷ vb **-lets, -leting, -leted** (tr) **12** to cut or prepare (meat or fish) as a fillet **13** to cut fillets from (meat or fish) **14** *anatomy* to surgically remove a bone from (part of the body) so that only soft tissue remains **15** to bind or decorate with or as if with a fillet ▷ Also (for senses 1–3): **filet** [C14: from Old French *filet*, from *fil* thread, from Latin *fīlum*]

fill in vb (adverb) **1** (tr) to complete (a form, drawing, etc) **2** (intr) to act as a substitute: *a girl is filling in while the typist is away* **3** (tr) to put material into (a hole or cavity), esp so as to make it level with a surface **4** (tr) *informal* to inform with facts or news **5** (tr) *Brit slang* to attack and injure severely ▷ n fill-in **6** a substitute **7** *US informal* a briefing to complete one's understanding

filling (ˈfɪlɪŋ) n **1** the substance or thing used to fill a space or container: *pie filling* **2** *dentistry* **a** any of various substances (metal, plastic, etc) for inserting into the prepared cavity of a tooth **b** the cavity of a tooth so filled **3** *textiles* another term for **weft** ▷ adj **4** (of food or a meal) substantial and satisfying

filling station n a place where petrol and other supplies for motorists are sold

fillip (ˈfɪlɪp) n **1** something that adds stimulation or enjoyment **2** the action of releasing a finger towards the palm with the thumb and suddenly releasing it outwards to produce a snapping sound **3** a quick blow or tap made by a finger snapped in this way ▷ vb **4** (tr) to stimulate or excite **5** (tr) to strike or project sharply with a fillip **6** (intr) to make a fillip [C15 *philippe*, of imitative origin]

Fillmore (ˈfɪlmɔː) n **Millard**. 1800–74, 13th president of the US (1850-53); a leader of the Whig Party

fill out vb (adverb) **1** to make or become fuller, thicker, or rounder: *her figure has filled out since her marriage* **2** to make more substantial: *the writers were asked to fill their stories out* **3** (tr) to complete (a form, application, etc)

fill up vb (adverb) **1** (tr) to complete (a form, application, etc) **2** to make or become completely full ▷ n fill-up **3** the act of filling something completely, esp the petrol tank of a car

filly (ˈfɪlɪ) n, pl **-lies 1** a female horse or pony under the age of four **2** *informal, rare* a spirited girl or young woman [C15: from Old Norse *fylja*; related to Old High German *fulīhha*; see FOAL]

film (fɪlm) n **1 a** a sequence of images of moving objects photographed by a camera and providing the optical illusion of continuous movement when projected onto a screen **b** a form of entertainment, information, etc, composed of such a sequence of images and shown in a cinema, etc **c** (as modifier): *film techniques* **2** a thin flexible strip of cellulose coated with a photographic emulsion, used to make negatives and transparencies **3** a thin coating or layer **4** a thin sheet of any material, as of plastic for packaging **5** a fine haze, mist, or blur **6** a gauzy web of filaments or fine threads **7** *pathol* an abnormally opaque tissue, such as the cornea in some eye diseases ▷ vb **8 a** to photograph with a cine camera **b** to make a film of (a screenplay, event, etc) **9** (often foll by over) to cover or become covered or coated with a film [Old English *filmen* membrane; related to Old Frisian *filmene*, Greek *pelma* sole of the foot; see FELL[4]]

filmi (ˈfɪlmɪ) adj *Hinglish* **1** of or relating to the Indian film industry or Indian films **2** containing the high drama typical of Indian films [Hindi]

filmic (ˈfɪlmɪk) adj **1** of or relating to films or the cinema **2** having characteristics that are suggestive of films or the cinema > **ˈfilmically** adv

film-maker n a person who directs or produces films for the cinema or television

film noir (nwɑː) n a gangster thriller, made esp in the 1940s in Hollywood characterized by contrasty lighting and often somewhat impenetrable plots [C20: French, literally: black film]

filmography (fɪlˈmɒgrəfɪ) n **1** a list of the films made by a particular director, actor, etc **2** any writing that deals with films or the cinema

filmset (ˈfɪlmˌsɛt) vb **-sets, -setting, -set** (tr) to set (type matter) by filmsetting > **ˈfilmˌsetter** n

filmsetting (ˈfɪlmˌsɛtɪŋ) n *printing* typesetting by exposing type characters onto photographic film from which printing plates are made

film speed n **1** the sensitivity to light of a photographic film, specified in terms of the film's ISO rating **2** the rate at which the film passes through a motion picture camera or projector

film strip n a strip of film composed of different images projected separately as slides

filmy (ˈfɪlmɪ) adj **filmier, filmiest 1** composed of or resembling film; transparent or gauzy **2** covered with or as if with a film; hazy; blurred > **ˈfilmily** adv > **ˈfilminess** n

filo (ˈfiːləʊ) n a type of Greek flaky pastry in very thin sheets [C20: Modern Greek *phullon* leaf]

Filofax (ˈfaɪləʊˌfæks) n *trademark* a type of loose-leaf ring binder with sets of different-coloured paper, used as a portable personal filing system, including appointments, addresses, etc

filter ('fɪltə) *n* **1** a porous substance, such as paper or sand, that allows fluid to pass but retains suspended solid particles: used to clean fluids or collect solid particles **2** any device containing such a porous substance for separating suspensions from fluids **3** any of various porous substances built into the mouth end of a cigarette or cigar for absorbing impurities such as tar **4** any electronic, optical, or acoustic device that blocks signals or radiations of certain frequencies while allowing others to pass. See also **band-pass filter 5** any transparent disc of gelatine or glass used to eliminate or reduce the intensity of given frequencies from the light leaving a lamp, entering a camera, etc **6** *Brit* a traffic signal at a road junction consisting of a green arrow which when illuminated permits vehicles to turn either left or right when the main signals are red ▷ *vb* **7** (often foll by *out*) to remove or separate (suspended particles, wavelengths of radiation, etc) from (a liquid, gas, radiation, etc) by the action of a filter **8** (*tr*) to obtain by filtering **9** (*intr* foll by *through*) to pass (through a filter or something like a filter): *dust filtered through the screen* **10** (*intr*) to flow slowly; trickle [C16 *filtre* from Medieval Latin *filtrum* piece of felt used as a filter, of Germanic origin; see FELT²]

filterable ('fɪltərəb³l) *or* **filtrable** ('fɪltrəb³l) *adj* **1** capable of being filtered **2** (of most viruses and certain bacteria) capable of passing through the pores of a fine filter

filter bed *n* a layer of sand or gravel in a tank or reservoir through which a liquid is passed so as to purify it

filter feeding *n* *zoology* a method of feeding occurring in some aquatic animals, such as planktonic invertebrates and whalebone whales, in which minute food particles are filtered from the surrounding water > filter feeder *n*

filter out *or* **filter through** *vb* (*intr, adverb*) to become known gradually; leak

filter paper *n* a porous paper used for filtering liquids

filter tip *n* **1** an attachment to the mouth end of a cigarette for trapping impurities such as tar during smoking. It consists of any of various dense porous substances, such as cotton **2** a cigarette having such an attachment > 'filter-,tipped *adj*

filth (fɪlθ) *n* **1** foul or disgusting dirt; refuse **2** extreme physical or moral uncleanliness; pollution **3** vulgarity or obscenity, as in language **4** the filth *derogatory, slang* the police [Old English *fȳlth*; related to Old Saxon, Old High German *fūlitha*; see FOUL, DEFILE]

filthy ('fɪlθɪ) *adj* filthier, filthiest **1** characterized by or full of filth; very dirty or obscene **2** offensive or vicious: *that was a filthy trick to play* **3** *informal, chiefly Brit* extremely unpleasant: *filthy weather* ▷ *adv* **4** extremely; disgustingly: *filthy rich* > 'filthily *adv* > 'filthiness *n*

filtrate ('fɪltreɪt) *n* **1** a liquid or gas that has been filtered ▷ *vb* **2** another name for **filter** (sense 7) [C17: from Medieval Latin *filtrāre* to FILTER]

filtration (fɪl'treɪʃən) *n* the act or process of filtering

fimbria ('fɪmbrɪə) *n, pl* -briae (-brɪ,iː) *anatomy* a fringe or fringelike margin or border, esp at the opening of the Fallopian tubes [C18: from Late Latin, from Latin *fimbriae* threads, shreds] > 'fimbrial *adj*

fin (fɪn) *n* **1** any of the firm appendages that are the organs of locomotion and balance in fishes and some other aquatic animals. Most fishes have paired and unpaired fins, the former corresponding to the limbs of higher vertebrates **2** a part or appendage that resembles a fin **3 a** *Brit* a vertical surface to which the rudder is attached, usually placed at the rear of an aeroplane to give stability about the vertical axis **b** a tail surface fixed to a rocket or missile to give stability **4** *nautical* a fixed or adjustable blade projecting under water from the hull of a vessel to give it stability or control **5** a projecting rib to dissipate heat from the surface of an engine cylinder, motor casing, or radiator ▷ *vb* fins, finning, finned **6** (*tr*) to provide with fins [Old English *finn*; related to Middle Dutch *vinne*, Old Swedish *fina*, Latin *pinna* wing] > 'finless *adj*

Fin *abbreviation* **1** Finland **2** Finnish

fin. *abbreviation* **1** finance **2** financial

finable *or* **fineable** ('faɪnəb³l) *adj* liable to a fine

> 'finableness *or* 'fineableness *n*

finagle (fɪ'neɪg³l) *vb informal* **1** (*tr*) to get or achieve by trickery, craftiness, or persuasion; wangle **2** to use trickery or craftiness on (a person) [C20: probably changed from dialect *fainaigue*] > fi'nagler *n*

final ('faɪn³l) *adj* **1** of or occurring at the end; concluding; ultimate; last **2** having no possibility for further discussion, action, or change; conclusive; decisive: *a final decree of judgment* **3** relating to or constituting an end or purpose: *a final clause may be introduced by "in order to"* **4** *music* another word for **perfect** (sense 9b) ▷ *n* **5** a terminal or last thing; end **6** a deciding contest between the winners of previous rounds in a competition ▷ See also **finals** [C14: from Latin *fīnālis*, from *fīnis* limit, boundary]

finale (fɪ'nɑːlɪ) *n* **1** the concluding part of any performance or presentation **2** the closing section or movement of a musical composition [C18: from Italian, n use of adj *finale*, from Latin *fīnālis* FINAL]

finalism ('faɪnə,lɪzəm) *n* *philosophy* the doctrine that final causes determine the course of all events

finalist ('faɪnəlɪst) *n* a contestant who has reached the last and decisive stage of a sports or other competition

finality (faɪ'nælɪtɪ) *n, pl* -ties **1** the condition or quality of being final or settled; conclusiveness: *the finality of death* **2** a final or conclusive act

finalize *or* **finalise** ('faɪnə,laɪz) *vb* **1** (*tr*) to put into final form; settle: *to finalize plans for the merger* **2** (*intr*) to complete arrangements or negotiations; reach agreement on a transaction > ,finali'zation *or* ,finali'sation *n*

finally ('faɪnəlɪ) *adv* **1** at the end or final point; lastly ▷ *sentence connector* **2** in the end; lastly: *finally, he put his tie on* **3** as the last or final point: linking what follows with the previous statements, as in a speech or argument

finals ('faɪn³lz) *pl n* **1** the deciding part or parts of a sports or other competition **2** *education* the last examination series in an academic or professional course

final-salary *adj* another name for **defined-benefit**

finance (fɪ'næns, 'faɪnæns) *n* **1** the system of money, credit, etc, esp with respect to government revenues and expenditures **2** funds or the provision of funds **3** (*plural*) funds; financial condition ▷ *vb* **4** (*tr*) to provide or obtain funds, capital, or credit for [C14: from Old French, from *finer* to end, settle by payment]

finance company *or* **finance house** *n* an enterprise engaged in the loan of money against collateral or speculatively to manufacturers and retailers, esp one specializing in the financing of hire-purchase contracts

financial (fɪ'nænʃəl, faɪ-) *adj* **1** of or relating to finance or finances **2** of or relating to persons who manage money, capital, or credit **3** *Austral & NZ informal* having money; in funds **4** *Austral & NZ* (of a club member) fully paid-up > fi'nancially *adv*

financial futures *pl n* futures in a stock-exchange index, currency exchange rate, or interest rate enabling banks, building societies, brokers, and speculators to hedge their involvement in these markets

Financial Ombudsman *n* any of five British ombudsmen: the **Banking Ombudsman**, set up in 1986 to investigate complaints from bank customers; the **Building Society Ombudsman**, set up in 1987 to investigate complaints from building society customers; the **Insurance Ombudsman**, set up in 1981 to investigate complaints by policyholders (since 1988 this ombudsman has also operated a **Unit Trust Ombudsman** scheme); the **Investment Ombudsman** set up in 1989 to investigate complaints by investors (the **Personal Investment Authority Ombudsman** is responsible for investigating complaints by personal investors); and the **Pensions Ombudsman**, set up in 1993 to investigate complaints regarding pension schemes

Financial Times Stock Exchange 100 Index *n* an index of share prices produced by the *Financial Times* based on an average of 100 securities and giving the best indication of daily movements. Abbreviation: FTSE 100 Index Also called: *informal* Footsie

financial year *n* *Brit* **1** any annual period at the end of which a firm's accounts are made up **2** the annual period ending April 5, over which Budget estimates are made by the British Government and which functions as the income-tax year ▷ US and Canadian equivalent: **fiscal year**

financier (fɪˈnænsɪə, faɪ-) *n* a person who is engaged or skilled in large-scale financial operations

financing gap *n* the difference between a country's requirements for foreign exchange to finance its debts and imports and its income from overseas

finback (ˈfɪnˌbæk) *n* another name for **rorqual**

finch (fɪntʃ) *n* any songbird of the family *Fringillidae*, having a short stout bill for feeding on seeds and, in most species, a bright plumage in the male. Common examples are the goldfinch, bullfinch, chaffinch, siskin, and canary [Old English *finc*; related to Old High German *finko*, Middle Dutch *vinker*, Greek *spingos*]

Finchley (ˈfɪntʃlɪ) *n* a residential district of N London, part of the Greater London borough of Barnet from 1965

find (faɪnd) *vb* **finds, finding, found** (faʊnd) (*mainly tr*) **1** to meet with or encounter by chance **2** to discover or obtain, esp by search or effort: *to find happiness* **3** (*may take a clause as object*) to become aware of; realize: *he found that nobody knew* **4** (*may take a clause as object*) to regard as being; consider: *I find this wine a little sour* **5** to look for and point out (something to be criticized): *to find fault* **6** (*also intr*) *law* to determine an issue after judicial inquiry and pronounce a verdict (upon): *the court found the accused guilty* **7** to regain (something lost or not functioning): *to find one's tongue* **8** to reach (a target): *the bullet found its mark* **9** to provide, esp with difficulty: *we'll find room for you too* **10** to be able to pay: *I can't find that amount of money* **11** find oneself to realize and accept one's real character; discover one's true vocation **12** find one's feet to become capable or confident, as in a new job ▷ *n* **13** a person, thing, etc, that is found, esp a valuable or fortunate discovery [Old English *findan*; related to Old Norse *finna*, Gothic *finthan*, Old High German *fintan* to find]
> ˈfindable *adj*

finder (ˈfaɪndə) *n* **1** a person or thing that finds **2** *physics* a small low-power wide-angle telescope fitted to a more powerful larger telescope, used to locate celestial objects to be studied by the larger instrument **3** *photog* short for **viewfinder** **4** finders keepers *informal* whoever finds something has the right to keep it

fin de siècle *French* (fɛ̃ də sjɛklə) *n* **1** the end of the 19th century, when traditional social, moral, and artistic values were in transition ▷ *adj* **fin-de-siècle 2** of or relating to the close of the 19th century **3** decadent, esp in artistic tastes

finding (ˈfaɪndɪŋ) *n* **1** a thing that is found or discovered **2** *law* the conclusion reached after a judicial inquiry; verdict **3** (*plural*) *US* the tools and equipment of an artisan

find out *vb* (*adverb*) **1** to gain knowledge of (something); learn: *he found out what he wanted* **2** to detect the crime, deception, etc, of (someone)

fine¹ (faɪn) *adj* **1** excellent or choice in quality; very good of its kind: *a fine speech* **2** superior in skill, ability, or accomplishment: *a fine violinist* **3** (of weather) clear and dry **4** enjoyable or satisfying: *a fine time* **5** (*postpositive*) *informal* quite well; in satisfactory health: *I feel fine* **6** satisfactory; acceptable: *that's fine by me* **7** of delicate composition or careful workmanship: *fine crystal* **8** (of precious metals) pure or having a high or specified degree of purity: *fine silver; gold 98 per cent fine* **9** subtle in perception; discriminating: *a fine eye for antique brasses* **10** abstruse or subtle: *a fine point in argument* **11** very thin or slender: *fine hair* **12** very small: *fine dust; fine print* **13** (of edges, blades, etc) sharp; keen **14** ornate, showy, or smart **15** good-looking; handsome: *a fine young woman* **16** polished, elegant, or refined: *a fine gentleman* **17** morally upright and commendable: *a fine man* **18** *cricket* (of a fielding position) oblique to and behind the wicket: *fine leg* **19** (*prenominal*) *informal* disappointing or terrible: *a fine mess* ▷ *adv* **20** *informal* quite well; all right: *that suits me fine* **21** a nonstandard word for **finely** **22** *billiards, snooker* (of a stroke on the cue ball) so as to merely brush the object ball **23** cut it fine to allow little margin of time,

space, etc ▷ *vb* **24** to make or become finer; refine **25** (often foll by *down* or *away*) to make or become smaller **26** (*tr*) to clarify (wine, etc) by adding finings **27** (*tr*) *billiards, snooker* to hit (a cue ball) fine **28** (*intr*; foll by *up*) *Austral & NZ informal* (of the weather) to become fine [C13: from Old French *fin*, from Latin *finis* end, boundary, as in *finis honōrum* the highest degree of honour] > ˈfineness *n*

fine² (faɪn) *n* **1** a certain amount of money exacted as a penalty: *a parking fine* **2** a payment made by a tenant at the start of his tenancy to reduce his subsequent rent; premium **3** *feudal law* a sum of money paid by a man to his lord, esp for the privilege of transferring his land to another 1833 **4** a method of transferring land in England by bringing a fictitious law suit: abolished 1833 **5** in fine **a** in short; briefly **b** in conclusion; finally ▷ *vb* **6** (*tr*) to impose a fine on [C12 (in the sense: conclusion, settlement): from Old French *fin*; see **FINE¹**]

fine³ (ˈfiːneɪ) *n music* **1** the point at which a piece is to end, usually after a *da capo* or *dal segno* **2** an ending or finale [Italian, from Latin *finis* end]

fine⁴ *French* (fin) *n* brandy of ordinary quality [literally: fine]

fine art *n* **1** art produced chiefly for its aesthetic value, as opposed to applied art **2** Also called: **beaux arts** (*often plural*) any of the fields in which such art is produced, such as painting, sculpture, and engraving

fine-draw *vb* **-draws, -drawing, -drew, -drawn** (*tr*) to sew together so finely that the join is scarcely noticeable

fine-drawn *adj* **1** (of arguments, distinctions, etc) precise or subtle **2** (of wire) drawn out until very fine; attenuated

fine-grain *adj photog* having or producing an image with grain of inconspicuous size: *a fine-grain image; a fine-grain developer*

fine-grained *adj* **1** (of wood, leather, etc) having a fine smooth even grain **2** detailed, in-depth, or involving fine detail

fine leg *n cricket* **a** a fielding position between long leg and square leg **b** a fielder in this position

finely (ˈfaɪnlɪ) *adv* **1** into small pieces; minutely **2** precisely or subtly **3** splendidly or delicately

fine print *n* matter set in small type, as in a contract, esp considered as containing unfavourable conditions that the signer might overlook. Also called: **small print**

finery¹ (ˈfaɪnərɪ) *n* elaborate or showy decoration, esp clothing and jewellery

finery² (ˈfaɪnərɪ) *n, pl* **-eries** a hearth for converting cast iron into wrought iron [C17: from Old French *finerie*, from *finer* to refine; see **FINE¹**]

fines herbes (*French* finz ɛrb) *pl n* a mixture of finely chopped herbs, used to flavour omelettes, salads, etc

finespun (ˈfaɪnˈspʌn) *adj* **1** spun or drawn out to a fine thread **2** excessively subtle or refined; not practical

finesse (fɪˈnɛs) *n* **1** elegant skill in style or performance **2** subtlety and tact in handling difficult situations **3** *bridge, whist* an attempt to win a trick when opponents hold a high card in the suit led by playing a lower card, hoping the opponent who has already played holds the missing card **4** a trick, artifice, or strategy ▷ *vb* **5** to manage or bring about with finesse **6** to play (a card) as a finesse [C15: from Old French, from *fin* fine, delicate; see **FINE¹**]

fine-tooth comb *or* **fine-toothed comb** *n* **1** a comb with fine teeth set closely together **2** go over with a fine-tooth comb, go over with a fine-toothed comb, go through with a fine-tooth comb *or* go through with a fine-toothed comb to examine very thoroughly

fine-tune *vb* (*tr*) to make fine adjustments to (something) in order to obtain optimum performance

finfoot (ˈfɪnˌfʊt) *n, pl* **-foots** any aquatic bird of the tropical and subtropical family *Heliornithidae*, having broadly lobed toes, a long slender head and neck, and pale brown plumage: order *Gruiformes* (cranes, rails etc). Also called: **sungrebe**

Fingal's Cave (ˈfɪŋɡᵊlz) *n* a cave in W Scotland, on Staffa Island in the Inner Hebrides: basaltic pillars. Length: 69 m (227 ft). Height: 36 m (117 ft)

finger (ˈfɪŋɡə) *n* **1 a** any of the digits of the hand, often excluding the thumb **b** (*as modifier*): *a finger bowl* **c** (in combination): *a fingernail*. Related adj: **digital 2** the part of a glove made to cover a finger **3** something that resembles a finger in shape or function: *a finger of land* **4** Also called: **digit** the length or width of a finger used as a unit of measurement **5** a quantity of liquid in a glass, etc, as deep as a finger is wide; **tot 6** a projecting machine part, esp one serving as an indicator, guide, or guard **7 burn one's fingers** to suffer from having meddled or been rash **8 get one's finger out** *or* **pull one's finger out** *Brit informal* to begin or speed up activity, esp after initial delay or slackness **9 have a finger in the pie** *or* **have one's finger in the pie a** to have an interest in or take part in some activity **b** to meddle or interfere **10 lay a finger on** (*usually negative*) to harm **11 lay one's finger on** *or* **put one's finger on** to indicate, identify, or locate accurately **12 not lift a finger** *or* **not raise a finger** (*foll by an infinitive*) not to make any effort (to do something) **13 let slip through one's fingers** to allow to escape; miss narrowly **14 point the finger at** to accuse or blame **15 put the finger on** *informal* **a** to inform on or identify, esp for the police **b** to choose (the victim or location of an intended crime) **16 twist around one's little finger** *or* **wrap around one's little finger** to have easy and complete control or influence over ▷ *vb* **17** (*tr*) to touch or manipulate with the fingers; handle **18** (*tr*) *informal, chiefly US* to identify as a criminal or suspect **19** (*intr*) to extend like a finger **20** to use one's fingers in playing (an instrument, such as a piano or clarinet) **21** to indicate on (a composition or part) the fingering required by a pianist, harpsichordist, etc **22** (*tr; usually passive*) to arrange the keys of (a clarinet, flute, etc) for playing in a certain way [Old English; related to Old Norse *fingr*, Gothic *figgrs*, Old High German *fingar*; see FIVE, FIST] > 'fingerless *adj*

fingerboard ('fɪŋgə,bɔːd) *n* the long strip of hard wood on a violin, guitar, or related stringed instrument upon which the strings are stopped by the fingers

finger bowl *n* a small bowl filled with water for rinsing the fingers at the table after a meal

finger buffet ('bʊfeɪ) *n* a buffet meal at which food that may be picked up with the fingers (**finger food**), such as canapés or vol-au-vents, is served

fingered ('fɪŋgəd) *adj* **1** marked or dirtied by handling **2 a** having a finger or fingers **b** (*in combination*): *nine-fingered; red-fingered* **3** (of a musical part) having numerals indicating the necessary fingering

fingering ('fɪŋgərɪŋ) *n* **1** the technique or art of using one's fingers in playing a musical instrument, esp the piano **2** the numerals in a musical part indicating this

fingerling ('fɪŋgəlɪŋ) *n* **1** a very young fish, esp the parr of salmon or trout **2** a diminutive creature or object

fingermark ('fɪŋgə,mɑːk) *n* a mark left by dirty or greasy fingers on paintwork, walls, etc

fingernail ('fɪŋgə,neɪl) *n* a thin horny translucent plate covering part of the dorsal surface of the end joint of each finger

finger painting *n* the process or art of painting with **finger paints** of starch, glycerine, and pigments, using the fingers, hand, or arm

finger post *n* a signpost showing a pointing finger or hand

fingerprint ('fɪŋgə,prɪnt) *n* **1** an impression of the pattern of ridges on the palmar surface of the end joint of each finger and thumb **2** any identifying characteristic **3** *biochem* the pattern of fragments obtained when a protein is digested by a proteolytic enzyme, usually observed following two-dimensional separation by chromatography and electrophoresis ▷ *vb* **4** (*tr*) to take an inked impression of the fingerprints of (a person) **5** to take a sample of (a person's) DNA

fingerstall ('fɪŋgə,stɔːl) *n* a protective covering for a finger. Also called: **cot, fingertip**

finger tight *adj* made as tight as possible by hand

fingertip ('fɪŋgə,tɪp) *n* **1** the end joint or tip of a finger **2** another term for **fingerstall 3 at one's fingertips** readily available and within one's mental grasp

finial ('faɪnɪəl) *n* **1** an ornament on top of a spire, gable, etc, esp in the form of a foliated fleur-de-lys **2** an ornament at the top of a piece of furniture, etc [c14:

from *finial* (adj), variant of FINAL] > 'finialed *adj*

finical ('fɪnɪk²l) *adj* another word for **finicky** > ,fini'cality *n* > 'finically *adv* > 'finicalness *n*

finicky ('fɪnɪkɪ) *or* **finicking** *adj* **1** excessively particular, as in tastes or standards; fussy **2** full of trivial detail; overelaborate [c19: from FINICAL]

finis ('fɪnɪs) *n* the end; finish: used at the end of books, films, etc [c15: from Latin]

finish ('fɪnɪʃ) *vb* (*mainly tr*) **1** to bring to an end; complete, conclude, or stop **2** (*intr; sometimes foll by up*) to be at or come to the end; use up **3** to bring to a desired or complete condition **4** to put a particular surface texture on (wood, cloth, etc) **5** (*often foll by off*) to destroy or defeat completely **6** to train (a person) in social graces and talents **7** (*intr; foll by with*) **a** to end a relationship or association **b** to stop punishing a person: *I haven't finished with you yet!* ▷ *n* **8** the final or last stage or part; end **9 a** the death, destruction, or absolute defeat of a person or one side in a conflict: *a fight to the finish* **b** the person, event, or thing that brings this about **10 a** the surface texture or appearance of wood, cloth, etc: *a rough finish* **b** a preparation, such as varnish, used to produce such a texture **11** a thing, event, etc, that completes **12** completeness and high quality of workmanship **13** refinement in social graces **14** *sport* ability to sprint at the end of a race: *he has a good finish* [c14: from Old French *finir*, from Latin *finīre* see FINE¹] > 'finisher *n*

finished ('fɪnɪʃt) *adj* **1** perfected **2** (*predicative*) at the end of a task, activity, etc: *they were finished by four* **3** (*predicative*) without further hope of success or continuation: *she was finished as a prima ballerina*

finishing school *n* a private school for girls that prepares them for society by teaching social graces and accomplishments

Finistère (,fɪnɪ'stɛə; *French* finistɛr) *n* a department of NW France, at the tip of the Breton peninsula. Capital: Quimper. Pop: 863 798 (2003 est). Area: 7029 sq km (2741 sq miles)

Finisterre (,fɪnɪ'stɛə) *n* **1 Cape Finisterre** a headland in NW Spain: the westernmost point of the Spanish mainland **2** an English name for **Finistère**

finite ('faɪnaɪt) *adj* **1** bounded in magnitude or spatial or temporal extent: *a finite difference* **2** *maths, logic* having a number of elements that is a natural number; able to be counted using the natural numbers less than some natural number **3 a** limited or restricted in nature: *human existence is finite* **b** (*as noun*): *the finite* **4** denoting any form or occurrence of a verb inflected for grammatical features such as person, number, and tense [c15: from Latin *finītus* limited, from *finīre* to limit, end] > 'finitely *adv* > 'finiteness *n*

fink (fɪŋk) *slang, chiefly US & Canadian* ▷ *n* **1 a** strikebreaker; blackleg **2** an informer, such as one working for the police; spy **3** an unpleasant, disappointing, or contemptible person ▷ *vb* **4** (*intr; often foll by on*) to inform (on someone), as to the police [c20: of uncertain origin]

Finland ('fɪnlənd) *n* **1** a republic in N Europe, on the Baltic Sea: ceded to Russia by Sweden in 1809; gained independence in 1917; Soviet invasion successfully withstood in 1939–40, with the loss of Karelia; a member of the European Union. It is generally low-lying, with about 50 000 lakes, extensive forests, and peat bogs. Official languages: Finnish and Swedish. Religion: Christian, Lutheran majority. Currency: euro. Capital: Helsinki. Pop: 5 216 000 (2004 est). Area: 337 000 sq km (130 120 sq miles). Finnish name: **Suomi 2 Gulf of Finland** an arm of the Baltic Sea between Finland, Estonia, and Russia

Finlandization *or* **Finlandisation** (,fɪnləndaɪ'zeɪʃən) *n* neutralization of a small country by a superpower, using conciliation, as the former Soviet Union did in relation to Finland

Finlay ('fɪnlɪ) *n* **Carlos Juan** ('karlos xwan). 1833–1915, Cuban physician: discovered that the mosquito was the vector of yellow fever

Finn¹ (fɪn) *n* a native, inhabitant, or citizen of Finland [Old English *Finnas* (plural); related to Old Norse *Finnr* Finn, Latin *Fennī* the Finns, Greek *Phinnoi*]

Finn² (fɪn) n known as *Finn MacCool*. (in Irish legend) chief of the Fianna, father of the heroic poet Ossian

Finn³ ('fɪn) n Neil (**Mullane**). born 1958, New Zealand singer and songwriter; lead singer with the group Crowded House (from 1985) with whom he recorded the albums *Crowded House* (1986), *Woodface* (1991), and *Time on Earth* (2007). Solo albums include *Try Whistling This* (1998)

finnan haddock ('fɪnən) or **finnan haddie** ('hædɪ) n smoked haddock [c18: *finnan* after *Findon*, a village in Scotland south of Aberdeen + HADDOCK]

Finney ('fɪnɪ) n 1 **Albert**. born 1936, British stage and film actor 2 **Tom**. born 1922, English footballer: won 76 international caps as a winger

Finnic ('fɪnɪk) n 1 one of the two branches of the Finno-Ugric family of languages, including Finnish and several languages of NE Europe. See Ugric ▷ adj 2 of or relating to this group of languages or to the Finns

Finnish ('fɪnɪʃ) adj 1 of, relating to, or characteristic of Finland, the Finns, or their language ▷ n 2 the official language of Finland, also spoken in Estonia and NW Russia, belonging to the Finno-Ugric family

Finnmark ('fɪn,mɑːk) n a county of N Norway: the largest, northernmost, and least populated county; mostly a barren plateau. Capital: Vadsø. Pop: 73 210 (2004 est). Area: 48 649 sq km (18 779 sq miles)

Finno-Ugric ('fɪnəʊ'uːgrɪk, -'juː-) or **Finno-Ugrian** n 1 a family of languages spoken in Scandinavia, Hungary, and NE Europe, including Finnish, Estonian, Hungarian, Ostyak, and Vogul: generally regarded as a subfamily of Uralic ▷ adj 2 of, relating to, speaking, or belonging to this family of languages

finny ('fɪnɪ) adj -nier, -niest 1 *poetic* relating to or containing many fishes 2 having or resembling a fin or fins

fino ('fiːnəʊ) n a very dry sherry [from Spanish: FINE¹]

Finsen (*Danish* 'fensən) n Niels Ryberg (neːls 'ryber). 1860–1904, Danish physician; founder of phototherapy: Nobel prize for physiology or medicine 1903

Finsteraarhorn (*German* ,fɪnstər'aːrhɔrn) n a mountain in S central Switzerland: highest peak in the Bernese Alps. Height: 4274 m (14 022 ft)

Finzi ('fɪnzɪ) n Gerald. 1901–56, British composer. His works include the cantata *Dies Natalis* (1940)

fiord (fjɔːd) n a variant spelling of **fjord**

fioritura (,fjɔːrɪ'tʊərə, ,fiːəri-) n, pl -ture (-'tʊəreɪ) *music* embellishment, esp ornamentation added by the performer [Italian: a blossoming]

fipple ('fɪpⁱl) n 1 a wooden plug forming a flue in the end of a pipe, as the mouthpiece of a recorder 2 a similar device in an organ pipe with a flutelike tone [c17: of unknown origin]

fipple flute n an end-blown flute provided with a fipple, such as the recorder or flageolet

fir (fɜː) n 1 any pyramidal coniferous tree of the N temperate genus *Abies*, having single needle-like leaves and erect cones: family *Pinaceae* 2 any of various other trees of the family *Pinaceae*, such as the Douglas fir 3 the wood of any of these trees [Old English *furh*; related to Old Norse *fura*, Old High German *foraha* fir, Latin *quercus* oak]

Firbank ('fɜːbæŋk) n (Arthur Annesley) Ronald. 1886–1926, English novelist, whose works include *Valmouth* (1919), *The Flower beneath the Foot* (1923), and *Concerning the Eccentricities of Cardinal Pirelli* (1926)

Firdausi (fɪə'daʊsɪ) or **Firdusi** (fɪə'duːsɪ) n pen name of *Abul Qasim Mansur* ?935–1020 AD, Persian epic poet; author of *Shah Nama* (*The Book of Kings*), a chronicle of the legends and history of Persia

fire (faɪə) n 1 the state of combustion in which inflammable material burns, producing heat, flames, and often smoke 2 a a mass of burning coal, wood, etc, used esp in a hearth to heat a room b (*in combination*): *firewood; firelighter* 3 a destructive conflagration, as of a forest, building, etc 4 a device for heating a room, etc 5 something resembling a fire in light or brilliance: *a diamond's fire* 6 a flash or spark of fire or as if of fire 7 a the act of discharging weapons, artillery, etc b the shells, etc, fired 8 a burst or rapid volley: *a fire of questions* 9 intense passion; ardour 10 liveliness, as of imagination, thought, etc 11 a burning sensation sometimes produced by drinking strong alcoholic liquor 12 fever and inflammation 13 a severe trial or torment (esp in the phrase **go through fire and water**) 14 catch fire to ignite 15 **draw someone's fire** to attract the criticism or censure of someone 16 **hang fire a** to delay firing **b** to delay or be delayed 17 **no smoke without fire** the evidence strongly suggests something has indeed happened 18 **on fire a** in a state of ignition **b** ardent or eager **c** *informal* playing or performing at the height of one's abilities 19 **open fire** to start firing a gun, artillery, etc 20 **play with fire** to be involved in something risky 21 **set fire to** or **set on fire** *Brit* **a** to ignite **b** to arouse or excite 22 **set the world on fire**, *Brit* **set the Thames on fire** or *Scot* **set the heather on fire** *informal* to cause a great sensation 23 **under fire** being attacked, as by weapons or by harsh criticism 24 (*modifier*) *astrology* of or relating to a group of three signs of the zodiac, Aries, Leo, and Sagittarius ▷ vb 25 to discharge (a firearm or projectile) or (of a firearm, etc) to be discharged 26 to detonate (an explosive charge or device) or (of such a charge or device) to be detonated 27 (tr) *informal* to dismiss from employment 28 (tr) *ceramics* to bake in a kiln to harden the clay, fix the glaze, etc 29 to kindle or be kindled; ignite 30 (tr) to provide with fuel: *oil fires the heating system* 31 (tr) to tend a fire 32 (tr) to subject to heat 33 (tr) to heat slowly so as to dry 34 (tr) to arouse to strong emotion 35 to glow or cause to glow 36 (intr) (of an internal-combustion engine) to ignite 37 (intr) (of grain) to become blotchy or yellow before maturity 38 *vet science* another word for: **cauterize** 39 (intr) *Austral informal* (of a sportsman, etc) to play well or with enthusiasm ▷ *sentence substitute* 40 a cry to warn others of a fire 41 the order to begin firing a gun, artillery, etc [Old English *fȳr*; related to Old Saxon *fiur*, Old Norse *fūrr*, Old High German *fūir*, Greek *pur*] > 'firer n

fire alarm n 1 a device to give warning of fire, esp a bell, siren, or hooter 2 a shout to warn that a fire has broken out

fire appliance n another name for **fire engine**

firearm ('faɪər,ɑːm) n a weapon, esp a portable gun or pistol, from which a projectile can be discharged by an explosion caused by igniting gunpowder, etc

fireback ('faɪə,bæk) n 1 Also called: reredos an ornamental iron slab against the back wall of a hearth 2 any pheasant of the genus *Lophura*, of SE Asia

fireball ('faɪə,bɔːl) n 1 a ball-shaped discharge of lightning 2 the bright spherical region of hot ionized gas at the centre of a nuclear explosion 3 *astronomy* a large bright meteor 4 *slang* an energetic person

firebase ('faɪə,beɪs) n an artillery base supporting advancing troops

fire blight n a disease of apples, pears, and similar fruit trees, caused by the bacterium *Erwinia amylovora* and characterized by blackening of the blossoms and leaves, and cankers on the branches

fireboat ('faɪə,bəʊt) n a motor vessel with fire-fighting apparatus

firebomb ('faɪə,bɒm) n another name for **incendiary** (sense 6)

firebox ('faɪə,bɒks) n 1 the furnace chamber of a boiler in a steam locomotive 2 an obsolete word for: **tinderbox**

firebreak ('faɪə,breɪk) n 1 Also called: fireguard or fire line a strip of open land in forest or prairie, to arrest the advance of a fire 2 a measure taken to arrest the advance of anything dangerous or harmful

firebrick ('faɪə,brɪk) n a refractory brick made of fire clay, used for lining furnaces, flues, etc

fire brigade n *chiefly Brit* an organized body of firefighters

firebug ('faɪə,bʌg) n *informal* a person who deliberately sets fire to property

fire clay n a heat-resistant clay used in the making of firebricks, furnace linings, etc

fire company n 1 an insurance company selling policies relating to fire risk 2 *US* an organized body of firemen

fire control n *military* the procedures by which weapons are brought to engage a target

firecracker ('faɪəˌkrækə) n a small cardboard container filled with explosive powder and lit by a fuse

firecrest ('faɪəˌkrɛst) n a small European warbler, *Regulus ignicapillus*, having a crown striped with yellow, black, and white

firedamp ('faɪəˌdæmp) n a mixture of hydrocarbons, chiefly methane, formed in coal mines. It forms explosive mixtures with air. See also **afterdamp**

firedog ('faɪəˌdɒg) n either of a pair of decorative metal stands used to support logs in an open fire

fire door n 1 a door made of noncombustible material, the purpose of which is to prevent a fire from spreading within a building 2 a similar door, leading to the outside of a building, that can be easily opened from inside; emergency exit

fire-eater n 1 a performer who simulates the swallowing of fire 2 a belligerent person

fire engine n a heavy road vehicle that carries firemen and fire-fighting equipment to a fire

fire escape n a means of evacuating persons from a building in the event of fire, esp a metal staircase outside the building

fire-extinguisher n a portable device for extinguishing fires, usually consisting of a canister with a directional nozzle used to direct a spray of water, chemically generated foam, inert gas, or fine powder onto the fire

firefighter ('faɪəˌfaɪtə) n a person who fights fires, usually a public employee or trained volunteer > 'fire,fighting n

firefly ('faɪəˌflaɪ) n, pl -flies 1 any nocturnal beetle of the family *Lampyridae*, common in warm and tropical regions, having luminescent abdominal organs 2 any tropical American click beetle of the genus *Pyrophorus*, esp *P. noctiluca*, that have luminescent thoracic organs

fireguard ('faɪəˌgɑːd) n Also called: **fire screen** a metal panel or meshed frame put before an open fire to protect against falling logs, sparks, etc

fire hall n US & Canadian a fire station

fire hydrant n a hydrant for use as an emergency supply for fighting fires, esp one in a street

fire insurance n insurance covering damage or loss caused by fire or lightning

fire irons pl n metal fireside implements, such as poker, shovel, and tongs

firelock ('faɪəˌlɒk) n 1 an obsolete type of gunlock with a priming mechanism ignited by sparks 2 a gun or musket having such a lock

fireman ('faɪəmən) n, pl -men 1 a man who fights fires, usually a public employee or trained volunteer. Gender-neutral form: **firefighter** 2 a (on steam locomotives) the man who stokes the fire and controls the injectors feeding water to the boiler b (on diesel and electric locomotives) the driver's assistant 3 a man who tends furnaces; stoker

Firenze (fi'rɛntse) n the Italian name for **Florence**

fire opal n an orange-red translucent variety of opal, valued as a gemstone

fireplace ('faɪəˌpleɪs) n 1 an open recess in a wall of a room, at the base of a chimney, etc, for a fire; hearth 2 Austral an authorized place or installation for outside cooking, esp by a roadside

fireplug ('faɪəˌplʌg) n another name (esp US and NZ) for **fire hydrant**

fire power n military 1 the amount of fire that may be delivered by a unit or weapon 2 the capability of delivering fire

fireproof ('faɪəˌpruːf) adj 1 capable of resisting damage by fire ▷ vb 2 (tr) to make resistant to fire

fire raiser n a person who deliberately sets fire to property > fire raising n

fire sale n 1 a sale of goods at reduced prices after a fire at a shop or factory 2 a any instance of offering goods or assets at greatly reduced prices to ensure a quick sale b (as modifier): fire-sale prices

fire screen n 1 a decorative screen placed in the hearth when there is no fire 2 a screen placed before a fire to protect the face from intense heat

fire ship n a vessel loaded with explosives and used, esp formerly, as a bomb by igniting it and directing it to

drift among an enemy's warships

fireside ('faɪəˌsaɪd) n 1 the hearth 2 family life; the home

fire station n a building where fire-fighting vehicles and equipment are stationed and where firefighters on duty wait. Also called (US): firehouse, station house

firestorm ('faɪəˌstɔːm) n an uncontrollable blaze sustained by violent winds that are drawn into the column of rising hot air over the burning area: often the result of heavy bombing

fire trail n Austral a permanent track cleared through the bush to provide access for fire-fighting

firetrap ('faɪəˌtræp) n a building that would burn easily or one without fire escapes

firewall n 1 a fireproof wall or partition used to impede the progress of a fire, as from one room or compartment to another 2 computing a computer system that isolates another computer from the internet in order to prevent unauthorized access

firewater ('faɪəˌwɔːtə) n any strong spirit, esp whisky

fireweed ('faɪəˌwiːd) n 1 any of various plants that appear as first vegetation in burnt-over areas, esp rosebay willowherb 2 Also called: pilewort a weedy North American plant, *Erechtites hieracifolia*, having small white or greenish flowers: family *Asteraceae* (composites) ▷ n 3 an Australian rainforest tree, *Stenocarpus sinuatus*, having whorls of bright red flowers

firework ('faɪəˌwɜːk) n a device, such as a Catherine wheel, Roman candle, or rocket, in which combustible materials are ignited and produce coloured flames, sparks, and smoke, sometimes accompanied by bangs

fireworks ('faɪəˌwɜːks) pl n 1 a show in which large numbers of fireworks are let off simultaneously 2 informal an exciting or spectacular exhibition, as of musical virtuosity or wit 3 informal a burst of temper

firie ('faɪəri) n Austral informal a firefighter

firing ('faɪərɪŋ) n 1 the process of baking ceramics, etc, in a kiln or furnace: a second firing 2 the act of stoking a fire or furnace 3 a discharge of a firearm 4 something used as fuel, such as coal or wood 5 US a scorching of plants, as a result of disease, drought, or heat

firing line n 1 military a the positions from which fire is delivered b the soldiers occupying these positions 2 the leading or most advanced position in an activity

firkin ('fɜːkɪn) n 1 a small wooden barrel or similar container 2 Brit a unit of capacity equal to nine gallons [C14 fir, from Middle Dutch *vierde* FOURTH + -KIN]

firm[1] (fɜːm) adj 1 not soft or yielding to a touch or pressure; rigid; solid 2 securely in position; stable or stationary 3 definitely established; decided; settled 4 enduring or steady; constant 5 having determination or strength; resolute 6 (of prices, markets, etc) tending to rise ▷ adv 7 in a secure, stable, or unyielding manner: he stood firm over his obligation to pay ▷ vb 8 (sometimes foll by up) to make or become firm 9 (intr) Austral horse racing (of a horse) to shorten in odds [C14: from Latin *firmus*] > 'firmly adv > 'firmness n

firm[2] (fɜːm) n 1 a business partnership 2 any commercial enterprise 3 a team of doctors and their assistants 4 Brit slang a a gang of criminals b a gang of football hooligans [C16 (in the sense: signature): from Spanish *firma* signature, title of a partnership or business concern, from *firmar* to sign, from Latin *firmāre* to confirm, from *firmus* firm]

firmament ('fɜːməmənt) n the expanse of the sky; heavens [C13: from Late Latin *firmāmentum* sky (considered as fixed above the earth), from Latin: prop, support, from *firmāre* to make FIRM[1]] > firmamental (ˌfɜːmə'mɛntəl) adj

firmware ('fɜːmˌwɛə) n computing a fixed form of software programmed into a read-only memory

first (fɜːst) adj (usually prenominal) 1 a coming before all others; earliest, best, or foremost b (as noun): I was the first to arrive 2 preceding all others in numbering or counting order; the ordinal number of one. Often written: 1st 3 rated, graded, or ranked above all other levels 4 denoting the lowest forward ratio of a gearbox in a motor vehicle 5 music a denoting the highest part assigned to one of the voice parts in a chorus or one of the sections of an orchestra: *first soprano; the first violins* **b** denoting the principal player in a specific orchestral section: *he plays first horn* **6** first thing as the first action of the day: *I'll see you first thing tomorrow* **7** first things is first things must be done in order of priority **8** the first thing (*in negative constructions*) even one thing: *he doesn't know the first thing about me* ▷ n **9** the beginning; outset: *I knew you were a rogue from the first; I couldn't see at first because of the mist* **10** *education chiefly Brit* an honours degree of the highest class **11** something which has not occurred before: *a first for the company* **12** the lowest forward ratio of a gearbox in a motor vehicle; low gear **13** *music* **a** the highest part in a particular section of a chorus or orchestra **b** the instrument or voice taking such a part **c** the chief or leading player in a section of an orchestra; principal **14** *music* **a** denoting the highest part assigned to one of the voice parts in a chorus or one of the sections of an orchestra: *the first violins* **b** denoting the principal player in a specific orchestral section: *he plays first horn* ▷ *adv* **15** before anything else in order, time, preference, importance, etc: *do this first; first, remove the head and tail of the fish* **16** first and last **on the whole; overall 17** from first to last throughout **18** for the first time: *I've loved you since I first saw you* **19** (*sentence modifier*) in the first place or beginning of a series of actions: *first I want to talk about criminality* [Old English *fyrest*; related to Old Saxon *furist*, Old Norse *fyrstr*, German *Fürst* prince, one who is first in rank]

first aid *n* **1 a** immediate medical assistance given in an emergency **b** (*as modifier*): *first-aid box* **2** (in Barbados) a small shop that sells domestic items after hours

first-born *adj* **1** eldest of the children in a family ▷ *n* **2** the eldest child in a family

first class *n* **1** the class or grade of the best or highest value, quality, etc ▷ *adj* (**first-class** *when prenominal*) **2** of the best or highest class or grade: *a first-class citizen* **3** excellent; first-rate **4** of or denoting the most comfortable and expensive class of accommodation in a hotel, aircraft, train, etc **5 a** (in Britain) of or relating to mail that is processed most quickly **b** (in the US and Canada) of or relating to mail that consists mainly of written letters, cards, etc **6** *education* See **first** (sense 10) ▷ *adv* **first-class 7** by first-class mail, means of transportation, etc

first-day cover *n philately* a cover, usually an envelope, postmarked on the first day of the issue of its stamps

first-degree burn *n pathol* See **burn¹** (sense 15)

first-foot *chiefly Scot* ▷ *n* Also: **first-footer 1** the first person to enter a household in the New Year. By Hogmanay tradition a dark-haired man who crosses the threshold at midnight brings good luck ▷ *vb* **2** to enter (a house) as first-foot > **'first-'footing** *n*

first fruits *pl n* **1** the first results, products, or profits of an undertaking **2** fruit that ripens first

first-hand *adj, adv* **1** from the original source; direct or directly: *first-hand news; he got the news first-hand* **2** at first hand from the original source; directly

first lady *n* (*often capitals*) **1** (in the US) the wife or official hostess of a chief executive, esp of a state governor or a president **2** a woman considered to be at the top of her profession or art: *the first lady of jazz*

first language *n* a person's native language

firstling ('fɜːstlɪŋ) *n* the first, esp the first offspring

first-loss policy *n* an insurance policy for goods in which a total loss is extremely unlikely and the insurer agrees to provide cover for a sum less than the total value of the property

firstly ('fɜːstlɪ) *adv* coming before other points, questions, etc

First Minister *n* **1** the chief minister of the Northern Ireland Assembly **2** the chief minister of the Scottish Parliament

first mortgage *n* a mortgage that has priority over other mortgages on the same property, except for taxation and other statutory liabilities

first name *n* a name given to a person at birth, as opposed to a surname

First Nation *n* (*also without capitals*) Canadian another name for **band¹** (sense 5)

first night *n* **a** the first public performance of a play or other production **b** (*as modifier*): *first-night nerves*

first offender *n* a person convicted of any criminal offence for the first time

first officer *n* the member of an aircraft crew who is second in command to the captain

first-past-the-post *n* (*modifier*) of or relating to a voting system in which a candidate may be elected by a simple majority rather than an absolute majority. See **proportional representation**

First Peoples *pl n Canadian* a collective term for the Native Canadian peoples, the Inuit, and the Métis

first person *n* a grammatical category of pronouns and verbs used by the speaker to refer to or talk about himself, either alone (**first person singular**) or together with others (**first person plural**)

first-person shooter *n* a type of computer game in which the player aims and shoots at targets, and the graphics displayed are seen from the viewpoint of the shooter. Abbreviation: **FPS**

first-rate *adj* **1** of the best or highest rated class or quality **2** *informal* very good; excellent ▷ *adv* **3** *not standard* very well; excellently

first reading *n* the introduction of a bill in a legislative assembly

first refusal *n* the chance of buying a house, merchandise, etc, before the offer is made to other potential buyers

first responder *n* a person who is trained to provide basic life support in a medical emergency

First Secretary *n* the chief minister of the National Assembly for Wales

first-strike *adj* (of a nuclear missile) intended for use in an opening attack calculated to destroy the enemy's nuclear weapons

first water *n* **1** the finest quality of diamond or other precious stone **2** the highest grade or best quality

firth (fɜːθ) *or* **frith** *n* a relatively narrow inlet of the sea, esp in Scotland [c15: from Old Norse *fjörthr* FIORD]

fisc (fɪsk) *n rare* a state or royal treasury [c16: from Latin *fiscus* treasury, originally money-bag]

fiscal ('fɪskəl) *adj* **1** of or relating to government finances, esp tax revenues **2** of or involving financial matters ▷ *n* **3 a** (in some countries) a public prosecutor **b** *Scot* short for **procurator fiscal 4** a postage or other stamp signifying payment of a tax [c16: from Latin *fiscālis* concerning the state treasury, from *fiscus* public money; see FISC] > **'fiscally** *adv*

fiscal year *n US & Canadian* **1** any annual period at the end of which a firm's accounts are made up **2** the annual period ending April 5, over which Budget estimates are made by the British Government and which functions as the income-tax year ▷ Also called (in Britain and certain other countries): **financial year**

Fischer ('fɪʃər) *n* **1 Emil Hermann** ('eːmiːl 'hɛrman). 1852–1919, German chemist, noted particularly for his work on synthetic sugars and the purine group: Nobel prize for chemistry 1902 **2 Ernst Otto**. 1918–94, German chemist: shared the Nobel prize for chemistry in 1973 with Geoffrey Wilkinson for his work on inorganic complexes **3 Hans** (hans). 1881–1945, German chemist, noted particularly for his work on chlorophyll, haemin, and the porphyrins: Nobel prize for chemistry 1930 **4 Robert James**, known as *Bobby*. 1943–2008, US chess player; world champion 1972–75

Fischer-Dieskau (*German* -'diːskau) *n* **Dietrich** ('diːtrɪç). born 1925, German baritone, noted particularly for his interpretation of Schubert's song cycles

Fischer von Erlach (*German* 'fɪʃər fɔn 'ɛrlax) *n* **Johann Bernhard** (jo'han 'bɛrnhart). 1656–1723, Austrian architect: a leading exponent of the German baroque

fish (fɪʃ) *n, pl* **fish** *or* **fishes 1 a** any of a large group of cold-blooded aquatic vertebrates having jaws, gills, and usually fins and a skin covered in scales: includes the sharks and rays (class *Chondrichthyes*: **cartilaginous fishes**) and the teleosts, lungfish, etc (class *Osteichthyes*: **bony fishes**) **b** (*in combination*): *fishpond*. Related adjs: **piscine 2** any of various similar but jawless vertebrates, such as the hagfish and lamprey **3** (*not in technical use*) any of various aquatic invertebrates, such as the cuttlefish, jellyfish, and crayfish **4** the flesh of fish used as food **5** *informal* a person of little emotion or intelligence: *a poor fish* **6** short for **fishplate 7** Also called: **tin fish** an informal word for **torpedo** (sense 1) **8 a fine kettle of fish** an awkward situation; mess **9 drink like a fish** to drink (esp alcohol) to excess **10 have other fish to fry** to have other activities to do, esp more important ones **11 like a fish out of water** out of one's usual place **12 neither fish, flesh, nor fowl** neither this nor that **13 make fish of one and flesh of another** *Irish* to discriminate unfairly between people ▷ *vb* **14** (*intr*) to attempt to catch fish, as with a line and hook or with nets, traps, etc **15** (*tr*) to fish in (a particular area of water) **16** to search (a body of water) for something or to search for something, esp in a body of water **17** (*intr*; foll by *for*) to seek something indirectly: *to fish for compliments* ▷ See also **fish out** [Old English *fisc*; related to Old Norse *fiskr*, Gothic *fiscs*, Russian *piskar*, Latin *piscis*] > **ˈfishˌlike** *adj*

fish and brewis *n Canadian* a Newfoundland dish of cooked salt cod and soaked hard bread

fish and chips *n* fish fillets coated with batter and deep-fried, eaten with potato chips

fishbone fern (ˈfɪʃˌbəʊn) *n* a common Australian fern, *Nephrolepsis cordifolia*, having fronds with many pinnae

fishcake (ˈfɪʃˌkeɪk) *n* a fried ball of flaked fish mixed with mashed potatoes

fisher (ˈfɪʃə) *n* **1** a person who fishes; fisherman **2** Also called: **pekan a** a large North American marten, *Martes pennanti*, having thick dark brown fur **b** the fur of this animal

Fisher (ˈfɪʃə) *n* **1 Andrew**. 1862–1928, Australian statesman, born in Scotland: prime minister of Australia (1908–09; 1910–13; 1914–15) **2 Saint John**. ?1469–1535, English prelate and scholar: executed for refusing to acknowledge Henry VIII as supreme head of the church. Feast day: June 22 **3 John Arbuthnot** 1st Baron Fisher of Kilverstone. 1841–1920, British admiral; First Sea Lord (1904–10; 1914–15); introduced the dreadnought

fisherman (ˈfɪʃəmən) *n, pl* **-men 1** a person who fishes as a profession or for sport **2** a vessel used for fishing

fishery (ˈfɪʃərɪ) *n, pl* **-eries 1 a** the industry of catching, processing, and selling fish **b** a place where this is carried on **2** a place where fish are reared **3** a fishing ground

Fishes (ˈfɪʃɪz) *n* **the Fishes** the constellation Pisces, the twelfth sign of the zodiac

fisheye lens (ˈfɪʃˌaɪ) *n photog* a lens of small focal length, having a highly curved protruding front element, that covers an angle of view of almost 180°. It yields a circular image having considerable linear distortion

fishfinger (ˈfɪʃˈfɪŋgə) *or US and Canadian* **fish stick** *n* an oblong piece of filleted or minced fish coated in breadcrumbs

fishgig (ˈfɪʃˌgɪg) *n* a pole with barbed prongs for impaling fish. Also called: **fizgig** [C17: of uncertain origin; perhaps altered from Spanish *fisga* harpoon]

Fishguard (ˈfɪʃˌgɑːd) *n* a port and resort in SW Wales, in Pembrokeshire: ferry connections to Cork and Rosslare. Pop: 3193 (2001)

fish hawk *n* another name for the **osprey**

fish-hook *n* **1** a sharp hook used in angling, esp one with a barb **2** *logic* a symbol (—⊃) for entailment

fishing (ˈfɪʃɪŋ) *n* **a** the occupation of catching fish **b** (*as modifier*): *a fishing match*

fishing ground *n* an area of water that is good for fishing

fishing rod *n* a long tapered flexible pole, often in jointed sections, for use with a fishing line and, usually, a reel

fish joint *n* a connection formed by fishplates at the meeting point of two rails, beams, etc, as on a railway

fishmeal (ˈfɪʃˌmiːl) *n* ground dried fish used as feed for farm animals, as a fertilizer, etc

fishmonger (ˈfɪʃˌmʌŋgə) *n chiefly Brit* a retailer of fish

fishnet (ˈfɪʃˌnɛt) *n* **1** *chiefly US & Canadian* a net for catching fish **2 a** an open mesh fabric resembling netting **b** (*as modifier*): *fishnet tights*

fish out *vb* (*tr, adverb*) to find or extract (something): *to fish keys out of a pocket*

fishplate (ˈfɪʃˌpleɪt) *n* a flat piece of metal joining one rail, stanchion, or beam to another

fishtail (ˈfɪʃˌteɪl) *n* **1** an aeroplane manoeuvre in which the tail is moved from side to side to reduce speed **2** a nozzle having a long narrow slot at the top, placed over a Bunsen burner to produce a thin fanlike flame

fishwife (ˈfɪʃˌwaɪf) *n, pl* **-wives 1** a woman who sells fish **2** a coarse scolding woman

fishy (ˈfɪʃɪ) *adj* **fishier, fishiest 1** of, involving, or suggestive of fish **2** abounding in fish **3** *informal* suspicious, doubtful, or questionable **4** dull and lifeless: *a fishy look* > **ˈfishily** *adv*

fissi- *combining form* indicating a splitting or cleft: *fissirostral* [from Latin *fissus*, past participle of *findere* to split]

fissile (ˈfɪsaɪl) *adj* **1** *Brit* capable of undergoing nuclear fission as a result of the impact of slow neutrons **2** *US & Canadian* capable of undergoing nuclear fission as a result of any process [C17: from Latin *fissilis*, from *fissus* split; see FISSI-]

fission (ˈfɪʃən) *n* **1** the act or process of splitting or breaking into parts **2** *biology* a form of asexual reproduction in single-celled animals and plants involving a division into two or more equal parts that develop into new cells **3** short for **nuclear fission** [C19: from Latin *fissiō* a cleaving]

fission-track dating *n* the dating of samples of minerals by comparing the tracks in them by fission fragments from the uranium nuclei they contain, before and after irradiation by neutrons

fissiparous (fɪˈsɪpərəs) *adj biology* reproducing by fission > **fisˈsiparously** *adv*

fissure (ˈfɪʃə) *n* **1** any long narrow cleft or crack, esp in a rock **2** a weakness or flaw indicating impending disruption or discord **3** *anatomy* a narrow split or groove that divides an organ such as the brain, lung, or liver into lobes ▷ *vb* **4** to crack or split apart [C14: from medical Latin *fissūra*, from Latin *fissus* split]

fist (fɪst) *n* **1** a hand with the fingers clenched into the palm, as for hitting **2** Also called: **fistful** the quantity that can be held in a fist or hand **3** an informal word for **hand index** (sense 9) ▷ *vb* **4** (*tr*) to hit with the fist [Old English *fȳst*; related to Old Frisian *fest*, Old Saxon, Old High German *fūst*; see FIVE]

fisticuffs (ˈfɪstɪˌkʌfs) *pl n* combat with the fists [C17: probably from *fisty* with the fist + CUFF²]

fistula (ˈfɪstjʊlə) *n, pl* **-las** *or* **-lae** (-ˌliː) *pathol* an abnormal opening between one hollow organ and another or between a hollow organ and the surface of the skin, caused by ulceration, congenital malformation, etc [C14: from Latin: pipe, tube, hollow reed, ulcer]

fistulous (ˈfɪstjʊləs), **fistular** (ˈfɪstjʊlə) *or* **fistulate** (ˈfɪstjʊlɪt) *adj* **1** *pathol* containing, relating to, or resembling a fistula **2** hollow, esp slender and hollow; reedlike or tubular **3** containing tubes or tubelike parts

fit¹ (fɪt) *vb* **fits, fitting, fitted** *or US* **fit** to be appropriate or suitable for (a situation, etc) **1** to be of the correct size or shape for (a connection, container, etc) **2** (*tr*) to adjust in order to render appropriate **3** (*tr*) to supply with that which is needed **4** (*tr*) to try clothes on (someone) in order to make adjustments if necessary **5** (*tr*) to make competent or ready **6** (*tr*) to locate with care **7** (*intr*) to correspond with the facts or circumstances ▷ *adj* **fitter, fittest 8** suitable to a purpose or design; appropriate **9** having the right qualifications; qualifying **10** in good health **11** worthy or deserving: *a book fit to be read* **12** (foll by an infinitive) in such an extreme condition that a specified consequence is likely: *she was fit to scream; you look fit to drop* ▷ *n* **13** the manner in which something fits **14** the act or process of fitting **15** *statistics* the correspondence between observed and predicted characteristics of a distribution or model. See **goodness of fit** [C14: probably from Middle Dutch *vitten*; related to Old Norse *fitja* to knit] > **ˈfittable** *adj*

fit² (fɪt) *n* **1** *pathol* a sudden attack or convulsion, such as an epileptic seizure **2** a sudden spell of emotion: *a fit of* anger **3** an impulsive period of activity or lack of activity; mood: *a fit of laziness* **4** give a person a **fit** to surprise a person in an outrageous manner **5** have a **fit** *or* throw a **fit** *informal* to become very angry or excited **6** in **fits and starts** *or* by **fits and starts** in spasmodic spells; irregularly [Old English *fitt* conflict]

fitch (fɪtʃ) *or* **fitchet** (ˈfɪtʃɪt) *n* **1** another name for **polecat** (sense 1) **2** the fur of the polecat or ferret [c16: probably from *ficheux* FITCHEW]

fitchew (ˈfɪtʃuː) *n* an archaic name for **polecat** [C14 *ficheux*, from Old French *ficheau*, from Middle Dutch *vitsau*, of obscure origin]

fitful (ˈfɪtfʊl) *adj* characterized by or occurring in irregular spells > **ˈfitfully** *adv*

fit in *vb* **1** (*tr*) to give a place or time to **2** (*intr, adverb*) to belong or conform, esp after adjustment: *he didn't fit in with their plans*

fitment (ˈfɪtmənt) *n* **1** *machinery* an accessory attached to an assembly of parts **2** *chiefly Brit* a detachable part of the furnishings of a room

fitness (ˈfɪtnɪs) *n* **1** the state of being fit **2** *biology* **a** the degree of adaptation of an organism to its environment, determined by its genetic constitution **b** the ability of an organism to produce viable offspring capable of surviving to the next generation

fit out *vb* (*tr, adverb*) to equip; supply with necessary or new equipment, clothes, etc

fitted (ˈfɪtɪd) *adj* **1** designed for excellent fit: *a fitted suit* **2** (of a carpet) cut, sewn, or otherwise adapted to cover a floor completely **3 a** (of furniture) built to fit a particular space: *a fitted cupboard* **b** (of a room) equipped with fitted furniture: *a fitted kitchen* **4** (of sheets) having ends that are elasticated and shaped to fit tightly over a mattress **5** having accessory parts

fitter (ˈfɪtə) *n* **1** a person who fits a garment, esp when it is made for a particular person **2** a person who is skilled in the assembly and adjustment of machinery, esp of a specified sort

fitting (ˈfɪtɪŋ) *adj* **1** appropriate or proper; suitable ▷ *n* **2** an accessory or part: *an electrical fitting* **3** (*plural*) furnishings or accessories in a building **4** work carried out by a fitter **5** the act of trying on clothes so that they can be adjusted to fit **6** *Brit* size in clothes or shoes: *a narrow fitting* > **ˈfittingly** *adv*

Fittipaldi (ˌfɪtɪˈpældɪ) *n* **Emerson.** born 1946, Brazilian motor-racing driver: world champion in 1972 and 1974

Fitzgerald (fɪtsˈdʒɛrəld) *n* **1 Edward.** 1809–83, English poet, noted particularly for his free translation of the *Rubáiyát of Omar Khayyám* (1859) **2 Ella.** 1918–96, US jazz singer, noted esp for her vocal range and scat singing **3 F(rancis) Scott (Key).** 1896–1940, US novelist and short-story writer, noted particularly for his portrayal of the 1920s in *The Great Gatsby* (1925) and *Tender is the Night* (1934) **4 Garret.** born 1926, Irish politician; leader of Fine Gael Party (1977–87); prime minister of the Republic of Ireland (1981–82; and 1982–87)

Fitzgerald-Lorentz contraction (fɪtsˈdʒɛrəldɔːˈrɛnts) *n physics* the contraction that a moving body exhibits when its velocity approaches that of light [c19: named after G. F. Fitzgerald (1851–1901), Irish physicist and H. A. Lorentz (1853–1928), Dutch physicist]

Fitzpatrick *n* **Sean** (ʃɔːn). born 1963, New Zealand Rugby Union footballer; captain of the All Blacks (1992–98)

Fitzrovia (fɪtsˈrəʊvɪə) *n informal* the district north of Oxford Street, London, around Fitzroy Square and its pubs, noted in the 1930s and 40s as a haunt of poets

Fitzsimmons (ˌfɪtˈsɪmənz) *n* **Bob.** 1862–1917, New Zealand boxer, born in England: world middleweight (1891–97), heavyweight (1897–99), and light-heavyweight (1903–05) champion

Fiume (ˈfiuːme) *n* the Italian name for **Rijeka**

five (faɪv) *n* **1** the cardinal number that is the sum of four and one **2** a numeral, 5, V, etc, representing this number **3** the amount or quantity that is one greater than four **4** something representing, represented by, or consisting of five units, such as a playing card with five symbols on it ▷ *determiner* **5 a** amounting to five: *five minutes; five nights* **b** (*as pronoun*): *choose any five you like* ▷ See also **fives** [Old English *fīf*; related to Old Norse *fimm*,

Gothic *fimf*, Old High German *finf*, Latin *quinque*, Greek *pente*, Sanskrit *pañca*]

five-a-side *n* a version of soccer with five players on each side

5BX *n* a fitness exercise programme originally devised in the Canadian Air Force [from 5 *b*(*asic*) (*e*)*x*(*ercises*)]

five-eighth *n* **1** *Austral* (in rugby) a player positioned between the scrum-half and the inside -centre **2** *NZ* (in rugby) either of two players positioned between the halfback and the centre

five-finger *n* any of various plants having five-petalled flowers or five lobed leaves, such as cinquefoil and Virginia creeper

fivefold (ˈfaɪvˌfəʊld) *adj* **1** equal to or having five times as many or as much **2** composed of five parts ▷ *adv* **3** by or up to five times as many or as much

Five Nations *pl n* (formerly) a confederacy of North American Indian peoples living mainly in and around present-day New York state, consisting of the Cayugas, Mohawks, Oneidas, Onondagas, and Senecas

five-o'clock shadow *n* beard growth visible late in the day on a man's shaven face

fivepins (ˈfaɪvˌpɪnz) *n* (*functioning as singular*) a bowling game using five pins, played esp in Canada. Also called: **five-pin bowling** > **ˈfiveˌpin** *adj*

fiver (ˈfaɪvə) *n informal* (in Britain) a five-pound note

fives (faɪvz) *n* (*functioning as singular*) a ball game similar to squash but played with bats or the hands

Five Towns *n* the **Five Towns** the name given in his fiction by Arnold Bennett to the Potteries towns (actually six in number) of Burslem, Fenton, Hanley, Longton, Stoke-upon-Trent, and Tunstall, now part of the city of Stoke-on-Trent

Five-Year Plan *n* (formerly in socialist economies) a government plan for economic development over a period of five years

fix (fɪks) *vb* (*mainly tr*) **1** (*also intr*) to make or become firm, stable, or secure **2** to attach or place permanently: *fix the mirror to the wall* **3** (often foll by *up*) to settle definitely; decide: *let us fix a date* **4** to hold or direct (eyes, attention, etc) steadily: *he fixed his gaze on the woman* **5** to call to attention or rivet **6** to make rigid: *to fix one's jaw* **7** to place or ascribe: *to fix the blame on someone* **8** to mend or repair **9** *informal* to provide with: *how are you fixed for supplies?* **10** *informal* to influence (a person, outcome of a contest, etc) unfairly, as by bribery **11** *slang* to take revenge on; get even with, esp by killing **12** *informal* to give (someone) his just deserts: *that'll fix him* **13** *informal* to prepare: *to fix a meal* **14** *dialect or informal* to spay or castrate (an animal) **15** *photog* to treat (a film, plate, or paper) with fixer to make permanent the image rendered visible by developer **16 a** to convert (atmospheric nitrogen) into nitrogen compounds, as in the manufacture of fertilizers or the action of bacteria in the soil **b** to convert (carbon dioxide) into organic compounds, esp carbohydrates, as occurs in photosynthesis in plants and some microorganisms **17** to reduce (a substance) to a solid or condensed state or a less volatile state **18** (*intr*) *slang* to inject a drug ▷ *n* **19** *informal* a predicament; dilemma **20** the ascertaining of the navigational position, as of a ship, by radar, observation, etc **21** *slang* an intravenous injection of a drug, esp heroin ▷ See also **fix up** [c15: from Medieval Latin *fīxāre*, from Latin *fīxus* fixed, from Latin *fīgere*] > **ˈfixable** *adj*

fixate (ˈfɪkseɪt) *vb* **1** to become or cause to become fixed **2** *psychol* to engage in fixation **3** (*tr; usually passive*) *informal* to obsess or preoccupy [c19: from Latin *fīxus* fixed + -ATE¹]

fixation (fɪkˈseɪʃən) *n* **1** the act of fixing or the state of being fixed **2** a preoccupation or obsession **3** *psychol* (in psychoanalytical schools) a strong attachment of a person to another person or an object in early life **4** *chem* the conversion of nitrogen in the air into a compound, esp a fertilizer **5** the reduction of a substance from a volatile or fluid form to a nonvolatile or solid form

fixative (ˈfɪksətɪv) *adj* **1** serving or tending to fix ▷ *n* **2 a** fluid usually consisting of a transparent resin, such as shellac, dissolved in alcohol and sprayed over drawings to prevent smudging **3** a substance added to a liquid, such as a perfume, to make it less volatile

fixed (fɪkst) *adj* **1** attached or placed so as to be immovable **2** not subject to change; stable: *fixed prices* **3** steadily directed: *a fixed expression* **4** established as to relative position: *a fixed point* **5** not fluctuating; always at the same time: *a fixed holiday* **6** (of ideas, notions, etc) firmly maintained **7** (of an element) held in chemical combination: *fixed nitrogen* **8** (of a substance) nonvolatile **9** arranged **10** *informal* equipped or provided for, as with money, possessions, etc **11** *informal* illegally arranged: *a fixed trial* > **fixedly** ('fɪksɪdlɪ) *adv* > 'fixedness *n*

fixed assets *pl n* nontrading business assets of a relatively permanent nature, such as plant, fixtures, or goodwill. Also called: **capital assets**

fixed oil *n* a natural animal or vegetable oil that is not volatile: a mixture of esters of fatty acids, usually triglycerides. Also called: **fatty oil** See **essential oil**

fixed-point representation *n computing* the representation of numbers by a single set of digits such that the radix point has a predetermined location, the value of the number depending on the position of each digit relative to the radix point. See **floating-point representation**

fixed satellite *n* a satellite in a geostationary orbit

fixed star *n* any of the stars in the Ptolemaic system, all of which were thought to be attached to an outer crystal sphere thus explaining their apparent lack of movement

fixer ('fɪksə) *n* **1** a person or thing that fixes **2** *photog* a solution containing one or more chemical compounds that is used, in fixing, to dissolve unexposed silver halides. It sometimes has an additive to stop the action of developer **3** *slang* a person who makes arrangements, esp by underhand or illegal means

fixing ('fɪksɪŋ) *n* a means of attaching one thing to another, as a pipe to a wall, slate to a roof, etc

fixity ('fɪksɪtɪ) *n, pl* -ties **1** the state or quality of being fixed; stability **2** something that is fixed; a fixture

fixture ('fɪkstʃə) *n* **1** an object firmly fixed in place, esp a household appliance **2** a person or thing regarded as fixed in a particular place or position **3** *property law* an article attached to land and regarded as part of it **4** *chiefly Brit* a sports match or social occasion **b** the date of such an event [c17: from Late Latin *fixūra* a fastening (with -t- by analogy with *mixture*)]

fix up *vb* (tr, adverb) **1** to arrange: *let's fix up a date* **2** (often foll by *with*) to provide: *I'm sure we can fix you up with a room*

fizgig ('fɪzˌgɪg) *n* **1** a frivolous or flirtatious girl **2** a firework or whirling top that fizzes as it moves [c16: probably from obsolete *fise* a breaking of wind + *gig* girl]

fizz (fɪz) *vb* (intr) **1** to make a hissing or bubbling sound **2** (of a drink) to produce bubbles of carbon dioxide, either through fermentation or aeration > *n* **3** a hissing or bubbling sound **4** the bubbly quality of a drink; effervescence **5** any effervescent drink [c17: of imitative origin] > 'fizzy *adj* > 'fizziness *n*

fizzle ('fɪzªl) *vb* (intr) **1** to make a hissing or bubbling sound **2** (often foll by *out*) *informal* to fail or die out, esp after a promising start > *n* **3** a hissing or bubbling sound; fizz **4** *informal* an outright failure; fiasco [c16: probably from obsolete *fist* to break wind]

fjord or fiord (fjɔːd) *n* (esp on the coast of Norway) a long narrow inlet of the sea between high steep cliffs formed by glacial action [c17: from Norwegian, from Old Norse *fjǫrthr*; see FIRTH, FORD]

FL *abbreviation* **1** Flight Lieutenant **2** Florida

fl. *abbreviation floruit*

Fla. *abbreviation* Florida

flab (flæb) *n* unsightly or unwanted fat on the body; flabbiness [c20: back formation from FLABBY]

flabbergast ('flæbəˌgɑːst) *vb* (tr) *informal* to overcome with astonishment; amaze utterly; astound [c18: of uncertain origin]

flabby ('flæbɪ) *adj* -bier, -biest **1** lacking firmness; loose or yielding: *flabby muscles* **2** having flabby flesh, esp through being overweight **3** lacking vitality; weak; ineffectual [c17: alteration of *flappy*, from FLAP + -Y¹; compare Dutch *flabbe* drooping lip] > 'flabbiness *n*

flaccid ('flæksɪd, 'flæs-) *adj* lacking firmness; soft and limp; flabby [c17: from Latin *flaccidus*, from *flaccus*] > **flac'cidity** or 'flaccidness *n*

flacon (French flakɔ̄) *n* a small stoppered bottle or flask, such as one used for perfume [c19: from French; see FLAGON]

flag¹ (flæg) *n* **1** a piece of cloth, esp bunting, often attached to a pole or staff, decorated with a design and used as an emblem, symbol, or standard or as a means of signalling **2** a small paper flag, emblem, or sticker sold on flag days **3** the conspicuously marked tail of a deer **4** *Austral & NZ* the part of a taximeter that is raised when a taxi is for hire **5** show the flag **a** to assert a claim, as to a territory or stretch of water, by military presence **b** *informal* to be present; make an appearance > *vb* flags, flagging, flagged (tr) **6** to decorate or mark with a flag or flags **7** (often foll by *down*) to warn or signal (a vehicle) to stop **8** to send or communicate (messages, information, etc) by flag [c16: of uncertain origin] > 'flagger *n*

flag² (flæg) *n* **1** any of various plants that have long swordlike leaves, esp the iris *Iris pseudacorus* (**yellow flag**) **2** the leaf of any such plant [c14: probably from Scandinavian origin; compare Dutch *flag*, Danish *flæg* yellow iris]

flag³ (flæg) *vb* flags, flagging, flagged (intr) **1** to hang down; become limp; droop **2** to decline in strength or vigour; become weak or tired [c16: of unknown origin]

flag⁴ (flæg) *n* **1** short for **flagstone** > *vb* flags, flagging, flagged **2** (tr) to furnish (a floor) with flagstones

flag day *n Brit* a day on which money is collected by a charity and small flags, emblems, or stickers are given to contributors

flagellant ('flædʒɪlənt, flə'dʒɛlənt) or **flagellator** ('flædʒɪˌleɪtə) *n* a person who whips himself or others either as part of a religious penance or for sexual gratification [c16: from Latin *flagellāre* to whip, from FLAGELLUM]

flagellate *vb* ('flædʒɪˌleɪt) **1** (tr) to whip; scourge; flog > *adj* ('flædʒɪlɪt, -ˌleɪt) Also called: **flagellated** **2** possessing one or more flagella **3** resembling a flagellum; whiplike > *n* ('flædʒɪlɪt, -ˌleɪt) **4** a flagellate organism, esp any protozoan of the phylum *Zoomastigina* > ˌflagel'lation *n*

flagellum (flə'dʒɛləm) *n, pl* -la (-lə) or -lums **1** *biology* a long whiplike outgrowth from a cell that acts as an organ of locomotion: occurs in some protozoans, gametes, spores, etc **2** *botany* a long thin supple shoot or runner [c19: from Latin: a little whip, from *flagrum* a whip, lash] > fla'gellar *adj*

flageolet¹ (ˌflædʒəˈlɛt) *n* a high-pitched musical instrument of the recorder family having six or eight finger holes [c17: from French, modification of Old French *flajolet* a little flute, from *flajol* flute, from Vulgar Latin *flabeolum* (unattested), from Latin *flāre* to blow]

flageolet² or **flageolet bean** ('flædʒəˌleɪ) *n* the pale green immature seed of a haricot bean, cooked and eaten as a vegetable [c19: from French *fageolet*, from Latin *phaseolus* bean; perhaps influenced by FLAGEOLET¹]

flag fall *n Austral* the minimum charge for hiring a taxi, to which the rate per kilometre is added

flag of convenience *n* a national flag flown by a ship registered in that country to gain financial or legal advantage

flag of truce *n* a white flag indicating the peaceful intent of its bearer or an invitation to an enemy to negotiate

flagon ('flægən) *n* **1** a large bottle of wine, cider, etc **2** a vessel having a handle, spout, and narrow neck [c15: from Old French *flascon*, from Late Latin *flascō*, probably of Germanic origin; see FLASK]

flagpole ('flægˌpəʊl) or **flagstaff** ('flægˌstɑːf) *n, pl* -poles, -staffs or -staves (-ˌsteɪvz) a pole or staff on which a flag is hoisted and displayed

flagrant ('fleɪgrənt) *adj* openly outrageous [c15: from Latin *flagrāre* to blaze, burn] > 'flagrancy, 'flagrance or 'flagrantly *adv*

flagrante delicto (flə'græntɪ dɪ'lɪktəʊ) *adv* See **in flagrante delicto**

flagship ('flægˌʃɪp) *n* **1** a ship, esp in a fleet, aboard which the commander of the fleet is quartered **2** the most important ship belonging to a shipping company **3** a single item from a related group considered as the most important, often in establishing a public image: *the nine o'clock news is the flagship of the BBC*

Flagstad ('flægstæd; *Norwegian* 'flaksta) *n* **Kirsten** ('çɪrstən). 1895–1962, Norwegian operatic soprano, noted particularly for her interpretations of Wagner

flagstone ('flæg,stəʊn) *or* **flag** *n* **1** a hard fine-textured rock, such as a sandstone or shale, that can be split up into slabs for paving **2** a slab of such a rock [C15 *flag* (in the sense: sod, turf), from Old Norse *flaga* slab; compare Old English *flæcg* plaster, poultice]

flag up *vb* (*tr; adverb*) to bring (something) to someone's attention; point out

flag-waving *n informal* an emotional appeal or display intended to arouse patriotic or nationalistic feeling

Flaherty ('flæhətɪ) *n* **Robert** (**Joseph**). 1884–1951, US film director, a pioneer of documentary film; his work includes *Nanook of the North* (1922) and *Elephant Boy* (1935)

flail (fleɪl) *n* **1** an implement used for threshing grain, consisting of a wooden handle with a free-swinging metal or wooden bar attached to it ▷ *vb* **2** (*tr*) to beat or thrash with or as if with a flail **3** to move or be moved like a flail; thresh about: *with arms flailing* [C12 *fleil*, ultimately from Late Latin *flagellum* flail, from Latin: whip]

flair (flɛə) *n* **1** natural ability; talent; aptitude **2** instinctive discernment; perceptiveness **3** stylishness or elegance; dash: *to dress with flair* [C19: from French, literally: sense of smell, from Old French: scent, from *flairier* to give off a smell, ultimately from Latin *frāgrāre* to smell sweet; see FRAGRANT]

flak *or* **flack** (flæk) *n* **1** anti-aircraft fire or artillery **2** *informal* a great deal of adverse criticism [C20: from German *Fl(ieger)a(bwehr)k(anone)*, literally: aircraft defence gun]

flake¹ (fleɪk) *n* **1** a small thin piece or layer chipped off or detached from an object or substance; scale **2** a small piece or particle: *a flake of snow* **3** *archaeol* a fragment removed by chipping or hammering from a larger stone used as a tool or weapon **4** *slang, chiefly US* an eccentric, crazy, or unreliable person ▷ *vb* **5** to peel or cause to peel off in flakes; chip **6** to cover or become covered with or as with flakes **7** (*tr*) to form into flakes [C14: of Scandinavian origin; compare Norwegian *flak* disc, Middle Dutch *vlacken* to flutter]

flake² (fleɪk) *n* a rack or platform for drying fish or other produce [C14: from Old Norse *flaki*; related to Dutch *vlaak* hurdle]

flake out *vb* (*intr, adverb*) *informal* to collapse or fall asleep as through extreme exhaustion

flake white *n* a pigment made from flakes of white lead

flak jacket *n* a reinforced sleeveless jacket for protection against gunfire or shrapnel worn by soldiers, policemen, etc

flaky ('fleɪkɪ) *adj* **flakier, flakiest 1** like or made of flakes **2** tending to peel off or break easily into flakes **3** Also: **flakey** *US slang* eccentric; crazy ▷ '**flakily** *adv* ▷ '**flakiness** *n*

flambé *or* **flambée** (flɑːmbeɪ, 'flæm-; *French* flãbe) *adj* **1** (of food, such as steak or pancakes) served in flaming brandy ▷ *vb* **-béing, -béeing, -béd, -béed 2** (*tr*) to pour brandy over (food) and ignite it [French, past participle of *flamber* to FLAME]

flambeau ('flæmbəʊ) *n, pl* **-beaux** (-bəʊ, -bəʊz) *or* **-beaus** a burning torch, as used in night processions [C17: from Old French: torch, literally: a little flame, from *flambe* FLAME]

Flamborough Head ('flæmbərə, -brə) *n* a chalk promontory in NE England, on the coast of the East Riding of Yorkshire

flamboyant (flæm'bɔɪənt) *adj* **1** elaborate or extravagant; florid; showy **2** rich or brilliant in colour; resplendent **3** exuberant or ostentatious **4** of, denoting, or relating to the French Gothic style of architecture characterized by flamelike tracery and elaborate carving [C19: from French: flaming, from *flamboyer* to FLAME] ▷ flam'**boyance** *or* flam'**boyancy** *n* ▷ flam'**boyantly** *adv*

flame (fleɪm) *n* **1** a hot usually luminous body of burning gas often containing small incandescent particles, typically emanating in flickering streams from burning material or produced by a jet of ignited gas **2** (*often plural*) the state or condition of burning with flames: *to burst into flames* **3** a brilliant light; fiery glow **4 a** a strong reddish-orange colour **b** (*as adjective*): *a flame carpet* **5** intense passion or ardour; burning emotion **6** *informal* a lover or sweetheart (esp in the phrase **an old flame**) **7** *informal* an abusive message sent by electronic mail, esp to express anger or criticism of an internet user by sending him or her large numbers of messages ▷ *vb* **8** to burn or cause to burn brightly; give off or cause to give off flame **9** (*intr*) to burn or glow as if with fire; become red or fiery: *his face flamed with anger* **10** (*intr*) to show great emotion; become angry or excited **11** (*tr*) to apply a flame to (something) **12** *informal* to send an abusive message by electronic mail [C14: from Anglo-French *flaume*, from Old French *flambe*, modification of *flamble*, from Latin *flammula* a little flame, from *flamma* flame] ▷ '**flame,like** *adj* ▷ '**flamy** *adj*

flame gun *n* a type of flame-thrower for destroying garden weeds

flamen ('fleɪmɛn) *n, pl* **flamens** *or* **flamines** ('flæmɪ,niːz) (in ancient Rome) any of 15 priests who each served a particular deity [C14: from Latin; probably related to Old English *blōtan* to sacrifice, Gothic *blotan* to worship]

flamenco (flə'mɛŋkəʊ) *n, pl* **-cos 1** a type of dance music for vocal soloist and guitar, characterized by elaborate melody and sad mood **2** the dance performed to such music [from Spanish: like a gipsy, literally: Fleming, from Middle Dutch *Vlaminc* Fleming]

flameout ('fleɪm,aʊt) *n* the failure of an aircraft jet engine in flight due to extinction of the flame

flame-thrower *n* a weapon that ejects a stream or spray of burning fluid

flame tree *n* any of various tropical trees with red or orange flowers, such as flame-of-the-forest

flaming ('fleɪmɪŋ) *adj* **1** burning with or emitting flames **2** glowing brightly; brilliant **3** intense or ardent; vehement; passionate: *a flaming temper* **4** *informal* (intensifier): *you flaming idiot*

flamingo (flə'mɪŋgəʊ) *n, pl* **-gos** *or* **-goes** any large wading bird of the family *Phoenicopteridae*, having a pink-and-red plumage and downward-bent bill and inhabiting brackish lakes: order *Ciconiiformes* [C16: from Portuguese *flamengo*, from Provençal *flamenc*, from Latin *flamma* flame + Germanic suffix *-ing* denoting descent from or membership of; compare -ING³]

Flaminian Way (flə'mɪnɪən) *n* an ancient road in Italy, extending north from Rome to Rimini: constructed in 220 BC by Gaius Flaminius. Length: over 322 km (200 miles)

Flamininus (,flæmɪ'naɪnəs) *n* **Titus Quinctius** ('taɪtəs 'kwɪŋktɪəs). ?230–?174 BC, Roman general and statesman: defeated Macedonia (197) and proclaimed the independence of the Greek states (196)

Flaminius (flə'mɪnɪəs) *n* **Gaius** ('gaɪəs). died 217 BC, Roman statesman and general: built the Flaminian Way; defeated by Hannibal at Trasimene (217)

flammable ('flæməb³l) *adj* liable to catch fire; readily combustible; inflammable ▷ ,**flamma'bility** *n*

● USAGE *Flammable* and *inflammable* are interchangeable
● when used of the properties of materials. *Flammable* is,
● however, often preferred for warning labels as there is
● less likelihood of misunderstanding (*inflammable*
● being sometimes taken to mean *not flammable*).
● *Inflammable* is preferred in figurative contexts: *this could*
● *prove to be an inflammable situation*

Flamsteed ('flæm,stiːd) *n* **John**. 1646–1719, English astronomer: the first Astronomer Royal and first director of the Royal Observatory, Greenwich (1675). He increased the accuracy of existing stellar catalogues, greatly aiding navigation

flan (flæn) *n* **1** an open pastry or sponge tart filled with fruit or a savoury mixture **2** a piece of metal ready to receive the die or stamp in the production of coins [C19: from French, from Old French *flaon*, from Late Latin *fladō* flat cake, of Germanic origin]

Flanders ('flɑːndəz) n a powerful medieval principality in the SW part of the Low Countries, now in the Belgian provinces of East and West Flanders, the Netherlands province of Zeeland, and the French department of the Nord; scene of battles in many wars

flange (flændʒ) n 1 a projecting disc-shaped collar or rim on an object for locating or strengthening it or for attaching it to another object 2 a flat outer face of a rolled-steel joist, esp of an I- or H-beam ▷ vb 3 (tr) to attach or provide (a component) with a flange [c17: probably changed from earlier *flaunche* curved segment at side of a heraldic field, from French *flanc* FLANK] > flanged adj > 'flangeless adj

flank (flæŋk) n 1 the side of a man or animal between the ribs and the hip 2 a cut of beef from the flank 3 the side of anything, such as a mountain or building 4 the side of a naval or military formation ▷ vb 5 (when intr, often foll by on or upon) to be located at the side of (an object, building, etc) 6 military to position or guard on or beside the flank of (a formation, etc) [c12: from Old French *flanc*, of Germanic origin]

flanker ('flæŋkə) n 1 one of a detachment of soldiers detailed to guard the flanks, esp of a formation 2 a projecting fortification, used esp to protect or threaten a flank 3 rugby a wing forward

flannel ('flænᵊl) n 1 a soft light woollen fabric with a slight nap, used for clothing 2 Brit a small piece of cloth used to wash the face and hands; face cloth. US and Canadian equivalent: washcloth 3 Brit informal indirect or evasive talk; deceiving flattery ▷ vb -nels, -nelling, -nelled or US -nels, -neling, -neled (tr) 4 to cover or wrap with flannel 5 to rub, clean, or polish with flannel 6 Brit informal to talk evasively to; flatter in order to mislead [c14: probably variant of *flanen* sackcloth, from Welsh *gwlanen* woollen fabric, from *gwlân* wool] > 'flannelly adj

flannelette (ˌflænᵊl'lɛt) n a cotton imitation of flannel

Flannery ('flænərɪ) n Tim, full name Timothy Fridtjof Flannery. born 1956, Australian zoologist, palaeontologist and environmentalist. His books include The Weather Makers (2006)

flap (flæp) vb flaps, flapping, flapped 1 to move (wings or arms) up and down, esp in or as in flying, or (of wings or arms) to move in this way 2 to move or cause to move noisily back and forth or up and down: the curtains flapped in the breeze 3 (intr) informal to become agitated or flustered; panic 4 to deal (a person or thing) a blow with a broad flexible object ▷ n 5 the action, motion, or noise made by flapping: with one flap of its wings the bird was off 6 a piece of material, etc, attached at one edge and usually used to cover an opening, as on a tent, envelope, or pocket 7 a blow dealt with a flat object; slap 8 a movable surface fixed to the trailing edge of an aircraft wing that increases lift during takeoff and drag during landing 9 informal a state of panic, distress, or agitation [c14: probably of imitative origin]

flapdoodle ('flæpˌduːdᵊl) n slang foolish talk; nonsense [c19: of unknown origin]

flapjack ('flæpˌdʒæk) n 1 a chewy biscuit made with rolled oats 2 US, Canadian & NZ another word for **pancake** [c17: from FLAP (in the sense: toss) + JACK¹]

flapper ('flæpə) n 1 a person or thing that flaps 2 (in the 1920s) a young woman, esp one flaunting her unconventional dress and behaviour

flare (flɛə) vb 1 to burn or cause to burn with an unsteady or sudden bright flame 2 to spread or cause to spread outwards from a narrow to a wider shape 3 (tr; sometimes foll by off) (in the oil industry) to burn off (unwanted gas) at an oil well ▷ n 4 an unsteady flame 5 a sudden burst of flame 6 a a blaze of light or fire used to illuminate, identify, alert, signal distress, etc b the device producing such a blaze 7 a spreading shape or anything with a spreading shape: a skirt with a flare 8 astronomy short for **solar flare** 9 an open flame used to burn off unwanted gas at an oil well [c16 (to spread out): of unknown origin]

flares (flɛəz) pl n informal trousers with legs that widen below the knee

flare-up n 1 a sudden burst of fire or light 2 informal a sudden burst of emotion or violence ▷ vb flare up (intr, adverb) 3 to burst suddenly into fire or light 4 informal to burst into anger

flash (flæʃ) n 1 a sudden short blaze of intense light or flame: a flash of sunlight 2 a very brief space of time: over in a flash 3 Also called: newsflash a short news announcement concerning a new event 4 Also called: patch chiefly Brit an insignia or emblem worn on a uniform, vehicle, etc, to identify its military formation 5 a volatile mixture of inorganic salts used to produce a glaze on bricks or tiles 6 a sudden rush of water down a river or watercourse 7 photog informal short for **flashlight** (sense 2) 8 (modifier) involving, using, or produced by a flash of heat, light, etc: flash blindness; flash distillation 9 **flash in the pan** a project, person, etc, that enjoys only short-lived success, notoriety, etc ▷ adj 10 informal ostentatious or vulgar 11 sham or counterfeit 12 informal relating to or characteristic of the criminal underworld 13 brief and rapid: flash freezing ▷ vb 14 to burst or cause to burst suddenly or intermittently into flame 15 to emit or reflect or cause to emit or reflect light suddenly or intermittently 16 (intr) to move very fast: he flashed by on his bicycle 17 (intr) to come rapidly (into the mind or vision) 18 (intr; foll by out or up) to appear like a sudden light 19 a to signal or communicate very fast b to signal by use of a light, such as car headlights 20 (tr) informal to display ostentatiously 21 (tr) informal to show suddenly and briefly 22 (intr) Brit slang to expose oneself indecently 23 to send a sudden rush of water down (a river, etc), or to carry (a vessel) down by this method [c14 (in the sense: to rush, as of water): of unknown origin]

flashback ('flæʃˌbæk) n a transition in a novel, film, etc, to an earlier scene or event

flashboard ('flæʃˌbɔːd) n a board or boarding that is placed along the top of a dam to increase its height and capacity

flashbulb ('flæʃˌbʌlb) n photog a small expendable glass light bulb formerly used to produce a bright flash of light

flashbulb memory n psychol the clear recollections that a person may have of the circumstances associated with a dramatic event

flash burn n pathol a burn caused by momentary exposure to intense radiant heat

flash card n a card on which are written or printed words for children to look at briefly, used as an aid to learning

flash drive n a pocket-sized portable computer hard drive and data storage device. See also **key drive, pen drive, USB drive**

flasher ('flæʃə) n 1 something that flashes, such as a direction indicator on a vehicle 2 Brit slang a person who indecently exposes himself

flash flood n a sudden short-lived torrent, usually caused by a heavy storm, esp in desert regions

flash gun n a type of electronic flash, attachable to or sometimes incorporated in a camera, that emits a very brief flash of light when the shutter is open

flashing ('flæʃɪŋ) n a weatherproof material, esp thin sheet metal, used to cover the valleys between the slopes of a roof, the junction between a chimney and a roof, etc

flashlight ('flæʃˌlaɪt) n 1 chiefly US & Canadian a small portable electric lamp powered by one or more dry batteries. Also called (in Britain and certain other countries): torch 2 photog the brief bright light emitted by an electronic flash unit. Sometimes shortened to: flash 3 chiefly US & Canadian a light that flashes, used for signalling, in a lighthouse, etc

flash mob n a group of people coordinated by email to meet to perform some predetermined action at a particular place and time and then disperse quickly > 'flashˌmobbing n

flash point or **flashing point** n 1 the lowest temperature at which the vapour above a liquid can be ignited in air 2 a critical moment beyond which a situation will inevitably erupt into violence

flashy ('flæʃɪ) adj flashier, flashiest 1 brilliant and dazzling, esp for a short time or in a superficial way

2 cheap and ostentatious ▷ **ˈflashily** *adv* ▷ **ˈflashiness** *n*

flask (flɑːsk) *n* 1 a bottle with a narrow neck, esp used in a laboratory or for wine, oil, etc 2 Also called: **hip flask** a small flattened container of glass or metal designed to be carried in a pocket, esp for liquor 3 See **powder flask** 4 See **vacuum flask** [c14: from Old French *flasque, flaske*, from Medieval Latin *flasca, flasco*, perhaps of Germanic origin; compare Old English *flasce, flaxe*]

flat¹ (flæt) *adj* **flatter, flattest** 1 horizontal; level: *flat ground; a flat roof* 2 even or smooth, without projections or depressions: *a flat surface* 3 lying stretched out at full length; prostrate: *he lay flat on the ground* 4 having little depth or thickness; shallow: *a flat dish* 5 (*postpositive; often foll by* against) having a surface or side in complete contact with another surface: *flat against the wall* 6 (of a tyre) deflated, either partially or completely 7 (of shoes) having an unraised or only slightly raised heel 8 *chiefly Brit* **a** (of races, racetracks, or racecourses) not having obstacles to be jumped **b** of, relating to, or connected with flat racing as opposed to steeplechasing and hurdling 9 without qualification; total: *a flat denial* 10 without possibility of change; fixed: *a flat rate* 11 (*prenominal or immediately postpositive*) neither more nor less; exact: *he did the journey in thirty minutes flat; a flat thirty minutes* 12 unexciting or lacking point or interest: *a flat joke* 13 without variation or resonance; monotonous: *a flat voice* 14 (of food) stale or tasteless 15 (of beer, sparkling wines, etc) having lost effervescence, as by exposure to air 16 (of trade, business, a market, etc) commercially inactive; sluggish 17 (of a battery) fully discharged; dead 18 (of a print, photograph, or painting) lacking contrast or shading between tones 19 (of paint) without gloss or lustre; matt 20 (of a painting) lacking perspective 21 (of lighting) diffuse 22 *music* **a** (*immediately postpositive*) denoting a note of a given letter name (or the sound it represents) that has been lowered in pitch by one chromatic semitone: *B flat* **b** (of an instrument, voice, etc) out of tune by being too low in pitch. See **sharp** (sense 12) 23 *phonetics* the vowel sound of *a* as in the usual US or S Brit pronunciation of *hand, cat*, usually represented by the symbol (æ) ▷ *adv* 24 in or into a prostrate, level, or flat state or position: *he held his hand out flat* 25 completely or utterly; absolutely 26 *music* **a** lower than a standard pitch **b** too low in pitch: *she sings flat*. See **sharp** (sense 17) 27 **fall flat** to fail to achieve a desired effect, etc 28 **flat out** *informal* **a** with the maximum speed or effort ▷ *n* 29 a flat object, surface, or part 30 (*often plural*) a low-lying tract of land, esp a marsh or swamp 31 (*often plural*) a mud bank exposed at low tide 32 *music* **a** an accidental that lowers the pitch of the following note by one chromatic semitone **b** a note affected by this accidental. See **sharp** (sense 18) 33 *theatre* a rectangular wooden frame covered with painted canvas, etc, used to form part of a stage setting 34 a punctured car tyre 35 *chiefly Brit* (*often cap; preceded by the*) **a** flat racing, esp as opposed to steeplechasing and hurdling **b** the season of flat racing 36 *nautical* a flatboat or lighter 37 *US & Canadian* a shallow box or container, used for holding plants, growing seedlings, etc ▷ *vb* **flats, flatting, flatted** 38 to make or become flat 39 *music* the usual US word for **flatten** (sense 3) [c14: from Old Norse *flatr*; related to Old High German *flaz* flat, Greek *platus* flat, broad] ▷ **ˈflatly** *adv* ▷ **ˈflatness** *n*

flat² (flæt) *n* 1 a set of rooms comprising a residence entirely on one floor of a building. Usual US and Canadian name: **apartment** ▷ *vb* **flats, flatting, flatted** (*intr*) 2 *Austral & NZ* to live in a flat (with someone) [Old English *flett* floor, hall, house; related to FLAT¹]

flat-bed lorry (ˈflætˌbɛd) *n* a lorry with a flat platform for its body

flat-bed scanner *n* a computer-controlled device which electronically scans images placed on its flat plate, allowing them to be stored in digital form

flatboat (ˈflætˌbəʊt) *n* any boat with a flat bottom, usually for transporting goods on a canal or river

flatbread (ˈflætˌbrɛd) *n* a type of thin unleavened bread

flatette (ˌflætˈɛt) *n* *Austral* a very small flat

flatfish (ˈflætˌfɪʃ) *n*, *pl* **-fish** or **-fishes** any marine spiny-finned fish of the order *Heterosomata*, including the halibut, plaice, turbot, and sole, all of which (when adult) swim along the sea floor on one side of the body, which is highly compressed and has both eyes on the uppermost side

flatfoot (ˈflætˌfʊt) *n* 1 Also called: **splayfoot** a condition in which the entire sole of the foot is able to touch the ground because of flattening of the instep arch 2 *pl* **-foots** or **-feet** a slang word (usually derogatory) for a: **policeman**

flat-footed (ˌflætˈfʊtɪd) *adj* 1 having flatfoot 2 *Brit informal* **a** clumsy or awkward **b** downright and uncompromising 3 *informal* off guard or unawares (often in the phrase **catch flat-footed**) ▷ ˌflat-ˈfootedly *adv* ▷ ˌflat-ˈfootedness *n*

flathead (ˈflætˌhɛd) *n*, *pl* **-head** or **-heads** any Pacific scorpaenoid food fish of the family *Platycephalidae*, which resemble gurnards

flatiron (ˈflætˌaɪən) *n* (formerly) an iron for pressing clothes that was heated by being placed on a stove, etc

flatlet (ˈflætlɪt) *n* a flat having only a few rooms

flatmate (ˈflætˌmeɪt) *n* *Brit* a person with whom one shares a flat

flat-pack *adj* (of a piece of furniture, equipment, or other construction) supplied in pieces packed into a flat box for assembly by the buyer

flat racing *n* **a** the racing of horses on racecourses without jumps **b** (*as modifier*): *the flat-racing season*

flats (flæts) or **flatties** (ˈflætɪz) *pl n* shoes with flat heels or no heels

flatscreen (ˈflætˌskriːn) *n* **a** a slimline television set or computer monitor with a flat screen **b** (*as modifier*): *a flatscreen television*

flat spin *n* 1 an aircraft spin in which the longitudinal axis is more nearly horizontal than vertical 2 *informal* a state of confusion; dither

flat spot *n* 1 *engineering* a region of poor acceleration over a narrow range of throttle openings, caused by a weak mixture in the carburettor 2 any narrow region of poor performance in a mechanical device

flatstick (ˈflætˌstɪk) *adv* *South African slang* with great speed or effort

flatten (ˈflætən) *vb* 1 (sometimes foll by *out*) to make or become flat or flatter 2 (*tr*) *informal* **a** to knock down or injure; prostrate **b** to crush or subdue 3 (*tr*) *music* to lower the pitch of (a note) by one chromatic semitone ▷ ˈflattener *n*

flatter (ˈflætə) *vb* 1 to praise insincerely, esp in order to win favour or reward 2 to show to advantage: *that dress flatters her* 3 (*tr*) to make to appear more attractive, etc, than in reality 4 to play upon or gratify the vanity of (a person) 5 (*tr*) to beguile with hope; encourage, esp falsely 6 (*tr*) to congratulate or deceive (oneself): *I flatter myself that I am the best* [c13: probably from Old French *flater* to lick, fawn upon, of Frankish origin] ▷ ˈflatterable *adj* ▷ ˈflatterer *n*

flattery (ˈflætərɪ) *n*, *pl* **-teries** 1 the act of flattering 2 excessive or insincere praise

flattie (ˈflætɪ) *n* *NZ informal* a flounder or other flatfish

flatties (ˈflætɪz) *pl n* another word for **flats**

flat top *n* a style of haircut in which the hair is cut shortest on the top of the head so that it stands up from the scalp and appears flat from the crown to the forehead

flat-track bully *n* a sportsperson who dominates inferior opposition, but who cannot beat top-level opponents

flatulent (ˈflætjʊlənt) *adj* 1 suffering from or caused by an excessive amount of gas in the alimentary canal, producing uncomfortable distension 2 generating excessive gas in the alimentary canal 3 pretentious or windy in style [c16: from New Latin *flātulentus*, from Latin: FLATUS] ▷ ˈflatulence or ˈflatulency *n* ▷ ˈflatulently *adv*

flatus (ˈfleɪtəs) *n*, *pl* **-tuses** gas generated in the alimentary canal [c17: from Latin: a blowing, snorting, from *flāre* to breathe, blow]

flatworm (ˈflætˌwɜːm) *n* any parasitic or free-living invertebrate of the phylum *Platyhelminthes*, including planarians, flukes, and tapeworms, having a flattened body with no circulatory system and only one opening to the intestine

Flaubert ('fləʊbɛə; *French* flobɛr) *n* **Gustave** (gystav). 1821–80, French novelist and short- story writer, regarded as a leader of the 19th-century naturalist school. His most famous novel, *Madame Bovary* (1857), for which he was prosecuted (and acquitted) on charges of immorality, and *L'Éducation sentimentale* (1869) deal with the conflict of romantic attitudes and bourgeois society. His other major works include *Salammbô* (1862), *La Tentation de Saint Antoine* (1874), and *Trois contes* (1877)

flaunt (flɔːnt) *vb* **1** to display (possessions, oneself, etc) ostentatiously; show off **2** to wave or cause to wave freely; flutter ▷ *n* **3** the act of flaunting [c16: perhaps of Scandinavian origin; compare Norwegian dialect *flanta* to wander about]

⬤ USAGE *Flaunt* is sometimes wrongly used where *flout* is
⬤ meant: *they must be prevented from flouting* (not *flaunting*)
⬤ *the law*

flautist ('flɔːtɪst) *or US and Canadian* **flutist** ('fluːtɪst) *n* a player of the flute [c19: from Italian *flautista*, from *flauto* FLUTE]

flavescent (flə'vɛsᵊnt) *adj* turning yellow; yellowish [c19: from Latin *flāvēscere* to become yellow, from *flāvēre* to be yellow, from *flāvus* yellow]

flavin *or* **flavine** ('fleɪvɪn) *n* **1** a heterocyclic ketone that forms the nucleus of certain natural yellow pigments, such as riboflavin. Formula: $C_{10}H_6N_4O_2$. See **flavoprotein** **2** any yellow pigment based on flavin [c19: from Latin *flāvus* yellow]

flavine ('fleɪvɪn) *n* another name for **acriflavine hydrochloride**

flavone ('fleɪvəʊn) *n* **1** a crystalline compound occurring in plants. Formula: $C_{15}H_{10}O_2$ **2** any of a class of yellow plant pigments derived from flavone [c19: from German *Flavon*, from Latin *flāvus* yellow + -ONE]

flavoprotein (,fleɪvəʊ'prəʊtiːn) *n* any of a group of enzymes that contain a derivative of riboflavin linked to a protein and catalyse oxidation in cells [c20: from FLAVIN + PROTEIN]

flavour *or US* **flavor** ('fleɪvə) *n* **1** taste perceived in food or liquid in the mouth **2** a substance added to food, etc, to impart a specific taste **3** a distinctive quality or atmosphere; suggestion **4** *physics* a property of quarks that enables them to be differentiated into six types: up, down, strange, charm, bottom (or beauty), and top (or truth) ▷ *vb* **5** (*tr*) to impart a flavour, taste, or quality to [c14: from Old French *flaour*, from Late Latin *flātor* (unattested) bad smell, breath, from Latin *flāre* to blow] > 'flavourless *or US* 'flavorless *adj* > 'flavoursome *or US* 'flavorsome *adj* > 'flavourful *or US* 'flavorful *adj*

flavour enhancer *n* another term for **monosodium glutamate**

flavouring *or* **flavoring** ('fleɪvərɪŋ) *n* a substance used to impart a particular flavour to food: *rum flavouring*

flaw¹ (flɔː) *n* **1** an imperfection, defect, or blemish **2** a crack, breach, or rift **3** *law* an invalidating fault or defect in a document or proceeding ▷ *vb* **4** to make or become blemished, defective, or imperfect [c14: probably from Old Norse *flaga* stone slab; related to Swedish *flaga* chip, flake, flaw] > 'flawless *adj*

flaw² (flɔː) *n* a sudden short gust of wind; squall [c16: of Scandinavian origin; related to Norwegian *flaga* squall, gust, Middle Dutch *vlāghe*]

flax (flæks) *n* **1** any herbaceous plant or shrub of the genus *Linum*, esp *L. usitatissimum*, which has blue flowers and is cultivated for its seeds (flaxseed) and for the fibres of its stems: family *Linaceae* **2** the fibre of this plant, made into thread and woven into linen fabrics **3** any of various similar plants **4** Also called: harakeke NZ a swamp plant producing a fibre that is used by Māoris for decorative work, baskets, etc [Old English *fleax*; related to Old Frisian *flax*, Old High German *flahs* flax, Greek *plekein* to plait]

flaxen ('flæksən) *or* **flaxy** *adj* **1** of, relating to, or resembling flax **2** of a soft yellow colour: *flaxen hair*

Flaxman ('flæksmən) *n* **John.** 1755–1826, English neoclassical sculptor and draughtsman, noted particularly for his monuments and his engraved illustrations for the *Iliad*, the *Odyssey*, and works by Dante and Aeschylus

flaxseed ('flæks,siːd) *n* the seed of the flax plant, which yields linseed oil. Also called: **linseed**

flay (fleɪ) *vb* (*tr*) **1** to strip off the skin or outer covering of, esp by whipping; skin **2** to attack with savage criticism [Old English *flēan*; related to Old Norse *flā* to peel, Lithuanian *plešti* to tear] > 'flayer *n*

flaysome ('fleɪsəm) *adj Northern English dialect* frightening

flea (fliː) *n* **1** any small wingless parasitic blood-sucking insect of the order *Siphonaptera*, living on the skin of mammals and birds and noted for its power of leaping **2** any of various invertebrates that resemble fleas, such as the water flea and flea beetle **3** flea in one's ear *informal* a sharp rebuke [Old English *flēah*; related to Old Norse *flō*, Old High German *flōh*]

fleabane ('fliː,beɪn) *n* **1** any of several plants of the related genus *Pulicaria*, esp the Eurasian *P. dysenterica*, which has yellow daisy-like flower heads **2** Canadian fleabane a related plant, *Conyza* (or *Erigeron*) *canadensis*, with small white tubular flower heads **3** any of various other plants reputed to ward off fleas

fleabite ('fliː,baɪt) *n* **1** the bite of a flea **2** a slight or trifling annoyance or discomfort

flea-bitten *adj* **1** bitten by or infested with fleas **2** *informal* shabby or decrepit; mean

flea market *n* an open-air market selling cheap and often second-hand goods

fleapit ('fliː,pɪt) *n informal* a shabby cinema or theatre

fleawort ('fliː,wɜːt) *n* **1** any of various plants of the genus *Senecio*, esp *S. integrifolius*, a European species with yellow daisy-like flowers and rosettes of downy leaves: family *Asteraceae* (composites) **2** a Eurasian plantain, *Plantago psyllium* (or *P. indica*), whose seeds resemble fleas and were formerly used as a flea repellent

flèche (fleɪʃ, flɛʃ) *n* Also called: **spirelet** a slender spire, esp over the intersection of the nave and transept ridges of a church roof [c18: from French: spire (literally: arrow), probably of Germanic origin; related to Middle Low German *flieke* long arrow]

fleck (flɛk) *n* **1** a small marking or streak; speckle **2** a small particle; speck: *a fleck of dust* ▷ *vb* **3** Also called: flecker (*tr*) to mark or cover with flecks; speckle [c16: probably from Old Norse *flekkr* stain, spot; related to Old High German *flec* spot, plot of land]

Flecker ('flɛkə) *n* **James Elroy.** 1884–1915, English poet and dramatist; author of *Hassan* (1922)

fled (flɛd) *vb* the past tense and past participle of **flee¹**

fledge (flɛdʒ) *vb* **1** (*tr*) to feed and care for (a young bird) until it is able to fly **2** Also called: fletch (*tr*) to fit (something, esp an arrow) with a feather or feathers **3** (*tr*) to cover or adorn with or as if with feathers [Old English *-flycge*, as in *unflycge* unfledged; related to Old High German *flucki* able to fly; see FLY¹]

fledgling *or* **fledgeling** ('flɛdʒlɪŋ) *n* **1** a young bird that has just fledged **2** a young and inexperienced person

flee (fliː) *vb* **flees, fleeing, fled 1** to run away from (a place, danger, etc); fly **2** (*intr*) to run or move quickly; rush; speed [Old English *flēon*; related to Old Frisian *fliā*, Old High German *fliohan*, Gothic *thliuhan*] > 'fleer *n*

fleece (fliːs) *n* **1** the coat of wool that covers the body of a sheep or similar animal and consists of a mass of crinkly hairs **2** the wool removed from a single sheep **3** something resembling a fleece in texture or warmth **4** sheepskin or a fabric with soft pile, used as a lining for coats, etc **5** a warm polyester fabric with a brushed nap, used for outdoor garments **6** a jacket or top made from such a fabric ▷ *vb* (*tr*) **7** to defraud or charge exorbitantly; swindle **8** another term for **shear** (sense 1) [Old English *flēos*; related to Middle High German *vlius*, Dutch *vlies* fleece, Latin *plūma* feather, down]

fleecie ('fliːsɪ) *n* NZ a person who collects fleeces after shearing and prepares them for baling. Also called: fleece-oh

fleecy ('fliːsɪ) *adj* **fleecier, fleeciest** of or resembling fleece; woolly > 'fleecily *adv*

fleer (flɪə) *archaic* ▷ *vb* **1** to grin or laugh at; scoff; sneer

▷ *n* **2** a derisory glance or grin [c14: of Scandinavian origin; compare Norwegian *flire* to snigger]

fleet[1] (fliːt) *n* **1** a number of warships organized as a tactical unit **2** all the warships of a nation **3** a number of aircraft, ships, buses, etc, operating together or under the same ownership [Old English *flēot* ship, flowing water, from *flēotan* to FLOAT]

fleet[2] (fliːt) *adj* **1** rapid in movement; swift **2** *poetic* fleeting; transient ▷ *vb* **3** (*intr*) to move rapidly **4** (*tr*) *obsolete* to cause (time) to pass rapidly [probably Old English *flēotan* to float, glide rapidly; related to Old High German *fliozzan* to flow, Latin *pluere* to rain] > 'fleetly *adv* > 'fleetness *n*

Fleet (fliːt) the Fleet *n* **1** a stream that formerly ran into the Thames between Ludgate Hill and Fleet Street and is now a covered sewer **2** Also called: **Fleet Prison** (formerly) a London prison, esp used for holding debtors

Fleet Air Arm *n* the aviation branch of the Royal Navy

fleet chief petty officer *n* a noncommissioned officer in the Royal Navy comparable in rank to a warrant officer in the British Army or Royal Air Force

fleeting ('fliːtɪŋ) *adj* rapid and transient: *a fleeting glimpse of the sea* > 'fleetingly *adv*

fleet rate *or* **fleet rating** *n* a reduced rate quoted by an insurance company to underwrite the risks to a fleet of vehicles, aircraft, etc

Fleet Street *n* **1** a street in central London in which many newspaper offices were formerly situated **2** British journalism or journalists collectively

Fleetwood ('fliːt,wʊd) *n* a fishing port in NW England, in Lancashire. Pop: 26 841 (2001)

Flémalle (*French* flemal) *n* **Master of.** See (Robert) **Campin**

Fleming[1] ('flɛmɪŋ) *n* a native or inhabitant of Flanders or a Flemish-speaking Belgian. See **Walloon** [c14: from Middle Dutch *Vlaminc*]

Fleming[2] ('flɛmɪŋ) *n* **1** Sir **Alexander**. 1881–1955, Scottish bacteriologist: discovered lysozyme (1922) and penicillin (1928): shared the Nobel prize for physiology or medicine in 1945 **2** Ian (**Lancaster**). 1908–64, English author of spy novels; creator of the secret agent James Bond **3** Sir **John Ambrose**. 1849–1945, English electrical engineer: invented the thermionic valve (1904) **4** Renée. born 1959, US operatic soprano and songwriter

Flemish ('flɛmɪʃ) *n* **1** one of the two official languages of Belgium, almost identical in form with Dutch **2** the Flemish (*functioning as plural*) the Flemings collectively ▷ *adj* **3** of, relating to, or characteristic of Flanders, the Flemings, or their language

Flemish Brabant *n* a province of central Belgium, formed in 1995 from the N part of Brabant province: densely populated and intensively farmed, with large industrial centres. Pop: 1 031 904 (2004 est). Area: 2106 sq km (813 sq miles)

Flensburg (*German* 'flɛnsbʊrk) *n* a port in N Germany, in Schleswig-Holstein: taken from Denmark by Prussia in 1864; voted to remain German in 1920. Pop: 85 300 (2003 est)

flense (flɛns), **flench** (flɛntʃ) *or* **flinch** (flɪntʃ) *vb* (*tr*) to strip (a whale, seal, etc) of (its blubber or skin) [c19: from Danish *flense*; related to Dutch *flensen*]

flesh (flɛʃ) *n* **1** the soft part of the body of an animal or human, esp muscular tissue, as distinct from bone and viscera **2** *informal* excess weight; fat **3** *archaic* the edible tissue of animals as opposed to that of fish or, sometimes, fowl; meat **4** the thick usually soft part of a fruit or vegetable, as distinct from the skin, core, stone, etc **5** the human body and its physical or sensual nature as opposed to the soul or spirit. Related adj: **carnal** **6** mankind in general **7** animate creatures in general **8** one's own family; kin (esp in the phrase **one's own flesh and blood**) **9** a yellowish-pink to greyish-yellow colour **10** in the flesh in person; actually present **11** press the flesh *informal* to shake hands, usually with large numbers of people, esp in political campaigning ▷ *vb* **12** (*tr*) *hunting* to stimulate the hunting instinct of (hounds or falcons) by giving them small quantities of raw flesh **13** *archaic or poetic* to accustom or incite to bloodshed or battle by initial experience **14** to fatten; fill

out [Old English *flǣsc*; related to Old Norse *flesk* ham, Old High German *fleisk* meat, flesh]

fleshings ('flɛʃɪŋz) *pl n* **1** flesh-coloured tights **2** bits of flesh scraped from the hides or skins of animals

fleshly ('flɛʃlɪ) *adj* **-lier, -liest** **1** relating to the body, esp its sensual nature; carnal: *fleshly desire* **2** worldly as opposed to spiritual **3** fleshy; fat > 'fleshliness *n*

flesh out *vb* (*adverb*) **1** (*tr*) to give substance to (an argument, description, etc) **2** (*intr*) to expand or become more substantial

fleshpots ('flɛʃ,pɒts) *pl n* *often facetious* **1** luxurious or self-indulgent living **2** places, such as striptease clubs, where bodily desires are gratified or titillated [c16: from the Biblical use as applied to Egypt (Exodus 16:3)]

flesh wound (wuːnd) *n* a wound affecting superficial tissues

fleshy ('flɛʃɪ) *adj* fleshier, fleshiest **1** fat; plump **2** related to or resembling flesh **3** *botany* (of some fruits, leaves, etc) thick and pulpy > 'fleshiness *n*

fletcher ('flɛtʃə) *n* a person who makes arrows [c14: from Old French *flechier*, from *fleche* arrow; see **FLÈCHE**]

Fletcher ('flɛtʃə) *n* **John**. 1579–1625, English Jacobean dramatist, noted for his romantic tragicomedies written in collaboration with Francis Beaumont, esp *Philaster* (1610) and *The Maid's Tragedy* (1611)

fleur-de-lys *or* **fleur-de-lis** (,flɜːdə'liː) *n, pl* fleurs-de-lys *or* fleurs-de-lis (,flɜːdə'liːz) **1** *heraldry* a charge representing a lily with three distinct petals **2** another name for: **iris** (sense 2) [c19: from Old French *flor de lis*, literally: lily flower]

fleurette *or* **fleuret** (flʊə'rɛt, flɜː-) *n* an ornament resembling a flower [c19: French, literally: a small flower, from *fleur* flower]

Fleury (*French* flœri) *n* **André Hercule de** (ɑ̃dre ɛrkyl də). 1653–1743, French cardinal and statesman: Louis XV's chief adviser and virtual ruler of France (1726–43)

flew (fluː) *vb* the past tense of **fly**[1] (sense 1)

flews (fluːz) *pl n* the fleshy hanging upper lip of a bloodhound or similar dog [c16: of unknown origin]

flex (flɛks) *n* **1** *Brit* a flexible insulated electric cable, used esp to connect appliances to mains. US and Canadian name: cord ▷ *vb* **2** to bend or be bent: *he flexed his arm; his arm flexed* **3** to contract (a muscle) or (of a muscle) to contract **4** (*intr*) to work according to flexitime [c16: from Latin *flexus* bent, winding, from *flectere* to bend, bow]

flexecutive (flɛg'zɛkjutɪv) *n* an executive to whom the employer allows flexibility about times and locations of working [c20: from FLEX(IBLE)+ (EX)ECUTIVE]

flex-fuel *adj* relating to cars or engines that can run on more than one type of fuel, usually petrol and ethanol

flexible ('flɛksɪb³l) *adj* **1** Also called: flexile ('flɛksaɪl) able to be bent easily without breaking; pliable **2** adaptable or variable: *flexible working hours* **3** able to be persuaded easily; tractable > ,flexi'bility *n* > 'flexibly *adv*

flexion ('flɛkʃən) *n* **1** the act of bending a joint or limb **2** the condition of the joint or limb so bent > 'flexional *adj*

flexitime ('flɛksɪ,taɪm) *or* **flextime** ('flɛks,taɪm) *n* a system permitting flexibility of working hours at the beginning or end of the day, provided an agreed period of each day (**core time**) is spent at work

flexor ('flɛksə) *n* any muscle whose contraction serves to bend a joint or limb. See **extensor** [c17: New Latin; see FLEX]

flexuous ('flɛksjʊəs) *or* **flexuose** ('flɛksjʊ,əʊs) *adj* full of bends or curves; winding [c17: from Latin *flexuōsus* full of bends, tortuous, from *flexus* a bending; see FLEX] > 'flexuously *adv*

flexure ('flɛkʃə) *n* **1** the act of flexing or the state of being flexed **2** a bend, turn, or fold

flex-wing *n* *aeronautics* a collapsible fabric delta wing, as used with hang-gliders

flibbert ('flɪbət) *n* *Southwest English dialect* a small piece or bit

flibbertigibbet ('flɪbətɪ,dʒɪbɪt) *n* an irresponsible, silly, or gossipy person [c15: of uncertain origin]

flick[1] (flɪk) *vb* **1** (*tr*) to touch with or as if with the finger or hand in a quick jerky movement **2** (*tr*) to propel or remove by a quick jerky movement, usually of the fingers or hand **3** to move or cause to move quickly or jerkily **4** (*intr*; foll by *through*) to read or look at (a book, newspaper, etc) quickly or idly ▷ *n* **5** a tap or quick stroke with the fingers, a whip, etc **6** the sound made by such a stroke **7** a fleck, streak, or particle **8** give someone the flick *informal* to dismiss someone from consideration [c15: of imitative origin; compare French *flicflac*]

flick² (flɪk) *n slang* **1** a cinema film **2** the flicks the cinema: *what's on at the flicks tonight?*

flicker¹ (ˈflɪkə) *vb* **1** (*intr*) to shine with an unsteady or intermittent light **2** (*intr*) to move quickly to and fro; quiver, flutter, or vibrate **3** (*tr*) to cause to flicker ▷ *n* **4** an unsteady or brief light or flame **5** a swift quivering or fluttering movement [Old English *flicorian*; related to Dutch *flikkeren*, Old Norse *flökra* to flutter]

flicker² (ˈflɪkə) *n* any North American woodpecker of the genus *Colaptes*, esp *C. auratus* (**yellow-shafted flicker**), which has a yellow undersurface to the wings and tail [c19: perhaps imitative of the bird's call]

flick knife *n* a knife with a retractable blade that springs out when a button is pressed. US and Canadian word: **switchblade**

flick-pass *n* **1** *rugby* a movement in which the ball is passed quickly to another player by flicking it out of the hand; often performed with only one hand **2** *hockey, ice hockey* an instance of passing the puck using a short backhand movement, esp over the stick of a defender **3** *Austral* an instance of passing of undesirable or unwanted duties, responsibility, etc, to someone else ▷ *vb* flick-pass (*tr*) **4** *rugby, hockey, ice hockey* to pass (a ball or puck) quickly with a flick-pass **5** *Austral* to pass (undesirable or unwanted duties, responsibility, etc) to someone else

flier (ˈflaɪə) *n* a variant spelling of **flyer**

flight¹ (flaɪt) *n* **1** the act, skill, or manner of flying **2** a journey made by a flying animal or object **3 a** a scheduled airline journey **b** an aircraft flying on such a journey **4** a group of flying birds or aircraft: *a flight of swallows* **5** the basic tactical unit of a military air force **6** a journey through space, esp of a spacecraft **7** a soaring mental journey above or beyond the normal everyday world: *a flight of fancy* **8** a feather or plastic attachment fitted to an arrow or dart to give it stability in flight **9** a set of steps or stairs between one landing or floor and the next ▷ *vb* **10** (*tr*) *sport* to cause (a ball, dart, etc) to float slowly or deceptively towards its target **11** (*tr*) to shoot (a bird) in flight **12** (*tr*) to fledge (an arrow or a dart) [Old English *flyht*; related to Middle Dutch *vlucht*, Old Saxon *fluht*]

flight² (flaɪt) *n* **1** the act of fleeing or running away, as from danger **2** put to flight to cause to run away; rout **3** take flight or take to flight to run away or withdraw hastily; flee [Old English *flyht* (unattested); related to Old Frisian *flecht*, Old High German *fluht*, Old Norse *flōtti*]

flight attendant *n* a person who attends to the needs of passengers on a commercial flight

flight deck *n* **1** the crew compartment in an airliner. See **cockpit** (sense 1) **2** the upper deck of an aircraft carrier from which aircraft take off and on which they land

flightless (ˈflaɪtlɪs) *adj* (of certain birds and insects) unable to fly. See also **ratite**

flight lieutenant *n* an officer holding a commissioned rank senior to a flying officer and junior to a squadron leader in the RAF and certain other air forces

flight path *n* the course through the air of an aircraft, rocket, or projectile. See **approach** (sense 9), **glide path**

flight recorder *n* an electronic device fitted to an aircraft for storing information concerning its performance in flight. It is often used to determine the cause of a crash. Also called: **black box**

flight sergeant *n* a noncommissioned officer in the Royal Air Force junior in rank to a master aircrew

flight simulator *n* a ground-training device that reproduces exactly the conditions experienced on the flight deck of an aircraft

flighty (ˈflaɪtɪ) *adj* flightier, flightiest **1** frivolous and irresponsible; capricious; volatile **2** mentally erratic, unstable, or wandering > ˈflightiness *n*

flim (flɪm) *n Northern English dialect* a five-pound note

flimflam (ˈflɪmˌflæm) *informal* ▷ *n* **1 a** nonsense; foolishness **b** (*as modifier*): *flimflam arguments* **2** a deception; swindle ▷ *vb* -flams, -flamming, -flammed **3** (*tr*) to deceive; trick; swindle; cheat [c16: probably of Scandinavian origin; compare Old Norse *flim* mockery, Norwegian *flire* to giggle] > ˈflimˌflammer *n*

flimsy (ˈflɪmzɪ) *adj* -sier, -siest **1** not strong or substantial; fragile: *a flimsy building* **2** light and thin: *a flimsy dress* **3** unconvincing or inadequate; weak: *a flimsy excuse* ▷ *n* **4** thin paper used for making carbon copies of a letter, etc **5** a copy made on such paper [c17: of uncertain origin] > ˈflimsiness *n*

flinch (flɪntʃ) *vb* (*intr*) **1** to draw back suddenly, as from pain, shock, etc; wince **2** (often foll by *from*) to avoid contact (with); shy away: *he never flinched from his duty* [c16: from Old French *flenchir*; related to Middle High German *lenken* to bend, direct] > ˈflinchingly *adv*

flinders (ˈflɪndəz) *pl n rare* small fragments or splinters (esp in the phrase **fly into flinders**) [c15: probably of Scandinavian origin; compare Norwegian *flindra* thin piece of stone]

Flinders Island *n* an island off the coast of NE Tasmania. The largest of the Furneaux Islands. Pop: 850 (2004 est). Area: 2077 sq km (802 sq miles)

Flinders Range *n* a mountain range in E South Australia, between Lake Torrens and Lake Frome. Highest peak: 1188 m (3898 ft)

fling (flɪŋ) *vb* flings, flinging, flung (flʌŋ) (*mainly tr*) **1** to throw, esp with force or abandon; hurl or toss **2** to put or send without warning or preparation: *to fling someone into jail* **3** (*also intr*) to move (oneself or a part of the body) with abandon or speed **4** (usually foll by *into*) to apply (oneself) diligently and with vigour (to) **5** to cast aside; disregard: *she flung away her scruples* ▷ *n* **6** the act or an instance of flinging; toss; throw **7** a period or occasion of unrestrained, impulsive, or extravagant behaviour **8** any of various vigorous Scottish reels full of leaps and turns, such as the Highland fling **9** a trial; try: *to have a fling at something different* [c13: of Scandinavian origin; related to Old Norse *flengja* to flog, Swedish *flänga*, Danish *flænge*] > ˈflinger *n*

flint (flɪnt) *n* **1** an impure opaque microcrystalline greyish-black form of quartz that occurs in chalk. It produces sparks when struck with steel and is used in the manufacture of pottery, flint glass, and road-construction materials. Formula: SiO_2 **2** any piece of flint, esp one used as a primitive tool or for striking fire **3** a small cylindrical piece of an iron alloy, used in cigarette lighters **4** Also called: **flint glass, white flint** colourless glass other than plate glass [Old English; related to Old High German *flins*, Old Swedish *flinta* splinter of stone, Latin *splendēre* to shine]

Flint (flɪnt) *n* **1** a town in NE Wales, in Flintshire, on the Dee estuary. Pop: 11 936 (2001) **2** a city in SE Michigan: closure of the car production plants led to a high level of unemployment. Pop: 120 292 (2003 est)

flintlock (ˈflɪntˌlɒk) *n* **1** an obsolete gunlock in which the charge is ignited by a spark produced by a flint in the hammer **2** a firearm having such a lock

Flintoff (ˈflɪntɒf) *n* **Andrew.** born 1977, English cricketer; played for Lancashire and England (from 1998)

Flintshire (ˈflɪntʃɪə, -ʃə) *n* a county of NE Wales, on the Irish Sea and the Dee estuary: became part of Clwyd in 1974, reinstated with reduced borders in 1996: includes the industrialized Deeside region in the E and the Clwydian Hills in the SW. Administrative centre: Mold. Pop: 149 400 (2003 est). Area: 437 sq km (169 sq miles)

flinty (ˈflɪntɪ) *adj* flintier, flintiest **1** of, relating to, or resembling flint **2** hard or cruel; obdurate; unyielding > ˈflintily *adv* > ˈflintiness *n*

flip (flɪp) *vb* flips, flipping, flipped **1** to throw (something light or small) carelessly or briskly; toss **2** to throw or flick (an object such as a coin) so that it turns or spins in the air **3** to propel by a sudden movement of the finger; flick: *to flip a crumb across the room* **4** (foll by *through*) to read or look at (a book, newspaper, etc) quickly, idly, or incompletely **5** (*intr*) to make a snapping movement or noise with the finger and thumb **6** (*intr*) *slang* to fly into a rage or an emotional outburst (also in the phrases **flip one's lid, flip one's top**) ▷ *n* **7** a snap or tap, usually with the fingers **8** a rapid jerk **9** same as **nog¹** (sense 1) ▷ *adj* **10** *informal* impertinent, flippant, or pert [c16: probably of imitative origin; see FILLIP]

flip chart *n* a pad, containing large sheets of paper that can be easily turned over, mounted on a stand and used to present reports, data, etc

flip-flop *n* **1** a backward handspring **2** Also called: **bistable** an electronic device or circuit that can assume either of two stable states by the application of a suitable pulse **3** *informal, chiefly US* a complete change of opinion, policy, etc **4** a repeated flapping or banging noise **5** a rubber-soled sandal attached to the foot by a thong between the big toe and the next toe. Also called (US, Canadian, Austral., and NZ): **thong** ▷ *vb* **-flops, -flopping, -flopped** (*intr*) **6** *informal, chiefly US* to make a complete change of opinion, policy, etc **7** to move with repeated flaps [c16: reduplication of FLIP]

flip-flopper *n US informal* a person who makes a complete change of policy, opinion, etc

flippant ('flɪpənt) *adj* **1** marked by inappropriate levity; frivolous or offhand **2** impertinent; saucy [c17: perhaps from FLIP] > 'flippancy *n* > 'flippantly *adv*

flipper ('flɪpə) *n* **1** the flat broad limb of seals, whales, penguins, and other aquatic animals, specialized for swimming **2** Also called: **fin** (*often plural*) either of a pair of rubber paddle-like devices worn on the feet as an aid in swimming, esp underwater

flip side *n* **1** another term for **B-side** **2** another, less familiar aspect of a person or thing

flirt (flɜːt) *vb* **1** (*intr*) to behave or act amorously without emotional commitment; toy or play with another's affections; dally **2** (*intr; usually foll by with*) to deal playfully or carelessly (with something dangerous or serious); trifle: *the motorcyclist flirted with death* **3** (*intr; usually foll by with*) to think casually (about); toy (with): *to flirt with the idea of leaving* **4** (*intr*) to move jerkily; dart; flit **5** (*tr*) to subject to a sudden swift motion; flick or toss ▷ *n* **6** a person who acts flirtatiously [c16: of uncertain origin] > 'flirter *n* > 'flirty *adj*

flirtation (flɜːˈteɪʃən) *n* **1** behaviour intended to arouse sexual feelings or advances without emotional commitment; coquetry **2** any casual involvement without commitment: *a flirtation with journalism*

flirtatious (flɜːˈteɪʃəs) *adj* **1** given to flirtation **2** expressive of playful sexual invitation: *a flirtatious glance* > flir'tatiously *adv* > flir'tatiousness *n*

flit (flɪt) *vb* **flits, flitting, flitted** (*intr*) **1** to move along rapidly and lightly; skim or dart **2** to fly rapidly and lightly; flutter **3** to pass quickly; fleet: *a memory flitted into his mind* **4** *Scot & Northern English dialect* to move house **5** *Brit informal* to depart hurriedly and stealthily in order to avoid obligations **6** an informal word for **elope** ▷ *n* **7** *Brit informal* a hurried and stealthy departure in order to avoid obligations (esp in the phrase **do a flit**) [c12: from Old Norse *flytja* to carry] > 'flitter *n*

flitch (flɪtʃ) *n* **1** a side of pork salted and cured **2** a piece of timber cut lengthways from a tree trunk, esp one that is larger than 4 by 12 inches [Old English *flicce*; related to Old Norse *flikki*, Middle Low German *vlicke*, Norwegian *flika*; see FLESH]

flitter ('flɪtə) *vb* a less common word for **flutter**

flittermouse ('flɪtəˌmaʊs) *n, pl* **-mice** a dialect name for **bat²** (sense 1) [c16: translation of German *Fledermaus*; see FLITTER, MOUSE]

float (fləʊt) *vb* **1** to rest or cause to rest on the surface of a fluid or in a fluid or space without sinking; be buoyant or cause to exhibit buoyancy: *oil floats on water; to float a ship* **2** to move or cause to move buoyantly, lightly, or freely across a surface or through air, water, etc; drift **3** to move about aimlessly, esp in the mind: *thoughts floated before him* **4** (*tr*) **a** to launch or establish (a commercial enterprise, etc) **b** to offer for sale (stock or bond issues, etc) on the stock market **5** (*tr*) *finance* to allow (a currency) to fluctuate against other currencies in accordance with market forces **6** (*tr*) to flood, inundate, or irrigate (land), either artificially or naturally ▷ *n* **7** something that floats **8** *angling* an

indicator attached to a baited line that sits on the water and moves when a fish bites **9** a small hand tool with a rectangular blade used for floating plaster, etc **10** Also called: **paddle** a blade of a paddle wheel **11** *Brit* a buoyant garment or device to aid a person in staying afloat **12** a hollow watertight structure fitted to the underside of an aircraft to allow it to land on water **13** a motor vehicle used to carry a tableau or exhibit in a parade, esp a civic parade **14** a small delivery vehicle, esp one powered by batteries: *a milk float* **15** *Austral & NZ* a vehicle for transporting horses **16** *chiefly US & Canadian* a sum to be applied to minor expenses; petty cash **17** a sum of money used by shopkeepers to provide change at the start of the day's business, this sum being subtracted from the total at the end of the day when calculating the day's takings **18** the hollow floating ball of a ballcock [Old English *flotian*; related to Old Norse *flota*, Old Saxon *flotōn*; see FLEET²] > 'floatable *adj* > ˌfloata'bility *n* > 'floaty *adj*

floatage ('fləʊtɪdʒ) *n* a variant spelling of **flotage**

floatation (fləʊˈteɪʃən) *n* a variant spelling of **flotation**

floatel (fləʊˈtɛl) *n* a variant spelling of **flotel**

floater ('fləʊtə) *n* **1** a person or thing that floats **2** any of a number of dark spots that appear in one's vision as a result of dead cells or fragments in the lens or vitreous humour of the eye **3** *US & Canadian* a person of no fixed political opinion **4** *US informal* a person who often changes employment, residence, etc; drifter

float glass *n* a type of flat polished transparent glass made by allowing the molten glass to harden as it floats on liquid of higher density

floating ('fləʊtɪŋ) *adj* **1** having little or no attachment **2** (of an organ or part) displaced from the normal position or abnormally movable: *a floating kidney* **3** not definitely attached to one place or policy; uncommitted or unfixed: *the floating vote* **4** *finance* **a** (of capital) not allocated or invested; available for current use **b** (of debt) short-term and unfunded, usually raised by a government or company to meet current expenses **c** (of a currency) free to fluctuate against other currencies in accordance with market forces

floating-point representation *n computing* the representation of numbers by two sets of digits (a, b), the set *a* indicating the significant digits, the set *b* giving the position of the radix point. The number is the product ar^b, where *r* is the base of the number system used. See **fixed-point representation**

floating rib *n* any rib of the lower two pairs of ribs in man, which are not attached to the breastbone

floats (fləʊts) *pl n theatre* another word for **footlights**

flob (flɒb) *vb* **flobs, flobbing, flobbed** (*intr*) *Brit informal* to spit [c20: probably of imitative origin]

flocculate ('flɒkjʊˌleɪt) *vb* to form or be formed into an aggregated flocculent mass > ˌfloccu'lation *n*

flocculent ('flɒkjʊlənt) *adj* **1** like wool; fleecy **2** *chem* aggregated in woolly cloudlike masses: *a flocculent precipitate* **3** *biology* covered with tufts or flakes of a waxy or wool-like substance > 'flocculence or 'flocculency *n*

flocculus ('flɒkjʊləs) *n, pl* **-li** (-ˌlaɪ) **1** a marking on the sun's surface or in its atmosphere, as seen on a spectroheliogram. It consists of calcium when lighter than the surroundings and of hydrogen when darker **2** *anatomy* a tiny ovoid prominence on each side of the cerebellum

flock¹ (flɒk) *n* (*sometimes functioning as plural*) **1** a group of animals of one kind, esp sheep or birds **2** a large number of people; crowd **3** a body of Christians regarded as the pastoral charge of a priest, a bishop, the pope, etc ▷ *vb* (*intr*) **4** to gather together or move in a flock **5** to go in large numbers: *people flocked to the church* [Old English *flocc*; related to Old Norse *flokkr* crowd, Middle Low German *vlocke*]

flock² (flɒk) *n* **1** a tuft, as of wool, hair, cotton, etc **2** waste from fabrics such as cotton, wool, or other cloth used for stuffing mattresses, upholstered chairs, etc **3** very small tufts of wool applied to fabrics, wallpaper, etc, to give a raised pattern [c13: from Old French *floc*, from Latin *floccus*; probably related to Old High German *floccho* down, Norwegian *flugsa* snowflake] > 'flocky *adj*

Flodden ('flɒdˀn) n a hill in Northumberland where invading Scots were defeated by the English in 1513 and James IV of Scotland was killed. Also called: **Flodden Field**

floe (fləʊ) n See **ice floe** [c19: probably from Norwegian *flo* slab, layer, from Old Norse; see FLAW[1]]

flog (flɒg) vb **flogs, flogging, flogged** 1 (tr) to beat harshly, esp with a whip, strap, etc 2 (tr) *Brit slang* to sell 3 (intr) to make progress by painful work 4 *NZ* to steal 5 **flog a dead horse** *chiefly Brit* **a** to harp on some long discarded subject **b** to pursue the solution of a problem long realized to be insoluble [c17: probably from Latin *flagellāre*; see FLAGELLANT] > '**flogger** n

flong (flɒŋ) n 1 *printing* a material, usually pulped paper or cardboard, used for making moulds in stereotyping 2 *journalism slang* material that is not urgently topical [c20: variant of FLAN]

flood (flʌd) n 1 **a** the inundation of land that is normally dry through the overflowing of a body of water, esp a river **b** the state of a river that is at an abnormally high level (esp in the phrase **in flood**). Related adj: **diluvial** 2 a great outpouring or flow: *a flood of words* 3 **a** the rising of the tide from low to high water **b** (as modifier): *the flood tide*. See **ebb** (sense 3) 4 *theatre* short for **floodlight** > vb 5 (of water) to inundate or submerge (land) or (of land) to be inundated or submerged 6 to fill or be filled to overflowing, as with a flood 7 (intr) to flow; surge: *relief flooded through him* 8 to supply an excessive quantity of petrol to (a carburettor or petrol engine) or (of a carburettor, etc) to be supplied with such an excess 9 (intr) to rise to a flood; overflow 10 (intr) to bleed profusely from the uterus, as following childbirth [Old English *flōd*; related to Old Norse *flōth*, Gothic *flōdus*, Old High German *fluot* flood, Greek *plōtos* navigable; see FLOW, FLOAT]

Flood[1] (flʌd) n **the Flood** *Old Testament* the flood extending over all the earth from which Noah and his family and livestock were saved in the ark. (Genesis 7–8); the Deluge

Flood[2] (flʌd) n Henry. 1732–91, Anglo-Irish politician: leader of the parliamentary opposition to English rule

floodgate ('flʌd,geɪt) n 1 Also called: **head gate, water gate** a gate in a sluice that is used to control the flow of water 2 (*often plural*) a control or barrier against an outpouring or flow

flooding ('flʌdɪŋ) n 1 the submerging of land under water, esp due to heavy rain, a lake or river overflowing, etc 2 *pathol* excessive bleeding from the uterus, as following childbirth 3 *psychol* a method of eliminating anxiety in a given situation, by exposing a person to the situation until the anxiety subsides

floodlight ('flʌd,laɪt) n 1 a broad intense beam of artificial light, esp as used in the theatre or to illuminate the exterior of buildings 2 the lamp or source producing such light > vb **-lights, -lighting, -lit** 3 (tr) to illuminate by or as if by a floodlight

flood plain n the flat area bordering a river, composed of sediment deposited during flooding

floor (flɔː) n 1 Also called: **flooring** the inner lower surface of a room 2 a storey of a building: *the second floor* 3 a flat bottom surface in or on any structure: *the floor of a lift; a dance floor* 4 the bottom surface of a tunnel, cave, river, sea, etc 5 that part of a legislative hall in which debate and other business is conducted 6 the right to speak in a legislative or deliberative body (esp in the phrases **get, have,** or **be given the floor**) 7 the earth; ground 8 a minimum price charged or paid 9 **take the floor** to begin dancing on a dance floor > vb 10 to cover with or construct a floor 11 (tr) to knock to the floor or ground 12 (tr) *informal* to disconcert, confound, or defeat: *to be floored by a problem* [Old English *flōr*; related to Old Norse *flōrr*, Middle Low German *vlōr* floor, Latin *plānus* level, Greek *planan* to cause to wander]

floorboard ('flɔː,bɔːd) n one of the boards forming a floor

flooring ('flɔːrɪŋ) n 1 the material used in making a floor, esp the surface material 2 another word for **floor** (sense 1)

floor manager n 1 the stage manager employed in the production of a television programme 2 a person in overall charge of one floor of a large shop or department store

floor plan n a drawing to scale of the arrangement of rooms on one floor of a building

floor show n a series of entertainments, such as singing, dancing, and comedy acts, performed in a nightclub

floozy, floozie or **floosie** ('fluːzɪ) n, pl **-zies** or **-sies** *slang* a disreputable woman [c20: of unknown origin]

flop (flɒp) vb **flops, flopping, flopped** 1 (intr) to bend, fall, or collapse loosely or carelessly: *his head flopped backwards* 2 (when intr, often foll by *into, onto*, etc) to fall, cause to fall, or move with a sudden noise 3 (intr) *informal* to fail; be unsuccessful: *the scheme flopped* 4 (intr) to fall flat onto the surface of water, hitting it with the front of the body 5 (intr; often foll by *out*) *slang* to go to sleep > n 6 the act of flopping 7 *informal* a complete failure 8 **the flop** *poker* the first three community cards dealt face-up in a round of several varieties of poker, including Texas holdem [c17: variant of FLAP]

floppy ('flɒpɪ) adj **-pier, -piest** 1 limp or hanging loosely > n, pl **-pies** 2 short for **floppy disk** > '**floppily** adv > '**floppiness** n

floppy disk n a flexible removable magnetic disk that stores information and can be used to store data for use in a microprocessor

flops or **FLOPS** n acronym for floating-point operations per second: used as a measure of computer processing power (in combination with a prefix)

flora ('flɔːrə) n, pl **-ras** or **-rae** (-riː) 1 all the plant life of a given place or time 2 a descriptive list of such plants, often including a key for identification [c18: from New Latin, from Latin *Flōra* goddess of flowers, from *flōs* FLOWER]

Flora ('flɔːrə) n the Roman goddess of flowers [c16: from Latin, from *flōs* flower]

floral ('flɔːrəl) adj 1 decorated with or consisting of flowers or patterns of flowers 2 of, relating to, or associated with flowers: *floral leaves* > '**florally** adv

Florence ('florəns) n a city in central Italy, on the River Arno in Tuscany: became an independent republic in the 14th century; under Austrian and other rule intermittently from 1737 to 1859; capital of Italy 1865–70. It was the major cultural and artistic centre of the Renaissance and is still one of the world's chief art centres. Pop: 356 118 (2001). Italian name: Firenze

Florentine ('florən,taɪn) adj 1 of or relating to Florence > n 2 a native or inhabitant of Florence 3 a biscuit containing nuts and dried fruit and coated with chocolate

Flores ('flɔːrɛs) n 1 an island in Indonesia, one of the Lesser Sunda Islands, between the Flores Sea and the Savu Sea: mountainous, with active volcanoes and unexplored forests. Chief town: Ende. Area: 17 150 sq km (6622 sq miles) 2 (Portuguese 'florɪʃ) an island in the Atlantic, the westernmost of the Azores. Chief town: Santa Cruz. Area: 142 sq km (55 sq miles)

florescence (flɔːˈrɛsəns) n the process, state, or period of flowering [c18: from New Latin *flōrēscentia*, from Latin *flōrēscere* to come into flower]

Flores Sea n a part of the Pacific Ocean in Indonesia between Celebes and the Lesser Sunda Islands

floret ('flɔːrɪt) n a small flower, esp one of many making up the head of a composite flower [c17: from Old French *florete* a little flower, from *flor* FLOWER]

Florey ('flɔːrɪ) n Howard Walter, Baron Florey. 1898–1968, British pathologist: shared the Nobel prize for physiology or medicine (1945) with E. B. Chain and Alexander Fleming for their work on penicillin

Florianópolis (Portuguese floriə'nɔpulis) n a port in S Brazil, capital of Santa Catarina state, on the W coast of Santa Catarina Island. Pop: 884 000 (2005 est)

floriated or **floreated** ('flɔːrɪ,eɪtɪd) adj *architect* having ornamentation based on flowers and leaves [c19: from Latin *flōs* FLOWER]

floribunda (,flɔːrɪ'bʌndə) n any of several varieties of cultivated hybrid roses whose flowers grow in large sprays [c19: from New Latin, feminine of *flōribundus* flowering freely]

floriculture ('flɔːrɪˌkʌltʃə) *n* the cultivation of flowering plants ▷ ˌflori'cultural *adj* ▷ ˌflori'culturist *n*

florid ('flɒrɪd) *adj* **1** having a red or flushed complexion **2** excessively ornate; flowery: *florid architecture* **3** an archaic word for **flowery** [c17: from Latin *flōridus* blooming] ▷ flo'ridity *or* 'floridness *n* ▷ 'floridly *adv*

Florida ('flɒrɪdə) *n* **1** a state of the southeastern US, between the Atlantic and the Gulf of Mexico: consists mostly of a low-lying peninsula ending in the **Florida Keys** a chain of small islands off the coast of S Florida, extending southwest for over 160 km (100 miles). Capital: Tallahassee. Pop: 17 019 068 (2003 est). Area: 143 900 sq km (55 560 sq miles). Abbreviation: Fla., FL **2** Straits of Florida a sea passage between the Florida Keys and Cuba, linking the Atlantic with the Gulf of Mexico

Floridian (flɒ'rɪdɪən) *n* **1** a native or inhabitant of Florida ▷ *adj* **2** of or relating to Florida or its inhabitants

floriferous (flɔː'rɪfərəs) *adj* bearing or capable of bearing many flowers

florin ('flɒrɪn) *n* **1** a former British coin, originally silver and later cupronickel, equivalent to ten (new) pence **2** (formerly) another name for **guilder** (sense 1) [c14: from French, from Old Italian *fiorino* Florentine coin, from *fiore* flower, from Latin *flōs*]

Florio ('flɔːrɪˌəʊ) *n* John. ?1553–?1625, English lexicographer, noted for his translation of Montaigne's *Essays* (1603)

florist ('flɒrɪst) *n* a person who grows or deals in flowers

floristic (flɒ'rɪstɪk) *adj* of or relating to flowers or a flora ▷ flo'ristically *adv*

-florous *adj combining form* indicating number or type of flowers: *tubuliflorous*

floruit *Latin* ('flɒruːɪt) *vb* (he or she) flourished: used to indicate the period when a historical figure, whose birth and death dates are unknown, was most active

floss (flɒs) *n* **1** the mass of fine silky fibres obtained from cotton and similar plants **2** any similar fine silky material, such as the hairlike styles and stigmas of maize or the fibres prepared from silkworm cocoons **3** untwisted silk thread used in embroidery, etc **4** See **dental floss** ▷ *vb* **5** (*tr*) to clean (between one's teeth) with dental floss [c18: perhaps from Old French *flosche* down]

flossy ('flɒsɪ) *adj* flossier, flossiest consisting of or resembling floss

flotage *or* **floatage** ('fləʊtɪdʒ) *n* **1** the act or state of floating; flotation **2** buoyancy; power or ability to float **3** objects or material that float on the surface of the water; flotsam

flotation *or* **floatation** (fləʊ'teɪʃən) *n* **1 a** the launching or financing of a commercial enterprise by bond or share issues **b** the raising of a loan or new capital by bond or share issues **2** power or ability to float; buoyancy **3** Also called: froth flotation a process to concentrate the valuable ore in low-grade ores. The ore is ground to a powder, mixed with water containing surface-active chemicals, and vigorously aerated. The bubbles formed trap the required ore fragments and carry them to the surface froth, which is then skimmed off

flotel *or* **floatel** (fləʊ'tɛl) *n* (in the oil industry) an oil rig or boat used as accommodation for workers in off-shore oil fields [c20: from *float* + *hotel*]

flotilla (flə'tɪlə) *n* a small fleet or a fleet of small vessels [c18: from Spanish *flota* fleet, from French *flotte*, ultimately from Old Norse *floti*]

Flotow (*German* 'floːto) *n* **Friedrich von** ('friːdrɪç fɒn). 1812–83, German composer of operas, esp *Martha* (1847)

flotsam ('flɒtsəm) *n* **1** wreckage from a ship found floating. See **jetsam** (sense 1) **2** useless or discarded objects; odds and ends (esp in the phrase **flotsam and jetsam**) **3** vagrants [c16: from Anglo-French *floteson*, from *floter* to FLOAT]

flounce¹ (flaʊns) *vb* **1** (*intr*; often foll by *about, away, out,* etc) to move or go with emphatic or impatient movements ▷ *n* **2** the act of flouncing [c16: of Scandinavian origin; compare Norwegian *flunsa* to

hurry, Swedish *flunsa* to splash]

flounce² (flaʊns) *n* an ornamental gathered ruffle sewn to a garment by its top edge [c18: from Old French *fronce* wrinkle, from *froncir* to wrinkle, of Germanic origin]

flounder¹ ('flaʊndə) *vb* (*intr*) **1** to struggle; to move with difficulty, as in mud **2** to behave awkwardly; make mistakes ▷ *n* **3** the act of floundering [c16: probably a blend of FOUNDER² + BLUNDER; perhaps influenced by FLOUNDER²]

● USAGE *Flounder* is sometimes wrongly used where
● *founder* is meant: *the project foundered* (not *floundered*)
● *because of a lack of funds*

flounder² ('flaʊndə) *n, pl* -der *or* -ders Also called: fluke a European flatfish, *Platichthys flesus* having a greyish-brown body covered with prickly scales: family Pleuronectidae: an important food fish [c14: probably of Scandinavian origin; compare Old Norse *flythra*, Norwegian *flundra*]

flour ('flaʊə) *n* **1** a powder, which may be either fine or coarse, prepared by sifting and grinding the meal of a grass, esp wheat **2** any finely powdered substance ▷ *vb* **3** (*tr*) to make (grain) into flour **4** (*tr*) to dredge or sprinkle (food or cooking utensils) with flour [c13 *flur* finer portion of meal, FLOWER] ▷ 'floury *adj*

flourish ('flʌrɪʃ) *vb* **1** (*intr*) to thrive; prosper **2** (*intr*) to be at the peak of condition **3** (*intr*) to be healthy: *plants flourish in the light* **4** to wave or cause to wave in the air with sweeping strokes **5** to display or make a display **6** to play (a fanfare, etc) on a musical instrument ▷ *n* **7** the act of waving or brandishing **8** a showy gesture: *he entered with a flourish* **9** an ornamental embellishment in writing **10** a display of ornamental language or speech **11** a grandiose passage of music **12** an ostentatious display or parade [c13: from Old French *florir*, ultimately from Latin *flōrēre* to flower, from *flōs* a flower] ▷ 'flourisher *n*

flout (flaʊt) *vb* (when *intr*, usually foll by *at*) to show contempt (for); scoff or jeer (at) [c16: perhaps from Middle English *flouten* to play the flute, from Old French *flauter* compare Dutch *fluiten*; see FLUTE] ▷ 'floutingly *adv*

● USAGE See at **flaunt**

flow (fləʊ) *vb* (*mainly intr*) **1** (of liquids) to move or be conveyed as in a stream **2** (of blood) to circulate around the body **3** to move or progress freely as if in a stream: *the crowd flowed into the building* **4** to proceed or be produced continuously and effortlessly: *ideas flowed from her pen* **5** to show or be marked by smooth or easy movement **6** to hang freely or loosely: *her hair flowed down her back* **7** to be present in abundance: *wine flows at their parties* **8** (of tide water) to advance or rise. See **ebb** (sense 1) **9** (of rocks such as slate) to yield to pressure without breaking so that the structure and arrangement of the constituent minerals are altered ▷ *n* **10** the act, rate, or manner of flowing: *a fast flow* **11** a continuous stream or discharge **12** continuous progression **13** the advancing of the tide **14** *Scot* **a** a marsh or swamp **b** an inlet or basin of the sea **c** (*capital when part of a name*): *Scapa Flow* [Old English *flōwan*; related to Old Norse *flōa*, Middle Low German *vlōien*, Greek *plein* to float, Sanskrit *plavate* he swims]

flow chart *or* **flow sheet** *n* a diagrammatic representation of the sequence of operations or equipment in an industrial process, computer program, etc

Flow Country *n* an area of moorland and peat bogs in northern Scotland known for its wildlife, now partly afforested

flower ('flaʊə) *n* **1 a** a bloom or blossom on a plant **b** a plant that bears blooms or blossoms **2** the reproductive structure of angiosperm plants, consisting normally of stamens and carpels surrounded by petals and sepals all borne on the receptacle (one or more of these structures may be absent). In some plants it is conspicuous and brightly coloured and attracts insects or other animals for pollination. Related adj: **floral 3** any similar reproductive structure in other plants **4** the prime; peak: *in the flower of his youth* **5** the choice or finest product, part, or representative **6** a decoration or embellishment **7** (*plural*) fine powder, usually produced by sublimation: *flowers of sulphur* ▷ *vb* **8** (*intr*) to produce flowers; bloom **9** (*intr*) to reach full growth or maturity **10** (*tr*) to deck or decorate with flowers or floral designs [c13: from Old French *flor*, from Latin *flōs*; see BLOW³] > 'flower-,like *adj* > 'flowerless *adj*

flowered ('flavəd) *adj* **1** having or abounding in flowers **2** decorated with flowers or a floral design

floweret ('flavərit) *n* another name for **floret**

flower girl *n* a girl or woman who sells flowers in the street

flowering ('flavərɪŋ) *adj* (of certain species of plants) capable of producing conspicuous flowers

flowerpot ('flavə,pɒt) *n* a pot in which plants are grown

flower power *n informal* a youth cult of the late 1960s advocating peace and love, using the flower as a symbol; associated with drug-taking. Its adherents were known as **flower children** or **flower people**

flowery ('flavərɪ) *adj* **1** abounding in flowers **2** decorated with flowers or floral patterns **3** like or suggestive of flowers **4** (of language or style) elaborate; ornate > 'floweriness *n*

flown (fləʊn) *vb* the past participle of **fly¹**

flow-on *n Austral & NZ* **a** a wage or salary increase granted to one group of workers as a consequence of a similar increase granted to another group **b** (*as modifier*): *a flow-on effect*

fl. oz. *abbreviation* fluid ounce

FLQ *abbreviation* (in Canada) Front de Libération du Québec: a Quebec separatist organization using terrorist tactics, esp in the 1960s and 1970s

flu (fluː) *n informal* **1** the flu short for **influenza** **2** any of various viral infections, esp a respiratory or intestinal infection

flub (flʌb) *informal* ▷ *n* **1** an embarrassing mistake or blunder ▷ *vb* **flubs**, **flubbing**, **flubbed** **2** (*intr*) to blunder or make an embarrassing mistake [c20: of origin unknown]

fluctuate ('flʌktjʊ,eɪt) *vb* **1** to change or cause to change position constantly; be or make unstable; waver or vary **2** (*intr*) to rise and fall like a wave; undulate [c17: from Latin *fluctuāre*, from *fluctus* a wave, from *fluere* to flow] > 'fluctuant *adj* > ,fluctu'ation *n*

flue (fluː) *n* a shaft, tube, or pipe, esp as used in a chimney, to carry off smoke, gas, etc [c16: of unknown origin]

fluent ('fluːənt) *adj* **1** able to speak or write a specified foreign language with facility **2** spoken or written with facility **3** easy and graceful in motion or shape **4** flowing or able to flow freely [c16: from Latin: flowing, from *fluere* to flow] > 'fluently *adv* > 'fluency *n*

flue pipe or **flue** *n* an organ pipe or tubular instrument of the flute family whose sound is produced by the passage of air across a sharp-edged fissure in the side. This sets in motion a vibrating air column within the pipe or instrument

fluff (flʌf) *n* **1** soft light particles, such as the down or nap of cotton or wool **2** any light downy substance **3** *informal* a mistake, esp in speaking or reading lines or performing music **4** *informal* a young woman (esp in the phrase **a bit of fluff**) ▷ *vb* **5** to make or become soft and puffy by shaking or patting; puff up **6** *informal* to make a mistake in performing (an action, dramatic speech, music, etc) [c18: perhaps from *flue* downy matter]

fluffy ('flʌfɪ) *adj* **fluffier**, **fluffiest** **1** of, resembling, or covered with fluff **2** soft and light > 'fluffily *adv* > 'fluffiness *n*

flugelhorn ('fluːgˌəlˌhɔːn) *n* a type of valved brass instrument consisting of a tube of conical bore with a cup-shaped mouthpiece, used esp in brass bands. It is a transposing instrument in B flat or C, and has the same range as the cornet in B flat [German *Flügelhorn*, from *Flügel* wing + *Horn* HORN]

fluid ('fluːɪd) *n* **1** a substance, such as a liquid or gas, that can flow, has no fixed shape, and offers little resistance to an external stress ▷ *adj* **2** capable of flowing and easily changing shape **3** of, concerned with, or using a fluid or fluids **4** constantly changing or apt to change **5** smooth in shape or movement; flowing [c15: from Latin *fluidus*, from *fluere* to flow] > 'fluidness *n*

fluidics (fluː'ɪdɪks) *n* (*functioning as singular*) the study and use of systems in which the flow of fluids in tubes simulates the flow of electricity in conductors. Such systems are used in place of electronics in certain applications, such as the control of apparatus > flu'idic *adj*

fluidize or **fluidise** ('fluːɪ,daɪz) *vb* (*tr*) to make fluid, esp to make (solids) fluid by pulverizing them so that they can be transported in a stream of gas as if they were liquids > ,fluidi'zation or ,fluidi'sation *n*

fluid mechanics *n* (*functioning as singular*) the study of the mechanical and flow properties of fluids, esp as they apply to practical engineering. Also called: hydraulics

fluid ounce *n* a unit of capacity equal to the volume of one avoirdupois ounce of distilled water at 62°F: there are twenty fluid ounces in an Imperial pint and sixteen in a US pint

fluke¹ (fluːk) *n* **1** Also called: flue a flat bladelike projection at the end of the arm of an anchor **2** either of the two lobes of the tail of a whale or related animal **3** Also called: flue the barb or barbed head of a harpoon, arrow, etc [c16: perhaps a special use of FLUKE³ (in the sense: a flounder)]

fluke² (fluːk) *n* **1** an accidental stroke of luck **2** any chance happening ▷ *vb* **3** (*tr*) to gain, make, or hit by a fluke [c19: of unknown origin]

fluke³ (fluːk) *n* any parasitic flatworm, such as the blood fluke and liver fluke, of the classes *Monogenea* and *Digenea* (formerly united in a single class *Trematoda*) [Old English *flōc*; related to Old Norse *flōki* flounder, Old Saxon *flaka* sole, Old High German *flah* smooth]

fluky or **flukey** ('fluːkɪ) *adj* **flukier**, **flukiest** *informal* **1** done or gained by an accident, esp a lucky one **2** variable; uncertain > 'flukiness *n*

flume (fluːm) *n* **1** a ravine through which a stream flows **2** a narrow artificial channel made for providing water for power, floating logs, etc **3** a slide in the form of a long and winding tube with a stream of water running through it that descends into a purpose-built pool ▷ *vb* **4** (*tr*) to transport (logs) in a flume [c12: from Old French *flum*, ultimately from Latin *flūmen* stream, from *fluere* to flow]

flummery ('flʌmərɪ) *n*, *pl* **-meries** **1** *informal* meaningless flattery; nonsense **2** *chiefly Brit* a cold pudding of oatmeal, etc [c17: from Welsh *llymru*]

flummox ('flʌməks) *vb* (*tr*) to perplex or bewilder [c19: of unknown origin]

flung (flʌŋ) *vb* the past tense and past participle of **fling**

flunitrazepam (,fluːnaɪ'træzə,pæm) *n* a drug similar to diazepam, used in treating long-term insomnia

flunk (flʌŋk) *informal*, *chiefly US, Canadian & NZ* ▷ *vb* **1** to fail or cause to fail to reach the required standard in (an examination, course, etc) **2** (*intr*; foll by *out*) to be dismissed from a school or college through failure in examinations [c19: perhaps from FLINCH¹ + FUNK¹]

flunky or **flunkey** ('flʌŋkɪ) *n*, *pl* **flunkies** or **flunkeys** **1** a servile or fawning person **2** a person who performs menial tasks **3** *usually derogatory* a manservant in livery [c18: of unknown origin]

fluor ('fluːɔː) *n* another name for **fluorspar** [c17: from Latin: a flowing; so called from its use as a metallurgical flux]

fluor- *combining form* a variant of **fluoro-** fluorene; fluorine

fluorene ('fluːərɪːn) *n* a white insoluble crystalline solid used in making dyes. Formula: $(C_6H_4)_2CH_2$

fluoresce (,fluə'rɛs) *vb* (*intr*) to exhibit fluorescence [c19: back formation from FLUORESCENCE]

fluorescence (,fluə'rɛsəns) *n* **1** *physics* **a** the emission of light or other radiation from atoms or molecules that are bombarded by particles, such as electrons, or by radiation from a separate source. The bombarding radiation produces excited atoms, molecules, or ions and these emit photons as they fall back to the ground state **b** such an emission of photons that ceases as soon as the bombarding radiation is discontinued **2** the radiation emitted as a result of fluorescence. See **phosphorescence** [c19: FLUOR + -escence (as in *opalescence*)] > ,fluo'rescent *adj*

fluorescent lamp *n* a type of lamp in which an

electrical gas discharge is maintained in a tube with a thin layer of phosphor on its inside surface. The gas, which is often mercury vapour, emits ultraviolet radiation causing the phosphor to fluoresce

fluoridate ('flʊərɪˌdeɪt) vb to subject (water) to fluoridation

fluoridation (ˌflʊərɪ'deɪʃən) n the addition of about one part per million of fluorides to the public water supply as a protection against tooth decay

fluoride ('flʊəˌraɪd) n 1 any salt of hydrofluoric acid, containing the fluoride ion, F⁻ 2 any compound containing fluorine, such as methyl fluoride

fluorinate ('flʊərɪˌneɪt) vb to treat or combine with fluorine > ˌfluori'nation n

fluorine ('flʊəriːn) or **fluorin** ('flʊərɪn) n a toxic pungent pale yellow gas of the halogen group that is the most electronegative and reactive of all the elements, occurring principally in fluorspar and cryolite: used in the production of uranium, fluorocarbons, and other chemicals. Symbol: F; atomic no: 9; atomic wt: 18.9984032; valency: 1; density: 1.696 kg/m³; relative density: 1.108; freezing pt: –219.62°C; boiling pt: –188.13°C

fluorite ('flʊəraɪt) n US & Canadian a white or colourless mineral sometimes fluorescent and often tinted by impurities, found in veins and as deposits from hot gases. It is used in the manufacture of glass, enamel, and jewellery, and is the chief ore of fluorine. Composition: calcium fluoride. Formula: CaF₂. Crystal structure: cubic. Also called (in Britain and certain other countries): fluorspar, fluor

fluoro- or before a vowel **fluor-** combining form 1 indicating the presence of fluorine: fluorocarbon 2 indicating fluorescence: fluoroscope

fluorocarbon (ˌflʊərəʊ'kɑːbən) n any compound derived by replacing all or some of the hydrogen atoms in hydrocarbons by fluorine atoms. Many of them are used as lubricants, solvents, and coatings. See also **Freon, CFC**

fluorometer (ˌflʊə'rɒmɪtə) or **fluorimeter** (ˌflʊə'rɪmɪtə) n a device for detecting and measuring ultraviolet radiation by determining the amount of fluorescence that it produces from a phosphor

fluoroscope ('flʊərəˌskəʊp) n a device consisting of a fluorescent screen and an X-ray source that enables an X-ray image of an object, person, or part to be observed directly

fluoroscopy (flʊə'rɒskəpɪ) n examination of a person or object by means of a fluoroscope

fluorosis (flʊə'rəʊsɪs) n fluoride poisoning, due to ingestion of too much fluoride in drinking water over a long period or to ingestion of pesticides containing fluoride salts. Chronic fluorosis results in mottling of the teeth of children

fluorspar ('flʊəˌspɑː) or **fluor** n a white or colourless mineral sometimes fluorescent and often tinted by impurities, found in veins and as deposits from hot gases. It is used in the manufacture of glass, enamel, and jewellery, and is the chief ore of fluorine. Composition: calcium fluoride. Formula: CaF₂. Crystal structure: cubic. Also called (US and Canadian) fluorite

flurry ('flʌrɪ) n, pl -ries 1 a sudden commotion or burst of activity 2 a light gust of wind or rain or fall of snow > vb -ries, -rying, -ried 3 to confuse or bewilder or be confused or bewildered [C17: from obsolete flurr to scatter, perhaps formed on analogy with HURRY]

flush¹ (flʌʃ) vb 1 to blush or cause to blush 2 to flow or flood or cause to flow or flood with or as if with water 3 to glow or shine or cause to glow or shine with a rosy colour 4 to send a volume of water quickly through (a pipe, channel, etc) or into (a toilet) for the purpose of cleansing, emptying, etc 5 (tr; usually passive) to excite or elate > n 6 a rosy colour, esp in the cheeks; blush 7 a sudden flow or gush, as of water 8 a feeling of excitement or elation: the flush of success 9 early bloom; freshness: the flush of youth 10 redness of the skin, esp of the face, as from the effects of a fever, alcohol, etc [C16 (in the sense: to gush forth): perhaps from FLUSH³] > 'flusher n

flush² (flʌʃ) adj (usually postpositive) 1 level or even with

another surface 2 directly adjacent; continuous 3 informal having plenty of money 4 informal abundant or plentiful, as money 5 full of vigour 6 full to the brim or to the point of overflowing > adv 7 so as to be level or even 8 directly or squarely > vb (tr) 9 to cause (surfaces) to be on the same level or in the same plane > n 10 a period of fresh growth of leaves, shoots, etc [C18: probably from FLUSH¹ (in the sense: spring out)] > 'flushness n

flush³ (flʌʃ) vb (tr) to rouse (game, wild creatures, etc) and put to flight [C13 flusshen, perhaps of imitative origin]

flush⁴ (flʌʃ) n (in poker and similar games) a hand containing only one suit [C16: from Old French flus, from Latin fluxus FLUX]

Flushing ('flʌʃɪŋ) n a port in the SW Netherlands, in Zeeland province, on Walcheren Island, at the mouth of the West Scheldt river: the first Dutch city to throw off Spanish rule (1572). Pop: 45 000 (2003 est). Dutch name: Vlissingen

fluster ('flʌstə) vb 1 to make or become confused, nervous, or upset > n 2 a state of confusion or agitation [C15: probably of Scandinavian origin; compare Icelandic flaustr to hurry, flaustra to bustle]

flute (fluːt) n 1 a wind instrument consisting of an open cylindrical tube of wood or metal having holes in the side stopped either by the fingers or by pads controlled by keys. The breath is directed across a mouth hole cut in the side, causing the air in the tube to vibrate. Range: about three octaves upwards from middle C 2 architect a rounded shallow concave groove on the shaft of a column, pilaster, etc 3 a tall narrow wineglass > vb 4 to produce or utter (sounds) in the manner or tone of a flute 5 (tr) to make grooves or furrows in [C14: from Old French flahute, via Old Provençal, from Vulgar Latin flabeolum (unattested); perhaps also influenced by Old Provençal laut lute; see FLAGEOLET] > 'flute,like adj > 'fluty adj

fluting ('fluːtɪŋ) n 1 a design or decoration of flutes on a column, pilaster, etc 2 grooves or furrows, as in cloth

flutist ('fluːtɪst) n Now chiefly US & Canadian a variant of flautist

flutter ('flʌtə) vb 1 to wave or cause to wave rapidly; flap 2 (intr) (of birds, butterflies, etc) to flap the wings 3 (intr) to move, esp downwards, with an irregular motion 4 (intr) pathol (of the auricles of the heart) to beat abnormally rapidly, esp in a regular rhythm 5 to be or make nervous or restless 6 (intr) to move about restlessly > n 7 a quick flapping or vibrating motion 8 a state of nervous excitement or confusion 9 excited interest; sensation; stir 10 Brit informal a modest bet or wager 11 pathol an abnormally rapid beating of the auricles of the heart (200 to 400 beats per minute), esp in a regular rhythm, sometimes resulting in heart block 12 electronics a slow variation in pitch in a sound-reproducing system, similar to wow but occurring at higher frequencies 13 a potentially dangerous oscillation of an aircraft, or part of an aircraft, caused by the interaction of aerodynamic forces, structural elastic reactions, and inertia 14 Also called: flutter tonguing music a method of sounding a wind instrument, esp the flute, with a rolling movement of the tongue [Old English floterian to float to and fro; related to German flattern; see FLOAT] > 'flutterer n > 'fluttery adj

fluvial ('fluːvɪəl) or **fluviatile** ('fluːvɪəˌtaɪl, -tɪl) adj of, relating to, or occurring in a river: fluvial deposits [C14: from Latin fluviālis, from fluvius river, from fluere to flow]

flux (flʌks) n 1 a flow or discharge 2 continuous change; instability 3 a substance, such as borax or salt, that gives a low melting-point mixture with a metal oxide. It is used for cleaning metal surfaces during soldering, etc, and for protecting the surfaces of liquid metals 4 metallurgy a chemical used to increase the fluidity of refining slags in order to promote the rate of chemical reaction 5 physics a the rate of flow of particles, energy, or a fluid, through a specified area, such as that of neutrons (**neutron flux**) or of light energy (**luminous flux**) b the strength of a field in a given area expressed as the product of the area and the component of the field strength at right angles to the area: *magnetic flux; electric flux* **6** *pathol* an excessive discharge of fluid from the body, such as watery faeces in diarrhoea ▷ *vb* **7** to make or become fluid **8** (*tr*) to apply flux to (a metal, soldered joint, etc) [C14: from Latin *fluxus* a flow, from *fluere* to flow]

flux density *n physics* the amount of flux per unit of cross-sectional area

fluxion ('flʌkʃən) *n maths obsolete* the rate of change of a function, especially the instantaneous velocity of a moving body; derivative [C16: from Late Latin *fluxiō* a flowing]

fly¹ (flaɪ) *vb* **flies, flying, flew, flown** **1** (*intr*) (of birds, aircraft, etc) to move through the air in a controlled manner using aerodynamic forces **2** to travel over (an area of land or sea) in an aircraft **3** to operate (an aircraft or spacecraft) **4** to float, flutter, or be displayed in the air or cause to float, etc, in this way: *to fly a kite; they flew the flag* **5** to transport or be transported by or through the air by aircraft, wind, etc **6** (*intr*) to move or be moved very quickly, forcibly, or suddenly: *she came flying towards me; the door flew open* **7** (*intr*) to pass swiftly: *time flies* **8** to escape from (an enemy, place, etc); flee **9** (*intr*; may be foll by *at* or *upon*) to move towards a person **10** fly a kite **a** to procure money by an accommodation bill **b** to release information or take a step in order to test public opinion **11** fly high *informal* **a** to have a high aim **b** to prosper or flourish **12** fly the coop *US & Canadian informal* to leave suddenly **13** let fly *informal* **a** to lose one's temper (with a person): *she really let fly at him* **b** to shoot or throw (an object) ▷ *n, pl* **flies 14** Also called: fly front (*often plural*) a closure that conceals a zip, buttons, or other fastening, by having one side overlapping, as on trousers **15** Also called: fly sheet **a** a flap forming the entrance to a tent **b** a piece of canvas drawn over the ridgepole of a tent to form an outer roof **16 a** the outer edge of a flag **b** the distance from the outer edge of a flag to the staff **17** *Brit* a light one-horse covered carriage formerly let out on hire **18** (*plural*) *theatre* the space above the stage out of view of the audience, used for storing scenery, etc **19** *rare* the act of flying [Old English *flēogan*; related to Old Frisian *fliāga*, Old High German *fliogan*, Old Norse *fljūga*] ▷ **'flyable** *adj*

fly² (flaɪ) *n, pl* **flies 1** any dipterous insect, esp the housefly, characterized by active flight **2** any of various similar but unrelated insects, such as the caddis fly, firefly, dragonfly, and chalcid fly **3** *angling* a lure made from a fish-hook dressed with feathers, tinsel, etc, to resemble any of various flies or nymphs: used in fly-fishing **4** fly in the ointment *informal* a slight flaw that detracts from value, completeness, or enjoyment **5** fly on the wall a person who watches others, while not being noticed himself **6** there are no flies on him *informal* he is no fool [Old English *flēoge*; related to Old Norse *fluga* Old High German *flioga*; see FLY¹] ▷ **'flyless** *adj*

fly³ (flaɪ) *adj* **flyer, flyest** *slang, chiefly Brit* knowing and sharp; smart [C19: of uncertain origin]

fly agaric *n* a saprotrophic agaricaceous woodland fungus, *Amanita muscaria*, having a scarlet cap with white warts and white gills: poisonous but rarely fatal [so named from its use as a poison on flypaper]

fly ash *n* fine solid particles of ash carried into the air during combustion, esp the combustion of pulverized fuel in power stations

flyaway ('flaɪəˌweɪ) *adj* **1** (of hair or clothing) loose and fluttering **2** frivolous or flighty; giddy ▷ *n* **3** a person who is frivolous or flighty

flyblow ('flaɪˌbləʊ) *vb* **-blows, -blowing, -blew, -blown** **1** (*tr*) to contaminate, esp with the eggs or larvae of the blowfly; taint ▷ *n* **2** (*usually plural*) the egg or young larva of a blowfly, deposited on meat, paper, etc

flyblown ('flaɪˌbləʊn) *adj* **1** covered with flyblows **2** contaminated; tainted

flybook ('flaɪˌbʊk) *n* a small case or wallet used by anglers for storing artificial flies

flyby ('flaɪˌbaɪ) *n, pl* **-bys** a flight past a particular position or target, esp the close approach of a spacecraft to a planet or satellite for investigation of conditions

fly-by-night *informal* ▷ *adj* **1** unreliable or untrustworthy,

esp in finance ▷ *n* Also: fly-by-nighter **2** an untrustworthy person, esp one who departs secretly or by night to avoid paying debts

flycatcher ('flaɪˌkætʃə) *n* **1** any small insectivorous songbird of the Old World subfamily *Muscicapinae*, having small slender bills fringed with bristles: family *Muscicapidae* **2** any American passerine bird of the family *Tyrannidae*

fly-drive *adj, adv* describing a type of package-deal holiday in which the price includes outward and return flights and car hire while away

flyer *or* **flier** ('flaɪə) *n* **1** a person or thing that flies or moves very fast **2** an aviator or pilot **3** *informal* a long flying leap; bound **4** a rectangular step in a straight flight of stairs. See **winder** (sense 5) **5** *athletics* an informal word for **flying start 6** *chiefly US* a speculative business transaction **7** a small handbill

fly-fish *vb* (*intr*) *angling* to fish using artificial flies as lures ▷ **'fly-ˌfishing** *n*

fly half *n rugby* another name for **stand-off half**

flying ('flaɪɪŋ) *adj* **1** (*prenominal*) hurried; fleeting: *a flying visit* **2** (*prenominal*) designed for fast action **3** (*prenominal*) moving or passing quickly on or as if on wings: *a flying leap; the flying hours* **4** hanging, waving, or floating freely: *flying hair* ▷ *n* **5** the act of piloting, navigating, or travelling in an aircraft **6** (*modifier*) relating to, capable of, accustomed to, or adapted for flight: *a flying machine*

flying boat *n* a seaplane in which the fuselage consists of a hull that provides buoyancy in the water

flying bridge *n* an auxiliary bridge of a vessel, usually built above or far outboard of the main bridge

flying buttress *n* a buttress supporting a wall or other structure by an arch or part of an arch that transmits the thrust outwards and downwards

flying colours *pl n* conspicuous success; triumph: *he passed his test with flying colours*

flying doctor *n* (in areas of sparse or scattered population) a doctor who visits patients by aircraft

flying fish *n* any marine teleost fish of the family *Exocetidae*, common in warm and tropical seas, having enlarged winglike pectoral fins used for gliding above the surface of the water

flying fox *n* **1** any large fruit bat, esp any of the genus *Pteropus* of tropical Africa and Asia: family *Pteropodidae* **2** *Austral & NZ* a cable mechanism used for transportation across a river, gorge, etc

flying gurnard *n* any marine spiny-finned gurnard-like fish of the mostly tropical family *Dactylopteridae*, having enlarged fan-shaped pectoral fins used to glide above the surface of the sea

flying jib *n* the jib set furthest forward or outboard on a vessel with two or more jibs

flying lemur *n* either of the two arboreal mammals of the genus *Cynocephalus*, family *Cynocephalidae*, and order *Dermoptera*, of S and SE Asia. They resemble lemurs but have a fold of skin between the limbs enabling movement by gliding leaps

flying officer *n* an officer holding commissioned rank senior to a pilot officer but junior to a flight lieutenant in the British and certain other air forces

flying phalanger *n* any nocturnal arboreal phalanger of the genus *Petaurus*, of E Australia and New Guinea, having black-striped greyish fur and moving with gliding leaps using folds of skin between the hind limbs and forelimbs

flying picket *n* (in industrial disputes) a member of a group of pickets organized to be able to move quickly from place to place

flying saucer *n* any disc-shaped flying object alleged to come from outer space

flying squad *n* a small group of police, soldiers, etc, ready to move into action quickly

flying squirrel *n* any nocturnal sciurine rodent of the subfamily *Petauristinae*, of Asia and North America. Furry folds of skin between the forelegs and hind legs enable these animals to move by gliding leaps

flying start *n* **1** (in sprinting) a start by a competitor anticipating the starting signal. Also called (*informal*): **flyer 2** a start to a race or time trial in which the competitor is already travelling at speed as he passes the starting line **3** any promising beginning **4** an initial advantage over others

flying wing n **1** an aircraft consisting mainly of one large wing and no fuselage or tailplane **2** (in Canadian football) the twelfth player, who has a variable position behind the scrimmage line

flyleaf ('flaɪ,liːf) n, pl -leaves the inner leaf of the endpaper of a book, pasted to the first leaf

Flynn (flɪn) n **1 Errol.** 1909–59, Australian-born Hollywood actor, who was noted for his swashbuckling roles; his films included *Captain Blood* (1935), *The Adventures of Robin Hood* (1938), and *Too Much Too Soon* (1958) **2 Rev. John.** 1880–1951, founder of the Australian flying doctor service

flyover ('flaɪ,əʊvə) n **1** Also called: **overpass** *Brit* an intersection of two roads at which one is carried over the other by a bridge **2** the US name for a **fly-past**

flypaper ('flaɪ,peɪpə) n paper with a sticky and poisonous coating, usually hung from the ceiling to trap flies

fly-past n a ceremonial flight of aircraft over a given area

flyposting ('flaɪ,pəʊstɪŋ) n the posting of advertising or political bills, posters, etc in unauthorized places

flyscreen ('flaɪ,skriːn) n a wire-mesh screen over a window to prevent flies from entering a room

fly sheet n **1** another name for **fly**[1] (sense 15) **2** a short handbill or circular

flyspeck ('flaɪ,spɛk) n **1** the small speck of the excrement of a fly **2** a small spot or speck ▷ vb **3** (tr) to mark with flyspecks

fly spray n a liquid used to destroy flies and other insects, sprayed from an aerosol

fly-tipping n the deliberate dumping of rubbish in an unauthorized place

flytrap ('flaɪ,træp) n **1** any of various insectivorous plants, esp Venus's flytrap **2** a device for catching flies

fly way n the usual route used by birds when migrating

flyweight ('flaɪ,weɪt) n **1 a** a professional boxer weighing not more than 112 pounds (51 kg) **b** an amateur boxer weighing 48–51 kg (106–112 pounds) **2** (in Olympic wrestling) a wrestler weighing not more than 115 pounds (52 kg)

flywheel ('flaɪ,wiːl) n a heavy wheel that stores kinetic energy and smooths the operation of a reciprocating engine by maintaining a constant speed of rotation over the whole cycle

fm abbreviation **1** fathom **2** from

Fm the chemical symbol for fermium

FM abbreviation **1** frequency modulation **2** Field Marshal

FMRI abbreviation functional magnetic resonance imaging: a technique that directly measures the blood flow in the brain, thereby providing information on brain activity

f-number or **f number** n photog the numerical value of the relative aperture. If the relative aperture is f8, 8 is the f-number and indicates that the focal length of the lens is 8 times the size of the lens aperture

Fo (fəʊ) n **Dario** ('dærɪəʊ). born 1926, Italian playwright and actor. His plays include *The Accidental Death of an Anarchist* (1970), *Trumpets and Raspberries* (1984), and *The Tricks of the Trade* (1991): Nobel prize for literature 1997

FO abbreviation **1** army Field Officer **2** air force Flying Officer **3** Foreign Office

fo. abbreviation folio

foal (fəʊl) n **1** the young of a horse or related animal ▷ vb **2** to give birth to (a foal) [Old English *fola*; related to Old Frisian *fola*, Old High German *folo* foal, Latin *pullus* young creature, Greek *pōlos* foal]

foam (fəʊm) n **1** a mass of small bubbles of gas formed on the surface of a liquid, such as the froth produced by agitating a solution of soap or detergent in water **2** frothy saliva sometimes formed in and expelled from the mouth, as in rabies **3** the frothy sweat of a horse or similar animal **4 a** any of a number of light cellular solids made by creating bubbles of gas in the liquid material and solidifying it: used as insulators and in packaging **b** (as modifier): *foam rubber; foam plastic* ▷ vb **5** to

produce or cause to produce foam; froth **6** (intr) to be very angry (esp in the phrase **foam at the mouth**) [Old English *fām*; related to Old High German *feim*, Latin *spūma*, Sanskrit *phena*] > 'foamless adj

foamy ('fəʊmɪ) adj **foamier, foamiest** of, resembling, consisting of, or covered with foam

fob[1] (fɒb) n **1** a chain or ribbon by which a pocket watch is attached to a waistcoat **2** any ornament hung on such a chain **3** a small pocket in a man's waistcoat, for holding a watch [C17: probably of Germanic origin; compare German dialect *Fuppe* pocket]

fob[2] (fɒb) vb **fobs, fobbing, fobbed** an archaic word for **cheat** [C15: probably from German *foppen* to trick]

fob[3] (fɒb) n NZ slang a Pacific Islander who has newly arrived in New Zealand [C20: from f(resh) o(ff) (the) b(oat)]

f.o.b. or **FOB** abbreviation commerce free on board

fob off vb (tr, adverb) **1** to appease or trick (a person) with lies or excuses **2** to dispose of (goods) by trickery

focaccia (fə'kætʃə) n a flat Italian bread made with olive oil and yeast [from Italian]

focal ('fəʊkəl) adj **1** of or relating to a focus **2** situated at, passing through, or measured from the focus

focalize or **focalise** ('fəʊkə,laɪz) vb a less common word for **focus** > ,focali'zation or ,focali'sation n

focal length or **focal distance** n the distance from the focal point of a lens or mirror to the reflecting surface of the mirror or the centre point of the lens

focal plane n the plane that is perpendicular to the axis of a lens or mirror and passes through the focal point

focal point n Also called: **principal focus, focus** the point on the axis of a lens or mirror to which parallel rays of light converge or from which they appear to diverge after refraction or reflection

Foch (French fɔʃ) n **Ferdinand** (fɛrdinã). 1851–1929, marshal of France; commander in chief of Allied armies on the Western front in World War I (1918)

fo'c's'le or **fo'c'sle** ('fəʊksəl) n a variant spelling of **forecastle**

focus ('fəʊkəs) n, pl **-cuses** or **-ci** (-saɪ, -kaɪ, -kiː) **1** a point of convergence of light or other electromagnetic radiation, particles, sound waves, etc, or a point from which they appear to diverge **2** another name for **focal point** (sense 1) **focal length** **3** optics the state of an optical image when it is distinct and clearly defined or the state of an instrument producing this image: *the picture is in focus; the telescope is out of focus* **4** a point upon which attention, activity, etc, is directed or concentrated **5** geometry a fixed reference point on the concave side of a conic section, used when defining its eccentricity **6** the point beneath the earth's surface at which an earthquake or underground nuclear explosion originates. See **epicentre** **7** pathol the main site of an infection or a localized region of diseased tissue ▷ vb **-cuses, -cusing, -cused** or **-cusses, -cussing, -cussed** **8** to bring or come to a focus or into focus **9** (tr; often foll by on) to fix attention (on); concentrate [C17: via New Latin from Latin: hearth, fireplace] > 'focuser n

focus group n a group of people brought together to give their opinions on a particular issue or product, often for the purpose of market research

focus puller n films the member of a camera crew who adjusts the focus of the lens as the camera is tracked in or out

fodder ('fɒdə) n **1** bulk feed for livestock, esp hay, straw, etc ▷ vb **2** (tr) to supply (livestock) with fodder [Old English *fōdor*; related to Old Norse *fōthr*, Old High German *fuotar*; see FOOD, FORAGE]

foe (fəʊ) n formal or literary another word for **enemy** [Old English *fāh* hostile; related to Old High German *fēhan* to hate, Old Norse *feikn* dreadful; see FEUD[1]]

FoE or **FOE** abbreviation Friends of the Earth

foehn (fɜːn; German føːn) n meteorol a variant spelling of **föhn**

foeman ('fəʊmən) n, pl **-men** archaic or poetic an enemy in war; foe

foetal ('fiːtəl) adj a variant spelling of **fetal**

foetid ('fɛtɪd, 'fiː-) adj a variant spelling of **fetid** > 'foetidly adv > 'foetidness n

foetus ('fiːtəs) n, pl **-tuses** a variant spelling of **fetus**

fog[1] (fɒg) n 1 a mass of droplets of condensed water vapour suspended in the air, often greatly reducing visibility, corresponding to a cloud but at a lower level 2 a cloud of any substance in the atmosphere reducing visibility 3 a state of mental uncertainty or obscurity 4 *photog* a blurred or discoloured area on a developed negative, print, or transparency caused by the action of extraneous light, incorrect development, etc ▷ vb **fogs**, **fogging**, **fogged** 5 to envelop or become enveloped with or as if with fog 6 to confuse or become confused: *to fog an issue* 7 *photog* to produce fog on (a negative, print, or transparency) or (of a negative, print, or transparency) to be affected by fog [C16: perhaps back formation from *foggy* damp, boggy, from FOG[2]]

fog[2] (fɒg) n a second growth of grass after the first mowing [C14: probably of Scandinavian origin; compare Norwegian *fogg* rank grass]

Fogarty ('fɒgɑːtɪ) n **Carl** (**George**). born 1965, British racing motorcyclist; Superbike world champion 1994, 1995, 1998, 1999

fog bank n a distinct mass of fog, esp at sea

fogbound ('fɒg,baʊnd) adj prevented from operation by fog: *the airport was fogbound*

fogbow ('fɒg,bəʊ) n a faint arc of light sometimes seen in a fog bank

fogey or **fogy** ('fəʊgɪ) n, pl **-geys** or **-gies** an extremely fussy, old-fashioned, or conservative person (esp in the phrase **old fogey**) [C18: of unknown origin] > **'fogeyish** or **'fogyish** adj

Foggia (Italian 'fɔddʒa) n a city in SE Italy, in Apulia: seat of Emperor Frederick II; centre for Carbonari revolutionary societies in the revolts of 1820, 1848, and 1860. Pop: 155 203 (2001)

foggy ('fɒgɪ) adj **-gier**, **-giest** 1 thick with fog 2 obscure or confused 3 not the foggiest, not the foggiest idea or not the foggiest notion no idea whatsoever: *I haven't the foggiest* > **'fogginess** n

foghorn ('fɒg,hɔːn) n 1 a mechanical instrument sounded at intervals to serve as a warning to vessels in fog 2 *informal* a loud deep resounding voice

fog signal n a signal used to warn railway engine drivers in fog, consisting of a detonator placed on the line

föhn or **foehn** (fɜːn; German føːn) n a warm dry wind blowing down the northern slopes of the Alps. It originates as moist air blowing from the Mediterranean, rising on reaching the Alps and cooling at the saturated adiabatic lapse rate, and descending on the leeward side, warming at the dry adiabatic lapse rate, thus gaining heat [German, from Old High German *phönno*, from Latin *favōnius*; related to *fovēre* to warm]

FOI abbreviation freedom of information

foible ('fɔɪbəl) n 1 a slight peculiarity or minor weakness; idiosyncrasy 2 the most vulnerable part of a sword's blade, from the middle to the tip [C17: from obsolete French, from obsolete adj: FEEBLE]

foie gras (French fwa gra) n See **pâté de foie gras**

foil[1] (fɔɪl) vb (tr) 1 to baffle or frustrate (a person, attempt, etc) 2 *hunting* (of hounds, hunters, etc) to obliterate the scent left by a hunted animal or (of a hunted animal) to run back over its own trail 3 *archaic* to repulse or defeat (an attack or assailant) [C13 *foilen* to trample, from Old French *fouler*, from Old French *fuler* tread down, FULL[2]] > **'foilable** adj

foil[2] (fɔɪl) n 1 metal in the form of very thin sheets: *gold foil; tin foil* 2 the thin metallic sheet forming the backing of a mirror 3 a thin leaf of shiny metal set under a gemstone to add brightness or colour 4 a person or thing that gives contrast to another 5 *architect* a small arc between cusps, as used in Gothic window tracery 6 short for **aerofoil**, **hydrofoil** ▷ vb (tr) 7 to back or cover with foil [C14: from Old French *foille* leaves, from Latin *folia* leaves, plural of *folium*]

foil[3] (fɔɪl) n a light slender flexible sword tipped by a button and usually having a bell-shaped guard [C16: of unknown origin]

foist (fɔɪst) vb (tr) 1 (often foll by off or on) to sell or pass off (something, esp an inferior article) as genuine,

valuable, etc 2 (usually foll by *in* or *into*) to insert surreptitiously or wrongfully [C16: probably from obsolete Dutch *vuisten* to enclose in one's hand, from Middle Dutch *vuist* fist]

Fokine (Russian 'fɔkin; French fɔkin) n **Michel** (miʃɛl). 1880–1942, US choreographer, born in Russia, regarded as the creator of modern ballet. He worked with Diaghilev as director of the Ballet Russe (1909–15), producing works such as *Les Sylphides* and *Petrushka*

Fokker ('fɒkə; Dutch 'fɔkər) n **Anthony Herman Gerard** (ɑn'toːni: 'hɜrman 'xeːrɑrt). 1890- -1939, Dutch designer and builder of aircraft, born in Java

fol. abbreviation 1 folio 2 following

fold[1] (fəʊld) vb 1 to bend or be bent double so that one part covers another: *to fold a sheet of paper* 2 (tr) to bring together and intertwine (the arms, legs, etc): *she folded her hands* 3 (tr) (of birds, insects, etc) to close (the wings) together from an extended position 4 (tr; often foll by *up* or *in*) to enclose in or as if in a surrounding material 5 (tr; foll by *in*) to clasp (a person) in the arms 6 (tr; usually foll by *round*, *about*, *etc*) to wind (around); entwine 7 Also called: **fold in** (tr) to mix (a whisked mixture) with other ingredients by gently turning one part over the other with a spoon 8 (intr; often foll by *up*) *informal* to collapse; fail: *the business folded* ▷ n 9 a piece or section that has been folded: *a fold of cloth* 10 a mark, crease, or hollow made by folding 11 a hollow in undulating terrain 12 a bend in stratified rocks that results from movements within the earth's crust and produces such structures as anticlines and synclines 13 a coil, as in a rope, etc [Old English *fealdan*; related to Old Norse *falda* , Old High German *faldan*, Latin *duplus* double, Greek *haploos* simple] > **'foldable** adj

fold[2] (fəʊld) n 1 a a small enclosure or pen for sheep or other livestock, where they can be gathered b a flock of sheep 2 a church or the members of it ▷ vb 3 (tr) to gather or confine (sheep or other livestock) in a fold [Old English *falod*; related to Old Saxon *faled*, Middle Dutch *vaelt*]

-fold suffix forming adjectives, suffix forming adverbs having so many parts, being so many times as much or as many, or multiplied by so much or so many: *threefold; three-hundredfold* [Old English *-fald*, *-feald*]

foldaway ('fəʊldə,weɪ) adj (prenominal) (of a bed) able to be folded and put away when not in use

folded dipole n a type of aerial, widely used with television and VHF radio receivers, consisting of two parallel dipoles connected together at their outer ends and fed at the centre of one of them. The length is usually half the operating wavelength

folder ('fəʊldə) n 1 a binder or file for holding loose papers, etc 2 a folded circular 3 a person or thing that folds

folderol ('fɒldə,rɒl) n a variant of **falderal**

folding door n a door in the form of two or more vertical hinged leaves that can be folded one against another

folding money n *informal* paper money

foley or **foley artist** ('fəʊlɪ) n *films* the US name for **footsteps editor** [C20: named after the inventor of the technique]

foliaceous (,fəʊlɪ'eɪʃəs) adj 1 having the appearance of the leaf of a plant 2 bearing leaves or leaflike structures 3 *geology* (of certain rocks, esp schists) consisting of thin layers; foliated [C17: from Latin *foliāceus*]

foliage ('fəʊliːdʒ) n 1 the green leaves of a plant 2 sprays of leaves used for decoration 3 an ornamental leaflike design [C15: from Old French *fuellage*, from *fuelle* leaf; influenced in form by Latin *folium*]

foliar ('fəʊlɪə) adj of or relating to a leaf or leaves [C19: from French *foliaire*, from Latin *folium* leaf]

foliate adj ('fəʊlɪɪt, -,eɪt) 1 a relating to, possessing, or resembling leaves b in combination: *trifoliate* ▷ vb ('fəʊlɪ,eɪt) 2 (tr) to ornament with foliage or with leaf forms such as foils 3 to hammer or cut (metal) into thin plates or foil 4 (tr) to number the leaves of (a book, manuscript, etc). See **paginate** 5 (intr) (of plants) to grow leaves [C17: from Latin *foliātus* leaved, leafy]

foliation (,fəʊlɪ'eɪʃən) n 1 *botany* a the process of producing leaves b the state of being in leaf c the arrangement of leaves in a leaf bud; vernation **2** *architect* ornamentation consisting of foliage **3** the consecutive numbering of the leaves of a book **4** *geology* the arrangement of the constituents of a rock in leaflike layers, as in schists

folic acid ('fəʊlɪk, 'fɒl-) *n* any of a group of vitamins of the B complex, including pteroylglutamic acid and its derivatives: used in the treatment of megaloblastic anaemia. Also called: folacin [C20: from Latin *folium* leaf; so called because it may be obtained from green leaves]

folio ('fəʊlɪəʊ) *n, pl* -lios **1** a sheet of paper folded in half to make two leaves for a book or manuscript **2** a book or manuscript of the largest common size made up of such sheets **3** a leaf of paper or parchment numbered on the front side only **4** a page number in a book **5** *law* a unit of measurement of the length of legal documents, determined by the number of words, generally 72 or 90 in Britain and 100 in the US ▷ *adj* **6** relating to or having the format of a folio: *a folio edition* [C16: from Latin phrase *in foliō* in a leaf, from *folium* leaf]

folk (fəʊk) *n, pl* folk or folks **1** (*functioning as plural; often plural in form*) people in general, esp those of a particular group or class: *country folk* **2** (*functioning as plural; usually plural in form*) informal members of a family **3** (*functioning as singular*) *informal* short for **folk music 4** a people or tribe **5** (*modifier*) relating to, originating from, or traditional to the common people of a country: *a folk song* [Old English *folc*; related to Old Saxon, Old Norse, Old High German *folk*] > **'folkish** *adj*

folk dance *n* **1** any of various traditional rustic dances often originating from festivals or rituals **2** a piece of music composed for such a dance > **folk dancing** *n*

Folkestone ('fəʊkstən) *n* a port and resort in SE England, in E Kent. Pop: 45 273 (2001)

folk etymology *n* the gradual change in the form of a word through the influence of a more familiar word or phrase with which it becomes associated, as for example *sparrow-grass* for *asparagus*

folkie or **folky** ('fəʊkɪ) *n, pl* -ies a devotee of folk music

folklore ('fəʊk,lɔː) *n* **1** the unwritten literature of a people as expressed in folk tales, proverbs, riddles, songs, etc **2** the body of stories and legends attached to a particular place, group, activity, etc: *Hollywood folklore; rugby folklore* **3** the anthropological discipline concerned with the study of folkloric materials > **'folk,loric** *adj* > **'folk,lorist** *n, adj*

folk medicine *n* the traditional art of medicine as practised among rustic communities and primitive peoples, consisting typically of the use of herbal remedies, fruits and vegetables thought to have healing power, etc

folk music *n* **1** music that is passed on from generation to generation by oral tradition in the idiom of this oral tradition **2** any music composed in the idiom of this oral tradition

folk-rock *n* a style of rock music influenced by folk, including traditional material arranged for electric instruments

folk song *n* **1** a song of which the music and text have been handed down by oral tradition among the common people **2** a modern song which employs or reflects the folk idiom

folksy ('fəʊksɪ) *adj* -sier, -siest **1** of or like ordinary people; sometimes used derogatorily to describe affected simplicity **2** *informal, chiefly US & Canadian* friendly; affable

folk tale or **folk story** *n* a tale or legend originating among a people and typically becoming part of an oral tradition

folk weave *n* a type of fabric with a loose weave

follicle ('fɒlɪkəl) *n* **1** any small sac or cavity in the body having an excretory, secretory, or protective function: *a hair follicle* **2** *botany* a dry fruit, formed from a single carpel, that splits along one side only to release its seeds: occurs in larkspur and columbine [C17: from Latin *folliculus* small bag, from *follis* pair of bellows, leather money-bag] > **follicular** (fɒ'lɪkjʊlə), **folliculate** (fɒ'lɪkjʊ,leɪt) or **fol'licu,lated** *adj*

follow ('fɒləʊ) *vb* **1** to go or come after in the same direction: *he followed his friend home* **2** (*tr*) to accompany;

attend: *she followed her sister everywhere* **3** to come after as a logical or natural consequence **4** (*tr*) to keep to the course or track of: *she followed the towpath* **5** (*tr*) to act in accordance with; obey: *to follow instructions* **6** (*tr*) to accept the ideas or beliefs of (a previous authority, etc): *he followed Donne in most of his teachings* **7** to understand (an explanation, argument, etc): *the lesson was difficult to follow* **8** to watch closely or continuously: *she followed his progress carefully* **9** (*tr*) to have a keen interest in: *to follow athletics* **10** (*tr*) to help in the cause of or accept the leadership of: *the men who followed Napoleon* [Old English *folgian*; related to Old Frisian *folgia*, Old Saxon *folgōn*, Old High German *folgēn*]

follower ('fɒləʊə) *n* **1** a person who accepts the teachings of another; disciple; adherent: *a follower of Marx* **2** an attendant or henchman **3** an enthusiast or supporter, as of a sport or team **4** (esp formerly) a male admirer

following ('fɒləʊɪŋ) *adj* **1 a** (*prenominal*) about to be mentioned, specified, etc: *the following items* **b** (*as noun*): *will the following please raise their hands?* **2** (of winds, currents, etc) moving in the same direction as the course of a vessel ▷ *n* **3** a group of supporters or enthusiasts: *he attracted a large following wherever he played* ▷ *prep* **4** as a result of: *he was arrested following a tip-off*

follow-on *cricket* ▷ *n* **1** an immediate second innings forced on a team scoring a prescribed number of runs fewer than its opponents in the first innings ▷ *vb* **follow on 2** (*intr, adverb*) (of a team) to play a follow-on

follow out *vb* (*tr, adverb*) to implement (an idea or action) to a conclusion

follow through *vb* (*adverb*) **1** *sport* to complete (a stroke or shot) by continuing the movement to the end of its arc **2** (*tr*) to pursue (an aim) to a conclusion ▷ *n* **follow-through 3** *sport* the act of following through

follow up *vb* (*tr, adverb*) **1** to pursue or investigate (a person, evidence, etc) closely **2** to continue (action) after a beginning, esp to increase its effect ▷ *n* **follow-up 3 a** something done to reinforce an initial action **b** (*as modifier*): *a follow-up letter* **4** *med* a routine examination of a patient at various intervals after medical or surgical treatment

folly ('fɒlɪ) *n, pl* -lies **1** the state or quality of being foolish; stupidity; rashness **2** a foolish action, mistake, idea, etc **3** a building in the form of a castle, temple, etc, built to satisfy a fancy or conceit, often an eccentric kind **4** (*plural*) *theatre* an elaborately costumed revue [C13: from Old French *folie* madness, from *fou* mad; see FOOL[1]]

foment (fə'mɛnt) *vb* (*tr*) **1** to encourage or instigate (trouble, discord, etc); stir up **2** *med* to apply heat and moisture to (a part of the body) to relieve pain and inflammation [C15: from Late Latin *fōmentāre*, from Latin *fōmentum* a poultice, ultimately from *fovēre* to foster] > **fomentation** (,fəʊmɛn'teɪʃən) *n* > **fo'menter** *n*

● **USAGE** Both *foment* and *ferment* can be used to talk
● about stirring up trouble: *he was accused of fomenting/*
● *fermenting unrest*. Only *ferment* can be used intransitively
● or as a noun: *his anger continued to ferment* (not *foment*);
● *rural areas were unaffected by the ferment in the cities*

fond (fɒnd) *adj* **1** (*postpositive; foll by of*) predisposed (to); having a liking (for) **2** loving; tender: *a fond embrace* **3** indulgent; doting: *a fond mother* **4** (of hopes, wishes, etc) cherished but unlikely to be realized: *he had fond hopes of starting his own business* **5** *archaic or dialect* **a** foolish **b** credulous [C14 *fonned*, from *fonnen* to be foolish, from *fonne* a fool] > **'fondly** *adv* > **'fondness** *n*

Fonda ('fɒndə) *n* **1 Henry**. 1905–82, US film actor. His many films include *Young Mr Lincoln* (1939), *The Grapes of Wrath* (1940), *Twelve Angry Men* (1957), and *On Golden Pond* (1981) for which he won an Oscar **2** his daughter **Jane**. born 1937, US film actress. Her films include *Klute* (1971) for which she won an Oscar, *Julia* (1977), *The China Syndrome* (1979), *On Golden Pond* (1981), and *The Old Gringo* (1989) **3** her brother, **Peter**. born 1939, US film actor, who made his name in *Easy Rider* (1969); later films include *Ulee's Gold* (1997)

fondant ('fɒndənt) *n* **1** a thick flavoured paste of sugar and water, used in sweets and icings **2** a sweet made of this mixture ▷ *adj* **3** (of a colour) soft; pastel [C19: from French, literally: melting, from *fondre* to melt, from

Latin *fundere*; see FOUND³]

fondle ('fɒndəl) *vb* (*tr*) to touch or stroke tenderly; caress [C17: from (obsolete) *vb fond* to fondle; see FOND¹] ▷ **'fondler** *n*

fondue ('fɒndjuː; *French* fɔ̃dy) *n* a Swiss dish, consisting of cheese melted in white wine or cider, into which small pieces of bread are dipped and then eaten [C19: from French, feminine of *fondu* melted, from *fondre* to melt; see FONDANT]

Fonseca (*Spanish* fɒnˈseka) *n* **Gulf of Fonseca** an inlet of the Pacific Ocean in W Central America

font¹ (fɒnt) *n* **1 a** a large bowl for baptismal water, usually mounted on a pedestal **b** a receptacle for holy water **2** the reservoir for oil in an oil lamp **3** *archaic or poetic* a fountain or well [Old English, from Church Latin *fons*, from Latin: fountain]

font² (fɒnt) *n printing* a complete set of type of one style and size. Also called: **fount** [C16: from Old French *fonte* a founding, casting, from Vulgar Latin *funditus* (unattested) a casting, from Latin *fundere* to melt; see FOUND³]

Fontainebleau ('fɒntɪnˌbləʊ; *French* fɔ̃tɛnblo) *n* a town in N France, in the **Forest of Fontainebleau**: famous for its palace (now a museum), one of the largest royal residences in France, built largely by Francis I (16th century). Pop: 15 942 (1999)

Fontane (*German* fɒnˈtaːnə) *n* **Theodor** ('teodɔːr). 1819–98, German novelist and journalist; his novels include *Vor dem Sturm* (1878) and *Effi Briest* (1898)

fontanelle *or chiefly US* **fontanel** (ˌfɒntəˈnɛl) *n anatomy* any of several soft membranous gaps between the bones of the skull in a fetus or infant [C16 (in the sense: hollow between muscles): from Old French *fontanele*, literally: a little spring, from *fontaine* FOUNTAIN]

Fontenelle (*French* fɔ̃tənɛl) *n* **Bernard le Bovier de** (bɛrnar lə bɔvje də). 1657–1757, French philosopher. His writings include *Digressions sur les anciens et les modernes* (1688) and *Éléments de la géométrie de l'infini* (1727)

Fonteyn (fɒnˈteɪn) *n* **Dame Margot**. real name *Margaret Hookham*. 1919–91, English classical ballerina

Foochow ('fuːˈtʃaʊ) *n* a variant transliteration of the Chinese name for **Fuzhou**

food (fuːd) *n* **1** any substance containing nutrients, such as carbohydrates, proteins, and fats, that can be ingested by a living organism and metabolized into energy and body tissue. Related adj: **alimentary 2** nourishment in more or less solid form as opposed to liquid form: *food and drink* **3** anything that provides mental nourishment or stimulus: *food for thought* [Old English *fōda*; related to Old Frisian *fōdia* to nourish, feed, Old Norse *fæthi*, Gothic *fōdeins* food; see FEED, FODDER]

food additive *n* any of various natural or synthetic substances, such as salt, monosodium glutamate, or citric acid, used in the commercial processing of food as preservatives, antioxidants, emulsifiers, etc, in order to preserve or add flavour, colour, or texture to processed food

food chain *n ecology* a sequence of organisms in an ecosystem in which each species is the food of the next member of the chain

food combining *n* the practice of keeping carbohydrates separate from proteins in one's daily diet, as a way of losing weight and also for some medical conditions

food group *n* any of the categories into which different foods may be placed according to the type of nourishment they supply, such as carbohydrates or proteins

foodie *or* **foody** ('fuːdɪ) *n*, *pl* -ies a person having an enthusiastic interest in the preparation and consumption of good food

food poisoning *n* an acute illness typically characterized by gastrointestinal inflammation, vomiting, and diarrhoea, caused by food that is either naturally poisonous or contaminated by pathogenic bacteria (esp *Salmonella*)

food processor *n cookery* an electric domestic appliance designed to speed the preparation and mixing of ingredients by automatic chopping, grating,

blending, etc

foodstuff ('fuːdˌstʌf) *n* any material, substance, etc, that can be used as food

fool¹ (fuːl) *n* **1** a person who lacks sense or judgement **2** a person who is made to appear ridiculous **3** (formerly) a professional jester living in a royal or noble household **4** *obsolete* an idiot or imbecile: *the village fool* **5 play the fool** *or* **act the fool** to deliberately act foolishly; indulge in buffoonery ▷ *vb* **6** (*tr*) to deceive (someone), esp in order to make him look ridiculous **7** (*intr*; foll by *with, around with,* or *about with*) *informal* to act or play (with) irresponsibly or aimlessly: *to fool around with a woman* **8** (*intr*) to speak or act in a playful, teasing, or jesting manner **9** (*tr*; foll by *away*) to squander; fritter: *he fooled away a fortune* ▷ *adj* **10** *informal* short for **foolish** [C13: from Old French *fol* mad person, from Late Latin *follis* empty-headed fellow, from Latin: bellows; related to Latin *flāre* to blow]

fool² (fuːl) *n chiefly Brit* a dessert made from a purée of fruit with cream or custard: *gooseberry fool* [C16: perhaps from FOOL¹]

foolery ('fuːlərɪ) *n*, *pl* -eries **1** foolish behaviour **2** an instance of this, esp a prank or trick

foolhardy ('fuːlˌhɑːdɪ) *adj* -hardier, -hardiest heedlessly rash or adventurous [C13: from Old French *fol hardi*, from *fol* foolish + *hardi* bold] ▷ **'fool,hardily** *adv* ▷ **'fool,hardiness** *n*

foolish ('fuːlɪʃ) *adj* **1** unwise; silly **2** resulting from folly or stupidity **3** ridiculous or absurd; not worthy of consideration **4** weak-minded; simple ▷ **'foolishly** *adv* ▷ **'foolishness** *n*

foolproof ('fuːlˌpruːf) *adj* **1** proof against failure; infallible: *a foolproof idea* **2** (esp of machines) proof against human misuse, error, etc

foolscap ('fuːlzˌkæp) *n chiefly Brit* a size of writing or printing paper, 13½ by 17 inches or 13½ by 16½ inches [C17: see FOOL¹, CAP; so called from the watermark formerly used on this kind of paper]

fool's cap *n* **1** a hood or cap with bells or tassels, worn by court jesters **2** a dunce's cap

fool's errand *n* a fruitless undertaking

fool's gold *n* any of various yellow minerals, esp pyrite or chalcopyrite, that can be mistaken for gold

fool's paradise *n* illusory happiness

fool's-parsley *n* an evil-smelling Eurasian umbelliferous plant, *Aethusa cynapium*, with small white flowers: contains the poison coniine

foosball ('fuːsˌbɔːl) *n US & Canadian* a game, often played in bars, in which opponents on either side of a purpose-built table attempt to strike a ball into the other side's goal by moving horizontal bars to which miniatures of footballers are attached. Also called (esp in Britain): table football

foot (fʊt) *n*, *pl* **feet** (fiːt) **1** the part of the vertebrate leg below the ankle joint that is in contact with the ground during standing and walking. Related adj: **pedal 2** the part of a garment that covers a foot **3** any of various organs of locomotion or attachment in invertebrates, including molluscs **4** *botany* the lower part of some plant structures, as of a developing moss sporophyte embedded in the parental tissue **5** a unit of length equal to one third of a yard or 12 inches. 1 Imperial foot is equivalent to 0.3048 metre. Abbreviation: ft **6** any part resembling a foot in form or function: *the foot of a chair* **7** the lower part of something; base; bottom: *the foot of the page*; *the foot of a hill* **8** the end of a series or group: *the foot of the list* **9** manner of walking or moving; tread; step: *a heavy foot* **10 a** infantry, esp in the British army **b** (*as modifier*): *a foot soldier* **11** any of various attachments on a sewing machine that hold the fabric in position, such as a presser foot for ordinary sewing and a zipper foot **12** *prosody* a group of two or more syllables in which one syllable has the major stress, forming the basic unit of poetic rhythm **13 a foot in the door** an action, appointment, etc, that provides an initial step towards a desired goal, esp one that is not easily attainable **14 my foot!** an expression of disbelief, often of the speaker's own preceding statement: *he didn't know, my foot! Of course he did!* **15 of foot** *archaic* in manner of movement: *fleet of*

foot 16 on foot a walking or running **b** in progress; astir; afoot **17 put a foot wrong** to make a mistake **18 put one's best foot forward a** to try to do one's best **b** to hurry **19 put one's foot down** *informal* to act firmly **20 put one's foot in it** *informal* to blunder **21 under foot** on the ground; beneath one's feet ▷ *vb* **22** to dance to music (esp in the phrase **foot it**) **23** (*tr*) to walk over or set foot on; traverse (esp in the phrase **foot it**) **24** (*tr*) to pay the entire cost (esp in the phrase **foot the bill**) ▷ See also **feet** [Old English *fōt*; related to Old Norse *fōtr*, Gothic *fōtus*, Old High German *fuoz*, Latin *pēs*, Greek *pous*, Sanskrit *pad*] > 'footless *adj*

● **USAGE** In front of another noun, the plural for the ● unit of length is *foot: a 20-foot putt; his 70-foot ketch. Foot* ● can also be used instead of *feet* when mentioning a ● quantity and in front of words like *tall: four foot of snow;* ● *he is at least six foot tall*

Foot (fʊt) *n* **Michael (Mackintosh).** born 1913, British Labour politician and journalist; secretary of state for employment (1974–76); leader of the House of Commons (1976–79); leader of the Labour Party (1980–83)

footage ('fʊtɪdʒ) *n* **1** a length or distance measured in feet **2** the extent of film material shot and exposed

foot-and-mouth disease *n* an acute highly infectious viral disease of cattle, pigs, sheep, and goats, characterized by the formation of vesicular eruptions in the mouth and on the feet, esp around the hoofs. Also called: hoof-and-mouth disease, aphtha, aphthous fever

football ('fʊt,bɔːl) *n* **1 a** any of various games played with a round or oval ball and usually based on two teams competing to kick, head, carry, or otherwise propel the ball into each other's goal, territory, etc **b** (*as modifier*): *a football ground; a football supporter* **2** the ball used in any of these games or their variants **3** a problem, issue, etc, that is continually passed from one group or person to another and treated as a pretext for argument instead of being resolved: *he accused the government of using the strike as a political football* > 'foot,baller *n*

footboard ('fʊt,bɔːd) *n* **1** a treadle or foot-operated lever on a machine **2** a vertical board at the foot of a bed

footbridge ('fʊt,brɪdʒ) *n* a narrow bridge for the use of pedestrians

-footed *adj* **1** having a foot or feet as specified: *four-footed* **2** having a tread as specified: *heavy-footed*

footer[1] ('fʊtə) *n* (*in combination*) a person or thing of a specified length or height in feet: *a six-footer*

footer[2] ('fʊtə) *n Brit informal* short for **football** (sense 1)

footfall ('fʊt,fɔːl) *n* the sound of a footstep

foot fault *n tennis* a fault that occurs when the server fails to keep both feet behind the baseline until he has served

foothill ('fʊt,hɪl) *n* (*often plural*) a lower slope of a mountain or a relatively low hill at the foot of a mountain

foothold ('fʊt,həʊld) *n* **1** a ledge, hollow, or other place affording a secure grip for the foot, as during climbing **2** a secure position from which further progress may be made

footing ('fʊtɪŋ) *n* **1** the basis or foundation on which something is established: *the business was on a secure footing* **2** the relationship or status existing between two persons, groups, etc: *the two countries were on a friendly footing* **3** a secure grip by or for the feet **4** the lower part of a foundation of a column, wall, building, etc

footle ('fuːtᵊl) *informal* ▷ *vb* (*intr*) (often foll by *around* or *about*) to loiter aimlessly; potter [c19: probably from French *foutre* to copulate with, from Latin *futuere*]

footlights ('fʊt,laɪts) *pl n theatre* lights set in a row along the front of the stage floor and shielded on the audience side

footling ('fuːtlɪŋ) *adj informal* silly, trivial, or petty

footloose ('fʊt,luːs) *adj* **1** free to go or do as one wishes **2** eager to travel; restless: *to feel footloose*

footman ('fʊtmən) *n, pl* -men **1** a male servant, esp one in livery **2** (*formerly*) a foot soldier

footnote ('fʊt,nəʊt) *n* **1** a note printed at the bottom of a page, to which attention is drawn by means of a reference mark in the body of the text ▷ *vb* **2** (*tr*) to supply (a page, book, etc) with footnotes

footpad ('fʊt,pæd) *n archaic* a robber or highwayman, on foot rather than horseback

footpath ('fʊt,pɑːθ) *n* **1** a narrow path for walkers only **2** *chiefly Brit, Austral & NZ* another word for **pavement**

footplate ('fʊt,pleɪt) *n chiefly Brit* a platform in the cab of a locomotive on which the crew stand to operate the controls

foot-pound-second *n* See **fps units**

footprint ('fʊt,prɪnt) *n* **1** an indentation or outline of the foot of a person or animal on a surface **2** the shape and size of the area something occupies: *enlarging the footprint of the building; a computer with a small footprint* **3** *computing* the amount of resources such as disk space and memory, that an application requires. See also **electronic footprint**

footrest ('fʊt,rɛst) *n* something that provides a support for the feet, such as a low stool, rail, etc

foot rot *n vet science* See **rot**[1] (sense 10)

footsie ('fʊtsɪ) *n informal* flirtation involving the touching together of feet, knees, etc (esp in the phrase **play footsie**)

Footsie ('fʊtsɪ) *n* an informal name for **Financial Times Stock Exchange 100 Index**

foot soldier *n* an infantryman

footsore ('fʊt,sɔː) *adj* having sore or tired feet, esp from much walking > 'foot,soreness *n*

footstep ('fʊt,stɛp) *n* **1** the action of taking a step in walking **2** the sound made by stepping or walking **3** the distance covered with a step; pace **4** a footmark **5** a single stair; step **6** to continue the tradition or example of another

footsteps editor *n Brit films* the technician who adds sound effects, such as doors closing, rain falling, etc, during the postproduction sound-dubbing process. US name: foley

footstool ('fʊt,stuːl) *n* a low stool used for supporting or resting the feet of a seated person

foot traffic *n* **1** the wear and tear caused to a surface by people walking on it **2** *US & Canadian* the activity of pedestrians in a particular area

footwear ('fʊt,wɛə) *n* anything worn to cover the feet

footwork ('fʊt,wɜːk) *n* **1** skilful use of the feet, as in sports, dancing, etc **2** *informal* clever manoeuvring: *deft political footwork* **3** *informal* preliminary groundwork: *many estate agents now do the footwork – you only need to visit*

footy or **footie** ('fʊtɪ) *n informal* **a** football **b** (*as modifier*): *footy boots*

fop (fɒp) *n* a man who is excessively concerned with fashion and elegance [c15: related to German *foppen* to trick; see FOB[2]] > 'foppish *adj* > 'foppery *n*

for (fɔː; *unstressed* fə) *prep* **1** intended to reach; directed or belonging to: *there's a phone call for you* **2** to the advantage of: *I only did it for you* **3** in the direction of: *heading for the border* **4** over a span of (time or distance): *working for six days; the river ran for six miles* **5** in favour of; in support of: *those for the proposal; vote for me* **6** in order to get or achieve: *I do it for money; he does it for pleasure; what did you do that for?* **7** appropriate to; designed to meet the needs of; meant to be used in: *these kennels are for puppies* **8** in exchange for; at a cost of; to the amount of: *I got it for hardly any money* **9** such as explains or results in: *his reason for changing his job was not given* **10** in place of: *a substitute for the injured player* **11** because of; through: *she wept for pure relief* **12** with regard or consideration to the usual characteristics of: *he's short for a man; it's cool for this time of year* **13** concerning; as regards: *desire for money* **14** as being: *we took him for the owner; I know that for a fact* **15** at a specified time: *a date for the next evening* **16** to do or partake of: *an appointment for supper* **17** in the duty or task of: *that's for him to say* **18** to allow of: *too big a job for us to handle* **19** despite; notwithstanding: *she's a good wife, for all her nagging* **20** in order to preserve, retain, etc: *to fight for survival* **21** as a direct equivalent to: *word for word; weight for weight* **22** in order to become or enter: *to go for a soldier; to train for the priesthood* **23** in recompense for: *I paid for it last week; he took the punishment for his crime* **24** for it *Brit informal* liable for punishment or blame: *you'll be for it if she catches you* ▷ *conj* **25** (*coordinating*) for the following reason; because; seeing that: *I couldn't stay, for the area was violent* [Old English;

related to Old Norse *fyr* for, Old High German *fora* before, Latin *per* through, *prō* before, Greek *pro* before, in front]

for- *prefix* **1** indicating rejection or prohibition: *forbear; forbid* **2** indicating falsity or wrongness: *forswear* **3** used to give intensive force: *forgive; forlorn* [Old English *for-*; related to German *ver-*, Latin *per-*, Greek *peri-*]

forage ('fɒrɪdʒ) *n* **1** food for horses or cattle, esp hay or straw **2** the act of searching for food or provisions ▷ *vb* **3** to search (the countryside or a town) for food, provisions, etc **4** (*intr*) military to carry out a raid **5** (*tr*) to obtain by searching about **6** (*tr*) to give food or other provisions to **7** (*tr*) to feed (cattle or horses) with such food [c14: from Old French *fourrage*, probably of Germanic origin; see FOOD, FODDER] > 'forager *n*

forage cap *n* a soldier's undress cap

foramen (fɒ'reɪmɛn) *n, pl* -ramina (-'ræmɪnə) *or* -ramens a natural hole, esp one in a bone through which nerves and blood vessels pass [c17: from Latin, from *forāre* to bore, pierce]

foraminifer (ˌfɒrə'mɪnɪfə) *n* any marine protozoan of the phylum *Foraminifera*, having a shell with numerous openings through which cytoplasmic processes protrude [c19: from New Latin, from FORAMEN + -FER]

forasmuch as (fərəz'mʌtʃ) *conj* (*subordinating*) archaic or legal seeing that; since

foray ('fɒreɪ) *n* **1** a short raid or incursion ▷ *vb* **2** to raid or ravage (a town, district, etc) [c14: from *forrayen* to pillage, from Old French *forreier*, from *forrier* forager, from *fuerre* fodder; see FORAGE]

forbade (fə'bæd, -'beɪd) *or* **forbad** (fə'bæd) *vb* the past tense of **forbid**

forbear¹ (fɔː'bɛə) *vb* -bears, -bearing, -bore, -borne **1** (when *intr*, often foll by *from* or an infinitive) to cease or refrain (from doing something) **2** archaic to tolerate or endure (misbehaviour, mistakes, etc) [Old English *forberan*; related to Gothic *frabairan* to endure]

forbear² ('fɔːˌbɛə) *n* a variant spelling of **forebear**

forbearance (fɔː'bɛərəns) *n* **1** the act of forbearing **2** self-control; patience

Forbes (fɔːbz) *n* **George William**. 1869–1947, New Zealand statesman; prime minister of New Zealand (1930–35)

forbid (fə'bɪd) *vb* -bids, -bidding, -bade *or* -bad, -bidden *or* -bid (*tr*) **1** to prohibit (a person) in a forceful or authoritative manner (from doing something or having something) **2** to make impossible; hinder **3** to shut out or exclude [Old English *forbēodan*; related to Old High German *farbiotan*, Gothic *faurbiudan*; see FOR-, BID] > for'bidder *n*

forbidden (fə'bɪd³n) *adj* **1** not permitted by order or law **2** physics involving a change in quantum numbers that is not permitted by certain rules derived from quantum mechanics, esp rules for changes in the electrical dipole moment of the system

Forbidden City *n* **the Forbidden City 1** Lhasa, Tibet: once famed for its inaccessibility and hostility to strangers **2** a walled section of Beijing, China, enclosing the Imperial Palace and associated buildings of the former Chinese Empire

forbidden fruit *n* any pleasure or enjoyment regarded as illicit, esp sexual indulgence

forbidding (fə'bɪdɪŋ) *adj* **1** hostile or unfriendly **2** dangerous or ominous

forbore (fɔː'bɔː) *vb* the past tense of **forbear¹**

forborne (fɔː'bɔːn) *vb* the past participle of **forbear¹**

force¹ (fɔːs) *n* **1** strength or energy; might; power: *the force of the blow; a gale of great force* **2** exertion or the use of exertion against a person or thing that resists; coercion **3** physics **a** a dynamic influence that changes a body from a state of rest to one of motion or changes its rate of motion. The magnitude of the force is equal to the product of the mass of the body and its acceleration **b** a static influence that produces an elastic strain in a body or system or bears weight. Symbol: F **4 a** intellectual, social, political, or moral influence or strength: *the force of his argument; the forces of evil* **b** a person or thing with such influence: *he was a force in the land* **5** vehemence or intensity: *he spoke with great force* **6** a group of persons organized for military or police functions: *armed forces* **7** the force (*sometimes capital*) informal the police force **8** a group of persons organized for particular duties or tasks: *a workforce* **9** criminal law violence unlawfully committed or threatened **10** in force **a** (of a law) having legal validity or binding effect **b** in great strength or numbers ▷ *vb* (*tr*) **11** to compel or cause (a person, group, etc) to do something through effort, superior strength, etc; coerce **12** to acquire, secure, or produce through effort, superior strength, etc: *to force a confession* **13** to propel or drive despite resistance: *to force a nail into wood* **14** to break down or open (a lock, safe, door, etc) **15** to impose or inflict: *he forced his views on them* **16** to cause (plants or farm animals) to grow or fatten artificially at an increased rate **17** to strain or exert to the utmost: *to force the voice* **18** to rape; ravish **19** cards **a** to compel a player by the lead of a particular suit to play (a certain card) **b** (in bridge) to induce (a bid) from one's partner by bidding in a certain way [c13: from Old French, from Vulgar Latin *fortia* (unattested), from Latin *fortis* strong] > 'forceable *adj* > 'forceless *adj* > 'forcer *n*

force² (fɔːs) *n* (in northern England) a waterfall [c17: from Old Norse *fors*]

forced (fɔːst) *adj* **1** done because of force; compulsory: *forced labour* **2** false or unnatural: *a forced smile* **3** due to an emergency or necessity: *a forced landing*

force de frappe (French fɔrs də frap) *n* a military strike force, esp the independent nuclear strike force of France [c20: literally: striking force]

force-feed *vb* -feeds, -feeding, -fed (*tr*) to force (a person or animal) to eat or swallow food

forceful ('fɔːsfʊl) *adj* **1** powerful **2** persuasive or effective > 'forcefully *adv* > 'forcefulness *n*

forcemeat ('fɔːsˌmiːt) *n* a mixture of chopped or minced ingredients used for stuffing. Also called: farce, farcemeat [c17: from *force* (see FARCE) + MEAT]

forceps ('fɔːsɪps) *n, pl* -ceps *or* -cipes (-sɪˌpiːz) **1 a** a surgical instrument in the form of a pair of pincers, used esp in the delivery of babies **b** (*as modifier*): *a forceps baby* **2** any part or structure of an organism shaped like a forceps [c17: from Latin, from *formus* hot + *capere* to seize]

force pump *n* a pump that ejects fluid under pressure. See **lift pump**

Forces ('fɔːsɪz) *pl n* **the Forces** the armed services of a nation

forcible ('fɔːsəb³l) *adj* **1** done by, involving, or having force **2** convincing or effective: *a forcible argument* > 'forcibly *adv*

ford (fɔːd) *n* **1** a shallow area in a river that can be crossed by car, horseback, etc ▷ *vb* **2** (*tr*) to cross (a river, brook, etc) over a shallow area [Old English; related to Old Frisian *forda*, Old High German *furt* ford, Latin *porta* door, *portus* PORT¹] > 'fordable *adj*

Ford (fɔːd) *n* **1 Ford Maddox** ('mædəks) original name *Ford Madox Hueffer*. 1873–1939, English novelist, editor, and critic; works include *The Good Soldier* (1915) and the war tetralogy *Parade's End* (1924–28). **2 Gerald R**(udolph). 1913–2006, US politician; 38th president of the US (1974–77) **3 Harrison**. born 1942, US film actor. His films include *Star Wars* (1977) and its sequels, *Raiders of the Lost Ark* (1981) and its sequels, *Bladerunner* (1982), *Clear and Present Danger* (1994), and *What Lies Beneath* (2000) **4 Henry**. 1863–1947, US car manufacturer, who pioneered mass production **5 John**. 1586–?1639, English dramatist; author of revenge tragedies such as *'Tis Pity She's a Whore* (1633) **6 John**, real name *Sean O'Feeney*. 1895–1973, US film director, esp of Westerns such as *Stagecoach* (1939) and *She Wore a Yellow Ribbon* (1949)

fore¹ (fɔː) *adj* **1** (*usually in combination*) located at, in, or towards the front: *the forelegs of a horse* ▷ *n* **2** the front part **3** something located at, in, or towards the front **4** fore and aft located at or directed towards both ends of a vessel: *a fore-and-aft rig* **5** to the fore to or into the front or conspicuous position ▷ *adv* **6** at or towards a ship's bow **7** obsolete before ▷ *prep, conj* **8** a less common word for **before** [Old English; related to Old Saxon, Old High German *fora*, Gothic *faura*, Greek *para*, Sanskrit *pura*]

fore² (fɔː) *interj* (in golf) a warning shout made by a player about to make a shot [c19: probably short for BEFORE]

fore- *prefix* **1** before in time or rank: *foresight; forefather;*

foreman **2** at or near the front; before in place: *forehead; forecourt* [Old English, from *fore* (adv)]

fore-and-after *n* nautical **1** any vessel with a fore-and-aft rig **2** a double-ended vessel

forearm[1] ('fɔ:r,ɑ:m) *n* the part of the arm from the elbow to the wrist [c18: from FORE- + ARM[1]]

forearm[2] (fɔ:r'ɑ:m) *vb* (*tr*) to prepare or arm (someone, esp oneself) in advance [c16: from FORE- + ARM[2]]

forebear *or* **forbear** ('fɔ:,bɛə) *n* an ancestor; forefather

forebode (fɔ:'bəʊd) *vb* **1** to warn of or indicate (an event, result, etc) in advance **2** to have an intuition or premonition of (an event)

foreboding (fɔ:'bəʊdɪŋ) *n* **1** a feeling of impending evil, disaster, etc **2** an omen or portent ▷ *adj* **3** presaging something

forebrain ('fɔ:,breɪn) *n* the nontechnical name for **prosencephalon**

forecast ('fɔ:,kɑ:st) *vb* **-casts, -casting, -cast** *or* **-casted** **1** to predict or calculate (weather, events, etc), in advance **2** (*tr*) to serve as an early indication of ▷ *n* **3** a statement of probable future weather conditions calculated from meteorological data **4** a prophecy or prediction **5** the practice or power of forecasting > 'fore,caster *n*

forecastle, fo'c's'le *or* **fo'c'sle** ('fəʊksᵊl) *n* the part of a vessel at the bow where the crew is quartered and stores, machines, etc, may be stowed

foreclose (fɔ:'kləʊz) *vb* **1** *law* to deprive (a mortgagor, etc) of the right to redeem (a mortgage or pledge) **2** (*tr*) to shut out; bar **3** (*tr*) to prevent or hinder [c15: from Old French *forclore*, from *for-* out + *clore* to close, from Latin *claudere*] > fore'closable *adj* > foreclosure (fɔ:'kləʊʒə) *n*

forecourt ('fɔ:,kɔ:t) *n* **1** a courtyard in front of a building, as one in a filling station **2** Also called: **front court** the front section of the court in tennis, badminton, etc, esp the area between the service line and the net

foredoom (fɔ:'du:m) *vb* (*tr*) to doom or condemn beforehand

forefather ('fɔ:,fɑ:ðə) *n* an ancestor, esp a male > 'fore,fatherly *adj*

forefinger ('fɔ:,fɪŋgə) *n* the finger next to the thumb. Also called: **index finger**

forefoot ('fɔ:,fʊt) *n*, *pl* **-feet** either of the front feet of a quadruped

forefront ('fɔ:,frʌnt) *n* **1** the extreme front **2** the position of most prominence, responsibility, or action

foregather *or* **forgather** (fɔ:'gæðə) *vb* (*intr*) **1** to gather together; assemble **2** (foll by *with*) to socialize

forego[1] (fɔ:'gəʊ) *vb* **-goes, -going, -went, -gone** to precede in time, place, etc [Old English *foregān*]

forego[2] (fɔ:'gəʊ) *vb* **-goes, -going, -went, -gone** (*tr*) a variant spelling of **forgo**

foregoing (fɔ:'gəʊɪŋ) *adj* (*prenominal*) (esp of writing or speech) going before; preceding

foregone (fɔ:'gɒn, 'fɔ:,gɒn) *adj* gone or completed; past > fore'goneness *n*

foregone conclusion *n* an inevitable result or conclusion

foreground ('fɔ:,graʊnd) *n* **1** the part of a scene situated towards the front or nearest to the viewer **2** a conspicuous or active position

forehand ('fɔ:,hænd) *adj* (*prenominal*) **1** *sport* (of a stroke) made with the racket held so that the wrist is facing the direction of the stroke ▷ *n* **2** *sport* **a** a forehand stroke **b** the side on which such strokes are made **3** the part of a horse in front of the saddle

forehead ('fɒrɪd, 'fɔ:,hɛd) *n* the part of the face between the natural hairline and the eyes, formed skeletally by the frontal bone of the skull; brow Related adj: **frontal** [Old English *forhēafod*; related to Old Frisian *forhāfd*, Middle Low German *vorhōved*]

foreign ('fɒrɪn) *adj* **1** of, involving, located in, or coming from another country, area, people, etc: *a foreign resident* **2** dealing or concerned with another country, area, people, etc: *a foreign office* **3** not pertinent or related: *a matter foreign to the discussion* **4** not familiar; strange **5** in an abnormal place or position: *foreign matter; foreign bodies* [c13: from Old French *forain*, from Vulgar Latin *forānus* (unattested) situated on the outside, from Latin *foris* outside] > 'foreignness *n*

foreign affairs *pl n* matters abroad that involve the homeland, such as relations with another country

foreigner ('fɒrɪnə) *n* **1** a person from a foreign country; alien **2** an outsider or interloper **3** something from a foreign country, such as a ship or product

foreign minister *or* **foreign secretary** *n* (*often capitals*) a cabinet minister who is responsible for a country's dealings with other countries. US equivalent: **secretary of state**

foreign office *n* the ministry of a country or state that is concerned with dealings with other states

foreknow (fɔ:'nəʊ) *vb* **-knows, -knowing, -knew, -known** (*tr*) to know in advance > fore'knowable *adj* > fore'knowledge *n*

foreland ('fɔ:lənd) *n* **1** a headland, cape, or coastal promontory **2** land lying in front of something, such as water

foreleg ('fɔ:,lɛg) *n* either of the front legs of a horse, sheep, or other quadruped

forelimb ('fɔ:,lɪm) *n* either of the front or anterior limbs of a four-limbed vertebrate: a foreleg, flipper, or wing

forelock ('fɔ:,lɒk) *n* a lock of hair growing or falling over the forehead

foreman ('fɔ:mən) *n*, *pl* **-men** **1** a person, often experienced, who supervises other workmen **2** *law* the principal juror, who presides at the deliberations of a jury

Foreman ('fɔ:mən) *n* **George.** born 1949, US boxer: WBA world heavyweight champion (1973–74); he regained the title in 1994 but refused to fight the WBA's top-ranked challenger and was stripped of the title in 1995; recognized as WBU champion until 1997

foremast ('fɔ:,mɑ:st; *nautical* 'fɔ:məst) *n* the mast nearest the bow on vessels with two or more masts

foremost ('fɔ:,məʊst) *adj*, *adv* first in time, place, rank, etc [Old English *formest*, from *forma* first; related to Old Saxon *formo* first, Old High German *fruma* advantage]

forename ('fɔ:,neɪm) *n* a first or Christian name

forenamed ('fɔ:,neɪmd) *adj* (*prenominal*) named or mentioned previously; aforesaid

forenoon ('fɔ:,nu:n) *n* the daylight hours before or just before noon

forensic (fə'rɛnsɪk) *adj* relating to, used in, or connected with a court of law: *forensic science* [c17: from Latin *forēnsis* public, from FORUM] > fo'rensically *adv*

forensic medicine *n* the applied use of medical knowledge or practice, esp pathology, to the purposes of the law, as in determining the cause of death. Also called: **medical jurisprudence, legal medicine**

foreordain (,fɔ:rɔ:'deɪn) *vb* (*tr*; *may take a clause as object*) to determine (events, results, etc) in the future > ,foreor'dainment *or* **foreordination** (,fɔ:rɔ:dɪ'neɪʃən) *n*

forepaw ('fɔ:,pɔ:) *n* either of the front feet of most land mammals that do not have hoofs

foreplay ('fɔ:,pleɪ) *n* mutual sexual stimulation preceding sexual intercourse

forequarter ('fɔ:,kwɔ:tə) *n* the front portion, including the leg, half of a carcass, as of beef or lamb

forequarters ('fɔ:,kwɔ:təz) *pl n* the part of the body of a horse or similar quadruped that consists of the forelegs, shoulders, and adjoining parts

forerun (fɔ:'rʌn) *vb* **-runs, -running, -ran, -run** (*tr*) **1** to serve as a herald for **2** to go before; precede **3** to prevent or forestall

forerunner ('fɔ:,rʌnə) *n* **1** a person or thing that precedes another; precursor **2** a person or thing coming in advance to herald the arrival of someone or something; harbinger **3** an indication beforehand of something to follow; omen; portent

foresail ('fɔ:,seɪl; *nautical* 'fɔ:sᵊl) *n* nautical **1** the aftermost headsail of a fore-and-aft rigged vessel **2** the lowest sail set on the foremast of a square-rigged vessel

foresee (fɔ:'si:) *vb* **-sees, -seeing, -saw, -seen** (*tr*; *may take a clause as object*) to see or know beforehand: *he did not foresee that* > fore'seeable *adj* > fore'seer *n*

foreshadow (fɔ:'ʃædəʊ) *vb* (*tr*) to show, indicate, or suggest in advance; presage

foreshank ('fɔ:,ʃæŋk) *n* **1** the top of the front leg of an animal **2** a cut of meat from this part

foresheet ('fɔːˌʃiːt) n 1 the sheet of a foresail 2 (plural) the part forward of the foremost thwart of a boat

foreshock ('fɔːˌʃɒk) n a relatively small earthquake heralding the arrival of a much larger one. Some large earthquakes are preceded by a series of foreshocks

foreshore ('fɔːˌʃɔː) n 1 the part of the shore that lies between the limits for high and low tides 2 the part of the shore that lies just above the high-water mark

foreshorten (fɔːˈʃɔːtᵊn) vb (tr) to represent (a line, form, object, etc) as shorter than actual length in order to give an illusion of recession or projection, in accordance with the laws of linear perspective

foreshow (fɔːˈʃəʊ) vb -shows, -showing, -showed, -shown (tr) archaic to indicate in advance; foreshadow

foresight ('fɔːˌsaɪt) n 1 provision for or insight into future problems, needs, etc 2 the act or ability of foreseeing 3 the act of looking forward 4 surveying a reading taken looking forwards to a new station, esp in levelling from a point of known elevation to a point the elevation of which is to be determined 5 the front sight on a firearm ▷ ˌfore'sighted adj ˌfore'sightedly adv ▷ ˌfore'sightedness n

foreskin ('fɔːˌskɪn) n anatomy the nontechnical name for **prepuce** (sense 1) Related adj: **preputial**

forest ('fɒrɪst) n 1 a large wooded area having a thick growth of trees and plants 2 the trees of such an area 3 NZ an area planted with exotic pines or similar trees. See **bush¹** (sense 4) 4 something resembling a large wooded area, esp in density: a forest of telegraph poles 5 law (formerly) an area of woodland, esp one owned by the sovereign and set apart as a hunting ground with its own laws and officers 6 (modifier) of, involving, or living in a forest or forests: a forest glade ▷ vb 7 (tr) to create a forest (in); plant with trees [c13: from Old French, from Medieval Latin forestis unfenced woodland, from Latin foris outside] ▷ 'forested adj

forestall (fɔːˈstɔːl) vb (tr) 1 to delay, stop, or guard against beforehand 2 to anticipate 3 to buy up (merchandise) for profitable resale [c14 forestallen to waylay, from Old English foresteall an ambush, from fore-in front of + steall place] ▷ fore'staller n ▷ fore'stalment or fore'stallment n

forestation (ˌfɒrɪˈsteɪʃən) n the planting of trees over a wide area

forestay ('fɔːˌsteɪ) n nautical an adjustable stay leading from the truck of the foremast to the deck, stem, or bowsprit, for controlling the motion or bending of the mast

forester ('fɒrɪstə) n 1 a person skilled in forestry or in charge of a forest 2 a person or animal that lives in a forest 3 (capital) a member of the Ancient Order of Foresters, a friendly society

Forester ('fɒrɪstə) n C(ecil) S(cott) 1899–1966, English novelist; creator of Captain Horatio Hornblower in a series of novels on the Napoleonic Wars

forest park n NZ a recreational reserve which may include bush and exotic trees

forestry ('fɒrɪstrɪ) n 1 the science of planting and caring for trees 2 the planting and management of forests 3 rare forest land

foretaste ('fɔːˌteɪst) n an early but limited experience or awareness of something to come

foretell (fɔːˈtɛl) vb -tells, -telling, -told (tr; may take a clause as object) to tell or indicate (an event, a result, etc) beforehand; predict

forethought ('fɔːˌθɔːt) n 1 advance consideration or deliberation 2 thoughtful anticipation of future events

foretoken n ('fɔːˌtəʊkən) 1 a sign of a future event ▷ vb (fɔːˈtəʊkən) 2 (tr) to foreshadow

foretop ('fɔːˌtɒp; nautical 'fɔːtəp) n nautical a platform at the top of the foremast

fore-topgallant (ˌfɔːtɒpˈɡælənt; nautical ˌfɔːtəˈɡælənt) adj nautical of, relating to, or being the topmost portion of a foremast, above the topmast

fore-topmast (fɔːˈtɒpˌmɑːst; nautical fɔːˈtɒpməst) n nautical a mast stepped above a foremast

fore-topsail (fɔːˈtɒpˌseɪl; nautical fɔːˈtɒpsᵊl) n nautical a sail set on a fore-topmast

forever (fɔːˈrɛvə, fə-) adv 1 Also: **for ever** without end;

everlastingly; eternally 2 at all times; incessantly 3 informal for a very long time: he went on speaking forever ▷ n 4 (as object) informal a very long time: it took him forever to reply

● USAGE Forever and for ever can both be used to say that
● something is without end. For all other meanings,
● forever is the preferred form

for evermore or **forevermore** (fɔːˌrɛvəˈmɔː, fə-) adv a more emphatic or emotive term for **forever**

forewarn (fɔːˈwɔːn) vb (tr) to warn beforehand ▷ fore'warner n

forewent (fɔːˈwɛnt) vb the past tense of **forego¹**

forewing ('fɔːˌwɪŋ) n either wing of the anterior pair of an insect's two pairs of wings

foreword ('fɔːˌwɜːd) n an introductory statement to a book [c19: literal translation of German Vorwort]

forfaiting ('fɔːˌfeɪtɪŋ) n the financial service of discounting, without recourse, a promissory note, bill of exchange, letter of credit, etc, received from an overseas buyer by an exporter; a form of debt discounting [c20: from French forfaire to forfeit or surrender]

Forfar ('fɔːfər, -fɑː) n a market town in E Scotland, the administrative centre of Angus: site of a castle, residence of Scottish kings between the 11th and 14th centuries. Pop: 13 206 (2001)

forfeit ('fɔːfɪt) n 1 something lost or given up as a penalty for a fault, mistake, etc 2 the act of losing or surrendering something in this manner 3 law something confiscated as a penalty for an offence, breach of contract, etc 4 (sometimes plural) a a game in which a player has to give up an object, perform a specified action, etc, if he commits a fault b an object so given up ▷ vb 5 (tr) to lose or be liable to lose in consequence of a mistake, fault, etc 6 (tr) law to confiscate as punishment ▷ adj 7 surrendered or liable to be surrendered as a penalty [c13: from Old French forfet offence, from forfaire to commit a crime, from Medieval Latin foris facere to act outside (what is lawful), from Latin foris outside + facere to do] ▷ 'forfeiter n

forfeiture ('fɔːfɪtʃə) n 1 something forfeited 2 the act of forfeiting or paying a penalty

forfend or **forefend** (fɔːˈfɛnd) vb (tr) 1 US to protect or secure 2 obsolete to prohibit or prevent

forgather (fɔːˈɡæðə) vb a variant spelling of **foregather**

forgave (fəˈɡeɪv) vb the past tense of **forgive**

forge¹ (fɔːdʒ) n 1 a place in which metal is worked by heating and hammering; smithy 2 a hearth or furnace used for heating metal ▷ vb 3 (tr) to shape (metal) by heating and hammering 4 (tr) to form, shape, make, or fashion (objects, articles, etc) 5 (tr) to invent or devise (an agreement, understanding, etc) 6 to make or produce a fraudulent imitation of (a signature, banknote, etc) or to commit forgery [c14: from Old French forgier to construct, from Latin fabricāre, from faber craftsman] ▷ 'forger n

forge² (fɔːdʒ) vb (intr) 1 to move at a steady and persevering pace 2 to increase speed; spurt [c17: of unknown origin]

forgery ('fɔːdʒərɪ) n, pl -geries 1 the act of reproducing something for a deceitful or fraudulent purpose 2 something forged, such as a work of art or an antique 3 criminal law a the false making or altering of any document, such as a cheque or character reference (and including a postage stamp), or any tape or disc on which information is stored, intending that anyone shall accept it as genuine and so act to his or another's prejudice b something forged

forget (fəˈɡɛt) vb -gets, -getting, -got, -gotten or archaic or dialect -got 1 (when tr, may take a clause as object or an infinitive) to fail to recall (someone or something once known); be unable to remember 2 (tr; may take a clause as object or an infinitive) to neglect, usually as the result of an unintentional error 3 (tr) to leave behind by mistake 4 forget oneself a to act in an improper manner b to be unselfish c to be deep in thought [Old English forgietan; related to Old Frisian forgeta, Old Saxon fargetan, Old High German firgezzan] ▷ for'gettable adj ▷ for'getter n

forgetful (fəˈɡɛtfʊl) adj 1 tending to forget 2 (often postpositive; foll by of) inattentive (to) or neglectful (of)

> for'getfully *adv* > for'getfulness *n*

forget-me-not *n* any temperate low-growing plant of the mainly European boraginaceous genus *Myosotis*, having clusters of small typically blue flowers. Also called: scorpion grass

forgive (fə'gɪv) *vb* **-gives, -giving, -gave, -given** **1** to cease to blame or hold resentment against (someone or something) **2** to grant pardon for (a mistake, wrongdoing, etc) **3** (*tr*) to free or pardon (someone) from penalty **4** (*tr*) to free from the obligation of (a debt, payment, etc) [Old English *forgiefan*; see FOR-, GIVE]
> for'givable *adj* > for'giver *n*

forgiveness (fə'gɪvnɪs) *n* **1** the act of forgiving or the state of being forgiven **2** willingness to forgive

forgiving (fə'gɪvɪŋ) *adj* willing to forgive; merciful

forgo *or* **forego** (fɔː'gəʊ) *vb* **-goes, -going, -went, -gone** (*tr*) to give up or do without [Old English *forgān*; see FOR-, GO[1]]

forgot (fə'gɒt) *vb* **1** the past tense of **forget** **2** *archaic or dialect* a past participle of **forget**

forgotten (fə'gɒtᵊn) *vb* a past participle of **forget**

forint (Hungarian 'forint) *n* the standard monetary unit of Hungary, divided into 100 fillér [from Hungarian, from Italian *fiorino* FLORIN]

fork (fɔːk) *n* **1** a small usually metal implement consisting of two, three, or four long thin prongs on the end of a handle, used for lifting food to the mouth or turning it in cooking, etc **2** an agricultural tool consisting of a handle and three or four metal prongs, used for lifting, digging, etc **3** a pronged part of any machine, device, etc **4** (of a road, river, etc) **a** a division into two or more branches **b** the point where the division begins **c** such a branch ▷ *vb* **5** (*tr*) to pick up, dig, etc, with a fork **6** (*tr*) *chess* to place (two enemy pieces) under attack with one of one's own pieces, esp a knight **7** (*intr*) to be divided into two or more branches **8** to take one or other branch at a fork in a road, river, etc [Old English *forca*, from Latin *furca*]

forked (fɔːkt, 'fɔːkɪd) *adj* **1 a** having a fork or forklike parts **b** (*in combination*): *two-forked* **2** having sharp angles; zigzag > forkedly ('fɔːkɪdlɪ) *adv*

fork-lift truck *n* a vehicle having two power-operated horizontal prongs that can be raised and lowered for loading, transporting, and unloading goods, esp goods that are stacked on wooden pallets. Often shortened to: forklift

fork out, fork over *or* **fork up** *vb* (*adverb*) *slang* to pay (money, goods, etc), esp with reluctance

forlorn (fə'lɔːn) *adj* **1** miserable, wretched, or cheerless; desolate **2** deserted; forsaken **3** (*postpositive*; foll by *of*) destitute; bereft: *forlorn of hope* **4** desperate: *the last forlorn attempt* [Old English *forloren* lost, from *forlēosan* to lose; related to Old Saxon *farliosan*, Gothic *fraliusan*, Greek *luein* to release] > for'lornness *n*

forlorn hope *n* **1** a hopeless or desperate enterprise **2** a faint hope **3** *obsolete* a group of soldiers assigned to an extremely dangerous duty [C16 (in the obsolete sense): changed (by folk etymology) from Dutch *verloren hoop* lost troop, from *verloren*, past participle of *verliezen* to lose + *hoop* troop (literally: heap)]

form (fɔːm) *n* **1** the shape or configuration of something as distinct from its colour, texture, etc **2** the particular mode, appearance, etc, in which a thing or person manifests itself: *water in the form of ice; in the form of a bat* **3** a type or kind: *imprisonment is a form of punishment* **4** a printed document, esp one with spaces in which to insert facts or answers: *an application form* **5** physical or mental condition, esp good condition, with reference to ability to perform: *off form* **6** the previous record of a horse, athlete, etc, esp with regard to fitness **7** *Brit slang* a criminal record **8** a fixed mode of artistic expression or representation in literary, musical, or other artistic works: *sonata form; sonnet form* **9** a mould, frame, etc, that gives shape to something **10** *education chiefly Brit* a group of children who are taught together; class **11** behaviour or procedure, esp as governed by custom or etiquette: *good form* **12** formality or ceremony **13** a prescribed set or order of words, terms, etc, as in a religious ceremony or legal document **14** *philosophy* **a** the structure of anything as opposed to its constitution or content **b** essence as opposed to matter **15** See **logical form** **16** *Brit* a bench, esp one that is long, low, and backless **17** the nest or hollow in which a hare lives ▷ *vb* **18** to give shape or form to or to take shape or form, esp a specified or particular shape **19** to come to or bring into existence: *a scum formed on the surface* **20** to make, produce, or construct or be made, produced, or constructed **21** to construct or develop in the mind: *to form an opinion* **22** (*tr*) to train, develop, or mould by instruction, discipline, or example **23** (*tr*) to acquire, contract, or develop: *to form a habit* **24** (*tr*) to be an element of, serve as, or constitute: *this plank will form a bridge* **25** (*tr*) to draw up; organize: *to form a club* [C13: from Old French *forme*, from Latin *forma* shape, model]

-form *adj combining form* having the shape or form of or resembling: *cruciform; vermiform* [from New Latin *-formis*, from Latin, from *fōrma* FORM]

formal ('fɔːməl) *adj* **1** of, according to, or following established or prescribed forms, conventions, etc: *a formal document* **2** characterized by observation of conventional forms of ceremony, behaviour, dress, etc: *a formal dinner* **3** methodical, precise, or stiff **4** suitable for occasions organized according to conventional ceremony: *formal dress* **5** denoting or characterized by idiom, vocabulary, etc, used by educated speakers and writers of a language **6** acquired by study in academic institutions: *a formal education* **7** regular or symmetrical in form: *a formal garden* **8** of or relating to the appearance, form, etc, of something as distinguished from its substance **9** logically deductive: *formal proof* **10** denoting a second-person pronoun in some languages used when the addressee is a stranger, social superior, etc: *in French the pronoun "vous" is formal, while "tu" is informal* [C14: from Latin *formālis*] > 'formally *adv* > 'formalness *n*

formaldehyde (fɔː'mældɪˌhaɪd) *n* a colourless poisonous irritating gas with a pungent characteristic odour, made by the oxidation of methanol and used as formalin and in the manufacture of synthetic resins. Formula: HCHO. Systematic name: **methanal** [C19: FORM(IC) + ALDEHYDE; on the model of German *Formaldehyd*]

formalin ('fɔːməlɪn) *or* **formol** ('fɔːmɒl) *n* a 40 per cent solution of formaldehyde in water, used as a disinfectant, preservative for biological specimens, etc

formalism ('fɔːməˌlɪzəm) *n* **1** scrupulous or excessive adherence to outward form at the expense of inner reality or content **2** the mathematical or logical structure of a scientific argument as distinguished from its subject matter **3** *theatre* a stylized mode of production **4** (in Marxist criticism) excessive concern with artistic technique at the expense of social values, etc > 'formalist *n* > ˌformal'istic *adj*

formality (fɔː'mælɪtɪ) *n, pl* **-ties** **1** a requirement of rule, custom, etiquette, etc **2** the condition or quality of being formal or conventional **3** strict or excessive observance of form, ceremony, etc

formalize *or* **formalise** ('fɔːməˌlaɪz) *vb* **1** to be or make formal **2** (*tr*) to make official or valid **3** (*tr*) to give a definite shape or form to > ˌformali'zation *or* ˌformali'sation *n*

formal language *n* a language designed for use in situations in which natural language is unsuitable, as for example in mathematics, logic, or computer programming. The symbols and formulas of such languages stand in precisely specified syntactic and semantic relations to one another

formal logic *n* Also called: **symbolic logic** the study of systems of deductive argument in which symbols are used to represent precisely defined categories of expressions

Forman ('fɔːmən) *n* **Miloš** ('miːləʊʃ). born 1932, Czech film director working in the USA. since 1968. His films include *One Flew over the Cuckoo's Nest* (1976), *Amadeus* (1985), and *The People vs Larry Flynt* (1996)

formant ('fɔːmənt) *n* *acoustics, phonetics* any of several frequency ranges within which the partials of a sound, esp a vowel sound, are at their strongest, thus imparting to the sound its own special quality, tone colour, or timbre

format ('fɔːmæt) *n* **1** the general appearance of a publication, including type style, paper, binding, etc **2** style, plan, or arrangement, as of a television programme **3** *computing* **a** the defined arrangement of data encoded in a file or for example on magnetic disk or CD-ROM, essential for the correct recording and recovery of data on different devices **b** the arrangement of text on printed output or a display screen, or a coded description of such an arrangement ▷ *vb* -mats, -matting, -matted (*tr*) **4** to arrange (a book, page, etc) into a specified format [c19: via French from German, from Latin *liber formātus* volume formed]

formation (fɔː'meɪʃən) *n* **1** the act of giving or taking form, shape, or existence **2** something that is formed **3** the manner in which something is formed or arranged **4 a** a formal arrangement of a number of persons or things acting as a unit, such as a troop of soldiers, aircraft in flight, or a football team **b** (*as modifier*): *formation dancing* **5** *geology* **a** the fundamental lithostratigraphic unit **b** a series of rocks with certain characteristics in common

formative ('fɔːmətɪv) *adj* **1** of or relating to formation, development, or growth: *formative years* **2** shaping; moulding: *a formative experience* **3** functioning in the formation of derived, inflected, or compound words ▷ *n* **4** an inflectional or derivational affix > **'formatively** *adv*

Formby ('fɔːmbɪ) *n* **George**. Real name *George Booth*. 1904–61, British comedian. He made many musical films in the 1930s, accompanying his songs on the ukulele

form class *n* **1** another term for **part of speech 2** a group of words distinguished by common inflections, such as the weak verbs of English

forme *or US* **form** (fɔːm) *n* *printing* type matter, blocks, etc, assembled in a chase and ready for printing [c15: from French: FORM]

former¹ ('fɔːmə) *adj* (*prenominal*) **1** belonging to or occurring in an earlier time: *former glory* **2** having been at a previous time: *a former colleague* **3** denoting the first or first mentioned of two: *in the former case* ▷ *n* **4** the former the first or first mentioned of two: distinguished from *latter*

former² ('fɔːmə) *n* **1** a person or thing that forms or shapes **2** *electrical engineering* a tool for giving a coil or winding the required shape, sometimes consisting of a frame on which the wire can be wound, the frame then being removed

formerly ('fɔːməlɪ) *adv* at or in a former time; in the past

formic ('fɔːmɪk) *adj* **1** of, relating to, or derived from ants **2** of, containing, or derived from formic acid [c18: from Latin *formīca* ant; the acid occurs naturally in ants]

Formica (fɔː'maɪkə) *n* *trademark* any of various laminated plastic sheets, containing melamine, used esp for heat-resistant surfaces that can be easily cleaned

formic acid *n* a colourless corrosive liquid carboxylic acid found in some insects, esp ants, and many plants: used in dyeing textiles and the manufacture of insecticides and refrigerants. Formula: HCOOH. Systematic name: methanoic acid

formidable ('fɔːmɪdəbəl) *adj* **1** arousing or likely to inspire fear or dread **2** extremely difficult to defeat, overcome, manage, etc: *a formidable problem* **3** tending to inspire awe or admiration because of great size, strength, excellence, etc [c15: from Latin *formīdābilis*, from *formīdāre* to dread, from *formīdō* fear] > **'formidably** *adv*

formless ('fɔːmlɪs) *adj* without a definite shape or form; amorphous > **'formlessly** *adv*

form letter *n* a single copy of a letter that has been mechanically reproduced in large numbers for circulation

Formosa (fɔː'məʊsə) *n* the former name of **Taiwan**

Formosa Strait *n* an arm of the Pacific between Taiwan and mainland China, linking the East and South China Seas. Also called: **Taiwan Strait**

formula ('fɔːmjʊlə) *n*, *pl* -las, -lae (-,liː) **1** an established form or set of words, as used in religious ceremonies, legal proceedings, etc **2** *maths, physics* a general

relationship, principle, or rule stated, often as an equation, in the form of symbols **3** *chem* a representation of molecules, radicals, ions, etc, expressed in the symbols of the atoms of their constituent elements **4 a** a method, pattern, or rule for doing or producing something, often one proved to be successful **b** (*as modifier*): *formula fiction* **5** a prescription for making up a medicine, baby's food, etc **6** *motor racing* the specific category in which a particular type of car competes, judged according to engine size, weight, and fuel capacity [c17: from Latin: diminutive of *forma* FORM] > **formulaic** (,fɔːmjʊ'leɪɪk) *adj*

Formula One *n* **1** the top class of professional motor racing **2** the most important world championship in motor racing

formulare *or* **formularise** ('fɔːmjʊlə,raɪz) *vb* a less common word for **formulate** (sense 1)

formulary ('fɔːmjʊlərɪ) *n*, *pl* -laries **1** a book or system of prescribed formulas, esp relating to religious procedure or doctrine **2** a formula **3** *pharmacol* a book containing a list of pharmaceutical products, with their formulas and means of preparation ▷ *adj* **4** of, relating to, or of the nature of a formula

formulate ('fɔːmjʊ,leɪt) *vb* (*tr*) **1** to put into or express in systematic terms; express in or as if in a formula **2** to devise > **,formu'lation** *n*

formyl ('fɔːmaɪl) *n* (*modifier*) of, consisting of, or containing the monovalent group HCO-: *a formyl group or radical* [c19: from FORM(IC) + -YL]

formwork ('fɔːm,wɜːk) *n* an arrangement of wooden boards, bolts, etc, used to shape reinforced concrete while it is setting

fornicate¹ ('fɔːnɪ,keɪt) *vb* (*intr*) to indulge in or commit fornication [c16: from Late Latin *fornicārī*, from Latin *fornix* vault, brothel situated therein] > **'forni,cator** *n*

fornicate² ('fɔːnɪkɪt, -,keɪt) *or* **fornicated** *adj* *biology* arched or hoodlike in form [c19: from Latin *fornicātus* arched, from *fornix* vault]

fornication (,fɔːnɪ'keɪʃən) *n* **1** voluntary sexual intercourse outside marriage **2** *Bible* sexual immorality in general, esp adultery

Forrest ('fɒrɪst) *n* **John**, 1st Baron Forrest 1847–1918, Australian statesman and explorer; first premier of Western Australia (1890–1901)

forsake (fə'seɪk) *vb* -sakes, -saking, -sook (-'sʊk), -saken (-'seɪkən) (*tr*) **1** to abandon **2** to give up (something valued or enjoyed) [Old English *forsacan*] > **for'saker** *n*

forsaken (fə'seɪkən) *vb* **1** the past participle of **forsake** ▷ *adj* **2** completely deserted or helpless; abandoned > **for'sakenly** *adv* > **for'sakenness** *n*

forsook (fə'sʊk) *vb* the past tense of **forsake**

forsooth (fə'suːθ) *adv* *archaic* in truth; indeed [Old English *forsōth*]

Forster ('fɔːstə) *n* **E(dward) M(organ)**. 1879–1970, English novelist, short-story writer, and essayist. His best-known novels are *A Room with a View* (1908), *Howard's End* (1910), and *A Passage to India* (1924), in all of which he stresses the need for sincerity and sensitivity in human relationships and criticizes English middle-class values

forswear (fɔː'swɛə) *vb* -swears, -swearing, -swore, -sworn **1** (*tr*) to reject or renounce with determination or as upon oath **2** (*tr*) to deny or disavow absolutely or upon oath: *he forswore any knowledge of the crime* **3** to perjure (oneself) [Old English *forswearian*] > **for'swearer** *n*

forsworn (fɔː'swɔːn) *vb* the past participle of **forswear** > **for'swornness** *n*

Forsyth (fə'saɪθ) *n* **1 Bill**. born 1947, Scottish writer and director. His films include *Gregory's Girl* (1981), *Local Hero* (1983), and *Gregory's Two Girls* (1999) **2 Frederick** born 1938, British thriller writer. His books include *The Day of the Jackal* (1970), *The Odessa File* (1972), and *The Fourth Protocol* (1984)

forsythia (fɔː'saɪθɪə) *n* any oleaceous shrub of the genus *Forsythia*, native to China, Japan, and SE Europe but widely cultivated for its showy yellow bell-shaped flowers, which appear in spring before the foliage [c19: New Latin, named after William *Forsyth* (1737–1804), English botanist]

fort (fɔːt) *n* **1** a fortified enclosure, building, or position able to be defended against an enemy **2** hold the fort *informal* to maintain or guard something temporarily [C15: from Old French, from *fort* (adj) strong, from Latin *fortis*]

Fortaleza (*Portuguese* forta'leza) *n* a port in NE Brazil, capital of Ceará state. Pop: 3 261 000 (2005 est). Also called: **Ceará**

Fort-de-France (*French* fɔrdəfrɑ̃s) *n* the capital of Martinique, a port on the W coast: commercial centre of the French Antilles. Pop: 94 049 (1999 est)

forte[1] (fɔːt, 'fɔːteɪ) *n* **1** something at which a person excels; strong point: *cooking is my forte* **2** fencing the stronger section of a sword blade, between the hilt and the middle [C17: from French *fort*, from *fort* (adj) strong, from Latin *fortis*]

forte[2] ('fɔːtɪ) *music* ▷ *adj, adv* **1** loud or loudly. Symbol: f ▷ *n* **2** a loud passage in music [C18: from Italian, from Latin *fortis* strong]

forte-piano (ˌfɔːtɪ'pjɑːnəʊ) *music* ▷ *adj, adv* **1** loud and then immediately soft. Symbol: fp ▷ *n* **2** a note played in this way

forth (fɔːθ) *adv* **1** forward in place, time, order, or degree **2** out, as from concealment, seclusion, or inaction **3** away, as from a place or country **4** and so on; et cetera ▷ *prep* **5** *archaic* out of; away from [Old English; related to Middle High German *vort*; see FOR, FURTHER]

Forth (fɔːθ) *n* **1** Firth of Forth an inlet of the North Sea in SE Scotland: spanned by a cantilever railway bridge 1600 m (almost exactly 1 mile) long (1889), and by a road bridge (1964) **2** a river in S Scotland, flowing generally east to the Firth of Forth. Length: about 104 km (65 miles)

forthcoming (ˌfɔːθ'kʌmɪŋ) *adj* **1** approaching in time: *the forthcoming debate* **2** about to appear: *his forthcoming book* **3** available or ready: *the money wasn't forthcoming* **4** open or sociable

forthright *adj* ('fɔːθˌraɪt) **1** direct and outspoken ▷ *adv* (ˌfɔːθ'raɪt, 'fɔːθˌraɪt) Also called: **forthrightly 2** in a direct manner; frankly **3** at once > 'forth,rightness *n*

forthwith (ˌfɔːθ'wɪθ, -'wɪð) *adv* at once; immediately

fortification (ˌfɔːtɪfɪ'keɪʃən) *n* **1** the act, art, or science of fortifying or strengthening **2 a** a wall, mound, etc, used to fortify a place **b** such works collectively

fortify ('fɔːtɪˌfaɪ) *vb* **-fies, -fying, -fied** (*mainly tr*) **1** (*also intr*) to make (a place) defensible, as by building walls, digging trenches, etc **2** to strengthen physically, mentally, or morally **3** to add spirits or alcohol to (wine), in order to produce sherry, port, etc **4** to increase the nutritious value of (a food), as by adding vitamins and minerals **5** to support or confirm: *to fortify an argument with facts* [C15: from Old French *fortifier*, from Late Latin *fortificāre*, from Latin *fortis* strong + *facere* to make] > 'forti,fiable *adj* > 'forti,fier *n*

fortissimo (fɔː'tɪsɪˌməʊ) *music* ▷ *adj, adv* **1** very loud. Symbol: ff ▷ *n* **2** a very loud passage in music [C18: from Italian, from Latin *fortissimus*, from *fortis* strong]

fortitude ('fɔːtɪˌtjuːd) *n* strength and firmness of mind; resolute endurance [C15: from Latin *fortitūdō* courage]

Fort Knox (nɒks) *n* a military reservation in N Kentucky: site of the US Gold Bullion Depository. Pop: 12 377 (2000)

Fort Lamy ('fɔːt 'lɑːmɪ; *French* fɔr lami) *n* the former name (until 1973) of **Ndjamena**

fortnight ('fɔːtˌnaɪt) *n* a period of 14 consecutive days; two weeks [Old English *fēowertiene niht* fourteen nights]

fortnightly ('fɔːtˌnaɪtlɪ) *chiefly Brit* ▷ *adj* **1** occurring or appearing once each fortnight ▷ *adv* **2** once a fortnight ▷ *n, pl* **-lies 3** a publication issued at intervals of two weeks

FORTRAN or **Fortran** ('fɔːtræn) *n* a high-level computer programming language for mathematical and scientific purposes, designed to facilitate and speed up the solving of complex problems [C20: from *for(mula)* tran*(slation)*]

fortress ('fɔːtrɪs) *n* **1** a large fort or fortified town **2** a place or source of refuge or support ▷ *vb* **3** (*tr*) to protect with or as if with a fortress [C13: from Old French *forteresse*, from Medieval Latin *fortalitia*, from Latin *fortis* strong]

Fort Sumter ('sʌmtə) *n* a fort in SE South Carolina, guarding Charleston Harbour. Its capture by Confederate forces (1861) was the first action of the Civil War

fortuitous (fɔː'tjuːɪtəs) *adj* happening by chance, esp by a lucky chance; unplanned; accidental [C17: from Latin *fortuitus* happening by chance, from *forte* by chance, from *fors* chance, luck] > for'tuitously *adv*

fortuity (fɔː'tjuːɪtɪ) *n, pl* **-ties 1** a chance or accidental occurrence **2** chance or accident

Fortuna (fɔː'tjuːnə) *n* the Roman goddess of fortune and good luck. Greek counterpart: **Tyche**

fortunate ('fɔːtʃənɪt) *adj* **1** having good luck; lucky **2** occurring by or bringing good fortune or luck; auspicious

fortune ('fɔːtʃən) *n* **1** an amount of wealth or material prosperity, esp when unqualified, a great amount **2** small fortune a large sum of money **3** a power or force, often personalized, regarded as being responsible for human affairs; chance **4** luck, esp when favourable **5** (*often plural*) a person's lot or destiny ▷ *vb* **6** *archaic* (*intr*) to happen by chance [C13: from Old French, from Latin *fortūna*, from *fors* chance]

fortune-hunter *n* a person who seeks to secure a fortune, esp through marriage

fortune-teller *n* a person who makes predictions about the future as by looking into a crystal ball, reading palms, etc > 'fortune-,telling *adj, n*

Fort William ('wɪljəm) *n* a town in W Scotland, in Highland at the head of Loch Linnhe: tourist centre; the fort itself, built in 1655 and renamed after William III in 1690, was demolished in 1866. Pop: 9908 (2001)

Fort Worth (wɜːθ) *n* a city in N Texas, at the junction of the Clear and West forks of the Trinity River: aircraft works, electronics. Pop: 585 122 (2003 est)

forty ('fɔːtɪ) *n, pl* **-ties 1** the cardinal number that is the product of ten and four. See also **number** (sense 1) **2** a numeral, 40, XL, etc, representing this number **3** something representing, represented by, or consisting of 40 units ▷ *determiner* **4 a** amounting to forty: *forty thieves* **b** (*as pronoun*): *there were forty in the herd* [Old English *fēowertig*] > 'fortieth *adj, n*

forty-five *n* a gramophone record played at 45 revolutions per minute

Forty-Five *n* the Forty-Five *Brit history* another name for the **Jacobite Rebellion** of 1745–46

forty-niner *n* (*sometimes capital*) *US history* a prospector who took part in the California gold rush of 1849

forty-ninth parallel *n* *Canadian* an informal name for the border with the USA., which is in part delineated by the parallel line of latitude at 49°N

forty winks *n* (*functioning as singular or plural*) *informal* a short light sleep; nap

forum ('fɔːrəm) *n, pl* **-rums, -ra** (-rə) **1** a meeting or assembly for the open discussion of subjects of public interest **2** a medium for open discussion, such as a magazine **3** a public meeting place for open discussion **4** a court; tribunal **5** (in South Africa) a pressure group of leaders or representatives, esp Black leaders or representatives **6** (in ancient Italy) an open space, usually rectangular in shape, serving as a city's marketplace and centre of public business [C15: from Latin: public place; related to Latin *foris* outside]

Forum or **Forum Romanum** (rəʊ'mɑːnəm) *n* the Forum the main forum of ancient Rome, situated between the Capitoline and the Palatine Hills

forward ('fɔːwəd) *adj* **1** directed or moving ahead **2** lying or situated in or near the front part of something **3** presumptuous, pert, or impudent: *a forward remark* **4** well developed or advanced, esp in physical, material, or intellectual growth or development **5** *archaic* (*often postpositive*) ready, eager, or willing **6 a** of or relating to the future or favouring change; progressive **b** (*in combination*): *forward-looking* **7** *commerce* realting to fulfilment at a future date ▷ *n* **8** an attacking player in any of various sports, such as soccer, hockey, or basketball ▷ *adv* **9** an email that has been sent to one recipient and then forwarded to another **10** a variant of **forwards 11** ('fɔːwəd; *Nautical* 'fɒrəd) towards the front or bow of an aircraft or ship **12** into prominence or a position of being subject to public scrutiny; out; forth: *the witness came forward* ▷ *vb* (*tr*) **13** to send forward or pass on to an ultimate destination: *the letter was forwarded from a previous address* **14** to advance, help, or promote: *to forward one's career* [Old English *foreweard*] > ˈforwardly *adv* > ˈforwarder *n* > ˈforwardness *n*

forwards (ˈfɔːwədz) *or* **forward** *adv* **1** towards or at a place ahead or in advance, esp in space but also in time **2** towards the front

forwent (fɔːˈwɛnt) *vb* the past tense of **forgo**

forza (ˈfɔːtsə) *n music* force [C19: Italian, literally: force]

FOS *abbreviation* fructooligosaccharide: a chain polymer of fructose found in a variety of plants, vegetables, and fruits and used as a sweetener

Foscolo (Italian ˈfoskolo) *n* **Ugo** (ˈuːgo), real name *Niccolò Foscolo*. 1778–1827, Italian poet and writer; his patriotic verse includes *Dei sepolcri* (1807)

Foshan (ˈfɔːˈʃɑːn) *or* **Fatshan** *n* a city in SE China, in W Guangdong province. Pop: 483 000 (2005 est). Also called: **Namhoi**

fossa (ˈfɒsə) *n*, *pl* **-sae** (-siː) an anatomical depression, trench, or hollow area [C19: from Latin: ditch, from *fossus* dug up, from *fodere* to dig up]

fosse *or* **foss** (fɒs) *n* a ditch or moat, esp one dug as a fortification [C14: from Old French, from Latin *fossa*; see FOSSA]

Fosse Way (fɒs) *n* a Roman road in Britain between Lincoln and Exeter, with a fosse on each side

fossick (ˈfɒsɪk) *vb Austral & NZ* **1** (*intr*) to search for gold or precious stones in abandoned workings, rivers, etc **2** to rummage or search for (something) [C19: Australian, probably from English dialect *fussock* to bustle about, from FUSS] > ˈfossicker *n*

fossil (ˈfɒsᵊl) *n* **1 a** a relic, remnant, or representation of an organism that existed in a past geological age, or of the activity of such an organism, occurring in the form of mineralized bones, shells, etc, as casts, impressions, and moulds, and as frozen perfectly preserved organisms **b** (*as modifier*): *fossil insects* **2** *informal, derogatory* a person, idea, thing, etc, that is outdated or incapable of change **3** *linguistics* a form once current but now appearing only in one or two special contexts, as for example *stead*, which is found now only in *instead* (*of*) and in phrases like *in his stead* [C17: from Latin *fossilis* dug up, from *fodere* to dig]

fossil fuel *n* any naturally occurring carbon or hydrocarbon fuel, such as coal, petroleum, peat, and natural gas, formed by the decomposition of prehistoric organisms

fossiliferous (ˌfɒsɪˈlɪfərəs) *adj* (of sedimentary rocks) containing fossils

fossilize *or* **fossilise** (ˈfɒsɪˌlaɪz) *vb* **1** to convert or be converted into a fossil **2** to become or cause to become antiquated or inflexible > ˌfossiliˈzation *or* ˌfossiliˈsation *n*

fossorial (fɒˈsɔːrɪəl) *adj* (of the forelimbs and skeleton of burrowing animals) adapted for digging [C19: from Medieval Latin *fossōrius* from Latin *fossor* digger, from *fodere* to dig]

foster (ˈfɒstə) *vb* (*tr*) **1** to promote the growth or development of **2** to bring up (a child, etc); rear **3** to cherish (a plan, hope, etc) in one's mind **4** *chiefly Brit* **a** to place (a child) in the care of foster parents **b** to bring up under fosterage ▷ *adj* **5** (*in combination*) indicating relationship through fostering and not through birth: *foster mother; foster child* **6** (*in combination*) of or involved in the rearing of a child by persons other than his natural or adopted parents: *foster home* [Old English *fōstrian* to feed, from *fōstor* FOOD] > ˈfosterer *n* > ˈfostering *n*

Foster (ˈfɒstə) *n* **1 Jodie**. born 1962, US film actress and director: her films include *Taxi Driver* (1976), *The Accused* (1988), *The Silence of the Lambs* (1990), *Little Man Tate* (1991; also directed), *Nell* (1995), and *Panic Room* (2002) **2 Norman**, Baron. born 1935, British architect. His works include the Willis Faber building (1978) in Ipswich, Stansted Airport, Essex (1991), Chek Lap Kok Airport, Hong Kong (1998), the renovation of the Reichstag, Berlin (1999), and City Hall, London (2002) **3 Stephen Collins**. 1826–64, US composer of songs such as *The Old*

Folks at Home and *Oh Susanna*

fosterage (ˈfɒstərɪdʒ) *n* **1** the act of caring for or bringing up a foster child **2** the condition or state of being a foster child **3** the act of encouraging or promoting

Fotheringhay (ˈfɒðərɪŋˌgeɪ) *n* a village in E England, in NE Northamptonshire: ruined castle, scene of the imprisonment and execution of Mary Queen of Scots (1587)

Foucault (French fuko) *n* **1 Jean Bernard Léon** (ʒɑ̃ bɛrnar leɔ̃). 1819–68, French physicist. He determined the velocity of light and proved that light travels more slowly in water than in air (1850). He demonstrated by means of the pendulum named after him the rotation of the earth on its axis (1851) and invented the gyroscope (1852) **2 Michel**. 1926–84, French philosopher and historian of ideas. His publications include *Histoire de la folie* (1961) and *Les Mots et les choses* (1966)

Foucquet (French fukɛ) *n* a variant spelling of (Nicolas) **Fouquet**

fought (fɔːt) *vb* the past tense and past participle of **fight**

foul (faʊl) *adj* **1** offensive to the senses; revolting **2** offensive in odour; stinking **3** charged with or full of dirt or offensive matter; filthy **4** (of food) putrid; rotten **5** morally or spiritually offensive; wicked; vile **6** obscene; vulgar: *foul language* **7** (esp of weather) unpleasant or adverse **8** blocked or obstructed with dirt or foreign matter: *a foul drain* **9** (of the bottom of a vessel) covered with barnacles and other growth that slow forward motion **10** *informal* unsatisfactory or uninteresting; bad: *a foul book* ▷ *n* **11** *sport* **a** a violation of the rules **b** (*as modifier*): *a foul shot; a foul blow* **12** an entanglement or collision, esp in sailing or fishing ▷ *vb* **13** to make or become dirty or polluted **14** to become or cause to become entangled or snarled **15** (*tr*) to disgrace or dishonour **16** to become or cause to become clogged or choked **17** (*tr*) *nautical* (of underwater growth) to cling to (the bottom of a vessel) so as to slow its motion **18** (*tr*) *sport* to commit a foul against (an opponent) **19** (*intr*) *sport* to infringe the rules **20** to collide with (a boat, etc) ▷ *adv* **21** in a foul or unfair manner **22 fall foul of a** to come into conflict with **b** *nautical* to come into collision with [Old English *fūl*; related to Old Norse *fūll*, Gothic *fūls* smelling offensively, Latin *pūs* PUS, Greek *puol* pus] > ˈfoully *adv*

foulard (fuːˈlɑːd, ˈfuːlɑː) *n* a soft light fabric of plain-weave or twill-weave silk or rayon, usually with a printed design [C19: from French, of unknown origin]

Foulness (faʊlˈnɛs) *n* a flat marshy island in SE England, in Essex north of the Thames estuary

foul play *n* **1** unfair or treacherous conduct esp with violence **2** a violation of the rules in a game or sport

foul up *vb* (*adverb*) **1** (*tr*) to bungle; mismanage **2** (*tr*) to make dirty; contaminate **3** to be or cause to be blocked, choked, or entangled ▷ *n* **foul-up 4** a state of confusion or muddle caused by bungling

found[1] (faʊnd) *vb* **1** the past tense and past participle of: **find** ▷ *adj* **2** furnished, or fitted out **3** *Brit* with meals, heating, bed linen, etc, provided without extra charge (esp in the phrase **all found**)

found[2] (faʊnd) *vb* **1** (*tr*) to bring into being, set up, or establish (something, such as an institution, society, etc) **2** (*tr*) to build or establish the foundation or basis of **3** (*also intr*; foll by *on* or *upon*) to have a basis (in); depend (on) [C13: from Old French *fonder*, from Latin *fundāre*, from *fundus* bottom]

found[3] (faʊnd) *vb* (*tr*) **1** to cast (a material, such as metal or glass) by melting and pouring into a mould **2** to shape or make (articles) in this way; cast [C14: from Old French *fondre*, from Latin *fundere* to melt]

foundation (faʊnˈdeɪʃən) *n* **1** that on which something is founded; basis **2** (*often plural*) a construction below the ground that distributes the load of a building, wall, etc **3** the base on which something stands **4** the act of founding or establishing or the state of being founded or established **5** an endowment or legacy for the perpetual support of an institution such as a school or hospital **6** an institution supported by an endowment, often one that provides funds for charities, research, etc **7** a cosmetic in cream or cake form used as a base for make-up > foun'dational *adj*

foundation garment *n* a woman's undergarment worn to shape and support the figure; brassiere or corset

foundation stone *n* a stone laid at a ceremony to mark the foundation of a new building

foundation subjects *pl n Brit education* the subjects studied as part of the National Curriculum, including the compulsory core subjects

founder¹ ('faʊndə) *n* a person who establishes an institution, company, society, etc [c14: see FOUND²]

founder² ('faʊndə) *vb* **1** (*intr*) (of a ship) to sink **2** to break down or fail: *the project foundered* **3** to sink into or become stuck in soft ground **4** to fall in or give way; collapse **5** (of a horse) to stumble or go lame [c13: from Old French *fondrer* to submerge, from Latin *fundus* bottom; see FOUND²]

● USAGE *Founder* is sometimes wrongly used where
● *flounder* is meant: *this unexpected turn of events left him*
● *floundering* (not foundering)

founder³ ('faʊndə) *n* **a** a person who makes metal castings **b** (*in combination*): *an iron founder* [c15: see FOUND³]

foundling ('faʊndlɪŋ) *n* an abandoned infant whose parents are not known [c13: *foundeling*; see FIND]

foundry ('faʊndrɪ) *n, pl* **-ries** a place in which metal castings are produced [c17: from Old French *fonderie*, from *fondre*; see FOUND³]

fount¹ (faʊnt) *n* **1** *poetic* a spring or fountain **2** source or origin [c16: back formation from FOUNTAIN]

fount² (faʊnt, font) *n printing* another word for **font²** [c16: from Old French *fonte* a founding, casting, from Vulgar Latin *funditus* (unattested) a casting, from Latin *fundere* to melt; see FOUND³]

fountain ('faʊntɪn) *n* **1** a jet or spray of water or some other liquid **2** a structure from which such a jet or a number of such jets spurt, often incorporating figures, basins, etc **3** a natural spring of water, esp the source of a stream **4** a stream, jet, or cascade of sparks, lava, etc **5** a principal source or origin **6** a reservoir or supply chamber, as for oil in a lamp [c15: from Old French *fontaine*, from Late Latin *fontāna*, from Latin *fons* spring, source] > 'fountained *adj*

fountainhead ('faʊntɪn,hɛd) *n* **1** a spring that is the source of a stream **2** a principal or original source

fountain pen *n* a pen the nib of which is supplied with ink from a cartridge or a reservoir in its barrel

Fouqué (*German* fuˈkeː) *n* Friedrich Heinrich Karl ('friːdrɪç 'haɪnrɪç karl), Baron de la Motte. 1777–1843, German romantic writer; author of *Undine* (1811)

Fouquet (*French* fukɛ) *n* **1** Jean (ʒɑ̃). ?1420–?80, French painter and miniaturist **2** Also: Foucquet **Nicolas** (nikɔla), *Marquis de Belle-Isle*. 1615–80, French statesman; superintendent of finance (1653–61) under Louis XIV. He was imprisoned for embezzlement, having been denounced by Colbert

Fouquier-Tinville (*French* fukjetɛ̃vil) *n* **Antoine Quentin** (ɑ̃twan kɑ̃tɛ̃). 1746–95, French revolutionary; as public prosecutor (1793–94) during the Reign of Terror, he sanctioned the guillotining of Desmoulins, Danton, and Robespierre

four (fɔː) *n* **1** the cardinal number that is the sum of three and one **2** a numeral, 4, IV, etc, representing this number **3** something representing, represented by, or consisting of four units, such as a playing card with four symbols on it **4** Also called: **four o'clock** four hours after noon or midnight **5** *cricket* **a** a shot that crosses the boundary after hitting the ground **b** the four runs scored for such a shot **6** *rowing* **a** a racing shell propelled by four oarsmen pulling one oar each, with or without a cox **b** the crew of such a shell ▷ *determiner* **7 a** amounting to four: *four thousand eggs; four times* **b** (*as pronoun*): *four are ready* [Old English *fēower*; related to Old Frisian *fiūwer*, Old Norse *fjōrir*, Old High German *fior*, Latin *quattuor*, Greek *tessares*, Sanskrit *catur*]

four-by-four *n* a vehicle equipped with four-wheel drive

four flush *n* a useless poker hand, containing four of a suit and one odd card

fourfold ('fɔː,fəʊld) *adj* **1** equal to or having four times as

many or as much **2** composed of four parts ▷ *adv* **3** by or up to four times as many or as much

Fourier ('fʊərɪˌeɪ; *French* furje) *n* **1** (**François Marie) Charles** (ʃarl). 1772–1837, French social reformer: propounded a system of cooperatives known as Fourierism, esp in his work *Le Nouveau monde industriel* (1829–30) **2 Jean Baptiste Joseph** (ʒɑ̃ batist ʒozɛf). 1768–1830, French mathematician, Egyptologist, and administrator, noted particularly for his research on the theory of heat and the method of analysis named after him

four-in-hand *n* **1** Also called: **tally-ho** a road vehicle drawn by four horses and driven by one driver **2** a four-horse team in a coach or carriage

four-leaf clover *or* **four-leaved clover** *n* a clover with four leaves rather than three, supposed to bring good luck

four-letter word *n* any of several short English words referring to sex or excrement: often used as swearwords and regarded generally as offensive or obscene

Fournier (*French* furnje) *n* See **Alain-Fournier**

four-o'clock *n* Also called: **marvel-of-Peru** a tropical American nyctaginaceous plant, *Mirabilis jalapa*, cultivated for its tubular yellow, red, or white flowers that open in late afternoon

four-poster *n* a bed with posts at each corner supporting a canopy and curtains

fourscore (ˌfɔːˈskɔː) *determiner* an archaic word for **eighty**

foursome ('fɔːsəm) *n* **1** a set or company of four **2** *sport* a game between two pairs of players, esp a form of golf in which each partner in a pair takes alternate strokes at the same ball

foursquare (ˌfɔːˈskwɛə) *adv* **1** squarely; firmly ▷ *adj* **2** solid and strong **3** forthright; honest **4** a rare word for **square**

four-stroke *adj* relating to or designating an internal-combustion engine in which the piston makes four strokes for every explosion

fourteen ('fɔːˈtiːn) *n* **1** the cardinal number that is the sum of ten and four **2** a numeral, 14, XIV, etc, representing this number **3** something represented by, representing, or consisting of 14 units ▷ *determiner* **4 a** amounting to fourteen: *fourteen cats* **b** (*as pronoun*): *the fourteen who remained* [Old English *fēowertīene*]

fourth (fɔːθ) *adj* (*usually prenominal*) **1 a** coming after the third in order, position, time, etc Often written: 4th **b** (*as noun*): *the fourth in succession* **2** denoting the fourth forward ratio of a gearbox in motor vehicles ▷ *n* **3** *music* **a** the interval between one note and another four notes away from it counting inclusively along the diatonic scale **b** one of two notes constituting such an interval in relation to the other **4** the fourth forward ratio of a gearbox in a motor vehicle **5** a less common word for **quarter** (sense 2) ▷ *adv* Also: **fourthly 6** after the third person, position, event, etc ▷ *sentence connector* Also: **fourthly 7** as the fourth point: linking what follows with the previous statements, as in a speech or argument

fourth dimension *n* **1** the dimension of time, which is necessary in addition to three spatial dimensions to specify fully the position and behaviour of a point or particle **2** the concept in science fiction of a dimension in addition to three spatial dimensions, used to explain supranatural phenomena, events, etc > ˌfourth-diˈmensional *adj*

fourth estate *n* (*sometimes capitals*) journalists or their profession; the press

four-wheel drive *n* a system used in motor vehicles in which all four wheels are connected to the source of power

fovea ('fəʊvɪə) *n, pl* **-veae** (-vɪˌiː) *anatomy* any small pit or depression in the surface of a bodily organ or part [c19: from Latin: a small pit]

Fowey (fɔɪ) *n* a resort and fishing village in SW England, in Cornwall, linked administratively with St Austell from 1968 to 1974. Pop: 2064 (2001)

fowl (faʊl) *n* **1** any other bird, esp any gallinaceous bird, that is used as food or hunted as game **2** the flesh or meat of fowl, esp of chicken **3** an archaic word for any:

bird ▷ *vb* **4** (*intr*) to hunt or snare wildfowl [Old English *fugol*; related to Old Frisian *fugel*, Old Norse *fogl*, Gothic *fugls*, Old High German *fogal*] > 'fowling *n* > 'fowler *n*

Fowler ('faʊlə) *n* **Henry Watson**. 1858–1933, English lexicographer and grammarian; compiler of *Modern English Usage* (1926)

Fowles (faʊlz) *n* **John** (**Martin**). 1926–2005, British novelist. His books include *The Collector* (1963), *The Magus* (1966), *The French Lieutenant's Woman* (1969), and *The Tree* (1991)

Fowliang or **Fou-liang** ('fuːˈljæŋ) *n* a variant transliteration of the Chinese name for **Jingdezhen**

fowl pest *n* an acute and usually fatal viral disease of domestic fowl, characterized by refusal to eat, high temperature, and discoloration of the comb and wattles

fox (fɒks) *n*, *pl* **foxes** or **fox** **1** any canine mammal of the genus *Vulpes* and related genera. They are mostly predators that do not hunt in packs and typically have large pointed ears, a pointed muzzle, and a bushy tail **2** the fur of any of these animals, usually reddish-brown or grey in colour **3** a person who is cunning and sly ▷ *vb* **4** (*tr*) to perplex or confound: *to fox a person with a problem* **5** to cause (paper, wood, etc) to become discoloured with spots, or (of paper, etc) to become discoloured, as through mildew **6** (*tr*) to trick; deceive **7** (*intr*) to act deceitfully or craftily [Old English; related to Old High German *fuhs*, Old Norse *fōa* fox, Sanskrit *puccha* tail; see VIXEN] > 'fox,like *adj*

Fox (fɒks) *n* **1 Charles James**. 1749–1806, British Whig statesman and orator. He opposed North over taxation of the American colonies and Pitt over British intervention against the French Revolution. He advocated parliamentary reform and the abolition of the slave trade **2 George**. 1624–91, English religious leader; founder (1647) of the Society of Friends (Quakers) **3 Terry**, full name *Terrance Stanley Fox* (1958–81). Canadian athlete: he lost a leg to cancer and subsequently attempted a coast-to-coast run across Canada to raise funds for cancer research **4 Vicente** (*Spanish* viˈθente). born 1942, Mexican politician; president of Mexico (2000–06) **5 Sir William**. 1812–93, New Zealand statesman, born in England: prime minister of New Zealand (1856; 1861–62; 1869–72; 1873)

Foxe (fɒks) *n* **John**. 1516–87, English Protestant clergyman; author of *History of the Acts and Monuments of the Church* (1563), popularly known as the *Book of Martyrs*

Foxe Basin (fɒks) *n* an arm of the Atlantic in NE Canada, between Melville Peninsula and Baffin Island

foxfire ('fɒks,faɪə) *n* a luminescent glow emitted by certain fungi on rotting wood

foxglove ('fɒks,ɡlʌv) *n* any Eurasian scrophulariaceous plant of the genus *Digitalis*, esp *D. purpurea*, having spikes of purple or white thimble-like flowers. The soft wrinkled leaves are a source of digitalis [Old English]

foxhole ('fɒks,həʊl) *n* *military* a small pit dug during an action to provide individual shelter against hostile fire

foxhound ('fɒks,haʊnd) *n* either of two breeds (the English and the American) of dog having a short smooth coat and pendent ears. Though not large (height about 60 cm or 23 in.) they have great stamina and are usually kept for hunting foxes

fox hunt *n* **1 a** the hunting of foxes with hounds **b** an instance of this **2** an organization for fox-hunting within a particular area > 'fox-,hunting *n* > 'fox-,hunter *n*

foxtail ('fɒks,teɪl) *n* any grass of the genus *Alopecurus*, esp *A. pratensis*, of Europe, Asia, and South America, having soft cylindrical spikes of flowers: cultivated as a pasture grass

Fox Talbot ('tɔːlbət) *n* **William Henry**. 1800–77, English physicist; a pioneer of photography

fox terrier *n* either of two breeds of small terrier, the wire-haired and the smooth, having a white coat with markings of black or tan or both

foxtrot ('fɒks,trɒt) *n* **1** a ballroom dance in quadruple time, combining short and long steps in various sequences ▷ *vb* -trots, -trotting, -trotted **2** (*intr*) to perform this dance

foxy ('fɒksɪ) *adj* **foxier, foxiest 1** of or resembling a fox, esp in craftiness **2** of a reddish-brown colour **3** (of

paper, wood, etc) spotted, esp by mildew **4** *slang* sexy; sexually attractive > 'foxily *adv* > 'foxiness *n*

foyer ('fɔɪeɪ, 'fɔɪə) *n* a hall, lobby, or anteroom, used for reception and as a meeting place, as in a hotel, theatre, cinema, etc [c19: from French: fireplace, from Medieval Latin *focārius*, from Latin *focus* fire]

fp *symbol for music* fortepiano

FP or **fp** *abbreviation* **1** former pupil **2** freezing point

FPA *abbreviation* Family Planning Association

fps *abbreviation* **1** feet per second **2** foot-pound-second **3** *photog* frames per second

FPS *abbreviation* first-person shooter

fps units *pl n* an Imperial system of units based on the foot, pound, and second as the units of length, mass, and time. For scientific and most technical purposes these units have been replaced by SI units

Fr *abbreviation* **1** *Christianity* **a** Frater **b** Father ▷ *the chemical symbol for* **2** francium [(for sense 1a) Latin: brother]

fr. *abbreviation* franc

Fr. *abbreviation* **1** *Christianity* Father **2** France [(sense 4) from German *Frau*]

Fra (frɑː) *n* brother: a title given to an Italian monk or friar [Italian, short for *frate* brother (in either natural or religious sense), from Latin *frāter* BROTHER]

fracas ('frækɑː) *n* a noisy quarrel; brawl [c18: from French, from *fracasser* to shatter, from *frangere* to break, influenced by *quassāre* to shatter]

fractal ('fræktəl) *n* *maths* a figure or surface generated by successive subdivisions of a simpler polygon or polyhedron, according to some iterative process [c20: from Latin *frāctus* past participle of *frangere* to break]

fraction ('frækʃən) *n* **1** *maths* a ratio of two expressions or numbers other than zero **2** any part or subdivision **3** a small piece; fragment **4** *chem* a component of a mixture separated by a fractional process, such as fractional distillation **5** *Christianity* the formal breaking of the bread in Communion [c14: from Late Latin *fractiō* a breaking into pieces, from Latin *fractus* broken, from *frangere* to break] > 'fractional or fractionary ('frækʃənərɪ) *adj* > 'fractionally *adv* > 'fractio,nize or 'fractio,nise *vb*

fractional crystallization *n* *chem* the process of separating the components of a solution on the basis of their different solubilities, by means of evaporating the solution until the least soluble component crystallizes out

fractional distillation *n* the process of separating the constituents of a liquid mixture by heating it and condensing separately the components according to their different boiling points

fractionate ('frækʃə,neɪt) *vb* **1** to separate or cause to separate into constituents or into fractions containing concentrated constituents **2** (*tr*) *chem* to obtain (a constituent of a mixture) by a fractional process > ,fraction'ation *n*

fractious ('frækʃəs) *adj* **1** irritable **2** unruly [c18: from (obsolete) *fraction* discord + -OUS] > 'fractiously *adv* > 'fractiousness *n*

fracture ('fræktʃə) *n* **1** the act of breaking or the state of being broken **2 a** the breaking or cracking of a bone or the tearing of a cartilage **b** the resulting condition **3** a division, split, or breach **4** *mineralogy* **a** the characteristic appearance of the surface of a freshly broken mineral or rock **b** the way in which a mineral or rock naturally breaks ▷ *vb* **5** to break or cause to break; split **6** to break or crack (a bone) or (of a bone) to become broken or cracked [c15: from Old French, from Latin *fractūra*, from *frangere* to break] > 'fractural *adj*

fraenum or **frenum** ('friːnəm) *n*, *pl* -na (-nə) a fold of membrane or skin, such as the fold beneath the tongue, that supports an organ [c18: from Latin: bridle]

fragile ('frædʒaɪl) *adj* **1** able to be broken easily **2** in a weakened physical state **3** delicate; light: *a fragile touch* **4** slight; tenuous [c17: from Latin *fragilis*, from *frangere* to break] > 'fragilely *adv* > fragility (frəˈdʒɪlɪtɪ) *n*

fragment *n* ('fræɡmənt) **1** a piece broken off or detached **2** an incomplete piece; portion: *fragments of a novel* **3** a scrap; morsel; bit ▷ *vb* (fræɡˈment) **4** to break or cause to break into fragments [c15: from Latin *fragmentum*, from *frangere* to break] > ,fragmen'tation *n*

fragmentary ('frægmən̩tərı, -trı) *adj* made up of fragments; disconnected; incomplete. Also called: **fragmental**

Fragonard (*French* fragɔnar) *n* **Jean-Honoré** (ʒɑ̃ ɔnɔre). 1732–1806, French artist, noted for richly coloured paintings typifying the frivolity of 18th- century French court life

fragrance ('freıgrəns) *or* **fragrancy** *n, pl* -grances *or* -grancies **1** a pleasant or sweet odour; scent; perfume **2** the state of being fragrant

fragrant ('freıgrənt) *adj* having a pleasant or sweet smell [C15: from Latin *frāgrāns*, from *frāgrāre* to emit a smell] > 'fragrantly *adv*

frail¹ (freıl) *adj* **1** physically weak and delicate **2** fragile: *a frail craft* **3** easily corrupted or tempted [C13: from Old French *frele*, from Latin *fragilis*, FRAGILE]

frail² (freıl) *n* **1** a rush basket for figs or raisins **2** a quantity of raisins or figs equal to between 50 and 75 pounds [C13: from Old French *fraiel*, of uncertain origin]

frailty ('freıltı) *n, pl* -ties **1** physical or moral weakness **2** (*often plural*) a fault symptomatic of moral weakness

framboesia *or US* **frambesia** (fræm'biːzıə) *n pathol* another name for **yaws** [C19: from New Latin, from French *framboise* raspberry; so called because of its raspberry-like excrescences]

framboise French (frɑ̃bwaz) *n* a brandy distilled from raspberries in the Alsace-Lorraine region [C16: from Old French: raspberry, probably of Germanic origin]

frame (freım) *n* **1** an open structure that gives shape and support to something, such as the transverse stiffening ribs of a ship's hull or an aircraft's fuselage or the skeletal beams and uprights of a building **2** an enclosing case or border into which something is fitted: *the frame of a picture* **3** the system around which something is built up: *the frame of government* **4** the structure of the human body **5** a condition; state (esp in the phrase **frame of mind**) **6 a** one of a series of individual exposures on a strip of film used in making motion pictures **b** an individual exposure on a film used in still photography **7** a television picture scanned by one or more electron beams at a particular frequency **8** *billiards, snooker* **a** the wooden triangle used to set up the balls **b** the balls when set up **c** a single game finished when all the balls have been potted **9** *computing* (on a website) a self-contained section that functions independently from other parts; by using frames, a website designer can make some areas of a website remain constant while others change according to the choices made by the internet user **10** short for **cold frame 11** one of the sections of which a beehive is composed, esp one designed to hold a honeycomb **12** *statistics* an enumeration of a population for the purposes of sampling, esp as the basis of a stratified sample **13** *slang* another word for **frame-up 14** *obsolete* shape; form ▷ *vb* (*mainly tr*) **15** to construct by fitting parts together **16** to draw up the plans or basic details for; outline: *to frame a policy* **17** to compose, contrive, or conceive: *to frame a reply* **18** to provide, support, or enclose with a frame: *to frame a picture* **19** to form (words) with the lips, esp silently **20** *slang* to conspire to incriminate (someone) on a false charge [Old English *framian* to avail; related to Old Frisian *framia* to carry out, Old Norse *frama*] > 'frameless *adj* > 'framer *n*

Frame (freım) *n* **Janet**. 1924–2004, and New Zealand writer: author of the novels *Owls Do Cry* (1957) and *Faces in the Water* (1961), the collection of verse *The Pocket* (1967), and volumes of autobiography including *An Angel at My Table* (1984), which was made into a film in 1990

frame house *n* a house that has a timber framework and cladding

frame of reference *n* **1** a set of basic assumptions or standards that determines and sanctions behaviour **2** any set of planes or curves, such as the three coordinate axes, used to locate or measure movement of a point in space

frame-up *n slang* **1** a conspiracy to incriminate someone on a false charge **2** a plot to bring about a dishonest result, as in a contest

framework ('freım,wɜːk) *n* **1** a structural plan or basis of

a project **2** a structure or frame supporting or containing something

franc (fræŋk; *French* frɑ̃) *n* **1** Also called: **French franc** the former standard monetary unit of France, most French dependencies, Andorra, and Monaco, divided into 100 centimes; replaced by the euro in 2002 **2** Also called: **franc CFA, CFA franc, franc of the African financial community** the standard monetary unit, comprising 100 centimes, of the following countries: Benin, Burkina Faso, Cameroon, the Central African Republic, Chad, Congo-Brazzaville, Côte d'Ivoire, Equatorial Guinea, Gabon, Guinea-Bissau, Mali, Niger, Senegal, and Togo **3** the standard monetary unit of Burundi (**Burundi franc**), Comoros (**Comorian franc**), Democratic Republic of Congo (formerly Zaïre; **Congolese franc**), Djibouti (**Djibouti franc**), Guinea (**Guinea franc**), Madagascar (**franc malgache**), Rwanda (**Rwanda franc**), and French Polynesia and New Caledonia (**French Pacific franc**)

France¹ (frɑːns) *n* a republic in W Europe, between the English Channel, the Mediterranean, and the Atlantic: the largest country wholly in Europe; became a republic in 1793 after the French Revolution and an empire in 1804 under Napoleon; reverted to a monarchy (1815–48), followed by the Second Republic (1848–52), the Second Empire (1852–70), the Third Republic (1870–1940), and the Fourth and Fifth Republics (1946 and 1958); a member of the European Union. It is generally flat or undulating in the north and west and mountainous in the south and east. Official language: French. Religion: Roman Catholic majority. Currency: euro. Capital: Paris. Pop: 60 434 000 (2004 est). Area: (including Corsica) 551 600 sq km (212 973 sq miles) Related adjs: **French¹, Gallic**

France² (*French* frɑ̃s) *n* **Anatole** (anatɔl), real name *Anatole François Thibault*. 1844–1924, French novelist, short-story writer, and critic. His works include *Le Crime de Sylvestre Bonnard* (1881), *L'Île des Pingouins* (1908), and *La Révolte des anges* (1914): Nobel prize for literature 1921

Francesca (*Italian* fran'tʃeska) *n* See **Piero Della Francesca**

Franche-Comté (*French* frɑ̃ʃkɔ̃te) *n* a region of E France, covering the Jura and the low country east of the Saône: part of the Kingdom of Burgundy (6th cent. AD–1137); autonomous as the Free County of Burgundy (1137–1384); under Burgundian rule (1384–1477) and Hapsburg rule (1493–1674); annexed by France (1678)

franchise ('fræntʃaız) *n* **1 the franchise** the right to vote, esp for representatives in a legislative body; suffrage **2** any exemption, privilege, or right granted to an individual or group by a public authority, such as the right to use public property for a business **3** *commerce* authorization granted by a manufacturing enterprise to a distributor to market the manufacturer's products **4** the full rights of citizenship ▷ *vb* **5** (*tr*) *commerce chiefly US & Canadian* to grant (a person, firm, etc) a franchise [C13: from Old French, from *franchir* to set free, from *franc* free; see FRANK] > 'franchi,see *n* > 'franchiser *n* > franchisement ('fræntʃızmənt) *n*

Francis ('frɑːnsıs) *n* **1 Dick**, full name *Richard Stanley Francis*. born 1920, British thriller writer, formerly a champion jockey. His books include *Dead Cert* (1962), *The Edge* (1988), and *Come to Grief* (1995) **2** Sir **Philip**. 1740–1818, British politician; probable author of the *Letters of Junius* (1769–72). He played an important part in the impeachment of Warren Hastings (1788–95)

Francis I *n* **1** 1494–1547, king of France (1515–47). His reign was dominated by his rivalry with Emperor Charles V for the control of Italy. He was a noted patron of the arts and learning **2** 1708–65, duke of Lorraine (1729–37), grand duke of Tuscany (1737–65), and Holy Roman Emperor (1745–65). His marriage (1736) to Maria Theresa led to the War of the Austrian Succession (1740–48) **3** title as emperor of Austria of **Francis II**

Francis II *n* **1** 1544–60 king of France (1559–60); son of Henry II and Catherine de' Medici; first husband of Mary, Queen of Scots **2** 1768–1835, last Holy Roman Emperor (1792–1806) and, as Francis I, first emperor of Austria (1804–35). The Holy Roman Empire was dissolved (1806) following his defeat by Napoleon at Austerlitz

Franciscan (fræn'sɪskən) *n* **a** a member of any of several Christian religious orders of mendicant friars or nuns tracing their origins back to Saint Francis of Assisi; a Grey Friar **b** (*as modifier*): *a Franciscan friar*

Francis of Assisi *n* **Saint** original name *Giovanni di Bernardone*. ?1181–1226, Italian monk; founder of the Franciscan order of friars. He is remembered for his humility and love for all creation and was the first person to exhibit stigmata (1224). Feast day: Oct 4

Francis of Sales (seɪlz; *French* sal) *n* **Saint**. 1567–1622, French ecclesiastic and theologian; bishop of Geneva (1602–22) and an opponent of Calvinism; author of *Introduction to a Devout Life* (1609) and founder of the Order of the Visitation (1610). Feast day: Jan 24

Francis Xavier (ˈzeɪvɪə) *n* Saint Francis Xavier See **Xavier**

francium (ˈfrænsɪəm) *n* an unstable radioactive element of the alkali-metal group, occurring in minute amounts in uranium ores. Symbol: Fr; atomic no: 87; half-life of most stable isotope, ²²³Fr: 22 minutes; valency: 1; melting pt: 27°C; boiling pt: 677°C [c20: from New Latin, from FRANCE + -IUM; so-called because first found in France]

francize *or* **francise** (ˈfrænsaɪz) *vb Canadian* to make or become French-speaking ⊳ ˌfranciˈzation *or* ˌfranciˈsation *n*

Franck *n* **1** (*French* frɑ̃k) **César** (**Auguste**) (sezar). 1822–90, French composer, organist, and teacher, born in Belgium. His works, some of which make use of cyclic form, include a violin sonata, a string quartet, the *Symphony in D Minor* (1888), and much organ music **2** (fræŋk) **James**. 1882–1964, US physicist, born in Germany: shared a Nobel prize for physics with Gustav Hertz (1925) for work on the quantum theory, particularly the effects of bombarding atoms with electrons

Franco (ˈfræŋkəʊ; *Spanish* ˈfraŋko) *n* **Francisco** (franˈθisko), called *el Caudillo*. 1892–1975, Spanish general and statesman; head of state (1939–1975). He was commander-in- chief of the Falangists in the Spanish Civil War (1936–39), defeating the republican government and establishing a dictatorship (1939). He kept Spain neutral in World War II

Franco- (ˈfræŋkəʊ-) *combining form* indicating France or French: *Franco-Prussian* [from Medieval Latin *Francus*, from Late Latin: FRANK]

francolin (ˈfræŋkəʊlɪn) *n* any African or Asian partridge of the genus *Francolinus* [c17: from French, from Old Italian *francolino*, of unknown origin]

Franconia (fræŋˈkəʊnɪə) *n* a medieval duchy of Germany, inhabited by the Franks from the 7th century, now chiefly in Bavaria, Hesse, and Baden-Württemberg

Franconian (fræŋˈkəʊnɪən) *n* **1** a group of medieval Germanic dialects spoken by the Franks in an area from N Bavaria and Alsace to the mouth of the Rhine. **Low Franconian** developed into Dutch; **Upper Franconian** contributed to High German, of which it remains a recognizable dialect. See also **Old Low German, Old High German, Frankish** ⊳ *adj* **2** of or relating to Franconia, the Franks, or their languages

Francophobe (ˈfræŋkəʊˌfəʊb) *n* (*sometimes not capital*) **1** a person who hates or despises France or its people **2** *Canadian* a person who hates or fears Canadian Francophones

Francophone (ˈfræŋkəʊˌfəʊn) *n* (*often not capital*) *n* **1** a person who speaks French, esp a native speaker ⊳ *adj* **2** speaking French as a native language **3** using French as a lingua franca

frangible (ˈfrændʒɪbᵊl) *adj* breakable or fragile [c15: from Old French, ultimately from Latin *frangere* to break] ⊳ ˌfrangiˈbility *or* ˈfrangibleness *n*

frangipane (ˈfrændʒɪˌpeɪn) *n* **1** a pastry filled with cream and flavoured with almonds **2** a variant of **frangipani** (sense 2)

frangipani (ˌfrændʒɪˈpɑːnɪ) *n*, *pl* -**panis**, -**pani 1** any tropical American apocynaceous shrub of the genus *Plumeria*, esp *P. rubra*, cultivated for its waxy typically white or pink flowers, which have a sweet overpowering scent **2** a perfume prepared from this plant or resembling the odour of its flowers **3** native frangipani *Austral* an Australian evergreen tree, *Hymenosporum flavum*, with large fragrant yellow flowers: family *Pittosporaceae* [c17: via French from Italian: perfume for scenting gloves, named after the Marquis Muzio Frangipani, 16th-century Roman nobleman who invented it]

Franglais (*French* frɑ̃glɛ) *n* informal French containing a high proportion of words of English origin [c20: from French *français* French + *anglais* English]

frank (fræŋk) *adj* **1** honest and straightforward in speech or attitude: *a frank person* **2** outspoken or blunt **3** open and avowed; undisguised: *frank interest* ⊳ *vb* (*tr*) **4** *chiefly Brit* to put a mark on (a letter, parcel, etc), either cancelling the postage stamp or in place of a stamp, ensuring free carriage **5** to mark (a letter, parcel, etc) with an official mark or signature, indicating the right of free delivery **6** to facilitate or assist (a person) to come and go, pass, or enter easily **7** to obtain immunity for or exempt (a person) ⊳ *n* **8** an official mark or signature affixed to a letter, parcel, etc, ensuring free delivery or delivery without stamps [c13: from Old French *franc*, from Medieval Latin *francus* free; identical with FRANK (in Frankish Gaul only members of this people enjoyed full freedom)] ⊳ ˈfrankable *adj* ⊳ ˈfranker *n* ⊳ ˈfrankness *n*

Frank¹ (fræŋk) *n* a member of a group of West Germanic peoples who spread from the east bank of the middle Rhine into the Roman Empire in the late 4th century AD, gradually conquering most of Gaul and Germany. The Franks achieved their greatest power under Charlemagne [Old English *Franca*; related to Old High German *Franko*; perhaps from the name of a typical Frankish weapon (compare Old English *franca* javelin)]

Frank² (*Dutch* fraŋk) *n* **1** **Anne**. 1929–45, German Jewess, whose *Diary* (1947) recorded the experiences of her family while in hiding from the Nazis in Amsterdam (1942–44). They were betrayed and she died in a concentration camp **2 Robert**. born 1924, US photographer and film maker, born in Switzerland; best known for his photographic book *The Americans* (1959)

Frankenstein (ˈfræŋkɪnˌstaɪn) *n* **1** a person who creates something that brings about his ruin **2** Also called: **Frankenstein's monster** a thing that destroys its creator [c19: after Baron *Frankenstein*, who created a destructive monster from parts of corpses in the novel by Mary Shelley (1818)] ⊳ ˌFrankenˈsteinian *adj*

Frankenstein food *or* **Frankenfood** (ˈfræŋkənˌfuːd) *n facetious* any foodstuff that has been genetically modified [c20: from FRANKENSTEIN, alluding to its unnatural origin]

Frankfort (ˈfræŋkfət) *n* **1** a city in N Kentucky: the state capital. Pop: 27 408 (2003 est) **2** *now rare* an English spelling of **Frankfurt¹**

Frankfurt¹ *or* **Frankfurt am Main** (*German* ˈfraŋkfʊrt ˌam ˈmain,) *n* a city in central Germany, in Hesse on the Main River: a Roman settlement in the 1st century; a free imperial city (1372–1806); seat of the federal assembly (1815–66); university (1914); trade fairs since the 13th century. Pop: 643 432 (2003 est)

Frankfurt² *or* **Frankfurt an der Oder** (*German* ˈfraŋkfʊrt ˌan der ˈoːdər,) *n* a city in E Germany on the Polish border: member of the Hanseatic League (1368–1450). Pop: 67 014 (2003 est)

frankfurter (ˈfræŋkˌfɜːtə) *n* a light brown smoked sausage, made of finely minced pork or beef, often served in a bread roll [c20: short for German *Frankfurter Wurst* sausage from FRANKFURT (AM MAIN)]

Frankfurter (ˈfræŋkˌfɜːtə) *n* an inhabitant or native of Frankfurt

frankincense (ˈfræŋkɪnˌsɛns) *n* an aromatic gum resin obtained from trees of the burseraceous genus *Boswellia*, which occur in Asia and Africa [c14: from Old French *franc* free, pure + *encens* INCENSE¹; see FRANK]

Frankish (ˈfræŋkɪʃ) *n* **1** the ancient West Germanic language of the Franks, esp the dialect that contributed to the vocabulary of modern French ⊳ *adj* **2** of or relating to the Franks or their language

franklin (ˈfræŋklɪn) *n* (in 14th- and 15th-century

England) a substantial landholder of free but not noble birth [C13: from Anglo-French *fraunclein*, from Old French *franc* free, on the model of CHAMBERLAIN]

Franklin ('fræŋklɪn) *n* **1 Aretha** (ə'riːθə) born 1942, US soul, pop, and gospel singer **2 Benjamin** 1706–90, American statesman, scientist, and author. He helped draw up the Declaration of Independence (1776) and, as ambassador to France (1776–85), he negotiated an alliance with France and a peace settlement with Britain. As a scientist, he is noted particularly for his researches in electricity, esp his invention of the lightning conductor **3 Sir John**. 1786–1847, English explorer of the Arctic: lieutenant-governor of Van Diemen's Land (now Tasmania) (1836–43): died while on a voyage to discover the Northwest Passage **4 Rosalind**. 1920–58, British x-ray crystallographer. She contributed to the discovery of the structure of DNA, before her premature death from cancer

frankly ('fræŋklɪ) *adv* **1** (*sentence modifier*) in truth; to be honest **2** in a frank manner

frantic ('fræntɪk) *adj* **1** distracted with fear, pain, joy, etc **2** marked by or showing frenzy: *frantic efforts* [C14: from Old French *frenetique*, from Latin *phreneticus* mad, FRENETIC] > 'frantically *or* 'franticly *adv*

Franz Ferdinand (*German* frants 'ferdinant) *n* English name *Francis Ferdinand*. 1863–1914, archduke of Austria; heir apparent of Franz Josef I. His assassination contributed to the outbreak of World War I

Franz Josef I (*German* frants 'joːzɛf) *n* English name *Francis Joseph I*. 1830–1916, emperor of Austria (1848–1916) and king of Hungary (1867–1916)

Franz Josef Land (*German* frants 'joːzɛf) *n* an archipelago of over 100 islands in the Arctic Ocean, administratively part of Russia. Area: about 21 000 sq km (8000 sq miles)

frap (fræp) *vb* **fraps, frapping, frapped** (*tr*) *nautical* to lash down or together [C14: from Old French *fraper* to hit, probably of imitative origin]

frappé ('fræpeɪ; *French* frape) *n* **1** a drink consisting of a liqueur, etc, poured over crushed ice ▷ *adj* **2** (*postpositive*) (esp of drinks) chilled; iced [C19: from French, from *frapper* to strike, hence, chill; see FRAP]

Fraser¹ ('freɪzə) *n* a river in SW Canada, in S central British Columbia, flowing northwest, south, and west through spectacular canyons in the Coast Mountains to the Strait of Georgia. Length: 1370 km (850 miles)

Fraser² ('freɪzə) *n* **1** (**John**) **Malcolm**. born 1930, Australian statesman; prime minister of Australia (1975–83) **2 Peter**. 1884–1950, New Zealand statesman, born in Scotland; prime minister (1940–49) **3 Simon**. (1776–1862), Canadian explorer: explored British Columbia and the river which was named after him

frater ('freɪtə) *n archaic* a refectory [C13: from Old French *fraiteur*, aphetic variant of *refreitor*, from Late Latin *refectōrium* REFECTORY]

fraternal (frə'tɜːnʰl) *adj* **1** of or suitable to a brother; brotherly **2** of or relating to a fraternity **3** designating either or both of a pair of twins of the same or opposite sex that developed from two separate fertilized ova. See **identical** (sense 3) [C15: from Latin *frāternus*, from *frāter* brother] > fra'ternalism *n*

fraternity (frə'tɜːnɪtɪ) *n*, *pl* **-ties 1** a body of people united in interests, aims, etc: *the teaching fraternity* **2** brotherhood **3** *US & Canadian* a secret society joined by male students, usually functioning as a social club

fraternize *or* **fraternise** ('frætəˌnaɪz) *vb* (*intr*; often foll by *with*) to associate on friendly terms > ˌfraterni'zation *or* ˌfraterni'sation > 'fraterˌnizer *or* 'fraterˌniser *n*

fratricide ('frætrɪˌsaɪd, 'freɪ-) *n* **1** the act of killing one's brother **2** a person who kills his brother [C15: from Latin *frātricīda*; see FRATER, -CIDE] > ˌfratri'cidal *adj*

Frau (frau) *n*, *pl* **Frauen** ('frauən) *or* **Fraus** a married German woman: usually used as a title equivalent to *Mrs* and sometimes extended to older unmarried women [from Old High German *frouwa*; related to Dutch *vrouw*]

fraud (frɔːd) *n* **1** deliberate deception, trickery, or cheating intended to gain an advantage **2** an act or instance of such deception **3** *informal* a person who acts in a false or deceitful way [C14: from Old French *fraude*,

from Latin *fraus* deception]

fraudster ('frɔːdstə) *n* a swindler

fraudulent ('frɔːdjʊlənt) *adj* **1** acting with or having the intent to deceive **2** relating to or proceeding from fraud or dishonest action [C15: from Latin *fraudulentus* deceitful] > 'fraudulence *or* 'fraudulency *n* > 'fraudulently *adv*

Frauenfeld (*German* 'frauənfɛlt) *n* a town in NE Switzerland, capital of Thurgau canton. Pop: 21 954 (2000)

fraught (frɔːt) *adj* **1** (*usually postpositive* and foll by *with*) filled or charged; attended: *a venture fraught with peril* **2** *informal* showing or producing tension or anxiety [C14: from Middle Dutch *vrachten*, from *vracht* FREIGHT]

Fräulein (*German* 'frɔylain; *English* 'frɔːlaɪn) *n*, *pl* **-lein** *or English* **-leins** an unmarried German woman: formerly used as a title equivalent to *Miss* [from Middle High German *vrouwelīn*, diminutive of *vrouwe* lady]

Fraunhofer (*German* 'fraunhoːfər) *n* **Joseph von** ('joːzɛf fɔn). 1787–1826, German physicist and optician, who investigated spectra of the sun, planets, and fixed stars, and improved telescopes and other optical instruments

Fraunhofer lines (*German* 'fraunhoːfər) *pl n* a set of dark lines appearing in the continuous emission spectrum of the sun. It is caused by the absorption of light of certain wavelengths coming from the hotter region of the sun by elements in the cooler outer atmosphere [named after J. von Fraunhofer (1787–1826), German physicist]

fraxinella (ˌfræksɪ'nɛlə) *n* another name for **gas plant** [C17: from New Latin: a little ash tree, from Latin *frāxinus* ash]

fray¹ (freɪ) *n* **1** a noisy quarrel **2** a fight or brawl [C14: short for AFFRAY]

fray² (freɪ) *vb* **1** to wear or cause to wear away into tatters or loose threads, esp at an edge or end **2** to make or become strained or irritated **3** to rub or chafe (another object) or (of two objects) to rub against one another [C14: from French *frayer* to rub, from Latin *fricāre*; see FRICTION, FRIABLE]

Fray Bentos (ˌfreɪ 'bɛntɒs) *n* a port in W Uruguay, on the River Uruguay: noted for meat-packing. Pop: 23 122 (2004 est)

Frayn (freɪn) *n* **Michael**. born 1933, British playwright, novelist, and translator; his plays include *The Two of Us* (1970), *Noises Off* (1982), *Copenhagen* (1998), and *Democracy* (2004); novels include *A Landing on the Sun* (1991) and *Spies* (2002)

Frazer ('freɪzə) *n* **Sir James George**. 1854–1941, Scottish anthropologist; author of many works on primitive religion, and magic, esp *The Golden Bough* (1890)

Frazier ('freɪzə) *n* **Joe**. born 1944, US boxer: won the world heavyweight title in 1970 and was the first to beat Muhammad Ali professionally (1971)

frazil ('freɪzɪl) *n* small pieces of ice that form in water moving turbulently enough to prevent the formation of a sheet of ice [C19: from Canadian French *frasil*, from French *fraisil* cinders, ultimately from Latin *fax* torch]

frazzle ('fræzʰl) *vb* **1** *informal* to make or become exhausted or weary; tire out ▷ *n* **2** *informal* the state of being frazzled or exhausted **3** to a frazzle *informal* absolutely; completely (esp in the phrase **burnt to a frazzle**) [C19: probably from Middle English *faselen* to fray, from *fasel* fringe; influenced by FRAY²]

freak (friːk) *n* **1** a person, animal, or plant that is abnormal or deformed; monstrosity **2 a** an object, event, etc, that is abnormal or extremely unusual **b** (*as modifier*): *a freak storm* **3** a personal whim or caprice **4** *informal* a person who acts or dresses in a markedly unconventional or strange way **5** *informal* a person who is obsessed with something specified: *a jazz freak* ▷ *vb* **6** See **freak out** [C16: of obscure origin]

freaking ('friːkɪŋ) *adj*, *adv* (*prenominal*) *slang, chiefly US* (*intensifier*): *his freaking mother; this is freaking weird* [C20: euphemism for FUCKING]

freak out *vb* (*adverb*) *informal* to be or cause to be in a heightened emotional state, such as that of fear, anger, or excitement

freckle ('frɛkʰl) *n* **1** a small brownish spot on the skin: a localized deposit of the pigment melanin, developed by exposure to sunlight **2** any small area of discoloration; a spot ▷ *vb* **3** to mark or become marked with freckles or spots [C14: from Old Norse *freknur* freckles; related to Swedish *fräkne*, Danish *fregne*] > 'freckled *or* 'freckly *adj*

Fredericia (*Danish* freðəˈrɛdsæ) *n* a port in Denmark, in E Jutland at the N end of the Little Belt. Pop: 37 054 (2004 est)

Frederick I (ˈfrɛdrɪk) *n* **1** See **Frederick Barbarossa** **2** 1657–1713, first king of Prussia (1701–13); son of Frederick William

Frederick II *n* **1** 1194–1250, Holy Roman Emperor (1220–50), king of Germany (1212–50), and king of Sicily (1198–1250) **2** See **Frederick the Great**

Frederick III *n* **1** 1415–93, Holy Roman Emperor (1452–93) and, as Frederick IV, king of Germany (1440–93) **2** called *the Wise*. 1463–1525, elector of Saxony (1486–1525). He protected Martin Luther in Wartburg Castle after the Diet of Worms (1521)

Frederick IV *n* See **Frederick III** (sense 1)

Frederick V *n* called *the Winter King*. 1596–1632, elector of the Palatinate (1610–23) and king of Bohemia (1619–20). He led the revolt of Bohemian Protestants at the beginning of the Thirty Years' War

Frederick IX *n* 1899–1972, king of Denmark (1947–72)

Frederick Barbarossa (ˌbɑːbəˈrɒsə) *n* official title *Frederick I*. ?1123–90, Holy Roman Emperor (1155–90), king of Germany (1152–90). His attempt to assert imperial rights in Italy ended in his defeat at Legnano (1176) and the independence of the Lombard cities (1183)

Frederick Henry *n* 1584–1647, prince of Orange and count of Nassau; son of William (I) the Silent

Frederick the Great *n* official title *Frederick II*. 1712–86, king of Prussia (1740–86); son of Frederick William I. He gained Silesia during the War of Austrian Succession (1740–48) and his military genius during the Seven Years' War (1756–63) established Prussia as a European power. He was also a noted patron of the arts

Frederick William *n* called *the Great Elector*. 1620–88, elector of Brandenburg (1640–88)

Frederick William I *n* 1688–1740, king of Prussia (1713–40); son of Frederick I: reformed the Prussian army

Frederick William II *n* 1744–97, king of Prussia (1786–97)

Frederick William III *n* 1770–1840, king of Prussia (1797–1840)

Frederick William IV *n* 1795–1861, king of Prussia (1840–61). He submitted to the 1848 Revolution but refused the imperial crown offered by the Frankfurt Parliament (1849). In 1857 he became insane and his brother, William I, became regent (1858–61)

Fredericton (ˈfrɛdrɪktən) *n* a city in SE Canada, capital of New Brunswick, on the St John River. Pop: 54 068 (2001)

Frederiksberg (*Danish* frɛðregsˈbɛr) *n* a city in E Denmark, within the area of greater Copenhagen: founded in 1651 by King Frederick III. Pop: 91 721 (2004 est)

Fredrikstad (*Norwegian* ˈfrɛdrɪkstad) *n* a port in SE Norway at the entrance to Oslo Fjord. Pop: 69 867 (2004 est)

free (friː) *adj* freer, freest **1** able to act at will; not under compulsion or restraint **2 a** having personal rights or liberty; not enslaved or confined **b** (*as noun*): *land of the free* **3** (*often postpositive* and foll by *from*) not subject (to) or restricted (by some regulation, constraint, etc); exempt: *a free market; free from pain* **4** (of a country, etc) autonomous or independent **5** exempt from external direction or restriction; not forced or induced: *free will* **6** not subject to conventional constraints **7** (of jazz) totally improvised, with no preset melodic, harmonic, or rhythmic basis **8** not exact or literal: *a free translation* **9** costing nothing; provided without charge: *free entertainment* **10** *law* (of property) **a** not subject to payment of rent or performance of services; freehold **b** not subject to any burden or charge, such as a mortgage or lien; unencumbered **11** (*postpositive*; often foll by *of* or *with*) ready or generous in using or giving; liberal; lavish: *free with advice* **12** not occupied or in use; available: *a free cubicle* **13** not occupied or busy; without previous engagements **14** open or available to all; public **15** without charge to the subscriber or user: *freepost;*

freephone **16** not fixed or joined; loose: *the free end of a chain* **17** without obstruction or impediment: *free passage* **18** *chem* chemically uncombined: *free nitrogen* **19** *logic* denoting an occurrence of a variable not bound by a quantifier. See **bound¹** (sense 7) **20** for free *not standard* without charge or cost **21** free and easy casual or tolerant; easy-going **22** make free with to take liberties with; behave too familiarly towards ▷ *adv* **23** in a free manner; freely **24** without charge or cost **25** *nautical* with the wind blowing from the quarter ▷ *vb* frees, freeing, freed (*tr*) **26** (sometimes foll by *up*) to set at liberty; release **27** to remove obstructions, attachments, or impediments from; disengage **28** (often foll by *of* or *from*) to relieve or rid (of obstacles, pain, etc) [Old English *frēo*; related to Old Saxon, Old High German *frī*, Gothic *freis* free, Sanskrit *priya* dear] > 'freely *adv* > 'freeness *n* **-free** *adj combining form* free from: *trouble-free; lead-free petrol*

free alongside ship *adj* (of a shipment of goods) delivered to the dock without charge to the buyer, but excluding the cost of loading onto the vessel. See **free on board**

free association *n* *psychoanal* a method of exploring a person's unconscious by eliciting words and thoughts that are associated with key words provided by a psychoanalyst

freebase (ˈfriːˌbeɪs) *n* **1** *slang* cocaine that has been refined by heating it in ether or some other solvent ▷ *vb* freebases, freebasing, freebased **2** to refine (cocaine) in this way **3** to smoke or inhale the fumes from (refined cocaine)

freebie (ˈfriːbɪ) *n* *slang* something provided without charge

freeboard (ˈfriːˌbɔːd) *n* the space or distance between the deck of a vessel and the waterline

freebooter (ˈfriːˌbuːtə) *n* a person, such as a pirate, living from plunder [C16: from Dutch *vrijbuiter*, from *vrijbuit* booty; see **FILIBUSTER**]

freeborn (ˈfriːˌbɔːn) *adj* **1** not born in slavery **2** of, relating to, or suitable for people not born in slavery

Free Church *n* *chiefly Brit* any Protestant Church, esp the Presbyterian, other than the Established Church

free city *n* a sovereign or autonomous city; city-state

freecycle (ˈfriːˌsaɪkᵊl) *n* **1** an informal network of citizens who cooperate online to promote recycling by offering one another unwanted items free of charge ▷ *vb* **2** (*tr*) to recycle (an unwanted item) by offering it to someone free of charge

freediving (ˈfriːdaɪvɪŋ) *n* the sport or activity of diving without the aid of breathing apparatus > freediver *n*

freedman (ˈfriːdˌmæn) *n, pl* -men a man who has been freed from slavery

freedom (ˈfriːdəm) *n* **1** personal liberty, as from slavery, bondage, serfdom, etc **2** liberation or deliverance, as from confinement or bondage **3** the quality or state of being free, esp to enjoy political and civil liberties **4** (usually foll by *from*) the state of being without something unpleasant or bad; exemption or immunity: *freedom from taxation* **5** the right or privilege of unrestricted use or access: *the freedom of a city* **6** autonomy, self-government, or independence **7** the power or liberty to order one's own actions **8** *philosophy* the quality, esp of the will or the individual, of not being totally constrained; able to choose between alternative actions in identical circumstances **9** ease or frankness of manner; candour: *she talked with complete freedom* **10** excessive familiarity of manner; boldness **11** ease and grace, as of movement; lack of effort [Old English *frēodōm*]

freedom fighter *n* a militant revolutionary

free energy *n* a thermodynamic property that expresses the capacity of a system to perform work under certain conditions

free enterprise *n* an economic system in which commercial organizations compete for profit with little state control

free fall *n* **1** free descent of a body in which the gravitational force is the only force acting on it **2** the part of a parachute descent before the parachute opens

free flight *n* the flight of a rocket, missile, etc, when its engine has ceased to produce thrust

free-for-all n *informal* a disorganized brawl or argument, usually involving all those present

free form *arts* ▷ n **1** an irregular flowing shape, often used in industrial or fabric design ▷ adj **free-form 2** freely flowing, spontaneous

free hand n **1** unrestricted freedom to act (esp in the phrase **give (someone) a free hand**) ▷ adj, adv **freehand 2** (done) by hand without the use of guiding instruments: *a freehand drawing*

free-handed adj generous or liberal; unstinting > ,free-'handedly adv

freehold ('fri:,həʊld) *property law* ▷ n **1 a** a tenure by which land is held in fee simple, fee tail, or for life **b** an estate held by such tenure ▷ adj **2** relating to or having the nature of freehold > 'free,holder n

free house n *Brit* a public house not bound to sell only one brewer's products

free kick n *soccer* a place kick awarded for a foul or infringement, either direct, from which a goal may be scored, or indirect, from which the ball must be touched by at least one other player for a goal to be allowed

freelance ('fri:,lɑːns) n **1 a** Also: **freelancer** a self-employed person, esp a writer or artist, who is not employed continuously but hired to do specific assignments **b** (*as modifier*): *a freelance journalist* **2** (in medieval Europe) a mercenary soldier or adventurer ▷ vb **3** to work as a freelance on (an assignment, etc) ▷ adv **4** as a freelance [C19 (in sense 3): later applied to politicians, writers, etc]

free-living adj **1** given to ready indulgence of the appetites **2** (of animals and plants) not parasitic; existing independently > ,free-'liver n

freeloader ('fri:,ləʊdə) n *slang* a person who habitually depends on the charity of others for food, shelter, etc

free love n the practice of sexual relationships without fidelity to a single partner or without formal or legal ties

freeman ('fri:mən) n, pl **-men 1** a person who is not a slave or in bondage **2** a person who enjoys political and civil liberties; citizen **3** a person who enjoys a privilege or franchise, such as the freedom of a city

Freeman ('fri:mən) n **Cathy,** full name *Catherine Astrid Salome Freeman.* born 1973, Australian sprinter; winner of the 200m and 400m in the 1994 Commonwealth Games and the 400m in the 2000 Olympic Games

free market n **a** an economic system that allows supply and demand to regulate prices, wages, etc, rather than government interference **b** (*as modifier*): *a free-market economy*

freemartin ('fri:,mɑːtɪn) n the female of a pair of twin calves of unlike sex that is imperfectly developed and sterile, probably due to the influence of the male hormones of its twin during development in the uterus [C17: of uncertain origin]

Freemason ('fri:,meɪsªn) n a member of the widespread secret order, constituted in London in 1717, of **Free and Accepted Masons,** pledged to brotherly love, faith, and charity. Sometimes shortened to: **Mason**

freemasonry ('fri:,meɪsªnrɪ) n natural or tacit sympathy and understanding

Freemasonry ('fri:,meɪsªnrɪ) n **1** the institutions, rites, practices, etc, of Freemasons **2** Freemasons collectively

free on board adj (of a shipment of goods) delivered on board ship or other carrier without charge to the buyer. See **free alongside ship**

Freeper ('fri:pə) n *chiefly US & Canadian informal* an active member of the Free Republic website, an American right-wing news and discussion forum

free port n **1** a port open to all commercial vessels on equal terms **2** Also called: **free zone** a zone adjoining a port that permits the duty-free entry of foreign goods intended for re-export

free radical n an atom or group of atoms containing at least one unpaired electron and existing for a brief period of time before reacting to produce a stable molecule

free-range adj *chiefly Brit* kept or produced in natural nonintensive conditions: *free-range hens; free-range eggs*

free-select vb (tr) *Austral history* to select (areas of crown

land) and acquire the freehold by a series of annual payments > ,free-se'lection n > ,free-se'lector n

freesia ('fri:zɪə, 'fri:ʒə) n any iridaceous plant of the genus *Freesia*, of southern Africa, cultivated for their white, yellow, or pink tubular fragrant flowers [C19: New Latin, named after F. H. T. *Freese* (died 1876), German physician]

free skating n either the short programme of specified movements or the long programme chosen by a skater in a figure-skating competition

free space n a region that has no gravitational and electromagnetic fields: used as an absolute standard. Also called (no longer in technical usage): vacuum

free-spoken adj speaking frankly or without restraint > ,free-'spokenly adv

freestanding (,fri:'stændɪŋ) adj standing apart; not attached to or supported by another object

Free State n a province of central South Africa; replaced the former province of Orange Free State in 1994: gold and uranium mining. Capital: Bloemfontein. Pop: 2 950 661 (2004 est). Area: 129 480 sq km (49 992 sq miles)

freestone ('fri:,stəʊn) n **1** any fine-grained stone, esp sandstone or limestone, that can be cut and worked in any direction without breaking **2** *botany* a fruit, such as a peach, in which the flesh separates readily from the stone

freestyle ('fri:,staɪl) n **1** a competition or race, as in swimming, in which each participant may use a style of his or her choice instead of a specified style **2 a** an amateur style of wrestling with an agreed set of rules **b** Also called: **all-in wrestling** a style of professional wrestling with no internationally agreed set of rules

freethinker (,fri:'θɪŋkə) n a person who forms his ideas and opinions independently of authority or accepted views, esp in matters of religion

Freetown ('fri:,taʊn) n the capital and chief port of Sierra Leone: founded in 1787 for slaves freed and destitute in England. Pop: 1 007 000 (2005 est)

free trade n **1** international trade that is free of such government interference as import quotas, export subsidies, protective tariffs, etc **2** *archaic* illicit trade; smuggling

free verse n unrhymed verse without a metrical pattern

freeware ('fri:,weə) n computer software that may be distributed and used without payment

freeway ('fri:,weɪ) n *US* **1** another name for **expressway 2** a major road that can be used without paying a toll

freewheel (,fri:'wi:l) n **1** a ratchet device in the rear hub of a bicycle wheel that permits the wheel to rotate freely while the pedals are stationary ▷ vb **2** (*intr*) to coast in a vehicle or on a bicycle using the freewheel

free will n **1 a** the apparent human ability to make choices that are not externally determined **b** the doctrine that such human freedom of choice is not illusory. See **determinism** (sense 1) **2** the ability to make a choice without coercion: *he left of his own free will: I did not influence him*

Free World n the Free World the non-Communist countries collectively, esp those that are actively anti-Communist

freeze (fri:z) vb **freezes, freezing, froze** (frəʊz), **frozen** ('frəʊzªn) **1** to change (a liquid) into a solid as a result of a reduction in temperature, or (of a liquid) to solidify in this way, esp to convert or be converted into ice **2** (when *intr*, sometimes foll by *over* or *up*) to cover, clog, or harden with ice, or become so covered, clogged, or hardened: *the lake froze over last week* **3** to fix fast or become fixed (to something) because of the action of frost **4** (tr) to preserve (food) by subjection to extreme cold, as in a freezer **5** to feel or cause to feel the sensation or effects of extreme cold **6** to die or cause to die of frost or extreme cold **7** to become or cause to become paralysed, fixed, or motionless, esp through fear, shock, etc **8** (tr) to cause (moving film) to stop at a particular frame **9** to make or become formal, haughty, etc, in manner **10** (tr) to fix (prices, incomes, etc) at a particular level, usually by government direction **11** (tr) to forbid by law the exchange, liquidation, or collection of (loans, assets, etc) **12** (tr) to stop (a process) at a particular stage of

development **13** (*intr; foll by onto*) *informal, chiefly US* to cling ▷ *n* **14** the act of freezing or state of being frozen **15** *meteorol* a spell of temperatures below freezing point, usually over a wide area **16** the fixing of incomes, prices, etc, by legislation ▷ *sentence substitute* **17** *chiefly US* a command to stop still instantly or risk being shot [Old English *frēosan*; related to Old Norse *frjōsa*, Old High German *friosan*, Latin *prūrīre* to itch; see FROST]
> '**freezable** *adj*

freeze-dry *vb* -dries, -drying, -dried (*tr*) to preserve (a substance) by rapid freezing and subsequently drying in a vacuum

freeze-frame *n* **1** *films, television* a single frame of a film repeated to give an effect like a still photograph **2** a single frame of a video recording viewed as a still by stopping the tape ▷ *vb* (*tr*) **3** to make a freeze-frame of (an image)

freeze out *vb* (*tr, adverb*) *informal* to force out or exclude, as by unfriendly behaviour, boycotting, etc

freezer ('fri:zə) *n* **1** Also called: **deepfreeze** a device that freezes or chills, esp an insulated cold-storage cabinet for long-term storage of perishable foodstuffs **2** a former name for a **refrigerator**

freeze-up *n* *US & Canadian* **a** the freezing of lakes, rivers, and topsoil in autumn or early winter **b** the time of year when this occurs

freezing ('fri:zɪŋ) *adj* *informal* extremely cold

freezing point *n* the temperature below which a liquid turns into a solid. It is equal to the melting point

freezing works *n* *Austral & NZ* a slaughterhouse at which animal carcasses are frozen for export

Frege (*German* 'freːɡə) *n* **Gottlob**. 1848–1925, German logician and philosopher, who laid the foundations of modern formal logic and semantics in his *Begriffsschrift* (1879)

Freiburg (*German* 'fraɪbʊrk) *n* **1** a city in SW Germany, in SW Baden-Württemberg: under Austrian rule (1368–1805); university (1457). Pop: 212 495 (2003 est) **2** the German name for **Fribourg**

freight (freit) *n* **1 a** commercial transport that is slower and cheaper than express **b** the price charged for such transport **c** goods transported by this means **d** (*as modifier*): *freight transport* **2** *chiefly Brit* a ship's cargo or part of it ▷ *vb* (*tr*) **3** to load with goods for transport [c16: from Middle Dutch *vrecht*; related to French *fret*, Spanish *flete*, Portuguese *frete*]

freightage ('freitidʒ) *n* **1** the commercial conveyance of goods **2** the goods so transported **3** the price charged for such conveyance

freighter ('freitə) *n* **1** a ship or aircraft designed for transporting cargo **2** a person concerned with the loading or chartering of a ship

Freightliner ('freit,lainə) *n* *trademark* a goods train carrying containers that can be transferred onto lorries or ships

Fremantle ('fri:,mæntəl) *n* a port in SW Western Australia, on the Indian Ocean. Pop: 25 197 (2001)

French[1] (frentʃ) *n* **1** the official language of France: also an official language of Switzerland, Belgium, Canada, and certain other countries. It is the native language of approximately 70 million people; also used for diplomacy. Historically, French is an Indo-European language belonging to the Romance group. See also **Old French, Anglo-French 2** the French (*functioning as plural*) the natives, citizens, or inhabitants of France collectively ▷ *adj* **3** relating to, denoting, or characteristic of France, the French, or their language. Related prefixes: **Franco-, Gallo- 4** (in Canada) of or relating to French Canadians [Old English *Frencisc* French, Frankish; see FRANK]

French[2] (frentʃ) *n* Sir **John Denton Pinkstone**, 1st Earl of Ypres. 1852–1925, British field marshal in World War I: commanded the British Expeditionary Force in France and Belgium (1914–15); Lord Lieutenant of Ireland (1918–21)

French bread *n* white bread in a long slender loaf that is made from a water dough and has a crisp brown crust

French Cameroons *pl n* the part of Cameroon formerly administered by France (1919–60)

French Canada *n* the areas of Canada, esp in the province of Quebec, where French Canadians predominate

French Canadian *n* **1** a Canadian citizen whose native language is French ▷ *adj* **French-Canadian 2** of or relating to French Canadians or their language

French chalk *n* a compact variety of talc used to mark cloth or remove grease stains from materials

French doors *pl n* *US & Canadian* a pair of casement windows extending to floor level and opening onto a balcony, garden, etc. Also called (in Britain and certain other countries): French windows

French dressing *n* a salad dressing made from oil and vinegar with seasonings; vinaigrette

French Equatorial Africa *n* the former French overseas territories of Chad, Gabon, Middle Congo, and Ubangi-Shari (1910–58)

French Foreign Legion *n* a unit of the French Army formerly serving esp in French North African colonies. It is largely recruited from foreigners, with French senior officers

French fried potatoes *pl n* a more formal name for **chips**. Also called (US and Canadian): French fries

French Guiana *n* a French overseas region in NE South America, on the Atlantic: colonized by the French in about 1637; tropical forests. Capital: Cayenne. Pop: 183 000 (2004 est). Area: about 91 000 sq km (23 000 sq miles)

French Guianese or **French Guianan** *adj* **1** of or relating to French Guiana or its inhabitants ▷ *n* **2** a native or inhabitant of French Guiana

French Guinea *n* a former French territory of French West Africa: became independent as Guinea in 1958

French horn *n* *music* a valved brass instrument with a funnel-shaped mouthpiece and a tube of conical bore coiled into a spiral. It is a transposing instrument in F. Range: about three and a half octaves upwards from B on the second leger line below the bass staff. See **horn**

Frenchify ('frentʃɪ,faɪ) *vb* -fies, -fying, -fied *informal* to make or become French in appearance, behaviour, etc

French India *n* a former French overseas territory in India, including Chandernagore and Pondicherry (now Puducherry): restored to India between 1949 and 1954

French Indochina *n* the territories of SE Asia that were colonized by France and held mostly until 1954: included Cochin China, Annam, and Tonkin (now largely Vietnam), Cambodia, Laos, and Kuang-Chou Wan (returned to China in 1945, now Zhanjiang)

French kiss *n* a kiss involving insertion of the tongue into the partner's mouth

French knickers *pl n* women's wide-legged underpants

French leave *n* an unauthorized or unannounced absence or departure [c18: alluding to a custom in France of leaving without saying goodbye to one's host or hostess]

French letter *n* *Brit* a slang term for **condom**

Frenchman ('frentʃmən) *n, pl* -men a native, citizen, or inhabitant of France > 'French,woman *fem n*

French Morocco *n* a former French protectorate in NW Africa, united in 1956 with Spanish Morocco and Tangier to form the kingdom of Morocco

French mustard *n* a mild mustard paste made with vinegar rather than water

French North Africa *n* the former French possessions of Algeria, French Morocco, and Tunisia

French Oceania *n* a former name (until 1958) of **French Polynesia**

French paradox *n* the theory that the lower incidence of heart disease in Mediterranean countries compared to that in the US is a consequence of the larger intake of flavonoids from red wine in these countries

French polish *n* **1** a varnish for wood consisting of shellac dissolved in alcohol **2** the gloss finish produced by repeated applications of this polish

French-polish *vb* to treat with French polish or give a French polish (to)

French Polynesia *n* a French Overseas Country (formerly Territory) in the S Pacific Ocean, including the Society Islands, the Tuamotu group, the Gambier group, the Tubuai Islands, and the Marquesas Islands. Capital: Papeete, on Tahiti. Pop: 248 000 (2004 est). Area: about 4000 sq km (1500 sq miles). Former name (until 1958): French Oceania

French Revolutionary calendar *n* the full name for the **Revolutionary calendar**

French seam *n* a seam in which the edges are not visible

French Somaliland *n* a former name (until 1967) of Djibouti

French Southern and Antarctic Territories *pl n* a French overseas territory, comprising Adélie Land in Antarctica, the islands of Amsterdam and St Paul and the Kerguelen and Crozet archipelagos in the S Indian Ocean, and (from 2007), the Îles Eparses ("scattered islands") previously administered from Réunion, consisting of Bassas da India, Europa, the Glorioso Islands (Îles Glorieuses), Juan de Nova, and Tromelin Island; no permanent population: all claims to the mainland of Antarctica are suspended under the Antarctic Treaty of 1959

French Sudan *n* a former name (1898–1959) of Mali

French toast *n* **1** *Brit* toast cooked on one side only **2** bread dipped in beaten egg and lightly fried

French Togoland *n* a former United Nations Trust Territory in W Africa, administered by France (1946–60), now the independent republic of Togo

French West Africa *n* a former group (1895–1958) of French Overseas Territories: consisted of Senegal, Mauritania, French Sudan, (now Mali), Upper Volta (now Burkina Faso), Niger, French Guinea, Côte d'Ivoire, and Dahomey (now Benin)

French windows *pl n* (*sometimes singular*) *Brit* a pair of casement windows extending to floor level and opening onto a balcony, garden, etc

Freneau ('frɛnəʊ) *n* **Philip.** 1752–1832, US poet, journalist, and patriot; editor of the *National Gazette* (1791–93)

frenetic (frɪ'nɛtɪk) *adj* distracted or frantic; frenzied [c14: via Old French *frenetique* from Latin *phrenēticus*, from Greek *phrenētikos*, from *phrenitis* insanity, from *phrēn* mind] > fre'netically *adv*

frenum ('friːnəm) *n, pl* -na (-nə) a variant spelling (esp US) of **fraenum**

frenzy ('frɛnzɪ) *n, pl* -zies **1** violent mental derangement **2** wild excitement or agitation; distraction **3** a bout of wild or agitated activity: *a frenzy of preparations* ▷ *vb* -zies, -zying, -zied **4** (*tr*) to make frantic; drive into a frenzy [c14: from Old French *frenesie*, from Late Latin *phrenēsis* madness, delirium, from Late Greek, ultimately from Greek *phrēn* mind; compare FRENETIC] > 'frenzied *adj*

Freon ('friːɒn) *n trademark* any of a group of chemically unreactive chlorofluorocarbons used as aerosol propellants, refrigerants, and solvents

frequency ('friːkwənsɪ) *n, pl* -cies **1** the state of being frequent; frequent occurrence **2** the number of times that an event occurs within a given period; rate of recurrence **3** *physics* the number of times that a periodic function or vibration repeats itself in a specified time, often 1 second. It is usually measured in hertz **4** *statistics* **a** the number of individuals in a class (**absolute frequency**) **b** the ratio of this number to the total number of individuals under survey (**relative frequency**) **5** *ecology* the number of individuals of a species within a given area [c16: from Latin *frequentia* a large gathering, from *frequēns* numerous, crowded]

frequency distribution *n statistics* the function of the distribution of a sample corresponding to the probability density function of the underlying population and tending to it as the sample size increases, the set of relative frequencies of sample points falling within given intervals of the range of the random variable

frequency modulation *n* a method of transmitting information using a radio-frequency carrier wave. The frequency of the carrier wave is varied in accordance with the amplitude and polarity of the input signal, the amplitude of the carrier remaining unchanged. Abbreviation: **FM** See **amplitude modulation**

frequent *adj* ('friːkwənt) **1** recurring at short intervals

2 constant or habitual ▷ *vb* (frɪ'kwɛnt) **3** (*tr*) to visit repeatedly or habitually [c16: from Latin *frequēns* numerous; perhaps related to Latin *farcīre* to stuff] > fre'quenter *n* > 'frequently *adv* > ,frequen'tation *n*

frequentative (frɪ'kwɛntətɪv) *grammar* ▷ *adj* **1** denoting an aspect of verbs in some languages used to express repeated or habitual action **2** (in English) denoting a verb or an affix having meaning that involves repeated or habitual action, such as the verb *wrestle*, from *wrest* ▷ *n* **3 a** a frequentative verb or affix **b** the frequentative aspect of verbs

fresco ('frɛskəʊ) *n, pl* -coes *or* -cos **1** a very durable method of wall-painting using watercolours on wet plaster or, less properly, dry plaster (**fresco secco**), with a less durable result **2** a painting done in this way [c16: from Italian: fresh plaster, coolness, from *fresco* (adj) fresh, cool, of Germanic origin]

Frescobaldi (*Italian* fresko'baldi) *n* **Girolamo** (dʒiˈrɔːlamo). 1583–1643, Italian organist and composer, noted esp for his organ and harpsichord music

fresh (frɛʃ) *adj* **1** not stale or deteriorated; newly made, harvested, etc: *fresh bread; fresh strawberries* **2** newly acquired, created, found, etc: *fresh publications* **3** novel; original: *a fresh outlook* **4** latest; most recent: *fresh developments* **5** further; additional; more: *fresh supplies* **6** not canned, frozen, or otherwise preserved: *fresh fruit* **7** (of water) not salt **8** bright or clear: *a fresh morning* **9** chilly or invigorating: *a fresh breeze* **10** not tired; alert; refreshed **11** not worn or faded: *fresh colours* **12** having a healthy or ruddy appearance **13** newly or just arrived; straight: *fresh from the presses* **14** youthful or inexperienced **15** *informal* presumptuous or disrespectful; forward ▷ *n* **16** the fresh part or time of something **17** another name for **freshet** ▷ *adv* **18** in a fresh manner; freshly [Old English *fersc* fresh, unsalted; related to Old High German *frisc*, Old French *freis*, Old Norse *ferskr*] > 'freshly *adv* > 'freshness *n*

fresh breeze *n* a fairly strong breeze of force five on the Beaufort scale

freshen ('frɛʃən) *vb* **1** to make or become fresh or fresher **2** (*often foll by up*) to refresh (oneself), esp by washing **3** (*intr*) (of the wind) to increase

fresher ('frɛʃə) *or* **freshman** ('frɛʃmən) *n, pl* -ers *or* -men a first-year student at college or university

freshet ('frɛʃɪt) *n* **1** the sudden overflowing of a river caused by heavy rain or melting snow **2** a stream of fresh water emptying into the sea

freshwater ('frɛʃ,wɔːtə) *n* (*modifier*) **1** of, relating to, or living in fresh water **2** (esp of a sailor who has not sailed on the sea) unskilled or inexperienced **3** *US* small and little known: *a freshwater school*

fresnel ('freɪnl; *French* frɛnɛl) *n* a unit of frequency equivalent to 10^{12} hertz [c20: named after Augustin Jean Fresnel (1788–1827), French physicist]

Fresnel (*French* frɛnɛl) *n* **Augustin Jean** (ogystɛ̃ ʒɑ̃). 1788–1827, French physicist: worked on the interference of light, contributing to the wave theory of light

Fresno ('freznəʊ) *n* a city in central California, in the San Joaquin Valley. Pop: 451 455 (2003 est)

fret¹ (frɛt) *vb* frets, fretting, fretted **1** to distress or be distressed; worry **2** to rub or wear away **3** to irritate or be irritated; feel or give annoyance or vexation **4** to eat away or be eaten away by chemical action; corrode **5** (*tr*) to make by wearing away; erode ▷ *n* **6** a state of irritation or anxiety [Old English *fretan* to EAT; related to Old High German *frezzan*, Gothic *fraitan*, Latin *peredere*]

fret² (frɛt) *n* **1** a repetitive geometrical figure, esp one used as an ornamental border **2** such a pattern made in relief and with numerous small openings; fretwork ▷ *vb* frets, fretting, fretted **3** (*tr*) to ornament with fret or fretwork [c14: from Old French *frete* interlaced design used on a shield, probably of Germanic origin] > 'fretless *adj*

fret³ (frɛt) *n* any of several small metal bars set across the fingerboard of a musical instrument of the lute, guitar, or viol family at various points along its length so as to produce the desired notes when the strings are stopped by the fingers [c16: of unknown origin] > 'fretless *adj*

fretboard ('frɛtbɔːd) n a fingerboard with frets on a stringed musical instrument

fretful ('frɛtfʊl) adj peevish, irritable, or upset > 'fretfully adv > 'fretfulness n

fret saw n a fine-toothed saw with a long thin narrow blade, used for cutting designs in thin wood or metal

fretwork ('frɛtˌwɜːk) n decorative geometrical carving or openwork

Freud (frɔɪd) n **1 Anna**. 1895–1982, Austrian psychiatrist: daughter of Sigmund Freud and pioneer of child psychoanalysis **2 Lucian**. born 1922, British painter, esp of nudes and portraits; grandson of Sigmund Freud **3 Sigmund** ('ziːkmʊnt). 1856–1939, Austrian psychiatrist: originator of psychoanalysis, based on free association of ideas and analysis of dreams. He stressed the importance of infantile sexuality in later development, evolving the concept of the Oedipus complex. His works include The Interpretation of Dreams (1900) and The Ego and the Id (1923)

Freudian ('frɔɪdɪən) adj **1** of or relating to Sigmund Freud (1856–1939), the Austrian psychiatrist, or his ideas ▷ n **2** a person who follows or believes in the basic ideas of Sigmund Freud > 'Freudianˌism n

Freudian slip n any action, such as a slip of the tongue, that may reveal an unconscious thought

Frey (freɪ) or **Freyr** (freɪə) n Norse myth the god of earth's fertility and dispenser of prosperity

Freya or **Freyja** ('freɪə) n Norse myth the goddess of love and fecundity, sister of Frey

Freytag (German 'fraɪtaːk) n **Gustav** ('ɡʊstaf). 1816–95, German novelist and dramatist; author of the comedy Die Journalisten (1853) and Soll und Haben (1855), a novel about German commercial life

Fri. abbreviation Friday

friable ('fraɪəbəl) adj easily broken up; crumbly [c16: from Latin friābilis, from friāre to crumble; related to Latin fricāre to rub down] > ˌfria'bility or 'friableness n

friar ('fraɪə) n a member of any of various chiefly mendicant religious orders of the Roman Catholic Church, the main orders being Black Friars (Dominicans), Grey Friars (Franciscans), White Friars (Carmelites), and Austin Friars (Augustinians) [c13 frere, from Old French: brother, from Latin frāter BROTHER]

friar's balsam n a compound containing benzoin, mixed with hot water, and used as an inhalant to relieve colds and sore throats

friary ('fraɪərɪ) n, pl -aries Christianity a convent or house of friars

Fribourg (French fribur) n **1** a canton in W Switzerland. Capital: Fribourg. Pop: 242 700 (2002 est). Area: 1676 sq km (645 sq miles) **2** a town in W Switzerland, capital of Fribourg canton: university (1889). Pop: 35 547 (2000) ▷ German name: Freiburg

fricandeau or **fricando** ('frɪkənˌdəʊ) n, pl -deaus, -deaux or -does (-ˌdəʊz) a larded and braised veal fillet [c18: from Old French, probably based on FRICASSEE]

fricassee (ˌfrɪkə'siː, 'frɪkəsɪ, 'frɪkəˌseɪ) n **1** stewed meat, esp chicken or veal, and vegetables, served in a thick white sauce ▷ vb -sees, -seeing, -seed **2** (tr) to prepare (meat) as a fricassee [c16: from Old French, from fricasser to fricassee; probably related to frire to FRY¹]

fricative ('frɪkətɪv) n **1** a continuant consonant produced by partial occlusion of the airstream, such as (f) or (z) ▷ adj **2** relating to or denoting a fricative [c19: from New Latin fricātīvus, from Latin fricāre to rub]

friction ('frɪkʃən) n **1** a resistance encountered when one body moves relative to another body with which it is in contact **2** the act, effect, or an instance of rubbing one object against another **3** disagreement or conflict; discord [c16: from French, from Latin frictiō a rubbing, from fricāre to rub, rub down; related to Latin friāre to crumble] > 'frictional adj > 'frictionless adj

Friday ('fraɪdɪ) n **1** the sixth day of the week; fifth day of the working week **2** See **man Friday** [Old English Frīgedæg, literally: Freya's day; related to Old Frisian frīadei, Old High German frīatag]

fridge (frɪdʒ) n informal short for **refrigerator**

fried (fraɪd) vb the past tense and past participle of **fry¹**

Friedan ('friːdən) n **Betty**. 1921–2006, US feminist,

founder and first president (1966–70) of the National Organization for Women. Her books include The Feminine Mystique (1963), The Second Stage (1982), and The Fountain of Life (1993)

Friedman ('friːdmən) n **Milton**. 1912–2006. US economist, particularly associated with monetarism; a forceful advocate of free market capitalism > 'Friedmanˌite n, adj

Friedrich (German 'friːdrɪç) n **Caspar David** ('kaspar 'daːfɪt). 1774–1840, German romantic landscape painter, noted for his skill in rendering changing effects of light

friend (frɛnd) n **1** a person known well to another and regarded with liking, affection, and loyalty; an intimate **2** an acquaintance or associate **3** an ally in a fight or cause; supporter **4** a fellow member of a party, society, etc **5** a patron or supporter **6** be friends to be friendly (with) **7** make friends to become friendly (with) ▷ vb **8** (tr) an archaic word for **befriend** [Old English frēond; related to Old Saxon friund, Old Norse frǣndi, Gothic frijōnds, Old High German friunt] > 'friendless adj > 'friendship n

Friend (frɛnd) n a member of the Religious Society of Friends; Quaker

friend at court n an influential acquaintance who can promote one's interests

friendly ('frɛndlɪ) adj -lier, -liest **1** showing or expressing liking, goodwill, or trust **2** on the same side; not hostile **3** tending or disposed to help or support; favourable: a friendly breeze helped them escape ▷ n, pl -lies **4** Also called: friendly match sport a match played for its own sake, and not as part of a competition, etc > 'friendlily adv > 'friendliness n

-friendly adj combining form helpful, easy, or good for the person or thing specified: ozone-friendly

friendly fire n military firing by one's own side, esp when it harms one's own personnel

Friendly Islands pl n another name for **Tonga¹**

friendly society n Brit an association of people who pay regular dues or other sums in return for old-age pensions, sickness benefits, etc

friend of Dorothy ('dɒrəθɪ) n informal a male homosexual [c20: after a character in the 1939 film The Wizard of Oz played by the US actress Judy Garland (1922–69), who has a large gay following]

Friends of the Earth n (functioning as singular or plural) an organization of environmentalists and conservationists whose aim is to promote the sustainable use of the earth's resources

frier ('fraɪə) n a variant spelling of **fryer**

fries (fraɪz) pl n another name for **French fried potatoes**

Friese-Greene (ˌfriːz'griːn) n **William**. 1855–1921, British photographer. He invented (with Mortimer Evans) the first practicable motion-picture camera

Friesian¹ ('friːʒən) n Brit any of several breeds of black-and-white dairy cattle having a high milk yield

Friesian² ('friːʒən) n, adj a variant of **Frisian**

Friesland ('friːzlənd; Dutch 'friːslɑnt) n **1** a province of the N Netherlands, on the IJsselmeer and the North Sea: includes four of the West Frisian Islands; flat, with sand dunes and fens (under reclamation), canals, and lakes. Capital: Leeuwarden. Pop: 640 000 (2003 est). Area: 3319 sq km (1294 sq miles) **2** an area comprising the province of Friesland in the Netherlands along with the regions of **East Friesland** and **North Friesland** in Germany

frieze¹ (friːz) n **1** architect **a** the horizontal band between the architrave and cornice of a classical entablature, esp one that is decorated with sculpture **b** the upper part of the wall of a room, below the cornice, esp one that is decorated **2** any ornamental band or strip on a wall [c16: from French frise, perhaps from Medieval Latin frisium, changed from Latin Phrygium Phrygian (work), from Phrygia Phrygia, famous for embroidery in gold]

frieze² (friːz) n a heavy woollen fabric with a long nap, used for coats, etc [c15: from Old French frise, from Middle Dutch friese, vriese, perhaps from Vriese Frisian]

frigate ('frɪɡɪt) n **1** a medium-sized square-rigged warship of the 18th and 19th centuries **2 a** Brit a warship larger than a corvette and smaller than a destroyer **b** US (formerly) a warship larger than a destroyer and smaller than a cruiser **c** *US* a small escort vessel [C16: from French *frégate*, from Italian *fregata*, of unknown origin]

frigate bird *n* any bird of the genus *Fregata* and family *Fregatidae*, of tropical and subtropical seas, having a long bill with a downturned tip, a wide wingspan, and a forked tail: order *Pelecaniformes* (pelicans, cormorants, etc)

Frigg (frɪg) *or* **Frigga** (ˈfrɪgə) *n Norse myth* the wife of Odin; goddess of the heavens and married love

fright (fraɪt) *n* **1** sudden intense fear or alarm **2** a sudden alarming shock **3** *informal* a horrifying, grotesque, or ludicrous person or thing: *she looks a fright in that hat* **4 take fright** to become frightened ▷ *vb* **5** a poetic word for **frighten** [Old English *fryhto*; related to Gothic *faurhtei*, Old Frisian *fruchte*, Old High German *forhta*]

frighten (ˈfraɪtən) *vb* (*tr*) **1** to cause fear in; terrify; scare **2** to drive or force to go (away, off, out, in, etc) by making afraid ▷ ˈ**frightening** *adj* ▷ ˈ**frighteningly** *adv* ▷ ˈ**frightener** *n*

frightful (ˈfraɪtfʊl) *adj* **1** very alarming, distressing, or horrifying **2** unpleasant, annoying, or extreme: *a frightful hurry* ▷ ˈ**frightfulness** *n* ▷ ˈ**frightfully** *adv*

frigid (ˈfrɪdʒɪd) *adj* **1** formal or stiff in behaviour or temperament; lacking in affection or warmth **2** (esp of a woman) lacking sexual responsiveness **3** characterized by physical coldness: *a frigid zone* [C15: from Latin *frigidus* cold, from *frīgēre* to be cold, freeze; related to Latin *frīgus* frost] ▷ fri**ˈgidity** *or* **ˈfrigidness** *n* ▷ ˈ**frigidly** *adv*

Frigid Zone *n archaic* the cold region inside the Arctic or Antarctic Circle where the sun's rays are very oblique

frijol (friːˈhəʊl; *Spanish* friˈxol) *n*, *pl* **-joles** (-ˈhəʊlz; *Spanish* -ˈxoles) a variety of bean, esp of the French bean, extensively cultivated for food in Mexico [C16: from Spanish, ultimately from Latin *phaseolus*, diminutive of *phasēlus*, from Greek *phasēlos* bean with edible pod]

frill (frɪl) *n* **1** a gathered, ruched, or pleated strip of cloth sewn on at one edge only, as on garments, as ornament, or to give extra body **2** a ruff of hair or feathers around the neck of a dog or bird or a fold of skin around the neck of a reptile or amphibian **3** (*often plural*) *informal* a superfluous or pretentious thing or manner; affectation: *he made a plain speech with no frills* ▷ *vb* **4** (*tr*) to adorn or fit with a frill or frills **5** to form into a frill or frills [C14: perhaps of Flemish origin] ▷ ˈ**frilliness** *n* ▷ ˈ**frilly** *adj*

frill-necked lizard *n* a large arboreal insectivorous Australian lizard, *Chlamydosaurus kingi*, having an erectile fold of skin around the neck: family *Agamidae* (agamas)

fringe (frɪndʒ) *n* **1** an edging consisting of hanging threads, tassels, etc **2** an outer edge; periphery **b** (*as modifier*): *fringe dwellers; a fringe area* **3** (*modifier*) unofficial; not conventional in form: *fringe theatre* **4** *chiefly Brit* a section of the front hair cut short over the forehead **5** an ornamental border or margin **6** *physics* any of the light and dark or coloured bands produced by diffraction or interference of light ▷ *vb* (*tr*) **7** to adorn or fit with a fringe or fringes **8** to be a fringe for [C14: from Old French *frenge*, ultimately from Latin *fimbria* fringe, border; see FIMBRIA] ▷ ˈ**fringeless** *adj*

fringe benefit *n* an incidental or additional advantage, esp a benefit provided by an employer to supplement an employee's regular pay, such as a pension, company car, luncheon vouchers, etc

fringing reef *n* a coral reef close to the shore to which it is attached, having a steep seaward edge

Frink (frɪŋk) *n* Dame **Elisabeth**. 1930–93, British sculptor

frippery (ˈfrɪpərɪ) *n*, *pl* **-peries 1** ornate or showy clothing or adornment **2** showiness; ostentation **3** unimportant considerations; trifles; trivia [C16: from Old French *freperie*, from *frepe* frill, rag, old garment, from Medieval Latin *faluppa* a straw, splinter, of obscure origin]

Frisbee (ˈfrɪzbiː) *n trademark* a light plastic disc, usually 20–25 centimetres in diameter, thrown with a spinning motion for recreation or in competition

Frisch (frɪʃ) *n* **1 Karl von**. 1886–1982, Austrian zoologist; studied animal behaviour, esp of bees; shared the Nobel

prize for physiology or medicine 1973 **2 Max** (maks). 1911–91, Swiss dramatist and novelist. His works are predominantly satirical and include the plays *Biedermann und die Brandstifter* (1953) and *Andorra* (1961), and the novel *Stiller* (1954) **3 Otto**. 1904–79, British nuclear physicist, born in Austria, who contributed to the development of the first atomic bomb **4 Ragnar** (**Anton Kittil**). 1895–1973, Norwegian economist, who pioneered the study of econometrics and greatly influenced the management of the Norwegian economy from 1945: shared the first Nobel prize for economics (1969) with Jan Tinbergen

Frisches Haff (ˈfrɪʃəs ˈhaf) *n* the German name for Vistula (sense 2)

frisette *or* **frizette** (frɪˈzɛt) *n* a curly or frizzed fringe, often an artificial hairpiece, worn by women on the forehead [C19: from French, literally: little curl, from *friser* to curl, shrivel up, probably from *frire* to FRY[1]]

Frisian (ˈfrɪʒən) *or* **Friesian** *n* **1 a** a language spoken in the NW Netherlands, parts of N Germany, and adjacent islands, belonging to the West Germanic branch of the Indo-European family: the nearest relative of the English language; it has three main dialects **2** a native or inhabitant of Friesland or a speaker of the Frisian language ▷ *adj* **3** of or relating to the Frisian language or its speakers [C16: from Latin *Frīsiī* people of northern Germany]

Frisian Islands *pl n* a chain of islands in the North Sea along the coasts of the Netherlands, Germany, and Denmark: separated from the mainland by shallows

frisk (frɪsk) *vb* **1** (*intr*) to leap, move about, or act in a playful manner; frolic **2** (*tr*) (esp of animals) to whisk or wave briskly: *the dog frisked its tail* **3** (*tr*) *informal* to search (someone) by feeling for concealed weapons, etc ▷ *n* **4** a playful antic or movement; frolic **5** *informal* the act or an instance of frisking a person [C16: from Old French *frisque*, of Germanic origin; related to Old High German *frisc* lively, FRESH] ▷ ˈ**frisker** *n*

frisky (ˈfrɪskɪ) *adj* **friskier, friskiest** lively, high-spirited, or playful ▷ ˈ**friskily** *adv*

frisson *French* (frisɔ̃) *n* a shudder or shiver; thrill [C18 (but in common use only from C20): literally: shiver]

frit *or* **fritt** (frɪt) *n* **1 a** the basic materials, partially or wholly fused, for making glass, glazes for pottery, enamel, etc **b** a glassy substance used in some soft-paste porcelain ▷ *vb* **frits** *or* **fritts, fritting, fritted 2** (*tr*) to fuse (materials) in making frit [C17: from Italian *fritta*, literally: fried, from *friggere* to fry, from Latin *frīgere*]

fritillary (frɪˈtɪlərɪ) *n*, *pl* **-laries 1** any N temperate liliaceous plant of the genus *Fritillaria*, having purple or white drooping bell-shaped flowers, typically marked in a chequered pattern **2** any of various nymphalid butterflies of the genera *Argynnis, Boloria*, etc, having brownish wings chequered with black and silver [C17: from New Latin *fritillāria*, from Latin *fritillus* dice box; probably with reference to the spotted markings]

fritter[1] (ˈfrɪtə) *vb* (*tr*) **1** (usually foll by *away*) to waste or squander: *to fritter away time* **2** to break or tear into small pieces; shred [C18: probably from obsolete *fitter* to break into small pieces, ultimately from Old English *fitt* a piece]

fritter[2] (ˈfrɪtə) *n* a piece of food, such as apple or clam, that is dipped in batter and fried in deep fat [C14: from Old French *friture*, from Latin *frictus* fried, roasted, from *frīgere* to fry, parch]

Friuli (Italian friˈuːli) *n* a historic region of SW Europe, between the Carnic Alps and the Gulf of Venice: the W part (**Venetian Friuli**) was ceded by Austria to Italy in 1866 and **Eastern Friuli** in 1919; in 1947 Eastern Friuli (except Gorizia) was ceded to Yugoslavia

Friulian (friˈuːlɪən) *n* **1** the Rhaetian dialect spoken in parts of Friuli. See also Romansch **2** an inhabitant of Friuli or a speaker of Friulian ▷ *adj* **3** of or relating to Friuli, its inhabitants, or their language

Friuli-Venezia Giulia (Italian ˈdʒuːlja) *n* a region of NE Italy, formed in 1947 from Venetian Friuli and part of Eastern Friuli. Capital: Trieste. Pop: 1 191 588 (2003 est). Area: 7851 sq km (3031 sq miles)

frivolous (ˈfrɪvələs) *adj* **1** not serious or sensible in content, attitude, or behaviour; silly **2** unworthy of

serious or sensible treatment; unimportant: *frivolous details* [C15: from Latin *frivolus* silly, worthless]
> '**frivolously** *adv* > '**frivolousness** *or* **frivolity** (frɪ'vɒlɪtɪ) *n*

frizz (frɪz) *vb* **1** (of the hair, nap, etc) to form or cause (the hair, etc) to form tight wiry curls or crisp tufts ▷ *n* **2** hair that has been frizzed **3** the state of being frizzed [C19: from French *friser* to curl, shrivel up (see FRISETTE): influenced by FRIZZLE¹]

frizzle¹ ('frɪzᵊl) *vb* **1** to form (the hair) into tight crisp curls; frizz ▷ *n* **2** a tight crisp curl [C16: probably related to Old English *frīs* curly, Old Frisian *frēsle* curl, ringlet]

frizzle² ('frɪzᵊl) *vb* **1** to scorch or be scorched, esp with a sizzling noise **2** (*tr*) to fry (bacon, etc) until crisp [C16: probably blend of FRY¹ + SIZZLE]

frizzy ('frɪzɪ) *or* **frizzly** ('frɪzlɪ) *adj* **-zier, -ziest** *or* **-zlier, -zliest** (of the hair) in tight crisp wiry curls > '**frizziness** *or* '**frizzliness** *n*

fro (frəʊ) *adv* back or from [C12: from Old Norse *frā*; related to Old English *fram* FROM]

Frobisher ('frəʊbɪʃə) *n* Sir **Martin**. ?1535–94, English navigator and explorer: made three unsuccessful voyages in search of the Northwest Passage (1576; 1577; 1578), visiting Labrador and Baffin Island

Frobisher Bay ('frəʊbɪʃə) *n* **1** an inlet of the Atlantic in NE Canada, in the SE coast of Baffin Island **2** the former name of **Iqaluit**

frock (frɒk) *n* **1** a girl's or woman's dress **2** a loose garment of several types, such as a peasant's smock **3** a coarse wide-sleeved outer garment worn by members of some religious orders ▷ *vb* **4** (*tr*) to invest (a person) with the office or status of a cleric [C14: from Old French *froc*; related to Old Saxon, Old High German *hroc* coat]

frock coat *n* a man's single- or double-breasted skirted coat, as worn in the 19th century

Fröding (Swedish 'frø:dɪn) *n* **Gustaf** ('gustav). 1860–1911, Swedish poet. His popular lyric verse includes the collections *Guitar and Concertina* (1891), *New Poems* (1894), and *Splashes and Rags* (1896)

Froebel *or* **Fröbel** (German 'frø:bəl) *n* **1** Friedrich (**Wilhelm August**) ('fri:drɪç). 1782– 1852, German educator: founded the first kindergarten (1840) ▷ *adj* **2** of, denoting, or relating to a system of kindergarten education developed by him or to the training and qualification of teachers to use this system

frog¹ (frɒg) *n* **1** any insectivorous anuran amphibian of the family *Ranidae*, such as *Rana temporaria* of Europe, having a short squat tailless body with a moist smooth skin and very long hind legs specialized for hopping **2** any of various similar amphibians of related families, such as the tree frog **3** any spiked or perforated object used to support plant stems in a flower arrangement **4 a frog in one's throat** phlegm on the vocal cords that affects one's speech [Old English *frogga*; related to Old Norse *froskr*, Old High German *forsk*] > '**froggy** *adj*

frog² (frɒg) *n* **1** (*often plural*) a decorative fastening of looped braid or cord, as on the front of a 19th-century military uniform **2** a loop or other attachment on a belt to hold the scabbard of a sword, etc [C18: perhaps ultimately from Latin *floccus* tuft of hair, FLOCK²]

frog³ (frɒg) *n* a tough elastic horny material in the centre of the sole of a horse's foot [C17: of uncertain origin]

frog⁴ (frɒg) *n* a grooved piece of iron or steel placed to guide train wheels over an intersection of railway lines [C19: of uncertain origin; perhaps a special use of FROG¹]

Frog (frɒg) *or* **Froggy** ('frɒgɪ) *n, pl* **Frogs** *or* **Froggies** a derogatory word for a French person

froghopper ('frɒg,hɒpə) *n* any small leaping herbivorous homopterous insect of the family *Cercopidae*, whose larvae secrete a protective spittle-like substance around themselves

frogman ('frɒgmən) *n, pl* **-men** a swimmer equipped with a rubber suit, flippers, and breathing equipment for working underwater

frogmarch ('frɒg,mɑ:tʃ) *n* **1** a method of carrying a resisting person in which each limb is held by one person and the victim is carried horizontally and face downwards **2** any method of making a resisting person move forward against his will ▷ *vb* **3** (*tr*) to carry in a

frogmarch or cause to move forward unwillingly

frogmouth ('frɒg,maʊθ) *n* any nocturnal insectivorous bird of the genera *Podargus* and *Batrachostomus*, of SE Asia and Australia, similar to the nightjars: family *Podargidae*, order *Caprimulgiformes*

frogspawn ('frɒg,spɔ:n) *n* a mass of fertilized frogs' eggs or developing tadpoles, each egg being surrounded by a protective nutrient jelly

frog spit *or* **frog spittle** *n* **1** another name for **cuckoo spit 2** a foamy mass of threadlike green algae floating on ponds

Froissart (French frwasar) *n* **Jean** (ʒɑ̃). ?1333–?1400, French chronicler and poet, noted for his *Chronique*, a vivid history of Europe from 1325 to 1400

frolic ('frɒlɪk) *n* **1** a light-hearted entertainment or occasion **2** light-hearted activity; gaiety; merriment ▷ *vb* **-ics, -icking, -icked 3** (*intr*) to caper about; act or behave playfully ▷ *adj* **4** *archaic or literary* full of merriment or fun [C16: from Dutch *vrolijk*, from Middle Dutch *vro* happy, glad; related to Old High German *frō* happy] > '**frolicker** *n*

frolicsome ('frɒlɪksəm) *or* **frolicky** *adj* given to frolicking; merry and playful > '**frolicsomely** *adv*

from (frɒm; *unstressed* frəm) *prep* **1** used to indicate the original location, situation, etc: *from Paris to Rome; from behind the bushes; from childhood to adulthood* **2** in a period of time starting at: *he lived from 1910 to 1970* **3** used to indicate the distance between two things or places: *a hundred miles from here* **4** used to indicate a lower amount: *from five to fifty pounds* **5** showing the model of: *painted from life* **6** used with the gerund to mark prohibition, restraint, etc: *nothing prevents him from leaving* **7** because of: *exhausted from his walk* [Old English *fram*; related to Old Norse *frā*, Old Saxon, Old High German, Gothic *fram* from, Greek *promos* foremost]

fromage frais ('frɒmɑːʒ 'freɪ) *n* a low-fat soft cheese with a smooth light texture [French, literally: fresh cheese]

Frome (frəʊm) *n* **Lake Frome** a shallow salt lake in NE South Australia: intermittently filled with water. Length: 100 km (60 miles). Width: 48 km (30 miles)

Fromm (frɒm) *n* **Erich** ('ɛrɪk). 1900–80, US psychologist and philosopher, born in Germany. His works include *The Art of Loving* (1956) and *To Have and To Be* (1976)

frond (frɒnd) *n* a large compound leaf, esp of a fern [C18: from Latin *frōns*]

front (frʌnt) *n* **1** that part or side that is forward, prominent, or most often seen or used **2** a position or place directly before or ahead: *a fountain stood at the front of the building* **3** the beginning, opening, or first part **4** the position of leadership; forefront; vanguard: *in the front of scientific knowledge* **5** land bordering a lake, street, etc **6** land along a seashore or large lake, esp a promenade **7** *military* **a** the total area in which opposing armies face each other **b** the lateral space in which a military unit or formation is operating: *to advance on a broad front* **8** *meteorol* the dividing line or plane between two air masses or water masses of different origins and having different characteristics **9** outward aspect or bearing, as when dealing with a situation: *a bold front* **10** *informal* a business or other activity serving as a respectable cover for another, usually criminal, organization **11** *chiefly US* a nominal leader of an organization, etc, who lacks real power or authority; figurehead **12** *informal* outward appearance of rank or wealth **13** a particular field of activity involving some kind of struggle: *on the wages front* **14** a group of people with a common goal: *a national liberation front* **15** a false shirt front; a dicky **16** *archaic* the forehead or the face ▷ *adj* (*prenominal*) **17** of, at, or in the front: *a front seat* **18** *phonetics* of, relating to, or denoting a vowel articulated with the blade of the tongue brought forward and raised towards the hard palate, as for the sound of *ee* in English *see* or *a* in English *hat* ▷ *vb* **19** (when *intr*, foll by *on* or *onto*) to be opposite (to); face (onto): *this house fronts the river* **20** (*tr*) to be a front of or for **21** (*tr*) *informal* to appear as a presenter in (a television show) **22** (*tr*) to be the lead singer or player in (a band) **23** (*tr*) to confront, esp in hostility or opposition **24** (*tr*) to supply a front for **25** (*intr; often foll by up*) *Austral & NZ*

f

informal to appear (at): *to front up at the police station* [C13 (in the sense: forehead, face): from Latin *frōns* forehead, foremost part] > **'frontless** *adj*

frontage ('frʌntɪdʒ) *n* **1** the façade of a building or the front of a plot of ground **2** the extent of the front of a shop, plot of land, etc, esp along a street, river, etc **3** the direction in which a building faces

frontal ('frʌnt°l) *adj* **1** of, at, or in the front **2** of or relating to the forehead ▷ *n* **3** a decorative hanging for the front of an altar [C14 (in the sense: adornment for forehead, altar cloth): via Old French *frontel*, from Latin *frontālia* (pl) ornament worn on forehead, *frontellum* altar cloth, both from *frōns* forehead, FRONT] > **'frontally** *adv*

frontal lobe *n anatomy* the anterior portion of each cerebral hemisphere, situated in front of the central sulcus

front bench *n* **1** *Brit* **a** the foremost bench of either the Government or Opposition in the House of Commons **b** the leadership (**frontbenchers**) of either group, who occupy this bench **2** the leadership of the government or opposition in various legislative assemblies

Frontenac *or* **Frontenac et Palluau** (French frɔ̃tnak ̩e palyo̩) *n* **Comte de** (kɔ̃t də). title of *Louis de Buade*. 1620–98, governor of New France (1672–82; 1689–98)

front-end *adj* (of money, costs, etc) required or incurred in advance of a project in order to get it under way

frontier ('frʌntɪə, frʌn'tɪə) *n* **1 a** the region of a country bordering on another or a line, barrier, etc, marking such a boundary **b** (*as modifier*): *a frontier post* **2** *US & Canadian* the edge of the settled area of a country **3** (*often plural*) the limit of knowledge in a particular field: *the frontiers of physics have been pushed back* [C14: from Old French *frontiere*, from *front* (in the sense: part which is opposite); see FRONT]

frontiersman ('frʌntɪəzmən, frʌn'tɪəz-) *n, pl* **-men** (formerly) a man living on a frontier, esp in a newly pioneered territory of the US

frontierswoman ('frʌntɪəzwʊmən, frʌn'tɪəz-) *n, pl* **-women** (formerly) a woman living on a frontier, esp in a newly pioneered territory of the US

frontispiece ('frʌntɪs,piːs) *n* **1** an illustration facing the title page of a book **2** the principal façade of a building; front **3** a pediment, esp an ornamented one, over a door, window, etc [C16 *frontispice*, from French, from Late Latin *frontispicium* façade, inspection of the forehead, from Latin *frōns* forehead + *specere* to look at; influenced by PIECE]

frontlet ('frʌntlɪt) *n* Also called: **frontal** a small decorative loop worn on a woman's forehead, projecting from under her headdress, in the 15th century [C15: from Old French *frontelet* a little FRONTAL]

front line *n* **1** *military* the most advanced military units or elements in a battle **2** frontline (*modifier*) **a** of, relating to, or suitable for the front line of a military formation: *frontline troops* **b** of or relating to a country bordering on or close to a hostile country or scene of armed conflict: *leaders of the frontline states attended the summit*

front loader *n* a washing machine with a door at the front which opens one side of the drum into which washing is placed

front-page *n* (*modifier*) important or newsworthy enough to be put on the front page of a newspaper

front row *n* (*functioning as singular or plural*) *rugby Union* **a** the forwards at the front of a scrum **b** (*as modifier*): *perhaps the finest front-row forward in the world*

frontrunner ('frʌnt,rʌnə) *n informal* the leader or a favoured contestant in a race, election, etc

frontrunning ('frʌnt,rʌnɪŋ) *n stock exchange* the practice by market makers of using advance information provided by their own investment analysts before it has been given to clients

front up *vb informal* **1** (*tr*) to pay (money) at the beginning of a business arrangement **2** to give one's best effort, esp in a physical contest: *We have to front up in the scrum if we want to beat the All Blacks*

frosh (frɒʃ) *n US & Canadian slang* a freshman [C20: altered from FRESHMAN]

frost (frɒst) *n* **1** a white deposit of ice particles, esp one formed on objects out of doors at night **2** an

atmospheric temperature of below freezing point, characterized by the production of this deposit **3** degrees below freezing point: *eight degrees of frost indicates a temperature of either −8°C or 24°F* **4** *informal* something given a cold reception; failure **5** *informal* coolness of manner **6** the act of freezing ▷ *vb* **7** to cover or be covered with frost **8** (*tr*) to give a frostlike appearance to (glass, etc), as by means of a fine-grained surface **9** (*tr*) *chiefly US & Canadian* to decorate (cakes, etc) with icing or frosting **10** (*tr*) to kill or damage (crops, etc) with frost [Old English *frost*; related to Old Norse, Old Saxon, Old High German *frost*; see FREEZE]

Frost (frɒst) *n* **1 Sir David** (**Paradine**). born 1939, British television presenter and executive, noted esp for political interviews **2 Robert** (**Lee**). 1874–1963, US poet, noted for his lyrical verse on country life in New England. His books include *A Boy's Will* (1913), *North of Boston* (1914), and *New Hampshire* (1923)

frostbite ('frɒst,baɪt) *n* destruction of tissues, esp those of the fingers, ears, toes, and nose, by freezing, characterized by tingling, blister formation, and gangrene > **'frost,bitten** *adj*

frosted ('frɒstɪd) *adj* **1** covered or injured by frost **2** covered with icing, as a cake **3** (of glass, etc) having a surface roughened, as if covered with frost, to prevent clear vision through it

frost hollow *n* a depression in a hilly area in which cold air collects, becoming very cold at night

frosting ('frɒstɪŋ) *n* **1** a soft icing based on sugar and egg whites **2** Also called: **icing** a sugar preparation, variously flavoured and coloured, for coating and decorating cakes, biscuits, etc **3** a rough or matt finish on glass, silver, etc

frosty ('frɒstɪ) *adj* **frostier, frostiest 1** characterized by frost: *a frosty night* **2** covered by or decorated with frost **3** lacking warmth or enthusiasm: *the new plan had a frosty reception* > **'frostily** *adv* > **'frostiness** *n*

froth (frɒθ) *n* **1** a mass of small bubbles of air or a gas in a liquid, produced by fermentation, detergent, etc **2** a mixture of saliva and air bubbles formed at the lips in certain diseases, such as rabies **3** trivial ideas, talk, or entertainment ▷ *vb* **4** to produce or cause to produce froth **5** (*tr*) to give out in the form of froth [C14: from Old Norse *frotha* or *frauth*; related to Old English *āfrēothan* to foam, Sanskrit *prothati* he snorts] > **'frothy** *adj* > **'frothily** *adv*

Froude (fruːd) *n* **1 James Anthony**. 1818–94, English historian; author of a controversial biography (1882–84) of Carlyle. **2** his brother **William**. 1810–79, English civil engineer

froufrou ('fruː,fruː) *n* a swishing sound, as made by a long silk dress [C19: from French, of imitative origin]

froward ('frəʊəd) *adj archaic* obstinate; contrary [C14: see FRO, -WARD] > **'frowardly** *adv* > **'frowardness** *n*

frown (fraʊn) *vb* **1** (*intr*) to draw the brows together and wrinkle the forehead, esp in worry, anger, or concentration **2** (*intr*; foll by *on* or *upon*) to have a dislike (of); look disapprovingly (upon) **3** (*tr*) to express (worry, etc) by frowning ▷ *n* **4** the act of frowning **5** a show of dislike or displeasure [C14: from Old French *froigner*, of Celtic origin; compare Welsh *ffroen* nostril, Middle Breton *froan*] > **'frowner** *n* > **'frowningly** *adv*

frowst (fraʊst) *n Brit informal* a hot and stale atmosphere; fug [C19: back formation from *frowsty* musty, stuffy, variant of FROWZY]

frowsty ('fraʊstɪ) *adj* **-stier, -stiest** ill-smelling; stale; musty > **'frowstiness** *n*

frowzy, frouzy *or* **frowsy** ('fraʊzɪ) *adj* **frowzier, frowziest, frouzier, frouziest, frowsier, frowsiest 1** untidy or unkempt in appearance; shabby **2** ill-smelling; frowsty [C17: of unknown origin] > **'frowziness, 'frouziness** *or* **'frowsiness** *n*

froze (frəʊz) *vb* the past tense of **freeze**

frozen ('frəʊz°n) *vb* **1** the past participle of **freeze** ▷ *adj* **2** turned into or covered with ice **3** killed, injured, or stiffened by extreme cold **4** (of a region or climate) icy or snowy **5** (of food) preserved by a freezing process **6 a** (of prices, wages, etc) arbitrarily pegged at a certain level **b** (of business assets) not convertible into cash, as by government direction or business conditions **7** frigid, unfeeling, or disdainful in manner **8** motionless or unyielding: *he was frozen with horror* ⊳ **'frozenly** *adv*

frozen shoulder *n pathol* a painful stiffness in a shoulder joint

FRS *abbreviation* (in Britain) Fellow of the Royal Society

FRSNZ *abbreviation* Fellow of the Royal Society of New Zealand

fructify ('frʌktɪˌfaɪ, 'fruk-) *vb* -**fies**, -**fying**, -**fied 1** to bear or cause to bear fruit **2** to make or become productive or fruitful [c14: from Old French *fructifier*, from Late Latin *frūctificāre* to bear fruit, from Latin *frūctus* fruit + *facere* to make, produce] ⊳ **'fructiˌfier** *n* ⊳ **fruc'tiferous** *adj* ⊳ ˌ**fructifi'cation** *n*

fructose ('frʌktəus, -təuz, 'fruk-) *n* a white crystalline water-soluble sugar occurring in honey and many fruits. Formula: $C_6H_{12}O_6$ [c19: from Latin *frūctus* fruit + -OSE²]

frugal ('fruːgəl) *adj* **1** practising economy; living without waste; thrifty **2** not costly; meagre [c16: from Latin *frūgālis*, from *frūgī* useful, temperate, from *frux* fruit] ⊳ **fru'gality** *or* **'frugalness** *n* ⊳ **'frugally** *adv*

frugivorous (fruː'dʒɪvərəs) *adj* feeding on fruit; fruit-eating [c18: from *frugi-* (as in FRUGAL) + -VOROUS]

fruit (fruːt) *n* **1** *botany* the ripened ovary of a flowering plant, containing one or more seeds. It may be dry, as in the poppy, or fleshy, as in the peach **2** any fleshy part of a plant, other than the above structure, that supports the seeds and is edible, such as the strawberry **3** any plant product useful to man, including grain, vegetables, etc **4** *(often plural)* the result or consequence of an action or effort **5** *slang, chiefly US & Canadian* a male homosexual **6** *archaic* offspring of man or animals; progeny ⊳ *vb* **7** to bear or cause to bear fruit [c12: from Old French, from Latin *frūctus* enjoyment, profit, fruit, from *fruī* to enjoy] ⊳ **'fruitˌlike** *adj*

fruit bat *n* any large Old World bat of the suborder *Megachiroptera*, occurring in tropical and subtropical regions and feeding on fruit

fruitcake ('fruːtˌkeɪk) *n* a rich cake containing mixed dried fruit, lemon peel, nuts, etc

fruit drop *n* **1** the premature shedding of fruit from a tree before fully ripe **2** a boiled sweet with a fruity flavour

fruiterer ('fruːtərə) *n chiefly Brit* a fruit dealer or seller

fruit fly *n* **1** any small dipterous fly of the family *Trypetidae*, which feed on and lay their eggs in plant tissues **2** any dipterous fly of the genus *Drosophila*. See **drosophila**

fruitful ('fruːtful) *adj* **1** bearing fruit in abundance **2** productive or prolific, esp in bearing offspring **3** producing results or profits: *a fruitful discussion* ⊳ **'fruitfully** *adv* ⊳ **'fruitfulness** *n*

fruition (fruː'ɪʃən) *n* **1** the attainment or realization of something worked for or desired; fulfilment **2** enjoyment of this **3** the act or condition of bearing fruit [c15: from Late Latin *fruitiō* enjoyment, from Latin *fruī* to enjoy]

fruitless ('fruːtlɪs) *adj* **1** yielding nothing or nothing of value; unproductive; ineffectual **2** without fruit ⊳ **'fruitlessly** *adv* ⊳ **'fruitlessness** *n*

fruit machine *n Brit* a gambling machine that pays out when certain combinations of diagrams, usually of fruit, are displayed

fruit salad *n* a dish consisting of sweet fruits cut up and served in a syrup: often sold canned

fruit sugar *n* another name for **fructose**

fruit tree *n* any tree that bears edible fruit

fruity ('fruːtɪ) *adj* **fruitier**, **fruitiest 1** of or resembling fruit **2** (of a voice) mellow or rich **3** *informal, chiefly Brit* erotically stimulating; salacious **4** *chiefly US & Canadian* a slang word for **homosexual** ⊳ **'fruitiness** *n* ⊳ **'fruitily** *adv*

frumenty ('fruːməntɪ), **fromenty**, **furmenty** *or* **furmity** *n Brit* a kind of porridge made from hulled wheat boiled with milk, sweetened, and spiced [c14: from Old French *frumentee*, from *frument* grain, from Latin *frūmentum*]

frump (frʌmp) *n* a woman who is dowdy, drab, or unattractive [c16 (in the sense: to be sullen); c19: dowdy woman): from Middle Dutch *verrompelen* to wrinkle,

RUMPLE] ⊳ **'frumpy** *or* **'frumpish** *adj*

Frunze (*Russian* 'frunzɪ) *n* the former name (until 1991) of **Bishkek**

frustrate (frʌ'streɪt) *vb* (*tr*) **1** to hinder or prevent (the efforts, plans, or desires) of; thwart **2** to upset, agitate, or tire ⊳ *adj* **3** *archaic* frustrated or thwarted; baffled [c15: from Latin *frustrāre* to cheat, from *frustrā* in error]

frustrated (frʌ'streɪtɪd) *adj* having feelings of dissatisfaction or lack of fulfilment

frustration (frʌ'streɪʃən) *n* **1** the condition of being frustrated **2** something that frustrates **3** *psychol* **a** the prevention or hindering of a potentially satisfying activity **b** the emotional reaction to such prevention that may involve aggression

frustum ('frʌstəm) *n*, *pl* -**tums** *or* -**ta** (-tə) *geometry* **a** the part of a solid, such as a cone or pyramid, contained between the base and a plane parallel to the base that intersects the solid **b** the part of such a solid contained between two parallel planes intersecting the solid [c17: from Latin: piece; probably related to Old English *brysan* to crush, BRUISE]

fry¹ (fraɪ) *vb* **fries**, **frying**, **fried 1** (when *tr*, sometimes foll by *up*) to cook or be cooked in fat, oil, etc, usually over direct heat **2** *slang, chiefly US* to kill or be killed by electrocution, esp in the electric chair ⊳ *n*, *pl* **fries 3** a dish of something fried, esp the offal of a specified animal: *pig's fry* **4** *Brit informal* the act of preparing a mixed fried dish or the dish itself [c13: from Old French *frire*, from Latin *frīgere* to roast, fry] ⊳ **'fryer** *or* **'frier** *n*

fry² (fraɪ) *pl n* **1** the young of various species of fish **2** the young of certain other animals, such as frogs [c14 (in the sense: young; offspring): perhaps via Norman French from Old French *freier* to spawn, rub, from Latin *fricāre* to rub]

Fry (fraɪ) *n* **1 Christopher**. 1907–2005, English dramatist; author of the verse dramas *A Phoenix Too Frequent* (1946), *The Lady's Not For Burning* (1948), and *Venus Observed* (1950) **2 Elizabeth**. 1780–1845, English prison reformer and Quaker **3 Roger Eliot**. 1866–1934, English art critic and painter who helped to introduce the postimpressionists to Britain. His books include *Vision and Design* (1920) and *Cézanne* (1927) **4 Stephen** (**John**). born 1957, British writer, actor, and comedian; his novels include *The Liar* (1991) and *The Stars' Tennis Balls* (2000)

frying pan *or esp US* **fry-pan** *n* **1** a long-handled shallow pan used for frying **2** out of the frying pan into the fire from a bad situation to a worse one

FSB *abbreviation* the Russian Federal Security Service, founded in 1995 [c20: Russian *Federalnaya sluzhba bezopasnosti*]

f-stop *n* any of the settings for the f-number of a camera

ft *abbreviation* foot or feet

fth. *or* **fthm.** *abbreviation* fathom

FTP *or* **ftp** *n* file transfer protocol; the standard protocol used to transfer files across the internet, or a similar network, between computer systems

Fuad I (fuː'ɑːd) *n* original name *Ahmed Fuad Pasha*. 1868–1936, sultan of Egypt (1917–22) and king (1922–36)

Fu-chou ('fuː'tʃau) *n* a variant transliteration of the Chinese name for **Fuzhou**

Fuchs (fuks, fuːks) *n* **1 Klaus Emil**. (klaus 'eːmiːl). 1911–88, East German physicist. He was born in Germany, became a British citizen (1942), and was imprisoned (1950–59) for giving secret atomic research information to the Soviet Union **2 Sir Vivian Ernest**. 1908–99, English explorer and geologist: led the Commonwealth Trans-Antarctic Expedition (1955–58)

fuchsia ('fjuːʃə) *n* **1** any onagraceous shrub of the mostly tropical genus *Fuchsia*, widely cultivated for their showy drooping purple, red, or white flowers **2 a** a reddish-purple to purplish-pink colour **b** (*as adjective*): *a fuchsia dress* [c18: from New Latin, named after Leonhard Fuchs (1501–66), German botanist]

fuchsin ('fuːksɪn) *or* **fuchsine** ('fuːksiːn, -sɪn) *n* a greenish crystalline substance, the quaternary chloride of rosaniline, forming a red solution in water: used as a textile dye and a biological stain. Formula: $C_{20}H_{19}N_3HCl$ [c19: from FUCHS(IA) + -IN; from its similarity in colour to the flower]

fuck (fʌk) *taboo* ▷ *vb* **1** to have sexual intercourse with (someone) ▷ *n* **2** an act of sexual intercourse **3** *slang* a partner in sexual intercourse, esp one of specified competence or experience **4** not care a fuck *or* not give a fuck not to care at all ▷ *interj* **5** *offensive* an expression of strong disgust or anger (often in exclamatory phrases such as **fuck you! fuck it!** etc) [c16: of Germanic origin; related to Middle Dutch *fokken* to strike]

fuck buddy *taboo, slang* a person with whom another person has a relationship based on casual sex only

fucking ('fʌkɪŋ) *adj, adv* (prenominal) *taboo, slang* (intensifier): *turn off that fucking phone; a fucking good time*

fuck off *offensive, taboo, slang* ▷ *interj* **1** a forceful expression of dismissal or contempt ▷ *vb* (adverb) **2** (intr) to go away ▷ *adj* **3** (prenominal) very large or impressive: *a huge fuck-off cigar*

fucus ('fjuːkəs) *n, pl* **-ci** (-saɪ) *or* **-cuses** any seaweed of the genus *Fucus*, common in the intertidal regions of many shores and typically having greenish-brown slimy fronds [c16: from Latin: rock lichen, from Greek *phukos* seaweed, dye, of Semitic origin]

fuddle ('fʌdə l) *vb* **1** (tr; often passive) to cause to be confused or intoxicated ▷ *n* **2** a muddled or confused state [c16: of unknown origin]

fuddy-duddy ('fʌdɪ,dʌdɪ) *n, pl* **-dies** *informal* a person, esp an elderly one, who is extremely conservative or dull [c20: of uncertain origin]

fudge[1] (fʌdʒ) *n* a soft variously flavoured sweet made from sugar, butter, cream, etc [c19: of unknown origin]

fudge[2] (fʌdʒ) *n* **1** foolishness; nonsense ▷ *interj* **2** a mild exclamation of annoyance [c18: of uncertain origin]

fudge[3] (fʌdʒ) *n* **1** a small section of type matter in a box in a newspaper allowing late news to be included without the whole page having to be remade **2** the late news so inserted **3** an unsatisfactory compromise reached to evade a difficult problem or controversial issue ▷ *vb* **4** (tr) to make or adjust in a false or clumsy way **5** (tr) to misrepresent; falsify **6** to evade (a problem, issue, etc); dodge; avoid [c19: see FADGE]

Fuegian (fjuːˈiːdʒɪən, ˈfweɪdʒ-) *adj* **1** of or relating to Tierra del Fuego or its indigenous Indians ▷ *n* **2** an Indian of Tierra del Fuego

fuel (fjʊəl) *n* **1** any substance burned as a source of heat or power, such as coal or petrol **2** the material, containing a fissile substance, such as uranium-235, that produces energy in a nuclear reactor **3** something that nourishes or builds up emotion, action, etc ▷ *vb* **fuels, fuelling, fuelled** *or US* **fuels, fueling, fueled 4** to supply with or receive fuel [c14: from Old French *feuaile*, from *feu* fire, ultimately from Latin *focus* fireplace, hearth]

fuel air bomb *n* a type of bomb that spreads a cloud of gas, which is then detonated, over the target area, causing extensive destruction

fuel cell *n* a cell in which the energy produced by oxidation of a fuel is converted directly into electrical energy

fuel injection *n* a system for introducing atomized liquid fuel under pressure directly into the combustion chambers of an internal-combustion engine without the use of a carburettor

fuel oil *n* a liquid petroleum product having a flash point above 37.8°C: used as a substitute for coal in industrial furnaces, domestic heaters, ships, and locomotives

Fuentes ('fwenteɪs) *n* **Carlos.** born 1928, Mexican novelist and writer. His novels include *A Change of Skin* (1967), *Terra Nostra* (1975), and *Cristóbal Nonato* (1987)

fug (fʌg) *n chiefly Brit* a hot, stale, or suffocating atmosphere [c19: perhaps variant of FOG[1]] ▷ **'fuggy** *adj*

fugacity (fjuːˈɡæsɪtɪ) *n Also called:* **escaping tendency** *thermodynamics* a property of a gas, related to its partial pressure, that expresses its tendency to escape or expand, given by $d(\log_e f) = d\mu/RT$, where μ is the chemical potential, R the gas constant, and T the thermodynamic temperature

Fugard ('fuːɡɑːd) *n* **Athol** ('æθəl). born 1932, South African dramatist and theatre director. His plays include *The Blood-Knot* (1961), *Sizwe Bansi is Dead* (1972), *Statements*

after an Arrest under the Immorality Act (1974), and *The Captain's Tiger* (1999)

-fuge *n combining form* indicating an agent or substance that expels or drives away: *vermifuge* [from Latin *fugāre* to expel, put to flight]

Fugger (*German* 'fʊɡər) *n* a German family of merchants and bankers, prominent in 15th- and 16th-century Europe

fugitive ('fjuːdʒɪtɪv) *n* **1** a person who flees **2** a thing that is elusive or fleeting ▷ *adj* **3** fleeing, esp from arrest or pursuit **4** not permanent; fleeting; transient [c14: from Latin *fugitīvus* fleeing away, from *fugere* to take flight, run away] ▷ **'fugitively** *adv*

fugleman ('fjuːɡəlmən) *n, pl* **-men 1** (formerly) a soldier used as an example for those learning drill **2** any person who acts as a leader or example [c19: from German *Flügelmann*, from *Flügel* wing, flank + *Mann* MAN]

fugly ('fʌɡlɪ) *adj* **-lier, -liest** *chiefly US & Austral offensive* extremely ugly [c20: FUCKING + UGLY]

fugu ('fuːɡuː) *n* any of various marine pufferfish of the genus *Tetraodontidae*, eaten as a delicacy in Japan once certain poisonous and potentially lethal parts have been removed [Japanese]

fugue (fjuːɡ) *n* **1** a musical form consisting essentially of a theme repeated a fifth above or a fourth below the continuing first statement **2** *psychiatry* a dreamlike altered state of consciousness, lasting from a few hours to several days, during which a person loses his memory for his previous life and often wanders away from home [c16: from French, from Italian *fuga*, from Latin: a running away, flight] ▷ **'fugal** *adj*

Führer *or* **Fuehrer** *German* ('fyːrər; *English* 'fjʊərə) *n* a leader: applied esp to Adolf Hitler (**der Führer**) while he was Chancellor [German, from *führen* to lead]

Fuji ('fuːdʒɪ) *n* Mount Fuji an extinct volcano in central Japan, in S central Honshu: the highest mountain in Japan, famous for its symmetrical snow-capped cone. Height: 3776 m (12 388 ft)

Fujian *or* **Fukien** ('fuːˈkjɛn) *n* **1** a province of SE China: mountainous and forested, drained chiefly by the Min River; noted for the production of flower-scented teas. Capital: Fuzhou. Pop: 34 880 000 (2003 est). Area: 123 000 sq km (47 970 sq miles) **2** any of the Chinese dialects of this province

Fukuoka (ˌfuːkuːˈəʊkə) *n* an industrial city and port in SW Japan, in N Kyushu: an important port in ancient times; site of Kyushu university. Pop: 1 302 454 (2002 est)

-ful *suffix* **1** (forming adjectives) full of or characterized by: *painful; spiteful; restful* **2** (forming adjectives) able or tending to: *helpful; useful* **3** (forming nouns) indicating as much as will fill the thing specified: *mouthful; spoonful* [Old English *-ful, -full*, from FULL[1]]

● USAGE Where the amount held by a spoon, etc, is used
● as a rough unit of measurement, the correct form is
● *spoonful*, etc: *take a spoonful of this medicine every day. Spoon*
● *full* is used in a sentence such as *he held out a spoon full of*
● *dark liquid*, where *full* of describes the spoon. A plural
● form such as *spoonfuls* is preferred by many speakers
● and writers to *spoonsful*

fulcrum ('fʊlkrəm, 'fʌl-) *n, pl* **-crums** *or* **-cra** (-krə) **1** the pivot about which a lever turns **2** something that supports or sustains; prop [c17: from Latin: foot of a couch, bedpost, from *fulcire* to prop up]

fulfil *or US* **fulfill** (fʊlˈfɪl) *vb* **-fils** *or US* **-fills, -filling, -filled** (tr) **1** to bring about the completion or achievement of (a desire, promise, etc) **2** to carry out or execute (a request, etc) **3** to conform with or satisfy (regulations, demands, etc) **4** to finish or reach the end of **5** fulfil oneself to achieve one's potential or desires [Old English *fulfyllan*] ▷ **ful'filment** *or US* **ful'fillment** *n*

fulgent ('fʌldʒənt) *or* **fulgid** ('fʌldʒɪd) *adj poetic* shining brilliantly; resplendent; gleaming [c15: from Latin *fulgēre* to shine, flash]

fulgurate ('fʌlɡjʊˌreɪt) *vb* (intr) *rare* to flash like lightning [c17: from Latin *fulgurāre*, from *fulgur* lightning]

fulgurite ('fʌlɡjʊˌraɪt) *n* a tube of glassy mineral matter found in sand and rock, formed by the action of lightning [c19: from Latin *fulgur* lightning]

Fulham ('fʊləm) *n* a district of the Greater London

borough of Hammersmith and Fulham (since 1965): contains **Fulham Palace** (16th century), residence of the Bishop of London

fuliginous (fjuː'lɪdʒɪnəs) *adj* 1 sooty or smoky 2 of the colour of soot; dull greyish-black or brown [c16: from Late Latin *fūlīginōsus* full of soot, from *fūlīgō* soot]

full[1] (fʊl) *adj* 1 holding or containing as much as possible; filled to capacity or near capacity 2 abundant in supply, quantity, number, etc: *full of energy* 3 having consumed enough food or drink 4 (esp of the face or figure) rounded or plump; not thin 5 (*prenominal*) with no part lacking; complete: *a full dozen* 6 (*prenominal*) with all privileges, rights, etc; not restricted: *a full member* 7 (*prenominal*) of, relating to, or designating a relationship established by descent from the same parents: *full brother* 8 filled with emotion or sentiment: *a full heart* 9 (*postpositive*; foll by *of*) occupied or engrossed (with): *full of his own projects* 10 *music* a powerful or rich in volume and sound b completing a piece or section; concluding: *a full close* 11 (of a garment, esp a skirt) containing a large amount of fabric; of ample cut 12 (of sails, etc) distended by wind 13 (of wine, such as a burgundy) having a heavy body 14 (of a colour) containing a large quantity of pure hue as opposed to white or grey; rich; saturated 15 *informal* drunk 16 full of oneself full of pride or conceit; egoistic 17 full up filled to capacity 18 in full swing at the height of activity: *the party was in full swing* ▷ *adv* 19 a completely; entirely b (*in combination*): *full-grown; full-fledged* 20 exactly; directly; right: *he hit him full in the stomach* 21 very; extremely (esp in the phrase **full well**) ▷ *n* 22 the greatest degree, extent, etc 23 in full without omitting, decreasing, or shortening: *we paid in full for our mistake* 24 to the full to the greatest extent; thoroughly; fully ▷ *vb* 25 (*tr*) *needlework* to gather or tuck 26 (*intr*) (of the moon) to be fully illuminated [Old English; related to Old Norse *fullr*, Old High German *foll*, Latin *plēnus*, Greek *plērēs*; see FILL] > 'fullness or fulness *esp US* 'fulness *n*

full[2] (fʊl) *vb* (of cloth, yarn, etc) to become or to make (cloth, yarn, etc) heavier and more compact during manufacture through shrinking and beating or pressing [c14: from Old French *fouler*, ultimately from Latin *fullō* a FULLER[1]]

fullback ('fʊl,bæk) *n* 1 *soccer, hockey* one of two defensive players positioned in front of the goalkeeper 2 the position held by any of these players

full-blooded *adj* 1 (esp of horses) of unmixed ancestry; thoroughbred 2 having great vigour or health; hearty; virile > ,full-'bloodedness *n*

full-blown *adj* 1 characterized by the fullest, strongest, or best development 2 in full bloom

full board *n* the provision by a hotel of a bed and all meals

full-bodied *adj* having a full rich flavour or quality

full-court press *n* *basketball* the tactic of harrying the opposing team in all areas of the court, as opposed to the more usual practice of trying to defend one's own basket

full dress *n* a a formal or ceremonial style of dress, such as white tie and tails for a man and a full-length evening dress for a woman b (*as modifier*): *full-dress uniform*

full employment *n* a state in which the labour force and other economic resources of a country are utilized to their maximum

fuller ('fʊlə) *n* a person who fulls cloth for his living [Old English *fullere*, from Latin *fullō*]

Fuller ('fʊlə) *n* 1 (**Richard**) **Buckminster**. 1895–1983, US architect and engineer: developed the geodesic dome 2 **Roy** (**Broadbent**). 1912–91, British poet and writer, whose collections include *The Middle of a War* (1942) and *A Lost Season* (1944), both of which are concerned with World War II, *Epitaphs and Occasions* (1949), and *Available for Dreams* (1989) 3 **Thomas**. 1608–61, English clergyman and antiquarian; author of *The Worthies of England* (1662)

fullerene ('fʊlə,riːn) *n* 1 short for **buckminster-fullerene** 2 any of various carbon molecules with a polyhedral structure similar to that of buckminsterfullerene, such as C_{70}, C_{76}, and C_{84}

fuller's earth *n* a natural absorbent clay used, after heating, for decolorizing oils and fats, fulling cloth, etc

full-faced *adj* Also called: **full face** facing towards the viewer, with the entire face visible

full-fledged *adj* See **fully fledged**

full forward *n* *Australian rules football, Gaelic football* an attacking player who plays in the centre of the forward line

full-frontal *adj* 1 *informal* (of a nude person or a photograph of a nude person) exposing the genitals to full view 2 all-out; unrestrained ▷ *n* **full frontal** 3 a full-frontal photograph

full house *n* 1 *poker* a hand with three cards of the same value and another pair 2 a theatre, etc, filled to capacity 3 (in bingo, etc) the set of numbers needed to win

full-length *n* (*modifier*) 1 extending to or showing the complete length 2 of the original length; not abridged

full monty ('mɒntɪ) *n* the full monty *informal* something in its entirety [of unknown origin]

full moon *n* one of the four phases of the moon, occurring when the earth lies between the sun and the moon so that the moon is visible as a fully illuminated disc

full nelson *n* a wrestling hold, illegal in amateur wrestling, in which a wrestler places both arms under his opponent's arms from behind and exerts pressure with both palms on the back of the neck

full-on *adj* *informal* complete; unrestrained: *full-on military intervention; full-on hard rock*

full sail *adv* 1 at top speed ▷ *adj, adv* (*postpositive*) 2 with all sails set

full-scale *n* (*modifier*) 1 (of a plan, etc) of actual size; having the same dimensions as the original 2 done with thoroughness or urgency; using all resources; all-out

full stop *or* **full point** *n* the punctuation mark (.) used at the end of a sentence that is not a question or exclamation, after abbreviations, etc. Also called (esp US and Canadian): period

full time *n* the end of a football or other match

full-time *adj* 1 for the entire time appropriate to an activity: *a full-time job; a full-time student* ▷ *adv* **full time** 2 on a full-time basis: *he works full time* ▷ See **part-time** > ,full-'timer *n*

full toss *or* **full pitch** *n* *cricket* a bowled ball that reaches the batsman without bouncing

fully ('fʊlɪ) *adv* 1 to the greatest degree or extent; totally; entirely 2 amply; sufficiently; adequately: *they were fully fed* 3 at least: *it was fully an hour before she came*

fully fashioned *adj* (of stockings, knitwear, etc) shaped and seamed so as to fit closely

fully fledged *or* **full-fledged** *adj* 1 (of a young bird) having acquired its adult feathers and thus able to fly 2 developed or matured to the fullest degree 3 of full rank or status

fulmar ('fʊlmə) *n* any heavily built short-tailed oceanic bird of the genus *Fulmarus* and related species, of polar regions: family *Procellariidae*, order *Procellariiformes* (petrels) [c17: of Scandinavian origin; related to Old Norse *fūlmār*, from *fūll* foul + *mār* gull]

fulminate ('fʌlmɪ,neɪt, 'fʊl-) *vb* 1 (*intr*; often foll by *against*) to make criticisms or denunciations; rail 2 to explode with noise and violence ▷ *n* 3 any salt or ester of fulminic acid, esp the mercury salt, which is used as a detonator [c15: from Medieval Latin *fulmināre*, from Latin: to cause lightning, from *fulmen* lightning that strikes] > ,fulmi'nation *n* > 'fulmi,natory *adj* > 'fulminant *adj*

fulsome ('fʊlsəm) *adj* 1 excessive or insincere, esp in an offensive or distasteful way: *fulsome compliments* 2 *not standard* extremely complimentary 3 *informal* full, rich or abundant: *a fulsome figure; a fulsome flavour; fulsome detail* > 'fulsomely *adv* > 'fulsomeness *n*

● USAGE The use of *fulsome* to mean *extremely*
● *complimentary* or *full, rich or abundant* is common in
● journalism, but should be avoided in other kinds of
● writing

Fulton ('fʊltən) *n* **Robert**. 1765–1815, US engineer: designed the first successful steamboat (1807) and steam warship (1814)

fulvous ('fʌlvəs, 'fʊl-) adj of a dull brownish-yellow colour; tawny [c17: from Latin *fulvus* reddish yellow, gold-coloured, tawny; probably related to *fulgēre* to shine]

fumarole ('fju:məˌrəʊl) n a vent in or near a volcano from which hot gases, esp steam, are emitted [c19: from French *fumerolle*, from Late Latin *fūmāriolum* smoke hole, from Latin *fūmus* smoke]

fumble ('fʌmbᵊl) vb 1 (intr; often foll by *for* or *with*) to grope about clumsily or blindly, esp in searching 2 (intr; foll by *at* or *with*) to finger or play with, esp in an absent-minded way 3 to say or do hesitantly or awkwardly: *he fumbled the introduction badly* 4 to fail to catch or grasp (a ball, etc) cleanly ▷ n 5 the act of fumbling [c16: probably of Scandinavian origin; related to Swedish *fumla*] > 'fumbler n > 'fumblingly adv

fume (fju:m) vb 1 (intr) to be overcome with anger or fury; rage 2 to give off (fumes) or (of fumes) to be given off, esp during a chemical reaction 3 (tr) to subject to or treat with fumes; fumigate ▷ n 4 (often plural) a pungent or toxic vapour 5 a sharp or pungent odour [c14: from Old French *fum*, from Latin *fūmus* smoke, vapour] > 'fumeless adj 'fumingly adv 'fumy adj

fumed (fju:md) adj (of wood, esp oak) having a dark colour and distinctive grain from exposure to ammonia fumes

fumigant ('fju:mɪgənt) n a substance used for fumigating

fumigate ('fju:mɪˌgeɪt) vb to treat (something contaminated or infected) with fumes or smoke [c16: from Latin *fūmigāre* to smoke, steam, from *fūmus* smoke + *agere* to drive, produce] > ˌfumi'gation n > 'fumiˌgator n

fuming sulphuric acid n a mixture of pyrosulphuric acid, $H_2S_2O_7$, and other condensed acids, made by dissolving sulphur trioxide in concentrated sulphuric acid. Also called: **oleum**

fumitory ('fju:mɪtərɪ, -trɪ) n, pl -ries any plant of the chiefly European genus *Fumaria*, esp *F. officinalis*, having spurred flowers and formerly used medicinally: family *Fumariaceae* [c14: from Old French *fumetere*, from Medieval Latin *fūmus terrae*, literally: smoke of the earth; see FUME]

fun (fʌn) n 1 a source of enjoyment, amusement, diversion, etc 2 pleasure, gaiety, or merriment 3 jest or sport (esp in the phrases **in** or **for fun**) 4 **fun and games** facetious, ironic amusement; frivolous activity 5 **make fun of** or **poke fun at** to ridicule or deride 6 (modifier) full of amusement, pleasure, gaiety, etc: *a fun sport* [c17: perhaps from obsolete *fon* to make a fool of; see FOND¹]

funambulist (fju:'næmbjʊlɪst) n a tightrope walker [c18: from Latin *fūnambulus* rope dancer, from *fūnis* rope + *ambulāre* to walk] > fu'nambulism n

Funchal (Portuguese f[˜u]'ʃal) n the capital and chief port of the Madeira Islands, on the S coast of Madeira. Pop: 103 962 (2001)

function ('fʌŋkʃən) n 1 the natural action or intended purpose of a person or thing in a specific role: *the function of a hammer is to hit nails into wood* 2 an official or formal social gathering or ceremony 3 a factor dependent upon another or other factors 4 Also called: **map, mapping** maths, logic a relation between two sets that associates a unique element (the value) of the second (the range) with each element (the argument) of the first (the domain): a many-one relation. Symbol: f(x) The value of f(x) for x = 2 is f(2) ▷ vb 5 (intr) to operate or perform as specified; work properly 6 (foll by *as*) to perform the action or role (of something or someone else): *a coin may function as a screwdriver* [c16: from Latin *functiō*, from *fungī* to perform, discharge]

functional ('fʌŋkʃənᵊl) adj 1 of, involving, or containing a function or functions 2 practical rather than decorative; utilitarian 3 capable of functioning; working 4 med affecting a function of an organ without structural change > 'functionally adv

functional food n a food containing additives which provide extra nutritional value. Also called: **nutraceutical**

functionalism ('fʌŋkʃənəˌlɪzəm) n 1 the theory of design that the form of a thing should be determined by its use 2 any doctrine that stresses utility or purpose > 'functionalist n, adj

functionality (ˌfʌŋkʃən'ælɪtɪ) n, pl -aries 1 the quality of being functional 2 computing a function or range of functions in a computer, program, package, etc

functionary ('fʌŋkʃənərɪ) n, pl -aries a person acting in an official capacity, as for a government; an official

function creep n the gradual widening of the use of a technology or system beyond the purpose for which it was originally intended, esp when this leads to potential invasion of privacy

fund (fʌnd) n 1 a reserve of money, etc, set aside for a certain purpose 2 a supply or store of something; stock: *it exhausted his fund of wisdom* ▷ vb (tr) 3 to furnish money to in the form of a fund 4 to place or store up in a fund 5 to convert (short-term floating debt) into long-term debt bearing fixed interest and represented by bonds 6 to accumulate a fund for the discharge of (a recurrent liability): *to fund a pension plan* 7 See also **funds** [c17: from Latin *fundus* the bottom, piece of land, estate] > 'funder n

fundament ('fʌndəmənt) n euphemistic or facetious the buttocks [c13: from Latin *fundāmentum* foundation, from *fundāre* to FOUND²]

fundamental (ˌfʌndə'mɛntᵊl) adj 1 of, involving, or comprising a foundation; basic 2 of, involving, or comprising a source; primary 3 music denoting or relating to the principal or lowest note of a harmonic series ▷ n 4 a principle, law, etc, that serves as the basis of an idea or system 5 a the principal or lowest note of a harmonic series b the bass note of a chord in root position > ˌfundamen'tality or ˌfunda'mentalness n > ˌfunda'mentally adv

fundamental interaction n any of the four basic interactions that occur in nature: the gravitational, electromagnetic, strong, and weak interactions

fundamentalism (ˌfʌndə'mɛntəˌlɪzəm) n 1 Christianity (esp among certain Protestant sects) the belief that every word of the Bible is divinely inspired and therefore true 2 Islam a movement favouring strict observance of the teachings of the Koran and Islamic law > ˌfunda'mentalist n, adj

fundamental particle n another name for **elementary particle**

fundamental unit n one of a set of unrelated units that form the basis of a system of units. For example, the metre, kilogram, and second are fundamental units of the SI system

funded debt n the part of the national debt, consisting mostly of consols, that the government has no obligation to repay by a specified date

fundholding ('fʌndˌhəʊldɪŋ) n (formerly, in the National Health Service in Britain) the system enabling general practitioners to receive a fixed budget from which to pay for primary care, drugs, and nonurgent hospital treatment for patients > 'fundˌholder n

fundi ('fʊndi:) n South African an expert [c20: from Nguni *umfindisi* a teacher]

fundie ('fʌndɪ) n Austral derogatory, slang a fundamentalist Christian

fundraise ('fʌndˌreɪz) vb (intr) to raise money for a cause > 'fundˌraising n, adj

fundraiser ('fʌndˌreɪzə) n 1 a person who raises money for a cause 2 an event held to raise money for a cause

funds (fʌndz) pl n 1 money that is readily available 2 British government securities representing national debt

fund supermarket n an online facility offering discounted investment opportunities and advice

fundus ('fʌndəs) n, pl -di (-daɪ) anatomy the base of an organ or the part farthest away from its opening [c18: from Latin, literally: the bottom, a farm, estate]

Fundy ('fʌndɪ) n **Bay of Fundy** an inlet of the Atlantic in SE Canada, between S New Brunswick and W Nova Scotia: remarkable for its swift tides of up to 21 m (70 ft)

Funen ('fu:nən) n the second largest island of Denmark, between the Jutland peninsula and the island of Zealand. Pop: 441 795 (2003 est). Area: 3481 sq km (1344 sq miles). Danish name: **Fyn**

funeral ('fju:nərəl) n 1 a a ceremony at which a dead person is buried or cremated b (as modifier): *a funeral service* 2 a procession of people escorting a corpse to burial

3 *informal* worry; concern; affair: *that's your funeral* [c14: from Medieval Latin *fūnerālia*, from Late Latin *fūnerālis* (adj), from Latin *fūnus* funeral] ▷ 'funerary *adj*

funeral director *n* an undertaker

funeral parlour *n* a place where the dead are prepared for burial or cremation

funereal (fjuːˈnɪərɪəl) *adj* suggestive of a funeral; gloomy or mournful. Also called: **funebrial** (fjuːˈniːbrɪəl) [c18: from Latin *fūnereus*] ▷ fu'nereally *adv*

funfair ('fʌnˌfɛə) *n Brit* an amusement park or fairground

fungible ('fʌndʒɪbəl) *n law (often plural)* moveable perishable goods of a sort that may be estimated by number or weight, such as grain, wine, etc [c18: from Medieval Latin *fungibilis*, from Latin *fungī* to perform; see FUNCTION] ▷ ˌfungi'bility *n*

fungicide ('fʌndʒɪˌsaɪd) *n* a substance or agent that destroys or is capable of destroying fungi ▷ ˌfungi'cidal *adj*

fungoid ('fʌŋgɔɪd) *adj* resembling a fungus or fungi

fungous ('fʌŋgəs) *adj* appearing suddenly and spreading quickly like a fungus, but not lasting

fungus ('fʌŋgəs) *n, pl* **fungi** ('fʌŋgaɪ, 'fʌndʒaɪ, 'fʌŋdʒɪ) *or* **funguses** *n* any member of a kingdom of organisms (Fungi) that lack chlorophyll, leaves, true stems, and roots, reproduce by spores, and live as saprotrophs or parasites. The group includes moulds, mildews, rusts, yeasts, and mushrooms **2** something resembling a fungus, esp in suddenly growing and spreading rapidly **3** *pathol* any soft tumorous growth [c16: from Latin: mushroom, fungus; probably related to Greek *spongos* SPONGE] ▷ 'fungal *adj*

funicular (fjuːˈnɪkjʊlə) *n* **1** Also called: **funicular railway** a railway up the side of a mountain, consisting of two counterbalanced cars at either end of a cable passing round a driving wheel at the summit ▷ *adj* **2** relating to or operated by a rope, cable, etc

funk¹ (fʌŋk) *informal, chiefly Brit* ▷ *n* **1** Also called: **blue funk** a state of nervousness, fear, or depression (esp in the phrase **in a funk**) **2** a coward ▷ *vb* **3** to flinch from (responsibility) through fear **4** (*tr; usually passive*) to make afraid [c18: university slang, perhaps related to FUNK²]

funk² (fʌŋk) *n informal* a type of polyrhythmic Black dance music with heavy syncopation [c20: back formation from FUNKY¹]

Funk (fʌŋk) *n* **Casimir** ('kæzɪˌmɪə). 1884–1967, US biochemist, born in Poland: studied and named vitamins

funky ('fʌŋkɪ) *adj* **funkier, funkiest** *informal* (of music) passionate, soulful; of or pertaining to funk [c20: from FUNK², perhaps alluding to music that was smelly, that is, earthy (like the early blues)]

funnel ('fʌnᵊl) *n* **1** a hollow utensil with a wide mouth tapering to a small hole, used for pouring liquids, powders, etc, into a narrow-necked vessel **2** something resembling this in shape or function **3** a smokestack for smoke and exhaust gases, as on a steamship or steam locomotive ▷ *vb* **-nels, -nelling, -nelled** *or US* **-nels, -neling, -neled 4** to move or cause to move or pour through or as if through a funnel [c15: from Old Provençal *fonilh*, ultimately from Latin *infundibulum* funnel, hopper (in a mill), from *infundere* to pour in] ▷ 'funnel-like *adj*

funnel-web *n Austral* any large poisonous black spider of the family Dipluridae, constructing funnel-shaped webs

funny ('fʌnɪ) *adj* **-nier, -niest 1** causing amusement or laughter; humorous; comical **2** peculiar; odd **3** suspicious or dubious (esp in the phrase **funny business**) **4** *informal* faint or ill ▷ *n, pl* **-nies 5** *informal* a joke or witticism ▷ 'funnily *adv* ▷ 'funniness *n*

funny bone *n* the area near the elbow where the ulnar nerve is close to the surface of the skin: when it is struck, a sharp tingling sensation is experienced along the forearm and hand

fun run *n* a long run or part-marathon run for exercise and pleasure, often by large numbers of people

fur (fɜː) *n* **1** the dense coat of fine silky hairs on such mammals as the cat, seal, and mink **2** a the dressed skin of certain fur-bearing animals, with the hair left on **b** (*as modifier*): *a fur coat* **3** a garment made of fur, such as a coat or stole **4** a pile fabric made in imitation of animal fur **5** *heraldry* any of various stylized representations of animal pelts or their tinctures, esp ermine or vair, used in coats of arms **6** **make the fur fly** to cause a scene or disturbance **7** *informal* a whitish coating of cellular debris on the tongue, caused by excessive smoking, an upset stomach, etc **8** *Brit* a whitish-grey deposit consisting chiefly of calcium carbonate precipitated from hard water onto the insides of pipes, boilers, and kettles ▷ *vb* **furs, furring, furred 9** (*tr*) to line or trim a garment, etc, with fur **10** (often foll by *up*) to cover or become covered with a furlike lining or deposit [c14: from Old French *forrer* to line a garment, from *fuerre* sheath, of Germanic origin; related to Old English *fōdder* case, Old Frisian *fōder* coat lining] ▷ 'furless *adj*

fur. *abbreviation* furlong

furbelow ('fɜːbɪˌləʊ) *n* **1** a flounce, ruffle, or other ornamental trim **2** (*often plural*) showy ornamentation ▷ *vb* **3** (*tr*) to put a furbelow on (a garment) [c18: by folk etymology from French dialect *farbella*; see FALBALA]

furbish ('fɜːbɪʃ) *vb* (*tr*) **1** to make bright by polishing; burnish **2** (often foll by *up*) to improve the appearance or condition of; renovate; restore [c14: from Old French *fourbir* to polish, of Germanic origin] ▷ 'furbisher *n*

furcate *vb* ('fɜːkeɪt) **1** to divide into two parts; fork ▷ *adj* ('fɜːkeɪt, -kɪt) **2** forked; divided: *furcate branches* [c19: from Late Latin *furcātus* forked, from Latin *furca* a fork] ▷ fur'cation *n*

furfuraceous (ˌfɜːfjʊˈreɪʃəs, -fəˈreɪ-) *adj* **1** relating to or resembling bran **2** *med* resembling dandruff; scaly

Furies ('fjʊərɪz) *pl n, sing* **Fury** *classical myth* the snake-haired goddesses of vengeance, usually three in number, who pursued unpunished criminals. Also called: **Erinyes, Eumenides**

furioso (ˌfjʊərɪˈəʊsəʊ) *music* ▷ *adj, adv* **1** in a frantically rushing manner ▷ *n, pl* **-sos 2** a passage or piece to be performed in this way [c19: Italian, literally: furious; see FURY]

furious ('fjʊərɪəs) *adj* **1** extremely angry or annoyed; raging **2** violent, wild, or unrestrained, as in speed, vigour, energy, etc ▷ 'furiously *adv* ▷ 'furiousness *n*

furl (fɜːl) *vb* **1** to roll up (an umbrella, a flag, etc) neatly and securely or (of an umbrella, flag, etc) to be rolled up in this way ▷ *n* **2** the act or an instance of furling **3** a single rolled-up section [c16: from Old French *ferlier* to bind tightly, from *ferm* tight (from Latin *firmus* FIRM¹) + *lier* to tie, bind, from Latin *ligāre*] ▷ 'furlable *adj*

furlong ('fɜːˌlɒŋ) *n* a unit of length equal to 220 yards (201.168 metres) [Old English *furlang*, from *furh* FURROW + *lang* LONG¹]

furlough ('fɜːləʊ) *n* **1** leave of absence from military duty ▷ *vb* (*tr*) **2** to grant a furlough to [c17: from Dutch *verlof*, from *ver-* FOR- + *lof* leave, permission; related to Swedish *förlof*]

furnace ('fɜːnɪs) *n* **1** an enclosed chamber in which heat is produced to generate steam, destroy refuse, smelt or refine ores, etc **2** a very hot or stifling place [c13: from Old French *fornais*, from Latin *fornax* oven, furnace; related to Latin *formus* warm]

Furness ('fɜːnɪs) *n* a region in NW England in Cumbria, forming a peninsula between the Irish Sea and Morecambe Bay

furnish ('fɜːnɪʃ) *vb* (*tr*) **1** to provide (a house, room, etc) with furniture, carpets, etc **2** to equip with what is necessary; fit out **3** to give; supply: *the records furnished the information required* [c15: from Old French *fournir*, of Germanic origin; related to Old High German *frummen* to carry out] ▷ 'furnisher *n*

furnishings ('fɜːnɪʃɪŋz) *pl n* furniture and accessories, including carpets and curtains, with which a room, house, etc, is furnished

furniture ('fɜːnɪtʃə) *n* **1** the movable, generally functional, articles that equip a room, house, etc **2** the equipment necessary for a ship, factory, etc **3** *printing* lengths of wood, plastic, or metal, used in assembling formes to create the blank areas and to surround the type **4** See **door furniture, street furniture** [c16: from French *fourniture*, from *fournir* to equip, FURNISH]

Furnivall ('fɜːnɪvəl) n **Frederick James**. 1825–1910, English philologist: founder of the Early English Text Society and one of the founders of the *Oxford English Dictionary*

furore (fjʊˈrɔːrɪ) *or esp US* **furor** ('fjʊərɔː) n **1** a public outburst; uproar **2** a sudden widespread enthusiasm for something; craze **3** frenzy; rage; madness [c15: from Latin: frenzy, rage, from *furere* to rave]

furphy ('fɜːfɪ) n, pl **-phies** *Austral slang* a rumour or fictitious story [c20: from *Furphy* carts (used for water or sewage in World War I), made at a foundry established by the Furphy family]

Furphy ('fɜːfɪ) n **Joseph**, pen name *Tom Collins*. 1843–1912, Australian author. His works include the classic Australian novel *Such is Life* (1903) and *The Buln-Buln and the Brolga* (1948)

furred (fɜːd) adj **1** made of, lined with, or covered in fur **2** wearing fur **3** (of animals) having fur **4** another word for **furry** (sense 3) **5** Also called: **furry** provided with furring strips **6** (of a pipe, kettle, etc) lined with hard lime or other salts deposited from water

furrier ('fʌrɪə) n a person whose occupation is selling, making, dressing, or repairing fur garments [c14: *furour*, from Old French *fourrer* to trim or line with FUR] > **'furriery** n

furring ('fɜːrɪŋ) n **1** short for **furring strip 2** the formation of fur on the tongue **3** trimming of animal fur, as on a coat or other garment, or furs collectively

furring strip n a strip of wood or metal fixed to a wall, floor, or ceiling to provide a surface for the fixing of plasterboard, floorboards, etc

furrow ('fʌrəʊ) n **1** a long narrow trench made in the ground by a plough or a trench resembling this **2** any long deep groove, esp a deep wrinkle on the forehead ▷ *vb* **3** to develop or cause to develop furrows or wrinkles **4** to make a furrow or furrows in (land) [Old English *furh*; related to Old Frisian *furch*, Old Norse *for*, Old High German *furuh* furrow, Latin *porca* ridge between furrows] > **'furrower** n > **'furrowless** adj > **'furrow-,like** or **'furrowy** adj

furry ('fɜːrɪ) adj **-rier, -riest 1** covered with fur or something furlike **2** of, relating to, or resembling fur **3** Also called: **furred** (of the tongue) coated with whitish cellular debris > **'furrily** adv > **'furriness** n

Fur Seal Islands pl n another name for the **Pribilof Islands**

further ('fɜːðə) adv **1** in addition; furthermore **2** to a greater degree or extent **3** to or at a more advanced point **4** to or at a greater distance in time or space; farther ▷ *adj* **5** additional; more **6** more distant or remote in time or space; farther ▷ *vb* **7** (tr) to assist the progress of; promote ▷ See also **far, furthest** [Old English *furthor*; related to Old Frisian *further*, Old Saxon *furthor*, Old High German *furdar*; see FORTH]
● USAGE See at **farther**

furtherance ('fɜːðərəns) n **1** the act of furthering; advancement **2** something that furthers or advances

further education n (in Britain) formal education beyond school other than at a university or polytechnic

furthermore ('fɜːðə,mɔː) adv in addition; moreover

furthermost ('fɜːðə,məʊst) adj most distant; furthest

furthest ('fɜːðɪst) adv **1** to the greatest degree or extent **2** to or at the greatest distance in time or space; farthest ▷ *adj* **3** most distant or remote in time or space; farthest

furtive ('fɜːtɪv) adj characterized by stealth; sly and secretive [c15: from Latin *furtīvus* stolen, clandestine, from *furtum* a theft, from *fūr* a thief; related to Greek *phōr* thief] > **'furtively** adv > **'furtiveness** n

Furtwängler (German 'fʊrtvɛŋlər) n **Wilhelm** ('vɪlhɛlm). 1886–1954, German conductor, noted for his interpretations of Wagner

furuncle ('fjʊərʌŋkəl) n *pathol* the technical name for **boil¹** [c17: from Latin *fūrunculus* pilferer, petty thief, sore on the body, from *fūr* thief] > **furuncular** (fjʊˈrʌŋkjʊlə) or **fu'runculous** adj

furunculosis (fjʊ,rʌŋkjʊˈləʊsɪs) n **1** a skin condition characterized by the presence of multiple boils **2** an infectious ulcerative disease of salmon and trout caused by the bacterium *Aeromonas salmonicida*

fury ('fjʊərɪ) n, pl **-ries 1** violent or uncontrolled anger; wild rage **2** an outburst of such anger **3** uncontrolled violence: *the fury of the storm* **4** a person, esp a woman, with a violent temper **5** See **Furies 6** like fury *informal* violently; furiously [c14: from Latin *furia* rage, from *furere* to be furious]

furze (fɜːz) n another name for **gorse** [Old English *fyrs*] > **'furzy** adj

fuscous ('fʌskəs) adj of a brownish-grey colour [c17: from Latin *fuscus* dark, swarthy, tawny]

fuse¹ *or US* **fuze** (fjuːz) n **1** a lead of combustible black powder in a waterproof covering (**safety fuse**), or a lead containing an explosive (**detonating fuse**), used to fire an explosive charge **2** any device by which an explosive charge is ignited ▷ *vb* **3** (tr) to provide or equip with such a fuse [c17: from Italian *fuso* spindle, from Latin *fūsus*] > **'fuseless** adj

fuse² (fjuːz) *vb* **1** to unite or become united by melting, esp by the action of heat **2** to become or cause to become liquid, esp by the action of heat; melt **3** to join or become combined; integrate **4** (tr) to equip (an electric circuit, plug, etc) with a fuse **5** *Brit* to fail or cause to fail as a result of the blowing of a fuse: *the lights fused* ▷ n **6** a protective device for safeguarding electric circuits, etc, containing a wire that melts and breaks the circuit when the current exceeds a certain value [c17: from Latin *fūsus* melted, cast, poured out, from *fundere* to pour out, shed; sense 5 influenced by FUSE¹]

fusee *or* **fuzee** (fjuːˈziː) n **1** (in early clocks and watches) a spirally grooved spindle, functioning as an equalizing force on the unwinding of the mainspring **2** a friction match with a large head, capable of remaining alight in a wind [c16: from French *fusée* spindleful of thread, from Old French *fus* spindle, from Latin *fūsus*]

fuselage ('fjuːzɪ,lɑːʒ) n the main body of an aircraft, excluding the wings, tailplane, and fin [c20: from French, from *fuseler* to shape like a spindle, from Old French *fusel* spindle; see FUSEE]

Fuseli ('fjuːzəlɪ) n **Henry**. original name *Johann Heinrich Füssli*. 1741–1825, British painter, born in Switzerland. His paintings include *Nightmare* (1782)

fusel oil *or* **fusel** ('fjuːzəl) n a mixture of amyl alcohols, propanol, and butanol: a by-product in the distillation of fermented liquors used as a source of amyl alcohols [c19: from German *Fusel* bad spirits]

Fushih *or* **Fu-shih** ('fuːˈʃiː) n another name for: **Yanan**

Fushun ('fuːˈʃʌn) n a city in NE China, in central Liaoning province near Shenyang: situated on one of the richest coalfields in the world; site of the largest thermal power plant in NE Asia. Pop: 1 425 000 (2005 est)

fusible ('fjuːzəbəl) adj capable of being fused or melted > **,fusi'bility** or **'fusibleness** n > **'fusibly** adv

fusiform ('fjuːzɪ,fɔːm) adj elongated and tapering at both ends; spindle-shaped [c18: from Latin *fūsus* spindle]

fusil ('fjuːzɪl) n a light flintlock musket [c16 (in the sense: steel for a tinderbox): from Old French *fuisil*, from Vulgar Latin *focīlis* (unattested), from Latin *focus* fire]

fusilier (,fjuːzɪˈlɪə) n **1** (formerly) an infantryman armed with a light musket **2** Also called: **fusileer a** a soldier, esp a private, serving in any of certain British or other infantry regiments **b** (pl; cap. when part of a name): *the Royal Welch Fusiliers* [c17: from French; see FUSIL]

fusillade (,fjuːzɪˈleɪd, -ˈlɑːd) n **1** a simultaneous or rapid continual discharge of firearms **2** a sudden outburst, as of criticism ▷ *vb* **3** (tr) to attack with a fusillade [c19: from French, from *fusiller* to shoot; see FUSIL]

fusilli (fʊˈziːlɪ, fjʊˈziːlɪ) n pasta in the form of short spirals [c20: Italian, literally: little spindles, from *fuso* a spindle]

fusion ('fjuːʒən) n **1** the act or process of fusing or melting together; union **2** the state of being fused **3** something produced by fusing **4** See **nuclear fusion 5** a coalition of political parties or other groups, esp to support common candidates at an election **6** a kind of popular music that is a blend of two or more styles, such as jazz and funk **7** (modifier) relating to a style of cooking which combines traditional Western techniques and ingredients with those used in Eastern cuisine: *fusion* *cuisine; fusion food* [C16: from Latin *fūsiō* a pouring out, melting, casting, from *fundere* to pour out, FOUND³]

fusion bomb *n* a type of bomb in which most of the energy is provided by nuclear fusion, esp the fusion of hydrogen isotopes. Also called: **thermonuclear bomb, fission-fusion bomb**

fuss (fʌs) *n* 1 nervous activity or agitation, esp when disproportionate or unnecessary 2 complaint or objection: *he made a fuss over the bill* 3 an exhibition of affection or admiration, esp if excessive: *they made a great fuss over the new baby* 4 a quarrel; dispute ▷ *vb* 5 (*intr*) to worry unnecessarily 6 (*intr*) to be excessively concerned over trifles 7 (when *intr*, usually foll by *over*) to show great or excessive concern, affection, etc (for) 8 (*tr*) to bother (a person) [C18: of uncertain origin] > 'fusser *n*

fusspot ('fʌs,pɒt) *n* Brit informal a person who fusses unnecessarily

fussy ('fʌsɪ) *adj* fussier, fussiest 1 inclined to fuss over minor points 2 very particular about detail 3 characterized by overelaborate detail > 'fussily *adv* > 'fussiness *n*

fustanella (,fʌstə'nɛlə) *or* **fustanelle** *n* a white knee-length pleated skirt worn by men in Greece and Albania [C19: from Italian, from Modern Greek *phoustani*, probably from Italian *fustagno* FUSTIAN]

fustian ('fʌstɪən) *n* 1 a a hard-wearing fabric of cotton mixed with flax or wool with a slight nap b (*as modifier*): *a fustian jacket* 2 pompous or pretentious talk or writing ▷ *adj* 3 cheap; worthless 4 pompous; bombastic [C12: from Old French *fustaigne*, from Medieval Latin *fustāneum*, from Latin *fustis* cudgel]

fustic ('fʌstɪk) *n* 1 Also called: **old fustic** a large tropical American moraceous tree, *Chlorophora tinctoria* 2 the yellow dye obtained from the wood of this tree 3 any of various trees or shrubs that yield a similar dye, esp *Rhus cotinus* (**young fustic**), a European sumach [C15: from French *fustoc*, from Spanish, from Arabic *fustuq*, from Greek *pistakē* pistachio tree]

fusty ('fʌstɪ) *n* -tier, -tiest 1 smelling of damp or mould; musty 2 old-fashioned in attitude [C14: from *fust* wine cask, from Old French: cask, tree trunk, from Latin *fūstis* cudgel, club] > 'fustily *adv* > 'fustiness *n*

futhark, futharc ('fu:θɑ:k) *or* **futhorc, futhork** ('fu:θɔ:k) *n* a phonetic alphabet consisting of runes [C19: from the first six letters: *f, u, th, a, r, k*; compare ALPHABET]

futile ('fju:taɪl) *adj* 1 having no effective result; unsuccessful 2 pointless; unimportant; trifling 3 inane or foolish [C16: from Latin *futtilis* pouring out easily, worthless, from *fundere* to pour out] > 'futilely *adv* > futility (fju:'tɪlɪtɪ) *n*

futon ('fu:tɒn) *n* a Japanese padded quilt, laid on the floor for use as a bed, or on a frame for use as a chair [C19: from Japanese]

futsal ('fʊt,sæl) *n* a form of association football, played indoors with five players on each side [C20: Spanish from *futbol* football + *sala* indoor]

futtock ('fʌtək) *n* nautical one of the ribs in the frame of a wooden vessel [C13: perhaps variant of *foothook*]

future ('fju:tʃə) *n* 1 the time yet to come 2 undetermined events that will occur in that time 3 the condition of a person or thing at a later date: *the future of the school is undecided* 4 likelihood of later improvement or advancement: *he has a future as a singer* 5 grammar a a tense of verbs used when the action or event described is to occur after the time of utterance b a verb in this tense 6 in future from now on; henceforth ▷ *adj* 7 that is yet to come or be 8 of or expressing time yet to come 9 (*prenominal*) destined to become 10 grammar in or denoting the future as a tense of verbs ▷ See also **futures** [C14: from Latin *fūtūrus* about to be, from *esse* to be] > 'futureless *adj*

future perfect grammar ▷ *adj* 1 denoting a tense of verbs describing an action that will have been performed by a

certain time. In English this is formed with *will have* or *shall have* plus the past participle ▷ *n* 2 a the future perfect tense b a verb in this tense

future-proof *adj* (of a system, computer, program, etc) guaranteed not to be superseded by future versions, developments, etc

futures ('fju:tʃəz) *pl n* a commodities or other financial products bought or sold at an agreed price for delivery at a specified future date. See also **financial futures** b (*as modifier*): *futures contract; futures market*

future value *n* the value that a sum of money invested at compound interest will have after a specified period

futurism ('fju:tʃə,rɪzəm) *n* an artistic movement that arose in Italy in 1909 to replace traditional aesthetic values with the characteristics of the machine age > 'futurist *n, adj*

futuristic (,fju:tʃə'rɪstɪk) *adj* 1 denoting or relating to design, technology, etc, that is thought likely to be current or fashionable at some future time; ultramodern 2 of or relating to futurism > ,futur'istically *adv*

futurity (fju:'tjʊərɪtɪ) *n, pl* -ties 1 a less common word for **future** 2 the quality of being in the future 3 a future event

futurology (,fju:tʃə'rɒlədʒɪ) *n* the study or prediction of the future of mankind > ,futur'ologist *n*

fuze (fju:z) *n* chiefly US a variant spelling of **fuse¹**

fuzee (fju:'zi:) *n* a variant spelling of **fusee**

Fuzhou ('fu:'dʒəʊ), **Foochow** *or* **Fuchou** *n* a port in SE China, capital of Fujian province on the Min Jiang: one of the original five treaty ports (1842). Pop: 1 398 000 (2005 est)

fuzz¹ (fʌz) *n* 1 a mass or covering of fine or curly hairs, fibres, etc 2 a blur ▷ *vb* 3 to make or become fuzzy 4 to make or become indistinct; blur [C17: perhaps from Low German *fussig* loose]

fuzz² (fʌz) *n* a slang word for **police, policeman** [C20: of uncertain origin]

fuzzy ('fʌzɪ) *adj* fuzzier, fuzziest 1 of, resembling, or covered with fuzz 2 indistinct; unclear or distorted 3 (of the hair) tightly curled or very wavy > 'fuzzily *adv* > 'fuzziness *n*

fuzzy logic *n* a branch of logic designed to allow degrees of imprecision in reasoning and knowledge, typified by terms such as 'very', 'quite possibly', and 'unlikely', to be represented in such a way that the information can be processed by computer

fuzzy-wuzzy ('fʌzɪ,wʌzɪ) *n, pl* -wuzzies *or* -wuzzy archaic, *offensive, slang* a Black fuzzy-haired native of any of various countries

fwd *abbreviation* forward

FWIW *abbreviation text messaging* for what it's worth

f-word *n* the f-word (*sometimes capital*) a euphemistic way of referring to the word **fuck**

FX *n* 1 *films informal* short for **special effects** ▷ *abbreviation* 2 *US & Canadian* foreign exchange

-fy *suffix forming verbs* to make or become: *beautify; simplify; liquefy* [from Old French *-fier*, from Latin *-ficāre*, verbal ending formed from *-ficus* -FIC]

FYI *abbreviation* for your information

Fylde (faɪld) *n* a region in NW England in Lancashire between the Wyre and Ribble estuaries

fylfot ('faɪlfɒt) *n* a rare word for **swastika** [C16 (apparently meaning: a sign or device for the lower part or foot of a painted window): from *fillen* to FILL + *fot* FOOT]

Fyn (Danish fyːn) *n* the Danish name for **Funen**

fynbos ('feɪnbɒs) *n* a type of vegetation unique to the Mediterranean-climate region of southern and southwestern South Africa, characterized by evergreen hard-leaved shrubs and almost no trees [Afrikaans: fine bush]

FYROM *abbreviation* Former Yugoslav Republic of Macedonia

Gg

g¹ *or* **G** (dʒiː) *n, pl* **g's, G's** *or* **Gs** **1** the seventh letter and fifth consonant of the modern English alphabet **2** a speech sound represented by this letter, in English usually either a voiced velar stop, as in *grass*, or a voiced palato-alveolar affricate, as in *page*

g² *symbol for* **1** gallon(s) **2** gram(s) **3** acceleration of free fall (due to gravity) near the surface of the earth **4** grav

G *symbol for* **1** *music* **a** a note having a frequency of 392 hertz (**G above middle** C) or this value multiplied or divided by any power of 2; the fifth note of the scale of C major **b** a key, string, or pipe producing this note **c** the major or minor key having this note as its tonic **2** gauss **3** gravitational constant **4** *physics* conductance **5** *biochem* guanine **6** German **7** Gibbs function **8** giga **9** good **10** *slang, chiefly US* grand (a thousand dollars or pounds) **11** (in Australia) **a** a general exhibition (used to describe a category of film certified as suitable for viewing by anyone) **b** (*as modifier*): *a G film*

G. *or* **g.** *abbreviation* **1** Gulf **2** guilder(s) **3** guinea(s)

2G *abbreviation* second-generation; a system for mobile phones, characterized by digital technology, internet access, and a short-message service

3G *abbreviation* third-generation; a system for mobile phones allowing fast connection, internet access, digital photography, graphics transmission and display, and other advanced features

4G *abbreviation* fourth generation: a stage in mobile phone technology when data can be provided more quickly and on broader bandwidths than previously

G3 *abbreviation* Group of Three

G5 *abbreviation* Group of Five

G7 *abbreviation* Group of Seven

G8 *abbreviation* Group of Eight

G10 *abbreviation* Group of Ten

G24 *abbreviation* Group of Twenty-Four

G77 *abbreviation* Group of Seventy-Seven

Ga *the chemical symbol for* gallium

GA *abbreviation* **1** General Assembly (of the United Nations) **2** general average **3** Georgia

Ga. *abbreviation* Georgia

gab (gæb) *informal* ▷ *vb* **gabs, gabbing, gabbed** **1** (*intr*) to talk excessively or idly, esp about trivial matters; gossip; chatter ▷ *n* **2** idle or trivial talk **3 gift of the gab** ability to speak effortlessly, glibly, or persuasively [c18: variant of Northern dialect *gob* mouth, probably from Irish Gaelic *gob* beak, mouth] > 'gabber *n*

gabardine *or* **gaberdine** ('gæbə,diːn, ,gæbə'diːn) *n* **1** a twill-weave worsted, cotton, or spun-rayon fabric **2** an ankle-length loose coat or frock worn by men, esp by Jews, in the Middle Ages **3** any of various other garments made of gabardine, esp a child's raincoat [c16: from Old French *gauvardine* pilgrim's garment, from Middle High German *wallewart* pilgrimage; related to Spanish *gabardina*]

gabble ('gæbᵊl) *vb* **1** to utter (words, etc) rapidly and indistinctly; jabber **2** (*intr*) (of geese and some other birds or animals) to utter rapid cackling noises ▷ *n* **3** rapid and indistinct speech or noises [c17: from Middle Dutch *gabbelen*, of imitative origin] > 'gabbler *n*

gabbro ('gæbrəʊ) *n, pl* **-bros** a dark coarse-grained basic plutonic igneous rock consisting of plagioclase feldspar, pyroxene, and often olivine [c19: from Italian, probably from Latin *glaber* smooth, bald] > gab'broic *or* ,gabbro'itic *adj*

gabby ('gæbɪ) *adj* **-bier, -biest** *informal* inclined to chatter; talkative

Gaberones (,gæbə'rəʊnɛs) *n* the former name for Gaborone

Gabès ('gɑːbɛs; *French* gabɛs) *n* **1** a port in E Tunisia. Pop: 116 000 (2005 est) **2 Gulf of Gabès** an inlet of the Mediterranean on the E coast of Tunisia ▷ Arabic name: Qabis

gabfest ('gæbfɛst) *n informal, chiefly US & Canadian* **1** prolonged gossiping or conversation **2** an informal gathering for conversation [c19: from GAB¹ + FEST]

gabion ('geɪbɪən) *n* **1** a cylindrical metal container filled with stones, used in the construction of underwater foundations **2** a wickerwork basket filled with stones or earth, used (esp formerly) as part of a fortification [c16: from French: basket, from Italian *gabbione*, from *gabbia* cage, from Latin *cavea*; see CAGE]

gable ('geɪbᵊl) *n* **1** the triangular upper part of a wall between the sloping ends of a pitched roof (**gable roof**) **2** a triangular ornamental feature in the form of a gable, esp as used over a door or window **3** the triangular wall on both ends of a gambrel roof [C14: Old French *gable*, probably from Old Norse *gafl*; related to Old English *geafol* fork, Old High German *gibil* gable] > **'gabled** *adj* > **'gable-ˌlike** *adj*

Gable ('geɪbᵊl) *n* (**William**) **Clark**. 1901–60, US film actor. His films include *It Happened One Night* (1934), *San Francisco* (1936), *Gone with the Wind* (1939), *Mogambo* (1953), and *The Misfits* (1960)

gable end *n* the end wall of a building on the side which is topped by a gable

Gabo ('gɑːbəʊ, -bɒ) *n* **Naum** (naʊm), original name *Naum Neemia Pevsner*. 1890–1977, US sculptor, born in Russia: a leading constructivist

Gabon (gəˈbɒn; *French* gabɔ̃) *n* a republic in W central Africa, on the Atlantic: settled by the French in 1839; made part of the French Congo in 1888; became independent in 1960; almost wholly forested. Official language: French. Religion: Christian majority; significant animist minority. Currency: franc. Capital: Libreville. Pop: 1 352 000 (2004 est). Area: 267 675 sq km (103 350 sq miles)

Gabonese (ˌgæbəˈniːz) *adj* **1** of or relating to Gabon or its inhabitants ▷ *n* **2** a native or inhabitant of Gabon

gaboon (gəˈbuːn) *n* the dark mahogany-like wood from a western and central African burseraceous tree, *Aucoumea klaineana*, used in plywood, for furniture, and as a veneer [C20: altered from GABON]

gaboon viper *n* a large venomous viper, *Bitis gabonica*, that occurs in African rainforests. It has brown and purple markings and hornlike projections on its snout

Gabor (gəˈbɔː) *n* **Dennis**. 1900–79, British electrical engineer, born in Hungary. He invented holography: Nobel prize for physics 1971

Gaborone (ˌhæbəˈrəʊnɪ) *n* the capital of Botswana (since 1964), in the extreme southeast. Pop: 186 007 (2001). Former name: **Gaberones**

Gabriel[1] ('geɪbrɪəl) *n Bible* one of the archangels, the messenger of good news (Daniel 8:16–26; Luke 1:11–20, 26–38)

Gabriel[2] (*French* gabriel) *n* **Jacques-Ange** (ʒakɑ̃ʒ). 1698–1782, French architect: designed the Petit Trianon at Versailles

Gabrieli (*Italian* gabriˈɛli) *or* **Gabrielli** *n* **1 Andrea** (anˈdrɛːa). 1520–86, Italian organist and composer; chief organist of St Mark's, Venice **2** his nephew, **Giovanni** (dʒoˈvanni). 1558–1612, Italian organist and composer

gaby ('geɪbɪ) *n, pl* **-bies** *archaic or dialect* a simpleton [C18: of unknown origin]

gad (gæd) *vb* **gads**, **gadding**, **gadded 1** (*intr*; often foll by *about* or *around*) to go out in search of pleasure, esp in an aimless manner; gallivant ▷ *n* **2** carefree adventure (esp in the phrase *on* or *upon the gad*) [C15: back formation from obsolete *gadling* companion, from Old English, from *gæd* fellowship; related to Old High German *gatuling*] > **'gadder** *n*

Gad (gæd) *n Old Testament* **1 a** Jacob's sixth son, whose mother was Zilpah, Leah's maid **b** the Israelite tribe descended from him **c** the territory of this tribe, lying to the east of the Jordan and extending southwards from the Sea of Galilee **2** a prophet and admonisher of David (I Samuel 22; II Samuel 24)

gadabout ('gædəˌbaʊt) *n informal* a person who restlessly seeks amusement

Gadarene ('gædəˌriːn) *adj* relating to or engaged in a headlong rush [C19: via Late Latin from Greek *Gadarēnos*, of Gadara (Palestine), alluding to the Biblical Gadarene swine (Matthew 8:28ff.)]

Gaddafi *or* **Qaddafi** (gəˈdɑːfɪ) *n* **Mu'ammar Muhammad al-** ('məʊəˌmɑː æl). born 1942, Libyan army officer and statesman; head of state from 1969

gadfly ('gædˌflaɪ) *n, pl* **-flies 1** any of various large dipterous flies, esp the horsefly, that annoy livestock by sucking their blood **2** a constantly irritating or harassing person [C16: from GAD[2] (sting) + FLY[2]]

gadget ('gædʒɪt) *n* **1** a small mechanical device or appliance **2** any object that is interesting for its ingenuity or novelty rather than for its practical use [C19: perhaps from French *gâchette* lock catch, trigger,

diminutive of *gâche* staple] > **'gadgety** *adj*

gadgetry ('gædʒɪtrɪ) *n* **1** gadgets collectively **2** use of or preoccupation with gadgets and their design

gado-gado ('gɑːdəʊˈgɑːdəʊ) *n* an Indonesian dish of cooked mixed vegetables and hard-boiled eggs served with a peanut sauce [Bahasa Indonesia]

gadolinite ('gædəlɪˌnaɪt) *n* a rare brown or black mineral consisting of a silicate of iron, beryllium, and yttrium in monoclinic crystalline form. Formula: $2BeO.FeO.Y_2O_3.2SiO_2$. Also called: **ytterbite** [C19: named after Johan *Gadolin* (1760–1852), Finnish mineralogist]

gadolinium (ˌgædəˈlɪnɪəm) *n* a ductile malleable silvery-white ferromagnetic element of the lanthanide series of metals: occurs principally in monazite and bastnaesite. Symbol: Gd; atomic no: 64; atomic wt: 157.25; valency: 3; relative density: 7.901; melting pt: 1313±°C; boiling pt: 3273°C (approx.) [C19: New Latin, from GADOLINITE] > ˌgado'linic *adj*

gadroon *or* **godroon** (gəˈdruːn) *n* **1** a moulding composed of a series of convex flutes and curves joined to form a decorative pattern, used esp as an edge to silver articles **2** *architect* a carved ornamental moulding having a convex cross section [C18: from French *godron*, perhaps from Old French *godet* cup, goblet, drinking vessel] > ga'drooned *or* go'drooned *adj*

Gadsden Purchase ('gædzdən) *n* an area of about 77 000 sq km (30 000 sq miles) in present-day Arizona and New Mexico, bought by the US from Mexico for 10 million dollars in 1853. The purchase was negotiated by James Gadsden (1788–1858), US diplomat

gadwall ('gædˌwɔːl) *n, pl* **-walls** *or* **-wall** a duck, *Anas strepera*, related to the mallard. The male has a grey body and black tail [C17: of unknown origin]

gadzooks (gædˈzuːks) *interj archaic* a mild oath [C17: perhaps from *God's hooks* (the nails of the cross), from *Gad* archaic euphemism for God]

Gaea ('dʒiːə) *n Greek myth* a variant of **Gaia**

Gael (geɪl) *n* a person who speaks a Gaelic language, esp a Highland Scot or an Irishman [C19: from Gaelic *Gaidheal*; related to Old Irish *goidel*, Old Welsh *gwyddel* Irishman] > **'Gaeldom** *n*

Gaelic ('geɪlɪk, 'gæl-) *n* **1** any of the closely related languages of the Celts in Ireland, Scotland, or (formerly) the Isle of Man ▷ *adj* **2** of, denoting, or relating to the Celtic people of Ireland, Scotland, or the Isle of Man or their language or customs

Gaelic coffee *n* another name for **Irish coffee**

Gaeltacht ('gɛːltəxt) *or* **Gaedhealtacht** ('geɪlˌtæxt, 'gæl-) *n* any of the regions in Ireland in which Irish Gaelic is the vernacular speech. The form *Gaeltacht* is sometimes also used to mean the region of Scotland in which Scottish Gaelic is spoken [C20: from Irish Gaelic]

gaff[1] (gæf) *n* **1** *angling* a stiff pole with a stout prong or hook attached for landing large fish **2** *nautical* a boom hoisted aft of a mast to support a gaffsail **3** a metal spur fixed to the leg of a gamecock ▷ *vb* (*tr*) **4** *angling* to hook or land (a fish) with a gaff **5** *slang* to cheat; hoax [C13: from French *gaffe*, from Provençal *gaf* boathook]

gaff[2] (gæf) *n* **1** *slang* foolish talk; nonsense **2** **blow the gaff** *Brit slang* to divulge a secret **3 stand the gaff** *slang, chiefly US & Canadian* to endure ridicule, difficulties, etc [C19: of unknown origin]

gaffe (gæf) *n* a social blunder, esp a tactless remark [C19: from French]

gaffer ('gæfə) *n* **1** an old man, esp one living in the country: often used affectionately or patronizingly **2** *informal, chiefly Brit* a boss, foreman, or owner of a factory, mine, etc **3** the senior electrician on a television or film set [C16: alteration of GODFATHER]

gag[1] (gæg) *vb* **gags**, **gagging**, **gagged 1** (*tr*) to stop up (a person's mouth), esp with a piece of cloth, etc, to prevent him or her from speaking or crying out **2** (*tr*) to suppress or censor (free expression, information, etc) **3** to retch or cause to retch **4** (*intr*) to struggle for breath; choke **5** (*tr*) to hold (the jaws) of (a person or animal) apart with a surgical gag **6** (*tr*) to apply a gag-bit to (a horse) **7 be gagging for** *or* **be gagging to** *slang* to be very eager to have or do something ▷ *n* **8** a piece of cloth, rope, etc, stuffed into or tied across the mouth **9** any restraint on or suppression of information, free speech, etc **10** a surgical device for keeping the jaws apart, as during a tonsillectomy [C15 *gaggen*; perhaps imitative of a gasping sound]

gag² (gæg) *informal* ▷ *n* **1** a joke or humorous story, esp one told by a professional comedian **2** a hoax, practical joke, etc: *he did it for a gag* ▷ *vb* gags, gagging, gagged **3** (*intr*) to tell jokes or funny stories, as comedians in nightclubs, etc **4** (often foll by *up*) *theatre* **a** to interpolate lines or business not in the actor's stage part, usually comic and improvised **b** to perform a stage jest, either spoken or based on movement [C19: perhaps special use of GAG¹]

gaga (ˈɡɑːɡɑː) *adj informal* **1** senile; doting **2** slightly crazy [C20: from French, of imitative origin]

Gagarin (*Russian* gaˈgarin) *n* **Yuri** (ˈjʊri). 1934–68, Soviet cosmonaut: made the first manned space flight (1961)

gage¹ (ɡeɪdʒ) *n* **1** something deposited as security against the fulfilment of an obligation; pledge **2** (formerly) a glove or other object thrown down to indicate a challenge to combat ▷ *vb* **3** *archaic* to stake, pledge, or wager [C14: from Old French *gage*, of Germanic origin; compare Gothic *wadi* pledge]

gage² (ɡeɪdʒ) *n* short for **greengage**

gage³ (ɡeɪdʒ) *n, vb* US a variant spelling (esp in technical senses) of **gauge**

Gage (ɡeɪdʒ) *n* **Thomas**. 1721–87, British general and governor in America; commander in chief of British forces at Bunker Hill (1775)

gaggle (ˈɡæɡəl) *vb* **1** (*intr*) (of geese) to cackle ▷ *n* **2** a flock of geese **3** *informal* a disorderly group of people **4** a gabbling or cackling sound [C14: of Germanic origin; compare Old Norse *gagl* gosling, Dutch *gaggelen* to cackle, all of imitative origin]

Gaia (ˈɡeɪə), **Gaea** or **Ge** *n* the goddess of the earth, who bore Uranus and by him Oceanus, Cronus, and the Titans [from Greek *gaia* earth]

Gaia hypothesis or **Gaia theory** (ˈɡeɪə) *n* the theory that the earth and everything on it constitutes a single self-regulating living entity

gaiety (ˈɡeɪətɪ) *n, pl* **-ties 1** the state or condition of being merry, bright, or lively **2** festivity; merrymaking ● USAGE See at **gay**

Gaillard Cut (ɡɪlˈjɑːd, ˈɡeɪləd) *n* the SE section of the Panama Canal, cut through Culebra Mountain. Length: about 13 km (8 miles). Former name: Culebra Cut [C19: named after David Du Bose *Gaillard* (1859–1913), US army engineer in charge of the work]

gaillardia (ɡeɪˈlɑːdɪə) *n* any plant of the North American genus *Gaillardia*, having ornamental flower heads with yellow or red rays and purple discs: family *Asteraceae* (composites) [C19: from New Latin, named after *Gaillard* de Marentonneau, 18th-century French amateur botanist]

gaily (ˈɡeɪlɪ) *adv* **1** in a lively manner; cheerfully **2** with bright colours; showily

gain (ɡeɪn) *vb* **1** (*tr*) to acquire (something desirable); obtain **2** (*tr*) to win in competition: *to gain the victory* **3** to increase, improve, or advance: *the car gained speed; the shares gained in value* **4** (*tr*) to earn (a wage, living, etc) **5** (*intr*; usually foll by *on* or *upon*) **a** to get nearer (to) or catch up (on) **b** to get farther away (from) **6** (*tr*) (esp of ships) to get to; reach: *the steamer gained port* **7** (of a timepiece) to operate too fast, so as to indicate a time ahead of the true time or to run fast by a specified amount: *this watch gains; it gains ten minutes a day* **8** gain ground to make progress or obtain an advantage **9** gain time **a** to obtain extra time by a delay or postponement **b** (of a timepiece) to operate too fast ▷ *n* **10** something won, acquired, earned, etc; profit; advantage **11** an increase in size, amount, etc **12** the act of gaining; attainment; acquisition **13** Also called: amplification *electronics* the ratio of the output signal of an amplifier to the input signal, usually measured in decibels [C15: from Old French *gaaignier*, of Germanic origin; related to Old High German *weidenen* to forage, hunt]

gainer (ˈɡeɪnə) *n* **1** a person or thing that gains **2** Also called: **full gainer** a type of dive in which the diver leaves the board facing forward and completes a full

backward somersault to enter the water feet first with his back to the diving board

gainful (ˈɡeɪnfʊl) *adj* profitable; lucrative: *gainful employment* ▷ **ˈgainfully** *adv* ▷ **ˈgainfulness** *n*

gainly (ˈɡeɪnlɪ) *obsolete, or dialect adj* **1** graceful or well-formed; shapely ▷ *adv* **2** conveniently or suitably ▷ **ˈgainliness** *n*

gainsay (ɡeɪnˈseɪ) *vb* **-says, -saying, -said** (*tr*) *archaic or literary* to deny (an allegation, a statement, etc); contradict [C13 *gainsaien*, from *gain-* AGAINST + *saien* to SAY¹] ▷ **gainˈsayer** *n*

Gainsborough (ˈɡeɪnzbərə, -brə) *n* **Thomas**. 1727–88, English painter, noted particularly for his informal portraits and for his naturalistic landscapes

'gainst or **gainst** (ɡɛnst, ɡeɪnst) *prep poetic* short for **against**

Gaiseric (ˈɡaɪzərɪk) *n* same as **Genseric**

gait (ɡeɪt) *n* **1** manner of walking or running; bearing **2** (used esp of horses and dogs) the pattern of footsteps at various speeds, as the walk, trot, canter, etc, each pattern being distinguished by a particular rhythm and footfall ▷ *vb* **3** (*tr*) to teach (a horse) a particular gait [C16: variant of GATE¹]

gaiter (ˈɡeɪtə) *n* **1** a cloth or leather covering for the leg or ankle buttoned on one side and usually strapped under the foot **2** Also called: **spat** a similar covering extending from the ankle to the instep **3** a waterproof covering for the ankle worn by climbers and walkers to prevent snow, mud, or gravel entering over the top of the boot [C18: from French *guêtre*, probably of Germanic origin and related to WRIST] ▷ **ˈgaiterless** *adj*

Gaitskell (ˈɡeɪtskɪl) *n* **Hugh** (**Todd Naylor**). 1906–63, British politician; leader of the Labour Party (1955–63)

Gaius (ˈɡaɪəs) or **Caius** *n* **1** ?110–?180 AD, Roman jurist. His *Institutes* were later used as the basis for those of Justinian **2** Gaius Caesar. See **Caligula**

gal (ɡæl) *n slang* a girl

gal. or **gall.** *abbreviation* gallon

Gal. *abbreviation Bible* Galatians

gala (ˈɡɑːlə, ˈɡeɪlə) *n* **1 a** a celebration; festive occasion **b** (*as modifier*): *a gala occasion* **2** *chiefly Brit* a sporting occasion involving competitions in several events: *a swimming gala* [C17: from French or Italian, from Old French *gale* pleasure, from Old French *galer* to make merry, probably of Germanic origin; compare GALLANT]

galactic (ɡəˈlæktɪk) *adj* **1** of or relating to a galaxy, esp the Galaxy: *the galactic plane* **2** *med* of or relating to milk [C19: from Greek *galaktikos*; see GALAXY]

galactic halo *n astronomy* a spheroidal aggregation of globular clusters, individual stars, dust, and gas that surrounds the Galaxy

galactic plane *n* the plane passing through the spiral arms of the Galaxy

galago (ɡəˈlɑːɡəʊ) *n, pl* **-gos** another name for **bushbaby** [C19: from New Latin, perhaps from Wolof *golokh* monkey]

galah (ɡəˈlɑː) *n* **1** an Australian cockatoo, *Kakatoe roseicapilla*, having grey wings, back, and crest and a pink body **2** *Austral slang* a fool or simpleton [C19: from a native Australian language]

Galahad (ˈɡæləˌhæd) *n* **1** Sir Galahad (in Arthurian legend) the most virtuous knight of the Round Table, destined to regain the Holy Grail; son of Lancelot and Elaine **2** a pure or noble man

galantine (ˈɡælənˌtiːn) *n* a cold dish of meat or poultry, which is boned, cooked, stuffed, then pressed into a neat shape and glazed [C14: from Old French, from Medieval Latin *galatina*, probably from Latin *gelātus* frozen, set; see GELATINE]

Galápagos Islands (ɡəˈlæpəɡəs; *Spanish* ɡaˈlapaɣɔs) *pl n* a group of 15 islands in the Pacific west of Ecuador, of which they form a province: discovered (1535) by the Spanish; main settlement on San Cristóbal. Pop: 18 640 (2001). Area: 7844 sq km (3028 sq miles)

Galashiels (ˌɡæləˈʃiːlz) *n* a town in SE Scotland, in central Scottish Borders. Pop: 14 361 (2001)

Galata (ˈɡælətə) *n* a port in NW Turkey, a suburb and the chief business section of Istanbul

Galatea (ˌɡæləˈtɪə) *n Greek myth* a statue of a maiden

brought to life by Aphrodite in response to the prayers of the sculptor Pygmalion, who had fallen in love with his creation

Galaţi (*Romanian* ga'latsj) *n* an inland port in SE Romania, on the River Danube. Pop: 251 000 (2005 est)

Galatia (gə'leɪʃə, -ʃɪə) *n* an ancient region in central Asia Minor, conquered by Gauls 278–277 BC: later a Roman province

Galatian (gə'leɪʃən, -ʃɪən) *adj* **1** of or relating to Galatia or its inhabitants ▷ *n* **2** a native or inhabitant of Galatia

galaxy ('gæləksɪ) *n, pl* **-axies** **1** any of a vast number of star systems held together by gravitational attraction in an asymmetric shape (an **irregular galaxy**) or, more usually, in a symmetrical shape (a **regular galaxy**), which is either a spiral or an ellipse **2** a splendid gathering, esp one of famous or distinguished people [C14 (in the sense: the Milky Way), from Medieval Latin *galaxia*, from Latin *galaxias*, from Greek, from *gala* milk; related to Latin *lac* milk]

Galaxy ('gæləksɪ) *n* the Galaxy the spiral galaxy, approximately 100 000 light years in diameter, that contains the solar system about three fifths of the distance from its centre

Galba ('gælbə) *n* **Servius Sulpicius** ('sɜːvɪəs sʌl'pɪʃəs). ?3 BC–69 AD, Roman emperor (68–69) after the assassination of Nero

galbanum ('gælbənəm) *n* a bitter aromatic gum resin extracted from any of several Asian umbelliferous plants of the genus *Ferula*, esp *F. galbaniflua*, and used in incense and medicinally as a counterirritant [C14: from Latin, from Greek *khalbanē*, from Hebrew *helbenāh*]

Galbraith (gæl'breɪθ) *n* **John Kenneth.** 1908–2006, US economist and diplomat born in Canada; author of *The Affluent Society* (1958), *The New Industrial State* (1967), and *The Culture of Contentment* (1992) ▷ **Gal'braithian** *adj*

gale (geɪl) *n* **1** a strong wind, specifically one of force seven to ten on the Beaufort scale or from 45 to 90 kilometres per hour **2** (*often plural*) a loud outburst, esp of laughter **3** *archaic, poetic* a gentle breeze [C16: of unknown origin]

galea ('geɪlɪə) *n, pl* **-leae** (-lɪ,iː) a part or organ shaped like a helmet or hood, such as the petals of certain flowers [C18: from Latin: helmet] ▷ '**gale,ate** or '**gale,ated** *adj* ▷ '**galei,form** *adj*

Galen ('geɪlən) *n* Latin name *Claudius Galenus*. ?130–?200 AD, Greek physician, anatomist, and physiologist. He codified existing medical knowledge and his authority continued until the Renaissance

galena (gə'liːnə) *or* **galenite** (gə'liːnaɪt) *n* a grey mineral, found in hydrothermal veins. It is the chief source of lead. Composition: lead sulphide. Formula: PbS. Crystal structure: cubic [C17: from Latin: lead ore, dross left after melting lead]

Galenic (geɪ'lɛnɪk, gə-) *adj* of or relating to Galen or his teachings or methods

Galerius (gə'lɛərɪəs) *n* full name *Gaius Galerius Valerius Maximianus*. ?250–311 AD, Eastern Roman Emperor (305–311): noted for his persecution of Christians

Galicia *n* **1** (gə'lɪʃɪə, -'lɪʃə) a region of E central Europe on the N side of the Carpathians, now in SE Poland and Ukraine **2** (*Spanish* ga'liθja) an autonomous region and former kingdom of NW Spain, on the Bay of Biscay and the Atlantic. Pop: 1 969 000 (2003 est)

Galician (gə'lɪʃɪən, -ʃən) *adj* **1** of or relating to Galicia in E central Europe **2** of or relating to Galicia in NW Spain ▷ *n* **3** a native or inhabitant of either Galicia **4** the Romance language or dialect of Spanish Galicia, sometimes regarded as a dialect of Spanish, although historically it is more closely related to Portuguese

Galilean¹ (,gælɪ'liːən) *n* **1** a native or inhabitant of Galilee **2** a the Galilean an epithet of Jesus Christ (?4 BC–?29 AD), the founder of Christianity **b** (*often plural*) a Christian ▷ *adj* **3** of Galilee

Galilean² (,gælɪ'leɪən) *adj* of or relating to Galileo Galilei

galilee ('gælɪ,liː) *n* a porch or chapel at the entrance to some medieval churches and cathedrals in England

Galilee ('gælɪ,liː) *n* **1** Sea of Galilee Also called: **Lake Tiberias, Lake Kinneret** a lake in NE Israel, 209 m (686 ft) below sea level, through which the River Jordan

flows. Area: 165 sq km (64 sq miles) **2** a northern region of Israel: scene of Christ's early ministry

Galileo (,gælɪ'leɪəʊ) *n* full name *Galileo Galilei*. 1564–1642, Italian mathematician, astronomer, and physicist. He discovered the isochronism of the pendulum and demonstrated that falling bodies of different weights descend at the same rate. He perfected the refracting telescope, which led to his discovery of Jupiter's satellites, sunspots, and craters on the moon. He was forced by the Inquisition to recant his support of the Copernican system

galingale ('gælɪŋ,geɪl) *or* **galangal** *n* a European cyperaceous plant, *Cyperus longus*, with rough-edged leaves, reddish spikelets of flowers, and aromatic roots [C13: from Old French *galingal*, from Arabic *khalanjān*, from Chinese *kaoliang-chiang*, from *Kaoliang* district in Guangdong province + *chiang* ginger]

galiot *or* **galliot** ('gælɪət) *n* **1** a small swift galley formerly sailed on the Mediterranean **2** a shallow-draught ketch formerly used along the coasts of Germany and the Netherlands [C14: from Old French *galiote*, from Italian *galeotta*, from Medieval Latin *galea* GALLEY]

galipot *or* **gallipot** ('gælɪ,pɒt) *n* a resin obtained from several species of pine, esp from the S European *Pinus pinaster* [C18: from French, of unknown origin]

gall¹ (gɔːl) *n* **1** *informal* impudence **2** bitterness; rancour **3** something bitter or disagreeable **4** *physiol* an obsolete term for **bile¹** **5** an obsolete term for **gall bladder** [from Old Norse, replacing Old English *gealla*; related to Old High German *galla*, Greek *kholē*]

gall² (gɔːl) *n* **1** a sore on the skin caused by chafing **2** something that causes vexation or annoyance: *a gall to the spirits* **3** irritation; exasperation ▷ *vb* **4** *pathol* to abrade (the skin, etc) as by rubbing **5** (*tr*) to irritate or annoy; vex [C14: of Germanic origin; related to Old English *gealla* sore on a horse, and perhaps to GALL¹]

gall³ (gɔːl) *n* an abnormal outgrowth in plant tissue caused by certain parasitic insects, fungi, bacteria, or mechanical injury [C14: from Old French *galle*, from Latin *galla*]

gall. *or* **gal.** *abbreviation* gallon

gallant ('gælənt) *adj* **1** brave and high-spirited; courageous and honourable; dashing: *a gallant warrior* **2** (gə'lænt, 'gælənt) (of a man) attentive to women; chivalrous **3** imposing; dignified; stately: *a gallant ship* **4** *archaic* showy in dress ▷ *n* ('gælənt, gə'lænt) *archaic* **5** a woman's lover or suitor **6** a dashing or fashionable young man, esp one who pursues women **7** a brave, high-spirited, or adventurous man ▷ *vb* (gə'lænt, 'gælənt) *rare* **8** (when *intr*, usually foll by *with*) to court or flirt (with) **9** (*tr*) to attend or escort (a woman) [C15: from Old French *galant*, from *galer* to make merry, from *gale* enjoyment, pleasure, of Germanic origin; related to Old English *wela* WEAL²] ▷ '**gallantly** *adv* ▷ '**gallantness** *n*

gallantry ('gæləntrɪ) *n, pl* **-ries** **1** conspicuous courage, esp in war: *the gallantry of the troops* **2** polite attentiveness to women **3** a gallant action, speech, etc

gall bladder *n* a muscular pear-shaped sac, lying underneath the right lobe of the liver, that stores bile and ejects it into the duodenum through the common bile duct

Galle ('gɔːl) *n* a port in SW Sri Lanka; along with other coastal settlements, it suffered badly in the Indian Ocean tsunami of December 2004. Pop: 90 270 (2001)

galleass *or* **galliass** ('gælɪ,æs) *n* *nautical* a three-masted lateen-rigged galley used as a warship in the Mediterranean from the 15th to the 18th centuries [C16: from French *galleasse*, from Italian *galeazza*, from *galea* GALLEY]

galleon ('gælɪən) *n* *nautical* a large sailing ship having three or more masts, lateen-rigged on the after masts and square-rigged on the foremast and mainmast, used as a warship or trader from the 15th to the 18th centuries [C16: from Spanish *galeón*, from French *galion*, from Old French *galie* GALLEY]

gallery ('gælərɪ) *n, pl* **-leries** **1** a room or building for exhibiting works of art **2** a covered passageway open on one side or on both sides **3** a a balcony running along or around the inside wall of a church, hall, etc **b** a covered balcony, sometimes with columns on the outside **4** *theatre* an upper floor that projects from the rear over the main floor and contains the cheapest seats **b** the seats there **c** the audience seated there **5** a long narrow room, esp one used for a specific purpose: *a shooting gallery* **6** *chiefly US* a building or room where articles are sold at auction **7** an underground passage, as in a mine, the burrow of an animal, etc **8** *theatre* a narrow raised platform at the side or along the back of the stage for the use of technicians and stagehands **9** (in a TV studio) a glass-fronted soundproof room high up to one side of the studio looking into it. One gallery is used by the director and an assistant and one is for lighting, etc **10** *nautical* a balcony or platform at the quarter or stern of a ship, sometimes used as a gun emplacement **11** a small ornamental metal or wooden balustrade or railing on a piece of furniture, esp one surrounding the top of a desk, table, etc **12** any group of spectators, as at a golf match **13** **play to the gallery** to try to gain popular favour, by crude appeals [c15: from Old French *galerie*, from Medieval Latin *galeria*, probably from *galilea* GALILEE, a porch or chapel at entrance to medieval church] > **'galleried** *adj*

galley ('gælɪ) *n* **1** any of various kinds of ship propelled by oars or sails used in ancient or medieval times as a warship or as a trader **2** the kitchen of a ship, boat, or aircraft **3** any of various long rowing boats **4** *printing* **a** (in hot-metal composition) a tray open at one end for holding composed type **b** short for **galley proof** [c13: from Old French *galie*, from Medieval Latin *galea*, from Greek *galaia*, of unknown origin; the sense development apparently is due to the association of a galley or slave ship with a ship's kitchen and hence with a hot furnace, trough, printer's tray, etc]

galley proof *n* a printer's proof, esp one taken on a long strip of paper from type in a galley, used to make corrections before the matter has been split into pages. Often shortened to: **galley**

galley slave *n* **1** a criminal or slave condemned to row in a galley **2** *informal* a drudge

gallfly ('gɔːlˌflaɪ) *n*, *pl* -flies any of several small insects that produce galls in plant tissues, such as the gall wasp and gall midge

Gallia ('gælɪə) *n* the Latin name of **Gaul**

galliard ('gæljəd) *n* **1** a spirited dance in triple time for two persons, popular in the 16th and 17th centuries **2** a piece of music composed for this dance ▷ *adj* **3** *archaic* lively; spirited [c14: from Old French *gaillard* valiant, perhaps of Celtic origin]

gallic¹ ('gælɪk) *adj* of or containing gallium in the trivalent state [c18: from GALL(IUM) + -IC]

gallic² ('gælɪk) *adj* of, relating to, or derived from plant galls [c18: from French *gallique*; see GALL³]

Gallic ('gælɪk) *adj* **1** of or relating to France **2** of or relating to ancient Gaul or the Gauls

gallic acid *n* a colourless crystalline compound obtained from tannin: used as a tanning agent and in making inks, paper, and pyrogallol; 3,4,5-trihydroxybenzoic acid. Formula: $C_6H_2(OH)_3COOH$ [c18: from French *gallique*; see GALL³]

Gallicism ('gælɪˌsɪzəm) *n* a word or idiom borrowed from French

Gallicize *or* **Gallicise** ('gælɪˌsaɪz) *vb* to make or become French in attitude, language, etc > **,Galli'zation** *or* **,Gallici'sation** *n* > **'Galli,cizer** *or* **'Galli,ciser** *n*

galligaskins *or* **gallygaskins** (,gælɪ'gæskɪnz) *pl n* **1** loose wide breeches or hose, esp as worn by men in the 17th century **2** leather leggings, as worn in the 19th century [c16: from obsolete French *garguesques*, from Italian *grechesco* Greek, from Latin *Graecus*]

gallimaufry (,gælɪ'mɔːfrɪ) *n*, *pl* -fries a jumble; hotchpotch [c16: from French *galimafrée* ragout, hash, of unknown origin]

gallinacean (,gælɪ'neɪʃən) *n* any gallinaceous bird

gallinaceous (,gælɪ'neɪʃəs) *adj* **1** of, relating to, or belonging to the *Galliformes*, an order of birds, including domestic fowl, pheasants, grouse, etc, having a heavy rounded body, short bill, and strong legs **2** of, relating

to, or resembling the domestic fowl [c18: from Latin *gallīnāceus*, from *gallīna* hen]

Gallinas Point (gɑː'jiːnəs) *n* a cape in NE Colombia: the northernmost point of South America

galling ('gɔːlɪŋ) *adj* **1** irritating, exasperating, or bitterly humiliating **2** *obsolete* rubbing painfully; chafing > **'gallingly** *adv*

gallinule ('gælɪˌnjuːl) *n* any of various aquatic birds of the genera *Porphyrio* and *Porphyrula*, typically having a dark plumage, red bill, and a red shield above the bill: family *Rallidae* (rails) [c18: from New Latin *Gallīnula* genus name, from Late Latin: pullet, chicken, from Latin *gallīna* hen]

galliot ('gælɪət) *n* a variant spelling of **galiot**

Gallipoli (gə'lɪpəlɪ) *n* **1** a peninsula in NW Turkey, between the Dardanelles and the Gulf of Saros: scene of a costly but unsuccessful Allied campaign in 1915 **2** a port in NW Turkey, at the entrance to the Sea of Marmara: historically important for its strategic position. Pop: 22 000 (latest est) ▷ Turkish name: Gelibolu

gallipot ('gælɪˌpɒt) *n* a small earthenware pot used by pharmacists as a container for ointments, etc [c16: probably from GALLEY + POT¹; so called because imported in galleys]

gallium ('gælɪəm) *n* a silvery metallic element that is liquid for a wide temperature range. It occurs in trace amounts in some ores and is used in high-temperature thermometers and low-melting alloys. **Gallium arsenide** is a semiconductor. Symbol: Ga; atomic no: 31; atomic wt: 69.723; valency: 2 or 3; relative density: 5.904; melting pt: 29.77°C; boiling pt: 2205°C [c19: from New Latin, from Latin *gallus* cock, translation of French *coq* in the name of its discoverer, *Lecoq* de Boisbaudran, 19th-century French chemist]

gallivant, galivant *or* **galavant** ('gælɪˌvænt) *vb* (*intr*) to go about in search of pleasure; gad about [c19: perhaps whimsical modification of GALLANT]

Gällivare (*Swedish* 'jeliˌvaːrə) *n* a town in N Sweden, within the Arctic Circle: iron mines. Pop: 19 191 (2004 est)

galliwasp ('gælɪˌwɒsp) *n* any lizard of the Central American genus *Diploglossus*, esp *D. monotropis* of the Caribbean: family *Anguidae* [c18: of unknown origin]

gallnut ('gɔːlˌnʌt) *or* **gall-apple** *n* a type of plant gall that resembles a nut

Gallo- ('gæləʊ) *combining form* denoting Gaul or France: *Gallo-Roman* [from Latin *Gallus* a Gaul]

gallon ('gælən) *n* **1** Also called: **imperial gallon** *Brit* a unit of capacity equal to 277.42 cubic inches. 1 Brit gallon is equivalent to 1.20 US gallons or 4.55 litres **2** a US a unit of capacity equal to 231 cubic inches. 1 US gallon is equivalent to 0.83 imperial gallon or 3.79 litres **3** (*plural*) great quantities [c13: from Old Northern French *galon* (Old French *jalon*), perhaps of Celtic origin]

gallonage ('gælənɪdʒ) *n* a capacity measured in gallons

galloon (gə'luːn) *n* a narrow band of cord, embroidery, silver or gold braid, etc, used on clothes and furniture [c17: from French *galon*, from Old French *galonner* to trim with braid, of unknown origin] > **gal'looned** *adj*

gallop ('gæləp) *vb* -lops, -loping, -loped **1** (*intr*) (of a horse or other quadruped) to run fast with a two-beat stride in which all four legs are off the ground at once **2** to ride (a horse, etc) at a gallop **3** (*intr*) to move, read, talk, etc, rapidly; hurry ▷ *n* **4** the fast two-beat gait of horses and other quadrupeds **5** an instance of galloping [c16: from Old French *galoper*, of uncertain origin] > **'galloper** *n*

Gallovidian (,gæləʊ'vɪdɪən) *n* **1** a native or inhabitant of Galloway ▷ *adj* **2** of or relating to Galloway ▷ Also called: Galwegian

Galloway ('gæləˌweɪ) *n* **1** an area of SW Scotland, on the Solway Firth: consists of the former counties of Kirkcudbright and Wigtown, now part of Dumfries and Galloway; in the west is a large peninsula, the **Rhinns of Galloway**, with the **Mull of Galloway**, a promontory, at the south end of it (the southernmost point of Scotland). Related adjs: **Gallovidian, Galwegian 2** a breed of hardy beef cattle, usually black, originally bred in Galloway

gallows ('gæləʊz) *n*, *pl* **-lowses** *or* **-lows** **1** a wooden structure usually consisting of two upright posts with a crossbeam from which a rope is suspended, used for hanging criminals **2** any timber structure resembling this, such as (in Australia and New Zealand) a frame for hoisting up the bodies of slaughtered cattle **3** the **gallows** execution by hanging [C13: from Old Norse *galgi*, replacing Old English *gealga*; related to Old High German *galgo*]

gallows bird *n informal* a person considered deserving of hanging

gallows humour *n* sinister and ironic humour

gallows tree *or* **gallow tree** *n* another name for **gallows** (sense 1)

gallsickness ('gɔːl,sɪknɪs) *n* a disease of cattle and sheep, caused by infection with rickettsiae of the genus *Anaplasma*, resulting in anaemia and jaundice. Also called: **anaplasmosis**

gallstone ('gɔːl,stəʊn) *n pathol* a small hard concretion of cholesterol, bile pigments, and lime salts, formed in the gall bladder or its ducts. Also called: **bilestone**

Gallup ('gæləp) *n* **George Horace**. 1901–84, US statistician: devised the Gallup Poll; founded the American Institute of Public Opinion (1935) and its British counterpart (1936)

Gallup Poll ('gæləp) *n* a sampling by the American Institute of Public Opinion or its British counterpart of the views of a representative cross section of the population, used esp as a means of forecasting voting

gall wasp *n* any small solitary wasp of the family *Cynipidae* and related families that produces galls in plant tissue, which provide shelter and food for the larvae

galoot *or* **galloot** (gə'luːt) *n slang, chiefly US* a clumsy or uncouth person [C19: of unknown origin]

galop ('gæləp) *n* **1** a 19th-century couple dance in quick duple time **2** a piece of music composed for this dance ▷ Also called: **gallopade** [C19: from French; see GALLOP]

galore (gə'lɔː) *determiner* (*immediately postpositive*) in great numbers or quantity: *there were daffodils galore in the park* [C17: from Irish Gaelic *go leór* to sufficiency]

galoshes *or* **goloshes** (gə'lɒʃɪz) *pl n* (*sometimes singular*) a pair of waterproof overshoes [C14 (in the sense: wooden shoe): from Old French *galoche*, from Late Latin *gallicula* Gallic shoe]

Galsworthy ('gɔːlz,wɜːðɪ) *n* **John**. 1867–1933, English novelist and dramatist, noted for *The Forsyte Saga* (1906–28): Nobel prize for literature 1932

Galt (gɔːlt) *n* **John**. 1779–1839, Scottish novelist, noted for his ironic humour, esp in *Annals of the Parish* (1821), *The Provost* (1822), and *The Entail* (1823)

Galton ('gɔːltən) *n* **Sir Francis**. 1822–1911, English explorer and scientist, a cousin of Charles Darwin, noted for his researches in heredity, meteorology, and statistics. He founded the study of eugenics and the theory of anticyclones

galumph (gə'lʌmpf, -'lʌmf) *vb* (*intr*) *informal* to leap or move about clumsily or joyfully [C19 (coined by Lewis Carroll): probably a blend of GALLOP + TRIUMPH]

Galvani (*Italian* gal'vaːni) *n* **Luigi** (lu'iːdʒi). 1737–98, Italian physiologist: observed that muscles contracted on contact with dissimilar metals. This led to the galvanic cell and the electrical theory of muscle control by nerves

galvanic (gæl'vænɪk) *or* **galvanical** *adj* **1** Also called: **voltaic** of, producing, or concerned with an electric current, esp a direct current produced chemically: *a galvanic cell* **2** *informal* resembling the effect of an electric shock; convulsive, startling, or energetic: *galvanic reflexes* ▷ gal'vanically *adv*

galvanism ('gælvə,nɪzəm) *n* **1** *obsolete* electricity, esp when produced by chemical means as in a cell or battery **2** *med* treatment involving the application of electric currents to tissues [C18: via French from Italian *galvanismo*, after Luigi Galvani (1737–98), Italian physiologist]

galvanize *or* **galvanise** ('gælvə,naɪz) *vb* (*tr*) **1** to stimulate to action; excite; startle **2** to cover (iron, steel, etc) with a protective zinc coating by dipping into

molten zinc or by electrodeposition **3** to stimulate by application of an electric current ▷ *n* **4** *Caribbean* galvanized iron, usually in the form of corrugated sheets as used in roofing > ,galvani'zation *or* ,galvani'sation *n* > 'galva,nizer *or* 'galva,niser *n*

galvanized iron *or* **galvanised iron** *n building trades* iron, esp a sheet of corrugated iron, covered with a protective coating of zinc

galvano- *combining form* indicating a galvanic current: *galvanometer*

galvanometer (,gælvə'nɒmɪtə) *n* any sensitive instrument for detecting or measuring small electric currents > galvanometric (,gælvənəʊ'mɛtrɪk, gæl,vænə-) *or* ,galvano'metrical *adj* > ,galvano'metrically *adv* > ,galva'nometry *n*

Galway ('gɔːlweɪ) *n* **1** a county of W Republic of Ireland, in S Connacht, on **Galway Bay** and the Atlantic: it has a deeply indented coastline and many offshore islands, including the Aran Islands. County town: Galway. Pop: 209 077 (2002). Area: 5939 sq km (2293 sq miles) **2** a port in W Republic of Ireland, county town of Co Galway, on Galway Bay: important fisheries (esp for salmon). Pop: 66 163 (2002) **3** a breed of sheep with long wool, originally from W Ireland. Former name: **Roscommon**

Galwegian (gæl'wiːdʒən) *n* **1** another word for **Gallovidian** (sense 1) **2** a native or inhabitant of the town or county of Galway in W Republic of Ireland ▷ *adj* **3** another word for **Gallovidian** (sense 2) [C18: influenced by *Norway, Norwegian*]

gam (gæm) *n slang* a leg, esp a woman's shapely leg [C18: probably from Old Northern French *gambe* or Lingua Franca *gambe*; see JAMB]

Gama ('gaːmə) *n* **Vasco da** ('væskəʊ də). ?1469–1524, Portuguese navigator, who discovered the sea route from Portugal to India around the Cape of Good Hope (1498)

gambado[1] (gæm'beɪdəʊ) *n*, *pl* **-dos** *or* **-does** **1** either of two leather holders for the feet attached to a horse's saddle like stirrups **2** either of a pair of leggings [C17: from Italian *gamba* leg, from Late Latin: leg, hoof; see JAMB]

gambado[2] (gæm'beɪdəʊ) *or* **gambade** (gæm'beɪd, -'baːd) *n*, *pl* **-bados**, **-badoes** *or* **-bades** **1** *dressage* another word for **curvet 2** a leap or gambol; caper [C19: from French *gambade* spring (of a horse), ultimately from Spanish or Italian *gamba* leg]

Gambetta (gæm'betə; *French* gãbɛta) *n* **Léon** (leɔ̃). 1838–82, French statesman; prime minister (1881–82). He organized resistance during the Franco-Prussian War (1870–71) and was a founder of the Third Republic (1871)

Gambia ('gæmbɪə) *n* **The Gambia** a republic in W Africa, entirely surrounded by Senegal except for an outlet to the Atlantic: sold to English merchants by the Portuguese in 1588; became a British colony in 1843; gained independence and became a member of the Commonwealth in 1965; joined with Senegal to form the Confederation of Senegambia (1982–89): consists of a strip of land about 16 km (10 miles) wide, on both banks of the **Gambia River,** extending inland for about 480 km (300 miles). Official language: English. Religion: Muslim majority. Currency: dalasi. Capital: Banjul. Pop: 1 462 000 (2004 est). Area: 11 295 sq km (4361 sq miles)

Gambian ('gæmbɪən) *adj* **1** of or relating to Gambia or its inhabitants ▷ *n* **2** a native or inhabitant of Gambia

gambier *or* **gambir** ('gæmbɪə) *n* an astringent resinous substance obtained from a rubiaceous tropical Asian woody climbing plant, *Uncaria gambir* (or *U. gambier*): used as an astringent and tonic and in tanning [C19: from Malay]

Gambier Islands ('gæmbɪə) *pl n* a group of islands in the S Pacific Ocean, in French Polynesia. Chief settlement: Rikitéa. Pop: 1097 (2002). Area: 30 sq km (11 sq miles)

gambit ('gæmbɪt) *n* **1** *chess* an opening move in which a chessman, usually a pawn, is sacrificed to secure an advantageous position **2** an opening comment, manoeuvre, etc, intended to secure an advantage or promote a point of view [C17: from French, from Italian *gambetto* a tripping up, from *gamba* leg]

gamble ('gæmbᵊl) *vb* **1** (*intr*) to play games of chance to win money **2** to risk or bet (money) on the outcome of an event, sport, etc **3** (*intr*; often foll by *on*) to act with the expectation of: *to gamble on its being a sunny day* **4** (often foll by *away*) to lose by or as if by betting; squander ▷ *n* **5** a risky act or venture **6** a bet, wager, or other risk or chance taken for possible monetary gain [c18: probably variant of GAME¹] > 'gambler *n* > 'gambling *n*

gamboge (gæm'bəʊdʒ, -'buːʒ) *n* **1 a** a gum resin used as the source of a yellow pigment and as a purgative **b** the pigment made from this resin **2 gamboge tree** any of several tropical Asian trees of the genus *Garcinia*, esp *G. hanburyi*, that yield this resin: family *Clusiaceae* **3** a strong yellow colour [c18: from New Latin *gambaugium*, from CAMBODIA] > gam'bogian *adj*

gambol ('gæmbᵊl) *vb* **-bols, -bolling, -bolled** or *US* **-bols, -boling, -boled 1** (*intr*) to skip or jump about in a playful manner; frolic ▷ *n* **2** a playful antic; frolic [c16: from French *gambade*; see JAMB]

gambrel ('gæmbrəl) *n* **1** the hock of a horse or similar animal **2** a frame of wood or metal shaped like a horse's hind leg, used by butchers for suspending carcasses of meat **3** short for **gambrel roof** [c16: from Old Northern French *gamberel*, from *gambe* leg]

gambrel roof *n* **1** *chiefly Brit* a hipped roof having a small gable at both ends **2** *chiefly US & Canadian* a roof having two slopes on both sides, the lower slopes being steeper than the upper. See **mansard** (sense 1) ▷ Sometimes shortened to: **gambrel** > 'gambrel-,roofed *adj*

game¹ (geɪm) *n* **1** an amusement or pastime; diversion **2** a contest with rules, the result being determined by skill, strength, or chance **3** a single period of play in such a contest, sport, etc **4** the score needed to win a contest **5** a single contest in a series; match **6** (*plural; often capital*) an event consisting of various sporting contests, esp in athletics: *Olympic Games; Highland Games* **7** equipment needed for playing certain games **8** short for **computer game 9** style or ability in playing a game: *he is a keen player but his game is not good* **10** a scheme, proceeding, etc, practised like a game: *the game of politics* **11** an activity undertaken in a spirit of levity; joke: *marriage is just a game to him* **12** wild animals, including birds and fish, hunted for sport, food, or profit **b** (*as modifier*): *game laws* **13** the flesh of such animals, used as food: generally taken not to include fish **14** an object of pursuit; quarry; prey (esp in the phrase **fair game**) **15** *informal* work or occupation **16** *informal* a trick, strategy, or device: *I can see through your little game* **17** *obsolete* pluck or courage; bravery **18** *slang, chiefly Brit* prostitution (esp in the phrase **on the game**) **19** **give the game away** to reveal one's intentions or a secret **20 make game of** or **make a game of** to make fun of; ridicule **21 off one's game** playing badly **22 on one's game** playing well **23 play the game** to behave fairly or in accordance with rules **24 the game is up** there is no longer a chance of success ▷ *adj* **25** *informal* full of fighting spirit; plucky; brave **26 game as Ned Kelly** or **as game as Ned Kelly** *Austral informal* extremely brave; indomitable **27** (usually foll by *for*) *informal* prepared or ready; willing: *I'm game for a try* ▷ *vb* **28** (*intr*) to play games of chance for money, stakes, etc; gamble [Old English *gamen*; related to Old Norse *gaman*, Old High German *gaman* amusement] > 'game,like *adj* > 'gamely *adv* > 'gameness *n*

game² (geɪm) *adj* a less common word for **lame¹**: *game leg* [c18: probably from Irish *cam* crooked]

gamecock ('geɪm,kɒk) *n* a cock bred and trained for fighting. Also called: **fighting cock**

game fish *n* any fish providing sport for the angler

gamekeeper ('geɪm,kiːpə) *n* a person employed to take care of game and wildlife, as on an estate > 'game,keeping *n*

gamelan ('gæmɪ,læn) *n* a type of percussion orchestra common in the East Indies [from Javanese]

game laws *pl n* laws governing the hunting and preservation of game

game plan *n* **1** a strategy **2** a plan of campaign, esp in politics

game point *n tennis, squash, badminton* a stage at which winning one further point would enable one player or side to win a game

gamer ('geɪmə) *n* a person who plays computer games or participates in a role-playing game

gamesmanship ('geɪmzmən,ʃɪp) *n informal* the art of winning games or defeating opponents by clever or cunning practices without actually cheating > 'gamesman *n*

gamesome ('geɪmsəm) *adj* full of merriment; sportive > 'gamesomely *adv* > 'gamesomeness *n*

gamester ('geɪmstə) *n* a person who habitually plays games for money; gambler

gametangium (,gæmɪ'tændʒɪəm) *n, pl* **-gia** (-dʒɪə) *biology* an organ or cell in which gametes are produced, esp in algae and fungi [c19: New Latin, from GAMETO- + Greek *angeion* vessel] > ,game'tangial *adj*

gamete ('gæmiːt, gə'miːt) *n* a haploid germ cell, such as a spermatozoon or ovum, that fuses with another germ cell during fertilization [c19: from New Latin, from Greek *gametē* wife, from *gamos* marriage] > ga'metal or gametic (gə'mɛtɪk) *adj*

gamete intrafallopian transfer (,ɪntrəfə'ləʊpɪən) *n* the full name for GIFT

game theory *n* mathematical theory concerned with the optimum choice of strategy in situations involving a conflict of interest. Also called: **theory of games** > ,game-,theo'retic *adj*

gameto- *or sometimes before a vowel* **gamet-** *combining form* gamete: *gametocyte*

gametophyte (gə'miːtəʊ,faɪt) *n* the plant body, in species showing alternation of generations, that produces the gametes. See **sporophyte** > gametophytic (,gæmɪtəʊ'fɪtɪk) *adj*

gamey or **gamy** ('geɪmɪ) *adj* **gamier, gamiest 1** having the smell or flavour of game, esp high game **2** *informal* spirited; plucky; brave > 'gamily *adv* > 'gaminess *n*

gamin ('gæmɪn; *French* gamɛ̃) *n* a street urchin; waif [from French]

gamine ('gæmiːn; *French* gamin) *n* **a** a slim and boyish girl or young woman; an elfish tomboy **b** (*as modifier*): *a gamine style of haircut* [from French]

gaming ('geɪmɪŋ) *n* **a** gambling on games of chance **b** (*as modifier*): *gaming house; gaming losses*

gamma ('gæmə) *n* **1** the third letter in the Greek alphabet (Γ, γ), a consonant, transliterated as *g*. When double, it is transcribed and pronounced as *ng* **2** the third highest grade or mark, as in an examination **3** a unit of magnetic field strength equal to 10^{-5} oersted. 1 gamma is equivalent to $0.795\ 775 \times 10^{-3}$ ampere per metre **4** *photog, television* the numerical value of the slope of the characteristic curve of a photographic emulsion or television camera; a measure of the contrast reproduced in a photographic or television image **5** (*modifier*) **a** involving or relating to photons of very high energy: *a gamma detector* **b** relating to one of two or more allotropes or crystal structures of a solid: *gamma iron* **c** relating to one of two or more isomeric forms of a chemical compound, esp one in which a group is attached to the carbon atom next but one to the atom to which the principal group is attached [c14: from Greek; related to Hebrew *gīmel* third letter of the Hebrew alphabet (probably: camel)]

gamma distribution *n statistics* a continuous two-parameter distribution from which the chi-square and exponential distributions are derived, written Gamma (α, β), where α and β are greater than zero, and defined in terms of the gamma function

gamma globulin *n* any of a group of proteins in blood plasma that includes most known antibodies

gamma hydroxybutyrate (,gæməhaɪ,drɒksɪ'bjuːtɪreɪt) *n* a substance that occurs naturally in the brain, used medically as a sedative but also as a recreational drug and alleged aphrodisiac: known as 'liquid ecstasy' when mixed with alcohol. Abbreviation: **GHB**

gamma knife *n* an machine that uses radiation with extreme accuracy to destroy abnormal tissue, esp in the brain

gamma radiation *n* **1** electromagnetic radiation

emitted by atomic nuclei; the wavelength is generally in the range 1×10^{-10} to 2×10^{-13} metres **2** electromagnetic radiation of very short wavelength emitted by any source, esp that portion of the electromagnetic spectrum with a wavelength less than about 1×10^{-11} metres

gamma-ray astronomy *n* the investigation of cosmic gamma rays, such as those from quasars

gamma-ray burst *n* *astronomy* an intense but short-lived burst of gamma rays from an unknown celestial source. First detected in 1970, they have since been found to be widely distributed in the sky

gamma rays *pl n* streams of gamma radiation

gamma stock *n* any of the third rank of active securities on the London Stock Exchange. Prices displayed by market makers are given as an indication rather than an offer to buy or sell

gammer ('gæmə) *n* *rare, chiefly Brit* a dialect word for an old woman: now chiefly humorous or contemptuous. See **gaffer** (sense 1) [c16: probably alteration of GODMOTHER or GRANDMOTHER]

gammon¹ ('gæmən) *n* **1** a cured or smoked ham **2** the hindquarter of a side of bacon, cooked either whole or cut into large rashers [c15: from Old Northern French *gambon*, from *gambe* leg; see GAMBREL]

gammon² ('gæmən) *n* **1** a double victory in backgammon in which one player throws off all his pieces before his opponent throws any **2** *archaic* the game of backgammon ▷ *vb* **3** (*tr*) to score a gammon over [c18: probably special use of Middle English *gamen* GAME¹]

gammon³ ('gæmən) *Brit informal* ▷ *n* **1** deceitful nonsense; humbug ▷ *vb* **2** to deceive (a person) [c18: perhaps special use of GAMMON²] > **'gammoner** *n*

gammy ('gæmɪ) *adj* **-mier, -miest** *Brit slang* (esp of the leg) malfunctioning, injured, or lame; game [c19: from Shelta *gyamyath* bad, altered form of Irish *cam* crooked; see GAME²]

gamo- or before a vowel **gam-** *combining form* **1** indicating sexual union or reproduction: *gamogenesis* **2** united or fused: *gamopetalous* [from Greek *gamos* marriage]

gamopetalous (,gæməʊ'petələs) *adj* (of flowers) having petals that are united or partly united, as the primrose. Also called: **sympetalous**. Compare **polypetalous**

gamp (gæmp) *n* *Brit informal* an umbrella [c19: after Mrs Sarah *Gamp*, a nurse in Dickens' *Martin Chuzzlewit*, who carried a faded cotton umbrella]

gamut ('gæmət) *n* **1** entire range or scale, as of emotions **2** *music* **a** a scale, esp (in medieval theory) one starting on the G on the bottom line of the bass staff **b** the whole range of notes **3** *physics* the range of chromaticities that can be obtained by mixing three colours [c15: from Medieval Latin, changed from *gamma ut*, from *gamma*, the lowest note of the hexachord as established by Guido d'Arezzo + *ut* (now, *doh*), the first of the notes of the scale *ut, re, mi, fa, sol, la, si*, derived from a Latin hymn to St John: *Ut queant laxis resonare fibris, Mira gestorum famuli tuorum, Solve polluti labi reatum, Sancte Iohannes*]

-gamy *n combining form* denoting marriage or sexual union: *bigamy* [from Greek *-gamia*, from *gamos* marriage] > **-gamous** *adj combining form* [from Greek *gamos*; see -CAMY]

ganache (gə'næʃ) *n* a smooth mixture of chocolate and cream, used in cakes, truffles, and chocolates [c20: from French]

Gance (*French* gãs) *n* **Abel** (abɛl). 1889–1981, French film director, whose works include *J'accuse* (1919, 1937) and *Napoléon* (1927), which introduced the split-screen technique

Gand (gã) *n* the French name for **Ghent**

gander ('gændə) *n* **1** a male goose **2** *informal* a quick look (esp in the phrase **take** or **have a gander**) **3** *informal* a simpleton [Old English *gandra, ganra*; related to Low German and Dutch *gander* and to GANNET]

Gandhi ('gændɪ) *n* **1 Indira** (**Priyadarshini**) (ɪn'dɪərə, 'ɪndərə), daughter of Jawaharlal Nehru. 1917–84, Indian stateswoman; prime minister of India (1966–77; 1980–84); assassinated **2 Mohandas Karamchand** (,məʊhən'dʌs ,kʌrəm'tʃʌnd), known as *Mahatma Gandhi*.

1869–1948, Indian political and spiritual leader and social reformer. He played a major part in India's struggle for home rule and was frequently imprisoned by the British for organizing acts of civil disobedience. He advocated passive resistance and hunger strikes as means of achieving reform, campaigned for the untouchables, and attempted to unite Muslims and Hindus. He was assassinated by a Hindu extremist **3 Rajiv** (ræ'dʒiːv), son of Indira Gandhi. 1944–91, Indian statesman; prime minister of India (1984–89); assassinated

Gandhian ('gændɪən) *adj* **1** of or relating to Mohandas Karamchand Gandhi or his ideas ▷ *n* **2** a follower of Gandhi or his ideas

G & S *abbreviation for* Gilbert and Sullivan

Gandzha (*Russian* gan'dʒa) or **Gäncä** *n* a city in NW Azerbaijan: annexed by the Russians in 1804; centre of a cotton-growing region. Pop: 314 000 (2005 est). Former names: **Yelisavetpol, Kirovabad**

Ganesh (gæ'niːʃ) *n* the Hindu god of prophecy, represented as having an elephant's head

gang¹ (gæŋ) *n* **1** a group of people who associate together or act as an organized body, esp for criminal or illegal purposes **2** an organized group of workmen **3** a herd of buffaloes or elks or a pack of wild dogs **4** *NZ* a group of shearers who travel to different shearing sheds, shearing, classing, and baling wool **5 a** a series of similar tools arranged to work simultaneously in parallel **b** (*as modifier*): *a gang saw* ▷ *vb* **6** to form into, become part of, or act as a gang **7** (*tr*) *electronics* to mount (two or more components, such as variable capacitors) on the same shaft, permitting adjustment by a single control ▷ See also **gang up** [Old English *gang* journey; related to Old Norse *gangr*, Old High German *gang*, Sanskrit *jangha* foot] > **ganged** *adj*

gang² (gæŋ) *vb* *Scot* to go [Old English *gangan* to GO¹]

gang³ (gæŋ) *n* a variant spelling of **gangue**

gangbang ('gæŋ,bæŋ) *slang* ▷ *n* **1** an instance of sexual intercourse between one woman and several men one after the other, esp against her will ▷ *vb* **2** (*tr*) to force (a woman) to take part in a gangbang **3** (*intr*) to take part in a gangbang ▷ Also called: **gangshag** ('gæŋ,ʃæg)

gang-banger *n* *US slang* a member of a street gang > **'gang-,banging** *n*

ganger ('gæŋə) *n* *chiefly Brit* the foreman of a gang of labourers

Ganges ('gændʒiːz) *n* the great river of N India and central Bangladesh: rises in two headstreams in the Himalayas and flows southeast to Allahabad, where it is joined by the Jumna; continues southeast into Bangladesh, where it enters the Bay of Bengal in a great delta; the most sacred river to Hindus, with many places of pilgrimage, esp Varanasi. Length: 2507 km (1557 miles)

Gangetic (gæn'dʒetɪk) *adj* of or relating to the river Ganges

gangland ('gæŋ,lænd, -lənd) *n* the criminal underworld

gangling ('gæŋglɪŋ) or **gangly** ('gæŋglɪ) *adj* tall, lanky, and awkward in movement [perhaps related to GANGREL; see GANG²]

ganglion ('gæŋglɪən) *n, pl* **-glia** (-glɪə) or **-glions 1** an encapsulated collection of nerve-cell bodies, usually located outside the brain and spinal cord **2** any concentration of energy, activity, or strength **3** a cystic tumour on a tendon sheath or joint capsule [c17: from Late Latin: swelling, from Greek: cystic tumour] > **'ganglial** or **'gangliar** *adj* > ,**gangli'onic** or **'gangli,ated** *adj*

gangplank ('gæŋ,plæŋk) or **gangway** *n* *nautical* a portable bridge for boarding and leaving a vessel at dockside

gangrel ('gæŋgrəl, 'gæŋrəl) *n* *Scot archaic, or literary* **1** a wandering beggar **2** a child just able to walk; toddler [c16: from Old English *gangan* to GO¹]

gangrene ('gæŋgriːn) *n* **1** death and decay of tissue as the result of interrupted blood supply, disease, or injury **2** moral decay or corruption ▷ *vb* **3** to become or cause to become affected with gangrene [c16: from Latin *gangraena*, from Greek *gangraina* an eating sore; related to Greek *gran* to gnaw] > **gangrenous** ('gæŋgrɪnəs) *adj*

g

gang saw n a saw having several parallel blades making simultaneous cuts ▷ **gang sawyer** n

gangsta rap ('gæŋstə) n a style of rap music, usually characterized by lyrics about Black street gangs in the US, often with violent, nihilistic, and misogynistic themes [C20: phonetic rendering of GANGSTER] ▷ **gangsta rapper** n

gangster ('gæŋstə) n a member of an organized gang of criminals, esp one who resorts to violence

gangsterism ('gæŋstərɪzəm) n the culture of belonging to organized gangs of criminals, esp involving violence

Gangtok ('gʌŋtɒk) n a town in NE India: capital of Sikkim state. Pop: 29 162 (2001)

gangue or **gang** (gæŋ) n valueless and undesirable material, such as quartz in small quantities, in an ore [C19: from French gangue, from German Gang vein of metal, course; see GANG¹]

gang up vb (often foll by on or against) informal to combine in a group (against)

gangway ('gæŋˌweɪ) n 1 an opening in a ship's side to take a gangplank 2 another word for **gangplank** 3 Brit an aisle between rows of seats 4 Also called: **logway** chiefly US a ramp for logs leading into a sawmill 5 a main passage in a mine 6 temporary planks over mud or earth, as on a building site ▷ sentence substitute 7 clear a path!

ganister or **gannister** ('gænɪstə) n 1 a highly refractory siliceous sedimentary rock occurring beneath coal seams: used for lining furnaces 2 a similar material synthesized from ground quartz and fireclay [C19: of unknown origin]

gannet ('gænɪt) n 1 any of several heavily built marine birds of the genus Morus (or Sula), having a long stout bill and typically white plumage with dark markings: family Sulidae, order Pelecaniformes (pelicans, cormorants, etc). See also **booby** (sense 3) 2 slang a gluttonous or greedy person [Old English ganot; related to Old High German gannazzo gander]

ganoid ('gænɔɪd) adj 1 (of the scales of certain fishes) consisting of an inner bony layer and an outer layer of an enamel-like substance (ganoin) 2 denoting fishes, including the sturgeon and bowfin, having such scales ▷ n 3 a ganoid fish [C19: from French ganoïde, from Greek ganos brightness + -OID]

Gansu ('gæn'su:) or **Kansu** n a province of NW China, between Tibet and Inner Mongolia: mountainous, with desert regions; forms a corridor, the Old Silk Road, much used in early and medieval times for trade with Turkestan, India, and Persia. Capital: Lanzhou. Pop: 26 030 000 (2003 est). Area: 366 500 sq km (141 500 sq miles)

gantlet¹ ('gæntlɪt, 'gɔ:nt-) n 1 a section of a railway where two tracks overlap 2 US a variant spelling of **gauntlet²** [C17 gantlope (modern spelling influenced by GAUNTLET¹), from Swedish gatlopp, literally: passageway, from gata way (related to GATE³) + lop course]

gantlet² ('gæntlɪt, 'gɔ:nt-) n a variant of **gauntlet¹**

gantry ('gæntrɪ) or **gauntry** n, pl **-tries** 1 a bridgelike framework used to support a travelling crane, signals over a railway track, etc 2 Also called: **gantry scaffold** the framework tower used to attend to a large rocket on its launching pad 3 a supporting framework for a barrel or cask 4 a the area behind a bar where bottles, esp spirit bottles mounted in optics, are kept for use or display b the range or quality of the spirits on view: this pub's got a good gantry [C16 (in the sense: wooden platform for barrels): from Old French chantier, from Medieval Latin cantārius, changed from Latin cantherius supporting frame, pack ass; related to Greek kanthēlios pack ass]

Gantt chart (gænt) n a chart showing, in horizontal lines, activity planned to take place during specified periods, which are indicated in vertical bands [C20: named after Henry L. Gantt (1861–1919), US management consultant]

Ganymede ('gænɪˌmiːd) n classical myth a beautiful Trojan youth who was abducted by Zeus to Olympus and made the cupbearer of the gods

Gao ('gɑːəʊ, gaʊ) n a town in E Mali, on the River Niger: a small river port. Pop: 57 978 (2005 est)

gaol (dʒeɪl) n, vb Brit a variant spelling of: **jail** ▷ **'gaoler** n

Gao Xingjian (gaʊ 'ʃɪŋ'dʒjæn) n born 1940, Chinese dramatist, novelist, and dissident, living in France from 1987; his works include the play Chezhan (Bus Stop, 1983) and the novel Lingshan (Soul Mountain, 1989): Nobel prize for literature 2000

Gaoxiong (ˌjaʊə'ʃɒŋ) n a variant transliteration of the Chinese name for **Kaohsiung**

gap (gæp) n 1 a break or opening in a wall, fence, etc 2 a break in continuity; interruption; hiatus: there is a serious gap in the accounts 3 a break in a line of hills or mountains affording a route through 4 chiefly US a gorge or ravine 5 a divergence or difference; disparity: there is a gap between his version of the event and hers; the generation gap 6 electronics a a break in a magnetic circuit that increases the inductance and saturation point of the circuit b See **spark gap** 7 bridge a gap, close a gap, fill a gap or stop a gap to remedy a deficiency ▷ vb **gaps**, **gapping**, **gapped** 8 (tr) to make a breach or opening in [C14: from Old Norse gap chasm; related to gapa to GAPE, Swedish gap, Danish gab open mouth, opening] ▷ **'gapless** adj ▷ **'gappy** adj

gape (geɪp) vb (intr) 1 to stare in wonder or amazement, esp with the mouth open 2 to open the mouth wide, esp involuntarily, as in yawning or hunger 3 to be or become wide open: the crater gaped under his feet ▷ n 4 the act of gaping 5 a wide opening; breach 6 the width of the widely opened mouth of a vertebrate 7 a stare or expression of astonishment ▷ See also **gapes** [C13: from Old Norse gapa; related to Middle Dutch gapen, Danish gabe] ▷ **'gaper** n ▷ **'gaping** adj

gapes (geɪps) n (functioning as singular) 1 a disease of young domestic fowl, characterized by gaping or gasping for breath and caused by parasitic worms (**gapeworms**) 2 informal a fit of yawning ▷ **'gapy** adj

gapper ('gæpə) n Brit a person who is taking a gap year

gap year n Brit a year's break taken by a student between leaving school and starting further education

gar (gɑː) n, pl **gar** or **gars** short for **garpike**, **garfish**

garage ('gærɑːʒ, -rɪdʒ) n 1 a building or part of a building used to house a motor vehicle 2 a commercial establishment in which motor vehicles are repaired, serviced, bought, and sold, and which usually also sells motor fuels 3 a a rough-and-ready style of rock music b a type of disco music based on soul ▷ vb 4 (tr) to put into, keep in, or take to a garage [C20: from French, from garer to dock (a ship), from Old French: to protect, from Old High German warōn; see BEWARE]

garage band n a rough-and-ready amateurish rock group [perhaps from the practice of such bands rehearsing in a garage]

garage sale n a sale of personal belongings or household effects held at a person's home, usually in the garage

garb (gɑːb) n 1 clothes, esp the distinctive attire of an occupation or profession: clerical garb 2 style of dress; fashion 3 external appearance, covering, or attire ▷ vb 4 (tr) to clothe or cover; attire [C16: from Old French garbe graceful contour, from Old Italian garbo grace, probably of Germanic origin] ▷ **'garbless** adj

garbage ('gɑːbɪdʒ) n 1 worthless, useless, or unwanted matter 2 Also called: **rubbish** discarded or waste matter; refuse 3 computing invalid data 4 informal nonsense [C15: probably from Anglo-French garbelage removal of discarded matter, of uncertain origin; compare Old Italian garbuglio confusion]

garbage collection n computing a systems routine for eliminating invalid or out-of-date data and releasing storage locations

garble ('gɑːbʰl) vb (tr) 1 to jumble (a story, quotation, etc), esp unintentionally 2 to distort the meaning of (an account, text, etc), as by making misleading omissions; corrupt 3 rare to select the best part of ▷ n 4 a the act of garbling b garbled matter [C15: from Old Italian garbellare to strain, sift, from Arabic gharbala from ghirbāl sieve, from Late Latin crībellum small sieve, from crībrum sieve] ▷ **'garbler** n

Garbo ('gɑːbəʊ) n **Greta** ('grɛtə), real name Greta Lovisa Gustafson. 1905–90, US film actress, born in Sweden. Her films include *Grand Hotel* (1932), *Queen Christina* (1933), *Anna Karenina* (1935), *Camille* (1936), and *Ninotchka* (1939)

garboard ('gɑːˌbɔːd) *n nautical* the bottommost plank of a vessel's hull. Also called: **garboard plank, garboard strake** [c17: from Dutch *gaarboord*, probably from Middle Dutch *gaderen* to GATHER + *boord* BOARD]

garbology (gɑːˈbɒlədʒɪ) *n* the study of the contents of domestic dustbins to analyse the consumption patterns of households [c20: from GARB(AGE) + OLOGY]
> gar'bologist *n*

García Lorca (*Spanish* gar'θia 'lɔrka) *n* See **Lorca¹**

García Márquez (*Spanish* gar'sia 'markes) *n* **Gabriel.** born 1928, Colombian novelist and short-story writer. His novels include *One Hundred Years of Solitude* (1967), *The Autumn of the Patriarch* (1977), *Love in the Time of Cholera* (1984), and *News of a Kidnapping* (1996). Nobel prize for literature 1982

garçon ('gɑːsɒn; *French* garsɔ̃) *n* a waiter or male servant, esp if French [c19: from Old French *gars* lad, probably of Germanic origin]

Gard (*French* gar) *n* a department of S France, in Languedoc-Roussillon region. Capital: Nîmes. Pop: 648 522 (2003 est). Area: 5881 sq km (2294 sq miles)

garda ('gɑːrdə) *n, pl* **gardaí** ('gɑːrdiː) a member of **Garda Síochána**

Garda ('gɑːdə) *n* Lake Garda a lake in N Italy: the largest lake in the country. Area: 370 sq km (143 sq miles)

Garda Síochána ('gɑːrdə ʃɪəˈxɑːnə) *n* the police force of the Republic of Ireland [c20: from Irish Gaelic *garda* guard + *síochána* of the peace, from *síocháin* peace]

garden ('gɑːdᵊn) *n* **1** *Brit* **a** an area of land, usually planted with grass, trees, flowerbeds, etc, adjoining a house. US and Canadian word: **yard** **b** (*as modifier*): *a garden chair* **2 a** an area of land used for the cultivation of ornamental plants, herbs, fruit, vegetables, trees, etc **b** (*as modifier*): *garden tools*. Related adj: **horticultural** **3** (*often plural*) such an area of land that is open to the public, sometimes part of a park: *botanical gardens* **4 a** a fertile and beautiful region **b** (*as modifier*): *a garden paradise* **5** (*modifier*) provided with or surrounded by a garden or gardens: *a garden flat* **6 lead a person up the garden path** *informal* to mislead or deceive a person ▷ *adj* **7 common** or garden *informal* ordinary; unexceptional ▷ *vb* **8** to work in, cultivate, or take care of (a garden, plot of land, etc) [c14: from Old French *gardin*, of Germanic origin; compare Old High German *gart* enclosure; see YARD² (sense 1)] > 'gardenless *adj* > 'garden-like *adj* > 'gardener *n* > 'gardening *n*

garden centre *n* a place where gardening tools and equipment, plants, seeds, etc, are sold

garden city *n* *Brit* a planned town of limited size with broad streets and spacious layout, containing trees and open spaces and surrounded by a rural belt

gardenia (gɑːˈdiːnɪə) *n* **1** any evergreen shrub or tree of the Old World tropical rubiaceous genus *Gardenia*, cultivated for their large fragrant waxlike typically white flowers **2** the flower of any of these shrubs [c18: New Latin, named after Dr Alexander *Garden* (1730–91), American botanist]

gardening leave *or* **garden leave** *n* *Brit informal* a period during which an employee who is about to leave a company continues to receive a salary but does not work

Garden of Eden *n* the full name for **Eden¹**

garderobe ('gɑːdˌrəʊb) *n archaic* a wardrobe or the contents of a wardrobe **1** a bedroom or private room **2** a privy [c14: from French, from *garder* to keep + *robe* dress, clothing; see WARDROBE]

Gardiner ('gɑːdnə) *n* **1** Sir **John Eliot.** born 1943, British conductor, noted for performances using period instruments; founded the Monteverdi Choir in 1965 and the Orchestre Révolutionnaire et Romantique in 1990 **2 Stephen.** ?1483–1555, English bishop and statesman; lord chancellor (1553–55). He opposed Protestantism, supporting the anti-Reformation policies of Mary I

Gardner ('gɑːdnə) *n* **Ava.** 1922–90, US film actress. Her films include *The Killers* (1946), *The Sun also Rises* (1957), and *The Night of the Iguana* (1964)

Garfield ('gɑːfiːld) *n* **James Abram.** 1831–81, 20th president of the US (1881); assassinated in office

garfish ('gɑːˌfɪʃ) *n, pl* -**fish** or -**fishes** **1** another name for **garpike** (sense 1) **2** an elongated European marine teleost fish, *Belone belone*, with long toothed jaws: related to the flying fishes **3** any of various marine or estuarine fish with a long needle-like lower jaw [Old English *gār* spear + FISH]

garganey ('gɑːgənɪ) *n* a small Eurasian duck, *Anas querquedula*, closely related to the mallard. The male has a white stripe over each eye [c17: from Italian dialect *garganei*, of imitative origin]

Gargantua (gɑːˈgæntjʊə) *n* a gigantic king noted for his great capacity for food and drink, in Rabelais' satire *Gargantua and Pantagruel* (1534)

gargantuan (gɑːˈgæntjʊən) *adj* (*sometimes capital*) huge; enormous

⦿ **USAGE** Some people think that *gargantuan* should only
⦿ be used to describe things connected with food: *a*
⦿ *gargantuan meal*; *his gargantuan appetite*

gargle ('gɑːgᵊl) *vb* **1** to rinse (the mouth and throat) with a liquid, esp a medicinal fluid by slowly breathing out through the liquid **2** to utter (words, sounds, etc) with the throaty bubbling noise of gargling ▷ *n* **3** the liquid used for gargling **4** the sound produced by gargling [c16: from Old French *gargouiller* to gargle, make a gurgling sound, from *gargouille* throat, perhaps of imitative origin] **5** *Brit informal* an alcoholic drink: *what was her favourite gargle?* > 'gargler *n*

gargoyle ('gɑːgɔɪl) *n* **1** a waterspout carved in the form of a grotesque face or creature and projecting from a roof gutter, esp of a Gothic church **2** any grotesque ornament or projection, esp on a building **3** a person with a grotesque appearance [c15: from Old French *gargouille* gargoyle, throat; see GARGLE] > 'gargoyled *adj*

garibaldi (ˌgærɪˈbɔːldɪ) *n Brit* a type of biscuit having a layer of currants in the centre

Garibaldi (ˌgærɪˈbɔːldɪ) *n* **Giuseppe** (dʒuˈzɛppe). 1807–82, Italian patriot; a leader of the Risorgimento. He fought against the Austrians and French in Italy (1848– 49; 1859) and, with 1000 volunteers, conquered Sicily and Naples for the emerging kingdom of Italy (1860)

garish ('gɛərɪʃ) *adj* gay or colourful in a crude or vulgar manner; gaudy [c16: from earlier *gaure* to stare + -ISH] > 'garishly *adv* > 'garishness *n*

garland ('gɑːlənd) *n* **1** a wreath or festoon of flowers, leaves, etc, worn round the head or neck or hung up **2** a representation of such a wreath, as in painting, sculpture, etc **3** a collection of short literary pieces, such as ballads or poems; miscellany or anthology **4** *nautical* a ring or grommet of rope ▷ *vb* **5** (*tr*) to deck or adorn with a garland or garlands [c14: from Old French *garlande*, perhaps of Germanic origin]

Garland ('gɑːlənd) *n* **Judy,** real name *Frances Gumm*. 1922–69, US singer and film actress. Already a child star, she achieved international fame with *The Wizard of Oz* (1939). Later films included *Meet Me in St Louis* (1944) and *A Star is Born* (1954)

garlic ('gɑːlɪk) *n* **1** a hardy widely cultivated Asian alliaceous plant, *Allium sativum*, having a stem bearing whitish flowers and bulbils **2 a** the bulb of this plant, made up of small segments (cloves) that have a strong odour and pungent taste and are used in cooking **b** (*as modifier*): *a garlic taste* **3** any of various other plants of the genus *Allium* [Old English *gārlēac*, from *gār* spear + *lēac* LEEK] > 'garlicky *adj*

garment ('gɑːmənt) *n* **1** (*often plural*) an article of clothing **2** outer covering ▷ *vb* **3** (*tr; usually passive*) to cover or clothe [c14: from Old French *garniment*, from *garnir* to equip; see GARNISH] > 'garmentless *adj*

garner ('gɑːnə) *vb* (*tr*) **1** to gather or store in or as if in a granary ▷ *n* **2** an archaic word for **granary** **3** *archaic* a place for storage or safekeeping [c12: from Old French *gernier* granary, from Latin *grānārium*, from *grānum* grain]

Garner ('gɑːnə) *n* **1 Erroll.** 1921–77, US jazz pianist and composer **2 Helen.** born 1942, Australian novelist and journalist. Her books include the novels *Monkey Grip* (1977), *The Idea of Perfection* (2002) and *The Children's Bach* (1984) and the nonfiction *The First Stone* (1995)

garnet ('gɑːnɪt) *n* any of a group of hard glassy red, yellow, or green minerals consisting of the silicates of calcium, iron, manganese, chromium, magnesium, and aluminium in cubic crystalline form: used as a gemstone and abrasive. Formula: $A_3B_2(SiO_4)_3$ where A is a divalent metal and B is a trivalent metal [c13: from Old French *grenat*, from *grenat* (adj) red, from *pome grenate* POMEGRANATE] > 'garnet-‚like *adj*

Garnett ('gɑːnɪt) *n* 1 **Constance**. 1862–1946, British translator of Russian novels 2 her son, **David**. 1892–1981, British novelist and editor. His novels include *Lady Into Fox* (1922) and *Aspects of Love* (1955)

garnish ('gɑːnɪʃ) *vb* (*tr*) 1 to decorate; trim 2 to add something to (food) in order to improve its appearance or flavour 3 *law* **a** to serve with notice of proceedings; warn **b** *obsolete* to summon to proceedings already in progress **c** to attach (a debt) 4 *slang* to extort money from ▷ *n* 5 a decoration; trimming 6 something, such as parsley, added to a dish for its flavour or decorative effect 7 *obsolete, slang* a payment illegally extorted, as from a prisoner by his jailer [c14: from Old French *garnir* to adorn, equip, of Germanic origin; compare Old High German *warnōn* to pay heed] > 'garnisher *n*

garnishee (‚gɑːnɪˈʃiː) *law* ▷ *n* 1 a person upon whom a garnishment has been served ▷ *vb* -nishees, -nisheeing, -nisheed (*tr*) 2 to attach (a debt or other property) by garnishment 3 to serve (a person) with a garnishment

garnishment ('gɑːnɪʃmənt) *n* 1 the act of garnishing 2 decoration or embellishment; garnish 3 *law* **a** a notice or warning **b** *obsolete* a summons to court proceedings already in progress **c** a notice warning a person holding money or property belonging to a debtor whose debt has been attached to hold such property until directed by the court to apply it

garniture ('gɑːnɪtʃə) *n* decoration or embellishment [c16: from French, from *garnir* to GARNISH]

Garonne (*French* garɔn) *n* a river in SW France, rising in the central Pyrenees in Spain and flowing northeast then northwest into the Gironde estuary. Length: 580 km (360 miles)

garpike ('gɑːˌpaɪk) *n* 1 Also called: **garfish, gar** any primitive freshwater elongated bony fish of the genus *Lepisosteus*, of North and Central America, having very long toothed jaws and a body covering of thick scales 2 another name for **garfish** (sense 2)

garret ('gærɪt) *n* another word for **attic** (sense 1) [c14: from Old French *garite* watchtower, from *garir* to protect, of Germanic origin; see WARY]

Garrett ('gærət) *n* **Lesley**. born 1955, British soprano; principal soprano with the English National Opera from 1984

garret window *n* a skylight that lies along the slope of the roof

Garrick ('gærɪk) *n* **David**. 1717–79, English actor and theatre manager

garrison ('gærɪsən) *n* 1 the troops who maintain and guard a base or fortified place 2 **a** the place itself **b** (*as modifier*): *a garrison town* ▷ *vb* 3 (*tr*) to station (troops) in (a fort) [c13: from Old French *garison*, from *garir* to defend, of Germanic origin; compare Old Norse *verja* to defend, Old English, Old High German *werian*]

garron ('gærən) *n* a small sturdy pony bred and used chiefly in Scotland and Ireland [c16: from Gaelic *gearran*]

garrotte, garrote *or* **garote** (gəˈrɒt) *n* 1 a Spanish method of execution by strangulation or by breaking the neck 2 the device, usually an iron collar, used in such executions 3 *obsolete* strangulation of one's victim while committing robbery ▷ *vb* (*tr*) 4 to execute by means of the garrotte 5 to strangle, esp in order to commit robbery [c17: from Spanish *garrote*, perhaps from Old French *garrot* cudgel; of obscure origin] > gar'rotter *or* ga'rotter *n*

garrulous ('gærʊləs) *adj* 1 given to constant and frivolous chatter; loquacious; talkative 2 wordy or diffuse; prolix [c17: from Latin *garrulus*, from *garrīre* to chatter] > 'garrulously *adv* > 'garrulousness, *or* garrulity (gæˈruːlɪtɪ) *n*

garryowen (‚gærɪˈəʊɪn) *n* (in rugby union) another term for **up-and-under** [c20: named after *Garryowen* RFC, Ireland]

garter ('gɑːtə) *n* 1 a band, usually of elastic, worn round

the arm or leg to hold up a shirtsleeve, sock, or stocking 2 *US & Canadian* **a** an elastic strap attached to a belt or corset having a fastener at the end, for holding up women's stockings **b** a similar fastener attached to a garter belt worn by men in order to support socks. Also called (in Britain and certain other countries): **suspender** ▷ *vb* 3 (*tr*) to fasten, support, or secure with or as if with a garter [c14: from Old Northern French *gartier*, from *garet* bend of the knee, probably of Celtic origin]

Garter ('gɑːtə) the Garter *n* 1 See **Order of the Garter** 2 (*sometimes not capital*) **a** the badge of this Order **b** membership of this Order

garter snake *n* any nonvenomous North American colubrid snake of the genus *Thamnophis*, typically marked with longitudinal stripes

garter stitch *n* knitting in which all the rows are knitted in plain stitch instead of alternating with purl rows

garth (gɑːθ) *n* 1 a courtyard surrounded by a cloister 2 *archaic* a yard or garden [c14: from Old Norse *garthr*; related to Old English *geard* YARD²]

Garvey ('gɑːvɪ) *n* **Marcus**. 1887–1940, Jamaican Black nationalist leader, active in the US He founded (1914) the Universal Negro Improvement Association and led the Back-to-Africa movement: gaoled for fraud (1925–27)

Gary ('gærɪ) *n* a port in NW Indiana, on Lake Michigan: a major world steel producer. Pop: 99 961 (2003 est)

gas (gæs) *n, pl* **gases** *or* **gasses** 1 a substance in a physical state in which it does not resist change of shape and will expand indefinitely to fill any container. If very high pressure is applied a gas may become liquid or solid, otherwise its density tends towards that of the condensed phase. See **liquid** (sense 1), **solid** (sense 1) 2 any substance that is gaseous at room temperature and atmospheric pressure 3 any gaseous substance that is above its critical temperature and therefore not liquefiable by pressure alone. See **vapour** (sense 2) 4 **a** a fossil fuel in the form of a gas, used as a source of domestic and industrial heat. See also **coal gas, natural gas b** (*as modifier*): *a gas cooker; gas fire* 5 a gaseous anaesthetic, such as nitrous oxide 6 *mining* firedamp or the explosive mixture of firedamp and air 7 the usual US, Canadian, and New Zealand word for **petrol, gasoline** 8 step on the gas *informal* **a** to increase the speed of a motor vehicle; accelerate **b** to hurry 9 a toxic or suffocating substance in suspension in air used against an enemy 10 *informal* idle talk or boasting 11 *slang* a delightful or successful person or thing: *his latest record is a gas* 12 *US* an informal name for **flatus** ▷ *vb* **gases** *or* **gasses, gassing, gassed** 13 (*tr*) to provide or fill with gas 14 (*tr*) to subject to gas fumes, esp so as to asphyxiate or render unconscious 15 (*intr*) to give off gas, as in the charging of a battery 16 (*tr*) (in textiles) to singe (fabric) with a flame from a gas burner to remove unwanted fibres 17 (*intr*; foll by *to*) *informal* to talk in an idle or boastful way (to a person) 18 (*tr*) *slang, chiefly US & Canadian* to thrill or delight [C17 (coined by J. B. van Helmont (1577–1644), Flemish chemist): modification of Greek *khaos* atmosphere] > 'gasless *adj*

gasbag ('gæsˌbæg) *informal* ▷ *n* 1 a person who talks in a voluble way, esp about unimportant matters ▷ *vb* -bags, -bagging, -bagged 2 (*intr*) Irish to talk in a voluble way, esp about unimportant matters

gas chamber *or* **gas oven** *n* an airtight room into which poison gas is introduced to kill people or animals

gas chromatography *n* a technique for analysing a mixture of volatile substances in which the mixture is carried by an inert gas through a column packed with a selective adsorbent and a detector records on a moving strip the conductivity of the gas leaving the tube. Peaks on the resulting graph indicate the presence of a particular component. Also called: gas-liquid chromatography

Gascoigne ('gæskɔɪn) *n* **Paul**, known as *Gazza*. born 1967, English footballer

Gascon ('gæskən) *n* 1 a native or inhabitant of Gascony 2 the dialect of French spoken in Gascony ▷ *adj* 3 of or relating to Gascony, its inhabitants, or their dialect of French

gasconade (ˌgæskəˈneɪd) *rare* ▷ *n* **1** boastful talk, bragging, or bluster ▷ *vb* **2** (*intr*) to boast, brag, or bluster [c18: from French *gasconnade*, from *gasconner* to chatter, boast like a Gascon] > ˌgasconˈader *n*

gas constant *n* the constant in the gas equation. It is equal to 8.31472 joules per kelvin per mole. Symbol: R Also called: universal gas constant

Gascony (ˈgæskənɪ) *n* a former province of SW France

gas-cooled reactor *n* a nuclear reactor using a gas as the coolant. In the Mark I type the coolant is carbon dioxide, the moderator is graphite, and the fuel is uranium cased in magnox. See also **advanced gas-cooled reactor**

gas-discharge tube *n electronics* any tube in which an electric discharge takes place through a gas

gaseous (ˈgæsɪəs, -ʃəs, -ʃɪəs, ˈgeɪ-) *adj* of, concerned with, or having the characteristics of a gas > ˈgaseousness *n*

gas equation *n* an equation that equates the product of the pressure and the volume of one mole of a gas to the product of its thermodynamic temperature and the **gas constant**. The equation is exact for an ideal gas and is a good approximation for real gases at low pressures. Also called: ideal gas equation, ideal gas law

gas gangrene *n* gangrene resulting from infection of a wound by anaerobic bacteria (esp *Clostridium welchii*) that cause gas bubbles and swelling in the surrounding tissues

gas giant *n* one of the four planets in our solar system that are composed chiefly of hydrogen and helium, namely Jupiter, Saturn, Uranus, and Neptune [c20: coined by James Blish (1921–75), US science fiction writer]

gas guzzler *n informal* a large car with very high petrol consumption

gash (gæʃ) *vb* **1** (*tr*) to make a long deep cut or wound in; slash ▷ *n* **2** a long deep cut or wound [c16: from Old French *garser* to scratch, wound, from Vulgar Latin *charissāre* (unattested), from Greek *kharassein* to scratch]

gasholder (ˈgæsˌhəʊldə) *n* **1** Also called: **gasometer** a large tank for storing coal gas or natural gas prior to distribution to users **2** any vessel for storing or measuring a gas

gasify (ˈgæsɪˌfaɪ) *vb* **-fies, -fying, -fied** **1** to make into or become a gas **2** to subject (coal, etc) to destructive distillation to produce gas, esp for use as a fuel > ˈgasiˌfiable *adj* > ˌgasifiˈcation *n* > ˈgasiˌfier *n*

Gaskell (ˈgæskᵊl) *n* **Mrs.** married name of *Elizabeth Cleghorn Stevenson*. 1810–65, English novelist. Her novels include *Mary Barton* (1848), an account of industrial life in Manchester, and *Cranford* (1853), a social study of a country village

gasket (ˈgæskɪt) *n* **1** a compressible packing piece of paper, rubber, asbestos, etc, sandwiched between the faces or flanges of a joint to provide a seal **2** *nautical* a piece of line used as a sail stop **3 blow a gasket** *slang* to burst out in anger [c17 (in the sense: rope lashing a furled sail): probably from French *garcette* rope's end, literally: little girl, from Old French *garce* girl, feminine of *gars* boy, servant]

gaslight (ˈgæsˌlaɪt) *n* **1** a type of lamp in which the illumination is produced by an incandescent mantle heated by a jet of gas **2** the light produced by such a lamp

gasman (ˈgæsˌmæn) *n, pl* **-men** a man employed to read household gas meters, supervise gas fittings, etc

gas mantle *n* a mantle for use in a gaslight. See **mantle** (sense 4)

gas mask *n* a mask fitted with a chemical filter to enable the wearer to breathe air free of poisonous or corrosive gases: used for military or industrial purposes. Also called (in Britain): respirator

gas meter *n* an apparatus for measuring and recording the amount of gas passed through it

gasoline or **gasolene** (ˈgæsəˌliːn) *n US & Canadian* any one of various volatile flammable liquid mixtures of hydrocarbons, mainly hexane, heptane, and octane, obtained from petroleum and used as a solvent and a fuel for internal-combustion engines. Usually petrol also contains additives such as antiknock compounds

and corrosion inhibitors. Also called (esp in Britain): petrol > **gasolinic** (ˌgæsəˈlɪnɪk) *adj*

gasometer (gæsˈɒmɪtə) *n* a nontechnical name for **gasholder**

gasp (gɑːsp) *vb* **1** (*intr*) to draw in the breath sharply, convulsively, or with effort, esp in expressing awe, horror, etc **2** (*intr*; foll by *after* or *for*) to crave **3** (*tr*; often foll by *out*) to utter or emit breathlessly ▷ *n* **4** a short convulsive intake of breath **5** a short convulsive burst of speech **6 at the last gasp a** at the point of death **b** at the last moment [c14: from Old Norse *geispa* to yawn; related to Swedish dialect *gispa*, Danish *gispe*] > ˈgaspingly *adv*

Caspar (ˈgæspə, ˈgæspɑː) *n* a variant of **Caspar**

Gasparovic (gæsˈpærəvɪtʃ) *n* **Ivan.** born 1941, Slovakian politician, president of Slovakia from 2004

Gaspé Peninsula (gæˈspeɪ; *French* gaspe) *n* a peninsula in E Canada, in SE Quebec between the St Lawrence River and New Brunswick: mountainous and wooded with many lakes and rivers. Area: about 29 500 sq km (11 400 sq miles). Also called: **the Gaspé**

gasper (ˈgɑːspə) *n* **1** a person who gasps **2** *Brit dated, slang* a cheap cigarette **3** *informal* something that shocks one or causes one to gasp in astonishment

gaspereau (ˈgæspərəʊ) *n Canadian* another name for **alewife** [from Canadian French]

gas plant *n* an aromatic white-flowered Eurasian rutaceous plant, *Dictamnus albus*, that emits a vapour capable of being ignited. Also called: burning bush, dittany, fraxinella

gas ring *n* a circular assembly of gas jets, used esp for cooking

Gassendi (*French* gasɛndi) *n* **Pierre.** 1592–1655, French physicist and philosopher, who promoted an atomic theory of matter

Gasser (ˈgæsə) *n* **Herbert Spencer.** 1888–1963, US physiologist: shared a Nobel prize for physiology or medicine (1944) with Erlanger for work on electrical signs of nervous activity

gassy (ˈgæsɪ) *adj* **-sier, -siest** **1** filled with, containing, or resembling gas **2** *informal* full of idle or vapid talk > ˈgassiness *n*

gasteropod (ˈgæstərəˌpɒd) *n, adj* a variant of **gastropod**

gas thermometer *n* a device for measuring temperature by observing the pressure of gas at a constant volume or the volume of a gas kept at a constant pressure

gastric (ˈgæstrɪk) *adj* of, relating to, near, or involving the stomach: *gastric pains*

gastric juice *n* a digestive fluid secreted by the stomach, containing hydrochloric acid, pepsin, rennin, etc

gastric ulcer *n* an ulcer of the mucous membrane lining the stomach. See **peptic ulcer**

gastritis (gæsˈtraɪtɪs) *n* inflammation of the lining of the stomach > gastritic (gæsˈtrɪtɪk) *adj*

gastro- or often before a vowel **gastr-** *combining form* stomach: *gastroenteritis; gastritis* [from Greek *gastēr*]

gastrocolic (ˌgæstrəʊˈkɒlɪk) *adj* of or relating to the stomach and colon: *gastrocolic reflex*

gastroenteritis (ˌgæstrəʊˌɛntəˈraɪtɪs) *n* inflammation of the stomach and intestines > gastroenteritic (ˌgæstrəʊˌɛntəˈrɪtɪk) *adj*

gastrointestinal (ˌgæstrəʊɪnˈtɛstɪnᵊl) *adj* of or relating to the stomach and intestinal tract

gastronome (ˈgæstrəˌnəʊm), **gastronomer** (gæsˈtrɒnəmə) or **gastronomist** *n* less common words for **gourmet**

gastronomy (gæsˈtrɒnəmɪ) *n* **1** the art of good eating **2** the type of cookery of a particular region: *the gastronomy of Provence* [c19: from French *gastronomie*, from Greek *gastronomia*, from *gastēr* stomach; see -NOMY] > ˌgastroˈnomic or ˌgastroˈnomical *adj* > ˌgastroˈnomically *adv*

gastropod (ˈgæstrəˌpɒd) or **gasteropod** *n* **1** any mollusc of the class Gastropoda, typically having a flattened muscular foot for locomotion and a head that bears stalked eyes. The class includes the snails, whelks, limpets, and slugs ▷ *adj* **2** of, relating to, or belonging to

g

the *Gastropoda* > **gastropodan** (gæs'trɒpəd°n) *adj, n* > gas'tropodous *adj*

gastroscope ('gæstrə,skəʊp) *n* a medical instrument for examining the interior of the stomach > **gastroscopic** (,gæstrə'skɒpɪk) *adj* > **gastroscopist** (gæs'trɒskəpɪst) *n* > gas'troscopy *n*

gastrula ('gæstrʊlə) *n, pl* **-las** or **-lae** (-,liː) a saclike animal embryo consisting of three layers of cells (ectoderm, mesoderm, and endoderm) surrounding a central cavity (archenteron) with a small opening (blastopore) to the exterior. See also **ectoderm, mesoderm, endoderm** [C19: New Latin: little stomach, from Greek *gastēr* belly] > 'gastrular *adj*

gas turbine *n* an internal-combustion engine in which the expanding gases emerging from one or more combustion chambers drive a turbine. A rotary compressor driven by the turbine compresses the air used for combustion, power being taken either as torque from the turbine or thrust from the expanding gases

gasworks ('gæs,wɜːks) *n* (*functioning as singular*) a plant in which gas, esp coal gas, is made

gat (gæt) *vb archaic* a past tense of **get**

gate (geɪt) *n* **1** a movable barrier, usually hinged, for closing an opening in a wall, fence, etc **2** an opening to allow passage into or out of an enclosed place **3** any means of entrance or access **4** a mountain pass or gap, esp one providing entry into another country or region **5 a** the number of people admitted to a sporting event or entertainment **b** the total entrance money received from them **6** (in a large airport) any of the numbered exits leading to the airfield or aircraft: *passengers for Paris should proceed to gate 14* **7** *horse racing* short for **starting gate 8** *electronics* **a** a logic circuit having one or more input terminals and one output terminal, the output being switched between two voltage levels determined by the combination of input signals **b** a circuit used in radar that allows only a fraction of the input signal to pass **9** the electrode region or regions in a field-effect transistor that is biased to control the conductivity of the channel between the source and drain **10 a** a component in a motion-picture camera or projector that holds each frame flat and momentarily stationary behind the lens **11** a slotted metal frame that controls the positions of the gear lever in a motor vehicle **12** *rowing* a hinged clasp to prevent the oar from jumping out of a rowlock **13** a frame surrounding the blade or blades of a saw ▷ *vb* (*tr*) **14** to provide with a gate or gates **15** *Brit* to restrict (a student) to the school or college grounds as a punishment **16** to select (part of a waveform) in terms of amplitude or time [Old English *geat*; related to Old Frisian *jet* opening, Old Norse *gat* opening, passage] > 'gateless *adj* > 'gate,like *adj*

gateau or **gâteau** ('gætəʊ) *n, pl* **-teaux** (-təʊz) any of various elaborate cakes, usually layered with cream and richly decorated [French: cake]

gate-crash *vb* to gain entry to (a party, concert, etc) without invitation or payment > 'gate-,crasher *n*

gatefold ('geɪt,fəʊld) *n* an oversize page in a book or magazine that is folded in. Also called: **foldout**

gatehouse ('geɪt,haʊs) *n* **1** a building above or beside an entrance gate to a city, university, etc, often housing a porter or guard, or (formerly) used as a fortification **2** a small house at the entrance to the grounds of a country mansion **3** a structure that houses the controls operating lock gates or dam sluices

gatekeeper ('geɪt,kiːpə) *n* **1** a person who has charge of a gate and controls who may pass through it **2** any of several Eurasian butterflies of the genus *Pyronia*, esp *P. tithonus*, having brown-bordered orange wings with a black-and-white eyespot on each forewing: family *Satyridae* **3** a manager in a large organization who controls the flow of information, esp to parent and subsidiary companies

gate-leg table or **gate-legged table** *n* a table with one or two drop leaves that are supported when in use by a hinged leg swung out from the frame

gatepost ('geɪt,pəʊst) *n* **1 a** the post on which a gate is hung **b** the post to which a gate is fastened when closed **2 between you, me, and the gatepost** confidentially

Gates (geɪts) *n* **1 Bill,** full name *William Henry Gates*. born 1955, US computer-software executive; founder (1976) of Microsoft Corporation **2 Henry Louis.** born 1950, US scholar and critic, who pioneered African-American studies in such works as *Figures in Black* (1987) **3 Horatio.** ?1728–1806, American Revolutionary general: defeated the British at Saratoga (1777)

Gateshead ('geɪts,hɛd) *n* **1** a port in NE England, in Gateshead unitary authority, Tyne and Wear: engineering works, cultural centre. Pop: 78 403 (2001) **2** a unitary authority in NE England, in Tyne and Wear. Pop: 191 000 (2003 est). Area: 142 sq km (55 sq miles)

gateway ('geɪt,weɪ) *n* **1** an entrance that may be closed by or as by a gate **2** a means of entry or access: *Mumbai, gateway to India* **3** (*modifier*) allowing entry, access, or progress to a more extreme form: *gateway drug; gateway drink* **4** *computing* hardware and software that connect incompatible computer networks, allowing information to be passed from one to another **5** a software utility that enables text messages to be sent and received over digital cellular telephone networks

Gath (gæθ) *n Old Testament* one of the five cities of the Philistines, from which Goliath came (I Samuel 17:4) and near which Saul fell in battle (II Samuel 1:20)

gather ('gæðə) *vb* **1** to assemble or cause to assemble **2** to collect or be collected gradually; muster **3** (*tr*) to learn from information given; conclude or assume **4** (*tr*) to pick or harvest (flowers, fruit, etc) **5** (*tr*; foll by *to* or *into*) to clasp or embrace: *the mother gathered the child into her arms* **6** (*tr*) to bring close (to) or wrap (around): *she gathered her shawl about her shoulders* **7** to increase or cause to increase gradually, as in force, speed, intensity, etc **8** to contract (the brow) or (of the brow) to become contracted into wrinkles; knit **9** (*tr*) to assemble (sections of a book) in the correct sequence for binding **10** (*tr*) to collect by making a selection **11** (*tr*) to prepare or make ready: *to gather one's wits* **12** to draw (material) into a series of small tucks or folds by passing a thread through it and then pulling it tight **13** (*intr*) (of a boil or other sore) to come to a head; form pus ▷ *n* **14 a** the act of gathering **b** the amount gathered **15** a small fold in material, as made by a tightly pulled stitch; tuck **16** *printing* an informal name for **section** (sense 16) [Old English *gadrian*; related to Old Frisian *gaderia*, Middle Low German *gaderen*] > 'gatherable *adj* > 'gatherer *n*

gathering ('gæðərɪŋ) *n* **1** a group of people, things, etc, that are gathered together; assembly **2** *sewing* a gather or series of gathers in material **3 a** the formation of pus in a boil **b** the pus so formed **4** *printing* an informal name for **section** (sense 16)

Gatling gun ('gætlɪŋ) *n* a hand-cranked automatic machine gun equipped with a rotating cluster of barrels that are fired in succession using brass cartridges [C19: named after R. J. *Gatling* (1818–1903), its US inventor]

gator or **gater** ('geɪtə) *n chiefly US informal* an alligator [C19]

GATT (gæt) *n acronym for* General Agreement on Tariffs and Trade: a multilateral international treaty signed in 1947 to promote trade, esp by means of the reduction and elimination of tariffs and import quotas; replaced in 1995 by the World Trade Organization

Gatún Lake (*Spanish* ga'tun) *n* a lake in Panama, part of the Panama Canal: formed in 1912 on the completion of the **Gatún Dam** across the Chagres River. Area: 424 sq km (164 sq miles)

gauche (gəʊʃ) *adj* lacking ease of manner; tactless [C18: French: awkward, left, from Old French *gauchir* to swerve, ultimately of Germanic origin; related to Old High German *wankōn* to stagger] > 'gauchely *adv* > 'gaucheness *n*

gaucherie (,gəʊʃə'riː, 'gəʊʃərɪ; *French* goʃri) *n* **1** the quality of being gauche **2** a gauche act

gaucho ('gaʊtʃəʊ) *n, pl* **-chos** a cowboy of the South American pampas, usually one of mixed Spanish and Indian descent [C19: from American Spanish, probably from Quechuan *wáhcha* orphan, vagabond]

gaud (gɔːd) *n* an article of cheap finery; trinket; bauble [C14: probably from Old French *gaudir* to be joyful, from Latin *gaudēre*]

Gaudí ('gaʊdɪ; *Spanish* gau'ði) *n* **Antonio** (an'tonjo). 1852–1926, Spanish architect, regarded as one of the most original exponents of Art Nouveau in Europe and noted esp for the church of the Sagrada Familia, Barcelona

Gaudier-Brzeska (*French* godjebʒeska) *n* **Henri** (ɑ̃ri), original name *Henri Gaudier*. 1891–1915, French vorticist sculptor

gaudy[1] ('gɔːdɪ) *adj* **gaudier, gaudiest** gay, bright, or colourful in a crude or vulgar manner; garish [c16: from GAUD] > 'gaudily *adv* > 'gaudiness *n*

gaudy[2] ('gɔːdɪ) *n, pl* **gaudies** *Brit* a celebratory festival or feast held at some schools and colleges [c16: from Latin *gaudium* joy, from *gaudēre* to rejoice]

gauge *or* **gage** (geidʒ) *vb* (*tr*) **1** to measure or determine the amount, quantity, size, condition, etc, of **2** to estimate or appraise; judge **3** to check for conformity or bring into conformity with a standard measurement, dimension, etc ▷ *n* **4** a standard measurement, dimension, capacity, or quantity **5** any of various instruments for measuring a quantity: *a pressure gauge* **6** any of various devices used to check for conformity with a standard measurement **7** a standard or means for assessing; test; criterion **8** scope, capacity, or extent **9** the diameter of the barrel of a gun, esp a shotgun **10** the thickness of sheet metal or the diameter of wire **11** the distance between the rails of a railway track: in Britain 4 ft 8½ in. (1.435 m) **12** the distance between two wheels on the same axle of a vehicle, truck, etc **13** *nautical* the position of a vessel in relation to the wind and another vessel. One vessel may be windward (**weather gauge**) or leeward (**lee gauge**) of the other **14** the proportion of plaster of Paris added to mortar to accelerate its setting **15** the distance between the nails securing the slates, tiles, etc, of a roof **16** a measure of the fineness of woven or knitted fabric, usually expressed as the number of needles used per inch **17** the width of motion-picture film or magnetic tape ▷ *adj* **18** (of a pressure measurement) measured on a pressure gauge that registers zero at atmospheric pressure; above or below atmospheric pressure: *5 bar gauge* [c15: from Old Northern French, probably of Germanic origin] > 'gaugeable *or* 'gageable *adj* > 'gaugeably *or* 'gageably *adv*

gauge boson *n physics* a boson that mediates the interaction between elementary particles. There are several types: photons for electromagnetic interactions, W and Z intermediate vector bosons for weak interactions, and gravitons for gravitational interactions

gauge theory *n physics* a type of theory of elementary particles designed to explain the strong, weak, and electromagnetic interactions in terms of exchange of virtual particles

Gauguin (*French* gogɛ̃) *n* **Paul** (pɔl). 1848–1903, French postimpressionist painter, who worked in the South Pacific from 1891. Inspired by primitive art, his work is characterized by flat contrasting areas of pure colours

Gauhati (gaʊ'hɑːtɪ) *n* a city in NE India, in Assam on the River Brahmaputra: centre of British administration in Assam (1826–74). Pop: 808 021 (2001)

Gaul (gɔːl) *n* **1** an ancient region of W Europe corresponding to N Italy, France, Belgium, part of Germany, and the S Netherlands: divided into Cisalpine Gaul, which became a Roman province before 100 BC, and Transalpine Gaul, which was conquered by Julius Caesar (58–51 BC). Latin name: **Gallia 2** a native of ancient Gaul **3** a Frenchman

Gauleiter ('gaʊ,laɪtə) *n* **1** a provincial governor in Germany under Hitler **2** (*sometimes not capital*) *informal* a person in a position of petty or local authority who behaves in an overbearing authoritarian manner [from German, from *Gau* district + *Leiter* LEADER]

Gaulish ('gɔːlɪʃ) *n* **1** the extinct language of the pre-Roman Gauls, belonging to the Celtic branch of the Indo-European family ▷ *adj* **2** of or relating to ancient Gaul, the Gauls, or their language

Gaulle (gəʊl, gɔːl; *French* gol) *n* See **de Gaulle**

Gaultier (*French* gotje) *n* **Jean-Paul** (ʒɑ̃pɔl). born 1952, French fashion designer

gaunt (gɔːnt) *adj* **1** bony and emaciated in appearance **2** (of places) bleak or desolate [c15: perhaps of Scandinavian origin; compare Norwegian dialect *gand* tall lean person] > 'gauntly *adv* > 'gauntness *n*

gauntlet[1] ('gɔːntlɪt) *or* **gantlet** *n* **1** a medieval armoured leather glove **2** a heavy glove with a long cuff **3** take up the gauntlet to accept a challenge **4** throw down the gauntlet to offer a challenge [c15: from Old French *gantelet*, diminutive of *gant* glove, of Germanic origin]

gauntlet[2] ('gɔːntlɪt) *n* **1** a punishment in which the victim is forced to run between two rows of men who strike at him as he passes: formerly a military punishment **2** run the gauntlet a to suffer this punishment **b** to endure an onslaught or ordeal, as of criticism **3** a testing ordeal; trial [c15: changed (through influence of GAUNTLET[1]) from earlier *gantlope*; see GANTLET[1]]

gaur (gaʊə) *n* a large wild member of the cattle tribe, *Bos gaurus*, inhabiting mountainous regions of S Asia [c19: from Hindi, from Sanskrit *gāura*]

gauss (gaʊs) *n, pl* **gauss** the cgs unit of magnetic flux density; the flux density that will induce an emf of 1 abvolt (10^{-8} volt) per centimetre in a wire moving across the field at a velocity of 1 centimetre per second. 1 gauss is equivalent to 10^{-4} tesla [after Karl Friedrich GAUSS]

Gauss (*German* gaus) *n* **Karl Friedrich** (karl 'friːdrɪç). 1777–1855, German mathematician: developed the theory of numbers and applied mathematics to astronomy, electricity and magnetism, and geodesy > **Gaussian** ('gaʊsɪən) *adj*

Gauteng (xaʊ'teŋ) *n* a province of N South Africa; formed in 1994 from part of the former province of Transvaal: service industries, mining, and manufacturing. Capital: Johannesburg. Pop: 8 847 740 (2004 est). Area: 18 810 sq km (7262 sq miles)

Gautier (*French* gotje) *n* **Théophile** (teɔfil). 1811–72, French poet, novelist, and critic. His early extravagant romanticism gave way to a preoccupation with poetic form and expression that anticipated the Parnassians

gauze (gɔːz) *n* **1** a transparent cloth of loose plain or leno weave **2** a surgical dressing of muslin or similar material **3** any thin openwork material, such as wire **4** a fine mist or haze [c16: from French *gaze*, perhaps from GAZA, where it was believed to originate]

gauzy ('gɔːzɪ) *adj* **gauzier, gauziest** resembling gauze; thin and transparent > 'gauzily *adv* > 'gauziness *n*

Gavaskar (gæ'væskɑː) *n* **Sunil Manohar** ('sʊnɪl 'mænəohɑː). born 1949, Indian cricketer. He captained India 1978–83 and 1984–85

gave (geɪv) *vb* the past tense of **give**

gavel ('gævəl) *n* a small hammer used by a chairman, auctioneer, etc, to call for order or attention [c19: of unknown origin]

gavial ('geɪvɪəl), **gharial** *or* **garial** ('gærɪəl) *n* a large fish-eating Indian crocodilian, *Gavialis gangeticus*, with a very long slender snout: family *Gavialidae* [c19: from French, from Hindi *ghariyāl*]

Gävle (*Swedish* 'jɛːvlə) *n* a port in E Sweden, on an inlet of the Gulf of Bothnia. Pop: 92 025 (2004 est)

gavotte *or* **gavot** (gə'vɒt) *n* **1** an old formal dance in quadruple time **2** a piece of music composed for or in the rhythm of this dance [c17: from French, from Provençal *gavoto*, from *gavot* mountaineer, dweller in the Alps (where the dance originated), from Old Latin *gaba* goitre (widespread in the Alps), from Old Latin *gaba* goitre (unattested) throat]

gawk (gɔːk) *n* **1** a clumsy stupid person; lout ▷ *vb* **2** (*intr*) to stare in a stupid way; gape [c18: from Old Danish *gaukr*; probably related to GAPE]

gawky ('gɔːkɪ) *or* **gawkish** *adj* **gawkier, gawkiest** clumsy or ungainly; awkward > 'gawkily *or* 'gawkishly *adv* > 'gawkiness *or* 'gawkishness *n*

gawp *or* **gaup** (gɔːp) *vb* (*intr; often foll by at*) *Brit slang* to stare stupidly; gape [c14 *galpen*; probably related to Old English *gielpan* to boast, YELP. Compare Dutch *galpen* to yelp] > 'gawper *n*

gay (geɪ) *adj* **1 a** a homosexual **b** of or for homosexuals: *a gay club* **2 a** carefree and merry: *a gay temperament* **b** brightly coloured; brilliant: *a gay hat* **c** given to pleasure, esp in social entertainment: *a gay life* ▷ *n* **3** a homosexual [C13: from Old French *gai*, from Old Provençal, of Germanic origin] > **'gayness** *n*

● USAGE *Gayness* is the word used to refer to
● homosexuality. The noun which refers to being
● carefree and merry is *gaiety*

Gay (geɪ) *n* **John.** 1685–1732, English poet and dramatist; author of *The Beggar's Opera* (1728)

Gaya ('gɑːjə, 'gaɪə) *n* a city in NE India, in Bihar: Hindu place of pilgrimage and one of the holiest sites of Buddhism. Pop: 383 197 (2001)

gaydar ('geɪdɑː) *n informal* the ability of a homosexual person to recognize whether another person is homosexual [C20 from GAY + (RA)DAR]

Gaye (geɪ) *n* **Marvin.** 1939–84, US soul singer and songwriter; recordings include "I Heard It Through the Grapevine" (1969), *What's Going On* (1971), and "Sexual Healing" (1982): shot dead by his father

Gay-Lussac ('geɪ'luːsæk; *French* gɛlysak) *n* **Joseph Louis** (ʒɔzɛf lwi). 1778–1850, French physicist and chemist: discovered the law named after him (1808), investigated the effects of terrestrial magnetism, isolated boron and cyanogen, and discovered methods of manufacturing sulphuric and oxalic acids

Gaza ('gɑːzə) *n* a city in the Gaza Strip: a Philistine city in biblical times. It was under Egyptian administration from 1949 until occupied by Israel (1967). Pop: 787 000 (2005 est). Arabic name: **Ghazzah**

gazania (gə'zeɪnɪə) *n* any plant of the S. African genus *Gazania*, grown for their rayed flowers in variegated colours; the flowers close in the afternoon: family *Asteraceae* [named after Theodore of Gaza, 1398–1478, translator of the botanical treatises of Theophrastus]

Gazankulu (,gazan'kuːluː) *n* (formerly) a Bantu homeland in South Africa; abolished in 1993. Capital: Giyani

Gaza Strip *n* a coastal region on the SE corner of the Mediterranean: administered by Egypt from 1949; occupied by Israel from 1967; granted autonomy in 1993 and administered by the Palestinian National Authority from 1994. Pop: 1 406 423 (2004 est). Area: 363 sq km (140 sq miles)

gaze (geɪz) *vb* **1** (*intr*) to look long and fixedly, esp in wonder or admiration ▷ *n* **2** a fixed look; stare [C14: from Swedish dialect *gasa* to gape at] > **'gazer** *n*

gazebo (gə'ziːbəʊ) *n*, *pl* **-bos** *or* **-boes** a summerhouse, garden pavilion, or belvedere, sited to command a view [C18: perhaps a pseudo-Latin coinage based on GAZE]

gazelle (gə'zɛl) *n*, *pl* **-zelles** *or* **-zelle** any small graceful usually fawn-coloured antelope of the genera *Gazella* and *Procapra*, of Africa and Asia, such as *G. thomsoni* (**Thomson's gazelle**) [C17: from Old French, from Arabic *ghazāl*]

gazette (gə'zɛt) *n* **1** a newspaper or official journal **2** *Brit* an official document containing public notices, appointments, etc ▷ *vb* **3** (*tr*) *Brit* to announce or report (facts or an event) in a gazette [C17: from French, from Italian *gazzetta*, from Venetian dialect *gazeta* news-sheet costing one *gazet*, small copper coin, perhaps from *gaza* magpie, from Latin *gaia, gaius* jay]

gazetteer (,gæzɪ'tɪə) *n* **1** a book or section of a book that lists and describes places **2** *archaic* a writer for a gazette or newspaper; journalist

Gaziantep (,gɑːziːɑːn'tɛp) *n* a city in S Turkey: base for Ibrahim Pasha's campaign against the Turks (1839) and centre of Turkish resistance to French forces (1921). Pop: 1 004 000 (2005 est)

gazillion (gə'zɪljən) *informal* ▷ *n*, *pl* **-lions** *or* **-lion** **1** (*often pl*) an extremely large but unspecified number, quantity, or amount: *gazillions of people turned up* ▷ *determiner* **2 a** amounting to a gazillion: *a gazillion types to choose from* **b** (*as pronoun*): *I found a gazillion under the sink* [C20: on the model of *million*]

gazillionaire (gə'zɪljə,nɛə) *n informal* a person who is enormously rich

gazpacho (gəz'pɑːtʃəʊ, gæs-) *n* a Spanish soup made from tomatoes, peppers, etc, and served cold [from Spanish]

gazump (gə'zʌmp) *Brit* ▷ *vb* **1** to raise the price of

something, esp a house, after agreeing a price verbally with (an intending buyer) **2** (*tr*) to swindle or overcharge ▷ *n* **3** the act or an instance of gazumping [C20: of uncertain origin] > **ga'zumper** *n*

gazunder (gə'zʌndə) *Brit* ▷ *vb* **1** to reduce an offer on a property immediately before exchanging contracts, having previously agreed a higher price with (the seller) ▷ *n* **2** an act or instance of gazundering [C20: modelled on GAZUMP] > **ga'zunderer** *n*

GB *abbreviation* Great Britain

GBE *abbreviation* (Knight or Dame) Grand Cross of the British Empire (a Brit title)

GBH *abbreviation* grievous bodily harm

GC *abbreviation* George Cross (a Brit award for bravery)

GCB *abbreviation* (Knight) Grand Cross of the Bath (a Brit title)

GCE *abbreviation* General Certificate of Education: a public examination in specified subjects taken in English and Welsh schools at the ages of 17 and 18. The GCSE has replaced the former GCE O-level for 16-year-olds. See also **AS level, S level**

GCHQ *abbreviation* (in Britain) Government Communications Headquarters

G clef *n* another name for **treble clef**

GCMG *abbreviation* (Knight or Dame) Grand Cross of the Order of St Michael and St George (a Brit title)

GCSE *abbreviation* (in Britain) General Certificate of Secondary Education: a public examination in specified subjects for 16-year-old schoolchildren. It replaced the GCE O-level and CSE

GCVO *abbreviation* (Knight or Dame) Grand Cross of the Royal Victorian Order (a Brit title)

Gd *the chemical symbol for* gadolinium

Gdańsk (*Polish* gdajinsk) *n* **1** the chief port of Poland, on the Baltic: a member of the Hanseatic league; under Prussian rule (1793–1807 and 1814–1919); a free city under the League of Nations from 1919 until annexed by Germany in 1939; returned to Poland in 1945. Pop: 851 000 (2005 est). German name: **Danzig 2 Bay of Gdańsk** a wide inlet of the Baltic Sea on the N coast of Poland

g'day *or* **gidday** (gə'daɪ) *sentence substitute* an Austral and NZ informal variant of **good day**

Gdns *abbreviation* Gardens

GDR *abbreviation* German Democratic Republic (East Germany; DDR)

Gdynia (*Polish* 'gdɪnja) *n* a port in N Poland, near Gdańsk: developed 1924–39 as the outlet for trade through the Polish Corridor; naval base. Pop: 251 183 (2007 est)

Ge¹ (dʒiː) *n* another name for **Gaia**

Ge² *the chemical symbol for* germanium

gean (giːn) *n* Also called: **wild cherry** a white-flowered rosaceous tree, *Prunus avium*, of Europe, W Asia, and N Africa, the ancestor of the cultivated sweet cherries [C16: from Old French *guine*]

gear (gɪə) *n* **1** a toothed wheel that engages with another toothed wheel or with a rack in order to change the speed or direction of transmitted motion **2** a mechanism for transmitting motion by gears, esp for a specific purpose **3** the engagement or specific ratio of a system of gears: *in gear; high gear* **4** personal equipment and accoutrements; belongings **5** equipment and supplies for a particular operation, sport, etc **6** *nautical* all equipment or appurtenances belonging to a certain vessel, sailor, etc **7** short for **landing gear 8** *informal* up-to-date clothes and accessories, esp those bought by young people **9** *slang* illegal drugs **10** a less common word for **harness** (sense 1) **11** **out of gear** out of order; not functioning properly ▷ *vb* **12** (*tr*) to adjust or adapt (one thing) so as to fit in or work with another: *to gear our output to current demand* **13** (*tr*) to equip with or connect by gears **14** (*intr*) to be in or come into gear **15** (*tr*) to equip with harness [C13: from Old Norse *gervi*; related to Old High German *garawi* equipment, Old English *gearwe*]

gearbox ('gɪə,bɒks) *n* **1** the metal casing within which a train of gears is sealed **2** this metal casing and its contents, esp in a motor vehicle

gearing ('gɪərɪŋ) *n* **1** an assembly of gears designed to transmit motion **2** the act or technique of providing gears to transmit motion **3** Also called: **capital gearing** *accounting, Brit* the ratio of a company's debt capital to its equity capital. US word: **leverage**

gear lever *or US and Canadian* **gearshift** ('gɪəˌʃɪft) *n* a lever used to move gearwheels relative to each other, esp in a motor vehicle

gear train *n engineering* a system of gears that transmits power from one shaft to another

gearwheel ('gɪəˌwiːl) *n* another name for **gear** (sense 1)

Geber ('dʒiːbə) *n* Latinized form of Jabir, assumed in honour of Jabir ibn Hayyan by a 14th-century alchemist, probably Spanish: he described the preparation of nitric and sulphuric acids

Gebrselassie (ˌgɛbrəsə'læsɪ) *n* **Haile** ('haɪlɪ). born 1973, Ethiopian athlete; Olympic gold medallist in the 10 000 metres in 1996 and 2000

gecko ('gɛkəʊ) *n, pl* **-os** *or* **-oes** any small insectivorous terrestrial lizard of the family *Gekkonidae*, of warm regions. The digits have adhesive pads, which enable these animals to climb on smooth surfaces [c18: from Malay *ge'kok*, of imitative origin]

gee[1] (dʒiː) *interj* **1** Also called: **gee up!** an exclamation, as to a horse or draught animal, to encourage it to turn to the right, go on, or go faster ▷ *vb* **gees, geeing, geed** **2** (usually foll by *up*) to move (an animal, esp a horse) ahead; urge on **3** (foll by *up*) to encourage (someone) to greater effort or activity [c17: origin uncertain]

gee[2] (dʒiː) *interj* US & Canadian informal a mild exclamation of surprise, admiration, etc. Also called: **gee whizz** [c20: euphemism for JESUS]

Gee (dʒiː) *n* **Maurice**. born 1931, New Zealand novelist

geebung ('dʒiːbʌŋ) *n* **1** any of various trees and shrubs of the genus *Persoonia* of Australia having an edible but tasteless fruit **2** the fruit of these trees [from a native Australian language]

geek (giːk) *n slang* **1** a person who is preoccupied with or very knowledgeable about computing **2** a boring and unattractive social misfit **3** a degenerate [c19: probably variant of Scottish *geck* fool, from Middle Low German *geck*] ▷ '**geeky** *adj*

geelbek ('xɪəlˌbɛk) *n South African* a yellow-jawed edible marine fish [from Afrikaans *geel* yellow + *bek* mouth]

Geelong (dʒə'lɒŋ) *n* a port in SE Australia, in S Victoria on Port Phillip Bay. Pop: 130 194 (2001)

geese (giːs) *n* the plural of **goose**[1]

geezer ('giːzə) *n informal* a man [c19: probably from dialect pronunciation of *guiser*, from GUISE + -ER[1]]

Gehenna (gɪ'hɛnə) *n* **1** *Old Testament* the valley below Jerusalem, where children were sacrificed and where idolatry was practised (II Kings 23:10; Jeremiah 19:6) and where later offal and refuse were slowly burned **2** *New Testament, Judaism* a place where the wicked are punished after death **3** a place or state of pain and torment [c16: from Late Latin, from Greek *Geena*, from Hebrew *Gê' Hinnōm*, literally: valley of Hinnom, symbolic of hell]

Gehry ('gɛɪrɪ) *n* **Frank O**(**wen**). born 1929, US architect and furniture designer, born in Canada; best known for the Guggenheim Museum in Bilbao, Spain (1997)

Geiger ('gaɪgə) *n* **Hans** (hans). 1882–1945, German physicist: developed the Geiger counter

Geiger counter *or* **Geiger-Müller counter** ('gaɪgə'mʊlə) *n* an instrument for detecting and measuring the intensity of ionizing radiation. It consists of a gas-filled tube containing a fine wire anode along the axis of a cylindrical cathode with a potential difference of several hundred volts. Any particle or photon which ionizes any number of gas molecules in the tube causes a discharge which is registered by electronic equipment. The magnitude of the discharge does not depend upon the nature or the energy of the ionizing particle [c20: named after Hans *Geiger* (1882–1945), German physicist and W. *Müller*, 20th-century German physicist]

Geikie ('giːkɪ) *n* Sir **Archibald**. 1835–1924, Scottish geologist noted for his study of British volcanic rocks

geisha ('geɪʃə) *n, pl* **-sha** *or* **-shas** a professional female companion for men in Japan, trained in music, dancing, and the art of conversation [c19: from Japanese, from *gei* art + *sha* person, from Ancient Chinese *ngi* and *che*]

Geissler tube ('gaɪslə) *n* a glass or quartz vessel, usually having two bulbs containing electrodes separated by a capillary tube, for maintaining an electric discharge in a low-pressure gas as a source of visible or ultraviolet light for spectroscopy [c19: named after Heinrich *Geissler* (1814–79), German mechanic]

gel (dʒɛl) *n* **1** a semirigid jelly-like colloid in which a liquid is dispersed in a solid: *nondrip paint is a gel* **2** See **hair gel** ▷ *vb* **gels, gelling, gelled** **3** to become or cause to become a gel **4** a variant spelling of **jell** [c19: by shortening from GELATINE]

gelatine ('dʒɛləˌtiːn) *or* **gelatin** ('dʒɛlətɪn) *n* **1** a colourless or yellowish water-soluble protein prepared by boiling animal hides and bones: used in foods, glue, photographic emulsions, etc **2** an edible jelly made of this substance, sweetened and flavoured [c19: from French *gélatine*, from Medieval Latin *gelātina*, from Latin *gelāre* to freeze]

gelatinize *or* **gelatinise** (dʒɪ'lætɪˌnaɪz) *vb* **1** to make or become gelatinous **2** (*tr*) *photog* to coat (glass, paper, etc) with gelatine ▷ ge,latini'zation *or* ge,latini'sation *n*

gelatinous (dʒɪ'lætɪnəs) *adj* **1** consisting of or resembling jelly; viscous **2** of, containing, or resembling gelatine ▷ ge'latinously *adv* ▷ ge'latinousness *n*

gelation (dʒɪ'leɪʃən) *n* the act or process of freezing a liquid [c19: from Latin *gelātiō* a freezing; see GELATINE]

geld (gɛld) *vb* **gelds, gelding, gelded** *or* **gelt** (*tr*) **1** to castrate (a horse or other animal) **2** to deprive of virility or vitality; emasculate; weaken [c13: from Old Norse *gelda*, from *geldr* barren]

Gelderland *or* **Guelderland** ('gɛldəˌlænd; *Dutch* 'xɛldərlɑnt) *n* a province of the E Netherlands: formerly a duchy, belonging successively to several different European powers. Capital: Arnhem. Pop: 1 960 000 (2003 est). Area: 5014 sq km (1955 sq miles). Also called: **Guelders**

gelding ('gɛldɪŋ) *n* a castrated male horse [c14: from Old Norse *geldingr*; see GELD[1], -ING[1]]

Geldof ('gɛldɒf) *n* **Bob**. Full name *Robert Frederick Zenon Geldof*. born 1954, Irish rock singer and philanthropist: formerly lead vocalist with the Boomtown Rats (1977–86): organizer of the Band Aid charity for famine relief in Africa. He received an honorary knighthood in 1986

Gelée (*French* ʒəle) *n* **Claude** (klod). the original name of: **Claude Lorrain**

Gelibolu (gɛ'libolu) *n* the Turkish name for: **Gallipoli**

gelid ('dʒɛlɪd) *adj* very cold, icy, or frosty [c17: from Latin *gelidus* icy cold, from *gelu* frost] ▷ ge'lidity *or* 'gelidness *n*

gelignite ('dʒɛlɪgˌnaɪt) *n* a type of dynamite in which the nitrogelatine is absorbed in a base of wood pulp and potassium or sodium nitrate [c19: from GEL(ATINE) + Latin *ignis* fire + -ITE[1]]

Gelligaer (*Welsh* ˌgɛhliː'gaɪr) *n* a town in S Wales, in Caerphilly county borough. Pop (including Ystrad Mynach): 17 185 (2001)

Gell-Mann ('gɛl'mæn) *n* **Murray**. born 1929, US physicist, noted for his research on the interaction and classification of elementary particles: Nobel prize for physics in 1969

Gelsenkirchen (*German* gɛlzən'kɪrçən) *n* an industrial city in W Germany, in North Rhine-Westphalia. Pop: 272 445 (2003 est)

gem (dʒɛm) *n* **1** a precious or semiprecious stone used in jewellery as a decoration; jewel **2** a person or thing held to be a perfect example; treasure ▷ *vb* **gems, gemming, gemmed** **3** (*tr*) to set or ornament with gems [c14: from Old French *gemme*, from Latin *gemma* bud, precious stone] ▷ 'gem,like *adj* ▷ 'gemmy *adj*

Gemara (gɛ'mɔːrə; *Hebrew* gɛma'ra) *n* *Judaism* the main body of the Talmud, consisting of a record of ancient rabbinical debates about the interpretation of the Mishna and constituting the primary source of Jewish religious law [c17: from Aramaic *gemārā* completion, from *gemār* to complete]

gemclip ('dʒɛmˌklɪp) *n* *South African* a paperclip

geminate *adj* ('dʒɛmɪnɪt, -ˌneɪt) Also called: **geminated** **1** combined in pairs; doubled: *a geminate leaf; a geminate consonant* ▷ *vb* ('dʒɛmɪˌneɪt) **2** to arrange or be arranged in pairs: *the "t"s in "fitted" are geminated* [C17: from Latin *gemināre* to double, from *geminus* born at the same time, twin] > **'geminately** *adv* > **,gemi'nation** *n*

Gemini ('dʒɛmɪ,naɪ, -,niː) *n, Latin genitive* **Geminorum** (,dʒɛmɪ'nɔːrəm) **1** *astronomy* a zodiacal constellation in the N hemisphere lying between Taurus and Cancer on the ecliptic and containing the stars Castor and Pollux **2** *classical myth* another name for **Castor and Pollux** **3** *astrology* Also called: **the Twins** the third sign of the zodiac, symbol ♊, having a mutable air classification and ruled by the planet Mercury. The sun is in this sign between about May 21 and June 20

gemma ('dʒɛmə) *n, pl* **-mae** (-miː) **1** a small asexual reproductive structure in liverworts, mosses, etc, that becomes detached from the parent and develops into a new individual **2** *zoology* another name for **gemmule** (sense 1) [C18: from Latin: bud, GEM]

gemmate ('dʒɛmeɪt) *adj* **1** (of some plants and animals) having or reproducing by gemmae ▷ *vb* **2** (*intr*) to produce or reproduce by gemmae > **gem'mation** *n*

gemmiparous (dʒɛ'mɪpərəs) *adj* (of plants and animals) reproducing by gemmae or buds. Also called: **gemmiferous** (dʒɛ'mɪfərəs)

gemmule ('dʒɛmjuːl) *n* **1** *zoology* a cell or mass of cells produced asexually by sponges and developing into a new individual; bud **2** *botany* a small gemma [C19: from French, from Latin *gemmula* a little bud; see GEM]

gemology *or* **gemmology** (dʒɛ'mɒlədʒɪ) *n* the branch of mineralogy that is concerned with gems and gemstones > **gemological** *or* **gemmological** (,dʒɛmə'lɒdʒɪkᵊl) *adj* > **gem'ologist** *or* **gem'mologist** *n*

gemsbok *or* **gemsbuck** ('gɛmz,bʌk) *n, pl* **-bok, -boks** *or* **-buck, -bucks** *South African* another word for **oryx** [C18: from Afrikaans, from German *Gemsbock*, from *Gemse* chamois + *Bock* BUCK¹]

gemstone ('dʒɛm,stəʊn) *n* a precious or semiprecious stone, esp one cut and polished for setting in jewellery

gen (dʒɛn) *n informal* information: *give me the gen on your latest project.* See also **gen up** [C20: from gen(eral information)]

Gen. *abbreviation* **1** General **2** *Bible* Genesis

-gen *suffix forming nouns* **1** producing or that which produces: *hydrogen* **2** something produced: *carcinogen* [via French *-gène*, from Greek *-genēs* born]

Genck (*Flemish* xɛŋk) *n* a variant spelling of **Genk**

gendarme ('ʒɒndɑːm; *French* ʒɑ̃darm) *n* **1** a member of the police force in France or in countries formerly influenced or controlled by France **2** a sharp pinnacle of rock on a mountain ridge, esp in the Alps [C16: from French, from *gens d'armes* people of arms]

gendarmerie *or* **gendarmery** (ʒɒn'dɑːmərɪ; *French* ʒɑ̃darməri) *n* **1** the whole corps of gendarmes **2** the headquarters or barracks of a body of gendarmes

gender ('dʒɛndə) *n* **1** a set of two or more grammatical categories into which the nouns of certain languages are divided, sometimes but not necessarily corresponding to the sex of the referent when animate **2** any of the categories, such as masculine, feminine, neuter, or common, within such a set **3** *informal* the state of being male, female, or neuter **4** *informal* all the members of one sex: *the female gender* [C14: from Old French *gendre*, from Latin *genus* kind]

gender-bender *n* **1** *informal* a person who adopts an androgynous style of dress, hair, make-up, etc **2** a male-male or female-female adaptor, used esp for computer hardware

gender dysphoria *n* a condition in which a person feels uncertainty or anxiety about his or her birth gender

gene (dʒiːn) *n* a unit of heredity composed of DNA occupying a fixed position on a chromosome (some viral genes are composed of RNA). A gene may determine a characteristic of an individual by specifying a polypeptide chain that forms a protein or part of a protein (**structural gene**); or encode an RNA molecule; or regulate the operation of other genes or repress such operation [C20: from German *Gen*, shortened from *Pangen*; see PAN-, -GEN]

-gene *suffix forming nouns* a variant of **-gen**

genealogy (,dʒiː'nɪ'ælədʒɪ) *n, pl* **-gies** **1** the direct descent

of an individual or group from an ancestor **2** the study of the evolutionary development of animals and plants from earlier forms **3** a chart showing the relationships and descent of an individual, group, genes, etc [C13: from Old French *genealogie*, from Late Latin *geneālogia*, from Greek, from *genea* race] > **genealogical** (,dʒiː,nɪə'lɒdʒɪkᵊl) *or* **,genea'logic** *adj* > **,genea'logically** *adv* > **,gene'alogist** *n*

gene bank *n botany* a collection of seeds, plants, tissue cultures, etc, of potentially useful species, esp species containing genes of significance to the breeding of crops

gene clone *n* See **clone** (sense 2)

genecology (,dʒɛnɪ'kɒlədʒɪ) *n* the study of the gene frequency of a species in relation to its population distribution within a particular environment

gene doping *n* a form of drug abuse in sport in which genetic material is injected into muscle to enhance performance or stimulate muscle growth

gene flow *n* the movement and exchange of genes between interbreeding populations

gene library *n* a collection of gene clones that represents the genetic material of an organism: used in genetic engineering

gene pool *n* the sum of all the genes in an interbreeding population

genera ('dʒɛnərə) *n* a plural of **genus**

general ('dʒɛnərəl, 'dʒɛnrəl) *adj* **1** common; widespread **2** of, including, applying to, or participated in by all or most of the members of a group, category, or community **3** relating to various branches of an activity, profession, etc; not specialized: *general office work* **4** including various or miscellaneous items: *general knowledge; a general store* **5** not specific as to detail; overall: *a general description of the merchandise* **6** not definite; vague: *give me a general idea of when you will finish* **7** applicable or true in most cases; usual **8** (*prenominal or immediately postpositive*) having superior or extended authority or rank: *general manager; consul general* ▷ *n* **9** an officer of a rank senior to lieutenant general, esp one who commands a large military formation **10** any person acting as a leader and applying strategy or tactics **11** a general condition or principle: *opposed to particular* **12** a title for the head of a religious order, congregation, etc **13** *archaic* the people; public **14** in general generally; mostly or usually [C13: from Latin *generālis* of a particular kind, from *genus* kind]

general anaesthetic *n* a drug producing anaesthesia of the entire body, with loss of consciousness

General Assembly *n* **1** the deliberative assembly of the United Nations. Abbreviation: GA **2** the supreme governing body of certain religious denominations, esp of the Presbyterian Church

general average *n insurance* loss or damage to a ship or its cargo that is shared among the shipowners and all the cargo owners. Abbreviation: GA See **particular average**

General Certificate of Education *n* See GCE

General Certificate of Secondary Education *n* See GCSE

general election *n* **1** an election in which representatives are chosen in all constituencies of a state **2** *US* a final election from which successful candidates are sent to a legislative body **3** *US & Canadian* (in the US) a national or state election or (in Canada) a federal or provincial election in contrast to a local election

generalissimo (,dʒɛnərə'lɪsɪ,məʊ, ,dʒɛnrə-) *n, pl* **-mos** a supreme commander of combined military, naval, and air forces, esp one who wields political as well as military power [C17: from Italian, superlative of *generale* GENERAL]

generality (,dʒɛnə'rælɪtɪ) *n, pl* **-ties** **1** a principle or observation having general application, esp when imprecise or unable to be proved **2** the state or quality of being general **3** *archaic* the majority

generalization *or* **generalisation** (,dʒɛnərəlaɪ'zeɪʃən) *n* **1** a principle, theory, etc, with general application **2** the act or an instance of generalizing **3** *logic* the derivation of a general statement from a particular one, formally by prefixing a quantifier and replacing a subject term by a bound variable. If the quantifier is universal (**universal generalization**) the argument is not in general valid; if it is existential (**existential generalization**) it is valid

generalize or **generalise** ('dʒɛnrə,laɪz) vb 1 to form (general principles or conclusions) from (detailed facts, experience, etc); infer 2 (intr) to think or speak in generalities, esp in a prejudiced way 3 (tr; usually passive) to cause to become widely used or known

generally ('dʒɛnrəlɪ) adv 1 usually; as a rule 2 commonly or widely 3 without reference to specific details or facts; broadly

general practitioner n a physician who does not specialize but has a medical practice (**general practice**) in which he deals with all illnesses. Informal name: family doctor Abbreviation: GP

general-purpose adj having a range of uses or applications; not restricted to one function

generalship ('dʒɛnrəl,ʃɪp) n 1 the art or duties of exercising command of a major military formation or formations 2 tactical or administrative skill

general staff n officers assigned to advise commanders in the planning and execution of military operations

general strike n a strike by all or most of the workers of a country, province, city, etc, esp (caps.) such a strike that took place in Britain in 1926

General Synod n the governing body, under Parliament, of the Church of England, made up of the bishops and elected clerical and lay representatives

generate ('dʒɛnə,reɪt) vb (mainly tr) 1 to produce or bring into being; create 2 (also intr) to produce (electricity), esp in a power station 3 to produce (a substance) by a chemical process 4 maths, linguistics to provide a precise criterion or specification for membership in (a set) 5 geometry to trace or form by moving a point, line, or plane in a specific way: circular motion of a line generates a cylinder [c16: from Latin generāre to beget, from genus kind]

generation (,dʒɛnə'reɪʃən) n 1 the act or process of bringing into being; production or reproduction, esp of offspring 2 a a successive stage in natural descent of organisms: the time between when an organism comes into being and when it reproduces b the individuals produced at each stage 3 the normal or average time between two such generations of a species: about 35 years for humans 4 all the people of approximately the same age, esp when considered as sharing certain attitudes, etc 5 production of electricity, heat, etc 6 (modifier, in combination) a belonging to a generation specified as having been born in or as having parents, grandparents, etc, born in a given country: a third-generation American b belonging to a specified stage of development in manufacture, usually implying improvement: a second-generation computer

generation gap n the years separating one generation from the generation that precedes or follows it, esp when regarded as representing the difference in outlook and the lack of understanding between them

Generation X n members of the generation of people born between the mid-1960s and the mid-1970s who are highly educated and underemployed, reject consumer culture, and have little hope for the future [c20: from the novel Generation X: Tales for an Accelerated Culture by Douglas Coupland]

generative ('dʒɛnərətɪv) adj 1 of or relating to the production of offspring, parts, etc 2 capable of producing or originating

generative grammar n a description of a language in terms of explicit rules that ideally generate all and only the grammatical sentences of the language

generator ('dʒɛnə,reɪtə) n 1 physics a any device for converting mechanical energy into electrical energy by electromagnetic induction, esp a large one as in a power station b a device for producing a voltage electrostatically 2 an apparatus for producing a gas 3 a person or thing that generates

generatrix ('dʒɛnə,reɪtrɪks) n, pl generatrices ('dʒɛnə,reɪtrɪ,siːz) a point, line, or plane that is moved in a specific way to produce a geometric figure

generic (dʒɪ'nɛrɪk) or **generical** adj 1 applicable or referring to a whole class or group; general 2 biology of, relating to, or belonging to a genus: the generic name 3 denoting the nonproprietary name of a drug, food product, etc [c17: from French; see GENUS] > ge'nerically adv

generosity (,dʒɛnə'rɒsɪtɪ) n, pl -ties 1 willingness and liberality in giving away one's money, time, etc; magnanimity 2 freedom from pettiness in character and mind 3 a generous act 4 abundance; plenty

generous ('dʒɛnərəs, 'dʒɛnrəs) adj 1 willing and liberal in giving away one's money, time, etc; munificent 2 free from pettiness in character and mind 3 full or plentiful: a generous portion 4 (of wine) rich in alcohol [c16: via Old French from Latin generōsus nobly born, from genus race; see GENUS] > 'generously adv > 'generousness n

genesis ('dʒɛnɪsɪs) n, pl -ses (-,siːz) a beginning or origin of anything [Old English: via Latin from Greek; related to Greek gignesthai to be born]

Genesis ('dʒɛnɪsɪs) n the first book of the Old Testament recounting the events from the Creation of the world to the sojourning of the Israelites in Egypt

-genesis n combining form indicating genesis, development, or generation: biogenesis; parthenogenesis [New Latin, from Latin: GENESIS] > -genetic or -genic adj combining form

genet¹ ('dʒɛnɪt) or **genette** (dʒɪ'nɛt) n 1 any agile catlike viverrine mammal of the genus Genetta, inhabiting wooded regions of Africa and S Europe, having an elongated head, thick spotted or blotched fur, and a very long tail 2 the fur of such an animal [c15: from Old French genette, from Arabic jarnayt]

genet² ('dʒɛnɪt) n an obsolete spelling of **jennet**

Genet (French ʒəne) n **Jean** (ʒɑ̃). 1910–86, French dramatist and novelist; his novels include Notre-Dame des Fleurs (1944) and his plays Les Bonnes (1947) and Le Balcon (1956)

gene therapy n the replacement or alteration of defective genes in order to prevent the occurrence of such inherited diseases as haemophilia. Effected by genetic engineering techniques, it is still at the experimental stage

genetic (dʒɪ'nɛtɪk) or **genetical** adj of or relating to genetics, genes, or the origin of something [c19: from GENESIS] > ge'netically adv

genetically modified adj denoting or derived from an organism whose DNA has been altered for the purpose of improvement or correction of defects: genetically modified food. Abbreviation: GM > genetic modification n

genetic code n biochem the order in which the nitrogenous bases of DNA are arranged in the molecule, which determines the type and amount of protein synthesized in the cell. The four bases are arranged in groups of three in a specific order, each group acting as a unit (codon), which specifies a particular amino acid

genetic counselling n the provision of advice for couples with a history of inherited disorders who wish to have children, including the likelihood of having affected children and the course and management of the disorder, etc

genetic engineering n alteration of the DNA of a cell for purposes of research, as a means of manufacturing animal proteins, correcting genetic defects, or making improvements to plants and animals bred by man

genetic fingerprint n the pattern of DNA unique to each individual that can be analysed in a sample of blood, saliva, or tissue: used as a means of identification

genetic map n a graphic representation of the order of genes within chromosomes by means of detailed analysis of the DNA. See also **chromosome map** > genetic mapping n

genetic marker n a gene with two or more alternative forms, producing readily identifiable variations in a particular character, used in studies of linkage, genetic mapping, and identification of the presence of other genes that are closely linked to, and therefore usually inherited with, it

genetics (dʒɪ'nɛtɪks) n 1 (functioning as singular) the branch of biology concerned with the study of heredity and variation in organisms **2** the genetic features and constitution of a single organism, species, or group >ge'neticist *n*

Geneva (dʒɪ'niːvə) *n* **1** a city in SW Switzerland, in the Rhône valley on Lake Geneva: centre of Calvinism; headquarters of the International Red Cross (1864), the International Labour Office (1925), the League of Nations (1929–46), the World Health Organization, and the European office of the United Nations; banking centre. Pop: 177 500 (2002 est) **2** a canton in SW Switzerland. Capital: Geneva. Pop: 419 300 (2002 est). Area: 282 sq km (109 sq miles). French name: **Genève**. German name: **Genf 3 Lake Geneva** a lake between SW Switzerland and E France: fed and drained by the River Rhône, it is the largest of the Alpine lakes; the surface is subject to considerable changes of level. Area: 580 sq km (224 sq miles). French name: **Lac Léman**. German name: **Genfersee**

Geneva bands *pl n* a pair of white lawn or linen strips hanging from the front of the neck or collar of some ecclesiastical and academic robes [C19: named after GENEVA, where originally worn by Swiss Calvinist clergy]

Geneva Convention *n* the international agreement, first formulated in 1864 at Geneva, establishing a code for wartime treatment of the sick or wounded: revised and extended on several occasions to cover maritime warfare and prisoners of war

Geneva gown *n* a long loose black gown with very wide sleeves worn by academics or Protestant clerics [C19: named after GENEVA; see GENEVA BANDS]

Genevan (dʒɪ'niːvᵊn) *or* **Genevese** (ˌdʒɛnɪ'viːz) *adj* **1** of, relating to, or characteristic of Geneva **2** of, adhering to, or relating to the teachings of Calvin or the Calvinists ▷ *n*, *pl* -vans *or* -vese **3** a native or inhabitant of Geneva

Geneva protocol *n* the agreement in 1925 to ban the use of asphyxiating, poisonous, or other gases in war. It does not ban the development or manufacture of such gases

Genève (ʒənɛv) *n* the French name for **Geneva**

Geneviève ('dʒɛnɪˌviːv; *French* ʒənvjɛv) *n* **Saint**. ?422–?512 AD, French nun; patron saint of Paris. Feast day: Jan 3

Genf (gɛnf) *n* the German name for: **Geneva** (senses 1, 2)

Genfersee ('gɛnfərzeː) *n* the German name for (Lake) **Geneva**

Genghis Khan ('dʒɛŋgɪs kɑːn) *n* original name *Temuchin or Temujin*. ?1162–1227, Mongol ruler, whose empire stretched from the Black Sea to the Pacific. Also called: **Jinghis Khan, Jenghis Khan**

genial¹ ('dʒiːnjəl, -nɪəl) *adj* **1** cheerful, easy-going, and warm in manner or behaviour **2** pleasantly warm, so as to give life, growth, or health [C16: from Latin *geniālis* relating to birth or marriage, from *genius* tutelary deity; see GENIUS] > geniality (ˌdʒiːnɪ'ælɪtɪ) *or* 'genialness *n* > 'genially *adv*

genial² (dʒɪ'niːəl) *adj* anatomy of or relating to the chin [C19: from Greek *geneion*, from *genus* jaw]

genic ('dʒɛnɪk) *adj* of or relating to a gene or genes

-genic *adj combining form* **1** relating to production or generation: *carcinogenic* **2** well suited to or suitable for: *photogenic* [from -GEN + -IC]

genie ('dʒiːnɪ) *n* **1** (in fairy tales and stories) a servant who appears by magic and fulfils a person's wishes **2** another word for **jinni** [C18: from French *génie*, from Arabic *jinni* demon, influenced by Latin *genius* attendant spirit; see GENIUS]

Genie ('dʒiːnɪ) *n Canadian* an award given by the Academy of Canadian Cinema and Television in recognition of Canadian cinematic achievements

genital ('dʒɛnɪtᵊl) *adj* **1** of or relating to the sexual organs or to reproduction **2** *psychoanal* relating to the mature stage of psychosexual development in which an affectionate relationship with one's sex partner is established [C14: from Latin *genitālis* concerning birth, from *gignere* to beget]

genital herpes *n* a sexually transmitted disease caused by a variety of the herpes simplex virus in which painful blisters occur in the genital region

genitals ('dʒɛnɪtᵊlz) *or* **genitalia** (ˌdʒɛnɪ'teɪlɪə, -'teɪljə) *pl n* the sexual organs; the testicles and penis of a male or the labia, clitoris, and vagina of a female

genitive ('dʒɛnɪtɪv) *grammar* ▷ *adj* **1** denoting a case of nouns, pronouns, and adjectives in inflected languages used to indicate a relation of ownership or association, usually translated by English *of* ▷ *n* **2 a** the genitive case **b** a word or speech element in this case [C14: from Latin *genetīvus* relating to birth, from *gignere* to produce] > genitival (ˌdʒɛnɪ'taɪvᵊl) *adj*

genitourinary (ˌdʒɛnɪtəʊ'jʊərɪnərɪ) *adj* of or relating to both the reproductive and excretory organs; urogenital

genius ('dʒiːnɪəs, -njəs) *n*, *pl* -uses *or for senses 5, 6* genii ('dʒiːnɪˌaɪ) **1** a person with exceptional ability, esp of a highly original kind **2** such ability or capacity **3** the distinctive spirit or creative nature of a nation, era, language, etc **4** a person considered as exerting great influence of a certain sort: *an evil genius* **5** *Roman myth* **a** the guiding spirit who attends a person from birth to death **b** the guardian spirit of a place, group of people, or institution **6** *Arabic myth* (*usually plural*) a demon; jinn [C16: from Latin, from *gignere* to beget]

genizah (gɛ'niːzə) *n*, *pl* genizahs, genizoth (gɛ'niːzəʊ) *Judaism* a repository (usually in a synagogue) for books and other sacred objects which can no longer be used but which may not be destroyed [C19: from Hebrew, literally: a hiding place, from *gānaz* to hide, set aside]

Genk *or* **Genck** (*Flemish* xɛŋk) *n* a town in NE Belgium, in Limburg province: coal-mining. Pop: 106 213 (2004 est)

genoa ('dʒɛnəʊə) *n yachting* a large triangular jib sail, often with a foot that extends as far aft as the clew of the mainsail

Genoa ('dʒɛnəʊə) *n* a port in NW Italy, capital of Liguria, on the **Gulf of Genoa**: Italy's main port; an independent commercial city with many colonies in the Middle Ages; university (1243); heavy industries. Pop: 610 307 (2001). Italian name: **Genova**

genocide ('dʒɛnəʊˌsaɪd) *n* the policy of deliberately killing a nationality or ethnic group [C20: from *geno-*, from Greek *genos* race + -CIDE] > genoˈcidal *adj*

Genoese (ˌdʒɛnəʊ'iːz) *or* **Genovese** (ˌdʒɛnə'viːz) *n*, *pl* -ese *or* -vese **1** a native or inhabitant of Genoa ▷ *adj* **2** of or relating to Genoa or its inhabitants

genome *or* **genom** ('dʒiːnəʊm) *n* the full complement of genetic material within an organism [C20: from German *Genom*, from *Gen* GENE + (CHROMOS)OME] > genomic (dʒɪ'nɒmɪk) *adj*

genomics (dʒɪ'nɒmɪks) *n* (*functioning as singular*) the branch of molecular genetics concerned with the study of genomes, specifically the identification and sequencing of their constituent genes and the application of this knowledge in medicine, pharmacy, agriculture, etc

genotoxic (ˌdʒɛnəʊ'tɒksɪk) *adj* harmful to genetic material

genotype ('dʒɛnəʊˌtaɪp) *n* **1** the genetic constitution of an organism **2** a group of organisms with the same genetic constitution > genotypic (ˌdʒɛnəʊ'tɪpɪk) *or* ˌgenoˈtypical *adj*

-genous *adj combining form* **1** yielding or generating: *androgenous*; *erogenous* **2** generated by or issuing from: *endogenous* [from -GEN + -OUS]

Genova ('dʒɛːnova) *n* the Italian name for **Genoa**

genre ('ʒɑːnrə) *n* **1 a** kind, category, or sort, esp of literary or artistic work **b** (*as modifier*): *genre fiction* **2 a** category of painting in which domestic scenes or incidents from everyday life are depicted [C19: from French, from Old French *gendre*; see GENDER]

gens (dʒɛnz) *n*, *pl* gentes ('dʒɛntiːz) **1** (in ancient Rome) any of a group of aristocratic families, having a common name and claiming descent from a common ancestor in the male line **2** *anthropol* a group based on descent in the male line [C19: from Latin: race; compare GENUS, GENDER]

Genseric ('gɛnsərɪk, 'dʒɛn-) *or* **Gaiseric** *n* ?390–477 AD, king of the Vandals (428–77). He seized Roman lands, esp extensive parts of N Africa, and sacked Rome (455)

gent (dʒɛnt) *n informal* short for **gentleman**

Gent (xɛnt) *n* the Flemish name for **Ghent**

gentamicin (ˌdʒɛntəˈmaɪsɪn) n a broad-spectrum antibiotic used in the treatment of serious infections [C20: from *genta* (of unknown origin) + -MYCIN]

genteel (dʒɛnˈtiːl) adj 1 affectedly proper or refined; excessively polite 2 respectable, polite, and well-bred 3 appropriate to polite or fashionable society [C16: from French *gentil* well-born; see GENTLE] > gen'teelly adv > gen'teelness n

gentian (ˈdʒɛnʃən) n 1 any gentianaceous plant of the genera *Gentiana* or *Gentianella*, having blue, yellow, white, or red showy flowers 2 the bitter-tasting dried rhizome and roots of *Gentiana lutea* (**European** or **yellow gentian**), which can be used as a tonic [C14: from Latin *gentiāna*; perhaps named after *Gentius*, a second-century BC Illyrian king, reputedly the first to use it medicinally]

gentian violet n a greenish crystalline substance, obtained from rosaniline, that forms a violet solution in water, used as an indicator, antiseptic, and in the treatment of burns

Gentile[1] (ˈdʒɛntaɪl) n 1 a person who is not a Jew 2 a Christian, as contrasted with a Jew 3 a person who is not a member of one's own church: used esp by Mormons 4 a heathen or pagan ⊳ adj 5 of or relating to a race or religion that is not Jewish 6 Christian, as contrasted with Jewish 7 not being a member of one's own church: used esp by Mormons 8 pagan or heathen

Gentile[2] (Italian dʒɛnˈtiːle) n **Giovanni** (dʒoˈvanni). 1875–1944, Italian Idealist philosopher and Fascist politician: minister of education (1922–24)

Gentile da Fabriano (Italian dʒɛnˈtiːle da fabriˈaːno) n original name *Niccolo di Giovanni di Massio*. ?1370–1427, Italian painter. His works, in the International Gothic style, include the *Adoration of the Magi* (1423)

gentility (dʒɛnˈtɪlɪtɪ) n, pl -ties 1 respectability and polite good breeding 2 affected politeness 3 noble birth or ancestry 4 people of noble birth [C14: from Old French *gentilite*, from Latin *gentīlitās* relationship of those belonging to the same tribe or family; see GENS]

gentle (ˈdʒɛntᵊl) adj 1 having a mild or kindly nature or character 2 soft or temperate; mild; moderate 3 gradual: *a gentle slope* 4 easily controlled; tame 5 archaic of good breeding; noble: *gentle blood* 6 archaic gallant; chivalrous ⊳ vb (tr) 7 to tame or subdue (a horse) 8 to appease or mollify ⊳ n 9 a maggot, esp when used as bait in fishing [C13: from Old French *gentil* noble, from Latin *gentīlis* belonging to the same family; see GENS] > 'gently adv > 'gentleness n

gentle breeze n meteorol a light breeze of force three on the Beaufort scale, blowing at 8–12 mph

gentlefolk (ˈdʒɛntᵊlˌfəʊk) or **gentlefolks** pl n persons regarded as being of good breeding

gentleman (ˈdʒɛntᵊlmən) n, pl -men 1 a man regarded as having qualities of refinement associated with a good family 2 a man who is cultured, courteous, and well-educated 3 a polite name for a man 4 the personal servant of a gentleman (esp in the phrase **gentleman's gentleman**) > 'gentlemanly adj > 'gentlemanliness n

gentleman-farmer n, pl gentlemen-farmers 1 a person who engages in farming but does not depend on it for his living 2 a person who owns farmland but does not farm it personally

gentlemen's agreement or **gentleman's agreement** n a personal understanding or arrangement based on honour and not legally binding

gentlewoman (ˈdʒɛntᵊlˌwʊmən) n, pl -women 1 archaic a woman regarded as being of good family or breeding; lady 2 history a woman in personal attendance on a high-ranking lady

gentrification (ˌdʒɛntrɪfɪˈkeɪʃən) n Brit a process by which middle-class people take up residence in a traditionally working-class area of a city, changing the character of the area [C20: from *gentrify* (to become GENTRY)] > 'gentriˌfier n

gentry (ˈdʒɛntrɪ) n 1 Brit persons just below the nobility in social rank 2 informal, often derogatory people, esp of a particular group or kind [C14: from Old French *genterie*, from *gentil* GENTLE]

gents (dʒɛnts) n (functioning as singular) Brit informal a men's public lavatory

genuflect (ˈdʒɛnjʊˌflɛkt) vb (intr) 1 to act in a servile or deferential manner 2 RC Church to bend one or both knees as a sign of reverence, esp when passing before the Blessed Sacrament [C17: from Medieval Latin *genūflectere*, from Latin *genu* knee + *flectere* to bend] > ˌgenu'flection or esp Brit ˌgenu'flexion n > 'genuˌflector n

genuine (ˈdʒɛnjʊɪn) adj 1 not fake or counterfeit; original; real; authentic 2 not pretending; frank; sincere 3 being of authentic or original stock [C16: from Latin *genuīnus* inborn, hence (in Late Latin) authentic, from *gignere* to produce] > 'genuinely adv > 'genuineness n

gen up vb gens up, genning up, genned up (adverb; often passive; when intr, usually foll by on) Brit informal to brief (someone) or study (something) in detail; make or become fully conversant with

genus (ˈdʒiːnəs) n, pl genera (ˈdʒɛnərə) or genuses 1 biology any of the taxonomic groups into which a family is divided and which contains one or more species. For example, *Vulpes* (foxes) is a genus of the dog family (*Canidae*) 2 logic a class of objects or individuals that can be divided into two or more groups or species 3 a class, group, etc, with common characteristics [C16: from Latin: race]

-geny n combining form indicating origin or manner of development: *phylogeny* [from Greek *-geneia*, from *-genēs* born] > -**genic** adj combining form

geo- combining form indicating earth: *geomorphology* [from Greek, from *gē* earth]

geocaching (ˈdʒiːəʊˌkæʃɪŋ) n a game in which the object is to identify and find items deposited by other players, using GPS navigation [C20: from GEO(GRAPHY) + *caching*]

geocentric (ˌdʒiːəʊˈsɛntrɪk) adj 1 having the earth at its centre: *the Ptolemaic system postulated a geocentric universe* 2 measured from or relating to the centre of the earth > ˌgeo'centrically adv

geochronology (ˌdʒiːəʊkrəˈnɒlədʒɪ) n the branch of geology concerned with ordering and dating of events in the earth's history, including the origin of the earth itself > geochronological (ˌdʒiːəʊˌkrɒnᵊˈlɒdʒɪkᵊl) adj

geode (ˈdʒiːəʊd) n a cavity, usually lined with crystals, within a rock mass or nodule [C17: from Latin *geōdēs* a precious stone, from Greek: earthlike; see GEO-, -ODE[1]] > geodic (dʒiːˈɒdɪk) adj

geodesic (ˌdʒiːəʊˈdɛsɪk, -ˈdiː-) adj 1 Also called: geodetic, geodesical relating to or involving the geometry of curved surfaces ⊳ n 2 Also called: geodesic line the shortest line between two points on a curved or plane surface

geodesic dome n a light structural framework arranged as a set of polygons in the form of a shell and covered with sheeting made of plastic, plywood, metal, etc; developed by Buckminster Fuller

geodesy (dʒiːˈɒdɪsɪ) n the branch of science concerned with determining the exact position of geographical points and the shape and size of the earth [C16: from French *géodésie*, from Greek *geōdaisia*, from GEO- + *daiein* to divide] > ge'odesist n

geodetic (ˌdʒiːəʊˈdɛtɪk) adj 1 of or relating to geodesy 2 another word for **geodesic** > ˌgeo'detically adv

geoduck (ˈdʒiːəʊˌdʌk) n Canadian a large edible clam [from Chinook jargon]

Geoffrey of Monmouth (ˈdʒɛfrɪ) n ?1100–54, Welsh bishop and chronicler; author of *Historia Regum Britanniae*, the chief source of Arthurian legends

geog. abbreviation 1 geographic(al) 2 geography

geographical mile n a former name for **nautical mile**

geography (dʒɪˈɒgrəfɪ) n, pl -phies 1 the study of the natural features of the earth's surface, including topography, climate, soil, vegetation, etc, and man's response to them 2 the natural features of a region > ge'ographer n > geographical (ˌdʒɪəˈgræfɪkᵊl) or ˌgeo'graphic adj > ˌgeo'graphically adv

geoid (ˈdʒiːɔɪd) n 1 a hypothetical surface that corresponds to mean sea level and extends at the same level under the continents 2 the shape of the earth

geol. abbreviation 1 geologic(al) 2 geology

geology (dʒɪˈɒlədʒɪ) n 1 the scientific study of the origin, history, structure, and composition of the earth 2 the geological features of a district or country > **geological** (ˌdʒɪəˈlɒdʒɪkəl) *or* ˌgeoˈlogic *adj* > ˌgeoˈlogically *adv* > geˈologist *or* geˈologer *n*

geom. *abbreviation* **1** geometric(al) **2** geometry

geomagnetism (ˌdʒiːəʊˈmægnɪˌtɪzəm) *n* **1** the magnetic field of the earth **2** the branch of physics concerned with this > **geomagnetic** (ˌdʒiːəʊmægˈnɛtɪk) *adj*

geometric (ˌdʒɪəˈmɛtrɪk) *or* **geometrical** *adj* **1** of, relating to, or following the methods and principles of geometry **2** consisting of, formed by, or characterized by points, lines, curves, or surfaces **3** (of design or ornamentation) composed predominantly of simple geometric forms, such as circles, rectangles, triangles, etc > ˌgeoˈmetrically *adv*

geometric mean *n* the average value of a set of *n* integers, terms, or quantities, expressed as the *n*th root of their product

geometric progression *n* a sequence of numbers, each of which differs from the succeeding one by a constant ratio, as 1, 2, 4, 8, ... See **arithmetic progression**

geometric series *n* a geometric progression written as a sum, as in $1 + 2 + 4 + 8$

geometrid (dʒɪˈɒmɪtrɪd) *n* any moth of the family *Geometridae*, the larvae of which are called measuring worms, inchworms, or loopers [C19: from New Latin *Geōmetridae*, from Latin, from Greek *geometrēs*: land measurer, from the looping gait of the larvae]

geometry (dʒɪˈɒmɪtrɪ) *n* **1** the branch of mathematics concerned with the properties, relationships, and measurement of points, lines, curves, and surfaces **2** a shape, configuration, or arrangement [C14: from Latin *geōmetria*, from Greek, from *geōmetrein* to measure the land] > geˈometer *or* geometrician (dʒɪˌɒmɪˈtrɪʃən, ˌdʒiːəʊmɪ-)

geomorphology (ˌdʒiːəʊmɔːˈfɒlədʒɪ) *n* the branch of geology that is concerned with the structure, origin, and development of the topographical features of the earth's surface > **geomorphological** (ˌdʒiːəʊˌmɔːfəˈlɒdʒɪkəl) *or* ˌgeoˌmorphoˈlogic *adj*

geophysics (ˌdʒiːəʊˈfɪzɪks) *n* (*functioning as singular*) the study of the earth's physical properties and of the physical processes acting upon, above, and within the earth. It includes seismology, geomagnetism, meteorology, and oceanography > ˌgeoˈphysicist *n* > ˌgeoˈphysical *adj*

geopolitics (ˌdʒiːəʊˈpɒlɪtɪks) *n* **1** (*functioning as singular*) the study of the effect of geographical factors on politics, esp international politics; political geography **2** (*functioning as plural*) the combination of geographical and political factors affecting a country or area **3** (*functioning as plural*) politics as they affect the whole world; global politics > **geopolitical** (ˌdʒiːəʊpəˈlɪtɪkəl) *adj*

geoponics (ˌdʒiːəʊˈpɒnɪks) *n* (*functioning as singular*) the science of agriculture

Geordie (ˈdʒɔːdɪ) *Brit* ▷ *n* **1** a person who comes from or lives in Tyneside **2** the dialect spoken by these people ▷ *adj* **3** of or relating to these people or their dialect [C19: a diminutive of *George*]

George (dʒɔːdʒ) *n* **1** David Lloyd. See: **Lloyd George 2** Sir Edward (**Alan John**), known as *Eddie*. born 1938, British economist; governor of the Bank of England (1993–2003) **3** Henry. 1839–97, US economist: advocated a single tax on land values, esp in *Progress and Poverty* (1879) **4** Saint. died ?303 AD, Christian martyr, the patron saint of England; the hero of a legend in which he slew a dragon. Feast day: April 23 **5** (*German* geˈɔrgə) **Stefan** (**Anton**) (ˈʃtɛfan). 1868–1933, German poet and aesthete. Influenced by the French Symbolists, esp Mallarmé and later by Nietzsche, he sought for an idealized purity of form in his verse. He refused Nazi honours and went into exile in 1933

George I *n* 1660–1727, first Hanoverian king of Great Britain and Ireland (1714–27) and elector of Hanover (1698–1727). His dependence in domestic affairs on his ministers led to the emergence of Walpole as the first prime minister

George II *n* 1 1683–1760, king of Great Britain and Ireland and elector of Hanover (1727–60); son of George I. His victory over the French at Dettingen (1743) in the War of

the Austrian Succession was the last appearance on a battlefield by a British king **2** 1890–1947, king of Greece (1922–24; 1935–47). He was overthrown by the republicans (1924) and exiled during the German occupation of Greece (1941–45)

George III *n* 1738–1820, king of Great Britain and Ireland (1760–1820) and of Hanover (1814–20). During his reign the American colonies were lost. He became insane in 1811, and his son acted as regent for the rest of the reign

George IV *n* 1762–1830, king of Great Britain and Ireland and also of Hanover (1820–30); regent (1811–20). His father (George III) disapproved of his profligate ways, which undermined the prestige of the crown, and of his association with the Whig opposition

George V *n* 1865–1936, king of Great Britain and Northern Ireland and emperor of India (1910–36)

George VI *n* 1895–1952, king of Great Britain and Northern Ireland (1936–52) and emperor of India (1936–47). The second son of George V, he succeeded to the throne after the abdication of his brother, Edward VIII

George Cross *n* a British award for bravery, esp of civilians: instituted 1940. Abbreviation: GC

Georgetown (ˈdʒɔːdʒˌtaʊn) *n* the capital and chief port of Guyana, at the mouth of the Demerara River: became capital of the Dutch colonies of Essequibo and Demerara in 1784; seat of the University of Guyana. Pop: 237 000 (2005 est). Former name (until 1812): Stabroek

George Town *n* **1** Also called: Penang a port in NW Malaysia, capital of Penang state, in NE Penang Island: the first chartered city of the Malayan federation. Pop: 162 000 (2005 est) **2** the capital of the Cayman Islands: a port on Grand Cayman Island. Pop: 30 600 (2004 est)

georgette *or* **georgette crepe** (dʒɔːˈdʒɛt) *n* a thin silk or cotton crepe fabric with a mat finish [C20: from the name Mme *Georgette*, a French modiste]

Georgia (ˈdʒɔːdʒə) *n* **1** a republic in NW Asia, on the Black Sea: an independent kingdom during the middle ages, it was divided by Turkey and Persia in 1555; became part of Russia in 1918 and a separate Soviet republic in 1936; its independence was recognized internationally in 1992. It is rich in minerals and has hydroelectric resources. Official language: Georgian. Religion: believers are mainly Christian or Muslim. Currency: lari. Capital: Tbilisi. Pop: 5 074 000 (2004 est). Area: 69 493 sq km (26 831 sq miles) **2** a state of the southeastern US, on the Atlantic: consists of coastal plains with forests and swamps, rising to the Cumberland Plateau and the Appalachians in the northwest Capital: Atlanta. Pop: 8 684 715 (2003 est). Area: 152 489 sq km (58 876 sq miles). Abbreviations: Ga *or* (with zip code) GA

Georgian (ˈdʒɔːdʒən) *adj* **1** of, characteristic of, or relating to any or all of the four kings who ruled Great Britain and Ireland from 1714 to 1830, or to their reigns **2** of or relating to George V of Great Britain and Northern Ireland and his reign (1910–36): *the Georgian poets* **3** of or relating to the republic of Georgia, its people, or their language **4** of or relating to the American State of Georgia or its inhabitants **5** in or imitative of the style prevalent in England during the 18th century (reigns of George I, II, and III); in architecture, dominated by the ideas of Palladio, and in furniture represented typically by the designs of Sheraton ▷ *n* **6** the official language of Georgia, belonging to the South Caucasian family **7** a native or inhabitant of Georgia **8** a native or inhabitant of the American State of Georgia

Georgian Bay *n* a bay in S central Canada, in Ontario, containing many small islands: the NE part of Lake Huron. Area: 15 000 sq km (5800 sq miles)

geostatics (ˌdʒiːəʊˈstætɪks) *n* (*functioning as singular*) the branch of physics concerned with the statics of rigid bodies, esp the balance of forces within the earth

geostationary (ˌdʒiːəʊˈsteɪʃənərɪ) *adj* (of a satellite) in a circular equatorial orbit in which it circles the earth once per sidereal day so that it appears stationary in relation to the earth's surface. Also called: geosynchronous

geostrophic (ˌdʒiːəʊˈstrɒfɪk) *adj* of, relating to, or caused by the force produced by the rotation of the earth: *geostrophic wind*

geosynchronous (ˌdʒiːəʊˈsɪŋkrənəs) *adj* another word for **geostationary**

geosyncline (ˌdʒiːəʊˈsɪŋklaɪn) *n* a broad elongated depression in the earth's crust containing great thicknesses of sediment

geotextile (ˌdʒiːəʊˈtɛkstaɪl) *n* any strong synthetic fabric used in civil engineering, as to retain an embankment

geothermal (ˌdʒiːəʊˈθɜːməl) *or* **geothermic** *adj* of or relating to the heat in the interior of the earth

geotropism (dʒɪˈɒtrəˌpɪzəm) *n* the response of a plant part to the stimulus of gravity. Plant stems, which grow upwards irrespective of the position in which they are placed, show **negative geotropism** > geotropic (ˌdʒiːəʊˈtrɒpɪk) *adj*

Ger. *abbreviation* 1 German 2 Germany

Gera (*German* ˈɡeːra) *n* an industrial city in E central Germany, in Thuringia. Pop: 106 365 (2003 est)

geranium (dʒɪˈreɪnɪəm) *n* 1 any cultivated geraniaceous plant of the genus *Pelargonium*, having scarlet, pink, or white showy flowers. See also **pelargonium** 2 any geraniaceous plant of the genus *Geranium*, such as cranesbill and herb Robert, having divided leaves and pink or purplish flowers [c16: from Latin: cranesbill, from Greek *geranion*, from *geranos* CRANE]

Gérard (*French* ʒerar) *n* **François** (**Pascal Simon**), Baron. 1770–1837, French painter, court painter to Napoleon I and Louis XVIII

gerbera (ˈdʒɜːbərə) *n* any plant of the perennial genus *Gerbera*, esp the Barberton daisy from S. Africa, *G. jamesonii*, grown, usually as a greenhouse plant, for its large brightly coloured daisy-like flowers: family *Asteraceae* [named after Traugott *Gerber* (died 1743), German naturalist]

gerbil *or* **gerbille** (ˈdʒɜːbɪl) *n* any burrowing rodent of the subfamily *Gerbillinae*, inhabiting hot dry regions of Asia and Africa and having soft pale fur: family *Cricetidae* [c19: from French *gerbille*, from New Latin *gerbillus* a little JERBOA]

gerfalcon (ˈdʒɜːˌfɔːlkən, -ˌfɔːkən) *n* a variant spelling of **gyrfalcon**

Gergiev (ˈɡɛədʒɛf) *n* **Valery Abesalovich**. born 1953, Russian conductor; musical director of the Kirov (now the Mariinsky) Opera from 1988

geriatric (ˌdʒɛrɪˈætrɪk) *adj* 1 of or relating to geriatric medicine or to older people 2 *offensive* (of people or machines) old, obsolescent, worn out, or useless ▷ *n* 3 *old-fashioned, offensive* an elderly person [c20: from Greek *gēras* old age + IATRIC]

geriatrics (ˌdʒɛrɪˈætrɪks) *n* (*functioning as singular*) the branch of medical science concerned with the diagnosis and treatment of diseases affecting older people > ˌgeriaˈtrician *or* geriatrist (ˌdʒɛrɪˈætrɪst) *n*

Géricault (*French* ʒeriko) *n* (**Jean Louis André**) **Théodore** (teɔdɔr). 1791–1824, French romantic painter, noted for his skill in capturing movement, esp of horses

Gerlachovka (*Slovak* ˈɡɛrlaxɔfka) *n* a mountain in N Slovakia, in the Tatra Mountains: the highest peak of the Carpathian Mountains. Height: 2663 m (8737 ft)

germ (dʒɜːm) *n* 1 a microorganism, esp one that produces disease in animals or plants 2 (*often plural*) the rudimentary or initial form of something: *the germs of revolution* 3 a simple structure, such as a fertilized egg, that is capable of developing into a complete organism [c17: from French *germe*, from Latin *germen* sprig, bud, sprout, seed]

german (ˈdʒɜːmən) *adj* 1 (used in combination) **a** having the same parents as oneself: *a brother-german* **b** having a parent that is a brother or sister of either of one's own parents: *cousin-german* 2 a less common word for **germane** [c14: via Old French *germain*, from Latin *germānus* of the same race, from *germen* sprout, offshoot]

German (ˈdʒɜːmən) *n* 1 the official language of Germany and Austria and one of the official languages of Switzerland; the native language of approximately 100 million people. It is an Indo-European language belonging to the West Germanic branch, closely related to English and Dutch. There is considerable diversity of dialects; modern standard German is a development of Old High German, influenced by Martin Luther's translation of the Bible 2 a native, inhabitant, or citizen of Germany 3 a person whose native language is German ▷ *adj* 4 denoting, relating to, or using the German language 5 relating to, denoting, or characteristic of any German state or its people

German Democratic Republic *n* (formerly) the official name of East Germany. Abbreviation: **GDR** *or* **DDR**

germander (dʒɜːˈmændə) *n* any of several plants of the genus *Teucrium*, esp *T. chamaedrys* (**wall germander**) of Europe, having two-lipped flowers with a very small upper lip: family *Lamiaceae* (labiates) [c15: from Medieval Latin *germandrea*, from Late Greek *khamandrua*, from Greek *khamaidrus*, from *khamai* on the ground + *drus* oak tree]

germane (dʒɜːˈmeɪn) *adj* (*postpositive; usually foll by to*) related (to the topic being considered); akin; relevant [variant of GERMAN] > **gerˈmanely** *adv* > **gerˈmaneness** *n*

German East Africa *n* a former German territory in E Africa, consisting of Tanganyika and Ruanda-Urundi: divided in 1919 between Great Britain and Belgium; now in Tanzania, Rwanda, and Burundi

Germanic (dʒɜːˈmænɪk) *n* 1 a branch of the Indo-European family of languages that includes English, Dutch, German, the Scandinavian languages, and Gothic. Abbreviation: **Gmc** 2 the unrecorded language from which all of these languages developed; Proto-Germanic ▷ *adj* 3 of, denoting, or relating to this group of languages 4 of, relating to, or characteristic of Germany, the German language, or any people that speaks a Germanic language

Germanicus Caesar (dʒɜːˈmænɪkəs) *n* 15 BC–19 AD, Roman general; nephew of the emperor Tiberius; waged decisive campaigns against the Germans (14–16)

germanium (dʒɜːˈmeɪnɪəm) *n* a brittle crystalline grey element that is a semiconducting metalloid, occurring principally in zinc ores and argyrodite: used in transistors, as a catalyst, and to strengthen and harden alloys. Symbol: Ge; atomic no: 32; atomic wt: 72.61; valency: 2 or 4; relative density: 5.323; melting pt: 938.35°C; boiling pt: 2834°C [c19: New Latin, named after GERMANY]

German measles *n* (*functioning as singular*) a nontechnical name for **rubella**

German Ocean *n* a former name for the **North Sea**

German shepherd *or* **German shepherd dog** *n* another name for **Alsatian** (sense 1)

German silver *n* another name for **nickel silver**

Germany (ˈdʒɜːmənɪ) *n* a country in central Europe: in the Middle Ages the centre of the Holy Roman Empire; dissolved into numerous principalities; united under the leadership of Prussia in 1871 after the Franco-Prussian War; became a republic with reduced size in 1919 after being defeated in World War I; under the dictatorship of Hitler from 1933 to 1945; defeated in World War II and divided by the Allied Powers into four zones, which became established as East and West Germany in the late 1940s; reunified in 1990: a member of the European Union. It is flat and low-lying in the north with plateaus and uplands (including the Black Forest and the Bavarian Alps) in the centre and south. Official language: German. Religion: Christianity, Protestant majority. Currency: euro. Capital: Berlin. Pop: 82 526 000 (2004 est). Area: 357 041 sq km (137 825 sq miles). German name: **Deutschland**. Official name: **Federal Republic of Germany**

germ cell *n* a sexual reproductive cell; gamete

germicide (ˈdʒɜːmɪˌsaɪd) *n* any substance that kills germs or other microorganisms > ˌgermiˈcidal *adj*

germinal (ˈdʒɜːmɪnˀl) *adj* 1 of, relating to, or like germs or a germ cell 2 of, or in the earliest stage of development; embryonic [c19: from New Latin *germinālis*, from Latin *germen* bud; see GERM] > ˈgerminally *adv*

germinate (ˈdʒɜːmɪˌneɪt) *vb* 1 to cause (seeds or spores) to sprout or (of seeds or spores) to sprout or form new tissue following increased metabolism 2 to grow or cause to grow; develop 3 to come or bring into existence; originate: *the idea germinated with me* [c17: from Latin

g

germ*in*āre to sprout; see GERM] ▷ 'germinable *or* 'germinative *adj* ▷ ,germi'nation *n* ▷ 'germi,nator *n*

Germiston (ˈdʒɜːmɪstən) *n* a city in South Africa, southeast of Johannesburg: industrial centre, with the world's largest gold refinery, serving the Witwatersrand mines. Pop: 139 721 (2001)

germ plasm *n* **a** the part of a germ cell that contains hereditary material; the chromosomes and genes **b** the germ cells collectively

germ warfare *n* the military use of disease-spreading bacteria against an enemy

Gerona (*Spanish* xeˈrona) *n* a city in NE Spain: city walls and 14th-century cathedral; often besieged, in particular by the French (1809). Pop: 81 220 (2003 est)

Geronimo (dʒəˈrɒnɪˌməʊ) *n* **1** 1829–1909, Apache Indian chieftain: led a campaign against the White settlers until his final capture in 1886 ▷ *interj* **2** US a shout given by paratroopers as they jump into battle **3** an exclamation expressing exhilaration, esp when jumping from a great height

gerontology (ˌdʒɛrɒnˈtɒlədʒɪ) *n* the scientific study of ageing and the problems associated with older people ▷ gerontological (ˌdʒɛrɒntəˈlɒdʒɪkˀl) *adj* ▷ ,geron'tologist *n*

-gerous *adj combining form* bearing or producing: *armigerous* [from Latin *-ger* bearing + -OUS]

gerrymander (ˈdʒɛrɪˌmændə) *vb* **1** to divide the constituencies of (a voting area) so as to give one party an unfair advantage **2** to manipulate or adapt to one's advantage ▷ *n* **3** an act or result of gerrymandering [C19: from Elbridge *Gerry*, US politician + (SALA)MANDER; from the salamander-like outline of an electoral district reshaped (1812) for political purposes while Gerry was governor of Massachusetts]

Gers (*French* ʒɛr) *n* a department of SW France, in Midi-Pyrénées region. Capital: Auch. Pop: 175 055 (2003 est). Area: 6291 sq km (2453 sq miles)

Gershwin (ˈɡɜːʃwɪn) *n* **1 George**, original name *Jacob Gershvin*. 1898–1937, US composer: incorporated jazz into works such as *Rhapsody in Blue* (1924) for piano and jazz band and the opera *Porgy and Bess* (1935) **2** his brother, **Ira**, original name *Israel Gershvin*. 1896–1983, US song lyricist, noted esp for his collaboration with George Gershwin

gerund (ˈdʒɛrənd) *n* a noun formed from a verb, denoting an action or state. In English, the gerund, like the present participle, ends in *-ing*: *the living is easy* [C16: from Late Latin *gerundium*, from Latin *gerundum* something to be carried on, from *gerere* to wage] ▷ gerundial (dʒɪˈrʌndɪəl) *adj*

gerundive (dʒɪˈrʌndɪv) *n* **1** (in Latin grammar) an adjective formed from a verb, expressing the desirability of the activity denoted by the verb ▷ *adj* **2** of or relating to the gerund or gerundive [C17: from Late Latin *gerundīvus*, from *gerundium* GERUND] ▷ **gerundival** (ˌdʒɛrənˈdaɪvˀl) *adj*

Gervais (ˌdʒɜːˈveɪz) *n* **Ricky**. born 1962, British comedian and actor, best known for his starring role in the TV series *The Office* (2001–02), which he also co-wrote and co-directed

Geryon (ˈɡɛrɪən) *n Greek myth* a winged monster with three bodies joined at the waist, killed by Hercules, who stole the monster's cattle as his tenth labour

gesso (ˈdʒɛsəʊ) *n* **1** a white ground of plaster and size, used esp in the Middle Ages and Renaissance to prepare panels or canvas for painting or gilding **2** any white substance, esp plaster of Paris, that forms a ground when mixed with water [C16: from Italian: chalk, GYPSUM]

gest *or* **geste** (dʒɛst) *n archaic* **1** a notable deed or exploit **2** a tale of adventure or romance, esp in verse [C14: from Old French, from Latin *gesta* deeds, from *gerere* to carry out]

Gestalt psychology *n* a system of thought, derived from experiments carried out by German psychologists, that regards all mental phenomena as being arranged in perceptual patterns or structures possessing qualities as a whole that cannot be described merely as a sum of their parts

Gestapo (ɡɛˈstɑːpəʊ; *German* ɡeˈʃtɑːpo) *n* the secret state police in Nazi Germany, noted for its brutal methods of interrogation [from German *Ge(heime) Sta(ats)po(lizei)*, literally: secret state police]

gestate (ˈdʒɛsteɪt) *vb* **1** (*tr*) to carry (developing young) in the uterus during pregnancy **2** (*tr*) to develop (a plan or idea) in the mind **3** (*intr*) to be in the process of gestating [C19: back formation from GESTATION]

gestation (dʒɛˈsteɪʃən) *n* **1 a** the development of the embryo of a viviparous mammal, between conception and birth: about 266 days in humans, 624 days in elephants, and 63 days in cats **b** (*as modifier*): *gestation period* **2** the development of an idea or plan in the mind **3** the period of such a development [C16: from Latin *gestātiō* a bearing, from *gestāre* to bear, frequentative of *gerere* to carry]

gesticulate (dʒɛˈstɪkjʊˌleɪt) *vb* to express by or make gestures [C17: from Latin *gesticulārī*, from Latin *gesticulus* (unattested except in Late Latin) gesture, diminutive of *gestus* gesture, from *gerere* to bear, conduct] ▷ ges'ticulative *adj* ▷ ges'ticu,lator *n* ▷ geˌsticu'lation *n* ▷ ges'ticulatory *adj*

gesture (ˈdʒɛstʃə) *n* **1** a motion of the hands, head, or body to emphasize an idea or emotion, esp while speaking **2** something said or done as a formality or as an indication of intention ▷ *vb* **3** to express by or make gestures; gesticulate [C15: from Medieval Latin *gestūra* bearing, from Latin *gestus*, past participle of *gerere* to bear] ▷ 'gestural *adj*

Gesualdo (*Italian* dʒezuˈaldo) *n* **Carlo** (ˈkarlo), Prince of Venosa. ?1560–1613, Italian composer, esp of madrigals

get (ɡɛt) *vb* **gets**, **getting**, **got** (ɡɒt) *or* **gotor** *esp* US **gotten** (*mainly tr*) **1** to come into possession of; receive or earn **2** to bring or fetch **3** to contract or be affected by: *he got a chill at the picnic* **4** to capture or seize: *the police finally got him* **5** (*also intr*) to become or cause to become or act as specified: *to get a window open; get one's hair cut; get wet* **6** (*intr*; foll by a preposition or adverbial particle) to succeed in going, coming, leaving, etc: *get off the bus* **7** (*takes an infinitive*) to manage or contrive: *how did you get to be captain?* **8** to make ready or prepare: *to get a meal* **9** to hear, notice, or understand: *I didn't get your meaning* **10** US & Canadian informal to learn or master by study **11** (*intr*; often foll by *to*) to come (to) or arrive (at): *we got home safely; to get to London* **12** to catch or enter: *to get a train* **13** to induce or persuade: *get him to leave at once* **14** to reach by calculation: *add 2 and 2 and you will get 4* **15** to receive (a broadcast signal) **16** to communicate with (a person or place), as by telephone **17** (*also intr*; foll by *to*) *informal* to have an emotional effect (on): *that music really gets me* **18** *informal* to annoy or irritate: *her high voice gets me* **19** *informal* to bring a person into a difficult position from which he or she cannot escape **20** *informal* to puzzle; baffle **21** *informal* to hit: *the blow got him in the back* **22** *informal* to be revenged on, esp by killing **23** *informal* to have the better of: *your extravagant habits will get you in the end* **24** (*intr*; foll by present participle) *informal* to begin: *get moving* **25** (used as a command) *informal* go! leave now! **26** *archaic* to beget or conceive **27** get with child *archaic* to make pregnant ▷ *n* **28** *rare* the act of begetting **29** *rare* something begotten; offspring **30** *Brit slang* a variant of *git* ▷ See also **get about, get across, get at, get away, get back, get by, get in, get off, get on, get out, get over, get round, get through, get-together, get up, got, gotten** [Old English *gietan*; related to Old Norse *geta* to get, learn, Old High German *bigezzan* to obtain] ▷ 'getable *or* 'gettable *adj* ▷ 'getter *n*

● USAGE The use of *off* after *get* as in *I got this chair off an antique dealer* is acceptable in conversation, but should
● not be used in formal writing

GeT *abbreviation* Greenwich Electronic Time

get about *or* **get around** *vb* (*intr, adverb*) **1** to move around, as when recovering from an illness **2** to be socially active **3** (of news, rumour, etc) to become known; spread

get across *vb* **1** to cross or cause or help to cross **2** (*adverb*) to be or cause to be readily understood

get at *vb* (*intr, preposition*) **1** to gain access to **2** to mean or intend: *what are you getting at when you look at me like that?* **3** to irritate or annoy persistently; criticize: *she is always* getting at him **4** to influence or seek to influence, esp illegally by bribery, intimidation, etc: *someone had got at the witness before the trial*

get away *vb* (*adverb, mainly intr*) **1** to make an escape; leave **2** to make a start **3 get away with a** to steal and escape (with money, goods, etc) **b** to do (something wrong, illegal, etc) without being discovered or punished or with only a minor punishment ▷ *interj* **4** an exclamation indicating mild disbelief ▷ *n* **getaway 5** the act of escaping, esp by criminals **6** a start or acceleration **7** (*modifier*) used for escaping: *a getaway car*

get back *vb* (*adverb*) **1** (*tr*) to recover or retrieve **2** (*intr; often foll by to*) to return, esp to a former position or activity **3** (*intr; foll by at*) to retaliate (against); wreak vengeance (on) **4 get one's own back** *informal* to obtain one's revenge

get by *vb* **1** to pass; go past or overtake **2** (*intr, adverb*) *informal* to manage, esp in spite of difficulties **3** (*intr*) to be accepted or permitted: *that book will never get by the authorities*

Gethsemane (gɛθ'sɛmənɪ) *n New Testament* the garden in Jerusalem where Christ was betrayed on the night before his Crucifixion (Matthew 26:36–56)

get in *vb* (*mainly adverb*) **1** (*intr*) to enter a car, train, etc **2** (*intr*) to arrive, esp at one's home or place of work **3** (*tr*) to bring in or inside: *get the milk in* **4** (*tr*) to insert or slip in: *he got his suggestion in before anyone else* **5** (*tr*) to gather or collect (crops, debts, etc) **6** to be elected or cause to be elected **7** (*intr*) to obtain a place at university, college, etc **8** (*foll by on*) to join or cause to join (an activity or organization)

get off *vb* **1** (*intr, adverb*) to escape the consequences of an action: *he got off very lightly in the accident* **2** (*adverb*) to be or cause to be acquitted: *a good lawyer got him off* **3** (*adverb*) to depart or cause to depart: *to get the children off to school* **4** (*intr*) to descend (from a bus, train, etc); dismount: *she got off at the terminus* **5** to move or cause to move to a distance (from): *get off the field* **6** (*tr, adverb*) to remove; take off: *get your coat off* **7** (*adverb*) to go or send to sleep **8** (*adverb*) to send (letters) or (of letters) to be sent **9 get off with** *Brit informal* to establish an amorous or sexual relationship with

get on *vb* (*mainly adverb*) **1** to board or cause or help to board (a bus, train, etc) **2** (*tr*) to dress in (clothes as specified) **3** (*intr*) to grow late or (of time) to elapse: *it's getting on and I must go* **4** (*intr*) to grow old **5** (*intr; foll by for*) to approach (a time, age, amount, etc): *she is getting on for seventy* **6** (*intr*) to make progress, manage, or fare: *how did you get on in your exam?* **7** (*intr; often foll by with*) to establish a friendly relationship: *he gets on well with other people* **8** (*intr; foll by with*) to continue to do: *get on with your homework!*

get out *vb* (*adverb*) **1** to leave or escape or cause to leave or escape: used in the imperative when dismissing a person **2** to make or become known; publish or be published **3** (*tr*) to express with difficulty **4** (*tr; often foll by of*) to extract (information or money) (from a person): *to get a confession out of a criminal* **5** (*tr*) to gain or receive something, esp something of significance or value **6** (*foll by of*) to avoid or cause to avoid: *she always gets out of swimming* **7** *cricket* to dismiss or be dismissed

get over *vb* **1** to cross or surmount (something) **2** (*intr, preposition*) to recover from (an illness, shock, etc) **3** (*intr, preposition*) to overcome or master (a problem) **4** (*intr, preposition*) to appreciate fully: *I just can't get over seeing you again* **5** (*tr, adverb*) to communicate effectively **6** (*tr, adverb; sometimes foll by with*) to bring (something necessary but unpleasant) to an end: *let's get this job over with quickly*

get round *or* **get around** *vb* (*intr*) **1** (*preposition*) to circumvent or overcome **2** (*preposition*) *informal* to have one's way with; cajole: *that girl can get round anyone* **3** (*preposition*) to evade (a law or rules) **4** (*adverb; foll by to*) to reach or come to at length: *I'll get round to that job in an hour*

get through *vb* **1** to succeed or cause or help to succeed in an examination, test, etc **2** to bring or come to a destination, esp after overcoming problems: *we got through the blizzards to the survivors* **3** (*intr, adverb*) to contact, as by telephone **4** (*intr, preposition*) to use, spend, or

consume (money, supplies, etc) **5** to complete or cause to complete (a task, process, etc): *to get a bill through Parliament* **6** (*adverb; foll by to*) to reach the awareness and understanding (of a person): *I just can't get the message through to him*

get-together *n* **1** *informal* a small informal meeting or social gathering ▷ *vb* **get together** (*adverb*) **2** (*tr*) to gather or collect **3** (*intr*) (of people) to meet socially **4** (*intr*) to discuss, esp in order to reach an agreement

Getty ('gɛtɪ) *n* J(**ean**) **Paul**. 1892–1976, US oil executive, millionaire, and art collector

Gettysburg ('gɛtɪz,bɜːg) *n* a small town in S Pennsylvania, southwest of Harrisburg: scene of a crucial battle (1863) during the American Civil War, in which Meade's Union forces defeated Lee's Confederate army; site of the national cemetery dedicated by President Lincoln. Pop: 7825 (2003 est)

get up *vb* (*mainly adverb*) **1** to wake and rise from one's bed or cause to wake and rise from bed **2** (*intr*) to rise to one's feet; stand up **3** (*also preposition*) to ascend or cause to ascend **4** to increase or cause to increase in strength: *the wind got up at noon* **5** (*tr*) *informal* to dress (oneself) in a particular way, esp showily or elaborately **6** (*tr*) *informal* to devise or create: *to get up an entertainment for Christmas* **7** (*tr*) *informal* to study or improve one's knowledge of: *I must get up my history* **8** (*intr; foll by to*) *informal* to be involved in: *he's always getting up to mischief* ▷ *n* **get-up 9** *informal* a costume or outfit, esp one that is striking or bizarre **10** *informal* the arrangement or production of a book, etc

get-up-and-go *n informal* energy, drive, or ambition

Getz (gɛts) *n* **Stanley**, known as *Stan*. 1927–91, US jazz saxophonist: leader of his own group from 1949

geum ('dʒiːəm) *n* any herbaceous plant of the rosaceous genus *Geum*, having compound leaves and red, orange, or white flowers [C19: New Latin, from Latin: herb bennet, avens]

gewgaw ('gjuːgɔː, 'guː-) *n* a showy but valueless trinket [C15: of unknown origin]

geyser ('giːzə; US 'gaɪzər) *n* **1** a spring that discharges steam and hot water **2** *Brit* a domestic gas water heater [C18: from Icelandic *Geysir*, from Old Norse *geysa* to gush]

Gezira (dʒəˈzɪərə) *n* a region of the E central Sudan between the Blue and White Niles: site of a large-scale irrigation scheme

G-force *n* the force of gravity

Ghana ('gɑːnə) *n* a republic in W Africa, on the Gulf of Guinea: a powerful empire from the 4th to the 13th centuries; a major source of gold and slaves for Europeans after 1471; British colony of the Gold Coast established in 1874; united with British Togoland in 1957 and became a republic and a member of the Commonwealth in 1960. Official language: English. Religions: Christian, Muslim, and animist. Currency: cedi. Capital: Accra. Pop: 21 377 000 (2004 est). Area: 238 539 sq km (92 100 sq miles)

Ghanaian (gɑːˈneɪən) *or* **Ghanian** ('gɑːnɪən) *adj* **1** of or relating to Ghana or its inhabitants ▷ *n* **2** a native or inhabitant of Ghana

gharry *or* **gharri** ('gærɪ) *n, pl* **-ries** (in India) a horse-drawn vehicle available for hire [C19: from Hindi *gārī*]

ghastly ('gɑːstlɪ) *adj* **-lier, -liest 1** *informal* very bad or unpleasant **2** deathly pale; wan **3** *informal* extremely unwell; ill **4** terrifying; horrible ▷ *adv* **5** unhealthily; sickly: *ghastly pale* [Old English *gāstlīc* spiritual; see GHOSTLY] > 'ghastliness *n*

ghat (gɔːt) *n* (in India) **1** stairs or a passage leading down to a river **2** a mountain pass or mountain range **3** a place of cremation [C17: from Hindi *ghāt*, from Sanskrit *ghatta*]

Ghats (gɔːts) *pl n* See **Eastern Ghats, Western Ghats**

Ghazali ('gɑːzˌɑːlɪ) *n* **al-**. 1058–1111, Muslim theologian, philosopher, and mystic

ghazi ('gɑːzɪ) *n, pl* **-zis 1** a Muslim fighter against infidels **2** (*often capital*) a Turkish warrior of high rank [C18: from Arabic, from *ghazā* he made war]

Ghazzah ('gɑːzə, 'gʌzə) *n* transliteration of the Arabic name for **Gaza**

GHB *abbreviation* gamma hydroxybutyrate

ghee (giː) *n* butter, clarified by boiling, used in Indian cookery [c17: from Hindi *ghī*, from Sanskrit *ghri* sprinkle]

Ghent (gɛnt) *n* an industrial city and port in NW Belgium, capital of East Flanders province, at the confluence of the Rivers Lys and Scheldt: formerly famous for its cloth industry; university (1816). Pop: 229 344 (2004 est). Flemish name: Gent. French name: Gand

Gheorgiu (ˈdʒɔdʒju) *n* **Angela**. born 1965, Romanian soprano: married to Roberto Alagna

gherkin (ˈɡɜːkɪn) *n* **1** the immature fruit of any of various cucumbers, used for pickling **2 a** a tropical American cucurbitaceous climbing plant, *Cucumis anguria* **b** the small edible fruit of this plant [c17: from early modern Dutch *agurkkijn*, diminutive of *gurk*, from Slavonic, ultimately from Greek *angourion*]

ghetto (ˈɡɛtəʊ) *n, pl* **-tos** *or* **-toes 1** *sociol* a densely populated slum area of a city inhabited by a socially and economically deprived minority **2** an area in a European city in which Jews were formerly required to live **3** a group or class of people that is segregated in some way [c17: from Italian, perhaps shortened from *borghetto*, diminutive of *borgo* settlement outside a walled city; or from the Venetian *ghetto* the medieval iron-founding district, largely inhabited by Jews]

ghetto blaster *n informal* a large portable cassette recorder or CD player with built-in speakers

ghettoize *or* **ghettoise** (ˈɡɛtəʊˌaɪz) *vb* (*tr*) to confine or restrict to a particular area, activity, or category: *to ghettoize women as housewives* > ˌghettoiˈzation *or* ˌghettoiˈsation *n*

Ghiberti (Italian ɡiˈbɛrti) *n* **Lorenzo** (loˈrɛntso). 1378–1455, Italian sculptor, painter, and goldsmith of the quattrocento: noted esp for the bronze doors of the baptistry of Florence Cathedral

ghillie (ˈɡɪli) *n* a variant spelling of **gillie** [from Scottish Gaelic *gille* boy]

Ghirlandaio *or* **Ghirlandajo** (Italian ɡirlanˈdaːjo) *n* **Domenico** (doˈmeːniko). original name *Domenico Bigordi*. 1449–94, Italian painter of frescoes

ghost (ɡəʊst) *n* **1** the disembodied spirit of a dead person, supposed to haunt the living as a pale or shadowy vision; phantom **2** a haunting memory: *the ghost of his former life rose up before him* **3** a faint trace or possibility of something; glimmer: *a ghost of a smile* **4** the spirit; soul (archaic, except in the phrase **the Holy Ghost**) **5** *physics* **a** a faint secondary image produced by an optical system **b** a similar image on a television screen, formed by reflection of the transmitting waves or by a defect in the receiver **6** (*modifier*) falsely recorded as doing a particular job or fulfilling a particular function in order that some benefit, esp money, may be obtained: *a ghost worker* **7** give up the ghost to die ▷ *vb* **8** See **ghostwrite 9** (*tr*) to haunt **10** (*intr*) to move effortlessly and smoothly, esp unnoticed: *he ghosted into the penalty area* [Old English *gāst*; related to Old Frisian *jēst*, Old High German *geist* spirit, Sanskrit *hēda* fury, anger] > ˈghostˌlike *adj* > ˈghostly *adj*

ghost car *n Canadian* an unmarked police car

ghost town *n* a deserted town, esp one in the western US that was formerly a boom town

ghost word *n* a word that has entered the language through the perpetuation, in dictionaries, etc, of an error

ghostwrite (ˈɡəʊstˌraɪt) *vb* **-writes**, **-writing**, **-wrote**, **-written** to write (an autobiographical or other article) on behalf of a person who is then credited as author. Often shortened to: **ghost** > ˈghostˌwriter *n*

ghoul (guːl) *n* **1** a malevolent spirit or ghost **2** a person interested in morbid or disgusting things **3** a person who robs graves **4** (in Muslim legend) an evil demon thought to eat human bodies, either stolen corpses or children [c18: from Arabic *ghūl*, from *ghāla* he seized] > ˈghoulish *adj* > ˈghoulishly *adv* > ˈghoulishness *n*

GHQ *abbreviation military* General Headquarters

ghrelin (ˈɡrɛlɪn) *n* a hormone produced in the body that stimulates appetite [c20: from *g(rowth) h(ormone) rel(easing)* + *-IN*]

ghyll (ɡɪl) *n* a variant spelling of **gill**[3]

Gi *electronics abbreviation* gilbert

GI *n US informal* ▷ **1** *pl* **GIs** *or* **GI's** a soldier in the US Army, esp an enlisted man ▷ *adj* **2** conforming to US Army regulations; of standard government issue [c20: abbrev. of *government issue*]

Giacometti (Italian dʒakoˈmetti) *n* **Alberto** (alˈbɛrto). 1901–66, Swiss sculptor and painter, noted particularly for his long skeletal statues of isolated figures

Giambologna (Italian dʒamboˈlɔɲa) *n* original name *Giovanni da Bologna* or *Jean de Boulogne*. 1529–1608, Italian mannerist sculptor, born in Flanders: noted for his fountains and such works as *Samson Slaying a Philistine* (1565)

giant (ˈdʒaɪənt) *n* **1** Also (*fem*): **giantess** (ˈdʒaɪəntɪs) a mythical figure of superhuman size and strength, esp in folklore or fairy tales **2** a person or thing of exceptional size, reputation, etc **3** a remarkably or supernaturally large ▷ *adj* **3** remarkably or supernaturally large [c13: from Old French *geant*, from Vulgar Latin *gagās* (unattested), from Latin *gigās*, *gigant-*, from Greek]

giant hogweed *n* an umbelliferous garden escape, *Heracleum mantegazzianum*, a tall species of cow parsley that grows up to 3½ metres (10 ft) and whose irritant hairs and sap can cause a severe reaction if handled

giantism (ˈdʒaɪənˌtɪzəm) *n* another term for **gigantism**

giant panda *n* See **panda** (sense 1)

Giant's Causeway *n* a promontory of columnar basalt on the N coast of Northern Ireland, in Antrim: consists of several thousand pillars, mostly hexagonal, that were formed by the rapid cooling of lava and the inward contraction of the lava flow

giant slalom *n skiing* a type of slalom in which the course is longer and the obstacles are further apart than in a standard slalom

giant star *n* any of a class of stars, such as Capella and Arcturus, that have swelled and brightened considerably as they approach the end of their life, their energy supply having changed

giaour (ˈdʒaʊə) *n* a derogatory term for a non-Muslim, esp a Christian, used esp by the Turks [c16: from Turkish *giaur* unbeliever, from Persian *gaur*, variant of *gäbr*]

gib (ɡɪb) *n* **1** a metal wedge, pad, or thrust bearing, esp a brass plate let into a steam engine crosshead ▷ *vb* **gibs**, **gibbing**, **gibbed 2** (*tr*) to fasten or supply with a gib [c18: of unknown origin]

Gib (dʒɪb) *n* an informal name for **Gibraltar**

gibber[1] (ˈdʒɪbə) *vb* **1** to utter rapidly and unintelligibly; prattle **2** (*intr*) (of monkeys and related animals) to make characteristic chattering sounds [c17: of imitative origin]

gibber[2] (ˈɡɪbə) *n Austral* **1** a stone or boulder **2** (*modifier*) of or relating to a dry flat area of land covered with wind-polished stones: *gibber plains* [c19: from a native Australian language]

Gibberd (ˈɡɪbəd) *n* Sir **Frederick**. 1908–84, British architect and town planner. His buildings include the Liverpool Roman Catholic cathedral (1960–67) and the Regent's Park Mosque in London (1977). Harlow in the U.K. and Santa Teresa in Venezuela were built to his plans

gibberellin (ˌdʒɪbəˈrɛlɪn) *n* any of several plant hormones, including gibberellic acid, whose main action is to cause elongation of the stem: used in promoting the growth of plants, in the malting of barley, etc

gibberish (ˈdʒɪbərɪʃ) *n* **1** rapid chatter like that of monkeys **2** incomprehensible talk; nonsense

gibbet (ˈdʒɪbɪt) *n* **1 a** a wooden structure resembling a gallows, from which the bodies of executed criminals were formerly hung to public view **b** a gallows ▷ *vb* (*tr*) **2** to put to death by hanging on a gibbet **3** to hang (a corpse) on a gibbet **4** to expose to public ridicule [c13: from Old French *gibet* gallows, literally: little cudgel, from *gibe* cudgel; of uncertain origin]

gibbon (ˈɡɪbən) *n* any small agile arboreal anthropoid ape of the genus *Hylobates*, inhabiting forests in S Asia [c18: from French, probably from an Indian dialect word]

Gibbon (ˈɡɪbən) *n* **1 Edward**. 1737–94, English historian; author of *The History of the Decline and Fall of the Roman*

Empire (1776–88), controversial in its historical criticism of Christianity **2 Lewis Grassic** ('græsɪk), real name James Leslie Mitchell. 1901–35, Scottish writer: best known for his trilogy of novels *Scots Quair* (1932–34)

Gibbons ('gɪbᵊnz) *n* **1 Grinling.** 1648–1721, English sculptor and woodcarver, noted for his delicate carvings of fruit, flowers, birds, etc **2 Orlando.** 1583–1625, English organist and composer, esp of anthems, motets, and madrigals

gibbous ('gɪbəs) *or* **gibbose** ('gɪbəʊs) *adj* **1** (of the moon or a planet) more than half but less than fully illuminated **2** having a hunchback; hunchbacked **3** bulging [c17: from Late Latin *gibbōsus* humpbacked, from Latin *gibba* hump] > 'gibbously *adv* > 'gibbousness *n*

Gibbs (gɪbz) *n* **1 James.** 1682–1754, British architect; his buildings include St Martin's-in-the-Fields, London (1722–26), and the Radcliffe Camera, Oxford (1737–49) **2 Josiah Willard.** 1839–1903, US physicist and mathematician: founder of chemical thermodynamics

gibe¹ *or* **jibe** (dʒaɪb) *vb* **1** to make jeering or scoffing remarks (at); taunt ▷ *n* **2** a derisive or provoking remark [c16: perhaps from Old French *giber* to treat roughly, of uncertain origin] > 'giber *or* 'jiber *n*

gibe² (dʒaɪb) *vb, n nautical* a variant spelling of **gybe**

Gibeon ('gɪbɪən) *n* an ancient town of Palestine: the excavated site thought to be its remains lies about 9 kilometres (6 miles) northwest of Jerusalem

giblets ('dʒɪblɪts) *pl n* (*sometimes singular*) the gizzard, liver, heart, and neck of a fowl [c14: from Old French *gibelet* stew of game birds, probably from *gibier* game, of Germanic origin]

Gibraltar (dʒɪˈbrɔːltə) *n* **1 City of Gibraltar** a city on the **Rock of Gibraltar,** a limestone promontory at the tip of S Spain: settled by Moors in 711 and taken by Spain in 1462; ceded to Britain in 1713; a British crown colony (1830–1969), still politically associated with Britain; a naval and air base of strategic importance. Pop: 27 000 (2003 est). Area: 6.5 sq km (2.5 sq miles). Ancient name: **Calpe 2 Strait of Gibraltar** a narrow strait between the S tip of Spain and the NW tip of Africa, linking the Mediterranean with the Atlantic

Gibraltarian (ˌdʒɪbrɔːlˈtɛərɪən) *adj* **1** of or relating to Gibraltar or its inhabitants ▷ *n* **2** a native or inhabitant of Gibraltar

Gibran (dʒɪˈbrɑːn) *n* **Kahlil** ('kɑːliːl). 1883–1931, Syro-Lebanese poet, mystic, and painter, resident in the US after 1910; author of *The Prophet* (1923)

Gibson ('gɪbsᵊn) *n* **Mel.** born 1956, Australian film actor and director: his films include *Mad Max* (1979), *Hamlet* (1990), *Braveheart* (1996; also directed), *What Women Want* (2000), and *The Passion of the Christ* (2004; director only)

Gibson Desert *n* a desert in W central Australia, between the Great Sandy Desert and the Victoria Desert: salt marshes, salt lakes, and scrub. Area: about 220 000 sq km (85 000 sq miles)

GIC *abbreviation* (in Canada) Guaranteed Investment Certificate: a form of investment that earns interest but is guaranteed not to incur loss

gidday (gəˈdaɪ) *sentence substitute* a variant spelling of: **g'day**

giddy ('gɪdɪ) *adj* **-dier, -diest 1** affected with a reeling sensation and feeling as if about to fall; dizzy **2** causing or tending to cause vertigo **3** impulsive; scatterbrained ▷ *vb* **-dies, -dying, -died 4** to make or become giddy [Old English *gydig* mad, frenzied, possessed by God; related to GOD] > 'giddily *adv* > 'giddiness *n*

Gide (French ʒid) *n* **André** (ãdre). 1869–1951, French novelist, dramatist, critic, diarist, and translator, noted particularly for his exploration of the conflict between self-fulfilment and conventional morality. His novels include *L'Immoraliste* (1902), *La Porte étroite* (1909), and *Les Faux-Monnayeurs* (1926): Nobel prize for literature 1947

Gideon ('gɪdɪən) *n Old Testament* a Hebrew judge who led the Israelites to victory over their Midianite oppressors (Judges 6:11–8:35)

gidgee *or* **gidjee** ('gɪdʒiː) *n Austral* any of various small acacia trees, *Acacia cambagei,* which at times emit an unpleasant smell [c19: from a native Australian language]

gie (giː) *vb* a Scot word for **give**

Gielgud ('giːlgʊd) *n* **Sir John.** 1904–2000, English stage, film, and television actor and director

Giessen (German 'giːsən) *n* a city in central Germany, in Hesse: university (1607). Pop: 74 001 (2003 est)

GIF (gɪf) *n computing* **a** a standard compressed file format used for pictures **b** a picture held in this format [c20: from *g(raphic) i(nterchange) f(ormat)*]

gift (gɪft) *n* **1** something given; a present **2** a special aptitude, ability, or power; talent **3** the power or right to give or bestow (esp in the phrases **in the gift of, in (someone's) gift**) **4** the act or process of giving **5 look a gift-horse in the mouth** (*usually negative*) to find fault with a free gift or chance benefit ▷ *vb* (*tr*) **6** to present (something) as a gift to (a person) [Old English *gift* payment for a wife, dowry; related to Old Norse *gipt*, Old High German *gift*, Gothic *fragifts* endowment, engagement; see GIVE]

GIFT (gɪft) *n acronym for* gamete intrafallopian transfer: a technique, similar to in vitro fertilization, that enables some women who are unable to conceive to bear children. Egg cells are removed from the woman's ovary, mixed with sperm, and introduced into one of her Fallopian tubes

gifted ('gɪftɪd) *adj* having or showing natural talent or aptitude: *a gifted musician; a gifted performance* > 'giftedly *adv* > 'giftedness *n*

gift of tongues *n* an utterance, partly or wholly unintelligible, believed by some to be produced under the influence of ecstatic religious emotion and conceived to be a manifestation of the Holy Ghost: practised in certain Christian churches, usually called Pentecostal. Also called: **glossolalia**

giftwrap ('gɪft.ræp) *vb* **-wraps, -wrapping, -wrapped** to wrap (an article intended as a gift) attractively

Gifu ('giːfuː) *n* a city in Japan, on central Honshu: hot springs, textile and paper lantern manufacturing. Pop: 401 296 (2002 est)

gig¹ (gɪg) *n* **1** a light two-wheeled one-horse carriage without a hood **2** *nautical* a light tender for a vessel, often for the personal use of the captain **3** a long light rowing boat, used esp for racing ▷ *vb* **gigs, gigging, gigged 4** (*intr*) to travel in a gig [c13 (in the sense: flighty girl, spinning top): perhaps of Scandinavian origin; compare Danish *gig* top, Norwegian *giga* to shake about]

gig² (gɪg) *n* **1** a cluster of barbless hooks drawn through a shoal of fish to try to impale them ▷ *vb* **gigs, gigging, gigged 2** to catch (fish) with a gig [c18: shortened from FISHGIG]

gig³ (gɪg) *informal* ▷ *n* **1** a job, esp a single booking for a musician, comedian, etc, to perform at a concert or club **2** the performance itself ▷ *vb* **gigs, gigging, gigged 3** (*intr*) to perform at a gig or gigs [c20: of unknown origin]

giga- ('gɪgə, 'gaɪgə) *combining form* **1** denoting 10⁹: *gigavolt.* Symbol: **G 2** (in computer technology) denoting 2³⁰: *gigabyte* [from Greek *gigas* GIANT]

gigabit ('gɪgə.bɪt, 'gaɪgə.bɪt) *n Computing* one million bits

gigaflop ('gɪgə.flɒp, 'gaɪgə.flɒp) *n computing* a measure of processing speed, consisting of a thousand million floating-point operations a second [c20: from GIGA- + *flo(ating) p(oint)*]

gigantic (dʒaɪˈgæntɪk) *adj* **1** very large; enormous **2** Also called: **gigantesque** (ˌdʒaɪɡænˈtɛsk) of or suitable for giants [c17: from Greek *gigantikos*, from *gigas* GIANT] > giˈgantically *adv*

gigantism ('dʒaɪɡænˌtɪzəm, dʒaɪˈɡæntɪzəm) *n* **1** Also called: **giantism** excessive growth of the entire body, caused by over-production of growth hormone by the pituitary gland during childhood or adolescence **2** the state or quality of being gigantic

giggle ('gɪɡᵊl) *vb* **1** (*intr*) to laugh nervously or foolishly ▷ *n* **2** such a laugh **3** *informal* something or someone that provokes amusement [c16: of imitative origin] > 'giggler *n* > 'giggling *n, adj* > 'giggly *adj*

Gigli (Italian 'dʒiʎi) *n* **Beniamino** (benjaˈmiːno). 1890–1957, Italian operatic tenor

gigolo ('ʒɪɡəˌləʊ) *n, pl* **-los 1** a man who is kept by a woman, esp an older woman **2** a man who is paid to dance with or escort women [c20: from French, back formation from *gigolette* girl for hire as a dancing partner, prostitute, from *giguer* to dance, from *gigue* a fiddle; compare GIGOT, GIGUE, JIG]

gigot ('ʒiːgəʊ, 'dʒɪgət) *n* **1** a leg of lamb or mutton **2** a leg-of-mutton sleeve [c16: from Old French: leg, a small fiddle, from *gigue* a fiddle, of Germanic origin]

gigue (ʒiːg) *n* a piece of music, usually in six-eight time and often fugal, incorporated into the classical suite [c17: from French, from Italian *giga*, literally: a fiddle; see GIGOT]

Gijón (giːˈhɔːn; *Spanish* xiˈxɔn) *n* a port in NW Spain, on the Bay of Biscay: capital of the kingdom of Asturias until 791. Pop: 270 875 (2003 est)

Gila monster ('hiːlə) *n* a large venomous brightly coloured lizard, *Heloderma suspectum*, inhabiting deserts of the southwestern US and Mexico and feeding mostly on eggs and small mammals: family *Helodermatidae* [c19: after the *Gila*, a river in New Mexico and Arizona]

gilbert ('gɪlbət) *n* a unit of magnetomotive force; the magnetomotive force resulting from the passage of 4π abamperes through one turn of a coil. 1 gilbert is equivalent to $10/4\pi$ = 0.795 775 ampere-turn. Symbols: Gi, Gb [c19: named after William Gilbert]

Gilbert ('gɪlbət) *n* **1 Grove Karl.** 1843–1918, US geologist who pioneered the study of river development and valley erosion **2 Sir Humphrey.** ?1539–83, English navigator: founded the colony at St John's, Newfoundland (1583) **3 William.** 1540–1603, English physician and physicist, noted for his study of terrestrial magnetism in *De Magnete* (1600) **4 Sir W(illiam) S(chwenck).** 1836–1911, English dramatist, humorist, and librettist. He collaborated (1871–96) with Arthur Sullivan on the famous series of comic operettas, including *The Pirates of Penzance* (1879), *Iolanthe* (1882), and *The Mikado* (1885)

Gilbert and George *n* a team of artists, **Gilbert Proesch**, Italian, born 1942, and **George Passmore**, British, born 1943: noted esp for their photomontages and performance works

Gilbert Islands *pl n* a group of islands in the W Pacific: with Banaba, the Phoenix Islands, and three of the Line Islands they constitute the independent state of Kiribati; until 1975 they formed part of the British colony of **Gilbert and Ellice Islands**; achieved full independence in 1979. Pop: 82 902 (2005). Area: 295 sq km (114 sq miles)

gild¹ (gɪld) *vb* **gilds, gilding, gilded** or **gilt** (gɪlt) (*tr*) **1** to cover with or as if with gold **2 gild the lily a** to adorn unnecessarily something already beautiful **b** to praise someone inordinately **3** to give a falsely attractive or valuable appearance to [Old English *gyldan*, from *gold* GOLD; related to Old Norse *gylla*, Middle High German *vergülden*] ▷ 'gilder *n*

gild² (gɪld) *n* a variant spelling of **guild** (sense 2)

gilding ('gɪldɪŋ) *n* **1** the act or art of applying gilt to a surface **2** the surface so produced **3** another word for **gilt¹** (sense 2)

Gilead¹ ('gɪlɪˌæd) *n* a historic mountainous region east of the River Jordan, rising over 1200 m (4000 ft)

Gilead² ('gɪlɪˌæd) *n Old Testament* a grandson of Manasseh; ancestor of the Coileadites (Numbers 26: 29–30)

Giles (dʒaɪlz) *n* **1 Saint.** 7th century AD, Greek hermit in France; patron saint of cripples, beggars, and lepers. Feast day: Sept 1 **2 William Ernest Powell.** 1835–97, Australian explorer, born in England. He was noted esp for his exploration of the western desert (1875–76)

gilet (dʒiˈleɪ) *n* **1** a bodice resembling a waistcoat in a woman's dress [c19: French, literally: waistcoat]

gill¹ (gɪl) *n* **1** the respiratory organ in many aquatic animals, consisting of a membrane or outgrowth well supplied with blood vessels. **External gills** occur in tadpoles, some molluscs, etc; **internal gills**, within gill slits, occur in most fishes **2** any of the radiating leaflike spore-producing structures on the undersurface of the cap of a mushroom [c14: of Scandinavian origin; compare Swedish *gäl*, Danish *gjælle*, Greek *khelunē* lip] ▷ **gilled** *adj*

gill² (dʒɪl) *n* a unit of liquid measure equal to one quarter of a pint [c14: from Old French *gille* vat, tub, from Late Latin *gillō* cooling vessel for liquids, of obscure origin]

gill³ or **ghyll** (gɪl) *n dialect* **1** a narrow stream; rivulet **2** a wooded ravine [c11: from Old Norse *gil* steep-sided valley]

Gill (gɪl) *n* (**Arthur**) **Eric** (**Rowton**). 1882–1940, British sculptor, engraver, and typographer: his sculptures include the *Stations of the Cross* in Westminster Cathedral, London

Gillespie (gɪˈlɛspɪ) *n* **Dizzy**, nickname of *John Birks Gillespie*. 1917–93, US jazz trumpeter

gillie, ghillie or **gilly** ('gɪlɪ) *n, pl* **-lies** *Scot* **1** an attendant or guide for hunting or fishing **2** (formerly) a Highland chieftain's male attendant or personal servant [c17: from Scottish Gaelic *gille* boy, servant]

Gillingham ('dʒɪlɪŋəm) *n* a town in SE England, in Medway unitary authority, Kent, on the Medway estuary: former dockyards. Pop: 98 403 (2001)

Gillray ('gɪlreɪ) *n* **James.** 1757–1815, English caricaturist

gills (gɪlz) *pl n* **1** (*sometimes singular*) the wattle of birds such as domestic fowl **2 green around the gills** or **green about the gills** *informal* looking or feeling nauseated

gillyflower or **gilliflower** ('dʒɪlɪˌflaʊə) *n* **1** any of several plants having fragrant flowers, such as the stock and wallflower **2** an archaic name for **carnation** [c14: changed (through influence of *flower*) from *gilofre*, from Old French *giroflé*, from Medieval Latin, from Greek *karuophullon* clove tree, from *karuon* nut + *phullon* leaf]

Gilolo (dʒaɪˈləʊləʊ, dʒɪ-) *n* See **Halmahera**

gilt¹ (gɪlt) *vb* **1** a past tense and past participle of **gild¹** ▷ *n* **2** gold or a substance simulating it, applied in gilding **3** another word for **gilding** (senses 1, 2) **4** superficial or false appearance of excellence; glamour **5** a gilt-edged security ▷ *adj* **6** covered with or as if with gold or gilt; gilded

gilt² (gɪlt) *n* a young female pig, esp one that has not had a litter [c15: from Old Norse *gyltr*; related to Old English *gelte*, Old High German *gelza*, Middle Low German *gelte*]

gilt-edged *adj* **1** *stock exchange* denoting government securities on which interest payments will certainly be met and that will certainly be repaid at par on the due date **2** of the highest quality: *the last track on the album is a gilt-edged classic* **3** (of books, papers, etc) having gilded edges

gimbals ('dʒɪmbᵊlz, 'gɪm-) *pl n* a device, consisting of two or three pivoted rings at right angles to each other, that provides free suspension in all planes for an object such as a gyroscope, compass, chronometer, etc. Also called: **gimbal ring** [c16: variant of earlier *gimmal* finger ring, from Old French *gemel*, from Latin *gemellus*, diminutive of *geminus* twin]

gimcrack ('dʒɪmˌkræk) *adj* **1** cheap; shoddy ▷ *n* **2** a cheap showy trifle or gadget [c18: changed from C14 *gibecrake* little ornament, of unknown origin] ▷ '**gim,crackery** *n*

gimlet ('gɪmlɪt) *n* **1** a small hand tool consisting of a pointed spiral tip attached at right angles to a handle, used for boring small holes in wood **2** *US* a cocktail consisting of half gin or vodka and half lime juice ▷ *vb* **3** (*tr*) to make holes in (wood) using a gimlet ▷ *adj* **4** penetrating; piercing (esp in the phrase **gimlet-eyed**) [c15: from Old French *guimbelet*, of Germanic origin, see WIMBLE]

gimmick ('gɪmɪk) *n* **1** something designed to attract extra attention, interest, or publicity **2** any clever device, gadget, or stratagem, esp one used to deceive [c20: originally US slang, of unknown origin] ▷ '**gimmickry** *n* ▷ '**gimmicky** *adj*

gimp or **guimpe** (gɪmp) *n* a tapelike trimming of silk, wool, or cotton, often stiffened with wire [c17: probably from Dutch *gimp*, of unknown origin]

gin¹ (dʒɪn) *n* an alcoholic drink obtained by distillation and rectification of the grain of malted barley, rye, or maize, flavoured with juniper berries [c18: shortened from Dutch *genever* juniper, via Old French from Latin *jūniperus* JUNIPER]

gin² (dʒɪn) *n* **1** a primitive engine in which a vertical shaft is turned by horses driving a horizontal beam or yoke in a circle **2** Also called: **cotton gin** a machine of this type used for separating seeds from raw cotton **3** a trap for catching small mammals, consisting of a noose of thin strong wire ▷ *vb* **gins, ginning, ginned** (*tr*) **4** to free (cotton) of seeds with a gin **5** to trap or snare (game) with a gin [C13 *gyn*, shortened from ENGINE]

gin³ (gɪn) *vb* **gins, ginning, gan, gun** an archaic word for **begin**

gin⁴ (dʒɪn) *n Austral offensive, slang* an Aboriginal woman [C19: from a native Australian language]

ginger ('dʒɪndʒə) *n* **1** any of several zingiberaceous plants of the genus *Zingiber*, esp *Z. officinale* of the East Indies, cultivated throughout the tropics for its spicy hot-tasting underground stem **2** the underground stem of this plant, which is used fresh or powdered as a flavouring or crystallized as a sweetmeat **3** a reddish-brown or yellowish-brown colour **b** (*as adjective*): *ginger hair* **4** *informal* liveliness; vigour [C13: from Old French *gingivre*, from Medieval Latin *gingiber*, from Latin *zinziberi*, from Greek *zingiberis*, probably from Sanskrit *śṛṅgaveram*, from *śṛṅga-* horn + *vera-* body, referring to its shape]

ginger ale *n* a sweetened effervescent nonalcoholic drink flavoured with ginger extract

ginger beer *n* a slightly alcoholic drink made by fermenting a mixture of syrup and root ginger

gingerbread ('dʒɪndʒə,brɛd) *n* **1** a moist brown cake, flavoured with ginger and treacle or syrup **2** a a rolled biscuit, similarly flavoured, cut into various shapes and sometimes covered with icing **b** (*as modifier*): *gingerbread man* **3** an elaborate but unsubstantial ornamentation

ginger group *n chiefly Brit* a group within a party, association, etc, that enlivens or radicalizes its parent body

gingerly ('dʒɪndʒəlɪ) *adv* **1** in a cautious, reluctant, or timid manner ▷ *adj* **2** cautious, reluctant, or timid [C16: perhaps from Old French *gensor* dainty, from *gent* of noble birth; see GENTLE]

ginger nut or **ginger snap** *n* a crisp biscuit flavoured with ginger

gingham ('gɪŋəm) *n textiles* a cotton fabric, usually woven of two coloured yarns in a checked or striped design [C17: from French *guingan*, from Malay *ginggang* striped cloth]

gingili, gingelli or **gingelly** ('dʒɪndʒɪlɪ) *n* **1** the oil obtained from sesame seeds **2** another name for **sesame** [C18: from Hindi *jingalī*]

gingiva ('dʒɪndʒɪvə, dʒɪn'dʒaɪvə) *n*, *pl* **-givae** (-dʒɪ,viː, -'dʒaɪviː) *anatomy* the technical name for the **gum²** [from Latin] > **gingival** *adj*

gingivitis (,dʒɪndʒɪ'vaɪtɪs) *n* inflammation of the gums

ginglymus ('dʒɪŋglɪməs, 'gɪŋ-) *n*, *pl* **-mi** (-,maɪ) *anatomy* a hinge joint [C17: New Latin, from Greek *ginglumos* hinge]

gink¹ (gɪŋk) *n slang* a man or boy, esp one considered to be odd [C20: of unknown origin]

gink² (gɪŋk) *NZ informal* a look, especially a brief one, at something

ginkgo ('gɪŋkgəʊ) or **gingko** ('gɪŋkəʊ) *n*, *pl* **-goes** or **-koes** a widely planted ornamental Chinese gymnosperm tree, *Ginkgo biloba*, with fan-shaped deciduous leaves and fleshy yellow fruit: phylum *Ginkgophyta*. It is used in herbal remedies and as a food supplement. Also called: **maidenhair tree** [C18: from Japanese *ginkyō*, from Ancient Chinese *yin* silver + *hang* apricot]

ginormous (dʒaɪ'nɔːməs) *adj informal* very large [C20: blend of *giant* or *gigantic* and *enormous*]

gin palace (dʒɪn) *n* (formerly) a gaudy drinking house

gin rummy (dʒɪn) *n* a version of rummy in which a player may go out if the odd cards outside his sequences total less than ten points [C20: from GIN¹ + RUMMY¹, apparently from a humorous allusion to gin and rum]

Ginsberg ('gɪnzbɜːg) *n* **Allen.** 1926–97, US poet of the Beat Generation. His poetry includes *Howl* (1956) and *Kaddish* (1960)

ginseng ('dʒɪnsɛŋ) *n* **1** either of two araliaceous plants, *Panax schinseng* of China or *P. quinquefolius* of North America, whose forked aromatic roots are used medicinally **2** the root of either of these plants, or a substance obtained from the roots, believed to possess

stimulant, tonic, and energy-giving properties [C17: from Mandarin Chinese *jen shen*, from *jen* man (from a resemblance of the roots to human legs) + *shen* ginseng]

Ginzburg (Italian 'gindzburg) *n* **Natalia** (nata'liːa). 1916–91, Italian writer and dramatist. Her books include *The Road to the City* (1942), *Voices in the Evening* (1961), and *Family Sayings* (1963)

Gioconda (Italian dʒo'konda) *n* **La Gioconda** See **Mona Lisa** [Italian: the smiling (lady)]

Giorgione (Italian dʒor'dʒoːne) *n* **Il.** original name *Giorgio Barbarelli*. ?1478–1511, Italian painter of the Venetian school, who introduced a new unity between figures and landscape

Giotto (Italian 'dʒɔtto) *n* also known as *Giotto di Bondone*. ?1267–1337, Florentine painter, who broke away from the stiff linear design of the Byzantine tradition and developed the more dramatic and naturalistic style characteristic of the Renaissance: his work includes cycles of frescoes in Assisi, the Arena Chapel in Padua, and the Church of Santa Croce, Florence

gip (dʒɪp) *vb* **gips, gipping, gipped 1** a variant spelling of **gyp¹** ▷ *n* **2** a variant spelling of **gyp²**

Gippsland ('gɪps,lænd) *n* a fertile region of SE Australia, in SE Victoria, extending east along the coast from Melbourne to the New South Wales border. Area: 35 200 sq km (13 600 sq miles)

gippy ('gɪpɪ) *n*, *pl* **-ies** *Northern English dialect* a starling

Gipsy ('dʒɪpsɪ) *n*, *pl* **-sies** (*sometimes not capital*) a variant spelling of **Gypsy**

gipsy moth *n* a European moth, *Lymantria dispar*, introduced into North America, where it is a serious pest of shade trees: family *Lymantriidae* (or *Liparidae*)

giraffe (dʒɪ'rɑːf, -'ræf) *n*, *pl* **-raffes** or **-raffe** a large ruminant mammal, *Giraffa camelopardalis*, inhabiting savannas of tropical Africa: the tallest mammal, with very long legs and neck and a colouring of regular reddish-brown patches on a beige ground: family *Giraffidae* [C17: from Italian *giraffa*, from Arabic *zarāfah*, probably of African origin]

Giraldus Cambrensis (dʒɪ'rældəs kæm'brɛnsɪs) *n* literary name of *Gerald de Barri*. ?1146–?1223, Welsh chronicler and churchman, noted for his accounts of his travels in Ireland and Wales

girandole ('dʒɪrən,dəʊl) or **girandola** (dʒɪ'rændələ) *n* **1** an ornamental branched wall candleholder, usually incorporating a mirror **2** an earring or pendant having a central gem surrounded by smaller ones **3** a kind of revolving firework **4** *artillery* a group of connected mines [C17: from French, from Italian *girandola*, from *girare* to revolve, from Latin *gȳrāre* to GYRATE]

girasol, girosol or **girasole** ('dʒɪrə,sɒl, -,səʊl) *n* a type of opal that has a red or pink glow in bright light; fire opal [C16: from Italian, from *girare* to revolve (see GYRATE) + *sole* the sun, from Latin *sōl*]

Giraud (French ʒiro) *n* **Henri Honoré** (ɑ̃rɪɔnɔre). 1879–1949, French general, who commanded French forces in North Africa (1942–43)

Giraudoux (French ʒirodu) *n* (**Hyppolyte**) **Jean** (ʒɑ̃). 1882–1944, French dramatist. His works include the novel *Suzanne et le Pacifique* (1921) and the plays *Amphitryon 38* (1929) and *La Guerre de Troie n'aura pas lieu* (1935)

gird¹ (gɜːd) *vb* **girds, girding, girded** or **girt** (*tr*) **1** to put a belt, girdle, etc, around (the waist or hips) **2** to bind or secure with or as if with a belt: *to gird on one's armour* **3** to surround; encircle **4** to prepare (oneself) for action (esp in the phrase **gird (up) one's loins**) [Old English *gyrdan*, of Germanic origin; related to Old Norse *gyrtha*, Old High German *gurten*]

gird² (gɜːd) *Northern English dialect* ▷ *vb* **1** (when *intr*, foll by *at*) to jeer (at someone); mock ▷ *n* **2** a taunt; gibe [C13 *girden* to strike, cut, of unknown origin]

girder ('gɜːdə) *n* a large beam, esp one made of steel, used in the construction of bridges, buildings, etc

girdle¹ ('gɜːdᵊl) *n* **1** a woman's elastic corset covering the waist to the thigh **2** anything that surrounds or encircles **3** a belt or sash **4** *jewellery* the outer edge of a gem **5** *anatomy* any encircling structure or part **6** the mark left on a tree trunk after the removal of a ring of bark ▷ *vb* (*tr*) **7** to put a girdle on or around **8** to

g

surround or encircle **9** to remove a ring of bark from (a tree or branch), thus causing it to die [Old English *gyrdel*, of Germanic origin; related to Old Norse *gyrthill*, Old Frisian *gerdel*, Old High German *gurtila*; see GIRD[1]]

girdle[2] ('gɜːd[a]l) *n Scot & northern English dialect* another word for **griddle**

Girgenti (*Italian* dʒir'dʒɛnti) *n* a former name (until 1927) of **Agrigento**

girl (gɜːl) *n* **1** a female child from birth to young womanhood **2** a young unmarried woman; lass; maid **3** *informal* a sweetheart or girlfriend **4** *informal* a woman of any age **5** a female employee, esp a female servant **6** *South African derogatory* a Black female servant of any age [c13: of uncertain origin; perhaps related to Low German *Göre* boy, girl] > 'girlish *adj*

girl Friday *n* a female employee who has a wide range of duties, usually including secretarial and clerical work [c20: coined on the pattern of MAN FRIDAY]

girlfriend ('gɜːl,frɛnd) *n* **1** a female friend with whom a man or boy is romantically or sexually involved; sweetheart **2** any female friend

Girl Guide *n* See **Guide**

girlhood ('gɜːl,hʊd) *n* the state or time of being a girl

girlie ('gɜːlɪ) *or* **girly** *adj* **1** displaying or featuring nude or scantily dressed women: *a girlie magazine* **2** suited to or designed to appeal to young women: *a girlie night out*

Girl Scout *n US* a member of the equivalent organization for girls to the Scouts

giro ('dʒaɪrəʊ) *n, pl* **-ros 1** a system of transferring money within the financial institutions of a country, such as banks and post offices, by which bills, etc may be paid by filling in a giro form authorizing the debit of a specified sum from one's own account to the credit of the payee's account **2** *Brit informal* an unemployment or income support payment by giro cheque, posted fortnightly [c20: ultimately from Greek *guros* circuit]

Girona (dʒi'rona) *n* the Catalan name for **Gerona**

Gironde (*French* ʒirɔ̃d) *n* **1** a department of SW France, in Aquitaine region. Capital: Bordeaux. Pop: 1 330 683 (2003 est). Area: 10 726 sq km (4183 sq miles) **2** an estuary in SW France, formed by the confluence of the Rivers Garonne and Dordogne. Length: 72 km (45 miles)

girt[1] (gɜːt) *vb* a past tense and past participle of **gird[1]**

girt[2] (gɜːt) *vb* **1** (*tr*) to bind or encircle; gird **2** to measure the girth of (something)

girth (gɜːθ) *n* **1** the distance around something; circumference **2** a band around a horse's belly to keep the saddle in position ▷ *vb* **3** (usually foll by *up*) to fasten a girth on (a horse) **4** (*tr*) to encircle or surround [c14: from Old Norse *gjörth* belt; related to Gothic *gairda* GIRDLE[1]; see GIRD[1]]

GIS *abbreviation* **1** geographic(al) information system: a system for storing, editing, and displaying geographical information on computer **2** (in Canada) guaranteed income supplement

Gisborne ('gɪzbən) *n* a port in N New Zealand, on E North Island on Poverty Bay. Pop: 44 900 (2004 est)

Giscard d'Estaing (*French* ʒiskardɛstɛ̃) *n* **Valéry** (valeri). born 1926, French politician; minister of finance and economic affairs (1962–66; 1969–74); president (1974–81)

Gish (gɪʃ) *n* **1 Dorothy.** 1898–1968, US film actress, chiefly in silent films **2** her sister, **Lillian.** 1896–1993, US film and stage actress, noted esp for her roles in such silent films as *The Birth of a Nation* (1915) and *Intolerance* (1916)

Gissing ('gɪsɪŋ) *n* **George (Robert).** 1857–1903, English novelist, noted for his depiction of middle-class poverty. His works include *Demos* (1886) and *New Grub Street* (1891)

gist (dʒɪst) *n* the point or substance of an argument, speech, etc [c18: from Anglo-French, as in *cest action gist en* this action consists in, literally: lies in, from Old French *gésir* to lie, from Latin *jacēre*, from *jacere* to throw]

git (gɪt) *Brit slang* **1** a contemptible person, often a fool **2** a bastard [c20: from GET (in the sense: *to beget*, hence a bastard, fool)]

gîte (ʒiːt) *n* a self-catering holiday cottage for let in France [c20: French]

Gitmo ('gɪtməʊ) *n informal, chiefly US* Guantánamo: referring more specifically to the detainment camp run here by the US military, in which suspected terrorists

are detained and questioned

gittern ('gɪtɜːn) *n music* an obsolete medieval stringed instrument resembling the guitar [c14: from Old French *guiterne*, ultimately from Old Spanish *guitarra* GUITAR; see CITTERN]

Giulini (*Italian* dʒuː'liːni) *n* **Carlo Maria** ('karlo ma'riːa). 1914–2005, Italian orchestral conductor, esp of opera

Giulio Romano (*Italian* 'dʒuːljo ro'maːno) *n* ?1499–1546, Italian architect and painter; a founder of mannerism

giusto ('dʒuːstəʊ) *music* ▷ *adv* **1** (of a tempo marking) **a** to be observed strictly **b** to be observed appropriately: *allegro giusto* ▷ *adj* **2** (of a tempo) **a** exact; strict **b** suitable [Italian: just, proper]

give (gɪv) *vb* **gives, giving, gave** (geɪv), **given** ('gɪv[a]n) (*mainly tr*) **1** (*also intr*) to present or deliver voluntarily (something that is one's own) to the permanent possession of another or others **2** (often foll by *for*) to transfer (something that is one's own, esp money) to the possession of another as part of an exchange: *to give fifty pounds for a painting* **3** to place in the temporary possession of another: *I gave him my watch while I went swimming* **4** (when *intr*, foll by *of*) to grant, provide, or bestow: *give me some advice* **5** to administer: *to give a reprimand* **6** to award or attribute: *to give blame, praise, etc* **7** to be a source of: *he gives no trouble* **8** to impart or communicate: *to give news; give a person a cold* **9** to utter or emit: *to give a shout* **10** to perform, make, or do: *the car gave a jolt and stopped* **11** to sacrifice or devote: *he gave his life for his country* **12** to surrender: *to give place to others* **13** to concede or yield: *I will give you this game* **14** (*intr*) *informal* to happen: *what gives?* **15** (often foll by *to*) to cause; lead: *she gave me to believe that she would come* **16** to perform or present as an entertainment: *to give a play* **17** to propose as a toast **18** (*intr*) to yield or break under force or pressure: *this surface will give if you sit on it; his courage will never give* **19 give as good as one gets** to respond to verbal or bodily blows to at least an equal extent as those received **20 give it up for someone** *slang* to applaud someone **21 give or take** plus or minus: *three thousand people came, give or take a few hundred* **22** a tendency to yield under pressure; resilience ▷ See also **give away, give in** [Old English *giefan*; related to Old Norse *gefa*, Gothic *giban*, Old High German *geban*, Swedish *giva*] > 'givable *or* 'giveable *adj* > 'giver *n*

give-and-take *n* **1** mutual concessions, shared benefits, and cooperation **2** a smoothly flowing exchange of ideas and talk ▷ *vb* **give and take** (*intr*) **3** to make mutual concessions

give away *vb* (*tr, adverb*) **1** to donate or bestow as a gift, prize, etc **2** to sell very cheaply **3** to reveal or betray (esp in the phrases **give the game** *or* **show away**) **4** to fail to use (an opportunity) through folly or neglect **5** to present (a bride) formally to her husband in a marriage ceremony ▷ *n* **giveaway 6** a betrayal or disclosure of information, esp when unintentional **7** (*modifier*) **a** very cheap (esp in the phrase **giveaway prices**) **b** free of charge: *a giveaway property magazine*

give in *vb* (*adverb*) **1** (*intr*) to yield; admit defeat **2** (*tr*) to submit or deliver (a document)

given ('gɪv[a]n) *vb* **1** the past participle of **give** ▷ *adj* **2** (*postpositive*; foll by *to*) tending (to); inclined or addicted (to) **3** specific or previously stated **4** assumed as a premise **5** *maths* known or determined independently: *a given volume* **6** (on official documents) issued or executed, as on a stated date

given name *n* another term for **first name**

give off *vb* (*tr, adverb*) to emit or discharge: *the mothballs gave off an acrid odour*

give out *vb* (*adverb*) **1** (*tr*) to emit or discharge **2** (*tr*) to publish or make known: *the chairman gave out that he would resign* **3** (*tr*) to hand out or distribute: *they gave out free chewing gum on the street* **4** (*intr*) to become exhausted; fail: *the supply of candles gave out*

give over *vb* (*adverb*) **1** (*tr*) to transfer, esp to the care or custody of another **2** (*tr*) to assign or resign to a specific purpose or function: *the day was given over to pleasure* **3** *informal* to cease (an activity): *give over fighting, will you!*

give up *vb* (*adverb*) **1** to abandon hope (for) **2** (*tr*) to renounce (an activity, belief, etc): *I have given up smoking*

3 (tr) to relinquish or resign from: *he gave up the presidency* **4** (tr; usually reflexive) to surrender: *the escaped convict gave himself up* **5** (intr) to admit one's defeat or inability to do something **6** (tr; often passive or reflexive) to devote completely (to): *she gave herself up to caring for the sick*

gizmo or **gismo** ('gɪzməʊ) *n, pl* **-mos** *slang* a device; gadget [C20: of unknown origin]

gizzard ('gɪzəd) *n* **1** the thick-walled part of a bird's stomach, in which hard food is broken up by muscular action and contact with grit and small stones **2** *informal* the stomach and entrails generally [C14: from Old North French *guisier* fowl's liver, alteration of Latin *gigēria* entrails of poultry when cooked, of uncertain origin]

Gk *abbreviation* Greek

glabella (glə'bɛlə) *n, pl* **-lae** (-liː) *anatomy* a smooth elevation of the frontal bone just above the bridge of the nose: a reference point in physical anthropology or craniometry [C19: New Latin, from Latin *glabellus* smooth, from *glaber* bald, smooth] > **gla'bellar** *adj*

glabrous ('gleɪbrəs) *adj biology* without hair or a similar growth; smooth [C17 *glabrous*, from Latin *glaber*]

glacé ('glæsɪ) *adj* **1** crystallized or candied: *glacé cherries* **2** covered in icing **3** (of leather, silk, etc) having a glossy finish ▷ *vb* **-cés**, **-céing**, **-céed** **4** (tr) to ice or candy (cakes, fruits, etc) [C19: from French *glacé*, literally: iced, from *glacer* to freeze, from *glace* ice, from Latin *glaciēs*]

glacial ('gleɪsɪəl, -ʃəl) *adj* **1** characterized by the presence of masses of ice **2** relating to, caused by, or deposited by a glacier **3** extremely cold; icy **4** cold or hostile in manner **5** (of a chemical compound) of or tending to form crystals that resemble ice > **'glacially** *adv*

glacial acetic acid *n* pure acetic acid (more than 99.8 per cent)

glacial period *n* **1** any period of time during which a large part of the earth's surface was covered with ice, due to the advance of glaciers, as in the late Carboniferous period, and during most of the Pleistocene; glaciation **2** (often capitals) the Pleistocene epoch ▷ Also called: **glacial epoch, ice age**

glaciate ('gleɪsɪˌeɪt) *vb* **1** to cover or become covered with glaciers or masses of ice **2** (tr) to subject to the effects of glaciers, such as denudation and erosion > **ˌglaci'ation** *n*

glacier ('glæsɪə, 'gleɪs-) *n* a slowly moving mass of ice originating from an accumulation of snow. It can either spread out from a central mass (**continental glacier**) or descend from a high valley (**alpine glacier**) [C18: from French (Savoy dialect), from Old French *glace* ice, from Late Latin *glacia*, from Latin *glaciēs* ice]

glaciology (ˌglæsɪ'ɒlədʒɪ, ˌgleɪ-) *n* the study of the distribution, character, and effects of glaciers > **glaciological** (ˌglæsɪə'lɒdʒɪkəl, ˌgleɪ-) *adj* > **ˌglaci'ologist** or **'glacialist** *n*

glacis ('glæsɪs, 'glæsɪ, 'gleɪ-) *n, pl* **-ises** or **-is** (-iːz, -ɪz) **1** a slight incline; slope **2** an open slope in front of a fortified place [C17: from French, from Old French *glacier* to freeze, slip, from Latin *glaciāre*, from *glaciēs* ice]

glad¹ (glæd) *adj* **gladder**, **gladdest** **1** happy and pleased; contented **2** causing happiness or contentment **3** (postpositive; foll by to) very willing: *he was glad to help* **4** (postpositive; foll by of) happy or pleased to have: *glad of her help* ▷ *vb* **glads**, **gladding**, **gladded** **5** an archaic word for **gladden** [Old English *glæd*; related to Old Norse *glathr*, Old High German *glat* smooth, shining, Latin *glaber* smooth, Lithuanian *glodùs* fitting closely] > **'gladly** *adv* > **'gladness** *n*

glad² (glæd) *n informal* short for **gladiolus**

Gladbeck (German 'glatbɛk) *n* a city in NW Germany, in North Rhine-Westphalia. Pop: Pop: 77 166 (2003 est)

gladden ('glædᵊn) *vb* to make or become glad and joyful > **'gladdener** *n*

glade (gleɪd) *n* an open place in a forest; clearing [C16: of uncertain origin; perhaps related to GLAD¹ (in obsolete sense: bright); see GLEAM]

glad eye *n informal* an inviting or seductive glance (esp in the phrase **give (someone) the glad eye**)

gladiator ('glædɪˌeɪtə) *n* **1** (in ancient Rome and Etruria) a man trained to fight in arenas to provide entertainment **2** a person who supports and fights publicly for a cause [C16: from Latin: swordsman, from

gladius sword] > **gladiatorial** (ˌglædɪə'tɔːrɪəl) *adj*

gladiolus (ˌglædɪ'əʊləs) *n, pl* **-lus**, **-li** (-laɪ) or **-luses** Also called: **sword lily, gladiola** any iridaceous plant of the widely cultivated genus *Gladiolus*, having sword-shaped leaves and spikes of funnel-shaped brightly coloured flowers [C16: from Latin: a small sword, sword lily, from *gladius* a sword]

glad rags *pl n informal* best clothes or clothes used on special occasions

gladsome ('glædsəm) *adj* an archaic word for **glad¹** > **'gladsomely** *adv* > **'gladsomeness** *n*

Gladstone ('glædstən) *n* **William Ewart.** 1809–98, British statesman. He became leader of the Liberal Party in 1867 and was four times prime minister (1868–74; 1880–85; 1886; 1892–94). In his first ministry he disestablished the Irish Church (1869) and introduced educational reform (1870) and the secret ballot (1872). He succeeded in carrying the Reform Act of 1884 but failed to gain support for a Home Rule Bill for Ireland, to which he devoted much of the latter part of his career

Gladstone bag *n* a piece of hand luggage consisting of two equal-sized hinged compartments [C19: named after William Ewart GLADSTONE]

Gladwrap ('glædˌræp) *n trademark NZ(sometimes not capital)* **1** a thin polythene material that clings closely to any surface around which it is placed: used for wrapping food ▷ *vb* **-wraps**, **-wrapping**, **-wrapped** **2** (tr) to cover (food) with Gladwrap

Glagolitic (ˌglægə'lɪtɪk) *adj* of, relating to, or denoting a Slavic alphabet whose invention is attributed to Saint Cyril, preserved only in certain Roman Catholic liturgical books found in Dalmatia [C19: from New Latin *glagoliticus*, from Serbo-Croat *glagolica* the Glagolitic alphabet; related to Old Church Slavonic *glagolŭ* word]

glair (gleə) *n* **1** white of egg, esp when used as a size, glaze, or adhesive, usually in bookbinding **2** any substance resembling this ▷ *vb* **3** (tr) to apply glair to (something) [C14: from Old French *glaire*, from Vulgar Latin *clāria* (unattested) CLEAR, from Latin *clārus*] > **'glairy** or **'glaireous** *adj*

glam (glæm) *adj slang* short for **glamorous**

Glamorgan (glə'mɔːgən) or **Glamorganshire** (glə'mɔːgənˌʃɪə, -ʃə) *n* a former county of SE Wales: divided into West Glamorgan, Mid Glamorgan, and South Glamorgan in 1974; since 1996 administered by the county of Swansea and the county boroughs of Neath Port Talbot, Bridgend, Rhondda Cynon Taff, Vale of Glamorgan, Merthyr Tydfil, and part of Caerphilly

glamorize, glamorise or *sometimes US* **glamourize** ('glæməˌraɪz) *vb* (tr) to cause to be or seem glamorous; romanticize or beautify > **ˌglamori'zation** or **ˌglamori'sation** *n*

glamorous or **glamourous** ('glæmərəs) *adj* **1** possessing glamour; alluring and fascinating **2** beautiful and smart, esp in a showy way: *a glamorous woman* > **'glamorously** or **'glamourously** *adv*

glamour or *sometimes US* **glamor** ('glæmə) *n* **1** charm and allure; fascination **2 a** fascinating or voluptuous beauty, often dependent on artifice **b** (as modifier): *a glamour girl* **3** *archaic* a magic spell; charm [C18: Scottish variant of GRAMMAR (hence a magic spell, because occult practices were popularly associated with learning)]

glance¹ (glɑːns) *vb* **1** (intr) to look hastily or briefly **2** (intr; foll by over, through, etc) to look over briefly: *to glance through a report* **3** (intr) to reflect, glint, or gleam: *the sun glanced on the water* **4** (intr; usually foll by off) to depart (from an object struck) at an oblique angle: *the arrow glanced off the tree* **5** (tr) *the arrow glanced the tree* ▷ *n* **6** a hasty or brief look; peep **7** a flash or glint of light; gleam **8** the act or an instance of an object glancing or glancing off another **9** a brief allusion or reference [C15: modification of *glacen* to strike obliquely, from Old French *glacier* to slide (see GLACIS); compare Middle English *glenten* to make a rapid sideways movement, GLINT] > **'glancing** *adj*

● USAGE *Glance* is sometimes wrongly used where *glimpse* is meant: *he caught a glimpse* (not *glance*) *of her making her way through the crowd*

glance² (glɑːns) *n* any mineral having a metallic lustre, esp a simple sulphide [C19: from German *Glanz* brightness, lustre]

gland¹ (glænd) *n* **1** a cell or organ in man and other animals that synthesizes chemical substances and secretes them for the body to use or eliminate, either through a duct exocrine gland) or directly into the bloodstream (endocrine gland). See also **exocrine gland, endocrine gland 2** a structure, such as a lymph node, that resembles a gland in form **3** a cell or organ in plants that synthesizes and secretes a particular substance [C17: from Latin *glāns* acorn]

gland² (glænd) *n* a device that prevents leakage of fluid along a rotating shaft or reciprocating rod passing through a boundary between areas of high and low pressure. It often consists of a flanged metal sleeve bedding into a stuffing box [C19: of unknown origin]

glanders ('glændəz) *n* (*functioning as singular*) a highly infectious bacterial disease of horses, sometimes transmitted to man, caused by *Actinobacillus mallei* and characterized by inflammation and ulceration of the mucous membranes of the air passages, skin, and lymph glands [C16: from Old French *glandres* enlarged glands, from Latin *glandulae*, literally: little acorns, from *glāns* acorn; see GLAND¹]

glandular ('glændjʊlə) *or* **glandulous** ('glændjʊləs) *adj* of, relating to, containing, functioning as, or affecting a gland [C18: from Latin *glandula*, literally: a little acorn; see GLANDERS] > 'glandularly *or* 'glandulously *adv*

glandular fever *n* another name for **infectious mononucleosis**

glandule ('glændjuːl) *n* a small gland

glans (glænz) *n, pl* **glandes** ('glændiːz) *anatomy* any small rounded body or glandlike mass, such as the head of the penis (**glans penis**) [C17: from Latin: acorn; see GLAND¹]

glare (glɛə) *vb* **1** (*intr*) to stare angrily; glower **2** (*tr*) to express by glowering **3** (*intr*) (of light, colour, etc) to be very bright and intense **4** (*intr*) to be dazzlingly ornamented or garish ⊳ *n* **5** an angry stare **6** a dazzling light or brilliance **7** garish ornamentation or appearance; gaudiness [C13: probably from Middle Low German, Middle Dutch *glaren* to gleam; probably related to Old English *glæren* glassy; see GLASS]

glaring ('glɛərɪŋ) *adj* **1** conspicuous: *a glaring omission* **2** dazzling or garish > 'glaringly *adv* > 'glaringness *n*

Glarus (German 'glaːrʊs) *n* **1** an Alpine canton of E central Switzerland. Capital: Glarus. Pop: 38 400 (2002 est). Area 684 sq km (264 sq miles) **2** a town in E central Switzerland, the capital of Glarus canton. Pop: 5556 (2000)

Glaser ('gleɪzə) *n* Donald Arthur. born 1926, US physicist: invented the bubble chamber; Nobel prize for physics 1960

Glasgow ('glaːzgəʊ, 'glæz-) *n* **1** a city in W central Scotland, in City of Glasgow council area on the River Clyde: the largest city in Scotland; centre of a major industrial region, formerly an important port; universities (1451, 1964, 1992). Pop: 629 501 (2001). Related adj: **Glaswegian 2 City of Glasgow** a council area in W central Scotland. Pop: 577 090 (2003 est). Area: 175 sq km (68 sq miles)

glasnost ('glæs,nɒst) *n* the policy of public frankness and accountability developed in the former Soviet Union under the leadership of Mikhail Gorbachov [C20: Russian, literally: openness]

glass (glaːs) *n* **1 a** a hard brittle transparent or translucent noncrystalline solid, consisting of metal silicates or similar compounds. It is made from a fused mixture of oxides, such as lime, silicon dioxide, etc, and is used for making windows, mirrors, bottles, etc **b** (*as modifier*): *a glass bottle*. Related adj: **vitreous 2** something made of glass, esp a drinking vessel, a barometer, or a mirror **3** Also called: **glassful** the amount contained in a drinking glass **4** glassware collectively **5** See **fibreglass** ⊳ *vb* (*tr*) **6** to cover with, enclose in, or fit with glass [Old English *glæs*; related to Old Norse *gler*, Old High German *glas*, Middle High German *glast* brightness; see GLARE¹] > 'glassless *adj* > 'glass,like *adj*

Glass (glaːs) *n* Philip. born 1937, US avant-garde

composer noted for his minimalist style: his works include *Music in Fifths* (1970), *Akhnaten* (1984), *The Voyage* (1992), and *Monsters of Grace* (1998)

glass-blowing *n* the process of shaping a mass of molten or softened glass into a vessel, shape, etc, by blowing air into it through a tube > 'glass-,blower *n*

glass ceiling *n* a situation in which progress, esp promotion, appears to be possible but restrictions or discrimination create a barrier that prevents it

glasses ('glaːsɪz) *pl n* a pair of lenses for correcting faulty vision, in a frame that rests on the bridge of the nose and hooks behind the ears. Also called: spectacles, eyeglasses

glass fibre *n* another name for **fibreglass**

glass harmonica *n* a musical instrument of the 18th century consisting of a set of glass bowls of graduated pitches, played by rubbing the fingers over the moistened rims or by a keyboard mechanism. Sometimes shortened to: harmonica. Also called: musical glasses

glasshouse ('glaːs,haʊs) *n* **1** Brit a glass building, esp a greenhouse, used for growing plants in protected or controlled conditions **2** obsolete, informal, chiefly Brit a military detention centre

glassine (glæ'siːn) *n* a glazed translucent paper used for book jackets

glass snake *n* any snakelike lizard of the genus *Ophisaurus*, of Europe, Asia, and North America, with vestigial hind limbs and a tail that breaks off easily: family *Anguidae*

glassware ('glaːs,wɛə) *n* articles made of glass

glass wool *n* fine spun glass massed into a wool-like bulk, used in insulation, filtering, etc

glasswort ('glaːs,wɜːt) *n* **1** Also called: marsh samphire any plant of the chenopodiaceous genus *Salicornia*, of salt marshes, having fleshy stems and scalelike leaves: formerly used as a source of soda for glass-making **2** another name for **saltwort** (sense 1)

glassy ('glaːsɪ) *adj* glassier, glassiest **1** resembling glass, esp in smoothness, slipperiness, or transparency **2** void of expression, life, or warmth: *a glassy stare* > 'glassily *adv* > 'glassiness *n*

Glastonbury ('glæstənbərɪ, -brɪ) *n* a town in SW England, in Somerset: remains of prehistoric lake villages; the reputed burial place of King Arthur; site of a ruined Benedictine abbey, probably the oldest in England. Pop: 8429 (2001)

Glaswegian (glæz'wiːdʒən) *adj* **1** of or relating to Glasgow or its inhabitants ⊳ *n* **2** a native or inhabitant of Glasgow [C19: influenced by *Norway, Norwegian*]

Glauber's salt ('glaʊbəz) *or* **Glauber salt** ('glaʊbə) *n* the crystalline decahydrate of sodium sulphate [C18: named after J. R. *Glauber* (1604–68), German chemist]

Glauce ('glɔːsɪ) *n* Greek myth **1** the second bride of Jason, murdered on her wedding day by Medea, whom Jason had deserted **2** a sea nymph, one of the Nereids

glaucoma (glɔː'kəʊmə) *n* a disease of the eye in which pressure within the eyeball damages the optic disc, impairing vision, sometimes progressing to blindness [C17: from Latin, from Greek *glaukōma*, from *glaukos*; see GLAUCOUS] > glau'comatous *adj*

glaucous ('glɔːkəs) *adj* **1** botany covered with a bluish waxy or powdery bloom **2** bluish-green [C17: from Latin *glaucus* silvery, bluish-green, from Greek *glaukos*]

glaze (gleɪz) *vb* **1** (*tr*) to fit or cover with glass **2** (*tr*) ceramics to cover with a vitreous solution, rendering impervious to liquid and smooth to the touch **3** (*tr*) to cover (foods) with a shiny coating by applying beaten egg, sugar, etc **4** (*tr*) to make glossy or shiny **5** (when *intr*, often foll by *over*) to become or cause to become glassy: *his eyes were glazing over* ⊳ *n* **6** ceramics **a** a vitreous or glossy coating **b** the substance used to produce such a coating **7** a smooth lustrous finish on a fabric produced by applying various chemicals **8** something used to give a glossy surface to foods: *a syrup glaze* [C14 *glasen*, from *glas* GLASS] > glazed *adj* > 'glazer *n*

glaze ice *or* **glazed frost** *n* Brit a thin clear layer of ice caused by the freezing of rain or water droplets in the air on impact with a cool surface or by refreezing after a thaw. Also called: **silver frost**

glazier ('gleɪzɪə) n a person who glazes windows, etc ▷ **'glaziery** n

glazing ('gleɪzɪŋ) n **1** the surface of a glazed object **2** glass fitted, or to be fitted, in a door, frame, etc

Glazunov ('glæzʊnɒf; Russian gləzu'nɔf) n **Aleksandr Konstantinovich** (alɪk'sandr kənstan'tinəvɪtʃ). 1865–1936, Russian composer, in France from 1928. A pupil of Rimsky-Korsakov, he wrote eight symphonies and concertos for piano and for violin among other works

GLC abbreviation Greater London Council, abolished 1986

gleam (gli:m) n **1** a small beam or glow of light, esp reflected light **2** a brief or dim indication: *a gleam of hope* ▷ vb (intr) **3** to send forth or reflect a beam of light **4** to appear, esp briefly [Old English *glǽm*; related to Old Norse *gljá* to flicker, Old High German *gleimo* glow-worm, *glīmo* brightness, Old Irish *glē* bright] ▷ **'gleaming** adj ▷ **'gleamy** adj

glean (gli:n) vb **1** to gather (something) slowly and carefully in small pieces: *to glean information from the newspapers* **2** to gather (the useful remnants of a crop) from the field after harvesting [c14: from Old French *glener*, from Late Latin *glennāre*, probably of Celtic origin] ▷ **'gleaner** n

gleanings ('gli:nɪŋz) pl n the useful remnants of a crop that can be gathered from the field after harvesting

glebe (gli:b) n **1** Brit land granted to a clergyman as part of his benefice **2** poetic land, esp when regarded as the source of growing things [c14: from Latin *glaeba*]

glee (gli:) n **1** great merriment or delight, often caused by someone else's misfortune **2** a type of song originating in 18th-century England, sung by three or more unaccompanied voices [Old English *glēo*; related to Old Norse *glȳ*]

glee club n Now chiefly US & Canadian a club or society organized for the singing of choral music

gleeful ('gli:fʊl) adj full of glee; merry ▷ **'gleefully** adv ▷ **'gleefulness** n

gleeman ('gli:mən) n, pl -men obsolete a minstrel

Gleiwitz ('glaɪvɪts) n the German name for **Gliwice**

glen (glɛn) n a narrow and deep mountain valley, esp in Scotland or Ireland [c15: from Scottish Gaelic *gleann*, from Old Irish *glend*]

Glen Albyn ('ælbɪn, 'ɔːl-) n another name for the **Great Glen**

Glencoe (glɛn'kəʊ) n a glen in W Scotland, in S Highland: site of a massacre of Macdonalds by Campbells and English troops (1692)

Glendower (glɛn'daʊə) n **Owen**, Welsh name *Owain Glyndŵr*. ?1350–?1416, Welsh chieftain, who led a revolt against Henry IV's rule in Wales (1400–1415)

glengarry (glɛn'gærɪ) n, pl -ries a brimless Scottish woollen cap with a crease down the crown, often with ribbons dangling at the back. Also called: **glengarry bonnet** [c19: after *Glengarry*, Scotland]

Glen More (mɔː) n another name for the **Great Glen**

Glenn (glɛn) n **John**. born 1921, US astronaut and politician. The first American to orbit the earth (Feb, 1962), he later became a senator (1975–99) and in 1998 returned to space at the age of 77

Glennie ('glɛnɪ) n **Dame Evelyn** (**Elizabeth Ann**). born 1965, British percussionist

Glenrothes (glɛn'rɒθɪs) n a new town in E central Scotland, the administrative centre of Fife: founded in 1948. Pop: 38 679 (2001)

glia ('gli:ə) n the delicate web of connective tissue that surrounds and supports nerve cells. Also called: **neuroglia** ▷ **'glial** adj

glib (glɪb) adj glibber, glibbest fluent and easy, often in an insincere or deceptive way [c16: probably from Middle Low German *glibberich* slippery] ▷ **'glibly** adv ▷ **'glibness** n

glib ice n Canadian ice that is particularly smooth and slippery

glide (glaɪd) vb **1** to move or cause to move easily without jerks or hesitations **2** (intr) to pass slowly or without perceptible change: *to glide into sleep* **3** to cause (an aircraft) to come into land without engine power, or (of an aircraft) to land in this way **4** (intr) to fly a glider

5 (intr) music to execute a portamento from one note to another **6** (intr) phonetics to produce a glide ▷ n **7** a smooth easy movement **8** a any of various dances featuring gliding steps **b** a step in such a dance **9** a manoeuvre in which an aircraft makes a gentle descent without engine power **10** the act or process of gliding **11** music a portamento or slur **12** phonetics a transitional sound as the speech organs pass from the articulatory position of one speech sound to that of the next, as the (w) sound in some pronunciations of the word *doing* [Old English *glīdan*; related to Old High German *glītan*] ▷ **'glidingly** adv

glide path or **glide slope** n the approach path of an aircraft when landing, usually defined by a radar beam

glider ('glaɪdə) n **1** an aircraft capable of gliding and soaring in air currents without the use of an engine **2** a person or thing that glides

glide time n NZ a system permitting flexibility of working hours at the beginning or end of the day, provided an agreed period of each day (**core time**) is spent at work. Also called (in Britain and certain other countries): **flexitime**

glimmer ('glɪmə) vb (intr) **1** (of a light, candle, etc) to glow faintly or flickeringly **2** to be indicated faintly: *hope glimmered in his face* ▷ n **3** a glow or twinkle of light **4** a faint indication [c14: compare Middle High German *glimmern*, Swedish *glimra*, Danish *glimre*] ▷ **'glimmeringly** adv

glimpse (glɪmps) n **1** a brief or incomplete view: *to catch a glimpse of the sea* **2** a vague indication **3** archaic a glimmer of light ▷ vb **4** (tr) to catch sight of briefly or momentarily [c14: of Germanic origin; compare Middle High German *glimsen* to glimmer] ▷ **'glimpser** n

● USAGE Glimpse is sometimes wrongly used where *glance* ● is meant: *he gave a quick glance (not glimpse) at his watch*

Glinka (Russian 'glinkə) n **Mikhail Ivanovich** (mixa'il i'vanəvɪtʃ). 1803–57, Russian composer who pioneered the Russian national school of music. His works include the operas *A Life for the Tsar* (1836) and *Russlan and Ludmilla* (1842)

glint (glɪnt) vb **1** to gleam or cause to gleam brightly ▷ n **2** a bright gleam or flash **3** brightness or gloss **4** a brief indication [c15: probably of Scandinavian origin; compare Swedish dialect *glänta*, *glinta* to gleam]

glioma (glaɪ'əʊmə) n, pl -mata (-mətə) or -mas a tumour of the brain and spinal cord, composed of neuroglia cells and fibres [c19: from New Latin, from Greek *glia* glue + -OMA]

glissade (glɪ'sɑːd, -'seɪd) n **1** a gliding step in ballet, in which one foot slides forwards, sideways, or backwards **2** a controlled slide down a snow slope ▷ vb **3** (intr) to perform a glissade [c19: from French, from *glisser* to slip, from Old French *glicier*, of Frankish origin; compare Old High German *glītan* to GLIDE]

glissando (glɪ'sændəʊ) n, pl -di (-diː) or -dos a rapidly executed series of notes on the harp or piano, each note of which is discretely audible [c19: probably Italianized variant of GLISSADE]

glisten ('glɪsᵊn) vb (intr) **1** (of a wet or glossy surface) to gleam by reflecting light **2** (of light) to reflect with brightness: *the sunlight glistens on wet leaves* ▷ n **3** rare a gleam or gloss [Old English *glisnian*; related to *glisian* to glitter, Middle High German *glistern*]

glister ('glɪstə) vb, n an archaic word for glitter [c14: probably from Middle Dutch *glisteren*]

glitch (glɪtʃ) n **1** a sudden instance of malfunctioning or irregularity in an electronic system **2** a change in the rotation rate of a pulsar [c20: of unknown origin]

glitter ('glɪtə) vb (intr) **1** (of a hard, wet, or polished surface) to reflect light in bright flashes **2** (of light) to be reflected in bright flashes **3** (usually foll by with) to be decorated or enhanced by the glamour (of): *the show glitters with famous actors* ▷ n **4** sparkle or brilliance **5** show and glamour **6** tiny pieces of shiny decorative material used for ornamentation, as on the skin **7** Also called: **silver thaw** Canadian ice formed from freezing rain [c14: from Old Norse *glitra*; related to Old High German *glīzan* to shine] ▷ **'glitteringly** adv ▷ **'glittery** adj

glitterati (ˌglɪtə'rɑːtiː) pl n informal the leaders of society, esp the rich and beautiful; fashionable celebrities [c20: from GLITTER + -ati as in LITERATI]

glitzy ('glɪtsɪ) *adj* **glitzier, glitziest** *slang* showily attractive; flashy or glittery [c20: originally US, probably via Yiddish from German *glitzern* to glitter]

Gliwice (*Polish* gli'vitsɛ) *n* an industrial city in S Poland. Pop: 197 874 (2007 est.). German name: **Gleiwitz**

gloaming ('gləʊmɪŋ) *n poetic* twilight or dusk [Old English *glōmung*, from *glōm*; related to Old Norse *glāmr* moon]

gloat (gləʊt) *vb* **1** (*intr*; often foll by *over*) to dwell (on) with malevolent smugness or exultation ▷ *n* **2** the act of gloating [c16: probably of Scandinavian origin; compare Old Norse *glotta* to grin, Middle High German *glotzen* to stare] > **'gloater** *n*

glob (glɒb) *n informal* a rounded mass of some thick fluid or pliable substance [c20: probably from GLOBE, influenced by BLOB]

global ('gləʊbᵊl) *adj* **1** covering, influencing, or relating to the whole world **2** comprehensive > **'globally** *adv*

globalization *or* **globalisation** (,gləʊbᵊlaɪ'zeɪʃən) *n* **1** the process enabling financial and investment markets to operate internationally, largely as a result of deregulation and improved communications **2** the emergence since the 1980s of a single world market dominated by multinational companies, leading to a diminishing capacity for national governments to control their economies **3** the process by which a company, etc, expands to operate internationally

globalize *or* **globalise** ('gləʊbᵊ,laɪz) *vb* (*tr*) to put into effect or spread worldwide

global product *n* a commercial product, such as Coca Cola, that is marketed throughout the world under the same brand name

global warming *n* an increase in the average temperature worldwide believed to be caused by the greenhouse effect

globe (gləʊb) *n* **1** a sphere on which a map of the world or the heavens is drawn or represented **2 the globe** the world; the earth **3** a planet or some other astronomical body **4** an object shaped like a sphere, such as a glass lampshade or fish-bowl **5** *Austral, NZ & South African* an electric light bulb **6** an orb, usually of gold, symbolic of authority or sovereignty ▷ *vb* **7** to form or cause to form into a globe [c16: from Old French, from Latin *globus*] > **'globe,like** *adj*

globefish ('gləʊb,fɪʃ) *n, pl* **-fish** *or* **-fishes** another name for **puffer** (sense 2)

globeflower ('gləʊb,flaʊə) *n* any ranunculaceous plant of the genus *Trollius*, having pale yellow, white, or orange globe-shaped flowers

globetrotter ('gləʊb,trɒtə) *n* a habitual worldwide traveller, esp a tourist or businessman > **'globe,trotting** *n, adj*

globigerina (gləʊ,bɪdʒə'raɪnə) *n, pl* **-nas** *or* **-nae** (-niː) **1** any marine protozoan of the genus *Globigerina*, having a rounded shell with spiny processes: phylum *Foraminifera* (foraminifers) **2 globigerina ooze** a deposit on the ocean floor consisting of the shells of these protozoans [c19: from New Latin, from Latin *globus* GLOBE + *gerere* to carry, bear]

globoid ('gləʊbɔɪd) *adj* **1** shaped approximately like a globe ▷ *n* **2** a globoid body, such as any of those occurring in certain plant granules

globose ('gləʊbəʊs, gləʊ'bəʊs) *or* **globous** ('gləʊbəs) *adj* spherical or approximately spherical [c15: from Latin *globōsus*; see GLOBE] > **'globosely** *adv*

globular ('glɒbjʊlə) *or* **globulous** *adj* **1** shaped like a globe or globule **2** having or consisting of globules

globule ('glɒbjuːl) *n* **1** a small globe, esp a drop of liquid **2** *astronomy* a small dark nebula thought to be a site of star formation [c17: from Latin *globulus*, diminutive of *globus* GLOBE]

globulin ('glɒbjʊlɪn) *n* any of a group of simple proteins, including gamma globulin, that are generally insoluble in water but soluble in salt solutions and coagulated by heat [c19: from GLOBULE + -IN]

Glock (glɒk) *n trademark* a type of pistol [c19: named after Gaston *Glock* (born 1929), Austrian manufacturer]

glockenspiel ('glɒkən,spiːl, -,ʃpiːl) *n* a percussion instrument consisting of a set of tuned metal plates played with a pair of small hammers [c19: German, from *Glocken* bells + *Spiel* play]

glom (glɒm) *vb slang* **1** (*tr*; foll by *on to*) to attach oneself to or associate oneself with **2** *US* to acquire, esp without paying [c20: from Scots *glaum*]

glomerate ('glɒmərɪt) *adj* **1** gathered into a compact rounded mass **2** *anatomy* (esp of glands) conglomerate in structure [c18: from Latin *glomerāre* to wind into a ball, from *glomus* ball]

glomerule ('glɒmə,ruːl) *n botany* a cymose inflorescence in the form of a ball-like cluster of flowers [c18: from New Latin GLOMERULUS]

glomerulus (glɒ'mɛrʊləs) *n, pl* **-li** (-,laɪ) **1** a knot of blood vessels in the kidney projecting into the capsular end of a urine-secreting tubule **2** any cluster or coil of blood vessels, nerve fibres, etc, in the body [c18: from New Latin, diminutive of *glomus* ball] > **glo'merular** *adj*

Glomma (*Norwegian* 'glɔma) *n* a river in SE Norway, rising near the border with Sweden and flowing generally south to the Skagerrak: the largest river in Scandinavia; important for hydroelectric power and floating timber. Length: 588 km (365 miles)

gloom (gluːm) *n* **1** partial or total darkness **2** a state of depression or melancholy **3** an appearance or expression of despondency or melancholy **4** *poetic* a dim or dark place ▷ *vb* **5** (*intr*) to look sullen or depressed **6** to make or become dark or gloomy [c14 *gloumben* to look sullen; related to Norwegian dialect *glome* to eye suspiciously]

gloomy ('gluːmɪ) *adj* **gloomier, gloomiest 1** dark or dismal **2** causing depression, dejection, or gloom: *gloomy news* **3** despairing; sad > **'gloomily** *adv* > **'gloominess** *n*

gloop (gluːp) *or esp US* **glop** (glɒp) *n informal* any messy sticky fluid or substance [c20: of uncertain origin] > **'gloopy** *or esp US* **'gloppy** *adj*

Glooscap, Gluscap *or* **Gluskap** ('gluː,skæp) *n* (among the Micmac and other Native North American peoples) a traditional trickster hero [of Algonquian origin]

gloria ('glɔːrɪə) *n* a halo or nimbus, esp as represented in art [c16: from Latin: GLORY]

Gloria ('glɔːrɪə, -,ɑː) *n* **1** any of several doxologies beginning with the word *Gloria*, esp the Greater and the Lesser Doxologies **2** a musical setting of one of these

glorify ('glɔːrɪ,faɪ) *vb* **-fies, -fying, -fied** (*tr*) **1** to make glorious **2** to make more splendid; adorn **3** to worship, exalt, or adore **4** to extol **5** to cause to seem more splendid or imposing than reality > **,glorifi'cation** *n*

gloriole ('glɔːrɪ,əʊl) *n* another name for a **halo** [c19: from Latin *glōriola*, literally: a small GLORY]

glorious ('glɔːrɪəs) *adj* **1** having or full of glory; illustrious **2** conferring glory or renown: *a glorious victory* **3** brilliantly beautiful **4** delightful or enjoyable > **'gloriously** *adv* > **'gloriousness** *n*

glory ('glɔːrɪ) *n, pl* **-ries 1** exaltation, praise, or honour, as that accorded by general consent **2** something that brings or is worthy of praise (esp in the phrase **crowning glory**) **3** thanksgiving, adoration, or worship: *glory be to God* **4** pomp; splendour: *the glory of the king's reign* **5** radiant beauty; resplendence: *the glory of the sunset* **6** the beauty and bliss of heaven **7** a state of extreme happiness or prosperity **8** another word for: **halo, nimbus** ▷ *vb* **-ries, -rying, -ried 9** (*intr*; often foll by *in*) to triumph or exult ▷ *interj* **10** *informal* a mild interjection to express pleasure or surprise (often in the exclamatory phrase **glory be!**) [c13: from Old French *glorie*, from Latin *glōria*, of obscure origin]

glory box *n Austral & NZ informal* a box in which a young woman stores clothes, etc, in preparation for marriage

glory hole *n* **1** *informal* a room, cupboard, or other storage space that contains an untidy and miscellaneous collection of objects **2** *nautical* another term for **lazaretto** (sense 1)

Glos *abbreviation* Gloucestershire

gloss¹ (glɒs) *n* **1 a** lustre or sheen, as of a smooth surface **b** (*as modifier*): *gloss paint* **2** a superficially attractive appearance **3** a cosmetic preparation applied to the skin to give it a faint sheen ▷ *vb* **4** to give a gloss to or obtain a gloss [C16: probably of Scandinavian origin; compare Icelandic *glossi* flame, Middle High German *glosen* to glow] > 'glosser *n*

gloss² (glɒs) *n* **1** a short or expanded explanation or interpretation of a word, expression, or foreign phrase in the margin or text of a manuscript, etc **2** an intentionally misleading explanation or interpretation **3** short for **glossary** ▷ *vb* (*tr*) **4** to add glosses to [C16: from Latin *glōssa* unusual word requiring explanatory note, from Ionic Greek]

glossary ('glɒsərɪ) *n*, *pl* **-ries** an alphabetical list of terms peculiar to a field of knowledge with definitions or explanations [C14: from Late Latin *glossārium*; see GLOSS²] > glossarial (glɒ'sɛərɪəl) *adj* > 'glossarist *n*

glosseme ('glɒsiːm) *n* the smallest meaningful unit of a language, such as stress, form, etc [C20: from Greek *glōssēma*; see GLOSS², -EME]

glossitis (glɒ'saɪtɪs) *n* inflammation of the tongue > glossitic (glɒ'sɪtɪk) *adj*

glosso- *or before a vowel* **gloss-** *combining form* indicating a tongue or language: *glossolaryngeal* [from Greek *glossa* tongue]

glossolalia (,glɒsə'leɪlɪə) *n* another term for **gift of tongues** [C19: New Latin, from GLOSSO- + Greek *lalein* to speak, babble]

gloss over *vb* (*tr, adverb*) **1** to hide under a deceptively attractive surface or appearance **2** to deal with (unpleasant facts) rapidly and cursorily, or to omit them altogether from an account of something

glossy ('glɒsɪ) *adj* **glossier, glossiest 1** smooth and shiny; lustrous **2** superficially attractive; plausible **3** (of a magazine) lavishly produced on shiny paper and usually with many colour photographs ▷ *n*, *pl* **glossies 4** an expensively produced magazine, typically a sophisticated fashion or glamour magazine, printed on shiny paper and containing high quality colour photography. Also called (US): **slick 5** a photograph printed on paper that has a smooth shiny surface > 'glossily *adv* > 'glossiness *n*

glottal ('glɒtᵊl) *adj* **1** of or relating to the glottis **2** *phonetics* articulated or pronounced at or with the glottis

glottal stop *n* a plosive speech sound produced as the sudden onset of a vowel in several languages, such as German, by first tightly closing the glottis and then allowing the air pressure to build up in the trachea before opening the glottis, causing the air to escape with force

glottis ('glɒtɪs) *n*, *pl* **-tises** *or* **-tides** (-tɪ,diːz) the vocal apparatus of the larynx, consisting of the two true vocal cords and the opening between them [C16: from New Latin, from Greek *glōttis*, from *glōtta*, Attic form of Ionic *glōssa* tongue; see GLOSS²]

Gloucester¹ ('glɒstə) *n* a city in SW England, administrative centre of Gloucestershire, on the River Severn; cathedral (founded 1100). Pop: 123 205 (2001).

Gloucester² ('glɒstə) *n* **1 Humphrey,** Duke of. 1391–1447, English soldier and statesman; son of Henry IV. He acted as protector during Henry VI's minority (1422– 29) and was noted for his patronage of humanists **2** Duke of. See: **Richard III 3** Duke of. See: **Thomas of Woodstock**

Gloucestershire ('glɒstəʃɪə, -ʃə) *n* a county of SW England, situated around the lower Severn valley: contains the Forest of Dean and the main part of the Cotswold Hills: the geographical and ceremonial county includes the unitary authority of South Gloucestershire (part of Avon county from 1974 to 1996). Administrative centre: Gloucester. Pop (excluding South Gloucestershire): 568 500 (2003 est). Area (excluding South Gloucestershire): 2643 sq km (1020 sq miles). Abbreviation: **Glos**

glove (glʌv) *n* **1** (*often plural*) a shaped covering for the hand with individual sheaths for the fingers and thumb, made of leather, fabric, etc **2** any of various large protective hand covers worn in sports, such as a boxing glove ▷ *vb* **3** (*tr; usually passive*) to cover or provide with or as if with gloves [Old English *glōfe*; related to Old Norse *glōfi*]

glove box *n* a closed box in which toxic or radioactive

substances can be handled by an operator who places his hands through protective gloves sealed to the box

glove compartment *n* a small compartment in a car dashboard for the storage of miscellaneous articles

glover ('glʌvə) *n* a person who makes or sells gloves

glow (gləʊ) *n* **1** light emitted by a substance or object at a high temperature **2** a steady even light without flames **3** brilliance or vividness of colour **4** brightness or ruddiness of complexion **5** a feeling of wellbeing or satisfaction **6** intensity of emotion; ardour ▷ *vb* (*intr*) **7** to emit a steady even light without flames **8** to shine intensely, as if from great heat **9** to be exuberant or high-spirited, as from excellent health or intense emotion **10** to experience a feeling of wellbeing or satisfaction: *to glow with pride* **11** (esp of the complexion) to show a strong bright colour, esp a shade of red **12** to be very hot [Old English *glōwan*; related to Old Norse *glōa*, Old High German *gluoen*, Icelandic *glōra* to sparkle]

glow discharge *n* a silent luminous discharge of electricity through a low-pressure gas

glower ('glaʊə) *vb* **1** (*intr*) to stare hard and angrily ▷ *n* **2** a sullen or angry stare [C16: probably of Scandinavian origin; related to Middle Low German *glūren* to watch] > 'gloweringly *adv*

glowing ('gləʊɪŋ) *adj* **1** emitting a steady bright light without flames: *glowing embers* **2** warm and rich in colour: *the room was decorated in glowing shades of gold and orange* **3** flushed and rosy, as from exercise or excitement: *glowing cheeks* **4** displaying or indicative of extreme satisfaction, pride, or emotion: *he gave a glowing account of his son's achievements*

glow-worm *n* a European beetle, *Lampyris noctiluca*, the females and larvae of which bear luminescent organs producing a greenish light: family *Lampyridae*

gloxinia (glɒk'sɪnɪə) *n* any of several tropical plants of the genus *Sinningia*, esp the South American *S. speciosa*, cultivated for its large white, red, or purple bell-shaped flowers: family *Gesneriaceae* [C19: named after Benjamin P. Gloxin, 18th-century German physician and botanist who first described it]

gloze (gləʊz) *vb archaic* **1** (*tr*; often foll by *over*) to explain away; minimize the effect or importance of **2** to make explanatory notes or glosses on (a text) **3** to use flattery (on) [C13: from Old French *gloser* to comment; see GLOSS²]

Gluck (German glʊk) *n* **Christoph Willibald von** ('krɪstɔf 'vɪlibalt fɔn). 1714– 87, German composer, esp of operas, including *Orfeo ed Euridice* (1762) and *Alceste* (1767)

glucose ('gluːkəʊz, -kəʊs) *n* **1** a white crystalline monosaccharide sugar that has several optically active forms, the most abundant being dextrose: a major energy source in metabolism. Formula: $C_6H_{12}O_6$ **2** a yellowish syrup (or, after desiccation, a solid) containing dextrose, maltose, and dextrin, obtained by incomplete hydrolysis of starch: used in confectionery, fermentation, etc [C19: from French, from Greek *gleukos* sweet wine; related to Greek *glukus* sweet]

glucoside ('gluːkəʊˌsaɪd) *n biochem* any of a large group of glycosides that yield glucose on hydrolysis > ˌgluco'sidal *or* gluco'sidic (ˌgluːkəʊ'sɪdɪk) *adj*

glue (gluː) *n* **1** any natural or synthetic adhesive, esp a sticky gelatinous substance prepared by boiling animal products such as bones, skin, and horns **2** any other sticky or adhesive substance ▷ *vb* **glues, glueing** *or* **glued 3** (*tr*) to join or stick together with or as if with glue [C14: from Old French *glu*, from Late Latin *glūs*; compare Greek *gloios*] > 'glue,like *adj* > 'gluer *n* > 'gluey *adj*

glue ear *n* accumulation of fluid in the middle ear in children, caused by infection and sometimes resulting in deafness

glue-sniffing *n* the practice of inhaling the fumes of certain types of glue to produce intoxicating or hallucinatory effects > 'glue-,sniffer *n*

gluhwein ('gluː,vaɪn) *n* mulled wine [German]

glum (glʌm) *adj* **glummer, glummest** silent or sullen, as from gloom [C16: variant of GLOOM] > 'glumly *adv* > 'glumness *n*

glume (gluːm) *n botany* one of a pair of dry membranous bracts at the base of the spikelet of grasses [C18: from

Latin *glūma* husk of corn; related to Latin *glūbere* to remove the bark from] > glu'maceous *adj*

gluon ('glu:ɒn) *n* a hypothetical particle believed to be exchanged between quarks in order to bind them together to form particles [C20: from GLUE + -ON]

glurge (glɜ:dʒ) *n* stories, often sent by email, that are supposed to be true and uplifting, but which are often fabricated and sentimental [C20: of unknown origin]

glut (glʌt) *n* 1 an excessive amount, as in the production of a crop, often leading to a fall in price 2 the act of glutting or state of being glutted ▷ *vb* gluts, glutting, glutted (*tr*) 3 to feed or supply beyond capacity 4 to supply (a market) with a commodity in excess of the demand for it [C14: probably from Old French *gloutir*, from Latin *gluttīre*; see GLUTTON[1]]

glutamic acid (glu:'tæmɪk) *n* a nonessential amino acid, occurring in proteins, that acts as a neurotransmitter and plays a part in nitrogen metabolism

glute (glu:t) *n informal* short for **gluteus** [C20]

gluten ('glu:tᵊn) *n* a protein consisting of a mixture of glutelin and gliadin, present in cereal grains, esp wheat. A gluten-free diet is used in cases of coeliac disease [C16: from Latin: GLUE] > 'glutenous *adj*

gluteus or **glutaeus** (glʊ'ti:əs) *n*, *pl* -tei or -taei (-'ti:aɪ) any one of the three large muscles that form the human buttock and move the thigh, esp the **gluteus maximus** [C17: from New Latin, from Greek *gloutos* buttock, rump] > glu'teal or glu'taeal *adj*

glutinous ('glu:tɪnəs) *adj* resembling glue in texture; sticky > 'glutinously *adv*

glutton[1] ('glʌtᵊn) *n* 1 a person devoted to eating and drinking to excess; greedy person 2 *often ironic* a person who has or appears to have a voracious appetite for something: *a glutton for punishment* [C13: from Old French *glouton*, from Latin *glutto*, from *gluttīre* to swallow] > 'gluttonous *adj* > 'gluttonously *adv*

glutton[2] ('glʌtᵊn) *n* another name for **wolverine** [C17: from GLUTTON[1], apparently translating German *Vielfrass* great eater]

gluttony ('glʌtᵊnɪ) *n* the act or practice of eating to excess

glycaemia or *US* **glycemia** (,glaɪ'si:mɪə) *n* the presence of glucose in blood [C20: from GLYCO- + -AEMIA] > glycaemic or *US* glycemic (,glaɪ'si:mɪk) *adj*

glycaemic load or *US* **glycemic load** *n* an index indicating the amount of carbohydrate contained in a specified serving of a particular food. It is calculated by multiplying the food's glycaemic index by its carbohydrate content in grams and then dividing by 100

glyceride ('glɪsə,raɪd) *n* any fatty-acid ester of glycerol

glycerine ('glɪsərɪn, ,glɪsə'ri:n) or **glycerin** ('glɪsərɪn) *n* another name (not in technical usage) for **glycerol** [C19: from French *glycérine*, from Greek *glukeros* sweet + -*ine* -IN; related to Greek *glukus* sweet]

glycerol ('glɪsə,rɒl) *n* a colourless or pale yellow odourless sweet-tasting syrupy liquid; 1,2,3-propanetriol: a by-product of soap manufacture, used as a solvent, antifreeze, plasticizer, and sweetener (**E422**). Formula: $C_3H_8O_3$ [C19: from GLYCER(INE) + -OL[1]]

glycine ('glaɪsi:n, glaɪ'si:n) *n* a nonessential amino acid occurring in most proteins that acts as a neurotransmitter; aminoacetic acid [C19: GLYCO- + -INE[2]]

glyco- or before a vowel **glyc-** *combining form* indicating sugar: *glycogen* [from Greek *glukus* sweet]

glycogen ('glaɪkəʊdʒən, -dʒɛn) *n* a polysaccharide consisting of glucose units: the form in which carbohydrate is stored in the liver and muscles in man and animals. It can easily be hydrolysed to glucose > glycogenic (,glaɪkəʊ'dʒɛnɪk) *adj* > ,glyco'genesis *n*

glycol ('glaɪkɒl) *n* another name (not in technical usage) for **ethanediol**

glycolic acid *n* a colourless crystalline soluble hygroscopic compound found in sugar cane and sugar beet: used in tanning and in the manufacture of pharmaceuticals, pesticides, adhesives, and plasticizers; hydroxyacetic acid. Formula: $CH_2(OH)COOH$

glycolysis (glaɪ'kɒlɪsɪs) *n biochem* the breakdown of glucose by enzymes into pyruvic and lactic acids with the liberation of energy

glycoside ('glaɪkəʊ,saɪd) *n* any of a group of substances, such as digitoxin, derived from monosaccharides by replacing the hydroxyl group by another group. Many are important medicinal drugs > glycosidic (,glaɪkəʊ'sɪdɪk) *adj*

glycosuria (,glaɪkəʊ'sjʊərɪə) or **glucosuria** *n* the presence of excess sugar in the urine, as in diabetes [C19: from New Latin, from French *glycose* GLUCOSE + -URIA]

Glyndebourne ('glaɪnd,bɔ:n) *n* an estate in SE England, in East Sussex: site of a famous annual festival of opera founded in 1934 by John Christie

glyph (glɪf) *n* 1 a carved channel or groove, esp a vertical one as used on a Doric frieze 2 *now rare* another word for **hieroglyphic** [C18: from French *glyphe*, from Greek *gluphē* carving, from *gluphein* to carve] > 'glyphic *adj*

glyptic ('glɪptɪk) *adj* of or relating to engraving or carving, esp on precious stones [C19: from French *glyptique*, from Greek *gluptikos*, from *gluptos*, from *gluphein* to carve]

glyptodont ('glɪptə,dɒnt) *n* any extinct late Cenozoic edentate mammal of the genus *Glyptodon* and related genera, of South America, which resembled giant armadillos [C19: from Greek *gluptos* carved + -ODONT]

GM *abbreviation* 1 general manager 2 genetically modified 3 (in Britain) George Medal 4 Grand Master 5 grant-maintained

G-man *n*, *pl* G-men 1 *US slang* an FBI agent 2 *Irish* a political detective

Gmc *abbreviation* Germanic

GMDSS *abbreviation* Global Marine Distress and Safety System: a worldwide satellite communication system used for transmitting messages (esp distress messages) at sea; officially superseded Morse code in 1999

GMO *abbreviation* genetically modified organism

GMT *abbreviation* Greenwich Mean Time

GMTA *abbreviation* text messaging great minds think alike

gnarl (nɑ:l) *n* 1 any knotty protuberance or swelling on a tree ▷ *vb* 2 (*tr*) to knot or cause to knot [C19: back formation from *gnarled*, probably variant of *knurled*; see KNURL]

gnarled (nɑ:ld) *adj* 1 having gnarls 2 (esp of hands) rough, twisted, and weather-beaten in appearance

gnarly ('nɑ:lɪ) *adj* 1 another word for **gnarled** 2 *NZ informal* good; great

gnash (næʃ) *vb* 1 to grind (the teeth) together, as in pain or anger 2 (*tr*) to bite or chew as by grinding the teeth ▷ *n* 3 the act of gnashing the teeth [C15: probably of Scandinavian origin; compare Old Norse *gnastan* gnashing of teeth, *gnesta* to clatter]

gnat (næt) *n* any of various small fragile biting dipterous insects of the suborder *Nematocera*, esp *Culex pipiens* (**common gnat**), which abounds near stagnant water [Old English *gnætt*; related to Middle High German *gnaz* scurf, German dialect *Gnitze* gnat]

gnathic ('næθɪk) *adj anatomy* of or relating to the jaw [C19: from Greek *gnathos* jaw]

-gnathous *adj combining form* indicating or having a jaw of a specified kind: *prognathous* [from New Latin -*gnathus*, from Greek *gnathos* jaw]

gnaw (nɔ:) *vb* gnaws, gnawing, gnawed or gnawn (nɔ:n) 1 (when *intr*, often foll by *at* or *upon*) to bite (at) or chew (upon) constantly so as to wear away little by little 2 (*tr*) to form by gnawing: *to gnaw a hole* 3 to cause erosion of (something) 4 (when *intr*, often foll by *at*) to cause constant distress or anxiety (to) ▷ *n* 5 the act or an instance of gnawing [Old English *gnagan*; related to Old Norse *gnaga*, Old High German *gnagan*] > 'gnawing *adj*, *n*

gneiss (naɪs) *n* any coarse-grained metamorphic rock that is banded and foliated: represents the last stage in the metamorphism of rocks before melting [C18: from German *Gneis*, probably from Middle High German *ganeist* spark; related to Old Norse *gneista* to give off sparks] > 'gneissic, 'gneissoid or 'gneissose *adj*

gnocchi ('nɒkɪ, gə'nɒkɪ, 'gnɒkɪ) *pl n* dumplings made of pieces of semolina pasta, or sometimes potato, used to garnish soup or served alone with sauce [Italian, plural of *gnocco* lump, probably of Germanic origin; compare

Middle High German *knoche* bone]

gnome (nəum) *n* **1** one of a species of legendary creatures, usually resembling small misshapen old men, said to live in the depths of the earth and guard buried treasure **2** the statue of a gnome, esp in a garden **3** a very small or ugly person **4** *facetious or derogatory* an international banker or financier (esp in the phrase *gnomes of Zürich*) [c18: from French, from New Latin *gnomus*, coined by Paracelsus, of obscure origin] > 'gnomish *adj*

gnomic ('nəumɪk, 'nɒm-) or **gnomical** *adj* consisting of, containing, or relating to gnomes or aphorisms > 'gnomically *adv*

gnomon ('nəumɒn) *n* **1** the stationary arm that projects the shadow on a sundial **2** a geometric figure remaining after a parallelogram has been removed from one corner of a larger parallelogram [c16: from Latin, from Greek: interpreter, from *gignōskein* to know] > gno'monic *adj*

gnosis ('nəusɪs) *n, pl* **-ses** (-siːz) supposedly revealed knowledge of various spiritual truths, esp that said to have been possessed by ancient Gnostics [c18: ultimately from Greek: knowledge, from *gignōskein* to know]

-gnosis *n combining form* (esp in medicine) recognition or knowledge [via Latin from Greek: GNOSIS] > **-gnostic** *adj combining form*

gnostic ('nɒstɪk) *adj* of, relating to, or possessing knowledge, esp esoteric spiritual knowledge

Gnostic ('nɒstɪk) *n* **1** an adherent of Gnosticism ▷ *adj* **2** of or relating to Gnostics or to Gnosticism [c16: from Late Latin *Gnosticī* the Gnostics, from Greek *gnōstikos* relating to knowledge, from *gnōstos* known, from *gignōskein* to know]

Gnosticism ('nɒstɪˌsɪzəm) *n* a religious movement characterized by a belief in gnosis, through which the spiritual element in man could be released from its bondage in matter: regarded as a heresy by the Christian Church

GNP *abbreviation* gross national product

gnu (nuː) *n, pl* **gnus** or **gnu** either of two sturdy antelopes, *Connochaetes taurinus* (**brindled gnu**) or the much rarer *C. gnou* (**white-tailed gnu**), inhabiting the savannas of Africa, having an oxlike head and a long tufted tail. Also called: **wildebeest** [c18: from Xhosa *nqu*]

GNVQ *abbreviation* (in Britain) general national vocational qualification: a qualification which rewards the development of skills which are likely to be of use to employers

go (gəu) *vb* **goes**, **going**, **went**, **gone** (*mainly intr*) **1** to move or proceed, esp to or from a point or in a certain direction: *to go to London; to go home* **2** (*tr; takes an infinitive, often with* **to** *omitted or replaced by* **and**) to proceed towards a particular person or place with some specified intention or purpose: *I must go and get that book* **3** to depart: *we'll have to go at eleven* **4** to start, as in a race: *often used in commands* **5** to make regular journeys: *this train service goes to the east coast* **6** to operate or function effectively: *the radio won't go* **7** (*copula*) to become: *his face went red with embarrassment* **8** to make a noise as specified: *the gun went bang* **9** to enter into a specified state or condition: *to go into hysterics; to go into action* **10** to be or continue to be in a specified state or condition: *to go in rags; to go in poverty* **11** to lead, extend, or afford access: *this route goes to the north* **12** to proceed towards an activity: *to go to supper; to go to sleep* **13** (*tr; takes an infinitive*) to serve or contribute: *this letter goes to prove my point* **14** to follow a course as specified; fare: *the lecture went badly* **15** to be applied or allotted to a particular purpose or recipient: *her wealth went to her son; his money went on drink* **16** to be sold or otherwise transferred to a recipient: *the necklace went for three thousand pounds* **17** to be ranked; compare: *this meal is good as my meals go* **18** to blend or harmonize: *these chairs won't go with the rest of your furniture* **19** (foll by **by** or **under**) to be known (by a name or disguise) **20** to have a usual or proper place: *those books go on this shelf* **21** (of music, poetry, etc) to be sounded; expressed, etc: *how does that song go?* **22** to fail or give way: *my eyesight is going* **23** to break down or collapse abruptly: *the ladder went at the critical moment* **24** to die: *the old man went at 2 a.m* **25** (often

foll by **by**) **a** (of time) to elapse: *the hours go by so slowly at the office* **b** to travel past: *the train goes by her house at four* **c** to be guided (by) **26** to occur: *happiness does not always go with riches* **27** to be eliminated, abolished, or given up: *this entry must go to save space* **28** to be spent or finished: *all his money has gone* **29** to attend: *go to school; go to church* **30** to join a stated profession: *go to the bar; go on the stage* **31** (foll by **to**) to have recourse (to); turn: *to go to arbitration* **32** (foll by **to**) to subject or put oneself (to): *she goes to great pains to please him* **33** to proceed, esp up to or beyond certain limits: *you will go too far one day and then you will be punished* **34** to be acceptable or tolerated: *anything goes in this place* **35** to carry the weight of final authority: *what the boss says goes* **36** (foll by **into**) to be contained in: *four goes into twelve three times* **37** (often foll by **for**) to endure or last out: *we can't go for much longer without water in this heat* **38** (*tr*) *cards* to bet or bid: *I go two hearts* **39** (*tr*) *not standard* to say: widely used, esp in the historic present, in reporting dialogue: *Then she goes, "Give it to me!" and she just snatched it* **40** **go and** *informal* to be so foolish or unlucky as to: *then she had to go and lose her hat* **41** **be going** to intend or be about to start (to do or be doing something): often used as an alternative future construction: *what's going to happen to us?* **42** **go it** *slang* to do something or move energetically **43** **go it alone** *informal* to act or proceed without allies or help **44** **go one better** *informal* to surpass or outdo (someone) **45** **let go a** to relax one's hold (on); release **b** to discuss or consider no further **46** **let oneself go a** to act in an uninhibited manner **b** to lose interest in one's appearance, manners, etc **47** **to go a** remaining **b** *US & Canadian informal* (of food served by a restaurant) for taking away ▷ *n, pl* **goes** **48** the act of going **49** *informal* **a** an attempt or try: *he had a go at the stamp business* **b** an attempt at stopping a person suspected of a crime: *the police are not always in favour of the public having a go* **c** an attack, esp verbal: *she had a real go at them* **50 a** a turn: *it's my go next* **51** *informal* the quality of being active and energetic: *she has much more go than I* **52** *informal* hard or energetic work: *it's all go* **53** *informal* a successful venture or achievement: *he made a go of it* **54** *informal* a bargain or agreement **55** **from the word go** *informal* from the very beginning **56** **no go** *informal* impossible; abortive or futile: *it's no go, I'm afraid* **57** **on the go** *informal* active and energetic ▷ *adj* **58** (*postpositive*) *informal* functioning properly and ready for action: esp used in astronautics: *all systems are go* ▷ See also **go about**, **go against** [Old English *gān*; related to Old High German *gēn*, Greek *kikhanein* to reach, Sanskrit *jahāti* he forsakes]

Goa ('gəuə) *n* a state on the W coast of India: a Portuguese overseas territory from 1510 until annexed by India in 1961. Capital: Panjim (or Panaji). Pop: 1 343 998 (2001). Area: 3702 sq km (1430 sq miles)

go about *vb* (*intr*) **1** (*preposition*) to busy oneself with: *to go about one's duties* **2** (*preposition*) to tackle (a problem or task) **3** to circulate (in): *there's a lot of flu going about* **4** (*adverb*) (of a sailing ship) to change from one tack to another

goad (gəud) *n* **1** a sharp pointed stick for urging on cattle, etc **2** anything that acts as a spur or incitement ▷ *vb* **3** (*tr*) to drive with or as if with a goad; spur; incite [Old English *gād*, of Germanic origin, related to Old English *gār*, Old Norse *geirr* spear]

Goa, Daman, and Diu *n* a former Union Territory of India consisting of the widely separated districts of Goa and Daman and the island of Diu. Capital: Panjim (or Panaji). Area: 3814 sq km (1472 sq miles)

go against *vb* (*intr, preposition*) **1** to be contrary to (principles or beliefs) **2** to be unfavourable to (a person): *the case went against him*

go ahead *vb* **1** (*intr, adverb*) to start or continue, often after obtaining permission ▷ *n* **go-ahead 2** the **go-ahead** *informal* permission to proceed ▷ *adj* **go-ahead 3** enterprising or ambitious

goal (gəul) *n* **1** the aim or object towards which an endeavour is directed **2** the terminal point of a journey or race **3** (in various sports) the net, basket, etc into or over which players try to propel the ball, puck, etc, to score **4** *sport* **a** a successful attempt at scoring **b** the score so made **5** (in soccer, hockey, etc) the position of goalkeeper [c16: perhaps related to Middle English *gol*

boundary, Old English *gǣlan* to hinder, impede]
> 'goalless *adj*

goalball ('gəʊl,bɔːl) *n* **1** a game played by two teams who compete to score goals by throwing a ball that emits audible sound when in motion. Players, who may be blind or sighted, are blindfolded during play **2** the ball used in this game

goalie ('gəʊlɪ) *n informal* short for **goalkeeper**

goalkeeper ('gəʊl,kiːpə) *n sport* a player in the goal whose duty is to prevent the ball, puck, etc, from entering or crossing it

goal kick *n soccer* a kick taken from the six-yard line by the defending team after the ball has been put out of play by an opposing player

goal line *n sport* the line marking each end of the pitch, on which the goals stand

go along *vb* (*intr, adverb*; often foll by *with*) to refrain from disagreement; assent

goalpost ('gəʊl,pəʊst) *n* **1** either of two upright posts supporting the crossbar of a goal **2 move the goalposts** to change the aims of an activity to ensure the desired results

goanna (gəʊ'ænə) *n* any of various Australian monitor lizards [C19: changed from IGUANA]

go around *or* **go round** *vb* **1** (*adverb*) to move about **2** (*adverb*; foll by *with*) to frequent the society (of a person or group of people): *she went around with older men* **3** (*adverb*) to be sufficient: *are there enough sweets to go round?* **4** to circulate (in): *measles is going round the school* **5** (*preposition*) to be actively and constantly engaged in (doing something): *she went around caring for the sick* **6** to be long enough to encircle: *will that belt go round you?*

goat (gəʊt) *n* **1** any sure-footed agile bovid mammal of the genus *Capra*, naturally inhabiting rough stony ground in Europe, Asia, and N Africa, typically having a brown-grey colouring and a beard. Domesticated varieties (*C. hircus*) are reared for milk, meat, and wool **2** *informal* a lecherous man **3 get someone's goat** *slang* to cause annoyance to someone [Old English *gāt*; related to Old Norse *geit*, Old High German *geiz*, Latin *haedus* kid] > 'goatish *adj*

Goat (gəʊt) *n* **the Goat** the constellation Capricorn, the tenth sign of the zodiac

go at *vb* (*intr, preposition*) **1** to make an energetic attempt at (something) **2** to attack vehemently

goatee (gəʊ'tiː) *n* a pointed tuftlike beard on the chin [C19: from GOAT + *-ee* (see -Y²)]

goatherd ('gəʊt,hɜːd) *n* a person employed to tend or herd goats

goatsbeard *or* **goat's-beard** ('gəʊts,bɪəd) *n* **1** Also called: Jack-go-to-bed-at-noon a Eurasian plant, *Tragopogon pratensis*, with woolly stems and large heads of yellow rayed flowers surrounded by large green bracts: family Asteraceae (composites) **2** an American rosaceous plant, *Aruncus sylvester*, with long spikes of small white flowers

goatskin ('gəʊt,skɪn) *n* **1** the hide of a goat **2** something made from the hide of a goat, such as leather or a container for wine

goatsucker ('gəʊt,sʌkə) *n US & Canadian* any nocturnal bird of the family Caprimulgidae, esp *Caprimulgus europaeus* (**European nightjar**): order Caprimulgiform es.. Also called (in Britain and certain other countries): nightjar

go-away bird *n South African* a common name for a grey-plumaged lourie of the genus *Corythaixoides*. See also lourie [C19: imitative of its call]

gob¹ (gɒb) *n* **1** a lump or chunk, esp of a soft substance **2** (*often plural*) *informal* a great quantity or amount **3** a lump of molten glass used to make a piece of glassware **4** *informal* a globule of spittle or saliva ▷ *vb* **gobs, gobbing, gobbed 5** (*intr*) *Brit informal* to spit [C14: from Old French *gobe* lump, from *gober* to gulp down; see GOBBET]

gob² (gɒb) *n US slang* an enlisted ordinary seaman in the US Navy [C20: of unknown origin]

go back *vb* (*intr, adverb*) **1** to return **2** (*often foll by to*) to originate (in): *the links with France go back to the Norman Conquest* **3** (foll by *on*) to change one's mind about; repudiate (esp in the phrase **go back on one's word**)

gobbet ('gɒbɪt) *n* a chunk, lump, or fragment, esp of

raw meat [C14: from Old French *gobet*, from *gober* to gulp down]

Gobbi (*Italian* 'gɔbbi) *n* Tito ('tiːto). 1915–84, Italian operatic baritone

gobble¹ ('gɒbªl) *vb* **1** (when *tr*, often foll by *up*) to eat or swallow (food) hastily and in large mouthfuls **2** (*tr*; often foll by *up*) *informal* to snatch [C17: probably from GOB¹]

gobble² ('gɒbªl) *n* **1** the loud rapid gurgling sound made by male turkeys ▷ *vb* **2** (*intr*) (of a turkey) to make this sound [C17: probably of imitative origin]

gobbledegook *or* **gobbledygook** ('gɒbªldɪ,guːk) *n* pretentious or unintelligible jargon, such as that used by officials [C20: whimsical formation from GOBBLE²]

gobbler ('gɒblə) *n informal* a male turkey

Gobelin ('gəʊbəlɪn; *French* gɔblɛ̃) *adj* **1** of or resembling tapestry made at the Gobelins' factory in Paris, having vivid pictorial scenes ▷ *n* **2** a tapestry of this kind [C19: from the *Gobelin* family, who founded the factory]

go-between *n* a person who acts as agent or intermediary for two people or groups in a transaction or dealing

Gobi ('gəʊbɪ) *n* a desert in E Asia, mostly in Mongolia and the Inner Mongolian Autonomous Region of China: sometimes considered to include all the arid regions east of the Pamirs and north of the plateau of Tibet and the Great Wall of China: one of the largest deserts in the world. Length: about 1600 km (1000 miles). Width: about 1000 km (625 miles). Average height: 900 m (3000 ft). Chinese name: Shamo > 'Gobian *adj*

Gobind Singh ('gəʊbɪnd sɪŋ) *or* **Govind Singh** *n* 1666–1708, tenth and last guru of the Sikhs (1675–1708): assassinated

goblet ('gɒblɪt) *n* **1** a vessel for drinking, usually of glass or metal, with a base and stem but without handles **2** *archaic* a large drinking cup shaped like a bowl [C14: from Old French *gobelet* a little cup, from *gobel* ultimately of Celtic origin]

goblin ('gɒblɪn) *n* (in folklore) a small grotesque supernatural creature, regarded as malevolent towards human beings [C14: from Old French, from Middle High German *kobolt*; compare COBALT]

gobo ('gəʊbəʊ) *n, pl* **-bos** *or* **-boes 1** a shield placed around a microphone to exclude unwanted sounds **2** a black screen placed around a camera lens, television lens, etc, to reduce the incident light [C20: of unknown origin]

gobshite ('gɒb,ʃaɪt) *n slang* a stupid person [C20: from *gob* mouth + *shite* excrement; see SHIT]

gobsmacked ('gɒb,smækt) *adj Brit slang* astounded; astonished [C20: from *gob* mouth + SMACK²]

goby ('gəʊbɪ) *n, pl* **-by** *or* **-bies** any small spiny-finned fish of the family Gobiidae, of coastal or brackish waters, having a large head, an elongated tapering body, and the ventral fins modified as a sucker [C18: from Latin *gōbius* gudgeon, fish of little value, from Greek *kōbios*]

go-by *n slang* a deliberate snub or slight (esp in the phrase **give (a person) the go-by**)

go by *vb* (*intr*) **1** to pass: *the cars went by; as the years go by we all get older; don't let those opportunities go by!* **2** (*preposition*) to be guided by: *in the darkness we could only go by the stars* **3** (*preposition*) to use as a basis for forming an opinion or judgment: *it's wise not to go only by appearances*

go-cart *n motor racing* See **kart**

god (gɒd) *n* **1** a supernatural being, who is worshipped as the controller of some part of the universe or some aspect of life in the world or is the personification of some force **2** an image, idol, or symbolic representation of such a deity **3** any person or thing to which excessive attention is given: *money was his god* **4** a man who has qualities regarded as making him superior to other men **5** (*in plural*) the gallery of a theatre [Old English *god*; related to Old Norse *goth*, Old High German *got*, Old Irish *guth* voice]

God (gɒd) *n* **1** *theol* the sole Supreme Being, eternal, spiritual, and transcendent, who is the Creator and ruler of all and is infinite in all attributes; the object of worship in monotheistic religions ▷ *interj* **2** an oath or exclamation used to indicate surprise, annoyance, etc

(and in such expressions as **My God!** or **God Almighty!**)

Godard (*French* ɡɔdar) *n* **Jean-Luc** (ʒãlyk). born 1930, French film director and writer associated with the New Wave of the 1960s. His works include *À bout de souffle* (1960), *Weekend* (1967), *Sauve qui peut* (1980), *Nouvelle Vague* (1990), and *Éloge de l'amour* (2003)

Godavari (ɡəʊˈdɑːvərɪ) *n* a river in central India, rising in the Western Ghats and flowing southeast to the Bay of Bengal: extensive delta, linked by canal with the Krishna delta; a sacred river to Hindus. Length: about 1500 km (900 miles)

God-botherer (ˈɡɒdˌbɒðərə) *n* *informal* an over-zealous Christian

godchild (ˈɡɒdˌtʃaɪld) *n*, *pl* **-children** (-ˌtʃɪldrən) a person, usually an infant, who is sponsored by adults at baptism

Goddard (ˈɡɒdɑːd) *n* **Robert Hutchings**. 1882–1945, US physicist. He made the first workable liquid-fuelled rocket

goddaughter (ˈɡɒdˌdɔːtə) *n* a female godchild

goddess (ˈɡɒdɪs) *n* **1** a female divinity **2** a woman who is adored or idealized, esp by a man

Godefroy de Bouillon (*French* ɡɔdfrwa də bujɔ̃) *n* ?1060–1100, French leader of the First Crusade (1096–99), becoming first ruler of the Latin kingdom of Jerusalem

Gödel (ˈɡɜːdᵊl) *n* **Kurt** (kʊrt). 1906–78, US logician and mathematician, born in Austria-Hungary. He showed (**Gödel's proof**) that in a formal axiomatic system, such as logic or mathematics, it is impossible to prove consistency without using methods from outside the system

Goderich (ˈɡəʊdrɪtʃ) *n* **Viscount**, title of *Frederick John Robinson*, 1st Earl of Ripon. 1782–1859, British statesman; prime minister (1827–28)

Godesberg (*German* ˈɡoːdəsbɛrk) *n* a town and spa in W Germany, in North Rhine-Westphalia on the Rhine: a SE suburb of Bonn. Official name: **Bad Godesberg**

godetia (ɡəˈdiːʃə) *n* any plant of the American onagraceous genus *Godetia*, esp one grown as a showy-flowered annual garden plant [C19: named after C. H. *Godet* (died 1879), Swiss botanist]

godfather (ˈɡɒdˌfɑːðə) *n* **1** a male godparent **2** the head of a Mafia family or other organized criminal ring **3** an originator or leading exponent: *the godfather of South African pop*

godfather offer *n* *informal* a takeover bid pitched so high that the management of the target company is unable to dissuade shareholders from accepting it [C20: from the 1972 film *The Godfather*, in which a character was made an offer he could not refuse by a threatening mafioso]

God-fearing *adj* pious; devout

godforsaken (ˈɡɒdfəˌseɪkən, ˌɡɒdfəˈseɪkən) *adj* (*sometimes capital*) **1** (*usually prenominal*) desolate; dreary; forlorn **2** wicked

Godhead (ˈɡɒdˌhɛd) *n* (*sometimes not capital*) **1** the essential nature and condition of being God **2** the Godhead God

godhood (ˈɡɒdˌhʊd) *n* the state of being divine

Godiva (ɡəˈdaɪvə) *n* **Lady**. ?1040–1080, wife of Leofric, Earl of Mercia. According to legend, she rode naked through Coventry in order to obtain remission for the townspeople from the heavy taxes imposed by her husband

godless (ˈɡɒdlɪs) *adj* **1** wicked or unprincipled **2** lacking a god **3** refusing to acknowledge God > **ˈgodlessly** *adv* > **ˈgodlessness** *n*

godlike (ˈɡɒdˌlaɪk) *adj* resembling or befitting a god or God; divine

godly (ˈɡɒdlɪ) *adj* **-lier, -liest** having a religious character; pious; devout > **ˈgodliness** *n*

godmother (ˈɡɒdˌmʌðə) *n* a female godparent

Godolphin (ɡəˈdɒlfɪn) *n* **Sidney**. 1st Earl of Godolphin. 1645–1712, English statesman; as Lord Treasurer, he managed the financing of Marlborough's campaigns in the War of the Spanish Succession

godown (ˈɡəʊˌdaʊn) *n* (in East Asia and India) a warehouse [C16: from Malay *godong*]

go down *vb* (*intr, mainly adverb*) **1** (*also preposition*) to move

or lead to or as if to a lower place or level; sink, decline, decrease, etc **2** to be defeated; lose **3** to be remembered or recorded (esp in the phrase **go down in history**) **4** to be received: *his speech went down well* **5** (of food) to be swallowed **6** *Brit* to leave a college or university at the end of a term or the academic year **7** (usually foll by *with*) to fall ill; be infected **8** (of a celestial body) to sink or set **9** *slang, chiefly US* to happen **10 go down on** *slang* to perform cunnilingus or fellatio on

Godoy (*Spanish* ɡoˈðoɪ) *n* **Manuel de**. 1767–1851, Spanish statesman: Charles IV's unpopular chief minister (1792–97; 1801–08)

godparent (ˈɡɒdˌpɛərənt) *n* a person who stands sponsor to another at baptism

God's acre *n* *literary* a churchyard or burial ground [C17: translation of German *Gottesacker*]

godsend (ˈɡɒdˌsɛnd) *n* a person or thing that comes unexpectedly but is particularly welcome [C19: changed from C17 *God's send*, alteration of *goddes sand* God's message, from Old English *sand*; see SEND¹]

godslot (ˈɡɒdˌslɒt) *n* *informal* a time in a television or radio schedule traditionally reserved for religious broadcasts

godson (ˈɡɒdˌsʌn) *n* a male godchild

Godspeed (ˈɡɒdˈspiːd) *interj, n* an expression of one's good wishes for a person's success and safety [C15: from *God spede* may God prosper (you)]

godsquad (ˈɡɒdˌskwɒd) *n* *informal, derogatory* any group of evangelical Christians, members of which are regarded as intrusive and exuberantly pious

Godthaab or **Godthåb** (ˈɡɒdhɔːb) *n* the Danish and former official name for: Nuuk

Godunov (ˈɡɒdəˌnɒf, 'ɡʊd-; *Russian* ɡədʊˈnɒf) *n* **Boris Fyodorovich** (baˈris ˈfjɔdərəvitʃ). ?1551–1605, Russian regent (1584–98) and tsar (1598–1605)

Godwin (ˈɡɒdwɪn) *n* **1** died 1053, Earl of Wessex. He was chief adviser to Canute and Edward the Confessor. His son succeeded Edward to the throne as Harold II **2 Mary**. See (Mary): **Wollstonecraft 3 William**. 1756–1836, British political philosopher and novelist. In *An Enquiry concerning Political Justice* (1793), he rejected government and social institutions, including marriage. His views greatly influenced English romantic writers

Godwin-Austen *n* another name for: **K2**

godwit (ˈɡɒdwɪt) *n* any large shore bird of the genus *Limosa*, of northern and arctic regions, having long legs and a long upturned bill: family *Scolopacidae* (sandpipers, etc), order *Charadriiformes* [C16: of unknown origin]

Godzone (ˈɡɒdzəʊn) *n* *Austral informal* one's home country [from *God's own country*]

Goebbels (*German* ˈɡœbəls) *n* **Paul Joseph** (paul ˈjoːzɛf). 1897–1945, German Nazi politician; minister of propaganda (1933–45)

goer (ˈɡəʊə) *n* **1 a** a person who attends something regularly **b** (*in combination*): *filmgoer* **2** an energetic person **3** *informal* an acceptable or feasible idea, proposal, etc

Goering (*German* ˈɡøːrɪŋ) *n* See **Göring**

Goes (ɡuːs) *n* **Hugo van der**. ?1440–82, Flemish painter: works include the *Pontinari Altarpiece* and *The Death of a Virgin*

Goethe (*German* ˈɡøːtə) *n* **Johann Wolfgang von** (joˈhan ˈvɔlfɡaŋ fɔn). 1749–1832, German poet, novelist, and dramatist, who settled in Weimar in 1775. His early works of the *Sturm und Drang* period include the play *Götz von Berlichingen* (1773) and the novel *The Sorrows of Young Werther* (1774). After a journey to Italy (1786–88) his writings, such as the epic play *Iphigenie auf Tauris* (1787) and the epic idyll *Hermann und Dorothea* (1797), showed the influence of classicism. Other works include the *Wilhelm Meister* novels (1796–1829) and his greatest masterpiece *Faust* (1808; 1832)

go-faster stripe *n* *informal* a decorative line, often suggestive of high speed, on the bodywork of a car

gofer (ˈɡəʊfə) *n* *slang, chiefly US & Canadian* an employee or assistant whose duties include menial tasks such as running errands [C20: originally US: alteration of *go for*]

goffer or **gauffer** (ˈɡəʊfə) *vb* (*tr*) **1** to press pleats into (a frill) **2** to decorate (the gilt edges of a book) with a repeating pattern ▷ *n* **3** an ornamental frill made by pressing pleats **4** the decoration formed by goffering books **5** the iron or tool used in making goffers [c18: from French *gaufrer* to impress a pattern, from *gaufre*, from Middle Low German *wāfel*; see WAFFLE¹, WAFER]

go for *vb* (*intr, preposition*) **1** to go somewhere in order to have or fetch: *he went for a drink; shall I go for a doctor?* **2** to seek to obtain: *I'd go for that job if I were you* **3** to prefer or choose; like: *I really go for that new idea of yours* **4** to make a physical or verbal attack on **5** to be considered to be of a stated importance or value: *his twenty years went for nothing when he was made redundant* **6** go for it *informal* to make the maximum effort to achieve a particular goal

Gog and Magog (gɒg, 'meɪgɒg) *n* **1** *Old Testament* a hostile prince and the land from which he comes to attack Israel (Ezekiel 38) **2** *New Testament* two kings, who are to attack the Church in a climactic battle, but are then to be destroyed by God (Revelation 20:8–10) **3** *Brit folklore* two giants, the only survivors of a race of giants destroyed by Brutus, the legendary founder of Britain

go-getter *n informal* an ambitious enterprising person >'go-,getting *adj*

gogga ('xɒxə) *n South African informal* any small animal that crawls or flies, esp an insect [c20: from Khoikhoi *xoxon* insects collectively]

goggle ('gɒgªl) *vb* **1** (*intr*) to stare stupidly or fixedly, as in astonishment **2** to cause (the eyes) to roll or bulge or (of the eyes) to roll or bulge ▷ *n* **3** a fixed or bulging stare **4** (*plural*) spectacles, often of coloured glass or covered with gauze: used to protect the eyes [c14: from *gogelen* to look aside, of uncertain origin; see AGOG] >'goggle-,eyed *adj*

gogglebox ('gɒgªl,bɒks) *n Brit slang* a television set

Gogh (gɒx; *Dutch* xɔx) *n* See **Van Gogh**

gogo ('gɒgɒ) *n South African* grandmother [from Zulu]

go-go dancer *n* a dancer, usually scantily dressed, who performs rhythmic and often erotic modern dance routines, esp in a nightclub or disco

Gogol ('gəʊgɒl; *Russian* 'gɔgəlj) *n* Nikolai Vasilievich (nika'laj va'siljivitʃ). 1809–52, Russian novelist, dramatist, and short-story writer. His best-known works are *The Government Inspector* (1836), a comedy satirizing bureaucracy, and the novel *Dead Souls* (1842)

Gogra ('gɒgrə) *n* a river in N India, rising in Tibet, in the Himalayas, and flowing southeast through Nepal as the Karnali, then through Uttar Pradesh to join the Ganges. Length: about 1000 km (600 miles)

Goiânia (gɔɪ'ɑːnɪə; *Portuguese* go'jənja) *n* a city in central Brazil, capital of Goiás state: planned in 1933 to replace the old capital, Goiás; two universities. Pop: 1 878 000 (2005 est)

Goiás (*Portuguese* gɔ'jas) *n* a state of central Brazil, in the Brazilian Highlands: contains Brasília, the capital of Brazil. Capital: Goiânia. Pop: 5 210 335 (2002). Area: 341 289 sq km (131 772 sq miles)

Goidelic *or* **Goidhelic** (gɔɪ'dɛlɪk) *n* **1** the N group of Celtic languages, consisting of Irish Gaelic, Scottish Gaelic, and Manx ▷ *adj* **2** of, relating to, or characteristic of this group of languages [c19: from Old Irish *Goidel* a Celt, from Old Welsh *gwyddel*, from *gwydd* savage]

go in *vb* (*intr, mainly adverb*) **1** to enter **2** (*preposition*) See **go into 3** (of the sun) to become hidden behind a cloud **4** go in for **a** to enter as a competitor or contestant **b** to adopt as an activity, interest, or guiding principle: *she went in for nursing; some men go in for football in a big way*

going ('gəʊɪŋ) *n* **1** a departure or farewell **2** the condition of a surface such as a road or field with regard to walking, riding, etc: *muddy going* **3** *informal* speed, progress, etc: *we made good going on the trip* ▷ *adj* **4** thriving (esp in the phrase **a going concern**) **5** current or accepted, as from past negotiations or commercial operation: *the going rate for electricians; the going value of the firm* **6** (*postpositive*) available: *the best going*

going-over *n*, *pl* **goings-over** *informal* **1** a check, examination, or investigation **2** a castigation or thrashing

goings-on *pl n informal* **1** actions or conduct, esp when regarded with disapproval **2** happenings or events, esp when mysterious or suspicious

go into *vb* (*intr, preposition*) **1** to enter **2** to start a career in:

to go into publishing **3** to investigate or examine **4** to discuss: *we won't go into that now* **5** to go to live in or be admitted to, esp temporarily: *she went into hospital on Tuesday* **6** to enter a specified state: *she went into fits of laughter*

goitre *or US* **goiter** ('gɔɪtə) *n pathol* a swelling of the thyroid gland, in some cases nearly doubling the size of the neck, usually caused by under- or overproduction of hormone by the gland [c17: from French *goitre*, from Old French *goitron*, ultimately from Latin *guttur* throat] >'goitred *or US* 'goitered *adj* >'goitrous *adj*

goji ('gəʊdʒi) *n* another name for **wolfberry** [c21: Tibetan]

go-kart *or* **go-cart** *n* See **kart**

Golan Heights ('gəʊlæn) *pl n* a range of hills in the Middle East, possession of which is disputed between Israel and Syria: under Syrian control until 1967 when they were stormed by Israeli forces; Jewish settlements have since been established. Highest peak: 2224 m (7297 ft)

Golconda (gɒl'kɒndə) *n* **1** a ruined town and fortress in S central India, in W Andhra Pradesh near Hyderabad city: capital of one of the five Muslim kingdoms of the Deccan from 1512 to 1687, then annexed to the Mogul empire; renowned for its diamonds **2** (*sometimes not capital*) a source of wealth or riches, esp a mine

gold (gəʊld) *n* **1 a** a dense inert bright yellow element that is the most malleable and ductile metal, occurring in rocks and alluvial deposits: used as a monetary standard and in jewellery, dentistry, and plating. The radioisotope gold-198 (**radiogold**), with a half-life of 2.69 days, is used in radiotherapy. Symbol: Au; atomic no: 79; atomic wt: 196.96654; valency: 1 or 3; relative density: 19.3; melting pt: 1064.43°C; boiling pt: 2857°C. Related adj: **auric b** (*as modifier*): *a gold mine* **2** a coin or coins made of this metal **3** money; wealth **4** something precious, beautiful, etc, such as a noble nature (esp in the phrase **heart of gold**) **5 a** a deep yellow colour, sometimes with a brownish tinge **b** (*as adjective*): *a gold carpet* **6** short for **gold medal** [Old English *gold*; related to Old Norse *gull*, Gothic *gulth*, Old High German *gold*]

Gold (gəʊld) *n* Thomas. 1920–2004, Austrian-born astronomer, working in England and the US: with Bondi and Hoyle he proposed the steady-state theory of the universe

gold card *n* a credit card issued by credit-card companies to favoured clients, entitling them to high unsecured overdrafts, some insurance cover, etc

Gold Coast *n* **1** the former name (until 1957) of **Ghana 2** a line of resort towns and beaches in E Australia, extending for over 30 km (20 miles) along the SE coast of Queensland and the NE coast of New South Wales

goldcrest ('gəʊld,krɛst) *n* a small Old World warbler, *Regulus regulus*, having a greenish plumage and a bright yellow-and-black crown

gold-digger *n* **1** a person who prospects or digs for gold **2** *informal* a woman who uses her sexual attractions to accumulate gifts and wealth or advance her social position

gold disc *n* **a** (in Britain) an LP record certified to have sold 250 000 copies or a single certified to have sold 500 000 copies **b** (in the US) an LP record or single certified to have sold 1 000 000 copies or a single certified to have sold 500 000 copies

gold dust *n* gold in the form of small particles or powder, as found in placer-mining

golden ('gəʊldən) *adj* **1** of the yellowish or brownish-yellow metallic colour of gold: *golden hair* **2** made from or largely consisting of gold: *a golden statue* **3** happy or prosperous: *golden days* **4** (*sometimes capital*) (of anniversaries) the 50th in a series: *Golden Jubilee; golden wedding* **5** *informal* very successful or destined for success: *the golden girl of tennis* **6** extremely valuable or advantageous: *a golden opportunity* >'goldenly *adv* >'goldenness *n*

golden age *n* **1** *classical myth* the first and best age of mankind, when existence was happy, prosperous, and innocent **2** the most flourishing and outstanding period, esp in the history of an art or nation: *the golden age of poetry*

golden eagle *n* a large eagle, *Aquila chrysaetos*, of mountainous regions of the N hemisphere, having a plumage that is golden brown on the back and brown elsewhere

goldeneye ('gəʊldən,aɪ) *n*, *pl* -eyes *or* -eye either of two black-and-white diving ducks, *Bucephala clangula* or *B. islandica*, of northern regions

Golden Fleece *n Greek myth* the fleece of a winged ram that rescued Phrixus and brought him to Colchis, where he sacrificed it to Zeus. Phrixus gave the fleece to King Aeëtes who kept it in a sacred grove, whence Jason and the Argonauts stole it with the help of Aeëtes' daughter

Golden Gate *n* a strait between the Pacific and San Francisco Bay: crossed by the **Golden Gate Bridge**, with a central span of 1280 m (4200 ft)

golden goal *n soccer* (in certain matches) the first goal scored in extra time, which wins the match for the side scoring it

golden goose *n* a goose in folklore that laid a golden egg a day until its greedy owner killed it in an attempt to get all the gold at once

golden handcuffs *pl n informal* payments deferred over a number of years that induce a person to stay with a particular company or in a particular job

golden handshake *n informal* a sum of money, usually large, given to an employee, either on retirement in recognition of long or excellent service or as compensation for loss of employment

golden hello *n informal* a payment made to a sought-after recruit on signing a contract of employment with a company

Golden Horn *n* an inlet of the Bosporus in NW Turkey, forming the harbour of Istanbul. Turkish name: **Haliç**

golden hour *n* the first hour after a serious accident, when it is crucial that the victim receives medical treatment in order to have a chance of surviving

golden mean *n* **1** the middle course between extremes **2** another term for **golden section**

golden number *n* a number between 1 and 19, used to indicate the position of any year in the Metonic cycle, calculated as the remainder when 1 is added to the given year and the sum is divided by 19. If the remainder is zero the number is 19

golden parachute *n informal* a clause in the employment contract of a senior executive providing for special benefits if the executive's employment is terminated as a result of a takeover

golden retriever *n* a compact large breed of dog having a silky coat of flat or wavy hair of a gold or dark-cream colour, well-feathered on the legs and tail

goldenrod (,gəʊldən'rɒd) *n* any plant of the genus *Solidago*, of North America, Europe, and Asia, having spikes made up of inflorescences of minute yellow florets: family *Asteraceae* (composites)

golden rule *n* **1** any of a number of rules of fair conduct, such as *Whatsoever ye would that men should do to you, do ye even so to them* (Matthew 7:12) or *thou shalt love thy neighbour as thyself* (Leviticus 19:28) **2** another name for **rule of three**

golden section *or* **golden mean** *n* the proportion of the two divisions of a straight line or the two dimensions of a plane figure such that the smaller is to the larger as the larger is to the sum of the two. If the sides of a rectangle are in this proportion and a square is constructed internally on the shorter side, the rectangle that remains will also have sides in the same proportion

golden share *n* a share in a company that controls at least 51% of the voting rights, esp one retained by the UK government in some privatization issues

golden syrup *n Brit* a light golden-coloured treacle produced by the evaporation of cane sugar juice, used to sweeten and flavour cakes, puddings, etc

golden triangle *n* the Golden Triangle an opium-producing area of SE Asia, comprising parts of Myanmar, Laos, and Thailand

golden wattle *n* **1** an Australian yellow-flowered leguminous plant, *Acacia pycnantha*, that yields a useful gum and bark **2** any of several similar and related plants, esp *Acacia longifolia* of Australia

goldfinch ('gəʊld,fɪntʃ) *n* a common European finch, *Carduelis carduelis*, the adult of which has a red-and-white face and yellow-and-black wings

goldfish ('gəʊld,fɪʃ) *n*, *pl* -fish *or* -fishes a freshwater cyprinid fish, *Carassius auratus*, of E Europe and Asia, esp China, widely introduced as a pond or aquarium fish. It resembles the carp and has a typically golden or orange-red coloration

gold foil *n* thin gold sheet that is thicker than gold leaf

Golding ('gəʊldɪŋ) *n* Sir **William** (**Gerald**). 1911–93, English novelist noted for his allegories of man's proclivity for evil. His novels include *Lord of the Flies* (1954), *Darkness Visible* (1979), *Rites of Passage* (1980), *Close Quarters* (1987), and *Fire Down Below* (1989). Nobel prize for literature 1983

gold leaf *n* very thin gold sheet with a thickness usually between 0.076 and 0.127 micrometre, produced by rolling or hammering gold and used for gilding woodwork, etc

gold medal *n* a medal of gold, awarded to the winner of a competition or race

Goldoni (Italian gol'do:ni) *n* **Carlo** ('karlo). 1707–93, Italian dramatist; author of over 250 plays in Italian or French, including *La Locandiera* (1753). His work introduced realistic Italian comedy, superseding the commedia dell'arte

gold plate *n* **1** a thin coating of gold, usually produced by electroplating **2** vessels or utensils made of gold

gold reserve *n* the gold reserved by a central bank to support domestic credit expansion, to cover balance of payments deficits, and to protect currency

gold rush *n* a large-scale migration of people to a territory where gold has been found

Goldschmidt ('gəʊld,ʃmɪt) *n* **Richard Benedikt**. 1878–1958, US geneticist, born in Germany. He advanced the theory that heredity is determined by the chemical configuration of the chromosome molecule rather than by the qualities of the individual genes

goldsmith ('gəʊld,smɪθ) *n* **a** a dealer in articles made of gold **b** an artisan who makes such articles

Goldsmith ('gəʊld,smɪθ) *n* **Oliver**. ?1730–74, Irish poet, dramatist, and novelist. His works include the novel *The Vicar of Wakefield* (1766), the poem *The Deserted Village* (1770), and the comedy *She Stoops to Conquer* (1773)

gold standard *n* **1** a monetary system in which the unit of currency is defined with reference to gold **2** the supreme example of something against which others are judged or measured: *the current gold standard for breast cancer detection*

golf (gɒlf) *n* **1** a game played on a large open course, the object of which is to hit a ball using clubs, with as few strokes as possible, into each of usually 18 holes ▷ *vb* **2** (*intr*) to play golf [C15: perhaps from Middle Dutch *colf* CLUB] ▷**'golfer** *n*

golf ball *n* **1** a small resilient, usually white, ball of either two-piece or three-piece construction, the former consisting of a solid inner core with a thick covering of toughened material, the latter consisting of a liquid centre, rubber-wound core, and a thin layer of balata **2** (in some electric typewriters) a small detachable metal sphere, around the surface of which type characters are arranged

golf club *n* **1** any of various long-shafted clubs with wood or metal heads used to strike a golf ball **2 a** an association of golf players, usually having its own course and facilities **b** the premises of such an association

golf course *or* **golf links** *n* a general term for an area of ground, either inland or beside the sea, laid out for the playing of golf

Golgi (Italian 'gɔldʒi) *n* **Camillo** (ka'millo). 1844–1926, Italian neurologist and histologist, noted for his work on the central nervous system and his discovery in animal cells of the bodies known by his name: shared the Nobel prize for physiology or medicine 1906

Golgotha ('gɒlgəθə) *n* **1** another name for **Calvary** **2** (*sometimes not capital*) *now rare* a place of burial [C17: from Late Latin, from Greek, from Aramaic, based on Hebrew *gulgōleth* skull]

g

g

Goliath (gə'laɪəθ) n *Old Testament* a Philistine giant from Gath who terrorized the Hebrews until he was killed by David with a stone from his sling (I Samuel 17)

golliwog or **golliwogg** ('gɒlɪˌwɒg) n a soft doll with a black face, usually made of cloth or rags [C19: from the name of a doll character in children's books by Bertha Upton (died 1912), US writer, and Florence Upton (died 1922), US illustrator]

gollop ('gɒləp) vb to eat or drink (something) quickly or greedily [dialect variant of GULP]

golly ('gɒlɪ) interj an exclamation of mild surprise or wonder [C19: originally a euphemism for GOD]

goloshes (gə'lɒʃɪz) pl n a less common spelling of galoshes

Gomberg ('gɒmbɜːg) n **Moses**. 1866–1947, US chemist, born in Russia, noted for his work on free radicals

Gomel (*Russian* 'gɒmɪlj) n an industrial city in SE Belarus, on the River Sozh; an industrial centre. Pop: 480 000 (2005 est)

Gomorrah or **Gomorrha** (gə'mɒrə) n 1 *Old Testament* one of two ancient cities near the Dead Sea, the other being Sodom, that were destroyed by God as a punishment for the wickedness of their inhabitants (Genesis 19:24) 2 any place notorious for vice and depravity > Go'morrean or Go'morrhean adj

Gompers ('gɒmpəz) n **Samuel**. 1850–1924, US labour leader, born in England; a founder of the American Federation of Labor and its president (1886–94; 1896–1924)

Gomulka (gə'mʊlkə) n **Władysław** (vwa'diswaf). 1905–82, Polish statesman; first secretary of the Polish Communist Party (1956–70)

-gon n combining form indicating a figure having a specified number of angles: *pentagon* [from Greek *-gōnon*, from *gōnia* angle]

gonad ('gɒnæd) n an animal organ in which gametes are produced, such as a testis or an ovary [C19: from New Latin *gonas*, from Greek *gonos* seed] > 'gonadal or gonadial (gɒ'neɪdɪəl)

gonadotrophin (ˌgɒnədəʊ'trəʊfɪn) or **gonadotropin** (ˌgɒnədəʊ'trəʊpɪn) n any of several glycoprotein hormones secreted by the pituitary gland and placenta that stimulate the gonads and control reproductive activity. See chorionic gonadotrophin > ˌgonado'trophic or ˌgonado'tropic adj

Gonaïves (*French* gɒnaiv) n a port in W Haiti, on the Gulf of Gonaïves; scene of the proclamation of Haiti's independence (1804). Pop: 104 825 (2003)

Goncharov (ˌgʌntʃə'rɒf) n **Ivan Aleksandrovich** (ɪ'van alɛksan'drɒvɪtʃ). 1812–91, Russian novelist: his best-known work is *Oblomov* (1859)

Goncourt (*French* gōkur) n **Edmond Louis Antoine Huot de** (ɛdmɔ̃ lwi ātwan yo də), 1822–96, and his brother, **Jules Alfred Huot de** (ʒyl alfrɛd), 1830–70, French writers, noted for their collaboration, esp on their *Journal*, and for the Académie Goncourt founded by Edmond's will

Gondar ('gɒndɑː) n a city in NW Ethiopia: capital of Ethiopia from the 17th century until 1868. Pop: 191 000 (2005 est)

gondola ('gɒndələ) n 1 a long narrow flat-bottomed boat with a high ornamented stem and a platform at the stern where an oarsman stands and propels the boat by sculling or punting: traditionally used on the canals of Venice 2 a a car or cabin suspended from an airship or balloon b a moving cabin suspended from a cable across a valley, etc 3 a flat-bottomed barge used on canals and rivers of the US as far west as the Mississippi 4 US & Canadian a low open flat-bottomed railway goods wagon 5 a set of island shelves in a self-service shop: used for displaying goods 6 Canadian a broadcasting booth built close to the roof over an ice-hockey arena, used by commentators [C16: from Italian (Venetian dialect), from Medieval Latin *gondula*, perhaps ultimately from Greek *kondu* drinking vessel]

gondolier (ˌgɒndə'lɪə) n a man who propels a gondola

Gondwanaland (gɒnd'wɑːnəˌlænd) or **Gondwana** n one of the two ancient supercontinents produced by the first split of the even larger supercontinent Pangaea about 200 million years ago, comprising chiefly what

are now Africa, South America, Australia, Antarctica, and the Indian subcontinent [C19: from *Gondwana* region in central north India, where the rock series was originally found]

gone (gɒn) vb 1 the past participle of go¹ ⊳ adj (*usually postpositive*) 2 ended; past 3 lost; ruined (esp in the phrases **gone goose** or **gosling**) 4 dead or near to death 5 spent; consumed; used up 6 *informal* faint or weak 7 *informal* having been pregnant (for a specified time): *six months gone* 8 (usually foll by *on*) *slang* in love (with)

goner ('gɒnə) n *slang* a person or thing beyond help or recovery, esp a person who is dead or about to die

gonfalon ('gɒnfələn) or **gonfanon** ('gɒnfənən) n 1 a banner hanging from a crossbar, used esp by certain medieval Italian republics or in ecclesiastical processions 2 a battle flag suspended crosswise on a staff, usually having a serrated edge to give the appearance of streamers [C16: from Old Italian *gonfalone*, from Old French *gonfalon*, of Germanic origin; compare Old English *gūthfana* war banner, Old Norse *gunnfani*]

gong (gɒŋ) n 1 Also called: **tam-tam** a percussion instrument of indefinite pitch, consisting of a metal platelike disc struck with a soft-headed drumstick 2 a rimmed metal disc, hollow metal hemisphere, or metal strip, tube, or wire that produces a note when struck. It may be used to give alarm signals when operated electromagnetically 3 a fixed saucer-shaped bell, as on an alarm clock, struck by a mechanically operated hammer 4 *Brit slang* a medal, esp a military one ⊳ vb 5 (*intr*) to sound a gong 6 (*tr*) (of traffic police) to summon (a driver) to stop by sounding a gong [C17: from Malay, of imitative origin]

Góngora y Argote (*Spanish* 'gɔŋgora i ar'ɣote) n **Luis de** (lwis de). 1561–1627, Spanish lyric poet, noted for the exaggerated pedantic style of works such as *Las Soledades*

goniometer (ˌgəʊnɪ'ɒmɪtə) n 1 an instrument for measuring the angles between the faces of a crystal 2 an instrument consisting of a transformer circuit connected to two directional aerials, used to determine the bearing of a distant radio station [C18: via French from Greek *gōnia* angle] > goniometric (ˌgəʊnɪə'mɛtrɪk) or ˌgonio'metrical adj

-gonium n combining form indicating a seed or reproductive cell: *archegonium* [from New Latin *gonium*, from Greek *gonos* seed]

gonococcus (ˌgɒnəʊ'kɒkəs) n, pl **-cocci** (-'kɒksaɪ) a spherical Gram-negative bacterium, *Neisseria gonorrhoeae*, that causes gonorrhoea: family Neisseriaceae

gonorrhoea or *esp US* **gonorrhea** (ˌgɒnə'rɪə) n an infectious venereal disease caused by a gonococcus, characterized by a burning sensation when urinating and a mucopurulent discharge from the urethra or vagina [C16: from Late Latin, from Greek, from *gonos* seed + *rhoia* flux, flow] > ˌgonor'rhoeal, ˌgonor'rhoeic or *esp US* ˌgonor'rheal adj

-gony n combining form genesis, origin, or production: *cosmogony* [from Latin *-gonia*, from Greek, *-goneia*, from *gonos* seed, procreation]

González (*Spanish* gɔn'θaleθ) n **Julio** ('xuljo). 1876–1942, Spanish sculptor: one of the first to create abstract geometric forms with soldered iron

González Márquez (*Spanish* gɔn'θaleθ 'markeθ) n **Felipe** (fe'lipe). born 1942, Spanish statesman; prime minister of Spain (1982–96)

gonzo ('gɒnzəʊ) adj *slang* 1 wild or crazy 2 (of journalism) explicitly including the writer's feelings at the time of witnessing the events or undergoing the experiences written about [C20: perhaps from Italian, literally: fool, or Spanish *ganso* idiot, bumpkin (literally: goose)]

goo (guː) n *informal* 1 a sticky or viscous substance 2 coy or sentimental language or ideas [C20: of uncertain origin]

Gooch (guːtʃ) n **Graham (Alan)**. born 1953, English cricketer; captain of England (1988, 1989–93)

good (gʊd) adj better, best 1 having admirable, pleasing, superior, or positive qualities; not negative, bad or mediocre: *a good idea; a good teacher* 2 a morally excellent or admirable; virtuous; righteous: *a good man*

b (*as collective noun; preceded by the*): *the good* **3** suitable or efficient for a purpose: *a good secretary; a good winter coat* **4** beneficial or advantageous: *vegetables are good for you* **5** not ruined or decayed; sound or whole: *the meat is still good* **6** kindly, generous, or approving: *you are good to him* **7** valid or genuine: *I would not do this without good reason* **8** honourable or held in high esteem: *a good family* **9** commercially or financially secure, sound, or safe: *good securities; a good investment* **10** (of a draft) drawn for a stated sum **11** (of debts) expected to be fully paid **12** clever, competent, or talented: *he's good at science* **13** obedient or well-behaved: *a good dog* **14** reliable, safe, or recommended: *a good make of clothes* **15** affording material pleasure or indulgence: *the good things in life; the good life* **16** having a well-proportioned, beautiful, or generally fine appearance: *a good figure; a good complexion* **17** complete; full: *I took a good look round the house* **18** propitious; opportune: *a good time to ask the manager for a rise* **19** satisfying or gratifying: *a good rest* **20** comfortable: *did you have a good night?* **21** newest or of the best quality: *to keep the good plates for important guests* **22** fairly large, extensive, or long: *a good distance away* **23** sufficient; ample: *we have a good supply of food* **24 a good one a** an unbelievable assertion **b** a very funny joke **25 as good as** virtually; practically: *it's as good as finished* **26 good and** *informal* (intensifier): *good and mad* **27** (intensifier; used in mild oaths): *good grief!; good heavens!* ▷ *interj* **28** an exclamation of approval, agreement, pleasure, etc ▷ *n* **29** moral or material advantage or use; benefit or profit: *for the good of our workers; what is the good of worrying?* **30** positive moral qualities; goodness; virtue; righteousness; piety **31** (*sometimes capital*) moral qualities seen as a single abstract entity: *we must pursue the Good* **32** a good thing **33** *economics* a commodity or service that satisfies a human need **34 for good or for good and all** forever; permanently: *I have left them for good* **35 make good a** to recompense or repair damage or injury **b** to be successful **c** to demonstrate or prove the truth of (a statement or accusation) **d** to secure and retain (a position) **e** to effect or fulfil (something intended or promised) ▷ See also **goods** [Old English *gōd*; related to Old Norse *gōthr*, Old High German *guot* good]
> 'goodish *adj*

Good Book *n* a name for the **Bible**

goodbye (,gʊd'baɪ) *sentence substitute* **1** farewell: a conventional expression used at leave-taking or parting with people and at the loss or rejection of things or ideas ▷ *n* **2** a leave-taking; parting **3** a farewell: *they said goodbyes to each other* [c16: contraction of *God be with ye*]

good cholesterol *n* a nontechnical name for **high-density lipoprotein**

good day *sentence substitute* a conventional expression of greeting or farewell used during the day

good-for-nothing *n* **1** an irresponsible or worthless person ▷ *adj* **2** irresponsible; worthless

Good Friday *n* the Friday before Easter, observed as a commemoration of the Crucifixion of Jesus

Good Hope *n* Cape of Good Hope See **Cape of Good Hope**

good-humoured *adj* being in or expressing a pleasant, tolerant, and kindly state of mind > ,good-'humouredly *adv*

goodies ('gʊdɪz) *pl n* any objects, rewards, prizes, etc, considered particularly desirable, attractive, or pleasurable

good-looking *adj* handsome or pretty

goodly ('gʊdlɪ) *adj* **-lier, -liest** **1** considerable: *a goodly amount of money* **2** *obsolete* attractive, pleasing, or fine
> 'goodliness *n*

goodman ('gʊdmən) *n, pl* **-men** *archaic* **1** a husband **2** a man not of gentle birth: used as a title **3** a master of a household

Goodman ('gʊdmən) *n* **Benny,** full name *Benjamin David Goodman.* 1909–86, US jazz clarinetist and bandleader, whose treatment of popular songs created the jazz idiom known as swing

good morning *sentence substitute* a conventional expression of greeting or farewell used in the morning

good-natured *adj* of a tolerant and kindly disposition > ,good-'naturedly *adv*

goodness ('gʊdnɪs) *n* **1** the state or quality of being good **2** generosity; kindness **3** moral excellence; piety; virtue ▷ *interj* **4** a euphemism for God: *goodness knows!; thank goodness!*

goodness of fit *n statistics* the extent to which observed sample values of a variable approximate to values derived from a theoretical density, often measured by a chi-square test

good night *sentence substitute* a conventional expression of farewell, or, rarely, of greeting, used in the late afternoon, the evening, or at night, esp when departing to bed

good-oh *or* **good-o** ('gʊd'əʊ) *interj Brit & Austral informal* an exclamation of pleasure, agreement, approval, etc

good oil *n* **the good oil** *Austral slang* true or reliable facts, information, etc

good people *pl n* **the good people** *folklore* fairies

goods (gʊdz) *pl n* **1** possessions and personal property **2** (*sometimes singular*) *economics* commodities that are tangible, usually movable, and generally not consumed at the same time as they are produced **3** articles of commerce; merchandise **4** *chiefly Brit* a merchandise when transported, esp by rail; freight **b** (*as modifier*): *a goods train* **5 the goods a** *informal* that which is expected or promised: *to deliver the goods* **b** *slang* the real thing **c** *US & Canadian slang* incriminating evidence (esp in the phrase **have the goods on someone**)

Good Samaritan *n* **1** *New Testament* a figure in one of Christ's parables (Luke 10:30–37) who is an example of compassion towards those in distress **2** a kindly person who helps another in difficulty or distress

Good Shepherd *n New Testament* a title given to Jesus Christ in John 10:11–12

good-sized *adj* quite large

good-tempered *adj* of a kindly and generous disposition

good turn *n* a helpful and friendly act; good deed; favour

goodwife ('gʊd,waɪf) *n, pl* **-wives** *archaic* **1** the mistress of a household **2** a woman not of gentle birth: used as a title

goodwill (,gʊd'wɪl) *n* **1** a feeling of benevolence, approval, and kindly interest **2** willingness or acquiescence **3** *accounting* an intangible asset taken into account in assessing the value of an enterprise and reflecting its commercial reputation, customer connections, etc

Goodwin Sands ('gʊdwɪn) *pl n* a dangerous stretch of shoals at the entrance to the Strait of Dover: separated from the E coast of Kent by the Downs roadstead

Goodwood ('gʊd,wʊd) *n* an area in SE England, in Sussex: site of a famous racecourse and of **Goodwood House,** built 1780–1800

goody¹ ('gʊdɪ) *interj* **1** a child's exclamation of pleasure and approval ▷ *n, pl* **goodies** **2** short for **goody-goody 3** *informal* the hero in a film, book, etc **4** See also **goodies**

goody² ('gʊdɪ) *n, pl* **goodies** *archaic or literary* a married woman of low rank: used as a title: *Goody Two-Shoes* [c16: shortened from GOODWIFE]

Goodyear ('gʊd,jɪə) *n* **Charles.** 1800–60, US inventor of vulcanized rubber

goody-goody *n, pl* **-goodies** **1** a smugly virtuous or sanctimonious person ▷ *adj* **2** smug and sanctimonious

gooey ('guːɪ) *adj* **gooier, gooiest** *informal* **1** sticky, soft, and often sweet **2** oversweet and sentimental
> 'gooiness *n*

goof (guːf) *informal* ▷ *n* **1** a foolish error or mistake **2** a stupid person ▷ *vb* **3** to bungle (something); botch **4** (*intr; often foll by about or around*) to fool (around); mess (about) [c20: probably from (dialect) *goff* simpleton, from Old French *goffe* clumsy, from Italian *goffo*, of obscure origin]

go off *vb* (*intr*) **1** (*adverb*) (of power, a water supply, etc) to cease to be available, running, or functioning: *the lights suddenly went off* **2** (*adverb*) to be discharged or activated; explode **3** (*adverb*) to occur as specified: *the meeting went off well* **4** to leave (a place): *the actors went off stage* **5** (*adverb*) (of a sensation) to gradually cease to be felt or perceived **6** (*adverb*) to fall asleep **7** (*adverb*) (of concrete, mortar, etc) to harden **8** (*adverb*) *Brit informal* (of food, milk, etc) to become stale or rotten **9** (*preposition*) *Brit informal* to cease to like

goofy ('gu:fɪ) *adj* goofier, goofiest *informal* foolish; silly; stupid > **'goofily** *adv* > **'goofiness** *n*

goog (gʊg) *n Austral informal* **1** an egg **2 full as a goog** drunk

Google ('gu:gºl) *n trademark* **1** a popular search engine on the internet ▷ *vb* (*without a cap*) **2** to search for (something on the internet) using a search engine **3** to check (the credentials of someone) by searching for websites containing his or her name [C20: a play on GOOGOL]

google-bombing *n informal* the practice of attempting to affect the ranking of websites provided by the Google website

googlewhack ('gu:gºl,wæk) *n* a search of the internet, using the Google search engine and without using quote marks, for a combination of two legitimate words that yields only one result [C21: from GOOGLE + *whack* attempt]

googly ('gu:glɪ) *n, pl* -lies *cricket* an off break bowled with a leg break action [C20: Australian, of unknown origin]

googol ('gu:gɒl, -gºl) *n* the number represented as one followed by 100 zeros (10¹⁰⁰) [C20: coined by E. Kasner (1878–1955), American mathematician]

Goolagong ('gu:lə,gɒn) *n* Evonne. See (Evonne) **Cawley**

Goole (gu:l) *n* an inland port in NE England, in the East Riding of Yorkshire at the confluence of the Ouse and Don Rivers, 75 km (47 miles) from the North Sea. Pop: 18 741 (2001)

goolie *or* **gooly** ('gu:lɪ) *n, pl* -lies **1** (*usually plural*) *slang* a testicle **2** *Austral slang* a stone or pebble [from Hindustani *goli* a ball, bullet]

goon (gu:n) *n* **1** a stupid or deliberately foolish person **2** *US informal* a thug hired to commit acts of violence or intimidation, esp in an industrial dispute [C20: partly from dialect *gooney* fool, partly after the character Alice the *Goon*, created by E. C. Segar (1894–1938), American cartoonist]

go on *vb* (*intr, mainly adverb*) **1** to continue or proceed **2** to happen or take place: *there's something peculiar going on here* **3** (*preposition*) to mount or board and ride on, esp as a treat: *children love to go on donkeys at the seaside* **4** *theatre* to make an entrance on stage **5** to talk excessively; chatter **6** to continue talking, esp after a short pause **7** (foll by *at*) to criticize or nag: *stop going on at me all the time!* ▷ *interj* **8** I don't believe what you're saying

gooney bird ('gu:nɪ) *n* an informal name for the albatross, esp the black-footed albatross (*Diomedea nigripes*) [C19 *gony* (originally sailors' slang), probably from dialect *gooney* fool, of obscure origin; compare GOON]

goop (gu:p) *n US & Canadian slang* **1** a rude or ill-mannered person **2** any sticky or semiliquid substance [C20: coined by G. Burgess (1866–1951), American humorist] > **'goopy** *adj*

goorie *or* **goory** ('gu:rɪ) *n, pl* -ries See **kuri**

goosander (gu:'sændə) *n* a common merganser (a duck), *Mergus merganser*, of Europe and North America, having a dark head and white body in the male [C17: probably from GOOSE¹ + Old Norse *önd* (genitive *andar*) duck]

goose¹ (gu:s) *n, pl* geese (gi:s) **1** any of various web-footed long-necked birds of the family *Anatidae*: order *Anseriformes*. They are typically larger and less aquatic than ducks and are gregarious and migratory **2** the female of such a bird, as opposed to the male (gander) **3** *informal* a silly person **4** *pl* gooses a pressing iron with a long curving handle, used esp by tailors **5** the flesh of the goose, used as food **6 cook someone's goose** *informal* **a** to spoil someone's plans **b** to bring about someone's ruin, downfall, etc **7 kill the goose that lays the golden eggs**. See also **golden goose** [Old English *gōs*; related to Old Norse *gās*, Old High German *gans*, Old Irish *gēiss* swan, Greek *khēn*, Sanskrit *hainsas*]

goose² (gu:s) *slang* ▷ *vb* **1** (*tr*) to prod (a person) playfully in the behind ▷ *n, pl* gooses **2** a playful prod in the

behind [C19: from GOOSE¹, probably from a comparison with the jabbing of a goose's bill]

gooseberry ('gʊzbərɪ, -brɪ) *n, pl* -ries **1** a Eurasian shrub, *Ribes uva-crispa* (or *R. grossularia*), having greenish, purple-flowered and ovoid yellow-green or red-purple berries: family *Grossulariaceae* **2 a** the berry of this plant **b** (*as modifier*): *gooseberry jam* **3** *Brit informal* an unwanted single person in a group of couples, esp a third person with a couple (often in the phrase **play gooseberry**)

goose flesh *n* the bumpy condition of the skin induced by cold, fear, etc, caused by contraction of the muscles at the base of the hair follicles with consequent erection of papillae: so called because of the resemblance to the skin of a freshly-plucked fowl. Also called: **goose bumps**, **goose pimples**, **goose skin**

goosefoot ('gu:s,fʊt) *n, pl* -foots any typically weedy chenopodiaceous plant of the genus *Chenopodium*, having small greenish flowers and leaves shaped like a goose's foot

goosegog ('gʊzgɒg) *or* **goosegob** *n Brit* a dialect or informal word for **gooseberry** [from *goose* in GOOSEBERRY + *gog*, variant of GOB¹]

goosegrass ('gu:s,grɑ:s) *n* another name for **cleavers**

Goosen ('gu:sən) *n* Retief. born 1969; South African golfer: won the British Open Championship (2005) and the US Open Championship (2001, 2004)

gooseneck ('gu:s,nɛk) *n* something in the form of a neck of a goose

goose step *n* **1** a military march step in which the leg is swung rigidly to an exaggerated height, esp as in the German army in the Third Reich ▷ *vb* **goose-step** -steps, -stepping, -stepped **2** (*intr*) to march in goose step

Goossens ('gu:sənz) *n* **1** Sir Eugene. 1893–1962, British composer and conductor, born in Belgium **2** his brother, Leon. 1896–1988, British oboist

go out *vb* (*intr, adverb*) **1** to depart from a room, house, country, etc **2** to cease to illuminate, burn, or function: *the fire has gone out* **3** to cease to be fashionable or popular: *that style went out ages ago!* **4** (of a broadcast) to be transmitted **5** to go to entertainments, social functions, etc **6** (*usually foll by* with *or* together) to associate (with a person of the opposite sex) regularly; date **7** (of workers) to begin to strike **8** *cards* to get rid of the last card, token, etc, in one's hand

go over *vb* (*intr*) **1** to be received in a specified manner: *the concert went over very well* **2** Also called: **go through** (*preposition*) to examine and revise as necessary: *he went over the accounts* **3** (*preposition*) to check and repair: *can you go over my car please?* **4** Also called: **go through** (*preposition*) to rehearse: *I'll go over my lines before the play*

gopak ('gəʊ,pæk) *n* a spectacular high-leaping Russian peasant dance for men [from Russian, from Ukrainian *hopak*, from *hop!* a cry in the dance, from German *hopp!*]

Go-Ped ('gəʊ,pɛd) *n trademark* a motorized vehicle consisting of a low footboard on wheels, steered by handlebars

gopher ('gəʊfə) *n* **1** Also called: **pocket gopher** any burrowing rodent of the family *Geomyidae*, of North and Central America, having a thickset body, short legs, and cheek pouches **2** another name for **ground squirrel** **3** any burrowing tortoise of the genus *Gopherus*, of SE North America [C19: shortened from earlier *megopher* or *magopher*, of obscure origin]

gora ('gɔ:rə) *n Hinglish informal* a White or fair-skinned male [C21: from Hindi]

Gorakhpur ('gɔ:rək,pʊə) *n* a city in N India, in SE Uttar Pradesh: formerly an important Muslim garrison. Pop: 624 570 (2001)

goral ('gɔ:rəl) *n* a small goat antelope, *Naemorhedus goral*, inhabiting mountainous regions of S Asia. It has a yellowish-grey and black coat and small conical horns [C19: from Hindi, probably of Sanskrit origin]

Gorbachov *or* **Gorbachev** (gɜ:bə'tʃɒf) *n* Mikhail Sergeevich (mixa'il sir'gjejivitʃ). born 1931, Soviet statesman; general secretary of the Soviet Communist Party (1985–91): president (1988–91). Nobel peace prize 1990. His reforms ended the Communist monopoly of power and led to the break-up of the Soviet Union

Gorbals ('gɔ:bºlz) *n* **the Gorbals** a district of Glasgow, formerly known for its slums

Gordian knot ('gɔːdɪən) n 1 (in Greek legend) a complicated knot, tied by King Gordius of Phrygia, that Alexander the Great cut with a sword 2 a complicated and intricate problem (esp in the phrase **cut the Gordian knot**)

Gordimer ('gɔːdɪmə) n **Nadine.** born 1923, South African novelist. Her books include *The Lying Days* (1952), *The Conservationist* (1974), which won the Booker prize, *None to Accompany Me* (1994), and *The House Gun* (1998). Her works were banned in South Africa for their condemnation of apartheid. Nobel prize for literature 1991

Gordon ('gɔːdᵊn) n 1 **Adam Lindsay.** 1833–70, Australian poet and horseman, born in the Azores, who developed the bush ballad as a literary form, esp in *Bush Ballads and Galloping Rhymes* (1870) 2 **Charles George,** known as *Chinese Gordon.* 1833–85, British general and administrator. He helped to crush the Taiping rebellion (1863–64), and was governor of the Sudan (1877–80), returning in 1884 to aid Egyptian forces against the Mahdi. He was killed in the siege of Khartoum 3 **Sir Donald.** born 1930; South African businessman 4 **Dexter (Keith).** 1923–90, US jazz tenor saxophonist 5 **Lord George.** 1751–93, English religious agitator. He led the Protestant opposition to legislation relieving Roman Catholics of certain disabilities, which culminated in the Gordon riots (1780) 6 **George Hamilton.** See (4th Earl of) **Aberdeen**[1]

gore[1] (gɔː) n 1 blood shed from a wound, esp when coagulated 2 *informal* killing, fighting, etc [Old English *gor* dirt; related to Old Norse *gor* half-digested food, Middle Low German *göre*, Dutch *goor*]

gore[2] (gɔː) vb (tr) (of an animal, such as a bull) to pierce or stab (a person or another animal) with a horn or tusk [c16: probably from Old English *gār* spear]

gore[3] (gɔː) n 1 a tapering or triangular piece of material used in making a shaped skirt, umbrella, etc ▷ vb 2 (tr) to make into or with a gore or gores [Old English *gāra*; related to Old Norse *geiri* gore, Old High German *gēro*]

Gore (gɔː) n **Al(bert) Jr.** born 1948, US Democrat politician; vice president of the US (1993–2001); defeated in the disputed presidential election of 2000; leading environmental campaigner; shared the 2007 Nobel Peace Prize with the Intergovernmental Panel For Climate Change

Górecki (gɔˈrɛkɪ) n **Henryk (Mikołaj).** born 1933, Polish composer, best known for his sombre third symphony (1979)

Gorey ('gɔːrɪ) n **Edward St John.** 1925–2000, US illustrator and author, noted for his bizarre humour in such works as *The Unstrung Harp* (1953) and *The Wuggly Ump* (1963)

gorge (gɔːdʒ) n 1 a deep ravine, esp one through which a river runs 2 the contents of the stomach 3 feelings of disgust or resentment (esp in the phrase **one's gorge rises**) 4 an obstructing mass: *an ice gorge* 5 fortifications a narrow rear entrance to a work 6 *archaic* the throat or gullet ▷ vb Also: **engorge** 7 to swallow (food) ravenously 8 (tr) to stuff (oneself) with food [c14: from Old French *gorger* to stuff, from *gorge* throat, from Late Latin *gurga*, modification of Latin *gurges* whirlpool]

gorgeous ('gɔːdʒəs) adj 1 strikingly beautiful or magnificent: *gorgeous array; a gorgeous girl* 2 *informal* extremely pleasing, fine, or good: *gorgeous weather* [c15: from Old French *gorgias* elegant, from *gorgias* wimple, from *gorge*; see GORGE] > **'gorgeously** adv > **'gorgeousness** n

gorget ('gɔːdʒɪt) n 1 a collar-like piece of armour worn to protect the throat 2 a part of a wimple worn by women to cover the throat and chest, esp in the 14th century 3 a band of distinctive colour on the throat of an animal, esp a bird [c15: from Old French, from *gorge*; see GORGE]

Gorgias ('gɔːdʒɪəs) n ?485–?380 BC, Greek sophist and rhetorician, subject of a dialogue by Plato

Gorgio ('gɔːdʒəʊ, -dʒɪəʊ) n, pl -gios (*sometimes not capital*) a word used by Gypsies for a non-Gypsy [from Romany]

Gorgon ('gɔːgən) n 1 *Greek myth* any of three winged monstrous sisters, Stheno, Euryale, and Medusa, who had live snakes for hair, huge teeth, and brazen claws 2 (*often not capital*) *informal* a fierce or unpleasant woman [via Latin *Gorgō* from Greek, from *gorgos* terrible]

gorgonian (gɔːˈgəʊnɪən) n any coral of the order *Gorgonacea*, having a horny or calcareous branching skeleton: includes the sea fans and red corals

Gorgonzola or **Gorgonzola cheese** (,gɔːgənˈzəʊlə) n a semihard blue-veined cheese of sharp flavour, made from pressed milk [c19: named after *Gorgonzola*, Italian town where it originated]

Gorica ('gɔːritsa) n the Croatian name for **Gorizia**

gorilla (gəˈrɪlə) n 1 the largest anthropoid ape, *Gorilla gorilla*, inhabiting the forests of central W Africa. It is stocky and massive, with a short muzzle and coarse dark hair 2 *informal* a large, strong, and brutal-looking man [c19: New Latin, from Greek *Gorillai*, an African tribe renowned for their hirsute appearance]

Göring or **Goering** (German 'gøːrɪŋ) n **Hermann Wilhelm** ('hɛrman 'vɪlhɛlm). 1893–1946, German Nazi leader and field marshal. He commanded Hitler's storm troops (1923) and as Prussian prime minister and German commissioner for aviation (1933–45) he founded the Gestapo and mobilized Germany for war. Sentenced to death at Nuremberg, he committed suicide

Gorizia (Italian goˈrittsja) n a city in NE Italy, in Friuli-Venezia Giulia, on the Isonzo River: cultural centre under the Hapsburgs. Pop: 35 667 (2001). German name: Görz. Croatian name: Gorica

Gorki[1] or **Gorky** (Russian 'gorjkij) n the former name (until 1991) of **Nizhni Novgorod**

Gorki[2] or **Gorky** (Russian 'gorjkij) n **Maxim** (mak'sim), pen name of *Aleksey Maximovich Peshkov.* 1868–1936, Russian novelist, dramatist, and short-story writer, noted for his depiction of the outcasts of society. His works include the play *The Lower Depths* (1902), the novel *Mother* (1907), and an autobiographical trilogy (1913–23)

Gorky ('gɔːkɪ) n **Arshile** ('aːʃɪl). 1904–48, US abstract expressionist painter, born in Armenia. Influenced by Picasso and Miró, his style is characterized by fluid lines and resonant colours

Görlitz (German 'gœrlɪts) n a city in E Germany, in Saxony on the Neisse River: divided in 1945, the area on the E bank of the river becoming the Polish town of **Zgorzelec.** Pop: 58 518 (2003 est)

Gorlovka (Russian 'gorləfkə) n a city in SE Ukraine in the centre of the Donets Basin: a major coal-mining centre. Pop: 280 000 (2005 est)

gormand ('gɔːmənd) n a less common variant of **gourmand**

gormandize or **gormandise** ('gɔːmənˌdaɪz) vb to eat (food) greedily and voraciously > **'gormand,izer** or **'gormand,iser** n

gormless ('gɔːmlɪs) adj *Brit informal* stupid; dull [c19: variant of c18 *gaumless*, from dialect *gome*, from Old English *gom, gome,* from Old Norse *gaumr* heed]

Gorno-Altai Republic ('gɔːnəʊælˈtaɪ, -ˈæltaɪ) n a constituent republic of S Russia: mountainous, rising over 4350 m (14 500 ft) in the Altai Mountains of the south. Capital: Gorno-Altaisk. Pop: 202 900 (2002). Area: 92 600 sq km (35 740 sq miles). Also called: Altai Republic

Gorno-Badakhshan Autonomous Republic (-bəˈdækʃaːn) n an administrative division of Tajikistan: generally mountainous and inaccessible. Capital: Khorog. Pop: 206 000 (2000 est). Area: 63 700 sq km (24 590 sq miles). Also called: Badakhshan

go round vb (intr) same as **go around**

gorse (gɔːs) n any evergreen shrub of the leguminous genus *Ulex*, esp the European species *U. europaeus*, which has yellow flowers and thick green spines instead of leaves. Also called: **furze, whin** [Old English *gors*; related to Old Irish *garb* rough, Latin *horrēre* to bristle, Old High German *gersta* barley, Greek *khēr* hedgehog] > **'gorsy** adj

Gorton ('gɔːtᵊn) n **Sir John Grey.** 1911–2002, Australian statesman; prime minister (1968–71)

gory ('gɔːrɪ) adj **gorier, goriest** 1 horrific or bloodthirsty: *a gory story* 2 involving bloodshed and killing: *a gory battle* 3 covered in gore > **'gorily** adv > **'goriness** n

Görz (gœrts) n the German name for **Gorizia**

gosh (gɒʃ) interj an exclamation of mild surprise or wonder [c18: euphemistic for *God,* as in *by gosh!*]

goshawk ('gɒsˌhɔːk) n a large hawk, *Accipiter gentilis*, of

Europe, Asia, and North America, having a bluish-grey back and wings and paler underparts: used in falconry [Old English *gōshafoc*; see GOOSE[1], HAWK[1]]

Goshen ('gəʊʃən) *n* **1** a region of ancient Egypt, east of the Nile delta: granted to Jacob and his descendants by the king of Egypt and inhabited by them until the Exodus (Genesis 45:10) **2** a place of comfort and plenty

gosling ('gɒzlɪŋ) *n* **1** a young goose **2** an inexperienced or youthful person [c15: from Old Norse *gæslingr*; related to Danish *gäsling*; see GOOSE[1], -LING[1]]

go-slow *n* **1** *Brit* a deliberate slackening of the rate of production by organized labour as a tactic in industrial conflict ▷ *vb* **go slow 2** (*intr*) to work deliberately slowly as a tactic in industrial conflict

gospel ('gɒspəl) *n* **1** Also called: **gospel truth** an unquestionable truth: *to take someone's word as gospel* **2** a doctrine maintained to be of great importance **3** Black religious music originating in the churches of the Southern states of the United States **4** the message or doctrine of a religious teacher **5 a** the story of Christ's life and teachings as narrated in the Gospels **b** the good news of salvation in Jesus Christ **c** (*as modifier*): *the gospel story* [Old English *gōdspell*, from *gōd* GOOD + *spell* message; see SPELL[2]; compare Old Norse *guthspjall*, Old High German *guotspell*]

Gospel ('gɒspəl) *n* **1** any of the first four books of the New Testament, namely Matthew, Mark, Luke, and John **2** a reading from one of these in a religious service

Gosport ('gɒs,pɔːt) *n* a town in S England, in Hampshire on Portsmouth harbour: naval base since the 16th century. Pop: 69 348 (2001)

goss (gɒs) *n informal* short for **gossip**

gossamer ('gɒsəmə) *n* **1** a gauze or silk fabric of the very finest texture **2** a filmy cobweb often seen on foliage or floating in the air **3** anything resembling gossamer in fineness or filminess [c14 (in the sense: a filmy cobweb): probably from *gos* GOOSE[1] + *somer* SUMMER[1]; the phrase refers to *St Martin's summer*, a period in November when goose was traditionally eaten; from the prevalence of the cobweb in the autumn; compare German *Gänsemonat*, literally: goosemonth, used for November] > 'gossamery *adj*

Gosse (gɒs) *n* Sir **Edmund William.** 1849–1928, English critic and poet, noted particularly for his autobiographical work *Father and Son* (1907)

gossip ('gɒsɪp) *n* **1** casual and idle chat **2** a conversation involving malicious chatter or rumours about other people **3** Also called: **gossipmonger** a person who habitually talks about others, esp maliciously **4** light easy communication: *to write a letter full of gossip* **5** *archaic* a close woman friend ▷ *vb* **-sips, -siping, -siped 6** (*intr*; often foll by *about*) to talk casually or maliciously (about other people) [Old English *godsibb* godparent, from GOD + SIB; the term came to be applied to familiar friends, esp a woman's female friends at the birth of a child, hence a person, esp a woman, fond of light talk] > 'gossiper *n* > 'gossipy *adj*

gossypol ('gɒsɪ,pɒl) *n* a toxic crystalline pigment that is a constituent of cottonseed oil [c19: from Modern Latin *gossypium* cotton plant + -OL[1]]

got (gɒt) *vb* **1** the past tense and past participle of **get 2 have got a** to possess **b** (*takes an infinitive*) used as an auxiliary to express compulsion felt to be imposed by or upon the speaker: *I've got to get a new coat*

Göta (*Swedish* 'jøːta) *n* a river in S Sweden, draining Lake Vänern and flowing south-southwest to the Kattegat: forms part of the **Göta Canal**, which links Göteborg with Stockholm. Length: 93 km (58 miles)

Göteborg (*Swedish* jœtə'bɔrj) or **Gothenburg** *n* a port in SW Sweden, at the mouth of the Göta River: the largest port and second largest city in the country; developed through the Swedish East India Company and grew through Napoleon's continental blockade and with the opening of the Göta Canal (1832); university (1891). Pop: 481 523 (2004 est)

Goth (gɒθ) *n* **1** a member of an East Germanic people from Scandinavia who settled south of the Baltic early in the first millennium AD. They moved on to the Ukrainian steppes and raided and later invaded many

parts of the Roman Empire from the 3rd to the 5th century **2** a rude or barbaric person **3** (*sometimes not capital*) an aficionado of Goth music and fashion ▷ *adj* **4** Also called: **Gothic** (*sometimes not capital*) **a** (of music) in a style of guitar-based rock with some similarities to heavy metal and punk and usually characterized by depressing or mournful lyrics **b** (of fashion) characterized by black clothes and heavy make-up, often creating a ghostly appearance [c14: from Late Latin (plural) *Gothī* from Greek *Gothoi*]

Gotha ('gəʊθə; *German* 'goːta) *n* a town in central Germany, in Thuringia on the N edge of the Thuringian forest: capital of Saxe-Coburg-Gotha (1826–1918); noted for the *Almanach de Gotha* (a record of the royal and noble houses of Europe, first published in 1764). Pop: 47 158 (2003 est)

Gothenburg ('gɒθən,bɜːg) *n* the English name for **Göteborg**

Gothic ('gɒθɪk) *adj* **1** denoting, relating to, or resembling the style of architecture that was used in W Europe from the 12th to the 16th centuries, characterized by the lancet arch, the ribbed vault, and the flying buttress. See also **Gothic Revival 2** of or relating to the style of sculpture, painting, or other arts as practised in W Europe from the 12th to the 16th centuries **3** (*sometimes not capital*) of or relating to a literary style characterized by gloom, the grotesque, and the supernatural, popular esp in the late 18th century **4** of, relating to, or characteristic of the Goths or their language **5** (*sometimes not capital*) primitive and barbarous in style, behaviour, etc **6** of or relating to the Middle Ages ▷ *n* **7** Gothic architecture or art **8** the extinct language of the ancient Goths, known mainly from fragments of a translation of the Bible made in the 4th century by Bishop Wulfila **9** the family of heavy script typefaces > 'Gothically *adv*

Gothic Revival *n* a Gothic style of architecture popular between the late 18th and late 19th centuries, exemplified by the Houses of Parliament in London (1840). Also called: **neogothic**

go through *vb* (*intr*) **1** (*adverb*) to be approved or accepted: *the amendment went through* **2** (*preposition*) to consume; exhaust: *we went through our supplies in a day; some men go through a pair of socks in no time* **3** Also called: **go over** (*preposition*) to examine and revise as necessary: *he went through the figures* **4** (*preposition*) to suffer: *she went through tremendous pain* **5** Also called: **go over** (*preposition*) to rehearse: *let's just go through the details again* **6** Also called: **go over** (*preposition*) to clean: *she went through the cupboards in the spring-cleaning* **7** (*adverb*; foll by *with*) to bring to a successful conclusion, often by persistence

Gotland ('gɒtlənd; *Swedish* 'gɔtlant), **Gothland** ('gɒθlənd) or **Gottland** ('gɒtlənd) *n* an island in the Baltic Sea, off the SE coast of Sweden: important trading centre since the Bronze Age; long disputed between Sweden and Denmark, finally becoming Swedish in 1645; tourism and agriculture now important. Capital: Visby. Pop: (including associated islands) 57 677 (2004 est). Area: 3140 sq km (1212 sq miles)

go together *vb* (*intr*, *adverb*) **1** to be mutually suited; harmonize: *the colours go well together* **2** *informal* (of two people) to have a romantic or sexual relationship: *they had been going together for two years*

gotten ('gɒtᵊn) *vb US* a past participle of **get**

Götterdämmerung (,gɒtə'dɛmə,rʊŋ; *German* gœtər'dɛmərʊŋ) *n German myth* the twilight of the gods; their ultimate destruction in a battle with the forces of evil. Norse equivalent: **Ragnarök**

Gottfried von Strassburg (*German* 'gɔtfriːt fɔn 'ʃtraːsbʊrk) *n* early 13th-century German poet; author of the incomplete epic *Tristan and Isolde*, the version of the legend that served as the basis of Wagner's opera

Göttingen ('gœtɪŋən) *n* a city in central Germany, in Lower Saxony: important member of the Hanseatic League (14th century); university, founded in 1734 by George II of England. Pop: 122 883 (2003 est)

Gottsched (*German* 'gɔtʃed) *n* **Johann Christoph.** 1700–66, German critic, dramatist, and translator

Götz von Berlichingen (*German* gœts fɔn 'bɛrlɪçɪŋən) *n* See **Berlichingen**

g

gouache (guˈɑːʃ) *n* 1 Also called: **body colour** a painting technique using opaque watercolour paint in which the pigments are bound with glue and the lighter tones contain white 2 the paint used in this technique 3 a painting done by this method [C19: from French, from Italian *guazzo* puddle, from Latin *aquātiō* a watering place, from *aqua* water]

Gouda (ˈgaʊdə; *Dutch* ˈxɔudaː) *n* 1 a town in the W Netherlands, in South Holland province: important medieval cloth trade; famous for its cheese. Pop: 72 000 (2003 est) 2 a large round Dutch cheese, mild and similar in taste to Edam

gouge (gaʊdʒ) *vb* (*mainly tr*) 1 (usually foll by *out*) to scoop or force (something) out of its position, esp with the fingers or a pointed instrument 2 (sometimes foll by *out*) to cut (a hole or groove) in (something) with a sharp instrument or tool 3 *US & Canadian informal* to extort from 4 (*also intr*) *Austral* to dig for (opal) ▷ *n* 5 a type of chisel with a blade that has a concavo-convex section 6 a mark or groove made with, or as if with, a gouge 7 *geology* a fine deposit of rock fragments, esp clay, occurring between the walls of a fault or mineral vein 8 *US & Canadian informal* extortion; swindling [C15: from French, from Late Latin *gulbia* a chisel, of Celtic origin] > ˈgouger *n*

goujon (ˈguːʒɒn) *n* a small strip of fish or chicken, coated in breadcrumbs and deep-fried [French, literally: gudgeon]

goulash (ˈguːlæʃ) *n* 1 Also called: **Hungarian goulash** a rich stew, originating in Hungary, made of beef, lamb, or veal highly seasoned with paprika 2 *bridge* a method of dealing in threes and fours without first shuffling the cards, to produce freak hands [C19: from Hungarian *gulyás hus* herdsman's meat, from *gulya* herd]

Gould (guːld) *n* 1 **Benjamin Apthorp**. 1824–96, US astronomer: the first to use the telegraph to determine longitudes; founded the *Astronomical Journal* (1849) 2 **Glenn**. 1932–82, Canadian pianist

go under *vb* (*intr, mainly adverb*) 1 (*also preposition*) to sink below (a surface) 2 to be conquered or overwhelmed: *the firm went under in the economic crisis*

Gounod (ˈguːnəʊ; *French* guno) *n* **Charles François** (ʃarl frɑ̃swa). 1818–93, French composer of the operas *Faust* (1859) and *Romeo and Juliet* (1867)

go up *vb* (*intr, mainly adverb*) 1 (*also preposition*) to move or lead to or as if to a higher place or level; rise; increase: *prices are always going up; the curtain goes up at eight o'clock; new buildings are going up all around us* 2 to be destroyed: *the house went up in flames* 3 *Brit* to go or return (to college or university) at the beginning of a term or academic year

gourami (ˈgʊərəmɪ) *n, pl* **-mi** or **-mis** 1 a large SE Asian labyrinth fish, *Osphronemus goramy*, used for food and (when young) as an aquarium fish 2 any of various other labyrinth fishes, such as *Helostoma temmincki* (**kissing gourami**), many of which are brightly coloured and popular aquarium fishes [from Malay *gurami*]

gourd (gʊəd) *n* 1 the fruit of any of various cucurbitaceous or similar plants, esp the bottle gourd and some squashes, whose dried shells are used for ornament, drinking cups, etc 2 any plant that bears this fruit 3 a bottle or flask made from the dried shell of the bottle gourd [C14: from Old French *gourde*, ultimately from Latin *cucurbita*]

gourmand (ˈgʊəmənd; *French* gurmɑ̃) *or* **gormand** *n* a person devoted to eating and drinking, esp to excess [C15: from Old French *gourmant*, of uncertain origin] > ˈgourmand,ism *n*

gourmet (ˈgʊəmeɪ; *French* gurmɛ) *n* a person who cultivates a discriminating palate for the enjoyment of good food and drink [C19: from French, from Old French *gromet* serving boy]

Gourmont (*French* gurmɔ̃) *n* **Remy de** (rəmi də). 1858–1915, French symbolist critic and novelist

gout (gaʊt) *n* 1 a metabolic disease characterized by painful inflammation of certain joints, esp the big toe and foot, caused by deposits of sodium urate in them 2 *archaic* a drop or splash, esp of blood [C13: from Old French *goute* gout (thought to result from drops of humours), from Latin *gutta* a drop] > ˈgouty *adj* > ˈgoutily

adv > ˈgoutiness *n*

goutweed (ˈgaʊt,wiːd) *n* a widely naturalized Eurasian umbelliferous plant, *Aegopodium podagraria*, with white flowers and creeping underground stems. Also called: bishop's weed, ground elder, herb Gerard

Gov. *or* **gov.** *abbreviation* governor

govern (ˈgʌvᵊn) *vb* (*mainly tr*) 1 (*also intr*) to direct and control the actions, affairs, policies, functions, etc, of (a political unit, organization, nation, etc); rule 2 to exercise restraint over; regulate or direct: *to govern one's temper* 3 to be a predominant influence on (something); decide or determine (something): *his injury governed his decision to avoid sports* 4 to control the speed of (an engine, machine, etc) using a governor 5 to control the rate of flow of (a fluid) by using an automatic valve 6 (of a word) to determine the inflection of (another word): *Latin nouns govern adjectives that modify them* [C13: from Old French *gouverner*, from Latin *gubernāre* to steer, from Greek *kubernan*] > ˈgovernable *adj*

governance (ˈgʌvənəns) *n* 1 government, control, or authority 2 the action, manner, or system of governing

governess (ˈgʌvənɪs) *n* a woman teacher employed in a private household to teach and train the children

government (ˈgʌvənmənt, ˈgʌvəmənt) *n* 1 the exercise of political authority over the actions, affairs, etc, of a political unit, people, etc, as well as the performance of certain functions for this unit or body; the action of governing; political rule and administration 2 the system or form by which a community, etc, is ruled: *tyrannical government* 3 a the executive policy-making body of a political unit, community, etc; ministry or administration b (*capital when of a specific country*): *the British Government* 4 a the state and its administration: *blame it on the government* b (*as modifier*): *a government agency* 5 regulation; direction 6 *grammar* the determination of the form of one word by another word > **governmental** (ˌgʌvənˈmentᵊl, ˌgʌvəˈmentᵊl) *adj* > ˌgovernˈmentally *adv*

Government House *n* the official residence of a representative of the British Crown (such as a Canadian Lieutenant-Governor or an Australian Governor General) in a state or province that recognizes the British sovereign as Head of the Commonwealth

governor (ˈgʌvənə) *n* 1 a person who governs 2 the ruler or chief magistrate of a colony, province, etc 3 the representative of the Crown in a British colony 4 *Brit* the senior administrator or head of a society, prison, etc 5 the chief executive of any state in the US 6 a device that controls the speed of an engine, esp by regulating the supply of fuel, etc, either to limit the maximum speed or to maintain a constant speed 7 *Brit informal* a name or title of respect for a father, employer, etc > ˈgovernorship *n*

governor general *n, pl* **governors general** *or* **governor generals** 1 the representative of the Crown in a dominion of the Commonwealth or a British colony; vicegerent 2 *Brit* a governor with jurisdiction or precedence over other governors > ˌgovernor-ˈgeneralˌship *n*

Govind Singh (ˈgəʊvɪnd sɪŋ) *n* See **Gobind Singh**

Govt *or* **govt** *abbreviation* government

Gower[1] (ˈgaʊə) *n* **the Gower** a peninsula in S Wales, in Swansea county on the Bristol Channel: mainly agricultural with several resorts

Gower[2] (ˈgaʊə) *n* 1 **David** (**Ivon**). born 1957, English cricketer 2 **John**. ?1330–1408, English poet, noted particularly for his tales of love, the *Confessio Amantis*, and his account of the Peasants' Revolt of 1381

go with *vb* (*intr, preposition*) 1 to accompany 2 to blend or harmonize: *that new wallpaper goes well with the furniture* 3 to be a normal part of: *three acres of land go with the house* 4 (of two people) to associate frequently with (each other)

go without *vb* (*intr*) *chiefly Brit* to be denied or deprived of (something, esp food): *if you don't like your tea you can go without*

gowk (gaʊk) *n Scot & northern English dialect* 1 a stupid person; fool 2 a cuckoo [from Old Norse *gaukr* cuckoo; related to Old High German *gouh*]

gown (gaʊn) *n* 1 any of various outer garments, such as a woman's elegant or formal dress, a dressing robe, or a protective garment, esp one worn by surgeons during operations **2** a loose wide garment indicating status, such as worn by academics **3** the members of a university as opposed to the other residents of the university town ▷ *vb* **4** (*tr*) to supply with or dress in a gown [c14: from Old French *goune*, from Late Latin *gunna* garment made of leather or fur, of Celtic origin]

goy (gɔɪ) *n, pl* **goyim** (ˈgɔɪɪm) *or* **goys** a Jewish word for a gentile [from Yiddish, from Hebrew *goi* people] ▷ **ˈgoyish** *adj*

Goya (ˈgɔɪə; *Spanish* ˈgoja) *n* **Francisco de** (franˈθisko de), full name *Francisco José de Goya y Lucientes*. 1746–1828, Spanish painter and etcher; well known for his portraits, he became court painter to Charles IV of Spain (1799). He recorded the French invasion of Spain in a series of etchings *The Disasters of War* (1810–14) and two paintings *2 May 1808* and *3 May 1808* (1814)

Goyen (ˈgɔɪən) *n* **Jan Josephszoon van** (dʒæn ˈdʒəʊzɪfsˌzʊn væn). 1596–1656, Dutch landscape painter and etcher

GP *abbreviation* **1** general practitioner **2** Gallup Poll **3** (in Britain) graduated pension **4** Grand Prix **5** *music* general pause

GPMU *abbreviation* (in Britain) Graphical, Paper and Media Union

GPO *abbreviation* general post office

GPRS *abbreviation* general packet radio service: a telecommunications system providing very fast internet connections for mobile phones

GPS *abbreviation* global positioning system

Gr. *abbreviation* **1** Grecian **2** Greece

Graafian follicle (ˈgrɑːfɪən) *n* a fluid-filled vesicle in the mammalian ovary containing a developing egg cell [c17: named after R. de *Graaf* (1641–73), Dutch anatomist]

grab (græb) *vb* **grabs, grabbing, grabbed 1** to seize hold of (something) **2** (*tr*) to seize illegally or unscrupulously **3** (*tr*) to arrest; catch **4** (*tr*) *informal* to catch the attention or interest of; impress ▷ *n* **5** the act or an instance of grabbing **6** a mechanical device for gripping objects, esp the hinged jaws of a mechanical excavator **7** something that is grabbed [c16: probably from Middle Low German or Middle Dutch *grabben*; related to Swedish *grabba*, Sanskrit *grbhnāti* he seizes] ▷ **ˈgrabber** *n*

grab bag *n* **1** a collection of miscellaneous things **2** *US, Canadian & Austral* a bag or other container from which gifts are drawn at random

grabby (ˈgræbɪ) *adj* **-bier, -biest 1** greedy or selfish **2** direct, stimulating, or attention-grabbing: *grabbier opening paragraphs*

Gracchus (ˈgrækəs) *n* **Tiberius Sempronius** (taɪˈbɪərɪəs semˈprəʊnɪəs). ?163–133 BC, and his younger brother, **Gaius Sempronius** (ˈgaɪəs), 153–121 BC, known as *the Gracchi*. Roman tribunes and reformers. Tiberius attempted to redistribute public land among the poor but was murdered in the ensuing riot. Violence again occurred when the reform was revived by Gaius, and he too was killed

grace (greɪs) *n* **1** elegance and beauty of movement, form, expression, or proportion **2** a pleasing or charming quality **3** goodwill or favour **4** the granting of a favour or the manifestation of goodwill, esp by a superior **5** a sense of propriety and consideration for others **6** (*plural*) **a** affectation of manner (esp in the phrase **airs and graces**) **b** in someone's good graces regarded favourably and with kindness by someone **7** mercy; clemency **8** *Christianity* **a** the free and unmerited favour of God shown towards man **b** the divine assistance and power given to man in spiritual rebirth and sanctification **c** the condition of being favoured or sanctified by God **d** an unmerited gift, favour, etc, granted by God **9** a short prayer recited before or after a meal to invoke a blessing upon the food or give thanks for it **10** *music* a melodic ornament or decoration **11** **with bad grace** or **with a bad grace** unwillingly or grudgingly **12** **with good grace** or **with a good grace** willingly or cheerfully ▷ *vb* **13** (*tr*) to add elegance and beauty to: *flowers graced the room* **14** (*tr*) to honour or favour: *to grace a party with one's presence* **15** to ornament or decorate (a melody, part, etc) with

nonessential notes [c12: from Old French, from Latin *grātia*, from *grātus* pleasing]

Grace¹ (greɪs) *n* (preceded by *your, his*, or *her*) a title used to address or refer to a duke, duchess, or archbishop

Grace² (greɪs) *n* **W(illiam) G(ilbert)**. 1848–1915, English cricketer

grace-and-favour *n* (*modifier*) *Brit* (of a house, flat, etc) owned by the sovereign and granted free of rent to a person to whom the sovereign wishes to express gratitude

graceful (ˈgreɪsfʊl) *adj* characterized by beauty of movement, style, form, etc ▷ **ˈgracefully** *adv* ▷ **ˈgracefulness** *n*

graceless (ˈgreɪslɪs) *adj* **1** lacking any sense of right and wrong; depraved **2** lacking grace or excellence ▷ **ˈgracelessly** *adv* ▷ **ˈgracelessness** *n*

grace note *n* *music* a note printed in small type to indicate that it is melodically and harmonically nonessential

Graces (ˈgreɪsɪz) *pl n Greek myth* three sisters, the goddesses Aglaia, Euphrosyne, and Thalia, givers of charm and beauty

gracious (ˈgreɪʃəs) *adj* **1** characterized by or showing kindness and courtesy **2** condescendingly courteous, benevolent, or indulgent **3** characterized by or suitable for a life of elegance, ease, and indulgence: *gracious living; gracious furnishings* **4** merciful or compassionate ▷ *interj* **5** an expression of mild surprise or wonder (often in exclamatory phrases such as **good gracious!, gracious me!**) ▷ **ˈgraciously** *adv* ▷ **ˈgraciousness** *n*

grackle (ˈgrækəl) *n* **1** Also called: **crow blackbird** any American songbird of the genera *Quiscalus* and *Cassidix*, having a dark iridescent plumage: family *Icteridae* (American orioles) **2** any of various starlings of the genus *Gracula*, such as *G. religiosa* (**Indian grackle** or **hill mynah**) [c18: from New Latin *Grācula*, from Latin *grāculus* jackdaw]

grad. *abbreviation* **1** *maths* gradient **2** *education* graduate(d)

gradate (grəˈdeɪt) *vb* **1** to change or cause to change imperceptibly, as from one colour, tone, or degree to another **2** (*tr*) to arrange in grades or ranks

gradation (grəˈdeɪʃən) *n* **1** a series of systematic stages; gradual progression **2** (*often plural*) a stage or degree in such a series or progression **3** the act or process of arranging or forming in stages, grades, etc, or of progressing evenly **4** (in painting, drawing, or sculpture) transition from one colour, tone, or surface to another through a series of very slight changes **5** *linguistics* any change in the quality or length of a vowel within a word indicating certain distinctions, such as inflectional or tense differentiations. See **ablaut** ▷ **graˈdational** *adj*

grade (greɪd) *n* **1** a position or degree in a scale, as of quality, rank, size, or progression: *small-grade eggs; high-grade timber* **2** a group of people or things of the same category **3** *chiefly US* a military or other rank **4** a stage in a course of progression **5** a mark or rating indicating achievement or the worth of work done, as at school **6** *US & Canadian* a unit of pupils of similar age or ability taught together at school **7** **make the grade** *informal* **a** to reach the required standard **b** to succeed ▷ *vb* **8** (*tr*) to arrange according to quality, rank, etc **9** (*tr*) to determine the grade of or assign a grade to **10** (*intr*) to achieve or deserve a grade or rank **11** to change or blend (something) gradually; merge **12** (*tr*) to level (ground, a road, etc) to a suitable gradient [c16: from French, from Latin *gradus* step, from *gradī* to step]

-grade *adj combining form* indicating a kind or manner of movement or progression: *plantigrade; retrograde* [via French from Latin *-gradus*, from *gradus* a step, from *gradī* to walk]

grade inflation *n* an apparently continual increase in numbers of students attaining high examination grades, or the practice of awarding grades in this way

gradely (ˈgreɪdlɪ) *adj* **-lier, -liest** *Midland English dialect* fine; excellent [c13 *greithlic, greithli*, from Old Norse *greithligr*, from *greithr* ready]

grader (ˈgreɪdə) *n* **1** a person or thing that grades **2** a machine, either self-powered or towed by a tractor, that levels earth, rubble, etc, as in road construction

gradient ('greɪdɪənt) n 1 a part of a railway, road, etc, that slopes upwards or downwards; inclination. Also called (esp US): **grade** 2 a measure of such a slope, esp the ratio of the vertical distance between two points on the slope to the horizontal distance between them. Also called (esp US and Canadian): **grade** 3 physics a measure of the change of some physical quantity, such as temperature or electric potential, over a specified distance 4 maths (of a curve) the slope of the tangent at any point on a curve with respect to the horizontal axis ▷ adj 5 sloping uniformly [C19: from Latin gradiēns stepping, from gradī to go]

gradin ('greɪdɪn) or **gradine** (grə'diːn) n 1 a ledge above or behind an altar on which candles, a cross, or other ornaments stand 2 one of a set of steps or seats arranged on a slope, as in an amphitheatre [C19: from French, from Italian gradino, a little step, from grado step; see GRADE]

gradual ('grædjʊəl) adj 1 occurring, developing, moving, etc, in small stages: a gradual improvement in health 2 not steep or abrupt: a gradual slope ▷ n 3 (often capital) Christianity a an antiphon or group of several antiphons, usually from the Psalms, sung or recited immediately after the epistle at Mass b a book of plainsong containing the words and music of the parts of the Mass that are sung by the cantors and choir [C16: from Medieval Latin graduālis relating to steps, from Latin gradus a step] > 'gradually adv > 'gradualness n

gradualism ('grædjʊə,lɪzəm) n 1 the policy of seeking to change something or achieve a goal gradually rather than quickly or violently, esp in politics 2 the theory that explains major changes in rock strata, fossils, etc in terms of gradual evolutionary processes rather than sudden violent catastrophes > 'gradualist n, adj > ,gradual'istic adj

graduand ('grædjʊ,ænd) n chiefly Brit a person who is about to graduate [C19: from Medieval Latin graduandus, gerundive of graduārī to GRADUATE]

graduate n ('grædjʊɪt) 1 a person who has been awarded a first degree from a university or college 2 US & Canadian a student who has completed a course of studies at a high school and received a diploma ▷ vb ('grædjʊ,eɪt) 3 to receive or cause to receive a degree or diploma 4 (tr) chiefly US & Canadian to confer a degree, diploma, etc upon 5 (tr) to mark (a thermometer, flask, etc) with units of measurement; calibrate 6 (tr) to arrange or sort into groups according to type, quality, etc 7 (intr; often foll by to) to change by degrees (from something to something else) [C15: from Medieval Latin graduārī to take a degree, from Latin gradus a step] > 'gradu,ator n

graduation (,grædjʊ'eɪʃən) n 1 the act of graduating or the state of being graduated 2 the ceremony at which school or college degrees and diplomas are conferred 3 a mark or division or all the marks or divisions that indicate measure on an instrument or vessel

Graeae ('griːiː) or **Graiae** pl n Greek myth three aged sea deities, having only one eye and one tooth among them, guardians of their sisters, the Gorgons

Graecism or esp US **Grecism** ('griːsɪzəm) n 1 Greek characteristics or style 2 admiration for or imitation of these, as in sculpture or architecture 3 a form of words characteristic or imitative of the idiom of the Greek language

Graeco- or esp US **Greco-** ('griːkəʊ, 'grɛkəʊ) combining form Greek: Graeco-Roman

Graeco-Roman or esp US **Greco-Roman** adj of, characteristic of, or relating to Greek and Roman influences, as found in Roman sculpture

Graf (græf) n **Steffi.** born 1969, German tennis player: Wimbledon champion 1988, 1989, 1991, 1992, 1993, 1995, and 1996

graffiti (græ'fiːtiː) pl n, sing -to (-təʊ) 1 (sometimes with singular verb) drawings, messages, etc, often obscene, scribbled on the walls of public lavatories, advertising posters, etc 2 archaeol inscriptions or drawings scratched or carved onto a surface, esp rock or pottery [C19: graffito from Italian: a little scratch, from graffio,

from Latin graphium stylus, from Greek grapheion; see GRAFT¹]

graft¹ (grɑːft) n 1 horticulture a a piece of plant tissue (the scion), normally a stem, that is made to unite with an established plant (the stock), which supports and nourishes it b the plant resulting from the union of scion and stock c the point of union between the scion and the stock 2 surgery a piece of tissue or an organ transplanted from a donor or from the patient's own body to an area of the body in need of the tissue 3 the act of joining one thing to another by or as if by grafting ▷ vb 4 horticulture a to induce (a plant or part of a plant) to unite with another part or (of a plant or part of a plant) to unite in this way b to produce (fruit, flowers, etc) by this means or (of fruit, flowers, etc) to grow by this means 5 to transplant (tissue) or (of tissue) to be transplanted 6 to attach or incorporate or become attached or incorporated: to graft a happy ending onto a sad tale [C15: from Old French graffe, from Medieval Latin graphium, from Latin: stylus, from Greek grapheion, from graphein to write] > 'grafting n

graft² (grɑːft) informal ▷ n 1 work (esp in the phrase hard graft) 2 a the acquisition of money, power, etc, by dishonest or unfair means, esp by taking advantage of a position of trust b something gained in this way, such as profit from government business c a payment made to a person profiting by such a practice ▷ vb 3 (intr) to work 4 to acquire by or practise graft [C19: of uncertain origin] > 'grafter n

Graham ('greɪəm) n 1 **Martha.** 1893–1991, US dancer and choreographer 2 **Thomas.** 1805–69, British physicist: proposed **Graham's law** (1831) of gaseous diffusion and coined the terms osmosis, crystalloids, and colloids 3 **William Franklin**, known as Billy Graham. born 1918, US evangelist

Grahame ('greɪəm) n **Kenneth.** 1859–1932, Scottish author, noted for the children's classic The Wind in the Willows (1908)

Graham Land n the N part of the Antarctic Peninsula: became part of the British Antarctic Territory in 1962 (formerly part of the Falkland Islands Dependencies; Claims are suspended under the Antarctic Treaty)

Graiae ('greɪiː, 'graɪiː) pl n a variant of Graeae

Graian Alps ('greɪən, 'graɪ-) pl n the N part of the Western Alps, in France and NW Piedmont, Italy. Highest peak: Gran Paradiso, 4061 m (13 323 ft)

Grail (greɪl) n See Holy Grail

grain (greɪn) n 1 the small hard seedlike fruit of a grass, esp a cereal plant 2 a mass of such fruits, esp when gathered for food 3 the plants, collectively, from which such fruits are harvested 4 a small hard particle: a grain of sand 5 a the general direction or arrangement of the fibrous elements in paper or wood: to saw across the grain b the pattern or texture of wood resulting from such an arrangement: the attractive grain of the table 6 the relative size of the particles of a substance: sugar of fine grain 7 a the granular texture of a rock, mineral, etc b the appearance of a rock, mineral, etc, determined by the size and arrangement of its constituents 8 the outer (hair-side) layer of a hide or skin from which the hair or wool has been removed 9 the smallest unit of weight in the avoirdupois, Troy, and apothecaries' systems, based on the average weight of a grain of wheat: in the avoirdupois system it equals 1/7000 of a pound, and in the Troy and apothecaries' systems it equals 1/5760 of a pound. 1 grain is equal to 0.0648 gram 10 the threads or direction of threads in a woven fabric 11 photog any of a large number of particles in a photographic emulsion, the size of which limit the extent to which an image can be enlarged without serious loss of definition 12 cleavage lines in crystalline material, parallel to growth planes 13 chem any of a large number of small crystals forming a polycrystalline solid, each having a regular array of atoms that differs in orientation from that of the surrounding crystallites 14 a very small amount: a grain of truth 15 natural disposition, inclination, or character (esp in the phrase **go against the grain**) 16 astronautics a homogenous mass of solid propellant in a form designed to give the required combustion characteristics for a particular rocket **17** (*not in technical usage*) kermes or a red dye made from this insect ▷ *vb* (*mainly tr*) **18** (*also intr*) to form grains or cause to form into grains; granulate; crystallize **19** to give a granular or roughened appearance or texture to **20** to paint, stain, etc, in imitation of the grain of wood or leather **21 a** to remove the hair or wool from (a hide or skin) before tanning **b** to raise the grain pattern on (leather) [c13: from Old French, from Latin *grānum*]

grain alcohol *n* ethanol containing about 10 per cent of water, made by the fermentation of grain

grain elevator *n* a machine for raising grain to a higher level, esp one having an endless belt fitted with scoops

Grainger ('greɪndʒə) *n* **Percy Aldridge.** 1882–1961, Australian pianist, composer, and collector of folk music on which many of his works are based

graining ('greɪnɪŋ) *n* **1** the pattern or texture of the grain of wood, leather, etc **2** the process of painting, printing, staining, etc, a surface in imitation of a grain **3** a surface produced by such a process

grainy ('greɪnɪ) *adj* **grainier, grainiest 1** resembling, full of, or composed of grain; granular **2** resembling the grain of wood, leather, etc **3** *photog* having poor definition because of large grain size > '**graininess** *n*

grallatorial (ˌgrælə'tɔːrɪəl) *adj* of or relating to long-legged wading birds, such as cranes, herons, and storks [c19: from New Latin *grallātōrius*, from Latin *grallātor* one who walks on stilts, from *grallae* stilts]

gram¹ (græm) *n* a metric unit of mass equal to one thousandth of a kilogram. It is equivalent to 15.432 grains or 0.002 205 pounds. Symbol: **g²** [c18: from French *gramme*, from Late Latin *gramma*, from Greek: small weight, from *graphein* to write]

gram² (græm) *n* **1** any of several leguminous plants, such as the beans *Phaseolus mungo* (**black gram** or **urd**) and *P. aureus* (**green gram**), whose seeds are used as food in India **2** the seed of any of these plants [c18: from Portuguese *gram* (modern spelling *grão*), from Latin *grānum* GRAIN]

gram. *abbreviation* **1** grammar **2** grammatical

-gram *n combining form* indicating a drawing or something written or recorded: *hexagram; telegram* [from Latin *-gramma*, from Greek, from *gramma* letter and *grammē* line]

gram atom *or* **gram-atomic weight** *n* an amount of an element equal to its atomic weight expressed in grams: now replaced by the mole. See **mole³**

gramineous (grə'mɪnɪəs) *adj* resembling a grass; grasslike. Also called: **graminaceous** (ˌgræmɪ'neɪʃəs) [c17: from Latin *grāmineus* of grass, grassy, from *grāmen* grass]

graminivorous (ˌgræmɪ'nɪvərəs) *adj* (of animals) feeding on grass [c18: from Latin *grāmen* grass + -VOROUS]

grammar ('græmə) *n* **1** the branch of linguistics that deals with syntax and morphology, sometimes also phonology and semantics **2** the abstract system of rules in terms of which a person's mastery of his native language can be explained **3** a systematic description of the grammatical facts of a language **4** a book containing an account of the grammatical facts of a language or recommendations as to rules for the proper use of a language **5** the use of language with regard to its correctness or social propriety, esp in syntax: *the teacher told him to watch his grammar* [c14: from Old French *gramaire*, from Latin *grammatica*, from Greek *grammatikē* (*tekhnē*) the grammatical (art), from *grammatikos* concerning letters, from *gramma* letter]

grammarian (grə'mɛərɪən) *n* **1** a person whose occupation is the study of grammar **2** the author of a grammar

grammar school *n* **1** *Brit* (esp formerly) a state-maintained secondary school providing an education with an academic bias for children who are selected by the eleven-plus examination, teachers' reports, or other means **2** *US* another term for **elementary school** **3** *Austral* a private school, esp one controlled by a church **4** *NZ* a secondary school forming part of the public education system

grammatical (grə'mætɪkᵊl) *adj* **1** of or relating to

grammar **2** (of a sentence) well formed; regarded as correct and acceptable by native speakers of the language > gram'matically *adv* > gram'maticalness *n*

gram molecule *or* **gram-molecular weight** *n* an amount of a compound equal to its molecular weight expressed in grams: now replaced by the mole. See **mole³**

Grammy ('græmɪ) *n, pl* -**mys** *or* -**mies** (in the US) one of the gold-plated discs awarded annually for outstanding achievement in the record industry [c20: from GRAM(OPHONE) + *my* as in EMMY]

gramophone ('græmə,fəʊn) *n* **1** Also called: **acoustic gramophone** a device for reproducing the sounds stored on a record: now usually applied to the nearly obsolete type that uses a clockwork motor and acoustic horn. US and Canadian name: **phonograph b** (*as modifier*): *a gramophone record* **2** the technique and practice of recording sound on disc: *the gramophone has made music widely available* [c19: originally a trademark, perhaps based on an inversion of *phonogram*; see PHONO-, -GRAM]

Grampian Mountains ('græmpɪən) *pl n* **1** a mountain system of central Scotland, extending from the southwest to the northeast and separating the Highlands from the Lowlands. Highest peak: Ben Nevis, 1344 m (4408 ft) **2** a mountain range in SE Australia, in W Victoria ▷ Also called: **the Grampians**

Grampian Region *n* a former local government region in NE Scotland, formed in 1975 from Aberdeenshire, Kincardineshire, and most of Banffshire and Morayshire; replaced in 1996 by the council areas of Aberdeenshire, City of Aberdeen, and Moray

grampus ('græmpəs) *n, pl* -**puses 1** a widely distributed slaty-grey dolphin, *Grampus griseus*, with a blunt snout **2** another name for **killer whale** [c16: from Old French *graspois*, from *gras* fat (from Latin *crassus*) + *pois* fish (from Latin *piscis*)]

Gramsci (Italian 'gramʃi) *n* **Antonio.** 1891–1937, Italian politician and Marxist theorist: founder (1921) of the Italian Communist party. His important works were written during his imprisonment (1926–37) by the Fascists

Gram's method *n bacteriol* a staining technique used to classify bacteria, based on their ability to retain or lose a violet colour, produced by crystal violet and iodine, after treatment with a decolorizing agent [c19: named after Hans Christian Joachim Gram (1853–1938), Danish physician]

gran (græn) *n* an informal word for **grandmother**

Granada (grə'nɑːdə) *n* **1** a former kingdom of S Spain, in Andalusia: founded in the 13th century and divided in 1833 into the present-day provinces of Granada, Almería, and Málaga **2** a city in S Spain, in Andalusia: capital of the Moorish kingdom of Granada from 1238 to 1492 and a great commercial and cultural centre, containing the Alhambra palace (13th and 14th centuries); university (1531). Pop: 237 663 (2003 est) **3** a city in SW Nicaragua, on the NW shore of Lake Nicaragua: the oldest city in the country, founded in 1523 by Córdoba; attacked frequently by pirates in the 17th century. Pop: 95 000 (2005 est)

granadilla (ˌgrænə'dɪlə) *n* **1** any of various passionflowers, such as *Passiflora quadrangularis* (**giant granadilla**), that have edible egg-shaped fleshy fruit **2** Also called: **passion fruit** the fruit of such a plant [c18: from Spanish, diminutive of *granada* pomegranate, from Late Latin *grānātum*]

Granados (Spanish gra'naðos) *n* **Enrique** (en'rrike), full name *Enrique Granados y Campina*. 1867–1916, Spanish composer, noted for the *Goyescas* (1911) for piano, which formed the basis for an opera of the same name

Grana Padano (ˌgrɑːnə pə'dɑːnəʊ) *n* a rich semifat hard cheese with a granular texture, often used grated, esp on pasta dishes and soups [c21: from Italian *grana* grain + *Padano* from the Po Valley]

granary ('grænərɪ; US 'greɪnərɪ) *n, pl* -**ries 1** a building or store room for storing threshed grain, farm feed, etc **2** a region that produces a large amount of grain [c16: from Latin *grānārium*, from *grānum* GRAIN]

Granary ('grænərɪ) *adj trademark* (of bread, flour, etc)

g

containing malted wheat grain

Gran Canaria (graŋ ka'narja) *n* the Spanish name for **Grand Canary**

Gran Chaco (*Spanish* gran 'tʃako) *n* a plain of S central South America, between the Andes and the Paraguay River in SE Bolivia, E Paraguay, and N Argentina: huge swamps and scrub forest Area: about 780 000 sq km (300 000 sq miles). Often shortened to: **Chaco**

grand (grænd) *adj* **1** large or impressive in size, extent, or consequence: *grand mountain scenery* **2** characterized by or attended with magnificence or display; sumptuous: *a grand feast* **3** of great distinction or pretension; dignified or haughty **4** designed to impress: *he punctuated his story with grand gestures* **5** very good; wonderful **6** comprehensive; complete: *a grand total* **7** worthy of respect; fine: *a grand old man* **8** large or impressive in conception or execution: *grand ideas* **9** most important; chief: *the grand arena* ▷ *n* **10** short for **grand piano** **11** *pl* **grand** *slang* a thousand pounds or dollars [c16: from Old French, from Latin *grandis*] > **'grandly** *adv* > **'grandness** *n*

grand- *prefix* (in designations of kinship) one generation removed in ascent or descent: *grandson; grandfather* [from French *grand-*, on the model of Latin *magnus* in such phrases as *avunculus magnus* great-uncle]

grandad, granddad ('græn,dæd) *or* **grandaddy, granddaddy** ('græn,dædɪ) *n, pl* **-dads** *or* **-daddies** informal words for **grandfather**

grandam ('grændəm, -dæm) *or* **grandame** ('grændeɪm, -dəm) *n* an archaic word for **grandmother** [c13: from Anglo-French *grandame*, from Old French GRAND- + *dame* lady, mother]

grandaunt ('grænd,ɑ:nt) *n* another name for **great-aunt**

Grand Bahama *n* an island in the Atlantic, in the W Bahamas. Pop: 46 994 (2000). Area: 1114 sq km (430 sq miles)

Grand Banks *pl n* a part of the continental shelf in the Atlantic, extending for about 560 km (350 miles) off the SE coast of Newfoundland: meeting place of the cold Labrador Current and the warm Gulf Stream, producing frequent fogs and formerly rich fishing grounds

Grand Canal *n* **1** a canal in E China, extending north from Hangzhou to Tianjin: the longest canal in China, now partly silted up; central section, linking the Yangtze and Yellow Rivers, finished in 486 BC; north section finished by Kublai Khan between 1282 and 1292. Length: about 1600 km (1000 miles). Chinese name: **Da Yunhe 2** a canal in Venice, forming the main water thoroughfare: noted for its bridges, the Rialto, and the fine palaces along its banks

Grand Canary *n* an island in the Atlantic, in the Canary Islands: part of the Spanish province of Las Palmas. Capital: Las Palmas. Pop: 771 333 (2002 est). Area: 1533 sq km (592 sq miles). Spanish name: **Gran Canaria**

Grand Canyon *n* a gorge of the Colorado River in N Arizona, extending from its junction with the Little Colorado River to Lake Mead; cut by vertical river erosion through the multicoloured strata of a high plateau; partly contained in the **Grand Canyon National Park**, covering 2610 sq km (1008 sq miles). Length: 451 km (280 miles). Width: 6 km (4 miles) to 29 km (18 miles). Greatest depth: over 1.5 km (1 mile)

grandchild ('græn,tʃaɪld) *n, pl* **-children** (-,tʃɪldrən) the son or daughter of one's child

Grand Coulee ('ku:lɪ) *n* a canyon in central Washington State, over 120 m (400 ft) deep, at the N end of which is situated the **Grand Coulee Dam**, on the Columbia River. Height of dam: 168 m (550 ft). Length of dam: 1310 m (4300 ft)

granddaughter ('græn,dɔ:tə) *n* a daughter of one's son or daughter

grand duchess *n* **1** the wife or a widow of a grand duke **2** a woman who holds the rank of grand duke in her own right

grand duchy *n* the territory, state, or principality of a grand duke or grand duchess

grand duke *n* **1** a prince or nobleman who rules a territory, state, or principality **2** a son or a male descendant in the male line of a Russian tsar **3** a medieval Russian prince who ruled over other princes

grande dame *French* (grɑ̃d dam) *n* a woman regarded as the most experienced, prominent, or venerable member of her profession, etc

grandee (græn'di:) *n* **1** a Spanish or Portuguese prince or nobleman of the highest rank **2** a man of great rank or eminence [c16: from Spanish *grande*]

Grande-Terre (*French* grɑ̃dtɛr) *n* a French island in the Caribbean, in the Lesser Antilles: one of the two main islands which constitute Guadeloupe. Chief town: Pointe-à-Pitre

grandeur ('grændʒə) *n* **1** personal greatness, esp when based on dignity, character, or accomplishments **2** magnificence; splendour **3** pretentious or bombastic behaviour

Grand Falls *pl n* the former name (until 1965) of **Churchill Falls**

grandfather ('græn,fɑ:ðə, 'grænd-) *n* **1** the father of one's father or mother **2** (*often plural*) a male ancestor **3** (*often capital*) a familiar term of address for an old man > **'grand,fatherly** *adj*

grandfather clock *n* any of various types of long-pendulum clocks in tall standing wooden cases, usually between six and eight feet tall

Grand Guignol *French* (grɑ̃ giɲɔl) *n* **a** a brief sensational play intended to horrify **b** (*modifier*) of, relating to, or like plays of this kind [c20: after *Le Grand Guignol*, a small theatre in Montmartre, Paris]

grandiloquent (græn'dɪləkwənt) *adj* inflated, pompous, or bombastic in style or expression [c16: from Latin *grandiloquus*, from *grandis* great + *loquī* to speak] > **gran'diloquence** *n* > **gran'diloquently** *adv*

grandiose ('grændɪ,əʊs) *adj* **1** pretentiously grand or stately **2** imposing in conception or execution [c19: from French, from Italian *grandioso*, from *grande* great; see GRAND] > **'grandi,osely** *adv* > **grandiosity** (,grændɪ'ɒsɪtɪ) *n*

grand jury *n law* (esp in the US and, now rarely, in Canada) a jury of between 12 and 23 persons summoned to inquire into accusations of crime and ascertain whether the evidence is adequate to found an indictment. Abolished in Britain in 1948

grand larceny *n* **1** (formerly in England) the theft of property valued at over 12 pence. Abolished in 1827 **2** (in some states of the US) the theft of property of which the value is above a specified figure, varying from state to state but usually being between $25 and $60

grandma ('græn,mɑ:, 'grænd-, 'græm-), **grandmama** *or* **grandmamma** ('grænmə,mɑ:, 'grænd-) *n* informal words for **grandmother**

grand mal (grɒn mæl; *French* grɑ̃ mal) *n* a form of epilepsy characterized by loss of consciousness for up to five minutes and violent convulsions. See **petit mal** [French: great illness]

Grandma Moses *n* the nickname of (Anna Mary Robertson) **Moses²**

Grand Manan (mə'næn) *n* a Canadian island, off the SW coast of New Brunswick: separated from the coast of Maine by the **Grand Manan Channel**. Area: 147 sq km (57 sq miles)

grandmaster ('grænd,mɑ:stə) *n* **1** *chess* one of the top chess players of a particular country **2** a leading exponent of any of various arts

Grand Master *n* the title borne by the head of any of various societies, orders, and other organizations, such as the Templars or Freemasons, or the various martial arts

grandmother ('græn,mʌðə, 'grænd-) *n* **1** the mother of one's father or mother **2** (*often plural*) a female ancestor > **'grand,motherly** *adj*

Grand National *n* the Grand National an annual steeplechase run at Aintree, Liverpool, since 1839

grandnephew ('græn,nɛvju:, -,nɛfju:, 'grænd-) *n* another name for **great-nephew**

grandniece ('græn,ni:s, 'grænd-) *n* another name for **great-niece**

grand opera *n* an opera that has a serious plot and is entirely in musical form, with no spoken dialogue

grandpa ('græn,pɑ:, 'grænd-, 'græm-) *or* **grandpapa** ('grænpə,pɑ:, 'grænd-) *n* informal words for: **grandfather**

grandparent ('græn,pɛərənt, 'grænd-) *n* the father or

mother of either of one's parents

grand piano *n* a form of piano in which the strings are arranged horizontally. Grand pianos exist in three sizes

Grand Pré (*French* grā pre) *n* a village in SE Canada, in W Nova Scotia: setting of Longfellow's *Evangeline*

Grand Prix (*French* grā pri) *n* **1** any of a series of formula motor races held to determine the annual Drivers' World Championship **2** a very important competitive event in various other sports, such as athletics, snooker, or powerboating [French: great prize]

Grand Rapids *n* (*functioning as singular*) a city in SW Michigan: electronics, car parts. Pop: 195 601 (2003 est)

grandsire ('græn,saɪə, 'grænd-) *n* an archaic word for **grandfather**

grand slam *n* **1** *bridge* the winning of 13 tricks by one player or side or the contract to do so **2** the winning of all major competitions in a season, esp in tennis and golf **3** (*often capital*) *rugby Union* the winning of all five games in the annual Six Nations Championship involving England, Scotland, Wales, Ireland, France, and Italy

grandson ('grænsʌn, 'grænd-) *n* a son of one's son or daughter

grandstand ('græn,stænd, 'grænd-) *n* **1** a terraced block of seats, usually under a roof, commanding the best view at racecourses, football pitches, etc **2** the spectators in a grandstand

grand tour *n* **1** (formerly) an extended tour through the major cities of Europe, esp one undertaken by a rich or aristocratic Englishman to complete his education **2** *informal* an extended sightseeing trip, tour of inspection, etc

granduncle ('grænd,ʌŋkᵊl) *n* another name for **great-uncle**

grand unified theory *n* *physics* any of a number of theories of elementary particles and fundamental interactions designed to explain the gravitational, electromagnetic, strong, and weak interactions in terms of a single mathematical formalism. Abbreviation: GUT

Grand Union Canal *n* a canal in S England linking London and the Midlands: opened in 1801

grange (greɪndʒ) *n* **1** *chiefly Brit* a farm, esp a farmhouse or country house with its various outbuildings **2** *history* an outlying farmhouse in which a religious establishment or feudal lord stored crops and tithes in kind **3** *archaic* a granary or barn [C13: from Anglo-French *graunge*, from Medieval Latin *grānica*, from Latin *grānum* GRAIN]

Grangemouth ('greɪndʒmaʊθ, -məθ) *n* a port in Scotland, in Falkirk council area: now Scotland's second port, with oil refineries, shipyards, and chemical industries. Pop: 17 771 (2001)

Granicus (grə'naɪkəs) *n* an ancient river in NW Asia Minor where Alexander the Great won his first major battle against the Persians (334 BC)

granita (grə'niːtə) *n* a type of Italian dessert, similar to a sorbet [from Italian *granito* grainy]

granite ('grænɪt) *n* **1** a light-coloured coarse-grained acid plutonic igneous rock consisting of quartz, feldspars, and such ferromagnesian minerals as biotite or hornblende: widely used for building **2** great hardness, endurance, or resolution [C17: from Italian *granito* grained, from *granire* to grain, from *grano* grain, from Latin *grānum*] > granitic (grə'nɪtɪk) or 'granit,oid *adj*

graniteware ('grænɪt,wɛə) *n* **1** iron vessels coated with enamel of a granite-like appearance **2** a type of pottery with a speckled glaze

granivorous (græ'nɪvərəs) *adj* (of animals) feeding on seeds and grain > granivore ('grænɪ,vɔː) *n*

granny *or* **grannie** ('grænɪ) *n, pl* -nies **1** *informal* words for **grandmother 2** *informal* an irritatingly fussy person **3** See **granny knot**

granny bond *n* (in Britain) an informal name for **retirement issue certificate,** an index-linked savings certificate, originally available only to people over retirement age

granny flat *n* self-contained accommodation within or built onto a house, suitable for an elderly parent

granny knot *or* **granny's knot** *n* a reef knot with the ends crossed the wrong way, making it liable to slip or jam

granola (grə'nəʊlə) *n* *US & Canadian* a mixture of rolled oats, brown sugar, nuts, fruit, etc, eaten with milk [C20: originally *Granola* a trademark]

Gran Paradiso (*Italian* gram para'diːzo) *n* a mountain in NW Italy, in NW Piedmont: the highest peak of the Graian Alps. Height: 4061 m (13 323 ft)

grant (grɑːnt) *vb* (*tr*) **1** to consent to perform or fulfil: *to grant a wish* **2** (*may take a clause as object*) to permit as a favour, indulgence, etc: *to grant an interview* **3** (*may take a clause as object*) to acknowledge the validity of; concede: *I grant what you say is true* **4** to bestow, esp in a formal manner **5** to transfer (property) to another, esp by deed; convey **6** take for granted **a** to accept or assume without question: *one takes certain amenities for granted* **b** to fail to appreciate the value, merit, etc, of (a person) ▷ *n* **7** a sum of money provided by a government, local authority, or public fund to finance educational study, overseas aid, building repairs, etc **8** a privilege, right, etc, that has been granted **9** the act of granting **10** a transfer of property by deed or other written instrument; conveyance [C13: from Old French *graunter*, from Vulgar Latin *credentāre* (unattested), from Latin *crēdere* to believe] > 'grantable *adj* > 'granter *n*

Grant (grɑːnt) *n* **1** Cary, real name *Alexander Archibald Leach.* 1904–86, US film actor, born in England. His many films include *Bringing up Baby* (1938), *The Philadelphia Story* (1940), *Arsenic and Old Lace* (1944), and *Mr Blandings Builds his Dream House* (1948) **2** Duncan (James Corrowr). 1885–1978, British painter and designer **3** Ulysses S(impson), real name *Hiram Ulysses Grant.* 1822–85, 18th president of the US (1869–77); commander in chief of Union forces in the American Civil War (1864–65)

Granta ('græntə, 'grɑːntə) *n* the original name, still in use locally, for the River Cam

grantee (grɑː'niː) *n* *law* a person to whom a grant is made

Grantham ('grænθəm) *n* a town in E England, in Lincolnshire: birthplace of Sir Isaac Newton and Margaret Thatcher. Pop: 34 592 (2001)

grant-in-aid *n, pl* grants-in-aid a sum of money granted by one government to a lower level of government or to a dependency for a programme, etc

grant-maintained *adj* (grant maintained *when postpositive*) (of schools or educational institutions) funded directly by central government

grantor (grɑː'tɔː, 'grɑːntə) *n* *law* a person who makes a grant

gran turismo ('græn tʊə'rɪzməʊ) *n, pl* gran turismos the full form of: GT [C20: Italian, literally: great touring (i.e., touring on a grand scale)]

granular ('grænjʊlə) *adj* **1** of, like, containing, or resembling a granule or granules **2** having a grainy or granulated surface > 'granularly *adv* > granularity (,grænjʊ'lærɪtɪ) *n*

granulate ('grænjʊ,leɪt) *vb* **1** (*tr*) to make into grains **2** to make or become roughened in surface texture > 'granulative *adj* > 'granu,lator *or* 'granu,later *n* > ,granu'lation *n*

granulation tissue *n* a mass of new connective tissue and capillaries formed on the surface of a healing ulcer or wound, usually leaving a scar. Nontechnical name: proud flesh

granule ('grænjuːl) *n* a small grain [C17: from Late Latin *grānulum* a small GRAIN]

granulocyte ('grænjʊlə,saɪt) *n* any of a group of phagocytic leucocytes having cytoplasmic granules that take up various dyes

Granville ('grænvɪl) *n* **1** 1st Earl, title of John Carteret. 1690–1763, British statesman: secretary of state (1742–44); a leading opponent of Walpole **2** 2nd Earl, title of *Granville George Leveson-Gower.* 1815–91, British Liberal politician: Gladstone's foreign secretary (1870–74; 1880–85) and a supporter of Irish Home Rule

Granville-Barker ('grænvɪl'bɑːkə) *n* Harley. 1877–1946, English dramatist, theatre director, and critic, noted particularly for his *Prefaces to Shakespeare* (1927–47)

grape (greɪp) n **1** the fruit of the grapevine, which has a purple or green skin and sweet flesh: eaten raw, dried to make raisins, currants, or sultanas, or used for making wine **2** See **grapevine** (sense 1) **3 the grape** an informal term for: **wine 4** See **grapeshot** [C13: from Old French *grape* bunch of grapes, of Germanic origin; compare Old High German *krāpfo*; related to CRAMP², GRAPPLE]
> 'grapey *or* 'grapy *adj*

grapefruit ('greɪpˌfruːt) n, pl **-fruit** *or* **-fruits 1** a tropical or subtropical cultivated evergreen rutaceous tree, *Citrus paradisi* **2** the large round edible fruit of this tree, which has yellow rind and juicy slightly bitter pulp

grape hyacinth n any of various Eurasian liliaceous plants of the genus *Muscari*, esp *M. botryoides*, with clusters of rounded blue flowers resembling tiny grapes

grapeshot ('greɪpˌʃɒt) n ammunition for cannons consisting of a canvas tube containing a cluster of small iron or lead balls that scatter after firing

grape sugar n another name for **dextrose**

grapevine ('greɪpˌvaɪn) n **1** any of several vitaceous vines of the genus *Vitis*, esp *V. vinifera* of E Asia, widely cultivated for its fruit (grapes): family *Vitaceae* **2** *informal* an unofficial means of relaying information, esp from person to person

graph (grɑːf, græf) n **1** Also called: **chart** a drawing depicting the relation between certain sets of numbers or quantities by means of a series of dots, lines, etc, plotted with reference to a set of axes **2** *maths* a drawing depicting a functional relation between two or three variables by means of a curve or surface containing only those points whose coordinates satisfy the relation **3** *linguistics* a symbol in a writing system not further subdivisible into other such symbols ▷ *vb* **4** (*tr*) to draw or represent in a graph [C19: short for *graphic formula*]

-graph n *combining form* **1** an instrument that writes or records: *telegraph* **2** a writing, record, or drawing: *autograph; lithograph* [via Latin from Greek *-graphos*, from *graphein* to write] > **-graphic** *or* **-graphical** *adj combining form*
> **-graphically** *adv combining form*

grapheme ('græfiːm) n *linguistics* one of a set of orthographic symbols (letters or combinations of letters) in a given language that serve to distinguish one word from another and usually correspond to or represent phonemes, e.g. the *f* in *fun*, the *ph* in *phantom*, and the *gh* in *laugh* [C20: from Greek *graphēma* a letter]
> gra'phemically *adv*

-grapher n *combining form* **1** indicating a person who writes about or is skilled in a subject: *geographer; photographer* **2** indicating a person who writes, records, or draws in a specified way: *stenographer; lithographer*

graphic ('græfɪk) *or* **graphical** *adj* **1** vividly or clearly described: *a graphic account of the disaster* **2** of or relating to writing or other inscribed representations: *graphic symbols* **3** *maths* using, relating to, or determined by a graph: *a graphic representation of the figures* **4** of or relating to the graphic arts **5** *geology* having or denoting a texture formed by intergrowth of the crystals to resemble writing: *graphic granite* [C17: from Latin *graphicus*, from Greek *graphikos*, from *graphein* to write; see CARVE]
> 'graphically *adv* > 'graphicalness *or* 'graphicness *n*

graphicacy ('græfɪkəsɪ) n the ability to understand and use maps, plans, symbols, etc [C20: formed on the model of *literacy*]

graphical user interface n an interface between a user and a computer system that involves the use of a mouse-controlled screen cursor to select options from menus, make choices with buttons, start programs by clicking icons, etc

graphic arts *pl* n any of the fine or applied visual arts based on drawing or the use of line, as opposed to colour or relief, on a plane surface, esp illustration and printmaking of all kinds

graphic equalizer n an electronic device for cutting or boosting selected frequencies, using small linear faders

graphic novel n a novel in the form of a comic strip

graphics ('græfɪks) n **1** (*functioning as singular*) the process or art of drawing in accordance with mathematical principles **2** (*functioning as singular*) the study of writing systems **3** (*functioning as plural*) the drawings, photographs, etc, in the layout of a magazine or book, or in a television or film production **4** (*functioning as plural*) the information displayed on a visual display unit or on a computer printout in the form of diagrams, graphs, pictures, and symbols

graphics adapter n *computing* (on a computer) the hardware that controls the way graphics appear on the monitor

graphite ('græfaɪt) n a blackish soft allotropic form of carbon in hexagonal crystalline form: used in pencils, crucibles, and electrodes, as a lubricant, as a moderator in nuclear reactors, and, in a carbon fibre form, as a tough lightweight material for sporting equipment [C18: from German *Graphit*; from Greek *graphein* to write + -ITE¹]
> graphitic (grə'fɪtɪk) *adj*

graphology (græ'fɒlədʒɪ) n **1** the study of handwriting, esp to analyse the writer's character **2** *linguistics* the study of writing systems > graphologic (ˌgræfə'lɒdʒɪk) *or* ˌgrapho'logical *adj* > gra'phologist *n*

graph paper n paper printed with intersecting lines, usually horizontal and vertical and equally spaced, for drawing graphs, diagrams, etc

-graphy n *combining form* **1** indicating a form or process of writing, representing, etc: *calligraphy; photography* **2** indicating an art or descriptive science: *choreography; oceanography* [via Latin from Greek *-graphia*, from *graphein* to write]

grapnel ('græpnəl) n **1** a device with a multiple hook at one end and attached to a rope, which is thrown or hooked over a firm mooring to secure an object attached to the other end of the rope **2** a light anchor for small boats [C14: from Old French *grapin* a little hook, from *grape* a hook; see GRAPE]

grappa ('græpə) n a spirit distilled from the fermented remains of grapes after pressing [Italian: grape stalk, of Germanic origin; see GRAPE]

Grappelli *or* **Grappelly** (grə'pelɪ) n **Stéphane** ('stefˀn) 1908–97, French jazz violinist: with Django Reinhardt, he led the Quintet of the Hot Club of France between 1934 and 1939

grapple ('græpˀl) *vb* **1** to come to grips with (one or more persons), esp to struggle in hand-to-hand combat **2** (*intr; foll by with*) to cope or contend: *to grapple with a financial problem* **3** (*tr*) to secure with a grapple ▷ *n* **4** any form of hook or metal instrument by which something is secured, such as a grapnel **5 a** the act of gripping or seizing, as in wrestling **b** a grip or hold [C16: from Old French *grappelle* a little hook, from *grape* hook; see GRAPNEL] > 'grappler *n*

grappling iron *or* **grappling hook** n a grapnel, esp one used for securing ships

graptolite ('græptəˌlaɪt) n any extinct Palaeozoic colonial animal of the class *Graptolithina*, usually regarded as related to either the hemichordates or the coelenterates: a common fossil, used to determine the age of sedimentary rocks [C19: from Greek *graptos* written, from *graphein* to write + -LITE]

Grasmere ('grɑːsˌmɪə) n a village in NW England, in Cumbria at the head of **Lake Grasmere**: home of William Wordsworth and of Thomas de Quincey

grasp (grɑːsp) *vb* **1** to grip (something) firmly with or as if with the hands **2** (when *intr*, often foll by *at*) to struggle, snatch, or grope (for) **3** (*tr*) to understand, esp with effort ▷ *n* **4** the act of grasping **5** a grip or clasp, as of a hand **6** total rule or possession **7** understanding; comprehension [C14: from Low German *grapsen*; related to Old English *græppian* to seize, Old Norse *grāpa* to steal] > 'graspable *adj* > 'grasper *n*

grasping ('grɑːspɪŋ) *adj* greedy; avaricious; rapacious > 'graspingly *adv*

grass (grɑːs) n **1** any monocotyledonous plant of the family *Poaceae* (formerly *Gramineae*), having jointed stems sheathed by long narrow leaves, flowers in spikes, and seedlike fruits. The family includes cereals, bamboo, etc **2** such plants collectively, in a lawn, meadow, etc. Related adj: **verdant 3** ground on which such plants grow; a lawn, field, etc **4** ground on which animals are grazed; pasture **5** a slang word for **marijuana 6** *Brit slang* a person who informs, esp on criminals **7 let the grass**

grow under one's feet to squander time or opportunity ▷ *vb* **8** to cover or become covered with grass **9** to feed or be fed with grass **10** (*tr*) to spread (cloth) out on grass for drying or bleaching in the sun **11** (*intr; usually foll by on*) *Brit slang* to inform, esp to the police. See also **grass up** [Old English *græs*; related to Old Norse, Gothic, Old High German *gras*, Middle High German *gruose* sap] > 'grass,like *adj*

Grass (*German* gras) *n* **Günter** (**Wilhelm**) ('gyntər). born 1927, German novelist, dramatist, and poet. His novels include *The Tin Drum* (1959), *Dog Years* (1963), *The Rat* (1986), *Crabwalk* (2002), and *Peeling the Onion* (2007). Nobel prize for literature 1999

grass hockey *n Canadian* field hockey, as contrasted with ice hockey

grasshopper ('grɑːs,hɒpə) *n* any orthopterous insect of the families *Acrididae* (**short-horned grasshoppers**) and *Tettigoniidae* (**long-horned grasshoppers**), typically terrestrial, feeding on plants, and producing a ticking sound by rubbing the hind legs against the leathery forewings

grassland ('grɑːs,lænd) *n* **1** land, such as a prairie, on which grass predominates **2** land reserved for natural grass pasture

grass roots *pl n* **1** the ordinary people as distinct from the active leadership of a party or organization: used esp of the rank-and-file members of a political party, or of the voters themselves **2** the origin or essentials [C20: sense 1 originally US, with reference to rural areas in contrast to the towns]

grass snake *n* **1** a harmless nonvenomous European colubrid snake, *Natrix natrix*, having a brownish-green body with variable markings **2** any of several similar related European snakes, such as *Natrix maura* (**viperine grass snake**)

grass tree *n* **1** Also called: **black boy, yacca, yacka** any plant of the Australian genus *Xanthorrhoea*, having a woody stem, stiff grasslike leaves, and a spike of small white flowers: family *Xanthorrhoeaceae*. Some species produce fragrant resins **2** any of several similar Australasian plants

grass up *vb* (*tr, adverb*) *slang* to inform on (someone), esp to the police

grass widow *n* a woman whose spouse is regularly away for short periods [C16, meaning a discarded mistress: perhaps an allusion to a grass bed as representing an illicit relationship; compare BASTARD; C19 in the modern sense]

grassy ('grɑːsɪ) *adj* **grassier, grassiest** covered with, containing, or resembling grass > 'grassiness *n*

grate¹ (greɪt) *vb* **1** (*tr*) to reduce to small shreds by rubbing against a rough or sharp perforated surface: *to grate carrots* **2** to scrape (an object) against something or (objects) together, producing a harsh rasping sound, or (of objects) to scrape with such a sound **3** (*intr*; foll by *on* or *upon*) to annoy [C15: from Old French *grater* to scrape, of Germanic origin; compare Old High German *krazzōn*] > 'grater *n*

grate² (greɪt) *n* **1** a framework of metal bars for holding fuel in a fireplace, stove, or furnace **2** a less common word for **fireplace 3** another name for **grating¹** (sense 1) ▷ *vb* **4** (*tr*) to provide with a grate or grates [C14: from French *grate*, from Latin *crātis* hurdle]

grateful ('greɪtfʊl) *adj* **1** thankful for gifts, favours, etc; appreciative **2** showing gratitude: *a grateful letter* **3** favourable or pleasant: *a grateful rest* [C16: from obsolete *grate*, from Latin *grātus* + -FUL] > 'gratefully *adv* > 'gratefulness *n*

Gratian ('greɪʃɪən) *n* Latin name *Flavius Gratianus*. 359–383 AD, Roman emperor (367–383): ruled with his father Valentinian I (367–375); ruled the Western Roman Empire with his brother Valentinian II (375-83); appointed Theodosius I emperor of the Eastern Roman Empire (379)

graticule ('græti,kjuːl) *n* **1** the grid of intersecting lines, esp of latitude and longitude on which a map is drawn **2** another name for **reticle** [C19: from French, from Latin *crāticula*, from *crātis* wickerwork]

gratify ('græti,faɪ) *vb* **-fies, -fying, -fied** (*tr*) **1** to satisfy or please **2** to yield to or indulge (a desire, whim, etc) [C16: from Latin *grātificārī* to do a favour to, from *grātus* grateful + *facere* to make] > 'grati,fier *n* > ,gratifi'cation *n* > 'grati,fying *adj* > 'grati,fyingly *adv*

gratin (*French* gratɛ̃) *adj* See **au gratin**

grating¹ ('greɪtɪŋ) *n* Also called: **grate** a framework of metal bars set into the form of a grille set into a wall, pavement, etc, serving as a cover or guard but admitting air and sometimes light

grating² ('greɪtɪŋ) *adj* **1** (of sounds) harsh and rasping **2** annoying; irritating ▷ *n* **3** (*often plural*) something produced by grating > 'gratingly *adv*

gratis ('greɪtɪs, 'grætɪs, 'grɑːtɪs) *adv, adj* (*postpositive*) without payment; free of charge [C15: from Latin: out of kindness, from *grātiīs*, ablative pl of *grātia* favour]

gratitude ('græti,tjuːd) *n* a feeling of thankfulness or appreciation, as for gifts or favours [C16: from Medieval Latin *grātitūdō*, from Latin *grātus* GRATEFUL]

Grattan ('græt°n) *n* **Henry**. 1746–1820, Irish statesman and orator: led the movement that secured legislative independence for Ireland (1782), opposed union with England (1800), and campaigned for Catholic emancipation

gratuitous (grə'tjuːɪtəs) *adj* **1** given or received without payment or obligation **2** without cause; unjustified [C17: from Latin *grātuītus*, from *grātia* favour] > gra'tuitously *adv* > gra'tuitousness *n*

gratuity (grə'tjuːɪtɪ) *n, pl* **-ties 1** a gift or reward, usually of money, for services rendered; tip **2** *military* a financial award granted for long or meritorious service

Graubünden (*German* grau'bʏndən) *n* an Alpine canton of E Switzerland: the largest of the cantons, but sparsely populated. Capital: Chur. Pop: 186 100 (2002 est). Area: 7109 sq km (2773 sq miles). Italian name: Grigioni. Romansch name: Grishun. French name: Grisons

grav (græv) *n* a unit of acceleration equal to the standard acceleration of free fall. 1 grav is equivalent to 9.806 65 metres per second per second. Symbol: $g²$

gravadlax ('grævəd,læks) *n* another name for **gravlax**

gravamen (grə'veɪmən) *n, pl* **-vamina** (-'væmɪnə) **1** *law* that part of an accusation weighing most heavily against an accused **2** *law* the substance or material grounds of a complaint **3** a rare word for **grievance** [C17: from Late Latin: trouble, from Latin *gravāre* to load, from *gravis* heavy; see GRAVE²]

grave¹ (greɪv) *n* **1** a place for the burial of a corpse, esp beneath the ground and usually marked by a tombstone. Related adj: **sepulchral 2** something resembling a grave or resting place: *the ship went to its grave* **3 the grave** poetic term for **death 4** to make someone turn in his grave *or* to make someone turn over in his grave to do something that would have shocked or distressed (someone now dead) [Old English *græf*; related to Old Frisian *gref*, Old High German *grab*, Old Slavonic *grobŭ*; see GRAVE³]

grave² (greɪv) *adj* **1** serious and solemn: *a grave look* **2** full of or suggesting danger: *a grave situation* **3** important; crucial: *grave matters of state* **4** (of colours) sober or dull **5** (*also* grɑːv) *phonetics* of or relating to an accent (`) over vowels, denoting a pronunciation with lower or falling musical pitch (as in ancient Greek), with certain special quality (as in French), or in a manner that gives the vowel status as a syllable nucleus not usually possessed by it in that position (as in English *agèd*) ▷ *n* **6** (*also* grɑːv) a grave accent [C16: from Old French, from Latin *gravis*; related to Greek *barus* heavy; see GRAVAMEN] > 'gravely *adv* > 'graveness *n*

grave³ (greɪv) *vb* **graves, graving, graved, graved** *or* **graven** (*tr*) *archaic* **1** to cut, carve, sculpt, or engrave **2** to fix firmly in the mind [Old English *grafan*; related to Old Norse *grafa*, Old High German *graban* to dig]

grave⁴ ('grɑːvɪ) *adj, adv music* to be performed in a solemn manner [C17: from Italian: heavy, from Latin *gravis*]

grave clothes *pl n* the wrappings in which a dead body is interred

gravel ('græv°l) *n* **1** an unconsolidated mixture of rock fragments that is coarser than sand **2** *pathol* small rough calculi in the kidneys or bladder ▷ *vb* **-els, -elling,**

-elled or US -els, -eling, -eled (tr) **3** to cover with gravel **4** to confound or confuse **5** US informal to annoy or disturb [c13: from Old French gravele, diminutive of grave gravel, perhaps of Celtic origin]

gravel-blind adj literary almost entirely blind [c16: from GRAVEL + BLIND, formed on the model of SAND-BLIND]

gravelly ('grævəlɪ) adj **1** consisting of or abounding in gravel **2** of or like gravel **3** (esp of a voice) harsh and grating

graven ('greɪvᵊn) vb **1** a past participle of **grave³** ▷ adj **2** strongly fixed

Gravenhage (xra:vən'ha:xə) n 's Gravenhage a Dutch name for (The) Hague¹

graven image n chiefly Bible a carved image used as an idol

graver ('greɪvə) n any of various engraving, chasing, or sculpting tools, such as a burin

Graves¹ (gra:v) n (sometimes not capital) a white or red wine from the district around Bordeaux, France

Graves² (greɪvz) n **Robert (Ranke)**. 1895–1985, English poet, novelist, and critic, whose works include his World War I autobiography, Goodbye to All That (1929), and the historical novels I, Claudius (1934) and Claudius the God (1934)

Gravesend (,greɪvz'end) n a river port in SE England, in NW Kent on the Thames. Pop: 53 045 (2001)

gravestone ('greɪv,stəʊn) n a stone marking a grave and usually inscribed with the name and dates of the person buried

graveyard ('greɪv,jɑːd) n a place for graves; a burial ground, esp a small one or one in a churchyard

graveyard shift n US the working shift between midnight and morning

graveyard slot n television the hours from late night until early morning when the number of people watching television is at its lowest

gravid ('grævɪd) adj the technical word for **pregnant** [c16: from Latin gravidus, from gravis heavy]

gravimeter (grə'vɪmɪtə) n **1** an instrument for measuring the earth's gravitational field at points on its surface **2** an instrument for measuring relative density [c18: from French gravimètre, from Latin gravis heavy] > gra'vimetry n

gravimetric (,grævɪ'mɛtrɪk) or **gravimetrical** adj of, concerned with, or using measurement by weight

graving dock n another term for **dry dock**

gravitas ('grævɪ,tæs) n seriousness, solemnity, or importance [c20: from Latin gravitās weight, from gravis heavy]

gravitate ('grævɪ,teɪt) vb (intr) **1** physics to move under the influence of gravity **2** (usually foll by to or towards) to be influenced or drawn, as by strong impulses **3** to sink or settle > 'gravi,tater n > 'gravi,tative adj

gravitation (,grævɪ'teɪʃən) n **1** the force of attraction that bodies exert on one another as a result of their mass **2** any process or result caused by this interaction, such as the fall of a body to the surface of the earth ▷ Also called: gravity > ,gravi'tational adj > ,gravi'tationally adv

gravitational constant n the factor relating force to mass and distance in Newton's law of gravitation. It is a universal constant with the value 6.673×10^{-11} N m² kg⁻². Symbol: G

gravitational field n the field of force surrounding a body of finite mass in which another body would experience an attractive force that is proportional to the product of the masses and inversely proportional to the square of the distance between them

gravitational mass n the mass of a body determined by its response to the force of gravity. See **inertial mass**

graviton ('grævɪ,tɒn) n a postulated quantum of gravitational energy, usually considered to be a particle with zero charge and rest mass and a spin of 2

gravity ('grævɪtɪ) n, pl -ties **1** the force of attraction that moves or tends to move bodies towards the centre of a celestial body, such as the earth or moon **2** the property of being heavy or having weight **3** another name for **gravitation 4** seriousness or importance, esp as a consequence of an action or opinion **5** manner or conduct that is solemn or dignified **6** lowness in pitch **7** (modifier) of or relating to gravity or gravitation or their effects: gravity wave; gravity feed [c16: from Latin gravitās weight, from gravis heavy]

gravity wave n physics **1** a wave propagated in a gravitational field, predicted to occur as a result of an accelerating mass **2** a surface wave on water or other liquid propagated because of the weight of liquid in the crests ▷ Also called: gravitational wave

gravlax ('græv,læks) or **gravadlax** n dry-cured salmon, marinated in salt, sugar, and spices, as served in Scandinavia [c20: from Norwegian, from grav grave (because the salmon is left to ferment) + laks or Swedish lax salmon]

gravure (grə'vjʊə) n **1** a method of intaglio printing using a plate with many small etched recesses. See also **rotogravure 2** See **photogravure 3** matter printed by this process [c19: from French, from graver to engrave, of Germanic origin; see GRAVE³]

gravy ('greɪvɪ) n, pl -vies **1 a** the juices that exude from meat during cooking **b** the sauce made by thickening and flavouring such juices **2** slang money or gain acquired with little effort, esp above that needed for ordinary living [c14: from Old French gravé, of uncertain origin]

gravy boat n a small often boat-shaped vessel for serving gravy or other sauces

gray¹ (greɪ) adj, n, vb a variant spelling (now esp US) of grey

gray² (greɪ) n the derived SI unit of absorbed ionizing radiation dose or kerma equivalent to an absorption per unit mass of one joule per kilogram of irradiated material. 1 gray is equivalent to 100 rads. Abbreviation: Gy [c20: named after Louis Harold Gray (1905–65), English physicist]

Gray (greɪ) n **1 Simon (James Holiday)**. born 1936, British writer: his plays include Butley (1971), The Common Pursuit (1988), Life Support (1997), and Japes (2001) **2 Thomas**. 1716–71, English poet, best known for his Elegy written in a Country Churchyard (1751)

grayling ('greɪlɪŋ) n, pl -ling or -lings **1** any freshwater salmonoid food fish of the genus Thymallus and family Thymallidae, of the N hemisphere, having a long spiny dorsal fin, a silvery back, and greyish-green sides **2** any butterfly of the satyrid genus Hipparchia and related genera, esp H. semele of Europe, having grey or greyish-brown wings

Graz (German gra:ts) n an industrial city in SE Austria, capital of Styria province: the second largest city in the country. Pop: 226 244 (2001)

graze¹ (greɪz) vb **1** to allow (animals) to consume the vegetation on (an area of land), or (of animals, esp cows and sheep) to feed thus **2** (tr) to tend (livestock) while at pasture **3** informal to eat snacks throughout the day rather than formal meals **4** US to pilfer and eat sweets, vegetables, etc, from supermarket shelves while shopping [Old English grasian, from græs GRASS; related to Old High German grasōn, Dutch grazen, Norwegian grasa]

graze² (greɪz) vb **1** (when intr, often foll by against or along) to brush or scrape (against) gently, esp in passing **2** (tr) to break the skin of (a part of the body) by scraping ▷ n **3** the act of grazing **4** a scrape or abrasion made by grazing [c17: probably special use of GRAZE¹; related to Swedish gräsa]

grazier ('greɪzɪə) n a rancher or farmer who rears or fattens cattle or sheep on grazing land

grazing ('greɪzɪŋ) n **1** the vegetation on pastures that is available for livestock to feed upon **2** the land on which this is growing

grease n (gri:s, gri:z) **1** animal fat in a soft or melted condition **2** any thick fatty oil, esp one used as a lubricant for machinery, etc ▷ vb (gri:z, gri:s) (tr) **3** to soil, coat, or lubricate with grease **4 grease the palm of** or **grease the hand of** slang to bribe; influence by giving money to [c13: from Old French craisse, from Latin crassus thick] > 'greaser n

grease gun n a device for forcing grease through nipples into bearings, usually consisting of a cylinder with a plunger and nozzle fitted to it

grease monkey n informal a mechanic, esp one who works on cars or aircraft

grease nipple n a metal nipple designed to engage with a grease gun for injecting grease into a bearing, etc

greasepaint ('gri:s,peint) n 1 a waxy or greasy substance used as make-up by actors 2 theatrical make-up

greaseproof paper ('gri:s,pru:f) n any paper that is resistant to penetration by greases and oils

greasies ('gri:sɪz) pl n NZ informal fish and chips

greasy ('gri:zɪ, -sɪ) adj greasier, greasiest 1 coated or soiled with or as if with grease 2 composed of or full of grease 3 resembling grease 4 unctuous or oily in manner > 'greasily adv > 'greasiness n

greasy wool n untreated wool, still retaining the lanolin, which is used for waterproof clothing

great (greit) adj 1 relatively large in size or extent; big 2 relatively large in number; having many parts or members: a great assembly 3 of relatively long duration: a great wait 4 of larger size or more importance than others of its kind: the great auk 5 extreme or more than usual: great worry 6 of significant importance or consequence: a great decision 7 a of exceptional talents or achievements; remarkable: a great writer b (as noun): the great; one of the greats 8 arising from or possessing idealism in thought, action, etc; heroic: great deeds 9 illustrious or eminent: a great history 10 impressive or striking: a great show of wealth 11 active or enthusiastic: a great walker 12 doing or exemplifying (a characteristic or pursuit) on a large scale: what a great buffoon; he's not a great one for reading 13 (often foll by at) skilful or adroit: a great carpenter; you are great at singing 14 informal excellent; fantastic ▷ n 15 Also called: great organ the principal manual on an organ [Old English grēat; related to Old Frisian grāt, Old High German grōz; see GRIT, GROAT] > 'greatly adv > 'greatness n

great- prefix 1 being the parent of a person's grandparent (in the combinations **great-grandfather**, **great-grandmother**, **great-grandparent**) 2 being the child of a person's grandchild (in the combinations **great-grandson**, **great-granddaughter**, **great-grandchild**)

great auk n a large flightless auk, Pinguinus impennis, extinct since the middle of the 19th century

great-aunt or **grandaunt** n an aunt of one's father or mother; sister of one's grandfather or grandmother

Great Australian Bight n a wide bay of the Indian Ocean, in S Australia, extending from Cape Pasley to the Eyre Peninsula: notorious for storms

Great Barrier Reef n a coral reef in the Coral Sea, off the NE coast of Australia, extending for about 2000 km (1250 miles) from the Torres Strait along the coast of Queensland; the largest coral reef in the world

Great Basin n a semiarid region of the western US, between the Wasatch and the Sierra Nevada Mountains, having no drainage to the ocean: includes Nevada, W Utah, and parts of E California, S Oregon, and Idaho. Area: about 490 000 sq km (189 000 sq miles)

Great Bear n the Great Bear the English name for **Ursa Major**

Great Bear Lake n a lake in NW Canada, in the Northwest Territories: the largest freshwater lake entirely in Canada; drained by the **Great Bear River**, which flows to the Mackenzie River. Area: 31 792 sq km (12 275 sq miles)

Great Belt n a strait in Denmark, between Zealand and Funen islands, linking the Kattegat with the Baltic. Danish name: **Store Bælt**

Great Britain n England, Wales, and Scotland including those adjacent islands governed from the mainland (i.e. excluding the Isle of Man and the Channel Islands). The United Kingdom of Great Britain was formed by the Act of Union (1707), although the term Great Britain had been in use since 1603, when James VI of Scotland became James I of England (including Wales). Later unions created the United Kingdom of Great Britain and Ireland (1801) and the United Kingdom of Great Britain and Northern Ireland (1922). Pop: 57 851 100 (2003 est). Area: 229 523 sq km (88 619 sq miles). See also **United Kingdom**

great circle n a circular section of a sphere that has a radius equal to that of the sphere

greatcoat ('greit,kəut) n a heavy overcoat, now worn esp by men in the armed forces

Great Dane n one of a very large powerful yet graceful breed of dog with a short smooth coat

Great Dividing Range pl n a series of mountain ranges and plateaus roughly parallel to the E coast of Australia, in Queensland, New South Wales, and Victoria; the highest range is the Australian Alps, in the south

Greater ('greitə) adj (of a city) considered with the inclusion of the outer suburbs: Greater London

Greater Antilles pl n the Greater Antilles a group of islands in the Caribbean, including Cuba, Jamaica, Hispaniola, and Puerto Rico

Greater London n See **London¹** (sense 2)

Greater Manchester n a metropolitan county of NW England, administered since 1986 by the unitary authorities of Wigan, Bolton, Bury, Rochdale, Salford, Manchester, Oldham, Trafford, Stockport, and Tameside. Area: 1286 sq km (496 sq miles)

Greater Sunda Islands pl n a group of islands in the W Malay Archipelago, forming the larger part of the Sunda Islands: consists of Borneo, Sumatra, Java, and Sulawesi

Great Glen n the Great Glen a fault valley across the whole of Scotland, extending southwest from the Moray Firth in the east to Loch Linnhe and containing Loch Ness and Loch Lochy. Also known as: **Glen More**, **Glen Albyn**

great gross n a unit of quantity equal to one dozen gross (or 1728)

great-hearted adj benevolent or noble; magnanimous > ,great-'heartedness n

Great Indian Desert n another name for the **Thar Desert**

Great Lakes pl n a group of five lakes in central North America with connecting waterways: the largest group of lakes in the world: consists of Lakes Superior, Huron, Erie, and Ontario, which are divided by the border between the US and Canada and Lake Michigan, which is wholly in the US; constitutes the most important system of inland waterways in the world, discharging through the St Lawrence into the Atlantic. Total length: 3767 km (2340 miles). Area: 246 490 sq km (95 170 sq miles)

great-nephew or **grandnephew** n a son of one's nephew or niece; grandson of one's brother or sister

great-niece or **grandniece** n a daughter of one's nephew or niece; granddaughter of one's brother or sister

Great Ouse n See **Ouse** (sense 1)

Great Plains pl n a vast region of North America east of the Rocky Mountains, extending from the lowlands of the Mackenzie River (Canada), south to the Big Bend of the Rio Grande

Great Red Spot n a large long-lived oval feature, south of Jupiter's equator, that is an anticyclonic disturbance in the atmosphere

Great Rift Valley n the most extensive rift in the earth's surface, extending from the Jordan valley in Syria to Mozambique; marked by a chain of steep-sided lakes, volcanoes, and escarpments

Great Russian n 1 linguistics the technical name for **Russian** 2 a member of the chief East Slavonic people of Russia ▷ adj 3 of or relating to this people or their language

Greats (greits) pl n (at Oxford University) 1 the Honour School of Literae Humaniores, involving the study of Greek and Roman history and literature and philosophy 2 the final examinations at the end of this course

Great Salt Lake n a shallow salt lake in NW Utah, in the Great Basin at an altitude of 1260 m (4200 ft): the area has fluctuated from less than 2500 sq km (1000 sq miles) to over 5000 sq km (2000 sq miles)

Great Sandy Desert n 1 a desert in NW Australia. Area: about 415 000 sq km (160 000 sq miles) 2 an English name for the **Rub' al Khali**

Great Satan n any force, person, organization, or country that is regarded as evil, used esp of the United States by radical Islamists

great seal n (*often capitals*) the principal seal of a nation, sovereign, etc, used to authenticate signatures and documents of the highest importance

Great Slave Lake n a lake in NW Canada, in the Northwest Territories: drained by the Mackenzie River into the Arctic Ocean. Area: 28 440 sq km (10 980 sq miles)

Great Slave River n another name for the **Slave River**

Great Smoky Mountains or **Great Smokies** pl n the W part of the Appalachians, in N North Carolina and E Tennessee. Highest peak: Clingman's Dome, 2024 m (6642 ft)

Great St Bernard Pass n a pass over the W Alps, between SW central Switzerland and N Italy: noted for the hospice at the summit, founded in the 11th century. Height: 2469 m (8100 ft)

Great Stour n another name for **Stour** (sense 1)

great tit n a large common Eurasian tit, *Parus major*, with yellow-and-black underparts and a black-and-white head

Great Trek n the Great Trek *South African history* the migration of Boer farmers with their slaves and African servants from the Cape Colony to the north and east from about 1836 to 1845 to escape British authority

great-uncle or **granduncle** n an uncle of one's father or mother; brother of one's grandfather or grandmother

Great Victoria Desert n a desert in S Australia, in SE Western Australia and W South Australia. Area: 323 750 sq km (125 000 sq miles)

Great Wall of China n a defensive wall in N China, extending from W Gansu to the Gulf of Liaodong: constructed in the 3rd century BC as a defence against the Mongols; substantially rebuilt in the 15th century. Length: over 2400 km (1500 miles). Average height: 6 m (20 ft). Average width: 6 m (20 ft)

Great War n another name for **World War I**

Great Yarmouth ('jɑ:məθ) n a port and resort in E England, in E Norfolk. Pop: 58 032 (2001)

Great Zimbabwe n another name for **Zimbabwe** (sense 2)

greave (gri:v) n (*often plural*) a piece of armour worn to protect the shin from the ankle to the knee [C14: from Old French *greve*, perhaps from *graver* to part the hair, of Germanic origin]

Greaves (gri:vz) n **Jimmy.** born 1940, English footballer and television commentator on the sport

grebe (gri:b) n any aquatic bird, such as *Podiceps cristatus* (**great crested grebe**), of the order *Podicipediformes*, similar to the divers but with lobate rather than webbed toes and a vestigial tail [C18: from French *grèbe*, of unknown origin]

Grecian ('gri:ʃən) adj 1 (esp of beauty or architecture) conforming to Greek ideals, esp in being classically simple ▷ n 2 a scholar of or expert in the Greek language or literature ▷ adj, n 3 another word for **Greek**

Grecism ('gri:ˌsɪzəm) n a variant spelling (esp US) of **Graecism**

Greco ('grɛkəʊ) n **El.** See **El Greco**

Greco- ('gri:kəʊ, 'grɛkəʊ) *combining form* a variant (esp US) of **Graeco-**

Greece (gri:s) n a republic in SE Europe, occupying the S part of the Balkan Peninsula and many islands in the Ionian and Aegean Seas; site of two of Europe's earliest civilizations (the Minoan and Mycenaean); in the classical era divided into many small independent city-states, the most important being Athens and Sparta; part of the Roman and Byzantine Empires; passed under Turkish rule in the late Middle Ages; became an independent kingdom in 1827; taken over by a military junta (1967–74); the monarchy was abolished in 1973; became a republic in 1975; a member of the European Union. Official language: Greek. Official religion: Eastern (Greek) Orthodox. Currency: euro. Capital: Athens. Pop: 10 977 000 (2004 est). Area: 131 944 sq km (50 944 sq miles). Modern Greek name: **Ellás.** Related adj: **Hellenic**

greed (gri:d) n 1 excessive consumption of or desire for food; gluttony 2 excessive desire, as for wealth or power [C17: back formation from GREEDY]

greedy ('gri:dɪ) adj greedier, greediest 1 excessively desirous of food or wealth, esp in large amounts; voracious 2 (*postpositive; foll by for*) eager (for): *a man greedy for success* [Old English *grǣdig*; related to Old Norse *grāthugr*, Gothic *grēdags* hungry, Old High German *grātac*] > 'greedily adv > 'greediness n

greegree ('gri:gri:) n a variant spelling of **grigri**

Greek (gri:k) n 1 the official language of Greece, constituting the Hellenic branch of the Indo-European family of languages. See **Late Greek, Medieval Greek** 2 a native or inhabitant of Greece or a descendant of such a native 3 a member of the Greek Orthodox Church 4 *informal* anything incomprehensible (esp in the phrase **it's (all) Greek to me**) 5 **Greek meets Greek** equals meet ▷ adj 6 denoting, relating to, or characteristic of Greece, the Greeks, or the Greek language; Hellenic 7 of, relating to, or designating the Greek Orthodox Church [from Old English *Grēcas* (plural), or Latin *Graecus*, from Greek *Graikos*] > 'Greekness n

Greek cross n a cross with each of the four arms of the same length

Greek fire n a Byzantine weapon employed in naval warfare from 670 AD. It consisted of an unknown mixture that, when wetted, exploded and was projected, burning, from tubes

Greek gift n a gift given with the intention of tricking and causing harm to the recipient [C19: in allusion to Virgil's *Aeneid* ii 49; see also TROJAN HORSE]

Greek Orthodox Church n 1 Also called: **Greek Church** the established Church of Greece, governed by the holy synod of Greece, in which the Metropolitan of Athens has primacy of honour 2 another name for **Orthodox Church**

Greeley ('gri:lɪ) n **Horace.** 1811–72, US journalist and political leader: founder (1841) and editor of the *New York Tribune*, which championed the abolition of slavery

green (gri:n) n 1 any of a group of colours, such as that of fresh grass, that lie between yellow and blue in the visible spectrum in the wavelength range 575–500 nanometres. Green is the complementary colour of magenta and with red and blue forms a set of primary colours. Related adj: **verdant** 2 a dye or pigment of or producing these colours 3 something of the colour green 4 a small area of grassland, esp in the centre of a village 5 an area of ground used for a purpose: *a putting green* 6 (*plural*) **a** the edible leaves and stems of certain plants, eaten as a vegetable **b** freshly cut branches of ornamental trees, shrubs, etc, used as a decoration 7 (*sometimes capital*) a person, esp a politician, who supports environmentalist issues (see sense 13) ▷ adj 8 of the colour green 9 greenish in colour or having parts or marks that are greenish 10 (*sometimes capital*) concerned with or relating to conservation of the world's natural resources and improvement of the environment 11 vigorous; not faded: *a green old age* 12 envious or jealous 13 immature, unsophisticated, or gullible 14 characterized by foliage or green plants: *a green wood; a green salad* 15 fresh, raw, or unripe: *green bananas* 16 unhealthily pale in appearance: *he was green after his boat trip* 17 denoting a unit of account that is adjusted in accordance with fluctuations between the currencies of the EU nations and is used to make payments to agricultural producers within the EU: *green pound; green franc* 18 (of meat) not smoked or cured; unprocessed: *green bacon* 19 (of timber) freshly felled; not dried or seasoned ▷ vb 20 to make or become green [Old English *grēne*; related to Old High German *gruoni*; see CROW] > 'greenish adj > 'greenly adv > 'greenness n > 'greeny adj

Green (gri:n) n 1 **Henry,** real name *Henry Vincent Yorke*. 1905–73, British novelist: author of *Living* (1929), *Loving* (1945), and *Back* (1946) 2 **John Richard.** 1837–83, British historian: author of *A Short History of the English People* (1874) 3 **T**(**homas**) **H**(**ill**). 1836–82, British idealist philosopher. His chief work, *Prolegomena to Ethics*, was unfinished at his death

Greenaway ('gri:nəˌweɪ) n 1 **Kate.** 1846–1901, English painter, noted as an illustrator of children's books 2 **Peter.** born 1942, British film director; noted for such cerebral films as *The Draughtsman's Contract* (1982), *Prospero's*

g

Books (1990), and Eight and a Half Women (1999)

greenback ('gri:n,bæk) n 1 US informal an inconvertible legal-tender US currency note originally issued during the Civil War in 1862 2 US slang a dollar bill

green ban n Austral a trade union ban on any development that might be considered harmful to the environment

green bean n any bean plant, such as the French bean, having narrow green edible pods when unripe

green belt n a zone of farmland, parks, and open country surrounding a town or city: usually officially designated as such and preserved from urban development

Green Cross Code n (in Britain) a code for children giving rules for road safety: first issued in 1971

Greene (gri:n) n 1 **Graham**. 1904–91, English novelist and dramatist; his works include the novels Brighton Rock (1938), The Power and the Glory (1940), The End of the Affair (1951), and Our Man in Havana (1958), and the film script The Third Man (1949) 2 **Robert**. ?1558–92, English poet, dramatist, and prose writer, noted for his autobiographical tract A Groatsworth of Wit bought with a Million of Repentance (1592), which contains an attack on Shakespeare

greenery ('gri:nərɪ) n, pl -ries green foliage or vegetation, esp when used for decoration

green-eyed adj 1 jealous or envious 2 the green-eyed monster jealousy or envy

greenfield ('gri:n,fi:ld) n (modifier) denoting or located in a rural area which has not previously been built on

greenfinch ('gri:n,fɪntʃ) n a common European finch, Carduelis chloris, the male of which has a dull green plumage with yellow patches on the wings and tail

green fingers pl n considerable talent or ability to grow plants

Green Flag n an award given to a bathing beach that meets EU standards of cleanliness

greenfly ('gri:n,flaɪ) n, pl -flies a greenish aphid commonly occurring as a pest on garden and crop plants

greengage ('gri:n,geɪdʒ) n 1 a cultivated variety of plum tree, Prunus domestica italica, with edible green plumlike fruits 2 the fruit of this tree [c18: GREEN + -gage, after Sir W. Gage (1777–1864), English botanist who brought it from France]

Greengrass ('gri:n,grɑ:s) n **Paul**. born 1955, English film director and writer; his films include The Bourne Supremacy (2004), United 93 (2006), and The Bourne Ultimatum (2007)

greengrocer ('gri:n,grəʊsə) n chiefly Brit a retail trader in fruit and vegetables > 'green,grocery n

Greenham Common ('gri:nəm) n a village in West Berkshire unitary authority, Berkshire; site of a US cruise missile base, and, from 1981, a camp of women protesters against nuclear weapons; although the base had closed by 1991 a small number of women remained until 2000

greenheart ('gri:n,hɑ:t) n 1 Also called: bebeeru a tropical American lauraceous tree, Ocotea (or Nectandra) rodiaei, that has dark green durable wood and bark that yields the alkaloid bebeerine 2 any of various similar trees 3 the wood of any of these trees

greenhorn ('gri:n,hɔ:n) n 1 an inexperienced person, esp one who is extremely gullible 2 chiefly US a newcomer or immigrant [c17: originally an animal with green (that is, young) horns]

greenhouse ('gri:n,haʊs) n 1 a building with transparent walls and roof, usually of glass, for the cultivation and exhibition of plants under controlled conditions ▷ adj 2 relating to or contributing to the greenhouse effect: greenhouse gases such as carbon dioxide

greenhouse effect n 1 an effect occurring in greenhouses, etc, in which radiant heat from the sun passes through the glass warming the contents in the process, the radiant heat from inside being trapped by the glass 2 the application of this effect to a planet's atmosphere; carbon dioxide and some other gases in the planet's atmosphere can absorb the infrared radiation emitted by the planet's surface as a result of exposure to solar radiation, thus increasing the mean temperature

of the planet

greenie ('gri:nɪ) n Austral informal a conservationist

green keeper n a person in charge of a golf course or bowling green

Greenland ('gri:nlənd) n a large island, lying mostly within the Arctic Circle off the NE coast of North America: first settled by Icelanders in 986; resettled by Danes from 1721 onwards; integral part of Denmark (1953–79); granted internal autonomy 1979; mostly covered by an icecap up to 3300 m (11 000 ft) thick, with ice-free coastal strips and coastal mountains; the population is largely Inuit, with a European minority; fishing, hunting, and mining. Capital: Nuuk (Godthåb). Pop: 57 000 (2003 est). Area: 175 600 sq km (840 000 sq miles). Danish name: Grønland

Greenlandic (gri:n'lændɪk) adj 1 of, relating to, or characteristic of Greenland, the Greenlanders, or the Inuit dialect spoken in Greenland ▷ n 2 the dialect of Inuktitut spoken in Greenland

Greenland Sea n the S part of the Arctic Ocean, off the NE coast of Greenland

Greenland whale n an arctic right whale, Balaena mysticetus, that is black with a cream-coloured throat

green leek n any of several Australian parrots with a green or mostly green plumage

green light n 1 a signal to go, esp a green traffic light 2 permission to proceed with a project ▷ vb greenlight -lights, -lighting, -lighted (tr) 3 to permit (a project, etc) to proceed

green line n (sometimes capitals) a line of demarcation between two hostile communities

greenmail ('gri:n,meɪl) n (esp in the US) the practice of a company buying sufficient shares in another company to threaten takeover and making a quick profit as a result of the threatened company buying back its shares at a higher price

green monkey disease n another name for **Marburg disease**

Green Mountains pl n a mountain range in E North America, extending from Canada through Vermont into W Massachusetts: part of the Appalachian system. Highest peak: Mount Mansfield, 1338 m (4393 ft)

Greenock ('gri:nək) n a port in SW Scotland, in Inverclyde on the Firth of Clyde: shipbuilding and other marine industries. Pop: 45 467 (2001)

Greenough ('gri:nəʊ) n **George Bellas**. 1778–1855, English geologist, founder of the Geological Society of London

green paper n (often capitals) (in Britain) a command paper containing policy proposals to be discussed, esp by Parliament

Green Party n a political party whose policies are based on concern for the environment

Greenpeace ('gri:n,pi:s) n an organization founded in 1971 that stresses the need to maintain a balance between human progress and environmental conservation. Members take active but nonviolent measures against what are regarded as threats to environmental safety, such as the dumping of nuclear waste in the sea

green pepper n the green unripe fruit of the sweet pepper, eaten raw or cooked

green pound n a unit of account used in calculating Britain's contributions to and payments from the Community Agricultural Fund of the EU

Green River n a river in the western US, rising in W central Wyoming and flowing south into Utah, east through NW Colorado, re-entering Utah before joining the Colorado River. Length: 1175 km (730 miles)

green roof n a roof covered with vegetation, designed for its aesthetic value and to optimize energy conservation

greenroom ('gri:n,ru:m, -,rʊm) n (esp formerly) a backstage room in a theatre where performers may rest or receive visitors [c18: probably from its original colour]

greensand ('gri:n,sænd) n an olive-green sandstone consisting mainly of quartz and glauconite

Greensboro ('gri:nzbərə, -brə) n a city in N central North Carolina. Pop: 229 110 (2003 est)

greenshank ('gri:n,ʃæŋk) n a large European sandpiper,

Tringa nebularia, with greenish legs and a slightly upturned bill

greensickness ('gri:n,sɪknɪs) *n* another name for: **chlorosis**

green soap *n* *med* a soft or liquid alkaline soap made from vegetable oils, used in treating certain chronic skin diseases. Also called: **soft soap**

greenstick fracture ('gri:n,stɪk) *n* a fracture in children in which the bone is partly bent and splinters only on the convex side of the bend [c20: alluding to the similar way in which a green stick splinters]

greenstone ('gri:n,stəun) *n* **1** any basic igneous rock that is dark green because of the presence of chlorite, actinolite, or epidote **2** a variety of jade used in New Zealand for ornaments and tools

greensward ('gri:n,swɔ:d) *n* *archaic or literary* fresh green turf or an area of such turf

green tax *n* any tax imposed with the aim of regulating activity in a way that benefits the environment

green tea *n* a sharp tea made from tea leaves that have been steamed and dried quickly without fermenting

green turtle *n* a mainly tropical edible turtle, *Chelonia mydas*, with greenish flesh used to prepare turtle soup: family *Chelonidae*

greenwash ('gri:n,wɒʃ) *n* a superficial or insincere display of concern for the environment that is shown by an organization

greenway ('gri:nweɪ) *n* *US* a corridor of protected open space that is maintained for conservation, recreation, and non-motorized transportation

green-wellie *n* (*modifier*) characterizing or belonging to the upper-class set devoted to hunting, shooting, and fishing: *the green-wellie brigade*

Greenwich ('grɪnɪdʒ, -ɪtʃ, 'gren-) *n* a Greater London borough on the Thames: site of a Royal Naval College (now used as the National Maritime Museum), including Inigo Jones' Queen's House (1617), and of the original Royal Observatory designed by Christopher Wren (1675), accepted internationally as the prime meridian of longitude since 1884, and the basis of Greenwich Mean Time; also site of the Millennium Dome. Pop: 223 700 (2003 est). Area: 46 sq km (18 sq miles)

Greenwich Mean Time *or* **Greenwich Time** *n* mean solar time on the 0° meridian passing through Greenwich, England, measured from midnight: formerly a standard time in Britain and a basis for calculating times throughout most of the world, it has been replaced by an atomic timescale. See **universal time** Abbreviation: **GMT**

● USAGE The name **Greenwich mean time** is ambiguous,
● having been measured from mean midday in
● astronomy up to 1925, and is not used for scientific
● purposes. It is generally and incorrectly used in the
● sense of **universal coordinated time**, an atomic
● timescale available since 1972 from broadcast signals,
● in addition to the earliest sense of **universal time**,
● adopted internationally in 1928 as the name for GMT
● measured from midnight

Greenwich Village ('grenɪtʃ, 'grɪn-) *n* a part of New York City in the lower west side of Manhattan; traditionally the home of many artists and writers

greenwood ('gri:n,wʊd) *n* a forest or wood when the leaves are green: the traditional setting of stories about English outlaws, esp Robin Hood

green woodpecker *n* a European woodpecker, *Picus viridis*, with a dull green back and wings and a red crown

Green Zone *n* (since the invasion of Iraq by US-led forces, and the fall of Saddam Hussein in 2003) the area of central Baghdad used by the coalition and civilian authorities, subject to high security

Greer ('grɪə) *n* **Germaine**. born 1939, Australian writer and feminist. Her books include *The Female Eunuch* (1970), *Sex and Destiny* (1984), and *The Whole Woman* (1998)

greet¹ (gri:t) *vb* (*tr*) **1** to meet or receive with expressions of gladness or welcome **2** to send a message of friendship to **3** to receive in a specified manner: *her remarks were greeted by silence* **4** to become apparent to: *the smell of bread greeted him* [Old English *grētan*; related to Old

greet² (gri:t) *Scot* ▷ *vb* **1** (*intr*) to weep; lament ▷ *n* **2** weeping; lamentation [from Old English *grētan*, northern dialect variant of *grætan*; compare Old Norse *grāta*, Middle High German *grazen*]

greeting ('gri:tɪŋ) *n* **1** the act or an instance of welcoming or saluting on meeting **2** (*often plural*) **a** an expression of friendly salutation **b** (*as modifier*): *a greetings card*

gregarious (grɪ'gɛərɪəs) *adj* **1** enjoying the company of others **2** (of animals) living together in herds or flocks **3** (of plants) growing close together but not in dense clusters **4** of, relating to, or characteristic of crowds or communities [c17: from Latin *gregārius* belonging to a flock, from *grex* flock] > gre'gariously *adv* > gre'gariousness *n*

Gregorian calendar *n* the revision of the Julian calendar introduced in 1582 by Pope Gregory XIII and still in force, whereby the ordinary year is made to consist of 365 days and a leap year occurs in every year whose number is divisible by four, except those centenary years, such as 1900, whose numbers are not divisible by 400

Gregorian chant *n* another name for **plainsong**

Gregorian telescope *n* a form of reflecting astronomical telescope with a concave ellipsoidal secondary mirror and the eyepiece set behind the centre of the parabolic primary mirror [c18: named after J. Gregory (died 1675), Scottish mathematician who invented it]

Gregory ('gregərɪ) *n* Lady (**Isabella**) **Augusta** (**Persse**). 1852–1932, Irish dramatist; a founder and director of the Abbey Theatre, Dublin

Gregory I *n* **Saint**, known as *Gregory the Great*. ?540–604 AD, pope (590–604), who greatly influenced the medieval Church. He strengthened papal authority by centralizing administration, tightened discipline, and revised the liturgy. He appointed Saint Augustine missionary to England. Feast day: March 12 or Sept 3

Gregory VII *n* **Saint**, monastic name *Hildebrand*. ?1020–85, pope (1073–85), who did much to reform abuses in the Church. His assertion of papal supremacy and his prohibition (1075) of lay investiture was opposed by the Holy Roman Emperor Henry IV, whom he excommunicated (1076). He was driven into exile when Henry captured Rome (1084). Feast day: May 25

Gregory IX *n* original name *Ugolino of Segni*. ?1148–1241, pope (1227–41). He excommunicated and waged war against Emperor Frederick II

Gregory XIII *n* 1502–85, pope (1572–85). He promoted the Counter-Reformation and founded seminaries. His reformed (Gregorian) calendar was issued in 1582

Gregory of Nazianzus (,næzɪ'ænzəs) *n* **Saint**. ?329–89 AD, Cappadocian theologian: bishop of Caesarea (370–79). Feast days: Jan 2, 25, and 30

Gregory of Nyssa ('nɪsə) *n* **Saint**. ?335–394 AD, Cappadocian theologian and brother of St Basil: bishop of Nyssa. Feast day: March 9

Gregory of Tours *n* **Saint**. ?538–?594 AD, Frankish bishop and historian. His *Historia Francorum* is the chief source of knowledge of 6th-century Gaul. Feast day: Nov 17

gremial ('gri:mɪəl) *n* *RC Church* a cloth spread upon the lap of a bishop when seated during Mass [c17: from Latin *gremium* lap]

gremlin ('gremlɪn) *n* **1** an imaginary imp jokingly said to be responsible for malfunctions in machinery **2** any mischievous troublemaker [c20: perhaps a corruption of GOBLIN]

Grenache (grɪ'nɑ:ʃ) *n* (*sometimes not capital*) **1** a black grape originally grown in the Languedoc-Roussillon region of France and now in other wine-producing areas **2** any of various red wines made from this grape [French]

Grenada (grɛ'neɪdə) *n* an island state in the Caribbean, in the Windward Islands: formerly a British colony (1783–1967); since 1974 an independent state within the Commonwealth; occupied by US troops (1983–85); mainly agricultural. Official language: English. Religion: Christian majority. Currency: East Caribbean dollar. Capital: St George's. Pop: 80 000 (2003 est). Area: 344 sq km (133 sq miles)

grenade (grɪˈneɪd) n **1** a small container filled with explosive thrown by hand or fired from a rifle **2** a sealed glass vessel that is thrown and shatters to release chemicals, such as tear gas or a fire extinguishing agent [c16: from French, from Spanish *granada* pomegranate, from Late Latin *grānāta*, from Latin *grānātus* seedy; see GRAIN]

Grenadian (grɛˈneɪdɪən) adj **1** of or relating to Grenada or its inhabitants ▷ n **2** a native or inhabitant of Grenada

grenadier (ˌɡrɛnəˈdɪə) n **1** military **a** (in the British Army) a member of the senior regiment of infantry in the Household Brigade **b** (formerly) a member of a special formation, usually selected for strength and height **c** (formerly) a soldier trained to throw grenades **2** Also called: **rat-tail** any deep-sea gadoid fish of the family *Macrouridae*, typically having a large head and trunk and a long tapering tail [c17: from French; see GRENADE]

grenadine¹ (ˌɡrɛnəˈdiːn) n a light thin leno-weave fabric of silk, wool, rayon, or nylon, used esp for dresses [c19: from French, from earlier *grenade* silk with a grained texture, from *grenu* grained; see GRAIN]

grenadine² (ˌɡrɛnəˈdiːn, ˈɡrɛnəˌdiːn) n a syrup made from pomegranate juice, used as a sweetening and colouring agent in various drinks [c19: from French: a little pomegranate, from *grenade* pomegranate; see GRENADE]

Grenadines (ˌɡrɛnəˈdiːnz, ˈɡrɛnəˌdiːnz) pl n the Grenadines a chain of about 600 islets in the Caribbean, part of the Windward Islands, extending for about 100 km (60 miles) between St Vincent and Grenada and divided administratively between the two states. Largest island: Carriacou

Grendel (ˈɡrɛndəl) n (in Old English legend) a man-eating monster defeated by the hero Beowulf

Grenfell (ˈɡrɛnfəl) n Joyce, real name Joyce Irene Phipps. 1910–79, British comedy actress and writer

Grenoble (grəˈnəʊbəl; French ɡrənɔblə) n a city in SE France, on the Isère River: university (1339). Pop: 153 317 (1999)

Grenville (ˈɡrɛnvɪl) n **1** George. 1712–70, British statesman; prime minister (1763–65). His policy of taxing the American colonies precipitated the War of Independence **2** Kate. born 1950. Australian writer. Her novels include *Lilian's Story* (1985), *The Idea of Perfection* (2002) and *The Secret River* (2005) **3** Sir Richard. ?1541–91, English naval commander. He was fatally wounded aboard his ship, the *Revenge*, during a lone battle with a fleet of Spanish treasure ships **4** William Wyndham, Baron Grenville, son of George Grenville. 1759–1834, British statesman; prime minister (1806–07) of the coalition government known as the "ministry of all the talents"

Gresham (ˈɡrɛʃəm) n Sir Thomas. ?1519–79, English financier, who founded the Royal Exchange in London (1568)

Gresham's law or **Gresham's theorem** (ˈɡrɛʃəmz) n the economic hypothesis that bad money drives good money out of circulation; the superior currency will tend to be hoarded and the inferior will thus dominate the circulation [c16: named after Sir Thomas GRESHAM]

gressorial (ɡrɛˈsɔːrɪəl) or **gressorious** adj **1** (of the feet of certain birds) specialized for walking **2** (of birds, such as the ostrich) having such feet [c19: from New Latin *gressōrius*, from *gressus* having walked, from *gradī* to step]

Gretna Green (ˈɡrɛtnə) n a village in S Scotland, in Dumfries and Galloway on the border with England: famous smithy where eloping couples were married by the blacksmith from 1754 until 1940, when such marriages became illegal. Pop: 2705 (2001)

Gretzky (ˈɡrɛtzkɪ) n Wayne. born 1961, Canadian ice-hockey player and coach, based in the US

Greuze (French ɡrøz) n Jean Baptiste (ʒɑ̃ batist). 1725–1805, French genre and portrait painter

Greville (ˈɡrɛvɪl) n Fulke (fʊlk), 1st Baron Brooke. 1554–1628, English poet, writer, politician, and diplomat: Chancellor of the Exchequer (1614–22); author of *The Life*

of the Renowned Sir Philip Sidney (1652)

grew (ɡruː) vb the past tense of **grow**

grey or now esp US **gray** (ɡreɪ) adj **1** of a neutral tone, intermediate between black and white, that has no hue and reflects and transmits only a little light **2** greyish in colour or having parts or marks that are greyish **3** dismal or dark, esp from lack of light; gloomy **4** neutral or dull, esp in character or opinion **5** having grey hair **6** of or relating to people of middle age or above: *grey power* **7** ancient; venerable ▷ n **8** any of a group of grey tones **9** grey cloth or clothing **10** an animal, esp a horse, that is grey or whitish ▷ vb **11** to become or make grey [Old English *grǣg*; related to Old High German *grāo*, Old Norse *grar*] > **'greyish** or now esp US **'grayish** adj > **'greyness** or now esp US **'grayness** n

Grey (ɡreɪ) n **1** Charles, 2nd Earl Grey. 1764–1845, British statesman. As Whig prime minister (1830–34), he carried the Reform Bill of 1832 and the bill for the abolition of slavery throughout the British Empire (1833) **2** Sir Edward, 1st Viscount Grey of Fallodon. 1862–1933, British statesman; foreign secretary (1905–16) **3** Sir George. 1812–98, British statesman and colonial administrator; prime minister of New Zealand (1877–79) **4** Lady Jane. 1537–54, queen of England (July 9–19, 1553); great-granddaughter of Henry VII. Her father-in-law, the Duke of Northumberland, persuaded Edward VI to alter the succession in her favour, but after ten days as queen she was imprisoned and later executed **5** Zane. 1875–1939, US author of Westerns, including *Riders of the Purple Sage* (1912)

grey area n **1** an area or part of something existing between two extremes and having mixed characteristics of both **2** an area, situation, etc, lacking clearly defined characteristics

greybeard or US **graybeard** (ˈɡreɪˌbɪəd) n **1** an old man, esp a sage **2** a large stoneware or earthenware jar or jug for spirits

grey eminence n the English equivalent of **éminence grise**

grey-faced petrel a dark-coloured New Zealand petrel, *Pterodroma macroptera gouldi*. Also called: **North Island muttonbird, oi**

Grey Friar n a Franciscan friar

greyhen (ˈɡreɪˌhɛn) n the female of the black grouse

greyhound (ˈɡreɪˌhaʊnd) n a tall slender fast-moving dog of an ancient breed originally used for coursing

grey knight n informal an ambiguous intervener in a takeover battle, who makes a counterbid for the shares of the target company without having made his intentions clear. See **black knight, white knight**

greylag or **greylag goose** (ˈɡreɪˌlæɡ) n a large grey Eurasian goose, *Anser anser*: the ancestor of many domestic breeds of goose [c18: from GREY + LAG¹, from its migrating later than other species]

grey market n **1** stock exchange a market in the shares of a new issue, in which market makers deal with investors who have applied for shares but not yet received an allotment **2** the market for goods and services created by older people with a comfortable disposable income and increased opportunities for spending it

grey matter n **1** the greyish tissue of the brain and spinal cord, containing nerve cell bodies, dendrites, and bare (unmyelinated) axons **2** informal brains or intellect

grey nurse shark n a common greyish Australian shark, *Odontaspis arenarius*

Grey Owl n Grey Owl, original name *Archibald Belaney* (1888–1938). Canadian writer and conservationist, born in England; adopted Native American identity

grey squirrel n a grey-furred squirrel, *Sciurus carolinensis*, native to E North America but now widely established

Grey-Thompson (ˈɡreɪˈtɒmpsən) n Dame Tanni (Carys Davina). born 1969, British wheelchair athlete; eleven gold medals in the Paralympics (1988–2004)

grey vote n the body of elderly people's votes, or elderly people regarded collectively as voters

greywacke or US **graywacke** (ˈɡreɪˌwækə) n any dark sandstone or grit having a matrix of clay minerals [c19: partial translation of German *Grauwacke*; see WACKE]

grey water n water that has been used for one purpose but can be used again without repurification, e.g. bath water, which can be used to water plants

grey wolf n another name for **timber wolf**

grid (grɪd) n 1 See **gridiron** 2 a network of horizontal and vertical lines superimposed over a map, building plan, etc, for locating points 3 a grating consisting of parallel bars 4 **the grid** the national network of transmission lines, pipes, etc, by which electricity, gas, or water is distributed 5 Also called: **control grid** electronics an electrode situated between the cathode and anode of a valve usually consisting of a cylindrical mesh of wires, that controls the flow of electrons between cathode and anode. See also **screen grid** 6 See **starting grid** 7 a plate in an accumulator that carries the active substance 8 any interconnecting system of links: the bus service formed a grid across the country [c19: back formation from GRIDIRON]

grid bias n the fixed voltage applied between the control grid and cathode of a valve

griddle ('grɪdᵊl) n 1 Also called: **girdle** Brit a thick round iron plate with a half hoop handle over the top, for making scones, etc 2 any flat heated surface, esp on the top of a stove, for cooking food ▷ vb 3 (tr) to cook (food) on a griddle [c13: from Old French gridil, from Late Latin crāticulum (unattested) fine wickerwork; see GRILL¹]

gridiron ('grɪd,aɪən) n 1 a utensil of parallel metal bars, used to grill meat, fish, etc 2 any framework resembling this utensil 3 a framework above the stage in a theatre from which suspended scenery, lights, etc, are manipulated 4 a the field of play in American football b an informal name for American football ▷ Often shortened to grid [c13 gredire, perhaps variant (through influence of ire IRON) of gredile GRIDDLE]

gridlock ('grɪd,lɒk) chiefly US ▷ n 1 obstruction of urban traffic caused by queues of vehicles forming across junctions and causing further queues to form in the intersecting streets 2 a point in a dispute at which no agreement can be reached: deadlock: political gridlock ▷ vb 3 (tr) (of traffic) to block or obstruct (an area)

grid road n (in Canada) a road that follows a surveyed division between areas of a township, municipality, etc

grief (griːf) n 1 deep or intense sorrow or distress, esp at the death of someone 2 something that causes keen distress or suffering 3 informal trouble or annoyance: people were giving me grief for leaving ten minutes early 4 **come to grief** informal to end unsuccessfully or disastrously [c13: from Anglo-French gref, from grever to GRIEVE¹]

Grieg (griːg) n 1 **Edvard** (**Hagerup**) ('ɛdvard). 1843–1907, Norwegian composer. His works, often inspired by Norwegian folk music, include the incidental music for Peer Gynt (1876), a piano concerto, and many songs

Grierson ('grɪəsᵊn) n **John**. 1898–1972, Scottish film director. He coined the noun documentary, of which genre his Industrial Britain (1931) and Song of Ceylon (1934) are notable examples

grievance ('griːvᵊns) n 1 a real or imaginary wrong causing resentment and regarded as grounds for complaint 2 a feeling of resentment or injustice at having been unfairly treated [c15 grevance, from Old French, from grever to GRIEVE¹]

grieve (griːv) vb to feel or cause to feel great sorrow or distress, esp at the death of someone [c13: from Old French grever, from Latin gravāre to burden, from gravis heavy] > **griever** n > **grieving** n

grievous ('griːvəs) adj 1 very severe or painful: a grievous injury 2 very serious; heinous: a grievous sin 3 showing or marked by great pain or suffering 4 causing great pain or suffering > **grievously** adv > **grievousness** n

grievous bodily harm n criminal law really serious injury caused by one person to another

griffin ('grɪfɪn), **griffon** or **gryphon** n a winged monster with an eagle-like head and the body of a lion [c14: from Old French grifon, from Latin grȳphus, from Greek grups, from grupos hooked]

Griffith ('grɪfɪθ) n 1 **Arthur**. 1872–1922, Irish journalist and nationalist: founder of Sinn Féin (1905); president of the Free State assembly (1922) 2 **D**(avid **Lewelyn**) **W**(ark). 1875–1948, US film director and producer. He introduced several cinematic techniques, including the flashback and the fade-out, in his masterpiece The Birth of a Nation (1915)

Griffith-Joyner (,grɪfɪθ'dʒɔɪnə) n **Florence**, known as Flojo. 1959–98, US sprinter, winner of two gold medals at the 1988 Olympic Games

griffon¹ ('grɪfᵊn) n 1 any of various small wire-haired breeds of dog, originally from Belgium 2 any large vulture of the genus Gyps, of Africa, S Europe, and SW Asia, having a pale plumage with black wings: family Accipitridae (hawks) [c19: from French GRIFFIN¹]

griffon² ('grɪfᵊn) n a variant of **griffin¹**

Crigioni (grɪ'dʒoːni) n the Italian name for: **Graubünden**

grigri, gris-gris or **greegree** ('griːgriː) n, pl -gris (-griːz) or -grees an African talisman, amulet, or charm [of African origin]

grill (grɪl) vb 1 to cook (meat, fish, etc) by direct heat, as under a grill or over a hot fire, or (of meat, fish, etc) to be cooked in this way. Usual US and Canadian word: broil 2 (tr; usually passive) to torment with or as if with extreme heat: the travellers were grilled by the scorching sun 3 (tr) informal to subject to insistent or prolonged questioning ▷ n 4 a device with parallel bars of thin metal on which meat, fish, etc, may be cooked by a fire; gridiron 5 a device on a cooker that radiates heat downwards for grilling meat, fish, etc 6 food cooked by grilling 7 See **grillroom** [c17: from French gril gridiron, from Latin crāticula fine wickerwork; see GRILLE] > **griller** n > **grilled** adj

grillage ('grɪlɪdʒ) n an arrangement of beams and crossbeams used as a foundation on soft ground [c18: from French, from griller to furnish with a grille]

grille or **grill** (grɪl) n 1 Also called: **grillwork** a framework, esp of metal bars arranged to form an ornamental pattern, used as a screen or partition 2 Also called: **radiator grille** a grating, often chromium-plated, that admits cooling air to the radiator of a motor vehicle 3 a metal or wooden openwork grating used as a screen or divider 4 a protective screen, usually plastic or metal, in front of the loudspeaker in a radio, record player, etc [c17: from Old French, from Latin crāticula fine hurdlework, from crātis a hurdle]

Grillparzer (German 'grɪlpartsər) n **Franz** (frants). 1791–1872, Austrian dramatist and poet, noted for his historical and classical tragedies, which include Sappho (1818), the trilogy The Golden Fleece (1819–22), and The Jewess of Toledo (1872)

grillroom ('grɪl,ruːm, -,rʊm) n a restaurant or room in a restaurant, etc, where grilled steaks and other meat are served

grilse (grɪls) n, pl grilses or grilse a young salmon that returns to fresh water after one winter in the sea [c15 grilles (plural), of uncertain origin]

grim (grɪm) adj grimmer, grimmest 1 stern; resolute: grim determination 2 harsh or formidable in manner or appearance 3 harshly ironic or sinister: grim laughter 4 cruel, severe, or ghastly: a grim accident 5 archaic or poetic fierce: a grim warrior 6 informal unpleasant; disagreeable [Old English grimm; related to Old Norse grimmr, Old High German grimm savage, Greek khremizein to neigh] > **grimly** adv > **grimness** n

grimace (grɪ'meɪs) n 1 an ugly or distorted facial expression, as of wry humour, disgust, etc ▷ vb 2 (intr) to contort the face [c17: from French grimace, of Germanic origin; related to Spanish grimazo caricature; see GRIM] > **gri'macer** n

Grimaldi (grɪ'mɔːldɪ) n **Joseph**. 1779–1837, English actor, noted as a clown in pantomime

grimalkin (grɪ'mælkɪn, -'mɔːl-) n 1 an old cat, esp an old female cat 2 a crotchety or shrewish old woman [c17: from GREY + MALKIN]

grime (graɪm) n 1 dirt, soot, or filth, esp when thickly accumulated or ingrained ▷ vb 2 (tr) to make dirty or coat with filth [c15: from Middle Dutch grime; compare Flemish grijm, Old English grīma mask] > **grimy** adj > **griminess** n

Grimm (grɪm) n **Jakob Ludwig Karl** ('jaːkɔp 'luːtvɪç karl), 1785–1863, and his brother, **Wilhelm Karl** ('vɪlhɛlm karl), 1786–1859, German philologists and folklorists, who collaborated on *Grimm's Fairy Tales* (1812–22) and began a German dictionary. Jakob is noted also for his philological work *Deutsche Grammatik* (1819–37), in which he formulated the law named after him

Grimsby ('grɪmzbɪ) *n* a port in E England, in North East Lincolnshire unitary authority, Lincolnshire, formerly important for fishing. Pop: 87 574 (2001)

grin (grɪn) *vb* **grins, grinning, grinned 1** to smile with the lips drawn back revealing the teeth or express (something) by such a smile: *to grin a welcome* **2** (*intr*) to draw back the lips revealing the teeth, as in a snarl or grimace **3 grin and bear it** *informal* to suffer trouble or hardship without complaint ▷ *n* **4** a broad smile **5** a snarl or grimace [Old English *grennian*; related to Old High German *grennen* to snarl, Old Norse *grenja* to howl; see GRUNT] > 'grinning *adj*, *n*

grinch (grɪntʃ) *n US informal* a person whose lack of enthusiasm or bad temper has a depressing effect on others [c20: from a character in the 1957 children's book *How the Grinch stole Christmas* by Dr Seuss (1904–91), US writer and illustrator, whose full name was Theodor Seuss Geisel]

grind (graɪnd) *vb* **grinds, grinding, ground 1** to reduce or be reduced to small particles by pounding or abrading: *to grind corn; to grind flour* **2** (*tr*) to smooth, sharpen, or polish by friction or abrasion: *to grind a knife* **3** to scrape or grate together (two things, esp the teeth) with a harsh rasping sound or (of such objects) to be scraped together **4** (*tr*; foll by *out*) to speak or say (something) in a rough voice **5** (*tr*; often foll by *down*) to hold down; oppress; tyrannize **6** (*tr*) to operate (a machine) by turning a handle **7** (*tr*; foll by *out*) to produce in a routine or uninspired manner: *he ground out his weekly article for the paper* **8** (*intr*) *informal* to study or work laboriously ▷ *n* **9** *informal* laborious or routine work or study **10** a specific grade of pulverization, as of coffee beans: *coarse grind* **11** the act or sound of grinding [Old English *grindan*; related to Latin *frendere*, Lithuanian *gréndu* I rub, Low German *grand* sand] > 'grindingly *adv*

Grindelwald (German 'grɪndəlvalt) *n* a valley and resort in central Switzerland, in the Bernese Oberland: mountaineering centre, with the Wetterhorn and the Eiger nearby

grinder ('graɪndə) *n* **1** a person who grinds, esp one who grinds cutting tools **2** a machine for grinding **3** a molar tooth

grindhouse ('graɪnd,haʊs) *n chiefly US* **a** a cinema specializing in violent or exploitative films such as martial arts movies from Japan and Hong Kong **b** (*as modifier*): *a grindhouse film*

grindstone ('graɪnd,stəʊn) *n* **1 a** a machine having a circular block of stone or composite abrasive rotated for sharpening tools or grinding metal **b** the stone used in this machine **c** any stone used for sharpening; whetstone **2 keep one's nose to the grindstone** *or* **have one's nose to the grindstone** to work hard and perseveringly

gringo ('grɪŋgəʊ) *n*, *pl* **-gos** a person from an English-speaking country: used as a derogatory term by Latin Americans [c19: from Spanish: foreigner, probably from *griego* Greek, hence an alien]

grip (grɪp) *n* **1** the act or an instance of grasping and holding firmly: *he lost his grip on the slope* **2** Also called: **handgrip** the strength or pressure of such a grasp, as in a handshake **3** the style or manner of grasping an object, such as a tennis racket **4** understanding, control, or mastery of a subject, problem, etc (esp in such phrases as **get** *or* **have a grip on**) **5** Also called: **handgrip** a part by which an object is grasped; handle **6** Also called: **handgrip** a travelling bag or holdall **7** See **hairgrip 8** any device that holds by friction, such as certain types of brake **9** a worker in a camera crew or a stagehand who shifts sets and props, etc **10 get to grips** *or* **come to grips** (often foll by *with*) **a** to deal with (a problem or subject) **b** to tackle (an assailant) ▷ *vb* **grips, gripping, gripped 11** to take hold of firmly or tightly, as by a clutch **12** to hold the interest or attention of: *to grip an audience* [Old English *gripe* grasp; related to Old Norse *gripr* property, Old High German *grif*] > 'gripper *n*

gripe (graɪp) *vb* **1** (*intr*) *informal* to complain, esp in a persistent nagging manner **2** to cause sudden intense pain in the intestines of (a person) or (of a person) to experience this pain **3** *archaic* to clutch; grasp **4** (*tr*) *archaic* to afflict ▷ *n* **5** (*usually plural*) a sudden intense pain in the intestines; colic **6** *informal* a complaint or grievance **7** *now rare* **a** the act of gripping **b** a firm grip **c** a device that grips [Old English *grīpan*; related to Gothic *greipan*, Old High German *grīfan* to seize, Lithuanian *greibiu*] > 'griper *n*

gripe water *n Brit* a solution given to infants to relieve colic

grippe *or* **grip** (grɪp) *n* a former name for **influenza** [c18: from French *grippe*, from *gripper* to seize, of Germanic origin; see GRIP[1]]

Griqualand East ('gri:kwə,lænd, 'grɪk-) *n* an area of central South Africa: settled in 1861 by Griquas led by Adam Kok III; annexed to the Cape Colony in 1879; part of the Transkei, 1903–93. Chief town: Kokstad. Area: 17 100 sq km (6602 sq miles)

Griqualand West *n* an area of N South Africa, north of the Orange river: settled after 1803 by the Griquas; annexed by the British in 1871 following a dispute with the Orange Free State; became part of the Cape Colony in 1880. Chief town: Kimberley. Area: 39 360 sq km (15 197 sq miles)

Gris (*Spanish* gris) *n* **Juan** (xwan). 1887–1927, Spanish cubist painter, resident in France from 1906

grisaille (grɪ'zeɪl; *French* grizaj) *n* **1** a technique of monochrome painting in shades of grey, as in an oil painting or a wall decoration, imitating the effect of relief **2** a painting, stained glass window, etc, in this manner [c19: from French, from *gris* grey]

griseofulvin (,grɪzɪəʊ'fʊlvɪn) *n* an antibiotic used to treat fungal infections [c20: from New Latin, from *Penicillium griseofulvum dierckx* (fungus from which it was isolated), from Medieval Latin *griseus* grey + Latin *fulvus* reddish yellow]

grisette (grɪ'zɛt) *n* (esp formerly) a French working-class girl, esp a pretty or flirtatious one [c18: from French, from *grisette* grey fabric used for dresses, from *gris* grey]

gris-gris ('gri:gri:) *n*, *pl* **-gris** (-gri:z) a variant spelling of **grigri**

Grisham ('grɪʃəm) *n* **John.** born 1955, US novelist and lawyer; his legal thrillers, many of which have been filmed, include *A Time to Kill* (1989), *The Pelican Brief* (1992), and *The Summons* (2002)

Grishun (gri:'ʃʊn) *n* the Romansch name for **Graubünden**

grisly ('grɪzlɪ) *adj* **-lier, -liest** causing horror or dread; gruesome [Old English *grislic*; related to Old Frisian *grislik*, Old High German *grīsenlīh*] > 'grisliness *n*

● USAGE See at **grizzly**

Grisons (grizɔ̃) *n* the French name for **Graubünden**

grissini (grɪ'si:nɪ) *pl n* thin crisp breadsticks [c20: from Italian]

grist (grɪst) *n* **1 a** grain intended to be or that has been ground **b** the quantity of such grain processed in one grinding **2** *brewing* malt grains that have been cleaned and cracked **3 grist to the mill, grist to one's mill, grist for the mill** *or* **grist for one's mill** anything that can be turned to profit or advantage [Old English *grīst*; related to Old Saxon *grist-grimmo* gnashing of teeth, Old High German *grist-grimmōn*]

gristle ('grɪsəl) *n* cartilage, esp when in meat [Old English *gristle*; related to Old Frisian, Middle Low German *gristel*] > 'gristly *adj* > 'gristliness *n*

grit (grɪt) *n* **1** small hard particles of sand, earth, stone, etc **2** Also called: **gritstone** any coarse sandstone that can be used as a grindstone or millstone **3** indomitable courage, toughness, or resolution ▷ *vb* **grits, gritting, gritted 4** to clench or grind together (two objects, esp the teeth) **5** to cover (a surface, such as icy roads) with grit [Old English *grēot*; related to Old Norse *grjōt* pebble, Old High German *grioz*; see GREAT, GROATS, GRUEL] > 'gritter *n*

Grit (grɪt) *n, adj Canadian* an informal word for **Liberal**

grits (grɪts) *pl n* **1** hulled and coarsely ground grain **2** *US*

See **hominy grits** [Old English *grytt*; related to Old High German *gruzzi*; see GREAT, GRIT]

gritty ('grɪtɪ) *adj* **-tier, -tiest 1** courageous; hardy; resolute **2** of, like, or containing grit > **'grittily** *adv* > **'grittiness** *n*

grivet ('grɪvɪt) *n* an E African variety of a common guenon monkey, *Cercopithecus aethiops*, having long white tufts of hair on either side of the face [C19: from French, of unknown origin]

grizzle[1] ('grɪzəl) *vb* **1** to make or become grey ▷ *n* **2** a grey colour **3** grey or partly grey hair [C15: from Old French *grisel*, from *gris*, of Germanic origin; compare Middle High German *grîs* grey]

grizzle[2] ('grɪzəl) *vb* (*intr*) informal, chiefly Brit (esp of a child) to fret; whine [C18: of Germanic origin; compare Old High German *grist-grimmōn* gnashing of teeth, German *Griesgram* unpleasant person] > **'grizzler** *n*

grizzled ('grɪzəld) *adj* **1** streaked or mixed with grey; grizzly; griseous **2** having grey or partly grey hair

grizzly ('grɪzlɪ) *adj* **-zlier, -zliest 1** somewhat grey; grizzled ▷ *n, pl* **-zlies 2** See **grizzly bear**

● USAGE *Grizzly* is sometimes wrongly used where *grisly* is meant: *a grisly* (not *grizzly*) *murder*

grizzly bear *n* a variety of the brown bear, *Ursus arctos horribilis*, formerly widespread in W North America; its brown fur has cream or white hair tips on the back, giving a grizzled appearance. Often shortened to: **grizzly**

groan (grəʊn) *n* **1** a prolonged stressed dull cry expressive of agony, pain, or disapproval **2** a loud harsh creaking sound, as of a tree bending in the wind **3** informal a grumble or complaint, esp a persistent one ▷ *vb* **4** to utter (low inarticulate sounds) expressive of pain, grief, disapproval, etc **5** (*intr*) to make a sound like a groan **6** (*intr*, usually foll by *beneath* or *under*) to be weighed down (by) or suffer greatly (under) **7** (*intr*) informal to complain or grumble [Old English *grānian*; related to Old Norse *grīna*, Old High German *grīnan*; see GRIN] > **'groaning** *n, adj* > **'groaningly** *adv* > **'groaner** *n*

groat (grəʊt) *n* an English silver coin worth four pennies, taken out of circulation in the 17th century [C14: from Middle Dutch *groot*, from Middle Low German *gros*, from Medieval Latin (*denarius*) *grossus* thick (coin); see GROSCHEN]

groats (grəʊts) *pl n* the hulled and crushed grain of oats, wheat, or certain other cereals [Old English *grot* particle; related to *grota* fragment, as in *meregrota* pearl; see GRIT, GROUT]

grocer ('grəʊsə) *n* a dealer in foodstuffs and other household supplies [C15: from Old French *grossier*, from *gros* large; see GROSS]

groceries ('grəʊsərɪz) *pl n* merchandise, esp foodstuffs, sold by a grocer

grocery ('grəʊsərɪ) *n, pl* **-ceries** the business or premises of a grocer

Grodno (*Russian* 'grɔdnə) *n* a city in W Belarus on the Neman River: part of Poland (1921–39); an industrial centre. Pop: 318 000 (2005 est)

Groening ('greɪnɪŋ) *n* **Matt(hew)**. born 1954, US cartoonist and writer, creator and producer of *The Simpsons* television series from 1989

grog (grɒg) *n* **1** diluted spirit, usually rum, as an alcoholic drink **2** informal, chiefly Austral & NZ alcoholic drink in general, esp spirits [C18: from Old *Grog*, nickname of Edward Vernon (1684–1757), British admiral, who in 1740 issued naval rum diluted with water; his nickname arose from his grogram cloak]

groggy ('grɒgɪ) *adj* **-gier, -giest** informal **1** dazed or staggering, as from exhaustion, blows, or drunkenness **2** faint or weak > **'groggily** *adv* > **'grogginess** *n*

grogram ('grɒgrəm) *n* a coarse fabric of silk, wool, or silk mixed with wool or mohair, often stiffened with gum, formerly used for clothing [C16: from French *gros grain* coarse grain; see GROSGRAIN]

groin (grɔɪn) *n* **1** the depression or fold where the legs join the abdomen **2** euphemistic the genitals, esp the testicles **3** a variant spelling (esp US) of **groyne 4** architect a curved arris formed where two intersecting vaults meet ▷ *vb* **5** (*tr*) architect to provide or construct with groins [C15: perhaps from English *grynde* abyss;

related to GROUND[1]]

grommet ('grɒmɪt) *or* **grummet** *n* **1** a ring of rubber or plastic or a metal eyelet designed to line a hole to prevent a cable or pipe passed through it from chafing **2** med a small tube inserted into the eardrum in cases of glue ear in order to allow air to enter the middle ear **3** Austral informal a young or inexperienced surfer [C15: from obsolete French *gourmette* chain linking the ends of a bit, from *gourmer* bridle, of unknown origin]

Gromyko (*Russian* gra'mikə) *n* **Andrei Andreyevich** (an'drjej an'drjejɪvɪtʃ). 1909–89, Soviet statesman and diplomat; foreign minister (1957–85); president (1985–88)

Groningen ('grəʊnɪŋən; *Dutch* 'xro:nɪŋə) *n* **1** a province in the NE Netherlands: mainly agricultural. Capital: Groningen. Pop: 573 000 (2003 est). Area: 2336 sq km (902 sq miles) **2** a city in the NE Netherlands, capital of Groningen province. Pop: 177 000 (2003 est)

Grønland ('grœnlan) *n* the Danish name for **Greenland**

groom (gru:m, grʊm) *n* **1** a person employed to clean and look after horses **2** See **bridegroom 3** any of various officers of a royal or noble household **4** archaic a male servant or attendant ▷ *vb* (*tr*) **5** to make or keep (clothes, appearance, etc) clean and tidy **6** to rub down, clean, and smarten (a horse, dog, etc) **7** to train or prepare for a particular task, occupation, etc: *to groom someone for the Presidency* [C13: *grom* manservant; perhaps related to Old English *grōwan* to GROW]

groomsman ('gru:mzmən, 'grʊmz-) *n, pl* **-men** a man who attends the bridegroom at a wedding, usually the best man

groove (gru:v) *n* **1** a long narrow channel or furrow, esp one cut into wood by a tool **2** the spiral channel, usually V-shaped, in a gramophone record **3** a settled existence, routine, etc, to which one is suited or accustomed: *one from which it is difficult to escape* **4** slang an experience, event, etc, that is groovy **5** **in the groove a** jazz playing well and apparently effortlessly, with a good beat, etc **b** US fashionable ▷ *vb* (*tr*) **6** to form or cut a groove in **7** (*intr*) dated, slang to enjoy oneself or feel in rapport with one's surroundings **8** (*intr*) jazz to play well, with a good beat, etc [C15: from obsolete Dutch *groeve*, of Germanic origin; compare Old High German *gruoba* pit, Old Norse *grof*]

groovy ('gru:vɪ) *adj* **groovier, grooviest** slang, often jocular attractive, fashionable, or exciting

grope (grəʊp) *vb* **1** (*intr*; usually foll by *for*) to feel or search about uncertainly (for something) with the hands **2** (*intr*; usually foll by *for* or *after*) to search uncertainly or with difficulty (for a solution, answer, etc) **3** (*tr*) to find or make (one's way) by groping **4** (*tr*) slang to feel or fondle the body of (someone) for sexual gratification ▷ *n* **5** the act of groping [Old English *grāpian*; related to Old High German *greifōn*, Norwegian *greipa*; compare GRIPE] > **'gropingly** *adv*

groper ('grəʊpə) *or* **grouper** *n, pl* **-er** *or* **-ers** any large marine serranid fish of the genus *Epinephelus* and related genera, of warm and tropical seas [C17: from Portuguese *garupa*, probably from a South American Indian word]

Gropius ('grəʊpɪəs) *n* **Walter**. 1883–1969, US architect, designer, and teacher, born in Germany. He founded (1919) and directed (1919–28) the Bauhaus in Germany. His influence stemmed from his adaptation of architecture to modern social needs and his pioneering use of industrial materials, such as concrete and steel. His buildings include the Fagus factory at Alfeld (1911) and the Bauhaus at Dessau (1926)

Gros (*French* gro) *n* Baron **Antoine Jean** (ātwan ʒā). 1771–1835, French painter, noted for his battle scenes

grosbeak ('grəʊs,bi:k, 'grɒs-) *n* any of various finches, such as *Pinicola enucleator* (**pine grosbeak**), that have a massive powerful bill [C17: from French *grosbec*, from Old French *gros* large, thick + *bec* BEAK[1]]

groschen ('grəʊʃən; *German* 'grɔʃən) *n, pl* **-schen 1** a former Austrian monetary unit worth one hundredth of a schilling **2** a former German coin worth ten pfennigs **3** a former German silver coin [C17: from German: Bohemian dialect alteration of Middle High German *grosse*, from Medieval Latin (*denarius*) *grossus* thick (penny); see GROSS, GROAT]

grosgrain ('grəʊ,greɪn) *n* a heavy ribbed silk or rayon fabric or tape for trimming clothes, etc [C19: from French *gros grain* coarse grain; see GROSS, GRAIN]

gros point ('grəʊ 'pɔɪnt; *French* gro pwɛ̃) *n* **1** a needlepoint stitch covering two horizontal and two vertical threads **2** work done in this stitch [C20: from Old French: large point]

gross (grəʊs) *adj* **1** repellently or excessively fat or bulky **2** with no deductions for expenses, tax, etc; total: *gross sales; gross income.* See **net²** (sense 1) **3** (of personal qualities, tastes, etc) conspicuously coarse or vulgar **4** obviously or exceptionally culpable or wrong; flagrant: *gross inefficiency* **5** lacking in perception, sensitivity, or discrimination: *gross judgments* **6** (esp of vegetation) dense; thick; luxuriant ▷ *interj slang* **7** an exclamation indicating disgust ▷ *n* **8** *pl* **gross** a unit of quantity equal to 12 dozen **9** *pl* **gross** **a** the entire amount **b** the great majority ▷ *vb* (*tr*) **10** to earn as total revenue, before deductions for expenses, tax, etc [C14: from Old French *gros* large, from Late Latin *grossus* thick] > '**grossly** *adv* > '**grossness** *n*

gross domestic product *n* the total value of all goods and services produced domestically by a nation during a year. It is equivalent to gross national product minus net investment incomes from foreign nations. Abbreviation: **GDP**

Grosseteste ('grəʊs,test) *n* **Robert.** ?1175–1253, English prelate and scholar; bishop of Lincoln (1235–53). He attacked ecclesiastical abuses and wrote commentaries on Aristotle and treatises on theology, philosophy, and science

gross national product *n* the total value of all final goods and services produced annually by a nation. Abbreviation: **GNP**

gross profit *n* *accounting* the difference between total revenue from sales and the total cost of purchases or materials, with an adjustment for stock

Grosswardein (gro:svar'dain) *n* the German name for **Oradea**

gross weight *n* total weight of an article inclusive of the weight of the container and packaging

Grosz (grəʊs; *German* grɔs) *n* **George.** 1893–1959, German painter, in the US from 1932, whose works satirized German militarism and bourgeois society

grot (grɒt) *n* *slang* rubbish; dirt [C20: from GROTTY]

Grote (grəʊt) *n* **George.** 1794–1871, English historian, noted particularly for his *History of Greece* (1846–56)

grotesque (grəʊ'tesk) *adj* **1** strangely or fantastically distorted; bizarre **2** of or characteristic of the grotesque in art **3** absurdly incongruous; in a ludicrous context ▷ *n* **4** a 16th-century decorative style in which parts of human, animal, and plant forms are distorted and mixed **5** a decorative device, as in painting or sculpture, in this style **6** *printing* the family of 19th-century sans serif display types **7** any grotesque person or thing [C16: from French, from Old Italian (*pittura*) *grottesca* cave painting, from *grottesco* of a cave, from *grotta* cave; see GROTTO] > gro'**tesquely** *adv* > gro'**tesqueness** *n* > gro'**tesquery** *or* gro'**tesquerie** *n*,

Grotius ('grəʊtɪəs) *n* **Hugo,** original name *Huig de Groot.* 1583–1645, Dutch jurist and statesman, whose *De Jure Belli ac Pacis* (1625) is regarded as the foundation of modern international law > '**Grotian** *adj* > '**Grotianism** *n*

grotto ('grɒtəʊ) *n, pl* **-toes** *or* **-tos** **1** a small cave, esp one with attractive features **2** a construction in the form of a cave, esp as in landscaped gardens during the 18th century [C17: from Old Italian *grotta*, from Late Latin *crypta* vault; see CRYPT]

grotty ('grɒtɪ) *adj* **-tier, -tiest** *Brit slang* **1** unpleasant, nasty, or unattractive **2** of poor quality or in bad condition; unsatisfactory or useless [C20: from GROTESQUE]

grouch (graʊtʃ) *informal* ▷ *vb* (*intr*) **1** to complain; grumble ▷ *n* **2** a complaint, esp a persistent one **3** a person who is always grumbling [C20: from obsolete *grutch*, from Old French *grouchier* to complain; see GRUDGE] > '**grouchy** *adj* > '**grouchily** *adv* > '**grouchiness** *n*

ground¹ (graʊnd) *n* **1** the land surface **2** earth or soil **3** (*plural*) the land around a dwelling house or other building **4** (*sometimes plural*) an area of land given over to a purpose: *football ground; burial grounds* **5** land having a particular characteristic: *level ground; high ground* **6** matter for consideration or debate; field of research or inquiry: *the lecture was familiar ground to him; the report covered a lot of ground* **7** a position or viewpoint, as in an argument or controversy (esp in the phrases **give ground, hold, stand,** *or* **shift one's ground**) **8** position or advantage, as in a subject or competition (esp in the phrases **gain ground, lose ground,** etc) **9** (*often plural*) reason; justification: *grounds for complaint* **10** *arts* **a** the prepared surface applied to the support of a painting, such as a wall, canvas, etc, to prevent it reacting with or absorbing the paint **b** the background of a painting or main surface against which the other parts of a work of art appear superimposed **11 a** the first coat of paint applied to a surface **b** (*as modifier*): *ground colour* **12** the bottom of a river or the sea **13** (*plural*) sediment or dregs, esp from coffee **14** *chiefly Brit* the floor of a room **15** *cricket* the area from the popping crease back past the stumps, in which a batsman may legally stand **16** *electrical, US & Canadian* a connection between an electrical circuit or device and the earth, which is at zero potential **17 break new ground** to do something that has not been done before **18 cut the ground from under someone's feet** to anticipate someone's action or argument and thus make it irrelevant or meaningless **19 to the ground** *or* **down to the ground** *Brit informal* completely; absolutely: *it suited him down to the ground* **20 into the ground** beyond what is requisite or can be endured; to exhaustion **21** (*modifier*) concerned with or operating on the ground, esp as distinct from in the air ▷ *vb* **22** (*tr*) to put or place on the ground **23** (*tr*) to instruct in fundamentals **24** (*tr*) to provide a basis or foundation for; establish **25** (*tr*) to confine (an aircraft, pilot, etc) to the ground **26** (*tr*) *informal* to confine (a child) to the house as a punishment **27** the usual US word for **earth** (sense 14) **28** (*tr*) *nautical* to run (a vessel) aground **29** (*intr*) to hit or reach the ground [Old English *grund*; related to Old Norse *grunn* shallow, *grunnr, grund* plain, Old High German *grunt*]

ground² (graʊnd) *vb* **1** the past tense and past participle of **grind** ▷ *adj* **2** having the surface finished, thickness reduced, or an edge sharpened by grinding **3** reduced to fine particles by grinding

groundage ('graʊndɪdʒ) *n* *Brit* a fee levied on a vessel entering a port or anchored off a shore

groundbait ('graʊnd,beɪt) *n* *angling* bait, such as scraps of bread, maggots, etc, thrown into an area of water to attract fish

ground bass *or* **ground** (beɪs) *n* *music* a short melodic bass line that is repeated over and over again

ground-breaking *adj* innovative: *a ground-breaking novel*

ground control *n* **1** the personnel, radar, computers, etc, on the ground that monitor the progress of aircraft or spacecraft **2** a system for feeding continuous radio messages to an aircraft pilot to enable him to make a blind landing

ground cover *n* dense low herbaceous plants and shrubs that grow over the surface of the ground, esp in a forest, preventing soil erosion or, in a garden, stifling weeds

grounded ('graʊndɪd) *adj* sensible and down-to-earth; having one's feet on the ground

ground elder *n* another name for **goutweed**

ground floor *n* the floor of a building level or almost level with the ground **1 get in on the ground floor** *or* **start from the ground floor** *informal* to be in a project, undertaking, etc, from its inception

ground frost *n* the condition resulting from a temperature reading of 0°C or below on a thermometer in contact with a grass surface

ground glass *n* **1** glass that has a rough surface produced by grinding, used for diffusing light **2** glass in the form of fine particles produced by grinding, used as an abrasive

groundhog ('graʊnd,hɒg) *n* another name for **woodchuck**

grounding ('graʊndɪŋ) *n* a basic knowledge of or training in a subject

ground ivy n a creeping or trailing Eurasian aromatic herbaceous plant, *Glechoma* (or *Nepeta*) *hederacea*, with scalloped leaves and purplish-blue flowers: family *Lamiaceae* (labiates)

groundless ('graʊndlɪs) *adj* without reason or justification: *his suspicions were groundless* > **'groundlessly** *adv* > **'groundlessness** n

groundling ('graʊndlɪŋ) n 1 any animal or plant that lives close to the ground or at the bottom of a lake, river, etc 2 (in Elizabethan theatre) a spectator standing in the yard in front of the stage and paying least 3 a person on the ground as distinguished from one in an aircraft

groundnut ('graʊnd,nʌt) n 1 a North American climbing leguminous plant, *Apios tuberosa*, with fragrant brown flowers and small edible underground tubers 2 the tuber of this plant 3 *Brit* another name for **peanut**

ground plan n 1 a drawing of the ground floor of a building, esp one to scale 2 a preliminary or basic outline

ground plate n a joist forming the lowest member of a timber frame. Also called: **groundsill, soleplate**

ground rule n a procedural rule or principle

groundsel ('graʊnsəl) n any of certain plants of the genus *Senecio*, esp *S. vulgaris*, a Eurasian weed with heads of small yellow flowers: family *Asteraceae* (composites) [Old English *grundeswelge*, changed from *gundeswilge*, from *gund* pus + *swelgan* to swallow; after its use in poultices on abscesses]

groundshare ('graʊnd,ʃeə) *vb* 1 (*intr*) to share the facilities and running costs of a single stadium with another team ▷ n 2 an arrangement, often temporary, whereby two sporting clubs share one stadium

groundsheet ('graʊnd,ʃiːt) or **ground cloth** n a waterproof rubber, plastic, or polythene sheet placed on the ground in a tent, etc, to keep out damp

groundsill ('graʊnd,sɪl) n another name for **ground plate**

groundsman ('graʊndzmən) n, *pl* **-men** a person employed to maintain a sports ground, park, etc

groundspeed ('graʊnd,spiːd) n the speed of an aircraft relative to the ground

ground squirrel n any burrowing sciurine rodent of the genus *Citellus* and related genera, resembling chipmunks and occurring in North America, E Europe, and Asia. Also called: **gopher**

groundswell ('graʊnd,swɛl) n 1 a considerable swell of the sea, often caused by a distant storm or earthquake or by the passage of waves into shallow water 2 a strong public feeling or opinion that is detectable even though not openly expressed

ground water n underground water that has come mainly from the seepage of surface water and is held in pervious rocks

groundwork ('graʊnd,wɜːk) n 1 preliminary work as a foundation or basis 2 the ground or background of a painting, etc

ground zero n a point on the surface of land or water at or directly above or below the centre of a nuclear explosion

group (gruːp) n 1 a number of persons or things considered as a collective unit 2 a a number of persons bound together by common social standards, interests, etc b (*as modifier*): *group behaviour* 3 a small band of players or singers, esp of pop music 4 a number of animals or plants considered as a unit because of common characteristics, habits, etc 5 an association of companies under a single ownership and control, consisting of a holding company, subsidiary companies, and sometimes associated companies 6 two or more figures or objects forming a design or unit in a design, in a painting or sculpture 7 a military formation comprising complementary arms and services, usually for a purpose: *a brigade group* 8 an air force organization of higher level than a squadron 9 Also called: **radical** *chem* two or more atoms that are bound together as a single unit in a molecule and behave as a single unit: *a methyl group* -CH$_3$ 10 a vertical column of elements in the periodic table that all have similar electronic structures, properties, and valencies 11 *maths* a set that has an associated operation that combines any two members of the set to give another member and that also contains an identity element and an inverse for each element 12 See **blood group** ▷ *vb* 13 to arrange or place (things, people, etc) in or into a group or (of things, etc) to form into a group [c17: from French *groupe*, of Germanic origin; compare Italian *gruppo*; see **CROP**]

group captain n an officer holding commissioned rank senior to a wing commander but junior to an air commodore in the RAF and certain other air forces

group dynamics n (*functioning as singular*) *psychol* a field of social psychology concerned with the nature of human groups, their development, and their interactions with individuals, other groups, and larger organizations

grouper ('gruːpə) n a variant of **groper**

groupie ('gruːpɪ) n *slang* 1 an ardent fan of a celebrity, esp a pop star: originally, often a girl who followed the members of a pop group on tour in order to have sexual relations with them 2 an enthusiastic follower of some activity: *a political groupie*

Group of Eight n the Group of Seven nations and Russia, whose heads of government meet to discuss economic matters and international relations. Abbreviation: **G8**

Group of Five n France, Japan, UK, US, and Germany acting as a group to stabilize their currency exchange rates. Abbreviation: **G5**

Group of Seven n the seven leading industrial nations, Canada, France, Germany, Italy, Japan, UK, and the US, whose heads of government and finance ministers meet regularly to coordinate economic policy. Abbreviation: **G7**

Group of Seventy-Seven n the developing countries of the world. Abbreviation: **G77**

Group of Ten n the ten nations who met in Paris in 1961 to arrange the special drawing rights of the IMF; Belgium, Canada, France, Italy, Japan, Netherlands, Sweden, UK, US, and West Germany. Abbreviation: **G10**

Group of Three n Japan, US, and Germany (formerly West Germany), regarded as the largest western industrialized nations. Abbreviation: **G3**

Group of Twenty-Four n the twenty-four richest and most industrialized countries of the world. Abbreviation: **G24**

group practice n a medical practice undertaken by a group of associated doctors who work together as partners or as specialists in different areas

group therapy n *psychol* the simultaneous treatment of a number of individuals who are members of a natural group or who are brought together to share their problems in group discussion

groupuscule ('gruːpə,skjuːl) n *usually derogatory* a small group within a political party or movement [c20: from French: small group]

groupware ('gruːp,weə) n software that enables computers within a group or organization to work together, allowing users to exchange electronic-mail messages, access shared files and databases, use video conferencing, etc

grouse¹ (graʊs) n, *pl* **grouse** or **grouses** 1 any gallinaceous bird of the family *Tetraonidae*, occurring mainly in the N hemisphere, having a stocky body and feathered legs and feet. They are popular game birds ▷ *adj* 2 *Austral & NZ slang* excellent [c16: of unknown origin]

grouse² (graʊs) *vb* 1 (*intr*) to grumble; complain ▷ n 2 a persistent complaint [c19: of unknown origin] > **'grouser** n

grout (graʊt) n 1 a thin mortar for filling joints between tiles, masonry, etc 2 a fine plaster used as a finishing coat ▷ *vb* 3 (*tr*) to fill (joints) or finish (walls, etc) with grout [Old English *grūt*; related to Old Frisian *grēt* sand, Middle High German *grūz*, Middle Dutch *grūte* coarse meal; see **GRIT, GROATS**] > **'grouter** n

grove (grəʊv) n 1 a small wooded area or plantation 2 a road lined with houses and often trees, esp in a suburban area [Old English *grāf*; related to *grǣfa* thicket, **GREAVE**, Norwegian *greivla* to intertwine]

grovel ('grɒvᵊl) *vb* **-els, -elling, -elled** or *US* **-els, -eling,**

-eled (*intr*) **1** to humble or abase oneself, as in making apologies or showing respect **2** to lie or crawl face downwards, as in fear or humility **3** (often foll by *in*) to indulge or take pleasure (in sensuality or vice) [c16: back formation from obsolete *groveling* (adv), from Middle English *on grufe* on the face, of Scandinavian origin; compare Old Norse *ā grūfu*, from *grūfa* prone position; see -LING²] > 'groveller *n*

Groves (grəʊvz) *n* Sir **Charles**. 1915–92, English orchestral conductor

grow (grəʊ) *vb* **grows, growing, grew** (gruː), **grown** (grəʊn) **1** (of an organism or part of an organism) to increase in size or develop (hair, leaves, or other structures) **2** (*intr*; usually foll by *out of* or *from*) to originate, as from an initial cause or source: *the federation grew out of the Empire* **3** (*intr*) to increase in size, number, degree, etc: *the population is growing rapidly* **4** (*intr*) to change in length or amount in a specified direction: *some plants grow downwards; profits over the years grew downwards* **5** (*copula; may take an infinitive*) (esp of emotions, physical states, etc) to develop or come into existence or being gradually: *to grow cold; to grow morose; he grew to like her* **6** (*intr*; foll by *together*) to be joined gradually by or as by growth **7** (when *intr*, foll by *with*) to become covered with a growth: *the path grew with weeds* **8** to produce (plants) by controlling or encouraging their growth, esp for home consumption or on a commercial basis ▷ See also **grow into, grow on, grow out of, grow up** [Old English *grōwan*; related to Old Norse *grōa*, Old Frisian *grōia*, Old High German *gruoen*; see GREEN, GRASS] > 'grower *n*

grow bag *n* a plastic bag containing a sufficient amount of a sterile growing medium and nutrients to enable a plant, such as a tomato or pepper, to be grown to full size in it, usually for one season only [c20: from *Gro-bag*, trademark for the first ones marketed]

growing pains *pl n* **1** pains in muscles or joints sometimes experienced by children during a period of unusually rapid growth **2** difficulties besetting a new enterprise in its early stages

grow into *vb* (*intr, preposition*) to become big or mature enough for: *his clothes were always big enough for him to grow into*

growl (graʊl) *vb* **1** (of animals, esp when hostile) to utter (sounds) in a low inarticulate manner: *the dog growled at us* **2** to utter (words) in a gruff or angry manner **3** (*intr*) to make sounds suggestive of an animal growling: *the thunder growled around the lake* ▷ *n* **4** the act or sound of growling [c18: from earlier *grolle*, from Old French *grouller* to grumble] > 'growler *n* (ˈgraʊlə)

grown (grəʊn) *adj* **a** developed or advanced: *fully grown* **b** (*in combination*): *half-grown*

grown-up *adj* **1** having reached maturity; adult **2** suitable for or characteristic of an adult ▷ *n* **3** an adult

grow on *vb* (*intr, preposition*) to become progressively more acceptable or pleasant to

grow out of *vb* (*intr, adverb + preposition*) to become too big or mature for: *she soon grew out of her girlish ways*

growth (grəʊθ) *n* **1** the process or act of growing, esp in organisms following assimilation of food **2** an increase in size, number, significance, etc **3** something grown or growing: *a new growth of hair* **4** a stage of development **5** any abnormal tissue, such as a tumour **6** (*modifier*) of, relating to, causing or characterized by growth: *a growth industry; growth hormone*

growth curve *n* a curve on a graph in which a variable is plotted against time to illustrate the growth of the variable

growth hormone *n* a hormone synthesized in and secreted by the anterior lobe of the pituitary gland that promotes growth of the long bones in the limbs and increases the synthesis of protein essential for growth. Also called: **somatotrophin, human growth hormone**

grow up *vb* (*intr, adverb*) **1** to reach maturity; become adult **2** to come into existence; develop

groyne *or esp US* **groin** (grɔɪn) *n* a wall or jetty built out from a riverbank or seashore to control erosion. Also called: **spur, breakwater** [c16: origin uncertain: perhaps altered from GROIN]

Grozny (*Russian* 'grɔznij) *n* a city in S Russia, capital of the Chechen Republic: a major oil centre: it was badly damaged during fighting between separatists and Russian troops (1994–95, 1999–2000). Pop: 199 000 (2005 est)

grub (grʌb) *vb* **grubs, grubbing, grubbed 1** (when *tr*, often foll by *up* or *out*) to search for and pull up (roots, stumps, etc) by digging in the ground **2** to dig up the surface of (ground, soil, etc), esp to clear away roots, stumps, etc **3** (*intr*; often foll by *in* or *among*) to search carefully **4** (*intr*) to work unceasingly, esp at a dull task or research ▷ *n* **5** the short legless larva of certain insects, esp beetles **6** *slang* food; victuals **7** a person who works hard, esp in a dull plodding way [c13: of Germanic origin; compare Old High German *grubilōn* to dig, German *grübeln* to rack one's brain, Middle Dutch *grobben* to scrape together; see GRAVE³, GROOVE]

grubber ('grʌbə) *n* **1** a person who grubs **2** *rugby* a kick of the ball along the ground

grubby ('grʌbɪ) *adj* **-bier, -biest 1** dirty; slovenly **2** mean; beggarly **3** infested with grubs > 'grubbily *adv* > 'grubbiness *n*

grub screw *n* a small headless screw having a slot cut for a screwdriver or a socket for a hexagon key and used to secure a sliding component in a determined position

grubstake ('grʌb,steɪk) *n* **1** *US & Canadian informal* supplies provided for a prospector on the condition that the donor has a stake in any finds ▷ *vb* (*tr*) **2** *US informal* to furnish with such supplies **3** *chiefly US & Canadian* to supply (a person) with a stake in a gambling game > 'grub,staker *n*

Grub Street *n* **1** a former street in London frequented by literary hacks and needy authors **2** the world or class of literary hacks, etc. Also called: 'Grub,street *adj* **3** (*sometimes not capital*) relating to or characteristic of hack literature

grudge (grʌdʒ) *n* **1** a persistent feeling of resentment, esp one due to some cause, such as an insult or injury **2** (*modifier*) planned or carried out in order to settle a grudge: *a grudge fight* ▷ *vb* **3** (*tr*) to give or allow unwillingly **4** to feel resentful or envious about (someone else's success, possessions, etc) [c15: from Old French *grouchier* to grumble, probably of Germanic origin; compare Old High German *grunnizōn* to grunt] > 'grudging *adj* > 'grudgingly *adv*

grue (gruː) *Scot n* **1** a shiver or shudder; a creeping of the flesh ▷ *vb* (*intr*) **2** to shiver or shudder **3** to feel strong aversion [c14: of Scandinavian origin; compare Old Swedish *grua*, Old Danish *grue*; related to German *graven*, Dutch *gruwen* to abhor]

gruel ('gruːəl) *n* a drink or thin porridge, made by boiling meal, esp oatmeal, in water or milk [c14: from Old French, of Germanic origin; see GROUT]

gruelling *or US* **grueling** ('gruːəlɪŋ) *adj* **1** severe or tiring ▷ *n* **2** *informal* a severe experience, esp punishment [c19: from now obsolete *vb gruel* to exhaust, punish]

gruesome ('gruːsəm) *adj* inspiring repugnance and horror; ghastly [c16: originally Northern English and Scottish; see GRUE, -SOME¹] > 'gruesomely *adv* > 'gruesomeness *n*

gruff (grʌf) *adj* **1** rough or surly in manner, speech, etc: *a gruff reply* **2** (of a voice, bark, etc) low and throaty [c16: originally Scottish, from Dutch *grof*, of Germanic origin; compare Old High German *girob*; related to Old English *hrēof*, Lithuanian *kraupùs*] > 'gruffly *adv* > 'gruffness *n*

grumble ('grʌmbᵊl) *vb* **1** to utter (complaints) in a nagging or discontented way **2** (*intr*) to make low dull rumbling sounds ▷ *n* **3** a complaint; grouse **4** a low rumbling sound [c16: from Middle German *grommelen*, of Germanic origin; see GRIM] > 'grumbler *n* > 'grumblingly *adv* > 'grumbly *adj*

grumbling appendix *n informal* a condition in which the appendix causes intermittent pain but appendicitis has not developed

grummet ('grʌmɪt) *n* another word for **grommet**

grump (grʌmp) *informal* ▷ *n* **1** a surly or bad-tempered person **2** (*plural*) a sulky or morose mood (esp in the phrase **have the grumps**) ▷ *vb* **3** (*intr*) to complain or grumble: *is he grumping again?* [c18: dialect *grump* surly

remark, probably of imitative origin]

grumpy ('grʌmpɪ) or **grumpish** ('grʌmpɪʃ) adj grumpier, grumpiest peevish; sulky [c18: from GRUMP + -Y¹] > 'grumpily or 'grumpishly adv > 'grumpiness, 'grumpishness n

Grundy ('grʌndɪ) n a narrow-minded person who keeps critical watch on the propriety of others [c18: named after Mrs Grundy, the character in T. Morton's play Speed the Plough (1798)] > 'Grundy,ism > 'Grundyist or 'Grundyite n

Grünewald (German 'gry:nəvalt) n **Matthias** (ma'ti:as), original name Mathis Gothardt. ?1470–1528, German painter, the greatest exponent of late Gothic art in Germany. The Isenheim Altarpiece is regarded as his masterpiece

grunge (grʌndʒ) n **1** US slang dirt or rubbish **2** a style of rock music originating in the US in the late 1980s, featuring a distorted guitar sound **3** a deliberately untidy and uncoordinated fashion style [c20: possibly a coinage imitating GRIME + SLUDGE]

grungy ('grʌndʒɪ) adj -gier, -giest slang **1** chiefly US & Canadian squalid or seedy **2** (of pop music) characterized by a loud fuzzy guitar sound

grunion ('grʌnjən) n a Californian marine teleost fish, Leuresthes tenuis, that spawns on beaches: family Atherinidae (silversides) [c20: probably from Spanish gruñón a grunter]

grunt (grʌnt) vb **1** (intr) (esp of pigs and some other animals) to emit a low short gruff noise **2** (when tr, may take a clause as object) to express something gruffly: he grunted his answer ▷ n **3** the characteristic low short gruff noise of pigs, etc, or a similar sound, as of disgust **4** any of various mainly tropical marine sciaenid fishes, such as Haemulon macrostomum (**Spanish grunt**), that utter a grunting sound when caught [Old English grunnettan, probably of imitative origin; compare Old High German grunnizōn, grunni moaning, Latin grunnīre] > 'grunter n

Gruyère or **Gruyère cheese** ('gru:jɛə; French gryjɛr) n a hard flat whole-milk cheese, pale yellow in colour and with holes [c19: after Gruyère, Switzerland where it originated]

gr. wt. abbreviation gross weight

gryphon ('grɪfᵊn) n a variant of **griffin¹**

grysbok ('graɪs,bɒk) n either of two small antelopes, Raphicerus melanotis or R. sharpei, of central and southern Africa, having small straight horns [c18: Afrikaans, from Dutch grijs grey + bok BUCK¹]

GS abbreviation **1** General Secretary **2** General Staff

GSM abbreviation Global System for Mobile Communications

GST abbreviation (in Australia, New Zealand, and Canada) goods and services tax

G-string n **1** a piece of cloth attached to a narrow waistband covering the pubic area, worn esp by strippers **2** a strip of cloth attached to the front and back of a waistband and covering the loins **3** music a string tuned to G, such as the lowest string of a violin

G-suit n a close-fitting garment covering the legs and abdomen that is worn by the crew of high-speed aircraft and can be pressurized to prevent blackout during certain manoeuvres [c20: from g(ravity) suit]

GSVQ abbreviation (in Britain) General Scottish Vocational Qualification. See GNVQ

GT abbreviation gran turismo: a high-performance luxury sports car with a hard fixed roof, designed for covering long distances

GTA abbreviation for Greater Toronto Area

gtd abbreviation guaranteed

Guadalajara (,gwɑ:dᵊlə'hɑ:rə; Spanish gwaðala'xara) n **1** a city in W Mexico, capital of Jalisco state: the second largest city of Mexico: centre of the Indian slave trade until its abolition, declared here in 1810; two universities (1792 and 1935). Pop: 3 905 000 (2005 est) **2** a city in central Spain, in New Castile. Pop: 70 732 (2003 est)

Guadalcanal (,gwɑ:dᵊlkə'næl; Spanish gwaðalka'nal) n a mountainous island in the SW Pacific, the largest of the Solomon Islands: under British protection until 1978; occupied by the Japanese (1942–43). Pop: 109 382 (1999).

Area: 6475 sq km (2500 sq miles)

Guadalquivir (,gwɑ:dᵊlkwɪ'vɪə; Spanish gwaðalki'βir) n the chief river of S Spain, rising in the Sierra de Segura and flowing west and southwest to the Gulf of Cádiz: navigable by ocean-going vessels to Seville. Length: 560 km (348 miles)

Guadalupe Hidalgo (,gwɑ:dᵊlu:p hɪ'dælgəʊ; Spanish gwaða'lupe i'ðalɣo) n the former name (until 1931) of Gustavo A. Madero

Guadeloupe (,gwɑ:dᵊlu:p) n an overseas region of France in the E Caribbean, in the Leeward Islands, formed by the islands of Basse-Terre and Grande-Terre and several offlying islands; in 2007 the island of Saint-Barthélemy and the part-island dependency of Saint-Martin were separated from Guadeloupe to become Overseas Collectivities directly subordinate to France. Capital: Basse-Terre. Pop: 443 000 (2004 est). Area: 1780 sq km (687 sq miles)

Guadiana (Spanish gwa'ðjana; Portuguese gwa'ðjɐnə) n a river in SW Europe, rising in S central Spain and flowing west, then south as part of the border between Spain and Portugal, to the Gulf of Cádiz. Length: 578 km (359 miles)

guaiacum or **guaiocum** ('gwaɪəkəm) n **1** any tropical American evergreen tree of the zygophyllaceous genus Guaiacum, such as the lignum vitae **2** the hard heavy wood of any of these trees **3** Also called: guaiac ('gwaɪæk) a brownish resin obtained from the lignum vitae, used medicinally and in making varnishes [c16: New Latin, from Spanish guayaco, of Taino origin]

Guam (gwɑ:m) n an island in the N Pacific, the largest and southernmost of the Marianas: belonged to Spain from the 17th century until 1898, when it was ceded to the US; site of naval and air force bases. Capital: Agana (now officially spelt Hagåtña). Pop: 165 000 (2004 est). Area: 541 sq km (209 sq miles)

Guamanian (gwɑ:'meɪnɪən) adj **1** of or relating to Guam or its inhabitants ▷ n **2** a native or inhabitant of Guam

Guanabara (Portuguese gwənə'bara) n (until 1975) a state of SE Brazil, on the Atlantic and **Guanabara Bay**, now amalgamated with the state of Rio de Janeiro

guanaco (gwɑ:'nɑ:kəʊ) n, pl -cos a cud-chewing South American artiodactyl mammal, Lama guanicoe, closely related to the domesticated llama: family Camelidae [c17: from Spanish, from Quechuan huanacu]

Guanajuato (Spanish gwana'xwato) n **1** a state of central Mexico, on the great central plateau: mountainous in the north, with fertile plains in the south; important mineral resources. Capital: Guanajuato. Pop: 4 656 761 (2000). Area: 30 588 sq km (11 810 sq miles) **2** a city in central Mexico, capital of Guanajuato state: founded in 1554, it became one of the world's richest silver-mining centres. Pop: 80 000 (2005 est)

Guangdong ('gwæŋ'dʊŋ) or **Kwangtung** n a province of SE China, on the South China Sea: includes the Leizhou Peninsula, with densely populated river valleys; traditionally also including Macao and Hong Kong; the only true tropical climate in China. Capital: Canton. Pop: Pop: 79 540 000 (2003 est). Area: 197 100 sq km (76 100 sq miles)

Guangxi Zhuang Autonomous Region ('gwæŋ'si: 'dʒwæŋ) or **Kwangsi-Chuang Autonomous Region** n an administrative division of S China. Capital: Nanning. Pop: 48 570 000 (2003 est). Area: 220 400 sq km (85 100 sq miles)

Guangzhou ('gwæŋ'dzəʊ) n the Pinyin transliteration of the Chinese name for **Canton**

guanine ('gwa:ni:n, 'gu:ə,ni:n) n a white almost insoluble compound: one of the purine bases in nucleic acids. Formula: $C_5H_5N_5O$ [c19: from GUANO + -INE²]

guano ('gwa:nəʊ) n, pl -nos **1 a** a dried excrement of fish-eating sea birds, deposited in rocky coastal regions of South America: contains the urates, oxalates, and phosphates of ammonium and calcium; used as a fertilizer **b** the accumulated droppings of bats and seals **2** any similar but artificial substance used as a fertilizer [c17: from Spanish, from Quechuan huano dung]

Guantánamo (Spanish gwan'tanamo) n a city in SE Cuba, on **Guantánamo Bay**. Pop: 214 000 (2005 est)

Guantánamo Bay Naval Base n a US naval base on Guantánamo Bay; since 2002, a detainment camp for suspected al-Qaeda and Taliban operatives

guanxi (ˌgwænˈsiː) n a Chinese social concept based on the exchange of favours, in which personal relationships are considered more important than laws and written agreements [C20: Chinese: relationships]

Guaporé (Portuguese gwapoˈrɛ) n 1 a river in W central South America, rising in SW Brazil and flowing northwest as part of the border between Brazil and Bolivia, to join the Mamoré River. Length: 1750 km (1087 miles). Spanish name: **Iténez** 2 the former name (until 1956) of: **Rondônia**

Guarani (ˌgwaːrəˈniː) n 1 pl -ni or -nis a member of a South American Indian people of Paraguay, S Brazil, and Bolivia 2 the language of this people, belonging to the Tupi-Guarani family; one of the official languages of Paraguay, along with Spanish

guarantee (ˌgærənˈtiː) n 1 a formal assurance, esp in writing, that a product, service, etc, will meet certain standards or specifications 2 law a promise, esp a collateral agreement, to answer for the debt, default, or miscarriage of another 3 a a person, company, etc, to whom a guarantee is made b a person, company, etc, who gives a guarantee 4 a person who acts as a guarantor 5 something that makes a specified condition or outcome certain 6 a variant spelling of **guaranty** ▷ vb -tees, -teeing, -teed (mainly tr) 7 (also tr) to take responsibility for (someone else's debts, obligations, etc) 8 to serve as a guarantee for 9 to secure or furnish security for: a small deposit will guarantee any dress 10 (usually foll by from or against) to undertake to protect or keep secure, as against injury, loss, etc 11 to ensure: good planning will guarantee success 12 (may take a clause as object or an infinitive) to promise or make certain [C17: perhaps from Spanish garante or French garant, of Germanic origin; compare WARRANT]

guarantor (ˌgærənˈtɔː) n a person who gives or is bound by a guarantee or guaranty; surety

guaranty (ˈgærəntɪ) n, pl -ties 1 a pledge of responsibility for fulfilling another person's obligations in case of that person's default 2 a thing given or taken as security for a guaranty 3 the act of providing security 4 a person who acts as a guarantor ▷ vb -ties, -tying, -tied 5 a variant of **guarantee** [C16: from Old French garantie, variant of warantie, of Germanic origin; see WARRANTY]

guard (gaːd) vb 1 to watch over or shield (a person or thing) from danger or harm; protect 2 to keep watch over (a prisoner or other potentially dangerous person or thing), as to prevent escape 3 (tr) to control: to guard one's tongue 4 (intr; usually foll by against) to take precautions 5 to control entrance and exit through (a gate, door, etc) 6 (tr) to provide (machinery, etc) with a device to protect the operator 7 (tr) a chess, cards to protect or cover (a chess man or card) with another b curling, bowling to protect or cover (a stone or bowl) by placing one's own stone or bowl between it and another player ▷ n 8 a person or group who keeps a protecting, supervising, or restraining watch or control over people, such as prisoners, things, etc. Related adj: **custodial** 9 a person or group of people, such as soldiers, who form a ceremonial escort 10 Brit the official in charge of a train 11 a the act or duty of protecting, restraining, or supervising b (as modifier): guard duty 12 a device, part, or attachment on an object, such as a weapon or machine tool, designed to protect the user against injury, as on the hilt of a sword or the trigger of a firearm 13 anything that provides or is intended to provide protection: a guard against infection 14 sport an article of light tough material worn to protect any of various parts of the body 15 the posture of defence or readiness in fencing, boxing, cricket, etc 16 off one's guard having one's defences down; unprepared 17 on one's guard prepared to face danger, difficulties, etc 18 stand guard (of a military sentry, etc) to keep watch 19 mount guard a (of a sentry) to begin to keep watch b (with over) to take up a protective or defensive stance (over something) [C15: from Old French garde, from garder to

protect, of Germanic origin; compare Spanish guardar; see WARD] ▷ 'guarder n

Guardafui (ˌgwaːdəˈfuːɪ) n Cape Guardafui a cape at the NE tip of Somalia, extending into the Indian Ocean

guarded (ˈgaːdɪd) adj 1 protected or kept under surveillance 2 prudent, restrained, or noncommittal: a guarded reply ▷ 'guardedly adv ▷ 'guardedness n

guard hair n any of the coarse hairs that form the outer fur in certain mammals, rising above the underfur

guardhouse (ˈgaːdˌhaʊs) n military a building serving as the headquarters or a post for military police and in which military prisoners are detained

Guardi (Italian ˈgwardi) n **Francesco** (franˈtʃesko). 1712–93, Venetian landscape painter

guardian (ˈgaːdɪən) n 1 one who looks after, protects, or defends: the guardian of public morals 2 law someone legally appointed to manage the affairs of a person incapable of acting for himself, as a minor or person of unsound mind ▷ adj 3 protecting or safeguarding ▷ 'guardianˌship n

Guardian Angels pl n vigilante volunteers who patrol the underground railway in New York, London, and elsewhere, wearing red berets, to deter violent crime

guard ring n 1 Also called: guard, keeper ring jewellery an extra ring worn to prevent another from slipping off the finger 2 an electrode used to counteract distortion of the electric fields at the edges of other electrodes in a capacitor or electron lens

Guards (gaːdz) pl n (esp in European armies) any of various regiments responsible for ceremonial duties and, formerly, the protection of the head of state: the Life Guards; the Grenadier Guards

guardsman (ˈgaːdzmən) n, pl -men 1 (in Britain) a member of a Guards battalion or regiment 2 (in the US) a member of the National Guard 3 a guard

guard's van n railways, Brit & NZ the van in which the guard travels, usually attached to the rear of a train. US and Canadian equivalent: caboose

Guarneri[1] (gwaːˈnɪərɪ; Italian gwarˈnɛːri), **Guarnieri** (Italian gwarˈnjeːri) or **Guarnerius** (gwaːˈnɛərɪəs) n, pl Guarneris, Guarnieris, Guarneriuses 1 an Italian family of 17th- and 18th-century violin-makers 2 any violin made by a member of this family

Guarneri[2] (gwaːˈnɪərɪ; Italian gwarˈnɛːri), **Guarnieri** (Italian gwarˈnjeːri) or **Guarnerius** (gwaːˈnɛərɪəs) n, pl Guarneris, Guarnieris or Guarneriuses any violin made by a member of the Guarneri family (active in Italy in the 17th and 18th centuries)

Guat. abbreviation Guatemala

Guatemala (ˌgwaːtəˈmaːlə) n a republic in Central America: original Maya Indians conquered by the Spanish in 1523; became the centre of Spanish administration in Central America; gained independence and was annexed to Mexico in 1821, becoming an independent republic in 1839. Official language: Spanish. Religion: Roman Catholic majority. Currency: quetzal and US dollar. Capital: Guatemala City. Pop: 12 661 000 (2004 est). Area: 108 889 sq km (42 042 sq miles)

Guatemala City n the capital of Guatemala, in the southeast: founded in 1776 to replace the former capital, Antigua Guatemala, after an earthquake; university (1676). Pop: 982 000 (2005 est)

Guatemalan (ˌgwaːtəˈmaːlən) adj 1 of or relating to Guatemala or its inhabitants ▷ n 2 a native or inhabitant of Guatemala

guava (ˈgwaːvə) n 1 any of various tropical American trees of the myrtaceous genus Psidium, esp P. guajava, grown in tropical regions for their edible fruit 2 the fruit of such a tree, having yellow skin and pink pulp: used to make jellies, jams, etc [C16: from Spanish guayaba, from a South American Indian word]

Guayaquil (Spanish gwaja'kil) n a port in W Ecuador: the largest city in the country and its chief port; university (1867). Pop: 2 387 000 (2005 est)

guayule (gwəˈjuːlɪ) n 1 a bushy shrub, Parthenium argentatum, of the southwestern US: family Asteraceae (composites) 2 rubber derived from the sap of this plant [from American Spanish, from Nahuatl cuauhuli, from *cuahuitl* tree + *uli* gum]

gubbins ('gʌbɪnz) *n informal* **1** (*functioning as singular*) an object of little or no value **2** (*functioning as singular*) a small device or gadget **3** (*functioning as plural*) odds and ends; litter or rubbish **4** (*functioning as singular*) a silly person [C16 (meaning: fragments): from obsolete *gobbon*, probably related to GOBBET]

gubernatorial (,gju:bənə'tɔ:rɪəl, ,gu:-) *adj chiefly US* of or relating to a governor [C18: from Latin *gubernātor* governor]

guddle ('gʌdəl) *Scot* ▷ *vb* **1** to catch (fish) by groping with the hands under the banks or stones of a stream ▷ *n* **2** a muddle; confusion [C19: of unknown origin]

gudgeon¹ ('gʌdʒən) *n* **1** a small slender European freshwater cyprinid fish, *Gobio gobio*, with a barbel on each side of the mouth: used as bait by anglers **2** any of various other fishes, such as the goby **3** *slang* a person who is easy to trick or cheat ▷ *vb* **4** (*tr*) *slang* to trick or cheat [C15: from Old French *gougon*, probably from Latin *gōbius*; see GOBY]

gudgeon² ('gʌdʒən) *n* **1** the female or socket portion of a pinned hinge **2** *nautical* one of two or more looplike sockets, fixed to the transom of a boat, into which the pintles of a rudder are fitted [C14: from Old French *goujon*, perhaps from Late Latin *gulbia* chisel]

gudgeon pin *n Brit* the pin through the skirt of a piston in an internal-combustion engine, to which the little end of the connecting rod is attached. US and Canadian name: **wrist pin**

Gudrun ('gʊdru:n), **Guthrun** ('gʊðru:n) *or* **Kudrun** ('kudru:n) *n Norse myth* the wife of Sigurd and, after his death, of Atli, whom she slew for his murder of her brother Gunnar. She corresponds to Kriemhild in the *Nibelungenlied*

guelder-rose ('gɛldə,rəʊz) *n* a Eurasian caprifoliaceous shrub, *Viburnum opulus*, with clusters of white flowers and small red fruits [C16: from Dutch *geldersche roos*, from *Gelderland* or *Gelders*, province of Holland]

Guelders ('gɛldəz) *n* another name for **Gelderland**

Guelph (gwelf) *n* a city in Canada, in SE Ontario. Pop: 106 920 (2001)

guenon (gə'nɒn) *n* any slender agile Old World monkey of the genus *Cercopithecus*, inhabiting wooded regions of Africa and having long hind limbs and tail and long hair surrounding the face [C19: from French, of unknown origin]

guerdon ('gɜ:dʰn) *poetic* ▷ *n* **1** a reward or payment ▷ *vb* **2** (*tr*) to give a guerdon to [C14: from Old French *gueredon*, of Germanic origin; compare Old High German *widarlōn*, Old English *witherlēan*; final element influenced by Latin *dōnum* gift]

Guericke (*German* 'ge:rɪkə) *n* **Otto von**. 1602–86, German physicist: invented the air pump (1650) and demonstrated the power of a vacuum with the Magdeburg hemispheres

Guernica (gɜ:'ni:kə, 'gɜ:nɪkə; *Spanish* gɛr'nika) *n* a town in N Spain: formerly the seat of a Basque parliament; destroyed in 1937 by German bombers during the Spanish Civil War, an event depicted in one of Picasso's most famous paintings. Pop: 15 454 (2003 est)

Guernsey ('gɜ:nzɪ) *n* **1** an island in the English Channel: the second largest of the Channel Islands, which, with Alderney and Sark, Herm, Jethou, and some islets, forms the bailiwick of Guernsey; finance, market gardening, dairy farming, and tourism. Capital: St Peter Port. Pop: 59 710 (2001). Area: 63 sq km (24.5 sq miles) **2** a breed of dairy cattle producing rich creamy milk, originating from the island of Guernsey **3** (*sometimes not capital*) a seaman's knitted woollen sweater **4** (*not capital*) *Austral* a sleeveless woollen shirt or jumper worn by a football player **5 get a guernsey** *Austral* to be selected or gain recognition for something

Guerrero (*Spanish* gɛ'rrɛro) *n* a mountainous state of S Mexico, on the Pacific: rich mineral resources. Capital: Chilpancingo. Pop: 3 075 083 (2000 est). Area: 63 794 sq km (24 631 sq miles)

guerrilla *or* **guerilla** (gə'rɪlə) *n* **a** a member of an irregular usually politically motivated armed force that combats stronger regular forces, such as the army or police **b** (*as modifier*): *guerrilla warfare* [C19: from Spanish, diminutive of *guerra* WAR]

Guesclin (*French* gɛklɛ̃) *n* **Bertrand du** *?*1320–80, French commander during the Hundred Years' War

guess (gɛs) *vb* (*when tr, may take a clause as object*) **1** (*when intr, often foll by at or about*) to form or express an uncertain estimate or conclusion (about something), based on insufficient information: *guess what we're having for dinner* **2** to arrive at a correct estimate of (something) by guessing **3** *informal, chiefly US & Canadian* to believe, think, or suppose (something): *I guess I'll go now* ▷ *n* **4** an estimate or conclusion arrived at by guessing: *a bad guess* **5** the act of guessing [C13: probably of Scandinavian origin; compare Old Swedish *gissa*, Old Danish *gitse*, Middle Dutch *gissen*; see GET] > 'guesser *n*

guesstimate *or* **guestimate** *informal* ▷ *n* **1** an estimate calculated mainly or only by guesswork ▷ *vb* ('gɛstɪ,meɪt) **2** to form a guesstimate of

guesswork ('gɛs,wɜ:k) *n* **1** a set of conclusions, estimates, etc, arrived at by guessing **2** the process of making guesses

guest (gɛst) *n* **1** a person who is entertained, taken out to eat, etc, and paid for by another **2 a** a person who receives hospitality at the home of another **b** (*as modifier*): *the guest room* **3 a** a person who receives the hospitality of a government, establishment, or organization **b** (*as modifier*): *a guest speaker* **4 a** an actor, contestant, entertainer, etc, taking part as a visitor in a programme in which there are also regular participants **b** (*as modifier*): *a guest appearance* **5** a patron of a hotel, boarding house, restaurant, etc ▷ *vb* **6** (*intr*) (in theatre and broadcasting) to be a guest: *to guest on a show* [Old English *giest* guest, stranger, enemy; related to Old Norse *gestr*, Gothic *gasts*, Old High German *gast*, Old Slavonic *gostĭ*, Latin *hostis* enemy]

guest beer *n* a draught beer stocked by a bar, often for a limited period, in addition to its usual range

guestbook ('gɛst,bʊk) *n* **1** a book in a museum, hotel, etc, in which a visitor can comment on his or her visit to that place **2** a page on a website where visitors may leave messages or greetings

guesthouse ('gɛst,haʊs) *n* a private home or boarding house offering accommodation, esp to travellers

guest rope *n nautical* any line sent or trailed over the side of a vessel as a convenience for boats drawing alongside, as an aid in warping or towing, etc

Guevara (gə'vɑ:rə; *Spanish* ge'βara) *n* **Ernesto** (ɛr'nesto), known as *Che Guevara*. 1928–67, Latin American politician and soldier, born in Argentina. He developed guerrilla warfare as a tool for revolution and was instrumental in Castro's victory in Cuba (1959), where he held government posts until 1965. He was killed while training guerrillas in Bolivia

guff (gʌf) *n slang* ridiculous or insolent talk [C19: imitative of empty talk; compare dialect Norwegian *gufs* puff of wind]

guffaw (gʌ'fɔ:) *n* **1** a crude and boisterous laugh ▷ *vb* **2** to laugh crudely and boisterously or express (something) in this way [C18: of imitative origin]

Guggenheim Museum ('gʊgən,haɪm) *n* an international chain of art museums, some of which are architecturally important buildings in their own right, most notably one in New York, designed by Frank Lloyd Wright (1956–59), and one in Bilbao, desgned by Frank O Gehry (1997)

Guiana (gaɪ'ænə, gɪ'ɑ:nə) *or* **The Guianas** *n* a region of NE South America, including Guyana, Surinam, French Guiana, and the **Guiana Highlands** (largely in SE Venezuela and partly in N Brazil). Area: about 1 787 000 sq km (690 000 sq miles) > **Guianese** (,gaɪə'ni:z, ,gɪə-) *or* **Guianan** (gaɪ'ænən, gɪ'ɑ:nən) *adj, n*

guidance ('gaɪdʰns) *n* **1** leadership, instruction, or direction **2 a** counselling or advice on educational, vocational, or psychological matters **b** (*as modifier*): *the marriage-guidance counsellor* **3** something that guides **4** any process by which the flight path of a missile is controlled in flight

guide (gaɪd) *vb* **1** to lead the way for (a person) **2** to control the movement or course of (an animal, vehicle, etc) by physical action; steer **3** to supervise or instruct (a person) **4** (*tr*) to direct the affairs of (a person, company, nation, etc) **5** (*tr*) to advise or influence (a person) in his standards or opinions: *let truth guide you always* ▷ *n* **6 a** a person, animal, or thing that guides **b** (*as modifier*): *a guide dog* **7** a person, usually paid, who conducts tour expeditions, etc **8** a model or criterion, as in moral standards or accuracy **9** a book that instructs or explains the fundamentals of a subject or skill **10** any device that directs the motion of a tool or machine part **11** a mark, sign, etc, that points the way **12 a** *naval* a ship in a formation used as a reference for manoeuvres, esp with relation to maintaining the correct formation and disposition **b** *military* a soldier stationed to one side of a column or line to regulate alignment, show the way, etc [c14: from (Old) French *guider*, of Germanic origin; compare Old English *wītan* to observe] > 'guidable *adj* > 'guider *n*

Guide (gaɪd) *n* (*sometimes not capital*) a member of an organization for girls equivalent to the Scouts. US equivalent: Girl Scout

guided missile *n* a missile, esp one that is rocket-propelled, having a flight path controlled during flight either by radio signals or by internal preset or self-actuating homing devices

guide dog *n* a dog that has been specially trained to live with and accompany someone who is blind, enabling the blind person to move about safely

guideline ('gaɪd,laɪn) *n* a principle put forward to set standards or determine a course of action

guidepost ('gaɪd,pəʊst) *n* **1** a sign on a post by a road indicating directions **2** a principle or guideline

Guider ('gaɪdə) *n* (*sometimes not capital*) **1** a woman leader of a company of Guides **2 Brownie Guider** a woman leader of a pack of Brownie Guides

Guido d'Arezzo (Italian 'gwi:do da'rettso) *n* ?995–?1050 AD, Italian Benedictine monk and musical theorist: reputed inventor of solmization

guidon ('gaɪdᵊn) *n* **1** a small pennant, used as a marker or standard, esp by cavalry regiments **2** the man or vehicle that carries this [c16: from French, from Old Provençal *guidoo*, from *guida* GUIDE]

Guienne or **Guyenne** (French gɥijɛn) *n* a former province of SW France: formed, with Gascony, the duchy of Aquitaine during the 12th century

guild or **gild** (gɪld) *n* **1** an organization, club, or fellowship **2** (esp in medieval Europe) an association of men sharing the same interests, such as merchants or artisans: formed for mutual aid and protection and to maintain craft standards or pursue some other purpose such as communal worship [c14: of Scandinavian origin; compare Old Norse *gjald* payment, *gildi* guild; related to Old English *gield* offering, Old High German *gelt* money]

guilder, gilder ('gɪldə) or **gulden** *n*, *pl* -ders, -der or -dens, -den **1** Also called: **florin** the former standard monetary unit of the Netherlands, divided into 100 cents; replaced by the euro in 2002 **2** any of various former gold or silver coins of Germany, Austria, or the Netherlands [c15: changed from Middle Dutch *gulden*, literally: GOLDEN]

Guildford ('gɪlfəd) *n* a city in S England, in Surrey: cathedral (1936–68); seat of the University of Surrey (1966). Pop: 69 400 (2001)

guildhall ('gɪld,hɔːl) *n* Brit **a** the hall of a guild or corporation **b** a town hall

guile (gaɪl) *n* clever or crafty character or behaviour [c18: from Old French *guile*, of Germanic origin; see WILE] > 'guileful *adj* > 'guilefully *adv* > 'guilefulness *n* > 'guileless *adj* > 'guilelessly *adv* > 'guilelessness *n*

Guilin ('gwer'lɪn), **Kweilin** or **Kuei-lin** *n* a city in S China, in Guangxi on the Li River: noted for the unusual caves and formations of the surrounding karst scenery; trade and manufacturing centre. Pop: 631 000 (2005 est)

Guillaume de Lorris (French gijom də lɔris) *n* 13th century, French poet who wrote the first 4058 lines of the allegorical romance, the *Roman de la rose*, continued by Jean de Meung

Guillem (French giem) *n* **Sylvie.** born 1965, French ballet dancer based in Britain; with the Royal Ballet from 1989

guillemot ('gɪlɪ,mɒt) *n* any northern oceanic diving bird of the genera *Uria* and *Cepphus*, having a black-and-white plumage and long narrow bill: family *Alcidae* (auks, etc), order *Charadriiformes* [c17: from French, diminutive of *Guillaume* William]

guilloche (gɪ'lɒʃ) *n* an ornamental band or border with a repeating pattern of two or more interwoven wavy lines, as in architecture [c19: from French: tool used in ornamental work, perhaps from *Guillaume* William]

guillotine *n* ('gɪlə,tiːn) **1 a** a device for beheading persons, consisting of a weighted blade set between two upright posts **b** the guillotine execution by this instrument **2** a device for cutting or trimming sheet material, such as paper or sheet metal, consisting of a blade inclined at a small angle that descends onto the sheet **3** a surgical instrument for removing tonsils, growths in the throat, etc **4** Also called: **closure by compartment** (in Parliament, etc) a form of closure under which a bill is divided into compartments, groups of which must be completely dealt with each day ▷ *vb* (,gɪlə'tiːn) (*tr*) **5** to behead (a person) by guillotine **6** (in Parliament, etc) to limit debate on (a bill, motion, etc) by the guillotine [c18: from French, named after Joseph Ignace *Guillotin* (1738–1814), French physician, who advocated its use in 1789] > ,guillo'tiner *n*

guilt (gɪlt) *n* **1** the fact or state of having done wrong or committed an offence **2** responsibility for a criminal or moral offence deserving punishment or a penalty **3** remorse or self-reproach caused by feeling that one is responsible for a wrong or offence **4** *archaic* sin or crime [Old English *gylt*, of obscure origin]

guiltless ('gɪltlɪs) *adj* free of all responsibility for wrongdoing or crime; innocent > 'guiltlessly *adv* > 'guiltlessness *n*

guilty ('gɪltɪ) *adj* guiltier, guiltiest **1** responsible for an offence or misdeed **2** *law* having committed an offence or adjudged to have done so: *the accused was found guilty* **3** of, showing, or characterized by guilt > 'guiltily *adv* > 'guiltiness *n*

guimpe (gɪmp, gæmp) *n* a variant spelling of gimp¹ [c19: variant of GIMP]

Guin. *abbreviation* Guinea

guinea ('gɪnɪ) *n* **1 a** a British gold coin taken out of circulation in 1813, worth 21 shillings **b** the sum of 21 shillings (£1.05), still used in some contexts, as in quoting professional fees **2** See guinea fowl [c16: the coin was originally made of gold from Guinea]

Guinea ('gɪnɪ) *n* **1** a republic in West Africa, on the Atlantic: established as the colony of French Guinea in 1890 and became an independent republic in 1958. Official language: French. Religion: Muslim majority and animist. Currency: franc. Capital: Conakry. Pop: 8 620 000 (2004 est). Area: 245 855 sq km (94 925 sq miles) **2** (formerly) the coastal region of West Africa, between Cape Verde and Namibe (formerly Moçâmedes; Angola): divided by a line of volcanic peaks into **Upper Guinea** (between The Gambia and Cameroon) and **Lower Guinea** (between Cameroon and S Angola) **3 Gulf of Guinea** a large inlet of the S Atlantic on the W coast of Africa, extending from Cape Palmas, Liberia, to Cape Lopez, Gabon: contains two large bays, the Bight of Bonny and the Bight of Benin, separated by the Niger delta

Guinea-Bissau *n* a republic in West Africa, on the Atlantic: first discovered by the Portuguese in 1446 and of subsequent importance in the slave trade; made a colony in 1879; became an independent republic in 1974. Official language: Portuguese; Cape Verde creole is widely spoken. Religion: animist majority and Muslim. Currency: franc. Capital: Bissau. Pop: 1 537 000 (2004 est). Area: 36 125 sq km (13 948 sq miles). Former name (until 1974): **Portuguese Guinea**

guinea fowl or **guinea** *n* any gallinaceous bird, esp *Numida meleagris*, of the family *Numididae* of Africa and SW Asia, having a dark plumage mottled with white, a naked head and neck, and a heavy rounded body

guinea hen *n* a guinea fowl, esp a female

guinea pig *n* **1** a domesticated cavy, probably descended from *Cavia porcellus*, commonly kept as a pet and used in scientific experiments **2** a person or thing used for experimentation [C17: origin uncertain: perhaps from old use of the name *Guinea* to mean any remote unknown land]

Guinevere ('gwɪnɪ,vɪə), **Guenevere** ('gwɛnɪ,vɪə) or **Guinever** ('gwɪnɪvə) *n* (in Arthurian legend) the wife of King Arthur and paramour of Lancelot

Guinness ('gɪnɪs) *n* Sir **Alec**. 1914–2000, British stage and film actor. His films include *Kind Hearts and Coronets* (1949), *The Bridge on the River Kwai* (1957), for which he won an Oscar, and *Star Wars* (1977); TV roles include Le Carré's George Smiley

guipure (gɪ'pjʊə) *n* **1** Also called: **guipure lace** any of many types of heavy lace that have their pattern connected by brides, rather than supported on a net mesh **2** a heavy corded trimming; gimp [C19: from Old French *guipure*, from *guiper* to cover with cloth, of Germanic origin; see WIPE, WHIP]

Guiscard (*French* giskar) *n* **Robert** (rɔbɛr). ?1015–85, Norman conqueror in S Italy

guise (gaɪz) *n* **1** semblance or pretence: *under the guise of friendship* **2** external appearance in general **3** *archaic* manner or style of dress [C13: from Old French *guise*, of Germanic origin; see WISE²]

guising ('gaɪzɪŋ) *n* (in Scotland and N England) the practice or custom of disguising oneself in fancy dress, often with a mask, and visiting people's houses, esp at Halloween > 'guiser *n*

guitar (gɪ'tɑː) *n music* a plucked stringed instrument originating in Spain, usually having six strings, a flat sounding board with a circular sound hole in the centre, a flat back, and a fretted fingerboard. Range: more than three octaves upwards from E on the first leger line below the bass staff [C17: from Spanish *guitarra*, from Arabic *qītār*, from Greek *kithara* CITHARA] > gui'tarist *n*

Guitry (*French* gitri) *n* **Sacha** (saʃa). 1885–1957, French actor, dramatist, and film director, born in Russia: plays include *Nono* (1905)

Guiyang ('gweɪ'jæn), **Kweiyang** or **Kuei-yang** *n* a city in S China, capital of Guizhou province: reached by rail in 1959, with subsequent industrial growth. Pop: 2 467 000 (2005 est)

Guizhou ('gweɪ'dʒəʊ), **Kweichow** or **Kueichow** *n* a province of SW China, between the Yangtze and Xi Rivers: a high plateau. Capital: Guiyang. Pop: 38 700 000 (2003 est). Area: 174 000 sq km (69 278 sq miles)

Guizot (*French* gizo) *n* **François Pierre Guillaume** (frɑ̃swa pjɛr ɡijɔm). 1787–1874, French statesman and historian. As chief minister (1840–48), his reactionary policies contributed to the outbreak of the revolution of 1848

Gujarat or **Gujerat** (,ɡʊdʒə'rɑːt) *n* **1** a state of W India: formed in 1960 from the N and W parts of the former Bombay State; one of India's most industrialized states. Capital: Gandhinagar. Pop: 50 596 992 (2001). Area: 196 024 sq km (75 268 sq miles) **2** a region of W India, north of the Narmada River: generally includes the areas north of Mumbai city where Gujarati is spoken

Gujarati or **Gujerati** (,ɡʊdʒə'rɑːtɪ) *n* **1** *pl* -**ti** a member of a people of India living chiefly in Gujarat **2** the state language of Gujarat, belonging to the Indic branch of the Indo-European family ▷ *adj* **3** of or relating to Gujarat, its people, or their language

Gujranwala (ɡuːdʒ'rɑːn,wʌlə) *n* a city in NE Pakistan: textile manufacturing. Pop: 1 466 000 (2005 est)

Gulag ('ɡuːlæɡ) *n* **1** (formerly) the central administrative department of the Soviet security service, established in 1930, responsible for maintaining prisons and forced labour camps **2** (*not capital*) any system used to silence dissents [C20: from Russian G(*lavnoye*) U(*pravleniye Ispravitelno-Trudovykh*) *Lag*(*erei*) Main Administration for Corrective Labour Camps]

Gulbenkian (ɡʊl'bɛŋkɪən) *n* **1** **Calouste Sarkis** (kæ'luːst 'sɑːkɪz). 1869–1955, British industrialist, born in Turkey. He endowed the international Gulbenkian Foundation for the advancement of the arts, science, and education **2** his son, **Nubar Sarkis** ('nuːbɑː 'sɑːkɪz). 1896–1972, British industrialist, diplomat, and philanthropist

gulch (ɡʌltʃ) *n US & Canadian* a narrow ravine cut by a fast stream [C19: of obscure origin]

gulden ('ɡʊldən) *n*, *pl* -**dens** or -**den** a variant of **guilder**

Gülek Bogaz (ɡuː'lɛk bəʊ'ɡɑːz) *n* the Turkish name for the **Cilician Gates**

gules (ɡjuːlz) *adj*, *n* (*usually postpositive*) *heraldry* red [C14: from Old French *gueules* red fur worn around the neck, from *gole* throat, from Latin *gula* GULLET]

gulf (ɡʌlf) *n* **1** a large deep bay **2** a deep chasm **3** something that divides or separates, such as a lack of understanding **4** something that engulfs, such as a whirlpool ▷ *vb* **5** (*tr*) to swallow up; engulf [C14: from Old French *golfe*, from Italian *golfo*, from Greek *kolpos*]

Gulf (ɡʌlf) *n* **1** the Persian Gulf **2** *Austral* **a** the Gulf of Carpentaria **b** (*modifier*) of, relating to, or adjoining the Gulf: *Gulf country* **3** NZ the Hauraki Gulf

Gulf States the Gulf States *pl n* **1** the oil-producing states around the Persian Gulf: Iran, Iraq, Kuwait, Saudi Arabia, Bahrain, Qatar, the United Arab Emirates, and Oman **2** the states of the US that border on the Gulf of Mexico: Alabama, Florida, Louisiana, Mississippi, and Texas

Gulf Stream *n* **1** a relatively warm ocean current flowing northeastwards off the Atlantic coast of the US from the Gulf of Mexico **2** another name for **North Atlantic Drift**

Gulf War *n* **1** the war (1991) between US-led UN forces and Iraq, following Iraq's invasion of Kuwait **2** See **Iran-Iraq War**

Gulf War syndrome *n* a group of various debilitating symptoms experienced by many soldiers who served in the Gulf War of 1991. It is claimed to be associated with damage to the central nervous system, caused by exposure to pesticides containing organophosphates

gulfweed ('ɡʌlf,wiːd) *n* any brown seaweed of the genus *Sargassum*, esp *S. bacciferum*, having air bladders and forming dense floating masses in tropical Atlantic waters, esp the Gulf Stream. Also called: **sargasso**, **sargasso weed**

gull¹ (ɡʌl) *n* any aquatic bird of the genus *Larus* and related genera, such as *L. canus* (**common gull** or **mew**) having long pointed wings, short legs, and a mostly white plumage: family *Laridae*, order *Charadriiformes* [C15: of Celtic origin; compare Welsh *gwylan*]

gull² (ɡʌl) *archaic* ▷ *n* **1** a person who is easily fooled or cheated ▷ *vb* **2** (*tr*) to fool, cheat, or hoax [C16: perhaps from dialect *gull* unfledged bird, probably from *gul*, from Old Norse *gulr* yellow]

gullet ('ɡʌlɪt) *n* **1** a less formal name for the **oesophagus** **2** the throat or pharynx [C14: from Old French *goulet*, diminutive of *goule* throat, from Latin *gula* throat]

gullible ('ɡʌləb³l) *adj* easily taken in or tricked > ,gulli'bility *n* > 'gullibly *adv*

gully or **gulley** ('ɡʌlɪ) *n*, *pl* -**lies** or -**leys** **1** a channel or small valley, esp one cut by heavy rainwater **2** NZ a small bush-clad valley **3** *cricket* **a** a fielding position between the slips and point **b** a fielder in this position ▷ *vb* -**lies**, -**lying**, -**lied** **4** (*tr*) to make (channels) in (the ground, sand, etc) [C16: from French *goulet* neck of a bottle; see GULLET]

gulp (ɡʌlp) *vb* **1** (*tr*; often foll by *down*) to swallow rapidly, esp in large mouthfuls **2** (*tr*; often foll by *back*) to stifle or choke: *to gulp back sobs* **3** (*intr*) to swallow air convulsively, as while drinking, because of nervousness, surprise, etc **4** (*intr*) to make a noise, as when swallowing too quickly ▷ *n* **5** the act of gulping **6** the quantity taken in a gulp [C15: from Middle Dutch *gulpen*, of imitative origin] > 'gulper *n* > 'gulpingly *adv* > 'gulpy *adj*

gum¹ (ɡʌm) *n* **1** any of various sticky substances that exude from certain plants, hardening on exposure to air and dissolving or forming viscous masses in water **2** any of various products, such as adhesives, that are made from such exudates **3** any sticky substance used as an adhesive; mucilage; glue **4** NZ short for **kauri gum** **5** See **chewing gum**, **bubble gum**, **gumtree 6** *chiefly Brit* a gumdrop ▷ *vb* **gums**, **gumming**, **gummed 7** to cover or become covered, clogged, or stiffened with or as if with gum **8** (*tr*) to stick together or in place with gum **9** (*intr*) to emit or form gum ▷ See also **gum up** [C14: from Old French *gomme*, from Latin *gummi*, from Greek *kommi*, from Egyptian *kemai*]

gum² (ɡʌm) *n* the fleshy tissue that covers the jawbones around the bases of the teeth. Technical name: **gingiva**.

Related adj: **gingival** [Old English *gōma* jaw; related to Old Norse *gōmr*, Middle High German *gūme*, Lithuanian *gomurīs*]

gum ammoniac *n* another name for **ammoniac**[1]

gum arabic *n* a gum exuded by certain acacia trees, esp *Acacia senegal*: used in the manufacture of ink, food thickeners, pills, emulsifiers, etc. Also called: **gum acacia**

gumbo *or* **gombo** ('gʌmbəʊ) *n*, *pl* -bos *US & Canadian* **1** the mucilaginous pods of okra **2** another name for **okra 3** a soup or stew thickened with okra pods **4** a fine soil in the W prairies that becomes muddy when wet [c19: from Louisiana French *gombo*, of Bantu origin]

gumboil ('gʌm,bɔɪl) *n* an abscess on the gums, often at the root of a decayed tooth. Also called: **parulis**

gumboots ('gʌm,buːts) *pl n* another name for **Wellington boots** (sense 1)

gumdrop ('gʌm,drɒp) *n* a small jelly-like sweet containing gum arabic and various colourings and flavourings. Also called (esp Brit): **gum**

gummy[1] ('gʌmɪ) *adj* -mier, -miest **1** sticky or tacky **2** consisting of, coated with, or clogged by gum or a similar substance **3** producing gum [c14: from GUM[1] + -Y[1]] > **'gumminess** *n*

gummy[2] ('gʌmɪ) *adj* -mier, -miest **1** toothless; not showing one's teeth ▷ *n*, *pl* -mies **2** *Austral* a small crustacean-eating shark, *Mustelus antarcticus*, with bony ridges resembling gums in its mouth [c20: from GUM[2] + -Y[1]]

gum nut *n Austral* the hardened seed container of the gum tree *Eucalyptus gummifera*

gumption ('gʌmpʃən) *n informal* **1** *Brit* common sense or resourcefulness **2** initiative or courage: *you haven't the gumption to try* [c18: originally Scottish, of unknown origin]

gum resin *n* a mixture of resin and gum obtained from various plants and trees

gumtree ('gʌm,triː) *n* **1** any of various trees that yield gum, such as the eucalyptus, sweet gum, and sour gum. Sometimes shortened to: **gum 2 up a gumtree** *informal* in a very awkward position; in difficulties

gum up *vb* (*tr, adverb*) **1** to cover, dab, or stiffen with gum **2** *informal* to make a mess of; bungle (often in the phrase **gum up the works**)

gun (gʌn) *n* **1 a** a weapon with a metallic tube or barrel from which a missile is discharged, usually by force of an explosion. It may be portable or mounted. In a military context the term applies specifically to a flat-trajectory artillery piece **b** (*as modifier*): *a gun barrel* **2** the firing of a gun as a salute or signal, as in military ceremonial **3** a member of or a place in a shooting party or syndicate **4** any device used to project something under pressure: *a grease gun; a spray gun* **5** *US slang* an armed criminal; gunman **6** *Austral & NZ slang* **a** an expert **b** (*as modifier*): *a gun shearer; a gun batsman* **7** **go great guns** *slang* to act or function with great speed, intensity, etc **8 jump the gun** *or* **beat the gun a** (of a runner, etc) to set off before the starting signal is given **b** *informal* to act prematurely **9 stick to one's guns** *informal* to maintain one's opinions or intentions in spite of opposition ▷ *vb* guns, gunning, gunned **10** (when *tr*, often foll by *down*) to shoot (someone) with a gun **11** (*tr*) to press hard on the accelerator of (an engine): *to gun the engine of a car* **12** (*intr*) to hunt with a gun ▷ See also **gun for** [c14: probably from a female pet name shortened from the Scandinavian name *Gunnhildr* (from Old Norse *gunnr* war + *hildr* war)]

gunboat ('gʌn,bəʊt) *n* a small shallow-draft vessel carrying mounted guns and used by coastal patrols, etc

gunboat diplomacy *n* diplomacy conducted by threats of military intervention, esp by a major power against a militarily weak state

guncotton ('gʌn,kɒtᵊn) *n* cellulose nitrate containing a relatively large amount of nitrogen: used as an explosive

gun dog *n* **1** a dog trained to work with a hunter or gamekeeper, esp in retrieving, pointing at, or flushing game **2** a dog belonging to any breed adapted to these activities

gunfight ('gʌn,faɪt) *n chiefly US* a fight between persons using firearms > **'gun,fighter** *n*

gunfire ('gʌn,faɪə) *n* **1** the firing of one or more guns, esp when done repeatedly **2** the use of firearms, as contrasted with other military tactics

gun for *vb* (*intr, preposition*) **1** to search for in order to reprimand, punish, or kill **2** to try earnestly for: *he was gunning for promotion*

gunge (gʌndʒ) *informal* ▷ *n* **1** sticky, rubbery, or congealed matter ▷ *vb* **2** (*tr, usually passive*; foll by *up*) to block or encrust with gunge; clog [c20: of imitative origin, perhaps influenced by GOO and SPONGE] > **'gungy** *adj*

gunk (gʌŋk) *n informal* slimy, oily, or filthy matter [c20: perhaps of imitative origin]

gunlock ('gʌn,lɒk) *n* the mechanism in some firearms that causes the charge to be exploded

gunman ('gʌnmən) *n*, *pl* -men **1** a man who is armed with a gun, esp unlawfully **2** a man who is skilled with a gun

gunmetal ('gʌn,metᵊl) *n* **1 a** a type of bronze containing copper (88 per cent), tin (8–10 per cent), and zinc (2–4 per cent): used for parts that are subject to wear or to corrosion, esp by sea water **2 a** a dark grey colour with a purplish or bluish tinge **b** (*as adjective*): *gunmetal chiffon*

Gunn (gʌn) *n* **Thom(son William)**. 1929–2004, British poet who lived in the USA. His works include *Fighting Terms* (1954), *My Sad Captains* (1961), *Jack Straw's Castle* (1976), *The Man with the Night Sweats* (1992), and *Boss Cupid* (2000)

Gunnar ('gʊnɑː) *n Norse myth* brother of Gudrun and husband of Brynhild, won for him by Sigurd. He corresponds to Gunther in the *Nibelungenlied*

gunnel[1] ('gʌnᵊl) *n* any eel-like blennioid fish of the family *Pholidae*, occurring in coastal regions of northern seas [c17: of unknown origin]

gunnel[2] ('gʌnᵊl) *n* a variant spelling of **gunwale** [c15: from GUN + WALE[1] from its use to support guns]

Gunnell ('gʌnᵊl) *n* **Sally**. born 1966, British athlete: Olympic 400-metre hurdles gold medallist (1992)

gunner ('gʌnə) *n* **1** a serviceman who works with, uses, or specializes in guns **2** *naval* (formerly) a warrant officer responsible for the training of gun crews, their performance in action, and accounting for ammunition **3** (in the British Army) an artilleryman, esp a private **4** a person who hunts with a rifle or shotgun

gunnery ('gʌnərɪ) *n* **1** the art and science of the efficient design and use of ordnance, esp artillery **2** guns collectively **3** the use and firing of guns

gunny ('gʌnɪ) *n*, *pl* -nies *chiefly US* **1** a coarse hard-wearing fabric usually made from jute and used for sacks, etc **2** Also called: **gunny sack** a sack made from this fabric [c18: from Hindi *gōnī*, from Sanskrit *gonī* sack, probably of Dravidian origin]

gunplay ('gʌn,pleɪ) *n chiefly US* the use of firearms, as by criminals

gunpoint ('gʌn,pɔɪnt) *n* **1** the muzzle of a gun **2 at gunpoint** being under or using the threat of being shot

gunpowder ('gʌn,paʊdə) *n* an explosive mixture of potassium nitrate, charcoal, and sulphur (typical proportions are 75:15:10): used in time fuses, blasting, and fireworks

gun room *n* **1** (esp in the Royal Navy) the mess allocated to subordinate or junior officers **2** a room where guns are stored

gunrunning ('gʌn,rʌnɪŋ) *n* the smuggling of guns and ammunition or other weapons of war into a country > **'gun,runner** *n*

gunshot ('gʌn,ʃɒt) *n* **1 a** a shot fired from a gun **b** (*as modifier*): *gunshot wounds* **2** the range of a gun **3** the shooting of a gun

gunslinger ('gʌn,slɪŋə) *n slang* a gunfighter or gunman, esp in the Old West

gunsmith ('gʌn,smɪθ) *n* a person who manufactures or repairs firearms, esp portable guns

gunstock ('gʌn,stɒk) *n* the wooden or metallic handle or support to which is attached the barrel of a rifle

Gunter ('gʌntə) *n* **Edmund**. 1581–1626, English mathematician and astronomer, who invented various measuring instruments, including Gunter's chain

Gunter's chain *n surveying* a measuring chain 22 yards

in length, or this length as a unit [C17: named after Edmund **Gunter**]

Gunther ('gʊntə) n (in the *Nibelungenlied*) a king of Burgundy, allied with Siegfried, who won for him his wife Brunhild. He corresponds to Gunnar in Norse mythology

Guntur (gʊn'tʊə) n a city in E India, in central Andhra Pradesh: founded by the French in the 18th century; ceded to Britain in 1788. Pop: 514 707 (2001)

gunwale or **gunnel** ('gʌnᵊl) n *nautical* the top of the side of a boat or the topmost plank of a wooden vessel

gunyah ('gʌnjə) n *Austral* a bush hut or shelter [C19: from a native Australian language]

guppy ('gʌpɪ) n, pl **-pies** a small brightly coloured freshwater viviparous cyprinodont fish, *Lebistes reticulatus*, of N South America and the Caribbean: a popular aquarium fish [C20: named after R. J. L. *Guppy*, 19th-century clergyman of Trinidad who first presented specimens to the British Museum]

Gurdjieff ('ɡɜːdjef) n Georgei Ivanovitch ('dʒɔːdʒɪ ɪ'vanə͵vɪtʃ). ?1877– 1949, Russian mystic: founded a teaching centre in Paris (1922)

gurdwara ('ɡɜːdwɑːrə) n a Sikh place of worship [C20: from Punjabi *gurduārā*, from Sanskrit *guru* teacher + *dvārā* **door**]

gurgle ('ɡɜːɡᵊl) vb (intr) **1** (of liquids, esp of rivers, streams, etc) to make low bubbling noises when flowing **2** to utter low throaty bubbling noises, esp as a sign of contentment: *the baby gurgled with delight* ▷ n **3** the act or sound of gurgling [C16: perhaps from Vulgar Latin *gurgulāre*, from Latin *gurguliō* gullet]

Gurkha ('ɡʊəkɑː, 'ɡɜːkə) n, pl **-khas** or **-kha 1** a member of a Hindu people, descended from Brahmins and Rajputs, living chiefly in Nepal, where they achieved dominance after being driven from India by the Muslims **2** a member of this people serving as a soldier in the Indian or British army

gurnard ('ɡɜːnəd) or **gurnet** ('ɡɜːnɪt) n, pl **-nard, -nards** or **-net, -nets** any European marine scorpaenoid fish of the family *Triglidae*, such as *Trigla lucerna* (**tub** or **yellow gurnard**), having a heavily armoured head and finger-like pectoral fins [C14: from Old French *gornard* grunter, from *grognier* to grunt, from Latin *grunnīre*]

Gurney ('ɡɜːnɪ) n Ivor (**Bertie**). 1890–1937, British poet and composer, noted esp for his songs and his poems of World War I

guru ('ɡʊruː, 'ɡuːruː) n **1** a Hindu or Sikh religious teacher or leader, giving personal spiritual guidance to his disciples **2** *often derogatory* a leader or chief theoretician of a movement, esp a spiritual or religious cult **3** *often facetious* a leading authority in a particular field [C17: from Hindi *gurū*, from Sanskrit *guruh* weighty]

Guru Granth or **Guru Granth Sahib** (ɡrʌnt) n the sacred scripture of the Sikhs, believed by them to be the embodiment of the gurus. Also called: **Adi Granth** [from Punjabi, from Sanskrit *grantha* a book]

Guru Nanak ('nɑːˌnʌk) n 1469–1539, Indian religious leader and founder of Sikhism. Born near Lahore in India, he spent many years as a missionary before returning to the Punjab, where he gained many followers. See also **Ten Gurus**

gush (ɡʌʃ) vb **1** to pour out or cause to pour out suddenly and profusely, usually with a rushing sound **2** to act or utter in an overeffusive, affected, or sentimental manner ▷ n **3** a sudden copious flow or emission, esp of liquid **4** something that flows out or is emitted **5** an extravagant and insincere expression of admiration, sentiment, etc [C14: probably of imitative origin; compare Old Norse *gjōsa*, Icelandic *gusa*] > **'gushing** adj > **'gushingly** adv

gusher ('ɡʌʃə) n **1** a person who gushes, as in being unusually effusive or sentimental **2** something, such as a spurting oil well, that gushes

gushy ('ɡʌʃɪ) adj **gushier, gushiest** *informal* displaying excessive admiration or sentimentality > **'gushily** adv > **'gushiness** n

gusset ('ɡʌsɪt) n **1** an inset piece of material used esp to strengthen or enlarge a garment **2** a triangular metal plate for strengthening a corner joist between two structural members ▷ vb **3** (tr) to put a gusset in (a garment) [C15: from Old French *gousset* a piece of mail, a diminutive of *gousse* pod, of unknown origin] > **'gusseted** adj

gust (ɡʌst) n **1** a sudden blast of wind **2** a sudden rush of smoke, sound, etc **3** an outburst of emotion ▷ vb (intr) **4** to blow in gusts [C16: from Old Norse *gustr*; related to *gjōsa* to **gush**; see **geyser**]

gustation (ɡʌ'steɪʃən) n the act of tasting or the faculty of taste [C16: from Latin *gustātiō*, from *gustāre* to taste] > **gustatory** ('ɡʌstətərɪ, -trɪ) or **'gustative** adj

Gustavo A. Madero (Spanish ɡus'taβo a ma'ðero) n a city in central Mexico, northeast of Mexico City: became a pilgrimage centre after an Indian convert had a vision of the Virgin Mary here in 1531. Pop: 668 500 (2000 est). Former name (until 1931): **Guadalupe Hidalgo**

Gustavus I (ɡʊ'stɑːvəs) n called *Gustavus Vasa*. ?1496–1560, king of Sweden (1523–60). He was elected king after driving the Danes from Sweden (1520–23)

Gustavus II n See **Gustavus Adolphus**

Gustavus VI n title of *Gustaf Adolf*. 1882–1973, king of Sweden (1950–73)

Gustavus Adolphus (ə'dɒlfəs) or **Gustavus II** n 1594–1632, king of Sweden (1611–32). A brilliant general, he waged successful wars with Denmark, Russia, and Poland and in the Thirty Years' War led a Protestant army against the Catholic League and the Holy Roman Empire (1630–32). He defeated Tilly at Leipzig (1631) and Lech (1632) but was killed at the battle of Lützen

gusto ('ɡʌstəʊ) n vigorous enjoyment, zest, or relish, esp in the performance of an action: *the aria was sung with great gusto* [C17: from Spanish: taste, from Latin *gustus* a tasting; see **gustation**]

gusty ('ɡʌstɪ) adj **gustier, gustiest 1** blowing or occurring in gusts or characterized by blustery weather: *a gusty wind* **2** given to sudden outbursts, as of emotion or temperament > **'gustily** adv > **'gustiness** n

gut (ɡʌt) n **1 a** the lower part of the alimentary canal; intestine **b** the entire alimentary canal. Related adj: **visceral 2** (often plural) the bowels or entrails, esp of an animal **3** *slang* the belly; paunch **4** See **catgut 5** a silky fibrous substance extracted from silkworms, used in the manufacture of fishing tackle **6** a narrow channel or passage **7** (plural) *informal* courage, willpower, or daring; forcefulness **8** (plural) *informal* the essential part: *the guts of a problem* ▷ vb **guts, gutting, gutted** (tr) **9** to remove the entrails from (fish, etc) **10** (esp of fire) to destroy the inside of (a building) **11** to take out the central points of (an article), esp in summary form ▷ adj **12** *informal* arising from or characterized by what is basic, essential, or natural: *a gut problem; a gut reaction* [Old English *gutt*; related to *gēotan* to flow; see **fusion**]

GUT (ɡʌt) n acronym for grand unified theory

Gutenberg ('ɡuːtᵊn͵bɜːɡ; German 'ɡuːtənbɛrk) n Johann (jo'han), original name *Johannes Gensfleisch*. ?1398–1468, German printer; inventor of printing by movable type

Gütersloh (German 'ɡyːtərsloː) n a town in NW Germany, in North Rhine-Westphalia. Pop: 95 928 (2003 est)

Guthrie ('ɡʌθrɪ) n **1 Samuel**. 1782–1848, US chemist: invented percussion priming powder and a punch lock for exploding it, and discovered chloroform (1831) **2 Sir (William) Tyrone**. 1900–71, English theatrical director **3 Woody**, full name *Woodrow Wilson Guthrie*. 1912–67, US folk singer and songwriter. His songs include "So Long, it's been Good to Know you" (1940) and "This Land is your Land" (1944)

Guthrun ('ɡʊðruːn) n a variant of **Gudrun**

gutless ('ɡʌtlɪs) adj *informal* lacking courage or determination

gut reaction n a reaction to a situation derived from a person's instinct and experience

gutsy ('ɡʌtsɪ) adj **gutsier, gutsiest** *slang* **1** gluttonous; greedy **2** full of courage, determination, or boldness

gutta-percha ('ɡʌtə'pɜːtʃə) n **1** any of several tropical trees of the sapotaceous genera *Palaquium* and *Payena*, esp *Palaquium gutta* **2** a whitish rubber substance derived from the coagulated milky latex of any of these trees: used in electrical insulation and dentistry [C19: from Malay *getah* gum + *percha* name of a tree that produces it]

g

g

guttate ('gʌteɪt) or **guttated** adj biology (esp of plants) covered with small drops or droplike markings, esp oil glands [c19: from Latin guttātus dappled, from gutta a drop]

gutted ('gʌtɪd) adj informal disappointed and upset

gutter ('gʌtə) n 1 a channel along the eaves or on the roof of a building, used to collect and carry away rainwater 2 a channel running along the kerb or the centre of a road to collect and carry away rainwater 3 a trench running beside a canal lined with clay puddle 4 either of the two channels running parallel to a tenpin bowling lane 5 printing the white space between the facing pages of an open book 6 surfing a dangerous deep channel formed by currents and waves 7 the gutter a poverty-stricken, degraded, or criminal environment ▷ vb 8 (tr) to make gutters in 9 (intr) to flow in a stream or rivulet 10 (intr) (of a candle) to melt away by the wax forming channels and running down in drops 11 (intr) (of a flame) to flicker and be about to go out [c13: from Anglo-French goutiere, from Old French goute a drop, from Latin gutta] > 'guttering n

gutter press n the section of the popular press that seeks sensationalism in its coverage

guttersnipe ('gʌtə,snaɪp) n a child who spends most of his time in the streets, esp in a slum area [c19: originally a name applied to the common snipe (the bird), then to a person who gathered refuse from gutters in city streets]

guttural ('gʌtərəl) adj 1 anatomy of or relating to the throat 2 phonetics pronounced in the throat or the back of the mouth; velar or uvular 3 raucous ▷ n 4 phonetics a guttural consonant [c16: from New Latin gutturālis concerning the throat, from Latin guttur gullet] > 'gutturally adv

gut-wrenching adj informal causing great distress or suffering: gut-wrenching scenes

guy[1] (gaɪ) n 1 informal a man or youth 2 Brit a crude effigy of Guy Fawkes, usually made of old clothes stuffed with straw or rags, that is burnt on top of a bonfire on Guy Fawkes Day 3 Brit a person in shabby or ludicrously odd clothes 4 (plural) informal persons of either sex ▷ vb 5 (tr) to make fun of; ridicule [c19: short for Guy Fawkes (1570–1606), English conspirator in the Gunpowder Plot]

guy[2] (gaɪ) n 1 a rope, chain, wire, etc, for anchoring an object, such as a radio mast, in position or for steadying or guiding it while being hoisted or lowered ▷ vb 2 (tr) to anchor, steady, or guide with a guy or guys [c14: probably from Low German; compare Dutch gei brail, geiblok pulley, Old French guie guide, from guier to GUIDE]

Guy (gaɪ) n **Buddy**, real name George Guy. born 1936, US blues singer and guitarist

Guyana (gaɪˈænə) n a republic in NE South America, on the Atlantic: colonized chiefly by the Dutch in the 17th and 18th centuries; became a British colony in 1831 and an independent republic within the Commonwealth in 1966. Official language: English. Religions: Christian and Hindu. Currency: dollar. Capital: Georgetown. Pop: 767 000 (2004 est). Area: about 215 000 sq km (83 000 sq miles). Former name (until 1966): **British Guiana**

Guyanese (,gaɪəˈniːz) or **Guyanan** (gaɪˈænən) adj 1 of or relating to Guyana or its inhabitants ▷ adj 2 a native or inhabitant of Guyana

Guyenne (French gɥijɛn) n a variant spelling of **Guienne**

Guzmán Blanco (Spanish guðˈman ˈblaŋko) n **Antonio** (anˈtonjo). 1829–99, Venezuelan statesman; president (1873–77; 1879–84; 1886–87). He was virtual dictator of Venezuela from 1870 until his overthrow (1889)

guzzle ('gʌzəl) vb to consume (food or drink) excessively or greedily [c16: of unknown origin]

Gwalior ('gwɑːlɪ,ɔː) n 1 a city in N central India, in Madhya Pradesh: built around the fort, which dates from before 525; industrial and commercial centre. Pop: 826 919 (2001) 2 a former princely state of central India, established in the 18th century: merged with Madhya Bharat in 1948, which in turn merged with Madhya Pradesh in 1956

Gwent (gwɛnt) n a former county of SE Wales: formed in 1974 from most of Monmouthshire and part of Breconshire; replaced in 1996 by Monmouthshire and the county boroughs of Newport, Torfaen, Blaenau Gwent, and part of Caerphilly

Gweru ('gweɪruː) n a city in central Zimbabwe. Pop: 140 000 (2005 est)

Gwich'in ('gwɪtʃɪn) n 1 a member of a North American Indian people from northwest Canada and northeast Alaska 2 the languge of these people

Gwyn (gwɪn) n **Nell**, original name Eleanor Gwynne. 1650–87, English actress; mistress of Charles II

Gwynedd ('gwɪnɛð) n a county of NW Wales, formed in 1974 from Anglesey, Caernarvonshire, part of Denbighshire, and most of Merionethshire; lost Anglesey and part of the NE in 1996: generally mountainous with many lakes, much of it lying in Snowdonia National Park. Administrative centre: Caernarfon. Pop: 117 500 (2003 est). Area: 2550 sq km (869 sq miles)

gybe or **jibe** (dʒaɪb) nautical ▷ vb 1 (intr) (of a fore-and-aft sail) to shift suddenly from one side of the vessel to the other when running before the wind, as the result of allowing the wind to catch the leech 2 to cause (a sailing vessel) to gybe or (of a sailing vessel) to undergo gybing ▷ n 3 an instance of gybing [c17: from obsolete Dutch gijben (now gijpen), of obscure origin]

gym (dʒɪm) n, adj short for **gymnasium, gymnastics, gymnastic**

gym bunny n informal a person who spends a lot of time exercising at a gymnasium

gymkhana (dʒɪmˈkɑːnə) n 1 chiefly Brit an event in which horses and riders display skill and aptitude in various races and contests 2 (esp in Anglo-India) a place providing sporting and athletic facilities [c19: from Hindi gend-khānā, literally: ball house, from khāna house; influenced by GYMNASIUM]

gymnasium (dʒɪmˈneɪzɪəm) n, pl -siums or -sia (-zɪə) 1 a large room or hall equipped with bars, weights, ropes, etc, for games or physical training 2 (in various European countries) a secondary school that prepares pupils for university [c16: from Latin: school for gymnastics, from Greek gumnasion, from gumnazein to exercise naked, from gumnos naked]

gymnast ('dʒɪmnæst) n a person who is skilled or trained in gymnastics

gymnastic (dʒɪmˈnæstɪk) adj of, relating to, like, or involving gymnastics > gymˈnastically adv

gymnastics (dʒɪmˈnæstɪks) n 1 (functioning as singular) practice or training in exercises that develop physical strength and agility or mental capacity 2 (functioning as plural) gymnastic exercises

gymno- combining form naked, bare, or exposed: gymnosperm [from Greek gumnos naked]

gymnosperm ('dʒɪmnəʊ,spɜːm, 'gɪm-) n any seed-bearing plant in which the ovules are borne naked on the surface of the megasporophylls, which are often arranged in cones. Gymnosperms, which include conifers and cycads, are traditionally classified in the division Gymnospermae but in modern classifications are split into separate phyla. See angiosperm > ,gymno'spermous adj

gympie ('gɪmpɪ) n Austral a tall tree with stinging hairs on its leaves [c19: from a native Australian language]

gym shoe n another name for plimsoll

gymslip ('dʒɪm,slɪp) n a tunic or pinafore dress worn by schoolgirls, often part of a school uniform

gyn- combining form variant of gyno-

gynaeco- or US **gyneco-** combining form relating to women; female: gynaecology [from Greek, from gunē, gunaik- woman, female]

gynaecology or US **gynecology** (,gaɪnɪˈkɒlədʒɪ) n the branch of medicine concerned with diseases in women, esp those of the genitourinary tract > gynaecological (,gaɪnɪkəˈlɒdʒɪkəl) or ,gynaeco'logic or US ,gyneco'logical or ,gyneco'logic adj > ,gynae'cologist or US ,gyne'cologist n

gynandromorph (dʒɪˈnændrəʊ,mɔːf, gaɪ-, dʒaɪ-) n an organism, esp an insect, that has both male and female physical characteristics

gynandrous (dʒaɪˈnændrəs, dʒɪ-, gaɪ-) adj (of flowers

such as the orchid) having the stamens and styles united in a column [C19: from Greek *gunandros* of uncertain sex, from *gunē* woman + *anēr* man]

gyno- *or before a vowel* **gyn-** *combining form* **1** relating to women; female: *gynarchy* **2** denoting a female reproductive organ: *gynophore* [from Greek, from *gunē* woman]

gynoecium, gynaeceum, gynaecium *or esp US* **gynecium** (dʒaɪ'niːsɪəm, gaɪ-) *n, pl* **-cia** *or* **-cea** (-sɪə) the carpels of a flowering plant collectively [C18: New Latin, from Greek *gunaikeion* women's quarters, from *gunaik-, gunē* woman + *-eion*, suffix indicating place]

gynophore (dʒaɪnəʊˌfɔː, 'gaɪ-) *n* a stalk in some plants that bears the gynoecium above the level of the other flower parts

-gynous *adj combining form* **1** of or relating to women or females: *androgynous; misogynous* **2** relating to female organs: *epigynous* [from New Latin *-gynus*, from Greek *-gunos*, from *gunē* woman] > **-gyny** *n combining form*

Győr (Hungarian djøːr) *n* an industrial town in NW Hungary: medieval Benedictine abbey. Pop: 128 913 (2003 est)

gyp¹ *or* **gip** (dʒɪp) *slang* ▷ *vb* **gyps, gypping, gypped** *or* **gips, gipping, gipped** **1** (*tr*) to swindle, cheat, or defraud ▷ *n* **2** an act of cheating **3** a person who gyps [C18: back formation from GYPSY]

gyp² (dʒɪp) *n* Brit & NZ slang severe pain; torture: *his arthritis gave him gyp* [C19: probably a contraction of *gee up!*; see GEE¹]

gyp³ (dʒɪp) *n* a college servant at the universities of Cambridge and Durham [C18: perhaps from GYPSY, or from obsolete *gippo* a scullion]

Gyprock ('dʒɪprɒk) *n trademark Austral* the brand name of a type of plasterboard [from GYPSUM + ROCK]

gypsophila (dʒɪp'sɒfɪlə) *n* any caryophyllaceous plant of the mainly Eurasian genus *Gypsophila*, such as baby's-breath, having small white or pink flowers [C18: New Latin, from Greek *gupsos* chalk + *philos* loving]

gypsum ('dʒɪpsəm) *n* a colourless or white mineral sometimes tinted by impurities, found in beds as an evaporite. It is used in the manufacture of plaster of Paris, cement, paint, school chalk, glass, and fertilizer. Composition: hydrated calcium sulphate. Formula: $CaSO_4.2H_2O$. Crystal structure: monoclinic [C17: from Latin, from Greek *gupsos* chalk, plaster, cement, of Semitic origin] > **gypseous** ('dʒɪpsɪəs) *adj*

Gypsy *or* **Gipsy** ('dʒɪpsɪ) *n, pl* **-sies** (*sometimes not capital*) **1 a** a member of a people scattered throughout Europe and North America, who maintain a nomadic way of life in industrialized societies. They migrated from NW India from about the 9th century onwards **b** (*as modifier*): *a Gypsy fortune-teller* **2** the language of the Gypsies; Romany **3** a person who looks or behaves like a Gypsy [C16: from EGYPTIAN, since they were thought to have come originally from Egypt] > **'Gypsyish** *or* **'Gipsyish** *adj* > **'Gypsy-ˌlike** *or* **'Gipsy-ˌlike** *adj*

gypsy moth *n* a variant spelling of **gipsy moth**

gyrate *vb* (dʒɪ'reɪt, dʒaɪ-) **1** (*intr*) to rotate or spiral, esp about a fixed point or axis ▷ *adj* ('dʒaɪrɪt, -reɪt) **2** biology curved or coiled into a circle; circinate [C19: from Late Latin *gȳrāre*, from Latin *gȳrus* circle, from Greek *guros*] > **gyratory** ('dʒaɪrətərɪ, -trɪ, dʒaɪ'reɪtərɪ) *adj* > **gy'ration** *n* > **gy'rator** *n*

gyre (dʒaɪə) *chiefly literary* ▷ *n* **1** a circular or spiral movement or path **2** a ring, circle, or spiral ▷ *vb* **3** (*intr*) to whirl [C16: from Latin *gȳrus* circle, from Greek *guros*]

gyrfalcon *or* **gerfalcon** ('dʒɜː,fɔːlkən or -,fɔːkən) *n* a very large rare falcon, *Falco rusticolus*, of northern and arctic regions: often used for hunting [C14: from Old French *gerfaucon*, perhaps from Old Norse *geirfalki*, from *geirr* spear + *falki* falcon]

gyro ('dʒaɪrəʊ) *n, pl* **-ros** **1** See **gyrocompass** **2** See **gyroscope**

gyro- *or before a vowel* **gyr-** *combining form* **1** indicating rotating or gyrating motion: *gyroscope* **2** indicating a spiral **3** indicating a gyroscope: *gyrocompass* [via Latin from Greek *guro-*, from *guros* circle]

gyrocompass ('dʒaɪrəʊ,kʌmpəs) *n* navigation a nonmagnetic compass that uses a motor-driven gyroscope to indicate true north

gyrodyne ('dʒaɪrəʊ,daɪn) *n* an aircraft that uses a powered rotor to take off and manoeuvre, but uses autorotation when cruising

gyromagnetic (ˌdʒaɪrəʊmæg'nɛtɪk) *adj* of or caused by magnetic properties resulting from the spin of a charged particle, such as an electron

gyroscope ('dʒaɪrə,skəʊp) *or* **gyrostat** *n* a device containing a disc rotating on an axis that can turn freely in any direction so that the disc resists the action of an applied couple and tends to maintain the same orientation in space irrespective of the movement of the surrounding structure > **gyroscopic** (ˌdʒaɪrə'skɒpɪk) *adj* > **ˌgyro'scopically** *adv*

gyrostabilizer *or* **gyrostabiliser** (ˌdʒaɪrəʊ'steɪbɪ,laɪzə) *n* a gyroscopic device used to stabilize the rolling motion of a ship

gyve (dʒaɪv) *archaic* ▷ *vb* **1** (*tr*) to shackle or fetter ▷ *n* **2** (*usually plural*) fetters [C13: of unknown origin]

Hh

h[1] *or* **H** (eɪtʃ) *n, pl* **h's, H's** *or* **Hs** **1** the eighth letter and sixth consonant of the modern English alphabet **2** a speech sound represented by this letter, in English usually a voiceless glottal fricative, as in *hat* **3 a** something shaped like an H **b** (*in combination*): *an H-beam*
h[2] *symbol for* **1** *physics* Planck constant **2** hecto-
H *symbol for* **1** *chem* hydrogen **2** *physics* magnetic field strength **3** *electronics* henry or henries **4** (on Brit pencils, signifying degree of hardness of lead) hard
h. *or* **H.** *abbreviation* **1** harbour **2** height **3** hour **4** husband
ha[1] *or* **hah** (hɑː) *interj* **1** an exclamation expressing derision, triumph, surprise, etc, according to the intonation of the speaker **2** (*reiterated*) a representation of the sound of laughter
ha[2] *symbol for* hectare
Haakon IV (ˈhɑːkɒn) *n* surnamed *Haakonsson*. 1204–63, king of Norway (1217–63). He strengthened the monarchy and extended Norwegian territory to include Iceland and Greenland
Haakon VII *n* 1872–1957, king of Norway (1905–57). During the Nazi occupation of Norway (1940–45) he led Norwegian resistance from England
haar (hɑː) *n Eastern Brit* a cold sea mist or fog off the North Sea [C17: related to Dutch dialect *harig* damp]
Haarlem (*Dutch* ˈhaːrlɛm) *n* a city in the W Netherlands, capital of North Holland province. Pop: 147 000 (2003 est)
Hab. *abbreviation Bible* Habakkuk
Habakkuk (ˈhæbəkək) *n Old Testament* **1** a Hebrew prophet **2** the book containing his oracles and canticle
Habana[1] (aˈβana) *n* the Spanish name for **Havana**
Habana[2] (həˈbænə) *n* **Bryan**. born 1983; South African Rugby Union football player: in national side from 2004
habanera (ˌhæbəˈnɛərə) *n* **1** a slow Cuban dance in duple time **2** a piece of music composed for or in the rhythm of this dance [from Spanish *danza habanera* dance from Havana]
habeas corpus (ˈheɪbɪəs ˈkɔːpəs) *n law* a writ ordering a person to be brought before a court or judge, esp so that the court may ascertain whether his detention is lawful [C15: from the opening of the Latin writ, literally: you may have the body]
haberdasher (ˈhæbəˌdæʃə) *n* **1** *Brit* a dealer in small articles for sewing, such as buttons, zips, and ribbons **2** *US* a men's outfitter [C14: from Anglo-French *hapertas* small items of merchandise, of obscure origin]
haberdashery (ˈhæbəˌdæʃərɪ) *n, pl* **-eries** the goods or business kept by a haberdasher
habergeon (ˈhæbədʒən) *or* **haubergeon** *n* a light sleeveless coat of mail worn in the 14th century under the plated hauberk [C14: from Old French *haubergeon* a little HAUBERK]
Habermas (ˈhɑːbərmas) *n* **Jürgen** (ˈjyrgən). born 1929, German social theorist: his chief works are *Theory and Practice* (1963) and *Knowledge and Human Interests* (1968)
Haber process (ˈhɑːbə) *n* an industrial process for producing ammonia by reacting atmospheric nitrogen with hydrogen at about 200 atmospheres (2×10^7 pascals) and 500°C in the presence of a catalyst, usually iron [named after Fritz *Haber* (1868–1934), German chemist]
habiliment (həˈbɪlɪmənt) *n* (*often plural*) dress or attire [C15: from Old French *habillement*, from *habiller* to dress, from *bille* log; see BILLET[2]]
habilitate (həˈbɪlɪˌteɪt) *vb* **1** (*tr*) *chiefly Western US* to equip and finance (a mine) **2** (*intr*) to qualify for office [C17: from Medieval Latin *habilitāre* to make fit, from Latin *habilitās* aptness, readiness; see ABILITY] > **haˌbiliˈtation** *n*
habit (ˈhæbɪt) *n* **1** a tendency or disposition to act in a particular way **2** established custom, usual practice, etc **3** *psychol* a learned behavioural response that has become associated with a particular situation, esp one frequently repeated **4** mental disposition or attitude: *a good working habit of mind* **5 a** a practice or substance to which a person is addicted: *drink has become a habit with him* **b** the state of being dependent on something, esp a drug **6** *botany, zoology* the method of growth, type of existence, behaviour, or general appearance of a plant or animal: *a climbing habit; a burrowing habit* **7** the customary apparel of a particular occupation, rank, etc, now esp the costume of a nun or monk **8** Also called: **riding habit** a woman's riding dress ▷ *vb* (*tr*) **9** to clothe **10** an archaic word for **inhabit** [C13: from Latin *habitus* custom,

from *habēre* to have]

habitable ('hæbɪtəbəl) *adj* able to be lived in > ˌhabita'bility *or* 'habitableness > 'habitably *adv*

habitant ('hæbɪtᵊnt) *n* **1** a less common word for **inhabitant 2** ('hæbɪtᵊnt; *French* abitã) **a** an early French settler in Canada or Louisiana, esp a small farmer **b** a descendant of these settlers, esp a farmer

habitat ('hæbɪˌtæt) *n* **1** the environment in which an animal or plant normally lives or grows **2** the place in which a person, group, class, etc, is normally found [c18: from Latin: it inhabits, from *habitāre* to dwell, from *habēre* to have]

habitation (ˌhæbɪ'teɪʃən) *n* **1** a dwelling place **2** occupation of a dwelling place

habit-forming *adj* (of an activity, indulgence, etc) tending to become a habit or addiction

habitual (hə'bɪtjʊəl) *adj* **1** (*usually prenominal*) done or experienced regularly and repeatedly: *the habitual Sunday walk* **2** (*usually prenominal*) by habit: *a habitual drinker* **3** customary; usual > ha'bitually *adv* > ha'bitualness *n*

habituate (hə'bɪtjʊˌeɪt) *vb* **1** to accustom; make used (to) **2** *US & Canadian archaic* to frequent > haˌbitu'ation *n*

habitude ('hæbɪˌtjuːd) *n rare* habit or tendency

habitué (hə'bɪtjʊˌeɪ) *n* a frequent visitor to a place [c19: from French, from *habituer* to frequent]

Habsburg ('haːpsbʊrk) *n* the German name for **Hapsburg**

HAC *abbreviation* Honourable Artillery Company

hachure (hæ'ʃjʊə) *n* shading of short lines drawn on a relief map to indicate gradients [c19: from French, from *hacher* to chop up, HATCH³]

hacienda (ˌhæsɪ'ɛndə) *n* (in Spain or Spanish-speaking countries) **1 a** a ranch or large estate **b** any substantial stock-raising, mining, or manufacturing establishment in the country **2** the main house on such a ranch or plantation [c18: from Spanish, from Latin *facienda* things to be done, from *facere* to do]

hack¹ (hæk) *vb* **1** (when *intr*, usually foll by *at* or *away*) to cut or chop (at) irregularly, roughly, or violently **2** to cut and clear (a way, path, etc), as through undergrowth **3** (in sport, esp rugby) to foul (an opposing player) by kicking or striking his shins **4** *basketball* to commit the foul of striking (an opposing player) on the arm **5** (*intr*) to cough in short dry spasmodic bursts **6** (*tr*) to reduce or cut (a story, article, etc) in a damaging way **7** to manipulate a computer program skilfully, esp, to gain unauthorized access to another computer system **8** (*tr*) *slang* to tolerate; cope with: *I joined the army but I couldn't hack it* ⊳ *n* **9** a cut, chop, notch, or gash, esp as made by a knife or axe **10** any tool used for shallow digging, such as a mattock or pick **11** a chopping blow **12** a dry spasmodic cough **13** a kick on the shins, as in rugby [Old English *haccian*; related to Old Frisian *hackia*, Middle High German *hacken*]

hack² (hæk) *n* **1** a horse kept for riding or (more rarely) for driving **2** an old, ill-bred, or overworked horse **3** a horse kept for hire **4** *Brit* a country ride on horseback **5** a drudge **6** a person who produces mediocre literary or journalistic work **7** Also called: **US** *informal* **hackie** a cab driver **b** a taxi ⊳ *vb* **8** (*tr*) *informal* to write (an article) as or in the manner of a hack ⊳ *adj* **9** (*prenominal*) banal, mediocre, or unoriginal: *hack writing* [c17: short for HACKNEY]

hack³ (hæk) *n* **1** a rack used for fodder for livestock **2** a board on which meat is placed for a hawk **3** a pile or row of unfired bricks stacked to dry [c16: variant of HATCH²]

hackamore ('hækəˌmɔː) *n US & NZ* a rope or rawhide halter used for unbroken foals [c19: by folk etymology from Spanish *jáquima* headstall, from Old Spanish *xaquima*, from Arabic *shaqīmah*]

hackberry ('hækˌbɛrɪ) *n, pl* -ries **1** any American tree or shrub of the ulmaceous genus *Celtis*, having edible cherry-like fruits **2** the fruit or soft yellowish wood of such a tree [c18: variant of C16 *hagberry*, of Scandinavian origin; compare Old Norse *heggr* hackberry]

hacker ('hækə) *n* **1** a person that hacks **2** *slang* a computer fanatic, esp one who through a personal computer breaks into the computer system of a company, government, etc

hackery ('hækərɪ) *n ironic* journalism; hackwork

hacking ('hækɪŋ) *adj* (of a cough) harsh, dry, and spasmodic

hackle ('hækᵊl) *n* **1** any of the long slender feathers on the necks of poultry and other birds **2** *angling* parts of an artificial fly made from hackle feathers, representing the legs and sometimes the wings of a real fly **3** a feathered ornament worn in the headdress of some British regiments **4** a steel flax comb ⊳ *vb* **5** to comb (flax) using a hackle [c15 *hakell*, probably from Old English; variant of HECKLE; see HATCHEL]

hackles ('hækᵊlz) *pl n* **1** the hairs on the back of the neck and the back of a dog, cat, etc, which rise when the animal is angry or afraid **2** anger or resentment (esp in the phrases **get one's hackles up**, **make one's hackles rise**)

Hackman ('hækmən) *n* **Gene**. born 1930, US film actor; his films include *The French Connection* (1971), *Mississippi Burning* (1988), *Absolute Power* (1997), and *The Royal Tenenbaums* (2001)

hackney ('hæknɪ) *n* **1** a compact breed of harness horse with a high-stepping trot **2** a coach or carriage that is for hire **3** a popular term for hack² (sense 1) ⊳ *vb* **4** (*tr; usually passive*) to make commonplace and banal by too frequent use [c14: probably after HACKNEY, where horses were formerly raised; sense 4 meaning derives from the allusion to a weakened hired horse]

Hackney ('hæknɪ) *n* a borough of NE Greater London: formed in 1965 from the former boroughs of Shoreditch, Stoke Newington, and Hackney; nearby are **Hackney Marshes**, the largest recreation ground in London. Pop: 208 400 (2003 est). Area: 19 sq km (8 sq miles)

hackneyed ('hæknɪd) *adj* (of phrases, fashions, etc) used so often as to be trite, dull, and stereotyped

hack off *vb* (*adv*) *informal* (*tr; often passive*) to annoy, irritate, or disappoint

hacksaw ('hækˌsɔː) *n* a handsaw for cutting metal, with a hard-steel blade in a frame under tension

hackwork ('hækˌwɜːk) *n* undistinguished literary work produced to order

had (hæd) *vb* the past tense and past participle of **have**

haddock ('hædək) *n, pl* -docks *or* -dock a North Atlantic gadoid food fish, *Melanogrammus aeglefinus*: similar to but smaller than the cod [c14: of uncertain origin]

hade (heɪd) *geology* ⊳ *n* **1** the angle made to the vertical by the plane of a fault or vein ⊳ *vb* **2** *obsolete* (*intr*) (of faults or veins) to incline from the vertical [c18: of unknown origin]

hadedah ('haːdɪˌdaː) *n South African* a large greyish-green ibis, *Hagedeshia hagedash*, having a greenish metallic sheen on the wing coverts and shoulders [probably imitative of the bird's call]

Haden ('heɪdən) *n* **Charles (Edward)**. born 1937, US jazz bassist

Hades ('heɪdiːz) *n* **1** *Greek myth* **a** the underworld abode of the souls of the dead **b** Pluto, the god of the underworld, brother of Zeus and husband of Persephone **2** (*often not capital*) *informal* hell

Hadhramaut *or* **Hadramaut** (ˌhɑːdrə'mɔːt) *n* a plateau region of the S Arabian Peninsula, in SE Yemen on the Indian Ocean; formerly in South Yemen: corresponds roughly to the former East Aden Protectorate. Area: about 151 500 sq km (58 500 sq miles)

Hadith ('hædɪθ, hɑː'diːθ) *n* the body of tradition and legend about Mohammed and his followers, used as a basis of Islamic law [Arabic]

hadj (hædʒ) *n, pl* hadjes a variant spelling of **hajj**

hadji ('hædʒɪ) *n, pl* hadjis a variant spelling of **hajji**

Hadlee ('hædlɪ) *n* **Sir Richard (John)**. born 1951, New Zealand cricketer

hadn't ('hædᵊnt) *vb* contraction of had not

Hadrian ('heɪdrɪən) *or* **Adrian** *n* Latin name *Publius Aelius Hadrianus*. 76–138 AD, Roman emperor (117–138); adopted son and successor of Trajan. He travelled throughout the Roman Empire, strengthening its frontiers and encouraging learning and architecture, and in Rome he reorganized the army and codified Roman law

Hadrian's Wall *n* a fortified Roman wall, of which substantial parts remain, extending across N England from the Solway Firth in the west to the mouth of the River Tyne in the east. It was built in 120–123 AD on the orders of the emperor Hadrian as a defence against the N British tribes

hadron ('hædrɒn) *n* any elementary particle capable of taking part in a strong nuclear interaction and therefore excluding leptons and photons [C20: from Greek *hadros* heavy, from *hadēn* enough + -ON] > **had'ronic** *adj*

hadst (hædst) *vb archaic or dialect* (used with the pronoun *thou*) a singular form of the past tense (indicative mood) of **have**

haecceity (hɛkˈsiːɪtɪ, hiːk-) *n, pl* **-ties** *philosophy* the property that uniquely identifies an object [C17: from Medieval Latin *haecceitas*, literally: thisness, from *haec*, feminine of *hic* this]

Haeckel (German 'hɛkəl) *n* **Ernst Heinrich** (ɛrnst 'hainrıç). 1834–1919, German biologist and philosopher. He formulated the recapitulation theory of evolution and was an exponent of the philosophy of materialistic monism > **Haeckelian** (hɛ'kiːlɪən) *adj*

haem *or US* **heme** (hiːm) *n biochem* a complex red organic pigment containing ferrous iron, present in haemoglobin [C20: shortened from HAEMATIN]

haem- *combining form* a variant of **haemo-** before a vowel. Also (US): **hem-**

haemal *or US* **hemal** ('hiːməl) *adj* **1** of or relating to the blood or the blood vessels **2** denoting or relating to the region of the body containing the heart

haematemesis *or US* **hematemesis** (,hiːmə'tɛmɪsɪs, ,hɛm-) *n* vomiting of blood, esp as the result of a bleeding ulcer [C19: from HAEMATO- + Greek *emesis* vomiting]

haematic *or US* **hematic** (hiː'mætɪk) *adj* Also: **haemic** relating to, acting on, having the colour of, or containing blood

haematin *or US* **hematin** ('hɛmətɪn, 'hiː-) *n biochem* a dark bluish or brownish pigment containing iron in the ferric state, obtained by the oxidation of haem

haematite ('hiːmə,taɪt, 'hɛm-) *n* a variant spelling of **hematite**

haemato- *or before a vowel* **haemat-** *combining form* indicating blood: *haematolysis*. Also: **haemo-**, (US) **hemato-**, (US) **hemat-** [from Greek *haima, haimat-* blood]

haematocrit *or US* **hematocrit** ('hɛmətəʊkrɪt, 'hiː-) *n* **1** a centrifuge for separating blood cells from plasma **2** Also called: **packed cell volume** the ratio of the volume occupied by these cells, esp the red cells, to the total volume of blood, expressed as a percentage [C20: from HAEMATO- + Greek *kritēs* judge, from *krinein* to separate]

haematology *or US* **hematology** (,hiːmə'tɒlədʒɪ) *n* the branch of medical science concerned with diseases of the blood and blood-forming tissues > **haematologic** (,hiːmətə'lɒdʒɪk) *or* ,**haemato'logical** *or US* ,**hemato'logic** *or* ,**hemato'logical** *adj*

haematoma *or US* **hematoma** (,hiːmə'təʊmə, ,hɛm-) *n, pl* **-mas** *or* **-mata** (-mətə) *pathol* a tumour of clotted or partially clotted blood

haematuria *or esp US* **hematuria** (,hiːmə'tjʊərɪə, ,hɛm-) *n pathol* the presence of blood or red blood cells in the urine

-haemia *or esp US* **-hemia** *n combining form* variants of **-aemia**

haemo-, haema- *or before a vowel* **haem-** *combining form* denoting blood. Also called: **haemato-**, (US) **hemo-**, (US) **hema-**, (US) **hem-** [from Greek *haima* blood]

haemocyanin *or US* **hemocyanin** (,hiːməʊ'saɪənɪn) *n* a blue copper-containing respiratory pigment in crustaceans and molluscs that functions as haemoglobin

haemocytometer (,hiːməʊsaɪ'tɒmɪtə), **haemacytometer**, *US* **hemocytometer** *or* **hemacytometer** *n med* an apparatus for counting the number of cells in a quantity of blood, typically consisting of a graduated pipette for drawing and diluting the blood and a ruled glass slide on which the cells are counted under a microscope

haemodialysis *or US* **hemodialysis** (,hiːməʊdaɪ'ælɪsɪs) *n, pl* **-ses** (-,siːz) *med* the filtering of circulating blood through a semipermeable membrane in an apparatus (haemodialyser or artificial kidney) to remove waste products: performed in cases of kidney failure [C20: from HAEMO- + DIALYSIS]

haemoglobin *or US* **hemoglobin** (,hiːməʊ'gləʊbɪn, ,hɛm-) *n* a conjugated protein, consisting of haem and the protein globin, that gives red blood cells their characteristic colour. It combines reversibly with oxygen and is thus very important in the transportation of oxygen to tissues [C19: shortened from *haematoglobulin*, from HAEMATIN + GLOBULIN the two components]

haemolysis (hɪ'mɒlɪsɪs), **haematolysis**, *US* **hemolysis** *or* **hematolysis** *n, pl* **-ses** (-,siːz) the disintegration of red blood cells, with the release of haemoglobin, occurring in the living organism or in a blood sample > **haemolytic** *or* (US) **hemolytic** (,hiːməʊ'lɪtɪk, ,hɛm-) *adj*

haemophilia *or US* **hemophilia** (,hiːməʊ'fɪlɪə, ,hɛm-) *n* an inheritable disease, usually affecting only males but transmitted by women to their male children, characterized by loss or impairment of the normal clotting ability of blood so that a minor wound may result in fatal bleeding > **haemophiliac** *or* (US) **hemophiliac** (,hiːməʊ'fɪlɪ,æk, ,hɛm-) *n* > **haemophilic** *or* (US) **hemophilic** (,hiːməʊ'fɪlɪk, ,hɛm-) *adj*

haemoptysis *or US* **hemoptysis** (hɪ'mɒptɪsɪs) *n, pl* **-ses** (-,siːz) spitting or coughing up of blood or blood-streaked mucus, as in tuberculosis [C17: from HAEMO- + -*ptysis*, from Greek *ptyein* to spit]

haemorrhage *or US* **hemorrhage** ('hɛmərɪdʒ) *n* **1** profuse bleeding from ruptured blood vessels **2** a steady or severe loss or depletion of resources, staff, etc ▷ *vb* **3** (*intr*) to bleed profusely [C17: from Latin *haemorrhagia*; see HAEMO-, -RRHAGIA]

haemorrhoids *or US* **hemorrhoids** ('hɛmə,rɔɪdz) *pl n pathol* swollen and twisted veins in the region of the anus and lower rectum, often painful and bleeding. Nontechnical name: **piles** [C14: from Latin *haemorrhoidae* (plural), from Greek, from *haimorrhoos* discharging blood, from *haimo-* HAEMO- + *rhein* to flow] > ,**haemor'rhoidal**, *US* **hemor'rhoidal** *adj*

haemostasis (,hiːməʊ'steɪsɪs, ,hɛm-), **haemostasia**, (,hiːməʊ'steɪʒɪə, -ʒə, ,hɛm-) *US* **hemostasis** *or* **hemostasia** *n* the stopping of bleeding or arrest of blood circulation in an organ or part, as during a surgical operation [C18: from New Latin, from HAEMO- + Greek *stasis* a standing still] > **haemostatic** *or* (US) **hemostatic** (,hiːməʊ'stætɪk, ,hɛm-) *adj, n*

haemostat *or US* **hemostat** ('hiːməʊ,stæt, 'hɛm-) *n* a surgical instrument that stops bleeding by compression of a blood vessel

haeremai ('haɪrə,maɪ) *NZ* ▷ *interj* **1** a Māori expression of welcome ▷ *n* **2** the act of saying "haeremai" [C18: Māori, literally: come hither]

Ha-erh-pin ('haː'ɛə'pɪn) *n* a transliteration of the Chinese name for **Harbin**

hafiz ('haːfɪz) *n Islam* a title for a person who knows the Koran by heart [from Persian, from Arabic *hāfiz*, from *hafiza* to guard]

Hafiz ('haːfɪz) *n* **Shams al-Din Muhammad** (,shæmz æl,dɪn məʊ'hæmɪd) ?1326–90, Persian lyric poet, best known for his many short poems about love and wine, often treated as religious symbols

hafnium ('hæfnɪəm) *n* a bright metallic element found in zirconium ores: used in tungsten filaments and as a neutron absorber in nuclear reactors. Symbol: Hf; atomic no: 72; atomic wt: 178.49; valency: 4; relative density: 13.31; melting pt: 2231±20°C; boiling pt: 4603°C [C20: New Latin, named after *Hafnia*, Latin name of Copenhagen + -IUM]

haft (haːft) *n* **1** the handle of an axe, knife, etc ▷ *vb* **2** (*tr*) to provide with a haft [Old English *hæft*; related to Old Norse *hapt*, Old High German *haft* fetter, *hefti* handle]

hag[1] (hæg) *n* **1** an unpleasant or ugly old woman **2** a witch **3** short for **hagfish** [Old English *hægtesse* witch; related to Old High German *hagazussa*, Middle Dutch *haghetisse*] > '**haggish** *adj*

hag[2] (hæg, haːg) *n Scot & northern English dialect* **1** a firm spot in a bog **2** a soft place in a moor [C13: of Scandinavian origin; compare Old Norse *högg* gap; see HEW]

Hag. *abbreviation Bible* Haggai

Hagar ('heɪgɑː, -gə) *n Old Testament* an Egyptian maid of Sarah, who bore Ishmael to Abraham, Sarah's husband

Hagåtña (hə'gɑtɲə) *n* the capital of the Pacific island of Guam, on its W coast. Pop: 1100 (2000). Former name: Agana

Hagen¹ ('hɑːgən) *n* (in the *Nibelungenlied*) Siegfried's killer, who in turn is killed by Siegfried's wife, Kriemhild

Hagen² (*German* 'haːgən) *n* an industrial city in NW Germany, in North Rhine-Westphalia. Pop: 200 039 (2003 est)

Hagen³ ('heɪgən) *n* **Walter**. 1892–1969, US golfer

hagfish ('hæg,fɪʃ) *n, pl* -fish *or* -fishes any eel-like marine cyclostome vertebrate of the family *Myxinidae*, having a round sucking mouth and feeding on the tissues of other animals and on dead organic material

Haggadah *or* **Haggadoth** (hə'gɑːdə; *Hebrew* haga'dɑː, -gɔ'dɔ) *n, pl* **-dahs**, **-das** *or* **-doth** (*Hebrew* -'dɔːt) *Judaism* **a** a book containing the order of service of the traditional Passover meal **b** the narrative of the Exodus from Egypt that constitutes the main part of that service. See also **Seder** [c19: from Hebrew *haggādāh* a story, from *hagged* to tell] > **haggadic** (hə'gædɪk, -'gɑː-) *or* **hag'gadical** *adj*

Haggai ('hægeɪ,aɪ) *n Old Testament* **1** a Hebrew prophet, whose oracles are usually dated between August and December of 520 BC **2** the book in which these oracles are contained, chiefly concerned with the rebuilding of the Temple after the Exile

haggard ('hægəd) *adj* **1** careworn or gaunt, as from lack of sleep, anxiety, or starvation **2** wild or unruly **3** (of a hawk) having reached maturity in the wild before being caught ▷ *n* **4** *falconry* a hawk that has reached maturity before being caught [c16: from Old French *hagard* wild; perhaps related to HEDGE] > **'haggardly** *adv* > **'haggardness** *n*

Haggard ('hægəd) *n* Sir (**Henry**) **Rider**. 1856–1925, British author of romantic adventure stories, including *King Solomon's Mines* (1885)

haggis ('hægɪs) *n* a Scottish dish made from sheep's or calf's offal, oatmeal, suet, and seasonings boiled in a skin made from the animal's stomach [c15: perhaps from *haggen* to HACK¹]

haggle ('hægᵊl) *vb* (*intr*; often foll by *over*) to bargain or wrangle (over a price, terms of an agreement, etc); barter [c16: of Scandinavian origin; compare Old Norse *haggva* to HEW] > **'haggler** *n*

hagio- *or before a vowel* **hagi-** *combining form* indicating a saint, saints, or holiness: *hagiography* [via Late Latin from Greek, from *hagios* holy]

Hagiographa (,hægɪ'ɒgrəfə) *n* the third of the three main parts into which the books of the Old Testament are divided in Jewish tradition (the other two parts being the Law and the Prophets), comprising Psalms, Proverbs, Job, the Song of Solomon, Ruth, Lamentations, Ecclesiastes, Esther, Daniel, Ezra, Nehemiah, and Chronicles

hagiographer (,hægɪ'ɒgrəfə) *or* **hagiographist** *n* **1** a person who writes about the lives of the saints **2** one of the writers of the Hagiographa

hagiography (,hægɪ'ɒgrəfɪ) *n, pl* -phies **1** the writing of the lives of the saints **2** any biography that idealizes or idolizes its subject > **hagiographic** (,hægɪə'græfɪk) *or* ,hagio'graphical *adj*

hagiolatry (,hægɪ'ɒlətrɪ) *n* worship or veneration of saints

hagiology (,hægɪ'ɒlədʒɪ) *n, pl* -gies literature concerned with the lives and legends of saints > **hagiologic** (,hægɪə'lɒdʒɪk) *or* ,hagio'logical *adj* > ,hagi'ologist *n*

hag-ridden *adj* tormented or worried, as if by a witch

Hague¹ (heɪg) *n* **The Hague** the seat of government of the Netherlands and capital of South Holland province, situated about 3 km (2 miles) from the North Sea. Pop: 464 000 (2003 est). Dutch names: 's Gravenhage, Den Haag

Hague² (heɪg) *n* **William Jefferson**. born 1961, British politician; leader of the Conservative party (1997–2001)

hah (hɑː) *interj* a variant spelling of **ha¹**

ha-ha¹ ('hɑː 'hɑː) *or* **haw-haw** *interj* **1** a representation of the sound of laughter **2** an exclamation expressing derision, mockery, surprise, etc

ha-ha² ('hɑː hɑː) *or* **haw-haw** *n* a wall or other boundary marker that is set in a ditch so as not to interrupt the landscape [c18: from French *haha*, probably based on *ha!* ejaculation denoting surprise]

Hahn (*German* haːn) *n* **1 Kurt**. 1886–1974, German educationalist. During the Nazi era he escaped to Britain, where he founded Gordonstoun School (1935) and helped to establish the Duke of Edinburgh's award scheme **2 Otto** ('ɔto). 1879–1968, German physicist: discovered the radioactive element protactinium with Meitner (1917); with Strassmann, demonstrated the nuclear fission of uranium, when it is bombarded with neutrons: Nobel prize for chemistry 1944

Hahnemann (*German* 'haːnəman) *n* (**Christian Friedrich**) **Samuel** ('zaːmueːl). 1755–1843, German physician; founder of homeopathy

hahnium ('haːnɪəm) *n* a name once advanced by the American Chemical Society for a transuranic element, artificially produced from californium, atomic no: 105; half-life of most stable isotope, ^{262}Ha: 40 seconds. now called **dubnium** [c20: named after Otto Hahn (1879–1968), German physicist]

Haidar Ali ('haɪdər 'ɑːlɪ) *n* a variant spelling of **Hyder Ali**

Haifa ('haɪfə) *n* a port in NW Israel, near Mount Carmel, on the Bay of Acre: Israel's chief port, with an oil refinery and other heavy industry. Pop: 269 400 (2003 est)

Haig (heɪg) *n* **Douglas**, 1st Earl Haig. 1861–1928, British field marshal; commander in chief of the British forces in France and Flanders (1915–18)

haik *or* **haick** (haɪk, heɪk) *n* an Arab's outer garment of cotton, wool, or silk, for the head and body [c18: from Arabic *hā'ik*]

haiku ('haɪkuː) *or* **hokku** *n, pl* -ku an epigrammatic Japanese verse form in 17 syllables [from Japanese, from *hai* amusement + *ku* verse]

hail¹ (heɪl) *n* **1** small pellets of ice falling from cumulonimbus clouds when there are very strong rising air currents **2** a shower or storm of such pellets **3** words, ideas, etc, directed with force and in great quantity: *a hail of abuse* ▷ *vb* **4** (*intr*; with *it* as subject) to be the case that hail is falling **5** (often with *it* as subject) to fall or cause to fall as or like hail [Old English *hægl*; related to Old Frisian *heil*, Old High German *hagal* hail, Greek *kakhlēx* pebble]

hail² (heɪl) *vb* (*mainly tr*) **1** to greet, esp enthusiastically: *the crowd hailed the actress with joy* **2** to acclaim or acknowledge: *they hailed him as their hero* **3** to attract the attention of by shouting or gesturing: *to hail a taxi; to hail a passing ship* **4** (*intr*; foll by *from*) to be a native (of): *she hails from India* ▷ *n* **5** the act or an instance of hailing **6** distance across which one can attract attention (esp in the phrase **within hail**) ▷ *sentence substitute* **7** *poetic* an exclamation of greeting [c12: from Old Norse *heill* WHOLE; see HALE¹, WASSAIL]

Haile Selassie ('haɪlɪ sə'læsɪ) *n* title of *Ras Tafari Makonnen*. 1892–1975, emperor of Ethiopia (1930–36; 1941–74). During the Italian occupation of Ethiopia (1936–41), he lived in exile in England. He was a prominent figure in the Pan-African movement: deposed 1974

hail-fellow-well-met *adj* genial and familiar, esp in an offensive or ingratiating way

Hail Mary *n* **1** Also called: **Ave Maria** *RC Church* a prayer to the Virgin Mary, based on the salutations of the angel Gabriel (Luke 1:28) and Elizabeth (Luke 1:42) to her **2** *American football slang* a very long high pass into the end zone, made in the final seconds of a half or of a game

Hailsham of St Marylebone ('heɪlʃəm) *n* Baron, title of Quintin (**McGarel**) **Hogg** ('kwɪntɪn). 1907–2001, British Conservative politician; Lord Chancellor (1970–74; 1979–87). He renounced his viscountcy in 1963 when he made an unsuccessful bid for the Conservative Party leadership; he became a life peer in 1970

hailstone ('heɪl,stəʊn) *n* a pellet of hail

hailstorm ('heɪl,stɔ:m) *n* a storm during which hail falls

Hailwood ('heɪlwʊd) *n* **Mike,** full name *Stanley Michael Bailey Hailwood.* 1940–81, English racing motorcyclist: world champion (250 cc.) 1961 and 1966–67; (350 cc.) 1966–67; and (500 cc.) 1962–65

Hainan ('haɪ'næn) *or* **Hainan Tao** (taʊ) *n* an island and province in the South China Sea, separated from the mainland of S China by the **Hainan Strait**: part of Guangdong province until 1988; mainland China's largest offshore island. Pop: 8 110 000 (2003 est). Area: 33 572 sq km (12 962 sq miles)

Hainaut *or* **Hainault** (*French* ɛno) *n* a province of SW Belgium: stretches from the Flanders Plain in the north to the Ardennes in the south. Capital: Mons. Pop: 1 283 200 (2004 est). Area: 3797 sq km (1466 sq miles)

Haiphong ('haɪ'fɒŋ) *n* a port in N Vietnam, on the Red River delta: a major industrial centre. Pop: 1 817 000 (2005 est)

hair (hɛə) *n* **1** any of the threadlike pigmented structures that grow from follicles beneath the skin of mammals and consist of layers of dead keratinized cells **2** a growth of such structures, as on the human head or animal body, which helps prevent heat loss from the body **3** *botany* any threadlike outgrowth from the epidermis, such as a root hair **4** a fabric or material made from the hair of some animals **5** another word for **hair's-breadth** to *lose by a hair* **6** *get in someone's hair informal* to annoy someone persistently **7** *hair of the dog* or *hair of the dog that bit one* an alcoholic drink taken as an antidote to a hangover **8** *keep your hair on! Brit informal* keep calm **9** *let one's hair down* to behave without reserve **10** *not turn a hair* to show no surprise, anger, fear, etc **11** *split hairs* to make petty and unnecessary distinctions [Old English *hær*; related to Old Norse *hār*, Old High German *hār* hair, Norwegian *herren* stiff, hard, Lettish *sari* bristles, Latin *crescere* to grow] ▷ '**hair,like** *adj*

haircloth ('hɛə,klɒθ) *n* a cloth woven from horsehair, used in upholstery

haircut ('hɛə,kʌt) *n* **1** the act or an instance of cutting the hair **2** the style in which hair has been cut

hairdo ('hɛə,du:) *n, pl* **-dos** the arrangement of a person's hair, esp after styling and setting

hairdresser ('hɛə,drɛsə) *n* **1** a person whose business is cutting, curling, colouring and arranging hair, esp that of women **2** a hairdresser's establishment. Related adjective: **tonsorial** ▷ '**hair,dressing** *n*

hairdryer treatment *n Brit informal* (esp in sport) the practice of shouting at someone at close quarters in order to express one's displeasure at something he or she has done [C21: from the supposed similarity between this experience and having a hot hairdryer too close to one's head]

-haired *adj* having hair as specified: *long-haired*

hair gel *n* a jelly-like substance applied to the hair before styling in order to retain the shape of the style

hairgrip ('hɛə,grɪp) *n chiefly Brit* a small tightly bent metal hair clip. Also called (esp US, Canadian, and NZ): **bobby pin**

hairline ('hɛə,laɪn) *n* **1** the natural margin formed by hair on the head **2 a** a very narrow line **b** (*as modifier*): *a hairline crack*

hairline fracture *n* a very fine crack in a bone

hairnet ('hɛə,nɛt) *n* any of several kinds of light netting worn over the hair to keep it in place

hairpiece ('hɛə,pi:s) *n* **1** a wig or toupee **2** Also called: **postiche** a section of extra hair attached to a woman's real hair to give it greater bulk or length

hairpin ('hɛə,pɪn) *n* **1** a thin double-pronged pin used by women to fasten the hair **2** (*modifier*) (esp of a bend in a road) curving very sharply

hair-raising *adj* inspiring horror; terrifying

hair's-breadth *n* **a** a very short or imperceptible margin or distance **b** (*as modifier*): *a hair's-breadth escape*

hair shirt *n* **1** a shirt made of haircloth worn next to the skin as a penance **2** a secret trouble or affliction

hair slide *n* a hinged clip with a tortoiseshell, bone, or similar back, used to fasten the hair

hairsplitting ('hɛə,splɪtɪŋ) *n* **1** the making of petty

distinctions ▷ *adj* **2** occupied with or based on petty distinctions > '**hair,splitter** *n*

hairspring ('hɛə,sprɪŋ) *n horology* a very fine spiral spring in some timepieces, which, in combination with the balance wheel, controls the timekeeping

hairstreak ('hɛə,stri:k) *n* any small butterfly of the genus *Callophrys* and related genera, having fringed wings marked with narrow white streaks: family *Lycaenidae*

hairstyle ('hɛə,staɪl) *n* a particular mode of arranging, cutting, or setting the hair > '**hair,stylist** *n*

hair trigger *n* **1** a trigger of a firearm that responds to very slight pressure **2** *informal* any mechanism, reaction, etc, set in operation by slight provocation

hairy ('hɛərɪ) *adj* **hairier, hairiest 1** having or covered with hair **2** *slang* **a** difficult or problematic **b** scaring, dangerous, or exciting > '**hairiness** *n*

Haiti ('heɪtɪ, hɑː'i:tɪ) *n* **1** a republic occupying the W part of the island of Hispaniola in the Caribbean, the E part consisting of the Dominican Republic: ceded by Spain to France in 1697 and became one of the richest colonial possessions in the world, with numerous plantations; slaves rebelled under Toussaint L'Ouverture in 1793 and defeated the French; taken over by the US (1915–41) after long political and economic chaos; under the authoritarian regimes of François Duvalier ('Papa Doc') (1957–71) and his son Jean-Claude Duvalier ('Baby Doc') (1971–86); returned to civilian rule in 1990, but another coup in 1991 brought military rule, which was ended in 1994 with US intervention. Official languages: French and Haitian creole. Religions: Roman Catholic and voodoo. Currency: gourde. Capital: Port-au-Prince. Pop: 8 437 000 (2004 est). Area: 27 749 sq km (10 714 sq miles) **2** a former name for **Hispaniola**

Haitian ('heɪʃɪən, hɑː'i:ʃən) *adj* **1** relating to or characteristic of Haiti, its inhabitants, or their language ▷ *n* **2** a native, citizen, or inhabitant of Haiti **3** the creolized French spoken in Haiti

Haitink ('haɪtɪŋk) *n* **Bernard.** born 1929, Dutch orchestral conductor; received an honorary knighthood in 1977

Haji-Ioannou ('hadʒijɒ'anu) *n* **Stelios.** born 1967, British businessman, born in Greece; founder (1995) and chairman (until 2002) of the low-cost airline company Easyjet

hajj *or* **hadj** (hædʒ) *n, pl* **hajjes** *or* **hadjes** the pilgrimage to Mecca that every Muslim is required to make at least once in his life, provided he has enough money and the health to do so [from Arabic *hajj* pilgrimage]

hajji, hadji *or* **haji** ('hædʒɪ) *n, pl* **hajis, hadjis** *or* **hajis 1** a Muslim who has made a pilgrimage to Mecca: also used as a title **2** a Christian of the Greek Orthodox or Armenian Churches who has visited Jerusalem

haka ('hɑːkə) *n NZ* **1** a Māori war chant accompanied by gestures **2** a similar performance by a rugby team [Māori]

hake (heɪk) *n, pl* **hake** *or* **hakes 1** any gadoid food fish of the genus *Merluccius,* such as *M. merluccius* (European hake), of the N hemisphere, having an elongated body with a large head and two dorsal fins **2** any North American fish of the genus *Urophycis,* similar and related to *Merluccius* species [C15: perhaps from Old Norse *haki* hook; compare Old English *hacod* pike; see **HOOK**]

hakim *or* **hakeem** (hɑː'ki:m, 'hɑː:ki:m) *n* **1** a Muslim judge, ruler, or administrator **2** a Muslim physician [C17: from Arabic, from *hakama* to rule]

Hakluyt ('hæklu:t) *n* **Richard.** ?1552–1616, English geographer, who compiled *The Principal Navigations, Voyages, and Discoveries of the English Nation* (1589)

Hakodate (,hɑ:kəʊ'dɑːteɪ) *n* a port in N Japan, on S Hokkaido: fishing industry and shipbuilding. Pop: 284 690 (2002 est)

hakuna mathata (,hɑ:'ku:nə ,mɑ:'tɑ:tə) *sentence substitute* no problem [from Swahili, there is no difficulty]

Halabja (hə'læbdʒə) *n* a Kurdish town in NE Iraq; in March 1998 Iraqi forces used poison gas on the population, killing hundreds of civilians. Pop: estimates vary between 45 000 and 80 000

Halacha, Halaka *or* **Halakha** (*Hebrew* hɑlɑ'xɑ:; *Yiddish* haʹloxə) n that part of the Talmud which is concerned with legal matters as distinct from homiletics [from Hebrew *hălākhāh* way]

halal or**hallal** (hɑːˈlɑːl) n 1 meat from animals that have been killed according to Muslim law ▷ adj 2 of or relating to such meat: *a halal butcher* ▷ vb -als, -alling, -alled (tr) 3 to kill (animals) in this way [from Arabic: lawful]

halation (həˈleɪʃən) n *photog* fogging usually seen as a bright ring surrounding a source of light: caused by reflection from the back of the film [C19: from HALO + -ATION]

halberd (ˈhælbəd) or**halbert** (ˈhælbət) n a weapon consisting of a long shaft with an axe blade and a pick, topped by a spearhead: used in 15th- and 16th-century warfare [C15: from Old French *hallebarde*, from Middle High German *helm* handle, HELM¹ + *barde* axe, from Old High German *bart* BEARD] ▷ ˌhalberˈdier n

Halberstadt (ˈhælbəˌʃtat) n a town in central Germany, in Saxony-Anhalt: industrial centre noted for its historic buildings. Pop: 40 014 (2003 est)

halcyon (ˈhælsɪən) Also:**halcyonian** (ˌhælsɪˈəʊnɪən), adj **halcyonic** (ˌhælsɪˈɒnɪk) 1 peaceful, gentle, and calm n 2 *Greek myth* a fabulous bird associated with the winter solstice 3 **halcyon days** a a fortnight of calm weather during the winter solstice b a period of peace and happiness 4 a poetic name for the **kingfisher** [C14: from Latin *alcyon*, from Greek *alkuōn* kingfisher, of uncertain origin]

Haldane (ˈhɔːldeɪn) n 1 J(ohn) B(urdon) S(anderson) 1892–1964, Scottish biochemist, geneticist, and writer on science 2 his father, **John Scott**. 1860–1936, Scottish physiologist, noted particularly for his research into industrial diseases 3 his brother, **Richard Burdon**, 1st Viscount Haldane of Cloan. 1856–1928, British statesman and jurist. As secretary of state for war (1905–12) he reorganized the army and set up the territorial reserve

hale¹ (heɪl) adj healthy and robust (esp in the phrase **hale and hearty**) [Old English *hæl* WHOLE] ▷ ˈhaleness n

hale² (heɪl) vb (tr) to pull or drag; haul [C13: from Old French *haler*, of Germanic origin; compare Old High German *halōn* to fetch, Old English *geholian* to acquire] ▷ ˈhaler n

Hale (heɪl) n 1 **George Ellery**. 1868–1938, US astronomer: undertook research into sunspots and invented the spectroheliograph 2 **Sir Matthew**. 1609–76, English judge and scholar; Lord Chief Justice (1671–76)

Haleakala (ˌhɑːliːˌɑːkɑːˈlɑː) n a volcano in Hawaii, on E Maui island. Height: 3057 m (10 032 ft). Area of crater: 49 sq km (19 sq miles). Depth of crater: 829 m (2720 ft)

Halesowen (heɪlzˈəʊɪn) n a town in W central England, in Dudley unitary authority, West Midlands. Pop: 55 273 (2001)

Halévy (French alevi) n 1 (**Jacques François**) **Fromental** (frɔmɛtal), original name *Elias Levy*. 1799–1862, French composer, noted for his operas, which include *La Juive* (1835) 2 his nephew, **Ludovic** (lydɔvik). 1834–1908, French dramatist and novelist, who collaborated with Meilhac on opera libretti

Haley (ˈheɪlɪ) n **Bill**, full name *William John Clifton Haley*. 1925–81, US rock and roll singer, best known for his recording of "Rock Around the Clock" (1955)

half (hɑːf) n, pl **halves** (hɑːvz) 1 a either of two equal or corresponding parts that together comprise a whole b a quantity equalling such a part: *half a dozen* 2 half a pint, esp of beer 3 *Scot* a small drink of spirits, esp whisky 4 *sport* the half of the pitch regarded as belonging to one team 5 *golf* an equal score on a hole or round with an opponent 6 (in various games) either of two periods of play separated by an interval (the **first half** and **second half**) 7 a half-price ticket on a bus, train, etc 8 short for **half-hour** 9 *sport* short for **halfback** 10 *obsolete* a half-year period 11 **by half** by an excessive amount or to an excessive degree: *he's too arrogant by half* 12 **by halves** (*used with a negative*) without being thorough or exhaustive: *we don't do things by halves* 13 **go halves** (often foll by *on*, *in*, etc) a to share the expenses (of something with one other person) b to share the whole amount (of something with another person): *to go halves on an orange*

▷ *determiner* 14 a being a half or approximately a half: *half the kingdom* b (*as pronoun; functioning as sing or plural*): *half of them came* ▷ adj 15 not perfect or complete; partial: *he only did a half job on it* ▷ adv 16 to the amount or extent of a half 17 to a great amount or extent 18 partially; to an extent 19 **half two** *informal* 30 minutes after two o'clock 20 **not half** *informal* a not in any way: *he's not half clever enough* b *Brit* really; very; indeed: *he isn't half stupid* c certainly; yes, indeed [Old English *healf*; related to Old Norse *halfr*, Old High German *halb*, Dutch *half*]

half- *prefix* 1 one of two equal parts: *half-moon* 2 related by one parent only: *half-sister* 3 not completely; partly: *half-hardy*

half-and-half n 1 a mixture of half one thing and half another thing 2 a drink consisting of equal parts of beer and stout, or equal parts of bitter and mild

halfback (ˈhɑːfˌbæk) n 1 *rugby* either the scrum half or the stand-off half 2 *soccer old-fashioned* any of three players positioned behind the line of forwards and in front of the fullbacks 3 any of certain similar players in other team sports

half-baked adj 1 insufficiently baked 2 *informal* foolish; stupid 3 *informal* poorly planned or conceived

halfbeak (ˈhɑːfˌbiːk) n any marine and freshwater teleost fish of the tropical and subtropical family *Hemiramphidae*, having an elongated body with a short upper jaw and a long protruding lower jaw

half-binding n a type of hardback bookbinding in which the spine and corners are bound in one material, such as leather, and the sides in another, such as cloth

half-blood n 1 a the relationship between individuals having only one parent in common b an individual having such a relationship 2 a less common name for a **half-breed** ▷ **half-blooded** adj

half board n the daily provision by a hotel of bed, breakfast, and one main meal. Also called: demi-pension

half-boot n a boot reaching to the midcalf

half-bottle n a bottle half the size of a standard bottle of wine, spirits, etc

half-breed adj 1 *offensive* a person whose parents are of different races, esp the offspring of a White person and an American Indian ▷ adj Also: **half-bred** 2 of, relating to, or designating offspring of people or animals of different races or breeds

half-brother n the son of either of one's parents by another partner

half-butt n a snooker cue longer than an ordinary cue, usually used with a long rest

half-caste n 1 *highly offensive* a person having parents of different races, esp the offspring of a European and an Indian ▷ adj 2 of, relating to, or designating such a person

half-century n, pl -ies 1 a period of 50 years 2 a score or grouping of 50: *a half-century of points*

half-cock n 1 on a single-action firearm, a halfway position in which the hammer can be set for safety; in this position the trigger is cocked by the hammer which cannot reach the primer to fire the weapon 2 **go off at half-cock** or **go off half-cocked** to fail as a result of inadequate preparation or premature starting

half-crown n a British silver or cupronickel coin worth two shillings and sixpence (now equivalent to 12½p), taken out of circulation in 1970. Also called: half-a-crown

half-cut adj informal intoxicated with alcohol

half-dozen determiner (preceded by *a*) six or a group of six

half gainer n a type of dive in which the diver completes a half backward somersault to enter the water headfirst facing the diving board

half-hardy adj (of a cultivated plant) able to survive out of doors except during severe frost

half-hearted adj without enthusiasm or determination ▷ ˌhalf-ˈheartedly adv

half-hitch n a knot made by passing the end of a piece of rope around itself and through the loop thus made

half-hour n 1 a period of 30 minutes 2 the point of time 30 minutes after the beginning of an hour ▷ ˌhalf-ˈhourly adv, adj

half-hunter n a watch with a hinged lid in which a

small circular opening or crystal allows the approximate time to be read

half landing *n* a landing halfway up a flight of stairs

half-life *n* the time taken for half of the atoms in a radioactive material to undergo decay

half-light *n* a dim light, as at dawn or dusk

half-mast *n* the lower than normal position to which a flag is lowered on a mast as a sign of mourning or distress

half measure *n* (*often plural*) an inadequate measure

half-moon *n* **1** the moon at first or last quarter when half its face is illuminated **2** the time at which a half-moon occurs **3** something shaped like a half-moon

half-nelson *n* a wrestling hold in which a wrestler places an arm under one of his opponent's arms from behind and exerts pressure with his palm on the back of his opponent's neck

half-note *n US & Canadian* a note having the time value of half a semibreve. Also called: **minim**

halfpenny *or* **ha'penny** ('heɪpnɪ; *for sense* 1 'hɑːfˌpɛnɪ) *n* **1** Also called: **half a** small British coin worth half a new penny, withdrawn from circulation in 1985 **2** *pl* **-pennies** an old British coin worth half an old penny **3** *pl* **-pence** something of negligible value > **'halfpenny₁worth** *or* **ha'p'orth** ('heɪpəθ) *n*

half-pie *adj NZ informal* poorly planned or conceived [from Māori *pai* good]

half-pipe *n* a structure with a U-shaped cross-section, used in performing stunts in skateboarding, snowboarding, rollerblading, etc

half-plate *n photog* a size of plate measuring 6½ × 4⅝4 inches

half seas over *adj Brit informal* drunk

half-section *n engineering* a scale drawing of a section through a symmetrical object that shows only half the object

half-sister *n* the daughter of either of one's parents by another partner

half-size *n* any size, esp in clothing, that is halfway between two sizes

half-sole *n* a sole from the shank of a shoe to the toe

half-step *n music, US & Canadian* another word for **semitone**

half term *n Brit education* a short holiday midway through an academic term

half-timbered *or* **half-timber** *adj* (of a building, wall, etc) having an exposed timber framework filled with brick, stone, or plastered laths, as in Tudor architecture > ₁half-'timbering *n*

half-time *n sport* **a** a rest period between the two halves of a game **b** (*as modifier*): *the half-time score*

half-title *n* **1** the short title of a book as printed on the right-hand page preceding the title page **2** a title on a separate page preceding a section of a book

halftone ('hɑːfˌtəʊn) *n* **1 a** a process used to reproduce an illustration by photographing it through a fine screen to break it up into dots **b** the print obtained from such a plate **2** *music, US & Canadian* another word for **semitone**

half-track *n* a vehicle with caterpillar tracks on the wheels that supply motive power only

half-truth *n* a partially true statement intended to mislead > 'half-'true *adj*

half volley *n sport* a stroke or shot in which the ball is hit immediately after it bounces

halfway (₁hɑːf'weɪ) *adv, adj* **1** at or to half the distance; at or to the middle **2** in or of an incomplete manner or nature **3** meet halfway to compromise with

halfway house *n* **1** a place to rest midway on a journey **2** the halfway point in any progression **3** a centre or hostel designed to facilitate the readjustment to private life of released prisoners, mental patients, etc

halfwit ('hɑːfˌwɪt) *n* **1** a feeble-minded person **2** a foolish or inane person > ₁half'witted *adj*

half-year *n* a period of 6 months

halibut ('hælɪbət) *or* **holibut** ('hɒlɪbət) *n, pl* **-buts** *or* **-but** the largest flatfish: a dark green North Atlantic species, *Hippoglossus hippoglossus*, that is a very important food fish: family *Pleuronectidae* [C15: from *hali* HOLY (because it was customarily eaten on holy days) + *butte* flat fish,

from Middle Dutch *butte*]

Haliç (ha'liːtʃ) *n* the Turkish name for the **Golden Horn**

Halicarnassian (₁hælɪkɑː'næsɪən) *adj* of or relating to the ancient Greek city of Halicarnassus

Halicarnassus (₁hælɪkɑː'næsəs) *n* a Greek colony on the SW coast of Asia Minor: one of the major Hellenistic cities

halide ('hælaɪd) *or* **halid** ('hælɪd) *n* a binary compound containing a halogen atom or ion in combination with a more electropositive element

Halifax¹ ('hælɪˌfæks) *n* **1** a port in SE Canada, capital of Nova Scotia, on the Atlantic: founded in 1749 as a British stronghold. Pop: 276 221 (2001) **2** a town in N England, in Calderdale unitary authority, West Yorkshire: textiles. Pop: 83 570 (2001)

Halifax² ('hælɪˌfæks) *n* **1 Charles Montagu**, Earl of Halifax. 1661–1715, British statesman; founder of the National Debt (1692) and the Bank of England (1694) **2 Edward Frederick Lindley Wood**, Earl of Halifax. 1881–1959, British Conservative statesman. He was viceroy of India (1926–31), foreign secretary (1938–40), and ambassador to the US (1941–46) **3 George Savile**, 1st Marquess of Halifax, known as *the Trimmer*. 1633–95, British politician, noted for his wavering opinions. He opposed the exclusion of the Catholic James II from the throne but later supported the Glorious Revolution

Haligonian ('hælɪ₁gəʊnɪən) *n* **1** a native or resident of Halifax, Canada ▷ *adj* **2** of or relating to Halifax, Canada

halite ('hælaɪt) *n* a colourless or white mineral sometimes tinted by impurities, found in beds as an evaporite. It is used to produce common salt and chlorine. Composition: sodium chloride. Formula: NaCl. Crystal structure: cubic. Also called: **rock salt** [C19: from New Latin *halītes*, from HALO-, -ITE²]

halitosis (₁hælɪ'təʊsɪs) *n* the state or condition of having bad breath [C19: New Latin, from Latin *hālitus* breath, from *hālāre* to breathe]

hall (hɔːl) *n* **1** a room serving as an entry area within a house or building **2** (*sometimes capital*) a building for public meetings **3** (*often capital*) the great house of an estate; manor **4** a large building or room used for assemblies, worship, concerts, dances, etc **5** a residential building, esp in a university; hall of residence **6 a** a large room, esp for dining, in a college or university **b** a meal eaten in this room **7** the large room of a house, castle, etc **8** *US & Canadian* a passage or corridor into which rooms open **9** (*often plural*) *informal* short for **music hall** [Old English *heall*; related to Old Norse *höll*, Old High German *halla* hall, Latin *cela* CELL¹, Old Irish *cuile* cellar, Sanskrit *śālā* hut; see HELL]

Hall (hɔːl) *n* **1 Charles Martin**. 1863–1914, US chemist: discovered the electrolytic process for producing aluminium **2 Sir John**. 1824–1907, New Zealand statesman, born in England: prime minister of New Zealand (1879–82) **3 Sir Peter**. born 1930, English stage director: director of the Royal Shakespeare Company (1960–73) and of the National Theatre (1973–88) **4** (**Margueritte**) **Radclyffe**. 1883–1943, British novelist and poet. Her frank treatment of a lesbian theme in the novel *The Well of Loneliness* (1928) led to an obscenity trial

Halle (German 'halə) *n* a city in E central Germany, in Saxony-Anhalt, on the River Saale: early saltworks; a Hanseatic city in the late Middle Ages; university (1694). Pop: 240 119 (2003 est)

Hallé ('hæleɪ) *n* **Sir Charles**, original name *Karl Hallé*. 1819–95, German conductor and pianist, in Britain from 1848. In 1857 he founded the Hallé Orchestra in Manchester

hallelujah, halleluiah (₁hælɪ'luːjə) *or* **alleluia** (₁ælɪ'luːjə) *interj* **1** an exclamation of praise to God ▷ *n* **2** an exclamation of "Hallelujah" **3** a musical composition that uses the word *Hallelujah* as its text [C16: from Hebrew *hallelūyāh* praise the Lord, from *hellēl* to praise + *yāh* the Lord, YAHWEH]

Haller (German 'halər) *n* **Albrecht von** ('albrɛçt fɔn). 1708–77, Swiss biologist: founder of experimental physiology

Halley ('hælɪ) *n* **Edmund**. 1656–1742, English astronomer and mathematician. He predicted the return of the comet now known as **Halley's comet**, constructed charts of magnetic declination, and produced the first wind maps

halliard ('hæljəd) *n* a variant spelling of **halyard**

Hall-Jones ('hɔːl'dʒəʊnz) *n* Sir **William**. 1851–1936, New Zealand statesman, born in England: prime minister of New Zealand (1906)

hallmark ('hɔːlˌmɑːk) *n* 1 *Brit* an official series of marks, instituted by statute in 1300, and subsequently modified, stamped by the Guild of Goldsmiths at one of its assay offices on gold, silver, or platinum (since 1975) articles to guarantee purity, date of manufacture, etc 2 a mark or sign of authenticity or excellence 3 an outstanding or distinguishing feature ▷ *vb* 4 (*tr*) to stamp with or as if with a hallmark [c18: named after Goldsmiths' *Hall* in London, where items were graded and stamped]

hallo (hə'ləʊ) *sentence substitute, n* 1 a variant spelling of **hello** ▷ *sentence substitute, n, vb* 2 a variant spelling of **halloo**

halloo (hə'luː), **hallo** or **halloa** (hə'ləʊ) *sentence substitute* 1 a shout to attract attention, esp to call hounds at a hunt ▷ *n*, *pl* **-loos**, **-los** or **-loas** 2 a shout of "halloo" ▷ *vb* **-loos**, **-looing**, **-looed**, **-los**, **-loing**, **-loed** or **-loas**, **-loaing**, **-loaed** 3 to shout (something) to (someone) 4 (*tr*) to urge on or incite (dogs) with shouts [c16: perhaps variant of *hallow* to encourage hounds by shouting]

halloumi or **haloumi** (hə'luːmɪ) *n* a salty white sheep's-milk cheese from Greece or Turkey, usually eaten grilled [probably from Arabic *haluma* be mild]

hallow ('hæləʊ) *vb* (*tr*) 1 to consecrate or set apart as being holy 2 to venerate as being holy [Old English *hālgian*, from HOLY] > **'hallower** *n*

hallowed ('hæləʊd; *liturgical* 'hæləʊɪd) *adj* 1 set apart as sacred 2 consecrated or holy

Halloween or **Hallowe'en** (ˌhæləʊ'iːn) *n* the eve of All Saints' Day celebrated on Oct 31 by masquerading; Allhallows Eve [c18: see ALLHALLOWS, EVEN²]

hall stand or *esp US* **hall tree** *n* a piece of furniture on which are hung coats, hats, etc

Hallstatt ('hælstæt) or **Hallstattian** (hæl'stætɪən) *adj* of or relating to a late Bronze Age culture extending from central Europe to Britain and lasting from the 9th to the 5th century BC, characterized by distinctive burial customs, bronze and iron tools, etc [c19: named after *Hallstatt*, Austrian village where remains were found]

hallucinate (hə'luːsɪˌneɪt) *vb* (*intr*) to experience hallucinations [c17: from Latin *ālūcinārī* to wander in mind; compare Greek *aluein* to be distraught] > **hal'luci,nator** *n*

hallucination (həˌluːsɪ'neɪʃən) *n* the alleged perception of an object when no object is present, occurring under hypnosis, in some mental disorders, etc > **halˌluci'national**, **hal'lucinative** or **hal'lucinatory** *adj*

hallucinogen (hə'luːsɪnəˌdʒɛn) *n* any drug, such as LSD or mescaline, that induces hallucinations > **halˌlucino'genic** *adj*

hallux ('hæləks) *n* the first digit on the hind foot of a mammal, bird, reptile, or amphibian; the big toe of man [c19: New Latin, from Late Latin *allex* big toe]

hallway ('hɔːlˌweɪ) *n* a hall or corridor

halm (hɔːm) *n* a variant spelling of **haulm**

halma ('hælmə) *n* a board game in which players attempt to transfer their pieces from their own to their opponents' bases [c19: from Greek *halma* leap, from *hallesthai* to leap]

Halmahera (ˌhælmə'hɪərə) *n* an island in NE Indonesia, the largest of the Moluccas: consists of four peninsulas enclosing three bays; mountainous and forested. Area: 17 780 sq km (6865 sq miles). Former names: Djailolo, Gilolo

Halmstad (*Swedish* 'halmstɑːd) *n* a port in SW Sweden, on the Kattegat. Pop: 88 032 (2004 est)

halo ('heɪləʊ) *n*, *pl* **-loes** or **-los** 1 a disc or ring of light around the head of an angel, saint, etc, as in painting or sculpture 2 the aura surrounding an idealized, famous, or admired person, thing, or event 3 a circle of light around the sun or moon, caused by the refraction of light by particles of ice ▷ *vb* **-loes** or **-los**, **-loing**, **-loed**

4 to surround with or form a halo [c16: from Medieval Latin, from Latin *halōs* circular threshing floor, from Greek]

halo-, **hali-** or before a vowel **hal-** *combining form* 1 indicating salt or the sea 2 relating to or containing a halogen [from Greek *hals*, *hal-* sea, salt]

halogen ('hælədʒɛn) *n* any of the chemical elements fluorine, chlorine, bromine, iodine, and astatine. They are all monovalent and readily form negative ions [c19: from Swedish; see HALO-, -GEN] > **halogenous** (hə'lɒdʒɪnəs) *adj*

halogenate ('hælədʒəˌneɪt) *vb* *chem* to treat or combine with a halogen > **ˌhalogen'ation** *n*

haloid ('hælɔɪd) *chem* ▷ *adj* 1 resembling or derived from a halogen: *a haloid salt* ▷ *n* 2 a compound containing halogen atoms in its molecules; halide

halon ('hælɒn) *n* any of a class of chemical compounds derived from hydrocarbons by replacing one or more hydrogen atoms by bromine atoms and other hydrogen atoms by other halogen atoms (chlorine, fluorine, or iodine). Halons are stable compounds that are used in fire extinguishers, although they may contribute to depletion of the ozone layer

Hals (*Dutch* hɑls) *n* **Frans** (frɑns). ?1580–1666, Dutch portrait and genre painter: his works include *The Laughing Cavalier* (1624)

Hälsingborg (*Swedish* hɛlsɪn'bɔrj) *n* the former name (until 1971) of **Helsingborg**

halt¹ (hɔːlt) *n* 1 an interruption or end to activity, movement, or progress 2 *chiefly Brit* a minor railway station, without permanent buildings 3 **call a halt** to put an end (to something); stop ▷ *n*, *sentence substitute* 4 a command to halt, esp as an order when marching ▷ *vb* 5 to come or bring to a halt [c17: from the phrase *to make halt*, translation of German *halt machen*, from *halten* to HOLD¹, STOP]

halt² (hɔːlt) *vb* (*intr*) 1 (esp of logic or verse) to falter or be defective 2 to waver or be unsure 3 *archaic* to be lame ▷ *adj* 4 *archaic* a lame b (*as collective noun; preceded by the*): *the halt* [Old English *healt* lame; related to Old Norse *haltr*, Old High German *halz* lame, Greek *kólos* maimed, Old Slavonic *kladivo* hammer]

halter ('hɔːltə) *n* 1 a rope or canvas headgear for a horse, usually with a rope for leading 2 Also called: **halterneck** a style of woman's top fastened behind the neck and waist, leaving the back and arms bare 3 a rope having a noose for hanging a person 4 death by hanging ▷ *vb* (*tr*) 5 to secure with a halter or put a halter on 6 to hang (someone) [Old English *hælfter*; related to Old High German *halftra*, Middle Dutch *heliftra*]

haltere ('hæltɪə) or **halter** ('hæltə) *n*, *pl* **halteres** (hæl'tɪəriːz) one of a pair of short projections in dipterous insects that are modified hind wings, used for maintaining equilibrium during flight [c18: from Greek *haltēres* (plural) hand-held weights used as balancers or to give impetus in leaping, from *hallesthai* to leap]

halting ('hɔːltɪŋ) *adj* 1 hesitant: *halting speech* 2 lame > **'haltingly** *adv*

Halton ('hɔːltən) *n* a unitary authority in NW England, in N Cheshire. Pop: 118 400 (2003 est). Area: 75 sq km (29 sq miles)

halvah, halva ('hælvɑː) or **halavah** ('hæləvɑː) *n* an Eastern Mediterranean, Middle Eastern, or Indian sweetmeat made of honey and containing sesame seeds, nuts, rose water, saffron, etc [from Yiddish *halva*, from Romanian *halva*, from Turkish *helve*, from Arabic *halwā* sweetmeat]

halve (hɑːv) *vb* (*tr*) 1 to divide into two approximately equal parts 2 to share equally 3 to reduce by half, as by cutting 4 *golf* to take the same number of strokes on (a hole or round) as one's opponent [Old English *hielfan*; related to Middle High German *helben*; see HALF]

halyard or **halliard** ('hæljəd) *n* *nautical* a line for hoisting or lowering a sail, flag, or spar [c14 *halier*, influenced by YARD¹; see HALE²]

ham¹ (hæm) *n* 1 the part of the hindquarters of a pig or similar animal between the hock and the hip 2 the meat of this part, esp when salted or smoked 3 *informal* the back of the leg above the knee [Old English *hamm*;

related to Old High German *hamma* haunch, Old Irish *cnáim* bone, *camm* bent, Latin *camur* bent]

ham² (hæm) *n* **1** *theatre, informal* **a** an actor who overacts or relies on stock gestures or mannerisms **b** overacting or clumsy acting **c** (*as modifier*): *a ham actor* **2** *informal* a licensed amateur radio operator ▷ *vb* **hams, hamming, hammed 3** *informal* to overact [c19: special use of HAM¹; in some senses probably influenced by AMATEUR]

Hama ('hɑːmɑː) *n* a city in W Syria, on the Orontes River: an early Hittite settlement; famous for its huge water wheels, used for irrigation since the Middle Ages. Pop: 439 000 (2005 est)

Hamadān *or* **Hamedān** ('hæmə,dæn) *n* city in W central Iran, at an altitude of over 1830 m (6000 ft): changed hands several times from the 17th century between Iraq, Persia, and Turkey; trading centre. Pop: 508 000 (2005 est)

hamadryad (,hæmə'draɪəd, -æd) *n* **1** *classical myth* one of a class of nymphs, each of which inhabits a tree and dies with it **2** another name for **king cobra** [c14: from Latin *Hamādryas*, from Greek *Hamadruas*, from *hama* together with + *drus* tree; see DRYAD]

hamadryas (,hæmə'draɪəs) *n* a baboon, *Papio* (or *Comopithecus*) *hamadryas*, of Arabia and NE Africa, having long silvery hair on the head, neck, and chest: regarded as sacred by the ancient Egyptians: family *Cercopithecidae* [c19: via New Latin from Latin; see HAMADRYAD]

Hamamatsu (,hæmə'mætsuː) *n* a city in central Japan, in S central Honshu: cotton textiles and musical instruments. Pop: 573 504 (2002 est)

hamba ('hæmbə) *interj South African, usually offensive* go away; be off [from Nguni *ukuttamba* to go]

Hamburg ('hæmbɜːg) *n* a city-state and port in NW Germany, on the River Elbe: the largest port in Germany; a founder member of the Hanseatic League; became a free imperial city in 1510 and a state of the German empire in 1871; university (1919); extensive shipyards. Pop: 1 734 083 (2003 est)

hamburger ('hæm,bɜːgə) *or* **hamburg** *n* a flat fried cake of minced beef, often served in a bread roll [c20: shortened from *Hamburger steak* (that is, steak in the fashion of HAMBURG)]

hame (heɪm) *n* either of the two curved bars holding the traces of the harness, attached to the collar of a draught animal [c14: from Middle Dutch *hame*; related to Middle High German *hame* fishing rod]

Hameln (German 'haːməln) *n* an industrial town in N Germany, in Lower Saxony on the Weser River: famous for the legend of the Pied Piper (supposedly took place in 1284). Pop: 58 902 (2003 est). English name: **Hamelin**

Hamersley Range ('hæməzlɪ) *n* a mountain range in N Western Australia: iron-ore deposits. Highest peak: 1236 m (4056 ft)

ham-fisted *or* **ham-handed** *adj informal* lacking dexterity or elegance; clumsy

Hamhung *or* **Hamheung** ('hɑːm'hʊŋ) *n* an industrial city in central North Korea: commercial and governmental centre of NE Korea during the Yi dynasty (1392–1910). Pop: 753 000 (2004 est)

Hamilcar Barca (hæ'mɪlkɑː 'bɑːkə, 'hæmɪl,kɑː) *n* died ?228 BC, Carthaginian general; father of Hannibal. He held command (247–41) during the first Punic War and established Carthaginian influence in Spain (237–?228)

Hamilton¹ ('hæməltən) *n* **1** a port in central Canada, in S Ontario on Lake Ontario: iron and steel industry. Pop: 618 820 (2001) **2** a city in New Zealand, on central North Island. Pop: 129 300 (2004 est) **3** a town in S Scotland, in South Lanarkshire near Glasgow. Pop: 48 546 (2001) **4** the capital and chief port of Bermuda. Pop: 3461 (2000) **5** the former name of **Churchill¹** (sense 1)

Hamilton² ('hæməltən) *n* **1 Alexander**. ?1757–1804, American statesman. He was a leader of the Federalists and as first secretary of the Treasury (1789–95) established a federal bank **2 Lady Emma**. ?1765–1815, mistress of Nelson **3 James**, 1st Duke of Hamilton. 1606–49, Scottish supporter of Charles I in the English Civil War: defeated by Cromwell at the Battle of Preston and executed **4 Lewis Carl**. born 1985, English formula 1 racing driver **5 Richard**. born 1922, British artist: a

pioneer of the pop art style **6 Sir William Rowan**. 1805–65, Irish mathematician: founded Hamiltonian mechanics and formulated the theory of quaternions

Hamitic (hæ'mɪtɪk, hə-) *n* **1** a group of N African languages related to Semitic. They are now classified in four separate subfamilies of the Afro-Asiatic family: Egyptian, Berber, Cushitic, and Chadic ▷ *adj* **2** denoting, relating to, or belonging to this group of languages **3** denoting, belonging to, or characteristic of the Hamites

hamlet ('hæmlɪt) *n* a small village or group of houses [c14: from Old French *hamelet*, diminutive of *hamel*, from *ham*, of Germanic origin; compare Old English *hamm* plot of pasture, Low German *hamm* enclosed land; see HOME]

Hamlisch ('hæmlɪʃ) *n* **Marvin**. born 1944, US composer, best known for the musical *A Chorus Line* (1975)

Hamlyn ('hæmlɪn) *n* Baron **Paul**. 1926–2001, British businessman and publisher

Hamm (German ham) *n* an industrial city in NW Germany, in North Rhine-Westphalia: a Hanse town from 1417; severely damaged in World War II. Pop: 184 961 (2003 est)

Hammarskjöld ('hæmə,ʃʊld; Swedish 'hamarʃœld) *n* **Dag** (**Hjalmar Agne Carl**) (dɑːg). 1905–61, Swedish statesman; secretary-general of the United Nations (1953–61): Nobel peace prize 1961

hammer ('hæmə) *n* **1** a hand tool consisting of a heavy usually steel head held transversely on the end of a handle, used for driving in nails, beating metal, etc **2** any tool or device with a similar function, such as the moving part of a door knocker, the striking head on a bell, etc **3** a power-driven striking tool, esp one used in forging. A pneumatic hammer delivers a repeated blow from a pneumatic ram, a drop hammer uses the energy of a falling weight **4** a part of a gunlock that rotates about a fulcrum to strike the primer or percussion cap, either directly or via a firing pin **5** *athletics* **a** a heavy metal ball attached to a flexible wire: thrown in competitions **b** the event or sport of throwing the hammer **6** an auctioneer's gavel **7** a device on a piano that is made to strike a string or group of strings causing them to vibrate **8** *anatomy* the nontechnical name for **malleus 9 go under the hammer** *or* **come under the hammer** to be offered for sale by an auctioneer **10 hammer and tongs** with great effort or energy: *fighting hammer and tongs* **11 on someone's hammer** *Austral & NZ slang* persistently demanding and critical of someone ▷ *vb* **12** to strike or beat (a nail, wood, etc) with or as if with a hammer **13** (*tr*) to shape or fashion with or as if with a hammer **14** (*tr*; foll by *in* or *into*) to impress or force (facts, ideas, etc) into (someone) through constant repetition **15** (*intr*) to feel or sound like hammering **16** (*intr*; often foll by *away*) to work at constantly **17** (*tr*) *Brit* to criticize severely **18** *informal* to inflict a defeat on **19** (*tr*) *stock exchange* **a** to announce the default of (a member) **b** to cause prices of (securities, the market, etc) to fall by bearish selling [Old English *hamor*; related to Old Norse *hamarr* crag, Old High German *hamar* hammer, Old Slavonic *kamy* stone] > **'hammer-,like** *adj*

hammer and sickle *n* the emblem on the flag of the former Soviet Union, representing the industrial workers and the peasants respectively

hammer beam *n* either of a pair of short horizontal beams that project from opposite walls to support arched braces and struts

Hammerfest (Norwegian 'hamərfɛst) *n* a port in N Norway, on the W coast of Kvalöy Island: the northernmost town in Europe, with uninterrupted daylight from May 17 to July 29 and no sun between Nov 21 and Jan 21; fishing and tourist centre. Pop: 9157 (2004 est)

hammerhead ('hæmə,hɛd) *n* **1** any shark of the genus *Sphyrna* and family *Sphyrnidae*, having a flattened hammer-shaped head **2** a heavily built tropical African wading bird, *Scopus umbretta*, related to the herons, having a dark plumage and a long backward-pointing crest: family *Scopidae*, order *Ciconiiformes* **3** a large African fruit bat, *Hypsignathus monstrosus*, with a large square head and hammer-shaped muzzle ▷ 'hammer,headed adj

hammerlock ('hæmə,lɒk) n a wrestling hold in which a wrestler twists his opponent's arm upwards behind his back

hammer out vb (tr, adverb) 1 to shape or remove with or as if with a hammer 2 to form or produce (an agreement, plan, etc) after much discussion or dispute

Hammersmith and Fulham ('hæmə,smiθ) n a borough of Greater London on the River Thames: established in 1965 by the amalgamation of Fulham and Hammersmith. Pop: 174 200 (2003 est). Area: 16 sq km (6 sq miles)

Hammerstein II ('hæmə,staɪn) n Oscar. 1895–1960, US librettist and songwriter: collaborated with the composer Richard Rodgers in musicals such as *South Pacific* (1949) and *The Sound of Music* (1959)

hammertoe ('hæmə,təʊ) n a deformity of the bones of a toe causing the toe to be bent in a clawlike arch

Hammett ('hæmət) n Dashiell. 1894–1961, US writer of detective novels. His books include *The Maltese Falcon* (1930) and *The Thin Man* (1932)

hammock ('hæmək) n a length of canvas, net, etc, suspended at the ends and used as a bed [c16: from Spanish *hamaca*, of Taino origin]

Hammond¹ ('hæmənd) n a city in NW Indiana, adjacent to Chicago. Pop: 80 547 (2003 est)

Hammond² ('hæmənd) n 1 Dame Joan. 1912–96, Australian operatic singer, born in New Zealand 2 Walter Reginald, known as Wally. 1903–65, English cricketer. An all-rounder, he played for England 85 times between 1928 and 1946

Hammurabi (,hæmʊ'rɑːbɪ) or **Hammurapi** n ?18th century bc, king of Babylonia; promulgator of one of the earliest known codes of law

hammy ('hæmɪ) adj -mier, -miest informal 1 (of an actor) overacting or tending to overact 2 (of a play, performance, etc) overacted or exaggerated

Hampden ('hæmpdən, 'hæmdən) n John. 1594–1643, English statesman; one of the leaders of the Parliamentary opposition to Charles I

hamper¹ ('hæmpə) vb 1 (tr) to prevent the progress or free movement of ▷ n 2 nautical gear aboard a vessel that, though essential, is often in the way [c14: of obscure origin; perhaps related to Old English *hamm* enclosure, *hemm* HEM¹]

hamper² ('hæmpə) n 1 a large basket, usually with a cover 2 Brit such a basket and its contents, usually food [c14: variant of HANAPER]

Hampshire¹ ('hæmp,ʃɪə, -ʃə) n a county of S England, on the English Channel: crossed by the **Hampshire Downs** and the South Downs, with the New Forest in the southwest and many prehistoric and Roman remains: the geographical and ceremonial county includes Portsmouth and Southampton, which became independent unitary authorities in 1997. Administrative centre: Winchester. Pop (excluding unitary authorities): 1 251 000 (2003 est). Area (excluding unitary authorities): 3679 sq km (1420 sq miles). Abbreviation: Hants

Hampshire² ('hæmpʃə) n Sir Stuart. 1914–2004, British philosopher: his publications include *Thought and Action* (1959), *Two Theories of Morality* (1977), and *Innocence and Experience* (1989)

Hampstead ('hæmpstɪd) n a residential district in N London: part of the Greater London borough of Camden since 1965; nearby is **Hampstead Heath**, a popular recreation area

Hampton¹ ('hæmptən) n 1 a city in SE Virginia, on the harbour of **Hampton Roads** on Chesapeake Bay. Pop: 146 878 (2003 est) 2 a district of the Greater London borough of Richmond-upon-Thames, on the River Thames: famous for **Hampton Court Palace** (built in 1515 by Cardinal Wolsey)

Hampton² ('hæmptən) n 1 Christopher James. born 1946, British playwright: his works include *When Did You Last See My Mother?* (1964), the screenplay for the film *Dangerous Liaisons* (1988), and the book for the musical *Sunset Boulevard* (1993) 2 Lionel. 1913–2002, US jazz-band leader and vibraphone player

hamster ('hæmstə) n any Eurasian burrowing rodent of the tribe Cricetini, such as *Mesocricetus auratus* (**golden hamster**), having a stocky body, short tail, and cheek pouches: family Cricetidae. They are popular pets [c17: from German, from Old High German *hamustro*, of Slavic origin]

hamstring ('hæm,strɪŋ) n 1 anatomy any of the tendons at the back of the knee ▷ vb -strings, -stringing, -strung (tr) 2 to cripple by cutting the hamstring of 3 to ruin or thwart [c16: HAM¹ + STRING]

Hamsun (Norwegian 'hamsun) n Knut, (knuːt), pen name of Knut Pedersen. 1859– 1952, Norwegian novelist, whose works include *The Growth of the Soil* (1917): Nobel prize for literature 1920

hamulus ('hæmjʊləs) n, pl -li (-,laɪ) biology a hook or hooklike process at the end of some bones or between the fore and hind wings of a bee or similar insect [c18: from Latin: a little hook, from *hāmus* hook]

Han¹ (hæn) n 1 the imperial dynasty that ruled China for most of the time from 206 bc to 221 ad, expanding its territory and developing its bureaucracy 2 the Chinese people as contrasted to Mongols, Manchus, etc

Han² (hæn) n a river in E central China, rising in S Shaanxi and flowing southeast through Hubei to the Yangtze River at Wuhan. Length: about 1450 km (900 miles)

hanaper ('hænəpə) n a small wickerwork basket, often used to hold official papers [c15: from Old French *hanapier*, from *hanap* cup, of Germanic origin; compare Old High German *hnapf* bowl, Old English *hnæp*]

Hanau (German 'haːnau) n a city in central Germany, in Hesse east of Frankfurt am Main: a centre of the jewellery industry. Pop: 88 897 (2003 est)

Han Cities pl n a group of three cities in E central China (Hanyang, Hankow, and Wuchang), in SE Hubei at the confluence of the Han and Yangtze Rivers; united in 1950 to form the conurbation of Wuhan, the capital of Hubei province

Hancock ('hænkɒk) n 1 Anthony John, known as Tony. 1924–68, British comedian, noted for his radio series *Hancock's Half Hour* 2 John. 1737–93, American statesman; first signatory of the Declaration of Independence

hand (hænd) n 1 a the prehensile part of the body at the end of the arm, consisting of a thumb, four fingers, and a palm b the bones of this part 2 the corresponding or similar part in animals 3 something resembling this in shape or function 4 a the cards dealt to one or all players in one round of a card game b a player holding such cards c one round of a card game 5 agency or influence: *the hand of God* 6 a part in something done: *he had a hand in the victory* 7 assistance: *to give someone a hand with his work* 8 a pointer on a dial, indicator, or gauge, esp on a clock 9 acceptance or pledge of partnership, as in marriage: *he asked for her hand; he gave me his hand on the merger* 10 a position or direction indicated by its location to the side of an object or the observer: *on the right hand; on every hand* 11 a contrastive aspect, condition, etc (in the phrases on the one hand, on the other hand) 12 (preceded by an ordinal number) source or origin: *a story heard at third hand* 13 a person, esp one who creates something: *a good hand at painting* 14 a labourer or manual worker: *we've just taken on a new hand at the farm* 15 a member of a ship's crew: *all hands on deck* 16 a person's handwriting: *the letter was in his own hand* 17 a round of applause: *give him a hand* 18 a manner or characteristic way of doing something: *the hand of a master* 19 a unit of length measurement equalling four inches, used for measuring the height of horses, usually from the front hoof to the withers 20 a cluster or bundle, esp of bananas 21 a free hand freedom to do as desired 22 a hand's turn (usually used with a negative) a small amount of work: *he hasn't done a hand's turn* 23 a heavy hand tyranny, persecution, or oppression: *he ruled with a heavy hand* 24 a high hand an oppressive or dictatorial manner 25 at hand or near at hand very near or close, esp in time 26 by hand a by manual rather than mechanical means b by messenger or personally: *the letter was delivered by hand* 27 from hand to mouth a in poverty: *living from hand to mouth* b without preparation or planning **28 hand and foot** in all ways possible; completely: *they waited on him hand and foot* **29 hand in glove** in an intimate relationship or close association **30 hand over fist** steadily and quickly; with rapid progress: *he makes money hand over fist* **31 hold one's hand** to stop or postpone a planned action or punishment **32 hold someone's hand** to support, help, or guide someone, esp by giving sympathy or moral support **33 in hand a** under control **b** receiving attention or being acted on **c** available for use; in reserve **d** with deferred payment: *he works a week in hand* **34 keep one's hand in** to continue or practise **35 on hand** close by; present: *I'll be on hand to help you* **36 out of hand a** beyond control **b** without reservation or deeper examination: *he condemned him out of hand* **37 show one's hand** to reveal one's stand, opinion, or plans **38 to hand** accessible **39 try one's hand** to attempt to do something **40** (*modifier*) **a** of or involving the hand: *a hand grenade* **b** made to be carried in or worn on the hand: *hand luggage* **c** operated by hand: *a hand drill* **41** (*in combination*) made by hand rather than by a machine: *hand-sewn* ▷ *vb* (*tr*) **42** to transmit or offer by the hand or hands **43** to help or lead with the hand **44** *nautical* to furl (a sail) **45 hand it to someone** to give credit to someone ▷ See also **hand down, hand in, hand-off, hand on, hand-out, hand over, hands** [Old English *hand*; related to Old Norse *hönd*, Gothic *handus*, Old High German *hant*] > 'handless *adj* > 'hand,like *adj*

HAND *abbreviation text messaging* have a nice day

handbag ('hænd,bæg) *n* **1** Also called: bag, (*US and Canadian*) purse, (*chiefly US*) pocketbook a woman's small bag carried to contain personal articles **2** a small suitcase that can be carried by hand **3** a commercial style of House music [(for sense 3) C20: humorous allusion to the trend for groups of women to dance round their handbags in discos, nightclubs, etc]

handball ('hænd,bɔːl) *n* **1** a game in which two teams of seven players try to throw a ball into their opponent's goal **2** a game in which two or four people strike a ball against a wall or walls with the hand, usually gloved **3** *soccer* the offence committed when a player other than a goalkeeper in his own penalty area touches the ball with a hand ▷ *vb* **4** *Australian rules football* to pass (the ball) with a blow of the fist

handbarrow ('hænd,bærəʊ) *n* a flat tray for transporting loads, usually carried by two men

handbill ('hænd,bɪl) *n* a small printed notice for distribution by hand

handbook ('hænd,bʊk) *n* a reference book listing brief facts on a subject or place or directions for maintenance or repair, as of a car

handbrake ('hænd,breɪk) *n* **1** a brake operated by a hand lever **2** the lever that operates the handbrake

handbrake turn *n* a turn sharply reversing the direction of a vehicle by speedily applying the handbrake while turning the steering wheel

handbreadth ('hænd,bretθ, -,bredθ) or **hand's-breadth** *n* the width of a hand used as an indication of length

h and c *abbreviation* hot and cold (water)

handcart ('hænd,kɑːt) *n* a simple cart, usually with one or two wheels, pushed or drawn by hand

handcraft ('hænd,krɑːft) *n* **1** another word for **handicraft** ▷ *vb* **2** (*tr*) to make by handicraft

handcrafted ('hænd,krɑːftɪd) *adj* made by handicraft

handcuff ('hænd,kʌf) *vb* **1** (*tr*) to put handcuffs on (a person); manacle ▷ *n* **2** (*plural*) a pair of locking metal rings joined by a short bar or chain for securing prisoners, etc

hand down *vb* (*tr, adverb*) **1** to leave to a later period or generation; bequeath **2** to pass (an outgrown garment) on from one member of a family to a younger one **3** *law* to announce or deliver (a verdict)

-handed *adj* having a hand or hands as specified: *broad-handed; a four-handed game of cards*

Handel ('hænd³l) *n* **George Frederick.** German name *Georg Friedrich Händel.* 1685–1759, German composer, resident in England, noted particularly for his oratorios, including the *Messiah* (1741) and *Samson* (1743). Other works include over 40 operas, 12 concerti grossi, organ concertos, chamber and orchestral music, esp *Water Music* (1717)

handful ('hændfʊl) *n, pl* **-fuls 1** the amount or number that can be held in the hand **2** a small number or quantity **3** *informal* a person or thing difficult to manage or control

handgun ('hænd,gʌn) *n* a firearm that can be held, carried, and fired with one hand, such as a pistol

hand-held *adj* **1** held in position by the hand **2** (of a film camera) held rather than mounted, as in close-up action shots **3** (of a computer) able to be held in the hand and not requiring connection to a fixed power source ▷ *n* **4** a computer that can be held in the hand

handicap ('hændɪ,kæp) *n* **1** something that hampers or hinders **2 a** a contest, esp a race, in which competitors are given advantages or disadvantages of weight, distance, time, etc, in an attempt to equalize their chances of winning **b** the advantage or disadvantage prescribed **3** *golf* the number of strokes by which a player's averaged score exceeds the standard scratch score for the particular course: used as the basis for handicapping in competitive play **4** any physical disability or disadvantage resulting from physical, mental, or social impairment or abnormality ▷ *vb* **-caps, -capping, -capped** (*tr*) **5** to be a hindrance or disadvantage to **6** to assign a handicap or handicaps to **7** to organize (a contest) by handicapping [c17: probably from *hand in cap*, a lottery game in which players drew forfeits from a cap or deposited money in it] > 'handi,capper *n*

handicapped ('hændɪ,kæpt) *adj* **1** physically disabled **2** (of a competitor) assigned a handicap

handicraft ('hændɪ,krɑːft) *n* **1** skill or dexterity in working with the hands **2** a particular skill or art performed with the hands, such as weaving, pottery, etc **3** Also called: handcraft the work produced by such a skill or art [c15: changed from HANDCRAFT through the influence of HANDIWORK, which was analysed as if HANDY + WORK]

hand in *vb* (*tr, adverb*) to return or submit (something, such as an examination paper)

handism ('hænd,ɪzəm) *n* discriminination against people on the grounds of whether they are left-handed or right-handed

handiwork ('hændɪ,wɜːk) *n* **1** work performed or produced by hand, such as embroidery or pottery **2** the result of the action or endeavours of a person or thing [Old English *handgeweorc*, from HAND + *geweorc*, from *ge-* (collective prefix) + *weorc* WORK]

handkerchief ('hæŋkətʃɪf, -,tʃiːf) *n* a small square of soft absorbent material, such as linen, silk, or soft paper, carried and used to wipe the nose, etc

handlanger ('hænd,læŋə) *n* *South African* an unskilled assistant to a tradesman [from Dutch]

handle ('hænd³l) *n* **1** the part of a utensil, drawer, etc, designed to be held in order to move, use, or pick up the object **2** NZ a glass beer mug with a handle **3** *slang* a person's name or title **4** a CB radio slang name for **call sign 5** an opportunity, reason, or excuse for doing something: *his background served as a handle for their mockery* **6** the quality, as of textiles, perceived by touching or feeling **7 fly off the handle** *informal* to become suddenly extremely angry ▷ *vb* (*mainly tr*) **8** to pick up and hold, move, or touch with the hands **9** to operate or employ using the hands: *the boy handled the reins well* **10** to have power or control over: *my wife handles my investments* **11** to manage successfully: *a secretary must be able to handle clients* **12** to discuss (a theme, subject, etc) **13** to deal with or treat in a specified way: *I was handled with great tact* **14** to trade or deal in (specified merchandise) **15** (*intr*) to react or respond in a specified way to operation or control: *the car handles well on bends* [Old English; related to Old Saxon *handlon* (vb), Old High German *hantilla* towel] > 'handled *adj*

handlebar moustache ('hænd³l,bɑː) *n* a bushy extended moustache with curled ends that resembles handlebars

handlebars ('hænd³l,bɑːz) *pl n* (*sometimes singular*) a metal tube having its ends curved to form handles, used for steering a bicycle, motorcycle, etc

handler ('hændlə) *n* **1** a person, esp a police officer, in charge of a specially trained dog **2** the trainer or second of a boxer

Handler ('hændlə) *n* Daniel. born 1970, US writer for older children, best known for the macabre humour of his *A Series of Unfortunate Events*, a sequence of books written in the persona of Lemony Snicket

Handley Page *n* Sir Frederick. See (Sir Frederick Handley) **Page**

handling ('hændlɪŋ) *n* **1** the act or an instance of picking up, turning over, or touching something **2** treatment, as of a theme in literature **3 a** the process by which a commodity is packaged, transported, etc **b** (*as modifier*): *handling charges* **4** *law* the act of receiving property that one knows or believes to be stolen

handmade (ˌhænd'meɪd) *adj* made by hand, not by machine, esp with care or craftsmanship

handmaiden ('hændˌmeɪdᵊn) *or* **handmaid** *n* **1** a person or thing that serves a useful but subordinate purpose **2** *archaic* a female servant or attendant

hand-me-down *n informal* **1** something, esp an outgrown garment, passed down from one person to another **2** anything that has already been used by another

hand-off *rugby* ▷ *n* **1** the act of warding off an opposing player with the open hand ▷ *vb* **hand off 2** (*tr, adverb*) to ward off (an opponent) using a hand-off

hand on *vb* (*tr, adverb*) to pass to the next in a succession

hand organ *n* another name for **barrel organ**

hand-out *n, pl* **hand-outs 1** clothing, food, or money given to a needy person **2** a leaflet, free sample, etc, given out to publicize something **3** a statement or other document distributed to the press or an audience to confirm, supplement, or replace an oral presentation ▷ *vb* **hand out** (*tr, adverb*) **4** to distribute

hand over *vb* (*tr, adverb*) **1** to surrender possession of; transfer ▷ *n* **handover 2** a transfer or surrender

hand-pick *vb* (*tr*) to choose or select with great care, as for a special job or purpose > ˌhand-'picked *adj*

handrail ('hændˌreɪl) *n* a rail alongside a stairway, etc, at a convenient height to be grasped to provide support

hands (hændz) *pl n* **1** power or keeping: *your welfare is in his hands* **2** Also called: **handling** *soccer* the infringement of touching the ball with any part of the hand or arm **3 change hands** to pass from the possession of one person or group to another **4 hands down** without effort; easily **5 have one's hands full a** to be completely occupied **b** to be beset with problems **6 have one's hands tied** to be wholly unable to act **7 lay hands on** *or* **lay hands upon a** to seize or get possession of **b** to beat up; assault **c** to find *Christianity* to confirm or ordain by the imposition of hands **8 off one's hands** for which one is no longer responsible **9 on one's hands a** for which one is responsible: *I've got too much on my hands to help* **b** to spare: *time on my hands* **10 wash one's hands of** to have nothing more to do with

Hands (hænz) *n* Terence David, known as *Terry*. born 1941, British theatre director: chief executive and artistic director (1986–91) of the Royal Shakespeare Company

handsaw ('hændˌsɔː) *n* any saw designed for use in one hand only

hand's-breadth *n* another name for **handbreadth**

handsel *or* **hansel** ('hænsᵊl) *archaic or dialect* ▷ *n* **1** a gift for good luck at the beginning of a new year, new venture, etc ▷ *vb* **-sels, -selling, -selled** *or US* **-sels, -seling, -seled** (*tr*) **2** to give a handsel to (a person) **3** to begin (a venture) with ceremony; inaugurate [Old English *handselen* delivery into the hand; related to Old Norse *handsal* promise sealed with a handshake, Swedish *handsöl* gratuity; see HAND, SELL]

handset ('hændˌset) *n* a telephone mouthpiece and earpiece mounted so that they can be held simultaneously to mouth and ear

handshake ('hændˌʃeɪk) *n* the act of grasping and shaking a person's hand, as when being introduced or agreeing on a deal

hands-off *adj* **1** (of a machine, device, etc) without need of manual operation **2** denoting a policy, etc, of

deliberate noninvolvement: *a hands-off strategy towards industry*

handsome ('hændsəm) *adj* **1** (of a man) good-looking, esp in having regular, pleasing, and well-defined features **2** (of a woman) fine-looking in a dignified way **3** well-proportioned, stately, or comely: *a handsome room* **4** liberal or ample: *a handsome allowance* **5** gracious or generous: *a handsome action* [C15 *handsom* easily handled; compare Dutch *handzaam*; see HAND, -SOME¹] > 'handsomely *adv* > 'handsomeness *n*

hands-on *adj* involving practical experience of equipment, etc: *hands-on training in the use of computers*

handspring ('hændˌsprɪŋ) *n* a gymnastic feat in which a person starts from a standing position and leaps forwards or backwards into a handstand and then onto his feet

handstand ('hændˌstænd) *n* the act or instance of supporting the body on the hands alone in an upside down position

hand-to-hand *adj, adv* at close quarters

hand-to-mouth *adj, adv* with barely enough money or food to satisfy immediate needs

handwork ('hændˌwɜːk) *n* work done by hand rather than by machine > 'handˌworked *adj*

handwriting ('hændˌraɪtɪŋ) *n* **1** writing by hand rather than by typing or printing **2** a person's characteristic writing style: *that signature is in my handwriting* > 'handˌwritten *adj*

handy ('hændɪ) *adj* **handier, handiest 1** conveniently or easily within reach **2** easy to manoeuvre, handle, or use: *a handy tool* **3** skilful with one's hands > 'handiness *n* > 'handily *adv*

Handy ('hændɪ) *n* W(illiam) C(hristopher). 1873–1958, US blues musician and singer, esp noted for the song "St Louis Blues"

handyman ('hændɪˌmæn) *n, pl* **-men** a man employed to do various tasks

Hanepoot ('hɑːnəˌpʊət) *n South African* a variety of muscat grape used as a dessert fruit and in making wine [from Afrikaans *hane* cock + *poot* claw]

Han Fei Zu ('hæn 'feɪ 'tʃuː) *n* died 233 BC, Chinese diplomat and philosopher of law

hang (hæŋ) *vb* **hangs, hanging, hung** (hʌŋ) **1** to fasten or be fastened from above, esp by a cord, chain, etc; suspend **2** to place or be placed in position as by a hinge so as to allow free movement around or at the place of suspension: *to hang a door* **3** (*intr; sometimes foll by over*) to be suspended or poised; hover: *a pall of smoke hung over the city* **4** (*intr; sometimes foll by over*) to be imminent; threaten **5** (*intr*) to be or remain doubtful or unresolved (esp in the phrase **hang in the balance**) **6** (*past tense and past participle* **hanged**) to suspend or be suspended by the neck until dead **7** (*tr*) to decorate, furnish, or cover with something suspended or fastened **8** (*tr*) to fasten to or suspend from a wall: *to hang wallpaper* **9** to fall or droop or allow to fall or droop: *to hang one's head in shame* **10** (*tr*) to suspend (game such as pheasant) so that it becomes slightly decomposed and therefore more tender and tasty **11** (of a jury) to prevent or be prevented from reaching a verdict **12** (*past tense and past participle* **hanged**) *slang* to damn or be damned: used in mild curses or interjections: *I'll be hanged before I'll go out in that storm* **13** (*intr*) to pass slowly (esp in the phrase **time hangs heavily**) **14 hang fire** to be delayed ▷ *n* **15** the way in which something hangs **16** (*usually used with a negative*) *slang* a damn: *I don't care a hang for what you say* **17 get the hang of** *informal* **a** to understand the technique of doing something **b** to perceive the meaning or significance of ▷ See also **hang about, hang back** [Old English *hangian*; related to Old Norse *hanga*, Old High German *hangēn*]

hang about *or* **hang around** *vb* (*intr*) **1** to waste time; loiter **2** (*adverb; foll by with*) to frequent the company (of someone)

hangar ('hæŋə) *n* a large workshop or building for storing and maintaining aircraft [C19: from French: shed, perhaps from Medieval Latin *angārium* shed used as a smithy, of obscure origin]

hang back *vb* (*intr, adverb; often foll by from*) to be reluctant to go forward or carry on (with some activity)

Hangchow *n* a variant transliteration of the Chinese name for **Hangzhou**

hangdog ('hæŋ,dɒg) *adj* downcast, furtive, or guilty in appearance or manner

hanger ('hæŋə) *n* **1 a** any support, such as a hook, strap, peg, or loop, on or by which something may be hung **b** See **coat hanger 2 a** a person who hangs something **b** (*in combination*): *paperhanger* **3** a wood on a steep hillside, characteristically beech growing on chalk in southern England **4** a loop or strap on a sword belt from which a short sword or dagger was hung

hanger-on *n*, *pl* **hangers-on** a sycophantic follower or dependant, esp one hoping for personal gain

hang-glider *n* an unpowered aircraft consisting of a large cloth wing stretched over a light framework from which the pilot hangs in a harness, using a horizontal bar to control the flight > **'hang-gliding** *n*

hangi ('hʌŋi:) *n* NZ **1** Also called: **Māori oven, umu** an open-air cooking pit **2** the food cooked in it **3** the social gathering at the resultant meal [Māori]

hang in *vb* (*intr, preposition*) *informal* to persist: *just hang in there for a bit longer*

hanging ('hæŋɪŋ) *n* **1 a** the putting of a person to death by suspending the body by the neck from a noose **b** (*as modifier*): *a hanging offence* **2** (*often plural*) a decorative textile such as a tapestry or drapery hung on a wall or over a window **3** the act of a person or thing that hangs ▷ *adj* **4** not supported from below; suspended **5** undecided; still under discussion **6** inclining or projecting downwards; overhanging **7** situated on a steep slope or in a high place **8** (*prenominal*) given to issuing harsh sentences: *a hanging judge*

Hanging Gardens of Babylon *n* (in ancient Babylon) gardens, probably planted on terraces of a ziggurat: one of the Seven Wonders of the World

hanging valley *n* *geography* a tributary valley entering a main valley at a much higher level because of overdeepening of the main valley, esp by glacial erosion

hangman ('hæŋmən) *n*, *pl* **-men** an official who carries out a sentence of hanging on condemned criminals

hangnail ('hæŋ,neɪl) *n* a piece of skin torn away from, but still attached to, the base or side of a fingernail [c17: from Old English *angnægl*, from *enge* tight + *nægl* NAIL; influenced by HANG]

hang on *vb* (*intr*) **1** (*adverb*) to continue or persist in an activity, esp with effort or difficulty **2** (*adverb*) to cling, grasp, or hold **3** (*preposition*) to be conditioned or contingent on; depend on: *everything hangs on this business deal* **4** Also called: **hang onto, hang upon** (*preposition*) to listen attentively to **5** (*adverb*) *informal* to wait or remain: *hang on for a few minutes*

hang out *vb* (*adverb*) **1** to suspend, be suspended, or lean, esp from an opening, as for display or airing **2** (*intr*) *informal* to live at or frequent a place **3** *slang* to relax completely in an unassuming way (esp in the phrase **let it all hang out**) **4** (*intr*) US *informal* to act or speak freely, in an open, cooperative, or indiscreet manner ▷ *n* **hang-out 5** *informal* a place where one lives or that one frequently visits

hangover ('hæŋ,əʊvə) *n* **1** the delayed aftereffects of drinking too much alcohol in a relatively short period of time, characterized by headache and sometimes nausea and dizziness **2** a person or thing left over from or influenced by a past age

Hang Seng Index (hæŋ sɛŋ) *n* an index of share prices based on an average of 33 stocks quoted on the Hong Kong Stock Exchange [name of a Hong Kong bank]

hang together *vb* (*intr, adverb*) **1** to be cohesive or united **2** to be consistent: *your statements don't quite hang together*

Hanguk ('hæn'gʊk) *n* the Korean name for **South Korea**

hang up *vb* (*adverb*) **1** (*tr*) to put on a hook, hanger, etc **2** to replace (a telephone receiver) on its cradle at the end of a conversation, often breaking a conversation off abruptly **3** (*tr; usually passive; usually foll by on*) *informal* to cause to have an emotional or psychological preoccupation or problem: *he's really hung up on his mother* ▷ *n* **hang-up** *informal* **4** an emotional or psychological preoccupation or problem **5** a persistent cause of annoyance

Hangzhou ('hæŋ'dʒəʊ) *or* **Hangchow** *n* a port in E China, capital of Zhejiang province, on Hangzhou Bay (an inlet of the East China Sea), at the foot of the Eye of Heaven Mountains: regarded by Marco Polo as the finest city in the world; seat of two universities (1927, 1959). Pop: 1 955 000 (2005 est)

hank (hæŋk) *n* **1** a loop, coil, or skein, as of rope, wool, or yarn **2** *nautical* a ringlike fitting that can be opened to admit a stay for attaching the luff of a sail **3** a unit of measurement of cloth, yarn, etc, such as a length of 840 yards (767 m) of cotton or 560 yards (512 m) of worsted yarn [c13: of Scandinavian origin; compare Old Norse *hanka* to coil, Swedish *hank* string]

hanker ('hæŋkə) *vb* (foll by *for, after*, or an infinitive) to have a yearning (for something or to do something) [c17: probably from Dutch dialect *hankeren*] > **'hankering** *n*

Hankow *or* **Han-k'ou** ('hæn'kaʊ) *n* a former city in SE China, in SE Hubei at the confluence of the Han and Yangtze Rivers: one of the Han Cities; merged with Hanyang and Wuchang in 1950 to form the conurbation of Wuhan

Hanks (hæŋks) *n* **Tom.** born 1956, US film actor: his films include *Splash* (1984), *Philadelphia* (1993), *Forrest Gump* (1994), *Saving Private Ryan* (1998), and *The Terminal* (2004)

hanky *or* **hankie** ('hæŋkɪ) *n*, *pl* **hankies** *informal* short for **handkerchief**

hanky-panky ('hæŋkɪ'pæŋkɪ) *n* *informal* **1** dubious or suspicious behaviour **2** foolish behaviour or talk **3** illicit sexual relations [c19: variant of HOCUS-POCUS]

Hanna ('hænə) *n* **William.** 1910–2001, US animator and film producer who with **Joseph Barbera** (born 1911) created the cartoon characters Tom and Jerry in the 1940s; the Hanna–Barbera company later produced numerous cartoon series for television

Hannah ('hænə) *n* *Old Testament* the woman who gave birth to Samuel (I Samuel 1–2)

Hannibal ('hænɪbºl) *n* 247–182 BC, Carthaginian general; son of Hamilcar Barca. He commanded the Carthaginian army in the Second Punic War (218–201). After capturing Sagunto in Spain, he invaded Italy (218), crossing the Alps with an army of about 40 000 men and defeating the Romans at Trasimene (217) and Cannae (216). In 203 he was recalled to defend Carthage and was defeated by Scipio at Zama (202). He was later forced into exile and committed suicide to avoid capture

Hannover (German ha'no:fər) *n* a city in N Germany, capital of Lower Saxony: capital of the kingdom of Hannover (1815–66); situated on the Mittelland canal. Pop: 516 160 (2003 est). English spelling: **Hanover**

Hanoi (hæ'nɔɪ) *n* the capital of Vietnam, on the Red River: became capital of Tonkin in 1802, of French Indochina in 1887, of Vietnam in 1945, and of North Vietnam (1954–75); university (1917); industrial centre. Pop: 4 147 000 (2005 est)

Hanover¹ ('hænəʊvə) *n* the English spelling of **Hannover**

Hanover² ('hænəʊvə) *n* **1** a princely house of Germany (1692–1815), the head of which succeeded to the British throne as George I in 1714 **2** the royal house of Britain (1714–1901)

Hanoverian (,hænə'vɪərɪən) *adj* **1** of, relating to, or situated in Hannover **2** of or relating to the princely house of Hanover or to the monarchs of England or their reigns from 1714 to 1901 ▷ *n* **3** a member or supporter of the house of Hanover

Hanratty (hæn'rætɪ) *n* **James.** 1936–62, Englishman executed, despite conflicting evidence, for a murder on the A6 road. Subsequent public concern played a major part in the abolition of capital punishment in Britain. New DNA evidence led to an appeal by Hanratty's supporters being dismissed in 2002

Hansard ('hænsɑːd) *n* **1** the official report of the proceedings of the British Parliament **2** a similar report kept by other legislative bodies [c19: named after T.C. *Hansard* (1752–1828) and his son, who compiled the reports until 1889]

Hanse (hæns) *or* **Hansa** ('hænsə, -zə) *n* **1** a medieval guild of merchants **2** a fee paid by the new members of a medieval trading guild **3** another name for the

Hanseatic League [c12: of Germanic origin; compare Old High German *hansa*, Old English *hōs* troop]

Hanseatic (ˌhænsɪˈætɪk) *adj* **1** of or relating to the Hanseatic League ▷ *n* **2** a member of the Hanseatic League

Hanseatic League *n* a commercial association of towns in N Germany formed in the mid-14th century to protect and control trade. It was at its most powerful in the 15th century

hansel (ˈhænsəl) *n, vb* a variant spelling of **handsel**

hansom (ˈhænsəm) *n* (*sometimes capital*) a two-wheeled one-horse carriage with a fixed hood. The driver sits on a high outside seat at the rear. Also called: **hansom cab** [c19: short for *hansom cab*, named after its designer J. A. Hansom (1803–82)]

hantavirus (ˈhæntəˌvaɪrəs) *n* any one of a group of viruses that are transmitted to humans by rodents and cause disease of varying severity, ranging from a mild form of influenza to respiratory or kidney failure [c20: from *Hanta(an)*, river in North and South Korea where the disease was first reported + VIRUS]

Hants (hænts) *abbreviation* Hampshire

Hanukkah, Hanukah *or* **Chanukah** (ˈhɑːnəkə, -nʊˌkɑː; *Hebrew* xanuˈka) *n* the eight-day Jewish festival of lights beginning on the 25th of Kislev and commemorating the rededication of the temple by Judas Maccabaeus in 165 BC. Also called: **Feast of Dedication, Feast of Lights** [from Hebrew, literally: a dedication]

Hanuman (ˌhʌnʊˈmɑːn) *n* **1** (*sometimes not capital*) another word for **entellus** **2** the monkey chief of Hindu mythology and devoted helper of Rama [from Hindi *Hanumān*, from Sanskrit *hanumant* having (conspicuous) jaws, from *hanu* jaw]

Hanyang *or* **Han-yang** (ˈhænˈjæn) *n* a former city in SE China, in SE Hubei at the confluence of the Han and Yangtze Rivers: one of the Han Cities; merged with Hankow and Wuchang in 1950 to form the conurbation of Wuhan

hap (hæp) *n* *archaic* **1** luck; chance **2** an occurrence ▷ *vb* **haps, happing, happed** **3** (*intr*) an archaic word for **happen** [c13: from Old Norse *happ* good luck; related to Old English *gehæplic* convenient, Old Slavonic *kobŭ* fate]

ha'penny (ˈheɪpnɪ) *n, pl* **-nies** *Brit* a variant spelling of **halfpenny**

haphazard (hæpˈhæzəd) *adv, adj* **1** at random ▷ *adj* **2** careless; slipshod > **hapˈhazardly** *adv* > **hapˈhazardness** *n*

hapless (ˈhæplɪs) *adj* unfortunate; wretched > **ˈhaplessly** *adv* > **ˈhaplessness** *n*

haplography (hæpˈlɒɡrəfɪ) *n, pl* **-phies** the accidental writing of only one letter or syllable where there should be two similar letters or syllables, as in spelling *endodontics* as *endontics* [c19: from Greek, from *haplous* single + -GRAPHY]

haploid (ˈhæplɔɪd) *biology* ▷ *adj* Also: **haploidic** **1** (esp of gametes) having a single set of unpaired chromosomes ▷ *n* **2** a haploid cell or organism [c20: from Greek *haploeidēs* single, from *haplous* single] > **ˈhaploidy** *n*

haplology (hæpˈlɒlədʒɪ) *n* omission of a repeated occurrence of a sound or syllable in fluent speech, as for example in the pronunciation of *library* as (ˈlaɪbrɪ)

haply (ˈhæplɪ) *adv* (*sentence modifier*) an archaic word for **perhaps**

happen (ˈhæpən) *vb* **1** (*intr*) (of an event in time) to come about or take place; occur **2** (*intr*; foll by *to*) (of some unforeseen circumstance or event, esp death), to fall to the lot (of); be a source of good or bad fortune (to): *if anything happens to me it'll be your fault* **3** (*tr*) to chance (to be or do something): *I happen to know him* **4** (*tr*; *takes a clause as object*) to be the case, esp if by chance, that: *it happens that I know him* ▷ *adv, sentence substitute* **5** *Northern English dialect* another word for **perhaps** [c14: see HAP¹, -EN¹]

● USAGE See at **occur**

happening (ˈhæpənɪŋ, ˈhæpnɪŋ) *n* **1** an occurrence; event **2** an improvised or spontaneous display or performance consisting of bizarre and haphazard events ▷ *adj* **3** *informal* fashionable and up-to-the-minute

happen on *or* **happen upon** *vb* (*intr, preposition*) to find by chance

happy (ˈhæpɪ) *adj* **-pier, -piest** **1** feeling, showing, or expressing joy; pleased **2** willing: *I'd be happy to show you around* **3** causing joy or gladness **4** fortunate; lucky: *the happy position of not having to work* **5** aptly expressed; appropriate: *a happy turn of phrase* **6** (*postpositive*) *informal* slightly intoxicated [c14: see HAP¹, -Y¹] > **ˈhappily** *adv* > **ˈhappiness** *n*

happy event *n* *informal* the birth of a child

happy-go-lucky *adj* carefree or easy-going

happy hour *n* a time, usually in the early evening, when some pubs or bars sell drinks at reduced prices

happy hunting ground *n* **1** (in American Indian legend) the paradise to which a person passes after death **2** a productive or profitable area for a person with a particular interest or requirement

happy medium *n* a course or state that avoids extremes

Hapsburg (ˈhæpsˌbɜːɡ) *n* a German princely family founded by Albert, count of Hapsburg (1153). From 1440 to 1806, the Hapsburgs wore the imperial crown of the Holy Roman Empire almost uninterruptedly. They also provided rulers for Austria, Spain, Hungary, Bohemia, etc The line continued as the royal house of **Hapsburg-Lorraine**, ruling in Austria (1806–48) and Austria-Hungary (1848–1918). German name: **Habsburg**

haptic (ˈhæptɪk) *adj* relating to or based on the sense of touch [from Greek, from *haptein* to touch]

hapuka *or* **hapuku** (həˈpuːkə, ˈhɑːpʊkə) *n* NZ another name for **groper** [Māori]

hara-kiri (ˌhærəˈkɪrɪ) *or* **hari-kari** (ˌhærɪˈkɑːrɪ) *n* (formerly, in Japan) ritual suicide by disembowelment with a sword when disgraced or under sentence of death. Also called: **seppuku** [c19: from Japanese taboo slang, from *hara* belly + *kiri* cutting]

Harald I (ˈhærəld) *n* called *Harald Fairhair*. ?850–933, first king of Norway: his rule caused emigration to the British Isles

Harald III *n* surname *Hardraade*. 1015–66, king of Norway (1047–66); invaded England (1066) and died at the battle of Stamford Bridge

harangue (həˈræŋ) *vb* **1** to address (a person or crowd) in an angry, vehement, or forcefully persuasive way ▷ *n* **2** a loud, forceful, or angry speech [c15: from Old French, from Old Italian *aringa* public speech, probably of Germanic origin; related to Medieval Latin *harenga*; see HARRY, RING] > **haˈranguer** *n*

Harappa (həˈræpə) *n* an ancient city in the Punjab in NW Pakistan: one of the centres of the Indus civilization that flourished from 2500 to 1700 BC; probably destroyed by Indo-European invaders

Harappan (həˈræpən) *adj* **1** of or relating to Harappa (an ancient city in the Punjab) or its inhabitants ▷ *n* **2** a native or inhabitant of Harappa

Harar *or* **Harrer** (ˈhɑːrə) *n* a city in E Ethiopia: former capital of the Muslim state of Adal. Pop: 96 000 (2005 est)

Harare (həˈrɑːrɪ) *n* the capital of Zimbabwe, in the northeast: University of Zimbabwe (1957); industrial and commercial centre. Pop: 1 527 000 (2005 est). Former name (until 1982): Salisbury

harass (ˈhærəs, həˈræs) *vb* (*tr*) to trouble, torment, or confuse by continual persistent attacks, questions, etc [c17: from French *harasser*, variant of Old French *harer* to set a dog on, of Germanic origin; compare Old High German *harēn* to cry out] > **ˈharassed** *adj* > **ˈharassment** *n*

Harbin (hɑːˈbiːn, -ˈbɪn) *n* a city in NE China, capital of Heilongjiang province on the Songhua River: founded by the Russians in 1897; centre of tsarist activities after the October Revolution in Russia (1917). Pop: 2 989 000 (2005 est). Also called: **Ha-erh-pin**

harbinger (ˈhɑːbɪndʒə) *n* **1** a person or thing that announces or indicates the approach of something; forerunner ▷ *vb* **2** (*tr*) to announce the approach or arrival of [c12: from Old French *herbergere*, from *herberge* lodging, from Old Saxon *heriberga*; compare Old High German *heriberga* army shelter; see HARRY, BOROUGH]

harbour *or US* **harbor** (ˈhɑːbə) *n* **1** a sheltered port **2** a place of refuge or safety ▷ *vb* **3** (*tr*) to give shelter to: *to harbour a criminal* **4** (*tr*) to maintain secretly: *to harbour a grudge* **5** to shelter (a vessel) in a harbour or (of a vessel) to seek shelter [Old English *herebeorg*, from *here* troop, army + *beorg* shelter; related to Old High German *heriberga* hostelry, Old Norse *herbergi*]

harbourage *or US* **harborage** ('hɑːbərɪdʒ) *n* shelter or refuge, as for a ship, or a place providing shelter

harbour master *n* an official in charge of a harbour

hard (hɑːd) *adj* **1** firm or rigid; not easily dented, crushed, or pierced **2** toughened by or as if by physical labour; not soft or smooth: *hard hands* **3** difficult to do or accomplish; arduous: *a hard task* **4** difficult to understand or perceive: *a hard question* **5** showing or requiring considerable physical or mental energy, effort, or application: *hard work; a hard drinker* **6** exacting; demanding: *a hard master* **7** harsh; cruel: *a hard fate* **8** inflicting pain, sorrow, distress, or hardship: *hard times* **9** tough or adamant: *a hard man* **10** forceful or violent: *a hard knock* **11** cool or uncompromising: *we took a long hard look at our profit factor* **12** indisputable; real: *hard facts* **13** *chem* (of water) impairing the formation of a lather by soap **14** practical, shrewd, or calculating: *he is a hard man in business* **15** too harsh to be pleasant: *hard light* **16 a** (of currency) in strong demand, esp as a result of a good balance of payments situation **b** (of credit) difficult to obtain; tight **17** (of alcoholic drink) being a spirit rather than a wine, beer, etc **18** (of a drug such as heroin, morphine, or cocaine) highly addictive **19** *physics* (of radiation, such as gamma rays and X-rays) having high energy and the ability to penetrate solids **20** *chiefly US* (of goods) durable **21** *phonetics* (not in modern technical usage) denoting the consonants *c* and *g* in English when they are pronounced as velar stops (k, g) **22 a** being heavily fortified and protected **b** (of nuclear missiles) located underground in massively reinforced silos **23** politically extreme: *the hard left* **24** *Brit & NZ informal* incorrigible or disreputable (esp in the phrase **a hard case**) **25 a hard nut to crack a** a person not easily persuaded or won over **b** a thing not easily understood **26 hard by** near; close by **27 hard up** *informal* **a** in need of money; poor **b** (foll by *for*) in great need (of): *hard up for suggestions* ▷ *adv* **28** with great energy, force, or vigour: *the team always played hard* **29** as far as possible; all the way: *hard left* **30** with application; earnestly or intently: *she thought hard about the formula* **31** with great intensity, force, or violence: *his son's death hit him hard* **32** (foll by *on*, *upon*, *by*, or *after*) close; near: *hard on his heels* **33** (foll by *at*) assiduously; devotedly **34 a** with effort or difficulty: *their victory was hard won* **b** (in combination): *hard-earned* **35** slowly and reluctantly: *prejudice dies hard* **36 go hard with** to cause pain or difficulty to (someone) **37 hard put** *or* **hard put to it** scarcely having the capacity (to do something) ▷ *n* **38** *Brit* a roadway across a foreshore **39** *slang* hard labour **40** *slang* an erection of the penis (esp in the phrase **get** or **have a hard on**) [Old English *heard*; related to Old Norse *harthr*, Old Frisian *herd*, Old High German *herti*, Gothic *hardus* hard, Greek *kratus* strong]

hard and fast *adj* (**hard-and-fast** *when prenominal*) (esp of rules) invariable or strict

hardback ('hɑːd,bæk) *n* **1** a book or edition with covers of cloth, cardboard, or leather ▷ *adj* **2** Also called: **casebound, hardbound** ('hɑːd,baʊnd), **hardcover** ('hɑːd,kʌvə) of or denoting a hardback or the publication of hardbacks

hard-bitten *adj* tough and realistic

hardboard ('hɑːd,bɔːd) *n* a thin stiff sheet made of compressed sawdust and wood pulp bound together with plastic adhesive or resin under heat and pressure

hard-boiled *adj* **1** (of an egg) boiled until the yolk and white are solid **2** *informal* **a** tough, realistic **b** cynical

hard cash *n* money or payment in the form of coins or notes rather than cheques or credit

hard coal *n* another name for **anthracite**

hard copy *n* computer output printed on paper, as contrasted with machine-readable output such as magnetic tape

hardcore ('hɑːd,kɔː) *n* **1** a style of rock music characterized by short fast numbers with minimal melody and aggressive delivery **2** a type of dance music with a very fast beat

hard core *n* **1** the members of a group or movement who

form an intransigent nucleus resisting change **2** material, such as broken bricks, stones, etc, used to form a foundation for a road, paving, building, etc ▷ *adj* **hard-core 3** (of pornography) describing or depicting sexual acts in explicit detail **4** extremely committed or fanatical: *a hard-core Communist*

hard disk *n* a disk of rigid magnetizable material that is used to store data for computers: it is permanently mounted in its disk drive and usually has a storage capacity of a few gigabytes

hard drive *or* **hard disk drive** *n* *computing* (on a computer) the mechanism that handles the reading, writing, and storage of data on the hard disk

Hardecanute ('hɑːdɪkə,njuːt) *n* same as **Harthacanute**

harden ('hɑːdᵊn) *vb* **1** to make or become hard or harder; freeze, stiffen, or set **2** to make or become more hardy, tough, or unfeeling **3** to make or become stronger or firmer **4** (*intr*) *commerce* **a** (of prices, a market, etc) to cease to fluctuate **b** (of price) to rise higher > **'hardener** *n*

Hardenberg (German 'hɑːdənbɛrk) *n* **Friedrich von** ('friːdrɪç fɔn). the original name of Novalis. See **Novalis**

Hardenburg ('hɑːdᵊn,bɜːg) *n* **Fürst Karl (August) von**. 1750–1822, Prussian statesman: foreign minister (1804–06): prime minister (1807; 1810–22). His reforms enabled Prussia to break away from Napoleonic control in 1813

hardened ('hɑːdᵊnd) *adj* **1** rigidly set, as in a mode of behaviour **2** toughened, as by custom; seasoned

harden off *vb* (*adverb*) to accustom (a cultivated plant) or (of such a plant) to become accustomed to outdoor conditions by repeated exposure

hard feeling *n* (*often plural; often used with a negative*) resentment; ill will: *no hard feelings?*

hard hat *n* **1** a hat made of a hard material for protection, worn esp by construction workers, equestrians, etc **2** *informal, chiefly US & Canadian* a construction worker

hard-headed *adj* tough, realistic, or shrewd; not moved by sentiment

hardhearted (,hɑːd'hɑːtɪd) *adj* unkind or intolerant > ,hard'heartedness *n*

Hardicanute ('hɑːdɪkə,njuːt) *n* same as **Harthacanute**

Hardie ('hɑːdɪ) *n* (**James**) **Keir** (kɪə). 1856–1915, British Labour leader and politician, born in Scotland; the first parliamentary leader of the Labour Party

hardihood ('hɑːdɪ,hʊd) *n* courage, daring, or audacity

Harding ('hɑːdɪŋ) *n* **Warren G(amaliel)**. 1865–1923, 29th president of the US (1921–23)

Hardinge ('hɑːdɪŋ) *n* **Henry**, 1st Viscount Hardinge of Lahore. 1785–1856, British politician, soldier, and colonial administrator; governor general of India (1844–48)

hard labour *n* *criminal law* (formerly) the penalty of compulsory physical labour imposed in addition to a sentence of imprisonment: abolished in England in 1948

hard landing *n* a landing by a rocket or spacecraft in which the vehicle is destroyed on impact

hard line *n* an uncompromising course or policy > ,hard'liner *n*

hardly ('hɑːdlɪ) *adv* **1** scarcely; barely: *we hardly knew the family* **2** just; only just: *he could hardly hold the cup* **3** often used ironically almost or probably not or not at all: *he will hardly incriminate himself* **4** with difficulty or effort **5** *rare* harshly or cruelly

● USAGE Since *hardly*, *scarcely*, and *barely* already have
● negative force, it is redundant to use another negative
● in the same clause: *he had hardly had* (not *he hadn't hardly*
● *had*) *time to think; there was scarcely any* (not *scarcely no*)
● bread left

hard-nosed *adj* *informal* tough, shrewd, and practical

hard of hearing *adj* **a** deaf or partly deaf **b** (*as collective noun; preceded by the*): *the hard of hearing*

Hardouin Mansart (French ardwɛ̃ mɑ̃saːr) *n* See **Mansart** (sense 2)

hard pad *n* (in dogs) an abnormal increase in the thickness of the foot pads: one of the clinical signs of canine distemper. See **distemper¹** (sense 1)

hard palate *n* the anterior bony portion of the roof of the mouth, extending backwards to the soft palate

hardpan ('hɑːd,pæn) n a hard impervious layer of clay below the soil, resistant to drainage and root growth

hard paste n **a** porcelain made with kaolin and petuntse, of Chinese origin and made in Europe from the early 18th century **b** (as modifier): hard-paste porcelain

hard-pressed adj **1** in difficulties **2** subject to severe competition **3** closely pursued

hard rock n music a rhythmically simple and usually highly amplified style of rock and roll

hard sauce n another name for **brandy butter**

hard science n one of the natural or physical sciences, such as physics, chemistry, biology, geology, or astronomy > hard scientist n

hard sell n an aggressive insistent technique of selling or advertising

hard-shell adj Also hard-shelled **1** zoology having a shell or carapace that is thick, heavy, or hard **2** US strictly orthodox

hardship ('hɑːdʃɪp) n **1** conditions of life difficult to endure **2** something that causes suffering or privation

hard shoulder n Brit a surfaced verge running along the edge of a motorway for emergency stops

hardtack ('hɑːd,tæk) n a kind of hard saltless biscuit, formerly eaten esp by sailors as a staple aboard ship. Also called: ship's biscuit, sea biscuit

hardtop ('hɑːd,tɒp) n a car equipped with a metal or plastic roof that is sometimes detachable

hardware ('hɑːd,wɛə) n **1** metal tools, implements, etc, esp cutlery or cooking utensils **2** computing the physical equipment used in a computer system, such as the central processing unit, peripheral devices, and memory ▷ See **software** **3** mechanical equipment, components, etc **4** heavy military equipment, such as tanks and missiles or their parts **5** informal a gun or guns collectively

hard-wired adj **1** (of a circuit or instruction) permanently wired into a computer, replacing separate software **2** (of human behaviour) innate; not learned: humans have a hard-wired ability for acquiring language

hardwood ('hɑːd,wʊd) n **1** the wood of any of numerous broad-leaved dicotyledonous trees, such as oak, beech, ash, etc, as distinguished from the wood of a conifer **2** any tree from which this wood is obtained

hardy ('hɑːdɪ) adj **-dier, -diest** **1** having or demanding a tough constitution; robust **2** bold; courageous **3** foolhardy; rash **4** (of plants) able to live out of doors throughout the winter [c13: from Old French hardi bold, past participle of hardir to become bold, of Germanic origin; compare Old English hierdan to HARDEN[1], Old Norse hertha, Old High German herten]

Hardy ('hɑːdɪ) n **1** Oliver. See **Laurel and Hardy** **2** Thomas. 1840–1928, British novelist and poet. Most of his novels are set in his native Dorset (part of his fictional Wessex) and include Far from the Madding Crowd (1874), The Return of the Native (1878), The Mayor of Casterbridge (1886), Tess of the d'Urbervilles (1891), and Jude the Obscure (1895), after which his work consisted chiefly of verse **3** Sir **Thomas Masterman**. 1769–1839, British naval officer, flag captain under Nelson (1799–1805): 1st Sea Lord (1830)

hare (hɛə) n, pl hares or hare **1** any solitary leporid mammal of the genus Lepus, such as L. europaeus (**European hare**). Hares are larger than rabbits, having longer ears and legs, and live in shallow nests (forms) **2** run with the hare and hunt with the hounds to be on good terms with both sides ▷ vb **3** (intr; often foll by off, after, etc) Brit informal to go or run fast or wildly [Old English hara; related to Old Norse heri, Old High German haso, Swedish hare, Sanskrit śaśá] > 'hare,like adj

Hare[1] (hɛə) n a member of a Dene Native Canadian people of northern Canada [of Athaspascan origin]

Hare[2] (hɛə) n **1** Sir **David**. born 1947, British dramatist and theatre director: his plays include Plenty (1978), Pravda (with Howard Brenton, 1985), The Secret Rapture (1989), Racing Demon (1990), and The Permanent Way (2003) **2** **William**. 19th century Irish murderer and bodysnatcher: associate of William Burke

hare and hounds n (functioning as singular) a game in which certain players (**hares**) run across country scattering pieces of paper that the other players (**hounds**) follow in an attempt to catch the hares

harebell ('hɛə,bɛl) n a N temperate campanulaceous plant, Campanula rotundifolia, having slender stems and leaves, and bell-shaped pale blue flowers

harebrained or **hairbrained** ('hɛə,breɪnd) adj rash, foolish, or badly thought out

Hare Krishna ('hɑːrɪ 'krɪʃnə) n **1** a Hindu sect devoted to a form of Hinduism (**Krishna Consciousness**) based on the worship of the god Krishna **2** pl Hare Krishnas a member or follower of this sect [c20: from Hindi, literally: Lord Krishna (vocative): the opening words of a sacred verse often chanted in public by adherents of the movement]

harelip ('hɛə,lɪp) n a congenital cleft or fissure in the midline of the upper lip, resembling the cleft upper lip of a hare, often occurring with cleft palate > 'hare,lipped adj

harem ('hɛərəm, hɑː'riːm) or **hareem** (hɑː'riːm) n **1** the part of an Oriental house reserved strictly for wives, concubines, etc **2** a Muslim's wives and concubines collectively **3** a group of female animals of the same species that are the mates of a single male [c17: from Arabic harīm forbidden (place)]

hare's-foot n a leguminous annual plant, Trifolium arvense, that grows on sandy soils in Europe and NW Asia and has downy heads of white or pink flowers

Harfleur ('hɑːflɜːr, French arflœr) n a port in N France, in Seine-Maritime department: important centre in the Middle Ages. Pop: 8517 (1999)

Hargeisa (hɑː'geɪsə) n a city in NW Somalia: former capital of British Somaliland (1941–60) and functioning as the capital of the separatist republic of Somaliland; trading centre for nomadic herders. Pop: reliable recent estimates are not available

Hargreaves ('hɑːgriːvz) n **James**. died 1778, English inventor of the spinning jenny

haricot ('hærɪkəʊ) n a variety of French bean with light-coloured edible seeds, which can be dried and stored [c17: from French, perhaps from Nahuatl ayecotli]

Harijan ('hʌrɪdʒən) n a member of certain classes in India, formerly considered inferior and untouchable [Hindi, literally: man of God (so called by Mahatma Gandhi), from Hari god + jan man]

hari-kari (,hærɪ'kɑːrɪ) n a non-Japanese variant of **hara-kiri**

Haringey ('hærɪŋ,geɪ) n a borough of N Greater London. Pop: 224 700 (2003 est). Area: 30 sq km (12 sq miles)

Harishchandra (,hærɪʃ'tʃændrə) n also known as Bharatendu. 1850–85, Indian poet, dramatist, and essayist, who established Hindi as a literary language

harissa (hə'rɪsə) n (in Tunisian cookery) a hot paste or sauce made from chilli peppers, tomatoes, spices, and olive oil, often served with couscous [c20: from Arabic]

hark (hɑːk) vb (intr; usually imperative) to listen; pay attention [Old English heorcnian to HEARKEN; related to Old Frisian herkia, Old High German hōrechen; see HEAR]

hark back vb (intr, adverb) to return to an earlier subject, point, or position, as in speech or thought

harken ('hɑːkən) vb a variant spelling (esp US) of **hearken** > 'harkener n

harl (hɑːl) n angling a variant of **herl**

Harlech ('hɑːlɪk) n a town in N Wales, in Gwynedd: noted for its ruined 13th-century castle overlooking Cardigan Bay: tourism. Pop: 1233 (2001)

Harlem ('hɑːləm) n a district of New York City, in NE Manhattan: now largely a Black ghetto

harlequin ('hɑːlɪkwɪn) n **1** (sometimes capital) theatre a stock comic character originating in the commedia dell'arte; the foppish lover of Columbine in the English harlequinade. He is usually represented in diamond-patterned multicoloured tights, wearing a black mask **2** a clown or buffoon ▷ adj **3** varied in colour or decoration: a harlequin suit **4** (of certain animals) having a white coat with irregular patches of black or other dark colour [c16: from Old French Herlequin, Hellequin leader of band of demon horsemen, perhaps from Middle English Herle king (unattested) King Herle, mythical being identified with Woden]

harlequinade (ˌhɑːlɪkwɪˈneɪd) n 1 (*sometimes capital*) *theatre* a play or part of a pantomime in which harlequin has a leading role 2 buffoonery

Harley (ˈhɑːlɪ) n **Robert**, 1st Earl of Oxford. 1661–1724, British statesman; head of the government (1710–14), negotiated the treaty of Utrecht (1713)

Harley Street (ˈhɑːlɪ) n a street in central London famous for its large number of medical specialists' consulting rooms

harlot (ˈhɑːlət) n a prostitute or promiscuous woman [c13: from Old French *herlot* rascal, of obscure origin] > ˈharlotry n

Harlow¹ (ˈhɑːləʊ) n a town in SE England, in W Essex: designated a new town in 1947. Pop: 78 389 (2001 est)

Harlow² (ˈhɑːləʊ) n **Jean**, real name *Harlean Carpentier*. 1911–37, US film actress, whose films include *Hell's Angels* (1930), *Red Dust* (1932), and *Bombshell* (1933)

harm (hɑːm) n 1 physical or mental injury or damage 2 moral evil or wrongdoing ▷ vb 3 (tr) to injure physically, morally, or mentally [Old English *hearm*; related to Old Norse *harmr* grief, Old High German *harm* injury, Old Slavonic *sramŭ* disgrace]

harmattan (hɑːˈmætᵊn) n a dry dusty wind from the Sahara blowing towards the W African coast, esp from November to March [c17: from Twi *haramata*, perhaps from Arabic *harām* forbidden thing; see HAREM]

harmful (ˈhɑːmfʊl) adj causing or tending to cause harm; injurious > ˈharmfully adv

harmless (ˈhɑːmlɪs) adj 1 not causing any physical or mental damage or injury 2 unlikely to annoy or worry people: *a harmless sort of man* > ˈharmlessly adv

harmonic (hɑːˈmɒnɪk) adj 1 of, involving, producing, or characterized by harmony; harmonious 2 *music* of, relating to, or belonging to harmony 3 *maths* a capable of expression in the form of sine and cosine functions b of or relating to numbers whose reciprocals form an arithmetic progression 4 *physics* of or concerned with an oscillation that has a frequency that is an integral multiple of a fundamental frequency ▷ n 5 *physics, music* a component of a periodic quantity, such as a musical tone, with a frequency that is an integral multiple of the fundamental frequency. The **first harmonic** is the fundamental, the **second harmonic** (twice the fundamental frequency) is the **first overtone**, the **third harmonic** (three times the fundamental frequency) is the **second overtone**, etc 6 *music* (not in technical use) overtone: in this case, the first overtone is the first harmonic, etc ▷ See also **harmonics** [c16: from Latin *harmonicus* relating to HARMONY] > harˈmonically adv

harmonica (hɑːˈmɒnɪkə) n 1 Also called: **mouth organ** a small wind instrument of the reed organ family in which reeds of graduated lengths set into a metal plate enclosed in a narrow oblong box are made to vibrate by blowing and sucking 2 See **glass harmonica** [c18: from Latin *harmonicus* relating to HARMONY]

harmonic analysis n the representation of a periodic function by means of the summation and integration of simple trigonometric functions

harmonic mean n the reciprocal of the arithmetic mean of the reciprocals of a set of specified numbers: the harmonic mean of 2, 3, and 4 is $3(\frac{1}{2} + 1\frac{5}{63} + 1\frac{5}{64})^{-1} = 36/13$

harmonic minor scale n *music* a minor scale modified from the state of being natural by the sharpening of the seventh degree

harmonic motion n a periodic motion in which the displacement is symmetrical about a point or a periodic motion that is composed of such motions

harmonic progression n a sequence of numbers whose reciprocals form an arithmetic progression, as 1, $\frac{1}{2}$, 1$\frac{5}{63}$, ...

harmonics (hɑːˈmɒnɪks) n 1 (*functioning as singular*) the science of musical sounds and their acoustic properties 2 (*functioning as plural*) the overtones of a fundamental note, as produced by lightly touching the string of a stringed instrument at one of its node points while playing

harmonic series n 1 *maths* a series whose terms are in

harmonic progression, as in $1 + \frac{1}{2} + \frac{1}{3} + ...$ 2 *acoustics* the series of tones with frequencies strictly related to one another and to the fundamental tone, as obtained by touching lightly the node points of a string while playing it. Its most important application is in the playing of brass instruments

harmonious (hɑːˈməʊnɪəs) adj 1 (esp of colours or sounds) fitting together well 2 having agreement or consensus 3 tuneful, consonant, or melodious

harmonist (ˈhɑːmənɪst) n 1 a person skilled in the art and techniques of harmony 2 a person who combines and collates parallel narratives

harmonium (hɑːˈməʊnɪəm) n a musical keyboard instrument of the reed organ family, in which air from pedal-operated bellows causes the reeds to vibrate [c19: from French, from *harmonie* HARMONY]

harmonize or **harmonise** (ˈhɑːmənaɪz) vb 1 to make or become harmonious 2 (tr) *music* to provide a harmony for (a melody, tune, etc) 3 (intr) to sing in harmony, as with other singers 4 to collate parallel narratives > ˌharmonizˈation or ˌharmoniˈsation n

harmony (ˈhɑːmənɪ) n, pl -nies 1 agreement in action, opinion, feeling, etc; accord 2 order or congruity of parts to their whole or to one another 3 agreeable sounds 4 *music* a any combination of notes sounded simultaneously b the vertically represented structure of a piece of music. See **melody** (sense 1b) c the art or science concerned with the structure and combinations of chords 5 a collation of the material of parallel narratives, esp of the four Gospels [c14: from Latin *harmonia* concord of sounds, from Greek: harmony, from *harmos* a joint]

Harmsworth (ˈhɑːmzwɜːθ) n 1 **Alfred Charles William**. See (Viscount) **Northcliffe** 2 **Harold Sydney**. See (1st Viscount) **Rothermere**

Harnack (German ˈharnak) n **Adolf von**. 1851–1930, German Protestant theologian, author of the influential *History of Dogma* (1886–90)

harness (ˈhɑːnɪs) n 1 an arrangement of leather straps buckled or looped together, fitted to a draught animal in order that the animal can be attached to and pull a cart 2 something resembling this, esp for attaching something to the body: *a parachute harness* 3 *weaving* the part of a loom that raises and lowers the warp threads, creating the shed 4 *archaic* armour collectively 5 **in harness** at one's routine work ▷ vb (tr) 6 to put harness on (a horse) 7 (usually foll by to) to attach (a draught animal) by means of harness to (a cart, etc) 8 to control so as to employ the energy or potential power of: *to harness the atom* 9 to equip or clothe with armour [c13: from Old French *harneis* baggage, probably from Old Norse *hernest* (unattested) provisions, from *herr* army + *nest* provisions] > ˈharnesser n

harness race n *horse racing* a trotting or pacing race for standard-bred horses driven in sulkies and harnessed in a special way to cause them to use the correct gait

Harney Peak (ˈhɑːnɪ) n a mountain in SW South Dakota: the highest peak in the Black Hills. Height: 2207 m (7242 ft)

Harnoncourt (anɔːˈcur) n **Nikolaus**. born 1929, Austrian conductor and cellist, noted for his performances using period instruments

Harold I (ˈhærəld) n surname *Harefoot*. died 1040, king of England (1037–40); son of Canute

Harold II n ?1022–66, king of England (1066); son of Earl Godwin and successor of Edward the Confessor. His claim to the throne was disputed by William the Conqueror, who defeated him at the Battle of Hastings (1066)

harp (hɑːp) n 1 a large triangular plucked stringed instrument consisting of a soundboard connected to an upright pillar by means of a curved crossbar from which the strings extend downwards. The strings are tuned diatonically and may be raised in pitch either one or two semitones by the use of pedals (**double-action harp**). Basic key: B major; range: nearly seven octaves ▷ vb 2 (intr) to play the harp 3 (tr) *archaic* to speak; utter; express 4 (intr; foll by *on* or *upon*) to speak or write in a persistent and tedious manner [Old English *hearpe*;

related to Old Norse *harpa*, Old High German *harfa*, Latin *corbis* basket, Russian *korobit* to warp] > 'harper *or* 'harpist *n*

Harper ('hɑːpə) *n* **Stephen (Joseph)**. born 1959. Canadian statesman; prime minister from 2006

Harper's Ferry ('hɑːpəz) *n* a village in NE West Virginia, at the confluence of the Potomac and Shenandoah Rivers: site of an arsenal seized by John Brown (1859). Pop: 302 (2003 est)

harpoon (hɑːˈpuːn) *n* **1 a** a barbed missile attached to a long cord and hurled or fired from a gun when hunting whales, etc **b** (*as modifier*): *a harpoon gun* ▷ *vb* **2** (*tr*) to spear with or as if with a harpoon [C17: probably from Dutch *harpoen*, from Old French *harpon* clasp, from *harper* to seize, perhaps of Scandinavian origin] > har'pooner *or* ‚harpoon'eer *n*

harp seal *n* a brownish-grey earless seal, *Pagophilus groenlandicus*, of the North Atlantic and Arctic Oceans

harpsichord ('hɑːpsɪˌkɔːd) *n* a horizontally strung stringed keyboard instrument, triangular in shape, consisting usually of two manuals controlling various sets of strings plucked by pivoted plectrums mounted on jacks. Some harpsichords have a pedal keyboard and stops by which the tone colour may be varied [C17: from New Latin *harpichordium*, from Late Latin *harpa* HARP + Latin *chorda* CHORD¹] > 'harpsi‚chordist *n*

harpy ('hɑːpɪ) *n, pl* -pies a cruel grasping woman [C16: from Latin *Harpyia*, from Greek *Harpuiai* the Harpies, literally: snatchers, from *harpazein* to seize]

Harpy ('hɑːpɪ) *n, pl* -pies *Greek myth* a ravenous creature with a woman's head and trunk and a bird's wings and claws

harquebus ('hɑːkwɪbəs) *n, pl* -buses a variant of **arquebus**

Harrer ('hɑːrə) *n* a variant spelling of **Harar**

harridan ('hærɪdən) *n* a scolding old woman; nag [C17: of uncertain origin; perhaps related to French *haridelle*, literally: broken-down horse; of obscure origin]

harrier¹ ('hærɪə) *n* **1** a person or thing that harries **2** any diurnal bird of prey of the genus *Circus*, having broad wings and long legs and tail and typically preying on small terrestrial animals: family *Accipitridae* (hawks, etc)

harrier² ('hærɪə) *n* **1** a smallish breed of hound used originally for hare-hunting **2** a cross-country runner [C16: from HARE + -ER¹; influenced by HARRIER¹]

Harriman ('hærɪmən) *n* **W(illiam) Averell**. 1891–1986, US diplomat: negotiated the Nuclear Test Ban Treaty with the Soviet Union (1963); governor of New York (1955–58)

Harrington ('hærɪŋtən) *n* **James**. 1611–77, English republican and writer. He described his ideal form of government in *Oceana* (1656)

Harris¹ ('hærɪs) *n* the S part of the island of Lewis with Harris, in the Outer Hebrides. Pop: about 3000 (2001). Area: 500 sq km (190 sq miles)

Harris² ('hærɪs) *n* **1 Sir Arthur Travers**, known as *Bomber Harris*. 1892–1984, British air marshal. He was commander-in-chief of Bomber Command of the RAF (1942–45) **2 Frank**. 1856–1931, British writer and journalist; his books include his autobiography *My Life and Loves* (1923–27) and *Contemporary Portraits* (1915–30) **3 Joel Chandler**. 1848–1908, US writer; creator of Uncle Remus **4 Roy**. 1898–1979, US composer, esp of orchestral and choral music incorporating American folk tunes

Harrisburg ('hærɪsˌbɜːg) *n* a city in S Pennsylvania, on the Susquehanna River: the state capital. Pop: 48 322 (2003 est)

Harrison ('hærɪsən) *n* **1 Benjamin**. 1833–1901, 23rd president of the US (1889–93) **2 George**. 1943–2001, British rock singer, guitarist, and songwriter: a member of the Beatles (1962–70). His solo recordings include *All Things Must Pass* (1970) and *Cloud Nine* (1987) **3 Rex (Carey)**. 1908–90, British actor. His many films include *Major Barbara* (1940), *Blithe Spirit* (1945), and *My Fair Lady* (1964) **4 Tony**. born 1937, British poet, dramatist, and translator: best known for his poems for television and his translations for the stage **5** grandfather of Benjamin, **William Henry**. 1773–1841, 9th president of the US (1841)

Harris Tweed *n trademark* a loose-woven tweed made in the Outer Hebrides, esp Lewis and Harris

Harrogate ('hærəgɪt) *n* a town in N England, in North Yorkshire: a former spa, now a centre for tourism and conferences. Pop: 70 811 (2001 est)

harrow ('hærəʊ) *n* **1** any of various implements used to level the ground, stir the soil, break up clods, destroy weeds, etc, in soil ▷ *vb* **2** (*tr*) to draw a harrow over (land) **3** (*tr*) to distress; vex [C13: of Scandinavian origin; compare Danish *harv*, Swedish *harf*; related to Middle Dutch *harke* rake] > 'harrower *n* > 'harrowing *adj, n*

Harrow ('hærəʊ) *n* a borough of NW Greater London; site of an English boys' public school founded in 1571 at **Harrow-on-the-Hill**, a part of this borough. Pop: 210 700 (2003 est). Area: 51 sq km (20 sq miles)

harrumph (həˈrʌmf) *vb* (*intr*) to clear or make the noise of clearing the throat

harry ('hærɪ) *vb* -ries, -rying, -ried **1** (*tr*) to harass; worry **2** to ravage (a town, etc), esp in war [Old English *hergian*; related to *here* army, Old Norse *herja* to lay waste, Old High German *heriōn*]

harsh (hɑːʃ) *adj* **1** rough or grating to the senses **2** stern, severe, or cruel [C16: probably of Scandinavian origin; compare Middle Low German *harsch*, Norwegian *harsk* rancid] > 'harshly *adv* > 'harshness *n*

hart (hɑːt) *n, pl* **harts** *or* **hart** the male of the deer, esp the red deer aged five years or more [Old English *heorot*; related to Old Norse *hjörtr*, Old High German *hiruz* hart, Latin *cervus* stag, Lithuanian *kárve* cow; see HORN]

Hart (hɑːt) *n* **1 Lorenz**. 1895–1943, US lyricist: collaborated with Richard Rodgers in writing musicals **2 Moss**. 1904–61, US dramatist: collaborated with George Kaufman on Broadway comedies and wrote libretti for musicals

hartal (hɑːˈtɑːl) *n* (in India) the act of closing shops or suspending work, esp in political protest [C20: from Hindi *hartāl*, from *hāt* shop (from Sanskrit *hatta*) + *tālā* bolt for a door (from Sanskrit: latch)]

Harte (hɑːt) *n* **(Francis) Bret**. 1836–1902, US poet and short-story writer, noted for his sketches of Californian gold miners, such as *The Luck of Roaring Camp* (1870)

hartebeest ('hɑːtɪˌbiːst) *or* **hartbeest** ('hɑːtˌbiːst) *n* either of two large African antelopes, *Alcelaphus buselaphus* or *A. lichtensteini*, having an elongated muzzle, lyre-shaped horns, and a fawn-coloured coat [C18: via Afrikaans from Dutch; see HART, BEAST]

Hartford ('hɑːtfəd) *n* a port in central Connecticut, on the Connecticut River: the state capital. Pop: 124 387 (2003 est)

Harthacanute ('hɑːθəkəˌnjuːt), **Hardecanute** *or* **Hardicanute** *n* ?1019–42, king of Denmark (1035–42) and of England (1040–42); son of Canute

Hartington ('hɑːtɪŋtən) *n* **Lord**. See (8th Duke of) **Devonshire**

Hartlepool ('hɑːtlɪˌpuːl) *n* **1** a port in NE England, in Hartlepool unitary authority, Co Durham, on the North Sea: greatly enlarged in 1967 by its amalgamation with West Hartlepool; engineering, clothing, food processing. Pop: 86 075 (2001) **2** a unitary authority in NE England, in Co Durham: formerly (1974–96) part of the county of Cleveland. Pop: 90 200 (2003 est). Area: 93 sq km (36 sq miles)

Hartley ('hɑːtlɪ) *n* **1 David**. 1705–57, English philosopher and physician. In *Observations of Man* (1749) he introduced the theory of psychological associationism **2 L(eslie) P(oles)**. 1895–1972, British novelist. His novels include the trilogy *The Shrimp and the Anemone* (1944), *The Sixth Heaven* (1946), and *Eustace and Hilda* (1947) as well as *The Go-Between* (1953)

Hartnell ('hɑːtnəl) *n* **Sir Norman**. 1901–79, English couturier

hartshorn ('hɑːtsˌhɔːn) *n* an obsolete name for: **sal volatile** (sense 2) [Old English *heortes horn* hart's horn (formerly a chief source of ammonia)]

hart's-tongue *n* an evergreen Eurasian fern, *Asplenium scolopendrium*, with narrow undivided fronds bearing rows of sori: family *Polypodiaceae*

harum-scarum ('hɛərəmˈskɛərəm) *adj, adv* **1** in a reckless way or of a reckless nature ▷ *n* **2** a person who is impetuous or rash [C17: perhaps from *hare* (in obsolete sense: harass) + *scare*, variant of STARE[1]; compare HELTER-SKELTER]

Harun al-Rashid (hæˈruːn ælræˈʃiːd) *n* ?763–809 AD, Abbasid caliph of Islam (786–809), whose court at Baghdad was idealized in the *Arabian Nights*

haruspex (həˈrʌspɛks) *n, pl* haruspices (həˈrʌspɪˌsiːz) (in ancient Rome) a priest who practised divination, esp by examining the entrails of animals [c16: from Latin, probably from *hīra* gut + *specere* to look] > haruspicy (həˈrʌspɪsɪ) *n*

harvest (ˈhɑːvɪst) *n* **1** the gathering of a ripened crop **2** the crop itself or the yield from it in a single growing season **3** the season for gathering crops **4** the product of an effort, action, etc: *a harvest of love* ▷ *vb* **5** to gather or reap (a ripened crop) from (the place where it has been growing) **6** (*tr*) to receive or reap (benefits, consequences, etc) [Old English *hærfest*; related to Old Norse *harfr* harrow, Old High German *herbist* autumn, Latin *carpere* to pluck, Greek *karpos* fruit, Sanskrit *krpāna* shears] > 'harvesting *n*

harvester (ˈhɑːvɪstə) *n* **1** a person who harvests **2** a harvesting machine, esp a combine harvester

harvest home *n* **1** the bringing in of the harvest **2** *chiefly Brit* a harvest supper

harvestman (ˈhɑːvɪstmən) *n, pl* -men **1** a person engaged in harvesting **2** any arachnid of the order *Opiliones* (or *Phalangida*), having a small rounded body and very long thin legs. Also called (*US and Canadian*): daddy-longlegs

harvest moon *n* the full moon occurring nearest to the autumnal equinox

harvest mouse *n* a very small reddish-brown Eurasian mouse, *Micromys minutus*, inhabiting cornfields, hedgerows, etc, and feeding on grain and seeds: family *Muridae*

Harvey (ˈhɑːvɪ) *n* **William**. 1578–1657, English physician who discovered the mechanism of blood circulation, expounded in *On the motion of the heart* (1628)

Harwell (ˈhɑːˌwɛl) *n* a village in S England, in Oxfordshire: atomic research station (1947)

Harwich (ˈhærɪtʃ) *n* a port in SE England, in NE Essex on the North Sea. Pop: 20 130 (2001)

Haryana (hərˈjɑːnə) *n* a state of NE India, formed in 1966 from the Hindi-speaking parts of the state of Punjab. Capital: Chandigarh (shared with Punjab). Pop: 21 082 989 (2001 est). Area: 44 506 sq km (17 182 sq miles)

Harz *or* **Harz Mountains** (hɑːts) *pl n* a range of wooded hills in central Germany, between the Rivers Weser and Elbe: source of many legends. Highest peak: Brocken, 1142 m (3746 ft)

has (hæz) *vb* (used with *he*, *she*, *it*, or a singular noun) a form of the present tense (indicative mood) of **have**

Hasan al-Basri (hæˈsæn æl ˈbæzrɪ) *n* died 728 AD, Muslim religious thinker

has-been *n informal* a person or thing that is no longer popular, successful, effective, etc

hasbian (ˈhæzbɪən) *n* a former lesbian who has become heterosexual or bisexual [c20: HAS-BEEN + LESBIAN]

Hasdrubal (ˈhæzdrʊbªl) *n* died 207 BC, Carthaginian general: commanded the Carthaginian army in Spain (218–211); joined his brother Hannibal in Italy and was killed at the Metaurus

Hašek (*Czech* ˈhaʃɛk) *n* **Jaroslav** (ˈjarɔslaf). 1883–1923, Czech novelist and short-story writer; author of *The Good Soldier Schweik* (1923)

hash¹ (hæʃ) *n* **1** a dish of diced cooked meat, vegetables, etc, reheated in a sauce **2** a reuse or rework of old material **3** make a hash of *informal* **a** to mix or mess up **b** to defeat or destroy **4** settle someone's hash *or* fix someone's hash *informal* to subdue or silence someone ▷ *vb* (*tr*) **5** to chop into small pieces **6** to mix or mess up [c17: from Old French *hacher* to chop up, from *hache* HATCHET]

hash² (hæʃ) *n slang* short for **hashish**

hash browns *pl n* diced boiled potatoes mixed with chopped onion, shaped and fried until brown

Hashemite Kingdom of Jordan (ˈhæʃɪˌmaɪt) *n* the official name of **Jordan¹**

hashish (ˈhæʃiːʃ, -ɪʃ) *or* **hasheesh** (ˈhæʃiːʃ) *n* a purified resinous extract of the dried flower tops of the female hemp plant, used as a hallucinogenic. See also **cannabis** [c16: from Arabic *hashīsh* hemp, dried herbage]

haslet (ˈhæzlɪt) *or* **harslet** *n* a loaf of cooked minced pig's offal, eaten cold [c14: from Old French *hastelet* piece of spit roasted meat, from *haste* spit, of Germanic origin; compare Old High German *harsta* frying pan]

hasn't (ˈhæzªnt) *vb contraction of* has not

hasp (hɑːsp) *n* **1** a metal fastening consisting of a hinged strap with a slot that fits over a staple and is secured by a pin, bolt, or padlock ▷ *vb* **2** (*tr*) to secure (a door, window, etc) with a hasp [Old English *hæpse*; related to Old Norse *hespa*, Old High German *haspa* hasp, Dutch *haspel* reel, Sanskrit *capa* bow]

Hassan II (hæˈsɑːn, ˈhæsªn) *n* 1929–1999, king of Morocco (1961–99)

Hasselt (*Flemish* ˈhasəlt; *French* asɛlt) *n* a market town in E Belgium, capital of Limburg province. Pop: 69 127 (2004 est)

Hassid *or* **Hasid** (ˈhæsɪd; *Hebrew* xaˈsid) *n* variant spellings of **Chassid**

hassium (ˈhæsɪəm) *n* a synthetic element produced in small quantities by high-energy ion bombardment. Symbol: Hs; atomic no 108 [c20: from Latin, from Hesse, German state where it was discovered]

hassle (ˈhæsªl) *informal* ▷ *n* **1** a prolonged argument; wrangle **2** a great deal of trouble; difficulty; nuisance ▷ *vb* **3** (*intr*) to quarrel or wrangle **4** (*tr*) to cause annoyance or trouble to (someone); harass [c20: of unknown origin]

hassock (ˈhæsək) *n* **1** a firm upholstered cushion used for kneeling on, esp in church **2** a thick clump of grass [Old English *hassuc* matted grass]

hast (hæst) *vb archaic or dialect* (used with the pronoun *thou* or its relative equivalent) a singular form of the present tense (indicative mood) of **have**

hastate (ˈhæsteɪt) *adj* (of a leaf) having a pointed tip and two outward-pointing lobes at the base [c18: from Latin *hastātus* with a spear, from *hasta* spear]

haste (heɪst) *n* **1** speed, esp in an action; swiftness; rapidity **2** the act of hurrying in a careless or rash manner **3** a necessity for hurrying; urgency **4** make haste to hurry; rush ▷ *vb* **5** a poetic word for **hasten** [c14: from Old French *haste*, of Germanic origin; compare Old Norse *heifst* hate, Old English *hǣst* strife, Old High German *heisti* powerful]

hasten (ˈheɪsªn) *vb* **1** (*may take an infinitive*) to hurry or cause to hurry; rush **2** (*tr*) to be anxious (to say something) > 'hastener *n*

Hastings¹ (ˈheɪstɪŋz) *n* **1** a port in SE England, in East Sussex on the English Channel: near the site of the **Battle of Hastings** (1066), in which William the Conqueror defeated King Harold; chief of the Cinque Ports. Pop: 85 828 (2001) **2** a town in New Zealand, on E North Island: centre of a rich agricultural and fruit-growing region. Pop: 71 100 (2004 est)

Hastings² (ˈheɪstɪŋz) *n* **1 Gavin**. born 1962, Scottish Rugby Union footballer; played for Scotland 1986–95 **2 Warren**. 1732–1818, British administrator in India; governor general of Bengal (1773–85). He implemented important reforms but was impeached by parliament (1788) on charges of corruption; acquitted in 1795

hasty (ˈheɪstɪ) *adj* -tier, -tiest **1** rapid; swift; quick **2** excessively or rashly quick **3** short-tempered **4** showing irritation or anger > 'hastily *adv* > 'hastiness *n*

hat (hæt) *n* **1** any of various head coverings, esp one with a brim and a shaped crown **2** *informal* a role or capacity **3** I'll eat my hat *informal* I will be greatly surprised if (something that proves me wrong) happens **4** keep something under one's hat to keep something secret **5** pass the hat round *or* send the hat round to collect money, as for a cause **6** take off one's hat to to admire or congratulate **7** talk through one's hat **a** to talk foolishly **b** to deceive or bluff ▷ *vb* hats, hatting, hatted **8** (*tr*) to supply (a person, etc) with a hat or put a hat on (someone) [Old English *hætt*; related to Old Norse *höttr* cap, Latin *cassis* helmet; see HOOD¹] > 'hatless *adj*

hatband (ˈhætˌbænd) *n* a band or ribbon around the base of the crown of a hat

hatbox ('hætˌbɒks) n a box or case for a hat or hats

hatch¹ (hætʃ) vb 1 to cause (the young of various animals, esp birds) to emerge from the egg or (of young birds, etc) to emerge from the egg 2 to cause (eggs) to break and release the fully developed young or (of eggs) to break and release the young animal within 3 (tr) to contrive or devise (a scheme, plot, etc) ▷ n 4 the act or process of hatching 5 a group of newly hatched animals [c13: of Germanic origin; compare Middle High German *hecken* to mate (used of birds), Swedish *häcka* to hatch, Danish *hække*]

hatch² (hætʃ) n 1 a covering for a hatchway 2 a short for **hatchway** b a door in an aircraft or spacecraft 3 Also called: **serving hatch** an opening in a wall between a kitchen and a dining area 4 the lower half of a divided door 5 a sluice or sliding gate in a dam, dyke, or weir 6 **down the hatch** *slang* (used as a toast) drink up! 7 **under hatches** a below decks b out of sight c brought low; dead [Old English *hæcc*; related to Middle High German *heck*, Dutch *hek* gate]

hatch³ (hætʃ) vb art to mark (a figure, shade, etc) with fine parallel or crossed lines to indicate shading [c15: from Old French *hacher* to chop, from *hache* HATCHET] ▷ 'hatching n

hatch⁴ (hætʃ) n informal short for **hatchback**

hatchback ('hætʃˌbæk) n 1 a sloping rear end of a car having a single door that is lifted to open 2 a car having such a rear end

hatchel ('hætʃəl) vb -els, -elling, -elled or US -els, -eling, -eled 1 another word for **heckle** ▷ n 2 another word for **heckle** [c13 *hechele*, of Germanic origin; related to Old High German *hāko* hook, Middle Dutch *hekele* HACKLE] ▷ 'hatcheller n

hatchery ('hætʃəri) n, pl -eries a place where eggs are hatched under artificial conditions

hatchet ('hætʃit) n 1 a short axe used for chopping wood, etc 2 a tomahawk 3 (modifier) of narrow dimensions and sharp features: a hatchet face 4 **bury the hatchet** to cease hostilities and become reconciled [c14: from Old French *hachette*, from *hache* axe, of Germanic origin; compare Old High German *happa* knife]

hatchet job n informal a malicious or devastating verbal or written attack

hatchet man n informal 1 a person carrying out unpleasant assignments for an employer or superior 2 a severe or malicious critic

hatchling ('hætʃlɪŋ) n a young animal that has newly emerged from an egg [c19: from HATCH¹ + -LING¹]

hatchment ('hætʃmənt) n heraldry a diamond-shaped tablet displaying the coat of arms of a dead person [c16: changed from ACHIEVEMENT]

hatchway ('hætʃˌweɪ) n 1 an opening in the deck of a vessel to provide access below 2 a similar opening in a wall, floor, ceiling, or roof, usually fitted with a lid or door

hate (heɪt) vb 1 to dislike (something) intensely; detest 2 (intr) to be unwilling (to be or do something) ▷ n 3 intense dislike 4 informal a person or thing that is hated (esp in the phrase **pet hate**) 5 (modifier) expressing or arousing feelings of hatred: hate mail [Old English *hatian*; related to Old Norse *hata*, Old Saxon *hatōn*, Old High German *hazzēn*] ▷ 'hateable or 'hatable adj ▷ 'hater n

hate crime n a crime, esp of violence, in which the victim is targeted because of his or her race, religion, sexuality, etc

hateful ('heɪtfʊl) adj 1 causing or deserving hate; loathsome; detestable 2 full of or showing hate ▷ 'hatefully adv ▷ 'hatefulness n

hate speech n speech disparaging a racial, sexual, or ethnic group or a member of such a group

Hatfield ('hætˌfiːld) n a market town in S central England, in Hertfordshire, with a new town of the same name built on the outskirts: university (1992); site of **Hatfield House** (1607–11), the seat of the Cecil family. Pop: 32 281 (2001)

hath (hæθ) vb archaic or dialect (used with the pronouns *he*, *she*, or *it* or a singular noun) a form of the present tense (indicative mood) of **have**

Hathaway ('hæθəˌweɪ) n Anne. ?1557–1623, wife of William Shakespeare

Hathor ('hæθɔː) n (in ancient Egyptian religion) the mother of Horus and goddess of creation > **Hathoric** (hæ'θɔːrɪk, -'θɒr-) adj

hatred ('heɪtrɪd) n a feeling of intense dislike; enmity

Hatshepsut (hæt'ʃepsuːt) or **Hatshepset** n queen of Egypt of the 18th dynasty (?1512–1482 BC). She built a great mortuary temple at Deir el Bahri near Thebes

hat stand or esp US **hat tree** n a frame or pole equipped with hooks or arms for hanging up hats, coats, etc

hatter ('hætə) n 1 a person who makes and sells hats 2 **mad as a hatter** crazily eccentric

Hatteras ('hætərəs) n **Cape Hatteras** a promontory off the E coast of North Carolina, on **Hatteras Island**, which is situated between Pamlico Sound and the Atlantic: known as the "Graveyard of the Atlantic" for its danger to shipping

Hattersley ('hætəzlɪ) n **Roy (Sydney George)**, Baron Hattersley of Sparkbrook. born 1932, British Labour politician; deputy leader of the Labour Party (1983–92); shadow home secretary (1980–83; 1987–92)

hat-trick n 1 cricket the achievement of a bowler in taking three wickets with three successive balls 2 any achievement of three points, victories, awards, etc within a given period, esp three goals scored by the same player in a soccer match

hauberk ('hɔːbɜːk) n a long coat of mail, often sleeveless [c13: from Old French *hauberc*, of Germanic origin; compare Old High German *halsberc*, Old English *healsbeorg*, from *heals* neck + *beorg* protection, shelter]

Haughey ('hɔːxɪ; Irish 'hʌhiː) n **Charles James**. 1925–2006, Irish politician; leader of the Fianna Fáil party; prime minister of the Republic of Ireland (1979–81; 1982; 1987–92)

haughty ('hɔːtɪ) adj -tier, -tiest having or showing arrogance [c16: from Old French *haut*, literally: lofty, from Latin *altus* high] ▷ 'haughtily adv ▷ 'haughtiness n

haul (hɔːl) vb 1 to drag or draw (something) with effort 2 (tr) to transport, as in a lorry 3 nautical to alter the course of (a vessel), esp so as to sail closer to the wind 4 (intr) nautical (of the wind) to blow from a direction nearer the bow ▷ n 5 the act of dragging with effort 6 (esp of fish) the amount caught at a single time 7 something that is hauled 8 the goods obtained from a robbery 9 a distance of hauling 10 the amount of a contraband seizure: arms haul; drugs haul [c16: from Old French *haler*, of Germanic origin; see HALE²]

haulage ('hɔːlɪdʒ) n 1 the act or labour of hauling 2 a rate or charge levied for the transportation of goods, esp by rail

haulier ('hɔːljə) n 1 a person or firm that transports goods by lorry; one engaged in road haulage 2 a person that hauls 3 a mine worker who conveys coal from the workings to the foot of the shaft

haulm or **halm** (hɔːm) n 1 the stems or stalks of beans, peas, potatoes, grasses, etc, collectively, as used for thatching, bedding, etc 2 a single stem of such a plant [Old English *healm*; related to Old Norse *halmr*, Old High German *halm* stem, straw, Latin *culmus* stalk, Greek *kalamos* reed, Old Slavonic *slama* straw]

haul up vb (adverb) 1 (tr) informal to call to account or criticize 2 nautical to sail (a vessel) closer to the wind

haunch (hɔːntʃ) n 1 the human hip or fleshy hindquarter of an animal, esp a horse or similar quadruped 2 the leg and loin of an animal, used for food 3 Also called: **hance** architect the part of an arch between the impost and the apex [c13: from Old French *hanche*; related to Spanish, Italian *anca*, of Germanic origin; compare Low German *hanke*]

haunt (hɔːnt) vb 1 to visit (a person or place) in the form of a ghost 2 (tr) to intrude upon or recur to (the memory, thoughts, etc): he was haunted by the fear of insanity 3 to visit (a place) frequently 4 to associate with (someone) frequently ▷ n 5 (often plural) a place visited frequently 6 a place to which animals habitually resort for food, drink, shelter, etc [c13: from Old French *hanter*, of Germanic origin; compare Old Norse *heimta* to bring home, Old English *hāmettan* to give a home to; see HOME]

haunted ('hɔːntɪd) adj 1 frequented or visited by ghosts

2 (*postpositive*) obsessed or worried

haunting ('hɔ:ntɪŋ) *adj* **1** (of memories) poignant or persistent **2** poignantly sentimental; enchantingly or eerily evocative ▷ '**haunted** *adv*

Hauptmann (*German* 'hauptman) *n* **Gerhart** ('ge:rhart). 1862–1946, German naturalist, dramatist, novelist, and poet. His works include the historical drama *The Weavers* (1892): Nobel prize for literature 1912

Hauraki Gulf (hau'ræki) *n* an inlet of the Pacific in New Zealand, on the N coast of North Island

Hausa ('hausə) *n* **1** *pl* **-sas** *or* **-sa** a member of a Negroid people of W Africa, living chiefly in N Nigeria **2** the language of this people: the chief member of the Chadic subfamily of the Afro-Asiatic family of languages. It is widely used as a trading language throughout W Africa and the S Sahara

hausfrau ('haus,frau) *n* a German housewife [German, from *Haus* HOUSE + *Frau* woman, wife]

Haussmann (*French* əsman) *n* **Georges-Eugène**, Baron. 1809–91, French town planner, noted for his major rebuilding of Paris in the reign of Napoleon III

hautboy ('əubɔɪ) *n* **1** Also called: **hautbois strawberry**, **haubois** ('əubɔɪ) a strawberry, *Fragaria moschata*, of central Europe and Asia, with large fruit **2** an archaic word for **oboe** [C16: from French *hautbois*, from *haut* high + *bois* wood, of Germanic origin; see BUSH[1]]

haute couture *French* (ot kutyr) *n* high fashion [literally: high dressmaking]

haute cuisine *French* (ot kwizin) *n* high-class cooking [literally: high cookery]

haute école *French* (ot ekɔl) *n* the classical art of riding [literally: high school]

Haute-Garonne (*French* otgarɔn) *n* a department of SW France, in Midi-Pyrénées region. Capital: Toulouse. Pop: 1 102 919 (2003 est). Area: 6367 sq km (2483 sq miles)

Haute-Loire (*French* otlwar) *n* a department of S central France, in Auvergne region. Capital: Le Puy. Pop: 213 993 (2003 est). Area: 5001 sq km (1950 sq miles)

Haute-Marne (*French* otmarn) *n* a department of NE France, in Champagne-Ardenne region. Capital: Chaumont. Pop: 190 983 (2003 est). Area: 6257 sq km (2440 sq miles)

Haute-Normandie (*French* otnɔrmãdi) *n* a region of NW France, on the English Channel: generally fertile and flat

Hautes-Alpes (*French* otzalp) *n* a department of SE France in Provence-Alpes-Côte d'Azur region. Capital: Gap. Pop: 126 810 (2003 est). Area: 5643 sq km (2201 sq miles)

Haute-Saône (*French* otson) *n* a department of E France, in Franche-Comté region. Capital: Vesoul. Pop: 232 283 (2003 est). Area: 5375 sq km (2096 sq miles)

Haute-Savoie (*French* otsavwa) *n* a department of E France, in Rhône-Alpes region. Capital: Annecy. Pop: 663 810 (2003 est). Area: 4958 sq km (1934 sq miles)

Hautes-Pyrénées (*French* otpirene) *n* a department of SW France, in Midi-Pyrénées region. Capital: Tarbes. Pop: 224 053 (2003 est). Area: 4534 sq km (1768 sq miles)

hauteur (əu'tɜ:) *n* pride; haughtiness [C17: from French, from *haut* high; see HAUGHTY]

Haute-Vienne (*French* otvjɛn) *n* a department of W central France, in Limousin region. Capital: Limoges. Pop: 353 788 (2003 est). Area: 5555 sq km (2166 sq miles)

haut monde *French* (o mɔ̃d) *n* high society [literally: high world]

Haut-Rhin (*French* orɛ̃) *n* a department of E France in Alsace region. Capital: Colmar. Pop: 722 692 (2003 est). Area: 3566 sq km (1377 sq miles)

Hauts-de-Seine (*French* odəsɛn) *n* a department of N central France, in Île-de-France region just west of Paris: formed in 1964. Capital: Nanterre. Pop: 1 470 706 (2003 est). Area: 175 sq km (68 sq miles)

Havana (hə'vænə) *n* the capital of Cuba, a port in the northwest on the Gulf of Mexico: the largest city in the Caribbean; founded in 1514 as San Cristóbal de la Habana by Diego Velásquez. Pop: 2 192 000 (2005 est). Spanish name: Habana. Related adjective: **Habanero**

Havana cigar *n* any of various cigars hand rolled in Cuba or made with Cuban tobacco, known esp for their high quality. Also called: Havana

Havant ('hæv°nt) *n* a market town in S England, in SE Hampshire. Pop: 45 435 (2001)

have (hæv) *vb* has, having, had (*mainly tr*) **1** to be in material possession of; own: *he has two cars* **2** to possess as a characteristic quality or attribute: *he has dark hair* **3** to receive, take, or obtain: *she had a present from him; have a look* **4** to hold or entertain in the mind: *to have an idea* **5** to possess a knowledge or understanding of: *I have no German* **6** to experience or undergo: *to have a shock* **7** to be infected with or suffer from: *to have a cold* **8** to gain control of or advantage over: *you have me on that point* **9** (*usually passive*) *slang* to cheat or outwit: *he was had by that dishonest salesman* **10** (foll by *on*) to exhibit (mercy, compassion, etc, towards) **11** to engage or take part in: *to have a conversation* **12** to arrange, carry out, or hold: *to have a party* **13** to cause, compel, or require to (be, do, or be done): *have my shoes mended* **14** (takes an infinitive with *to*) used as an auxiliary to express compulsion or necessity: *I had to run quickly to escape him* **15** to eat, drink, or partake of **16** *slang* to have sexual intercourse with **17** (*used with a negative*) to tolerate or allow: *I won't have all this noise* **18** to declare, state, or assert: *rumour has it that they will marry* **19** to put or place: *I'll have the sofa in this room* **20** to receive as a guest: *to have three people to stay* **21** to beget or bear (offspring) **22** (takes a past participle) used as an auxiliary to form compound tenses expressing completed action: *I have gone; I shall have gone; I would have gone; I had gone* **23** had rather *or* had sooner to consider or find preferable that: *I had rather you left at once* **24** have had it *informal* **a** to be exhausted, defeated, or killed **b** to have lost one's last chance **c** to become unfashionable **25** have it away *or* have it off *Brit slang* to have sexual intercourse **26** have it so good to have so many benefits, esp material benefits **27** have to do with **a** to have dealings or associate with **b** to be of relevance to **28** let someone have it *slang* to launch or deliver an attack on, esp to discharge a firearm at someone ▷ *n* **29** (*usually plural*) a person or group of people in possession of wealth, security, etc: *the haves and the have-nots* ▷ See also **have at**, **have on** [Old English *habban*; related to Old Norse *hafa*, Old Saxon *hebbian*, Old High German *habēn*, Latin *habēre*]

have-a-go *adj informal* (of people attempting arduous or dangerous tasks) brave or spirited: *a have-a-go pensioner*

have at *vb* (*intr, preposition*) *archaic* to make an opening attack on, esp in fencing

Havel[1] (*German* 'ha:fəl) *n* a river in E Germany, flowing south to Berlin, then west and north to join the River Elbe. Length: about 362 km (225 miles)

Havel[2] (*Czech* 'havɛl) *n* **Václav** ('vatslav). born 1936, Czech dramatist and statesman: founder of the Civil Forum movement for political change: president of Czechoslovakia (1989–92) and of the Czech Republic (1993–2003). His plays include *The Garden Party* (1963) and *Redevelopment* (1989)

havelock ('hævlɒk) *n* a light-coloured cover for a service cap with a flap extending over the back of the neck to protect the head and neck from the sun [C19: named after Sir H. Havelock (1795–1857), English general in India]

haven ('heɪv°n) *n* **1** a port, harbour, or other sheltered place for shipping **2** a place of safety or sanctuary; shelter ▷ *vb* **3** (*tr*) to secure or shelter in or as if in a haven [Old English *hæfen*, from Old Norse *höfn*; related to Middle Dutch *havene*, Old Irish *cuan* to bend]

have-not *n* (*usually plural*) a person or group of people in possession of relatively little material wealth

haven't ('hæv°nt) *vb* contraction of have not

have on *vb* (*tr*) **1** (*usually adverb*) to wear **2** (*usually adverb*) to have (a meeting or engagement) arranged as a commitment: *what does your boss have on this afternoon?* **3** (*adverb*) *informal* to trick or tease (a person) **4** (*preposition*) to have available (information or evidence, esp when incriminating) about (a person)

have out *vb* (*tr, adverb*) **1** to settle (a matter) or come to (a final decision), esp by fighting or by frank discussion (often in the phrase **have it out**) **2** to have extracted or removed

haver ('heɪvə) *vb* (*intr*) *Brit* **1** to dither **2** *Scot & northern*

English *dialect* to talk nonsense; babble ▷ *n* **3** (*usually plural*) *Scot* nonsense [c18: of unknown origin]

Havering ('heɪvərɪŋ) *n* a borough of NE Greater London, formed in 1965 from Romford and Hornchurch (both previously in Essex). Pop: 224 600 (2003 est). Area: 120 sq km (46 sq miles)

haversack ('hævə,sæk) *n* a canvas bag for provisions or equipment, carried on the back or shoulder [c18: from French *havresac*, from German *Habersack* oat bag, from Old High German *habaro* oats + *Sack* SACK¹]

haversine ('hævə,saɪn) *n* *obsolete* half the value of the versed sine [c19: combination of *half* + *versed* + SINE¹]

have up *vb* (*tr, adverb; usually passive*) to cause to appear for trial: *he was had up for breaking and entering*

havildar ('hævɪl,dɑ:) *n* a noncommissioned officer in the Indian army, equivalent in rank to sergeant [c17: from Hindi, from Persian *hawāldār* one in charge]

havoc ('hævək) *n* **1** destruction; devastation; ruin **2** *informal* confusion; chaos **3** cry havoc *archaic* to give the signal for pillage and destruction **4** play havoc (often foll by *with*) to cause a great deal of damage, distress, or confusion (to) [c15: from Old French *havot* pillage, probably of Germanic origin]

Havre ('hɑ:vrə; *French* ɑvrə) *n* See **Le Havre**

haw¹ (hɔ:) *n* **1** the round or oval fruit (a pome) of the hawthorn, usually red or yellow, containing one to five seeds **2** another name for **hawthorn** [Old English *haga*, identical with *haga* HEDGE; related to Old Norse *hagi* pasture]

haw² (hɔ:) *n, interj* **1** an inarticulate utterance, as of hesitation, embarrassment, etc; hem ▷ *vb* **2** (*intr*) to make this sound [c17: of imitative origin]

haw³ (hɔ:) *n* the nictitating membrane of a horse or other domestic animal [c15: of unknown origin]

Hawaii (hə'waɪɪ) *n* a state of the US in the central Pacific, consisting of over 20 volcanic islands and atolls, including Hawaii, Maui, Oahu, Kauai, and Molokai: discovered by Captain Cook in 1778; annexed by the US in 1898; naval base at Pearl Harbor attacked by the Japanese in 1941, a major cause of US entry into World War II; became a state in 1959. Capital: Honolulu. Pop: 1 257 608 (2003 est). Area: 16 640 sq km (6425 sq miles). Former name: Sandwich Islands. Abbreviations: Ha *or* (with zip code) HI

Hawaiian (hə'waɪən) *adj* **1** of or relating to Hawaii, its people, or their language ▷ *n* **2** a native or inhabitant of Hawaii, esp one descended from Melanesian or Tahitian immigrants **3** a language of Hawaii belonging to the Malayo-Polynesian family

Hawaiki ('hɑ:waɪki:) *n* NZ a legendary Pacific island from which the Māoris migrated to New Zealand by canoe [Māori]

Hawes Water (hɔ:z) *n* a lake in NW England, in the Lake District: provides part of Manchester's water supply; extended by damming from 4 km (2.5 miles) to 6 km (4 miles)

hawfinch ('hɔ:,fɪntʃ) *n* an uncommon European finch, *Coccothraustes coccothraustes*, having a very stout bill and brown plumage with black-and-white wings

Haw-Haw ('hɔ:,hɔ:) *n* Lord Haw-Haw See **Joyce** (sense 2)

Hawick ('hɔ:ɪk) *n* a town in SE Scotland, in S central Scottish Borders: knitwear industry. Pop: 14 573 (2001)

hawk¹ (hɔ:k) *n* **1** any of various diurnal birds of prey of the family *Accipitridae*, such as the goshawk and Cooper's hawk, typically having short rounded wings and a long tail **2** a person who advocates or supports war or warlike policies. See **dove¹** (sense 2) **3** a ruthless or rapacious person ▷ *vb* **4** (*intr*) to hunt with falcons, hawks, etc **5** (*intr*) (of falcons or hawks) to fly in quest of prey **6** to pursue or attack on the wing, as a hawk [Old English *hafoc*; related to Old Norse *haukr*, Old Frisian *havek*, Old High German *habuh*, Polish *kobuz*] > 'hawk,like *adj* > 'hawking *n* > 'hawkish *adj*

hawk² (hɔ:k) *vb* **1** to offer (goods) for sale, as in the street **2** (*tr; often foll by about*) to spread (news, gossip, etc) [c16: back formation from HAWKER¹]

hawk³ (hɔ:k) *vb* **1** (*intr*) to clear the throat noisily **2** (*tr*) to force (phlegm) up from the throat [c16: of imitative origin; see HAW²]

hawk⁴ (hɔ:k) *n* a small square board with a handle underneath, used for carrying wet plaster or mortar. Also called: **mortar board** [of unknown origin]

Hawke (hɔ:k) *n* **1 Edward**, 1st Baron. 1705–81, British admiral. He destroyed the French fleet in Quiberon Bay (1759), preventing a French invasion of England **2 Robert** (**James Lee**), known as *Bob*. born 1929, Australian statesman; prime minister of Australia (1983–91)

hawker¹ ('hɔ:kə) *n* a person who travels from place to place selling goods [c16: probably from Middle Low German *hōker*, from *hōken* to peddle; see HUCKSTER]

hawker² ('hɔ:kə) *n* a person who hunts with hawks, falcons, etc [Old English *hafecere*; see HAWK¹, -ER¹]

hawk-eyed *adj* **1** having extremely keen sight **2** vigilant, watchful, or observant

Hawking ('hɔ:kɪŋ) *n* **Stephen William**. born 1942, British physicist. Stricken with a progressive nervous disease since the 1960s, he has nevertheless been a leader in cosmological theory. His *A Brief History of Time* (1987) was a bestseller

Hawkins ('hɔ:kɪnz) *n* **1 Coleman**. 1904–69, US pioneer of the tenor saxophone for jazz **2 Sir John**. 1532–95, English naval commander and slave trader, treasurer of the navy (1577–89); commander of a squadron in the fleet that defeated the Spanish Armada (1588)

hawk moth *n* any of various moths of the family *Sphingidae*, having long narrow wings and powerful flight, with the ability to hover over flowers when feeding from the nectar

Hawks (hɔ:ks) *n* **Howard** (**Winchester**). 1896–1977, US film director. His films include *Sergeant York* (1941) and *The Big Sleep* (1946)

hawksbill turtle *or* **hawksbill** ('hɔ:ks,bɪl) *n* a small tropical turtle, *Eretmochelys imbricata*, with a hooked beaklike mouth: a source of tortoiseshell: family *Chelonidae*

Hawksmoor ('hɔ:ks,mɔ:) *n* **Nicholas**. 1661–1736, English architect. His designs include All Souls', Oxford, and a number of London churches, notably St Anne's, Limehouse

hawkweed ('hɔ:k,wi:d) *n* any typically hairy plant of the genus *Hieracium*, with clusters of dandelion-like flowers: family *Asteraceae* (composites)

Haworth¹ ('hauəθ) *n* a village in N England, in Bradford unitary authority, West Yorkshire: home of Charlotte, Emily, and Anne Brontë. Pop: 6078 (2001)

Haworth² ('hauəθ) *n* Sir **Walter Norman**. 1883–1950, British biochemist, who shared the Nobel prize for chemistry (1937) for being the first to synthesize ascorbic acid (vitamin C)

hawse (hɔ:z) *nautical* ▷ *n* **1** the part of the bows of a vessel where the hawseholes are **2** short for **hawsehole, hawsepipe 3** the distance from the bow of an anchored vessel to the anchor **4** the arrangement of port and starboard anchor ropes when a vessel is riding on both anchors [c14: from earlier *halse*, probably from Old Norse *háls*; related to Old English *heals* neck]

hawsehole ('hɔ:z,həʊl) *n* *nautical* one of the holes in the upper part of the bows of a vessel through which the anchor ropes pass

hawsepipe ('hɔ:z,paɪp) *n* *nautical* a strong metal pipe through which an anchor rope passes

hawser ('hɔ:zə) *n* *nautical* a large heavy rope [c14: from Anglo-French *hauceour*, from Old French *haucier* to hoist, ultimately from Latin *altus* high]

hawthorn ('hɔ:,θɔ:n) *n* any of various thorny trees or shrubs of the N temperate rosaceous genus *Crataegus*, esp *C. oxyacantha*, having white or pink flowers and reddish fruits (haws). Also called (in Britain): **may, may tree, mayflower** [Old English *haguthorn* from *haga* hedge + *thorn* thorn; related to Old Norse *hagthorn*, Middle High German *hagendorn*, Dutch *haagdoorn*]

Hawthorne ('hɔ:,θɔ:n) *n* **Nathaniel**. 1804–64, US novelist and short-story writer: his works include the novels *The Scarlet Letter* (1850) and *The House of the Seven Gables* (1851) and the children's stories *Tanglewood Tales* (1853)

hay (heɪ) *n* **1 a** grass, clover, etc, cut and dried as fodder **b** (*in combination*): *a hayfield; a hayloft* **2** hit the hay *slang* to go to bed **3 make hay of** to throw into confusion **4 make hay while the sun shines** to take full advantage of an opportunity **5 roll in the hay** *informal* sexual intercourse or heavy petting ▷ *vb* **6** to cut, dry, and store (grass, clover, etc) as fodder [Old English *hieg*; related to Old Norse *hey*, Gothic *hawi*, Old Frisian *hē*, Old High German *houwi*; see HEW]

Hay (heɪ) *n* Will. 1888–1949, British music-hall comedian, who later starred in films, such as *Oh, Mr Porter!* (1937)

haybox ('heɪ,bɒks) *n* an airtight box full of hay or other insulating material used to keep partially cooked food warm and allow cooking by retained heat

haycock ('heɪ,kɒk) *n* a small cone-shaped pile of hay left in the field until dry enough to carry to the rick or barn

Haydn ('haɪdᵊn) *n* **1** (Franz) **Joseph** ('jɔːzɛf). 1732–1809, Austrian composer, who played a major part in establishing the classical forms of the symphony and the string quartet. His other works include the oratorios *The Creation* (1796–98) and *The Seasons* (1798–1801) **2** his brother, **Johann Michael** (German joˈhan ˈmɪçaːl). 1737–1806, Austrian composer, esp of Church music

Haydon ('heɪdᵊn) *n* **Benjamin** (**Robert**). 1786–1846, British historical painter and art critic, best known for his *Autobiography and Journals* (1853)

Hayek ('haɪjək) *n* **Friedrich August von**. 1899–1992, British economist and political philosopher, born in Austria: noted for his advocacy of free-market ideas; shared the Nobel prize for economics 1974

Hayes (heɪz) *n* **Rutherford B**(irchard). 1822–93, 19th president of the US (1877–81)

hay fever *n* an allergic reaction to pollen, dust, etc, characterized by sneezing, runny nose, and watery eyes due to inflammation of the mucous membranes of the eyes and nose

haymaker ('heɪ,meɪkə) *n* **1** a person who helps to cut, turn, toss, spread, or carry hay **2** Also called: **hay conditioner** either of two machines, one designed to crush stems of hay, the other to break and bend them, in order to cause more rapid and even drying **3** *boxing slang* a wild swinging punch > 'hay,making *adj, n*

haymow ('heɪ,maʊ) *n* **1** a part of a barn where hay is stored **2** a quantity of hay stored in a barn or loft

hayseed ('heɪ,siːd) *n* **1** seeds or fragments of grass or straw **2** *US & Canadian informal, derogatory* a yokel

haystack ('heɪ,stæk) *or* **hayrick** ('heɪ,rɪk) *n* a large pile of hay, esp one built in the open air and covered with thatch

haywire ('heɪ,waɪə) *adj* (*postpositive*) *informal* **1** (of things) not functioning properly; disorganized (esp in the phrase **go haywire**) **2** (of people) erratic or crazy [c20: alluding to the disorderly tangle of wire removed from bales of hay]

hazard ('hæzəd) *n* **1** exposure or vulnerability to injury, loss, evil, etc **2 at hazard** at risk; in danger **3** a thing likely to cause injury, etc **4** *golf* an obstacle such as a bunker, a road, rough, water, etc **5** chance; accident (esp in the phrase **by hazard**) **6** a gambling game played with two dice **7** *real tennis* **a** the receiver's side of the court **b** one of the winning openings **8** *billiards* a scoring stroke made either when a ball other than the striker's is pocketed (**winning hazard**) or the striker's cue ball itself (**losing hazard**) ▷ *vb* (*tr*) **9** to chance or risk **10** to venture (an opinion, guess, etc) **11** to expose to danger [c13: from Old French *hasard*, from Arabic *az-zahr* the die]

hazard lights *adj, pl n* the indicator lights of a motor vehicle when flashing simultaneously to indicate that the vehicle is stationary and temporarily obstructing the traffic. Also called: **hazard warning lights, hazards**

hazardous ('hæzədəs) *adj* **1** involving great risk **2** depending on chance > 'hazardously *adv* > 'hazardousness *n*

hazard warning device *n* an appliance fitted to a motor vehicle to operate the hazard lights

haze¹ (heɪz) *n* **1** *meteorol* reduced visibility in the air as a result of condensed water vapour, dust, etc, in the atmosphere **2** obscurity of perception, feeling, etc ▷ *vb* **3** (when *intr*, often foll by *over*) to make or become hazy [c18: back formation from HAZY]

haze² (heɪz) *vb* (*tr*) **1** *chiefly US & Canadian* to subject (fellow students) to ridicule or abuse **2** *nautical* to harass with humiliating tasks [c17: of uncertain origin]

hazel ('heɪzᵊl) *n* **1** Also called: **cob** any of several shrubs of the N temperate genus *Corylus*, esp *C. avellana*, having oval serrated leaves and edible rounded brown nuts: family *Corylaceae* **2** the wood of any of these trees **3** short for **hazelnut 4 a** a light yellowish-brown colour **b** (*as adjective*): *hazel eyes* [Old English *hæsel*; related to Old Norse *hasl*, Old High German *hasala*, Latin *corylus*, Old Irish *coll*]

hazelhen ('heɪzᵊl,hɛn) *n* a European woodland gallinaceous bird, *Tetrastes bonasia*, with a speckled brown plumage and slightly crested crown: family *Tetraonidae* (grouse)

hazelnut ('heɪzᵊl,nʌt) *n* the nut of a hazel shrub, having a smooth shiny hard shell. Also called: **filbert**, (*Brit*) **cobnut**, (*Brit*) **cob**

Hazlitt ('hæzlɪt) *n* **William**. 1778–1830, English critic and essayist: works include *Characters of Shakespeare's Plays* (1817), *Table Talk* (1821), and *The Plain Speaker* (1826)

hazy ('heɪzɪ) *adj* **-zier, -ziest 1** characterized by reduced visibility; misty **2** indistinct; vague [c17: of unknown origin] > 'hazily *adv* > 'haziness *n*

Hb *symbol for* haemoglobin

HB *symbol for* (on Brit pencils) hard-black: denoting a medium-hard pencil lead

HBC (in Canada) *abbreviation* Hudson's Bay Company

HBM (in Britain) *abbreviation* His (*or* Her) Britannic Majesty

H-bomb *n* short for **hydrogen bomb**

HC *abbreviation* **1** Holy Communion **2** (in Britain) House of Commons

HCF *or* **hcf** *abbreviation* highest common factor

HCG *abbreviation* human chorionic gonadotrophin

hcp *abbreviation* handicap

HDCP *abbreviation* high-bandwidth digital content protection

HDD *abbreviation* computing hard disk drive

HD-DVD *abbreviation* High Definition DVD: a DVD capable of storing between two and four times as much data as a standard DVD

HDMI *abbreviation* high definition multimedia interface

hdqrs *abbreviation* headquarters: replaced in military use by **HQ**

HDTV *abbreviation* high definition television

he (hiː; *unstressed* i:) *pron* (*subjective*) **1** refers to a male person or animal **2** refers to an indefinite antecedent such as *one, whoever*, or *anybody*: *everybody can do as he likes in this country* **3** refers to a person or animal of unknown or unspecified sex: *a member of the party may vote as he sees fit* ▷ *n* **4 a** a male person or animal **b** (*in combination*): *he-goat* **5** a children's game in which one player chases the others in an attempt to touch one of them, who then becomes the chaser. See **tag²** [Old English *hē*; related to Old Saxon *hie*, Old High German *her* he, Old Slavonic *sĭ* this, Latin *cis* on this side]

He *the chemical symbol for* helium

HE *abbreviation* **1** high explosive **2** His Eminence **3** His (*or* Her) Excellency

head (hɛd) *n* **1** the upper or front part of the body in vertebrates, including man, that contains and protects the brain, eyes, mouth, and nose and ears when present **2** the corresponding part of an invertebrate animal **3** something resembling a head in form or function, such as the top of a tool **4 a** the person commanding most authority within a group, organization, etc **b** (*in modifier*): *head buyer* **c** (*in combination*): *headmaster* **5** the position of leadership or command **6** the most forward part of a thing; a part that juts out; front: *the head of a queue* **7** the highest part of a thing; upper end: *the head of the pass* **8** the froth on the top of a glass of beer **9** aptitude, intelligence, and emotions (esp in the phrases **above** or **over one's head, have a head for, keep one's head, lose one's head**, etc): *she has a good head for figures; a wise old head* **10** *pl* **head** a person or animal considered as a unit: *the show was two pounds per head; six hundred head of cattle* **11** the head considered as a measure of length or height: *he's a head taller than his mother*

12 *botany* **a** a dense inflorescence such as that of the daisy and other composite plants **b** any other compact terminal part of a plant, such as the leaves of a cabbage or lettuce **13** a culmination or crisis (esp in the phrase **bring** or **come to a head**) **14** the pus-filled tip or central part of a pimple, boil, etc **15** the source or origin of a river or stream **16** (*capital when part of name*) a headland or promontory, esp a high one **17** the obverse of a coin, usually bearing a portrait of the head or a full figure of a monarch, deity, etc **18** a main point or division of an argument, discourse, etc **19** (*often plural*) the headline at the top of a newspaper article or the heading of a section within an article **20** *nautical* (*often plural*) a slang word for **lavatory 21** the taut membrane of a drum, tambourine, etc **22 a** the height of the surface of liquid above a specific point, esp when considered or used as a measure of the pressure at that point: *a head of four feet* **b** pressure of water, caused by height or velocity, measured in terms of a vertical column of water **c** any pressure: *a head of steam in the boiler* **23** *slang* **a** a person who regularly takes drugs, esp LSD or cannabis **b** (*in combination*): *an acidhead; a pothead* **24** *mining* a road driven into the coal face **25 a** the terminal point of a route **b** (*in combination*): *railhead* **26** a device on a turning or boring machine, such as a lathe, that is equipped with one or more cutting tools held to the work by this device **27** an electromagnet that can read, write, or erase information on a magnetic medium such as a magnetic tape, disk, or drum, used in computers, tape recorders, etc **28** *informal* short for **headmaster** or **headmistress 29** any narrow margin of victory (in the phrase (**win**) **by a head**) **30** *informal* short for **headache 31 bite someone's head off** or **snap someone's head off** to speak sharply and angrily to someone **32 give someone his head** to allow a person greater freedom or responsibility **33 give a horse its head** to allow a horse to gallop by lengthening the reins **34 go to one's head a** to make one dizzy or confused, as might an alcoholic drink **b** to make one conceited: *his success has gone to his head* **35 head and shoulders above** greatly superior to **36 head over heels a** turning a complete somersault **b** completely; utterly (esp in the phrase **head over heels in love**) **37 hold up one's head** to be unashamed **38 keep one's head** to remain calm **39 keep one's head above water** to manage to survive a difficult experience **40 make head or tail of** (*used with a negative*) to attempt to understand (a problem, etc) **41 off one's head** or **out of one's head** *slang* insane or delirious **42 on one's head** or **on one's own head** at one's (own) risk or responsibility **43 over someone's head a** without a person in the obvious position being considered, esp for promotion: *the graduate was promoted over the heads of several of his seniors* **b** without consulting a person in the obvious position but referring to a higher authority: *in making his complaint he went straight to the director, over the head of his immediate boss* **c** beyond a person's comprehension **44 put their heads together** *informal* to consult together **45 take it into one's head** to conceive a notion, desire, or wish (to do something) **46 turn someone's head** to make someone vain, conceited, etc ⊳ *vb* **47** (*tr*) to be at the front or top of: *to head the field* **48** (*tr; often foll by up*) to be in the commanding or most important position **49** (*often foll by for*) or **cause to go** (towards): *where are you heading?* **50** to turn or steer (a vessel) as specified: *to head into the wind* **51** *soccer* to propel (the ball) by striking it with the head **52** (*tr*) to provide with or be a head or heading **53** (*tr*) to cut the top branches or shoots off (a tree or plant) **54** (*intr*) to form a head, as a boil or plant **55** (*intr; often foll by in*) (of streams, rivers, etc) to originate or rise in ⊳ See also **head off, heads** [Old English *hēafod*; related to Old Norse *haufuth*, Old Frisian *hāved*, Old Saxon *hōbid*, Old High German *houbit*] > ˈ**head**ˌ**like** *adj* > ˈ**headless** *adj*

Head (hɛd) *n* Edith. 1907–81, US dress designer: won many Oscars for her Hollywood film costume designs

-head *combining form* indicating a person having a preoccupation as specified: *breadhead*

headache (ˈhɛdˌeɪk) *n* **1** pain in the head, caused by dilation of cerebral arteries, muscle contraction, insufficient oxygen in the cerebral blood, reaction to drugs, etc **2** *informal* any cause of worry, difficulty, or annoyance > ˈ**head**ˌ**achy** or ˈ**head**ˌ**achey** *adj*

headband (ˈhɛdˌbænd) *n* **1** a ribbon or band worn around the head **2** a narrow cloth band attached to the top of the spine of a book for protection or decoration

headbang (ˈhɛdˌbæŋ) *vb* (*intr*) *slang* to nod one's head violently to the beat of loud rock music

head-banger *n* *slang* **1** a heavy-metal rock fan **2** a crazy or stupid person

headboard (ˈhɛdˌbɔːd) *n* a vertical board or terminal at the head of a bed

head-butt *vb* (*tr*) **1** to deliberately strike (someone) with the head ⊳ *n* **head butt 2** an act or an instance of deliberately striking someone with the head

headdress (ˈhɛdˌdrɛs) *n* any head covering, esp an ornate one or one denoting a rank or occupation

headed (ˈhɛdɪd) *adj* **1 a** having a head or heads **b** (*in combination*): *two-headed; bullet-headed* **2** having a heading: *headed notepaper*

header (ˈhɛdə) *n* **1** Also called: **header tank** a reservoir, tank, or hopper that maintains a gravity feed or a static fluid pressure in an apparatus **2** a brick or stone laid across a wall so that its end is flush with the outer surface **3** the action of striking a ball with the head **4** *informal* a headlong fall or dive

headfirst (ˈhɛdˈfɜːst) *adj, adv* **1** with the head foremost; headlong ⊳ *adv* **2** rashly or carelessly

headfuck (ˈhɛdfʌk) *n* *taboo slang* an experience that is wildly exciting or impressive

headgear (ˈhɛdˌɡɪə) *n* **1** any head covering, esp a hat **2** any part of a horse's harness that is worn on the head **3** the hoisting mechanism at the pithead of a mine

headguard (ˈhɛdˌɡɑːd) *n* a padded helmet worn to protect the head in contact sports such as rugby and boxing

head-hunting *n* **1** the practice among certain peoples of removing the heads of slain enemies and preserving them as trophies **2** the recruitment, esp through an agency, of executives from one company to another, often rival, company **3** *US slang* the destruction or neutralization of political opponents > ˈ**head-**ˌ**hunter** *n*

heading (ˈhɛdɪŋ) *n* **1** a title for a page, paragraph, chapter, etc **2** a main division, as of a lecture, speech, essay, etc **3** *mining* **a** a horizontal tunnel **b** the end of such a tunnel **4** the angle between the direction of an aircraft and a specified meridian, often due north **5** the compass direction parallel to the keel of a vessel **6** the act of heading

headland *n* **1** (ˈhɛdlənd) a narrow area of land jutting out into a sea, lake, etc **2** (ˈhɛdˌlænd) a strip of land along the edge of an arable field left unploughed to allow space for machines

headless (ˈhɛdlɪs) *adj* **1** without a head **2** without a leader **3** foolish

headlight (ˈhɛdˌlaɪt) *or* **headlamp** *n* a powerful light, equipped with a reflector and attached to the front of a motor vehicle, locomotive, etc

headline (ˈhɛdˌlaɪn) *n* **1** Also called: **head, heading a a** phrase at the top of a newspaper or magazine article indicating the subject of the article, usually in larger and heavier type **b** a line at the top of a page indicating the title, page number, etc **2** (*usually plural*) the main points of a television or radio news broadcast, read out before the full broadcast and summarized at the end **3 hit the headlines** to become prominent in the news ⊳ *vb* **4** (*tr*) to furnish (a story or page) with a headline **5** to have top billing (in)

headlong (ˈhɛdˌlɒŋ) *adv, adj* **1** with the head foremost; headfirst **2** with great haste ⊳ *adj* **3** *archaic* (of slopes, etc) very steep; precipitous

headman (ˈhɛdmən) *n, pl* **-men 1** *anthropol* a chief or leader **2** a foreman or overseer

headmaster (ˌhɛdˈmɑːstə) *n* a male principal of a school

headmistress (ˌhɛdˈmɪstrəs) *n* a female principal of a school

headmost (ˈhɛdˌməʊst) *adj* a less common word for **foremost**

head off *vb* (*tr, adverb*) **1** to intercept and force to change direction **2** to prevent or forestall (something that is likely to happen)

head-on *adv, adj* **1** with the front or fronts foremost: *a head-on collision* **2** with directness or without compromise: *in his usual head-on fashion*

headphones ('hɛd,fəʊnz) *pl n* an electrical device consisting of two earphones held in position by a flexible metallic strap passing over the head. Also called: *informal* cans

headpiece ('hɛd,piːs) *n* **1** *printing* a decorative band at the top of a page, chapter, etc **2** any covering for the head, esp a helmet **3** *archaic* the intellect

headpin ('hɛd,pɪn) *n* *tenpin bowling* another word for kingpin

headquarters (,hɛd'kwɔːtəz) *pl n* (*sometimes functioning as singular*) **1** any centre or building from which operations are directed, as in the military, the police, etc **2** a military formation comprising the commander, his staff, and supporting echelons ▷ Abbreviation: HQ

headrace ('hɛd,reɪs) *n* a channel that carries water to a water wheel, turbine, etc

headrest ('hɛd,rɛst) *n* a support for the head, as on a dentist's chair or car seat

head restraint *n* an adjustable support for the head, attached to a car seat, to prevent the neck from being jolted backwards sharply in the event of a crash or sudden stop

headroom ('hɛd,rʊm, -,ruːm) *or* **headway** *n* the height of a bridge, room, etc; clearance

heads (hɛdz) *interj, adv* with the obverse side of a coin uppermost, esp if it has a head on it: used as a call before tossing a coin

headscarf ('hɛd,skɑːf) *n, pl* **-scarves** (-,skɑːvz) a scarf for the head, often worn tied under the chin

headset ('hɛd,sɛt) *n* a pair of headphones, esp with a microphone attached

headship ('hɛdʃɪp) *n* **1** the position or state of being a leader; command; leadership **2** *education Brit* the position of headmaster or headmistress of a school

headshrinker ('hɛd,ʃrɪŋkə) *n* **1** Often shortened to **shrink** a psychiatrist **2** a head-hunter who shrinks the heads of his victims

headsman ('hɛdzmən) *n, pl* **-men** (formerly) an executioner who beheaded condemned persons

head start *n* an initial advantage in a competitive situation [originally referring to a horse's having its head in front of others at the start of a race]

headstock ('hɛd,stɒk) *n* the part of a machine that supports and transmits the drive to the chuck

headstone ('hɛd,stəʊn) *n* **1** a memorial stone at the head of a grave **2** *architect* another name for **keystone**

headstream ('hɛd,striːm) *n* a stream that is the source or a source of a river

headstrong ('hɛd,strɒŋ) *adj* **1** self-willed; obstinate **2** (of an action) heedless; rash

head-to-head *informal* ▷ *adj* **1** in direct competition ▷ *n* **2** a competition involving two people, teams, etc

head-up display *n* the projection of readings from instruments onto a windscreen, enabling an aircraft pilot or car driver to see them without looking down

head voice *or* **head register** *n* the high register of the human voice, in which the vibrations of sung notes are felt in the head

headwaters ('hɛd,wɔːtəz) *pl n* the tributary streams of a river in the area in which it rises; headstreams

headway ('hɛd,weɪ) *n* **1** motion in a forward direction: *the vessel made no headway* **2** progress or rate of progress: *he made no headway with the problem* **3** another name for **headroom 4** the distance or time between consecutive trains, buses, etc, on the same route

headwind ('hɛd,wɪnd) *n* a wind blowing directly against the course of an aircraft or ship

headword ('hɛd,wɜːd) *n* a key word placed at the beginning of a line, paragraph, etc, as in a dictionary entry

headwork ('hɛd,wɜːk) *n* **1** mental work **2** the ornamentation of the keystone of an arch

heady ('hɛdɪ) *adj* **headier, headiest 1** (of alcoholic drink) intoxicating **2** strongly affecting the mind or senses;

extremely exciting **3** rash; impetuous > 'headily *adv* > 'headiness *n*

heal (hiːl) *vb* **1** to restore or be restored to health **2** (*intr; often foll by over or up*) (of a wound, burn, etc) to repair by natural processes, as by scar formation **3** (*tr*) to cure (a disease or disorder) **4** to restore or be restored to friendly relations, harmony, etc [Old English *hælan*; related to Old Norse *heila*, Gothic *hailjan*, Old High German *heilen*; see HALE¹, WHOLE] > 'healer *n* > 'healing *n, adj*

Healey ('hiːlɪ) *n* Denis (Winston), Baron Healey. born 1917, British Labour politician; Chancellor of the Exchequer (1974–79); deputy leader of the Labour Party (1980–83)

health (hɛlθ) *n* **1** the state of being bodily and mentally vigorous and free from disease **2** the general condition of body and mind: *in poor health* **3** the condition of any unit, society, etc: *the economic health of a nation* **4** a toast to a person, wishing him or her good health, happiness, etc **5** (*modifier*) of or relating to food or other goods reputed to be beneficial to the health: *health food; a health store* **6** (*modifier*) of or relating to health, esp to the administration of health: *a health committee; health resort; health service* [Old English *hælth*; related to *hāl* HALE¹]

health card *n* *Canadian* an identity card required to obtain public health insurance services

health centre *n* (in Britain) premises, owned by a local authority, providing health care for the local community and usually housing a group practice, nursing staff, a child-health clinic, X-ray facilities, etc

health farm *n* a residential establishment, often in the country, visited by those who wish to improve their health by losing weight, eating healthy foods, taking exercise, etc

health food *n* **a** vegetarian food organically grown and with no additives, eaten for its dietary value and benefit to health **b** (*as modifier*): *a health-food shop*

healthful ('hɛlθfʊl) *adj* a less common word for **healthy** (senses 1–3)

health salts *pl n* magnesium sulphate or similar salts taken as a mild laxative

health visitor *n* (in Britain) a nurse employed by a district health authority to visit people in their homes and give help and advice on health and social welfare, esp to mothers of preschool children, to the handicapped, and to elderly people

healthy ('hɛlθɪ) *adj* **healthier, healthiest 1** enjoying good health **2** functioning well or being sound: *the company's finances are not very healthy* **3** conducive to health; salutary **4** indicating soundness of body or mind: *a healthy appetite* **5** *informal* considerable in size or amount: *a healthy sum* > 'healthily *adv* > 'healthiness *n*

Healy ('hiːlɪ) *n* Ian. born 1964, Australian cricketer; holds the record for the highest number of wicketkeeping dismissals in Test matches

Heaney ('hiːnɪ) *n* Seamus (Justin) ('ʃeɪməs). born 1939, Irish poet and critic, born in Northern Ireland. His collections include *Death of a Naturalist* (1966), *North* (1975), *The Haw Lantern* (1987), *The Spirit Level* (1996), and *District and Circle* (2006). Nobel prize for literature 1995

heap (hiːp) *n* **1** a collection of articles or mass of material gathered together in one place **2** (*often plural; usually foll by of*) *informal* a large number or quantity **3** give it heaps NZ slang to try very hard **4** *informal* a place or thing that is very old, untidy, unreliable, etc: *the car was a heap* ▷ *adv* **5** heaps (intensifier): *he said he was feeling heaps better* ▷ *vb* **6** (often foll by *up* or *together*) to collect or be collected into or as if into a heap or pile **7** (*tr; often foll by with, on, or upon*) to load or supply (with) abundantly: *to heap with riches* [Old English *héap*; related to Old Frisian *hāp*, Old Saxon *hōp*, Old High German *houf*] > 'heaper *n*

hear (hɪə) *vb* **hears, hearing, heard** (hɜːd) **1** (*tr*) to perceive (a sound) with the sense of hearing **2** (*tr; may take a clause as object*) to listen to: *did you hear what I said?* **3** (when *intr*, sometimes foll by *of* or *about*; when *tr*, may take a clause as object) to be informed (of); receive information (about) **4** *law* to give a hearing to (a case) **5** (when *intr*, usually foll by *of* and used with a negative)

to listen (to) with favour, assent, etc: *she wouldn't hear of it*
6 (*intr*; foll by *from*) to receive a letter, news, etc (from)
7 hear! hear! an exclamation used to show approval of
something said **8 hear tell** *dialect* to be told (about);
learn (of) [Old English *hieran*; related to Old Norse *heyra*,
Gothic *hausjan*, Old High German *hōren*, Greek *akouein*]
> 'hearer *n*

Heard and McDonald Islands (hɜ:d, mək'dɒnəld) *pl n* a
group of islands in the S Indian Ocean: an external
territory of Australia from 1947. Area: 412 sq km (159 sq
miles)

hearing ('hɪərɪŋ) *n* **1** the faculty or sense by which sound
is perceived **2** an opportunity to be listened to **3** the
range within which sound can be heard; earshot **4** the
investigation of a matter by a court of law, esp the
preliminary inquiry into an indictable crime by
magistrates

hearing aid *n* a device for assisting the hearing of
partially deaf people, typically consisting of a small
battery-powered electronic amplifier with microphone
and earphone, worn by a deaf person in or behind
the ear

hearing dog *n* a dog that has been specially trained to
help deaf or partially deaf people by alerting them to
sounds such as a ringing doorbell, an alarm, etc

hearken *or sometimes US* **harken** ('hɑ:kən) *vb archaic* to
listen to (something) [Old English *heorcnian*; see HARK]

hear out *vb* (*tr, adverb*) to listen in regard to every detail
and give a proper or full hearing to

hearsay ('hɪə,seɪ) *n* gossip; rumour

hearsay evidence *n law* evidence based on what has
been reported to a witness by others rather than what
he has himself observed or experienced (not generally
admissible as evidence)

hearse (hɜ:s) *n* a vehicle, such as a specially designed
car or carriage, used to carry a coffin to a place of
worship and ultimately to a cemetery or crematorium
[c14: from Old French *herce*, from Latin *hirpex* harrow]

Hearst (hɜ:st) *n* **William Randolph**. 1863–1951, US
newspaper publisher, whose newspapers were noted for
their sensationalism

heart (hɑ:t) *n* **1** the hollow muscular organ in
vertebrates whose contractions propel the blood
through the circulatory system. In mammals it consists
of a right and left atrium and a right and left ventricle.
Related adj: **cardiac 2** the corresponding organ or part
in invertebrates **3** this organ considered as the seat of
life and emotions, esp love **4** emotional mood or
disposition: *a happy heart; a change of heart* **5** tenderness or
pity: *you have no heart* **6** courage or spirit; bravery **7** the
inmost or most central part of a thing: *the heart of the city*
8 the most important or vital part: *the heart of the matter*
9 (of vegetables such as cabbage) the inner compact part
10 the part nearest the heart of a person; breast: *she held
him to her heart* **11** a dearly loved person: usually used as a
term of address: *dearest heart* **12** a conventionalized
representation of the heart, having two rounded lobes at
the top meeting in a point at the bottom **13 a** a red
heart-shaped symbol on a playing card **b** a card with
one or more of these symbols or (*when pl.*) the suit of
cards so marked **14** a fertile condition in land, conducive
to vigorous growth in crops or herbage (esp in the
phrase **in good heart**) **15** after one's own heart
appealing to one's own disposition, taste, or tendencies
16 break one's heart *or* **break someone's heart** to grieve
or cause to grieve very deeply, esp through love **17 by
heart** by committing to memory **18 eat one's heart out**
to brood or pine with grief or longing **19 from one's
heart** *or* **from the bottom of one's heart** very sincerely or
deeply **20 have one's heart in one's mouth** *or* **have one's
heart in one's throat** to be full of apprehension,
excitement, or fear **21 have one's heart in the right place**
to be kind, thoughtful, or generous **22 have the heart**
(*usually used with a negative*) to have the necessary will,
callousness, etc, (to do something): *I didn't have the heart to
tell him* **23 heart of hearts** the depths of one's conscience
or emotions **24 heart of oak** a brave person **25 lose
heart** to become despondent or disillusioned (over
something) **26 lose one's heart to** to fall in love with

27 set one's heart on to have as one's ambition to
obtain; covet **28 take heart** to become encouraged
29 take to heart to take seriously or be upset about
30 wear one's heart on one's sleeve to show one's
feelings openly **31 with all one's heart** *or* **with one's
whole heart** very willingly ▷ *vb* **32** (*intr*) (of vegetables)
to form a heart ▷ See also **hearts** [Old English *heorte*;
related to Old Norse *hjarta*, Gothic *hairtō*, Old High
German *herza*, Latin *cor*, Greek *kardia*, Old Irish *cride*]

heartache ('hɑ:t,eɪk) *n* intense anguish or mental
suffering

heart attack *n* any sudden severe instance of abnormal
heart functioning, esp coronary thrombosis

heartbeat ('hɑ:t,bi:t) *n* one complete pulsation of the
heart

heart block *n* impaired conduction or blocking of the
impulse that regulates the heartbeat, resulting in a lack
of coordination between the beating of the atria and the
ventricles

heartbreak ('hɑ:t,breɪk) *n* intense and overwhelming
grief, esp through disappointment in love
> 'heart,breaker *n* > 'heart,breaking *adj*

heartburn ('hɑ:t,bɜ:n) *n* a burning sensation beneath
the breastbone caused by irritation of the oesophagus,
as from regurgitation of the contents of the stomach.
Technical names: cardialgia, pyrosis

-hearted *adj* having a heart or disposition as specified:
good-hearted; cold-hearted; great-hearted; heavy-hearted

hearten ('hɑ:tᵊn) *vb* to make or become cheerful

heartening ('hɑ:tᵊnɪŋ) *adj* causing cheerfulness;
encouraging

heart failure *n* **1** a condition in which the heart is
unable to pump an adequate amount of blood to the
tissues, usually resulting in breathlessness, swollen
ankles, etc **2** sudden and permanent cessation of the
heartbeat, resulting in death

heartfelt ('hɑ:t,fɛlt) *adj* sincerely and strongly felt

hearth (hɑ:θ) *n* **1 a** the floor of a fireplace, esp one that
extends outwards into the room **b** (*as modifier*): *hearth rug*
2 this part of a fireplace as a symbol of the home, etc
3 the bottom part of a metallurgical furnace in which
the molten metal is produced or contained [Old English
heorth; related to Old High German *herd* hearth, Latin
carbō charcoal]

hearthstone ('hɑ:θ,stəʊn) *n* **1** a stone that forms a
hearth **2** soft stone used to clean and whiten floors,
steps, etc

heartily ('hɑ:tɪlɪ) *adv* **1** thoroughly or vigorously: *to eat
heartily* **2** in a sincere manner

heartland ('hɑ:t,lænd) *n* the central region of a country
or continent

heartless ('hɑ:tlɪs) *adj* unkind or cruel; hard-hearted
> 'heartlessly *adv* > 'heartlessness *n*

heart-lung machine *n* a machine used to maintain the
circulation and oxygenation of the blood during heart
surgery

heart-rending *adj* causing great mental pain and
sorrow > 'heart-,rendingly *adv*

hearts (hɑ:ts) *n* (*functioning as singular*) a card game in
which players must avoid winning tricks containing
hearts or the queen of spades. Also called: **Black Maria**

heart-searching *n* examination of one's feelings or
conscience

heartsease *or* **heart's-ease** ('hɑ:ts,i:z) *n* **1** another
name for the **wild pansy 2** peace of mind

heartsick ('hɑ:t,sɪk) *adj* deeply dejected or despondent
> 'heart,sickness *n*

heartstrings ('hɑ:t,strɪŋz) *pl n often facetious* deep
emotions or feelings [c15: originally referring to the
tendons supposed to support the heart]

heart-throb *n* **1** an object of infatuation **2** a heart beat

heart-to-heart *adj* **1** (esp of a conversation or
discussion) concerned with personal problems or
intimate feelings ▷ *n* **2** an intimate conversation or
discussion

heart-warming *adj* **1** pleasing; gratifying **2** emotionally
moving

heartwood ('hɑ:t,wʊd) *n* the central core of dark hard
wood in tree trunks, consisting of nonfunctioning

h

xylem tissue that has become blocked with resins, tannins, and oils

hearty ('hɑːtɪ) *adj* **heartier, heartiest 1** warm and unreserved in manner or behaviour **2** sincere and heartfelt: *hearty dislike* **3** healthy and strong (esp in the phrase **hale and hearty**) **4** substantial and nourishing ▷ *n informal* **5** a comrade, esp a sailor **6** a vigorous sporting man: *a rugby hearty* > 'heartiness *n*

heat (hiːt) *n* **1** the energy transferred as a result of a difference in temperature. Related adjs: **thermal, calorific 2** the sensation caused in the body by heat energy; warmth **3** the state or quality of being hot **4** hot weather: *the heat of summer* **5** intensity of feeling; passion: *the heat of rage* **6** pressure: *the political heat on the government over the economy* **7** the most intense or active part: *the heat of the battle* **8** a period or condition of sexual excitement in female mammals that occurs at oestrus **9** *sport* **a** a preliminary eliminating contest in a competition **b** a single section of a contest **10** *slang* police activity after a crime: *the heat is off* **11** *chiefly US slang* criticism or abuse: *he took a lot of heat for that mistake* **12** in the heat of the moment without pausing to think **13** on heat *or* in heat *Also called:* in season (of some female mammals) sexually receptive **b** in a state of sexual excitement ▷ *vb* **14** to make or become hot or warm **15** to make or become excited or intense [Old English *hǣtu*; related to *hāt* HOT, Old Frisian *hēte* heat, Old High German *heizī*]

heat barrier *n* another name for **thermal barrier**

heat capacity *n* the heat required to raise the temperature of a substance by unit temperature interval under specified conditions, usually measured in joules per kelvin. Symbol: C_p (for constant pressure) or C_v (for constant volume)

heat death *n thermodynamics* the condition of any closed system when its total entropy is a maximum and it has no available energy. If the universe is a closed system it should eventually reach this state

heated ('hiːtɪd) *adj* **1** made hot; warmed **2** impassioned or highly emotional > 'heatedly *adv*

heat engine *n* an engine that converts heat energy into mechanical energy

heater ('hiːtə) *n* **1** any device for supplying heat, such as a hot-air blower, radiator, convector, etc **2** *US slang* a pistol **3** *electronics* a conductor carrying a current that indirectly heats the cathode in some types of valve

heat exchanger *n* a device for transferring heat from one fluid to another without allowing them to mix

heat exhaustion *n* a condition resulting from exposure to intense heat, characterized by dizziness, abdominal cramp, and prostration

heath (hiːθ) *n* **1** *Brit* a large open area, usually with sandy soil and scrubby vegetation, esp heather **2** *Also called:* heather any low-growing evergreen ericaceous shrub of the Old World genus *Erica* and related genera, having small bell-shaped typically pink or purple flowers **3** any of several nonericaceous heathlike plants, such as sea heath [Old English *hǣth*; related to Old Norse *heithr* field, Old High German *heida* heather] > 'heath,like *adj* > 'heathy *adj*

Heath (hiːθ) *n* **Sir Edward** (**Richard George**). 1916–2005, British statesman; leader of the Conservative Party (1965–75); prime minister (1970–74)

heathen ('hiːðən) *n, pl* -**thens** *or* -**then 1** a person who does not acknowledge the God of Christianity, Judaism, or Islam; pagan **2** an uncivilized or barbaric person ▷ *adj* **3** irreligious; pagan **4** unenlightened; uncivilized; barbaric **5** of or relating to heathen peoples or their religious, moral, and other customs, practices, and beliefs [Old English *hǣthen*; related to Old Norse *heithinn*, Old Frisian *hēthin*, Old High German *heidan*] > 'heathenism *or* 'heathenry *n* > 'heathendom *n*

heathenish ('hiːðənɪʃ) *adj* of, relating to, or resembling a heathen or heathen culture

heathenize *or* **heathenise** ('hiːðə,naɪz) *vb* **1** to render or become heathen, or bring or come under heathen influence **2** (*intr*) to engage in heathen practices

heather ('hɛðə) *n* **1** *Also called:* ling, heath a low-growing evergreen Eurasian ericaceous shrub, *Calluna*

vulgaris, that grows in dense masses on open ground and has clusters of small bell-shaped typically pinkish-purple flowers **2** any of certain similar plants **3** a purplish-red to pinkish-purple colour ▷ *adj* **4** of a heather colour **5** of or relating to interwoven yarns of mixed colours: *heather mixture* [C14: originally Scottish and Northern English, probably from HEATH] > 'heathered *adj* > 'heathery *adj*

Heath Robinson ('rɒbɪnsən) *adj* (of a mechanical device) absurdly complicated in design and having a simple function [C20: named after William *Heath Robinson* (1872–1944), British cartoonist]

heating ('hiːtɪŋ) *n* **1** a device or system for supplying heat, esp central heating, to a building **2** the heat supplied

heat pump *n* a device, as used in a refrigerator, for extracting heat from a source and delivering it elsewhere at a much higher temperature

heat rash *n* a nontechnical name for **miliaria**

heat-seeking *adj* (of a missile) able to detect and follow a source of heat, as from an aircraft engine: *a heat-seeking missile* > heat seeker *n*

heat shield *n* a coating or barrier for shielding from excessive heat, such as that experienced by a spacecraft on re-entry into the earth's atmosphere

heat sink *n* **1** a metal plate specially designed to conduct and radiate heat from an electrical component **2** a layer of material placed within the outer skin of high-speed aircraft to absorb heat

heatstroke ('hiːt,strəʊk) *n* a condition resulting from prolonged exposure to intense heat, characterized by high fever and in severe cases convulsions and coma

heat-treat *vb* (*tr*) to apply heat to (a metal or alloy) in one or more temperature cycles to give it desirable properties > heat treatment *n*

heat wave *n* **1** a continuous spell of abnormally hot weather **2** (*not in technical use*) an extensive slow-moving air mass at a relatively high temperature

heave (hiːv) *vb* **heaves, heaving, heaved** *or chiefly nautical* **hove 1** (*tr*) to lift or move with a great effort **2** (*tr*) to throw (something heavy) with effort **3** to utter (sounds, sighs, etc) or breathe noisily or unhappily: *to heave a sigh* **4** to rise and fall or cause to rise and fall heavily **5** (*past tense and past participle* **hove**) *nautical* **a** to move or cause to move in a specified way, direction, or position: *to heave in sight* **b** (*intr*) (of a vessel) to pitch or roll **6** (*tr*) to displace (rock strata, mineral veins, etc) in a horizontal direction **7** (*intr*) to retch ▷ *n* **8** the act or an instance of heaving **9** a fling **10** the horizontal displacement of rock strata at a fault ▷ *See also* **heaves, heave to** [Old English *hebban*; related to Old Norse *hefja*, Old Saxon *hebbian*, Old High German *heffen* to raise, Latin *capere* to take, Sanskrit *kapaṭī* two hands full] > 'heaver *n*

heave-ho *sentence substitute* a sailors' cry, as when hoisting anchor

heaven ('hɛvən) *n* **1** (*sometimes capital*) Christianity **a** the abode of God and the angels **b** a place or state of communion with God after death **2** (*usually plural*) the sky, firmament or space surrounding the earth **3** (in any of various mythologies) a place, such as Elysium or Valhalla, to which those who have died in the gods' favour are brought to dwell in happiness **4** a place or state of joy and happiness **5** (*singular or plural; sometimes capital*) God or the gods, used in exclamatory phrases of surprise, exasperation, etc: *for heaven's sake; heavens above* **6** in seventh heaven ecstatically happy **7** move heaven and earth to do everything possible (to achieve something) [Old English *heofon*; related to Old Saxon *heban*]

heavenly ('hɛvənlɪ) *adj* **1** *informal* alluring, wonderful, or sublime **2** of or occurring in space: *a heavenly body* **3** divine; holy > 'heavenliness *n*

heavenward ('hɛvənwəd) *adj* **1** directed towards heaven or the sky ▷ *adv* **2** *Also* **heavenwards** towards heaven or the sky

heaves (hiːvz) *n* (*functioning as singular or plural*) *Also called:* broken wind a chronic respiratory disorder of animals of the horse family caused by allergies and dust

heave to *vb* (*adverb*) to stop (a vessel) or (of a vessel) to stop, as by trimming the sails, etc. Also called: **lay to**

Heaviside ('hɛvɪˌsaɪd) n **Oliver**. 1850–1925, English physicist. Independently of Kennelly, he predicted (1902) the existence of an ionized gaseous layer in the upper atmosphere (the **Heaviside layer**); he also contributed to telegraphy

Heaviside layer ('hɛvɪˌsaɪd) n the E region of the ionosphere, predicted by English physicist Oliver Heaviside (1850–1925) in 1902. See **E region**

heavy ('hɛvɪ) adj **heavier**, **heaviest 1** of comparatively great weight: *a heavy stone* **2** having a relatively high density: *lead is a heavy metal* **3** great in yield, quality, or quantity: *heavy rain; heavy traffic* **4** great or considerable: *heavy emphasis* **5** hard to bear, accomplish, or fulfil: *heavy demands* **6** sad or dejected in spirit or mood: *heavy at heart* **7** coarse or broad: *a heavy line; heavy features* **8** (of soil) having a high clay content; cloggy **9** solid or fat: *heavy legs* **10** (of an industry) engaged in the large-scale complex manufacture of capital goods or extraction of raw materials **11** serious; grave **12** military **a** armed or equipped with large weapons, armour, etc **b** (of guns, etc) of a large and powerful type **13** (of a syllable) having stress or accentuation **14** dull and uninteresting: *a heavy style* **15** prodigious: *a heavy drinker* **16** (of cakes, bread, etc) insufficiently leavened **17** deep and loud: *a heavy thud* **18** (of music, literature, etc) **a** dramatic and powerful; grandiose **b** not immediately comprehensible or appealing **19** slang **a** unpleasant or tedious **b** wonderful **c** (of rock music) having a powerful beat; hard **20** weighted; burdened: *heavy with child* **21** clumsy and slow: *heavy going* **22** permeating: *a heavy smell* **23** cloudy or overcast, esp threatening rain: *heavy skies* **24** not easily digestible: *a heavy meal* **25** (of an element or compound) being or containing an isotope with greater atomic weight than that of the naturally occurring element: *heavy hydrogen; heavy water* **26** horse racing (of the going on a racecourse) soft and muddy **27** slang using, or prepared to use, violence or brutality: *the heavy mob* **28** heavy on informal using large quantities of: *this car is heavy on petrol* ▷ n, pl **heavies 29 a** a villainous role **b** an actor who plays such a part **30** military **a** a large fleet unit, esp an aircraft carrier or battleship **b** a large calibre or weighty piece of artillery **31** the **heavies** (usually plural) informal a serious newspaper: *the Sunday heavies* **32** informal a heavyweight boxer, wrestler, etc **33** informal a man hired to threaten violence or deter others by his presence **34** Scot strong bitter beer ▷ adv **35 a** in a heavy manner; heavily: *time hangs heavy* **b** (in combination): *heavy-laden* [Old English *hefig*; related to HEAVE, Old High German *hebīg*] > 'heavily adv > 'heaviness n

heavy-duty n (modifier) made to withstand hard wear, bad weather, etc: *heavy-duty uniforms*

heavy-handed adj **1** clumsy **2** harsh and oppressive > ˌheavy-'handedly adv > ˌheavy-'handedness n

heavy-hearted adj sad; melancholy

heavy hitter n informal another term for **big hitter** (sense 2)

heavy hydrogen n another name for **deuterium**

heavy metal n a type of rock music characterized by a strong beat and amplified instrumental effects, often with violent, nihilistic, and misogynistic lyrics

heavy middleweight n a professional wrestler weighing 177–187 pounds (81–85 kg)

heavy spar n another name for **barytes**

heavy water n water that has been electrolytically decomposed to enrich it in the deuterium isotope in the form HDO or D₂O

heavyweight ('hɛvɪˌweɪt) n **1** a person or thing that is heavier than average **2 a** a professional boxer weighing more than 175 pounds (79 kg) **b** an amateur boxer weighing more than 81 kg (179 pounds) **c** (as modifier): *the world heavyweight championship* **3** a wrestler in a similar weight category (usually over 214 pounds (97 kg)) **4** informal an important or highly influential person

Heb. or **Hebr.** abbreviation **1** Hebrew (language) **2** Bible Hebrews

Hebbel (German 'hɛbəl) n **Christian Friedrich** ('krɪstian 'friːdrɪç). 1813–63, German dramatist and lyric poet, whose historical works were influenced by Hegel; his major plays are *Maria Magdalena* (1844), *Herodes und Mariamne* (1850), and the trilogy *Die Nibelungen* (1862)

hebdomadal (hɛb'dɒmədəl) adj a rare word for **weekly**

Hebe ('hiːbɪ) n Greek myth the goddess of youth and spring, daughter of Zeus and Hera and wife of Hercules

Hebei ('hʌ'beɪ), **Hopeh** or **Hopei** n a province of NE China, on the Gulf of Chihli: important for the production of winter wheat, cotton, and coal. Capital: Shijiazhuang. Pop: 67 690 000 (2003 est). Area: 202 700 sq km (79 053 sq miles)

Hébert (French ebɛr) n **Jacques René** (ʒak rəne). 1755–94, French journalist and revolutionary: a leader of the sans-culottes during the French Revolution. He was guillotined under Robespierre

hebetate ('hɛbɪˌteɪt) adj **1** (of plant parts) having a blunt or soft point ▷ vb **2** rare to make or become blunted [C16: from Latin *hebetāre* to make blunt, from *hebes* blunt] > ˌhebe'tation n > 'hebeˌtative adj

Hebraic (hɪ'breɪɪk), **Hebraical** or **Hebrew** adj of, relating to, or characteristic of the Hebrews or their language or culture > He'braically adv

Hebraism ('hiːbreɪˌɪzəm) n a linguistic usage, custom, or other feature borrowed from or particular to the Hebrew language, or to the Jewish people or their culture

Hebrew ('hiːbruː) n **1** the ancient language of the Hebrews, revived as the official language of Israel. It belongs to the Canaanitic branch of the Semitic subfamily of the Afro-Asiatic family of languages **2** a member of an ancient Semitic people claiming descent from Abraham; an Israelite **3** archaic or offensive a Jew ▷ adj **4** of or relating to the Hebrews or their language **5** archaic, or offensive Jewish [C13: from Old French *Ebreu*, from Latin *Hebraeus*, from Greek *Hebraios*, from Aramaic *'ibhray*, from Hebrew *'ibhrī* one from beyond (the river)]

Hebrews ('hiːbruːz) n (functioning as singular) a book of the New Testament

Hebridean (ˌhɛbrɪ'diːən) or **Hebridian** (hɛ'brɪdɪən) adj **1** of or relating to the Hebrides or their inhabitants ▷ n **2** a native or inhabitant of the Hebrides

Hebrides ('hɛbrɪˌdiːz) pl n the **Hebrides** a group of over 500 islands off the W coast of Scotland: separated by the North Minch, Little Minch, and the Sea of the Hebrides: the chief islands are Skye, Raasay, Rum, Eigg, Coll, Tiree, Mull, Jura, Colonsay, and Islay (**Inner Hebrides**), and Lewis with Harris, North Uist, Benbecula, South Uist, and Barra (**Outer Hebrides**)

Hebron ('hɛbrɒn, 'hiː-) n a city in the West Bank: famous for the Haram, which includes the cenotaphs of Abraham and Sarah, Isaac and Rebecca, and Jacob and Leah. Pop: 168 000 (2005 est). Arabic name: **El Khalil**

Hecate or **Hekate** ('hɛkətɪ) n Greek myth a goddess of the underworld

hecatomb ('hɛkəˌtəʊm, -ˌtuːm) n **1** (in ancient Greece or Rome) any great public sacrifice and feast, originally one in which 100 oxen were sacrificed **2** a great sacrifice [C16: from Latin *hecatombē*, from Greek *hekatombē*, from *hekaton* hundred + *bous* ox]

heck (hɛk) interj a mild exclamation of surprise, irritation, etc [C19: euphemistic for *hell*]

heckelphone ('hɛkəlˌfəʊn) n music a type of bass oboe [C20: named after W. *Heckel* (1856–1909), German inventor]

heckle ('hɛkəl) vb **1** to interrupt (a public speaker, performer, etc) by comments, questions, or taunts **2** Also called: **hackle**, **hatchel** (tr) to comb (hemp or flax) ▷ n **3** an instrument for combing flax or hemp [C15: Northern and East Anglian form of HACKLE] > 'heckler n

hectare ('hɛktɑː) n one hundred ares. 1 hectare is equivalent to 10 000 square metres or 2.471 acres. Symbol: **ha¹** [C19: from French; see HECTO-, ARE²]

hectic ('hɛktɪk) adj **1** characterized by extreme activity or excitement **2** associated with, peculiar to, or symptomatic of tuberculosis (esp in the phrases **hectic fever**, **hectic flush**) ▷ n **3** a hectic fever or flush **4** rare a person who is consumptive or who experiences a hectic fever or flush [C14: from Late Latin *hecticus*, from Greek *hektikos* habitual, from *hexis* state, from *ekhein* to have] > 'hectically adv

hecto- or before a vowel **hect-** prefix denoting 100: *hectogram*

Symbol: h² [via French from Greek *hekaton* hundred]

hectogram *or* **hectogramme** ('hɛktəʊ,græm) *n* one hundred grams. 1 hectogram is equivalent to 3.527 ounces. Symbol: hg

hectograph ('hɛktəʊ,grɑːf, -,græf) *n* **1** Also called: copygraph a process for copying type or manuscript from a glycerine-coated gelatine master to which the original has been transferred **2** a machine using this process

hector ('hɛktə) *vb* **1** to bully or torment ▷ *n* **2** a blustering bully [c17: after HECTOR (the son of Priam), in the sense: a bully]

Hector ('hɛktə) *n* classical myth a son of King Priam of Troy, who was killed by Achilles

Hecuba ('hɛkjʊbə) *n* classical myth the wife of King Priam of Troy, and mother of Hector and Paris

he'd (hiːd; *unstressed* iːd, hɪd, ɪd) *contraction of* he had or he would

heddle ('hɛdᵊl) *n* one of a set of frames of vertical wires on a loom, each wire having an eye through which a warp thread can be passed [Old English *hefeld* chain; related to Old Norse *hafald*, Middle Low German *hevelte*]

hedera ('hɛdərə) *n* See ivy (sense 1) [Latin: ivy]

hedge (hɛdʒ) *n* **1** a row of shrubs, bushes, or trees forming a boundary to a field, garden, etc **2** a barrier or protection against something **3** the act or a method of reducing the risk of financial loss on an investment, bet, etc **4** a cautious or evasive statement **5** (*modifier; often in combination*) low, inferior, or illiterate: *a hedge lawyer* ▷ *vb* **6** (*tr*) to enclose or separate with or as if with a hedge **7** (*intr*) to make or maintain a hedge, as by cutting and laying **8** (*tr; often foll by* in, about, *or* around) to hinder, obstruct, or restrict **9** (*intr*) to evade decision or action, esp by making noncommittal statements **10** (*tr*) to guard against the risk of loss in (a bet, the paying out of a win, etc), esp by laying bets with other bookmakers **11** (*intr*) to protect against financial loss through future price fluctuations, as by investing in futures [Old English *hecg*; related to Old High German *heckia*, Middle Dutch *hegge*; see HAW¹] > 'hedger *n* > 'hedging *n* > 'hedgy *adj*

hedge fund *n* a largely unregulated speculative fund which offers substantial returns for high-risk investments

hedgehog ('hɛdʒ,hɒg) *n* any small nocturnal Old World mammal of the genus *Erinaceus*, such as *E. europaeus*, and related genera, having a protective covering of spines on the back: family *Erinaceidae*, order *Insectivora* (insectivores)

hedgehop ('hɛdʒ,hɒp) *vb* -hops, -hopping, -hopped (*intr*) (of an aircraft) to fly close to the ground, as in crop spraying > 'hedge,hopper *n* > 'hedge,hopping *n, adj*

hedgerow ('hɛdʒ,rəʊ) *n* a hedge of shrubs or low trees growing along a bank, esp one bordering a field or lane

hedge sparrow *n* a small brownish European songbird, *Prunella modularis*: family *Prunellidae* (accentors). Also called: dunnock

hedonics (hiː'dɒnɪks) *n* (*functioning as singular*) **1** the branch of psychology concerned with the study of pleasant and unpleasant sensations **2** (*in philosophy*) the study of pleasure, esp in its relation to duty

hedonism ('hiːdᵊ,nɪzəm, 'hɛd-) *n* **1** ethics **a** the doctrine that moral value can be defined in terms of pleasure **b** the doctrine that the pursuit of pleasure is the highest good **2** indulgence in sensual pleasures [c19: from Greek *hēdonē* pleasure] > he'donic *or* ,hedon'istic *adj* > 'hedonist *n*

-hedron *n combining form* indicating a geometric solid having a specified number of faces or surfaces: *tetrahedron* [from Greek *-edron* -sided, from *hedra* seat, base] > -hedral *adj combining form*

heebie-jeebies ('hiːbɪ'dʒiːbɪz) *pl n* the heebie-jeebies slang apprehension and nervousness [c20: coined by W. De Beck (1890–1942), American cartoonist]

heed (hiːd) *n* **1** close and careful attention; notice (often in the phrases **give, pay,** *or* **take heed**) ▷ *vb* **2** to pay close attention to (someone or something) [Old English *hēdan*; related to Old Saxon *hōdian*, Old High German *huoten*] > 'heeder *n* > 'heedful *adj* > 'heedfully *adv* > 'heedfulness *n*

heedless ('hiːdlɪs) *adj* taking little or no notice; careless

or thoughtless > 'heedlessly *adv* > 'heedlessness *n*

heehaw (,hiː'hɔː) *interj* an imitation or representation of the braying sound of a donkey

heel¹ (hiːl) *n* **1** the back part of the human foot from the instep to the lower part of the ankle **2** the corresponding part in other vertebrates **3** the part of a shoe, stocking, etc, designed to fit the heel **4** the outer part of a shoe underneath the heel **5** the lower, end, or back section of something: *the heel of a loaf* **6** horticulture the small part of the parent plant that remains attached to a young shoot cut for propagation and that ensures more successful rooting **7** the back part of a golf club head where it bends to join the shaft **8** slang a contemptible person **9** at one's heels *or* on one's heels just behind or following closely **10** down at heel **a** shabby or worn **b** slovenly or careless **11** kick one's heels *or* cool one's heels to be kept waiting **12** take to one's heels to run off **13** to heel disciplined or under control, as a dog walking by a person's heel ▷ *vb* **14** (*tr*) to repair or replace the heel of (shoes, boots, etc) **15** (*tr*) golf to strike (the ball) with the heel of the club **16** to follow at the heels of (a person) [Old English *hēla*; related to Old Norse *hæll*, Old Frisian *hēl*] > 'heelless *adj*

heel² (hiːl) *vb* **1** (*of a vessel*) to lean over; list ▷ *n* **2** inclined position from the vertical: *the boat is at ten degrees of heel* [Old English *hieldan*; related to Old Norse *hallr* inclined, Old High German *helden* to bow]

heelball ('hiːl,bɔːl) *n* **a** a black waxy substance used by shoemakers to blacken the edges of heels and soles **b** a similar substance used to take rubbings, esp brass rubbings

heeler ('hiːlə) *n* **1** US See **ward heeler 2** a person or thing that heels **3** Austral & NZ a dog that herds cattle by biting at their heels

heel in *or dialect* **hele in** *vb* (*tr, adverb*) to insert (cuttings, shoots, etc) into the soil before planting to keep them moist

heeltap ('hiːl,tæp) *n* **1** Also called: lift a layer of leather, etc, in the heel of a shoe **2** a small amount of alcoholic drink left at the bottom of a glass after drinking

Heerlen ('hɪələn; *Dutch* 'heːrlə) *n* a city in the SE Netherlands, in Limburg province: industrial centre of a coal-mining region. Pop: 94 000 (2003 est)

Hefei ('hʌ'feɪ) *or* **Hofei** *n* a city in SE China, capital of Anhui province: administrative and commercial centre in a rice- and cotton-growing region. Pop: 1 320 000 (2005 est)

heft (hɛft) *vb* (*tr*) **1** to assess the weight of (something) by lifting **2** to lift ▷ *n* **3** US weight **4** US the main part [c19: probably from HEAVE, by analogy with *thieve, theft, cleave, cleft*] > 'hefter *n*

hefty ('hɛftɪ) *adj* heftier, heftiest informal **1** big and strong **2** characterized by vigour or force: *a hefty blow* **3** large, bulky, or heavy **4** sizable; involving a large amount of money: *a hefty bill; a hefty wage* > 'heftily *adv* > 'heftiness *n*

Hegel ('heɪgᵊl) *n* **Georg Wilhelm Friedrich** (geˈɔrk ˈvɪlhɛlm ˈfriːdrɪç). 1770–1831, German philosopher, who created a fundamentally influential system of thought. His view of man's mind as the highest expression of the Absolute is expounded in *The Phenomenology of Mind* (1807). He developed his concept of dialectic, in which the contradiction between a proposition (thesis) and its antithesis is resolved at a higher level of truth (synthesis), in *Science of Logic* (1812–16) > Hegelian (hɪ'geɪlɪən, heɪ'giː-) *adj* > He'gelian,ism *n*

hegemony (hɪ'gɛmənɪ) *n, pl* -nies ascendancy or domination of one power or state within a league, confederation, etc, or of one social class over others [c16: from Greek *hēgemonia* authority, from *hēgemōn* leader, from *hēgeisthai* to lead] > hegemonic (,hɛgə'mɒnɪk) *adj*

Hegira *or* **Hejira** ('hɛdʒɪrə) *n* **1** the departure of Mohammed from Mecca to Medina in 622 AD; the starting point of the Muslim era **2** the Muslim era itself **3** (*often not capital*) an emigration escape or flight [c16: from Medieval Latin, from Arabic *hijrah* emigration or flight]

Heidegger (*German* 'haidɛgər) *n* **Martin** ('martiːn). 1889–1976, German existentialist philosopher: he expounded his ontological system in *Being and Time* (1927)

Heidelberg ('haɪdəl,bɜːɡ; *German* 'haɪdəlbɛrk) *n* a city in SW Germany, in NW Baden-Württemberg on the River Neckar: capital of the Palatinate from the 13th century until 1719; famous castle (begun in the 12th century) and university (1386), the oldest in Germany. Pop: 142 959 (2003 est)

heifer ('hɛfə) *n* a young cow [Old English *heahfore*; related to Greek *poris* calf; see HIGH]

Heifetz ('haɪfɪts) *n* **Jascha** ('jæʃə). 1901–87, US violinist, born in Russia

heigh-ho ('heɪ'həʊ) *interj* an exclamation of weariness, disappointment, surprise, or happiness

height (haɪt) *n* **1** the vertical distance from the bottom or lowest part of something to the top or apex **2** the vertical distance of an object or place above the ground or above sea level; altitude **3** relatively great altitude or distance from the bottom to the top **4** the topmost point; summit **5** *astronomy* the angular distance of a celestial body above the horizon **6** the period of greatest activity or intensity: *the height of the battle* **7** an extreme example of its kind: *the height of rudeness* **8** (*often plural*) an area of high ground [Old English *hīehthu*; related to Old Norse *hæthe*, Gothic *hauhitha*, Old High German *hōhida*; see HIGH]

heighten ('haɪtˀn) *vb* **1** to make or become high or higher **2** to make or become more extreme or intense > **'heightened** *adj* > **'heightener** *n*

height of land *n* *US & Canadian* a watershed

Heilbronn (*German* hail'brɔn) *n* a city in SW Germany, in N Baden-Württemberg on the River Neckar. Pop: 120 705 (2003 est)

Heilongjiang ('heɪ'lʊŋdʒaɪ'æŋ) *or* **Heilungkiang** ('heɪ'lʊŋ'kjæŋ, -kaɪ'æŋ) *n* a province of NE China, in Manchuria: coal-mining, with placer gold in some rivers. Capital: Harbin. Pop: 38 150 000 (2003 est). Area: 464 000 sq km (179 000 sq miles)

Heilong Jiang ('heɪ'lʊŋ 'dʒaɪ'æŋ) *n* the Pinyin transliteration of the Chinese name for the **Amur**

Heiltsuk ('haɪl,stʊk) *n* a member of a coastal Native Canadian people living in British Columbia [of Wakashan origin]

Heimdall, Heimdal ('heɪm,dɑːl) *or* **Heimdallr** ('heɪm,dɑːlə) *n* *Norse myth* the god of light and the dawn, and the guardian of the rainbow bridge Bifrost

Heine (*German* 'haɪnə) *n* **Heinrich** ('haɪnrɪç). 1797–1856, German poet and essayist, whose chief poetic work is *Das Buch der Lieder* (1827). Many of his poems have been set to music, notably by Schubert and Schumann

Heinkel (*German* 'haɪŋkəl) *n* **Ernst Heinrich** (ɛrnst 'haɪnrɪç). 1888–1958, German aircraft designer. His company provided many military aircraft in World Wars I and II, including the first jet-powered plane

heinous ('heɪnəs, 'hiː-) *adj* evil; atrocious [C14: from Old French *haineus*, from *haine* hatred, from *hair* to hate, of Germanic origin; see HATE] > **'heinously** *adv* > **'heinousness** *n*

heir (ɛə) *n* **1** *civil law* the person legally succeeding to all property of a deceased person, irrespective of whether such person died testate or intestate, and upon whom devolves as well as the rights the duties and liabilities attached to the estate **2** any person or thing that carries on some tradition, circumstance, etc, from a forerunner [C13: from Old French, from Latin *hērēs*; related to Greek *khēros* bereaved]

heir apparent *n, pl* **heirs apparent** *property law* a person whose right to succeed to certain property cannot be defeated, provided such person survives his ancestor

heiress ('ɛərɪs) *n* **1** a woman who inherits or expects to inherit great wealth **2** *property law* a female heir

heirloom ('ɛə,luːm) *n* **1** an object that has been in a family for generations **2** *property law* a chattel inherited by special custom or in accordance with the terms of a will [C15: from HEIR + *lome* tool; see LOOM¹]

heir presumptive *n* *property law* a person who expects to succeed to an estate but whose right may be defeated by the birth of one nearer in blood to the ancestor

Heisenberg ('haɪzˀn,bɜːɡ; *German* 'haɪzənbɛrk) *n* **Werner Karl** ('vɛrnər karl). 1901–76, German physicist. He

contributed to quantum mechanics and formulated the uncertainty principle (1927): Nobel prize for physics 1932

heist (haɪst) *slang, chiefly US & Canadian* ▷ *n* **1** a robbery ▷ *vb* **2** (*tr*) to steal or burgle [variant of HOIST] > **'heister** *n*

Heitler (*German* 'haitlər) *n* **Walter** ('valtər). 1904–81, German physicist, noted for his work on chemical bonds

Hejaz, Hedjaz *or* **Hijaz** (hiːˈdʒæz) *n* a region of W Saudi Arabia, along the Red Sea and the Gulf of Aqaba: formerly an independent kingdom; united with Nejd in 1932 to form Saudi Arabia. Area: about 348 600 sq km (134 600 sq miles)

Hejira ('hedʒɪrə) *n* a variant spelling of **Hegira**

Hekate ('hɛkətɪ) *n* a variant spelling of **Hecate**

Hekla ('hɛklə) *n* a volcano in SW Iceland: several craters, subject to fairly frequent eruptions in recent times. Height: 1491 m (4892 ft)

Hel (hɛl) *or* **Hela** ('hɛlɑː) *n* *Norse myth* **1** the goddess of the dead **2** the underworld realm of the dead

held (hɛld) *vb* the past tense and past participle of **hold¹**

Helen ('hɛlɪn) *n* *Greek myth* the beautiful daughter of Zeus and Leda, whose abduction by Paris from her husband Menelaus caused the Trojan War

Helena¹ ('hɛlənə) *n* a city in W Montana: the state capital. Pop: 26 718 (2003 est)

Helena² (hɛlənə) *n* **Saint.** ?248–?328 AD, Roman empress, mother of Constantine I. After converting to Christianity (313) she made a pilgrimage to the Holy Land (?326) where she supposedly discovered the cross on which Christ died. Feast day: May 21

helenium (hə'liːnɪəm) *n* any plant of the American genus *Helenium*, up to 1.6 m (5 ft) tall, some species of which are grown as border plants for their daisy-like yellow or variegated flowers: family *Asteraceae* [New Latin, from Greek *helenion*, a plant name]

Helgoland ('hɛlgolant) *n* the German name for **Heligoland**

heli- *combining form* helicopter: heliport [C20: shortened from HELICOPTER]

heliacal rising (hɪ'laɪək²l) *n* **1** the rising of a celestial object at approximately the same time as the rising of the sun **2** the date at which such a celestial object first becomes visible in the dawn sky [C17: from Late Latin *hēliacus* relating to the sun, from Greek *hēliakos*, from *hēlios* the sun]

helianthemum (hiːlɪ'ænθəməm) *n* any plant of the dwarf evergreen genus *Helianthemum*, some species of which are grown as rock-garden plants for their numerous papery yellow or orange flowers; related to the rockrose, which they resemble: family *Cistaceae*. Also called: Cape primrose [New Latin, from Greek *hēlios* sun + *anthemon* flower]

helianthus (ˌhiːlɪ'ænθəs) *n, pl* **-thuses** any plant of the genus *Helianthus*, such as the sunflower and Jerusalem artichoke, typically having large yellow daisy-like flowers with yellow, brown, or purple centres: family *Asteraceae* (composites) [C18: New Latin, from Greek *hēlios* sun + *anthos* flower]

heli-boarding *n* *NZ* the sport of snowboarding on mountains or glaciers accessible only by helicopter or skiplane

helical ('hɛlɪk²l) *adj* of or shaped like a helix; spiral > **'helically** *adv*

helical gear *n* a cylindrical gearwheel having the tooth form generated on a helical path about the axis of the wheel

helices ('hɛlɪˌsiːz) *n* a plural of **helix**

helichrysum (ˌhɛlɪ'kraɪzəm) *n* any plant of the widely cultivated genus *Helichrysum*, whose flowers retain their shape and colour when dried: family *Asteraceae* (composites) [C16: from Latin, from Greek *helikhrusos*, from *helix* spiral + *khrusos* gold]

helico- *or before a vowel* **helic-** *combining form* spiral or helical [from Latin, from Greek *helix* spiral]

helicoid ('hɛlɪˌkɔɪd) *adj* Also: helicoidal **1** *biology* shaped like a spiral: *a helicoid shell* ▷ *n* **2** *geometry* any surface resembling that of a screw thread > ˌheli'coidally *adv*

helicon ('hɛlɪkən) *n* a bass tuba made to coil over the shoulder of a band musician [C19: probably from HELICON, associated with Greek *helix* spiral]

Helicon ('hɛlɪkən) *n* a mountain in Greece, in Boeotia: location of the springs of Hippocrene and Aganippe, believed by the Ancient Greeks to be the source of poetic inspiration and the home of the Muses. Height: 1749 m (5738 ft). Modern Greek name: Elikón

helicopter ('hɛlɪ,kɒptə) *n* an aircraft capable of hover, vertical flight, and horizontal flight in any direction. Most get all of their lift and propulsion from the rotation of overhead blades [c19: from French *hélicoptère*, from HELICO- + Greek *pteron* wing]

helicopter gunship *n* a large heavily armed helicopter used for ground attack

helicopter view *n* an overview of a situation without any details

Heligoland ('hɛlɪgəʊ,lænd) *n* a small island in the North Sea, one of the North Frisian Islands, separated from the coast of NW Germany by the **Heligoland Bight**: administratively part of the German state of Schleswig-Holstein: a large island in early medieval times, now eroded to an area of about 150 hectares (380 acres); ceded by Britain to Germany in 1890 in exchange for Zanzibar. German name: Helgoland

helio- *or before a vowel* **heli-** *combining form* indicating the sun: *heliocentric; heliolithic* [from Greek, from *hēlios* sun]

heliocentric (,hi:lɪəʊ'sɛntrɪk) *adj* **1** having the sun at its centre **2** measured from or in relation to the centre of the sun > ,helio'centrically *adv* > ,heliocen'tricity (,hi:lɪəʊsɛn'trɪsɪtɪ) *or* ,helio'centri,cism (,hi:lɪəʊ'sɛntrɪ,sɪzəm) *n*

Heliogabalus (,hi:lɪəʊ'gæbələs) *or* **Elagabalus** *n* original name *Varius Avitus Bassianus.* ?204–222 AD, Roman emperor (218–222). His reign was notorious for debauchery and extravagance

heliograph ('hi:lɪəʊ,grɑːf, -,græf) *n* **1** an instrument with mirrors and a shutter used for sending messages in Morse code by reflecting the sun's rays **2** a device used to photograph the sun > **heliographer** (,hi:lɪ'ɒgrəfə) *n* > ,helio'graphic *or* ,helio'graphical *adj* > ,heli'ography *n*

heliometer (,hi:lɪ'ɒmɪtə) *n* a refracting telescope having a split objective lens that is used to determine very small angular distances between celestial bodies > **heliometric** (,hi:lɪəʊ'mɛtrɪk) *or* ,helio'metrical *adj* > ,helio'metrically *adv* > ,heli'ometry *n*

heliopause ('hi:lɪəʊ,pɔːz) *n* the boundary between the region of space dominated by the solar wind and the interstellar medium

Heliopolis (,hi:lɪ'ɒpəlɪs) *n* **1** (in ancient Egypt) a city near the apex of the Nile delta: a centre of sun worship. Ancient Egyptian name: On **2** the Ancient Greek name for **Baalbek**

Helios ('hi:lɪ,ɒs) *n Greek myth* the god of the sun, who drove his chariot daily across the sky. Roman counterpart: Sol

heliostat ('hi:lɪəʊ,stæt) *n* an astronomical instrument used to reflect the light of the sun in a constant direction > ,helio'static *adj*

heliotrope ('hi:lɪə,trəʊp, 'hɛljə-) *n* **1** any boraginaceous plant of the genus *Heliotropium,* esp the South American *H. arborescens,* cultivated for its small fragrant purple flowers **2 garden heliotrope** a widely cultivated valerian, *Valeriana officinalis,* with clusters of small pink, purple, or white flowers **3** any of various plants that turn towards the sun **4 a** a bluish-violet to purple colour **b** (*as adjective*): *a heliotrope dress* **5** an instrument used in geodetic surveying employing the sun's rays reflected by a mirror as a signal for the sighting of stations over long distances **6** another name for **bloodstone** [c17: from Latin *hēliotropium,* from Greek *hēliotropion,* from *hēlios* sun + *trepein* to turn]

heliotropism (,hi:lɪ'ɒtrə,pɪzəm) *n* the growth of plants or plant parts (esp flowers) in response to the stimulus of sunlight, so that they turn to face the sun > **heliotropic** (,hi:lɪəʊ'trɒpɪk) *adj* > ,helio'tropically *adv*

heliport ('hɛlɪ,pɔːt) *n* an airport for helicopters [c20: from HELI- + PORT¹]

heli-skiing *n* skiing in which skiers are transported by helicopter to remote slopes > 'heli-,skier *n*

helium ('hi:lɪəm) *n* a very light nonflammable colourless odourless element that is an inert gas, occurring in certain natural gases: used in balloons and in cryogenic research. Symbol: He; atomic no: 2; atomic wt: 4.002602; density: 0.1785 kg/m³; at normal pressures it is liquid down to absolute zero; melting pt: below −272.2°C; boiling pt: −268.90°C [c19: New Latin, from HELIO- + -IUM; named from its having first been detected in the solar spectrum]

helix ('hi:lɪks) *n, pl* **helices** ('hɛlɪ,si:z) *or* **helixes** **1** a curve that lies on a cylinder or cone, at a constant angle to the line segments making up the surface; spiral **2** a spiral shape or form **3** the incurving fold that forms the margin of the external ear **4** another name for **volute** (sense 2) **5** any terrestrial gastropod mollusc of the genus *Helix,* which includes the garden snail (*H. aspersa*) [c16: from Latin, from Greek: spiral; probably related to Greek *helissein* to twist]

hell (hɛl) *n* **1** *Christianity* (*sometimes capital*) **a** the place or state of eternal punishment of the wicked after death, with Satan as its ruler **b** forces of evil regarded as residing there **2** (*sometimes capital*) (in various religions and cultures) the abode of the spirits of the dead **3** pain, extreme difficulty, etc **4** *informal* a cause of such difficulty or suffering: *war is hell* **5** *US & Canadian* high spirits or mischievousness **6** *now rare* a gambling house, booth, etc **7 for the hell of it** *informal* for the fun of it **8 from hell** *informal* denoting a person or thing that is particularly bad or alarming: *neighbour from hell; hangover from hell* **9 give someone hell** *informal* **a** to give someone a severe reprimand or punishment **b** to be a source of annoyance or torment to someone **10 hell for leather** at great speed **11 hell to pay** *informal* serious consequences, as of a foolish action **12 the hell** *informal* **a** (intensifier) used in such phrases as **what the hell, who the hell,** etc **b** an expression of strong disagreement or disfavour: *the hell I will* ▷ *interj* **13** *informal* an exclamation of anger, annoyance, surprise, etc (Also in exclamations such as **hell's bells, hell's teeth,** etc) [Old English *hell;* related to *helan* to cover, Old Norse *hel,* Gothic *halja* hell, Old High German *hella*]

he'll (hi:l; *unstressed* i:l, hɪl, ɪl) *contraction of* he will *or* he shall

hellacious (hɛ'leɪʃəs) *adj US slang* **1** remarkable; horrifying **2** wonderful; excellent [c20: from HELL + -*acious* as in AUDACIOUS]

Helladic (hɛ'lædɪk) *adj* of, characteristic of, or related to the Bronze Age civilization that flourished about 2900 to 1100 BC on the Greek mainland and islands

Hellas ('hɛləs) *n* transliteration of the Ancient Greek name for **Greece**

hellbent (,hɛl'bɛnt) *adj* (*postpositive* and foll by *on*) *informal* strongly or rashly intent

hellcat ('hɛl,kæt) *n* a spiteful fierce-tempered woman

Helle ('hɛlɪ) *n Greek myth* a daughter of King Athamas, who was borne away with her brother Phrixus on the golden winged ram. She fell from its back and was drowned in the Hellespont. See also **Phrixus, Golden Fleece**

hellebore ('hɛlɪ,bɔː) *n* **1** any plant of the Eurasian ranunculaceous genus *Helleborus,* esp *H. niger* (black hellebore), typically having showy flowers and poisonous parts ▷ See also **Christmas rose 2** any of various liliaceous plants of the N temperate genus *Veratrum,* esp *V. album,* that have greenish flowers and yield alkaloids used in the treatment of heart disease [c14: from Greek *helleboros,* of uncertain origin]

Hellen ('hɛlɪn) *n* (in Greek legend) a Thessalian king and eponymous ancestor of the Hellenes

Hellene ('hɛli:n) *or* **Hellenian** (hɛ'li:nɪən) *n* another name for a **Greek**

Hellenic (hɛ'lɛnɪk, -'li:-) *adj* **1** of or relating to the ancient or modern Greeks or their language **2** of or relating to ancient Greece or the Greeks of the classical period (776–323 BC). See **Hellenistic** ▷ *n* **3** a branch of the Indo-European family of languages consisting of Greek in its various ancient and modern dialects

Hellenism ('hɛlɪ,nɪzəm) *n* **1** the principles, ideals, and pursuits associated with classical Greek civilization **2** the spirit or national character of the Greeks **3** conformity to, imitation of, or devotion to the culture of ancient Greece **4** the cosmopolitan civilization of the Hellenistic world

Hellenistic (ˌhɛlɪˈnɪstɪk) or **Hellenistical** adj **1** characteristic of or relating to Greek civilization in the Mediterranean world, esp from the death of Alexander the Great (323 BC) to the defeat of Antony and Cleopatra (30 BC) **2** of or relating to the Greeks or to Hellenism ▷ ˌHellenˈistically adv

Hellenize or **Hellenise** (ˈhɛlɪˌnaɪz) vb to make or become like the ancient Greeks ▷ ˌHelleniˈzation or ˌHelleniˈsation n ▷ ˈHellenˌizer or ˈHellenˌiser n

Heller (ˈhɛlə) n **Joseph.** 1923–99, US novelist. His works include Catch 22 (1961), God Knows (1984), Picture This (1988), and Closing Time (1994)

Helles (ˈhɛlɪs) n **Cape Helles** a cape in NW Turkey, at the S end of the Gallipoli Peninsula

Hellespont (ˈhɛlɪˌspɒnt) n the ancient name for the **Dardanelles**

hellfire (ˈhɛlˌfaɪə) n **1** the torment and punishment of hell, envisaged as eternal fire **2** (modifier) characterizing sermons or preachers that emphasize this aspect of Christian belief: hellfire evangelism

hellion (ˈhɛljən) n US informal a rough or rowdy person, esp a child; troublemaker. Also called: heller [C19: probably from dialect hallion rogue, of unknown origin]

hellish (ˈhɛlɪʃ) adj **1** of or resembling hell; cruel **3** informal very difficult or unpleasant ▷ adv **4** Brit informal (intensifier): a hellish good idea ▷ ˈhellishly adv ▷ ˈhellishness n

Hellman (ˈhɛlmən) n **Lillian.** 1905–84, US dramatist. Her works include the plays The Little Foxes (1939), The Searching Wind (1944), and the autobiographical Scoundrel Time (1976)

hello, hallo or **hullo** (hɛˈləʊ, hə-, ˈhɛləʊ) sentence substitute **1** an expression of greeting used on meeting a person or at the start of a telephone call **2** a call used to attract attention **3** an expression of surprise **4** an expression used to indicate that the speaker thinks his or her listener is naive or slow to realize something: Hello? Have you been on Mars for the past two weeks or something? ▷ n, pl -los **5** the act of saying or calling "hello" [C19: see HALLO]

Hell's Angel n a member of a motorcycle gang of a kind originating in the US in the 1950s, who typically dress in denim and Nazi-style paraphernalia and are noted for their initiation rites, lawless behaviour, etc

helluva (ˈhɛləvə) adj, adv informal **1** (intensifier): a helluva difficult job; he's a helluva guy **2** South African (intensifier): it's helluva tough out here

helm¹ (hɛlm) n **1** nautical **a** the wheel, tiller, or entire apparatus by which a vessel is steered **b** the position of the helm: that is, on the side of the keel opposite from that of the rudder **2** a position of leadership or control (esp in the phrase **at the helm**) ▷ vb **3** (tr) to direct or steer [Old English helma; related to Old Norse hjalm rudder, Old High German halmo] ▷ ˈhelmless adj

helm² (hɛlm) n an archaic or poetic word for **helmet** [Old English helm; related to helan to cover, Old Norse hjalmr, Gothic hilms, Old High German helm helmet, Sanskrit śárman protection]

Helmand (ˈhɛlmənd) n a river in S Asia, rising in E Afghanistan and flowing generally southwest to a marshy lake, Hamun Helmand, on the border with Iran. Length: 1400 km (870 miles)

helmer (ˈhɛlmə) n informal a film director

helmet (ˈhɛlmɪt) n **1** a piece of protective or defensive armour for the head worn by soldiers, policemen, firemen, divers, etc **2** biology a part or structure resembling a helmet, esp the upper part of the calyx of certain flowers [C15: from Old French, diminutive of helme, of Germanic origin] ▷ ˈhelmeted adj

Helmholtz (German ˈhɛlmhɔlts) n Baron **Hermann Ludwig Ferdinand von** (ˈhɛrman ˈluːtvɪç ˈfɛrdinand fɔn). 1821–94, German physiologist, physicist, and mathematician: helped to found the theory of the conservation of energy; invented the ophthalmoscope (1850); and investigated the mechanics of sight and sound

helminth (ˈhɛlmɪnθ) n any parasitic worm, esp a nematode or fluke [C19: from Greek helmins parasitic worm] ▷ helminthoid (ˈhɛlmɪnˌθɔɪd, hɛlˈmɪnθɔɪd) adj

helminthiasis (ˌhɛlmɪnˈθaɪəsɪs) n infestation of the body with parasitic worms [C19: from New Latin, from Greek helminthian to be infested with worms]

Helmont (Flemish ˈhɛlmɔnt) n **Jean Baptiste van** (ʒã batist van). 1577–1644, Flemish chemist and physician. He was the first to distinguish gases and claimed to have coined the word gas

Héloïse (ˈɛləʊˌiːz; French elɔiz) n ?1101–64, pupil, mistress, and wife of Abelard

Helot (ˈhɛlət, ˈhiː-) n **1** (in ancient Greece, esp Sparta) a member of the class of unfree men above slaves owned by the state **2** (usually not capital) a serf or slave [C16: from Latin Hēlotēs, from Greek Heilōtes, alleged to have meant originally: inhabitants of Helos, who, after its conquest, were serfs of the Spartans]

help (hɛlp) vb **1** to assist or aid (someone to do something), esp by sharing the work, cost, or burden of something: he helped his friend to escape; she helped him climb out of the boat **2** to alleviate the burden of (someone else) by giving assistance **3** (tr) to assist (a person) to go in a specified direction: help the old lady up from the chair **4** to promote or contribute to: to help the relief operations **5** to cause improvement in (a situation, person, etc): crying won't help **6** (tr; preceded by can, could, etc; usually used with a negative) **a** to avoid or refrain from: we can't help wondering who he is **b** (usually foll by it) to prevent or be responsible for: I can't help it if it rains **7** to alleviate (an illness, etc) **8** (tr) to serve (a customer): can I help you, madam? **9** (tr; foll by to) **a** to serve (someone with food, etc) (usually in the phrase **help oneself**): may I help you to some more vegetables?; help yourself to peas **b** to provide (oneself with) without permission: he's been helping himself to money out of the petty cash **10** cannot help but to be unable to do anything else except: I cannot help but laugh **11** help a person off with to assist a person in the removal of (clothes) **12** help a person on with to assist a person in the putting on of (clothes) **13** so help me **a** on my honour **b** no matter what: so help me, I'll get revenge ▷ n **14** the act of helping, or being helped, or a person or thing that helps: she's a great help **15** a helping **16 a** a person hired for a job; employee, esp a farm worker or domestic servant **b** (functioning as singular) several employees collectively **17** a means of remedy: there's no help for it ▷ interj **18** used to ask for assistance ▷ See also **help out** [Old English helpan; related to Old Norse hjalpa, Gothic hilpan, Old High German helfan] ▷ ˈhelpable adj ▷ ˈhelper n

helper T-cell n See **T-lymphocyte**

helpful (ˈhɛlpfʊl) adj serving a useful function; giving help ▷ ˈhelpfully adv ▷ ˈhelpfulness n

helping (ˈhɛlpɪŋ) n a single portion of food taken at a meal

helping hand n assistance: many people lent a helping hand in making arrangements for the party

helpless (ˈhɛlplɪs) adj **1** unable to manage independently **2** made powerless or weak: they were helpless from so much giggling **3** without help ▷ ˈhelplessly adv ▷ ˈhelplessness n

helpline (ˈhɛlpˌlaɪn) n **1** a telephone line operated by a charitable organization for people in distress **2** a telephone line operated by a commercial organization to provide information

Helpmann (ˈhɛlpmən) n Sir **Robert.** 1909–86, Australian ballet dancer and choreographer: his ballets include Miracle in the Gorbals (1944), Display (1965), and Yugen (1965)

helpmate (ˈhɛlpˌmeɪt) n a companion and helper, esp a wife

helpmeet (ˈhɛlpˌmiːt) n a less common word for **helpmate** [C17: from the phrase an helpe meet (suitable) for him Genesis 2:18]

help out vb (adverb) **1** to assist or aid (someone), esp by sharing the burden **2** to share the burden or cost of something with (another person)

Helsingborg (Swedish hɛlsɪŋˈbɔrj) n a port in SW Sweden, on the Sound opposite Helsingør, Denmark: changed hands several times between Denmark and Sweden, finally becoming Swedish in 1710; shipbuilding. Pop: 121 097 (2004 est). Former name (until 1971): Hälsingborg

Helsingør (Danish hɛlseŋˈøːr) n a port in NE Denmark, in NE Zealand: site of Kronborg Castle (16th century), famous as the scene of Shakespeare's *Hamlet*. Pop: 35 002 (2004 est). English name: Elsinore

Helsinki ('hɛlsɪŋkɪ, hɛl'sɪŋ-) *n* the capital of Finland, a port in the south on the Gulf of Finland: founded by Gustavus I of Sweden in 1550; replaced Turku as capital in 1812, while under Russian rule; university. Pop: 559 330 (2003 est)

helter-skelter ('hɛltə'skɛltə) *adj* 1 haphazard or carelessly hurried ▷ *adv* 2 in a helter-skelter manner ▷ *n* 3 *Brit* a high spiral slide, as at a fairground 4 disorder or haste [c16: probably of imitative origin]

helve (hɛlv) *n* 1 the handle of a hand tool such as an axe or pick ▷ *vb* 2 (*tr*) to fit a helve to (a tool) [Old English *hielfe*; related to Old Saxon *hëlvi*, Old High German *halb*, Lithuanian *kílpa* stirrup; see HALTER]

Helvellyn (hɛl'vɛlɪn) *n* a mountain in NW England, in the Lake District. Height: 949 m (3114 ft)

Helvetia (hɛl'viːʃə) *n* 1 the Latin name for Switzerland 2 a Roman province in central Europe (1st century BC to the 5th century AD), corresponding to part of S Germany and parts of W and N Switzerland

Helvetian (hɛl'viːʃən) *adj* 1 another word for Swiss ▷ *n* 2 a native or citizen of Switzerland

Helvétius (hɛl'viːʃɪəs; *French* ɛlvesjys) *n* **Claude Adrien** (klod adriɛ̃). 1715–71, French philosopher. In his chief work *De l'Esprit* (1758), he asserted that the mainspring of human action is self-interest and that differences in human intellects are due only to differences in education

hem¹ (hɛm) *n* 1 an edge to a piece of cloth, made by folding the raw edge under and stitching it down 2 short for **hemline** ▷ *vb* **hems**, **hemming**, **hemmed** (*tr*) 3 to provide with a hem 4 (usually foll by *in*, *around*, or *about*) to enclose or confine [Old English *hemm*; related to Old Frisian *hemme* enclosed land]

hem² (hɛm) *n, interj* 1 a representation of the sound of clearing the throat, used to gain attention, express hesitation, etc ▷ *vb* **hems**, **hemming**, **hemmed** 2 (*intr*) to utter this sound 3 **hem and haw** *or* **hum and haw** to hesitate in speaking or in making a decision

he-man *n, pl* **-men** *informal* a strongly built muscular man

hematite ('hɛmətaɪt) *or* **haematite** ('hɛmətaɪt, 'hiːm-) *n* a red, grey, or black mineral, found as massive beds and in veins and igneous rocks. It is the chief source of iron. Composition: iron (ferric) oxide. Formula: Fe₂O₃. Crystal structure: hexagonal (rhombohedral). Also called: iron glance [c16: via Latin from Greek *haimatitēs* resembling blood, from *haima* blood] > **hematitic** *or* **haematitic** (,hɛmə'tɪtɪk, ,hiː-) *adj*

hemato- *or before a vowel* **hemat-** *combining form* US variants of **haemato-**

Hemel Hempstead ('hɛməl 'hɛmstɪd) *n* a town in SE England, in W Hertfordshire: designated a new town in 1947. Pop: 83 118 (2001)

hemeralopia (,hɛmərə'ləupɪə) *n* inability to see clearly in bright light. See **nyctalopia** [c18: New Latin, from Greek *hēmeralōps*, from *hēmera* day + *alaos* blind + *ōps* eye] > **hemeralopic** (,hɛmərə'lɒpɪk) *adj*

hemerocallis (,hɛmərəʊ'kælɪs) *n* See **day lily** [from Greek *hemera* day + *kallos* beautiful]

hemi- *prefix* half: *hemicycle*; *hemisphere* [from Latin, from Greek *hēmi-*]

-hemia *n combining form* US variant of **-aemia**

hemidemisemiquaver (,hɛmɪ,dɛmɪ'sɛmɪ,kweɪvə) *n* *music* a note having the time value of one sixty-fourth of a semibreve. Usual US and Canadian name: **sixty-fourth note**

Hemingway ('hɛmɪŋ,weɪ) *n* **Ernest** 1899–1961, US novelist and short-story writer. His novels include *The Sun Also Rises* (1926), *A Farewell to Arms* (1929), *For Whom the Bell Tolls* (1940), and *The Old Man and the Sea* (1952): Nobel prize for literature 1954

Hemingwayesque (,hɛmɪŋ,weɪ'ɛsk) *adj* of, relating to, or like Ernest Hemingway (1899–1961), the US novelist and short-story writer, his works, ideas, etc

hemiplegia (,hɛmɪ'pliːdʒɪə) *n* paralysis of one side of the body, usually as the result of injury to the brain > ,hemi'plegic *adj*

hemipode ('hɛmɪ,pəʊd) *or* **hemipod** ('hɛmɪ,pɒd) *n* other names for **button quail**

hemipteran (hɪ'mɪptərən) *n* Also called: **hemipteron** (hɪ'mɪptə,rɒn) any hemipterous insect [c19: from HEMI- + Greek *pteron* wing]

hemipterous (hɪ'mɪptərəs) *or* **hemipteran** *adj* of, relating to, or belonging to the *Hemiptera*, a large order of insects having sucking or piercing mouthparts specialized as a beak (rostrum). The group is divided into the suborders *Homoptera* (aphids, cicadas, etc) and *Heteroptera* (water bugs, bedbugs, etc)

hemisphere ('hɛmɪ,sfɪə) *n* 1 one half of a sphere 2 a half of the terrestrial globe, divided into **northern** and **southern hemispheres** by the equator or into **eastern** and **western hemispheres** by some meridians, usually 0° and 180° b a map or projection of one of the hemispheres 3 either of the two halves of the celestial sphere that lie north or south of the celestial equator 4 *anatomy* short for **cerebral hemisphere**, a half of the cerebrum > hemispheric (,hɛmɪ'sfɛrɪk) *or* ,hemi'spherical *adj*

hemistich ('hɛmɪ,stɪk) *n* *prosody* a half line of verse

hemline ('hɛm,laɪn) *n* the level to which the hem of a skirt or dress hangs; hem: *knee-length hemlines*

hemlock ('hɛm,lɒk) *n* 1 an umbelliferous poisonous Eurasian plant, *Conium maculatum*, having finely divided leaves, spotted stems, and small white flowers 2 a poisonous drug derived from this plant 3 Also called: **hemlock spruce** any coniferous tree of the genus *Tsuga*, of North America and E Asia, having short flat needles: family *Pinaceae* [Old English *hymlic*; perhaps related to *hymele* hop plant, Middle Low German *homele*, Old Norwegian *humli*, Old Slavonic *chŭmelī*]

hemo- *combining form* a US variant of **haemo-**

hemp (hɛmp) *n* 1 Also called: **cannabis**, **marijuana** an annual strong-smelling Asian plant, *Cannabis sativa*, having tough fibres, deeply lobed leaves, and small greenish flowers: family *Cannabidaeceae*. See also **Indian hemp** 2 the fibre of this plant, used to make canvas, rope, etc 3 any of several narcotic drugs obtained from some varieties of this plant, esp from Indian hemp [Old English *hænep*; related to Old Norse *hampr*, Old High German *hanaf*, Greek *kannabis*, Dutch *hennep*] > 'hempen *or* 'hemp,like *adj*

hemstitch ('hɛm,stɪtʃ) *n* 1 a decorative edging stitch, usually for a hem, in which the cross threads are stitched in groups ▷ *vb* 2 to decorate (a hem, etc) with hemstitches > 'hem,stitcher *n*

hen (hɛn) *n* 1 the female of any bird, esp the adult female of the domestic fowl 2 the female of certain other animals, such as the lobster 3 *informal* a woman regarded as gossipy or foolish 4 *Scot dialect* a term of address (often affectionate), used to women and girls 5 **scarce as hen's teeth** extremely rare [Old English *henn*; related to Old High German *henna*, Old Frisian *henne*]

Henan ('hʌ'næn) *or* **Honan** *n* a province of N central China: the chief centre of early Chinese culture; mainly agricultural (the largest wheat-producing province in China). Capital: Zhengzhou. Pop: 96 670 000 (2003 est)

henbane ('hɛn,beɪn) *n* a poisonous solanaceous European plant, *Hyoscyamus niger*, with sticky hairy leaves and funnel-shaped greenish flowers: yields the drug hyoscyamine

hence (hɛns) *sentence connector* 1 for this reason; following from this; therefore ▷ *adv* 2 from this time: *a year hence* 3 *archaic* a from here or from this world; away b from this origin or source ▷ *interj* 4 *archaic* begone! away! [Old English *hionane*; related to Old High German *hinana* away from here, Old Irish *cen* on this side]

henceforth ('hɛns'fɔːθ), **henceforwards** *or* **henceforward** *adv* from this time forward; from now on

henchman ('hɛntʃmən) *n, pl* **-men** 1 a faithful attendant or supporter 2 *archaic* a squire; page [c14 *hengestman*, from Old English *hengest* stallion + MAN; related to Old Norse *hestr* horse, Old High German *hengist* gelding]

hendeca- *combining form* eleven: *hendecagon*; *hendecahedron*; *hendecasyllable* [from Greek *hendeka*, from *hen*, neuter of *heis* one + *deka* ten]

hendecagon (hɛnˈdɛkəgən) *n* a polygon having 11 sides
> **hendecagonal** (ˌhɛndɪˈkægənᵊl) *adj*

hendecasyllable (ˈhɛndɛkəˌsɪləbᵊl) *n prosody* a verse line of 11 syllables [c18: via Latin from Greek *hendekasullabos*]
> **hendecasyllabic** (ˌhɛndɛkəsɪˈlæbɪk) *adj*

Henderson (ˈhɛndəsən) *n* **Arthur**. 1863–1935, British Labour politician. As foreign secretary (1929–31) he supported the League of Nations and international disarmament; Nobel peace prize 1934

hendiadys (hɛnˈdaɪədɪs) *n* a rhetorical device by which two nouns joined by a conjunction, usually *and*, are used instead of a noun and a modifier, as in *to run with fear and haste* instead of *to run with fearful haste* [c16: from Medieval Latin, changed from Greek phrase *hen dia duoin*, literally: one through two]

Hendra (ˈhɛndrə) *n* a virus that affects humans and horses, causing a fatal, influenza-like illness [c20: after the suburb of Brisbane, the location of the outbreak during which the virus was first isolated]

Hendrix (ˈhɛndrɪks) *n* **Jimi**, full name *James Marshall Hendrix*. 1942–70, US rock guitarist, singer, and songwriter, noted for his innovative guitar technique. His recordings include "Purple Haze" (1967) and *Are you Experienced?* (1967)

Hendry (ˈhɛndrɪ) *n* **Stephen**. born 1969, British snooker player: world champion 1990, 1992–96, and 1999

henequen, henequin *or* **heniquen** (ˈhɛnɪkɪn) *n* **1** an agave plant, *Agave fourcroydes*, that is native to Yucatán **2** the fibre of this plant, used in making rope, twine, and coarse fabrics [c19: from American Spanish *henequén*, probably of Taino origin]

henge (hɛndʒ) *n* a circular area, often containing a circle of stones or sometimes wooden posts, dating from the Neolithic and Bronze Ages [back formation from STONEHENGE]

Hengelo (*Dutch* ˈhɛŋəlo:) *n* a city in the E Netherlands, in Overijssel province on the Twente Canal: industrial centre, esp for textiles. Pop: 81 000 (2003 est)

Hengist (ˈhɛŋgɪst) *n* died ?488 AD, a leader, with his brother Horsa, of the first Jutish settlers in Britain; he is thought to have conquered Kent (?455)

Hengyang (ˈhɛŋˈjæŋ) *n* a city in SE central China, in Hunan province on the Xiang River. Pop: 853 000 (2005 est)

hen harrier *n* a common harrier, *Circus cyaneus*, that flies over fields and marshes and nests in marshes and open land

henhouse (ˈhɛnˌhaʊs) *n* a coop for hens

Henie (ˈhɛnɪ) *n* **Sonja** (ˈsɒnjə). 1912–69, Norwegian figure-skater

Henley-on-Thames (ˈhɛnlɪ-) *n* a town in S England, in SE Oxfordshire on the River Thames: a riverside resort with an annual regatta. Pop: 10 513 (2001). Often shortened to **Henley**

henna (ˈhɛnə) *n* **1** a lythraceous shrub or tree, *Lawsonia inermis*, of Asia and N Africa, with white or reddish fragrant flowers **2** a reddish dye obtained from the powdered leaves of this plant, used as a cosmetic and industrial dye **3** a reddish-brown or brown colour ▷ *vb* **4** (*tr*) to dye with henna [c16: from Arabic *hinnā*; see ALKANET]

hen night *n informal* a party for women only, esp held for a woman shortly before she is married. See **hen party**, **stag night**

henotheism (ˈhɛnəʊθiːˌɪzəm) *n* the worship of one deity (of several) as the special god of one's family, clan, or tribe [c19: from Greek *heis* one + *theos* god] > ˈhenotheist *n* > ˌhenotheˈistic *adj*

hen party *n informal* a party at which only women are present. See **hen night, stag night**

henpeck (ˈhɛnˌpɛk) *vb* (*tr*) (of a woman) to harass or torment (a man, esp her husband) by persistent nagging

henpecked (ˈhɛnˌpɛkd) *adj* (of a man) continually harassed or tormented by the persistent nagging of a woman (esp his wife)

Henrietta Maria (ˌhɛnrɪˈɛtə məˈriːə) *n* 1609–69, queen of England (1625–49), the wife of Charles I; daughter of Henry IV of France. Her Roman Catholicism contributed to the unpopularity of the crown in the period leading to the Civil War

henry (ˈhɛnrɪ) *n, pl* **-ry, -ries** *or* **-rys** the derived SI unit of electric inductance; the inductance of a closed circuit in which an emf is produced when the current varies uniformly at the rate of 1 ampere per second. Symbol: H [c19: named after Joseph *Henry* (1797–1878), US physicist]

Henry (ˈhɛnrɪ) *n* **1 Joseph**. 1797–1878, US physicist. He discovered the principle of electromagnetic induction independently of Faraday and constructed the first electromagnetic motor (1829). He also discovered self-induction and the oscillatory nature of electric discharges (1842) **2 O**. See: **O. Henry 3 Patrick**. 1736–99, American statesman and orator, a leading opponent of British rule during the War of American Independence **4 Prince**, known as **Harry**. born 1984, second son of Charles, Prince of Wales, and Diana, Princess of Wales

Henry I *n* **1** known as *Henry the Fowler*. ?876–936 AD, duke of Saxony (912–36) and king of Germany (919–36): founder of the Saxon dynasty (918–1024) **2** 1068–1135, king of England (1100–35) and duke of Normandy (1106–35); son of William the Conqueror: crowned in the absence of his elder brother, Robert II, duke of Normandy; conquered Normandy (1106)

Henry II *n* **1** known as *Henry the Saint*. 973–1024, king of Germany and Holy Roman Emperor (1014–24): canonized in 1145 **2** 1133–89, first Plantagenet king of England (1154–89): extended his Anglo-French domains and instituted judicial and financial reforms. His attempts to control the church were opposed by Becket **3** 1519–59, king of France (1547–59); husband of Catherine de' Medici. He recovered Calais from the English (1558) and suppressed the Huguenots

Henry III *n* **1** 1017–56, king of Germany and Holy Roman Emperor (1046–56). He increased the power of the Empire but his religious policy led to rebellions **2** 1207–72, king of England (1216–72); son of John. His incompetent rule provoked the Barons' War (1264–67), during which he was captured by Simon de Montfort **3** 1551–89, king of France (1574–89). He plotted the massacre of Huguenots on St Bartholomew's Day (1572) with his mother Catherine de' Medici, thus exacerbating the religious wars in France

Henry IV *n* **1** 1050–1106, Holy Roman Emperor (1084–1105) and king of Germany (1056–1105). He was excommunicated by Pope Gregory VII, whom he deposed (1084) **2** surnamed *Bolingbroke*. 1367–1413, first Lancastrian king of England (1399–1413); son of John of Gaunt: deposed Richard II (1399) and suppressed rebellions led by Owen Glendower and the Earl of Northumberland **3** known as *Henry of Navarre*. 1553–1610, first Bourbon king of France (1589–1610). He obtained toleration for the Huguenots with the Edict of Nantes (1598) and restored prosperity to France following the religious wars (1562–98)

Henry V *n* **1** 1081–1125, king of Germany (1089–1125) and Holy Roman Emperor (1111–25) **2** 1387–1422, king of England (1413–22); son of Henry IV. He defeated the French at the Battle of Agincourt (1415), conquered Normandy (1419), and was recognized as heir to the French throne (1420)

Henry VI *n* **1** 1165–97, king of Germany (1169–97) and Holy Roman Emperor (1190–97): added Sicily to the Empire **2** 1421–71, last Lancastrian king of England (1422–61; 1470–71); son of Henry V. His weak rule was blamed for the loss by 1453 of all his possessions in France except Calais; from 1454 he suffered periods of insanity which contributed to the outbreak of the Wars of the Roses (1455–85). He was deposed by Edward IV (1461) but was briefly restored to the throne (1470)

Henry VII *n* **1** ?1275–1313, Holy Roman Emperor (1312–13) and, as Henry VI, count of Luxembourg (1288–1313). He became king of the Lombards in 1313 **2** 1457–1509, first Tudor king of England (1485–1509). He came to the throne (1485) after defeating Richard III at the Battle of Bosworth Field, ending the Wars of the Roses. Royal power and the prosperity of the country greatly increased during his reign

Henry VIII *n* 1491–1547, king of England (1509–47); second son of Henry VII. The declaration that his marriage to Catherine of Aragon was invalid and his marriage to Anne Boleyn (1533) precipitated the Act of Supremacy, making Henry supreme head of the Church in England. Anne Boleyn was executed (1536) and Henry subsequently married Jane Seymour, Anne of Cleves, Catherine Howard, and Catherine Parr. His reign is also noted for the fame of his succession of advisers, Cardinal Wolsey, Sir Thomas More, and Thomas Cromwell

Henryson ('hɛnrɪsᵊn) *n* **Robert**. ?1430–?1506, Scottish poet. His works include *Testament of Cresseid* (1593), a sequel to Chaucer's *Troilus and Cressida*, the 13 *Moral Fables of Esope the Phrygian*, and the pastoral dialogue *Robene and Makyne*

Henry the Lion *n* ?1129–95, duke of Saxony (1142–81). His ambitions led to conflict with the Holy Roman Emperors, notably Frederick Barbarossa

Henry the Navigator *n* 1394–1460, prince of Portugal, noted for his patronage of Portuguese voyages of exploration of the W coast of Africa

Henslowe ('hɛnzləʊ) *n* **Philip**. died 1616, English theatre manager, noted also for his diary

Henze (*German* 'hɛntsə) *n* **Hans Werner** (hans 'vɛrnər). born 1926, German composer, whose works, in many styles, include the operas *The Stag King* (1956), *The Bassarids* (1965), *The English Cat* (1983), and *Das verratene Meer* (1990) and the oratorio *The Raft of the Medusa* (1968)

hep¹ (hɛp) *adj* **hepper, heppest** *slang* an earlier word for **hip⁴**

hep² (hɛp) *n informal* short for **hepatitis**

heparin ('hɛpərɪn) *n* a polysaccharide, containing sulphate groups, present in most body tissues: an anticoagulant used in the treatment of thrombosis [c20: from Greek *hēpar* the liver + -ɪɴ] > 'heparin,oid *adj*

hepatic (hɪ'pætɪk) *adj* 1 of or relating to the liver 2 having the colour of liver ▷ *n* 3 *obsolete* any of various drugs for use in treating diseases of the liver [c15: from Latin *hēpaticus*, from Greek *hēpar* liver]

hepatica (hɪ'pætɪkə) *n* any ranunculaceous woodland plant of the N temperate genus *Hepatica*, having three-lobed leaves and white, mauve, or pink flowers [c16: from Medieval Latin: liverwort, from Latin *hēpaticus* of the liver]

hepatitis (ˌhɛpə'taɪtɪs) *n* inflammation of the liver, characterized by fever, jaundice, and weakness

hepatitis A *n* a form of hepatitis caused by a virus transmitted in contaminated food or drink

hepatitis B *n* a form of hepatitis caused by a virus transmitted by infected blood (as in transfusions), contaminated hypodermic needles, sexual contact, or by contact with any other body fluid. Former name: serum hepatitis

hepatitis C *n* a form of hepatitis caused by a virus that is transmitted in the same ways as that responsible for hepatitis B

hepatology (ˌhɛpə'tɒlədʒɪ) *n* the branch of medicine concerned with the liver and its diseases > ˌhepa'tologist *n*

Hepburn ('hɛp,bɜːn) *n* 1 **Audrey**. 1929–93, US actress, born in Belgium. Her films include *Roman Holiday* (1955), *Funny Face* (1957), and *My Fair Lady* (1964) 2 **Katharine**. 1907–2003, US film actress, whose films include *The Philadelphia Story* (1940), *Adam's Rib* (1949), *The African Queen* (1951), *The Lion in Winter* (1968) for which she won an Oscar, and *On Golden Pond* (1981)

Hephaestus (hɪ'fiːstəs) *or* **Hephaistos** (hɪ'faɪstɒs) *n* Greek myth the lame god of fire and metal-working. Roman counterpart: Vulcan

Hepplewhite ('hɛpᵊl,waɪt) *adj* of, denoting, or made in a style of ornamental and carved 18th-century English furniture, of which oval or shield-shaped open chairbacks are characteristic [c18: named after George Hepplewhite (1727–86), English cabinetmaker]

hepta- *or before a vowel* **hept-** *combining form* seven: *heptameter* [from Greek]

heptad ('hɛptæd) *n* 1 a group or series of seven 2 the number or sum of seven 3 an atom or element with a valency of seven [c17: from Greek *heptas* seven]

heptagon ('hɛptəgən) *n* a polygon having seven sides > heptagonal (hɛp'tægənᵊl) *adj*

heptahedron (ˌhɛptə'hiːdrən) *n* a solid figure having seven plane faces

heptameter (hɛp'tæmɪtə) *n prosody* a verse line of seven metrical feet > heptametrical (ˌhɛptə'mɛtrɪkᵊl) *adj*

heptane ('hɛpteɪn) *n* an alkane existing in nine isomeric forms, esp the isomer with a straight chain of carbon atoms (*n*-heptane), which is found in petroleum and used as an anaesthetic. Formula: C_7H_{16} [c19: from HEPTA- + -ANE, so called because it has seven carbon atoms]

heptarchy ('hɛptɑːkɪ) *n, pl* -chies 1 government by seven rulers 2 a state divided into seven regions each under its own ruler 3 the seven kingdoms into which Anglo-Saxon England is thought to have been divided from about the 7th to the 9th centuries AD: Kent, East Anglia, Essex, Sussex, Wessex, Mercia, and Northumbria > 'heptarch *n* > hep'tarchic *or* hep'tarchal *adj*

heptathlon (hɛp'tæθlɒn) *n* an athletic contest for women in which each athlete competes in seven different events [c20: from HEPTA- + Greek *athlon* contest] > hep'tathlete *n*

heptavalent (hɛp'tævələnt, ˌhɛptə'veɪlənt) *adj chem* having a valency of seven. Also called: septivalent

Hepworth ('hɛpwəθ) *n* Dame **Barbara**. 1903–75, British sculptor of abstract works

her (hɜː; *unstressed* hə, ə) *pron* (*objective*) 1 refers to a female person or animal: *he loves her; they sold her a bag; something odd about her; lucky her!* 2 refers to things personified as feminine or traditionally to ships and nations ▷ *determiner* 3 of, belonging to, or associated with her: *her silly ideas; her hair; her smoking annoys me* [Old English *hire*, genitive and dative of *hēo* SHE, feminine of *hēo* HE¹; related to Old High German *ira*, Gothic *izōs*, Middle Dutch *hare*]
● USAGE See at **me¹**

Hera *or* **Here** ('hɪərə) *n* Greek myth the queen of the Olympian gods and sister and wife of Zeus. Roman counterpart: **Juno¹**

Heraclea (ˌhɛrə'kliːə) *n* any of several ancient Greek colonies. The most famous is the S Italian site where Pyrrhus of Epirus defeated the Romans (280 BC)

Heracleides *or* **Heraclides of Pontus** (ˌhɛrə'klaɪdiːz, 'pɒntəs) *n* ?390–?322 BC, Greek astronomer and philosopher: the first to state that the earth rotates on its axis

Heracles *or* **Herakles** ('hɛrə,kliːz) *n* the usual name (in Greek) for **Hercules** > ˌHera'clean *or* ˌHera'klean *adj*

Heraclitus (ˌhɛrə'klaɪtəs) *n* ?535–?475 BC, Greek philosopher, who held that fire is the primordial substance of the universe and that all things are in perpetual flux

Heraclius (hɛ'ræklɪəs) *n* ?575–641 AD, Byzantine emperor, who restored the Holy Cross to Jerusalem (629)

Herakleion *or* **Heraklion** (*Greek* he'ra:klɪɔn) *n* variants of **Iráklion**

herald ('hɛrəld) *n* 1 a a person who announces important news b (*as modifier*): *herald angels* 2 *often literary* a forerunner; harbinger 3 the intermediate rank of heraldic officer, between king-of-arms and pursuivant 4 (in the Middle Ages) an official at a tournament ▷ *vb* (*tr*) 5 to announce publicly 6 to precede or usher in [c14: from Old French *herault*, of Germanic origin; compare Old English *here* war; see WIELD]

heraldic (hɛ'rældɪk) *adj* 1 of or relating to heraldry 2 of or relating to heralds > he'raldically *adv*

heraldry ('hɛrəldrɪ) *n, pl* -ries 1 the occupation or study concerned with the classification of armorial bearings, the allocation of rights to bear arms, the tracing of genealogies, etc 2 the duties and pursuit of a herald 3 armorial bearings, insignia, devices, etc 4 heraldic symbols or symbolism 5 the show and ceremony of heraldry > 'heraldist *n*

Herat (he'ræt) *n* a city in NW Afghanistan, on the Hari Rud River: on the site of several ancient cities; at its height as a cultural centre in the 15th century. Pop: 344 000 (2005 est)

Hérault (*French* ero) *n* a department of S France, in

Languedoc-Roussillon region. Capital: Montpellier. Pop: 945 901 (2003 est). Area: 6224 sq km (2427 sq miles)

herb (hɜːb; *US* ɜːrb) *n* **1** a seed-bearing plant whose aerial parts do not persist above ground at the end of the growing season; herbaceous plant **2** any of various usually aromatic plants, such as parsley, rue, and rosemary, that are used in cookery and medicine [c13: from Old French *herbe*, from Latin *herba* grass, green plants] > 'herb,like *adj*

herbaceous (hɜːˈbeɪʃəs) *adj* **1** designating or relating to plants or plant parts that are fleshy as opposed to woody: *a herbaceous plant* **2** (of petals and sepals) green and leaflike **3** of or relating to herbs > her'baceously *adv*

herbaceous border *n* a flower bed that primarily contains nonwoody perennials rather than annuals

herbage (hɜːbɪdʒ) *n* **1** herbaceous plants collectively, esp the edible parts on which cattle, sheep, etc, graze **2** the vegetation of pasture land; pasturage

herbal (hɜːbᵊl) *adj* **1** of or relating to herbs, usually culinary or medicinal herbs ▷ *n* **2** a book describing and listing the properties of plants

herbalism (hɜːbᵊlɪzəm) *n* the study or use of the medicinal properties of plants

herbalist (hɜːbᵊlɪst) *n* **1** a person who grows, collects, sells, or specializes in the use of herbs, esp medicinal herbs **2** (formerly) a descriptive botanist

herbarium (hɜːˈbeərɪəm) *n, pl* -iums *or* -ia (-ɪə) **1** a collection of dried plants that are mounted and classified systematically **2** a building, room, etc, in which such a collection is kept > her'barial *adj*

herb bennet *n* a Eurasian and N African rosaceous plant, *Geum urbanum*, with yellow flowers. Also called: wood avens, bennet [c13 *herbe beneit*, from Old French *herbe benoite*, literally: blessed herb, from Medieval Latin *herba benedicta*]

Herbert (hɜːbət) *n* **1 Edward**, 1st Baron Herbert of Cherbury. 1583–1648, English philosopher and poet, noted for his deistic views **2** his brother, **George**. 1593–1633, English Metaphysical poet. His chief work is *The Temple: Sacred Poems and Private Ejaculations* (1633) **3 Zbigniew** (ᵊzˈbɪgnɪəf), 1924–98, Polish poet and dramatist, noted esp for his dramatic monologues

herbicide (hɜːbɪˌsaɪd) *n* a chemical that destroys plants, esp one used to control weeds > ˌherbi'cidal *adj*

herbivore (hɜːbɪˌvɔː) *n* **1** an animal that feeds on grass and other plants **2** *informal* a liberal, idealistic, or nonmaterialistic person [c19: from New Latin *herbivora* grass-eaters]

herb Paris *n, pl* herbs Paris a Eurasian woodland plant, *Paris quadrifolia*, with a whorl of four leaves and a solitary yellow flower; formerly used medicinally: family *Trilliaceae* [c16: from Medieval Latin *herba paris*, literally: herb of a pair: so called because the four leaves on the stalk look like a true lovers' knot; associated in folk etymology with *Paris*, France]

herb Robert *n, pl* herbs Robert a low-growing N temperate geraniaceous plant, *Geranium robertianum*, with strongly scented divided leaves and small pink flowers [c13: from Medieval Latin *herba Roberti* herb of Robert, probably named after St *Robert*, 11th-century French ecclesiastic]

Hercegovina (Bosnian ˈhɛrtsɛgɔvina) *n* a variant of **Herzegovina**

Herceptin (hərˈsɛptɪn) *n trademark* a monoclonal antibody that inhibits the protein that can fuel tumour growth, used in the treatment of breast cancer

Herculaneum (ˌhɜːkjʊˈleɪnɪəm) *n* an ancient city in SW Italy, of marked Greek character, on the S slope of Vesuvius: buried along with Pompeii by an eruption of the volcano (79 AD). Excavation has uncovered well preserved streets, houses, etc

herculean (ˌhɜːkjʊˈliːən) *adj* **1** requiring tremendous effort, strength, etc: *a herculean task* **2** (*sometimes capital*) resembling Hercules in strength, courage, etc

Hercules (hɜːkjʊˌliːz), **Heracles** *or* **Herakles** *n* **1** Also called: **Alcides** *classical myth* a hero noted for his great strength, courage, and for the performance of twelve immense labours **2** a man of outstanding strength or size

herd[1] (hɜːd) *n* **1** a large group of mammals living and feeding together, esp a group of cattle, sheep, etc **2** *often disparaging* a large group of people **3** *derogatory* the large mass of ordinary people ▷ *vb* **4** to collect or be collected into or as if into a herd [Old English *heord*; related to Old Norse *hjörth*, Gothic *hairda*, Old High German *herta*, Greek *kórthus* troop]

herd[2] (hɜːd) *n* **1 a** *archaic or dialect* a man or boy who tends livestock; herdsman **b** (*in combination*): *goatherd; swineherd* ▷ *vb* (*tr*) **2** to drive forwards in a large group **3** to look after (livestock) [Old English *hirde*; related to Old Norse *hirthir*, Gothic *hairdeis*, Old High German *hirti*, Old Saxon *hirdi*, *herdi*; see HERD[1]]

Herder (German ˈhɛrdər) *n* **Johann Gottfried von** (joˈhan ˈgɔtfriːt fɔn). 1744–1803, German philosopher, critic, and poet, the leading figure in the *Sturm und Drang* movement in German literature. His chief work is *Outlines of a Philosophy of the History of Man* (1784–91)

herd instinct *n psychol* the inborn tendency to associate with others and follow the group's behaviour

herdsman (hɜːdzmən) *n, pl* -men *chiefly Brit* a person who breeds, rears, or cares for cattle or (rarely) other livestock in the herd

here (hɪə) *adv* **1** in, at, or to this place, point, case, or respect: *we come here every summer; here, the policemen do not usually carry guns; here comes Roy* **2** here and there at several places in or throughout an area **3** here's to a formula used in proposing a toast to someone or something **4** neither here nor there of no relevance or importance ▷ *n* **5** this place: *they leave here tonight* [Old English *hēr*; related to Old Norse *hēr*, Old High German *hiar*, Old Saxon *hīr*]

hereabouts (ˈhɪərəˌbauts) *or* **hereabout** *adv* in this region or neighbourhood; near this place

hereafter (ˌhɪərˈɑːftə) *adv* **1** *formal* in a subsequent part of this document, matter, case, etc **2** a less common word for **henceforth** **3** at some time in the future **4** in a future life after death the hereafter *n* **5** life after death **6** the future

hereat (ˌhɪərˈæt) *adv archaic* because of this

hereby (ˌhɪəˈbaɪ) *adv* (used in official statements, proclamations, etc) by means of or as a result of this

hereditable (hɪˈrɛdɪtəbᵊl) *adj* a less common word for **heritable** > heˌredita'bility *n* > he'reditably *adv*

hereditament (ˌhɛrɪˈdɪtəmənt) *n property law* any kind of property capable of being inherited

hereditary (hɪˈrɛdɪtərɪ, -trɪ) *adj* **1** of, relating to, or denoting factors that can be transmitted genetically from one generation to another **2** *law* **a** descending or capable of descending to succeeding generations by inheritance **b** transmitted or transmissible according to established rules of descent **3** derived from one's ancestors; traditional: *hereditary feuds* **4** *maths, logic* **a** (of a set) containing all those elements which have a given relation to any element of the set **b** (of a property) transferred by the given relation, so that if x has the property P and xRy, then y also has the property P > he'reditarily *adv* > he'reditariness *n*

heredity (hɪˈrɛdɪtɪ) *n, pl* -ties **1** the transmission from one generation to another of genetic factors that determine individual characteristics: responsible for the resemblances between parents and offspring **2** the sum total of the inherited factors or their characteristics in an organism [c16: from Old French *heredite*, from Latin *hērēditās* inheritance; see HEIR]

Hereford (hɛrɪfəd) *n* **1** a city in W England, in Herefordshire on the River Wye: trading centre for agricultural produce; cathedral (begun 1079). Pop: 56 373 (2001) **2** a hardy breed of beef cattle characterized by a red body, red and white head, and white markings

Hereford and Worcester *n* a former county of the W Midlands of England, created in 1974 from the historic counties of Herefordshire and (most of) Worcestershire: abolished in 1998 when Herefordshire became an independent unitary authority

Herefordshire (hɛrɪfədˌʃɪə, -ʃə) *n* a county of W England: from 1974 to 1998 part of Hereford and Worcester: drained chiefly by the River Wye; agricultural (esp fruit and cattle). Administrative centre: Hereford. Pop: 176 900 (2003 est). Area: 2180 sq km (842 sq miles)

herein (ˌhɪərˈɪn) *adv* **1** *formal* in or into this place, thing, document, etc **2** *rare* in this respect, circumstance, etc

hereinafter (ˌhɪərɪnˈɑːftə) *adv* *formal or law* in a subsequent part or from this point on in this document, statement, etc

hereinto (ˌhɪərˈɪntuː) *adv* *formal or law* into this place, circumstance, etc

hereof (ˌhɪərˈɒv) *adv* *formal or law* of or concerning this

hereon (ˌhɪərˈɒn) *adv* an archaic word for **hereupon**

heresiarch (hɪˈriːzɪˌɑːk) *n* the leader or originator of a heretical movement or sect

heresy (ˈhɛrəsɪ) *n*, *pl* **-sies** **1 a** an opinion or doctrine contrary to the orthodox tenets of a religious body or church **b** the act of maintaining such an opinion or doctrine **2** any opinion or belief that is or is thought to be contrary to official or established theory **3** belief in or adherence to unorthodox opinion [c13: from Old French *eresie*, from Late Latin *haeresis*, from Latin: sect, from Greek *hairesis* a choosing, from *hairein* to choose]

heretic (ˈhɛrətɪk) *n* **1** *now chiefly RC Church* a person who maintains beliefs contrary to the established teachings of the Church **2** a person who holds unorthodox opinions in any field > **heretical** (hɪˈrɛtɪkᵊl) *adj* > he·**ret**ically *adv*

hereto (ˌhɪəˈtuː) *adv* *formal or law* to this place, thing, matter, document, etc

heretofore (ˌhɪətʊˈfɔː) *adv* *formal or law* until now; before this time

hereunder (ˌhɪərˈʌndə) *adv* *formal or law* **1** (in documents, etc) below this; subsequently; hereafter **2** under the terms or authority of this

hereupon (ˌhɪərəˈpɒn) *adv* **1** following immediately after this; at this stage **2** *formal* upon this thing, point, subject, etc

Hereward (ˈhɛrɪwəd) *n* called *Hereward the Wake*. 11th-century Anglo-Saxon rebel, who defended the Isle of Ely against William the Conqueror (1070–71): a subject of many legends

herewith (ˌhɪəˈwɪð, -ˈwɪθ) *adv* *formal* together with this: *we send you herewith your statement of account*

Hering (ˈherɪŋ) *n* *Ewald* (ˈevalt). 1834–1918, German physiologist and experimental psychologist who studied vision and propounded the doctrine of nativism, the policy of favouring the natives of a country over the immigrants

heriot (ˈhɛrɪət) *n* (in medieval England) a death duty paid by villeins and free tenants to their lord, often consisting of the dead man's best beast or chattel [Old English *heregeatwa*, from *here* army + *geatwa* equipment]

Herisau (German ˈheːrizau) *n* a town in NE Switzerland, capital of Appenzell Outer Rhodes demicanton. Pop: 15 882 (2000)

heritable (ˈhɛrɪtəbᵊl) *adj* **1** capable of being inherited; inheritable **2** *chiefly law* capable of inheriting [c14: from Old French, from *heriter* to **INHERIT**] > ˌherita·**bil**ity *n* > **herit**ably *adv*

heritage (ˈhɛrɪtɪdʒ) *n* **1** something inherited at birth, such as personal characteristics, status, and possessions **2** anything that has been transmitted from the past or handed down by tradition **3 a** the evidence of the past, such as historical sites, buildings, and the unspoilt natural environment, considered collectively as the inheritance of present-day society **b** (*as modifier; cap. as part of name*): *Bannockburn Heritage Centre* **4** something that is reserved for a particular person or group or the outcome of an action, way of life, etc: *the sea was their heritage; the heritage of violence* **5** *law* any property, esp land, that by law has descended or may descend to an heir **6** *Bible* **a** the Israelites regarded as belonging inalienably to God **b** the land of Canaan regarded as God's gift to the Israelites [c13: from Old French; see **HEIR**]

herl (hɜːl) *or* **harl** *n* *angling* **1** the barb or barbs of a feather, used to dress fishing flies **2** an artificial fly dressed with such barbs [c15: from Middle Low German *herle*, of obscure origin]

Hermann (ˈhɜːmən; German ˈhɛrman) *n* another name for **Arminius** (sense 1)

Hermannstadt (ˈhɛrmanʃtat) *n* the German name for **Sibiu**

hermaphrodite (hɜːˈmæfrəˌdaɪt) *n* **1** *biology* an individual animal or flower that has both male and female reproductive organs **2** a person having both male and female sexual characteristics and genital tissues **3** a person or thing in which two opposite forces or qualities are combined ▷ *adj* **4** having the characteristics of a hermaphrodite [c15: from Latin *hermaphrodītus*, from Greek, after **HERMAPHRODITUS**] > herˌmaphro·**dit**ic *or* herˌmaphro·**dit**ical *adj* > herˌmaphro·**dit**ically *adv* > her'maphroditˌism *n*

hermaphrodite brig *n* a sailing vessel with two masts, rigged square on the foremast and fore-and-aft on the aftermast. Also called: **brigantine**

Hermaphroditus (hɜːˌmæfrəˈdaɪtəs) *n* *Greek myth* a son of Hermes and Aphrodite who merged with the nymph Salmacis to form one body

hermeneutic (ˌhɜːmɪˈnjuːtɪk) *or* **hermeneutical** *adj* **1** of or relating to the interpretation of Scripture; using or relating to hermeneutics **2** interpretive > ˌherme·**neut**ically *adv* > ˌherme·**neut**ist *n*

hermeneutics (ˌhɜːmɪˈnjuːtɪks) *n* (*functioning as singular*) **1** the science of interpretation, esp of Scripture **2** the branch of theology that deals with the principles and methodology of exegesis **3** *philosophy* **a** the study and interpretation of human behaviour and social institutions **b** (in existentialist thought) discussion of the purpose of life [c18: from Greek *hermēneutikos* expert in interpretation, from *hermēneuein* to interpret, from *hermēneus* interpreter, of uncertain origin]

Hermes (ˈhɜːmiːz) *n* *Greek myth* the messenger and herald of the gods; the divinity of commerce, cunning, theft, travellers, and rascals. He was represented as wearing winged sandals. Roman counterpart: **Mercury**

Hermes Trismegistus (ˌtrɪsməˈdʒɪstəs) *n* a Greek name for the Egyptian god Thoth, credited with various works on mysticism and magic [Greek: Hermes thrice-greatest]

hermetic (hɜːˈmɛtɪk) *or* **hermetical** *adj* **1** sealed so as to be airtight **2** hidden or protected from the outside world [c17: from Medieval Latin *hermēticus* belonging to **HERMES TRISMEGISTUS**, traditionally the inventor of a magic seal] > her**met**ically *adv*

Hermetic¹ (hɜːˈmɛtɪk) *adj* **1** of or relating to Hermes Trismegistus or the writings and teachings ascribed to him **2** of or relating to ancient science, esp alchemy

Hermetic² (hɜːˈmɛtɪk) *adj* **1** of or relating to ancient science, esp alchemy **2** esoteric or recondite [see **HERMETIC¹**]

hermit (ˈhɜːmɪt) *n* **1** one of the early Christian recluses **2** any person living in solitude [c13: from Old French *hermite*, from Late Latin *erēmīta*, from Greek *erēmītēs* living in the desert, from *erēmia* desert, from *erēmos* lonely] > her·**mit**ic *or* her·**mit**ical *adj* > her·**mit**ically *adv* > **hermit**-ˌlike *adj*

hermitage (ˈhɜːmɪtɪdʒ) *n* **1** the abode of a hermit **2** any place where a person may live in seclusion; retreat

hermit crab *n* any small soft-bodied decapod crustacean of the genus *Pagurus* and related genera, living in and carrying about the empty shells of whelks or similar molluscs

Hermon (ˈhɜːmən) *n* *Mount* a mountain on the border between Lebanon and SW Syria, in the Anti-Lebanon Range: represented the NE limits of Israeli conquests under Moses and Joshua. Height: 2814 m (9232 ft)

Hermosillo (Spanish ɛrmoˈsiʎo) *n* a city in NW Mexico, capital of Sonora state, on the Sonora River: university (1938); winter resort and commercial centre for an agricultural and mining region. Pop: 668 000 (2005 est)

Hermoupolis (hɜːˈmuːpəlɪs) *n* a port in Greece, capital of Cyclades department, on the E coast of Syros Island. Pop: (municipality): 13 496 (2001).

Herne (German ˈhɛrnə) *n* an industrial city in W Germany, in North Rhine-Westphalia, in the Ruhr on the Rhine-Herne Canal. Pop: 172 870 (2003 est)

hernia (ˈhɜːnɪə) *n*, *pl* **-nias** *or* **-niae** (-nɪˌiː) the projection of an organ or part through the lining of the cavity in which it is normally situated, esp the protrusion of intestine through the front wall of the abdominal cavity. It is caused by muscular strain, injury, etc. Also called: rupture [c14: from Latin] > 'hernial *adj* > 'herni‚ated *adj*

hero ('hɪərəʊ) *n*, *pl* **-roes** 1 a man distinguished by exceptional courage, nobility, fortitude, etc 2 a man who is idealized for possessing superior qualities in any field 3 *classical myth* a being of extraordinary strength and courage, often the offspring of a mortal and a god, who is celebrated for his exploits 4 the principal male character in a novel, play, etc [c14: from Latin *hērōs*, from Greek]

Hero[1] ('hɪərəʊ) *n Greek myth* a priestess of Aphrodite, who killed herself when her lover Leander drowned while swimming the Hellespont to visit her

Hero[2] ('hɪərəʊ) *or* **Heron** *n* 1st century AD, Greek mathematician and inventor

Herod ('hɛrəd) *n* called *the Great*. ?73–4 BC, king of Judaea (37–4). The latter part of his reign was notable for his cruelty: according to the New Testament he ordered the Massacre of the Innocents

Herod Agrippa I *n* 10 BC–44 AD, king of Judaea (41–44), grandson of Herod (the Great). A friend of Caligula and Claudius, he imprisoned Saint Peter and executed Saint James

Herod Agrippa II *n* died ?93 AD, king of territories in N Palestine (50–?93 AD). He presided (60) at the trial of Saint Paul and sided with the Roman authorities in the Jewish rebellion of 66

Herod Antipas ('æntɪˌpæs) *n* died ?40 AD, tetrarch of Galilee and Peraea (4 BC–40 AD); son of Herod the Great. At the instigation of his wife Herodias, he ordered the execution of John the Baptist

Herodias (hɛ'rəʊdɪˌæs) *n* ?14 BC–?40 AD, niece and wife of Herod Antipas and mother of Salome, whom she persuaded to ask for the head of John the Baptist. Her ambition led to the banishment of her husband

Herodotus (hɪ'rɒdətəs) *n* called *the Father of History*. ?485–?425 BC, Greek historian, famous for his *History* dealing with the causes and events of the wars between the Greeks and the Persians (490–479)

heroic (hɪ'rəʊɪk) *or* **heroical** *adj* 1 of, like, or befitting a hero 2 courageous but desperate 3 relating to or treating of heroes and their deeds 4 of, relating to, or resembling the heroes of classical mythology 5 (of language, manner, etc) extravagant 6 *prosody* relating to, or resembling heroic verse 7 (of the arts, esp sculpture) larger than life-size; smaller than colossal > he'roically *adv*

heroic age *n* the period in an ancient culture, when legendary heroes are said to have lived

heroic couplet *n prosody* a verse form consisting of two rhyming lines in iambic pentameter

heroics (hɪ'rəʊɪks) *pl n* 1 *prosody* short for **heroic verse** 2 extravagant or melodramatic language, behaviour, etc

heroic verse *n prosody* a type of verse suitable for epic or heroic subjects, such as the classical hexameter, the French Alexandrine, or the English iambic pentameter

heroin ('hɛrəʊɪn) *n* a white odourless bitter-tasting crystalline powder related to morphine: a highly addictive narcotic. Formula: $C_{21}H_{23}NO_5$ [c19: coined in German as a trademark, probably from HERO, referring to its aggrandizing effect on the personality]

heroine ('hɛrəʊɪn) *n* 1 a woman possessing heroic qualities 2 a woman idealized for possessing superior qualities 3 the main female character in a novel, play, film, etc

heroism ('hɛrəʊˌɪzəm) *n* the state or quality of being a hero

heron ('hɛrən) *n* any of various wading birds of the genera *Butorides*, *Ardea*, etc, having a long neck, slim body, and a plumage that is commonly grey or white: family *Ardeidae*, order *Ciconiiformes* [c14: from Old French *hairon*, of Germanic origin; compare Old High German *heigaro*, Old Norse *hegri*]

Heron ('hɪərɒn) *n* 1 same as **Hero**[1] 2 **Patrick.** 1920–99, British abstract painter and art critic

heronry ('hɛrənrɪ) *n*, *pl* **-ries** a colony of breeding herons

Herophilus (hɪə'rɒfɪləs) *n* died ?280 BC, Greek anatomist in Alexandria. He was the first to distinguish sensory

from motor nerves

hero worship *n* 1 admiration for heroes or idealized persons 2 worship by the ancient Greeks and Romans of heroes ▷ *vb* **hero-worship**, **-ships**, **-shipping**, **-shipped** *or* US **-ships**, **-shiping**, **-shiped** 3 (*tr*) to feel admiration or adulation for > 'hero-ˌworshipper *n*

herpes ('hɜːpiːz) *n* any of several inflammatory diseases of the skin, esp herpes simplex, characterized by the formation of small watery blisters [c17: via Latin from Greek: a creeping, from *herpein* to creep]

herpes simplex ('sɪmplɛks) *n* an acute viral disease characterized by formation of clusters of watery blisters, esp on the margins of the lips and nostrils or on the genitals. It can be sexually transmitted and may recur fitfully [New Latin: simple herpes]

herpes zoster ('zɒstə) *n* a technical name for **shingles** [New Latin: girdle herpes, from HERPES + Greek *zōstēr* girdle]

herpetology (ˌhɜːpɪ'tɒlədʒɪ) *n* the study of reptiles and amphibians [c19: from Greek *herpeton* creeping animal, from *herpein* to creep] > herpetologic (ˌhɜːpɪtə'lɒdʒɪk) *or* ˌherpeto'logical *adj* > ˌherpeto'logically *adv* > ˌherpe'tologist *n*

Herr (*German* hɛr) *n*, *pl* **Herren** ('hɛrən) a German man: used before a name as a title equivalent to *Mr* [German, from Old High German *herro* lord]

Herrenvolk *German* ('hɛrənfɒlk) *n* See **master race**

Herrick ('hɛrɪk) *n* **Robert.** 1591–1674, English poet. His chief work is the *Hesperides* (1648), a collection of short, delicate, sacred, and pastoral lyrics

herring ('hɛrɪŋ) *n*, *pl* **-rings** *or* **-ring** any marine soft-finned teleost fish of the family *Clupeidae*, esp *Clupea harengus*, an important food fish of northern seas, having an elongated body covered, except in the head region, with large fragile silvery scales [Old English *hæring*; related to Old High German *hāring*, Old Frisian *hēring*, Dutch *haring*]

herringbone ('hɛrɪŋˌbəʊn) *n* 1 a a pattern used in textiles, brickwork, etc, consisting of two or more rows of short parallel strokes slanting in alternate directions to form a series of parallel Vs or zigzags b (*as modifier*): *a herringbone jacket; a herringbone pattern of very long, narrow bricks* 2 *skiing* a method of ascending a slope by walking with the skis pointing outwards and one's weight on the inside edges ▷ *vb* 3 to decorate (textiles, brickwork, etc) with herringbone 4 (*intr*) *skiing* to ascend a slope in herringbone fashion

herring gull *n* a common gull, *Larus argentatus*, that has a white plumage with black-tipped wings and pink legs

Herriot *n* 1 (*French* ɛrjo) **Édouard** (edwar). 1872–1957, French Radical statesman and writer; premier (1924–25; 1932) 2 ('hɛrɪət) **James.** real name *James Alfred Wight*. 1916–95, British veterinary surgeon and writer. His books based on his experiences in Yorkshire have been adapted for television and films

hers (hɜːz) *pron* 1 something or someone belonging to or associated with her: *hers is the nicest dress; that cat is hers* 2 of hers belonging to or associated with her [c14 *hires*; see HER]

Herschel ('hɜːʃəl) *n* 1 **Caroline Lucretia.** 1750–1848, British astronomer, born in Germany, noted for her catalogue of nebulae and star clusters: sister of Sir William Herschel 2 Sir **John Frederick William.** 1792–1871, British astronomer. He discovered and catalogued over 525 nebulae and star clusters 3 his father, Sir (**Frederick**) **William,** original name *Friedrich Wilhelm Herschel*. 1738–1822, British astronomer, born in Germany. He constructed a reflecting telescope, which led to his discovery of the planet Uranus (1781), two of its satellites, and two of the satellites of Saturn. He also discovered the motions of binary stars

herself (hə'sɛlf) *pron* 1 a the reflexive form of *she* or *her* b (intensifier): *the queen herself signed the letter* 2 (preceded by a copula) her normal or usual self: *she looks herself again after the operation* 3 *Irish & Scot* the wife or woman of the house: *is herself at home?*

Herstmonceux *or* **Hurstmonceux** ('hɜːstmənˌsjuː, -ˌsəʊ) *n* a village in S England, in E Sussex north of Eastbourne: 15th-century castle, site of the Royal

Observatory, which was transferred from Greenwich between 1948 and 1958, until 1990

Hertford ('hɑːtfəd) n a town in SE England, administrative centre of Hertfordshire. Pop: 24 460 (2001)

Hertfordshire ('hɑːtfədˌʃɪə, -fə) n a county of S England, bordering on Greater London in the south: mainly low-lying, with the Chiltern Hills in the northwest; largely agricultural; light industries, esp in the new towns. Administrative centre: Hertford. Pop: 1 040 900 (2003 est). Area: 1634 sq km (631 sq miles)

Hertogenbosch (Dutch hɛrto:xən'bɔs) n See 's Hertogenbosch

Herts (hɑːts) abbreviation Hertfordshire

hertz (hɜːts) n, pl hertz the derived SI unit of frequency; the frequency of a periodic phenomenon that has a periodic time of 1 second; 1 cycle per second. Symbol: Hz [c20: named after Heinrich Rudolph Hertz (1857–94), German physicist]

Hertz (hɜːts; German hɛrts) n 1 **Gustav** ('gʊstaf). 1887–1975, German atomic physicist. He provided evidence for the quantum theory by his research with Franck on the effects produced by bombarding atoms with electrons: they shared the Nobel prize for physics (1925) 2 **Heinrich Rudolph** ('hainrɪç 'ruːdɔlf). 1857–94, German physicist. He was the first to produce electromagnetic waves artificially > **'Hertzian** adj

Hertzian wave n an electromagnetic wave with a frequency in the range from about 3×10^{10} hertz to about 1.5×10^5 hertz [c19: named after Heinrich Rudolph Hertz (1857–94), German physicist]

Hertzog ('hɜːtsɒg) n **James Barry Munnik**. 1866–1942, South African statesman; prime minister (1924–39): founded the Nationalist Party (1913), advocating complete South African independence from Britain; opposed South African participation in World Wars I and II

Hertzsprung (Danish hɛrdsbrɔŋ) n **Ejnar** ('ainar). 1873–1967, Danish astronomer: he discovered the existence of giant and dwarf stars, originating one form of the Hertzsprung-Russell diagram

Hertzsprung-Russell diagram ('hɜːtssprʌŋ'rʌsəl) n a graph in which the spectral types of stars are plotted against their absolute magnitudes. Stars fall into different groupings in different parts of the graph [c20: named after Ejnar Hertzsprung (1873–1967), Danish astronomer, and Henry Norris Russell (1877–1957), US astronomer and astrophysicist]

Herzegovina (ˌhɜːtsəgəʊ'viːnə) or **Hercegovina** n a region in Bosnia-Herzegovina: originally under Austro-Hungarian rule; became part of the province of Bosnia-Herzegovina (1878), which was a constituent republic of Yugoslavia (1946–92)

Herzen (Russian 'gjɛrtsən) n **Aleksandr** (**Ivanovich**) (alek'sandr i'va:novitʃ). 1812–70, Russian socialist political philosopher: best known for his autobiography My Past and Thoughts (1861–67)

Herzl (German 'hɛrtsəl) n **Theodor** ('te:odo:r). 1860–1904, Austrian writer, born in Hungary; founder of the Zionist movement. In The Jewish State (1896), he advocated resettlement of the Jews in a state of their own

Herzog (German 'hɛrtso:k) n 1 **Roman**. born 1934, German politician; president of Germany (1994–99) 2 **Werner** ('vɛrnər). born 1942, German film director. His films include Signs of Life (1967), Fata Morgana (1970), Fitzcarraldo (1982), Little Dieter Needs to Fly (1997), and Grizzly Man (2005)

he's (hiːz) contraction of he is or he has

hESC abbreviation human embryonic stem cell

Heseltine ('hɛzəlˌtain) n 1 **Michael** (**Ray Dibden**) Baron. born 1933, British Conservative politician; secretary of state for defence (1983–86); secretary of state for the environment (1990–92); secretary of state for trade and industry (1992–95); deputy prime minister (1995–97) 2 **Philip Arnold** Heseltine the real name of composer Peter Warnock

Hesiod ('hɛsɪˌɒd) n 8th century BC, Greek poet and the earliest author of didactic verse. His two complete extant works are the Works and Days, dealing with the agricultural seasons, and the Theogony, concerning the origin of the world and the genealogies of the gods > ˌHesi'odic adj

Hesione (hɪ'saɪənɪ) n Greek myth daughter of King Laomedon, rescued by Hercules from a sea monster

hesitant ('hɛzɪt³nt) adj wavering, hesitating, or irresolute > **'hesitance** or **'hesitancy** n > **'hesitantly** adv

hesitate ('hɛzɪˌteɪt) vb (intr) 1 to hold back or be slow in acting; be uncertain 2 to be unwilling or reluctant (to do something) 3 to stammer or pause in speaking [c17: from Latin haesitāre, from haerēre to cling to] > **'hesi,tater** or **'hesi,tator** n > **'hesi,tatingly** adv > ˌhesi'tation n > **'hesi,tative** adj

Hesperia (hɛ'spɪərɪə) n a poetic name used by the ancient Greeks for Italy and by the Romans for Spain or beyond [Latin, from Greek: land of the west, from hesperos western]

Hesperian (hɛ'spɪərɪən) adj 1 poetic western 2 of or relating to the Hesperides

Hesperides (hɛ'spɛrɪˌdiːz) pl n Greek myth 1 the daughters of Hesperus, nymphs who kept watch with a dragon over the garden of the golden apples in the Islands of the Blessed 2 (functioning as singular) the gardens themselves 3 another name for the **Islands of the Blessed** > Hesperidian (ˌhɛspə'rɪdɪən) or ˌHesper'idean adj

hesperidium (ˌhɛspə'rɪdɪəm) n botany the fruit of citrus plants, in which the flesh consists of fluid-filled hairs and is protected by a tough rind [c19: New Latin; alluding to the fruit in the garden of the HESPERIDES]

Hesperus ('hɛspərəs) n an evening star, esp Venus [from Latin, from Greek Hesperos, from hesperos western]

Hess (hɛs) n 1 Dame **Myra**. 1890–1965, English pianist 2 (**Walther Richard**) Rudolf ('ruːdɔlf). 1894–1987, German Nazi leader. He made a secret flight to Scotland (1941) to negotiate peace with Britain but was held as a prisoner of war; later sentenced to life imprisonment at the Nuremberg trials (1946); committed suicide 3 **Victor Francis**. 1883–1964, US physicist, born in Austria: pioneered the investigation of cosmic rays: shared the Nobel prize for physics (1936)

Hesse[1] (hɛs) n a state of central Germany, formed in 1945 from the former Prussian province of Hesse-Nassau and part of the former state of Hesse; part of West Germany until 1990. Capital: Wiesbaden. Pop: 6 089 000 (2003 est). Area: 21 111 sq km (8151 sq miles)

Hesse[2] (hɛs; German 'hɛsə) n **Hermann** ('hɛrman). 1877–1962, German novelist, short-story writer, and poet. His novels include Der Steppenwolf (1927) and Das Glasperlenspiel (1943): Nobel prize for literature 1946

Hesse-Nassau n a former province of Prussia, now part of the state of Hesse, Germany

hessian ('hɛsɪən) n a coarse jute fabric similar to sacking, used for bags, upholstery, etc [c18: from HESSE + -IAN]

Hessian ('hɛsɪən) n 1 a native or inhabitant of Hesse 2 a a Hessian soldier in any of the mercenary units of the British Army in the War of American Independence or the Napoleonic Wars b US any German mercenary in the British Army during the War of American Independence 3 chiefly US a mercenary or ruffian ▷ adj 4 of or relating to Hesse or its inhabitants

Hessian fly n a small dipterous fly, Mayetiola destructor, whose larvae damage wheat, barley, and rye: family Cecidomyidae (gall midges) [c18: so called because it was thought to have been introduced into America by Hessian soldiers]

hest (hɛst) n an archaic word for **behest** [Old English hǣs; related to hātan to promise, command]

Hestia ('hɛstɪə) n Greek myth the goddess of the hearth. Roman counterpart: **Vesta**[1]

hetaera (hɪ'tɪərə) or **hetaira** (hɪ'taɪrə) n, pl -taerae (-'tɪəriː) or -tairai (-'taɪraɪ) (esp in ancient Greece) a female prostitute, esp an educated courtesan [c19: from Greek hetaira concubine] > he'taeric or he'tairic adj

hetaerism (hɪ'tɪərɪzəm) or **hetairism** (hɪ'taɪrɪzəm) n 1 the state of being a concubine 2 sociol, anthropol a social system attributed to some primitive societies, in which women are communally shared > he'taerist or he'tairist n > ˌhetae'ristic or ˌhetai'ristic adj

hetero- combining form other, another, or different:

heterodyne; heterophony; heterosexual [from Greek *heteros* other]

heteroclite ('hɛtərəˌklaɪt) *Also called:* heteroclitic (ˌhɛtərə'klɪtɪk) *adj* **1** (esp of the form of a word) irregular or unusual ▷ *n* **2** an irregularly formed word [c16: from Late Latin *heteroclitus* declining irregularly, from Greek *heteroklitos*, from HETERO- + *klinein* to bend, inflect]

heterocyclic (ˌhɛtərəʊ'saɪklɪk, -'sɪk-) *adj* (of an organic compound) containing a closed ring of atoms, at least one of which is not a carbon atom

heterodox ('hɛtərəʊˌdɒks) *adj* **1** at variance with established, orthodox, or accepted doctrines or beliefs **2** holding unorthodox opinions [c17: from Greek *heterodoxos* holding another opinion, from HETERO- + *doxa* opinion] > 'hetero,doxy *n*

heterodyne ('hɛtərəˌdaɪn) *vb* **1** *electronics* to combine by intermodulation (two alternating signals, esp radio signals) to produce two signals having frequencies corresponding to the sum and the difference of the original frequencies ▷ *adj* **2** produced by, operating by, or involved in heterodyning two signals

heteroecious (ˌhɛtə'riːʃəs) *adj* (of parasites, esp rust fungi) undergoing different stages of the life cycle on different host species [from HETERO- + -*oecious*, from Greek *oikia* house] > ,heter'oecism *n*

heterogamete (ˌhɛtərəʊgæ'miːt) *n* a gamete that differs in size and form from the one with which it unites in fertilization

heterogamy (ˌhɛtə'rɒgəmɪ) *n* **1** a type of sexual reproduction in which the gametes differ in both size and form **2** a condition in which different types of reproduction occur in successive generations of an organism **3** the presence of both male and female flowers in one inflorescence > ,heter'ogamous *adj*

heterogeneous (ˌhɛtərəʊ'dʒiːnɪəs) *adj* **1** composed of unrelated or differing parts or elements **2** not of the same kind or type [c17: from Medieval Latin *heterogeneus*, from Greek *heterogenēs*, from HETERO- + *genos* sort] > heterogeneity (ˌhɛtərəʊdʒɪ'niːɪtɪ) *or* ,hetero'geneousness *n*

heterogony (ˌhɛtə'rɒgənɪ) *n* **1** *biology* the alternation of parthenogenetic and sexual generations in rotifers and similar animals **2** the condition in plants, such as the primrose, of having flowers that differ from each other in the length of their stamens and styles > ,heter'ogonous *adj*

heterologous (ˌhɛtə'rɒləgəs) *adj* **1** *pathol* of, relating to, or designating cells or tissues not normally present in a particular part of the body **2** (esp of parts of an organism or of different organisms) differing in structure or origin > ,heter'ology *n*

heteromerous (ˌhɛtə'rɒmərəs) *adj* *biology* having or consisting of parts that differ, esp in number

heteromorphic (ˌhɛtərəʊ'mɔːfɪk) *or* **heteromorphous** *adj* *biology* **1** differing from the normal form in size, shape, and function **2** (esp of insects) having different forms at different stages of the life cycle > ,hetero'morphism *or* ,hetero'morphy *n*

heteronomous (ˌhɛtə'rɒnɪməs) *adj* **1** subject to an external law, rule, or authority **2** (of the parts of an organism) differing in the manner of growth, development, or specialization > ,heter'onomously *adv* > ,heter'onomy *n*

heteronym ('hɛtərəʊˌnɪm) *n* one of two or more words pronounced differently but spelt alike: *the two English words spelt "bow" are heteronyms.* See **homograph** [c17: from Late Greek *heteronumos*, from Greek HETERO- + *onoma* name]

heterophyllous (ˌhɛtərəʊ'fɪləs, ˌhɛtə'rɒfɪləs) *adj* (of plants such as arrowhead) having more than one type of leaf on the same plant > 'hetero,phylly *n*

heteropterous (ˌhɛtə'rɒptərəs) *or* **heteropteran** *adj* of, relating to, or belonging to the *Heteroptera*, a suborder of hemipterous insects, including bedbugs, water bugs, etc, in which the forewings are membranous but have leathery tips [c19: from New Latin *Heteroptera*, from HETERO- + Greek *pteron* wing]

heterosexism (ˌhɛtərəʊ'sɛkˌsɪzəm) *n* discrimination on the basis of sexual orientation, practised by heterosexuals against homosexuals > ,hetero'sexist *adj, n*

heterosexual (ˌhɛtərəʊ'sɛksjʊəl) *n* **1** a person who is sexually attracted to the opposite sex ▷ *adj* **2** of or relating to heterosexuality > ,hetero,sexu'ality *n*

heterosocial (ˌhɛtərəʊ'səʊʃəl) *adj* relating to or denoting mixed-sex social relationships > heterosociality (ˌhɛtərəʊˌsəʊʃɪ'ælɪtɪ) *n* See **homosocial**

heterotaxis (ˌhɛtərəʊ'tæksɪs), **heterotaxy** *or* **heterotaxia** *n* an abnormal or asymmetrical arrangement of parts, as of the organs of the body or the constituents of a rock

heterotrophic (ˌhɛtərəʊ'trɒfɪk) *adj* (of organisms, such as animals) obtaining carbon for growth and energy from complex organic compounds [c20: from HETERO- + Greek *trophikos* concerning food, from *trophē* nourishment] > 'hetero,troph *n*

heterozygote (ˌhɛtərəʊ'zaɪgəʊt, -'zɪgəʊt) *n* an animal or plant that is heterozygous; a hybrid

heterozygous (ˌhɛtərəʊ'zaɪgəs) *adj genetics* (of an organism) having different alleles for any one gene: *heterozygous for eye colour*

heth *or* **cheth** (hɛt; *Hebrew* xɛt) *n* the eighth letter of the Hebrew alphabet (ח), transliterated as *ḥ* and pronounced as a pharyngeal fricative [from Hebrew]

hetman ('hɛtmən) *n, pl* -mans another word for **ataman** [c18: from Polish, from German *Hauptmann* headman]

hettie ('hɛtɪ) *informal* ▷ *adj* **1** heterosexual ▷ *n* **2** a heterosexual person [c20: shortened from HETEROSEXUAL]

het up *adj* angry; excited

heuchera ('hjuːkərə) *n* any plant of the N. American genus *Heuchera*, with low-growing heart-shaped leaves and mostly red flowers carried in sprays on slender graceful stems: family *Saxifragaceae* [named after J. H. Heucher (1677–1747), German doctor and botanist]

heuristic (hjʊə'rɪstɪk) *adj* **1** helping to learn; guiding in discovery or investigation **2** (of a method of teaching) allowing pupils to learn things for themselves **3** a *maths, science, philosophy* using or obtained by exploration of possibilities rather than by following set rules **b** *computing* denoting a rule of thumb for solving a problem without the exhaustive application of an algorithm: *a heuristic solution* ▷ *n* **4** (*plural*) the science of heuristic procedure [c19: from New Latin *heuristicus*, from Greek *heuriskein* to discover] > heu'ristically *adv*

Hevelius (*German* he've:lius) *n* **Johannes** (jo'hanəs). 1611–87, German astronomer, who published one of the first detailed maps of the lunar surface

Hevesy (*Hungarian* 'hɛvɛʃi) *n* **Georg von** ('geːɔrg fɔn). 1885–1966, Hungarian chemist. He worked on radioactive tracing and, with D. Coster, discovered the element hafnium (1923): Nobel prize for chemistry 1943

hew (hjuː) *vb* hews, hewing, hewed, hewed *or* hewn (hjuːn) **1** to strike (something, esp wood) with cutting blows, as with an axe **2** (*tr; often foll by out*) to shape or carve from a substance **3** (*tr; often foll by away, down, from, off, etc*) to sever from a larger or another portion **4** (*intr; often foll by to*) *US & Canadian* to conform (to a code, principle, etc) [Old English *hēawan*; related to Old Norse *heggva*, Old Saxon *hāwa*, Old High German *houwan*, Latin *cūdere* to beat] > 'hewer *n*

Hewish ('hjuːɪʃ) *n* **Antony.** born 1924, British radio astronomer, noted esp for his role in the discovery of pulsars (1967): shared the Nobel prize for physics 1974

Hewitt ('hjuːɪt) *n* **Lleyton** ('leɪtən). born 1981, Australian tennis player; US Open champion 2001, Wimbledon singles champion 2002

hex[1] (hɛks) *n* **a** short for **hexadecimal notation b** (*as modifier*): *hex code*

hex[2] (hɛks) *informal* ▷ *vb* **1** (*tr*) to bewitch ▷ *n* **2** an evil spell or symbol of bad luck **3** a witch [c19: via Pennsylvania Dutch from German *Hexe* witch, from Middle High German *hecse*, perhaps from Old High German *hagzissa*; see HAG[1]]

hexa- *or before a vowel* **hex-** *combining form* six: *hexachord; hexameter* [from Greek, from *hex* SIX]

hexachlorophene (ˌhɛksə'klɔːrəfiːn) *n* an insoluble almost odourless white bactericidal substance used in antiseptic soaps, deodorants, etc. Formula: $(C_6HCl_3OH)_2CH_2$

hexachord ('hɛksə,kɔːd) *n* (in medieval musical theory) any of three diatonic scales based upon C, F, and G, each consisting of six notes, from which solmization was developed

hexad ('hɛksæd) *n* a group or series of six [c17: from Greek *hexas*, from *hex* six]

hexadecane ('hɛksədɛ,keɪn, ,hɛksə'dɛkeɪn) *n* the systematic name for **cetane** [c19: from HEXA- + DECA- + -ANE]

hexadecanoic acid ('hɛksə,dɛkənəʊɪk) *n* the systematic name for **palmitic acid**

hexadecimal notation *or* **hexadecimal** (,hɛksə'dɛsɪməl) *n* a number system having a base 16; the symbols for the numbers 0–9 are the same as those used in the decimal system, and the numbers 10–15 are usually represented by the letters A–F. The system is used as a convenient way of representing the internal binary code of a computer

hexagon ('hɛksəgən) *n* a polygon having six sides

hexagram ('hɛksə,græm) *n* a star-shaped figure formed by extending the sides of a regular hexagon to meet at six points

hexahedron (,hɛksə'hiːdrən) *n* a solid figure having six plane faces. A **regular hexahedron** (cube) has square faces > ,hexa'hedral *adj*

hexameter (hɛk'sæmɪtə) *n prosody* **1** a verse line consisting of six metrical feet **2** (in Greek and Latin epic poetry) a verse line of six metrical feet, of which the first four are usually dactyls or spondees, the fifth almost always a dactyl, and the sixth a spondee or trochee > hexametric (,hɛksə'mɛtrɪk) *or* hex'ametral *or* ,hexa'metrical *adj*

hexane ('hɛkseɪn) *n* a liquid alkane existing in five isomeric forms that are found in petroleum and used as solvents, esp the isomer with a straight chain of carbon atoms (*n*-hexane). Formula: C_6H_{14} [c19: from HEXA- + -ANE]

hexapla ('hɛksəplə) *n* an edition of the Old Testament compiled by Origen, containing six versions of the text [c17: from Greek *hexaploos* sixfold] > 'hexaplar *or* hexaplaric (,hɛksə'plærɪk) *or* hexaplarian (,hɛksə'plɛərɪən) *adj*

hexapod ('hɛksə,pɒd) *n* any arthropod of the class *Hexapoda* (or *Insecta*); an insect

hexavalent (,hɛksə'veɪlənt) *adj chem* having a valency of six. Also called: **sexivalent**

hexose ('hɛksəʊs, -əʊz) *n* a monosaccharide, such as glucose, that contains six carbon atoms per molecule

hey (heɪ) *interj* **1** an expression indicating surprise, dismay, discovery, etc, or calling for another's attention **2** *South African* an exclamation used for emphasis at the end of a statement, or alone to seek repetition or confirmation of another person's statement **3** hey presto an exclamation used by conjurors to herald the climax of a trick [c13: compare Old French *hay*, German *hei*, Swedish *hej*]

heyday ('heɪ,deɪ) *n* the time of most power, popularity, vigour, etc; prime [c16: probably based on HEY]

Heyer ('heɪə) *n* **Georgette**. 1902–74, British historical novelist and writer of detective stories, noted esp for her romances of the Regency period

Heyerdahl (*Norwegian* 'heɪərdaːl) *n* **Thor** (tɔː). 1914–2002, Norwegian anthropologist. In 1947 he demonstrated that the Polynesians could originally have been migrants from South America, by sailing from Peru to the Pacific Islands of Tuamotu in the *Kon-Tiki*, a raft made of balsa wood. DNA testing in the late 1990s indicated that such a migration did not take place

Heysham ('hiːʃəm) *n* a port in NW England, in NW Lancashire. Pop (with Morecambe): 16 136 (2001)

Heywood[1] ('heɪ,wʊd) *n* a town in NW England, in Rochdale unitary authority, Greater Manchester, near Bury. Pop: 28 024 (2001))

Heywood[2] ('heɪ,wʊd) *n* **1 John**. ?1497–?1580, English dramatist, noted for his comic interludes **2 Thomas**. ?1574–1641, English dramatist, noted esp for his domestic drama *A Woman Killed with Kindness* (1607)

Hezekiah (,hɛzə'kaɪə) *n* a king of Judah ?715–?687 BC, noted for his religious reforms (II Kings 18–19) [from Hebrew *hizqīyyāh ū* God has strengthened]

hf *abbreviation* half

Hf *the chemical symbol for* hafnium

HF *or* **h.f.** *abbreviation* high frequency

HFEA (in Britain) *abbreviation* Human Fertilization and Embryology Authority

hg *abbreviation* hectogram

Hg *the chemical symbol for* mercury [from New Latin HYDRARGYRUM]

HG *abbreviation* His (*or* Her) Grace

hgt *abbreviation* height

HGV (formerly, in Britain) *abbreviation* heavy goods vehicle

HH *abbreviation* **1** His (*or* Her) Highness **2** His Holiness (title of the Pope) ▷ *symbol for* **3** double hard (on Brit pencils)

H-hour *n military* the specific hour at which any operation commences. Also called: **zero hour**

hi (haɪ) *sentence substitute* an informal word for **hello** [c20: originally US, from HIYA]

HI *abbreviation* **1** Hawaii (state) **2** Hawaiian Islands

Hialeah (,haɪə'liːə) *n* a city in SE Florida, near Miami: racetrack. Pop: 226 401 (2003 est)

hiatus (haɪ'eɪtəs) *n, pl* **-tuses** *or* **-tus** **1** a break or interruption in continuity **2** a break between adjacent vowels in the pronunciation of a word [c16: from Latin: gap, cleft, aperture, from *hiāre* to gape, yawn]

hiatus hernia *or* **hiatal hernia** *n* protrusion of part of the stomach through the diaphragm at the oesophageal opening

Hiawatha (,haɪə'wɒθə) *n* a 16th-century Onondaga Indian chief: credited with the organization of the Five Nations

Hib (hɪb) *n acronym for* Haemophilus influenzae type b: a vaccine against a type of bacterial meningitis, administered to children

hibachi (hɪ'baːtʃɪ) *n* a portable brazier for heating and cooking food [from Japanese, from *hi* fire + *bachi* bowl]

hibakusha (hɪ'baːkʊʃə) *n, pl* **-sha** *or* **-shas** a survivor of either of the atomic-bomb attacks on Hiroshima and Nagasaki in 1945 [c20: from Japanese, from *hibaku* exposed + *-sha* -person]

hibernal (haɪ'bɜːnəl) *adj* of or occurring in winter [c17: from Latin *hībernālis*, from *hiems* winter]

hibernate ('haɪbə,neɪt) *vb* (*intr*) **1** (of some mammals, reptiles, and amphibians) to pass the winter in a dormant condition with metabolism greatly slowed down **2** to cease from activity [c19: from Latin *hībernāre* to spend the winter, from *hībernus* of winter, from *hiems* winter] > ,hiber'nation *n* > 'hiber,nator *n*

Hibernia (haɪ'bɜːnɪə, hɪ'bɜːnɪə) *n* the Roman name for **Ireland**[1] > Hi'bernian *adj, n*

Hibernicism (haɪ'bɜːnɪ,sɪzəm) *n* an Irish expression, idiom, trait, custom, etc

Hiberno- (haɪ'bɜːnəʊ, hɪ'bɜːnəʊ) *combining form* denoting Irish or Ireland: *Hiberno-English*

hibiscus (haɪ'bɪskəs) *n, pl* **-cuses** any plant of the chiefly tropical and subtropical malvaceous genus *Hibiscus*, esp *H. rosa-sinensis*, cultivated for its large brightly coloured flowers [c18: from Latin, from Greek *hibiskos* marsh mallow]

hiccup *or* **hiccough** ('hɪkʌp) *n* **1** a spasm of the diaphragm producing a sudden breathing in followed by a closing of the glottis, resulting in a sharp sound **2** the state or condition of having such spasms **3** *informal* a minor difficulty or problem ▷ *vb* **-cups, -cuping, -cuped** *or* **-cups, -cupping, -cupped, -coughs, -coughing, -coughed 4** (*intr*) to make a hiccup or hiccups **5** (*tr*) to utter with a hiccup or hiccups [c16: of imitative origin]

hic jacet *Latin* (hɪk 'jækɛt) (on gravestones) here lies

hick (hɪk) *n* **1** *informal* **a** a country person; bumpkin **b** (*as modifier*): *hick ideas* [c16: after Hick, familiar form of *Richard*]

Hickok ('hɪkɒk) *n* **James Butler**, known as *Wild Bill Hickok*. 1837–76, US frontiersman and marshal

hickory ('hɪkərɪ) *n, pl* **-ries 1** any juglandaceous tree of the chiefly North American genus *Carya*, having nuts with edible kernels and hard smooth shells **2** the hard tough wood of any of these trees [c17: from earlier *pohickery*, from Algonquian *pawcohiccora* food made from ground hickory nuts]

Hickox ('hɪkɒks) *n* **Richard** (**Sidney**). born 1948, British conductor; musical director of the City of London Sinfonia and Singers since 1971

hid (hɪd) *vb* the past tense and a past participle of **hide**[1]

hidalgo (hɪ'dælgəʊ; *Spanish* i'ðalɣo) *n*, *pl* **-gos** (-gəʊz; *Spanish* -ɣos) a member of the lower nobility in Spain [c16: from Spanish, from Old Spanish *fijo dalgo* nobleman, from Latin *filius* son + *dē* of + *aliquid* something]

Hidalgo (hɪ'dælgəʊ; *Spanish* i'ðalɣo) *n* a state of central Mexico: consists of a high plateau, with the Sierra Madre Oriental in the north and east; ancient remains of Teltec culture (at Tula); rich mineral resources. Capital: Pachuca. Pop: 2 231 392 (2000). Area: 20 987 sq km (8103 sq miles)

hidden ('hɪdən) *vb* **1** a past participle of **hide**[1] ▷ *adj* **2** concealed or obscured: *a hidden cave; a hidden meaning*

hidden agenda *n* a hidden motive or intention behind an overt action, policy, etc

hide[1] (haɪd) *vb* **hides**, **hiding**, **hid** (hɪd), **hidden** ('hɪdən) *or* **hid** **1** to put or keep (oneself or an object) in a secret place; conceal (oneself or an object) from view or discovery: *to hide a pencil; to hide from the police* **2** (*tr*) to conceal or obscure: *the clouds hid the sun* **3** (*tr*) to keep secret **4** (*tr*) to turn (one's head, eyes, etc) away ▷ *n* **5** *Brit* a place of concealment, usually disguised to appear as part of the natural environment, used by hunters, birdwatchers, etc. US and Canadian equivalent: **blind** [Old English *hȳdan*; related to Old Frisian *hēda*, Middle Low German *hüden*, Greek *keuthein*] ▷ **'hider** *n*

hide[2] (haɪd) *n* **1** the skin of an animal, esp the tough thick skin of a large mammal, either tanned or raw **2** *informal* the human skin ▷ *vb* **hides**, **hiding**, **hided** **3** (*tr*) *informal* to flog [Old English *hȳd*; related to Old Norse *hūth*, Old Frisian *hēd*, Old High German *hūt*, Latin *cutis* skin, Greek *kutos*; see **CUTICLE**]

hide[3] (haɪd) *n* an obsolete Brit unit of land measure, varying in magnitude from about 60 to 120 acres [Old English *hīgid*; related to *hīw* family, household, Latin *cīvis* citizen]

hide-and-seek *or US and Canadian* **hide-and-go-seek** *n* a game in which one player covers his eyes and waits while the others hide, and then he tries to find them

hideaway ('haɪdəˌweɪ) *n* a hiding place or secluded spot

hidebound ('haɪdˌbaʊnd) *adj* **1** restricted by petty rules, a conservative attitude, etc **2** (of cattle, etc) having the skin closely attached to the flesh as a result of poor feeding

hideous ('hɪdɪəs) *adj* **1** extremely ugly; repulsive **2** terrifying and horrific [c13: from Old French *hisdos*, from *hisde* fear; of uncertain origin] ▷ **'hideously** *adv* ▷ **'hideousness** *or* **hideosity** (ˌhɪdɪ'ɒsɪtɪ) *n*

hideout ('haɪdˌaʊt) *n* a hiding place, esp a remote place used by outlaws, etc; hideaway

Hideyoshi Toyotomi (ˌhiːdeˈjɔːʃi ˌtɔːjɔːˈtɔːmi) *n* 1536–98, Japanese military dictator (1582–98). He unified all Japan (1590)

hiding[1] ('haɪdɪŋ) *n* **1** the state of concealment (esp in the phrase **in hiding**) **2** hiding place a place of concealment

hiding[2] ('haɪdɪŋ) *n* *informal* a flogging; beating

hidrosis (hɪ'drəʊsɪs) *n* a technical word for **sweat** *or* **sweating** [c18: via New Latin from Greek: sweating, from *hidrōs* sweat] ▷ **hidrotic** (hɪ'drɒtɪk) *adj*

hidy-hole *or* **hidey-hole** ('haɪdɪˌhəʊl) *n* *informal* a hiding place

hie (haɪ) *vb* **hies**, **hieing** *or* **hying**, **hied** *archaic or poetic* to hurry; hasten; speed [Old English *hīgian* to strive]

hieland ('hiːlənd) *adj* *Scot dialect* **1** a variant of **Highland** **2** characteristic of Highlanders, esp alluding to their supposed gullibility or foolishness in towns or cities

hierarch ('haɪəˌrɑːk) *n* **1** a a person in a position of high priestly authority **b** a person holding high rank in a religious hierarchy **2** a person at a high level in a hierarchy ▷ **ˌhier'archal** *adj*

hierarchy ('haɪəˌrɑːkɪ) *n*, *pl* **-chies** **1** a system of persons or things arranged in a graded order **2** a body of persons

in holy orders organized into graded ranks **3** the collective body of those so organized **4** a series of ordered groupings within a system, such as the arrangement of plants and animals into classes, orders, families, etc **5** government by an organized priesthood [c14: from Medieval Latin *hierarchia*, from Late Greek *hierarkhia*, from *hierarkhēs* high priest; see **HIERO-**, **-ARCHY**] ▷ **ˌhier'archical** *or* **ˌhier'archic** *adj* ▷ **'hierˌarchism** *n*

hieratic (ˌhaɪə'rætɪk) *adj* Also: **hieratical** **1** of or relating to priests **2** of or relating to a cursive form of hieroglyphics used by priests in ancient Egypt **3** of or relating to styles in art that adhere to certain fixed types or methods, as in ancient Egypt ▷ *n* **4** the hieratic script of ancient Egypt [c17: from Latin *hierāticus*, from Greek *hieratikos*, from *hiereus* a priest, from *hieros* holy] ▷ **ˌhier'atically** *adv*

hiero- *or before a vowel* **hier-** *combining form* holy or divine: *hierocracy; hierarchy* [from Greek, from *hieros*]

hieroglyphic (ˌhaɪərə'glɪfɪk) *adj* Also: **hieroglyphical** **1** of or relating to a form of writing using picture symbols, esp as used in ancient Egypt **2** difficult to read or decipher ▷ *n* Also: **hieroglyph** **3** a picture or symbol representing an object, concept, or sound **4** a symbol or picture that is difficult to read or decipher [c16: from Late Latin *hieroglyphicus*, from Greek *hierogluphikos*, from **HIERO-** + *gluphē* carving, from *gluphein* to carve] ▷ **ˌhiero'glyphically** *adv*

hieroglyphics (ˌhaɪərə'glɪfɪks) *n* (*functioning as singular or plural*) **1** a form of writing, esp as used in ancient Egypt, in which pictures or symbols are used to represent objects, concepts, or sounds **2** difficult or undecipherable writing

Hieronymus (ˌhaɪə'rɒnɪməs) *n* **Eusebius** (juː'siːbɪəs). the Latin name of Saint Jerome. See **Jerome** (sense 1) ▷ **Hieronymic** (ˌhaɪərə'nɪmɪk) *or* **Hiero'nymian** *adj*

hierophant ('haɪərəˌfænt) *n* **1** (in ancient Greece) an official high priest of religious mysteries, esp those of Eleusis **2** a person who interprets and explains esoteric mysteries [c17: from Late Latin *hierophanta*, from Greek *hierophantēs*, from **HIERO-** + *phainein* to reveal] ▷ **ˌhiero'phantic** *adj*

hi-fi ('haɪˌfaɪ) *n* *informal* **1** a short for **high fidelity** **b** (*as modifier*): *hi-fi equipment* **2** a set of high-quality sound-reproducing equipment

Higgins ('hɪgɪnz) *n* **1** **Alex**, known as **Hurricane Higgins**. born 1949, Northern Irish snooker player **2** **Jack**, real name *Harry Patterson*. born 1929, British novelist; his thrillers include *The Eagle Has Landed* (1975), *Confessional* (1985), and *Midnight Runner* (2002)

higgledy-piggledy ('hɪgəldɪ'pɪgəldɪ) *informal* ▷ *adj, adv* **1** in a jumble ▷ *n* **2** a muddle

high (haɪ) *adj* **1** being a relatively great distance from top to bottom; tall: *a high building* **2** situated at or extending to a relatively great distance above the ground or above sea level: *a high plateau* **3** (*postpositive*) being a specified distance from top to bottom: *three feet high* **4** extending from an elevation: *a high dive* **5** (*in combination*) coming up to a specified level: *knee-high* **6** being at its peak or point of culmination: *high noon* **7** of greater than average height: *a high collar* **8** greater than normal in degree, intensity, or amount: *high prices; a high temperature; a high wind* **9** (of sound) acute in pitch; having a high frequency **10** (of latitudes) situated relatively far north or south from the equator **11** (of meat) slightly decomposed or tainted, regarded as enhancing the flavour of game **12** of great eminence; very important: *the high priestess* **13** exalted in style or character; elevated: *high drama* **14** expressing or feeling contempt or arrogance: *high words* **15** elated; cheerful: *high spirits* **16** (*predicative*) *informal* overexcited: *by the end of term the children are really high* **17** *informal* being in a state of altered consciousness, characterized esp by euphoria and often induced by the use of alcohol, narcotics, etc **18** luxurious or extravagant: *high life* **19** advanced in complexity or development: *high finance* **20** (of a gear) providing a relatively great forward speed for a given engine speed **21** *phonetics* of, relating to, or denoting a vowel whose articulation is produced by raising the back of the tongue towards the soft palate or the blade towards the hard palate, such as for the *ee* in English *see* or *oo* in English *moon* **22** (*capital when part of name*) formal and elaborate in style: *High Mass* **23** (*usually capital*) of or relating to the High Church **24** *cards* having a relatively great value in a suit **25** high and dry stranded; helpless; destitute **26** high and mighty *informal* arrogant **27** high opinion a favourable opinion ▷ *adv* **28** at or to a height: *he jumped high* **29** in a high manner **30** *nautical* close to the wind with sails full ▷ *n* **31** a high place or level **32** *informal* a state of altered consciousness, often induced by alcohol, narcotics, etc **33** another word for **anticyclone 34** on high **a** at a height **b** in heaven [Old English *hēah*; related to Old Norse *hār*, Gothic *hauhs*, Old High German *hōh* high, Lithuanian *kaũkas* bump, Russian *kúchča* heap, Sanskrit *kuča* bosom]

High Arctic *n* the regions of Canada, esp the northern islands, within the Arctic Circle

highball ('haɪ,bɔːl) *n chiefly US* a long iced drink consisting of a spirit base with water, soda water, etc

highborn ('haɪ,bɔːn) *adj* of noble or aristocratic birth

highboy ('haɪ,bɔɪ) *n US & Canadian* a tall chest of drawers in two sections, the lower section being a lowboy. Brit equivalent: **tallboy**

highbrow ('haɪ,braʊ) *often disparaging n* **1** a person of scholarly and erudite tastes ▷ *adj* Also: **highbrowed 2** appealing to highbrows

highchair ('haɪ,tʃeə) *n* a long-legged chair for a child, esp one with a table-like tray used at meal times

High Church *n* **1** the party or movement within the Church of England stressing continuity with Catholic Christendom, the authority of bishops, and the importance of sacraments, rituals, and ceremonies ▷ *adj* **High-Church 2** of or relating to this party or movement > 'High-'Churchman *n*

high-class *adj* **1** of very good quality; superior: *a high-class grocer* **2** belonging to, associated with, or exhibiting the characteristics of an upper social class

high-coloured *adj* (of the complexion) deep red or purplish; florid

high comedy *n* comedy set largely among cultured and articulate people and featuring witty dialogue

high commissioner *n* the senior diplomatic representative sent by one Commonwealth country to another instead of an ambassador

high-context *adj* preferring to communicate in person, rather than by electronic methods such as email. See **low-context**

high country *n* the high country sheep pastures in the foothills of the Southern Alps, New Zealand

High Court *n* **1** (in England and Wales) a shortened form of High Court of Justice **2** (in Australia) the highest court of appeal, deciding esp constitutional issues **3** (in New Zealand) a court of law inferior to the Court of Appeal. Formerly called: Supreme Court

high definition television *n* a television system offering a picture with superior definition, using 1000 or more scanning lines, and possibly a higher field repetition rate to reduce flicker effects. Abbreviation: HDTV

high-density lipoprotein *n* a lipoprotein that is the form in which cholesterol is transported in the bloodstream from the tissues to the liver. Abbreviation: HDL

high-dependency *adj* needing or providing a more than usually high level of healthcare: *a shortage of high-dependency beds*

high-energy physics *n* another name for **particle physics**

higher ('haɪə) *adj* **1** the comparative of **high** ▷ *n* (*usually capital*) (in Scotland) **2 a** the advanced level of the Scottish Certificate of Education **b** (*as modifier*): *Higher Latin* **3** a pass in a particular subject at Higher level: *she has four Highers*

higher education *n* education and training at colleges, universities, polytechnics, etc

higher mathematics *n* (*functioning as singular*) abstract mathematics, including number theory and topology, that is more advanced than basic arithmetic, algebra, geometry, and trigonometry

higher rate *n* (in Britain) a rate of income tax that is higher than the basic rate and becomes payable on taxable income in excess of a specified limit

Higher Still *n* (in Scotland) a system of post-Standard Grade qualifications offered at five levels including Higher and Advanced Higher

higher-up *n informal* a person of higher rank or in a superior position

highest common factor *n* the largest number or quantity that is a factor of each member of a group of numbers or quantities

high explosive *n* an extremely powerful chemical explosive, such as TNT or gelignite

highfalutin, hifalutin (,haɪfə'luːtɪn) *or* **highfaluting** *adj informal* pompous or pretentious [C19: from HIGH + -*falutin*, perhaps variant of *fluting*, from FLUTE]

high fidelity *n* **a** the reproduction of sound using electronic equipment that gives faithful reproduction with little or no distortion **b** (*as modifier*): *a high-fidelity amplifier* Often shortened to **hi-fi**

high-five *n slang* a gesture of greeting or congratulation in which two people slap raised right palms together

high-flown *adj* extravagant or pretentious in conception or intention: *high-flown ideas*

high-flyer *or* **high-flier** *n* **1** a person who is extreme in aims, ambition, etc **2** a person of great ability, esp in a career > 'high-'flying *adj*

high frequency *n* a radio-frequency band or radio frequency lying between 3 and 30 megahertz. Abbreviation: HF

High German *n* the standard German language, historically developed from the form of West Germanic spoken in S Germany

high-handed *adj* tactlessly overbearing and inconsiderate > ,high-'handedness *n*

high-hat *adj* **1** *informal* snobbish and arrogant ▷ *vb* -hats, -hatting, -hatted (*tr*) **2** *informal, chiefly US & Canadian* to treat in a snobbish or offhand way ▷ *n* **3** *informal* a snobbish person

high hurdles *n* (*functioning as singular*) a race in which competitors leap over hurdles 42 inches (107 cm) high

high-impact *adj* (*prenominal*) **1** (of a plastic or other material) able to withstand great force **2** (of aerobic or other exercise) placing great stress on various areas of the body **3** *informal* having great effect: *high-impact sound*

highjack ('haɪ,dʒæk) *vb, n* a less common spelling of **hijack** > 'high,jacker *n*

high jump *n* **1** the high jump an athletic event in which a competitor has to jump over a high bar set between two vertical supports **2** be for the high jump *Brit informal* to be liable to have a severe reprimand or punishment > high jumper *n* > high jumping *n*

high-key *adj* (of a photograph, painting, etc) having a predominance of light grey tones or light colours. See **low-key** (sense 3)

highland ('haɪlənd) *n* **1** relatively high ground **2** (*modifier*) of or relating to a highland > 'highlander *n*

Highland ('haɪlənd) *n* **1** a council area in N Scotland, formed in 1975 (as Highland Region) from Caithness, Sutherland, Nairnshire, most of Inverness-shire, and Ross and Cromarty except for the Outer Hebrides. Administrative centre: Inverness. Pop: 209 080 (2003 est). Area: 25 149 sq km (9710 sq miles) **2** (*modifier*) of, relating to, or denoting the Highlands of Scotland

Highland cattle *n* a breed of cattle with shaggy hair, usually reddish-brown in colour, and long horns

Highland dress *n* **1** the historical costume, including the plaid, kilt or filibeg, and bonnet, as worn by Highland clansmen and soldiers **2** a modern version of this worn for formal occasions

Highland fling *n* a vigorous Scottish solo dance

Highland Games *n* (*functioning as singular or plural*) a meeting in which competitions in sport, piping, and dancing are held: originating in the Highlands of Scotland

Highlands ('haɪləndz) the Highlands *n* **1 a** the part of Scotland that lies to the northwest of the great fault that runs from Dumbarton to Stonehaven **b** a smaller area consisting of the mountainous north of Scotland:

distinguished by Gaelic culture **2** (*often not capital*) the highland region of any country

high-level *adj* (of conferences, talks, etc) involving very important people

high-level language *n* a computer programming language that resembles natural language or mathematical notation and is designed to reflect the requirements of a problem; examples include Ada, BASIC, C, COBOL, FORTRAN, Pascal

high-level waste *n* radioactive waste material, such as spent nuclear fuel initially having a high activity and thus needing constant cooling for several decades by its producers before it can be reprocessed or treated. See **intermediate-level waste, low-level waste**

highlight ('haɪˌlaɪt) *n* **1** an area of the lightest tone in a painting, drawing, photograph, etc **2** the most exciting or memorable part of an event or period of time **3** (*often plural*) a bleached blond streak in the hair ▷ *vb* (*tr*) **4** *painting, drawing, photog* to mark (any brightly illuminated or prominent part of a form or figure) with light tone **5** to bring notice or emphasis to **6** to produce blond streaks in the (hair) by bleaching

highlighter ('haɪˌlaɪtə) *n* **1** a cosmetic cream or powder applied to the face to highlight the cheekbones, eyes, etc **2** a fluorescent felt-tip pen used as a marker to emphasize a section of text without obscuring it

highly ('haɪlɪ) *adv* **1** (intensifier): *highly pleased; highly disappointed* **2** with great approbation or favour: *we spoke highly of it* **3** in a high position: *placed highly in class* **4** at or for a high price or cost

highly strung *or US and Canadian* **high-strung** *adj* tense and easily upset; excitable; nervous

high-maintenance *adj* **1** (of a piece of equipment, motor vehicle, etc) requiring regular maintenance to keep it in working order **2** *informal* (of a person) requiring a high level of care and attention; demanding

High Mass *n* a solemn and elaborate sung Mass

high-minded *adj* **1** having or characterized by high moral principles **2** *archaic* arrogant; haughty > ˌhigh-'mindedness *n*

high-muck-a-muck *n* a conceited or haughty person [c19: from Chinook Jargon *hiu muckamuck*, literally: plenty (of) food]

highness ('haɪnɪs) *n* the condition of being high or lofty

Highness ('haɪnɪs) *n* (preceded by *Your, His,* or *Her*) a title used to address or refer to a royal person

high-octane *adj* **1** (of petrol) having a high octane number **2** *informal* dynamic, forceful, or intense: *high-octane drive and efficiency*

high-pass filter *n electronics* a filter that transmits all frequencies above a specified value, substantially attenuating frequencies below this value

high-pitched *adj* **1** pitched high in volume or tone **2** (of a roof) having steeply sloping sides **3** (of an argument, style, etc) lofty or intense

high-powered *adj* **1** (of an optical instrument or lens) having a high magnification **2** dynamic and energetic; highly capable

high-pressure *adj* **1** having, using, involving, or designed to withstand a pressure above normal pressure **2** *informal* (of selling) persuasive in an aggressive and persistent manner

high priest *n* **1** *Judaism* the priest of highest rank who alone was permitted to enter the holy of holies of the tabernacle and Temple **2** Also (*feminine*): **high priestess** the head of a group or cult > **high priesthood** *n*

high profile *n* a position or approach characterized by a deliberate seeking of prominence or publicity

high-rise *adj* (*prenominal*) of or relating to a building that has many storeys, esp one used for flats or offices: *a high-rise block*

high-risk *adj* denoting a group, part, etc, that is particularly subject or exposed to a danger

highroad ('haɪˌrəʊd) *n* **1** a main road; highway **2** (*the highroad*) the sure way: *the highroad to fame*

high school *n* **1** *Brit* another term for **grammar school 2** *US & NZ* a secondary school from grade 7 to grade 12

high seas *pl n* (*sometimes singular*) the open seas of the world, outside the jurisdiction of any one nation

high season *n* the most popular time of year at a holiday resort, etc

Highsmith ('haɪˌsmɪθ) *n* **Patricia.** 1921–95, US author of crime fiction. Her novels include *Strangers on a Train* (1950) and *Ripley's Game* (1974)

high-sounding *adj* another term for **high-flown**

high-spirited *adj* vivacious, bold, or lively > ˌhigh-'spiritedness *n*

High Street (*often not capitals*) the High Street *n Brit* the main street of a town, usually where the principal shops are situated

high table *n* (*sometimes capitals*) the table, sometimes elevated, in the dining hall of a school, college, etc, at which the principal teachers, fellows, etc, sit

hightail ('haɪˌteɪl) *vb* (*intr*) *informal, chiefly US & Canadian* to go or move in a great hurry

High Tatra *n* another name for the **Tatra Mountains**

high tea *n Brit* See **tea** (sense 4b)

high tech (tɛk) *n* a variant spelling of **hi tech**

high technology *n* highly sophisticated, often electronic, techniques used in manufacturing and other processes

high-tension *n* (*modifier*) subjected to, carrying, or capable of operating at a relatively high voltage

high tide *n* **1** the tide at its highest level **2** a culminating point

high time *informal* ▷ *adv* **1** the latest possible time; a time that is almost too late: *it's high time you mended this shelf* ▷ *n* **2** Also called: **high old time** an enjoyable and exciting time

high-toned *adj* **1** having a superior social, moral, or intellectual quality **2** affectedly superior **3** high in tone

high tops *pl n* training shoes that reach above the ankles

high treason *n* an act of treason directly affecting a sovereign or state

high-up *n informal* a person who holds an important or influential position

highveld ('haɪˌfɛlt, -ˌvɛlt) *n* the highveld the high-altitude grassland region of E South Africa

high water *n* **1** another name for **high tide** (sense 1) **2** the state of any stretch of water at its highest level, as during a flood

high-water mark *n* **1** the level reached by sea water at high tide or by other stretches of water in flood **2** the highest point

highway ('haɪˌweɪ) *n* **1** a public road that all may use **2** *chiefly US & Canadian except in legal contexts* a main road, esp one that connects towns or cities **3** a direct path or course

Highway Code *n* (in Britain) an official government booklet giving guidance to users of public roads

highwayman ('haɪˌweɪmən) *n, pl* -men (formerly) a robber, usually on horseback, who held up travellers

high wire *n* a tightrope stretched high in the air for balancing acts

High Wycombe ('wɪkəm) *n* a town in S central England, in S Buckinghamshire: furniture industry. Pop: 77 178 (2001)

HIH *abbreviation* His (*or* Her) Imperial Highness

hijack *or* **highjack** ('haɪˌdʒæk) *vb* **1** (*tr*) to seize, divert, or appropriate (a vehicle or the goods it carries) while in transit: *to hijack an aircraft* ▷ *n* **2** the act or an instance of hijacking [c20: of unknown origin] > 'hiˌjacker *or* 'highˌjacker *n*

Hijaz (hiːˈdʒæz) *n* a variant spelling of **Hejaz**

hike (haɪk) *vb* **1** (*intr*) to walk a long way, usually for pleasure or exercise, esp in the country **2** (usually foll by *up*) to pull or be pulled; hitch **3** (*tr*) to increase (a price) ▷ *n* **4** a long walk **5** a rise in prices, wages, etc [c18: of uncertain origin] > 'hiker *n*

hikoi ('hiːˌkɔɪ) *NZ* ▷ *n* **1** a walk or march, esp a Māori protest march ▷ *vb* **2** (*intr*) to take part in such a march [Māori]

hilarious (hɪˈlɛərɪəs) *adj* very funny or merry [c19: from Latin *hilaris* glad, from Greek *hilaros*] > hi'lariously *adv* > hi'lariousness *n*

hilarity (hɪˈlærɪtɪ) *n* mirth and merriment; cheerfulness

Hilary of Poitiers ('hɪlərɪ) *n* **Saint.** ?315–?367 AD, French bishop, an opponent of Arianism. Feast day: Jan 13 or 14

Hilary term ('hɪlərɪ) n the spring term at Oxford University, the Inns of Court, and some other educational establishments [c16: named after Saint Hilary of Poitiers (?315–?367 AD), French bishop, whose feast day is Jan 13 or 14]

Hilbert ('hɪlbət) n **David** ('da:fɪt). 1862–1943, German mathematician, who made outstanding contributions to the theories of number fields and invariants and to geometry

Hildebrand ('hɪldə,brænd) n the monastic name of **Gregory VII** > ,Hilde'brandian adj, n > 'Hilde,brandine adj

Hildegard of Bingen ('hɪldəga:d, 'bɪŋən) n **Saint**. 1098–1179, German abbess, poet, composer, and mystic

Hildesheim (German 'hɪldəshaim) n a city in N central Germany, in Lower Saxony: a member of the Hanseatic League. Pop: 103 245 (2003 est)

hill (hɪl) n **1 a** a conspicuous and often rounded natural elevation of the earth's surface, less high or craggy than a mountain **b** (in combination): a hillside; a hilltop **2 a** a heap or mound made by a person or animal **b** (in combination): a dunghill **3** an incline; slope **4** over the hill **a** informal beyond one's prime **b** military slang absent without leave or deserting ▷ vb (tr) **5** to form into a hill or mound **6** to cover or surround with a mound or heap of earth [Old English hyll; related to Old Frisian holla head, Latin collis hill, Low German hull hill] > 'hilly adj

Hill (hɪl) n **1 Archibald Vivian**. 1886–1977, British biochemist, noted for his research into heat loss in muscle contraction: shared the Nobel prize for physiology or medicine (1922) **2 Damon Graham Devereux**, son of Graham Hill. born 1960, British motor-racing driver; Formula One world champion (1996) **3 David Octavius** 1802–70, Scottish painter and portrait photographer, noted esp for his collaboration with the chemist Robert Adamson (1821–48) **4 Geoffrey (William)**. born 1932, British poet: his books include King Log (1968), Mercian Hymns (1971), The Mystery of the Charity of Charles Péguy (1983), and The Orchards of Syon (2002) **5 Graham**. 1929–75, British motor-racing driver: world champion (1962, 1968) **6 Octavia**. 1838–1912, British housing reformer; a founder of the National Trust **7 Sir Rowland**. 1795–1879, British originator of the penny postage **8 Susan (Elizabeth)**. born 1942, British novelist and writer of short stories: her books include I'm the King of the Castle (1970) The Woman in Black (1983), and Felix Derby (2002)

Hilla ('hɪlə) n a market town in central Iraq, on a branch of the Euphrates: built partly of bricks from the nearby site of Babylon. Pop: 364 000 (2005 est). Also called: Al Hillah

Hillary ('hɪlərɪ) n Sir **Edmund**. 1919–2008, New Zealand explorer and mountaineer. He and his Sherpa guide, Tenzing Norgay, were the first to reach the summit of Mount Everest (1953); New Zealand ambassador to India (1984–89)

hillbilly ('hɪl,bɪlɪ) n, pl -lies **1** usually disparaging an unsophisticated person, esp from the mountainous areas in the southeastern US **2** another name for **country and western** [c20: from HILL + Billy (the nickname)]

Hillel ('hɪlɛl, -ləl) n ?60 BC–?9 AD, rabbi, born in Babylonia; president of the Sanhedrin. He was the first to formulate principles of biblical interpretation

Hiller ('hɪlə) n Dame **Wendy**. 1912–2003, British actress. Her many films include Pygmalion (1938), Major Barbara (1940), and Separate Tables (1958)

Hilliard ('hɪliəd) n **Nicholas**. 1537–1619, English miniaturist, esp of portraits

Hillingdon ('hɪlɪŋdən) n a residential borough of W Greater London. Pop: 247 600 (2003 est). Area: 110 sq km (43 sq miles)

hillock ('hɪlək) n a small hill or mound [C14 hilloc, from HILL + -OCK] > 'hillocked or 'hillocky adj

hills (hɪlz) pl n **1** the hills a hilly and often remote region **2** as old as the hills very old

hill station (in northern India) a settlement or resort at a high altitude

hilt (hɪlt) n **1** the handle or shaft of a sword, dagger, etc

2 to the hilt to the full [Old English; related to Old Norse hjalt, Old Saxon helta oar handle, Old High German helza]

Hilton ('hɪltən) n **Walter**. died 1396, English mystical writer: author of The Scale of Perfection

hilum ('haɪləm) n, pl -la (-lə) **1** botany a scar on the surface of a seed marking its point of attachment to the seed stalk (funicle) **2** a deep fissure or depression on the surface of a bodily organ around the point of entrance or exit of vessels, nerves, or ducts [C17: from Latin: trifle; see NIHIL]

Hilversum ('hɪlvəsəm; Dutch 'hɪlvərsym) n a city in the central Netherlands, in North Holland province: Dutch radio and television centre. Pop: 83 000 (2003 est))

him (hɪm; unstressed ɪm) pron (objective) refers to a male person or animal: they needed him; she baked him a cake; not him again! [Old English him, dative of hē HE[1]]
● USAGE See at me[1]

HIM abbreviation His (or Her) Imperial Majesty

Himachal Pradesh (hɪ'mɑːtʃəl prɑː'dɛʃ) n a state of N India, in the W Himalayas: rises to about 6700 m (22 000 ft) and is densely forested. Capital: Simla. Pop: 6 077 248 (2001). Area: 55 658 sq km (21 707 sq miles)

Himalayan (,hɪmə'leɪən) adj of or relating to the Himalayas or their inhabitants

Himalayas (,hɪmə'leɪəz, hɪ'mɑːljəz) pl n the Himalayas a vast mountain system in S Asia, extending 2400 km (1500 miles) from Kashmir (west) to Assam (east), between the valleys of the Rivers Indus and Brahmaputra: covers most of Nepal, Sikkim, Bhutan, and the S edge of Tibet; the highest range in the world, with several peaks over 7500 m (25 000 ft). Highest peak: Mount Everest, 8848 m (29 028 ft)

himation (hɪ'mætɪ,ɒn) n, pl -ia (-ɪə) (in ancient Greece) a cloak draped around the body [c19: from Greek: a little garment, from heima dress, from hennunai to clothe]

himbo ('hɪmbəʊ) n, pl -bos slang, usually derogatory an attractive, but empty-headed man [c20: from HIM + (BIM)BO]

Himeji ('hi:mɛ,dʒi:) n a city in central Japan, on W Honshu: cotton textile centre. Pop: 475 892 (2002 est)

Himmler (German 'hɪmlər) n **Heinrich** ('haɪnrɪç). 1900–45, German Nazi leader, head of the SS and the Gestapo (1936–45); committed suicide

Hims (hɪmz) n a former name of **Homs**

himself (hɪm'sɛlf; medially often ɪm'sɛlf) pron **1 a** the reflexive form of he or him **b** (intensifier): the king himself waved to me **2** (preceded by a copula) his normal or usual self: he seems himself once more [Old English him selfum, dative singular of hē self; see HE[1], SELF]

Himyarite ('hɪmjə,raɪt) n **1** a member of an ancient people of SW Arabia, sometimes regarded as including the Sabeans ▷ adj **2** of or relating to this people or their culture [c19: named after Himyar legendary king in ancient Yemen]

Hinayana (,hi:nə'jɑːnə) n any of various early forms of Buddhism [from Sanskrit hīnayāna, from hīna lesser + yāna vehicle]

Hinckley ('hɪŋklɪ) n a town in central England, in Leicestershire. Pop: 43 246 (2001)

hind[1] (haɪnd) adj hinder, hindmost or hindermost (prenominal) (esp of parts of the body) situated at the back or rear: a hind leg [Old English hindan at the back, related to German hinten; see BEHIND, HINDER[2]]

hind[2] (haɪnd) n, pl hinds or hind **1** the female of the deer, esp the red deer when aged three years or more **2** any of several marine serranid fishes of the genus Epinephelus, closely related and similar to the gropers [Old English hind; related to Old High German hinta, Greek kemas young deer, Lithuanian szmúlas hornless]

hind[3] (haɪnd) n (formerly) **1** a simple peasant **2** (in N Britain) a skilled farm worker **3** a steward [Old English hīne, from hīgna, genitive plural of hīgan servants]

Hindemith (German 'hɪndəmɪt) n **Paul** (paul). 1895–1963, German composer and musical theorist, who opposed the twelve-tone technique. His works include the song cycle Das Marienleben (1923) and the opera Mathis der Maler (1938)

Hindenburg[1] ('hɪndənbʊrk) n the German name for **Zabrze**

Hindenburg² ('hɪndən‚bɜːg; German 'hɪndənbʊrk) n **Paul von Beneckendorff und von** (paul fɔn 'bɛnəkəndɔrf ʊnt fɔn). 1847–1934, German field marshal and statesman; president (1925–34). During World War I he directed German strategy together with Ludendorff (1916–18)

hinder¹ ('hɪndə) vb **1** to be or get in the way of (someone or something); hamper **2** (tr) to prevent [Old English hindrian; related to Old Norse hindra, Old High German hintarōn]

hinder² ('haɪndə) adj (prenominal) situated at or further towards the back or rear; posterior [Old English; related to Old Norse hindri latter, Gothic hindar beyond, Old High German hintar behind]

Hindi ('hɪndɪ) n **1** a language or group of dialects of N central India. It belongs to the Indic branch of the Indo-European family and is closely related to Urdu. See also **Hindustani 2** a formal literary dialect of this language, the official language of India, usually written in Nagari script **3** a person whose native language is Hindi [c18: from Hindi hindī, from Hind India, from Old Persian Hindu the river Indus]

hindmost ('haɪnd‚məʊst) or **hindermost** ('haɪndə‚məʊst) adj furthest back; last

Hindoo ('hɪnduː, hɪnˈduː) n, pl **-doos** an older spelling of **Hindu** ▷ **Hindooism** ('hɪndʊ‚ɪzəm) n

hindquarter ('haɪnd‚kwɔːtə) n **1** one of the two back quarters of a carcass of beef, lamb, etc **2** (plural) the rear, esp of a four-legged animal

hindrance ('hɪndrəns) n **1** an obstruction or snag; impediment **2** the act of hindering; prevention

hindsight ('haɪnd‚saɪt) n **1** the ability to understand, after something has happened, what should have been done or what caused the event **2** a firearm's rear sight

Hindu or **Hindoo** ('hɪnduː, hɪnˈduː) n, pl **-dus, -doos 1** a person who adheres to Hinduism **2** an inhabitant or native of Hindustan or India, esp one adhering to Hinduism ▷ adj **3** relating to Hinduism, Hindus, or India [c17: from Persian Hindū, from Hind India; see HINDI]

Hinduism or **Hindooism** ('hɪndʊ‚ɪzəm) n the complex of beliefs, values, and customs comprising the dominant religion of India, characterized by the worship of many gods, including Brahma as supreme being, a caste system, belief in reincarnation, etc

Hindu Kush (kʊʃ, kuːʃ) pl n a mountain range in central Asia, extending about 800 km (500 miles) east from the Koh-i-Baba Mountains of central Afghanistan to the Pamirs. Highest peak: Tirich Mir, 7690 m (25 230 ft)

Hindustan (‚hɪndʊˈstaːn) n **1** the land of the Hindus, esp India north of the Deccan and excluding Bengal **2** the general area around the Ganges where Hindi is the predominant language **3** the areas of India where Hinduism predominates, as contrasted with those areas where Islam predominates

Hindustani, Hindoostani (‚hɪndʊˈstaːnɪ) or **Hindostani** (‚hɪndəʊˈstaːnɪ) n **1** the dialect of Hindi spoken in Delhi: used as a lingua franca throughout India **2** a group of languages or dialects consisting of all spoken forms of Hindi and Urdu considered together ▷ adj **3** of or relating to these languages or Hindustan

Hindutva (hɪnˈdʊtvə) n (in India) a political movement advocating Hindu nationalism and the establishment of a Hindu state [c21: Hindi, literally: Hinduness]

Hines (haɪnz) n **Earl**, known as **Earl "Fatha" Hines.** 1905–83, US jazz pianist, conductor, and songwriter

hinge (hɪndʒ) n **1** a device for holding together two parts such that one can swing relative to the other, typically having two interlocking metal leaves held by a pin about which they pivot **2** anatomy a type of joint, such as the knee joint, that moves only backwards and forwards; a joint that functions in only one plane **3** a similar structure in invertebrate animals, such as the joint between the two halves of a bivalve shell **4** something on which events, opinions, etc, turn **5** Also called: **mount** philately a small thin transparent strip of gummed paper for affixing a stamp to a page ▷ vb **6** (tr) to attach or fit a hinge to (something) **7** (intr; usually foll by on or upon) to depend (on) **8** (intr) to hang or turn on or as if on a hinge [c13: probably of Germanic origin; compare Middle Dutch henge; see HANG] ▷ **hinged** adj

Hinglish ('hɪŋlɪʃ) n a variety of English incorporating elements of Hindi [c20: a blend of HINDI + ENGLISH]

hinny¹ ('hɪnɪ) n, pl **-nies** the sterile hybrid offspring of a male horse and a female donkey or ass [c17: from Latin hinnus, from Greek hinnos]

hinny² ('hɪnɪ) n Scot & northern English dialect a term of endearment, esp for a woman or child [variant of HONEY]

Hinshelwood ('hɪnʃəl‚wʊd) n Sir **Cyril Norman.** 1897–1967, English chemist, who shared the Nobel prize for chemistry (1956) for the study of reaction kinetics

hint (hɪnt) n **1** a suggestion or implication given in an indirect or subtle manner **2** a helpful piece of advice or practical suggestion **3** a small amount; trace ▷ vb **4** (when intr, often foll by at; when tr, takes a clause as object) to suggest or imply indirectly [c17: of uncertain origin]

hinterland ('hɪntə‚lænd) n **1** land lying behind something, esp a coast or the shore of a river **2** remote or undeveloped areas of a country **3** an area located near and dependent on a large city, esp a port [c19: from German, from hinter behind + land LAND; see HINDER²]

hip¹ (hɪp) n **1** (often plural) either side of the body below the waist and above the thigh, overlying the lateral part of the pelvis and its articulation with the thighbones **2** another name for **pelvis** (sense 1) **3** short for **hip joint 4** the angle formed where two sloping sides of a roof meet or where a sloping side meets a sloping end [Old English hype; related to Old High German huf, Gothic hups, Dutch heup] ▷ **'hipless** adj

hip² (hɪp) n the berry-like brightly coloured fruit of a rose plant: a swollen receptacle, rich in vitamin C, containing several small hairy achenes. Also called: rosehip [Old English héopa; related to Old Saxon hiopo, Old High German hiufo, Dutch joop, Norwegian dialect hjūpa]

hip³ (hɪp) interj an exclamation used to introduce cheers (in the phrase **hip, hip, hurrah**) [c18: of unknown origin]

hip⁴ (hɪp) adj **hipper, hippest** or **hepper, heppest** slang **1** aware of or following the latest trends in music, ideas, fashion, etc **2** (often postpositive; foll by to) informed (about) [c20: variant of earlier hep]

HIP (hɪp) n acronym for (in England and Wales) home information pack: a set of documents that a seller must possess before his or her property can be put on the market

hip bath n a portable bath in which the bather sits

hipbone ('hɪp‚bəʊn) n the nontechnical name for **innominate bone**

hip flask n a small metal flask for spirits, etc, often carried in a hip pocket

hip-hop ('hɪp‚hɒp) n a US pop culture movement originating in the 1980s comprising rap music, graffiti, and break dancing

hip joint n the ball-and-socket joint that connects each leg to the trunk of the body, in which the head of the femur articulates with the socket (acetabulum) of the pelvis

Hipparchus (hɪˈpɑːkəs) n **1** 2nd century BC, Greek astronomer. He discovered the precession of the equinoxes, calculated the length of the solar year, and developed trigonometry **2** died 514 BC, tyrant of Athens (527–514)

hippeastrum (hɪpɪˈæstrəm) n any plant of the South American amaryllidaceous genus Hippeastrum: cultivated for their large funnel-shaped typically red flowers [c19: New Latin, from Greek hippeus knight + astron star]

hipped¹ (hɪpt) adj **1 a** having a hip or hips **b** (in combination): broad-hipped; low-hipped **2** (esp of cows, sheep, reindeer, elk, etc) having an injury to the hip, such as a dislocation of the bones **3** architect having a hip or hips

hipped² (hɪpt) adj (often postpositive; foll by on) US & Canadian dated slang very enthusiastic (about) [c20: from HIP⁴]

hippie ('hɪpɪ) n a variant spelling of **hippy¹**

hippo ('hɪpəʊ) n, pl **-pos** informal short for **hippopotamus**

hippocampus (‚hɪpəʊˈkæmpəs) n, pl **-pi** (-paɪ) **1** a mythological sea creature with the forelegs of a horse and the tail of a fish **2** any marine teleost fish of the genus *Hippocampus*, having a horselike head. See **sea horse** **3** an area of cerebral cortex that forms a ridge in the floor of the lateral ventricle of the brain, which in cross section has the shape of a sea horse. It functions as part of the limbic system [c16: from Latin, from Greek *hippos* horse + *kampos* a sea monster]

hippocras ('hɪpəʊˌkræs) *n* an old English drink of wine flavoured with spices [c14 *ypocras*, from Old French: Hippocrates (?460–?377 BC), Greek physician, probably referring to a filter called *Hippocrates' sleeve*]

Hippocrates (hɪ'pɒkrəˌtiːz) *n* ?460–?377 BC, Greek physician, commonly regarded as the father of medicine > ˌHippo'cratic *or* ˌHippo'cratical *adj*

Hippocratic oath (ˌhɪpəʊ'krætɪk) *n* an oath taken by a doctor to observe a code of medical ethics supposedly derived from that of Hippocrates (?460–?337), Greek physician commonly regarded as the father of medicine

Hippocrene ('hɪpəʊˌkriːn, ˌhɪpəʊ'kriːnɪ) *n* a spring on Mount Helicon in Greece, said to engender poetic inspiration [c17: via Latin from Greek *hippos* horse + *krēnē* spring] > ˌHippo'crenian *adj*

hippodrome ('hɪpəˌdrəʊm) *n* **1** a music hall, variety theatre, or circus **2** (in ancient Greece or Rome) an open-air course for horse and chariot races [c16: from Latin *hippodromos*, from Greek *hippos* horse + *dromos* a race]

hippogriff *or* **hippogryph** ('hɪpəʊˌgrɪf) *n* a monster of Greek mythology with a griffin's head, wings, and claws and a horse's body [c17: from Italian *ippogrifo*, from *ippo-* horse (from Greek *hippos*) + *grifo* GRIFFIN[1]]

Hippolyta (hɪ'pɒlɪtə) *or* **Hippolyte** (hɪ'pɒlɪˌtiː) *n Greek myth* a queen of the Amazons, slain by Hercules in battle for her belt, which he obtained as his ninth labour

Hippolytus (hɪ'pɒlɪtəs) *n Greek myth* a son of Theseus, killed after his stepmother Phaedra falsely accused him of raping her > Hip'polytan *adj*

Hippomenes (hɪ'pɒmɪˌniːz) *n Greek myth* the husband, in some traditions, of Atalanta

hippopotamus (ˌhɪpə'pɒtəməs) *n, pl* **-muses** *or* **-mi** (-ˌmaɪ) a very large massive gregarious artiodactyl mammal, *Hippopotamus amphibius*, living in or around the rivers of tropical Africa: family Hippopotamidae. It has short legs and a thick skin sparsely covered with hair [c16: from Latin, from Greek *hippopotamos* river horse, from *hippos* horse + *potamos* river]

Hippo Regius ('hɪpəʊ 'riːdʒɪəs) *n* an ancient Numidian city, adjoining present-day Annaba, Algeria

hippy[1] *or* **hippie** ('hɪpɪ) *n, pl* **-pies** (esp during the 1960s) a person whose behaviour, dress, use of drugs, etc, implied a rejection of conventional values [c20: see HIP[4]]

hippy[2] ('hɪpɪ) *adj* **-pier**, **-piest** *informal* (esp of a woman) having large hips

hip roof *n* a roof having sloping ends and sides

hipster ('hɪpstə) *n* **1** *slang, now rare* **a** an enthusiast of modern jazz **b** an outmoded word for **hippy**[1] **2** (*modifier*) (of trousers) cut so that the top encircles the hips

hipsters ('hɪpstəz) *pl n Brit* trousers cut so that the top encircles the hips

Hiram ('haɪərəm) *n* 10th century BC, king of Tyre, who supplied Solomon with materials and craftsmen for the building of the Temple (II Samuel 5:11; I Kings 5:1–18)

hircine ('hɜːsaɪn, -sɪn) *adj* **1** *archaic* of or like a goat, esp in smell **2** *literary* lustful; lascivious [c17: from Latin *hircīnus*, from *hircus* goat]

hire ('haɪə) *vb* (*tr*) **1** to acquire the temporary use of (a thing) or the services of (a person) in exchange for payment **2** to employ (a person) for wages **3** (often foll by *out*) to provide (something) or the services of (oneself or others) for an agreed payment, usually for an agreed period **4** (*tr*; foll by *out*) chiefly Brit to pay independent contractors for (work to be done) ▷ *n* **5 a** the act of hiring or the state of being hired **b** (*as modifier*): *a hire car* **6** the price paid or payable for a person's services or the temporary use of something **7 for hire** or **on hire** available for service or temporary use in exchange for payment [Old English *hȳrian*; related to Old Frisian *hēra* to lease, Middle Dutch *hūren*] > 'hirable *or* 'hireable *adj* > 'hirer *n*

hireling ('haɪəlɪŋ) *n derogatory* a person who works only for money, esp one paid to do something unpleasant

[Old English *hȳrling*; related to Dutch *huurling*; see HIRE, -LING[1]]

hire-purchase *n Brit, Austral, NZ & South African* a system for purchasing merchandise, such as cars or furniture, in which the buyer takes possession of the merchandise on payment of a deposit and completes the purchase by paying a series of regular instalments while the seller retains ownership until the final instalment is paid Abbreviation: **HP**. US and Canadian equivalents: **installment plan**, **instalment plan**

Hirohito (ˌhɪərəʊ'hiːtəʊ) *n* 1901–89, emperor of Japan 1926–89. In 1946 he became a constitutional monarch

Hiroshige (ˌhɪərəʊ'ʃiːgeɪ) *n* Ando ('aːndəʊ). 1797–1858, Japanese artist, esp of colour wood-block prints

Hiroshima (ˌhɪrɒ'ʃiːmə, hɪ'rɒʃɪmə) *n* a port in SW Japan, on SW Honshu on the delta of the Ota River: largely destroyed on August 6, 1945, by the first atomic bomb to be used in warfare, dropped by the US, which killed over 75 000 of its inhabitants. Pop: 1 113 786 (2002 est)

Hirst (hɜːst) *n* Damien. born 1965, British artist, noted esp for his works featuring dead animals preserved in tanks of formaldehyde, and for his 2007 sculpture, *For the Love of God*, a human skull encrusted with flawless diamonds

hirsute ('hɜːsjuːt) *adj* **1** covered with hair **2** (of plants or their parts) covered with long but not stiff hairs **3** (of a person) having long, thick, or untrimmed hair [c17: from Latin *hirsūtus* shaggy; related to Latin *horrēre* to bristle, *hirtus* hairy; see HORRID[1]] > 'hirsuteness *n*

his (hɪz; *unstressed* ɪz) *determiner* **1 a** of, belonging to, or associated with him: *his own fault; his knee; I don't like his being out so late* **b** *as pronoun*: *his is on the left; that book is his* **2 his and hers** (of paired objects) for a man and woman respectively ▷ *pron* **3** of his belonging to or associated with him [Old English *his*, genitive of *hē* HE[1] and of *hit* IT]

Hispania (hɪ'spænɪə) *n* the Iberian peninsula in the Roman world

Hispanic (hɪ'spænɪk) *adj* **1** relating to, characteristic of, or derived from Spain or Spanish-speaking countries ▷ *n* **2** a person of Latin-American or Spanish descent living in the US > Hi'spaniˌcism *n*

Hispaniola (ˌhɪspən'jəʊlə; *Spanish* ispa'ɲola) *n* the second largest island in the Caribbean, in the Greater Antilles: divided politically into Haiti and the Dominican Republic; discovered in 1492 by Christopher Columbus, who named it La Isla Española. Area: 18 703 sq km (29 418 sq miles). Former name: **Santo Domingo**

hispid ('hɪspɪd) *adj biology* covered with stiff hairs or bristles [c17: from Latin *hispidus* bristly]

hiss (hɪs) *n* **1** a voiceless fricative sound like that of a prolonged *s* **2** such a sound uttered as an exclamation of derision, contempt, etc, esp by an audience or crowd ▷ *vb* **3** (*intr*) to produce or utter a hiss **4** (*tr*) to express with a hiss, usually to indicate derision or anger **5** (*tr*) to show derision or anger towards (a speaker, performer, etc) by hissing [c14: of imitative origin]

Hiss (hɪs) *n* Alger. 1904–96, US government official: imprisoned (1950–54) for perjury in connection with alleged espionage activities

hissy fit ('hɪsɪ) *n informal* a childish temper tantrum

hist (hɪst) *interj* an exclamation used to attract attention or as a warning to be silent

histamine ('hɪstəˌmiːn, -mɪn) *n* an amine formed from histidine and released by the body tissues in allergic reactions, causing irritation. It also stimulates gastric secretions, dilates blood vessels, and contracts smooth muscle. Formula: $C_5H_9N_3$ [c20: from HIST(IDINE) + -AMINE] > histaminic (ˌhɪstə'mɪnɪk) *adj*

histidine ('hɪstɪˌdiːn, -dɪn) *n* a nonessential amino acid that occurs in most proteins: a precursor of histamine

histo- *or before a vowel* **hist-** *combining form* indicating animal or plant tissue: *histology; histamine* [from Greek, from *histos* web]

histogenesis (ˌhɪstəʊ'dʒɛnɪsɪs) *n* the formation of tissues and organs from undifferentiated cells > histogenetic (ˌhɪstəʊdʒə'nɛtɪk) *or* ˌhisto'genic *adj*

histogram ('hɪstəˌgræm) *n* a statistical graph that represents the frequency of values of a quantity by vertical rectangles of varying heights and widths. The width of the rectangles is in proportion to the class interval under consideration, and their areas represent the relative frequency of the phenomenon in question [c20: perhaps from HISTO(RY) + -GRAM]

histology (hɪˈstɒlədʒɪ) n the study, esp the microscopic study, of the tissues of an animal or plant > histological (ˌhɪstəˈlɒdʒɪkᵉl) or ˌhistoˈlogic adj

histolysis (hɪˈstɒlɪsɪs) n the disintegration of organic tissues > histolytic (ˌhɪstəˈlɪtɪk) adj

historian (hɪˈstɔːrɪən) n a person who writes or studies history, esp one who is an authority on it

historic (hɪˈstɒrɪk) adj 1 famous or likely to become famous in history; significant 2 Also called: secondary linguistics (of Latin, Greek, or Sanskrit verb tenses) referring to past time
 ● USAGE A distinction is usually made between historic
 ● (important, significant) and historical (pertaining to
 ● history): a historic decision; a historical perspective

historical (hɪˈstɒrɪkᵉl) adj 1 belonging to or typical of the study of history: historical methods 2 concerned with or treating of events of the past: historical accounts 3 based on or constituting factual material as distinct from legend or supposition 4 based on or inspired by history: a historical novel 5 occurring or prominent in history > hisˈtorically adv

historical-cost accounting n a method of accounting that values assets at the original cost. In times of high inflation profits can be overstated. See current-cost accounting

historical linguistics n (functioning as singular) the study of language as it changes in the course of time, with a view either to discovering general principles of linguistic change or to establishing the correct genealogical classification of particular languages

historical present n the present tense used to narrate past events, usually employed in English for special effect or in informal use, as in a week ago I'm walking down the street and I see this accident

historicism (hɪˈstɒrɪˌsɪzəm) n 1 the belief that natural laws govern historical events which in turn determine social and cultural phenomena 2 the doctrine that each period of history has its own beliefs and values inapplicable to any other, so that nothing can be understood independently of its historical context 3 excessive emphasis on history, historicism, past styles, etc > hisˈtoricist n, adj

historicity (ˌhɪstəˈrɪsɪtɪ) n historical authenticity

historiographer (hɪˌstɔːrɪˈɒɡrəfə) n 1 a historian, esp one concerned with historical method and the writings of other historians 2 a historian employed to write the history of a group or public institution > ˌhistoriˈography n

history (ˈhɪstərɪ, ˈhɪstrɪ) n, pl -ries 1 a record or account, often chronological in approach, of past events, developments, etc 2 all that is preserved or remembered of the past, esp in written form 3 the discipline of recording and interpreting past events involving human beings 4 past events, esp when considered as an aggregate 5 an event in the past, esp one that has been forgotten or reduced in importance: their quarrel was just history 6 the past, background, previous experiences, etc, of a thing or person: the house had a strange history 7 a play that depicts or is based on historical events 8 a narrative relating the events of a character's life: the history of Joseph Andrews [c15: from Latin historia, from Greek: enquiry, from historein to narrate, from histōr judge]

histrionic (ˌhɪstrɪˈɒnɪk) adj 1 excessively dramatic, insincere, or artificial: histrionic gestures 2 now rare dramatic ▷ n 3 (plural) melodramatic displays of temperament 4 rare (plural, functioning as singular) dramatics [c17: from Late Latin histriōnicus of a player, from histriō actor] > ˌhistriˈonically adv

hit (hɪt) vb hits, hitting, hit (mainly tr) 1 (also intr) to deal (a blow or stroke) to (a person or thing); strike 2 to come into violent contact with: the car hit the tree 3 to reach or strike with a missile, thrown object, etc: to hit a target 4 to make or cause to make forceful contact; knock or bump: I hit my arm on the table 5 to propel or cause to move by striking: to hit a ball 6 cricket to score (runs) 7 to affect

(a person, place, or thing) suddenly or adversely: his illness hit his wife very hard 8 to achieve or reach: to hit the jackpot; unemployment hit a new high 9 to experience or encounter: I've hit a slight snag here 10 slang to murder (a rival criminal) in fulfilment of an underworld contract or vendetta 11 informal to set out on (a road, path, etc): let's hit the road 12 informal to arrive or appear in: he will hit town tomorrow night 13 informal, chiefly US & Canadian to demand or request from: he hit me for a pound 14 slang to drink an excessive amount of (alcohol): to hit the bottle ▷ n 15 an impact or collision 16 a shot, blow, etc, that reaches its object 17 an apt, witty, or telling remark 18 informal a person or thing that gains wide appeal: she's a hit with everyone b (as modifier): a hit record 19 informal a stroke of luck 20 slang a a murder carried out as the result of an underworld vendetta or rivalry b (as modifier): a hit squad 21 computing a single visit to a website 22 make a hit with or score a hit with informal to make a favourable impression on ▷ See also hit off, hit on, hit out [Old English hittan, from Old Norse hitta]

Hitachi (hɪˈtætʃɪ) n a city in Japan, in E Honshu: a centre of the electronics industry. Pop: 193 080 (2002 est)

hit-and-miss adj informal random; haphazard: a hit-and-miss affair; the technique is very hit and miss. Also called: hit or miss

hit-and-run adj (prenominal) 1 involved in or denoting a motor-vehicle accident in which the driver leaves the scene without stopping to give assistance, inform the police, etc 2 (of an attack, raid, etc) relying on surprise allied to a rapid departure from the scene of operations for the desired effect: hit-and-run tactics

hitch (hɪtʃ) vb 1 to fasten or become fastened with a knot or tie, esp temporarily 2 (tr; often foll by up) to pull up (the trousers, a skirt, etc) with a quick jerk 3 (intr) chiefly US to move in a halting manner 4 (tr; passive) slang to marry (esp in the phrase get hitched) 5 informal to obtain (a ride or rides) by hitchhiking ▷ n 6 an impediment or obstacle, esp one that is temporary or minor 7 a knot for fastening a rope to posts, other ropes, etc, that can be undone by pulling against the direction of the strain that holds it 8 a sudden jerk; tug; pull: he gave it a hitch and it came loose 9 informal a ride obtained by hitchhiking [c15: of uncertain origin] > ˈhitcher n

Hitchcock (ˈhɪtʃˌkɒk) n Sir Alfred (Joseph). 1899–1980, English film director, noted for his mastery in creating suspense. His films include The Thirty-Nine Steps (1935), Rebecca (1940), Psycho (1960), and The Birds (1963)

hitchhike (ˈhɪtʃˌhaɪk) vb (intr) to travel by obtaining free lifts in motor vehicles > ˈhitchˌhiker n

hi tech or **high tech** (tɛk) n 1 short for high technology 2 a style of interior design using features of industrial equipment ▷ adj hi-tech or high-tech 3 designed for or using high technology 4 of or in the interior design style ▷ See low tech

hither (ˈhɪðə) adv 1 to or towards this place (esp in the phrase come hither) 2 hither and thither this way and that, as in a state of confusion ▷ adj 3 archaic or dialect (of a side or part, esp of a hill or valley) nearer; closer [Old English hider; related to Old Norse hethra here, Gothic hidrē, Latin citrā on this side, citrō]

hithermost (ˈhɪðəˌməʊst) adj now rare nearest to this place or in this direction

hitherto (ˈhɪðəˈtuː) adv 1 until this time: hitherto, there have been no problems ▷ adj 2 until this time: a hitherto unoccupied house

Hitler (ˈhɪtlə) n 1 Adolf. (ˈaːdɔlf). Grandmother's maiden name and father's original surname Schicklgrüber. 1889–1945, German dictator, born in Austria. After becoming president of the National Socialist German Workers' Party (Nazi party), he attempted to overthrow the government of Bavaria (1923). While in prison he wrote Mein Kampf, expressing his philosophy of the superiority of the Aryan race and the inferiority of the Jews. He was appointed chancellor of Germany (1933), transforming it from a democratic republic into the totalitarian Third Reich, of which he became Führer in 1934. He established concentration camps to exterminate the Jews, rearmed the Rhineland (1936), annexed Austria (1938) and Czechoslovakia, and invaded

h

Poland (1939), which precipitated World War II. He committed suicide **2** a person who displays dictatorial characteristics

Hitlerism ('hɪtlə,rɪzəm) *n* the policies, principles, and methods of the Nazi party as developed by its leader Adolf Hitler (1889–1945)

hit list *n informal* **1** a list of people to be murdered: *a terrorist hit list* **2** a list of targets to be eliminated in some way: *a hit list of pits to be closed*

hit man *n slang* a hired assassin, esp one employed by gangsters

hit off *vb* **1** (*tr, adverb*) to represent or mimic accurately **2** hit it off *informal* to have a good relationship with

hit on *vb* (*tr, preposition*) **1** Also called: hit upon to discover unexpectedly or guess correctly **2** *US & Canadian slang* to make sexual advances to (a person)

hit out *vb* (*intr, adverb; often foll by at*) **1** to direct blows forcefully and vigorously **2** to make a verbal attack (upon someone)

Hittite ('hɪtaɪt) *n* **1** a member of an ancient people of Anatolia, who built a great empire in N Syria and Asia Minor in the second millennium BC **2** the extinct language of this people, deciphered from cuneiform inscriptions found at Boğazköy and elsewhere. It is clearly related to the Indo-European family of languages, although the precise relationship is disputed ▷ *adj* **3** of or relating to this people, their civilization, or their language

hit wicket *n cricket* an instance of a batsman breaking the wicket with the bat or a part of the body while playing a stroke and so being out

HIV *abbreviation* human immunodeficiency virus; the cause of AIDS. Two strains have been identified: HIV-1 and HIV-2

hive (haɪv) *n* **1** a structure in which social bees live and rear their young **2** a colony of social bees **3** a place showing signs of great industry (esp in the phrase **a hive of activity**) **4** a teeming crowd; multitude ▷ *vb* **5** to cause (bees) to collect or (of bees) to collect inside a hive **6** to live or cause to live in or as if in a hive **7** (*tr*) (of bees) to store (honey, pollen, etc) in the hive [Old English *hȳf*; related to Westphalian *hüwe*, Old Norse *hūfr* ship's hull, Latin *cūpa* barrel, Greek *kupē*, Sanskrit *kūpa* cave]

hive off *vb* (*adverb*) **1** to transfer or be transferred from a larger group or unit **2** (*usually tr*) to transfer (profitable activities of a nationalized industry) back to private ownership

hives (haɪvz) *n* (*functioning as singular or plural*) *pathol* a nontechnical name for **urticaria** [c16: of uncertain origin]

hiya ('haɪjə, ˌhaɪ'jɑː) *sentence substitute* an informal term of greeting [c20: shortened from *how are you?*]

hl *symbol for* hectolitre

HL (in Britain) *abbreviation* House of Lords

hm *symbol for* hectometre

HM *abbreviation* **1** His (or Her) Majesty **2** headmaster; headmistress

h'm (*spelling pron* hmmm) *interj* used to indicate hesitation, doubt, assent, pleasure, etc

HMAS *abbreviation* His (or Her) Majesty's Australian Ship

HMCS *abbreviation* His (or Her) Majesty's Canadian Ship

HMI (in Britain) *abbreviation* Her Majesty's Inspector; a government official who examines and supervises schools

H.M.S. or **HMS** *abbreviation* **1** His (or Her) Majesty's Service **2** His (or Her) Majesty's Ship

HMSO (formerly, in Britain) *abbreviation* His (or Her) Majesty's Stationery Office, now The Stationery Office (TSO)

HNC (in Britain) *abbreviation* Higher National Certificate; a qualification recognized by many national technical and professional institutions

HND (in Britain) *abbreviation* Higher National Diploma; a qualification in technical subjects equivalent to an ordinary degree

ho¹ (həʊ) *interj* **1** Also called: ho-ho an imitation or representation of the sound of a deep laugh **2** an exclamation used to attract attention, announce a destination, etc [c13: of imitative origin; compare Old

Norse *hó*, Old French *ho! halt!*]

ho² (həʊ) *n US Black slang* a derogatory term for a woman [c20: from Black or Southern US pronunciation of WHORE]

Ho *the chemical symbol for* holmium

hoar (hɔː) *n* **1** short for **hoarfrost** ▷ *adj* **2** *rare* covered with hoarfrost **3** *archaic* a poetic variant of **hoary** [Old English *hār*; related to Old Norse *hārr*, Old High German *hēr*, Old Slavonic *sěrŭ* grey]

hoard (hɔːd) *n* **1** an accumulated store hidden away for future use **2** a cache of ancient coins, treasure, etc ▷ *vb* **3** to gather or accumulate (a hoard) [Old English *hord*; related to Old Norse *hodd*, Gothic *huzd*, German *Hort*, Swedish *hydda* hut] > 'hoarder *n*

hoarding ('hɔːdɪŋ) *n* **1** a large board used for displaying advertising posters, as by a road. Also called (esp US and Canadian): billboard **2** a temporary wooden fence erected round a building or demolition site [c19: from c15 *hoard* fence, from Old French *hourd* palisade, of Germanic origin, related to Gothic *haurds*, Old Norse *hurth* door]

hoarfrost ('hɔːˌfrɒst) *n* a deposit of needle-like ice crystals formed on the ground by direct condensation at temperatures below freezing point. Also called: white frost

hoarhound ('hɔːˌhaʊnd) *n* a variant spelling of **horehound**

hoarse (hɔːs) *adj* **1** gratingly harsh or raucous in tone **2** having a husky voice, as through illness, shouting, etc [c14: of Scandinavian origin; related to Old Norse *hās*, Old Saxon *hēs*] > 'hoarsely *adv* > 'hoarseness *n*

hoarsen ('hɔːsⁿn) *vb* to make or become hoarse

hoary ('hɔːrɪ) *adj* hoarier, hoariest **1** having grey or white hair **2** white or whitish-grey in colour **3** ancient or venerable > 'hoariness *n*

hoatzin (həʊˈætsɪn) *or* **hoactzin** *n* a unique South American gallinaceous bird, *Opisthocomus hoazin*, with a brownish plumage, a very small crested head, and clawed wing digits in the young: family *Opisthocomidae* [c17: from American Spanish, from Nahuatl *uatzin* pheasant]

hoax (həʊks) *n* **1** a deception, esp a practical joke ▷ *vb* **2** (*tr*) to deceive or play a joke on (someone) [c18: probably from HOCUS] > 'hoaxer *n*

hob¹ (hɒb) *n* **1** the flat top part of a cooking stove, or a separate flat surface, containing hotplates or burners **2** a shelf beside an open fire, for keeping kettles, etc, hot **3** a steel pattern used in forming a mould or die in cold metal [c16: variant of obsolete *hubbe*, of unknown origin; perhaps related to HUB]

hob² (hɒb) *n* **1** a hobgoblin or elf **2** raise hob *or* play hob *US informal* to cause mischief or disturbance **3** a male ferret [c14: variant of *Rob*, short for *Robin* or *Robert*]

Hobart ('həʊbɑːt) *n* a port in Australia, capital of the island state of Tasmania on the estuary of the Derwent: excellent natural harbour; University of Tasmania (1890). Pop: 126 048 (2001)

Hobbema ('hɒbɪmə; *Dutch* 'hɔbəmɑː) *n* **Meindert** ('maɪndərt). 1638–1709, Dutch painter of peaceful landscapes, usually including a watermill

Hobbes (hɒbz) *n* **Thomas.** 1588–1679, English political philosopher. His greatest work is the *Leviathan* (1651), which contains his defence of absolute sovereignty > 'Hobbesian *n, adj*

hobbit ('hɒbɪt) *n* one of an imaginary race of half-size people living in holes [c20: coined by British writer J. R. R. Tolkien (1892–1973), with the meaning "hole-builder"]

hobble ('hɒbⁿl) *vb* **1** (*intr*) to walk with a lame awkward movement **2** (*tr*) to fetter the legs of (a horse) in order to restrict movement **3** to progress unevenly or with difficulty ▷ *n* **4** a strap, rope, etc, used to hobble a horse **5** a limping gait [c14: probably from Low German; compare Flemish *hoppelen*, Middle Dutch *hobbelen* to stammer] > 'hobbler *n*

hobbledehoy (ˌhɒbⁿldɪˈhɔɪ) *n archaic or dialect* a clumsy or bad-mannered youth [c16: from earlier *hobbard de hoy*, of uncertain origin]

Hobbs (hɒbz) *n* Sir **John Berry**, known as *Jack Hobbs*. 1882–1963, English cricketer: scored 197 centuries

hobby¹ ('hɒbɪ) *n*, *pl* **-bies 1** an activity pursued in spare time for pleasure or relaxation **2** *archaic or dialect* a small horse or pony **3** short for **hobbyhorse** (sense 1) **4** an early form of bicycle, without pedals [C14 *hobyn*, probably variant of proper name *Robin*; compare DOBBIN] > **'hobbyist** *n*

hobby² ('hɒbɪ) *n*, *pl* **-bies** any of several small Old World falcons, esp the European *Falco subbuteo*, formerly used in falconry [C15: from Old French *hobet*, from *hobe* falcon; probably related to Middle Dutch *hobbelen* to roll, turn]

hobbyhorse ('hɒbɪ,hɔːs) *n* **1** a toy consisting of a stick with a figure of a horse's head at one end **2** another word for **rocking horse 3** a figure of a horse attached to a performer's waist in a pantomime, morris dance, etc **4** a favourite topic or obsessive fixed idea (esp in the phrase **on one's hobbyhorse**) [C16: from HOBBY¹, originally a small horse, hence sense 3; then generalized to apply to any pastime]

hobgoblin (,hɒb'gɒblɪn) *n* **1** an evil or mischievous goblin **2** a bogey; bugbear [C16: from HOB² + GOBLIN]

hobnail ('hɒb,neɪl) *n* **a** a short nail with a large head for protecting the soles of heavy footwear **b** (*as modifier*): *hobnail boots* [C16: from HOB¹ (in the archaic sense: peg) + NAIL] > **'hob,nailed** *adj*

hobnob ('hɒb,nɒb) *vb* **-nobs**, **-nobbing**, **-nobbed** (*intr*; often foll by *with*) **1** to socialize or talk informally **2** *obsolete* to drink (with) [C18: from *hob* or *nob* to drink to one another in turns, hence, to be familiar, ultimately from Old English *habban* to HAVE + *nabban* not to have]

hobo ('həʊbəʊ) *n*, *pl* **-bos** *or* **-boes** *chiefly US & Canadian* **1** a tramp; vagrant **2** a migratory worker, esp an unskilled labourer [C19 (US): origin unknown] > **'hoboism** *n*

Hoboken ('həʊbəʊkən) *n* a city in N Belgium, in Antwerp province, on the River Scheldt. Pop: 33 476 (2002 est)

Hobson's choice ('hɒbsªnz) *n* the choice of taking what is offered or nothing at all [C16: named after Thomas *Hobson* (1544–1631), English liveryman who gave his customers no choice but had them take the nearest horse]

Hochheimer ('hɒk,haɪmə; *German* 'hɔːxhaɪmər) *n* a German white wine from the area around Hochheim near Mainz. Also called: **Hochheim**

Hochhuth (*German* 'hɔːxhuːt) *n* **Rolf** (rɔlf). born 1933, Swiss dramatist. His best-known works are the controversial documentary drama *The Representative* (1963), on the papacy's attitude to the Jews in World War II, *Soldiers* (1967), *German Love Story* (1980), and *Wessis in Weimar* (1992)

Ho Chi Minh ('həʊ 'tʃiː 'mɪn) *n* original name *Nguyen That Tan*. 1890–1969, Vietnamese statesman; president of North Vietnam (1954–69). He headed the Vietminh (1941), which won independence for Vietnam from the French (1954)

Ho Chi Minh City ('həʊ 'tʃiː 'mɪn) *n* a port in S Vietnam, 97 km (60 miles) from the South China Sea, on the Saigon River: captured by the French in 1859; merged with adjoining Cholon in 1932; capital of the former Republic of Vietnam (South Vietnam) from 1954 to 1976; university (1917); US headquarters during the Vietnam War. Pop: 5 030 000 (2005 est). Former name (until 1976): **Saigon**

hock¹ (hɒk) *n* **1** the joint at the tarsus of a horse or similar animal, pointing backwards and corresponding to the human ankle ⊳ *vb* **2** another word for **hamstring** [C16: short for *hockshin*, from Old English *hōhsinu* heel sinew]

hock² (hɒk) *n* any of several white wines from the German Rhine [C17: short for obsolete *hockamore* HOCHHEIMER]

hock³ (hɒk) *informal, chiefly US & Canadian* ⊳ *vb* **1** (*tr*) to pawn or pledge ⊳ *n* **2** the state of being in pawn (esp in the phrase **in hock**) **3** in hock **a** in prison **b** in debt **c** in pawn [C19: from Dutch *hok* prison, debt]

hockey ('hɒkɪ) *n* **1** Also called (esp US and Canadian): **field hockey a** a game played on a field by two opposing teams of 11 players each, who try to hit a ball into their opponents' goal using long sticks curved at the end **b** (*as modifier*): *hockey stick* 2 See **ice hockey** [C19: from earlier *hawkey*, of unknown origin]

Hockney ('hɒknɪ) *n* **David**. born 1937, English painter, best known for his etchings, such as those to Cavafy's poems (1966), naturalistic portraits such as *Mr and Mrs Clark and Percy* (1971), and for paintings of water, swimmers, and swimming pools

hocus ('həʊkəs) *vb* **-cuses**, **-cusing**, **-cused** *or* **-cuses**, **-cussing**, **-cussed** (*tr*) *now rare* **1** to take in; trick **2** to stupefy, esp with a drug **3** to add a drug to (a drink)

hocus-pocus ('həʊkəs'pəʊkəs) *n* **1** trickery or chicanery **2** an incantation used by conjurors or magicians when performing tricks **3** conjuring skill or practice ⊳ *vb* **-cuses**, **-cusing**, **-cused** *or* **-cuses**, **-cussing**, **-cussed 4** to deceive or trick (someone) [C17: perhaps a dog-Latin formation invented by jugglers]

hod (hɒd) *n* **1** an open metal or plastic box fitted with a handle, for carrying bricks, mortar, etc **2** a tall narrow coal scuttle [C14: perhaps alteration of C13 dialect *hot*, from Old French *hotte* pannier, creel, probably from Germanic]

Hodeida (hɒ'deɪdə) *n* a port in N Yemen, on the Red Sea. Pop: 547 000 (2005 est)

hodgepodge ('hɒdʒ,pɒdʒ) *n US & Canadian* **1** a jumbled mixture **2** a thick soup or stew made from meat and vegetables ⊳ Also called (in Britain and certain other countries): **hotchpotch** [C15: variant of HOTCHPOT]

Hodgkin ('hɒdʒkɪn) *n* **1** Sir **Alan Lloyd**. 1914–98, English physiologist. With A. F. Huxley, he explained the conduction of nervous impulses in terms of the physical and chemical changes involved: shared the Nobel prize for physiology or medicine (1963) **2** **Dorothy Crowfoot**. 1910–94, English chemist and crystallographer, who determined the three-dimensional structure of insulin: Nobel prize for chemistry (1964) **3** Sir **Howard**. born 1932, British painter, noted for his brightly coloured semi-abstract works

Hodgkin's disease ('hɒdʒkɪnz) *n* a malignant disease, a form of lymphoma, characterized by painless enlargement of the lymph nodes, spleen, and liver [C19: named after Thomas *Hodgkin* (1798–1866), London physician, who first described it]

hodograph ('hɒdə,grɑːf, -græf) *n* a curve of which the radius vector represents the velocity of a moving particle [C19: from Greek *hodos* way + -GRAPH]

hodometer (hɒ'dɒmɪtə) *n US* another name for **odometer** > **ho'dometry** *n*

hoe (həʊ) *n* **1** any of several kinds of long-handled hand implement equipped with a light blade and used to till the soil, eradicate weeds, etc ⊳ *vb* **hoes**, **hoeing**, **hoed 2** to dig, scrape, weed, or till (surface soil) with or as if with a hoe [C14: via Old French *houe* from Germanic: compare Old High German *houwā*, *houwan* to HEW, German *Haue* hoe] > **'hoer** *n*

hoedown ('həʊ,daʊn) *n US & Canadian* **1** a boisterous square dance **2** a party at which hoedowns are danced

Hoek van Holland ('huːk fɑn 'hɔlɑnt) *n* the Dutch name for the **Hook of Holland**

Hofei ('həʊ'feɪ) *n* a variant transliteration of the Chinese name for **Hefei**

Hoffman ('hɒfmən) *n* **Dustin** (**Lee**) ('dʌstɪn). born 1937, US stage and film actor. His films include *The Graduate* (1967), *Midnight Cowboy* (1969), *All the President's Men* (1976), *Kramer vs Kramer* (1979), *Rain Man* (1989), *Accidental Hero* (1992), and *Moonlight Mile* (2002)

Hofmann ('hɒfmən) *n* **Hans**. 1880–1966, US painter, born in Germany: a pioneer of the abstract expressionist style

Hofmannsthal (*German* 'hoːfmanstaːl) *n* **Hugo von** ('huːgo fɔn). 1874–1929, Austrian lyric poet and dramatist, noted as the librettist for Richard Strauss' operas, esp *Der Rosenkavalier* (1911), *Elektra* (1909), and *Ariadne auf Naxos* (1912)

Hofuf (hɒ'fuːf) *n* another name for **Al Hufuf**

hog (hɒg) *n* **1** a domesticated pig, esp a castrated male weighing more than 102 kg **2** *US & Canadian* any artiodactyl mammal of the family *Suidae*; pig **3** Also called: **hogg** *Brit dialect*, *Austral & NZ* another name for **hogget 4** *informal* a selfish, greedy or slovenly person **5** **go the whole hog** *informal* to do something thoroughly or unreservedly ⊳ *vb* **hogs**, **hogging**, **hogged** (*tr*) **6** *slang* to take more than one's share of **7** to arch (the back) like a hog **8** to cut (the mane) of (a horse) very short [Old English *hogg*, from Celtic; compare Cornish *hoch*] ▷ **'hogger** *n* ▷ **'hog,like** *adj*

hogan ('həʊgən) *n* a wooden dwelling covered with earth, typical of the Navaho Indians of N America [from Navaho]

Hogan ('həʊgən) *n* **Ben,** full name *William Benjamin Hogan.* 1912–97, US golfer

Hogarth ('həʊgɑː:θ) *n* **William.** 1697–1764, English engraver and painter. He is noted particularly for his series of engravings satirizing the vices and affectations of his age, such as *A Rake's Progress* (1735) and *Marriage à la Mode* (1745) ▷ **Ho'garthian** *adj*

hogback ('hɒg,bæk) *n* **1** Also called: **hog's back** a narrow ridge that consists of steeply inclined rock strata **2** *archaeol* a Saxon or Scandinavian tomb with sloping sides

hogfish ('hɒg,fɪʃ) *n, pl* **-fish** or **-fishes** a wrasse, *Lachnolaimus maximus,* that occurs in the Atlantic off the SE coast of North America. The head of the male resembles a pig's snout

Hogg (hɒg) *n* **1 James,** known as *the Ettrick Shepherd.* 1770–1835, Scottish poet and writer. His works include the volume of poems *The Queen's Wake* (1813) and the novel *The Confessions of a Justified Sinner* (1824) **2** Quintin See **Hailsham of St Marylebone**

hogget ('hɒgɪt) *n Brit dialect, Austral & NZ* a sheep up to the age of one year that has yet to be sheared

hoggish ('hɒgɪʃ) *adj* selfish, gluttonous, or dirty

Hogmanay (,hɒgmə'neɪ) *n* (*sometimes not capital*) New Year's Eve in Scotland [c17: Scottish and Northern English, perhaps from Norman French *hoguinane,* from Old French *aguillanneuf* the last day of the year; also, a New Year's eve gift]

hognose snake ('hɒg,nəʊz) *n* any North American nonvenomous colubrid snake of the genus *Heterodon,* having a trowel-shaped snout and inflating the body when alarmed. Also called: **puff adder**

hogshead ('hɒgz,hɛd) *n* **1** a unit of capacity, used esp for alcoholic beverages. It has several values, being 54 imperial gallons in the case of beer and 52.5 imperial gallons in the case of wine **2** a large cask used for shipment of wines and spirits [c14: of obscure origin]

hogtie ('hɒg,taɪ) *vb* **-ties, -tying, -tied** (*tr*) *chiefly US* **1** to tie together the legs or the arms and legs of **2** to impede, hamper, or thwart

Hogtown ('hɒg,taʊn) *n Canadian* a slang name for **Toronto**

hogwash ('hɒg,wɒʃ) *n* **1** *informal* nonsense **2** pigswill

hogweed ('hɒg,wiːd) *n* any of several coarse weedy umbelliferous plants, esp cow parsnip

Hogwood ('hɒgwʊd) *n* **Christopher (Jarvis Haley).** born 1941, British harpsichordist, conductor, and musicologist; founder and director of the Academy of Ancient Music (1973–2006)

Hohenlohe ('həʊən,ləʊə; *German* 'kloːtvɪç) *n* **Chlodwig,** Prince of Hohenlohe-Schillingsfürst. 1819–1901, Prussian statesman; chancellor of the German empire (1894–1900)

Hohenstaufen ('həʊən,ʃtaʊfən; *German* hoːən'ʃtaufən) *n* a German princely family that provided rulers of Germany (1138–1208, 1215–54), Sicily (1194–1268), and the Holy Roman Empire (1138–1254)

Hohenzollern ('həʊən,zɒlən; *German* hoːən'tsɔlərn) *n* a German noble family, the younger (Franconian) branch of which provided rulers of Brandenburg (1417–1701) and Prussia (1701–1918). The last kings of Prussia (1871–1918) were also emperors of Germany

Hohhot ('hɒ'hɒt), **Huhehot** *or* **Hu-ho-hao-t'e** *n* a city in N China, capital of Inner Mongolia (since 1954); previously capital of the former Suiyüan province; Inner Mongolia University (1957). Pop: 998 000 (2005 est)

ho-hum ('həʊ,hʌm) *adj informal* lacking interest or inspiration; dull; mediocre: *a ho-hum album*

hoick (hɔɪk) *vb informal* to rise or raise abruptly and sharply [c20: perhaps a variant of *hike*]

hoi polloi (,hɔɪ pə'lɔɪ) *pl n often derogatory* the masses; common people [Greek, literally: the many]

hoisin (,hɔɪ'sɪn) *n* (in Chinese cookery) a sweet spicy reddish-brown sauce made from soya beans, sugar, vinegar, and garlic. Also called: **Peking sauce** [c20: from Cantonese]

hoist (hɔɪst) *vb* **1** (*tr*) to raise or lift up, esp by mechanical means ▷ *n* **2** any apparatus or device for hoisting **3** the act of hoisting **4** *nautical* a group of signal flags **5** the inner edge of a flag next to the staff [c16: variant of *hoise,* probably from Low German; compare Dutch *hijschen,* German *hissen*] ▷ **'hoister** *n*

hoity-toity (,hɔɪtɪ'tɔɪtɪ) *adj informal* arrogant or haughty [c17: rhyming compound based on C16 *hoit* to romp, of obscure origin]

hokey cokey ('həʊkɪ 'kəʊkɪ) *n* a Cockney song with a traditional dance routine to match the words

hokey-pokey (,həʊkɪ'pəʊkɪ) *n NZ* a brittle toffee sold in lumps

hoki ('həʊkiː) *n, pl* **hoki** an edible saltwater fish, *Macruronus novaezeelandiae,* of southern New Zealand waters [Māori]

Hokkaido (hɒ'kaɪdəʊ) *n* the second largest and northernmost of the four main islands of Japan, separated from Honshu by the Tsugaru Strait and from the island of Sakhalin, Russia, by La Pérouse Strait: constitutes an autonomous administrative division. Capital: Sapporo. Pop: 5 670 000 (2002 est). Area: 78 508 sq km (30 312 sq miles)

hokonui (həʊkə'nuːiː) *n NZ obsolete* illicit whisky [from *Hokonui,* district of Southland region, NZ]

hokum ('həʊkəm) *n slang* **1** claptrap; bunk **2** obvious or hackneyed material of a sentimental nature in a play, film, etc [c20: probably a blend of HOCUS-POCUS and BUNKUM]

Hokusai ('həʊkʊ,saɪ, ,həʊkʊ'saɪ) *n* **Katsushika** (,kætsu:'ʃiːkə). 1760–1849, Japanese artist, noted for the draughtsmanship of his colour wood-block prints, which influenced the impressionists

Holarctic (hɒʊ'lɑːktɪk) *adj* of or denoting a zoogeographical region consisting of the Palaearctic and Nearctic regions [c19: from HOLO- + ARCTIC]

Holbein (*German* 'hɔlbain) *n* **1 Hans** (hans), known as *Holbein the Elder.* 1465– 1524, German painter **2** his son, **Hans,** known as *Holbein the Younger.* 1497–1543, German painter and engraver; court painter to Henry VIII of England (1536–43). He is noted particularly for his portraits, such as those of Erasmus (1524; 1532) and Sir Thomas More (1526)

Holberg ('hɒlbɜːg) *n* **Ludvig,** Baron. 1684–1754, Danish playwright, poet, and historian, born in Norway: considered the founder of modern Danish literature

hold¹ (həʊld) *vb* **holds, holding, held** (hɛld) **1** to have or keep (an object) with or within the hands, arms, etc; clasp **2** (*tr*) to support or bear: *to hold a drowning man's head above water* **3** to maintain or be maintained in a specified state or condition: *to hold one's emotions in check; hold firm* **4** (*tr*) to set aside or reserve: *they will hold our tickets until tomorrow* **5** (when *intr, usually used in commands*) to restrain or be restrained from motion, action, departure, etc: *hold that man until the police come* **6** (*intr*) to remain fast or unbroken: *that cable won't hold much longer* **7** (*intr*) (of the weather) to remain dry and bright **8** (*tr*) to keep the attention of **9** (*tr*) to engage in or carry on: *to hold a meeting* **10** (*tr*) to have the ownership, possession, etc, of: *he holds a law degree from London; who's holding the ace of spades?* **11** (*tr*) to have the use of or responsibility for: *to hold the office of director* **12** (*tr*) to have the space or capacity for: *the carton will hold only eight books* **13** (*tr*) to be able to control the outward effects of drinking beer, spirits, etc **14** (often foll by *to* or *by*) to remain or cause to remain committed to: *hold him to his promise; he held by his views in spite of opposition* **15** (*tr; takes a clause as object*) to claim: *he holds that the theory is incorrect* **16** (*intr*) to remain relevant, valid, or true: *the old philosophies don't hold nowadays* **17** (*tr*) to regard or consider in a specified manner: *I hold him very dear* **18** (*tr*) to guard or defend successfully: *hold the fort against the attack* **19** (sometimes foll by *on*) *music* to sustain the sound of (a note) throughout its specified duration **20** (*tr*) *computing* to retain (data) in a storage device after copying onto another storage device or onto another location in the same device **21 hold for** or **hold good for** to apply or be relevant to: *the same rules hold for everyone* **22 there is no holding him** he is so spirited or resolute that he cannot be restrained ▷ *n* **23** the act or method of holding fast or grasping, as with the hands **24** something to hold onto, as for support or control **25** an object or device that holds fast or grips something else so as to hold it fast **26** controlling force or influence: *she has a hold on him* **27** a short delay or pause **28** a prison or a cell in a prison **29** *wrestling* a way of seizing one's opponent **30** *music* a pause or fermata **31 a** a tenure or holding, esp of land **b** (*in combination*): *leasehold; freehold; copyhold* **32** *archaic* a fortified place **33 no holds barred** all limitations removed ▷ *See also* **hold back, hold down, hold forth, hold in, hold off, hold on, hold out, hold over, hold-up, hold with** [Old English *healdan*; related to Old Norse *halla*, Gothic *haldan*, German *halten*] ▷ **'holdable** *adj*

hold² ('həʊld) *n* the space in a ship or aircraft for storing cargo [c16: variant of HOLE]

holdall ('həʊld,ɔːl) *n Brit* a large strong bag with handles

hold back *vb* (*adverb*) **1** to restrain or be restrained **2** (*tr*) to withhold: *he held back part of the payment*

hold down *vb* (*tr, adverb*) **1** to restrain or control **2** *informal* to manage to retain or keep possession of: *to hold down two jobs at once*

holder ('həʊldə) *n* **1 a** a person or thing that holds **2 a a** person, such as an owner, who has possession or control of something **b** (*in combination*): *householder* **3** *law* a person who has possession of a bill of exchange, cheque, or promissory note that he is legally entitled to enforce

Hölderlin (German 'hœldərliːn) *n* **Friedrich** ('friːdrɪç). 1770–1843, German lyric poet, whose works include the poems *Menon's Lament for Diotima* and *Bread and Wine* and the novel *Hyperion* (1797–99)

holdfast ('həʊld,faːst) *n* **1** the act of gripping strongly **2** any device used to secure an object, such as a hook, clamp, etc **3** the organ of attachment of a seaweed or related plant

hold forth *vb* (*adverb*) **1** (*intr*) to speak for a long time or in public **2** (*tr*) to offer (an attraction or enticement)

hold in *vb* (*tr, adverb*) **1** to curb, control, or keep in check **2** to conceal or restrain (feelings)

holding ('həʊldɪŋ) *n* **1** land held under a lease and used for agriculture or similar purposes **2** (*often plural*) property to which the holder has legal title, such as land, stocks, shares, and other investments **3** *sport* the obstruction of an opponent with the hands or arms, esp in boxing ▷ *adj* **4** *Austral informal* in funds; having money

holding company *n* a company with controlling shareholdings in one or more other companies

holding operation *n* a plan or procedure devised to prolong the existing situation

holding paddock *n Austral & NZ* a paddock in which cattle or sheep are kept temporarily, as before shearing, etc

holding pattern *n* the oval or circular path of an aircraft flying around an airport awaiting permission to land

hold off *vb* (*adverb*) **1** (*tr*) to keep apart or at a distance **2** (*intr*; often foll by *from*) to refrain (from doing something)

hold on *vb* (*intr, adverb*) **1** to maintain a firm grasp **2** to continue or persist **3** (foll by *to*) to keep or retain: *hold on to those stamps as they'll soon be valuable* **4** to keep a telephone line open ▷ *interj* **5** *informal* stop! wait!

hold out *vb* (*adverb*) **1** (*tr*) to offer or present **2** (*intr*) to last or endure **3** (*intr*) to continue to resist or stand firm, as a city under siege or a person refusing to succumb to persuasion **4** *chiefly US* to withhold (something due or expected) **5 hold out for** to wait patiently or uncompromisingly for (the fulfilment of one's demands) **6 hold out on** *informal* to delay in or keep from telling (a person) some new or important information

hold over *vb* (*tr, mainly adverb*) **1** to defer consideration of or action on **2** (*preposition*) to intimidate (a person) with (a threat)

hold-up *n* **1** a robbery, esp an armed one **2** a delay;

stoppage ▷ *vb* **hold up** (*adverb*) **3** (*tr*) to delay; hinder **4** (*tr*) to keep from falling; support **5** (*tr*) to stop forcibly or waylay in order to rob, esp using a weapon **6** (*tr*) to exhibit or present

hold with *vb* (*intr, preposition*) to support; approve of

hole (həʊl) *n* **1** an area hollowed out in a solid **2** an opening made in or through something **3** an animal's hiding place or burrow **4** *informal* an unattractive place, such as a town or a dwelling **5** a fault (esp in the phrase **pick holes in**) **6** *slang* a difficult and embarrassing situation **7** the cavity in various games into which the ball must be thrust **8** (on a golf course) **a** each of the divisions of a course (usually 18) represented by the distance between the tee and a green **b** the score made in striking the ball from the tee into the hole **9** *physics* a vacancy in a nearly full band of quantum states of electrons in a semiconductor or an insulator. Under the action of an electric field holes behave as carriers of positive charge **10 in holes** so worn as to be full of holes **11 make a hole in** to consume or use a great amount of (food, drink, money, etc) ▷ *vb* **12** to make a hole or holes in (something) **13** (when *intr*, often foll by *out*) *golf* to hit (the ball) into the hole [Old English *hol*; related to Gothic *hulundi*, German *Höhle*, Old Norse *hylr* pool, Latin *caulis* hollow stem; see HOLLOW]

hole-and-corner *adj* (usually prenominal) *informal* furtive or secretive

hole in one *n golf* a shot from the tee that finishes in the hole. Also called (esp US): **ace**

hole in the heart *n* a defect of the heart in which there is an abnormal opening in any of the walls dividing the four heart chambers

hole in the wall *n informal* **1** *chiefly Brit* another name for: **cash dispenser 2** a small dingy place, esp one difficult to find

hole up *vb* (*intr, adverb*) **1** (of an animal) to hibernate, esp in a cave **2** *informal* to hide or remain secluded

Holguín (Spanish ɔl'ɣin) *n* a city in NE Cuba, in Holguín province: trading centre. Pop: 278 000 (2005 est)

Holi ('hɒˌliː) *n* a Hindu spring festival, celebrated for two to five days, commemorating Krishna's dalliance with the cowgirls. Bonfires are lit and coloured powder and water thrown over celebrants [named after *Holika*, legendary female demon]

-holic *suffix forming nouns* indicating a person having an abnormal desire for or dependence on: *workaholic; chocoholic* [c20: on the pattern of *alcoholic*]

holiday ('hɒlɪˌdeɪ, -dɪ) *n* **1** (*often plural*) *chiefly Brit* a period in which a break is taken from work or studies for rest, travel, or recreation. US and Canadian word: **vacation 2** a day on which work is suspended by law or custom, such as a religious festival, bank holiday, etc. Related adj: **ferial** ▷ *vb* **3** (*intr*) *chiefly Brit* to spend a holiday [Old English *hāligdæg*, literally: holy day]

Holiday ('hɒlɪˌdeɪ) *n* **Billie**. real name *Eleanora Fagan*; known as *Lady Day*. 1915–59, US jazz singer

holiday camp *n Brit* a place, esp one at the seaside, providing accommodation, recreational facilities, etc, for holiday-makers

holiday-maker *n Brit* a person who goes on holiday. US and Canadian equivalents: **vacationer, vacationist**

holily ('həʊlɪlɪ) *adv* in a holy, devout, or sacred manner

holiness ('həʊlɪnɪs) *n* the state or quality of being holy

Holiness ('həʊlɪnɪs) *n* (preceded by *his* or *your*) a title once given to all bishops, but now reserved for the pope

Holinshed ('hɒlɪnˌʃed) or **Holingshed** *n* **Raphael**. died ?1580, English chronicler. His *Chronicles of England, Scotland, and Ireland* (1577) provided material for Shakespeare's historical and legendary plays

holism ('həʊlɪzəm) *n* **1** any doctrine that a system may have properties over and above those of its parts and their organization **2** the treatment of any subject as a whole integrated system, esp, in medicine, the consideration of the complete person, physically and psychologically, in the treatment of a disease [c20: from HOLO- + -ISM]

holistic (həʊ'lɪstɪk) *adj* **1** of or relating to a doctrine of holism **2** of or relating to the medical consideration of the complete person, physically and psychologically,

h

in the treatment of a disease ▷ ho'listically *adv*

Holkar State (ˈhɒlˈkɑː) *n* a former state of central India, ruled by the Holkar dynasty of Maratha rulers of Indore (18th century until 1947)

holland (ˈhɒlənd) *n* a coarse linen cloth, used esp for furnishing [c15: after HOLLAND, where it was made]

Holland¹ (ˈhɒlənd) *n* 1 another name for the **Netherlands** 2 a county of the Holy Roman Empire, corresponding to the present-day North and South Holland provinces of the Netherlands 3 Parts of an area in E England constituting a former administrative division of Lincolnshire

Holland² (ˈhɒlənd) *n* 1 Henry. 1745–1806, British neoclassical architect. His work includes Brooks's Club (1776) and Carlton House (1783), both in London 2 Sir **Sidney George.** 1893–1961, New Zealand statesman; prime minister of New Zealand (1949–57)

hollandaise sauce (ˌhɒlənˈdeɪz, ˈhɒlənˌdeɪz) *n* a rich sauce of egg yolks, butter, vinegar, etc, served esp with fish [c19: from French *sauce hollandaise* Dutch sauce]

Hollandia (hɒˈlændɪə) *n* a former name of **Jayapura**

Hollands (ˈhɒləndz) *n* Dutch gin, often sold in stone bottles [c18: from Dutch *hollandsch genever*]

holler (ˈhɒlə) *informal* ▷ *vb* 1 to shout or yell (something) ▷ *n* 2 a shout; call [variant of C16 *hollow*, from *holla*, from French *holà* stop! (literally: ho there!)]

Holliger (German ˈhɔlɪgə) *n* **Heinz** (haints). born 1939, Swiss oboist and composer

hollo (ˈhɒləʊ), **holla** (ˈhɒlə) *or* **holloa** (həˈləʊ) *n*, *pl* -los, -las *or* -loas (-ˈləʊz) 1 a cry for attention, or of encouragement ▷ *vb* 2 (*intr*) to shout [c16: from French *holà* ho there!]

hollow (ˈhɒləʊ) *adj* 1 having a sunken area; concave 2 recessed or deeply set: *hollow cheeks* 3 (of sounds) as if resounding in a hollow place 4 without substance or validity 5 hungry or empty 6 insincere; cynical ▷ *adv* 7 beat someone hollow *Brit informal* to defeat someone thoroughly and convincingly ▷ *n* 8 a cavity, opening, or space in or within something 9 a depression or dip in the land ▷ *vb* (often foll by *out*, usually when *tr*) 10 to make or become hollow 11 to form (a hole, cavity, etc) or (of a hole, etc) to be formed [c12: from *holu*, inflected form of Old English *holh* cave; related to Old Norse *holr*, German *hohl*; see HOLE] ▷ 'hollowly *adv* ▷ 'hollowness *n*

hollow-eyed *adj* with the eyes appearing to be sunk into the face, as from excessive fatigue

holly (ˈhɒlɪ) *n*, *pl* -lies 1 any tree or shrub of the genus *Ilex*, such as the Eurasian *I. aquifolium*, having bright red berries and shiny evergreen leaves with prickly edges 2 branches of any of these trees, used for Christmas decorations 3 holly oak another name for **holm oak** ▷ See also **sea holly** [Old English *holegn*; related to Old Norse *hulfr*, Old High German *hulis*, German *Hulst*, Old Slavonic *kolja* prick]

Holly (ˈhɒlɪ) *n* **Buddy.** real name *Charles Harden Holley.* 1936–59, US rock-and-roll singer, guitarist, and songwriter. His hits (all 1956–59) include "That'll be the Day", "Maybe Baby", "Peggy Sue", "Oh, Boy", "Think it over", and "It doesn't Matter anymore"

hollyhock (ˈhɒlɪˌhɒk) *n* a tall widely cultivated malvaceous plant, *Althaea rosea*, with stout hairy stems and spikes of white, yellow, red, or purple flowers [c16: from HOLY + *hock*, from Old English *hoc* mallow]

Hollywood (ˈhɒlɪˌwʊd) *n* 1 a NW suburb of Los Angeles, California: centre of the American film industry. Pop: 167 664 (2000) 2 a the American film industry b (*as modifier*): *a Hollywood star*

holm¹ (həʊm) *n* *dialect, chiefly Northwestern English* 1 an island in a river, lake, or estuary 2 low flat land near a river [Old English *holm* sea, island; related to Old Saxon *holm* hill, Old Norse *holmr* island, Latin *culmen* tip]

holm² (həʊm) *n* 1 short for **holm oak** 2 *chiefly Brit* a dialect word for **holly** [c14: variant of obsolete *holin*, from Old English *holegn* HOLLY]

Holmes (həʊmz) *n* 1 **Oliver Wendell.** 1809–94, US author, esp of humorous essays, such as *The Autocrat of the Breakfast Table* (1858) and its sequels 2 his son, **Oliver Wendell.** 1841–1935, US jurist, noted for his liberal judgments 3 **Paul.** born 1950, New Zealand radio and

television broadcaster; presenter of *The Paul Holmes Breakfast*, a popular breakfast radio show, since 1987

holmium (ˈhɒlmɪəm) *n* a malleable silver-white metallic element of the lanthanide series. Symbol: Ho; atomic no: 67; atomic wt: 164.93032; valency: 3; relative density: 8.795; melting pt: 1474°C; boiling pt: 2700°C [c19: from New Latin *Holmia* Stockholm]

holm oak *n* an evergreen Mediterranean oak tree, *Quercus ilex*, widely planted for ornament: the leaves are holly-like when young but become smooth-edged with age. Also called: **holm, holly oak, ilex**

holo- *or before a vowel* **hol-** *combining form* whole or wholly: *holograph*; *holotype*; *Holarctic* [from Greek *holos*]

holocaust (ˈhɒləˌkɔːst) *n* 1 great destruction or loss of life or the source of such destruction, esp fire 2 (*usually capital*) the Holocaust Also called: Churban, Shoah the mass murder of Jews and members of many other ethnic, social, and political groups in continental Europe between 1940 and 1945 by the Nazi regime 3 a rare word for **burnt offering** [c13: from Late Latin *holocaustum* whole burnt offering, from Greek *holokauston*, from HOLO- + *kaustos*, from *kaiein* to burn]

Holocene (ˈhɒləˌsiːn) *adj* 1 of, denoting, or formed in the second and most recent epoch of the Quaternary period, which began 10 000 years ago at the end of the Pleistocene ▷ *n* 2 the Holocene the Holocene epoch or rock series ▷ Also called: Recent

Holofernes (ˌhɒləˈfɜːniːz, həˈlɒfəˌniːz) *n* the Assyrian general, who was killed by the biblical heroine Judith

hologram (ˈhɒləˌgræm) *n* a photographic record produced by illuminating the object with coherent light (as from a laser) and, without using lenses, exposing a film to light reflected from this object and to a direct beam of coherent light. When interference patterns on the film are illuminated by the coherent light a three-dimensional image is produced

holograph (ˈhɒləˌgrɑːf, -ˌgrɑːf) *n* a book or document handwritten by its author; original manuscript; autograph

holography (hɒˈlɒgrəfɪ) *n* the science or practice of producing holograms ▷ ˌholoˈgraphic *adj* ▷ ˌholoˈgraphically *adv*

holohedral (ˌhɒləˈhiːdrəl) *adj* (of a crystal) exhibiting all the planes required for the symmetry of the crystal system

holophytic (ˌhɒləˈfɪtɪk) *adj* (of plants) capable of synthesizing their food from inorganic molecules, esp by photosynthesis

holothurian (ˌhɒləˈθjʊərɪən) *n* 1 any echinoderm of the class *Holothuroidea*, including the sea cucumbers, having a leathery elongated body with a ring of tentacles around the mouth ▷ *adj* 2 of, relating to, or belonging to the *Holothuroidea* [c19: from New Latin *Holothūria* name of type genus, from Latin: water polyp, from Greek *holothourion*, of obscure origin]

hols (hɒlz) *pl n* *Brit school slang* holidays

Holst (həʊlst) *n* 1 **Alison.** born 1938, New Zealand chef. 2 **Gustav (Theodore).** 1874–1934, English composer. His works include operas, choral music, and orchestral music such as the suite *The Planets* (1917)

Holstein (German ˈhɔlʃtain) *n* a region of N Germany, in S Schleswig-Holstein: in early times a German duchy of Saxony; became a duchy of Denmark in 1474; finally incorporated into Prussia in 1866

holster (ˈhəʊlstə) *n* a sheathlike leather case for a pistol, attached to a belt or saddle [c17: via Dutch *holster* from Germanic; compare Old Norse *hulstr* sheath, Old English *heolstor* darkness, Gothic *hulistr* cover]

holt¹ (həʊlt) *n* *archaic or poetic* a wood or wooded hill [Old English *holt*; related to Old Norse *holt*, Old High German *holz*, Old Slavonic *kladū* log, Greek *klados* twig]

holt² (həʊlt) *n* the burrowed lair of an animal, esp an otter [c16: a phonetic variant of HOLD²]

Holt (həʊlt) *n* **Harold Edward.** 1908–67, Australian statesman; prime minister (1966–67); believed drowned

holy (ˈhəʊlɪ) *adj* holier, holiest 1 of, relating to, or associated with God or a deity; sacred 2 endowed or invested with extreme purity or sublimity 3 devout, godly, or virtuous 4 holier-than-thou offensively sanctimonious or self-righteous ▷ *n, pl* -lies **5** a sacred place [Old English *hālig, hǣlig*; related to Old Saxon *hēlag*, Gothic *hailags*, German *heilig*; see HALLOW]

Holy Communion *n* **1** the celebration of the Eucharist **2** the consecrated elements of the Eucharist

holy day *n* a day on which a religious festival is observed

Holy Father *n RC Church* a title of the pope

Holy Ghost *n* another name for the **Holy Spirit**

Holy Grail *n* **1** Also called: Grail, Sangraal (in medieval legend) the bowl used by Jesus at the Last Supper. It was allegedly brought to Britain by Joseph of Arimathea, where it became the quest of many knights **2** *informal* any desired ambition or goal: *the Holy Grail of infrared astronomy* [C14 *grail* from Old French *graal*, from Medieval Latin *gradālis* bowl, of unknown origin]

Holyhead ('hɒlɪ,hɛd) *n* a town in NW Wales, in Anglesey, the chief town of Holy Island: a port on the N coast. Pop: 11 237 (2001)

Holy Island *n* **1** Also called: Lindisfarne an island off the NE coast of Northumberland, linked to the mainland by road but accessible only at low water: site of a monastery founded by St Aidan in 635 **2** an island off the NW coast of Anglesey. Area: about 62 sq km (24 sq miles)

Holy Land *n* the another name for **Palestine** (sense 1)

Holyoake ('həʊlɪ,əʊk) *n* Sir **Keith Jacka** ('dʒækə). 1904–83, New Zealand politician; prime minister (1957; 1960–72); governor general (1977–80)

holy of holies *n* **1** any place of special sanctity **2** (*capitals*) the innermost compartment of the Jewish tabernacle, and later of the Temple, where the Ark was enshrined

holy orders *pl n* **1** the sacrament or rite whereby a person is admitted to the Christian ministry **2** the grades of the Christian ministry **3** the rank or status of an ordained Christian minister ▷ See also **orders**

Holy Roman Empire *n* the complex of European territories under the rule of the Frankish or German king who bore the title of Roman emperor, beginning with the coronation of Charlemagne in 800 AD. The last emperor, Francis II, relinquished his crown in 1806

Holyrood ('hɒlɪ,ruːd, 'həʊlɪ,ruːd) *n* **1** the Scottish Parliament building in Edinburgh, located beside Holyroodhouse **2** *informal* the Scottish Government

Holy Scripture *n* another term for **Scripture**

Holy See *n RC Church* **1** the see of the pope as bishop of Rome and head of the Church **2** the Roman curia

Holy Spirit *or* Holy Ghost *n Christianity* the third person of the Trinity

holystone ('həʊlɪ,stəʊn) *n* **1** a soft sandstone used for scrubbing the decks of a vessel ▷ *vb* **2** (*tr*) to scrub (a vessel's decks) with a holystone [C19: perhaps so named from its being used in a kneeling position]

holy synod *n* the governing body of any of the Orthodox Churches

holy water *n* water that has been blessed by a priest for use in symbolic rituals of purification

Holy Week *n* the week preceding Easter Sunday

Holy Willie ('wɪlɪ) *n* a person who is hypocritically pious [c18: from Burns' *Holy Willie's Prayer*]

Holy Writ *n* another term for **Scripture**

homage ('hɒmɪdʒ) *n* **1** a public show of respect or honour towards someone or something (esp in the phrases **pay** *or* **do homage to**) **2** (in feudal society) the act of respect and allegiance made by a vassal to his lord [c13: from Old French, from *home* man, from Latin *homo*]

homburg ('hɒmbɜːɡ) *n* a man's hat of soft felt with a dented crown and a stiff upturned brim [c20: named after *Homburg*, in Germany, town where it was originally made]

home (həʊm) *n* **1** the place or a place where one lives **2** a house or other dwelling **3** a family or other group living in a house or other place **4** a person's country, city, etc, esp viewed as a birthplace, a residence during one's early years, or a place dear to one **5** the environment or habitat of a person or animal **6** the place where something is invented, founded, or developed **7** a building or organization set up to care for orphans, the aged, etc **8** *sport* one's own ground: *the match is at home*

9 a the objective towards which a player strives in certain sports **b** an area where a player is safe from attack **10** *NZ informal, obsolete* Britain, esp England **11** a home from home a place other than one's own home where one can be at ease **12** at home **a** in one's own home or country **b** at ease, as if at one's own home **c** giving an informal party at one's own home **13** at home in, at home on *or* at home with familiar or conversant with **14** home and dry *Brit informal* definitely safe or successful: *we will not be home and dry until the votes have been counted* **15** near home concerning one deeply ▷ *adj* (*usually prenominal*) **16** of, relating to, or involving one's home, country, etc; domestic **17** (of an activity) done in one's home area **18** *sport* relating to one's own ground: *a home game* **19** *US* central; principal: *the company's home office* ▷ *adv* **20** to or at home: *I'll be home tomorrow* **21** to or on the point **22** to the fullest extent: *hammer the nail home* **23** bring home to **a** to make clear to **b** to place the blame on **24** nothing to write home about *informal* to be of no particular interest: *the film was nothing to write home about* ▷ *vb* **25** (*intr*) (of birds and other animals) to return home accurately from a distance **26** (often foll by *on* or *onto*) to direct or be directed onto a point or target, esp by automatic navigational aids **27** to send or go home **28** to furnish with or have a home **29** (*intr*; often foll by *in* or *in on*) to be directed towards a goal, target, etc [Old English *hām*; related to Old Norse *heimr*, Gothic *haims*, Old High German *heim*, Dutch *heem*, Greek *kōmi* village] > 'home,like *adj*

Home (hjuːm) *n* Baron See (Baron) **Home of the Hirsel**

home-alone *adj informal* (esp of a young child) left in a house, flat, etc unattended

home banking *n* a system whereby a person at home or in an office can use a computer with a modem to call up information from a bank or to transfer funds electronically

homebirth ('həʊm,bɜːθ) *n* **1** the act of giving birth to a child in one's own home **2** an instance of a woman giving birth to a child at home: *a large increase in homebirths*

homeboy ('həʊm,bɔɪ) *n slang, chiefly US* **1** a close friend **2** a person from one's home town or neighbourhood [c20: US rap-music usage]

home brand *n Austral* **a** an item packaged and marketed under the brand name of a particular retailer, usually a large supermarket chain, rather than that of the manufacturer **b** (*as modifier*): *home-brand products* Also called (in certain other countries): **own brand**

home-brew *n* **1** a beer or other alcoholic drink brewed at home rather than commercially **2** *Canad informal* a professional football player who was born in Canada and is not an import > 'home-'brewed *adj*

homecoming ('həʊm,kʌmɪŋ) *n* **1** the act of coming home **2** *US* an annual celebration held by a university, college, or school, for former students

Home Counties *pl n* the counties surrounding London

home economics *n* (*functioning as singular or plural*) the study of diet, budgeting, child care, textiles, and other subjects concerned with running a home

home farm *n Brit* (esp formerly) a farm belonging to and providing food for a large country house

home ground *n* a familiar area or topic

Home Guard *n* a volunteer part-time military force recruited for the defence of the United Kingdom in World War II

home help *n social welfare* (in Britain and New Zealand) a person who is paid to do domestic chores for persons unable to look after themselves adequately

home invasion *n Austral & NZ* aggravated burglary

homeland ('həʊm,lænd) *n* **1** the country in which one lives or was born **2** the official name for a **Bantustan**

homeless ('həʊmlɪs) *adj* **a** having nowhere to live **b** (*as collective noun; preceded by the*): *the homeless* > 'homelessness *n*

homely ('həʊmlɪ) *adj* -lier, -liest **1** characteristic of or suited to the ordinary home; unpretentious **2** (of a person) **a** *Brit* warm and domesticated in manner or appearance **b** *chiefly US & Canadian* plain or ugly > 'homeliness *n*

home-made *adj* **1** (esp of cakes, jam, and other foods) made at home or on the premises, esp of high-quality ingredients **2** crudely fashioned

homeo-, homoeo- *or* **homoio-** *combining form* like or similar: *homeomorphism* [from Latin *homoeo-*, from Greek *homoio-*, from *homos* same]

Home Office *n Brit government* the national department responsible for the maintenance of law and order, immigration control, and all other domestic affairs not specifically assigned to another department

Home of the Hirsel (hjuːm, 'hɜːsəl) *n* Baron, title of *Sir Alec Douglas-Home*, formerly 14th Earl of Home. 1903–95, British Conservative statesman: he renounced his earldom to become prime minister of Great Britain and Northern Ireland (1963–64); foreign secretary (1970–74)

homeopathy *or* **homoeopathy** (ˌhəʊmɪˈɒpəθɪ) *n* a method of treating disease by the use of small amounts of a drug that, in healthy persons, produces symptoms similar to those of the disease being treated
> homeopathic *or* homoeopathic (ˌhəʊmɪəˈpæθɪk) *adj*
> homeopathist, homoeopathist (ˌhəʊmɪˈɒpəθɪst) *or* homeopath, homoeopath (ˈhəʊmɪəˌpæθ) *n*

homeostasis *or* **homoeostasis** (ˌhəʊmɪəʊˈsteɪsɪs) *n*
1 the maintenance of metabolic equilibrium within an animal by a tendency to compensate for disrupting changes **2** the maintenance of equilibrium within a social group, person, etc

homeowner (ˈhəʊmˌəʊnə) *n* a person who owns the house in which he or she lives > ˌhome'ownership *n*

home page *n computing* (on a website) the main document relating to an individual or institution that provides introductory information about a website with links to the actual details of services or information provided

homer (ˈhəʊmə) *n* another word for **homing pigeon**

Homer (ˈhəʊmə) *n* **1** c. 800 BC, Greek poet to whom are attributed the *Iliad* and the *Odyssey*. Almost nothing is known of him, but it is thought that he was born on the island of Chios and was blind **2 Winslow**. 1836–1910, US painter, noted for his seascapes and scenes of working life

Homeric (həʊˈmɛrɪk) *adj* **1** of, relating to, or resembling Homer (c. 800 BC), the Greek poet to whom are attributed the *Iliad* and the *Odyssey*, or his poems **2** imposing or heroic

homeroom (ˈhəʊmˌruːm, -ˌrʊm) *n US* **1** a room in a school used by a particular group of students as a base for registration, notices, etc **2** a group of students who use the same room as a base in school

home rule *n* the partial autonomy sometimes granted to a national minority or a colony

Home Rule *n* self-government for Ireland: the goal of the Irish Nationalists from about 1870 to 1920

home run *n baseball* a hit that enables the batter to run round all four bases, usually by hitting the ball out of the playing area

Home Secretary *n Brit government* short for **Secretary of State for the Home Department**; the head of the Home Office

homesick (ˈhəʊmˌsɪk) *adj* depressed or melancholy at being away from home and family > ˈhomeˌsickness *n*

homespun (ˈhəʊmˌspʌn) *adj* **1** having plain or unsophisticated character **2** woven or spun at home ▷ *n* **3** cloth made at home or made of yarn spun at home **4** a cloth resembling this but made on a power loom

homestead (ˈhəʊmˌstɛd, -stɪd) *n* **1** a house or estate and the adjoining land, buildings, etc, esp a farm **2** (in the US) a house and adjoining land designated by the owner as his fixed residence and exempt under the homestead laws from seizure and forced sale for debts **3** (in western Canada) a piece of land, usually 160 acres, granted to a settler by the federal government **4** *Austral & NZ* the owner's or manager's residence on a sheep or cattle station; in New Zealand the term includes all outbuildings

Homestead Act *n* **1** an act passed by the US Congress in 1862 making available to settlers 160-acre tracts of public land for cultivation **2** (in Canada) a similar act passed by the Canadian Parliament in 1872

homesteader (ˈhəʊmˌstɛdə) *n* **1** a person owning a

homestead **2** *US & Canadian* a person who acquires or possesses land under a homestead law

homestead law *n* (in the US and Canada) any of various laws conferring certain privileges on owners of homesteads

home straight *n* **1** *horse racing* the section of a racecourse forming the approach to the finish **2** the final stage of an undertaking or journey

home truth *n* (*often plural*) an unpleasant fact told to a person about himself

home unit *n Austral & NZ* a self-contained residence which is part of a series of similar residences. Often shortened to **unit**

homeward (ˈhəʊmwəd) *adj* **1** directed or going home **2** (of a ship, part of a voyage, etc) returning to the home port ▷ *adv* Also: **homewards 3** towards home

homeware (ˈhəʊmwɛə) *n* crockery, furniture, and furnishings with which a house, room, etc, is furnished [C20: HOME + WARE¹]

homework (ˈhəʊmˌwɜːk) *n* **1** school work done out of lessons, esp at home **2** any preparatory study **3** work done at home for pay

homey (ˈhəʊmɪ) *adj* homier, homiest a variant spelling (esp US) of **homy** > ˈhomeyness *n*

homicide (ˈhɒmɪˌsaɪd) *n* **1** the killing of a human being by another person **2** a person who kills another [C14: from Old French, from Latin *homo* man + *caedere* to slay] > ˌhomi'cidal *adj*

homicide bomber *n* another name for **suicide bomber**

homiletics (ˌhɒmɪˈlɛtɪks) *n* (*functioning as singular*) the art of preaching or writing sermons [C17: from Greek *homilētikos* cordial, from *homilein* to converse with; see HOMILY] > ˌhomi'letic *or* homiletical *adj*

homily (ˈhɒmɪlɪ) *n, pl* **-lies 1** a sermon or discourse on a moral or religious topic **2** moralizing talk or writing [C14: from Church Latin *homīlia*, from Greek: discourse, from *homilein* to converse with, from *homilos* crowd, from *homou* together + *ílē* crowd] > ˈhomilist *n*

homing (ˈhəʊmɪŋ) *n* (*modifier*) **1** *zoology* relating to the ability to return home after travelling great distances **2** (of an aircraft, a missile, etc) capable of guiding itself onto a target or to a specified point

homing pigeon *n* any breed of pigeon developed for its homing instinct, used for carrying messages or for racing. Also called: **homer**

hominid (ˈhɒmɪnɪd) *n* **1** any primate of the family Hominidae, which includes modern man (*Homo sapiens*) and the extinct precursors of man ▷ *adj* **2** of, relating to, or belonging to the Hominidae. [C19: via New Latin from Latin *homo* man + -ID¹]

hominoid (ˈhɒmɪˌnɔɪd) *adj* **1** of or like man; manlike **2** of, relating to, or belonging to the primate superfamily Hominoidea, which includes the anthropoid apes and man ▷ *n* **3** a hominoid animal [C20: from Latin *homin-*, *homo* man + -OID]

hominy (ˈhɒmɪnɪ) *n chiefly US* coarsely ground maize prepared as a food by boiling in milk or water [C17: probably of Algonquian origin]

hominy grits *pl n US* finely ground hominy

homo¹ (ˈhəʊməʊ) *n, pl* **-mos** *informal, derogatory* short for **homosexual**

homo² (ˈhəʊməʊ) *n Canadian informal* short for **homogenized milk**

Homo (ˈhəʊməʊ) *n* a genus of hominids including modern man (see **Homo sapiens**) and several extinct species of primitive man, including *H. habilis* and *H. erectus* [Latin: man]

homo- *combining form* being the same or like: *homologous*; *homosexual* [via Latin from Greek, from *homos* same]

homocyclic (ˌhəʊməʊˈsaɪklɪk, -ˈsɪk-, ˌhɒm-) *adj* (of an organic compound) containing a closed ring of atoms of the same kind, esp carbon atoms. See **heterocyclic**

homocysteine (ˌhəʊməʊˈsɪstiːn) *n* an amino acid occurring as an intermediate in the metabolism of methionine. Elevated levels in the blood may indicate increased risk of cardiovascular disease

homoeo- *combining form* a variant of **homeo-**

homogamy (hɒˈmɒɡəmɪ) *n* **1** a condition in which all the flowers of an inflorescence are either of the same sex or hermaphrodite **2** the maturation of the anthers and stigmas of a flower at the same time, ensuring self-pollination > ho'mogamous *adj*

homogeneous (ˌhɒʊməˈdʒiːnɪəs, ˌhɒm-) *adj* **1** composed of similar or identical parts or elements **2** of uniform nature **3** similar in kind or nature > homogeneity (ˌhɒʊmɜʊdʒɪˈniːɪtɪ, ˌhɒm-) *n*

homogenize *or* **homogenise** (hʊˈmɒdʒɪˌnaɪz) *vb* **1** (*tr*) to break up the fat globules in (milk or cream) so that they are evenly distributed **2** to make or become homogeneous > hoˌmogeniˈzation *or* hoˌmogeniˈsation *n* > hoˈmogeˌnizer *or* hoˈmogeˌniser *n*

homogenous (həˈmɒdʒɪnəs) *adj* of, relating to, or exhibiting homogeny

homogeny (hʊˈmɒdʒɪnɪ) *n biology* similarity in structure of individuals or parts because of common ancestry [C19: from Greek *homogeneia* community of origin, from *homogenēs* of the same kind]

homograph (ˈhɒməˌɡrɑːf, -ˌɡrɑːf) *n* one of a group of words spelt in the same way but having different meanings > ˌhomoˈgraphic *adj*

homoiothermic (həʊˌmɔɪəˈθɜːmɪk) *or* **homothermal** *adj* (of birds and mammals) having a constant body temperature, usually higher than the temperature of the surroundings; warm-blooded > hoˈmoioˌthermy *or* ˈhomoˌthermy *n*

homologate (hʊˈmɒləˌɡeɪt) *vb* (*tr*) **1** *law, chiefly Scots* to approve or ratify (a deed or contract, esp one that is defective) **2** *law* to confirm (a proceeding, etc) [C17: from Medieval Latin *homologāre* to agree, from Greek *homologein* to approve, from *homologos* agreeing, from HOMO- + *legein* to speak] > hoˌmoloˈgation *n*

homologize *or* **homologise** (hʊˈmɒləˌdʒaɪz) *vb* to be, show to be, or make homologous

homologous (hɒʊˈmɒləɡəs, hɒ-), **homological** (ˌhəʊməˈlɒdʒɪkəl, ˌhɒm-) *or* **homologic** *adj* **1** having a related or similar position, structure, etc **2** *chem* (of a series of organic compounds) having similar characteristics and structure but differing by a number of CH₂ groups **3** *biology* (of organs and parts) having the same evolutionary origin but different functions: *the wing of a bat and the paddle of a whale are homologous* > ˌhomoˈlogically *adv* > ˈhomoˌlogue *or* ˈhomoˌlog *n*

homolographic (həʊˌmɒləˈɡræfɪk) *or* **homalographic** *adj cartography* (of a map projection) showing area accurately and therefore distorting shape and direction

homology (hɒʊˈmɒlədʒɪ) *n, pl* **-gies** the condition of being homologous [C17: from Greek *homologia* agreement, from *homologos* agreeing; see HOMOLOGATE]

homolosine projection (hʊˈmɒləˌsaɪn) *n* a map projection of the world on which the oceans are distorted to allow for greater accuracy in representing the continents, combining the sinusoidal and equal-area projections [C20: from HOMOLOGRAPHIC + SINE¹]

homomorphism (ˌhəʊməʊˈmɔːfɪzəm, ˌhɒm-) *or* **homomorphy** *n biology* similarity in form > ˌhomoˈmorphic *or* ˌhomoˈmorphous *adj*

homonym (ˈhɒmənɪm) *n* **1** one of a group of words pronounced or spelt in the same way but having different meanings. See **homograph**, **homophone** **2** *biology* a name for a species or genus that should be unique but has been used for two or more different organisms [C17: from Latin *homōnymum*, from Greek *homōnumon*, from *homōnumos* of the same name; see HOMO-, -ONYM] > ˌhomoˈnymic *or* hoˈmonymous *adj*

homophobia (ˌhəʊməʊˈfəʊbɪə) *n* intense hatred or fear of homosexuals or homosexuality [C20: from HOMO(SEXUAL) + -PHOBIA] > ˈhomoˌphobe *n* > ˌhomoˈphobic *adj*

homophone (ˈhɒməˌfəʊn) *n* **1** one of a group of words pronounced in the same way but differing in meaning or spelling or both, as for example *bear* and *bare* **2** a written letter or combination of letters that represents the same speech sound as another: *"ph" is a homophone of "f" in English*

homophonic (ˌhɒməˈfɒnɪk) *adj* **1** of or relating to homophony **2** of or relating to music in which the parts move together rather than independently

homopterous (həʊˈmɒptərəs) *or* **homopteran** *adj* of,

relating to, or belonging to the *Homoptera*, a suborder of hemipterous insects, including cicadas, aphids, and scale insects, having wings of a uniform texture held over the back at rest. See **heteropterous** [C19: from Greek *homopteros*, from HOMO- + *pteron* wing]

Homo sapiens (ˈsæpɪˌɛnz) *n* the specific name of modern man; the only extant species of the genus *Homo*. This species also includes extinct types of primitive man such as Cro-Magnon man [New Latin, from Latin *homo* man + *sapiens* wise]

homosexual (ˌhəʊməʊˈsɛksjʊəl, ˌhɒm-) *n* **1** a person who is sexually attracted to members of the same sex ▷ *adj* **2** of or relating to homosexuals or homosexuality **3** of or relating to the same sex. See **heterosexual**

homosexuality (ˌhəʊməʊˌsɛksjʊˈælɪtɪ, ˌhɒm-) *n* sexual attraction to or sexual relations with members of the same sex. See **heterosexuality**

homosocial (ˌhəʊməʊˈsəʊʃəl) *adj* relating to or denoting same-sex social relationships. See **heterosocial** > ˌhomosociality (ˌhəʊməʊˌsəʊʃɪˈælɪtɪ) *n*

homozygote (ˌhəʊməʊˈzaɪɡəʊt, -ˈzɪɡ-, ˌhɒm-) *n* an animal or plant that is homozygous and breeds true to type > homozygotic (ˌhəʊməʊzaɪˈɡɒtɪk, -ˈzɪ-, ˌhɒm-) *adj*

homozygous (ˌhəʊməʊˈzaɪɡəs, -ˈzɪɡ-, ˌhɒm-) *adj genetics* (of an organism) having identical alleles for any one gene: *these two fruit flies are homozygous for red eye colour*

Homs (hɒms) *or* **Hums** (hʊms) *n* a city in W Syria, near the Orontes River: important in Roman times as the capital of Phoenicia-Lebanesia. Pop: 915 000 (2005 est). Former name: Hims

homunculus (hʊˈmʌŋkjʊləs) *n, pl* **-li** (-ˌlaɪ) a miniature man; midget. Also called: homuncule (həʊˈmʌŋkjuːl) [C17: from Latin, diminutive of *homo* man] > hoˈmuncular *adj*

homy *or esp US* **homey** (ˈhəʊmɪ) *adj* homier, homiest like a home, esp in comfort or informality; cosy > ˈhominess *or esp US* ˈhomeyness *n*

hon. *abbreviation* **1** honorary **2** honourable

Hon. *abbreviation* Honourable (title)

Honan (ˈhəʊˈnæn) *n* a variant transliteration of the Chinese name for: **Henan**

honcho (ˈhɒntʃəʊ) *n, pl* **-chos** *informal, chiefly US* the person in charge; the boss [C20: from Japanese *han'chō* group leader]

Hond. *abbreviation* Honduras

Hondo (ˈhɒndəʊ) *n* another name for **Honshu**

Honduran (hɒnˈdjʊərən) *adj* **1** of or relating to Honduras or its inhabitants ▷ *n* **2** a native or inhabitant of Honduras

Honduras (hɒnˈdjʊərəs) *n* **1** a republic in Central America: an early centre of Mayan civilization; colonized by the Spanish from 1524 onwards; gained independence in 1821. Official language: Spanish; English is also widely spoken. Religion: Roman Catholic majority. Currency: lempira. Capital: Tegucigalpa. Pop: 7 100 000 (2004 est). Area: 112 088 sq km (43 277 sq miles) **2** Gulf of Honduras an inlet of the Caribbean, on the coasts of Honduras, Guatemala, and Belize

hone (həʊn) *n* **1** a fine whetstone, esp for sharpening razors ▷ *vb* **2** (*tr*) to sharpen or polish with or as if with a hone [Old English *hān* stone; related to Old Norse *hein*]
 ● USAGE *Hone* is sometimes wrongly used where *home* is
 ● meant: *this device makes it easier to home in on* (not *hone in*
 ● *on*) *the target*

Honecker (German ˈhɒnɛkər) *n* Erich (ˈeːrɪç). 1912–94, German statesman; head of state of East Germany (1976–89)

Honegger (ˈhɒnɪɡə; French ɔnɛɡɛr) *n* Arthur (artyr). 1892–1955, French composer, one of Les Six. His works include the oratorios *King David* (1921) and *Joan of Arc at the Stake* (1935), and *Pacific 231* (1924) for orchestra

honest (ˈɒnɪst) *adj* **1** not given to lying, cheating, stealing, etc; trustworthy **2** not false or misleading; genuine **3** just or fair: *honest wages* **4** characterized by sincerity and candour: *an honest appraisal* **5** without pretensions or artificial traits: *honest farmers* **6** *archaic* (of a woman) respectable **7** honest broker a mediator in disputes, esp international ones **8** make an honest woman of to marry (a woman, esp one who is pregnant)

h

to prevent scandal [c13: from Old French *honeste*, from Latin *honestus* distinguished, from *honōs* HONOUR]

honestly ('ɒnɪstlɪ) *adv* **1** in an honest manner **2** (intensifier): *I honestly don't believe it*

honesty ('ɒnɪstɪ) *n, pl* -ties **1** the condition of being honest **2** *archaic* virtue or chastity **3** Also called: moonwort, satinpod a purple-flowered SE European plant, *Lunaria annua*, cultivated for its flattened silvery pods, which are used for indoor decoration: family *Brassicaceae* (crucifers)

honey ('hʌnɪ) *n* **1 a** a sweet viscid substance made by bees from nectar and stored in their nests or hives as food. It is spread on bread or used as a sweetening agent **2** any similar sweet substance, esp the nectar of flowers **3** (*often capital*) *chiefly US & Canadian* a term of endearment **4** *informal, chiefly US & Canadian* something considered to be very good of its kind: *a honey of a car* ▷ *vb* honeys, honeying, honeyed *or* honied **5** (*tr*) to sweeten with or as if with honey **6** (often foll by *up*) to talk to (someone) in a fond or flattering way [Old English *huneg*; related to Old Norse *hunang*, Old Saxon *hanig*, German *Honig*, Greek *knēkos* yellowish, Sanskrit *kánaka-* gold] > 'honey-,like *adj*

honey badger *n* another name for **ratel**

honeybee ('hʌnɪ,biː) *n* any of various social honey-producing bees of the genus *Apis*, esp *A. mellifera*, which has been widely domesticated as a source of honey and beeswax. Also called: hive bee

honey buzzard *n* a common European bird of prey, *Pernis apivorus*, having broad wings and a typically dull brown plumage with white-streaked underparts: family *Accipitridae* (hawks, buzzards, etc). It feeds on grubs and honey from bees' nests

honeycomb ('hʌnɪ,kəʊm) *n* **1** a waxy structure, constructed by bees in a hive, that consists of adjacent hexagonal cells in which honey is stored, eggs are laid, and larvae develop **2** something resembling this in structure or appearance **3** *zoology* another name for **reticulum** (sense 2) ▷ *vb* (*tr*) **4** to pierce or fill with holes, cavities, etc **5** to permeate: *honeycombed with spies*

honey creeper *n* any small tropical American songbird of the genus *Dacnis* and related genera, closely related to the tanagers and buntings, having a slender downward-curving bill and feeding on nectar

honeydew ('hʌnɪ,djuː) *n* **1** a sugary substance excreted by aphids and similar insects **2** a similar substance exuded by certain plants

honeydew melon *n* a variety of muskmelon with a smooth greenish-white rind and sweet greenish flesh

honey-eater ('hʌnɪ,iːtə) *n* any small arboreal songbird of the Australasian family *Meliphagidae*, having a downward-curving bill and a brushlike tongue specialized for extracting nectar from flowers

honeyed *or* **honied** ('hʌnɪd) *adj poetic* **1** flattering or soothing **2** made sweet or agreeable: *honeyed words* **3** of, full of, or resembling honey

honey guide *n* any small bird of the family *Indicatoridae*, inhabiting tropical forests of Africa and Asia and feeding on beeswax, honey, and insects: order *Piciformes* (woodpeckers, etc)

honeymoon ('hʌnɪ,muːn) *n* **1** a holiday taken by a newly married couple **2** a holiday considered to resemble a honeymoon: *a second honeymoon* **3** the early, usually calm period of a relationship, such as a political or business one ▷ *vb* **4** (*intr*) to take a honeymoon [c16: traditionally explained as an allusion to the feelings of married couples as changing with the phases of the moon] > 'honey,mooner *n*

honey mouse *or* **honey phalanger** *n* a small agile Australian marsupial, *Tarsipes spenserae*, having dark-striped pale brown fur, a long prehensile tail, and a very long snout and tongue with which it feeds on honey, pollen, and insects: family *Phalangeridae*. Also called: honeysucker

honeypot ('hʌnɪ,pɒt) *n* **1** a container for honey **2** something which attracts people in great numbers: *Cornwall is a honeypot for tourists*

honeysuckle ('hʌnɪ,sʌkᵊl) *n* **1** any temperate caprifoliaceous shrub or vine of the genus *Lonicera*: cultivated for their fragrant white, yellow, or pink

tubular flowers **2** any of various Australian trees or shrubs of the genus *Banksia*, having flowers in dense spikes: family *Proteaceae* [Old English *hunigsūce*, from HONEY + SUCK; see SUCKLE]

honeytrap ('hʌnɪ,træp) *n informal* a scheme in which a victim is lured into a compromising sexual situation to provide an opportunity for blackmail

hongi ('hɒŋiː) *n NZ* a form of salutation expressed by touching noses [Māori]

Hong Kong (,hɒŋ 'kɒŋ) *n* **1** a Special Administrative Region of China, in the south of the country, with some autonomy; formerly a British Crown Colony: consists of Hong Kong Island, leased by China to Britain from 1842 until 1997, Kowloon Peninsula, Stonecutters Island, the New Territories (mainland), leased by China in 1898 for a 99-year period, and over 230 small islands; important entrepôt trade and manufacturing centre, esp for textiles and other consumer goods; university (1912). It retains its own currency, the Hong Kong dollar. Administrative centre: Victoria. Pop: 7 182 000 (2005 est). Area: 1046 sq km (404 sq miles) **2** an island in Hong Kong region, south of Kowloon Peninsula: contains the capital, Victoria. Pop: 1 337 800 (2001). Area: 75 sq km (29 sq miles)

Hong-wu ('hɒŋ'wuː) *or* **Hung-wu** *n* title of *Chu Yuan-Zhang* (or *Chu Yüan-Chang*), 1328–98, first emperor (1368–98) of the Ming dynasty, uniting China under his rule by 1382

Hong Xiu Quan ('hɒŋ 'ʃjuː 'tʃwaːn) *or* **Hung Hsiu-Ch'uan** *n* 1814–64, Chinese religious leader and revolutionary. Claiming (1851) to be Christ's brother, he led the Taiping rebellion; committed suicide when it was defeated

Honiara (,həʊnɪ'aːrə) *n* the capital of the Solomon Islands, on NW Guadalcanal Island. Pop: 61 000 (2005 est)

honk (hɒŋk) *n* **1** a representation of the sound made by a goose **2** any sound resembling this, esp a motor horn **3** *Brit & Austral slang* a bad smell ▷ *vb* **4** to make or cause (something) to make such a sound **5** (*intr*) *Brit* a slang word for **vomit** **6** *Brit & Austral slang* to have a bad smell

honky ('hɒŋkɪ) *n, pl* honkies *derogatory, slang, chiefly US* a White man or White men collectively [c20: of unknown origin]

honky-tonk ('hɒŋkɪ,tɒŋk) *n* **1** *US & Canadian slang* a cheap disreputable nightclub, bar, etc **2** a style of ragtime piano-playing, esp on a tinny-sounding piano **3** (*as modifier*): *honky-tonk music* [c19: rhyming compound based on HONK]

Honolulu (,hɒnə'luːluː) *n* a port in Hawaii, on S Oahu island: the state capital. Pop: 380 149 (2003 est)

honorarium (,ɒnə'rɛərɪəm) *n, pl* -iums *or* -ia (-ɪə) a fee paid for a nominally free service [c17: from Latin: something presented on being admitted to a post of HONOUR]

honorary ('ɒnərərɪ, 'ɒnrərɪ) *adj* (*usually prenominal*) **1 a** (esp of a position, title, etc) held or given only as an honour, without the normal privileges or duties: *an honorary degree* **b** (of a secretary, treasurer, etc) unpaid **2** having such a position or title **3** depending on honour rather than legal agreement

honorific (,ɒnə'rɪfɪk) *adj* **1** showing or conferring honour or respect **2 a** (of a pronoun, verb inflection, etc) indicating the speaker's respect for the addressee or his acknowledgment of inferior status **b** (*as noun*): *a Japanese honorific* > ,honor'ifically *adv*

honour *or US* **honor** ('ɒnə) *n* **1** personal integrity; allegiance to moral principles **2** fame or glory **3** (*often plural*) great respect, regard, esteem, etc, or an outward sign of this **4** (*often plural*) high or noble rank **5** a privilege or pleasure: *it is an honour to serve you* **6** a woman's virtue or chastity **7 a** *bridge, poker* any of the top five cards in a suit or any of the four aces at no trumps **b** *whist* any of the top four cards **8** *golf* the right to tee off first **9 do the honours a** to serve as host or hostess **b** to perform a social act, such as carving meat, proposing a toast, etc **10 in honour bound** under a moral obligation **11 in honour of** out of respect for **12 on one's honour** *or* **upon one's honour** on the pledge of one's word or good name ▷ *vb* (*tr*) **13** to hold in respect or esteem **14** to show courteous behaviour towards **15** to worship **16** to confer a distinction upon **17** to accept and then pay when due (a cheque, draft, etc) **18** to keep (one's promise); fulfil (a previous agreement) **19** to bow or curtsy to (one's dancing partner) [c12: from Old French *onor*, from Latin *honor* esteem]

Honour ('ɒnə) *n* (preceded by *Your, His*, or *Her*) a title used to or of certain judges

honourable *or US* **honorable** ('ɒnrəbəl, 'ɒnrəb-l) *adj* **1** possessing or characterized by high principles **2** worthy of or entitled to honour or esteem **3** consistent with or bestowing honour ▷ **'honourably** *or US* **'honorably** *adv*

Honourable *or US* **Honorable** ('ɒnərəbəl, 'ɒnrəb-l) *adj* the (*prenominal*) a title of respect placed before a name: employed before the names of various officials in the English-speaking world, as a courtesy title in Britain for the children of viscounts and barons and the younger sons of earls, and in Parliament by one member speaking of another. Abbreviation: **Hon.**

honour killing *n* a murder committed by a male on a female relative considered to have brought dishonour to the family, usually through sexual activity forbidden by religion or tradition

honours *or US* **honors** ('ɒnəz) *pl n* **1** observances of respect **2** (*often capital*) **a** (in a university degree or degree course) a rank of the highest academic standard **b** (*as modifier*): *an honours degree*. Abbreviation: **Hons 3** a high mark awarded for an examination; distinction **4** last honours *or* funeral honours observances of respect at a funeral **5** military honours ceremonies performed by troops in honour of royalty, at the burial of an officer, etc

honours of war *pl n military* the honours granted by the victorious to the defeated, esp as of marching out with all arms and flags flying

Honshu ('hɒnʃu:) *n* the largest of the four main islands of Japan, between the Pacific and the Sea of Japan; regarded as the Japanese mainland; includes a number of offshore islands and contains most of the main cities. Pop: 102 324 961 (2000). Area: 230 448 sq km (88 976 sq miles). Also called: **Hondo**

hooch *or* **hootch** (hu:tʃ) *n informal, chiefly US & Canadian* alcoholic drink, esp illicitly distilled spirits [c20: shortened from Tlingit *Hootchinoo*, name of a tribe that distilled a type of liquor]

Hooch *or* **Hoogh** (hu:tʃ; *Dutch* ho:x) *n* **Pieter de** ('pi:tər də). 1629–?1684, Dutch genre painter, noted esp for his light effects

hood¹ (hʊd) *n* **1** a loose head covering either attached to a cloak or coat or made as a separate garment **2** something resembling this in shape or use **3** the US and Canadian name for **bonnet** (sense 3) **4** the folding roof of a convertible car **5** a hoodlike garment worn over an academic gown, indicating its wearer's degree and university **6** *biology* a structure or marking, such as the fold of skin on the head of a cobra, that covers or appears to cover the head or some similar part ▷ *vb* **7** (*tr*) to cover or provide with or as if with a hood [Old English *hōd*; related to Old High German *huot* hat, Middle Dutch *hoet*, Latin *cassis* helmet; see HAT] ▷ **'hood,like** *adj*

hood² (hʊd) *n slang* short for **hoodlum** (sense 1)

-hood *suffix forming nouns* **1** indicating state or condition of being: *manhood; adulthood* **2** indicating a body of persons: *knighthood; priesthood* [Old English *-hād*]

Hood (hʊd) *n* **1 Robin** See **Robin Hood 2 Samuel**, 1st Viscount. 1724–1816, British admiral. He fought successfully against the French during the American Revolution and the French Revolutionary Wars **3 Thomas**. 1799–1845, British poet and humorist: his work includes protest poetry, such as *The Song of the Shirt* (1843) and *The Bridge of Sighs* (1844)

hooded ('hʊdɪd) *adj* **1** covered with, having, or shaped like a hood **2** (of eyes) having heavy eyelids that appear to be half closed

hooded crow *n* a subspecies of the carrion crow, *Corvus corone cornix*, that has a grey body and black head, wings, and tail. Also called: (*Scot*): **hoodie** ('hʊdɪ), **hoodie crow**

hoodie ('hʊdɪ) *n informal* **1** a hooded sweatshirt **2** a young person who wears a hooded sweatshirt, regarded by some as a potential hooligan

hoodlum ('hu:dləm) *n* **1** a petty gangster or ruffian **2** a lawless youth [c19: perhaps from Southern German dialect *Haderlump* ragged good-for-nothing]

hoodman-blind *n Brit archaic* blind man's buff

hoodoo ('hu:du:) *n, pl* **-doos 1** a variant of **voodoo 2** *informal* a person or thing that brings bad luck **3** *informal* bad luck ▷ *vb* **-doos, -dooing, -dooed 4** (*tr*) *informal* to bring bad luck to [c19: variant of VOODOO]

hoodwink ('hʊd,wɪŋk) *vb* (*tr*) **1** to dupe; trick **2** *obsolete* to cover or hide [c16: originally, to cover the eyes with a hood, blindfold]

hooey ('hu:ɪ) *n, interj slang* nonsense; rubbish [c20: of unknown origin]

hoof (hu:f) *n, pl* **hooves** (hu:vz) *or* **hoofs 1 a** the horny covering of the end of the foot in the horse, deer, and all other ungulate mammals **b** (*in combination*): *a hoofbeat*. Related adj: **ungular 2** the foot of an ungulate mammal **3** a hoofed animal **4** *facetious* a person's foot **5** on the hoof **a** (of livestock) alive **b** in an impromptu manner: *he did his thinking on the hoof* ▷ *vb* **6** hoof it *slang* **a** to walk **b** to dance [Old English *hōf*; related to Old Norse *hōfr*, Old High German *huof* (German *Huf*), Sanskrit *saphás*] ▷ **hoofed** *adj*

hoofer ('hu:fə) *n slang* a professional dancer, esp a tap-dancer

Hooft (*Dutch* ho:ft) *n* **Pieter Corneliszoon** ('pi:tər kɔr'ne:liso:n). 1581–1647, Dutch poet, historian, and writer: noted esp for his love poetry and his 27-volume *History of the Netherlands* (1626–47)

Hoogh (*Dutch* ho:x) *n* See (Pieter de) **Hooch**

Hooghly ('hu:glɪ) *n* a river in NE India, in West Bengal: the westernmost and commercially most important channel by which the River Ganges enters the Bay of Bengal. Length: 232 km (144 miles)

hoo-ha ('hu:,ha:) *n* a noisy commotion or fuss [c20: of unknown origin]

hook (hʊk) *n* **1 a** piece of material, usually metal, curved or bent and used to suspend, catch, hold, or pull something **2** short for **fish-hook 3** a trap or snare **4** *chiefly US* something that attracts or is intended to be an attraction **5** something resembling a hook in design or use **6 a** a sharp bend or angle in a geological formation, esp a river **b** a sharply curved spit of land **7** *boxing* a short swinging blow delivered from the side with the elbow bent **8** *cricket* a shot in which the ball is hit square on the leg side with the bat held horizontally **9** *golf* a shot that causes the ball to swerve sharply from right to left **10** *surfing* the top of a breaking wave **11** Also called: **hookcheck** *ice hockey* the act of hooking an opposing player **12** *music* a stroke added to the stem of a written or printed note to indicate time values shorter than a crotchet **13** another name for a **sickle 14** a nautical word for **anchor 15** by hook or crook *or* by hook or by crook by any means **16** hook, line, and sinker *informal* completely: *he fell for it hook, line, and sinker* **17** off the hook *slang* out of danger; free from obligation or guilt **18** sling one's hook *Brit slang* to leave ▷ *vb* **19** (often foll by *up*) to hook or be fastened with or as if with a hook or hooks **20** (*tr*) to catch (something, such as a fish) on a hook **21** to curve like or into the shape of a hook **22** (*tr*) to make (a rug) by hooking yarn through a stiff fabric backing with a special instrument **23** *boxing* to hit (an opponent) with a hook **24** *cricket* to play (a ball) with a hook [Old English *hōc*; related to Middle Dutch *hōk*, Old Norse *haki*]

hookah *or* **hooka** ('hʊkə) *n* an oriental pipe for smoking marijuana, tobacco, etc, consisting of one or more long flexible stems connected to a container of water or other liquid through which smoke is drawn and cooled. Also called: **hubble-bubble, water pipe** [c18: from Arabic *huqqah*]

Hooke (hʊk) *n* **Robert**. 1635–1703, English physicist, chemist, and inventor. He formulated Hooke's law (1678), built the first Gregorian telescope, and invented a balance spring for watches

hooked (hʊkt) *adj* **1** bent like a hook **2** having a hook or hooks **3** caught or trapped **4** a slang word for **married** **5** *slang* addicted to a drug **6** (often foll by *on*) obsessed (with)

hooker ('hʊkə) *n* **1** a person or thing that hooks **2** *US & Canadian slang* a prostitute **3** *rugby* the central forward in the front row of a scrum whose main job is to hook the ball

Hooker ('hʊkə) *n* **1 John Lee.** 1917–2001, US blues singer and guitarist **2 Sir Joseph Dalton.** 1817–1911, British botanist; director of Kew Gardens (1865–85) **3 Richard.** 1554–1600, British theologian, who influenced Anglican theology with *The Laws of Ecclesiastical Polity* (1593–97) **4** Sir **William Jackson.** 1785–1865, British botanist; first director of Kew Gardens: father of Sir Joseph Dalton Hooker

Hooke's law (hʊks) *n* the principle that the stress imposed on a solid is directly proportional to the strain produced, within the elastic limit [c18: named after Robert *Hooke* (1635–1703), English physicist, chemist, and inventor]

Hook of Holland *n* the *n* **1** a cape on the SW coast of the Netherlands, in South Holland province **2** a port on this cape ▷ Dutch name: Hoek van Holland

hook-up *n* **1** the contact of an aircraft in flight with the refuelling hose of a tanker aircraft **2** an alliance or relationship, esp an unlikely one, between people, countries, etc **3** the linking of broadcasting equipment or stations to transmit a special programme ▷ *vb* hook up (*adverb*) **4** to connect (two or more people or things)

hookworm ('hʊk,wɜːm) *n* any parasitic blood-sucking nematode worm of the family *Ancylostomatidae*, esp *Ancylostoma duodenale* or *Necator americanus*, both of which cause disease. They have hooked mouthparts and enter their hosts by boring through the skin

hooky *or* **hookey** ('hʊkɪ) *n informal, chiefly US, Canadian & NZ* truancy, usually from school (esp in the phrase **play hooky**) [c20: perhaps from *hook* it to escape]

hooligan ('huːlɪɡən) *n slang* a rough lawless young person [c19: perhaps variant of *Houlihan*, Irish surname] ▷ **'hooliganism** *n*

hoon (huːn) *n Austral & NZ informal* a hooligan [of unknown origin]

hoop¹ (huːp) *n* **1** a rigid circular band of metal or wood **2** something resembling this **3** a band of iron that holds the staves of a barrel or cask together **4** a child's toy shaped like a hoop and rolled on the ground or whirled around the body **5** *croquet* any of the iron arches through which the ball is driven **6 a** a light curved frame to spread out a skirt **b** (*as modifier*): *a hoop skirt; a hoop petticoat* **7** *basketball* the round metal frame to which the net is attached to form the basket **8** a large ring through which performers or animals jump **9** go through the hoop *or* be put through the hoop to be subjected to an ordeal ▷ *vb* **10** (*tr*) to surround with or as if with a hoop [Old English *hōp*; related to Dutch *hoep*, Old Norse *hōp* bay, Lithuanian *kabė* hook] ▷ **hooped** *adj*

hoop² (huːp) *n, vb* a variant spelling of **whoop**

hoopla ('huːplɑː) *n* **1** *Brit* a fairground game in which a player tries to throw a hoop over an object and so win it **2** *US & Canadian slang* noise; bustle **3** *US slang* nonsense; ballyhoo [c20: see WHOOP, LA²]

hoopoe ('huːpuː) *n* an Old World bird, *Upupa epops*, having a pinkish-brown plumage with black-and-white wings and an erectile crest: family *Upupidae*, order *Coraciiformes* (kingfishers, etc) [c17: from earlier *hoopoop*, of imitative origin; compare Latin *upupa*]

hoop pine *n* a fast-growing timber tree of Australia, *Araucaria cunninghamii*, having rough bark with hoop-like cracks around the trunk and branches: family *Araucariaceae*

Hooray Henry ('huː,reɪ) *n, pl* Hooray Henries *or* -rys a young upper-class man, often with affectedly hearty voice and manners

hoosegow *or* **hoosgow** ('huːsɡaʊ) *n US* a slang word for jail [c20: from Mexican Spanish *jusgado* prison, from Spanish: court of justice, from *juzgar* to judge, from Latin *judicāre*, from *judex* a judge; compare JUDGE; compare JUG]

hoot¹ (huːt) *n* **1** the mournful wavering cry of some owls **2** a similar sound, such as that of a train whistle **3** a jeer

of derision **4** *informal* an amusing person or thing ▷ *vb* **5** (often foll by *at*) to jeer or yell (something) contemptuously (at someone) **6** (*tr*) to drive (political speakers, actors on stage, etc) off or away by hooting **7** (*intr*) to make a hoot **8** (*intr*) *Brit* to blow a horn [c13 *hoten*, of imitative origin]

hoot² (huːt) *n Austral & NZ* a slang word for **money** [from Māori *utu* price]

hootenanny ('huːtᵊ,nænɪ) *or* **hootnanny** ('huːt,nænɪ) *n, pl* -nies an informal performance by folk singers [c20: of unknown origin]

hooter ('huːtə) *n chiefly Brit* **1** a person or thing that hoots, esp a car horn **2** *slang* a nose

Hoover¹ ('huːvə) *n* **1** *trademark* a type of vacuum cleaner ▷ *vb* (*usually not capital*) **2** to vacuum-clean (a carpet, furniture, etc) **3** (*tr*; often foll by *up*) to consume or dispose of (something) quickly and completely: *he hoovered up his grilled fish*

Hoover² ('huːvə) *n* **1 Herbert (Clark).** 1874–1964, US statesman; 31st president of the US (1929–33). He organized relief for Europe during and after World War I, but as president he lost favour after his failure to alleviate the effects of the Depression **2 J(ohn) Edgar.** 1895–1972, US lawyer: director of the FBI (1924–72). He used new scientific methods to combat crime, including the first fingerprint file

Hoover Dam *n* a dam in the western US, on the Colorado River on the border between Nevada and Arizona; forms Lake Mead. Height: 222 m (727 ft). Length: 354 m (1180 ft). Former name (1933–47): Boulder Dam

hooves (huːvz) *n* a plural of **hoof**

hop¹ (hɒp) *vb* hops, hopping, hopped **1** (*intr*) to make a jump forwards or upwards, esp on one foot **2** (*intr*) (esp of frogs, birds, rabbits, etc) to move forwards in short jumps **3** (*intr*) *informal* to move or proceed quickly (in, on, out of, etc): *hop on a bus* **4** (*tr*) *informal* to cross (an ocean) in an aircraft **5** (*tr*) *US & Canadian informal* to travel by means of (an aircraft, bus, etc): *he hopped a train to Chicago* **6** (*intr*) another word for **limp¹** **7** hop it *or* hop off *Brit slang* to go away ▷ *n* **8** the act or an instance of hopping **9** on the hop *informal* **a** active or busy **b** *Brit* unawares or unprepared [Old English *hoppian*; related to Old Norse *hoppa* to hop, Middle Low German *hupfen*]

hop² (hɒp) *n* **1** any climbing plant of the N temperate genus *Humulus*, esp *H. lupulus*, which has green conelike female flowers and clusters of small male flowers: family *Cannabiaceae* (or *Cannabidaceae*) ▷ See also **hops** **2** hop garden a field of hops **3** *obsolete, slang* opium or any other narcotic drug [c15: from Middle Dutch *hoppe*; related to Old High German *hopfo*, Norwegian *hupp* tassel]

hope (həʊp) *n* **1** (*sometimes plural*) a feeling of desire for something and confidence in the possibility of its fulfilment: *his hope for peace was justified; their hopes were dashed* **2** a reasonable ground for this feeling: *there is still hope* **3** a person or thing that gives cause for hope **4** a thing, situation, or event that is desired: *my hope is that prices will fall* **5** not a hope *or* some hope used ironically to express little confidence that expectations will be fulfilled ▷ *vb* **6** (*tr*; takes a clause as object or an infinitive) to desire (something) with some possibility of fulfilment: *we hope you can come; I hope to tell you* **7** (*intr*; often foll by *for*) to have a wish (for a future event, situation, etc) **8** (*tr*; takes a clause as object) to trust, expect, or believe: *we hope that this is satisfactory* [Old English *hopa*; related to Old Frisian *hope*, Dutch *hoop*, Middle High German *hoffe*]

Hope (həʊp) *n* **1 Anthony,** real name *Sir Anthony Hope Hawkins*. 1863–1933, English novelist; author of *The Prisoner of Zenda* (1894) **2 Bob,** real name *Leslie Townes Hope*. 1903–2003, US comedian and comic actor, born in England. His films include *The Cat and the Canary* (1939), *Road to Morocco* (1942), and *The Paleface* (1947). He was awarded an honorary knighthood in 1998 **3 David (Michael).** Baron. born 1940, British churchman, Archbishop of York (1995–2005)

hope chest *n US & Canadian* a young woman's collection of clothes, linen, cutlery, etc, in anticipation of marriage. Also called (esp in Britain): **bottom drawer**

hopeful ('həʊpfʊl) *adj* **1** having or expressing hope

2 giving or inspiring hope; promising ▷ *n* **3** a person considered to be on the brink of success (esp in the phrase **a young hopeful**) > 'hopefulness *n*

hopefully ('həʊpfʊlɪ) *adv* **1** in a hopeful manner **2** *informal* it is hoped: *hopefully they will be here soon*
● USAGE The use of *hopefully* to mean *it is hoped* used to be
● considered incorrect by some people but has now
● become acceptable in informal contexts

Hopeh or **Hopei** ('həʊ'peɪ) *n* a variant transliteration of the Chinese name for **Hebei**

hopeless ('həʊplɪs) *adj* **1** having or offering no hope **2** impossible to analyse or solve **3** unable to learn, function, etc **4** *informal* without skill or ability > 'hopelessly *adv* > 'hopelessness *n*

Hopi ('həʊpɪ) *n* **1** *pl* **-pis** or **-pi** a member of a North American Indian people of NE Arizona **2** the language of this people, belonging to the Shoshonean subfamily of the Uto-Aztecan family [from Hopi *Hópi* peaceful]

Hopkins ('hɒpkɪnz) *n* **1** Sir **Anthony**. born 1937, Welsh actor: his films include *Bounty* (1984), *The Silence of the Lambs* (1991), *Shadowlands* (1994), and *Hannibal* (2000) **2** Sir **Frederick Gowland** ('gaʊlənd). 1861–1947, British biochemist, who pioneered research into what came to be called vitamins: shared the Nobel prize for physiology or medicine (1929) **3** Gerard Manley. 1844–89, British poet and Jesuit priest, who experimented with sprung rhythm in his highly original poetry **4** Harry L(loyd). 1890–1946, US administrator. During World War II he was a personal aide to President Roosevelt and administered the lend-lease programme

hoplite ('hɒplaɪt) *n* (in ancient Greece) a heavily armed infantryman [c18: from Greek *hoplitēs*, from *hoplon* weapon, from *hepein* to prepare]

hopper ('hɒpə) *n* **1** a person or thing that hops **2** a funnel-shaped chamber or reservoir from which solid materials can be discharged under gravity into a receptacle below, esp for feeding fuel to a furnace, loading a railway truck with grain, etc **3** a machine used for picking hops **4** any of various long-legged hopping insects, esp the grasshopper, leaf hopper, and immature locust **5** Also called: **hoppercar** an open-topped railway truck for bulk transport of loose minerals, etc, unloaded through doors on the underside **6** *South African* another name for **cocopan** **7** *computing* a device formerly used for holding punched cards and feeding them to a card punch or card reader

Hopper ('hɒpə) *n* **Edward**. 1882–1967, US painter, noted for his realistic depiction of everyday scenes

hopping ('hɒpɪŋ) *adj* **hopping mad** in a terrible rage

hops (hɒps) *pl n* the dried ripe flowers, esp the female flowers, of the hop plant, used to give a bitter taste to beer

hopsack ('hɒp,sæk) *n* **1** a roughly woven fabric of wool, cotton, etc, used for clothing **2** Also called: **hopsacking** a coarse fabric used for bags, etc, made generally of hemp or jute

hopscotch ('hɒp,skɒtʃ) *n* a children's game in which a player throws a small stone or other object to land in one of a pattern of squares marked on the ground and then hops over to it to pick it up [c19: HOP¹ + SCOTCH¹]

Horace ('hɒrɪs) *n* Latin name *Quintus Horatius Flaccus*. 65–8 BC, Roman poet and satirist: his verse includes the lyrics in the *Epodes* and the *Odes*, the *Epistles* and *Satires*, and the *Ars Poetica*

Horae ('hɔːriː) *pl n* *classical myth* the goddesses of the seasons. Also called: the **Hours** [Latin: hours]

horary ('hɔːrərɪ) *adj archaic* **1** relating to the hours **2** hourly [c17: from Medieval Latin *hōrārius*; see HOUR]

Horatian (hə'reɪʃən) *adj* of, relating to, or characteristic of the Roman poet Horace (Latin name *Quintus Horatius Flaccus*; (65–8 BC) or his poetry

Horatius Cocles (hɒ'reɪʃɪəs 'kəʊkliːz) *n* a legendary Roman hero of the 6th century BC, who defended a bridge over the Tiber against Lars Porsena

horde (hɔːd) *n* **1** a vast crowd; throng; mob **2** a nomadic group of people, esp an Asiatic group **3** a large moving mass of animals, esp insects [from Polish *horda*, from Turkish *ordü* camp; compare *Urdu*]

Hordern ('hɔːdən) *n* Sir **Michael** (**Murray**). 1911–95,

British stage and film actor

Horeb ('hɔːrɛb) *n* *Bible* a mountain, probably Mount Sinai

horehound or **hoarhound** ('hɔː,haʊnd) *n* Also called: **white horehound** a downy perennial herbaceous Old World plant, *Marrubium vulgare*, with small white flowers that contain a bitter juice formerly used as a cough medicine and flavouring: family *Lamiaceae* (labiates) [Old English *hārhūne*, from *hār* grey + *hūne* horehound, of obscure origin]

hori ('hɔːri) *NZ informal, derogatory* ▷ *n*, *pl* **horis** **1** a Māori ▷ *adj* **2** of or relating to the Māori [Māori]

horizon (hə'raɪzⁿn) *n* **1** Also called: **visible horizon**, **apparent horizon** the apparent line that divides the earth and the sky **2** *astronomy* **a** Also called: **sensible horizon** the circular intersection with the celestial sphere of the plane tangential to the earth at the position of the observer **b** Also called: **celestial horizon** the great circle on the celestial sphere, the plane of which passes through the centre of the earth and is parallel to the sensible horizon **3** the range or limit of scope, interest, knowledge, etc **4** a thin layer of rock within a stratum that has a distinct composition, esp of fossils, by which the stratum may be dated [c14: from Latin, from Greek *horizōn* limiting circle, from *horizein* to limit, from *horos* limit]

horizontal (,hɒrɪ'zɒntⁿl) *adj* **1** parallel to the plane of the horizon; level; flat. See **vertical** (sense 1) **2** of or relating to the horizon **3** measured or contained in a plane parallel to that of the horizon **4** applied uniformly or equally to all members of a group **5** *economics* relating to identical stages of commercial activity: *horizontal integration* ▷ *n* **6** a horizontal plane, position, line, etc > ,horizon'tality or ,hori'zontalness *n* > ,hori'zontally *adv*

horizontal bar *n* *gymnastics* a raised bar on which swinging and vaulting exercises are performed

Horkheimer (German 'hɔrkhaɪmər) *n* **Max**. 1895–1973, German social theorist of the Frankfurt school. His books include *Eclipse of Reason* (1947) and *Critical Theory* (1968)

horlicks ('hɔːlɪks) *n* **make a horlicks** *Brit informal* to make a mistake or a mess: *his boss is making a horlicks of his job* [c20: from *Horlicks*, a drink meant to induce sleep]

hormone ('hɔːməʊn) *n* **1** a chemical substance produced in an endocrine gland and transported in the blood to a certain tissue, on which it exerts a specific effect **2** any synthetic substance having the same effects [c20: from Greek *hormōn*, from *horman* to stir up, urge on, from *hormē* impulse, assault] > hor'monal *adj*

hormone replacement therapy *n* a form of oestrogen treatment used to control menopausal symptoms and in the prevention of osteoporosis. Abbreviation: **HRT**

Hormuz (hɔː'muːz, 'hɔːmʌz) or **Ormuz** *n* an island off the SE coast of Iran, in the **Strait of Hormuz**: ruins of the ancient city of Hormuz, a major trading centre in the Middle Ages. Area: about 41 sq km (16 sq miles)

horn (hɔːn) *n* **1** either of a pair of permanent outgrowths on the heads of cattle, antelopes, sheep, etc, consisting of a central bony core covered with layers of keratin **2** the outgrowth from the nasal bone of a rhinoceros, consisting of a mass of fused hairs **3** any hornlike projection or process, such as the eyestalk of a snail **4** the antler of a deer **5 a** the constituent substance, mainly keratin, of horns, hooves, etc **b** (*in combination*): *horn-rimmed spectacles* **6** a container or device made from this substance or an artificial substitute: *a shoe horn*; *a drinking horn* **7** an object or part resembling a horn in shape, such as the points at either end of a crescent, the point of an anvil, the pommel of a saddle, or a cornucopia **8** a primitive musical wind instrument made from the horn of an animal **9** any musical instrument consisting of a pipe or tube of brass fitted with a mouthpiece, with or without valves. See **French horn**, **cor anglais** **10** *jazz slang* any wind instrument **11 a** a device for producing a warning or signalling noise **b** (*in combination*): *a foghorn* **12** (*usually plural*) the imaginary hornlike parts formerly supposed to appear on the forehead of a cuckold **13 a** Also called: **acoustic horn**, **exponential horn** a hollow conical device coupled to the diaphragm of a gramophone to control the direction and quality of the sound **b** any such device used to spread or focus sound, such as the device attached to an electrical loudspeaker in a public address system **14** a stretch of land or water shaped like a horn **15** *Brit slang* an erection of the penis ▷ *vb* (*tr*) **16** to provide with a horn or horns **17** to gore or butt with a horn [Old English; related to Old Norse *horn*, Gothic *haurn*, Latin *cornu* horn] > 'hornless *adj*

Horn (hɔːn) *n* Cape See **Cape Horn**

hornbag ('hɔːn,bæg) *n Austral slang* a promiscuous woman [C20: from HORNY]

hornbeam ('hɔːn,biːm) *n* any tree of the betulaceous genus *Carpinus*, such as *C. betulus* of Europe and Asia, having smooth grey bark and hard white wood. Also called: ironwood [C14: from HORN + BEAM, referring to its tough wood]

hornbill ('hɔːn,bɪl) *n* any bird of the family *Bucerotidae* of tropical Africa and Asia, having a very large bill with a basal bony protuberance: order *Coraciiformes* (kingfishers, etc)

hornblende ('hɔːn,blɛnd) *n* a black or greenish-black mineral of the amphibole group, found in igneous and metamorphic rocks. Composition: calcium magnesium iron sodium aluminium aluminosilicate. General formula: $(Ca,Na)_{2,3}(Mg,Fe,Al)_5Si_6(Si,Al)_2O_{22}(OH)_2$ [C18: from German *Horn* horn + BLENDE]

hornbook ('hɔːn,bʊk) *n* a page bearing a religious text or the alphabet, held in a frame with a thin window of flattened cattle horn over it

Hornby ('hɔːnbɪ) *n* Nick. born 1958, British writer; his books include the memoir *Fever Pitch* (1992; filmed 1997) and the bestselling novels *About a Boy* (1998; filmed 2002) and *How To Be Good* (2001)

horned toad *or* **horned lizard** *n* any small insectivorous burrowing lizard of the genus *Phrynosoma*, inhabiting desert regions of America, having a flattened toadlike body covered with spines: family *Iguanidae* (iguanas)

horned viper *n* a venomous snake, *Cerastes cornutus*, that occurs in desert regions of N Africa and SW Asia and has a small horny spine above each eye: family *Viperidae* (vipers)

hornet ('hɔːnɪt) *n* **1** any of various large social wasps of the family *Vespidae*, esp *Vespa crabro* of Europe, that can inflict a severe sting **2** **hornet's nest** a strongly unfavourable reaction (often in the phrase **stir up a hornet's nest**) [Old English *hyrnetu*; related to Old Saxon *hornut*, Old High German *hornuz*]

horn in *vb* (*intr, adverb*; often foll by *on*) *slang* to interrupt or intrude: *don't horn in on our conversation*

Horn of Africa *n* a region of NE Africa, comprising Somalia and adjacent territories

horn of plenty *n* another term for **cornucopia**

hornpipe ('hɔːn,paɪp) *n* **1** an obsolete reed instrument with a mouthpiece made of horn **2** an old British solo dance to a hornpipe accompaniment, traditionally performed by sailors **3** a piece of music for such a dance

hornswoggle ('hɔːn,swɒgᵊl) *vb* (*tr*) *slang* to cheat or trick; bamboozle [C19: of unknown origin]

horny ('hɔːnɪ) *adj* hornier, horniest **1** of, like, or hard as horn **2** *slang* **a** sexually aroused **b** provoking or intended to provoke sexual arousal **c** sexually eager or lustful > 'horniness *n*

horologe ('hɒrə,lɒdʒ) *n* a rare word for **timepiece** [C14: from Latin *hōrologium*, from Greek *hōrologion*, from *hōra* HOUR + *-logos* from *legein* to tell]

horologist (hɒ'rɒlədʒɪst) *or* **horologer** (hɒ'rɒlədʒə) *n* a person skilled in horology, esp an expert maker of timepieces

horology (hɒ'rɒlədʒɪ) *n* the art or science of making timepieces or of measuring time > horologic (,hɒrə'lɒdʒɪk) *or* ,horo'logical *adj*

horoscope ('hɒrə,skəʊp) *n* **1** the prediction of a person's future based on a comparison of the zodiacal data for the time of birth with the data from the period under consideration **2** the configuration of the planets, the sun, and the moon in the sky at a particular moment **3** Also called: chart a diagram showing the positions of the planets, sun, moon, etc, at a particular time and

place [Old English *horoscopus*, from Latin, from Greek *hōroskopos* ascendant birth sign, from *hōra* HOUR + -SCOPE] > ,horo'scopic *adj* > horoscopy (hɒ'rɒskəpɪ) *n*

Horowitz ('hɒrəvɪts) *n* Vladimir. 1904–89, Russian virtuoso pianist, in the US from 1928

horrendous (hɒ'rɛndəs) *adj* another word for **horrific** [C17: from Latin *horrendus* fearful, from *horrēre* to bristle, shudder, tremble; see HORROR] > hor'rendously *adv*

horrible ('hɒrəbᵊl) *adj* **1** causing horror; dreadful **2** disagreeable; unpleasant **3** *informal* cruel or unkind [C14: via Old French from Latin *horribilis*, from *horrēre* to tremble] > 'horribleness *n* > 'horribly *adv*

horrid ('hɒrɪd) *adj* **1** disagreeable; unpleasant: *a horrid meal* **2** repulsive or frightening **3** *informal* unkind [C16 (in the sense: bristling, shaggy): from Latin *horridus* prickly, rough, from *horrēre* to bristle] > 'horridly *adv* > 'horridness *n*

horrific (hɒ'rɪfɪk, hə-) *adj* provoking horror; horrible > hor'rifically *adv*

horrified ('hɒrɪ,faɪd) *adj* **1** terrified; frightened **2** dismayed or shocked

horrify ('hɒrɪ,faɪ) *vb* -fies, -fying, -fied (*tr*) **1** to cause feelings of horror in; terrify; frighten **2** to dismay or shock greatly > ,horrifi'cation *n*

horrifying ('hɒrɪ,faɪɪŋ) *adj* **1** causing feelings of horror in; awful; terrifying; **2** dismaying or greatly shocking; dreadful > 'horri,fyingly *adv*

horripilation (hɒ,rɪpɪ'leɪʃən) *n physiol* a technical name for **goose flesh** [C17: from Late Latin *horripilātiō* a bristling, from Latin *horrēre* to stand on end + *pilus* hair]

horror ('hɒrə) *n* **1** extreme fear; terror; dread **2** intense loathing; hatred **3** (*often plural*) a thing or person causing fear, loathing, etc **4** (*modifier*) having a frightening subject, esp a supernatural one: *a horror film* [C14: from Latin: a trembling with fear; compare HIRSUTE]

horrors ('hɒrəz) *pl n* **1** *slang* a fit of depression or anxiety **2** *informal* See **delirium tremens** ▷ *interj* **3** an expression of dismay, sometimes facetious

Horsa ('hɔːsə) *n* died ?455 AD, leader, with his brother Hengist, of the first Jutish settlers in Britain. See also **Hengist**

hors de combat French (ɔr də kɔ̃ba) *adj, adv* (*postpositive*,) disabled or injured [literally: out of (the) fight]

hors d'oeuvre (ɔː 'dɜːvr; *French* ɔr dœvr) *n, pl* hors d'oeuvre *or* hors d'oeuvres ('dɜːvr; *French* dœvrə) an additional dish served as an appetizer, usually before the main meal [C18: from French, literally: outside the work, not part of the main course]

horse (hɔːs) *n* **1** a domesticated perissodactyl mammal, *Equus caballus*, used for draught work and riding: family *Equidae*. Related adj: **equine** **2** the adult male of this species; stallion **3** wild horse **a** a horse (*Equus caballus*) that has become feral **b** another name for **Przewalski's horse** **4** (*functioning as plural*) horsemen, esp cavalry: *a regiment of horse* **5** Also called: buck *gymnastics* a padded apparatus on legs, used for vaulting, etc **6** a narrow board supported by a pair of legs at each end, used as a frame for sawing or as a trestle, barrier, etc **7** a contrivance on which a person may ride and exercise **8** a slang word for **heroin** **9** *mining* a mass of rock within a vein of ore **10** *nautical* a rod, rope, or cable, fixed at the ends, along which something may slide by means of a thimble, shackle, or other fitting; traveller **11** *chess* an informal name for **knight** **12** *informal* short for **horsepower** **13** (*modifier*) drawn by a horse or horses: *a horse cart* **14** be on one's high horse *or* get on one's high horse *informal* to be disdainfully aloof **15** a horse of another colour *or* a horse of a different colour a completely different topic, argument, etc **16** horses for courses a policy, course of action, etc modified slightly to take account of specific circumstances without departing in essentials from the original **17** the horse's mouth the most reliable source ▷ *vb* **18** to put or be put on horseback [Old English *hors*; related to Old Frisian *hors*, Old High German *hros*, Old Norse *hross*] > 'horse,like *adj*

horse around *or* **horse about** *vb* (*intr, adverb*) *informal* to indulge in horseplay

horseback ('hɔːs,bæk) *n* **a** a horse's back (esp in the phrase **on horseback** **b** (*as modifier*): *horseback riding*

horsebox ('hɔːs,bɒks) *n* *Brit* a van or trailer used for carrying horses

horse brass *n* a decorative brass ornament, usually circular, originally attached to a horse's harness

horse chestnut *n* **1** any of several trees of the genus *Aesculus*, esp the Eurasian *A. hippocastanum*, having palmate leaves, erect clusters of white, pink, or red flowers, and brown shiny inedible nuts enclosed in a spiky bur: family *Hippocastanaceae* **2** Also called: **conker** the nut of this tree [c16: so called from its having been used in the treatment of respiratory disease in horses]

horseflesh ('hɔːs,flɛʃ) *n* **1** horses collectively **2** the flesh of a horse, esp edible horse meat

horsefly ('hɔːs,flaɪ) *n*, *pl* **-flies** any large stout-bodied dipterous fly of the family *Tabanidae*, the females of which suck the blood of mammals, esp horses, cattle, and man. Also called: **gadfly, cleg**

horsehair ('hɔːs,hɛə) *n* hair taken chiefly from the tail or mane of a horse, used in upholstery and for fabric, etc

horsehide ('hɔːs,haɪd) *n* **1** the hide of a horse **2** leather made from this hide **3** (*modifier*) made of horsehide

horse latitudes *pl n* *nautical* the latitudes near 30°N or 30°S at sea, characterized by baffling winds, calms, and high barometric pressure [c18: referring either to the high mortality of horses on board ship in these latitudes or to *dead horse* (nautical slang: advance pay), which sailors expected to work off by this stage of a voyage]

horse laugh *n* a coarse, mocking, or raucous laugh; guffaw

horseleech ('hɔːs,liːtʃ) *n* **1** any of several large carnivorous freshwater leeches of the genus *Haemopis*, esp *H. sanguisuga* **2** an archaic name for a **veterinary surgeon**

horse mackerel *n* **1** Also called: **scad** a mackerel-like carangid fish, *Trachurus* of European Atlantic waters, with a row of bony scales along the lateral line **2** any of various large tunnies or related fishes

horseman ('hɔːsmən) *n*, *pl* **-men 1** a person who is skilled in riding or horsemanship **2** a person who rides a horse > 'horse,woman *fem n*

horse mushroom *n* a large edible agaricaceous field mushroom, *Agaricus arvensis*, with a white cap and greyish gills

Horsens (*Danish* 'hɔrsəns) *n* a port in Denmark, in E Jutland at the head of **Horsens Fjord**. Pop: 49 652 (2004 est)

horse pistol *n* a large holstered pistol formerly carried by horsemen

horseplay ('hɔːs,pleɪ) *n* rough, boisterous, or rowdy play

horsepower ('hɔːs,paʊə) *n* **1** an fps unit of power, equal to 550 foot-pounds per second (equivalent to 745.7 watts) **2** a US standard unit of power, equal to 746 watts ▷ Abbreviation: **HP**

horse racing *n* an organized sport, closely associated with gambling, in which riders race horses over dedicated courses, often incorporating hurdles.

horseradish ('hɔːs,rædɪʃ) *n* **1** a coarse Eurasian plant, *Armoracia rusticana*, cultivated for its thick white pungent root: family *Brassicaceae* (crucifers) **2** the root of this plant, which is ground and combined with vinegar, etc, to make a sauce

horse sense *n* another term for **common sense**

horseshoe ('hɔːs,ʃuː) *n* **1** a piece of iron shaped like a U with the ends curving inwards that is nailed to the underside of the hoof of a horse to protect the soft part of the foot from hard surfaces: commonly thought to be a token of good luck **2** an object of similar shape

horseshoe bat *n* any of numerous large-eared Old World insectivorous bats, mostly of the genus *Rhinolophus*, with a fleshy growth around the nostrils, used in echolocation: family *Rhinolophidae*

horseshoe crab *n* any marine chelicerate arthropod of the genus *Limulus*, of North America and Asia, having a rounded heavily armoured body with a long pointed tail: class *Merostomata*. Also called: **king crab**

horsetail ('hɔːs,teɪl) *n* **1** any tracheophyte plant of the genus *Equisetum*, having jointed stems with whorls of small dark toothlike leaves and producing spores within

conelike structures at the tips of the stems: phylum *Sphenophyta* **2** a stylized horse's tail formerly used as the emblem of a pasha, the number of tails increasing with rank

horse trading *n* hard bargaining to obtain equal concessions by both sides in a dispute

horsewhip ('hɔːs,wɪp) *n* **1** a whip, usually with a long thong, used for managing horses ▷ *vb* **-whips, -whipping, -whipped 2** (*tr*) to flog with such a whip > 'horse,whipper *n*

horsey or **horsy** ('hɔːsɪ) *adj* **horsier, horsiest 1** of or relating to horses: *a horsey smell* **2** dealing with or devoted to horses **3** like a horse: *a horsey face* > 'horsily *adv* > 'horsiness *n*

horst (hɔːst) *n* a ridge of land that has been forced upwards between two parallel faults [c20: from German: thicket]

Horta¹ (*Portuguese* 'ɔrtə) *n* a port in the Azores, on the SE coast of Fayal Island

Horta² ('ɔːtə) *n* Victor. 1861–1947, Belgian architect, best known for his early buildings in Art Nouveau style

hortatory ('hɔːtətərɪ, -trɪ) or **hortative** ('hɔːtətɪv) *adj* tending to exhort; encouraging [c16: from Late Latin *hortātōrius*, from Latin *hortārī* to EXHORT] > hor'tation *n* > 'hortatorily or 'hortatively *adv*

Hortense (*French* ɔrtɑs) *n* See (Eugénie Hortense de) **Beauharnais** (sense 3)

Horthy (*Hungarian* 'horti) *n* **Miklós** ('miklɔːʃ), full name *Horthy de Nagybánya*. 1868–1957, Hungarian admiral: suppressed Kun's Communist republic (1919); regent of Hungary (1920–44)

horticulture ('hɔːtɪ,kʌltʃə) *n* the art or science of cultivating gardens [c17: from Latin *hortus* garden + CULTURE, on the model of AGRICULTURE] > ,horti'culturist *n* > ,horti'cultural *adj* > ,horti'culturally *adv* > ,horti'culturalist *n*

Horus ('hɔːrəs) *n* a solar god of Egyptian mythology, usually depicted with a falcon's head [via Late Latin from Greek *Hōros*, from Egyptian *Hur* hawk]

Hos. *abbreviation* Bible Hosea

hosanna (həʊ'zænə) *interj* an exclamation of praise, esp one to God [Old English *osanna*, via Late Latin from Greek, from Hebrew *hōshi 'āh nnā* save now, we pray]

hose¹ (həʊz) *n* **1** a flexible pipe, for conveying a liquid or gas ▷ *vb* **2** (sometimes foll by *down*) to wash, water, or sprinkle (a person or thing) with or as if with a hose [c15: later use of HOSE²]

hose² (həʊz) *n*, *pl* **hose** or **hosen 1** stockings, socks, and tights collectively **2** *history* a man's garment covering the legs and reaching up to the waist; worn with a doublet **3** half-hose socks [Old English *hosa*; related to Old High German *hosa*, Dutch *hoos*, Old Norse *hosa*]

Hosea (həʊ'zɪə) *n* Old Testament **1** a Hebrew prophet of the 8th century BC **2** the book containing his oracles

hoser ('həʊzə) *n* Canadian slang an unsophisticated, esp rural, person

hosier ('həʊzɪə) *n* a person who sells stockings, etc

hosiery ('həʊzɪərɪ) *n* stockings, socks, and knitted underclothing collectively

hospice ('hɒspɪs) *n*, *pl* **hospices 1** a nursing home that specializes in caring for the terminally ill **2** Also called: **hospitium** (hɒ'spɪtɪəm) *pl* **hospitia** (hɒ'spɪtɪə) *archaic* a place of shelter for travellers, esp one kept by a monastic order [c19: from French, from Latin *hospitium* hospitality, from *hospes* guest, HOST¹]

hospitable ('hɒspɪtəbəl, hɒ'spɪt-) *adj* **1** welcoming to guests or strangers **2** fond of entertaining [c16: from Medieval Latin *hospitāre* to receive as a guest, from Latin *hospes* guest, HOST¹] > 'hospitableness *n* > 'hospitably *adv*

hospital ('hɒspɪtəl) *n* **1** an institution for the medical, surgical, obstetric, or psychiatric care and treatment of patients **2** (*modifier*) having the function of a hospital: *a hospital ship* **3** a repair shop for something specified: *a dolls' hospital* **4** archaic a charitable home, hospice, or school [c13: from Medieval Latin *hospitāle* hospice, from Latin *hospitālis* relating to a guest, from *hospes*, hospit-guest, HOST¹]

Hospitalet (*Spanish* ɔspita'lɛt) *n* a city in NE Spain, a SW suburb of Barcelona. Pop: 246 415 (2003 est)

hospitality (ˌhɒspɪˈtælɪtɪ) *n, pl* -ties kindness in welcoming strangers or guests

hospitality suite *n* a room or suite, as at a conference, where free drinks are offered

hospitalization *or* **hospitalisation** (ˌhɒspɪtəlaɪˈzeɪʃən) *n* **1** the act or an instance of being hospitalized **2** the duration of a stay in a hospital

hospitalize *or* **hospitalise** (ˈhɒspɪtəˌlaɪz) *vb* (*tr*) to admit or send (a person) into a hospital

hospitaller *or US* **hospitaler** (ˈhɒspɪtələ) *n* a person, esp a member of certain religious orders, dedicated to hospital work, ambulance services, etc [C14: from Old French *hospitalier*, from Medieval Latin *hospitālārius*, from *hospitāle* hospice; see HOSPITAL]

Hospitaller *or US* **Hospitaler** (ˈhɒspɪtələ) *n* a member of the order of the Knights Hospitallers

hospital pass *n informal* **1** *sport* a pass made to a team-mate who will be tackled heavily as soon as the ball is received **2** a task or project that will inevitably bring heavy criticism on the person to whom it has been assigned

host[1] (həʊst) *n* **1** a person who receives or entertains guests, esp in his own home **2 a** a country or organization which provides facilities for and receives visitors to an event **b** (*as modifier*): *the host nation* **3** the compere of a show or television programme **4** *biology* **a** an animal or plant that nourishes and supports a parasite **b** an animal, esp an embryo, into which tissue is experimentally grafted **5** *computing* a computer connected to a network and providing facilities to other computers and their users **6** the owner or manager of an inn ▷ *vb* **7** to be the host of (a party, programme, etc): *to host one's own show* [C13: from French *hoste*, from Latin *hospes* guest, foreigner, from *hostis* enemy]

host[2] (həʊst) *n* **1** a great number; multitude **2** an archaic word for **army** [C13: from Old French *hoste*, from Latin *hostis* stranger, enemy]

Host (həʊst) *n* the bread consecrated in the Eucharist [C14: from Old French *oiste*, from Latin *hostia* victim]

hosta (ˈhɒstə) *n* any plant of the liliaceous genus *Hosta*, of China and Japan: cultivated esp for their ornamental foliage [C19: New Latin, named after N. T. Host (1761–1834), Austrian physician]

hostage (ˈhɒstɪdʒ) *n* **1** a person given to or held by a person, organization, etc, as a security or pledge or for ransom, release, exchange for prisoners, etc **2** the state of being held as a hostage **3** any security or pledge **4 give hostages to fortune** to place oneself in a position in which misfortune may strike through the loss of what one values most [C13: from Old French, from *hoste* guest, HOST[1]]

hostel (ˈhɒstəl) *n* **1** a building providing overnight accommodation, as for the homeless, etc **2** See **youth hostel** **3** *Brit* a supervised lodging house for nurses, workers, etc **4** *archaic* another word for **hostelry** [C13: from Old French, from Medieval Latin *hospitāle* hospice; see HOSPITAL]

hosteller *or US* **hosteler** (ˈhɒstələ) *n* **1** a person who stays at youth hostels **2** an archaic word for **innkeeper**

hostelling *or US* **hosteling** (ˈhɒstəlɪŋ) *n* the practice of staying at youth hostels when travelling

hostelry (ˈhɒstəlrɪ) *n, pl* -ries *archaic or facetious* an inn

hostess (ˈhəʊstɪs) *n* **1** a woman acting as host **2** a woman who receives and entertains patrons of a club, restaurant, etc **3** See **air hostess**

hostile (ˈhɒstaɪl) *adj* **1** antagonistic; opposed **2** of or relating to an enemy **3** unfriendly [C16: from Latin *hostīlis*, from *hostis* enemy] ▷ ˈhostilely *adv*

hostility (hɒˈstɪlɪtɪ) *n, pl* -ties **1** enmity or antagonism **2** an act expressing enmity or opposition **3** (*plural*) fighting; warfare

hostler (ˈɒslə) *n* another name (esp Brit) for **ostler**

hot (hɒt) *adj* hotter, hottest **1** having a relatively high temperature **2** having a temperature higher than desirable **3** causing or having a sensation of bodily heat **4** causing a burning sensation on the tongue: *hot mustard; a hot curry* **5** expressing or feeling intense emotion, such as embarrassment, anger, or lust **6** intense or vehement **7** recent; fresh; new: *a hot trial; hot*

from the press **8** *ball games* (of a ball) thrown or struck hard, and so difficult to respond to **9** much favoured or approved: *a hot tip; a hot favourite* **10** *informal* having a dangerously high level of radioactivity **11** *slang* (of goods or money) stolen, smuggled, or otherwise illegally obtained **12** *slang* (of people) being sought by the police **13** (of a colour) intense; striking: *hot pink* **14** close or following closely: *hot on the scent* **15** *informal* at a dangerously high electric potential **16** *slang* impressive or good of its kind (esp in the phrase **not so hot**) **17** *jazz slang* arousing great excitement or enthusiasm by inspired improvisation, strong rhythms, etc **18** *informal* dangerous or unpleasant (esp in the phrase **make it hot for someone**) **19** (in various searching or guessing games) very near the answer or object to be found **20** *metallurgy* (of a process) at a sufficiently high temperature for metal to be in a soft workable state **21** *Austral & NZ informal* (of a price, charge, etc) excessive **22** **hot on** *informal* **a** very severe: *the police are hot on drunk drivers* **b** particularly skilled at or knowledgeable about **23 hot under the collar** *informal* aroused with anger, annoyance, etc **24 in hot water** *informal* in trouble, esp with those in authority ▷ *adv* **25** in a hot manner; hotly ▷ See also **hots, hot up** [Old English *hāt*; related to Old High German *heiz*, Old Norse *heitr*, Gothic *heito* fever] > ˈhotly *adv* > ˈhotness *n* > ˈhotish *adj*

hot air *n informal* empty and usually boastful talk

Hotan (ˈhəʊˌtæn), **Hotien** *or* **Ho-t'ien** (ˈhəʊˌtjɛn) *n* **1** an oasis in W China, in the Taklimakan Shamo desert of central Xinjiang, around the seasonal Hotan River **2** the chief town of this oasis, situated at the foot of the Kunlun Mountains. Pop: 114 000 (2006 est) ▷ Also called: Khotan, Hetian

hotbed (ˈhɒtˌbɛd) *n* **1** a glass-covered bed of soil, usually heated by fermenting material, used for propagating plants, forcing early vegetables, etc **2** a place offering ideal conditions for the growth of an idea, activity, etc, esp one considered bad

hot-blooded *adj* **1** passionate or excitable **2** (of a horse) being of thoroughbred stock

hot button *n informal* **a** a controversial subject or issue that is likely to arouse strong emotions **b** (*as modifier*): *the hot-button issue of abortion*

hotchpot (ˈhɒtʃˌpɒt) *n property law* the collecting of property so that it may be redistributed in equal shares, esp on the intestacy of a parent who has given property to his children in his lifetime [C14: from Old French *hochepot*, from *hocher* to shake, of Germanic origin + POT[1]]

hotchpotch (ˈhɒtʃˌpɒtʃ) *or esp US and Canadian* **hodgepodge** *n* **1** a jumbled mixture **2** a thick soup or stew made from meat and vegetables [C15: a variant of HOTCHPOT]

hot cross bun *n* a yeast bun with spices, currants, and sometimes candied peel, marked with a cross and traditionally eaten on Good Friday

hot-desking (ˈdɛskɪŋ) *n* the practice of not assigning permanent desks in a workplace, so that employees may work at any available desk

hot dog[1] *n* a sausage, esp a frankfurter, served hot in a long roll split lengthways [C20: from the supposed resemblance of the sausage to a dachshund]

hot dog[2] *n* **1** *chiefly US* a person who performs showy acrobatic manoeuvres when skiing or surfing ▷ *vb* hot-dog, -dogs, -dogging, -dogged **2** (*intr*) to perform a series of manoeuvres in skiing, surfing, etc, esp in a showy manner [C20: from US *hot dog!*, exclamation of pleasure, approval, etc]

hotel (həʊˈtɛl) *n* a commercially run establishment providing lodging and usually meals for guests, and often containing a public bar [C17: from French *hôtel*, from Old French *hostel*; see HOSTEL]

hotelier (həʊˈtɛljeɪ) *n* an owner or manager of one or more hotels

Hotere (həʊˈtɛərɪ) *n* **Ralph**. born 1931, New Zealand artist of Māori origin, noted esp for his minimalist *Black Paintings*

hot flush *or US* **hot flash** *n* a sudden unpleasant hot feeling in the skin, caused by endocrine imbalance, esp experienced by women at menopause

hotfoot ('hɒt,fʊt) *adv* with all possible speed; quickly

hothead ('hɒt,hɛd) *n* an excitable or fiery person

hot-headed *adj* impetuous, rash, or hot-tempered > ,hot-'headedness *n*

hothouse ('hɒt,haʊs) *n* **1 a** a greenhouse in which the temperature is maintained at a fixed level above that of the surroundings **b** (*as modifier*): *a hothouse plant* **2 a** an environment that encourages rapid development **b** (*as modifier*): *a hot-house atmosphere* **3** (*modifier*) informal, often *pejorative* sensitive or delicate: *a hothouse temperament*

Hotien or **Ho-t'ien** ('həʊ'tjɛn) *n* a variant transliteration of the Chinese name for **Hotan**

hot key *n computing* a single key or combination of keys on the keyboard of a computer that carries out a series of commands

hotline ('hɒt,laɪn) *n* **1** a direct telephone, teletype, or other communications link between heads of government, for emergency use **2** any such direct line kept for urgent use

hot link *n* a word or phrase in a hypertext document that when selected by mouse or keyboard causes information that has been associated with that word or phrase to be displayed

hot money *n* capital transferred from one financial centre to another seeking the highest interest rates or the best opportunity for short-term gain, esp from changes in exchange rates

hotplate ('hɒt,pleɪt) *n* **1** an electrically heated plate on a cooker **2** a portable device, heated electrically or by spirit lamps, etc, on which food can be kept warm

hot pool *n* a pool or spring that is heated geothermally

hotpot ('hɒt,pɒt) *n* **1** Brit a baked stew or casserole made with meat or fish and covered with a layer of potatoes **2** Austral slang a heavily backed horse

hot potato *n slang* an awkward or delicate matter

hot-press *n* **1** a machine for applying a combination of heat and pressure to give a smooth surface to paper, to express oil from it, etc ▷ *vb* **2** (*tr*) to subject (paper, cloth, etc) to heat and pressure to give it a smooth surface or extract oil

hot rod *n* a car with an engine that has been radically modified to produce increased power

hots (hɒts) *pl n* the slang intense sexual desire; lust (esp in the phrase **have the hots for someone**)

hot seat *n* **1** informal a precarious, difficult, or dangerous position **2** US a slang term for **electric chair**

hot spot *n* **1** an area of potential violence or political unrest **2** a lively nightclub or other place of entertainment **3** an area of great activity of a specific type: *the world's economic hot spots* **4** any local area of high temperature in a part of a machine, etc **5** computing a company that provides wireless access to the internet for users of portable computers or a place from which the internet can be accessed in this manner **6** med **a** a small area on the surface of or within a body with an exceptionally high concentration of radioactivity or of some chemical or mineral considered harmful **b** a similar area that generates an abnormal amount of heat, as revealed by thermography

hotspot ('hɒt,spɒt) *n* a place where wireless broadband services are provided to users through a wireless local area network, such as in an airport, railway station, or library

hot spring *n* a natural spring of mineral water at a temperature of 21°C (70°F) or above, found in areas of volcanic activity. Also called: **thermal spring**

hotspur ('hɒt,spɜː) *n* an impetuous or fiery person [c15: from *Hotspur*, nickname of Sir Henry Percy (1364–1403), English rebel]

Hotspur ('hɒt,spɜː) *n* Harry Hotspur the nickname of Sir Henry Percy. See **Percy** (sense 1)

hot stuff *n* informal **1** a person, object, etc, considered important, attractive, sexually exciting, etc **2** a pornographic or erotic book, play, film, etc

hot-swappable *adj computing* (of devices, disks, etc) capable of being inserted or removed from a computer system that is running, without causing damage to or affecting performance

hot swapping *n computing* the insertion or removal of peripheral devices, disks, etc while a computer is still running without either causing damage to the system or affecting performance

Hottentot ('hɒt³n,tɒt) *n offensive* pl -tot or -tots a former name for **Khoikhoi** (sense 1) [c17: from Afrikaans, of uncertain origin]

hotting ('hɒtɪŋ) *n* informal the practice of stealing fast cars and putting on a show of skilful but dangerous driving > 'hotter *n*

hot up *vb* (*adverb*) informal **1** to make or become more exciting, active, or intense **2** (*tr*) another term for **soup up**

hot-water bottle *n* a receptacle, now usually made of rubber, designed to be filled with hot water, used for warming a bed or parts of the body

hot-wire *vb* (*tr*) slang to start the engine of (a motor vehicle) by bypassing the ignition switch

Houdini (huː'diːnɪ) *n* **Harry**, real name *Ehrich Weiss*. 1874–1926, US magician and escapologist

Houdon (*French* udɔ̃) *n* **Jean Antoine** (ʒɑ̃ ɑ̃twan). 1741–1828, French neoclassical portrait sculptor

hough (hɒk) Brit ▷ *n* **1** another word for **hock¹** ▷ *vb* (*tr*) **2** to hamstring (cattle, horses, etc) [c14: from Old English *hōh* heel]

Houghton-le-Spring ('haʊt³nlə'sprɪŋ) *n* a town in N England, in Sunderland unitary authority, Tyne and Wear: coal-mining. Pop: 36 746 (2001)

hound (haʊnd) *n* **1 a** any of several breeds of dog used for hunting **b** (*in combination*): *an otterhound; a deerhound* **2 the hounds** a pack of foxhounds, etc **3** a dog, esp one regarded as annoying **4** a despicable person **5** (in hare and hounds) a runner who pursues a hare **6** slang, chiefly US & Canadian an enthusiast **7 ride to hounds** or **follow the hounds** to take part in a fox hunt with hounds ▷ *vb* (*tr*) **8** to pursue or chase relentlessly **9** to urge on [Old English *hund*; related to Old High German *hunt*, Old Norse *hundr*, Gothic *hunds*] > 'hounder *n*

houndfish ('haʊnd,fɪʃ) *n*, pl -fish or -fishes a name given to various small sharks or dogfish

hound's-tongue *n* any boraginaceous weedy plant of the genus *Cynoglossum*, esp the Eurasian *C. officinale*, which has small reddish-purple flowers and spiny fruits. Also called: dog's-tongue [Old English *hundestunge*, translation of Latin *cynoglōssos*, from Greek *kunoglōssos*, from *kuōn* dog + *giōssa* tongue; referring to the shape of its leaves]

hound's-tooth check *n* a pattern of broken or jagged checks, esp one printed on or woven into cloth. Also called: dog's-tooth check, dogtooth check

Hounslow ('haʊnzləʊ) *n* a borough of Greater London, on the River Thames: site of London's first civil airport (1919). Pop: 212 900 (2003 est). Area: 59 sq km (23 sq miles)

Houphouet-Boigny (*French* ufwɛwaɲi) *n* **Félix** (feliks). 1905–93, Côte d'Ivoire statesman; president of the Côte d'Ivoire (1960–93)

hour (aʊə) *n* **1** a period of time equal to 3600 seconds; 1/24th of a calendar day **2** any of the points on the face of a timepiece that indicate intervals of 60 minutes **3 the hour** an exact number of complete hours: *the bus leaves on the hour* **4** the period of time allowed for or used for something: *the lunch hour; the hour of prayer* **5** a special moment or period: *our finest hour* **6** the distance covered in an hour: *we live an hour from the city* **7** astronomy an angular measurement of right ascension equal to 15° or a 24th part of the celestial equator **8 one's hour a** a time of success, fame, etc **b** Also called: one's last hour the time of one's death ▷ See also **hours** [c13: from Old French *hore*, from Latin *hōra*, from Greek: season]

hour circle *n* a great circle on the celestial sphere passing through the celestial poles and a specified point, such as a star

hourglass ('aʊə,glɑːs) *n* **1** a device consisting of two transparent chambers linked by a narrow channel, containing a quantity of sand that takes a specified time to trickle to one chamber from the other **2** (*modifier*) well-proportioned with a small waist: *an hourglass figure*

hour hand *n* the pointer on a timepiece that indicates the hour

houri ('hʊərɪ) *n*, pl -ris **1** (in Muslim belief) any of the nymphs of Paradise **2** any alluring woman [c18: from French, from Persian *hūri*, from Arabic *hūr*, plural of *haurā'* woman with dark eyes]

hourly ('aʊəlı) *adj* **1** of, occurring, or done every hour **2** done in or measured by the hour: *we are paid an hourly rate* **3** continual or frequent ▷ *adv* **4** every hour **5** at any moment or time

hours (aʊəz) *pl n* **1** a period regularly or customarily appointed for work, business, etc **2** one's times of rising and going to bed (esp in the phrases **keep regular, irregular,** or **late hours**) **3** the small hours the hours just after midnight **4** an indefinite period of time **5** *Roman Catholic Church* Also called: **canonical hours a** the seven times of the day laid down for the recitation of the prayers of the divine office **b** the prayers recited at these times

Hours (aʊəz) *pl n* another word for the **Horae**

house (haʊs) *n, pl* **houses** ('haʊzɪz) **1 a** a building used as a home; dwelling **b** (*as modifier*): *house dog* **2** the people present in a house, esp its usual occupants **3 a** a building used for some specific purpose **b** (*in combination*): *a schoolhouse* **4** (*often capital*) a family line including ancestors and relatives, esp a noble one: *the House of York* **5 a** a commercial company; firm: *a publishing house* **b** (*as modifier*): *house style; a house journal* **6** an official deliberative or legislative body, such as one chamber of a bicameral legislature **7** a quorum in such a body (esp in the phrase **make a house**) **8** a dwelling for a religious community **9** *astrology* any of the 12 divisions of the zodiac **10** any of several divisions, esp residential, of a large school **11** a hotel, restaurant, bar, inn, club, etc, or the management of such an establishment **12** (*modifier*) (of wine) sold unnamed by a restaurant, at a lower price than wines specified on the wine list: *the house red* **13** the audience in a theatre or cinema **14** an informal word for **brothel 15** a hall in which an official deliberative or legislative body meets **16** See **full house 17** *nautical* any structure or shelter on the weather deck of a vessel **18 bring the house down** *theatre* to win great applause **19 like a house on fire** *informal* very well, quickly, or intensely **20 on the house** (usually of drinks) paid for by the management of the hotel, bar, etc **21 put one's house in order** to settle or organize one's affairs **22 safe as houses** *Brit* very secure *vb* (haʊz) **23** (*tr*) to provide with or serve as accommodation **24** to give or receive shelter or lodging **25** (*tr*) to contain or cover, esp in order to protect **26** (*tr*) to fit (a piece of wood) into a mortise, joint, etc [Old English *hūs*; related to Old High German *hūs*, Gothic *gudhūs* temple, Old Norse *hūs* house] ▷ **'houseless** *adj*

House (haʊs) the *n* **1** See **House of Commons 2** *Brit informal* the Stock Exchange

house agent *n Brit* another name for **estate agent**

house arrest *n* confinement to one's own home

houseboat ('haʊs,bəʊt) *n* a stationary boat or barge used as a home

housebound ('haʊs,baʊnd) *adj* unable to leave one's house because of illness, injury, etc

housebreaking ('haʊs,breɪkɪŋ) *n criminal law* the act of entering a building as a trespasser for an unlawful purpose. Assimilated with burglary, 1968 ▷ **'house,breaker** *n*

housecoat ('haʊs,kəʊt) *n* a woman's loose robelike informal garment

house-craft *n* skill in domestic management

housefly ('haʊs,flaɪ) *n, pl* **-flies** a common dipterous fly, *Musca domestica*, that frequents human habitations, spreads disease, and lays its eggs in carrion, decaying vegetables, etc: family *Muscidae*

household ('haʊs,həʊld) *n* **1** the people living together in one house collectively **2** (*modifier*) of, relating to, or used in the running of a household; domestic: *household management*

householder ('haʊs,həʊldə) *n* a person who owns or rents a house ▷ **'house,holder,ship** *n*

household name *or* **household word** *n* a person or thing that is very well known

housekeeper ('haʊs,kiːpə) *n* a person, esp a woman, employed to run a household

housekeeping ('haʊs,kiːpɪŋ) *n* **1** the running of a household **2** money allocated for the running of a household **3** the general maintenance of a computer storage system, including removal of obsolete files, documentation, security copying, etc

houseleek ('haʊs,liːk) *n* any Old World crassulaceous plant of the genus *Sempervivum*, esp *S. tectorum*, which has a rosette of succulent leaves and pinkish flowers: grows on walls

house lights *pl n* the lights in the auditorium of a theatre, cinema, etc

housemaid ('haʊs,meɪd) *n* a girl or woman employed to do housework, esp one who is resident in the household

housemaid's knee *n* inflammation and swelling of the bursa in front of the kneecap, caused esp by constant kneeling on a hard surface

house martin *n* a Eurasian swallow, *Delichon urbica*, with a slightly forked tail and a white and bluish-black plumage

house mouse *n* any of various greyish mice of the Old World genus *Mus*, esp *M. musculus*, a common household pest in most parts of the world: family *Muridae*

House music *or* **House** *n* a type of disco music originating in the late 1980s, based on funk, with fragments of other recordings edited in electronically

House of Assembly *n* a legislative assembly or the lower chamber of such an assembly, esp in various British colonies and countries of the Commonwealth

house of cards *n* **1** a tiered structure created by balancing playing cards on their edges **2** an unstable situation, plan, etc

House of Commons *n* (in Britain, Canada, etc) the lower chamber of Parliament

house of correction *n* (formerly) a place of confinement for persons convicted of minor offences

house officer *or* **houseman** ('haʊsmən) *n, pl* **-men** *med* a doctor who is the most junior member of the medical staff of a hospital, usually resident in the hospital. US and Canadian equivalent: **intern**

house of ill repute *or* **house of ill fame** *n* a euphemistic name for **brothel**

House of Keys *n* the lower chamber of the legislature of the Isle of Man

House of Lords *n* (in Britain) the upper chamber of Parliament, composed of the peers of the realm

House of Representatives *n* **1** (in the US) the lower chamber of Congress **2** (in Australia) the lower chamber of Parliament **3** the sole chamber of New Zealand's Parliament: formerly the lower chamber

house party *n* **1** a party, usually in a country house, at which guests are invited to stay for several days **2** the guests who are invited

house plant *n* a plant that can be grown indoors

house-proud *adj* proud of the appearance, cleanliness, etc, of one's house, sometimes excessively so

houseroom ('haʊs,rʊm, -,ruːm) *n* **1** room for storage or lodging **2 give something houseroom** (*used with a negative*) to have or keep something in one's house

house-sit *vb* **-sits, -sitting, -sat** (*intr*) to live in and look after a house during the absence of its owner or owners ▷ **'house-,sitter** *n*

Houses of Parliament *n* (in Britain) **1** the building in which the House of Commons and the House of Lords assemble **2** these two chambers considered together

house sparrow *n* a small Eurasian weaverbird, *Passer domesticus*, now established in North America and Australia. It has a brown streaked plumage with grey underparts

house-train *vb* (*tr*) *Brit* to train (pets) to urinate and defecate outside the house or in a special place, such as a litter tray ▷ **'house-,trained** *adj*

housewares ('haʊs,wɛəz) *pl n US & Canadian* kitchenware and other utensils for use in the home

house-warming *n* a party given after moving into a new home

housewife ('haʊs,waɪf) *n, pl* **-wives 1** a woman, typically a married woman, who keeps house, usually without having paid employment **2** Also called: **hussy, huswife** ('hʌzɪf) *chiefly Brit* a small sewing kit issued to soldiers

> **housewifery** ('haʊs,wɪfərɪ, -,wɪfrɪ) *n* > **'house,wifely** *adj*
housework ('haʊs,wɜːk) *n* the work of running a home, such as cleaning, cooking, etc
housey-housey ('haʊzɪ'haʊzɪ) *n* another name for **bingo**, **lotto** [C20: so called from the cry of "house!" shouted by the winner of a game, probably from FULL HOUSE]
housing[1] ('haʊzɪŋ) *n* **1 a** houses or dwellings collectively **b** (*as modifier*): *a housing problem* **2** the act of providing with accommodation **3** a hole, recess, groove, or slot made in one wooden member to receive another **4** a part designed to shelter, cover, contain, or support a component, such as a bearing, or a mechanism, such as a pump or wheel: *a bearing housing; a motor housing; a wheel housing*
housing[2] ('haʊzɪŋ) *n* (*often plural*) *archaic* another word for **trappings** (sense 2) [C14: from Old French *houce* covering, of Germanic origin]
housing estate *n* a planned area of housing, often with its own shops and other amenities
housing scheme *n Brit* **1** a local authority housing plan **2** the houses built according to such a plan; housing estate ▷ Often shortened to **scheme**
Housman ('haʊsmən) *n* **A(lfred) E(dward)**. 1859–1936, English poet and classical scholar, author of *A Shropshire Lad* (1896) and *Last Poems* (1922)
Houston ('hjuːstən) *n* an inland port in SE Texas, linked by the **Houston Ship Canal** to the Gulf of Mexico and the Gulf Intracoastal Waterway: capital of the Republic of Texas (1837–39; 1842–45); site of the Manned Spacecraft Center (1964). Pop: 2 009 690 (2003 est)
hove (həʊv) *vb chiefly nautical* a past tense and past participle of **heave**
Hove (həʊv) *n* a town and coastal resort in S England, in Brighton and Hove unitary authority, East Sussex. Pop: 72 335 (2001)
hovel ('hʌvəl, 'hɒv-) *n* **1** a ramshackle dwelling place **2** an open shed for livestock, carts, etc **3** the conical building enclosing a kiln [C15: of unknown origin]
hover ('hɒvə) *vb* **1** (*intr*) to remain suspended in one place **2** (*intr*) (of certain birds, esp hawks) to remain in one place in the air by rapidly beating the wings **3** (*intr*) to linger uncertainly in a nervous or solicitous way **4** (*intr*) to be in a state of indecision ▷ *n* **5** the act of hovering [C14: *hoveren*, variant of *hoven*, of obscure origin]
> **'hoverer** *n*
hovercraft ('hɒvə,krɑːft) *n* a vehicle that is able to travel across both land and water on a cushion of air. The cushion is produced by a fan continuously forcing air under the vehicle
hover fly *n* any dipterous fly of the family *Syrphidae*, with a typically hovering flight, esp *Syrphus ribesii*, which mimics a wasp
hoverport ('hɒvə,pɔːt) *n* a port for hovercraft
hovertrain ('hɒvə,treɪn) *n* a train that moves over a concrete track and is supported while in motion by a cushion of air supplied by powerful fans
how (haʊ) *adv* **1** in what way? in what manner? by what means?: *how did it happen?* Also used in indirect questions: *tell me how he did it* **2** to what extent?: *how tall is he?* **3** how good? how well? what...like?: *how did she sing?; how was the holiday?* **4** how about? used to suggest something: *how about asking her?; how about a cup of tea?* **5** how are you? what is your state of health? **6** how come? *informal* what is the reason (that)?: *how come you told him?* **7** how's that? **a** what is your opinion? **b** *cricket* Also written: **howzat** (an appeal to the umpire) is the batsman out? **8** how now? or how so? *archaic* what is the meaning of this? **9** in whatever way: *do it how you wish* **10** and how! (*intensifier*) very much so! ▷ *n* **11** the way a thing is done: *the how of it* [Old English *hu*; related to Old Frisian *hū*, Old High German *hweo*]
Howard ('haʊəd) *n* **1 Catherine**. ?1521–42, fifth wife of Henry VIII of England; beheaded **2 Charles**, Lord Howard of Effingham and 1st Earl of Nottingham. 1536–1624, Lord High Admiral of England (1585–1618). He commanded the fleet that defeated the Spanish Armada (1588) **3 Sir Ebenezer**. 1850–1928, English town planner, who introduced garden cities **4** Henry Howard See

Surrey[2] **5 John**. 1726–90, English prison reformer **6 John Winston**. born 1939, Australian politician; prime minister of Australia (1996–2007) **7 Leslie**. real name *Leslie Howard Stainer*. 1890–1943, British actor of Hungarian descent. His many films included *The Scarlet Pimpernel* (1938), *Pygmalion* (1938), and *Gone With the Wind* (1939) **8 Trevor**. 1916-88, British actor. His many films include *Brief Encounter* (1946), *The Third Man* (1949), *Ryan's Daughter* (1970), and *White Mischief* (1987)
howbeit (haʊ'biːɪt) *archaic* ▷ *sentence connector* **1** however ▷ *conj* **2** (*subordinating*) though; although
howdah or **houdah** ('haʊdə) *n* a seat for riding on an elephant's back, esp one with a canopy [C18: from Hindi *haudah*, from Arabic *haudaj* load carried by elephant or camel]
how do you do *sentence substitute* **1** Also called: **how do?**, **how d'ye do?** a formal greeting said by people who are being introduced to each other or are meeting for the first time ▷ *n* **how-do-you-do 2** *informal* a difficult situation
howdy ('haʊdɪ) *sentence substitute chiefly US* an informal word for **hello** [C16: from the phrase *how d'ye do*]
Howe (haʊ) *n* **1 Elias**. 1819–67, US inventor of the sewing machine (1846) **2 Gordon**, known as *Gordie*. born 1928, US ice-hockey player, who scored a record 1071 goals in a professional career lasting 32 years. **3 Howe of Aberavon**, Baron, title of (*Richard Edward*) *Geoffrey Howe*. born 1926, British Conservative politician; Chancellor of the Exchequer (1979–83); foreign secretary (1983–89); deputy prime minister (1989–90) **4 Richard**, 4th Viscount Howe. 1726–99, British admiral: served (1776–78) in the War of American Independence and commanded the Channel fleet against France, winning the Battle of the Glorious First of June (1794) **5** his brother, **William**, 5th Viscount Howe. 1729–1814, British general; commander in chief (1776–78) of British forces in the War of American Independence
Howel Dda ('haʊəl 'dɑː) *n* See **Hywel Dda**
however (haʊ'ɛvə) *sentence connector* **1** still; nevertheless **2** on the other hand; yet ▷ *adv* **3** by whatever means; in whatever manner **4** (*used with adjectives expressing or admitting of quantity or degree*) no matter how: *however long it takes, finish it* **5** an emphatic form of **how**[1] (sense 1)
howitzer ('haʊɪtsə) *n* a cannon having a short or medium barrel with a low muzzle velocity and a steep angle of fire [C16: from Dutch *houwitser*, from German *Haubitze*, from Czech *houfnice* stone-sling]
howl (haʊl) *n* **1** a long plaintive cry or wail characteristic of a wolf or hound **2** a similar cry of pain or sorrow **3** *slang* a prolonged outburst of laughter **4** *electronics* an unwanted prolonged high-pitched sound produced by a sound-producing system as a result of feedback ▷ *vb* **5** to express in a howl or utter such cries **6** (*intr*) (of the wind, etc) to make a wailing noise **7** (*intr*) *informal* to shout or laugh [C14: *houlen*; related to Middle High German *hiuweln*, Middle Dutch *hūlen*, Danish *hyle*]
Howland Island ('haʊlənd) *n* a small island in the central Pacific, near the equator northwest of Phoenix Island: US airfield. Area: 2.6 sq km (1 sq mile)
howl down *vb* (*tr, adverb*) to prevent (a speaker) from being heard by shouting disapprovingly
howler ('haʊlə) *n* **1** Also called: **howler monkey** any large New World monkey of the genus *Alouatta*, inhabiting tropical forests in South America and having a loud howling cry **2** *informal* a glaring mistake **3** a person or thing that howls
howling ('haʊlɪŋ) *adj* (*prenominal*) *informal* (intensifier): *a howling success; a howling error*
Howlin' Wolf ('haʊlɪn) *n* real name *Chester Burnett*. 1910–76, US blues singer and songwriter
Howrah ('haʊrə) *n* an industrial city in E India, in West Bengal on the Hooghly River opposite Kolkata (Calcutta). Pop: 1 008 704 (2001)
howsoever (,haʊsəʊ'ɛvə) *sentence connector, adv* a less common word for **however**
how-to *adj* (of a book or guide) giving basic instructions to the lay person on how to do or make something, esp as a hobby or for practical purposes: *a how-to book on carpentry*

howzit ('haʊzɪt) *sentence substitute South African* an informal word for **hello** [c20: from the phrase *how is it?*]

Hoxha (*Albanian* 'hodʒa) *n* **Enver** ('emver). 1908–85, Albanian statesman: founded the Albanian Communist Party in 1941 and was its first secretary (1954–85)

hoy¹ (hɔɪ) *n nautical* **1** a freight barge **2** a coastal fishing and trading vessel, usually sloop-rigged, used during the 17th and 18th centuries [c15: from Middle Dutch *hoei*]

hoy² (hɔɪ) *interj* a cry used to attract attention or drive animals [c14: variant of HEY]

hoya ('hɔɪə) *n* any plant of the asclepiadaceous genus *Hoya*, of E Asia and Australia, esp the waxplant popular as a house plant [c19: named after Thomas *Hoy* (died 1821), English gardener]

hoyden *or* **hoiden** ('hɔɪdᵊn) *n* a wild boisterous girl; tomboy [c16: perhaps from Middle Dutch *heidijn* heathen] > 'hoydenish *or* 'hoidenish *adj*

Hoylake ('hɔɪˌleɪk) *n* a town and resort in NW England, in Wirral unitary authority, Merseyside, on the Irish Sea. Pop: 25 524 (2001)

Hoyle (hɔɪl) *n* Sir **Fred**. 1915–2001, English astronomer and writer: his books include *The Nature of the Universe* (1950) and *Frontiers of Astronomy* (1955), and science-fiction writings

HP *or* **h.p.** *abbreviation* **1** *Brit* hire-purchase **2** horsepower **3** high pressure **4** (in Britain) Houses of Parliament

HPV *abbreviation* human papilloma virus

HQ *or* **h.q.** *abbreviation* headquarters

hr *abbreviation* hour

Hradec Králové (*Czech* 'hradɛts 'kraːlɔvɛː) *n* a town in the N Czech Republic, on the Elbe River. Pop: 97 000 (2005 est). German name: Königgrätz

HRH *abbreviation* His (*or* Her) Royal Highness

HRT *abbreviation* hormone replacement therapy

Hrvatska ('hrvaːtskaː) *n* the Croatian name for **Croatia**

HS *abbreviation* (in Britain) Home Secretary

HSE *abbreviation* (in Britain) Health and Safety Executive

HSH *abbreviation* His (*or* Her) Serene Highness

Hsia Kuei ('ʃja: 'kweɪ) *n* See **Xia Gui**

Hsia-men ('ʃjaː'mɛn) *n* a transliteration of the modern Chinese name for **Amoy**

Hsian (ʃjaːn) *n* a variant transliteration of the Chinese name for **Xi'an**

Hsiang (ʃjaːŋ) *n* a variant transliteration of the Chinese name for **Xiang**

Hsin-hai-lien ('ʃɪn 'haɪ 'ljɛn) *n* a variant transliteration of the alternative name of **Lianyungang**

Hsining ('ʃiː'nɪŋ) *n* a variant transliteration of the Chinese name for **Xining**

Hsinking ('ʃɪn'kɪŋ) *n* the former name (1932–45) of **Changchun**

Hsüan-tsang ('ʃwaːn 'tsæn) *n* a variant transliteration of the Chinese name for **Xuan Zang**

Hsüan-tsung ('ʃwaːn 'tsʊŋ) *n* a variant transliteration of the Chinese name for **Xuan Zong**

Hsüan T'ung ('ʃwaːn 'tʊŋ) *n* a variant transliteration of the Chinese name for **Xuan-tong**

Hsü-chou ('ʃuː'tʃaʊ) *n* a variant transliteration of the Chinese name for **Xuzhou**

Hsün-tzu ('tʃun 'dʒɪ) *n* a variant transliteration of the Chinese name for **Xun Zi**

ht *abbreviation* height

HT *abbreviation physics* high tension

HTLV *abbreviation* human T-cell lymphotrophic virus: any one of a small family of viruses that cause certain rare diseases in the T-cells of human beings; for instance, HTLV I causes a form of leukaemia

HTML *abbreviation* hypertext markup language: a text description language that is used for electronic publishing, esp on the World Wide Web

HTTP *abbreviation* hypertext transfer protocol, used esp on the World Wide Web. See also **hypertext**

Hua Guo Feng ('hwa: gwəʊ 'fʌʃ) *or* **Hua Kuo-feng** ('hwa: kwəʊ 'fɛŋ) *n* born c. 1920, Chinese Communist statesman; prime minister of China 1976–80

Huainan ('hwaɪ'næn) *n* a city in E China, in Anhui province north of Hefei. Pop: 1 422 000 (2005 est)

Huambo (*Portuguese* 'wambu) *n* a town in central Angola: designated at one time by the Portuguese as the future capital of the country. Pop: 756 000 (2005 est). Former name (1928–73): Nova Lisboa

Huang Hai ('hwæŋ 'haɪ) *n* the Pinyin transliteration of the Chinese name for the **Yellow Sea**

Huang Hua (hwæŋ hwaː) *n* born 1913, Chinese Communist statesman; minister for foreign affairs (1976–83)

Huáscar (*Spanish* uaskar) *n* died 1533, Inca ruler (1525–33): murdered by his half brother Atahualpa

Huascarán (*Spanish* uaska'ran) *or* **Huascán** (*Spanish* uas'kan) *n* an extinct volcano in W Peru, in the Peruvian Andes: the highest peak in Peru; avalanche in 1962 killed over 3000 people. Height: 6768 m (22 205 ft)

hub (hʌb) *n* **1** the central portion of a wheel, propeller, fan, etc, through which the axle passes **2** the focal point **3** *computing* a device for connecting computers in a network [c17: probably variant of HOB¹]

hub-and-spoke *n* (*modifier*) denoting a method of organizing intercontinental air traffic in which one major airport is used as a feeder for local airports. Sometimes shortened to **hub**

Hubble ('hʌbᵊl) *n* **Edwin Powell**. 1889–1953, US astronomer, noted for his investigations of nebulae and the recession of the galaxies

hubble-bubble ('hʌbᵊl'bʌbᵊl) *n* **1** another name for **hookah 2** hubbub; turmoil **3** a bubbling or gargling sound [c17: rhyming jingle based on BUBBLE]

Hubble's law *n astronomy* a law stating that the velocity of recession of a galaxy is proportional to its distance from the observer

Hubble telescope *n* a telescope launched into orbit around the earth in 1990 to provide information about the universe in the visible, infrared, and ultraviolet ranges. Also called: Hubble space telescope

hubbub ('hʌbʌb) *n* **1** a confused noise of many voices **2** uproar [c16: probably from Irish *hooboobbes*; compare Scottish Gaelic *ubub!* an exclamation of contempt]

hubby ('hʌbɪ) *n, pl* -bies an informal word for **husband** [c17: by shortening and altering]

hubcap ('hʌbˌkæp) *n* a metal cap fitting onto the hub of a wheel, esp a stainless steel or chromium-plated one

Hubei ('huː'beɪ), **Hupeh** *or* **Hupei** *n* a province of central China: largely low-lying with many lakes. Capital: Wuhan. Pop: 60 020 000 (2003 est). Area: 187 500 sq km (72 394 sq miles)

Hubli ('huːblɪ) *n* a city in W India, in NW Mysore: incorporated with Dharwar in 1961; educational and trading centre. Pop (with Dharwar): 786 018 (2001)

hubris ('hjuːbrɪs) *or* **hybris** ('haɪbrɪs) *n* **1** pride or arrogance **2** (in Greek tragedy) an excess of ambition, pride, etc, ultimately causing the transgressor's ruin [c19: from Greek] > hu'bristic *or* hy'bristic *adj*

huckaback ('hʌkəˌbæk) *n* a coarse absorbent linen or cotton fabric used for towels and informal shirts, etc. Also called: huck (hʌk) [c17: of unknown origin]

huckleberry ('hʌkᵊlˌbɛrɪ) *n, pl* -ries **1** any American ericaceous shrub of the genus *Gaylussacia*, having edible dark blue berries with large seeds **2** the fruit of any of these shrubs **3** a Brit name for **whortleberry** (sense 1) [c17: probably a variant of *hurtleberry*, of unknown origin]

huckster ('hʌkstə) *n* **1** a person who uses aggressive or questionable methods of selling **2** *now rare* a person who sells small articles or fruit in the street **3** *US* a person who writes for radio or television advertisements ▷ *vb* **4** (*tr*) to peddle **5** (*tr*) to sell or advertise aggressively or questionably **6** to haggle (over) [c12: perhaps from Middle Dutch *hoekster*, from *hoeken* to carry on the back]

Huddersfield ('hʌdəzˌfiːld) *n* a town in N England, in Kirklees unitary authority, West Yorkshire, on the River Colne: former textile centre, now with varied manufacturing and services; university 1992. Pop: 146 234 (2001)

huddle ('hʌdᵊl) *n* **1** a heaped or crowded mass of people or things **2** *informal* a private or impromptu conference (esp in the phrase **go into a huddle**) ▷ *vb* **3** to crowd or cause to crowd together or nestle closely together **4** (often foll by *up*) to draw or hunch (oneself), as through cold **5** (*intr*) *informal* to meet and confer privately **6** (*tr*) *chiefly Brit* to do (something) in a careless way **7** (*tr*) *rare* to put on

h

(clothes) hurriedly [c16: of uncertain origin; compare Middle English *hoderen* to wrap up] > 'huddler *n*

Huddleston ('hʌdᵊlstən) *n* Trevor. 1913–98, British Anglican prelate; suffragan bishop of Stepney (1968–78) and bishop of Mauritius (1978–83); president of the Anti-Apartheid Movement (1981–94)

hudna ('hʊdnə) *n* Islam a truce or ceasefire for a fixed duration [c21: Arabic]

Hudson ('hʌdsən) *n* **1 Henry.** died 1611, English navigator: he explored the Hudson River (1609) and Hudson Bay (1610), where his crew mutinied and cast him adrift to die **2 W(illiam) H(enry).** 1841–1922, British naturalist and novelist, born in Argentina, noted esp for his romance *Green Mansions* (1904) and the autobiographical *Far Away and Long Ago* (1918)

Hudson Bay *n* an inland sea in NE Canada: linked with the Atlantic by **Hudson Strait**; the S extension forms James Bay; discovered in 1610 by Henry Hudson. Area (excluding James Bay): 647 500 sq km (250 000 sq miles)

Hudson River *n* a river in E New York State, flowing generally south into Upper New York Bay: linked to the Great Lakes, the St Lawrence Seaway, and Lake Champlain by the New York State Barge Canal and the canalized Mohawk River. Length: 492 km (306 miles)

Hudson's Bay blanket *n* Canadian a woollen blanket with wide stripes [c19: from a type of blanket originally sold by the Hudson's Bay Company]

hue (hju:) *n* **1** the attribute of colour that enables an observer to classify it as red, green, blue, purple, etc, and excludes white, black, and shades of grey **2** a shade of a colour **3** aspect; complexion: *a different hue on matters* [Old English *hīw* beauty; related to Old Norse *hȳ* fine hair, Gothic *hiwi* form] > **hued** *adj*

Hué (French ɥe) *n* a port in central Vietnam, on the delta of the **Hué River** near the South China Sea: former capital of the kingdom of Annam, of French Indochina (1883–1946), and of Central Vietnam (1946–54). Pop: 377 000 (2005 est)

hue and cry *n* **1** (formerly) the pursuit of a suspected criminal with loud cries in order to raise the alarm **2** any loud public outcry [c16: from Anglo-French *hu et cri*, from Old French *hue* outcry, from *huer* to shout, from *hu!* shout of warning + *cri* CRY]

Huelva (Spanish 'uɛlβa) *n* a port in SW Spain, between the estuaries of the Odiel and Tinto Rivers: exports copper and other ores. Pop: 144 831 (2003 est)

Huesca (Spanish 'ueska) *n* a city in NE Spain: Roman town, site of Quintus Sertorius' school (76 BC); 15th-century cathedral and ancient palace of Aragonese kings. Pop: 47 609 (2003 est)

huff (hʌf) *n* **1** a passing mood of anger or pique (esp in the phrase **in a huff**) > *vb* **2** to make or become angry or resentful **3** (intr) to blow or puff heavily **4** Also called: **blow draughts** to remove (an opponent's draught) from the board for failure to make a capture **5** (tr) obsolete to bully **6** huffing and puffing empty threats or objections; bluster [c16: of imitative origin; compare PUFF] > 'huffish or 'huffy *adj* > 'huffily or 'huffishly *adv*

Hufuf (hʊ'fu:f) *n* See **Al Hufuf**

hug (hʌg) *vb* hugs, hugging, hugged (mainly tr) **1** (also intr) to clasp (another person or thing) tightly or (of two people) to cling close together; embrace **2** to keep close to a shore, kerb, etc **3** to cling to (beliefs, etc); cherish **4** to congratulate (oneself); be delighted with (oneself) > *n* **5** a tight or fond embrace [c16: probably of Scandinavian origin; related to Old Norse *hugga* to comfort, Old English *hogian* to take care of] > 'huggable *adj*

huge (hju:dʒ) *adj* extremely large in size, amount, or scope [c13: from Old French *ahuge*, of uncertain origin] > 'hugeness *n* > 'hugely *adv*

hugger-mugger ('hʌgə,mʌgə) *n* **1** confusion **2** rare secrecy > *adj, adv* archaic **3** with secrecy **4** in confusion > *vb* obsolete **5** (tr) to keep secret **6** (intr) to act secretly [c16: of uncertain origin]

Huggins ('hʌgɪnz) *n* Sir **William.** 1824–1910, British astronomer. He pioneered the use of spectroscopy in astronomy and discovered the red shift in the lines of a stellar spectrum

huggy ('hʌgɪ) *adj* -gier, -giest informal sensitive and caring: *a soft, lovely, huggy person*

Hugh Capet ('hju: 'kæpɪt, 'keɪpɪt) *n* See **Capet**

Hughes (hju:z) *n* **1 Howard.** 1905–76, US industrialist, aviator, and film producer. He became a total recluse during the last years of his life **2** (James Mercer) Langston. 1902–67, US Black poet and writer. His collections include *The Weary Blues* (1926) and *The Panther and the Lash* (1967) **3 Richard** (Arthur Warren). 1900–76, British novelist. He wrote *A High Wind in Jamaica* (1929), *In Hazard* (1938), and *The Fox in the Attic* (1961) **4 Robert** (Studley Forrest). born 1938, Australian art critic, writer, and broadcaster; his work includes the television series *The Shock of the New* (1981) and the book *The Culture of Complaint* (1993) **5 Ted,** full name *Edward James Hughes*. 1930–98, British poet: his works include *The Hawk in the Rain* (1957), *Crow* (1970), and *Birthday Letters* (1998). Poet laureate (1984–98) **6 Thomas.** 1822–96, British novelist; author of *Tom Brown's Schooldays* (1857) **7 William Morris.** 1864–1952, Australian statesman, born in England: prime minister of Australia (1915–23)

Hughes syndrome (hju:z) *n* a condition of the autoimmune system caused by antibodies reacting against phospholipids, leading to thrombosis [c20: after Graham *Hughes*, British rheumatologist who described it in 1983]

Hughie ('hju:ɪ) *n* Austral & NZ informal the god of rain and of surf (esp in the phrases **send her down, Hughie!** and **send 'em up, Hughie!**) [c20: of uncertain origin]

Hugo ('hju:gəʊ; French ygo) *n* **Victor** (Marie) (viktɔr). 1802–85, French poet, novelist, and dramatist; leader of the romantic movement in France. His works include the volumes of verse *Les Feuilles d'automne* (1831) and *Les Contemplations* (1856), the novels *Notre-Dame de Paris* (1831) and *Les Misérables* (1862), and the plays *Hernani* (1830) and *Ruy Blas* (1838)

Huguenot ('hju:gə,nəʊ, -,nɒt) *n* **1** a French Calvinist, esp of the 16th or 17th centuries > *adj* **2** designating the French Protestant Church [c16: from French, from Genevan dialect *eyguenot* one who opposed annexation by Savoy, ultimately from Swiss German *Eidgenoss* confederate; influenced by *Hugues*, surname of 16th-century Genevan burgomaster]

huh (spelling pron hʌ) *interj* an exclamation of derision, bewilderment, inquiry, etc

Huhehot (,hu:hɪ'hɒt ,hu:ɪ-) *or* **Hu-ho-hao-t'e** (,hu:həʊ-haʊ'teɪ) *n* a variant transliteration of the Chinese name for **Hohhot**

huhu ('hu:hu:) *n* a New Zealand beetle, *Prionoplus reticularis*, with a hairy body [Māori]

hui ('hu:ɪ) *n, pl* hui *or* huis NZ a conference, meeting, or other gathering [Māori]

huia ('hu:ɪjə) *n* an extinct bird of New Zealand, *Heteralocha acutirostris*, prized by early Māoris for its distinctive tail feathers [Māori]

hula ('hu:lə) *or* **hula-hula** *n* a Hawaiian dance performed by a woman [from Hawaiian]

Hula Hoop *n* trademark a light hoop that is whirled around the body by movements of the waist and hips

hulk (hʌlk) *n* **1** the body of an abandoned vessel **2** disparaging a large or unwieldy vessel **3** disparaging a large ungainly person or thing **4** (often plural) the frame or hull of a ship, used as a storehouse, etc, or (esp in 19th-century Britain) as a prison [Old English *hulc*, from Medieval Latin *hulca*, from Greek *holkas* barge, from *helkein* to tow]

hulking ('hʌlkɪŋ) *adj* big and ungainly

hull (hʌl) *n* **1** the main body of a vessel, tank, flying boat, etc **2** the shell or pod of peas or beans; the outer covering of any fruit or seed; husk **3** the persistent calyx at the base of a strawberry, raspberry, or similar fruit **4** the outer casing of a missile, rocket, etc > *vb* **5** to remove the hulls from (fruit or seeds) **6** (tr) to pierce the hull of (a vessel, tank, etc) [Old English *hulu*; related to Old High German *helawa*, Old English *helan* to hide]

Hull¹ (hʌl) *n* **1** a city and port in NE England, in Kingston upon Hull unitary authority, East Riding of Yorkshire: fishing, food processing; two universities. Pop: 301 416 (2001). Official name: **Kingston upon Hull 2** a city in SE

h

Canada, in SW Quebec on the River Ottawa: a centre of the timber trade and associated industries. Pop: 66 246 (2001)

Hull² (hʌl) n **Cordell.** 1871–1955, US statesman; secretary of state (1933– 44). He helped to found the U.N.: Nobel peace prize 1945

hullabaloo or **hullaballoo** (ˌhʌləbəˈluː) n, pl -loos loud confused noise, esp of protest; commotion [c18: perhaps from interjection HALLO + Scottish baloo lullaby]

hullo (hʌˈləʊ) sentence substitute, n a variant of **hello**

Hulme (hjuːm) n T(**homas**) E(**rnest**). 1883–1917, English literary critic and poet; a proponent of imagism

hum (hʌm) vb hums, humming, hummed **1** (intr) to make a low continuous vibrating sound like that of a prolonged m **2** (intr) (of a person) to sing with the lips closed **3** (intr) to utter an indistinct sound, as in hesitation; hem **4** (intr) informal to be in a state of feverish activity **5** (intr) Brit & Irish slang to smell unpleasant **6** hum and haw See hem² (sense 3) ▷ n **7** a low continuous murmuring sound **8** electronics an undesired low-frequency noise in the output of an amplifier or receiver, esp one caused by the power supply ▷ interj, n **9** an indistinct sound of hesitation, embarrassment, etc; hem [c14: of imitative origin; compare Dutch hommelen, Old High German humbal bumblebee]

human (ˈhjuːmən) adj **1** of, characterizing, or relating to man and mankind: human nature **2** consisting of people: the human race; a human chain **3** having the attributes of man as opposed to animals, divine beings, or machines: human failings **4 a** kind or considerate **b** natural ▷ n **5** a human being; person [c14: from Latin hūmānus; related to Latin homō man] > 'humanness n

human being n a member of any of the races of Homo sapiens; person; man, woman, or child

humane (hjuːˈmeɪn) adj **1** characterized by kindness, mercy, sympathy, etc **2** inflicting as little pain as possible: a humane killing **3** civilizing or liberal (esp in the phrases **humane studies, humane education**) [c16: variant of HUMAN] > hu'manely adv > hu'maneness n

human embryonic stem cell n a stem cell obtained from the blastocyst of a human embryo. Abbreviation: hESC

human growth hormone n another name for **growth hormone.** Abbreviation: HGH

human immunodeficiency virus n the full name for HIV

human interest n (in a newspaper story, news broadcasting, etc) reference to individuals and their emotions

humanism (ˈhjuːməˌnɪzəm) n **1** the denial of any power or moral value superior to that of humanity; the rejection of religion in favour of a belief in the advancement of humanity by its own efforts **2** (often capital) a cultural movement of the Renaissance, based on classical studies **3** interest in the welfare of people > 'humanist n > ˌhuman'istic adj

humanitarian (hjuːˌmænɪˈtɛərɪən) adj **1** having the interests of mankind at heart ▷ n **2** a philanthropist > huˌmani'tarianism n

humanity (hjuːˈmænɪtɪ) n, pl -ties **1** the human race **2** the quality of being human **3** kindness or mercy **4** the humanities (plural) the study of literature, philosophy, and the arts

humanize or **humanise** (ˈhjuːməˌnaɪz) vb **1** to make or become human **2** to make or become humane > ˌhumani'zation or ˌhumani'sation n

humankind (ˌhjuːmənˈkaɪnd) n the human race; humanity

● USAGE See at mankind

humanly (ˈhjuːmənlɪ) adv **1** by human powers or means **2** in a human or humane manner

human nature n the qualities common to humanity

humanoid (ˈhjuːməˌnɔɪd) adj **1** like a human being in appearance ▷ n **2** a being with human rather than anthropoid characteristics **3** (in science fiction) a robot or creature resembling a human being

human papilloma virus n any one of a class of viruses that cause tumours, including warts, in humans.

Certain strains infect the cervix and have been implicated as a cause of cervical cancer. Abbreviation: HPV

human rights pl n the rights of individuals to liberty, justice, etc

Humber (ˈhʌmbə) n an estuary in NE England, into which flow the Rivers Ouse and Trent: flows east into the North Sea; navigable for large ocean-going ships as far as Hull; crossed by the **Humber Bridge** (1981), a single-span suspension bridge with a main span of 1410 m (4626 ft). Length: 64 km (40 miles)

Humberside (ˈhʌmbəˌsaɪd) n a former county of N England around the Humber estuary, formed in 1974 from parts of the East and West Ridings of Yorkshire and N Lincolnshire: replaced in 1996 by the unitary authorities of East Riding of Yorkshire, Kingston upon Hull, North Lincolnshire, and North East Lincolnshire

humble (ˈhʌmbəl) adj **1** conscious of one's failings **2** unpretentious; lowly: a humble cottage; my humble opinion **3** deferential or servile ▷ vb (tr) **4** to cause to become humble; humiliate **5** to lower in status [c13: from Old French, from Latin humilis low, from humus the ground] > 'humbleness n > 'humbly adv

humblebee (ˈhʌmbəlˌbiː) n another name for the **bumblebee** [c15: related to Middle Dutch hommel bumblebee, Old High German humbal; see HUM]

humble pie n **1** (formerly) a pie made from the heart, entrails, etc, of a deer **2** eat humble pie to behave or be forced to behave humbly; be humiliated [c17: earlier an umble pie, by mistaken word division from a numble pie, from numbles offal of a deer, from Old French nombles, ultimately from Latin lumbulus a little loin, from lumbus loin]

Humboldt (ˈhʌmbəʊlt; German ˈhʊmbɔlt) n **1** Baron (**Friedrich Heinrich**) **Alexander von** (alɛˈksandər fɔn). 1769–1859, German scientist, who made important scientific explorations in Central and South America (1799–1804). In Kosmos (1845–62), he provided a comprehensive description of the physical universe **2** his brother, Baron (**Karl**) **Wilhelm von** (ˈvɪlhɛlm fɔn). 1767–1835, German philologist and educational reformer

Humboldt Current (ˈhʌmbəʊlt) n a cold ocean current of the S Pacific, flowing north along the coasts of Chile and Peru. Also called: Peru Current

humbug (ˈhʌmˌbʌg) n **1** a person or thing that tricks or deceives **2** nonsense; rubbish **3** Brit a hard boiled sweet, usually flavoured with peppermint and often having a striped pattern ▷ vb -bugs, -bugging, -bugged **4** to cheat or deceive (someone) [c18: of unknown origin] > 'hum,bugger n > 'hum,buggery n

humdinger (ˈhʌmˌdɪŋə) n slang an excellent person or thing [c20: of unknown origin]

humdrum (ˈhʌmˌdrʌm) adj **1** ordinary; dull ▷ n **2** a monotonous routine, task, or person [c16: rhyming compound, probably based on HUM]

Hume (hjuːm) n **1** (**George**) **Basil.** 1923–99, English Roman Catholic Benedictine monk and cardinal; archbishop of Westminster (1976–99) **2** David. 1711–76, Scottish empiricist philosopher, economist, and historian, whose sceptic philosophy restricted human knowledge to that which can be perceived by the senses. His works include A Treatise of Human Nature (1740), An Enquiry concerning the Principles of Morals (1751), Political Discourses (1752), and History of England (1754–62) **3** John. born 1937, Northern Ireland politician; leader of the Social Democratic and Labour Party (SDLP) (1979–2001). Nobel peace prize jointly with David Trimble in 1998 > 'Humism n

humectant (hjuːˈmɛktənt) adj **1** producing moisture ▷ n **2** a substance added to another substance to keep it moist [c17: from Latin ūmectāre to wet, from ūmēre to be moist, from ūmor moisture; see HUMOUR]

humerus (ˈhjuːmərəs) n, pl -meri (-məˌraɪ) **1** the bone that extends from the shoulder to the elbow **2** the corresponding bone in other vertebrates [c17: from Latin umerus; related to Gothic ams shoulder, Greek ōmos] > 'humeral adj

humid (ˈhjuːmɪd) adj moist; damp [c16: from Latin ūmidus, from ūmēre to be wet; see HUMECTANT, HUMOUR]

> 'humidly *adv* > 'humidness *n*

humidex ('hju:mɪˌdɛks) *n Canadian* a scale indicating the levels of heat and humidity in current weather conditions [C20: from HUMID + (IN)DEX]

humidifier (hju:'mɪdɪˌfaɪə) *n* a device for increasing or controlling the water vapour in a room, building, etc

humidify (hju:'mɪdɪˌfaɪ) *vb* -fies, -fying, -fied (*tr*) to make (air) humid or damp > huˌmidifi'cation *n*

humidity (hju:'mɪdɪtɪ) *n* **1** the state of being humid; dampness **2** a measure of the amount of moisture in the air

humidor ('hju:mɪˌdɔ:) *n* a humid place or container for storing cigars, tobacco, etc

humify ('hju:mɪˌfaɪ) *vb* -fies, -fying, -fied to convert or be converted into humus > ˌhumifi'cation *n*

humiliate (hju:'mɪlɪˌeɪt) *vb* (*tr*) to lower or hurt the dignity or pride of [C16: from Late Latin *humiliāre*, from Latin *humilis* HUMBLE] > hu'miliˌatingly *adv* > huˌmili'ation *n* > hu'miliˌator *n*

humility (hju:'mɪlɪtɪ) *n, pl* -ties the state or quality of being humble

humint ('hju:mɪnt) *n* human intelligence: military intelligence gained from human sources with knowledge of the target area

Hummel ('hʊməl) *n* **Johann Nepomuk** (joˈhan 'ne:pomʊk). 1778–1837, German composer and pianist

hummingbird ('hʌmɪŋˌbɜ:d) *n* any very small American bird of the family *Trochilidae*, having a brilliant iridescent plumage, long slender bill, and wings specialized for very powerful vibrating flight: order *Apodiformes*

hummock ('hʌmək) *n* **1** a hillock; knoll **2** a ridge or mound of ice in an ice field **3** Also called: **hammock** *chiefly Southern US* a wooded area lying above the level of an adjacent marsh [C16: of uncertain origin; compare HUMP, HAMMOCK] > 'hummocky *adj*

hummus, hoummos or **houmous** ('hʊməs) *n* a creamy dip originating in the Middle East, made from puréed chickpeas, tahina, etc [from Turkish *humus*]
● USAGE **humus**

humongus (ˌhju:'mʌŋgəs) *adj* exceptionally large; huge [C20: of uncertain origin]

humoral ('hju:mərəl) *adj* **1** *immunol* denoting or relating to a type of immunity caused by free antibodies circulating in the blood **2** *obsolete* of or relating to the four bodily fluids (humours)

humoresque (ˌhju:mə'rɛsk) *n* a short lively piece of music [C19: from German *Humoreske*, ultimately from English HUMOUR]

humorist ('hju:mərɪst) *n* a person who acts, speaks, or writes in a humorous way

humorous ('hju:mərəs) *adj* **1** funny; comical; amusing **2** displaying or creating humour **3** *archaic* another word for **capricious** > 'humorously *adv* > 'humorousness *n*

humour or *US* **humor** ('hju:mə) *n* **1** the quality of being funny **2** Also called: **sense of humour** the ability to appreciate or express that which is humorous **3** situations, speech, or writings that are thought to be humorous **4 a** a state of mind; temper; mood **b** (*in combination*): *ill humour; good humour* **5** temperament or disposition **6** a caprice or whim **7** any of various fluids in the body, esp the aqueous humour and vitreous humour **8** Also called: **cardinal humour** *archaic* any of the four bodily fluids (blood, phlegm, choler or yellow bile, melancholy or black bile) formerly thought to determine emotional and physical disposition **9** out of humour in a bad mood ▷ *vb* (*tr*) **10** to attempt to gratify; indulge: *he humoured the boy's whims* **11** to adapt oneself to: *to humour someone's fantasies* [C14: from Latin *humor* liquid; related to Latin *ūmēre* to be wet, Old Norse *vökr* moist, Greek *hugros* wet] > 'humourless or *US* 'humorless *adj*

hump ('hʌmp) *n* **1** a rounded protuberance or projection, as of earth, sand, etc **2** *pathol* a rounded deformity of the back in persons with kyphosis, consisting of a convex spinal curvature **3** a rounded protuberance on the back of a camel or related animal **4** the hump *Brit informal* a fit of depression or sulking (esp in the phrase **it gives me the hump**) ▷ *vb* **5** to form or become a hump; hunch; arch **6** (*tr*) *Brit slang* to carry or heave **7** *slang* to have sexual intercourse with (someone) [C18: probably from

earlier HUMPBACKED] > 'humpy *adj*

humpback ('hʌmpˌbæk) *n* **1** another word for **hunchback** **2** Also called: **humpback whale** a large whalebone whale, *Megaptera novaeangliae*, closely related and similar to the rorquals but with a humped back and long flippers: family *Balaenopteridae* **3** a Pacific salmon, *Oncorhynchus gorbuscha*, the male of which has a humped back and hooked jaws **4** Also called: **humpback bridge** *Brit* a road bridge having a sharp incline and decline and usually a narrow roadway [C17: alteration of earlier *crumpbacked*, perhaps influenced by HUNCHBACK; perhaps related to Dutch *homp* lump] > 'humpˌbacked *adj*

Humperdinck (German 'hʊmpərdɪŋk) *n* **Engelbert** ('ɛŋəlbɛrt). 1854–1921, German composer, esp of operas, including *Hansel and Gretel* (1893)

humph (*spelling pron* hʌmf) *interj* an exclamation of annoyance, dissatisfaction, scepticism, etc

Humphrey ('hʌmfrɪ) *n* **1** Duke Humphrey See **Gloucester²** (sense 1) **2 Hubert Horatio.** 1911–78, US statesman; vice-president of the US under President Johnson (1965–69)

Humphreys Peak ('hʌmfrɪz) *n* a mountain in N central Arizona, in the San Francisco Peaks: the highest peak in the state. Height: 3862 m (12 670 ft)

Humphries ('hʌmfrɪz) *n* (**John**) **Barry.** born 1934, Australian comic actor and writer, best known for creating the character Dame Edna Everage

humpty dumpty ('hʌmptɪ 'dʌmptɪ) *n chiefly Brit* **1** a short fat person **2** a person or thing that once overthrown or broken cannot be restored or mended [C18: after the nursery rhyme *Humpty Dumpty*]

humpy ('hʌmpɪ) *n, pl* humpies *Austral* a primitive hut [C19: from a native Australian language]

Hums (hums) *n* a variant of **Homs**

humus ('hju:məs) *n* a dark brown or black colloidal mass of partially decomposed organic matter in the soil. It improves the fertility and water retention of the soil and is therefore important for plant growth [C18: from Latin: soil, earth]
● USAGE Avoid confusion with **hummus**

humvee ('hʌmˌvi:) *n* a four-wheel drive military vehicle [from h(igh-mobility) + m(ulti-purpose) v(ehicle) + -EE]

Hun (hʌn) *n* **1** a member of any of several Asiatic nomadic peoples speaking Mongoloid or Turkic languages who dominated much of Asia and E Europe from before 300 BC, invading the Roman Empire in the 4th and 5th centuries AD **2** *informal* (esp in World War I) a derogatory name for a **German 3** *informal* a vandal [Old English *Hūnas*, from Late Latin *Hūnī*, from Turkish *Hun-yū*] > 'Hunˌlike *adj* > 'Hunnish *adj*

Hunan ('hu:'næn) *n* a province of S China, between the Yangtze River and the Nan Ling Mountains: drained chiefly by the Xiang and Yüan Rivers; valuable mineral resources. Capital: Changsha. Pop: 66 630 000 (2003 est). Area: 210 500 sq km (82 095 sq miles)

hunch (hʌntʃ) *n* **1** an intuitive guess or feeling **2** another word for **hump 3** a lump or large piece ▷ *vb* **4** to bend or draw (oneself or a part of the body) up or together **5** (*intr*; usually foll by *up*) to sit in a hunched position [C16: of unknown origin]

hunchback ('hʌntʃˌbæk) *n* **1** a person having an abnormal convex curvature of the thoracic spine **2** such a curvature ▷ Also called: **humpback** [C18: from earlier *hunchbacked, huckbacked* humpbacked; influenced by *bunchbacked*, from *bunch* (in obsolete sense of *hump*) + BACKED] > 'hunchˌbacked *adj*

hundred ('hʌndrəd) *n, pl* -dreds or -dred **1** the cardinal number that is the product of ten and ten; five score **2** a numeral, 100, C, etc, representing this number **3** (*often plural*) a large but unspecified number, amount, or quantity **4** (*plural*) the 100 years of a specified century: *in the sixteen hundreds* **5** something representing, represented by, or consisting of 100 units **6** *maths* the position containing a digit representing that number followed by two zeros: *in 4376, 3 is in the hundred's place* **7** an ancient division of a county in England, Ireland, and parts of the US ▷ *determiner* **8** amounting to or approximately a hundred: *a hundred reasons for that* [Old English; related to Old Frisian *hunderd*, Old Norse hundrath, German *hundert*, Gothic *hund*, Latin *centum*, Greek *hekaton*] > 'hundredth *adj, n*

hundreds and thousands *pl n* tiny beads of brightly coloured sugar, used in decorating cakes, sweets, etc

hundredweight ('hʌndrəd,weɪt) *n, pl* -weights *or* -weight **1** Also called: **long hundredweight** *Brit* a unit of weight equal to 112 pounds or 50.802 35 kilograms **2** Also called: **short hundredweight** *US & Canadian* a unit of weight equal to 100 pounds or 45.359 24 kilograms **3** Also called: **metric hundredweight** a metric unit of weight equal to 50 kilograms > Abbreviation (for senses 1, 2): **cwt**

hung (hʌŋ) *vb* **1** the usual past tense and past participle of: **hang** > *adj* **2** (of a legislative assembly) not having a party with a working majority: *a hung parliament* **3** hung over *informal* suffering from the effects of a hangover **4** hung up *slang* **a** impeded by some difficulty or delay **b** in a state of confusion; emotionally disturbed **5** hung up on *slang* obsessively or exclusively interested in

Hung. *abbreviation* **1** Hungarian **2** Hungary

Hungarian (hʌŋ'gɛərɪən) *n* **1** the official language of Hungary, also spoken in Romania and elsewhere, belonging to the Finno-Ugric family and most closely related to the Ostyak and Vogul languages of NW Siberia **2** a native, inhabitant, or citizen of Hungary > *adj* **3** of or relating to Hungary, its people, or their language > See **Magyar**

Hungary ('hʌŋgərɪ) *n* a republic in central Europe: Magyars first unified under Saint Stephen, the first Hungarian king (1001–38); taken by the Hapsburgs from the Turks at the end of the 17th century; gained autonomy with the establishment of the dual monarchy of Austria-Hungary (1867) and became a republic in 1918; passed under Communist control in 1949; a popular rising in 1956 was suppressed by Soviet troops; a multi-party democracy replaced Communism in 1989 after mass protests; joined the EU in 2004. It consists chiefly of the Middle Danube basin and plains. Official language: Hungarian. Religion: Christian majority. Currency: forint. Capital: Budapest. Pop: 9 831 000 (2004 est). Area: 93 030 sq km (35 919 sq miles). Hungarian name: **Magyarország**

hunger ('hʌŋgə) *n* **1** a feeling of pain, emptiness, or weakness induced by lack of food **2** an appetite, desire, need, or craving: *hunger for a woman* > *vb* **3** (*intr; usually foll by for or after*) to have a great appetite or desire (for) [Old English *hungor*; related to Old High German *hungar*, Old Norse *hungr*, Gothic *hūhrus*]

hunger march *n* a procession of protest or demonstration by the unemployed

hunger strike *n* a voluntary fast undertaken, usually by a prisoner, as a means of protest > **hunger striker** *n*

Hung Hsiu-ch'uan (hʌŋ 'ʃjuː 'tʃwaːn) *n* See **Hong Xiu Quan**

Hungnam (,hʊŋ'næm) *n* a port in E North Korea, on the Sea of Japan (East Sea) southeast of Hamhung. Pop: about 200 000 (latest est), but the city was merged administratively with Hamhung in 2005 and figures are not normally published separately

hungry ('hʌŋgrɪ) *adj* -grier, -griest **1** desiring food **2** (*postpositive; foll by for*) having a craving, desire, or need (for) **3** expressing or appearing to express greed, craving, or desire **4** lacking fertility; poor **5** *Austral & NZ informal* **a** greedy; grasping **b** stingy; mean **6** *NZ* (of timber) dry and bare > **hungrily** *or* **hungeringly** *adv* > **hungriness** *n*

Hung-wu (hʌŋ 'wuː) *n* See **Hong-wu**

hunk (hʌŋk) *n* **1** a large piece **2** Also called: **hunk of a man** *slang* a well-built, sexually attractive man [C19: probably related to Flemish *hunke*; compare Dutch *homp* lump]

hunkers ('hʌŋkəz) *pl n* haunches [C18: of uncertain origin]

hunky-dory (,hʌŋkɪ'dɔːrɪ) *adj informal* very satisfactory; fine [C20: of uncertain origin]

hunt (hʌnt) *vb* **1** to seek out and kill or capture (game or wild animals) for food or sport **2** (*intr; often foll by for*) to look (for); search (for): *to hunt for a book; to hunt up a friend* **3** (*tr*) to use (hounds, horses, etc) in the pursuit of wild animals, game, etc: *to hunt a pack of hounds* **4** (*tr*) to search

or draw (country) to hunt wild animals, game, etc: *to hunt the parkland* **5** (*tr; often foll by down*) to track or chase diligently, esp so as to capture: *to hunt down a criminal* **6** (*tr; usually passive*) to persecute; hound **7** (*intr*) (of a gauge indicator, engine speed, etc) to oscillate about a mean value or position **8** (*intr*) (of an aircraft, rocket, etc) to oscillate about a flight path > *n* **9** the act or an instance of hunting **10** chase or search, esp of animals or game **11** the area of a hunt **12** a party or institution organized for the pursuit of wild animals or game, esp for sport **13** the participants in or members of such a party or institution **14** in the hunt *informal* having a chance of success: *that result keeps us in the hunt* [Old English *huntian*; related to Old English *hentan*, Old Norse *henda* to grasp]

Hunt (hʌnt) *n* **1 Henry**, known as *Orator Hunt*. 1773–1835, British radical, who led the mass meeting that ended in the Peterloo Massacre (1819) **2** (**William**) **Holman**. 1827–1910, British painter; a founder of the Pre-Raphaelite Brotherhood (1848) **3 James**. 1947–93, British motor-racing driver: world champion 1976 **4** (**Henry Cecil**) **John**, Baron. 1910–98, British army officer and mountaineer. He planned and led the expedition that first climbed Mount Everest (1953) **5** (**James Henry**) **Leigh** (liː). 1784–1859, British poet and essayist: a founder of *The Examiner* (1808) in which he promoted the work of Keats and Shelley

huntaway ('hʌntə,weɪ) *n NZ* a dog trained to drive sheep at a long distance from the shepherd

hunted ('hʌntɪd) *adj* harassed and worn: *he has a hunted look*

hunter ('hʌntə) *n* **1** a person or animal that seeks out and kills or captures game. Female equivalent: **huntress** ('hʌntrɪs) **2 a** a person who looks diligently for something **b** (*in combination*): *a fortune-hunter* **3** a specially bred horse used in hunting, usually characterized by strength and stamina **4** Also called: **hunting watch** a watch with a hinged metal lid or case (**hunting case**) to protect the crystal

Hunter ('hʌntə) *n* **1 John**. 1728–93, British physician, noted for his investigation of venereal and other diseases **2** his brother, **William**. 1718–83, British anatomist and obstetrician

hunter-killer *adj* denoting a type of naval vessel, esp a submarine, designed and equipped to pursue and destroy enemy craft

hunter's moon *n* the full moon following the harvest moon

hunting ('hʌntɪŋ) *n* **a** the pursuit and killing or capture of game and wild animals, regarded as a sport **b** (*as modifier*): *hunting boots; hunting lodge*

Huntingdon[1] ('hʌntɪŋdən) *n* a town in E central England, in Cambridgeshire: birthplace of Oliver Cromwell. Pop (with Godmanchester): 20 600 (2001)

Huntingdon[2] ('hʌntɪŋdən) *n* **Selina**, Countess of Huntingdon. 1707–91, English religious leader, who founded a Calvinistic Methodist sect

Huntingdonshire ('hʌntɪŋdənˌʃɪə, -ʃə) *n* (until 1974) a former county of E England, now part of Cambridgeshire

hunting horn *n* a long straight metal tube with a flared end and a cylindrical bore, used in giving signals in hunting

Huntington's disease ('hʌntɪŋtən) *n* a rare hereditary type of chorea, marked by involuntary jerky movements, impaired speech, and increasing dementia [C19: named after George *Huntington* (1850–1916), US neurologist]

huntsman ('hʌntsmən) *n, pl* -men **1** a person who hunts **2** a person who looks after and trains hounds, and manages them during a hunt

Huntsville ('hʌntsvɪl) *n* a city in NE Alabama: space-flight and guided-missile research centre. Pop: 164 237 (2003 est)

Hunyadi (Hungarian 'hunjɔdi) *n* **János** ('jaːnoʃ). ?1387–1456, Hungarian general, who led Hungarian resistance to the Turks, defeating them notably at Belgrade (1456)

Huon pine ('hjuːɒn) *n* a Tasmanian coniferous tree,

Dacrydium franklinii, with scalelike leaves and cup-shaped berry-like fruits: family *Podocarpaceae*. It is among the oldest living individual plants, thought to be up to 10 000 years old [named after the *Huon* River, Tasmania]

Hupeh *or* **Hupei** ('xuː'peɪ) *n* a variant transliteration of the Chinese name for **Hubei**

Hurd (hɜːd) *n* **Douglas** (**Richard**), Baron Hurd of Westwell. born 1930, British Conservative politician; home secretary (1985–89); foreign secretary (1989–95)

hurdle ('hɜːdᵊl) *n* **1 a** *athletics* one of a number of light barriers over which runners leap in certain events **b** a low barrier used in certain horse races **2** an obstacle to be overcome **3** a light framework of interlaced osiers, wattle, etc, used as a temporary fence **4** *Brit* a sledge on which criminals were dragged to their executions ▷ *vb* **5** to jump (a hurdle, etc), as in racing **6** (*tr*) to surround with hurdles **7** (*tr*) to overcome [Old English *hyrdel*; related to Gothic *haurds* door, Old Norse *hurth* door, Old High German *hurd*, Latin *crātis*, Greek *kurtos* basket]
▷ 'hurdler *n*

hurdy-gurdy ('hɜːdɪ'ɡɜːdɪ) *n*, *pl* -dies any mechanical musical instrument, such as a barrel organ [c18: rhyming compound, probably of imitative origin]

hurl (hɜːl) *vb* **1** (*tr*) to throw or propel with great force **2** (*tr*) to utter with force; yell: *to hurl insults* ▷ *n* **3** the act or an instance of hurling [c13: probably of imitative origin]

hurling ('hɜːlɪŋ) *n* a traditional Irish game resembling hockey and lacrosse, played with sticks and a ball between two teams of 15 players each

hurly-burly ('hɜːlɪ'bɜːlɪ) *n*, *pl* hurly-burlies confusion or commotion [c16: from earlier *hurling and burling*, rhyming phrase based on *hurling* in obsolete sense of uproar]

Huron ('hjʊərən) *n* **1** Lake a lake in North America, between the US and Canada: the second largest of the Great Lakes. Area: 59 570 sq km (23 000 sq miles) **2** *pl* -rons *or* -ron a member of a North American Indian people formerly living in the region east of Lake Huron **3** the Iroquoian language of this people

hurrah (hʊ'rɑː), **hooray** (huː'reɪ) *or* **hurray** (hʊ'reɪ) *interj*, *n* **1** a cheer of joy, victory, etc ▷ *vb* **2** to shout "hurrah" [c17: probably from German *hurra*; compare HUZZAH]

hurricane ('hʌrɪkᵊn, -keɪn) *n* **1** a severe, often destructive storm, esp a tropical cyclone **2** a wind of force 12 or above on the Beaufort scale [c16: from Spanish *huracán*, from Taino *hurakán*, from *hura* wind]

hurricane deck *n* a ship's deck that is covered by a light deck as a sunshade

hurricane lamp *n* a paraffin lamp, with a glass covering to prevent the flame from being blown out. Also called: storm lantern

hurried ('hʌrɪd) *adj* performed with great or excessive haste ▷ 'hurriedly *adv* ▷ 'hurriedness *n*

hurry ('hʌrɪ) *vb* -ries, -rying, -ried **1** (*intr*; often foll by *up*) to hasten (to do something); rush **2** (*tr*; often foll by *along*) to speed up the completion, progress, etc, of ▷ *n* **3** haste **4** urgency or eagerness **5** in a hurry *informal* **a** easily: *you won't beat him in a hurry* **b** willingly: *we won't go there again in a hurry* [c16 *horyen*, probably of imitative origin; compare Middle High German *hurren*; see SCURRY]

hurst (hɜːst) *n* *archaic* **1** a wood **2** a sandbank [Old English *hyrst*; related to Old High German *hurst*]

Hurstmonceux ('hɜːstmənˌsuː, -ˌsəʊ) *n* a variant spelling of **Herstmonceux**

hurt (hɜːt) *vb* hurts, hurting, hurt **1** to cause physical pain to (someone or something) **2** to cause emotional pain or distress to (someone) **3** to produce a painful sensation in (someone): *the bruise hurts* **4** (*intr*) *informal* to feel pain ▷ *n* **5** physical, moral, or mental pain or suffering **6** a wound, cut, or sore **7** damage or injury; harm ▷ *adj* **8** injured or pained physically or emotionally: *a hurt knee; a hurt look* [c12 *hurten* to hit, from Old French *hurter* to knock against, probably of Germanic origin; compare Old Norse *hrútr* ram, Middle High German *hurt* a collision]

hurtful ('hɜːtfʊl) *adj* causing distress or injury: *to say hurtful things* ▷ 'hurtfully *adv*

hurtle ('hɜːtᵊl) *vb* **1** to project or be projected very quickly, noisily, or violently **2** (*intr*) *rare* to collide [c13 *hurtlen*, from

hurten to strike; see HURT¹]

Hus (*Czech* hʊs) *n* **Jan** (jan). the Czech name of John Huss. See **Huss**

Husain (hʊ'seɪn, -'saɪn) *n* **1** ?629–680 AD, Islamic caliph, the son of Ali and Fatima and the grandson of Mohammed **2** same as **Hussein**

husband ('hʌzbənd) *n* **1** a woman's partner in marriage **2** *archaic* a manager of an estate ▷ *vb* **3** to manage or use (resources, finances, etc) thriftily **4** *archaic* (*tr*) to find a husband for **5** (*tr*) *obsolete* to till (the soil) [Old English *hūsbonda*, from Old Norse *hūsbōndi*, from *hūs* house + *bōndi* one who has a household, from *bōa* to dwell]
▷ 'husbander *n*

husbandman ('hʌzbəndmən) *n*, *pl* -men a farmer

husbandry ('hʌzbəndrɪ) *n* **1** farming, esp when regarded as a science, skill, or art **2** management of affairs and resources

Husein ibn-Ali (hʊ'seɪn 'ɪbᵊn'ɑːlɪ, ˌælɪ, hʊ'saɪn) *n* 1856–1931, first king of Hejaz (1916–24): initiated the Arab revolt against the Turks (1916–18); forced to abdicate by ibn-Saud

hush (hʌʃ) *vb* **1** to make or become silent; quieten ▷ *n* **2** stillness; silence ▷ *interj* **3** a plea or demand for silence [c16: probably from earlier *husht* quiet!, the -t being thought to indicate a past participle] ▷ hushed *adj*

hushaby ('hʌʃəˌbaɪ) *interj*, *pl* -bies **1** used in quietening a baby or child to sleep ▷ *n* **2** a lullaby [c18: from HUSH¹ + *by*, as in BYE-BYE]

hush-hush *adj* *informal* (esp of official work, documents, etc) secret; confidential

hush money *n* *slang* money given to a person, such as an accomplice, to ensure that something is kept secret

hush up *vb* (*tr, adverb*) to suppress information or rumours about

husk (hʌsk) *n* **1** the external green or membranous covering of certain fruits and seeds **2** any worthless outer covering ▷ *vb* **3** (*tr*) to remove the husk from [c14: probably based on Middle Dutch *huusken* little house, from *hūs* house; related to Old English *hosu* husk, *hūs* HOUSE]

husky¹ ('hʌskɪ) *adj* huskier, huskiest **1** (of a voice, an utterance, etc) slightly hoarse or rasping **2** of, like, or containing husks **3** *informal* big, strong, and well-built [c19: probably from HUSK, from the toughness of a corn husk] ▷ 'huskily *adv* ▷ 'huskiness *n*

husky² ('hʌskɪ) *n*, *pl* huskies **1** a breed of Arctic sled dog with a thick dense coat, pricked ears, and a curled tail **2** *Canad slang* **a** a member of the Inuit people **b** the Inuit language [c19: probably based on ESKIMO]

Huss (hʌs) *n* **John**, Czech name Jan Hus. ?1372–1415, Bohemian religious reformer. Influenced by Wycliffe, he anticipated the Reformation in denouncing doctrines and abuses of the Church. His death at the stake precipitated the Hussite wars in Bohemia and Moravia

Hussain (hʊ'seɪn) *n* **Nasser** ('næsə). born 1968, British cricketer born in India, captain of England (1999–2003)

hussar (hʊ'zɑː) *n* **1** a member of any of various light cavalry regiments in European armies, renowned for their elegant dress **2** a Hungarian horseman of the 15th century [c15: from Hungarian *huszár* hussar, formerly freebooter, from Old Serbian *husar*, from Old Italian *corsaro* CORSAIR]

Hussein (hʊ'seɪn) *n* **1** Also called: Husain 1935–99, king of Jordan (1952–99) **2 Saddam** (sæ'dæm). 1937–2006, Iraqi politician: president (1979–2003) and prime minister (1994–2003) of Iraq. He led Iraq into the Iran-Iraq War (1980–88) and the Gulf War (1991) but was deposed and captured in the US-led invasion of 2003; executed 2006

Husserl (*German* 'hʊsərl) *n* **Edmund** ('etmʊnt). 1859–1938, German philosopher; founder of phenomenology

Hussite ('hʌsaɪt) *n* **1** an adherent of the religious ideas of John Huss (?1372–1415), the Bohemian religious reformer, or a member of the movement initiated by him ▷ *adj* **2** of or relating to John Huss, his teachings, followers, etc ▷ 'Hussism *or* 'Hussitism *n*

hussy ('hʌsɪ, -zɪ) *n*, *pl* -sies a shameless or promiscuous woman [c16 (in the sense: housewife): from *hussif* HOUSEWIFE]

hustings ('hʌstɪŋz) *n* (functioning as plural or singular) **1** Brit (before 1872) the platform on which candidates were nominated for Parliament and from which they addressed the electors **2** the proceedings at a parliamentary election [C11: from Old Norse *hūsthing*, from *hūs* HOUSE + *thing* assembly]

hustle ('hʌsªl) *vb* **1** to shove or crowd (someone) roughly **2** to move or cause to move hurriedly or furtively: *he hustled her out of sight* **3** (*tr*) to deal with or cause to proceed hurriedly: *to hustle legislation through* **4** *slang* to earn or obtain (something) forcefully **5** *US & Canadian slang* (of procurers and prostitutes) to solicit ▷ *n* **6** an instance of hustling [C17: from Dutch *husselen* to shake, from Middle Dutch *hutsen*] > 'hustler *n*

Huston ('hjuːstən) *n* **John**. 1906–87, US film director. His films include *The Treasure of the Sierra Madre* (1947), for which he won an Oscar, *The African Queen* (1951), *The Man Who Would Be King* (1975), *Prizzi's Honour* (1985), and *The Dead* (1987)

hut (hʌt) *n* **1** a small house or shelter, usually made of wood or metal ▷ *vb* **2** to furnish with or live in a hut [C17: from French *hutte*, of Germanic origin; related to Old High German *hutta* a crude dwelling] > 'hut,like *adj*

hutch (hʌtʃ) *n* **1** a cage, usually of wood and wire mesh, for small animals **2** *informal, derogatory* a small house **3** a cart for carrying ore [C14 *hucche*, from Old French *huche*, from Medieval Latin *hutica*, of obscure origin]

Hutcheson ('hʌtʃɪsən) *n* **1 Francis**. 1694–1746, Scottish philosopher: he published books on ethics and aesthetics, including *System of Moral Philosophy* (1755)

hutment ('hʌtmənt) *n* *chiefly military* a number or group of huts

Hutterite ('hʌtə,raɪt) *n* a member of an Anabaptist Christian sect founded in Moravia, branches of which established farming communities in western Canada and the northwest US [C19: after Jacob *Hutter* (died 1536), Moravian Anabaptist]

Hutton ('hʌtªn) *n* **1 James**. 1726–97, Scottish geologist, regarded as the founder of modern geology **2 Sir Leonard**, known as *Len Hutton*. 1916–90, English cricketer; the first professional captain of England (1953)

Huxley ('hʌkslɪ) *n* **1 Aldous (Leonard)** ('ɔːldəs). 1894–1963, British novelist and essayist, noted particularly for his novel *Brave New World* (1932), depicting a scientifically controlled civilization of human robots **2** his half-brother, **Sir Andrew Fielding**, born 1917, English biologist: noted for his research into nerve cells and the mechanism by which nerve impulses are transmitted; Nobel prize for physiology or medicine shared with Alan Hodgkin and John Eccles 1963; president of the Royal Society (1980–85) **3** brother of Aldous, **Sir Julian (Sorrel)**. 1887–1975, English biologist; first director-general of UNESCO (1946–48). His works include *Essays of a Biologist* (1923) and *Evolution: the Modern Synthesis* (1942) **4** their grandfather, **Thomas Henry**. 1825–95, English biologist, the leading British exponent of Darwin's theory of evolution; his works include *Man's Place in Nature* (1863) and *Evolution and Ethics* (1893)

Hu Yaobang (xuː jaʊˈbɑːŋ) `*n* 1915–89, Chinese statesman; leader of the Chinese Communist Party (1981–87)

Huygens ('haɪɡənz; *Dutch* 'hœixəns) *n* **Christiaan** ('kristiˌaːn). 1629–95, Dutch physicist: first formulated the wave theory of light

Huysmans (*French* Λismɑ̃s) *n* **Joris Karl** (ʒɔris karl). 1848–1907, French novelist of the Decadent school, whose works include *À rebours* (1884)

huzzah (həˈzɑː) *interj, n, vb* an archaic word for **hurrah** [C16: of unknown origin]

HV *or* **h.v.** *abbreviation* high voltage

Hwange ('hwæŋɡeɪ) *n* a town in W Zimbabwe: coal mines. Pop: 42 581 (1992). Former name (until 1982): **Wankie**

Hwang Hai ('wæŋ 'haɪ) *n* a former transliteration of the Chinese name for **Yellow Sea**

Hwang Ho ('wæŋ 'həʊ) *n* a former transliteration of the Chinese name for **Yellow River**

HWM *abbreviation* high-water mark

hwyl ('huːɪl) *n* emotional fervour, as in the recitation of poetry [C19: Welsh]

hyacinth ('haɪəsɪnθ) *n* **1** any liliaceous plant of the Mediterranean genus *Hyacinthus*, esp any cultivated variety of *H. orientalis*, having a thick flower stalk bearing white, blue, or pink fragrant flowers **2** the flower or bulb of such a plant **3** any similar or related plant, such as the grape hyacinth **4** Also called: **jacinth** a red or reddish-brown transparent variety of the mineral zircon, used as a gemstone **5 a** any of the varying colours of the hyacinth flower or stone **b** (*as modifier*): *hyacinth eyes* [C16: from Latin *hyacinthus*, from Greek *huakinthos*] > **hyacinthine** (ˌhaɪəˈsɪnθaɪn) *adj*

Hyacinthus (ˌhaɪəˈsɪnθəs) *n Greek myth* a youth beloved of Apollo and inadvertently killed by him. At the spot where the youth died, Apollo caused a flower to grow

Hyades[1] ('haɪəˌdiːz) *or* **Hyads** ('haɪædz) *pl n* an open cluster of stars in the constellation Taurus [C16: via Latin from Greek *huades*, perhaps from *huein* to rain]

Hyades[2] ('haɪəˌdiːz) *pl n Greek myth* seven nymphs, daughters of Atlas, whom Zeus placed among the stars after death

hyaena (haɪˈiːnə) *n* a variant spelling of **hyena**

hyaline ('haɪəlɪn) *adj biology* clear and translucent, with no fibres or granules [C17: from Late Latin *hyalinus*, from Greek *hualinos* of glass, from *hualos* glass]

hyalite ('haɪəˌlaɪt) *n* a clear and colourless variety of opal in globular form

hyaloid ('haɪəˌlɔɪd) *adj anatomy, zoology* clear and transparent; glassy; hyaline [C19: from Greek *hualoeidēs*]

hyaloid membrane *n* the delicate transparent membrane enclosing the vitreous humour of the eye

hybrid ('haɪbrɪd) *n* **1** an animal or plant resulting from a cross between genetically unlike individuals. Hybrids between different species are usually sterile **2** anything of mixed ancestry **3** a vehicle that is powered by an internal-combustion engine and another source of power such as a battery **4** a word, part of which is derived from one language and part from another, such as *monolingual*, which has a prefix of Greek origin and a root of Latin origin ▷ *adj* **5** (of a vehicle) powered by more than one source **6** denoting or being a hybrid; of mixed origin [C17: from Latin *hibrida* offspring of a mixed union (human or animal)] > **'hybridism** *n* > **hy'bridity** *n*

hybrid computer *n* a computer that uses both analogue and digital techniques

hybridize *or* **hybridise** ('haɪbrɪˌdaɪz) *vb* to produce or cause to produce hybrids; crossbreed > **,hybridi'zation** *or* **,hybridi'sation** *n*

hybridoma (ˌhaɪbrəˈdəʊmə) *n* a hybrid cell formed by the fusion of two different types of cell, esp one capable of producing antibodies, but of limited lifespan, fused with an immortal tumour cell [C20: from HYBRID + -OMA]

hybrid vigour *n biology* the increased size, strength, etc, of a hybrid as compared to either of its parents. Also called: **heterosis**

hydatid ('haɪdətɪd) *n* **1** a large bladder containing encysted larvae of the tapeworm *Echinococcus*: causes serious disease in man **2** Also called: **hydatid cyst** a sterile fluid-filled cyst produced in man and animals during infestation by *Echinococcus* larval forms [C17: from Greek *hudatis* watery vesicle, from *hudōr, hudat-* water]

Hyde[1] (haɪd) *n* a town in NW England, in Tameside unitary authority, Greater Manchester; textiles, footwear, engineering. Pop: 31 253 (2001)

Hyde[2] (haɪd) *n* **1 Douglas**. 1860–1949, Irish scholar and author; first president of Eire (1938–45) **2** Edward Hyde See **Clarendon**[2]

Hyde Park *n* a park in W central London: popular for open-air meetings

Hyderabad ('haɪdərəˌbɑːd, -ˌbæd, 'haɪdrə-) *n* **1** a city in S central India, capital of Andhra Pradesh state and capital of former Hyderabad state; university (1918). Pop: 3 449 878 (2001) **2** a former state of S India: divided in 1956 between the states of Andhra Pradesh, Mysore, and Maharashtra **3** a city in SW Pakistan, on the River Indus: seat of the University of Sind (1947). Pop: 1 392 000 (2005 est)

Hyder Ali *or* **Haidar Ali** ('haɪdər 'ɑːlɪ) *n* 1722–82, Indian ruler of Mysore (1766–82), who waged two wars against the British in India (1767–69; 1780–82)

hydr- *combining form* a variant of **hydro-**

hydra ('haɪdrə) *n, pl* **-dras, -drae** (-driː) **1** any solitary freshwater hydroid coelenterate of the genus *Hydra*, in which the body is a slender polyp with tentacles around the mouth **2** a persistent trouble or evil [c16: from Latin, from Greek *hudra* water serpent; compare OTTER]

Hydra ('haɪdrə) *n* Greek myth a monster with nine heads, each of which, when struck off, was replaced by two new ones

hydracid (haɪ'dræsɪd) *n* an acid, such as hydrochloric acid, that does not contain oxygen

hydrangea (haɪ'dreɪndʒə) *n* any shrub or tree of the Asian and American genus *Hydrangea*, cultivated for their large clusters of white, pink, or blue flowers: family Hydrangeaceae [c18: from New Latin, from Greek *hudōr* water + *angeion* vessel: probably from the cup-shaped fruit]

hydrant ('haɪdrənt) *n* an outlet from a water main, usually consisting of an upright pipe with a valve attached, from which water can be tapped for fighting fires [c19: from HYDRO- + -ANT]

hydrargyrum (haɪ'drɑːdʒɪrəm) *n* an obsolete name for mercury (sense 1) [c16: from New Latin, from Latin *hydrargyrus* from Greek *hydrarguros*, from HYDRO- + *arguros* silver] ▷ **hydrargyric** (,haɪdrɑː'dʒɪrɪk) *adj*

hydrate ('haɪdreɪt) *n* **1** a chemical compound containing water that is chemically combined with a substance and can usually be expelled without changing the constitution of the substance (*not in technical usage*) **2** a chemical compound, such as a carbohydrate, that contains hydrogen and oxygen atoms in the ratio two to one ▷ *vb* **3** to undergo or cause to undergo treatment or impregnation with water [c19: from HYDRO- + -ATE[1]] ▷ hy'dration *n* ▷ 'hydrator *n*

hydrated ('haɪdreɪtɪd) *adj* (of a compound) chemically bonded to water molecules

hydraulic (haɪ'drɒlɪk) *adj* **1** operated by pressure transmitted through a pipe by a liquid, such as water or oil **2** of, concerned with, or employing liquids in motion **3** of or concerned with hydraulics **4** hardening under water: *hydraulic cement* [c17: from Latin *hydraulicus* of a water organ, from Greek *hudraulikos*, from *hudraulos* water organ, from HYDRO- + *aulos* pipe, reed instrument] ▷ hy'draulically *adv*

hydraulic brake *n* a type of brake, used in motor vehicles, in which the braking force is transmitted from the brake pedal to the brakes by a liquid under pressure

hydraulic coupling *n* another name for **torque converter**

hydraulic press *n* a press that utilizes liquid pressure to enable a small force applied to a small piston to produce a large force on a larger piston. The small piston moves through a proportionately greater distance than the larger

hydraulic ram *n* **1** any large device involving the displacement of a piston or plunger driven by fluid pressure **2** a form of water pump utilizing the kinetic energy of running water to provide static pressure to raise water to a reservoir higher than the source

hydraulics (haɪ'drɒlɪks) *n* (*functioning as singular*) another name for **fluid mechanics**

hydraulic suspension *n* a system of motor-vehicle suspension using hydraulic members, often with hydraulic compensation between front and rear systems (**hydroelastic suspension**)

hydrazine ('haɪdrə,ziːn, -zɪn) *n* a colourless basic liquid made from sodium hypochlorite and ammonia: a strong reducing agent, used chiefly as a rocket fuel. Formula: N_2H_4 [c19: from HYDRO- + AZO- + -INE[2]]

hydric ('haɪdrɪk) *adj* **1** of or containing hydrogen **2** containing or using moisture

hydride ('haɪdraɪd) *n* any compound of hydrogen with another element, including ionic compounds such as sodium hydride (NaH), covalent compounds such as borane (B_2H_6), and the transition metal hydrides formed when certain metals, such as palladium, absorb hydrogen

hydrilla (haɪ'drɪlə) *n* any aquatic plant of the Eurasian

genus *Hydrilla*, growing underwater and forming large masses: used as an oxygenator in aquaria and pools. It was introduced in the S US where it has become a serious problem, choking fish and hindering navigation [c20: New Latin, probably from HYDRA]

hydriodic acid (,haɪdrɪ'ɒdɪk) *n* the colourless or pale yellow aqueous solution of hydrogen iodide: a strong acid [c19: from HYDRO- + IODIC]

hydro[1] ('haɪdrəʊ) *n, pl* **-dros** Brit (*esp formerly*) a hotel or resort, often near a spa, offering facilities for hydropathic treatment

hydro[2] ('haɪdrəʊ) *adj* **1** short for **hydroelectric** ▷ *n* **2** a Canadian name for electricity when it is supplied to a residence, business, institution, etc

Hydro ('haɪdrəʊ) *n* (*esp in Canada*) a hydroelectric power company or board

hydro- *or sometimes before a vowel* **hydr-** *combining form* **1** indicating or denoting water, liquid, or fluid: *hydrolysis; hydrodynamics* **2** indicating the presence of hydrogen in a chemical compound: *hydrochloric acid* **3** indicating a hydroid: *hydrozoan* [from Greek *hudōr* water]

hydrobromic acid (,haɪdrəʊ'brəʊmɪk) *n* the colourless or faintly yellow aqueous solution of hydrogen bromide: a strong acid

hydrocarbon (,haɪdrəʊ'kɑːbən) *n* any organic compound containing only carbon and hydrogen, such as the alkanes, alkenes, alkynes, terpenes, and arenes

hydrocele ('haɪdrəʊ,siːl) *n* an abnormal collection of fluid in any saclike space, esp around the testicles [c16: from HYDRO- + -CELE]

hydrocephalus (,haɪdrəʊ'sɛfələs) *or* **hydrocephaly** (,haɪdrəʊ'sɛfəlɪ) *n* accumulation of cerebrospinal fluid within the ventricles of the brain because its normal outlet has been blocked by congenital malformation or disease. In infancy it usually results in great enlargement of the head ▷ **hydrocephalic** (,haɪdrəʊsɪ'fælɪk) *or* ,hydro'cephalous *adj*

hydrochloric acid (,haɪdrə'klɒrɪk) *n* the colourless or slightly yellow aqueous solution of hydrogen chloride: a strong acid used in many industrial and laboratory processes

hydrochloride (,haɪdrə'klɔːraɪd) *n* a quaternary salt formed by the addition of hydrochloric acid to an organic base, such as aniline hydrochloride, $[C_6H_5NH_3]^+Cl^-$

hydrocyanic acid (,haɪdrəʊsaɪ'ænɪk) *n* another name for hydrogen cyanide, esp when in aqueous solution

hydrodynamics (,haɪdrəʊdaɪ'næmɪks, -dɪ-) *n Also called*: hydromechanics (*functioning as singular*) the branch of science concerned with the mechanical properties of fluids, esp liquids

hydroelastic suspension (,haɪdrəʊɪ'læstɪk) *n* See hydraulic suspension

hydroelectric (,haɪdrəʊɪ'lɛktrɪk) *adj* **1** generated by the pressure of falling water: *hydroelectric power* **2** of or concerned with the generation of electricity by water pressure: *a hydroelectric scheme* ▷ **hydroelectricity** (,haɪdrəʊɪlɛk'trɪsɪtɪ, -,iːlɛk-) *n*

hydrofluoric acid (,haɪdrəʊflʊ'ɒrɪk) *n* the colourless aqueous solution of hydrogen fluoride: a strong acid that attacks glass

hydrofoil ('haɪdrə,fɔɪl) *n* **1** a fast light vessel the hull of which is raised out of the water on one or more pairs of fixed vanes **2** any of these vanes

hydroforming ('haɪdrəʊ,fɔːmɪŋ) *n* **chem 1** the catalytic reforming of petroleum to increase the proportion of aromatic and branched-chain hydrocarbons **2** **engineering** a forming process in which a metal component is shaped by a metal punch forced against a die, consisting of a flexible bag containing a fluid

hydrogen ('haɪdrɪdʒən) *n* **a** a flammable colourless gas that is the lightest and most abundant element in the universe. It occurs mainly in water and in most organic compounds and is used in the production of ammonia and other chemicals, in the hydrogenation of fats and oils, and in welding. Symbol: H; atomic no: 1; atomic wt: 1.00794; valency: 1; density: 0.08988 kg/m³; melting pt: –259.34°C; boiling pt: –252.87°C **b** (*as modifier*): *hydrogen bomb* [c18: from French *hydrogène*, from HYDRO- + -GEN; SO

called because its combustion produces water]
> hydrogenous (haɪˈdrɒdʒɪnəs) *adj*

hydrogenate (ˈhaɪdrədʒɪˌneɪt, haɪˈdrɒdʒɪˌneɪt), **hydrogenize** *or* **hydrogenise** (ˈhaɪdrədʒɪˌnaɪz, haɪˈdrɒdʒɪˌnaɪz) *vb* to undergo or cause to undergo a reaction with hydrogen: *to hydrogenate ethylene* > ˌhydrogenˈation, ˌhydrogeniˈzation *or* ˌhydrogeniˈsation *n*

hydrogen bomb *n* a type of bomb in which energy is released by fusion of hydrogen nuclei to give helium nuclei. The energy required to initiate the fusion is provided by the detonation of an atomic bomb, which is surrounded by a hydrogen-containing substance such as lithium deuteride. Also called: **H-bomb**

hydrogen bond *n* a weak chemical bond between an electronegative atom, such as fluorine, oxygen, or nitrogen, and a hydrogen atom bound to another electronegative atom. Hydrogen bonds are responsible for the properties of water and many biological molecules

hydrogen bromide *n* **1** a colourless pungent gas used in organic synthesis. Formula: HBr **2** an aqueous solution of hydrogen bromide; hydrobromic acid

hydrogen carbonate *n* another name for **bicarbonate**

hydrogen chloride *n* **1** a colourless pungent corrosive gas obtained by the action of sulphuric acid on sodium chloride: used in making vinyl chloride and other organic chemicals. Formula: HCl **2** an aqueous solution of hydrogen chloride; hydrochloric acid

hydrogen cyanide *n* a colourless poisonous liquid with a faint odour of bitter almonds, usually made by a catalysed reaction between ammonia, oxygen, and methane. It forms prussic acid in aqueous solution and is used for making plastics and dyes and as a war gas. Formula: HCN. Also called: hydrocyanic acid

hydrogen fluoride *n* **1** a colourless poisonous corrosive gas or liquid made by reaction between calcium fluoride and sulphuric acid: used as a fluorinating agent and catalyst. Formula: HF **2** an aqueous solution of hydrogen fluoride; hydrofluoric acid

hydrogen iodide *n* **1** a colourless poisonous corrosive gas obtained by a catalysed reaction between hydrogen and iodine vapour: used in making iodides. Formula: HI **2** an aqueous solution of this gas; hydriodic acid

hydrogen ion *n* an ionized hydrogen atom, occurring in plasmas and in aqueous solutions of acids, in which it is solvated by one or more water molecules; proton. Formula: H^+

hydrogenize *or* **hydrogenise** (ˈhaɪdrədʒɪˌnaɪz, haɪˈdrɒdʒɪˌnaɪz) *vb* variants of **hydrogenate**

hydrogen peroxide *n* a colourless oily unstable liquid, usually used in aqueous solution. It is a strong oxidizing agent used as a bleach for textiles, wood pulp, hair, etc, and as an oxidizer in rocket fuels. Formula: H_2O_2

hydrogen sulphide *n* a colourless poisonous soluble flammable gas with an odour of rotten eggs: used as a reagent in chemical analysis. Formula: H_2S. Also called: sulphuretted hydrogen

hydrography (haɪˈdrɒɡrəfɪ) *n* the study, surveying, and mapping of the oceans, seas, and rivers > hyˈdrographer *n* > hydrographic (ˌhaɪdrəˈɡræfɪk) *adj*

hydroid (ˈhaɪdrɔɪd) *adj* **1** of or relating to the *Hydroida*, an order of colonial hydrozoan coelenterates that have the polyp phase dominant **2** (of coelenterate colonies or individuals) having or consisting of hydra-like polyps ▷ *n* **3** a hydroid colony or individual [C19: from HYDRA + -OID]

hydrokinetics (ˌhaɪdrəʊkɪˈnɛtɪks, -kaɪ-) *n* (functioning as singular) the branch of science concerned with the mechanical behaviour and properties of fluids in motion, esp of liquids. Also called: hydrodynamics

hydrolase (ˈhaɪdrəˌleɪz) *n* an enzyme, such as an esterase, that controls hydrolysis

hydrology (haɪˈdrɒlədʒɪ) *n* the study of the distribution, conservation, use, etc, of the water of the earth and its atmosphere, particularly at the land surface > hydrologic (ˌhaɪdrəˈlɒdʒɪk) *or* ˌhydroˈlogical *adj* > hyˈdrologist *n*

hydrolyse *or US* **hydrolyze** (ˈhaɪdrəˌlaɪz) *vb* to subject to or undergo hydrolysis

hydrolysis (haɪˈdrɒlɪsɪs) *n* a chemical reaction in which a compound reacts with water to produce other compounds > hydrolytic (ˌhaɪdrəˈlɪtɪk) *adj*

hydrolyte (ˈhaɪdrəˌlaɪt) *n* a substance subjected to hydrolysis

hydromel (ˈhaɪdrəʊˌmɛl) *n archaic* another word for **mead**[1] [C15: from Latin, from Greek *hudromeli*, from HYDRO- + *meli* honey]

hydrometer (haɪˈdrɒmɪtə) *n* an instrument for measuring the relative density of a liquid, usually consisting of a sealed graduated tube with a weighted bulb on one end, the relative density being indicated by the length of the unsubmerged stem > hydrometric (ˌhaɪdrəʊˈmɛtrɪk) *or* ˌhydroˈmetrical *adj*

hydronaut (ˈhaɪdrəʊˌnɔːt) *n US navy* a person trained to operate deep submergence vessels [C20: from Greek, from HYDRO- + -*naut*, as in *aeronaut, astronaut*]

hydropathy (haɪˈdrɒpəθɪ) *n* a pseudoscientific method of treating disease by the use of large quantities of water both internally and externally > hydropathic (ˌhaɪdrəʊˈpæθɪk) *adj*

hydrophilic (ˌhaɪdrəʊˈfɪlɪk) *adj chem* tending to dissolve in, mix with, or be wetted by water: *a hydrophilic colloid* > ˈhydroˌphile *n*

hydrophobia (ˌhaɪdrəˈfəʊbɪə) *n* **1** another name for **rabies 2** a fear of drinking fluids, esp that of a person with rabies, because of painful spasms when trying to swallow > ˌhydroˈphobic *adj*

hydrophone (ˈhaɪdrəˌfəʊn) *n* an electroacoustic transducer that converts sound or ultrasonic waves travelling through water into electrical oscillations

hydrophyte (ˈhaɪdrəʊˌfaɪt) *n* a plant that grows only in water or very moist soil

hydroplane (ˈhaɪdrəʊˌpleɪn) *n* **1** a motorboat equipped with hydrofoils or with a shaped bottom that raises its hull out of the water at high speeds **2** an attachment to an aircraft to enable it to glide along the surface of water **3** another name (esp US) for a **seaplane 4** a horizontal vane on the hull of a submarine for controlling its vertical motion ▷ *vb* **5** (intr) (of a boat) to rise out of the water in the manner of a hydroplane

hydroponics (ˌhaɪdrəʊˈpɒnɪks) *n* (functioning as singular) a method of cultivating plants by growing them in gravel, etc, through which water containing dissolved inorganic nutrient salts is pumped [C20: from HYDRO- + (GEO)PONICS] > ˌhydroˈponic *adj* > ˌhydroˈponically *adv*

hydropower (ˈhaɪdrəʊˌpaʊə) *n* hydroelectric power

hydroquinone (ˌhaɪdrəʊkwɪˈnəʊn) *or* **hydroquinol** (ˌhaɪdrəʊˈkwɪnɒl) *n* a white crystalline soluble phenol used as a photographic developer; 1,4-dihydroxybenzene. Formula: $C_6H_4(OH)_2$

hydrosol (ˈhaɪdrəˌsɒl) *n chem* a sol that has water as its liquid phase

hydrosphere (ˈhaɪdrəˌsfɪə) *n* the watery part of the earth's surface, including oceans, lakes, water vapour in the atmosphere, etc

hydrostatics (ˌhaɪdrəʊˈstætɪks) *n* (functioning as singular) the branch of science concerned with the mechanical properties and behaviour of fluids that are not in motion > ˌhydroˈstatic *or* ˌhydroˈstatical *adj*

hydrotherapeutics (ˌhaɪdrəʊˌθɛrəˈpjuːtɪks) *n* (functioning as singular) the branch of medical science concerned with hydrotherapy

hydrotherapy (ˌhaɪdrəʊˈθɛrəpɪ) *n med* the treatment of certain diseases by the external use of water, esp by exercising in water in order to mobilize stiff joints or strengthen weakened muscles

hydrothermal (ˌhaɪdrəʊˈθɜːməl) *adj* of or relating to the action of water under conditions of high temperature, esp in forming rocks and minerals

hydrotropism (haɪˈdrɒtrəˌpɪzəm) *n* the directional growth of plants in response to the stimulus of water

hydrous (ˈhaɪdrəs) *adj* containing water

hydrovane (ˈhaɪdrəʊˌveɪn) *n* a vane on a seaplane conferring stability on water (a sponson) or facilitating take off (a hydrofoil)

hydroxide (haɪˈdrɒksaɪd) *n* **1** a base or alkali containing the ion OH^- **2** any compound containing an -OH group

hydroxy (haɪ'drɒksɪ) *adj* (of a chemical compound) containing one or more hydroxyl groups [C19: HYDRO- + OXY(GEN)]

hydroxyl (haɪ'drɒksɪl) *n* (*modifier*) of, consisting of, or containing the monovalent group -OH or the ion OH⁻: *a hydroxyl group or radical*

hydroxytryptamine (haɪˌdrɒksɪ'trɪptəmiːn) *n* 5-hydroxytryptamine another name for **serotonin**

hydrozoan (ˌhaɪdrə'zəʊən) *n* **1** any colonial or solitary coelenterate of the class *Hydrozoa*, which includes the hydra, Portuguese man-of-war, and the sertularians ▷ *adj* **2** of, relating to, or belonging to the *Hydrozoa*

hyena *or* **hyaena** (haɪ'iːnə) *n* any of several long-legged carnivorous doglike mammals of the genera *Hyaena* and *Crocuta*, such as *C. crocuta* (**spotted** or **laughing hyena**), of Africa and S Asia: family *Hyaenidae*, order *Carnivora* (carnivores) [C16: from Medieval Latin, from Latin *hyaena*, from Greek *huaina*, from *hus* hog] > **hy'enic** *or* **hy'aenic** *adj*

Hygeia (haɪ'dʒiːə) *n* the Greek goddess of health > **Hy'geian** *adj*

hygiene ('haɪdʒiːn) *n* **1** Also called: hygienics the science concerned with the maintenance of health **2** clean or healthy practices or thinking: *personal hygiene* [C18: from New Latin *hygiēna*, from Greek *hugieinē*, from *hugiēs* healthy]

hygienic (haɪ'dʒiːnɪk) *adj* promoting health or cleanliness; sanitary > **hy'gienically** *adv*

hygienics (haɪ'dʒiːnɪks) *n* (*functioning as singular*) another word for **hygiene** (sense 1)

hygienist (haɪ'dʒiːnɪst), **hygeist** *or* **hygieist** ('haɪdʒiːɪst) *n* a person skilled in the practice of hygiene

hygro- *or before a vowel* **hygr-** *combining form* indicating moisture: *hygrometer* [from Greek *hugros* wet]

hygrometer (haɪ'grɒmɪtə) *n* any of various instruments for measuring humidity > **hygrometric** (ˌhaɪgrə'mɛtrɪk) *adj*

hygrophyte ('haɪgrəˌfaɪt) *n* any plant that grows in wet or waterlogged soil > **hygrophytic** (ˌhaɪgrə'fɪtɪk) *adj*

hygroscope ('haɪgrəˌskəʊp) *n* any device that indicates the humidity of the air without necessarily measuring it

hygroscopic (ˌhaɪgrə'skɒpɪk) *adj* (of a substance) tending to absorb water from the air > **hygro'scopically** *adv*

hying ('haɪɪŋ) *vb* a present participle of **hie**

hyla ('haɪlə) *n* any tree frog of the genus *Hyla*, such as *H. leucophyllata* (**white-spotted hyla**) of tropical America [C19: from New Latin, from Greek *hulē* forest, wood]

hylo- *or before a vowel* **hyl-** *combining form* **1** indicating matter (as distinguished from spirit): *hylozoism* **2** indicating wood [from Greek *hulē* wood]

hylomorphism (ˌhaɪlə'mɔːfɪzəm) *n* the philosophical doctrine that identifies matter with the first cause of the universe

hylozoism (ˌhaɪlə'zəʊɪzəm) *n* the philosophical doctrine that life is one of the properties of matter [C17: HYLO- + Greek *zōē* life] > **hylo'zoic** *adj* > **hylo'zoist** *n* > **hylozo'istic** *adj* > **hylozo'istically** *adv*

hymen ('haɪmɛn) *n* anatomy a fold of mucous membrane that partly covers the entrance to the vagina and is usually ruptured when sexual intercourse takes place for the first time [C17: from Greek: membrane] > **'hymenal** *adj*

Hymen ('haɪmɛn) *n* the Greek and Roman god of marriage

hymeneal (ˌhaɪmɪ'niːəl) *adj* **1** chiefly poetic of or relating to marriage ▷ *n* **2** a wedding song or poem

hymenopteran (ˌhaɪmɪ'nɒptərən) *or* **hymenopteron** *n*, *pl* **-terans** *or* **-tera** (-tərə) *or* **-terons** any hymenopterous insect

hymenopterous (ˌhaɪmɪ'nɒptərəs) *or* **hymenopteran** *adj* of, relating to, or belonging to the *Hymenoptera*, an order of insects, including bees, wasps, ants, and sawflies, having two pairs of membranous wings and an ovipositor specialized for stinging, sawing, or piercing [C19: from Greek *humenopteros* membrane wing; see HYMEN, -PTEROUS]

Hymettian (haɪ'mɛtɪən) *or* **Hymettic** (haɪ'mɛtɪk) *adj* of

or relating to Hymettus, a mountain in SE Greece

Hymettus (haɪ'mɛtəs) *n* a mountain in SE Greece, in Attica east of Athens: famous for its marble and for honey. Height: 1032 m (3386 ft). Modern Greek name: Imittós

hymn (hɪm) *n* **1** a Christian song of praise sung to God or a saint **2** a similar song praising other gods, a nation, etc ▷ *vb* **3** to express (praises, thanks, etc) by singing hymns [C13: from Latin *hymnus*, from Greek *humnos*] > **hymnic** ('hɪmnɪk) *adj*

hymnal ('hɪmnəl) *n* **1** a book of hymns ▷ *adj* **2** of, relating to, or characteristic of hymns

hymnody ('hɪmnədɪ) *n* **1** the composition or singing of hymns **2** hymns collectively ▷ Also called: hymnology [C18: from Medieval Latin *hymnōdia*, from Greek *humnōidia*, from *humnōidein* to chant a hymn, from HYMN + *aeidein* to sing]

hymnology (hɪm'nɒlədʒɪ) *n* **1** the study of hymn composition **2** another word for **hymnody** > **hym'nologist** *n*

hyoid ('haɪɔɪd) Also called: hyoidal *adj* hyoidean **1** of or relating to the hyoid bone *n* Also: hyoid bone **2** the horseshoe-shaped bone that lies at the base of the tongue and above the thyroid cartilage [C19: from New Latin *hyoïdes*, from Greek *huoeidēs* having the shape of the letter UPSILON, from *hu* upsilon + -OID]

hyoscine ('haɪəˌsiːn) *n* another name for **scopolamine** [C19: from HYOSC(YAMUS) + -INE²]

hyoscyamine (ˌhaɪə'saɪəˌmiːn, -mɪn) *n* a poisonous alkaloid occurring in henbane and related plants: an optically active isomer of atropine, used in medicine in a similar way. Formula: $C_{17}H_{23}NO_3$ [C19: from New Latin, from Greek *huoskuamos* (from *hus* pig + *kuamos* bean) + AMINE]

hyoscyamus (ˌhaɪə'saɪəməs) *n* any plant of the solanaceous genus *Hyoscyamus*, of Europe, Asia, and N Africa, including henbane [C18: from New Latin, from Greek *huoskuamos*, from *hus* pig + *kuamos* bean; the plant was thought to be poisonous to pigs]

hyp. *abbreviation* **1** hypotenuse **2** hypothetical

hypaethral *or US* **hypethral** (hɪ'piːθrəl, haɪ-) *adj* (esp of a classical temple) having no roof [C18: from Latin *hypaethrus* uncovered, from Greek *hupaithros*, from HYPO- + *aithros* clear sky]

hypallage (haɪ'pæləˌdʒiː) *n* rhetoric a figure of speech in which the natural relations of two words in a statement are interchanged, as in *the fire spread the wind* [C16: via Late Latin from Greek *hupallagē* interchange, from HYPO- + *allassein* to exchange]

Hypatia (haɪ'peɪʃɪə) *n* died 415 AD, Neo-Platonist philosopher and politician, who lectured at Alexandria. She was murdered by a Christian mob

hype¹ (haɪp) *slang n* **1** a hypodermic needle or injection ▷ *vb* **2** (*intr*; usually foll by *up*) to inject oneself with a drug **3** (*tr*) to stimulate artificially or excite [C20: shortened from HYPODERMIC]

hype² (haɪp) *n* **1** a deception or racket **2** intensive or exaggerated publicity or sales promotion ▷ *vb* (*tr*) **3** to market or promote (a product) using exaggerated or intensive publicity [C20: of unknown origin]

hyped up *adj slang* stimulated or excited by or as if by the effect of a stimulating drug

hyper ('haɪpə) *adj informal* overactive; overexcited [C20: probably independent use of HYPER-]

hyper- *prefix* **1** above, over, or in excess: *hypercritical* **2** (in medicine) denoting an abnormal excess: *hyperacidity* **3** indicating that a chemical compound contains a greater than usual amount of an element: *hyperoxide* [from Greek *huper* over]

hyperacidity (ˌhaɪpərə'sɪdɪtɪ) *n* excess acidity of the gastrointestinal tract, esp the stomach, producing a burning sensation

hyperactive (ˌhaɪpər'æktɪv) *adj* abnormally active > **hyper'action** *n* > **hyperac'tivity** *n*

hyperaemia *or US* **hyperemia** (ˌhaɪpər'iːmɪə) *n* pathol an excessive amount of blood in an organ or part

hyperaesthesia *or US* **hyperesthesia** (ˌhaɪpərɪs'θiːzɪə) *n* pathol increased sensitivity of any of the sense organs, esp of the skin to cold, heat, pain, etc > **hyperaesthetic** *or*

US hyperesthetic (ˌhaɪpəriːsˈθɛtɪk) *adj*

hyperbaton (haɪˈpɜːbəˌtɒn) *n rhetoric* a figure of speech in which the normal order of words is reversed, as in *cheese I love* [c16: via Latin from Greek, literally: an overstepping, from HYPER- + *bainein* to step]

hyperbola (haɪˈpɜːbələ) *n, pl* -las, -le (-ˌliː) a conic section formed by a plane that cuts both bases of a cone; it consists of two branches asymptotic to two intersecting fixed lines and has two foci. Standard equation: $x^2/a^2 - y^2/b^2 = 1$ where $2a$ is the distance between the two intersections with the x-axis and $b = a\sqrt{(e^2 - 1)}$, where e is the eccentricity [c17: from Greek *huperbolē*, literally: excess, extravagance, from HYPER- + *ballein* to throw]

hyperbole (haɪˈpɜːbəlɪ) *n* a deliberate exaggeration used for effect: *he embraced her a thousand times* [c16: from Greek: from HYPER- + *bolē* a throw, from *ballein* to throw] > hyˈperbolism *n*

hyperbolic (ˌhaɪpəˈbɒlɪk) *or* **hyperbolical** *adj* **1** of or relating to a hyperbola **2** *rhetoric* of or relating to a hyperbole > ˌhyperˈbolically *adv*

hyperbolic function *n* any of a group of functions of an angle expressed as a relationship between the distances of a point on a hyperbola to the origin and to the coordinate axes. The group includes sinh (**hyperbolic sine**), cosh (**hyperbolic cosine**), tanh (**hyperbolic tangent**), sech (**hyperbolic secant**), cosech (**hyperbolic cosecant**), and coth (**hyperbolic cotangent**)

hyperbolize *or* **hyperbolise** (haɪˈpɜːbəˌlaɪz) *vb* to express (something) by means of hyperbole

hyperboloid (haɪˈpɜːbəˌlɔɪd) *n* a geometric surface consisting of one sheet, or of two sheets separated by a finite distance, whose sections parallel to the three coordinate planes are hyperbolas or ellipses. Equations $x^2/a^2 + y^2/b^2 - z^2/c^2 = 1$ (one sheet) or $x^2/a^2 - y^2/b^2 - z^2/c^2 = 1$ (two sheets) where a, b, and c are constants

Hyperborean (ˌhaɪpəˈbɔːrɪən) *n* **1** *Greek myth* one of a people believed to have lived beyond the North Wind in a sunny land **2** an inhabitant of the extreme north ▷ *adj* **3** (*sometimes not capital*) of or relating to the extreme north [c16: from Latin *hyperboreus*, from Greek *huperboreos*, from HYPER- + *Boreas* the north wind]

hypercharge (ˈhaɪpəˌtʃɑːdʒ) *n* a property of baryons that is used to account for the absence of certain strong interaction decays

hypercholesterolaemia *or US* **hypercholesterolemia** (ˌhaɪpəkəˌlɛstərɒlˈiːmɪə) *n* the condition of having a high concentration of cholesterol in the blood

hypercorrect (ˌhaɪpəkəˈrɛkt) *adj* **1** excessively correct or fastidious **2** resulting from or characterized by hypercorrection

hypercorrection (ˌhaɪpəkəˈrɛkʃən) *n* a mistaken correction to text or speech made through a desire to avoid nonstandard pronunciation or grammar: *"between you and I" is a hypercorrection of "between you and me"*

hypercritical (ˌhaɪpəˈkrɪtɪkəl) *adj* excessively or severely critical; carping; captious > ˌhyperˈcritically *adv*

hyperfocal distance (ˌhaɪpəˈfəʊkəl) *n* the distance from a camera lens to the point beyond which all objects appear sharp and clearly defined

hyperglycaemia *or US* **hyperglycemia** (ˌhaɪpəglaɪˈsiːmɪə) *n pathol* an abnormally large amount of sugar in the blood [c20: from HYPER- + GLYCO- + -AEMIA] > ˌhyperglyˈcaemic *or US* ˌhyperglyˈcemic *adj*

hypergolic (ˌhaɪpəˈgɒlɪk) *adj* (of a rocket fuel) able to ignite spontaneously on contact with an oxidizer [c20: from German *Hypergol* (perhaps from HYP(ER-) + ERG¹ + -OL²) + -IC]

hypericum (haɪˈpɛrɪkəm) *n* any herbaceous plant or shrub of the temperate genus *Hypericum*: family Hypericaceae. See **rose of Sharon** (sense 1), **Saint John's wort** [c16: via Latin from Greek *hupereikon*, from HYPER- + *ereikē* heath]

hyperinflation (ˌhaɪpəɪnˈfleɪʃən) *n* extremely high inflation, usually over 50 per cent per month, often involving social disorder

Hyperion (haɪˈpɪərɪən) *n Greek myth* a Titan, son of Uranus and Gaea, father of Helios (sun), Selene (moon), and Eos (dawn)

hyperlink (ˈhaɪpəˌlɪŋk) *n* **1** a word, phrase, picture, icon, etc, in a computer document on which a user may click to move to another part of the document or to another document ▷ *vb* **2** (*tr*) to link (files) in this way ▷ Often shortened to **link¹**

hypermarket (ˈhaɪpəˌmɑːkɪt) *n Brit* a huge self-service store, usually built on the outskirts of a town [c20: translation of French *hypermarché*]

hypermedia (ˈhaɪpəˌmiːdɪə) *n* computer software and hardware that allows users to interact with text, graphics, sound, and video, each of which can be accessed from within any of the others. See **hypertext**

hypermetropia (ˌhaɪpəmɪˈtrəʊpɪə) *or* **hypermetropy** (ˌhaɪpəˈmɛtrəpɪ) *n pathol* variants of **hyperopia** [c19: from Greek *hupermetros* beyond measure (from HYPER- + *metron* measure) + -OPIA]

hyperon (ˈhaɪpəˌrɒn) *n physics* any baryon that is not a nucleon [c20: from HYPER- + -ON]

hyperopia (ˌhaɪpəˈrəʊpɪə) *n* inability to see near objects clearly because the images received by the eye are focused behind the retina; long-sightedness > hyperopic (ˌhaɪpəˈrɒpɪk) *adj*

hyperphysical (ˌhaɪpəˈfɪzɪkəl) *adj* beyond the physical; supernatural or immaterial

hyperpyrexia (ˌhaɪpəpaɪˈrɛksɪə) *n pathol* an extremely high fever, with a temperature of 41°C (106°F) or above

hyperreal (ˌhaɪpəˈrɪəl) *adj* **1** involving or characterized by particularly realistic graphic representation **2** distorting or exaggerating reality **3** pertaining to or creating a hyperreality ▷ *n* **4** the hyperreal that which constitutes hyperreality **5** short for **hyperreal number**

hyperreal number *n* any of the set of numbers formed by the addition of infinite numbers and infinitesimal numbers to the set of real numbers

hypersensitive (ˌhaɪpəˈsɛnsɪtɪv) *adj* **1** having unduly vulnerable feelings **2** abnormally sensitive to an allergen, a drug, or other agent > ˌhyperˈsensitiveness *or* ˌhyperˌsensiˈtivity *n*

hypersonic (ˌhaɪpəˈsɒnɪk) *adj* concerned with or having a velocity of at least five times that of sound in the same medium under the same conditions

hyperspace (ˌhaɪpəˈspeɪs) *n* **1** *maths* space having more than three dimensions: often used to describe a multi-dimensional environment **2** (in science fiction) a theoretical dimension within which conventional space-time relationship does not apply

hypersthene (ˈhaɪpəˌsθiːn) *n* a green, brown, or black pyroxene mineral consisting of magnesium iron silicate in orthorhombic crystalline form. Formula: $(Mg,Fe)_2Si_2O_6$ [c19: from HYPER- + Greek *sthenos* strength]

hypertension (ˌhaɪpəˈtɛnʃən) *n pathol* abnormally high blood pressure > hypertensive (ˌhaɪpəˈtɛnsɪv) *adj, n*

hypertext (ˈhaɪpəˌtɛkst) *n* computer software and hardware that allows users to create, store, and view text and move between related items easily and in a nonsequential way; a word or phrase can be selected to link users to another part of the same document or to a different document

hypertext markup language *n* the full name for **HTML**

hyperthermia (ˌhaɪpəˈθɜːmɪə) *or* **hyperthermy** (ˌhaɪpəˈθɜːmɪ) *n pathol* variants of **hyperpyrexia** > ˌhyperˈthermal *adj*

hyperthermophile (ˌhaɪpəˈθɜːməʊˌfaɪl) *n* an organism, esp a bacterium, that lives at high temperatures (above 80°C), found in some hot springs [c20: from HYPER- + -THERMOPHILE] > hyperthermophilic (ˌhaɪpəˌθɜːməʊˈfɪlɪk) *adj*

hyperthyroidism (ˌhaɪpəˈθaɪrɔɪˌdɪzəm) *n* overproduction of thyroid hormone by the thyroid gland, causing nervousness, insomnia, sweating, palpitation, and sensitivity to heat > ˌhyperˈthyroid *adj, n*

hypertonic (ˌhaɪpəˈtɒnɪk) *adj* **1** (esp of muscles) being in a state of abnormally high tension **2** (of a solution) having a higher osmotic pressure than that of a specified, generally physiological, solution

hypertrophy (haɪˈpɜːtrəfɪ) *n, pl* -phies **1** enlargement of an organ or part resulting from an increase in the size of the cells ▷ *vb* -phies, -phying, -phied **2** to undergo or cause to undergo this condition

hyperventilate (ˌhaɪpəˈvɛntɪleɪt) *vb* (*intr*) to breathe in an abnormally deep, long, and rapid manner, sometimes resulting in cramp and dizziness

hyperventilation (ˌhaɪpəˌvɛntɪˈleɪʃən) *n* an increase in the depth, duration, and rate of breathing, sometimes resulting in cramp and dizziness

hypha (ˈhaɪfə) *n*, *pl* -phae (-fiː) any of the filaments that constitute the body (mycelium) of a fungus [C19: from New Latin, from Greek *huphē* web] > ˈhyphal *adj*

hyphen (ˈhaɪfən) *n* 1 the punctuation mark (-), used to separate the parts of some compound words, to link the words of a phrase, and between syllables of a word split between two consecutive lines of writing or printing ▷ *vb* 2 (*tr*) another word for **hyphenate** [C17: from Late Latin (meaning: the combining of two words), from Greek *huphen* (adv) together, from HYPO- + *heis* one]

hyphenate (ˈhaɪfəˌneɪt) *or* **hyphen** *vb* (*tr*) to separate (syllables, words, etc) with a hyphen > ˌhyphenˈation *n*

hyphenated (ˈhaɪfəˌneɪtɪd) *adj* 1 containing or linked with a hyphen 2 *chiefly US* having a nationality denoted by a hyphenated word, as in *American-Irish*

hypno- *or before a vowel* **hypn-** *combining form* 1 indicating sleep: *hypnophobia* 2 relating to hypnosis: *hypnotherapy* [from Greek *hupnos* sleep]

hypnoid (ˈhɪpnɔɪd) *or* **hypnoidal** (hɪpˈnɔɪdəl) *adj psychol* of or relating to a state resembling sleep or hypnosis

hypnology (hɪpˈnɒlədʒɪ) *n psychol* the study of sleep and hypnosis > hypˈnologist *n*

hypnopaedia (ˌhɪpnəʊˈpiːdɪə) *n* the learning of lessons heard during sleep [C20: from HYPNO- + Greek *paideia* education]

hypnopompic (ˌhɪpnəʊˈpɒmpɪk) *adj psychol* relating to the state existing between sleep and full waking, characterized by the persistence of dreamlike imagery [C20: from HYPNO- + Greek *pompē* a sending forth, escort + -IC; see POMP]

Hypnos (ˈhɪpnɒs) *n Greek myth* the god of sleep. Roman counterpart: Somnus. See **Morpheus** [Greek: sleep]

hypnosis (hɪpˈnəʊsɪs) *n*, *pl* -ses (-siːz) an artificially induced state of relaxation and concentration in which deeper parts of the mind become more accessible: used clinically to reduce reaction to pain, to encourage free association, etc

hypnotherapy (ˌhɪpnəʊˈθɛrəpɪ) *n* the use of hypnosis in the treatment of emotional and psychogenic problems > ˌhypnoˈtherapist *n*

hypnotic (hɪpˈnɒtɪk) *adj* 1 of, relating to, or producing hypnosis or sleep 2 (of a person) susceptible to hypnotism ▷ *n* 3 a drug or agent that induces sleep 4 a person susceptible to hypnosis [C17: from Late Latin *hypnōticus*, from Greek *hupnōtikos*, from *hupnoun* to put to sleep, from *hupnos* sleep] > hypˈnotically *adv*

hypnotism (ˈhɪpnəˌtɪzəm) *n* 1 the scientific study and practice of hypnosis 2 the process of inducing hypnosis > ˈhypnotist *n*

hypnotize *or* **hypnotise** (ˈhɪpnəˌtaɪz) *vb* (*tr*) 1 to induce hypnosis in (a person) 2 to charm or beguile; fascinate > ˌhypnotiˈzation *or* ˌhypnotiˈsation *n* > ˈhypnoˌtizer *or* ˈhypnoˌtiser *n*

hypo¹ (ˈhaɪpəʊ) *n* another name for sodium thiosulphate, esp when used as a fixer in photographic developing [C19: shortened from HYPOSULPHITE]

hypo² (ˈhaɪpəʊ) *n*, *pl* -pos *informal* short for **hypodermic syringe**

hypo- *or before a vowel* **hyp-** *prefix* 1 under, beneath, or below: *hypodermic* 2 lower; at a lower point: *hypogastrium* 3 less than: *hypoploid* 4 (in medicine) denoting a deficiency or an abnormally low level: *hypothyroid*; *hypoglycaemia* [from Greek, from *hupo* under]

hypoallergenic (ˈhaɪpəʊˌæləˈdʒɛnɪk) *adj* (of cosmetics, earrings, etc) not likely to cause an allergic reaction

hypoblast (ˈhaɪpəˌblæst) *n* Also called: endoblast *embryol* the inner layer of an embryo at an early stage of development that becomes the endoderm at gastrulation

hypocaust (ˈhaɪpəˌkɔːst) *n* an ancient Roman heating system in which hot air circulated under the floor and between double walls [C17: from Latin *hypocaustum*, from Greek *hupokauston* room heated from below, from

hupokaiein to light a fire beneath, from HYPO- + *kaiein* to burn]

hypocentre (ˈhaɪpəʊˌsɛntə) *n* 1 Also called: ground zero the point on the ground immediately below the centre of explosion of a nuclear bomb in the atmosphere 2 another term for **focus** (sense 6)

hypochlorite (ˌhaɪpəˈklɔːraɪt) *n* any salt or ester of hypochlorous acid

hypochlorous acid (ˌhaɪpəˈklɔːrəs) *n* an unstable acid known only in solution and in the form of its salts, formed when chlorine dissolves in water: a strong oxidizing and bleaching agent. Formula: HOCl

hypochondria (ˌhaɪpəˈkɒndrɪə) *n* chronic abnormal anxiety concerning the state of one's health, even in the absence of any evidence of disease on medical examination. Also called: hypochondriasis (ˌhaɪpəʊkɒnˈdraɪəsɪs) [C18: from Late Latin: the abdomen, supposedly the seat of melancholy, from Greek *hupokhondria*, from *hupokhondrios* of the upper abdomen, from HYPO- + *khondros* cartilage]

hypochondriac (ˌhaɪpəˈkɒndrɪˌæk) *n* 1 a person suffering from hypochondria ▷ *adj* Also: hypochondriacal (ˌhaɪpəkɒnˈdraɪəkəl) 2 relating to or suffering from hypochondria

hypocorism (haɪˈpɒkəˌrɪzəm) *n* a pet name, esp one using a diminutive affix: *"Sally" is a hypocorism for "Sarah"* [C19: from Greek *hupokorisma*, from *hupokorizesthai* to use pet names, from *hupo*- beneath + *korizesthai*, from *korē* girl, *koros* boy] > hypocoristic (ˌhaɪpəkɒˈrɪstɪk) *adj*

hypocotyl (ˌhaɪpəˈkɒtɪl) *n* the part of an embryo plant between the cotyledons and the radicle [C19: from HYPO- + COTYL(EDON)]

hypocrisy (hɪˈpɒkrəsɪ) *n*, *pl* -sies 1 the practice of professing standards, beliefs, etc, contrary to one's real character or actual behaviour, esp the pretence of virtue and piety 2 an act or instance of this

hypocrite (ˈhɪpəkrɪt) *n* a person who pretends to be what he is not [C13: from Old French *ipocrite*, via Late Latin, from Greek *hupokritēs* one who plays a part, from *hupokrinein* to feign, from *krinein* to judge] > ˌhypoˈcritical *adj* > ˌhypoˈcritically *adv*

hypocycloid (ˌhaɪpəˈsaɪklɔɪd) *n* a curve described by a point on the circumference of a circle as the circle rolls around the inside of a fixed coplanar circle > ˌhypocyˈcloidal *adj*

hypodermic (ˌhaɪpəˈdɜːmɪk) *adj* 1 of or relating to the region of the skin beneath the epidermis 2 injected beneath the skin ▷ *n* 3 a hypodermic syringe or needle > ˌhypoˈdermically *adv*

hypodermic syringe *n med* a type of syringe consisting of a hollow cylinder, usually of glass or plastic, a tightly fitting piston, and a hollow needle (**hypodermic needle**), used for withdrawing blood samples, injecting medicine, etc

hypodermis (ˌhaɪpəˈdɜːmɪs) *or* **hypoderm** *n* 1 *botany* a layer of thick-walled supportive or water-storing cells beneath the epidermis in some plants 2 *zoology* the epidermis of arthropods, annelids, etc, which secretes and is covered by a cuticle [C19: from HYPO- + EPIDERMIS]

hypogastrium (ˌhaɪpəˈgæstrɪəm) *n*, *pl* -tria (-trɪə) *anatomy* the lower front central region of the abdomen, below the navel [C17: from New Latin, from Greek *hupogastrion*, from HYPO- + *gastrion*, diminutive of *gastēr* stomach]

hypogeal (ˌhaɪpəˈdʒiːəl) *or* **hypogeous** *adj* occurring or living below the surface of the ground [C19: from Latin *hypogēus*, from Greek *hupogeios*, from HYPO- + *gē* earth]

hypogene (ˈhaɪpəˌdʒiːn) *adj* formed, taking place, or originating beneath the surface of the earth

hypogeum (ˌhaɪpəˈdʒiːəm) *n*, *pl* -gea (-ˈdʒiːə) an underground vault, esp one used for burials [C18: from Latin, from Greek *hupogeion*; see HYPOGEAL]

hypoid gear (ˈhaɪpɔɪd) *n* a gear having a tooth form generated by a hypocycloidal curve; used extensively in motor vehicle transmissions to withstand a high surface loading [C20: *hypoid*, shortened from HYPOCYCLOID]

hyponasty (ˈhaɪpəˌnæstɪ) *n* increased growth of the lower surface of a plant part, resulting in an upward bending of the part > ,hypo'nastic *adj*

hypophosphate (,haɪpə'fɒsfeɪt) *n* any salt or ester of hypophosphoric acid

hypophosphite (,haɪpə'fɒsfaɪt) *n* any salt of hypophosphorous acid

hypophosphoric acid (,haɪpəfɒs'fɒrɪk) *n* a crystalline odourless deliquescent solid: a tetrabasic acid produced by the slow oxidation of phosphorus in moist air. Formula: $H_4P_2O_6$

hypophosphorous acid (,haɪpə'fɒsfərəs) *n* a colourless or yellowish oily liquid or white deliquescen.t solid: a monobasic acid and a reducing agent. Formula: H_3PO_2

hypophysis (haɪ'pɒfɪsɪs) *n, pl* -ses (-,siːz) the technical name for **pituitary gland** [c18: from Greek: outgrowth, from HYPO- + *phuein* to grow] > **hypophyseal** *or* **hypophysial** (,haɪpə'fɪzɪəl, haɪ,pɒfɪ'sɪəl) *adj*

hypostasis (haɪ'pɒstəsɪs) *n, pl* -ses (-,siːz) 1 *metaphysics* the essential nature of a substance as opposed to its attributes 2 *Christianity* a any of the three persons of the Godhead, together constituting the Trinity b the one person of Christ in which the divine and human natures are united 3 the accumulation of blood in an organ or part, under the influence of gravity as the result of poor circulation [c16: from Late Latin: substance, from Greek *hupostasis* foundation, from *huphistasthai* to stand under, from HYPO- + *histanai* to cause to stand] > **hypostatic** (,haɪpə'stætɪk) *or* ,hypo'statical *adj*

hypostyle ('haɪpəʊ,staɪl) *adj* 1 having a roof supported by columns ▷ *n* 2 a building constructed in this way

hyposulphite (,haɪpə'sʌlfaɪt) *n* another name for sodium thiosulphate, esp when used as a photographic fixer. Often shortened to: **hypo**

hyposulphurous acid (,haɪpə'sʌlfərəs) *n* another name for **dithionous acid**

hypotension (,haɪpəʊ'tɛnʃən) *n pathol* abnormally low blood pressure > **hypotensive** (,haɪpəʊ'tensɪv) *adj*

hypotenuse (haɪ'pɒtɪ,njuːz) *n* the side in a right-angled triangle that is opposite the right angle [c16: from Latin *hypotēnūsa*, from Greek *hupoteinousa grammē* subtending line, from *hupoteinein* to subtend, from HYPO- + *teinein* to stretch]

hypothalamus (,haɪpə'θæləməs) *n, pl* -mi (-,maɪ) a neural control centre at the base of the brain, concerned with hunger, thirst, satiety, and other autonomic functions > **hypothalamic** (,haɪpəθə'læmɪk) *adj*

hypothec (haɪ'pɒθɪk) *n Roman law, Scots law* a charge on property in favour of a creditor [c16: from Late Latin *hypotheca* a security, from Greek *hupothēkē* deposit, pledge, from *hupotithenai* to deposit as a security, place under, from HYPO- + *tithenai* to place]

hypothecate (haɪ'pɒθɪ,keɪt) *vb* 1 (*tr*) *law* to pledge (personal property or a ship) as security for a debt without transferring possession or title 2 to allocate the revenue raised by a tax for a specified purpose [c17: *hypothēcātus*, past participle of *hypothēcāre*; see HYPOTHEC, -ATE¹] > hy,pothe'cation *n* > hy'pothe,cator *n*

hypothermia (,haɪpəʊ'θɜːmɪə) *n* 1 *pathol* an abnormally low body temperature, as induced in the elderly by exposure to cold weather 2 *med* the intentional reduction of normal body temperature, as by ice packs, to reduce the patient's metabolic rate: performed esp in heart and brain surgery

hypothesis (haɪ'pɒθɪsɪs) *n, pl* -ses (-,siːz) 1 a suggested explanation for a group of facts or phenomena, either accepted as a basis for further verification (**working hypothesis**) or accepted as likely to be true 2 an assumption used in an argument without its being endorsed; a supposition [c16: from Greek, from *hupotithenai* to propose, suppose, literally: put under; see HYPO-, THESIS] > hy'pothesist *n*

hypothesize *or* **hypothesise** (haɪ'pɒθɪ,saɪz) *vb* to form or assume as a hypothesis > hy'pothe,sizer *or* hy'pothe,siser *n*

hypothetical (,haɪpə'θɛtɪkᵊl) *or* **hypothetic** *adj* 1 having the nature of a hypothesis 2 assumed or thought to exist 3 *logic* another word for **conditional** (sense 3) > ,hypo'thetically *adv*

hypothyroidism (,haɪpəʊ'θaɪrɔɪ,dɪzəm) *n pathol*

1 insufficient production of thyroid hormones by the thyroid gland 2 any disorder, such as cretinism or myxoedema, resulting from this > ,hypo'thyroid *n, adj*

hypotonic (,haɪpə'tɒnɪk) *adj* 1 *pathol* (of muscles) lacking normal tone or tension 2 (of a solution) having a lower osmotic pressure than that of a specified, generally physiological, solution

hypoxia (haɪ'pɒksɪə) *n* deficiency in the amount of oxygen delivered to the body tissues [c20: from HYPO- + OXY-² +-IA]

Hypsilantis *or* **Hypsilantes** (Greek ,ipsi'landis) *n* variants of **Ypsilanti**

hypso- *or before a vowel* **hyps-** *combining form* indicating height: *hypsometry* [from Greek *hupsos*]

hypsography (hɪp'sɒɡrəfɪ) *n* the study and mapping of the earth's topography above sea level

hypsometer (hɪp'sɒmɪtə) *n* 1 an instrument for measuring altitudes by determining the boiling point of water at a given altitude 2 any instrument used to calculate the heights of trees by triangulation

hypsometry (hɪp'sɒmɪtrɪ) *n* (in mapping) the establishment of height above sea level

hyrax ('haɪræks) *n, pl* **hyraxes** *or* **hyraces** ('haɪrə,siːz) any agile herbivorous mammal of the family *Procaviidae* and order *Hyracoidea*, of Africa and SW Asia, such as *Procavia capensis* (**rock hyrax**). They resemble rodents but have feet with hooflike toes. Also called: **dassie** [c19: from New Latin, from Greek *hurax* shrewmouse; probably related to Latin *sōrex*]

Hyrcania (hɜː'keɪnɪə) *n* an ancient district of Asia, southeast of the Caspian Sea > Hyr'canian *adj*

hyson ('haɪsᵊn) *n* a Chinese green tea, the early crop of which is known as **young hyson** and the inferior leaves as **hyson skin** [c18: from Chinese (Cantonese) *hei-ch'un* bright spring]

hyssop ('hɪsəp) *n* 1 a widely cultivated Asian plant, *Hyssopus officinalis*, with spikes of small blue flowers and aromatic leaves, used as a condiment and in perfumery and folk medicine: family *Lamiaceae* (labiates) 2 a Biblical plant, used for sprinkling in the ritual practices of the Hebrews [Old English *ysope*, from Latin *hyssōpus*, from Greek *hussōpos*, of Semitic origin; compare Hebrew *ēzōv*]

hysterectomy (,hɪstə'rɛktəmɪ) *n, pl* -mies surgical removal of the uterus

hysteresis (,hɪstə'riːsɪs) *n physics* the lag in a variable property of a system with respect to the effect producing it as this effect varies, esp the phenomenon in which the magnetic flux density of a ferromagnetic material lags behind the changing external magnetic field strength [c19: from Greek *husterēsis* coming late, from *husteros* coming after] > **hysteretic** (,hɪstə'rɛtɪk) *adj*

hysteresis loop *n* a closed curve showing the variation of the magnetic flux density of a ferromagnetic material with the external magnetic field producing it, when this field is changed through a complete cycle

hysteria (hɪ'stɪərɪə) *n* 1 a mental disorder characterized by emotional outbursts, susceptibility to autosuggestion, and, often, symptoms such as paralysis that mimic the effects of physical disorders 2 any frenzied emotional state, esp of laughter or crying [c19: from New Latin, from Latin *hystericus* HYSTERIC]

hysteric (hɪ'stɛrɪk) *n* 1 a hysterical person ▷ *adj* 2 hysterical [c17: from Latin *hystericus* literally: of the womb, from Greek *husterikos*, from *hustera* the womb; from the belief that hysteria in women originated in disorders of the womb]

hysterical (hɪ'stɛrɪkᵊl) *or* **hysteric** *adj* 1 of or suggesting hysteria: *hysterical cries* 2 suffering from hysteria 3 *informal* wildly funny > hys'terically *adv*

hysterics (hɪ'stɛrɪks) *n* (*functioning as plural or singular*) 1 an attack of hysteria 2 *informal* wild uncontrollable bursts of laughter

hystero- *or before a vowel* **hyster-** *combining form* indicating the uterus: *hysterotomy* [from Greek *hustera* womb]

hysteron proteron ('hɪstə,rɒn 'prɒtə,rɒn) *n* 1 *logic* a fallacious argument in which the proposition to be proved is assumed as a premise 2 *rhetoric* a figure of speech in which the normal order of two sentences, clauses, etc, is reversed, as in *bred and born* (for *born and bred*) [c16: from Late Latin, from Greek *husteron proteron* the latter (placed as) former]

hystricomorph (hɪ'straɪkəʊˌmɔːf) *n* **1** any rodent of the suborder *Hystricomorpha*, which includes porcupines, cavies, agoutis, and chinchillas ▷ *adj* Also: **hystricomorphic** (hɪˌstraɪkəʊ'mɔːfɪk) **2** of, relating to, or belonging to the *Hystricomorpha* [c19: from Latin *hystrix* porcupine, from Greek *hustrix*]

Hywel Dda or **Howel Dda** ('haʊəl 'ðɑː) *n* known as *Hywel the Good.* died 950 AD, Welsh prince. He united S and N Wales and oversaw the codification of Welsh law at the conference of Whitland (945)

Hz *symbol for* hertz

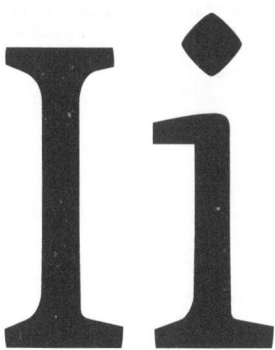

Ii

i¹ or **I** (aɪ) *n, pl* **i's, I's** or **Is** **1** the ninth letter and third vowel of the modern English alphabet **2** any of several speech sounds represented by this letter, in English as in *bite* or *hit* **3 a** something shaped like an I **b** (*in combination*): *an I-beam*

i² *symbol for* the imaginary number √–1

I¹ (aɪ) *pron* (*subjective*) refers to the speaker or writer [C12: reduced form of Old English *ic*; compare Old Saxon *ik*, Old High German *ih*, Sanskrit *ahám*]

I² *symbol for* **1** *chem* iodine **2** *physics* current **3** *physics* isospin **4** *the Roman numeral for* one. See **Roman numerals**

I. *abbreviation* **1** International **2** Island *or* Isle

Ia. *or* **IA** *abbreviation* Iowa

-ia *suffix forming nouns* **1** occurring in place names: *Albania; Columbia* **2** occurring in names of diseases and pathological disorders: *pneumonia; aphasia* **3** occurring in words denoting condition or quality: *utopia* **4** occurring in names of botanical genera **5** occurring in names of zoological classes: *Reptilia* **6** occurring in collective nouns borrowed from Latin: *marginalia; memorabilia; regalia* [(for senses 1–4) New Latin, from Latin and Greek, suffix of feminine nouns; (for senses 5–6) from Latin, neuter plural suffix]

IAA *abbreviation* indoleacetic acid

IAAF *abbreviation* International Amateur Athletic Federation

IAEA *abbreviation* International Atomic Energy Agency

-ial *suffix forming adjectives* of; relating to; connected with: *managerial* [from Latin *-iālis*, adj suffix; compare -AL¹]

iamb (ˈaɪæm, ˈaɪæmb) *or* **iambus** (aɪˈæmbəs) *n, pl* **iambs, iambi** (aɪˈæmbaɪ) *or* **iambuses** *prosody* **1** a metrical foot consisting of two syllables, a short one followed by a long one (--) **2** a line of verse of such feet [C16 *iambus*, from Latin, from Greek *iambos*]

iambic (aɪˈæmbɪk) *prosody* ▷ *adj* **1** of, relating to, consisting of, or using an iamb or iambs **2** (in Greek literature) denoting a type of satirical verse written in iambs ▷ *n* **3** a metrical foot, line, or stanza of verse consisting of iambs **4** a type of ancient Greek satirical verse written in iambs

-ian *suffix* a variant of **-an**: *Etonian; Johnsonian* [from Latin *-iānus*]

-iana *suffix forming nouns* a variant of **-ana**

IAP *abbreviation* internet access provider: a company that provides organizations or individuals with access to the internet

Iaşi (Romanian ˈiaʃj) *n* a city in NE Romania: capital of Moldavia (1565–1859); university (1860). Pop: 280 000 (2005 est). German name: **Jassy**

-iasis *or* **-asis** *n combining form* (in medicine) indicating a diseased condition: *psoriasis*. See **-osis** (sense 2) [from New Latin, from Greek, suffix of action]

IATA (aɪˈɑːtə, iːˈɑːtə) *n acronym for* International Air Transport Association

iatric (aɪˈætrɪk) *or* **iatrical** *adj* relating to medicine or physicians; medical [C19: from Greek *iatrikos* of healing, from *iasthai* to heal]

-iatrics *n combining form* indicating medical care or treatment: *paediatrics* [from IATRIC]

iatrogenic (aɪˌætrəʊˈdʒɛnɪk) *adj med* (of an illness or symptoms) induced in a patient as the result of a physician's words or actions, esp as a consequence of taking a drug prescribed by the physician ▷ **iatrogenicity** (aɪˌætrəʊdʒɪˈnɪsɪtɪ) *n*

-iatry *n combining form* indicating healing or medical treatment: *psychiatry*. See **-iatrics** [from New Latin *-iatria*, from Greek *iatreia* the healing art, from *iatros* healer, physician] ▷ **-iatric** *adj combining form*

IBA *abbreviation* (in Britain) Independent Broadcasting Authority

Ibadan (ɪˈbædⁿn) *n* a city in SW Nigeria, capital of Oyo state: university (1948). Pop: 2 375 000 (2005 est)

Ibagué (Spanish iβaˈɣe) *n* a city in W central Colombia. Pop: 440 000 (2005 est)

Ibáñez (Spanish iˈβaɲeθ) *n* See **Blasco Ibáñez**

Ibarruri (Spanish iˈβarruri) *n* **Dolores** (doˈlores). real name of (La) **Pasionaria**

I-beam *n* a rolled steel joist or a girder with a cross section in the form of a capital letter I

Iberia (aɪˈbɪərɪə) *n* **1** the Iberian Peninsula **2** an ancient region in central Asia, south of the Caucasus corresponding approximately to present-day Georgia

Iberian (aɪˈbɪərɪən) *n* **1 a** a member of a group of ancient Caucasoid peoples who inhabited the Iberian Peninsula in preclassical and classical times **2** a native or inhabitant of the Iberian Peninsula; a Spaniard or Portuguese **3** a native or inhabitant of ancient Iberia in the Caucasus ▷ *adj* **4** denoting, or relating to the pre-Roman peoples of the Iberian Peninsula or Caucasian Iberia **5** of or relating to the Iberian Peninsula, its inhabitants, or any of their languages

Iberian Peninsula *n* a peninsula of SW Europe, occupied by Spain and Portugal

iberis (aɪˈbɪərɪs) *n* any plant of the annual or perennial Eurasian genus *Iberis*, 12 to 25 cm (6–12 in.) in height, with white or purple flowers. *I. amara* and *I. umbellata* are the garden candytuft Family *Brassicaceae* (crucifers) [New Latin, from *Iberia* Spain, where many species are common]

Ibert (French ibɛr) *n* Jacques (François Antoine) (ʒak). 1890–1962, French composer; his works include the humorous orchestral *Divertissement* (1930)

Iberville (French ibɛrvil) *n* Pierre le Moyne (pjɛr lə mwan), Sieur d'. 1661–1706, French-Canadian explorer, who founded (1700) the first French colony in Louisiana

ibex (ˈaɪbɛks) *n*, *pl* **ibexes**, **ibices** (ˈɪbɪˌsiːz, ˈaɪ-) or **ibex** any of three wild goats, *Capra ibex*, *C. caucasica*, or *C. pyrenaica*, of mountainous regions of Europe, Asia, and North Africa, having large backward-curving horns [C17: from Latin: chamois]

IBF *abbreviation* International Boxing Federation

ibid. or **ib.** *abbreviation* (in annotations, bibliographies, etc, when referring to a book, article, chapter, or page previously cited) ibidem [Latin: in the same place]

ibis (ˈaɪbɪs) *n*, *pl* **ibises** or **ibis** any of various wading birds of the family *Threskiornithidae*, such as *Threskiornis aethiopica* (**sacred ibis**), that occur in warm regions and have a long thin down-curved bill: order *Ciconiiformes* (herons, storks, etc) [C14: via Latin from Greek, from Egyptian *hby*]

Ibiza or **Iviza** (Spanish iˈβiθa) *n* **1** a Spanish island in the W Mediterranean, one of the Balearic Islands: hilly, with a rugged coast; tourism. Pop: 40 175 (2003 est). Area: 541 sq km (209 sq miles) **2** the capital of Ibiza, a port on the south of the island. Pop: 16 000 (latest est)

-ible *suffix forming adjectives* a variant of **-able** > **-ibly** *suffix forming adverbs* > **-ibility** *suffix forming nouns*

ibn-al-Arabi (ˌɪbᵊnˈæləˈrɑːbɪ) *n* Muhyi-l-din. 1165–1240, Muslim mystic and poet, born in Spain, noted for his influence on Sufism

ibn-Batuta (ˌɪbᵊnbæˈtuːtɑː) *n* 1304–?68, Arab traveller, who wrote the *Rihlah*, an account of his travels (1325–54) in Africa and Asia

ibn-Ezra (ˌɪbᵊnˈɛzrə) *n* Abraham Ben Meir. 1093–1167, Jewish poet, scholar, and traveller, born in Spain

ibn-Gabirol (ˌɪbᵊnˌɡɑːˈbiːrɔːl) *n* Solomon. ?1021–?58, Jewish philosopher and poet, born in Spain. His work *The Fountain of Life* influenced Western medieval philosophers

ibn-Khaldun (ˌɪbᵊnˌkɑːlˈduːn) *n* 1332–1406, Arab historian and philosopher. His *Kitab al-'ibar* (Book of Examples) is a history of Islam

ibn-Rushd (ˌɪbᵊnˈrʊʃt) *n* the Arabic name of **Averroës**

ibn-Saud (ˌɪbᵊnˈsaʊd) *n* Abdul-Aziz (æbˈdʊlæˈziːz). 1880–1953, first king of Saudi Arabia (1932–53)

ibn-Sina (ˌɪbᵊnˈsiːnə) *n* the Arabic name of **Avicenna**

Ibo or **Igbo** (ˈiːbəʊ) *n* **1** *pl* **-bos** or **-bo** a member of a Negroid people of W Africa, living chiefly in S Nigeria **2** the language of this people, belonging to the Kwa branch of the Niger-Congo family: one of the chief literary and cultural languages of S Nigeria

Ibrahim Pasha (ˌɪbrəˈhiːm ˈpɑːʃə) *n* 1789–1848, Albanian general; son of Mehemet Ali, whom he succeeded as viceroy of Egypt (1848)

IBRD *abbreviation* International Bank for Reconstruction and Development (the World Bank)

IBS *abbreviation* irritable bowel syndrome

Ibsen (ˈɪbsən) *n* Henrik (ˈhɛnrɪk). 1828–1906, Norwegian dramatist and poet. After his early verse plays *Brand* (1866) and *Peer Gynt* (1867), he began the series of social dramas in prose, including *A Doll's House* (1879), *Ghosts* (1881), and *The Wild Duck* (1886), which have had a profound influence on modern drama. His later plays, such as *Hedda Gabler* (1890) and *The Master Builder* (1892),

are more symbolic

ibuprofen (aɪˈbjuːprəʊfən) *n* a drug, isobutylphenylpropionic acid, that relieves pain and reduces inflammation: used to treat arthritis and muscular strains. Formula: $C_{13}H_{18}O_2$

i/c *abbreviation* in charge (of)

-ic *suffix forming adjectives* **1** of, relating to, or resembling: *allergic*; *Germanic*; *periodic*. See also **-ical 2** (in chemistry) indicating that an element is chemically combined in the higher of two possible valence states: *ferric*; *stannic*. See **-ous** (sense 2) [from Latin *-icus* or Greek *-ikos*; *-ic* also occurs in nouns that represent a substantive use of adjectives (*magic*) and in nouns borrowed directly from Latin or Greek (*critic, music*)]

Içá (ˈiːsɑ:; Portuguese iˈsa) *n* the Brazilian part of the **Putumayo River**

ICA *abbreviation* (in Britain) Institute of Contemporary Arts

-ical *suffix forming adjectives* a variant of **-ic** *economical*; *fanatical* [from Latin *-icālis*] > **-ically** *suffix forming adverbs*

ICAO *abbreviation* International Civil Aviation Organization

Icaria (aɪˈkɛərɪə, ɪ-) *n* a Greek island in the Aegean Sea, in the Southern Sporades group. Area: 256 sq km (99 sq miles). Modern Greek name: Ikaría Also called: Nikaria

Icarian Sea *n* the part of the Aegean Sea between the islands of Patmos and Leros and the coast of Asia Minor, where, according to legend, Icarus fell into the sea

Icarus (ˈɪkərəs, ˈaɪ-) *n Greek myth* the son of Daedalus, with whom he escaped from Crete, flying with wings made of wax and feathers. Heedless of his father's warning he flew too near the sun, causing the wax to melt, and fell into the Aegean and drowned

ICBM *abbreviation* intercontinental ballistic missile: a missile with a range greater than 5500 km

ice (aɪs) *n* **1** water in the solid state, formed by freezing liquid water. Related adj: glacial **2** a portion of ice cream **3** *slang* a diamond or diamonds **4** *slang* a concentrated and highly potent form of methamphetamine with dangerous side effects **5** break the ice **a** to relieve shyness, etc, esp between strangers **b** to be the first of a group to do something **6** on ice in abeyance; pending **7** on thin ice unsafe or unsafely; vulnerable or vulnerable **8** the Ice NZ informal Antarctica ▷ *vb* **9** (often foll by *up*, *over*, etc) to form or cause to form ice; freeze **10** (tr) to mix with ice or chill (a drink, etc) **11** (tr) to cover (a cake, etc) with icing [Old English *īs*; compare Old High German *īs*, Old Norse *īss*] > **iced** *adj*

ICE *abbreviation* (in Britain) Institution of Civil Engineers

Ice. *abbreviation* Iceland(ic)

ice age *n* another name for **glacial period**

ice axe *n* a light axe used by mountaineers for cutting footholds in snow or ice, to provide an anchor point, or to control a slide on snow; it has a spiked tip and a head consisting of a pick and an adze

ice bag *n* a waterproof bag used as an ice pack

iceberg (ˈaɪsbɜːɡ) *n* **1** a large mass of ice floating in the sea, esp a mass that has broken off a polar glacier **2** *slang*, *chiefly US* a person considered to have a cold or reserved manner [C18: probably part translation of Middle Dutch *ijsberg* ice mountain; compare Norwegian *isberg*]

iceberg lettuce *n* a type of lettuce with very crisp pale leaves tightly enfolded

iceblink (ˈaɪsˌblɪŋk) *n* Also called: blink a yellowish-white reflected glare in the sky over an ice field

icebound (ˈaɪsˌbaʊnd) *adj* covered or made immobile by ice; frozen in: *an icebound ship*

icebox (ˈaɪsˌbɒks) *n* **1** a compartment in a refrigerator for storing or making ice **2** an insulated cabinet packed with ice for storing food **3** *US & Canad* a refrigerator

icebreaker (ˈaɪsˌbreɪkə) *n* **1** Also called: iceboat a vessel with a reinforced bow for breaking up the ice in bodies of water to keep channels open for navigation **2** any tool or device for breaking ice into smaller pieces **3** something intended to relieve mutual shyness at a gathering of strangers

ice bridge *n Canadian* a body of ice that forms across the width of a river and is strong enough to bear traffic

icecap ('aɪs,kæp) *n* a thick mass of glacial ice and snow that permanently covers an area of land, such as either of the polar regions or the peak of a mountain

ice cream *n* a kind of sweetened frozen liquid, properly made from cream and egg yolks but often made from milk or a custard base, flavoured in various ways

ice dance *n* any of a number of dances, mostly based on ballroom dancing, performed by a couple skating on ice ▷ **ice dancer** *n* ▷ **ice dancing** *n*

icefall ('aɪs,fɔːl) *n* a very steep part of a glacier that has deep crevasses and resembles a frozen waterfall

ice field *n* **1** a very large flat expanse of ice floating in the sea; large ice floe **2** a large mass of ice permanently covering an extensive area of land

ice floe *n* a sheet of ice, of variable size, floating in the sea ▷ See also **ice field** (sense 1)

ice hockey *n* a game played on ice by two opposing teams of six players each, who wear skates and try to propel a flat puck into their opponents' goal with long sticks having an offset flat blade at the end

ice house *n* a building for storing ice

İçel (iː'tʃɛl) *n* another name for **Mersin**

Iceland ('aɪslənd) *n* an island republic in the N Atlantic, regarded as part of Europe: settled by Norsemen, who established a legislative assembly in 930; under Danish rule (1380–1918); gained independence in 1918 and became a republic in 1944; contains large areas of glaciers, snowfields, and lava beds with many volcanoes and hot springs (the chief source of domestic heat); inhabited chiefly along the SW coast. The economy is based largely on fishing and tourism. Official language: Icelandic. Official religion: Evangelical Lutheran. Currency: króna. Capital: Reykjavik. Pop: 291 000 (2004 est). Area: 102 828 sq km (39 702 sq miles)

Icelander ('aɪs,lændə, 'aɪsləndə) *n* a native, citizen, or inhabitant of Iceland

Icelandic (aɪs'lændɪk) *adj* **1** of, relating to, or characteristic of Iceland, its people, or their language ▷ *n* **2** the official language of Iceland, belonging to the North Germanic branch of the Indo-European family

Iceland poppy *n* any of various widely cultivated arctic poppies, esp *Papaver nudicaule*, with white or yellow nodding flowers

Iceland spar *n* a pure transparent variety of calcite with double-refracting crystals used in making polarizing microscopes

ice lolly *n* *Brit informal* an ice cream or water ice on a stick. Also called: **lolly**

ice pack *n* **1** a bag or folded cloth containing ice, applied to a part of the body, esp the head, to cool, reduce swelling, etc **2** another name for **pack ice** **3** a sachet containing a gel that can be frozen or heated and that retains its temperature for an extended period of time, used esp in cool bags

ice pick *n* a pointed tool used for breaking ice

ice plant *n* a low-growing plant, *Mesembryanthemum* (or *Cryophytum*) *crystallinum*, of southern Africa, with fleshy leaves covered with icelike hairs and pink or white rayed flowers: family *Aizoaceae*

ice point *n* the temperature at which a mixture of ice and water are in equilibrium at a pressure of one atmosphere. It is 0° on the Celsius scale and 32° on the Fahrenheit scale ▷ See **steam point**

ice sheet *n* a thick layer of ice covering a large area of land for a long time, esp those in Antarctica and Greenland

ice shelf *n* a thick mass of ice that is permanently attached to the land but projects into and floats on the sea

ice skate *n* **1** a boot having a steel blade fitted to the sole to enable the wearer to glide swiftly over ice **2** the steel blade on such a boot or shoe ▷ *vb* **ice-skate** **3** (*intr*) to glide swiftly over ice on ice skates ▷ **ice-,skater** *n*

ice station *n* a scientific research station in polar regions, where ice movement, weather, and environmental conditions are monitored

icewine ('aɪswaɪn) *n* *Canadian* a dessert wine made from grapes that have frozen before being harvested

Ichang or **I-ch'ang** ('iː'tʃæŋ) *n* a variant transliteration of the Chinese name for **Yichang**

I.Chem.E. *abbreviation* Institution of Chemical Engineers

I Ching ('iː 'tʃɪŋ) *n* an ancient Chinese book of divination and a source of Confucian and Taoist philosophy. Answers to questions and advice may be obtained by referring to the text accompanying one of 64 hexagrams, selected at random

ichneumon (ɪk'njuːmən) *n* a mongoose, *Herpestes ichneumon*, of Africa and S Europe, having greyish-brown speckled fur [c16: via Latin from Greek, literally: tracker, hunter, from *ikhneuein* to track, from *ikhnos* a footprint; so named from the animal's alleged ability to locate the eggs of crocodiles]

ichneumon fly or **ichneumon wasp** *n* any hymenopterous insect of the family *Ichneumonidae*, whose larvae are parasitic in caterpillars and other insect larvae

ichnography (ɪk'nɒɡrəfɪ) *n* **1** the art of drawing ground plans **2** the ground plan of a building, factory, etc [c16: from Latin *ichnographia*, from Greek *ikhnographia*, from *ikhnos* trace, track] ▷ **ichnographic** (,ɪknə'ɡræfɪk) or ,**ichno'graphical** *adj*

ichor ('aɪkɔː) *n* **1** *Greek myth* the fluid said to flow in the veins of the gods **2** *pathol* a foul-smelling watery discharge from a wound or ulcer [c17: from Greek *ikhōr*, of obscure origin] ▷ **'ichorous** *adj*

ichthyo- or before a vowel **ichthy-** *combining form* indicating or relating to fishes: *ichthyology* [from Latin, from Greek *ikhthus* fish]

ichthyoid ('ɪkθɪ,ɔɪd) *adj* Also: **ichthyoidal** **1** resembling a fish ▷ *n* **2** a fishlike vertebrate

ichthyology (,ɪkθɪ'ɒlədʒɪ) *n* the study of the physiology, history, economic importance, etc, of fishes ▷ **ichthyologic** (,ɪkθɪə'lɒdʒɪk) or ,**ichthyo'logical** *adj* ▷ ,**ichthy'ologist** *n*

ichthyosaur ('ɪkθɪə,sɔː) or **ichthyosaurus** (,ɪkθɪə'sɔːrəs) *n*, *pl* -saurs, -sauruses or -sauri (-'sɔːraɪ) any extinct marine Mesozoic reptile of the order *Ichthyosauria*, which had a porpoise-like body with dorsal and tail fins and paddle-like limbs. See also **plesiosaur**

ichthyosis (,ɪkθɪ'əʊsɪs) *n* a congenital disease in which the skin is coarse, dry, and scaly ▷ **ichthyotic** (,ɪkθɪ'ɒtɪk) *adj*

ICI *abbreviation* Imperial Chemical Industries

-ician *suffix forming nouns* indicating a person skilled or involved in a subject or activity: *physician; beautician* [from French -*icien*; see -IC, -IAN]

icicle ('aɪsɪkᵊl) *n* a hanging spike of ice formed by the freezing of dripping water [c14: from ICE + *ickel*, from Old English *gicel* icicle, related to Old Norse *jökull* large piece of ice, glacier]

icing ('aɪsɪŋ) *n* **1** a sugar preparation, variously flavoured and coloured, for coating and decorating cakes, biscuits, etc. Also called (esp US and Canadian): **frosting** **2** the formation of ice, as on a ship or aircraft, due to the freezing of moisture in the atmosphere **3** any unexpected extra or bonus (esp in **icing on the cake**)

icing sugar *n* *Brit* a very finely ground sugar used for icings, confections, etc

icky ('ɪkɪ) *adj* ickier, ickiest **1** sticky **2** excessively sentimental or emotional ▷ **'ickiness** *n*

icon or **ikon** ('aɪkɒn) *n* **1** a representation of Christ, the Virgin Mary, or a saint, esp one painted in oils on a wooden panel, depicted in a traditional Byzantine style and venerated in the Eastern Church **2** an image, picture, representation, etc **3** a symbol resembling or analogous to the thing it represents **4** a person regarded as a sex symbol or as a symbol of a belief or cultural movement **5** a pictorial representation of a facility available on a computer system, that enables the facility to be activated by means of a screen cursor rather than by a textual instruction [c16: from Latin, from Greek *eikōn* image, from *eikenai* to be like] ▷ **i'conic** *adj*

Iconium (aɪ'kəʊnɪəm) *n* the ancient name for **Konya**

icono- or before a vowel **icon-** *combining form* indicating an image or likeness: *iconology* [from Greek: ICON]

iconoclast (aɪ'kɒnə,klæst) *n* **1** a person who attacks established or traditional concepts, principles, laws, etc **2** **a** a destroyer of religious images or sacred objects **b** an adherent of the heretical movement within the Greek Orthodox Church from 725 to 842 AD, which aimed at the destruction of icons and religious images [c16: from Late Latin *iconoclastes*, from Late Greek *eikonoklastes*, from *eikōn* icon + *klastēs* breaker] > i'cono,clastic *adj* > i'cono,clasm *n*

iconography (,aɪkɒ'nɒɡrəfɪ) *n*, *pl* -phies **1 a** the symbols used in a work of art or art movement **b** the conventional significance attached to such symbols **2 a** collection of pictures of a particular subject, such as Christ **3** the representation of the subjects of icons or portraits, esp on coins > ,ico'nographer *n* > iconographic (aɪ,kɒnə'ɡræfɪk) or i,cono'graphical *adj*

iconolatry (,aɪkɒ'nɒlətrɪ) *n* the worship or adoration of icons as idols > ,ico'nolater *n* > ,ico'nolatrous *adj*

iconology (,aɪkɒ'nɒlədʒɪ) *n* **1** the study or field of art history concerning icons **2** the symbolic representation or symbolism of icons > iconological (aɪ,kɒnə'lɒdʒɪkᵊl) *adj* > ,ico'nologist *n*

iconoscope (aɪ'kɒnə,skəʊp) *n* a television camera tube in which an electron beam scans a photoemissive surface, converting an optical image into electrical pulses

iconostasis (,aɪkəʊ'nɒstəsɪs) or **iconostas** (aɪ'kɒnə,stæs) *n*, *pl* iconostases (,aɪkəʊ'nɒstə,siːz, aɪ'kɒnə,stæsɪz) *Eastern Church* a screen with doors and icons set in tiers, which separates the bema (sanctuary) from the nave [c19: Church Latin, from Late Greek *eikonostasion* shrine, literally: area where images are placed, from ICONO- + *histanai* to stand]

icosahedron (,aɪkəsə'hiːdrən) *n*, *pl* -drons or -dra (-drə) a solid figure having 20 faces. The faces of a **regular icosahedron** are equilateral triangles [c16: from Greek *eikosaedron*, from *eikosi* twenty + *-edron* -HEDRON] > ,icosa'hedral *adj*

-ics *suffix forming nouns* (functioning as singular) **1** indicating a science, art, or matters relating to a particular subject: *aeronautics*; *politics* **2** indicating certain activities or practices: *acrobatics* [plural of *-ic*, representing Latin *-ica*, from Greek *-ika*, as in *mathēmatika* mathematics]

ICSI *abbreviation* intracytoplasmic sperm injection: a method of in vitro fertilization in which a spermatozoon is injected into an ovum for implantation within the womb

ICT *abbreviation* Information and Communications Technology

Ictinus (ɪk'taɪnəs) *n* 5th century BC, Greek architect, who designed the Parthenon with Callicrates

ictus ('ɪktəs) *n*, *pl* -tuses or -tus **1** *prosody* metrical or rhythmic stress in verse feet, as contrasted with the stress accent on words **2** *med* a sudden attack or stroke [c18: from Latin *icere* to strike] > 'ictal *adj*

ICU *abbreviation* intensive care unit

icy ('aɪsɪ) *adj* icier, iciest **1** made of, covered with, or containing ice **2** resembling ice **3** freezing or very cold **4** cold or reserved in manner; aloof > 'icily *adv*

id (ɪd) *n psychoanal* the mass of primitive instincts and energies in the unconscious mind that, modified by the ego and the superego, underlies all psychic activity [c20: New Latin, from Latin: it; used to render German *Es*]

ID *abbreviation* **1** Idaho **2** identification (document) **3** Also called: i.d. intradermal(ly)

id. *abbreviation* idem

Id. *abbreviation* Idaho

I'd (aɪd) *contraction of* I had *or* I would

-id¹ *suffix forming adjectives, suffix forming nouns* indicating members of a zoological family: *cyprinid* [from New Latin *-idae* or *-ida*, from Greek *-idēs* suffix indicating offspring]

-id² *suffix forming nouns* a variant of **-ide**

Ida ('aɪdə) *n* **1 a** mountain in central Crete: the highest on the island; in ancient times associated with the worship of Zeus. Height: 2456 m (8057 ft). Modern Greek name: **Idhi 2** a mountain in NW Turkey, southeast of the site of ancient Troy. Height: 1767 m (5797 ft). Turkish name: **Kaz Daği**

IDA *abbreviation* International Development Association

-idae *suffix forming nouns* indicating names of zoological families: *Felidae*; *Hominidae* [New Latin, from Latin, from Greek *-idai*, suffix indicating offspring]

Idaho ('aɪdə,həʊ) *n* a state of the northwestern US: consists chiefly of ranges of the Rocky Mountains, with the Snake River basin in the south; important for agriculture (**Idaho potatoes**), livestock, and silver-mining. Capital: Boise. Pop: 1 366 332 (2003 est). Area: 216 413 sq km (83 557 sq miles). Abbreviations: Ida, (with zip code) ID

-ide or **-id** *suffix forming nouns* **1** (added to the combining form of the nonmetallic or electronegative elements) indicating a binary compound: *sodium chloride* **2** indicating an organic compound derived from another: *acetanilide* **3** indicating one of a class of compounds or elements: *peptide*; *lanthanide* [from German *-id*, from French *oxide* OXIDE, based on the suffix of *acide* ACID]

idea (aɪ'dɪə) *n* **1** any content of the mind, esp the conscious mind **2** the thought of something: *the very idea appals me* **3** an individual's conception of something: *his idea of honesty is not the same as yours and mine* **4** the belief that something is the case **5** a scheme, intention, plan, etc **6** a vague notion or indication; inkling: *he had no idea of what life would be like in Africa* **7** significance or purpose: *the idea of the game is to discover the murderer* **8** *philosophy* a private mental object, regarded as the immediate object of thought or perception **9 get ideas** to become ambitious, restless, etc **10** not one's idea of not what one regards as (hard work, a holiday, etc) **11** that's an idea that is worth considering **12 the very idea!** that is preposterous, unreasonable, etc [c16: via Late Latin from Greek: model, pattern, notion, from *idein* to see]

● **USAGE** It is usually considered correct to say that
● someone has *the idea of doing* something, rather than
● *the idea to do* it: *he had the idea of taking* (not *the idea to*
● *take*) *a short holiday*

idea hamster or **ideas hamster** *n slang* a person who is employed as a source of new ideas

ideal (aɪ'dɪəl) *n* **1** a conception of something that is perfect, esp that which one seeks to attain **2** a person or thing considered to represent perfection **3** something existing only as an idea **4** a pattern or model, esp of ethical behaviour ▷ *adj* **5** conforming to an ideal **6** of, involving, or existing in the form of an idea **7** *philosophy* **a** of or relating to a highly desirable and possible state of affairs **b** of or relating to idealism > i'deally *adv* > i'dealness *n*

ideal element *n* any element added to a mathematical theory in order to eliminate special cases. The ideal element $i = \sqrt{-1}$ allows all algebraic equations to be solved and the point at infinity (**ideal point**) ensures that any two lines in projective geometry intersect

ideal gas *n* a hypothetical gas which obeys Boyle's law exactly at all temperatures and pressures, and which has internal energy that depends only upon the temperature. Measurements upon real gases are extrapolated to zero pressure to obtain results in agreement with theories relating to an ideal gas, especially in thermometry

idealism (aɪ'dɪə,lɪzəm) *n* **1** belief in or pursuance of ideals **2** the tendency to represent things in their ideal forms, rather than as they are **3** any of a group of philosophical doctrines that share the monistic view that material objects and the external world do not exist in reality independently of the human mind but are variously creations of the mind or constructs of ideas ▷ See **materialism** (sense 2) > i'dealist *n* > i,deal'istic *adj* > i,deal'istically *adv*

idealize or **idealise** (aɪ'dɪə,laɪz) *vb* **1** to consider or represent (something) as ideal **2** (tr) to portray as ideal; glorify **3** (intr) to form an ideal or ideals > i'deal,izer or i'deal,iser *n* > i,deali'zation or i,deali'sation *n*

idée fixe (ide fiks) *n*, *pl* **idées fixes** (ide fiks) a fixed idea; obsession

idem Latin ('aɪdɛm, 'ɪdɛm) the same: used to refer to an article, chapter, etc, previously cited

identic (aɪ'dɛntɪk) *adj diplomacy* (esp of opinions expressed by two or more governments) having the same wording or intention regarding another power

identical (aɪ'dɛntɪkᵊl) *adj* **1** Also called: numerically identical being one and the same individual: *Cicero and Tully are identical* **2** Also called: quantitatively identical exactly alike, equal, or agreeing **3** designating either or both of a pair of twins of the same sex who developed from a single fertilized ovum that split into two. See **fraternal** (sense 3) > i'dentically *adv* [c17: from Medieval Latin *identicus*, from Latin *idem* the same]

identification (aɪ,dɛntɪfɪ'keɪʃən) *n* **1** the act of identifying or the state of being identified **2 a** something that identifies a person or thing **b** (*as modifier*): *an identification card* **3** *psychol* **a** the process of recognizing specific objects as the result of remembering **b** the process by which one incorporates aspects of another person's personality **c** the transferring of a response from one situation to another because the two bear similar features

identification parade *n* a group of persons including one suspected of having committed a crime assembled for the purpose of discovering whether a witness can identify the suspect

identify (aɪ'dɛntɪ,faɪ) *vb* **-fies, -fying, -fied** (*mainly tr*) **1** to prove or recognize as being a certain person or thing; determine the identity of **2** to consider as the same or equivalent **3** (*also intr; often foll by* *with*) to consider (oneself) as similar to another **4** to determine the taxonomic classification of (a plant or animal) **5** (*intr; usually foll by* *with*) *psychol* to engage in identification > i'denti,fiable *adj* > i'denti,fier *n*

Identikit (aɪ'dɛntɪ,kɪt) *n trademark* **1 a** a set of transparencies of various typical facial characteristics that can be superimposed on one another to build up, on the basis of a description, a picture of a person sought by the police **b** (*as modifier*): *an Identikit picture* **2** (*modifier*) artificially created by copying different elements in an attempt to form a whole: *an identikit pop group*

identity (aɪ'dɛntɪtɪ) *n, pl* **-ties 1** the state of having unique identifying characteristics held by no other person or thing **2** the individual characteristics by which a person or thing is recognized **3** *Also called:* **qualitative identity** the state of being the same in nature, quality, etc: *they were linked by the identity of their tastes* **4** the state of being the same as a person or thing described or claimed: *the identity of the stolen goods has not yet been established* **5** *maths* **a** an equation that is valid for all values of its variables, as in $(x − y)(x + y) = x^2 − y^2$. Often denoted by the symbol ≡ **b** *Also called:* **identity element** a member of a set that when operating on another member, *x*, produces that member *x*: *the identity for multiplication of numbers is 1 since x.1 = 1.x = x* **6** *Austral & NZ informal* a well-known person, esp in a specified locality; figure (esp in the phrase **an old identity**) [c16: from Late Latin *identitās*, from Latin *idem* the same]

identity card *n* a card that establishes a person's identity, esp one issued to all members of the population in wartime, to the staff of an organization, etc

identity theft *n* the crime of setting up and using bank accounts and credit facilities fraudulently in another person's name without his or her knowledge

ideo- *combining form* indicating idea or ideas: *ideology* [from French *idéo-*, from Greek *idea* IDEA]

ideogram ('ɪdɪəʊ,græm) *or* **ideograph** ('ɪdɪəʊ,gra:f, -,græf) *n* **1** a sign or symbol, used in such writing systems as those of China or Japan, that directly represents a concept, idea, or thing rather than a word or set of words for it **2** any graphic sign or symbol, such as %, @, &, etc

ideography (,ɪdɪ'ɒgrəfɪ) *n* the use of ideograms to communicate ideas

ideology (,aɪdɪ'ɒlədʒɪ) *n, pl* **-gies 1** a body of ideas that reflects the beliefs and interests of a nation, political system, etc and underlies political action **2** speculation that is imaginary or visionary **3** the study of the nature and origin of ideas > **ideological** (,aɪdɪə'lɒdʒɪkəl) *or* ,ideo'logic *adj* > ,ideo'logically *adv* > ,ide'ologist *or* ideologue ('aɪdɪə,lɒg) *n*

ides (aɪdz) *n* (*functioning as singular*) (in the Roman calendar) the 15th day in March, May, July, and October and the 13th day of each other month [c15: from Old French, from Latin *īdūs* (plural), of uncertain origin]

id est *Latin* ('ɪd 'ɛst) the full form of **i.e.**

Idhi ('ɪðɪ) *n* a transliteration of the Modern Greek name for (Mount) Ida (sense 1)

idio- *combining form* indicating peculiarity, isolation, or that which pertains to an individual person or thing: *idiolect* [from Greek *idios* private, separate]

idiocy ('ɪdɪəsɪ) *n, pl* **-cies 1** (*not in technical usage*) severe mental retardation **2** foolishness or senselessness; stupidity **3** a foolish act or remark

idiom ('ɪdɪəm) *n* **1** a group of words whose meaning cannot be predicted from the meanings of the constituent words, as for example (*It was raining*) *cats and dogs* **2** linguistic usage that is grammatical and natural to native speakers of a language **3** the characteristic artistic style of an individual, school, period, etc [c16: from Latin *idiōma* peculiarity of language, from Greek; see IDIO-] > idiomatic (,ɪdɪə'mætɪk) *adj* > ,idio'matically *adv*

idiosyncrasy (,ɪdɪəʊ'sɪŋkrəsɪ) *n, pl* **-sies 1** a tendency, type of behaviour, mannerism, etc, of a specific person; quirk **2** the composite physical or psychological make-up of a specific person **3** an abnormal reaction of an individual to specific foods, drugs, or other agents [c17: from Greek *idiosunkrasia*, from *idios* + *sunkrasis* mixture, temperament, from *sun-* SYN- + *kerannunai* to mingle]

idiosyncratic (,ɪdɪəʊsɪŋ'krætɪk) *adj* of or relating to idiosyncrasy; characteristic of a specific person > ,idiosyn'cratically *adv*

idiot ('ɪdɪət) *n* **1** a person with severe mental retardation **2** a foolish or senseless person [c13: from Latin *idiōta* ignorant person, from Greek *idiōtēs* private person, one who lacks professional knowledge, ignoramus; see IDIO-]

idiot board *n* a slang name for **Autocue**

idiot box *n slang* a television set

idiotic (,ɪdɪ'ɒtɪk) *adj* of or resembling an idiot; foolish; senseless > ,idi'otically *adv*

idiot savant ('i:djəʊ sæ'vɑ̃, 'ɪdɪət 'sævənt) *n, pl* **idiots savants** ('i:djəʊ sæ'vɑ̃) *or* **idiot savants** a person with learning difficulties who performs brilliantly at some specialized intellectual task, such as giving the day of the week for any calendar date past or present [c19: from French: knowledgeable idiot]

idiot strings *pl n Canadian informal* strings attached to children's mittens to prevent the wearer from losing them

idiot tape *n printing* an input tape for a typesetting machine that contains text only, the typographical instructions being supplied by the typesetting machine itself

idle ('aɪdəl) *adj* **1** unemployed or unoccupied; inactive **2** not operating or being used **3** (of money) not being used to earn interest or dividends **4** not wanting to work; lazy **5** (*usually prenominal*) frivolous or trivial: *idle pleasures* **6** ineffective or powerless; fruitless; vain **7** without basis; unfounded ▷ *vb* **8** (when *tr*, often foll by *away*) to waste or pass (time) fruitlessly or inactively **9** (*intr*) (of a shaft, engine, etc) to turn without doing useful work **10** (*intr*) (of an engine) to run at low speed with the transmission disengaged [Old English *īdel*; compare Old High German *ītal* empty, vain] > 'idleness *n* > 'idly *adv*

idle pulley *or* **idler pulley** *n* a freely rotating trolley used to control the tension or direction of a belt. *Also called:* **idler**

idler ('aɪdlə) *n* **1** a person who idles **2** another name for **idle pulley**, **idle wheel**

idle wheel *n* a gearwheel interposed between two others to transmit torque without changing the direction of rotation to the velocity ratio. *Also called:* **idler**

idol ('aɪdəl) *n* **1** a material object, esp a carved image, that is worshipped as a god **2** *Christianity, Judaism* any being (other than the one God) to which divine honour is paid **3** a person who is revered, admired, or highly loved [c13: from Late Latin *īdōlum*, from Latin: image, from Greek *eidōlon*, from *eidos* shape, form]

idolatry (aɪ'dɒlətrɪ) *n* **1** the worship of idols **2** great devotion or reverence > i'dolater *n* *or* i'dolatress *fem n* > i'dolatrous *adj*

idolize or **idolise** ('aɪdə,laɪz) vb **1** (tr) to admire or revere greatly **2** (tr) to worship as an idol **3** (intr) to worship idols > i'dolism, ,idoli'zation or ,idoli'sation n > 'idolist, 'idol,izer or 'idol,iser n

idolum (ɪ'dəʊlʊm) n **1** a mental picture; idea **2** a false idea, fallacy [c17: from Latin: IDOL]

Idomeneus (aɪ'dɒmɪ,njuːs) n Greek myth a king of Crete who fought on the Greek side in the Trojan War

IDP abbreviation integrated data processing

Idun ('iːdʊn) or **Ithunn** n Norse myth the goddess of spring who guarded the apples that kept the gods eternally young; wife of Bragi

idyll or sometimes US **idyl** ('ɪdɪl) n **1** a poem or prose work describing an idealized rural life, pastoral scenes, etc **2** a charming or picturesque scene or event **3** a piece of music with a calm or pastoral character [c17: from Latin *īdyllium*, from Greek *eidullion*, from *eidos* shape, (literary) form] > i'dyllic adj > i'dyllically adv

IE abbreviation Indo-European (languages)

i.e. abbreviation id est [Latin: that is (to say); in other words]

-ie suffix forming nouns a variant of -y²

IEA abbreviation International Energy Agency

IED abbreviation improvised explosive device

IEE abbreviation Institution of Electrical Engineers

Ieper ('iːpər) n the Flemish name for **Ypres**

-ier suffix forming nouns a variant of -eer: brigadier [from Old English -ere -ER¹ or (in some words) from Old French -ier, from Latin -ārius -ARY]

Ieyasu (,iːjeˈjɑːsuː) n a variant spelling of (Tokugawa) **Iyeyasu**

if (ɪf) conj (subordinating) **1** in case that, or on condition that: *if you try hard it might work; if he were poor, would you marry him?* **2** used to introduce an indirect question. In this sense, if approaches the meaning of whether **3** even though: *an attractive if awkward girl* **4 a** used to introduce expressions of desire, with only: *if I had only known* **b** used to introduce exclamations of surprise, dismay, etc: *if this doesn't top everything!* ▷ n **5** an uncertainty or doubt: *the big if is whether our plan will work at all* **6** a condition or stipulation: *I won't have any ifs or buts* [Old English *gif*; related to Old Saxon *ef* if, Old High German *iba* whether, if]

IF or **i.f.** abbreviation electronics intermediate frequency

IFA abbreviation independent financial adviser

IFAD abbreviation International Fund for Agricultural Development

IFC abbreviation International Finance Corporation

Ife ('iːfɪ) n a town in W central Nigeria: one of the largest and oldest Yoruba towns; university (1961); centre of the cocoa trade. Pop: 229 000 (2005 est)

-iferous suffix forming adjectives containing or yielding: carboniferous

iffy ('ɪfɪ) adj iffier, iffiest informal uncertain or subject to contingency [c20: from IF + -Y¹]

Ifni (Spanish 'ifni) n a former Spanish province in S Morocco, on the Atlantic: returned to Morocco in 1969

IFP abbreviation Inkatha Freedom Party

IFS abbreviation Irish Free State (now called Republic of Ireland)

-ify suffix forming verbs a variant of -fy intensify > -ification suffix forming nouns

Igbo ('iːbəʊ) n, pl -bo or -bos a variant spelling of **Ibo**

IGC abbreviation inter-governmental conference (esp in the European Union)

Igdrasil ('ɪgdrəsɪl) n a variant spelling of **Yggdrasil**

igloo or **iglu** ('ɪgluː) n, pl -loos or -lus **1** a dome-shaped Inuit house, usually built of blocks of solid snow **2** a hollow made by a seal in the snow over its breathing hole in the ice [c19: from Inuktitut *igdlu* house]

Ignatiev (ɪg'nɑː,tjef) n Count **Nikolai Pavlovich**. 1832–1908, Russian diplomat and politician. As ambassador to Turkey (1864–77), he negotiated the Treaty of San Stefano (1878) ending the Russo-Turkish War

Ignatius (ɪg'neɪʃəs) n **Saint**, surnamed *Theophorus*. died ?110 AD, bishop of Antioch. His seven letters, written on his way to his martyrdom in Rome, give valuable insight into the early Christian Church. Feast day: Oct 17 or Dec 17 or 20

Ignatius Loyola (lɔɪ'əʊlə) n **Saint**. 1491–1556, Spanish ecclesiastic. He founded the Society of Jesus (1534) and was its first general (1541–56). His *Spiritual Exercises* (1548) remains the basic manual for the training of Jesuits. Feast day: July 31

igneous ('ɪgnɪəs) adj **1** (of rocks) derived by solidification of magma or molten lava emplaced on or below the earth's surface **2** of or relating to fire [c17: from Latin *igneus* fiery, from *ignis* fire]

ignis fatuus ('ɪgnɪs 'fætjʊəs) n, pl ignes fatui ('ɪgniːz 'fætjʊ,aɪ) another name for **will-o'-the-wisp** [c16: from Medieval Latin, literally: foolish fire]

ignite (ɪg'naɪt) vb **1** to catch fire or set fire to; burn or cause to burn **2** (tr) chem to heat strongly **3** (tr) to stimulate or provoke [c17: from Latin *ignīre* to set alight, from *ignis* fire] > ig'nitable or ig'nitible adj > ig,nita'bility or ig,niti'bility n

igniter (ɪg'naɪtə) n **1** a person or thing that ignites **2** a fuse to fire explosive charges **3** an electrical device for lighting a gas turbine **4** a subsidiary electrode in an ignitron

ignition (ɪg'nɪʃən) n **1** the act or process of initiating combustion **2** the process of igniting the fuel in an internal-combustion engine **3** the the devices used to ignite the fuel in an internal-combustion engine

ignition coil n an induction coil that supplies the high voltage to the sparking plugs of an internal-combustion engine

ignition key n the key used in a motor vehicle to turn the switch that connects the battery to the ignition system and other electrical devices

ignitron (ɪg'naɪtrɒn, 'ɪgnɪ,trɒn) n a mercury-arc rectifier controlled by a subsidiary electrode, the igniter, partially immersed in a mercury cathode. A current passed between igniter and cathode forms a hot spot sufficient to strike an arc between cathode and anode [c20: from IGNITER + ELECTRON]

ignoble (ɪg'nəʊbªl) adj **1** dishonourable; base; despicable **2** of low birth or origins; humble; common **3** of low quality; inferior [c16: from Latin *ignōbilis*, from IN-¹ + Old Latin *gnōbilis* NOBLE] > ,igno'bility or ig'nobleness n > ig'nobly adv

ignominy ('ɪgnə,mɪnɪ) n, pl -minies **1** disgrace or public shame; dishonour **2** a cause of disgrace; a shameful act [c16: from Latin *ignōminia* disgrace, from *ig-* (see IN-²) + *nōmen* name, reputation] > ,igno'minious adj > ,igno'miniously adv > ,igno'miniousness n

ignoramus (,ɪgnə'reɪməs) n, pl -muses an ignorant person; fool [c16: from legal Latin, literally: we have no knowledge of, from Latin *ignōrāre* to be ignorant of; see IGNORE; modern usage originated from the use of *Ignoramus* as the name of an unlettered lawyer in a play by G. Ruggle, 17th-century English dramatist]

ignorance ('ɪgnərəns) n lack of knowledge, information, or education; the state of being ignorant

ignorant ('ɪgnərənt) adj **1** lacking in knowledge or education; unenlightened **2** (postpositive; often foll by of) lacking in awareness or knowledge (of): *ignorant of the law* **3** resulting from or showing lack of knowledge or awareness: *an ignorant remark* > 'ignorantly adv

ignore (ɪg'nɔː) vb (tr) to fail or refuse to notice; disregard [c17: from Latin *ignōrāre* not to know, from *ignārus* ignorant of, from *i-* IN-¹ + *gnārus* knowing; related to Latin *noscere* to know] > ig'norer n

Iguaçu or **Iguassú** (Portuguese igua'su) n a river in SE South America, rising in S Brazil and flowing west to join the Paraná River, forming part of the border between Brazil and Argentina. Length: 1200 km (745 miles)

Iguaçu Falls n a waterfall on the border between Brazil and Argentina, on the Iguaçu River: divided into hundreds of separate falls by forested rocky islands. Width: about 4 km (2.5 miles). Height: 82 m (269 ft)

iguana (ɪ'gwɑːnə) n either of two large tropical American arboreal herbivorous lizards of the genus *Iguana*, esp *I. iguana* (**common iguana**), having a greyish-green body with a row of spines along the back: family Iguanidae [c16: from Spanish, from Arawak *iwana*] > i'guanian n, adj

iguanodon (ɪˈgwɑːnəˌdɒn) *n* a massive herbivorous long-tailed bipedal dinosaur of the genus *Iguanodon*, common in Europe and N Africa in Jurassic and Cretaceous times: suborder *Ornithopoda* (ornithopods) [C19: New Latin, from IGUANA + Greek *odōn* tooth]

IHC *abbreviation* (in New Zealand) Intellectually Handicapped Children

Ihimaera (ɪhɪˈmɑːrə) *n* **Witi** (ˈwɪtɪ), full name *Witi Tame Ihimaera-Smiler*. born 1944, New Zealand Māori novelist and short-story writer; his novels include *The Whale Rider* (1987) and *The Uncle's Story* (2002)

IHS *n* the first three letters of the name Jesus in Greek (ΙΗΣΟΥΣ), often used as a Christian emblem

IJssel *or* **Yssel** (ˈaɪsəl; *Dutch* ˈɛisəl) *n* a river in the central Netherlands: a distributary of the Rhine, flowing north to the IJsselmeer. Length: 116 km (72 miles)

Ikaría (ika'ria) *n* a transliteration of the Modern Greek name for **Icaria**

ikat (ˈaɪkæt) *n* a method of creating patterns in fabric by tie-dyeing the yarn before weaving [C20: from Malay, literally: to tie, bind]

ikebana (ˌiːkəˈbɑːnə) *n* the Japanese decorative art of flower arrangement

Ikeja (ɪˈkeɪjə) *n* a town in SW Nigeria, capital of Lagos state: residential and industrial suburb of Lagos. Pop (local government area): 313 196 (2006)

Ikhnaton (ɪkˈnɑːtən) *n* same as **Akhenaten**

ikon (ˈaɪkɒn) *n* a variant spelling of **icon**

IL *abbreviation* Illinois

il- *prefix* variant of in-[1,2]

-ile *suffix forming adjectives, suffix forming nouns* indicating capability, liability, or a relationship with something: *agile; fragile; juvenile* [via French from Latin or directly from Latin *-ilis*]

Île-de-France (*French* ildəfrɑs) *n* **1** a region of N France, in the Paris Basin: part of the duchy of France in the 10th century **2** a former name (1715–1810) for **Mauritius**

Île du Diable (il dy djablə) *n* the French name for **Devil's Island**

ileitis (ˌɪlɪˈaɪtɪs) *n* inflammation of the ileum

ileostomy (ˌɪlɪˈɒstəmɪ) *n, pl* -mies the surgical formation of a permanent opening through the abdominal wall into the ileum

Îles Comores (il kɔmɔr) *pl n* the French name for the **Comoros**

Îles du Salut (il dy saly) *pl n* the French name for the **Safety Islands**

Ilesha (ɪˈleɪʃə) *n* a town in W Nigeria. Pop: 500 000 (2005 est)

Îles Mascareignes (il maskarɛɲ) *pl n* the French name for the **Mascarene Islands**

Îles sous le Vent (il su lə vã) *pl n* the French name for the **Leeward Islands** (sense 3)

ileum (ˈɪlɪəm) *n* the part of the small intestine between the jejunum and the caecum [C17: New Latin, from Latin *ilium, ileum* flank, groin, of obscure origin]

ilex (ˈaɪlɛks) *n* **1** any of various trees or shrubs of the widely distributed genus *Ilex*, such as the holly and inkberry: family *Aquifoliaceae* **2** another name for the **holm oak** [C16: from Latin]

Ilia (ˈɪlɪə) *n* (in Roman legend) the daughter of Aeneas and Lavinia, who, according to some traditions, was the mother of Romulus and Remus. See also **Rhea Silvia**

Ilía (iˈlia) *n* a transliteration of the Modern Greek name for **Elia**[1]

Iliamna (ˌɪlɪˈæmnə) *n* **1** a lake in SW Alaska: the largest lake in Alaska. Length: about 130 km (80 miles). Width: 40 km (25 miles) **2** a volcano in SW Alaska, northwest of Iliamna Lake. Height: 3076 m (10 092 ft)

Iligan (ɪˈliːgən) *n* a city in the Philippines, a port on the N coast of Mindanao. Pop: 306 000 (2005 est)

Ilion (ˈɪlɪən) *n* a transliteration of the Greek name for ancient **Troy**

ilium (ˈɪlɪəm) *n, pl* -ia (-ɪə) the uppermost and widest of the three sections of the hipbone

Ilium (ˈɪlɪəm) *n* the Latin name for ancient **Troy**

ilk (ɪlk) *n* **1** a type; class; sort (esp in the phrase **of that, his, her**, etc, **ilk**): *people of that ilk should not be allowed here* **2** of that ilk *Scot* of the place of the same name: used to indicate that the person named is proprietor or laird of the place named: *Moncrieff of that ilk* [Old English *ilca* the same family, same kind; related to Gothic *is* he, Latin *is*, Old English *gelīc* like]

● USAGE Although the use of *ilk* in the sense of sense 1 is
● sometimes condemned as being the result of a
● misunderstanding of the original Scottish expression
● *of that ilk*, it is nevertheless well established and
● generally acceptable

Ilkeston (ˈɪlkɪstən) *n* a town in N central England, in SE Derbyshire. Pop: 37 270 (2001)

Ilkley (ˈɪlklɪ) *n* a town in N England, in Bradford unitary authority, West Yorkshire: nearby is **Ilkley Moor** (to the south). Pop: 13 472 (2001)

ill (ɪl) *adj* worse, worst **1** (*usually postpositive*) not in good health; sick **2** characterized by or intending evil, harm, etc; hostile: *ill deeds* **3** causing or resulting in pain, harm, adversity, etc **4** ascribing or imputing evil to something referred to: *ill repute* **5** promising an unfavourable outcome; unpropitious: *an ill omen* **6** harsh; lacking kindness: *ill will* **7** not up to an acceptable standard; faulty: *ill manners* **8** ill at ease unable to relax; uncomfortable ▷ *n* **9** evil or harm **10** a mild disease **11** misfortune; trouble ▷ *adv* **12** badly: *the title ill befits him* **13** with difficulty; hardly: *he can ill afford the money* **14** not rightly: *she ill deserves such good fortune* [C11 (in the sense: evil): from Old Norse *illr* bad]

Ill. *abbreviation* Illinois

I'll (aɪl) *contraction of* I will *or* I shall

ill-advised *adj* **1** acting without reasonable care or thought: *you would be ill-advised to sell your house now* **2** badly thought out; not or insufficiently considered: *an ill-advised plan of action* ▷ ˌill-adˈvisedly *adv*

ill-affected *adj* (*often foll by* *towards*) not well disposed; disaffected

Illampu (*Spanish* iʎamˈpu) *n* one of the two peaks of Mount Sorata

ill-assorted *adj* badly matched; incompatible

illative (ɪˈleɪtɪv) *adj* **1** of or relating to illation; inferential **2** *grammar* denoting a word or morpheme used to signal inference, for example *so* or *therefore* **3** (in the grammar of Finnish and other languages) denoting a case of nouns expressing a relation of motion or direction, usually translated by the English prepositions *into* or *towards* ▷ *n* **4** *grammar* **a** the illative case **b** an illative word or speech element [C16: from Late Latin *illātīvus* inferring, concluding] ▷ ilˈlatively *adv*

Illawarra (ˌɪləˈwɒrə) *n* **1** a coastal district of E Australia, in S New South Wales. Pop: 404 626 (2002 est) **2** an Australian breed of shorthorn dairy cattle noted for its high milk yield and ability to survive on poor pastures

ill-bred *adj* badly brought up; lacking good manners ▷ ˌill-ˈbreeding *n*

ill-considered *adj* done without due consideration; not thought out: *an ill-considered decision*

ill-defined *adj* imperfectly defined; having no clear outline

ill-disposed *adj* (*often foll by* *towards*) not kindly disposed

Ille-et-Vilaine (*French* ilevilɛn) *n* a department of NW France, in E Brittany. Capital: Rennes. Pop: 894 625 (2003 est). Area: 6992 sq km (2727 sq miles)

illegal (ɪˈliːgəl) *adj* **1** forbidden by law; unlawful; illicit **2** unauthorized or prohibited by a code of official or accepted rules ▷ *n* **3** a person who has entered or attempted to enter a country illegally ▷ ilˈlegally *adv* ▷ ˌilleˈgality *n*

illegible (ɪˈlɛdʒɪbəl) *adj* unable to be read or deciphered ▷ ilˌlegiˈbility *or* ilˈlegibleness *n* ▷ ilˈlegibly *adv*

illegitimate (ˌɪlɪˈdʒɪtɪmɪt) *adj* **1** born of parents who were not married to each other at the time of birth; bastard **2** forbidden by law; illegal; unlawful **3** contrary to logic; incorrectly reasoned ▷ *n* **4** an illegitimate person; bastard ▷ ˌilleˈgitimacy *or* ˌilleˈgitimateness *n* ▷ ˌilleˈgitimately *adv*

ill-fated *adj* doomed or unlucky

ill-favoured *or US* **ill-favored** *adj* **1** unattractive or repulsive in appearance; ugly **2** offensive, disagreeable, or objectionable ▷ ˌill-ˈfavouredly *or US* ˌill-ˈfavoredly *adv*

> ˌill-'favouredness or US ˌill-'favoredness n

ill feeling n hostile feeling; animosity

ill-founded adj not founded on true or reliable premises; unsubstantiated

ill-gotten adj obtained dishonestly or illegally (esp in the phrase **ill-gotten gains**)

ill humour n a disagreeable or sullen mood; bad temper
> ˌill-'humoured adj > ˌill-'humouredly adv

illiberal (ɪˈlɪbərəl) adj **1** narrow-minded; prejudiced; bigoted; intolerant **2** not generous; mean **3** lacking in culture or refinement > il,liber'ality, il'liberalness or il'liberalism n > il'liberally adv

Illich ('ɪlɪtʃ) n **Ivan**. 1926–2002. US teacher and writer, born in Austria. His books include *Deschooling Society* (1971), *Medical Nemesis* (1975), and *In the Mirror of the Past* (1991)

illicit (ɪˈlɪsɪt) adj **1** another word for **illegal 2** not allowed or approved by common custom, rule, or standard: *illicit sexual relations* > il'licitly adv > illicitness n

Illimani (*Spanish* iˌʎiˈmani) n a mountain in W Bolivia, in the Andes near La Paz. Height: 6882 m (22 580 ft)

illimitable (ɪˈlɪmɪtəbəl) adj limitless; boundless
> il,limita'bility or il'limitableness n

Illinois (ˌɪlɪˈnɔɪ) n **1** a state of the N central US, in the Midwest: consists of level prairie crossed by the Illinois and Kaskaskia Rivers; mainly agricultural. Capital: Springfield. Pop: 12 653 544 (2003 est). Area: 144 858 sq km (55 930 sq miles). Abbreviations: Ill., (with zip code) IL **2** a river in Illinois, flowing SW to the Mississippi. Length: 439 km (273 miles)

illiterate (ɪˈlɪtərɪt) adj **1** unable to read and write **2** violating accepted standards in reading and writing: *an illiterate scrawl* **3** uneducated, ignorant, or uncultured: *scientifically illiterate* ▷ n **4** an illiterate person > il'literacy or il'literateness n > il'literately adv

ill-judged adj rash; ill-advised

ill-mannered adj having bad manners; rude; impolite
> ˌill-'manneredly adv

ill-natured adj naturally unpleasant and mean > ˌill-'naturedly adv > ˌill-'naturedness n

illness ('ɪlnɪs) n **1** a disease or indisposition; sickness **2** a state of ill health

illogical (ɪˈlɒdʒɪkəl) adj **1** characterized by lack of logic; senseless or unreasonable **2** disregarding logical principles > illogicality (ɪ,lɒdʒɪ'kælɪtɪ) or il'logicalness n > il'logically adv

ill-starred adj unlucky; unfortunate; ill-fated

ill temper n bad temper; irritability

ill-timed adj occurring at or planned for an unsuitable time

ill-treat vb (tr) to behave cruelly or harshly towards; misuse; maltreat > ˌill-'treatment n

illude (ɪˈluːd) vb *literary* to trick or deceive [C15: from Latin *illūdere* to sport with, from *lūdus* game]

illuminance (ɪˈluːmɪnəns) n the luminous flux incident on unit area of a surface. It is measured in lux. Sometimes called: **illumination**. Compare **irradiance**

illuminant (ɪˈluːmɪnənt) n **1** something that provides or gives off light ▷ adj **2** giving off light; illuminating

illuminate (ɪˈluːmɪ,neɪt) **1** (tr) to throw light in or into; light up **2** (tr) to make easily understood; clarify **3** to adorn, decorate, or be decorated with lights **4** (tr) to decorate (a letter, page, etc) by the application of colours, gold, or silver **5** (intr) to become lighted up ▷ adj (ɪ'luːmɪnɪt, -,neɪt) **6** *archaic* made clear or bright with light; illuminated ▷ n (ɪ'luːmɪnɪt, -,neɪt) **7** a person who has or claims to have special enlightenment [C16: from Latin *illūmināre* to light up, from *lūmen* light]
> il'luminative adj > il'lumi,nator n

illuminati (ɪ,luːmɪˈnɑːtiː) pl n, sing **-to** (-təʊ) a group of persons claiming exceptional enlightenment on some subject, esp religion [C16: from Latin, literally: the enlightened ones, from *illūmināre* to ILLUMINATE]

Illuminati (ɪ,luːmɪˈnɑːtiː) pl n, sing **-to** (-təʊ) any of several groups of illuminati, esp in 18th-century France

illumination (ɪ,luːmɪˈneɪʃən) n **1** the act of illuminating or the state of being illuminated **2** a source of light **3** (*often plural*) *chiefly Brit* a light or lights, esp coloured lights, used as decoration in streets, parks, etc

4 spiritual or intellectual enlightenment; insight or understanding **5** the act of making understood; clarification **6** decoration in colours, gold, or silver used on some manuscripts or printed works **7** *physics* another name (not in technical usage) for **illuminance**

illumine (ɪˈluːmɪn) vb a literary word for **illuminate** [C14: from Latin *illūmināre* to make light; see ILLUMINATE]
> il'luminable adj

ill-use vb (ˈɪlˈjuːz) **1** to use badly or cruelly; abuse; maltreat ▷ n (ˈɪlˈjuːs) Also called: **ill-usage 2** harsh or cruel treatment; abuse

illusion (ɪˈluːʒən) n **1** a false appearance or deceptive impression of reality **2** a false or misleading perception or belief; delusion **3** *psychol* a perception that is not true to reality, having been altered subjectively in some way in the mind of the perceiver. See also **hallucination** [C14: from Latin *illūsiō* deceit, from *illūdere*; see ILLUDE]
> il'lusionary or il'lusional adj

illusionism (ɪˈluːʒə,nɪzəm) n **1** *philosophy* the doctrine that the external world exists only in illusory sense perceptions **2** the use of highly illusory effects in art or decoration, esp the use of perspective in painting to create an impression of three-dimensional reality

illusionist (ɪˈluːʒənɪst) n **1** a person given to illusions; visionary; dreamer **2** *philosophy* a person who believes in illusionism **3** an artist who practises illusionism **4** a conjuror; magician > il,lusion'istic adj

illusory (ɪˈluːsərɪ) or **illusive** (ɪˈluːsɪv) adj producing, produced by, or based on illusion; deceptive or unreal
> il'lusorily or il'lusively adv > il'lusoriness or il'lusiveness n

● USAGE **Illusive** is sometimes wrongly used where *elusive* is meant: *they fought hard, but victory remained elusive* (not *illusive*)

illust. or illus. abbreviation **1** illustrated **2** illustration

illustrate ('ɪlə,streɪt) vb **1** to clarify or explain by use of examples, analogy, etc **2** (tr) to be an example or demonstration of **3** (tr) to explain or decorate (a book, text, etc) with pictures [C16: from Latin *illustrāre* to make light, explain, from *lustrāre* to purify, brighten; see LUSTRUM] > 'illus,trative adj > 'illus,trator n

illustration (,ɪlə'streɪʃən) n **1** pictorial matter used to explain or decorate a text **2** an example or demonstration **3** the act of illustrating or the state of being illustrated > ,illus'trational adj

illustrious (ɪˈlʌstrɪəs) adj **1** of great renown; famous and distinguished **2** glorious or great: *illustrious deeds* [C16: from Latin *illustris* bright, distinguished, famous, from *illustrāre* to make light; see ILLUSTRATE] > il'lustriously adv > il'lustriousness n

ill will n hostile feeling; enmity; antagonism

Illyria (ɪˈlɪrɪə) n an ancient region of uncertain boundaries on the E shore of the Adriatic Sea, including parts of present-day Croatia, Montenegro, and Albania
> Il'lyrian n, adj

Illyricum (ɪˈlɪrɪkəm) n a Roman province founded after 168 BC, based on the coastal area of Illyria

Ilmen ('ɪlmən) n **Lake** a lake in NW Russia, in the Novgorod Region: drains through the Volkhov River into Lake Ladoga. Area: between 780 sq km (300 sq miles) and 2200 sq km (850 sq miles), according to the season

ILO abbreviation International Labour Organisation

Iloilo (,iːləˈiːləʊ) n a port in the W central Philippines, on SE Panay Island. Pop: 408 000 (2005 est)

Ilorin (ɪˈlɒrɪn) n a city in W Nigeria, capital of Kwara state: agricultural trade centre. Pop: 714 000 (2005 est)

ILU abbreviation text messaging I love you

Ilves ('iːlvɛs) n **Toomas Hendrik**. born 1953, Estonian politician, president of Estonia from 2006

Ilyushin (*Russian* il'juːʃɪn) n **Sergei Vladimirovich** (sɛr'ɡɛi vladi'mirovɪtʃ). 1894– 1977, Soviet aircraft designer. He designed the dive bomber Il-2 Stormovik and the jet airliner Il-62

IM or i.m. abbreviation **1** intramuscular **2** *computing* instant messaging

I'm (aɪm) *contraction of* I am

im- prefix a variant of **in-¹** and **in-²** before *b, m,* and *p*

image ('ɪmɪdʒ) n **1** a representation or likeness of a person or thing, esp in sculpture **2** an optically formed reproduction of an object, such as one formed by a lens or mirror **3** a person or thing that resembles another closely; double or copy **4** a mental representation or picture; idea produced by the imagination **5** the personality presented to the public by a person, organization, etc: *a criminal charge is not good for a politician's image* **6** the pattern of light that is focused on to the retina of the eye **7** *psychol* the mental experience of something that is not immediately present to the senses, often involving memory. See also **imagery 8** a personification of a specified quality; epitome: *the image of good breeding* **9** a mental picture or association of ideas evoked in a literary work, esp in poetry **10** a figure of speech, such as a simile or metaphor ▷ *vb* (*tr*) **11** to picture in the mind; imagine **12** to make or reflect an image of **13** *computing* to project or display on a screen or visual display unit **14** to portray or describe **15** to be an example or epitome of; typify [C13: from Old French *imagene*, from Latin *imāgō* copy, representation; related to Latin *imitārī* to IMITATE] > 'imageable *adj* > 'imageless *adj*

image converter *or* **image tube** *n* a device for producing a visual image formed by other electromagnetic radiation such as infrared or ultraviolet radiation or X-rays

image enhancement *n* a method of improving the definition of a video picture by a computer program, which reduces the lowest grey values to black and the highest to white: used for pictures from microscopes, surveillance cameras, and scanners

image intensifier *or* **image tube** *n* any of various devices for amplifying the intensity of an optical image, sometimes used in conjunction with an image converter

image orthicon *n* a television camera tube in which electrons, emitted from a photoemissive surface in proportion to the intensity of the incident light, are focused onto the target causing secondary emission of electrons

image processing *n* the manipulation or modification of a digitized image, esp in order to enhance its quality

imager ('ımıdʒə) *n* an electronic device that records images: *a thermal imager*

imagery ('ımıdʒrı, -dʒərı) *n, pl* -ries **1** figurative or descriptive language in a literary work **2** images collectively **3** *psychol* **a** the materials or general processes of the imagination **b** the characteristic kind of mental images formed by a particular individual. See also **image** (sense 7), **imagination** (sense 1)

image tube *n* another name for **image converter, image intensifier**

imaginary (ı'mædʒınərı, -dʒınrı) *adj* **1** existing in the imagination; unreal; illusory **2** *maths* involving or containing imaginary numbers. The imaginary part of a complex number, *z*, is usually written Imz > im'aginarily *adv*

imaginary number *n* any complex number of the form *ib*, where $i = \sqrt{-1}$

imagination (ı,mædʒı'neıʃən) *n* **1** the faculty or action of producing ideas, esp mental images of what is not present or has not been experienced **2** mental creative ability **3** the ability to deal resourcefully with unexpected or unusual problems, circumstances, etc

imaginative (ı'mædʒınətıv) *adj* **1** produced by or indicative of a vivid or creative imagination **2** having a vivid imagination > im'aginatively *adv* > im'aginativeness *n*

imagine (ı'mædʒın) *vb* **1** (when *tr*, may take a clause as object) to form a mental image of **2** (when *tr*, may take a clause as object) to think, believe, or guess **3** (*tr*; takes a clause as object) to suppose; assume: *I imagine he'll come* **4** (*tr*; takes a clause as object) to believe or assume without foundation: *he imagines he knows the whole story* [C14: from Latin *imāginārī* to fancy, picture mentally, from *imāgō* likeness; see IMAGE] > im'aginable *adj* > im'aginably *adv* > im'aginer *n*

imagism ('ımı,dʒızəm) *n* a poetic movement in England and America between 1912 and 1917, initiated chiefly by Ezra Pound, the US poet, translator, and critic (1885–1972), advocating the use of ordinary speech and the precise presentation of images > 'imagist *n, adj*

> ,imag'istic *adj* > ,imag'istically *adv*

imago (ı'meıgəʊ) *n, pl* imagoes *or* imagines (ı'mædʒə,ni:z) **1** an adult sexually mature insect produced after metamorphosis **2** *psychoanal* an idealized image of another person, usually a parent, acquired in childhood and carried in the unconscious in later life [C18: New Latin, from Latin: likeness; see IMAGE]

imam (ı'mɑ:m) *or* **imaum** (ı'mɑ:m, ı'mɔ:m) *n Islam* **1** a leader of congregational prayer in a mosque **2** a caliph, as leader of a Muslim community **3** any of a succession of either seven or twelve religious leaders of the Shiites, regarded by their followers as divinely inspired [C17: from Arabic: leader, from *amma* he guided]

imamate (ı'mɑ:meıt) *n Islam* **1** the region or territory governed by an imam **2** the office, rank, or period of office of an imam

IMAP ('aı,mæp) *abbreviation* **a** Internet Message Access Protocol: a way of accessing e-mail messages which are held on an internet server, rather than on an individual's computer **b** (*as modifier*): *an IMAP account/server*

IMAX ('aımæks) *n trademark* a process of film projection using a giant screen on which an image approximately ten times larger than standard is projected [C20: from IMAGE + MAXIMUM]

imbalance (ım'bæləns) *n* a lack of balance, as in emphasis, proportion, etc: *the political imbalance of the programme*

imbecile *n* ('ımbı,si:l, -,saıl) **1** *psychol* a person of very low intelligence (IQ of 25 to 50), usually capable only of guarding himself against danger and of performing simple mechanical tasks under supervision **2** *informal* an extremely stupid person; dolt ▷ *adj* Also: imbecilic (,ımbı'sılık) **3** of or like an imbecile; mentally deficient; feeble-minded **4** stupid or senseless: *an imbecile thing to do* [C16: from Latin *imbēcillus* feeble (physically or mentally)] > 'imbe,cilely *or* ,imbe'cilically *adv* > ,imbe'cility *n*

imbed (ım'bɛd) *vb* -beds, -bedding, -bedded a less common spelling of **embed**

imbibe (ım'baıb) *vb* **1** to drink (esp alcoholic drinks) **2** *literary* to take in or assimilate (ideas, facts, etc): *to imbibe the spirit of the Renaissance* **3** (*tr*) to take in as if by drinking: *to imbibe fresh air* **4** to absorb or cause to absorb liquid or moisture; assimilate or saturate [C14: from Latin *imbibere*, from *bibere* to drink] > im'biber *n*

imbizo (ım'bi:zɒ) *n, pl* -zos *South African* a meeting, esp a gathering of the Zulu people called by the king or a traditional leader [from Zulu *biza* to call or summon]

imbricate *adj* ('ımbrıkıt, -,keıt) Also called: imbricated **1** *architect* relating to or having tiles, shingles, or slates that overlap **2** *botany* (of leaves, scales, etc) overlapping each other ▷ *vb* ('ımbrı,keıt) **3** (*tr*) to decorate with a repeating pattern resembling scales or overlapping tiles [C17: from Latin *imbricāre* to cover with overlapping tiles, from *imbrex* pantile] > 'imbricately *adv* > ,imbri'cation *n*

imbroglio (ım'brəʊlı,əʊ) *n, pl* -glios **1** a confused or perplexing political or interpersonal situation **2** *obsolete* a confused heap; jumble [C18: from Italian, from *imbrogliare* to confuse, EMBROIL]

Imbros ('ımbrəs) *n* a Turkish island in the NE Aegean Sea, west of the Gallipoli Peninsula: occupied by Greece (1912–14) and Britain (1914–23). Area: 280 sq km (108 sq miles). Turkish name: Imroz

imbrue *or* **embrue** (ım'bru:) *vb* -brues, -bruing, -brued (*tr*) *rare* **1** to stain, esp with blood **2** to permeate or impregnate [C15: from Old French *embreuver*, from Latin *imbibere* IMBIBE] > im'bruement *or* em'bruement *n*

imbue (ım'bju:) *vb* -bues, -buing, -bued (*tr*; usually foll by *with*) **1** to instil or inspire (with ideals, principles, etc) **2** *rare* to soak, esp with moisture, dye, etc [C16: from Latin *imbuere* to stain, accustom] > im'buement *n*

IMechE *abbreviation* Institution of Mechanical Engineers

IMF *abbreviation* International Monetary Fund

IMHO *abbreviation text messaging* in my humble *or* honest opinion

Imhotep (ım'həʊtɛp) *n c.* 2600 BC, Egyptian physician and architect. After his death he was worshipped as a god; the Greeks identified him with Asclepius

imide ('ımaıd) *n* any of a class of organic compounds

819 | **immoral**

whose molecules contain the divalent group -CONHCO- [C19: alteration of AMIDE] > imidic (ɪ'mɪdɪk) adj

imitate ('ɪmɪˌteɪt) vb (tr) **1** to try to follow the manner, style, character, etc, of or take as a model: *many writers imitated the language of Shakespeare* **2** to pretend to be or to impersonate, esp for humour; mimic **3** to make a copy or reproduction of; duplicate; counterfeit [C16: from Latin *imitārī*; see IMAGE] > 'imitable *adj* > ˌimita'bility *or* 'imitableness *n* > 'imiˌtator *n*

imitation (ˌɪmɪ'teɪʃən) *n* **1** the act, practice, or art of imitating; mimicry **2** an instance or product of imitating, such as a copy of the manner of a person; impression **3 a** a copy or reproduction of a genuine article; counterfeit **b** (*as modifier*): *imitation jewellery* **4** (in contrapuntal or polyphonic music) the repetition of a phrase or figure in one part after its appearance in another, as in a fugue > ˌimi'tational *adj*

imitative ('ɪmɪtətɪv) *adj* **1** imitating or tending to imitate or copy **2** characterized by imitation **3** copying or reproducing the features of an original, esp in an inferior manner: *imitative painting* **4** another word for **onomatopoeic** > 'imitatively *adv* > 'imitativeness *n*

Imittós (ˌimi'tɔs) *n* a transliteration of the Modern Greek name for **Hymettus**

immaculate (ɪ'mækjʊlɪt) *adj* **1** completely clean; extremely tidy: *his clothes were immaculate* **2** completely flawless, exact: *an immaculate rendering of the symphony* **3** morally pure; free from sin or corruption **4** biology of only one colour, with no spots or markings [C15: from Latin *immaculātus*, from IM- (not) + *macula* blemish] > im'maculacy *or* im'maculateness *n* > im'maculately *adv*

Immaculate Conception *n* Christian theol, RC Church the doctrine that the Virgin Mary was conceived without any stain of original sin

immanent ('ɪmənənt) *adj* **1** existing, operating, or remaining within; inherent **2** of or relating to the pantheistic conception of God, as being present throughout the universe [C16: from Latin *immanēre* to remain in, from IM- (in) + *manēre* to stay] > 'immanence *or* 'immanency *n* > 'immanently *adv* > 'immanenˌtism *n*

Immanuel *or* **Emmanuel** (ɪ'mænjʊəl) *n* Bible the child whose birth was foretold by Isaiah (Isaiah 7:14) and who in Christian tradition is identified with Jesus [from Hebrew 'immānū'el, literally: God with us]

immaterial (ˌɪmə'tɪərɪəl) *adj* **1** of no real importance; inconsequential **2** not formed of matter; incorporeal; spiritual > ˌimma'teri'ality *or* ˌimma'terialness *n* > ˌimma'terially *adv*

immaterialism (ˌɪmə'tɪərɪəˌlɪzəm) *n* philosophy the doctrine that the material world exists only in the mind > ˌimma'terialist *n*

immature (ˌɪmə'tjʊə, -'tʃʊə) *adj* **1** not fully grown or developed **2** deficient in maturity; lacking wisdom, insight, emotional stability, etc > ˌimma'turity *or* ˌimma'tureness *n* > ˌimma'turely *adv*

immeasurable (ɪ'mɛʒərəbᵊl) *adj* incapable of being measured, esp by virtue of great size; limitless > imˌmeasura'bility *or* im'measurableness *n* > im'measurably *adv*

immediate (ɪ'mi:dɪət) *adj* (*usually prenominal*) **1** taking place or accomplished without delay: *an immediate reaction* **2** closest or most direct in effect or relationship: *the immediate cause of his downfall* **3** having no intervening medium; direct in effect: *an immediate influence* **4** contiguous in space, time, or relationship: *our immediate neighbour* **5** present; current: *the immediate problem is food* **6** philosophy of or relating to an object or concept that is directly known or intuited [C16: from Medieval Latin *immediātus*, from Latin IM- (not) + *mediāre* to be in the middle; see MEDIATE] > im'mediacy *or* im'mediateness *n*

immediately (ɪ'mi:dɪətlɪ) *adv* **1** without delay or intervention; at once; instantly **2** very closely or directly: *this immediately concerns you* **3** near or close by: *he's somewhere immediately in this area* ▷ *conj* **4** (*subordinating*) chiefly Brit at the same time as; as soon as: *immediately he opened the door, there was a gust of wind*

immemorial (ˌɪmɪ'mɔ:rɪəl) *adj* originating in the distant past; ancient (postpositive in the phrase **time**

immemorial) [C17: from Medieval Latin *immemoriālis*, from Latin IM- (not) + *memoria* MEMORY] > ˌimme'morially *adv*

immense (ɪ'mɛns) *adj* **1** unusually large; huge; vast **2** without limits; immeasurable **3** informal very good; excellent [C15: from Latin *immensus*, literally: unmeasured, from IM- (not) + *mensus* measured, from *mētīrī* to measure] > im'mensely *adv* > im'menseness *n*

immensity (ɪ'mɛnsɪtɪ) *n*, *pl* -ties **1** the state or quality of being immense; vastness; enormity **2** enormous expanse, distance, or volume **3** informal a huge amount: *an immensity of wealth*

immerse (ɪ'mɜːs) *vb* (tr) **1** (often foll by *in*) to plunge or dip into liquid **2** (often passive; often foll by *in*) to involve deeply; engross: *to immerse oneself in a problem* **3** to baptize by immersion [C17: from Latin *immergere*, from IM- + *mergere* to dip] > im'mersible *adj* > i'mmersion *n*

immerser (ɪ'mɜːsə) *n* an informal term for **immersion heater**

immersion heater *n* an electrical device, usually thermostatically controlled, for heating the liquid in which it is immersed, esp as a fixture in a domestic hot-water tank

immersive (ɪ'mɜːsɪv) *adj* providing information or stimulation for a number of senses, not only sight and sound: *immersive television sets*

immigrant ('ɪmɪgrənt) *n* **a** a person who comes to a country in order to settle there **b** (*as modifier*): *an immigrant community*

immigrate ('ɪmɪˌgreɪt) *vb* **1** (intr) to come to a place or country of which one is not a native in order to settle there **2** (tr) to introduce or bring in as an immigrant [C17: from Latin *immigrāre* to go into, from IM- + *migrāre* to move] > 'immiˌgratory *adj* > 'immiˌgrator *n*

immigration (ˌɪmɪ'greɪʃən) *n* **1** the movement of non-native people into a country in order to settle there **2** the part of a port, airport, etc where government employees examine the passports, visas, etc of foreign nationals entering the country

imminent ('ɪmɪnənt) *adj* **1** liable to happen soon; impending **2** obsolete jutting out or overhanging [C16: from Latin *imminēre* to project over, from IM- (in) + *-minēre* to project; related to *mons* mountain] > 'imminence *or* 'imminentness *n* > 'imminently *adv*

Immingham ('ɪmɪŋəm) *n* a port in NE England, in North East Lincolnshire unitary authority, Lincolnshire: docks opened in 1912, principally for the exporting of coal; now handles chiefly bulk exports, esp imported iron ore. Pop: 11 090 (2001)

immiscible (ɪ'mɪsɪbᵊl) *adj* (of two or more liquids) incapable of being mixed to form a homogeneous substance: *oil and water are immiscible* > imˌmisci'bility *n* > im'miscibly *adv*

immitigable (ɪ'mɪtɪgəbᵊl) *adj* rare unable to be mitigated; relentless; unappeasable > im'mitigably *adv* > imˌmitiga'bility *n*

immobile (ɪ'məʊbaɪl) *adj* **1** not moving; motionless **2** not able to move or be moved; fixed > immobility (ˌɪməʊ'bɪlɪtɪ) *n*

immobilize *or* **immobilise** (ɪ'məʊbɪˌlaɪz) *vb* (tr) **1** to make or become immobile: *to immobilize a car* **2** finance to convert (circulating capital) into fixed capital > imˌmobili'zation *or* imˌmobili'sation *n* > im'mobiˌlizer *or* im'mobiˌliser *n*

immoderate (ɪ'mɒdərɪt, ɪ'mɒdrɪt) *adj* lacking in moderation; excessive: *immoderate demands* > im'moderately *adv* > imˌmoder'ation *or* im'moderateness *n*

immodest (ɪ'mɒdɪst) *adj* **1** indecent, esp with regard to sexual propriety; improper **2** bold, impudent, or shameless > im'modestly *adv* > im'modesty *n*

immolate ('ɪməʊˌleɪt) *vb* (tr) **1** to kill or offer as a sacrifice, esp by fire **2** literary to sacrifice (something highly valued) [C16: from Latin *immolāre* to sprinkle an offering with sacrificial meal, sacrifice, from IM- (in) + *mola* spelt grain; see MILL¹] > ˌimmo'lation *n* > 'immoˌlator *n*

immoral (ɪ'mɒrəl) *adj* **1** transgressing accepted moral rules; corrupt **2** sexually dissolute; profligate or promiscuous **3** unscrupulous or unethical: *immoral trading* **4** tending to corrupt or resulting from corruption: *an immoral film; immoral earnings* > im'morally *adv*

immorality (ˌɪməˈrælɪtɪ) *n*, *pl* **-ties 1** the quality, character, or state of being immoral **2** immoral behaviour, esp in sexual matters; licentiousness; profligacy or promiscuity **3** an immoral act

immortal (ɪˈmɔːtʰl) *adj* **1** not subject to death or decay; having perpetual life **2** having everlasting fame; remembered throughout time **3** everlasting; perpetual; constant **4** of or relating to immortal beings or concepts ▷ *n* **5** an immortal being **6** (*often plural*) a person who is remembered enduringly, esp an author > immor'tality *n* > im'mortally *adv*

immortalize *or* **immortalise** (ɪˈmɔːtəˌlaɪz) *vb* (*tr*) **1** to give everlasting fame to, as by treating in a literary work: *Macbeth was immortalized by Shakespeare* **2** to give immortality to > im,mortali'zation *or* im,mortali'sation *n* > im'mortal,izer *or* im'mortal,iser *n*

immortelle (ˌɪmɔːˈtɛl) *n* any of various plants, mostly of the family *Asteraceae* (composites), that retain their colour when dried, esp *Xeranthemum annuum*. Also called: everlasting, everlasting flower [c19: from French (*fleur*) *immortelle* everlasting (flower)]

immovable *or* **immoveable** (ɪˈmuːvəbʰl) *adj* **1** unable to move or be moved; fixed; immobile **2** unable to be diverted from one's intentions; steadfast **3** unaffected by feeling; impassive **4** unchanging; unalterable **5** *law* **a** (of property) not liable to be removed; fixed **b** of or relating to immoveables > im,mova'bility, im,movea'bility *or* im'movableness *or* im'moveableness *n* > im'movably, im'moveably *adv*

immune (ɪˈmjuːn) *adj* **1** protected against a specific disease by inoculation or as the result of innate or acquired resistance **2** relating to or conferring immunity: *an immune body*. See **antibody 3** (*usually postpositive*; foll by *to*) unsusceptible (to) or secure (against): *immune to inflation* **4** exempt from obligation, penalty, etc ▷ *n* **5** an immune person or animal [c15: from Latin *immūnis* exempt from a public service, from IM- (not) + *mūnus* duty]

immune response *n* the reaction of an organism's body to foreign materials (antigens), including the production of antibodies

immunity (ɪˈmjuːnɪtɪ) *n*, *pl* **-ties 1** the ability of an organism to resist disease, either through the activities of specialized blood cells or antibodies produced by them in response to natural exposure or inoculation (**active immunity**) or by the injection of antiserum or the transfer of antibodies from a mother to her baby via the placenta or breast milk (**passive immunity**). See also **acquired immunity, natural immunity 2** freedom from obligation or duty, esp exemption from tax, duty, legal liability, etc

immunize *or* **immunise** (ˈɪmjʊˌnaɪz) *vb* to make immune, esp by inoculation > ,immuni'zation *or* ,immuni'sation *n* > 'immu,nizer *or* 'immu,niser *n*

immuno- *or before a vowel* **immun-** *combining form* indicating immunity or immune: *immunology*

immunoassay (ˌɪmjʊnəʊˈæseɪ) *n immunol* a technique of identifying a substance by its ability to bind to an antibody

immunocompromised (ˌɪmjʊnəʊˈkɒmprəmaɪzd) *adj* having an impaired immune system and therefore incapable of an effective immune response, usually as a result of disease, such as AIDS, that damages the immune system

immunodeficiency (ˌɪmjʊnəʊdɪˈfɪʃənsɪ) *n* a deficiency in or breakdown of a person's immune system

immunogenic (ˌɪmjʊnəʊˈdʒɛnɪk) *adj* causing or producing immunity or an immune response > ,immuno'genically *adv*

immunoglobulin (ˌɪmjʊnəʊˈɡlɒbjʊlɪn) *n* any of five classes of proteins, all of which show antibody activity. The most abundant ones are **immunoglobulin G (IgG)** and **immunoglobulin A (IgA)**

immunology (ˌɪmjʊˈnɒlədʒɪ) *n* the branch of biological science concerned with the study of immunity

> immunologic (ˌɪmjʊnəˈlɒdʒɪk) *or* ,immuno'logical *adj* > ,immuno'logically *adv* > ,immu'nologist *n*

immunopharmacology (ˌɪmjʊnəʊˌfɑːməˈkɒlədʒɪ) *n* the branch of pharmacology concerned with the immune system > ,immuno,pharma'cologist *n*

immunoreaction (ˌɪmjuːnəʊrɪˈækʃən) *n* the reaction between an antigen and its antibody

immunosuppression (ˌɪmjʊnəʊsəˈprɛʃən) *n* medical suppression of the body's immune system, esp in order to reduce the likelihood of rejection of a transplanted organ

immunosuppressive (ˌɪmjʊnəʊsəˈprɛsɪv) *n* **1** any drug used for immunosuppression ▷ *adj* **2** of or relating to such a drug

immunotherapy (ˌɪmjʊnəʊˈθɛrəpɪ) *n med* the treatment of disease by stimulating the body's production of antibodies > immunotherapeutic (ˌɪmjʊnəʊˌθɛrəˈpjuːtɪk) *adj*

immure (ɪˈmjʊə) *vb* (*tr*) **1** *archaic or literary* to enclose within or as if within walls; imprison **2** to shut (oneself) away from society [c16: from Medieval Latin *immūrāre*, from Latin IM- (in) + *mūrus* a wall] > im'murement *n*

immutable (ɪˈmjuːtəbəl) *adj* unchanging through time; unalterable; ageless: *immutable laws* > im,muta'bility *or* im'mutableness *n*

Imo (ˈiːməʊ) *n* a state of SE Nigeria. Capital: Owerri. Pop: 3 934 899 (2006). Area: 5100 sq km (1969 sq miles)

IMO *abbreviation* International Maritime Organization

imp (ɪmp) *n* **1** a small demon or devil; mischievous sprite **2** a mischievous child ▷ *vb* **3** (*tr*) *falconry* to insert (new feathers) into the stumps of broken feathers in order to repair the wing of a hawk or falcon [Old English *impa* bud, graft, hence offspring, child, from *impian* to graft, ultimately from Greek *emphutos* implanted, from *emphuein* to implant, from *phuein* to plant]

imp. *abbreviation* **1** imperative **2** imperfect **3** imperial

impact *n* (ˈɪmpækt) **1** the act of one body, object, etc, striking another; collision **2** the force with which one thing hits another or with which two objects collide **3** the impression made by an idea, cultural movement, social group, etc ▷ *vb* (ɪmˈpækt) **4** to drive or press (an object) firmly into (another object, thing, etc) or (of two objects) to be driven or pressed firmly together **5** to have an impact or strong effect (on) [c18: from Latin *impactus* pushed against, fastened on, from *impingere* to thrust at, from *pangere* to drive in] > im'paction *n*

impacted (ɪmˈpæktɪd) *adj* **1** (of a tooth) unable to erupt, esp because of being wedged against another tooth below the gum **2** (of a fracture) having the jagged broken ends wedged into each other

impair (ɪmˈpɛə) *vb* (*tr*) to reduce or weaken in strength, quality, etc: *his hearing was impaired by an accident* [c14: from Old French *empeirer* to make worse, from Late Latin *pējōrāre*, from Latin *pejor* worse; see PEJORATIVE] > im'pairable *adj* > im'pairer *n* > im'pairment *n*

impala (ɪmˈpɑːlə) *n*, *pl* **-las** *or* **-la** an antelope, *Aepyceros melampus*, of southern and eastern Africa, having lyre-shaped horns and able to move with enormous leaps when disturbed [from Zulu]

impale *or* **empale** (ɪmˈpeɪl) *vb* (*tr*) **1** (*often foll by* on, upon, *or* with) to pierce with a sharp instrument: *they impaled his severed head on a spear* **2** *heraldry* to charge (a shield) with two coats of arms placed side by side [c16: from Medieval Latin *impālāre*, from Latin IM- (in) + *pālus* PALE²] > im'palement *or* em'palement *n*

impalpable (ɪmˈpælpəbʰl) *adj* **1** imperceptible, esp to the touch: *impalpable shadows* **2** difficult to understand; abstruse > im,palpa'bility *n* > im'palpably *adv*

impanel (ɪmˈpænʰl) *vb* **-els, -elling, -elled** *or US* **-els, -eling, -eled** a variant spelling (esp US) of **empanel** > im'panelment *n*

impart (ɪmˈpɑːt) *vb* (*tr*) **1** to communicate (information); relate **2** to give or bestow (something, esp an abstract quality): *to impart wisdom* [c15: from Old French *impartir*, from Latin *impertīre*, from IM- (in) + *partīre* to share, from *pars* part] > im'partable *adj* > ,impar'tation *or* im'partment *n*

impartial (ɪmˈpɑːʃəl) *adj* not prejudiced towards or

against any particular side or party; fair; unbiased > im,parti'ality *or* im'partialness *n* > im'partially *adv*

impartible (ɪmˈpɑːtəbəl) *adj law* (of land, an estate, etc) incapable of partition; indivisible > im,parti'bility *n* > im'partibly *adv*

impassable (ɪmˈpɑːsəbəl) *adj* (of terrain, roads, etc) not able to be travelled through or over > im'passably *adv*

impasse (æmˈpɑːs, ˈæmpɑːs, ɪmˈpɑːs, ˈɪmpɑːs) *n* a situation in which progress is blocked; an insurmountable difficulty; stalemate; deadlock [c19: from French; see IM-, PASS]

impassible (ɪmˈpæsəbəl) *adj rare* **1** not susceptible to pain or injury **2** impassive or unmoved > im,passi'bility *or* im'passibleness *n* > im'passibly *adv*

impassion (ɪmˈpæʃən) *vb* (*tr*) to arouse the passions of; inflame

impassioned (ɪmˈpæʃənd) *adj* filled with passion; fiery; inflamed: *an impassioned appeal* > im'passionedly *adv* > im'passionedness *n*

impassive (ɪmˈpæsɪv) *adj* **1** not revealing or affected by emotion; reserved **2** calm; serene; imperturbable > im'passively *adv* > im'passiveness *or* impassivity (,ɪmpæˈsɪvɪtɪ) *n*

impaste (ɪmˈpeɪst) *vb* (*tr*) to apply paint thickly to [c16: from Italian *impastare*, from *pasta* PASTE¹] > impastation (,ɪmpæsˈteɪʃən) *n*

impasto (ɪmˈpæstəʊ) *n* **1** paint applied thickly, so that brush and palette knife marks are evident **2** the technique of applying paint in this way [c18: from Italian, from *impastare*; see IMPASTE]

impatience (ɪmˈpeɪʃəns) *n* **1** lack of patience; intolerance of or irritability with anything that impedes or delays **2** restless desire for change and excitement

impatiens (ɪmˈpeɪʃɪˌɛnz) *n, pl* -ens any balsaminaceous plant of the genus *Impatiens*, such as balsam, touch-me-not, busy Lizzie, and policeman's helmet [c18: New Latin from Latin: impatient; from the fact that the ripe pods burst open when touched]

impatient (ɪmˈpeɪʃənt) *adj* **1** lacking patience; easily irritated at delay, opposition, etc **2** exhibiting lack of patience **3** (*postpositive*; foll by *of*) intolerant (of) or indignant (at): *impatient of indecision* **4** (*postpositive*; often foll by *for*) restlessly eager (for something or to do something) > im'patiently *adv*

impeach (ɪmˈpiːtʃ) *vb* (*tr*) **1** *criminal law* to bring a charge or accusation against **2** *Brit criminal law* to accuse of a crime, esp of treason or some other offence against the state **3** *chiefly US* to charge (a public official) with an offence committed in office **4** to challenge or question (a person's honesty, integrity, etc) [c14: from Old French *empeechier*, from Late Latin *impedicāre* to entangle, catch, from Latin IM- (in) + *pedica* a fetter, from *pēs* foot] > im'peachable *adj* > im'peachment *n*

impeccable (ɪmˈpɛkəbəl) *adj* **1** without flaw or error; faultless: *an impeccable record* **2** *rare* incapable of sinning [c16: from Late Latin *impeccābilis* sinless, from Latin IM- (not) + *peccāre* to sin] > im,pecca'bility *n* > im'peccably *adv*

impecunious (,ɪmpɪˈkjuːnɪəs) *adj* without money; penniless [c16: from IM- (not) + -*pecunious*, from Latin *pecūniōsus* wealthy, from *pecūnia* money] > ,impe'cuniously *adv* > ,impe'cuniousness *or* impecuniosity (,ɪmpɪkjuːnɪˈɒsɪtɪ) *n*

impedance (ɪmˈpiːdəns) *n* **1** a measure of the opposition to the flow of an alternating current equal to the square root of the sum of the squares of the resistance and the reactance, expressed in ohms **2** Also called: acoustic impedance the ratio of the sound pressure in a medium to the rate of alternating flow of the medium through a specified surface due to the sound wave **3** Also called: mechanical impedance the ratio of the mechanical force, acting in the direction of motion, to the velocity of the resulting vibration

impede (ɪmˈpiːd) *vb* (*tr*) to restrict or retard in action, progress, etc; hinder; obstruct [c17: from Latin *impedīre* to hinder, literally: shackle the feet, from *pēs* foot] > im'peder *n* > im'pedingly *adv*

impediment (ɪmˈpɛdɪmənt) *n* **1** a hindrance or obstruction **2** a physical defect, esp one of speech, such as a stammer **3** *pl* -ments *or* -menta (-ˈmɛntə) *law* an

obstruction to the making of a contract, esp a contract of marriage by reason of closeness of blood or affinity > im,pedi'mental *or* im,pedi'mentary *adj*

impedimenta (ɪm,pɛdɪˈmɛntə) *pl n* **1** the baggage and equipment carried by an army **2** a plural of impediment (sense 3) [c16: from Latin, plural of *impedīmentum* hindrance; see IMPEDE]

impel (ɪmˈpɛl) *vb* -pels, -pelling, -pelled (*tr*) **1** to urge or force (a person) to an action; constrain or motivate **2** to push, drive, or force into motion [c15: from Latin *impellere* to push against, drive forward, from IM- (in) + *pellere* to drive, push, strike] > im'pellent *n, adj*

impeller (ɪmˈpɛlə) *n* the vaned rotating disc of a centrifugal pump, compressor, etc

impend (ɪmˈpɛnd) *vb* (*intr*) **1** (esp of something threatening) to be about to happen; be imminent **2** (foll by *over*) *rare* to be suspended; hang [c16: from Latin *impendēre* to overhang, from *pendēre* to hang] > im'pendence *or* im'pendency *n*

impending (ɪmˈpɛndɪŋ) *adj* about to happen; imminent

impenetrable (ɪmˈpɛnɪtrəbəl) *adj* **1** incapable of being pierced through or penetrated: *an impenetrable forest* **2** incapable of being understood; incomprehensible **3** incapable of being seen through: *impenetrable gloom* **4** not susceptible to ideas, influence, etc: *impenetrable ignorance* **5** *physics* (of a body) incapable of occupying the same space as another body > im,penetra'bility *n* > im'penetrableness *n* > im'penetrably *adv*

impenitent (ɪmˈpɛnɪtənt) *adj* not sorry or penitent; unrepentant > im'penitence, im'penitence *or* im'penitentness *n* > im'penitently *adv*

imperative (ɪmˈpɛrətɪv) *adj* **1** extremely urgent or important; essential **2** peremptory or authoritative: *an imperative tone of voice* **3** Also called: imperatival (ɪm,pɛrəˈtaɪvəl) *grammar* denoting a mood of verbs used in giving orders, making requests, etc. In English the verb root without any inflections is the usual form, as for example *leave* in *Leave me alone* ▷ *n* **4** something that is urgent or essential **5** an order or command **6** *grammar* **a** the imperative mood **b** a verb in this mood [c16: from Late Latin *imperātīvus*, from Latin *imperāre* to command] > im'peratively *adv* > im'perativeness *n*

imperator (,ɪmpəˈrɑːtɔː) *n* (in imperial Rome) a title of the emperor [c16: from Latin: commander, from *imperāre* to command] > imperatorial (ɪm,pɛrəˈtɔːrɪəl) *adj* > ,impe'rator,ship *n*

imperceptible (,ɪmpəˈsɛptɪbəl) *adj* too slight, subtle, gradual, etc, to be perceived > ,imper,cepti'bility *or* ,imper'ceptibleness *n* > ,imper'ceptibly *adv*

imperceptive (,ɪmpəˈsɛptɪv) Also called: impercipient (,ɪmpə-ˈsɪpɪənt) *adj* lacking in perception; obtuse > ,imper'ception *n* > ,imper'ceptively *adv* > ,impercep'tivity, ,imper'ceptiveness *or* ,imper'cipience *n*

imperf. *abbreviation* **1** Also called: impf imperfect **2** (of stamps) imperforate

imperfect (ɪmˈpɜːfɪkt) *adj* **1** exhibiting or characterized by faults, mistakes, etc; defective **2** not complete or finished; deficient **3** *grammar* denoting a tense of verbs used most commonly in describing continuous or repeated past actions or events, as for example *was walking* as opposed to *walked* **4** *law* (of a trust, an obligation, etc) lacking some necessary formality to make effective or binding; incomplete; legally unenforceable **5** *music* **a** (of a cadence) proceeding to the dominant from the tonic, subdominant, or any chord other than the dominant **b** of or relating to all intervals other than the fourth, fifth, and octave. See **perfect** (sense 9) ▷ *n* **6** *grammar* **a** the imperfect tense **b** a verb in this tense > im'perfectly *adv* > im'perfectness *n*

imperfection (,ɪmpəˈfɛkʃən) *n* **1** the condition or quality of being imperfect **2** a fault or defect

imperfective (,ɪmpəˈfɛktɪv) *grammar* ▷ *adj* **1** denoting an aspect of the verb in some languages, including English, used to indicate that the action is in progress without regard to its completion. See **perfective** ▷ *n* **2** **a** the imperfective aspect of a verb **b** a verb in this aspect > ,imper'fectively *adv*

imperforate (ɪmˈpɜːfərɪt, -,reɪt) *adj* **1** not perforated **2** (of a postage stamp) not provided with perforation or any other means of separation **3** *anatomy* (of a bodily part, such as the anus) without the normal opening > im,perfo'ration *n*

imperial (ɪm'pɪərɪəl) *adj* **1** of or relating to an empire, emperor, or empress **2** characteristic of or befitting an emperor; majestic; commanding **3** characteristic of or exercising supreme authority; imperious **4** (esp of products and commodities) (of a superior size or quality **5** (*usually prenominal*) (of weights, measures, etc) conforming to standards or definitions legally established in Britain ▷ *n* **6** any of various book sizes, esp 7½ by 11 inches (**imperial octavo**) or (chiefly Brit) 11 by 15 inches (**imperial quarto**) **7** a size of writing or printing paper, 23 by 31 inches (US and Canadian) or 22 by 30 inches (Brit) **8** *US* **a** the top of a carriage, such as a diligence **b** a luggage case carried there **9** a small tufted beard popularized by the emperor Napoleon III [c14: from Late Latin *imperiālis*, from Latin *imperium* command, authority, empire] > im'perially *adv* > im'perialness *n*

imperialism (ɪm'pɪərɪə,lɪzəm) *n* **1** the policy or practice of extending a state's rule over other territories **2** the extension or attempted extension of authority, influence, power, etc, by any person, country, institution, etc: *cultural imperialism* **3** a system of imperial government or rule by an emperor **4** the spirit, character, authority, etc, of an empire > im'perialist *adj*, *n* > im,perial'istic *adj* > im,perial'istically *adv*

imperil (ɪm'pɛrɪl) *vb* -rils, -rilling, -rilled, *or US* -rils, -riling, -riled (*tr*) to place in danger or jeopardy; endanger > im'perilment *n*

imperious (ɪm'pɪərɪəs) *adj* **1** domineering; arrogant; overbearing **2** *rare* urgent; imperative [c16: from Latin *imperiōsus* from *imperium* command, power] > im'periously *adv* > im'periousness *n*

imperishable (ɪm'pɛrɪʃəbᵊl) *adj* **1** not subject to decay or deterioration **2** not likely to be forgotten: *imperishable truths* > im,perisha'bility *or* im'perishableness *n* > im'perishably *adv*

impermanent (ɪm'pɜːmənənt) *adj* not permanent; fleeting; transitory > im'permanence *or* im'permanency *n* > im'permanently *adv*

impermeable (ɪm'pɜːmɪəbᵊl) *adj* (of a substance) not allowing the passage of a fluid through interstices; not permeable > im,permea'bility *or* im'permeableness *n* > im'permeably *adv*

impermissible (,ɪmpə'mɪsɪbᵊl) *adj* not permissible; not allowed > ,imper,missi'bility *n*

impersonal (ɪm'pɜːsənᵊl) *adj* **1** without reference to any individual person; objective: *an impersonal assessment* **2** devoid of human warmth or sympathy; cold: *an impersonal manner* **3** not having human characteristics: *an impersonal God* **4** *grammar* (of a verb) having no logical subject. Usually in English the pronoun *it* is used in such cases as a grammatical subject, as for example in *It is raining* **5** *grammar* (of a pronoun) not denoting a person > im,person'ality *n* > im'personally *adv*

impersonalize *or* **impersonalise** (ɪm'pɜːsənə,laɪz) *vb* (*tr*) to make impersonal, esp to rid of such human characteristics as sympathy, warmth, etc; dehumanize > im,personali'zation *or* im,personali'sation *n*

impersonate (ɪm'pɜːsə,neɪt) *vb* (*tr*) **1** to pretend to be (another person) **2** to imitate the character, mannerisms, etc, of (another person) **3** *rare* to play the part or character of **4** an archaic word for **personify** > im,person'ation *n* > im'person,ator *n*

impertinence (ɪm'pɜːtɪnəns) *or* **impertinency** *n* **1** disrespectful behaviour or language; rudeness; insolence **2** an impertinent act, gesture, etc **3** *rare* lack of pertinence; irrelevance; inappropriateness

impertinent (ɪm'pɜːtɪnənt) *adj* **1** rude; insolent; impudent **2** irrelevant or inappropriate [c14: from Latin *impertinēns* not belonging, from Latin ɪm- (not) + *pertinēre* to be relevant; see PERTAIN] > im'pertinently *adv*

imperturbable (,ɪmpɜː'tɜːbᵊl) *adj* not easily perturbed; calm; unruffled > ,imper,turba'bility *or* ,imper'turbableness *n* > ,imper'turbably *adv*

impervious (ɪm'pɜːvɪəs) *or* **imperviable** *adj* **1** not able to be penetrated, as by water, light, etc; impermeable **2** (*often postpositive*; foll by *to*) not able to be influenced

(by) or not receptive (to): *impervious to argument* > im'perviously *adv* > im'perviousness *n*

impetigo (,ɪmpɪ'taɪgəʊ) *n* a contagious bacterial skin disease characterized by the formation of pustules that develop into yellowish crusty sores [c16: from Latin: scabby eruption, from *impetere* to assail; see IMPETUS; for form, compare VERTIGO] > impetiginous (,ɪmpɪ'tɪdʒɪnəs) *adj*

impetuous (ɪm'pɛtjʊəs) *adj* **1** liable to act without consideration; rash; impulsive **2** resulting from or characterized by rashness or haste **3** *poetic* moving with great force or violence; rushing: *the impetuous stream hurtled down the valley* [c14: from Late Latin *impetuōsus* violent; see IMPETUS] > im'petuously *adv* > im'petuousness *or* impetuosity (ɪm,pɛtjʊ'ɒsɪtɪ) *n*

impetus (ɪm'pɪtəs) *n, pl* -tuses **1** an impelling movement or force; incentive or impulse; stimulus **2** *physics* the force that sets a body in motion or that tends to resist changes in a body's motion [c17: from Latin: attack, from *impetere* to assail, from ɪm- (in) + *petere* to make for, seek out]

Imphal (ɪm'fɑːl, 'ɪmfəl) *n* a city in NE India, capital of Manipur Territory, on the Manipur River: formerly the seat of the Manipur kings: site of a major Anglo-Indian victory over the Japanese (1944), which was a turning point in the British recovery of Burma (now officially called Myanmar). Pop: 217 275 (2001)

impi ('ɪmpɪ) *n, pl* -pi *or* -pies a group of Bantu warriors [c19: Nguni: regiment, army]

impiety (ɪm'paɪɪtɪ) *n, pl* -ties **1** lack of reverence or proper respect for a god **2** any lack of proper respect **3** an impious act

impinge (ɪm'pɪndʒ) *vb* **1** (*intr*; usually foll by *on* or *upon*) to encroach or infringe; trespass: *to impinge on someone's time* **2** (*intr*; usually foll by *on*, *against*, or *upon*) to collide (with); strike [c16: from Latin *impingere* to drive at, dash against, from *pangere* to fasten, drive in] > im'pingement *n* > im'pinger *n*

impious ('ɪmpɪəs) *adj* **1** lacking piety or reverence for a god; ungodly **2** lacking respect; undutiful > 'impiously *adv* > 'impiousness *n*

impish ('ɪmpɪʃ) *adj* of or resembling an imp; mischievous > 'impishly *adv* > 'impishness *n*

implacable (ɪm'plækəbᵊl) *adj* **1** incapable of being placated or pacified; unappeasable **2** inflexible; intractable > im,placa'bility *or* im'placableness *n* > im'placably *adv*

implant *vb* (ɪm'plɑːnt) (*tr*) **1** to establish firmly; inculcate; instil: *to implant sound moral principles* **2** to plant or embed; infix; entrench **3** *surgery* **a** to graft (a tissue) into the body **b** to insert (a radioactive substance, hormone, etc) into the tissues ▷ *n* ('ɪm,plɑːnt) **4** anything implanted, esp surgically, such as a tissue graft or hormone > ,implan'tation *n*

implausible (ɪm'plɔːzəbᵊl) *adj* not plausible; provoking disbelief; unlikely > im,plausi'bility *or* im'plausibleness *n* > im'plausibly *adv*

implement *n* ('ɪmplɪmənt) **1** a piece of equipment; tool or utensil: *gardening implements* **2** something used to achieve a purpose; agent ▷ *vb* ('ɪmplɪ,mɛnt) (*tr*) **3** to carry out; put into action; perform: *to implement a plan* **4** *archaic* to complete, satisfy, or fulfil [c17: from Late Latin *implēmentum*, literally: a filling up, from Latin *implēre* to fill up, satisfy, fulfil] > ,imple'mental *adj* > ,implemen'tation *n* > 'imple,menter *or* 'imple,mentor *n*

implicate ('ɪmplɪ,keɪt) *vb* (*tr*) **1** to show to be involved, esp in a crime **2** to involve as a necessary inference; imply: *his protest implicated censure by the authorities* **3** to affect intimately: *this news implicates my decision* **4** *rare* to intertwine or entangle [c16: from Latin *implicāre* to involve, from ɪm- + *plicāre* to fold] > implicative (ɪm'plɪkətɪv) *adj* > im'plicatively *adv*

implication (,ɪmplɪ'keɪʃən) *n* **1** the act of implicating or the state of being implicated **2** something that is implied; suggestion

implicit (ɪm'plɪsɪt) *adj* **1** not explicit; implied; indirect **2** absolute and unreserved; unquestioning: *you have implicit trust in him* **3** (*when postpositive*, foll by *in*) contained or inherent: *to bring out the anger implicit in the argument* [c16:

from Latin *implicitus*, variant of *implicātus* interwoven; see IMPLICATE] > im'plicitly *adv* > im'plicitness or im'plicity *n*

implied (ɪm'plaɪd) *adj* hinted at or suggested; not directly expressed: *an implied criticism*

implode (ɪm'pləʊd) *vb* to collapse or cause to collapse inwards in a violent manner as a result of external pressure. See **explode** [C19: from IM- + (EX)PLODE] > im'plosion *n*

implore (ɪm'plɔː) *vb* (*tr*) to beg or ask (someone) earnestly (to do something); plead with; beseech [C16: from Latin *implōrāre*, from IM- + *plōrāre* to bewail] > ˌimplo'ration *n* > im'ploringly *adv*

imply (ɪm'plaɪ) *vb* -plies, -plying, -plied (*tr; may take a clause as object*) **1** to express or indicate by a hint; suggest **2** to suggest or involve as a necessary consequence [C14: from Old French *emplier*, from Latin *implicāre* to involve; see IMPLICATE]
● USAGE See at **infer**

impolder (ɪm'pəʊldə) or **empolder** *vb rare* to make into a polder; reclaim (land) from the sea [C19: from Dutch *inpolderen*, see IN-², POLDER]

impolite (ˌɪmpə'laɪt) *adj* discourteous; rude; uncivil > ˌimpo'litely *adv* > ˌimpo'liteness *n*

impolitic (ɪm'pɒlɪtɪk) *adj* not politic or expedient; unwise > im'politicly *adv*

imponderable (ɪm'pɒndərəbᵊl, -drəbᵊl) *adj* **1** unable to be weighed or assessed ▷ *n* **2** something difficult or impossible to assess > imˌpondera'bility or im'ponderableness *n* > im'ponderably *adv*

import *vb* (ɪm'pɔːt, 'ɪmpɔːt) **1** to buy or bring in (goods or services) from a foreign country **2** (*tr*) to bring in from an outside source: *to import foreign words into the language* **3** *rare* to signify or be significant; mean; convey: *to import doom* ▷ *n* ('ɪmpɔːt) **4** (*often plural*) **a** goods (**visible imports**) or services (**invisible imports**) that are bought from foreign countries **b** (*as modifier*): *an import licence* **5** significance or importance: *a man of great import* **6** meaning or signification **7** *Canadian informal* a sportsman or -woman who is not native to the country in which he or she plays [C15: from Latin *importāre* to carry in, from IM- + *portāre* to carry] > im'portable *adj* > im'porter *n*

importance (ɪm'pɔːtᵊns) *n* **1** the state of being important; significance **2** social status; standing; esteem: *a man of importance* **3** *obsolete* **a** meaning or signification **b** an important matter **c** importunity

important (ɪm'pɔːtᵊnt) *adj* **1** of great significance or value; outstanding **2** of social significance; notable; eminent; esteemed: *an important man in the town* **3** (*when postpositive, usually foll by to*) specially relevant or of great concern (to); valued highly (by): *your wishes are important to me* [C16: from Old Italian *importante*, from Medieval Latin *importāre* to signify, be of consequence, from Latin: to carry in; see IMPORT] > im'portantly *adv*
● USAGE The use of *more importantly* as in *more importantly, the local council is opposed to this proposal* has become very common, but many people still prefer to use *more important*

importation (ˌimpɔː'teɪʃən) *n* **1** the act, business, or process of importing goods or services **2** an imported product or service

importunate (ɪm'pɔːtjʊnɪt) *adj* **1** persistent or demanding; insistent **2** *rare* troublesome; annoying > im'portunately *adv* > im'portunateness *n*

importune (ɪm'pɔːtjuːn) *vb* (*tr*) **1** to harass with persistent requests; demand of (someone) insistently **2** to beg for persistently; request with insistence [C16: from Latin *importūnus* tiresome, from im- IN-¹ + -*portūnus* as in *opportūnus* OPPORTUNE] > im'portuner *n* > ˌimpor'tunity or im'portunacy *n*

impose (ɪm'pəʊz) *vb* (*usually foll by on or upon*) **1** (*tr*) to establish as something to be obeyed or complied with; enforce **2** to force (oneself, one's presence, etc) on another or others; obtrude **3** (*intr*) to take advantage, as of a person or quality: *to impose on someone's kindness* **4** (*tr*) *printing* to arrange pages so that after printing and folding the pages will be in the correct order **5** (*tr*) to pass off deceptively; foist [C15: from Old French *imposer*, from Latin *impōnere* to place upon, from *pōnere* to place,

set] > im'posable *adj* > im'poser *n*

imposing (ɪm'pəʊzɪŋ) *adj* grand or impressive: *an imposing building* > im'posingly *adv* > im'posingness *n*

imposition (ˌimpə'zɪʃən) *n* **1** the act of imposing **2** something that is imposed unfairly on someone **3** (in Britain) a task set as a school punishment **4** the arrangement of pages for printing so that the finished work will have its pages in the correct order

impossibility (ɪmˌpɒsə'bɪlɪtɪ, ˌimpɒs-) *n*, *pl* -ties **1** the state or quality of being impossible **2** something that is impossible

impossible (ɪm'pɒsəbᵊl) *adj* **1** incapable of being done, undertaken, or experienced **2** incapable of occurring or happening **3** absurd or inconceivable; unreasonable **4** *informal* intolerable; outrageous: *those children are impossible* > im'possibleness *n* > im'possibly *adv*

impossible figure *n* a picture of an object that at first sight looks three-dimensional but cannot be a two-dimensional projection of a real three-dimensional object, for example a picture of a staircase that re-enters itself while appearing to ascend continuously

impost¹ ('ɪmpəʊst) *n* **1** a tax, esp a customs duty **2** *horse racing* the specific weight that a particular horse must carry in a handicap race ▷ *vb* **3** (*tr*) *US* to classify (imported goods) according to the duty payable on them [C16: from Medieval Latin *impostus* tax, from Latin *impositus* imposed; see IMPOSE] > 'imposter *n*

impost² ('ɪmpəʊst) *n architect* a member at the top of a wall, pier, or column that supports an arch, esp one that has a projecting moulding [C17: from French *imposte*, from Latin *impositus* placed upon; see IMPOSE]

impostor or **imposter** (ɪm'pɒstə) *n* a person who deceives others, esp by assuming a false identity; charlatan [C16: from Late Latin: deceiver; see IMPOSE]

imposture (ɪm'pɒstʃə) *n* the act or an instance of deceiving others, esp by assuming a false identity [C16: from French, from Late Latin *impostūra*, from Latin *impōnere*; see IMPOSE] > impostrous (ɪm'pɒstrəs), impostorous (ɪm'pɒstərəs) or im'posturous *adj*

impotent ('ɪmpətənt) *adj* **1** (*when postpositive, often takes an infinitive*) lacking sufficient strength; powerless **2** (*esp of males*) unable to perform sexual intercourse > 'impotence, 'impotency or 'impotentness *n* > 'impotently *adv*

impound (ɪm'paʊnd) *vb* (*tr*) **1** to confine (stray animals, illegally parked cars, etc) in a pound **2** to take possession of (a document, evidence, etc) and hold in legal custody **3** to collect (water) in a reservoir or dam, as for irrigation > im'poundable *adj* > im'poundage or im'poundment *n* > im'pounder *n*

impoverish (ɪm'pɒvərɪʃ) *vb* (*tr*) **1** to make poor or diminish the quality of: *to impoverish society by cutting the grant to the arts* **2** to deprive (soil, etc) of fertility [C15: from Old French *empovrir*, from *povre* POOR] > im'poverishment *n*

impracticable (ɪm'præktɪkəbᵊl) *adj* **1** incapable of being put into practice or accomplished; not feasible **2** unsuitable for a desired use; unfit > imˌpractica'bility or im'practicableness *n* > im'practicably *adv*

impractical (ɪm'præktɪkᵊl) *adj* **1** not practical or workable: *an impractical solution* **2** not given to practical matters or gifted with practical skills > imˌpracti'cality or im'practicalness *n* > im'practically *adv*

imprecate ('ɪmprɪˌkeɪt) *vb* **1** (*intr*) to swear, curse, or blaspheme **2** (*tr*) to invoke or bring down (evil, a curse, etc) [C17: from Latin *imprecārī* to invoke, from im- IN-² + *precārī* to PRAY] > 'impreˌcatory *adj*

imprecation (ˌimprɪ'keɪʃən) *n* **1** the act of imprecating **2** a malediction; curse

imprecise (ˌimprɪ'saɪs) *adj* not precise; inexact or inaccurate > ˌimpre'cisely *adv* > imprecision (ˌimprɪ'sɪʒən) or ˌimpre'ciseness *n*

impregnable¹ (ɪm'pregnəbᵊl) *adj* **1** unable to be broken into or taken by force: *an impregnable castle* **2** unable to be shaken or overcome: *impregnable self-confidence* **3** incapable of being refuted: *an impregnable argument* [C15 *imprenable*, from Old French, from IM- (not) + *prenable* able to be taken, from *prendre* to take] > imˌpregna'bility or im'pregnableness *n* > im'pregnably *adv*

impregnable² (ɪmˈprɛɡnəbəl) *or* **impregnatable** (ˌɪmprɛɡˈneɪtəbəl) *adj* able to be impregnated; fertile

impregnate *vb* (ˈɪmprɛɡˌneɪt) (*tr*) **1** to saturate, soak, or infuse **2** to imbue or permeate; pervade **3** to cause to conceive; make pregnant **4** to make (land, soil, etc) fruitful ▷ *adj* (ɪmˈprɛɡnɪt, -ˌneɪt) **5** pregnant or fertilized [C17: from Late Latin *impraegnāre* to make pregnant, from Latin *im-* IN-² + *praegnans* PREGNANT] > ˌimpregˈnation *n* > imˈpregnator *n*

impresa (ɪmˈpreɪzə) *or* **imprese** (ɪmˈpriːz) *n* an emblem or device, usually a motto, as on a coat of arms [C16: from Italian, literally: undertaking, hence deed of chivalry, motto, from *imprendere* to undertake]

impresario (ˌɪmprəˈsɑːrɪˌəʊ) *n, pl* **-sarios** the director or manager of an opera, ballet, or other performing company [C18: from Italian, literally: one who undertakes; see IMPRESA]

imprescriptible (ˌɪmprɪˈskrɪptəbəl) *adj law* immune or exempt from prescription > ˌimpreˌscriptiˈbility *n* > ˌimpreˈscriptibly *adv*

impress¹ *vb* (ɪmˈprɛs) (*tr*) **1** to make an impression on; have a strong, lasting, or favourable effect on: *I am impressed by your work* **2** to produce (an imprint, etc) by pressure in or on (something): *to impress a seal in wax; to impress wax with a seal* **3** (often foll by *on*) to stress (something to a person); urge; emphasize **4** to exert pressure on; press ▷ *n* (ˈɪmprɛs) **5** the act or an instance of impressing **6** a mark, imprint, or effect produced by impressing [C14: from Latin *imprimere* to press into, imprint, from *premere* to PRESS¹] > imˈpresser *n* > imˈpressible *adj*

impress² *vb* (ɪmˈprɛs) **1** to commandeer or coerce (men or things) into government service; press-gang ▷ *n* (ˈɪmprɛs) **2** the act of commandeering or coercing into government service; impressment [C16: see *im-* IN-², PRESS²]

impression (ɪmˈprɛʃən) *n* **1** an effect produced in the mind by a stimulus; sensation: *he gave the impression of wanting to help* **2** an imprint or mark produced by pressing **3** a vague idea, consciousness, or belief: *I had the impression we had met before* **4** a strong, favourable, or remarkable effect **5** the act of impressing or the state of being impressed **6** *printing* **a** the act, process, or result of printing from type, plates, etc **b** the total number of copies of a publication printed at one time **7** *dentistry* an imprint of the teeth and gums, esp in wax or plaster, for use in preparing crowns, inlays, or dentures **8** an imitation or impersonation: *he did a funny impression of the politician* > imˈpressional *adj* > imˈpressionally *adv*

impressionable (ɪmˈprɛʃənəbəl, -ˈprɛʃnə-) *adj* easily influenced or characterized by susceptibility to influence: *an impressionable child; an impressionable age* > imˌpressionaˈbility *or* imˈpressionableness *n*

impressionism (ɪmˈprɛʃəˌnɪzəm) *n* (*often capital*) a movement in French painting, developed in the 1870s chiefly by Monet, Renoir, Pissarro, and Sisley, having the aim of objectively recording experience by a system of fleeting impressions, esp of natural light effects > imˈpressionist *n, adj*

impressive (ɪmˈprɛsɪv) *adj* capable of impressing, esp by size, magnificence, etc; awe-inspiring; commanding > imˈpressively *adv* > imˈpressiveness *n*

imprest (ɪmˈprɛst) *n* **1** a fund of cash from which a department or other unit pays incidental expenses, topped up periodically from central funds **2** *chiefly Brit* an advance from government funds for the performance of some public business or service [C16: probably from Italian *imprestare* to lend, from Latin *in-* towards + *praestāre* to pay, from *praestō* at hand; see PRESTO]

imprimatur (ˌɪmprɪˈmeɪtə, -ˈmɑː-) *n* **1** *RC Church* a licence granted by a bishop certifying the Church's approval of a book to be published **2** sanction, authority, or approval, esp for something to be printed [C17: New Latin, literally: let it be printed]

imprimis (ɪmˈpraɪmɪs) *adv archaic* in the first place [C15: from Latin phrase *in prīmīs*, literally: among the first things]

imprint *n* (ˈɪmprɪnt) **1** a mark or impression produced by pressure, printing, or stamping **2** a characteristic mark

or indication; stamp: *the imprint of great sadness on his face* **3** the publisher's name and address, usually with the date of publication, in a book, pamphlet, etc **4** the printer's name and address on any printed matter ▷ *vb* (ɪmˈprɪnt) **5** to produce (a mark, impression, etc) on (a surface) by pressure, printing, or stamping: *to imprint a seal on wax; to imprint wax with a seal* **6** to establish firmly; impress; stamp: *to imprint the details on one's mind*

imprinting (ɪmˈprɪntɪŋ) *n* the development through exceptionally fast learning in young animals of recognition of and attraction to members of their own species or to surrogates

imprison (ɪmˈprɪzən) *vb* (*tr*) to confine in or as if in prison > imˈprisonment *n*

improbable (ɪmˈprɒbəbəl) *adj* not likely or probable; doubtful; unlikely > imˌprobaˈbility *or* imˈprobableness *n* > imˈprobably *adv*

improbity (ɪmˈprəʊbɪtɪ) *n, pl* **-ties** dishonesty, wickedness, or unscrupulousness

impromptu (ɪmˈprɒmptjuː) *adj* **1** unrehearsed; spontaneous; extempore **2** produced or done without care or planning; improvised ▷ *adv* **3** in a spontaneous or improvised way: *he spoke impromptu* ▷ *n* **4** something that is impromptu **5** a short piece of instrumental music, sometimes improvisatory in character [C17: from French, from Latin *in promptū* in readiness, from *promptus* (*adj*) ready, PROMPT]

improper (ɪmˈprɒpə) *adj* **1** lacking propriety; not seemly or fitting **2** unsuitable for a certain use or occasion; inappropriate: *an improper use for a tool* **3** irregular or abnormal > imˈproperly *adv* > imˈproperness *n*

improper fraction *n* a fraction in which the numerator has a greater absolute value or degree than the denominator, as $7/6$ or $(x^2 + 3)/(x + 1)$

impropriate *vb* (ɪmˈprəʊprɪˌeɪt) **1** (*tr*) to transfer (property, rights, etc) from the Church into lay hands ▷ *adj* (ɪmˈprəʊprɪɪt, -ˌeɪt) **2** transferred in this way [C16: from Medieval Latin *impropriāre* to make one's own, from Latin *im-* IN-² + *propriāre* to APPROPRIATE] > imˌpropriˈation *n* > imˈpropriˌator *n*

impropriety (ˌɪmprəˈpraɪɪtɪ) *n, pl* **-ties** **1** lack of propriety; indecency; indecorum **2** an improper act or use **3** the state of being improper

improve (ɪmˈpruːv) *vb* **1** to make or become better in quality; ameliorate **2** (*tr*) to make (buildings, land, etc) more valuable by additions or betterment **3** (*intr*; usually foll by *on* or *upon*) to achieve a better standard or quality in comparison (with): *to improve on last year's crop* [C16: from Anglo-French *emprouer* to turn to profit, from *en prou* into profit, from *prou* profit, from Late Latin *prōde* beneficial, from Latin *prōdesse* to be advantageous, from PRO-¹ + *esse* to be] > imˈprovable *adj* > imˌprovaˈbility *or* imˈprovableness *n* > imˈprovably *adv* > imˈprover *n* > imˈprovingly *adv*

improvement (ɪmˈpruːvmənt) *n* **1** the act of improving or the state of being improved **2** something that improves, esp an addition or alteration **3** (*usually plural*) *Austral & NZ* a building or other works on a piece of land, adding to its value

improvident (ɪmˈprɒvɪdənt) *adj* **1** not provident; thriftless, imprudent, or prodigal **2** heedless or incautious; rash > imˈprovidence *n* > imˈprovidently *adv*

improvise (ˈɪmprəˌvaɪz) *vb* **1** to perform or make quickly from materials and sources available, without previous planning **2** to perform (a poem, play, piece of music, etc), composing as one goes along [C19: from French, from Italian *improvvisare*, from Latin *imprōvīsus* unforeseen, from *im-* (not) + *prōvīsus*, from *prōvidēre* to foresee; see PROVIDE] > ˈimproˌviser *n* > ˌimproviˈsation *n* > ˌimproviˈsational *or* improvisatory (ˌɪmprəˈvaɪzətərɪ, -ˈvɪz-, ˌɪmprəvaɪˈzeɪtərɪ, -trɪ) *adj*

imprudent (ɪmˈpruːdənt) *adj* not prudent; rash, heedless, or indiscreet > imˈprudence *n* > imˈprudently *adv*

impudence (ˈɪmpjʊdəns) *or* **impudency** *n* **1** the quality of being impudent **2** an impudent act or statement [C14: from Latin *impudēns* shameless, from IM- (not) + *pudēns* modest; see PUDENCY]

impudent (ˈɪmpjʊdənt) *adj* **1** mischievous, impertinent, or disrespectful **2** an obsolete word for **immodest** > 'impudently *adv* > 'impudentness *n*

impugn (ɪmˈpjuːn) *vb* (*tr*) to challenge or attack as false; assail; criticize [c14: from Old French *impugner*, from Latin *impugnāre* to fight against, attack, from ɪM- + *pugnāre* to fight] > imˈpugnable *adj* > impugnation (ˌɪmpʌgˈneɪʃən) or imˈpugnment *n* > imˈpugner *n*

impulse (ˈɪmpʌls) *n* **1** an impelling force or motion; thrust; impetus **2** a sudden desire, whim, or inclination **3** an instinctive drive; urge **4** tendency; current; trend **5** *physics* **a** the product of the average magnitude of a force acting on a body and the time for which it acts **b** the change in the momentum of a body as a result of a force acting upon it for a short period of time **6** *physiol* See **nerve impulse** **7** on impulse spontaneously or impulsively [c17: from Latin *impulsus* a pushing against, incitement, from *impellere* to strike against; see IMPEL]

impulse buying *n* the buying of retail merchandise prompted by a whim on seeing the product displayed > **impulse buyer** *n*

impulsion (ɪmˈpʌlʃən) *n* **1** the act of impelling or the state of being impelled **2** motion produced by an impulse; propulsion **3** a driving force; compulsion

impulsive (ɪmˈpʌlsɪv) *adj* **1** characterized by actions based on sudden desires, whims, or inclinations rather than careful thought: *an impulsive man* **2** based on emotional impulses or whims; spontaneous **3** forceful, inciting, or impelling **4** (of physical forces) acting for a short time; not continuous **5** (of a sound) brief, loud, and having a wide frequency range > imˈpulsively *adv* > imˈpulsiveness *n*

impunity (ɪmˈpjuːnɪtɪ) *n*, *pl* -ties **1** exemption or immunity from punishment or recrimination **2** with impunity **a** with no unpleasant consequences **b** with no care or heed for such consequences [c16: from Latin *impūnitās* freedom from punishment, from *impūnis* unpunished, from ɪM- (not) + *poena* punishment]

impure (ɪmˈpjʊə) *adj* **1** not pure; mixed with something else; tainted or sullied **2** (in certain religions) (of persons) ritually unclean and as such debarred from certain religious ceremonies **3** (of a colour) mixed with another colour or with black or white **4** of more than one origin or style, as of architecture or other design > imˈpurely *adv* > imˈpureness *n*

impurity (ɪmˈpjʊərɪtɪ) *n*, *pl* -ties **1** the quality of being impure **2** an impure thing, constituent, or element: *impurities in the water* **3** *electronics* a small quantity of an element added to a pure semiconductor crystal to control its electrical conductivity

impute (ɪmˈpjuːt) *vb* (*tr*) **1** to attribute or ascribe (something dishonest or dishonourable, esp a criminal offence) to a person **2** to attribute to a source or cause: *I impute your success to nepotism* **3** *commerce* to give (a notional value) to goods or services when the real value is unknown [c14: from Latin *imputāre* to think, calculate] > impuˈtation *n* > imˈputative *adj* > imˈputer *n* > imˈputable *adj*

Imran Khan (ˈɪmrɑːn ˈkɑːn) *n* full name *Imran Ahmad Khan Niazi*. born 1952, Pakistani cricketer: played for Worcestershire (1971–76) and Sussex (1977–88); captained Pakistan (1982–84; 1985–87; 1988–92)

Imroz (ˈɪmrɒz) *n* the Turkish name for **Imbros**

IMunE *abbreviation* Institution of Municipal Engineers

in (ɪn) *prep* **1** inside; within: *no smoking in the auditorium* **2** at a place where there is: *lying in the shade; walking in the rain* **3** indicating a state, situation, or condition: *in a deep sleep; standing in silence* **4** before or when (a period of time) has elapsed: *come back in one year* **5** using (a language, etc) as a means of communication: *written in code* **6** concerned or involved with, esp as an occupation: *in journalism* **7** while or by performing the action of; as a consequence of or by means of: *in crossing the street he was run over* **8** used to indicate goal or purpose: *in honour of the president* **9** (used of certain animals) about to give birth to; pregnant with (specified offspring): *in foal; in calf* **10** a variant of *into*: *she fell in the water; he tore the paper in two* **11** have it in one (often foll by an infinitive) to have the ability (to do something) **12** in that or in so far as

(*conjunction*) because or to the extent that; inasmuch as: *I regret my remark in that it upset you* **13** nothing in it no difference or interval between two things ▷ *adv* (*particle*) **14** in or into a particular place; inward or indoors: *come in; bring him in* **15** so as to achieve office, power, or authority: *the Conservatives got in at the last election* **16** so as to enclose: *block in; cover in* **17** (in certain games) so as to take one's turn or one's team's turn at a certain aspect of the play; taking one's innings: *you have to get the other side out before you go in* **18** *Brit* (of a fire) alight **19** (*in combination*) indicating an activity or gathering, esp one organized to protest against something: *teach-in; work-in* **20** in at present at (the beginning, end, etc) **21** in for about to be affected by (something, esp something unpleasant): *you're in for a shock* **22** in on acquainted with or sharing in: *I was in on all his plans* **23** in with associated with; friendly with; regarded highly by **24** have it in for or have got it in for *informal* to wish or intend harm towards ▷ *adj* **25** (*stressed*) fashionable; modish: *the in thing to do* **26** *NZ* competing: *you've got to be in to win* ▷ *n* **27** ins and outs intricacies or complications; details: *the ins and outs of a computer system* [Old English; compare Old High German *in*, Welsh *yn*, Old Norse *ī*, Latin *in*, Greek *en*]

In the chemical symbol for **indium**

in. *abbreviation* inch(es)

in-¹, **il-**, **im-** or **ir-** *prefix* not; non-: *incredible; insincere; illegal; imperfect; irregular*. See **un-¹** [from Latin *in-*; related to *ne-*, *nōn* not]

in-², **il-**, **im-** or **ir-** *prefix* **1** in; into; towards; within; on: *infiltrate; immigrate* **2** having an intensive or causative function: *inflame; imperil* [from IN (prep, adv)]

-in *suffix* forming nouns **1** indicating a neutral organic compound, including proteins, glucosides, and glycerides: *insulin; digitoxin; tripalmitin* **2** indicating an enzyme in certain nonsystematic names: *pepsin* **3** indicating a pharmaceutical substance: *penicillin; riboflavin; aspirin* **4** indicating a chemical substance in certain nonsystematic names: *coumarin* [from New Latin *-ina*; compare -INE²]

in absentia *Latin* (ɪn æbˈsɛntɪə) *adv* in the absence of (someone indicated): *he was condemned in absentia*

inaccessible (ˌɪnækˈsɛsəbəl) *adj* not accessible; unapproachable > ˌinacˌcessiˈbility or ˌinacˈcessibleness *n* > ˌinacˈcessibly *adv*

inaccuracy (ɪnˈækjʊrəsɪ) *n*, *pl* -cies **1** lack of accuracy; imprecision **2** an error, a mistake, or a slip

inaccurate (ɪnˈækjʊrɪt) *adj* not accurate; imprecise, inexact, or erroneous

inaction (ɪnˈækʃən) *n* lack of action; idleness; inertia

inactivate (ɪnˈæktɪˌveɪt) *vb* (*tr*) to render inactive > inˌactiˈvation *n*

inactive (ɪnˈæktɪv) *adj* **1** idle or inert; not active **2** sluggish, passive, or indolent **3** *military* of or relating to persons or equipment not in active service **4** *chem* (of a substance) having little or no reactivity **5** (of an element, isotope, etc) having little or no radioactivity > inˈactively *adv* > inacˈtivity or inˈactiveness *n*

inadequate (ɪnˈædɪkwɪt) *adj* **1** not adequate; insufficient **2** not capable or competent; lacking > inˈadequacy *n* > inˈadequately *adv*

inadvertence (ˌɪnədˈvɜːtəns) or **inadvertency** *n* **1** lack of attention; heedlessness **2** an instance or an effect of being inadvertent; oversight; slip

inadvertent (ˌɪnədˈvɜːtənt) *adj* **1** failing to act carefully or considerately; inattentive **2** resulting from heedless action; unintentional > ˌinadˈvertently *adv*

-inae *suffix* forming plural proper nouns occurring in names of zoological subfamilies: *Felinae* [New Latin, from Latin, feminine plural of *-īnus* -INE¹]

inalienable (ɪnˈeɪljənəbəl) *adj* not able to be transferred to another; not alienable: *the inalienable rights of the citizen* > inˌalienaˈbility or inˈalienableness *n* > inˈalienably *adv*

inalterable (ɪnˈɔːltərəbəl) *adj* not alterable; unalterable > inˌalteraˈbility or inˈalterableness *n* > inˈalterably *adv*

inamorata (ɪnˌæməˈrɑːtə, ˌɪnæmə-) *n*, *pl* -tas a woman with whom one is in love; a female lover [c17: see INAMORATO]

inamorato (ɪnˌæməˈrɑːtəʊ, ˌɪnæmə-) *n*, *pl* -tos or -ti (-tɪ) a man with whom one is in love; a male lover [c16: from

Italian *innamorato, innamorata*, from *innamorare* to cause to fall in love, from *amore* love, from Latin *amor*]

inane (ɪˈneɪn) *adj* senseless, unimaginative, or empty; unintelligent: *inane remarks* [c17: from Latin *inānis* empty] > in'anely *adv*

inanimate (ɪnˈænɪmɪt) *adj* 1 lacking the qualities or features of living beings; not animate: *inanimate objects* 2 lacking any sign of life or consciousness; appearing dead 3 lacking vitality; spiritless; dull > in'animately *adv* > in'animateness *or* inanimation (ɪnˌænɪˈmeɪʃən) *n*

inanition (ˌɪnəˈnɪʃən) *n* 1 exhaustion resulting from lack of food 2 mental, social, or spiritual weakness or lassitude [c14: from Late Latin *inānītio* emptiness, from Latin *inānis* empty; see INANE]

inanity (ɪˈnænɪtɪ) *n, pl* -ties 1 lack of intelligence or imagination; senselessness; silliness 2 a senseless action, remark, etc

inapposite (ɪnˈæpəzɪt) *adj* not appropriate or pertinent; unsuitable > in'appositely *adv* > in'appositeness *n*

inapt (ɪnˈæpt) *adj* 1 not apt or fitting; inappropriate 2 lacking skill; inept > in'apti,tude *or* in'aptness *n* > in'aptly *adv*

inarch (ɪnˈɑːtʃ) *vb* (tr) to graft (a plant) by uniting stock and scion while both are still growing independently

inasmuch as (ˌɪnəzˈmʌtʃ) *conj* (subordinating) 1 in view of the fact that; seeing that; since 2 to the extent or degree that; in so far as

inaugural (ɪnˈɔːɡjʊrəl) *adj* 1 characterizing or relating to an inauguration ▷ *n* 2 a speech made at an inauguration, esp by a president of the US

inaugurate (ɪnˈɔːɡjʊˌreɪt) *vb* (tr) 1 to commence officially or formally; initiate 2 to place in office formally and ceremonially; induct 3 to open ceremonially; dedicate formally: *to inaugurate a factory* [c17: from Latin *inaugurāre*, literally: to take omens, practise augury, hence to install in office after taking auguries; see IN-², AUGUR] > in,augu'ration *n* > in'augu,rator *n* > inauguratory (ɪnˈɔːɡjʊrətərɪ, -trɪ) *adj*

inauthentic (ˌɪnɔːˈθɛntɪk) *adj* not authentic; false

in-between *adj* intermediate: *he's at the in-between stage, neither a child nor an adult*

inboard (ˈɪnˌbɔːd) *adj* 1 (esp of a boat's motor or engine) situated within the hull 2 situated between the wing tip of an aircraft and its fuselage: *an inboard engine* ▷ *adv* 3 towards the centre line of or within a vessel, aircraft, etc

inborn (ˈɪnˈbɔːn) *adj* existing from birth; congenital; innate

inbound (ˈɪnˌbaʊnd) *adj* coming in; inward bound: *an inbound ship*

inbred (ˈɪnˈbrɛd) *adj* 1 produced as a result of inbreeding 2 deeply ingrained; innate: *inbred good manners*

inbreed (ˈɪnˈbriːd) *vb* -breeds, -breeding, -bred 1 to breed from unions between closely related individuals, esp over several generations 2 (tr) to develop within; engender > 'in'breeding *n, adj*

in-built *adj* built-in, integral

inc. *abbreviation* including

Inc. *abbreviation* incorporated

Inca (ˈɪŋkə) *n, pl* -ca *or* -cas 1 a member of a South American Indian people whose great empire centred on Peru lasted from about 1100 AD to the Spanish conquest in the early 1530s and is famed for its complex culture 2 the language of the Incas. See also **Quechua** [c16: from Spanish, from Quechua *inka* king] > 'Incan *adj*

incalculable (ɪnˈkælkjʊləbəl) *adj* beyond calculation; unable to be predicted or determined > in,calcula'bility *or* in'calculableness *n* > in'calculably *adv*

in camera (ɪn ˈkæmərə) *adv, adj* in a private or secret session; not in public [Latin: in the chamber]

incandesce (ˌɪnkænˈdɛs) *vb* (intr) to exhibit incandescence

incandescent (ˌɪnkænˈdɛsənt) *adj* 1 emitting light as a result of being heated to a high temperature; red-hot or white-hot 2 informal extremely angry; raging [c18: from Latin *incandescere* to become hot, glow, from IN-² + *candescere* to grow bright, from *candēre* to be white; see CANDID] > ,incan'descently *adv* > ,incan'descence *n*

incandescent lamp *n* a source of light that contains a heated solid, such as an electrically heated filament

incantation (ˌɪnkænˈteɪʃən) *n* 1 ritual recitation of magic words or sounds 2 the formulaic words or sounds used; a magic spell [c14: from Late Latin *incantātio* an enchanting, from *incantāre* to repeat magic formulas, from Latin, from IN-² + *cantāre* to sing; see ENCHANT] > ,incan'tational *adj*

incapacitate (ˌɪnkəˈpæsɪˌteɪt) *vb* (tr) 1 to deprive of power, strength, or capacity; disable 2 to deprive of legal capacity or eligibility > ,inca,paci'tation *n*

incapacity (ˌɪnkəˈpæsɪtɪ) *n, pl* -ties 1 lack of power, strength, or capacity; inability 2 law legal disqualification or ineligibility

in-car *adj* installed or provided within a car: *an in-car hi-fi system*

incarcerate (ɪnˈkɑːsəˌreɪt) *vb* (tr) to confine or imprison [c16: from Medieval Latin *incarcerāre*, from Latin IN-² + *carcer* prison] > in,carcer'ation *n* > in'carcer,ator *n*

incarnadine (ɪnˈkɑːnəˌdaɪn) *archaic or literary* ▷ *vb* 1 (tr) to tinge or stain with red ▷ *adj* 2 of a pinkish or reddish colour similar to that of flesh or blood [c16: from French *incarnadin* flesh-coloured, from Italian, from Late Latin *incarnātus* made flesh, INCARNATE]

incarnate *adj* (ɪnˈkɑːnɪt, -neɪt) (usually immediately postpositive) 1 possessing bodily form, esp the human form: *a devil incarnate* 2 personified or typified: *stupidity incarnate* ▷ *vb* (ɪnˈkɑːneɪt) (tr) 3 to give a bodily or concrete form to 4 to be representative or typical of [c14: from Late Latin *incarnāre* to make flesh, from Latin IN-² + *carō* flesh]

incarnation (ˌɪnkɑːˈneɪʃən) *n* 1 the act of manifesting or state of being manifested in bodily form, esp human form 2 a bodily form assumed by a god, etc 3 a person or thing that typifies or represents some quality, idea, etc

Incarnation (ˌɪnkɑːˈneɪʃən) *n* Christian theol the assuming of a human body by the Son of God

incarvillea (ˌɪnkɑːˈvɪlɪə) *n* any plant of the genus *Incarvillea*, native to China, of which some species are grown as garden or greenhouse plants for their large usually carmine-coloured trumpet-shaped flowers, esp *I. delavayi*: family Bignoniaceae [named after Pierre d'Incarville (1706–57), French missionary]

incase (ɪnˈkeɪs) *vb* a variant spelling of **encase** > in'casement *n*

incautious (ɪnˈkɔːʃəs) *adj* not careful or cautious > in'cautiously *adv* > in'cautiousness *or* in'caution *n*

incendiary (ɪnˈsɛndɪərɪ) *adj* 1 of or relating to the illegal burning of property, goods, etc 2 tending to create strife, violence, etc; inflammatory 3 (of a substance) capable of catching fire, causing fires, or burning readily ▷ *n, pl* -aries 4 a person who illegally sets fire to property, goods, etc; arsonist 5 (esp formerly) a person who stirs up civil strife, violence, etc, for political reasons; agitator 6 Also called: incendiary bomb a bomb that is designed to start fires 7 an incendiary substance, such as phosphorus [c17: from Latin *incendiārius* setting alight, from *incendium* fire, from *incendere* to kindle] > in'cendia,rism *n*

incense¹ (ˈɪnsɛns) *n* 1 any of various aromatic substances burnt for their fragrant odour, esp in religious ceremonies 2 the odour or smoke so produced 3 any pleasant fragrant odour; aroma ▷ *vb* 4 to burn incense in honour of (a deity) 5 (tr) to perfume or fumigate with incense [c13: from Old French *encens*, from Church Latin *incensum*, from Latin *incendere* to kindle]

incense² (ɪnˈsɛns) *vb* (tr) to enrage greatly [c15: from Latin *incensus* set on fire, from *incendere* to kindle] > in'censement *n*

incensory (ˈɪnsɛnsərɪ) *n, pl* -ries a less common name for a **censer** [c17: from Medieval Latin *incensorium*]

incentive (ɪnˈsɛntɪv) *n* 1 a motivating influence; stimulus 2 a an additional payment made to employees as a means of increasing production b (as modifier): *an incentive scheme* ▷ *adj* 3 serving to incite to action [c15: from Late Latin *incentīvus* (adj), from Latin: striking up, setting the tune, from *incinere* to sing, from IN-² + *canere* to sing]

incentivize *or* **incentivise** (ɪnˈsɛntɪˌvaɪz) *vb* (tr) a to provide (someone) with a good reason for wanting to do something: *why not incentivize companies to relocate?* **b** to promote (something) with a particular incentive: *an incentivized share option scheme*

incept (ɪnˈsɛpt) *vb* (*tr*) **1** (of organisms) to ingest (food) **2** Brit (formerly) to take a master's or doctor's degree at a university [C19: from Latin *inceptus* begun, attempted, from *incipere* to begin, take in hand, from IN-² + *capere* to take] > inˈceptor *n*

inception (ɪnˈsɛpʃən) *n* the beginning, as of a project or undertaking

inceptive (ɪnˈsɛptɪv) *adj* **1** beginning; incipient; initial **2** Also called: inchoative *grammar* denoting an aspect of verbs in some languages used to indicate the beginning of an action ▷ *n* **3** *grammar* the inceptive aspect of verbs > inˈceptively *adv*

incertitude (ɪnˈsɜːtɪˌtjuːd) *n* **1** uncertainty; doubt **2** a state of mental or emotional insecurity

incessant (ɪnˈsɛsᵊnt) *adj* not ceasing; continual [C16: from Late Latin *incessāns*, from Latin IN-¹ + *cessāre* to CEASE] > inˈcessancy *or* inˈcessantness *n* > inˈcessantly *adv*

incest (ˈɪnsɛst) *n* sexual intercourse between two persons commonly regarded as too closely related to marry [C13: from Latin *incestus* incest (from *adj*: impure, defiled), from IN-¹ + *castus* CHASTE]

incestuous (ɪnˈsɛstjʊəs) *adj* **1** relating to or involving incest: *an incestuous union* **2** guilty of incest **3** resembling incest in excessive or claustrophobic intimacy > inˈcestuously *adv* > inˈcestuousness *n*

inch¹ (ɪntʃ) *n* **1** a unit of length equal to one twelfth of a foot or 0.0254 metre **2** *meteorol* **a** an amount of precipitation that would cover a surface with water one inch deep **b** a unit of pressure equal to a mercury column one inch high in a barometer **3** a very small distance, degree, or amount **4 every inch** in every way; completely: *he was every inch an aristocrat* **5 inch by inch** gradually; little by little **6 within an inch of** very close to ▷ *vb* **7** to move or be moved very slowly or in very small steps: *the car inched forward* **8** (*tr*; foll by **out**) to defeat (someone) by a very small margin [Old English *ynce*, from Latin *uncia* twelfth part; see OUNCE¹]

inch² (ɪntʃ) *n* Scot & Irish a small island [C15: from Gaelic *innis* island; compare Welsh *ynys*]

inchoate *adj* (ɪnˈkəʊeɪt, -ˈkəʊɪt) **1** just beginning; incipient **2** undeveloped; immature; rudimentary ▷ *vb* (ɪnˈkəʊeɪt) (*tr*) **3** to begin [C16: from Latin *incohāre* to make a beginning, literally: to hitch up (from IN-² + *cohum* yokestrap] > inˈchoately *adv* > inˈchoateness *n* > ˌinchoˈation *n* > inchoative (ɪnˈkəʊətɪv) *adj*

Inchon *or* **Incheon** (ˈɪntʃɒn) *n* a port in W South Korea, on the Yellow Sea: the chief port for Seoul: site of a major strategic amphibious assault by UN troops, liberating Seoul (Sept 15, 1950). Pop: 2 642 000 (2005 est). Former name: Chemulpo

inchworm (ˈɪntʃˌwɜːm) *n* another name for a **measuring worm**

incidence (ˈɪnsɪdəns) *n* **1** degree, extent, or frequency of occurrence; amount: *a high incidence of death from pneumonia* **2** the act or manner of impinging on or affecting by proximity or influence **3** *physics* the arrival of a beam of light or particles at a surface. See also **angle of incidence** **4** *geometry* the partial coincidence of two configurations, such as a point that lies on a circle

incident (ˈɪnsɪdənt) *n* **1** a distinct or definite occurrence; event **2** a minor, subsidiary, or related event or action **3** a relatively insignificant event that might have serious consequences, esp in international politics **4** a public disturbance **5** the occurrence of something interesting or exciting: *the trip was not without incident* ▷ *adj* **6** (*postpositive*; foll by **to**) related (to) or dependent (on) **7** (when *postpositive*, often foll by **to**) having a subsidiary or minor relationship (with) **8** (esp of a beam of light or particles) arriving at or striking a surface [C15: from Medieval Latin *incidens* an event, from Latin *incidere*, literally: to fall into, hence befall, happen, from IN-² + *cadere* to fall]

incidental (ˌɪnsɪˈdɛntᵊl) *adj* **1** happening in connection with or resulting from something more important; casual or fortuitous **2** (*postpositive*; foll by **to**) found in

connection (with); related (to) **3** (*postpositive*; foll by **upon**) caused (by) **4** occasional or minor: *incidental expenses* ▷ *n* **5** (*often plural*) an incidental or minor expense, event, or action > ˌinciˈdentalness *n*

incidentally (ˌɪnsɪˈdɛntəlɪ) *adv* **1** as a subordinate or chance occurrence **2** (*sentence modifier*) by the way

incidental music *n* background music for a film, television programme, etc

incinerate (ɪnˈsɪnəˌreɪt) *vb* to burn up completely; reduce to ashes [C16: from Medieval Latin *incinerāre*, from Latin IN-² + *cinis* ashes] > inˌcinerˈation *n*

incinerator (ɪnˈsɪnəˌreɪtə) *n* a furnace or apparatus for incinerating something, esp refuse

incipient (ɪnˈsɪpɪənt) *adj* just starting to be or happen; beginning [C17: from Latin *incipiēns*, from *incipere* to begin, take in hand, from IN-² + *capere* to take] > inˈcipience *or* inˈcipiency *n* > inˈcipiently *adv*

incise (ɪnˈsaɪz) *vb* (*tr*) to produce (lines, a design, etc) by cutting into the surface of (something) with a sharp tool [C16: from Latin *incīdere* to cut into, from IN-² + *caedere* to cut]

incision (ɪnˈsɪʒən) *n* **1** the act of incising **2** a cut, gash, or notch **3** a cut made with a knife during a surgical operation

incisive (ɪnˈsaɪsɪv) *adj* **1** keen, penetrating, or acute **2** biting or sarcastic; mordant: *an incisive remark* **3** having a sharp cutting edge: *incisive teeth* > inˈcisively *adv* > inˈcisiveness *n*

incisor (ɪnˈsaɪzə) *n* a chisel-edged tooth at the front of the mouth. In man there are four in each jaw

incite (ɪnˈsaɪt) *vb* (*tr*) to stir up or provoke to action [C15: from Latin *incitāre*, from IN-² + *citāre* to excite] > ˌinciˈtation *n* > inˈcitement *n* > inˈciter *n* > inˈcitingly *adv*

incivility (ˌɪnsɪˈvɪlɪtɪ) *n, pl* -ties **1** lack of civility or courtesy; rudeness **2** an impolite or uncivil act or remark

incl. *abbreviation* **1** including **2** inclusive

inclement (ɪnˈklɛmənt) *adj* **1** (of weather) stormy, severe, or tempestuous **2** harsh, severe, or merciless > inˈclemency *or* inˈclementness *n* > inˈclemently *adv*

inclination (ˌɪnklɪˈneɪʃən) *n* **1** (often foll by **for, to, towards**, or an infinitive) a particular disposition, esp a liking or preference; tendency: *I've no inclination for such dull work* **2** the degree of deviation from a particular plane, esp a horizontal or vertical plane **3** a sloping or slanting surface; incline **4** the act of inclining or the state of being inclined **5** the act of bowing or nodding the head **6** *physics* another name for **dip** (sense 25) > ˌincliˈnational *adj*

incline *vb* (ɪnˈklaɪn) **1** to deviate or cause to deviate from a particular plane, esp a vertical or horizontal plane; slope or slant **2** (when *tr*, may take an infinitive) to be disposed or cause to be disposed (towards some attitude or to do something) **3** to bend or lower (part of the body, esp the head), as in a bow or in order to listen **4 incline one's ear** to listen favourably (to) ▷ *n* (ˈɪnklaɪn, ɪnˈklaɪn) **5** an inclined surface or slope; gradient [C13: from Latin *inclīnāre* to cause to lean, from *clīnāre* to bend; see LEAN¹] > inˈcliner *n*

inclined (ɪnˈklaɪnd) *adj* **1** (*postpositive*; often foll by **to**) having a disposition; tending **2** sloping or slanting

inclined plane *n* a plane whose angle to the horizontal is less than a right angle

inclinometer (ˌɪnklɪˈnɒmɪtə) *n* an aircraft instrument for indicating the angle that an aircraft makes with the horizontal

inclose (ɪnˈkləʊz) *vb* a less common spelling of **enclose** > inˈclosure *n*

include (ɪnˈkluːd) *vb* (*tr*) **1** to have as contents or part of the contents; be made up of or contain **2** to add as part of something else; put in as part of a set, group, or category **3** to contain as a secondary or minor ingredient or element [C15 (in the sense: to enclose): from Latin *inclūdere* to enclose, from IN-² + *claudere* to close] > inˈcludable *or* inˈcludible *adj*

include out *vb* (*tr, adverb*) *informal* to exclude: *you can include me out of that deal*

inclusion (ɪnˈkluːʒən) *n* **1** the act of including or the state of being included **2** something included

inclusion body *n pathol* any of the small particles found in the nucleus and cytoplasm of cells infected with certain viruses

inclusive (ɪnˈkluːsɪv) *adj* **1** (*postpositive; foll by of*) considered together (with): *capital inclusive of profit* **2** (*postpositive*) including the limits specified: *Monday to Friday inclusive is five days* **3** comprehensive **4** *logic* (of a disjunction) true if at least one of its component propositions is true > inˈclusively *adv* > inˈclusiveness *n*

inclusive language *n* language that avoids the use of certain expressions or words that might be considered to exclude particular groups of people, esp gender-specific words, such as "man", "mankind", and masculine pronouns, the use of which might be considered to exclude women

incognito (ˌɪnkɒɡˈniːtəʊ, ɪnˈkɒɡnɪtəʊ) *adv, adj* (*postpositive*) **1** under an assumed name or appearance; in disguise ▷ *n, pl* -tos **2** a person who is incognito **3** the assumed name or disguise of such a person [C17: from Italian, from Latin *incognitus* unknown, from ɪN-¹ + *cognitus* known]

incognizant (ɪnˈkɒɡnɪzənt) *adj* (*when postpositive, often foll by of*) unaware (of) > inˈcognizance *n*

incoherent (ˌɪnkəʊˈhɪərənt) *adj* **1** lacking in clarity or organization; disordered **2** unable to express oneself clearly; inarticulate **3** *physics* (of two or more waves) having the same frequency but not the same phase: *incoherent light* > ˌincoˈherence *or* ˌincoˈherency *n* > ˌincoˈherently *adv*

income (ˈɪnkʌm, ˈɪnkəm) *n* **1** the amount of monetary or other returns, either earned or unearned, accruing over a given period of time **2** receipts; revenue [C13 (in the sense: arrival, entrance): from Old English *incumen* a coming in]

incomer (ˈɪnkʌmə) *n* a person who comes to live in a place in which he was not born

incomes policy *n* See **prices and incomes policy**

income support *n* (in Britain, formerly) a social security payment for people on very low incomes

income tax *n* a personal tax, usually progressive, levied on annual income subject to certain deductions

incoming (ˈɪnˌkʌmɪŋ) *adj* **1** coming in; entering **2** about to come into office; succeeding **3** (of interest, dividends, etc) being received; accruing ▷ *n* **4** the act of coming in; entrance **5** (*usually plural*) income or revenue

incommensurable (ˌɪnkəˈmɛnʃərəbəl) *adj* **1** incapable of being judged, measured, or considered comparatively **2** (*postpositive; foll by with*) not in accordance; incommensurate **3** *maths* not having units of the same dimension ▷ *n* **4** something incommensurable > ˌincomˌmensuraˈbility *or* ˌincomˈmensurableness *n* > ˌincomˈmensurably *adv*

incommensurate (ˌɪnkəˈmɛnʃərɪt) *adj* **1** (*when postpositive, often foll by with*) not commensurate; disproportionate **2** incommensurable > ˌincomˈmensurately *adv* > ˌincomˈmensurateness *n*

incommode (ˌɪnkəˈməʊd) *vb* (*tr*) to bother, disturb, or inconvenience [C16: from Latin *incommodāre* to be troublesome, from *incommodus* inconvenient, from ɪN-¹ + *commodus* convenient; see COMMODE]

incommodious (ˌɪnkəˈməʊdɪəs) *adj* **1** insufficiently spacious; cramped **2** troublesome or inconvenient > ˌincomˈmodiously *adv*

incommodity (ˌɪnkəˈmɒdɪtɪ) *n, pl* -ties a less common word for **inconvenience**

incommunicado (ˌɪnkəˌmjuːnɪˈkɑːdəʊ) *adv, adj* (*postpositive*) deprived of communication with other people, as while in solitary confinement [C19: from Spanish *incomunicado*, from *incomunicar* to deprive of communication; see ɪN-¹, COMMUNICATE]

incomparable (ɪnˈkɒmpərəbəl, -prəbəl) *adj* **1** beyond or above comparison; matchless; unequalled **2** lacking a basis for comparison; not having qualities or features that can be compared > inˌcomparaˈbility *or* inˈcomparableness *n* > inˈcomparably *adv*

incompatible (ˌɪnkəmˈpætəbəl) *adj* **1** incapable of living or existing together in peace or harmony; conflicting or antagonistic **2** opposed in nature or quality; inconsistent **3** *med* (esp of two drugs or two types of blood) incapable of being combined or used together; antagonistic **4** *logic* (of two propositions) unable to be both true at the same time **5** (of plants) incapable of fertilizing each other ▷ *n* **6** (*often plural*) a person or thing that is incompatible with another > ˌincomˌpatiˈbility *or* ˌincomˈpatibleness *n* > ˌincomˈpatibly *adv*

incompetent (ɪnˈkɒmpɪtənt) *adj* **1** not possessing the necessary ability, skill, etc to do or carry out a task; incapable **2** marked by lack of ability, skill, etc **3** *law* not legally qualified: *an incompetent witness* ▷ *n* **4** an incompetent person > inˈcompetence *or* inˈcompetency *n* > inˈcompetently *adv*

incomplete (ˌɪnkəmˈpliːt) *adj* **1** not complete or finished **2** not completely developed; imperfect > ˌincomˈpletely *adv* > ˌincomˈpleteness *or* ˌincomˈpletion *n*

incomprehensible (ˌɪnkɒmprɪˈhɛnsəbəl, ɪnˌkɒm-) *adj* **1** incapable of being understood; unintelligible **2** *archaic* limitless; boundless > ˌincompreˌhensiˈbility *or* ˌincompreˈhensibleness *n* > ˌincompreˈhensibly *adv*

inconceivable (ˌɪnkənˈsiːvəbəl) *adj* incapable of being conceived, imagined, or considered > ˌinconˌceivaˈbility *or* ˌinconˈceivableness *n* > ˌinconˈceivably *adv*

inconclusive (ˌɪnkənˈkluːsɪv) *adj* not conclusive or decisive; not finally settled; indeterminate > ˌinconˈclusively *adv* > ˌinconˈclusiveness *n*

incongruous (ɪnˈkɒŋɡrʊəs) *or* **incongruent** *adj* **1** (*when postpositive, foll by with or to*) incompatible with (what is suitable); inappropriate **2** containing disparate or discordant elements or parts > inˈcongruously *or* inˈcongruently *adv* > inˈcongruousness *or* inˈcongruence *n*

inconnu (ˈɪnkənuː) *n* a North American freshwater food and game fish, *Stenodus leucichthys*, related to the salmon [C19: from French, literally: unknown]

inconsequential (ˌɪnkɒnsɪˈkwɛnʃəl, ɪnˌkɒn-) *or* **inconsequent** (ɪnˈkɒnsɪkwənt) *adj* **1** not following logically as a consequence **2** trivial or insignificant **3** not in a logical sequence; haphazard > ˌinconseˌquentiˈality, ˌinconseˈquentialness *or* inˈconsequence *or* inˈconsequentness *n* > ˌinconseˈquentially *or* inˈconsequently *adv*

inconsiderable (ˌɪnkənˈsɪdərəbəl) *adj* **1** relatively small **2** not worthy of consideration; insignificant > ˌinconˈsiderableness *n* > ˌinconˈsiderably *adv*

inconsiderate (ˌɪnkənˈsɪdərɪt) *adj* lacking in care or thought for others; heedless; thoughtless > ˌinconˈsiderately *adv* > ˌinconˈsiderateness *or* ˌinconˌsiderˈation *n*

inconsistency (ˌɪnkənˈsɪstənsɪ) *n, pl* -cies **1** lack of consistency or agreement; incompatibility **2** an inconsistent feature or quality

inconsistent (ˌɪnkənˈsɪstənt) *adj* **1** lacking in consistency, agreement, or compatibility; at variance **2** containing contradictory elements **3** irregular or fickle in behaviour or mood **4** *logic* (of a set of propositions) enabling an explicit contradiction to be validly derived > ˌinconˈsistently *adv*

inconsolable (ˌɪnkənˈsəʊləbəl) *adj* incapable of being consoled or comforted; disconsolate > ˌinconˌsolaˈbility *or* ˌinconˈsolableness *n* > ˌinconˈsolably *adv*

inconsonant (ɪnˈkɒnsənənt) *adj* lacking in harmony or compatibility; discordant > inˈconsonance *n* > inˈconsonantly *adv*

inconspicuous (ˌɪnkənˈspɪkjʊəs) *adj* not easily noticed or seen; not prominent or striking > ˌinconˈspicuously *adv* > ˌinconˈspicuousness *n*

incontinent¹ (ɪnˈkɒntɪnənt) *adj* **1** lacking in restraint or control, esp sexually **2** relating to or exhibiting involuntary urination or defecation **3** (*foll by of*) having little or no control (over) **4** unrestrained; uncontrolled [C14: from Old French, from Latin *incontinens*, from ɪN-¹ + *continere* to hold, restrain] > inˈcontinence *or* inˈcontinency *n* > inˈcontinently *adv*

incontinent² (ɪnˈkɒntɪnənt) *or* **incontinently** *adv* obsolete words for **immediately** [C15: from Late Latin *in continentī tempore*, literally: in continuous time, that is, with no interval]

incontrovertible (ˌɪnkɒntrəˈvɜːtəbəl, ɪnˌkɒn-) *adj* incapable of being contradicted or disputed; undeniable > ˌincontroˌvertiˈbility *or* ˌincontroˈvertibleness *n*

> ˌincontro'vertibly *adv*

inconvenience (ˌɪnkən'viːnjəns, -'viːnɪəns) *n* **1** the state or quality of being inconvenient **2** something inconvenient; a hindrance, trouble, or difficulty ▷ *vb* **3** (*tr*) to cause inconvenience to; trouble or harass

inconvenient (ˌɪnkən'viːnjənt, -'viːnɪənt) *adj* not convenient; troublesome, awkward, or difficult > ˌincon'veniently *adv*

incorporate *vb* (ɪn'kɔːpəˌreɪt) **1** to include or be included as a part or member of a united whole **2** to form or cause to form a united whole or mass; merge or blend **3** to form (individuals, an unincorporated enterprise, etc) into a corporation or other organization with a separate legal identity from that of its owners or members ▷ *adj* (ɪn'kɔːpərɪt, -prɪt) **4** combined into a whole; incorporated **5** formed into or constituted as a corporation [C14 (in the sense: put into the body of something else): from Late Latin *incorporāre* to embody, from Latin IN-² + *corpus* body] > in'corporative *adj* > inˌcorpo'ration *n*

incorporeal (ˌɪnkɔː'pɔːrɪəl) *adj* **1** without material form, body, or substance **2** spiritual or metaphysical **3** *law* having no material existence but existing by reason of its annexation of something material, such as an easement, touchline, copyright, etc: *an incorporeal hereditament* > ˌincor'poreally *adv* > incorporeity (ɪnˌkɔːpə'riːɪtɪ) or ˌincorpore'ality *n*

incorrect (ˌɪnkə'rɛkt) *adj* **1** false; wrong: *an incorrect calculation* **2** not fitting or proper: *incorrect behaviour* > ˌincor'rectly *adv* > ˌincor'rectness *n*

incorrigible (ɪn'kɒrɪdʒəb³l) *adj* **1** beyond correction, reform, or alteration **2** firmly rooted; ineradicable ▷ *n* **3** a person or animal that is incorrigible > inˌcorrigi'bility or in'corrigibleness *n* > in'corrigibly *adv*

incorruptible (ˌɪnkə'rʌptəb³l) *adj* **1** incapable of being corrupted; honest; just **2** not subject to decay or decomposition > inˌcorrupti'bility or ˌincor'ruptibleness *n* > ˌincor'ruptibly *adv*

incrassate *adj* (ɪn'kræsɪt, -eɪt) Also called: incrassated **1** *biology* thickened or swollen ▷ *vb* (ɪn'kræseɪt) **2** *obsolete* to make or become thicker [C17: from Late Latin *incrassāre*, from Latin *crassus* thick, dense] > ˌincras'sation *n*

increase *vb* (ɪn'kriːs) **1** to make or become greater in size, degree, frequency, etc; grow or expand ▷ *n* ('ɪnkriːs) **2** the act of increasing; augmentation **3** the amount by which something increases **4** on the increase increasing, esp becoming more frequent [C14: from Old French *encreistre*, from Latin *incrēscere*, from IN-² + *crēscere* to grow] > in'creasable *adj* > increasedly (ɪn'kriːsɪdlɪ) or in'creasingly *adv* > in'creaser *n*

incredible (ɪn'krɛdəb³l) *adj* **1** beyond belief or understanding; unbelievable **2** *informal* marvellous; amazing > inˌcredi'bility or in'credibleness *n* > in'credibly *adv*

incredulity (ˌɪnkrɪ'djuːlɪtɪ) *n* lack of belief; scepticism

incredulous (ɪn'krɛdjʊləs) *adj* (often foll by *of*) not prepared or willing to believe (something); unbelieving > in'credulously *adv* > in'credulousness *n*

increment ('ɪnkrɪmənt) *n* **1** an increase or addition, esp one of a series **2** the act of increasing; augmentation **3** *maths* a small positive or negative change in a variable or function. Symbol: Δ, as in Δx or Δf [C15: from Latin *incrēmentum* growth, INCREASE] > ˌincre'mental *adj*

incremental plotter *n* a device that plots graphs on paper from computer-generated information

incriminate (ɪn'krɪmɪˌneɪt) *vb* (*tr*) **1** to imply or suggest the guilt or error of (someone) **2** to charge with a crime or fault [C18: from Late Latin *incrīmināre* to accuse, from Latin *crīmen* accusation; see CRIME] > inˌcrimi'nation *n* > in'crimiˌnator *n* > in'criminatory *adj*

incrust (ɪn'krʌst) *vb* a variant spelling of **encrust** > in'crustant *n*, *adj* > ˌincrus'tation *n*

incubate ('ɪnkjʊˌbeɪt) *vb* **1** (of birds) to supply (eggs) with heat for their development, esp by sitting on them **2** to cause (eggs, embryos, bacteria, etc) to develop, esp in an incubator or culture medium **3** (*intr*) (of eggs, embryos, bacteria, etc) to develop in favourable conditions, esp in an incubator **4** (*intr*) (of disease germs) to remain inactive in an animal or human before causing disease

5 to develop or cause to develop gradually; foment or be fomented [C18: from Latin *incubāre* to lie upon, hatch, from IN-² + *cubāre* to lie down] > ˌincu'bation *n* > ˌincu'bational *adj* > 'incuˌbative or 'incuˌbatory *adj*

incubation period *n med* the time between exposure to an infectious disease and the appearance of the first signs or symptoms

incubator ('ɪnkjʊˌbeɪtə) *n* **1** *med* an enclosed transparent boxlike apparatus for housing prematurely born babies under optimum conditions until they are strong enough to survive in the normal environment **2** a container kept at a constant temperature in which birds' eggs can be artificially hatched or bacterial cultures grown **3** a person, animal, or thing that incubates

incubus ('ɪnkjʊbəs) *n*, *pl* -bi (-ˌbaɪ) or -buses **1** a demon believed in folklore to lie upon sleeping persons, esp to have sexual intercourse with sleeping women. See **succubus 2** something that oppresses, worries, or disturbs greatly, esp a nightmare or obsession [C14: from Late Latin, from *incubāre* to lie upon; see INCUBATE]

inculcate ('ɪnkʌlˌkeɪt, ɪn'kʌlkeɪt) *vb* (*tr*) to instil by forceful or insistent repetition [C16: from Latin *inculcāre* to tread down, ram down, from IN-² + *calcāre* to trample, from *calx* heel] > ˌincul'cation *n* > 'inculˌcator *n*

inculpate ('ɪnkʌlˌpeɪt, ɪn'kʌlpeɪt) *vb* (*tr*) to incriminate; cause blame to be imputed to [C18: from Late Latin *inculpāre*, from Latin *culpāre* to blame, from *culpa* fault, blame] > ˌincul'pation *n* > inculpative (ɪn'kʌlpətɪv) or inculpatory (ɪn'kʌlpətərɪ, -trɪ) *adj*

incumbency (ɪn'kʌmbənsɪ) *n*, *pl* -cies **1** the state or quality of being incumbent **2** the office, duty, or tenure of an incumbent

incumbent (ɪn'kʌmbənt) *adj* **1** *formal* (often *postpositive* and foll by *on* or *upon* and an infinitive) morally binding or necessary; obligatory: *it is incumbent on me to attend* **2** (usually *postpositive* and foll by *on*) resting or lying (on) ▷ *n* **3** a person who holds an office, esp a clergyman holding a benefice [C16: from Latin *incumbere* to lie upon, devote one's attention to, from IN-² + *-cumbere*, related to Latin *cubāre* to lie down]

incunabula (ˌɪnkjʊ'næbjʊlə) *pl n*, *sing* -lum (-ləm) **1** any book printed before 1501 **2** the infancy or earliest stages of something; beginnings [C19: from Latin, originally: swaddling clothes, hence beginnings, from IN-² + *cūnābula* cradle] > ˌincu'nabular *adj*

incur (ɪn'kɜː) *vb* -curs, -curring, -curred (*tr*) **1** to make oneself subject to (something undesirable); bring upon oneself **2** to run into or encounter [C16: from Latin *incurrere* to run into, from *currere* to run] > in'currable *adj*

incurable (ɪn'kjʊərəb³l) *adj* **1** (esp of a disease) not curable; unresponsive to treatment ▷ *n* **2** a person having an incurable disease > inˌcura'bility or in'curableness *n* > in'curably *adv*

incurious (ɪn'kjʊərɪəs) *adj* not curious; indifferent or uninterested > incuriosity (ɪnˌkjʊərɪ'ɒsɪtɪ) or in'curiousness *n* > in'curiously *adv*

incursion (ɪn'kɜːʃən) *n* **1** a sudden invasion, attack, or raid **2** the act of running or leaking into; penetration [C15: from Latin *incursiō* onset, attack, from *incurrere* to run into; see INCUR] > in'cursive (ɪn'kɜːsɪv) *adj*

incus ('ɪŋkəs) *n*, *pl* incudes (ɪn'kjuːdiːz) the central of the three small bones in the middle ear of mammals. See **malleus**, **stapes** [C17: from Latin: anvil, from *incūdere* to forge]

incuse (ɪn'kjuːz) *n* **1** a design stamped or hammered onto a coin ▷ *vb* **2** to impress (a design) in a coin or to impress (a coin) with a design by hammering or stamping ▷ *adj* **3** stamped or hammered onto a coin [C19: from Latin *incūsus* hammered; see INCUS]

Ind (ɪnd) *n* **1** a poetic name for **India 2** an obsolete name for the **Indies**

Ind. *abbreviation* **1** Independent **2** India **3** Indian

Indaba (ɪn'dɑːbə) *n* **1** *anthropol, history* (among Bantu peoples of southern Africa) a meeting to discuss a serious topic **2** *South African informal* a matter of concern or for discussion [C19: from Zulu: topic]

indebted (ɪn'dɛtɪd) *adj* (*postpositive*) **1** owing gratitude for help, favours, etc; obligated **2** owing money

indebtedness (ɪnˈdɛtɪdnɪs) n 1 the state of being indebted 2 the total of a person's debts

indecency (ɪnˈdiːsənsɪ) n, pl -cies 1 the state or quality of being indecent 2 an indecent act, etc

indecent (ɪnˈdiːsənt) adj 1 offensive to standards of decency, esp in sexual matters 2 unseemly or improper (esp in the phrase **indecent haste**) > inˈdecently adv

indecent assault n the act of taking indecent liberties with a person without his or her consent

indecent exposure n the offence of indecently exposing parts of one's body in public, esp the genitals

indecisive (ˌɪndɪˈsaɪsɪv) adj 1 (of a person) vacillating; irresolute 2 not decisive or conclusive > ˌindeˈcision or ˌindeˈcisiveness n > ˌindeˈcisively adv

indecorous (ɪnˈdɛkərəs) adj improper or ungraceful; unseemly > inˈdecorously adv

indecorum (ˌɪndɪˈkɔːrəm) n indecorous behaviour or speech; unseemliness

indeed (ɪnˈdiːd) sentence connector 1 certainly; actually: *indeed, it may never happen* ▷ adv 2 (intensifier): *that is indeed amazing* 3 or rather; what is more: *a comfortable, indeed extremely wealthy family* ▷ interj 4 an expression of doubt, surprise, etc

indef. abbreviation indefinite

indefatigable (ˌɪndɪˈfætɪgəbəl) adj unable to be tired out; unflagging [c16: from Latin *indēfatigābilis*, from IN-¹ + *dēfatigāre*, from *fatīgāre* to tire] > ˌindeˌfatigaˈbility or ˌindeˈfatigableness n > ˌindeˈfatigably adv

indefeasible (ˌɪndɪˈfiːzəbəl) adj law not liable to be annulled or forfeited > ˌindeˌfeasiˈbility or ˌindeˈfeasibleness n > ˌindeˈfeasibly adv

indefensible (ˌɪndɪˈfɛnsəbəl) adj 1 not justifiable or excusable 2 capable of being disagreed with; untenable 3 incapable of defence against attack > ˌindeˌfensiˈbility or ˌindeˈfensibleness n > ˌindeˈfensibly adv

indefinite (ɪnˈdɛfɪnɪt) adj 1 not certain or determined; unsettled 2 without exact limits; indeterminate: *an indefinite number* 3 vague, evasive, or unclear > inˈdefiniteness n > inˈdefinitely adv

indefinite article n grammar a determiner that expresses nonspecificity of reference, such as *a*, *an*, or *some*

indehiscent (ˌɪndɪˈhɪsənt) adj (of fruits) not dehiscent; not opening to release seeds > ˌindeˈhiscence n

indelible (ɪnˈdɛlɪbəl) adj 1 incapable of being erased or obliterated 2 making indelible marks: *indelible ink* [c16: from Latin *indēlēbilis* indestructible, from IN-¹+ *dēlēre* to destroy] > inˌdeliˈbility or inˈdelibleness n > inˈdelibly adv

indelicate (ɪnˈdɛlɪkɪt) adj 1 coarse, crude, or rough 2 offensive, embarrassing, or tasteless > inˈdelicacy or inˈdelicateness n > inˈdelicately adv

indemnify (ɪnˈdɛmnɪˌfaɪ) vb -fies, -fying, -fied (tr) 1 to secure against future loss, damage, or liability; give security for; insure 2 to compensate for loss, injury, expense, etc; reimburse > inˌdemnifiˈcation n > inˈdemniˌfier n

indemnity (ɪnˈdɛmnɪtɪ) n, pl -ties 1 compensation for loss or damage; reimbursement 2 protection or insurance against future loss or damage 3 legal exemption from penalties or liabilities incurred through one's acts or defaults 4 (in Canada) the salary paid to a member of Parliament or of a legislature [c15: from Late Latin *indemnitās*, from *indemnis* uninjured, from Latin IN-¹ + *damnum* damage]

indene (ˈɪndiːn) n a colourless liquid hydrocarbon extracted from petroleum and coal tar and used in making synthetic resins. Formula: C_9H_8 [c20: from INDOLE + -ENE]

indent¹ vb (ɪnˈdɛnt) (mainly tr) 1 to place (written or printed matter, etc) in from the margin, as at the beginning of a paragraph 2 to cut or tear (a document, esp a contract or deed in duplicate) so that the irregular lines may be matched to confirm its authenticity 3 chiefly Brit (in foreign trade) to place an order for (foreign goods), usually through an agent 4 (when intr, foll by for, on, or upon) chiefly Brit to make an order on (a source or supply) or for (something) 5 to notch (an edge, border, etc); make jagged 6 to bind (an apprentice, etc) by indenture ▷ n (ˈɪndɛnt) 7 chiefly Brit (in foreign trade)

an order for foreign merchandise, esp one placed with an agent 8 chiefly Brit an official order for goods [c14: from Old French *endenter*, from EN-¹ + *dent* tooth, from Latin *dēns*] > inˈdenter or inˈdentor n

indent² vb (ɪnˈdɛnt) 1 (tr) to make a dent or depression in ▷ n (ˈɪndɛnt) 2 a dent or depression [c15: from IN-² + DENT¹]

indentation (ˌɪndɛnˈteɪʃən) n 1 a hollowed, notched, or cut place, as on an edge or on a coastline 2 a series of hollows, notches, or cuts 3 the act of indenting or the condition of being indented 4 Also called: indention, indent the leaving of space or the amount of space left between a margin and the start of an indented line

indention (ɪnˈdɛnʃən) n another word for **indentation** (sense 4)

indenture (ɪnˈdɛntʃə) n 1 any deed, contract, or sealed agreement between two or more parties 2 (formerly) a deed drawn up in duplicate, each part having correspondingly indented edges for identification and security 3 (often plural) a contract between an apprentice and his master 4 a less common word for **indentation** ▷ vb 5 (intr) to enter into an agreement by indenture 6 (tr) to bind (an apprentice, servant, etc) by indenture > inˈdenture,ship n

independence (ˌɪndɪˈpɛndəns) n the state or quality of being independent. Also called: independency

Independence (ˌɪndɪˈpɛndəns) n a city in W Missouri, near Kansas City: starting point for the Santa Fe, Oregon, and California Trails (1831–44). Pop: 112 079 (2003 est)

independency (ˌɪndɪˈpɛndənsɪ) n, pl -cies 1 a territory or state free from the control of any other power 2 another word for **independence**

independent (ˌɪndɪˈpɛndənt) adj 1 free from control in action, judgment, etc; autonomous 2 not dependent on anything else for function, validity, etc; separate: *two independent units make up this sofa* 3 not reliant on the support, esp financial support, of others 4 capable of acting for oneself or on one's own: *a very independent little girl* 5 providing a large unearned sum towards one's support (esp in the phrases **independent income, independent means**) 6 living on an unearned income 7 maths (of a system of equations) not linearly dependent. See also **independent variable** 8 statistics (of two or more variables) distributed so that the value taken by one variable will have no effect on that taken by another or others ▷ n 9 an independent person or thing 10 a person who is not affiliated to or who acts independently of a political party > ˌindeˈpendently adv

Independent (ˌɪndɪˈpɛndənt) n 1 (in England) a member of the Congregational Church ▷ adj 2 of or relating to Independency

independent clause n grammar a main or coordinate clause. See **dependent clause**

independent school n 1 (in Britain) a school that is neither financed nor controlled by the government or local authorities 2 (in Australia) a school that is not part of the state system

independent variable n Also called: argument a variable in a mathematical equation or statement whose value determines that of the dependent variable: in $y = f(x)$, x is the independent variable

in-depth adj carefully worked out, detailed and thorough: *an in-depth study*

indescribable (ˌɪndɪˈskraɪbəbəl) adj beyond description; too intense, extreme, etc, for words > ˌindeˌscribaˈbility or ˌindeˈscribableness n > ˌindeˈscribably adv

indestructible (ˌɪndɪˈstrʌktəbəl) adj incapable of being destroyed; very durable > ˌindeˌstructiˈbility or ˌindeˈstructibleness n > ˌindeˈstructibly adv

indeterminate (ˌɪndɪˈtɜːmɪnɪt) adj 1 uncertain in extent, amount, or nature 2 not definite; inconclusive: *an indeterminate reply* 3 unable to be predicted, calculated, or deduced 4 maths a having no numerical meaning, as 0.00 or 0/0 b (of an equation) having more than one variable and an unlimited number of solutions > ˌindeˈterminacy, ˌindeˌtermiˈnation or ˌindeˈterminateness n > ˌindeˈterminately adv

indeterminism (ˌɪndɪˈtɜːmɪˌnɪzəm) n the philosophical

doctrine that behaviour is not entirely determined by motives > ˌindeˈterminist n, adj > ˌindeˌterminˈistic adj

index (ˈɪndɛks) n, pl **-dexes** or **-dices** (-dɪˌsiːz) **1** an alphabetical list of persons, places, subjects, etc, mentioned in the text of a printed work, usually at the back, and indicating where in the work they are referred to **2** See **thumb index 3** library science a systematic list of book titles or author's names, giving cross-references and the location of each book; catalogue **4** an indication, sign, or token **5** a pointer, needle, or other indicator, as on an instrument **6** maths **a** another name for **exponent** (sense 4) **b** a number or variable placed as a superscript to the left of a radical sign indicating by its value the root to be extracted, as in $^3\sqrt{8} = 2$ **7** a numerical scale by means of which variables, such as levels of the cost of living, can be compared with each other or with some base number **8** a number or ratio indicating a specific characteristic, property, etc: refractive index **9** Also called: fist a printer's mark (☞) used to indicate notes, paragraphs, etc ▷ vb (tr) **10** to put an index in (a book) **11** to enter (a word, item, etc) in an index **12** to point out; indicate **13** to index-link **14** to move (a machine or a workpiece held in a machine tool) so that one particular operation will be repeated at certain defined intervals [C16: from Latin: pointer, hence forefinger, title, index, from indicāre to disclose, show; see INDICATE]

indexation (ˌɪndɛkˈseɪʃən) or **index-linking** n the act of making wages, interest rates, etc, index-linked

index case n med the first case of a disease, or the primary case referred to in a report

index finger n the finger next to the thumb. Also called: forefinger

index fossil n a fossil species that characterizes and is used to delimit a geological zone. Also called: zone fossil

index futures pl n a form of financial futures based on projected movement of a share price index, such as the Financial Times Stock Exchange 100 Share Index

indexical (ɪnˈdɛksɪkᵊl) adj **1** arranged as or relating to an index or indexes ▷ n **2** Also called: deictic logic, linguistics a term whose reference depends on the context of utterance, such as I, you, here, now, or tomorrow

Index Librorum Prohibitorum Latin (ˈɪndɛks laɪˈbrɔːrʊm prəʊˌhɪbɪˈtɔːrʊm) n RC Church (formerly) an official list of proscribed books [C17, literally: list of forbidden books]

index-linked adj (of wages, interest rates, etc) directly related to the cost-of-living index and rising or falling accordingly

index number n statistics a statistic indicating the relative change occurring in each successive period of time in the price, volume, or value of a commodity or in a general economic variable, such as the price level, national income, or gross output, with reference to a previous base period conventionally given the number 100

India (ˈɪndɪə) n **1** a republic in S Asia: history dates from the Indus Valley civilization (3rd millennium BC); came under British supremacy in 1763 and passed to the British Crown in 1858; nationalist movement arose under Gandhi (1869–1948); Indian subcontinent divided into Pakistan (Muslim) and India (Hindu) in 1947; became a republic within the Commonwealth in 1950. It consists chiefly of the Himalayas, rising over 7500 m (25 000 ft) in the extreme north, the Ganges plain in the north, the Thar Desert in the northwest, and the Chota Nagpur plateau in the northeast, and the Deccan Plateau in the south. Official and administrative languages: Hindi and English; each state has its own language. Parts of the SE coast suffered badly in the Indian Ocean tsunami of December 2004. Religion: Hindu majority, Muslim minority. Currency: rupee. Capital: New Delhi. Pop: 1 081 229 000 (2004 est). Area: 3 268 100 sq km (1 261 813 sq miles). Hindi name: Bharat **2** communications a code word for the letter i

Indiaman (ˈɪndɪəmən) n, pl **-men** (formerly) a large merchant ship engaged in trade with India

Indian (ˈɪndɪən) n **1** a native, citizen, or inhabitant of the Republic of India **2** old-fashioned, highly offensive a Native American **3** (not in scholarly usage) any of the languages of Native Americans ▷ adj **4** of, relating to, or characteristic of India, its inhabitants, or any of their languages **5** (Not in scholarly usage) of, relating to, or characteristic of Native Americans or any of their languages

Indianapolis (ˌɪndɪəˈnæpəlɪs) n a city in central Indiana: the state capital. Pop: 783 438 (2003 est)

Indian club n a bottle-shaped club, usually used in pairs by gymnasts, jugglers, etc

Indian corn n another name for **maize** (sense 1)

Indian Desert n another name for the **Thar Desert**

Indian Empire n British India and the Indian states under indirect British control, which gained independence as India and Pakistan in 1947

Indian file n another term for **single file**

Indian hemp n another name for hemp, esp the variety Cannabis indica, from which several narcotic drugs are obtained

Indian ink or esp US and Canadian **India ink** n **1** a black pigment made from a mixture of lampblack and a binding agent such as gelatine or glue: usually formed into solid cakes and sticks **2** a black liquid ink made from this pigment ▷ Also called: China ink, Chinese ink

Indian liquorice n a woody leguminous climbing plant, Abrus precatorius, native to tropical Asia and naturalized elsewhere, having scarlet black-spotted poisonous seeds, used as beads, and roots used as a substitute for liquorice. Also called: jequirity

Indian list n informal (in Canada) a list of persons to whom spirits may not be sold

Indian meal n another name for **corn meal**

Indian Ocean n an ocean bordered by Africa in the west, Asia in the north, and Australia in the east and merging with the Antarctic Ocean in the south. Average depth: 3900 m (13 000 ft). Greatest depth (off the Sunda Islands): 7450 m (24 442 ft). In December 2004 a major undersea earthquake off Sumatra triggered a tsunami which affected large areas of the ocean as far away as east Africa, and killed an estimated 226 435 people. Area: about 73 556 000 sq km (28 400 000 sq miles)

Indian rice n **1** an annual erect aquatic North American grass, Zizania aquatica, with edible purplish-black grain **2** the grain of this plant ▷ Also called: wild rice

Indian rope-trick n the supposed Indian feat of climbing an unsupported rope

Indian States and Agencies pl n another name for the **Native States**

Indian summer n **1** a period of unusually settled warm weather after the end of summer proper **2** a period of ease and tranquillity or of renewed productivity towards the end of a person's life or of an epoch [originally US: probably so named because it was first noted in regions occupied by American Indians]

Indian Territory n the territory established in the early 19th century in present-day Oklahoma, where Indians were forced to settle by the US government. The last remnant was integrated into the new state of Oklahoma in 1907

Indian tobacco n a poisonous North American campanulaceous plant, Lobelia inflata, with small pale blue flowers and rounded inflated seed capsules

India paper n a thin soft opaque printing paper made in the Orient

India rubber n another name for **rubber¹** (sense 1)

Indic (ˈɪndɪk) adj **1** denoting, belonging to, or relating to a branch of Indo-European consisting of the Indo-European languages of India, including Sanskrit, Hindi and Urdu, Punjabi, Gujerati, Bengali, and Sinhalese ▷ n **2** this group of languages ▷ Also called: Indo-Aryan

indicate (ˈɪndɪˌkeɪt) vb (tr) **1** (may take a clause as object) to be or give a sign or symptom of; imply: cold hands indicate a warm heart **2** to point out or show **3** (may take a clause as object) to state briefly; suggest **4** (of instruments) to show a reading of **5** (usually passive) to recommend or require: surgery seems to be indicated for this patient [C17: from Latin indicāre to point out, from IN-² + dicāre to proclaim; compare INDEX] > ˈindiˌcatable adj > indicatory (ɪnˈdɪkətərɪ, -trɪ) adj

indication (ˌɪndɪˈkeɪʃən) n **1** something that serves to indicate or suggest; sign: an indication of foul play **2** the degree or quantity represented on a measuring instrument or device **3** the action of indicating **4** something that is indicated as advisable, necessary, or expedient

indicative (ɪnˈdɪkətɪv) *adj* **1** (*usually postpositive*; *foll by of*) serving as a sign; suggestive: *indicative of trouble ahead* **2** *grammar* denoting a mood of verbs used chiefly to make statements ▷ *n* **3** *grammar* **a** the indicative mood **b** a verb in the indicative mood > inˈdicatively *adv*

indicator (ˈɪndɪˌkeɪtə) *n* **1** something that provides an indication, esp of trends. See **economic indicator 2** a device to attract attention, such as the pointer of a gauge or a warning lamp **3** an instrument that displays certain operating conditions in a machine, such as a gauge showing temperature, speed, pressure, etc **4** a device that records or registers something, such as the movements of a lift, or that shows information, such as arrival and departure times of trains **5** Also called: blinker a device for indicating that a motor vehicle is about to turn left or right, esp two pairs of lights that flash when operated or a pair of trafficators **6** Also called: dial gauge a delicate measuring instrument used to determine small differences in the height of mechanical components. It consists of a spring-loaded plunger that operates a pointer moving over a circular scale **7** *chem* a substance used in titrations to indicate the completion of a chemical reaction, usually by a change of colour **8** Also called: indicator species *ecology* a plant or animal species that thrives only under particular environmental conditions and therefore indicates these conditions where it is found

indices (ˈɪndɪˌsiːz) *n* a plural of **index**

indicia (ɪnˈdɪʃɪə) *pl nor sing* -cium (-ʃɪəm) distinguishing markings or signs; indications [C17: from Latin, plural of *indicium* a notice, from INDEX] > inˈdicial *adj*

indict (ɪnˈdaɪt) *vb* (*tr*) to charge (a person) with crime, esp formally in writing; accuse [C14: alteration of *enditen* to INDITE] > ˌindictˈee *n* > inˈdicter *or* inˈdictor *n* > inˈdictable *adj*

● USAGE See at **indite**

indictment (ɪnˈdaɪtmənt) *n criminal law* **1** a formal written charge of crime formerly referred to and presented on oath by a grand jury **2** any formal accusation of crime **3** the act of indicting or the state of being indicted

indie (ˈɪndɪ) *n informal* **a** an independent film or record company **b** (*as modifier*): *an indie producer; the indie charts*

Indies (ˈɪndɪz) *the Indies n* **1** the territories of S and SE Asia included in the East Indies, India, and Indochina **2** See **East Indies 3** See **West Indies**

indifference (ɪnˈdɪfrəns, -fərəns) *n* **1** the fact or state of being indifferent; lack of care or concern **2** lack of quality; mediocrity **3** lack of importance; insignificance

indifferent (ɪnˈdɪfrənt, -fərənt) *adj* **1** (*often foll by to*) showing no care or concern; uninterested: *he was indifferent to my pleas* **2** unimportant; immaterial **3 a** of only average or moderate size, extent, quality, etc **b** not at all good; poor **4** showing or having no preferences; impartial [C14: from Latin *indifferēns* making no distinction] > inˈdifferently *adv*

indifferentism (ɪnˈdɪfrənˌtɪzəm, -fərən-) *n* systematic indifference, esp in matters of religion > inˈdifferentist *n*

indigenous (ɪnˈdɪdʒɪnəs) *adj* (*when postpositive, foll by to*) **1** originating or occurring naturally (in a country, region, etc); native **2** innate to (in) [C17: from Latin *indigenus*, from *indigena* indigene, from *indi-* in + *gignere* to beget] > inˈdigenously *adv* > inˈdigenousness *or* indigenity (ˌɪndɪˈdʒɛnɪtɪ) *n*

indigent (ˈɪndɪdʒənt) *adj* **1** so poor as to lack even necessities; very needy **2** (*usually foll by of*) *archaic* lacking (in) or destitute (of) ▷ *n* **3** an impoverished person [C14: from Latin *indigēre* to need, from *egēre* to lack] > ˈindigence *n* > ˈindigently *adv*

indigestible (ˌɪndɪˈdʒɛstəbᵊl) *adj* **1** incapable of being digested or difficult to digest **2** difficult to understand or absorb mentally: *an indigestible book* > ˌindiˌgestiˈbility *or* ˌindiˈgestibleness *n* > ˌindiˈgestibly *adv*

indigestion (ˌɪndɪˈdʒɛstʃən) *n* difficulty in digesting food, accompanied by abdominal pain, heartburn, and belching. Technical name: **dyspepsia**

indignant (ɪnˈdɪɡnənt) *adj* feeling or showing indignation [C16: from Latin *indignārī* to be displeased with] > inˈdignantly *adv*

indignation (ˌɪndɪɡˈneɪʃən) *n* anger or scorn aroused by something felt to be unfair, unworthy, or wrong

indignity (ɪnˈdɪɡnɪtɪ) *n, pl* -ties injury to one's self-esteem or dignity; humiliation

indigo (ˈɪndɪˌɡəʊ) *n, pl* -gos *or* -goes **1** Also called: indigotin a blue vat dye originally obtained from plants but now made synthetically **2** any of various tropical plants of the leguminous genus *Indigofera*, such as the anil, that yield this dye **3 a** any of a group of colours that have the same blue-violet hue; a spectral colour **b** (*as adjective*): *an indigo carpet* [C16: from Spanish *indico*, via Latin from Greek *Indikos* of India] > indigotic (ˌɪndɪˈɡɒtɪk) *adj*

indigo blue *n, adj* (**indigo-blue** *when prenominal*) the full name for **indigo** (senses 1, 3)

indirect (ˌɪndɪˈrɛkt) *adj* **1** deviating from a direct course or line; roundabout; circuitous **2** not coming as a direct effect or consequence; secondary: *indirect benefits* **3** not straightforward, open, or fair; devious or evasive > ˌindiˈrectly *adv* > ˌindiˈrectness *n*

indirect costs *pl n* another name for **overheads**

indirection (ˌɪndɪˈrɛkʃən) *n* **1** indirect procedure, courses, or methods **2** lack of direction or purpose; aimlessness **3** indirect dealing; deceit

indirect lighting *n* reflected or diffused light from a concealed source

indirect object *n grammar* a noun, pronoun, or noun phrase indicating the recipient or beneficiary of the action of a verb and its direct object, as *John* in the sentence *I bought John a newspaper*

indirect proof *n logic, maths* proof of a conclusion by showing its negation to be self-contradictory; reductio ad absurdum. See **direct** (sense 17)

indirect question *n* a question reported in indirect speech, as in *She asked why you came*

indirect speech *or esp US* **indirect discourse** *n* the reporting of something said or written by conveying what was meant rather than repeating the exact words, as in the sentence *He asked me whether I would go* as opposed to *He asked me, "Will you go?"*. Also called: reported speech

indirect tax *n* a tax levied on goods or services rather than on individuals or companies

indiscreet (ˌɪndɪˈskriːt) *adj* not discreet; imprudent or tactless > ˌindisˈcreetly *adv* > ˌindisˈcreetness *n*

indiscrete (ˌɪndɪˈskriːt) *adj* not divisible or divided into parts

indiscretion (ˌɪndɪˈskrɛʃən) *n* **1** the characteristic or state of being indiscreet **2** an indiscreet act, remark, etc

indiscriminate (ˌɪndɪˈskrɪmɪnɪt) *adj* **1** lacking discrimination or careful choice; random or promiscuous **2** jumbled; confused > ˌindisˈcriminately *adv* > ˌindisˈcriminateness *n* > ˌindisˌcrimiˈnation *n*

indispensable (ˌɪndɪˈspɛnsəbᵊl) *adj* **1** absolutely necessary; essential **2** not to be disregarded or escaped: *an indispensable role* ▷ *n* **3** an indispensable person or thing > ˌindisˌpensaˈbility *or* ˌindisˈpensableness *n* > ˌindisˈpensably *adv*

indispose (ˌɪndɪˈspəʊz) *vb* (*tr*) **1** to make unwilling or opposed; disincline **2** to cause to feel ill **3** to make unfit (for something or to do something)

indisposed (ˌɪndɪˈspəʊzd) *adj* **1** sick or ill **2** unwilling [C15: from Latin *indispositus* disordered] > indisposition (ˌɪndɪspəˈzɪʃən) *n*

indisputable (ˌɪndɪˈspjuːtəbᵊl) *adj* beyond doubt; not open to question > ˌindisˌputaˈbility *or* ˌindisˈputableness *n* > ˌindisˈputably *adv*

indissoluble (ˌɪndɪˈsɒljʊbᵊl) *adj* incapable of being dissolved or broken; permanent > ˌindisˈsolubly *adv*

indistinct (ˌɪndɪˈstɪŋkt) *adj* incapable of being clearly distinguished, as by the eyes, ears, or mind; not distinct > ˌindisˈtinctly *adv* > ˌindisˈtinctness *n*

indistinguishable (ˌɪndɪˈstɪŋɡwɪʃəbᵊl) *adj* **1** (*often postpositive*; *foll by from*) identical or very similar (to): *twins indistinguishable from one another* **2** not easily perceptible;

indiscernible > ,indis,tinguisha'bility or
,indis'tinguishableness n > ,indis'tinguishably adv

indite (ɪn'daɪt) vb (tr) archaic to write [c14: from Old French enditer, from Latin indīcere to declare, from IN-² + dīcere to say] > in'ditement n > in'diter n

• **USAGE** Indite and inditement are sometimes wrongly
• used where indict and indictment are meant: he was
• indicted (not indited) for fraud

indium ('ɪndɪəm) n a rare soft silvery metallic element associated with zinc ores: used in alloys, electronics, and electroplating. Symbol: In; atomic no: 49; atomic wt: 114.82; valency: 1, 2, or 3; relative density: 7.31; melting pt: 156.63°C; boiling pt: 2073°C [c19: New Latin, from INDIGO + -IUM]

individual (,ɪndɪ'vɪdjʊəl) adj 1 of, relating to, characteristic of, or meant for a single person or thing 2 separate or distinct, esp from others of its kind; particular: please mark the individual pages 3 characterized by unusual and striking qualities; distinctive 4 obsolete indivisible; inseparable ▷ n 5 a single person, esp when regarded as distinct from others 6 biology a single animal or plant, esp as distinct from a species [c15: from Medieval Latin indivīduālis, from Latin indīviduusindivisible, from IN-¹ + dīviduus divisible, from dīvidere to DIVIDE] > ,indi'vidually adv

individualism (,ɪndɪ'vɪdjʊə,lɪzəm) n 1 the action or principle of asserting one's independence and individuality; egoism 2 an individual quirk or peculiarity 3 another word for **laissez faire** (sense 1) 4 philosophy the doctrine that only individual things exist and that therefore classes or properties have no reality > ,indi'vidualist n

individuality (,ɪndɪ,vɪdjʊ'ælɪtɪ) n, pl -ties 1 distinctive or unique character or personality: a work of great individuality 2 the qualities that distinguish one person or thing from another; identity 3 the state or quality of being a separate entity; discreteness

individualize or **individualise** (,ɪndɪ'vɪdjʊə,laɪz) vb (tr) 1 to make or mark as individual or distinctive in character 2 to consider or treat individually; particularize 3 to make or modify so as to meet the special requirements of a person > ,indi,viduali'zation or ,indi,viduali'sation n > ,indi'vidual,izer or ,indi'vidual,iser n

individuate (,ɪndɪ'vɪdjʊ,eɪt) vb (tr) 1 to give individuality or an individual form to 2 to distinguish from others of the same species or group; individualize > ,indi'vidu,ator n

indivisible (,ɪndɪ'vɪzəb³l) adj 1 unable to be divided 2 maths leaving a remainder when divided by a given number > ,indi,visi'bility or ,indi'visibleness n > ,indi'visibly adv

Indo- ('ɪndəʊ-) combining form denoting India or Indian: Indo-European

Indo-Canadian n 1 a Canadian of Indian descent ▷ adj 2 of or relating to Canadians of Indian descent

Indo-Caribbean n, adj another word for **East Indian**

Indochina or **Indo-China** ('ɪndəʊ'tʃaɪnə) n 1 Also called: Farther India a peninsula in SE Asia, between India and China: consists of Myanmar, Thailand, Laos, Cambodia, Vietnam, and Malaysia 2 the former French colonial possessions of Cochin China, Annam, Tonkin, Laos, and Cambodia

indoctrinate (ɪn'dɒktrɪ,neɪt) vb (tr) 1 to teach (a person or group of people) systematically to accept doctrines, esp uncritically 2 rare to impart learning to; instruct > in,doctri'nation n > in'doctri,nator n

Indo-European adj 1 denoting, belonging to, or relating to a family of languages that includes English and many other culturally and politically important languages of the world: a characteristic feature, esp of the older languages such as Latin, Greek, and Sanskrit, is inflection showing gender, number, and case 2 denoting or relating to the hypothetical parent language of this family, primitive Indo-European 3 denoting, belonging to, or relating to any of the peoples speaking these languages ▷ n 4 the Indo-European family of languages 5 Also called: primitive Indo-European, Proto-Indo-European the reconstructed hypothetical parent language of this family

Indo-Iranian adj 1 of or relating to the Indic and Iranian branches of the Indo-European family of languages ▷ n 2 this group of languages, sometimes considered as forming a single branch of Indo-European

indole ('ɪndəʊl) or **indol** ('ɪndəʊl, -dɒl) n a white or yellowish crystalline heterocyclic compound extracted from coal tar and used in perfumery, medicine, and as a flavouring agent; 1-benzopyrrole. Formula: C_8H_7N [c19: from IND(IGO) + -OLE¹]

indolent ('ɪndələnt) adj 1 disliking work or effort; lazy; idle 2 pathol causing little pain: an indolent tumour 3 (esp of a painless ulcer) slow to heal [c17: from Latin indolēns not feeling pain, from IN-¹ + dolēns, from dolēre to grieve, cause distress] > 'indolence n > 'indolently adv

indomitable (ɪn'dɒmɪtəb³l) adj (of courage, pride, etc) difficult or impossible to defeat or subdue [c17: from Late Latin indomitābilis, from Latin indomitus untamable, from IN-¹ + domitus subdued, from domāre to tame] > in,domita'bility or in'domitableness n > in'domitably adv

Indonesia (,ɪndəʊ'niːzɪə) n a republic in SE Asia, in the Malay Archipelago, consisting of the main islands of Sumatra, Java and Madura, Bali, Sulawesi (Celebes), Lombok, Sumbawa, Flores, the Moluccas, part of Timor, part of Borneo (Kalimantan), Papua (formerly Irian Jaya), and over 3000 small islands in the Indian and Pacific Oceans: became the Dutch East Indies in 1798; declared independence in 1945; became a republic in 1950; East Timor (illegally annexed in 1975) became independent in 2002. Parts of Sumatra suffered badly in the Indian Ocean tsunami of December 2004. Official language: Bahasa Indonesia. Religion: Muslim majority. Currency: rupiah. Capital: Jakarta. Pop: 222 611 000 (2004 est). Area: 1 919 317 sq km (741 052 sq miles). Former names (1798–1945): Dutch East Indies, Netherlands East Indies

Indonesian (,ɪndəʊ'niːzɪən) adj 1 of or relating to Indonesia, its people, or their language ▷ n 2 a native or inhabitant of Indonesia

indoor ('ɪn,dɔː) adj (prenominal) of, situated in, or appropriate to the inside of a house or other building: an indoor tennis court; indoor amusements

indoors (,ɪn'dɔːz) adv, adj (postpositive) inside or into a house or other building

Indo-Pak adj of or relating to India and Pakistan: the future of Indo-Pak relations

Indore (ɪn'dɔː) n 1 a city in central India, in W Madhya Pradesh. Pop: 1 597 441 (2001) 2 a former state of central India: became part of Madhya Bharat in 1948, which in turn became part of Madhya Pradesh in 1956

indorse (ɪn'dɔːs) vb a variant spelling of **endorse**

Indra ('ɪndrə) n Hinduism the most celebrated god of the Rig-Veda, governing the weather and dispensing rain

indraught or US **indraft** ('ɪn,drɑːft) n 1 the act of drawing or pulling in 2 an inward flow, esp of air

indrawn (,ɪn'drɔːn) adj 1 drawn or pulled in 2 inward-looking or introspective

Indre (French ɛ̃drə) n a department of central France in the Centre region. Capital: Châteauroux. Pop: 230 954 (2003 est). Area: 6906 sq km (2693 sq miles)

Indre-et-Loire (French ɛ̃drelwar) n a department of W central France in the Centre region: contains many famous châteaux along the Loire. Capital: Tours. Pop: 563 062 (2003 est). Area: 6158 sq km (2402 sq miles)

indris ('ɪndrɪs) or **indri** ('ɪndrɪ) n, pl -dris 1 a large Madagascan arboreal lemuroid primate, Indri indri, with thick silky fur patterned in black, white, and fawn: family Indriidae 2 woolly indris a related nocturnal Madagascan animal, Avahi laniger, with thick grey-brown fur and a long tail [c19: from French: lemur, from Malagasy indry! look! mistaken for the animal's name]

indubitable (ɪn'djuːbɪtəb³l) adj incapable of being doubted; unquestionable [c18: from Latin indubitābilis, from IN-¹ + dubitāre to doubt] > in'dubitably adv

induce (ɪn'djuːs) vb (tr) 1 (often foll by an infinitive) to persuade or use influence on 2 to cause or bring about 3 med to initiate or hasten (labour), as by administering a drug to stimulate uterine contractions 4 logic obsolete to assert or establish (a general proposition, hypothesis, etc) by induction 5 to produce (an electromotive force or electrical current) by induction **6** to transmit (magnetism) by induction [C14: from Latin *indūcere* to lead in, from *dūcere* to lead] > in'ducer *n* > in'ducible *adj*

inducement (ɪn'djuːsmənt) *n* **1** the act of inducing **2** a means of inducing; persuasion; incentive **3** *law* (in pleading) the introductory part that leads up to and explains the matter in dispute

induct (ɪn'dʌkt) *vb* (*tr*) **1** to bring in formally or install in an office, place, etc; invest **2** (foll by *to* or *into*) to initiate in knowledge (of) **3** *US* to enlist for military service; conscript **4** *physics* another word for **induce** (senses 5, 6) [C14: from Latin *inductus* led in, past participle of *indūcere* to introduce; see INDUCE]

inductance (ɪn'dʌktəns) *n* Also called: induction the property of an electric circuit as a result of which an electromotive force is created by a change of current in the same circuit (self-inductance) or in a neighbouring circuit (mutual inductance). It is usually measured in henries

induction (ɪn'dʌkʃən) *n* **1** the act of inducting or state of being inducted **2** the act of inducing **3** (in an internal-combustion engine) the part of the action of a piston by which mixed air and fuel are drawn from the carburettor to the cylinder **4** *logic* **a** a process of reasoning, used esp in science, by which a general conclusion is drawn from a set of premises, based mainly on experience or experimental evidence. The conclusion goes beyond the information contained in the premises, and does not follow necessarily from them. Thus an inductive argument may be highly probable, yet lead from true premises to a false conclusion **b** a conclusion reached by this process of reasoning **5** the process by which electrical or magnetic properties are transferred, without physical contact, from one circuit or body to another. See also **inductance 6** *maths, logic* a method of proving a proposition that all integers have a property, by first proving that 1 has the property and then that if the integer *n* has it so has $n + 1$ **7 a** a formal introduction or entry into an office or position **b** (*as modifier*): *induction course; induction period* **8** *US* the formal enlistment of a civilian into military service > in'ductional *adj*

induction coil *n* a transformer for producing a high voltage from a low voltage. It consists of a cylindrical primary winding of few turns, a concentric secondary winding of many turns, and often a common soft-iron core. Sometimes shortened to: coil

induction heating *n* the heating of a conducting material as a result of the electric currents induced in it by an externally applied alternating magnetic field

induction loop system *n* a system enabling partially deaf people to hear dialogue and sound in theatres, cinemas, etc, consisting of a loop of wire placed round the perimeter of a designated area. This emits an electromagnetic signal which is picked up by a hearing aid

induction motor *n* a type of brushless electric motor in which an alternating supply fed to the windings of the stator creates a magnetic field that induces a current in the windings of the rotor. Rotation of the rotor results from the interaction of the magnetic field created by the rotor current with the field of the stator

inductive (ɪn'dʌktɪv) *adj* **1** relating to, involving, or operated by electrical or magnetic induction: *an inductive reactance* **2** *logic, maths* of, relating to, or using induction: *inductive reasoning* **3** serving to induce or cause > in'ductively *adv* > in'ductiveness *n*

inductor (ɪn'dʌktə) *n* **1** a person or thing that inducts **2** a component, such as a coil, in an electrical circuit the main function of which is to produce inductance

indue (ɪn'djuː) *vb* **-dues, -duing, -dued** a variant spelling of **endue**

indulge (ɪn'dʌldʒ) *vb* **1** (when *intr*, often foll by *in*) to yield to or gratify (a whim or desire for): *to indulge a desire for new clothes; to indulge in new clothes* **2** (*tr*) to yield to the wishes of; pamper: *to indulge a child* **3** (*tr*) to allow oneself the pleasure of something: *at Christmas he liked to indulge himself* **4** (*intr*) *informal* to take alcoholic drink, esp to excess [C17: from Latin *indulgēre* to concede, from -*dulgēre*,

probably related to Greek *dolikhos* long, Gothic *tulgus* firm] > in'dulger *n* > in'dulgingly *adv*

indulgence (ɪn'dʌldʒəns) *n* **1** the act of indulging or state of being indulgent **2** a pleasure, habit, etc, indulged in; extravagance **3** liberal or tolerant treatment **4** something granted as a favour or privilege **5** *RC Church* a remission of the temporal punishment for sin after its guilt has been forgiven **6** Also called: Declaration of Indulgence a royal grant during the reigns of Charles II and James II of England giving Nonconformists and Roman Catholics a measure of religious freedom

indulgent (ɪn'dʌldʒənt) *adj* showing or characterized by indulgence > in'dulgently *adv*

induna (ɪn'duːnə) *n* (in South Africa) a Black African overseer in a factory, mine, etc [C20: from Zulu *nduna* an official]

indurate *rare* ▷ *vb* ('ɪndjʊˌreɪt) **1** to make or become hard or callous **2** to make or become hardy ▷ *adj* ('ɪndjʊrɪt) **3** hardened, callous, or unfeeling [C16: from Latin *indūrāre* to make hard; see ENDURE] > ˌindu'ration *n* > 'induˌrative *adj*

Indus ('ɪndəs) *n* a river in S Asia, rising in SW Tibet in the Kailas Range of the Himalayas and flowing northwest through Kashmir, then southwest across Pakistan to the Arabian Sea: important throughout history, esp for the Indus Civilization (about 3000 to 1500 BC), and for irrigation. Length: about 2900 km (1800 miles)

indusium (ɪn'djuːzɪəm) *n, pl* **-sia** (-zɪə) **1** a membranous outgrowth on the undersurface of fern leaves that covers and protects the developing sporangia **2** an enveloping membrane, such as the amnion [C18: New Latin, from Latin: tunic, from *induere* to put on] > in'dusial *adj*

industrial (ɪn'dʌstrɪəl) *adj* **1** of, relating to, derived from, or characteristic of industry **2** employed in industry: *the industrial workforce* **3** relating to or concerned with workers in industry: *industrial conditions* **4** used in industry: *industrial chemicals* > in'dustrially *adv*

industrial action *n* *Brit* any action, such as a strike or go-slow, taken by employees in industry to protest against working conditions, redundancies, etc

industrial archaeology *n* the study of past industrial machines, works, etc

industrial design *n* the art or practice of designing any object for manufacture > industrial designer *n*

industrial diamond *n* a small often synthetic diamond, valueless as a gemstone, used in cutting tools, abrasives, etc

industrial disease *n* any disease to which workers in a particular industry are prone

industrial espionage *n* attempting to obtain trade secrets by dishonest means, as by telephone- or computer-tapping, infiltration of a competitor's workforce, etc

industrial estate *n* *Brit* another name for **trading estate**

industrialism (ɪn'dʌstrɪəˌlɪzəm) *n* an organization of society characterized by large-scale mechanized manufacturing industry rather than trade, farming, etc

industrialist (ɪn'dʌstrɪəlɪst) *n* a person who has a substantial interest in the ownership or control of industrial enterprise

industrialize *or* **industrialise** (ɪn'dʌstrɪəˌlaɪz) *vb* **1** (*tr*) to develop industry on an extensive scale in (a country, region, etc) **2** (*intr*) (of a country, region, etc) to undergo the development of industry on an extensive scale > inˌdustriali'zation *or* inˌdustriali'sation *n*

industrial medicine *n* the study and practice of the health care of employees of large organizations, including measures to prevent accidents, industrial diseases, and stress in the workforce and to monitor the health of executives

industrial relations *n* **1** (*functioning as plural*) those aspects of collective relations between management and workers' representatives which are normally covered by collective bargaining **2** (*functioning as singular*) the management of relations between the employers or managers of an enterprise and their employees

Industrial Revolution n the the transformation in the 18th and 19th centuries of first Britain and then other W European countries and the US into industrial nations

industrial tribunal n (in Northern Ireland and formerly elsewhere in the UK) a tribunal that rules on disputes between employers and employees regarding unfair dismissal, redundancy, etc

industrious (ɪn'dʌstrɪəs) adj hard-working, diligent, or assiduous > in'dustriously adv > in'dustriousness n

industry ('ɪndəstrɪ) n, pl -tries 1 organized economic activity concerned with manufacture, extraction and processing of raw materials, or construction 2 a branch of commercial enterprise concerned with the output of a specified product or service: the steel industry 3 a industrial ownership and management interests collectively, as contrasted with labour interests b manufacturing enterprise collectively, as opposed to agriculture 4 diligence; assiduity [c15: from Latin industria diligence, from industrius active, of uncertain origin]

indwell (ɪn'dwɛl) vb -dwells, -dwelling, -dwelt 1 (tr) (of a spirit, principle, etc) to inhabit; suffuse 2 (intr) to dwell; exist > in'dweller n

Indy (French ēdi) n See **d'Indy**

-ine¹ suffix forming adjectives 1 of, relating to, or belonging to: saturnine 2 consisting of or resembling: crystalline [from Latin -īnus, from Greek -inos]

-ine² suffix forming nouns 1 indicating a halogen: chlorine 2 indicating a nitrogenous organic compound, including amino acids, alkaloids, and certain other bases: alanine; nicotine; purine 3 Also used: -in indicating a chemical substance in certain nonsystematic names: glycerine 4 indicating a mixture of hydrocarbons: benzine 5 indicating a feminine form: heroine [via French from Latin -ina (from -inus) and Greek -inē]

Ine ('ɪnə, 'ɪnɪ) n died after 726, king of Wessex (688–726)

inebriate vb (ɪn'iːbrɪˌeɪt) (tr) 1 to make drunk; intoxicate 2 to arouse emotionally; make excited ▷ adj (ɪn'iːbrɪɪt) 3 a person who is drunk, esp habitually ▷ adj (ɪn'iːbrɪɪt) Also called: inebriated 4 drunk, esp habitually [c15: from Latin inēbriāre, from ɪN-² + ēbriāre to intoxicate, from ēbrius drunk] > in,ebri'ation n > inebriety (,ɪnɪ'braɪɪtɪ) n

inedible (ɪn'ɛdɪbəl) adj not fit to be eaten; uneatable > in,edi'bility n

ineducable (ɪn'ɛdjʊkəbəl) adj incapable of being educated, esp on account of mental retardation > in,educa'bility n

ineffable (ɪn'ɛfəbəl) adj 1 too great or intense to be expressed in words; unutterable 2 too sacred to be uttered 3 indescribable; indefinable [c15: from Latin ineffābilis unutterable, from ɪN-¹ + effābilis, from effārī to utter, from fārī to speak] > in,effa'bility or in'effableness n > in'effably adv

ineffective (,ɪnɪ'fɛktɪv) adj 1 having no effect 2 incompetent or inefficient > ,ineffectively adv > ,ineffectiveness n

ineffectual (,ɪnɪ'fɛktʃʊəl) adj 1 having no effect or an inadequate effect 2 lacking in power or forcefulness; impotent: an ineffectual ruler > ,inef,fectu'ality or ,ineffectualness n > ,ineffectually adv

inefficacious (,ɪnɛfɪ'keɪʃəs) adj failing to produce the desired effect > ,ineffi'caciously adv > inefficacy (ɪn'ɛfɪkəsɪ) ,ineffi'caciousness or inefficacity (,ɪnɛfɪ'kæsɪtɪ) n

inefficient (,ɪnɪ'fɪʃənt) adj 1 unable to perform a task or function to the best advantage; wasteful or incompetent 2 unable to produce the desired result > ,inefficiency n > ,inefficiently adv

ineligible (ɪn'ɛlɪdʒəbəl) adj 1 (often foll by for or an infinitive) not fit or qualified: ineligible for a grant; ineligible to vote ▷ n 2 an ineligible person > in,eligi'bility or in'eligibleness n > in'eligibly adv

ineluctable (,ɪnɪ'lʌktəbəl) adj (esp of fate) incapable of being avoided; inescapable [c17: from Latin inēluctābilis, from ɪN-¹ + ēluctārī to escape, from luctārī to struggle] > ,ine,lucta'bility n > ,ine'luctably adv

inept (ɪn'ɛpt) adj 1 awkward, clumsy, or incompetent 2 not suitable, appropriate, or fitting; out of place [c17: from Latin ineptus, from ɪN-¹ + aptus fitting, suitable]

> in'epti,tude n > in'eptly adv > in'eptness n

inequable (ɪn'ɛkwəbəl) adj 1 uneven 2 not uniform 3 changeable

inequality (,ɪnɪ'kwɒlɪtɪ) n, pl -ties 1 the state or quality of being unequal; disparity 2 an instance of disparity 3 lack of smoothness or regularity 4 social or economic disparity 5 maths a a statement indicating that the value of one quantity or expression is not equal to another, as in x ≠ y b a relationship between real numbers involving inequality: x may be greater than y, denoted by x > y, or less than y, denoted by x < y 6 astronomy a departure from uniform orbital motion

inert (ɪn'ɜːt) adj 1 having no inherent ability to move or to resist motion 2 inactive, lazy, or sluggish 3 having only a limited ability to react chemically; unreactive [c17: from Latin iners unskilled, from ɪN-¹ + ars skill; see ART¹] > in'ertly adv > in'ertness n

inert gas n 1 Also called: noble gas, rare gas, argonon any of the unreactive gaseous elements helium, neon, argon, krypton, xenon, and radon 2 (loosely) any gas, such as carbon dioxide, that is nonoxidizing

inertia (ɪn'ɜːʃə, -ʃɪə) n 1 the state of being inert; disinclination to move or act 2 physics a the tendency of a body to preserve its state of rest or uniform motion unless acted upon by an external force b an analogous property of other physical quantities that resist change: thermal inertia > in'ertial adj

inertial guidance or **inertial navigation** n a method of controlling the flight path of a missile by instruments contained within it. Velocities or distances covered, computed from the acceleration measured by these instruments, are compared with stored data and used to control the speed and direction of the missile

inertial mass n the mass of a body as determined by its momentum, as opposed to gravitational mass. The acceleration of a falling body is inversely proportional to its inertial mass but directly proportional to its gravitational mass: as all falling bodies have the same constant acceleration the two types of mass must be equal. See **gravitational mass**

inertia-reel seat belt n a type of car seat belt in which the belt is free to unwind from a metal drum except when the drum locks as a result of rapid deceleration

inertia selling n (in Britain) the illegal practice of sending unrequested goods to householders followed by a bill for the price of the goods if they do not return them

inescapable (,ɪnɪ'skeɪpəbəl) adj incapable of being escaped or avoided > ,ines'capably adv

inestimable (ɪn'ɛstɪməbəl) adj 1 not able to be estimated; immeasurable 2 of immeasurable value > in,estima'bility or in'estimableness n > in'estimably adv

inevitable (ɪn'ɛvɪtəbəl) adj 1 unavoidable 2 sure to happen; certain ▷ n 3 the inevitable something that is unavoidable [c15: from Latin inēvītābilis, from ɪN-¹ + ēvītābilis, from ēvītāre to shun, from vītāre to avoid] > in,evita'bility or in'evitableness n > in'evitably adv

inexcusable (,ɪnɪk'skjuːzəbəl) adj not able to be excused or justified > ,inex,cusa'bility or ,inex'cusableness n > ,inex'cusably adv

inexhaustible (,ɪnɪg'zɔːstəbəl) adj 1 incapable of being used up; endless 2 incapable or apparently incapable of becoming tired; tireless > ,inex,hausti'bility or ,inex'haustibleness n > ,inex'haustibly adv

inexorable (ɪn'ɛksərəbəl) adj 1 not able to be moved by entreaty or persuasion 2 relentless [c16: from Latin inexōrābilis, from ɪN-¹ + exōrābilis, from exōrāre to prevail upon, from ōrāre to pray] > in,exora'bility or in'exorableness n > in'exorably adv

inexpensive (,ɪnɪk'spɛnsɪv) adj not expensive; cheap > ,inex'pensively adv > ,inex'pensiveness n

inexperience (,ɪnɪk'spɪərɪəns) n lack of experience or of the knowledge and understanding derived from experience > ,inex'perienced adj

inexpiable (ɪn'ɛkspɪəbəl) adj 1 incapable of being expiated; unpardonable 2 archaic implacable > in'expiableness n

inexplicable (,ɪnɪk'splɪkəbəl, ɪn'ɛksplɪkəbəl) or **inexplainable** adj not capable of explanation;

unexplainable ▷ ,inexplica'bility, ,inex'plicableness,
,inex,plaina'bility *or* ,inex'plainableness *n* ▷ ,inex'plicably,
,inex'plainably *adv*

in extenso *Latin* (ɪn ɪk'stɛnsəʊ) *adv* at full length

in extremis *Latin* (ɪn ɪk'striːmɪs) *adv* **1** in extremity; in
dire straits **2** at the point of death [literally: in the
furthest reaches]

inextricable (,ɪnɛks'trɪkəb°l) *adj* **1** not able to be escaped
from: *an inextricable dilemma* **2** not able to be disentangled,
etc: *an inextricable knot* **3** extremely involved or intricate
▷ ,inextrica'bility *or* ,inex'tricableness *n*
▷ ,inex'tricably *adv*

inf *abbreviation* **1** infinitive **2** informal [Latin: below;
after; later]

infallible (ɪn'fæləb°l) *adj* **1** not fallible; not liable to error
2 not liable to failure; certain; sure: *an infallible cure* ▷ *n*
3 a person or thing that is incapable of error or failure
▷ in,falli'bility *or* in'fallibleness *n* ▷ in'fallibly *adv*

infamous ('ɪnfəməs) *adj* **1** having a bad reputation;
notorious **2** causing or deserving a bad reputation;
shocking: *infamous conduct* ▷ 'infamously *adv*
▷ 'infamousness *n*

infamy ('ɪnfəmɪ) *n, pl* -mies **1** the state or condition of
being infamous **2** an infamous act or event [c15: from
Latin *infāmis* of evil repute, from IN-¹ + *fāma* FAME]

infancy ('ɪnfənsɪ) *n, pl* -cies **1** the state or period of being
an infant; childhood **2** an early stage of growth or
development **3** infants collectively **4** the period of life
prior to attaining legal majority (reached at 21 under
common law, at 18 by statute); minority nonage

infant ('ɪnfənt) *n* **1** a child at the earliest stage of its life;
baby **2** *law* another word for **minor** (sense 9) **3** *Brit* a
young schoolchild, usually under the age of seven **4** a
person who is beginning or inexperienced in an activity
5 (*modifier*) **a** of or relating to young children or infancy
b designed or intended for young children ▷ *adj* **6** in an
early stage of development; nascent: *an infant science or
industry* **7** *law* of or relating to the legal status of infancy
[c14: from Latin *infāns*, literally: speechless, from IN-¹ +
fārī to speak] ▷ 'infant,hood *n*

infanta (ɪn'fæntə) *n* **1** a daughter of a king of Spain or
(formerly) Portugal **2** (formerly) the wife of an infante
[c17: from Spanish or Portuguese, feminine of INFANTE]

infante (ɪn'fæntɪ) *n* (formerly) a son of a king of Spain
or Portugal, esp one not heir to the throne [c16: from
Spanish or Portuguese, literally: INFANT]

infanticide (ɪn'fæntɪ,saɪd) *n* **1** the killing of an infant
2 the practice of killing newborn infants, still prevalent
in some primitive tribes **3** a person who kills an infant
▷ in,fanti'cidal *adj*

infantile ('ɪnfən,taɪl) *adj* **1** like a child in action or
behaviour; childishly immature; puerile **2** of, relating
to, or characteristic of infants or infancy **3** in an early
stage of development ▷ infantility (,ɪnfən'tɪlɪtɪ) *n*

infantile paralysis *n* a former name for **poliomyelitis**

infantilism (ɪn'fæntɪ,lɪzəm) *n* **1** *psychol* a condition in
which an older child or adult is mentally or physically
undeveloped **2** childish speech; baby talk

infantry ('ɪnfəntrɪ) *n, pl* -tries **a** soldiers or units of
soldiers who fight on foot with small arms **b** (*as
modifier*): *an infantry unit* [c16: from Italian *infanteria*, from
infante boy, foot soldier; see INFANT]

infantryman ('ɪnfəntrɪmən) *n, pl* -men a soldier
belonging to the infantry

infant school *n* (in England and Wales) a school for
children aged between 5 and 7

infarct (ɪn'fɑːkt) *n* a localized area of dead tissue
(necrosis) resulting from obstruction of the blood supply
to that part, esp by an embolus. Also called: infarction
[c19: via New Latin from Latin *infarctus* stuffed into, from
farcīre to stuff] ▷ in'farcted *adj*

infatuate *vb* (ɪn'fætjʊ,eɪt) (*tr*) **1** to inspire or fill with
foolish, shallow, or extravagant passion **2** to cause to act
foolishly ▷ *n* (ɪn'fætjʊɪt, -,eɪt) **3** *literary* a person who is
infatuated [c16: from Latin *infatuāre*, from IN-² + *fatuus*
FATUOUS]

infatuated (ɪn'fætjʊ,eɪtɪd) *adj* (often foll by *with*)
possessed by a foolish or extravagant passion, esp for
another person

infatuation (ɪn,fætjʊ'eɪʃən) *n* **1** the act of infatuating or
state of being infatuated **2** foolish or extravagant
passion **3** an object of foolish or extravagant passion

infect (ɪn'fɛkt) *vb* (*mainly tr*) **1** to cause infection in;
contaminate (an organism, wound, etc) with
pathogenic microorganisms **2** (*also intr*) to affect or
become affected with a communicable disease **3** to
taint, pollute, or contaminate **4** to affect, esp adversely,
as if by contagion **5** *computing* to affect with a computer
virus ▷ *adj* **6** *archaic* contaminated or polluted with or as
if with a disease; infected [c14: from Latin *inficere* to dip
into, stain, from *facere* to make] ▷ in'fector *or* in'fecter *n*

infection (ɪn'fɛkʃən) *n* **1** invasion of the body by
pathogenic microorganisms **2** the resulting condition
in the tissues **3** an infectious disease **4** the act of
infecting or state of being infected **5** an agent or
influence that infects **6** persuasion or corruption, as by
ideas, perverse influences, etc

infectious (ɪn'fɛkʃəs) *adj* **1** (of a disease) capable of being
transmitted **2** (of a disease) caused by microorganisms,
such as bacteria, viruses, or protozoa **3** causing or
transmitting infection **4** tending or apt to spread, as
from one person to another: *infectious mirth* ▷ in'fectiously
adv ▷ in'fectiousness *n*

infectious hepatitis *n* any form of hepatitis caused by
viruses. See **hepatitis A, hepatitis B, hepatitis C**

infectious mononucleosis *n* an acute infectious
disease, caused by Epstein-Barr virus, characterized by
fever, sore throat, swollen and painful lymph nodes,
and abnormal lymphocytes in the blood. Also called:
glandular fever

infective (ɪn'fɛktɪv) *adj* **1** capable of causing infection
2 a less common word for **infectious** ▷ in'fectively *adv*
▷ in'fectiveness *or* ,infec'tivity *n*

infelicity (,ɪnfɪ'lɪsɪtɪ) *n, pl* -ties **1** the state or quality of
being unhappy or unfortunate **2** an instance of bad luck
or mischance; misfortune **3** something, esp a remark or
expression, that is inapt or inappropriate
▷ ,infe'licitous *adj*

infer (ɪn'fɜː) *vb* -fers, -ferring, -ferred (when *tr*, *may take a
clause as object*) **1** to conclude (a state of affairs,
supposition, etc) by reasoning from evidence; deduce
2 (*tr*) to have or lead to as a necessary or logical
consequence; indicate **3** (*tr*) to hint or imply [c16: from
Latin *inferre* to bring into, from *ferre* to bear, carry]
▷ in'ferable, in'ferible, in'ferrable *or* in'ferrible *adj*
▷ in'ferrer *n*

● **USAGE** The use of *infer* to mean *imply* is becoming more
● and more common in both speech and writing. There
● is nevertheless a useful distinction between the two
● which many people would be in favour of
● maintaining. To *infer* means 'to deduce', and is used in
● the construction *to infer something from something*: I
● *inferred from what she said that she had not been well.* To *imply*
● (sense 1) means 'to suggest, to insinuate' and is
● normally followed by a clause: *are you implying that I was
● responsible for the mistake?*

inference ('ɪnfərəns, -frəns) *n* **1** the act or process of
inferring **2** an inferred conclusion, deduction, etc **3** any
process of reasoning from premises to a conclusion
4 *logic* the specific mode of reasoning used

inferential (,ɪnfə'rɛnʃəl) *adj* of, relating to, or derived
from inference ▷ ,infer'entially *adv*

inferior (ɪn'fɪərɪə) *adj* **1** lower in value or quality **2** lower
in rank, position, or status; subordinate **3** not of the
best; mediocre; commonplace **4** lower in position;
situated beneath **5** (of a plant ovary) enclosed by and
fused with the receptacle so that it is situated below the
other floral parts **6** *astronomy* **a** orbiting or occurring
between the sun and the earth: *an inferior planet; inferior
conjunction* **b** lying below the horizon **7** *printing* (of a
character) printed at the foot of an ordinary character,
as the 2 in H_2O ▷ *n* **8** an inferior person **9** *printing* an
inferior character [c15: from Latin: lower, from *inferus*
low] ▷ inferiority (ɪn,fɪərɪ'ɒrɪtɪ) *n* ▷ in'feriorly *adv*

inferiority complex *n* *psychiatry* a disorder arising from
the conflict between the desire to be noticed and the
fear of being humiliated, characterized by
aggressiveness or withdrawal into oneself

infernal (ɪnˈfɜːnəl) *adj* **1** of or relating to an underworld of the dead **2** deserving hell or befitting its occupants; diabolic; fiendish **3** *informal* irritating; confounded [c14: from Late Latin *infernālis*, from *infernus* hell, from Latin (adj): lower, hellish; related to Latin *inferus* low]
> ˌinferˈnality *n* > inˈfernally *adv*

infernal machine *n archaic* a usually disguised explosive device or booby trap

inferno (ɪnˈfɜːnəʊ) *n*, *pl* **-nos 1** the (*sometimes capital*) hell; the infernal region **2** any place or state resembling hell, esp a conflagration [c19: from Italian, from Late Latin *infernus* hell]

infertile (ɪnˈfɜːtaɪl) *adj* **1** not capable of producing offspring; sterile **2** (of land) not productive; barren
> inˈfertilely *adv* > infertility (ˌɪnfəˈtɪlɪtɪ) *n*

infest (ɪnˈfɛst) *vb* (*tr*) **1** to inhabit or overrun in dangerously or unpleasantly large numbers **2** (of parasites such as lice) to invade and live on or in (a host) [c15: from Latin *infestāre* to molest, from *infestus* hostile]
> ˌinfesˈtation *n* > inˈfester *n*

infeudation (ˌɪnfjʊˈdeɪʃən) *n* **1** (in feudal society) the act of putting a vassal in possession of a fief **2** the granting of tithes to laymen

infidel (ˈɪnfɪdəl) *n* **1** a person who has no religious belief; unbeliever ▷ *adj* **2** rejecting a specific religion, esp Christianity or Islam **3** of, characteristic of, or relating to unbelievers or unbelief [c15: from Medieval Latin *infidēlis*, from Latin (adj): unfaithful, from ɪN⁻¹ + *fidēlis* faithful; see FEAL]

infidelity (ˌɪnfɪˈdɛlɪtɪ) *n*, *pl* **-ties 1** lack of faith or constancy, esp sexual faithfulness **2** lack of religious faith; disbelief **3** an act or instance of disloyalty

infield (ˈɪnˌfiːld) *n* **1** *cricket* the area of the field near the pitch. See **outfield 2** *baseball* the area of the playing field enclosed by the base lines and extending beyond them towards the outfield **3** *agriculture* the part of a farm nearest to the farm buildings > ˈinˌfielder *n*

infighting (ˈɪnˌfaɪtɪŋ) *n* **1** *boxing* combat at close quarters in which proper blows are inhibited and the fighters try to wear down each other's strength **2** intense competition, as between members of the same organization, esp when kept secret from outsiders
> ˈinˌfighter *n*

infill (ˈɪnfɪl) *or* **infilling** (ˈɪnfɪlɪŋ) *n* **1** the act of filling or closing gaps, etc, in something, such as a row of buildings **2** material used to fill a cavity, gap, hole, etc

infiltrate (ˈɪnfɪlˌtreɪt) *vb* **1** to undergo or cause to undergo the process in which a fluid passes into the pores or interstices of a solid; permeate **2** *military* to pass undetected through (an enemy-held line or position) **3** to gain or cause to gain entrance or access surreptitiously: *they infiltrated the party structure* ▷ *n* **4** something that infiltrates [c18: from ɪN⁻² + FILTRATE]
> ˌinfilˈtration *n* > ˈinfilˌtrative *adj* > ˈinfilˌtrator *n*

infin. *abbreviation* infinitive

infinite (ˈɪnfɪnɪt) *adj* **1 a** having no limits or boundaries in time, space, extent, or magnitude **b** (*as noun*; preceded by *the*): *the infinite* **2** extremely or immeasurably great or numerous: *infinite wealth* **3** all-embracing, absolute, or total: *God's infinite wisdom* **4** *maths* having an unlimited number of digits, factors, terms, members, etc
> ˈinfinitely *adv* > ˈinfiniteness *n*

infinitesimal (ˌɪnfɪnɪˈtɛsɪməl) *adj* **1** infinitely or immeasurably small **2** *maths* of, relating to, or involving a small change in the value of a variable that approaches zero as a limit ▷ *n* **3** *maths* an infinitesimal quantity > ˌinfiniˈtesimally *adv*

infinitesimal calculus *n* another name for **calculus** (sense 1)

infinitive (ɪnˈfɪnɪtɪv) *n grammar* a form of the verb not inflected for grammatical categories such as tense and person and used without an overt subject. In English, the infinitive usually consists of the word *to* followed by the verb > infinitival (ˌɪnfɪnɪˈtaɪvəl) *adj* > inˈfinitively *or* ˌinfiniˈtivally *adv*

infinitude (ɪnˈfɪnɪˌtjuːd) *n* **1** the state or quality of being infinite **2** an infinite extent, quantity, degree, etc

infinity (ɪnˈfɪnɪtɪ) *n*, *pl* **-ties 1** the state or quality of being infinite **2** endless time, space, or quantity **3** an infinitely or indefinitely great number or amount **4** *maths* the concept of a value greater than any finite numerical value

infirm (ɪnˈfɜːm) *adj* **1 a** weak in health or body, esp from old age **b** (*as collective noun*; preceded by *the*): *the infirm* **2** lacking moral certainty; indecisive or irresolute **3** not stable, sound, or secure: *an infirm structure; an infirm claim* **4** *law* (of a law, custom, etc) lacking legal force; invalid
> inˈfirmly *adv* > inˈfirmness *n*

infirmary (ɪnˈfɜːmərɪ) *n*, *pl* **-ries** a place for the treatment of the sick or injured; dispensary; hospital

infirmity (ɪnˈfɜːmɪtɪ) *n*, *pl* **-ties 1** the state or quality of being infirm **2** physical weakness or debility; frailty **3** a moral flaw or failing

infix *vb* (ɪnˈfɪks, ˈɪnˌfɪks) **1** (*tr*) to fix firmly in **2** (*tr*) to instil or inculcate **3** *grammar* to insert (an affix) or (of an affix) to be inserted into the middle of a word ▷ *n* (ˈɪnˌfɪks) **4** *grammar* an affix inserted into the middle of a word > ˌinfixˈation *or* infixion (ɪnˈfɪkʃən) *n*

in flagrante delicto (ɪn fləˈɡræntɪ dɪˈlɪktəʊ) *adv chiefly law* while committing the offence; red-handed. Also called: **flagrante delicto** [Latin, literally: with the crime still blazing]

inflame (ɪnˈfleɪm) *vb* **1** to arouse or become aroused to violent emotion **2** (*tr*) to increase or intensify; aggravate **3** to produce inflammation in (a tissue, organ, or part) or (of a tissue, etc) to become inflamed **4** to set or be set on fire; kindle **5** (*tr*) to cause to redden > inˈflamer *n*

inflammable (ɪnˈflæməbəl) *adj* **1** liable to catch fire; flammable **2** readily aroused to anger or passion ▷ *n* **3** something that is liable to catch fire > inˌflammaˈbility *or* inˈflammableness *n* > inˈflammably *adv*

● USAGE See at **flammable**

inflammation (ˌɪnfləˈmeɪʃən) *n* **1** the reaction of living tissue to injury or infection, characterized by heat, redness, swelling, and pain **2** the act of inflaming or the state of being inflamed

inflammatory (ɪnˈflæmətərɪ, -trɪ) *adj* **1** characterized by or caused by inflammation **2** tending to arouse violence, strong emotion, etc > inˈflammatorily *adv*

inflatable (ɪnˈfleɪtəbəl) *n* **1** any of various large air-filled objects made of strong plastic or rubber, used for children to play on at fairs, carnivals, etc ▷ *adj* **2** capable of being inflated

inflate (ɪnˈfleɪt) *vb* **1** to expand or cause to expand by filling with gas or air **2** (*tr*) to cause to increase excessively; puff up; swell: *to inflate one's opinion of oneself* **3** (*tr*) to cause inflation of (prices, money, etc) **4** (*tr*) to raise in spirits; elate **5** (*intr*) to undergo economic inflation [c16: from Latin *inflāre* to blow into, from *flāre* to blow] > inˈflatedly *adv* > inˈflatedness *n* > inˈflater *or* inˈflator *n*

inflation (ɪnˈfleɪʃən) *n* **1** the act of inflating or state of being inflated **2** *economics* a progressive increase in the general level of prices brought about by an expansion in demand or the money supply (**demand-pull inflation**) or by autonomous increases in costs (**cost-push inflation**). See **deflation 3** *informal* the rate of increase of prices > inˈflationary *adj*

inflationary spiral *n* the situation in which price and income increases may each induce further rises in the other

inflationary universe *n* a variation of the cosmological big-bang theory in which the early stage of the evolution of the universe is postulated to include a period of accelerated expansion

inflationism (ɪnˈfleɪʃəˌnɪzəm) *n* the advocacy or policy of inflation through expansion of the supply of money and credit > inˈflationist *n*, *adj*

inflect (ɪnˈflɛkt) *vb* **1** (*grammar*) to change (the form of a word) or (of a word) to change in form by inflection **2** (*tr*) to change (the voice) in tone or pitch; modulate **3** (*tr*) to cause to deviate from a straight or normal line or course; bend [c15: from Latin *inflectere* to curve round, alter, from *flectere* to bend] > inˈflectedness *n* > inˈflective *adj* > inˈflector *n*

inflection *or* **inflexion** (ɪnˈflɛkʃən) *n* **1** modulation of the voice **2** (*grammar*) a change in the form of a word, usually modification or affixation, signalling change in such grammatical functions as tense, voice, mood, person, gender, number, or case **3** an angle or bend **4** the act of inflecting or the state of being inflected **5** *maths* a change in curvature from concave to convex or vice versa ▷ in'flectional *or* in'flexional *adj* ▷ in'flectionally *or* in'flexionally *adv* ▷ in'flectionless *or* in'flexionless *adj*

inflexible (ɪn'flɛksəb³l) *adj* **1** not flexible; rigid; stiff **2** obstinate; unyielding **3** without variation; unalterable; fixed [c14: from Latin *inflexibilis*; see INFLECT] ▷ in,flexi'bility *or* in'flexibleness *n* ▷ in'flexibly *adv*

inflict (ɪn'flɪkt) *vb* (*tr*) **1** (often foll by *on or upon*) to impose (something unwelcome, such as pain, oneself, etc) **2** to deal out (blows, lashes, etc) [c16: from Latin *infligere* to strike (something) against, dash against, from *flīgere* to strike] ▷ in'flictable *adj* ▷ in'flicter *or* in'flictor *n* ▷ in'fliction *n*

in-flight *adj* provided during flight in an aircraft: *in-flight meals*

inflorescence (,ɪnflɔː'rɛsəns) *n* **1** the part of a plant that consists of the flower-bearing stalks **2** the arrangement of the flowers on the stalks **3** the process of flowering; blossoming [c16: from New Latin *inflōrēscentia*, from Late Latin *inflōrēscere* to blossom, from *flōrēscere* to bloom] ▷ ,inflo'rescent *adj*

inflow ('ɪn,fləʊ) *n* **1** something, such as a liquid or gas, that flows in **2** Also called: inflowing the act of flowing in; influx

influence ('ɪnfluəns) *n* **1** an effect of one person or thing on another **2** the power of a person or thing to have such an effect **3** power or sway resulting from ability, wealth, position, etc **4** a person or thing having influence **5** *astrology* an ethereal fluid or occult power regarded as emanating from the stars and affecting a person's actions, future, etc **6** under the influence *informal* drunk ▷ *vb* (*tr*) **7** to persuade or induce **8** to have an effect upon (actions, events, etc); affect [c14: from Medieval Latin *influentia* emanation of power from the stars, from Latin *influere* to flow into, from *fluere* to flow] ▷ 'influenceable *adj* ▷ 'influencer *n*

influent ('ɪnfluənt) *adj* Also: inflowing **1** flowing in ▷ *n* **2** something flowing in, esp a tributary **3** *ecology* an organism that has a major effect on the nature of its community

influential (,ɪnflu'ɛnʃəl) *adj* having or exerting influence ▷ ,influ'entially *adv*

influenza (,ɪnflu'ɛnzə) *n* a highly contagious and epidemic viral disease characterized by fever, prostration, muscular aches and pains, and inflammation of the respiratory passages [c18: from Italian, literally: INFLUENCE, hence, incursion, epidemic (first applied to influenza in 1743)] ▷ ,influ'enzal *adj*

influx ('ɪn,flʌks) *n* **1** the arrival or entry of many people or things **2** the act of flowing in; inflow **3** the mouth of a stream or river [c17: from Late Latin *influxus*, from *influere*; see INFLUENCE]

info ('ɪnfəʊ) *n informal* short for **information**

infold (ɪn'fəʊld) *vb* a variant spelling of **enfold**

inform (ɪn'fɔːm) *vb* **1** (*tr*; often foll by *of or about*) to give information to; tell **2** (*tr*; often foll by *of or about*) to make conversant (with) **3** (*intr*; often foll by *against or on*) to give information regarding criminals, as to the police, etc **4** to give form to **5** to impart some essential or formative characteristic to **6** (*tr*) to animate or inspire [c14: from Latin *informāre* to give form to, describe, from *formāre* to FORM] ▷ in'formable *adj*

informal (ɪn'fɔːməl) *adj* **1** not of a formal, official, or stiffly conventional nature **2** appropriate to everyday life or use **3** denoting or characterized by idiom, vocabulary, etc, appropriate to everyday conversational language rather than to formal written language **4** denoting a second-person pronoun in some languages used when the addressee is regarded as a friend or social inferior ▷ in'formally *adv*

informality (,ɪnfɔː'mælɪtɪ) *n, pl* -ties **1** the condition or quality of being informal **2** an informal act

informal settlement *n South African euphemistic* a squatter camp

informal vote *n Austral & NZ* an invalid vote or ballot

informant (ɪn'fɔːmənt) *n* a person who gives

information about a thing, a subject being studied, etc

informatics (,ɪnfə'mætɪks) *n* (*functioning as singular*) the science of the collection, evaluation, organization, and dissemination of information, often employing computers

information (,ɪnfə'meɪʃən) *n* **1** knowledge acquired through experience or study **2** knowledge of specific and timely events or situations; news **3** the act of informing or the condition of being informed **4 a** an office, agency, etc, providing information **b** (*as modifier*): *information service* **5** a charge or complaint made before justices of the peace, usually on oath, to institute summary criminal proceedings **6** *computing* **a** the meaning given to data by the way in which it is interpreted **b** another word for **data** (sense 2) ▷ ,infor'mational *adj*

information architecture *n computing* the practice of structuring information for particular purposes

information retrieval *n computing* the process of recovering specific information from stored data

information superhighway *n* **1** the concept of a worldwide network of computers capable of transferring all types of digital information at high speed **2** another name for the **internet** ▷ Also called: information highway

information technology *n* the technology of the production, storage, and communication of information using computers and microelectronics

information theory *n* a collection of mathematical theories, based on statistics, concerned with methods of coding, transmitting, storing, retrieving, and decoding information

information warfare *n* the use of electronic communications and the internet to disrupt a country's telecommunications, power supply, transport system, etc

informative (ɪn'fɔːmətɪv) *or* **informatory** *adj* providing information; instructive ▷ in'formatively *adv* ▷ in'formativeness *n*

informed (ɪn'fɔːmd) *adj* **1** having much knowledge or education; learned or cultured **2** based on information: *an informed judgment*

informer (ɪn'fɔːmə) *n* **1** a person who informs against someone, esp a criminal **2** a person who provides information

infotainment (,ɪnfəʊ'teɪnmənt) *n* (in television) the practice of presenting serious or instructive subjects in a style designed primarily to be entertaining [c20: from INFO + (ENTER)TAINMENT]

infra- *prefix* below; beneath; after: *infrasonic; infralapsarian* [from Latin *infrā*]

infract (ɪn'frækt) *vb* (*tr*) to violate or break (a law, an agreement, etc) [c18: from Latin *infractus* broken off, from *infringere*; see INFRINGE] ▷ in'fraction *n* ▷ in'fractor *n*

infra dig ('ɪnfrə 'dɪg) *adj* (*postpositive*) *informal* beneath one's dignity [c19: from Latin phrase *infrā dignitātem*]

infrangible (ɪn'frændʒɪb³l) *adj* **1** incapable of being broken **2** not capable of being violated or infringed [c16: from Late Latin *infrangibilis*, from Latin IN-¹ + *frangere* to break] ▷ in,frangi'bility *or* in'frangibleness *n* ▷ in'frangibly *adv*

infrared (,ɪnfrə'rɛd) *n* **1** the part of the electromagnetic spectrum with a longer wavelength than light but a shorter wavelength than radio waves; radiation with wavelength between 0.8 micrometres and 1 millimetre ▷ *adj* **2** of, relating to, using, or consisting of radiation lying within the infrared

infrared astronomy *n* the study of radiations from space in the infrared region of the electromagnetic spectrum

infrared photography *n* photography using film with an emulsion that is sensitive to infrared light, enabling it to be used in misty weather, in darkened interiors, or at night. It has applications in aerial surveys, the detection of forgeries, etc

infrasound ('ɪnfrə,saʊnd) *n* soundlike waves having a frequency below the audible range, that is, below about 16Hz ▷ infrasonic (,ɪnfrə'sɒnɪk) *adj*

infrastructure ('ɪnfrə,strʌktʃə) *n* **1** the basic structure of an organization, system, etc **2** the stock of fixed capital equipment in a country, including factories, roads, schools, etc, considered as a determinant of economic growth

infrequent (ɪnˈfriːkwənt) *adj* rarely happening or present; only occasional > in'frequency *or* in'frequence *n* > in'frequently *adv*

infringe (ɪnˈfrɪndʒ) *vb* **1** (*tr*) to violate or break (a law, an agreement, etc) **2** (*intr*; foll by *on or upon*) to encroach or trespass [C16: from Latin *infringere* to break off, from *frangere* to break] > in'fringement *n* > in'fringer *n*

infundibular (ˌɪnfʌnˈdɪbjʊlə) *adj* funnel-shaped [C18: from INFUNDIBULUM]

infundibulum (ˌɪnfʌnˈdɪbjʊləm) *n, pl* **-la** (-lə) *anatomy* any funnel-shaped part, esp the stalk connecting the pituitary gland to the base of the brain [C18: from Latin: funnel, from *infundere* to INFUSE] > ˌinfun'dibulate *adj*

infuriate *vb* (ɪnˈfjʊərɪˌeɪt) **1** (*tr*) to anger; annoy ▷ *adj* (ɪnˈfjʊərɪɪt) **2** *archaic* furious; infuriated [C17: from Medieval Latin *infuriāre* (vb); see IN-², FURY] > in'furiating *adj* > in'furiatingly *adv*

infuse (ɪnˈfjuːz) *vb* **1** (*tr*; often foll by *into*) to instil or inculcate **2** (*tr*; foll by *with*) to inspire; emotionally charge **3** to soak or be soaked in order to extract flavour or other properties **4** *rare* (foll by *into*) to pour [C15: from Latin *infundere* to pour into]

infusible¹ (ɪnˈfjuːzəbªl) *adj* not fusible; not easily melted; having a high melting point [C16: from IN-¹ + FUSIBLE] > inˌfusi'bility *or* in'fusibleness *n*

infusible² (ɪnˈfjuːzəbªl) *adj* capable of being infused [C17: from INFUSE + -IBLE] > inˌfusi'bility *or* in'fusibleness *n*

infusion (ɪnˈfjuːʒən) *n* **1** the act of infusing **2** something infused **3** an extract obtained by soaking > infusive (ɪnˈfjuːsɪv) *adj*

infusorian (ˌɪnfjʊˈzɔːrɪən) *n obsolete* **1** any of the microscopic organisms, such as protozoans and rotifers, found in infusions of organic material ▷ *adj* **2** of or relating to infusorians [C18: from New Latin *Infusoria* former class name; see INFUSE] > ˌinfu'sorial *adj*

-ing¹ *suffix forming nouns* **1** (*from verbs*) the action of, process of, result of, or something connected with the verb: *coming; meeting; a wedding; winnings* **2** (*from other nouns*) something used in, consisting of, involving, etc: *tubing; soldiering* **3** (*from other parts of speech*): *an outing* [Old English *-ing, -ung*]

-ing² *suffix* **1** forming the present participle of verbs: *walking; believing* **2** forming participial adjectives: *a growing boy; a sinking ship* **3** forming adjectives not derived from verbs: *swashbuckling* [Middle English *-ing, -inde*, from Old English *-ende*]

-ing³ *suffix forming nouns* a person or thing having a certain quality or being of a certain kind: *sweeting; whiting* [Old English *-ing*; related to Old Norse *-ingr*]

ingather (ɪnˈgæðə) *vb* (*tr*) to gather together or in (a harvest) > in'gatherer *n*

Inge (ɪŋ) *n* **William Ralph**, known as the *Gloomy Dean*. 1860–1954, English theologian, noted for his pessimism; dean of St Paul's Cathedral (1911–34)

ingeminate (ɪnˈdʒɛmɪˌneɪt) *vb* (*tr*) *rare* to repeat; reiterate [C16: from Latin *ingemināre* to redouble, from IN-² + *gemināre* to GEMINATE]

Ingenhousz (ˈɪngənˌhaʊs) *n* **Jan** (jɑn). 1730–99, Dutch plant physiologist and physician, who discovered photosynthesis

ingenious (ɪnˈdʒiːnjəs, -nɪəs) *adj* possessing or done with ingenuity; skilful or clever [C15: from Latin *ingeniōsus*, from *ingenium* natural ability; see ENGINE] > in'geniously *adv* > in'geniousness *n*

ingénue (ˌænʒeɪˈnjuː; *French* ɛ̃ʒeny) *n* an artless, innocent, or inexperienced girl or young woman [C19: from French, feminine of *ingénu* INGENUOUS]

ingenuity (ˌɪndʒɪˈnjuːɪtɪ) *n, pl* **-ties** **1** inventive talent; cleverness **2** an ingenious device, act, etc **3** *archaic* frankness; candour [C16: from Latin *ingenuitās* a freeborn condition, outlook consistent with such a condition, from *ingenuus* native, freeborn (see INGENUOUS); meaning influenced by INGENIOUS]

ingenuous (ɪnˈdʒɛnjʊəs) *adj* **1** naive, artless, or innocent **2** candid; frank; straightforward [C16: from Latin *ingenuus*

freeborn, worthy of a freeman, virtuous, from IN-² + *-genuus*, from *gignere* to beget] > in'genuously *adv* > in'genuousness *n*

ingest (ɪnˈdʒɛst) *vb* (*tr*) to take (food or liquid) into the body [C17: from Latin *ingerere* to put into, from IN-² + *gerere* to carry; see GEST] > in'gestible *adj* > in'gestion *n* > in'gestive *adj*

ingle (ˈɪŋgªl) *n archaic or dialect* a fire in a room or a fireplace [C16: probably from Scots Gaelic *aingeal* fire]

Ingleborough (ˈɪŋglˌbərə, -brə) *n* a mountain in N England, in North Yorkshire: potholes. Height: 723 m (2373 ft)

inglenook (ˈɪŋglˌnʊk) *n Brit* a corner by a fireplace; chimney corner

ingoing (ˈɪnˌgəʊɪŋ) *adj* coming or going in; entering

Ingolstadt (*German* ˈɪŋɔlʃtat) *n* a city in S central Germany, in Bavaria on the River Danube: oil-refining. Pop: 119 528 (2003 est)

ingot (ˈɪŋgət) *n* a piece of cast metal obtained from a mould in a form suitable for storage, transporting, and further use [C14: perhaps from IN-² + Old English *goten*, past participle of *geotan* to pour]

ingraft (ɪnˈgrɑːft) *vb* a variant spelling of **engraft** > in'graftment *or* ˌingraf'tation *n*

ingrain *or* **engrain** *vb* (ɪnˈgreɪn) (*tr*) **1** to impress deeply on the mind or nature; instil **2** to dye into the fibre of (a fabric) ▷ *adj* (ˈɪnˌgreɪn) **3** (of woven or knitted articles, esp rugs and carpets) made of dyed yarn or of fibre that is dyed before being spun into yarn ▷ *n* (ˈɪnˌgreɪn) **4** a carpet made from ingrained yarn [C18: from the phrase *dyed in grain* dyed with kermes through the fibre]

ingrained *or* **engrained** (ɪnˈgreɪnd) *adj* **1** deeply impressed or instilled **2** (*prenominal*) complete or inveterate; utter **3** (esp of dirt) worked into or through the fibre, grain, pores, etc > ingrainedly *or* engrainedly (ɪnˈgreɪnɪdlɪ) *adv* > in'grainedness *or* en'grainedness *n*

ingrate (ˈɪngreɪt, ɪnˈgreɪt) *archaic* ▷ *n* **1** an ungrateful person ▷ *adj* **2** ungrateful [C14: from Latin *ingrātus* (adj), from IN-¹ + *grātus* GRATEFUL] > 'ingrately *adv*

ingratiate (ɪnˈgreɪʃɪˌeɪt) *vb* (*tr*; often foll by *with*) to place (oneself) purposely in the favour (of another) [C17: from Latin, from IN-² + *grātia* grace, favour] > in'gratiating *or* in'gratiatory *adj* > in'gratiˌatingly *adv* > inˌgrati'ation *n*

ingredient (ɪnˈgriːdɪənt) *n* a component of a mixture, compound, etc, esp in cooking [C15: from Latin *ingrediēns* going into, from *ingredī* to enter; see INGRESS]

Ingres (*French* ɛ̃grə) *n* **Jean Auguste Dominique** (ʒɑ̃ ogyst dɔminik). 1780– 1867, French classical painter, noted for his draughtsmanship

ingress (ˈɪngrɛs) *n* **1** the act of going or coming in; an entering **2** a way in; entrance **3** the right or permission to enter [C15: from Latin *ingressus*, from *ingredī* to go in, from *gradī* to step, go] > ingression (ɪnˈgrɛʃən) *n*

in-group *n sociol* a highly cohesive and relatively closed social group characterized by the preferential treatment reserved for its members and the strength of loyalty between them

ingrowing (ˈɪnˌgrəʊɪŋ) *adj* **1** (esp of a toenail) growing abnormally into the flesh **2** growing within or into > 'inˌgrowth *n*

ingrown (ˈɪnˌgrəʊn, ɪnˈgrəʊn) *adj* **1** (esp of a toenail) grown abnormally into the flesh; covered by adjacent tissues **2** grown within; native; innate

inguinal (ˈɪŋgwɪnªl) *adj anatomy* of or relating to the groin [C17: from Latin *inguinālis*, from *inguen* groin]

ingulf (ɪnˈgʌlf) *vb* a variant spelling of **engulf**

ingurgitate (ɪnˈgɜːdʒɪˌteɪt) *vb* to swallow (food) with greed or in excess; gorge [C16: from Latin *ingurgitāre* to flood, from IN-² + *gurges* abyss] > inˌgurgi'tation *n*

Ingush Republic *n* a constituent republic of S Russia: part of the Checheno-Ingush Autonomous Republic from 1936 until 1992. Capital: Magas (formerly at Nazran). Pop: 468 900 (2002). Area: 3600 sq km (1390 sq miles). Also called: Ingushetia (ˌɪnguːˈʃɛtɪə)

inhabit (ɪnˈhæbɪt) *vb* **-its, -iting, -ited** (*tr*) to live or dwell in; occupy [C14: from Latin *inhabitāre*, from *habitāre* to dwell] > in'habitable *adj* > inˌhabita'bility *n* > inˌhabi'tation *n*

inhabitant (ɪnˈhæbɪtənt) n a person or animal that is a permanent resident of a particular place or region ▷ inˈhabitancy or inˈhabitance n

inhalant (ɪnˈheɪlənt) adj 1 (esp of a volatile medicinal formulation) inhaled for its soothing or therapeutic effect 2 inhaling ▷ n 3 an inhalant medicinal formulation

inhale (ɪnˈheɪl) vb to draw (breath) into the lungs; breathe in [c18: from IN-² + Latin halāre to breathe] ▷ ˌinhaˈlation n

inhaler (ɪnˈheɪlə) n 1 a device for breathing in therapeutic vapours through the nose or mouth, esp one for relieving nasal congestion or asthma 2 a person who inhales

Inhambane (ˌɪnjəmˈbɑːnə) n a port in SE Mozambique on an inlet of the Mozambique Channel (**Inhambane Bay**). Pop: about 70 000 (latest est)

inhere (ɪnˈhɪə) vb (intr; foll by in) to be an inseparable part (of) [c16: from Latin inhaerēre to stick in, from haerēre to stick]

inherent (ɪnˈhɪərənt, -ˈhɛr-) adj existing as an inseparable part; intrinsic ▷ inˈherently adv

inherit (ɪnˈhɛrɪt) vb -its, -iting, -ited 1 to receive (property, a right, title, etc) by succession or under a will 2 (intr) to succeed as heir 3 (tr) to possess (a characteristic) through genetic transmission 4 (tr) to receive (a position, attitude, property, etc) from a predecessor [c14: from Old French enheriter, from Late Latin inhērēditāre to appoint an heir, from Latin hērēs HEIR] ▷ inˈherited adj ▷ inˈheritor n ▷ inˈheritress or inˈheritrix fem n

inheritable (ɪnˈhɛrɪtəbᵊl) adj 1 capable of being transmitted by heredity from one generation to a later one 2 capable of being inherited 3 rare capable of inheriting; having the right to inherit ▷ inˌheritaˈbility or inˈheritableness n ▷ inˈheritably adv

inheritance (ɪnˈhɛrɪtəns) n 1 law a a hereditary succession to an estate, title, etc b the right of an heir to succeed to property on the death of an ancestor c something that may legally be transmitted to an heir 2 the act of inheriting 3 something inherited; heritage 4 the derivation of characteristics of one generation from an earlier one by heredity

inheritance tax n 1 (in Britain) a tax introduced in 1986 to replace capital transfer tax, consisting of a percentage levied on that part of an inheritance exceeding a specified allowance, and scaled charges on gifts made within seven years of death 2 (in the US) a state tax imposed on an inheritance according to its size and the relationship of the beneficiary to the deceased

inhibit (ɪnˈhɪbɪt) vb -its, -iting, -ited (tr) 1 to restrain or hinder (an impulse, a desire, etc) 2 to prohibit; forbid 3 to stop, prevent, or decrease the rate of (a chemical reaction) [c15: from Latin inhibēre to restrain, from IN-² + habēre to have] ▷ inˈhibitable adj ▷ inˈhibitive or inˈhibitory adj

inhibition (ˌɪnɪˈbɪʃən, ˌɪnhɪ-) n 1 the act of inhibiting or the condition of being inhibited 2 psychol a mental state or condition in which the varieties of expression and behaviour of an individual become restricted 3 the process of stopping or retarding a chemical reaction 4 physiol the suppression of the function or action of an organ or part, as by stimulation of its nerve supply

inhibitor (ɪnˈhɪbɪtə) n 1 Also called: **inhibiter** a person or thing that inhibits 2 Also called: **anticatalyst** a substance that retards or stops a chemical reaction 3 biochem a a substance that inhibits the action of an enzyme b a substance that inhibits a metabolic or physiological process: a plant growth inhibitor

inhospitable (ɪnˈhɒspɪtəbᵊl, ˌɪnhɒˈspɪt-) adj 1 not hospitable; unfriendly 2 (of a region, an environment, etc) lacking a favourable climate, terrain, etc ▷ inˈhospitableness n ▷ inˈhospitably adv

in-house adj, adv within an organization or group: an in-house job; the job was done in-house

inhuman (ɪnˈhjuːmən) adj 1 Also called: **inhumane** (ˌɪnhjuːˈmeɪn) lacking humane feelings, such as sympathy, understanding, etc; cruel; brutal 2 not human ▷ ˌinhuˈmanely adv ▷ inˈhumanly adv

▷ inˈhumanness n

inhumanity (ˌɪnhjuːˈmænɪtɪ) n, pl -ties 1 lack of humane qualities 2 an inhumane act, decision, etc

inhume (ɪnˈhjuːm) vb (tr) to inter; bury [c17: from Latin inhumāre, from IN-² + humus ground] ▷ ˌinhuˈmation n ▷ inˈhumer n

inimical (ɪˈnɪmɪkᵊl) adj 1 adverse or unfavourable 2 not friendly; hostile [c17: from Late Latin inimīcālis, from inimīcus, from IN-¹ + amīcus friendly; see ENEMY] ▷ inˈimically adv ▷ inˈimicalness or inˌimiˈcality n

inimitable (ɪˈnɪmɪtəbᵊl) adj incapable of being duplicated or imitated; unique ▷ inˌimitaˈbility or inˈimitableness n ▷ inˈimitably adv

iniquity (ɪˈnɪkwɪtɪ) n, pl -ties 1 lack of justice or righteousness; wickedness; injustice 2 a wicked act; sin [c14: from Latin inīquitās, from inīquus unfair, from IN-¹ + aequus even, level; see EQUAL] ▷ inˈiquitous adj ▷ inˈiquitously adv ▷ inˈiquitousness n

initial (ɪˈnɪʃəl) adj 1 of, at, or concerning the beginning ▷ n 2 the first letter of a word, esp a person's name 3 printing a large sometimes highly decorated letter set at the beginning of a chapter or work 4 botany a cell from which tissues and organs develop by division and differentiation; a meristematic cell ▷ vb -tials, -tialling, -tialled or US -tials, -tialing, -tialed 5 (tr) to sign with one's initials, esp to indicate approval; endorse [c16: from Latin initiālis of the beginning, from initium beginning, literally: an entering upon, from inīre to go in, from IN-² + īre to go] ▷ inˈitialer or inˈitialler n ▷ inˈitially adv

initialize or **initialise** (ɪˈnɪʃəˌlaɪz) vb (tr) to assign an initial value to (a variable or storage location) in a computer program ▷ inˌitialiˈzation or inˌitialiˈsation n

initiate vb (ɪˈnɪʃɪˌeɪt) (tr) 1 to begin or originate 2 to accept (new members) into an organization such as a club, through often secret ceremonies 3 to teach fundamentals to ▷ adj (ɪˈnɪʃɪɪt, -ˌeɪt) 4 initiated; begun ▷ n (ɪˈnɪʃɪɪt, -ˌeɪt) 5 a person who has been initiated, esp recently 6 a beginner; novice [c17: from Latin initiāre (vb), from initium; see INITIAL]

initiation (ɪˌnɪʃɪˈeɪʃən) n 1 the act of initiating or the condition of being initiated 2 the often secret ceremony initiating new members into an organization

initiative (ɪˈnɪʃɪətɪv, -ˈnɪʃətɪv) n 1 the first step or action of a matter; commencing move: he took the initiative; a peace initiative 2 the right or power to begin or initiate something: he has the initiative 3 the ability or attitude required to begin or initiate something 4 government the right or power to introduce legislation, etc, in a legislative body 5 on one's own initiative without being prompted ▷ adj 6 of or concerning initiation or serving to initiate; initiatory ▷ inˈitiatively adv

initiator (ɪˈnɪʃɪˌeɪtə) n 1 a person or thing that initiates 2 chem a substance that starts a chain reaction 3 chem an explosive used in detonators

inject (ɪnˈdʒɛkt) vb (tr) 1 med to introduce (a fluid) into (the body of a person or animal) by means of a syringe or similar instrument 2 (foll by into) to introduce (a new aspect or element): to inject humour into a scene 3 to interject (a comment, idea, etc) [c17: from Latin injicere to throw in, from jacere to throw] ▷ inˈjectable adj ▷ inˈjector n

injection (ɪnˈdʒɛkʃən) n 1 fluid injected into the body, esp for medicinal purposes 2 something injected 3 the act of injecting 4 a the act or process of introducing fluid under pressure, such as fuel into the combustion chamber of an engine b (as modifier): injection moulding ▷ inˈjective adj

injunction (ɪnˈdʒʌŋkʃən) n 1 law an instruction or order issued by a court to a party to an action, esp to refrain from some act, such as causing a nuisance 2 a command, admonition, or act of enjoining [c16: from Late Latin injunctiō, from Latin injungere to ENJOIN] ▷ inˈjunctive adj ▷ inˈjunctively adv

injure (ˈɪndʒə) vb (tr) 1 to cause physical or mental harm or suffering to; hurt or wound 2 to offend, esp by an injustice [c16: back formation from INJURY] ▷ ˈinjurable adj ▷ ˈinjured adj ▷ ˈinjurer n

injurious (ɪnˈdʒʊərɪəs) adj 1 causing damage or harm;

deleterious; hurtful **2** abusive, slanderous, or libellous > in'juriously *adv* > in'juriousness *n*

injury ('ɪndʒərɪ) *n*, *pl* -ries **1** physical damage or hurt **2** a specific instance of this: *a leg injury* **3** harm done to a reputation **4** *law* a violation or infringement of another person's rights that causes him harm and is actionable at law [c14: from Latin *injūria* injustice, wrong, from *injūriōsus* acting unfairly, wrongful, from IN-¹ + *jūs* right]

injury list *n* the people who are unable to participate in a sport as expected, due to illness or injury

injury time *n* *sport* extra playing time added on to compensate for time spent attending to injured players during the match. Also called: **stoppage time**

injustice (ɪn'dʒʌstɪs) *n* **1** the condition or practice of being unjust or unfair **2** an unjust act

ink (ɪŋk) *n* **1** a fluid or paste used for printing, writing, and drawing **2** a dark brown fluid ejected into the water for self-concealment by an octopus or related mollusc from a gland (**ink sac**) near the anus ▷ *vb* (*tr*) **3** to mark with ink **4** to coat (a printing surface) with ink [c13: from Old French *enque*, from Late Latin *encaustum* a purplish-red ink, from Greek *enkauston* purple ink, from *enkaustos* burnt in, from *enkaiein* to burn in; see EN-², CAUSTIC] > 'inker *n*

Inkatha (ɪn'kɑːtə) *n* a South African Zulu organization founded by Chief Mangosuthu Buthelezi in 1975 as a paramilitary group seeking nonracial democracy; won four seats in South Africa's first nonracial elections in 1994 [c20: Zulu name for the grass coil used by Zulu women carrying loads on their heads, the many strands of which provide its strength and cohesion]

inkblot ('ɪŋk,blɒt) *n* *psychol* an abstract patch of ink, one of ten commonly used in the Rorschach test

ink-cap *n* any of several saprotrophic agaricaceous fungi of the genus *Coprinus*, whose caps disintegrate into a black inky fluid after the spores mature. It includes the **shaggy ink-cap** (*Coprinus comatus*), also called **lawyer's wig**, a distinctive fungus having a white cylindrical cap covered with shaggy white or brownish scales

Inkerman ('ɪŋkəmən, *Russian* ɪnkɪr'man) *n* a village in Ukraine, in the S Crimea east of Sevastopol: scene of a battle during the Crimean War in which British and French forces defeated the Russians (1854)

inkhorn ('ɪŋk,hɔːn) *n* (formerly) a small portable container for ink, usually made from horn

ink in *vb* (*adverb*) **1** (*tr*) to use ink to go over pencil lines in (a drawing) **2** to apply ink to (a printing surface) in preparing to print from it **3** to arrange or confirm definitely

inkling ('ɪŋklɪŋ) *n* a slight intimation or suggestion; suspicion [c14: probably from *inclen* to hint at; related to Old English *inca*]

inkstand ('ɪŋk,stænd) *n* a stand or tray on which are kept writing implements and containers for ink

inkwell ('ɪŋk,wɛl) *n* a small container for pen ink, often let into the surface of a desk

inky ('ɪŋkɪ) *adj* inkier, inkiest **1** resembling ink, esp in colour; dark or black **2** of, containing, or stained with ink > 'inkiness *n*

INLA *abbreviation* Irish National Liberation Army; a Republican paramilitary organization in Ireland

inlaid ('ɪn,leɪd, ɪn'leɪd) *adj* **1** set in the surface, as a design in wood **2** having such a design or inlay: *an inlaid table*

inland ('ɪnlənd) *adj* **1** of, concerning, or located in the interior of a country or region away from a sea or border **2** *chiefly Brit* operating within a country or region; domestic; not foreign ▷ *n* ('ɪn,lænd, -lənd) **3** the interior of a country or region ▷ *adv* ('ɪn,lænd, -lənd) **4** towards or into the interior of a country or region > 'inlander *n*

Inland Revenue *n* (in Britain and New Zealand) a government board that administers and collects major direct taxes, such as income tax, corporation tax, and capital gains tax

Inland Sea *n* a sea in SW Japan, between the islands of Honshu, Shikoku, and Kyushu. Japanese name: **Seto Naikai**

in-law *n* **1** a relative by marriage ▷ *adj* **2** (*postpositive; in combination*) related by marriage: *a father-in-law* [c19: back formation from *father-in-law*, etc]

inlay *vb* (ɪn'leɪ) -lays, -laying, -laid (*tr*) **1** to decorate (an article, esp of furniture, or a surface) by inserting pieces of wood, ivory, etc, into prepared slots in the surface ▷ *n* ('ɪn,leɪ) **2** *dentistry* a filling, made of gold, porcelain, etc, inserted into a cavity and held in position by cement **3** decoration made by inlaying **4** an inlaid article, surface, etc > 'in,layer *n*

inlet *n* ('ɪn,lɛt) **1** a narrow inland opening of the coastline **2** an entrance or opening **3** the act of letting someone or something in **4** something let in or inserted **5 a** a passage, valve, or part through which a substance, esp a fluid, enters a device or machine **b** (*as modifier*): *an inlet valve* ▷ *vb* (ɪn'lɛt) -lets, -letting, -let **6** (*tr*) to insert or inlay

inlier ('ɪn,laɪə) *n* an outcrop of rocks that is entirely surrounded by younger rocks

in-line skate *n* another name for **Rollerblade**

in loco parentis *Latin* (ɪn 'ləʊkəʊ pə'rɛntɪs) in place of a parent: said of a person acting in a parental capacity

inly ('ɪnlɪ) *adv* *poetic* inwardly; intimately

inmate ('ɪn,meɪt) *n* a person who is confined to an institution such as a prison or hospital

in medias res *Latin* (ɪn 'miːdɪ,æs 'reɪs) in or into the middle of events or a narrative [literally: into the midst of things, taken from a passage from Horace's *Ars Poetica*]

in memoriam (ɪn mɪ'mɔːrɪəm) in memory of; as a memorial to: used in obituaries, epitaphs, etc [Latin]

inmost ('ɪn,məʊst) *adj* another word for **innermost**

inn (ɪn) *n* a pub or small hotel providing food and accommodation [Old English; compare Old Norse *inni* inn, house, place of refuge]

Inn (ɪn) *n* a river in central Europe, rising in Switzerland in Graubünden and flowing northeast through Austria and Bavaria to join the River Danube at Passau: forms part of the border between Austria and Germany. Length: 514 km (319 miles)

innards ('ɪnədz) *pl n* *informal* **1** the internal organs of the body, esp the viscera **2** the interior parts or components of anything, esp the working parts [c19: colloquial variant of *inwards*]

innate (ɪ'neɪt) *adj* **1** existing in a person or animal from birth; congenital; inborn **2** being an essential part of the character of a person or thing **3** instinctive; not learned: *innate capacities* **4** (in rationalist philosophy) (of ideas) present in the mind before any experience and knowable by pure reason [c15: from Latin, from *innascī* to be born in, from *nascī* to be born] > in'nately *adv* > in'nateness *n*

inner ('ɪnə) *adj* (*prenominal*) **1** being or located further inside: *an inner room* **2** happening or occurring inside **3** relating to the soul, mind, spirit, etc **4** more profound or obscure; less apparent: *the inner meaning* **5** exclusive or private: *inner regions of the party* ▷ *n* **6** Also called: **red** *archery* **a** the red innermost ring on a target **b** a shot which hits this ring > 'innerly *adv* > 'innerness *n*

inner bar *n* *Brit* all Queen's or King's Counsel collectively

inner child *n* *psychol* the part of the psyche believed to retain feelings as they were experienced in childhood

inner city *n* **a** the parts of a city in or near its centre, esp when they are associated with poverty, unemployment, substandard housing, etc **b** (*as modifier*): *inner-city schools*

Inner Hebrides *pl n* See **Hebrides**

inner man *n* **1** a man's mind, soul, or nature **2** *jocular* the stomach or appetite

Inner Mongolia *n* an autonomous region of NE China: consists chiefly of the Mongolian plateau, with the Gobi Desert in the north and the Great Wall of China in the south. Capital: Hohhot. Pop: 23 800 000 (2003 est). Area: 1 177 500 sq km (459 225 sq miles)

innermost ('ɪnə,məʊst) *adj* **1** being or located furthest within; central **2** intimate; private

inner tube *n* an inflatable rubber tube that fits inside a pneumatic tyre casing

innervate ('ɪnɜː,veɪt) *vb* (*tr*) **1** to supply nerves to (a bodily organ or part) **2** to stimulate (a bodily organ or part) with nerve impulses > ,inner'vation *n*

innings ('ɪnɪŋz) *n* **1** (*functioning as singular*) *cricket* **a** the batting turn of a player or team **b** the runs scored during such a turn **2** (*sometimes singular*) a period of opportunity or action

Inniskilling (,ɪnɪs'kɪlɪŋ) *n* the former name of **Enniskillen**

innkeeper ('ɪn,ki:pə) *n* an owner or manager of an inn

innocence ('ɪnəsəns) *n* the quality or state of being innocent [c14: from Latin *innocentia* harmlessness, from *innocēns* doing no harm, blameless, from IN-¹ + *nocēns* harming, from *nocēre* to hurt, harm; see NOXIOUS]

innocent ('ɪnəsənt) *adj* **1** not corrupted or tainted with evil or unpleasant emotion; sinless; pure **2** not guilty of a particular crime; blameless **3** (*postpositive*; foll by *of*) free (of); lacking: *innocent of all knowledge of history* **4 a** harmless or innocuous: *an innocent game* **b** not cancerous: *an innocent tumour* **5** credulous, naive, or artless **6** simple-minded; slow-witted ▷ *n* **7** an innocent person, esp a young child or an ingenuous adult **8** a simple-minded person; simpleton > **'innocently** *adv*

Innocent II *n* original name *Gregorio Papareschi*. died 1143, pope (1130–43). He condemned Abelard's teachings

Innocent III *n* original name *Giovanni Lotario de' Conti*. ?1161–1216, pope (1198–1216), under whom the temporal power of the papacy reached its height. He instituted the Fourth Crusade (1202) and a crusade against the Albigenses (1208), and called the fourth Lateran Council (1215)

Innocent IV *n* original name *Sinibaldo de' Fieschi*. died 1254, pope (1243–54); an unrelenting enemy of Emperor Frederick II and his heirs

innocuous (ɪ'nɒkjʊəs) *adj* having little or no adverse or harmful effect; harmless [c16: from Latin *innocuus* harmless, from IN-¹ + *nocēre* to harm] > **in'nocuously** *adv* > **in'nocuousness** or **innocuity** (,ɪnə'kju:ɪtɪ) *n*

innominate bone *n* either of the two bones that form the sides of the pelvis, consisting of three fused components, the ilium, ischium, and pubis. Nontechnical name: **hipbone**

innovate ('ɪnə,veɪt) *vb* to invent or begin to apply (methods, ideas, etc) [c16: from Latin *innovāre* to renew, from IN-² + *novāre* to make new, from *novus* new] > **'inno,vative** or **'inno,vatory** *adj* > **'inno,vator** *n*

innovation (,ɪnə'veɪʃən) *n* **1** something newly introduced, such as a new method or device **2** the act of innovating > **,inno'vational** *adj* > **,inno'vationist** *n*

Innsbruck ('ɪnzbrʊk) *n* a city in W Austria, on the River Inn at the foot of the Brenner Pass: tourist centre. Pop: 113 392 (2001)

Innu ('ɪnu:) *n* **1** a member of an Algonquian people living in Labrador and northern Quebec **2** the Algonquian language of this people

innuendo (,ɪnjʊ'ɛndəʊ) *n*, *pl* **-dos** or **-does 1** an indirect or subtle reference, esp one made maliciously or indicating criticism or disapproval; insinuation **2** *law* (in an action for defamation) an explanation of the construction put upon words alleged to be defamatory where the defamatory meaning is not apparent [c17: from Latin, literally: by hinting, from *innuendum*, gerund of *innuere* to convey by a nod, from IN-² + *nuere* to nod]

Innuit ('ɪnju:ɪt) *n* a variant spelling of **Inuit**

innumerable (ɪ'nju:mərəbəl, ɪ'nju:mrəbəl) or **innumerous** *adj* so many as to be uncountable; extremely numerous > **in,numera'bility** or **in'numerableness** *n* > **in'numerably** *adv*

innumerate (ɪ'nju:mərɪt) *adj* **1** having neither knowledge nor understanding of mathematics or science ▷ *n* **2** an innumerate person > **in'numeracy** *n*

inoculate (ɪ'nɒkjʊ,leɪt) *vb* **1** to introduce (the causative agent of a disease) into the body of (a person or animal), in order to induce immunity **2** (*tr*) to introduce (microorganisms, esp bacteria) into (a culture medium) **3** (*tr*) to cause to be influenced or imbued, as with ideas or opinions [c15: from Latin *inoculāre* to implant, from IN-² + *oculus* eye, bud] > **in,ocu'lation** *n* > **in'oculative** *adj* > **in'ocu,lator** *n*

inoculum (ɪ'nɒkjʊləm) or **inoculant** *n*, *pl* **-la** (-lə) or **-lants** *med* the substance used in giving an inoculation [c20: New Latin; see INOCULATE]

in-off *n* billiards, snooker a shot that goes into a pocket after striking another ball

Inönü ('i:nɜ:,nʊ, ,ɪnɜ:'nu:) *n* **Ismet** (ɪs'mɛt, 'ɪsmɛt).

1884–1973, Turkish statesman; president of Turkey (1938–50) and prime minister (1923–37; 1961–65)

inoperable (ɪn'ɒpərəbəl, -'ɒprə-) *adj* **1** incapable of being implemented or operated; unworkable **2** surgery not suitable for operation without risk, esp (of a malignant tumour) because metastasis has rendered surgery useless > **in,opera'bility** or **in'operableness** *n* > **in'operably** *adv*

inordinate (ɪn'ɔ:dɪnɪt) *adj* **1** exceeding normal limits; immoderate **2** unrestrained, as in behaviour or emotion; intemperate **3** irregular or disordered [c14: from Latin *inordinātus* disordered, from IN-¹ + *ordināre* to put in order] > **in'ordinacy** or **in'ordinateness** *n* > **in'ordinately** *adv*

inorganic (,ɪnɔ:'gænɪk) *adj* **1** not having the structure or characteristics of living organisms; not organic **2** relating to or denoting chemical compounds that do not contain carbon **3** not having a system, structure, or ordered relation of parts; amorphous **4** not resulting from or produced by growth; artificial > **,inor'ganically** *adv*

inorganic chemistry *n* the branch of chemistry concerned with the elements and all their compounds except those containing carbon. Some simple carbon compounds, such as oxides, carbonates, etc, are treated as inorganic

inosculate (ɪn'ɒskjʊ,leɪt) *vb* **1** physiol (of small blood vessels) to communicate by anastomosis **2** to unite or be united so as to be continuous; blend **3** to intertwine or cause to intertwine [c17: from IN-² + Latin *ōsculāre* to equip with an opening, from *ōsculum*, diminutive of *ōs* mouth] > **in,oscu'lation** *n*

inositol (ɪ'nəʊsɪ,tɒl) *n* a cyclic alcohol, one isomer of which (i-inositol) is present in yeast and is a growth factor for some organisms; cyclohexanehexol. Formula: $C_6H_{12}O_6$ [c19: from Greek *in-*, *is* sinew + -OSE² + -ITE¹ + -OL¹]

inpatient ('ɪn,peɪʃənt) *n* a hospital patient who occupies a bed for at least one night in the course of treatment, examination, or observation

in perpetuum Latin (ɪn pɜ:'pɛtjʊəm) *adv* for ever

input ('ɪn,pʊt) *n* **1** the act of putting in **2** that which is put in **3** (*often plural*) a resource required for industrial production, such as capital goods, labour services, raw materials, etc **4** electronics the signal or current fed into a component or circuit **5** computing the data fed into a computer from a peripheral device **6** (*modifier*) of or relating to electronic, computer, or other input ▷ *vb* **-puts**, **-putting**, **-put** or **-putted 7** (*tr*) to insert (data) into a computer

input/output *n* computing **1** the data or information that is passed into or out of a computer **2** (*modifier*) concerned with or relating to such passage of data or information

inquest ('ɪn,kwɛst) *n* **1** an inquiry into the cause of an unexplained, sudden, or violent death, or as to whether or not property constitutes treasure trove, held by a coroner, in certain cases with a jury **2** informal any inquiry or investigation [c13: from Medieval Latin *inquēsta*, from Latin IN-² + *quaesītus* investigation, from *quaerere* to examine]

inquietude (ɪn'kwaɪɪ,tju:d) *n* restlessness, uneasiness, or anxiety > **inquiet** (ɪn'kwaɪət) *adj* > **in'quietly** *adv*

inquiline ('ɪnkwɪ,laɪn) *n* **1** an animal that lives in close association with another animal without harming it. See also **commensal** (sense 1) ▷ *adj* **2** of or living as an inquiline [c17: from Latin *inquilīnus* lodger, from IN-² + *colere* to dwell] > **inquilinous** (,ɪnkwɪ'laɪnəs) *adj*

inquire or **enquire** (ɪn'kwaɪə) *vb* **1 a** to seek information; ask: *she inquired his age; she inquired about rates of pay* **b** (foll by *of*) to ask (a person) for information: *I'll inquire of my aunt when she is coming* **2** (*intr*; often foll by *into*) to make a search or investigation [c13: from Latin *inquīrere* from IN-² + *quaerere* to seek] > **in'quirer** or **en'quirer** *n*

inquiry or **enquiry** (ɪn'kwaɪərɪ) *n*, *pl* **-ries 1** a request for information; a question **2** an investigation, esp a formal one conducted into a matter of public concern by a body constituted for that purpose by a government, local authority, or other organization

inquisition (,ɪnkwɪ'zɪʃən) *n* **1** the act of inquiring deeply or searchingly; investigation **2** a deep or searching inquiry, esp a ruthless official investigation of individuals in order to suppress revolt or root out the unorthodox **3** an official inquiry, esp one held by a jury before an officer of the Crown [c14: from legal Latin *inquīsītiō*, from *inquīrere* to seek for; see INQUIRE] > ˌinqui'sitional *adj* > ˌinqui'sitionist *n*

Inquisition (ˌɪnkwɪ'zɪʃən) *n history* a judicial institution of the Roman Catholic Church (1232–1820) founded to discover and suppress heresy

inquisitive (ɪn'kwɪzɪtɪv) *adj* **1** excessively curious, esp about the affairs of others; prying **2** eager to learn; inquiring > in'quisitively *adv* > in'quisitiveness *n*

inquisitor (ɪn'kwɪzɪtə) *n* **1** a person who inquires, esp deeply, searchingly, or ruthlessly **2** (*often capital*) an official of the ecclesiastical court of the Inquisition

inquisitorial (ɪnˌkwɪzɪ'tɔːrɪəl) *adj* **1** of, relating to, or resembling inquisition or an inquisitor **2** offensively curious; prying **3** *law* denoting criminal procedure in which one party is both prosecutor and judge, or in which the trial is held in secret. See **accusatorial** (sense 2) > inˌquisi'torially *adv* > inˌquisi'torialness *n*

inquorate (ɪn'kwɔːreɪt) *adj Brit* not consisting of or being a quorum: *this meeting is inquorate*

in re (ɪn 'reɪ) *prep* in the matter of: used esp in bankruptcy proceedings [c17: from Latin]

INRI *abbreviation* Iesus Nazarenus Rex Iudaeorum (the inscription placed over Christ's head during the Crucifixion) [Latin: Jesus of Nazareth, King of the Jews]

inroad ('ɪnˌrəʊd) *n* **1** an invasion or hostile attack; raid or incursion **2** an encroachment or intrusion

inrush ('ɪnˌrʌʃ) *n* a sudden usually overwhelming inward flow or rush; influx > 'inˌrushing *n, adj*

ins. *abbreviation* inches

insane (ɪn'seɪn) *adj* **1 a** mentally deranged; crazy; of unsound mind **b** (*as collective noun; preceded by the*): *the insane* **2** characteristic of a person of unsound mind: *an insane stare* **3** irresponsible; very foolish; stupid > in'sanely *adv* > in'saneness *n*

insanitary (ɪn'sænɪtərɪ, -trɪ) *adj* not sanitary; dirty or infected

insanity (ɪn'sænɪtɪ) *n, pl* **-ties 1** relatively permanent disorder of the mind; state or condition of being insane **2** utter folly; stupidity

insatiable (ɪn'seɪʃəbəl, -ʃɪə-) *or* **insatiate** (ɪn'seɪʃɪɪt) *adj* not able to be satisfied or satiated; greedy or unappeasable > inˌsatia'bility, in'satiableness *or* in'satiateness *n* > in'satiably *or* in'satiately *adv*

inscape ('ɪnskeɪp) *n* the essential inner nature of a person, an object, etc [c19: from IN-² + *-scape*, as in LANDSCAPE; coined by Gerard Manley *Hopkins* (1844–89), British poet and Jesuit priest]

inscribe (ɪn'skraɪb) *vb* (*tr*) **1** to make, carve, or engrave (writing, letters, a design, etc) on (a surface such as wood, stone, or paper) **2** to enter (a name) on a list or in a register **3** to sign one's name on (a book, photograph, etc) before presentation to another person **4** to draw (a geometric construction such as a circle, polygon, etc) inside another construction so that the two are in contact but do not intersect [c16: from Latin *inscrībere*; see INSCRIPTION] > in'scribable *adj* > in'scribableness *n* > in'scriber *n*

inscription (ɪn'skrɪpʃən) *n* **1** something inscribed, esp words carved or engraved on a coin, tomb, etc **2** a signature or brief dedication in a book or on a work of art **3** the act of inscribing [c14: from Latin *inscrīptiō* a writing upon, from *inscrībere* to write upon, from IN-² + *scrībere* to write] > in'scriptional *or* in'scriptive *adj* > in'scriptively *adv*

inscrutable (ɪn'skruːtəbəl) *adj* incomprehensible; mysterious or enigmatic [c15: from Late Latin *inscrūtābilis*, from IN-¹ + *scrūtārī* to examine] > inˌscruta'bility *or* in'scrutableness *n* > in'scrutably *adv*

insect ('ɪnsɛkt) *n* **1** any small air-breathing arthropod of the class *Insecta*, having a body divided into head, thorax, and abdomen, three pairs of legs, and (in most species) two pairs of wings. Insects comprise about five sixths of all known animal species, with a total of over one million named species **2** (*loosely*) any similar

invertebrate, such as a spider, tick, or centipede **3** a contemptible, loathsome, or insignificant person [c17: from Latin *insectum* (animal that has been) cut into, insect, from *insecāre*, from IN-² + *secāre* to cut; translation of Greek *entomon* insect] > in'sectean *or* in'sectile *adj* > 'insect-ˌlike *adj*

insectarium (ˌɪnsɛk'tɛərɪəm) *or* **insectary** (ɪn'sɛktərɪ) *n, pl* **-tariums, -taria** (-'tɛərɪə) *or* **-taries** a place where living insects are kept, bred, and studied

insecticide (ɪn'sɛktɪˌsaɪd) *n* a substance used to destroy insect pests > inˌsecti'cidal *adj*

insectivore (ɪn'sɛktɪˌvɔː) *n* **1** any placental mammal of the order *Insectivora*, being typically small, with simple teeth, and feeding on invertebrates. The group includes shrews, moles, and hedgehogs **2** any animal or plant that derives nourishment from insects

insectivorous (ˌɪnsɛk'tɪvərəs) *adj* **1** feeding on or adapted for feeding on insects: *insectivorous plants* **2** of or relating to the order *Insectivora*

insecure (ˌɪnsɪ'kjʊə) *adj* **1** anxious or afraid; not confident or certain **2** not adequately protected: *an insecure fortress* **3** unstable or shaky > inse'curely *adv* > ˌinse'cureness *n* > ˌinse'curity *n*

inselberg ('ɪnzəlˌbɜːg) *n* an isolated rocky hill rising abruptly from a flat plain [from German, from *Insel* island + *Berg* mountain]

inseminate (ɪn'sɛmɪˌneɪt) *vb* (*tr*) **1** to impregnate (a female) with semen **2** to introduce (ideas or attitudes) into the mind of (a person or group) [c17: from Latin *insēmināre*, from IN-² + *sēmināre* to sow, from *sēmen* seed] > inˌsemi'nation *n* > in'semiˌnator *n*

insensate (ɪn'sɛnseɪt, -sɪt) *adj* **1** lacking sensation or consciousness **2** insensitive; unfeeling **3** foolish; senseless > in'sensately *adv* > in'sensateness *n*

insensible (ɪn'sɛnsəbəl) *adj* **1** lacking sensation or consciousness **2** (foll by *of* or *to*) unaware (of) or indifferent (to): *insensible to suffering* **3** thoughtless or callous **4** a less common word for **imperceptible** > inˌsensi'bility *or* in'sensibleness *n* > in'sensibly *adv*

insensitive (ɪn'sɛnsɪtɪv) *adj* **1** lacking sensitivity; unfeeling **2** lacking physical sensation **3** (*postpositive; foll by to*) not sensitive (to) or affected (by): *insensitive to radiation* > in'sensitively *adv* > in'sensitiveness *or* inˌsensi'tivity *n*

insentient (ɪn'sɛnʃɪənt) *adj rare* lacking consciousness or senses; inanimate > in'sentience *or* in'sentiency *n*

inseparable (ɪn'sɛpərəbəl, -'sɛprə-) *adj* incapable of being separated or divided > inˌsepara'bility *or* in'separableness *n* > in'separably *adv*

insert *vb* (ɪn'sɜːt) (*tr*) **1** to put in or between; introduce **2** to introduce, as into text, such as a newspaper; interpolate ▷ *n* (ˈɪnsɜːt) **3** something inserted **4 a a** folded section placed in another for binding in with a book **b** a printed sheet, esp one bearing advertising, placed loose between the leaves of a book, periodical, etc [c16: from Latin *inserere* to plant in, ingraft, from IN-² + *serere* to join] > in'sertable *adj* > in'serter *n*

insertion (ɪn'sɜːʃən) *n* **1** the act of inserting or something that is inserted **2** a word, sentence, correction, etc, inserted into text, such as a newspaper **3** a strip of lace, embroidery, etc, between two pieces of material **4** *anatomy* the point or manner of attachment of a muscle to the bone that it moves > in'sertional *adj*

in-service *adj* denoting training that is given to employees during the course of employment: *an in-service course*

insessorial (ˌɪnsɛ'sɔːrɪəl) *adj* **1** (of feet or claws) adapted for perching **2** (of birds) having insessorial feet [c19: from New Latin *Insessōrēs* birds that perch, from Latin: perchers, from *insidēre* to sit upon, from *sedēre* to sit]

inset *vb* (ɪn'sɛt) **-sets, -setting, -set 1** (*tr*) to set or place in or within; insert ▷ *n* (ˈɪnˌsɛt) **2** something inserted **3** *printing* **a** a small map or diagram set within the borders of a larger one **b** another name for **insert** (sense 4) **4** a piece of fabric inserted into a garment, as to shape it or for decoration > 'inˌsetter *n*

inshallah (ɪn'ʃælə) *sentence substitute Islam* if Allah wills it [c19: from Arabic]

inshore ('ɪn'ʃɔː) *adj* **1** in or on the water, but close to the shore: *inshore weather* ▷ *adv, adj* **2** towards the shore from the water: *an inshore wind; we swam inshore*

inside *n* ('ɪn'saɪd) **1** the interior; inner or enclosed part or surface **2** the side of a path away from the road or adjacent to a wall **3** (*also plural*) *informal* the internal organs of the body, esp the stomach and bowels **4** inside of in a period of time less than; within **5** inside out with the inside facing outwards **6** know something inside out to know something thoroughly or perfectly ▷ *prep* (ˌɪn'saɪd) **7** in or to the interior of; within or to within; on the inside of ▷ *adj* ('ɪn'saɪd) **8** on or of an interior; on the inside: *an inside door* **9** (*prenominal*) arranged or provided by someone within an organization or building, esp illicitly: *the raid was an inside job; inside information* ▷ *adv* (ˌɪn'saɪd) **10** within or to within a thing or place; indoors
● USAGE See at **outside**

inside job *n informal* a crime committed with the assistance of someone associated with the victim, such as a person employed on the premises burgled

inside lane *n athletics* the inside, and therefore the shortest, route around a circular or oval multi-lane running track

insider (ˌɪn'saɪdə) *n* **1** a member of a specified group **2** a person with access to exclusive information

insider dealing *or* **insider trading** *n* dealing in company securities on a recognized stock exchange, with a view to making a profit or avoiding a loss, by a person who has confidential information about the securities that, if generally known, would affect their price. Its practice by those connected with a company is illegal ▷ insider dealer *or* insider trader *n*

insidious (ɪn'sɪdɪəs) *adj* **1** stealthy, subtle, cunning, or treacherous **2** working in a subtle or apparently innocuous way, but nevertheless deadly: *an insidious illness* [c16: from Latin *insidiōsus* cunning, from *insidiae* an ambush, from *insidēre* to sit in; see INSESSORIAL] ▷ in'sidiously *adv* ▷ in'sidiousness *n*

insight ('ɪn'saɪt) *n* **1** the ability to perceive clearly or deeply; penetration **2** a penetrating and often sudden understanding, as of a complex situation or problem **3** *psychol* the capacity for understanding one's own or another's mental processes **4** *psychiatry* the ability to understand one's own problems, sometimes used to distinguish between psychotic and neurotic disorders ▷ 'in,sightful *adj*

insignia (ɪn'sɪgnɪə) *n, pl* -nias *or* -nia **1** a badge or emblem of membership, office, or dignity **2** a distinguishing sign or mark [c17: from Latin: marks, badges, from *insignis* distinguished by a mark, prominent, from IN-² + *signum* mark]

insignificant (ˌɪnsɪg'nɪfɪkənt) *adj* **1** having little or no importance; trifling **2** almost or relatively meaningless **3** small or inadequate: *an insignificant wage* **4** not distinctive in character, etc ▷ ,insig'nificance *or* ,insig'nificancy *n* ▷ ,insig'nificantly *adv*

insincere (ˌɪnsɪn'sɪə) *adj* lacking sincerity; hypocritical ▷ ,insin'cerely *adv* ▷ insincerity (ˌɪnsɪn'sɛrɪtɪ) *n*

insinuate (ɪn'sɪnjʊˌeɪt) *vb* **1** (*may take a clause as object*) to suggest by indirect allusion, hints, innuendo, etc **2** (*tr*) to introduce subtly or deviously **3** (*tr*) to cause (someone, esp oneself) to be accepted by gradual approaches or manoeuvres [c16: from Latin *insinuāre* to wind one's way into, from IN-² + *sinus* curve] ▷ in'sinuative *or* in'sinuatory *adj* ▷ in'sinu,ator *n*

insinuation (ɪnˌsɪnjʊ'eɪʃən) *n* **1** an indirect or devious hint or suggestion **2** the act or practice of insinuating

insipid (ɪn'sɪpɪd) *adj* **1** lacking spirit; boring **2** lacking taste; unpalatable [c17: from Latin *insipidus*, from IN-¹ + *sapidus* full of flavour, SAPID] ▷ ,insi'pidity *or* in'sipidness *n* ▷ in'sipidly *adv*

insist (ɪn'sɪst) *vb* (*when tr, takes a clause as object; when intr, usually foll by on or upon*) **1** to make a determined demand (for): *he insisted that his rights be respected; he insisted on his rights* **2** to express a convinced belief (in) or assertion (of) [c16: from Latin *insistere* to stand upon, urge, from IN-² + *sistere* to stand] ▷ in'sister *n* ▷ in'sistingly *adv*

insistent (ɪn'sɪstənt) *adj* **1** making continual and persistent demands **2** demanding notice or attention; compelling: *the insistent cry of a bird* ▷ in'sistence *or* in'sistency *n* ▷ in'sistently *adv*

in situ Latin (ɪn 'sɪtjuː) *adv, adj* (*postpositive*) in the natural, original, or appropriate position

in so far as *or* **insofar as** (ˌɪnsəʊ'fɑː) *adv* to the degree or extent that

insolation (ˌɪnsəʊ'leɪʃən) *n* **1** the quantity of solar radiation falling upon a body or planet, esp per unit area **2** exposure to the sun's rays **3** former name for **sunstroke**

insole ('ɪn,səʊl) *n* **1** the inner sole of a shoe or boot **2** a loose additional inner sole used to give extra warmth, comfort, etc

insolent ('ɪnsələnt) *adj* offensive, impudent, or disrespectful [c14: from Latin *insolens*, from IN-¹ + *solēre* to be accustomed] ▷ 'insolence *n* ▷ 'insolently *adv*

insoluble (ɪn'sɒljʊbəl) *adj* **1** incapable of being dissolved; incapable of forming a solution, esp in water **2** incapable of being solved ▷ in,solu'bility *or* in'solubleness *n* ▷ in'solubly *adv*

insolvent (ɪn'sɒlvənt) *adj* **1** (of a person, company, etc) having insufficient assets to meet debts and liabilities; bankrupt **2** of or relating to bankrupts or bankruptcy ▷ *n* **3** a person who is insolvent; bankrupt ▷ in'solvency *n*

insomnia (ɪn'sɒmnɪə) *n* chronic inability to fall asleep or to enjoy uninterrupted sleep [c18: from Latin, from *insomnis* sleepless, from *somnus* sleep] ▷ in'somnious *adj* ▷ in'somni,ac *adj, n*

insomuch (ˌɪnsəʊ'mʌtʃ) *adv* **1** (foll by *as* or *that*) to such an extent or degree **2** (foll by *as*) because of the fact (that); inasmuch (as)

insouciant (ɪn'suːsɪənt) *adj* carefree or unconcerned; light-hearted [c19: from French, from IN-¹ + *souciant* worrying, from *soucier* to trouble, from Latin *sollicitāre*; compare SOLICITOUS] ▷ in'souciance *n* ▷ in'souciantly *adv*

insourcing ('ɪn,sɔːsɪŋ) *n* the practice of subcontracting work to another company that is under the same general ownership ▷ 'in,source *vb*

inspan (ɪn'spæn) *vb* -spans, -spanning, -spanned (*tr*) *chiefly South African* **1** to harness (animals) to (a vehicle); yoke **2** to press (people) into service [c19: from Afrikaans, from Middle Dutch *inspannen*, from *spannen* to stretch, yoke; see SPAN¹]

inspect (ɪn'spɛkt) *vb* (*tr*) **1** to examine closely, esp for faults or errors **2** to scrutinize officially (a document, military personnel on ceremonial parade, etc) [c17: from Latin *inspicere*, from *specere* to look] ▷ in'spectable *adj* ▷ in'spection *n* ▷ in'spective *adj*

inspector (ɪn'spɛktə) *n* **1** a person who inspects, esp an official who examines for compliance with regulations, standards, etc **2** a police officer ranking below a superintendent or chief inspector and above a sergeant ▷ in'spectoral *or* inspectorial (ˌɪnspɛk'tɔːrɪəl) *adj* ▷ in'spector,ship *n*

inspectorate (ɪn'spɛktərɪt) *n* **1** the office, rank, or duties of an inspector **2** a body of inspectors **3** a district under an inspector

inspiration (ˌɪnspɪ'reɪʃən) *n* **1** stimulation or arousal of the mind, feelings, etc, to special or unusual activity or creativity **2** the state or quality of being so stimulated or aroused **3** someone or something that causes this state **4** an idea or action resulting from such a state **5** the act or process of inhaling; breathing in

inspirational (ˌɪnspɪ'reɪʃənəl) *adj* **1** of, relating to, or tending to arouse inspiration; inspiring **2** resulting from inspiration; inspired ▷ ,inspi'rationally *adv*

inspiratory (ɪn'spaɪərətɪ, -trɪ) *adj* of or relating to inhalation or the drawing in of air

inspire (ɪn'spaɪə) *vb* **1** to exert a stimulating or beneficial effect upon (a person); animate or invigorate **2** (*tr*; foll by *with* or *to*; *may take an infinitive*) to arouse (with a particular emotion or to a particular action); stir **3** (*tr*) to prompt or instigate; give rise to **4** (*tr*; *often passive*) to guide or arouse by divine influence or inspiration **5** to take or draw (air, gas, etc) into the lungs; inhale **6** (*tr*) *archaic* to breathe into or upon [c14 (in the sense: to breathe upon, blow into): from Latin *inspīrāre*, from *spīrāre* to breathe] ▷ in'spirable *adj* ▷ in'spirative *adj* ▷ in'spirer *n*

> in'spiringly *adv*

inspirit (ɪn'spɪrɪt) *vb* (*tr*) to fill with vigour; inspire
> in'spiriter *n* > in'spiriting *adj* > in'spiritment *n*

inspissate (ɪn'spɪseɪt) *vb archaic* to thicken, as by
evaporation [C17: from Late Latin *inspissātus* thickened,
from Latin *spissāre* to thicken, from *spissus* thick]
> ,inspis'sation *n* > 'inspis,sator *n*

Inst. *abbreviation* 1 Institute 2 Institution

instability (,ɪnstə'bɪlɪtɪ) *n*, *pl* -ties 1 lack of stability or
steadiness 2 tendency to variable or unpredictable
behaviour

install *or* **instal** (ɪn'stɔːl) *vb* -stalls, -stalling, -stalled *or*
-stals, -stalling, -stalled (*tr*) 1 to place (machinery,
equipment, etc) in position and connect and adjust for
use 2 to transfer (computer software) from a
distribution file to a permanent location on disk, and
prepare it for its particular environment and application
3 to put in a position, rank, etc 4 to settle (a person, esp
oneself) in a position or state: *she installed herself in an
armchair* [C16: from Medieval Latin *installāre*, from IN-² +
stallum STALL¹] > in'staller *n*

installation (,ɪnstə'leɪʃən) *n* 1 the act of installing or the
state of being installed 2 a large device, system, or piece
of equipment that has been installed

installment plan *or esp Canadian* **instalment plan** *n US &
Canadian* a system for purchasing merchandise, such as
cars or furniture, in which the buyer takes possession of
the merchandise on payment of a deposit and completes
the purchase by paying a series of regular instalments
while the seller retains ownership until the final
instalment is paid. Also called (in Britain and certain
other countries): hire-purchase

instalment *or US* **installment** (ɪn'stɔːlmənt) *n* 1 one of
the portions, usually equal, into which a debt is divided
for payment at specified intervals over a fixed period 2 a
portion of something that is issued, broadcast, or
published in parts, such as a serial in a magazine [C18:
from obsolete *estallment*, probably from Old French *estaler*
to fix, hence to agree rate of payment, from *estal*
something fixed, place, from Old High German *stal*
STALL¹]

instance ('ɪnstəns) *n* 1 a case or particular example 2 for
instance for or as an example 3 a specified stage in
proceedings; step (in the phrases **in the first, second,**
etc, **instance**) 4 urgent request or demand (esp in the
phrase **at the instance of**) ▷ *vb* 5 to cite as an
example [C14 (in the sense: case, example): from
Medieval Latin *instantia* example, (in the sense: urgency)
from Latin: a being close upon, presence, from *instāns*
pressing upon, urgent; see INSTANT]

instant ('ɪnstənt) *n* 1 a very brief time; moment 2 a
particular moment or point in time: *at the same instant*
3 on the instant immediately; without delay ▷ *adj*
4 immediate; instantaneous 5 (esp of foods) prepared or
designed for preparation with very little time and effort:
instant coffee 6 urgent or imperative 7 (*postpositive*) (when
abbreviated in formal correspondence) of the present
month: *a letter of the 7th instant*. Abbreviation: inst [C15:
from Latin *instāns*, from *instāre* to be present, press
closely, from IN-² + *stāre* to stand]

instantaneous (,ɪnstən'teɪnɪəs) *adj* 1 occurring with
almost no delay; immediate 2 happening or completed
within a moment: *instantaneous death* > ,instan'taneously
adv > ,instan'taneousness *or* instantaneity
(ɪn,stæntə'niːɪtɪ) *n*

instanter (ɪn'stæntə) *adv law* without delay; (in
connection with pleading) the same day or within 24
hours [C17: from Latin: urgently, from *instans* INSTANT]

instantly ('ɪnstəntlɪ) *adv* 1 immediately; at once 2 *archaic*
urgently or insistently

instant messaging *n computing* the online facility that
allows the instant exchange of written messages
between two or more people using different computers
or mobile phones. Abbreviation: IM

instar ('ɪnstɑː) *n* the stage in the development of an
insect between any two moults [C19: New Latin from
Latin: image]

instate (ɪn'steɪt) *vb* (*tr*) to place in a position or office;
install > in'statement *n*

instead (ɪn'stɛd) *adv* 1 as a replacement, substitute, or
alternative 2 instead of (*preposition*) in place of or as an
alternative to [C13: from phrase *in stead* in place]

instep ('ɪn,stɛp) *n* 1 the middle section of the human
foot, forming the arch between the ankle and toes 2 the
part of a shoe, stocking, etc, covering this [C16: probably
from IN-² + STEP]

instigate ('ɪnstɪ,geɪt) *vb* (*tr*) 1 to bring about, as by
incitement or urging: *to instigate rebellion* 2 to urge on to
some drastic or inadvisable action [C16: from Latin
instīgāre to stimulate, incite; compare Greek *stizein* to
prick] > ,insti'gation *n* > 'insti,gative *adj* > 'insti,gator *n*

instil *or US* **instill** (ɪn'stɪl) *vb* -stils *or* -stills, -stilling,
-stilled (*tr*) 1 to introduce gradually; implant or infuse
2 *rare* to pour in or inject in drops [C16: from Latin
instillāre to pour in a drop at a time, from *stillāre* to drip]
> in'stiller *n* > in'stilment *or US* in'stillment *or*
,instil'lation *n*

instinct *n* ('ɪnstɪŋkt) 1 the innate capacity of an animal
to respond to a given stimulus in a relatively fixed way
2 inborn intuitive power ▷ *adj* (ɪn'stɪŋkt) 3 *rare*
(*postpositive*; often foll by *with*) **a** animated or impelled
(by) **b** imbued or infused (with) [C15: from Latin
instinctus roused, from *instinguere* to incite; compare
INSTIGATE]

instinctive (ɪn'stɪŋktɪv) *or* **instinctual** *adj* 1 of, relating
to, or resulting from instinct 2 conditioned so as to
appear innate: *an instinctive movement in driving*
> in'stinctively *or* in'stinctually *adv*

institute ('ɪnstɪ,tjuːt) *vb* (*tr*) 1 to organize; establish 2 to
initiate: *to institute a practice* 3 to establish in a position or
office; induct ▷ *n* 4 an organization founded for
particular work, such as education, promotion of the
arts, or scientific research 5 the building where such an
organization is situated 6 something instituted, esp a
rule, custom, or precedent [C16: from Latin *instituere*,
from *statuere* to place, stand] > 'insti,tutor *or* 'insti,tuter *n*

institutes ('ɪnstɪ,tjuːts) *pl n* a digest or summary, esp of
laws

institution (,ɪnstɪ'tjuːʃən) *n* 1 the act of instituting 2 an
organization or establishment founded for a specific
purpose, such as a hospital, church, company, or college
3 the building where such an organization is situated
4 an established custom, law, or relationship in a society
or community 5 Also called: institutional investor a
large organization, such as an insurance company,
bank, or pension fund, that has substantial sums to
invest on a stock exchange 6 *informal* a constant feature
or practice: *Jones' drink at the bar was an institution* 7 the
appointment or admission of an incumbent to an
ecclesiastical office or pastoral charge
> ,insti'tutionary *adj*

institutional (,ɪnstɪ'tjuːʃənəl) *adj* 1 of, relating to, or
characteristic of institutions 2 dull, routine, and
uniform: *institutional meals* 3 relating to principles or
institutes, esp of law > ,insti'tutionally *adv*

institutionalize *or* **institutionalise** (,ɪnstɪ'tjuːʃənə,laɪz)
vb 1 (*tr*; *often passive*) to subject to the deleterious effects
of confinement in an institution 2 (*tr*) to place in an
institution 3 to make or become an institution
> ,insti,tutionali'zation *or* ,insti,tutionali'sation *n*

in-store *adj* available or taking place within a
supermarket or other large shop: *in-store banking facilities*

instruct (ɪn'strʌkt) *vb* (*tr*) 1 to direct to do something;
order 2 to teach (someone) how to do (something) 3 to
furnish with information; apprise 4 *law chiefly Brit* (esp
of a client to his solicitor or a solicitor to a barrister) to
give relevant facts or information to [C15: from Latin
instruere to construct, set in order, equip, teach, from
struere to build] > in'structible *adj*

instruction (ɪn'strʌkʃən) *n* 1 a direction; order 2 the
process or act of imparting knowledge; teaching;
education 3 *computing* a part of a program consisting of a
coded command to the computer to perform a specified
function > in'structional *adj*

instructions (ɪn'strʌkʃənz) *pl n* 1 directions, orders, or
recommended rules for guidance, use, etc 2 *law* the
facts and details relating to a case given by a client to
his solicitor or by a solicitor to a barrister with

directions to conduct the case

instructive (ɪnˈstrʌktɪv) *adj* serving to instruct or enlighten; conveying information ▷ in'structively *adv* ▷ in'structiveness *n*

instructor (ɪnˈstrʌktə) *n* 1 someone who instructs; teacher 2 *US & Canadian* a university teacher ranking below assistant professor ▷ in'structor,ship *n* ▷ instructress (ɪnˈstrʌktrɪs) *fem n*

instrument *n* (ˈɪnstrəmənt) 1 a mechanical implement or tool, esp one used for precision work 2 *music* any of various contrivances or mechanisms that can be played to produce musical tones or sounds 3 an important factor or agency in something: *her evidence was an instrument in his arrest* 4 *informal* a person used by another to gain an end; dupe; tool 5 a measuring device, such as a pressure gauge or ammeter 6 a a device or system for use in navigation or control, esp of aircraft b (*as modifier*): *instrument landing* 7 a formal legal document ▷ *vb* (ˈɪnstrəˌmɛnt) (*tr*) 8 another word for **orchestrate** (sense 1) 9 to equip with instruments [c13: from Latin *instrūmentum* tool, equipment, from *instruere* to erect, furnish; see INSTRUCT]

instrumental (ˌɪnstrəˈmɛntəl) *adj* 1 serving as a means or influence; helpful 2 of, relating to, or characterized by an instrument or instruments 3 played by or composed for musical instruments 4 *grammar* denoting a case of nouns, etc, in certain inflected languages, indicating the instrument used in performing an action, usually translated into English using the prepositions *with* or *by means of* ▷ *n* 5 a piece of music composed for instruments rather than for voices 6 *grammar* the instrumental case ▷ ,instrumen'tality *n* ▷ ,instru'mentally *adv*

instrumentalist (ˌɪnstrəˈmɛntəlɪst) *n* a person who plays a musical instrument

instrumentation (ˌɪnstrəmɛnˈteɪʃən) *n* 1 the instruments specified in a musical score or arrangement 2 the study of the characteristics of musical instruments 3 the use of instruments or tools

instrument panel *or* **instrument board** *n* 1 a panel on which instruments are mounted, as on a car. See also **dashboard** 2 an array of instruments, gauges, etc, mounted to display the condition or performance of a machine or process

insubordinate (ˌɪnsəˈbɔːdɪnɪt) *adj* 1 not submissive to authority; disobedient or rebellious 2 not in a subordinate position or rank ▷ *n* 3 an insubordinate person ▷ ,insub'ordinately *adv* ▷ ,insub,ordi'nation *n*

insubstantial (ˌɪnsəbˈstænʃəl) *adj* 1 not substantial; flimsy, tenuous, or slight 2 imaginary; unreal ▷ ,insub,stanti'ality *n* ▷ ,insub'stantially *adv*

insufferable (ɪnˈsʌfərəbəl) *adj* intolerable; unendurable ▷ in'sufferableness *n* ▷ in'sufferably *adv*

insufficiency (ˌɪnsəˈfɪʃənsɪ) *n* 1 Also called: insufficience the state of being insufficient 2 *pathol* failure in the functioning of an organ, tissue, etc: *cardiac insufficiency*

insufficient (ˌɪnsəˈfɪʃənt) *adj* not sufficient; inadequate or deficient ▷ ,insuf'ficiently *adv*

insufflate (ˈɪnsʌˌfleɪt) *vb* 1 (*tr*) to breathe or blow (something) into (a room, area, etc) 2 *med* to blow (air, medicated powder, etc) into the lungs or into a body cavity 3 (*tr*) to breathe or blow upon (someone or something) as a ritual or sacramental act, esp so as to symbolize the influence of the Holy Spirit ▷ ,insuf'flation *n* ▷ 'insuf,flator *n*

insular (ˈɪnsjʊlə) *adj* 1 of, relating to, or resembling an island 2 remote, detached, or aloof 3 illiberal or narrow-minded 4 isolated or separated [c17: from Late Latin *insulāris*, from Latin *insula* island, ISLE] ▷ 'insularism *or* insularity (ˌɪnsjʊˈlærɪtɪ) *n* ▷ 'insularly *adv*

insulate (ˈɪnsjʊˌleɪt) *vb* (*tr*) 1 to prevent or reduce the transmission of electricity, heat, or sound to or from (a body, device, or region) by surrounding with a nonconducting material 2 to isolate or detach [c16: from Late Latin *insulātus*: made into an island]

insulation (ˌɪnsjʊˈleɪʃən) *n* 1 Also called: insulant (ˈɪnsjʊlənt) material used to insulate a body, device, or region 2 the act or process of insulating

insulator (ˈɪnsjʊˌleɪtə) *n* any material or device that insulates, esp a material with a very low electrical conductivity or thermal conductivity or something made of such a material

insulin (ˈɪnsjʊlɪn) *n* a protein hormone, secreted in the pancreas by the islets of Langerhans, that controls the concentration of glucose in the blood. Insulin deficiency results in diabetes mellitus [c20: from New Latin *insula* islet (of the pancreas) + -IN]

insult *vb* (ɪnˈsʌlt) (*tr*) 1 to treat, mention, or speak to rudely; offend; affront ▷ *n* (ˈɪnsʌlt) 2 an offensive or contemptuous remark or action; affront; slight 3 a person or thing producing the effect of an affront: *some television is an insult to intelligence* 4 *med* an injury or trauma [c16: from Latin *insultāre* to jump upon, from IN-² + *saltāre* to jump] ▷ in'sulter *n*

insuperable (ɪnˈsuːpərəbəl, -prəbəl, -ˈsjuː-) *adj* incapable of being overcome; insurmountable ▷ in,supera'bility *or* in'superableness *n* ▷ in'superably *adv*

insupportable (ˌɪnsəˈpɔːtəbəl) *adj* 1 incapable of being endured; intolerable; insufferable 2 incapable of being supported or justified; indefensible ▷ ,insup'portableness *n* ▷ ,insup'portably *adv*

insurance (ɪnˈʃʊərəns, -ˈʃɔː-) *n* 1 a the act, system, or business of providing financial protection for property, life, health, etc, against specified contingencies, such as death, loss, or damage, and involving payment of regular premiums in return for a policy guaranteeing such protection b the state of having such protection c Also called: insurance policy the policy providing such protection d the pecuniary amount of such protection e the premium payable in return for such protection f (*as modifier*): *insurance agent; insurance broker; insurance company* 2 a means of protecting or safeguarding against risk or injury

insure (ɪnˈʃʊə, -ˈʃɔː) *vb* 1 (often foll by *against*) to guarantee or protect (against risk, loss, etc) 2 (often foll by *against*) to issue (a person) with an insurance policy or take out an insurance policy (on): *his house was heavily insured against fire; after all his car accidents the company refuses to insure him again* 3 another word (esp US) for **ensure** (senses 1, 2) ▷ Also (rare) (for senses 1, 2) **ensure** ▷ in'surable *adj* ▷ in,sura'bility *n*

insured (ɪnˈʃʊəd, -ˈʃɔːd) *adj* 1 covered by insurance: *an insured risk* ▷ *n* 2 the person, persons, or organization covered by an insurance policy

insurer (ɪnˈʃʊərə, -ˈʃɔː-) *n* 1 a person or company offering insurance policies in return for premiums 2 a person or thing that insures

insurgence (ɪnˈsɜːdʒəns) *n* rebellion, uprising, or riot

insurgent (ɪnˈsɜːdʒənt) *adj* 1 rebellious or in revolt, as against a government in power or the civil authorities ▷ *n* 2 a person who takes part in an uprising or rebellion; insurrectionist [c18: from Latin *insurgēns* rising upon or against, from *insurgere* to rise up, from *surgere* to rise] ▷ in'surgency *n*

insurmountable (ˌɪnsəˈmaʊntəbəl) *adj* incapable of being overcome; insuperable ▷ ,insur,mounta'bility *or* ,insur'mountableness *n* ▷ ,insur'mountably *adv*

insurrection (ˌɪnsəˈrɛkʃən) *n* the act or an instance of rebelling against a government in power or the civil authorities; insurgency [c15: from Late Latin *insurrectiō*, from *insurgere* to rise up] ▷ ,insur'rectional *adj*

intact (ɪnˈtækt) *adj* untouched or unimpaired; left complete or perfect [c15: from Latin *intactus* not touched, from *tangere* to touch] ▷ in'tactness *n*

intaglio (ɪnˈtɑːlɪˌəʊ) *n, pl* -lios *or* -li (-lɪː) 1 a seal, gem, etc, ornamented with a sunken or incised design, as opposed to a design in relief 2 the art or process of incised carving 3 a design, figure, or ornamentation carved, engraved, or etched into the surface of the material used 4 any of various printing techniques using an etched or engraved plate. The whole plate is smeared with ink, the surface wiped clean, and the ink in the recesses then transferred to the paper or other material 5 an incised die used to make a design in relief [c17: from Italian, from *intagliare* to engrave, from *tagliare* to cut, from Late Latin *tāliāre*; see TAILOR] ▷ intagliated (ɪnˈtɑːlɪˌeɪtɪd) *adj*

intake (ˈɪnˌteɪk) *n* 1 a thing or a quantity taken in: *an* *intake of students* **2** the act of taking in **3** the opening through which fluid enters a duct or channel, esp the air inlet of a jet engine **4** a ventilation shaft in a mine **5** a contraction or narrowing: *an intake in a garment*

intangible (ɪnˈtændʒɪbªl) *adj* **1** incapable of being perceived by touch; impalpable **2** imprecise or unclear to the mind: *intangible ideas* **3** (of property or a business asset) saleable though not possessing intrinsic productive value ▷ *n* **4** something that is intangible > inˌtangiˈbility or inˈtangibleness *n* > inˈtangibly *adv*

intarsia (ɪnˈtɑːsɪə) or **tarsia** *n* **1** a decorative or pictorial mosaic of inlaid wood or sometimes ivory of a style developed in the Italian Renaissance and used esp on wooden wall panels **2** (in knitting) an individually worked motif [C19: changed from Italian *intarsio*]

integer (ˈɪntɪdʒə) *n* **1** any rational number that can be expressed as the sum or difference of a finite number of units, being a member of the set ...−3, −2, −1, 0, 1, 2, 3... **2** an individual entity or whole unit [C16: from Latin: untouched, entire, from *tangere* to touch]

integral (ˈɪntɪɡrəl, ɪnˈtɛɡrəl) **1** (often foll by *to*) being an essential part (of); intrinsic (to) **2** intact; entire **3** formed of constituent parts; united **4** *maths* **a** of or involving an integral **b** involving or being an integer ▷ *n* (ˈɪntɪɡrəl) **5** *maths* the limit of an increasingly large number of increasingly smaller quantities, related to the function that is being integrated (the *integrand*). The independent variable may be confined within certain limits (**definite integral**) or in the absence of limits (**indefinite integral**) **6** a complete thing; whole > integrality (ˌɪntɪˈɡrælɪtɪ) *n* > ˈintegrally *adv*

integral calculus *n* the branch of calculus concerned with the determination of integrals and their application to the solution of differential equations, the determination of areas and volumes, etc

integrand (ˈɪntɪˌɡrænd) *n* a mathematical function to be integrated [C19: from Latin: to be integrated]

integrant (ˈɪntəɡrənt) *adj* **1** part of a whole; integral; constituent ▷ *n* **2** an integrant thing or part

integrate (ˈɪntɪˌɡreɪt) *vb* **1** to make or be made into a whole; incorporate or be incorporated **2** (*tr*) to designate (a school, park, etc) for use by all races or groups; desegregate **3** to amalgamate or mix (a racial or religious group) with an existing community *adj* (ˈɪntɪɡrɪt) **4** made up of parts; integrated [C17: from Latin *integrāre*; see INTEGER] > **integrable** (ˈɪntəɡrəbªl) *adj* > ˌintegraˈbility *n* > ˈinteˌgrative *adj* > ˈinteˈgration *n*

integrated circuit *n* a very small electronic circuit consisting of an assembly of elements made from a chip of semiconducting material, such as crystalline silicon

integrity (ɪnˈtɛɡrɪtɪ) *n* **1** adherence to moral principles; honesty **2** the quality of being unimpaired; soundness **3** unity; wholeness [C15: from Latin *integritās*; see INTEGER]

integument (ɪnˈtɛɡjʊmənt) *n* the outer protective layer or covering of an animal, such as skin or a cuticle [C17: from Latin *integumentum*, from *tegere* to cover] > inˌteguˈmental or inˌteguˈmentary *adj*

intel (ˈɪntɛl) *n informal* **a** *US* military intelligence **b** information in general

intellect (ˈɪntɪˌlɛkt) *n* **1** the capacity for understanding, thinking, and reasoning, as distinct from feeling or wishing **2** a mind or intelligence, esp a brilliant one: *his intellect is wasted on that job* **3** *informal* a person possessing a brilliant mind; brain [C14: from Latin *intellectus* comprehension, intellect, from *intellegere* to understand; see INTELLIGENCE] > ˌintelˈlective *adj* > ˌintelˈlectively *adv*

intellection (ˌɪntɪˈlɛkʃən) *n* **1** mental activity; thought **2** an idea or thought

intellectual (ˌɪntɪˈlɛktʃʊəl) *adj* **1** of or relating to the intellect, as opposed to the emotions **2** appealing to or characteristic of people with a developed intellect: *intellectual literature* **3** expressing or enjoying mental activity ▷ *n* **4** a person who enjoys mental activity and has highly developed tastes in art, literature, etc **5** a person who uses or works with his intellect **6** a highly intelligent person > ˌintelˈlectuˈality or ˌintelˈlectualness *n* > ˌintelˈlectually *adv* > ˌintelˈlectualize or ˌintelˈlectualise *vb*

intellectualism (ˌɪntɪˈlɛktʃʊəˌlɪzəm) *n* **1** development and exercise of the intellect **2** *philosophy* the doctrine that reason is the ultimate criterion of knowledge > ˌintelˈlectualist *n, adj* > ˌintelˌlectualˈistic *adj*

intellectually handicapped *adj Austral* mentally handicapped

intellectual property *n* an intangible asset, such as a copyright or patent

intelligence (ɪnˈtɛlɪdʒəns) *n* **1** the capacity for understanding; ability to perceive and comprehend meaning **2** *old-fashioned* news; information **3** military information about enemies, spies, etc **4** a group or department that gathers or deals with such information **5** (*often capital*) an intelligent being, esp one that is not embodied **6** (*modifier*) of or relating to intelligence: *an intelligence network* [C14: from Latin *intelligentia*, from *intellegere* to discern, comprehend, literally: choose between, from INTER- + *legere* to choose] > inˌtelliˈgential *adj*

intelligence quotient *n* a measure of the intelligence of an individual derived from results obtained from specially designed tests. The quotient is traditionally derived by dividing an individual's mental age by his chronological age and multiplying the result by 100. Abbreviation: IQ

intelligence test *n* any of a number of tests designed to measure a person's mental skills

intelligent (ɪnˈtɛlɪdʒənt) *adj* **1** having or indicating intelligence **2** indicating high intelligence; perceptive: *an intelligent guess* **3** (of computerized functions) able to modify action in the light of ongoing events **4** (*postpositive; foll by of*) *archaic* having knowledge or information > inˈtelligently *adv*

intelligent card *n* another name for **smart card**

intelligent design *n* a theory that rejects the theory of natural selection, arguing that the complexities of the universe and of all life suggest an intelligent cause in the form of a supreme creator

intelligentsia (ɪnˌtɛlɪˈdʒɛntsɪə) *n* (usually preceded by *the*) the educated or intellectual people in a society or community [C20: from Russian *intelligentsiya*, from Latin *intelligentia* INTELLIGENCE]

intelligible (ɪnˈtɛlɪdʒəbªl) *adj* **1** able to be understood; comprehensible **2** *philosophy* capable of being apprehended by the mind or intellect alone [C14: from Latin *intellegibilis*; see INTELLECT] > inˌtelligiˈbility or inˈtelligibleness *n* > inˈtelligibly *adv*

intemperate (ɪnˈtɛmpərɪt, -prɪt) *adj* **1** consuming alcoholic drink habitually or to excess **2** unrestrained: *intemperate rage* **3** extreme or severe: *an intemperate climate* > inˈtemperance or inˈtemperateness *n* > inˈtemperately *adv*

intend (ɪnˈtɛnd) *vb* **1** (*may take a clause as object*) to propose or plan (something or to do something); have in mind; mean **2** (*tr; often foll by for*) to design or destine (for a certain purpose, person, etc) **3** (*tr*) to mean to express or indicate: *what do his words intend?* **4** (*intr*) to have a purpose as specified; mean: *he intends well* [C14: from Latin *intendere* to stretch forth, give one's attention to, from *tendere* to stretch] > inˈtender *n*

intendancy (ɪnˈtɛndənsɪ) *n* **1** the position or work of an intendant **2** intendants collectively

intendant (ɪnˈtɛndənt) *n* a senior administrator in some countries, esp in Latin America

intended (ɪnˈtɛndɪd) *adj* **1** planned or future ▷ *n* **2** *informal* a person whom one is to marry; fiancé or fiancée

intense (ɪnˈtɛns) *adj* **1** of extreme force, strength, degree, or amount: *intense heat* **2** characterized by deep or forceful feelings: *an intense person* [C14: from Latin *intensus* stretched, from *intendere* to stretch out; see INTEND] > inˈtensely *adv* > inˈtenseness *n*

● USAGE *Intense* is sometimes wrongly used where
● *intensive* is meant: *the land is under intensive* (not *intense*)
● *cultivation*. *Intensely* is sometimes wrongly used where
● *intently* is meant: *he listened intently* (not *intensely*)

intensifier (ɪnˈtɛnsɪˌfaɪə) *n* **1** a person or thing that intensifies **2** a word, esp an adjective or adverb, that has little semantic content of its own but that serves to intensify the meaning of the word or phrase that it modifies: *awfully* and *up* are intensifiers in the phrases *awfully sorry* and *cluttered up* **3** a substance, esp one containing silver or uranium, used to increase the density of a photographic film or plate

intensify (ɪnˈtɛnsɪˌfaɪ) *vb* **-fies, -fying, -fied 1** to make or become intense or more intense **2** (*tr*) to increase the density of (a photographic film or plate) > inˌtensifiˈcation *n*

intension (ɪnˈtɛnʃən) *n logic* the set of characteristics or properties by which the referent or referents of a given word are determined: thus, the intension of *marsupial* is the set containing the characteristics *suckling its young* and *having a pouch* > inˈtensional *adj*

intensity (ɪnˈtɛnsɪtɪ) *n, pl* -ties **1** the state or quality of being intense **2** extreme force, degree, or amount **3** *physics* **a** a measure of field strength or of the energy transmitted by radiation **b** (of sound in a specified direction) the average rate of flow of sound energy, usually in watts, for one period through unit area at right angles to the specified direction

intensive (ɪnˈtɛnsɪv) *adj* **1** involving the maximum use of land, time, or some other resource: *intensive agriculture; an intensive course* **2** (*usually in combination*) using one factor of production proportionately more than others, as specified: *capital-intensive; labour-intensive* **3** *agriculture* involving or farmed using large amounts of capital or labour to increase production from a particular area. See **extensive** (sense 3) **4** denoting or relating to a grammatical intensifier **5** denoting or belonging to a class of pronouns used to emphasize a noun or personal pronoun, such as *himself* in the sentence *John himself did it.* In English, intensive pronouns are identical in form with reflexive pronouns **6** of or relating to intension ▷ *n* **7** an intensifier or intensive pronoun or grammatical construction > inˈtensively *adv* > inˈtensiveness *n*

intensive care *n* extensive and continuous care and treatment provided for an acutely ill patient, usually in a specially designated section (**intensive care unit**) of a hospital

intent (ɪnˈtɛnt) *n* **1** something that is intended; aim; purpose; design **2** the act of intending **3** *law* the will or purpose with which one does an act **4** implicit meaning; connotation **5** to all intents and purposes for all practical purposes; virtually ▷ *adj* **6** firmly fixed; determined; concentrated: *an intent look* **7** (*postpositive; usually foll by on or upon*) having the fixed intention (of); directing one's mind or energy (to): *intent on committing a crime* [C13 (in the sense: intention): from Late Latin *intentus* aim, intent, from Latin: a stretching out; see INTEND] > inˈtently *adv* > inˈtentness *n*

intention (ɪnˈtɛnʃən) *n* **1** a purpose or goal; aim: *it is his intention to reform* **2** *med* a natural healing process, as by **first intention**, in which the edges of a wound cling together with no tissue between, or by **second intention**, in which the wound edges adhere with granulation tissue **3** (*usually plural*) design or purpose with respect to a proposal of marriage (esp in the phrase **honourable intentions**)

intentional (ɪnˈtɛnʃənəl) *adj* **1** performed by or expressing intention; deliberate **2** of or relating to intention or purpose > inˌtentionˈality *n* > inˈtentionally *adv*

inter (ɪnˈtɜː) *vb* **-ters, -terring, -terred** (*tr*) to place (a body) in the earth; bury, esp with funeral rites [C14: from Old French *enterrer*, from Latin IN-² + *terra* earth]

inter- *prefix* **1** between or among: *international* **2** together, mutually, or reciprocally: *interdependent; interchange* [from Latin]

interact (ˌɪntərˈækt) *vb* (*intr*) to act on or in close relation with each other

Interact (ˈɪntərˌækt) *n Canadian* a system of electronic bank payments or withdrawals

interaction (ˌɪntərˈækʃən) *n* **1** a mutual or reciprocal action or influence **2** *physics* the transfer of energy between elementary particles, between a particle and a field, or between fields. See **fundamental interaction**

interactive (ˌɪntərˈæktɪv) *adj* **1** allowing or relating to continuous two-way transfer of information between a

user and the central point of a communication system, such as a computer or television **2** (of two or more persons, forces, etc) acting upon or in close relation with each other; interacting

inter alia *Latin* (ˈɪntər ˈeɪlɪə) *adv* among other things

interbreed (ˌɪntəˈbriːd) *vb* **-breeds, -breeding, -bred 1** (*intr*) to breed within a single family or strain so as to produce particular characteristics in the offspring **2** another term for **crossbreed** (sense 1)

interbroker dealer (ˌɪntəˈbrəʊkə) *n stock exchange* a specialist who matches the needs of different market makers and facilitates dealings between them

intercalary (ɪnˈtɜːkələrɪ) *adj* **1** (of a day, month, etc) inserted in the calendar **2** (of a particular year) having one or more days inserted **3** inserted, introduced, or interpolated [C17: from Latin *intercalārius*; see INTERCALATE]

intercalate (ɪnˈtɜːkəˌleɪt) *vb* (*tr*) **1** to insert (one or more days) into the calendar **2** to interpolate or insert [C17: from Latin *intercalāre* to insert, proclaim that a day has been inserted, from INTER- + *calāre* to proclaim] > inˌtercaˈlation *n* > inˈtercalative *adj*

intercede (ˌɪntəˈsiːd) *vb* (*intr*)(often foll by *in*) to come between parties or act as mediator or advocate: *to intercede in the strike* [C16: from Latin *intercēdere* to intervene, from INTER- + *cēdere* to move] > ˌinterˈceder *n*

intercensal (ˌɪntəˈsɛnsəl) *adj* (of population figures, etc) estimated at a time between official censuses [C19: from INTER- + *censal*, irregularly formed from CENSUS]

intercept *vb* (ˌɪntəˈsɛpt) (*tr*) **1** to stop, deflect, or seize on the way from one place to another; prevent from arriving or proceeding **2** *sport* to seize or cut off (a pass) on its way from one opponent to another **3** *maths* to cut off, mark off, or bound (some part of a line, curve, plane, or surface) ▷ *n* (ˈɪntəˌsɛpt) **4** *maths* **a** a point at which two figures intersect **b** the distance from the origin to the point at which a line, curve, or surface cuts a coordinate axis **5** *sport, US & Canadian* the act of intercepting an opponent's pass [C16: from Latin *intercipere* to seize before arrival, from INTER- + *capere* to take] > ˌinterˈception *n* > ˌinterˈceptive *adj*

interceptor *or* **intercepter** (ˌɪntəˈsɛptə) *n* **1** a person or thing that intercepts **2** a fast highly manoeuvrable fighter aircraft used to intercept enemy aircraft

intercession (ˌɪntəˈsɛʃən) *n* **1** the act or an instance of interceding **2** the act of interceding or offering petitionary prayer to God on behalf of others **3** such petitionary prayer [C16: from Latin *intercessio*; see INTERCEDE] > ˌinterˈcessional *or* ˌinterˈcessory *adj* > ˌinterˈcessor *n* > ˌintercesˈsorial *adj*

interchange *vb* (ˌɪntəˈtʃeɪndʒ) **1** to change places or cause to change places; alternate; exchange; switch ▷ *n* (ˈɪntəˌtʃeɪndʒ) **2** the act of interchanging; exchange or alternation **3** a motorway junction of interconnecting roads and bridges designed to prevent streams of traffic crossing one another > ˌinterˈchangeable *adj* > ˌinterˌchangeaˈbility *or* ˌinterˈchangeableness *n* > ˌinterˈchangeably *adv*

Intercity (ˌɪntəˈsɪtɪ) *adj trademark* (in Britain) denoting a fast train or passenger rail service, esp between main towns

intercom (ˈɪntəˌkɒm) *n informal* an internal telephone system for communicating within a building, an aircraft, etc [C20: short for *intercommunication*]

intercommunicate (ˌɪntəkəˈmjuːnɪˌkeɪt) *vb* (*intr*) **1** to communicate mutually **2** to interconnect, as two rooms > ˌintercomˈmunicable *adj* > ˌintercomˌmuniˈcation *n* > ˌintercomˈmunicative *adj*

intercommunion (ˌɪntəkəˈmjuːnjən) *n* association between Churches, involving esp mutual reception of Holy Communion

intercontinental (ˌɪntəˌkɒntɪˈnɛntəl) *adj* relating to travel, commerce, relations, etc, between continents

intercostal (ˌɪntəˈkɒstəl) *adj anatomy* between the ribs: *intercostal muscles* [C16: via New Latin from Latin INTER- + *costa* rib]

intercourse (ˈɪntəˌkɔːs) *n* **1** communication or exchange between individuals; mutual dealings **2** See **sexual intercourse** [C15: from Medieval Latin *intercursus* business, from Latin *intercurrere* to run between, from *currere* to run]

intercurrent (ˌɪntəˈkʌrənt) *adj* **1** occurring during or in between; intervening **2** *pathol* (of a disease) occurring during the course of another disease > ˌinterˈcurrence *n*

interdependent (ˌɪntədɪˈpɛndənt) *adj* relating to two or more people or things dependent on each other

interdict *n* (ˈɪntəˌdɪkt, -ˌdaɪt) **1** *RC Church* the exclusion of a person or all persons in a particular place from certain sacraments and other benefits, although not from communion **2** *civil law* any order made by a court or official prohibiting an act **3** *Scots law* an order having the effect of an injunction ▷ *vb* (ˌɪntəˈdɪkt, -ˈdaɪt) (*tr*) **4** to place under legal or ecclesiastical sanction; prohibit; forbid **5** *military* to destroy (an enemy's lines of communication) by firepower [C13: from Latin *interdictum* prohibition, from *interdicere* to forbid, from INTER- + *dīcere* to say] > ˌinterˈdictive *or* ˌinterˈdictory *adj* > ˌinterˈdictively *adv* > ˌinterˈdictor *n* > ˌinterˈdiction *n*

interdigitate (ˌɪntəˈdɪdʒɪˌteɪt) *vb* (*intr*) to interlock like the fingers of clasped hands [C19: from INTER- + Latin *digitus* (see DIGIT) + -ATE[1]]

interdisciplinary (ˌɪntəˈdɪsɪˌplɪnərɪ) *adj* involving two or more academic disciplines

interest (ˈɪntrɪst, -tərɪst) *n* **1** the sense of curiosity about or concern with something or someone **2** the power of stimulating such a sense: *to have great interest* **3** the quality of such stimulation **4** something in which one is interested; a hobby or pursuit **5** (*often plural*) benefit; advantage: *in one's own interest* **6** (*often plural*) a right, share, or claim, esp in a business or property **7 a** a charge for the use of credit or borrowed money **b** such a charge expressed as a percentage per time unit of the sum borrowed or used **8** (*often plural*) a section of a community, etc, whose members have common aims: *we must not offend the landed interest* **9** declare an interest to make known one's connection, esp a prejudicial connection, with an affair ▷ *vb* (*tr*) **10** to arouse or excite the curiosity or concern of **11** to cause to become involved in something; concern [C15: from Latin: it concerns, from *interesse*; from INTER- + *esse* to be]

interested (ˈɪntrɪstɪd, -tərɪs-) *adj* **1** showing or having interest **2** (*usually prenominal*) personally involved or implicated: *the interested parties met to discuss the business* > ˈinterestedly *adv* > ˈinterestedness *n*

interesting (ˈɪntrɪstɪŋ, -tərɪs-) *adj* inspiring interest; absorbing > ˈinterestingly *adv* > ˈinterestingness *n*

interest-rate futures *pl n* financial futures based on projected movements of interest rates

interface *n* (ˈɪntəˌfeɪs) **1** *chem* a surface that forms the boundary between two bodies, liquids, or chemical phases **2** a common point or boundary between two things, subjects, etc **3** an electrical circuit linking one device, esp a computer, with another ▷ *vb* (ˌɪntəˈfeɪs) **4** (*tr*) to design or adapt the input and output configurations of (two electronic devices) so that they may work together compatibly **5** to be or become an interface (with) **6** to be or become interactive (with) > interfacial (ˌɪntəˈfeɪʃəl) *adj* > ˌinterˈfacially *adv*

interfacing (ˈɪntəˌfeɪsɪŋ) *n* **1** a piece of fabric sewn beneath the facing of a garment, usually at the inside of the neck, armholes, etc, to give shape and firmness **2** another name for **interlining**

interfaith (ˌɪntəˈfeɪθ) *adj* relating to, between, or involving different religions: *to forward interfaith relations*

interfere (ˌɪntəˈfɪə) *vb* (*intr*) **1** (often foll by *in*) to interpose, esp meddlesomely or unwarrantedly; intervene **2** (often foll by *with*) to come between or in opposition; hinder; obstruct **3** (foll by *with*) *euphemistic* to assault sexually **4** to strike one against the other, as a horse's legs **5** *physics* to cause or produce interference [C16: from Old French *s'entreferir* to collide, from *entre-* INTER- + *ferir* to strike, from Latin *ferīre*] > ˌinterˈfering *adj*

interference (ˌɪntəˈfɪərəns) *n* **1** the act or an instance of interfering **2** *physics* the process in which two or more coherent waves combine to form a resultant wave in which the displacement at any point is the vector sum of the displacements of the individual waves. If the individual waves converge the resultant is a system of

fringes. Two waves of equal or nearly equal intensity moving in opposite directions combine to form a standing wave **3** Also called: **radio interference** any undesired signal that tends to interfere with the reception of radio waves > interferential (ˌɪntəfəˈrɛnʃəl) *adj*

interferometer (ˌɪntəfəˈrɒmɪtə) *n physics* any acoustic, optical, or microwave instrument that uses interference patterns or fringes to make accurate measurements of wavelength, wave velocity, distance, etc > interferometric (ˌɪntəˌfɛrəˈmɛtrɪk) *adj* > ˌinterˌferoˈmetrically *adv* > ˌinterferˈometry *n*

interferon (ˌɪntəˈfɪərɒn) *n biochem* any of a family of proteins made by cells in response to virus infection that prevent the growth of the virus. Some interferons can prevent cell growth and have been tested for use in cancer therapy [C20: from INTERFERE + -ON]

interfuse (ˌɪntəˈfjuːz) *vb* **1** to diffuse or mix throughout or become so diffused or mixed; intermingle **2** to blend or fuse or become blended or fused > ˌinterˈfusion *n*

intergovernmental (ˌɪntəˌgʌvəˈmɛntəl) *adj* conducted between or involving two or more governments

interim (ˈɪntərɪm) *adj* **1** (*prenominal*) temporary, provisional, or intervening: *interim measures to deal with the emergency* ▷ *n* **2** the interim the intervening time; the meantime (esp in the phrase **in the interim**) ▷ *adv* **3** *rare* meantime [C16: from Latin: meanwhile]

interior (ɪnˈtɪərɪə) *n* **1** a part, surface, or region that is inside or on the inside: *the interior of Africa* **2** inner character or nature **3** a film or scene shot inside a building, studio, etc **4** a picture of the inside of a room or building, as in a painting or stage design **5** the inside of a building or room, with respect to design and decoration ▷ *adj* **6** of, situated on, or suitable for the inside; inner **7** coming or acting from within; internal **8** of or involving a nation's domestic affairs; internal **9** (esp of one's spiritual or mental life) secret or private; not observable [C15: from Latin (adj), comparative of *inter* within] > inˈteriorly *adv*

interior angle *n* an angle of a polygon contained between two adjacent sides

interior decoration *n* **1** the colours, furniture, etc, of the interior of a house, etc **2** Also called: **interior design** the art or business of an interior decorator > **interior decorator** *n*

interiority (ɪnˌtɪərɪˈɒrɪtɪ) *n* the quality of being focused on one's inner life and identity

interiorize *or* **interiorise** (ɪnˈtɪərɪəˌraɪz) *vb* (*tr*) another word for **internalize**

interj. *abbreviation* interjection

interject (ˌɪntəˈdʒɛkt) *vb* (*tr*) to interpose abruptly or sharply; interrupt with; throw in: *she interjected clever remarks* [C15: from Latin *interjicere* to place between, from *jacere* to throw] > ˌinterˈjector *n*

interjection (ˌɪntəˈdʒɛkʃən) *n* **1** the act of interjecting **2** a word or phrase that is characteristically used in syntactic isolation and that usually expresses sudden emotion; expletive. Abbreviation: **interj** > ˌinterˈjectional *or* ˌinterˈjectory *adj* > ˌinterˈjectionally *adv*

Interlaken (ˈɪntəˌlɑːkən) *n* a town and resort in central Switzerland, situated between Lakes Brienz and Thun on the River Aar. Pop: 5119 (2000)

interlard (ˌɪntəˈlɑːd) *vb* **1** to scatter thickly in or between; intersperse: *to interlard one's writing with foreign phrases* **2** to occur frequently in; be scattered in or through: *foreign phrases interlard his writings*

interlay (ˌɪntəˈleɪ) *vb* -lays, -laying, -laid (-ˈleɪd) (*tr*) to insert (layers) between; interpose

interleaf (ˈɪntəˌliːf) *n*, *pl* -leaves a blank leaf inserted between the leaves of a book

interleave (ˌɪntəˈliːv) *vb* (*tr*) **1** (often foll by *with*) to intersperse (with), esp alternately, as the illustrations in a book (with protective leaves) **2** to provide (a book) with blank leaves for notes, etc, or to protect illustrations

interleukin (ˌɪntəˈluːkɪn) *n* a substance extracted from white blood cells that stimulates their activity against infection and may be used to combat some forms of cancer

interline[1] (ˌɪntəˈlaɪn) *or* **interlineate** (ˌɪntəˈlɪnɪˌeɪt) *vb*

interline (tr) to write or print (matter) between the lines of (a text, book, etc) > 'inter,lining or ,inter,line'ation n

interline² (,ɪntə'laɪn) vb (tr) to provide (a part of a garment, such as a collar or cuff) with a second lining, esp of stiffened material > 'inter,liner n

interlinear (,ɪntə'lɪnɪə) or **interlineal** adj 1 written or printed between lines of text 2 written or printed with the text in different languages or versions on alternate lines > ,inter'linearly or ,inter'lineally adv

interlining ('ɪntə,laɪnɪŋ) n the material used to interline parts of garments, now often made of reinforced paper

interlock vb (,ɪntə'lɒk) 1 to join or be joined firmly, as by a mutual interconnection of parts ▷ n ('ɪntə,lɒk) 2 the act of interlocking or the state of being interlocked 3 a device, esp one operated electromechanically, used in a logic circuit or electrical safety system to prevent an activity being initiated unless preceded by certain events 4 a closely knitted fabric ▷ adj ('ɪntə,lɒk) 5 (of fabric) closely knitted > 'inter,locker n

interlocutor (,ɪntə'lɒkjʊtə) n 1 a person who takes part in a conversation 2 Also called: middleman the man in the centre of a troupe of minstrels who engages the others in talk or acts as announcer 3 Scots law a decree by a judge > ,inter'locutress, ,inter'locutrice or ,inter'locutrix fem n

interlocutory (,ɪntə'lɒkjʊtərɪ, -trɪ) adj 1 law pronounced during the course of proceedings; provisional: an interlocutory injunction 2 interposed, as into a conversation, narrative, etc 3 of, relating to, or characteristic of dialogue > ,inter'locutorily adv

interloper ('ɪntə,ləʊpə) n 1 an intruder 2 a person who introduces himself into professional or social circles where he does not belong 3 a person who interferes in matters that are not his concern [C17: from INTER- + loper, from Middle Dutch loopen to leap]

interlude ('ɪntə,luːd) n 1 a period of time or different activity between longer periods, processes, or events; episode or interval 2 theatre a short dramatic piece played separately or as part of a longer entertainment, common in 16th-century England 3 a brief piece of music, dance, etc, given between the sections of another performance [C14: from Medieval Latin interlūdium, from Latin INTER- + lūdus play]

intermarry (,ɪntə'mærɪ) vb -ries, -rying, -ried (intr) 1 (of different groups, races, religions, creeds, etc) to become connected by marriage 2 to marry within one's own family, clan, group, etc > ,inter'marriage n

intermediary (,ɪntə'miːdɪərɪ) n, pl -aries 1 a person who acts as a mediator or agent between parties 2 something that acts as a medium or means ▷ adj 3 acting as an intermediary 4 situated, acting, or coming between; intermediate

intermediate adj (,ɪntə'miːdɪɪt) 1 occurring or situated between two points, extremes, places, etc; in between 2 (of a class, course, etc) suitable for learners with some degree of skill or competence ▷ n (,ɪntə'miːdɪɪt) 3 something intermediate 4 a substance formed during one of the stages of a chemical process before the desired product is obtained ▷ vb (,ɪntə'miːdɪ,eɪt) 5 (intr) to act as an intermediary or mediator [C17: from Medieval Latin intermediāre to intervene, from Latin INTER- + medius middle] > ,inter'mediacy or ,inter'mediateness n > ,inter'mediately adv > ,inter,medi'ation n > ,inter'medi,ator n

intermediate-acting adj (of a drug) intermediate in its effects between long- and short-acting drugs. See **long-acting**, **short-acting**

intermediate frequency n electronics the frequency to which the signal carrier frequency is changed in a superheterodyne receiver and at which most of the amplification takes place

intermediate-level waste n radioactive waste material, such as reactor and processing-plant components, that is solidified before being mixed with concrete and stored in steel drums in deep mines or beneath the seabed in concrete chambers. See **high-level waste**, **low-level waste**

intermediate technology n technology which combines sophisticated ideas with cheap and readily available materials, especially for use in developing countries

intermediate vector boson n physics a hypothetical particle believed to mediate the weak interaction between elementary particles

interment (ɪn'tɜːmənt) n burial, esp with ceremonial rites

intermezzo (,ɪntə'mɛtsəʊ) n, pl -zos or -zi (-tsiː) 1 a short piece of instrumental music composed for performance between the acts or scenes of an opera, drama, etc 2 an instrumental piece either inserted between two longer movements in an extended composition or intended for independent performance [C19: from Italian, from Late Latin intermedium interval; see INTERMEDIATE]

interminable (ɪn'tɜːmɪnəb°l) adj endless or seemingly endless because of monotony or tiresome length > in'termina'bility or in'terminableness n > in'terminably adv

intermission (,ɪntə'mɪʃən) n 1 an interval, as between parts of a film 2 a period between events or activities; pause 3 the act of intermitting or the state of being intermitted [C16: from Latin intermissiō, from intermittere to leave off, INTERMIT] > ,inter'missive adj

intermit (,ɪntə'mɪt) vb -mits, -mitting, -mitted to suspend (activity) or (of activity) to be suspended temporarily or at intervals [C16: from Latin intermittere to leave off, from INTER- + mittere to send] > ,inter'mittor n

intermittent (,ɪntə'mɪt°nt) adj occurring occasionally or at regular or irregular intervals; periodic > ,inter'mittence or ,inter'mittency n > ,inter'mittently adv

intermix (,ɪntə'mɪks) vb 1 (tr) to mix (ingredients, liquids, etc) together 2 (intr) to become or have the capacity to become combined, joined, etc

intermixture (,ɪntə'mɪkstʃə) n 1 the act of intermixing or state of being intermixed 2 an additional constituent or ingredient

intern vb 1 (ɪn'tɜːn) (tr) to detain or confine (foreign or enemy citizens, ships, etc), esp during wartime 2 ('ɪntɜːn) (intr) chiefly US to serve or train as an intern ▷ n ('ɪntɜːn) 3 another word for **internee** 4 Also called: interne med, US & Canadian a graduate in the first year of training after medical school, resident in a hospital and under supervision by senior doctors. British equivalent: house officer 5 chiefly US a student teacher 6 chiefly US a student or recent graduate receiving practical training in a working environment [C19: from Latin internus internal] > in'ternment n > 'internship n

internal (ɪn'tɜːn°l) adj 1 of, situated on, or suitable for the inside; inner 2 coming or acting from within; interior 3 involving the spiritual or mental life; subjective 4 of or involving a nation's domestic as opposed to foreign affairs 5 situated within, affecting, or relating to the inside of the body ▷ n 6 a medical examination of the vagina, uterus, or rectum [C16: from Medieval Latin internālis, from Late Latin internus inward] > ,inter'nality or in'ternalness n > in'ternally adv

internal-combustion engine n a heat engine in which heat is supplied by burning the fuel in the working fluid (usually air)

internal energy n the thermodynamic property of a system that changes by an amount equal to the work done on the system when it suffers an adiabatic change. It is the sum of the kinetic and potential energies of its constituent atoms, molecules, etc

internalize or **internalise** (ɪn'tɜːnə,laɪz) vb (tr) psychol, sociol to make internal, esp to incorporate within oneself (values, attitudes, etc) through learning or socialization. Also: interiorize > in,ternali'zation or in,ternali'sation n

internal market n a system in which goods and services are sold by the provider to a range of purchasers within the same organization, who compete to establish the price of the product

internal medicine n the branch of medical science concerned with the diagnosis and nonsurgical treatment of disorders of the internal structures of the body

international (,ɪntə'næʃən°l) adj 1 of, concerning, or

involving two or more nations or nationalities **2** established by, controlling, or legislating for several nations: *an international court; international fishing rights* **3** available for use by all nations: *international waters* ▷ *n* **4** *sport* **a** a contest between two national teams **b** a member of these teams > ˌinterˌnation'ality *n* > ˌinter'nationally *adv*

International (ˌɪntəˈnæʃənʲl) *n* **1** any of several international socialist organizations **2** a member of any of these organizations

International Atomic Time *n* the scientific standard of time based on the SI unit, the second, used by means of atomic clocks and satellites to synchronize the time standards of the major nations. Abbreviation: TAI

International Bank for Reconstruction and Development *n* the official name for the **World Bank**

International Court of Justice *n* a court established in the Hague to settle disputes brought by nations that are parties to the Statute of the Court. Also called: World Court

International Date Line *n* the line approximately following the 180° meridian from Greenwich on the east side of which the date is one day earlier than on the west

internationalism (ˌɪntəˈnæʃənəˌlɪzəm) *n* **1** the ideal or practice of cooperation and understanding between nations **2** the state or quality of being international

internationalize *or* **internationalise** (ˌɪntəˈnæʃənəˌlaɪz) *vb* (*tr*) **1** to make international **2** to put under international control > ˌinterˌnationaliˈzation *or* ˌinterˌnationaliˈsation *n*

international law *n* the body of rules generally recognized by civilized nations as governing their conduct towards each other and towards each other's subjects

International Modernism *n* See **International Style**

International Phonetic Alphabet *n* a series of signs and letters propagated by the Association Phonétique Internationale for the representation of human speech sounds. It is based on the Roman alphabet but supplemented by modified signs or symbols from other writing systems, and is usually employed in its revised form of 1951

International Practical Temperature Scale *n* a temperature scale adopted by international agreement in 1968, and revised in 1990, based on thermodynamic temperature and using experimental values to define 16 fixed points. The lowest is the triple point of an equilibrium mixture of orthohydrogen and parahydrogen (−259.34°C) and the highest the freezing point of copper (1084.62°C)

International Space Station *n* an orbiting space station construction of which began in 2001 with the cooperation of 16 nations; used for scientific and space research. Abbreviation: ISS

International Style *or* **Modernism** *n* a 20th-century architectural style characterized by undecorated rectilinear forms and the use of glass, steel, and reinforced concrete

International Telecommunications Union *n* a special agency of the United Nations, founded in 1947, that is responsible for the international allocation and registration of frequencies for communications and the regulation of telegraph, telephone, and radio services: originally established in 1865 as the International Telegraph Union

interne (ˈɪntɜːn) *n* a variant spelling of **intern** (sense 4)

internecine (ˌɪntəˈniːsaɪn) *adj* **1** mutually destructive or ruinous; maiming both or all sides: *internecine war* **2** of or relating to slaughter or carnage; bloody **3** of or involving conflict within a group or organization [C17: from Latin *internecīnus*, from *internecāre* to destroy, from *necāre* to kill]

internee (ˌɪntɜːˈniː) *n* a person who is interned, esp an enemy citizen in wartime or a terrorism suspect

internet (ˈɪntəˌnɛt) *n* the (*sometimes with a capital*) the single worldwide computer network that interconnects other computer networks, on which end-user services, such as World Wide Web sites or data archives, are located, enabling data and other information to be exchanged. Also called: the Net

internist (ˈɪntɜːnɪst, ɪnˈtɜːnɪst) *n chiefly* US a physician who specializes in internal medicine

interoperable (ˌɪntərˈɒprəbʲl) *adj* of or relating to the ability to share data between different computer systems, esp on different machines: *interoperable network management systems* > ˌinterˌopera'bility *n*

interpellate (ɪnˈtɜːpɛˌleɪt) *vb* (*tr*) *parliamentary procedure* (in European legislatures) to question (a member of the government) on a point of government policy, often interrupting the business of the day [C16: from Latin *interpellāre* to disturb, from INTER- + *pellere* to push] > ˌinterpelˈlation *n* > inˈterpelˌlator *n*

interpenetrate (ˌɪntəˈpɛnɪˌtreɪt) *vb* **1** to penetrate (something) thoroughly; pervade **2** to penetrate each other or one another mutually > ˌinterˈpenetrable *adj* > ˌinterˈpenetrant *adj* > ˌinterˌpeneˈtration *n* > ˌinterˈpenetrative *adj* > ˌinterˈpenetratively *adv*

interplay (ˈɪntəˌpleɪ) *n* reciprocal and mutual action and reaction, as in circumstances, events, or personal relations

interpleader (ˌɪntəˈpliːdə) *n law* **1** a process by which a person holding money or property claimed by two or more parties and having no interest in it himself can require the claimants to litigate with each other to determine the issue **2** a person who interpleads

Interpol (ˈɪntəˌpɒl) *n acronym for* International Criminal Police Organization, an association of over 100 national police forces, devoted chiefly to fighting international crime

interpolate (ɪnˈtɜːpəˌleɪt) *vb* **1** to insert or introduce (a comment, passage, etc) into (a conversation, text, etc) **2** to falsify or alter (a text, manuscript, etc) by the later addition of (material, esp spurious or valueless passages) **3** (*intr*) to make additions, interruptions, or insertions **4** *maths* to estimate (a value of a function) between the values already known or determined. See **extrapolate** (sense 1) [C17: from Latin *interpolāre* to give a new appearance to, from INTER- + *polīre* to POLISH] > inˈterpoˌlater *or* inˈterpoˌlator *n* > inˈterpolative *adj*

interpose (ˌɪntəˈpəʊz) *vb* **1** to put or place between or among other things **2** to introduce (comments, questions, etc) into a speech or conversation; interject **3** to exert or use power, influence, or action in order to alter or intervene in (a situation) [C16: from Old French *interposer*, from Latin *interpōnere*, from INTER- + *pōnere* to put] > ˌinterˈposal *n* > ˌinterˈposer *n* > ˌinterpoˈsition *n*

interpret (ɪnˈtɜːprɪt) *vb* **1** (*tr*) to clarify or explain the meaning of; elucidate **2** (*tr*) to construe the significance or intention of **3** (*tr*) to convey or represent the spirit or meaning of (a poem, song, etc) in performance **4** (*intr*) to act as an interpreter; translate orally [C14: from Latin *interpretārī*, from *interpres* negotiator, one who explains, from INTER- + *-pres*, probably related to *pretium* PRICE] > inˈterpretable *adj* > inˌterpreta'bility *or* inˈterpretableness *n* > inˈterpretably *adv* > inˈterpretative *or* inˈterpretive *adj*

interpretation (ɪnˌtɜːprɪˈteɪʃən) *n* **1** the act or process of interpreting or explaining; elucidation **2** the result of interpreting; an explanation **3** a particular view of an artistic work, esp as expressed by stylistic individuality in its performance **4** explanation, as of the environment, a historical site, etc, provided by the use of original objects, personal experience, visual display material, etc > inˌterpre'tational *adj*

interpreter (ɪnˈtɜːprɪtə) *n* **1** a person who translates orally from one language into another **2** a person who interprets the work of others **3** *computing* a program that translates a second program to machine code one statement at a time and causes the execution of the resulting code as soon as the translation is completed > inˈterpreterˌship *n* > inˈterpretress *fem n*

interpretive centre *n* (at a place of interest, such as a country park, historical site, etc) a building or group of buildings that provides interpretation of the place of interest through a variety of media, such as video displays and exhibitions of material, and, often, includes facilities such as refreshment rooms and gift shops

interregnum (ˌɪntəˈrɛgnəm) *n, pl* -nums *or* -na (-nə) **1** an interval between two reigns, governments, incumbencies, etc **2** any period in which a state lacks a ruler, government, etc **3** a period of absence of some control, authority, etc **4** a gap in a continuity [c16: from Latin, from INTER- + *regnum* REIGN] > ˌinterˈregnal *adj*

interrelate (ˌɪntərɪˈleɪt) *vb* to place in or come into a mutual or reciprocal relationship > ˌinterreˈlation *n* > ˌinterreˈlationˌship *n*

interrogate (ɪnˈtɛrəˌgeɪt) *vb* to ask questions (of), esp to question (a witness in court, spy, etc) closely [c15: from Latin *interrogāre* to question, examine, from *rogāre* to ask]

interrogation (ɪnˌtɛrəˈgeɪʃən) *n* **1** the technique, practice, or an instance of interrogating **2** a question or query **3** *telecomm* the transmission of one or more triggering pulses to a transponder > inˌterroˈgational *adj*

interrogation mark *n* a less common term for **question mark**

interrogative (ˌɪntəˈrɒgətɪv) *adj* **1** asking or having the nature of a question **2** denoting a form or construction used in asking a question **3** denoting or belonging to a class of words, such as *which* and *whom*, that are determiners, adjectives, or pronouns and serve to question which individual referent or referents are intended ▷ *n* **4** an interrogative word, phrase, sentence, or construction **5** a question mark > ˌinterˈrogatively *adv*

interrogator (ɪnˈtɛrəˌgeɪtə) in'terro,gator *n* **1** a person who interrogates **2** a radio or radar transmitter used to send interrogating signals

interrogatory (ˌɪntəˈrɒgətərɪ, -trɪ) *adj* **1** expressing or involving a question ▷ *n, pl* -tories **2** a question or interrogation

interrupt (ˌɪntəˈrʌpt) *vb* **1** to break the continuity of (an action, event, etc) or hinder (a person) by intrusion **2** (*tr*) to cease to perform (some action) **3** (*tr*) to obstruct (a view) **4** to prevent or disturb (a conversation, discussion, etc) by questions, interjections, or comment [c15: from Latin *interrumpere*, from INTER- + *rumpere* to break] > ˌinterˈruptible *adj* > ˌinterˈruptive *adj* > ˌinterˈruptively *adv* > ˌinterˈrupted *adj*

interrupted screw *n* a screw with a slot or slots cut into the thread, esp one used in the breech of some guns permitting both engagement and release of the block by a partial turn of the screw

interrupter *or* **interruptor** (ˌɪntəˈrʌptə) *n* **1** a person or thing that interrupts **2** an electromechanical device for opening and closing an electric circuit

interruption (ˌɪntəˈrʌpʃən) *n* **1** something that interrupts, such as a comment, question, or action **2** an interval or intermission **3** the act of interrupting or the state of being interrupted

interscholastic (ˌɪntəskəˈlæstɪk) *adj* **1** (of sports events, competitions, etc) occurring between two or more schools **2** representative of various schools

intersect (ˌɪntəˈsɛkt) *vb* **1** to divide, cut, or mark off by passing through or across **2** (esp of roads) to cross (each other) **3** *maths* (often foll by *with*) to have one or more points in common (with another configuration) [c17: from Latin *intersecāre* to divide, from INTER- + *secāre* to cut]

intersection (ˌɪntəˈsɛkʃən, ˈɪntəˌsɛk-) *n* **1** a point at which things intersect, esp a road junction **2** the act of intersecting or the state of being intersected **3** *maths* **a** a point or set of points common to two or more geometric configurations **b** Also called: product the set of elements that are common to two sets **c** the operation that yields that set from a pair of given sets. Symbol: ∩, as in *A* ∩ *B* > ˌinterˈsectional *adj*

intersex (ˈɪntəˌsɛks) *n* the condition of having characteristics intermediate between those of a male and a female

intersexual (ˌɪntəˈsɛksjʊəl) *adj* **1** occurring or existing between the sexes **2** relating to or being an intersex > ˌinterˌsexuˈality *or* ˌinterˈsexualism *n* > ˌinterˈsexually *adv*

interspace (ˌɪntəˈspeɪs) *vb* **1** (*tr*) to make or occupy a space between *n* (ˈɪntəˌspeɪs) **2** space between or among things > interspatial (ˌɪntəˈspeɪʃəl) *adj* > ˌinterˈspatially *adv*

intersperse (ˌɪntəˈspɜːs) *vb* (*tr*) **1** to scatter or distribute among, between, or on **2** to diversify (something) with other things scattered here and there [c16: from Latin *interspargere*, from INTER- + *spargere* to sprinkle] > interspersedly (ˌɪntəˈspɜːsɪdlɪ) *adv* > interspersion (ˌɪntəˈspɜːʃən) *or* ˌinterˈspersal *n*

interstate (ˈɪntəˌsteɪt) *adj* **1** between or involving two or more of the states of the US, Australia, etc ▷ *vb* **2** *US* a motorway crossing between states

interstellar (ˌɪntəˈstɛlə) *adj* conducted, or existing between two or more stars

interstice (ɪnˈtɜːstɪs) *n* (*usually plural*) **1** a minute opening or crevice between things **2** *physics* the space between adjacent atoms in a crystal lattice [c17: from Latin *interstitium* interval, from *intersistere*, from INTER- + *sistere* to stand]

interstitial (ˌɪntəˈstɪʃəl) *adj* **1** of or relating to an interstice or interstices **2** *physics* forming or occurring in an interstice: *an interstitial atom* **3** *anatomy, zoology* occurring in the spaces between organs, tissues, etc: *interstitial cells* ▷ *n* **4** *chem* an atom or ion situated in the interstices of a crystal lattice > ˌinterˈstitially *adv*

intertrigo (ˌɪntəˈtraɪgəʊ) *n* chafing between two moist closely opposed skin surfaces, as under the breasts or at the armpit [c18: from INTER- + -*trigo*, from Latin *terere* to rub]

interval (ˈɪntəvəl) *n* **1** the period of time marked off by or between two events, instants, etc **2** the distance between two points, objects, etc **3** a pause or interlude, as between periods of intense activity **4** *Brit* a short period between parts of a play, concert, film, etc; intermission **5** *music* the difference of pitch between two notes, either sounded simultaneously (**harmonic interval**) or in succession as in a musical part (**melodic interval**). An interval is calculated by counting the (inclusive) number of notes of the diatonic scale between the two notes **6** the ratio of the frequencies of two sounds **7** at intervals **a** occasionally or intermittently **b** with spaces between [c13: from Latin *intervallum*, literally: space between two palisades, from INTER- + *vallum* palisade, rampart] > intervallic (ˌɪntəˈvælɪk) *adj*

intervene (ˌɪntəˈviːn) *vb* (*intr*) **1** (often foll by *in*) to take a decisive or intrusive role (in) in order to modify or determine events or their outcome **2** (foll by *in* or *between*) to come or be (among or between) **3** (of a period of time) to occur between events or points in time **4** (of an event) to disturb or hinder a course of action **5** *economics* to take action to affect the market forces of an economy, esp to maintain the stability of a currency **6** *law* to interpose and become a party to a legal action between others, esp in order to protect one's interests [c16: from Latin *intervenīre* to come between, from INTER- + *venīre* to come] > ˌinterˈvener *or* ˌinterˈvenor *n*

intervention (ˌɪntəˈvɛnʃən) *n* **1** the act of intervening **2** any interference in the affairs of others, esp by one state in the affairs of another **3** *economics* the action of a central bank in supporting the international value of a currency by buying large quantities of the currency to keep the price up **4** *commerce* the action of the EU in buying up surplus produce when the market price drops to a certain value

interventionist (ˌɪntəˈvɛnʃənɪst) *adj* **1** of, relating to, or advocating intervention, esp in the affairs of a foreign country ▷ *n* **2** an interventionist person or state

intervertebral disc (ˌɪntəˈvɜːtəbrəl) *n* any of the cartilaginous discs between individual vertebrae, acting as shock absorbers

interview (ˈɪntəˌvjuː) *n* **1** a conversation with or questioning of a person, usually conducted for television, radio, or a newspaper **2** a formal discussion, esp one in which an employer assesses an applicant for a job ▷ *vb* **3** to conduct an interview with (someone) [c16: from Old French *entrevue*; see INTER-, VIEW] > ˈinterviewˌee *n* > ˈinterˌviewer *n*

inter vivos (ˈɪntə ˈviːvɒs) *Latin adj law* between living people: *an inter vivos gift*

interwar (ˌɪntəˈwɔː) *adj* of or happening in the period between World War I and World War II

intestate (ɪnˈtɛsteɪt, -tɪt) *adj* **1 a** (of a person) not having made a will **b** (of property) not disposed of by will ▷ *n* **2** a person who dies without having made a will [c14: from Latin *intestātus*, from IN-¹ + *testātus*, from *testārī* to bear witness, make a will, from *testis* a witness] > inˈtestacy *n*

intestine (ɪnˈtɛstɪn) *n* (*usually plural*) the part of the alimentary canal between the stomach and the anus. See **large intestine, small intestine** [c16: from Latin *intestīnum* gut, from *intestīnus* internal, from *intus* within] > **intestinal** (ɪnˈtɛstɪnˀl, ˌɪntɛsˈtaɪnˀl) *adj*

inti (ˈɪntɪ) *n* a former monetary unit of Peru [c20: from Quechua]

intifada (ˌɪntɪˈfɑːdə) *n* the Palestinian uprising against Israel in the West Bank and Gaza Strip that started at the end of 1987 [c20: Arabic, literally: uprising]

intimacy (ˈɪntɪməsɪ) *n*, *pl* -cies **1** close or warm friendship or understanding; personal relationship **2** (*often plural*) *euphemistic* sexual relations

intimate¹ (ˈɪntɪmɪt) *adj* **1** characterized by a close or warm personal relationship: *an intimate friend* **2** deeply personal, private, or secret **3** (*often postpositive*; foll by *with*) *euphemistic* having sexual relations (with) **4 a** (*postpositive*; foll by *with*) having a deep or unusual knowledge (of) **b** (of knowledge) deep; extensive **5** having a friendly, warm, or informal atmosphere: *an intimate nightclub* **6** of or relating to the essential part or nature of something; intrinsic ▷ *n* **7** a close friend [c17: from Latin *intimus* very close friend, from (adj): innermost, deepest, from *intus* within] > **intimately** *adv* > **intimateness** *n*

intimate² (ˈɪntɪˌmeɪt) *vb* (*tr; may take a clause as object*) **1** to hint; suggest **2** to proclaim; make known [c16: from Late Latin *intimāre* to proclaim, from Latin *intimus* innermost] > **intiˌmater** *n* > **intiˈmation** *n*

intimidate (ɪnˈtɪmɪˌdeɪt) *vb* (*tr*) **1** to make timid or frightened; scare **2** to discourage, restrain, or silence illegally or unscrupulously, as by threats or blackmail [c17: from Medieval Latin *intimidāre*, from Latin IN-² + *timidus* fearful, from *timor* fear] > inˈtimiˌdating *adj* > inˌtimiˈdation *n* > inˈtimiˌdator *n*

intinction (ɪnˈtɪŋkʃən) *n* *Christianity* the practice of dipping the Eucharistic bread into the wine at Holy Communion [c16: from Late Latin *intinctiō* a dipping in, from Latin *intingere* to dip in, from *tingere* to dip]

intitule (ɪnˈtɪtjuːl) *vb* (*tr*) *parliamentary procedure* (in Britain) to entitle (an Act) [c15: from Old French *intituler*, from Latin *titulus* TITLE]

intl *abbreviation* international

into (ˈɪntuː; *unstressed* ˈɪntə) *prep* **1** to the interior or inner parts of: *to look into a case* **2** to the middle or midst of so as to be surrounded by: *into the water; into the bushes* **3** against; up against: *he drove into a wall* **4** used to indicate the result of a transformation or change: *he changed into a monster* **5** *maths* used to indicate a dividend: *three into six is two* **6** *informal* interested or enthusiastically involved in: *I'm really into Freud these days*

intonation (ˌɪntəʊˈneɪʃən) *n* **1** the sound pattern of phrases and sentences produced by pitch variation in the voice **2** the act or manner of intoning **3** an intoned, chanted, or monotonous utterance; incantation **4** *music* the opening of a piece of plainsong, sung by a soloist **5** *music* the capacity to play or sing in tune > ˌintoˈnational *adj*

intone (ɪnˈtəʊn) *vb* **1** to utter, recite, or sing (a chant, prayer, etc) in a monotonous or incantatory tone **2** (*intr*) to speak with a particular or characteristic intonation or tone **3** to sing (the opening phrase of a psalm, etc) in plainsong [c15: from Medieval Latin *intonare*, from IN-² + TONE] > inˈtoner *n*

in toto *Latin* (ɪn ˈtəʊtəʊ) *adv* totally; entirely; completely

intoxicant (ɪnˈtɒksɪkənt) *n* **1** anything that causes intoxication ▷ *adj* **2** causing intoxication

intoxicate (ɪnˈtɒksɪˌkeɪt) *vb* (*tr*) **1** (of an alcoholic drink) to produce in (a person) a state ranging from euphoria to stupor, usually accompanied by loss of inhibitions and control; make drunk; inebriate **2** to stimulate, excite, or elate so as to overwhelm **3** (of a drug) to poison [c16: from Medieval Latin, from *intoxicāre* to poison, from Latin *toxicum* poison; see TOXIC] > inˈtoxicable *adj*

intoxicating (ɪnˈtɒksɪˌkeɪtɪŋ) *adj* **1** (of an alcoholic drink) producing in a person a state ranging from euphoria to stupor, usually accompanied by loss of inhibitions and control; inebriating **2** stimulating, exciting, or producing great elation > inˈtoxiˌcatingly *adv*

intoxication (ɪnˌtɒksɪˈkeɪʃən) *n* **1** drunkenness; inebriation **2** great elation **3** the act of intoxicating **4** poisoning

intr *abbreviation* intransitive

intra- *prefix* within; inside: *intravenous* [from Latin *intrā* on the inside, within; see INTERIOR]

Intracoastal Waterway (ˌɪntrəˈkəʊstˀl) *n* short for **Atlantic Intracoastal Waterway**

intractable (ɪnˈtræktəbˀl) *adj* **1** difficult to influence or direct: *an intractable disposition* **2** (of a problem, illness, etc) difficult to solve, alleviate, or cure **3** difficult to shape or mould, esp with the hands > inˌtractaˈbility or inˈtractableness *n* > inˈtractably *adv*

intradermal (ˌɪntrəˈdɜːməl) or **intradermic** *adj* *anatomy* within the skin. Abbreviation (esp of an injection): ID > ˌintraˈdermally or ˌintraˈdermically *adv*

intrados (ɪnˈtreɪdɒs) *n*, *pl* -dos or -doses *architect* the inner curve or surface of an arch or vault [c18: from French, from INTRA- + *dos* back, from Latin *dorsum*]

intramural (ˌɪntrəˈmjʊərəl) *adj* *education chiefly US & Canadian* operating within or involving those in a single establishment > ˌintraˈmurally *adv*

intramuscular (ˌɪntrəˈmʌskjʊlə) *adj* *anatomy* within a muscle: *an intramuscular injection*. Abbreviation (esp of an injection): IM > ˌintraˈmuscularly *adv*

intranet (ˈɪntrəˌnɛt) *n* *computing* an internal network that makes use of internet technology [c20: from INTRA- + NET¹ (sense 8), modelled on INTERNET]

intrans. *abbreviation* intransitive

intransigent (ɪnˈtrænsɪdʒənt) *adj* **1** not willing to compromise; obstinately maintaining an attitude ▷ *n* Also: **intransigentist 2** an intransigent person, esp in politics [c19: from Spanish *los intransigentes* the uncompromising (ones), a name adopted by certain political extremists, from IN-¹ + *transigir* to compromise, from Latin *transigere* to settle; see TRANSACT] > inˈtransigence or inˈtransigency *n* > inˈtransigently *adv*

intrapreneur (ˌɪntrəprəˈnɜː) *n* a person who while remaining within a larger organization uses entrepreneurial skills to develop a new product or line of business as a subsidiary of the organization [c20: from INTRA- + (ENTRE)PRENEUR]

intrauterine (ˌɪntrəˈjuːtəraɪn) *adj* within the womb

intrauterine device *n* a metal or plastic device, in the shape of a loop, coil, or ring, inserted into the uterus to prevent conception. Abbreviation: IUD

intravenous (ˌɪntrəˈviːnəs) *adj* *anatomy* within a vein: *an intravenous injection*. Abbreviations: i.v., IV > ˌintraˈvenously *adv*

in-tray *n* a tray for incoming papers requiring attention

intrench (ɪnˈtrɛntʃ) *vb* a less common spelling of **entrench** > inˈtrencher *n* > inˈtrenchment *n*

intrepid (ɪnˈtrɛpɪd) *adj* fearless; daring; bold [c17: from Latin *intrepidus*, from IN-¹ + *trepidus* fearful, timid] > ˌintreˈpidity or inˈtrepidness *n* > inˈtrepidly *adv*

intricate (ˈɪntrɪkɪt) *adj* **1** difficult to understand; obscure; complex; puzzling **2** entangled or involved: *intricate patterns* [c15: from Latin *intrīcāre* to entangle, perplex, from IN-² + *trīcae* trifles, perplexities] > ˈintricacy or ˈintricateness *n* > ˈintricately *adv*

intrigue *vb* (ɪnˈtriːg) -trigues, -triguing, -trigued **1** (*tr*) to make interested or curious **2** (*intr*) to make secret plots or employ underhand methods; conspire **3** (*intr*; often foll by *with*) to carry on a clandestine love affair ▷ *n* (ɪnˈtriːg, ˈɪntriːg) **4** the act or an instance of secret plotting, etc **5** a clandestine love affair **6** the quality of arousing interest or curiosity; beguilement [c17: from French *intriguer*, from Italian *intrigare*, from Latin *intrīcāre*; see INTRICATE] > inˈtriguer *n* > inˈtriguing *adj* > inˈtriguingly *adv*

intrinsic (ɪnˈtrɪnsɪk) or **intrinsical** *adj* **1** of or relating to the essential nature of a thing; inherent **2** *anatomy* situated within or peculiar to a part: *intrinsic muscles* [c15: from Late Latin *intrinsecus* from Latin, inwardly, from

intrā within + *secus* alongside; related to *sequī* to follow]
> in'trinsically *adv*

intro ('ɪntrəʊ) *n, pl* -tros *informal* short for **introduction**

intro. or **introd.** *abbreviation* **1** introduction
2 introductory

intro- *prefix* in, into, or inward: introvert [from Latin *intrō* towards the inside, inwardly, within]

introduce (ˌɪntrə'djuːs) *vb (tr)* **1** (often foll by *to*) to present (someone) by name (to another person) or (two or more people to each other) **2** (foll by *to*) to cause to experience for the first time: *to introduce a visitor to beer* **3** to present for consideration or approval, esp before a legislative body: *to introduce a draft bill* **4** to bring in; establish: *to introduce decimal currency* **5** to present (a radio or television programme, etc) verbally **6** (foll by *with*) to start: *he introduced his talk with some music* **7** (often foll by *into*) to insert or inject: *he introduced the needle into his arm* **8** to place (members of a species of plant or animal) in a new environment with the intention of producing a resident breeding population [c16: from Latin *intrōdūcere* to bring inside, from INTRO- + *dūcere* to lead]
> ˌintro'ducer *n* > ˌintro'ducible *adj*

introduction (ˌɪntrə'dʌkʃən) *n* **1** the act of introducing or fact of being introduced **2** a presentation of one person to another or others **3** a means of presenting a person to another person, group, etc, such as a letter of introduction or reference **4** a preliminary part, as of a book, speech, etc **5** *music* **a** an instrumental passage preceding the entry of a soloist, choir, etc **b** an opening passage in a movement or composition that precedes the main material **6** something that has been or is introduced, esp something that is not native to an area, country, etc **7** a basic or elementary work of instruction, reference, etc

introductory (ˌɪntrə'dʌktərɪ, -trɪ) *adj* serving as an introduction; preliminary; prefatory

introit ('ɪntrɔɪt) *n* RC Church, Church of England a short prayer said or sung as the celebrant is entering the sanctuary to celebrate Mass or Holy Communion [c15: from Church Latin *introitus* introit, from Latin: entrance, from *introīre* to go in, from INTRO- + *īre* to go]
> in'troital *adj*

intromit (ˌɪntrə'mɪt) *vb* -mits, -mitting, -mitted *(tr) rare* to enter or insert or allow to enter or be inserted [c15: from Latin *intrōmittere* to send in, from INTRO- + *mittere* to send] > ˌintro'missible *adj* > ˌintro'mittent *adj*
> ˌintro'mission *n*

introspection (ˌɪntrə'spɛkʃən) *n* the examination of one's own thoughts, impressions, and feelings, esp for long periods [c17: from Latin *intrōspicere* to look within, from INTRO- + *specere* to look] > ˌintro'spectional or ˌintro'spective *adj* > ˌintro'spectively *adv*

introversion (ˌɪntrə'vɜːʃən) *n* psychol the directing of interest inwards towards one's own thoughts and feelings rather than towards the external world or making social contacts > ˌintro'versive or ˌintro'vertive

introvert ('ɪntrəˌvɜːt) **1** psychol a person prone to introversion ▷ *adj* ('ɪntrəˌvɜːt) **2** Also called: introverted characterized by introversion ▷ *vb* (ˌɪntrə'vɜːt) **3** *(tr) pathol* to turn (a hollow organ or part) inside out [c17: see INTRO-, INVERT]

intrude (ɪn'truːd) *vb* **1** (often foll by *into, on,* or *upon*) to put forward or interpose (oneself, one's views, something) abruptly or without invitation **2** *geology* to force or thrust (rock material, esp molten magma) or (of rock material) to be thrust between solid rocks [c16: from Latin *intrūdere* to thrust in, from IN-² + *trūdere* to thrust]
> in'trudingly *adv* > in'truder *n*

intrusion (ɪn'truːʒən) *n* **1** the act or an instance of intruding; an unwelcome visit, interjection, etc: *an intrusion on one's privacy* **2 a** the movement of magma from within the earth's crust into spaces in the overlying strata to form igneous rock **b** any igneous rock formed in this way **3** *property law* an unlawful entry onto land by a stranger after determination of a particular estate of freehold and before the remainderman or reversioner has made entry > in'trusional *adj*

intrusive (ɪn'truːsɪv) *adj* **1** characterized by intrusion or tending to intrude **2** (of igneous rocks) formed by

intrusion **3** *phonetics* relating to or denoting a speech sound that is introduced into a word or piece of connected speech for a phonetic rather than a historical or grammatical reason, such as the (r) often pronounced between *idea* and *of* in *the idea of it* > in'trusively *adv*
> in'trusiveness *n*

intrust (ɪn'trʌst) *vb* a less common spelling of **entrust**

intubate ('ɪntjʊˌbeɪt) *vb (tr) med* to insert a tube or cannula into (a hollow organ); cannulate
> ˌintu'bation *n*

intuit (ɪn'tjuːɪt) *vb* to know or discover by intuition
> in'tuitable *adj*

intuition (ˌɪntjʊ'ɪʃən) *n* **1** knowledge or belief obtained neither by reason nor by perception **2** instinctive knowledge or belief **3** a hunch or unjustified belief [c15: from Late Latin *intuitiō* a contemplation, from Latin *intuērī* to gaze upon, from *tuērī* to look at] > ˌintu'itional *adj* > ˌintu'itionally *adv*

intuitionism (ˌɪntjʊ'ɪʃəˌnɪzəm) or **intuitionalism** *n* **1** (in ethics) the doctrine that there are moral truths discoverable by intuition **2** the doctrine that knowledge, esp of the external world, is acquired by intuition > ˌintu'itionist or ˌintu'itionalist *n*

intuitive (ɪn'tjuːɪtɪv) *adj* **1** resulting from intuition: *an intuitive awareness* **2** of, characterized by, or involving intuition > in'tuitively *adv* > in'tuitiveness *n*

intumesce (ˌɪntjʊ'mɛs) *vb (intr)* to swell or become swollen; undergo intumescence [c18: from Latin *intumescere*, from *tumescere* to begin to swell, from *tumēre* to swell] > ˌintu'mescence *n*

intussusception (ˌɪntəssə'sɛpʃən) *n* **1** *pathol* invagination of a tubular organ or part, esp the telescoping of one section of the intestinal tract into a lower section, causing obstruction **2** *biology* growth in the surface area of a cell by the deposition of new material between the existing components of the cell wall [c18: from Latin *intus* within + *susceptiō* a taking up]

Inuit or **Innuit** ('ɪnjuːɪt) *n, pl* -it or -its **1** any of several Native peoples of N America or Greenland, as distinguished from those from Asia or the Aleutian Islands (who are still generally referred to as Eskimos); the preferred term for *Eskimo* in N America **2** the language of these peoples; Inuktitut [from Inuktitut *inuit* the people, pl of *inuk* a man]

Inuk (ɪ'nʊk) *n* a member of any Inuit people [from Inuktitut *inuk* man]

inukshuk (ɪ'nʊkʃʊk) *n, pl* inukshuks or inukshuit (ɪ'nʊkʃuːɪt) a stone used by the Inuit to mark a location [from Inuktitut, literally: something in the shape of a man]

Inuktitut (ɪ'nʊktɪˌtʊt) *n* Canadian the language of the Inuit [from Inuktitut *inuk* man + *titut* speech]

inunction (ɪn'ʌŋkʃən) *n* **1** the application of an ointment to the skin, esp by rubbing **2** the ointment so used **3** the act of anointing; anointment [c15: from Latin *inunguere* to anoint, from *unguere*; see UNCTION]

inundate ('ɪnʌnˌdeɪt) *vb (tr)* **1** to cover completely with water; overflow; flood; swamp **2** to overwhelm, as if with a flood: *to be inundated with requests* [c17: from Latin *inundāre* to flood, from *unda* wave] > 'inundant or in'undatory *adj* > ˌinun'dation *n* > 'inunˌdator *n*

inure or **enure** (ɪ'njʊə) *vb* **1** *(tr; often passive; often foll by to)* to cause to accept or become hardened to; habituate **2** *(intr)* (esp of a law, etc) to come into operation; take effect [c15: *enuren* to accustom, from *ure* use, from Old French *euvre* custom, work, from Latin *opera* works, plural of *opus*] > in'urement or en'urement *n*

in utero Latin (ɪn 'juːtəˌrəʊ) *adv* within the womb

in vacuo Latin (ɪn 'vækjʊˌəʊ) *adv* in a vacuum

invade (ɪn'veɪd) *vb* **1** to enter (a country, territory, etc) by military force **2** *(tr)* to occupy in large numbers; overrun; infest **3** *(tr)* to trespass or encroach upon (privacy, etc) **4** *(tr)* to enter and spread throughout, esp harmfully; pervade [c15: from Latin *invādere*, from *vādere* to go]
> in'vadable *adj* > in'vader *n*

invaginate *vb* (ɪn'vædʒɪˌneɪt) **1** *pathol* to push one section of (a tubular organ or part) back into itself so that it becomes ensheathed; intussuscept **2** *(intr)* (of the outer layer of an organism or part) to undergo

invagination ▷ *adj* (ɪnˈvædʒɪnɪt, -ˌneɪt) **3** (of an organ or part) folded back upon itself [C19: from Medieval Latin *invāgināre*, from Latin IN-² + *vāgīna* sheath] ▷ in'vaginable *adj* ▷ in ˌvagiˈnation *n*

invalid¹ (ˈɪnvəˌliːd, -lɪd) *n* **1 a** a person suffering from disablement or chronic ill health **b** (*as modifier*): *an invalid chair* ▷ *adj* **2** suffering from or disabled by injury, sickness, etc ▷ *vb* (*tr*) **3** to cause to become an invalid; disable **4** (*usually foll by* out; *often passive*) *chiefly Brit* to require (a member of the armed forces) to retire from active service through wounds or illness [C17: from Latin *invalidus* infirm, from IN-¹ + *validus* strong] ▷ ˌinvaˈlidity *n*

invalid² (ɪnˈvælɪd) *adj* **1** not valid; having no cogency or legal force **2** *logic* (of an argument) having a conclusion that does not follow from the premises: it may be false when the premises are all true; not valid [C16: from Medieval Latin *invalidus* without legal force; see INVALID¹] ▷ invalidity (ˌɪnvəˈlɪdɪtɪ) *or* inˈvalidness *n* ▷ inˈvalidly *adv*

invalidate (ɪnˈvælɪˌdeɪt) *vb* (*tr*) **1** to render weak or ineffective, as an argument **2** to take away the legal force or effectiveness of; annul, as a contract ▷ inˌvaliˈdation *n* ▷ inˈvaliˌdator *n*

invaluable (ɪnˈvæljʊəbᵊl) *adj* having great value that is impossible to calculate; priceless ▷ inˈvaluableness *n* ▷ inˈvaluably *adv*

Invar (ɪnˈvɑː) *n trademark* an alloy containing iron (63.8 per cent), nickel (36 per cent), and carbon (0.2 per cent). It has a very low coefficient of expansion and is used for the balance springs of watches, etc [C20: shortened from INVARIABLE]

invariable (ɪnˈvɛərɪəbᵊl) *adj* **1** not subject to alteration; unchanging ▷ *n* **2** a mathematical quantity having an unchanging value; a constant ▷ inˌvariaˈbility *or* inˈvariableness *n*

invariably (ɪnˈvɛərɪəblɪ) *adv* always; without exception

invariant (ɪnˈvɛərɪənt) *n* **1** *maths* an entity, quantity, etc, that is unaltered by a particular transformation of coordinates: *a point in space, rather than its coordinates, is an invariant* ▷ *adj* **2** *maths* (of a relationship or a property of a function, configuration, or equation) unaltered by a particular transformation of coordinates ▷ inˈvariance *or* inˈvariancy *n*

invasion (ɪnˈveɪʒən) *n* **1** the act of invading with armed forces **2** any encroachment or intrusion: *an invasion of rats* **3** the onset or advent of something harmful, esp a disease **4** *pathol* the spread of cancer from its point of origin into surrounding tissues **5** the movement of plants to a new area or to an area to which they are not native

invasive (ɪnˈveɪsɪv) *adj* **1** of or relating to an invasion, intrusion, etc **2** (of surgery) involving making a relatively large incision in the body to gain access to the target of the surgery, as opposed to making a small incision or gaining access endoscopically through a natural orifice

invective (ɪnˈvɛktɪv) *n* **1** vehement accusation or denunciation, esp of a bitterly abusive or sarcastic kind ▷ *adj* **2** characterized by or using abusive language, bitter sarcasm, etc [C15: from Late Latin *invectīvus* reproachful, scolding, from Latin *invectus* carried in; see INVEIGH] ▷ inˈvectively *adv* ▷ inˈvectiveness *n*

inveigh (ɪnˈveɪ) *vb* (*intr*; *foll by* against) to speak with violent or invective language; rail [C15: from Latin *invehī*, literally: to be carried in, hence, assail physically or verbally, from IN-² + *vehī* to be carried, ride] ▷ inˈveigher *n*

inveigle (ɪnˈviːgᵊl, -ˈveɪ-) *vb* (*tr*; *often foll by* into or an infinitive) to lead (someone into a situation) or persuade (to do something) by cleverness or trickery; cajole: *to inveigle customers into spending more* [C15: from Old French *avogler* to blind, deceive, from *avogle* blind, from Medieval Latin *ab oculis* without eyes] ▷ inˈveiglement *n* ▷ inˈveigler *n*

invent (ɪnˈvɛnt) *vb* **1** to create or devise (new ideas, machines, etc) **2** to make up (falsehoods); fabricate [C15: from Latin *invenīre* to find, come upon, from IN-² + *venīre* to come] ▷ inˈventable *or* inˈventible *adj*

invention (ɪnˈvɛnʃən) *n* **1** the act or process of inventing **2** something that is invented **3** *patent law* the discovery or production of some new or improved process or machine that is both useful and is not obvious to persons skilled in the particular field **4** creative power or ability; inventive skill **5** *euphemistic* a fabrication; lie **6** *music* a short piece consisting of two or three parts usually in imitative counterpoint ▷ inˈventional *adj* ▷ inˈventionless *adj*

inventive (ɪnˈvɛntɪv) *adj* **1** skilled or quick at contriving; ingenious; resourceful **2** characterized by inventive skill: *an inventive programme of work* **3** of or relating to invention ▷ inˈventively *adv* ▷ inˈventiveness *n*

inventor (ɪnˈvɛntə) *n* a person who invents, esp as a profession ▷ inˈventress *fem n*

inventory (ˈɪnvəntərɪ, -trɪ) *n* **1** a detailed list of articles, goods, property, etc **2** (*often plural*) *accounting chiefly US* **a** the amount or value of a firm's current assets that consist of raw materials, work in progress, and finished goods; stock **b** such assets individually ▷ *vb* -tories, -torying, -toried **3** (*tr*) to enter (items) in an inventory; make a list of [C16: from Medieval Latin *inventōrium*; see INVENT] ▷ 'inventoriable *adj* ▷ ˌinven'torial *adj* ▷ ˌinven'torially *adv*

Inveraray (ˌɪnvəˈrɛərɪ) *n* a town in W Scotland, in Argyll and Bute: Inveraray Castle is the seat of the Dukes of Argyll. Pop: about 700 (2001)

Invercargill (ˌɪnvəˈkɑːgɪl) *n* a city in New Zealand, on South Island: regional trading centre for sheep and agricultural products. Pop: 51 700 (2004 est)

Inverclyde (ˌɪnvəˈklaɪd) *n* a council area of W central Scotland: created in 1996 from part of Strathclyde region. Administrative centre: Greenock. Pop: 83 050 (2003 est). Area: 162 sq km (63 sq miles)

Inverness (ˌɪnvəˈnɛs) *n* **1 a** a city in N Scotland, administrative centre of Highland: tourism and specialized engineering. Pop: 40 949 (2001) **2** (*sometimes not capital*) an overcoat with a removable cape

Inverness-shire (ˌɪnvəˈnɛsˌʃɪə, -ʃə) *n* (until 1975) a county of NW Scotland, now part of Highland

inverse (ɪnˈvɜːs, ˈɪnvɜːs) *adj* **1** opposite or contrary in effect, sequence, direction, etc **2** *maths* **a** (of a relationship) containing two variables such that an increase in one results in a decrease in the other **b** (of an element) operating on a specified member of a set to produce the identity of the set: *the additive inverse element of x is –x, the multiplicative inverse element of x is 1/x* **3** (*usually prenominal*) upside-down; inverted: *in an inverse position* ▷ *n* **4** *maths* an inverse element [C17: from Latin *inversus*, from *invertere* to INVERT] ▷ inˈversely *adv*

inversion (ɪnˈvɜːʃən) *n* **1** the act of inverting or state of being inverted **2** something inverted, esp a reversal of order, mutual functions, etc: *an inversion of their previous relationship* **3** *Also called:* anastrophe *rhetoric* the reversal of a normal order of words **4** *chem* **a** the conversion of a dextrorotatory solution of sucrose into a laevorotatory solution of glucose and fructose by hydrolysis **b** any similar reaction in which the optical properties of the reactants are opposite to those of the products **5** *music* **a** the process or result of transposing the notes of a chord (esp a triad) such that the root, originally in the bass, is placed in an upper part. When the bass note is the third of the triad, the resulting chord is the **first inversion**; when it is the fifth, the resulting chord is the **second inversion** **b** the modification of an interval in which the higher note becomes the lower or the lower one the higher **6** *pathol* abnormal positioning of an organ or part, as in being upside down or turned inside out **7** *psychiatry* **a** the adoption of the role or characteristics of the opposite sex **b** another word for **homosexuality 8** *meteorol* an abnormal condition in which the layer of air next to the earth's surface is cooler than an overlying layer **9** *computing* an operation by which each digit of a binary number is changed to the alternative digit, as 10110 to 01001 ▷ inˈversive *adj*

invert *vb* (ɪnˈvɜːt) **1** to turn or cause to turn upside down or inside out **2** (*tr*) to reverse in effect, sequence, direction, etc **3** (*tr*) *phonetics* **a** to turn (the tip of the tongue) up and back **b** to pronounce (a speech sound) by retroflexion ▷ *n* (ˈɪnvɜːt) **4** *psychiatry* **a** a person who adopts the role of the opposite sex **b** another word for **homosexual 5** *architect* **a** the lower inner surface of a drain, sewer, etc **b** an arch that is concave upwards, esp one used in foundations [C16: from Latin *invertere*, from IN-² + *vertere* to turn] > in'vertible *adj* > in,verti'bility *n*

invertase (ɪn'vɜːteɪz) *n* an enzyme, occurring in the intestinal juice of animals and in yeasts, that hydrolyses sucrose to glucose and fructose

invertebrate (ɪn'vɜːtɪbrɪt, -,breɪt) *n* **1** any animal lacking a backbone, including all species not classified as vertebrates ▷ *adj* Also: in'vertebral **2** of, relating to, or designating invertebrates

inverted comma *n* another term for **quotation mark**

inverted mordent *n music* a melodic ornament consisting of the rapid single or double alternation of a principal note with a note one degree higher

inverter *or* **invertor** (ɪn'vɜːtə) *n* any device for converting a direct current into an alternating current

invert sugar ('ɪnvɜːt) *n* a mixture of fructose and glucose obtained by the inversion of sucrose

invest (ɪn'vɛst) *vb* **1** (often foll by *in*) to lay out (money or capital in an enterprise, esp by purchasing shares) with the expectation of profit **2** (*tr*; often foll by *in*) to devote (effort, resources, etc, to a project) **3** (*tr*; often foll by *in* or *with*) *mainly archaic* to clothe or adorn (in some garment, esp the robes of an office) **4** (*tr*; often foll by *in*) to install formally or ceremonially (in an official position, rank, etc) **5** (*tr*; foll by *in* or *with*) to place (power, authority, etc, in) or provide (with power or authority): *to invest new rights in the monarchy* **6** (*tr*; usually passive; foll by *in* or *with*) to provide or endow (a person with qualities, characteristics, etc) **7** (*tr*; foll by *with*) *usually poetic* to cover or adorn, as if with a coat or garment: *when spring invests the trees with leaves* **8** (*tr*) *rare* to surround with military forces; besiege **9** (*intr*; foll by *in*) *informal* to purchase; buy [C16: from Medieval Latin *investīre* to clothe, from Latin, from *vestīre*, from *vestis* a garment] > in'vestable *or* in'vestible *adj* > in'vestor *n*

investigate (ɪn'vɛstɪ,geɪt) *vb* to inquire into (a situation or problem, esp a crime or death) thoroughly; examine systematically, esp in order to discover the truth [C16: from Latin *investīgāre* to search after, from IN-² + *vestīgium* track; see VESTIGE] > in'vestigative *or* in'vestigatory *adj* > in'vesti,gator *n*

investigation (ɪn,vɛstɪ'geɪʃən) *n* the act or process of investigating; a careful search or examination in order to discover facts, etc

investiture (ɪn'vɛstɪtʃə) *n* **1** the act of presenting with a title or with the robes and insignia of an office or rank **2** (in feudal society) the formal bestowal of the possessory right to a fief or other benefice > in'vestitive *adj*

investment (ɪn'vɛstmənt) *n* **1 a** the act of investing money **b** the amount invested **c** an enterprise, asset, etc, in which money is or can be invested **2 a** the act of investing effort, resources, etc **b** the amount invested **3** *biology* the outer layer or covering of an organ, part, or organism **4** a less common word for **investiture** (sense 1) **5** the act of investing or state of being invested, as with an official robe, a specific quality, etc **6** *rare* the act of besieging with military forces, works, etc

investment analyst *n* a specialist in forecasting the prices of stocks and shares

investment bond *n* a single-premium life-assurance policy in which a fixed sum is invested in an asset-backed fund

investment trust *n* a financial enterprise that invests its subscribed capital in securities for its investors' benefit

inveterate (ɪn'vɛtərɪt) *adj* **1** long established, esp so as to be deep-rooted or ingrained: *an inveterate feeling of hostility* **2** (*prenominal*) settled or confirmed in a habit or practice, esp a bad one; hardened [C16: from Latin *inveterātus* of long standing, from *inveterāre* to make old, from IN-² + *vetus* old] > in'veteracy *or* in'veterateness *n* > in'veterately *adv*

invidious (ɪn'vɪdɪəs) *adj* **1** incurring or tending to arouse resentment, unpopularity, etc: *an invidious task* **2** (of comparisons or distinctions) unfairly or offensively discriminating [C17: from Latin *invidiōsus* full of envy, from *invidia* ENVY] > in'vidiously *adv* > in'vidiousness *n*

invigilate (ɪn'vɪdʒɪ,leɪt) *vb* (*intr*) **1** *Brit* to watch examination candidates, esp to prevent cheating. US word: proctor **2** *archaic* to keep watch [C16: from Latin *invigilāre* to watch over, from IN-² + *vigilāre* to keep watch; see VIGIL] > in,vigi'lation *n* > in'vigi,lator *n*

invigorate (ɪn'vɪgə,reɪt) *vb* (*tr*) to give vitality and vigour to; animate; brace; refresh: *to be invigorated by fresh air* [C17: from IN-² + Latin *vigor* vigour] > in'vigor,ating *adj* > in,vigor'ation *n* > in'vigorative *adj* > in'vigor,ator *n*

invincible (ɪn'vɪnsəb°l) *adj* incapable of being defeated; unconquerable [C15: from Late Latin *invincibilis*, from Latin IN-¹ + *vincere* to conquer] > in,vinci'bility *or* in'vincibleness *n* > in'vincibly *adv*

inviolable (ɪn'vaɪələb°l) *adj* that must not or cannot be transgressed, dishonoured, or broken; to be kept sacred: *an inviolable oath* > in,viola'bility *or* in'violableness *n* > in'violably *adv*

inviolate (ɪn'vaɪəlɪt, -,leɪt) *adj* **1** free from violation, injury, disturbance, etc **2** a less common word for **inviolable** > in'violacy *or* in'violateness *n* > in'violately *adv*

invisible (ɪn'vɪzəb°l) *adj* **1** not visible; not able to be perceived by the eye: *invisible rays* **2** concealed from sight; hidden **3** not easily seen or noticed: *invisible mending* **4** kept hidden from public view; secret; clandestine **5** *economics* of or relating to services rather than goods in relation to the invisible balance: *invisible earnings* ▷ *n* **6** *economics* an invisible item of trade; service > in,visi'bility *or* in'visibleness *n* > in'visibly *adv*

invitation (,ɪnvɪ'teɪʃən) *n* **1 a** the act of inviting, such as an offer of entertainment or hospitality **b** (*as modifier*): *an invitation dance; an invitation race* **2** the act of enticing or attracting; allurement

invite *vb* (ɪn'vaɪt) (*tr*) **1** to ask (a person or persons) in a friendly or polite way (to do something, attend an event, etc) **2** to make a request for, esp publicly or formally: *to invite applications* **3** to bring on or provoke; give occasion for: *you invite disaster by your actions* **4** to welcome or tempt ▷ *n* ('ɪnvaɪt) **5** an informal word for **invitation** [C16: from Latin *invītāre* to invite, entertain, from IN-² + *-vītāre*, probably related to Greek *hiesthai* to be desirous of] > in'viter *n*

inviting (ɪn'vaɪtɪŋ) *adj* tempting; alluring; attractive > in'vitingness *n*

in vitro (ɪn 'viːtrəʊ) *adv, adj* (of biological processes or reactions) made to occur outside the living organism in an artificial environment, such as a culture medium [New Latin, literally: in glass]

in vitro fertilization *n* a technique enabling some women who are unable to conceive to bear children. Egg cells removed from a woman's ovary are fertilized by sperm in vitro; some of the resulting fertilized egg cells are incubated until the blastocyst stage, which are then implanted into her uterus. Abbreviation: IVF

in vivo (ɪn 'viːvəʊ) *adv, adj* (of biological processes or experiments) occurring or carried out in the living organism [New Latin, literally: in a living (thing)]

invocation (,ɪnvə'keɪʃən) *n* **1** the act of invoking or calling upon some agent for assistance **2** a prayer asking God for help, forgiveness, etc, esp as part of a religious service **3** an appeal for inspiration and guidance from a Muse or deity at the beginning of a poem **4 a** the act of summoning a spirit or demon from another world by ritual incantation or magic **b** the incantation used in this act > ,invo'cational *adj* > invocatory (ɪn'vɒkətərɪ, -trɪ) *adj*

invoice ('ɪnvɔɪs) *n* **1** a document issued by a seller to a buyer listing the goods or services supplied and stating the sum of money due ▷ *vb* **2** (*tr*) **a** to present (a customer) with an invoice **b** to list (merchandise sold) on an invoice [C16: from earlier *invoyes*, from Old French *envois*, plural of *envoi* message; see ENVOY¹]

invoke (ɪn'vəʊk) *vb* (*tr*) **1** to call upon (an agent, esp God or another deity) for help, inspiration, etc **2** to put (a law, penalty, etc) into use: *the union invoked the dispute procedure* **3** to appeal to (an outside agent or authority) for confirmation, corroboration, etc **4** to implore or beg (help, etc) **5** to summon (a spirit, demon, etc); conjure up [C15: from Latin *invocāre* to call upon, appeal to, from

vocāre to call] ▷ in'vocable *adj* ▷ in'voker *n*
● USAGE *Invoke* is sometimes wrongly used where *evoke* is
● meant: *this proposal evoked* (not *invoked*) *a strong reaction*

involucre ('ɪnvə,luːkə) *or* **involucrum** (,ɪnvə'luːkrəm) *n*,
pl -cres *or* -cra (-krə) a ring of bracts at the base of an
inflorescence in such plants as the composites [C16 (in
the sense: envelope): from New Latin *involucrum*, from
Latin: wrapper, from *involvere* to wrap; see INVOLVE]
▷ ,invo'lucral *adj* ▷ ,invo'lucrate *adj*

involuntary (ɪn'vɒləntərɪ, -trɪ) *adj* **1** carried out without
one's conscious wishes; not voluntary; unintentional
2 *physiol* (esp of a movement or muscle) performed or
acting without conscious control ▷ in'voluntarily *adv*
▷ in'voluntariness *n*

involute *adj* ('ɪnvə,luːt) Also called: **involuted 1** complex,
intricate, or involved **2** *botany* (esp of petals, leaves, etc,
in bud) having margins that are rolled inwards **3** (of
certain shells) closely coiled so that the axis is obscured
▷ *n* ('ɪnvə,luːt) **4** *geometry* the curve described by the free
end of a thread as it is wound around another curve, the
evolute, such that its normals are tangential to the
evolute. See also **evolute** ▷ *vb* (,ɪnvə'luːt) **5** (*intr*) to
become involute [C17: from Latin *involūtus*, from *involvere*;
see INVOLVE] ▷ 'invo,lutely *adv* ▷ ,invo'lutedly *adv*

involution (,ɪnvə'luːʃən) *n* **1** the act of involving or
complicating or the state of being involved or
complicated **2** something involved or complicated
3 *zoology* degeneration or structural deformation
4 *biology* an involute formation or structure **5** *physiol*
reduction in size of an organ or part, as of the uterus
following childbirth or as a result of ageing **6** an
algebraic operation in which a number, variable,
expression etc, is raised to a specified power
▷ ,invo'lutional *adj*

involve (ɪn'vɒlv) *vb* (*tr*) **1** to include or contain as a
necessary part **2** to have an effect on; affect: *the
investigation involved many innocent people* **3** (often passive;
usually foll by *in* or *with*) to concern or associate
significantly: *many people were involved in the crime* **4** (often
passive) to make complicated; tangle **5** *rare, often poetic* to
wrap or surround **6** *maths obsolete* to raise to a specified
power [C14: from Latin *involvere* to roll in, surround, from
IN-² + *volvere* to roll] ▷ in'volvement *n* ▷ in'volver *n*

invulnerable (ɪn'vʌlnərəb³l, -'vʌlnrəb³l) *adj* **1** incapable
of being wounded, hurt, damaged, etc, either physically
or emotionally **2** incapable of being damaged or
captured: *an invulnerable fortress* ▷ in,vulnera'bility *or*
in'vulnerableness *n* ▷ in'vulnerably *adv*

inward ('ɪnwəd) *adj* **1** going or directed towards the
middle of or into something **2** situated within; inside
3 of, relating to, or existing in the mind or spirit: *inward
meditation* **4** of one's own country or a specific country:
inward investment ▷ *adv* **5** a variant of **inwards** (sense 1) ▷ *n*
6 the inward part; inside ▷ 'inwardness *n*

inwardly ('ɪnwədlɪ) *adv* **1** within the private thoughts or
feelings; secretly **2** not aloud: *to laugh inwardly* **3** with
reference to the inside or inner part; internally

inwards *adv* ('ɪnwədz) Also called: **inward 1** towards the
interior or middle of something **2** in, into, or towards
the mind or spirit ▷ *pl n* ('ɪnədz) **3** a variant spelling of
innards

inweave (ɪn'wiːv) *vb* -weaves, -weaving, -wove *or*
-weaved, -woven *or* -weaved (*tr*) to weave together into
or as if into a design, fabric, etc; interweave

inwrap (ɪn'ræp) *vb* -wraps, -wrapping, -wrapped a less
common spelling of **enwrap**

inwrought (,ɪn'rɔːt) *adj* **1** worked or woven into material,
esp decoratively **2** *rare* blended with other things

in-your-face *adj slang* aggressive and confrontational:
provocative in-your-face activism

Io¹ ('aɪəʊ) *n Greek myth* a maiden loved by Zeus and
turned into a white heifer by either Zeus or Hera

Io² *the chemical symbol for* **ionium**

Ioánnina (Greek jo'anina) *or* **Yanina** *n* a city in NW
Greece: belonged to the Serbs (1349–1430) and then the
Turks (until 1913); seat of Ali Pasha, the "Lion of Janina",
from 1788 to 1822. Pop: 78 000 (2005 est). Serbian name:
Janina

IOC *abbreviation* International Olympic Committee

iodic (aɪ'ɒdɪk) *adj* of or containing iodine, esp in the
pentavalent state

iodide ('aɪə,daɪd) *n* **1** a salt of hydriodic acid, containing
the iodide ion, I⁻ **2** a compound containing an iodine
atom, such as methyl iodide, CH_3I

iodine ('aɪə,diːn) *n* a bluish-black element of the
halogen group that sublimates into a violet irritating
gas. Its compounds are used in medicine and
photography and in dyes. The radioisotope **iodine-131
(radioiodine)**, with a half-life of 8 days, is used in the
diagnosis and treatment of thyroid disease. Symbol: I;
atomic no: 53; atomic wt: 126.90447; valency: 1, 3, 5, or 7;
relative density: 4.93; melting pt: 113.5°C; boiling pt:
184.35°C [C19: from French *iode*, from Greek *iōdēs* rust-
coloured, but taken to mean violet-coloured, through a
mistaken derivation from *ion* violet]

iodize *or* **iodise** ('aɪə,daɪz) *vb* (*tr*) to treat or react with
iodine or an iodine compound. Also called: **iodate**
▷ ,iodi'zation *or* ,iodi'sation *n* ▷ 'io,dizer *or* 'io,diser *n*

iodoform (aɪ'ɒdə,fɔːm) *n* a yellow crystalline insoluble
volatile solid with a penetrating sweet odour made by
heating alcohol with iodine and an alkali: used as an
antiseptic. Formula: CHI_3

iodopsin (,aɪə'dɒpsɪn) *n* a violet light-sensitive pigment
in the cones of the retina of the eye that is responsible
for colour vision. See also **rhodopsin**

IOM *abbreviation* Isle of Man

ion ('aɪən, -ɒn) *n* an electrically charged atom or group
of atoms formed by the loss or gain of one or more
electrons. See also **cation, anion** [C19: from Greek,
literally: going, from *ienai* to go]

-ion *suffix forming nouns* indicating an action, process, or
state: *creation*; *objection*. See **-ation, -tion** [from Latin -iōn-,
-io]

Iona (aɪ'əʊnə) *n* an island off the W coast of Scotland, in
the Inner Hebrides: site of St Columba's monastery
(founded in 563) and an important early centre of
Christianity. Area: 854 ha (2112 acres)

Ionesco (,iːə'nɛskəʊ; *French* jɔnɛsko) *n* **Eugène** (øʒɛn)
1912–94, French dramatist, born in Romania; a leading
exponent of the theatre of the absurd. His plays include
The Bald Prima Donna (1950) and *Rhinoceros* (1960)

ion exchange *n* the process in which ions are
exchanged between a solution and an insoluble solid,
usually a resin. It is used to soften water, to separate
radioactive isotopes, and to purify certain industrial
chemicals

Ionia (aɪ'əʊnɪə) *n* an ancient region of W central Asia
Minor, including adjacent Aegean islands: colonized by
Greeks in about 1100 BC ▷ I'onian *n*, *adj*

Ionian Islands *pl n* a group of Greek islands in the
Ionian Sea, consisting of Corfu, Cephalonia, Zante,
Levkas, Ithaca, Cythera, and Paxos: ceded to Greece in
1864. Pop: 212 984 (2001). Area: 2307 sq km (891 sq miles)

Ionian Sea *n* the part of the Mediterranean Sea between
SE Italy, E Sicily, and Greece

ionic (aɪ'ɒnɪk) *adj* of, relating to, or occurring in the
form of ions

Ionic (aɪ'ɒnɪk) *adj* **1** of, denoting, or relating to one of the
five classical orders of architecture, characterized by
fluted columns and capitals with scroll-like ornaments
2 of or relating to Ionia, its inhabitants, or their dialect
of Ancient Greek ▷ *n* **3** one of four chief dialects of
Ancient Greek; the dialect spoken in Ionia

ionium (aɪ'əʊnɪəm) *n obsolete* a naturally occurring
radioisotope of thorium with a mass number of 230.
Symbol: Io [C20: from New Latin, from ION + -IUM]

ionization *or* **ionisation** (,aɪənaɪ'zeɪʃən) *n* **a** the
formation of ions as a result of a chemical reaction,
high temperature, electrical discharge, particle
collisions, or radiation **b** (*as modifier*): *ionization temperature*;
ionization current

ionize *or* **ionise** ('aɪə,naɪz) *vb* to change or become
changed into ions ▷ 'ion,izable *or* 'ion,isable *adj* ▷ 'io,nizer
or 'io,niser *n*

ionosphere (aɪ'ɒnə,sfɪə) *n* a region of the earth's
atmosphere, extending from about 60 kilometres to
1000 km above the earth's surface, in which there is a
high concentration of free electrons formed as a result

of ionizing radiation entering the atmosphere from space > **ionospheric** (ˌaɪˌɒnəˈsfɛrɪk) *adj*

iota (aɪˈəʊtə) *n* **1** the ninth letter in the Greek alphabet (Ι, ι), a vowel or semivowel, transliterated as *i* or *j* **2** (*usually used with a negative*) a very small amount; jot (*esp* in the phrase **not one** *or* **an iota**) [c16: via Latin from Greek, of Semitic origin; see JOT]

IOU *n* a written promise or reminder to pay a debt [c17: representing *I owe you*]

-ious *suffix forming adjectives from nouns* characterized by or full of: *ambitious; religious; suspicious* [from Latin *-ius* and *-iōsus* full of]

IOW *abbreviation* Isle of Wight

Iowa (ˈaɪəʊə) *n* a state in the N central US, in the Midwest: consists of rolling plains crossed by many rivers, with the Missouri forming the western border and the Mississippi the eastern. Capital: Des Moines. Pop: 2 944 062 (2003 est). Area: 144 887 sq km (55 941 sq miles). Abbreviations: Ia., (with zip code) IA

IP *abbreviation* **1** internet protocol: a code used to label packets of data sent across the internet, identifying both the sending and the receiving computers **2** *law* intellectual property

IPA *abbreviation* International Phonetic Alphabet

IP address *n computing* internet protocol address: the numeric code that identifies all computers that are connected to the internet

Ipatieff (ˈpætjɛf) *n* **Vladimir Nikolaievich** (ˈvlædɪmɪə ˌnɪkəˈlaɪəvɪtʃ). 1867–1952, US physicist, born in Russia. He discovered the structure of isoprene (1897) and later developed high-octane fuels

ipecacuanha (ˌɪpɪˌpætjɛf) *or* **ipecac** (ˈɪpɪˌkæk) *n* **1** a low-growing South American rubiaceous shrub, *Cephaelis ipecacuanha* **2** a drug prepared from the dried roots of this plant, used as a purgative and emetic [c18: from Portuguese, from Tupi *ipekaaguéne*, from *ipeh* low + *kaa* leaves + *guéne* vomit]

Iphigenia (ˌɪfɪdʒɪˈnaɪə) *n* Greek *myth* the daughter of Agamemnon, taken by him to be sacrificed to Artemis, who saved her life and made her a priestess

I-pin (ˈɪpɪn) *n* a variant transliteration of the Chinese name for **Yibin**

IPO *stock exchange abbreviation* initial public offering

iPod, iPOD *or* **IPod** (ˈaɪˌpɒd) *n trademark* a small portable digital audio player capable of storing thousands of tracks downloaded from the internet or transferred from a CD > **ˈiˌPodder** *n*

Ipoh (ˈiːpəʊ) *n* a city in Malaysia, capital of Perak state: tin-mining centre. Pop: 643 000 (2005 est)

ipomoea (ˌɪpəˈmɪə, -aɪ-) *n* **1** any tropical or subtropical convolvulaceous plant of the genus *Ipomoea*, such as the morning-glory, sweet potato, and jalap, having trumpet-shaped flowers **2** the dried root of a Mexican species, *I. orizabensis*, which yields a cathartic resin [c18: New Latin, from Greek *ips* worm + *homoios* like]

ippon (ˈɪpɒn) *n judo, karate* a winning point awarded in a sparring competition for a perfectly executed technique [c20: Japanese, literally: one point]

Ipsambul (ˌɪpsæmˈbuːl) *n* another name for **Abu Simbel**

ipse dixit Latin (ˈɪpseɪ ˈdɪksɪt) *n* an arbitrary and unsupported assertion [c16, literally: he himself said it]

ipso facto (ˈɪpsəʊ ˈfæktəʊ) *adv* by that very fact or act [from Latin]

Ipsus (ˈɪpsəs) *n* an ancient town in Asia Minor, in S Phrygia: site of a decisive battle (301 BC) in the Wars of the Diadochi in which Lysimachus and Seleucus defeated Antigonus and Demetrius

Ipswich (ˈɪpswɪtʃ) *n* a town in E England, administrative centre of Suffolk, a port at the head of the Orwell estuary: financial services, telecommunications. Pop: 138 718 (2001)

IQ *abbreviation* intelligence quotient

Iqaluit (ɪˈkæluɪt) *n* a town in N Canada, capital of Nunavut. Pop: 5236 (2001). Former name: Frobisher Bay

Iqbal (ˈɪkbal) *n* **Sir Muhammad** (mʊˈhæməd). 1875–1938, Indian Muslim poet, philosopher, and political leader, who advocated the establishment of separate nations for Indian Hindus and Muslims and is generally regarded as the originator of Pakistan

Iquique (*Spanish* iˈkike) *n* a port in N Chile: oil refineries. Pop: 243 000 (2005 est)

Iquitos (*Spanish* iˈkitɔs) *n* an inland port in NE Peru, on the Amazon 3703 km (2300 miles) from the Atlantic: head of navigation for large steamers. Pop: 389 000 (2005 est)

Ir *the chemical symbol for* iridium

Ir. *abbreviation* **1** Ireland **2** Irish

ir- *prefix* a variant of **in-**¹,²

IRA *abbreviation* Irish Republican Army

irade (ɪˈrɑːdɛ) *n* a written edict of a Muslim ruler [c19: from Turkish: will, desire, from Arabic *irādah*]

Iráklion (*Greek* iˈraklɪɔn) *n* a port in Greece, in N Crete: former capital of Crete (until 1841); ruled by Venetians (13th–17th centuries). Pop: 150 000 (2005 est). Italian name: Candia Also called: Heraklion, Herakleion

Iran (ɪˈrɑːn) *n* a republic in SW Asia, between the Caspian Sea and the Persian Gulf: a monarchy until an Islamic revolution in 1979 headed by the Ayatollah Khomeini when the Shah was obliged to leave the country. Consists chiefly of a high central desert plateau almost completely surrounded by mountains, a semitropical fertile region along the Caspian coast, and a hot and dry area beside the Persian Gulf. Oil is the most important export. Official language: Persian (Iranian or Farsi). Official religion: Muslim majority. Currency: rial. Capital: Tehran. Pop: 68 789 000 (2004 est). Area: 1 647 050 sq km (635 932 sq miles). Former name (until 1935): Persia, Persian Empire

Iranian (ɪˈreɪnɪən) *n* **1** a native, citizen, or inhabitant of Iran **2** a branch of the Indo-European family of languages, divided into **West Iranian** (including Old Persian, Pahlavi, modern Persian, Kurdish, Baluchi, and Tajik) and **East Iranian** (including Avestan, Sogdian, Pashto, and Ossetic) **3** Also called: Persian, Farsi the modern Persian language ▷ *adj* **4** relating to, denoting, or characteristic of Iran, its inhabitants, or their language; Persian **5** belonging to or relating to the Iranian branch of Indo-European

Iran-Iraq War *n* the war (1980–88) fought by Iran and Iraq, following the Iraqi invasion of disputed border territory in Iran. It ended indecisively with no important gains on either side: Iraq subsequently (1990) conceded the disputed territory. Also called: Gulf War

Iraq (ɪˈrɑːk) *n* a republic in SW Asia, on the Persian Gulf: coextensive with ancient Mesopotamia; became a British mandate in 1920, independent in 1932, and a republic in 1958. The Iraqi invasion of Kuwait (1990) led to their defeat in the first Gulf War (1991) by US-led UN forces. The second Gulf War (2003) took place when Iraq was invaded by a coalition of US, UK and other forces; government elected in 2005, although there is continuing violence and resistance to the coalition presence. Iraq consists chiefly of the mountains of Kurdistan in the northeast, part of the Syrian Desert, and the lower basin of the Rivers Tigris and Euphrates. Oil is the major export. Official language: Arabic; Kurdish is official in the Kurdish Autonomous Region only. Official religion: Muslim. Currency: dinar. Capital: Baghdad. Pop: 25 856 000 (2004 est). Area: 438 446 sq km (169 284 sq miles) > **Iˈraqi** *adj, n*

irascible (ɪˈræsɪbᵊl) *adj* **1** easily angered; irritable **2** showing irritability: *an irascible action* [c16: from Late Latin *īrascibilis*, from Latin *īra* anger] > **iˌrasciˈbility** *or* **iˈrascibleness** *n* > **iˈrascibly** *adv*

irate (aɪˈreɪt) *adj* **1** incensed with anger; furious **2** marked by extreme anger: *an irate letter* [c19: from Latin *īrātus* enraged, from *īrascī* to be angry] > **iˈrately** *adv*

Irbid (ˈɪrbɪd) *n* a town in NW Jordan. Pop: 280 000 (2005 est)

Irbil (ˈɪəbɪl) *n* a variant of **Erbil**

IRBM *abbreviation* intermediate range ballistic missile

IRC *abbreviation* **1** International Red Cross **2** International Red Crescent

IRD *abbreviation* (in New Zealand) Inland Revenue Department

ire (aɪə) *n literary* anger; wrath [c13: from Old French, from Latin *īra*] > **ˈireful** *adj* > **ˈirefulness** *n*

Ire. *abbreviation* Ireland

Ireland[1] ('aɪələnd) n **1** an island off NW Europe: part of the British Isles, separated from Britain by the North Channel, the Irish Sea, and St George's Channel; contains large areas of peat bog, with mountains that rise over 900 m (3000 ft) in the southwest and several large lakes. It was conquered by England in the 16th and early 17th centuries and ruled as a dependency until 1801, when it was united with Great Britain until its division in 1921 into the Irish Free State and Northern Ireland. Latin name: Hibernia **2** Republic of Ireland Also called: Irish Republic, Southern Ireland a republic in NW Europe occupying most of Ireland: established as the Irish Free State (a British dominion) in 1921 and declared a republic in 1949; joined the European Community (now the European Union) in 1973. Official languages: Irish (Gaelic) and English. Currency: euro. Capital: Dublin. Pop: 3 999 000 (2004 est). Area: 70 285 sq km (27 137 sq miles) ▷ See also **Northern Ireland**

Ireland[2] ('aɪələnd) n **John** (**Nicholson**). 1879–1962, English composer, esp of songs

Irene (aɪˈriːnɪ) n **1** ?752–803 AD, Byzantine ruler (780–90, 792–97), joint ruler with her son Constantine VI; 797–802). She is venerated as a saint in the Greek Orthodox Church **2** Greek myth the goddess of peace

irenic or **eirenic** (aɪˈriːnɪk, -ˈrɛn-), **irenical** or **eirenical** adj tending to conciliate or promote peace [C19: from Greek eirēnikos, from eirēnē peace] ▷ **i'renically** or **ei'renically** adv

Ireton ('aɪətᵊn) n **Henry**. 1611–51, English Parliamentarian general in the Civil War; son-in-law of Oliver Cromwell. His plan for a constitutional monarchy was rejected by Charles I (1647), whose death warrant he signed; lord deputy of Ireland (1650–51)

Irian Barat ('ɪərɪən 'bærɑːt) n a former Indonesian name for **Papua** (sense 2)

Irian Jaya n a former Indonesian name (1973–2001) for **Papua** (sense 2)

iridaceous (ˌɪrɪˈdeɪʃəs, ˌaɪ-) adj of, relating to, or belonging to the Iridaceae, a family of monocotyledonous plants, including iris, crocus, and gladiolus, having swordlike leaves and showy flowers

iridescent (ˌɪrɪˈdɛsᵊnt) adj displaying a spectrum of colours that shimmer and change due to interference and scattering as the observer's position changes [C18: from IRIDO- + -ESCENT] ▷ ˌiri'descence n ▷ ˌiri'descently adv

iridium (aɪˈrɪdɪəm, ɪˈrɪd-) n a very hard inert yellowish-white transition element that is the most corrosion-resistant metal known. It occurs in platinum ores and is used as an alloy with platinum. Symbol: Ir; atomic no: 77; atomic wt: 192.22; valency: 3 or 4; relative density: 22.42; melting pt: 2447°C; boiling pt: 4428°C [C19: New Latin, from IRIDO- + -IUM; from its colourful appearance when dissolving in certain acids]

irido- or before a vowel **irid-** combining form **1** denoting the iris of the eye or the genus of plants: iridaceous **2** denoting a rainbow: iridescent [from Latin irid-, IRIS]

iris ('aɪrɪs) n, pl **irises** or **irides** ('aɪrɪˌdiːz, 'ɪrɪ-) **1** the coloured muscular diaphragm that surrounds and controls the size of the pupil **2** Also called: fleur-de-lys any plant of the iridaceous genus Iris, having brightly coloured flowers composed of three petals and three drooping sepals **3** a rare or poetic word for **rainbow** **4** short for **iris diaphragm** [C14: from Latin: rainbow, iris (flower), crystal, from Greek]

Iris ('aɪrɪs) n the goddess of the rainbow along which she travelled to earth as a messenger of the gods

iris diaphragm n an adjustable diaphragm that regulates the amount of light entering an optical instrument, esp a camera. It usually consists of a number of thin metal leaves arranged so that they open out into an approximately circular aperture

Irish ('aɪrɪʃ) adj **1** of, relating to, or characteristic of Ireland, its people, their Celtic language, or their dialect of English **2** informal, offensive ludicrous or illogical ▷ n **3** the Irish (functioning as plural) the natives or inhabitants of Ireland **4** another name for **Irish Gaelic**

Irish coffee n hot coffee mixed with Irish whiskey and topped with double cream

Irish Free State n a former name (1921–37) for the (Republic of) **Ireland**[1]

Irish Gaelic n the Goidelic language of the Celts of Ireland, now spoken mainly along the west coast; an official language of the Republic of Ireland since 1921

Irishman ('aɪrɪʃmən) n, pl **-men** a male native, citizen, or inhabitant of Ireland or a male descendant of someone Irish

Irish pipes n another name for **uillean pipes**

Irish Republic n See **Ireland**[1] (sense 2)

Irish Republican Army n a militant organization of Irish nationalists founded with the aim of striving for a united independent Ireland by means of guerrilla warfare. Abbreviation: IRA

Irish Sea n an arm of the North Atlantic Ocean between Great Britain and Ireland

Irish stew n a white stew made of mutton, lamb, or beef, with potatoes, onions, etc

Irish wolfhound n a very large breed of hound with a rough thick coat

iritis (aɪˈraɪtɪs) n inflammation of the iris of the eye ▷ **iritic** (aɪˈrɪtɪk) adj

irk (ɜːk) vb (tr) to irritate, vex, or annoy [C13 irken to grow weary; probably related to Old Norse yrkja to work]

irksome ('ɜːksəm) adj causing vexation, annoyance, or boredom; troublesome or tedious ▷ **'irksomely** adv ▷ **'irksomeness** n

Irkutsk (Russian ir'kutsk) n a city in S Russia; situated on the Trans-Siberian railway; university (1918); one of the largest industrial centres in Siberia, esp for heavy engineering. Pop: 587 000 (2005 est)

IRO abbreviation **1** (in Britain) Inland Revenue Office **2** International Refugee Organization

iron ('aɪən) n **1** **a** a malleable ductile silvery-white ferromagnetic metallic element occurring principally in haematite and magnetite. It is widely used for structural and engineering purposes. Symbol: Fe; atomic no: 26; atomic wt: 55.847; valency: 2,3,4, or 6; relative density: 7.874; melting pt: 1538°C; boiling pt: 2862°C. Related adjs: **ferric, ferrous** Related prefix: **ferro-** **b** (as modifier): iron railings **2** any of certain tools or implements made of iron or steel, esp for use when hot: a grappling iron; a soldering iron **3** an appliance for pressing fabrics using dry heat or steam, esp a small electrically heated device with a handle and a weighted flat bottom **4** any of various golf clubs with narrow metal heads, numbered from 1 to 9 according to the slant of the face, used esp for approach shots **5** US slang a splintlike support for a malformed leg **6** great hardness, strength, or resolve: a will of iron **7** strike while the iron is hot to act at an opportune moment ▷ adj **8** very hard, immovable, or implacable: iron determination **9** very strong; extremely robust: an iron constitution **10** cruel or unyielding: he ruled with an iron hand ▷ vb **11** to smooth (clothes or fabric) by removing (creases or wrinkles) using a heated iron; press **12** (tr) to furnish or clothe with iron **13** (tr) rare to place (a prisoner) in irons ▷ See also **iron out, irons** [Old English īren; related to Old High German īsan, Old Norse jārn; compare Old Irish īarn] ▷ **'ironer** n ▷ **'ironless** adj ▷ **'iron,like** adj

Iron Age n **a** the period following the Bronze Age characterized by the extremely rapid spread of iron tools and weapons, which began in the Middle East about 1100 BC **b** (as modifier): an Iron-Age weapon

ironbark ('aɪənˌbɑːk) n any of several Australian eucalyptus trees that have hard rough bark

ironbound ('aɪənˌbaʊnd) adj **1** bound with iron **2** unyielding; inflexible **3** (of a coast) rocky; rugged

Iron Chancellor n **the**. nickname of (Prince Otto Eduard Leopold von) **Bismarck**[1]

ironclad ('aɪənˌklæd) **1** covered or protected with iron: an ironclad warship **2** inflexible; rigid: an ironclad rule ▷ n ('aɪənˌklæd) **3** a large wooden 19th-century warship with armoured plating

Iron Curtain n **a** (formerly) the guarded border between the countries of the Soviet bloc and the rest of Europe **b** (as modifier): Iron Curtain countries

Iron Duke n **the**. nickname of (1st Duke of) **Wellington**[1]

Iron Gate or **Iron Gates** n a gorge of the River Danube on the border between Romania and Serbia. Length: 3 km (2 miles). Romanian name: Porțile de Fier

iron hand *n* harsh or rigorous control; overbearing or autocratic force

iron horse *n* *archaic* a steam-driven railway locomotive

ironic (aɪˈrɒnɪk) *or* **ironical** *adj* of, characterized by, or using irony ⊳ iˈronicalness *n* ⊳ iˈronically *adv*

ironing (ˈaɪənɪŋ) *n* **1** the act of ironing washed clothes **2** clothes that are to be or that have been ironed

ironing board *n* a board, usually on legs, with a suitable covering on which to iron clothes

iron lung *n* an airtight metal cylinder enclosing the entire body up to the neck and providing artificial respiration when the respiratory muscles are paralysed, as by poliomyelitis

iron maiden *n* a medieval instrument of torture, consisting of a hinged case (often shaped in the form of a woman) lined with iron spikes, which was forcibly closed on the victim

iron man *n* *Austral* **1** an event at a surf carnival in which contestants compete at swimming, surfing, running, etc **2** *Austral* a competitor at such an event

ironmaster (ˈaɪənˌmɑːstə) *n* *Brit* a manufacturer of iron, esp (formerly) the owner of an ironworks

ironmonger (ˈaɪənˌmʌŋɡə) *n* *Brit* a dealer in metal utensils, hardware, locks, etc ⊳ ˈironˌmongery *n*

iron out *vb* (*tr, adverb*) **1** to smooth, using a heated iron **2** to put right or settle (a problem or difficulty) as a result of negotiations or discussions **3** *Austral informal* to knock unconscious

iron pyrites (ˈpaɪraɪts) *n* another name for **pyrite**

iron rations *pl n* emergency food supplies, esp for military personnel in action

irons (ˈaɪənz) *pl n* **1** fetters or chains (often in the phrase **in** *or* **into irons**) **2** have several irons in the fire to be involved in many projects, activities, etc

Irons (ˈaɪənz) *n* **Jeremy.** born 1948, British film and stage actor. His films include *The French Lieutenant's Woman* (1981), *The Mission* (1986), *Reversal of Fortune* (1990), and *Lolita* (1997)

Ironside (ˈaɪənˌsaɪd) *n* nickname of Edmund II of England. See **Edmund II**

ironsides (ˈaɪənˌsaɪdz) *n* **1** a person with great stamina or resistance **2** an ironclad ship **3** (*often capital*) (in the English Civil War) **a** the cavalry regiment trained and commanded by Oliver Cromwell **b** Cromwell's entire army

ironstone (ˈaɪənˌstəʊn) *n* **1** any rock consisting mainly of an iron-bearing ore **2** Also called: **ironstone china** a tough durable earthenware

ironware (ˈaɪənˌwɛə) *n* domestic articles made of iron

ironwood (ˈaɪənˌwʊd) *n* **1** any of various betulaceous trees, such as hornbeam, that have very hard wood **2** a Californian rosaceous tree, *Lyonothamnus floribundus*, with very hard wood **3** any of various other trees with hard wood, such as the mopani **4** the wood of any of these trees

ironwork (ˈaɪənˌwɜːk) *n* **1** work done in iron, esp decorative work **2** the craft or practice of working in iron

ironworks (ˈaɪənˌwɜːks) *n* (*sometimes functioning as singular*) a building in which iron is smelted, cast, or wrought

irony¹ (ˈaɪrənɪ) *n*, *pl* **-nies 1** the humorous or mildly sarcastic use of words to imply the opposite of what they normally mean **2** an instance of this, used to draw attention to some incongruity or irrationality **3** incongruity between what is expected to be and what actually is, or a situation or result showing such incongruity **4** See **dramatic irony 5** *philosophy* See **Socratic irony** [C16: from Latin *ironia*, from Greek *eirōneia*, from *eirōn* dissembler, from *eirein* to speak]

irony² (ˈaɪənɪ) *adj* of, resembling, or containing iron

Iroquoian (ˌɪrəˈkwɔɪən) *n* **1** a family of North American Indian languages including Cherokee, Mohawk, Seneca, Oneida, and Onondaga: probably related to Siouan ⊳ *adj* **2** of or relating to the Iroquois, their culture, or their languages

Iroquois (ˈɪrəˌkwɔɪ, -ˌkwɔɪz) *n*, *pl* **-quois 1** a member of any of a group of North American Indian peoples

formerly living between the Hudson River and the St Lawrence and Lake Erie **2** any of the Iroquoian languages

irradiance (ɪˈreɪdɪəns) *n* the radiant flux incident on unit area of a surface. It is measured in watts per square metre. Also called: **irradiation** See **illuminance**

irradiate (ɪˈreɪdɪˌeɪt) *vb* **1** *physics* to subject to or treat with light or other electromagnetic radiation or with beams of particles **2** (*tr*) to expose (food) to electromagnetic radiation to kill bacteria and retard deterioration **3** (*tr*) to make clear or bright intellectually or spiritually; illumine **4** a less common word for: **radiate** (sense 1) **5** (*intr*) *obsolete* to become radiant ⊳ irˈradiative *adj* ⊳ irˈradiˌator *n*

irrational (ɪˈræʃənəl) *adj* **1** inconsistent with reason or logic; illogical; absurd **2** incapable of reasoning **3** *maths* **a** not rational **b** (*as noun*): *an irrational* ⊳ irˈrationally *adv* ⊳ iˌrrtioˈnality *n*

irrational number *n* any real number that cannot be expressed as the ratio of two integers, such as π

Irrawaddy (ˌɪrəˈwɒdɪ) *n* the main river in Myanmar, rising in the north in two headstreams and flowing south through the whole length of Myanmar, to enter the Andaman Sea by nine main mouths. Length: 2100 km (1300 miles)

irreclaimable (ˌɪrɪˈkleɪməbəl) *adj* not able to be reclaimed ⊳ ˌirreˌclaimaˈbility *or* ˌirreˈclaimableness *n* ⊳ ˌirreˈclaimably *adv*

irreconcilable (ɪˈrɛkənˌsaɪləbəl, ɪˌrɛkənˈsaɪ-) *adj* **1** not able to be reconciled; uncompromisingly conflicting; incompatible ▷ *n* **2** a person or thing that is implacably hostile or uncompromisingly opposed **3** (*usually plural*) one of various principles, ideas, etc, that are incapable of being brought into agreement ⊳ irˌreconˌcilaˈbility *or* irˈreconˌcilableness *n* ⊳ irˈreconˌcilably *adv*

irrecoverable (ˌɪrɪˈkʌvərəbəl, -ˈkʌvrə-) *adj* **1** not able to be recovered or regained **2** not able to be remedied or rectified ⊳ ˌirreˈcoverableness *n* ⊳ ˌirreˈcoverably *adv*

irrecusable (ˌɪrɪˈkjuːzəbəl) *adj* not able to be rejected or challenged, as evidence, etc

irredeemable (ˌɪrɪˈdiːməbəl) *adj* **1** (of bonds, debentures, shares, etc) without a date of redemption of capital; incapable of being bought back directly or paid off **2** (of paper money) not convertible into specie **3** (of a loss) not able to be recovered; irretrievable **4** not able to be improved or rectified; irreparable ⊳ ˌirreˌdeemaˈbility *or* ˌirreˈdeemableness *n* ⊳ ˌirreˈdeemably *adv*

irredentist (ˌɪrɪˈdɛntɪst) *n* **1** a person who favours the acquisition of territory that once was part of his country or is considered to have been ▷ *adj* **2** of, relating to, or advocating this belief [C19: from Italian *irredentista*, from the phrase *Italia irredenta*, literally: Italy unredeemed, from *ir- IN-¹* + *redento* redeemed, from Latin *redemptus* bought back; see REDEEM] ⊳ irreˈdentism *n*

irreducible (ˌɪrɪˈdjuːsəbəl) *adj* **1** not able to be reduced or lessened **2** not able to be brought to a simpler or reduced form **3** *maths* **a** (of a polynomial) unable to be factorized into polynomials of lower degree, as $(x^2 + 1)$ **b** (of a radical) incapable of being reduced to a rational expression, as $\sqrt{(x + 1)}$ ⊳ ˌirreˌduciˈbility *or* ˌirreˈducibleness *n* ⊳ ˌirreˈducibly *adv*

irrefragable (ɪˈrɛfrəɡəbəl) *adj* not able to be denied or refuted; indisputable [C16: from Late Latin *irrefrāgābilis*, from Latin *IR-* + *refrāgārī* to resist, thwart] ⊳ irˌrefragaˈbility *or* irˈrefragableness *n* ⊳ irˈrefragably *adv*

irrefrangible (ˌɪrɪˈfrændʒəbəl) *adj* **1** not to be broken or transgressed; inviolable **2** *physics* incapable of being refracted ⊳ ˌirreˌfrangiˈbility *or* ˌirreˈfrangibleness *n* ⊳ ˌirreˈfrangibly *adv*

irrefutable (ɪˈrɛfjʊtəbəl, ˌɪrɪˈfjuːtəbəl) *adj* impossible to deny or disprove; incontrovertible ⊳ irˌrefutaˈbility *or* irˈrefutableness *n* ⊳ irˈrefutably *adv*

irreg. *abbreviation* irregular(ly)

irregular (ɪˈrɛɡjʊlə) *adj* **1** lacking uniformity or symmetry; uneven in shape, position, arrangement, etc **2** not occurring at expected or equal intervals: *an irregular pulse* **3** differing from the normal or accepted practice or routine **4** (of the formation, inflections, or derivations of a word) not following the usual pattern of formation in a language, as English plurals ending other than in -*s* or -*es* **5** of or relating to guerrillas or volunteers not belonging to regular forces: *irregular troops* **6** (of flowers) having any of their parts, esp petals, differing in size, shape, etc; asymmetric **7** *US* (of merchandise) not up to the manufacturer's standards or specifications; flawed; imperfect ▷ *n* **8** a soldier not in a regular army **9** (*often plural*) *US* imperfect or flawed merchandise > ir'regularly *adv* > i‚regu'larity *n*

irrelevant (ɪ'rɛləvənt) *adj* not relating or pertinent to the matter at hand; not important > ir'relevance *or* ir'relevancy *n* > ir'relevantly *adv*

irreligion (‚ɪrɪ'lɪdʒən) *n* **1** lack of religious faith **2** indifference or opposition to religion > ‚irre'ligionist *n* > ‚irre'ligious *adj* > ‚irre'ligiously *adv* > ‚irre'ligiousness *n*

irremediable (‚ɪrɪ'miːdɪəbəl) *adj* not able to be remedied; incurable or irreparable > ‚irre'mediableness *n* > ‚irre'mediably *adv*

irremissible (‚ɪrɪ'mɪsəbəl) *adj* **1** unpardonable; inexcusable **2** that must be done, as through duty or obligation > ‚irre‚missi'bility *or* ‚irre'missibleness *n* > ‚irre'missibly *adv*

irremovable (‚ɪrɪ'muːvəbəl) *adj* not able to be removed > ‚irre‚mova'bility *or* ‚irre'movableness *n* > ‚irre'movably *adv*

irreparable (ɪ'rɛpərəbəl, ɪ'rɛprəbəl) *adj* not able to be repaired or remedied; beyond repair > ir‚repara'bility *or* ir'reparableness *n* > ir'reparably *adv*

irreplaceable (‚ɪrɪ'pleɪsəbəl) *adj* not able to be replaced: *an irreplaceable antique* > ‚irre'placeably *adv*

irrepressible (‚ɪrɪ'prɛsəbəl) *adj* not capable of being repressed, controlled, or restrained > ‚irre‚pressi'bility *or* ‚irre'pressibleness *n* > ‚irre'pressibly *adv*

irreproachable (‚ɪrɪ'prəʊtʃəbəl) *adj* not deserving reproach; blameless > ‚irre‚proacha'bility *or* ‚irre'proachableness *n* > ‚irre'proachably *adv*

irresistible (‚ɪrɪ'zɪstəbəl) *adj* **1** not able to be resisted or refused; overpowering: *an irresistible impulse* **2** very fascinating or alluring: *an irresistible woman* > ‚irre‚sisti'bility *or* ‚irre'sistibleness *n* > ‚irre'sistibly *adv*

irresolute (ɪ'rɛzə‚luːt) *adj* lacking resolution; wavering; hesitating > ir'reso‚lutely *adv* > ir'reso‚luteness *or* ir‚reso'lution *n*

irrespective (‚ɪrɪ'spɛktɪv) *adj* **1** irrespective of (*preposition*) without taking account of; regardless of ▷ *adv* **2** *informal* regardless; without due consideration: *he carried on with his plan irrespective* > ‚irre'spectively *adv*

irresponsible (‚ɪrɪ'spɒnsəbəl) *adj* **1** not showing or done with due care for the consequences of one's actions or attitudes; reckless **2** not capable of bearing responsibility > ‚irre‚sponsi'bility *or* ‚irre'sponsibleness *n* > ‚irre'sponsibly *adv*

irresponsive (‚ɪrɪ'spɒnsɪv) *adj* not responsive > ‚irre'sponsively *adv* > ‚irre'sponsiveness *n*

irretrievable (‚ɪrɪ'triːvəbəl) *adj* not able to be retrieved, recovered, or repaired > ‚irre‚trieva'bility *or* ‚irre'trievableness *n* > ‚irre'trievably *adv*

irreverence (ɪ'rɛvərəns, ɪ'rɛvrəns) *n* **1** lack of due respect or veneration; disrespect **2** a disrespectful remark or act > i'reverent *or* irreverential (ɪ‚rɛvə'rɛnʃəl) *adj* > i'reverently *adv*

irreversible (‚ɪrɪ'vɜːsəbəl) *adj* **1** not able to be reversed: *the irreversible flow of time* **2** not able to be revoked or repealed; irrevocable **3** *chem, physics* capable of changing or producing a change in one direction only: *an irreversible reaction* > ‚irre‚versi'bility *or* ‚irre'versibleness *n* > ‚irre'versibly *adv*

irrevocable (ɪ'rɛvəkəbəl) *adj* not able to be revoked, changed, or undone; unalterable > ir‚revoca'bility *or* ir'revocableness *n* > ir'revocably *adv*

irrigate ('ɪrɪ‚ɡeɪt) *vb* **1** to supply (land) with water by means of artificial canals, ditches, etc, esp to promote the growth of food crops **2** *med* to bathe or wash out a bodily part, cavity, or wound **3** (*tr*) to make fertile, fresh, or vital by or as if by watering [c17: from Latin *irrigāre*, from *rigāre* to moisten, conduct water] > 'irrigable *adj* > ‚irri'gation *n* > ‚irri'gational *or* 'irri‚gative *adj* > 'irri‚gator *n*

irritable ('ɪrɪtəbəl) *adj* **1** quickly irritated; easily annoyed;

peevish **2** (of all living organisms) capable of responding to such stimuli as heat, light, and touch **3** *pathol* abnormally sensitive > ‚irrita'bility *n* > 'irritableness *n* > 'irritably *adv*

irritable bowel syndrome *n med* a chronic condition of recurring abdominal pain with constipation or diarrhoea or both

irritant ('ɪrɪtənt) *adj* **1** causing irritation; irritating ▷ *n* **2** something irritant > 'irritancy *n*

irritate ('ɪrɪ‚teɪt) *vb* **1** to annoy or anger (someone) **2** (*tr*) *biology* to stimulate (an organism or part) to respond in a characteristic manner **3** (*tr*) *pathol* to cause (a bodily organ or part) to become excessively stimulated, resulting in inflammation, tenderness, etc [c16: from Latin *irrītāre* to provoke, exasperate] > 'irri‚tator *n*

irritation (‚ɪrɪ'teɪʃən) *n* **1** something that irritates **2** the act of irritating or the condition of being irritated > 'irri‚tative *adj*

irrupt (ɪ'rʌpt) *vb* (*intr*) **1** to enter forcibly or suddenly **2** (of a plant or animal population) to enter a region suddenly and in very large numbers **3** (of a population) to increase suddenly and greatly [c19: from Latin *irrumpere* to rush into, invade, from *rumpere* to break, burst] > ir'ruption *n* > i'rruptive *adj*

IRS *abbreviation* **1** (in the US) Internal Revenue Service **2** insulin resistance syndrome: a condition associated with diabetes mellitus in which higher than normal levels of insulin are present in the blood to compensate for the failure of normal insulin levels to perform their function

Irtysh *or* **Irtish** (ɪə'tɪʃ) *n* a river in central Asia, rising in China in the Altai Mountains and flowing west through Kazakhstan, then northwest into Russia to join the Ob River as its chief tributary. Length: 4444 km (2760 miles)

Irvine[1] ('ɜːvɪn) *n* a town on the W coast of Scotland, the administrative centre of North Ayrshire: designated a new town in 1966. Pop: 33 090 (2001)

Irvine[2] ('ɜːvɪn) *n* **Alexander Andrew Mackay,** Baron, known as *Derry*. born 1940, British lawyer and Labour politician; Lord Chancellor (1997–2003)

Irving ('ɜːvɪŋ) *n* **1** Sir **Henry.** real name *John Henry Brodribb*. 1838–1905, English actor and manager of the Lyceum Theatre in London (1878–1902) **2 Washington.** 1783–1859, US essayist and short-story writer, noted for *The Sketch Book of Geoffrey Crayon* (1820), which contains the stories *Rip Van Winkle* and *The Legend of Sleepy Hollow*

Irwin ('ɜːwɪn) *n* **Steve,** full name *Stephen Robert Irwin*, known as 'The Crocodile Hunter'. 1962–2006, Australian zoologist, environmentalist and maker of television wildlife documentaries; died following wounding by a stingray

is (ɪz) *vb* (used with *he, she, it,* and with singular nouns) a form of the present tense (indicative mood) of **be**[1] [Old English; compare Old Norse *es*, German *ist*, Latin *est*, Greek *esti*]

Is. *abbreviation* **1** *Bible* Isaiah. Also: Isa **2** Island(s) *or* Isle(s)

is- *combining form* variant of **iso-**: *isentropic*

ISA ('aɪsə) *n acronym for* individual savings account: a tax-free savings scheme introduced in Britain in 1999

Isaac ('aɪzək) *n* an Old Testament patriarch, the son of Abraham and Sarah and father of Jacob and Esau (Genesis 17; 21–27)

Isabella (‚ɪzə'bɛlə) *n* original name *Elizabeth Farnese*. 1692–1766, second wife (1714–46) of Philip V of Spain and mother of Charles III of Spain

Isabella I *n* known as *Isabella the Catholic*. 1451–1504, queen of Castile (1474–1504) and, with her husband, Ferdinand V, joint ruler of Castile and Aragon (1479–1504)

Isabella II *n* 1830–1904, queen of Spain (1833–68), whose accession precipitated the first Carlist war (1833–39). She was deposed in a revolution

Isabella of France *n* 1292–1358, wife (1308–27) of Edward II of England, whom, aided by her lover, Roger de Mortimer, she deposed; mother of Edward III

isagogics (‚aɪsə'ɡɒdʒɪks) *n* (*usually functioning as singular*) introductory studies, esp in the history of the Bible

Isaiah (aɪ'zaɪə) *n Old Testament* **1** the first of the major Hebrew prophets, who lived in the 8th century BC **2** the book of his and others' prophecies

isallobar (aɪˈsæləˌbaː) n meteorol a line on a map running through places experiencing equal pressure changes

Isar (ˈiːzaː) n a river in central Europe, rising in W Austria and flowing generally northeast through S Germany into the Danube. Length: over 260 km (160 miles)

isatin (ˈaɪsətɪn) or **isatine** (ˈaɪsəˌtiːn) n a yellowish-red crystalline compound soluble in hot water, used for the preparation of vat dyes. Formula: $C_8H_5NO_2$ [c19: from Latin isatis woad + -IN] > ˌisaˈtinic adj

Isauria (aɪˈsɔːrɪə) n an ancient district of S central Asia Minor, chiefly on the N slopes of the W Taurus Mountains > Iˈsaurian adj, n

ISBN abbreviation International Standard Book Number

Iscariot (ɪˈskærɪət) n See **Judas** (sense 1)

ischaemia or **ischemia** (ɪˈskiːmɪə) n pathol an inadequate supply of blood to an organ or part, as from an obstructed blood flow [c19: from Greek iskhein to restrict, + -EMIA] > ischaemic or ischemic (ɪˈskɛmɪk) adj

Ischia (ˈiːskjaː, ˈɪskɪə) n a volcanic island in the Tyrrhenian Sea, at the N end of the Bay of Naples. Area: 47 sq km (18 sq miles)

ischium (ˈɪskɪəm) n, pl -chia (-kɪə) one of the three sections of the hipbone, situated below the ilium [c17: from Latin: hip joint, from Greek iskhion] > ˈischial adj

iSCSI abbreviation internet Small Computer System Interface: an internet Protocol-based storage networking standard used for linking data storage facilities

ISDN abbreviation integrated services digital network: a rapid telecommunications network, combining data transfer and telephony

-ise suffix forming verbs a variant of **-ize**
● USAGE See at **-ize**

isentropic (ˌaɪsɛnˈtrɒpɪk) adj having or taking place at constant entropy

Isère (French izɛr) n 1 a department of SE France, in Rhône-Alpes region. Capital: Grenoble. Pop: 1 128 755 (2003 est). Area: 7904 sq km (3083 sq miles) 2 a river in SE France, rising in the Graian Alps and flowing west and southwest to join the River Rhône near Valence. Length: 290 km (180 miles)

Iseult, Yseult (ɪˈsuːlt) or **Isolde** (ɪˈzəʊldə) n (in Arthurian legend) 1 an Irish princess wed to Mark, king of Cornwall, but in love with his knight Tristan 2 (in another account) the daughter of the king of Brittany, married to Tristan

Isfahan (ˌɪsfəˈhaːn) or **Eşfahān** n a city in central Iran: the second largest city in the country; capital of Persia in the 11th century and from 1598 to 1722. Pop: 1 547 000 (2005 est)

-ish suffix forming adjectives 1 of or belonging to a nationality or group: Scottish 2 often derogatory having the manner or qualities of; resembling: slavish; prudish; boyish 3 somewhat; approximately: yellowish; sevenish 4 concerned or preoccupied with: bookish [Old English -isc; related to German -isch, Greek -iskos]

Isherwood (ˈɪʃəˌwʊd) n **Christopher**, full name Christopher William Bradshaw-Isherwood. 1904–86, US novelist and dramatist, born in England. His works include the novel Goodbye to Berlin (1939) and three verse plays written in collaboration with W.H. Auden

Ishiguro (ˌɪʃɪˈɡʊrəʊ) n **Kazuo** (kætˈzuːəʊ). born 1954, British novelist, born in Japan. His novels include An Artist of the Floating World (1986), the Booker-prizewinning The Remains of the Day (1989), and Never Let Me Go (2005)

Ishmael (ˈɪʃmeɪəl) n 1 the son of Abraham and Hagar, Sarah's handmaid: the ancestor of 12 Arabian tribes (Genesis 21:8–21; 25:12–18) 2 a bandit chieftain, who defied the Babylonian conquerors of Judah and assassinated the governor appointed by Nebuchadnezzar (II Kings 25:25; Jeremiah 40:13–41:18) 3 rare an outcast

Ishtar (ˈɪʃtaː) n the principal goddess of the Babylonians and Assyrians; divinity of love, fertility, and war

Isidore of Seville (ˈɪzɪdɔː) n **Saint**, Latin name Isidorus Hispalensis. ?560–636 AD, Spanish archbishop and scholar, noted for his Etymologies, an encyclopedia. Feast day: April 4

isinglass (ˈaɪzɪŋˌglaːs) n a gelatine made from the air bladders of freshwater fish, used as a clarifying agent and adhesive [c16: from Middle Dutch huysenblase, literally: sturgeon bladder; influenced by English GLASS]

Isis¹ (ˈaɪsɪs) n the local name for the River Thames at Oxford

Isis² (ˈaɪsɪs) n an ancient Egyptian fertility goddess, depicted as a woman with a cow's horns, between which was the disc of the sun; wife and sister of Osiris

Iskander Bey (ɪsˈkændə beɪ) n the Turkish name for **Scanderbeg**

Iskenderun (ɪsˈkɛndəˌruːn) n a port in S Turkey, on the Gulf of Iskenderun. Pop: 161 000 (2005 est). Former name: Alexandretta

Isl. abbreviation 1 Island 2 Isle

Islam (ˈɪzlaːm) n 1 the religion of Muslims, having the Koran as its sacred scripture and teaching that there is only one God and that Mohammed is his prophet; Mohammedanism 2 a Muslims collectively and their civilization b the countries where the Muslim religion is predominant [c19: from Arabic: surrender (to God), from aslama to surrender] > Isˈlamic adj

Islamabad (ɪzˈlaːməˌbaːd) n the capital of Pakistan, in the north on the Potwar Plateau: site chosen in 1959; surrounded by the Capital Territory of Islamabad for 909 sq km (351 sq miles). Pop: 770 000 (2005 est)

Islamism (ˈɪzləmɪzm) n support of or advocacy for Islamic fundamentalism

Islamist (ˈɪzləmɪst) adj 1 supporting or advocating Islamic fundamentalism ▷ n 2 a supporter or advocate of Islamic fundamentalism

Islamize or **Islamise** (ˈɪzləˌmaɪz) vb (tr) to convert to or bring under the influence of Islam > ˌIslamiˈzation or ˌIslamiˈsation n

Islamophobia (ˌɪzlɑːməˈfəʊbɪə) n hatred or fear of Muslims or of their politics or culture > ˌIslamoˈphobic adj

island (ˈaɪlənd) n 1 a mass of land that is surrounded by water and is smaller than a continent 2 anatomy a part, structure, or group of cells distinct in constitution from its immediate surroundings. Related adjective: **insular** ▷ vb (tr) rare 3 to cause to become an island 4 to intersperse with islands 5 to place on an island; insulate; isolate [Old English īgland, from īg island + LAND; s inserted through influence of ISLE] > ˈisland-ˌlike adj

islander (ˈaɪləndə) n 1 a native or inhabitant of an island 2 (capital) NZ a native or inhabitant of the Pacific Islands

Islands (ˈaɪləndz) pl n the NZ the islands of the South Pacific

Islands of the Blessed pl n Greek myth lands where the souls of heroes and good men were taken after death. Also called: Hesperides

island universe n a former name for **galaxy**

Islay (ˈaɪlə, ˈaɪleɪ) n an island off the W coast of Scotland: the southernmost of the Inner Hebrides; separated from the island of Jura by the Sound of Islay. Pop: 3457 (2001). Area: 606 sq km (234 sq miles)

isle (aɪl) n an island, esp a small one: used in literature and (when cap) in place names [c13: from Old French isle, from Latin insula island]

Isle of Dogs n See (Isle of) **Dogs**

Isle of Man n See (Isle of) **Man**

Isle of Pines n the former name of the (Isle of) **Youth**

Isle of Sheppey n See (Isle of) **Sheppey**

Isle of Wight n See (Isle of) **Wight**

Isle of Youth n See (Isle of) **Youth**

Isle Royale (ˈrɔɪəl) n an island in the northeast US, in NW Lake Superior: forms, with over 100 surrounding islands, **Isle Royale National Park**. Area: 541 sq km (209 sq miles)

islet (ˈaɪlɪt) n a small island [c16: from Old French islette; see ISLE]

islets of Langerhans or **islands of Langerhans** (ˈlæŋəˌhæns) pl n small groups of endocrine cells in the pancreas that secrete the hormones insulin and glucagon [c19: named after Paul Langerhans (1847–88), German physician]

Islington ('ɪzlɪŋtən) *n* a borough of N Greater London. Pop: 180 100 (2003 est). Area: 16 sq km (6 sq miles)

ism ('ɪzəm) *n informal, often derogatory* an unspecified doctrine, system, or practice

-ism *suffix forming nouns* **1** indicating an action, process, or result: *criticism; terrorism* **2** indicating a state or condition: *paganism* **3** indicating a doctrine, system, or body of principles and practices: *Leninism; spiritualism* **4** indicating behaviour or a characteristic quality: *heroism* **5** indicating a characteristic usage, esp of a language: *colloquialism; Scotticism* **6** indicating prejudice on the basis specified: *sexism; ageism* [from Old French *-isme*, from Latin *-ismus*, from Greek *-ismos*]

Ismaili or **Isma'ili** (,ɪzmɑː'iːlɪ) *n Islam* **1** a Shiah sect whose adherents believe that Ismail, son of the sixth imam, was the rightful seventh imam **2** Also called: **Ismailian** (,ɪzmɑː'iːliːən) *pl* -lis a member of this sect

Ismailia (,ɪzmaɪ'lɪə) *n* a city in NE Egypt, on the Suez Canal: founded in 1863 by the former Suez Canal Company; devastated by Israeli troops in the October War (1973). Pop: 299 000 (2005 est)

Ismoil Somoni ('ɪsmɔiːl sɒ'mɒniː) *n* a mountain in SE Tajikistan in the Pamirs: the highest mountain in the former Soviet Union. Height: 7495 m (24 590 ft). Former names: Stalin Peak, Communism Peak

Ismail Pasha (,ɪzmɑː'iːl 'paːʃə) *n* 1830–95, viceroy (1863–66) and khedive (1867–79) of Egypt, who brought his country close to bankruptcy. He was forced to submit to Anglo-French financial control (1876) and to abdicate (1879)

isn't ('ɪzªnt) *vb contraction of* is not

ISO *n* International Organization for Standardization [Greek *isos* equal; often wrongly thought to be an abbreviation for *International Standards Organization*]

iso- *or before a vowel* **is-** *combining form* **1** equal or identical: *isomagnetic* **2** indicating that a chemical compound is an isomer of a specified compound: *isobutane; isocyanic acid* [from Greek *isos* equal]

isobar ('aɪsəʊ,bɑː) *n* **1** a line on a map connecting places of equal atmospheric pressure, usually reduced to sea level for purposes of comparison, at a given time or period **2** *physics* any of two or more atoms that have the same mass number but different atomic numbers. See **isotope** [C19: from Greek *isobarēs* of equal weight, from ISO- + *baros* weight] > **isobar,ism** *n* > **,iso'baric** *adj*

isocheim or **isochime** ('aɪsəʊ,kaɪm) *n* a line on a map connecting places with the same mean winter temperature [C19: from ISO- + Greek *kheima* winter weather] > ,iso'cheimal or ,iso'cheimenal or ,iso'chimal *adj*

isochronal (aɪ'sɒkrənªl) or **isochronous** *adj* **1** having the same duration; equal in time **2** occurring at equal time intervals; having a uniform period of vibration or oscillation [C17: from New Latin *isochronus*, from Greek *isokhronos*, from ISO- + *khronos* time] > i'sochronally or i'sochronously *adv* > i'sochro,nism *n*

isoclinal (,aɪsəʊ'klaɪnªl) or **isoclinic** (,aɪsəʊ'klɪnɪk) *adj* **1** sloping in the same direction and at the same angle **2** *geology* (of folds) having limbs that are parallel to each other ▷ *n* **3** Also called: **isocline, isoclinal line** an imaginary line connecting points on the earth's surface having equal angles of dip

isocline ('aɪsəʊ,klaɪn) *n* **1** a series of rock strata with isoclinal folds **2** another name for **isoclinal** (sense 3)

Isocrates (aɪ'sɒkrə,tiːz) *n* 436–338 BC, Athenian rhetorician and teacher

isodynamic (,aɪsəʊdaɪ'næmɪk) *adj physics* **1** having equal force or strength **2** of or relating to an imaginary line on the earth's surface connecting points of equal horizontal magnetic intensity

isoflavone (,aɪsəʊ'fleɪvəʊn) *n* one of a class of phytoestrogens, found in soya beans and marketed as a health supplement

isogeotherm (,aɪsəʊ'dʒiː,əʊ,θɜːm) *n* an imaginary line below the surface of the earth connecting points of equal temperature > ,iso,geo'thermal or ,iso,geo'thermic *adj*

isogloss ('aɪsəʊ,glɒs) *n* a line drawn on a map around the area in which a linguistic feature is to be found, such as a particular pronunciation of a given word

> ,iso'glossal *or* ,iso'glottic *adj*

isogonic (,aɪsəʊ'gɒnɪk) or **isogonal** (aɪ'sɒgənªl) *adj* **1** *maths* having, making, or involving equal angles ▷ *n* **2** Also called: **isogonic line, isogonal line, isogone** *physics* an imaginary line connecting points on the earth's surface having equal magnetic declination

isohel ('aɪsəʊ,hɛl) *n* a line on a map connecting places with an equal period of sunshine [C20: from ISO- + Greek *hēlios* sun]

isohyet (,aɪsəʊ'haɪɪt) *n* a line on a map connecting places having equal rainfall [C19: from ISO- + *-hyet*, from Greek *huetos* rain]

isolate *vb* ('aɪsə,leɪt) (*tr*) **1** to place apart; cause to be alone **2** *med* to quarantine (a person or animal) having or suspected of having a contagious disease **3** to obtain (a compound) in an uncombined form **4** to obtain pure cultures of (bacteria, esp those causing a particular disease) **5** *electronics* to prevent interaction between (circuits, components, etc); insulate ▷ *n* ('aɪsəlɪt) **6** an isolated person or group [C19: back formation from *isolated*, via Italian from Latin *insulātus*, literally: made into an island; see INSULATE] > 'isolable *adj* > ,isola'bility *n* > 'iso,lator *n* > ,iso'lation *n*

ISO Latin-1 or **ISO-8859-1** *n computing* a standard set of characters for Western European languages put together by the International Organization for Standardization

isolationism (,aɪsə'leɪʃə,nɪzəm) *n* **1** a policy of nonparticipation in or withdrawal from international affairs **2** an attitude favouring such a policy > ,iso'lationist *n, adj*

Isolde (i'zɔldə) *n* the German name of **Iseult**

isomer ('aɪsəmə) *n* **1** *chem* a compound that exhibits isomerism with one or more other compounds **2** *physics* a nuclide that exhibits isomerism with one or more other nuclides > **isomeric** (,aɪsə'mɛrɪk) *adj*

isomerism (aɪ'sɒmə,rɪzəm) *n* **1** the existence of two or more compounds having the same molecular formula but a different arrangement of atoms within the molecule **2** the existence of two or more nuclides having the same atomic numbers and mass numbers but different energy states

isomerous (aɪ'sɒmərəs) *adj* (of flowers) having floral whorls with the same number of parts

isometric (,aɪsəʊ'mɛtrɪk) *adj Also:* **isometrical 1** having equal dimensions or measurements **2** *physiol* of or relating to muscular contraction that does not produce shortening of the muscle **3** (of a crystal or system of crystallization) having three mutually perpendicular equal axes **4** (of a method of projecting a drawing in three dimensions) having the three axes equally inclined and all lines drawn to scale ▷ *n* **5** Also called: **isometric drawing** a drawing made in this way [C19: from Greek *isometria* (see ISO- + -METRY) + -IC] > ,iso'metrically *adv*

isometrics (,aɪsəʊ'mɛtrɪks) *n* (*functioning as singular*) physical exercise involving isometric contraction of muscles

isomorphism (,aɪsəʊ'mɔːfɪzəm) *n* **1** *biology* similarity of form, as in different generations of the same life cycle **2** *chem* the existence of two or more substances of different composition in a similar crystalline form **3** *maths* a one-to-one correspondence between the elements of two or more sets, such as those of Arabic and Roman numerals, and between the sums or products of the elements of one of these sets and those of the equivalent elements of the other set or sets

isophote ('aɪsə,fəʊt) *n astronomy* a line on a diagram or image of a galaxy, nebula, or other celestial object joining points of equal surface brightness

isopleth ('aɪsəʊ,plɛθ) *n* a line on a map connecting places registering the same amount or ratio of some geographical or meteorological phenomenon or phenomena. Also called: **isogram, isoline** [C20: from Greek *isoplēthēs* equal in number, from ISO- + *plēthos* multitude, great number]

isopod ('aɪsəʊ,pɒd) *n* **1** any crustacean of the order *Isopoda*, including woodlice and pill bugs, in which the body is flattened dorsoventrally ▷ *adj* **2** of, relating to, or belonging to the *Isopoda* > isopodan (aɪ'sɒpədən) *or* i'sopodous *adj*

isoprene ('aɪsəʊ,priːn) *n* a colourless volatile liquid with a penetrating odour: used in making synthetic rubbers. Formula: $CH_2:CHC(CH_3):CH_2$ [C20: from ISO- + PR(OPYL) + -ENE]

ISO rating *n photog* a classification of film speed in which a doubling of the ISO number represents a doubling in sensitivity; for example, ISO 400 film requires half the exposure of ISO 200 under the same conditions. The system uses identical numbers to the obsolete ASA rating [C20: from International Standards Organization]

isosceles (aɪ'sɒsɪ,liːz) *adj* (of a triangle) having two sides of equal length [C16: from Late Latin, from Greek *isoskelēs*, from ISO- + *skelos* leg]

isoseismal (,aɪsəʊ'saɪzməl) *adj* 1 of or relating to equal intensity of earthquake shock ▷ *n* 2 a line on a map connecting points at which earthquake shocks are of equal intensity ▷ Also called: isoseismic

isostasy (aɪ'sɒstəsɪ) *n* the state of balance, or equilibrium, which sections of the earth's lithosphere (whether continental or oceanic) are thought ultimately to achieve when the vertical forces upon them remain unchanged. The lithosphere floats upon the semifluid asthenosphere below. If a section of lithosphere is loaded, as by ice, it will slowly subside to a new equilibrium position; if a section of lithosphere is reduced in mass, as by erosion, it will slowly rise to a new equilibrium position [C19: ISO- + -*stasy*, from Greek *stasis* a standing] > isostatic (,aɪsəʊ'stætɪk) *adj*

isothere ('aɪsəʊ,θɪə) *n* a line on a map linking places with the same mean summer temperature. See **isocheim** [C19: from ISO- + Greek *theros* summer] > isotheral (aɪ'sɒθərəl) *adj*

isotherm ('aɪsəʊ,θɜːm) *n* 1 a line on a map linking places of equal temperature 2 *physics* a curve on a graph that connects points of equal temperature ▷ Also called: isothermal, isothermal line

isothermal (,aɪsəʊ'θɜːməl) *adj* 1 (of a process or change) taking place at constant temperature 2 of or relating to an isotherm ▷ *n* 3 another word for **isotherm** > ,iso'thermally *adv*

isotonic (,aɪsəʊ'tɒnɪk) *adj* 1 *physiol* (of two or more muscles) having equal tension 2 (of a drink) designed to replace the fluid and salts lost from the body during strenuous exercise 3 Also called: isosmotic (of two solutions) having the same osmotic pressure, commonly having physiological osmotic pressure. See **hypertonic**, **hypotonic** > isotonicity (,aɪsəʊtəʊ'nɪsɪtɪ) *n*

isotope ('aɪsə,təʊp) *n* one of two or more atoms with the same atomic number that contain different numbers of neutrons [C20: from ISO- + Greek *topos* place] > isotopic (,aɪsə'tɒpɪk) *adj* > ,iso'topically *adv* > isotopy (aɪ'sɒtəpɪ) *n*

isotropic (,aɪsəʊ'trɒpɪk) *or* **isotropous** (aɪ'sɒtrəpəs) *adj* 1 having uniform physical properties in all directions 2 *biology* not having predetermined axes: *isotropic eggs* > ,iso'tropically *adv* > i'sotropy *n*

ISP *abbreviation* internet service provider, a business providing its customers with connection to the internet and other related services

I-spy *n* a game in which one player specifies the initial letter of the name of an object that he can see, which the other players then try to guess

Israel ('ɪzreɪəl, -rɪəl) *n* 1 a republic in SW Asia, on the Mediterranean Sea: established in 1948, in the former British mandate of Palestine, as a primarily Jewish state; 8 disputes with Arab neighbours (who did not recognize the state of Israel), erupted into full-scale wars in 1948, 1956, 1967 (the Six Day War), and 1973 (the Yom Kippur War). In 1993 Israel agreed to grant autonomous status to the Gaza Strip and the West Bank, according to the terms of a peace agreement with the PLO. Official languages: Hebrew and Arabic. Religion: Jewish majority, Muslim and Christian minorities. Currency: shekel. Capital: Jerusalem (international recognition withheld as East Jerusalem was annexed (1967) by Israel: UN recognized capital: Tel Aviv). Pop: 6 560 000 (2004 est). Area (including Golan Heights and

East Jerusalem): 21 946 sq km (8473 sq miles) 2 a the ancient kingdom of the 12 Hebrew tribes at the SE end of the Mediterranean b the kingdom in the N part of this region formed by the ten northern tribes of Israel in the 10th century BC and destroyed by the Assyrians in 721 BC 3 *informal* the Jewish community throughout the world

Israeli (ɪz'reɪlɪ) *n, pl* -lis *or* -li 1 a citizen or inhabitant of the state of Israel ▷ *adj* 2 of, relating to, or characteristic of the state of Israel or its inhabitants

Israelite ('ɪzrɪə,laɪt, -rə-) *n* 1 *Bible* a member of the ethnic group claiming descent from Jacob; a Hebrew 2 a member of any of various Christian sects who regard themselves as God's chosen people 3 an archaic and sometimes offensive word for a *Jew*

ISS *abbreviation* International Space Station

Issachar ('ɪsə,kɑː) *n Old Testament* 1 the fifth son of Jacob by his wife Leah (Genesis 30:17–18) 2 the tribe descended from this patriarch 3 the territory of this tribe

Isserlis ('ɪsəlɪs) *n* **Steven (John)**. born 1958, British cellist

Issigonis (,ɪsɪ'gəʊnɪs) *n* **Sir Alec (Arnold Constantine)**. 1906–88, British car designer born in Smyrna. He is noted for his designs for the Morris Minor (1948) and the Mini (1959)

ISSN *abbreviation* International Standard Serial Number

issuance ('ɪʃʊəns) *n* the act of issuing

issue ('ɪʃjuː) *n* 1 the act of sending or giving out something; supply; delivery 2 something issued; an edition of stamps, a magazine, etc 3 the number of identical items, such as banknotes or shares in a company, that become available at a particular time 4 the act of emerging; outflow; discharge 5 something flowing out, such as a river 6 a place of outflow; outlet 7 the descendants of a person; offspring; progeny 8 a topic of interest or discussion 9 an important subject requiring a decision 10 an outcome or consequence; result 11 *pathol* a a suppurating sore b discharge from a wound 12 *law* the matter remaining in dispute between the parties to an action after the pleadings 13 the yield from or profits arising out of land or other property 14 *military* the allocation of items of government stores, such as food, clothing, and ammunition 15 *library science* a the system for recording current loans b the number of books loaned in a specified period 16 *obsolete* an act, deed, or proceeding 17 at issue a under discussion b in disagreement 18 force the issue to compel decision on some matter 19 join issue a to join in controversy b to submit an issue for adjudication 20 take issue to disagree ▷ *vb* -sues, -suing, -sued 21 to come forth or emerge or cause to come forth or emerge 22 to publish or deliver (a newspaper, magazine, etc) 23 (*tr*) to make known or announce 24 (*intr*) to originate or proceed 25 (*intr*) to be a consequence; result 26 (*intr;* foll by *in*) to end or terminate 27 (*tr*) a to give out or allocate (equipment, a certificate, etc) officially to someone b (foll by *with*) to supply officially (with) [C13: from Old French *eissue* way out, from *eissir* to go out, from Latin *exīre*, from EX-¹ + *īre* to go] > 'issueless *adj* > 'issuer *n*

issue price *n stock exchange* the price at which a new issue of shares is offered to the public

Issus ('ɪsəs) *n* an ancient town in S Asia Minor, in Cilicia north of present-day Iskenderun: scene of a battle (333 BC) in which Alexander the Great defeated the Persians

Issyk-Kul (Russian is'sik'kulj) *n* a lake in NE Kyrgyzstan in the Tian Shan mountains, at an altitude of 1609 m (5280 ft): one of the largest mountain lakes in the world. Area: 6200 sq km (2390 sq miles)

-ist *suffix* 1 (*forming nouns*) a person who performs a certain action or is concerned with something specified: *motorist; soloist* 2 (*forming nouns*) a person who practises in a specific field: *physicist; typist* 3 (*forming nouns and adjectives*) a person who advocates a particular doctrine, system, etc, or relating to such a person or the doctrine advocated: *socialist* 4 (*forming nouns and adjectives*) a person characterized by a specified trait, tendency, etc, or relating to such a person or trait: *purist* 5 (*forming nouns and adjectives*) a person who is prejudiced on the basis specified: *sexist; ageist* [via Old French from Latin -*ista*, -*istēs*, from Greek -*istēs*]

Istanbul (,ɪstæn'buːl) *n* a port in NW Turkey, on the

western (European) shore of the Bosporus: the largest city in Turkey; founded in about 660 BC by Greeks; refounded by Constantine the Great in 330 AD as the capital of the Eastern Roman Empire; taken by the Turks in 1453 and remained capital of the Ottoman Empire until 1922; industrial centre for shipbuilding, textiles, etc Pop: 9 760 000 (2005 est). Ancient name: Byzantium. Former name (330–1926): Constantinople

isthmian ('ısθmıən) *adj* relating to or situated in an isthmus

isthmus ('ısməs) *n, pl* -muses *or* -mi (-maı) **1** a narrow strip of land connecting two relatively large land areas **2** *anatomy* **a** a narrow band of tissue connecting two larger parts of a structure **b** a narrow passage connecting two cavities [C16: from Latin, from Greek *isthmos*] > 'isthmoid *adj*

-istic *suffix forming adjectives* equivalent to a combination of **-ist** and **-ic** but in some words having a less specific or literal application and sometimes a mildly pejorative force, as compared with corresponding adjectives ending in **-ist**: *communistic; impressionistic* [from Latin *-isticus*, from Greek *istikos*]

istle ('ıstlı) *or* **ixtle** *n* a fibre obtained from various tropical American agave and yucca trees used in making carpets, cord, etc [C19: from Mexican Spanish *ixtle*, from Nahuatl *ichtli*]

Istria ('ıstrıə) *n* a peninsula in the N Adriatic Sea: passed from Italy to Yugoslavia (except for Trieste) in 1947 and to Croatia in 1991 > 'Istrian *adj, n*

it (ıt) *pron* (*subjective or objective*) **1** refers to a nonhuman, animal, plant, or inanimate thing, or sometimes to a small baby: *it looks dangerous; give it a bone* **2** refers to an unspecified or implied antecedent or to a previous or understood clause, phrase, etc: *it is impossible; I knew it* **3** used to represent human life or experience either in totality or in respect of the present situation: *how's it going?; I've had it; to brazen it out* **4** used as a formal subject (or object), referring to a following clause, phrase, or word: *it helps to know the truth; I consider it dangerous to go on* **5** used in the nominative as the formal grammatical subject of impersonal verbs. When *it* functions absolutely in such sentences, not referring to any previous or following clause or phrase, the context is nearly always a description of the environment or of some physical sensation: *it is raining; it hurts* **6** (used as complement with *be*) *informal* the crucial or ultimate point: *the steering failed and I thought that was it* ⊳ *n* **7** (in children's games) the player whose turn it is to try to touch another **8** *informal* **a** sexual intercourse **b** sex appeal **9** *informal* a desirable quality or ability: *he's really got it* [Old English *hit*]

IT *abbreviation* information technology

It. *abbreviation* **1** Italian **2** Italy

i.t.a. *or* **ITA** *abbreviation* initial teaching alphabet, a partly phonetic alphabet used to teach reading

ital. *abbreviation* italic

Ital. *abbreviation* **1** Italian **2** Italy

Italia (i'ta:lja) *n* the Italian name for **Italy**

Italian (ı'tæljən) *n* **1** the official language of Italy and one of the official languages of Switzerland: the native language of approximately 60 million people. It belongs to the Romance group of the Indo-European family, and there is a considerable diversity of dialects **2** a native, citizen, or inhabitant of Italy, or a descendant of one ⊳ *adj* **3** relating to, denoting, or characteristic of Italy, its inhabitants, or their language

Italianate (ı'tæljənıt, -,neıt) *or* **Italianesque** (ı,tæljə'nɛsk) *adj* Italian in style or character

Italian East Africa *n* a former Italian territory in E Africa, formed in 1936 from the possessions of Eritrea, Italian Somaliland, and Ethiopia: taken by British forces in 1941

Italian Somaliland *n* a former Italian colony in E Africa, united with British Somaliland in 1960 to form the independent republic of Somalia

italic (ı'tælık) *adj* **1** Also called: **Italian** of, relating to, or denoting a style of handwriting with the letters slanting to the right ⊳ *n* **2** a style of printing type modelled on this, chiefly used to indicate emphasis, a foreign word, etc. See **roman**³ **3** (*often plural*) italic type or print [C16 (after an edition of Virgil (1501) printed in Venice and dedicated to Italy): from Latin *Italicus* of Italy, from Greek *Italikos*]

Italic (ı'tælık) *n* **1** a branch of the Indo-European family of languages that includes many of the ancient languages of Italy, such as Venetic and the Osco-Umbrian group, Latin, which displaced them, and the Romance languages ⊳ *adj* **2** denoting, relating to, or belonging to this group of languages, esp the extinct ones

italicize *or* **italicise** (ı'tælı,saız) *vb* **1** to print (textual matter) in italic type **2** (*tr*) to underline (letters, words, etc) with a single line to indicate italics > i,talici'zation *or* i,talici'sation *n*

Italy ('ıtəlı) *n* a republic in S Europe, occupying a peninsula in the Mediterranean between the Tyrrhenian and the Adriatic Seas, with the islands of Sardinia and Sicily to the west: first united under the Romans but became fragmented into numerous political units in the Middle Ages; united kingdom proclaimed in 1861; under the dictatorship of Mussolini (1922–43); became a republic in 1946; a member of the European Union. It is generally mountainous, with the Alps in the north and the Apennines running the length of the peninsula. Official language: Italian. Religion: Roman Catholic majority. Currency: euro. Capital: Rome. Pop: 57 346 000 (2004 est) Area: 301 247 sq km (116 312 sq miles). Italian name: **Italia**

ITC (in Britain) *abbreviation* Independent Television Commission

itch (ıtʃ) *n* **1** an irritation or tickling sensation of the skin causing a desire to scratch **2** a restless desire **3** any skin disorder, such as scabies, characterized by intense itching ⊳ *vb* **4** (*intr*) to feel or produce an irritating or tickling sensation **5** (*intr*) to have a restless desire (to do something) **6** *not standard* to scratch (the skin) **7** *itching palm* a grasping nature; avarice **8** *have itchy feet* to be restless; have a desire to travel [Old English *gicean* to itch, of Germanic origin] > 'itchy *adj* > 'itchiness *n*

-ite¹ *suffix forming nouns* **1** a native or inhabitant of: *Israelite* **2** a follower or advocate of; a member or supporter of a group: *Luddite; labourite* **3** (in biology) indicating a division of a body or organ: *somite* **4** indicating a mineral or rock: *nephrite; peridotite* **5** indicating a commercial product: *vulcanite* [via Latin *-ita* from Greek *-itēs* or directly from Greek]

-ite² *suffix forming nouns* indicating a salt or ester of an acid having a name ending in *-ous*: *a nitrite is a salt of nitrous acid* [from French, arbitrary alteration of *-ATE*¹]

item *n* **1** a thing or unit, esp included in a list or collection **2** *book-keeping* an entry in an account **3** a piece of information, detail, or note: *a news item* **4** *informal* two people having a romantic or sexual relationship ⊳ *vb* ('aıtəm) **5** (*tr*) an archaic word for **itemize** ⊳ *adv* ('aıtɛm) **6** likewise; also [C14 (adv): from Latin: in like manner]

itemize *or* **itemise** ('aıtə,maız) *vb* (*tr*) to put on a list or make a list of > ,itemi'zation *or* ,itemi'sation *n*

Iténez (i'teneθ) *n* the Spanish name for the **Guaporé**

iterate ('ıtə,reıt) *vb* (*tr*) to say or do again; repeat [C16: from Latin *iterāre*, from *iterum* again] > 'iterant *adj* > ,iter'ation *or* 'iterance *n* > 'iterative *adj*

Ithaca ('ıθəkə) *n* a Greek island in the Ionian Sea, the smallest of the Ionian Islands: regarded as the home of Homer's Odysseus. Area: 93 sq km (36 sq miles) > 'Ithacan *adj, n*

Ithunn ('i:ðʊn) *n* a variant of **Idun**

itinerancy (ı'tınərənsı, aı-) *or* **itineracy** *n* **1** the act of itinerating **2** *chiefly Methodist Church* the system of appointing a minister to a circuit of churches or chapels **3** itinerants collectively

itinerant (ı'tınərənt, aı-) *adj* **1** itinerating **2** working for a short time in various places, esp as a casual labourer ⊳ *n* **3** an itinerant worker or other person [C16: from Late Latin *itinerārī* to travel, from *iter* a journey] > i'tinerantly *adv*

itinerary (aı'tınərərı, ı-) *n, pl* -aries **1** a plan or line of travel; route **2** a record of a journey **3** a guidebook for travellers ⊳ *adj* **4** of or relating to travel or routes of travel **5** a less common word for **itinerant**

itinerate (aɪˈtɪnəˌreɪt, ɪ-) *vb* (*intr*) to travel from place to place > iˌtinerˈation *n*

-itis *suffix forming nouns* **1** indicating inflammation of a specified part: *tonsillitis* **2** *informal* indicating a preoccupation with or imaginary condition of illness caused by: *computeritis; telephonitis* [New Latin, from Greek, feminine of *-itēs* belonging to; see -ITE¹]

it'll (ˈɪtəl) *contraction of* it will *or* it shall

ITN (in Britain) *abbreviation* Independent Television News

Ito (ˈiːtəʊ) *n* Prince **Hirobumi** (ˌhɪərəˈbuːmɪ). 1841–1909, Japanese statesman; premier (1884–88; 1892–96; 1898; 1900–01). He led the movement to modernize Japan and helped to draft the Meiji constitution (1889); assassinated

ITO *abbreviation* International Trade Organization

-itol *suffix forming nouns* indicating that certain chemical compounds are polyhydric alcohols: *inisitol; sorbitol* [from -ITE² + -OL¹]

its (ɪts) *determiner* **a** of, belonging to, or associated in some way with it: *its left rear wheel* **b** (*as pronoun*): *each town claims its is the best*

it's (ɪts) *contraction of* it is *or* it has

- ◉ USAGE One of the commonest mistakes made in
- ◉ written English is the confusion of *its* and *it's*. You can
- ◉ see examples of this every day in books, magazines,
- ◉ and newspapers: *its good for us; a smart case with it's own*
- ◉ *mirror*, and even *Cheng, and its' subsidiaries*. *Its* refers to
- ◉ something belonging to or relating to a thing that
- ◉ has already been mentioned: *the baby threw its rattle out*
- ◉ *of the pram); it's* is a shortened way of saying *it is* or *it*
- ◉ *has* (the apostrophe indicates that a letter has been
- ◉ omitted): *it's a lovely day; it's been a great weekend*.

itself (ɪtˈsɛlf) *pron* **1 a** the reflexive form of **it¹** **b** (*intensifier*): *even the money itself won't convince me* **2** (*preceded by a copula*) its normal or usual self: *my cat isn't itself today*

itsy-bitsy (ˈɪtsɪˈbɪtsɪ) *or* **itty-bitty** (ˈɪtɪˈbɪtɪ) *adj informal* very small; tiny [C20: baby talk alteration of *little bit*]

ITU *abbreviation* **1** Intensive Therapy Unit **2** International Telecommunications Union

iTunes (ˈaɪˌtjuːnz) *n trademark* a computer application enabling users to download music from the internet, create and order playlists, etc

Itúrbide (*Spanish* ˈiβtureðe) *n* **Agustín de** (aˈɣustin de). 1783–1824, Mexican nationalist and emperor (1822–23). He was forced to abdicate and later executed

ITV (in Britain) *abbreviation* Independent Television

-ity *suffix forming nouns* indicating state or condition: *technicality* [from Old French *-ite*, from Latin *-itās*]

IU *abbreviation* **1** immunizing unit **2** international unit

IUD *or* **IUCD** *abbreviation* intrauterine device or intrauterine contraceptive device

IUI *abbreviation* **1** intrauterine insemination: a form of fertility treatment in which sperm are injected directly into the uterus **2** intelligent user interface: a system enabling and facilitating interaction between humans and computers

Iulus (aɪˈjuːləs) *n* **1** *Roman myth* another name for **Ascanius 2** *Roman myth* the son of Ascanius, founder of the Julian gens or clan

-ium *or sometimes* **-um** *suffix forming nouns* **1** indicating a metallic element: *platinum; barium* **2** (in chemistry) indicating groups containing positive ions: *ammonium chloride; hydroxonium ion* **3** indicating a biological structure: *syncytium* [New Latin, from Latin, from Greek *-ion*, diminutive suffix]

i.v. *or* **IV** *abbreviation* intravenous(ly)

Ivan III (ˈaɪvən) *n* known as *Ivan the Great*. 1440–1505, grand duke of Muscovy (1462–1505). He expanded Muscovy, defeated the Tatars (1480), and assumed the title of Ruler of all Russia (1472)

Ivan IV *n* known as *Ivan the Terrible*. 1530–84, grand duke of Muscovy (1533–47) and first tsar of Russia (1547–84). He conquered Kazan (1552), Astrakhan (1556), and Siberia (1581), but was defeated by Poland in the Livonian War (1558–82) after which his rule became increasingly oppressive

Ivanovo (*Russian* ɪˈvanəvə) *n* a city in W central Russia,

on the Uvod River: textile centre. Pop: 423 000 (2005 est)

I've (aɪv) *contraction of* I have

-ive *suffix* **1** (*forming adjectives*) indicating a tendency, inclination, character, or quality: *divisive; prohibitive; festive; massive* **2** (*forming nouns of adjectival origin*): *detective; expletive* [from Latin *-ivus*]

Ives (aɪvz) *n* **1 Charles Edward**. 1874–1954, US composer, noted for his innovative use of polytonality, polyrhythms, and quarter tones. His works include *Second Piano Sonata: Concord* (1915), five symphonies, chamber music, and songs **2 Frederick Eugene**. 1856–1937, US inventor of halftone photography

IVF *abbreviation* in vitro fertilization

ivied (ˈaɪvɪd) *adj* covered with ivy

Ivorian (aɪˈvɔːrɪən) *n* **1** a native or inhabitant of the Côte d'Ivoire ▷ *adj* **2** of or relating to the Côte d'Ivoire or its inhabitants

ivories (ˈaɪvərɪz, -vrɪz) *pl n slang* **1** the keys of a piano **2** another word for **teeth 3** another word for **dice**

ivory (ˈaɪvərɪ, -vrɪ) *n, pl* **-ries 1 a** a hard smooth creamy white variety of dentine that makes up a major part of the tusks of elephants, walruses, and similar animals **b** (*as modifier*): *ivory ornaments* **2** a tusk made of ivory **3 a** a yellowish-white colour; cream **b** (*as adjective*): *ivory shoes* **4** a substance resembling elephant tusk **5** an ornament, etc, made of ivory **6** black ivory *obsolete* Black slaves collectively [C13: from Old French *ivurie*, from Latin *evoreus* made of ivory, from *ebur* ivory; related to Greek *elephas* ivory, ELEPHANT] > ˈivory-ˌlike *adj*

Ivory (ˈaɪvərɪ) *n* **James**. born 1928, US film director. With the producer Ismael Merchant, his films include *Shakespeare Wallah* (1964), *Heat and Dust* (1983), *A Room With a View* (1986), and *The Golden Bowl* (2000)

ivory black *n* a black pigment obtained by grinding charred scraps of ivory in oil

Ivory Coast *n* the Ivory Coast the former name (until 1986) of **Côte d'Ivoire**

ivory nut *n* **1** the seed of the ivory palm, which contains an ivory-like substance used to make buttons, etc **2** any similar seed from other palms ▷ Also called: **vegetable ivory**

ivory tower (ˈtaʊə) *n* a seclusion or remoteness of attitude regarding real problems, everyday life, etc **b** (*as modifier*): *ivory-tower aestheticism* > ˌivory-ˈtowered *adj*

ivorywood (ˈaɪvərɪˌwʊd) *n* **1** the yellowish-white wood of an Australian tree, *Siphonodon australe*, used for engraving, inlaying, and turnery **2** the tree itself: family *Celastraceae*

IVR *abbreviation* International Vehicle Registration

ivy (ˈaɪvɪ) *n, pl* **ivies 1** any woody climbing or trailing araliaceous plant of the Old World genus *Hedera*, esp *H. helix*, having lobed evergreen leaves and black berry-like fruits **2** any of various other climbing or creeping plants, such as Boston ivy, poison ivy, and ground ivy [Old English *īfig*; related to Old High German *ebah*, perhaps to Greek *iphuon* a plant] > ˈivy-ˌlike *adj*

iwi (ˈiːwiː) *n NZ* a Māori tribe [Māori, literally: bone(s)]

iwis *or* **ywis** (ɪˈwɪs) *adv* an archaic word for **certainly** [C12: from Old English *gewiss* certain]

Iwo (ˈiːwəʊ) *n* a city in SW Nigeria. Pop: 479 000 (2005 est)

Iwo Jima (ˈdʒiːmə) *n* an island in the W Pacific, about 1100 km (700 miles) south of Japan: one of the Volcano Islands; scene of prolonged fighting between US and Japanese forces until taken by the US in 1945; returned to Japan in 1968. Area: 20 sq km (8 sq miles)

IWW *abbreviation* Industrial Workers of the World

ixia (ˈɪksɪə) *n* any plant of the iridaceous genus *Ixia* of southern Africa, having showy ornamental funnel-shaped flowers [C18: New Latin from Greek *ixos* mistletoe, birdlime prepared from mistletoe berries]

Ixion (ɪkˈsaɪən) *n Greek myth* a Thessalian king punished by Zeus for his love of Hera by being bound to a perpetually revolving wheel > **Ixionian** (ˌɪksɪˈəʊnɪən) *adj*

Ixtaccihuatl *or* **Iztaccihuatl** (ˌiːstəkˈsiːwətəl) *n* a dormant volcano in central Mexico, southeast of Mexico City. Height: (central peak) 5286 m (17 342 ft)

ixtle (ˈɪkstlɪ, ˈɪst-) *n* a variant of **istle**

Iyeyasu *or* **Ieyasu** (ˌiːjeɪˈjɑːsuː) *n* **Tokugawa**

(ˌtɒkuːˈɡɑːwə). 1542–1616, Japanese general and statesman; founder of the Tokugawa shogunate (1603–1867)

IYKWIMAITYD *abbreviation text messaging* if you know what I mean and I think you do

izard (ˈɪzəd) *n* (esp in the Pyrenees) another name for **chamois**

-ize *or* **-ise** *suffix forming verbs* **1** to cause to become, resemble, or agree with: *legalize* **2** to become; change into: *crystallize* **3** to affect in a specified way; subject to: *hypnotize* **4** to act according to some practice, principle, policy, etc: *economize* [from Old French *-iser*, from Late Latin *-izāre*, from Greek *-izein*]

● **USAGE** In Britain and the US *-ize* is the preferred
● ending for many verbs, but *-ise* is equally acceptable in
● British English. Certain words (chiefly those not
● formed by adding the suffix to an existing word) are,
● however, always spelt with *-ise* in both Britain and the
● US: *advertise, revise*

Izetbegović (ˌɪzətˈbɛɡəvɪtʃ) *n* **Alija** (ˈæljə). 1925–2003, Bosnia and Herzegovinian politician: president (1992–2000), he led the country to independence and during the subsequent civil war

Izhevsk (*Russian* iˈʒefsk) *n* an industrial city in central Russia, capital of the Udmurt Republic. Pop: 632 000 (2005 est)

Izmir (ˈɪzmɪə) *n* a port in W Turkey, on the **Gulf of Izmir**: the third largest city in the country; university (1955). Pop: 2 500 000 (2005 est). Former name: **Smyrna**

Izmit (ˈɪzmɪt) *n* a town in NW Turkey, on the **Gulf of Izmit**. Pop: 306 000 (2005 est)

Iznik (ɪzˈnɪk) *n* the modern Turkish name of **Nicaea**

Iztaccihuatl (ˌiːstəkˈsiːwətᵊl) *n* a variant spelling of **Ixtaccihuatl**

Jj

j¹ or **J** (dʒeɪ) *n, pl* **j's, J's** or **Js 1** the tenth letter and seventh consonant of the modern English alphabet **2** a speech sound represented by this letter, in English usually a voiced palato-alveolar affricate, as in *jam*

j² *symbol for* **1** *maths* the unit vector along the *y*-axis **2** Also called: **i** *obsolete* the imaginary number √–1

J *symbol for* **1** *cards* jack **2** joule(s) **3** current density

ja (jɑː) *sentence substitute South African* yes [from Afrikaans]

jab (dʒæb) *vb* **jabs, jabbing, jabbed 1** to poke or thrust sharply **2** to strike with a quick short blow or blows ▷ *n* **3** a sharp poke or stab **4** a quick short blow, esp (in boxing) a straight punch with the leading hand **5** *informal* an injection: *polio jabs* [c19: originally Scottish variant of JOB] > ˈjabbing *adj*

Jabalpur or **Jubbulpore** (ˌdʒʌbəlˈpʊə) *n* a city in central India, in central Madhya Pradesh. Pop: 951 469 (2001)

jabber (ˈdʒæbə) *vb* **1** to speak or say rapidly, incoherently, and without making sense; chatter ▷ *n* **2** such talk [c15: of imitative origin; compare GIBBER¹]

jabberwocky (ˈdʒæbəˌwɒkɪ) *n, pl* -**wockies** nonsense verse [c19: coined by Lewis Carroll as the title of a poem in *Through the Looking Glass* (1871)]

Jabir ibn Hayyan (ˈdʒɑːbɪə ˌiːbʰn hɑːˈjɑːn) *n* ?721–?815. Arab alchemist, whose many works enjoyed enormous esteem among later alchemists, such as Geber

jabiru (ˈdʒæbɪˌruː) *n* **1** a large white tropical American stork, *Jabiru mycteria*, with a dark naked head and a dark bill **2** Also called: **black-necked stork, policeman bird** a large Australian stork, *Xenorhyncus asiaticus*, having a white plumage, dark green back and tail, and red legs **3** another name for **saddlebill** [c18: via Portuguese from Tupi-Guarani]

jabot (ˈʒæbəʊ) *n* a frill or ruffle on the breast or throat of a garment, originally to hide the closure of a shirt [c19: from French: bird's crop, jabot; compare Old French *gave* throat]

jaçana (ˌʒɑːsəˈnɑː, ˌdʒæ-) *n* any bird of the family *Jacanidae*, of tropical and subtropical marshy regions, having long legs and very long toes that enable walking on floating plants: order *Charadriiformes* [c18: from Portuguese *jaçanã*, from Tupi-Guarani *jasaná*]

jacaranda (ˌdʒækəˈrændə) *n* **1** any bignoniaceous tree of the tropical American genus *Jacaranda*, having fernlike leaves and pale purple flowers and widely cultivated in temperate areas of Australia **2** the fragrant ornamental wood of any of these trees **3** any of several related or similar trees or their wood [c18: from Portuguese, from Tupi-Guarani *yacarandá*]

jacaré (ˈdʒækəreɪ) *n* another name for **cayman** [c18: from Portuguese, from Tupi *jacaré*]

jacinth (ˈdʒæsɪnθ) *n* another name for **hyacinth** (sense 4) [c13: from Medieval Latin *jacinthus*, from Latin *hyacinthus* plant, precious stone; see HYACINTH]

jack (dʒæk) *n* **1** a man or fellow **2** a sailor **3** the male of certain animals, esp of the ass or donkey **4** a mechanical or hydraulic device for exerting a large force, esp to raise a heavy weight such as a motor vehicle **5** any of several mechanical devices that replace manpower, such as a contrivance for rotating meat on a spit **6** one of four playing cards in a pack, one for each suit, bearing the picture of a young prince; knave **7** *bowls* a small usually white bowl at which the players aim with their own bowls **8** *electrical engineering* a female socket with two or more terminals designed to receive a male plug (**jack plug**) that either makes or breaks the circuit or circuits **9** a flag, esp a small flag flown at the bow of a ship indicating the ship's nationality **10** a part of the action of a harpsichord, consisting of a fork-shaped device on the end of a pivoted lever on which a plectrum is mounted **11** any of various tropical and subtropical carangid fishes, esp those of the genus *Caranx*, such as *C. hippos* (**crevalle jack**) **12** Also called: **jackstone** one of the pieces used in the game of jacks **13** *US* a slang word for **money 14** every man jack everyone without exception **15** the jack *Austral slang* venereal disease ▷ *adj* **16** jack of *Austral slang* tired or fed up with (something) ▷ *vb* (*tr*) **17** to lift or push (an object) with a jack ▷ See also **jack in, jack up** [c16 *jakke*, variant of *Jankin*, diminutive of *John*]

Jack (dʒæk) *n* **I'm all right, Jack** *Brit informal* a remark indicating smug and complacent selfishness

jackal (ˈdʒækɔːl) *n* **1** any of several African or S Asian canine mammals of the genus *Canis*, closely related to the dog, having long legs and pointed ears and muzzle:

predators and carrion-eaters **2** a person who does menial tasks for another [c17: from Turkish *chakāl*, from Persian *shagāl*, from Sanskrit *srgāla*]

jackanapes ('dʒækə,neɪps) *n* **1** a conceited impertinent person **2** a mischievous child **3** *archaic* a monkey [c16: variant of *Jakken-apes*, literally: Jack of the ape, nickname of William de la Pole (1396–1450), first Duke of Suffolk, whose badge showed an ape's ball and chain]

jackass ('dʒæk,æs) *n* **1** a male donkey **2** a stupid person; fool [c18: from JACK¹ (male) + ASS¹]

jackboot ('dʒæk,buːt) *n* **1** an all-leather military boot, extending up to or above the knee **2** arbitrary, cruel, and authoritarian rule or behaviour ▷ 'jack,booted *adj*

jackdaw ('dʒæk,dɔː) *n* a large common Eurasian passerine bird, *Corvus monedula*, in which the plumage is black and dark grey: noted for its thieving habits: family *Corvidae* (crows) [c16: from JACK¹ + DAW]

jackeroo or **jackaroo** (,dʒækə'ruː) *n, pl* **-roos** *Austral informal* a young male management trainee on a sheep or cattle station [c19: from JACK¹ + (KANG)AROO]

jacket ('dʒækɪt) *n* **1** a short coat, esp one that is hip-length and has a front opening and sleeves **2** something that resembles this or is designed to be worn around the upper part of the body: *a life jacket* **3** any exterior covering or casing, such as the insulating cover of a boiler **4** See **dust jacket 5 a** the skin of a baked potato **b** (*as modifier*): *jacket potatoes* ▷ *vb* **6** (*tr*) to put a jacket on (someone or something) [c15: from Old French *jaquet* short jacket, from *jacque* peasant, from proper name *Jacques* James] ▷ 'jacketed *adj*

Jack Frost *n* a personification of frost or winter

Jackie or **Jacky** ('dʒækɪ) *n, pl* **Jackies** *Austral, offensive slang* **1** a native Australian **2** native Australians collectively **3** sit up like Jackie to sit bolt upright, esp cheekily

jack in *vb* (*tr, adverb*) *slang* to abandon or leave (an attempt or enterprise)

jack-in-office *n* a self-important petty official

jack-in-the-box *n, pl* **jack-in-the-boxes** or **jacks-in-the-box** a toy consisting of a figure on a compressed spring in a box, which springs out when the lid is opened

Jack Ketch (ketʃ) *n Brit archaic* a hangman [c18: after John Ketch (died 1686), public executioner in England]

jackknife ('dʒæk,naɪf) *n, pl* **-knives 1** a knife with the blade pivoted to fold into a recess in the handle **2** a former name for a type of dive in which the diver bends at the waist in midair, with his legs straight and his hands touching his feet, finally straightening out and entering the water headfirst: forward pike dive ▷ *vb* (*intr*) **3** (of an articulated lorry) to go out of control in such a way that the trailer swings round at an angle to the cab

Jacklin ('dʒæklɪn) *n* **Tony**, full name *Anthony Jacklin*. born 1944, English golfer: won the British Open Championship (1969) and the US Open Championship (1970)

jack of all trades *n, pl* **jacks of all trades** a person who undertakes many different kinds of work

jack-o'-lantern *n* **1** a lantern made from a hollowed pumpkin, which has holes cut in it to represent a human face **2** a will-o'-the-wisp or similar phenomenon

jack plane *n* a carpenter's plane, usually with a wooden body, used for rough planing of timber

jack plug *n* another name for **jack** (sense 8)

jackpot ('dʒæk,pɒt) *n* **1** any large prize, kitty, or accumulated stake that may be won in gambling, such as a pool in poker that accumulates until the betting is opened with a pair of jacks or higher **2** hit the jackpot **a** to win a jackpot **b** *informal* to achieve great success, esp through luck [c20: probably from JACK¹ (playing card) + POT¹]

jack rabbit *n* any of various W North American hares, such as *Lepus townsendi* (**white-tailed jack rabbit**), having long hind legs and large ears [c19: shortened from *jackass-rabbit*, referring to its long ears]

Jack Robinson *n* before you could say Jack Robinson or before you can say Jack Robinson extremely quickly or suddenly

Jack Russell *n* a small short-legged terrier having a

white coat with tan, black, or lemon markings: there are rough- and smooth-haired varieties [named after John *Russell* (1795–1883), English clergyman who developed the breed]

jacks (dʒæks) *n* (*functioning as singular*) a game in which bone, metal, or plastic pieces (**jackstones**) are thrown and then picked up in various groups between bounces or throws of a small ball [c19: shortened from *jackstones*, variant of *checkstones* pebbles]

jacksie or **jacksy** ('dʒæksɪ) *n Brit slang* the buttocks or anus. Also called: jaxie, jaxy [c19: probably from JACK¹]

jacksnipe ('dʒæk,snaɪp) *n, pl* **-snipe** or **-snipes** a small Eurasian short-billed snipe, *Lymnocryptes minima*

Jackson¹ ('dʒæksən) *n* a city in and state capital of Mississippi, on the Pearl River. Pop: 179 599 (2003 est)

Jackson² ('dʒæksən) *n* **1 Andrew**. 1767–1845, US statesman, general, and lawyer; seventh president of the US (1829–37). He became a national hero after successfully defending New Orleans from the British (1815). During his administration the spoils system was introduced and the national debt was fully paid off **2 Colin** (**Ray**). born 1967, British athlete, broke world record for 110 m hurdles in 1993 (12.91 seconds) and for the 60 m hurdles in 1994 (7.3 seconds) **3 Glenda**. born 1936, British stage, film, and television actress, and Labour politician. Her films include *Women in Love* (1969) for which she won an Oscar, *The Music Lovers* (1970), *Sunday Bloody Sunday* (1971), and *Turtle Diary* (1985); became a member of parliament in 1992 **4 Jesse** (**Louis**). born 1941, US Democrat politician and clergyman; Black campaigner for minority rights **5 Michael** (**Joe**). born 1958, US pop singer, lead vocalist with the Jacksons (originally the Jackson 5) (1969–86). His solo albums include *Thriller* (1982), *Bad* (1989), and *Invincible* (2001) **6 Peter**. born 1961, New Zealand film director, screenwriter, and producer; his films include *Heavenly Creatures* (1994), *The Lord of the Rings* trilogy (2001–03), and *King Kong* (2005) **7 Thomas Jonathan**, known as *Stonewall Jackson*. 1824–63, Confederate general in the American Civil War, noted particularly for his command at the first Battle of Bull Run (1861) ▷ Jacksonian (dʒæk'səʊnɪən) *adj, n*

Jacksonville ('dʒæksən,vɪl) *n* a port in NE Florida: the leading commercial centre of the southeast. Pop: 773 781 (2003 est)

jackstraws ('dʒæk,strɔːz) *n* (*functioning as singular*) another name for **spillikins**

Jack Tar *n now chiefly literary* a sailor

Jack the Ripper *n* an unidentified murderer who killed at least seven prostitutes in London's East End between August and November 1888

jack up *vb* (*adverb*) **1** (*tr*) to increase (prices, salaries, etc) **2** (*tr*) to raise an object, such as a car, with or as with a jack **3** (*intr*) *slang* to inject oneself with a drug, usually heroin **4** (*intr*) *Austral informal* to refuse to comply; rebel, esp collectively **5** *NZ informal* to initiate, organize, or procure ▷ *n* **jack-up 6** *NZ* something that has been contrived or achieved by dishonest means

Jacob ('dʒeɪkəb) *n Old Testament* the son of Isaac, twin brother of Esau, and father of the twelve patriarchs of Israel

Jacobean (,dʒækə'biən) *adj* **1** *history* characteristic of or relating to James I (1566–1625) of England or to the period of his rule (1603–25) **2** of or relating to the style of furniture current at this time, characterized by the use of dark brown carved oak **3** denoting, relating to, or having the style of architecture used in England during this period, characterized by a combination of late Gothic and Palladian motifs [c18: from New Latin *jacōbaeus*, from *Jacōbus* James]

Jacobi *n* **1** (dʒə'kəʊbɪ) Sir **Derek** (**George**). born 1938, British actor **2** (German ja'koːbi) **Karl Gustav Jacob** (karl 'ɡʊstaf 'jaːkɔp). 1804–51, German mathematician. Independently of N. H. Abel, he discovered elliptic functions (1829). He also made important contributions to the study of determinants and differential equations

Jacobin ('dʒækəbɪn) *n* **1** a member of the most radical club founded during the French Revolution, which overthrew the Girondists in 1793 and, led by Maximilien

Robespierre (1758–94), instituted the Reign of Terror **2** a leftist or extreme political radical **3** a French Dominican friar ▷ *adj* **4** of, characteristic of, or relating to the Jacobins or their policies [c14: from Old French, from Medieval Latin *Jacōbīnus*, from Late Latin *Jacōbus* James; applied to the Dominicans, from the proximity of the church of St Jacques (St James) to their first convent in Paris; the political club originally met in the convent in 1789] ▷ Jaco'binic or Jaco'binical *adj* ▷ 'Jacobinism *n*

Jacobite ('dʒækə,baɪt) *n Brit history* an adherent of James II (1633–1701, king of England, Ireland, and, as James VII, of Scotland, 1685–88) after his overthrow in 1688, or of his descendants in their attempts to regain the throne [c17: from Late Latin *Jacōbus* James + -ITE[1]] ▷ Jacobitic (,dʒækə'bɪtɪk) *adj*

Jacobite Rebellion *n* the Jacobite Rebellion *Brit history* **1** the unsuccessful Jacobite rising of 1715 led by James Francis Edward Stuart **2** the last Jacobite rising (1745-46) led by Charles Edward Stuart, the Young Pretender, which after initial successes was crushed at Culloden

Jacobsen (*Danish* 'jakɔbsən) *n* **Arne** ('arnə). 1902–71, Danish architect and designer. His buildings include the Town Hall at Rodovre (1955)

Jacob's ladder *n* **1** *Old Testament* the ladder reaching up to heaven that Jacob saw in a dream (Genesis 28:12–17) **2** Also called: **jack ladder** a ladder made of wooden or metal steps supported by ropes or chains **3** a North American polemoniaceous plant, *Polemonium caeruleum*, with blue flowers and a ladder-like arrangement of leaves

Jacob's staff *n* a medieval instrument for measuring heights and distances

jaconet ('dʒækənɪt) *n* a light cotton fabric used for clothing, bandages, etc [c18: from Urdu *jagannāthī*, from *Jagannāthpūrī*, India, where it was originally made]

Jacopo della Quercia (*Italian* 'ja:kopo ,dela 'kwɛrtʃa) *n* ?1374–1438, Italian Renaissance sculptor: best known for his marble reliefs of scenes from Genesis around the portal of S. Petronio, Bologna (1425–35)

Jacquard ('dʒækɑːd, dʒə'kɑːd; *French* ʒakar) *n* **1** Also called: **Jacquard weave** a fabric in which the design is incorporated into the weave instead of being printed or dyed on **2** Also called: **Jacquard loom** the loom that produces this fabric [c19: named after Joseph M. *Jacquard* (1752–1834), French inventor]

jactation (dʒæk'teɪʃən) *n* **1** *rare* the act of boasting **2** *pathol* another word for **jactitation** (sense 3) [c16: from Latin *jactātiō* bragging, from *jactāre* to flourish, from *jacere* to throw]

jactitation (,dʒæktɪ'teɪʃən) *n* **1** the act of boasting **2** a false boast or claim that tends to harm another person, esp a false assertion that one is married to another, formerly actionable at law **3** Also called: **jactation** *pathol* restless tossing in bed, characteristic of severe fevers and certain mental disorders [c17: from Medieval Latin *jactitātiō*, from Latin *jacitāre* to utter publicly, from *jactitāre* to toss about; see JACTATION]

Jacuzzi (dʒə'kuːzɪ) *n*, *pl* -zis **1** *trademark* a system of underwater jets that keep the water in a bath or pool constantly agitated **2** (*sometimes not capital*) a bath or pool equipped with this [c20: named after Candido and Roy *Jacuzzi*, who developed and marketed it]

jade[1] (dʒeɪd) *n* **1** a semiprecious stone consisting of either jadeite or nephrite. It varies in colour from white to green and is used for making ornaments and jewellery **2 a** the green colour of jade **b** (*as modifier*): *a jade skirt* [c18: from French, from Italian *giada*, from obsolete Spanish *piedra de ijada* colic stone (literally: stone of the flank, because it was believed to cure renal colic); *ijada*, from Vulgar Latin *īliata* (unattested) flanks, from Latin *īlia*, plural of *īlium*; see ILEUM]

jade[2] (dʒeɪd) *n* **1** an old overworked horse; nag; hack **2** *derogatory or facetious* a woman considered to be ill-tempered or disreputable ▷ *vb* **3** to exhaust or make exhausted from work or use [c14: of unknown origin] ▷ 'jadish *adj*

jaded ('dʒeɪdɪd) *adj* **1** exhausted or dissipated **2** satiated ▷ 'jadedly *adv* ▷ 'jadedness *n*

jadeite ('dʒeɪdaɪt) *n* a usually green or white mineral of the clinopyroxene group, found in igneous and metamorphic rocks. It is used as a gemstone (jade). Composition: sodium aluminium silicate. Formula: $NaAlSi_2O_6$. Crystal structure: monoclinic

Jadotville (*French* ʒadovil) *n* the former name of **Likasi**

j'adoube *French* (ʒadub) *interj chess* an expression of an intention to touch a piece in order to adjust its placement rather than to make a move [literally: I adjust]

jaeger ('jeɪgə) *n US & Canadian* any of several skuas of the genus *Stercorarius* [c18: from German *Jäger* hunter, from *jagen* to hunt; see YACHT]

Jael ('dʒeɪəl) *n Old Testament* the woman who killed Sisera when he took refuge in her tent (Judges 4:17–21)

Jaén (xa'en) *n* a city in S Spain. Pop: 115 638 (2003 est)

Jaffa ('dʒæfə, 'dʒɑː-) *n* **1** a port in W Israel, on the Mediterranean: incorporated into Tel Aviv in 1950; an old Canaanite city. Biblical name: Joppa. Hebrew name: Yafo **2** a large variety of orange, having a thick skin

Jaffna ('dʒæfnə) *n* a port in N Sri Lanka: for many centuries the capital of a Tamil kingdom. Pop: 149 000 (2005 est)

jag[1] *or* **jagg** (dʒæg) *vb* jags, jagging, jagged **1** (*tr*) to cut unevenly; make jagged **2** *Austral* to catch (fish) by impaling them on an unbaited hook ▷ *n*, *vb* **3** *Scot* an informal word for **jab** (sense 3) ▷ *n* **4** a jagged notch or projection [c14: of unknown origin]

jag[2] (dʒæg) *n slang* **1 a** intoxication from drugs or alcohol **b** a bout of drinking or drug taking **2** a period of uncontrolled activity: *a crying jag* [of unknown origin]

jagged ('dʒægɪd) *adj* having sharp projecting notches; ragged; serrate ▷ 'jaggedly *adv*

Jagger ('dʒægə) *n* Sir **Mick**, full name *Michael Philip Jagger*. born 1943, English rock singer and songwriter: lead vocalist with the Rolling Stones

jaggy ('dʒægɪ) *adj* -gier, -giest **1** a less common word for **jagged** **2** *Scot* prickly

jaguar ('dʒægjʊə) *n* a large feline mammal, *Panthera onca*, of S North America, Central America, and N South America, similar to the leopard but with a shorter tail and larger spots on its coat [c17: from Portuguese, from Tupi *jaguara*, Guarani *yaguara*]

Jahwism ('jɑː,wɪz[ə]m) *or* **Jahvism** ('jɑː,vɪzəm) *n* variants of Yahwism ▷ Jah'wistic *or* Jah'vistic *adj*

jai alai ('haɪ 'laɪ, 'haɪ ə,laɪ, ,haɪ ə'laɪ) *n* a version of pelota played by two or four players [via Spanish from Basque, from *jai* game, festival + *alai* merry]

jail *or* **gaol** (dʒeɪl) *n* **1** a place for the confinement of persons convicted and sentenced to imprisonment or of persons awaiting trial to whom bail is not granted ▷ *vb* **2** (*tr*) to confine in prison [c13: from Old French *jaiole* cage, from Vulgar Latin *caveola* (unattested), from Latin *cavea* enclosure; see CAGE: the two spellings derive from the forms of the word that developed in two different areas of France, and the spelling *gaol* represents a pronunciation in use until the 17th century]

jailbait ('dʒeɪl,beɪt) *n slang* a young woman, or young women collectively, considered sexually attractive but below the age of consent

jailbird *or* **gaolbird** ('dʒeɪl,bɜːd) *n* a person who is or has been confined to jail, esp repeatedly; convict

jailbreak *or* **gaolbreak** ('dʒeɪl,breɪk) *n* an escape from jail

jailer, jailor *or* **gaoler** ('dʒeɪlə) *n* a person in charge of prisoners in a jail

Jain (dʒaɪn) *or* **Jaina** ('dʒaɪnə) *n* **1** an adherent of Jainism ▷ *adj* **2** of or relating to Jainism or the Jains [c19: from Hindi *jaina* saint, literally: overcomer, from Sanskrit]

Jainism ('dʒaɪ,nɪzəm) *n* an ancient Hindu religion, which has its own scriptures and believes that the material world is eternal, progressing endlessly in a series of vast cycles ▷ 'Jainist *n*, *adj*

Jaipur (dʒaɪ'pʊə) *n* a city of great beauty in N India, capital of Rajasthan state: University of Rajasthan (1947). Pop: 2 324 319 (2001)

Jakarta (dʒə'kɑːtə) *n* the capital of Indonesia, in N West Java: founded in 1619 and ruled by the Dutch until 1945; the chief trading centre of the East in the 17th century; University of Indonesia (1947). Pop: 8 347 083 (2000).

Former name (until 1949): Batavia. Former spelling: Djakarta

jake (dʒeɪk) *adj Austral & NZ slang* **1** satisfactory; all right **2** she's jake everything is under control [probably from the name *Jake*]

jakey ('dʒeɪkɪ) *n Scot slang, derogatory* a homeless alcoholic [c20: from *jake* a tramps' word for a drinker of meths]

Jakobson ('jɑːkəbsən) *n* **Roman** (**Osipovič**). 1896–1982, US linguist, born in Russia. His publications include *Children's Speech* (1941) and *Fundamentals of Language* (1956)

Jalalabad (dʒə'læləbæd) *n* a city in NE Afghanistan, capital of Nangarhar province; a trading, military, and tourist centre on the main route between Kabul and the Khyber Pass. Pop: 96 000 (2004 est)

Jalandhar ('dʒælən,dɑː) *n* a city in NW India, in central Punjab. Pop: 701 223 (2001)

jalap *or* **jalop** ('dʒæləp) *n* **1** a Mexican convolvulaceous plant, *Exogonium* (or *Ipomoea*) *purga* **2** the dried and powdered root of any of these plants, used as a purgative [c17: from French, from Mexican Spanish *jalapa*, short for *purga de Jalapa* purgative of Jalapa] > **jalapic** (dʒə'læpɪk) *adj*

Jalapa (Spanish xa'lapa) *n* a city in E central Mexico, capital of Veracruz State, at an altitude of 1427 m (4681 ft): resort. Pop: 525 000 (2005 est)

jalapeño (dʒælə'piːnəʊ; Spanish xala'penjo) *n* a very hot type of green chilli pepper, used esp in Mexican cookery [Mexican Spanish]

Jalisco (Spanish xa'lisko) *n* a state of W Mexico, on the Pacific: crossed by the Sierra Madre; valuable mineral resources. Capital: Guadalajara. Pop: 6 321 278 (2000). Area: 80 137 sq km (30 934 sq miles)

jalopy *or* **jaloppy** (dʒə'lɒpɪ) *n, pl* **-lopies** *or* **-loppies** *informal* a dilapidated old car [c20: of unknown origin]

jalousie ('ʒæluˌziː) *n* **1** a window blind or shutter constructed from angled slats of wood, plastic, etc **2** a window made of similarly angled slats of glass [c19: from Old French *gelosie* latticework screen, literally: JEALOUSY, perhaps because one can look through the screen without being seen]

jam¹ (dʒæm) *vb* **jams, jamming, jammed** **1** (*tr*) to cram or wedge into or against something: *to jam paper into an incinerator* **2** (*tr*) to crowd or pack: *cars jammed the roads* **3** to make or become stuck or locked **4** (*tr*; often foll by *on*) to activate suddenly (esp in the phrase **jam on the brakes**) **5** (*tr*) to block; congest **6** (*tr*) to crush, bruise, or squeeze; smash **7** *radio* to prevent the clear reception of (radio communications or radar signals) by transmitting other signals on the same frequency **8** (*intr*) *slang* to play in a jam session ▷ *n* **9** a crowd or congestion in a confined space: *a traffic jam* **10** the act of jamming or the state of being jammed **11** *informal* a difficult situation; predicament: *to help a friend out of a jam* **12** See **jam session** [c18: probably of imitative origin; compare CHAMP¹] > **'jammer** *n*

jam² (dʒæm) *n* **1** a preserve containing fruit, which has been boiled with sugar until the mixture sets **2** *slang* something desirable: *you want jam on it* [c18: perhaps from JAM¹ (the act of squeezing)]

Jam. *abbreviation* **1** Jamaica **2** *Bible* James

jamaat (dʒɑː'mɑːt) *n* an Islamic council or assembly [from Arabic *jama'at* group, congregation]

Jamaica (dʒə'meɪkə) *n* an island and state in the Caribbean: colonized by the Spanish from 1494 onwards, large numbers of Black slaves being imported; captured by the British in 1655 and established as a colony in 1866; gained full independence in 1962; a member of the Commonwealth. Exports: chiefly bauxite and alumina, sugar, and bananas. Official language: English. Religion: Protestant majority. Currency: Jamaican dollar. Capital: Kingston. Pop: 2 676 000 (2004 est). Area: 10 992 sq km (4244 sq miles) > **Ja'maican** *adj, n*

jamb *or* **jambe** (dʒæm) *n* a vertical side member of a doorframe, window frame, or lining [c14: from Old French *jambe* leg, jamb, from Late Latin *gamba* hoof, hock, from Greek *kampē* joint]

Jambi ('dʒæmbɪ) *n* a port in W Indonesia, in SE Sumatra on the Hari River. Pop: 417 507 (2000). Also called:

Telanaipura

jamboree (ˌdʒæmbə'riː) *n* **1** a large and often international gathering of Scouts **2** a party or spree [c19: of uncertain origin]

James (dʒeɪmz) *n* **1 Clive**. born 1939, Australian journalist, critic and broadcaster. His books include the memoirs *Unreliable Memoirs* (1980) and *North Face of Soho* (2006) and the novel *Brilliant Creatures* **2 Henry** 1843–1916, British novelist, short-story writer, and critic, born in the US Among his novels is *Washington Square* (1880), *The Portrait of a Lady* (1881), *The Bostonians* (1886), *The Wings of the Dove* (1902), *The Ambassadors* (1903), and *The Golden Bowl* (1904) **3 Jesse** (**Woodson**). 1847–82, US outlaw **4 P(hyllis) D(orothy)**, Baroness James of Holland Park. born 1920, British detective novelist. Her books include *Death of an Expert Witness* (1977), *Original Sin* (1994), and *Death in Holy Orders* (2001) **5 William**, brother of Henry James. 1842–1910, US philosopher and psychologist, whose theory of pragmatism is expounded in *Essays in Radical Empiricism* (1912). His other works include *The Will to Believe* (1897), *The Principles of Psychology* (1890), and *The Varieties of Religious Experience* (1902) **6** *New Testament* **a** known as *James the Great*. one of the twelve apostles, a son of Zebedee and brother to John the apostle (Matthew 4:21). Feast day: July 25 or April 30 **b** known as *James the Less*. one of the twelve apostles, son of Alphaeus (Matthew 10:3). Feast day: May 3 or Oct 9 **c** known as *James the brother of the Lord*. a brother or close relative of Jesus (Mark 6:3; Galatians 1:19). Feast day: Oct 23 **d** the book ascribed to his authorship (in full **The Epistle of James**)

James I *n* **1** called the *Conqueror*. 1208–76, king of Aragon (1216–76). He captured the Balearic Islands and Valencia from the Muslims, thus beginning Aragonese expansion in the Mediterranean **2** 1394–1437, king of Scotland (1406–37), second son of Robert III **3** 1566–1625, king of England and Ireland (1603–25) and, as James VI, king of Scotland (1567–1625), in succession to Elizabeth I of England and his mother, Mary Queen of Scots, respectively. He alienated Parliament by his assertion of the divine right of kings, his favourites, esp the Duke of Buckingham, and his subservience to Spain

James II *n* **1** 1430–60, king of Scotland (1437–60), son of James I **2** 1633–1701, king of England, Ireland, and, as James VII, of Scotland (1685–88); son of Charles I. His pro-Catholic sympathies and arbitrary rule caused the Whigs and Tories to unite in inviting his eldest surviving daughter, Mary, and her husband, William of Orange, to take the throne as joint monarchs. James was defeated at the Boyne (1690) when he attempted to regain the throne

James III *n* 1451–88, king of Scotland (1460–88), son of James II

James IV *n* 1473–1513, king of Scotland (1488–1513), son of James III; he invaded England (1496) in support of Perkin Warbeck; he was killed at Flodden

James V *n* 1512–42, king of Scotland (1513–42), son of James IV

James VI *n* title as king of Scotland of James I of England and Ireland. See **James I** (sense 3)

James VII *n* title as king of Scotland of James II of England and Ireland. See **James II** (sense 2)

James Bay *n* the S arm of Hudson Bay, in central Canada. Area: 108 780 sq km (42 000 sq miles)

Jameson ('dʒeɪmsᵊn) *n* **Sir Leander Starr**. 1853–1917, British administrator in South Africa, who led an expedition into the Transvaal in 1895 in an unsuccessful attempt to topple its Boer regime (the **Jameson Raid**); prime minister of Cape Colony (1904–08)

Jamestown ('dʒeɪmz,taʊn) *n* a ruined village in E Virginia, on **Jamestown Island** (a peninsula in the James River): the first permanent settlement by the English in America (1607); capital of Virginia (1607–98); abandoned in 1699

Jammu ('dʒʌmuː) *n* a city in N India, winter capital of the state of Jammu and Kashmir. Pop: 378 431 (2001)

Jammu and Kashmir *n* the official name for the part of Kashmir under Indian control

jammy ('dʒæmɪ) *adj* **-mier, -miest** **1** covered with or tasting like jam **2** *Brit slang* lucky

Jamnagar (ˌdʒæmnəˈgɑː) n a city in India, in Gujarat: noted for its palaces and temples: cement, pottery, textiles. Pop: 447 734 (2001)

jam-packed adj crowded, packed, or filled to capacity

jam session n slang an unrehearsed or improvised jazz or rock performance [c20: probably from JAM¹]

Jamshedpur (ˌdʒʌmʃɛdˈpʊə) n a city in NE India, in Jharkhand: large iron and steel works (1907–11); a major industrial centre. Pop: 570 349 (2001)

Jamshid or **Jamshyd** (dʒæmˈʃiːd) n Persian myth a ruler of the peris who was punished for bragging that he was immortal by being changed into human form. He then became a great king of Persia. See also **peri**

Jan abbreviation January

Janáček (Czech ˈjanaːtʃɛk) n Leoš (ˈlɛɔʃ). 1854–1928, Czech composer. His music is influenced by Czech folksong and speech rhythms and is remarkable for its integration of melody and language. His works include the operas Jenufa (1904) and The Cunning Little Vixen (1924), the Glagolitic Mass (1927), as well as orchestral and chamber music and songs

Jandal (ˈdʒændəl) n trademark NZ a type of sandal with a strip of material between the big toe and the other toes and over the foot

Janet (French ʒanɛ) n Pierre Marie Félix (pjɛr mari feliks). 1859–1947, French psychologist and neurologist, noted particularly for his work on the origins of hysteria

jangle (ˈdʒæŋgəl) vb 1 to sound or cause to sound discordantly, harshly, or unpleasantly 2 (tr) to produce a jarring effect on: the accident jangled his nerves 3 an archaic word for **wrangle** ▷ n 4 a harsh, unpleasant ringing noise 5 an argument or quarrel [c13: from Old French jangler, of Germanic origin; compare Middle Dutch jangelen to whine, complain] > ˈjangler n

Janiculum (dʒəˈnɪkjʊləm) n a hill in Rome across the River Tiber from the Seven Hills

Janina (ˈjaniːna) n the Serbian name for **Ioánnina**

janissary (ˈdʒænɪsərɪ) or **janizary** (ˈdʒænɪzərɪ) n, pl -saries or -zaries an infantryman in the Turkish army, originally a member of the sovereign's personal guard, from the 14th to the early 19th century [c16: from French janissaire, from Italian giannizzero, from Turkish yeniçeri, from yeni new + çeri soldiery]

janitor (ˈdʒænɪtə) n 1 Scot, US & Canadian the caretaker of a building, esp a school 2 chiefly US & Canadian a person employed to clean and maintain a building, esp the public areas in a block of flats or office building; porter [c17: from Latin: doorkeeper, from jānua door, entrance, from jānus covered way (compare JANUS); related to Latin īre to go] > janitorial (ˌdʒænɪˈtɔːrɪəl) adj

Janjaweed or **Janjawid** (ˈdʒænˌdʒəwɪd) n an armed tribal militia group in the Darfur region of western Sudan [Arabic: a man with a horse and a gun]

Jan Mayen (ˈjæn ˈmaɪən) n an island in the Arctic Ocean, between Iceland and N Norway: volcanic, with large glaciers; former site of Dutch whaling stations; annexed to Norway in 1929. Area: 373 sq km (144 sq miles)

Jansen (ˈdʒænsən) n Cornelis (kɔːˈniːlɪs). Latin name Cornelius Jansenius. 1585–1638, Dutch Roman Catholic theologian. In Augustinus (1640) he defended the teachings of St Augustine, esp on free will, grace, and predestination

Jansenism (ˈdʒænsəˌnɪzəm) n RC Church the doctrine of the Dutch Roman Catholic theologian Cornelis Jansen (1585–1638), and his disciples, who maintained that salvation was limited to those subject to a supernatural determinism, the rest being destined to perdition > ˈJansenist n, adj > Jansenˈistic or ˈJansenˌistical adj

jansky (ˈdʒænskɪ) n, pl -skys a unit of flux density equal to 10^{-26} W m^{-2} Hz^{-1}, used predominantly in radio and infrared astronomy [c20: named after Karl Guthe Jansky (1905–50), US electrical engineer]

Jansky (ˈdʒænskɪ) n Karl Guthe 1905–50, US electrical engineer. He discovered a source of radio waves outside the solar system (1932) and pioneered radio astronomy

January (ˈdʒænjʊərɪ) n, pl -aries the first month of the year, consisting of 31 days [c14: from Latin Jānuārius, from adj: (month) of JANUS]

Janus (ˈdʒeɪnəs) n the Roman god of doorways, passages, and bridges. In art he is depicted with two heads facing opposite ways [c16: from Latin, from jānus archway]

Jap. abbreviation Japan(ese)

japan (dʒəˈpæn) n 1 a glossy durable black lacquer originally from the Orient, used on wood, metal, etc 2 work decorated and varnished in the Japanese manner ▷ vb -pans, -panning, -panned 3 (tr) to lacquer with japan or any similar varnish

Japan (dʒəˈpæn) n an archipelago and empire in E Asia, extending for 3200 km (2000 miles) between the Sea of Japan and the Pacific and consisting of the main islands of Hokkaido, Honshu, Shikoku, and Kyushu and over 3000 smaller islands: feudalism abolished in 1871, followed by industrialization and expansion of territories, esp during World Wars I and II, when most of SE Asia came under Japanese control; dogma of the emperor's divinity abolished in 1946 under a new democratic constitution; rapid economic growth has made Japan the most industrialized nation in the Far East. Official language: Japanese. Religion: Shintoist majority, large Buddhist minority. Currency: yen. Capital: Tokyo. Pop: 127 799 000 (2004 est). Area: 369 660 sq km (142 726 sq miles). Japanese names: Nippon, Nihon

Japan Current n a warm ocean current flowing northeastwards off the E coast of Japan towards the North Pacific. Also called: Kuroshio

Japanese (ˌdʒæpəˈniːz) adj 1 of, relating to, or characteristic of Japan, its people, or their language ▷ n 2 pl -nese a native or inhabitant of Japan or a descendant of one 3 the official language of Japan: the native language of approximately 100 million people: considered by some scholars to be part of the Altaic family of languages

Japanese stranglehold n a wrestling hold in which an opponent's wrists are pulled to cross his arms in front of his own neck and exert pressure on his windpipe

jape (dʒeɪp) n 1 a jest or joke ▷ vb 2 to joke or jest (about) [c14: perhaps from Old French japper to bark, yap, of imitative origin] > ˈjaper n > ˈjapery n

Japheth (ˈdʒeɪfɛθ) n Old Testament the second son of Noah, traditionally regarded as the ancestor of a number of non-Semitic nations (Genesis 10:1–5)

Japlish (ˈdʒæplɪʃ) n the adoption and adaptation of English words into the Japanese language [c20: from a blend of JAPANESE + ENGLISH]

japonica (dʒəˈpɒnɪkə) n 1 Also called: Japanese quince, flowering quince a Japanese rosaceous shrub, Chaenomeles japonica, cultivated for its red flowers and yellowish fruit 2 another name for the **camellia** [c19: from New Latin, feminine of japonicus Japanese, from Japonia JAPAN]

Japurá (Portuguese ʒapuˈra) n a river in NW South America, rising in SW Colombia and flowing southeast across Colombia and Brazil to join the Amazon near Tefé: known as the Caquetá in Colombia. Length: about 2800 km (1750 miles). Spanish name: Yapurá

Jaques-Dalcroze (French ʒakdalkroz) n Émile (emil). 1865–1950, Swiss composer and teacher: invented eurythmics

jar¹ (dʒɑː) n 1 a wide-mouthed container that is usually cylindrical, made of glass or earthenware, and without handles 2 Also called: jarful the contents or quantity contained in a jar 3 Brit informal a glass of alcoholic drink, esp beer [c16: from Old French jarre, from Old Provençal jarra, from Arabic jarrah large earthen vessel]

jar² (dʒɑː) vb jars, jarring, jarred 1 to vibrate or cause to vibrate 2 to make or cause to make a harsh discordant sound 3 (often foll by on) to have a disturbing or painful effect (on the nerves, mind, etc) 4 (intr) to disagree; clash ▷ n 5 a jolt or shock 6 a harsh discordant sound [c16: probably of imitative origin; compare Old English cearran to creak] > ˈjarring adj > ˈjarringly adv

jar³ (dʒɑː) n on a jar or on the jar (of a door) slightly open; ajar [C17 (in the sense: turn): from earlier char, from Old English cierran to turn; see AJAR]

jardinière (ˌʒɑːdɪˈnjɛə) n 1 an ornamental pot or trough for plants 2 a garnish of fresh vegetables, cooked, diced, and served around a dish of meat [c19: from French, feminine of *jardinier* gardener, from *jardin* GARDEN]

jargon ('dʒɑːgən) *n* **1** specialized language concerned with a particular subject, culture, or profession **2** language characterized by pretentious syntax, vocabulary, or meaning **3** gibberish [c14: from Old French, perhaps of imitative origin; see GARGLE]

jarhead ('dʒɑːˌhɛd) *n* *US military slang* a member of the United States Marine Corps [c20: so called because of their distinctive haircut]

jarl (jɑːl) *n* *medieval history* a Scandinavian chieftain or noble [c19: from Old Norse; see EARL] > 'jarldom *n*

Jarman ('jɑːmən) *n* **Derek.** 1942–94, British film director and writer; his films include *Jubilee* (1977), *Caravaggio* (1986), and *Wittgenstein* (1993)

jarrah ('dʒærə) *n* a widely planted Australian eucalyptus tree, *Eucalyptus marginata*, that yields a valuable timber [from a native Australian language]

Jarrett ('dʒærɪt) *n* **Keith** born 1945, US jazz pianist and composer

Jarrow ('dʒærəʊ) *n* a port in NE England, in South Tyneside unitary authority, Tyne and Wear: ruined monastery where the Venerable Bede lived and died; its unemployed marched on London in the 1930s; shipyards, oil installations, iron and steel works. Pop: 27 526 (2001)

Jarry (*French* ʒari) *n* **Alfred** (alfrɛd). 1873–1907, French dramatist and poet, who anticipated the theatre of the absurd with his play *Ubu Roi* (1896)

Jaruzelski (*Polish* jaruːˈʒɛlski) *n* **Wojciech** ('vɔɪtʃɛk). born 1923, Polish statesman and soldier; prime minister (1981–85); head of state 1985–90 (as president from 1989)

Jas. *abbreviation* James

jasmine ('dʒæsmɪn, 'dʒæz-) *n* **1** Also called: **jessamine** any oleaceous shrub or climbing plant of the tropical and subtropical genus *Jasminum*, esp *J. officinalis*: widely cultivated for their white, yellow, or red fragrant flowers, which are used in making perfume and in flavouring tea **2** any of several other fragrant shrubs with fragrant flowers, such as the Cape jasmine, yellow jasmine, and frangipani (**red jasmine**) [c16: from Old French *jasmin*, from Arabic *yāsamīn*, from Persian *yāsmīn*]

Jason ('dʒeɪsᵊn) *n* *Greek myth* the hero who led the Argonauts in quest of the Golden Fleece. He became the husband of Medea, whom he later abandoned for Glauce

jaspé ('dʒæspeɪ) *adj* resembling jasper; variegated [c19: from French, from *jasper* to marble]

jasper ('dʒæspə) *n* **1** an opaque impure microcrystalline form of quartz, red, yellow, brown, or dark green in colour, used as a gemstone and for ornamental decoration **2** Also called: **jasper ware** a dense hard stoneware, invented in 1775 by Wedgwood, capable of being stained throughout its substance with metallic oxides and used as background for applied classical decoration [c14: from Old French *jaspe*, from Latin *jaspis*, from Greek *iaspis*, of Semitic origin; related to Assyrian *ashpū*, Arabic *yashb*, Hebrew *yāshpheh*]

Jasper National Park ('dʒæspə) *n* a national park in SW Canada, in W Alberta in the Rockies: wildlife sanctuary. Area: 10 900 sq km (4200 sq miles)

Jaspers (*German* 'jaspərs) *n* **Karl** (karl). 1883–1969, German existentialist philosopher

Jassy ('jasi) *n* the German name for **Iaşi**

jato ('dʒeɪtəʊ) *n, pl* **-tos** *aeronautics* jet-assisted takeoff [C20 *j(et-)a(ssisted) t(ake)o(ff)*]

jaundice ('dʒɔːndɪs) *n* **1** Also called: **icterus** yellowing of the skin and whites of the eyes due to the abnormal presence of bile pigments in the blood, as in hepatitis **2** a mental state of bitterness, jealousy, and ill humour resulting in distorted judgment ▷ *vb* **3** to distort (the judgment, etc) adversely: *jealousy had jaundiced his mind* **4** to affect with or as if with jaundice [c14: from Old French *jaunisse*, from *jaune* yellow, from Latin *galbinus* yellowish, from *galbus*] > 'jaundiced *adj*

jaunt (dʒɔːnt) *n* **1** a short pleasurable excursion; outing ▷ *vb* **2** (*intr*) to go on such an excursion [c16: of unknown origin]

jaunty ('dʒɔːntɪ) *adj* **-tier, -tiest** **1** sprightly, self-confident, and cheerful; brisk: *a jaunty step* **2** smart; trim: *a jaunty hat* [c17: from French *gentil* noble; see GENTEEL]

> 'jauntily *adv* > 'jauntiness *n*

Jaurès (*French* ʒɔrɛs) *n* **Jean Léon** (ʒɑ̃ leɔ̃). 1859–1914, French politician and writer, who founded the socialist paper *l'Humanité* (1904), and united the French socialist movement into a single party (1905); assassinated

Java¹ ('dʒɑːvə) *n* an island of Indonesia, south of Borneo, from which it is separated by the **Java Sea**: politically the most important island of Indonesia; it consists chiefly of active volcanic mountains and is densely forested. It came under Dutch control in 1596 and became part of Indonesia in 1949. It is one of the most densely populated areas in the world. Capital: Jakarta. Pop (with Madura): 121 352 608 (2000 est). Area: 132 174 sq km (51 032 sq miles) > 'Javan *adj, n*

Java² ('dʒɑːvə) *n* *trademark* a programming language especially applicable to the World Wide Web [c20: named after *Java* coffee, said to be consumed in large quantities by the language's creators]

Java man *n* a type of primitive man, *Homo erectus* (formerly called *Pithecanthropus erectus*), that lived in the middle Palaeolithic Age in Java

Javanese (ˌdʒɑːvəˈniːz) *adj* **1** of, relating to, or characteristic of Java, its people, or the Javanese language ▷ *n* **2** *pl* **-nese** a native or inhabitant of Java **3** a Malayo-Polynesian language of Central and Eastern Java

Javari *or* **Javary** (*Portuguese* ʒavaˈri) *n* a river in South America, flowing northeast as part of the border between Peru and Brazil to join the Amazon. Length: about 1050 km (650 miles). Spanish name: Yavarí

javelin ('dʒævlɪn) *n* **1** a long pointed spear thrown as a weapon or in competitive field events **2** the javelin the event or sport of throwing the javelin [c16: from Old French *javeline*, variant of *javelot*, of Celtic origin]

javelin fish *n* a fish of the genus *Pomadasys* of semitropical Australian seas with a long spine on its anal fin

jaw (dʒɔː) *n* **1** the part of the skull of a vertebrate that frames the mouth and holds the teeth. In higher vertebrates it consists of the **upper jaw** (maxilla) fused to the cranium and the **lower jaw** (mandible) **2** the corresponding part of an invertebrate, esp an insect **3** a pair or either of a pair of hinged or sliding components of a machine or tool designed to grip an object **4** *slang* **a** impudent talk; cheek **b** idle conversation; chat **c** moralizing talk; a lecture ▷ *vb* **5** (*intr*) *slang* **a** to talk idly; chat; gossip **b** to lecture [c14: probably from Old French *joue* cheek; related to Italian *gota* cheek]

Jawara ('dʒɑːwərə) *n* **Sir Dawda** ('dɔːdə). born 1924, Gambian statesman; president of The Gambia (1970–94); overthrown in a military coup

jawbone ('dʒɔːˌbəʊn) *n* a nontechnical name for **mandible** or (less commonly) **maxilla**

jawbreaker ('dʒɔːˌbreɪkə) *n* **1** Also called: **jawcrusher** a device having hinged jaws for crushing rocks and ores **2** *informal* a word that is hard to pronounce

> 'jaw,breaking *adj*

jaw-dropping *adj* *informal* amazing > 'jaw-,droppingly *adv*

ja well no fine *sentence substitute* *South African* used to indicate reluctant acceptance

jaws (dʒɔːz) *pl n* **1** the narrow opening of some confined place such as a gorge **2** the jaws a dangerously close position: *the jaws of death*

Jaxartes (dʒækˈsɑːtiːz) *n* the ancient name for **Syr Darya**

jay (dʒeɪ) *n* **1** any of various passerine birds of the family Corvidae (crows), esp the Eurasian *Garrulus glandarius*, with a pinkish-brown body, blue-and-black wings, and a black-and-white crest **2** a foolish or gullible person [c13: from Old French *jai*, from Late Latin *gāius*, perhaps from proper name *Gāius*]

Jay (dʒeɪ) *n* **John** 1745–1829, American statesman, jurist, and diplomat; first chief justice of the Supreme Court (1789–95). He negotiated the treaty with Great Britain (**Jay's treaty**, 1794), that settled outstanding disputes

Jaya ('dʒɑːjə) *n* **Mount Jaya** a mountain in E Indonesia, in Papua (formerly Irian Jaya) in the Sudirman Range: the highest mountain in New Guinea. Height: 5039 m (16 532 ft). Former name: Sukarno Peak

Jayapura (ˌdʒɑːjɑːˈpʊərə) *n* a port in NE Indonesia,

capital of Papua (formerly Irian Jaya), on the N coast. Pop: 155 548 (2000). Former names: Sukarnapura, Kotabaru, Hollandia

Jayawardene (ˌdʒeɪəˈwɑːdɪnə) *n* **Junius Richard.** 1906–96, Sri Lankan statesman; prime minister (1977–78) and first president of Sri Lanka (1978–89)

Jaycee (ˈdʒeɪˈsiː) *n* *Austral, NZ, US & Canadian* a young person who belongs to a junior chamber of commerce [c20: from the initials of J(unior) C(hamber), short for *United States Junior Chamber of Commerce*]

jaywalk (ˈdʒeɪˌwɔːk) *vb* (*intr*) to cross or walk in a street recklessly or illegally [c20: from JAY (sense 2)] > ˈjayˌwalker *n* > ˈjayˌwalking *n*

jazz (dʒæz) *n* **1 a** a kind of music of African-American origin, characterized by syncopated rhythms, solo and group improvisation, and a variety of harmonic idioms and instrumental techniques. It exists in a number of styles **b** (*as modifier*): *a jazz band* **c** (*in combination*): *a jazzman* **2** *slang* rigmarole; paraphernalia: *legal papers and all that jazz* ▷ *vb* **3** (*intr*) to play or dance to jazz music [c20: of unknown origin] > ˈjazzy *adj* > ˈjazzily *adv* > ˈjazziness *n*

jazzed (dʒæzd) *adj* *US & Canadian slang* excited or delighted

jazz up *vb* (*tr, adverb*) *informal* **1** to imbue (a piece of music) with jazz qualities, esp by improvisation or a quicker tempo **2** to make more lively, gaudy, or appealing

J.C. *abbreviation for* **1** Jesus Christ **2** Julius Caesar

JCB *n trademark* a type of construction machine with a hydraulically operated shovel on the front and an excavator arm on the back [named from the initials of J(oseph) C(yril) B(amford) (1916–2001), its English manufacturer]

jealous (ˈdʒɛləs) *adj* **1** suspicious or fearful of being displaced by a rival **2** (often *postpositive* and foll by *of*) resentful (of) or vindictive (towards), esp through envy **3** (often *postpositive* and foll by *of*) possessive and watchful in the maintenance or protection (of) **4** characterized by or resulting from jealousy **5** *obsolete* or *biblical* demanding exclusive loyalty: *a jealous God* [c13: from Old French *gelos*, from Medieval Latin *zēlōsus*, from Late Latin *zēlus* emulation, jealousy, from Greek *zēlos* ZEAL] > ˈjealously *adv*

jealousy (ˈdʒɛləsɪ) *n, pl* -ousies the state or quality of being jealous

jean (dʒiːn) *n* a tough twill-weave cotton fabric used for hard-wearing trousers, overalls, etc [c16: short for *jean fustian*, from *Gene* GENOA]

Jean[1] (*French* ʒɑ̃) *n* **Michaelle.** born 1957, in Haiti. Canadian stateswoman and broadcaster; governor-general from 2005

Jean[2] (*French* ʒɑ̃) *n* born 1921, grand duke of Luxembourg from 1964

Jean de Meung (*French* ʒɑ̃ də mœ̃) *n* real name *Jean Clopinel.* ?1250–?1305, French poet, who continued Guillaume de Lorris' *Roman de la Rose.* His portion of the poem consists of some 18 000 lines and contains satirical attacks on women and the Church

Jeanne d'Arc (ʒɑn dark) *n* the French name of **Joan of Arc**

Jean Paul (*French* ʒɑ̃ pɔl) *n* real name *Johann Paul Friedrich Richter.* 1763–1825, German novelist

jeans (dʒiːnz) *pl n* informal trousers for casual wear, made esp of denim or corduroy [plural of JEAN]

Jeans (dʒiːnz) *n* Sir **James Hopwood.** 1877–1946, English astronomer, physicist, and mathematician, best known for his popular books on astronomy. He made important contributions to the kinetic theory of gases and the theory of stellar evolution

Jebel Musa (ˈdʒɛbəl ˈmuːsə) *n* a mountain in NW Morocco, near the Strait of Gibraltar: one of the Pillars of Hercules. Height: 850 m (2790 ft)

Jedda (ˈdʒɛdə) *n* another name for **Jiddah**

jedi or **Jedi** (ˈdʒɛdaɪ) *n* a person who claims to live according to a philosophy based on that of the fictional Jedi, a caste of wizards in the *Star Wars* series of films by George Lucas, US film director

Jeep (dʒiːp) *n trademark* a small military road vehicle with four-wheel drive [c20: probably from the initials GP, for *general purpose* (vehicle)]

jeepers or **jeepers creepers** (ˈdʒiːpəz ˈkriːpəz) *interj* *US & Canadian slang* a mild exclamation of surprise [c20: euphemism for *Jesus*]

jeepney (ˈdʒiːpnɪ) *n* (in the Philippines) a jeep that has been customized and converted into a taxi [c20: from JEEP + JIT(NEY)]

Jeeps (dʒiːps) *n* **Dickie.** born 1931, English Rugby Union footballer: halfback for England (1956–62) and the British Lions (1959–62)

jeer (dʒɪə) *vb* **1** (often foll by *at*) to laugh or scoff (at a person or thing); mock ▷ *n* **2** a remark or cry of derision; gibe; taunt [c16: of unknown origin] > ˈjeerer *n* > ˈjeering *adj, n* > ˈjeeringly *adv*

jeff (dʒɛf) *vb* (*tr*) *Austral slang* **1** to downsize or close down (an organization) **2** to reduce (staff numbers) or dismiss (an employee) **3** to spoil or destroy ruthlessly. ▷ *Also called:* kennett [c20: named after *Jeff Kennett,* former premier of the state of Victoria, Australia]

Jefferies (ˈdʒɛfrɪz) *n* **Richard.** 1848–87, British writer and naturalist, noted for his observation of English country life: his books include *Bevis* (1882) and collections of essays such as *The Open Air* (1885)

Jefferson (ˈdʒɛfəsən) *n* **Thomas.** 1743–1826, US statesman: secretary of state (1790–93); third president (1801–09). He was the chief drafter of the Declaration of Independence (1776), the chief opponent of the centralizing policies of the Federalists under Hamilton, and effected the Louisiana Purchase (1803) > Jeffersonian (ˌdʒɛfəˈsəʊnɪən) *adj, n*

Jefferson City *n* a city in central Missouri, the state capital, on the Missouri River. Pop: 37 550 (2003 est)

Jeffrey (ˈdʒɛfrɪ) *n* **Francis, Lord.** 1773–1850, Scottish judge and literary critic. As editor of the *Edinburgh Review* (1803–29), he was noted for the severity of his criticism of the romantic poets, esp Wordsworth

Jeffreys (ˈdʒɛfrɪz) *n* **George, 1st Baron Jeffreys of Wem.** ?1645–89, English judge, notorious for his brutality at the "Bloody Assizes" (1685), where those involved in Monmouth's rebellion were tried

jehad (dʒɪˈhæd) *n* a variant spelling of **jihad**

Jehol (dʒəˈhɒl) *n* **1** a former province of NE China, north of the Great Wall: divided among Hebei, Liaoning, and Inner Mongolia in 1956. Area: 192 380 sq km (74 278 sq miles) **2** a region of NE China, in Hebei and Liaoning provinces: mountainous

Jehoshaphat (dʒɪˈhɒʃəˌfæt, -ˈhɒs-) *n* *Old Testament* **1** the king of Judah (?873–?849 BC) (I Kings 22:41–50) **2** the site of Jehovah's apocalyptic judgment upon the nations (Joel 4:14)

Jehovah (dʒɪˈhəʊvə) *n* *Old Testament* the personal name of God, revealed to Moses on Mount Horeb (Exodus 3) [c16: from Medieval Latin, from Hebrew YHVH: the original vocalization was considered too sacred to be pronounced and the vowels of Eloah (God) were therefore substituted in the Masoretic text, whence Yetto Vah]

Jehovah's Witness *n* a member of a Christian Church of American origin, the followers of which believe that the end of the present world system of government is near, that all other Churches and religions are false or evil, that all war is unlawful, and that the civil law must be resisted whenever it conflicts with their Church's own religious principles

Jehu (ˈdʒiːhjuː) *n* **1** *Old Testament* the king of Israel (?842–?815 BC); the slayer of Jezebel (II Kings 9:11–30) **2** a fast driver, esp one who is reckless (from the phrase **to drive like Jehu.** II Kings 9:20)

jejune (dʒɪˈdʒuːn) *adj* **1** simple; naive; unsophisticated **2** insipid; dull; dry **3** lacking nourishment; insubstantial or barren [c17: from Latin *jējūnus* hungry, empty] > jeˈjunely *adv* > jeˈjuneness *or* jeˈjunity *n*

jejunum (dʒɪˈdʒuːnəm) *n* the part of the small intestine between the duodenum and the ileum [c16: from Latin, from *jējūnus* empty; from the belief that the jejunum is empty after death]

Jekyll (ˈdʒɛkəl) *n* **Gertrude.** 1843–1932, British landscape gardener: noted for her simplicity of design and use of indigenous plants

Jekyll and Hyde (ˈdʒɛkəl, haɪd) *n* **a** a person with two distinct personalities, one good, the other evil **b** (as modifier): a Jekyll-and-Hyde personality [c19: after the principal character of Robert Louis Stevenson's novel *The Strange Case of Dr Jekyll and Mr Hyde* (1886)]

jell or **gel** (dʒɛl) vb **jells, jelling, jelled** or **gels, gelling, gelled 1** to make or become gelatinous; congeal **2** (intr) to assume definite form: his ideas have jelled [c19: back formation from JELLY¹]

jellaba or **jellabah** ('dʒɛləbə) n variant spellings of **djellaba** [from Arabic jallabah]

Jellicoe ('dʒɛlɪ,kəʊ) n **John Rushworth**, 1st Earl Jellicoe. 1859–1935, British admiral, who commanded the Grand Fleet at the Battle of Jutland (1916), which incapacitated the German fleet for the rest of World War I

jellies ('dʒɛlɪz) pl n **1** Brit slang gelatine capsules of temazepam, dissolved and injected as a recreational drug **2** Also called: **jelly shoes** shoes made from brightly coloured transparent plastic [c20: shortened from GELATINE]

jellify ('dʒɛlɪ,faɪ) vb **-fies, -fying, -fied** to make into or become jelly > jellifiˈcation n

jelly¹ ('dʒɛlɪ) n, pl **-lies 1** a fruit-flavoured clear dessert set with gelatine **2** a preserve made from the juice of fruit boiled with sugar and used as jam **3** a savoury food preparation set with gelatine or with a strong gelatinous stock and having a soft elastic consistency: calf's-foot jelly ▷ vb **-lies, -lying, -lied 4** to jellify [c14: from Old French gelee frost, jelly, from gel to set hard, from Latin gelāre, from gelu frost] > 'jelly-,like adj > 'jellied adj

jelly² ('dʒɛlɪ) n Brit a slang name for **gelignite**

jelly baby n Brit a small sweet made from a gelatinous substance formed to resemble a baby in shape

jellyfish ('dʒɛlɪ,fɪʃ) n, pl **-fish** or **-fishes 1** any marine medusoid coelenterate of the class Scyphozoa, having a gelatinous umbrella-shaped body with trailing tentacles **2** informal a weak indecisive person

jelly fungus n a member of any of three orders (Auriculariales, Tremellales, and Dacrymycetales) of basidiomycetous fungi that grow on trees and have a jelly-like consistency when wet. They include the conspicuous **yellow brain fungus** (Tremella mesenterica), the black **witch's butter** (Exidia plana), and the pinky-red **jew's-ear** (Auricularia auricula-judae)

Jemappes (French ʒəmap) n a town in SW Belgium, in Hainaut province west of Mons: scene of a battle (1792) during the French Revolutionary Wars, in which the French defeated the Austrians

jemmy ('dʒɛmɪ) or US **jimmy** n, pl **-mies 1** a short steel crowbar used, esp by burglars, for forcing doors and windows ▷ vb **-mies, -mying, -mied 2** (tr) to prise (something) open with a jemmy [c19: from the pet name for James]

Jena (German 'jeːna) n a city in E central Germany, in Thuringia: university (1558), at which Hegel and Schiller taught; site of the battle (1806) in which Napoleon Bonaparte defeated the Prussians; optical and precision instrument industry. Pop: 102 634 (2003 est)

Jenghis Khan ('dʒɛŋgɪs 'kaːn) n See **Genghis Khan**

Jenkins ('dʒɛŋkɪnz) n **Roy (Harris)**, Baron Jenkins of Hillhead. 1920–2003, British statesman and author; Labour home secretary (1965–67, 1974–76) and chancellor of the exchequer (1967–70); president of the European Commission (1977–80); cofounder of the Social Democratic Party (1981); leader of party (1982–83); Chancellor of Oxford University (1987–2003)

Jenner ('dʒɛnə) n **1 Edward** 1749–1823, English physician, who discovered vaccination by showing that injections of cowpox virus produce immunity against smallpox (1796) **2 Sir William**. 1815–98, English physician and pathologist, who differentiated between typhus and typhoid fevers (1849)

jennet, genet or **gennet** ('dʒɛnɪt) n a small Spanish riding horse [c15: from Old French genet, from Catalan ginet, horse of the type used by the Zenete, from Arabic Zanātah the Zenete, a Moorish people renowned for their horsemanship]

jenny ('dʒɛnɪ) n, pl **-nies 1** a hand-operated machine for turning up the edge of a piece of sheet metal in preparation for making a joint **2** the female of certain

animals or birds, esp a donkey, ass, or wren **3** short for **spinning jenny 4** billiards, snooker an in-off [c17: from the name Jenny, diminutive of Jane]

Jensen (Danish 'jɛnsən) n **Johannes Vilhelm** (jo'hanəs 'vɪlhɛlm). 1873–1950, Danish novelist, poet, and essayist: best known for his novel sequence about the origins of mankind The Long Journey (1908–22). Nobel prize for literature 1944

jeopardize or **jeopardise** ('dʒɛpə,daɪz) vb (tr) **1** to risk; hazard: he jeopardized his job by being persistently unpunctual **2** to put in danger; imperil

jeopardy ('dʒɛpədɪ) n (usually preceded by in) **1** danger of injury, loss, death, etc; risk; peril; hazard: his health was in jeopardy **2** law danger of being convicted and punished for a criminal offence [c14: from Old French jeu parti, literally: divided game, hence uncertain issue, from jeu game, from Latin jocus joke, game + partir to divide, from Latin partīrī]

Jephthah ('dʒɛfθə) n Old Testament a judge of Israel, who sacrificed his daughter in fulfilment of a vow (Judges 11:12–40)

jequirity or **jequerity** (dʒɪ'kwɪrɪtɪ) n, pl **-ties 1** other names for **Indian liquorice 2** the seed of the Indian liquorice [c19: from Portuguese jequirití, from Tupi-Guarani jekirití]

Jer. abbreviation Bible Jeremiah

jerbil ('dʒɜːbɪl) n a variant spelling of **gerbil**

jerboa (dʒɜː'bəʊə) n any small nocturnal burrowing rodent of the family Dipodidae, inhabiting dry regions of Asia and N Africa, having pale sandy fur, large ears, and long hind legs specialized for jumping [c17: from New Latin, from Arabic yarbū']

jeremiad (,dʒɛrɪ'maɪəd) n a long mournful lamentation or complaint

Jeremiah (,dʒɛrɪ'maɪə) n **1** Old Testament **a** a major prophet of Judah from about 626 to 587 BC **b** the book containing his oracles **2** a person who habitually prophesies doom or denounces contemporary society

jerepigo (,dʒɛrə'piːgəʊ) n South African a usually red heavy dessert wine [from Portuguese geropiga]

Jerez (Spanish xe'rɛθ) n a town in SW Spain: famous for the making of sherry. Pop: 191 002 (2003 est). Former name: Xeres

Jericho ('dʒɛrɪ,kəʊ) n a town in the West Bank near the N end of the Dead Sea, 251 m (825 ft) below sea level: on the site of an ancient city, the first place to be taken by the Israelites under Joshua after entering the Promised Land in the 14th century BC (Joshua 6)

jerk¹ (dʒɜːk) vb **1** to move or cause to move with an irregular or spasmodic motion **2** to throw, twist, pull, or push (something) abruptly or spasmodically **3** (tr; often foll by out) to utter (words, sounds, etc) in a spasmodic, abrupt, or breathless manner ▷ n **4** an abrupt or spasmodic movement **5** an irregular jolting motion: the car moved with a jerk **6** Also called: **physical jerks** (plural) Brit informal physical exercises **7** slang, chiefly US & Canadian a person regarded with contempt, esp a stupid or ignorant person [c16: probably variant of yerk to pull stitches tight in making a shoe; compare Old English gearcian to make ready] > 'jerker n

jerk² (dʒɜːk) vb (tr) **1** to preserve (venison, beef, etc) by cutting into thin strips and curing by drying in the sun ▷ n **2** Also called: **jerky** jerked meat, esp beef [c18: back formation from jerky, from CHARQUI]

jerkin ('dʒɜːkɪn) n **1** a sleeveless and collarless short jacket worn by men or women **2** a man's sleeveless and collarless fitted jacket, often made of leather, worn in the 16th and 17th centuries [c16: of unknown origin]

jerk off or US **jack off** vb (adverb often reflexive) slang (of a male) to masturbate

jerky ('dʒɜːkɪ) adj **jerkier, jerkiest** characterized by jerks; spasmodic > 'jerkily adv > 'jerkiness n

jeroboam (,dʒɛrə'bəʊəm) n a wine bottle holding the equivalent of four normal bottles (approximately 104 ounces) [c19: humorous allusion to JEROBOAM (sense 1), described as a "mighty man of valour" (I Kings 11:28) who "made Israel to sin" (I Kings 14:16)]

Jeroboam (,dʒɛrə'bəʊəm) n Old Testament **1** the first king of the northern kingdom of Israel (?922–?901 BC) **2** king of the northern kingdom of Israel (?786–?746 BC)

Jerome (dʒəˈrəʊm) n 1 Latin name *Eusebius Hieronymus*. ?347–?420 AD, Christian monk and scholar, whose outstanding work was the production of the Vulgate. Feast day: Sept 30 2 **Jerome K(lapka)**. 1859–1927, English humorous writer; author of *Three Men in a Boat* (1889)

jerry (ˈdʒɛrɪ) n, pl -ries Brit an informal word for **chamber pot**

Jerry (ˈdʒɛrɪ) n, pl -ries Brit slang 1 a German, esp a German soldier 2 the Germans collectively

jerry-build vb -builds, -building, -built (tr) to build (houses, flats, etc) badly using cheap materials > ˈjerry-ˌbuilder n

jerry can n a flat-sided can with a capacity of between 4.5 and 5 gallons used for storing or transporting liquids, esp motor fuel: originally a German design adopted by the British Army during World War II [C20: from JERRY]

jersey (ˈdʒɜːzɪ) n 1 a knitted garment covering the upper part of the body 2 a a machine-knitted slightly elastic cloth of wool, silk, nylon, etc, used for clothing b (as modifier): *a jersey suit* 3 a football shirt [C16: from JERSEY, from the woollen sweaters traditionally worn by the fishermen]

Jersey (ˈdʒɜːzɪ) n 1 an island in the English Channel, the largest of the Channel Islands: forms, with two other islands, the bailiwick of Jersey; colonized from Normandy in the 11th century and still officially French-speaking; noted for finance, market gardening, dairy farming, and tourism. Capital: St Helier. Pop: 87 500 (2003 est). Area: 116 sq km (45 sq miles) 2 a breed of dairy cattle producing milk with a high butterfat content, originating from the island of Jersey

Jersey City n an industrial city in NE New Jersey, opposite Manhattan on a peninsula between the Hudson and Hackensack Rivers: part of the Port of New York; site of one of the greatest railway terminals in the world. Pop: 239 097 (2003 est)

Jerusalem (dʒəˈruːsələm) n 1 the de facto capital of Israel (recognition of this has been withheld by the United Nations), situated in the Judaean hills: became capital of the Hebrew kingdom after its capture by David around 1000 BC; destroyed by Nebuchadnezzar of Babylon in 586 BC; taken by the Romans in 63 BC; devastated in 70 AD and 135 AD during the Jewish rebellions against Rome; fell to the Arabs in 637 and to the Seljuk Turks in 1071; ruled by Crusaders from 1099 to 1187 and by the Egyptians and Turks until conquered by the British (1917); centre of the British mandate of Palestine from 1920 to 1948, when the Arabs took the old city and the Jews held the new city; unified after the Six Day War (1967) under the Israelis; the holy city of Jews, Christians, and Muslims. Pop: 693 200 (2003 est) 2 a the New Jerusalem Christianity Heaven b any ideal city

Jerusalem artichoke n 1 a North American sunflower, *Helianthus tuberosus*, widely cultivated for its underground edible tubers 2 the tuber of this plant, which is cooked and eaten as a vegetable [C17: by folk etymology from Italian *girasole articiocco*; see GIRASOL]

Jervis Bay (ˈdʒɑːvɪs) n an inlet of the Pacific in SE Australia, in Jervis Bay Territory on the coast of S New South Wales: regarded for some purposes as part of the Australian Capital Territory: site of the Royal Australian Naval College

Jespersen (ˈjɛspəsᵊn, ˈdʒɛs-) n (**Jens**) **Otto** (**Harry**). 1860–1943, Danish philologist: author of *Modern English Grammar* (1909–31)

jess (dʒɛs) n falconry a short leather strap, one end of which is permanently attached to the leg of a hawk or falcon while the other can be attached to a leash [C14: from Old French *ges*, from Latin *jactus* a throw, from *jacere* to throw] > jessed adj

jessamine (ˈdʒɛsəmɪn) n another name for **jasmine** (sense 1)

Jesse (ˈdʒɛsɪ) n Old Testament the father of David (I Samuel 16)

Jesselton (ˈdʒɛsəltən) n the former name of **Kota Kinabalu**

jessie (ˈdʒɛsɪ) n slang an effeminate, weak, or cowardly

boy or man

jest (dʒɛst) n 1 something done or said for amusement; joke 2 a frivolous mood or attitude; playfulness; fun: *to act in jest* 3 a jeer or taunt 4 an object of derision; laughing stock; butt ▷ vb 5 to act or speak in an amusing, teasing, or frivolous way; joke 6 to make fun of (a person or thing); scoff or mock [C13: variant of GEST] > ˈjesting adj, n ˈjestingly adv

jester (ˈdʒɛstə) n a professional clown employed by a king or nobleman, esp at courts during the Middle Ages

Jesu (ˈdʒiːzjuː) n a poetic name for or vocative form of **Jesus** [C17: from Late Latin, vocative of JESUS]

Jesuit (ˈdʒɛzjʊɪt) n 1 a member of a Roman Catholic religious order (the **Society of Jesus**) founded by the Spanish ecclesiastic Saint Ignatius Loyola (1491–1556) in 1534 with the aims of defending the papacy and Catholicism against the Reformation and to undertake missionary work among the heathen 2 (sometimes not capital) informal, offensive a person given to subtle and equivocating arguments; casuist [C16: from New Latin *Jēsuita*, from Late Latin *Jēsus* + -ita -ITE¹] > Jesuˈitic or Jesuˈitical adj

Jesus (ˈdʒiːzəs) n 1 Also called: Jesus Christ, Jesus of Nazareth ?4 BC–?29 AD, founder of Christianity, born in Bethlehem and brought up in Nazareth as a Jew. He is believed by Christians to be the Son of God and to have been miraculously conceived by the Virgin Mary, wife of Joseph. With 12 disciples, he undertook two missionary journeys through Galilee, performing miracles, teaching, and proclaiming the coming of the Kingdom of God. After the Last Supper with his disciples, he was betrayed by Judas and crucified. He is believed by Christians to have risen from his tomb after three days, appeared to his disciples several times, and ascended to Heaven after 40 days ▷ interj Also: Jesus wept 2 taboo, slang used to express intense surprise, etc [via Latin from Greek *Iēsous*, from Hebrew *Yeshūa'*, shortened from *Yehōshūa'* God is help, JOSHUA]

Jesus freak n informal a member of any of various Christian groups that combine a hippy communal way of life with zealous evangelicalism

jet¹ (dʒɛt) n 1 a thin stream of liquid or gas forced out of a small aperture or nozzle 2 an outlet or nozzle for emitting such a stream 3 a jet-propelled aircraft ▷ vb jets, jetting, jetted 4 to issue or cause to issue in a jet: *water jetted from the hose; he jetted them with water* 5 to transport or be transported by jet aircraft [C16: from Old French *jeter* to throw, from Latin *jactāre* to toss about, frequentative of *jacere* to throw]

jet² (dʒɛt) n a a hard black variety of coal that takes a brilliant polish and is used for jewellery, ornaments, etc b (as modifier): *jet earrings* [C14: from Old French *jaiet*, from Latin *gagātēs*, from Greek *lithos gagatēs* stone of Gagai, a town in Lycia, Asia Minor]

jet black n a a deep black colour b (as adjective): *jet-black hair*

jet boat n NZ a power boat that is powered and steered by a jet of water under pressure

jeté (ʒəˈteɪ) n ballet a step in which the dancer springs from one leg and lands on the other [French, literally: thrown, from *jeter*; see JET¹]

jet engine n a gas turbine, esp one fitted to an aircraft

jetfoil (ˈdʒɛtˌfɔɪl) n a type of hydrofoil that is propelled by water jets [C20: from a blend of JET¹ + (HYDRO)FOIL]

Jethro (ˈdʒɛθrəʊ) n Old Testament a Midianite priest, the father-in-law of Moses (Exodus 3:1; 4:18)

jet lag n a general feeling of fatigue and disorientation often experienced by travellers by jet aircraft who cross several time zones in relatively few hours

jet-propelled adj 1 driven by jet propulsion 2 informal very fast

jet propulsion n 1 propulsion by means of a jet of fluid 2 propulsion by means of a gas turbine, esp when the exhaust gases provide the propulsive thrust

jetsam or **jetsom** (ˈdʒɛtsəm) n 1 that portion of the equipment or cargo of a vessel thrown overboard to lighten her, as during a storm. See **flotsam** (sense 1) 2 another word for **flotsam** (sense 2) [C16: shortened from JETTISON]

jet set *n* **a** a rich and fashionable social set the members of which travel widely for pleasure **b** (*as modifier*): *jet-set travellers* ▷ 'jet-ˌsetter *n* ▷ 'jet-ˌsetting *adj*

Jet Ski *n* **1** *trademark* a small self-propelled vehicle for one person resembling a scooter, which skims across water on a flat keel, and is steered by means of handlebars ▷ *vb* jet-ski, -skis, -skiing, -skied *or* -ski'd (*intr; usually not capital*) **2** to ride a Jet Ski ▷ Jet Skier *n* ▷ Jet Skiing *n*

jet stream *n* **1** *meteorol* a narrow belt of high-altitude winds (about 12 000 metres high) moving east at high speeds and having an important effect on frontogenesis **2** the jet of exhaust gases produced by a gas turbine, rocket motor, etc

jettison ('dʒɛtɪsᵊn, -zᵊn) *vb* -sons, -soning, -soned (*tr*) **1** to throw away; abandon: *to jettison old clothes* **2** to throw overboard ▷ *n* **3** another word for **jetsam** (sense 1) [c15: from Old French *getaison*, ultimately from Latin *jactātiō* a tossing about; see JACTATION]

jetton ('dʒɛtᵊn) *n* a counter or token, esp a chip used in such gambling games as roulette [c18: from French *jeton*, from *jeter* to cast up (accounts); see JET¹]

jetty ('dʒɛtɪ) *n, pl* -ties **1** a structure built from a shore out into the water to direct currents or protect a harbour **2** a landing pier; dock [c15: from Old French *jetee* projecting part, literally: something thrown out, from *jeter* to throw; see JET¹]

jeu d'esprit *French* (ʒø dɛspri) *n, pl* jeux d'esprit (ʒø dɛspri) a light-hearted display of wit or cleverness, esp in literature [literally: play of spirit]

Jevons ('dʒɛvᵊnz) *n* **William Stanley**. 1835–82, English economist and logician: introduced the concept of final or marginal utility in *The Theory of Political Economy* (1871)

Jew (dʒuː) *n* **1** a member of the Semitic people who claim descent from the ancient Hebrew people of Israel, are spread throughout the world, and are linked by cultural or religious ties **2** a person whose religion is Judaism [c12: from Old French *juiu*, from Latin *jūdaeus*, from Greek *ioudaios*, from Hebrew *yehūdī*, from *yehūdāh* JUDAH]

jewel ('dʒuːᵊl) *n* **1** a precious or semiprecious stone; gem **2** a person or thing resembling a jewel in preciousness, brilliance, etc **3** a gemstone, often synthetically produced, used as a bearing in a watch **4** a piece of jewellery ▷ *vb* -els, -elling, -elled *or US* -els, -eling, -eled **5** (*tr*) to fit or decorate with a jewel or jewels [c13: from Old French *jouel*, perhaps from *jeu* game, from Latin *jocus*]

jewelfish ('dʒuːᵊlˌfɪʃ) *n, pl* -fish *or* -fishes an African cichlid, *Hemichromis bimaculatus*: a beautifully coloured and popular aquarium fish

jeweller *or US* **jeweler** ('dʒuːᵊlə) *n* a person whose business is the cutting, polishing, or setting of gemstones or the making, repairing, or selling of jewellery

jeweller's rouge *n* a finely powdered form of ferric oxide used as a metal polish

jewellery *or US* **jewelry** ('dʒuːᵊlrɪ) *n* objects that are worn for personal adornment, such as bracelets, rings, necklaces, etc, considered collectively

Jewess ('dʒuːɪs) *n often offensive* a Jewish girl or woman

jewfish ('dʒuːˌfɪʃ) *n, pl* -fish *or* -fishes **1** any of various large dark serranid fishes, as *Mycteroperca bonaci*, of warm or tropical seas **2** *Austral* a large food fish of W Australian waters *Glaucosama hebraicum* [c17: of uncertain origin]

jewie ('dʒuːɪ) *n Austral informal* a jewfish

Jewish ('dʒuːɪʃ) *adj* of, relating to, or characteristic of Jews ▷ 'Jewishly *adv* ▷ 'Jewishness *n*

Jewish Autonomous Region *n* an administrative division of SE Russia, in E Siberia: colonized by Jews in 1928; largely agricultural. Capital: Birobidzhan. Pop: 190 900 (2002). Area: 36 000 sq km (13 895 sq miles). Also called: Birobidzhan, Birobijan

jew lizard *n* another name for **bearded dragon**

Jewry ('dʒʊərɪ) *n, pl* -ries **1 a** Jews collectively **b** the Jewish religion or culture **2** *archaic* (sometimes found in street names in England) a quarter of a town inhabited by Jews

jew's-ear *n* See **jelly fungus**

jew's-harp *n* a musical instrument consisting of a small lyre-shaped metal frame held between the teeth, with a steel tongue plucked with the finger. Changes in pitch are produced by varying the size of the mouth cavities

Jezebel ('dʒɛzəˌbɛl, -bᵊl) *n* **1** *Old Testament* the wife of Ahab, king of Israel: she fostered the worship of Baal and tried to destroy the prophets of Israel (I Kings 18:4–13); she was killed by Jehu (II Kings 9:29–37) **2** (*sometimes not capital*) a shameless or scheming woman

Jezreel ('dʒɛzrɪəl) *n* Plain of Jezreel another name for **Esdraelon**

JFK *abbreviation for* John Fitzgerald Kennedy

Jhabvala ('dʒæb'vɑːlə) *n* **Ruth Prawer**, original name **Ruth Prawer**. born 1927, British writer living in India and the US, born in Germany to Polish parents: author of the Booker-prizewinning novel *Heat and Dust* (1975) and scripts for films by James Ivory

Jhansi ('dʒɑːnsɪ) *n* a city in central India, in SW Uttar Pradesh: scene of a mutiny against the British in 1857. Pop: 383 248 (2001)

Jharkhand ('dʒɑːkɑːnd) *n* a state of NE India, created in 2000 from the S part of Bihar: consists of part of the Chota Nagpur plateau; mineral extraction, including coal and mica. Capital: Ranchi. Pop: 26 909 428 (2001). Area: 74 677 sq km (28 833 sq miles)

Jhelum ('dʒiːləm) *n* a river in Pakistan and Kashmir, rising in W central Kashmir and flowing northwest through the Vale of Kashmir, then southwest into NW Punjab to join the Chenab River: important for irrigation, having the Mangla Dam (Pakistan), completed in 1967. Length: about 720 km (450 miles)

JHVH *or* **JHWH** *n Old Testament* variants of YHVH

-ji (-dziː) *suffix Indian* a suffix placed after a person's name or title as a mark of respect [Hindi]

Jiang Jie Shi ('dʒjæŋ 'dʒjː 'ʃː) *n* See **Chiang Kai-shek**

Jiang Jing Guo ('dʒjæŋ 'dʒɪŋ 'gwəʊ) *n* See **Chiang Ching-kuo**

Jiang Qing ('dʒjæŋ 'tʃɪŋ) *or* **Chiang Ch'ing** *n* 1913–91, Chinese Communist actress and politician; widow of Mao Tse-tung. She was a leading member of the Gang of Four

Jiangsu ('dʒjæŋ'suː) *or* **Kiangsu** *n* a province of E China, on the Yellow Sea: consists mostly of the marshy delta of the Yangtze River, with some of China's largest cities and most densely populated areas. Capital: Nanjing. Pop: 74 060 000 (2003 est). Area: 102 200 sq km (39 860 sq miles)

Jiangxi ('dʒjæŋ'ʃiː) *or* **Kiangsi** *n* a province of SE central China, in the basins of the Kan River and Poyang Lake: mineral resources include coal and tungsten. Capital: Nanchang. Pop: 42 220 000 (2003 est). Area: 164 800 sq km (64 300 sq miles)

Jiang Zemin ('dʒjæŋ ʒeɪ'mɪn) *n* born 1926, Chinese Communist politician: president (1993–2003)

Jiazhou ('dʒjæ'dʒəʊ) *or* **Kiaochow** *n* a territory of NE China, in SE Shandong province, surrounding Jiazhou Bay (an inlet of the Yellow Sea): leased to Germany from 1898 to 1914. Area: about 520 sq km (200 sq miles)

jib¹ (dʒɪb) *n* **1** *nautical* any triangular sail set forward of the foremast of a vessel **2** cut of someone's jib someone's manner, behaviour, style, etc [c17: of unknown origin]

jib² (dʒɪb) *vb* jibs, jibbing, jibbed (*intr*) *chiefly Brit* **1** (often foll by *at*) to be reluctant (to); hold back (from); balk (at) **2** (of an animal) to stop short and refuse to go forwards **3** *nautical* variant of **gybe** [c19: of unknown origin] ▷ 'jibber *n*

jib³ (dʒɪb) *n* the projecting arm of a crane or the boom of a derrick, esp one that is pivoted to enable it to be raised or lowered [c18: probably based on GIBBET]

jib boom *n nautical* a spar forming an extension of the bowsprit

jibe¹ (dʒaɪb), **jib** *or* **jibb** (dʒɪb) *vb, n nautical* variants of **gybe**

jibe² (dʒaɪb) *vb* a variant spelling of **gibe¹**

jibe³ (dʒaɪb) *vb* (*intr*) *informal* to agree; accord; harmonize [c19: of unknown origin]

Jibouti *or* **Jibuti** (dʒɪ'buːtɪ) *n* variant spellings of **Djibouti**

Jiddah ('dʒɪdə) *or* **Jedda** *n* a port in W Saudi Arabia, on the Red Sea: the diplomatic capital of the country; the port of entry for Mecca, 80 km (50 miles) east. Pop: 3 807 000 (2005 est)

jiffy ('dʒɪfɪ) *or* **jiff** (dʒɪf) *n, pl* **jiffies** *or* **jiffs** *informal* a very short time: *wait a jiffy* [c18: of unknown origin]

Jiffy bag *n trademark* a thickly padded but light envelope in which articles such as books are placed for protection in the post

jig (dʒɪg) *n* **1** any of several old rustic kicking and leaping dances **2** a piece of music composed for or in the rhythm of this dance, usually in six-eight time **3** a mechanical device designed to hold and locate a component during machining and to guide the cutting tool **4** *angling* any of various spinning lures that wobble when drawn through the water **5** *Also called:* **jigger** *mining* a device for separating ore or coal from waste material by agitation in water ▷ *vb* **jigs, jigging, jigged 6** to dance (a jig) **7** to jerk or cause to jerk up and down rapidly **8** (often foll by *up*) to fit or be fitted in a jig **9** (*tr*) to drill or cut (a workpiece) in a jig **10** *mining* to separate ore or coal from waste material using a jig [c16 (originally: a dance or the music for it; applied to various modern devices because of the verbal sense: to jerk up and down rapidly): of unknown origin]

Jigawa (ˌdʒɪ'gɑːwə) *n* a state of N Nigeria. Capital: Dutse. Pop: 4 348 649 (2006). Area: 23 154 sq km (8940 sq miles)

jigger¹ ('dʒɪgə) *n* **1** a person or thing that jigs **2** *golf* an iron, now obsolete, with a thin blade, used for hitting long shots from a bare lie **3** any of a number of mechanical devices having a vibratory or jerking motion **4** a light lifting tackle used on ships **5** a small glass, esp for whisky, with a capacity of about one and a half ounces **6** NZ a light hand- or power-propelled vehicle used on railway lines **7** *billiards* another word for **bridge¹** (sense 10)

jigger² *or* **jigger flea** ('dʒɪgə) *n* other names for the **chigoe** (sense 1)

jiggered ('dʒɪgəd) *adj* (*postpositive*) *informal* damned; blowed [c19: probably euphemism for *buggered;* see **BUGGER**]

jiggermast ('dʒɪgəˌmɑːst) *n nautical* any small mast on a sailing vessel, esp the mizzenmast of a yawl

jiggery-pokery ('dʒɪgərɪ'pəʊkərɪ) *n informal, chiefly Brit* dishonest or deceitful behaviour or business; trickery [c19: from Scottish dialect *joukery-pawkery*]

jiggle ('dʒɪgəl) *vb* **1** to move or cause to move up and down or to and fro with a short jerky motion ▷ *n* **2** a short jerky motion [c19: frequentative of JIG; compare JOGGLE] > **'jiggly** *adj*

jigsaw ('dʒɪgˌsɔː) *n* **1** a mechanical saw with a fine steel blade for cutting intricate curves in sheets of material **2** See **jigsaw puzzle** [c19: from JIG (to jerk up and down rapidly) + SAW¹]

jigsaw puzzle *n* a puzzle in which the player has to reassemble a picture that has been mounted on a wooden or cardboard base and cut into a large number of irregularly shaped interlocking pieces

jihad *or* **jehad** (dʒɪ'hæd) *n Islam* a holy war against infidels undertaken by Muslims in defence of the Islamic faith [c19: from Arabic *jihād* a conflict]

jihadi *or* **jehadi** (dʒɪ'hædɪ) *n Islam* **a** a person who takes part in a jihad **b** (*as modifier*): *jihadi groups*

jihadism *or* **jehadism** (dʒɪ'hædˌɪzəm) *n Islam* an Islamic fundamentalist movement that favours the pursuit of jihads in defence of the Islamic faith [c21: Arabic] > **ji'hadist** *or* **je'hadist** *adj, n*

Jilin ('dʒiː'lɪn) *or* **Kirin** (ˌ) *n* **1** a province of NE China, in central Manchuria. Capital: Changchun. Pop: 27 040 000 (2003 est). Area: 187 000 sq km (72 930 sq miles) **2** *Also called:* **Chi-lin** ('tʃiː'lɪn) a river port in NE China, in N central Jilin province on the Songhua River. Pop: 1 496 000 (2005 est)

Jilong ('dʒiː'lʊŋ) *n* the Pinyin transliteration of the Chinese name for: **Chilung**

jilt (dʒɪlt) *vb* **1** (*tr*) to leave or reject (a lover), esp without previous warning ▷ *n* **2** a woman who jilts a lover [c17: from dialect *jillet* flighty girl, diminutive of proper name *Gill*]

jim crow ('dʒɪm 'krəʊ) *n* (*often capitals*) *US* **1 a** the policy or practice of segregating Black people **b** (*as modifier*): jim-

crow laws **2** a derogatory term for a Black person **3** an implement for bending iron bars or rails [c19: from *Jim Crow,* name of song made the basis of an act by Thomas Rice (1808–60), American entertainer] > **'jim-'crowism** *n*

Jiménez (*Spanish* xi'meneθ) *n* **Juan Ramón** (xwan ra'mɔn). 1881–1958, Spanish lyric poet. His most famous work is *Platero y yo* (1917), a prose poem: Nobel prize for literature 1956

Jiménez de Cisneros (*Spanish* xi'meneð ðe θiz'nerɔs) *n* **Francisco** (fran'θisko). 1436–1517, Spanish cardinal and statesman; regent of Castile (1506–07) and Spain (1516–17) and grand inquisitor for Castile and León (1507–17). *Also called:* **Ximenes de Cisneros, Ximenez de Cisneros**

jimjams (ˌdʒɪmˌdʒæmz) *pl n* **1** a slang word for **delirium tremens 2** a state of nervous tension, excitement, or anxiety **3** *informal* pyjamas [c19: whimsical formation based on JAM¹]

jimmy ('dʒɪmɪ) *n, pl* -mies **1** the US word for **jemmy** ▷ *vb* -mies, -mying, -mied **2** the US word for **jemmy**

Jinan ('dʒiː'næn), **Chinan** *or* **Tsinan** *n* an industrial city in NE China, capital of Shandong province; probably over 3000 years old. Pop: 2 654 000 (2005 est)

Jingdezhen ('dʒɪŋ'dedʒen), **Fowliang** *or* **Fou-liang** *n* a city in SE China, in NE Jiangxi province east of Poyang Lake: famous for its porcelain industry, established in the sixth century. Pop: 416 000 (2005 est)

Jinghis Khan ('dʒɪŋgɪs 'kɑːn) *n* See **Genghis Khan**

jingle ('dʒɪŋgəl) *vb* **1** to ring or cause to ring lightly and repeatedly **2** (*intr*) to sound in a manner suggestive of jingling: *a jingling verse* ▷ *n* **3** a sound of metal jingling **4** a catchy and rhythmic verse, song, etc, esp one used in advertising [c16: probably of imitative origin; compare Dutch *jengelen*] > **'jingly** *adj*

jingo ('dʒɪŋgəʊ) *n, pl* -goes **1** a loud and bellicose patriot; chauvinist **2** jingoism **3** *informal* an exclamation of surprise [c17: originally perhaps a euphemism for *Jesus;* applied to bellicose patriots after the use of *by Jingo!* in the refrain of a 19th-century music-hall song]

jingoism ('dʒɪŋgəʊˌɪzəm) *n* the belligerent spirit or foreign policy of jingoes; chauvinism > **'jingoist** *n, adj* > **jingo'istic** *adj*

Jinja ('dʒɪndʒə) *n* a town in Uganda, on the N shore of Lake Victoria. Pop: 86 520 (2002 est)

Jinjiang ('dʒɪn'dʒæŋ) *n* a former spelling of **Zhenjiang**

jink (dʒɪŋk) *vb* **1** to move swiftly or jerkily or make a quick turn in order to dodge or elude ▷ *n* **2** a jinking movement [c18: of Scottish origin, imitative of swift movement]

jinker ('dʒɪŋkə) *n Austral* a vehicle for transporting timber, consisting of a tractor and two sets of wheels for supporting the logs [of unknown origin]

jinks (dʒɪŋks) *pl n* boisterous or mischievous play (esp in the phrase **high jinks**) [c18: of unknown origin]

jinn (dʒɪn) *n* (*often functioning as singular*) the plural of **jinni**

Jinnah ('dʒɪnə) *n* **Mohammed Ali** 1876–1948, Indian Muslim statesman. He campaigned for the partition of India into separate Hindu and Muslim states, becoming first governor general of Pakistan (1947–48)

jinni, jinnee, djinni *or* **djinny** (dʒɪ'niː, 'dʒɪn) *n, pl* **jinn** *or* **djinn** (dʒɪn) a being or spirit in Muslim belief who could assume human or animal form and influence man by supernatural powers [c17: from Arabic]

jinrikisha, jinricksha, jinrickshaw *or* **jinriksha** (dʒɪn'rɪkʃɔː, -ʃə) *n* other names for **rickshaw** [c19: from Japanese, from *jin* man + *riki* power + *sha* carriage]

jinx (dʒɪŋks) *n* **1** an unlucky or malevolent force, person, or thing ▷ *vb* **2** (*tr*) to be or put a jinx on [c20: perhaps from New Latin *Jynx* genus name of the wryneck, from Greek *iunx* wryneck, the name of a bird used in magic]

Jinzhou ('dʒɪn'dʒəʊ), **Chin-Chou** *or* **Chin-chow** *n* a city in NE China, in SW Liaoning province. Pop: 888 000 (2005 est)

JIT *abbreviation* just-in-time

jitter ('dʒɪtə) *informal* ▷ *vb* **1** (*intr*) to be anxious or nervous ▷ *n* **2** the jitters nervousness and anxiety [c20: of unknown origin]

jitterbug ('dʒɪtəˌbʌg) *n* **1** a fast jerky American dance, usually to a jazz accompaniment, that was popular in the 1940s **2** a person who dances the jitterbug ▷ *vb* -bugs, -bugging, -bugged **3** (*intr*) to perform such a dance

jittery ('dʒɪtərɪ) *adj informal* nervous and anxious > 'jitteriness *n*

jiujitsu *or* **jiujutsu** (dʒuː'dʒɪtsuː) *n* variant spellings of **jujitsu**

Jivaro ('hiːvərəu) *n* **1 a** a member of a group of sub-tribes native to the Amazonian forests of Peru and Ecuador, formerly noted for their warlike nature and head-shrinking rituals **b** *as modifier*: *Jivaro rituals* **2** any of the languages spoken by the Jivaro people [C19: from Spanish *jíbaro*, from Shuar *shuar* people]

jive (dʒaɪv) *n* **1** a style of lively and jerky dance performed to jazz and, later, to rock and roll, popular esp in the 1940s and 1950s **2 a** *slang, chiefly US* deliberately misleading or deceptive talk **b** (*as modifier*): *jive talk* ▷ *vb* **3** (*intr*) to dance the jive **4** *slang, chiefly US* to mislead; tell lies (to) [C20: of unknown origin] > 'jiver *n*

Joab ('dʒəuæb) *n Old Testament* the successful commander of King David's forces and the slayer of Abner and Absalom (II Samuel 2:18–23; 3:24–27; 18:14–15)

Joachim *n* **1** ('joːaxɪm) Joseph ('joːzɛf). 1831–1907, Hungarian violinist and composer **2** ('dʒəuəkɪm) **Saint**. 1st century BC, traditionally the father of the Virgin Mary; feast day: July 25 or Sept 9

Joachim of Fiore ('fjɔːreɪ) *n* ?1132–1202 AD, Italian mystic and philosopher, best known for teaching that history can be divided into three ages, those of the Father, Son, and Holy Ghost

Joan (dʒəun) *n* **1** known as *the Fair Maid of Kent*. 1328–85, wife of Edward the Black Prince; mother of Richard II **2 Pope** legendary female pope, first mentioned in the 13th century: said to have been elected while disguised as a man and to have died in childbirth

Joan of Arc *n* **Saint** known as *the Maid of Orléans*; French name *Jeanne d'Arc*. ?1412–31, French national heroine, who led the army that relieved Orléans in the Hundred Years' War, enabling Charles VII to be crowned at Reims (1429). After being captured (1430), she was burnt at the stake as a heretic. She was canonized in 1920. Feast day: May 30

João Pessoa (Portuguese 'ʒuəm pe'soa) *n* a port in NE Brazil, capital of Paraíba state. Pop: 931 000 (2005 est)

job (dʒɒb) *n* **1** an individual piece of work or task **2** an occupation; post of employment **3** an object worked on or a result produced from working **4** a duty or responsibility: *her job was to cook the dinner* **5** *informal* a difficult task or problem: *I had a job to contact him* **6** a state of affairs: *make the best of a bad job; it's a good job I saw you* **7** *informal* a crime, esp a robbery or burglary **8** *informal* an article or specimen: *the new car was a nice little job* **9** *computing* a unit of work for a computer consisting of a single complete task submitted by a user **10** jobs for the boys appointments given to or created for allies or favourites **11** on the job actively engaged in one's employment **12** just the job exactly what was required ▷ *vb* jobs, jobbing, jobbed **13** (*intr*) to work by the piece or at casual jobs **14** to make a private profit out of (a public office, etc) **15** (*intr*; usually foll by *in*) to buy and sell (goods or services) as a middleman: *he jobs in government surplus* **b** *Brit* to buy and sell stocks and shares as a stockjobber [C16: of uncertain origin] > 'jobless *adj*

Job (dʒəub) *n* **1** *Old Testament* **a** a Jewish patriarch, who maintained his faith in God in spite of the afflictions sent by God to test him **b** the book containing Job's pleas to God under these afflictions, attempted explanations of them by his friends, and God's reply to him **2** any person who withstands great suffering without despairing

jobber ('dʒɒbə) *n* **1** *Brit* short for **stockjobber** (sense 1) **2** a person who jobs

jobbery ('dʒɒbərɪ) *n* the practice of making private profit out of a public office; corruption or graft

jobbing ('dʒɒbɪŋ) *adj* working on occasional jobs or by the piece rather than in a regular job: *a jobbing gardener*

Jobcentre ('dʒɒb,sɛntə) *n Brit* any of a number of government offices having premises usually situated in or near the main shopping area of a town in which people seeking jobs can consult displayed advertisements in informal surroundings

Jobclub ('dʒɒb,klʌb) *n* a group of unemployed people organized through a Jobcentre, which meets every day and is given advice on job seeking to increase its members' chances of finding employment

job description *n* a detailed written account, agreed between management and worker, of all the duties and responsibilities which together make up a particular job

job lot *n* **1** a miscellaneous collection of articles sold as a lot **2** a collection of cheap or trivial items

job satisfaction *n* the extent to which a person's hopes, desires, and expectations about the employment he is engaged in are fulfilled

Job's comforter *n* a person who, while purporting to give sympathy, succeeds only in adding to distress

jobseeker's allowance ('dʒɒb,siːkəz) *n* (in Britain) a National Insurance or social security payment for unemployed people; replaced unemployment benefit in 1996. Abbreviation: JSA

job sharing *n* the division of a job between two or more people such that each covers the same job for complementary parts of the day or week > job sharer *n*

jobsworth ('dʒɒbz,wɜːθ) *n informal* a person in a position of minor authority who invokes the letter of the law in order to avoid any action requiring initiative, cooperation, etc [C20: from *it's more than my job's worth to …*]

Joburg ('dʒəu,bɜːg) *n informal* Johannesburg

Jocasta (dʒəu'kæstə) *n Greek myth* a queen of Thebes, the wife of Laius, who married Oedipus without either of them knowing he was her son

Jochum (German 'joxum) *n* Eugen ('ɔygeːn). 1902–87, German orchestral conductor

jock (dʒɒk) *n* **1** *informal* short for **disc jockey 2** *informal* short for **jockstrap**

Jock (dʒɒk) *n* a slang word or term of address for a Scot

jockey ('dʒɒkɪ) *n* **1** a person who rides horses in races, esp as a profession or for hire ▷ *vb* **2 a** (*tr*) to ride (a horse) in a race **b** (*intr*) to ride as a jockey **3** (*intr*; often foll by *for*) to try to obtain an advantage by manoeuvring, esp literally in a race or metaphorically, as in a struggle for power (esp in the phrase *jockey for position*) **4** to trick or cheat (a person) [C16 (in the sense: lad): from name *Jock* + -EY]

jockstrap ('dʒɒk,stræp) *n* an elasticated belt with a pouch worn by men, esp athletes, to support the genitals. Also called: **athletic support** [C20: from slang *jock* penis + STRAP]

jocose (dʒə'kəus) *adj* characterized by humour; merry [C17: from Latin *jocōsus* given to jesting, from *jocus* JOKE] > jo'cosely *adv* > jo'coseness *or* jocosity (dʒə'kɒsɪtɪ) *n*

jocular ('dʒɒkjulə) *adj* **1** characterized by joking and good humour **2** meant lightly or humorously; facetious [C17: from Latin *joculāris*, from *joculus* little JOKE] > jocularity (,dʒɒkju'lærɪtɪ) *n* > 'jocularly *adv*

jocund ('dʒɒkənd) *adj* of a humorous temperament; merry [C14: from Late Latin *jocundus*, from Latin *jūcundus* pleasant, from *juvāre* to please] > jocundity (dʒəu'kʌndɪtɪ) *n* > 'jocundly *adv*

Jodhpur (,dʒɒd'puə) *n* **1** a former state of NW India, one of the W Rajputana states: now part of Rajasthan **2** a walled city in NW India, in W Rajasthan: university (1962). Pop: 846 408 (2001) > Jodhpuri ('dʒɒdpurɪ) *adj*

jodhpurs ('dʒɒdpəz) *pl n* riding breeches, loose-fitting around the hips and tight-fitting from the thighs to the ankles [C19: from the town JODHPUR]

Jodl (German 'jodəl) *n* Alfred ('alfreːt). 1890–1946, German general, largely responsible for German strategy during World War II: executed as a war criminal

Joe Blake *n Austral* **1** *rhyming slang* a snake **2** the Joe Blakes the DT's

Joe Bloggs (blɒgz) *n Brit slang* an average or typical man. US, Canadian and Austral equivalent: Joe Blow See also **Joe Six-Pack**

joe job *n Canadian informal* a dull unrewarding job or task

Joel ('dʒəuəl) *n Old Testament* **1** a Hebrew prophet **2** the book containing his oracles

Joe Public *n slang* the general public

joes (dʒəuz) *pl n* **the joes** *Austral informal* a fit of depression [short for *the Joe Blakes*]

Joe Six-Pack ('sɪks,pæk) *n US slang* an average or typical man

joey ('dʒəʊɪ) *n Austral informal* **1** a young kangaroo or possum **2** a young animal or child [C19: from a native Australian language]

Joffre (French ʒɔfrə) *n* **Joseph Jacques Césaire** (ʒɔzɛf ʒak sezɛr). 1852– 1931, French marshal. He commanded the French army (1914–16) and was largely responsible for the Allies' victory at the Marne (1914), which halted the German advance on Paris

jog (dʒɒg) *vb* **jogs, jogging, jogged 1** (*intr*) to run or move slowly or at a jog trot, esp for physical exercise **2** (*intr; foll by on or along*) to continue in a plodding way **3** (*tr*) to jar or nudge slightly; shake lightly **4** (*tr*) to remind; stimulate: *please jog my memory* ▷ *n* **5** the act of jogging **6** a slight jar or nudge **7** a jogging motion; trot [C14: probably variant of *shog* to shake, influenced by dialect *jot* to jolt]

jogger ('dʒɒgə) *n* **1** a person who runs at a jog trot over some distance for exercise, usually regularly **2** *NZ* a cart with rubber-tyred wheels used on a farm

jogger's nipple *n informal* painful inflammation of the nipple, caused by friction with a garment when running for long distances

jogging ('dʒɒgɪŋ) *n* running at a slow regular pace usually over a long distance as part of an exercise routine

joggle ('dʒɒgəl) *vb* **1** to shake or move (someone or something) with a slightly jolting motion **2** (*tr*) to join or fasten (two pieces of building material) by means of a joggle ▷ *n* **3** the act of joggling **4** a slight irregular shake; jolt **5** a joint between two pieces of building material by means of a projection on one piece that fits into a notch in the other; dowel [C16: frequentative of JOG¹] > **'joggler** *n*

Jogjakarta (,dʒɒʊɡjɑː'kɑːtɑː, ,dʒɒg-) *n* a former spelling of **Yogyakarta**

jog trot *n* **1** an easy bouncy gait, esp of a horse, midway between a walk and a trot **2** a monotonous or regular way of living or doing something

Johannesburg (dʒəʊ'hænɪs,bɜːg) *n* a city in N South Africa; the capital of Gauteng province: South Africa's largest city and chief industrial centre; grew with the establishment in 1886 of the gold-mining industry; University of Witwatersrand (1922). Pop: 1 009 036 (2001)

john (dʒɒn) *n* **1** *chiefly US & Canadian* a slang word for lavatory (sense 1) **2** *slang, chiefly US* a prostitute's client [C20: special use of the proper name]

John (dʒɒn) *n* **1** *New Testament* **a** the apostle John, the son of Zebedee, identified with the author of the fourth Gospel, three epistles, and the book of Revelation. Feast day: Dec 27 or Sept 26 **b** the fourth Gospel **c** any of three epistles (in full **The First, Second,** and **Third Epistles of John**) **2** See **John the Baptist 3** known as *John Lackland*. 1167–1216, king of England (1199–1216); son of Henry II. He succeeded to the throne on the death of his brother Richard I, having previously tried to usurp the throne. War with France led to the loss of most of his French possessions. After his refusal to recognize Stephen Langton as archbishop of Canterbury an interdict was imposed on England (1208–14). In 1215 he was compelled by the barons to grant the Magna Carta **4** called *the Fearless*. 1371–1419, duke of Burgundy (1404–19). His attempt to control the mad king Charles VI and his murder of the king's brother led to civil war: assassinated **5 Augustus** (Edwin). 1878–1961, British painter, esp of portraits **6 Barry** born 1945, Welsh Rugby Union footballer: halfback for Wales (1966–72) and the British Lions (1968–71) **7** Sir **Elton** (**Hercules**). original name *Reginald Dwight*. born 1947, British rock pianist, composer, and singer; his hits include "Goodbye Yellow Brick Road" (1973) and "Candle in the Wind 1997" (1997), a tribute to Diana, Princess of Wales **8 Gwen**, sister of Augustus John. 1876–1939, British painter, working in France: noted esp for her portraits of women

John I *n* **1** surnamed *Tzimisces*. 925–976 AD, Byzantine emperor (969–976): extended Byzantine power into Bulgaria and Syria **2** called *the Great*. 1357–1433, king of

Portugal (1385–1433). He secured independence for Portugal by his victory over Castile (1385) and initiated Portuguese overseas expansion

John II *n* **1** called *the Good*. 1319–64, king of France (1350–64): captured by the English at Poitiers (1356) and forced to sign treaties (1360) surrendering SW France to England **2** called *the Perfect*. 1455–95, king of Portugal (1481–95): sponsored Portuguese expansion in the New World and reduced the power of the aristocracy **3** surnamed *Casimir Vasa*. 1609–72, king of Poland (1648–68), who lost much territory to neighbouring countries: abdicated

John III *n* **1** 1507–57, king of Portugal (1521–57): his reign saw the expansion of the Portuguese empire overseas but the start of economic decline at home **2** surnamed *Sobieski*. 1624–96, king of Poland (1674–96). He raised the Turkish siege of Vienna (1683)

John IV *n* called *the Fortunate*. 1604–56, king of Portugal (1640–56). As duke of Braganza he led a revolt against Spanish rule and became king: lost most of Portugal's Asian possessions to the Dutch

John VI *n* ?1769–1826, king of Portugal (1816–26): recognized the independence of Brazil (1825)

John XXII *n* original name *Jacques Duèse*. ?1244–1334, pope (1316–34), residing at Avignon; involved in a long conflict with the Holy Roman Emperor Louis IV and opposed the Franciscan Spirituals

John XXIII *n* original name *Angelo Giuseppe Roncalli*. 1881–1963, pope (1958–63). He promoted ecumenism and world peace and summoned the second Vatican Council (1962–65)

John Barleycorn *n usually humorous* the personification of alcohol, esp of malt spirits

John Bull *n* **1** a personification of England or the English people **2** a typical Englishman [C18: name of a character intended to be representative of the English nation in *The History of John Bull* (1712) by John Arbuthnot]

John Chrysostom ('krɪsəstəm) *n* Saint. ?345–407 AD, Greek bishop and theologian; one of the Fathers of the Greek Church, noted for his eloquence. Feast day: Sept 13

John Doe *n* See **Doe**

John Dory ('dɔːrɪ) *n* **1 a** a European dory (the fish), *Zeus faber*, having a deep compressed body, spiny dorsal fins, and massive mobile jaws **2** *Austral* a related fish, *Zeus australis*, which is a valued food fish of Australia [C18: from proper name *John* + DORY¹; on the model of DOE]

John Hop *n Austral slang* a policeman [rhyming slang for COP¹]

johnny ('dʒɒnɪ) *n, pl* -nies *Brit* (*often capital*) *informal* a man or boy; chap

Johnny Canuck ('dʒɒnɪ kə'nʌk) *n Canadian* **1** an informal name for a **Canadian 2** a personification of Canada

Johnny-come-lately *n, pl* Johnny-come-latelies *or* Johnnies-come-lately a brash newcomer, novice, or recruit

John of Austria *n* called *Don John*. 1547–78, Spanish general: defeated the Turks at Lepanto (1571)

John of Damascus *n* Saint. ?675–749 AD, Syrian theologian, who defended the veneration of icons and images against the iconoclasts. Feast day: Dec 4

John of Gaunt (gɔːnt) *n* Duke of Lancaster. 1340–99, son of Edward III: virtual ruler of England during the last years of his father's reign and during Richard II's minority [*Gaunt*, variant of GHENT, where he was born]

John of Leyden ('laɪdən) *n* original name *Jan Bockelson*. ?1509–36, Dutch Anabaptist leader. He established a theocracy in Münster (1534) but was tortured to death after the city was recaptured (1535) by its prince bishop

John of Salisbury *n* died 1180, English ecclesiastic and scholar; bishop of Chartres (1176–80). He supported Thomas à Becket against Henry II

John of the Cross *n* Saint. original name *Juan de Yepis y Alvarez*. 1542–91, Spanish Carmelite monk, poet, and mystic. He founded the Discalced Carmelites with Saint Teresa (1568). Feast day: Dec 14

John o'Groats (ə'grəʊts) *n* a village at the northeasternmost tip of the Scottish mainland: considered to be the northernmost point of the mainland of Great Britain although Dunnet Head, slightly to the west, lies further north. See also **Land's End**

John Paul I original name *Albino Luciani*. 1912–78, pope (1978) whose brief 33-day reign was characterized by a simpler papal style and anticipated an emphasis on pastoral rather than administrative priorities

John Paul II *n* original name *Karol Wojtyla*. 1920–2005, pope from 1978, born in Poland: the first non-Italian to be elected since 1522

Johns (dʒɒnz) *n* **1 Andrew (Gary)**. born 1974, Australian Rugby League footballer: halfback for Australia (1995–2006) **2 Jasper**. born 1930, US artist, noted for his collages and constructions

Johnson ('dʒɒnsən) *n* **1 Amy** 1903–41, British aviator, who made several record flights, including those to Australia (1930) and to Cape Town and back (1936) **2 Andrew** 1808–75, US Democrat statesman who was elected vice president under the Republican Abraham Lincoln; 17th president of the US (1865–69), became president after Lincoln's assassination. His lenience towards the South after the American Civil War led to strong opposition from radical Republicans, who tried to impeach him **3 Earvin** ('ɜːvɪn), known as *Magic*. born 1959, US basketball player **4 Eyvind** ('evɪnt). 1900–76, Swedish novelist and writer, whose novels include the *Krilon* trilogy (1941–43): joint winner of the Nobel prize for literature 1974 **5 Jack** 1878–1946, US boxer; world heavyweight champion (1908–15) **6 Lionel (Pigot)** 1867–1902, British poet and critic, best known for his poems "Dark Angel" and "By the Statue of King Charles at Charing Cross" **7 Lyndon Baines** known as *LBJ*. 1908–73, US Democrat statesman; 36th president of the US (1963–69). His administration carried the Civil Rights Acts of 1964 and 1965, but he lost popularity by increasing US involvement in the Vietnam war **8 Martin**. born 1970, English Rugby Union footballer; captain of the England team that won the World Cup in 2003. **9 Michael (Duane)** born 1967, US athlete: world (1995) and Olympic (1996) 200- and 400-metre gold medallist **10 Philip (Cortelyou)**. 1906–2005, US architect and writer; his buildings include the New York State Theater (1964) and the American Telephone and Telegraph building (1978–83), both in New York **11 Robert** ?1898–1937, US blues singer and guitarist **12 Samuel** known as *Dr. Johnson*. 1709–84, British lexicographer, critic, and conversationalist, whose greatest works are his *Dictionary* (1755), his edition of Shakespeare (1765), and his *Lives of the Most Eminent English Poets* (1779–81). His fame, however, rests as much on Boswell's biography of him as on his literary output

Johnsonian (dʒɒn'səʊnɪən) *adj* of, relating to, or characteristic of the British lexicographer, critic, poet, and conversationalist Samuel *Johnson* (1709–84), his works, or his style of writing

John the Baptist *n* Saint John the Baptist *New Testament* the son of Zacharias and Elizabeth and the cousin and forerunner of Jesus, whom he baptized. He was beheaded by Herod (Matthew 14:1–2). Feast day: June 24

John Thomas *n* a name for **penis**

Johore *or* **Johor** (dʒəʊ'hɔː) *n* a state of Malaysia, on the S Malay Peninsula: mostly forested, with large swamps; bauxite- and iron-mining. Capital: Johore Bahru. Pop: 2 740 625 (2000). Area: 18 986 sq km (7331 sq miles)

Johore Bahru *or* **Johor Bahru** ('baːruː) *n* a city in S Malaysia, capital of Johore state: important trading centre, situated at the sole crossing point of **Johore Strait** (between Malaya and Singapore Island). Pop: 719 000 (2005 est)

joie de vivre French (ʒwa də vivrə) *n* joy of living; enjoyment of life; ebullience

join (dʒɔɪn) *vb* **1** to come or bring together; connect **2** to become a member of (a club, organization, etc) **3** (*intr; often foll by with*) to become associated or allied **4** (*intr; usually foll by in*) to take part **5** (*tr*) to meet (someone) as a companion **6** (*tr*) to become part of; take a place in or with **7** (*tr*) to unite (two people) in marriage **8** (*tr*) *geometry* to connect with a straight line or a curve **9** join hands **a** to hold one's own hands together **b** (of two people) to hold each other's hands **c** (usually foll by

with) to work together in an enterprise or task ▷ *n* **10** a joint; seam **11** the act of joining ▷ See also **join up** [c13: from Old French *joindre* from Latin *jungere* to yoke]

joinder ('dʒɔɪndə) *n* **1** the act of joining, esp in legal contexts **2** *law* **a** (in pleading) the stage at which the parties join issue (**joinder of issue**) **b** the joining of two or more persons as coplaintiffs or codefendants (**joinder of parties**) [c17: from French *joindre* to **JOIN**]

joined-up *adj* **1** with all departments or sections communicating efficiently with each other and acting together purposefully and effectively: *joined-up government* **2 a** focusing on or producing an integrated and coherent result, strategy, etc: *joined-up thinking* **b** forming an integrated and coherent whole: *joined-up policies*

joiner ('dʒɔɪnə) *n* **1** *chiefly Brit* a person trained and skilled in making finished woodwork, such as windows, doors, and stairs **2** a person or thing that joins **3** *informal* a person who joins many clubs, causes, etc

joinery ('dʒɔɪnərɪ) *n* **1** the skill or craft of a joiner **2** work made by a joiner

joint (dʒɔɪnt) *n* **1 a** a junction of two or more parts or objects **2** *anatomy* the junction between two or more bones, usually formed of connective tissue and cartilage **3** the point of connection between movable parts in invertebrates, esp insects and other arthropods **4** the part of a plant stem from which a branch or leaf grows **5** one of the parts into which a carcass of meat is cut by the butcher, esp for roasting **6** *geology* a crack in a rock along which no displacement has occurred **7** *slang* **a** a disreputable establishment, such as a bar or nightclub **b** *often facetious* a dwelling or meeting place **8** *slang* a cannabis cigarette **9 out of joint a** dislocated **b** out of order or disorganized ▷ *adj* **10** shared by or belonging to two or more: *joint property* **11** created by combined effort **12** sharing with others or with one another: *joint rulers* ▷ *vb* (*tr*) **13** to provide with or fasten by a joint or joints **14** to plane the edge of (a board, etc) into the correct shape for a joint **15** to cut or divide (meat, fowl, etc) into joints or at a joint ▷ 'jointly *adv* ▷ 'jointed *adj*

joint account *n* a bank account registered in the name of two or more persons, any of whom may make deposits and withdrawals

joint stock *n* capital funds held in common and usually divided into shares between the owners

joint-stock company *n* **1** *Brit* a business enterprise characterized by its separate legal existence and the sharing of ownership between shareholders, whose liability is limited **2** *US* a business enterprise whose owners are issued shares of transferable stock but do not enjoy limited liability

jointure ('dʒɔɪntʃə) *n* *law* **a** a provision made by a husband for his wife by settling property upon her at marriage for her use after his death **b** the property so settled [c14: from Old French, from Latin *junctūra* a joining]

join up *vb* (*adverb*) **1** (*intr*) to become a member of a military or other organization; enlist **2** (*often foll by with*) to unite or connect

Joinville (French ʒwɛ̃vil) *n* **Jean de** (ʒɑ̃ də). ?1224–1317, French chronicler, noted for his *Histoire de Saint Louis* (1309)

joist (dʒɔɪst) *n* a beam made of timber, steel, or reinforced concrete, used in the construction of floors, roofs, etc [c14: from Old French *giste* beam supporting a bridge, from Vulgar Latin *jacitum* (unattested) support, from *jacēre* to lie]

jojoba (həʊ'həʊbə) *n* a shrub or small tree of SW North America, *Simmondsia californica*, that has edible seeds containing a valuable oil used in cosmetics [Mexican Spanish]

joke (dʒəʊk) *n* **1** a humorous anecdote **2** something that is said or done for fun; prank **3** a ridiculous or humorous circumstance **4** a person or thing inspiring ridicule or amusement; butt **5 joking apart** or **aside**: said to recall a discussion to seriousness after there has been joking **6 no joke** something very serious ▷ *vb* **7** (*intr*) to tell jokes **8** (*intr*) to speak or act facetiously or in fun **9** to make fun of (someone); tease; kid [c17: from Latin *jocus* a jest] ▷ 'jokingly *adv* ▷ 'jokey *or* 'joky *adj*

joker ('dʒəʊkə) n **1** a person who jokes, esp in an obnoxious manner **2** *slang, often derogatory* a person: *who does that joker think he is?* **3** an extra playing card in a pack, which in many card games can substitute for or rank above any other card

Jokjakarta (ˌdʒɒkjəˈkɑːtɑː, ˌdʒɒk-) n a former spelling of **Yogyakarta**

jol (dʒɒl) *South African slang* ▷ n **1** a party ▷ vb jolling, jolled **2** (intr) to have a good time

Jolie (ʒɒli) n **Angelina Jolie** (Voight), born 1975, US actor; her films include *Girl Interrupted* (1999), *Lara Croft, Tomb Raider* (2001), and *A Mighty Heart* (2007)

Joliot-Curie (French ʒɔljɔkyri) n **Jean-Frédéric** (ʒɑ̃frederik), 1900–58, and his wife, **Irène** (irɛn), 1897–1956, French physicists: shared the Nobel prize for chemistry in 1935 for discovering artificial radioactivity

Jolliet (French ʒɔljɛ) n **Louis**. 1645–1700, French-Canadian explorer, with Jaques Marquette, of the Mississippi river

jollification (ˌdʒɒlɪfɪˈkeɪʃən) n a merry festivity

jollify ('dʒɒlɪˌfaɪ) vb **-fies, -fying, -fied** to be or cause to be jolly

jollity ('dʒɒlɪtɪ) n, pl **-ties** the condition of being jolly

jolly ('dʒɒlɪ) adj **-lier, -liest 1** full of good humour; jovial **2** having or provoking gaiety and merrymaking; festive **3** greatly enjoyable; pleasing ▷ adv **4** *Brit* (intensifier): *you're jolly nice* ▷ vb **-lies, -lying, -lied** (tr) *informal* **5** (often foll by *up* or *along*) to try to make or keep (someone) cheerful **6** to make goodnatured fun of [c14: from Old French *jolif*, probably from Old Norse *jōl* YULE]
▷ 'jolliness n

jolly boat n a small boat used as a utility tender for a vessel [c18: *jolly* probably from Danish *jolle* YAWL¹]

Jolly Jumper n *trademark Canadian* a type of fixed sprung baby harness in which an infant may be placed and allowed to bounce up and down for exercise

Jolly Roger n the traditional pirate flag, consisting of a white skull and crossbones on a black field

Jolo (həʊˈləʊ) n an island in the SW Philippines: the main island of the Sulu Archipelago. Pop: 87 998 (2000). Area: 893 sq km (345 sq miles)

Jolson ('dʒəʊlsən) n **Al**, real name *Asa Yoelson*. 1886–1950, US singer and film actor, born in Russia; star of the first talking picture *The Jazz Singer* (1927)

jolt (dʒəʊlt) vb (tr) **1** to bump against with a jarring blow; jostle **2** to move in a jolting manner **3** to surprise or shock ▷ n **4** a sudden jar or blow **5** an emotional shock [c16: probably blend of dialect *jot* to jerk and dialect *joll* to bump]

Jon. *abbreviation Bible* Jonah

Jonah ('dʒəʊnə) or **Jonas** ('dʒəʊnəs) n **1** *Old Testament* a Hebrew prophet who, having been thrown overboard from a ship in which he was fleeing from God, was swallowed by a great fish and vomited onto dry land **2** a person believed to bring bad luck to those around him; a jinx

Jonathan n *Old Testament* the son of Saul and David's close friend, who was killed in battle (I Samuel 31; II Samuel 1:19–26)

Jones (dʒəʊnz) n **1 Daniel**. 1881–1967, British phonetician **2 Daniel**. 1912–93, Welsh composer. He wrote nine symphonies and much chamber music **3 David**. 1895–1974, British artist and writer: his literary works, which combine poetry and prose, include *In Parenthesis* (1937), an account of World War I, and *The Anathemata* (1952) **4 Digby** (**Marritt**). born 1956, British businessman; director-general of the Confederation of British Industry (2000–06) **5 Inigo** ('ɪnɪgəʊ). 1573–1652, English architect and theatrical designer, who introduced Palladianism to England. His buildings include the Banqueting Hall of Whitehall. He also designed the settings for court masques, being the first to use the proscenium arch and movable scenery in England **6 John Paul**, original name *John Paul*. 1747–92, US naval commander, born in Scotland: noted for his part in the War of American Independence **7** (**Everett**) **Le Roi** ('liːrɔɪ), Muslim name *Imanu Amiri Baraka*. born 1934, US Black poet, dramatist, and political figure **8 Quincy**. born 1933, US composer, arranger, conductor, record producer, and trumpeter, noted esp for his film scores **9 Robert Tyre**, known as

Bobby Jones. 1902–71, US golfer

jong (jɒŋ) n *South African informal* a friend, often used in direct address [from Afrikaans]

Jongkind (Dutch 'jɒŋkɪnt) n **Johann Barthold** (joːˈhan 'bartɔlt). 1819–91, Dutch landscape painter and etcher, working in Paris: best known for his atmospheric seascapes

jongleur (French ʒɔ̃glœr) n (in medieval France) an itinerant minstrel [c18: from Old French *jogleour*, from Latin *joculator* joker, jester; see JUGGLE]

Jönköping (Swedish 'jœntɕøːpiŋ) n a city in S Sweden, on the S shore of Lake Vättern: scene of the conclusion of peace between Sweden and Denmark in 1809. Pop: 119 971 (2004 est)

jonquil ('dʒɒŋkwɪl) n **1** a Eurasian amaryllidaceous plant, *Narcissus jonquilla* with long fragrant yellow or white short-tubed flowers **2** any of various other small daffodil-like plants [c17: from French *jonquille*, from Spanish *junquillo*, diminutive of *junco* reed; see JUNCO]

Jonson ('dʒɒnsən) n **Ben**. 1572–1637, English dramatist and poet, who developed the "comedy of humours", in which each character is used to satirize one particular humour or temperament. His plays include *Volpone* (1606), *The Alchemist* (1610), and *Bartholomew Fair* (1614), and he also wrote court masques

jook (dʒʊk) or **chook** *Caribbean informal* vb **1** (tr) to poke or puncture (the skin) ▷ n **2** a jab or the resulting wound [c20: of uncertain origin]

Joplin ('dʒɒplɪn) n **1 Janis** 1943–70, US rock singer, noted for her hoarse and passionate style. Her albums include *Cheap Thrills* (1968) and *Pearl* (1971) **2 Scott** 1868–1917, US pianist and composer: creator of ragtime

Joppa ('dʒɒpə) n the biblical name of Jaffa, the port from which Jonah embarked (Jonah 1:3)

Jordaens (Flemish jɔrˈdaːns) n **Jacob** ('jaːkɔp). 1593–1678, Flemish painter, noted for his naturalistic depiction of peasant scenes

Jordan¹ ('dʒɔːdᵊn) n **1** a kingdom in SW Asia: coextensive with the biblical Moab, Gilead, and Edom; made a League of Nations mandate and emirate under British control in 1922 and became an independent kingdom in 1946; territories west of the River Jordan and the Jordanian part of Jerusalem (intended to be part of an autonomous Palestine) were occupied by Israel after the war of 1967. It contains part of the Great Rift Valley and consists mostly of desert. Official language: Arabic. Official religion: (Sunni) Muslim. Currency: dinar. Capital: Amman. Pop: 5 613 000 (2004 est). Area: 89 185 sq km (34 434 sq miles). Official name: Hashemite Kingdom of Jordan. Former name (1922–49): Trans-Jordan **2** the chief and only perennial river of Israel and Jordan, rising in several headstreams in Syria and Lebanon, and flowing south through the Sea of Galilee to the Dead Sea: occupies the N end of the Great Rift Valley system and lies mostly below sea level. Length: over 320 km (200 miles) ▷ Jor'danian adj, n

Jordan² ('dʒɔːdᵊn) n **1 Michael** (**Jeffrey**). born 1963, US basketball player **2 Neil**. born 1950, Irish film director and writer; his films include *The Company of Wolves* (1984), *Mona Lisa* (1986), *The Crying Game* (1992), *Michael Collins* (1996), *The End of the Affair* (2000), and *The Brave One* (2007)

jorum ('dʒɔːrəm) n a large drinking bowl or vessel or its contents [c18: probably named after *Jorum*, who brought vessels of silver, gold, and brass to King David (II Samuel 8:10)]

Jos (dʒɒs) n a city in central Nigeria, capital of Plateau state on the **Jos Plateau**: major centre of the tin-mining industry. Pop: 685 000 (2005 est)

Joseph ('dʒəʊzɪf) n **1** *Old Testament* **a** the eleventh son of Jacob and one of the 12 patriarchs of Israel (Genesis 30:2–24) **b** either or both of two tribes descended from his sons Ephraim and Manasseh **2** *Saint Joseph New Testament* the husband of Mary the mother of Jesus (Matthew 1:16–25). Feast day: Mar 19

Joseph Bonaparte Gulf n an inlet of the Timor Sea in N Australia. Width: 360 km (225 miles)

Joseph II n 1741–90, Holy Roman emperor (1765–90); son of Francis I. He ruled Austria jointly with his mother, Maria Theresa, until her death (1780). He reorganized taxation, abolished serfdom, curtailed the feudal power of the nobles, and asserted his independence from the pope

Josephine (ˈdʒəʊzəˌfiːn) *n* **Empress,** previous name *Joséphine de Beauharnais*; real name *Marie Joséphine Tascher de la Pagerie*. 1763–1814, empress of France as wife of Napoleon Bonaparte (1796–1809)

Joseph of Arimathea (ˌærɪməˈθiːə) *n* Saint Joseph of Arimathea *New Testament* a wealthy member of the Sanhedrin, who obtained the body of Jesus after the Crucifixion and laid it in his own tomb (Matthew 27:57–60). Feast day: Mar 17 or July 31

Josephus (dʒəʊˈsiːfəs) *n* **Flavius** (ˈfleɪvɪəs). real name *Joseph ben Matthias*. ?37–?100 AD, Jewish historian and general; author of *History of the Jewish War* and *Antiquities of the Jews*

josh (dʒɒʃ) *slang vb* ▷ 1 to tease (someone) in a bantering way ▷ *n* 2 a teasing or bantering joke [C19: perhaps from JOKE, influenced by BOSH[1]] > ˈjosher *n*

Josh. *abbreviation Bible* Joshua

Joshua (ˈdʒɒʃʊə) *n Old Testament* 1 Moses' successor, who led the Israelites in the conquest of Canaan 2 the book recounting his deeds

Josiah (dʒəʊˈsaɪə) *n* died ?609 BC, king of Judah (?640–?609). After the discovery of a book of law (probably Deuteronomy) in the Temple he began a programme of religious reform

Jospin (*French* ʒɔspɛ̃) *n* **Lionel (Robert)** born 1937, French politician; prime minister (1997–2002)

Josquin des Prés (*French* ʒɔskɛ̃ de pre) *n* See des Prés

joss (dʒɒs) *n* a Chinese deity worshipped in the form of an idol [C18: from pidgin English, from Portuguese *deos* god, from Latin *deus*]

joss house *n* a Chinese temple or shrine where an idol or idols are worshipped

joss stick *n* a stick of dried perfumed paste, giving off a fragrant odour when burnt as incense

jostle (ˈdʒɒsəl) *vb* 1 to bump or push (someone) roughly 2 to come or bring into contact 3 to force (one's way) by pushing ▷ *n* 4 the act of jostling 5 a rough bump or push [C14: see JOUST]

jot (dʒɒt) *vb* jots, jotting, jotted 1 (*tr*; usually foll by *down*) to write a brief note of ▷ *n* 2 (*used with a negative*) a little bit (in phrases such as **not to care** (*or* **give**) **a jot**) [C16: from Latin *jota*, from Greek *iōta*, of Semitic origin; see IOTA]

jota (*Spanish* ˈxɔta) *n* a Spanish dance with castanets in fast triple time, usually to a guitar and voice accompaniment [Spanish, probably modification of Old Spanish *sota*, from *sotar* to dance, from Latin *saltāre*]

jotter (ˈdʒɒtə) *n* a small notebook

jotting (ˈdʒɒtɪŋ) *n* something jotted down

Jotun *or* **Jotunn** (ˈjɔːtʊn) *n Norse myth* any of a race of giants [from Old Norse *jötunn* giant; related to EAT]

Jotunheim *or* **Jotunnheim** (ˈjɔːtʊnˌheɪm) *n Norse myth* the home of the giants in the northeast of Asgard [from Old Norse *jötunn* giant + *heimr* world, HOME]

joual (ʒwɑːl) *n* nonstandard Canadian French dialect, esp as associated with ill-educated speakers [from the pronunciation in this dialect of French *cheval* horse]

joule (dʒuːl) *n* the derived SI unit of work or energy; the work done when the point of application of a force of 1 newton is displaced through a distance of 1 metre in the direction of the force. 1 joule is equivalent to 1 watt-second, 10^7 ergs, 0.2390 calories, or 0.738 foot-pound. Symbol: J [C19: named after James Prescott *Joule* (1818–89), English physicist]

Joule (dʒuːl) *n* **James Prescott**. 1818–89, English physicist, who evaluated the mechanical equivalent of heat and contributed to the study of heat and electricity

jounce (dʒaʊns) *vb* 1 to shake or jolt or cause to shake or jolt; bounce ▷ *n* 2 a jolting movement; shake; bump [C15: probably a blend of dialect *joll* to bump + BOUNCE]

journal (ˈdʒɜːnəl) *n* 1 a newspaper or periodical 2 a book in which a daily record of happenings, etc, is kept 3 an official record of the proceedings of a legislative body 4 *book-keeping* Also called: **Book of Original Entry** one of several books in which transactions are initially recorded to facilitate subsequent entry in the ledger

5 the part of a shaft or axle in contact with or enclosed by a bearing [C14: from Old French: daily, from Latin *diurnālis*; see DIURNAL]

journal box *n machinery* a case enclosing or supporting a journal, often used as a means of retaining the lubricant

journalese (ˌdʒɜːnəˈliːz) *n derogatory* a superficial cliché-ridden style of writing regarded as typical of newspapers

journalism (ˈdʒɜːnəˌlɪzəm) *n* 1 the profession or practice of reporting about, photographing, or editing news stories for one of the mass media 2 newspapers and magazines collectively; the press

journalist (ˈdʒɜːnəlɪst) *n* 1 a person whose occupation is journalism 2 a person who keeps a journal > ˌjournaˈlistic *adj* > ˌjournalˈistically *adv*

journalize *or* **journalise** (ˈdʒɜːnəˌlaɪz) *vb* to record (daily events) in a journal > ˌjournaliˈzation *or* ˌjournaliˈsation *n*

journey (ˈdʒɜːnɪ) *n* 1 a travelling from one place to another; trip or voyage 2 a the distance travelled in a journey b the time taken to make a journey ▷ *vb* 3 (*intr*) to make a journey [C13: from Old French *journee* a day, a day's travelling, from Latin *diurnum* day's portion; see DIURNAL] > ˈjourneyer *n*

journeyman (ˈdʒɜːnɪmən) *n, pl* -men 1 a craftsman, artisan, etc, who is qualified to work at his trade in the employment of another 2 a competent workman [C15: from JOURNEY (in obsolete sense: a day's work) + MAN]

joust (dʒaʊst) *history* ▷ *n* 1 a combat between two mounted knights tilting against each other with lances. A tournament consisted of a series of such engagements ▷ *vb* 2 (*intr*; often foll by *against* or *with*) to encounter or engage in such a tournament: *he jousted with five opponents* [C13: from Old French *jouste*, from *jouster* to fight on horseback, from Vulgar Latin *juxtāre* (unattested) to come together, from Latin *juxtā* close] > ˈjouster *n*

Jove (dʒəʊv) *n* 1 another name for **Jupiter**[1] 2 **by Jove** an exclamation of surprise or excitement [C14: from Old Latin *Jovis* Jupiter] > ˈJovian *adj* [C16: from Old Latin *Jovis* Jupiter]

jovial[1] (ˈdʒəʊvɪəl) *adj* having or expressing convivial humour; jolly [C16: from Latin *joviālis* of (the planet) Jupiter, considered by astrologers to foster good humour] > ˌjoviˈality *or* ˈjovialness *n* > ˈjovially *adv*

Jovian[2] (ˈdʒəʊvɪən) *n* full name *Flavius Claudius Jovianus*. ?331–364 AD, Roman emperor (363–64): he made peace with Persia, relinquishing Roman provinces beyond the Tigris, and restored privileges to the Christians

Jowett (ˈdʒaʊɪt) *n* **Benjamin**. 1817–93, British classical scholar and educator: translated the works of Plato

jowl[1] (dʒaʊl) *n* 1 the jaw, esp the lower one 2 (*often plural*) a cheek, esp a prominent one 3 **cheek by jowl** See **cheek** (sense 6) [Old English *ceafl* jaw; related to Middle High German *kivel*, Old Norse *kjaptr*] > jowled *adj*

jowl[2] (dʒaʊl) *n* 1 fatty flesh hanging from the lower jaw 2 a similar fleshy part in animals, such as the wattle of a fowl or the dewlap of a bull [Old English *ceole* throat; compare Old High German *kela*]

joy (dʒɔɪ) *n* 1 a deep feeling or condition of happiness or contentment 2 something causing such a feeling; a source of happiness 3 an outward show of pleasure or delight; rejoicing 4 *Brit informal* success; satisfaction: *I went to the bank for a loan, but got no joy* ▷ *vb* 5 (*intr*) to feel joy 6 (*tr*) *obsolete* to make joyful; gladden [C13: from Old French *joie*, from Latin *gaudium* joy, from *gaudēre* to be glad]

Joyce (dʒɔɪs) *n* 1 **James (Augustine Aloysius)**. 1882–1941, Irish novelist and short-story writer. He profoundly influenced the development of the modern novel by his use of complex narrative techniques, esp stream of consciousness and parody, and of compound and coined words. His works include the novels *Ulysses* (1922) and *Finnegans Wake* (1939) and the short stories *Dubliners* (1914) 2 **William**, known as **Lord Haw-Haw**. 1906–46, British broadcaster of Nazi propaganda to Britain, who was executed for treason

Joycean (ˈdʒɔɪsɪən) *adj* 1 of, relating to, or like, the Irish novelist and short-story writer James Joyce or his works ▷ *n* 2 a student or admirer of Joyce or his works

joyful ('dʒɔɪfʊl) *adj* 1 full of joy; elated 2 expressing or producing joy: *a joyful look; a joyful occasion* > 'joyfully *adv* > 'joyfulness *n*

joyless ('dʒɔɪlɪs) *adj* having or producing no joy or pleasure > 'joylessly *adv* > 'joylessness *n*

joyous ('dʒɔɪəs) *adj* 1 having a happy nature or mood 2 joyful > 'joyously *adv*

joyride *n* 1 a ride taken for pleasure in a car, esp in a stolen car driven recklessly ▷ *vb* joy-ride, -rides, -riding, -rode, -ridden 2 (*intr*) to take such a ride > 'joy,rider *n* > 'joy,riding *n*

joystick ('dʒɔɪ,stɪk) *n* 1 *informal* the control stick of an aircraft or of any of various machines 2 *computing* a lever by means of which the display on a screen may be controlled used esp for games, flight simulators, etc

Jozi ('dʒəʊsɪ) *n South African informal* Johannesburg

JP *abbreviation* Justice of the Peace

JPEG ('dʒeɪ,pɛg) *n computing* a a standard file format for compressing pictures by disposing of redundant pixels b a picture held in this file format c (*as modifier*): *a JPEG image* [c20: technique devised by the J(oint) P(hotographic) E(xperts) G(roup)]

J/psi particle *n* a type of elementary particle (meson) thought to be formed from charmed quarks

Jr *or* **jr** *abbreviation* junior

JSA *abbreviation* (in Britain) jobseeker's allowance

Juan Carlos (*Spanish* xwan 'karlɔs) *n* born 1938, king of Spain from 1975: nominated by Franco as the first king of the restored Spanish monarchy that was to follow his death

Juan de Fuca ('dʒuːən dɪ 'fjuːkə; *Spanish* xwan de 'fuka) *n* Strait of Juan de Fuca a strait between Vancouver Island (Canada) and NW Washington (US). Length: about 129 km (80 miles). Width: about 24 km (15 miles)

Juan Fernández Islands ('dʒuːən fəˈnændez; *Spanish* xwan fɛr'nandeθ) *pl n* a group of three islands in the S Pacific Ocean, administered by Chile: volcanic and wooded. Area: about 180 sq km (70 sq miles)

Juantorena (*Spanish* xwantoˈrena) *n* **Alberto** (alˈβɛrto). born 1951, Cuban runner: won the 400 metres and the 800 metres in the 1976 Olympic Games

Juárez¹ (*Spanish* 'xwarεθ) *n* short for **Ciudad Juárez**

Juárez² (*Spanish* 'xwarεθ) *n* **Benito Pablo** (be'nito 'paβlo). 1806–72, Mexican statesman. As president (1861–65; 1867–72) he thwarted Napoleon III's attempt to impose an empire under Maximilian and introduced many reforms

Juba ('dʒuːbə) *n* a river in NE Africa, rising in S central Ethiopia and flowing south across Somalia to the Indian Ocean: the chief river of Somalia. Length: about 1660 km (1030 miles)

Jubal ('dʒuːbᵊl) *n Old Testament* the alleged inventor of musical instruments (Genesis 4:21)

jubbah ('dʒʊbə) *n* a long loose outer garment with wide sleeves, worn by Muslim men and women, esp in India [c16: from Arabic]

jube ('dʒuːb) *n Austral & NZ informal* any jelly-like sweet [c20: shortened from JUJUBE]

jubilant ('dʒuːbɪlənt) *adj* feeling or expressing great joy [c17: from Latin *jūbilāns* shouting for joy, from *jūbilāre* to give a joyful cry, from *jūbilum* a shout, wild cry] > 'jubilance *or* 'jubilancy *n* > 'jubilantly *adv*

jubilate ('dʒuːbɪ,leɪt) *vb* (*intr*) 1 to have or express great joy; rejoice 2 to celebrate a jubilee [c17: from Latin *jūbilāre* to raise a shout of joy; see JUBILANT]

jubilation (,dʒuːbɪˈleɪʃən) *n* a feeling of great joy and celebration

jubilee ('dʒuːbɪ,liː:, ,dʒuːbɪˈliː:) *n* 1 a time or season for rejoicing 2 a special anniversary, esp a 25th or 50th one 3 *RC Church* a specially appointed period, now ordinarily every 25th year, in which special indulgences are granted 4 *Old Testament* a year that was to be observed every 50th year, during which Hebrew slaves were to be liberated, alienated property was to be restored, etc 5 a less common word for jubilation [c14: from Old French *jubile*, from Late Latin *jubilaeus*, from Late Greek *iōbēlaios*, from Hebrew *yōbhēl* ram's horn, used for the proclamation of the year of jubilee; influenced by Latin *jūbilāre* to shout for joy]

Jud. *abbreviation Bible* 1 Also called: Judg Judges 2 Judith

Judaea *or* **Judea** (dʒuːˈdɪə) *n* the S division of ancient Palestine, succeeding the kingdom of Judah: a Roman province during the time of Christ > Judaean *or* Judean (dʒuːˈdɪən) *adj, n*

Judah ('dʒuːdə) *n Old Testament* 1 the fourth son of Jacob, one of whose descendants was to be the Messiah (Genesis 29:35; 49:8–12) 2 the tribe descended from him 3 the tribal territory of his descendants which became the nucleus of David's kingdom and, after the kingdom had been divided into Israel and Judah, the southern kingdom of Judah, with Jerusalem as its centre

Judah ha-Levi (haːˈliːvaɪ) *n* ?1075–1141, Jewish poet and philosopher, born in Spain; his major works include the collection in *Diwan* and the prose work *Sefer ha-Kuzari*, which presented his philosophy of Judaism in dialogue form

Judah ha-Nasi (haːnaːˈsiː:) *n* ?135–?220 AD, rabbi and patriarch of the Sanhedrin, who compiled the Mishnah

Judaic (dʒuːˈdeɪɪk) *or* **Judaical** *adj* of or relating to the Jews or Judaism > Juˈdaically *adv*

Judaism ('dʒuːdeɪ,ɪzəm) *n* 1 the religion of the Jews, based on the Old Testament and the Talmud and having as its central point a belief in the one God as transcendent creator of all things and the source of all righteousness 2 the religious and cultural traditions, customs, attitudes, and way of life of the Jews > Juda'istic *adj*

Judaize *or* **Judaise** ('dʒʊdeɪ,aɪz) *vb* 1 to conform or bring into conformity with Judaism 2 (*tr*) to convert to Judaism 3 (*tr*) to imbue with Jewish principles > ,Judai'zation *or* ,Judai'sation *n*

Judas ('dʒuːdəs) *n* 1 *New Testament* the apostle who betrayed Jesus to his enemies for 30 pieces of silver (Luke 22:3–6, 47–48). Full name: Judas Iscariot 2 a person who betrays a friend; traitor 3 a brother or relative of James and also of Jesus (Matthew 13:55). This figure, Thaddaeus, and Jude were probably identical

Judas Maccabaeus (,mækəˈbiːəs) *n* Jewish leader, whose revolt (166–161 BC) against the Seleucid kingdom of Antiochus IV (Epiphanes) enabled him to recapture Jerusalem and rededicate the Temple

judder ('dʒʌdə) *informal, chiefly Brit* ▷ *vb* 1 (*intr*) to shake or vibrate ▷ *n* 2 abnormal vibration in a mechanical system, esp due to grabbing between friction surfaces, as in the clutch of a motor vehicle 3 a juddering motion [probably blend of JAR² + SHUDDER]

judder bar *n NZ* a bump built across roads, esp in housing estates, to reduce speeding. Also called: ramp, (*chiefly Brit*) sleeping policeman

Jude (dʒuːd) *n* 1 a book of the New Testament (in full **The Epistle of Jude**) 2 Also called: Judas, Saint Jude the author of this, stated to be the brother of James (Jude 1) and almost certainly identical with Thaddaeus (Matthew 10:2–4). Feast day: Oct 28 or June 19

Judea (dʒuːˈdɪə) *n* a variant spelling of **Judaea**

judge (dʒʌdʒ) *n* 1 a public official with authority to hear cases in a court of law and pronounce judgment upon them 2 a person who is appointed to determine the result of contests or competitions 3 a person qualified to comment critically: *a good judge of antiques* 4 a leader of the peoples of Israel from Joshua's death to the accession of Saul ▷ *vb* 5 to hear and decide upon (a case at law) 6 (*tr*) to pass judgment on; sentence 7 (when *tr*, *may take a clause as object or an infinitive*) to decide or deem (something) after inquiry or deliberation 8 to determine the result of (a contest or competition) 9 to appraise (something) critically 10 (*tr*; *takes a clause as object*) to believe (something) to be the case; suspect [c14: from Old French *jugier*, from Latin *jūdicāre* to pass judgment, from *jūdex* a judge] > 'judge,like *adj* > 'judger *n* > 'judgeship *n*

judge advocate *n*, *pl* judge advocates an officer who superintends proceedings at a military court martial

judges' rules *pl n* (in English law, formerly) a set of rules, not legally binding, governing the behaviour of police towards suspects, as in administering a caution to a person under arrest

judgment or **judgement** ('dʒʌdʒmənt) n **1** the faculty of being able to make critical distinctions and achieve a balanced viewpoint; discernment **2 a** the decision or verdict pronounced by a court of law **b** an obligation arising as a result of such a decision or verdict, such as a debt **c** (as modifier): a judgment debtor **3** the formal decision of one or more judges at a contest or competition **4** a particular decision or opinion formed in a case in dispute or doubt **5** an estimation: a good judgment of distance **6** criticism or censure **7** against one's better judgment contrary to a more appropriate or preferred course of action **8** sit in judgment **a** to preside as judge **b** to assume the position of critic **9** in someone's judgment in someone's opinion

Judgment ('dʒʌdʒmənt) n **1** the estimate by God of the ultimate worthiness or unworthiness of the individual (the **Particular Judgment**) or of all mankind (the **General Judgment** or **Last Judgment**) **2** God's subsequent decision determining the final destinies of all individuals

judgmental or **judgemental** (dʒʌdʒˈmɛntˀl) adj of or denoting an attitude in which judgments about other people's conduct are made

Judgment Day n the occasion of the Last (or General) Judgment by God at the end of the world. Also called: **Day of Judgment** See **Last Judgment**

judicatory ('dʒuːdɪkətərɪ) adj **1** of or relating to the administration of justice ▷ n **2** a court of law **3** the administration of justice

judicature ('dʒuːdɪkətʃə) n **1** the administration of justice **2** the office, function, or power of a judge **3** the extent of authority of a court or judge **4** a body of judges or persons exercising judicial authority; judiciary **5** a court of justice or such courts collectively

judicial (dʒuːˈdɪʃəl) adj **1** of or relating to the administration of justice **2** of or relating to judgment in a court of law or to a judge exercising this function **3** allowed or enforced by a court of law: a decree of judicial separation **4** having qualities appropriate to a judge **5** giving or seeking judgment, esp determining or seeking determination of a contested issue [c14: from Latin jūdiciālis belonging to the law courts, from jūdicium judgment, from jūdex a judge] > ju'dicially adv

judiciary (dʒuːˈdɪʃɪərɪ, -ˈdɪʃərɪ) adj **1** of or relating to courts of law, judgment, or judges ▷ n, pl -aries **2** the branch of the central authority in a state concerned with the administration of justice **3** the system of courts in a country **4** the judges collectively; bench

judicious (dʒuːˈdɪʃəs) adj having or proceeding from good judgment > ju'diciously adv > ju'diciousness n

Judith ('dʒuːdɪθ) n **1** the heroine of one of the books of the Apocrypha, who saved her native town by decapitating Holofernes **2** the book recounting this episode

judo ('dʒuːdəʊ) n **a** the modern sport derived from jujitsu, in which the object is to throw, hold to the ground, or otherwise force an opponent to submit, using the minimum of physical effort **b** (as modifier): a judo throw [Japanese, from jū gentleness + dō way] > 'judoist n

Judy ('dʒuːdɪ) n, pl -dies **1** See **Punch 2** (often not capital) Brit slang a girl or woman

jug (dʒʌg) n **1 a** a vessel for holding or pouring liquids, usually having a handle and a spout or lip. US equivalent: pitcher **2** Austral & NZ such a vessel used as a kettle **3** US a large vessel with a narrow mouth **4** Also called: **jugful** the amount of liquid held by a jug **5** Brit informal a glass of alcoholic drink, esp beer **6** a slang word for **jail** ▷ vb jugs, jugging, jugged **7** to stew or boil (meat, esp hare) in an earthenware container **8** (tr) slang to put in jail [c16: probably from **Jug**, nickname from girl's name Joan]

jugate ('dʒuːgeɪt, -gɪt) adj (esp of compound leaves) having parts arranged in pairs [c19: from New Latin jugātus (unattested), from Latin jugum a yoke]

juggernaut ('dʒʌgəˌnɔːt) n **1** any terrible force, esp one that destroys or that demands complete self-sacrifice **2** Brit a very large lorry for transporting goods by road, esp one that travels throughout Europe

juggins ('dʒʌgɪnz) n Brit informal a silly person; simpleton [c19: special use of the surname Juggins]

juggle ('dʒʌgᵊl) vb **1** to throw and catch (several objects) continuously so that most are in the air all the time, as an entertainment **2** to arrange or manipulate (facts, figures, etc) so as to give a false or misleading picture **3** (tr) to keep (several activities) in progress, esp with difficulty ▷ n **4** an act of juggling [c14: from Old French jogler to perform as a jester, from Latin joculārī to jest, from jocus a jest] > 'juggler n

Jugoslav ('juːgəʊˌslɑːv) or **Jugoslavian** (juːgəʊˈslɑːvɪən) adj, n a variant spelling of **Yugoslav, Yugoslavian**

Jugoslavia (juːgəʊˈslɑːvɪə) n a variant spelling of **Yugoslavia**

jugular ('dʒʌgjʊlə) adj **1** of, relating to, or situated near the throat or neck ▷ n **2** short for **jugular vein**, any of three large veins in the neck that return blood to the heart from the head and face [c16: from Late Latin jugulāris, from Latin jugulum throat]

Jugurtha (dʒuːˈgɜːθə) n died 104 BC, king of Numidia (?112–104), who waged war against the Romans (the **Jugurthine War**, 112–105) and was defeated and executed

juice (dʒuːs) n **1** any liquid that occurs naturally in or is secreted by plant or animal tissue: the juice of an orange; digestive juices **2** informal **a** a fuel for an engine, esp petrol **b** electricity **c** alcoholic drink **3** vigour or vitality [c13: from Old French jus, from Latin] > 'juiceless adj

juice up vb (tr, adverb) US slang to make lively: to juice up a party

juicy ('dʒuːsɪ) adj juicier, juiciest **1** full of juice **2** provocatively interesting; spicy: juicy gossip **3** chiefly US & Canadian profitable: a juicy contract > 'juicily adv > 'juiciness n

Juiz de Fora (Portuguese ʒuˈiʃ di ˈfɔra) n a city in SE Brazil, in Minas Gerais state on the Rio de Janeiro–Belo Horizonte railway: textiles. Pop: 502 000 (2005 est)

jujitsu, jujutsu or **jiujitsu** (dʒuːˈdʒɪtsuː) n the traditional Japanese system of unarmed self-defence perfected by the samurai. See also **judo** [c19: from Japanese, from jū gentleness + jutsu art]

juju ('dʒuːdʒuː) n **1** an object superstitiously revered by certain W African peoples and used as a charm or fetish **2** the power associated with a juju **3** a taboo effected by a juju [c19: probably from Hausa djudju evil spirit, fetish]

jujube ('dʒuːdʒuːb) n **1** any of several Old World spiny rhamnaceous trees of the genus Ziziphus, esp Z. jujuba, that have small yellowish flowers and dark red edible fruits **2** the fruit of any of these trees **3** a chewy sweet made of flavoured gelatine and sometimes medicated to soothe sore throats [c14: from Medieval Latin jujuba, modification of Latin zīzyphum, from Greek zizuphon]

jukebox ('dʒuːkˌbɒks) n a coin-operated machine, usually found in pubs, clubs, etc, that contains records, CDs, or videos, which are played when selected by a customer [c20: from Gullah juke bawdy (as in juke house brothel) + BOX¹]

jukskei ('jʊkˌskeɪ) n South African a game in which a peg is thrown over a fixed distance at a stake driven into the ground [from Afrikaans juk yoke + skei pin]

julep ('dʒuːlɪp) n **1** a sweet drink, variously prepared and sometimes medicated **2** chiefly US short for **mint julep** [c14: from Old French, from Arabic julāb, from Persian gulāb rose water, from gul rose + āb water]

Julian¹ ('dʒuːljən, -lɪən) n known as Julian the Apostate; Latin name Flavius Claudius Julianus. 331–363 AD, Roman emperor (361–363), who attempted to revive paganism in the Roman empire while remaining tolerant to Christians and Jews

Julian² ('dʒuːljən, -lɪən) adj **1** of or relating to Julius Caesar (100–44 BC), the Roman general, statesman, and historian **2** denoting or relating to the Julian calendar

Juliana (ˌdʒuːlɪˈɑːnə; Dutch jyːliːˈaːnaː) n full name Juliana Louise Emma Marie Wilhelmina. 1909–2004, queen of the Netherlands (1948–80). She abdicated in favour of her eldest daughter Beatrix

Julian Alps pl n a mountain range in Slovenia: an E range of the Alps

Julian calendar n the calendar introduced by Julius Caesar in 46 BC, identical to the present calendar in all but two aspects: the beginning of the year was not fixed on Jan 1 and leap years occurred every fourth year and in every centenary year. See **Gregorian calendar**

Julian of Norwich *n* ?1342–?1413, English mystic and anchoress: best known for the *Revelations of Divine Love* describing her visions

julienne (ˌdʒuːlɪˈɛn) *adj* **1** (of vegetables) cut into thin shreds ▷ *n* **2** a clear consommé to which a mixture of such vegetables has been added [French, from name *Jules*, *Julien*, or *Julienne*]

Julius II (ˈdʒuːljəs, -lɪəs) *n* original name *Guiliano della Rovere*. 1443–1513, pope (1503–13). He completed the restoration of the Papal States to the Church, began the building of St Peter's, Rome (1506), and patronized Michelangelo, Raphael, and Bramante

Julius Caesar *n* See **Caesar**

Jullundur (ˈdʒʌləndə) *n* the former name of **Jalandhar**

July (dʒuːˈlaɪ, dʒə-, dʒʊ-) *n, pl* -lies the seventh month of the year, consisting of 31 days [c13: from Anglo-French *julie*, from Latin *Jūlius*, after Gaius Julius Caesar (100–44 BC), Roman statesman in whose honour it was named]

jumble (ˈdʒʌmbᵊl) *vb* **1** to mingle (objects, papers, etc) in a state of disorder **2** (*tr; usually passive*) to remember in a confused form; muddle ▷ *n* **3** a disordered mass, state, etc **4** *Brit* articles donated for a jumble sale [c16: of uncertain origin] > ˈjumbly *adj*

jumble sale *n* a sale of miscellaneous articles, usually cheap and predominantly secondhand, in aid of charity. US and Canadian equivalent: rummage sale

jumbo (ˈdʒʌmbəʊ) *n, pl* -bos **1** *informal* **a** a very large person or thing **b** (*as modifier*): *a jumbo box of detergent* **2** See **jumbo jet** [c19: after the name of a famous elephant exhibited by P. T. Barnum, from Swahili *jumbe* chief]

jumbo jet *n* *informal* a type of large jet-propelled airliner that carries several hundred passengers

jumbuck (ˈdʒʌmˌbʌk) *n* *Austral archaic* an informal word for **sheep** [c19: from a native Australian language]

Jumna (ˈdʒʌmnə) *n* a river in N India, rising in Uttarakhand in the Himalayas and flowing south and southeast to join the Ganges just below Allahabad (a confluence held sacred by Hindus). Length: 1385 km (860 miles)

jump (dʒʌmp) *vb* **1** (*intr*) to leap or spring clear of the ground or other surface by using the muscles in the legs and feet **2** (*tr*) to leap over or clear (an obstacle): *to jump a gap* **3** (*tr*) to cause to leap over an obstacle: *to jump a horse over a hedge* **4** (*intr*) to move or proceed hastily (into, onto, out of, etc): *she jumped into a taxi and was off* **5** (*tr*) *informal* to board so as to travel illegally on: *he jumped the train as it was leaving* **6** (*intr*) to parachute from an aircraft **7** (*intr*) to jerk or start, as with astonishment, surprise, etc **8** (*tr*) to rise or cause to rise suddenly or abruptly **9** to pass or skip over (intervening objects or matter): *she jumped a few lines and then continued reading* **10** (*intr*) to change from one thing to another, esp from one subject to another **11** *draughts* to capture (an opponent's piece) by moving one of one's own pieces over it to an unoccupied square **12** (*intr*) *bridge* to bid in response to one's partner at a higher level than is necessary, to indicate a strong hand **13** (*tr*) to come off (a track, rail, etc): *the locomotive jumped the rails* **14** (*intr*) (of the stylus of a record player) to be jerked out of the groove **15** (*intr*) *slang* to be lively: *the party was jumping when I arrived* **16** (*tr*) *informal* to attack without warning: *thieves jumped the old man as he walked through the park* **17** (*tr*) *informal* (of a driver or a motor vehicle) to pass through (a red traffic light) or move away from (traffic lights) before they change to green **18** jump down someone's throat *informal* to address or reply to someone with unexpected sharpness **19** jump ship to desert, esp to leave a ship in which one is legally bound to serve **20** jump the queue See **queue-jump** **21** jump to it *informal* to begin something quickly and efficiently ▷ *n* **22** an act or instance of jumping **23** a space, distance, or obstacle to be jumped or that has been jumped **24** a descent by parachute from an aircraft **25** *sport* any of several contests involving a jump: *the high jump* **26** a sudden rise: *the jump in prices last month* **27** a sudden or abrupt transition **28** a sudden jerk or involuntary muscular spasm, esp as a reaction of

surprise **29** a step or degree: *one jump ahead* **30** *draughts* a move that captures an opponent's piece by jumping over it **31** *films* **a** a break in continuity in the normal sequence of shots **b** (*as modifier*): *a jump cut* **32** *Brit slang* an act of sexual intercourse **33** on the jump *informal, chiefly US & Canadian* **a** in a hurry **b** busy and energetic **34** take a running jump *Brit informal* a contemptuous expression of dismissal ▷ See also **jump at**, **jump-off** [c16: probably of imitative origin; compare Swedish *gumpa* to jump]

jump at *vb* (*intr, preposition*) to be glad to accept: *I would jump at the chance of going*

jumped-up *adj* *informal* suddenly risen in significance, esp when appearing arrogant

jumper¹ (ˈdʒʌmpə) *n* **1** *chiefly Brit* a knitted or crocheted garment covering the upper part of the body **2** Also called: pinafore dress *US & Canadian* a sleeveless dress worn over a blouse or sweater [c19: from obsolete *jump* man's loose jacket, variant of *jupe*, from Old French, from Arabic *jubbah* long cloth coat]

jumper² (ˈdʒʌmpə) *n* **1** a boring tool that works by repeated impact, such as a steel bit in a hammer drill used in boring rock **2** Also called: jumper cable, jumper lead a short length of wire used to make a connection, usually temporarily, between terminals or to bypass a component **3** a person or animal that jumps

jumping bean *n* a seed of any of several Mexican euphorbiaceous plants, esp species of *Sebastiania*, that contains a moth caterpillar whose movements cause it to jerk about

jumping jack *n* a toy figure of a man with jointed limbs that can be moved by pulling attached strings

jump jet *n* a fixed-wing jet aircraft that is capable of landing and taking off vertically

jump jockey *n* *Brit* a jockey who rides in steeplechases (as opposed to one who rides in flat races)

jump leads (liːdz) *pl n* two heavy cables fitted with crocodile clips used to start a motor vehicle with a discharged battery by connecting the battery to an external battery

jump-off *n* **1** an extra round in a showjumping contest when two or more horses are equal first, the fastest round deciding the winner ▷ *vb* jump off **2** (*intr, adverb*) to begin or engage in a jump-off

jump on *vb* (*intr, preposition*) *informal* to reprimand or attack suddenly and forcefully

jump seat *n* **1** a folding seat for temporary use, as on the flight deck of some aircraft for an additional crew member **2** *Brit* a folding seat in a motor vehicle such as in a London taxi

jump-start *vb* **1** to start the engine of (a car) by connecting it to another engine with jump leads or (of a car) to start in this way ▷ *n* **2** the act of starting a car in this way

jump suit *n* a one-piece garment of combined trousers and jacket or shirt

jumpy (ˈdʒʌmpɪ) *adj* jumpier, jumpiest **1** nervous or apprehensive **2** moving jerkily or fitfully > ˈjumpily *adv* > ˈjumpiness *n*

Jun *abbreviation* **1** June **2** Also called: jun junior

Junagadh (ˌdʒuːnəˈgæd) *n* a town in India, in Gujarat: noted for its Buddhist caves and temples. Pop: 168 686 (2001)

junco (ˈdʒʌŋkəʊ) *n, pl* -cos or -coes any North American bunting of the genus *Junco*, having a greyish plumage with white outer tail feathers [c18: from Spanish: a rush, a marsh bird, from Latin *juncus* rush]

junction (ˈdʒʌŋkʃən) *n* **1** a place where several routes, lines, or roads meet, or cross each other: *a railway junction* **2** a point on a motorway where traffic may leave or join in **3** *electronics* **a** a contact between two different metals or other materials: *a thermocouple junction* **b** a transition region between regions of differing electrical properties in a semiconductor **4** the act of joining or the state of being joined [c18: from Latin *junctiō* a joining, from *junctus* joined, from *jungere* to join]

junction box *n* an earthed enclosure within which wires or cables can be safely connected

junction transistor *n* a bipolar transistor consisting of two p-n junctions combined to form either an n-p-n or a p-n-p transistor, having the three electrodes, the emitter, base, and collector

juncture ('dʒʌŋktʃə) n 1 a point in time, esp a critical one (often in the phrase **at this juncture**) 2 *linguistics* the set of phonological features signalling a division between words, such as those that distinguish *a name* from *an aim* 3 a less common word for **junction**

Jundiaí (*Portuguese* ʒundia'i) n an industrial city in SE Brazil, in São Paulo state. Pop: 332 000 (2005 est)

June (dʒuːn) n the sixth month of the year, consisting of 30 days [Old English *iunius*, from Latin *junius*, probably from *Junius* name of Roman gens]

Juneau ('dʒuːnəʊ) n a port in SE Alaska: state capital. Pop: 31 187 (2003 est)

Jung (jʊŋ) n **Carl Gustav** (karl 'gʊstaf). 1875–1961, Swiss psychologist. His criticism of Freud's emphasis on the sexual instinct ended their early collaboration. He went on to found analytical psychology, developing the concepts of the collective unconscious and its archetypes and of the extrovert and introvert as the two main psychological types

Jungfrau (*German* 'jʊŋfraʊ) n a mountain in S Switzerland, in the Bernese Alps south of Interlaken. Height: 4158 m (13 642 ft)

Junggar Pendi ('dʒʊŋ'gɛər 'pɛn'di:), **Dzungaria** or **Zungaria** n an arid region of W China, in N Xinjiang between the Altai Mountains and the Tian Shan

jungle ('dʒʌŋg°l) n 1 an equatorial forest area with luxuriant vegetation, often almost impenetrable 2 any dense or tangled thicket or growth 3 a place of intense competition or ruthless struggle for survival: *the concrete jungle* 4 a type of fast electronic dance music, originating in the early 1990s, which combines elements of techno and ragga [c18: from Hindi *jangal*, from Sanskrit *jāngala* wilderness] > 'jungly *adj*

jungle fever n a serious malarial fever occurring in the East Indies

jungle fowl n 1 any small gallinaceous bird of the genus *Gallus*, the males of which have an arched tail and a combed and wattled head: family *Phasianidae* (pheasants). *G. gallus* (**red jungle fowl**) is thought to be the ancestor of the domestic fowl 2 *Austral* any of several megapodes, esp *Megapodius freycinet*

jungle juice n a slang name for alcoholic liquor, esp home-made liquor

junior ('dʒuːnjə) *adj* 1 lower in rank or length of service; subordinate 2 younger in years 3 of or relating to youth or childhood 4 *Brit* of or relating to schoolchildren between the ages of 7 and 11 approximately 5 *US* of, relating to, or designating the third year of a four-year course at college or high school ▷ n 6 *law* (in England) any barrister below the rank of Queen's Counsel 7 a junior person 8 *Brit* a junior schoolchild 9 *US* a junior student [c17: from Latin: younger, from *juvenis* young]

Junior ('dʒuːnjə) *adj* being the younger: usually used after a name to distinguish the son from the father with the same first name or names: *Charles Parker, Junior* Abbreviations: Jr, Jun, Jnr

junior common room n (in certain universities and colleges) a common room for the use of students

junior lightweight n **a** a professional boxer weighing 126–130 pounds (57–59 kg) **b** (*as modifier*): *a junior-lightweight bout*

junior middleweight n **a** a professional boxer weighing 147–154 pounds (66.5–70 kg) **b** *the junior-middleweight championship*

junior school n (in England and Wales) a school for children aged between 7 and 11

junior technician n a rank in the RAF senior to aircraftman: comparable to that of private in the army

junior welterweight n **a** a professional boxer weighing 135–140 pounds (61–63.5 kg) **b** (*as modifier*): *a junior-welterweight fight*

juniper ('dʒuːnɪpə) n any coniferous shrub or small tree of the genus *Juniperus*, of the N hemisphere, having purple berry-like cones. The cones of *J. communis* (**common** or **dwarf juniper**) are used as a flavouring in making gin [c14: from Latin *jūniperus*, of obscure origin]

Junius ('dʒuːnjəs) n pen name of the anonymous author

of a series of letters (1769–72) attacking the ministries of George III of England: now generally believed to have been written by Sir Philip Francis

junk¹ (dʒʌŋk) n 1 discarded or secondhand objects, etc, collectively 2 *informal* **a** rubbish generally **b** nonsense: *the play was absolute junk* 3 *slang* any narcotic drug, esp heroin ▷ vb 4 (*tr*) *informal* to discard as junk; scrap [c15: *jonke* old useless rope]

junk² (dʒʌŋk) n a sailing vessel used in Chinese waters and characterized by a very high poop, flat bottom, and square sails supported by battens [c17: from Portuguese *junco*, from Javanese *jon*; related to Dutch *jonk*]

junk bond n *finance* a security that offers a high yield but often involves a high risk of default

Junker ('jʊŋkə) n 1 *history* any of the aristocratic landowners of Prussia who were devoted to maintaining their identity and extensive social and political privileges 2 an arrogant, narrow-minded, and tyrannical German army officer or official 3 (*formerly*) a young German nobleman [c16: from German, from Old High German *junchērro* young lord, from *junc* young + *hērro* master, lord] > 'Junkerdom n

Junkers ('jʊŋkəz) n **Hugo.** 1859–1935, German aircraft designer. His military aircraft were used in both World Wars

junket ('dʒʌŋkɪt) n 1 an excursion, esp one made for pleasure at public expense by a public official or committee 2 a sweet dessert made of flavoured milk set to a curd with rennet 3 a feast or festive occasion ▷ vb 4 (*intr*) (of a public official, committee, etc) to go on a junket 5 to have or entertain with a feast or festive gathering [c14 (in the sense: rush basket, hence custard served on rushes): from Old French (dialect) *jonquette*, from *jonc* rush, from Latin *juncus* reed] > 'junketing n

junk food n food that is low in nutritional value, often highly processed or ready-prepared, and eaten instead of or in addition to well-balanced meals

junkie or **junky** ('dʒʌŋkɪ) n, pl **junkies** an informal word for a drug addict, esp one who injects heroin into himself

junk mail n untargeted mail advertising goods or services

junk shop n a shop selling miscellaneous secondhand goods

Juno¹ ('dʒuːnəʊ) n 1 (in Roman tradition) the queen of the Olympian gods. Greek counterpart: Hera 2 a woman of stately bearing and regal beauty

Juno² ('dʒuːnəʊ) n *astronomy* the fourth largest known asteroid (approximate diameter 240 kilometres) and one of the four brightest

Juno³ n an award given for achievements in the Canadian music industry [c20: originally after Pierre Juneau (born 1922) Canadian broadcaster]

junta ('dʒʊntə, 'dʒʌn-; *US* 'hʊntə) n 1 a group of military officers holding the power in a country, esp after a coup d'état 2 Also called: **junto** a small group of men; cabal, faction, or clique 3 a legislative or executive council in some parts of Latin America [c17: from Spanish: council, from Latin *junctus* joined, from *jungere* to join]

junto ('dʒʊntəʊ, 'dʒʌn-) n, pl **-tos** a variant of **junta** (sense 2) [c17: variant of **junta**]

Jupiter¹ ('dʒuːpɪtə) n (in Roman tradition) the king and ruler of the Olympian gods

Jupiter² ('dʒuːpɪtə) n the largest of the planets and the fifth from the sun. It has 16 satellites and is surrounded by a transient planar ring system consisting of dust particles. Mean distance from sun: 778 million km; period of revolution around sun: 11.86 years; period of axial rotation: 9.83 hours; diameter and mass: 11.2 and 317.9 times that of earth respectively

Jura ('dʒʊərə) n 1 a department of E France, in Franche-Comté region. Capital: Lons-le-Saunier. Pop: 253 309 (2003 est)). Area: 5055 sq km (1971 sq miles) 2 a canton of Switzerland, bordering the French frontier: formed in 1979 from part of Bern. Capital: Delémont. Pop: 69 200 (2002 est). Area: 838 sq km (323 sq miles) 3 an island off the W coast of Scotland, in the Inner Hebrides, separated from the mainland by the **Sound of Jura**. Pop: 200 (2004 est). Area: 381 sq km (147 sq miles) 4 a mountain range in W central Europe, between the Rivers Rhine and Rhône: mostly in E France, extending into W Switzerland **5** a range of mountains in the NE quadrant of the moon lying on the N border of the Mare Imbrium

Jurassic (dʒʊˈræsɪk) *adj* **1** of, denoting, or formed in the second period of the Mesozoic era, between the Triassic and Cretaceous periods, lasting for 55 million years during which dinosaurs and ammonites flourished ▷ *n* **2 the Jurassic** the Jurassic period or rock system [c19: from French *jurassique*, after the JURA (Mountains)]

jurat (ˈdʒʊəræt) *n* **1** *law* a statement at the foot of an affidavit, naming the parties, stating when, where, and before whom it was sworn, etc **2** (in England) a municipal officer of the Cinque Ports, having a similar position to that of an alderman **3** (in France and the Channel Islands) a magistrate [c16: from Medieval Latin *jūrātus* one who has been sworn, from Latin *jūrāre* to swear]

juridical (dʒʊˈrɪdɪkʰl) *adj* of or relating to law, to the administration of justice, or to the office or function of a judge; legal [c16: from Latin *jūridicus*, from *iūs* law + *dicere* to say] ▷ juˈridically *adv*

jurisdiction (ˌdʒʊərɪsˈdɪkʃən) *n* **1** the right or power to administer justice and to apply laws **2** the exercise or extent of such right or power **3** power or authority in general [c13: from Latin *jūrisdictiō* administration of justice; see JUS, DICTION] ▷ jurisˈdictional *adj*

jurisprudence (ˌdʒʊərɪsˈpruːdʰns) *n* **1** the science or philosophy of law **2** a system or body of law **3** a branch of law: *medical jurisprudence* [c17: from Latin *jūris prūdentia*; see JUS, PRUDENCE] ▷ jurisprudential (ˌdʒʊərɪspruːˈdɛnʃəl) *adj*

jurist (ˈdʒʊərɪst) *n* a person versed in the science of law, esp Roman or civil law [c15: from French *juriste*, from Medieval Latin *jūrista*; see JUS]

juristic (dʒʊˈrɪstɪk) *or* **juristical** *adj* **1** of or relating to jurists **2** of, relating to, or characteristic of the study of law or the legal profession

juror (ˈdʒʊərə) *n* **1** a member of a jury **2** a person who takes an oath [c14: from Anglo-French *jurour*, from Old French *jurer* to take an oath, from Latin *jūrāre*]

Juruá (Portuguese ʒuˈrua) *n* a river in South America, rising in E central Peru and flowing northeast across NW Brazil to join the Amazon. Length: 1900 km (1200 miles)

jury¹ (ˈdʒʊərɪ) *n*, *pl* **-ries 1** a group of, usually twelve, people sworn to deliver a true verdict according to the evidence upon a case presented in a court of law **2** a body of persons appointed to judge a competition and award prizes [c14: from Old French *juree*, from *jurer* to swear; see JUROR]

jury² (ˈdʒʊərɪ) *adj chiefly nautical* (in combination) makeshift: *jury-rigged* [c17: of unknown origin]

jury box *n* an enclosure where the jury sit in court

juryman (ˈdʒʊərɪmən) *n*, *pl* **-men** a member of a jury, esp a man

jury-rigged *adj chiefly nautical* set up in a makeshift manner, usually as a result of the loss of regular gear

jus (ʒuː; French ʒy) *n* a sauce [French: literally, juice]

just (dʒʌst) *adj* **1 a** fair or impartial in action or judgment **b** (*as collective noun; preceded by the*): *the just* **2** conforming to high moral standards; honest **3** consistent with justice: *a just action* **4** rightly applied or given; deserved: *a just reward* **5** legally valid; lawful: *a just inheritance adv* (dʒʌst; *unstressed* dʒəst) **6** used with forms of *have* to indicate an action performed in the very recent past: *I have just closed the door* **7** at this very instant: *he's just coming in to land* **8** no more than; merely; only: *just an ordinary car* **9** exactly; precisely: *that's just what I mean* **10** by a small margin; barely: *he just got there in time* **11** just about **a** at the point of starting (to do something) **b** very nearly; almost: *I've just about had enough* **12** just a moment, just a second *or* just a minute an expression requesting the hearer to wait or pause for a brief period of time **13** just now **a** a very short time ago **b** at this moment **c** *South African informal* in a little while **14** just so arranged with precision [c14: from Latin *jūstus* righteous, from *jūs* justice] ▷ ˈjustly *adv* ▷ ˈjustness *n*

justice (ˈdʒʌstɪs) *n* **1** the quality or fact of being just **2** *ethics* the principle of fairness that like cases should be treated alike **3** the administration of law according to prescribed and accepted principles **4** conformity to the law; legal validity **5** a judge of the Supreme Court of Judicature **6** short for **justice of the peace 7** good reason (esp in the phrase **with justice**): *he was disgusted by their behaviour, and with justice* **8 do justice to a** to show to full advantage: *the picture did justice to her beauty* **b** to show full appreciation of by action: *he did justice to the meal* **c** to treat or judge fairly **9 do oneself justice** to make full use of one's abilities **10 bring to justice** to capture, try, and usually punish (a criminal, an outlaw, etc) [c12: from Old French, from Latin *jūstitia*, from *jūstus* JUST]

justice of the peace *n* **1** (in Britain) a lay magistrate, appointed by the crown or acting *ex officio*, whose function is to preserve the peace in his area, try summarily such cases as are within his jurisdiction, and perform miscellaneous administrative duties **2** (in Australia and New Zealand) a person authorised to administer oaths, attest instruments, and take declarations

justiciar (dʒʌˈstɪʃɪˌɑː) *n English legal history* the chief political and legal officer from the time of William I to that of Henry III, who deputized for the king in his absence and presided over the kings' courts. Also called: **justiciary** ▷ jusˈticiarˌship *n*

justiciary (dʒʌˈstɪʃɪərɪ) *adj* **1** of or relating to the administration of justice ▷ *n*, *pl* **-aries 2** an officer or administrator of justice; judge

justifiable (ˈdʒʌstɪˌfaɪəbʰl) *adj* capable of being justified; understandable ▷ justiˌfiaˈbility *or* ˈjustiˌfiableness *n* ▷ ˈjustiˌfiably *adv*

justifiable homicide *n* lawful killing, as in self-defence or to prevent a crime

justification (ˌdʒʌstɪfɪˈkeɪʃən) *n* **1** reasonable grounds for complaint, defence, etc **2** the act of justifying; proof, vindication, or exculpation **3** *theol* **a** the act of justifying **b** the process of being justified or the condition of having been justified

justificatory (ˈdʒʌstɪfɪˌkeɪtərɪ, -trɪ) ˈjustiˌcatory *adj* serving as justification or capable of justifying; vindicatory

justify (ˈdʒʌstɪˌfaɪ) *vb* **-fies, -fying, -fied** (*mainly tr*) **1** (*often passive*) to prove or see to be just or valid; vindicate **2** to show to be reasonable; warrant or substantiate: *his behaviour justifies our suspicion* **3** to declare or show to be free from blame or guilt; absolve **4** *law* to show good reason in court for (some action taken) **5** (*also intr*) *printing, computing* to adjust the spaces between words in (a line of type or data) so that it is of the required length or (of a line of type or data) to fit exactly **6 a** *Protestant theol* to account or declare righteous by the imputation of Christ's merits to the sinner **b** *RC theol* to change from sinfulness to righteousness by the transforming effects of grace **7** (*also intr*) *law* to prove (a person) to have sufficient means to act as surety, etc, or (of a person) to qualify to provide bail or surety [c14: from Old French *justifier*, from Latin *justificāre*, from *jūstus* JUST + *facere* to make] ▷ ˈjustiˌfier *n*

Justinian Code *n* a compilation of Roman imperial law made by order of Justinian I, forming part of the Corpus Juris Civilis

Justinian I (dʒʌˈstɪnɪən) *n* called *the Great*; Latin name *Flavius Anicius Justinianus*. 483–565 AD, Byzantine emperor (527–565). He recovered North Africa, SE Spain, and Italy, largely owing to the brilliance of generals such as Belisarius. He sponsored the Justinian Code

Justinian II *n* 669–711 AD, Byzantine emperor (685–95, 705–11). Banished (695) after a revolt against his oppressive rule, he regained the throne with the help of the Bulgars. He was killed in a second revolt

Justin Martyr (ˈdʒʌstɪn) *n* Saint. ?100–?165 AD, Christian apologist and philosopher. Feast day: June 1

just-in-time *adj* denoting or relating to an industrial method in which waste of resources is eliminated or reduced by producing production-line components, etc, as they are required, rather than holding large stocks. Abbreviation: JIT

justle ('dʒʌsᵊl) *vb* a less common word for **jostle**

jut (dʒʌt) *vb* **juts, jutting, jutted** **1** (*intr*; often foll by *out*) to stick out or overhang beyond the surface or main part; protrude or project ▷ *n* **2** something that juts out [c16: variant of JET¹] > 'jutting *adj*

jute (dʒuːt) *n* **1** either of two Old World tropical yellow-flowered herbaceous plants, *Corchorus capsularis* or *C. olitorius*, cultivated for their strong fibre: family *Tiliaceae* **2** this fibre, used in making sacks, rope, etc [c18: from Bengali *jhuto*, from Sanskrit *jūta* braid of hair, matted hair]

Jutland ('dʒʌtlənd) *n* a peninsula of N Europe: forms the continental portion of Denmark and geographically includes the N part of the German province of Schleswig-Holstein, while politically it includes only the mainland of Denmark and the islands north of Limfjorden; a major but inconclusive naval battle was fought off its NW coast in 1916 between the British and German fleets. Danish name: Jylland

Juvenal ('dʒuːvɪnᵊl) *n* Latin name *Decimus Junius Juvenalis.* ?60–?140 AD, Roman satirist. In his 16 verse satires, he denounced the vices of imperial Rome

juvenescence (,dʒuːvɪ'nesəns) *n* **1** youth or immaturity **2** the act or process of growing from childhood to youth [c19: from Latin *juvenēscere* to grow up, regain strength, from *juvenis* youthful] > juve'nescent *adj*

juvenile ('dʒuːvɪ,naɪl) *adj* **1** young, youthful, or immature **2** suitable or designed for young people: *juvenile pastimes* ▷ *n* **3** a juvenile person, animal, or plant **4** an actor who performs youthful roles **5** a book intended for young readers [c17: from Latin *juvenīlis* youthful, from *juvenis* young] > 'juve,nilely *adv*

juvenile delinquency *n* antisocial or criminal conduct by juvenile delinquents

juvenile delinquent *n* a child or young person guilty of some offence, act of vandalism, or antisocial behaviour or whose conduct is beyond parental control and who may be brought before a juvenile court

juvenilia (,dʒuːvɪ'nɪlɪə) *pl n* works of art, literature, or music produced in youth or adolescence, before the artist, author, or composer has formed a mature style [c17: from Latin, literally: youthful things; see JUVENILE]

juxtapose (,dʒʌkstə'pəʊz) *vb* (*tr*) to place close together or side by side [c19: back formation from *juxtaposition*, from Latin *juxta* next to + POSITION] > juxtapo'sition *n* > juxtapo'sitional *adj*

Jylland ('jylan) *n* the Danish name for **Jutland**

j

Kk

k¹ or **K** (keɪ) *n, pl* **k's**, **K's** or **Ks** **1** the 11th letter and 8th consonant of the modern English alphabet **2** a speech sound represented by this letter, usually a voiceless velar stop, as in *kitten*

k² *symbol for* **1** kilo(s) **2** *maths* the unit vector along the z-axis

K¹ *symbol for* **1** kelvin(s) **2** *chess* king **3** *chem* potassium **4** *physics* kaon **5** *currency* **a** kina **b** kip **c** kopeck **d** kwacha **e** kyat **6** one thousand **7** *computing* **a** a unit of 1024 words, bits, or bytes **b** (not in technical usage) 1000 [(for sense 3) from New Latin *kalium*; (for sense 6) from KILO-]

K² or **K.** *abbreviation* Köchel: indicating the serial number in the catalogue (1862) of the works of Mozart made by Ludwig von Köchel (1800–77)

K2 *n* a mountain in the Karakoram Range on the Kashmir-Xinjiang border: the second highest mountain in the world. Height: 8611 m (28 250 ft). Also called: Godwin-Austen, Dapsang

Kaaba or **Caaba** (ˈkɑːbə) *n* a cube-shaped building in Mecca, the most sacred Muslim pilgrim shrine, into which is built the black stone believed to have been given by Gabriel to Abraham. Muslims turn in its direction when praying [from Arabic *ka'bah*, from *ka'b* cube]

kaal (ˈkɑːl) or **kaal gat** (ˈkɑːl gæt) *adj South African informal* naked [from Afrikaans, literally: bare (arsed)]

kabaddi (kəˈbɑːdɪ) *n* a game played between two teams of seven players, in which individuals take turns to chase and try to touch members of the opposing team without being captured by them [Tamil]

Kabalega Falls (ˌkɑːbəˈleɪgə) *pl n* rapids on the lower Victoria Nile, about 35 km (22 miles) east of Lake Albert, where the Nile drops 120 m (400 ft)

Kabardino-Balkar Republic (ˌkæbəˈdiːnəʊˌbælkə) *n* a constituent republic of S Russia, on the N side of the Caucasus Mountains. Capital: Nalchik. Pop: 900 500 (2002). Area: 12 500 sq km (4825 sq miles). Also called: Kabardino-Balkaria (ˌkæbəˌdiːnəʊˈbælkɑːrɪə)

kabbalah, kabbala, kabala, cabbala, cabala or **qabalah** (kəˈbɑːlə) *n* **1** an ancient Jewish mystical tradition based on an esoteric interpretation of the Old Testament **2** any secret or occult doctrine or science [c16: from Medieval Latin, from Hebrew *qabbālāh* tradition, what is received, from *qābal* to receive] **> kabbalism, kabalism, cabbalism, cabalism,** or **qabalism** (ˈkæbəˌlɪzəm) *n* **> 'kabbalist, 'kabalist, 'cabbalist, 'cabalist** or **'qabalist** *n* **> ˌkabba'listic, ˌkaba'listic, ˌcabba'listic, ˌcaba'listic** or **ˌqaba'listic** *adj*

kabeljou (ˈkɑːbəlˌjəʊ) *n South African* a large marine sciaenid fish, *Argyrosomus hololepidotus*, that is an important food fish of South African waters [c18: from Afrikaans, from Dutch, cod]

Kabila (kæˈbiːlə) *n* **Laurent** (*French* lorã). 1940–2001, Congolese politician and guerrilla leader: he overthrew the Mobutu regime in Zaïre, becoming president of the renamed Democratic Republic of Congo (1997–2001): assassinated

Kabir (kəˈbɪə) *n* 1440–1518, Indian religious leader who pioneered a religious movement that combined elements of Islam and Hinduism and is considered the precursor of Sikhism

kabuki (kæˈbuːkɪ) *n* a form of Japanese drama based on popular legends and characterized by elaborate costumes, stylized acting, and the use of male actors for all roles [Japanese, from *ka* singing + *bu* dancing + *ki* art]

Kabul (kəˈbʊl, ˈkɑːbᵊl) or **Kabol** *n* **1** the capital of Afghanistan, in the northeast of the country at an altitude of 1800 m (5900 ft) on the **Kabul River**: over 3000 years old, with a strategic position commanding passes through the Hindu Kush and main routes to the Khyber Pass; destroyed and rebuilt many times; capital of the Mogul Empire from 1504 until 1738 and of Afghanistan from 1773; university (1932). Pop: 3 288 000 (2005 est) **2** a river in Afghanistan and Pakistan, rising in the Hindu Kush and flowing east into the Indus at Attock, Pakistan. Length: 700 km (435 miles)

Kabyle (kəˈbaɪl) *n* **1** *pl* **-byles** or **-byle** a member of a Berber people inhabiting the E Atlas Mountains in Tunisia and Algeria **2** the dialect of Berber spoken by this people [c19: from Arabic *qabā'il*, plural of *qabīlah* tribe]

Kaczynski (kæˈtʃɪnskɪ) *n* **Lech.** born 1949, Polish politician, president of Poland from 2005

Kádár ('ka:da:r) *n* János ('ja:noʃ). 1912–89, Hungarian statesman; Communist prime minister of Hungary (1956–58; 1961–65) and first secretary of the Communist Party (1956–88)

kadi ('ka:dɪ, 'keɪdɪ) *n*, *pl* -dis a variant spelling of **cadi**

Kaduna (kə'du:nə) *n* **1** a state of N Nigeria. Capital: Kaduna. Pop: 6 066 562 (2006). Area: 46 053 sq km (17 781 sq miles) **2** a city in N central Nigeria, capital of Kaduna state on the **Kaduna River** (a principal tributary of the Niger). Pop: 1 329 000 (2005 est)

Kaesŏng ('keɪ'sɒŋ) *n* a city in SW North Korea: former capital of Korea (938–1392). Pop: 621 000 (2005 est)

Kaffir *or* **Kafir** ('kæfə) *n*, *pl* -firs *or* -fir **1** *taboo* (in southern Africa) any Black African **2** *offensive* (among Muslims) a non-Muslim or infidel [c19: from Arabic *kāfir* infidel, from *kafara* to deny, refuse to believe]

kaffir beer *n South African* a former, taboo name for **sorghum beeer**

kaffirboom ('kæfə,buəm) *n South African* a former, taboo name for *Erythrina caffra*, now known as **coral tree** [from KAFFIR + Afrikaans *boom* tree]

kaffir corn *or sometimes US* **kafir corn** an old-fashioned and now taboo name for a Southern African variety of sorghum, cultivated in dry regions for its grain and as fodder

Kaffraria (kæ'frɛərɪə) *n* a former region of S central South Africa: inhabited chiefly by people then known as the Kaffirs; British Kaffraria was a crown colony established in 1853 in the southwest of the region and annexed to Cape Colony in 1865 ▷ **Kaffrarian** *adj, n*

Kafir ('kæfə) *n*, *pl* -irs *or* -ir another name for the **Nuri** [c19: from Arabic; see KAFFIR]

Kafiristan (,kæfɪrɪ'sta:n) *n* the former name of **Nuristan**

Kafka ('kæfkə; *Czech* 'kafka) *n* Franz (frants). 1883–1924, Czech novelist writing in German. In his two main novels *The Trial* (1925) and *The Castle* (1926), published posthumously against his wishes, he portrays man's fear, isolation, and bewilderment in a nightmarish dehumanized world ▷ **Kafkaesque** (,kæfkə'ɛsk) *adj*

kaftan *or* **caftan** ('kæftæn, -,ta:n) *n* **1** a long coatlike garment, usually worn with a belt and made of rich fabric, worn in the East **2** an imitation of this, worn, esp by women, in the West, consisting of a loose dress with long wide sleeves [c16: from Turkish *qaftān*]

Kagera (kæ'gɛrə) *n* a river in E Africa, rising in headstreams on the border between Tanzania and Rwanda and flowing east to Lake Victoria: the most remote headstream of the Nile and largest tributary of Lake Victoria. Length: about 480 km (300 miles)

Kagoshima (,kægʊ'ʃi:mə) *n* a port in SW Japan, on S Kyushu. Pop: 544 840 (2002 est)

kagoul *or* **kagoule** (kə'gu:l) *n* variant spellings of: **cagoule**

kahawai ('ka:hə,waɪ) *n* a large food and game fish of Australian and New Zealand coastal waters, *Arripis trutta*, that is greenish grey to silvery underneath and spotted with brown: resembles a salmon but is in fact a marine perch [Māori]

Kahn (ka:n) *n* **1** Herman. 1922–83, US mathematician and futurologist; director of the Hudson Institute (1961–83) **2** Louis I(sadore). 1901–74, US architect, noted for his art museums at Yale (1951–53), Fort Worth (1966–72), and New Haven (1969–74)

kai (kaɪ) *n NZ* food [Māori, from Melanesian pidgin *kaikai*]

kaiak ('kaɪæk) *n* a variant of **kayak**

Kaieteur Falls (,kaɪə'tʊə) *pl n* a waterfall in Guyana, on the Potaro River. Height: 226 m (741 ft). Width: about 107 m (350 ft)

Kaifeng ('kaɪ'fɛŋ) *n* a city in E China, in N Henan on the Yellow River: one of the oldest cities in China and its capital (as Pien-liang) from 907 to 1126. Pop: 810 000 (2005 est)

kail (keɪl) *n* a variant spelling of **kale¹**

kai moana (mɒʊ'ænə) *n NZ* seafood [Māori, from KAI + *moana* sea]

kainite ('kaɪnaɪt) *n* a white mineral consisting of potassium chloride and magnesium sulphate: a fertilizer and source of potassium salts. Formula:

$KCl.MgSO_4.3H_2O$ [c19: from German *Kainit*, from Greek *kainos* new + -ITE¹]

Kairouan (*French* kɛrwã), **Kairwan** *or* **Qairwan** (kaɪə'wa:n) *n* a city in NE Tunisia: one of the holy cities of Islam; pilgrimage and trading centre. Pop: 124 000 (2005 est)

Kaiser¹ ('kaɪzə) *n* (*sometimes not capital*) *history* **1** any German emperor, esp Wilhelm II (1888–1918) **2** *obsolete* any Austro-Hungarian emperor [c16: from German, ultimately from Latin *Caesar* emperor, from the cognomen of Gaius Julius Caesar (100–44 BC), Roman general, statesman, and historian]

Kaiser² (*German* 'kaɪzər) *n* Georg ('ge:ɔrk). 1878–1945, German expressionist dramatist

Kaiserslautern (*German* kaɪzərs'laʊtərn) *n* a city in W Germany, in S Rhineland-Palatinate. Pop: 999 095 (2003 est)

kaizen *Japanese* (kaɪ'zɛn) *n* a philosophy of continuous improvement of working practices that underlies total quality management and just-in-time business techniques [literally: improvement]

kak ('kʌk) *n South African taboo* **1** faeces **2** rubbish [Afrikaans]

kaka ('ka:kə) *n* a New Zealand parrot, *Nestor meridionalis*, with a long compressed bill [c18: from Māori, perhaps imitative of its call]

kaka beak *n* an evergreen climbing shrub, *Clianthus puniceus*, having pinnate leaves and clusters of bright red flowers in the shape of a parrot's beak. It is native to New Zealand but now rare except in cultivation

kakapo ('ka:kə,pəʊ) *n*, *pl* -pos a ground-living nocturnal parrot, *Strigops habroptilus*, of New Zealand, resembling an owl [c19: from Māori, literally: night kaka]

kakariki ('ka:ka:,ri:ki:) *n*, *pl* kakariki any of various green-feathered New Zealand parrots of the genus *Cyanoramphus* [Māori]

kakemono (,kækɪ'məʊnəʊ) *n*, *pl* -nos a Japanese paper or silk wall hanging, usually long and narrow, with a picture or inscription on it and a roller at the bottom [c19: from Japanese, from *kake* hanging + *mono* thing]

kala-azar (,ka:lə'za:) *n* a tropical infectious disease caused by the protozoan *Leishmania donovani* in the liver, spleen, etc, characterized by fever and weight loss; visceral leishmaniasis [from Assamese *kālā* black + *āzār* disease]

Kalahari (,kælə'ha:rɪ) *n* the Kalahari an extensive arid plateau of South Africa, Namibia, and Botswana. Area: 260 000 sq km (100 000 sq miles). Also called: **Kalahari Desert**

Kalamazoo (,kæləmə'zu:) *n* a city in SW Michigan, midway between Detroit and Chicago: aircraft, missile parts. Pop: 75 312 (2003 est)

Kalashnikov (,kə'læʃnɪ,kɒf) *n* a Russian-made automatic rifle. See also **AK-47** [c20: named after Mikhail *Kalashnikov* (born 1919), its designer]

Kalat *or* **Khelat** (kə'la:t) *n* a region of SW Pakistan, in S Baluchistan: formerly a princely state ruled by the Khan of Kalat, which joined Pakistan in 1948

kale *or* **kail** (keɪl) *n* **1** a cultivated variety of cabbage, *Brassica oleracea acephala*, with crinkled leaves: used as a potherb **2** *Scot* a cabbage ▷ Compare **sea kale** [Old English *cāl*; see COLE]

kaleidoscope (kə'laɪdə,skəʊp) *n* **1** an optical toy for producing symmetrical patterns by multiple reflections in inclined mirrors enclosed in a tube. Loose pieces of coloured glass, paper, etc, are placed between transparent plates at the far end of the tube, which is rotated to change the pattern **2** any complex pattern of frequently changing shapes and colours [c19: from Greek *kalos* beautiful + *eidos* form + -SCOPE] ▷ **kaleidoscopic** (kə,laɪdə'skɒpɪk) *adj*

kalends ('kælɪndz) *pl n* a variant spelling of **calends**

Kalevala (,ka:lə'va:lə; *Finnish* 'kɑlevɑlɑ) *n Finnish legend* **1** the land of the hero Kaleva, who performed legendary exploits **2** the Finnish national epic in which these exploits are recounted, compiled by Elias Lönnrot from folk poetry in 1835 to 1849 [Finnish, from *kaleva* of a hero + -*la* dwelling place, home]

kaleyard *or* **kailyard** ('keɪl,ja:d; *Scot* -,jard) *n Scot* a vegetable garden [c19: literally: cabbage garden]

kaleyard school *or* **kailyard school** *n* a group of writers who depicted the sentimental and homely aspects of life in the Scottish Lowlands from about 1880 to 1914. The best known contributor to the school was J. M. Barrie

Kalgan ('kɑ:l'gɑ:n) *n* a former name of **Zhangjiakou**

Kalgoorlie (kæl'guəlɪ) *n* a city in Western Australia, adjoining the town of Boulder: a centre of the Coolgardie gold rushes of the early 1890s; declining gold resources superseded by the discovery of nickel ore in 1966. Pop: 28 281 (including Boulder) (2001)

Kali ('kɑ:lɪ) *n* the Hindu goddess of destruction, consort of Siva. Her cult was characterized by savagery and cannibalism

Kalidasa (ˌkælɪ'dɑ:sə) *n* ?5th century AD, Indian dramatist and poet, noted for his romantic verse drama *Sakuntala*

Kalimantan (ˌkælɪ'mæntən) *n* the Indonesian name for Borneo: applied to the Indonesian part of the island only, excluding the Malaysian states of Sabah and Sarawak and the sultanate of Brunei. Pop: 11 341 558 (2000)

Kalinin¹ (*Russian* ka'linin) *n* the former name (until 1991) of **Tver**

Kalinin² (*Russian* ka'linin) *n* **Mikhail Ivanovich** (mixa'il i'vanəvitʃ). 1875–1946, Soviet statesman: titular head of state (1919–46); a founder of *Pravda* (1912)

Kaliningrad (*Russian* kəlinin'grat) *n* a port in W Russia, on the Pregolya River: severely damaged in World War II as the chief German naval base on the Baltic; ceded to the Soviet Union in 1945 and is now Russia's chief Baltic naval base. Pop: 436 000 (2005 est). Former name (until 1946): Königsberg

Kalisz (*Polish* 'kaliʃ) *n* a town in central Poland, on an island in the Prosna River: textile industry. Pop: 110 000 (2005 est)

Kalmar (*Swedish* 'kalmar) *n* a port in SE Sweden, partly on the mainland and partly on a small island in the **Sound of Kalmar** opposite Öland: scene of the signing of the Union of Kalmar, which united Sweden, Denmark, and Norway into a single monarchy (1397–1523). Pop: 60 734 (2004 est)

kalmia ('kælmɪə) *n* any evergreen ericaceous shrub of the North American genus *Kalmia*, having showy clusters of white or pink flowers. See also **mountain laurel** [c18: named after Peter *Kalm* (1715–79), Swedish botanist and pupil of Linnaeus]

Kalmuck ('kælmʌk) *or* **Kalmyk** ('kælmɪk) *n* **1** *pl* -mucks, -muck *or* -myks, -myk a member of a Mongoloid people of Buddhist tradition, who migrated from W China in the 17th century **2** the language of this people, belonging to the Mongolic branch of the Altaic family

Kalmuck Republic *or* **Kalmyk Republic** *n* a constituent republic of S Russia, on the Caspian Sea: became subject to Russia in 1646. Capital: Elista. Pop: 292 400 (2002). Area: 76 100 sq km (29 382 sq miles). Also called: Kalmykia

kalong ('kɑ:lɒŋ) *n* any fruit bat of the genus *Pteropus*; a flying fox [Javanese]

kalpa ('kælpə) *n* (in Hindu cosmology) a period in which the universe experiences a cycle of creation and destruction [c18: Sanskrit]

Kaluga (*Russian* ka'lugə) *n* a city in central Russia, on the Oka River. Pop: 340 000 (2005 est)

Kama¹ (*Russian* 'kamə) *n* a river in central Russia, rising in the Ural Mountains and flowing to the River Volga, of which it is the largest tributary. Length: 2030 km (1260 miles)

Kama² ('kɑ:mə) *n* the Hindu god of love [from Sanskrit]

Kamakura (ˌkæmə'kuərə) *n* a city in central Japan, on S Honshu: famous for its Great Buddha (Daibutsu), a 13th-century bronze, 15 m (49 ft) high. Pop: 169 714 (2002 est)

Kama Sutra (ˌkɑ:mə 'su:trə) *n* the Kama Sutra an ancient Hindu text on erotic pleasure and other topics [Sanskrit: book on love, from *kāma* love + *sūtra* thread]

Kamchatka (*Russian* kam'tʃatka) *n* a peninsula in E Russia, between the Sea of Okhotsk and the Bering Sea. Length: about 1200 km (750 miles) > **Kamchatkan**

(*Russian* kam'tʃatkən) *adj, n*

kame (keɪm) *n* an irregular mound or ridge of gravel, sand, etc, deposited by water derived from melting glaciers [c19: Scottish and northern English variant of COMB]

kameez (kə'mi:z) *n pl* -meez *or* -meezes a long tunic worn in the Indian subcontinent, often with shalwar [Urdu *kamis*, from Arabic *qamīṣ*]

Kamensk-Uralski (*Russian* 'kaminsku'raljskij) *n* an industrial city in S Russia. Pop: 183 000 (2005 est)

Kamerlingh-Onnes (*Dutch* 'kamərlɪŋ'ɔnəs) *n* **Heike** ('haɪkə). 1853–1926, Dutch physicist: a pioneer of the physics of low-temperature materials and discoverer (1911) of superconductivity. Nobel prize for physics 1913

Kamerun ('kaməru:n) *n* the German name for **Cameroon**

Kamet ('kʌmɛt, 'kʌmeɪt) *n* a mountain on the border of China and India, west of Nepal in the Himalayas. Height: 7756 m (25 447 ft)

kamik ('kɑ:mɪk) *n* *Canadian* a traditional Inuit boot made of caribou hide or sealskin [from Inuktitut]

kamikaze (ˌkæmɪ'kɑ:zɪ) *n* (*often capital*) **1** (in World War II) one of a group of Japanese pilots who performed suicidal missions by crashing their aircraft, loaded with explosives, into an enemy target, esp a ship **2** (*modifier*) (of an action) undertaken or (of a person) undertaking an action in the knowledge that it will result in the death of the person performing it in order that maximum damage may be inflicted on an enemy: *a kamikaze attack; a kamikaze bomber* **3** (*modifier*) extremely foolhardy and possibly self-defeating: *kamikaze pricing* [c20: from Japanese, from *kami* divine + *kaze* wind, referring to the winds that, according to Japanese tradition, destroyed a Mongol invasion fleet in 1281]

Kamilaroi ('kæmələrɔɪ) *n* an Australian Aboriginal language formerly used in NW New South Wales

Kamloops trout ('kæmˌlu:ps) *n* *Canadian* a variety of rainbow trout found in Canadian lakes

Kammerer (*German* 'kamərər) *n* **Paul**. 1880–1926, Austrian zoologist: noted for his controversial experiments, esp with the midwife toad, apparently demonstrating the inheritance of acquired characteristics. Accused of fraud, he committed suicide

Kampala (kæm'pɑ:lə) *n* the capital and largest city of Uganda, in Central region on Lake Victoria: Makerere University (1961). Pop: 1 208 544 (2002 est)

kampong ('kæmpɒŋ, kæm'pɒŋ) *n* (in Malaysia) a village [c19: from Malay]

Kampuchea (ˌkæmpu'tʃɪə) *n* the name (1976–89) of **Cambodia**

Kan. *abbreviation* Kansas

Kanak (kə'næk) *n* a native or inhabitant of New Caledonia who seeks independence from France [c20: from Hawaiian: man]

Kanaka (kə'nækə, 'kænəkə) *n* **1** (esp in Hawaii) a native Hawaiian **2** (*often not capital*) *Austral* any native of the South Pacific islands, esp (formerly) one abducted to work in Australia [c19: from Hawaiian: man, human being]

Kananga (kə'næŋgə) *n* a city in the SW Democratic Republic of Congo (formerly Zaïre): a commercial centre on the railway from Lubumbashi to Port Francqui. Pop: 424 000 (2005 est). Former name (until 1966): Luluabourg

Kanara *or* **Canara** (kə'nɑ:rə) *n* a region of SW India, in Karnataka on the Deccan Plateau and the W Coast. Area: about 155 000 sq km (60 000 sq miles)

Kanarese *or* **Canarese** (ˌkænə'ri:z) *n* **1** *pl* -rese a member of a people of S India living chiefly in Kanara **2** the language of this people; Kannada

Kanazawa (ˌkænə'zɑ:wə) *n* a port in central Japan, on W Honshu: textile and porcelain industries. Pop: 439 892 (2002 est)

kanban *Japanese* ('kænbæn) *n* **1** a just-in-time manufacturing process in which the movements of materials through a process are recorded on specially designed cards **2** any of the cards used for ordering materials in such a system [literally: advertisement hoarding]

Kanchenjunga (ˌkæntʃənˈdʒʌŋɡə) *n* a variant spelling of **Kangchenjunga**

Kanchipuram (kɑːnˈtʃiːpərəm) *n* a city in SE India, in Tamil Nadu: a sacred Hindu town known as "the Benares of the South"; textile industries. Pop: 152 984 (2001)

Kandahar (ˌkændəˈhɑː) *n* a city in S Afghanistan: an important trading centre, built by Ahmad Shah Durrani (1724–73) as his capital on the site of several former cities. Pop: 436 000 (2005 est)

Kandinsky (*Russian* kanˈdinskij) *n* **Vasili** (vaˈsilij). 1866–1944, Russian expressionist painter and theorist, regarded as the first to develop an entirely abstract style: a founder of *der Blaue Reiter*

Kandy (ˈkændɪ) *n* a city in central Sri Lanka: capital of the kingdom of Kandy from 1480 until 1815, when occupied by the British; sacred Buddhist temple; University of Sri Lanka. Pop: 112 000 (2005 est)

kanga *or* **khanga** (ˈkɑːŋɡə) *n* a piece of gaily decorated thin cotton cloth used as a garment by women in E Africa [from Swahili]

kangaroo (ˌkæŋɡəˈruː) *n, pl* -roos **1** any large herbivorous marsupial of the genus *Macropus* and related genera, of Australia and New Guinea, having large powerful hind legs, used for leaping, and a long thick tail: family *Macropodidae* **2** (*usually plural*) *stock exchange* an Australian share, esp in mining, land, or a tobacco company [c18: probably from a native Australian language] > ˌkangaˈroo-like *adj*

kangaroo closure *n parliamentary procedure* a form of closure in which the chairman or speaker selects certain amendments for discussion and excludes others

kangaroo court *n* an irregular court, esp one set up by prisoners in a jail or by strikers to judge strikebreakers

Kangaroo Island *n* an island in the Indian Ocean, off South Australia. Area: 4350 sq km (1680 sq miles)

kangaroo paw *n* any plant of the Australian genus *Anigozanthos*, resembling a kangaroo's paw, esp the red-and-green flowered *A.manglesii*, which is the floral emblem of Western Australia: family *Haemodoraceae*

kangaroo rat *n* **1** any small leaping rodent of the genus *Dipodomys*, related to the squirrels and inhabiting desert regions of North America, having a stocky body and very long hind legs and tails: family *Heteromyidae* **2** Also called: kangaroo mouse any of several leaping murine rodents of the Australian genus *Notomys*

Kangchenjunga, Kanchenjunga (ˌkæntʃənˈdʒʌŋɡə) *or* **Kinchinjunga** *n* a mountain on the border between Nepal and Sikkim, in the Himalayas: the third highest mountain in the world. Height: 8598 m (28 208 ft)

Kang-de (ˈkæŋˈdeɪ) *or* **Kang-te** (ˈkæŋˈteɪ) *n* title as emperor of Manchukuo of (Henry) **Pu-yi**

KaNgwane (ˌkɑːʔŋˈɡwɑːneɪ) *n* (formerly) a Bantu homeland in South Africa; abolished in 1994. Capital: Schoemansdal. Former name: Swazi Territory

kanji (ˈkændʒɪ, ˈkɑːn-) *n, pl* -ji *or* -jis **1** a Japanese writing system using characters mainly derived from Chinese ideograms **2** a character in this system [Japanese, from Chinese *han* Chinese + *zi* character]

Kano (ˈkɑːnəʊ, ˈkeɪnəʊ) *n* **1** a state of N Nigeria: consists of wooded savanna in the south and scrub vegetation in the north. Capital: Kano. Pop: 9 383 682 (2006). Area: 20 131 sq km (7773 sq miles) **2** a city in N Nigeria, capital of Kano state: transport and market centre. Pop: 674 100 (1996 est)

Kanpur (kɑːnˈpʊə) *n* an industrial city in NE India, in S Uttar Pradesh on the River Ganges: scene of the massacre by Nana Sahib of British soldiers and European families and his later defeat by British forces in 1857. Pop: 2 532 138 (2001). Former name: Cawnpore

Kansas (ˈkænzəs) *n* a state of the central US: consists of undulating prairie, drained chiefly by the Arkansas, Kansas, and Missouri Rivers; mainly agricultural. Capital: Topeka. Pop: 2 723 507 (2003 est). Area: 213 096 sq km (82 277 sq miles). Abbreviations: Kan., Kans. *or* (with zip code) KS

Kansas City *n* **1** a city in W Missouri, at the confluence of the Missouri and Kansas Rivers: important centre of livestock and meat-packing industry. Pop: 442 768 (2003

est) **2** a city in NE Kansas, adjacent to Kansas City, Missouri. Pop: 145 757 (2003 est)

Kansu (ˈkænˈsuː) *n* a variant transliteration of the Chinese name for **Gansu**

Kant (kænt; *German* kant) *n* **Immanuel** (ɪˈmaːnuel). 1724–1804, German idealist philosopher. He sought to determine the limits of man's knowledge in *Critique of Pure Reason* (1781) and propounded his system of ethics as guided by the categorical imperative in *Critique of Practical Reason* (1788)

KANU (ˈkaːnuː) *n acronym for* Kenya African National Union

Kaohsiung, Kao-hsiung (ˈkaʊˈʃjʊŋ) *or* **Gaoxiong** *n* a port in SW Taiwan, on the South China Sea: the chief port of the island. Pop: 1 506 000 (2005 est). Japanese name: Takao

Kaolack (ˈkɑːəʊˌlæk, ˈkaʊlæk) *n* a port in SW Senegal, on the Saloum River. Pop: 299 000 (2005 est)

kaolin *or* **kaoline** (ˈkeɪəlɪn) *n* a fine white clay used for the manufacture of hard-paste porcelain and bone china and in medicine as a poultice and gastrointestinal absorbent. Also called: china clay, china stone [c18: from French, from Chinese *Kaoling* Chinese mountain where supplies for Europe were first obtained, from *kao* high + *ling* hill] > ˈkaoˈlinic *adj*

kaon (ˈkeɪɒn) *n* a meson that has a positive or negative charge and a rest mass of about 966 electron masses, or no charge and a rest mass of 974 electron masses. Also called: K-meson [c20: *ka* representing the letter *k* + (MES)ON]

kapa haka (ˈkɑːpə ˈhɑːkə) *n* NZ the traditional Māori performing arts, often performed competitively [Māori, literally: traditional dance performed by groups in a line]

ka pai (ˌkə ˈpaɪ) *sentence substitute* NZ good! well done! [Māori]

kapellmeister (kæˈpɛlˌmaɪstə) *n, pl* -ter a variant spelling of **capellmeister**

Kapfenberg (*German* ˈkapfənbɛrk) *n* an industrial town in E Austria, in Styria. Pop: 22 234 (2001)

Kapil Dev (ˈkæpɪl ˈdev) *n* (**Ramlal**) **Nikhanj** (nɪˈkændʒ). born 1959, Indian cricketer: captain of India (1983–84)

Kapitza (kəˈpitsə) *n* **Piotr Leonidovich** (ˈpjɒtᵊr lioˌnidovitʃ). 1894–1984, Russian physicist. He worked in England and the USSR, doing research in several areas, particularly cryogenics; Nobel prize for physics in 1978

kapok (ˈkeɪpɒk) *n* a silky fibre obtained from the hairs covering the seeds of a tropical bombacaceous tree, *Ceiba pentandra* (**kapok tree** *or* **silk-cotton tree**): used for stuffing pillows, etc, and for sound insulation [c18: from Malay]

Kaposi's sarcoma (kæˈpəʊsɪz) *n* a form of skin cancer found in Africans and more recently in victims of AIDS [c20: named after Moritz Kohn *Kaposi* (1837–1902), Austrian dermatologist who first described the sores that characterize the disease]

kappa (ˈkæpə) *n* the tenth letter in the Greek alphabet (Κ, κ), a consonant, transliterated as *c* or *k* [Greek, of Semitic origin]

kaput (kæˈpʊt) *adj* (*postpositive*) *informal* ruined, broken, or not functioning [c20: from German *kaputt* done for, from French *être capot* to have made no tricks (literally: to be hoodwinked), from *capot* hooded cloak]

karabiner (ˌkærəˈbiːnə) *n* *mountaineering* a metal clip with a spring for attaching to a piton, belay, etc. Also called: snaplink, krab [shortened from German *Karabinerhaken*, literally: carbine hook, that is, one used to attach carbines to a belt]

Karachai-Cherkess Republic (kərʌˈtʃɛəˈkɛs) *or* **Karachayevo-Cherkess Republic** (kərʌˈtʃaɪɛvəʊtʃɛəˈkɛs) *n* a constituent republic of W Russia, on the N side of the Caucasus Mountains. Capital: Cherkessk. Pop: 439 700 (2002). Area: 14 100 sq km (5440 sq miles). Also called: Karachai-Cherkessia (kærəˌtʃaɪtʃɛəˈkɛsɪə)

Karachi (kəˈrɑːtʃɪ) *n* a port in S Pakistan, on the Arabian Sea: capital of Pakistan (1947–60); university (1950); chief port: commercial and industrial centre. Pop: 11 819 000 (2005 est)

k

Karadžić (ˈkærədʒjɪtʃ) n **Radovan** (ˈrædəvæn). born 1945, Bosnian Serb political leader and psychiatrist; charged with genocide by the International War Crimes Tribunal for his role in the Bosnian civil war of 1992–95; in hiding

Karafuto (ˌkɑːrɑːˈfuːtɔ) n transliteration of the Japanese name for **Sakhalin**

Karaganda (Russian kərəganˈda) n a city in E central Kazakhstan, founded in 1857: a major coal-mining and industrial centre. Pop: 412 000 (2005 est). Also called: Qaraghandy

Karajan (German ˈkaːrajan) n **Herbert von** (ˈhɛrbɛrt fɔn). 1908–89, Austrian conductor

Kara-Kalpak Autonomous Republic (kəˈrɑːkəlˈpaːk) n an administrative division in NW Uzbekistan, on the Aral Sea: came under Russian rule by stages from 1873 until Uzbekistan became independent in 1991. Capital: Nukus. Pop: 1 633 900 (2002 est). Area: 165 600 sq km (63 900 sq miles). Also called: Kara-Kalpakia (kəˈrɑːkəlˈpaːkɪə), Kara-Kalpakstan (kəˈrɑːkəlˌpaːkˌstæn, -ˈstaːn)

karakia (ˌkɑːrəˈkiːə) n NZ a prayer [Māori]

Karakoram or **Karakorum** (ˌkærəˈkɔːrəm) n a mountain system in N Kashmir, extending for about 480 km (300 miles) from northwest to southeast: contains the second highest peak in the world (K2); crossed by several high passes, notably the **Karakoram Pass** 5575 m (18 290 ft)

Karakorum (ˌkærəˈkɔːrəm) n a ruined city in Mongolia: founded in 1220 by Ghenghis Khan; destroyed by Kublai Khan when his brother rebelled against him, after Kublai Khan had moved his capital to Peking (now Beijing)

karakul or **caracul** (ˈkærəkᵊl) n **1** a breed of sheep of central Asia having coarse black, grey, or brown hair: the lambs have soft curled usually black hair **2** the fur prepared from these lambs ▷ See also **Persian lamb** [c19: from Russian, from the name of a region in Bukhara where the sheep originated]

Kara Kum (Russian kərə ˈkum) n a desert in Turkmenistan, covering most of the country: extensive areas now irrigated. Area: about 300 000 sq km (120 000 sq miles)

Karamanlis (Greek karamanˈlis) n **Konstantinos** (kɔnstanˈtinɔs). 1907–98, Greek statesman; prime minister of Greece (1955–58; 1958–61; 1961–63; 1974–80): president of Greece (1980–85; 1990–95)

Karan (ˈkærən) n **Donna**. born 1948, US fashion designer

karanga (kəˈræŋə) n NZ a call or chant of welcome, sung by a female elder [Māori]

karaoke (ˌkɑːrəˈəʊkɪ) n **a** an entertainment of Japanese origin in which people take it in turns to sing well-known songs over a prerecorded backing tape **b** (as modifier): a karaoke bar [from Japanese, from kara empty + ōkesutora orchestra]

Kara Sea (ˈkɑːrə) n a shallow arm of the Arctic Ocean off the N coast of Russia: ice-free for about three months of the year

karat (ˈkærət) n US & Canadian a measure of the proportion of gold in an alloy, expressed as the number of parts of gold in 24 parts of the alloy. Also spelt (in Britain and certain other countries): **carat** [c16: from Old French, from Medieval Latin carratus, from Arabic qīrāt weight of four grains, carat, from Greek keration a little horn, from keras horn]

karate (kəˈrɑːtɪ) n **a** a traditional Japanese system of unarmed combat, employing smashes, chops, kicks, etc, made with the hands, feet, elbows, or legs **b** (as modifier): a karate chop to the head [Japanese, literally: empty hand, from kara empty + te hand]

karateka (kəˈrɑːtɪˌkæ) n a competitor or expert in karate [Japanese; see KARATE]

Karbala (ˈkɑːbələ) or **Kerbela** n a town in central Iraq: the chief holy city of Iraq and centre of Shiah Muslim pilgrimage; burial place of Mohammed's grandson Husain. Pop: 460 000 (2005 est)

Karelia (kəˈriːlɪə; Russian kaˈreljə) n **1** a region of NE Europe comprising areas of both Finland and Russia. Following the Russo-Finnish War (1939–40) a large part of what had been Finnish Karelia was annexed by the former Soviet Union; together with the part of Karelia which already belonged to Russia at that time, it corresponds roughly to the modern Karelian Republic in Russia **2** another name for the **Karelian Republic** ▷ Ka'relian adj, n

Karelian Isthmus n a strip of land, now in Russia, between the Gulf of Finland and Lake Ladoga: annexed by the former Soviet Union after the Russo-Finnish War (1939–40)

Karelian Republic n a constituent republic of NW Russia between the White Sea and Lakes Onega and Ladoga. Capital: Petrozavodsk. Pop: 716 700 (2002). Area: 172 400 sq km (66 560 sq miles). Also called: Karelia

Kariba (kɑːˈriːbə) **Lake Kariba** n a lake on the Zambia-Zimbabwe border, created by the building of the **Kariba Dam** across the Zambezi for hydroelectric power. Length: 282 km (175 miles)

Karitane (ˌkærɪˈtɑːnɪ) n short for **Karitane nurse**

Karitane nurse n NZ a nurse trained in the care of young babies and their mothers according to the principles of the Plunket Society. Often shortened to: Karitane

Karl-Marx-Stadt (German karlˈmarksʃtat) n the former name (1953–90) of **Chemnitz**

Karloff (ˈkɑːlɒf) n **Boris**, real name William Pratt 1887–1969, English film actor, famous for his roles in horror films, esp Frankenstein (1931)

Karlovy Vary (Czech ˈkarlɔvi ˈvari) n a city in the W Czech Republic, at the confluence of the Tepla and Ohře Rivers: warm mineral springs. Pop: 50 691 (2007 est)

Karlskrona (ˈkaɪlsˌkrəʊnə) n a port in S Sweden: Sweden's main naval base since 1680. Pop: 61 097 (2004 est)

Karlsruhe (German ˈkarlsruːə) n a city in SW Germany, in Baden-Württemberg: capital of the former Baden state. Pop: 282 595 (2003 est)

karma (ˈkɑːmə) n **1** Hinduism, Buddhism the principle of retributive justice determining a person's state of life and the state of his reincarnations as the effect of his past deeds **2** destiny or fate [c19: from Sanskrit: action, effect, from karoti he does] ▷ 'karmic adj

Karnak (ˈkɑːnæk) n a village in E Egypt, on the Nile: site of the N part of the ruins of ancient Thebes

Karnataka (kəˈnɑːtəkə) n a state of S India, on the Arabian Sea: consists of a narrow coastal plain rising to the South Deccan plateau; mainly agricultural. Capital: Bangalore. Pop: 52 733 958 (2001). Area: 191 791 sq km (74 051 sq miles). Former name (1956–73): Mysore

Kärnten (ˈkɛrntən) n the German name for: **Carinthia**

Karoo or **Karroo** (kəˈruː) n, pl -roos (often not capital) **1** any of several high arid plateaus in South Africa, esp the **Central Karoo** and the **Little Karoo**. The highveld, north of the Central Karoo, is sometimes called the **Northern Karoo 2** a period or rock system in Southern Africa equivalent to the period or system extending from the Upper Carboniferous to the Lower Jurassic: divided into **Lower** and **Upper Karoo** ▷ adj **3** of, denoting, or formed in the Karoo period [c18: from Afrikaans karo, probably from Khoikhoi garo desert]

kaross (kəˈrɒs) n a garment of skins worn by indigenous peoples in southern Africa [c18: from Afrikaans karos, perhaps from Dutch kuras, from French cuirasse CUIRASS]

Karpov (Russian ˈkarpəf) n **Anatoly** (anaˈtɔlij). born 1951, Russian chess player: world champion (1975–85); FIDE world champion (1993–99)

karri (ˈkærɪ) n, pl -ris **1** an Australian eucalyptus tree, Eucalyptus diversifolia **2** the durable wood of this tree, used esp for construction [from a native Australian language]

Karsh (kɑːʃ) n **Yousuf**. 1908–2002, Canadian photographer noted for portraits, especially of famous subjects

karst (kɑːst) n (modifier) denoting the characteristic scenery of a limestone region, including underground streams, gorges, etc [c19: German, from Karst, limestone plateau near Trieste]

kart (kɑːt) n a light low-framed vehicle with small wheels and engine used for recreational racing. Also called: go-cart, go-kart

karyo- or **caryo-** combining form indicating the nucleus of a cell [from New Latin, from Greek *karuon* kernel, nut]

karyotype ('kærɪəˌtaɪp) *n* **1** the appearance of the chromosomes in a somatic cell of an individual or species, with reference to their number, size, shape, etc ▷ *vb* (*tr*) **2** to determine the karyotype of (a cell) > karyotypic (ˌkærɪə'tɪpɪk) *or* ˌkaryo'typical *adj*

Karzai ('kɑːzdɪ) *n* **Hamid.** born 1957, Afghan military and political leader: president from 2002

Kasai (kɑ'saɪ) *n* a river in southwestern Africa, rising in central Angola and flowing east then north as part of the border between Angola and the Democratic Republic of Congo (formerly Zaïre), continuing northwest through the Democratic Republic of Congo to the River Congo. Length: 2154 km (1338 miles)

kasbah *or* **casbah** ('kæzbɑː) *n* (*sometimes capital*) **1** the citadel of any of various North African cities **2** the quarter in which a kasbah is located [from Arabic *qasba* citadel]

kasha ('kɑːʃə) *n* a dish originating in Eastern Europe, consisting of boiled or baked buckwheat [from Russian]

Kashi ('kɑːʃiː) *or* **Kashgar** ('kɑːʃgɑː) *n* an oasis city in W China, in W Xinjiang. Pop: 318 000 (2005 est)

Kashmir (kæʃ'mɪə) *n* a region of SW central Asia: from the 16th century ruled by the Moguls, Afghans, Sikhs, and British successively; since 1947 disputed between India, Pakistan, and China; 84 000 sq km (33 000 sq miles) in the northwest are held by Pakistan and in part known as Azad Kashmir (Free Kashmir), part as the Northern Areas; an area of 42 735 sq km (16 496 sq miles) in the east (the Aksai Chin) is held by China; the remainder was in 1956 officially incorporated into India as the state of Jammu and Kashmir; traversed by the Himalaya and Karakoram mountain ranges and the Rivers Jhelum and Indus; a fruit-growing and cattle-grazing region, with a woollen industry. Capitals: (Jammu and Kashmir) Srinagar (summer), Jammu (winter); (Azad Kashmir) Muzaffarabad; (Northern Areas) Gilgit ▷ Kash'miri *adj*, *n* ▷ Kash'mirian *adj*, *n*

kashruth *or* **kashrut** *Hebrew* (kaʃ'ruːt) *n* **1** the condition of being fit for ritual use in general **2** the system of dietary laws which require ritual slaughter, the removal of excess blood from meat, and the complete separation of milk and meat, and prohibit such foods as pork and shellfish ▷ See also **kosher** (sense 1) [literally: appropriateness, fitness]

Kasparov ('kæspərɒf) *n* **Garry** ('gærɪ), real name *Garik Weinstein*. born 1963, Armenian-Jewish chess player, born in Azerbaijan: world champion (1985–93); PCA world champion (1993–2000)

Kassa ('kɒʃʃɔ) *n* the Hungarian name for **Košice**

Kassala (kə'sɑːlə) *n* a city in the E Sudan: founded as a fort by the Egyptians in 1834. Pop: 430 000 (2005 est)

Kassel *or* **Cassel** (*German* 'kasəl) *n* a city in central Germany, in Hesse; capital of Westphalia (1807–13) and of the Prussian province of Hesse-Nassau (1866–1945). Pop: 194 322 (2003 est)

kata ('kætə) *n* an exercise consisting of a sequence of the specific movements of a martial art, used in training and designed to show skill in technique [c20: Japanese, literally: shape, pattern]

kata- *prefix* a variant of **cata-**

katabatic (ˌkætə'bætɪk) *adj* (of winds) blowing downhill through having become denser with cooling, esp at night when heat is lost from the earth's surface

Katanga (kə'tæŋɡə) *n* a region of SE Democratic Republic of Congo: site of a secessionist movement during the 1960s and again in 1993; important for hydroelectric power and rich mineral resources (copper and tin ore). Pop: estimates vary between 4 000 000 (1998) and 8 000 000 (2006). Area: 496 964 sq km (191 878 sq miles). Former name (1972–97): **Shaba**

Katar (kæ'tɑː) *n* a variant spelling of **Qatar**

Kathiawar (ˌkætɪə'wɑː) *n* a large peninsula of W India, in Gujarat between the Gulf of Kutch and the Gulf of Cambay. Area: about 60 690 sq km (23 430 sq miles)

katipo ('kætɪˌpəʊ, 'kɑːd-) *n*, *pl* -pos a small venomous spider, *Latrodectus katipo*, of New Zealand, commonly black with a red or orange stripe on the abdomen [Māori]

Katmai ('kætmaɪ) *n* Mount Katmai a volcano in SW Alaska, in the Aleutian Range: erupted in 1912 forming the Valley of Ten Thousand Smokes, a region with numerous fumaroles; established as **Katmai National Monument**, 10 917 sq km (4215 sq miles), in 1918. Height: 2100 m (7000 ft). Depth of crater: 1130 m (3700 ft). Width of crater: about 4 km (2.5 miles)

Katmandu *or* **Kathmandu** (ˌkætmæn'duː) *n* the capital of Nepal, in the east at the confluence of the Baghmati and Vishnumati Rivers. Pop: 814 000 (2005 est)

Katowice (*Polish* katɔ'vitsɛ) *n* an industrial city in S Poland. Pop: 2 914 000 (2005 est). Former name (1953–56): Stalinogrod

Katrine ('kætrɪn) *n* Loch Katrine a lake in central Scotland, east of Loch Lomond: noted for its associations with Sir Walter Scott's *Lady of the Lake*. Length: about 13 km (8 miles)

Katsina (kæt'siːnə) *n* **1** a state of N Nigeria. Capital: Katsina. Pop: 5 792 578 (2006). Area: 24 192 sq km (9341 sq miles) **2** a city in N Nigeria, in Katsina state: a major intellectual and cultural centre of the Hausa people (16th–18th centuries). Pop: 530 000 (2005 est)

Kattegat ('kætɪˌgæt) *n* a strait between Denmark and Sweden: linked by the Sound, the Great Belt, and the Little Belt with the Baltic Sea and by the Skagerrak with the North Sea

katydid ('keɪtɪˌdɪd) *n* any typically green long-horned grasshopper of the genus *Microcentrum* and related genera, living among the foliage of trees in North America [c18: of imitative origin]

Katz ('kæts) *n* Sir **Bernard.** 1911–2003, British neurophysiologist, born in Germany. Shared the Nobel prize for physiology or medicine (1970) with Julius Axelrod and Ulf von Euler

Kauai (kɑː'wɑːiː) *n* a volcanic island in NW Hawaii, northwest of Oahu. Chief town: Lihue. Pop (Kauai county): 60 747 (2003 est). Area (island): 1433 sq km (553 sq miles)

Kauffmann ('kaʊfmən) *n* **Angelica** (andʒe'likə). 1741–1807, Swiss painter, who worked chiefly in England

Kaufman ('kaʊfmən) *n* **George S(imon).** 1889–1961, US dramatist who, with Moss Hart, collaborated on many Broadway comedy hits

kaumatua (kaʊ'mɑːtuːə) *n* NZ a senior member of a tribe; elder [Māori]

Kaunas ('kaʊnəs) *n* a city in central Lithuania at the confluence of the Neman and Viliya Rivers: ceded by Poland to Russia in 1795; became the provisional capital of Lithuania (1920–40); incorporated into the Soviet Union 1944–91; university (1922). Pop: 364 000 (2005 est). Russian name: Kovno

Kaunda (kɑː'ʊndə) *n* **Kenneth (David).** born 1924, Zambian statesman. He became Zambia's first president (1964–91)

kaupapa (kaʊ'pɑːpə) *n* NZ a strategy, policy, or cause [Māori]

kauri ('kaʊrɪ) *n*, *pl* -ris **1** a New Zealand coniferous tree, *Agathis australis*, with oval leaves and round cones: family Araucariaceae **2** the wood or resin of this tree [c19: Māori]

kauri gum *n* a hard resin from the kauri tree, found usually as a fossil in the soil where an extinct tree once grew: used chiefly in making varnishes

kava ('kɑːvə) *n* **1** a Polynesian shrub, *Piper methysticum*: family Piperaceae **2** a drink prepared from the aromatic roots of this shrub [c18: from Polynesian (Tongan): bitter]

Kaválla (kə'vælə; *Greek* ka'vala) *n* a port in E Greece, in Macedonia East and Thrace region on the **Bay of Kaválla** an important Macedonian fortress of the Byzantine empire; ceded to Greece by Turkey after the Balkan War (1912–13). Pop (municipality): 63 572 (2001)

Kavir Desert (kæ'vɪə) *n* another name for the **Dasht-i-Kavir**

Kawabata (ˌkæwə'bɑːtə) *n* **Yasunari** (ˌjæsʊ'nɑːrɪ). 1899–1972, Japanese novelist, author of *Yukiguni* (*Snow Country*, 1948) and *Yama no oto* (*The Sound of the Mountain*, 1954): Nobel prize for literature 1968

Kawasaki (ˌkɑːwə'sɑːkɪ) *n* an industrial port in central

k

Japan, on SE Honshu, between Tokyo and Yokohama. Pop: 1 245 780 (2002 est)

Kawasaki's disease (ˌkæwəˈsækɪ) *n* a disease of children that causes a rash, fever, and swelling of the lymph nodes and often damages the heart muscle [c20: named after T. *Kawasaki*, Japanese physician who first described it]

Kay (keɪ) *n* **Sir Kay** (in Arthurian legend) the braggart foster brother and steward of King Arthur

kayak *or* **kaiak** (ˈkaɪæk) *n* **1** a small light canoe-like boat used by the Inuit, consisting of a light frame covered with watertight animal skins **2** a fibreglass or canvas-covered canoe of similar design [c18: from Inuktitut (Greenland dialect)]

kaylied (ˈkeɪliːd) *adj Brit slang* intoxicated; drunk

kayo *or* **KO** (ˈkeɪˈəʊ) *slang n, pl* kayos **1** *boxing* another term for **knockout** ▷ *vb* kayoes *or* kayos, kayoing, kayoed **2** *boxing* another term for **knock out** [c20: from the initial letters of *knock out*]

Kayseri (ˌkaɪsɛˈriː; *Turkish* ˈkaiseri) *n* a city in central Turkey: trading centre since ancient times as the chief city of Cappadocia. Pop: 605 000 (2005 est)

Kazakh *or* **Kazak** (kəˈzɑːk, kɑː-) *n* **1** *pl* -zakhs *or* -zaks a member of a traditionally Muslim Mongoloid people of Kazakhstan **2** the language of this people, belonging to the Turkic branch of the Altaic family

Kazakhstan *or* **Kazakstan** (ˌkɑːzɑːkˈstæn, -ˈstɑːn) *n* a republic in central Asia: conquered by Mongols in the 13th century; came under Russian control in the 18th and 19th centuries; was a Soviet republic from 1936 until it gained independence in 1991. It has rich mineral deposits and agriculture is important. Official language: Kazakh. Religion: nonreligious, Muslim, and Christian. Official currency: tenge. Capital: Astana (formerly Akmola, Akmolinsk, or Tselinograd); capital functions moved from Almaty (formerly Alma-Ata) in 1997. Pop: 15 403 000 (2004 est). Area: 2 715 100 sq km (1 048 030 sq miles)

Kazan¹ (kəˈzæn, -ˈzɑːn; *Russian* kaˈzanj) *n* a city in W Russia, capital of the Tatar Autonomous Republic on the River Volga: capital of an independent khanate in the 15th century; university (1804); a major industrial centre. Pop: 1 108 000 (2005 est)

Kazan² (kəˈzɑːn) *n* **Elia** (ˈiːljə), real name *Elia Kazanjoglous* 1909–2003, US stage and film director and writer, born in Turkey. His films include *Gentleman's Agreement* (1947) and *On the Waterfront* (1954) for both of which he won Oscars, and *East of Eden* (1955).

Kazan Retto (kɑːˈzɑːn ˈrɛtəʊ) *n* transliteration of the Japanese name for the **Volcano Islands**

Kazantzakis (*Greek* kazanˈdzakis) *n* **Nikos** (ˈnikɔs). 1885–1957, Greek novelist, poet, and dramatist, noted esp for his novels *Zorba the Greek* (1946) and *Christ Recrucified* (1954) and his epic poem *The Odyssey* (1938).

Kazbek (kɑːzˈbɛk) *n* **Mount Kazbek** an extinct volcano in N Georgia in the central Caucasus Mountains. Height: 5047 m (16 558 ft)

Kaz Daği (ˈkaz ˈdaj) *n* the Turkish name for (Mount) **Ida** (sense 2)

kazoo (kəˈzuː) *n, pl* -zoos a cigar-shaped musical instrument of metal or plastic with a membranous diaphragm of thin paper that vibrates with a nasal sound when the player hums into it [c20: probably imitative of the sound produced]

Kb *or* **kb** *computing abbreviation* kilobit

KB *abbreviation* **1** King's Bench (in Britain) **2** *computing* kilobyte

KBE *abbreviation* Knight (Commander of the Order) of the British Empire

Kbps *or* **kbps** *computing abbreviation* kilobits per second

kbyte *abbreviation computing* kilobyte

kc *abbreviation* kilocycle

KC *abbreviation* (in Britain) **1** King's Counsel **2** Kennel Club

kcal *abbreviation* kilocalorie

KCB *abbreviation* Knight Commander of the Bath (a Brit title)

KCMG *abbreviation* Knight Commander (of the Order) of St Michael and St George (a Brit title)

KE *abbreviation* kinetic energy

kea (ˈkeɪə) *n* a large New Zealand parrot, *Nestor notabilis*, with brownish-green plumage [c19: from Māori, imitative of its call]

Kea *n, pl* Kea (in New Zealand) a member of the junior branch of the Scouts [from KEA]

Kéa (ˈkɛə) *n* transliteration of the Modern Greek name for **Keos**

Kean (kiːn) *n* **Edmund**. ?1789–1833, English actor, noted for his Shakespearean roles

Keating (ˈkiːtɪŋ) *n* **Paul**. born 1944, Australian Labor politician; prime minister of Australia (1991–96)

Keaton (ˈkiːtən) *n* **Buster**, real name *Joseph Francis Keaton* 1895–1966, US film comedian who starred in silent films such as *The Navigator* (1924), *The General* (1926), and *Steamboat Bill Junior* (1927)

Keats (kiːts) *n* **John**. 1795–1821, English poet. His finest poetry is contained in *Lamia and other Poems* (1820), which includes *The Eve of St Agnes, Hyperion*, and the odes *On a Grecian Urn, To a Nightingale, To Autumn*, and *To Psyche*

kebab (kəˈbæb) *n* a dish consisting of small pieces of meat, tomatoes, onions, etc, threaded onto skewers and grilled, generally over charcoal. Also called: shish kebab [c17: via Urdu from Arabic *kabāb* roast meat]

Keble (ˈkiːbəl) *n* **John**. 1792–1866, English clergyman. His sermon on national apostasy (1833) is considered to have inspired the Oxford Movement

kecks *or* **keks** (kɛks) *pl n* *Northern English dialect* trousers [c19: from obsolete *kicks* breeches]

Kecskemét (*Hungarian* ˈkɛtʃkɛmeːt) *n* a city in central Hungary: vineyards and fruit farms. Pop: 107 604 (2003 est)

Kedah (ˈkɛdə) *n* a state of NW Malaysia: under Thai control until it came under the British in 1909; the chief exports are rice, tin, and rubber. Capital: Alor Star. Pop: 1 648 756 (2000). Area: 9426 sq km (3639 sq miles)

kedge (kɛdʒ) *nautical vb* **1** to draw (a vessel) along by hauling in on the cable of a light anchor that has been dropped at some distance from it, or (of a vessel) to be drawn in this fashion ▷ *n* **2** a light anchor, used esp for kedging [c15: from *caggen* to fasten]

kedgeree (ˌkɛdʒəˈriː) *n* *chiefly Brit* a lightly curried dish consisting of rice, cooked flaked fish, and hard-boiled eggs [c17: from Hindi *khicarī*, from Sanskrit *khiccā*, of obscure origin]

Kediri (kɪˈdɪərɪ) *n* a city in Indonesia, in E Java: commercial centre. Pop: 244 519 (2000)

Kedron (ˈkɛdrɒn) *or* **Kidron** *n* *Bible* a ravine under the eastern wall of Jerusalem

Keegan (ˈkiːgən) *n* **Kevin**. born 1951, English footballer; manager of Newcastle United (1992–97; 2008); England coach (1999–2000)

keek (kiːk) *n, vb* a Scot word for **peep¹** [c18: probably from Middle Dutch *kīken* to look]

keel¹ (kiːl) *n* **1** one of the main longitudinal structural members of a vessel to which the frames are fastened and that may extend into the water to provide lateral stability **2** on an even keel well-balanced; steady **3** any structure corresponding to or resembling the keel of a ship, such as the central member along the bottom of an aircraft fuselage **4** *biology* a ridgelike part; carina ▷ *vb* **5** to capsize ▷ See also **keel over** [c14: from Old Norse *kjǫlr*; related to Middle Dutch *kiel*, KEEL²]

keel² (kiːl) *n* *Eastern English dialect* **1** a flat-bottomed vessel, esp one used for carrying coal **2** a measure of coal equal to about 21 tons [c14 *kele*, from Middle Dutch *kiel*; compare Old English *cēol* ship]

keelage (ˈkiːlɪdʒ) *n* a fee charged by certain ports to allow a ship to dock

keelhaul (ˈkiːlˌhɔːl) *vb* (*tr*) **1** to drag (a person) by a rope from one side of a vessel to the other through the water under the keel **2** to rebuke harshly [c17: from Dutch *kielhalen*; see KEEL¹, HAUL]

Keeling Islands (ˈkiːlɪŋ) *pl n* another name for the **Cocos Islands**

keel over *vb* (*adverb*) **1** to turn upside down; capsize **2** (*intr*) *informal* to collapse suddenly

keelson (ˈkɛlsən, ˈkiːl-) *or* **kelson** *n* a longitudinal beam fastened to the keel of a vessel for strength and stiffness

[C17: probably from Low German *kielswin*, keel swine, ultimately of Scandinavian origin]

Keelung ('ki:'lʊŋ) *n* another name for **Chilung**

keen[1] (ki:n) *adj* **1** eager or enthusiastic **2** (*postpositive*; foll by *on*) fond (of); devoted (to): *keen on a girl; keen on golf* **3** intellectually acute: *a keen wit* **4** (of sight, smell, hearing, etc) capable of recognizing fine distinctions **5** having a sharp cutting edge or point **6** extremely cold and penetrating: *a keen wind* **7** intense or strong: *a keen desire* **8** *chiefly Brit* extremely low so as to be competitive: *keen prices* [Old English *cēne*; related to Old High German *kuoni* brave, Old Norse *koenn* wise; see CAN[1], KNOW] ▷ **'keenly** *adv* ▷ **'keenness** *n*

keen[2] (ki:n) *vb* (*intr*) **1** to lament the dead ▷ *n* **2** a dirge or lament for the dead [C19: from Irish Gaelic *caoine*, from Old Irish *coínim* I wail] ▷ **'keener** *n*

keener ('ki:nə) *n* *Canadian informal* a person, esp a student, who is keen, enthusiastic, or zealous

keep (ki:p) *vb* **keeps**, **keeping**, **kept** (kɛpt) **1** (*tr*) to have or retain possession of **2** (*tr*) to have temporary possession or charge of: *keep my watch for me during the game* **3** (*tr*) to store in a customary place: *I keep my books in the desk* **4** to remain or cause to remain in a specified state or condition: *keep the dog quiet; keep ready* **5** to continue or cause to continue: *keep the beat; keep in step* **6** (*tr*) to have or take charge or care of: *keep the shop for me till I return* **7** (*tr*) to look after or maintain for use, pleasure, etc: *to keep chickens; keep two cars* **8** (*tr*) to provide for the upkeep or livelihood of **9** (*tr*) to support financially, esp in return for sexual favours **10** to confine or detain or be confined or detained **11** to withhold or reserve or admit of withholding or reserving: *your news will keep till later* **12** (*tr*) to refrain from divulging or violating: *to keep a secret; keep one's word* **13** to preserve or admit of preservation **14** (*tr*; sometimes foll by *up*) to observe with due rites or ceremonies **15** (*tr*) to maintain by writing regular records in: *to keep a diary* **16** (when *intr*, foll by *in*, *on*, *to*, etc) to stay in, on, or at (a place or position): *please keep your seats; keep to the path* **17** (*tr*) to associate with (esp in the phrase **keep bad company**) **18** (*tr*) to maintain in existence: *to keep court in the palace* **19** (*tr*) *chiefly Brit* to have habitually in stock: *this shop keeps all kinds of wool* **20** *how are you keeping?* ▷ *n* **21** living or support **22** *archaic* charge or care **23** Also called: **dungeon** or **donjon** the main tower within the walls of a medieval castle or fortress **24** *informal* **a** completely; permanently **b** for the winner or possessor to keep permanently ▷ See also **keep at**, **keep away** [Old English *cēpan* to observe; compare Old Saxon *kapōn* to look, Old Norse *kōpa* to stare]

keep at *vb* (*preposition*) **1** (*intr*) to persevere with or persist in **2** (*tr*) to constrain (a person) to continue doing (a task)

keep away *vb* (*adverb*; often foll by *from*) to refrain or prevent from coming (near)

keep back *vb* (*adverb*; often foll by *from*) **1** (*tr*) to refuse to reveal or disclose **2** to prevent, be prevented, or refrain from advancing, entering, etc

keep down *vb* (*adverb*, mainly *tr*) **1** to repress; hold in submission **2** to restrain or control: *he had difficulty keeping his anger down* **3** to cause not to increase or rise **4** (*intr*) not to show oneself to one's opponents; lie low **5** to cause (food) to stay in the stomach; not vomit

keeper ('ki:pə) *n* **1** a person in charge of animals, esp in a zoo **2** a person in charge of a museum, collection, or section of a museum **3** a person in charge of other people, such as a warder in a jail **4** See **goalkeeper**, **wicketkeeper**, **gamekeeper** **5** a person who keeps something **6** a soft iron or steel bar placed across the poles of a permanent magnet to close the magnetic circuit when it is not in use

keep fit *n* exercises designed to promote physical fitness if performed regularly

keep from *vb* (*preposition*) **1** (foll by a gerund) to prevent or restrain (oneself or another); refrain or cause to refrain from **2** (*tr*) to protect or preserve from

keeping ('ki:pɪŋ) *n* **1** conformity or harmony (esp in the phrases **in** or **out of keeping**) **2** charge or care: *valuables in the keeping of a bank*

keepnet ('ki:p,nɛt) *n* a cylindrical net strung on wire hoops and sealed at one end, suspended in water by anglers to keep alive the fish they have caught

keep off *vb* **1** to stay or cause to stay at a distance (from) **2** (*preposition*) to not eat or drink or prevent from eating or drinking **3** (*preposition*) to avoid or cause to avoid (a topic)

keep on *vb* (*adverb*) **1** to continue or persist in (doing something): *keep on running* **2** (*tr*) to continue to wear **3** (*tr*) to continue to employ: *the firm kept on only ten men* **4** (*intr*; foll by *about*) to persist in talking (about) **5** (*intr*; foll by *at*) to nag (a person)

keep out *vb* (*adverb*) **1** to remain or cause to remain outside **2** *keep out of* **a** to remain or cause to remain unexposed to **b** to avoid or cause to avoid

keepsake ('ki:p,seɪk) *n* a gift that evokes memories of a person or event with which it is associated

keep to *vb* (*preposition*) **1** to adhere to or stand by or cause to adhere to or stand by **2** to confine or be confined to **3** *keep to oneself* **a** (*intr*) to avoid the society of others **b** (*tr*) to refrain from sharing or disclosing **4** *keep oneself to oneself* to avoid the society of others

keep up *vb* (*adverb*) **1** (*tr*) to maintain (prices, one's morale) at the present level **2** (*intr*) to maintain a pace or rate set by another **3** (*intr*; often foll by *with*) to remain informed: *to keep up with technological developments* **4** (*tr*) to maintain in good condition **5** (*tr*) to hinder (a person) from going to bed at night **6** *keep it up* to continue a good performance **7** *keep up with* to remain in contact with, esp by letter **8** *keep up with the Joneses* *informal* to compete with one's neighbours in material possessions, etc

Keewatin (ki:'weɪtɪn) *n* a former administrative district of the Northwest Territories of Canada stretching from the district of Mackenzie to Hudson Bay; became part of Nunavut in 1999: mostly tundra

kef (kɛf) *n* a variant of **kif**

Kefallonia (ˌkɛfə'ləʊnɪə) *n* another name for **Cephalonia**

keffiyeh (kɛ'fi:jə), **kaffiyeh** or **kufiyah** *n* a cotton headdress worn by Arabs [C19: from Arabic, perhaps from Late Latin *cofea* COIF]

Keflavík ('kɛflə,vɪk) *n* a port in SW Iceland: NATO airbase, fishing. Pop: 7963 (2003 est)

keg (kɛg) *n* **1** a small barrel with a capacity of between five and ten gallons **2** *Brit* an aluminium container in which beer is transported and stored [C17: variant of Middle English *kag*, of Scandinavian origin; related to Old Norse *kaggi* cask]

Keighley ('ki:θlɪ) *n* a town in N England, in Bradford unitary authority, West Yorkshire, on the River Aire: textile industry. Pop: 49 453 (2001)

Keijo (ˌkeɪ'dʒəʊ) *n* transliteration of the Japanese name for **Seoul**

Keitel ('kaɪtəl) *n* **Wilhelm** ('vɪlhɛlm). 1882–1946, German field marshal; chief of the supreme command of the armed forces (1938–45). He was convicted at the Nuremberg trials and executed

Kekkonen (*Finnish* 'kɛkkɔnɛn) *n* **Urho** ('urhɔ). (1900–86), Finnish statesman; president (1956–81)

keks (kɛks) *pl n* a variant spelling of **kecks**

Kekulé von Stradonitz (*German* 'kekule fɔn 'ʃtradonɪts) *n* (**Friedrich**) **August** ('ogʏst). 1829–96, German chemist. His elucidation of the concepts of valence and single, double, and triple bonds enabled him to suggest the structure of many molecules, notably benzene (**Kekulé structure**)

Kelantan (kɛ'læntən, kɪ,læn'tæn) *n* a state of NE Malaysia: under Thai control until it came under the British in 1909; produces rice and rubber. Capital: Kota Bharu. Pop: 1 313 014 (2000). Area: 14 920 sq km (5761 sq miles)

Keller ('kɛlə) *n* **1 Gottfried**. 1819–90, Swiss novelist and short-story writer, who wrote in German: noted esp for the novel *Der Grüne Heinrich* (1855, rewritten 1880) **2 Helen** (**Adams**). 1880–1968, US author and lecturer. Blind and deaf from infancy, she was taught to read, write, and speak and became noted for her work for the handicapped

Kells (kɛlz) *n* a town in the Republic of Ireland, in Co Meath: *The Book of Kells*, an illuminated manuscript of the Gospels, was produced at the monastery here in the 8th century. Pop: 4421 (2002)

Kelly ('kɛlı) n **1 Gene**, full name *Eugene Curran Kelly*. 1912–96, US dancer, choreographer, film actor, and director. His many films include *An American in Paris* (1951) and *Singin' in the Rain* (1952) **2 Grace**. 1929–82, US film actress. Her films included *High Noon* (1952) and *High Society* (1956). She married Prince Rainier III of Monaco in 1956 and died following a car crash **3 Ned**. 1855–80, Australian horse and cattle thief and bushranger, active in Victoria: captured by the police and hanged **4 game as Ned Kelly** or **as game as Ned Kelly** See **game¹** (sense 25)

keloid or **cheloid** ('ki:lɔɪd) n *pathol* a hard smooth pinkish raised growth of scar tissue at the site of an injury, tending to occur more frequently in dark-skinned races [c19: from Greek *khēlē* claw]

kelp (kɛlp) n **1** any large brown seaweed, esp any in the order *Laminariales* **2** the ash of such seaweed, used as a source of iodine and potash [c14: of unknown origin]

kelpie¹ or **kelpy** ('kɛlpɪ) n, *pl* **-pies** an Australian breed of sheepdog, originally developed from Scottish collies, having a smooth coat of various colours and erect ears [named after a particular specimen of the breed, c. 1870]

kelpie² ('kɛlpɪ) n (in Scottish folklore) a water spirit in the form of a horse that drowned its riders [c18: probably related to Scottish Gaelic *cailpeach* heifer, of obscure origin]

kelson ('kɛlsən) n a variant of **keelson**

kelt (kɛlt) n a salmon that has recently spawned and is usually in poor condition [c14: of unknown origin]

Kelt (kɛlt) n a variant of **Celt**

kelter ('kɛltə) n a variant of **kilter**

kelvin ('kɛlvɪn) n the basic SI unit of thermodynamic temperature; the fraction 1/273.16 of the thermodynamic temperature of the triple point of water. Symbol: K

Kelvin ('kɛlvɪn) n **William Thomson**, 1st Baron Kelvin. 1824–1907, British physicist, noted for his work in thermodynamics, inventing the Kelvin scale, and in electricity, pioneering undersea telegraphy

Kelvin scale n a thermodynamic temperature scale based upon the efficiencies of ideal heat engines. The zero of the scale is absolute zero. Originally the degree was equal to that on the Celsius scale but it is now defined so that the triple point of water is exactly 273.16 kelvins. The International Practical Temperature Scale (1968, revised 1990) realizes the Kelvin scale over a wide range of temperatures

Kemal Atatürk (kɛˈmɑːl ˈætəˌtɜːk) n See **Atatürk** > Ke'malism n > Ke'malist n, *adj*

kembla ('kɛmblə) n *Austral slang* small change [from rhyming slang *Kembla Grange*]

Kemble ('kɛmbªl) n **1 Frances Anne**, known as *Fanny*. 1809–93, English actress, in the US from 1832 **2** her uncle, **John Philip**. 1757–1823, English actor and theatrical manager

Kemerovo (*Russian* 'kjemɪrəvə) n a city in S Russia: a major coal-mining centre of the Kuznetsk Basin, with important chemical plants. Pop: 479 000 (2005 est). Former name (until 1932): Shcheglovsk

Kempe (kɛmp) n **1 Margery**. ?1373–?1440, English mystic. Her autobiography, *The Book of Margery Kempe*, describes her mystical experiences and pilgrimages in Europe and Palestine **2** (*German* 'kɛmpə) **Rudolf** ('ru:dɔlf). 1910–76, German orchestral conductor, noted esp for his interpretations of Wagner

Kempis ('kɛmpɪs) n **Thomas à.** ?1380–1471, German Augustinian monk, generally regarded as the author of the devotional work *The Imitation of Christ*

kempt (kɛmpt) *adj* (of hair) tidy; combed. See also **unkempt** [c20: back formation from *unkempt*; originally past participle of dialect *kemb* to **comb**]

ken (kɛn) n **1** range of knowledge or perception (esp in the phrases **beyond** or **in one's ken**) ▷ *vb* kens, kenning, kenned or kent (kɛnt) **2** *Scot & northern English dialect* to know **3** *Scot & northern English dialect* to understand; perceive **4** (*tr*) *archaic* to see [Old English *cennan*; related to Old Norse *kenna* to perceive, Old High German *kennen* to make known; see **can¹**]

Ken. *abbreviation* Kentucky

Kendal ('kɛndªl) n a town in NW England, in Cumbria: a gateway town to the Lake District, with an ancient woollen industry. Pop: 28 030 (2001)

Kendall ('kɛndəl) n **Edward Calvin**. 1886–1972, US biochemist, who isolated the hormone thyroxine (1916). He shared the Nobel prize for physiology or medicine (1950) with Phillip Hench and Tadeus Reichstein for their work on hormones

kendo ('kɛndəʊ) n the Japanese art of fencing with pliable bamboo staves or, sometimes, real swords: strict conventions are observed [from Japanese]

Kendrew ('kɛndru:) n **Sir John Cowdery**. 1917–97, British biochemist. Using X-ray diffraction he discovered the structure of myoglobin, for which he shared a Nobel Prize (1962) with Max Perutz

Keneally (kəˈnælɪ) n **Thomas (Michael)**. born 1935, Australian writer. His novels include the Booker prizewinner *Schindler's Ark* (1982); other works are *The Playmaker* (1987), *The Great Shame* (1998), and *The Woman and Her Hero* (2007)

Kenilworth ('kɛnɪlˌwɜːθ) n a town in central England, in Warwickshire: ruined 12th-century castle, subject of Sir Walter Scott's novel *Kenilworth*. Pop: 22 218 (2001)

Kénitra (*French* kenitra) n a port in NW Morocco, on the Sebou River 16 km (10 miles) from the Atlantic. Pop: 598 000 (2003). Also called: Mina Hassan Tani

Kennedy¹ ('kɛnɪdɪ) n **Cape Kennedy** a former name (1963–73) of (Cape) **Canaveral**

Kennedy² ('kɛnɪdɪ) n **1 Charles Peter**. born 1959, British politician, leader of the Liberal Democrats (1999–2006) **2 Edward (Moore)**, known as *Ted*. born 1932, US Democrat politician; senator since 1962 **3** his brother, **John (Fitzgerald)**, known as *JFK*. 1917–63, US Democrat statesman; 35th president of the US (1961–63), the first Roman Catholic and the youngest man ever to be president. He demanded the withdrawal of Soviet missiles from Cuba (1962) and prepared civil rights reforms; assassinated **4 Nigel (Paul)**. born 1956, British violinist, noted for his flamboyant style **5 Robert (Francis)**, known as *Bobby*, brother of John Kennedy. 1925–68, US Democrat statesman; attorney general (1961–64) and senator for New York (1965–68); assassinated

kennel ('kɛnªl) n **1** a hutlike shelter for a dog. US name: doghouse **2** (*usually plural*) an establishment where dogs are bred, trained, boarded, etc **3** a ramshackle house; hovel **4** a pack of hounds ▷ *vb* -nels, -nelling, -nelled or *US* -nels, -neling, -neled **5** to put or go into a kennel; keep or stay in a kennel [c14: from Old French *chenil*, from Vulgar Latin *canīle* (unattested), from Latin *canis* dog]

Kennelly ('kɛnəlɪ) n **Arthur Edwin**. 1861–1939, US electrical engineer: independently of Heaviside, he predicted the existence of an ionized layer in the upper atmosphere, known as the Kennelly-Heaviside layer or E region

Kenneth I ('kɛnɪθ) n surnamed *MacAlpine*. died 858, king of the Scots of Dalriada and of the Picts (?844–858): considered the first Scottish king

kennett ('kɛnɪt) *vb* (*tr*) *Austral slang* another word for **jeff**

kenning ('kɛnɪŋ) n a conventional metaphoric name for something, esp in Old Norse and Old English poetry, such as Old English *bānhūs* (bone house) for "body" [c14: from Old Norse, from *kenna*; see **ken**]

Kenny ('kɛnɪ) n **1 Brett**. born 1961, Australian rugby league player **2 Yvonne**, born 1950, Australian opera singer

Kensington and Chelsea ('kɛnzɪŋtən) n a borough of Greater London, on the River Thames: **Kensington Palace** (17th century) and gardens. Pop: 174 400 (2003 est). Area: 12 sq km (5 sq miles)

kenspeckle ('kɛnˌspɛkªl) *adj Scot* easily seen or recognized [c18: from dialect *kenspeck*, of Scandinavian origin; compare Old Norse *kennispecki* power of recognition; related to **ken**]

Kent¹ (kɛnt) n a county of SE England, on the English Channel: the first part of Great Britain to be colonized by the Romans; one of the seven kingdoms of Anglo-

Saxon England until absorbed by Wessex in the 9th century AD. Apart from the Downs it is mostly low-lying and agricultural, specializing in fruit and hops. The Medway towns of Rochester and Gillingham became an independent unitary authority in 1998. Administrative centre: Maidstone. Pop (excluding Medway): 1 348 800 (2003 est). Area (excluding Medway): 3526 sq km (1361 sq miles) > 'Kentish *adj, n*

Kent² (kɛnt) *n* **William**. ?1685–1748, English architect, landscape gardener, and interior designer

kentledge ('kɛntlɪdʒ) *n nautical* scrap metal used as ballast in a vessel [c17: perhaps from Old French *quintelage* ballast, from *quintal* hundredweight, ultimately from Arabic *qintār; see* KANTAR]

Kentucky (kɛn'tʌkɪ) *n* **1** a state of the S central US: consists of an undulating plain in the west, the Bluegrass region in the centre, the Tennessee and Ohio River basins in the southwest, and the Appalachians in the east. Capital: Frankfort. Pop: 4 117 827 (2003 est). Area: 102 693 sq km (39 650 sq miles). Abbreviations: Ken., Ky *or* (with zip code) KY **2** a river in central Kentucky, rising in the Cumberland Mountains and flowing northwest to the Ohio River. Length: 417 km (259 miles) > Ken'tuckian *n, adj*

Kenya ('kɛnjə, 'kiːnjə) *n* **1** a republic in E Africa, on the Indian Ocean: became a British protectorate in 1895 and a colony in 1920; gained independence in 1963 and is a member of the Commonwealth. Tea and coffee constitute about a third of the total exports. Official languages: Swahili and English. Religions: Christian majority, animist minority. Currency: shilling. Capital: Nairobi. Pop: 32 420 000 (2004 est). Area: 582 647 sq km (224 960 sq miles) **2** Mount Kenya an extinct volcano in central Kenya: the second highest mountain in Africa; girth at 2400 m (8000 ft) is about 150 km (95 miles). The regions above 3200 m (10 500 ft) constitute **Mount Kenya National Park**. Height: 5199 m (17 058 ft) > 'Kenyan *adj, n*

Kenyatta (kɛn'jætə) *n* **Jomo** ('dʒəʊməʊ). ?1891–1978, Kenyan statesman: imprisoned as a suspected leader of the Mau Mau revolt (1953–59); elected president of the Kenya African National Union (1961); prime minister of independent Kenya (1963) and president (1964–78)

Keos ('keɪɒs) *n* an island in the Aegean Sea, in the NW Cyclades. Pop: 2412 (2001). Area: 174 sq km (67 sq miles). Italian name: Zea. Modern Greek name: Kéa

kep (kɛp) *vb* keps, kepping, keppit ('kɛpɪt) *(tr) Scot & N English dialect* to catch [from KEEP (in obsolete sense: to put oneself in the way of)]

Kephallinía (ˌkɛfali'niːa; *English* ˌkɛfə'liːnɪə) *n* a transliteration of the Modern Greek name for **Cephalonia**

kepi ('keɪpiː) *n, pl* kepis a military cap with a circular top and a horizontal peak [c19: from French *képi*, from German (Swiss dialect) *käppi* a little cap, from *kappe* CAP]

Kepler ('kɛplə) *n* **Johannes** (joˈhanəs). 1571–1630, German astronomer. As discoverer of Kepler's laws of planetary motion he is regarded as one of the founders of modern astronomy

Kepler's laws *pl n* three laws of planetary motion published by Johannes Kepler between 1609 and 1619. The first states that the orbit of a planet describes an ellipse with the sun at one focus. The second states that, during one orbit, the straight line joining the sun and a planet sweeps out equal areas in equal times. The third states that the squares of the periods of any two planets are proportional to the cubes of their orbital major axes

kept (kɛpt) *vb* **1** the past tense and past participle of **keep 2** kept woman *censorious* a woman maintained by a man as his mistress

Kerala ('kɛrələ, kəˈrɑːlə) *n* a state of SW India, on the Arabian Sea: formed in 1956, it includes the former state of Travancore-Cochin; has the highest population density of any Indian state. Capital: Trivandrum (Thiruvananthapuram). Pop: 31 838 619 (2001). Area: 38 863 sq km (15 005 sq miles)

keratin ('kɛrətɪn) *or* **ceratin** *n* a fibrous protein that occurs in the outer layer of the skin and in hair, nails, feathers, hooves, etc

keratose ('kɛrəˌtəʊs, -ˌtəʊz) *adj* (esp of certain sponges) having a horny skeleton

kerb *or US and Canadian* **curb** (kɜːb) *n* a line of stone or concrete forming an edge between a pavement and a roadway, so that the pavement is some 15 cm above the level of the road [c17: from Old French *courbe* bent, from Latin *curvus; see* CURVE] > 'kerbing *or (US and Canadian)* 'curbing *n*

kerb crawling *n* the act of driving slowly along the edge of the pavement seeking to entice someone into the car for sexual purposes > kerb crawler *n*

kerb drill *n* a pedestrian's procedure for crossing a road safely, esp as taught to children

Kerbela ('kɜːbələ) *n* a variant of **Karbala**

kerbstone *or US and Canadian* **curbstone** ('kɜːbˌstəʊn) *n* one of a series of stones that form a kerb

Kerch (*Russian* kjertʃ) *n* a port in S Ukraine on the **Kerch Peninsula** and the **Strait of Kerch** (linking the Black Sea with the Sea of Azov): founded as a Greek colony in the 6th century BC; ceded to Russia in 1774; iron-mining, steel production, and fishing. Pop: 153 000 (2005 est)

kerchief ('kɜːtʃɪf) *n* a piece of cloth worn tied over the head or around the neck [c13: from Old French *cuevrechef*, from *covrir* to COVER + *chef* head; see CHIEF] > 'kerchiefed *adj*

kerel ('kɛrəl) *n South African* a chap or fellow [c19: Afrikaans]

Kerenski *or* **Kerensky** (kəˈrɛnskɪ; *Russian* 'kjerɪnskij) *n* **Aleksandr Fyodorovich** (alɪk'sandr 'fjɔdərəvitʃ). 1881–1970, Russian liberal revolutionary leader; prime minister (July–October 1917): overthrown by the Bolsheviks

kerf (kɜːf) *n* the cut made by a saw, an axe, etc [Old English *cyrf* a cutting; related to Old English *ceorfan* to CARVE]

kerfuffle, carfuffle *or* **kurfuffle** (kəˈfʌfᵊl) *n informal, chiefly Brit* commotion; disorder; agitation [from Scottish *curfuffle, carfuffle*, from Scottish Gaelic *car* twist, turn + *fuffle* to disarrange]

Kerguelen ('kɜːɡɪlɪn) *n* an archipelago in the S Indian Ocean: consists of one large volcanic island (Kerguelen or Desolation Island) and 300 small islands; part of the French Southern and Antarctic Territories

Kerkrade (*Dutch* 'kɛrkraːdə) *n* a town in the SE Netherlands, in Limburg: one of the oldest coal-mining centres in Europe. Pop: 50 000 (2003 est)

Kérkyra ('kɛrkira) *n* transliteration of the Modern Greek name for **Corfu**

Kerman (kəˈmɑːn) *n* a city in SE Iran: carpet-making centre. Pop: 546 000 (2005 est)

Kermanshah (ˌkɜːmænˈʃɑː) *n* a city in W Iran, in the valley of the Qareh Su: oil refinery. Pop: 832 000 (2005 est). Former name (1987–1995): Bakhtaran

kermes ('kɜːmɪz) *n* **1** the dried bodies of female scale insects of the genus *Kermes*, esp *K. ilices* of Europe and W Asia, used as a red dyestuff **2** a small evergreen Eurasian oak tree, *Quercus coccifera*, with prickly leaves resembling holly: the host plant of kermes scale insects [c16: from French *kermès*, from Arabic *qirmiz*, from Sanskrit *krmija-* red dye, literally: produced by a worm, from *krmi* worm + *ja-* produced]

kermis *or* **kirmess** ('kɜːmɪs) *n* **1** (formerly, esp in Holland and Northern Germany) an annual country festival or carnival **2** US & Canadian a similar event, esp one held to collect money for charity [c16: from Middle Dutch *kercmisse*, from *kerc* church + *misse* MASS; originally a festival held to celebrate the dedication of a church]

kern¹ *or* **kerne** (kɜːn) *n* the part of the character on a piece of printer's type that projects beyond the body [c17: from French *carne* corner of type, projecting angle, ultimately from Latin *cardō* hinge]

kern² (kɜːn) *n* **1** a lightly armed foot soldier in medieval Ireland or Scotland **2** *archaic* a loutish peasant [c14: from Middle Irish *cethern* band of foot soldiers, from *cath* battle]

Kern (kɜːn) *n* **Jerome** (**David**). 1885–1945, US composer of musical comedies, esp *Show Boat* (1927)

kernel ('kɜːnᵊl) *n* **1** the edible central part of a seed, nut, or fruit within the shell or stone **2** the grain of a cereal, esp wheat, consisting of the seed in a hard husk **3** the central or essential part of something [Old English *cyrnel* a little seed, from *corn* seed; see CORN¹] > **'kernel-less** *adj*

kerosene *or* **kerosine** ('kɛrə,siːn) *n* **1** Also called: paraffin a liquid mixture consisting mainly of alkane hydrocarbons with boiling points in the range 150°–300°C, used as an aircraft fuel, in domestic heaters, and as a solvent **2** the general name for paraffin as a fuel for jet aircraft [C19: from Greek *kēros* wax + -ENE]

Kerouac ('kɛru,æk) *n* **Jack**, real name *Jean-Louis Lebris de Kérouac*. 1922–69, US novelist and poet of the Beat Generation. His works include *On the Road* (1957) and *Big Sur* (1962)

Kerr (kɜː) *n* **Sir John Robert**. 1914–91, Australian public servant. As governor general of Australia (1974–77), he dismissed the Labor prime minister Gough Whitlam (1975) amid great controversy

Kerry¹ ('kɛrɪ) *n* **1** a county of SW Republic of Ireland, in W Munster province: mostly mountainous (including the highest peaks in Ireland), with a deeply indented coast and many offshore islands. County town: Tralee. Pop: 132 527 (2002). Area: 4701 sq km (1815 sq miles) **2** a small black breed of dairy cattle, originally from Kerry

Kerry² ('kɛrɪ) *n* **John Forbes**. born 1943, US politician; Democratic Party candidate in the presidential election of 2004

kersey ('kɜːzɪ) *n* a twilled woollen cloth with a cotton warp [C14: probably from *Kersey*, village in Suffolk]

kerseymere ('kɜːzɪ,mɪə) *n* a fine soft woollen cloth of twill weave [C18: from KERSEY + (CASSI)MERE]

Kesey ('kiːsɪ) *n* **Ken**. 1935–2001, US novelist, best-known for *One Flew Over the Cuckoo's Nest* (1962)

Kesselring ('kɛs°lrɪŋ) *n* **Albert** ('albɛrt). 1885–1960, German field marshal. He commanded the Luftwaffe attacks on Poland, France, and Britain (1939–40), and was supreme commander in Italy (1943–45) and on the western front (1945)

Kesteven ('kɛstɪv°n, kɛ'stiːv°n) *n* Parts of Kesteven an area in E England constituting a former administrative division of Lincolnshire

kestrel ('kɛstrəl) *n* any of several small falcons, esp the European *Falco tinnunculus*, that tend to hover against the wind and feed on small mammals on the ground [C15: changed from Old French *cresserele*, from *cressele* rattle, from Vulgar Latin *crepicella* (unattested), from Latin *crepitāre* to crackle, from *crepāre* to rustle]

Keswick ('kɛzɪk) *n* a market town in NW England, in Cumbria in the Lake District: tourist centre. Pop: 4984 (2001)

ketch (kɛtʃ) *n* a two-masted sailing vessel, fore-and-aft rigged, with a tall mainmast and a mizzen stepped forward of the rudderpost [C15 *cache*, probably from *cacchen* to hunt; see CATCH]

ketchup ('kɛtʃəp), **catchup** *or* **catsup** *n* any of various piquant sauces containing vinegar: *tomato ketchup* [C18: from Chinese (Amoy) *kōetsiap* brine of pickled fish, from *kōe* seafood + *tsiap* sauce]

ketone ('kiːtəʊn) *n* any of a class of compounds with the general formula R′COR, where R and R′ are alkyl or aryl groups [C19: from German *Keton*, from *Aketon* ACETONE] > **ketonic** (kɪ'tɒnɪk) *adj*

ketone body *n biochem* any of three compounds (acetoacetic acid, 3-hydroxybutanoic acid, and acetone) produced when fatty acids are broken down in the liver to provide a source of energy. Excess ketone bodies are present in the blood and urine of people unable to use glucose as an energy source, as in diabetes and starvation. Also called: acetone body

Kettering ('kɛtərɪŋ) *n* a town in central England, in Northamptonshire: footwear industry. Pop: 51 063 (2001)

kettle ('kɛt°l) *n* **1** a metal or plastic container with a handle and spout for boiling water **2** any of various metal containers for heating liquids, cooking fish, etc **3** a large metal vessel designed to withstand high temperatures, used in various industrial processes such as refining and brewing [C13: from Old Norse *ketill*; related to Old English *cietel* kettle, Old High German *kezzil*; all ultimately from Latin *catillus* a little pot, from *catīnus* pot]

kettledrum ('kɛt°l,drʌm) *n* a percussion instrument of definite pitch, consisting of a hollow bowl-like hemisphere covered with a skin or membrane, supported on a tripod or stand. The pitch may be adjusted by means of screws or pedals, which alter the tension of the skin > **'kettle,drummer** *n*

kettle hole *n* a round hollow formed by the melting of a mass of buried ice

kettle of fish *n* **1** a situation; state of affairs (often used ironically in the phrase **a pretty** or **fine kettle of fish**) **2** case; matter for consideration: *that's quite a different kettle of fish*

Kevlar ('kɛv,lɑː) *n trademark* a synthetic fibre, consisting of long-chain polyamides, having high tensile strength and temperate resistance

Kew (kjuː) *n* part of the Greater London borough of Richmond-upon-Thames, on the River Thames: famous for **Kew Gardens** (the Royal Botanic Gardens), established in 1759 and given to the nation in 1841

kewl (kuːl) *adj informal* a nonstandard variant spelling of: **cool** (sense 11)

key¹ (kiː) *n* **1** a metal instrument, usually of a specifically contoured shape, that is made to fit a lock and, when rotated, operates the lock's mechanism **2** any instrument that is rotated to operate a valve, clock winding mechanism, etc **3** a small metal peg or wedge inserted into keyways **4** any of a set of levers operating a typewriter, computer, etc **5** any of the visible parts of the lever mechanism of a musical keyboard instrument that when depressed set in motion the action that causes the instrument to sound **6 a** Also called: tonality any of the 24 major and minor diatonic scales considered as a corpus of notes upon which a piece of music draws for its tonal framework **b** the main tonal centre in an extended composition: *a symphony in the key of F major* **7** something that is crucial in providing an explanation or interpretation **8** a means of achieving a desired end: *the key to happiness* **9** a means of access or control: *Gibraltar is the key to the Mediterranean* **10** a list of explanations of symbols, codes, etc **11** a text that explains or gives information about a work of literature, art, or music **12** *electrical engineering* **a** a hand-operated device for opening or closing a circuit or for switching circuits **b** a hand-operated switch that is pressed to transmit coded signals, esp Morse code **13** the grooving or scratching of a surface or the application of a rough coat of plaster, etc, to provide a bond for a subsequent finish **14** pitch: *he spoke in a low key* **15** a characteristic mood or style: *a poem in a melancholy key* **16** short for **keystone** (sense 1) **17** *botany* any dry winged fruit, esp that of the ash **18** (*modifier*) of great importance: *a key issue* ▷ *vb* (*mainly tr*) **19** (foll by *to*) to harmonize (with): *to key one's actions to the prevailing mood* **20** to adjust or fasten with a key or some similar device **21** to provide with a key or keys **22** (*also intr*) another word for **keyboard** (sense 3) **23** to include a distinguishing device in (an advertisement, etc), so that responses to it can be identified [Old English *cǣg*; related to Old Frisian *kēi*, Middle Low German *keie* spear] > **'keyless** *adj*

key² (kiː) *n* a variant spelling of **cay**

keyboard ('kiː,bɔːd) *n* **1 a** a complete set of keys, usually hand-operated, as on a piano, organ, typewriter, or typesetting machine **b** (*as modifier*): *a keyboard instrument* **2** (*often plural*) a musical instrument, esp an electronic one, played by means of a keyboard ▷ *vb* **3** to set (a text, etc) in type, onto magnetic tape, or into some other medium, by using a keyboard machine > **'key,boarder** *n*

key drive *n computing* a very small, portable storage device that plugs into a computer and facilitates moving data between machines. Also called: pen drive

key grip *n chiefly US* the person in charge of moving and setting up camera tracks and scenery in a film or television studio

keyhole ('kiː,həʊl) *n* an aperture in a door or a lock case through which a key may be passed to engage the lock mechanism

keyhole surgery *n* surgery carried out through a very small incision

key in *vb* (*tr, adverb*) to enter (information or instructions)

that no-one else knows [C19: probably from KID[1]] > 'kidder n > 'kiddingly adv

Kid (kɪd) n a variant spelling of (Thomas) **Kyd**

Kidd (kɪd) n **William**, known as *Captain Kidd*. 1645–1701, Scottish privateer, pirate, and murderer; hanged

Kidderminster ('kɪdə,mɪnstə) n **1** a town in W central England, in N Worcestershire on the River Stour: carpet industry. Pop: 55 610 (2001) **2** a type of ingrain reversible carpet originally made at Kidderminster

kiddy or **kiddie** ('kɪdɪ) n, pl -dies informal an affectionate word for **child**

kid glove n **1** a glove made of kidskin **2** handle with kid gloves to treat with great tact or caution ▷ adj **kidglove 3** overdelicate or overrefined **4** diplomatic; tactful: a kidglove approach

Kidman ('kɪdmən) n **Nicole**. born 1967, Australian film actress, born in Hawaii. Her films include *To Die For* (1995), *Eyes Wide Shut* (1999), *The Hours* (2002), and *The Golden Compass* (2007): formerly married to Tom Cruise

kidnap ('kɪdnæp) vb -naps, -napping, -napped or US -naps, -naping, -naped (tr) to carry off and hold (a person), usually for ransom [C17: KID[1] + obsolete nap to steal; see NAB] > 'kidnapper or US 'kidnaper n

kidney ('kɪdnɪ) n **1** either of two bean-shaped organs at the back of the abdominal cavity in man, one on each side of the spinal column. They maintain water and electrolyte balance and filter waste products from the blood, which are excreted as urine. Related adj: **renal 2** the corresponding organ in other animals **3** the kidneys of certain animals used as food **4** class, type, or disposition (esp in the phrases **of the same** or **a different kidney**) [C14: of uncertain origin]

kidney bean n **1** any of certain bean plants having kidney-shaped seeds, esp the French bean and scarlet runner **2** the seed of any of these beans

kidney machine n See **haemodialysis**

kidney stone n **1** Also called: renal calculus pathol a hard mass formed in the kidney, usually composed of oxalates, phosphates, and carbonates **2** mineralogy another name for **nephrite**

kidology (kɪ'dɒlədʒɪ) n Brit informal the art or practice of bluffing or deception [C20: from KID[2] + OLOGY]

Kidron ('ki:drən) n a variant of **Kedron**

kidskin ('kɪd,skɪn) n a soft smooth leather made from the hide of a young goat. Often shortened to **kid[1]**

kids' stuff n slang **1** something considered fit only for children **2** something considered simple or easy

kidstakes ('kɪd,steɪks) pl n Austral informal pretence; nonsense: cut the kidstakes!

kiekie ('kɪə,kɪə, 'ki:,ki:) n a climbing bush plant, *Freycinetia banksii*, of New Zealand, having elongated leaves and edible berries [Māori]

Kiel (ki:l) n a port in N Germany, capital of Schleswig-Holstein state, on the **Kiel Canal** (connecting the North Sea with the Baltic): joined the Hanseatic League in 1284; became part of Denmark in 1773 and passed to Prussia in 1866; an important naval base in World Wars I and II; shipbuilding and engineering industries. Pop: 233 039 (2003 est)

Kielce (Polish 'kjɛltsɛ) n an industrial city in S Poland. Pop: 206 796 (2007 est)

Kierkegaard ('kɪəkə,gɑ:d; Danish 'kirgəgɔ:r) n **Søren Aabye** ('sø:rən 'ɔ:by). 1813–55, Danish philosopher and theologian. He rejected organized Christianity and anticipated the existentialists in emphasizing man's moral responsibility and freedom of choice. His works include *Either/Or* (1843), *The Concept of Dread* (1844), and *The Sickness unto Death* (1849) > ,Kierke'gaardian adj

kieselguhr ('ki:z[ə]l,gʊə) n an unconsolidated form of **diatomite** [C19: from German *Kieselgur*, from *Kiesel* flint, pebble + *Gur* loose earthy deposit]

Kieślowski (ki'ʃlɒfskɪ) n **Krzysztof** ('krɪʃtɔf). 1941–96, Polish film director, whose later films were made in France; his work includes the television series *Decalogue* (1988–89) and the film trilogy *Three Colours* (1993–94)

Kiev ('ki:ɛf; Russian 'kijɪf) n the capital of Ukraine, on the Dnieper River: formed the first Russian state by the late 9th century; university (1834). Pop: 2 623 000 (2005 est)

kif (kɪf, ki:f), **kaif**, **keef**, **kef** or **kief** n **1** another name for

marijuana **2** any drug or agent that when smoked is capable of producing a euphoric condition **3** the euphoric condition produced by smoking marijuana [C20: from Arabic *kayf* pleasure]

Kigali (kɪ'gɑ:lɪ) n the capital of Rwanda, in the central part. Pop: 782 000 (2005 est)

kike (kaɪk) n US & Canadian slang an offensive word for **Jew** [C20: probably variant of *kiki*, reduplication of -*ki*, common name-ending among Jews from Slavic countries]

Kikládhes (ki'klaðɛs) n a transliteration of the Modern Greek name for **Cyclades**

Kilauea (,ki:lɑː'uː'eɪə) n a crater on the E side of Mauna Loa volcano, on SE Hawaii island: the world's largest active crater. Height: 1247 m (4090 ft). Width: 3 km (2 miles)

Kildare (kɪl'dɛə) n a county of E Republic of Ireland, in Leinster province: mostly low-lying and fertile. County town: Naas. Pop: 163 944 (2002). Area: 1694 sq km (654 sq miles)

kilderkin ('kɪldəkɪn) n **1** an obsolete unit of liquid capacity equal to 16 or 18 Imperial gallons or of dry capacity equal to 16 or 18 wine gallons **2** a cask capable of holding a kilderkin [C14: from Middle Dutch *kindekijn*, from *kintal* hundredweight, from Medieval Latin *quintale*; see KENTLEDGE]

kilim (kɪ'lim, 'ki:lɪm) n a pileless woven rug of intricate design made in the Middle East [C19: from Turkish, from Persian *kilīm*]

Kilimanjaro (,kɪlɪmən'dʒɑ:rəʊ) n a volcanic massif in N Tanzania: the highest peak in Africa; extends from east to west for 80 km (50 miles). Height: 5895 m (19 340 ft)

Kilkenny (kɪl'kɛnɪ) n **1** a county of SE Republic of Ireland, in Leinster province: mostly agricultural. County town: Kilkenny. Pop: 80 339 (2002). Area: 2062 sq km (796 sq miles) **2** a market town in SE Republic of Ireland, county town of Co Kilkenny: capital of the ancient kingdom of Ossory. Pop: 8594 (latest est)

kill (kɪl) vb (mainly tr) **1** (also intr; when tr, sometimes foll by off) to cause the death of (a person or animal) **2** to put an end to; destroy: to kill someone's interest **3** to deaden (sound) **4** informal to tire out; exhaust: the effort killed him **5** informal to cause to suffer pain or discomfort: my shoes are killing me **6** informal to quash, defeat, or veto: the bill was killed in the House of Lords **7** informal to switch off; stop **8** (also intr) informal to overcome with attraction, laughter, surprise, etc: she was dressed to kill; his gags kill me **9** sport to hit (a ball) so hard or so accurately that the opponent cannot return it **10** soccer to bring (a moving ball) under control; trap **11** kill oneself informal to overexert oneself: don't kill yourself **12** kill two birds with one stone to achieve two results with one action ▷ n **13** the act of causing death, esp at the end of a hunt, bullfight, etc **14** the animal or animals killed during a hunt **15** NZ the seasonal tally of stock slaughtered at a freezing works **16** the destruction of a battleship, tank, etc **17** in at the kill present at the end or climax of some undertaking [C13 cullen; perhaps related to Old English cwellan to kill; compare German (Westphalian dialect) küllen; see QUELL]

Killarney (kɪ'lɑ:nɪ) n a town in SW Republic of Ireland, in Co Kerry: a tourist centre near the **Lakes of Killarney**. Pop: 13 137 (2002)

killdeer ('kɪl,dɪə) n, pl -deer or -deers a large brown-and-white North American plover, *Charadrius vociferus*, with two black breast bands and a noisy cry [C18: of imitative origin]

killer ('kɪlə) n **1 a** a person or animal that kills, esp habitually **b** (as modifier): a killer shark **2** something, esp a task or activity, that is particularly taxing or exhausting **3** Austral & NZ an animal selected to be slaughtered for food

killer application n a highly innovative, very powerful, or extremely useful computer application; esp one sufficiently important as to justify purchase of the equipment or software

killer bee n an African honeybee, or one of its hybrids originating in Brazil, that is extremely aggressive when disturbed

k

killer cell *n* a type of white blood cell that is able to kill cells, such as cancer cells and cells infected with viruses

killer whale *n* a predatory black-and-white toothed whale, *Orcinus orca*, with a large erect dorsal fin, most common in cold seas: family *Delphinidae*

killick ('kɪlɪk) *or* **killock** ('kɪlək) *n nautical* a small anchor, esp one made of a heavy stone [c17: of unknown origin]

Killiecrankie (ˌkɪlɪ'kræŋkɪ) *n* a pass in central Scotland, in the Grampians: scene of a battle (1689) in which the Jacobites defeated William III's forces but lost their leader, Viscount Dundee

killifish ('kɪlɪˌfɪʃ) *n, pl* -fish *or* -fishes any of various chiefly American minnow-like cyprinodont fishes of the genus *Fundulus* and related genera, of fresh and brackish waters: used as aquarium fishes, to control mosquitoes, and as anglers' bait [c19: from Middle Dutch *kille* river + FISH]

killing ('kɪlɪŋ) *adj* 1 *informal* very tiring; exhausting: *a killing pace* 2 *informal* extremely funny; hilarious 3 causing death; fatal ▷ *n* 4 the act of causing death; slaying 5 *informal* a sudden stroke of success, usually financial, as in speculations on the stock market (esp in the phrase **make a killing**)

killjoy ('kɪlˌdʒɔɪ) *n* a person who spoils other people's pleasure

Kilmarnock (kɪl'mɑːnək) *n* a town in SW Scotland, the administrative centre of East Ayrshire: associations with Robert Burns; engineering and textile industries; whisky blending. Pop: 43 588 (2001)

kiln (kɪln) *n* a large oven for burning, drying, or processing something, such as porcelain or bricks [Old English *cylen*, from Late Latin *culīna* kitchen, from Latin *coquere* to COOK]

kilo ('kiːləʊ) *n, pl* **kilos** short for **kilogram** *or* **kilometre**

kilo- *prefix* 1 denoting 10³ (1000): *kilometre*. Symbol: k 2 (in computer technology) denoting 2¹⁰ (1024): *kilobyte*: in computer usage, *kilo-* is restricted to sizes of storage (e.g. *kilobit*) when it means 1024; in other computer contexts it retains its usual meaning of 1000 [from French, from Greek *khilioi* thousand]

kilobit ('kɪləˌbɪt) *n computing* 1 (in general computer contexts, such as data transfer) 1000 bits 2 (in data-storage contexts) 1024 bits ▷ Abbreviation: Kb

kilobyte ('kɪləˌbaɪt) *n computing* 1024 bytes. Abbreviations: KB *or* kbyte See also **kilo-** (sense 2)

kilocalorie ('kɪləʊˌkælərɪ) *n* another name for **Calorie**

kilocycle ('kɪləʊˌsaɪkᵊl) *n* short for kilocycle per second: a former unit of frequency equal to 1 kilohertz

kilogram ('kɪləʊˌɡræm) *n* 1 one thousand grams 2 the basic SI unit of mass, equal to the mass of the international prototype held by the *Bureau International des Poids et Mesures*. One kilogram is equivalent to 2.204 62 pounds ▷ Symbol: kg

kilohertz ('kɪləʊˌhɜːts) *n* one thousand hertz; one thousand cycles per second. Symbol: kHz

kilolitre ('kɪləʊˌliːtə) *n* one thousand litres. Symbol: kl

kilometre *or US* **kilometer** (kɪ'lɒmɪtə, 'kɪləˌmiːtə) *n* one thousand metres, equal to 0.621371 miles. Symbol: km > kilometric (ˌkɪləʊ'mɛtrɪk) *adj*

kiloton ('kɪləʊˌtʌn) *n* 1 one thousand tons 2 an explosive power, esp of a nuclear weapon, equal to the power of 1000 tons of TNT ▷ Abbreviation: kt

kilovolt ('kɪləʊˌvəʊlt) *n* one thousand volts. Symbol: kV

kilowatt ('kɪləʊˌwɒt) *n* one thousand watts. Symbol: kW

kilowatt-hour *n* a unit of energy equal to the work done by a power of 1000 watts in one hour. Symbol: kWh

kilt (kɪlt) *n* 1 a knee-length pleated skirt-like garment, esp one in tartan, as worn by men in Highland dress ▷ *vb* (*tr*) 2 to tuck (a skirt) up around one's body 3 to put pleats in (cloth, a skirt, etc) [c18: of Scandinavian origin; compare Danish *kilte* to tuck up, Old Swedish *kilta* lap] > 'kilted *adj*

kilter ('kɪltə) *or* **kelter** *n* working order or alignment (esp in the phrases **off kilter, out of kilter**) [c17: origin unknown]

Kilung ('kiː'lʊŋ) *n* another name for **Chilung**

Kilvert ('kɪlvət) *n* **Francis.** 1840–79, British clergyman and diarist. His diary (published 1938–40) gives a vivid account of life in the Welsh Marches in the 1870s

Kimberley ('kɪmbəlɪ) *n* 1 a city in central South Africa; the capital of Northern Cape province: besieged (1899–1900) for 126 days during the Boer War; diamond-mining and -marketing centre, with heavy engineering works. Pop: 62 526 (2001) 2 Also called: the Kimberleys a plateau region of NW Australia, in N Western Australia: consists of rugged mountains surrounded by grassland. Area: about 360 000 sq km (140 000 sq miles)

kimberlite ('kɪmbəˌlaɪt) *n* an intrusive igneous rock generated at great depth in the earth's mantle and consisting largely of olivine and phlogopite. It often contains diamonds [c19: from KIMBERLEY + -ITE¹]

Kim Il Sung (kim iːl sʌn) *n* 1912–94, North Korean statesman and marshal; prime minister (1948–72) and president (1972–94) of North Korea

Kim Jong Il (kim dʒɒŋ iːl) *n* born 1942, Korean politician; ruler of North Korea from 1994, official head of state from 1998: son of Kim Il Sung

kimono (kɪ'məʊnəʊ) *n, pl* -nos a loose sashed ankle-length garment with wide sleeves, worn in Japan [c19: from Japanese: clothing, from *kiru* to wear + *mono* thing] > ki'monoed *adj*

kin (kɪn) *n* 1 a person's relatives collectively; kindred 2 a class or group with similar characteristics 3 See next of kin ▷ *adj* 4 (*postpositive*) related by blood [Old English *cyn*; related to Old Norse *kyn* family, Old High German *kind* child, Latin *genus* kind]

-kin *suffix forming nouns* small: *lambkin* [from Middle Dutch, of West Germanic origin; compare German *-chen*]

kina¹ ('kiːnə) *n* the standard monetary unit of Papua New Guinea, divided into 100 toea [from a Papuan language]

kina² ('kiːnə) *n, pl* kina a green sea urchin, *Evichinus chloroticus*, eaten in New Zealand. Also called: sea egg [Māori]

Kinabalu (ˌkɪnəbə'luː) *n* a mountain in Malaysia, on N Borneo in central Sabah: the highest peak in Borneo. Height: 4125 m (13 533 ft)

kinaesthesia (ˌkɪnɪs'θiːzɪə, ˌkaɪn-), **kinaesthesis**, *US* **kinesthesia** *or* **kinesthesis** *n* the sensation by which bodily position, weight, muscle tension, and movement are perceived [c19: from New Latin, from Greek *kinein* to move + AESTHESIA] > kinaesthetic *or US* kinesthetic (ˌkɪnɪs'θɛtɪk, ˌkaɪn-) *adj*

Kincardineshire (kɪn'kɑːdɪnˌʃɪə, -ʃə) *n* a former county of E Scotland: became part of Grampian region in 1975 and part of Aberdeenshire in 1996. Also called: the Mearns

Kinchinjunga (ˌkɪntʃɪn'dʒʌŋɡə) *n* a variant of **Kangchenjunga**

kincob ('kɪŋkɒb) *n* a fine silk fabric embroidered with threads of gold or silver, of a kind made in India [c18: from Urdu *kimkhāb*]

kind¹ (kaɪnd) *adj* 1 having a friendly or generous nature or attitude 2 helpful to others or to another: *a kind deed* 3 considerate or humane 4 cordial; courteous (esp in the phrase **kind regards**) 5 pleasant; agreeable; mild: *a kind climate* 6 *informal* beneficial or not harmful [Old English *gecynde* natural, native; see KIND²]

kind² (kaɪnd) *n* 1 a class or group having characteristics in common; sort; type: *two of a kind; what kind of creature?* 2 an instance or example of a class or group, esp a rudimentary one: *heating of a kind* 3 essential nature or character: *the difference is one of kind rather than degree* 4 *archaic* nature; the natural order 5 in kind a (of payment) in goods or produce rather than in money b with something of the same sort: *to return an insult in kind* [Old English *gecynd* nature; compare Old English *cyn* KIN, Gothic *kuni* race, Old High German *kikunt*, Latin *gens*]

kindergarten ('kɪndəˌɡɑːt'n) *n* a class or small school for young children, usually between the ages of four and six to prepare them for primary education [c19: from German, literally: children's garden]

kind-hearted *adj* characterized by kindness; sympathetic > ˌkind-'heartedly *adv* > ˌkind-'heartedness *n*

kindle ('kɪndᵊl) *vb* 1 to set alight or start to burn 2 to arouse or be aroused: *the project kindled his interest* 3 to make or become bright [C12: from Old Norse *kynda*, influenced by Old Norse *kyndill* candle] > 'kindler *n*

kindling ('kɪndlɪŋ) *n* material for starting a fire, such as dry wood, straw, etc

kindly ('kaɪndlɪ) *adj* **-lier, -liest** **1** having a sympathetic or warm-hearted nature **2** motivated by warm and sympathetic feelings **3** pleasant, mild, or agreeable: *a kindly climate* **4** *archaic* natural; normal ▷ *adv* **5** in a considerate or humane way **6** with tolerance or forbearance: *he kindly forgave my rudeness* **7** cordially; pleasantly: *he greeted us kindly* **8** please (often used to express impatience or formality): *will you kindly behave yourself?* **9** *archaic* in accordance with nature; appropriately **10** not take kindly to to react unfavourably towards > 'kindliness *n*

kindness ('kaɪndnɪs) *n* **1** the practice or quality of being kind **2** a kind, considerate, or helpful act

kindred ('kɪndrɪd) *adj* **1** having similar or common qualities, origin, etc **2** related by blood or marriage **3** kindred spirit a person with whom one has something in common ▷ *n* **4** relationship by blood **5** similarity in character **6** a person's relatives collectively [C12 *kinred*, from KIN + *-red*, from Old English *rǣden* rule, from *rǣdan* to rule]

kinematics (,kɪnɪ'mætɪks, ,kaɪ-) *n* (*functioning as singular*) the study of the motion of bodies without reference to mass or force [C19: from Greek *kinēma* movement; see CINEMA, -ICS] > ,kine'matic *adj* > ,kine'matically *adv*

kinematograph (,kɪnɪ'mætə,grɑːf, ,kaɪnɪ-, -,græf) *n* a variant of **cinematograph**

kinesis (kɪ'niːsɪs, kaɪ-) *n* *biology* the nondirectional movement of an organism or cell in response to a stimulus, the rate of movement being dependent on the strength of the stimulus

kinesthesia (,kɪnɪs'θiːzɪə, ,kaɪn-) *or* **kinesthesis** *n* the usual US spelling of **kinaesthesia**

kinetic (kɪ'nɛtɪk, kaɪ-) *adj* relating to, characterized by, or caused by motion [C19: from Greek *kinētikos*, from *kinein* to move] > ki'netically *adv*

kinetic art *n* art, esp sculpture, that moves or has moving parts

kinetic energy *n* the energy of motion of a body, equal to the work it would do if it were brought to rest. The **translational kinetic energy** depends on motion through space, and for a rigid body of constant mass is equal to the product of half the mass times the square of the speed. The **rotational kinetic energy** depends on rotation about an axis, and for a body of constant moment of inertia is equal to the product of half the moment of inertia times the square of the angular velocity. In relativistic physics kinetic energy is equal to the product of the increase of mass caused by motion times the square of the speed of light. The SI unit is the joule but the electronvolt is often used in atomic physics

kinetics (kɪ'nɛtɪks, kaɪ-) *n* (*functioning as singular*) **1** another name for **dynamics** (sense 2) **2** the branch of dynamics that excludes the study of bodies at rest

kinetic theory *n* the kinetic theory a theory of gases postulating that they consist of particles of negligible size moving at random and undergoing elastic collisions

king (kɪŋ) *n* **1** a male sovereign prince who is the official ruler of an independent state; monarch. Related adjs: **royal, regal, monarchical 2 a** a ruler or chief: *king of the fairies* **b** (*in combination*): *the pirate king* **3 a** a person, animal, or thing considered as the best or most important of its kind **b** (*as modifier*): *a king bull* **4** any of four playing cards in a pack, one for each suit, bearing the picture of a king **5** the most important chess piece, although theoretically the weakest, being able to move only one square at a time in any direction **6** *draughts* a piece that has moved entirely across the board and has been crowned, after which it may move backwards as well as forwards **7** king of kings **a** God **b** a title of any of various oriental monarchs ▷ *vb* (*tr*) **8** to make (someone) a king **9** king it to act in a superior fashion [Old English *cyning*; related to Old High German *kunig* king, Danish *konge*] > 'king,hood *n* > 'king,like *adj*

King (kɪŋ) *n* **1** B.B., real name *Riley B. King*. born 1925, US blues singer and guitarist **2 Billie Jean** (née *Moffitt*). born

1943, US tennis player: Wimbledon champion 1966–68, 1972–73, and 1975; US champion 1967, 1971–72, and 1974 **3 Martin Luther.** 1929–68, US Baptist minister and civil-rights leader. He advocated nonviolence in his campaigns against the segregation of Black people in the South: assassinated: Nobel Peace Prize 1964 **4 Stephen** (**Edwin**). born 1947, US writer esp of horror novels; his books, many of which have been filmed, include *Carrie* (1974), *The Shining* (1977), *Misery* (1988), and *Everything's Eventual* (2002) **5 William Lyon Mackenzie.** 1874–1950, Canadian Liberal statesman; prime minister (1921–26; 1926–30; 1935–48)

King Charles spaniel *n* **1** a toy breed of spaniel with a short turned-up nose and a domed skull **2** cavalier King Charles spaniel a similar breed that is slightly larger and has a longer nose [C17: named after Charles II of England, who popularized the breed]

king cobra *n* a very large venomous tropical Asian elapid snake, *Ophiophagus hannah*, that feeds on snakes and other reptiles and extends its neck into a hood when alarmed. Also called: hamadryad

King Country *n* the King Country an area in the centre of North Island, New Zealand: home of the King Movement, a nineteenth-century Māori separatist movement

king crab *n* another name for the **horseshoe crab**

kingdom ('kɪŋdəm) *n* **1** a territory, state, people, or community ruled or reigned over by a king or queen **2** any of the three groups into which natural objects may be divided: the animal, plant, and mineral kingdoms **3** *biology* any of the major categories into which living organisms of the domain *Eukarya* are classified. Modern systems recognize four kingdoms: *Protoctista* (algae, protozoans, etc), *Fungi*, *Plantae*, and *Animalia*. See also **domain** (sense 12) **4** *theol* the eternal sovereignty of God **5** an area of activity, esp mental activity, considered as being the province of something specified: *the kingdom of the mind*

kingfish ('kɪŋ,fɪʃ) *n*, *pl* **-fish** *or* **-fishes** **1** any marine sciaenid food and game fish of the genus *Menticirrhus*, occurring in warm American Atlantic coastal waters **2** another name for **opah** **3** any of various other large food fishes, esp the Spanish mackerel **4** Also called: (NZ) haku a large food and game fish, *Seriola lalandi lalandi*, of New Zealand waters

kingfisher ('kɪŋ,fɪʃə) *n* any coraciiform bird of the family *Alcedinidae*, esp the Eurasian *Alcedo atthis*, which has a greenish-blue and orange plumage. Kingfishers have a large head, short tail, and long sharp bill and tend to live near open water and feed on fish [C15: originally *king's fisher*]

King James Version *or* **King James Bible** *n* another name for the **Authorized Version**

kingklip ('kɪŋ,klɪp) *n* South African an edible eel-like marine fish

kinglet ('kɪŋlɪt) *n* **1** often derogatory the king of a small or insignificant territory **2** US & Canadian any of various small warblers of the genus *Regulus*, having a black-edged yellow crown: family *Muscicapidae*

kingly ('kɪŋlɪ) *adj* **-lier, -liest** **1** appropriate to a king; majestic **2** royal ▷ *adv* **3** poetic or archaic in a manner appropriate to a king > 'kingliness *n*

king penguin *n* a large penguin, *Aptenodytes patagonica*, found on islands bordering the Antarctic Circle

kingpin ('kɪŋ,pɪn) *n* **1** the most important person in an organization **2** a pivot pin that provides a steering joint in a motor vehicle by securing the stub axle to the axle beam. Also called (Brit): swivel pin **3** tenpin bowling the front pin in the triangular arrangement of the ten pins **4** (in ninepins) the central pin in the diamond pattern of the nine pins

king post *n* a vertical post connecting the apex of a triangular roof truss to the tie beam

King's Bench *n* (when the sovereign is male) another name for **Queen's Bench Division**

King's Counsel *n* (when the sovereign is male) another name for **Queen's Counsel**

King's English *n* (esp when the British sovereign is male) standard Southern British English

k

king's evidence *n* (when the sovereign is male) another name for **queen's evidence**

king's evil *n* the king's evil *pathol* a former name for **scrofula** [c14: from the belief that the king's touch would heal scrofula]

Kingsford-Smith ('kɪŋzfəd'smɪθ) *n* Sir **Charles** (**Edward**). 1897–1935, Australian aviator and pioneer (with Charles Ulm) of trans-Pacific and trans-Tasman flights

king's highway *n* (in Britain, esp when the sovereign is male) any public road or right of way

kingship ('kɪŋʃɪp) *n* **1** the position or authority of a king **2** the skill or practice of ruling as a king

king-size *or* **king-sized** *adj* larger or longer than a standard size

Kingsley ('kɪŋzlɪ) *n* **1** Sir **Ben**. born 1943, British actor. He won an Oscar for his performance in the title role of the film *Gandhi* (1982) **2** **Charles**. 1819–75, British clergyman and author. His works include the historical romances *Westward Ho!* (1855) and *Hereward the Wake* (1866) and the children's story *The Water Babies* (1863) **3** his brother, **Henry**. 1830–76, British novelist, editor, and journalist, who spent some time in Australia. His works include *Ravenshoe* (1861) and the Anglo-Australian novels *The Recollections of Geoffrey Hamlyn* (1859) and *The Hillyars and the Burtons* (1865)

King's Lynn ('kɪŋz 'lɪn) *n* a market town in E England, in Norfolk on the estuary of the Great Ouse near the Wash: a leading port in the Middle Ages. Pop: 40 921 (2001). Also called: **Lynn** *or* **Lynn Regis**

King-Smith ('kɪŋ'smɪθ) *n* **Ronald Gordon**, known as *Dick*. born 1922, British writer for children; his numerous books include *The Sheep Pig* (1984) and the *Sophie* series

Kingston ('kɪŋstən) *n* **1** the capital and chief port of Jamaica, on the SE coast: University of the West Indies. Pop: 574 000 (2005 est) **2** a port in SE Canada, in SE Ontario: the chief naval base of Lake Ontario and a large industrial centre; university (1841). Pop: 108 158 (2001) **3** the capital of Norfolk Island, in the S Pacific Ocean **4** short for **Kingston upon Thames**

Kingston upon Hull *n* **1** the official name of: **Hull**¹ **2** a unitary authority in NE England, in the East Riding of Yorkshire: formerly (1974–96) part of the county of Humberside. Pop: 247 900 (2003 est). Area: 71 sq km (27 sq miles)

Kingston upon Thames *n* a borough of SW Greater London, on the River Thames: formed in 1965 by the amalgamation of several former boroughs of Surrey; administrative centre of Surrey. Pop: 150 400 (2003 est). Area: 38 sq km (15 sq miles)

Kingstown ('kɪŋz,taun) *n* the capital of St Vincent and the Grenadines: a port and resort. p.: 31 000 (2005 est)

kinin ('kaɪnɪn) *n* **1** any of a group of polypeptides in the blood that cause dilation of the blood vessels and make smooth muscles contract **2** another name for **cytokinin** [c20: from Greek *kin(ēma)* motion + -IN]

kink (kɪŋk) *n* **1** a sharp twist or bend in a wire, rope, hair, etc, esp one caused when it is pulled tight **2** a crick in the neck or similar muscular spasm **3** a flaw or minor difficulty in some undertaking or project **4** a flaw or idiosyncrasy of personality; quirk [c17: from Dutch: a curl in a rope; compare Middle Low German *kinke* kink, Old Norse *kinka* to nod]

kinkajou ('kɪŋkə,dʒuː) *n* Also called: **honey bear**, **potto** an arboreal fruit-eating mammal, *Potos flavus*, of Central and South America, with a long prehensile tail: family Procyonidae (raccoons) order Carnivora (carnivores) [c18: from French *quincajou*, from Algonquian; related to Ojibwa *gwīngwâage* wolverine]

kinky ('kɪŋkɪ) *adj* **kinkier**, **kinkiest** **1** *slang* given to unusual, abnormal, or deviant sexual practices **2** *informal* exhibiting unusual idiosyncrasies of personality; quirky; eccentric **3** *informal* attractive or provocative in a bizarre way: *kinky clothes* **4** tangled or tightly looped, as a wire or rope **5** tightly curled, as hair > '**kinkily** *adv* > '**kinkiness** *n*

Kinnock ('kɪnək) *n* **Neil** (**Gordon**). Baron. born 1942, British Labour politician, born in Wales; leader of the Labour Party (1983–92); a European commissioner from 1994 and vice-president of the European Commission

(1999–2004)

kino ('kiːnəu) *n* a dark red resin obtained from various tropical plants, esp an Indian leguminous tree, *Pterocarpus marsupium*, used as an astringent and in tanning [c18: of West African origin; related to Mandingo *keno*]

Kinross-shire (kɪn'rɒs,ʃɪə, -,ʃə) *n* a former county of E central Scotland: became part of Tayside region in 1975 and part of Perth and Kinross in 1996

kin selection *n* *biology* natural selection resulting from altruistic behaviour by animals towards members of the same species, esp their offspring or other relatives

Kinsey ('kɪnzɪ) *n* **Alfred Charles**. 1894–1956, US zoologist, who directed a survey of human sexual behaviour

kinsfolk ('kɪnz,fəuk) *pl n* one's family or relatives

Kinshasa (kɪn'ʃaːzə, -'ʃaːsə) *n* the capital of the Democratic Republic of Congo (formerly Zaïre), on the River Congo opposite Brazzaville: became capital of the Belgian Congo in 1929 and of Zaïre in 1960; university (1954). Pop: 5 717 000 (2005 est). Former name (until 1966): **Léopoldville**

kinship ('kɪnʃɪp) *n* **1** blood relationship **2** the state of having common characteristics or a common origin

kinsman ('kɪnzmən) *n*, *pl* **-men** a blood relation or a relation by marriage > '**kins,woman** *fem n*

Kinyarwanda (,kɪnjəru'ændə) *n* one of the official languages of Rwanda, belonging to the Bantu group of the Niger-Congo family and closely related to Kirundi

kiore ('kiːɒre) *n*, *pl* **kiore** another name for **Māori rat** [Māori]

kiosk ('kiːɒsk) *n* a small sometimes movable booth from which cigarettes, newspapers, light refreshments, etc, are sold **1** *chiefly Brit* a telephone box **2** (in Turkey, Iran, etc, esp formerly) a light open-sided pavilion [c17: from French *kiosque* bandstand, from Turkish *kösk*, from Persian *kūshk* pavilion]

kip¹ (kɪp) *slang* ▷ *n* **1** *Brit* sleep or slumber: *to get some kip* **2** *Brit* a bed or lodging ▷ *vb* **kips**, **kipping**, **kipped** (*intr*) **3** *Brit* to sleep or take a nap **4** *Brit* (foll by *down*) to prepare for sleep [c18: of uncertain origin; apparently related to Danish *kippe* common alehouse]

kip² (kɪp) *or* **kipskin** ('kɪp,skɪn) *n* the hide of a young animal, esp a calf or lamb [c16: from Middle Dutch *kipp*; related to Middle Low German *kip*, Old Norse *kippa* bundle]

kip³ (kɪp) *n* *Austral* a small board used to spin the coins in two-up [c19: from KEP]

Kipling ('kɪplɪŋ) *n* (**Joseph**) **Rudyard** ('rʌdjəd). 1865–1936, English poet, short-story writer, and novelist, born in India. His works include *Barrack-Room Ballads* (1892), the two *Jungle Books* (1894, 1895), *Stalky and Co* (1899), *Kim* (1901), and the *Just So Stories* (1902): Nobel prize for literature 1907

kipper ('kɪpə) *n* **1** a fish, esp a herring, that has been cleaned, salted, and smoked **2** a male salmon during the spawning season ▷ *vb* **3** (*tr*) to cure (a fish, esp a herring) by salting and smoking [Old English *cypera*, perhaps from *coper* COPPER¹; referring to its colour]

kir (kɜː, kɪr) *n* a drink made from dry white wine and cassis [named after Canon F. Kir (1876–1968), mayor of Dijon, who is reputed to have invented it]

kirby grip ('kɜːbɪ) *n* *Brit* a hairgrip consisting of a piece of metal bent over to form a tight clip and having the upper part ridged to prevent it slipping on the hair [from *Kerbigrip*, trademark for the original such hairgrip]

Kirchhoff (German 'kɪrçhɔf) *n* **Gustav Robert** ('gustaf 'roːbɛrt). 1824–87, German physicist. With Bunsen he developed the method of spectrum analysis that led to their discovery of caesium (1860) and rubidium (1861): also worked on electrical networks

Kirchner (German kɪrçnər) *n* **Ernst Ludwig**. 1880–1938, German expressionist painter and printmaker; a founder of the group *die Brücke* (1905)

Kirghiz *or* **Kirgiz** ('kɜːgɪz) *n* a variant spelling of **Kyrgyz**

Kirghizia *or* **Kirgizia** (kɜː'gɪzɪə) *n* the former Russian name for **Kyrgyzstan**

Kirghiz Steppe *n* a variant spelling of **Kyrgyz Steppe**

Kiribati (,kɪrɪ'bæs, ,kɪrɪ'bætɪ) *n* an independent republic in the W Pacific: comprises 33 islands including Banaba

(Ocean Island), the Gilbert and Phoenix Islands, and eight of the Line Islands; part of the British colony of the Gilbert and Ellice Islands until 1975; became self-governing in 1977 and gained full independence in 1979 as the Republic of Kiribati; a member of the Commonwealth. Official languages: English, I-Kiribati (Gilbertese) is widely spoken. Religion: Christian majority. Currency: Australian dollar. Capital: Bairiki islet, in Tarawa atoll. Pop: 88 000 (2003 est). Area: 684 sq km (264 sq miles)

Kirin ('ki:'rɪn) n a variant transliteration of the Chinese name for **Jilin**

Kiritimati (kə'rısmæs) n an island in the central Pacific, in Kiribati: one of the Line Islands; the largest atoll in the world. Pop: 5115 (2005). Former name: **Christmas Island**

kirk (kɜːk; Scot kɪrk) n **1** a Scot word for **church 2** a Scottish church [c12: from Old Norse kirkja, from Old English cirice CHURCH]

Kirk (kɜːk) n **Norman.** 1923–74, prime minister of New Zealand (1972–74)

Kirkby¹ ('kɜːbɪ) n a town in NW England, in Knowsley unitary authority, Merseyside. Pop: 40 006 (2001)

Kirkby² (kɜːkbɪ) n **1** Dame **Emma.** born 1949, British soprano, specializing in performances of early music with period instruments

Kirkcaldy (kɜː'kɔːdɪ) n a port in E Scotland, in SE Fife on the Firth of Forth. Pop: 46 912 (2001)

Kirkcudbrightshire (kɜː'kuːbrɪˌʃɪə, -ʃə) n a former county of SW Scotland, part of Dumfries and Galloway since 1975

Kirklees (ˌkɜːk'liːz) n a unitary authority in N England, in West Yorkshire. Pop: 391 400 (2003 est). Area: 410 sq km (158 sq miles)

Kirkpatrick (kɜː'kpætrɪk) n Mount Kirkpatrick a mountain in Antarctica, in S Victoria Land in the Queen Alexandra Range. Height: 4528 m (14 856 ft)

kirk session n the lowest court of the Presbyterian Church

Kirkuk (kɜː'kuːk, 'kɜːkʊk) n a city in NE Iraq: centre of a rich oilfield with pipelines to the Mediterranean. Pop: 548 000 (2005 est)

Kirkwall ('kɜːkˌwɔːl) n a town on the N coast of Mainland in the Orkney Islands: administrative centre of the island authority of Orkney: cathedral built by Norsemen (begun in 1137). Pop: 6206 (2001)

kirmess ('kɜːmɪs) n a variant spelling of **kermis**

Kirov¹ (Russian 'kirəf) n a city in NW Russia, on the Vyatka River: an early trading centre; engineering industries. Pop: 454 000 (2005 est). Former name (1780–1934): Vyatka

Kirov² (Russian 'kirəf) n **Sergei Mironovich** (sɪr'gjej mi'rɒnəvitʃ). 1888–1934, Soviet politician; one of Stalin's chief aides. His assassination was the starting point for Stalin's purge of the Communist Party (1934–38)

Kirovabad (Russian kirəva'bat) n the former name (1936–91) of **Gandzha**

Kirovograd (Russian kirəva'grat) n a city in S central Ukraine on the Ingul River: manufacturing centre of a rich agricultural area. Pop: 250 000 (2005 est). Former names: Yelisavetgrad, Zinovievsk

Kirribilli House ('kɪrɪˌbɪlɪ) n the official Sydney residence of the Australian Prime Minister

Kirsch (kɪəʃ) or **Kirschwasser** ('kɪəʃˌvɑːsə) n a brandy distilled from cherries, made chiefly in the Black Forest in Germany and in the Jura and Vosges districts of France [German Kirschwasser cherry water]

kirtle ('kɜːtªl) n archaic **1** a woman's skirt or dress **2** a man's coat [Old English cyrtel, probably from cyrtan to shorten, ultimately from Latin curtus cut short]

Kiruna (Swedish 'kiːruna) n a town in N Sweden: iron-mining centre. Pop: 23 273 (2004 est)

Kisangani (ˌkiːsæŋ'gɑːnɪ) n a city in the N Democratic Republic of Congo (formerly Zaïre), at the head of navigation of the River Congo below Boyoma Falls (Stanley Falls): Université Libre du Congo (1963). Pop: 475 000 (2005 est). Former name (until 1966): Stanleyville

Kishinev (Russian kiʃi'njɔf) n the Russian name for **Chişinău**

Kismayu (kɪs'mɑːjuː) n another name for **Chisimaio**

kismet ('kɪzmɛt, 'kɪs-) n **1** Islam the will of Allah **2** fate or destiny [c19: from Turkish, from Persian qismat, from Arabic qasama he divided]

kiss (kɪs) vb **1** (tr) to touch with the lips or press the lips against as an expression of love, greeting, respect, etc **2** (intr) to join lips with another person in an act of love or desire **3** to touch (each other) lightly **4** billiards (of balls) to touch (each other) lightly while moving ▷ n **5** the act of kissing; a caress with the lips **6** a light touch ▷ See also **kiss off** [Old English cyssan, from coss; compare Old High German kussen, Old Norse kyssa] > 'kissable adj

KISS abbreviation text messaging keep it simple, stupid

kissagram ('kɪsəˌgræm) n a greetings service in which a person is employed to present greetings by kissing the person celebrating [c20: blend of kiss and telegram]

kiss-and-tell modifier denoting the practice of publicizing one's former sexual relationship with a celebrity, esp in the tabloid press: a kiss-and-tell interview

kiss curl n Brit a circular curl of hair pressed flat against the cheek or forehead

kisser ('kɪsə) n **1** a person who kisses, esp in a way specified **2** a slang word for **mouth** or **face**

Kissinger ('kɪsɪndʒə) n **Henry (Alfred).** born 1923, US academic and diplomat, born in Germany; assistant to President Nixon for national security affairs (1969–75); Secretary of State (1973–77): shared the Nobel peace prize 1973

kissing gate n a gate set in a U- or V-shaped enclosure, allowing only one person to pass through at a time

kiss off slang, chiefly US & Canadian ▷ vb **1** (tr) to ignore or dismiss rudely and abruptly ▷ n **kiss-off 2** a rude and abrupt dismissal

kiss of life the kiss of life n mouth-to mouth or mouth-to-nose resuscitation in which a person blows gently into the mouth or nose of an unconscious person, allowing the lungs to deflate after each blow

kist¹ (kɪst) n Scot & northern English dialect a large chest or coffer [c14: from Old Norse kista; see CHEST]

kist² (kɪst) n South African a large wooden chest in which linen is stored, esp one used to store a bride's trousseau [from Afrikaans, from Dutch: CHEST]

Kistna ('kɪstnə) n another name for the (River) **Krishna¹**

Kisumu (kɪ'suːmuː) n a port in W Kenya, in Nyanza province on the NE shore of Lake Victoria: fishing and trading centre. Pop: 433 000 (2005 est)

kit¹ (kɪt) n **1** a set of tools, supplies, construction materials, etc, for use together or for a purpose: a first-aid kit; a model aircraft kit **2** the case or container for such a set **3** a set of pieces of equipment ready to be assembled **4 a** clothing and other personal effects, esp those of a traveller or soldier: safari kit; battle kit **b** informal clothing in general (esp in the phrase **get one's kit off**) **5** NZ a flax basket ▷ See also **kit out** [c14: from Middle Dutch kitte tankard]

kit² (kɪt) n NZ a plaited flax basket [from Māori kete]

KIT abbreviation text messaging keep in touch

Kitagawa Utamaro n See **Utamaro**

Kitaj ('kaɪteɪ) n **R. B.** 1932–2007, US painter working in Britain, noted for such large figurative works as If Not, Not (1976)

Kitakyushu (ˌkiːtə'kjuːʃuː) n a port in Japan, on N Kyushu: formed by the amalgamation of the cities of Wakamatsu, Yawata, Tobata, Kokura, and Moji; one of Japan's largest industrial centres. Pop: 999 806 (2002 est)

kitbag ('kɪtˌbæg) n a canvas or other bag for a serviceman's kit

kitchen ('kɪtʃɪn) n **a** a room or part of a building equipped for preparing and cooking food **b** (as modifier): a kitchen table [Old English cycene, ultimately from Late Latin coquīna, from Latin coquere to COOK; see KILN]

kitchen cabinet n a group of unofficial advisers to a political leader, esp when considered to be more influential than the official cabinet

Kitchener¹ ('kɪtʃɪnə) n an industrial town in SE Canada, in S Ontario: founded in 1806 as Dutch Sand Hills, it was

k

renamed Berlin in 1830 and Kitchener in 1916. Pop: 190 399 (2001)

Kitchener² ('kɪtʃɪnə) n **Horatio Herbert, 1st Earl Kitchener of Khartoum.** 1850–1916, British field marshal. As head of the Egyptian army (1892–98), he expelled the Mahdi from the Sudan (1898), occupying Khartoum; he also commanded British forces (1900–02) in the Boer War and (1902–09) in India. He conducted the mobilization of the British army for World War I as war minister (1914–16); he was drowned on his way to Russia

kitchenette or **kitchenet** (,kɪtʃɪ'nɛt) n a small kitchen or part of another room equipped for use as a kitchen

kitchen garden n a garden where vegetables and sometimes also fruit are grown

kitchen midden n archaeol the site of a large mound of domestic refuse marking a prehistoric settlement

kitchen police pl n US soldiers who have been detailed to work in the kitchen, esp as a punishment

kitchen sink n 1 a sink in a kitchen for washing dishes, vegetables, etc 2 (modifier) denoting a type of drama or painting of the 1950s depicting the sordid aspects of domestic reality

kitchen tea n Austral & NZ a party held before a wedding to which female guests bring items of kitchen equipment as wedding presents

kitchenware ('kɪtʃɪn,wɛə) n pots and pans, knives, forks, spoons, and other utensils used in the kitchen

kite (kaɪt) n 1 a light frame covered with a thin material flown in the wind at the end of a length of string 2 Brit slang an aeroplane 3 (plural) nautical any of various light sails set in addition to the working sails of a vessel 4 any diurnal bird of prey of the genera Milvus, Elanus, etc, typically having a long forked tail and long broad wings and usually preying on small mammals and insects: family Accipitridae (hawks, etc) 5 archaic a person who preys on others 6 commerce a negotiable paper drawn without any actual transaction or assets and designed to obtain money on credit, give an impression of affluence, etc ▷ vb 7 to issue (fictitious papers) to obtain credit or money 8 (intr) to soar and glide [Old English cȳta; related to Middle High German küze owl, Old Norse kȳta to quarrel]

Kitemark n Brit the official mark of quality and reliability, in the form of a kite, on articles approved by the British Standards Institution

kitesurfing ('kaɪt,sɜːfɪŋ) n the sport of sailing standing up on a surfboard while being pulled along by a large kite > 'kite,surfer n

kith (kɪθ) n one's friends and acquaintances (esp in the phrase **kith and kin**) [Old English cȳthth, from cūth; see UNCOUTH]

Kíthira ('kiθira) n a transliteration of the Modern Greek name for **Cythera**

kit out or **kit up** vb kits, kitting, kitted 1 (tr, adverb) chiefly Brit to provide with (a kit of personal effects and necessities) 2 to provide with (an outfit of clothes)

kitsch (kɪtʃ) n tawdry, vulgarized, or pretentious art, literature, etc, usually with popular or sentimental appeal [c20: from German] > 'kitschy adj

kitset ('kɪt,sɛt) n NZ **a** a piece of furniture supplied in pieces for the purchaser to assemble himself or herself **b** (as modifier): a kitset kitchen

kitten ('kɪtⁿn) n 1 a young cat 2 **have kittens** Also called: **have a canary** Brit informal to react with disapproval, anxiety, etc: she had kittens when she got the bill ▷ vb 3 (of cats) to give birth to (young) [c14: from Old Northern French caton, from CAT¹; probably influenced by Middle English kiteling]

kitten heel n 1 a low stiletto heel on a woman's shoe 2 a woman's shoe with a low stiletto heel

kittenish ('kɪtⁿnɪʃ) adj 1 like a kitten; lively 2 (of a woman) flirtatious, esp coyly flirtatious

kittiwake ('kɪtɪ,weɪk) n either of two oceanic gulls of the genus Rissa, esp R. tridactyla, having a white plumage with pale grey black-tipped wings and a square-cut tail [c17: of imitative origin]

kitty¹ ('kɪtɪ) n, pl -ties a diminutive or affectionate name for a **kitten** or **cat¹** [c18]

kitty² ('kɪtɪ) n, pl -ties 1 the pool of bets in certain gambling games 2 any shared fund of money, etc 3 (in bowls) the jack [c19: see KIT¹]

kitty-cornered adj a variant of **cater-cornered**

Kitty Hawk ('kɪtɪ hɔːk) n a village in NE North Carolina, near Kill Devil Hill, where the Wright brothers made the world's first aeroplane flight (1903)

Kitwe ('kɪtweɪ) n a city in N Zambia: commercial centre of the Copper Belt. Pop: 545 000 (2005 est)

Kitzbühel ('kɪtsbʊəl) n a town in W Austria, in the Tirol: centre for winter sports. Pop: 8574 (2001)

Kivu ('kiːvuː) n **Lake Kivu** a lake in central Africa, between the Democratic Republic of Congo (formerly Zaïre) and Rwanda at an altitude of 1460 m (4790 ft). Area: 2698 sq km (1042 sq miles). Depth: (maximum) 475 m (1558 ft)

kiwi ('kiːwiː) n, pl kiwis 1 any nocturnal flightless New Zealand bird of the genus Apteryx, having a long beak, stout legs, and weakly barbed feathers: order Apterygiformes 2 informal except in New Zealand a New Zealander [c19: from Māori, of imitative origin]

Kiwiana (,kiːwɪ'ɑːnə) pl n Austral & NZ collectable objects, ornaments, etc, esp dating from the 1950s or 1960s, relating to the history or popular culture of New Zealand

kiwi fruit n the edible oval fruit of the kiwi plant, Actinidia chinensis, a climbing plant native to Asia but grown extensively in New Zealand; it has a brown fuzzy skin and pale green flesh. Also called: **Chinese gooseberry**

Kizil Irmak (kɪ'zɪl ɪə'mɑːk) n a river in Turkey, rising in the Kizil Dag and flowing southwest, northwest, and northeast to the Black Sea: the longest river in Asia Minor. Length: about 1150 km (715 miles)

KKK abbreviation Ku Klux Klan

Klagenfurt (German 'klɑːɡənfʊrt) n a city in S Austria, capital of Carinthia province: tourist centre. Pop: 90 141 (2001)

Klaipeda (Russian 'klajpɪdə) n a port in Lithuania on the Baltic: shipbuilding and fish canning. Pop: 190 000 (2005 est). German name: **Memel**

Klan (klæn) n **the Klan** short for **Ku Klux Klan** > 'Klanism n

Klaus (klaʊs) n **Vaclav.** born 1941, Czech politician, president of Czech Republic from 2003

klaxon or **claxon** ('klæksⁿn) n a type of loud horn formerly used on motor vehicles [c20: former trademark, from the name of the manufacturing company]

Kléber (French klebɛr) n **Jean Baptiste** (ʒɑ̃ batist). 1753–1800, French general, who succeeded Napoleon as commander in Egypt (1799); assassinated

klebsiella (,klɛbzɪ'ɛlə) n a Gram-negative bacteria found in the respiratory, intestinal, and urinogenital tracts of humans and animals, which can cause pneumonia and urinary infections [c20: after Edwin Klebs (1834–913), German bacteriologist]

Klee (German kleː) n **Paul** (paul). 1879–1940, Swiss painter and etcher. A founder member of der Blaue Reiter, he subsequently evolved an intensely personal style of unusual fantasy and wit

Kleenex ('kliːnɛks) n, pl -ex or -exes trademark a kind of soft paper tissue, used esp as a handkerchief

Klein (klaɪn) n 1 **Calvin (Richard).** born 1942, US fashion designer 2 **Melanie.** 1882–1960, Austrian psychoanalyst resident in England (from 1926), noted for her work on child behaviour

Klein bottle (klaɪn) n maths a surface formed by inserting the smaller end of an open tapered tube through the surface of the tube and making this end contiguous with the other end [named after Felix Klein (1849–1925) German mathematician]

kleinhuisie ('kleɪn'heɪsɪ) n South African an outside lavatory [c20: Afrikaans: literally, little house]

Kleist (klaɪst) n **Bernd) Heinrich (Wilhelm) von** ('haɪnrɪç fɔn). 1777–1811, German dramatist, poet, and short-story writer. His plays include The Broken Pitcher (1808), Penthesilea (1808), and The Prince of Homburg (published 1821)

Klemperer ('klɛmpərə) n **Otto**. 1885–1973, orchestral conductor, born in Germany. He was best known for his interpretations of Beethoven

kleptocracy or **cleptocracy** (,klɛp'tɒkrəsɪ) n, pl -cies informal a government where officials are politically corrupt and financially self-interested [c20: from KLEPTO(MANIA) + -CRACY]

kleptocratic (,klɛptəʊ'krætɪk) adj (of a government, state, etc) characterized by corruption amongst those in power

kleptomania (,klɛptəʊ'meɪnɪə) n psychol a strong impulse to steal, esp when there is no obvious motivation [c19: klepto- from Greek kleptēs thief, from kleptein to steal + -MANIA] > ,klepto'mani,ac n

klieg light (kliːg) n an intense carbon-arc light used for illumination in producing films [c20: named after John H. Kliegl (1869–1959) and his brother Anton (1872–1927), German-born American inventors in the field of lighting]

Klimt (klɪmt) n **Gustav** ('gʊstaf). 1862–1918, Austrian painter. He founded the Vienna Sezession (1897), a group of painters influenced by Art Nouveau

Kline (klaɪn) n **Franz** (frænts). 1910–62, US abstract expressionist painter. His works are characterized by heavy black strokes on a white or grey background

Klint (klɪnt) n **Kaara** (ka:rə). 1888–1954, Danish furniture designer; founder of the contemporary Scandinavian style

klipspringer ('klɪp,sprɪŋə) n a small agile antelope, Oreotragus oreotragus, inhabiting rocky regions of Africa south of the Sahara [c18: from Afrikaans, from Dutch klip rock (see CLIFF) + springer, from springen to SPRING]

Klondike ('klɒndaɪk) n **1** a region of NW Canada, in the Yukon in the basin of the Klondike River: site of rich gold deposits, discovered in 1896 but largely exhausted by 1910. Area: about 2100 sq km (800 sq miles) **2** a river in NW Canada, rising in the Yukon and flowing west to the Yukon River. Length: about 145 km (90 miles)

kloof (kluːf) n a mountain pass or gorge in southern Africa [c18: from Afrikaans, from Middle Dutch clove a cleft; see CLEAVE[1]]

Klopstock (German 'klɔpʃtɔk) n **Friedrich Gottlieb** ('friːdrɪç 'gɔtliːp). 1724–1803, German poet, noted for his religious epic Der Messias (1748–73) and for his odes

klystron ('klɪstrɒn, 'klaɪ-) n an electron tube for the amplification or generation of microwaves by means of velocity modulation [c20 klys-, from Greek klus-, kluzein to wash over, break over + -TRON]

km symbol for kilometre

K-meson n another name for **kaon**

km/h abbreviation kilometres per hour

knack (næk) n **1** a skilful, ingenious, or resourceful way of doing something **2** a particular talent or aptitude, esp an intuitive one [c14: probably variant of knak sharp knock, rap, of imitative origin]

knacker ('nækə) Brit ▷ n **1** a person who buys up old horses for slaughter **2** a person who buys up old buildings and breaks them up for scrap **3** Irish slang a despicable person ▷ vb **4** (tr; usually passive) slang to exhaust; tire [c16: probably from nacker saddler, probably of Scandinavian origin; compare Old Norse hnakkur saddle]

knackered ('nækəd) adj Brit slang **1** exhausted; tired out **2** worn out; no longer working, esp after long or hard use

knacker's yard n Brit **1** a slaughterhouse for horses **2** informal destruction because of being beyond all usefulness (esp in the phrase **ready for the knacker's yard**)

knag (næg) n **1** a knot in wood **2** a wooden peg [c15: perhaps from Low German knagge]

knap (næp) vb knaps, knapping, knapped (tr) dialect to hit, hammer, or chip [c15 (IN THE SENSE: TO STRIKE WITH A SHARP SOUND): OF IMITATIVE ORIGIN; COMPARE DUTCH knappen TO CRACK] > 'knapper n

knapping hammer n a hammer used for breaking and shaping stones

knapsack ('næp,sæk) n a canvas or leather bag carried strapped on the back or shoulder [c17: from Low German

knappsack, probably from knappen to bite, snap + sack bag; related to Dutch knapzak; see SACK[1]]

knapweed ('næp,wiːd) n any of several plants of the genus Centaurea, having purplish thistle-like flowers: family Asteraceae (composites) [c15 knopwed; see KNOP, WEED[1]]

knar (nɑː) n a variant of **knur** [c14 knarre rough stone, knot on a tree; related to Low German knarre]

knave (neɪv) n **1** archaic a dishonest man; rogue **2** another word for **jack** (sense 6) **3** obsolete a male servant [Old English cnafa; related to Old High German knabo boy] > 'knavish adj

knavery ('neɪvərɪ) n, pl -eries **1** a deceitful or dishonest act **2** dishonest conduct; trickery

knead (niːd) vb (tr) **1** to work and press (a soft substance, such as bread dough) into a uniform mixture with the hands **2** to squeeze, massage, or press with the hands **3** to make by kneading [Old English cnedan; related to Old Saxon knedan, Old Norse knotha] > 'kneader n

knee (niː) n **1** the joint of the human leg connecting the tibia and fibula with the femur and protected in front by the patella **2 a** the area surrounding and above this joint **b** (modifier) reaching or covering the knee: knee breeches; knee socks **3** a corresponding or similar part in other vertebrates **4** the part of a garment that covers the knee **5** the upper surface of a seated person's thigh: the child sat on her mother's knee **6** anything resembling a knee in shape, such as an angular bend in a pipe **7** any of the hollow rounded protuberances that project upwards from the roots of the swamp cypress: thought to aid respiration in waterlogged soil **8** bend the knee or bow the knee to kneel or submit **9** bring someone to his knees to force someone into submission **10** bring something to its knees to cause something to be in a weakened or impoverished state ▷ vb knees, kneeing, kneed **11** (tr) to strike, nudge, or push with the knee [Old English cnēow; compare Old High German kneo, Old Norse knē, Latin genu]

kneecap ('niː,kæp) n **1** anatomy a nontechnical name for **patella** ▷ vb -caps, -capping, -capped (tr) **2** (esp of certain terrorist groups) to shoot (a person) in the kneecap, esp as an act of retaliation

knee-deep adj **1** so deep as to reach or cover the knees **2** (postpositive; often foll by in) **a** sunk or covered to the knees: knee-deep in sand **b** immersed; deeply involved: knee-deep in work

knee-high adj another word for **knee-deep** (sense 1)

kneehole ('niː,həʊl) n a space for the knees, esp under a desk

knee jerk n **1** Also called: patellar reflex physiol an outward reflex kick of the lower leg caused by a sharp tap on the quadriceps tendon just below the patella ▷ modifier **2** made or occurring as a predictable and automatic response, without thought: kneejerk support

kneel (niːl) vb kneels, kneeling, knelt or kneeled **1** (intr) to rest, fall, or support oneself on one's knees ▷ n **2** the act or position of kneeling [Old English cnēowlian; see KNEE] > 'kneeler n

knees-up n, pl knees-ups a lively noisy party or celebration, esp one with dancing [c20: from the song "Knees up Mother Brown" to which the dance is performed]

knell (nɛl) n **1** the sound of a bell rung to announce a death or a funeral **2** something that precipitates or indicates death or destruction ▷ vb **3** (intr) to ring a knell **4** (tr) to proclaim or announce by or as if by a tolling bell [Old English cnyll; related to Middle High German knüllen to strike, Dutch knallen to bang]

Kneller ('nɛlə) n **Sir Godfrey**. ?1646–1723, portrait painter at the English court, born in Germany

knelt (nɛlt) vb a past tense and past participle of **kneel**

Knesset or **Knesseth** ('knɛsɪt) n the unicameral parliament of Israel [Hebrew, literally: gathering]

knew (njuː) vb the past tense of **know**

Knickerbocker ('nɪkə,bɒkə) n US **1** a descendant of the original Dutch settlers of New York **2** an inhabitant of New York [c19: named after Diedrich Knickerbocker, fictitious Dutchman alleged to be the author of

Washington Irving's *History of New York* (1809)]

knickerbocker glory *n* a rich confection consisting of layers of ice cream, jelly, cream, and fruit served in a tall glass

knickerbockers ('nɪkəˌbɒkəz) *pl n* baggy breeches fastened with a band at the knee or above the ankle. Also called (US): knickers [c19: regarded as the traditional dress of the Dutch settlers in America; see KNICKERBOCKER]

knickers ('nɪkəz) *pl n* an undergarment for women covering the lower trunk and sometimes the thighs and having separate legs or leg-holes [c19: contraction of KNICKERBOCKERS]

knick-knack *or* **nick-nack** ('nɪkˌnæk) *n* **1** a cheap ornament; trinket **2** an ornamental article of furniture, dress, etc [c17: by reduplication from *knack*, in obsolete sense: toy]

knife (naɪf) *n, pl* **knives** (naɪvz) **1** a cutting instrument consisting of a sharp-edged often pointed blade of metal fitted into a handle or onto a machine **2** a similar instrument used as a weapon **3** under the knife undergoing a surgical operation ▷ *vb* (*tr*) **4** to cut, stab, or kill with a knife **5** to betray, injure, or depose in an underhand way [Old English *cnīf*; related to Old Norse *knífr*, Middle Low German *knīf*] > 'knife,like *adj*

knife edge *n* **1** the sharp cutting edge of a knife **2** any sharp edge **3** a sharp-edged wedge of hard material on which the beam of a balance pivots or about which a pendulum is suspended **4** a critical point in the development of a situation, process of making a decision, etc

knifeman ('naɪfmən) *n, pl* -men a man who is armed with a knife, esp unlawfully

knight (naɪt) *n* **1** (in medieval Europe) **a** (originally) a person who served his lord as a mounted and heavily armed soldier **b** (later) a gentleman invested by a king or other lord with the military and social standing of this rank **2** (in modern times) a person invested by a sovereign with a nonhereditary rank and dignity usually in recognition of personal services, achievements, etc. A British knight bears the title *Sir* placed before his name, as in *Sir Winston Churchill* **3** a chess piece, usually shaped like a horse's head, that moves either two squares horizontally and one square vertically or one square horizontally and two squares vertically **4** a heroic champion of a lady or of a cause or principle **5** a member of the Roman class of the equites ▷ *vb* **6** (*tr*) to make (a person) a knight; dub [Old English *cniht* servant; related to Old High German *kneht* boy]

Knight (naɪt) *n* Dame **Laura**. 1887–1970, British painter, noted for her paintings of Gypsies, the ballet, and the circus

knight errant *n, pl* **knights errant** (esp in medieval romance) a knight who wanders in search of deeds of courage, chivalry, etc > knight errantry *n*

knighthood ('naɪthʊd) *n* **1** the order, dignity, or rank of a knight **2** the qualities of a knight; knightliness **3** knights collectively

knightly ('naɪtlɪ) *adj* of, relating to, resembling, or befitting a knight > 'knightliness *n*

knight of the road *n* informal or facetious **1** a tramp **2** a commercial traveller **3** a lorry driver **4** obsolete a highwayman

Knights Hospitallers *n* Also called: Knights of St John of Jerusalem a military religious order founded about the time of the first crusade (1096–99) among European crusaders. It took its name from a hospital and hostel in Jerusalem

Knight Templar *n, pl* **Knights Templars** *or* **Knights Templar** another term for **Templar**

kniphofia (nɪ'fəʊfɪə) *n* any plant of the perennial southern African genus *Kniphofia*, some species of which are cultivated for their conical spikes of bright red or yellow drooping tubular flowers: family *Liliaceae*. Also called: red-hot poker [named after J. H. *Kniphof* (1704–1763), German doctor and botanist]

knit (nɪt) *vb* **knits**, **knitting**, **knitted** *or* **knit 1** to make (a garment, etc) by looping and entwining (yarn, esp wool) by hand by means of long eyeless needles (**knitting**

needles) or by machine (**knitting machine**) **2** to join or be joined together closely **3** to draw (the brows) together or (of the brows) to come together, as in frowning or concentrating **4** (of a broken bone) to join together; heal ▷ *n* **5 a** a fabric or garment made by knitting **b** (*in combination*): *a heavy knit* [Old English *cnyttan* to tie in; related to Middle Low German *knütten* to knot together; see KNOT¹] > 'knitter *n*

knitting ('nɪtɪŋ) *n* knitted work or the process of producing it

knitwear ('nɪtˌwɛə) *n* knitted clothes, esp sweaters

knives (naɪvz) *n* the plural of **knife**

knob (nɒb) *n* **1** a rounded projection from a surface, such as a lump on a tree trunk **2** a handle of a door, drawer, etc, esp one that is rounded **3** a round hill or knoll or morainic ridge ▷ *vb* **knobs**, **knobbing**, **knobbed 4** (*tr*) to supply or ornament with knobs **5** (*intr*) to form into a knob; bulge [c14: from Middle Low German *knobbe* knot in wood; see KNOP] > 'knobby *adj* > 'knobbly *adj* -blier, -bliest

knobby ('nɒbɪ) *adj* -bier, -biest having or covered with small knobs; knobbly

knobkerrie ('nɒbˌkɛrɪ) *or* **knobstick** ('nɒbˌstɪk) *n* a stick with a round knob at the end, used as a club or missile by South African tribesmen [c19: from Afrikaans *knopkierie*, from *knop* knob, from Middle Dutch *cnoppe* + *kierie* stick, from Khoikhoi *kirri*]

knock (nɒk) *vb* **1** (*tr*) to give a blow or push to; strike **2** (*intr*) to rap sharply with the knuckles, a hard object, etc, esp to capture attention: *to knock at the door* **3** (*tr*) to make or force by striking **4** (*intr*; usually foll by *against*) to collide (with) **5** (*tr*) to bring into a certain condition by hitting or pushing: *to knock someone unconscious* **6** (*tr*) *informal* to criticize adversely; belittle: *to knock someone's work* **7** Also called: pink (*intr*) (of an internal-combustion engine) to emit a characteristic metallic noise as a result of faulty combustion **8** (*intr*) (of a bearing, esp one in an engine) to emit a regular characteristic sound as a result of wear **9** *Brit slang* to have sexual intercourse with (a person) **10** knock a person into the middle of next week *informal* to hit a person with a very heavy blow **11** knock on the head **a** to daze or kill (a person) by striking on the head **b** effectively to prevent the further development of (a plan) ▷ *n* **12 a** a blow, push, or rap: *he gave the table a knock* **b** the sound so caused **13** the sound of knocking in an engine or bearing **14** *informal* a misfortune, rebuff, or setback **15** *informal* unfavourable criticism ▷ See also **knock about**, **knock back** [Old English *cnocian*, of imitative origin; related to Old Norse *knoka* to hit]

knock about *or* **knock around** *vb* **1** (*intr, adverb*) to wander about aimlessly **2** (*intr, preposition*) to travel about, esp as resulting in varied or exotic experience: *he's knocked about the world a bit* **3** (*intr, adverb*; foll by *with*) to associate **4** (*tr, adverb*) to consider or discuss informally ▷ *adj* knockabout **5** rough; boisterous: *knockabout farce*

knock back *vb* (*tr, adverb*) **1** *informal* to drink, esp quickly **2** *informal* to cost **3** *slang* to reject or refuse ▷ *n* knock-back **4** *slang* a refusal or rejection **5** *prison slang* failure to obtain parole

knock down *vb* (*tr, adverb*) **1** to strike to the ground with a blow, as in boxing **2** (in auctions) to declare (an article) sold, as by striking a blow with a gavel **3** to demolish **4** to dismantle, for ease of transport **5** *informal* to reduce (a price, etc) **6** *Austral slang* to spend (a cheque) **7** *Austral slang* to drink ▷ *adj* knockdown (*prenominal*) **8** overwhelming; powerful: *a knockdown blow* **9** *chiefly Brit* cheap: *I got the table at a knockdown price* **10** easily dismantled: *knockdown furniture*

knocker ('nɒkə) *n* **1** an object, usually ornamental and made of metal, attached to a door by a hinge and used for knocking **2** *informal* a person who finds fault or disparages **3** (*usually plural*) *slang* a female breast **4** a person or thing that knocks **5** on the knocker *Austral & NZ informal* promptly; at once: *you pay on the knocker here*

knocking copy *n* advertising or publicity material designed to denigrate a competing product

knocking-shop *n* *Brit* a slang word for **brothel**

knock-knee *n* a condition in which the legs are bent

inwards causing the knees to touch when standing

knock off *vb* (*mainly adverb*) **1** (*intr, also preposition*) *informal* to finish work: *we knocked off an hour early* **2** (*tr*) *informal* to make or do hastily or easily: *to knock off a novel in a week* **3** (*tr; also preposition*) *informal* to reduce the price of (an article) by (a stated amount) **4** (*tr*) *slang* to kill **5** (*tr*) *slang* to rob or steal: *to knock off a bank; to knock off a watch* **6** (*tr*) *slang* to stop doing something, used as a command: *knock it off!* ▷ *n* **knockoff 7** *informal* an illegal imitation of a well-known product **b** (*as modifier*): *knockoff watches*

knock-on *n* **1** *rugby* the infringement of playing the ball forward with the hand or arm ▷ *vb* **knock on** (*adverb*) **2** *rugby* to play (the ball) forward with the hand or arm

knockout ('nɒk,aʊt) *n* **1** the act of rendering unconscious **2** a blow that renders an opponent unconscious **3 a** a competition in which competitors are eliminated progressively **b** (*as modifier*): *a knockout contest* **4** *informal* a person or thing that is overwhelmingly impressive or attractive: *she's a knockout* ▷ *vb* **knock out** (*tr, adverb*) **5** to render unconscious, esp by a blow **6** *boxing* to defeat (an opponent) by a knockout **7** to destroy, damage, or injure badly **8** to eliminate, esp in a knockout competition **9** *informal* to overwhelm or amaze, esp with admiration or favourable reaction: *I was knocked out by that new song*

knockout drops *pl n slang* a drug secretly put into someone's drink to cause stupefaction. See also **Mickey Finn**

knock up *vb* (*adverb, mainly tr*) **1** Also called: **knock together** *informal* to assemble quickly; improvise: *to knock up a set of shelves* **2** *Brit informal* to waken; rouse: *to knock someone up early* **3** *slang* to make pregnant **4** *Brit informal* to exhaust: *the heavy work knocked him up* **5** *cricket* to score (runs) **6** (*intr*) *tennis, squash, badminton* to practise or hit the ball about immediately before a match ▷ *n* **knock-up 7** a practice session at tennis, squash, or a similar game

knoll (nəʊl) *n* a small rounded hill [Old English *cnoll*; compare Old Norse *knollr* hilltop] > 'knolly *adj*

knop (nɒp) *n archaic* a knob, esp an ornamental one [c14: from Germanic; compare Middle Dutch *cnoppe* bud, Old High German *knopf*]

Knossos *or* **Cnossus** ('nɒsəs, 'knɒs-) *n* a ruined city in N central Crete: remains of the Minoan Bronze Age civilization

knot[1] (nɒt) *n* **1** any of various fastenings formed by looping and tying a piece of rope, cord, etc, in upon itself, to another piece of rope, or to another object **2** a prescribed method of tying a particular knot **3** a tangle, as in hair or string **4** a decorative bow or fastening, as of ribbon or braid **5** a small cluster or huddled group **6** a tie or bond: *the marriage knot* **7** a difficult problem **8 a** a hard mass of wood at the point where a branch joins the trunk of a tree **b** a cross section of this, usually roundish and cross-grained, visible in a piece of timber **9** a sensation of constriction, caused by tension or nervousness: *his stomach was tying itself in knots* **10** *pathol* a lump of vessels or fibres formed in a part, as in a muscle **11** a unit of speed used by nautical vessels and aircraft, being one nautical mile (about 1.15 statute miles or 1.85 km) per hour **12** at a rate of knots very fast **13** tie someone in knots to completely perplex or confuse someone ▷ *vb* **knots, knotting, knotted 14** (*tr*) to tie or fasten in a knot **15** to form or cause to form into a knot **16** (*tr*) to ravel or entangle or become ravelled or entangled **17** (*tr*) to make (an article or a design) by tying thread in an interlaced pattern of ornamental knots, as in macramé [Old English *cnotta*; related to Old High German *knoto*, Old Norse *knūtr*] > 'knotter *n* > 'knotless *adj* > 'knotted *adj*

knot[2] (nɒt) *n* a small northern sandpiper, *Calidris canutus*, with a short bill and grey plumage [c15: of unknown origin]

knot garden *n* (esp formerly) a formal garden of intricate design

knotgrass ('nɒt,grɑːs) *n* **1** Also called: **allseed** a polygonaceous weedy plant, *Polygonum aviculare*, whose small green flowers produce numerous seeds **2** any of several related plants

knothole ('nɒt,həʊl) *n* a hole in a piece of wood where a knot has been

knotty ('nɒtɪ) *adj* **-tier, -tiest 1** (of wood, rope, etc) full of or characterized by knots **2** extremely difficult or intricate

knout (naʊt) *n* a stout whip used formerly in Russia as an instrument of punishment [c17: from Russian *knut*, of Scandinavian origin; compare Old Norse *knūtr* knot]

know (nəʊ) *vb* **knows, knowing, knew** (njuː) **known** (nəʊn) (*mainly tr*) **1** (*also intr; may take a clause as object*) to be or feel certain of the truth or accuracy of (a fact, etc) **2** to be acquainted or familiar with: *she's known him five years* **3** to have a familiarity or grasp of, as through study or experience: *he knows French* **4** (*also intr; may take a clause as object*) to understand, be aware of, or perceive (facts, etc): *he knows the answer now* **5** (foll by *how*) to be sure or aware of (how to be or do something) **6** to experience, esp deeply: *to know poverty* **7** to be intelligent, informed, or sensible enough (to do something) **8** (*may take a clause as object*) to be able to distinguish or discriminate **9** *archaic* to have sexual intercourse with **10** know what's what to know how one thing or things in general work **11** you never know things are uncertain ▷ *n* **12** in the know *informal* aware or informed [Old English *gecnāwan*; related to Old Norse *knā* I can, Latin *noscere* to come to know] > 'knowable *adj* > 'knower *n*

know-all *n informal, disparaging* a person who pretends or appears to know a great deal

know-how *n informal* **1** ingenuity, aptitude, or skill; knack **2** commercial and saleable knowledge of how to do a particular thing; experience

knowing ('nəʊɪŋ) *adj* **1** suggesting secret information or knowledge **2** wise, shrewd, or clever **3** deliberate; intentional ▷ *n* **4** there is no knowing one cannot tell > 'knowingly *adv* > 'knowingness *n*

knowledge ('nɒlɪdʒ) *n* **1** the facts, feelings or experiences known by a person or group of people **2** the state of knowing **3** awareness, consciousness, or familiarity gained by experience or learning **4** erudition or informed learning **5** specific information about a subject **6** to my knowledge **a** as I understand it **b** as I know

knowledgeable *or* **knowledgable** ('nɒlɪdʒəbəl) *adj* possessing or indicating much knowledge > 'knowledgeably *or* 'knowledgably *adv*

knowledge-based system *n computing* an expert system

knowledge economy *n* an economy in which information services are dominant as an area of growth

knowledge worker *n* a person employed to produce or analyse ideas and information

Knowles (nəʃuəlz) *n* **Beyoncé** (beɪ'jɒnseɪ). born 1981, US singer, songwriter, and actress. A member of the hugely successful Destiny's Child, she later found solo success with *Dangerously in Love* (2003) and the single "Crazy in Love" (2003)

known (nəʊn) *vb* **1** the past participle of **know** ▷ *adj* **2** specified and identified: *a known criminal*

know-nothing *n informal, disparaging* an ignorant person

Knowsley ('nəʊzlɪ) *n* a unitary authority of NW England, in Merseyside. Pop: 150 200 (2003 est). Area: 97 sq km (38 sq miles)

Knox (nɒks) *n* **1 John.** ?1514–72, Scottish theologian and historian. After exile in England and on the Continent (1547–59), he returned to Scotland in 1559 and established the Presbyterian Church of Scotland (1560). His chief historical work was the *History of the Reformation in Scotland* (1586) **2 Ronald** (**Arbuthnott**). 1888–1957, British priest and author. A convert to Roman Catholicism, he is noted for his translation of the Vulgate (1945–49)

Knox-Johnston (,nɒks'dʒɒnstən) *n* **Sir Robin** (**William Robert Patrick**). born 1939, British yachtsman. He was the first to sail round the world alone nonstop (1968–69)

Knoxville ('nɒksvɪl) *n* an industrial city in E Tennessee, on the Tennessee River: state capital (1796–1812; 1817–19). Pop: 173 278 (2003 est)

knuckle ('nʌkəl) *n* **1 a** a joint of a finger, esp that connecting a finger to the hand **2** a joint of veal, pork, etc, consisting of the part of the leg below the knee joint, often used in making stews or stock **3** near the knuckle *informal* approaching indecency ▷ *vb* **4** (*tr*) to rub or press with the knuckles **5** (*intr*) to keep the knuckles on the ground while shooting a marble ▷ See also **knuckle down, knuckle under** [C14: related to Middle High German *knöchel*, Middle Low German *knoke* bone, Dutch *knok*] > 'knuckly *adj*

knucklebones ('nʌkəl,bəʊnz) *n* (*functioning as singular*) a less common name for **jacks**

knuckle down *vb* (*intr, adverb*) *informal* to apply oneself diligently: *to knuckle down to some work*

knuckle-duster *n* (*often plural*) a metal bar fitted over the knuckles, often with holes for the fingers, for inflicting injury by a blow with the fist

knucklehead ('nʌkəl,hed) *n informal* fool; idiot > 'knuckle,headed *adj*

knuckle under *vb* (*intr, adverb*) to give way under pressure or authority; yield

knur, knurr (nɜː) *or* **knar** *n* a knot or protuberance in a tree trunk or in wood [C16 *knor*; related to Middle High German *knorre* knot; compare KNAR]

knurl *or* **nurl** (nɜːl) *vb* (*tr*) **1** to impress with a series of fine ridges or serrations ▷ *n* **2** a small ridge, esp one of a series providing a rough surface that can be gripped [C17: probably from KNUR]

Knussen ('nʌsən) *n* (**Stuart**) **Oliver**. born 1952, British composer and conductor. His works include the opera *Where the Wild Things Are* (1981) and three symphonies

Knut (kə'njuːt) *n* a variant spelling of **Canute**

KO *or* **k.o.** ('keɪ'əʊ) *vb* KO's, KO'ing, KO'd, k.o.'s, k.o.'ing, k.o.'d **1** a slang term for **knockout** ▷ *n*, *pl* KO's or k.o.'s **2** a slang term for **knockout**

koala *or* **koala bear** (kəʊ'ɑːlə) *n* a slow-moving Australian arboreal marsupial, *Phascolarctus cinereus*, having dense greyish fur and feeding on eucalyptus leaves and bark. Also called (Austral.): native bear [from a native Australian language]

koan ('kəʊæn) *n* (in Zen Buddhism) a problem or riddle that admits no logical solution [from Japanese]

Kobarid ('kəʊbəˌriːd; *Slovene* 'kɔbaˌrid) *n* a village in Slovenia on the Isonzo River: part of Italy until 1947; scene of the defeat of the Italians by Austro-German forces (1917). Italian name: Caporetto

Kobe ('kəʊbɪ) *n* a port in S Japan, on S Honshu on Osaka Bay: formed in 1889 by the amalgamation of Hyogo and Kobe; a major industrial complex, producing ships, steel, and rubber goods. Pop: 1 478 380 (2002 est)

København (købən'haun) *n* the Danish name for **Copenhagen**

Koblenz *or* **Coblenz** (*German* 'koːblɛnts) *n* a city in W central Germany, in the Rhineland-Palatinate at the confluence of the Rivers Moselle and Rhine: ruled by the archbishop-electors of Trier from 1018 until occupied by the French in 1794; passed to Prussia in 1815, becoming capital of the Rhine Province (1824–1945) and of the Rhineland-Palatinate (1946–50); wine trade centre. Pop: 107 608 (2003 est)

kobold ('kɒbəʊld) *n German myth* a mischievous household sprite [C19: from German; see COBALT]

Koch (*German* kɔx) *n* **Robert**. ('roːbɛrt). 1843–1910, German bacteriologist, who isolated the anthrax bacillus (1876), the tubercle bacillus (1882), and the cholera bacillus (1883): Nobel prize for physiology or medicine 1905

Kochi (kəʊ'tʃiː) *n* a port in SW Japan, on central Shikoku on Urado Bay. Pop: 326 490 (2002 est)

kochia ('kəʊkɪə) *n* any plant of the widely distributed annual genus *Kochia*, esp *K. Scoparia trichophila*, grown for its foliage, which turns dark red in the late summer: family *Chenopodiaceae* [named after W. D. J. *Koch* (1771–1849), German botanist]

Kodály (*Hungarian* 'kodaːj) *n* **Zoltán** (zolta:n). 1882–1967, Hungarian composer. His works were often inspired by native folk songs and include the comic opera *Háry János* (1926) and *Psalmus Hungaricus* (1923) for chorus and orchestra

Kodiak ('kəʊdɪˌæk) *n* an island in S Alaska, in the Gulf of Alaska: site of the first European settlement in Alaska, made by Russians in 1784. Pop: 13 466 (2004 est). Area:

8974 sq km (3465 sq miles)

Kodiak bear *or* **Kodiak** *n* a large variety of the brown bear, *Ursus arctos*, inhabiting the west coast of Alaska and neighbouring islands, esp Kodiak

koeksister ('kʊkˌsɪstə) *n South African* a plaited doughnut deep-fried and soaked in syrup [Afrikaans, but possibly of Malay origin]

koel ('kəʊəl) *n* any of several parasitic cuckoos of the genus *Eudynamys*, esp *E. scolopacea*, of S and SE Asia and Australia [C19: from Hindi, from Sanskrit *kokila*]

Koestler ('kɜːstlə) *n* **Arthur**. 1905–83, British writer, born in Hungary. Of his early antitotalitarian novels *Darkness at Noon* (1940) is outstanding. His later works, *The Sleepwalkers* (1959), *The Act of Creation* (1964), and *The Ghost in the Machine* (1967) reflect his interest in science, philosophy, and psychology. He committed suicide

Kofu ('kəʊfuː) *n* a city in central Japan, on S Honshu: textiles. Pop: 190 098 (2002 est)

Kogi ('kəʊgɪ) *n* a state of W Nigeria. Capital: Lokoja. Pop: 3 278 487 (2006). Area: 29 833 sq km (11 519 sq miles)

koha ('kəʊhə) *n NZ* a gift or donation, esp of cash [Māori]

kohanga reo (kɔː'hɑːˌŋa 'reɪəʊ) *n NZ* an infant class in which the lessons are conducted in Māori [Māori, literally: language nest]

Kohima ('kəʊhɪˌmɑː) *n* a city in NE India, capital of Nagaland, near the Burmese border: centre of fierce fighting in World War II, when it was surrounded by the Japanese but not captured (1944). Pop: 78 584 (2001)

kohl (kəʊl) *n* a cosmetic powder used, originally esp in Muslim and Asian countries, to darken the area around the eyes. It is usually powdered antimony sulphide [C18: from Arabic *kohl*; see ALCOHOL]

Kohl (kəʊl) *n* **Helmut** ('hɛlmuːt). born 1930, German statesman: chancellor of West Germany (1982–90) and of Germany (1990–98)

Köhler (*German* 'køːlər) *n* **Wolfgang** ('vɔlfgaŋ). 1887–1967, German psychologist, a leading exponent of Gestalt psychology

kohlrabi (kəʊl'rɑːbɪ) *n*, *pl* -bies a cultivated variety of cabbage, *Brassica oleracea caulorapa* (or *gongylodes*), whose thickened stem is eaten as a vegetable. Also called: turnip cabbage [C19: from German, from Italian *cavoli rape* (pl), from *cavolo* cabbage (from Latin *caulis*) + *rapa* turnip (from Latin); influenced by German *Kohl* cabbage]

koi (kɔɪ) *n* any of various ornamental forms of the common carp [Japanese]

koine ('kɔɪniː) *n* a common language among speakers of different languages; lingua franca [from Greek *koinē dialektos* common language]

Koine ('kɔɪniː) *n* the Koine (*sometimes not capital*) the Ancient Greek dialect that was the lingua franca of the empire of Alexander the Great and was widely used throughout the E Mediterranean area in Roman times

Koizumi (ˌkɔɪ'zuːmɪ) *n* **Junichiro** (ˌjunɪ'kiro). born 1941, Japanese politician; prime minister (2001–06)

Kokand (*Russian* ka'kant) *n* a city in NE Uzbekistan, in the Fergana valley. Pop: 211 000 (2005 est)

kokanee (kəʊ'kænɪ) *n* a landlocked salmon, *Oncorhynchus nerka kennerlyi*, of lakes in W North America: a variety of sockeye [probably from *Kokanee* Creek, in SE British Columbia]

Koko Nor ('kəʊ'kəʊ 'nɔː) *or* **Kuku Nor** *n* a lake in W China, in Qinghai province in the NE Tibetan Highlands at an altitude of about 3000 m (10 000 ft): the largest lake in China. Area: about 4100 sq km (1600 sq miles). Chinese name: Qinghai

Kokoschka (*German* ko'kɔʃka) ('kɔkɔʃka) *n* **Oskar** ('ɔskar). 1886–1980, Austrian expressionist painter and dramatist, noted for his landscapes and portraits

kola ('kəʊlə) *n* a variant spelling of **cola¹**

kola nut *n* a variant spelling of **cola nut**

Kola Peninsula ('kəʊlə) *n* a peninsula in NW Russia, between the Barents and White Seas: forms most of the Murmansk region. Area: about 130 000 sq km (50 000 sq miles)

Kolar Gold Fields (kəʊ'lɑː) *n* a city in S India, in SE Karnataka: a major gold-mining centre since 1881. Pop: 176 000 (2005 est)

Kolding (*Danish* 'kɔlɛŋ) *n* a port in Denmark, in E Jutland at the head of **Kolding Fjord** (an inlet of the Little Belt). Pop: 54 941 (2004 est)

Kolhapur (ˌkəʊlhɑːˈpʊə) *n* a city in W India, in S Maharashtra: university (1963). Pop: 485 183 (2001)

kolinsky (kəˈlɪnskɪ) *n, pl -skies* **1** any of various Asian minks, esp *Mustela sibirica* of Siberia **2** the rich tawny fur of this animal [c19: from Russian *kolinski* of *Kola*: see KOLA PENINSULA]

Kolkata (ˈkɒlkɑːtə) *n* a port in E India, capital of West Bengal state, on the Hooghly River: former capital of the country (1833–1912); major commercial and industrial centre; many universities. Pop: 4 580 544 (2001). Former official name: **Calcutta**

kolkhoz, kolkhos (kɒlˈhɔːz; *Russian* kalˈxos) *or* **kolkoz** (kɒlˈkɔːz) *n* a Russian collective farm [c20: from Russian, short for *kollektivnoe khozyaistvo* collective farm]

Kollwitz (*German* ˈkɔlvɪts) *n* **Käthe** (ˈkɛːtə). 1867–1945, German lithographer and sculptress

Kolmar (ˈkɔlmar) *n* the German name for **Colmar**

Kolmogorov (ˌkɒlmɒˈɡɔːrɒf) *n* **Andrei Nikolaevich** (anˈdrjej nikaˈlajəvitʃ). (1903–87), Soviet mathematician, who made important contributions to the theoretical foundations of probability

Köln (kœln) *n* the German name for **Cologne**

Kol Nidre (kɔːl ˈnɪdreɪ; *Hebrew* kɔl niːˈdre) *n Judaism* **1** the evening service with which Yom Kippur begins **2** the opening prayer of that service, declaring null in advance any purely religious vows one may come to make in the coming year [Aramaic *kōl nidhrē* all the vows; the prayer's opening words]

Kolomna (*Russian* kaˈlɔmnə) *n* a city in the W central Russia, at the confluence of the Moskva and Oka Rivers: railway engineering centre. Pop: 151 500 (1999 est)

Kolyma (*Russian* kaliˈma) *n* a river in NE Russia, rising in the Kolyma Mountains north of the Sea of Okhotsk and flowing generally north to the East Siberian Sea. Length: 2600 km (1615 miles)

Kolyma Range *n* a mountain range in NE Russia, in NE Siberia, extending about 1100 km (700 miles) between the Kolyma River and the Sea of Okhotsk. Highest peak: 1862 m (6109 ft)

Komati (kəˈmɑːtɪ, ˈkəʊmətɪ) *n* a river in southern Africa, rising in E South Africa and flowing east through Swaziland and Mozambique to the Indian Ocean at Delagoa Bay. Length: about 800 km (500 miles)

komatik (ˈkəʊmætɪk) *n* a sledge having wooden runners and crossbars bound with rawhide, used by the Inuit and other related peoples [c20: from Inuktitut (Labrador)]

Komi Republic (ˈkəʊmɪ) *n* a constituent republic of NW Russia: annexed by the princes of Moscow in the 14th century. Capital: Syktyvkar. Pop: 1 019 000 (2002). Area: 415 900 sq km (160 540 sq miles)

Kommunarsk (*Russian* kəmuˈnarsk) *n* the Former name (until 1992) of **Alchevsk**

Komsomolsk (*Russian* kəmsaˈmɔljsk) *n* an industrial city in W Russia, on the Amur River: built by members of the Komsomol (Communist youth league) in 1932. Pop: 275 000 (2005 est)

Konakry *or* **Konakri** (*French* kɔnakri) *n* variant spellings of **Conakry**

Kongur Shan (ˈkʊŋʊə ˈʃæn), **Kungur** *or* **Qungur** *n* a mountain in China, in W Xinjiang: the highest peak in the Pamirs. Height: 7719 m (25 325 ft)

Kong Zi (ˈkʊŋ ziː) *n* the Pinyin transliteration of the Chinese name for **Confucius**

Königgrätz (køːnɪçˈɡrɛːts) *n* the German name for **Hradec Králové**

Königsberg (ˈkɜːnɪɡzˌbɜːɡ; *German* ˈkøːnɪçsbɛrk) *n* the former name (until 1946) of **Kaliningrad**

Königshütte (ˈkøːnɪçʃhytə) *n* the German name for **Chorzów**

Konstanz (ˈkɔnstants) *n* the German name for **Constance**

Konya *or* **Konia** (ˈkɔːnjɑː) *n* a city in SW central Turkey: in ancient times a Phrygian city and capital of Lycaonia. Pop: 883 000 (2005 est). Ancient name: **Iconium**

koodoo (ˈkuːduː) *n* a variant spelling of **kudu**

kook (kuːk) *n US & Canadian informal* an eccentric, crazy, or foolish person [c20: probably from CUCKOO] > **kooky** *or* **kookie** (ˈkuːkɪ) *adj* kookier, kookiest

kookaburra (ˈkʊkəˌbʌrə) *n* **1** Also called: laughing jackass a large arboreal Australian kingfisher, *Dacelo novaeguineae* (or *gigas*), with a cackling cry **2** Also called: blue-winged kookaburra a related smaller bird *D. Leachii*, of tropical Australia and New Guinea [c19: from a native Australian language]

Koolhaas (*Dutch* ˈkulhɑs) *n* **Rem.** Dutch architect and theorist, co-founder of the Office for Metropolitan Architecture (1975); buildings include the Grand Palais and associated developments in Lille, France (1989–96); books include *S, M, L, XL* (1996)

Kooning (ˈkuːnɪŋ) *n* See **de Kooning**

Kootenay *or* **Kootenai** (ˈkuːtəˈniː, ˈkuːtəneɪ) *n* a river in W North America, rising in SE British Columbia and flowing south into NW Montana, then north into Idaho before re-entering British Columbia, broadening into **Kootenay Lake**, then flowing to the Columbia River. Length: 655 km (407 miles)

kop (kɒp) *n* a prominent isolated hill or mountain in southern Africa [from Afrikaans: head, hence high part; compare German *Kopf* head; see COP²]

kopeck, kopek *or* **copeck** (ˈkəʊpɛk) *n* a monetary unit of Russia and Belarus worth one hundredth of a rouble: coins are still used as tokens for coin-operated machinery although the kopeck itself is virtually valueless [Russian *kopeika*, from *kopye* lance; so called because of the representation of Tsar Ivan IV on the coin with a lance in his hand]

Kopeisk *or* **Kopeysk** (*Russian* kaˈpjejsk) *n* a city in SW central Russia, in Chelyabinsk province: lignite mining. Pop: 24 000 (2005 est)

kopje *or* **koppie** (ˈkɒpɪ) *n* a small isolated hill [c19: from Afrikaans *koppie*, from Dutch *kopje*, literally: a little head, from *kop* head; see KOP]

kora (ˈkɔːrə) *n* a West African instrument with twenty-one strings, combining features of the harp and the lute

Koran (kɔːˈrɑːn) *n* the sacred book of Islam, believed by Muslims to be the infallible word of God dictated to Mohammed through the medium of the angel Gabriel. Also called: Qur'an [c17: from Arabic *qur'ān* reading, book; related to *qara'a* to read, recite] > **Ko'ranic** *adj*

Korbut (*Russian* ˈkɔrbʊt) *n* **Olga** (ˈɔljɡə). born 1955, Soviet gymnast: noted for her highly individualistic style, which greatly increased the popularity of the sport, esp following her performance in the 1972 Olympic Games

Korchnoi (ˈkɔːtʃˌnɔɪ) *n* **Victor.** born 1931, Soviet-born chess player: Soviet champion 1960, 1962, and 1964: defected to the West in 1976

Korda (ˈkɔːdə) *n* **Sir Alexander**, real name *Sandor Kellner*. 1893–1956, British film producer and director, born in Hungary: his films include *The Scarlet Pimpernel* (1934), *Anna Karenina* (1948), and *The Third Man* (1949)

Kordofan (ˌkɔːdəʊˈfæn) *n* a region of the central Sudan: consists of a plateau with rugged uplands (the Nuba Mountains). Area: 380 548 sq km (146 930 sq miles)

Korea (kəˈriːə) *n* a former country in E Asia, now divided into two separate countries, North Korea and South Korea. Korea occupied the peninsula between the Sea of Japan (East Sea) and the Yellow Sea: an isolated vassal of Manchu China for three centuries until the opening of ports to Japanese trade in 1876; gained independence in 1895; annexed to Japan in 1910 and divided in 1945 into two occupation zones (Russian in the north, American in the south), which became North Korea and South Korea in 1948. Japanese name (1910–45): Chosen See **North Korea, South Korea** > **Ko'rean** *adj, n*

Korea Strait *n* a strait between South Korea and SW Japan, linking the Sea of Japan (East Sea) with the East China Sea

korfball (ˈkɔːfˌbɔːl) *n* a game similar to basketball, in which each team consists of six men and six women [c20: from Dutch *korfbal* basketball]

Kórinthos (ˈkɔrinθɒs) *n* transliteration of the Modern Greek name for **Corinth**

korma *or* **qorma** (ˈkɔːmə) *n* any of a variety of Indian dishes consisting of meat or vegetables braised with water, stock, yogurt, or cream [from Urdu]

Korsakoffian (ˌkɔːsəˈkɒfiən) *adj* **1** relating to or suffering from Korsakoff's psychosis ▷ *n* **2** a person suffering from Korsakoff's psychosis

Korzybski (kɔːˈzɪbskɪ) *n* **Alfred (Habdank Skarbek).** 1879–1950, US originator of the theory and study of general semantics, born in Poland

Kos *or* **Cos** (kɒs) *n* an island in the SE Aegean Sea, in the Greek Dodecanese Islands: separated from SW Turkey by the **Kos Channel**; settled in ancient times by Dorians and became famous for literature and medicine. Pop: 30 947 (2001). Area: 282 sq km (109 sq miles)

Kosciusko (ˌkɒsɪˈʌskəʊ) *n* **Thaddeus,** Polish name *Tadeusz Kościuszko.* 1746–1817, Polish general: fought for the colonists in the American War of Independence and led an unsuccessful revolt against the partitioning of Poland (1794)

Kosciuszko (ˌkɒsɪˈʌskəʊ) *n* **Mount Kosciuszko** a mountain in Australia, in SE New South Wales in the Australian Alps: the highest peak in Australia. Height: 2230 m (7316 ft)

kosher (ˈkəʊʃə) *adj* **1** *Judaism* conforming to religious law; fit for use: esp, (of food) prepared in accordance with the dietary laws **2** *informal* **a** genuine or authentic **b** legitimate or proper [C19: from Yiddish, from Hebrew *kāshēr* right, proper]

kosher salt *n* *US* a coarse flaky salt that contains no additives, used in cooking and in preparing kosher meals

Košice (Czech ˈkɔʃitsɛ) *n* a city in E Slovakia: passed from Hungary to Czechoslovakia in 1920 and to Slovakia in 1993. Pop: 236 093 (2001). Hungarian name: Kassa

Kosovo (ˈkɒsəvəʊ; Serbian ˈkɔsɔvɔ) *or* **Kosova** (Albanian kɔˈsɔva) *n* an autonomous province of Serbia, in the SW: chiefly Albanian in population since the 13th century; Serb suppression of separatists escalated to a policy of ethnic cleansing in 1998, provoking NATO airstrikes against Serbia in 1999 and takeover by UN administration; unilaterally declared independence in 2008. Mainly a plateau. Capital: Priština. Pop: 2 325 000 (2001 est). Area: 10 887 sq km (4203 sq miles) > Kosovar (ˈkɒsəˌvɑː) *or* Kosovan (ˈkɒsəˌvæn) *adj, n*

Kossoff (ˈkɒsɒf) *n* **Leon.** born 1926, British painter, esp of London scenes

Kossuth (Hungarian ˈkoʃuːt) *n* **Lajos** (ˈlɒjɒʃ). 1802–94, Hungarian statesman. He led the revolution against Austria (1848) and was provisional governor (1849), but he fled when the revolt was suppressed (1849)

Kostroma (Russian kəstraˈma) *n* a city in W central Russia, on the River Volga: fought over bitterly by Novgorod, Tver, and Moscow, until annexed by Moscow in 1329; textile centre. Pop: 280 000 (2005 est)

Koštunica (ˌkɒstjʊˈniːkə) *n* **Vojislav** (ˈvɒjɪslæf). born 1944, Serbian politician; president of the Federal Republic of Yugoslavia (2000–03); prime minister of Serbia and Montenegro (2004–06); prime minister of Serbia from 2006

Kosygin (Russian kaˈsiɡin) *n* **Aleksei Nikolayevich** (alˈɪkˈsjej nikaˈlajɪvitʃ). 1904–80, Soviet statesman; premier of the Soviet Union (1964–80)

Kota *or* **Kotah** (ˈkəʊtə) *n* a city in NW India, in Rajasthan on the Chambal River: textile industry. op.: 695 899 (2001)

Kotabaru (ˌkəʊtəˈbɑːruː) *n* a former name of **Jayapura**

Kota Bharu *or* **Bahru** (ˈkəʊtə ˈbɑːruː) *n* a port in NE Peninsular Malaysia: capital of Kelantan state on the delta of the Kelantan River. Pop: 263 000 (2005 est)

Kota Kinabalu (ˈkəʊtə ˌkɪnəbəˈluː) *n* a port in Malaysia, capital of Sabah state on the South China Sea: exports timber and rubber. Pop: 439 000 (2005 est). Former name: Jesselton

koto (ˈkəʊtəʊ) *n, pl* kotos a Japanese stringed instrument, consisting of a rectangular wooden body over which are stretched silk strings, which are plucked with plectrums or a nail-like device [Japanese]

kotuku (ˈkəʊtʊkuː) *n, pl* -ku the white heron, *Egretta alba,* having brilliant white plumage, black legs and yellow eyes and bill [Māori]

kouprey (ˈkuːpreɪ) *n* a large wild member of the cattle

tribe, *Box sauveli,* of SE Asia, having a blackish-brown body and white legs: an endangered species [C20: from French, from a Cambodian native name, from Pali *gō* cow + Khmer *brai* forest]

Kourou (ˈkuːruː) *n* a town in N central French Guiana; site of the European Space Agency's launch and research base. Pop: 19 107 (1999)

Kovno (ˈkɒvnə) *n* transliteration of the Russian name for **Kaunas**

Kovrov (Russian kavˈrɒf) *n* a city in W central Russia, on the Klyazma River: textiles and heavy engineering. Pop: 155 000 (2005 est)

Koweit (kəʊˈweɪt) *n* a variant of **Kuwait**

kowhai (ˈkəʊwaɪ, ˈkəʊfaɪ) *n* NZ a small leguminous tree, *Sophora tetraptera,* of New Zealand and Chile, with clusters of yellow flowers [C19: from Māori]

Kowloon (ˈkaʊˈluːn) *n* **1** a peninsula of SE China, opposite Hong Kong Island: part of the former British colony of Hong Kong. Area: 10 sq km (3.75 sq miles) **2** a port in Hong Kong, on Kowloon Peninsula. Pop: 2 019 533 (2006 est)

kowtow (ˌkaʊˈtaʊ) *vb* (*intr*) **1** to touch the forehead to the ground as a sign of deference: a former Chinese custom **2** (often foll by *to*) to be servile or obsequious (towards) ▷ *n* **3** the act of kowtowing [C19: from Chinese *k'o t'ou,* from *k'o* to strike, knock + *t'ou* head]

Kozhikode (ˌkəʊʒɪˈkəʊd) *n* a port in SW India, in W Kerala on the Malabar coast: important European trading post (1511–1765): formerly calico-manufacturing. Pop: 436 527 (2001). Former name: Calicut

Kr *symbol for* **1** *currency* **a** krona **b** krone ▷ *the chemical symbol for* **2** krypton

kr. *abbreviation* **1** krona **2** krone

Kra (krɑː) *n* **Isthmus of Kra** an isthmus of SW Thailand, between the Bay of Bengal and the Gulf of Thailand: the narrowest part of the Malay Peninsula. Width: about 56 km (35 miles)

kraal (krɑːl) *South African* ▷ *n* **1** a hut village in southern Africa, esp one surrounded by a stockade **2** an enclosure for livestock [C18: from Afrikaans, from Portuguese *curral* pen; see **CORRAL**]

Krafft-Ebing (German ˈkraftˈeːbɪŋ) *n* **Richard** (ˈrɪçart), Baron von Krafft-Ebing. 1840–1902, German neurologist and psychiatrist who pioneered the systematic study of sexual behaviour in *Psychopathia Sexualis* (1886)

kraft (krɑːft) *n* strong wrapping paper, made from pulp processed with a sulphate solution [from German: force]

Kragujevac (Serbian ˈkraɡujɛvats) *n* a town in E central Serbia; capital of Serbia (1818–39); automobile industry. Pop: 145 890 (2002)

krait (kraɪt) *n* any nonaggressive brightly coloured venomous elapid snake of the genus *Bungarus,* of S and SE Asia [C19: from Hindi *karait,* of obscure origin]

Krakatoa (ˌkrɑːkəˈtəʊə, ˌkrækəˈtəʊə) *or* **Krakatau** (ˌkrɑːkəˈtaʊ, ˌkrækəˈtaʊ) *n* a volcanic island in Indonesia, in the Sunda Strait between Java and Sumatra: partially destroyed by its eruption in 1883, the greatest in recorded history. Further eruptions 44 years later formed a new island, **Anak Krakatau** ("Child of Krakatau"). Also called: Rakata

Krakau (ˈkrɑːkaʊ) *n* the German name for **Cracow**

kraken (ˈkrɑːkən) *n* a legendary sea monster of gigantic size believed to dwell off the coast of Norway [C18: from Norwegian, of obscure origin]

Kraków (ˈkrakuf) *n* the Polish name for **Cracow**

Kramatorsk (Russian krəmaˈtɔrsk) *n* a city in Ukraine: a major industrial centre of the Donets Basin. Pop: 177 000 (2005 est)

Kranj (krɑːnj) *n* the Slovene name for **Carniola**

krans (krɑːns) *n* *South African* a sheer rock face; precipice [C18: from Afrikaans]

Krasnodar (Russian krəsnaˈdar) *n* an industrial city in SW Russia, on the Kuban River. Pop: 650 000 (2005 est). Former names (until 1920): Yekaterinodar, Ekaterinodar

Krasnoyarsk (Russian krəsnaˈjarsk) *n* a city in E central Russia, on the Yenisei River: the country's largest hydroelectric power station is nearby. Pop: 912 000 (2005 est)

Krebs (krɛbz) *n* Sir **Hans Adolf.** 1900–81, British

biochemist, born in Germany, who shared a Nobel prize for physiology or medicine (1953) for the discovery of the Krebs cycle

Krefeld ('kreɪfeld; German 'kreːfɛlt) n a city in Germany, in E central North Rhine-Westphalia: textile industries. Pop: 238 565 (2003 est)

Kreisler (German 'kraɪslər) n **Fritz** (frɪts). 1875–1962, US violinist, born in Austria

Kremenchug (Russian krɪmɪn'tʃuk) n an industrial city in E central Ukraine on the Dnieper River. Pop: 234 000 (2005 est)

Kremer ('kreɪmə) n **Gidon**. born 1947, Latvian violinist, now based in the US

kremlin ('kremlɪn) n the citadel of any Russian city [c17: from obsolete German Kremelin, from Russian kreml]

Kremlin ('kremlɪn) n **1** the 12th-century citadel in Moscow, containing the former Imperial Palace, three Cathedrals, and the offices of the Russian government **2** (formerly) the central government of the Soviet Union

Krems (German krɛms) n a town in NE Austria, in Lower Austria on the River Danube. Pop: 23 713 (2001)

Kriemhild ('kriːmhɪlt) or **Kriemhilde** ('kriːmˌhɪldə) n (in the Nibelungenlied) the wife of Siegfried. She corresponds to Gudrun in Norse mythology

krill (krɪl) n, pl krill any small shrimplike marine crustacean of the order Euphausiacea: the principal food of whalebone whales [c20: from Norwegian kril young fish]

krimmer or **crimmer** ('krɪmə) n a tightly curled light grey fur obtained from the skins of lambs from the Crimean region [c20: from German, from Krim CRIMEA]

Kriol ('krɪvl) n a creole language used by Aboriginal communities in the northern regions of Australia, developed from Northern Territory pidgin

kris (krɪs) n a Malayan and Indonesian stabbing or slashing knife with a scalloped edge. Also called: crease, creese [c16: from Malay kris]

Krishna¹ ('krɪʃnə) n a river in S India, rising in the Western Ghats and flowing generally southeast to the Bay of Bengal. Length: 1300 km (800 miles). Also called: Kistna

Krishna² ('krɪʃnə) n Hinduism the most celebrated of the Hindu deities, whose life story is told in the Mahabharata [via Hindi from Sanskrit, literally: dark, black] > 'Krishnaism n

Krishna Menon (kriːʃnə 'menən) n See Menon

Kristeva (krɪs'teɪvə) n **Julia**. born 1941, French semiotician, born in Bulgaria. Her works include La Révolution du langage poétique (1974), Histoires d'amour (1983), and the autobiographical novel Les Samourais (1990)

Kristiania (ˌkrɪstɪ'ɑːnɪə) n a former name (1877–1924) of **Oslo**

Kristiansand or **Kristiansand** ('krɪstʃənˌsænd; Norwegian kristian'san) n a port in S Norway, on the Skagerrak: shipbuilding. Pop: 75 280 (2004 est)

Kristiansen ('krɪstʃənsən) n **Ingrid**. born 1956, Norwegian long-distance runner: former London marathon winner: world 10 000 metres record holder (1986–93)

Kristianstad ('krɪstʃənˌstɑːd; Swedish kri'ʃanstaːd) n a town in S Sweden: founded in 1614 as a Danish fortress, it was finally acquired by Sweden in 1678. Pop: 75 590 (2004 est)

Kríti ('kriti) n transliteration of the Modern Greek name for **Crete**

Krivoy Rog (Russian kri'vɔj 'rɔk) n a city in SE Ukraine: founded in the 17th century by Cossacks; iron-mining centre; iron- and steelworks. Pop: 658 000 (2005 est)

krona ('krəʊnə) n, pl kronor ('krəʊnə) the standard monetary unit of Sweden, divided into 100 öre

króna ('krəʊnə) n, pl -nur (-nə) the standard monetary unit of Iceland, divided into 100 aurar

krone ('krəʊnə) n, pl -ner (-nə) **1** the standard monetary unit of Denmark, the Faeroe Islands, and Greenland, divided into 100 øre **2** the standard monetary unit of Norway, divided into 100 øre [c19: from Danish or Norwegian, from Middle Low German krōne, ultimately from Latin corōna CROWN]

Kronos ('krəʊnɒs) n a variant of **Cronus**

Kronstadt n **1** (Russian kran'ʃtat) a port in NW Russia, on Kotlin island in the Gulf of Finland: naval base. Pop: 42 800 (2006 est) **2** ('kroːnʃtat) the German name for **Brașov**

Kropotkin (Russian kra'pɒtkin) n Prince **Peter**, Russian name Pyotr Alexeyevich. 1842–1921, Russian anarchist: his books include Mutual Aid (1902) and Modern Science and Anarchism (1903)

Kruger ('kruːgə) n **Stephanus Johannes Paulus** ('stefənʊs jəʊ'hænɪs 'pɔːlʊs), known as Oom Paul. 1825–1904, Boer statesman; president of the Transvaal (1883–1900). His opposition to Cecil Rhodes and his denial of civil rights to the Uitlanders led to the Boer War (1899–1902)

Kruger National Park n a wildlife sanctuary in NE South Africa: the world's largest game reserve. Area: over 21 700 sq km (8400 sq miles)

Krugerrand ('kruːgəˌrænd) n a South African coin used for investment only and containing 1 troy ounce of gold [c20: from Stephanus Johannes Paulus Kruger (1825–1904), Boer statesman + RAND¹]

Krugersdorp ('kruːgəzˌdɔːp) n a city in NE South Africa, in the Witwatersrand, at an altitude of 1720 m (5650 ft): a gold-, manganese-, and uranium-mining centre. Pop: 86 618 (2001)

krummhorn ('krʊmˌhɔːn) n a variant spelling of **crumhorn**

krumping ('krʌmpɪŋ) n a type of dancing in which participants, often wearing face paint, dance with one another in a fast and aggressive style mimicking a fight but without any physical contact [c21: origin unknown] > 'krumper n

Krupp (krʊp, krʌp) n a German family of steel and armaments manufacturers, including **Alfred**, 1812–87, his son **Friedrich Alfred**, 1854–1902, and the latter's son-in-law, **Gustav Krupp von Bohlen und Halbach**, 1870–1950

Krušné Hory ('krʊʃne 'hɔrɪ) n the Czech name for the **Erzgebirge**

Krym or **Krim** (krɪm) n transliteration of the Russian name for **Crimea**

krypton ('krɪptɒn) n an inert gaseous element occurring in trace amounts in air and used in fluorescent lights and lasers. Symbol: Kr; atomic no: 36; atomic wt: 83.80; valency: 0; density: 3.733 kg/m³; melting pt: -157.37°C; boiling pt: -153.23±0.10°C [c19: from Greek, from kruptos hidden; see CRYPT]

krytron ('kraɪtrɒn) n electronics a type of fast electronic gas-discharge switch, used as a trigger in nuclear weapons

KS abbreviation Kansas

Kshatriya ('kʃætrɪə) n a member of the second of the four main Hindu castes, the warrior caste [c18: from Sanskrit, from kshatra rule]

kt abbreviation **1** karat **2** nautical knot

Kt abbreviation **1** Also called: Knt knight ▷ symbol for **2** Also called: N chess knight

Kuala Lumpur ('kwɑːlə 'lʊmpʊə, -pə) n a city in Malaysia, in the SW Malay Peninsula: formerly (until 1999) the capital of Malaysia; became capital of the Federated Malay States in 1895, and of Malaysia in 1963; capital of Selangor state from 1880 to 1973, when it was made a federal territory. Pop: 1 392 000 (2005 est)

Kuban (Russian ku'banj) n a river in SW Russia, rising in the Caucasus Mountains and flowing north and northwest to the Sea of Azov. Length: 906 km (563 miles)

Kubelik (Czech 'kubeliːk) n **Raphael** ('raːfaɛl). 1914–96, Czech conductor and composer

Kublai Khan ('kuːblaɪ 'kɑːn) n ?1216–94, Mongol emperor of China: grandson of Genghis Khan. He completed his grandfather's conquest of China by overthrowing the Sung dynasty (1279) and founded the Yuan dynasty (1279–1368)

Kubrick ('kjuːbrɪk) n **Stanley**. 1928–99, US film writer, director, and producer. He directed Lolita (1962), Dr Strangelove (1963), 2001: A Space Odyssey (1968), A Clockwork Orange (1971), The Shining (1980), Full Metal Jacket (1987), and Eyes Wide Shut (1999)

Kuching ('kuːtʃɪŋ) n a port in E Malaysia, capital of Sarawak state, on the Sarawak River 24 km (15 miles)

from its mouth. Pop: 152 310 (2000)

kudlik ('ku:dlɪk) n *Canadian* an Inuit soapstone seal-oil lamp [Inuktitut]

kudos ('kju:dɒs) n *(functioning as singular)* acclaim, glory, or prestige: *the kudos of playing Carnegie Hall* [c18: from Greek]

kudu or **koodoo** ('ku:du:) n either of two spiral-horned antelopes, *Tragelaphus strepsiceros* (**greater kudu**) or *T. imberbis* (**lesser kudu**), which inhabit the bush of Africa [c18: from Afrikaans *koedoe*, probably from Khoi]

kugel (ku:gəl) *South African derogatory, slang* a young Jewish woman from a wealthy background who is seen as being excessively materialistic [c20 from Yiddish: pudding]

kuia ('ku:jə) n *NZ* a Māori female elder or elderly woman [Māori]

Kuibyshev or **Kuybyshev** (*Russian* 'kujbɪʃəf) n the former name (until 1991) of **Samara**

Ku Klux Klan ('ku: 'klʌks 'klæn) n **1** a secret organization of White Southerners formed after the US Civil War to fight Black emancipation and Northern domination **2** a secret organization of White Protestant Americans, mainly in the South, who use violence against Black people, Jewish people, and other minority groups [c19 *Ku Klux*, probably based on Greek *kuklos* CIRCLE + *Klan* CLAN] > Ku Kluxer or Ku Klux Klanner n > Ku Kluxism n

kukri ('kʊkrɪ) n, pl -ris a knife with a curved blade that broadens towards the point, esp as used by Gurkhas [from Hindi]

Kuku Nor ('ku:'ku: 'nɔ:) n a variant of **Koko Nor**

kulak ('ku:læk) n (in Russia after 1906) a member of the class of peasants who became proprietors of their own farms. After the October Revolution the kulaks opposed collectivization of land, but in 1929 Stalin initiated their liquidation [c19: from Russian: fist, hence, tightfisted person; related to Turkish *kol* arm]

kulfi ('kʊlfɪ) n an Indian dessert made by freezing milk which has been concentrated by boiling away some of the water in it, and flavoured with nuts and cardamom seeds

Kulun ('ku:'lu:n) n the Chinese name for **Ulan Bator**

Kum (kʊm) n a variant spelling of **Qom**

Kumamoto (,kʊmə'məʊtəʊ) n a city in SW Japan, on W central Kyushu: Kumamoto Medical University (1949). Pop: 653 835 (2002 est)

Kumaratunge (,kʊmə'rətʊŋgə) n **Chandrika** ('tʃʊn,drɪkə) **Bandaranaike**. born 1945, Sri Lankan politician: prime minister (1994); president (1994–2005)

Kumasi (ku:'mæsɪ) n a city in S Ghana: seat of Ashanti kings since 1663; university (1961); market town for a cocoa-producing region. Pop: 862 000 (2005 est)

Kumayri (*Russian* ,kʊmaɪ'rɪ) n a city in NW Armenia: textile centre. Pop: 144 000 (2005 est). Former names: Aleksandropol (1840–1924), Leninakan (1924–91)

Kumbh Mela (,kʊm 'meɪlə, ,kʊm mə'lɑ:) n a Hindu festival held once every twelve years in one of four sacred sites, where bathing for purification from sin is considered especially efficacious [from Hindi, literally: pitcher festival or Aquarius festival, from Sanskrit *kumbha* pot, Aquarius + *melā* assembly]

kumiss, koumiss, koumis or **koumyss** ('ku:mɪs) n a drink made from fermented mare's or other milk, drunk by certain Asian tribes, esp in Russia or used for dietetic and medicinal purposes [c17: from Russian *kumys*, from Kazan Tatar *kumyz*]

kumite ('ku:mɪ,teɪ) n martial arts freestyle sparring or fighting [c20: Japanese, literally: sparring]

kümmel ('kʊməl; *German* 'kyməl) n a German liqueur flavoured with aniseed and cumin [c19: from German *Kümmel*, from Old High German *kumil*, probably variant of *kumin* CUMIN]

kumquat or **cumquat** ('kʌmkwɒt) n **1** any of several small Chinese trees of the rutaceous genus *Fortunella* **2** the small round orange fruit of such a tree, with a sweet rind, used in preserves and confections [c17: from Chinese (Cantonese) *kam kwat*, representing Mandarin Chinese *chin chü* golden orange]

Kun (ku:n) n **Béla** ('be:lɒ). 1886–?1937, Hungarian Communist leader, president of the short-lived

Communist republic in Hungary (1919). He was forced into exile and died in a Stalinist purge

Kundera ('kʌndərə) n **Milan**. born 1929, Czech novelist living in France. His novels include *The Book of Laughter and Forgetting* (1979), *The Unbearable Lightness of Being* (1984), and *Ignorance* (2002)

Küng (kʊŋ) n **Hans**. born 1928, Swiss Roman Catholic theologian, who questioned the doctrine of infallibility: his licence to teach was withdrawn in 1979. His books include *Global Responsibility* (1991)

kung fu ('kʌŋ 'fu:) n any of various Chinese martial arts, some focusing on unarmed combat, others involving the use of weapons [from Chinese: skill, accomplishment]

K'ung Fu-tse ('kʊŋ 'fu:'tseɪ) n the Chinese name of **Confucius**

Kungur ('kʊŋgʊə) n a variant transliteration of the Chinese name for **Kongur Shan**

Kunlun ('kʊn'lʊn), **Kuenlun** or **Kwenlun** n a mountain range in China, between the Tibetan plateau and the Tarim Basin, extending over 1600 km (1000 miles): east from the Pamirs: the largest mountain system of Asia. Highest peak: Ulugh Muztagh, 7723 m (25 338 ft)

Kunming or **K'un-ming** ('kʊn'mɪŋ) n a city in SW China, capital of Yunnan province, near Lake Tien: important during World War II as a Chinese military centre, American air base, and transport terminus for the Burma Road; Yunnan University (1934). Pop: 1 748 000 (2005 est)

Kuopio (*Finnish* 'kwɔpjɔ) n a city in S central Finland. Pop: 88 250 (2003 est)

Kura (kʊ'rɑ:) n a river in W Asia, rising in NE Turkey and flowing across Georgia and Azerbaijan to the Caspian Sea. Length: 1515 km (941 miles)

kura kaupapa Māori (ku:rə ka:u:pɑ:pɑ:) n, pl **kura kaupapa Māori** *NZ* a primary school where teaching is based on Māori language and culture [Māori]

kurchatovium (,kɜ:tʃə'təʊvɪəm) n another name for rutherfordium, esp as used in the former Soviet Union [c20: from Russian, named after I. V. *Kurchatov* (1903–60), Soviet physicist]

Kurd (kɜ:d) n a member of a nomadic people living chiefly in E Turkey, N Iraq, and W Iran

Kurdish ('kɜ:dɪʃ) n **1** the language of the Kurds, belonging to the West Iranian branch of the Indo-European family ▷ adj **2** of or relating to the Kurds or their language

Kurdistan, Kurdestan or **Kordestan** (,kɜ:dɪ'stɑ:n) n a large plateau and mountainous region, between the Caspian Sea and the Black Sea, south of the Caucasus. Area: over 29 000 sq km (74 000 sq miles)

Kure (ku:'reɪ) n a port in SW Japan, on SW Honshu: a naval base; shipyards. Pop: 202 628 (2002 est)

Kurgan (*Russian* kur'gan) n a city in W Russia, on the Tobol River: industrial centre for an agricultural region. Pop: 344 000 (2005 est)

kuri ('ku:rɪ) n, pl -ris Also called: **goorie** *NZ* a mongrel dog [Māori]

Kuril Islands or **Kurile Islands** (kʊ'ri:l) pl n a chain of 56 volcanic islands off the NE coast of Asia, extending for 1200 km (750 miles) from the S tip of the Kamchatka Peninsula to NE Hokkaido. Area: 14 990 sq km (6020 sq miles). Japanese name: **Chishima**

Kurosawa (,kʊərə'sɑ:wə) n **Akira** (ə'kɪərə). 1910–99, Japanese film director. His works include *Rashomon* (1950), *The Seven Samurai* (1954), *The Throne of Blood* (1957), *Kagemusha* (1980), *Ran* (1985), and *Madadayo* (1993)

Kuroshio (kʊ'rəʊʃɪ,əʊ) n another name for **Japan Current**

kurrajong or **currajong** ('kʌrə,dʒɒŋ) n any of various Australian trees or shrubs, esp *Brachychiton populneum*, a sterculiaceous tree that yields a tough durable fibre [c19: from a native Australian language]

kursaal ('kɜ:z²l) n **1** a public room at a health resort **2** an amusement park at a seaside or other resort [from German, literally: cure room]

Kursk (*Russian* kursk) n a city in W Russia: industrial centre of an agricultural region: scene of a major Soviet victory (1943). Pop: 410 000 (2005 est)

kurtosis (kə'təʊsɪs) n *statistics* a measure of the

concentration of a distribution around its mean, esp the statistic $B_2 = m_4/m_2{}^2$ where m_2 and m_4 are respectively the second and fourth moment of the distribution around the mean. In a normal distribution $B_2 = 3$ [from Greek: *curvature*, from *kurtos* arched]

kuru ('kuru:) *n* a degenerative disease of the nervous system, restricted to certain tribes in New Guinea, marked by loss of muscular control and thought to be caused by a slow virus [C20: from a native name]

Kush (kʌʃ, kʊʃ) *n* a variant spelling of **Cush**

Kuskokwim ('kʌskə,kwɪm) *n* a river in SW Alaska, rising in the Alaska Range and flowing generally southwest to **Kuskokwim Bay** an inlet of the Bering Sea. Length: about 970 km (600 miles).

kuta (guː'ðɑː) *n* Hinglish 1 a male dog 2 derogatory a man or boy regarded as unpleasant or contemptible [C21: Hindi]

Kutaisi (*Russian* kuta'isi) *n* an industrial city in W Georgia on the Rioni River: one of the oldest towns of the Caucasus. Pop: 175 000 (2005 est)

Kutch or **Cutch** (kʌtʃ) *n* 1 a former state of W India, on the **Gulf of Kutch** (an inlet of the Arabian Sea): part of Gujarat state since 1960 2 **Rann of Kutch** an extensive salt waste in W central India, and S Pakistan: consists of the Great Rann in the north and the Little Rann in the southeast; seasonal alternation between marsh and desert; some saltworks. In 1968 an international tribunal awarded about 10 per cent of the border area to Pakistan. Area: 23 000 sq km (9000 sq miles)

kutu ('kuːtuː) *n* NZ slang a body louse. See **louse** (sense 1). Also called: cootie [Māori]

Kutuzov (*Russian* ku'tuzəf) *n* Prince **Mikhail Ilarionovich** (mixa'il iləri'ɔnəvitʃ). 1745–1813, Russian field marshal, who harried the French army under Napoleon throughout their retreat from Moscow (1812–13)

Kuwait (kʊ'weɪt) or **Koweit** *n* 1 a state on the NW coast of the Persian Gulf: came under British protection in 1899 and gained independence in 1961; invaded by Iraq in 1990; liberated by US-led UN forces 1991 in the Gulf War: mainly desert. The economy is dependent on oil. Official language: Arabic. Official religion: Muslim. Currency: dinar. Capital: Kuwait. Pop: 2 595 000 (2004 est). Area: 24 280 sq km (9375 sq miles) 2 the capital of Kuwait: a port on the Persian Gulf. Pop: 1 225 000 (2005 est) > **Kuwaiti** (kʊ'weɪtɪ) or **Koweiti** (kəʊ'weɪtɪ) *adj, n*

Kuznets ('kuznɪts) *n* **Simon**. 1901–85, US economist born in Russia. His books include *National Income and its Composition* (1919–1938) (1941) and *Economic Growth of Nations* (1971). He was awarded the Nobel Prize for economics in 1971

Kuznetsk Basin (*Russian* kuz'njɛtsk) or **Kuzbass** (*Russian* kuz'bas) *n* a region of S Russia, in the Kemerovo Region of W Siberia: the richest coalfield in the country, with reserves of iron ore. Chief industrial centre: Novokuznetsk. Area: about 69 900 sq km (27 000 sq miles)

Kvaløy (*Norwegian* 'kvaːlœj) *n* two islands in the Arctic Ocean, off the N coast of Norway: **North Kvaløy**, 329 sq km (127 sq miles), and **South Kvaløy**, 735 sq km (284 sq miles)

kvass, kvas or **quass** (kvɑːs) *n* an alcoholic drink of low strength made in Russia and E Europe from cereals and stale bread [C16: from Russian *kvas*; related to Old Slavic *kvasĭ* yeast, Latin *cāseus* cheese]

kvetch (kvɛtʃ) *vb* (*intr*) slang, chiefly US to complain or grumble, esp incessantly [C20: from Yiddish *kvetshn*, literally: to squeeze, press]

kW *abbreviation* kilowatt

kwacha ('kwɑːtʃɑː) *n* 1 the standard monetary unit of Zambia, divided into 100 ngwee 2 the standard monetary unit of Malawi, divided into 100 tambala [from a native word in Zambia]

kwaito ('kwaɪ,təʊ) *n* a type of South African pop music with lyrics spoken over an instrumental backing usually consisting of slowed-down house music layered with African percussion and melodies [C20: from *Amakwaito*, a gang in Sophiatown, South Africa, in the 1950s]

Kwajalein ('kwɑːdʒə,leɪn) *n* an atoll in the W Pacific, in the W Marshall Islands, in the central part of the Ralik

Chain. Length: about 125 km (78 miles)

Kwangchow ('kwæŋ'tʃaʊ) *n* a variant transliteration of the Chinese name for **Canton**

Kwangchowan ('kwæŋ'tʃaʊ'wɑːn) *n* a territory of SE China, in SW Kwantung province: leased to France as part of French Indochina from 1898 to 1945. Area: 842 sq km (325 sq miles)

Kwangju ('kwæŋ'dʒuː) *n* a city in SW South Korea: an important military base during the Korean War; cotton textile industry. Pop: 1 448 000 (2005 est)

Kwangsi-Chuang Autonomous Region ('kwæŋ'siː'tʃwæŋ) *n* another spelling of **Guangxi Zhuang Autonomous Region**

Kwangtung ('kwæŋ'tʊŋ) *n* a variant transliteration of the Chinese name for **Guangdong**

Kwantung Leased Territory (,kwæn'tʊŋ) *n* a strategic territory of NE China, at the S tip of the Liaodong Peninsula of Manchuria: leased forcibly by Russia in 1898; taken over by Japan in 1905; occupied by the Soviet Union in 1945 and subsequently returned to China on the condition of shared administration; made part of Liaoning province by China in 1954. Area: about 3400 sq km (1300 sq miles). Also called: Kuan-tung

Kwara ('kwɑːrə) *n* a state of W Nigeria: mainly wooded savanna. Capital: Ilorin. Pop: 2 371 089 (2006). Area: 36 825 sq km (14 218 sq miles)

kwashiorkor (,kwæʃɪ'ɔːkə) *n* severe malnutrition of infants and young children, esp soon after weaning, resulting from dietary deficiency of protein [C20: from a native word in Ghana]

KwaZulu-Natal (kwɑː,zuːluː nə'tæl, -'tɑːl) *n* a province of NE South Africa; replaced the former province of Natal in 1994: service industries. Capital: Pietermaritzburg. Pop: 9 665 875 (2004 est). Area: 92 180 sq km (35 591 sq miles)

Kweichow or **Kueichou** ('kweɪ'tʃaʊ) *n* a variant transliteration of the Chinese name for **Guizhou**

Kweilin or **Kuei-lin** ('kweɪ'lɪn) *n* a variant transliteration of the Chinese name for **Guilin**

Kweisui ('kweɪ'sweɪ) *n* the former name of **Hohhot**

Kweiyang or **Kuei-yang** ('kweɪ'jæŋ) *n* a variant transliteration of the Chinese name for **Guiyang**

kWh *abbreviation* kilowatt-hour

KWIC (kwɪk) *n acronym for* key word in context (esp in the phrase **KWIC index**)

KWOC (kwɒk) *n acronym for* key word out of context

Ky (kiː) *n* **Nguyen Kao** (ᵑ'ɡuːjɛn 'kaʊ). born 1930, Vietnamese military and political leader: premier of South Vietnam (1965–67); vice president (1967–71)

Ky. or **KY** *abbreviation* Kentucky

kyanite ('kaɪə,naɪt) or **cyanite** *n* a grey, green, or blue mineral consisting of aluminium silicate in triclinic crystalline form. It occurs in metamorphic rocks and is used as a refractory. Formula AL_2SiO_5 > **kyanitic** (,kaɪə'nɪtɪk) *adj*

kyanize or **kyanise** ('kaɪə,naɪz) *vb* (*tr*) to treat (timber) with corrosive sublimate to make it resistant to decay [C19: after J. H. *Kyan* (died 1850), English inventor of the process] > ,kyani'zation, ,kyani'sation *n*

Kyd or **Kid** (kɪd) *n* **Thomas**. 1558–94, English dramatist, noted for his revenge play *The Spanish Tragedy* (1586)

kyle (kaɪl) *n* Scot (esp in place names) a narrow strait or channel: *Kyle of Lochalsh* [C16: from Gaelic *caol*, from *caol* narrow]

kylie or **kiley** ('kaɪlɪ) *n* Austral a boomerang that is flat on one side and convex on the other [C19: from a native Australian language]

kyloe ('kaɪləʊ) *n* a breed of small long-horned long-haired beef cattle from NW Scotland [C19: of uncertain origin]

kymograph ('kaɪmə,grɑːf, -,græf) or **cymograph** *n* med a rotatable drum for holding paper on which a tracking stylus continuously records variations in blood pressure, respiratory movements, etc [C20: from Greek *kuma* wave + -GRAPH] > ,kymo'graphic, ,cymo'graphic *adj*

Kymric ('kɪmrɪk) *n, adj* a variant spelling of **Cymric**

Kymry ('kɪmrɪ) *pl n* a variant spelling of **Cymry**

Kynewulf ('kɪnə,wʊlf) *n* a variant spelling of **Cynewulf**

Kyongsong ('kjɔːŋ'sɔːŋ) *n* another name for **Seoul**

k

Kyoto or **Kioto** (kɪˈəʊtəʊ, ˈkjəʊ-) n a city in central Japan, on S Honshu: the capital of Japan from 794 to 1868; cultural centre, with two universities (1875, 1897). Pop: 1 387 264 (2002 est)

Kyoto protocol n an amendment to the United Nations international treaty on global warming in which participating nations commit to reducing their emissions of carbon dioxide, negotiated in Kyoto, Japan, in 1997

kyphosis (kaɪˈfəʊsɪs) n pathol backward curvature of the thoracic spine, of congenital origin or resulting from injury or disease; hunchback [c19: from New Latin, from Greek kuphōsis, from kuphos humpbacked] > **kyphotic** (kaɪˈfɒtɪk) adj

Kyrgyz (ˈkɪəɡɪz), **Kirghiz** or **Kirgiz** n 1 pl -gyz, -ghiz or -giz a member of a Mongoloid people of central Asia, inhabiting Kyrgyzstan and a vast area of central Siberia 2 the language of this people, belonging to the Turkic branch of the Altaic family

Kyrgyzstan (ˈkɪəɡɪzˌstɑːn, -ˌstæn), **Kirghizstan** or **Kirgizstan** n a republic in central Asia: came under Russian rule in the 19th century, became a Soviet republic in 1936 and gained independence in 1991; it has deposits of minerals, oil, and gas. Official languages: Kyrgyz and Russian. Religion: nonreligious, Muslim. Currency: som. Capital: Bishkek. Pop: 5 208 000 (2004 est). Area: 198 500 sq km (76 460 sq miles)

Kyrgyz Steppe n a vast steppe region in central Kazakhstan. Also called: **the Steppes**

Kyrie eleison (ˈkɪrɪɪ əˈleɪsᵊn) n 1 a formal invocation used in the liturgies of the Roman Catholic, Greek Orthodox, and Anglican Churches 2 a musical setting of this [c14: via Late Latin from Late Greek kurie, eleēson Lord, have mercy]

Kythera (ˈkɪθɪrə) n a variant spelling of **Cythera**

kyu (kjuː) n judo one of the five student grades for inexperienced competitors [from Japanese]

Kyushu or **Kiushu** (ˈkjuːʃuː) n an island of SW Japan: the southernmost of Japan's four main islands, with over 300 surrounding small islands; coalfield and chemical industries. Chief cities: Fukuoka, Kitakyushu, and Nagasaki. Pop: 14 786 000 (2002 est). Area: 35 659 sq km (13 768 sq miles)

Kyzyl Kum (Russian kiˈzil ˈkum) n a desert in Kazakhstan and Uzbekistan

KZN abbreviation (in South Africa) KwaZulu-Natal

k

L1

l¹ or **L** (ɛl) *n*, *pl* **l's**, **L's** or **Ls 1** the 12th letter and ninth consonant of the modern English alphabet **2** a speech sound represented by this letter, usually a lateral, as in *label* **3 a** something shaped like an L **b** (*in combination*): *an L-shaped room*

l² *symbol for* litre

L *symbol for* **1** lambert(s) **2** large **3** Latin **4** (on British motor vehicles) learner driver **5** *physics* length **6** live **7** *currency* **a** Usually written: **£** pound **b** lire **8** *electronics* inductor (in circuit diagrams) **9** *physics* latent heat **10** *physics* self-inductance **11** the Roman numeral for 50. See **Roman numerals** [(for sense 7a) Latin *libra* pound]

L. or **l.** *abbreviation* **1** lake **2** left **3** length

la¹ (lɑː) *n music* a variant spelling of **lah**

la² (lɔː) *interj* an exclamation of surprise or emphasis [Old English *lā* LO]

La *the chemical symbol for* lanthanum

laager or **lager** ('lɑːɡə) *n* **1** (in Africa) a camp, esp one defended by a circular formation of wagons **2** *military* a place where armoured vehicles are parked ▷ *vb* **3** to form (wagons) into a laager **4** (*tr*) to park (armoured vehicles) in a laager [c19: from Afrikaans *lager*, via German from Old High German *legar* bed, lair]

lab (læb) *n informal* short for **laboratory**

lab. *abbreviation* **1** laboratory **2** labour

Lab. *abbreviation* **1** *politics* Labour **2** Labrador

Laban ('leɪbᵊn) *n Old Testament* the father-in-law of Jacob, father of Leah and Rachel (Genesis 29:16)

labdanum ('læbdənəm) or **ladanum** *n* a dark resinous juice obtained from various rockroses of the genus *Cistus*, used in perfumery and in the manufacture of fumigants and medicinal plasters [c16: Latin, from Greek *ladanon*, from *lēdon* rockrose, from Semitic]

Labe ('labɛ) *n* the Czech name for the (River) **Elbe**

label ('leɪbᵊl) *n* **1 a** piece of paper, card, or other material attached to an object to identify it or give instructions or details concerning its ownership, use, nature, destination, etc; tag **2** a brief descriptive phrase or term given to a person, group, school of thought, etc: *the label "Romantic" is applied to many different kinds of poetry* **3** a word or phrase heading a piece of text to indicate or summarize its contents **4** a trademark or company or brand name on certain goods, esp on gramophone records **5** *computing* a group of characters, such as a number or a word, appended to a particular statement in a program to allow its unique identification **6** *chem* a radioactive element used in a compound to trace the mechanism of a chemical reaction ▷ *vb* **-bels**, **-belling**, **-belled** or *US* **-bels**, **-beling**, **-beled** (*tr*) **7** to fasten a label to **8** to mark with a label **9** to describe or classify in a word or phrase: *to label someone a liar* **10** to make (one or more atoms in a compound) radioactive, for use in determining the mechanism of a reaction [c14: from Old French, from Germanic; compare Old High German *lappa* rag] ▷ **'labeller** *n*

labia ('leɪbɪə) *n* the plural of **labium**

labial ('leɪbɪəl) *adj* **1** of, relating to, or near lips or labia **2** *music* producing sounds by the action of an air stream over a narrow liplike fissure, as in a flue pipe of an organ **3** *phonetics* relating to a speech sound whose articulation involves movement or use of the lips ▷ *n* **4** Also called: **labial pipe** *music* an organ pipe with a liplike fissure **5** *phonetics* a speech sound such as English *p* or *m*, whose articulation involves movement or use of the lips [c16: from Medieval Latin *labiālis*, from Latin *labium* lip] ▷ **'labially** *adv*

labiate ('leɪbɪ,eɪt, -ɪt) *n* **1** any plant of the family *Lamiaceae* (formerly *Labiatae*), having square stems, aromatic leaves, and a two-lipped corolla: includes mint, thyme, sage, rosemary, etc ▷ *adj* **2** of, relating to, or belonging to the family *Lamiaceae* [c18: from New Latin *labiātus*, from Latin *labium* lip]

Labiche (French labiʃ) *n* **Eugène Marin** (øʒɛn marɛ̃). 1815–88, French dramatist, noted for his farces of middle-class life, which include *Le Chapeau de paille d'Italie* (1851) and *Le Voyage de Monsieur Perrichon* (1860)

labile ('leɪbɪl) *adj* **1** *chem* (of a compound) prone to chemical change **2** liable to change or move [c15: via Late Latin *lābilis*, from Latin *lābī* to slide, slip] ▷ **lability** (lə'bɪlɪtɪ) *n*

labio- or before a vowel **labi-** *combining form* relating to or formed by the lips and (another organ or part): *labiodental* [from Latin *labium* lip]

labiodental (ˌleɪbɪəʊ'dɛntᵊl) *phonetics* ▷ *adj* **1** pronounced by bringing the bottom lip into contact or near contact with the upper teeth, as for the fricative (f) in English *fat*, *puff* ▷ *n* **2** a labiodental consonant

labium ('leɪbɪəm) *n*, *pl* **-bia** (-bɪə) **1** a lip or liplike structure **2** any one of the four lip-shaped folds of the female vulva [c16: New Latin, from Latin: lip]

laboratory (lə'bɒrətərɪ, -trɪ; *US* 'læbrə,tɔːrɪ) *n*, *pl* **-ries** **1 a** a building or room equipped for conducting scientific research or for teaching practical science **b** (*as modifier*): *laboratory equipment* **2** a place where chemicals or medicines are manufactured ▷ Often shortened to: lab [c17: from Medieval Latin *labōrātōrium* workshop, from Latin *labōrāre* to LABOUR]

Labor Day *n* **1** (in the US and Canada) a public holiday in honour of labour, held on the first Monday in September **2** (in Australia) a public holiday observed on different days in different states

laborious (lə'bɔːrɪəs) *adj* **1** involving great exertion or long effort **2** given to working hard **3** (of literary style, etc) not fluent > la'boriously *adv* > la'boriousness *n*

Labor Party *n* one of the chief political parties of Australia, generally supporting the interests of organized labour

labour *or US* **labor** ('leɪbə) *n* **1** productive work, esp physical toil done for wages **2 a** the people, class, or workers involved in this, esp in contrast to management, capital, etc **b** (*as modifier*): *a labour dispute; labour relations* **3** a difficult or arduous work or effort **b** (*in combination*): *labour-saving* **4** a particular job or task, esp of a difficult nature **5 a** the process or effort of childbirth or the time during which this takes place **b** (*as modifier*): *labour pains* ▷ *vb* **6** (*intr*) to perform labour; work **7** (*intr*; foll by *for*, etc) to strive or work hard (for something) **8** (*intr*; usually foll by *under*) to be burdened (by) or be at a disadvantage (because of): *to labour under a misapprehension* **9** (*intr*) to make one's way with difficulty **10** (*tr*) to deal with or treat too persistently: *to labour a point* **11** (*intr*) (of a woman) to be in labour **12** (*intr*) (of a ship) to pitch and toss [c13: via Old French from Latin *labor*; perhaps related to *lābī* to fall]

labour camp *n* **1** a penal colony involving forced labour **2** a camp for migratory labourers

Labour Day *n* a public holiday in many countries in honour of labour, usually held on May 1

laboured *or US* **labored** ('leɪbəd) *adj* **1** (of breathing) performed with difficulty **2** showing effort; contrived; lacking grace or fluency

labourer *or US* **laborer** ('leɪbərə) *n* a person engaged in physical work, esp of an unskilled kind

labour exchange *n Brit* a former name for **employment office**

labour-intensive *adj* of or denoting a task, organization, industry, etc, in which a high proportion of the costs are due to wages, salaries, etc

Labourite ('leɪbə,raɪt) *n* an adherent of the Labour Party

Labour Party *n* **1** a British political party, formed in 1900 as an amalgam of various trade unions and socialist groups, generally supporting the interests of organized labour and advocating democratic socialism and social equality **2** any similar party in any of various other countries

labradoodle ('læbrə,duːd°l) *n* a type of dog that is a cross between a labrador retriever and a poodle

Labrador ('læbrə,dɔː) *n* **1** Also called: Labrador-Ungava a large peninsula of NE Canada, on the Atlantic, the Gulf of St Lawrence, Hudson Strait, and Hudson Bay: contains most of Quebec and the mainland part of the province of Newfoundland and Labrador; geologically part of the Canadian Shield. Area: 1 619 000 sq km (625 000 sq miles) **2** Also called: Coast of Labrador a region of NE Canada, on the Atlantic and consisting of the mainland part of Newfoundland and Labrador province **3** (*often not capital*) short for **Labrador retriever**

Labrador retriever *n* a powerfully-built variety of retriever with a short dense usually black or golden-brown coat. Often shortened to: Labrador

labret ('leɪbrɛt) *n* a piece of bone, shell, etc, inserted into the lip as an ornament by certain peoples [c19: from Latin *labrum* lip]

labrum ('leɪbrəm, 'læb-) *n*, *pl* **-bra** (-brə) a lip or liplike part, such as the cuticular plate forming the upper lip of insects [c19: New Latin, from Latin]

La Bruyère (*French* la bryjɛr) *n* **Jean de** (ʒɑ̃ də). 1645–96, French moralist, noted for his *Caractères* (1688), satirical character studies, including portraits of contemporary public figures

Labuan (lə'buːən) *n* an island off the NW coast of Borneo, forming a federal territory of Malaysia: part of the Straits Settlements until 1946, when transferred to North Borneo. Chief town: Victoria (or Labuan). Area: 98 sq km (38 sq miles)

laburnum (lə'bɜːnəm) *n* any leguminous tree or shrub of the Eurasian genus *Laburnum*, having clusters of yellow drooping flowers: all parts of the plant are poisonous [c16: New Latin, from Latin]

labyrinth ('læbərɪnθ) *n* **1** a mazelike network of tunnels, chambers, or paths, either natural or man-made **2** any complex or confusing system of streets, passages, etc **3** a complex or intricate situation **4** any system of interconnecting cavities, esp those comprising the internal ear **5** *electronics* an enclosure behind a high-performance loudspeaker, consisting of a series of air chambers designed to absorb unwanted sound waves [c16: via Latin from Greek *laburinthos*, of obscure origin]

labyrinthine (,læbə'rɪnθaɪn) *adj* **1** of or relating to a labyrinth **2** resembling a labyrinth in complexity

lac¹ (læk) *n* a resinous substance secreted by certain lac insects, used in the manufacture of shellac [c16: from Dutch *lak* or French *laque*, from Hindi *lākh* resin, ultimately from Sanskrit *lākshā*]

lac² (lɑːk) *n* a variant spelling of **lakh**

Lacan (*French* lakɑ̃) *n* **Jacques** (ʒak). 1901–81, French psychoanalyst, who reinterpreted Freud in terms of structural linguistics: an important influence on poststructuralist thought

Laccadive, Minicoy, and Amindivi Islands ('lækədɪv, 'mɪnɪ,kɔɪ, ,əmən'diːviː) *pl n* the former name (until 1973) of the **Lakshadweep Islands**

laccolith ('lækəlɪθ) *or* **laccolite** ('lækə,laɪt) *n* a dome-shaped body of igneous rock between two layers of older sedimentary rock: formed by the intrusion of magma, forcing the overlying strata into the shape of a dome. See **lopolith** [c19: from Greek *lakkos* cistern + -LITH]

lace (leɪs) *n* **1** a delicate decorative fabric made from cotton, silk, etc, woven in an open web of different symmetrical patterns and figures **2** a cord or string drawn through holes or eyelets or around hooks to fasten a shoe or garment **3** ornamental braid often used on military uniforms, etc ▷ *vb* **4** to fasten (shoes, etc) with a lace **5** (*tr*) to draw (a cord or thread) through holes, eyes, etc, as when tying shoes **6** (*tr*) to compress the waist of (someone), as with a corset **7** (*tr*) to add a small amount of alcohol or drugs to (food or drink) **8** (*tr; usually passive* and foll by *with*) to streak or mark with lines or colours: *the sky was laced with red* **9** (*tr*) to intertwine; interlace **10** (*tr*) *informal* to give a sound beating to [c13 *las*, from Old French *laz*, from Latin *laqueus* noose]

lacebark ('leɪs,bɑːk) *n* another name for **ribbonwood**

Lacedaemon (,læsɪ'diːmən) *n* another name for **Sparta** *or* **Laconia** > ,Lacedae'monian *adj*, *n*

lacerate *vb* ('læsə,reɪt) (*tr*) **1** to tear (the flesh, etc) jaggedly **2** to hurt or harrow (the feelings, etc) ▷ *adj* ('læsə,reɪt, -rɪt) **3** having edges that are jagged or torn; lacerated: *lacerate leaves* [c16: from Latin *lacerāre* to tear, from *lacer* mangled] > ,lacer'ation *n*

lace up *vb* **1** (*tr*, *adverb*) to tighten or fasten (clothes or footwear) with laces ▷ *adj* lace-up **2** (of footwear) to be fastened with laces ▷ *n* lace-up **3** a lace-up shoe or boot

lacewing ('leɪs,wɪŋ) *n* any of various neuropterous insects, esp any of the families *Chrysopidae* (**green lacewings**) and *Hemerobiidae* (**brown lacewings**), having lacy wings and preying on aphids and similar pests

laches ('lætʃɪz) *n law* negligence or unreasonable delay in pursuing a legal remedy [c14 *lachesse*, via Old French *lasche* slack, from Latin *laxus* LAX]

Lachesis ('lækɪsɪs) *n Greek myth* one of the three Fates [via Latin from Greek, from *lakhesis* destiny, from *lakhein* to befall by lot]

Lachlan ('lɒklən) *n* a river in SE Australia, rising in central New South Wales and flowing northwest then southwest to the Murrumbidgee River. Length: about 1450 km (900 miles) [named after *Lachlan* Macquarie, governor of New South Wales (1809–21)]

lachrymal ('lækrɪməl) *adj* a variant spelling of **lacrimal**

lachrymatory ('lækrɪmətərɪ, -trɪ) *n, pl* -ries **1** a small vessel found in ancient tombs, formerly thought to hold the tears of mourners ▷ *adj* **2** a variant spelling of **lacrimatory**

lachrymose ('lækrɪˌməʊs, -ˌməʊz) *adj* **1** given to weeping; tearful **2** mournful; sad [c17: from Latin *lacrimōsus*, from *lacrima* a tear] > 'lachry,mosely *adv*

lacing ('leɪsɪŋ) *n* **1** *chiefly Brit* a course of bricks, stone, etc, for strengthening a rubble or flint wall **2** another word for **lace** (sense 2) **3** *informal* a severe beating (esp in the phrase **give someone a lacing**)

laciniate (lə'sɪnɪˌeɪt, -ɪt) *or* **laciniated** *adj* **1** *biology* jagged: *a laciniate leaf* **2** having a fringe [c17: from Latin *lacinia* flap] > la,cini'ation *n*

lack (læk) *n* **1** an insufficiency, shortage, or absence of something required or desired **2** something that is required but is absent or in short supply ▷ *vb* **3** (when *intr*, often foll by *in* or *for*) to be deficient (in) or have need (of) [c12: related to Middle Dutch *laken* to be wanting]

lackadaisical (ˌlækə'deɪzɪkᵊl) *adj* **1** lacking vitality and purpose **2** lazy or idle, esp in a dreamy way [c18: from earlier *lackadaisy*, extended form of LACKADAY] > ,lacka'daisically *adv*

lackaday ('lækəˌdeɪ) *interj archaic* another word for **alas** [c17: from *alack the day*]

lackey ('lækɪ) *n* **1** a servile follower; hanger-on **2** a liveried male servant or valet **3** a person who is treated like a servant ▷ *vb* **4** (when *intr*, often foll by *for*) to act as a lackey (to) [c16: via French *laquais*, from Old French, perhaps from Catalan *lacayo*, *alacayo*; perhaps related to ALCALDE]

lacklustre *or US* **lackluster** ('lækˌlʌstə) *adj* lacking force, brilliance, or vitality

Laclos (*French* laklo) *n* **Pierre Choderlos de** (pjɛr ʃɔdɛrlo də). 1741–1803, French soldier and writer, noted for his novel in epistolary form *Les Liaisons dangereuses* (1782)

Laconia (lə'kəʊnɪə) *n* an ancient country of S Greece, in the SE Peloponnese, of which Sparta was the capital: corresponds to the present-day department of Lakonia > La'conian *n, adj*

laconic (lə'kɒnɪk) *adj* (of a person's speech) using few words; terse [c16: via Latin from Greek *Lakōnikos*, from *Lakōn* Laconian, Spartan; referring to the Spartans' terseness of speech] > la'conically *adv*

La Coruña (*Spanish* la ko'ruɲa) *n* a port in NW Spain, on the Atlantic: point of departure for the Spanish Armada (1588); site of the defeat of the French by the British under Sir John Moore in the Peninsular War (1809). Pop: 243 902 (2003 est). English name: **Corunna**

lacquer ('lækə) *n* **1** a hard glossy coating made by dissolving cellulose derivatives or natural resins in a volatile solvent **2** a black resinous substance, obtained from certain trees, used to give a hard glossy finish to wooden furniture **3** *lacquer tree* an E Asian anacardiaceous tree, *Rhus verniciflua*, whose stem yields a toxic exudation from which black lacquer is obtained **4** Also called: **hair lacquer** a mixture of shellac and alcohol for spraying onto the hair to hold a style in place **5** *art* decorative objects coated with such lacquer, often inlaid ▷ *vb* **6** to apply lacquer to [c16: from obsolete French *lacre* sealing wax, from Portuguese *laca* LAC¹] > 'lacquerer *n*

lacrimal, lachrymal *or* **lacrymal** ('lækrɪməl) *adj* of or relating to tears or to the glands that secrete tears [c16: from Medieval Latin *lachrymālis*, from Latin *lacrima* a tear]

lacrimal duct *n* a short tube in the inner corner of the eyelid through which tears drain into the nose. Nontechnical name: **tear duct**

lacrimation (ˌlækrɪ'meɪʃən) *n* the secretion of tears

lacrimatory, lachrymatory *or* **lacrymatory** ('lækrɪmətərɪ, -trɪ) *adj* of, causing, or producing tears

lacrosse (lə'krɒs) *n* a ball game invented by Native

Americans, now played by two teams who try to propel a ball into each other's goal by means of long-handled hooked sticks that are loosely strung with a kind of netted pouch [c19: Canadian French: the hooked stick, crosier]

lactam ('læktæm) *n chem* any of a group of inner amides, derived from amino acids, having the characteristic group -CONH- [c20: from LACT(ONE) + AM(IDE)]

lactate¹ ('lækteɪt) *n* an ester or salt of lactic acid [c18: from LACTO- + -ATE¹]

lactate² ('lækteɪt) *vb* (*intr*) (of mammals) to produce or secrete milk

lactation (læk'teɪʃən) *n* **1** the secretion of milk from the mammary glands after parturition **2** the period during which milk is secreted

lacteal ('læktɪəl) *adj* **1** of, relating to, or resembling milk **2** (of lymphatic vessels) conveying or containing chyle ▷ *n* **3** any of the lymphatic vessels conveying chyle from the small intestine to the thoracic duct [c17: from Latin *lacteus* of milk, from *lac* milk]

lactescent (læk'tɛsᵊnt) *adj* **1** (of plants and certain insects) secreting a milky fluid **2** milky or becoming milky [c18: from Latin *lactescēns*, from *lactescēre* to become milky, from *lact-, lac* milk] > lac'tescence *n*

lactic ('læktɪk) *adj* relating to or derived from milk [c18: from Latin *lact-, lac* milk]

lactic acid *n* a colourless syrupy carboxylic acid found in sour milk and many fruits and used as a preservative (E270) for foodstuffs, such as soft margarine, and for making pharmaceuticals and adhesives. Formula: $CH_3CH(OH)COOH$

lactiferous (læk'tɪfərəs) *adj* producing, conveying, or secreting milk or a milky fluid [c17: from Latin *lactifer*, from *lact-, lac* milk]

lacto- *or before a vowel* **lact-** *combining form* indicating milk: *lactobacillus* [from Latin *lact-, lac* milk]

lactone ('læktəʊn) *n* any of a class of organic compounds formed from hydroxy acids and containing the group -C(CO)OC-, where the carbon atoms are part of a ring > **lactonic** (læk'tɒnɪk) *adj*

lactose ('læktəʊs, -təʊz) *n* a white crystalline disaccharide occurring in milk and used in the manufacture of pharmaceuticals and baby foods. Formula: $C_{12}H_{22}O_{11}$

lacto-vegetarian *n* a vegetarian whose diet includes dairy produce and eggs

La Cumbre (la 'ku:mbreɪ) *n* another name for the **Uspallata Pass**

lacuna (lə'kju:nə) *n, pl* -nae (-ni:) *or* -nas **1** a gap or space, esp in a book or manuscript **2** *biology* a cavity or depression, such as any of the spaces in the matrix of bone [c17: from Latin *lacūna* pool, cavity, from *lacus* lake] > la'cunose, la'cunal *or* la'cunary *adj*

lacustrine (lə'kʌstraɪn) *adj* **1** of or relating to lakes **2** living or growing in or on the shores of a lake [c19: from Italian *lacustre*, from Latin *lacus* lake]

lacy ('leɪsɪ) *adj* **lacier, laciest** made of or resembling lace > 'lacily *adv* > 'laciness *n*

lad (læd) *n* **1** a boy or young man **2** *informal* a familiar form of address for any male **3** a lively or dashing man or youth (esp in the phrase **a bit of a lad**) **4** a young man whose behaviour is characteristic of male adolescents, esp in being rowdy, macho, or immature **5** *Brit* a boy or man who looks after horses [c13 *ladde*; perhaps of Scandinavian origin]

ladanum ('lædənəm) *n* another name for **labdanum**

ladder ('lædə) *n* **1** a portable framework of wood, metal, rope, etc, in the form of two long parallel members connected by several parallel rungs or steps fixed to them at right angles, for climbing up or down **2** any hierarchy conceived of as having a series of ascending stages, levels, etc: *the social ladder* **3** Also called: **run** *chiefly Brit* a line of connected stitches that have come undone in knitted material, esp stockings ▷ *vb* **4** *chiefly Brit* to cause a line of interconnected stitches in (stockings, etc) to undo, as by snagging, or (of a stocking) to come undone in this way [Old English *hlǣdder*; related to Old High German *leitara*]

ladder back *n* a type of chair in which the back is constructed of horizontal slats between two uprights

laddie ('lædɪ) *n chiefly Scot* a familiar term for a male, esp a young man; lad

laddish ('lædɪʃ) *adj informal, usually derogatory* characteristic of male adolescents or young men, esp by being rowdy, macho, or immature: *laddish behaviour*

lade (leɪd) *vb* **lades, lading, laded, laden** ('leɪdᵊn) *or* **laded** **1** to put cargo or freight on board (a ship, etc) or (of a ship, etc) to take on cargo or freight **2** (*tr; usually passive* and foll by *with*) to burden or oppress **3** (*tr; usually passive* and foll by *with*) to fill or load **4** to remove (liquid) with or as if with a ladle [Old English *hladen* to load; related to Dutch *laden*]

laden ('leɪdᵊn) *vb* **1** a past participle of **lade¹** ▷ *adj* **2** weighed down with a load; loaded **3** encumbered; burdened

ladette (,læd'ɛt) *n informal* a young woman whose social behaviour is similar to that of male adolescents or young men

la-di-da, lah-di-dah *or* **la-de-da** (,lɑːdɪ'dɑː) *adj informal* affecting exaggeratedly genteel manners or speech [C19: mockingly imitative of affected speech]

ladies *or* **ladies' room** *n* (*functioning as singular*) *informal* a women's public lavatory

lading ('leɪdɪŋ) *n* a load; cargo; freight

Ladislaus I ('lædɪs,lɔːs) *or* **Ladislas I** ('lædɪs,læs) *n* **Saint.** 1040–95, king of Hungary (1077–95). He extended his country's boundaries and suppressed paganism. Feast day: June 27

ladle ('leɪdᵊl) *n* **1** a long-handled spoon having a deep bowl for serving or transferring liquids **2** a large bucket-shaped container for transferring molten metal ▷ *vb* **3** (*tr*) to lift or serve out with or as if with a ladle [Old English *hlædel*, from *hladan* to draw out] > 'ladle,ful *n*

ladle out *vb* (*tr, adverb*) *informal* to distribute (money, gifts, etc) generously

Ladoga (*Russian* 'ladəgə) *n* **Lake Ladoga** a lake in NW Russia, in the SW Karelian Republic: the largest lake in Europe; drains through the River Neva into the Gulf of Finland. Area: about 18 000 sq km (7000 sq miles)

Ladrone Islands (lə'drəʊn) *pl n* the former name (1521–1668) of the **Mariana Islands**

lady ('leɪdɪ) *n, pl* **-dies 1** a woman regarded as having the characteristics of a good family and high social position **2 a** a polite name for a woman **b** (*as modifier*): *a lady doctor* **3** an informal name for **wife 4 lady of the house** the female head of the household **5** *history* a woman with proprietary rights and authority, as over a manor [Old English *hlǣfdige*, from *hlāf* bread + *dige* kneader, related to *dāh* dough]

Lady ('leɪdɪ) *n, pl* **-dies 1** (in Britain) a title of honour borne by various classes of women of the peerage **2 my lady** a term of address to holders of the title Lady, used esp by servants **3 Our Lady** a title of the Virgin Mary

ladybird ('leɪdɪ,bɜːd) *n* any of various small brightly coloured beetles of the family *Coccinellidae*, such as *Adalia bipunctata* (**two-spotted ladybird**), which has red elytra marked with black spots [C18: named after Our *Lady*, the Virgin Mary]

lady bountiful *n* an ostentatiously charitable woman [after a character in George Farquhar's play *The Beaux' Stratagem* (1707)]

ladyboy ('leɪdɪ,bɔɪ) *n informal* a transvestite or transsexual, esp one from the Far East

Lady Chapel *n* a chapel within a church or cathedral, dedicated to the Virgin Mary

Lady Day *n* March 25, the feast of the Annunciation of the Virgin Mary; one of the four quarter days in England, Wales and Ireland. Also called: **Annunciation Day**

lady-in-waiting *n, pl* **ladies-in-waiting** a lady of a royal household who attends a queen or princess

lady-killer *n informal* a man who is, or thinks he is, irresistibly fascinating to women

ladylike ('leɪdɪ,laɪk) *adj* like or befitting a lady in manners and bearing; refined and fastidious

ladylove ('leɪdɪ,lʌv) *n now rare* a beloved woman

Lady Macbeth strategy *n informal* a strategy in a takeover battle in which a third party makes a bid acceptable to the target company, appearing to act as a white knight but subsequently joining forces with the original (unwelcome) bidder [C20: after *Lady Macbeth* in Shakespeare's *Macbeth* (1605)]

lady mayoress *n Brit* the wife of a lord mayor

Lady of the Lake *n* (in Arthurian legend) a mysterious supernatural being sometimes identified with Vivian

lady's bedstraw *n* a Eurasian rubiaceous plant, *Galium verum*, with clusters of small yellow flowers

lady's finger *n* another name for **bhindi**

Ladyship ('leɪdɪʃɪp) *n* (preceded by *your* or *her*) a title used to address or refer to any peeress except a duchess

lady's maid *n* a personal servant to a woman, esp in matters of dress and toilet

Ladysmith ('leɪdɪ,smɪθ) *n* a city in E South Africa: besieged by Boers for four months (1899–1900) during the Boer War. Pop: 41 427 (2001)

lady's-slipper *n* any of various orchids of the Eurasian genus *Cypripedium*, esp *C. calceolus*, having reddish or purple flowers

lady's-smock *n* a N temperate plant, *Cardamine pratensis*, with white or rose-pink flowers: family *Brassicaceae* (crucifers). Also called: **cuckooflower**

Laënnec (*French* laɛnɛk) *n* **René Théophile Hyacinthe** (rəne teofil jasɛt). 1781–1826, French physician, who invented the stethoscope

Laertes (leɪ'ɜːtiːz) *n Greek myth* the father of Odysseus

laevo- *or US* **levo-** *combining form* **1** on or towards the left: *laevorotation* **2** (in chemistry) denoting a laevorotatory compound [from Latin *laevus* left]

laevorotation (,liːvəʊrəʊ'teɪʃən) *n* **1** a rotation to the left **2** an anticlockwise rotation of the plane of polarization of plane-polarized light as a result of its passage through a crystal, liquid, or solution ▷ See **dextrorotation** ▷ **laevorotatory** (,liːvəʊ'rəʊtətərɪ, -trɪ) *adj*

Lafayette *or* **La Fayette** (*French* lafajɛt) *n* **1 Marie Joseph Paul Yves Roch Gilbert du Motier** (mari ʒozɛf pɔl iv rɔk ʒilber dy mɔtje), Marquis de Lafayette. 1757–1834, French general and statesman. He fought on the side of the colonists in the War of American Independence and, as commander of the National Guard (1789–91; 1830), he played a leading part in the French Revolution and the revolution of 1830 **2 Marie-Madeleine** (marimadlɛn), Comtesse de Lafayette. 1634–93, French novelist, noted for her historical romance *La Princesse de Clèves* (1678)

Laffer curve ('læfə) *n economics* a curve on a graph showing government tax revenue plotted against percentage tax rates. It has been used to show that a cut in a high tax rate can increase government revenue [C20: named after Arthur *Laffer* (born 1940), US economist]

La Fontaine (*French* la fɔ̃tɛn) *n* **Jean de** (ʒɑ̃ də). 1621–95, French poet, famous for his *Fables* (1668–94)

Laforgue (*French* lafɔrg) *n* **Jules** (ʒyl). 1860–87, French symbolist poet. An originator of free verse, he had a considerable influence on modern poetry

LAFTA ('læftə) *n acronym for* Latin American Free Trade Area, the name before 1981 of the Latin American Integration Association. See **LAIA**

lag¹ (læg) *vb* **lags, lagging, lagged** (*intr*) **1** (often foll by *behind*) to hang (back) or fall (behind) in movement, progress, development, etc **2** to fall away in strength or intensity ▷ *n* **3** the act or state of slowing down or falling behind **4** the interval of time between two events, esp between an action and its effect [C16: of obscure origin]

lag² (læg) *slang* ▷ *n* **1** a convict or ex-convict (esp in the phrase **old lag**) **2** a term of imprisonment ▷ *vb* **lags, lagging, lagged 3** (*tr*) to arrest or put in prison [C19: of unknown origin]

lag³ (læg) *vb* **lags, lagging, lagged 1** (*tr*) to cover (a pipe, cylinder, etc) with lagging to prevent loss of heat ▷ *n* **2** the insulating casing of a steam cylinder, boiler, etc; lagging **3** a stave or lath [C17: of Scandinavian origin; related to Swedish *lagg* stave]

lagan ('lægᵊn) *n* goods or wreckage on the sea bed, sometimes attached to a buoy to permit recovery [C16: from Old French *lagan*, probably of Germanic origin;

compare Old Norse *lögn* dragnet]

lager ('lɑːgə) *n* a light-bodied effervescent beer, fermented in a closed vessel using yeasts that sink to the bottom of the brew [c19: from German *Lagerbier* beer for storing, from *Lager* storehouse]

Lagerfeld ('lɑːgəˌfɛlt) *n* **Karl** (**Otto**). born 1938, German fashion designer working mainly in Paris

Lagerkvist (*Swedish* 'lɑːgərkvist) *n* **Pär** (**Fabian**) (pæːr). 1891–1974, Swedish novelist and dramatist. His works include the novels *The Dwarf* (1944) and *Barabbas* (1950): Nobel prize for literature 1951

Lagerlöf (*Swedish* 'lɑːgərlœːv) *n* **Selma** ('sɛlma). 1858–1940, Swedish novelist, noted esp for her children's classic *The Wonderful Adventures of Nils* (1906–07): Nobel prize for literature 1909

lager lout *n* a rowdy or aggressive young drunk male

laggard ('lægəd) *n* 1 a person who lags behind ▷ *adj* 2 *rare* sluggish, slow, or dawdling > 'laggardly *adv* > 'laggardness *n*

lagging ('lægɪŋ) *n* 1 insulating material wrapped around pipes, boilers, etc, or laid in a roof loft, to prevent loss of heat 2 the act or process of applying lagging

lagomorph ('lægəʊˌmɔːf) *n* any placental mammal of the order *Lagomorpha*, having two pairs of upper incisors specialized for gnawing: includes pikas, rabbits, and hares [c19: via New Latin from Greek *lagōs* hare; see -MORPH]

lagoon (lə'guːn) *n* 1 a body of water cut off from the open sea by coral reefs or sand bars 2 any small body of water, esp one adjoining a larger one [c17: from Italian *laguna*, from Latin *lacūna* pool; see LACUNA]

Lagoon Islands *pl n* a former name of **Tuvalu**

Lagos ('leɪgɒs) *n* 1 the former capital and chief port of Nigeria, on the Bight of Benin: first settled in the sixteenth century; a slave market until the nineteenth century; ceded to Britain (1861); university (1962). Pop: 11 135 000 (2005 est) 2 a state of SW Nigeria. Capital: Ikeja. Pop: 9 013 534 (2006). Area: 3345 sq km (1292 sq miles)

Lagrange (*French* lagrɑ̃ʒ) *n* Comte **Joseph Louis** (ʒozɛf lwi). 1736–1813, French mathematician and astronomer, noted particularly for his work on harmonics, mechanics, and the calculus of variations > Lagrangian (lə'greɪndʒɪən) *adj*

Lagrangian point *n* astronomy one of five points in the plane of revolution of two bodies in orbit around their common centre of gravity, at which a third body of negligible mass can remain in equilibrium with respect to the other two bodies [named after Comte Joseph Louis *Lagrange* (1736–1813), French mathematician and astronomer]

La Granja (*Spanish* la 'graŋxa) *n* another name for **San Ildefonso**

La Guaira or **La Guayra** (*Spanish* la 'gwaira) *n* the chief seaport of Venezuela, on the Caribbean. Pop: 26 669 (1990 est)

La Guardia (lə'gwɑːdɪə) *n* **Fiorello H**(**enry**) (ˌfɪə'rɛləʊ). 1882–1947, US politician. As mayor of New York (1933–45), he organized slum-clearance and labour safeguard schemes and suppressed racketeering

lah (lɑː) *n* music (in tonic sol-fa) the sixth note of any major scale; submediant [c14: see GAMUT]

lahar ('lɑːhɑː) *n* a landslide of volcanic debris mixed with water down the sides of a volcano, usually precipitated by heavy rainfall [c20: from Javanese: lava]

lah-di-dah (ˌlɑːdiː'dɑː) *adj, n* informal a variant spelling of **la-di-da**

Lahore (lə'hɔː) *n* 1 a city in NE Pakistan: capital of the former province of West Pakistan (1955–70); University of the Punjab (1882). Pop: 6 373 000 (2005 est) 2 a variety of large domestic fancy pigeon having a black-and-white plumage

Lahti (*Finnish* 'lɑhti) *n* a town in S Finland: site of the main Finnish radio and television stations; furniture industry. Pop: 98 253 (2003 est)

LAIA *abbreviation* Latin American Integration Association (before 1981, known as the Latin American Free Trade Area). An economic group, its members are Argentina, Bolivia, Brazil, Chile, Colombia, Ecuador, Mexico, Paraguay, Peru, Uruguay, and Venezuela

Laibach ('laibax) *n* the German name for **Ljubljana**

laic ('leɪɪk) *adj* 1 Also: laical of or involving the laity; secular ▷ *n* 2 a rare word for **layman** [c15: from Late Latin *lāicus* LAY³] > 'laically *adv*

laicize or **laicise** ('leɪɪˌsaɪz) *vb* (*tr*) to withdraw clerical or ecclesiastical character or status from (an institution, building, etc) > ˌlaici'zation or ˌlaici'sation *n*

laid (leɪd) *vb* the past tense and past participle of **lay¹**

laid-back *adj* informal relaxed in style, character, or behaviour; easy-going and unhurried

laid paper *n* paper with a regular mesh impressed upon it by the dandy roller on a paper-making machine

laik (leɪk) *vb* Northern English dialect 1 (when intr, often foll by *about*) to play (a game, etc) 2 (intr) to be on holiday, esp to take a day off work 3 (intr) to be unemployed [c14: *leiken*, from Old Norse *leika*; related to Old English *lacan* to manoeuvre; compare LARK²]

Lailat-ul-Qadr (ˌleɪlætʊl'kɑːdə) *n* a night of study and prayer observed annually by Muslims to mark the communication of the Koran: it usually follows the 27th day of Ramadan [from Arabic: night of determination]

lain (leɪn) *vb* the past participle of **lie²**

Laine (leɪn) *n* **Cleo** ('kliːəʊ), full name *Clementina Dinah Laine*. born 1927, British jazz singer, noted esp for her recordings with her husband John Dankworth

Laing (leɪŋ) *n* **R**(**onald**) **D**(**avid**). 1927–89, Scottish psychiatrist; his best known books include *The Divided Self* (1960), *The Politics of Experience and the Bird of Paradise* (1967), and *Knots* (1970)

Laingian ('læŋɪən) *adj* 1 of or based on the theory of Scottish psychiatrist R. D. Laing (1927–89) that mental illnesses are understandable as natural responses to stress in family and social situations ▷ *n* 2 a follower or adherent of Laing's teaching

lair¹ (leə) *n* 1 the resting place of a wild animal 2 informal a place of seclusion or hiding ▷ *vb* 3 (intr) (esp of a wild animal) to retreat to or rest in a lair 4 (tr) to drive or place (an animal) in a lair [Old English *leger*; related to LIE² and Old High German *leger* bed]

lair² (leə) *Austral slang* ▷ *n* 1 a flashy man who shows off ▷ *vb* 2 (intr; foll by *up* or *around*) to behave or dress like a lair [perhaps from LEER]

laird (lɛəd; *Scot* leɪrd) *n* Scot a landowner, esp of a large estate [c15: Scottish variant of LORD]

laissez faire or **laisser faire** (ˌleɪseɪ 'fɛə; *French* lese fɛr) *n* 1 **a** Also called: individualism the doctrine of unrestricted freedom in commerce, esp for private interests **b** (*as modifier*): *a laissez-faire economy* 2 indifference or noninterference, esp in the affairs of others [French, literally: let (them) act]

laissez passer or **laisser passer** *French* (lese pase) *n* a document granting unrestricted access or movement to its holder [literally: let pass]

laity ('leɪɪtɪ) *n* 1 laymen, as distinguished from clergymen 2 all people not of a specific occupation [c16: from LAY³]

Laius ('laɪəs) *n* Greek myth a king of Thebes, killed by his son Oedipus, who did not know of their relationship

lake¹ (leɪk) *n* 1 an expanse of water entirely surrounded by land and unconnected to the sea except by rivers or streams. Related adj: **lacustrine** 2 anything resembling this 3 a surplus of a liquid commodity: *a wine lake* [c13: *lac*, via Old French from Latin *lacus* basin]

lake² (leɪk) *n* 1 a bright pigment used in textile dyeing and printing inks, produced by the combination of an organic colouring matter with an inorganic compound, usually a metallic salt, oxide, or hydroxide 2 a red dye obtained by combining a metallic compound with cochineal [c17: variant of LAC¹]

Lake District *n* a region of lakes and mountains in NW England, in Cumbria: includes England's largest lake (Windermere) and highest mountain (Scafell Pike); national park; literary associations (the Lake Poets); tourist region. Also called: **Lakeland**

lake dwelling *n* a dwelling, esp in prehistoric villages, constructed on platforms supported by wooden piles driven into the bottom of a lake > lake dweller *n*

Lakeland ('leɪkˌlænd) *n* 1 another name for the **Lake**

District ▷ adj **2** of or relating to the Lake District

Lakeland terrier n a wire-haired breed of terrier, originally from the Lake District and used for hunting

Lake of the Woods n a lake in N central North America, mostly in W Northern Ontario, Canada: fed chiefly by the Rainy River; drains into Lake Winnipeg by the Winnipeg River; many islands; tourist region. Area: 3846 sq km (1485 sq miles)

Lake Poets pl n the English poets Wordsworth, Coleridge, and Southey, who lived in and drew inspiration from the Lake District at the beginning of the 19th century

Lake Success n a village in SE New York State, on W Long Island: headquarters of the United Nations Security Council from 1946 to 1951. Pop: 2832 (2003 est)

lakh or **lac** (laːk) n (in India and Pakistan) the number 100 000, esp when referring to this sum of rupees [C17: from Hindi lākh, ultimately from Sanskrit lakshā a sign]

Lakshadweep Islands (lækˈʃædwiːp) pl n a group of 26 coral islands and reefs in the Arabian Sea, off the SW coast of India: a union territory of India since 1956. Administrative centre: Kavaratti Island. Pop: 60 595 (2001). Area: 28 sq km (11 sq miles). Former name (until 1973): Laccadive, Minicoy, and Amindivi Islands

-lalia combining form indicating a speech defect or abnormality: coprolalia; echolalia [New Latin, from Greek lalia chatter, from lalein to babble]

La Línea (Spanish la ˈlinea) n a town in SW Spain, on the Bay of Gibraltar. Pop: 61 892 (2003 est)

Lalique (French lalik) n **René (Jules)** (rəne). 1860–1945, French Art- Nouveau jeweller, glass-maker, and designer: noted esp for his frosted glassware

Lallans (ˈlælənz) or **Lallan** (ˈlælən) n **1** a literary version of the variety of English spoken and written in the Lowlands of Scotland **2** (modifier) of or relating to the Lowlands of Scotland or their dialects [Scottish variant of LOWLANDS]

lallation (læˈleɪʃən) n phonetics a defect of speech consisting of the pronunciation of (r) as (l) [C17: from Latin lallāre to sing lullaby, of imitative origin]

Lalo (ˈlaːləʊ) n (**Victor-Antoine-)Édouard** (edwar). 1823–92, French composer of Spanish descent. His works include the Symphonie espagnole (1873) and the ballet Namouna (1882)

lam¹ (læm) vb **lams, lamming, lammed** slang **1** (tr) to thrash or beat **2** (intr; usually foll by into or out) to make a sweeping stroke or blow [C16: from Scandinavian; related to Old Norse lemja]

lam² (læm) US & Canadian slang ▷ n **1** a sudden flight or escape, esp to avoid arrest **2** on the lam making an escape [C19: perhaps from LAM¹ (hence, to be off)]

Lam. abbreviation Bible Lamentations

lama (ˈlaːmə) n a priest or monk of Lamaism [C17: from Tibetan blama]

Lamaism (ˈlaːmə,ɪzəm) n the Mahayana form of Buddhism of Tibet and Mongolia > ˈLamaist n, adj > ˌLamaˈistic adj

La Mancha (Spanish la ˈmantʃa) n a plateau of central Spain, between the mountains of Toledo and the hills of Cuenca: traditionally associated with episodes in Don Quixote. Average height: 600 m (2000 ft)

La Manche (French la maʃ) n See Manche (sense 2)

Lamarck (French lamark) n **Jean Baptiste Pierre Antoine de Monet** (ʒã batist pjɛr ãtwan də mɔnɛ), Chevalier de Lamarck. 1744–1829, French naturalist. He outlined his theory of organic evolution (Lamarckism) in Philosophie Zoologique (1809)

Lamarckism (laˈmaːkɪzəm) n the theory of organic evolution proposed by Jean Baptiste Pierre Antoine de Monet, Chevalier de Lamarck (1744–1829), the French naturalist, based on the principle that characteristics of an organism modified during its lifetime are inheritable

Lamartine (French lamartin) n **Alphonse Marie Louis de Prat de** (alfɔs mari lwi də pra də). 1790–1869, French romantic poet, historian, and statesman: his works include Méditations poétiques (1820) and Histoire des Girondins (1847)

lamasery (ˈlaːməsərɪ) n, pl **-series** a monastery of lamas [C19: from French lamaserie, from LAMA + French -serie, from Persian serāī palace]

lamb (læm) n **1** the young of a sheep **2** the meat of a young sheep **3** a person, esp a child, who is innocent, meek, good, etc **4** a person easily deceived ▷ vb **5** Also called: lamb down (intr) (of a ewe) to give birth **6** (intr) (of a shepherd) to tend the ewes and newborn lambs at lambing time [Old English lamb, from Germanic; compare German Lamm, Old High German and Old Norse lamb] > ˈlamb,like adj

Lamb¹ (læm) n the Lamb a title given to Christ in the New Testament

Lamb² (læm) n **1 Charles**, pen name Elia. 1775–1834, English essayist and critic. He collaborated with his sister Mary on Tales from Shakespeare (1807). His other works include Specimens of English Dramatic Poets (1808) and the largely autobiographical essays collected in Essays of Elia (1823; 1833) **2 William**. See (2nd Viscount) Melbourne¹ **3 Willis Eugene**. born 1913, US physicist. He detected the small difference in energy between two states of the hydrogen atom (Lamb shift). Nobel prize for physics 1955

lambada (læmˈbaːdə) n **1** an erotic dance, originating in Brazil, performed by two people who hold each other closely and gyrate their hips in synchronized movements **2** the music that accompanies the lambada, combining salsa, calypso, and reggae [C20: from Portuguese, literally: the snapping of a whip]

Lambaréné (French lãbarene) n a town in W Gabon on the Ogooué River: site of the hospital built by Albert Schweitzer, who died and was buried there (1965). Pop: 9000 (2003 est)

lambast (læmˈbæst) or **lambaste** (læmˈbeɪst) vb (tr) **1** to beat or whip severely **2** to reprimand or scold [C17: perhaps from LAM¹ + BASTE³]

lambda (ˈlæmdə) n the 11th letter of the Greek alphabet (Λ, λ), a consonant transliterated as l [C14: from Greek, from Semitic; related to LAMED]

lambent (ˈlæmbənt) adj **1** (esp of a flame) flickering softly over a surface **2** glowing with soft radiance **3** (of wit or humour) light or brilliant [C17: from the present participle of Latin lambere to lick] > ˈlambency n > ˈlambently adv

lambert (ˈlæmbət) n the cgs unit of illumination, equal to 1 lumen per square centimetre. Symbol: L [named after J. H. Lambert (1728–77), German mathematician and physicist]

Lambert (ˈlæmbət) n **Constant**. 1905–51, English composer and conductor. His works include much ballet music and The Rio Grande (1929), a work for chorus, orchestra, and piano, using jazz idioms

Lambeth (ˈlæmbəθ) n **1** a borough of S Greater London, on the Thames: contains **Lambeth Palace** (the London residence of the Archbishop of Canterbury). Pop: 268 500 (2003 est). Area: 27 sq km (11 sq miles) **2** the Archbishop of Canterbury in his official capacity

Lambic (ˈlæmbɪk) n **a** a type of Belgian beer brewed with raw wheat and wild yeast in wooden casks, and fermented for at least a year **b** (as modifier): Lambic beers [C20: probably from Lembeek a town near Brussels]

lambing (ˈlæmɪŋ) n **1** the birth of lambs **2** the shepherd's work of tending the ewes and newborn lambs at this time

lambkin (ˈlæmkɪn) n **1** a small or young lamb **2** a term of affection for a small endearing child

Lamb of God n a title given to Christ in the New Testament, probably with reference to his sacrificial death

lambrequin (ˈlæmbrɪkɪn, ˈlæmbə-) n **1** an ornamental hanging covering the edge of a shelf or the upper part of a window or door **2** (often plural) a scarf worn over a helmet [C18: from French, from Dutch lamperkin (unattested), diminutive of lamper veil]

Lambrusco (læmˈbrʊskəʊ) n **1** a red grape grown in Italy **2** a sparkling red wine made in Italy from this grape **3** a much less common white variety of this grape or wine

lambskin (ˈlæm,skɪn) n **1** the skin of a lamb, esp with the wool still on **2** a material or garment prepared from this skin

lamb's lettuce n another name for **corn salad**

lamb's tails *pl n* the pendulous catkins of the hazel tree

lame (leɪm) *adj* **1** disabled or crippled in the legs or feet **2** painful or weak: *a lame back* **3** weak; unconvincing: *a lame excuse* **4** not effective or enthusiastic: *a lame try* **5** *US slang* conventional or uninspiring ▷ *vb* **6** (*tr*) to make lame [Old English *lama*; related to Old Norse *lami*, German *lahm*] > **'lamely** *adv* > **'lameness** *n*

lamé ('lɑːmeɪ) *n* a fabric of silk, cotton, or wool interwoven with threads of metal [from French, from Old French *lame* gold or silver thread, thin plate, from Latin *lāmina* thin plate]

lame duck *n* **1** a person or thing that is disabled or ineffectual **2** *stock exchange* a speculator who cannot discharge his liabilities **3** *US* an elected official or body of officials remaining in office in the interval between the election and inauguration of a successor

lamed ('lɑːmɪd; *Hebrew* 'lɑmɛd) *n* the 12th letter in the Hebrew alphabet (ל), transliterated as *l*. Also called: **lamedh** ('lɑmɛd) [from Hebrew, literally: ox goad (from its shape)]

lamella (lə'mɛlə) *n, pl* **-lae** (-liː) *or* **-las** a thin layer, plate, or membrane, esp any of the calcified layers of which bone is formed [c17: New Latin, from Latin, diminutive of *lāmina* thin plate] > la'**mellar**, **lamellate** ('læmɪˌleɪt, -lɪt, lə'mɛleɪt, -lɪt) *or* **lamellose** (lə'mɛləʊs, 'læmɪˌləʊs) *adj*

lamellibranch (lə'mɛlɪˌbræŋk) *n, adj* another word for **bivalve** (sense 1) [c19: from New Latin *lamellibranchia* plate-gilled (animals); see LAMELLA, BRANCHIA]

lamellicorn (lə'mɛlɪˌkɔːn) *n* **1** any beetle of the superfamily *Lamellicornia*, having flattened terminal plates to the antennae: includes the scarabs and stag beetles ▷ *adj* **2** designating antennae with platelike terminal segments [c19: from New Latin *Lamellicornia* plate-horned (animals)]

lament (lə'mɛnt) *vb* **1** to feel or express sorrow, remorse, or regret (for or over) ▷ *n* **2** an expression of sorrow **3** a poem or song in which a death is lamented [c16: from Latin *lāmentum*] > la'**menter** *n* > la'**mentingly** *adv*

lamentable ('læməntəbəl) *adj* **1** wretched, deplorable, or distressing **2** an archaic word for **mournful** > '**lamentably** *adv*

lamentation (ˌlæmɛn'teɪʃən) *n* **1** a lament; expression of sorrow **2** the act of lamenting

lamented (lə'mɛntɪd) *adj* grieved for or regretted (often in the phrase **late lamented**): *our late lamented employer* > la'**mentedly** *adv*

Lamerie ('læmərɪ) *n* **Paul de.** 1688–1751, English silversmith of French Huguenot descent, noted for his lavish rococo designs

lamina ('læmɪnə) *n, pl* **-nae** (-ˌniː) *or* **-nas** **1** a thin plate or layer, esp of bone or mineral **2** *botany* the flat blade of a leaf, petal, or thallus [c17: New Latin, from Latin: thin plate] > '**laminar** *or* **laminose** ('læmɪˌnəʊs, -ˌnəʊz) *adj*

laminar flow *n* nonturbulent motion of a fluid in which parallel layers have different velocities relative to each other

laminate *vb* ('læmɪˌneɪt) **1** (*tr*) to make (material in sheet form) by bonding together two or more thin sheets **2** to split or be split into thin sheets **3** (*tr*) to beat, form, or press (material, esp metal) into thin sheets **4** (*tr*) to cover or overlay with a thin sheet of material ▷ *n* ('læmɪˌneɪt, -nɪt) **5** a material made by bonding together two or more sheets ▷ *adj* ('læmɪˌneɪt, -nɪt) **6** having or composed of lamina; laminated [c17: from New Latin *lāminātus* plated] > **laminable** ('læmɪnəbəl) *adj* > '**lami,nator** *n*

laminated ('læmɪˌneɪtɪd) *adj* **1** composed of thin sheets (of plastic, wood, etc) superimposed and bonded together by synthetic resins, usually under heat and pressure **2** covered with a thin protective layer of plastic or synthetic resin

lamington ('læmɪŋtən) *n* *Austral & NZ* a cube of sponge cake coated in chocolate and dried coconut [c20 (in the earlier sense: a homburg hat): named after Baron *Lamington*, governor of Queensland (1896–1901)]

Lammas ('læməs) *n* **1** *RC Church* Aug 1, held as a feast, commemorating St Peter's miraculous deliverance from prison **2** Also called: **Lammas Day** the same day formerly observed in England as a harvest festival. In Scotland Lammas is a quarter day [Old English *hlāfmæsse* loaf mass]

lammergeier *or* **lammergeyer** ('læməˌgaɪə) *n* a rare vulture, *Gypaetus barbatus*, of S Europe, Africa, and Asia, with dark wings, a pale breast, and black feathers around the bill: family *Accipitridae* (hawks) [c19: from German *Lämmergeier*, from *Lämmer* lambs + *Geier* vulture]

lamp (læmp) *n* **1 a** any of a number of devices that produce illumination: *an electric lamp; a gas lamp; an oil lamp* **b** (*in combination*): *lampshade* **2** a device for holding one or more electric light bulbs: *a table lamp* **3** a vessel in which a liquid fuel is burned to supply illumination **4** any of a variety of devices that produce radiation, esp for therapeutic purposes: *an ultraviolet lamp* [c13 *lampe*, via Old French from Latin *lampas*, from Greek, from *lampein* to shine]

lampblack ('læmp,blæk) *n* a finely divided form of almost pure carbon produced by the incomplete combustion of organic compounds, such as natural gas, used in making carbon electrodes and dynamo brushes and as a pigment

lamp chimney *n* a glass tube that surrounds the wick in an oil lamp

Lampedusa¹ (ˌlæmpɪ'djuːzə) *n* an island in the Mediterranean, between Malta and Tunisia. Area: about 21 sq km (8 sq miles)

Lampedusa² (ˌlæmpɪ'djuːzə) *n* **Giuseppe Tomasi di.** 1896–1957, Italian novelist: author of the historical novel *The Leopard* (1958)

lamplighter ('læmp,laɪtə) *n* **1** (formerly) a person who lit and extinguished street lamps, esp gas ones **2** *chiefly US & Canadian* any of various devices used to light lamps

lampoon (læm'puːn) *n* **1** a satire in prose or verse ridiculing a person, literary work, etc ▷ *vb* **2** (*tr*) to attack or satirize in a lampoon [c17: from French *lampon*, perhaps from *lampons* let us drink (frequently used as a refrain in poems)] > lam'**pooner** *or* lam'**poonist** *n* > lam'**poonery** *n*

lamppost ('læmp,pəʊst) *n* a post supporting a lamp, esp in a street

lamprey ('læmprɪ) *n* any eel-like cyclostome vertebrate of the family *Petromyzonidae*, having a round sucking mouth for clinging to and feeding on the blood of other animals. Also called: lamper eel [c13: from Old French *lamproie*, from Late Latin *lamprēda*; origin obscure]

Lanai (lɑː'nɑːɪ, lə'naɪ) *n* an island in central Hawaii, west of Maui island. Pop: 3193 (2000). Area: 363 sq km. (140 sq miles)

Lanarkshire ('lænəkˌʃɪə, -ʃə) *n* a historical county of S Scotland: became part of Strathclyde region in 1975; since 1996 administered by the council areas of North Lanarkshire, South Lanarkshire, and Glasgow

Lancashire ('læŋkəˌʃɪə, -ʃə) *n* a county of NW England, on the Irish Sea: became a county palatine in 1351 and a duchy attached to the Crown; much reduced in size after the 1974 boundary changes, losing the Furness district to Cumbria and much of the south to Greater Manchester, Merseyside, and Cheshire: Blackburn with Darwen and Blackpool became independent unitary authorities in 1998. It was traditionally a cotton textiles manufacturing region. Administrative centre: Preston. Pop (excluding unitary authorities): 1 147 000 (2003 est). Area (excluding unitary authorities): 2889 sq km (1115 sq miles). Abbreviation: Lancs

Lancaster¹ ('læŋkəstə, 'læŋˌkæstə) *n* the English royal house that reigned from 1399 to 1461

Lancaster² ('læŋkəstə) *n* a city in NW England, former county town of Lancashire, on the River Lune: castle (built on the site of a Roman camp); university (1964). Pop: 45 952 (2001)

Lancastrian (læŋ'kæstrɪən) *n* **1** a native or resident of Lancashire or Lancaster **2** an adherent of the house of Lancaster in the Wars of the Roses ▷ *adj* **3** of or relating to Lancashire or Lancaster **4** of or relating to the house of Lancaster

lance (lɑːns) *n* **1** a long weapon with a pointed head used by horsemen to unhorse or injure an opponent **2** a similar weapon used for hunting, whaling, etc **3** *surgery* another name for **lancet** ▷ *vb* (*tr*) **4** to pierce (an abscess or boil) with a lancet to drain off pus **5** to pierce with or as if with a lance [C13 *launce*, from Old French *lance*, from Latin *lancea*]

lance corporal *n* a noncommissioned officer of the lowest rank in the British Army

lancelet ('lɑːnslɪt) *n* any of several marine animals of the genus *Branchiostoma* (formerly *Amphioxus*), esp *B. lanceolatus*, that are closely related to the vertebrates: subphylum *Cephalochordata* (cephalochordates). Also called: amphioxus [C19: referring to the slender shape]

Lancelot ('lɑːnslət) *n* (in Arthurian legend) one of the Knights of the Round Table; the lover of Queen Guinevere

lanceolate ('lɑːnsɪəˌleɪt, -lɪt) *adj* narrow and tapering to a point at each end: *lanceolate leaves* [C18: from Late Latin *lanceolātus*, from *lanceola* small LANCE]

lancer ('lɑːnsə) *n* **1** (formerly) a cavalryman armed with a lance **2** a member of a regiment retaining such a title

lancers ('lɑːnsəz) *n* (*functioning as singular*) **1** a quadrille for eight or sixteen couples **2** a piece of music composed for this dance

lancet ('lɑːnsɪt) *n* **1** Also called: **lance** a pointed surgical knife with two sharp edges **2** short for **lancet arch, lancet window** [C15 *lancette*, from Old French: small LANCE]

lancet arch *n* a narrow acutely pointed arch having two centres of equal radii

lancet window *n* a narrow window having a lancet arch

lancewood ('lɑːnsˌwʊd) *n* Also called: **horoeka** a New Zealand forest tree, *Pseudopanax crassifolius*, with a small round head and a slender trunk

Lanchow or **Lan-chou** ('læn'tʃaʊ) *n* a variant transliteration of the Chinese name for **Lanzhou**

Lancs (læŋks) *abbreviation* Lancashire

land (lænd) *n* **1** the solid part of the surface of the earth as distinct from seas, lakes, etc. Related adj: **terrestrial** **2** ground, esp with reference to its use, quality, etc **3** rural or agricultural areas as contrasted with urban ones **4** farming as an occupation or way of life **5** *law* any tract of ground capable of being owned as property, together with any buildings on it, extending above and below the surface **6 a** a country, region, or area **b** the people of a country, etc **7** *economics* the factor of production consisting of all natural resources ▷ *vb* **8** to transfer (something) or go from a ship or boat to the shore: *land the cargo* **9** (*intr*) to come to or touch shore **10** to come down or bring (something) down to earth after a flight or jump **11** to come or bring to some point, condition, or state: *land the cargo* **12** (*tr*) *angling* to retrieve (a hooked fish) from the water **13** (*tr*) *informal* to win or obtain: *to land a job* **14** (*tr*) *informal* to deliver (a blow) ▷ See also **land up** [Old English; compare Old Norse, Gothic *land*, Old High German *lant*] > **landless** *adj*

Land[1] (lænd) *n* **Edwin Herbert.** 1909–91, US inventor of the Polaroid Land camera

Land[2] *German* (lant) *n*, *pl* **Länder** ('lendər) **a** any of the federal states of Germany **b** any of the provinces of Austria

land agent *n* **1** a person who administers a landed estate and its tenancies **2** a person who acts as an agent for the sale of land > **land agency** *n*

landau ('lændɔː) *n* a four-wheeled carriage, usually horse-drawn, with two folding hoods that meet over the middle of the passenger compartment [C18: named after *Landau* (a town in Bavaria), where it was first made]

Landau (*Russian* lan'dau) *n* **Lev Davidovich** (ljɛf da'vidəvitʃ). 1908–68, Soviet physicist, noted for his researches on quantum theory and his work on the theories of solids and liquids: Nobel prize for physics 1962

landaulet or **landaulette** (ˌlændɔːˈlɛt) *n* **1** a small landau **2** *US* an early type of car with a folding hood over the passenger seats and an open driver's seat

landed ('lændɪd) *adj* **1** owning land: *landed gentry* **2** consisting of or including land: *a landed estate*

landed immigrant *n* *Canadian* a former term for **permanent resident**

Landes (*French* lɑ̃d) *n* **1** a department of SW France, in

Aquitaine region. Capital: Mont-de-Marsan. Pop: 341 254 (2003 est). Area: 9364 sq km (3652 sq miles) **2** a region of SW France, on the Bay of Biscay: occupies most of the Landes department and parts of Gironde and Lot-et-Garonne; consists chiefly of the most extensive forest in France. Area: 14 000 sq km (5400 sq miles)

landfall ('lændˌfɔːl) *n* **1** the act of sighting or nearing land, esp from the sea **2** the land sighted or neared

landfill ('lændˌfɪl) *n* **a** disposal of waste material by burying it under layers of earth **b** (*as modifier*): *landfill sites*

landform ('lændˌfɔːm) *n* *geology* any natural feature of the earth's surface, such as valleys and mountains

land girl *n* a girl or woman who does farm work, esp in wartime

landgrave ('lændˌgreɪv) *n* *German history* **1** (from the 13th century to 1806) a count who ruled over a specified territory **2** (after 1806) the title of any of various sovereign princes in central Germany [C16: via German, from Middle High German *lantgrāve*, from *lant* land + *grāve* count]

land-holder *n* a person who owns or occupies land > 'land-ˌholding *adj*, *n*

landing ('lændɪŋ) *n* **1 a** the act of coming to land, esp after a flight or sea voyage **b** (*as modifier*): *landing place* **2** a place of disembarkation **3** the floor area at the top of a flight of stairs or between two flights of stairs

landing craft *n* *military* any small vessel designed for the landing of troops and equipment on beaches

landing field *n* an area of land on which aircraft land and from which they take off

landing gear *n* another name for **undercarriage** (sense 1)

landing net *n* *angling* a loose long-handled net on a triangular frame for lifting hooked fish from the water

landing stage *n* a platform used for landing goods and passengers from a vessel

landing strip *n* another name for **airstrip**

landlady ('lændˌleɪdɪ) *n*, *pl* **-dies** **1** a woman who owns and leases property **2** a woman who owns or runs a lodging house, pub, etc

ländler (*German* 'lentlər) *n* **1** an Austrian country dance in which couples spin and clap **2** a piece of music composed for or in the rhythm of this dance, in three-four time [German, from dialect *Landl* Upper Austria]

land line *n* a telecommunications wire or cable laid over land

landlocked ('lændˌlɒkt) *adj* **1** (of a country) completely surrounded by land **2** (esp of certain salmon) living in fresh water that is permanently isolated from the sea

landlord ('lændˌlɔːd) *n* **1** a man who owns and leases property **2** a man who owns or runs a lodging house, pub, etc

landlubber ('lændˌlʌbə) *n* *nautical* any person having no experience at sea [C18: LAND + LUBBER]

landmark ('lændˌmɑːk) *n* **1** a prominent or well-known object in or feature of a particular landscape **2** an important or unique decision, event, fact, discovery, etc **3** a boundary marker or signpost

landmass ('lændˌmæs) *n* a large continuous area of land, as opposed to seas or islands

land mine *n* *military* an explosive charge placed in the ground, usually detonated by stepping or driving on it

land of milk and honey *n* **1** *Old Testament* the land of natural fertility promised to the Israelites by God (Ezekiel 20:6) **2** any fertile land, state, etc

land of Nod *n* **1** *Old Testament* a region to the east of Eden to which Cain went after he had killed Abel (Genesis 4:14) **2** an imaginary land of sleep

Landor ('lændɔː) *n* **Walter Savage.** 1775–1864, English poet, noted also for his prose works, including *Imaginary Conversations* (1824–29)

landowner ('lændˌəʊnə) *n* a person who owns land > 'land,owner,ship *n* > 'land,owning *n, adj*

Landowska (*Polish* lan'dɔfska) *n* **Wanda** ('vanda). 1877–1959, US harpsichordist, born in Poland

land rail *n* another name for **corncrake**

land reform *n* the redistributing of large agricultural holdings among the landless

landscape ('lændˌskeɪp) *n* **1** an extensive area of land regarded as being visually distinct **2** a painting, drawing, photograph, etc, depicting natural scenery **3** the genre including such pictures **4** the distinctive features of a given area of intellectual activity, regarded as an integrated whole ▷ *adj* **5** *printing* **a** (of a publication or an illustration in a publication) of greater width than height. See **portrait** (sense 3) **b** (of a page) carrying an illustration or table printed at right angles to the normal text ▷ *vb* **6** (*tr*) to improve the natural features of (a garden, park, etc), as by creating contoured features and planting trees **7** (*intr*) to work as a landscape gardener [C16 *landskip* (originally a term in painting), from Middle Dutch *lantscap* region; related to Old English *landscipe* tract of land, Old High German *lantscaf* region]

landscape gardening *n* the art of laying out grounds in imitation of natural scenery. Also called: landscape architecture ▷ landscape gardener *n*

landscapist ('lænd,skeɪpɪst) *n* a painter of landscapes

Landseer ('lænsɪə) *n* Sir **Edwin Henry**. 1802–73, English painter, noted for his studies of animals

Land's End *n* a granite headland in SW England, on the SW coast of Cornwall: the westernmost point of England

Landshut (*German* 'lantshuːt) *n* a city in SE Germany, in Bavaria: Trausnitz castle (13th century); manufacturing centre for machinery and chemicals. Pop: 60 282 (2003 est)

landside ('lænd,saɪd) *n* **1** the part of an airport farthest from the aircraft, the boundary of which is the security check, customs, passport control, etc. See **airside** **2** the part of a plough that slides along the face of the furrow wall on the opposite side to the mouldboard

landslide ('lænd,slaɪd) *n* **1** Also called: landslip **a** the sliding of a large mass of rock material, soil, etc, down the side of a mountain or cliff **b** the material dislodged in this way **2** an overwhelming electoral victory

landsman ('lændzmən) *n*, *pl* -men a person who works or lives on land, as distinguished from a seaman

Landsteiner (*German* 'lant,ʃtaɪnər) *n* **Karl** (karl). 1868–1943, Austrian immunologist, who discovered (1900) human blood groups and introduced the ABO classification system. He also discovered (1940) the Rhesus (Rh) factor in blood and researched into poliomyelitis. Nobel prize for physiology or medicine (1930)

land up *vb* (*adverb, usually intr*) to arrive or cause to arrive at a final point

landward ('lændwəd) *adj* **1** lying, facing, or moving towards land **2** in the direction of the land ▷ *adv* **3** a variant of **landwards**

landwards ('lændwədz) *or* **landward** *adv* towards land

land yacht *n* a three-wheeled recreational vehicle with a sail, used on land and propelled by wind power

lane (leɪn) *n* **1** a narrow road or way between buildings, hedges, fences, etc **2** **a** any of the parallel strips into which the carriageway of a major road or motorway is divided **b** any narrow well-defined route or course for ships or aircraft **3** one of the parallel strips into which a running track or swimming bath is divided for races **4** the long strip of wooden flooring down which balls are bowled in a bowling alley [Old English *lane, lanu*, of Germanic origin; related to Middle Dutch *lāne* lane]

Lanfranc ('lænfræŋk) *n* ?1005–89, Italian ecclesiastic and scholar; archbishop of Canterbury (1070–89) and adviser to William the Conqueror. He instituted many reforms in the English Church

Lang (læŋ) *n* **1 Cosmo Gordon**, 1st Baron Lang of Lambeth. 1864–1945, British churchman; archbishop of Canterbury (1928–42) **2 Fritz**. 1890–1976, Austrian film director, later in the US, most notable for his silent films, such as *Metropolis* (1926), *M* (1931), and *The Testament of Dr. Mabuse* (1932) **3 Jack** (**John Thomas**). 1876–1975, controversial Labor premier of New South Wales from 1925–27 and from 1930–32, who introduced much social welfare legislation and was dismissed by the governor, Sir Philip Game, in 1932 for acting unconstitutionally

Lange ('lɒŋɪ) *n* **David** (**Russell**). 1942–2005, New Zealand statesman: leader of the Labour Party from 1983: prime minister (1984–89)

Langer ('læŋə) *n* **Bernhard** ('bɛrnhart). born 1957, German professional golfer: won the US Masters Championship (1985, 1993)

Langerhans islets ('læŋə,hæns) *or* **Langerhans islands** *n anatomy* See **islets of Langerhans**

Langland ('lænlənd) *n* **William**. ?1332–?1400, English poet. The allegorical religious poem in alliterative verse, *The Vision of William concerning Piers the Plowman*, is attributed to him

langlauf ('lɑːŋ,laʊf) *n* cross-country skiing [German, literally: long run] > langläufer ('lɑːŋ,lɔɪfə) *n*

Langley ('lænlɪ) *n* **Samuel Pierpont**. 1834–1906, US astronomer and physicist: invented the bolometer (1878) and pioneered the construction of heavier-than-air flying machines

Langmuir ('læŋmjʊə) *n* **Irving**. 1881–1957, US chemist. He developed the gas-filled tungsten lamp and the atomic hydrogen welding process: Nobel prize for chemistry 1932

langouste ('lɒŋguːst, lɒŋ'guːst) *n* another name for the spiny lobster [French, from Old Provençal *langosta*, perhaps from Latin *lōcusta* lobster, locust]

langoustine (,lɒŋguːs'tiːn) *n* a large prawn or small lobster [from French, diminutive of LANGOUSTE]

Langres Plateau (*French* lɑ̃grə) *n* a calcareous plateau of E France north of Dijon between the Seine and the Saône, reaching over 580 m (1900 ft): forms a watershed between rivers flowing to the Mediterranean and to the English Channel

langsyne (,læŋ'saɪn, -'saɪn) *Scot* ▷ *adv* **1** long ago; long since ▷ *n* **2** times long past, esp those fondly remembered [C16: Scottish: long since]

Langton ('læŋtən) *n* **Stephen**. ?1150–1228, English cardinal; archbishop of Canterbury (1213–28). He was consecrated archbishop by Pope Innocent III in 1207 but was kept out of his see by King John until 1213. He was partly responsible for the Magna Carta (1215)

Langtry ('læntrɪ) *n* **Lillie**, known as *the Jersey Lily*, real name Émilie Charlotte le Breton. 1852–1929, English actress, noted for her beauty and for her friendship with Edward VII

language ('læŋgwɪdʒ) *n* **1** a system for the expression of thoughts, feelings, etc, by the use of spoken sounds or conventional symbols **2** the faculty for the use of such systems, which is a distinguishing characteristic of man as compared with other animals **3** the language of a particular nation or people **4** any other systematic or nonsystematic means of communicating, such as gesture or animal sounds: *the language of love* **5** the specialized vocabulary used by a particular group: *medical language* **6** a particular manner or style of verbal expression: *your language is disgusting* **7** *computing* See **programming language** [C13: from Old French *langage*, ultimately from Latin *lingua* tongue]

language laboratory *n* a room equipped with tape recorders, etc, for learning foreign languages

langue (lɑːŋg) *n linguistics* language considered as an abstract system or a social institution, being the common possession of a speech community [C19: from French: language]

Languedoc (*French* lɑ̃gdɔk) *n* **1** a former province of S France, lying between the foothills of the Pyrenees and the River Rhône: formed around the countship of Toulouse in the 13th century; important production of bulk wines **2** a wine from this region

langue d'oc *French* (lɑ̃g dɔk) *n* the group of medieval French dialects spoken in S France: often regarded as including Provençal [literally: language of *oc* (the Provençal form for *yes*), ultimately from Latin *hoc* this]

Languedoc-Roussillon (*French* lɑ̃gdɔkrusijɔ̃) *n* a region of S France, on the Gulf of Lions: consists of the departments of Lozère, Gard, Hérault, Aude, and Pyrénées-Orientales; mainly mountainous with a coastal plain

langue d'oïl *French* (lɑ̃g dɔj) *n* the group of medieval French dialects spoken in France north of the Loire; the medieval basis of modern French [literally: language of *oïl* (the northern form for *yes*), ultimately from Latin *hoc ille* (*fecit*) this he (did)]

languid ('læŋgwɪd) *adj* **1** without energy or spirit **2** without interest or enthusiasm **3** sluggish; inactive [C16: from Latin *languidus*, from *languēre* to languish] > **'languidly** *adv* > **'languidness** *n*

languish ('læŋgwɪʃ) *vb* (*intr*) **1** to lose or diminish in strength or energy **2** (often foll by *for*) to be listless with desire; pine **3** to suffer deprivation, hardship, or neglect: *to languish in prison* **4** to put on a tender, nostalgic, or melancholic expression [C14 *languishen*, from Old French *languiss-*, stem of *languir*, ultimately from Latin *languēre*] > **'languishing** *adj* > **'languishingly** *adv*

languor ('læŋgə) *n* **1** physical or mental laziness or weariness **2** a feeling of dreaminess and relaxation **3** oppressive silence or stillness [C14 *langour*, via Old French from Latin *languor*, from *languēre* to languish; the modern spelling is directly from Latin] > **'languorous** *adj*

langur (lʌŋ'gʊə) *n* any of various agile arboreal Old World monkeys of the genus *Presbytis* and related genera, of S and SE Asia having a slender body, long tail and hands, and long hair surrounding the face [Hindi, perhaps related to Sanskrit *lāngūla* tailed]

laniard ('lænjəd) *n* a variant spelling of **lanyard**

laniary ('læniəri) *adj* **1** (esp of canine teeth) adapted for tearing ▷ *n*, *pl* **-aries** **2** a tooth adapted for tearing [C19: from Latin *lanius* butcher, from *laniāre* to tear]

laniferous (lə'nɪfərəs) or **lanigerous** (lə'nɪdʒərəs) *adj* *biology* bearing wool or fleecy hairs resembling wool [C17: from Latin *lānifer*, from *lāna* wool]

La Niña (læ 'niːnjə) *n* *meteorol* a cooling of the eastern tropical Pacific, occurring in certain years [C20: from Spanish: The Little Girl, to distinguish it from El Niño]

lank[1] (læŋk) *adj* **1** long and limp **2** thin or gaunt [Old English *hlanc* loose] > **'lankly** *adv* > **'lankness** *n*

lank[2] (læŋk) *adj, adv* *South African informal* a lot; a great deal [perhaps from Afrikaans *lank* long]

Lankester ('læŋkɪstə) *n* Sir **Edwin Ray**. 1847–1929, English zoologist, noted particularly for his work in embryology and study of protozoans

lanky ('læŋkɪ) *adj* **lankier, lankiest** tall, thin, and loose-jointed > **'lankily** *adv* > **'lankiness** *n*

lanner ('lænə) *n* **1 a** a large falcon, *Falco biarmicus*, of Mediterranean regions, N Africa, and S Asia **2** *falconry* the female of this falcon [C15: from Old French (*faucon*) *lanier* cowardly (falcon), from Latin *lanārius* wool worker, coward; referring to its sluggish flight and timid nature]

lanolin ('lænəlɪn) or **lanoline** ('lænəlɪn, -,liːn) *n* a yellowish viscous substance extracted from wool, consisting of a mixture of esters of fatty acids: used in some ointments [C19: via German from Latin *lāna* wool + *oleum* oil; see -IN]

Lansbury ('lænzbərɪ) *n* **George**. 1859–1940, British Labour politician, who led the Labour Party in opposition (1931–35). A committed pacifist, he resigned over the party's reaction to Mussolini's seizure of Ethiopia

Lansdowne ('lænzdaʊn) *n* **1st Marquess of**. See (William Petty Fitzmaurice) **Shelburne**

Lansing ('lænsɪŋ) *n* a city in S Michigan, on the Grand River: the state capital. Pop: 118 329 (2003 est)

lantern ('læntən) *n* **1** a light with a transparent or translucent protective case **2** a structure on top of a dome or roof having openings or windows to admit light or air **3** the upper part of a lighthouse that houses the light [C13: from Latin *lanterna*, from Greek *lamptēr* lamp, from *lampein* to shine]

lantern jaw *n* (when *plural*, refers to upper and lower jaw; when *singular* usually to lower jaw) a long hollow jaw that gives the face a drawn appearance > **'lantern-jawed** *adj*

lantern slide *n* (formerly) a photographic slide for projection, used in a magic lantern

lanthanide ('lænθə,naɪd) *n* any element of the lanthanide series [C19: from LANTHANUM + -IDE]

lanthanum ('lænθənəm) *n* a silvery-white ductile metallic element of the lanthanide series, occurring principally in bastnaesite and monazite: used in pyrophoric alloys, electronic devices, and in glass manufacture. Symbol: La; atomic no: 57; atomic wt: 138.9055; valency: 3; relative density: 6.145; melting pt: 918°C; boiling pt: 3464°C [C19: New Latin, from Greek *lanthanein* to lie unseen]

lanthorn ('lænt,hɔːn, 'læntən) *n* an archaic word for **lantern**

lanugo (lə'njuːgəʊ) *n*, *pl* **-gos** a layer of fine hairs, esp the covering of the human fetus before birth [C17: from Latin: down, from *lāna* wool]

Lanús (*Spanish* la'nus) *n* a city in E Argentina: a S suburb of Buenos Aires. Pop: 212 152 (2001)

lanyard or **laniard** ('lænjəd) *n* **1** a cord worn around the neck, shoulder, etc, to hold something such as a whistle or knife **2** a cord with an attached hook used in firing certain types of cannon **3** *nautical* a line rove through deadeyes for extending or tightening standing rigging [C15 *lanyer*, from French *lanière*, from *lasne* strap, probably of Germanic origin]

Lanzarote (,lænzə'rɒtɪ) *n* the most easterly of the Canary Islands; mountainous, with a volcanic landscape; tourism, fishing. Pop: 109 942 (2002 est). Area: 795 sq km (307 sq miles)

Lanzhou, Lanchow or **Lan-chou** ('læn'dʒəʊ) *n* a city in N China, capital of Gansu province, on the Yellow River: situated on the main route between China and the West op.: 1 788 000 (2005 est)

Laoag (laː'waːg) *n* a city in the N Philippines, on NW Luzon: trade centre for an agricultural region. Pop: 94 466 (2000)

Laocoon (leɪ'ɒkəʊ,ɒn) *n* *Greek myth* a priest of Apollo at Troy who warned the Trojans against the wooden horse left by the Greeks; killed with his twin sons by two sea serpents

Laodicea (,leɪəʊdɪ'sɪə) *n* the ancient name of several Greek cities in W Asia, notably of Latakia

laodicean (,leɪəʊdɪ'sɪən) *adj* **1** lukewarm and indifferent, esp in religious matters ▷ *n* **2** a person having a lukewarm attitude towards religious matters [C17: referring to the early Christians of Laodicea (Revelation 3:14–16)]

Laoighis ('liːʃ) *n* a variant spelling of **Laois**

Laois ('liːʃ) *n* a county of central Republic of Ireland, in Leinster province: formerly boggy but largely reclaimed for agriculture. County town: Portlaoise. Pop: 58 774 (2002). Area: 1719 sq km (664 sq miles). Also called: **Laoighis, Leix** Former name: **Queen's County**

Laomedon (leɪ'ɒmɪ,dɒn) *n* *Greek myth* the founder and ruler of Troy, who cheated Apollo and Poseidon of their wage for constructing the city's walls; the father of Priam

Laos (laʊz, laʊs) *n* a republic in SE Asia: first united as the kingdom of Lan Xang ("million elephants") in 1353, after being a province of the Khmer Empire for about four centuries; made part of French Indochina in 1893 and gained independence in 1949; became a republic in 1975. It is generally forested and mountainous, with the Mekong River running almost the whole length of the W border. Official language: Laotian. Religion: Buddhist majority, tribal religions. Currency: kip. Capital: Vientiane. Pop: 5 787 000 (2004 est). Area: 236 800 sq km (91 429 sq miles) > **Laotian** ('laʊʃən) *n, adj*

Lao Zi ('laʊ'zɪə) or **Lao-tzu** ('laʊ'tsuː) *n* ?604–?531 BC, Chinese philosopher, traditionally regarded as the founder of Taoism and the author of the *Tao-te Ching*

lap[1] (læp) *n* **1** the area formed by the upper surface of the thighs of a seated person **2** Also called: **lapful** the amount held in one's lap **3** a protected place or environment: *in the lap of luxury* **4** the part of one's clothing that covers the lap **5** drop in someone's lap to give someone the responsibility of [Old English *læppa* flap; see LOBE, LAPPET, LOP[2]]

lap[2] (læp) *n* **1** one circuit of a racecourse or track **2** a stage or part of a journey, race, etc **3 a** an overlapping part or projection **b** the extent of overlap **4** the length of material needed to go around an object **5** a rotating disc coated with fine abrasive for polishing gemstones ▷ *vb* **laps, lapping, lapped** **6** (*tr*) to wrap or fold (around or over): *he lapped a bandage around his wrist* **7** (*tr*) to enclose or envelop in: *he lapped his wrist in a bandage* **8** to place or lie partly or completely over or project beyond **9** (*tr,* *usually passive*) to envelop or surround with comfort, love, etc: *lapped in luxury* **10** (*intr*) to be folded **11** (*tr*) to overtake (an opponent) in a race so as to be one or more circuits ahead **12** (*tr*) to polish or cut (a workpiece, gemstone, etc) with a fine abrasive, esp to hone (mating metal parts) against each other with an abrasive [C13 (in the sense: to wrap): probably from LAP¹] > 'lapper *n*

lap³ (læp) *vb* **laps, lapping, lapped** **1** (of small waves) to wash against (a shore, boat, etc), usually with light splashing sounds **2** (often foll by *up*) (esp of animals) to scoop (a liquid) into the mouth with the tongue ▷ *n* **3** the act or sound of lapping **4** a thin food for dogs or other animals ▷ See also **lap up** [Old English *lapian*; related to Old High German *laffan*, Latin *lambere*, Greek *laptein*] > 'lapper *n*

La Palma (*Spanish* la 'palma) *n* an island in the N Atlantic, in the NW Canary Islands: administratively part of Spain. Chief town: Santa Cruz de la Palma. Pop: 85 547 (2002 est). Area: 725 sq km (280 sq miles)

laparoscope ('læpərə,skəʊp) *n* a medical instrument consisting of a tube that is inserted through the abdominal wall and illuminated to enable a doctor to view the internal organs [C19 (applied to various instruments used to examine the abdomen) and C20 (in the specific modern sense): from Greek *lapara* (see LAPAROTOMY) + -SCOPE] > ,lapa'roscopy *n*

laparotomy (,læpə'rɒtəmɪ) *n*, *pl* -mies surgical incision through the abdominal wall, esp to investigate the cause of an abdominal disorder [C19: from Greek *lapara* flank, from *laparos* soft + -TOMY]

La Paz (læ 'pæz; *Spanish* la 'paθ) *n* a city in W Bolivia, at an altitude of 3600 m (12 000 ft): seat of government since 1898 (though Sucre is still the official capital); the country's largest city; founded in 1548 by the Spaniards; university (1830). Pop: 1 533 000 (2005 est)

lap dancing *n* a form of entertainment in which scantily dressed women dance erotically for individual members of the audience

lap dissolve *n films* the technique of allowing the end of one scene to overlap the beginning of the next scene by fading out the former while fading in the latter

lapdog ('læp,dɒg) *n* a pet dog small and docile enough to be cuddled in the lap

lapel (lə'pɛl) *n* the continuation of the turned or folded back collar on a suit coat, jacket, etc [C18: from LAP¹] > la'pelled *adj*

lapheld ('læp,hɛld) *adj* (esp of a personal computer) small enough to be used on one's lap; portable

lapidary ('læpɪdərɪ) *n*, *pl* -daries **1** a person whose business is to cut, polish, set, or deal in gemstones ▷ *adj* **2** of or relating to gemstones or the work of a lapidary **3** Also called: **lapidarian** (,læpɪ'dɛərɪən) engraved, cut, or inscribed in a stone or gemstone **4** of sufficiently high quality to be engraved on a stone: *a lapidary inscription* [C14: from Latin *lapidārius*, from *lapid-*, *lapis* stone]

lapillus (lə'pɪləs) *n*, *pl* -li (-laɪ) a small piece of lava thrown from a volcano [C18: Latin: little stone]

lapis lazuli ('læpɪs 'læzjʊ,laɪ) *or* **lazuli** *n* **1** a brilliant blue variety of the mineral lazurite, used as a gemstone **2** the deep blue colour of lapis lazuli [C14: from Latin *lapis* stone + Medieval Latin *lazulī*, from *lazulum*, from Arabic *lāzaward*, from Persian *lāzhuward*, of obscure origin]

Lapith ('læpɪθ) *n*, *pl* **Lapithae** ('læpɪ,θiː) *or* **Lapiths** *Greek myth* a member of a people in Thessaly who at the wedding of their king, Pirithoüs, fought the drunken centaurs

lap joint *n* a joint made by placing one member over another and fastening them together. Also called: **lapped joint** > 'lap-jointed *adj*

Laplace (*French* laplas) *n* **Pierre Simon** (pjɛr simɔ̃), Marquis de Laplace. 1749– 1827, French mathematician, physicist, and astronomer. He formulated the nebular hypothesis (1796). He also developed the theory of probability

Laplace operator (læ'plɑːs) *n maths* the operator $\partial^2/\partial x^2 + \partial^2/\partial y^2 + \partial^2/\partial z^2$ Symbol: ∇^2 [named after Pierre Simon, Marquis de *Laplace* (1749–1827), the French mathematician, physicist, and astronomer]

Lapland ('læp,lænd) *n* an extensive region of N Europe, mainly within the Arctic Circle: consists of the N parts of Norway, Sweden, Finland, and the Kola Peninsula of the extreme NW of Russia > 'Lap,lander *n*

La Plata (*Spanish* la 'plata) *n* **1** a port in E Argentina, near the Río de la Plata estuary: founded in 1882 and modelled on Washington DC; university (1897). Pop: 758 000 (2005 est) **2** See (Río de la) **Plata**

lap of honour *n* a ceremonial circuit of a racing track, etc, by the winner of a race

Lapp (læp) *n* **1** a member of a nomadic people living chiefly in N Scandinavia and the Kola Peninsula of Russia **2** the language of this people, belonging to the Finno-Ugric family ▷ *adj* **3** of or relating to this people or their language > 'Lappish *adj*, *n*

● USAGE The indigenous people of Lapland prefer to be called *Sami*, although *Lapp* is still in widespread use

lappet ('læpɪt) *n* **1** a small hanging flap or piece of lace, etc, such as one dangling from a headdress **2** *zoology* a lobelike hanging structure, such as the wattle on a bird's head [C16: from LAP¹ + -ET]

lapse (læps) *n* **1** a drop in standard of an isolated or temporary nature: *a lapse of justice* **2** a break in occurrence, usage, etc: *a lapse of five weeks between letters* **3** a gradual decline or a drop to a lower degree, condition, or state: *a lapse from high office* **4** a moral fall **5** *law* the termination of some right, interest, or privilege, as by neglecting to exercise it or through failure of some contingency **6** *insurance* the termination of coverage following a failure to pay the premiums ▷ *vb* (*intr*) **7** to drop in standard or fail to maintain a norm **8** to decline gradually or fall in status, condition, etc **9** to be discontinued, esp through negligence or other failure **10** (usually foll by *into*) to drift or slide (into a condition): *to lapse into sleep* **11** (often foll by *from*) to turn away (from beliefs or norms) **12** (of time) to slip away [C15: from Latin *lāpsus* error, from *lābī* to glide] > 'lapsable *or* 'lapsible *adj* > lapsed *adj* > 'lapser *n*

lapse rate *n* the rate of change of any meteorological factor with altitude, esp atmospheric temperature, which usually decreases at a rate of 0.6°C per 100 metres (**environmental lapse rate**). Unsaturated air loses about 1°C per 100 m (**dry adiabatic lapse rate**), whereas saturated air loses an average 0.5°C per 100 m (**saturated adiabatic lapse rate**)

Laptev Sea ('læptɪf) *n* a shallow arm of the Arctic Ocean, along the N coast of Russia between the Taimyr Peninsula and the New Siberian Islands. Former name: Nordenskjöld Sea

laptop ('læp,tɒp) *or* **laptop computer** *n* a personal computer that is small and light enough to be operated on the user's lap. See **palmtop computer**

lap up *vb* (*tr, adverb*) **1** to eat or drink **2** to relish or delight in: *he laps up old horror films* **3** to believe or accept eagerly and uncritically: *he laps up tall stories*

lapwing ('læp,wɪŋ) *n* any of several plovers of the genus *Vanellus*, esp *V. vanellus*, typically having a crested head, wattles, and spurs. Also called: **green plover, peewit** [C17: altered form of Old English *hlēapewince* plover, from *hlēapan* to LEAP + *wincian* to jerk, WINK¹]

Lara ('lɑːrə) *n* **Brian Charles**. born 1970, Trinidadian cricketer: holder of records for highest individual score in first-class cricket and for highest Test innings score

larboard ('lɑːbəd) *n*, *adj nautical* a former word for **port²** [C14 *laddeborde* (changed to *larboard* by association with *starboard*), from *laden* to load + *borde* BOARD]

larceny ('lɑːsɪnɪ) *n*, *pl* -nies *law* (formerly) a technical word for **theft** [C15: from Old French *larcin*, from Latin *lātrōcinium* robbery, from *latrō* robber] > 'larcenist *or* 'larcener *n* > 'larcenous *adj*

larch (lɑːtʃ) *n* **1** any coniferous tree of the genus *Larix*, having deciduous needle-like leaves and egg-shaped cones: family *Pinaceae* **2** the wood of any of these trees [C16: from German *Lärche*, ultimately from Latin *larix*]

lard (lɑːd) *n* **1** the rendered fat from a pig, esp from the abdomen, used in cooking ▷ *vb* (*tr*) **2** to prepare (lean meat, poultry, etc) by inserting small strips of bacon or fat before cooking **3** to cover or smear (foods) with lard **4** to add extra material to (speech or writing); embellish [C15: via Old French from Latin *lāridum* bacon fat]

larder ('lɑːdə) n a room or cupboard, used as a store for food [c14: from Old French lardier, from LARD]

Lardner ('lɑːdnə) n Ring(old Wilmer). 1885–1933, US short-story writer and journalist, whose best-known works are collected in *How to Write Short Stories* (1924) and *The Love Nest* (1926)

lardon ('lɑːdᵊn) or **lardoon** (lɑːˈduːn) n a strip or cube of fat or bacon used in larding meat [c15: from Old French, from LARD]

lardy ('lɑːdɪ) adj **lardier, lardiest** fat; obese

lardy cake ('lɑːdɪ) n Brit a rich sweet cake made of bread dough, lard, sugar, and dried fruit

Laredo (ləˈreɪdəʊ) n a city in the US, in Texas, on the Mexican border: founded by the Spanish in 1755 on the Rio Grande. Pop: 197 488 (2003 est)

lares and penates ('lɛəriːz, 'lɑː-, -ˈpɛ, lɑː'neɪtiːz) pl n **1** Roman myth **a** household gods **b** statues of these gods kept in the home **2** the valued possessions of a household [Latin]

large (lɑːdʒ) adj **1** having a relatively great size, quantity, extent, etc; big **2** of wide or broad scope, capacity, or range; comprehensive **3** having or showing great breadth of understanding ▷ n **4** at large **a** (esp of a dangerous criminal or wild animal) free; not confined **b** roaming freely, as in a foreign country **c** as a whole; in general **d** in full detail; exhaustively **e** ambassador-at-large See **ambassador** (sense 4) [c12: (originally: generous): via Old French from Latin largus ample, abundant] > **largeness** n

large intestine n the part of the alimentary canal consisting of the caecum, colon, and rectum. It extracts moisture from food residues, which are later excreted as faeces

largely ('lɑːdʒlɪ) adv **1** principally; to a great extent **2** on a large scale or in a large manner

larger-than-life adj exceptionally striking or colourful

large-scale adj **1** wide-ranging or extensive **2** (of maps and models) constructed or drawn to a big scale

largesse or **largess** (lɑːˈdʒɛs) n **1** the generous bestowal of gifts, favours, or money **2** the things so bestowed **3** generosity of spirit or attitude [c13: from Old French, from LARGE]

largish ('lɑːdʒɪʃ) adj fairly large

largo ('lɑːgəʊ) music ▷ adj, adv **1** to be performed slowly and broadly ▷ n, pl **-gos** **2** a piece or passage to be performed in this way [c17: from Italian, from Latin largus LARGE]

Lariam ('lærɪæm) n trademark a brand of mefloquine, used in the treatment and prevention of malaria

lariat ('lærɪət) n US & Canadian **1** another word for **lasso** **2** a rope for tethering animals [c19: from Spanish la reata the LASSO]

Larisa or **Larissa** (ləˈrɪsə; Greek 'larisa) n a city in E Greece, in E Thessaly: fortified by Justinian; annexed to Greece in 1881. Pop: 130 000 (2005 est)

lark¹ (lɑːk) n **1** any brown songbird of the predominantly Old World family *Alaudidae*, esp the skylark: noted for their singing **2** short for **titlark** [Old English lāwerce, lǣwerce, of Germanic origin; related to German Lerche, Icelandic lǣvirki]

lark² (lɑːk) informal ▷ n **1** a carefree adventure or frolic **2** a harmless piece of mischief ▷ vb (intr) **3** (often foll by about) to have a good time by frolicking **4** to play a prank [c19: originally slang, perhaps related to LAIK] > **larkish** adj > **larky** adj

Larkin ('lɑːkɪn) n Philip. 1922–85, English poet: his verse collections include *The Less Deceived* (1955) and *The Whitsun Weddings* (1964)

larkspur ('lɑːkˌspɜː) n any of various ranunculaceous plants of the genus *Delphinium*, with spikes of blue, pink, or white irregular spurred flowers [c16: LARK¹ + SPUR]

larn (lɑːn) vb not standard **1** facetious to learn **2** (tr) to teach (someone) a lesson: *that'll larn you!* [c18: from a dialect form of LEARN]

Larne (lɒːn) n a district of NE Northern Ireland, in Co Antrim. Pop: 30 948 (2003 est). Area: 336 sq km (130 sq miles)

larney ('lɑːnɪ) adj South African (of clothes) smart [c20: probably from an Indian language]

La Rochefoucauld (French la rɔʃfuko) n **François** (frɑ̃swa), Duc de La Rochefoucauld. 1613–80, French writer. His best-known work is *Réflexions ou sentences et maximes morales* (1665), a collection of epigrammatic and cynical observations on human nature

La Rochelle (French la rɔʃɛl) n a port in W France, on the Bay of Biscay: a Huguenot stronghold until its submission through famine to Richelieu's forces after a long siege (1627–28). Pop: 76 584 (1999)

Larousse (French larus) n **Pierre Athanase** (pjɛr atanɑz). 1817–75, French grammarian, lexicographer, and encyclopedist. He edited and helped to compile the *Grand Dictionnaire universel du XIX siècle* (1866–76)

larrigan ('lærɪgən) n a knee-high oiled leather moccasin boot worn by trappers, etc [c19: of unknown origin]

larrikin ('lærɪkɪn) n Austral & NZ slang **1** a mischievous person **2** a hooligan [c19: from English dialect: a mischievous youth]

larrup ('lærəp) vb (tr) dialect to beat or flog [c19: of unknown origin]

Larry ('lærɪ) n happy as Larry or as happy as Larry Brit, Austral & NZ informal extremely happy [of uncertain origin]

larva ('lɑːvə) n, pl -vae (-viː) an immature free-living form of many animals that develops into a different adult form by metamorphosis [c18: (c17 in the original Latin sense: ghost): New Latin] > **larval** adj

Larwood ('lɑːwʊd) n **Harold**. 1904–95, English cricketer. An outstanding fast bowler, he played 21 times for England between 1926 and 1932

laryngeal (ˌlærɪnˈdʒiːəl, ləˈrɪndʒɪəl) or **laryngal** (ləˈrɪŋgᵊl) adj **1** of or relating to the larynx **2** phonetics articulated at the larynx; glottal [c18: from New Latin laryngeus of the LARYNX]

laryngitis (ˌlærɪnˈdʒaɪtɪs) n inflammation of the larynx > **laryngitic** (ˌlærɪnˈdʒɪtɪk) adj

laryngo- or before a vowel **laryng-** combining form indicating the larynx: laryngoscope

laryngoscope (ləˈrɪŋgəˌskəʊp) n a medical instrument for examining the larynx > **laryngoscopy** n

laryngotomy (ˌlærɪŋˈgɒtəmɪ) n, pl -mies surgical incision into the larynx

larynx ('lærɪŋks) n, pl larynges (ləˈrɪndʒiːz) or larynxes a cartilaginous and muscular hollow organ forming part of the air passage to the lungs: in higher vertebrates it contains the vocal cords [c16: from New Latin larynx, from Greek larunx]

lasagne or **lasagna** (ləˈzænjə, -ˈsæn-) n **1** a form of pasta consisting of wide flat sheets **2** any of several dishes made from layers of lasagne and meat, cheese, etc [from Italian lasagna, from Latin lasanum cooking pot]

La Salle¹ (lə ˈsæl) n a city in SE Canada, in Quebec: a S suburb of Montreal. Pop (with Émard): 100 327 (2006)

La Salle² (French la sal) n Sieur **Robert Cavelier de** (rɔbɛr kavəlje də). 1643–87, French explorer and fur trader in North America; founder of Louisiana (1682)

La Scala (la ˈskaːla) n the chief opera house in Italy, in Milan (opened 1776)

lascar ('læskə) n a sailor from the East Indies [c17: from Urdu lashkar soldier, from Persian: the army]

Lascaux (French lasko) n the site of a cave in SW France, in the Dordogne: contains Palaeolithic wall drawings and paintings

lascivious (ləˈsɪvɪəs) adj **1** lustful; lecherous **2** exciting sexual desire [c15: from Late Latin lascīviōsus, from Latin lascīvia wantonness, from lascīvus] > **las'civiously** adv > **las'civiousness** n

Lasdun ('læzdən) n Sir **Denys**. 1914–2001, British architect. He is best known for the University of East Anglia (1968) and the National Theatre in London (1976)

lase (leɪz) vb (intr) (of a substance, such as carbon dioxide or ruby) to be capable of acting as a laser

laser ('leɪzə) n **1** a source of high-intensity optical, infrared, or ultraviolet radiation produced as a result of stimulated emission maintained within a solid, liquid, or gaseous medium. The photons involved in the emission process all have the same energy and phase so that the laser beam is monochromatic and coherent, allowing it to be brought to a fine focus **2** any similar

source producing a beam of any electromagnetic radiation, such as infrared or microwave radiation [c20: from light amplification by stimulated emission of radiation]

laserdisc or esp US **laserdisk** ('leizə,dısk) n a disk similar in size to a long-playing record, on which data is stored in pits in a similar way to data storage on a compact disk, used esp for storing high-quality video

laser printer n a quiet high-quality computer printer that uses a laser beam shining on a photoconductive drum to produce characters, which are then transferred to paper

lash¹ (læʃ) n 1 a sharp cutting blow from a whip or other flexible object 2 the flexible end or ends of a whip 3 a cutting or hurtful blow to the feelings, as one caused by ridicule or scolding 4 a forceful beating or impact, as of wind, rain, or waves against something 5 See **eyelash** 6 have a lash Austral & NZ informal to make an attempt at or take part in (something) ▷ vb (tr) 7 to hit (a person or thing) sharply with a whip, rope, etc, esp as a punishment 8 (of rain, waves, etc) to beat forcefully against 9 to attack with words, ridicule, etc 10 to flick or wave sharply to and fro: the restless panther lashed his tail 11 to urge or drive with or as if with a whip: to lash the audience into a violent mood ▷ See also **lash out** [c14: perhaps imitative] ▷ 'lasher n

lash² (læʃ) vb (tr) to bind or secure with rope, string, etc [c15: from Old French lachier, ultimately from Latin laqueāre to ensnare, from laqueus noose]

-lashed adj having eyelashes as specified: long-lashed

lashing¹ ('læʃɪŋ) n 1 a whipping; flogging 2 a scolding 3 (plural; usually foll by of) Brit informal large amounts; lots

lashing² ('læʃɪŋ) n rope, cord, etc, used for binding or securing

Lashio ('læʃɪ,əʊ) n a town in NE central Myanmar: starting point of the Burma Road to Chongqing, China

Lashkar ('lʌʃkə) n a former city in N India, in Madhya Pradesh: capital of the former states of Gwalior and Madhya Bharat; now part of the city of Gwalior

lash out vb (intr, adverb) 1 to burst into or resort to verbal or physical attack 2 Brit informal to be extravagant, as in spending

lash-up ('læʃ,ʌp) n Also called: hook-up a temporary connection of equipment for experimental or emergency use

LASIK surgery ('leisik) n laser surgery to correct short sight [c20: from Laser-Assisted In Situ Keratomileusis]

Lasker ('læskə) n Emanuel. 1868–1941, German chess player: world champion (1894–1921)

Laski ('læskɪ) n Harold (Joseph). 1893–1950, English political scientist and socialist leader

Las Palmas (Spanish las 'palmas) n a port in the central Canary Islands, on NE Grand Canary: a major fuelling port on the main shipping route between Europe and South America. Pop: 377 600 (2003 est)

La Spezia (Italian la 'spettsia) n a port in NW Italy, in Liguria, on the **Gulf of Spezia**: the chief naval base in Italy. Pop: 91 391 (2001)

lass (læs) n 1 a girl or young woman 2 informal a familiar form of address for any female [c13: origin uncertain]

Lassa ('lɑːsə) n a variant spelling of **Lhasa**

Lassa fever n a serious viral disease of Central West Africa, characterized by high fever and muscular pains [named after Lassa, the village in Nigeria where it was first identified]

Lassalle (German la'sal) n Ferdinand ('fɛrdinant). 1825–64, German socialist and writer: a founder of the first German workers' political party (1863), which later became the Social Democratic Party

Lassen Peak ('læsᵊn) n a volcano in S California, in the S Cascade Range. An area of 416 sq km (161 sq miles) was established as **Lassen Volcanic National Park** in 1916. Height: 3187 m (10 457 ft)

lassi ('læsɪ) n a cold drink made with yoghurt or buttermilk and flavoured with sugar, salt, or a mild spice [from Hindi]

lassie ('læsɪ) n informal a little lass; girl

lassitude ('læsɪ,tjuːd) n physical or mental weariness

[c16: from Latin lassitūdō, from lassus tired]

lasso (læ'suː, 'læsəʊ) n, pl -sos or -soes 1 a long rope or thong with a running noose at one end, used (esp in America) for roping horses, cattle, etc; lariat ▷ vb -sos or -soes, -soing, -soed 2 (tr) to catch with or as if with a lasso [c19: from Spanish lazo, ultimately from Latin laqueus noose] ▷ las'soer n

Lassus ('læsəs) n Roland de. Italian name Orlando di Lasso. ?1532–94, Flemish composer, noted for his mastery in both sacred and secular music

last¹ (lɑːst) adj (often prenominal) 1 being, happening, or coming at the end or after all others: the last horse in the race 2 being or occurring just before the present; most recent: last Thursday 3 only remaining: one's last cigarette 4 most extreme; utmost 5 least suitable, appropriate, or likely: he was the last person I would have chosen 6 (esp relating to the end of a person's life or of the world) final or ultimate: last rites ▷ adv 7 after all others; or in the end: he came last 8 most recently: he was last seen in the mountains 9 (sentence modifier) as the last or latest item ▷ n 10 the last a a person or thing that is last b the final moment; end 11 one's last moments before death 12 the final appearance, mention, or occurrence: we've seen the last of him 13 at last in the end; finally 14 at long last finally, after difficulty, delay, or irritation [variant of Old English latest, lætest, superlative of LATE]

● USAGE Since last can mean either after all others or most ● recent, it is better to avoid using this word where ● ambiguity might arise as in her last novel. Final or latest ● should be used in such contexts to avoid ambiguity

last² (lɑːst) vb 1 (when intr, often foll by for) to remain in being (for a length of time); continue: his hatred lasted for several years 2 to be sufficient for the needs of (a person) for (a length of time): it will last us until Friday 3 (when intr, often foll by for) to remain fresh, uninjured, or unaltered (for a certain time or duration) ▷ See also **last out** [Old English lǣstan; related to Gothic laistjan to follow] ▷ 'laster n

last³ (lɑːst) n 1 the wooden or metal form on which a shoe or boot is fashioned or repaired ▷ vb 2 (tr) to fit (a shoe or boot) on a last [Old English lǣste, from lāst footprint; related to Old Norse leistr foot, Gothic laists] ▷ 'laster n

last-ditch n (modifier) made or done as a last desperate attempt or effort in the face of opposition

last-gasp n (modifier) done in desperation at the last minute: a last-gasp attempt to save the talks

lasting ('lɑːstɪŋ) adj permanent or enduring ▷ 'lastingly adv ▷ 'lastingness n

Last Judgment n the Last Judgment the occasion, after the resurrection of the dead at the end of the world, when, according to biblical tradition, God will decree the final destinies of all men according to the good and evil in their earthly lives. Also known as: Judgment Day

lastly ('lɑːstlɪ) adv 1 at the end or at the last point ▷ sentence connector 2 in the end; finally

last name n another term for surname (sense 1)

last out vb (adverb) 1 (intr) to be sufficient for one's needs: how long will our supplies last out? 2 (tr) to endure or survive: some old people don't last out the winter

last post n (in the British military services) 1 a bugle call that orders men to retire for sleep 2 a similar call sounded at military funerals

last rites pl n Christianity religious rites prescribed for those close to death

Last Supper n the Last Supper the meal eaten by Christ with his disciples on the night before his Crucifixion, during which he is believed to have instituted the Eucharist

Las Vegas (læs 'veigəs) n a city in SE Nevada: famous for luxury hotels and casinos. Pop: 517 017 (2003 est)

lat. abbreviation latitude

Lat. abbreviation Latin

latah ('lɑːtə) n a psychological condition, observed esp in Malaysian cultures, in which an individual, after experiencing a shock, becomes anxious and suggestible, often imitating the actions of another person [c19: from Malay]

Latakia or **Lattakia** (,lætə'kiːə) n the chief port of Syria, in the northwest: tobacco industry. Pop: 486 000 (2005 est)

latch (lætʃ) *n* **1** a fastening for a gate or door that consists of a bar that may be slid or lowered into a groove, hole, etc **2** a spring-loaded door lock that can be opened by a key from outside **3** Also called: **latch circuit** *electronics* a logic circuit that transfers the input states to the output states when signalled, the output thereafter remaining insensitive to changes in input status until signalled again ▷ *vb* **4** to fasten, fit, or be fitted with or as if with a latch [Old English *læccan* to seize, of Germanic origin; related to Greek *lazesthai*]

latchkey (ˈlætʃˌkiː) *n* **1** a key for an outside door or gate, esp one that lifts a latch **2** a supposed freedom from restrictions

latchkey child *n* a child who has to let himself or herself in at home on returning from school, as his or her parents are out at work

latch on *vb* (*intr, adverb; often foll by to*) *informal* **1** to attach oneself (to) **2** to understand

latchstring (ˈlætʃˌstrɪŋ) *n* a length of string fastened to a latch and passed through a hole in the door so that it can be opened from the other side

late (leɪt) *adj* **1** occurring or arriving after the correct or expected time: *the train was late* **2** (*prenominal*) occurring, scheduled for, or being at a relatively advanced time: *a late marriage* **3** (*prenominal*) towards or near the end: *the late evening* **4** at an advanced time in the evening or at night: *it was late* **5** (*prenominal*) occurring or being just previous to the present time: *his late remarks on industry* **6** (*prenominal*) having died, esp recently: *my late grandfather* **7** (*prenominal*) just preceding the present or existing person or thing; former: *the late manager of this firm* **8** of late recently; lately ▷ *adv* **9** after the correct or expected time: *he arrived late* **10** at a relatively advanced age: *she married late* **11** recently; lately: *as late as yesterday he was selling books* **12** late hours rising and going to bed later than is usual **13** late in the day **a** at a late or advanced stage **b** too late [Old English *læt*; related to Old Norse *latr*, Gothic *lats*] ▷ **ˈlateness** *n*

lateen (ləˈtiːn) *adj nautical* denoting a rig with a triangular sail (**lateen sail**) bent to a yard hoisted to the head of a low mast, used esp in the Mediterranean [c18: from French *voile latine* Latin sail]

Late Greek *n* the Greek language from about the 3rd to the 8th centuries AD

Late Latin *n* the form of written Latin used from the 3rd to the 7th centuries AD

lately (ˈleɪtlɪ) *adv* in recent times; of late

La Tène (læ ˈtɛn) *adj* of or relating to a Celtic culture in Europe from about the 5th to the 1st centuries BC, characterized by a distinctive type of curvilinear decoration [c20: from *La Tène*, a part of Lake Neuchâtel, Switzerland, where remains of this culture were first discovered]

latent (ˈleɪt³nt) *adj* **1** potential but not obvious or explicit **2** (of buds, spores, etc) dormant (esp of an infectious disease) not yet revealed or manifest **4** (of a virus) inactive in the host cell, its nucleic acid being integrated into, and replicated with, the host cell's DNA **5** *psychoanal* relating to that part of a dream expressive of repressed desires: *latent content*. See **manifest** (sense 2) [c17: from Latin *latent-*, from *latens* present participle of *latēre* to lie hidden] ▷ **ˈlatency** *n* ▷ **ˈlatently** *adv*

latent heat *n* (*no longer in technical usage*) the heat evolved or absorbed per unit mass (**specific latent heat**) or unit amount of substance (**molar latent heat**) when it changes phase without change of temperature

latent image *n photog* the invisible image produced by the action of light, etc, on silver halide crystals suspended in the emulsion of a photographic material. It becomes visible after development

later (ˈleɪtə) *adj, adv* **1** the comparative of **late** ▷ *adv* **2** afterwards; subsequently

lateral (ˈlætərəl) *adj* **1** of or relating to the side or sides: *a lateral blow* ▷ *n* **2** a lateral object, part, passage, or movement [c17: from Latin *laterālis*, from *latus* side] ▷ **ˈlaterally** *adv*

lateral thinking *n* a way of solving problems by

rejecting traditional methods and employing unorthodox and apparently illogical means

laterite (ˈlætəˌraɪt) *n* any of a group of deposits consisting of residual insoluble deposits of ferric and aluminium oxides: formed by weathering of rocks in tropical regions [c19: from Latin *later* brick, tile]

latest (ˈleɪtɪst) *adj, adv* **1** the superlative of **late** ▷ *adj* **2** most recent, modern, or new: *the latest fashions* ▷ *n* **3** at the latest no later than the time specified **4** the latest *informal* the most recent fashion or development

latex (ˈleɪtɛks) *n, pl* **latexes** or **latices** (ˈlætɪˌsiːz) **1** a whitish milky fluid containing protein, starch, alkaloids, etc, that is produced by many plants. Latex from the rubber tree is used in the manufacture of rubber **2** a suspension of synthetic rubber or plastic in water, used in the manufacture of synthetic rubber products, etc [c19: New Latin, from Latin: liquid, fluid]

lath (lɑːθ) *n, pl* **laths** (lɑːðz, lɑːθs) **1** one of several thin narrow strips of wood used to provide a supporting framework for plaster, tiles, etc **2** expanded sheet metal, wire mesh, etc, used to provide backing for plaster or rendering **3** any thin strip of wood ▷ *vb* **4** (*tr*) to attach laths to (a ceiling, roof, floor, etc) [Old English *lætt*; related to Dutch *lat*, Old High German *latta*]

lathe (leɪð) *n* **1** a machine for shaping, boring, facing, or cutting a screw thread in metal, wood, etc, in which the workpiece is turned about a horizontal axis against a fixed tool ▷ *vb* **2** (*tr*) to shape, bore, or cut a screw thread in or on (a workpiece) on a lathe [perhaps c15 *lath* a support, of Scandinavian origin; compare Old Danish *lad* lathe, Old English *hlæd* heap]

lather (ˈlɑːðə, ˈlæ-) *n* **1** foam or froth formed by the action of soap or a detergent in water **2** foam formed by other liquid, such as the sweat of a horse **3** *informal* a state of agitation or excitement ▷ *vb* **4** to cover or become coated with lather **5** (*intr*) to form a lather [Old English *lēathor* soap; related to Old Norse *lauthr* foam] ▷ **ˈlathery** *adj*

lathi (ˈlɑːtɪ) *n* a long heavy wooden stick used as a weapon in India, esp by the police [Hindi]

Latimer (ˈlætɪmə) *n* **Hugh.** ?1485–1555, English Protestant bishop: burnt at the stake for refusing to disavow his Protestant beliefs when Mary I assumed the throne

Latin (ˈlætɪn) *n* **1** the language of ancient Rome and the Roman Empire and the educated in medieval Europe, which achieved its classical form during the 1st century BC. Having originally been the language of Latium, belonging to the Italic branch of the Indo-European family, it later formed the basis of the Romance group **2** a member of any of those peoples whose languages are derived from Latin **3** an inhabitant of ancient Latium ▷ *adj* **4** of or relating to the Latin language, the ancient Latins, or Latium **5** characteristic of or relating to those peoples in Europe and Latin America whose languages are derived from Latin **6** of or relating to the Roman Catholic Church [Old English *latin* and *læden* Latin, language, from Latin *Latīnus* of Latium]

Latin-1 *n computing* another name for **ISO Latin-1**

Latina (Italian laˈtiːna) *n* a city in W central Italy, in Lazio: built as a planned town in 1932 on reclaimed land of the Pontine Marshes. Pop: 107 898 (2001)

Latin America *n* those areas of America whose official languages are Spanish and Portuguese, derived from Latin: South America, Central America, Mexico, and certain islands in the Caribbean ▷ **Latin American** *n, adj*

Latinate (ˈlætɪˌneɪt) *adj* (of writing, vocabulary, etc) imitative of or derived from Latin

Latinism (ˈlætɪˌnɪzəm) *n* a word, idiom, or phrase borrowed from Latin

Latinist (ˈlætɪnɪst) *n* a person who studies or is proficient in Latin

Latinize or **Latinise** (ˈlætɪˌnaɪz) *vb* (*tr*) **1** to translate into Latin or Latinisms **2** to cause to acquire Latin style or customs **3** to bring Roman Catholic influence to bear upon (the form of religious ceremonies, etc) ▷ **ˌLatiniˈzation** or **ˌLatiniˈsation** *n* ▷ **ˈLatinˌizer** or **ˈLatinˌiser** *n*

Latin Quarter *n* an area of Paris, on the S bank of the

River Seine: contains the city's main educational establishments; centre for students and artists

latish ('leɪtɪʃ) *adj* rather late

latitude ('lætɪˌtjuːd) *n* **1 a** an angular distance in degrees north or south of the equator (latitude 0°), equal to the angle subtended at the centre of the globe by the meridian between the equator and the point in question **b** (*often plural*) a region considered with regard to its distance from the equator **2** scope for freedom of action, thought, etc; freedom from restriction: *his parents gave him a great deal of latitude* [c14: from Latin *lātitūdō*, from *lātus* broad] > ˌlati'tudinal *adj* > ˌlati'tudinally *adv*

latitudinarian (ˌlætɪˌtjuːdɪ'nɛərɪən) *adj* **1** permitting or marked by freedom of attitude or behaviour, esp in religious matters ▷ *n* **2** a person with latitudinarian views [c17: from Latin *lātitūdō* breadth, LATITUDE, influenced in form by TRINITARIAN] > ˌlati,tudi'narianism *n*

Latium ('leɪʃɪəm) *n* an ancient territory in W central Italy, in modern Lazio, on the Tyrrhenian Sea: inhabited by the Latin people from the 10th century until dominated by Rome (4th century BC). Italian name: Lazio

Latona (lə'təʊnə) *n* the Roman name of Leto

Latour (*French* latur) *n* **Maurice Quentin de** (mɔris kɑ̃tɛ̃ də) 1704–88, French pastelist noted for the vivacity of his portraits

La Tour (*French* la tur) *n* **Georges de** (ʒɔrʒ də). ?1593–1652, French painter, esp of candlelit religious scenes

latria (lə'traɪə) *n RC Church, theol* the adoration that may be offered to God alone [c16: via Latin from Greek *latreia* worship]

latrine (lə'triːn) *n* a lavatory, as in a barracks, camp, etc [c17: from French, from Latin *lātrīna*, shortened form of *lavātrīna* bath, from *lavāre* to wash]

-latry *n combining form* indicating worship of or excessive veneration of: *idolatry; Mariolatry* [from Greek *-latria*, from *latreia* worship] > -latrous *adj combining form*

latte ('læteɪ, 'lɑːteɪ) *n* coffee made with hot milk [c20: from Italian (*caffè e*) *latte* (coffee and) milk]

latter ('lætə) *adj* (*prenominal*) **1 a** denoting the second or second mentioned of two: distinguished from *former* **b** (*as noun; functioning as sing or plural*): *the latter is not important* **2** near or nearer the end: *the latter part of a film* **3** more advanced in time or sequence; later

● USAGE *The latter should only be used to refer to the*
● *second of two items: many people choose to go by hovercraft*
● *rather than use the ferry, but I prefer the latter. The last of*
● *three or more items can be referred to as the last-named*

latter-day *adj* present-day; modern

Latter-day Saint *n* a more formal name for **Mormon**

latterly ('lætəlɪ) *adv* recently; lately

lattice ('lætɪs) *n* **1** Also called: latticework an open framework of strips of wood, metal, etc, arranged to form an ornamental pattern **2 a** a gate, screen, etc, formed of such a framework **b** (*as modifier*): *a lattice window* **3** something, such as a decorative or heraldic device, resembling such a framework **4** an array of objects or points in a periodic pattern in two or three dimensions, esp an array of atoms, ions, etc, in a crystal or an array of points indicating their positions in space ▷ *vb* **5** to make, adorn, or supply with a lattice or lattices [c14: from Old French *lattis*, from *latte* LATH] > 'latticed *adj*

Latvia ('lætvɪə) *n* a republic in NE Europe, on the Gulf of Riga and the Baltic Sea: ruled by Poland, Sweden, and Russia since the 13th century, Latvia was independent from 1919 until 1940 and was a Soviet republic (1940–91), gaining its independence after conflict with Soviet forces; it joined the EU in 2004. Latvia is mostly forested. Official language: Latvian. Religion: nonreligious, Christian. Currency: lats. Capital: Riga. Pop: 2 286 000 (2004 est). Area: 63 700 sq km (25 590 sq miles)

Latvian ('lætvɪən) *adj* **1** of or relating to Latvia, its people, or their language ▷ *n* **2** Also called: Lettish the official language of Latvia: closely related to Lithuanian and belonging to the Baltic branch of the Indo-European family **3** a native or inhabitant of Latvia

laud (lɔːd) *literary* ▷ *vb* **1** (*tr*) to praise or glorify ▷ *n* **2** praise or glorification [c14: vb from Latin *laudāre*; n from *laudēs*, pl of Latin *laus* praise]

Laud (lɔːd) *n* **William**. 1573–1645, English prelate; archbishop of Canterbury (1633–45). His persecution of Puritans and his High Church policies in England and Scotland were a cause of the Civil War; he was impeached by the Long Parliament (1640) and executed

Lauda (*German* 'lauda) *n* **Niki** ('nɪki). born 1949, Austrian motor-racing driver: world champion 1975, 1977, 1984

laudable ('lɔːdəbªl) *adj* deserving or worthy of praise; admirable; commendable > 'laudableness or ˌlauda'bility *n* > 'laudably *adv*

laudanum ('lɔːdªnəm) *n* **1** a tincture of opium **2** (*formerly*) any medicine of which opium was the main ingredient [c16: New Latin, name chosen by Paracelsus for a preparation probably containing opium, perhaps based on LABDANUM]

laudation (lɔː'deɪʃən) *n* a formal word for **praise**

laudatory ('lɔːdətərɪ, -trɪ) *or* **laudative** *adj* expressing or containing praise; eulogistic

Lauder ('lɔːdə) *n* **Sir Harry**. real name *Hugh MacLennan*. 1870–1950, Scottish ballad singer and music-hall comedian

lauds (lɔːdz) *n* (*functioning as singular or plural*) *chiefly RC Church* the traditional morning prayer of the Western Church, constituting with matins the first of the seven canonical hours [c14: see LAUD]

Laue (*German* 'lauə) *n* **Max Theodor Felix von** (maks 'teːodoːr 'feːlɪks fɔn). 1879–1960, German physicist. He pioneered the technique of measuring the wavelengths of X-rays by their diffraction by crystals and contributed to the theory of relativity: Nobel prize for physics 1914

laugh (lɑːf) *vb* **1** (*intr*) to express or manifest emotion, esp mirth or amusement, typically by expelling air from the lungs in short bursts to produce an inarticulate voiced noise, with the mouth open **2** (*intr*) (esp of certain mammals or birds) to make a noise resembling a laugh **3** (*tr*) to utter or express with laughter: *he laughed his derision at the play* **4** (*tr*) to bring or force (someone, esp oneself) into a certain condition by laughter: *he laughed himself sick* **5** (*intr*; foll by *at*) to make fun (of); jeer (at) **6** laugh up one's sleeve to laugh or have grounds for amusement, self-satisfaction, etc, secretly **7** laugh on the other side of one's face to show sudden disappointment or shame after appearing cheerful or confident ▷ *n* **8** the act or an instance of laughing **9** a manner of laughter **10** *informal* a person or thing that causes laughter: *that holiday was a laugh* **11** the last laugh the final success in an argument, situation, etc, after previous defeat ▷ See also **laugh off** [Old English *læhan, hliehhen*; related to Gothic *hlahjan*, Dutch *lachen*] > 'laugher *n* > 'laughing *n, adj* > 'laughingly *adv*

laughable ('lɑːfəbªl) *adj* **1** producing scorn; ludicrous: *he offered me a laughable sum for the picture* **2** arousing laughter > 'laughableness *n* > 'laughably *adv*

laughing gas *n* another name for **nitrous oxide**

laughing jackass *n* another name for **kookaburra** (sense 1)

laughing stock *n* an object of humiliating ridicule

laugh off *vb* (*tr, adverb*) to treat or dismiss lightly, esp with stoicism

laughter ('lɑːftə) *n* **1** the action of or noise produced by laughing **2** the experience or manifestation of mirth, amusement, scorn, or joy [Old English *hleahtor*; related to Old Norse *hlātr*]

laughter club *n* a group of people who meet regularly to take part in communal laughing for therapeutic effect

Laughton ('lɔːtªn) *n* **Charles**. 1899–1962, US actor, born in England: noted esp for his films of the 1930s, such as *The Private Life of Henry VIII* (1933), for which he won an Oscar, and *Mutiny on the Bounty* (1935)

Launceston ('lɔːnsəstən) *n* a city in Australia, the chief port of the island state of Tasmania on the Tamar River, 64 km (40 miles) from Bass Strait. Pop: 68 443 (2001)

launch¹ (lɔːntʃ) *vb* **1** to move (a vessel) into the water **2** to move (a newly built vessel) into the water for the first time **3** (*tr*) **a** to start off or set in motion: *to launch a scheme* **b** to put (a new product) on the market **4** (*tr*) to propel with force **5** to involve (oneself) totally and enthusiastically: *to launch oneself into work* **6** (*tr*) to set (a missile, spacecraft, etc) into motion **7** (*intr;* foll by *into*) to start talking or writing (about): *he launched into a story* **8** (*intr;* usually foll by *out*) to start (out) on a fresh course ▷ *n* **9** an act or instance of launching [C14: from Anglo-French *lancher,* from Late Latin *lanceāre* to use a lance, hence, to set in motion. See LANCE] > **'launcher** *n*

launch² (lɔːntʃ) *n* **1 a** a motor driven boat used chiefly as a transport boat **2** the largest of the boats of a man-of-war [C17: via Spanish *lancha* and Portuguese from Malay *lancharan* boat, from *lanchar* speed]

launch pad *or* **launching pad** *n* **1** a platform from which a spacecraft, rocket, etc, is launched **2** an effective starting point for a career, enterprise, or campaign

launch window *n* the limited period during which a spacecraft can be launched on a particular mission

launder ('lɔːndə) *vb* **1** to wash, sometimes starch, and often also iron (clothes, linen, etc) **2** (*intr*) to be capable of being laundered without shrinking, fading, etc **3** (*tr*) to process (something acquired illegally) to make it appear respectable, esp to process illegally acquired funds through a legitimate business or to send them to a foreign bank for subsequent transfer to a home bank [C14 (*n,* meaning: a person who washes linen): changed from *lavender* washerwoman, from Old French *lavandiere,* ultimately from Latin *lavāre* to wash] > **'launderer** *n*

Launderette (,lɔːndə'rɛt, lɔːn'drɛt) *n* trademark *Brit & NZ* a commercial establishment where clothes can be washed and dried, using coin-operated machines. Also called (US, Canadian and NZ): **Laundromat**

laundress ('lɔːndrɪs) *n* a woman who launders clothes, sheets, etc, for a living

laundry ('lɔːndrɪ) *n, pl* -dries **1** a place where clothes and linen are washed and ironed **2** the clothes or linen washed and ironed **3** the act of laundering [C16: changed from C14 *lavendry;* see LAUNDER]

laundry list *n US & Canadian* a list of items perceived as being long: *a laundry list of complaints*

laundryman ('lɔːndrɪmən) *n, pl* -men **1** a man who collects or delivers laundry **2** a man who works in a laundry

laundrywoman ('lɔːndrɪwʊmən) *n, pl* -women **1** a woman who collects or delivers laundry **2** a woman who works in a laundry

Laurasia (lɔː'reɪʃə) *n* one of the two ancient supercontinents produced by the first split of the even larger supercontinent Pangaea about 200 million years ago, comprising what are now North America, Greenland, Europe, and Asia (excluding India). See also **Gondwanaland** [C20: from New Latin *Laur(entia)* (referring to the ancient N American landmass, from *Laurentian* strata of the Canadian Shield) + (*Eur*)*asia*]

laureate ('lɔːrɪɪt) *adj* (*usually immediately postpositive*) **1** literary crowned with laurel leaves as a sign of honour ▷ *n* **2** short for **poet laureate 3** a person honoured with an award for art or science: *a Nobel laureate* **4** rare a person honoured with the laurel crown or wreath [C14: from Latin *laureātus,* from *laurea* LAUREL] > **'laureate,ship** *n*

laurel ('lɔːrəl) *n* **1** Also called: **bay, true laurel** any lauraceous tree of the genus *Laurus,* such as the bay tree (see **bay⁴**) and *L. canariensis,* of the Canary Islands and Azores **2** any lauraceous plant **3** spurge laurel a European thymelaeaceous evergreen shrub, *Daphne laureola,* with glossy leaves and small green flowers **4** (*plural*) a wreath of true laurel, worn on the head as an emblem of victory or honour in classical times **5** (*plural*) honour, distinction, or fame **6** look to one's laurels to be on guard against one's rivals **7** rest on one's laurels to be satisfied with distinction won by past achievements and cease to strive for further achievements ▷ *vb* -rels, -relling, -relled *or US* -rels, -reling, -reled **8** (*tr*) to crown with laurels [C13 *lorer,* from Old French *lorier* laurel tree, ultimately from Latin *laurus*]

Laurel and Hardy ('lɔːrəl, 'hɑːdɪ) *n* a team of US film comedians, **Stan Laurel,** 1890–1965, born in Britain, the thin one, and his partner, **Oliver Hardy,** 1892–1957, the

fat one

Lauren ('lɔːrən) *n* **Ralph.** born 1939, US fashion designer

Laurentian (lɔː'rɛnʃən) *adj* **1** Also called: **Lawrentian** of or resembling the style of D. H. Lawrence (1885–1930), the British novelist, poet, and short-story writer, or T. E. *Lawrence* "of Arabia" (1885–1935), the British soldier and writer **2** of, relating to, or situated near the St Lawrence River

Laurence ('lɒrəns) *n* Margaret, full name *Jean Margaret Laurence,* 1926–87, Canadian novelist and short story writer; her novels include *The Stone Angel* (1964)

Laurentian Mountains *pl n* a range of low mountains in E Canada, in Quebec between the St Lawrence River and Hudson Bay. Highest point: 1191 m (3905 ft). Also called: **Laurentides** ('lɔːrən,taɪdz)

Laurentian Shield *n* another name for the **Canadian Shield.** Also called: **Laurentian Plateau**

Laurier ('lɒrɪə) *n* Sir **Wilfrid.** 1841–1919, Canadian Liberal statesman; the first French-Canadian prime minister (1896–1911)

laurustinus (,lɔːrə'staɪnəs) *n* a Mediterranean caprifoliaceous shrub, *Viburnum tinus,* with glossy evergreen leaves and white or pink fragrant flowers [C17: from New Latin, from Latin *laurus* laurel]

Lausanne (ləʊ'zæn; *French* lozan) *n* a city in W Switzerland, capital of Vaud canton, on Lake Geneva; cultural and commercial centre; university (1537). Pop: 116 300 (2002 est)

Lautrec (*French* lo'trɛk) *n* See **Toulouse-Lautrec**

lav (læv) *n Brit informal* short for **lavatory**

lava ('lɑːvə) *n* **1** magma emanating from volcanoes and other vents **2** any extrusive igneous rock formed by the cooling and solidification of molten lava [C18: from Italian (Neapolitan dialect), from Latin *lavāre* to wash]

lavabo (lə'veɪbəʊ) *n, pl* -boes *or* -bos *chiefly RC Church* **1 a** the ritual washing of the celebrant's hands after the offertory at Mass **b** (*as modifier*): *lavabo basin; lavabo towel* **2** another name for **washbasin 3** a trough for washing in a convent or monastery [C19: from Latin: I shall wash, the opening of Psalm 26:6]

lavage ('lævɪdʒ, læ'vɑːʒ) *n med* the washing out of a hollow organ by flushing with water [C19: via French, from Latin *lavāre* to wash]

Laval¹ (lə'væl) *n* a city in SE Canada, in Quebec: a NW suburb of Montreal. Pop: 343 005 (2001)

Laval² (*French* laval) *n* **Pierre** (pjɛr). 1883–1945, French statesman. He was premier of France (1931–32; 1935–36) and premier of the Vichy government (1942–44). He was executed for collaboration with Germany

lavatorial (,lævə'tɔːrɪəl) *adj* characterized by excessive mention of lavatories and the excretory functions; vulgar or scatological: *lavatorial humour*

lavatory ('lævətərɪ, -trɪ) *n, pl* -ries Also called: **toilet, water closet, WC a** a sanitary installation for receiving and disposing of urine and faeces, consisting of a bowl fitted with a water-flushing device and connected to a drain **b** a room containing such an installation [C14: from Late Latin *lavātōrium,* from Latin *lavāre* to wash]

lavatory paper *n Brit* another name for **toilet paper**

lave (leɪv) *vb* an archaic word for **wash** [Old English *lafian,* perhaps from Latin *lavāre* to wash]

lavender ('lævəndə) *n* **1** any of various perennial shrubs or herbaceous plants of the genus *Lavandula,* esp *L. vera,* cultivated for its mauve or blue flowers and as the source of a fragrant oil (**oil of lavender**): family *Lamiaceae* (labiates) **2** the dried parts of *L. vera,* used to perfume clothes **3** a pale or light bluish-purple to a very pale violet colour **4** perfume scented with lavender [C13: *lavendre,* via French from Medieval Latin *lavendula,* of obscure origin]

laver ('leɪvə) *n Old Testament* a large basin of water used by the priests for ritual ablutions [C14: from Old French *laveoir,* from Late Latin *lavātōrium* washing place]

Laver ('leɪvə) *n* **Rod**(*ney*) (**George**). born 1938, Australian tennis player: Wimbledon champion 1961, 1962, 1968, 1969; US champion 1962, 1969

Lavigne (læ'viːn) *n* **Avril.** born 1984, Canadian rock singer and songwriter; her recordings include *Let Go* (2002), *Under My Skin* (2004) and *The Best Damn Thing* (2007)

lavish ('lævɪʃ) *adj* **1** prolific, abundant, or profuse **2** generous; unstinting; liberal **3** extravagant; prodigal; wasteful: *lavish expenditure* ▷ *vb* **4** (*tr*) to give, expend, or apply abundantly, generously, or in profusion [c15: adj use of *lavas* profusion, from Old French *lavasse* torrent, from Latin *lavāre* to wash] > 'lavisher *n* > 'lavishly *adv* > 'lavishness *n*

Lavoisier (*French* lavwazje) *n* **Antoine Laurent** (ɑ̃twan lɔrā). 1743–94, French chemist; one of the founders of modern chemistry. He disproved the phlogiston theory, named oxygen, and discovered its importance in respiration and combustion

law (lɔː) *n* **1 a** a rule or set of rules, enforceable by the courts, regulating the government of a state, the relationship between the organs of government and the subjects of the state, and the relationship or conduct of subjects towards each other **2 a** a rule or body of rules made by the legislature. See **statute law b** a rule or body of rules made by a municipal or other authority. See **bylaw 3 a** the condition and control enforced by such rules **b** (*in combination*): *lawcourt* **4** a rule of conduct: *a law of etiquette* **5** one of a set of rules governing a particular field of activity: *the laws of tennis* **6** the law **a** the legal or judicial system **b** the profession or practice of law **c** *informal* the police or a policeman **7** Also called: **law of nature** a generalization based on a recurring fact or event **8** the science or knowledge of law; jurisprudence **9** the principles originating and formerly applicable only in courts of common law. See **equity** (sense 3) **10** a general principle, formula, or rule describing a phenomenon in mathematics, science, philosophy, etc: *the laws of thermodynamics* **11** the Law Also called: **Law of Moses** *Judaism* the body of laws contained in the first five book of the Old Testament **12 go to law** to resort to legal proceedings on some matter **13 lay down the law** to speak in an authoritative or dogmatic manner Related adjectives: **judicial, juridical, legal** [Old English *lagu*, from Scandinavian; compare Icelandic *lög* (pl) things laid down, law]

Law (lɔː) *n* **1 Andrew Bonar** ('bɒnə). 1858–1923, British Conservative statesman, born in Canada; prime minister (1922–23) **2 Denis.** born 1940, Scottish footballer and television and radio commentator on the sport **3 John.** 1671–1729, Scottish financier. He founded the first bank in France (1716) and the Mississippi Scheme for the development of Louisiana (1717), which collapsed due to excessive speculation **4 Jude.** born 1972, British film actor, who starred in *The Talented Mr Ripley* (1999) and *Cold Mountain* (2003). **5 William.** 1686–1761, British Anglican divine, best known for *A Serious Call to a Holy and Devout Life* (1728)

law-abiding *adj* adhering more or less strictly to the laws: *a law-abiding citizen*

law agent *n* (in Scotland) a solicitor holding a certificate from the Law Society of Scotland and thereby entitled to appear for a client in any Sheriff Court

law-and-order *n* (*modifier*) favouring or advocating strong measures to suppress crime and violence: *a law-and-order candidate*

lawbreaker ('lɔːˌbreɪkə) *n* a person who breaks the law > 'law,breaking *n, adj*

law centre *n Brit* an office, usually staffed by professional volunteers, at which free legal advice and information are provided to the general public

Lawes (lɔːz) *n* **1 Henry.** 1596–1662, English composer, noted for his music for Milton's masque *Comus* (1634) and for his settings of some of Robert Herrick's poems **2** his brother, **William.** 1602–45, English composer, noted for his harmonically experimental instrumental music

lawful ('lɔːfʊl) *adj* allowed, recognized, or sanctioned by law; legal > 'lawfully *adv* > 'lawfulness *n*

lawgiver ('lɔːˌgɪvə) *n* **1** the giver of a code of laws **2** Also called: **lawmaker** a maker of laws > 'law,giving *n, adj*

lawks (lɔːks) *interj Brit* an expression of surprise or dismay [c18: variant of *Lord!*, probably influenced in form by ALACK]

lawless ('lɔːlɪs) *adj* **1** without law **2** disobedient to the law **3** contrary to or heedless of the law **4** uncontrolled; unbridled: *lawless rage* > 'lawlessly *adv* > 'lawlessness *n*

Law Lords *pl n* (in Britain) members of the House of Lords who sit as the highest court of appeal, although in theory the full House of Lords has this role

lawn[1] (lɔːn) *n* a flat and usually level area of mown and cultivated grass [c16: changed form of c14 *launde*, from Old French *lande*, of Celtic origin; compare Breton *lann* heath; related to LAND] > 'lawny *adj*

lawn[2] (lɔːn) *n* a fine linen or cotton fabric, used for clothing [c15: probably from *Laon*, a town in France where linen was made] > 'lawny *adj*

lawn mower *n* a hand-operated or power-operated machine with rotary blades for cutting grass on lawns

lawn tennis *n* **1** tennis played on a grass court **2** the formal name for **tennis**

law of averages *n* (popularly) the expectation that a possible event is bound to occur regularly with a frequency approximating to its probability, as in the (actually false) example

law of supply and demand *n* the theory that prices are determined by the interaction of supply and demand: an increase in supply will lower prices if not accompanied by increased demand, and an increase in demand will raise prices unless accompanied by increased supply

law of the jungle *n* a state of ruthless competition or self-interest

law of thermodynamics *n* any of three principles governing the relationships between different forms of energy. The **first law of thermodynamics** (law of conservation of energy) states that the change in the internal energy of a system is equal to the sum of the heat added to the system and the work done on it. The **second law of thermodynamics** states that heat cannot be transferred from a colder to a hotter body within a system without net changes occurring in other bodies within that system; in any irreversible process, entropy always increases. The **third law of thermodynamics** (Nernst heat theorem) states that it is impossible to reduce the temperature of a system to absolute zero in a finite number of steps

Lawrence ('lɒrəns) *n* **1 Saint.** died 258 AD, Roman martyr: according to tradition he was roasted to death on a gridiron. Feast day: Aug 10 **2 D**(avid) **H**(erbert). 1885–1930, British novelist, poet, and short-story writer. Many of his works deal with the destructiveness of modern industrial society, contrasted with the beauty of nature and instinct, esp the sexual impulse. His novels include *Sons and Lovers* (1913), *The Rainbow* (1915), *Women in Love* (1920), and *Lady Chatterley's Lover* (1928) **3 Ernest Orlando.** 1901–58, US physicist, who invented the cyclotron (1931): Nobel prize for physics 1939 **4 Gertrude.** 1898–1952, British actress, noted esp for her roles in comedies such as Noël Coward's *Private Lives* (1930) **5 Sir Thomas.** 1769–1830, British portrait painter **6 T**(homas) **E**(dward), known as *Lawrence of Arabia*. 1888–1935, British soldier and writer. He took a major part in the Arab revolt against the Turks (1916–18), proving himself an outstanding guerrilla leader. He described his experiences in *The Seven Pillars of Wisdom* (1926)

lawrencium (lɒˈrɛnsɪəm, lɔː-) *n* a transuranic element artificially produced from californium. Symbol: Lr; atomic no: 103; half-life of most stable isotope, ^{256}Lr: 35 seconds; valency: 3 [c20: named after Ernest Orlando Lawrence (1901–58), US physicist]

Lawrentian (lɔːˈrɛnʃən) *adj* relating to or characteristic of D(avid) H(erbert) Lawrence (1885-1930), the British novelist, poet, and short-story writer

Lawson ('lɔːsən) *n* **1 Henry Archibald.** 1867–1922, Australian poet and short-story writer, whose work is taken as being most representative of the Australian outback, esp in *While the Billy Boils* (1896) and *Joe Wilson and his Mates* (1901) **2 Nigel**, Baron. born 1932, British Conservative politician; Chancellor of the Exchequer (1983–89). **3** his daughter, **Nigella** (naɪˈdʒɛlə). born 1959, British journalist, broadcaster, and cookery writer

lawsuit ('lɔːˌsuːt, -ˌsjuːt) *n* a proceeding in a court of law brought by one party against another, esp a civil action

law term *n* **1** an expression or word used in law **2** any of various periods appointed for the sitting of law courts

lawyer ('lɔːjə, 'lɔɪə) *n* a member of the legal profession, esp a solicitor. See also **advocate, barrister, solicitor** [C14: from LAW¹]

lax (læks) *adj* **1** lacking firmness; not strict **2** lacking precision or definition **3** not taut **4** *phonetics* (of a speech sound) pronounced with little muscular effort and consequently having relatively imprecise accuracy of articulation and little temporal duration. In English the vowel *i* in *bit* is lax [C14 (originally used with reference to the bowels): from Latin *laxus* loose] > **'laxly** *adv* > **'laxity** *or* **'laxness** *n*

laxative ('læksətɪv) *n* **1** an agent stimulating evacuation of faeces ⊳ *adj* **2** stimulating evacuation of faeces [C14 (originally: relaxing): from Medieval Latin *laxātīvus*, from Latin *laxāre* to loosen]

Laxness ('laxsnɛs) *n* **Halldór (Kiljan)** (haldəʊr). 1902–98, Icelandic novelist, noted for his treatment of rural working life in Iceland. His works include *Salka Valka* (1932) and *Independent People* (1935). Nobel prize for literature 1955

lay¹ (leɪ) *vb* **lays, laying, laid** (leɪd) (*mainly tr*) **1** to put in a low or horizontal position; cause to lie: *to lay a cover on a bed* **2** to place, put, or be in a particular state or position: *he laid his finger on his lips* **3** (*intr*) *dialect or not standard* to be in a horizontal position; lie: *he often lays in bed all the morning* **4** (sometimes foll by *down*) to establish as a basis: *to lay a foundation for discussion* **5** to place or dispose in the proper position: *to lay a carpet* **6** to arrange (a table) for eating a meal **7** to prepare (a fire) for lighting by arranging fuel in the grate **8** (*also intr*) (of birds, esp the domestic hen) to produce (eggs) **9** to present or put forward: *he laid his case before the magistrate* **10** to impute or attribute: *all the blame was laid on him* **11** to arrange, devise, or prepare: *to lay a trap* **12** to place, set, or locate: *the scene is laid in London* **13** to make (a bet) with (someone): *I lay you five to one on Prince* **14** to cause to settle: *to lay the dust* **15** to allay; suppress: *to lay a rumour* **16** to bring down forcefully: *to lay a whip on someone's back* **17** *slang* to have sexual intercourse with **18** to press down or make smooth: *to lay the nap of cloth* **19** (*intr*) *nautical* to move or go, esp into a specified position or direction: *to lay close to the wind* **20** lay bare to reveal or explain: *he laid bare his plans* **21** lay hold of to seize or grasp **22** lay oneself open to make oneself vulnerable (to criticism, attack, etc) **23** lay open to reveal or disclose ⊳ *n* **24** the manner or position in which something is placed **25** *taboo, slang* **a** an act of sexual intercourse **b** a sexual partner ⊳ See also **lay aside, lay-by,** etc [Old English *lecgan*; related to Gothic *lagjan*, Old Norse *leggja*]

 ◉ USAGE In careful English, the verb *lay* is used with an
 ◉ object and *lie* without one: *the soldier laid down his arms;*
 ◉ *the Queen laid a wreath; the book was lying on the table; he was*
 ◉ *lying on the floor.* In informal English, *lay* is frequently
 ◉ used for *lie: the book was laying on the table.* All careful
 ◉ writers and speakers observe the distinction even in
 ◉ informal contexts

lay² (leɪ) *vb* the past tense of **lie²**

lay³ (leɪ) *adj* **1** of, involving, or belonging to people who are not clergy **2** nonprofessional or nonspecialist; amateur [C14: from Old French *lai*, from Late Latin *lāicus*, ultimately from Greek *laos* people]

lay⁴ (leɪ) *n* **1** a ballad or short narrative poem, esp one intended to be sung **2** a song or melody [C13: from Old French *lai*, perhaps of Germanic origin]

layabout ('leɪəˌbaʊt) *n* a lazy person; loafer

Layamon ('laɪəmən) *or* **Lawman** ('lɔːmən) *n* 12th-century English poet and priest; author of the *Brut*, a chronicle providing the earliest version of the Arthurian story in English

lay analyst *n* a person without medical qualifications who practises psychoanalysis

Layard (lɛəd) *n* Sir **Austen Henry.** 1817–94, English archaeologist, noted for his excavations at Nimrud and Nineveh

lay aside *vb* (*tr, adverb*) **1** to abandon or reject **2** to store or reserve for future use

lay brother *n* a man who has taken the vows of a religious order but is not ordained and not bound to divine office

lay-by *n* **1** *Brit* a place for drivers to stop at the side of a main road **2** *nautical* an anchorage in a narrow waterway, away from the channel **3** a small railway siding where rolling stock may be stored or parked **4** *Austral & NZ* a system of payment whereby a buyer pays a deposit on an article, which is reserved for him until he has paid the full price ⊳ *vb* **lay by** (*adverb*) **5** (*tr*) to set aside or save for future needs

lay days *pl n* **1** *commerce* the number of days permitted for the loading or unloading of a ship without payment of demurrage **2** *nautical* the time during which a ship is kept from sailing because of loading, bad weather, etc

lay down *vb* (*tr, adverb*) **1** to place on the ground, etc **2** to relinquish or discard: *to lay down one's life* **3** to formulate (a rule, principle, etc) **4** to build or begin to build: *the railway was laid down as far as Manchester* **5** to record (plans) on paper **6** to convert (land) into pasture **7** to store or stock: *to lay down wine* **8** *informal* to wager or bet **9** (*tr, adverb*) *informal* to record (tracks) in a studio

layer ('leɪə) *n* **1** a thickness of some homogeneous substance, such as a stratum or a coating on a surface **2** a laying hen **3** *horticulture* a shoot or branch rooted during layering ⊳ *vb* **4** to form or make a layer of (something) **5** to take root or cause to take root by layering [C14 *leyer, legger,* from LAY¹ + -ER¹]

layering ('leɪərɪŋ) *n* **1** *horticulture* a method of propagation that induces a shoot or branch to take root while it is still attached to the parent plant **2** *geology* the banded appearance of certain igneous and metamorphic rocks, each band being of a different mineral composition

layette (leɪˈɛt) *n* a complete set of articles, including clothing, bedclothes, and other accessories, for a newborn baby [C19: from French, from Old French, from *laie,* from Middle Dutch *laege* box]

lay figure *n* **1** an artist's jointed dummy, used in place of a live model, esp for studying effects of drapery **2** a person considered to be subservient or unimportant [C18: from obsolete *layman,* from Dutch *leeman,* literally: joint-man]

lay in *vb* (*tr, adverb*) to accumulate and store: *we must lay in food for the party*

lay into *vb* (*intr, preposition*) *informal* **1** to attack forcefully **2** to berate severely

layman ('leɪmən) *n, pl* -**men 1** a man who is not a member of the clergy **2** a person who does not have specialized or professional knowledge of a subject: *science for the layman*

lay off *vb* **1** (*tr, adverb*) to suspend (workers) from employment with the intention of re-employing them at a later date: *the firm had to lay off 100 men* **2** (*intr*) *informal* to leave (a person, thing, or activity) alone: *lay off me, will you!* **3** (*tr, adverb*) to mark off the boundaries of ⊳ *n* **lay-off 4** the act of suspending employees **5** a period of imposed unemployment

lay on *vb* (*tr, adverb*) **1** to provide or supply: *to lay on entertainment* **2** *Brit* to install: *to lay on electricity* **3** lay it on *informal* **a** to exaggerate, esp when flattering **b** to charge an exorbitant price **c** to punish or strike harshly

lay out *vb* (*tr, adverb*) **1** to arrange or spread out **2** to prepare (a corpse) for burial or cremation **3** to plan or contrive **4** *informal* to spend (money), esp lavishly **5** *informal* to knock unconscious ⊳ *n* **layout 6** the arrangement or plan of something, such as a building **7** the arrangement of written material, photographs, or other artwork on an advertisement or page in a book, newspaper, etc **8** a preliminary plan indicating this **9** a drawing showing the relative disposition of parts in a machine, etc **10** the act of laying out **11** something laid out

lay over *US & Canadian* ⊳ *vb* (*adverb*) **1** (*tr*) to postpone for future action **2** (*intr*) to make a temporary stop in a journey ⊳ *n* **layover 3** a break in a journey, esp in waiting for a connection

lay person *or* **layperson** *n, pl* **lay persons, lay people** *or* **laypersons, laypeople 1** a person who is not a member of the clergy **2** a person who does not have specialized or professional knowledge of a subject: *a lay person's guide to conveyancing*

lay reader n **1** Church of England a person licensed by a bishop to conduct religious services other than the Eucharist **2** RC Church a layman chosen from among the congregation to read the epistle at Mass and sometimes other prayers

lay up vb (tr, adverb) **1** to store or reserve for future use **2** (usually passive) informal to incapacitate or confine through illness

laywoman ('leɪwʊmən) n, pl **-women 1** a woman who is not a member of the clergy **2** a woman who does not have specialized or professional knowledge of a subject: a guide for the laywoman

lazar ('læzə) n an archaic word for leper [c14: via Old French and Medieval Latin, after LAZARUS]

lazaretto (,læzə'rɛtəʊ), **lazaret** or **lazarette** (,læzə'rɛt) n, pl **-rettos, -rets** or **-rettes 1** Also called: **glory hole** nautical a small locker at the stern of a boat or a storeroom between decks of a ship **2** Also called: **lazar house, pesthouse** (formerly) a hospital for persons with infectious diseases, esp leprosy [c16: Italian, from lazzaro LAZAR]

Lazarus ('læzərəs) n New Testament **1** the brother of Mary and Martha, whom Jesus restored to life (John 11–12) **2** the beggar who lay at the gate of the rich man Dives in Jesus' parable (Luke 16:19–31)

laze (leɪz) vb **1** (intr) to be indolent or lazy **2** (tr; often foll by away) to spend (time) in indolence ▷ n **3** the act or an instance of idling [c16: back formation from LAZY]

Lazio ('lattsjo) n **1** a region of W central Italy, on the Tyrrhenian Sea: includes the plain of the lower Tiber, the reclaimed Pontine Marshes, and Campagna. Capital: Rome. Pop: 5 145 805 (2003 est) **2** the Italian name for **Latium**

lazy ('leɪzɪ) adj **lazier, laziest 1** not inclined to work or exertion **2** conducive to or causing indolence **3** moving in a languid or sluggish manner: a lazy river [c16: origin uncertain] > 'lazily adv > 'laziness n

lazybones ('leɪzɪ,bəʊnz) n informal a lazy person

lazy Susan n a revolving tray, often divided into sections, for holding condiments, etc

lb abbreviation **1** cricket leg bye **2** Also called: **lb** pound (weight) [Latin: libra]

LBD abbreviation informal little black dress

LBJ abbreviation Lyndon Baines Johnson

LBO abbreviation leveraged buyout

lbw abbreviation cricket leg before wicket

lc abbreviation **1** left centre (of a stage, etc) **2** loco citato [Latin: in the place cited] **3** printing lower case

L/C, l/c or **lc** abbreviation letter of credit

LCD abbreviation liquid-crystal display

LCJ abbreviation Brit Lord Chief Justice

lcm or **LCM** abbreviation lowest common multiple

LCoS abbreviation liquid crystal on silicon: a technology used in television screens in which liquid crystals are applied to a silicon chip, allowing the production of high resolution images

L/Cpl abbreviation lance corporal

LD abbreviation lethal dosage: usually used with a subscript numeral showing what percentage of a test group of animals dies as a result of either being given a substance being tested on them or being exposed to ionizing radiation, esp in the median lethal dose: LD_{50}

LDL abbreviation low-density lipoprotein

L-dopa (ɛl'dəʊpə) n a substance occurring naturally in the body and used to treat Parkinson's disease. Formula: $C_9H_{11}NO_4$. Also called: **levodopa** [c20: from L-d(ihydr)o(xy)p(henyl)a(lanine)]

LDS abbreviation **1** Latter-day Saints **2** laus Deo semper [Latin: praise be to God for ever] **3** (in Britain) Licentiate in Dental Surgery

lea (li:) n **1** poetic a meadow or field **2** land that has been sown with grass seed [Old English lēah; related to German dialect loh thicket]

LEA abbreviation (in Britain) Local Education Authority

leach (li:tʃ) vb **1** to remove or be removed from a substance by a percolating liquid **2** to lose or cause to lose soluble substances by the action of a percolating liquid ▷ n **3** the act or process of leaching **4** a substance that is leached or the constituents removed by leaching

5 a porous vessel for leaching [c17: variant of obsolete letch to wet, perhaps from Old English leccan to water; related to LEAK] > 'leacher n

Leach (li:tʃ) n **Bernard (Howell)**. 1887–1979, British potter, born in Hong Kong

Leacock ('li:kɒk) n **Stephen Butler**. 1869–1944, Canadian humorist and economist: his comic works include Literary Lapses (1910) and Frenzied Fiction (1917)

lead¹ (li:d) vb **leads, leading, led** (lɛd) **1** to show the way to (an individual or a group) by going with or ahead: lead the party into the garden **2** to guide or be guided by holding, pulling, etc: he led the horse by its reins **3** (tr) to cause to act, feel, think, or behave in a certain way; induce; influence: he led me to believe that we would go **4** (when intr, foll by to) (of a road, route, etc) to serve as the means of reaching a place **5** (tr) to go ahead so as to indicate (esp in the phrase **lead the way**) **6** to guide, control, or direct: to lead an army **7** (tr) to direct the course of or conduct (water, a rope or wire, etc) along or as if along a channel **8** to initiate the action of (something); have the principal part in (something): to lead a discussion **9** to go at the head of or have the top position in (something): he leads his class in geography **10** (intr; foll by with) to have as the first or principal item: the newspaper led with the royal birth **11** music Brit to play first violin in (an orchestra) **12** to direct and guide (one's partner) in a dance **13** (tr) **a** to pass or spend: I lead a miserable life **b** to cause to pass a life of a particular kind: to lead a person a dog's life **14** (intr; foll by to) to tend (to) or result (in): this will only lead to misery **15** to initiate a round of cards by putting down (the first card) or to have the right to do this: she led a diamond **16** (intr) boxing to make an offensive blow, esp as one's habitual attacking punch ▷ n **17 a** the first, foremost, or most prominent place **b** (as modifier): lead singer **18** example, precedence, or leadership: the class followed the teacher's lead **19** an advance or advantage held over others: the runner had a lead of twenty yards **20** anything that guides or directs; indication; clue **21** another name for leash **22** the act or prerogative of playing the first card in a round of cards or the card so played **23** the principal role in a play, film, etc, or the person playing such a role **24 a** the principal news story in a newspaper: the scandal was the lead in the papers **b** (as modifier): lead story **25** music an important entry assigned to one part usually at the beginning of a movement or section **26** a wire, cable, or other conductor for making an electrical connection **27** boxing **a** one's habitual attacking punch **b** a blow made with this **28** a deposit of metal or ore; lode ▷ See also **lead off, lead on,** etc [Old English lǣdan; related to līthan to travel, Old High German līdan to go]

lead² (lɛd) n **1 a** a heavy toxic bluish-white metallic element that is highly malleable: occurs principally as galena and used in alloys, accumulators, cable sheaths, paints, and as a radiation shield. Symbol: Pb; atomic no: 82; atomic wt: 207.2; valency: 2 or 4; relative density: 11.35; melting pt: 327.502°C; boiling pt: 1750°C **2** a lead weight suspended on a line used to take soundings of the depth of water **3** lead weights or shot, as used in cartridges, fishing lines, etc **4** a thin grooved strip of lead for holding small panes of glass or pieces of stained glass **5** (plural) **a** thin sheets or strips of lead used as a roof covering **b** a flat or low-pitched roof covered with such sheets **6** printing a thin strip of type metal used for spacing between lines of hot-metal type **7 a** graphite or a mixture containing graphite, clay, etc, used for drawing **b** a thin stick of this material, esp the core of a pencil **8** (modifier) made of, consisting of, relating to, or containing lead ▷ vb (tr) **9** to fill or treat with lead **10** to surround, cover, or secure with lead or leads **11** printing to space (type) by use of leads [Old English; related to Dutch lood, German Lot]

lead acetate (lɛd) n a white crystalline toxic solid used in dyeing cotton and in making varnishes and enamels. Formula: $Pb(CH_3CO)_2$

Leadbelly ('lɛd,bɛlɪ) n real name Huddie Ledbetter. 1888–1949, US blues singer and guitarist

lead chromate (lɛd) n chem a yellow solid used as a pigment, as in chrome yellow. Formula: $PbCrO_4$

leaded ('lɛdɪd) *adj* (of windows) composed of small panes of glass held in place by thin grooved strips of lead: *leaded lights*

leaden ('lɛdᵊn) *adj* **1** heavy and inert **2** laboured or sluggish: *leaden steps* **3** gloomy, spiritless, or lifeless **4** made partly or wholly of lead **5** of a dull greyish colour: *a leaden sky* > **'leadenly** *adv* > **'leadenness** *n*

leader ('liːdə) *n* **1** a person who rules, guides, or inspires others; head **2** *music* **a** the principal first violinist of an orchestra, who plays solo parts, and acts as the conductor's deputy and spokesman for the orchestra. Also called (esp US and Canadian): **concertmaster b** US a conductor or director of an orchestra or chorus **3 a** the first man on a climbing rope **b** the leading horse or dog in a team **4** Also called: **leading article** *chiefly Brit* the leading editorial in a newspaper **5** *angling* another word for **trace²** (sense 2) **6** a strip of blank film or tape used to facilitate threading a projector, developing machine, etc, and to aid identification **7** (*plural*) *printing* rows of dots or hyphens used to guide the reader's eye across a page, as in a table of contents **8** *botany* any of the long slender shoots that grow from the stem or branch of a tree: usually removed during pruning **9** *Brit* a member of the Government having primary authority in initiating legislative business (esp in the phrases **Leader of the House of Commons** and **Leader of the House of Lords**) > **'leaderless** *adj*

leaderboard ('liːdəˌbɔːd) *n* a board displaying the names and current scores of the leading competitors, esp in a golf tournament

leadership ('liːdəʃɪp) *n* **1** the position or function of a leader **2** the period during which a person occupies the position of leader: *during her leadership very little was achieved* **3 a** the ability to lead **b** (*as modifier*): *leadership qualities* **4** the leaders as a group of a party, union, etc: *the union leadership is now very reactionary*

lead-free (ˌlɛd'friː) *adj* See **unleaded** (sense 1)

lead glass (lɛd) *n* glass that contains lead oxide as a flux

lead-in ('liːdˌɪn) *n* **1** an introduction to a subject **2** the connection between a radio transmitter, receiver, etc, and the aerial or transmission line

leading¹ ('liːdɪŋ) *adj* **1** guiding, directing, or influencing **2** (*prenominal*) principal or primary **3** in the first position

leading² ('lɛdɪŋ) *n* *printing* the spacing between lines of photocomposed or digitized type. Also called: **interlinear spacing**

leading aircraftman ('liːdɪŋ) *n* *Brit air force* the rank above aircraftman > **leading aircraftwoman** *fem n*

leading edge ('liːdɪŋ) *n* **1** the forward edge of a propeller blade, aerofoil, or wing. See **trailing edge 2** *electrical engineering* the part of a pulse signal that has an increasing amplitude **3 a** the leading position in any field **b** (*as modifier*): *leading-edge technology*

leading light ('liːdɪŋ) *n* an important or outstanding person, esp in an organization or cause

leading note ('liːdɪŋ) *n* *music* **1** another word for **subtonic 2** (esp in cadences) a note, usually the subtonic of a scale, that tends most naturally to resolve to the note lying one semitone above it

leading question ('liːdɪŋ) *n* a question phrased in a manner that tends to suggest the desired answer, such as *What do you think of the horrible effects of pollution?*

leading rating *n* a rank in the Royal Navy comparable but junior to that of a corporal in the army

leading reins *or US and Canadian* **leading strings** ('liːdɪŋ) *pl n* **1** straps or a harness and strap used to assist and control a child who is learning to walk **2** excessive guidance or restraint

lead monoxide (lɛd) *n* a poisonous insoluble oxide of lead existing in red and yellow forms: used in making glass, glazes, and cements, and as a pigment. Formula: PbO

lead off (liːd) *vb* (*adverb*) **1** to initiate the action of (something); begin ▷ *n* **lead-off 2** an initial move or action

lead on (liːd) *vb* (*tr, adverb*) to lure or entice, esp into trouble or wrongdoing

lead pencil (lɛd) *n* a pencil in which the writing material is a thin stick of a graphite compound

lead poisoning (lɛd) *n* **1** Also called: **plumbism, saturnism** acute or chronic poisoning by lead or its salts, characterized by abdominal pain, vomiting, convulsions, and coma **2** *US slang* death or injury resulting from being shot with bullets

lead screw (liːd) *n* a threaded rod that drives the tool carriage in a lathe when screw cutting, etc

lead tetraethyl (lɛd) *n* another name for **tetraethyl lead**

lead time (liːd) *n* **1** *manufacturing* the time between the design of a product and its production **2** *commerce* the time from the placing of an order to the delivery of the goods

lead up to (liːd) *vb* (*intr, adverb + preposition*) **1** to act as a preliminary or introduction to **2** to approach (a topic) gradually or cautiously

leaf (liːf) *n, pl* **leaves** (liːvz) **1** the main organ of photosynthesis and transpiration in higher plants, usually consisting of a flat green blade attached to the stem directly or by a stalk **2** foliage collectively **3** *in leaf* (of shrubs, trees, etc) having a full complement of foliage leaves **4** one of the sheets of paper in a book **5** a hinged, sliding, or detachable part, such as an extension to a table **6** metal in the form of a very thin flexible sheet: *gold leaf* **7** *take a leaf out of someone's book or take a leaf from someone's book* to imitate someone, esp in one particular course of action **8** *turn over a new leaf* to begin a new and improved course of behaviour ▷ *vb* **9** (when *intr*, usually foll by *through*) to turn (through pages, sheets, etc) cursorily **10** (*intr*) (of plants) to produce leaves [Old English; related to Gothic *laufs*, Icelandic *lauf*] > **'leafless** *adj* > **'leaf,like** *adj*

leafage ('liːfɪdʒ) *n* a less common word for **foliage**

leaflet ('liːflɪt) *n* **1** a printed and usually folded sheet of paper for distribution, usually free and containing advertising material or information about a political party, charity, etc **2** any of the subdivisions of a compound leaf such as a fern leaf **3** (*loosely*) any small leaf or leaflike part ▷ *vb* **4** to distribute printed leaflets (to)

leaf miner *n* **1** any of various insect larvae that bore into and feed on leaf tissue, esp the larva of dipterous flies of the genus *Philophylla* (family *Trypetidae*) and the caterpillar of moths of the family *Gracillariidae* **2** the adult insect of any of these larvae

leaf mould *n* **1** a nitrogen-rich material consisting of decayed leaves, etc, used as a fertilizer **2** any of various fungus diseases affecting the leaves of certain plants

leaf spring *n* **1** one of a number of metal strips bracketed together in length to form a compound spring **2** the compound spring so formed

leafstalk ('liːfˌstɔːk) *n* the stalk attaching a leaf to a stem or branch. Technical name: petiole

leafy ('liːfɪ) *adj* **leafier, leafiest 1** covered with or having leaves **2** resembling a leaf or leaves > **'leafiness** *n*

league¹ (liːg) *n* **1** an association or union of persons, nations, etc, formed to promote the interests of its members **2** an association of sporting clubs that organizes matches between member teams of a similar standard **3** a class, category, or level: *he is not in the same league* **4** *in league* working or planning together (with) **5** (*modifier*) of, involving, or belonging to a league: *a league game; a league table* ▷ *vb* **leagues, leaguing, leagued 6** to form or be formed into a league [c15: from Old French *ligue*, from Italian *liga*, ultimately from Latin *ligāre* to bind]

league² (liːg) *n* an obsolete unit of distance of varying length. It is commonly equal to 3 miles [C14 *leuge*, from Late Latin *leuga, leuca*, of Celtic origin]

league football *n* **1** Also called: **league** *chiefly Austral* rugby league football **2** *Austral* an Australian Rules competition conducted within a league rather than a football association

leaguer ('liːgə) *n* *chiefly US & Canadian* a member of a league

league table *n* *Brit* **1** a tabulated comparison of clubs or teams competing in a sporting league **2** a set of statistics used to compare the performance of a number of individuals, groups, or institutions

Leah ('lɪə) n Old Testament the first wife of Jacob and elder sister of Rachel, his second wife (Genesis 29)

leak (li:k) n **1 a** a crack, hole, etc, that allows the accidental escape or entrance of fluid, light, etc **b** such escaping or entering fluid, light, etc **2** spring a leak to develop a leak **3** something resembling this in effect: a leak in the defence system **4** the loss of current from an electrical conductor because of faulty insulation, etc **5** a disclosure, often intentional, of secret information **6** the act or an instance of leaking ▷ vb **7** to enter or escape or allow to enter or escape through a crack, hole, etc **8** (when intr, often foll by out) to disclose (secret information), often intentionally, or (of secret information) to be disclosed **9** (intr) a slang word for **urinate** [C15: from Scandinavian; compare Old Norse leka to drip] > 'leaker n

leakage ('li:kɪdʒ) n **1** the act or an instance of leaking **2** something that escapes or enters by a leak **3** physics an undesired flow of electric current, neutrons, etc

Leakey ('li:kɪ) n **1 Louis Seymour Bazett** ('bæzɪt). 1903-72, British anthropologist and archaeologist, settled in Kenya. He discovered fossil remains of manlike apes in E Africa **2** his son **Richard**. born 1944, Kenyan anthropologist, who discovered the remains of primitive man over 2 million years old in E Africa

leaky ('li:kɪ) adj leakier, leakiest leaking or tending to leak > 'leakiness n

leal (li:l) adj Scot loyal; faithful [C13: from Old French leial, from Latin lēgālis LEGAL; related to LOYAL] > 'leally adv > lealty ('li:əltɪ) n

Leamington Spa ('lemɪŋtən) n a town in central England, in central Warwickshire: saline springs. Pop: 61 595 (2001). Official name: Royal Leamington Spa

lean¹ (li:n) vb leans, leaning, leaned or leant **1** (foll by against, on, or upon) to rest or cause to rest against a support **2** to incline or cause to incline from a vertical position **3** (intr; foll by to or towards) to have or express a tendency or leaning ▷ n **4** the condition of inclining from a vertical position [Old English hleonian, hlinian; related to Old High German hlinēn, Latin clīnāre to INCLINE]

lean² (li:n) adj **1** (esp of a person or an animal) having no surplus flesh or bulk; not fat or plump **2** not bulky or full **3** (of meat) having little or no fat **4** not rich, abundant, or satisfying **5** (of a mixture of fuel and air) containing insufficient fuel and too much air ▷ n **6** the part of meat that contains little or no fat [Old English hlæne, of Germanic origin] > 'leanly adv > 'leanness n

Lean (li:n) n Sir **David**. 1908-91, English film director. His films include In Which We Serve (1942), Blithe Spirit (1945), Brief Encounter (1946), Great Expectations (1946), Oliver Twist (1948), The Bridge on the River Kwai (1957), Lawrence of Arabia (1962), Dr Zhivago (1965), and A Passage to India (1984)

lean-burn adj (esp of an internal-combustion engine) designed to use a lean mixture of fuel and air in order to reduce petrol consumption and exhaust emissions

Leander (lɪ'ændə) n (in Greek legend) a youth of Abydos, who drowned in the Hellespont in a storm on one of his nightly visits to Hero, his beloved. See also **Hero¹**

leaning ('li:nɪŋ) n a tendency or inclination

leant (lent) vb a past tense and past participle of **lean¹**

lean-to n, pl -tos **1** a roof that has a single slope with its upper edge adjoining a wall or building **2** a shed or outbuilding with such a roof

leap (li:p) vb leaps, leaping, leapt or leaped **1** (intr) to jump suddenly from one place to another **2** (intr; often foll by at) to move or react quickly **3** (tr) to jump over **4** to come into prominence rapidly: the thought leapt into his mind **5** (tr) to cause (an animal, esp a horse) to jump a barrier ▷ n **6** the act of jumping **7** a spot from which a leap was or may be made **8** an abrupt change or increase **9** a leap in the dark an action performed without knowledge of the consequences **10** by leaps and bounds with unexpectedly rapid progress [Old English hlēapan; related to Gothic hlaupan, German laufen] > 'leaper n

leapfrog ('li:p,frɒg) n **1** a children's game in which each player in turn leaps over the others' bent backs, leaning on them with the hands and spreading the legs wide ▷ vb -frogs, -frogging, -frogged **2 a** (intr) to play leapfrog **b** (tr) to leap in this way over (something) **3** to advance or cause to advance by jumps or stages

leap second n a second added to or removed from a scale for reckoning time on one particular occasion, to synchronize it with another scale

leapt (lept, li:pt) vb a past tense and past participle of **leap**

leap year n a calendar year of 366 days, February 29 (**leap day**) being the additional day, that occurs every four years (those whose number is divisible by four) except for century years whose number is not divisible by 400. It offsets the difference between the length of the solar year (365.2422 days) and the calendar year of 365 days

Lear (lɪə) n **Edward**. 1812-88, English humorist and painter, noted for his illustrated nonsense poems and limericks

learn (lɜ:n) vb learns, learning, learned (lɜ:nd) or learnt **1** (when tr, may take a clause as object) to gain knowledge of (something) or acquire skill in (some art or practice) **2** (tr) to commit to memory **3** (tr) to gain by experience, example, etc **4** (intr; often foll by of or about) to become informed; know **5** not standard to teach [Old English leornian; related to Old High German lirnen] > 'learnable adj > 'learner n

learned ('lɜ:nɪd) adj **1** having great knowledge or erudition **2** involving or characterized by scholarship **3** (prenominal) a title applied in referring to a member of the legal profession, esp to a barrister: my learned friend > 'learnedly adv > 'learnedness n

learning ('lɜ:nɪŋ) n **1** knowledge gained by study; instruction or scholarship **2** the act of gaining knowledge

learning curve n a graphical representation of progress in learning: I'm still only half way up the learning curve

learning support assistant n same as **classroom assistant**

learnt (lɜ:nt) vb a past tense and past participle of **learn**

lease (li:s) n **1** a contract by which property is conveyed to a person for a specified period, usually for rent **2** the instrument by which such property is conveyed **3** the period of time for which it is conveyed **4** a prospect of renewed health, happiness, etc: a new lease of life ▷ vb (tr) **5** to grant possession of (land, buildings, etc) by lease **6** to take a lease of (property); hold under a lease [C15: via Anglo-French from Old French lais (n), from laissier to let go, from Latin laxāre to loosen] > 'leasable adj > 'leaser n

leaseback ('li:s,bæk) n a property transaction in which the buyer leases the property to the seller

leasehold ('li:s,həʊld) n **1** land or property held under a lease **2** the tenure by which such property is held **3** (modifier) held under a lease > 'lease,holder n

leash (li:ʃ) n **1** a line or rope used to walk or control a dog or other animal; lead **2** something resembling this in function: he kept a tight leash on his emotions **3** straining at the leash eagerly impatient to begin something ▷ vb **4** (tr) to control or secure by or as if by a leash [C13: from Old French laisse, from laissier to loose (hence, to let a dog run on a leash), ultimately from Latin laxus LAX]

least (li:st) determiner **1 a** the least the superlative of **little** you have the least talent of anyone **b** (as pronoun; functioning as sing): least isn't necessarily worst **2 a** if nothing else: you should at least try **b** at the least **3** at the least Also called: at least at the minimum: at the least you should earn a hundred pounds **4** in the least (usually used with a negative) in the slightest degree; at all: I don't mind in the least ▷ adv **5** the least superlative of **little** they travel the least of all ▷ adj **6** of very little importance or rank [Old English læst, superlative of læssa LESS]

least common denominator n another name for **lowest common denominator**

least common multiple n another name for **lowest common multiple**

least squares n a method for determining the best value of an unknown quantity relating one or more sets of observations or measurements, esp to find a curve that best fits a set of data. It states that the sum of the squares of the deviations of the experimentally determined value from its optimum value should be a minimum

leastways ('liːstˌweɪz) *or US & Canadian* **leastwise** *adv informal* at least; anyway; at any rate

least-worst *adj informal* bad but better than any available alternative

leather ('lɛðə) *n* **1 a** a material consisting of the skin of an animal made smooth and flexible by tanning, removing the hair, etc **b** (*as modifier*): *leather goods* **2** (*plural*) leather clothes, esp as worn by motorcyclists ▷ *vb* (*tr*) **3** to cover with leather **4** to whip with or as if with a leather strap [Old English *lether-* (in compound words); related to Old High German *leder*, Old Norse *lethr-*]

Leatherhead ('lɛðəˌhɛd) *n* a town in S England, in Surrey. Pop: 42 885 (2001)

leatherjacket ('lɛðəˌdʒækɪt) *n* **1** any of various tropical carangid fishes of the genera *Oligoplites* and *Scomberoides*, having a leathery skin **2** the greyish-brown tough-skinned larva of certain craneflies, esp of the genus *Tipula*, which destroy the roots of grasses, etc

leathern ('lɛðən) *adj archaic* made of or resembling leather

leatherneck ('lɛðəˌnɛk) *n slang* a member of the US Marine Corps [from the custom of facing the neckband of their uniform with leather]

leathery ('lɛðərɪ) *adj* having the appearance or texture of leather, esp in toughness ▷ **'leatheriness** *n*

leave¹ (liːv) *vb* **leaves, leaving, left** (*mainly tr*) **1** (*also intr*) to go or depart (from a person or place) **2** to cause to remain behind, often by mistake, in a place: *he often leaves his keys in his coat* **3** to cause to be or remain in a specified state: *paying the bill left him penniless* **4** to renounce or abandon: *to leave a political movement* **5** to refrain from consuming or doing something: *the things we have left undone* **6** to result in; cause: *childhood problems often leave emotional scars* **7** to entrust or commit: *leave the shopping to her* **8** to pass in a specified direction: *flying out of the country, we left the cliffs on our left* **9** to be survived by (members of one's family): *he leaves a wife and two children* **10** to bequeath or devise: *he left his investments to his children* **11** (*tr*) to have as a remainder: *37 − 14 leaves 23* **12** *not standard* to permit; let **13 leave someone alone a** Also called: **let alone** See **let¹** (sense 7) **b** to permit to stay or be alone ▷ See also **leave off, leave out** [Old English *lǣfan*; related to *belīfan* to be left as a remainder] ▷ **'leaver** *n*

leave² (liːv) *n* **1** permission to do something: *he was granted leave to speak* **2 by your leave** *or* **with your leave** with your permission **3** permission to be absent, as from a place of work or duty: *leave of absence* **4** the duration of such absence: *ten days' leave* **5** a farewell or departure (esp in the phrase **take (one's) leave**) **6** on leave officially excused from work or duty **7 take leave** to say farewell (to) [Old English *lēaf*; related to *alȳfan* to permit, Middle High German *loube* permission]

leave³ (liːv) *vb* **leaves, leaving, leaved** (*intr*) to produce or grow leaves

leaved (liːvd) *adj* **a** having a leaf or leaves; leafed **b** (in combination): *a five-leaved stem*

leaven ('lɛvᵊn) *n* Also: **leavening 1** any substance that produces fermentation in dough or batter, such as yeast, and causes it to rise **2** a piece of such a substance kept to ferment a new batch of dough **3** an agency or influence that produces a gradual change ▷ *vb* (*tr*) **4** to cause fermentation in (dough or batter) **5** to pervade, causing a gradual change, esp with some moderating or enlivening influence [c14: via Old French ultimately from Latin *levāmen* relief, (hence, raising agent, leaven), from *levāre* to raise]

Leavenworth ('lɛvᵊnˌwɜːθ, -wəθ) *n* a city in NE Kansas, on the Missouri River: the state's oldest city, founded in 1854 by proslavery settlers from Missouri. Pop: 35 211 (2003 est)

leave off *vb* **1** (*intr*) to stop; cease **2** (*tr, adverb*) to stop wearing or using

leave out *vb* (*tr, adverb*) **1** to cause to remain in the open **2** to omit or exclude

leaves (liːvz) *n* the plural of **leaf**

leave-taking *n* the act of departing; a farewell

leavings ('liːvɪŋz) *pl n* something remaining, such as food on a plate, residue, refuse, etc

Leavis ('liːvɪs) *n* **F(rank) R(aymond).** 1895–1978, English literary critic. He edited *Scrutiny* (1932–53) and his books include *The Great Tradition* (1948) and *The Common Pursuit* (1952) ▷ **'Leavisˌite** *adj, n*

Lebanon ('lɛbənən) *n* **the Lebanon** a republic in W Asia, on the Mediterranean: an important centre of the Phoenician civilization in the third millennium BC; part of the Ottoman Empire from 1516 until 1919; gained independence in 1941 (effective by 1945). Official language: Arabic; French and English are also widely spoken. Religion: Muslim and Christian. Currency: Lebanese pound. Capital: Beirut. Pop: 3 708 000 (2004 est). Area: 10 400 sq km (4015 sq miles) ▷ **Lebanese** (ˌlɛbə'niːz) *adj, n*

Lebanon Mountains *pl n* a mountain range in central Lebanon, extending across the whole country parallel with the Mediterranean coast. Highest peak: 3104 m (10 184 ft)

Lebensraum ('leɪbənzˌraʊm) *n* territory claimed by a nation or state on the grounds that it is necessary for survival or growth [German, literally: living space]

Leblanc (*French* ləblɑ̃) *n* **Nicolas** (nikɔla). ?1742–1806, French chemist, who invented a process for the manufacture of soda from common salt

Lebrun (*French* ləbrœ̃) *n* **1 Albert** (albɛr). 1871–1950, French statesman; president (1932–40) **2** Also called: **Le Brun Charles** (ʃarl). 1619–90, French historical painter. He was court painter to Louis XIV and executed much of the decoration of the palace of Versailles

LEC (lɛk) *n acronym for* Local Enterprise Company. See **Training Agency**

Le Carré (lə 'kæreɪ) *n* **John,** real name *David John Cornwell.* born 1931, English novelist, esp of spy thrillers such as *The Spy who came in from the Cold* (1963), *Tinker, Tailor, Soldier, Spy* (1974), *Smiley's People* (1980), *The Tailor of Panama* (1996), and *The Mission Song* (2006)

Lecce (*Italian* 'lettʃe) *n* a walled city in SE Italy, in Puglia: Greek and Roman remains. Pop: 83 303 (2001)

lech *or* **letch** (lɛtʃ) *informal* ▷ *vb* **1** (*intr; usually foll by after*) to behave lecherously (towards); lust (after) ▷ *n* **2** a lecherous act or indulgence [c19: back formation from LECHER]

Lech (lɛk; *German* lɛç) *n* a river in central Europe, rising in SW Austria and flowing generally north through S Germany to the River Danube. Length: 285 km (177 miles)

lecher ('lɛtʃə) *n* a promiscuous or lewd man [c12: from Old French *lecheor* lecher, from *lechier* to lick, of Germanic origin; compare Old High German *leccōn* to lick]

lecherous ('lɛtʃərəs) *adj* characterized by or inciting lechery ▷ **'lecherously** *adv*

lechery ('lɛtʃərɪ) *n, pl* **-eries** unrestrained and promiscuous sexuality

lecithin ('lɛsɪθɪn) *n biochem* any of a group of phospholipids that are found in many plant and animal tissues, esp egg yolk: used in making candles, cosmetics, and inks, and as an emulsifier and stabilizer in foods (E322). Systematic name: phosphatidylcholine [c19: from Greek *lekithos* egg yolk]

Lecky ('lɛkɪ) *n* **William Edward Hartpole** ('haːtˌpəʊl). 1838–1903, Irish historian; author of *The History of England in the 18th Century* (1878–90)

Leclanché cell (lə'klɑːnʃeɪ) *n electrical engineering* a primary cell with a carbon anode, surrounded by crushed carbon and manganese dioxide in a porous container, immersed in an electrolyte of aqueous ammonium chloride into which the zinc cathode dips. The common dry battery is a form of Leclanché cell [c19: named after Georges *Leclanché* (1839–82), French engineer]

Leconte de Lisle (*French* ləkɔ̃t də lil) *n* **Charles Marie René** (ʃarl mari rəne). 1818–94, French Parnassian poet

Le Corbusier (*French* lə kɔrbyzje) *n* real name *Charles Édouard Jeanneret.* 1887–1965, French architect and town planner, born in Switzerland. He is noted for his use of reinforced concrete and for his modular system, which used units of a standard size. His works include Unité d'Habitation at Marseilles (1946–52) and the city of Chandigarh, India (1954)

Le Creusot (French lə krøzo) n a town in E central France: metal, machinery, and armaments industries. Pop: 26 283 (1999)

lectern ('lɛktən) n **1** a reading desk or support in a church **2** any similar desk or support [c14: from Old French lettrun, from Late Latin lectrum, ultimately from legere to read]

lection ('lɛkʃən) n a variant reading of a passage in a particular copy or edition of a text [c16: from Latin lectio a reading, from legere to read, select]

lectionary ('lɛkʃənərɪ) n, pl -aries a book containing readings appointed to be read at divine services [c15: from Church Latin lectiōnārium, from lectio LECTION]

lector ('lɛktɔ:) n **1** a lecturer or reader in certain universities **2** RC Church **a** a person appointed to read lessons at certain services **b** (in convents or monastic establishments) a member of the community appointed to read aloud during meals [c15: from Latin, from legere to read]

lecture ('lɛktʃə) n **1** a discourse on a particular subject given or read to an audience **2** the text of such a discourse **3** a method of teaching by formal discourse **4** a lengthy reprimand or scolding ▷ vb **5** to give or read a lecture (to an audience or class) **6** (tr) to reprimand at length [c14: from Medieval Latin lectūra reading, from legere to read] > **'lecturer** n > **'lectureship** n

led (lɛd) vb the past tense and past participle of **lead**¹

LED abbreviation electronics light-emitting diode

Leda ('li:də) n Greek myth a queen of Sparta who was the mother of Helen and Pollux by Zeus, who visited her in the form of a swan

Lederberg ('lɛdə,bɜːg) n Joshua. born 1925, US geneticist, who discovered the phenomenon of transduction in bacteria. Nobel prize for physiology or medicine 1958 with George Beadle and Edward Tatum

lederhosen ('leɪdə,həʊzən) pl n leather shorts with H-shaped braces, worn by men in Austria, Bavaria, etc [German: leather trousers]

ledge (lɛdʒ) n **1** a narrow horizontal surface resembling a shelf and projecting from a wall, window, etc **2** a layer of rock that contains an ore; vein **3** a ridge of rock that lies beneath the surface of the sea **4** a narrow shelflike rock projection on a cliff or mountain [c14 legge, perhaps from leggen to LAY¹] > **'ledgy** or **ledged** adj

ledger ('lɛdʒə) n **1** book-keeping the principal book in which the commercial transactions of a company are recorded **2** angling a wire trace that allows the weight to rest on the bottom and the bait to float freely ▷ vb **3** (intr) angling to fish using a ledger [c15 legger book retained in a specific place, probably from leggen to LAY¹]

Ledger ('lɛdʒə) n **Heath**, full name Heathcliff Andrew Ledger. 1979–2008, Australian film actor. His films include The Patriot (2000), A Knight's Tale (2001) and Brokeback Mountain (2005)

ledger line n music a short line placed above or below the staff to accommodate notes representing pitches above or below the staff

Led Zeppelin ('lɛd 'zɛpəlɪn) n British rock group (1968–80); comprised Jimmy Page (born 1944), Robert Plant (born 1948), John Paul Jones (born 1946), and John Bonham (1948–80): recordings include Led Zeppelin I (1969), Led Zeppelin IV (1971), and Physical Graffiti (1975)

lee (li:) n **1** a sheltered part or side; the side away from the direction from which the wind is blowing ▷ adj **2** (prenominal) nautical on, at, or towards the side or part away from the wind: on a lee shore. See **weather** (sense 4) [Old English hlēow shelter; related to Old Norse hle]

Lee¹ (li:) n a river in SW Republic of Ireland, flowing east into Cork Harbour. Length: about 80 km (50 miles)

Lee² (li:) n **1** Ang (æŋ). born 1954, Taiwanese film director; his films include Sense and Sensibility (1995), Crouching Tiger, Hidden Dragon (2000), and Brokeback Mountain (2005) **2** Bruce, original name Lee Yuen Kam. 1940–73, US film actor and kung fu expert who starred in such films as Enter the Dragon (1973) **3** Gypsy Rose, original name Rose Louise Hovick. 1914–70, US striptease and burlesque artiste, who appeared in the Ziegfeld

Follies (1936) and in films **4** Laurie ('lɒrɪ). 1914–97, British poet and writer, best known for the autobiographical Cider with Rosie (1959) **5** Richard Henry. 1732–94, American Revolutionary statesman, who moved the resolution in favour of American independence (1776) **6** Robert E(dward). 1807–70, American general; commander-in-chief of the Confederate armies in the Civil War **7** Spike, real name Shelton Jackson Lee. born 1957, US film director: his films include She's Gotta Have It (1985), Malcolm X (1992), and 25th Hour (2002) **8** T(sung)-D(ao) (tsu:ŋ daʊ). born 1926, US physicist, born in China. With Yang he disproved the principle that that parity is always conserved and shared the Nobel prize for physics in 1957

leech¹ (li:tʃ) n **1** any annelid worm of the class Hirudinea, which have a sucker at each end of the body and feed on the blood or tissues of other animals **2** a person who clings to or preys on another person **3 a** an archaic word for **physician b** (in combination): leechcraft ▷ vb **4** (tr) to use leeches to suck the blood of (a person), as a method of medical treatment [Old English lǣce, lœce; related to Middle Dutch lieke]

leech² or **leach** (li:tʃ) n nautical the after edge of a fore-and-aft sail or either of the vertical edges of a squaresail [c15: of Germanic origin; compare Dutch lijk]

Leeds¹ (li:dz) n **1** a city in N England, in Leeds unitary authority, West Yorkshire on the River Aire: linked with Liverpool and Goole by canals; a former centre of the clothing industry; two universities (1904, 1992). Pop: 443 247 (2001) **2** a unitary authority in N England, in West Yorkshire. Pop: 715 200 (2003 est). Area: 562 sq km (217 sq miles)

Leeds² (li:dz) n **1st Duke of**. See (1st Earl of) **Danby**

leek (li:k) n **1** Also called: scallion an alliaceous plant, Allium porrum, with a slender white bulb, cylindrical stem, and broad flat overlapping leaves: used in cooking **2** a leek, or a representation of one, as a national emblem of Wales [Old English lēac; related to Old Norse laukr, Old High German louh]

leer (lɪə) vb **1** (intr) to give an oblique, sneering, or suggestive look or grin ▷ n **2** such a look [c16: perhaps verbal use of obsolete leer cheek, from Old English hlēor] > **'leering** adj, n > **'leeringly** adv

leery or **leary** ('lɪərɪ) adj leerier, leeriest or learier, leariest **1** now chiefly dialect knowing or sly **2** slang (foll by of) suspicious or wary [c18: perhaps from obsolete sense (to look askance) of LEER] > **'leeriness** or **'leariness** n

lees (li:z) pl n the sediment from an alcoholic drink [c14: plural of obsolete lee, from Old French, probably from Celtic; compare Irish lige bed]

leet (li:t) n Scot a list of candidates for an office [c15: perhaps from Anglo-French litte, variant of LIST¹]

Leeuwarden (Dutch 'le:wardə) n a city in the N Netherlands, capital of Friesland province. Pop: 91 000 (2003 est)

Leeuwenhoek ('leɪvˀn,hu:k; Dutch 'le:wənhu:k) n Anton van ('antɔn van). 1632–1723, Dutch microscopist, whose microscopes enabled him to give the first accurate description of blood corpuscles, spermatozoa, and microbes

leeward ('li:wəd; Nautical 'lu:əd) chiefly nautical ▷ adj **1** of, in, or moving to the quarter towards which the wind blows ▷ n **2** the point or quarter towards which the wind blows **3** the side towards the lee ▷ adv **4** towards the lee ▷ See **windward**

Leeward Islands ('li:wəd) pl n **1** a group of islands in the Caribbean, in the N Lesser Antilles between Puerto Rico and Martinique **2** a former British colony in the E Caribbean (1871–1956), consisting of Antigua, Barbuda, Redonda, Saint Kitts, Nevis, Anguilla, Montserrat, and the British Virgin Islands **3** a group of islands in the S Pacific, in French Polynesia in the W Society Archipelago: Huahiné, Raiatéa, Tahaa, Bora-Bora, and Maupiti. Pop: 30 221 (2002). French name: Îles sous le Vent

lee wave n meteorol a stationary wave sometimes formed in an air stream on the leeward side of a hill or mountain range

leeway ('li:,weɪ) n **1** room for free movement within limits, as in action or expenditure **2** sideways drift of a boat or aircraft

Le Fanu ('lɛfənju:) n (**Joseph**) **Sheridan**. 1814–73, Irish writer, best known for his stories of mystery and the supernatural, esp *Uncle Silas* (1864) and the collection *In a Glass Darkly* (1872)

Lefkoşa (lɛf'kɔʃə) n the Turkish name for **Nicosia**

left¹ (lɛft) adj **1** (*usually prenominal*) of or designating the side of something or someone that faces west when the front is turned towards the north **2** (*usually prenominal*) worn on a left hand, foot, etc **3** (*sometimes capital*) of or relating to the political or intellectual left **4** (*sometimes capital*) radical or progressive, esp as compared to less radical or progressive groups, persons, etc ▷ adv **5** on or in the direction of the left ▷ n **6** a left side, direction, position, area, or part. Related adjs: **sinister, sinistral 7** (*often capital*) the supporters or advocates of varying degrees of social, political, or economic change, reform, or revolution designed to promote the greater freedom, power, welfare, or comfort of the common people **8** *boxing* **a** a blow with the left hand **b** the left hand [Old English *left* idle, weak, variant of *lyft-* (in *lyftādl* palsy, literally: left-disease); related to Middle Dutch *lucht* left]

left² (lɛft) vb the past tense and past participle of **leave¹**

Left Bank n a district of Paris, on the S bank of the River Seine; frequented by artists, students, etc

left brain n **a** the left hemisphere of the human brain, which is believed to control linear and analytical thinking, decision-making, and language **b** (*as modifier*): *a left-brain activity*

left-hand adj (*prenominal*) **1** of, relating to, located on, or moving towards the left **2** for use by the left hand; left-handed

left-handed adj **1** using the left hand with greater ease than the right **2** performed with the left hand **3** designed or adapted for use by the left hand **4** awkward or clumsy **5** ironically ambiguous: *a left-handed compliment* **6** turning from right to left; anticlockwise ▷ adv **7** with the left hand ▷ ˌleft-'handedly adv > ˌleft-'handedness n > ˌleft-'hander n

leftist ('lɛftɪst) adj **1** of, tending towards, or relating to the political left or its principles ▷ n **2** a person who supports or belongs to the political left > 'leftism n

left-luggage office n *Brit* a place at a railway station, airport, etc, where luggage may be left for a small charge with an attendant for safekeeping. US and Canadian name: checkroom

leftover ('lɛftˌəʊvə) n **1** (*often plural*) an unused portion or remnant, as of material or of cooked food ▷ adj **2** left as an unused portion or remnant

leftward ('lɛftwəd) adj **1** on or towards the left ▷ adv **2** a variant of **leftwards**

leftwards ('lɛftwədz) *or* **leftward** adv towards or on the left

left wing n **1** (*often capitals*) the leftist faction of an assembly, party, group, etc; the radical or progressive wing **2** *sport* **a** the left-hand side of the field of play from the point of view of either team facing its opponents' goal **b** a player positioned in this area in certain games ▷ adj **left-wing 3** of, belonging to, or relating to the political left wing > ˌleft-'winger n

lefty ('lɛftɪ) n, pl **lefties** *informal* **1** a left-winger **2** *chiefly US & Canadian* a left-handed person

leg (lɛg) n **1** either of the two lower limbs, including the bones and fleshy covering of the femur, tibia, fibula, and patella **2** this part of an animal, esp the thigh, used for food: *leg of lamb* **3** something similar to a leg in appearance or function, such as one of the four supporting members of a chair **4** a branch, limb, or part of a forked or jointed object **5** the part of a garment that covers the leg **6** a section or part of a journey or course **7** a single stage, lap, length, etc, in a relay race **8** either one of two races on which a cumulative bet has been placed **9** either the opposite or adjacent side of a right-angled triangle **10** one of a series of games, matches, or parts of games **11** *cricket* **a** the side of the field to the left of a right-handed batsman as he faces the bowler **b** (*as modifier*): *a leg slip; leg stump* **12** have legs *informal* to be successful or show the potential to succeed **13** not have a leg to stand on to have no reasonable or logical basis for an opinion or argument **14** on its last legs worn out; exhausted **15** pull someone's leg *informal* to tease, fool, or make fun of someone **16** shake a leg *informal* to hurry up: usually used in the imperative **17** stretch one's legs to stand up or walk around, esp after sitting for some time ▷ vb legs, legging, legged **18** leg it *informal* to walk, run, or hurry [C13: from Old Norse *leggr*, of obscure origin]

leg. *abbreviation* legato

legacy ('lɛgəsɪ) n, pl -cies **1** a gift by will, esp of money or personal property **2** something handed down or received from an ancestor or predecessor [C14 (meaning: office of a legate), C15 (meaning: bequest): from Medieval Latin *lēgātia* commission; see LEGATE]

legal ('li:gəl) adj **1** established by or founded upon law; lawful **2** of or relating to law **3** recognized, enforceable, or having a remedy at law rather than in equity **4** relating to or characteristic of the profession of law [C16: from Latin *lēgālis*, from *lēx* law] > 'legally adv

legal aid n a means-tested benefit in the form of financial assistance for persons to meet the cost of advice and representation in legal proceedings

legalese (ˌli:gə'li:z) n the conventional language in which legal documents, etc, are written

legalism ('li:gəˌlɪzəm) n strict adherence to the law, esp the stressing of the letter of the law rather than its spirit > 'legalist n, adj > ˌlega'listic adj

legality (lɪ'gælɪtɪ) n, pl -ties **1** the state or quality of being legal or lawful **2** adherence to legal principles

legalize *or* **legalise** ('li:gəˌlaɪz) vb (*tr*) to make lawful or legal > ˌlegali'zation *or* ˌlegali'sation n

legal tender n currency in specified denominations that a creditor must by law accept in redemption of a debt

Legaspi (lɛ'gæspɪ) n a port in the Philippines, on SE Luzon on the Gulf of Albay. Pop: 178 000 (2005 est)

legate ('lɛgɪt) n **1** a messenger, envoy, or delegate **2** *RC Church* an emissary to a foreign state representing the Pope [Old English, via Old French from Latin *lēgātus* deputy, from *lēgāre* to delegate; related to *lēx* law] > 'legateˌship n

legatee (ˌlɛgə'ti:) n a person to whom a legacy is bequeathed

legation (lɪ'geɪʃən) n **1** a diplomatic mission headed by a minister **2** the official residence and office of a diplomatic minister **3** the act of sending forth a diplomatic envoy **4** the mission or business of a diplomatic envoy **5** the rank or office of a legate [C15: from Latin *lēgātiō*, from *lēgātus* LEGATE]

legato (lɪ'gɑ:təʊ) *music* ▷ adj, adv **1** to be performed smoothly and connectedly ▷ n, pl -tos **2 a** a style of playing in which no perceptible gaps are left between notes **b** (*as modifier*): *a legato passage* [C19: from Italian, literally: bound]

leg before wicket n *cricket* a manner of dismissal on the grounds that a batsman has been struck on the leg by a bowled ball that otherwise would have hit the wicket. Abbreviation: lbw

leg break n *cricket* a bowled ball that spins from leg to off on pitching

legend ('lɛdʒənd) n **1** a popular story handed down from earlier times whose truth has not been ascertained **2** a group of such stories: *the Arthurian legend* **3** a modern story that has taken on the characteristics of a traditional legendary tale **4** a person whose fame or notoriety makes him a source of exaggerated or romanticized tales or exploits **5** an inscription or title, as on a coin or beneath a coat of arms **6** explanatory matter accompanying a table, map, chart, etc [C14 (in the sense: a saint's life or a collection of saints' lives): from Medieval Latin *legenda* passages to be read, from Latin *legere* to read]

legendary ('lɛdʒəndərɪ, -drɪ) adj **1** of or relating to legend **2** celebrated or described in a legend or legends **3** very famous or notorious

Legendre (*French* ləʒɑ̃drə) n **Adrien Marie** (adriɛ̃ mari). 1752–1833, French mathematician, noted for his work on the theory of numbers, the theory of elliptical functions, and the method of least squares

Léger (*French* leʒe) *n* **Fernand** (fɛrnɑ̃). 1881–1955, French cubist painter, influenced by industrial technology

legerdemain (ˌlɛdʒədəˈmeɪn) *n* **1** another name for **sleight of hand** **2** cunning deception or trickery [c15: from Old French: light of hand]

leger line (ˈlɛdʒə) *n* a variant spelling of **ledger line**

legged (ˈlɛɡɪd, lɛɡd) *adj* **a** having a leg or legs **b** (*in combination*): *three-legged; long-legged*

leggings (ˈlɛɡɪŋz) *pl n* **1** an extra outer covering for the lower legs **2** close-fitting trousers worn by women and children

leggy (ˈlɛɡɪ) *adj* **-gier, -giest 1** having unusually long legs **2** (of a woman) having long and shapely legs **3** (of a plant) having an unusually long and weak stem > **legginess** *n*

leghorn (ˈlɛɡˌhɔːn) *n* **1** a type of Italian wheat straw that is woven into hats **2** any hat made from this straw when plaited [c19: named after LEGHORN (Livorno)]

Leghorn *n* **1** (ˈlɛɡˌhɔːn) the English name for **Livorno 2** (lɛˈɡɔːn) a breed of domestic fowl laying white eggs

legible (ˈlɛdʒəbᵊl) *adj* (of handwriting, print, etc) able to be read or deciphered [c14: from Late Latin *legibilis*, from Latin *legere* to read] > ˌlegiˈbility *or* ˈlegibleness *n* > ˈlegibly *adv*

legion (ˈliːdʒən) *n* **1** a military unit of the ancient Roman army made up of infantry with supporting cavalry, numbering some three to six thousand men **2** any large military force: *the French Foreign Legion* **3** (*usually capital*) an association of ex-servicemen: *the British Legion* **4** (*often plural*) any very large number, esp of people ▷ *adj* **5** (*usually postpositive*) very large or numerous [c13: from Old French, from Latin *legio*, from *legere* to choose]

legionary (ˈliːdʒənərɪ) *adj* **1** of or relating to a legion ▷ *n*, *pl* **-aries 2** a soldier belonging to a legion

legionnaire (ˌliːdʒəˈnɛə) *n* (*often capital*) a member of certain military forces or associations, such as the French Foreign Legion or the British Legion

legionnaire's disease *or* **legionnaires' disease** *n* a serious, sometimes fatal, infection, caused by the bacterium *Legionella pneumophila*, which has symptoms similar to those of pneumonia: believed to be spread by inhalation of contaminated water vapour from showers and air-conditioning plants [c20: after the outbreak at a meeting of the American Legion at Philadelphia in 1976]

legislate (ˈlɛdʒɪsˌleɪt) *vb* **1** (*intr*) to make or pass laws **2** (*tr*) to bring into effect by legislation [c18: back formation from LEGISLATOR]

legislation (ˌlɛdʒɪsˈleɪʃən) *n* **1** the act or process of making laws; enactment **2** the laws so made

legislative (ˈlɛdʒɪslətɪv) *adj* **1** of or relating to legislation **2** having the power or function of legislating: *a legislative assembly* **3** of or relating to a legislature > ˈlegislatively *adv*

legislative assembly *n* (*often capitals*) **1** the bicameral legislature in 28 states of the US **2** the lower chamber of the bicameral state legislatures in several Commonwealth countries, such as Australia **3** the unicameral legislature in most Canadian provinces **4** any assembly with legislative powers

legislative council *n* (*often capitals*) **1** the upper chamber of certain bicameral legislatures, such as those of the Indian and Australian states **2** the unicameral legislature of certain colonies or dependent territories **3** (in the US) a committee composed of members of both chambers of a state legislature, that meets to discuss problems, construct a legislative programme, etc

legislator (ˈlɛdʒɪsˌleɪtə) *n* **1** a person concerned with the making or enactment of laws **2** a member of a legislature [c17: from Latin *lēgis lātor*, from *lēx* law + *lātor* from *lātus*, past participle of *ferre* to bring]

legislature (ˈlɛdʒɪslətʃə) *n* a body of persons vested with power to make, amend, and repeal laws

legit (lɪˈdʒɪt) *slang* ▷ *adj* **1** short for **legitimate** ▷ *n* **2** legitimate or professionally respectable drama

legitimate *adj* (lɪˈdʒɪtɪmɪt) **1** born in lawful wedlock; enjoying full filial rights **2** conforming to established standards of usage, behaviour, etc **3** based on correct or acceptable principles of reasoning **4** authorized, sanctioned by, or in accordance with law **5** of, relating

to, or ruling by hereditary right: *a legitimate monarch* **6** of or relating to a body of famous long-established plays as distinct from films, television, vaudeville, etc ▷ *vb* (lɪˈdʒɪtɪˌmeɪt) **7** (*tr*) to make, pronounce, or show to be legitimate [c15: from Medieval Latin *lēgitimātus* made legal, from *lēx* law] > leˈgitimacy *or* leˈgitimateness *n* > leˈgitimately *adv* > leˌgitiˈmation *n*

legitimist (lɪˈdʒɪtɪmɪst) *n* a monarchist who supports the rule of a legitimate dynasty or of its senior branch > leˈgitimism *n*

legitimize, legitimise (lɪˈdʒɪtɪˌmaɪz) *or* **legitimatize, legitimatise** (lɪˈdʒɪtɪməˌtaɪz) *vb* (*tr*) to make legitimate; legalize > leˌgitimiˈzation, leˌgitimiˈsation, leˌgitimatiˈzation *or* leˌgitimatiˈsation *n*

legless (ˈlɛɡlɪs) *adj* without legs

Legnica (*Polish* lɛɡˈnitsa) *n* an industrial town in SW Poland. Pop: 105 025 (2007 est). German name: **Liegnitz**

Lego (ˈlɛɡəʊ) *n trademark* a construction toy consisting of plastic bricks and other standardized components that fit together with studs [c20: from Danish *leg godt* play well]

leg-of-mutton *or* **leg-o'-mutton** *n* (*modifier*) (of a sail, sleeve, etc) tapering sharply or having a triangular profile

leg-pull *n Brit informal* a practical joke or mild deception

legroom (ˈlɛɡˌruːm) *n* room to move one's legs comfortably, as in a car

leg rope *n Austral & NZ* a rope used to secure an animal by its hind leg

leguaan (ˈlɛɡjʊən, ˈlɛɡʊˌɑːn) *n South African* a large amphibious monitor lizard of the genus *Varanus*, esp *V. niloticus* (the **water leguaan**), which can grow up to 2 or 3 m. Also called: iguana [c19: Dutch, from French *l'iguane* the iguana]

legume (ˈlɛɡjuːm, lɪˈɡjuːm) *n* **1** the long dry dehiscent fruit produced by leguminous plants; a pod **2** any table vegetable of the family *Fabaceae* (formerly *Leguminosae*), esp beans or peas **3** any leguminous plant [c17: from French *légume*, from Latin *legūmen* bean, from *legere* to pick (a crop)]

leguminous (lɪˈɡjuːmɪnəs) *adj* of, relating to, or belonging to the *Fabaceae* (formerly *Leguminosae*), a family of flowering plants having pods (or legumes) as fruits and root nodules enabling storage of nitrogen-rich material: includes peas, beans, clover, gorse, acacia, and carob [c17: from Latin *legūmen*; see LEGUME]

legwarmer (ˈlɛɡˌwɔːmə) *n* one of a pair of garments resembling stockings without feet, usually knitted and brightly coloured, often worn over jeans, tights, etc or during exercise

legwork (ˈlɛɡˌwɜːk) *n informal* work that involves travelling on foot or as if on foot

Lehár (ˈleɪhɑː, lɪˈhɑː) *n* **Franz** (frants). 1870–1948, Hungarian composer of operettas, esp *The Merry Widow* (1905)

Le Havre (lə ˈhɑːvrə; *French* lə avrə) *n* a port in N France, on the English Channel at the mouth of the River Seine: transatlantic trade; oil refining. Pop: 190 905 (1999)

Lehmann (ˈleɪmən) *n* **1 Lilli** (ˈlɪlɪ). 1848–1929, German soprano **2 Lotte** (ˈlɒtə). 1888–1976, US soprano, born in Germany **3 Rosamond** (Nina). 1903–90, British novelist. Her books include *Dusty Answer* (1927), *Invitation to the Waltz* (1932), and *The Echoing Grove* (1953)

Lehmbruck (*German* ˈleːmbrʊk) *n* **Wilhelm** (ˈvɪlhɛlm). 1881–1919, German sculptor and graphic artist

lei (leɪ) *n* (in Hawaii) a garland of flowers, worn around the neck [from Hawaiian]

Leibnitz *or* **Leibniz** (ˈlaɪbnɪts) *n* Baron **Gottfried Wilhelm von** (ˈɡɒtfriːt ˈvɪlhɛlm fɒn). 1646–1716, German rationalist philosopher and mathematician. He conceived of the universe as a hierarchy of independent units or monads, synchronized by pre-established harmony. His works include *Théodicée* (1710) and *Monadologia* (1714). He also devised a system of calculus, independently of Newton > Leibˈnitzian *adj*

Leibovitz (ˈlaɪbəvɪts) *n* **Annie**. born 1949, US photographer, known for her portraits of celebrities

Leicester[1] (ˈlɛstə) *n* **1** a city in central England, in Leicester unitary authority, on the River Soar:

administrative centre of Leicestershire: Roman remains and a ruined Norman castle; two universities (1957, 1992); light engineering, hosiery, and footwear industries. Pop: 283 900 (2003 est) **2** a unitary authority in central England, in Leicestershire. Pop: 330 574 (2001). Area: 73 sq km (28 sq miles) **3** short for **Leicestershire 4** a breed of sheep with long wool, originally from Leicestershire **5** a fairly mild dark orange whole-milk cheese, similar to Cheddar

Leicester² ('lɛstə) *n* **Earl of.** title of *Robert Dudley.* ?1532–88, English courtier; favourite of Elizabeth I. He led an unsuccessful expedition to the Netherlands (1585–87)

Leicestershire ('lɛstəʃɪə, -ʃə) *n* a county of central England: absorbed the small historical county of Rutland in 1974; Rutland and Leicester city became independent unitary authorities in 1997: largely agricultural. Administrative centre: Leicester. Pop (excluding Leicester city): 619 200 (2003 est). Area (excluding Leicester city): 2084 sq km (804 sq miles). Shortened form: Leicester Abbreviation: Leics

Leichhardt ('laɪkˌhɑːt; *German* 'laiçhart) *n* **Friedrich Wilhelm Ludwig** ('friːdrɪç 'vɪlhɛlm 'luːtvɪç). 1813–48, Australian explorer, born in Prussia. He disappeared during an attempt to cross Australia from East to West

Leics *abbreviation* Leicestershire

Leiden *or* **Leyden** ('laɪdªn; *Dutch* 'lɛidə) *n* a city in the W Netherlands, in South Holland province: residence of the Pilgrim Fathers for 11 years before they sailed for America in 1620; university (1575). Pop: 118 000 (2003 est)

Leif Ericson ('liːf 'ɛrɪksən) *n* See **Ericson**

Leigh¹ (liː) *n* a town in NW England, in Wigan unitary authority, Greater Manchester: engineering industries. Pop: 43 006 (2001)

Leigh² (liː) *n* **1 Mike.** born 1943, British dramatist and theatre, film, and television director, noted for his use of improvisation. His plays include *Abigail's Party* (1977), and his films include *High Hopes* (1988), *Secrets and Lies* (1996), and *Vera Drake* (2004) **2 Vivien**, real name Vivian Hartley. 1913–67, English stage and film actress. Her films include *Gone with the Wind* (1939) and *A Streetcar Named Desire* (1951), for both of which she won Oscars

Leigh Fermor ('fɜːmɔː) *n* See **Fermor**

Leighton ('leɪtən) *n* **Frederic**, 1st Baron Leighton of Stretton. 1830–96, British painter and sculptor of classical subjects: president of the Royal Academy (1878)

Leinster ('lɛnstə) *n* a province of E and SE Republic of Ireland: it consists of the counties of Carlow, Dublin, Kildare, Kilkenny, Laois, Longford, Louth, Meath, Offaly, Westmeath, Wexford, and Wicklow. Pop: 2 105 579 (2002). Area: 19 632 sq km (7580 sq miles)

Leipzig ('laɪpsɪg; *German* 'laiptsɪç) *n* a city in E central Germany, in Saxony: famous fairs, begun about 1170; publishing and music centre; university (1409); scene of a decisive defeat for Napoleon Bonaparte in 1813. Pop: 497 531 (2003 est)

Leiria (*Portuguese* lei'riə) *n* a city in central Portugal: site of the first printing press in Portugal (1466). Pop: 119 870 (2001)

leishmaniasis (ˌliːʃməˈnaɪəsɪs) *or* **leishmaniosis** (liːʃˌmeɪnɪˈəʊsɪs, -ˌmæn-) *n* any disease, such as kala-azar, caused by protozoa of the genus *Leishmania*

leister ('liːstə) *n* **1** a spear with three or more prongs for spearing fish, esp salmon ▷ *vb* **2** (*tr*) to spear (a fish) with a leister [c16: from Scandinavian; related to Old Norse *ljóstr*, from *ljósta* to stab]

leisure ('lɛʒə; *US* 'liːʒər) *n* **1 a** time or opportunity for ease, relaxation, etc **b** (*as modifier*): *leisure activities* **2** ease or leisureliness **3 at leisure a** having free time for ease, relaxation, etc **b** not occupied or engaged **c** without hurrying **4 at one's leisure** when one has free time [c14: from Old French *leisir*; ultimately from Latin *licēre* to be allowed] > **leisured** *adj*

leisure centre *n* a building designed to provide facilities for a range of leisure pursuits, such as a sports hall, café, and meeting rooms

leisurely ('lɛʒəlɪ) *adj* **1** unhurried; relaxed ▷ *adv* **2** without haste; in a relaxed way > **leisureliness** *n*

leisure sickness *n* a medical condition in which people who have been working become ill with symptoms such

as fatigue or muscular pains at a weekend or while on holiday

Leith (liːθ) *n* a port in SE Scotland, on the Firth of Forth: part of Edinburgh since 1920

leitmotif *or* **leitmotiv** ('laɪtməʊˌtiːf) *n* **1** *music* a recurring short melodic phrase or theme used, esp in Wagnerian music dramas, to suggest a character, thing, etc **2** an often repeated word, phrase, image, or theme in a literary work [c19: from German *leitmotiv* leading motif]

Leitrim ('liːtrɪm) *n* a county of N Republic of Ireland in Connacht province, on Donegal Bay: agricultural. County town: Carrick-on-Shannon. Pop: 25 799 (2002). Area: 1525 sq km (589 sq miles)

Leix (liːʃ) *n* another name for **Laois**

Leizhou Peninsula ('leɪˈdʒəʊ) *or* **Luichow Peninsula** *n* a peninsula of SE China, in SW Guangdong province, separated from Hainan Island by Hainan Strait

lek (lɛk) *n* a small area in which birds of certain species, notably the black grouse, gather for sexual display and courtship [c19: perhaps from dialect *lake* (vb) from Old English *lácan* to frolic, fight, or perhaps from Swedish *leka* to play]

lekgotla (lɛˈxʊtlə) *or* **kgotla** ('xʊtlə) *n* *South African* **1 a** meeting place for village assemblies, court cases, and meetings of village leaders **2** a conference or business meeting [from Sotho and Tswana *lekgotla* courtyard or court]

lekker ('lɛkə) *adj* *South African slang* **1** pleasing or enjoyable **2** tasty [c20: Afrikaans, from Dutch]

Lely ('liːlɪ) *n* Sir **Peter**. Dutch name *Pieter van der Faes*. 1618–80, Dutch portrait painter in England

LEM (lɛm) *n acronym for* lunar excursion module

Lemaître (*French* ləmɛtr) *n* Abbé **Georges** (**Édouard**) (ʒɔrʒ). 1894–1966, Belgian astronomer and priest, who first proposed the big-bang theory of the universe (1927)

Lemalu (ləˈmɑːluː) *n* **Jonathan** (**Fa'afetai**). born 1976, New Zealand singer of Samoan descent; a bass-baritone noted esp for his lieder recitals

Léman (lemã) *n* Lac Léman the French name for (Lake) Geneva

Le Mans (*French* lə mã) *n* a city in NW France: scene of the first experiments in motoring and flying; annual motor race. Pop: 146 105 (1999)

Lemberg ('lɛmbɛrk) *n* the German name for **Lvov**

lemma ('lɛmə) *n, pl* **-mas** *or* **-mata** (-mətə) **1** a subsidiary proposition, proved for use in the proof of another proposition **2** *linguistics* a word considered as its citation form together with all the inflected forms. For example, the lemma *go* consists of *go* together with *goes*, *going*, *went*, and *gone* **3** an argument or theme, esp when used as the subject or title of a composition [c16 (meaning: proposition), c17 (meaning: title, theme): via Latin from Greek: premise, from *lambanein* to take (for granted)]

lemming ('lɛmɪŋ) *n* **1** any of various volelike rodents of the genus *Lemmus* and related genera, of northern and arctic regions of Europe, Asia, and North America: family *Cricetidae*. The Scandinavian variety, *Lemmus lemmus*, migrates periodically when its population reaches a peak **2** a member of any large group following an unthinking course towards mass destruction [c17: from Norwegian; related to Latin *latrāre* to bark] > **lemming-like** *adj*

Lemnos ('lɛmnɒs) *n* a Greek island in the N Aegean Sea: famous for its medicinal earth (**Lemnian seal**). Chief town: Kastron. Pop: 18 104 (2001). Area: 477 sq km (184 sq miles). Modern Greek name: Límnos

lemon ('lɛmən) *n* **1** a small Asian evergreen tree, *Citrus limon*, widely cultivated in warm and tropical regions, having pale green glossy leaves and edible fruits. Related adjs: **citric, citrine 2 a** the yellow oval fruit of this tree, having juicy acidic flesh rich in vitamin C **b** (*as modifier*): *a lemon jelly* **3** Also called: **lemon yellow a** a greenish-yellow or strong yellow colour **b** (*as adjective*): *lemon wallpaper* **4** a distinctive tart flavour made from or in imitation of the lemon **5** *slang* a person or thing considered to be useless or defective [c14: from Medieval Latin *lemōn-*, from Arabic *laymūn*] > **lemonish** *adj* > **'lemon-ˌlike** *adj* > **'lemony** *adj*

lemonade (ˌlɛməˈneɪd) *n* a drink made from lemon juice, sugar, and water or from carbonated water, citric acid, etc

lemon balm *n* the full name of **balm** (sense 4)

lemon cheese *or* **lemon curd** *n* a soft paste made from lemons, sugar, eggs, and butter, used as a spread or filling

lemon grass *n* a perennial grass, *Cymbopogon citratus*, with a large flower spike: used in cooking and grown in tropical regions as the source of an aromatic oil (**lemon grass oil**)

lemon sole *n* a European flatfish, *Microstomus kitt*, with a variegated brown body: highly valued as a food fish: family *Pleuronectidae*

lemon squash *n Brit* a drink made from a sweetened lemon concentrate and water

Lemper (ˈlɛmpə) *n* **Ute** (ˈuːtɪ). born 1963, German singer and actress, noted esp for her performances of songs by Kurt Weill

lemur (ˈliːmə) *n* **1** any Madagascan prosimian primate of the family *Lemuridae*, such as *Lemur catta* (the **ring-tailed lemur**). They are typically arboreal, having foxy faces and long tails **2** any similar or closely related animal, such as a loris or indris [c18: New Latin, adapted from Latin *lemurēs* ghosts; so named by Linnaeus for its ghost-like face and nocturnal habits]

Lena (ˈliːnə; *Russian* ˈljɛnə) *n* a river in Russia, rising in S Siberia and flowing generally north through the Sakha Republic to the Laptev Sea by an extensive delta: the longest river in Russia. Length: 4271 km (2653 miles)

lend (lɛnd) *vb* **lends, lending, lent** (lɛnt) **1** (*tr*) to permit the use of (something) with the expectation of return of the same or an equivalent **2** to provide (money) temporarily, often at interest **3** (*intr*) to provide loans, esp as a profession **4** (*tr*) to impart or contribute (something, esp some abstract quality): *her presence lent beauty* **5** (*tr*) to provide, esp in order to assist or support: *he lent his skill to the company* **6** **lend an ear** to listen **7** **lend itself** to possess the right characteristics or qualities for: *the novel lends itself to serialization* **8** **lend oneself** to give support, cooperation, etc [c15 *lende* (originally the past tense), from Old English *lǣnan*, from *lǣn* LOAN¹; related to Icelandic *lāna*, Old High German *lēhanōn*] > **ˈlender** *n*

lending library *n* **1** the department of a public library providing books for use outside the building. Also called (esp US): circulating library **2** a small commercial library

Lendl (ˈlɛndəl) *n* **Ivan** (iːˈvæn, -ˈvɑːn). born 1960, Czech tennis player; US Open champion (1985–87)

lend-lease *n* (during World War II) the system organized by the US in 1941 by which equipment and services were provided for countries fighting Germany

Lenglen (*French* lɑ̃glɑ̃) *n* **Suzanne** (syzan). 1899–1938, French tennis player: Wimbledon champion (1919-25)

length (lɛŋkθ, lɛŋθ) *n* **1** the linear extent or measurement of something from end to end, usually being the longest dimension or, for something fixed, the longest horizontal dimension **2** the extent of something from beginning to end, measured in some more or less regular units or intervals: *the book was 600 pages in length* **3** a specified distance, esp between two positions or locations: *the length of a race* **4** a period of time, as between specified limits or moments **5** something of a specified, average, or known size or extent measured in one dimension, often used as a unit of measurement: *a length of cloth* **6** a piece or section of something narrow and long: *a length of tubing* **7** the quality, state, or fact of being long rather than short **8** (*usually plural*) the amount of trouble taken in pursuing or achieving something (esp in the phrase **to great lengths**) **9** (*often plural*) the extreme or limit of action (in phrases such as **to any length**(**s**), **to what length**(**s**) **would someone go**, etc) **10** *prosody, phonetics* the metrical quantity or temporal duration of a vowel or syllable **11** the distance from one end of a rectangular swimming bath to the other. See **width** (sense 4) **12** *prosody* the quality of a vowel, whether stressed or unstressed, that distinguishes it from another vowel of similar articulatory characteristics. Thus (i:) in English *beat* is of greater length than (ɪ) in English *bit* **13** **at length a** in

depth; fully **b** eventually **c** for a long time; interminably [Old English *lengthu*; related to Middle Dutch *lengede*, Old Norse *lengd*]

lengthen (ˈlɛŋkθən, ˈlɛŋθən) *vb* to make or become longer > **ˈlengthener** *n*

lengthways (ˈlɛŋkθ‚weɪz, ˈlɛŋθ-) *or* **lengthwise** *adv, adj* in, according to, or along the direction of length

lengthy (ˈlɛŋkθɪ, ˈlɛŋθɪ) *adj* **lengthier, lengthiest** of relatively great or tiresome extent or duration > **ˈlengthily** *adv* > **ˈlengthiness** *n*

lenient (ˈliːnɪənt) *adj* showing or characterized by mercy or tolerance [c17: from Latin *lēnīre* to soothe, from *lēnis* soft] > **ˈleniency** *or* **ˈlenience** *n* > **ˈleniently** *adv*

Lenin (ˈlɛnɪn) *n* Vladimir Ilyich (vlaˈdimir iljˈjitʃ), original surname *Ulyanov*. 1870–1924, Russian statesman and Marxist theoretician; first premier of the Soviet Union. He formed the Bolsheviks (1903) and led them in the October Revolution (1917), which established the Soviet Government. He adopted the New Economic Policy (1921) after the Civil War had led to the virtual collapse of the Russian economy, formed the Comintern (1919), and was the originator of the guiding doctrine of the Soviet Union, Marxism-Leninism. After the Soviet Union broke up in 1991, many statues of Lenin were demolished

Leninabad (*Russian* lɪninaˈbat) *n* the former name (1937–91) of **Khojent**

Leninakan (*Russian* lɪninaˈkan) *n* the former name (1925–91) of **Kumayri**

Leningrad (ˈlɛnɪn‚græd; *Russian* lɪninˈgrat) *n* the former name (1937–91) of **Saint Petersburg**

Leninism (ˈlɛnɪ‚nɪzəm) *n* the political and economic theories of Vladimir Ilyich Lenin (original surname *Ulyanov*; 1870–1924) the Russian statesman and Marxist theoretician > **ˈLeninist** *or* **ˈLeninite** *n, adj*

Lenin Peak *n* a mountain on the border of Kyrgyzstan and Tajikistan; the highest peak in the Trans Alai Range. Height: 7134 m (23 406 ft)

lenitive (ˈlɛnɪtɪv) *adj* **1** soothing or alleviating pain or distress ▷ *n* **2** *obsolete* a lenitive drug [c16: from Medieval Latin *lēnītīvus*, from Latin *lēnīre* to soothe]

lenity (ˈlɛnɪtɪ) *n, pl* **-ties** the state or quality of being lenient [c16: from Latin *lēnitās* gentleness, from *lēnis* soft]

Lennon (ˈlɛnən) *n* **John** (**Ono**), original name *John Winston Lennon*. 1940–80, English rock guitarist, singer, and songwriter: member of the Beatles (1962–70). His subsequent recordings, many in collaboration with his wife Yoko Ono, include "Instant Karma" (1970), *Imagine* (1971), and *Double Fantasy* (1980). He was shot dead by a demented fan

leno (ˈliːnəʊ) *n, pl* **-nos 1** (in textiles) a weave in which the warp yarns are twisted together in pairs between the weft or filling yarns **2** a fabric of this weave [c19: probably from French *linon* lawn, from *lin* flax, from Latin *līnum*. See LINEN]

Leno (ˈliːnəʊ) *n* **Dan**, original name *George Galvin*. 1860–1904, British music-hall entertainer, noted esp for his pantomime performances: he died insane

Le Nôtre (*French* lə notrə) *n* **André** (ɑ̃dre). 1613–1700, French landscape gardener, who created the gardens at Versailles for Louis XIV

lens (lɛnz) *n* **1** a piece of glass or other transparent material, used to converge or diverge transmitted light and form optical images **2** Also called: compound lens a combination of such lenses for forming images or concentrating a beam of light **3** a device that diverges or converges a beam of electromagnetic radiation, sound, or particles. See **electron lens 4** *anatomy* See **crystalline lens** [c17: from Latin *lēns* lentil, referring to the similarity of a lens to the shape of a lentil]

lent (lɛnt) *vb* the past tense and past participle of **lend**

Lent (lɛnt) *n Christianity* the period of forty weekdays lasting from Ash Wednesday to Holy Saturday, observed as a time of penance and fasting commemorating Jesus' fasting in the wilderness [Old English *lencten, lengten* spring, literally: lengthening (of hours of daylight)]

lentamente (ˌlɛntəˈmɛntɪ) *adv music* to be played slowly [c18: Italian, from LENTO]

lenten (ˈlɛntən) *adj* **1** (*often capital*) of or relating to Lent **2** *archaic or literary* spare, plain, or meagre: *lenten fare*

lenticel ('lɛntɪ,sɛl) *n* any of numerous pores in the stem of a woody plant allowing exchange of gases between the plant and the exterior [c19: from New Latin *lenticella*, from Latin *lenticula* diminutive of *lēns* LENTIL]

lenticular (lɛn'tɪkjʊlə) *adj* 1 Also called: **lentoid** ('lɛntɔɪd) shaped like a biconvex lens 2 of or concerned with a lens or lenses 3 shaped like a lentil seed [c17: from Latin *lenticulāris* like a LENTIL]

lentil ('lɛntɪl) *n* 1 a small annual leguminous plant, *Lens culinaris*, of the Mediterranean region and W Asia, having edible brownish convex seeds 2 any of the seeds of this plant, which are cooked and eaten as a vegetable, in soups, etc [c13: from Old French *lentille*, from Latin *lenticula*, diminutive of *lēns* lentil]

lentivirus ('lɛntɪ,vaɪrəs) *n* any of a group of slowly acting viruses that includes the human immunodeficiency virus (HIV), which causes AIDS [c20: from Latin *lentus* slow + VIRUS]

lent lily *n* another name for the **daffodil**

lento ('lɛntəʊ) *music* ▷ *adj, adv* 1 to be performed slowly ▷ *n, pl* **-tos** 2 a movement or passage performed in this way [c18: Italian, from Latin *lentus* slow]

Lent term *n* the spring term at Cambridge University and some other educational establishments

Lenya ('lɛnjə) *n* **Lotte** ('lɒtɪ), original name *Caroline Blamauer*. 1900–81, Austrian singer and actress, associated esp with the songs of her husband Kurt Weill

Leo ('liːəʊ) *n, Latin genitive* **Leonis** (liː'əʊnɪs) 1 *astronomy* a zodiacal constellation in the N hemisphere, lying between Cancer and Virgo on the ecliptic, that contains the star Regulus and the radiant of the Leonid meteor shower 2 *astrology* Also called: **the Lion** the fifth sign of the zodiac, symbol ♌, having a fixed fire classification and ruled by the sun. The sun is in this sign between about July 23 and Aug 22

Leo I ('liːəʊ) *n* **Saint,** known as *Leo the Great*. ?390–461 AD, pope (440–461). He extended the authority of the papacy in the West and persuaded Attila not to attack Rome (452). Feast day: Nov 10 or Feb 18

Leo III *n* 1 called *the Isaurian*. ?675–741 AD, Byzantine emperor (717–41): he checked Arab expansionism and began the policy of iconoclasm, which divided the empire for the next century 2 **Saint.** ?750–816 AD, pope (795–816). He crowned Charlemagne emperor of the Romans (800). Feast day: June 12

Leo IX *n* **Saint,** original name *Bruno of Egisheim*. 1002–54, pope (1049–54): first of the great medieval reforming popes. Conflict with the Eastern Church led to the schism between Rome and Constantinople (1054). Feast day: April 19

Leo X *n* original name *Giovanni de' Medici*. 1475–1521, pope (1513–21): noted for his patronage of Renaissance art and learning; excommunicated Luther (1521)

Leo XIII *n* original name *Gioacchino Pecci*. 1810–1903, pope (1878–1903). His many important encyclicals include *Rerum novarum* (1891) on the need for Roman Catholics to take action on various social problems

Leoben (*German* leˈoːbən) *n* a city in E central Austria, in Styria on the Mur River: lignite mining. Pop: 25 804 (2001)

León (*Spanish* leˈɔn) *n* 1 a region and former kingdom of NW Spain, which united with Castile in 1230 2 a city of NW Spain: capital of the kingdom of León (10th century). Pop: 135 634 (2003 est) 3 a city in central Mexico, in W Guanajuato state: commercial centre of a rich agricultural region. Pop: 1 438 000 (2005 est) 4 a city in W Nicaragua: one of the oldest towns of Central America, founded in 1524; capital of Nicaragua until 1855; university (1812). Pop: 168 000 (2005 est)

Leonard ('lɛnəd) *n* **Sugar Ray**, real name *Ray Charles Leonard*. born 1956, US boxer: the first man to have won world titles at five officially recognized weights

Leonardo da Vinci (,liːəˈnɑːdəʊ də ˈvɪntʃɪ) *n* 1452–1519, Italian painter, sculptor, architect, and engineer: the most versatile talent of the Italian Renaissance. His most famous paintings include *The Virgin of the Rocks* (1483–85), the *Mona Lisa* (or *La Gioconda*, 1503), and the *Last Supper* (?1495–97). His numerous drawings, combining scientific precision in observation with intense

imaginative power, reflect the breadth of his interests, which ranged over biology, physiology, hydraulics, and aeronautics. He invented the first armoured tank and foresaw the invention of aircraft and submarines ▷ **Leonardesque** (,liːənɑːˈdɛsk) *adj*

Leonardo of Pisa *n* See **Fibonacci**

Leoncavallo (*Italian* leoŋkaˈvallo) *n* **Ruggiero** (rudˈdʒɛːro). 1858–1919, Italian composer of operas, notably I Pagliacci (1892)

Leonid ('liːənɪd) *n, pl* **Leonids** or **Leonides** (lɪˈɒnɪ,diːz) any member of a meteor shower that is usually insignificant, but more spectacular every 33 years, and occurs annually in mid-November, appearing to radiate from a point in the constellation Leo [c19: from New Latin *Leōnīdes*, from *leō* lion]

Leonidas (lɪˈɒnɪ,dæs) *n* died 480 BC, king of Sparta (?490–480), hero of the Battle of Thermopylae, in which he was killed by the Persians under Xerxes

leonine ('liːə,naɪn) *adj* of, characteristic of, or resembling a lion [c14: from Latin *leōnīnus*, from *leō* lion]

Leonine ('liːə,naɪn) *adj* 1 connected with one of the popes called Leo 2 **Leonine City** a district of Rome on the right bank of the Tiber fortified by Pope Leo IV ▷ *n* 3 Also called: **Leonine verse a** a type of medieval hexameter or elegiac verse having internal rhyme **b** a type of English verse with internal rhyme

Leonov (*Russian* lɪˈɔnəf) *n* **Aleksei Arkhipovich** (alɪkˈsjej arˈxipivitʃ). born 1934, Soviet cosmonaut; the first man to walk in space (1965)

leopard ('lɛpəd) *n* 1 Also called: **panther** a large feline mammal, *Panthera pardus*, of forests of Africa and Asia, usually having a tawny yellow coat with black rosette-like spots 2 any of several similar felines, such as the snow leopard and cheetah 3 *heraldry* a stylized leopard, painted as a lion with the face turned towards the front [c13: from Old French *lepart*, from Late Latin *leōpardus*, from Late Greek *leópardos*, from *leōn* lion + *pardos* PARD (the leopard was thought at one time to be the result of cross-breeding)] ▷ **'leopardess** *fem n*

Leopardi (*Italian* leoˈpardi) *n* **Count Giacomo** ('dʒaːkomo). 1798–1837, Italian poet and philosopher, noted esp for his lyrics, collected in *I Canti* (1831)

Leopold I ('lɪə,pəʊld) *n* 1 1640–1705, Holy Roman Emperor (1658–1705). His reign was marked by wars with Louis XIV of France and with the Turks 2 1790–1865, first king of the Belgians (1831–65)

Leopold II *n* 1 1747–92, Holy Roman Emperor (1790–92). He formed an alliance with Prussia against France (1792) after the downfall of his brother-in-law Louis XVI 2 1835–1909, king of the Belgians (1865–1909); son of Leopold I. He financed Stanley's explorations in Africa, becoming first sovereign of the Congo Free State (1885)

Leopold III *n* 1901–83, king of the Belgians (1934–51); son of Albert I. His surrender to the Nazis (1940) forced his eventual abdication in favour of his son, Baudouin

Léopoldville ('lɪəpəʊld,vɪl; *French* leɔpɔlvil) *n* the former name (until 1966) of **Kinshasa**

leotard ('lɪə,tɑːd) *n* 1 a tight-fitting garment covering the body from the shoulders down to the thighs and worn by acrobats, ballet dancers, etc 2 (*plural*) US & *Canadian* another name for **tights** (sense 1b) [c19: named after Jules *Léotard*, French acrobat]

Lepanto *n* 1 (lɪˈpæntəʊ) a port in W Greece, between the Gulfs of Corinth and Patras: scene of a naval battle (1571) in which the Turkish fleet was defeated by the fleets of the Holy League. Pop (municipality): 18 259 (2001). Greek name: **Návpaktos** 2 **Gulf of Lepanto** another name for the (Gulf of) **Corinth**

Lepaya (lɪˈpɑːjə) *n* a variant spelling of **Liepāja**

Le Pen (*French* lə pɛ) *n* **Jean-Marie** (ʒɑ̃məri). born 1928, French politician; leader of the extreme right-wing Front National from 1972; runner-up in the presidential election of 2002

leper ('lɛpə) *n* 1 a person who has leprosy 2 a person who is ignored or despised [c14: via Late Latin from Greek *lepra*, noun use of *lepros* scaly, from *lepein* to peel]

lepido- or before a vowel **lepid-** combining form scale or scaly: *lepidopterous* [from Greek *lepis* scale; see LEPER]

lepidopteran (,lɛpɪˈdɒptərən) *n, pl* **-terans** or **-tera** (-tərə)

1 Also: lepidopteron, any of numerous insects of the order *Lepidoptera*, typically having two pairs of wings covered with fragile scales, mouthparts specialized as a suctorial proboscis, and caterpillars as larvae: comprises the butterflies and moths ▷ *adj* 2 Also: lepidopterous of, relating to, or belonging to the order *Lepidoptera* [C19: from New Latin *lepidoptera*, from LEPIDO- + Greek *pteron* wing]

lepidopterist (ˌlɛpɪˈdɒptərɪst) *n* a person who studies or collects moths and butterflies

Lepidus (ˈlɛpɪdəs) *n* **Marcus Aemilius** (ˈmɑːkəs iːˈmɪlɪəs). died ?13 BC, Roman statesman: formed the Second Triumvirate with Octavian (later Augustus) and Mark Antony

Lepontine Alps (lɪˈpɒntaɪn) *pl n* a range of the S central Alps, in S Switzerland and N Italy. Highest peak: Monte Leone, 3553 m (11 657 ft)

Leppard (ˈlɛpəd) *n* **Raymond**. born 1927, British conductor and musicologist, in the US from 1977: noted esp for his revivals of early opera

leprechaun (ˈlɛprəˌkɔːn) *n* (in Irish folklore) a mischievous elf, often believed to have a treasure hoard [C17: from Irish Gaelic *leipreachān*, from Middle Irish *lúchorpān*, from *lū* small + *corp* body, from Latin *corpus* body]

leprosy (ˈlɛprəsɪ) *n* *pathol* a chronic infectious disease occurring mainly in tropical and subtropical regions, characterized by the formation of painful inflamed nodules beneath the skin and disfigurement and wasting of affected parts, caused by the bacillus *Mycobacterium leprae* [C16: from LEPROUS + -Y³]

leprous (ˈlɛprəs) *adj* 1 having leprosy 2 relating to or resembling leprosy [C13: from Old French, from Late Latin *leprosus*, from *lepra* LEPER]

-lepsy *or sometimes* **-lepsia** *n combining form* indicating a seizure or attack: *catalepsy* [from New Latin *-lepsia*, from Greek *lēpsis* a seizure, from *lambanein* to seize] ▷ **-leptic** *adj combining form*

lepto- *or before a vowel* **lept-** *combining form* fine, slender, or slight: *leptosome* [from Greek *leptos* thin, literally: peeled, from *lepein* to peel]

leptodactylous (ˌlɛptəʊˈdæktɪləs) *adj* *zoology* having slender digits

lepton¹ (ˈlɛptɒn) *n*, *pl* **-ta** (-tə) 1 a former Greek monetary unit worth one hundredth of a drachma 2 a small coin of ancient Greece [from Greek *lepton* (*nomisma* small (coin)]

lepton² (ˈlɛptɒn) *n* *physics* any of a group of elementary particles and their antiparticles, such as an electron, muon, or neutrino, that participate in electromagnetic and weak interactions and have a half-integral spin [C20: from LEPTO- + -ON]

lepton number *n* *physics* a quantum number describing the behaviour of elementary particles, equal to the number of leptons present minus the number of antileptons. It is thought to be conserved in all processes

leptospirosis (ˌlɛptəʊspaɪˈrəʊsɪs) *n* any of several infectious diseases caused by spirochaete bacteria of the genus *Leptospira*, transmitted to man by animals and characterized by jaundice, meningitis, and kidney failure. Also called: Weil's disease [C20: from New Latin *Leptospira* (LEPTO- + Greek *speira* coil + -OSIS)]

Lérida (*Spanish* ˈleriða) *n* a city in NE Spain, in Catalonia: commercial centre of an agricultural region. Pop: 118 035 (2003 est)

Lermontov (*Russian* ˈljɛrməntəf) *n* **Mikhail Yurievich** (mixaˈil ˈjurjɪvitʃ). 1814–41, Russian novelist and poet: noted esp for the novel *A Hero of Our Time* (1840)

Lerner (ˈlɜːnə) *n* **Alan Jay**. 1914–86, US songwriter and librettist. With Frederick Loewe he wrote *My Fair Lady* (1956) and *Camelot* (1960) as well as a number of film scripts, including *Gigi* (1958)

Lerwick (ˈlɜːwɪk) *n* a town in Shetland, administrative centre of the island authority of Shetland, on the island of Mainland: the most northerly town in the British Isles; knitwear, oil refining. Pop: 6830 (2001)

Le Sage *or* **Lesage** (*French* lə saʒ) *n* **Alain-René** (alɛ̃rəne). 1668–1747, French novelist and dramatist, author of the picaresque novel *Gil Blas* (1715–35)

lesbian (ˈlɛzbɪən) *n* 1 a female homosexual ▷ *adj* 2 of or characteristic of lesbians [C19: from the homosexuality attributed to Sappho (6th century BC), poetess of Lesbos] ▷ **ˈlesbianism** *n*

Lesbos (ˈlɛzbɒs) *n* an island in the E Aegean, off the NW coast of Turkey: a centre of lyric poetry, led by Alcaeus and Sappho (6th century BC); annexed to Greece in 1913. Chief town: Mytilene. Pop: 90 642 (2001). Area: 1630 sq km (630 sq miles). Modern Greek name: Lésvos. Former name: Mytilene

Les Cayes (leɪ ˈkeɪ; *French* le kaj) *n* a port in SW Haiti, on the S Tiburon Peninsula. Pop: 45 904 (1995). Also called: Cayes Former name: Aux Cayes

lese-majesty (ˈliːzˈmædʒɪstɪ) *n* 1 any of various offences committed against the sovereign power in a state; treason 2 an attack on authority or position [C16: from French *lèse majesté*, from Latin *laesa mājestās* wounded majesty]

lesion (ˈliːʒən) *n* 1 any structural change in a bodily part resulting from injury or disease 2 an injury or wound [C15: via Old French from Late Latin *laesiō* injury, from Latin *laedere* to hurt]

Lesotho (lɪˈsuːtʊ, ləˈsəʊtəʊ) *n* a kingdom in southern Africa, forming an enclave in the Republic of South Africa: annexed to British Cape Colony in 1871; made a protectorate in 1884; gained independence in 1966; a member of the Commonwealth. It is generally mountainous, with temperate grasslands throughout. Languages: Sesotho and English. Religion: Christian majority. Currency: loti and South African rand. Capital: Maseru. Pop: 1 800 000 (2004 est). Area: 30 344 sq km (11 716 sq miles). Former name (1884–1966): Basutoland

less (lɛs) *determiner* 1 a the comparative of **little** (sense 1) *less sugar; less spirit than before* b (*as pronoun; functioning as sing or plural*): *she has less than she needs; the less you eat, the less you want* 2 (*often preceded by no*) lower in rank or importance: *no less a man than the president; St James the Less* 3 *less of* to a smaller extent or degree: *we see less of John these days; less of a success than I'd hoped* ▷ *adv* 4 the comparative of **little** (sense 1): *she walks less than she should; less quickly; less beautiful* ▷ *prep* 5 subtracting; minus: *three weeks less a day* [Old English *lǣssa* (adj), *lǣs* (adv, n)]

● USAGE *Less* should not be confused with *fewer. Less*
● refers strictly only to quantity and not to number:
● *there is less water than before. Fewer* means smaller in
● number: *there are fewer people than before*

-less *suffix forming adjectives* 1 without; lacking: *speechless* 2 not able to (do something) or not able to be (done, performed, etc): *countless* [Old English *-lās*, from *lēas* lacking]

lessee (lɛˈsiː) *n* a person to whom a lease is granted; a tenant under a lease [C15: via Anglo-French from Old French *lessé*, from *lesser* to LEASE¹]

lessen (ˈlɛsən) *vb* 1 to make or become less 2 (*tr*) to make little of

Lesseps (ˈlɛsəps; *French* lesɛps) *n* See **de Lesseps**

lesser (ˈlɛsə) *adj* not as great in quantity, size, or worth

Lesser Antilles *pl n* the Lesser Antilles a group of islands in the Caribbean, including the Leeward Islands, the Windward Islands, Barbados, and the Netherlands Antilles. Formerly called: (the) **Caribees**

lesser celandine *n* a Eurasian ranunculaceous plant, *Ranunculus ficaria*, having yellow flowers and heart-shaped leaves

lesser panda *n* See **panda** (sense 2)

Lesser Sunda Islands *pl n* the English name of **Nusa Tenggara**

Lessing (ˈlɛsɪŋ) *n* 1 **Doris** (**May**). born 1919, English novelist and short-story writer, brought up in Rhodesia: her novels include the five-novel sequence *Children of Violence* (1952–69), *The Golden Notebook* (1962), a series of science-fiction works (1979–83), *The Good Terrorist* (1985), and *The Sweetest Dream* (2001). Nobel prize for literature 2007 2 **Gotthold Ephraim** (ˈɡɔtɔlt ˈeːfraɪm). 1729–81, German dramatist and critic. His plays include *Miss Sara Sampson* (1755), the first German domestic tragedy, and *Nathan der Weise* (1779). He is noted for his criticism of French classical dramatists, and for his treatise on aesthetics *Laokoon* (1766)

lesson ('lɛsᵊn) *n* **1 a** a unit, or single period of instruction in a subject; class: *an hour-long music lesson* **b** the content of such a unit **2** material assigned for individual study **3** something from which useful knowledge or principles can be learned; example **4** the principles, knowledge, etc, gained **5** a reprimand or punishment intended to correct **6** a portion of Scripture appointed to be read at divine service [c13: from Old French *leçon*, from Latin *lēctiō*, from *legere* to read]

lessor ('lɛsɔ:, lɛ'sɔ:) *n* a person who grants a lease of property

lest (lɛst) *conj* (*subordinating*; takes *should* or a subjunctive verb) **1** so as to prevent any possibility that: *he fled the country lest he be captured and imprisoned* **2** (*after verbs or phrases expressing fear, worry, anxiety, etc*) for fear that; in case: *he was alarmed lest she should find out* [Old English *the lǣste*, earlier *thȳ lǣs the*, literally: whereby less that]

Lésvos ('lɛzvɔs) *n* transliteration of the Modern Greek name for **Lesbos**

let¹ (lɛt) *vb* **lets, letting, let** (*tr*; usually takes an infinitive without *to* or an implied infinitive) **1** to permit; allow: *she lets him roam around* **2** (*imperative or dependent imperative*) **a** used as an auxiliary to express a request, proposal, or command, or to convey a warning or threat: *let's get on; just let me catch you here again!* **b** (in mathematical or philosophical discourse) used as an auxiliary to express an assumption or hypothesis: *let "a" equal "b"* **c** used as an auxiliary to express resigned acceptance of the inevitable: *let the worst happen* **3 a** to allow the occupation of (accommodation) in return for rent **b** to assign (a contract for work) **4** to allow or cause the movement of (something) in a specified direction: *to let air out of a tyre* **5** *Irish informal* to utter: *to let a cry* **6 let alone a** (*conjunction*) much less; not to mention: *I can't afford wine, let alone champagne* **b** let be, let alone, leave alone *or* leave be to refrain from annoying or interfering with: *let the poor cat alone* **7** let go See **go¹** (sense 45) **8** let loose **a** to set free **b** *informal* to make (a sound or remark) suddenly: *he let loose a hollow laugh* **c** *informal* to discharge (rounds) from a gun or guns: *they let loose a couple of rounds of ammunition* ▷ *n* **9** *Brit* the act of letting property or accommodation: *the majority of new lets are covered by the rent regulations* ▷ See also **let down, let in, let off, let on, let out, let up** [Old English *lǣtan* to permit; related to Gothic *lētan*, German *lassen*]

let² (lɛt) *n* **1** an impediment or obstruction (esp in the phrase **without let or hindrance**) **2** *tennis, squash* **a** a minor infringement or obstruction of the ball, requiring a point to be replayed **b** the point so replayed ▷ *vb* **lets, letting, letted** *or* **let 3** (*tr*) *archaic* to hinder; impede [Old English *lettan* to hinder, from *lǣt* LATE; related to Old Norse *letja*]

-let *suffix forming nouns* **1** small or lesser: *booklet; starlet* **2** an article of attire or ornament worn on a specified part of the body: *anklet* [from Old French *-elet*, from Latin *-āle*, neuter of adj suffix *-ālis* or from Latin *-ellus*, diminutive suffix]

Letchworth ('lɛtʃwəθ, -,wɜ:θ) *n* a town in SE England, in N Hertfordshire: the first garden city in Great Britain (founded in 1903). Pop: 32 932 (2001)

let down *vb* (*tr, mainly adverb*) **1** (*also preposition*) to lower **2** to fail to fulfil the expectations of (a person); disappoint **3** to undo, shorten, and resew (the hem) so as to lengthen (a dress, skirt, etc) **4** to untie (long hair that is bound up) and allow to fall loose **5** to deflate: *to let down a tyre* ▷ *n* **6** a disappointment

lethal ('li:θəl) *adj* **1** able to cause or causing death **2** of or suggestive of death [c16: from Latin *lēthālis*, from *lētum* death] > **lethality** (li:'θælɪtɪ) *n* > '**lethally** *adv*

lethargy ('lɛθədʒɪ) *n, pl* **-gies 1** sluggishness, slowness, or dullness **2** an abnormal lack of energy, esp as the result of a disease [c14: from Late Latin *lēthargīa*, from Greek *lēthargos* drowsy, from *lēthē* forgetfulness] > **lethargic** (lɪ'θɑ:dʒɪk) *or* **le'thargical** *adj* > **le'thargically** *adv*

Lethbridge ('lɛθbrɪdʒ) *n* a city in Canada, in S Alberta: coal-mining. Pop: 67 374 (2001)

Lethe ('li:θɪ) *n* **1** *Greek myth* a river in Hades that caused

forgetfulness in those who drank its waters **2** forgetfulness [c16: via Latin from Greek, from *lēthē* oblivion] > Lethean (lɪ'θi:ən) *adj*

let in *vb* (*tr, adverb*) **1** to allow to enter **2** let in for to involve (oneself or another) in (something more than is expected): *he let himself in for a lot of extra work* **3** let in on to allow (someone) to know about or participate in

Leto ('li:təʊ) *n* the mother by Zeus of Apollo and Artemis. Roman name: Latona

let off *vb* (*tr, mainly adverb*) **1** (*also preposition*) to allow to disembark or leave **2** to explode or fire (a bomb, gun, etc) **3** (*also preposition*) to excuse from (work or other responsibilities): *I'll let you off for a week* **4** to allow to get away without the expected punishment, work, etc **5** to let (accommodation) in portions **6** to release (liquid, air, etc)

let on *vb* (*adverb; when tr, takes a clause as object*) *informal* **1** to allow (something, such as a secret) to be known; reveal: *he never let on that he was married* **2** (*tr*) to cause or encourage to be believed; pretend

let out *vb* (*adverb, mainly tr*) **1** to give vent to; emit: *to let out a howl* **2** to allow to go or run free; release **3** (*may take a clause as object*) to reveal (a secret) **4** to make available to tenants, hirers, or contractors **5** to permit to flow out: *to let air out of the tyres* **6** to make (a garment) larger, as by unpicking (the seams) and sewing nearer the outer edge ▷ *n* **7** a chance to escape

let's (lɛts) *contraction of* let us: used to express a suggestion, command, etc, by the speaker to himself and his hearers

Lett (lɛt) *n* another name for a **Latvian**

letter ('lɛtə) *n* **1** any of a set of conventional symbols used in writing or printing a language, each symbol being associated with a group of phonetic values in the language; character of the alphabet **2** a written or printed communication addressed to a person, company, etc, usually sent by post in an envelope **3** the letter the strict legalistic or pedantic interpretation of the meaning of an agreement, document, etc; exact wording as distinct from actual intention (esp in the phrase **the letter of the law**) **4** to the letter **a** following the literal interpretation or wording exactly **b** attending to every detail ▷ *vb* **5** to write or mark letters on (a sign, etc), esp by hand **6** (*tr*) to set down or print using letters [c13: from Old French *lettre*, from Latin *littera* letter of the alphabet] > '**letterer** *n*

letter bomb *n* a thin explosive device inside an envelope, detonated when the envelope is opened

letter box *n chiefly Brit* **1 a** a slot, usually covered with a hinged flap, through which letters, etc, are delivered to a building **b** a private box into which letters, etc, are delivered **2** Also called: postbox a public box into which letters, etc, are put for collection and delivery

lettered ('lɛtəd) *adj* **1** well educated in literature, the arts, etc **2** literate **3** of or characterized by learning or culture **4** printed or marked with letters

letterhead ('lɛtə,hɛd) *n* a sheet of paper printed with one's address, name, etc, for writing a letter on

lettering ('lɛtərɪŋ) *n* **1** the act, art, or technique of inscribing letters on to something **2** the letters so inscribed

letter of credit *n* a letter issued by a bank entitling the bearer to draw funds up to a specified maximum from that bank or its agencies

letter of intent *n* a letter indicating that the writer has the serious intention of doing something, such as signing a contract in the circumstances specified. It does not constitute either a promise or a contract

letter of marque *or* **letters of marque** *n* **1** a licence granted by a state to a private citizen to arm a ship and seize merchant vessels of another nation **2** a similar licence issued by a nation allowing a private citizen to seize goods or citizens of another nation ▷ Also called: letter of marque and reprisal

letter-perfect *adj* another term (esp in the US) for **word-perfect**

letterpress ('lɛtə,prɛs) *n* **1 a** a method of printing in which ink is transferred from raised surfaces to paper by pressure; relief printing **b** matter so printed **2** text matter as distinct from illustrations

letters ('lɛtəz) n (functioning as plural or singular) **1** literary knowledge, ability, or learning: a man of letters **2** literary culture in general **3** an official title, degree, etc, indicated by an abbreviation: letters after one's name

letters patent pl n See **patent** (sense 4)

Lettish ('lɛtɪʃ) n, adj another word for **Latvian**

lettuce ('lɛtɪs) n **1** any of various plants of the genus Lactuca, esp L. sativa, which is cultivated in many varieties for its large edible leaves: family Asteraceae (composites) **2** the leaves of any of these varieties, which are eaten in salads **3** any of various plants that resemble true lettuce, such as lamb's lettuce and sea lettuce [C13: probably from Old French laitues, pl of laitue, from Latin lactūca, from lac- milk, because of its milky juice]

let up vb (intr, adverb) **1** to diminish, slacken, or stop **2** (foll by on) informal to be less harsh (towards someone) ▷ n let-up **3** informal a lessening or abatement

Leucas ('lu:kəs) n a variant spelling of **Leukas**

Leucippus (lu:'sɪpəs) n 5th century BC Greek philosopher, who originated the atomist theory of matter, developed by his disciple, Democritus

leuco-, leuko-, or before a vowel **leuc-, leuk-** combining form white or lacking colour: leucocyte; leucorrhoea; leukaemia [from Greek leukos white]

leucoblast or esp US **leukoblast** ('lu:kəʊ,blɑ:st) n an immature leucocyte

leucocyte or esp US **leukocyte** ('lu:kə,saɪt) n any of the various large unpigmented cells in the blood of vertebrates. Also called: white blood cell, white blood corpuscle See also **lymphocyte, granulocyte, monocyte** ▷ **leucocytic** or esp US leukocytic (,lu:kə'sɪtɪk) adj

leucoma (lu:'kəʊmə) n pathol a white opaque scar of the cornea

leucotomy (lu:'kɒtəmɪ) n, pl **-tomies** the surgical operation of cutting some of the nerve fibres in the frontal lobes of the brain for treating intractable mental disorders [C20: from LEUCO- (with reference to the white brain tissue) + -TOMY]

Leuctra ('lu:ktrə) n an ancient town in Greece southwest of Thebes in Boeotia: site of a victory of Thebes over Sparta (371BC), which marked the end of Spartan military supremacy in Greece

leukaemia or esp US **leukemia** (lu:'ki:mɪə) n an acute or chronic disease characterized by a gross proliferation of leucocytes, which crowd into the bone marrow, spleen, lymph nodes, etc, and suppress the blood-forming apparatus [C19: from LEUCO- + Greek haima blood]

Leukas or **Leucas** ('lu:kəs) n another name for **Levkás**

Leuven ('lø:və) n the Flemish name for **Louvain**

Lev. abbreviation Bible Leviticus

levant (lɪ'vænt) n a type of leather made from the skins of goats, sheep, or seals, having a pattern of irregular creases [C19: shortened from Levant morocco (type of leather)]

Levant (lɪ'vænt) n the Levant a former name for the area of the E Mediterranean now occupied by Lebanon, Syria, and Israel [C15: from Old French, from the present participle of lever to raise (referring to the rising of the sun in the east), from Latin levāre] ▷ **Levan,tine** adj, n

levanter (lɪ'væntə) n (sometimes capital) **1** an easterly wind in the W Mediterranean area, esp in the late summer **2** an inhabitant of the Levant

levator (lɪ'veɪtə, -tɔ:) n anatomy any of various muscles that raise a part of the body [C17: New Latin, from Latin levāre to raise]

levee[1] ('lɛvɪ) n US **1** an embankment alongside a river, produced naturally by sedimentation or constructed by man to prevent flooding **2** an embankment that surrounds a field that is to be irrigated **3** a landing place on a river; quay [C18: from French, from Medieval Latin levāta, from Latin levāre to raise]

levee[2] ('lɛvɪ, 'lɛveɪ) n **1** a formal reception held by a sovereign just after rising from bed **2** (in Britain) a public court reception for men, held in the early afternoon [C17: from French, variant of lever a rising, from Latin levāre to raise]

level ('lɛvəl) adj **1** on a horizontal plane **2** having a

surface of completely equal height **3** being of the same height as something else **4** (of quantities to be measured, as in recipes) even with the top of the cup, spoon, etc **5** equal to or even with (something or someone else) **6** not having or showing inconsistency or irregularities **7** Also called: level-headed even-tempered; steady ▷ vb **-els, -elling, -elled** or US **-els, -eling, -eled** **8** (tr; sometimes foll by off) to make (a surface) horizontal, level, or even **9** to make (two or more people or things) equal, as in position or status **10** (tr) to raze to the ground **11** (tr) to knock (a person) down by or as if by a blow **12** (tr) to direct (a gaze, criticism, etc) emphatically at someone **13** (intr; often foll by with) informal to be straightforward and frank **14** (intr; foll by off or out) to manoeuvre an aircraft into a horizontal flight path after a dive, climb, or glide **15** (often foll by at) to aim (a weapon) horizontally ▷ n **16** a horizontal datum line or plane **17** a device, such as a spirit level, for determining whether a surface is horizontal **18** a surveying instrument consisting basically of a telescope with a spirit level attached, used for measuring relative heights of land **19** position or status in a scale of values **20** amount or degree of progress; stage **21** a specified vertical position; altitude **22** a horizontal line or plane with respect to which measurement of elevation is based: sea level **23** a flat even surface or area of land **24** do one's level best to make every possible effort; try one's utmost **25** on the level informal sincere, honest, or genuine [C14: from Old French livel, from Vulgar Latin libellum (unattested), from Latin lībella, diminutive of lībra scales] ▷ **'levelly** adv ▷ **'levelness** n ▷ **'leveller** or US **'leveler** n

level crossing n Brit a point at which a railway and a road cross, espe one with barriers that close the road when a train is scheduled to pass

level-headed adj even-tempered, balanced, and reliable; steady ▷ ,level-'headedly adv ▷ ,level-'headedness n

level of attainment n Brit education one of ten groupings, each with its own attainment criteria based on pupil age and ability, within which a pupil is assessed

level pegging Brit informal ▷ n **1** equality between two contestants ▷ adj **2** (of two contestants) equal

level playing field n a situation in which none of the competing parties has an advantage at the outset of a competitive activity

Leven ('li:vən) Loch Leven n **1** a lake in E central Scotland: one of the shallowest of Scottish lochs, with seven islands, on one of which Mary, Queen of Scots was imprisoned (1567–8). Length: 6 km (3.7 miles). Width: 4 km (2.5 miles) **2** a sea loch in W Scotland, extending for about 14 km (9 miles) east from Loch Linnhe

lever ('li:və) n **1** a rigid bar pivoted about a fulcrum, used to transfer a force to a load and usually to provide a mechanical advantage **2** any of a number of mechanical devices employing this principle **3** a means of exerting pressure in order to accomplish something; strategic aid ▷ vb **4** to prise or move (an object) with a lever [C13: from Old French leveour, from lever to raise, from Latin levāre, from levis light]

leverage ('li:vərɪdʒ, -vrɪdʒ) n **1** the action of a lever **2** the mechanical advantage gained by employing a lever **3** power to accomplish something; strategic advantage **4** the enhanced power available to a large company: the supermarket chains have greater leverage than single-outlet enterprises **5** the US word for **gearing** (sense 3) **6** the use made by a company of its limited assets to guarantee the substantial loans required to finance its business

leveraged buyout ('li:vərɪdʒd) n a takeover bid in which a small company makes use of its limited assets, and those of the usually larger target company, to raise the loans required to finance the takeover. Abbreviation: LBO

leveret ('lɛvərɪt, -vrɪt) n a young hare, esp one less than one year old [C15: from Norman French levrete, diminutive of levre, from Latin lepus hare]

Leverhulme ('li:və,hju:m) n **William Hesketh**, 1st Viscount. 1851–1925, English soap manufacturer and philanthropist, who founded (1881) the model industrial town Port Sunlight

Leverkusen (German ˈleːvərˌkuːzən) *n* a town in NW Germany, in North Rhine-Westphalia on the Rhine: chemical industries. Pop: 161 543 (2003 est)

Leverrier (French ləvɛrje) *n* **Urbain Jean Joseph** (yrbɛ̃ ʒɑ̃ ʒozɛf). 1811–77, French astronomer: calculated the existence and position of the planet Neptune

Levi[1] (ˈliːvaɪ) *n* **1** *Old Testament* **a** the third son of Jacob and Leah and the ancestor of the tribe of Levi (Genesis 29:34) **b** the priestly tribe descended from this patriarch (Numbers 18:21–24) **2** *New Testament* another name for Matthew the apostle

Levi[2] (Italian ˈleːvi) *n* **1 Carlo**. 1902–75, Italian physician, painter, and writer. Best known for his novel *Christ Stopped at Eboli* (1947), his other works include *The Watch* (1952) and *Words are Stones* (1958) **2 Primo** (ˈpriːməʊ). 1919–87, Italian novelist. His book *If This is a Man* (1947) relates his experiences in Auschwitz. Other books include *The Periodic Table* (1956) and *The Drowned and the Saved* (1988), published after his suicide

leviable (ˈlɛvɪəbəl) *adj* **1** (of taxes, tariffs, etc) liable to be levied **2** (of goods, etc) liable to bear a levy; taxable

leviathan (lɪˈvaɪəθən) *n* **1** *Bible* a monstrous beast, esp a sea monster **2** any huge or powerful thing [c14: from Late Latin, ultimately from Hebrew *liwyāthān*, of obscure origin]

levigate (ˈlɛvɪˌgeɪt) *vb chem* **1** (*tr*) to grind into a fine powder or a smooth paste **2** to form or cause to form a homogeneous mixture, as in the production of gels **3** (*tr*) to suspend (fine particles) by grinding in a liquid, esp as a method of separating fine from coarse particles [c17: from Latin *lēvigāre*, from *lēvis* smooth] ▷ ˌleviˈgation *n*

Levi's (ˈliːvaɪz) *pl n trademark* jeans, usually blue and made of denim

Lévi-Strauss (ˈlɛvɪˈstraʊs; French levistros) *n* **Claude** (klod). born 1908, French anthropologist, leading exponent of structuralism. His books include *The Elementary Structures of Kinship* (1969), *Totemism* (1962), *The Savage Mind* (1966), *Mythologies* (1964–71), and *Saudades do Brazil* (Memories of Brazil; 1994)

levitate (ˈlɛvɪˌteɪt) *vb* to rise or cause to rise and float in the air, without visible agency, attributed, esp formerly, to supernatural causes [c17: from Latin *levis* light + -*tate*, as in *gravitate*] ▷ ˌleviˈtation *n* ▷ ˈleviˌtator *n*

levity (ˈlɛvɪtɪ) *n, pl* -ties **1** inappropriate lack of seriousness **2** fickleness or instability **3** *archaic* lightness in weight [c16: from Latin *levitās* lightness, from *levis* light]

Levkás (lɛfˈkæs), **Leukas** or **Leucas** *n* a Greek island in the Ionian Sea, in the Ionian Islands. Pop: 20 751 (2001). Area: 295 sq km (114 sq miles). Italian name: **Santa Maura**

Levkosia (lɛfˈkaʊsɪə) or **Leukosia** *n* the Greek name for **Nicosia**

levodopa (ˌliːvəʊˈdəʊpə) *n* another name for **L-dopa**

levy (ˈlɛvɪ) *vb* levies, levying, levied (*tr*) **1** to impose and collect (a tax, tariff, fine, etc) **2** to conscript troops for service **3** to seize or attach (property) in accordance with the judgment of a court ▷ *pl* levies **4 a** the act of imposing and collecting a tax, tariff, etc **b** the money so raised **5 a** the conscription of troops for service **b** a person conscripted in this way [c15: from Old French *levée* a raising, from *lever*, from Latin *levāre* to raise]

Lévy-Bruhl (levibrul) *n* **Lucien** (lysjɛ̃). 1857–1939, French anthropologist and philosopher, noted for his study of the psychology of primitive peoples

lewd (luːd) *adj* characterized by or intended to excite crude sexual desire; obscene [c14: from Old English *lǣwde* lay, ignorant; see LAY³] ▷ ˈlewdly *adv* ▷ ˈlewdness *n*

Lewes (ˈluːɪs) *n* a market town in S England, administrative centre of East Sussex, on the River Ouse: site of a battle (1264) in which Henry III was defeated by Simon de Montfort. Pop: 15 988 (2001)

lewis (ˈluːɪs) or **lewisson** (ˈluːɪsən) *n* a lifting device for heavy stone or concrete blocks consisting of a number of curved pieces of metal or wedges fitting into a dovetailed recess cut into the block [c18: perhaps from the name of the inventor]

Lewis[1] (ˈluːɪs) *n* the N part of the island of Lewis with Harris, in the Outer Hebrides. Pop: about 17 000 (2001). Area: 1634 sq km (631 sq miles)

Lewis[2] (ˈluːɪs) *n* **1 Carl**. full name *Frederick Carleton Lewis*. born 1961, US athlete; winner of the long jump, 100 metres, 200 metres, and 4 × 100 metres relay at the 1984 Olympic Games; winner of the 100 metres in the 1988 Olympic Games; winner of the long jump in the 1992 and 1996 Olympic Games **2** See **Day-Lewis 3 C**(**live**) **S**(**taples**). 1898–1963, English novelist, critic, and Christian apologist, noted for his critical work, *Allegory of Love* (1936), his theological study, *The Screwtape Letters* (1942), and for his children's books chronicling the land of Narnia **4 Lennox**. born 1965, British boxer; undisputed world heavyweight champion (2000–01) **5 Matthew Gregory**, known as *Monk Lewis*. 1775–1818, English novelist and dramatist, noted for his Gothic horror story *The Monk* (1796) **6 Meriwether**. 1774–1807, American explorer who, with William Clark, led an overland expedition from St Louis to the Pacific Ocean (1804–06) **7** (**John**) **Saunders** (ˈsɔːndəz). 1893–1985, Welsh poet, dramatist, critic, and politician: founder (1926) and president (1926–39) of the Welsh Nationalist Party **8** (**Harry**) **Sinclair**. 1885–1951, US novelist. He satirized the complacency and philistinism of American small-town life, esp in *Main Street* (1920) and *Babbitt* (1922): Nobel prize for literature 1930 **9 Wally**. born 1959, Australian rugby league player **10** (**Percy**) **Wyndham**. 1884–1957, British painter, novelist, and critic, born in the US: founder of vorticism. His writings include *Time and Western Man* (1927), *The Apes of God* (1930), and the trilogy *The Human Age* (1928–55)

Lewis acid *n* a substance capable of accepting a pair of electrons from a base to form a covalent bond. See **Lewis base** [c20: named after G. N. *Lewis* (1875–1946), US chemist]

Lewis base *n* a substance capable of donating a pair of electrons to an acid to form a covalent bond. See **Lewis acid** [c20: named after G. N. *Lewis* (1875–1946), US chemist]

Lewis gun *n* a light air-cooled drum-fed gas-operated machine gun used chiefly in World War I [c20: named after I. N. *Lewis* (1858–1931), US soldier]

Lewisham (ˈluːɪʃəm) *n* a borough of S Greater London, on the River Thames. Pop: 248 300 (2003 est). Area: 35 sq km (13 sq miles)

lewisite (ˈluːɪˌsaɪt) *n* a colourless oily poisonous liquid with an odour resembling that of geraniums, having a powerful vesicant action and used as a war gas; 1-chloro-2-dichloroarsinoethene. Formula: $ClCH{:}CHAsCl_2$ [c20: named after W. L. *Lewis* (1878–1943), US chemist]

Lewis with Harris or **Lewis and Harris** *n* an island in the Outer Hebrides, separated from the NW coast of Scotland by the Minch: consists of Lewis in the north and Harris in the south; many lakes and peat moors; economy based chiefly on the Harris tweed industry, with some fishing. Chief town: Stornoway. Pop: 19 918 (2001). Area: 2134 sq km (824 sq miles)

lexeme (ˈlɛksiːm) *n linguistics* a minimal meaningful unit of language, the meaning of which cannot be understood from that of its component morphemes. *Take off* (in the senses to mimic, to become airborne, etc) is a lexeme, as well as the independent morphemes *take* and *off* [c20: from LEX(ICON) + -EME]

lexical (ˈlɛksɪkəl) *adj* **1** of or relating to items of vocabulary in a language **2** of or relating to a lexicon ▷ ˈlexically *adv*

lexicography (ˌlɛksɪˈkɒɡrəfɪ) *n* the process or profession of writing or compiling dictionaries ▷ ˌlexiˈcographer *n* ▷ lexicographic (ˌlɛksɪkəˈɡræfɪk) or ˌlexicoˈgraphical *adj*

lexicon (ˈlɛksɪkən) *n* **1 a** a dictionary, esp one of an ancient language such as Greek or Hebrew **2** a list of terms relating to a particular subject **3** the vocabulary of a language or of an individual **4** *linguistics* the set of all the morphemes of a language [c17: New Latin, from Greek *lexikon*, *n* use of *lexikos* relating to words, from Greek *lexis* word, from *legein* to speak]

lexigraphy (lɛkˈsɪɡrəfɪ) *n* a system of writing in which each word is represented by a sign [c19: from Greek *lexis*

Lexington ('lɛksɪŋtən) *n* **1** a city in NE central Kentucky, in the bluegrass region: major centre for horse-breeding. Pop (including Fayette): 266 798 (2003 est) **2** a city in Massachusetts, northwest of Boston: site of the first action (1775) of the War of American Independence. Pop: 30 631 (2003 est)

lexis ('lɛksɪs) *n* the totality of vocabulary items in a language, including all forms having lexical meaning or grammatical function [C20: from Greek *lexis* word]

ley (leɪ, liː) *n* **1** arable land put down to grass; grassland or pastureland **2** Also called: **ley line** a line joining two prominent points in the landscape, thought to be the line of a prehistoric track [C14: variant of LEA¹]

Leyden¹ ('laɪdᵊn; *Dutch* 'lɛidə) *n* a variant spelling of **Leiden**

Leyden² ('laɪdᵊn) *n* See **Lucas van Leyden**

Leyden jar *n physics* an early type of capacitor consisting of a glass jar with the lower part of the inside and outside coated with tin foil [C18: first made in Leiden]

Leyland cypress ('leɪlənd) *n* a fast-growing cypress, *Cupressocyparis leylandii*, that is a hybrid produced by crossing the macrocarpa with the Nootka cypress (*Chamaecyparis nootkatensis*): widely grown for hedging. Also called: **Leylandii** [C19: named after C. J. *Leyland* (1849–1926), British horticulturalist]

Leyte ('leɪteɪ) *n* an island in the central Philippines, in the Visayan Islands. Chief town: Tacloban. Pop: 1 592 336 (2000). Area: 7215 sq km (2786 sq miles)

Leyte Gulf *n* an inlet of the Pacific in the E Philippines, east of Leyte and south of Samar: scene of a battle (Oct 23–26, 1944) during World War II, in which the Americans defeated almost the entire Japanese navy, thereby ensuring ultimate Allied victory

lezzie ('lɛzɪ) *or* **lezza** ('lɛzə) *n slang* a lesbian

LF *abbreviation radio* low frequency

LG *abbreviation* Low German

LGBT *abbreviation* **1** lesbian, gay, bisexual, and transgender ▷ *n* ('ɛl'dʒiː'biː'tiː) *pl* LGBT's *or* LGBTs **2** a lesbian, gay, bisexual, or transgender person

LGV *abbreviation* (in Britain) large goods vehicle

lh *or* **LH** *abbreviation* left hand

Lhasa *or* **Lassa** ('lɑːsə) *n* a city in SW China, capital of Tibet, at an altitude of 3606 m (11 830 ft): for centuries the sacred city of Lamaism and residence of the Dalai Lamas from the 17th century until 1959; known as the Forbidden City because it was closed to Westerners until the beginning of the 20th century; annexed by China in 1951. The Dalai Lama fled after an unsuccessful revolt against Chinese rule in 1959. Pop: 131 000 (2005 est)

Li *the chemical symbol for* lithium

LI *abbreviation* **1** Long Island **2** Light Infantry

liabilities (ˌlaɪə'bɪlɪtɪz) *pl n accounting* business obligations incurred but not discharged and entered as claims on the assets shown on the balance sheet

liability (ˌlaɪə'bɪlɪtɪ) *n, pl* -ties **1** the state of being liable **2** a financial obligation **3** a hindrance or disadvantage

liable ('laɪəbᵊl) *adj* (*postpositive*) **1** legally obliged or responsible; answerable **2** susceptible or exposed; subject **3** probable, likely, or capable: *it's liable to happen soon* [C15: perhaps via Anglo-French, from French *lier* to bind, from Latin *ligāre*]
   ● **USAGE** The use of *liable to* to mean *likely to* was formerly considered incorrect, but is now acceptable

liaise (lɪ'eɪz) *vb* (*intr;* usually foll by *with*) to communicate and maintain contact (with) [C20: back formation from LIAISON]

liaison (lɪ'eɪzɒn) *n* **1** communication and contact between groups or units **2** a secretive or adulterous sexual relationship **3** one who acts as an agent between parties; intermediary **4** the relationship between military units necessary to ensure unity of purpose **5** (in the phonology of several languages, esp French) the pronunciation of a normally silent consonant at the end of a word immediately before another word commencing with a vowel, in such a way that the consonant is taken over as the initial sound of the following word. Liaison is seen between French *ils* (il) and *ont* (ɔ̃), to give *ils ont* (il zɔ̃) **6** any thickening for

soups, sauces, etc, such as egg yolks or cream [C17: via French from Old French, from *lier* to bind, from Latin *ligāre*]

Liákoura ('ljakura) *n* a transliteration of the Modern Greek name for (Mount) **Parnassus**

liana (lɪ'ɑːnə) *or* **liane** (lɪ'ɑːn) *n* any of various woody climbing plants mainly of tropical forests [C19: changed from earlier *liane* (through influence of French *lier* to bind), from French, of obscure origin]

Lianyungang ('ljæn'jʊŋ'gæn), **Sinhailien** *or* **Hsin-hai-lien** *n* a city in E China, near the coast of Jiangsu. Pop: 645 000 (2005 est)

Liao (ljaʊ) *n* a river in NE China, rising in SE Inner Mongolia and flowing northeast then southwest to the Gulf of Liaodong. Length: about 1100 km (700 miles)

Liaodong ('ljaʊ'dʊŋ) *or* **Liaotung** ('ljaʊ'tʊŋ) *n* **1** Liaodong Pensinula a peninsula of NE China, in S Manchuria extending south into the Yellow Sea: forms the S part of Liaoning province **2** Gulf of Liaodong the N part of the Gulf of Chihli, west of the Liaodong Peninsula

Liaoning ('ljaʊ'nɪŋ) *n* a province of NE China, in S Manchuria. Capital: Shenyang. Pop: 42 100 000 (2003 est). Area: 150 000 sq km (58 500 sq miles)

Liaoyang ('ljaʊ'jæn) *n* a city in NE China, in S Manchuria, in Liaoning province: a regional capital in the early dynasties. Pop: 752 000 (2005 est)

liar ('laɪə) *n* a person who has lied or lies repeatedly

Liard ('liːɑːd, liː'ɑːd, -'ɑː) *n* a river in W Canada, rising in the SE Yukon and flowing east and then northwest to the Mackenzie River. Length: 885 km (550 miles)

Lias ('laɪəs) *n* the lowest series of rocks of the Jurassic system [C15 (referring to a kind of limestone), C19 (geological sense) from Old French *liois*, perhaps from *lie* lees, dregs, so called from its appearance] ▷ **Liassic** (laɪˈæsɪk) *adj*

lib (lɪb) *n informal, sometimes derogatory* short for **liberation** (sense 2)

lib. *abbreviation* **1** librarian **2** library

Lib. *abbreviation* Liberal

libation (laɪ'beɪʃən) *n* **1 a** the pouring out of wine, etc, in honour of a deity **b** the liquid so poured out **2** *usually facetious* an alcoholic drink [C14: from Latin *lībātiō*, from *lībāre* to pour an offering of drink]

Libau ('liːbaʊ) *n* the German name for **Liepāja**

Libava (lɪ'bavə) *n* transliteration of the Russian name for **Liepāja**

Libby ('lɪbɪ) *n* Willard Frank. 1908–80, US chemist, who devised the technique of radiocarbon dating: Nobel prize for chemistry 1960

libel ('laɪbᵊl) *n* **1** *law* **a** the publication of defamatory matter in permanent form, as by a written or printed statement, picture, etc **b** the act of publishing such matter **2** any defamatory or unflattering representation or statement **3** *Scots law* the formal statement of a charge ▷ *vb* -bels, -belling, -belled *or US* -bels, -beling, -beled (*tr*) **4** *law* to make or publish a defamatory statement or representation about (a person) **5** to misrepresent injuriously [C13 (in the sense: written statement), hence C14 legal sense: from Old French from Latin *libellus* a little book, from *liber* a book] ▷ **libeller** *or US* **libelist** *n* ▷ **libellous** *or US* **libelous** *adj*

liberal ('lɪbᵊrəl, 'lɪbrəl) *adj* **1** relating to or having social and political views that favour progress and reform **2** relating to or having policies or views advocating individual freedom **3** giving and generous in temperament or behaviour **4** tolerant of other people **5** abundant; lavish: *a liberal helping of cream* **6** not strict; free: *a liberal translation* **7** of or relating to an education that aims to develop general cultural interests and intellectual ability ▷ *n* **8** a person who has liberal ideas or opinions [C14: from Latin *līberālis* of freedom, from *līber* free] ▷ **'liberally** *adv* ▷ **'liberalness** *n*

Liberal ('lɪbᵊrəl, 'lɪbrəl) *n* **1** a member or supporter of a Liberal Party or Liberal Democrat party ▷ *adj* **2** of or relating to a Liberal Party

liberal arts *pl n* the fine arts, humanities, sociology, languages, and literature. Often shortened to: **arts**

Liberal Democrat *n* a member or supporter of the Liberal Democrats

Liberal Democrats *pl n* (in Britain) a political party with centrist policies; established in 1988 as the Social and Liberal Democrats when the Liberal Party merged with the Social Democratic Party; renamed Liberal Democrats in 1989

liberalism ('lɪbərə,lɪzəm, 'lɪbrə-) *n* liberal opinions, practices, or politics

liberality (,lɪbə'rælɪtɪ) *n*, *pl* **-ties 1** generosity; bounty **2** the quality or condition of being liberal

liberalize *or* **liberalise** ('lɪbərə,laɪz, 'lɪbrə-) *vb* to make or become liberal ▷ ,liberali'zation *or* ,liberali'sation *n* ▷ 'liberal,izer *or* 'liberal,iser *n*

Liberal Party *n* **1** one of the former major political parties in Britain; in 1988 merged with the Social Democratic Party to form the Social and Liberal Democrats; renamed the Liberal Democrats in 1989 **2** one of the major political parties in Australia, a conservative party, generally opposed to the Labor Party **3** any other party supporting liberal policies

liberal studies *n* (*functioning as singular*) *Brit* a supplementary arts course for those specializing in scientific, technical, or professional studies

liberate ('lɪbə,reɪt) *vb* (*tr*) **1** to give liberty to; make free **2** to release (something, esp a gas) from chemical combination during a chemical reaction **3** to release from occupation or subjugation by a foreign power **4** to free from social prejudices or injustices **5** *euphemistic or facetious* to steal ▷ 'liber,ator *n*

liberated ('lɪbə,reɪtɪd) *adj* **1** given liberty; freed; released **2** released from occupation or subjugation by a foreign power **3** (esp in feminist theory) not bound by traditional sexual and social roles

liberation (,lɪbə'reɪʃən) *n* **1** a liberating or being liberated **2** the seeking of equal status or just treatment for or on behalf of any group believed to be discriminated against: *women's liberation; animal liberation* ▷ ,liber'ationist *n, adj*

liberation theology *n* the belief that Christianity involves not only faith in the teachings of the Church but also a commitment to change social and political conditions from within in societies in which it is considered exploitation and oppression exist

Liberec (*Czech* 'lɪbɛrɛts) *n* a city in the N Czech Republic, on the Neisse River: a centre of the German Sudeten movement in 1938. Pop: 97 000 (2005 est). German name: Reichenberg

Liberia (laɪ'bɪərɪə) *n* a republic in W Africa, on the Atlantic: originated in 1822 as a home for freed Afro-American slaves, with land purchased by the American Colonization Society; republic declared in 1847; exports are predominantly rubber and iron ore. Official language: English. Religion: Christian majority, also animist. Currency: dollar. Capital: Monrovia. Pop: 3 487 000 (2005 est). Area: 111 400 sq km (43 000 sq miles) ▷ Li'berian *adj, n*

libertarian (,lɪbə'tɛərɪən) *n* **1** a believer in freedom of thought, expression, etc **2** *philosophy* a believer in the doctrine of free will. Compare **determinism** ▷ *adj* **3** of, relating to, or characteristic of a libertarian [c18: from LIBERTY] ▷ ,liber'tarianism *n*

libertine ('lɪbə,tiːn, -,taɪn) *n* **1** a morally dissolute person ▷ *adj* **2** morally dissolute [C14 (in the sense: freedman, dissolute person): from Latin *lībertīnus* freedman, from *lībertus* freed, from *līber* free] ▷ 'liber,tinage *or* 'libertin,ism *n*

liberty ('lɪbətɪ) *n*, *pl* **-ties 1** the power of choosing, thinking, and acting for oneself; freedom from control or restriction **2** the right or privilege of access to a particular place; freedom **3** (*often plural*) a social action regarded as being familiar, forward, or improper **4** (*often plural*) an action that is unauthorized or unwarranted in the circumstances: *he took liberties with the translation* **5 a** authorized leave granted to a sailor **b** (*as modifier*): *liberty man; liberty boat* **6** at liberty free, unoccupied, or unrestricted **7** take liberties to be overfamiliar or overpresumptuous (with) [c14: from Old French *liberté*, from Latin *lībertās*, from *līber* free]

Liberty bodice *n* *trademark* a sleeveless vest-like undergarment made from thick cotton and covering the upper part of the body, formerly worn esp by young children

liberty hall *n* (*sometimes capitals*) *informal* a place or condition of complete liberty

Liberty Island *n* a small island in upper New York Bay: site of the Statue of Liberty. Area: 5 hectares (12 acres). Former name (until 1956): Bedloe's Island

Libeskind ('liːbəskɪnd) *n* **Daniel**. born 1946, US architect, born in Poland. Based in Berlin, he designed the Jewish Museum there (1999), the Imperial War Museum in Manchester (2000), the proposed spiral extension to London's Victoria and Albert Museum, and the "Freedom Tower" that will replace the World Trade Center in New York

Libia ('liːbja) *n* the Italian name for **Libya**

libidinous (lɪ'bɪdɪnəs) *adj* characterized by excessive sexual desire ▷ li'bidinously *adv* ▷ li'bidinousness *n*

libido (lɪ'biːdəʊ) *n*, *pl* **-dos 1** *psychoanal* psychic energy emanating from the id **2** sexual urge or desire [C20 (in psychoanalysis): from Latin: desire] ▷ libidinal (lɪ'bɪdɪn*ə*l) *adj* ▷ li'bidinally *adv*

libra ('laɪbrə) *n*, *pl* **-brae** (-briː) an ancient Roman unit of weight corresponding to 1 pound, but equal to about 12 ounces [c14: from Latin, literally: scales]

Libra ('liːbrə) *n*, *Latin genitive* Librae ('liːbriː) **1** *astronomy* a small faint zodiacal constellation in the S hemisphere, lying between Virgo and Scorpius on the ecliptic **2** *astrology* Also called: the Scales, the Balance the seventh sign of the zodiac, symbol ♎, having a cardinal air classification and ruled by the planet Venus. The sun is in this sign between about Sept 23 and Oct 22

librarian (laɪ'brɛərɪən) *n* a person in charge of or assisting in a library ▷ li'brarianship *or* library science *n*

library ('laɪbrərɪ) *n*, *pl* **-braries 1** a room or set of rooms where books and other literary materials are kept **2** a collection of literary materials, films, CDs, children's toys, etc, kept for borrowing or reference **3** the building or institution that houses such a collection: *a public library* **4** a set of books published as a series, often in a similar format **5** *computing* a collection of standard programs and subroutines for immediate use, usually stored on disk or some other storage device **6** a collection of specific items for reference or checking against: *a library of genetic material* [c14: from Old French *librairie*, from Medieval Latin *librāris*, n use of Latin *librārius* relating to books, from *liber* book]

libration (laɪ'breɪʃən) *n* **1** the act or an instance of oscillating **2** a real or apparent oscillation of the moon enabling approximately 59 per cent of the surface to be visible from the earth over a period of time [c17: from Latin *librātus*, from *librāre* to balance]

librettist (lɪ'brɛtɪst) *n* the author of a libretto

libretto (lɪ'brɛtəʊ) *n*, *pl* **-tos** *or* **-ti** (-tiː) a text written for and set to music in an opera, etc [c18: from Italian, diminutive of *libro* book]

Libreville (*French* librəvil) *n* the capital of Gabon, in the west on the estuary of the Gabon River: founded as a French trading post in 1843 and expanded with the settlement of freed slaves in 1848. Pop: 649 000 (2005 est)

Librium ('lɪbrɪəm) *n* *trademark* a brand of the drug chlordiazepoxide. See also **benzodiazepine**

Libya ('lɪbɪə) *n* a republic in N Africa, on the Mediterranean: became an Italian colony in 1912; divided after World War II into Tripolitania and Cyrenaica (under British administration) and Fezzan (under French); gained independence in 1951; monarchy overthrown by a military junta in 1969. It consists almost wholly of desert and is a major exporter of oil. Official language: Arabic. Official religion: (Sunni) Muslim. Currency: Libyan dinar. Capital: Tripoli. Pop: 5 659 000 (2004 est). Area: 1 760 000 sq km (680 000 sq miles) ▷ Libyan *adj, n*

Libyan Desert *n* a desert in N Africa, in E Libya, W Egypt, and the NW Sudan: the NE part of the Sahara

lice (laɪs) *n* the plural of **louse**

licence *or* *US* **license** ('laɪsəns) *n* **1** a certificate, tag, document, etc, giving official permission to do something **2** formal permission or exemption **3** liberty of action or thought; freedom **4** intentional disregard of or deviation from conventional rules to achieve a certain effect: *poetic licence* **5** excessive freedom [C14: via Old French and Medieval Latin *licentia* permission, from Latin: freedom, from *licet* it is allowed]

license ('laɪsəns) *vb* (*tr*) **1** to grant or give a licence for (something, such as the sale of alcohol) **2** to give permission to or for ▷ 'licensable *adj* ▷ 'licenser or 'licensor *n*

licensee (,laɪsən'siː) *n* a person who holds a licence, esp one to sell alcoholic drink

licentiate (laɪ'sɛnʃɪɪt) *n* **1** a person who has received a formal attestation of professional competence to practise a certain profession or teach a certain skill or subject **2** a degree between that of bachelor and doctor awarded now only by certain chiefly European universities **3** a person who holds this degree **4** *chiefly Presbyterian Church* a person holding a licence to preach [C15: from Medieval Latin *licentiātus*, from *licentiāre* to permit] ▷ li'centiate,ship *n*

licentious (laɪ'sɛnʃəs) *adj* **1** sexually unrestrained or promiscuous **2** *now rare* showing disregard for convention [C16: from Latin *licentiōsus* capricious, from *licentia* LICENCE] ▷ li'centiously *adv* ▷ li'centiousness *n*

lichee (,laɪ'tʃiː) *n* a variant spelling of **litchi**

lichen ('laɪkən, 'lɪtʃən) *n* an organism that is formed by the symbiotic association of a fungus and an alga or cyanobacterium and occurs as crusty patches or bushy growths on tree trunks, bare ground, etc. Lichens are now classified as a phylum of fungi (*Mycophycophyta*) [C17: via Latin from Greek *leikhēn*, from *leikhein* to lick] ▷ 'lichened *adj* ▷ 'lichenous or 'lichen,ose *adj*

Lichfield ('lɪtʃ,fiːld) *n* a city in central England, in SE Staffordshire: cathedral with three spires (13th-14th century); birthplace of Samuel Johnson, during whose lifetime the **Lichfield Group** (a literary circle) flourished. Pop: 28 435 (2001)

lich gate (lɪtʃ) *n* a variant spelling of **lych gate**

Lichtenstein ('lɪktən,staɪn) *n* **Roy.** 1923-97, US pop artist

licit ('lɪsɪt) *adj* a less common word for **lawful** [C15: from Latin *licitus* permitted, from *licēre* to be permitted] ▷ 'licitly *adv* ▷ 'licitness *n*

lick (lɪk) *vb* **1** (*tr*) to pass the tongue over, esp in order to taste or consume **2** to flicker or move lightly over or round (something): *the flames licked around the door* **3** (*tr*) *informal* **a** to defeat or vanquish **b** to flog or thrash **c** to be or do much better than **4** lick into shape to put into a satisfactory condition: from the former belief that bear cubs were born formless and had to be licked into shape by their mother **5** lick one's wounds to retire after a defeat or setback in order to husband one's resources ▷ *n* **6** an instance of passing the tongue over something **7** a small amount: *a lick of paint* **8** Also called: salt lick a block of compressed salt or chemical matter provided for domestic animals to lick for medicinal and nutritional purposes **9** *informal* a hit; blow **10** *slang* a musical phrase, usually on one instrument **11** *informal* speed; rate of movement: *he was going at quite a lick when he hit it* **12** a lick and a promise something hastily done, esp a hurried wash [Old English *liccian*; related to Old High German *leckon*, Latin *lingere*, Greek *leikhein*] ▷ 'licker *n*

lickerish or **liquorish** ('lɪkərɪʃ) *adj archaic* **1** lecherous or lustful **2** greedy; gluttonous **3** appetizing or tempting [C16: changed from C13 *lickerous*, via Norman French from Old French *lecherous* lecherous; see LECHER]

lickety-split ('lɪkɪtɪ'splɪt) *adv US & Canadian informal* very quickly; speedily [C19: from LICK + SPLIT]

licking ('lɪkɪŋ) *n informal* **1** a beating **2** a defeat

lickspittle ('lɪk,spɪtəl) *n* a flattering or servile person

licorice ('lɪkərɪs) *n* the usual US and Canadian spelling of **liquorice**

lictor ('lɪktə) *n* one of a group of ancient Roman officials, usually bearing fasces, who attended magistrates, etc [C16 *lictor*, C14 *littour*, from Latin *ligāre* to bind]

lid (lɪd) *n* **1** a cover, usually removable or hinged, for a receptacle: *a saucepan lid; a desk lid* **2** short for **eyelid 3** put

the lid on *informal* **a** *Brit* to be the final blow to **b** to curb, prevent, or discourage [Old English *hlid*; related to Old Friesian *hlid*, Old High German *hlit* cover] ▷ 'lidded *adj* ▷ 'lidless *adj*

Liddell Hart ('lɪdəl haːt) *n* Sir **Basil Henry.** 1895-1970, British military strategist and historian: he advocated the development of mechanized warfare before World War II

Lidice (Czech 'lidjtsɛ) *n* a mining village in the Czech Republic: destroyed by the Germans in 1942 in reprisal for the assassination of Reinhard Heydrich; rebuilt as a national memorial

lido ('liːdəʊ) *n, pl* -dos *Brit* a public place of recreation, including a pool for swimming or water sports [C20: after the *Lido*, island bathing beach near Venice, from Latin *litus* shore]

lie¹ (laɪ) *vb* lies, lying, lied **1** (*intr*) to speak untruthfully with intent to mislead or deceive **2** (*intr*) to convey a false impression or practise deception: *the camera does not lie* ▷ *n* **3** an untrue or deceptive statement deliberately used to mislead **4** something that is deliberately intended to deceive **5** give the lie to **a** to disprove **b** to accuse of lying Related adj: **mendacious** [Old English *lyge* (n), *lēogan* (vb); related to Old High German *liogan*, Gothic *liugan*]

lie² (laɪ) *vb* lies, lying, lay (leɪ), lain (leɪn) (*intr*) **1** (often foll by *down*) to place oneself or be in a prostrate position, horizontal to the ground **2** to be situated, esp on a horizontal surface: *the pencil is lying on the desk; India lies to the south of Russia* **3** to be buried: *here lies Jane Brown* **4** (*copula*) to be and remain (in a particular state or condition): *to lie dormant* **5** to stretch or extend: *the city lies before us* **6** (usually foll by *on* or *upon*) to rest or weigh: *my sins lie heavily on my mind* **7** (usually foll by *in*) to exist or consist inherently: *strength lies in unity* **8** (foll by *with*) **a** to be or rest (with): *the ultimate decision lies with you* **b** *archaic* to have sexual intercourse (with) **9** (of an action, claim, appeal, etc) to subsist; be maintainable or admissible **10** *archaic* to stay temporarily ▷ *n* **11** the manner, place, or style in which something is situated **12** the hiding place or lair of an animal **13** lie of the land **a** the topography of the land **b** the way in which a situation is developing or people are behaving ▷ See also **lie down, lie in, lie to** [Old English *licgan* akin to Old High German *ligen* to lie, Latin *lectus* bed]

● USAGE See at **lay¹**

Lie (liː) *n* **Trygve Halvdan** ('trygvə 'haldən). 1896-1968, Norwegian statesman; first secretary-general of the United Nations (1946-52)

Liebig (German 'liːbɪç) *n* **Justus** ('justus), Baron von Liebig. 1803-73, German chemist, who founded agricultural chemistry. He also contributed to organic chemistry, esp to the concept of radicals, and discovered chloroform

Liebig condenser (German 'liːbɪç) *n chem* a laboratory condenser consisting of a glass tube surrounded by a glass jacket through which cooling water flows [named after Justus, Baron von Liebig (1803-73), German chemist]

Liebknecht (German 'liːpknɛçt) *n* **1 Karl** (karl). 1871-1919, German socialist leader: with Rosa Luxemburg he led an unsuccessful Communist revolt (1919) and was assassinated **2** his father, **Wilhelm** ('vɪlhɛlm). 1826-1900, German socialist leader and journalist, a founder (1869) of what was to become (1891) the German Social Democratic Party

Liechtenstein ('lɪktən,staɪn; German 'lɪçtənʃtaɪn) *n* a small mountainous principality in central Europe on the Rhine: formed in 1719 by the uniting of the lordships of Schellenburg and Vaduz, which had been purchased by the Austrian family of Liechtenstein; customs union formed with Switzerland in 1924. Official language: German. Religion: Roman Catholic majority. Currency: Swiss franc. Capital: Vaduz. Pop: 34 000 (2003 est). Area: 160 sq km (62 sq miles)

lied (liːd; German liːt) *n, pl* lieder ('liːdə; German 'liːdər) *music* any of various musical settings for solo voice and piano of a romantic or lyrical poem, for which composers such as Schubert, Schumann, and Wolf are famous [from German: song]

lie detector *n* a polygraph used esp by a police interrogator to detect false or devious answers to questions, a sudden change in one or more involuntary physiological responses being considered a manifestation of guilt, fear, etc

lie down *vb* (*intr, adverb*) **1** to place oneself or be in a prostrate position in order to rest or sleep **2** to accept without protest or opposition (esp in the phrases **lie down under, take something lying down**) ▷ *n* lie-down **3** a rest

lief (liːf) *adv* **1** *now rare* gladly; willingly: *I'd as lief go today as tomorrow* ▷ *adj* **2** *archaic* **a** ready; glad **b** dear; beloved [Old English *lēof*; related to *lufu* love]

liege (liːdʒ) *adj* **1** (of a lord) owed feudal allegiance (esp in the phrase **liege lord**) **2** (of a vassal or servant) owing feudal allegiance: *a liege subject* **3** faithful; loyal ▷ *n* **4** a liege lord **5** a liegeman or true subject [c13: from Old French *lige*, from Medieval Latin *līticus*, from *lītus, laetus* serf, of Germanic origin]

Liège (lɪˈeɪʒ; *French* ljɛʒ) *n* **1** a province of E Belgium: formerly a principality of the Holy Roman Empire, much larger than the present-day province. Pop: 1 029 605 (2004 est). Area: 3877 sq km (1497 sq miles) **2** a city in E Belgium, capital of Liège province: the largest French-speaking city in Belgium; river port and industrial centre. Pop: 185 488 (2004 est) ▷ Flemish name: Luik

liegeman (ˈliːdʒˌmæn) *n, pl* -men **1** (formerly) the subject of a sovereign or feudal lord; vassal **2** a loyal follower

Liegnitz (ˈliːɡnɪts) *n* the German name for **Legnica**

lie in *vb* (*intr, adverb*) **1** to remain in bed late in the morning **2** to be confined in childbirth ▷ *n* lie-in **3** a long stay in bed in the morning

lien (ˈliːən, liːn) *n law* a right to retain possession of another's property pending discharge of a debt [c16: via Old French from Latin *ligāmen* bond, from *ligāre* to bind]

Liepāja *or* **Lepaya** (lɪˈpɑːjə) *n* a port in W Latvia on the Baltic Sea: founded by the Teutonic Knights in 1263: a naval and industrial centre, with a fishing fleet. Pop: 86 985 (2002 est). Russian name: Libava. German name: Libau

lierne (lɪˈɜːn) *n architect* a short secondary rib that connects the intersections of the primary ribs, esp as used in Gothic vaulting [c19: from French, perhaps related to *lier* to bind]

Liestal (*German* ˈliːstaːl) *n* a city in NW Switzerland, capital of Basel-Land demicanton. Pop: 12 930 (2000)

lie to *vb* (*intr, adverb*) *nautical* (of a vessel) to be hove to with little or no swinging

Lietuva (lɪəˈtuːvə) *n* the Lithuanian name for **Lithuania**

lieu (ljuː, luː) *n* stead; place (esp in the phrases **in lieu, in lieu of**) [c13: from Old French, ultimately from Latin *locus* place]

lieutenant (lɛfˈtɛnənt; *US* luːˈtɛnənt) *n* **1** a military officer holding commissioned rank immediately junior to a captain **2** a naval officer holding commissioned rank immediately junior to a lieutenant commander **3** *US* an officer in a police or fire department ranking immediately junior to a captain **4** a person who holds an office in subordination to or in place of a superior [c14: from Old French, literally: place-holding] ▷ lieu'tenancy *n*

lieutenant colonel *n* an officer holding commissioned rank immediately junior to a colonel in certain armies, air forces, and marine corps

lieutenant commander *n* an officer holding commissioned rank in certain navies immediately junior to a commander

lieutenant general *n* an officer holding commissioned rank in certain armies, air forces, and marine corps immediately junior to a general

lieutenant governor *n* **1** a deputy governor **2** (in the US) an elected official who acts as deputy to a state governor and succeeds him if he dies **3** lieutenant-governor (in Canada) the representative of the Crown in a province: appointed by the federal government acting for the Crown

Lifar (*Russian* ljiˈfar) *n* **Serge** (sɛrʒ). 1905–86, Russian ballet dancer and choreographer: ballet master at the Paris Opera Ballet (1932–58). His ballets include *Prométhée* (1929), *Icare* (1935), and *Phèdre* (1950)

life (laɪf) *n, pl* **lives** (laɪvz) **1** the state or quality that distinguishes living beings or organisms from dead ones and from inorganic matter, characterized chiefly by metabolism, growth, and the ability to reproduce and respond to stimuli. Related adj: **animate 2** the period between birth and death **3** a living person or being: *to save a life* **4** the time between birth and the present time **5 a** the remainder or extent of one's life **b** (as modifier): *a life sentence; life membership; life subscription; life work* **6** short for **life imprisonment 7** the amount of time that something is active or functioning: *the life of a battery* **8** a present condition, state, or mode of existence: *my life is very dull here* **9 a** a biography **b** (as modifier): *a life story* **10** a characteristic state or mode of existence: *town life* **11** the sum or course of human events and activities **12** liveliness or high spirits: *full of life* **13** a source of strength, animation, or vitality: *he was the life of the show* **14** all living things, taken as a whole: *there is no life on Mars; plant life* **15** (modifier) *arts* drawn or taken from a living model: *life drawing; a life mask* **16** (in certain games) one of a number of opportunities of participation **17** as large as life *informal* real and living **18** for the life of one though trying desperately **19** not on your life *informal* certainly not **20** the life and soul *informal* a person regarded as the main source of merriment and liveliness: *the life and soul of the party* **21** to the life (of a copy or image) resembling the original exactly **22** true to life faithful to reality [Old English *līf*; related to Old High German *lib*, Old Norse *líf* life, body]

life assurance *n* a form of insurance providing for the payment of a specified sum to a named beneficiary on the death of the policyholder. Also called: **life insurance**

life belt *n* a ring filled with buoyant material or air, used to keep a person afloat when in danger of drowning

lifeblood (ˈlaɪfˌblʌd) *n* **1** the blood, considered as vital to sustain life **2** the essential or animating force

lifeboat (ˈlaɪfˌbəʊt) *n* **1** a boat, propelled by oars or a motor, used for rescuing people at sea, escaping from a sinking ship, etc **2** *informal* a fund set up by the dealers in a market to rescue any member who may become insolvent as a result of a collapse in market prices

life buoy *n* any of various kinds of buoyant device for keeping people afloat in an emergency

life coach *n* a person whose job is to improve the quality of his or her client's life, by offering advice on professional and personal matters, such as career, health, personal relationships, etc

life cycle *n* the series of changes occurring in an animal or plant between one development stage and the identical stage in the next generation

life expectancy *n* the statistically determined average number of years of life remaining after a specified age for a given group of individuals

lifeguard (ˈlaɪfˌɡɑːd) *n* a person present at a beach or pool to guard people against the risk of drowning

life imprisonment *n* (in Britain) an indeterminate sentence always given for murder and as a maximum sentence in several other crimes. There is no remission, although the Home Secretary may order the prisoner's release on licence

life jacket *n* an inflatable sleeveless jacket worn to keep a person afloat when in danger of drowning

lifeless (ˈlaɪflɪs) *adj* **1** without life; inanimate; dead **2** not sustaining living organisms **3** having no vitality or animation **4** unconscious ▷ 'lifelessly *adv* ▷ 'lifelessness *n*

lifelike (ˈlaɪfˌlaɪk) *adj* closely resembling or representing life ▷ 'life,likeness *n*

lifeline (ˈlaɪfˌlaɪn) *n* **1** a line thrown or fired aboard a vessel for hauling in a hawser for a breeches buoy **2** a line by which a deep-sea diver is raised or lowered **3** a vital line of access or communication

lifelong (ˈlaɪfˌlɒŋ) *adj* lasting for or as if for a lifetime

lifelong learning *n* the provision or use of both formal and informal learning opportunities throughout people's lives in order to foster the continuous development and improvement of the knowledge and skills needed for employment and personal fulfilment

life partner *n* either member of a couple in a long-term relationship

life peer *n Brit* a peer whose title lapses at his or her death

life preserver *n* **1** *Brit* a club or bludgeon, esp one kept for self-defence **2** *US & Canadian* a life belt or life jacket

lifer ('laɪfə) *n informal* a prisoner sentenced to life imprisonment

life raft *n* a raft for emergency use at sea

life-saver *n* **1** the saver of a person's life **2** another name for **lifeguard 3** *informal* a person or thing that gives help in time of need > 'life-,saving *adj, n*

life science *n* any one of the branches of science concerned with the structure and behaviour of living organisms, such as biology, botany, zoology, physiology, or biochemistry

life-size *or* **life-sized** *adj* representing actual size

life span *n* the period of time during which a human being, animal, machine, etc, may be expected to live or function under normal conditions

lifestyle ('laɪf,staɪl) *n* **1** a set of attitudes, habits, or possessions associated with a particular person or group **2** such attitudes, etc, regarded as fashionable or desirable **3** *NZ* **a** a luxurious semirural manner of living **b** (*as modifier*): *a lifestyle property* ▷ *adj* **4** suggestive of a fashionable or desirable lifestyle: *a lifestyle café* **5** (of a drug) designed to treat problems, such as impotence or excess weight, which affect a person's quality of life rather than his or her health

lifestyle block *n NZ* a semi-rural property comprising a house and land for small-scale farming

lifestyle business *n* a small business in which the owner is more anxious to pursue interests that reflect his or her lifestyle than to make more than a comfortable living

lifestyle disease *n* a disease that potentially can be prevented by changes in diet, environment, and lifestyle, such as heart disease, stroke, obesity, and osteoporosis [C20]

lifestyler ('laɪf,staɪlə) *n informal* a person who adopts a particular lifestyle: *new lifestyler; vampire lifestyler*

life-support *adj* of or providing the equipment required to sustain human life in an unnatural environment, such as in space, or in severe illness or disability

lifetime ('laɪf,taɪm) *n* **1 a** the length of time a person or animal is alive **b** (*as modifier*): *a lifetime supply* **2** the length of time that something functions, is useful, etc **3** *physics* the average time of existence of an unstable or reactive entity, such as a nucleus, excited state, elementary particle, etc; mean life

Liffey ('lɪfɪ) *n* a river in E Republic of Ireland, rising in the Wicklow Mountains and flowing west, then northeast through Dublin into Dublin Bay. Length: 80 km (50 miles)

Lifford ('lɪfəd) *n* the county town of Donegal, Republic of Ireland; market town. Pop: 1395 (2002)

LIFO ('laɪfəʊ) *n acronym* last in, first out (as an accounting principle in sorting stock). See **FIFO**

lift (lɪft) *vb* **1** to rise or cause to rise upwards from the ground or another support to a higher place: *to lift a sack* **2** to move or cause to move upwards: *to lift one's eyes* **3** (*tr*) to take hold of in order to carry or remove: *to lift something down from a shelf* **4** (*tr*) to raise in status, spirituality, estimation, etc: *his position lifted him from the common crowd* **5** (*tr*) to revoke or rescind: *to lift tax restrictions* **6** (*tr*) to take (plants or underground crops) out of the ground for transplanting or harvesting **7** (*intr*) to disappear by lifting or as if by lifting: *the fog lifted* **8** (*tr*) *informal* to take unlawfully or dishonourably; steal **9** (*tr*) *informal* to make dishonest use of (another person's idea, writing, etc); plagiarize **10** (*tr*) *slang* to arrest **11** (*tr*) to perform a face-lift on ▷ *n* **12** the act or an instance of lifting **13** the power or force available or used for lifting **14 a** *Brit* a platform, compartment, or cage raised or lowered in a vertical shaft to transport persons or goods in a building. US and Canadian word: **elevator b** See **chairlift, ski lift 15** the distance or degree to which

something is lifted **16** a usually free ride as a passenger in a car or other vehicle **17** a rise in the height of the ground **18** a rise in morale or feeling of cheerfulness usually caused by some specific thing or event **19** the force required to lift an object **20** a layer of the heel of a shoe, etc, or a detachable pad inside the shoe to give the wearer added height **21** aid; help **22** the component of the aerodynamic forces acting on a wing, etc, at right angles to the airflow [C13: from Scandinavian; related to Old Norse *lypta*, Old English *lyft* sky; compare LOFT] > 'lifter *n*

liftoff ('lɪft,ɒf) *n* **1** the initial movement or ascent of a rocket from its launch pad **2** the instant at which this occurs ▷ *vb* **lift off 3** (*intr, adverb*) (of a rocket) to leave its launch pad

lift pump *n* a pump that raises a fluid to a higher level. It usually consists of a piston and vertical cylinder with flap or ball valves in both piston and cylinder base. See **force pump**

lig (lɪg) *Brit slang* ▷ *n* **1** (esp in the entertainment industry and the media) a function at which free entertainment and refreshments are available ▷ *vb* **ligs, ligging, ligged 2** (*intr*) to attend such a function in order to take advantage of free entertainment and refreshments; freeload [C20: origin uncertain] > 'ligger *n* > 'ligging *n*

ligament ('lɪgəmənt) *n* **1** *anatomy* any one of the bands or sheets of tough fibrous connective tissue that restrict movement in joints, connect various bones or cartilages, support muscles, etc **2** any physical or abstract connection or bond [C14: from Medieval Latin *ligāmentum*, from Latin (in the sense: bandage), from *ligāre* to bind]

ligand ('lɪgənd, 'laɪ-) *n chem* an atom, molecule, radical, or ion forming a complex with a central atom [C20: from Latin *ligandum*, gerund of *ligāre* to bind]

ligate ('laɪgeɪt) *vb* (*tr*) to tie up or constrict (something) with a ligature [C16: from Latin *ligātus*, from *ligāre* to bind] > li'gation *n*

ligature ('lɪgətʃə, -,tʃʊə) *n* **1** the act of binding or tying up **2** something used to bind **3** a link, bond, or tie **4** *surgery* a thread or wire for tying around a vessel, duct, etc, as for constricting the flow of blood to a part **5** *printing* a character of two or more joined letters, such as, fi, fl, ffi, ffl **6** *music* a slur or the group of notes connected by it ▷ *vb* **7** (*tr*) to bind with a ligature; ligate [C14: from Late Latin *ligātūra*, ultimately from Latin *ligāre* to bind]

liger ('laɪgə) *n* the hybrid offspring of a female tiger and a male lion

Ligeti (*Hungarian* 'lɪgeti) *n* **György** (djɔrdj). 1923–2006, Hungarian composer, resident in Vienna. His works, noted for their experimentalism, include *Atmosphères* (1961) for orchestra, *Volumina* (1962) for organ, and a requiem mass (1965)

light¹ (laɪt) *n* **1** the medium of illumination that makes sight possible **2** Also called: **visible radiation** electromagnetic radiation that is capable of causing a visual sensation and has wavelengths from about 380 to about 780 nanometres **3** (*not in technical usage*) electromagnetic radiation that has a wavelength outside this range, esp ultraviolet radiation: *ultraviolet light* **4** the sensation experienced when electromagnetic radiation within the visible spectrum falls on the retina of the eye **5** anything that illuminates, such as a lamp or candle **6** See **traffic light 7** a particular quality or type of light: *a good light for reading* **8 a** illumination from the sun during the day; daylight **b** the time this appears; daybreak; dawn **9** anything that allows the entrance of light, such as a window or compartment of a window **10** the condition of being visible or known (esp in the phrases **bring** *or* **come to light**) **11** an aspect or view: *he saw it in a different light* **12** mental understanding or spiritual insight **13** a person considered to be an authority or leader **14** brightness of countenance, esp a sparkle in the eyes **15 a** the act of igniting or kindling something, such as a cigarette **b** something that ignites or kindles, esp in a specified manner, such as a spark or flame **c** something used for igniting or kindling, such as a match **16** See **lighthouse 17 in light of** *or* **in the light of** in view of; taking into account; considering **18** see the light *or* see the light of day **a** to come into being **b** to come to public notice **19** strike a light (*verb*) **a** to ignite something, esp a match, by friction **b** (*interjection*) *Brit* an exclamation of surprise ▷ *adj* **20** full of light; well-lighted **21** (of a colour) reflecting or transmitting a large amount of light: *light yellow* ▷ *vb* lights, lighting, lighted *or* lit (lɪt) **22** to ignite or cause to ignite **23** (often foll by *up*) to illuminate or cause to illuminate **24** to make or become cheerful or animated **25** (*tr*) to guide or lead by light ▷ See also **lights¹**, **light up** [Old English *lēoht*; related to Old High German *lioht*, Gothic *liuhath*, Latin *lux*] > 'lightish *adj* > 'lightless *adj*

light² (laɪt) *adj* **1** not heavy; weighing relatively little **2** having relatively low density: *magnesium is a light metal* **3** lacking sufficient weight; not agreeing with standard or official weights **4** not great in degree, intensity, or number: *light rain; a light eater* **5** without burdens, difficulties, or problems; easily borne or done: *a light heart; light work* **6** graceful, agile, or deft: *light fingers* **7** not bulky or clumsy **8** not serious or profound; entertaining: *light verse* **9** without importance or consequence; insignificant: *no light matter* **10** frivolous or capricious **11** loose in morals **12** dizzy or unclear: *a light head* **13** (of bread, cake, etc) spongy or well leavened **14** easily digested: *a light meal* **15** relatively low in alcoholic content: *a light wine* **16** (of a soil) having a crumbly texture **17** (of a vessel, lorry, etc) **a** designed to carry light loads **b** not loaded **18** carrying light arms or equipment: *light infantry* **19** (of an industry) engaged in the production of small consumer goods using light machinery **20** *aeronautics* (of an aircraft) having a maximum take-off weight less than 5670 kilograms (12 500 pounds) **21** *chem* (of an oil fraction obtained from coal tar) having a boiling range between about 100° and 210°C **22** (of a railway) having a narrow gauge, or in some cases a standard gauge with speed or load restrictions not applied to a main line **23** *phonetics, prosody* (of a syllable, vowel, etc) unaccented or weakly stressed; short **24** light on *informal* lacking a sufficient quantity of (something) **25** make light of to treat as insignificant or trifling ▷ *adv* **26** with little equipment, baggage, etc: *to travel light* ▷ *vb* lights, lighting, lighted *or* lit (lɪt) (*intr*) **27** (esp of birds) to settle or land after flight **28** to get down from a horse, vehicle, etc **29** (foll by *on or upon*) to come upon unexpectedly **30** to strike or fall on: *the choice lighted on me* ▷ See also **light into**, **light out**, **lights²** [Old English *lēoht*; related to Dutch *licht*, Gothic *leihts*] > 'lightish *adj* > 'lightly *adv* > 'lightness *n*

light air *n* very light air movement of force one on the Beaufort scale

light box *n* a light source contained in a box and covered with a diffuser, used for viewing photographic transparencies, negatives, etc

light breeze *n* a very light wind of force two on the Beaufort scale

light bulb *n* a glass bulb containing a gas, such as argon or nitrogen, at low pressure and enclosing a thin metal filament that emits light when an electric current is passed through it. Sometimes shortened to: **bulb**

light bulb moment *n informal* a moment of sudden inspiration, revelation, or recognition [c20: from the cartoon image of a light bulb lighting up above a character's head when he or she has an idea]

light-emitting diode *n* a diode of semiconductor material, such as gallium arsenide, that emits light when a forward bias is applied, the colour depending on the semiconductor material: used as off/on indicators. Abbreviation: **LED**

lighten¹ ('laɪtᵊn) *vb* **1** to become or make light **2** (*intr*) to shine; glow **3** (*intr*) (of lightning) to flash

lighten² ('laɪtᵊn) *vb* **1** to make or become less heavy **2** to make or become less burdensome or oppressive; mitigate **3** to make or become more cheerful or lively

lightening ('laɪtᵊnɪŋ) *n obstetrics* the sensation, experienced by many women late in pregnancy when the head of the fetus enters the pelvis, of a reduction in pressure on the diaphragm, making it easier to breathe

lighter¹ ('laɪtə) *n* **1** a small portable device for providing a naked flame or red-hot filament to light cigarettes, etc

2 a person or thing that ignites something

lighter² ('laɪtə) *n* a flat-bottomed barge used for transporting cargo, esp in loading or unloading a ship [c15: probably from Middle Dutch; compare c16 Dutch *lichter*]

lighterage ('laɪtərɪdʒ) *n* **1** the conveyance or loading and unloading of cargo by means of a lighter **2** the charge for this service

light face *printing* ▷ *n* **1** a weight of type characterized by light thin lines ▷ *adj* Also: **light-faced 2** (of type) having this weight

light-fingered *adj* having nimble or agile fingers, esp for thieving or picking pockets

light flyweight *n* **1** an amateur boxer weighing not more than 48 kg (106 pounds) **2** a wrestler in a similar weight category

Lightfoot ('laɪtfʊt) *n* **Gordon.** born 1938, Canadian singer and songwriter; his recordings include 'If You Could Read My Mind' (1970), *Dream Street Rose* (1980) and *Harmony* (2004)

light-footed *adj* having a light or nimble tread > ,light-'footedly *adv*

light-headed *adj* **1** frivolous in disposition or behaviour **2** giddy; feeling faint or slightly delirious > ,light-'headedly *adv* > ,light-'headedness *n*

light-hearted *adj* cheerful or carefree in mood or disposition > ,light-'heartedly *adv* > ,light-'heartedness *n*

light heavyweight *n* **1** Also called (in Britain): cruiserweight **a** a professional boxer weighing 160–175 pounds (72.5–79.5 kg) **b** an amateur boxer weighing 75–81 kg (165–179 pounds) **2** a wrestler in a similar weight category (usually 192–214 pounds (87–97 kg))

lighthouse ('laɪt,haʊs) *n* a fixed structure in the form of a tower equipped with a light visible to mariners for warning them of obstructions, for marking harbour entrances, etc

lighting ('laɪtɪŋ) *n* **1** the act or quality of illumination or ignition **2** the apparatus for supplying artificial light effects to a stage, film, or television set **3** the distribution of light on an object or figure, as in painting, photography, etc

lighting cameraman *n films* the person who designs and supervises the lighting of scenes to be filmed

lighting-up time *n* the time when vehicles are required by law to have their lights switched on

light into *vb* (*intr, preposition*) *informal* to assail physically or verbally

light middleweight *n* an amateur boxer weighing 67–71 kg (148–157 pounds)

lightness ('laɪtnɪs) *n* the attribute of an object or colour that enables an observer to judge the extent to which the object or colour reflects or transmits incident light

lightning ('laɪtnɪŋ) *n* **1** a flash of light in the sky, occurring during a thunderstorm and caused by a discharge of electricity, either between clouds or between a cloud and the earth **2** (*modifier*) fast and sudden: *a lightning raid* [c14: variant of *lightening*]

lightning conductor *or* **lightning rod** *n* a metal strip terminating in a series of sharp points, attached to the highest part of a building, etc, to discharge the electric field before it can reach a dangerous level and cause a lightning strike

light opera *n* another term for **operetta**

light out *vb* (*intr, adverb*) *informal* to depart quickly, as if being chased

light pen *n computing* **a** a rodlike device which, when applied to the screen of a cathode-ray tube, can detect the time of passage of the illuminated spot across that point thus enabling a computer to determine the position on the screen being pointed at **b** a penlike device, used to read bar codes, that emits light and determines the intensity of that light as reflected from a small area of an adjacent surface

light pollution *n* the glow from street and domestic lighting that obscures the night sky and hinders the observation of faint stars

light rail *n* a transport system using small trains or trams, often serving parts of a large metropolitan area

lights¹ (laɪts) *pl n* a person's ideas, knowledge, or

lights² (laɪts) *pl n* the lungs, esp of sheep, bullocks, and pigs, used for feeding pets and occasionally in human food [C13: plural noun use of LIGHT², referring to the light weight of the lungs]

light-sensitive *adj physics* (of a surface) having a photoelectric property, such as the ability to generate a current, change its electrical resistance, etc, when exposed to light

lightship ('laɪtˌʃɪp) *n* a ship equipped as a lighthouse and moored where a fixed structure would prove impracticable

light show *n* a kaleidoscopic display of moving lights, etc, projected onto a screen, esp during pop concerts

lightsome ('laɪtsəm) *adj archaic or poetic* **1** lighthearted **2** airy or buoyant **3** not serious; frivolous

lights out *n* **1** the time when those resident at an institution, such as soldiers in barracks or children at a boarding school, are expected to retire to bed **2** a fanfare or other signal indicating or signifying this

light table *n printing* a translucent surface of ground glass or a similar substance, illuminated from below and used for the examination of positive or negative film, and for the make-up of photocomposed pages

light trap *n* any mechanical arrangement that allows some form of movement to take place while excluding light, such as a light-proof door or the lips of a film cassette

light up *vb* (*adverb*) **1** to light a cigarette, pipe, etc **2** to illuminate or cause to illuminate **3** to make or become cheerful or animated

lightweight ('laɪtˌweɪt) *adj* **1** of a relatively light weight **2** not serious; trivial ▷ *n* **3** a person or animal of a relatively light weight **4 a** a professional boxer weighing 130–135 pounds (59–61 kg) **b** an amateur boxer weighing 57–60 kg (126–132 pounds) **5** a wrestler in a similar weight category (usually 115–126 pounds (52–57 kg)) **6** *informal* a person of little importance or influence

light welterweight *n* an amateur boxer weighing 60–63.5 kg (132–140 pounds)

light year *n* a unit of distance used in astronomy, equal to the distance travelled by light in one year, i.e. 9.4607 × 10¹² kilometres or 0.3066 parsecs

ligneous ('lɪgnɪəs) *adj* of or resembling wood [C17: from Latin *ligneus*, from *lignum* wood]

lignin ('lɪgnɪn) *n* a complex polymer occurring in certain plant cell walls making the plant rigid

lignite ('lɪgnaɪt) *n* a brown carbonaceous sedimentary rock with woody texture that consists of accumulated layers of partially decomposed vegetation: used as a fuel. Fixed carbon content: 46–60 per cent; calorific value: 1.28 × 10⁷ to 1.93 × 10⁷ J/kg (5500 to 8300 Btu/lb). Also called: brown coal ▷ lignitic (lɪg'nɪtɪk) *adj*

lignum vitae ('lɪgnəm 'vaɪtɪ) *n* **1** either of two zygophyllaceous tropical American trees, *Guaiacum officinale* or *G. sanctum*, having blue or purple flowers **2** the heavy resinous wood of either of these trees, which is used in machine bearings, casters, etc: formerly thought to have medicinal properties ▷ See also **guaiacum** [New Latin, from Late Latin, literally: wood of life]

ligroin ('lɪgrəʊɪn) *n* a volatile fraction of petroleum containing aliphatic hydrocarbons of the paraffin series. It has an approximate boiling point range of 70°–130°C and is used as a solvent [origin unknown]

Liguria (lɪ'gjʊərɪə) *n* a region of NW Italy, on the **Ligurian Sea** (an arm of the Mediterranean): the third smallest of the regions of Italy. Pop: 1 572 197 (2003 est). Area: 5410 sq km (2089 sq miles) ▷ Li'gurian *adj, n*

likable *or* **likeable** ('laɪkəbᵊl) *adj* easy to like; pleasing > 'likableness *or* 'likeableness *n*

Likasi (lɪ'kɑːsɪ) *n* a city in the S Democratic Republic of Congo (formerly Zaïre): a centre of copper and cobalt production. Pop: 345 000 (2005 est). Former name: Jadotville

like¹ (laɪk) *adj* **1** (*prenominal*) similar; resembling ▷ *prep* **2** similar to; similarly to; in the manner of: *acting like a maniac; he's so like his father* **3** used correlatively to express similarity in certain proverbs: *like mother, like daughter*

4 such as: *there are lots of ways you might amuse yourself — like taking a long walk, for instance* ▷ *adv* **5** a dialect word for **likely 6** *not standard* as it were: often used as a parenthetic filler ▷ *conj* **7** *not standard* as though; as if: *you look like you've just seen a ghost* **8** in the same way as; in the same way that: *she doesn't dance like you do* ▷ *n* **9** the equal or counterpart of a person or thing, esp one respected or prized: *compare like with like; her like will never be seen again* **10** like similar things: *dogs, foxes, and the like* **11** the likes of *or* the like of people or things similar to (someone or something specified): *we don't want the likes of you around here* [shortened from Old English *gelīc*; compare Old Norse *glīkr* and *līkr* like]

● USAGE The use of *like* to mean *such as* was formerly
● thought to be undesirable in formal writing, but has
● now become acceptable. It was also thought that *as*
● rather than *like* should be used to mean *in the same way*
● *that*, but now both *as* and *like* are acceptable: *they hunt*
● *and catch fish as/like their ancestors used to*. The use of *look*
● *like* and *seem like* before a clause, although very
● common, is thought by many people to be incorrect or
● non-standard: *it looks as though he won't come* (not *it looks*
● *like he won't come*)

like² (laɪk) *vb* **1** (*tr*) to find (something) enjoyable or agreeable or find it enjoyable or agreeable (to do something): *he likes boxing; he likes to hear music* **2** (*tr*) to be fond of **3** (*tr*) to prefer or wish (to do something): *we would like you to go* **4** (*tr*) to feel towards; consider; regard: *how did she like it?* **5** (*intr*) to feel disposed or inclined; choose; wish ▷ *n* **6** (*usually plural*) a favourable feeling, desire, preference, etc (esp in the phrase **likes and dislikes**) [Old English *līcian*; related to Old Norse *līka*, Dutch *lijken*]

-like *suffix forming adjectives* **1** resembling or similar to: *lifelike; springlike* **2** having the characteristics of: *childlike; ladylike* [from LIKE¹ (prep)]

likelihood ('laɪklɪˌhʊd) *or* **likeliness** ('laɪklɪˌnɪs) *n* **1** the condition of being likely or probable; probability **2** something that is probable

likely ('laɪklɪ) *adj* **1** (usually foll by an infinitive) tending or inclined; apt: *likely to rain* **2** probable: *a likely result* **3** believable or feasible; plausible **4** appropriate for a purpose or activity **5** having good possibilities of success: *a likely candidate* ▷ *adv* **6** probably or presumably **7** as likely as not very probably [C14: from Old Norse *līkligr*]

● USAGE Likely as an adverb is preceded by another,
● intensifying adverb, as in *it will very likely rain* or *it will*
● *most likely rain*. Its use without an intensifier, as in *it*
● *will likely rain* is regarded as unacceptable by most users
● of British English, though it is common in colloquial
● US English

like-minded *adj* agreeing in opinions, goals, etc > ˌlike-'mindedly *adv* > ˌlike-'mindedness *n*

liken ('laɪkən) *vb* (*tr*) to see or represent as the same or similar; compare [C14: from LIKE¹ (adj)]

likeness ('laɪknɪs) *n* **1** the condition of being alike; similarity **2** a painted, carved, moulded, or graphic image of a person or thing **3** an imitative appearance; semblance

likewise ('laɪkˌwaɪz) *adv* **1** in addition; moreover; also **2** in like manner; similarly

liking ('laɪkɪŋ) *n* **1** the feeling of a person who likes; fondness **2** a preference, inclination, or pleasure

lilac ('laɪlək) *n* **1** Also called: syringa any of various Eurasian oleaceous shrubs or small trees of the genus *Syringa*, esp *S. vulgaris* (**common lilac**) which have large sprays of purple or white fragrant flowers **2 a** a light or moderate purple colour, sometimes with a bluish or reddish tinge **b** (as adjective): *a lilac carpet* [C17: via French from Spanish, from Arabic *līlak*, changed from Persian *nīlak* bluish, from *nīl* blue]

Lilburn ('lɪlˌbɜːn) *n* **Douglas** (**Gordon**). 1915–2001, New Zealand composer; noted esp for his pioneering use of electronic music in combination with more traditional orchestration

Lilburne ('lɪlˌbɜːn) *n* **John**. ?1614–57, English Puritan pamphleteer and leader of the Levellers, a radical group prominent during the Civil War

liliaceous (ˌlɪlɪˈeɪʃəs) *adj* of, relating to, or belonging to the *Liliaceae*, a family of plants having showy flowers and a bulb or bulblike organ: includes the lily, tulip, and bluebell [c18: from Late Latin *līliāceus*, from *līlium* lily]

Lilienthal (German 'liːliənˌtaːl) *n* **Otto** (ˈɔto). 1848–96, German aeronautical engineer, a pioneer of glider design

Lilith (ˈlɪlɪθ) *n* **1** (in the Old Testament and in Jewish folklore) a female demon, who attacks children **2** (in Talmudic literature) Adam's first wife **3** a witch notorious in medieval demonology

Liliuokalani (liːˌliːʊəkəˈlɑːni) *n* **Lydia Kamekeha** (ˌkɑːmeɪˈkeɪhɑː). 1838–1917, queen and last sovereign of the Hawaiian Islands (1891–95)

Lille (French lil) *n* an industrial city in N France: the medieval capital of Flanders; forms with Roubaix and Tourcoing one of the largest conurbations in France. Pop: 184 657 (1999)

Lille Bælt (ˈlilə ˈbɛld) *n* the Danish name for the **Little Belt**

Lillee (ˈlɪli) *n* **Dennis** (**Keith**). born 1949, Australian cricketer who, by the end of the 1982–83 season, had taken what was then world record total of 355 wickets in 65 tests

Lilliputian (ˌlɪlɪˈpjuːʃɪən) *n* **1** a tiny person or being ▷ *adj* **2** tiny; very small **3** petty or trivial [c18: from *Lilliput*, an imaginary country of tiny inhabitants in Swift's *Gulliver's Travels* (1726)]

Lilo (ˈlaɪləʊ) *n*, *pl* **-los** *trademark* a type of inflatable plastic or rubber mattress

Lilongwe (lɪˈlɒŋwɪ) *n* the capital of Malawi, in the central part west of Lake Malawi. Pop: 655 000 (2005 est)

lilt (lɪlt) *n* **1** (in music) a jaunty rhythm **2** a buoyant motion ▷ *vb* (*intr*) **3** (of a melody) to have a lilt **4** to move in a buoyant manner [c14 *lulten*, origin obscure] > **'lilting** *adj*

lily (ˈlɪli) *n*, *pl* **lilies** **1** any liliaceous perennial plant of the N temperate genus *Lilium*, such as the Turk's-cap lily and tiger lily, having scaly bulbs and showy typically pendulous flowers **2** the bulb or flower of any of these plants **3** any of various similar or related plants, such as the water lily, plantain lily, and day lily [Old English, from Latin *līlium*; related to Greek *leirion* lily] > **'lily-ˌlike** *adj*

lily-livered *adj* cowardly; timid

lily of the valley *n*, *pl* **lilies of the valley** a small liliaceous plant, *Convallaria majalis*, of Eurasia and North America cultivated as a garden plant, having two long oval leaves and spikes of white bell-shaped flowers

lily-white *adj* **1** of a pure white: *lily-white skin* **2** *informal* pure; irreproachable

Lima (ˈliːmə) *n* **1** the capital of Peru, near the Pacific coast on the Rímac River: the centre of Spanish colonization in South America; university founded in 1551 (the oldest in South America); an industrial centre with a port at nearby Callao. Pop: 8 180 000 (2005 est) **2** *communications* a code word for the letter L

lima bean (ˈlaɪmə, 'liː-) *n* **1** any of several varieties of the bean plant, *Phaseolus lunatus* (or *P. limensis*), native to tropical America but cultivated in the US for its flat pods containing pale green edible seeds **2** the seed of such a plant ▷ See also **butter bean** [c19: named after LIMA]

Limassol (ˈlɪməˌsɒl) *n* a port in S Cyprus: trading centre. Pop: 163 000 (2005 est)

Limavady (ˌlɪməˈvædɪ) *n* a district of N Northern Ireland, in Co Londonderry. Pop: 33 571 (2003 est). Area: 586 sq km (226 sq miles)

limb¹ (lɪm) *n* **1** an arm or leg, or the analogous part on an animal, such as a wing **2** any of the main branches of a tree **3** a branching or projecting section or member; extension **4** a person or thing considered to be a member, part, or agent of a larger group or thing **5** *chiefly Brit* a mischievous child (esp in **limb of Satan** or **limb of the devil**) **6** **out on a limb a** in a precarious or questionable position **b** *Brit* isolated, esp because of unpopular opinions [Old English *lim*; related to Old Norse *limr*] > **'limbless** *adj*

limb² (lɪm) *n* **1** the edge of the apparent disc of the sun, a moon, or a planet **2** a graduated arc attached to

instruments, such as the sextant, used for measuring angles **3** *botany* **a** the expanded upper part of a bell-shaped corolla **b** the expanded part of a leaf, petal, or sepal **4** either of the two halves of a bow **5** Also called: **fold limb** either of the sides of a geological fold [c15: from Latin *limbus* edge]

limbed (lɪmd) *adj* **a** having limbs **b** (*in combination*): *short-limbed; strong-limbed*

limber¹ (ˈlɪmbə) *adj* **1** capable of being easily bent or flexed; pliant **2** able to move or bend freely; agile [c16: origin uncertain] > **'limberness** *n*

limber² (ˈlɪmbə) *n* **1** part of a gun carriage, often containing ammunition, consisting of an axle, pole, and two wheels, that is attached to the rear of an item of equipment, esp field artillery ▷ *vb* **2** (usually foll by *up*) to attach the limber (to a gun, etc) [c15 *lymour* shaft of a gun carriage, origin uncertain]

limber up *vb* (*intr, adverb*) (esp in sports) to exercise in order to be limber and agile

limbic system (ˈlɪmbɪk) *n* the part of the brain bordering on the corpus callosum: concerned with basic emotion, hunger, and sex [c19 *limbic*, from French *limbique*, from *limbe* limbus, from New Latin *limbus*, from Latin: border]

limbo¹ (ˈlɪmbəʊ) *n*, *pl* **-bos** **1** (*often capital*) *Christianity* the supposed abode of infants dying without baptism and the just who died before Christ **2** an imaginary place for lost, forgotten, or unwanted persons or things **3** an unknown intermediate place or condition between two extremes: *in limbo* [c14: from Medieval Latin *in limbo* on the border (of hell)]

limbo² (ˈlɪmbəʊ) *n*, *pl* **-bos** a Caribbean dance in which dancers pass, while leaning backwards, under a bar [c20: origin uncertain]

Limburg¹ (ˈlɪmbɜːg; *Dutch* 'lɪmbyrx) *n* **1** a medieval duchy of W Europe: divided between the Netherlands and Belgium in 1839 **2** a province of the SE Netherlands: contains a coalfield and industrial centres. Capital: Maastricht. Pop: 1 142 000 (2003 est). Area: 2253 sq km (809 sq miles) **3** a province of NE Belgium: contains the industrial regions of the Kempen coalfield. Capital: Hasselt. Pop: 805 786 (2004 est). Area: 2422 sq km (935 sq miles)

Limburg² (*Dutch* 'lɪmbyrx) or **Limbourg** *n* **de Limburg**. active ?1400–?1416, a Dutch family of manuscript illuminators. The three brothers Pol, Herman, and Jehanequin are best known for illustrating the *Très Riches Heures du Duc de Berry*, one of the finest examples of the International Gothic style

lime¹ (laɪm) *n* **1** short for **quicklime, birdlime, slaked lime** **2** *agriculture* any of certain calcium compounds, esp calcium hydroxide, spread as a dressing on lime-deficient land ▷ *vb* (*tr*) **3** to spread (twigs, etc) with birdlime **4** to spread a calcium compound upon (land) to improve plant growth **5** to catch (animals, esp birds) with or as if with birdlime **6** to whitewash or cover (a wall, ceiling, etc) with a mixture of lime and water (**limewash**) [Old English *līm*; related to Icelandic *līm* glue, Latin *līmus* slime]

lime² (laɪm) *n* **1** a small Asian citrus tree, *Citrus aurantifolia*, with stiff sharp spines and small round or oval greenish fruits **2 a** the fruit of this tree, having acid fleshy pulp rich in vitamin C **b** (*as modifier*): *lime juice* ▷ *adj* **3** having the flavour of lime fruit [c17: from French, from Provençal, from Arabic *līmah*]

lime³ (laɪm) *n* any linden tree, such as *Tilia europaea*, planted in many varieties for ornament [c17: changed from obsolete *line*, from Old English *lind* LINDEN]

limeade (ˌlaɪmˈeɪd) *n* a drink made from sweetened lime juice and plain or carbonated water

lime green *n* **a** a moderate greenish-yellow colour **b** (*as adjective*): *a lime-green dress*

limekiln (ˈlaɪmˌkɪln) *n* a kiln in which calcium carbonate is calcined to produce quicklime

limelight (ˈlaɪmˌlaɪt) *n* **1** the limelight a position of public attention or notice (esp in the phrase **in the limelight**) **2 a** a type of lamp, formerly used in stage lighting, in which light is produced by heating lime to white heat **b** Also called: **calcium light** brilliant white light produced in this way

limerick ('lımərık) *n* a form of comic verse consisting of five anapaestic lines of which the first, second, and fifth have three metrical feet and rhyme together and the third and fourth have two metrical feet and rhyme together [C19: allegedly from *will you come up to Limerick?*, a refrain sung between nonsense verses at a party]

Limerick ('lımərık) *n* **1** a county of SW Republic of Ireland, in N Munster province: consists chiefly of an undulating plain with rich pasture and mountains in the south. County town: Limerick. Pop: 175 304 (2002). Area: 2686 sq km (1037 sq miles) **2** a port in SW Republic of Ireland, county town of Limerick, at the head of the Shannon estuary. Pop: 86 998 (2002)

limescale ('laımskeıl) *n* a flaky deposit left in containers such as kettles by the action of heat on water containing calcium salts. Often shortened to: scale [from LIME¹ (sense 1) + SCALE¹ (sense 3)]

limestone ('laım,stəʊn) *n* a sedimentary rock consisting mainly of calcium carbonate, deposited as the calcareous remains of marine animals or chemically precipitated from the sea: used as a building stone and in the manufacture of cement, lime, etc

limewater ('laım,wɔ:tə) *n* **1** a clear colourless solution of calcium hydroxide in water, formerly used in medicine as an antacid **2** water that contains dissolved lime or calcium salts, esp calcium carbonate or calcium sulphate

limey ('laımı) *US & Canadian slang ▷ n* **1** a British person **2** a British sailor or ship ▷ *adj* **3** British [abbreviated from C19 *lime-juicer*, because British sailors were required to drink lime juice as a protection against scurvy]

limit ('lımıt) *n* **1** (*sometimes plural*) the ultimate extent, degree, or amount of something: *the limit of endurance* **2** (*often plural*) the boundary or edge of a specific area: *the city limits* **3** (*often plural*) the area of premises within specific boundaries **4** the largest quantity or amount allowed **5** *maths* **a** a value to which a function f(x) approaches as closely as desired as the independent variable approaches a specified value (x = a) or approaches infinity **b** a value to which a sequence a_n approaches arbitrarily close as n approaches infinity **c** the limit of a sequence of partial sums of a convergent infinite series: *the limit of* $1 + \frac{1}{2} + \frac{1}{4} + \frac{1}{8} + \dots$ *is* 2 **6** *maths* one of the two specified values between which a definite integral is evaluated **7** the limit *informal* a person or thing that is intolerably exasperating ▷ *vb* **-its, -iting, -ited** (*tr*) **8** to restrict or confine, as to area, extent, time, etc [C14: from Latin *limes* boundary] > 'limitable *adj* > 'limitableness *n* > 'limitless *adj* > 'limitlessly *adv* > 'limitlessness *n*

limitary ('lımıtərı, -trı) *adj* **1** of, involving, or serving as a limit **2** restricted or limited

limitation (,lımı'teıʃən) *n* **1** something that limits a quality or achievement **2** the act of limiting or the condition of being limited **3** *law* a certain period of time, legally defined, within which an action, claim, etc, must be commenced

limited ('lımıtıd) *adj* **1** having a limit; restricted; confined **2** without fullness or scope; narrow **3** (of governing powers, sovereignty, etc) restricted or checked, by or as if by a constitution, laws, or an assembly: *limited government* **4** *chiefly Brit* (of a business enterprise) owned by shareholders whose liability for the enterprise's debts is restricted > 'limitedly *adv* > 'limitedness *n*

limited liability *n Brit* liability restricted to the unpaid portion (if any) of the par value of the shares of a limited company. It is a feature of share ownership

limited partner *n* a business partner who has no management authority and no personal liability

limiter ('lımıtə) *n* an electronic circuit that produces an output signal whose positive or negative amplitude, or both, is limited to some predetermined value above which the peaks become flattened. Also called: clipper

limn (lım) *vb* (*tr*) **1** to represent in drawing or painting **2** *archaic* to describe in words **3** an obsolete word for **illuminate** [C15: from Old French *enluminer* to illumine (a manuscript) from Latin *inlūmināre* to brighten, from

lūmen light] > limner ('lımnə) *n*

limnology (lım'nɒlədʒı) *n* the study of bodies of fresh water with reference to their plant and animal life, physical properties, geographical features, etc [C20: from Greek *limnē* lake] > limnological (,lımnə'lɒdʒıkᵊl) or ,limno'logic *adj* > ,limno'logically *adv* > lim'nologist *n*

Límnos ('lımnɒs) *n* transliteration of the Modern Greek name for **Lemnos**

Limoges (lı'məʊʒ; *French* limɔʒ) *n* a city in S central France, on the Vienne River: a centre of the porcelain industry since the 18th century. Pop: 133 968 (1999)

Limousin (*French* limuzɛ̃) *n* a region and former province of W central France, in the W part of the Massif Central

limousine ('lımə,zi:n, ,lımə'zi:n) *n* **1** any large and luxurious car, esp one that has a glass division between the driver and passengers **2** a former type of car in which the roof covering the rear seats projected over the driver's compartment [C20: from French, literally: cloak (originally one worn by shepherds in *Limousin*), hence later applied to the car]

limp¹ (lımp) *vb* (*intr*) **1** to walk with an uneven step, esp with a weak or injured leg **2** to advance in a labouring or faltering manner ▷ *n* **3** an uneven walk or progress [C16: probably a back formation from obsolete *limphalt* lame, from Old English *lemphealt*; related to Middle High German *limpfen* to limp] > 'limper *n* > 'limping *adj, n*

limp² (lımp) *adj* **1** not firm or stiff **2** not energetic or vital **3** (of the binding of a book) not stiffened with boards [C18: probably of Scandinavian origin; related to Icelandic *limpa* looseness] > 'limply *adv* > 'limpness *n*

limpet ('lımpıt) *n* **1** any of numerous marine gastropods, such as *Patella vulgata* (**common limpet**) and *Fissurella* (or *Diodora*) *apertura* (**keyhole limpet**), that have a conical shell and are found clinging to rocks **2** (*modifier*) relating to or denoting certain weapons that are attached to their targets by magnetic or adhesive properties and resist removal: *limpet mines* [Old English *lempedu*, from Latin *lepas*, from Greek]

limpid ('lımpıd) *adj* **1** clear or transparent **2** (esp of writings, style, etc) free from obscurity **3** calm; peaceful [C17: from French *limpide*, from Latin *limpidus* clear] > lim'pidity *or* 'limpidness *n* > 'limpidly *adv*

Limpopo (lım'pəʊpəʊ) *n* **1** a province of NE South Africa, comprising the N part of the former province of Transvaal: agriculture and service industries. Capital: Polokwane (formerly Pietersburg). Pop: 5 511 962 (2004 est). Area: 123 910 sq km (47 842 sq miles). Former name (1994–2002): Northern Province **2** a river in SE Africa, rising in E South Africa and flowing northeast, then southeast as the border between South Africa and Zimbabwe and through Mozambique to the Indian Ocean. Length: 1770 km (1100 miles)

limp-wristed *adj* ineffectual; effete

limy¹ ('laımı) *adj* limier, limiest of, like, or smeared with birdlime > 'liminess *n*

limy² ('laımı) *adj* limier, limiest of or tasting of lime (the fruit)

Linacre ('lınəkə) *n* **Thomas**. ?1460–1524, English humanist and physician: founded the Royal College of Physicians (1518)

linage *or* **lineage** ('laınıdʒ) *n* **1** the number of lines in a piece of written or printed matter **2** payment for written material calculated according to the number of lines

Linares (*Spanish* li'nares) *n* a city in S Spain: site of Scipio Africanus' defeat of the Carthaginians (208 BC); lead mines. Pop: 58 257 (2003 est)

Lin Biao ('lın 'bjaʊ) *n* See **Lin Piao**

linchpin *or* **lynchpin** ('lıntʃ,pın) *n* **1** a pin placed transversely through an axle to keep a wheel in position **2** a person or thing regarded as an essential or coordinating element: *the linchpin of the company* [C14 *lynspin*, from Old English *lynis*]

Lincoln¹ ('lıŋkən) *n* **1** a city in E central England, administrative centre of Lincolnshire: an important ecclesiastical and commercial centre in the Middle Ages; Roman ruins, a castle (founded by William the Conqueror) and a famous cathedral (begun in 1086). Pop: 85 963 (2001) **2** a city in SE Nebraska: state capital;

I

University of Nebraska (1869). Pop: 235 594 (2003 est) **3** short for **Lincolnshire** **4** a breed of long-woolled sheep, originally from Lincolnshire

Lincoln² ('lɪŋkən) n **Abraham.** 1809–65, US Republican statesman; 16th president of the US. His fame rests on his success in saving the Union in the Civil War (1861–65) and on his emancipation of slaves (1863); assassinated by John Wilkes Booth

Lincoln green n, **1 a** a yellowish-green or brownish-green colour **b** (as adjective): a Lincoln-green suit **2** a cloth of this colour [c16: so named after a green fabric formerly made at LINCOLN, England]

Lincolnshire ('lɪŋkənˌʃɪə, -ʃə) n a county of E England, on the North Sea and the Wash: mostly low-lying and fertile, with fenland around the Wash and hills (the **Lincoln Wolds**) in the east; one of the main agricultural counties of Great Britain: the geographical and ceremonial county includes the unitary authorities of North Lincolnshire and North East Lincolnshire (both part of Humberside county from 1974 to 1996). Administrative centre: Lincoln. Pop (excluding unitary authorities): 665 300 (2003 est). Area (excluding unitary authorities): 5880 sq km (2270 sq miles). Abbreviation: Lincs

Lincs (lɪŋks) abbreviation Lincolnshire

linctus ('lɪŋktəs) n, pl -tuses a syrupy medicinal formulation taken to relieve coughs and sore throats [C17 (in the sense: medicine to be licked with the tongue): from Latin, past participle of lingere to lick]

Lind (lɪnd) n **1 James.** 1716–94, British physician. He demonstrated (1754) that citrus fruits can cure and prevent scurvy, a remedy adopted by the British navy in 1796 **2 Jenny,** original name Johanna Maria Lind Goldschmidt. 1820–87, Swedish coloratura soprano

lindane ('lɪndeɪn) n a white poisonous crystalline powder with a slight musty odour: used as an insecticide, weedkiller, and, in low concentrations, in treating scabies; 1,2,3,4,5,6-hexachlorocyclohexane. Formula: $C_6H_6Cl_6$ [c20: named after T. van der Linden, Dutch chemist]

Lindbergh ('lɪndbɜːɡ, 'lɪnbɜːɡ) n **Charles Augustus.** 1902–74, US aviator, who made the first solo nonstop flight across the Atlantic (1927)

Lindemann ('lɪndəmən) n **Frederick Alexander,** 1st Viscount Cherwell. 1886–1957, British physicist, born in Germany; Churchill's scientific adviser during World War II

linden ('lɪndən) n any of various tiliaceous deciduous trees of the N temperate genus Tilia, having heart-shaped leaves and small fragrant yellowish flowers: cultivated for timber and as shade trees. See also **lime³** [c16: n use of obsolete adj linden, from Old English linde lime tree]

Lindesnes ('lɪndɪsˌnes) n a cape at the S tip of Norway, projecting into the North Sea. Also called: the Naze

Lindisfarne ('lɪndɪsˌfaːn) n another name for **Holy Island**

Lindsay ('lɪndzɪ) n **1** See (Sir David) **Lyndsay** **2** (Nicholas) **Vachel** ('veɪtʃəl). 1879–1931, US poet; best known for General William Booth (1913) and The Congo (1914) **3 Norman Alfred William.** 1879–1969, Australian artist and writer

Lindsey ('lɪndzɪ) n **Parts of Lindsey** an area in E England constituting a former administrative division of Lincolnshire

Lindwall ('lɪndˌwɔːl) n **Ray(mond Russell).** 1921–96, Australian cricketer. A fast bowler, he played for Australia 61 times between 1946 and 1958

line¹ (laɪn) n **1** a narrow continuous mark, as one made by a pencil, pen, or brush across a surface **2** such a mark cut into or raised from a surface **3** a thin indented mark or wrinkle **4** a straight or curved continuous trace having no breadth that is produced by a moving point **5** maths any straight one-dimensional geometrical element whose identity is determined by two points. A **line segment** lies between any two points on a line **b** a set of points (x, y) that satisfies the equation $y = mx + c$, where m is the gradient and c is the intercept with the y-axis **6** a border or boundary: the county line **7** sport **a** a white or coloured band indicating a boundary or division on a field, track, etc **b** a mark or imaginary

mark at which a race begins or ends **8** American football **a** See **line of scrimmage** **b** the players arranged in a row on either side of the line of scrimmage at the start of each play **9** a specified point of change or limit: the dividing line between sanity and madness **10 a** the edge or contour of a shape, as in sculpture or architecture, or a mark on a painting, drawing, etc, defining or suggesting this **b** the sum or type of such contours or marks, characteristic of a style or design: the line of a draughtsman; the line of a building **11** anything long, flexible, and thin, such as a wire or string: a washing line; a fishing line **12** a telephone connection: a direct line to New York **13** a conducting wire, cable, or circuit for making connections between pieces of electrical apparatus, such as a cable for electric-power transmission, telecommunications, etc **b** (as modifier): the line voltage **14** a system of travel or transportation, esp over agreed routes: a shipping line **15** a company operating such a system **16** a route between two points on a railway **17** chiefly Brit a railway track, including the roadbed, sleepers, etc **18** a course or direction of movement or advance: the line of flight of a bullet **19** a course or method of action, behaviour, etc: take a new line with him **20** a policy or prescribed course of action or way of thinking (often in the phrases **bring** or **come into line**) **21** a field of study, interest, occupation, trade, or profession: this book is in your line **22** alignment; true (esp in the phrases **in line, out of line**) **23** one kind of product or article: a nice line in hats **24** a row of persons or things: a line of cakes on the conveyor belt **25** a chronological or ancestral series, esp of people: a line of prime ministers **26** a row of words printed or written across a page or column **27** a unit of verse consisting of the number of feet appropriate to the metre being used and written or printed with the words in a single row **28** a short letter; note: just a line to say thank you **29** a piece of useful information or hint about something: give me a line on his work **30** one of a number of narrow horizontal bands forming a television picture **31** physics a narrow band in an electromagnetic spectrum, resulting from a transition in an atom, ion, or molecule of a gas or plasma **32** music **a** any of the five horizontal marks that make up the stave **b** the musical part or melody notated on one such set **c** a discernible shape formed by sequences of notes or musical sounds: a meandering melodic line **d** (in polyphonic music) a set of staves that are held together with a bracket or brace **33** a defensive or fortified position, esp one that marks the most forward position in war or a national boundary: the front line **34 line ahead** or **line abreast** a formation adopted by a naval unit for manoeuvring **35** a formation adopted by a body or a number of military units when drawn up abreast **36** the combatant forces of certain armies and navies, excluding supporting arms **37 a** the equator (esp in the phrase **crossing the line**) **b** any circle or arc on the terrestrial or celestial sphere **38** US & Canadian a line of people, vehicles, etc, waiting for something. Also called (in Britain and certain other countries): **queue 39** slang a portion of a powdered drug for snorting **40** slang something said for effect, esp to solicit for money, sex, etc **41 all along the line a** at every stage in a series **b** in every detail **42** draw the line to object reasonably (to) or set a limit (on): her father draws the line at her coming in after midnight **43** get a line on informal to obtain information about **44 hold the line a** to keep a telephone line open **b** football to prevent the opponents from taking the ball forward **c** (of soldiers) to keep formation, as when under fire **45 in line for** in the running for; a candidate for: he's in line for a directorship **46 in line with** conforming to **47** lay on the line or put on the line **a** to pay money **b** to speak frankly and directly **c** to risk (one's career, reputation, etc) on something **48 shoot a line** informal to try to create a false image, as by boasting or exaggerating ▷ vb **49** (tr) to mark with a line or lines **50** (tr) to draw or represent with a line or lines **51** (tr) to be or put as a border to: tulips lined the lawns **52** to place in or form a row, series, or alignment ▷ See also **lines, line-up** [c13: partly from Old French ligne, ultimately from Latin līnea, n use of līneus flaxen, from līnum flax; partly from Old English līn, ultimately also from Latin *līnum* flax] > 'linable *or* 'lineable *adj* > lined *adj*

line² (laɪn) *vb* (*tr*) **1** to attach an inside covering to (a garment, curtain, etc), as for protection, to hide the seaming, or so that it should hang well **2** to cover or fit the inside of: *to line the walls with books* **3** to fill plentifully: *a purse lined with money* [c14: ultimately from Latin *līnum* flax, since linings were often made of linen]

lineage¹ ('lɪnɪɪdʒ) *n* direct descent from an ancestor, esp a line of descendants from one ancestor [c14: from Old French *lignage*, from Latin *līnea* LINE¹]

lineage² ('laɪnɪdʒ) *n* a variant spelling of **linage**

lineal ('lɪnɪəl) *adj* **1** being in a direct line of descent from an ancestor **2** of, involving, or derived from direct descent **3** a less common word for **linear** [c14: via Old French from Late Latin *līneālis*, from Latin *līnea* LINE¹] > 'lineally *adv*

lineament ('lɪnɪəmənt) *n* (*often plural*) **1** a facial outline or feature **2** a distinctive characteristic or feature [c15: from Latin: line, from *līneāre* to draw a line]

linear ('lɪnɪə) *adj* **1** of, in, along, or relating to a line **2** of or relating to length **3** resembling, represented by, or consisting of a line or lines **4** having one dimension **5** designating a style in the arts, esp painting, that obtains its effects through line rather than colour or light and in which the edges of forms and planes are sharply defined **6** *maths* of or relating to the first degree: *a linear equation* **7** narrow and having parallel edges: *a linear leaf* **8** *electronics* **a** (of a circuit, etc) having an output that is directly proportional to input: *linear amplifier* **b** having components arranged in a line [c17: from Latin *līneāris* of or by means of lines] > linearity (ˌlɪnɪˈærɪtɪ) *n* > 'linearly *adv*

Linear A *n* a hitherto undeciphered script, partly syllabic and partly ideographic, found on tablets and pottery in Crete and dating mainly from the 15th century BC

linear accelerator *n* an accelerator in which charged particles are accelerated along a linear path by potential differences applied to a number of electrodes along their path

Linear B *n* an ancient system of writing, apparently a modified form of Linear A, found on clay tablets and jars of the second millennium BC. The earliest excavated examples, dating from about 1400, came from Knossos, in Crete, but all the later finds are at Pylos and Mycenae on the Greek mainland, dating from the 14th–12th centuries. The script is generally accepted as being an early representation of Mycenaean Greek

linear measure *n* a unit or system of units for the measurement of length. Also called: **long measure**

linear motor *n* a form of electric motor in which the stator and the rotor are linear and parallel. It can be used to drive a train, one part of the motor being in the locomotive, the other in the track

linear programming *n* *maths* a technique used in economics, etc, for determining the maximum or minimum of a linear function of non-negative variables subject to constraints expressed as linear equalities or inequalities

lineation (ˌlɪnɪˈeɪʃən) *n* **1** the act of marking with lines **2** an arrangement of or division into lines

line dancing *n* a form of dancing performed by rows of people to country and western music

line drawing *n* a drawing made with lines only, gradations in tone being provided by the spacing and thickness of the lines

Line Islands *pl n* a group of coral islands in the central Pacific, including Tabuaeran, Teraina, and Kiritimati; part of Kiribati, with Palmyra and Jarvis administered by the US

Lineker ('lɪnɪkə) *n* Gary Winston. born 1960, English footballer: played for England (1986–92; captain 1991–92); his clubs included Barcelona (1986–89) and Tottenham Hotspur (1989–92)

lineman ('laɪnmən) *n, pl* -men **1** another name for **platelayer 2** a person who does the chaining, taping, or marking of points for a surveyor **3** *Austral & NZ* (formerly) the member of a beach life-saving team who controlled the line used to help drowning swimmers

and surfers **4** *American football* a member of the row of players who start each down positioned on either side of the line of scrimmage **5** *US & Canadian* another word for **linesman** (sense 2)

line management *n* *commerce* those managers in an organization who are responsible for the main activity or product of the organization, as distinct from those, such as transport, accounting, or personnel, who provide services to the line management > line manager *n*

linen ('lɪnɪn) *n* **1 a** a hard-wearing fabric woven from the spun fibres of flax **b** (*as modifier*): *a linen tablecloth* **2** yarn or thread spun from flax fibre **3** clothes, sheets, tablecloths, etc, made from linen cloth or from a substitute such as cotton [Old English *linnen*, ultimately from Latin *līnum* flax, LINE²]

line of battle *n* a formation adopted by a military or naval force when preparing for action

line of fire *n* the flight path of a missile discharged or to be discharged from a firearm

line of force *n* an imaginary line representing a field of force, such as an electric or magnetic field, such that the tangent at any point is the direction of the field vector at that point

line of scrimmage *n* *American football* an imaginary line, parallel to the goal lines, on which the ball is placed at the start of a down and on either side of which the offense and defense line up

lineolate ('lɪnɪəˌleɪt) *or* **lineolated** *adj* *biology* marked with very fine parallel lines [c19: from Latin *līneola*, diminutive of *līnea* LINE¹]

line-out *n* *rugby union* the method of restarting play when the ball goes into touch, the forwards forming two parallel lines at right angles to the touchline and jumping for the ball when it is thrown in

line printer *n* an electromechanical device that prints a line of characters at a time rather than a character at a time, at speeds from about 200 to 3000 lines per minute: used in printing and in computer systems

liner¹ ('laɪnə) *n* **1 a** a passenger ship or aircraft, esp one that is part of a commercial fleet **2** See **Freightliner 3** Also called: **eye liner** a cosmetic used to outline the eyes, consisting of a liquid or cake mixed with water and applied by brush or a grease pencil **4** a person or thing that uses lines, esp in drawing or copying

liner² ('laɪnə) *n* **1 a** material used as a lining **2** a person who supplies or fits linings

lines (laɪnz) *pl n* **1** general appearance or outline: *a car with fine lines* **2** a plan of procedure or construction: *built on traditional lines* **3 a** the spoken words of a theatrical presentation **b** the words of a particular role: *he forgot his lines* **4** *informal, chiefly Brit* a marriage certificate: *marriage lines* **5** a defensive position, row of trenches, or other fortification: *we broke through the enemy lines* **6** a school punishment of writing the same sentence or phrase out a specified number of times **7** read between the lines to understand or find an implicit meaning in addition to the obvious one

linesman ('laɪnzmən) *n, pl* -men **1** an official who helps the referee or umpire in various sports, esp by indicating when the ball has gone out of play **2** *chiefly Brit* a person who installs, maintains, or repairs telephone or electric-power lines. US and Canadian name: **lineman**

line-up *n* **1** a row or arrangement of people or things assembled for a particular purpose: *the line-up for the football match* **2** the members of such a row or arrangement **3** an identity parade ▷ *vb* line up (*adverb*) **4** to form, put into, or organize a line-up **5** (*tr*) to produce, organize, and assemble: *they lined up some questions* **6** (*tr*) to align

ling¹ (lɪŋ) *n, pl* ling *or* lings **1** any of several gadoid food fishes of the northern coastal genus *Molva*, esp *M. molva*, having an elongated body with long fins **2** another name for **burbot** [c13: probably from Low German; related to LONG¹]

ling² (lɪŋ) *n* another name for **heather** (sense 1) [c14: from Old Norse *lyng*]

ling. *abbreviation* linguistics

-ling¹ *suffix forming nouns* **1** *often disparaging* a person or thing belonging to or associated with the group, activity, or quality specified: *nestling; underling* **2** used as a diminutive: *duckling* [Old English *-ling*, of Germanic origin; related to Icelandic *-lingr*, Gothic *-lings*]

-ling² *suffix forming adverbs* in a specified condition, manner, or direction: *darkling; sideling* [Old English *-ling*, adverbial suffix]

lingam ('lɪŋgəm) *or* **linga** ('lɪŋgə) *n* the Hindu phallic image of the god Siva [c18: from Sanskrit]

Lingayen Gulf ('lɪŋgaː'jɛn) *n* a large inlet of the South China Sea in the Philippines, on the NW coast of Luzon: site of the Japanese landing in the 1941 invasion

linger ('lɪŋgə) *vb* (*mainly intr*) **1** to delay or prolong departure **2** to go in a slow or leisurely manner; saunter **3** to remain just alive for some time prior to death **4** to persist or continue, esp in the mind **5** to be slow to act; dither; procrastinate [c13 (northern dialect) *lengeren* to dwell, from *lengen* to prolong, from Old English *lengan*; related to Old Norse *lengja*; see LONG¹] > **'lingerer** *n* > **'lingering** *adj* > **'lingeringly** *adv*

lingerie ('lænʒərɪ) *n* **1** women's underwear and nightwear **2** *archaic* linen goods collectively [c19: from French, from *linge*, from Latin *līneus* linen, from *līnum* flax]

lingo ('lɪŋgəʊ) *n*, *pl* **-goes** *informal* any foreign or unfamiliar language, jargon, etc [c17: perhaps from LINGUA FRANCA; compare Portuguese *lingoa* tongue]

lingua franca ('lɪŋgwə 'fræŋkə) *n*, *pl* **lingua francas** *or* **linguae francae** ('lɪŋgwi: 'frænsi:) **1** a language used for communication among people of different mother tongues **2** a hybrid language containing elements from several different languages used in this way **3** any system of communication providing mutual understanding [c17: Italian, literally: Frankish tongue]

Lingua Franca *n* a particular lingua franca spoken from the time of the Crusades to the 18th century in the ports of the Mediterranean, based on Italian, Spanish, French, Arabic, Greek, and Turkish

lingual ('lɪŋgwəl) *adj* **1** *anatomy* of or relating to the tongue or a part or structure resembling a tongue **2** a *rare* of or relating to language or languages **b** (*in combination*): *polylingual* **3** articulated with the tongue ▷ *n* **4** a lingual consonant, such as Scots (r) > **'lingually** *adv*

linguiform ('lɪŋgwɪˌfɔːm) *adj* shaped like a tongue

linguist ('lɪŋgwɪst) *n* **1** a person who has the capacity to learn and speak foreign languages **2** a person who studies linguistics [c16: from Latin *lingua* tongue]

linguistic (lɪŋ'gwɪstɪk) *adj* **1** of or relating to language **2** of or relating to linguistics > **lin'guistically** *adv*

linguistic atlas *n* an atlas showing the distribution of distinctive linguistic features of languages or dialects

linguistics (lɪŋ'gwɪstɪks) *n* (*functioning as singular*) the scientific study of language

liniment ('lɪnɪmənt) *n* a medicated liquid, usually containing alcohol, camphor, and an oil, applied to the skin to relieve pain, stiffness, etc [c15: from Late Latin *linīmentum*, from *linere* to smear, anoint]

lining ('laɪnɪŋ) *n* **1** material used to line a garment, curtain, etc **2** any material used as an interior covering

link¹ (lɪŋk) *n* **1** any of the separate rings, loops, or pieces that connect or make up a chain **2** something that resembles such a ring, loop, or piece **3** a road, rail, air, or sea connection, as between two main routes **4** a connecting part or episode **5** a connecting piece in a mechanism, often having pivoted ends **6** Also called: **radio link** a system of transmitters and receivers that connect two locations by means of radio and television signals **7** a unit of length equal to one hundredth of a chain. 1 link of a Gunter's chain is equal to 7.92 inches, and of an engineer's chain to 1 foot **8** *computing* short for **hyperlink** ▷ *vb* **9** (often foll by *up*) to connect or be connected with or as if with links **10** (*tr*) to connect by association, etc [c14: from Scandinavian; compare Old Norse *hlekkr* link]

link² (lɪŋk) *n* (formerly) a torch used to light dark streets [c16: perhaps from Latin *lychnus*, from Greek *lukhnos* lamp]

linkage ('lɪŋkɪdʒ) *n* **1** the act of linking or the state of being linked **2** a system of interconnected levers or rods for transmitting or regulating the motion of a mechanism **3** *electronics* the product of the total number of lines of magnetic flux and the number of turns in a coil or circuit through which they pass **4** *genetics* the occurrence of two genes close together on the same chromosome so that they are unlikely to be separated during crossing over and tend to be inherited as a single unit **5** the fact of linking separate but related issues in the course of political negotiations

linkman ('lɪŋkmən) *n*, *pl* **-men** a presenter of a television or radio programme, esp a sports transmission, consisting of a number of outside broadcasts from different locations

Linköping (*Swedish* 'lintɕøːpiŋ) *n* a city in S Sweden: a political and ecclesiastical centre in the Middle Ages; engineering industry. Pop: 137 004 (2004 est)

links (lɪŋks) *pl n* **1 a** short for **golf links b** (*as modifier*): *a links course* **2** *chiefly Scot* undulating sandy ground near the shore [Old English *hlincas* plural of *hlinc* ridge]

linkup ('lɪŋkˌʌp) *n* the establishing of a connection or union between objects, groups, organizations, etc

Linlithgow (lɪn'lɪθgəʊ) *n* **1** a town in SE Scotland, in West Lothian: ruined palace, residence of Scottish kings and birthplace of Mary, Queen of Scots. Pop: 13 370 (2001) **2** the former name of **West Lothian**

linn (lɪn) *n* *chiefly Scot* **1** a waterfall or a pool at the foot of it **2** a ravine or precipice [c16: probably from a confusion of two words, Scottish Gaelic *linne* pool and Old English *hlynn* torrent]

Linnaeus (lɪ'niːəs, -'neɪ-) *n* **Carolus** ('kærələs), original name *Carl von Linné*. 1707–78, Swedish botanist, who established the binomial system of biological nomenclature that forms the basis of modern classification

linnet ('lɪnɪt) *n* a brownish Old World finch, *Acanthis cannabina*: the male has a red breast and forehead [c16: from Old French *linotte*, ultimately from Latin *līnum* flax (because the bird feeds on flaxseeds)]

Linnhe ('lɪnɪ) *n* **Loch Linnhe** a sea loch of W Scotland, at the SW end of the Great Glen. Length: about 32 km (20 miles)

lino ('laɪnəʊ) *n* short for **linoleum**

linocut ('laɪnəʊˌkʌt) *n* **1** a design cut in relief on linoleum mounted on a wooden block **2** a print made from such a design

linoleum (lɪ'nəʊlɪəm) *n* a sheet material made of hessian, jute, etc, coated under pressure and heat with a mixture of powdered cork, linseed oil, rosin, and pigment, used as a floor covering. Often shortened to **lino** [c19: from Latin *līnum* flax + *oleum* oil]

Linotype ('laɪnəʊˌtaɪp) *n* **1** *trademark* a typesetting machine, operated by a keyboard, that casts an entire line on one solid slug of metal **2** type produced by such a machine

Lin Piao ('lɪn 'pjaʊ) *or* **Lin Biao** *n* 1908–71, Chinese Communist general and statesman. He became minister of defence (1959) and second in rank to Mao Tse-tung (1966). He fell from grace and is reported to have died in an air crash while attempting to flee to the Soviet Union

linseed ('lɪnˌsiːd) *n* another name for **flaxseed** [Old English *līnsǣd*, from *līn* flax + *sǣd* seed]

linseed oil *n* a yellow oil extracted from seeds of the flax plant. It has great drying qualities and is used in making oil paints, printer's ink, linoleum, etc

linsey-woolsey ('lɪnzɪ'wʊlzɪ) *n* **1** a thin rough fabric of linen warp and coarse wool or cotton filling **2** a strange nonsensical mixture or confusion [c15: probably from *Lindsey*, Suffolk village where the fabric was first made + WOOL (with rhyming suffix -*sey*)]

lint (lɪnt) *n* **1** an absorbent cotton or linen fabric with the nap raised on one side, used to dress wounds, etc **2** shreds of fibre, yarn, etc [c14: probably from Latin *linteus* made of linen, from *līnum* flax] > **'linty** *adj*

lintel ('lɪntᵊl) *n* a horizontal beam, as over a door or window [c14: via Old French probably from Late Latin *līmitāris* (unattested) of the boundary, influenced in meaning by *līminaris* of the threshold]

linter ('lɪntə) n 1 a machine for stripping the short fibres of ginned cotton seeds 2 (plural) the fibres so removed

Linz[1] (lɪnts) n a port in N Austria, capital of Upper Austria, on the River Danube: cultural centre; steelworks. Pop: 183 504 (2001)

Linz[2] (lɪnz) n acronym for Land Information New Zealand; the official body responsible for land registration, mapping, and surveying in New Zealand

lion ('laɪən) n 1 a large gregarious predatory feline mammal, *Panthera leo*, of open country in parts of Africa and India, having a tawny yellow coat and, in the male, a shaggy mane. Related adj: **leonine** 2 a conventionalized lion, the principal beast used as an emblem in heraldry. It has become the national emblem of Great Britain 3 a courageous, strong, or bellicose person 4 a celebrity or idol who attracts much publicity and a large following 5 the lion's share the largest portion [Old English līo, lēo (Middle English lioun, from Anglo-French liun), both from Latin leo, Greek leōn]

Lion ('laɪən) n the Lion the constellation Leo, the fifth sign of the zodiac

lioness ('laɪənɪs) n a female lion

lion-hearted adj very brave; courageous

lionize or **lionise** ('laɪə,naɪz) vb (tr) to treat as or make into a celebrity ⊳ ,lioni'zation or ,lioni'sation n ⊳ 'lion,izer or 'lion,iser n

Lions ('laɪənz) n Gulf of Lions a wide bay of the Mediterranean off the S coast of France, between the Spanish border and Toulon

lip (lɪp) n 1 anatomy a either of the two fleshy folds surrounding the mouth, playing an important role in the production of speech sounds, retaining food in the mouth, etc. Related adj: **labial** b (as modifier): lip salve 2 the corresponding part in animals, esp mammals 3 any structure resembling a lip, such as the rim of a crater, the margin of a gastropod shell, etc 4 a nontechnical word for **labium** 5 slang impudent talk or backchat 6 keep a stiff upper lip to maintain one's courage or composure during a time of trouble without giving way to or revealing one's emotions 7 lick one's lips or smack one's lips to anticipate or recall something with glee or relish ⊳ vb lips, lipping, lipped 8 (tr) to touch with the lip or lips 9 (tr) to form or be a lip or lips for 10 (tr) rare to murmur or whisper 11 (intr) to use the lips in playing a wind instrument [Old English lippa; related to Old Dutch leffur, Norwegian lepe, Latin labium] ⊳ 'lipless adj ⊳ 'lip,like adj

Lipari Islands ('lɪpərɪ) pl n a group of volcanic islands under Italian administration off the N coast of Sicily: remains that form a continuous record from Neolithic times. Chief town: Lipari. Pop: 10 554 (2001). Area: 114 sq km (44 sq miles). Also called: Aeolian Islands, Isole Eolie ('iːzole e'ɔːlje) (Italian name)

lipase ('laɪpeɪs, 'lɪpeɪs) n any of a group of fat-digesting enzymes produced in the stomach, pancreas, and liver and also occurring widely in the seeds of plants [c19: from Greek lipos fat + -ASE]

Lipchitz ('lɪpʃɪts) n **Jacques** (ʒɑːk). 1891–1973, US sculptor, born in Lithuania: he pioneered cubist sculpture

Li Peng ('liː 'pʊŋ) n born 1928, Chinese Communist politician: premier (1988–98)

Lipetsk (Russian 'lipitsk) n a city in central Russia, on the Voronezh River: steelworks. Pop: 518 000 (2005 est)

lip gloss n a cosmetic preparation applied to the lips to give a sheen

lipid or **lipide** ('laɪpɪd, 'lɪpɪd) n biochem any of a large group of organic compounds that are esters of fatty acids (**simple lipids**, such as fats and waxes) or closely related substances (**compound lipids**, such as phospholipids): usually insoluble in water but soluble in alcohol and other organic solvents. They are important structural materials in living organisms. Former name: lipoid [c20: from French lipide, from Greek lipos fat]

Lipizzaner (,lɪpɪt'sɑːnə) n a breed of riding and carriage horse used by the Spanish Riding School in Vienna and nearly always grey in colour [German, after Lipizza, near Trieste, where these horses were bred]

lipo ('lɪpəʊ, 'laɪpəʊ) n informal short for **liposuction**

lipo- or before a vowel **lip-** combining form fat or fatty:

lipoprotein [from Greek lipos fat]

Li Po or **Li T'ai-po** ('liː 'taɪ 'pəʊ) n ?700–762 AD, Chinese poet. His lyrics deal mostly with wine, nature, and women and are remarkable for their imagery

lipogram ('lɪpəʊ,græm) n a piece of writing from which all words containing a particular letter have been deliberately omitted

lipography (lɪ'pɒgrəfɪ) n the accidental omission of words or letters in writing [c19: from Greek lip-, stem of leipein to omit + -GRAPHY]

lipoid ('lɪpɔɪd, 'laɪ-) adj 1 Also: lipoidal resembling fat; fatty ⊳ n 2 a fatlike substance, such as wax 3 biochem a former name for **lipid**

lipoprotein (,lɪpəʊ'prəʊtiːn, ,laɪ-) n any of a group of proteins to which a lipid molecule is attached, important in the transport of lipids in the bloodstream. They exist in two main forms: high-density lipoproteins and low-density lipoproteins. See also **low-density lipoprotein**

liposculpture ('lɪpəʊ,skʌlptʃə, 'laɪpəʊ,skʌlptʃə) n a cosmetic surgical operation in which the shape of the body is altered by the removal by suction of excess body fat

liposuction ('lɪpəʊ,sʌkʃən, 'laɪpəʊ,sʌkʃən) n a cosmetic surgical operation in which subcutaneous fat is removed from the body by suction

Lippe ('lɪpə) n 1 a former state of NW Germany, now part of the German state of North Rhine-Westphalia 2 a river in NW Germany, flowing west to the Rhine. Length: about 240 km (150 miles)

-lipped adj having a lip or lips as specified: tight-lipped

Lippershey ('lɪpəs,haɪ) or **Lippersheim** ('lɪpəs,haɪm) n **Hans**. died ?1619, Dutch lens grinder, who built the first telescope

Lippi (Italian 'lippi) n 1 **Filippino** (filip'piːno). ?1457–1504, Italian painter of the Florentine school 2 his father, **Fra Filippo** (fra fi'lippo). ?1406–69, Italian painter of the Florentine school, noted particularly for his frescoes at Prato Cathedral (1452–64)

Lippizaner (,lɪpɪt'zɑːnə) n a variant spelling of **Lipizzaner**

Lippmann ('lɪpmən; French lipman) n **Gabriel** (gabriɛl). 1845–1921, French physicist. He devised the earliest process of colour photography: Nobel prize for physics 1908

lip-read ('lɪp,riːd) vb -reads, -reading, -read (-,red) to interpret (words) by lip-reading

lip-reading n a method used by deaf people to comprehend spoken words by interpreting movements of the speaker's lips. Also called: speech-reading ⊳ 'lip-,reader n

lip service n insincere support or respect expressed but not put into practice

lipstick ('lɪp,stɪk) n a cosmetic for colouring the lips, usually in the form of a stick

lipstick lesbian n slang a lesbian with a noticeably feminine appearance

lip-synch or **lip-sync** ('lɪp,sɪŋk) vb to mouth (prerecorded words) on television or film

liq. abbreviation liquid

liquefacient (,lɪkwɪ'feɪʃənt) n 1 a substance that liquefies or causes liquefaction ⊳ adj 2 becoming or causing to become liquid [c19: from Latin liquefacere to make LIQUID]

liquefied natural gas n a mixture of various gases, esp methane, liquefied under pressure for transportation and used as an engine fuel. Abbreviation: LNG

liquefied petroleum gas n a mixture of various petroleum gases, esp propane and butane, stored as a liquid under pressure and used as an engine fuel. Abbreviation: LPG See also **bottled gas**

liquefy ('lɪkwɪ,faɪ) vb -fies, -fying, -fied (esp of a gas) to become or cause to become liquid [c15: via Old French from Latin liquefacere to make liquid] ⊳ liquefaction (,lɪkwɪ'fækʃən) n ⊳ ,lique'factive adj ⊳ 'lique,fiable adj ⊳ 'lique,fier n

liquescent (lɪ'kwɛsᵊnt) adj (of a solid or gas) becoming or tending to become liquid [c18: from Latin liquescere] ⊳ li'quescence or li'quescency n

liqueur (lɪˈkjʊə; *French* likœr) *n* **1 a** any of several highly flavoured sweetened spirits such as kirsch or cointreau, intended to be drunk after a meal **b** (*as modifier*): *liqueur glass* **2** a small hollow chocolate sweet containing liqueur [c18: from French; see LIQUOR]

liquid (ˈlɪkwɪd) *n* **1** a substance in a physical state in which it does not resist change of shape but does resist change of size. See **gas** (sense 1), **solid** (sense 1) **2** a substance that is a liquid at room temperature and atmospheric pressure **3** *phonetics* a frictionless continuant, esp (l) or (r) ▷ *adj* **4** of, concerned with, or being a liquid or having the characteristic state of liquids: *liquid wax* **5** shining, transparent, or brilliant **6** flowing, fluent, or smooth **7** (of assets) in the form of money or easily convertible into money [c14: via Old French from Latin *liquidus*, from *liquēre* to be fluid] ▷ ˈliquidly *adv* ▷ ˈliquidness *n*

liquid air *n* air that has been liquefied by cooling. It is a pale blue and consists mainly of liquid oxygen (boiling pt: –182.9°C) and liquid nitrogen (boiling pt: –195.7°C): used in the production of pure oxygen, nitrogen, and the inert gases, and as a refrigerant

liquidambar (ˌlɪkwɪdˈæmbə) *n* **1** any deciduous tree of the hamamelidaceous genus *Liquidambar*, of Asia and North and Central America, with star-shaped leaves, and exuding a yellow aromatic balsam **2** the balsam of this tree, used in medicine [c16: New Latin, from Latin *liquidus* liquid + Medieval Latin *ambar* AMBER]

liquidate (ˈlɪkwɪˌdeɪt) *vb* **1 a** to settle or pay off (a debt, claim, etc) **b** to determine by litigation or agreement the amount of (damages, indebtedness, etc) **2 a** to terminate the operations of (a commercial firm, bankrupt estate, etc) by assessment of liabilities and appropriation of assets for their settlement **b** (of a commercial firm, etc) to terminate operations in this manner **3** (*tr*) to convert (assets) into cash **4** (*tr*) to eliminate or kill ▷ ˈliquiˌdator *n*

liquidation (ˌlɪkwɪˈdeɪʃən) *n* **1 a** the process of terminating the affairs of a business firm, etc, by realizing its assets to discharge its liabilities **b** the state of a business firm, etc, having its affairs so terminated (esp in the phrase **to go into liquidation**) **2** destruction; elimination

liquid-crystal display *n* a flat-screen display in which an array of liquid-crystal elements can be selectively activated to generate an image, an electric field applied to each element altering its optical properties; it is used, for example, in portable computers, digital watches, and calculators. Abbreviation: LCD

liquid ecstasy *n* another name for **gamma hydroxybutyrate**

liquidize *or* **liquidise** (ˈlɪkwɪˌdaɪz) *vb* **1** to make or become liquid; liquefy **2** (*tr*) to pulverize (food) in a liquidizer so as to produce a fluid

liquidizer *or* **liquidiser** (ˈlɪkwɪˌdaɪzə) *n* a kitchen appliance with blades for cutting and puréeing vegetables, blending liquids, etc. Also called: blender

liquid measure *n* a unit or system of units for measuring volumes of liquids or their containers

liquid oxygen *n* the clear pale blue liquid state of oxygen produced by liquefying air and allowing the nitrogen to evaporate: used in rocket fuels. Also called: lox

liquid paraffin *n* a colourless almost tasteless oily liquid obtained by petroleum distillation and used as a laxative. Also called (esp US and Canadian): mineral oil

liquor (ˈlɪkə) *n* **1** any alcoholic drink, esp spirits, or such drinks collectively **2** any liquid substance, esp that in which food has been cooked **3** *pharmacol* a solution of a pure substance in water **4** in liquor drunk; intoxicated [c13: via Old French from Latin, from *liquēre* to be liquid]

liquorice *or US and Canadian* **licorice** (ˈlɪkərɪs, -ərɪʃ) *n* **1 a** perennial Mediterranean leguminous shrub, *Glycyrrhiza glabra*, having spikes of pale blue flowers and flat red-brown pods **2** the dried root of this plant, used as a laxative and in confectionery **3** a sweet having a liquorice flavour [c13: via Anglo-Norman and Old French from Late Latin *liquiritia*, from Latin *glycyrrhīza*, from Greek *glukurrhiza*, from *glukus* sweet + *rhiza* root]

liquor store *n US & Canadian* See **package store**

lira (ˈlɪərə; *Italian* ˈliːra) *n, pl* **lire** (ˈlɪəri; *Italian* ˈliːre) *or* **liras** **1** the former standard monetary unit of Italy, San Marino, and the Vatican City, divided into 100 centesimi; replaced by the euro in 2002 **2** Also called: **pound** the standard monetary unit of Turkey, divided into 100 kuruş **3** the standard monetary unit of Malta, divided into 100 cents or 1000 mils [Italian, from Latin *lībra* pound]

liriodendron (ˌlɪrɪəʊˈdɛndrən) *n, pl* **-drons** *or* **-dra** (-drə) either of the two deciduous trees of the magnoliaceous genus *Liriodendron*, the tulip trees of North America or China [c18: New Latin, from Greek *leiron* lily + *dendron* tree]

Lisbon (ˈlɪzbən) *n* the capital and chief port of Portugal, in the southwest on the Tagus estuary: became capital in 1256; subject to earthquakes and severely damaged in 1755; university (1911). Pop: 1 892 891 (2001)

Lisburn (ˈlɪzbɜːn) *n* **1** a city in Northern Ireland in Lisburn district, Co Antrim, noted for its linen industry: headquarters of the British Army in Northern Ireland. Pop: 71 465 (2001) **2** a district of S Northern Ireland, in Co Antrim and Co Down. Pop: 109 565 (2003 est). Area: 446 sq km (172 sq miles)

Lisieux (*French* lizjø) *n* a town in NW France: Roman Catholic pilgrimage centre, for its shrine of St Thérèse, who lived there. Pop: 23 166 (1999)

lisle (laɪl) *n* **a** a strong fine cotton thread or fabric **b** (*as modifier*): *lisle stockings* [c19: named after *Lisle* (now Lille), town in France where this type of thread was originally manufactured]

lisp (lɪsp) *n* **1** the articulation of *s* and *z* like or nearly like the *th* sounds in English *thin* and *then* respectively **2** the habit or speech defect of pronouncing *s* and *z* in this manner **3** the sound of a lisp in pronunciation ▷ *vb* **4** to use a lisp in the pronunciation of (speech) **5** to speak or pronounce imperfectly or haltingly [Old English *āwlispian*, from *wlisp* lisping; of imitative origin; related to Old High German *lispen*] ▷ ˈlisper *n* ▷ ˈlisping *adj, n* ▷ ˈlispingly *adv*

lissom *or* **lissome** (ˈlɪsəm) *adj* **1** supple in the limbs or body; lithe; flexible **2** agile; nimble [c19: variant of LITHESOME] ▷ ˈlissomly *or* ˈlissomely *adv* ▷ ˈlissomness *or* ˈlissomeness *n*

list[1] (lɪst) *n* **1** an item-by-item record of names or things, usually written or printed one under the other **2** *computing* a linearly ordered data structure ▷ *vb* **3** (*tr*) to make a list of **4** (*tr*) to include in a list **5** (*tr*) *Brit* to declare to be a listed building **6** (*tr*) *stock exchange* to obtain an official quotation for (a security) so that it may be traded on the recognized market **7** an archaic word for **enlist** [c17: from French, ultimately related to LIST[2]; compare Italian *lista* list of names (earlier: border, strip, as of paper), Old High German *līsta* border] ▷ ˈlistable *adj*

list[2] (lɪst) *n* **1** a border or edging strip, esp of cloth **2** a less common word for **selvage** ▷ *vb* **3** (*tr*) to border with or as if with a list or lists ▷ See also **lists** [Old English *līst*; related to Old High German *līsta*]

list[3] (lɪst) *vb* **1** (esp of ships) to lean over or cause to lean over to one side ▷ *n* **2** the act or an instance of leaning to one side [c17: origin unknown]

list[4] (lɪst) *archaic* ▷ *vb* **1** to be pleasing to (a person) **2** (*tr*) to desire or choose ▷ *n* **3** a liking or desire [Old English *lystan*; related to Old High German *lusten* and Gothic *lūston* to desire]

list[5] (lɪst) *vb* an archaic or poetic word for **listen** [Old English *hlystan*; related to Old Norse *hlusta*]

listed building *n* (in Britain) a building officially recognized as having special historical or architectural interest and therefore protected from demolition or alteration

listed company *n stock exchange* a company whose shares are quoted on the main market of the London Stock Exchange

listed security *n stock exchange* a security that is quoted on the main market of the London Stock Exchange and appears in its *Official List of Securities*. See **Third Market**

listen (ˈlɪsən) *vb* (*intr*) **1** to concentrate on hearing something **2** to take heed; pay attention: *I told you many times but you wouldn't listen* [Old English *hlysnan*; related to Old High German *lūstrēn*] > **'listener** *n*

listenership ('lɪsnə,ʃɪp) *n* all the listeners collectively of a particular radio programme, station, or broadcaster

listen in *vb* (*intr, adverb*; often foll by *to*) **1** to listen to the radio **2** to intercept radio communications **3** to listen but not contribute (to a discussion), esp surreptitiously

listening post *n military* **1** a forward position set up to obtain early warning of enemy movement **2** any strategic position or place for obtaining information about another country or area

lister ('lɪstə) *n US & Canadian agriculture* a plough with a double mouldboard designed to throw soil to either side of a central furrow. Also called: **lister plough, middlebreaker, middle buster** [C19: from LIST²]

Lister ('lɪstə) *n* **Joseph**, 1st Baron Lister. 1827–1912, British surgeon, who introduced the use of antiseptics

listeriosis (lɪ,stɪərɪ'əʊsɪs) *n* a serious form of food poisoning, caused by bacteria of the genus *Listeria*. Its symptoms can include meningitis and in pregnant women it may cause damage to the fetus

listless ('lɪstlɪs) *adj* disinclined for any effort or exertion; lacking vigour, enthusiasm, or energy [C15: from *list* desire + -LESS] > **'listlessly** *adv* > **'listlessness** *n*

Liston ('lɪstən) *n* **Sonny**, real name *Charles*. 1922–70, US boxer: former world heavyweight champion

list price *n* the selling price of merchandise as quoted in a catalogue or advertisement

list renting *n* the practice of renting a list of potential customers to a direct-mail seller of goods or to the fundraisers of a charity

lists (lɪsts) *pl n* **1** *history* **a** the enclosed field of combat at a tournament **b** the barriers enclosing the field at a tournament **2** any arena or scene of conflict, controversy, etc **3** **enter the lists** to engage in a conflict, controversy, etc [C14: plural of LIST² (border, boundary)]

listserv ('lɪst,sɜ:v) *n* a service on the internet that provides an electronic mailing to subscribers with similar interests

Liszt (lɪst) *n* **Franz** (frants). 1811–86, Hungarian composer and pianist. The greatest piano virtuoso of the 19th century, he originated the symphonic poem, pioneered the one-movement sonata form, and developed new harmonic combinations. His works include the symphonies *Faust* (1861) and *Dante* (1867), piano compositions and transcriptions, songs, and church music

lit (lɪt) *vb* **1 a** past tense and past participle of **light¹ 2** an alternative past tense and past participle of **light²**

lit. *abbreviation* **1** literal(ly) **2** literary **3** literature

Li T'ai-po ('li: 'taɪ'pəʊ) *n* See **Li Po**

litany ('lɪtənɪ) *n, pl* **-nies 1** *Christianity* **a** a form of prayer consisting of a series of invocations, each followed by an unvarying response **b** **the Litany** the general supplication in this form included in the Book of Common Prayer **2** any long or tedious speech or recital [C13: via Old French from Medieval Latin *litanīa* from Late Greek *litaneia* prayer, ultimately from Greek *litē* entreaty]

litchi, lichee, lichi *or* **lychee** (,laɪ'tʃi:) *n* **1** a Chinese sapindaceous tree, *Litchi chinensis*, cultivated for its round edible fruits **2** the fruit of this tree, which has a whitish juicy edible aril [C16: from Cantonese *lai chi*]

lite (laɪt) *adj* **1** (of food and drink) containing few calories or little alcohol or fat **2** denoting a more restrained or less extreme version of a person or thing: *reggae lite* [C20: variant spelling of LIGHT²]

-lite *n combining form* (in names of minerals) stone: *chrysolite*. See **-lith** [from French *-lite* or *-lithe*, from Greek *lithos* stone]

liter ('li:tə) *n* the US spelling of **litre**

literacy ('lɪtərəsɪ) *n* **1** the ability to read and write **2** the ability to use language proficiently

literacy hour *n* (in England and Wales) a daily reading and writing lesson that was introduced into the national primary school curriculum in 1998 to raise standards of literacy

literae humaniores ('lɪtə,ri: hju:,mænɪ'ɔ:ri:z) *n* (at Oxford University) the faculty concerned with Greek

and Latin literature, ancient history, and philosophy; classics [Latin, literally: the more humane letters]

literal ('lɪtərəl) *adj* **1** in exact accordance with or limited to the primary or explicit meaning of a word or text **2** word for word **3** dull, factual, or prosaic **4** consisting of, concerning, or indicated by letters **5** true; actual ▷ *n* **6** Also called: **literal error** a misprint or misspelling in a text [C14: from Late Latin *litterālis* concerning letters, from Latin *littera* LETTER] > **'literalness** *or* **literality** (,lɪtə'rælɪtɪ) *n*

literalism ('lɪtərə,lɪzəm) *n* **1** the disposition to take words and statements in their literal sense **2** literal or realistic portrayal in art or literature > **'literalist** *n* > ,literal'istic *adj* > ,literal'istically *adv*

literally ('lɪtərəlɪ) *adv* **1** in a literal manner **2** (intensifier): *there were literally thousands of people* ● USAGE The use of *literally* as an intensifier is common, esp in informal contexts. In some cases, it provides emphasis without adding to the meaning: *the house was literally only five minutes walk away*. Often, however, its use results in absurdity: *the news was literally an eye-opener to me*. It is therefore best avoided in formal contexts

literary ('lɪtərərɪ, 'lɪtrərɪ) *adj* **1** of, relating to, concerned with, or characteristic of literature or scholarly writing: *a literary discussion; a literary style* **2** versed in or knowledgeable about literature **3** (of a word) formal; not colloquial [C17: from Latin *litterārius* concerning reading and writing. See LETTER] > **'literarily** *adv* > **'literariness** *n*

literate ('lɪtərɪt) *adj* **1** able to read and write **2** educated; learned ▷ *n* **3** a literate person [C15: from Latin *litterātus* learned. See LETTER] > **'literately** *adv*

literati (,lɪtə'rɑ:ti:) *pl n* literary or scholarly people [C17: from Latin]

literature ('lɪtərɪtʃə, 'lɪtrɪ-) *n* **1** written material such as poetry, novels, essays, etc, esp works of imagination characterized by excellence of style and expression and by themes of general and enduring interest **2** the body of written work of a particular culture or people: *Scandinavian literature* **3** written or printed matter of a particular type or on a particular subject: *scientific literature; the literature of the violin* **4** printed material giving a particular type of information: *sales literature* **5** the art or profession of a writer [C14: from Latin *litterātūra* writing; see LETTER]

Lith. *abbreviation* Lithuania(n)

-lith *n combining form* indicating stone or rock: *megalith*. See **-lite** [from Greek *lithos* stone]

litharge ('lɪθɑ:dʒ) *n* another name for **lead monoxide** [C14: via Old French from Latin *lithargyrus*, from Greek, from *lithos* stone + *arguros* silver]

lithe (laɪð) *adj* flexible or supple [Old English (in the sense: gentle; C15: supple); related to Old High German *lindi* soft, Latin *lentus* slow] > **'lithely** *adv* > **'litheness** *n*

lithesome ('laɪðsəm) *adj* a less common word for **lissom** [C18: from LITHE + -SOME¹]

lithia ('lɪθɪə) *n* **1** another name for **lithium oxide 2** lithium present in mineral waters as lithium salts [C19: New Latin, ultimately from Greek *lithos* stone]

lithic ('lɪθɪk) *adj* **1** of, relating to, or composed of stone **2** containing abundant fragments of previously formed rock: *a lithic sandstone* **3** *pathol* of or relating to a calculus or calculi, esp one in the urinary bladder **4** of or containing lithium [C18: from Greek *lithikos* stony]

-lithic *adj combining form* (in anthropology) relating to the use of stone implements in a specified cultural period: *Neolithic* [from Greek *lithikos*, from *lithos* stone]

lithium ('lɪθɪəm) *n* a soft silvery element of the alkali metal series: the lightest known metal, used as an alloy hardener, as a reducing agent, and in batteries. Symbol: Li; atomic no: 3; atomic wt: 6.941; valency: 1; relative density: 0.534; melting pt: 180.6°C; boiling pt: 1342°C [C19: New Latin, from LITHO- + -IUM]

lithium carbonate *n* a white crystalline solid used in the treatment of manic-depressive illness and mania. Formula: Li_2CO_3. Lithium citrate is also sometimes used for this purpose

lithium oxide *n* a white crystalline compound. It absorbs carbon dioxide and water vapour

litho ('laɪθəʊ) *n, pl* -thos **1** short for **lithography, lithograph** ▷ *adj* **2** short for **lithographic, lithographical** ▷ *adj* **3** short for **lithographically**

litho- *or before a vowel* **lith-** *combining form* stone: *lithograph* [from Latin, from Greek, from *lithos* stone]

lithograph ('lɪθəˌgrɑːf, -ˌgræf) *n* **1** a print made by lithography ▷ *vb* **2** (*tr*) to reproduce (pictures, text, etc) by lithography > **lithographic** (ˌlɪθəˈgræfɪk) *or* ˌlitho'graphical *adj* > ˌlitho'graphically *adv*

lithography (lɪˈθɒgrəfɪ) *n* a method of printing from a metal or stone surface on which the printing areas are not raised but made ink-receptive while the non-image areas are made ink-repellent [c18: from New Latin *lithographia*, from LITHO- + -GRAPHY] > li'thographer *n*

lithology (lɪˈθɒlədʒɪ) *n* **1** the physical characteristics of a rock, including colour, composition, and texture **2** the study of rocks

lithophyte ('lɪθəˌfaɪt) *n* **1** a plant that grows on rocky or stony ground **2** an organism, such as a coral, that is partly composed of stony material

lithosphere ('lɪθəˌsfɪə) *n* the rigid outer layer of the earth, having an average thickness of about 75 km and comprising the earth's crust and the solid part of the mantle above the asthenosphere

lithotomy (lɪˈθɒtəmɪ) *n, pl* -mies the surgical removal of a calculus, esp one in the urinary bladder [c18: via Late Latin from Greek, from LITHO- + -TOMY]

lithotripsy ('lɪθəʊˌtrɪpsɪ) *n* the use of ultrasound, often generated by a lithotripter, to pulverize kidney stones and gallstones *in situ* [c20: from LITHO- + Greek *thruptein* to crush]

Lithuania (ˌlɪθjʊˈeɪnɪə) *n* a republic in NE Europe, on the Baltic Sea: a grand duchy in medieval times; united with Poland in 1569; occupied by Russia in 1795 and by Germany during World War I; independent Lithuania formed in 1918, but occupied by Soviet troops in 1919 and then by Poland; became a Soviet republic in 1940; unilaterally declared independence from the Soviet Union in 1990; recognized as independent in 1991; joined the EU in 2004. Official language: Lithuanian. Religion: Roman Catholic majority. Currency: litas. Capital: Vilnius. Pop: 3 422 000 (2004 est). Area: 65 200 sq km (25 174 sq miles). Also called: **Lithuanian Republic** Lithuanian name: **Lietuva**

Lithuanian (ˌlɪθjʊˈeɪnɪən) *adj* **1** of, relating to, or characteristic of Lithuania, its people, or their language ▷ *n* **2** the official language of Lithuania: belonging to the Baltic branch of the Indo-European family **3** a native or inhabitant of Lithuania

litigable ('lɪtɪgəbəl) *adj law* that may be the subject of litigation

litigant ('lɪtɪgənt) *n* **1** a party to a lawsuit ▷ *adj* **2** engaged in litigation

litigate ('lɪtɪˌgeɪt) *vb* **1** to bring or contest (a claim, action, etc) in a lawsuit **2** (*intr*) to engage in legal proceedings [c17: from Latin *lītigāre*, from *līt-*, stem of *līs* lawsuit + *agere* to carry on] > 'liti,gator *n*

litigation (ˌlɪtɪˈgeɪʃən) *n* **1** the act or process of bringing or contesting a legal action in court **2** a judicial proceeding or contest

litigious (lɪˈtɪdʒəs) *adj* **1** excessively ready to go to law **2** of or relating to litigation **3** inclined to dispute or disagree [c14: from Latin *lītigiōsus* quarrelsome, from *lītigium* strife] > li'tigiously *adv* > li'tigiousness *n*

litmus ('lɪtməs) *n* a soluble powder obtained from certain lichens. It turns red under acid conditions and blue under basic conditions and is used as an indicator [c16: perhaps from Scandinavian; compare Old Norse *litmosi*, from *litr* dye + *mosi* moss]

litotes ('laɪtəʊˌtiːz) *n, pl* -tes understatement for rhetorical effect, esp when achieved by using negation with a term in place of using an antonym of that term, as in "She was not a little upset" for "She was extremely upset." [c17: from Greek, from *litos* small]

litre *or US* **liter** ('liːtə) *n* **1** one cubic decimetre **2** (formerly) the volume occupied by 1 kilogram of pure water at 4°C and 760 millimetres of mercury. This is equivalent to 1.000 028 cubic decimetres or about 1.76 pints [c19: from French, from Medieval Latin *litra*, from

Greek: a unit of weight]

LittD *or* **LitD** *abbreviation* Doctor of Letters *or* Doctor of Literature [Latin: *Litterarum Doctor*]

litter ('lɪtə) *n* **1 a** small refuse or waste materials carelessly dropped, esp in public places **b** (*as modifier*): *litter bin* **2** a disordered or untidy condition or a collection of objects in this condition **3** a group of offspring produced at one birth by a mammal such as a sow **4** a layer of partly decomposed leaves, twigs, etc, on the ground in a wood or forest **5** straw, hay, or similar material used as bedding, protection, etc, by animals or plants **6** See **cat litter 7** a means of conveying people, esp sick or wounded people, consisting of a light bed or seat held between parallel sticks ▷ *vb* **8** to make (a place) untidy by strewing (refuse) **9** to scatter (objects, etc) about or (of objects) to lie around or upon (anything) in an untidy fashion **10** (of pigs, cats, etc) to give birth to (offspring) **11** (*tr*) to provide (an animal or plant) with straw or hay for bedding, protection, etc [c13 (in the sense: bed): via Anglo-French, ultimately from Latin *lectus* bed]

littérateur (ˌlɪtərəˈtɜː; *French* literatœr) *n* an author, esp a professional writer [c19: from French from Latin *litterātor* a grammarian]

litter lout *or US and Canadian* **litterbug** ('lɪtəˌbʌg) *n slang* a person who tends to drop refuse in public places

little ('lɪtəl) *determiner* **1** (often preceded by *a*) **a** a small quantity, extent, or duration of: *the little hope there is left; very little milk* **b** (*as pronoun*): *save a little for me* **2** not much: *little damage was done* **3** make little of See **make of** (sense 3) **4** not a little **a** very **b** a lot **5** quite a little a considerable amount **6** think little of to have a low opinion of ▷ *adj* **7** of small or less than average size **8** young: *a little boy; our little ones* **9** endearingly familiar; dear: *my husband's little ways* **10** contemptible, mean, or disagreeable: *your filthy little mind* ▷ *adv* **11** (usually preceded by *a*) in a small amount; to a small extent or degree; not a lot: *to laugh a little* **12** (*used preceding a verb*) not at all, or hardly: *he little realized his fate* **13** not much or often: *we go there very little now* **14** little by little by small degrees ▷ See also **less, lesser, least** [Old English *lȳtel*; related to *lȳr* few, Old High German *luzzil*]

Little Bear *n* the Little Bear the English name for **Ursa Minor**

Little Belt *n* a strait in Denmark, between Jutland and Funen Island, linking the Kattegat with the Baltic. Length: about 48 km (30 miles). Width: up to 29 km (18 miles). Danish name: **Lille Bælt**

Little Bighorn *n* a river in the W central US, rising in N Wyoming and flowing north to the Bighorn River. Its banks were the scene of the defeat (1876) and killing of General Custer and his command by Indians

Little Diomede *n* the smaller of the two Diomede Islands in the Bering Strait: administered by the US Area: about 10 sq km (4 sq miles)

Little Dipper *n* the Little Dipper *US & Canadian* a small faint constellation, the brightest star of which is the Pole Star, lying 1° from the true celestial pole. Also known as: Ursa Minor, the Bear, the Little Bear

Little John *n* one of Robin Hood's companions, noted for his great size and strength

little people *or* **little folk** *pl n folklore* small supernatural beings, such as elves, pixies, or leprechauns

Little Rock *n* a city in central Arkansas, on the Arkansas River: state capital. Pop: 184 053 (2003 est)

Little Russia *n* a region of the former SW Soviet Union, consisting chiefly of Ukraine

little slam *n bridge* the winning of all tricks except one by one side, or the contract to do so. Also called: **small slam**

Little St Bernard Pass *n* a pass over the Savoy Alps, between Bourg-Saint-Maurice, France, and La Thuile, Italy: 11th-century hospice. Height: 2187 m (7177 ft)

Littlewood ('lɪtəlˌwʊd) *n* (**Maud**) **Joan**. 1914–2002, British theatre director, who founded the Theatre Workshop Company (1945) with the aim of bringing theatre to the working classes: noted esp for her production of *Oh, What a Lovely War!* (1963)

littlie ('lɪtlɪ) *n Austral informal* a young child

littoral ('lɪtərəl) *adj* **1** of or relating to the shore of a sea, lake, or ocean ▷ *n* **2** a coastal or shore region [c17: from Late Latin *littorālis*, from *lītorālis*, from *lītus* shore]

liturgical (lɪ'tɜːdʒɪkəl) *or* **liturgic** (lɪ'tɜːdʒɪk) *adj* **1** of or relating to public worship **2** of or relating to the liturgy ▷ **li'turgically** *adv*

liturgy ('lɪtədʒɪ) *n, pl* **-gies 1** the forms of public services officially prescribed by a Church **2** (*often capital*) Also called: **Divine Liturgy** *chiefly Eastern Churches* the Eucharistic celebration **3** a particular order or form of public service laid down by a Church [c16: via Medieval Latin, from Greek *leitourgia*, from *leitourgos* minister, from *leit-* people + *ergon* work]

Liu Shao Qi *or* **Liu Shao-ch'i** ('lju: 'ʃaʊ'tʃiː) *n* 1898–1974, Chinese Communist statesman; chairman of the People's Republic of China (1959–68); deposed during the Cultural Revolution

livable *or* **liveable** ('lɪvəbəl) *adj* **1** (of a room, house, etc) suitable for living in **2** worth living; tolerable **3** (foll by *with*) pleasant to live (with) ▷ **'livableness, 'liveableness** *or* ˌliva'bility, ˌlivea'bility *n*

live¹ (lɪv) *vb* (*mainly intr*) **1** to show the characteristics of life; be alive **2** to remain alive or in existence **3** to exist in a specified way: *to live poorly* **4** (usually foll by *in* or *at*) to reside or dwell: *to live in London* **5** (often foll by *on*) to continue or last: *the pain still lives in her memory* **6** (usually foll by *by*) to order one's life (according to a certain philosophy, religion, etc) **7** (foll by *on, upon,* or *by*) to support one's style of life; subsist: *to live by writing* **8** (foll by *with*) to endure the effects (of a crime, mistake, etc) **9** (foll by *through*) to experience and survive: *he lived through the war* **10** (*tr*) to pass or spend (one's life, etc) **11** to enjoy life to the full: *he knows how to live* **12** (*tr*) to put into practice in one's daily life; express: *he lives religion every day* **13 live and let live** to refrain from interfering in others' lives; to be tolerant ▷ See also **live down, live in,** etc [Old English *libban, lifian*; related to Old High German *libēn,* Old Norse *lifa*]

live² (laɪv) *adj* **1** (*prenominal*) showing the characteristics of life **2** (*usually prenominal*) of, relating to, or abounding in life: *the live weight of an animal* **3** (*usually prenominal*) of current interest; controversial: *a live issue* **4** actual: *a real live cowboy* **5** *informal* full of life and energy **6** (of a coal, ember, etc) glowing or burning **7** (esp of a volcano) not extinct **8** loaded or capable of exploding: *a live bomb* **9** *radio, television* transmitted or present at the time of performance, rather than being a recording: *a live show* **10** (of a record) **a** recorded in concert **b** recorded in one studio take, without overdubs or splicing **11** connected to a source of electric power: *a live circuit* **12** acoustically reverberant **13** being in a state of motion or transmitting power; positively connected to a driving member ▷ *adv* **14** during, at, or in the form of a live performance [c16: from *on live* ALIVE]

-lived (-lɪvd) *adj* having or having had a life as specified: *short-lived*

live data *n computing* data that is still relevant

lived-in *adj* having a comfortable, natural, or homely appearance, as if subject to regular use or habitation

live down (lɪv) *vb* (*tr, adverb*) to withstand the effects of (a crime, mistake, etc) by waiting until others forget or forgive it

live in (lɪv) *vb* (*intr, adverb*) **1** (of an employee, as in a hospital or hotel) to dwell at one's place of employment ▷ *adj* **live-in 2** living in the place at which one works: *a live-in maid* **3** living with someone else in that person's home: *a live-in lover*

livelihood ('laɪvlɪˌhʊd) *n* occupation or employment

livelong ('lɪvˌlɒŋ) *adj chiefly poetic* **1** (of time) long or seemingly long, esp in a tedious way (esp in the phrase **all the livelong day**) **2** whole; entire

lively ('laɪvlɪ) *adj* **-lier, -liest 1** full of life or vigour **2** vivacious or animated, esp when in company **3** busy; eventful **4** characterized by mental or emotional intensity; vivid **5** having a striking effect on the mind or senses **6** refreshing: *a lively breeze* **7** springy or bouncy or encouraging springiness: *a lively ball* **8** (of a boat or ship) readily responsive to the helm ▷ *adv* Also: 'livelily **9** in a brisk manner: *step lively* ▷ **'liveliness** *n*

liven ('laɪvᵊn) *vb* (usually foll by *up*) to make or become lively; enliven ▷ **'livener** *n*

live oak (laɪv) *n* a hard-wooded evergreen oak, *Quercus virginiana,* of S North America: used for shipbuilding

live out (lɪv) *vb* (*intr, adverb*) (of an employee, as in a hospital or hotel) to dwell away from one's place of employment

liver¹ ('lɪvə) *n* **1** a multilobed highly vascular reddish-brown glandular organ occupying most of the upper right part of the human abdominal cavity immediately below the diaphragm. It secretes bile, stores glycogen, detoxifies certain poisons, and plays an important part in the metabolism of carbohydrates, proteins, and fat, helping to maintain a correct balance of nutrients. Related adj: **hepatic 2** the corresponding organ in animals **3** the liver of certain animals used as food **4** a reddish-brown colour, sometimes with a greyish tinge [Old English *lifer*; related to Old High German *lebrav,* Old Norse *lefr,* Greek *liparos* fat]

liver² ('lɪvə) *n* a person who lives in a specified way: *a fast liver*

liveried ('lɪvərɪd) *adj* (esp of servants or footmen) wearing livery

liverish ('lɪvərɪʃ) *adj* **1** *informal* having a disorder of the liver **2** disagreeable; peevish ▷ **'liverishness** *n*

liver opal *n* a form of opal having a reddish-brown coloration. Also called: **menilite**

Liverpool¹ ('lɪvəˌpuːl) *n* **1** a city in NW England, in Liverpool unitary authority, Merseyside, on the Mersey estuary: second largest seaport in Great Britain; developed chiefly in the 17th century with the industrialization of S Lancashire; Liverpool University (1881) and John Moores University (1992). Pop: 469 017 (2001) **2** a unitary authority in NW England, in Merseyside. Pop: 441 800 (2003 est). Area: 113 sq km (44 sq miles)

Liverpool² ('lɪvəˌpuːl) *n* **Robert Banks Jenkinson,** 2nd Earl of Liverpool. 1770–1828, British Tory statesman; prime minister (1812–27). His government was noted for its repressive policies until about 1822, when more liberal measures were introduced by such men as Peel and Canning

Liverpudlian (ˌlɪvə'pʌdlɪən) *n* **1** a native or inhabitant of Liverpool ▷ *adj* **2** of or relating to Liverpool [c19: from LIVERPOOL, with humorous alteration of *pool* to *puddle*]

liver salts *pl n* a preparation of mineral salts used to treat indigestion

liver sausage *or esp US* **liverwurst** ('lɪvəˌwɜːst) *n* a sausage made of or containing liver

liverwort ('lɪvəˌwɜːt) *n* any bryophyte plant of the phylum *Hepatophyta,* growing in wet places and resembling green seaweeds or leafy mosses [late Old English *liferwyrt*]

livery ('lɪvərɪ) *n, pl* **-eries 1** the identifying uniform, badge, etc, of a member of a guild or one of the servants of a feudal lord **2** a uniform worn by some menservants and chauffeurs **3** an individual or group that wears such a uniform **4** distinctive dress or outward appearance **5 a** the stabling, keeping, or hiring out of horses for money **b** (*as modifier*): *a livery horse* **6** at livery being kept in a livery stable [c14: via Anglo-French from Old French *livrée* allocation, from *livrer* to hand over, from Latin *līberāre* to set free]

livery company *n Brit* one of the chartered companies of the City of London originating from the craft guilds

liveryman ('lɪvərɪmən) *n, pl* **-men 1** *Brit* a member of a livery company **2** a worker in a livery stable

livery stable *n* a stable where horses are accommodated and from which they may be hired out

lives (laɪvz) *n* the plural of **life**

livestock ('laɪvˌstɒk) *n* (*functioning as singular or plural*) cattle, horses, poultry, and similar animals kept for domestic use but not as pets, esp on a farm or ranch

live together (lɪv) *vb* (*intr, adverb*) (esp of an unmarried couple) to dwell in the same house or flat; cohabit

live up (lɪv) *vb* **1** (*intr, adverb*; foll by *to*) to fulfil (an expectation, obligation, principle, etc) **2 live it up** *informal* to enjoy oneself, esp flamboyantly

live wire (laɪv) *n* **1** *informal* an energetic or enterprising person **2** a wire carrying an electric current

live with (lɪv) *vb* (*tr, preposition*) to dwell with (a person to whom one is not married)

liveyer *or* **liveyere** ('lɪvjə) *n Canadian* (in Newfoundland) a full-time resident [altered from LIVER, a dweller]

Livia Drusilla ('lɪvɪə druː'sɪlə) *n* 58 BC–29 AD, Roman noblewoman: wife (from 39 BC) of Emperor Augustus and mother of Emperor Tiberius

livid ('lɪvɪd) *adj* **1** (of the skin) discoloured, as from a bruise or contusion **2** of a greyish tinge or colour: *livid pink* **3** *informal* angry or furious [C17: via French from Latin *līvidus*, from *līvēre* to be black and blue] > **'lividly** *adv* > **'lividness** *or* **li'vidity** *n*

living ('lɪvɪŋ) *adj* **1 a** possessing life; not dead **b** (*as collective noun* preceded by *the*): *the living* **2** having the characteristics of life (used esp to distinguish organisms from nonliving matter) **3** currently in use or valid: *living language* **4** seeming to be real: *a living image* **5** (of animals or plants) existing in the present age; extant **6** presented by actors before a live audience: *living theatre* **7** (*prenominal*) (intensifier): *the living daylights* ▷ *n* **8** the condition of being alive **9** the manner in which one conducts one's life: *fast living* **10** the means, esp the financial means, whereby one lives **11** *Church of England* another term for **benefice** **12** (*modifier*) of, involving, or characteristic of everyday life: *living area* **13** (*modifier*) of or involving those now alive (esp in the phrase **living memory**)

living death *n* a life or lengthy experience of constant misery

living history *n* any of various activities involving the re-enactment of historical events or the recreation of living conditions of the past

living room *n* a room in a private house or flat used for relaxation and entertainment of guests

Livingston ('lɪvɪŋstən) *n* a town in SE Scotland, the administrative centre of West Lothian: founded as a new town in 1962. Pop: 50 826 (2001)

Livingstone ('lɪvɪŋstən) *n* **1 David.** 1813–73, Scottish missionary and explorer in Africa. After working as a missionary in Botswana, he led a series of expeditions and was the first European to discover Lake Ngami (1849), the Zambezi River (1851), the Victoria Falls (1855), and Lake Malawi (1859). In 1866 he set out to search for the source of the Nile and was found in dire straits and rescued (1871) by the journalist H. M. Stanley **2 Kenneth Robert,** known as *Ken.* born 1945, mayor of London from 2000; Labour leader of the Greater London Council (1981–86)

living wage *n* a wage adequate to permit a wage earner to live and support a family in reasonable comfort

living will *n* a document stating that if its author becomes terminally ill, his or her life should not be prolonged by artificial means, such as a life-support machine

Livonia (lɪ'vəʊnɪə) *n* **1** a former Russian province on the Baltic, north of Lithuania: became Russian in 1721; divided between Estonia and Latvia in 1918 **2** a city in SE Michigan, west of Detroit. Pop: 99 487 (2003 est) > **Li'vonian** *adj, n*

Livorno (*Italian* li'vorno) *n* a port in W central Italy, in Tuscany on the Ligurian Sea: shipyards; oil-refining. Pop: 156 274 (2001). English name: **Leghorn**

Livy ('lɪvɪ) *n* Latin name *Titus Livius.* 59 BC–17 AD, Roman historian; of his history of Rome in 142 books, only 35 survive

lizard ('lɪzəd) *n* any reptile of the suborder *Lacertilia* (or *Sauria*), esp those of the family *Lacertidae* (Old World lizards), typically having an elongated body, four limbs, and a long tail: includes the geckos, iguanas, chameleons, monitors, and slow worms [C14: via Old French from Latin *lacerta*]

Lizard ('lɪzəd) *n* **the Lizard** a promontory in SW England, in SW Cornwall: the southernmost point in Great Britain

LJ *abbreviation Brit* Lord Justice

Ljubljana (luː'bljɑːnə) *n* the capital of Slovenia: capital of Illyria (1816–49); part of Yugoslavia (1918–91); university (1595). Pop: 265 881 (2002). German name: Laibach

LL *abbreviation* **1** Late Latin **2** Low Latin **3** Lord Lieutenant

ll. *abbreviation* lines (of written matter)

llama ('lɑːmə) *n* **1** a domesticated South American cud-chewing mammal, *Lama glama* (or *L. peruana*), that is used as a beast of burden and is valued for its hair, flesh, and hide: family *Camelidae* (camels) **2** the cloth made from the wool of this animal **3** any other animal of the genus *Lama*. See **alpaca¹, guanaco** [C17: via Spanish from Quechua]

Llandaff ('lændəf, -dæf) *or* **Llandaf** (*Welsh* hlan'dav) *n* a town in SE Wales, now a suburb of Cardiff; the oldest bishopric in Wales (6th century)

Llandudno (θlæn'dɪdnəʊ, læn'dɪdnəʊ; *Welsh* hlan'dɪdnɔ) *n* a town and resort in NW Wales, in Conwy county borough on the Irish Sea. Pop: 14 872 (2001)

Llanelli *or* **Llaneily** (θlæ'nɛθlɪ; *Welsh* hla'nɛhliː) *n* an industrial town in S Wales, in SE Carmarthenshire on an inlet of Carmarthen Bay. Pop: 46 357 (2001)

Llanfairpwllgwyngyll (*Welsh* hlan,vaɪrpʊhl'gwɪngɪhl), **Llanfairpwll** *or* **Llanfair P. G.** *n* a village in NW Wales, in SE Anglesey: reputed to be the longest place name in Great Britain when unabbreviated; means: St Mary's Church in the hollow of the white hazel near the rapid whirlpool of Llandysilio of the red cave Full name: Llanfairpwllgwyngyllgogerychwyrndrobwllllantysilio-gogogoch (*Welsh* hlah'vaɪrpʊhl'gwzngɪhlgɔ'gɛrəx-wɪrn'drɔbʊhl'hlantə'sɪljɔ'gɔgɔ'gɔx)

Llangollen (*Welsh* hlan'gɔhlɛn) *n* a town in NE Wales, in Denbighshire on the River Dee: International Musical Eisteddfod held annually since 1946. Pop: 2930 (2001)

llano ('lɑːnəʊ; *Spanish* 'ʎano) *n, pl* **-nos** (-nəʊz; *Spanish* -nɔs) an extensive grassy treeless plain, esp in South America [C17: Spanish, from Latin *plānum* level ground]

Llano Estacado ('lɑːnəʊ ‚ɛstəˈkɑːdəʊ) *n* the S part of the Great Plains of the US, extending over W Texas and E New Mexico: oil and natural gas resources. Chief towns: Lubbock and Amarillo. Area: 83 700 sq km (30 000 sq miles). Also called: **Staked Plain**

LLB *abbreviation* Bachelor of Laws [Latin: *Legum Baccalaureus*]

LLD *abbreviation* Doctor of Laws [Latin: *Legum Doctor*]

Lleida (*Catalan* 'ʎeiðə) *n* the Catalan name for **Lérida**

Llewellyn (luː'ɛlɪn) *n* Colonel **Harry.** 1911–99, Welsh show-jumping rider: on Foxhunter, he was a member of the British team that won the gold medal at the 1952 Olympic Games

Llewelyn I *n* See **Llywelyn ap Iorwerth**

Llewelyn II *n* See **Llywelyn ap Gruffudd**

Lleyn Peninsula (*Welsh* hliːn) *n* a peninsula in NW Wales between Cardigan Bay and Caernarfon Bay

LLM *abbreviation* Master of Laws [Latin: *Legum Magister*]

Lloyd (lɔɪd) *n* **1 Clive** (**Hubert**). born 1944, West Indian (Guyanese) cricketer; captained the West Indies (1974–88) **2 Harold** (**Clayton**). 1893–1971, US comic film actor **3 Marie,** real name *Matilda Alice Victoria Wood.* 1870–1922, English music-hall entertainer

Lloyd George *n* **David,** 1st Earl Lloyd George of Dwyfor. 1863–1945, British Liberal statesman: prime minister (1916–22). As chancellor of the exchequer (1908–15) he introduced old age pensions (1908), a radical budget (1909), and an insurance scheme (1911)

Lloyd's (lɔɪdz) *n* an association of London underwriters, set up in the late 17th century. Originally concerned exclusively with marine insurance and a shipping information service, it now subscribes a variety of insurance policies and publishes a daily list (**Lloyd's List**) of shipping data and news [C17: named after Edward Lloyd (died ?1726) at whose coffee house in London the underwriters originally carried on their business]

Lloyd Webber ('wɛbə) *n* **1 Andrew,** Baron Lloyd-Webber. born 1948, English composer. His musicals include *Joseph and the Amazing Technicolour Dreamcoat* (1968), *Jesus Christ Superstar* (1970), and *Evita* (1978), all with lyrics by Tim Rice, and *Cats* (1981), *Phantom of the Opera* (1986), *Sunset Boulevard* (1993), and *The Beautiful Game* (2000) **2** his brother, **Julian.** born 1951, British cellist

Llywelyn ap Gruffudd ('hləwɛlɪn æp 'grɪfɪθ) *n* died 1282, prince of Wales (1258–82): the only Welsh ruler to be recognized as such by the English

Llywelyn ap Iorwerth ('hləwɛlɪn æp 'jɔːrwɛərθ) *n* called **Llywelyn the Great.** died 1240, prince of Gwynedd, N Wales (1194–1238), who extended his rule over most of Wales

lm *symbol for* lumen

LMS *abbreviation* (in Britain) local management of schools: the system of making each school responsible for controlling its total budget, after the budget has been calculated by the Local Education Authority

LNG *abbreviation* liquefied natural gas

lo (ləʊ) *interj* look! see! (now often in the phrase **lo and behold**) [Old English *lā*]

loach (ləʊtʃ) *n* any carplike freshwater cyprinoid fish of the family *Cobitidae*, of Eurasia and Africa, having a long narrow body with barbels around the mouth [C14: from Old French *loche*, of obscure origin]

Loach (ləʊtʃ) *n* **Ken(neth).** born 1936, British television and film director; his works for television include *Cathy Come Home* (1966) and his films include *Kes* (1970), *Riff-Raff* (1991), *Bread and Roses* (2000), and *The Wind that Shakes the Barley* (2006)

load (ləʊd) *n* **1** something to be borne or conveyed; weight **2** a the usual amount borne or conveyed **b** (*in combination*): *a carload* **3** something that weighs down, oppresses, or burdens: *that's a load off my mind* **4** a single charge of a firearm **5** the weight that is carried by a structure **6** *electrical engineering, electronics* **a** a device that receives or dissipates the power from an amplifier, oscillator, generator, or some other source of signals **b** the power delivered by a machine, generator, circuit, etc **7** the resistance overcome by an engine or motor when it is driving a machine, etc **8** an external force applied to a component or mechanism **9** a load of *informal* a quantity of: *a load of nonsense* **10** get a load of *informal* pay attention to **11** have a load on *US & Canadian slang* to be intoxicated ▷ *vb* (*mainly tr*) **12** (*also intr*) to place or receive (cargo, goods, etc) upon (a ship, lorry, etc) **13** to burden or oppress **14** to supply or beset (someone) with in abundance or overwhelmingly: *they loaded her with gifts* **15** to cause to be biased: *to load a question* **16** (*also intr*) to put an ammunition charge into (a firearm) **17** *photog* to position (a film, cartridge, or plate) in (a camera) **18** to weight or bias (a roulette wheel, dice, etc) **19** *insurance* to increase (a premium) to cover expenses, etc **20** *computing* to transfer (a program) to a memory **21** load the dice **a** to add weights to dice in order to bias them **b** to arrange to have a favourable or unfavourable position ▷ See also **loads** [Old English *lād* course; in meaning, influenced by LADE[1]; related to LEAD[1]] > 'loader *n*

loaded (ləʊdɪd) *adj* **1** carrying a load **2** (of dice, a roulette wheel, etc) weighted or otherwise biased **3** (of a question or statement) containing a hidden trap or implication **4** charged with ammunition **5** (of concrete) containing heavy metals, esp iron or lead, for use in making radiation shields **6** *slang* wealthy **7** (*postpositive*) *slang, chiefly US & Canadian* **a** drunk **b** drugged; influenced by drugs

loading ('ləʊdɪŋ) *n* **1** a load or burden; weight **2** the addition of an inductance to electrical equipment, such as a transmission line or aerial, to improve its performance **3** *Austral & NZ* a payment made in addition to a basic wage or salary to reward special skills, compensate for unfavourable conditions, etc

load line *n nautical* a pattern of lines painted on the hull of a ship, approximately midway between the bow and the stern, indicating the various levels that the waterline should reach if the ship is properly loaded under given circumstances

loads (ləʊdz) *informal* ▷ *pl n* **1** (*often foll by of*) a lot: *loads to eat* ▷ *adv* **2** (*intensifier*): *loads better; thanks loads*

loadstar ('ləʊd,stɑː) *n* a variant spelling of **lodestar**

loadstone ('ləʊd,stəʊn) *n* a variant spelling of **lodestone**

loaf[1] (ləʊf) *n, pl* **loaves** (ləʊvz) **1** a shaped mass of baked bread **2** any shaped or moulded mass of food, such as cooked meat **3** *slang* the head; sense: *use your loaf!* [Old English *hlāf*; related to Old High German *hleib* bread, Old Norse *hleifr*, Latin *libum* cake]

loaf[2] (ləʊf) *vb* **1** (*intr*) to loiter or lounge around in an idle way **2** (*tr*; *foll by away*) to spend (time) idly: *he loafed away*

his life [C19: perhaps back formation from LOAFER]

loafer ('ləʊfə) *n* **1** a person who avoids work; idler **2** a moccasin-like shoe for casual wear [C19: perhaps from German *Landläufer* vagabond]

loam (ləʊm) *n* **1** rich soil consisting of a mixture of sand, clay, and decaying organic material **2** a paste of clay and sand used for making moulds in a foundry, plastering walls, etc ▷ *vb* **3** (*tr*) to cover, treat, or fill with loam [Old English *lām*; related to Old Swedish *lēmo* clay, Old High German *leimo*] > 'loamy *adj* > 'loaminess *n*

loan (ləʊn) *n* **1** the act of lending: *the loan of a car* **2** property lent, esp money lent at interest for a period of time **3** the adoption by speakers of one language of a form current in another language **4** short for **loan word** **5** on loan **a** lent out; borrowed **b** (esp of personnel) transferred from a regular post to a temporary one elsewhere ▷ *vb* **6** to lend (something, esp money) [C13 *loon, lan*, from Old Norse *lān*; related to Old English *lǣn* loan; compare German *Lehen* fief, *Lohn* wages] > 'loanable *adj* > 'loaner *n*

loanback ('ləʊn,bæk) *n* **1** a facility offered by some life-assurance companies in which an individual can borrow from his pension fund ▷ *vb* **loan back 2** to make use of this facility

Loan Council *n* (in Australia) a statutory body that controls borrowing by the states

Loanda (ləʊ'ændə) *n* a variant spelling of **Luanda**

loan shark *n informal* a person who lends funds at illegal or exorbitant rates of interest

loan translation *n* the adoption by one language of a phrase or compound word whose components are literal translations of the components of a corresponding phrase or compound in a foreign language: *English "superman" is a loan translation from German "Übermensch"*. Also called: calque

loan word *n* a word adopted, often with some modification of its form, from one language into another

loath or **loth** (ləʊθ) *adj* **1** (usually foll by *to*) reluctant or unwilling **2** nothing loath willing [Old English *lāth* (in the sense: hostile); related to Old Norse *leithr*]

loathe (ləʊð) *vb* (*tr*) to feel strong hatred or disgust for [Old English *lāthian*, from LOATH] > 'loather *n*

loathing ('ləʊðɪŋ) *n* abhorrence; disgust

loathly[1] ('ləʊθlɪ) *adv* with reluctance; unwillingly

loathly[2] ('ləʊðlɪ) *adj* an archaic word for **loathsome**

loathsome ('ləʊðsəm) *adj* causing loathing; abhorrent > 'loathsomely *adv* > 'loathsomeness *n*

loaves (ləʊvz) *n* the plural of **loaf**[1]

lob (lɒb) *sport* ▷ *n* **1** a ball struck in a high arc **2** *cricket* a ball bowled in a slow high arc ▷ *vb* **lobs, lobbing, lobbed 3** to hit or kick (a ball) in a high arc **4** *informal* to throw, esp in a high arc [C14: probably of Low German origin, originally in the sense: something dangling; compare Middle Low German *lobbe* hanging lower lip, Old English *loppe* spider]

Lobachevsky (*Russian* ləbɑ'tʃɛfskij) *n* **Nikolai Ivanovich** (nika'laj i'vanəvitʃ). 1793–1856, Russian mathematician; a founder of non-Euclidean geometry

lobar ('ləʊbə) *adj* of, relating to, or affecting a lobe

lobate ('ləʊbeɪt) *or* **lobated** *adj* **1** having or resembling lobes **2** (of birds) having separate toes that are each fringed with a weblike lobe > 'lobately *adv*

lobby ('lɒbɪ) *n, pl* **-bies 1** a room or corridor used as an entrance hall, vestibule, etc **2** *chiefly Brit* a hall in a legislative building used for meetings between the legislators and members of the public **3** Also called: **division lobby** *chiefly Brit* one of two corridors in a legislative building in which members vote **4** a group of persons who attempt to influence legislators on behalf of a particular interest ▷ *vb* **-bies, -bying, -bied 5** to attempt to influence (legislators, etc) in the formulation of policy **6** (*intr*) to act in the manner of a lobbyist **7** (*tr*) to apply pressure or influence for the passage of (a bill, etc) [C16: from Medieval Latin *lobia* portico, from Old High German *lauba* arbor, from *laub* leaf] > 'lobbyer *n*

lobbyist ('lɒbɪɪst) *n* a person employed by a particular interest to lobby > 'lobby,ism *n*

lobe (ləʊb) *n* **1** any rounded projection forming part of a larger structure **2** any of the subdivisions of a bodily organ or part, delineated by shape or connective tissue **3** short for **ear lobe 4** any of the parts, not entirely separate from each other, into which a flattened plant part, such as a leaf, is divided [c16: from Late Latin *lobus*, from Greek *lobos* lobe of the ear or of the liver]

lobectomy (ləʊˈbɛktəmɪ) *n, pl* **-mies** surgical removal of a lobe from any organ or gland in the body, esp removal of tissue from the frontal lobe of the brain in an attempt to alleviate mental disorder

lobelia (ləʊˈbiːlɪə) *n* any plant of the campanulaceous genus *Lobelia*, having red, blue, white, or yellow five-lobed flowers with the three lower lobes forming a lip [c18: from New Latin, named after Matthias de *Lobel* (1538–1616), Flemish botanist]

Lobengula (ˌləʊbənˈɡjuːlə) *n* ?1836–94, last Matabele king (1870–93); his kingdom was destroyed by the British

Lobito (Portuguese luˈβitu) *n* the chief port in Angola, in the west on **Lobito Bay**: terminus of the railway through Benguela to Mozambique. Pop: 470 000 (2005 est)

loblolly (ˈlɒbˌlɒlɪ) *n, pl* **-lies** a southern US pine tree, *Pinus taeda*, with bright red-brown bark, green needle-like leaves, and reddish-brown cones [c16: perhaps from dialect *lob* to boil + obsolete dialect *lolly* thick soup]

lobola or **lobolo** (lɔːˈbɔːlə, ləˈbəʊ-) *n* (in southern Africa) an African custom by which a bridegroom's family makes a payment in cattle or cash to the bride's family shortly before the marriage [from Nguni *ukulobola* to give the bride price]

lobotomy (ləʊˈbɒtəmɪ) *n, pl* **-mies 1** a surgical incision into a lobe of any organ **2** Also called: **prefrontal leucotomy** a surgical interruption of one or more nerve tracts in the frontal lobe of the brain: used in the treatment of intractable mental disorders [c20: from LOBE + -TOMY]

lobscouse (ˈlɒbˌskaʊs) *n* a sailor's stew of meat, vegetables, and hardtack [c18: perhaps from dialect *lob* to boil + *scouse*, broth; compare LOBLOLLY]

lobster (ˈlɒbstə) *n, pl* **-sters** or **-ster 1** any of several large marine decapod crustaceans of the genus *Homarus*, esp *H. vulgaris*, occurring on rocky shores and having the first pair of limbs modified as large pincers **2** any of several similar crustaceans, esp the spiny lobster **3** the flesh of any of these crustaceans, eaten as a delicacy [Old English *loppestre*, from *loppe* spider]

lobster pot or **lobster trap** *n* a round basket or trap made of open slats used to catch lobsters

lobule (ˈlɒbjuːl) *n* a small lobe or a subdivision of a lobe [c17: from New Latin *lobulus*, from Late Latin *lobus* LOBE] > **lobular** (ˈlɒbjʊlə), **lobulate** (ˈlɒbjʊlɪt), **ˈlobuˌlated** or **ˈlobulose** *adj* > ˌlobuˈlation *n*

lobworm (ˈlɒbˌwɜːm) *n* **1** another name for **lugworm 2** a large earthworm used as bait in fishing [c17: from obsolete *lob* lump + WORM]

local (ˈləʊkəl) *adj* **1** characteristic of or associated with a particular locality or area **2** of, concerned with, or relating to a particular place or point in space **3** *med* of, affecting, or confined to a limited area or part **4** (of a train, bus, etc) stopping at all stations or stops ▷ *n* **5** a train, bus, etc, that stops at all stations or stops **6** an inhabitant of a specified locality **7** *Brit informal* a pub close to one's home or place of work **8** *med* short for **local anaesthetic 9** *US & Canadian* an item of local interest in a newspaper [c15: via Old French from Late Latin *locālis*, from Latin *locus* place, LOCUS] > ˈlocalness *n* ˈlocally *adv*

local anaesthetic *n med* a drug that produces local anaesthesia. See **anaesthesia** (sense 2)

local authority *n Brit & NZ* the governing body of a county, district, etc. US equivalent: **local government**

locale (ləʊˈkɑːl) *n* a place or area, esp with reference to events connected with it [c18: from French *local* (n use of adj); see LOCAL]

local government *n* **1** government of the affairs of counties, towns, etc, by locally elected political bodies **2** the US equivalent of **local authority**

Local Group *n astronomy* the cluster of galaxies to which our galaxy and the Andromeda Galaxy belong

localism (ˈləʊkəˌlɪzəm) *n* **1** a pronunciation, phrase, etc, peculiar to a particular locality **2** another word for **provincialism**

locality (ləʊˈkælɪtɪ) *n, pl* **-ties 1** a neighbourhood or area **2** the site or scene of an event **3** the fact or condition of having a location or position in space

localize or **localise** (ˈləʊkəˌlaɪz) *vb* **1** to make or become local in attitude, behaviour, etc **2** (*tr*) to restrict or confine (something) to a particular area or part **3** (*tr*) to assign or ascribe to a particular region > ˈlocalˌizable or ˈlocalˌisable *adj* > ˌlocaliˈzation or ˌlocaliˈsation *n* > ˈlocalˌizer or ˈlocalˌiser *n*

local loan *n* (in Britain) a loan issued by a local government authority

local option *n* (esp in Scotland, New Zealand, and the US) the privilege of a municipality, county, etc, to determine by referendum whether a particular activity, esp the sale of liquor, shall be permitted there

Locarno (Italian loˈkarno) *n* a town in S Switzerland, in Ticino canton at the N end of Lake Maggiore: tourist resort. Pop: 14 561 (2000)

locate (ləʊˈkeɪt) *vb* **1** (*tr*) to discover the position, situation, or whereabouts of; find **2** (*tr; often passive*) to situate or place: *located on the edge of the city* **3** (*intr*) to become established or settled > loˈcater *n*

location (ləʊˈkeɪʃən) *n* **1** a site or position; situation **2** the act or process of locating or the state of being located **3** a place outside a studio where filming is done: *shot on location* **4** (in South Africa) **a** a Black African or Coloured township, usually located near a small town. See also **township** (sense 4) **b** (formerly) an African tribal reserve **5** *computing* a position in a memory capable of holding a unit of information, such as a word, and identified by its address **6** *Roman law, Scots law* the letting out on hire of a chattel or of personal services [c16: from Latin *locātiō*, from *locāre* to place]

locative (ˈlɒkətɪv) *grammar* ▷ *adj* **1** (of a word or phrase) indicating place or direction **2** denoting a case of nouns, etc, that refers to the place at which the action described by the verb occurs ▷ *n* **3 a** the locative case **b** a word or speech element in this case [c19: LOCATE + -IVE, on the model of *vocative*]

loc. cit. *abbreviation* (in textual annotation) loco citato

loch (lɒx, lɒk) *n* **1** a Scot word for **lake**[1] **2** Also called: **sea loch** a long narrow bay or arm of the sea in Scotland [c14: from Gaelic]

lochia (ˈlɒkɪə) *n* a vaginal discharge of cellular debris, mucus, and blood following childbirth [c17: New Latin from Greek *lokhia*, from *lokhios*, from *lokhos* childbirth] > ˈlochial *adj*

loci (ˈləʊsaɪ) *n* the plural of **locus**

lock[1] (lɒk) *n* **1** a device fitted to a gate, drawer, lid, etc, to keep it firmly closed and often to prevent access by unauthorized persons **2** a similar device attached to a machine, vehicle, etc, to prevent use by unauthorized persons: *a steering lock* **3 a** section of a canal or river that may be closed off by gates to control the water level and the raising and lowering of vessels that pass through it **b** (*as modifier*): *a lock gate* **4** the jamming, fastening, or locking together of parts **5** *Brit* the extent to which a vehicle's front wheels will turn to the right or left: *this car has a good lock* **6** a mechanism that detonates the charge of a gun **7** *US & Canadian informal* a person or thing that is certain to win or to succeed: *she is a lock for the Academy Award* **8 lock, stock, and barrel** completely; entirely **9** any wrestling hold in which a wrestler seizes a part of his opponent's body and twists it or otherwise exerts pressure upon it **10** Also called: **lock forward** *rugby* either of two players who make up the second line of the scrum and apply weight to the forwards in the front line **11** a gas bubble in a hydraulic system or a liquid bubble in a pneumatic system that stops or interferes with the fluid flow in a pipe, capillary, etc: *an air lock* ▷ *vb* **12** to fasten (a door, gate, etc) or (of a door, etc) to become fastened with a lock, bolt, etc, so as to prevent entry or exit **13** (*tr*) to secure (a building) by locking all doors, windows, etc **14** to fix or become fixed together securely or inextricably **15** to become or cause to become rigid or immovable: *the front wheels of the car locked* **16** (when *tr*, often *passive*) to clasp or entangle (someone or each other) in a struggle or embrace **17** (*tr*) to furnish (a canal) with locks **18** (*tr*) to move (a vessel) through a system of locks **19 lock horns** (esp of two equally matched opponents) to become engaged in argument or battle **20 lock the stable door after the horse has bolted** to take precautions after harm has been done ▷ See also **lock out, lock up** [Old English *loc*; related to Old Norse *lok*] > 'lockable *adj*

lock² (lɒk) *n* **1** a strand, curl, or cluster of hair **2** a tuft or wisp of wool, cotton, etc **3** (*plural*) *chiefly literary* hair, esp when curly or fine [Old English *loc*; related to Old Frisian *lok*, Old Norse *lokkr* lock of wool]

lockdown ('lɒk,daʊn) *n US* a security measure in which those inside a building such as a prison, school, or hospital are required to remain confined in it for a time: *many schools remained under lockdown yesterday*

Locke (lɒk) *n* **1 John.** 1632–1704, English philosopher, who discussed the concept of empiricism in his *Essay Concerning Human Understanding* (1690). He influenced political thought, esp in France and America, with his *Two Treatises on Government* (1690), in which he sanctioned the right to revolt **2 Matthew.** ?1630–77, English composer, esp of works for the stage

locked-in syndrome *n* a condition in which a person is conscious but unable to move any part of the body except the eyes: results from damage to the brainstem

locker ('lɒkə) *n* **1 a** a small compartment or drawer that may be locked, as one of several in a gymnasium, etc, for clothes and valuables **b** (*as modifier*): *a locker room* **2** a person or thing that locks **3** *US & Canadian* a refrigerated compartment for keeping frozen foods, esp one rented in an establishment

Lockerbie ('lɒkəbɪ) *n* a town in SW Scotland, in Dumfries and Galloway: scene (1988) of the UK's worst air disaster when a jumbo jet was brought down by a terrorist bomb, killing 270 people, including eleven residents of the town

locket ('lɒkɪt) *n* a small ornamental case, usually on a necklace or chain, that holds a picture, keepsake, etc [C17: from French *loquet* latch, diminutive of *loc* LOCK¹]

lockjaw ('lɒk,dʒɔː) *n pathol* a nontechnical name for **trismus** *or* **tetanus**

lock out *vb* (*tr, adverb*) **1** to prevent from entering by locking a door **2** to prevent (employees) from working during an industrial dispute, as by closing a factory ▷ *n* **lockout 3** the closing of a place of employment by an employer, in order to bring pressure on employees to agree to terms

locksmith ('lɒk,smɪθ) *n* a person who makes or repairs locks > 'lock,smithery *or* 'lock,smithing *n*

lockstep ('lɒk,stɛp) *n* **1** a method of marching in step such that the men follow one another as closely as possible **2** *chiefly US & Canadian* a standard procedure that is closely, often mindlessly, followed **3 in lockstep with** progressing at exactly the same speed and in the same direction as other people or things, esp as a matter of course rather than by choice

lock up *vb* (*adverb*) **1** Also called: **lock in, lock away** (*tr*) to imprison or confine **2** to lock or secure the doors, windows, etc, of (a building) **3** (*tr*) to keep or store securely: *secrets locked up in history* **4** (*tr*) to invest (funds) so that conversion into cash is difficult **5** *printing* to secure (type, etc) in a chase or in the bed of the printing machine by tightening the quoins ▷ *n* **lockup 6** the action or time of locking up **7** a jail or block of cells **8** *Brit* a small shop with no attached quarters for the owner or shopkeeper **9** *Brit* a garage or storage place separate from the main premises **10** *stock exchange* an investment that is intended to be held for a relatively long period **11** *printing* the pages of type held in a chase by the positioning of quoins ▷ *adj* **12 lock-up** *Brit & NZ* (of premises) without living accommodation: *a lock-up shop*

Lockyer ('lɒkjə) *n* Sir **Joseph Norman.** 1836–1920, English astronomer: a pioneer in solar spectroscopy, he was the first to observe helium in the sun's atmosphere (1868)

loco¹ ('ləʊkəʊ) *n informal* short for **locomotive**

loco² ('ləʊkəʊ) *adj* **1** *slang, chiefly US* insane **2** (of an animal) affected with loco disease ▷ *n, pl* -**cos 3** short for

locoweed ▷ *vb* (*tr*) **4** to poison with locoweed **5** *US slang* to make insane [C19: via Mexican Spanish from Spanish: crazy]

loco³ ('ləʊkəʊ) *adj* denoting a price for goods, esp goods to be exported, that are in a place specified or known, the buyer being responsible for all transport charges from that place: *loco Bristol; a loco price* [C20: from Latin *locō* from a place]

loco citato ('ləʊkəʊ sɪ'tɑːtəʊ) in the place or passage quoted. Abbreviations: **loc. cit., lc** [Latin: in the place cited]

loco disease *or* **loco poisoning** *n* a disease of cattle, sheep, and horses characterized by paralysis and faulty vision, caused by ingestion of locoweed

locomotion (,ləʊkə'məʊʃən) *n* the act, fact, ability, or power of moving [C17: from Latin *locō* from a place, ablative of *locus* place + MOTION]

locomotive (,ləʊkə'məʊtɪv) *n* **1 a** Also called: **locomotive engine** a self-propelled engine driven by steam, electricity, or diesel power and used for drawing trains along railway tracks **b** (*as modifier*): *a locomotive shed; a locomotive works* ▷ *adj* **2** of or relating to locomotion **3** moving or able to move, as by self-propulsion > ,loco'motively *adv* > ,loco'motiveness *n*

locomotor (,ləʊkə'məʊtə) *adj* of or relating to locomotion [C19: from Latin *locō* from a place, ablative of *locus* place + MOTOR (mover)]

locomotor ataxia *n pathol* another name for **tabes dorsalis**

locoweed ('ləʊkəʊ,wiːd) *n* any of several perennial leguminous plants of the genera *Oxytropis* and *Astragalus* of W North America that cause loco disease in horses, cattle, and sheep

Locris *or* **Lokris** ('ləʊkrɪs, 'lɒk-) *n* an ancient region of central Greece

locum tenens ('ləʊkəm 'tiːnɛnz) *n, pl* **locum tenentes** (tə'nɛntiːz) *chiefly Brit* a person who stands in temporarily for another member of the same profession, esp for a physician, chemist, or clergyman Often shortened to **locum** [C17: Medieval Latin: (someone) holding the place (of another)]

locus ('ləʊkəs) *n, pl* **loci** ('ləʊsaɪ) **1** (in many legal phrases) a place or area, esp the place where something occurred **2** *maths* a set of points whose location satisfies or is determined by one or more specified conditions: *the locus of points equidistant from a given point is a circle* **3** *genetics* the position of a particular gene on a chromosome [C18: Latin]

locust ('ləʊkəst) *n* **1** any of numerous orthopterous insects of the genera *Locusta, Melanoplus*, etc, such as L. *migratoria*, of warm and tropical regions of the Old World, which travel in vast swarms, stripping large areas of vegetation. See also **grasshopper** (sense 1) **2** Also called: **locust tree, false acacia** a North American leguminous tree, *Robinia pseudoacacia*, having prickly branches, hanging clusters of white fragrant flowers, and reddish-brown seed pods **3** the yellowish durable wood of this tree **4** any of several similar trees, such as the honey locust and carob [C13 (the insect): from Latin *locusta* locust; applied to the tree (C17) because the pods resemble locusts] > 'locust-,like *adj*

locution (ləʊ'kjuːʃən) *n* **1** a word, phrase, or expression **2** manner or style of speech or expression [C15: from Latin *locūtiō* an utterance, from *loquī* to speak]

Lod (lɒd) *n* a town in central Israel, southeast of Tel Aviv: Israel's chief airport. Pop: 66 800 (2003 est). Also called: **Lydda**

lode (ləʊd) *n* **1** a deposit of valuable ore occurring between definite limits in the surrounding rock; vein **2** a deposit of metallic ore filling a fissure in the surrounding rock [Old English *lād* course. Compare LOAD]

loden ('ləʊdⁿn) *n* **1** a thick heavy waterproof woollen cloth with a short pile, used to make garments, esp coats **2** a dark bluish-green colour, in which the cloth is often made [German, from Old High German *lodo* thick cloth, perhaps related to Old English *lotha* cloak]

lodestar *or* **loadstar** ('ləʊd,stɑː) *n* **1** a star, esp the North Star, used in navigation or astronomy as a point of reference **2** something that serves as a guide or model [c14: literally, guiding star. See LODE]

lodestone or **loadstone** ('ləʊdˌstəʊn) n **1 a** a rock that consists of pure or nearly pure magnetite and thus is naturally magnetic **b** a piece of such rock, which can be used as a magnet and which was formerly used as a primitive compass **2** a person or thing regarded as a focus of attraction [c16: literally: guiding stone]

lodge (lɒdʒ) n **1** chiefly Brit a small house at the entrance to the grounds of a country mansion, usually occupied by a gatekeeper or gardener **2** a house or cabin used occasionally, as for some seasonal activity **3** US & Canadian a central building in a resort, camp, or park **4** (capital when part of a name) a large house or hotel **5** a room for the use of porters in a university, college, etc **6** a local branch or chapter of certain societies **7** the building used as the meeting place of such a society **8** the dwelling place of certain animals, esp the dome-shaped den constructed by beavers **9** a hut or tent of certain North American Indian peoples **10** (at Cambridge University) the residence of the head of a college ▷ vb **11** to provide or be provided with accommodation or shelter, esp rented accommodation **12** (intr) to live temporarily, esp in rented accommodation **13** to implant, embed, or fix or be implanted, embedded, or fixed **14** (tr) to deposit or leave for safety, storage, etc **15** (tr) to bring (a charge or accusation) against someone **16** (tr; often foll by in or with) to place (authority, power, etc) in the control (of someone) **17** (intr; often foll by in) archaic to exist or be present (in) **18** (tr) (of wind, rain, etc) to beat down (crops) [c15: from Old French loge, perhaps from Old High German louba porch] > 'lodgeable adj

Lodge¹ (lɒdʒ) n the Lodge the official Canberra residence of the Australian Prime Minister

Lodge² (lɒdʒ) n **1** David (John). born 1935, British novelist and critic. His books include Changing Places (1975), Small World (1984), Nice Work (1988), Therapy (1995), and Thinks... (2001) **2** Sir Oliver (Joseph). 1851–1940, British physicist, who made important contributions to electromagnetism, radio reception, and attempted to detect the ether. He also studied allegedly psychic phenomena **3** Thomas. ?1558–1625, English writer. His romance Rosalynde (1590) supplied the plot for Shakespeare's As You Like It

lodger ('lɒdʒə) n a person who pays rent in return for accommodation in someone else's house

lodging ('lɒdʒɪŋ) n **1** a temporary residence **2** (sometimes plural) sleeping accommodation **3** (sometimes plural) (at Oxford University) the residence of the head of a college ▷ See also **lodgings**

lodging house n a private home providing accommodation and meals for lodgers

lodgings ('lɒdʒɪŋz) pl n a rented room or rooms in which to live, esp in another person's house

lodgment or **lodgement** ('lɒdʒmənt) n **1** the act of lodging or the state of being lodged **2** a blockage or accumulation **3** a small area gained and held in enemy territory

Lodi (Italian 'lɔːdi) n a town in N Italy, in Lombardy: scene of Napoleon's defeat of the Austrians in 1796. Pop: 40 805 (2001)

Łódź (Polish wudʒ) n a city in central Poland: the country's second largest city; major centre of the textile industry; university (1945). Pop: 943 000 (2005 est)

Loeb (lɜːb; German løːp) n Jacques (ʒɑːk). 1859–1924, US physiologist, born in Germany, noted esp for his pioneering work on artificial parthenogenesis

loess ('ləʊɪs; German lœs) n a light-coloured fine-grained accumulation of clay and silt particles that have been deposited by the wind [c19: from German Löss, from Swiss German dialect lösch loose] > loessial (ləʊ'ɛsɪəl) adj

Loewe¹ (ləʊ) n Frederick. 1904–88, US composer of such musical comedies as Brigadoon (1947), My Fair Lady (1956), and Camelot (1960), all with librettos by Alan Jay Lerner

Loewe² or **Löwe** (German 'løːvə) n (Johann) Karl (Gottfried). 1796–1869, German composer, esp of songs, such as Der Erlkönig (1818)

Loewi ('ləʊɪ) n Otto. 1873–1961, US pharmacologist, born

in Germany. He shared a Nobel prize for physiology or medicine (1936) with Dale for their work on the chemical transmission of nerve impulses

Lofoten and Vesterålen (Norwegian 'luːfutən, 'vɛstəroːlən) pl n a group of islands off the NW coast of Norway, within the Arctic Circle. Largest island: Hinnøy. Pop: 54 589 (2004 est). Area: about 5130 sq km (1980 sq miles)

loft (lɒft) n **1** the space inside a roof **2** a gallery, esp one for the choir in a church **3** a room over a stable used to store hay **4** an upper storey of a warehouse or factory, esp when converted into living space **5** a raised house or coop in which pigeons are kept **6** sport **a** (in golf) the angle from the vertical made by the club face to give elevation to a ball **b** elevation imparted to a ball **c** a lofting stroke or shot ▷ vb **7** sport to strike or kick (a ball) high in the air **8** to store or place in a loft **9** to lay out a full-scale working drawing of (the lines of a vessel's hull) [Late Old English, from Old Norse lopt air, ceiling; compare Old Danish and Old High German loft (German Luft air)]

lofty ('lɒftɪ) adj **loftier, loftiest** **1** of majestic or imposing height **2** exalted or noble in character or nature **3** haughty or supercilious **4** elevated, eminent, or superior > 'loftily adv > 'loftiness n

log¹ (lɒg) n **1 a** a section of the trunk or a main branch of a tree, when stripped of branches **b** (modifier) constructed out of logs: a log cabin **2 a** a detailed record of a voyage of a ship or aircraft **b** a record of the hours flown by pilots and aircrews **c** a book in which these records are made; logbook **3** a written record of information about transmissions kept by radio stations, amateur radio operators, etc **4 a** a device consisting of a float with an attached line, formerly used to measure the speed of a ship **b** heave the log to determine a ship's speed with such a device **5** Austral a claim for better pay and conditions presented by a trade union to an employer **6** like a log without stirring or being disturbed (in the phrase sleep like a log) ▷ vb logs, logging, logged **7** (tr) to fell the trees of (a forest, area, etc) for timber **8** (tr) to saw logs from (trees) **9** (intr) to work at the felling of timber **10** (tr) to enter (a distance, event, etc) in a logbook or log **11** (tr) to record the punishment received by (a sailor) in a logbook or log **12** (tr) to travel (a specified distance or time) or move at (a specified speed) [c14: origin obscure]

log² (lɒg) n short for **logarithm**

-log combining form a US variant of **-logue**

logan¹ ('ləʊgən) or **logan-stone** n other names for **rocking stone** [c18: from logging-stone, from dialect log to rock]

logan² ('ləʊgən) n Canadian another name for **bogan¹**

Logan ('ləʊgən) n Mount Logan a mountain in NW Canada, in SW Yukon in the St Elias Range: the highest peak in Canada and the second highest in North America. Height (after a re-survey in 1993): 5959 m (19 550 ft)

loganberry ('ləʊgənbərɪ, -brɪ) n, pl -ries **1** a trailing prickly hybrid rosaceous plant, Rubus loganobaccus, cultivated for its edible fruit: probably a hybrid between an American blackberry and a raspberry **2 a** the purplish-red acid fruit of this plant **b** (as modifier): loganberry pie [c19: named after James H. Logan (1841–1928), American judge and horticulturist who first grew it (1881)]

logarithm ('lɒgəˌrɪðəm) n the exponent indicating the power to which a fixed number, the base, must be raised to obtain a given number or variable. It is used esp to simplify multiplication and division: if $a^x = M$, then the logarithm of M to the base a (written $\log_a M$) is x. Often shortened to: **log** See also **natural logarithm** [c17: from New Latin logarithmus, coined 1614 by John Napier (1550–1617), Scottish mathematician who invented them, from Greek, logos ratio, reckoning + arithmos number] > logarithmic (ˌlɒgəˈrɪðmɪk) or ˌloga'rithmical adj

logarithmic function n **a** the mathematical function $y = \log x$ **b** a function that can be expressed in terms of this function

logbook ('lɒɡ,bʊk) *n* 1 a book containing the official record of trips made by a ship or aircraft; log 2 *Brit* (formerly) a document listing the registration, manufacture, ownership and previous owners, etc, of a motor vehicle. See **registration document**

log chip *n nautical* the chip of a chip log

loge (ləʊʒ) *n* 1 a small enclosure or box in a theatre or opera house 2 the upper section in a theatre or cinema [c18: French; see LODGE]

logger ('lɒɡə) *n* 1 another word for **lumberjack** 2 a tractor or crane for handling logs

loggerhead ('lɒɡə,hɛd) *n* 1 Also called: loggerhead turtle a large-headed turtle, *Caretta caretta*, occurring in most seas: family *Chelonidae* 2 loggerhead shrike a North American shrike, *Lanius ludovicianus*, having a grey head and body, black-and-white wings and tail, and black facial stripe 3 a tool consisting of a large metal sphere attached to a long handle, used for warming liquids, melting tar, etc 4 a strong round upright post in a whaleboat for belaying the line of a harpoon 5 *archaic or dialect* a blockhead; dunce 6 at loggerheads engaged in dispute or confrontation [c16: probably from dialect *logger* wooden block + HEAD] > 'logger,headed *adj*

loggia ('lɒdʒə, 'lɒdʒɪə) *n, pl* -gias or -gie (-dʒɛ) 1 a covered area on the side of a building, esp one that serves as a porch 2 an open balcony in a theatre [c17: Italian, from French *loge*. See LODGE]

logging ('lɒɡɪŋ) *n* the work of felling, trimming, and transporting timber

logic ('lɒdʒɪk) *n* 1 the branch of philosophy concerned with analysing the patterns of reasoning by which a conclusion is properly drawn from a set of premises, without reference to meaning or context. See also **formal logic, induction** (sense 4) 2 any particular formal system in which are defined axioms and rules of inference. See **formal language** 3 the system and principles of reasoning used in a specific field of study 4 a particular method of argument or reasoning 5 force or effectiveness in argument or dispute 6 reasoned thought or argument, as distinguished from irrationality 7 the relationship and interdependence of a series of events, facts, etc 8 chop logic to use excessively subtle or involved logic or argument 9 *electronics, computing* a the principles underlying the units in a computer system that perform arithmetical and logical operations. See also **logic circuit** b (*as modifier*): *a logic element* [c14: from Old French *logique* from Medieval Latin *logica* (neuter plural, treated in Medieval Latin as feminine singular), from Greek *logikos* concerning speech or reasoning]

logical ('lɒdʒɪkᵊl) *adj* 1 relating to, used in, or characteristic of logic 2 using, according to, or deduced from the principles of logic: *a logical conclusion* 3 capable of or characterized by clear or valid reasoning 4 reasonable or necessary because of facts, events, etc: *the logical candidate* 5 *computing* of, performed by, used in, or relating to the logic circuits in a computer > ,logi'cality *or* 'logicalness *n* > 'logically *adv*

logical form *n* the syntactic structure that may be shared by different expressions as abstracted from their content and articulated by the logical constants of a particular logical system, esp the structure of an argument by virtue of which it can be shown to be formally valid. Thus *John is tall and thin, so John is tall* has the same logical form as *London is large and dirty, so London is large*, namely *P & Q, so P*

logical positivism *n* a philosophical theory that holds to be meaningful only those propositions that can be analysed by the tools of logic into elementary propositions that are either tautological or are empirically verifiable. It therefore rejects metaphysics, theology, and sometimes ethics, as meaningless

logic bomb *n computing* an unauthorized program that is inserted into a computer system; when activated it interferes with the operation of the system

logic cell *n* a logic circuit forming part of a chip

logic circuit *n* an electronic circuit used in computers to perform a logical operation on its two or more input signals. There are six basic circuits, the AND, NOT, NAND, OR, NOR, and exclusive OR circuits, which can be combined into more complex circuits

logician (lɒ'dʒɪʃən) *n* a person who specializes in or is skilled at logic

logic programming *n* the study or implementation of computer programs capable of discovering or checking proofs of formal expressions or segments

Logie ('ləʊɡɪ) *n* (in Australia) one of the awards made annually for outstanding television performances [c20: after (John) *Logie* Baird (1888–1946), the Scottish inventor of the television]

log in *computing* ▷ *vb* 1 Also called: log on to enter (an identification number, password, etc) from a remote terminal to gain access to a multiaccess system ▷ *n* login 2 Also called: logon the process by which a computer user logs in

logistics (lɒ'dʒɪstɪks) *n* (*functioning as singular or plural*) 1 the science of the movement, supplying, and maintenance of military forces in the field 2 the management of materials flow through an organization, from raw materials through to finished goods 3 the detailed planning and organization of any large complex operation [c19: from French *logistique*, from *loger* to LODGE] > lo'gistic *or* lo'gistical *adj*

log jam *n chiefly US & Canadian* 1 blockage caused by the crowding together of a number of logs floating in a river 2 a deadlock; standstill

loglog ('lɒɡlɒɡ) *n* the logarithm of a logarithm (in equations, etc)

logo ('ləʊɡəʊ, 'lɒɡ-) *n, pl* -os short for **logotype** (sense 2)

logo- *combining form* indicating word or speech: *logogram* [from Greek; from LOGOS]

logogram ('lɒɡə,ɡræm) *or* **logograph** ('lɒɡə,ɡrɑːf, -,ɡræf) *n* a single symbol representing an entire morpheme, word, or phrase, as for example the symbol (%) meaning *per cent* > logogrammatic (,lɒɡəɡrə'mætɪk), logographic (,lɒɡə'ɡræfɪk) *or* 'logo,graphical *adj* > ,logogram'matically *or* ,logo'graphically *adv*

logorrhoea *or esp US* **logorrhea** (,lɒɡə'rɪə) *n* excessive, uncontrollable, or incoherent talkativeness

logos ('lɒɡɒs) *n philosophy* reason or the rational principle expressed in words and things, argument, or justification; esp personified as the source of order in the universe [c16: from Greek: word, reason, discourse, from *legein* to speak]

Logos ('lɒɡɒs) *n Christian theol* the divine Word; the second person of the Trinity incarnate in the person of Jesus

logotype ('lɒɡəʊ,taɪp) *n* 1 *printing* a piece of type with several uncombined characters cast on it 2 Also called: logo a trademark, company emblem, or similar device

log out *computing* ▷ *vb* 1 Also called: log off to disconnect a remote terminal from a multiaccess system by entering (an identification number, password, etc) ▷ *n* logout 2 Also called: logoff the process by which a computer user logs out

logroll ('lɒɡ,rəʊl) *vb chiefly US* to use logrolling in order to procure the passage of (legislation) > 'log,roller *n*

logrolling ('lɒɡ,rəʊlɪŋ) *n* 1 US the practice of undemocratic agreements between politicians involving mutual favours, the trading of votes, etc 2 another name for **birling**. See birl¹

Logroño (Spanish lo'ɣroɲo) *n* a walled city in N Spain, on the Ebro River: trading centre of an agricultural region noted for its wine. Pop: 139 615 (2003 est)

-logue *or US* **-log** *n combining form* indicating speech or discourse of a particular kind: *travelogue; monologue* [from French, from Greek *-logos*]

logwood ('lɒɡ,wʊd) *n* 1 a leguminous tree, *Haematoxylon campechianum*, of the Caribbean and Central America 2 the heavy reddish-brown wood of this tree, yielding the dye haematoxylin

-logy *n combining form* 1 indicating the science or study of: *musicology* 2 indicating writing, discourse, or body of writings: *trilogy; phraseology; martyrology* [from Latin *-logia*, from Greek, from *logos* word; see LOGOS] > -logical *or* -logic *adj combining form* > -logist *n combining form*

Lohengrin ('ləʊɪŋɡrɪn) *n* (in German legend) a son of Parzival and knight of the Holy Grail

loin (lɔɪn) n **1** Also called: **lumbus** anatomy the part of the lower back and sides between the pelvis and the ribs. Related adj: **lumbar 2** a cut of meat from this part of an animal ▷ See also **loins** [C14: from Old French loigne, perhaps from Vulgar Latin lumbra (unattested), from Latin lumbus loin]

loincloth (ˈlɔɪnˌklɒθ) n a piece of cloth worn round the loins

loins (lɔɪnz) pl n **1** the hips and the inner surface of the legs where they join the trunk of the body; crotch **2** a euphemistic the reproductive organs **b** chiefly literary the womb

Loire (French lwar) n **1** a department of E central France, in Rhône-Alpes region. Capital: St Étienne. Pop: 726 613 (2003 est). Area: 4799 sq km (1872 sq miles) **2** a river in France, rising in the Massif Central and flowing north and west in a wide curve to the Bay of Biscay: the longest river in France. Its valley is famous for its wines and châteaux. Length: 1020 km (634 miles)

Loire-Atlantique (French lwaratlɑ̃tik) n a department of W France, in Pays de la Loire region. Capital: Nantes. Pop: 1 174 120 (2003 est). Area: 6980 sq km (2722 sq miles)

Loiret (French lwarɛ) n a department of central France, in Centre region. Capital: Orléans. Pop: 629 377 (2003 est). Area: 6812 sq km (2657 sq miles)

Loir-et-Cher (French lwareʃer) n a department of N central France, in Centre region. Capital: Blois. Pop: 318 853 (2003 est). Area: 6422 sq km (2505 sq miles)

loiter (ˈlɔɪtə) vb (intr) to stand or act aimlessly or idly [C14: perhaps from Middle Dutch lōteren to wobble: perhaps related to Old English lūtian to lurk] > ˈloiterer n > ˈloitering n, adj

Loki (ˈləʊkɪ) n Norse myth the god of mischief and destruction

LOL abbreviation text messaging laughing out loud

loll (lɒl) vb **1** (intr) to lie, lean, or lounge in a lazy or relaxed manner **2** to hang or allow to hang loosely ▷ n **3** an act or instance of lolling [C14: perhaps imitative; perhaps related to Middle Dutch lollen to doze] > ˈloller n > ˈlolling adj

Lolland or **Laaland** (Danish ˈlɔlan) n an island of Denmark in the Baltic Sea, south of Sjælland. Pop: 69 796 (2003 est). Area: 1240 sq km (480 sq miles)

Lollard (ˈlɒləd) n English history a follower of John Wycliffe during the 14th, 15th, and 16th centuries [C14: from Middle Dutch; mutterer, from lollen to mumble (prayers)] > ˈLollardy or ˈLollardism n

lollipop (ˈlɒlɪˌpɒp) n **1** a boiled sweet or toffee stuck on a small wooden stick **2** Brit another word for **ice lolly** [C18: perhaps from Northern English dialect lolly the tongue (compare LOLL) + POP¹]

lollipop man or **lollipop lady** n (in Britain) a person who stops traffic by holding up a circular sign on a pole to allow children travelling to or from school to cross a road safely

lollop (ˈlɒləp) vb (intr) chiefly Brit **1** to walk or run with a clumsy or relaxed bouncing movement **2** a less common word for **lounge** [C18: probably from LOLL + -op as in GALLOP, to emphasize the contrast in meaning]

lollo rosso (ˈlɒləʊ ˈrɒsəʊ) n a variety of lettuce originating in Italy, having curly red-tipped leaves and a slightly bitter taste [Italian, literally: red husk]

lolly (ˈlɒlɪ) n, pl -lies **1** an informal word for **lollipop 2** Brit short for **ice lolly 3** Brit, Austral & NZ a slang word for money **4** Austral & NZ informal a sweet, esp a boiled one **5** do the lolly or do one's lolly Austral informal to lose one's temper [shortened from LOLLIPOP]

Lomax (ˈləʊmæks) n **Alan.** born 1915, and his father **John Avery** (ˈeɪvərɪ) (1867–1948), US folklorists

Lombard¹ (ˈlɒmbəd, -bɑːd, ˈlʌm-) n **1** a native or inhabitant of Lombardy **2** Also called: **Langobard** a member of an ancient Germanic people who settled in N Italy after 568 AD ▷ adj **3** Also: **Lombardic** of or relating to Lombardy or the Lombards

Lombard² (ˈlɒmbəd, -bɑːd, ˈlʌm-) n **Peter.** ?1100–?60, Italian theologian, noted for his Sententiarum libri quatuor

Lombardi (lɒmˈbɑːdɪ) n **Vincent Thomas.** 1913–70, American football coach, whose team won the first two Superbowls, and after whom the trophy awarded to the

winners of the Superbowl is named

Lombard Street n the British financial and banking world [C16: from a street in London once occupied by Lombard bankers]

Lombardy (ˈlɒmbədɪ, ˈlʌm-) n a region of N central Italy, bordering on the Alps: dominated by prosperous lordships and city-states during the Middle Ages; later ruled by Spain and then by Austria before becoming part of Italy in 1859; intensively cultivated and in parts highly industrialized. Pop: 9 108 645 (2003 est). Area: 23 804 sq km (9284 sq miles)

Lombardy poplar n an Italian poplar tree, Populus nigra italica, with upwardly pointing branches giving it a columnar shape

Lombok (ˈlɒmbɒk) n an island of Indonesia, in the Lesser Sunda Islands (Nusa Tenggara) east of Java: came under Dutch rule in 1894; important biologically as being transitional between Asian and Australian in flora and fauna, the line of demarcation beginning at **Lombok Strait** (a channel between Lombok and Bali, connecting the Flores Sea with the Indian Ocean). Chief town: Mataram. Pop: 2 536 000 (2004 est). Area: 4730 sq km (1826 sq miles)

Lombroso (Italian lomˈbroːso) n **Cesare** (ˈtʃeːzare). 1836–1909, Italian criminologist: he postulated the existence of a criminal type

Lomond (ˈləʊmənd) n **1** Loch Lomond a lake in W Scotland, north of Glasgow: the largest Scottish lake; designated a national park in 2002. Length: about 38 km (24 miles). Width: up to 8 km (5 miles) **2** See **Ben Lomond**

Lomu (ˈləʊmuː) n **Jonah.** born 1975, New Zealand Rugby Union football player

London¹ (ˈlʌndən) n **1** the capital of the United Kingdom, a port in S England on the River Thames near its estuary on the North Sea: consists of the **City** (the financial quarter), the **West End** (the entertainment and major shopping centre), the **East End** (the industrial and former dock area), and extensive suburbs. See also **City 2** Greater London the administrative area of London, consisting of the City of London and 32 boroughs (13 Inner London boroughs and 19 Outer London boroughs): formed in 1965 from the City, parts of Surrey, Kent, Essex, and Hertfordshire, and almost all of Middlesex, and abolished for administrative purposes in 1996: a Mayor of London and a new London Assembly took office in 2000. Pop: 7 387 900 (2003 est). Area: 1579 sq km (610 sq miles) **3** a city in SE Canada, in SE Ontario on the Thames River: University of Western Ontario (1878). Pop: 337 318 (2001) > ˈLondoner n

London² (ˈlʌndən) n **Jack,** full name John Griffith London. 1876–1916, US novelist, short-story writer, and adventurer. His works include Call of the Wild (1903), The Sea Wolf (1904), The Iron Heel (1907), and the semiautobiographical John Barleycorn (1913)

Londonderry (ˈlʌndənˌdɛrɪ) n **1** a historical county of NW Northern Ireland, on the Atlantic: in 1973 replaced for administrative purposes by the districts of Coleraine, Derry, Limavady, and Magherafelt. Area: 2108 sq km (814 sq miles) **2** a port in N Northern Ireland, second city of Northern Ireland: given to the City of London in 1613 to be colonized by Londoners; besieged by James II's forces (1688–89). Pop: 83 699 (2001) ▷ See also **Derry**

London pride n a saxifragaceous plant, a hybrid between Saxifraga spathularis and S. umbrosa, having a basal rosette of leaves and pinkish-white flowers

Londrina (Portuguese lonˈdrina) n a city in S Brazil, in Paraná: centre of a coffee-growing area. Pop: 679 000 (2005 est)

lone (ləʊn) adj (prenominal) **1** unaccompanied; solitary **2** single or isolated: a lone house **3** a literary word for **lonely 4** unmarried or widowed [C14: from the mistaken division of ALONE into a lone] > ˈloneness n

lonely (ˈləʊnlɪ) adj -lier, -liest **1** unhappy as a result of being without the companionship of others: alone; a lonely man **2** causing or resulting from the state of being alone: a lonely existence **3** isolated, unfrequented, or desolate **4** without companions; solitary > ˈloneliness n

lonely hearts adj (often capitals) of or for people who

wish to meet a congenial companion or marriage partner: *a lonely hearts advertisement*

loner ('ləʊnə) *n informal* a person or animal who avoids the company of others or prefers to be alone

lonesome ('ləʊnsəm) *adj* **1** *chiefly US & Canadian* another word for **lonely** ▷ *n* **2** on one's lonesome or *US* by one's lonesome *informal* on one's own > **'lonesomely** *adv* > **'lonesomeness** *n*

long¹ (lɒŋ) *adj* **1** having relatively great extent in space on a horizontal plane **2** having relatively great duration in time **3** (*postpositive*) of a specified number of units in extent or duration: *three hours long* **b** (*in combination*): *a two-foot-long line* **4** having or consisting of a relatively large number of items or parts: *a long list* **5** having greater than the average or expected range: *a long memory* **6** being the longer or longest of alternatives: *the long way to the bank* **7** having more than the average or usual quantity, extent, or duration: *a long match* **8** seeming to occupy a greater time than is really so: *she spent a long afternoon waiting in the departure lounge* **9** intense or thorough (esp in the phrase **a long look**) **10** (of drinks) containing a large quantity of nonalcoholic beverage **11** (of a garment) reaching to the wearer's ankles **12** *informal* (foll by *on*) plentifully supplied or endowed (with): *long on good ideas* **13** *phonetics* (of a speech sound, esp a vowel) **a** of relatively considerable duration **b** (in popular usage) denoting the qualities of the five English vowels in such words as *mate, mete, mite, moat, moot*, and *mute* **14** from end to end; lengthwise **15** unlikely to win, happen, succeed, etc: *a long chance* **16** *prosody* **a** denoting a vowel of relatively great duration or (esp in classical verse) followed by more than one consonant **b** denoting a syllable containing such a vowel **c** (in verse that is not quantitative) carrying the emphasis or ictus **17** *finance* having or characterized by large holdings of securities or commodities in anticipation of rising prices: *a long position* **18** *cricket* (of a fielding position) near the boundary: *long leg* **19** *informal* (of people) tall and slender **20** in the long run See **run** (sense 71) **21** long in the tooth *informal* old or ageing ▷ *adv* **22** for a certain time or period: *how long will it last?* **23** for or during an extensive period of time: *long into the next year* **24** at a distant time; quite a bit of time: *long before I met you; long ago* **25** *finance* into a position with more security or commodity holdings than are required by sale contracts and therefore dependent on rising prices for profit: *to go long* **26** as long as or so long as **a** for or during just the length of time that **b** inasmuch as; since **c** provided that; if **27** no longer not any more; formerly but not now ▷ *n* **28** a long time (esp in the phrase **for long**) **29** a relatively long thing, such as a signal in Morse code **30** a clothing size for tall people, esp in trousers **31** *phonetics* a long vowel or syllable **32** *finance* a person with large holdings of a security or commodity in expectation of a rise in its price; bull **33** *music* a note common in medieval music but now obsolete, having the time value of two breves **34** before long soon **35** the long and the short of it the essential points or facts ▷ See also **longs** [Old English *lang*; related to Old High German *lang*, Old Norse *langr*, Latin *longus*]

long² (lɒŋ) *vb* (*intr*; foll by *for* or an infinitive) to have a strong desire [Old English *langian*; related to LONG¹]

long³ (lɒŋ) *vb* (*intr*) *archaic* to belong, appertain, or be appropriate [Old English *langian* to belong, from *gelang* at hand, belonging to; compare ALONG]

Long (lɒŋ) *n* Crawford Williamson. 1815–78, US surgeon. He was the first to use ether as an anaesthetic

long *abbreviation* longitude

long- *adv* (*in combination*) for or lasting a long time: *long-awaited; long-established; long-lasting*

long-acting *adj* (of a drug) slowly effective after initial dosage, but maintaining its effects over a long period of time, being slowly absorbed and persisting in the tissues before being excreted. See **intermediate-acting**, **short-acting**

Long Beach *n* a city in SW California, on San Pedro Bay: resort and naval base; oil-refining. Pop: 475 460 (2003 est)

Longbenton (ˌlɒŋ'bɛntən) *n* a town in N England, in North Tyneside unitary authority, Tyne and Wear. Pop: 34 878 (2001)

longboard ('lɒŋˌbɔːd) *n* **1** a type of surfboard **2** a type of skateboard

longboat ('lɒŋˌbəʊt) *n* **1** the largest boat carried aboard a commercial sailing vessel **2** another term for **longship**

longbow ('lɒŋˌbəʊ) *n* a large powerful hand-drawn bow, esp as used in medieval England

longcase clock ('lɒŋˌkeɪs) *n* another name for **grandfather clock**

longcloth ('lɒŋˌklɒθ) *n* **1** a fine plain-weave cotton cloth made in long strips **2** *US* a light soft muslin

long-dated *adj* (of a gilt-edged security) having more than 15 years to run before redemption. See **medium-dated**, **short-dated**

long-day *adj* (of certain plants) able to mature and flower only if exposed to long periods of daylight (more than 12 hours), each followed by a shorter period of darkness. See **short-day**

long-distance *n* **1** (*modifier*) covering relatively long distances: *a long-distance driver* **2** (*modifier*) (of telephone calls, lines, etc) connecting points a relatively long way apart **3** *chiefly US & Canadian* a long-distance telephone call **4** a long-distance telephone system or its operator ▷ *adv* **5** by a long-distance telephone line: *he phoned long-distance*

long-drawn-out *adj* over-prolonged or extended

Long Eaton ('iːtᵊn) *n* a town in N central England, in SE Derbyshire. Pop: 46 490 (2001)

longeron ('lɒndʒərən) *n* a main longitudinal structural member of an aircraft [c20: from French: side support, ultimately from Latin *longus* LONG¹]

longevity (lɒn'dʒɛvɪtɪ) *n* **1** long life **2** relatively long duration of employment, service, etc [c17: from Late Latin *longaevitās*, from Latin *longaevus* long-lived, from *longus* LONG¹ + *aevum* age] > **longevous** (lɒn'dʒiːvəs) *adj*

long face *n* a disappointed, solemn, or miserable facial expression > **long-'faced** *adj*

Longfellow ('lɒŋˌfɛləʊ) *n* Henry Wadsworth. 1807–82, US poet, noted particularly for his long narrative poems *Evangeline* (1847) and *The Song of Hiawatha* (1855)

Longford ('lɒŋfəd) *n* **1** a county of N Republic of Ireland, in Leinster province. County town: Longford. Pop: 31 068 (2002). Area: 1043 sq km (403 sq miles) **2** a town in N Republic of Ireland, county town of Co Longford. Pop: 7557 (2002)

longhand ('lɒŋˌhænd) *n* ordinary handwriting, in which letters, words, etc, are set down in full, as opposed to shorthand or to typing

long haul *n* **1** a journey over a long distance, esp one involving the transport of goods **2** a lengthy job

long-headed *adj* astute; shrewd; sagacious > **ˌlong-'headedly** *adv* > **ˌlong-'headedness** *n*

longhorn ('lɒŋˌhɔːn) *n* **1** Also called: Texas longhorn a long-horned breed of beef cattle, usually red or variegated, formerly common in SW US **2** a now rare British breed of beef cattle with long curved horns

longing ('lɒŋɪŋ) *n* **1** a prolonged unfulfilled desire or need ▷ *adj* **2** having or showing desire or need: *a longing look* > **'longingly** *adv*

Longinus (lɒn'dʒaɪnəs) *n* Dionysius (ˌdaɪə'nɪsɪəs). ?2nd century AD, supposed author of the famous Greek treatise on literary criticism *On the Sublime* > Longinean (lɒn'dʒɪnɪən) *adj*

longish ('lɒŋɪʃ) *adj* rather long

Long Island *n* an island in SE New York State, separated from the S shore of Connecticut by **Long Island Sound** (an arm of the Atlantic): contains the New York City boroughs of Brooklyn and Queens in the west, many resorts (notably Coney Island), and two large airports (La Guardia and John F. Kennedy). Area: 4462 sq km (1723 sq miles)

longitude ('lɒndʒɪˌtjuːd, 'lɒŋg-) *n* distance in degrees east or west of the prime meridian at 0° measured by the angle between the plane of the prime meridian and that of the meridian through the point in question, or by the corresponding time difference. See **latitude** (sense 1) [c14: from Latin *longitūdō* length, from *longus* LONG¹]

I

longitudinal (ˌlɒndʒɪˈtjuːdɪnºl, ˌlɒŋɡ-) *adj* **1** of or relating to longitude or length **2** placed or extended lengthways. See **transverse** (sense 1) **3** *psychol* (of a study of behaviour) carried on over a protracted period of time > ˌlongiˈtudinally *adv*

longitudinal wave *n* a wave that is propagated in the same direction as the displacement of the transmitting medium. See **transverse wave**

long johns *pl n informal* underpants with long legs

long jump *n* an athletic contest in which competitors try to cover the farthest distance possible with a running jump from a fixed board or mark > **long jumping** *n*

long leg *n cricket* **a** a fielding position on the leg side near the boundary almost directly behind the batsman's wicket **b** a fielder in this position

long list *chiefly Brit* ▷ *n* **1** a list of suitable applicants for a job, post, etc, from which a short list will be selected ▷ *vb* **long-list 2** (*tr*) to put (someone) on a long list

long-lived *adj* having long life, existence, or currency > ˌlong-ˈlivedness *n*

longneck (ˈlɒŋˌnɛk) *n US, Canadian & Austral* **a** a 330-ml beer bottle with a long narrow neck **b** (*as modifier*): *a longneck bottle*

long-off *n cricket* **a** a fielding position on the off side near the boundary almost directly behind the bowler **b** a fielder in this position

long-on *n cricket* **a** a fielding position on the leg side near the boundary almost directly behind the bowler **b** a fielder in this position

long-playing *adj* of or relating to an LP (long-playing record)

long-range *adj* **1** of or extending into the future: *a long-range weather forecast* **2** (of vehicles, aircraft, etc) capable of covering great distances without refuelling **3** (of weapons) made to be fired at a distant target

longs (lɒŋz) *pl n* **1** full-length trousers **2** long-dated gilt-edged securities **3** *finance* unsold securities or commodities held in anticipation of rising prices

longship (ˈlɒŋˌʃɪp) *n* a narrow open vessel with oars and a square sail, used esp by the Vikings during medieval times

longshore (ˈlɒŋˌʃɔː) *adj* situated on, relating to, or along the shore [C19: shortened form of *alongshore*]

longshore drift *n* the process whereby beach material is gradually shifted laterally as a result of waves meeting the shore at an oblique angle

longshoreman (ˈlɒŋˌʃɔːmən) *n, pl* -men *US & Canadian* a man employed in the loading or unloading of ships. Also called (in Britain and certain other countries): **docker**

long shot *n* **1** a competitor, as in a race, considered to be unlikely to win **2** a bet against heavy odds **3** an undertaking, guess, or possibility with little chance of success **4** *films, television* a shot where the camera is or appears to be distant from the object to be photographed **5 by a long shot** by any means: *he still hasn't finished by a long shot*

long-sighted *adj* **1** related to or suffering from hyperopia **2** able to see distant objects in focus **3** having foresight > ˌlong-ˈsightedly *adv* > ˌlong-ˈsightedness *n*

Longs Peak *n* a mountain in N Colorado, in the Front Range of the Rockies: the highest peak in the Rocky Mountain National Park. Height: 4345 m (14 255 ft)

long-standing *adj* existing or in effect for a long time

long-suffering *adj* **1** enduring pain, unhappiness, etc, without complaint ▷ *n* **2** Also: **long-sufferance** long and patient endurance > ˌlong-ˈsufferingly *adv*

long suit *n* **1 a** the longest suit in a hand of cards **b** a holding of four or more cards of a suit **2** *informal* an outstanding advantage, personal quality, or talent

long-term *adj* **1** lasting, staying, or extending over a long time: *long-term prospects* **2** *finance* maturing after a long period of time: *a long-term bond*

long-termism *n* the tendency to focus attention on long-term gains

longtime (ˈlɒŋˌtaɪm) *adj* of long standing

long ton *n* the full name for **ton**[1] (sense 1)

Longueuil (lɒŋˈɡeɪl; *French* lɔ̃ɡœj) *n* a city in SE Canada,

in S Quebec: a suburb of Montreal. Pop: 128 016 (2001)

longueur (*French* lɔ̃ɡœr) *n* a period of boredom or dullness [literally: length]

Longus (ˈlɒŋɡəs) *n* ?3rd century AD, Greek author of the prose romance *Daphnis and Chloe*

long vacation *n* the long period of holiday in the summer during which universities, law courts, etc, are closed

long wave *n* **a** a radio wave with a wavelength greater than 1000 metres **b** (*as modifier*): *a long-wave broadcast*

longways (ˈlɒŋˌweɪz) *adv* another word for **lengthways**

long weekend *n* a weekend holiday extended by a day or days on either side

long-winded *adj* **1** tiresomely long **2** capable of energetic activity without becoming short of breath > ˌlong-ˈwindedly *adv* > ˌlong-ˈwindedness *n*

Longyearbyen (ˈlɒŋjɪəˌbjen) *n* a village on Spitsbergen island, administrative centre of the Svalbard archipelago: coal-mining

lonicera (lɒˈnɪsərə) *n* See **honeysuckle**

Lons-le-Saunier (*French* lɔ̃ləsonje) *n* a town in E France: saline springs; manufactures sparkling wines. Pop: 25 867 (1999)

loo[1] (luː) *n, pl* **loos** *Brit* an informal word for **lavatory** (sense 1) [C20: perhaps from French *lieux d'aisance* water closet]

loo[2] (luː) *n, pl* **loos 1** a gambling card game **2** a stake used in this game [C17: shortened form of *lanterloo*, via Dutch from French *lanterelu*, originally a meaningless word from the refrain of a popular song]

loofah (ˈluːfə) *n* the fibrous interior of the fruit of the dishcloth gourd, which is dried, bleached, and used as a bath sponge or for scrubbing [C19: from New Latin *luffa*, from Arabic *lūf*]

look (lʊk) *vb* (*mainly intr*) **1** (often foll by *at*) to direct the eyes (towards): *to look at the sea* **2** (often foll by *at*) to direct one's attention (towards): *let's look at the circumstances* **3** (often foll by *to*) to turn one's interests or expectations (towards): *to look to the future* **4** (*copula*) to give the impression of being by appearance to the eye or mind; seem: *that looks interesting* **5** to face in a particular direction: *the house looks north* **6** to expect, hope, or plan (to do something): *I look to hear from you soon; he's looking to get rich* **7** (foll by *for*) **a** to search or seek: *I looked for you everywhere* **b** to cherish the expectation (of); hope (for): *I look for success* **8** (foll by *to*) **a** to be mindful (of): *to look to the promise one has made* **b** to have recourse (to): *look to your swords, men!* **9** to be a pointer or sign: *these early inventions looked towards the development of industry* **10** (foll by *into*) to carry out an investigation: *to look into a mystery* **11** (*tr*) to direct a look at (someone) in a specified way: *she looked her rival up and down* **12** (*tr*) to accord in appearance with (something): *to look one's age* **13 look alive** or **look lively** to hurry up; get busy **14 look daggers** See **dagger** (sense 4) **15 look here** an expression used to attract someone's attention, add emphasis to a statement, etc **16 look sharp** or **look smart** (*imperative*) to hurry up; make haste **17 not look at** to refuse to consider: *they won't even look at my offer of £5000* **18 not much to look at** unattractive; plain ▷ *n* **19** the act or an instance of looking: *a look of despair* **20** a view or sight (of something): *let's have a look* **21** (often plural) appearance to the eye or mind; aspect: *the look of innocence; I don't like the looks of this place* **22** style; fashion ▷ *sentence connector* **23** an expression demanding attention or showing annoyance, determination, etc: *look, I've had enough of this* ▷ See also **look after, look back,** etc [Old English *lōcian*; related to Middle Dutch *læken*, Old High German *luogen* to look out] > **looker** *n*

● **USAGE** See at **like**[1]

look after *vb* (*intr, preposition*) **1** to take care of; be responsible for: *she looked after the child while I was out* **2** to follow with the eyes: *he looked after the girl thoughtfully*

lookalike (ˈlʊkəˌlaɪk) *n* **a** a person or thing that is the double of another **b** (*as modifier*): *a lookalike Minister; a lookalike newspaper*

look back *vb* (*intr, adverb*) **1** to cast one's mind to the past **2 to never look back** to become increasingly successful: *after his book was published, he never looked back* **3** *chiefly Brit* to pay another visit later

look down *vb* **1** (*intr, adverb*; foll by *on* or *upon*) to express or show contempt or disdain (for) **2** look down one's nose at *informal* to be contemptuous or disdainful of

look forward to *vb* (*intr, adverb + preposition*) to wait or hope for, esp with pleasure

look-in *informal* **1** a chance to be chosen, participate, etc **2** a short visit ▷ *vb* look in **3** (*intr, adverb*; often foll by *on*) to pay a short visit

looking glass *n* a mirror, esp a ladies' dressing mirror

look on *vb* (*intr*) **1** (*adverb*) to be a spectator at an event or incident **2** Also called: look upon (*preposition*) to consider or regard: *she looked on the whole affair as a joke; he looks on his mother-in-law with disapproval* ▷ ˌlooker-ˈon *n*

lookout ('lʊkˌaʊt) *n* **1** the act of keeping watch against danger, etc **2** a person or persons instructed or employed to keep such a watch, esp on a ship **3** a strategic point from which a watch is kept **4** *informal* worry or concern: *that's his lookout* **5** *chiefly Brit* outlook, chances, or view ▷ *vb* look out (*adverb, mainly intr*) **6** to heed one's behaviour; be careful: *look out for the children's health* **7** to be on the watch: *look out for my mother at the station* **8** (*tr*) to search for and find: *I'll look out some curtains for your new house* **9** (foll by *on* or *over*) to face in a particular direction: *the house looks out over the moor*

look over *vb* **1** (*intr, preposition*) to inspect by making a tour of (a factory, house, etc): *we looked over the country house* **2** (*tr, adverb*) to examine (a document, letter, etc): *please look the papers over quickly* ▷ *n* lookover **3** an inspection, often, specifically, a brief or cursory view

look-see *n informal* a brief inspection or look

look up *vb* (*adverb*) **1** (*tr*) to discover (something required to be known) by resorting to a work of reference, such as a dictionary **2** (*intr*) to increase, as in quality or value: *things are looking up* **3** (*intr*; foll by *to*) to have respect (for): *I've always wanted a girlfriend I could look up to* **4** (*tr*) to visit or make contact with (a person): *I'll look you up when I'm in town*

loom¹ (luːm) *n* **1** an apparatus, worked by hand (**hand loom**) or mechanically (**power loom**), for weaving yarn into a textile **2** the middle portion of an oar, which acts as a fulcrum swivelling in the rowlock [C13 (meaning any kind of tool): variant of Old English *gelōma* tool; compare HEIRLOOM]

loom² (luːm) *vb* (*intr*) **1** to come into view indistinctly with an enlarged and often threatening aspect **2** (of an event) to seem ominously close **3** (often foll by *over*) (of large objects) to dominate or overhang ▷ *n* **4** a rising appearance, as of something far away [C16: perhaps from East Frisian *lomen* to move slowly]

loon¹ (luːn) *n* the US and Canadian name for **diver** (sense 3) [C17: of Scandinavian origin; related to Old Norse *lōmr*]

loon² (luːn) *n* **1** *informal* a simple-minded or stupid person **2** *Northeast Scot dialect* a lad **3** *archaic* a person of low rank or occupation (esp in the phrase **lord and loon**) [C15: origin obscure]

loonie ('luːnɪ) *n Canadian slang* **a** a Canadian dollar coin with a loon bird on one of its faces **b** the Canadian currency

loony, looney or **luny** ('luːnɪ) *slang* ▷ *adj* loonier, looniest or lunier, luniest **1** lunatic; insane **2** foolish or ridiculous ▷ *n, pl* loonies, looneys or lunies **3** a foolish or insane person > 'looniness or 'luniness *n*

loony bin *n slang* a mental hospital or asylum

loop (luːp) *n* **1** the round or oval shape formed by a line, string, etc, that curves around to cross itself **2** any round or oval-shaped thing that is closed or nearly closed **3** a piece of material, such as string, curved round and fastened to form a ring or handle for carrying by **4** an intrauterine contraceptive device in the shape of a loop **5** *electronics* a closed electric or magnetic circuit through which a signal can circulate **6** a flight manoeuvre in which an aircraft flies one complete circle in the vertical plane **7** Also called: loop line *chiefly Brit* a railway branch line which leaves the main line and rejoins it after a short distance **8** *maths, physics* a closed curve on a graph: *hysteresis loop* **9** *anatomy* **a** the most common basic pattern of the human fingerprint, formed by several sharply rising U-shaped ridges. See

arch¹ (sense 4b) **b** a bend in a tubular structure, such as the U-shaped curve in a kidney tubule (**Henle's loop** or **loop of Henle**) **10** *computing* a series of instructions in a program, performed repeatedly until some specified condition is satisfied **11** *skating* a jump in which the skater takes off from a back outside edge, makes one, two, or three turns in the air, and lands on the same back outside edge **12** a group of people to whom information is circulated (esp in the phrases **in** or **out of the loop**) ▷ *vb* **13** (*tr*) to make a loop in or of (a line, string, etc) **14** (*tr*) to fasten or encircle with a loop or something like a loop **15** Also called: loop the loop to cause (an aircraft) to perform a loop or (of an aircraft) to perform a loop **16** (*intr*) to move in loops or in a path like a loop [C14: *loupe*, origin unknown] > 'looper *n*

loophole ('luːpˌhəʊl) *n* **1** an ambiguity, omission, etc, as in a law, by which one can avoid a penalty or responsibility **2** a small gap or hole in a wall, esp one in a fortified wall ▷ *vb* **3** (*tr*) to provide with loopholes

loopy ('luːpɪ) *adj* loopier, loopiest **1** full of loops; curly or twisted **2** *informal* slightly mad, crazy, or stupid

Loos (German luːs) *n* **Adolf** ('adolf). 1870–1933, Austrian architect: a pioneer of modern architecture, noted for his plain austere style in such buildings as Steiner House, Vienna (1910)

loose (luːs) *adj* **1** free or released from confinement or restraint **2** not close, compact, or tight in structure or arrangement **3** not fitted or fitting closely: *loose clothing is cooler* **4** not bundled, packaged, fastened, or put in a container: *loose nails* **5** inexact; imprecise: *a loose translation* **6** (of funds, cash, etc) not allocated or locked away; readily available **7 a** (esp of women) promiscuous or easy **b** (of attitudes, ways of life, etc) immoral or dissolute **8** lacking a sense of responsibility or propriety: *loose talk* **9 a** (of the bowels) emptying easily, esp excessively; lax **b** (of a cough) accompanied by phlegm, mucus, etc **10** (of a dye or dyed article) fading as a result of washing; not fast **11** *informal, chiefly US & Canadian* very relaxed; easy ▷ *n* **12** the loose *rugby* the part of play when the forwards close round the ball in a ruck or loose scrum. See **scrum** **13** on the loose **a** free from confinement or restraint **b** *informal* on a spree ▷ *adv* **14 a** in a loose manner; loosely **b** (*in combination*): *loose-fitting* **15** hang loose *informal, chiefly US* to behave in a relaxed, easy fashion ▷ *vb* **16** (*tr*) to set free or release, as from confinement, restraint, or obligation **17** (*tr*) to unfasten or untie **18** to make or become less strict, tight, firmly attached, compact, etc **19** (when *intr*, often foll by *off*) to let fly (a bullet, arrow, or other missile) [C13 (in the sense: not bound): from Old Norse *lauss* free; related to Old English *lēas* free from, -LESS] > 'loosely *adv* > 'looseness *n*

loosebox ('luːsˌbɒks) *n* an enclosed and covered stall with a door in which an animal can be confined

loose cannon *n* a person or thing that appears to be beyond control and is potentially a source of unintentional damage

loose cover *n* a fitted but easily removable cloth cover for a chair, sofa, etc. US and Canadian name: slipcover

loose end *n* **1** a detail that is left unsettled, unexplained, or incomplete **2** at a loose end without purpose or occupation

loose forward *n rugby* one of a number of forwards who play at the back or sides of the scrum and who are not bound wholly into it

loose head *n rugby* the prop on the hooker's left in the front row of a scrum. See **tight head**

loose-jointed *adj* **1** supple and easy in movement **2** loosely built; with ill-fitting joints > ˌloose-ˈjointedness *n*

loose-leaf *adj* **1** (of a binder, album, etc) capable of being opened to allow removal and addition of pages ▷ *n* **2** a serial publication published in loose leaves and kept in such a binder

loosen ('luːsᵊn) *vb* **1** to make or become less tight, fixed, etc **2** (often foll by *up*) to make or become less firm, compact, or rigid **3** (*tr*) to untie **4** (*tr*) to let loose; set free **5** (often foll by *up*) to make or become less strict, severe, etc **6** (*tr*) to rid or relieve (the bowels) of constipation

[C14: from LOOSE] > **'loosener** n

loosestrife ('luːsˌstraɪf) n **1** any of various primulaceous plants of the genus *Lysimachia*, esp the yellow-flowered *L. vulgaris* (**yellow loosestrife**) **2** purple loosestrife a purple-flowered lythraceous marsh plant, *Lythrum salicaria* **3** any of several similar or related plants, such as the primulaceous plant *Naumburgia thyrsiflora* (**tufted loosestrife**) [C16: LOOSE + STRIFE, an erroneous translation of Latin *lysimachia*, as if from Greek *lusimakhos* ending strife, instead of from the name of the supposed discoverer, *Lusimakhos*]

loot (luːt) n **1** goods stolen during pillaging, as in wartime, during riots, etc **2** goods, money, etc, obtained illegally **3** *informal* money or wealth **4** the act of looting or plundering ▷ vb **5** to pillage (a city, settlement, etc) during war or riots **6** to steal (money or goods), esp during pillaging [C19: from Hindi *lūt*] > **'looter** n

lop¹ (lɒp) vb **lops, lopping, lopped** (tr; usually foll by *off*) **1** to sever (parts) from a tree, body, etc, esp with swift strokes **2** to cut out or eliminate from as excessive ▷ n **3** a part or parts lopped off, as from a tree [C15 *loppe* branches cut off; compare LOB¹] > **'lopper** n

lop² (lɒp) vb **lops, lopping, lopped 1** to hang or allow to hang loosely **2** (intr) to slouch about or move awkwardly **3** (intr) a less common word for **lope** [C16: perhaps related to LOP¹; compare LOB¹]

lop³ (lɒp) n *Northern English dialect* a flea [probably from Old Norse *hloppa* (unattested) flea, from *hlaupa* to LEAP]

lope (ləʊp) vb **1** (intr) (of a person) to move or run with a long swinging stride **2** (intr) (of four-legged animals) to run with a regular bounding movement **3** to cause (a horse) to canter with a long easy stride or (of a horse) to canter in this manner ▷ n **4** a long steady gait or stride [C15: from Old Norse *hlaupa* to LEAP; compare Middle Dutch *lopen* to run] > **'loper** n

lop-eared adj (of animals) having ears that droop

Lope de Vega (*Spanish* 'lope ðe 'βeɣa) n full name *Lope Felíx de Vega Carpio*. 1562–1635, Spanish dramatist, novelist, and poet. He established the classic form of Spanish drama and was a major influence on European, esp French, literature. Some 500 of his 1800 plays are extant

Lopez ('ləʊpɛz) n **Jennifer**. born 1970, Puerto Rican singer and film actress, known as J-Lo; her films include *Out of Sight* (1998) and *The Wedding Planner* (2001) and her records include *On the 6* (1999) and *This is Me...Then* (2002)

lopolith ('lɒpəlɪθ) n a saucer- or lens-shaped body of intrusive igneous rock, formed by the penetration of magma between the beds or layers of existing rock and subsequent subsidence beneath the intrusion. See **laccolith** [C20: from Greek *lopas* dish + -LITH]

lopsided (ˌlɒp'saɪdɪd) adj **1** leaning or inclined to one side **2** greater in weight, height, or size on one side > **ˌlop'sidedly** adv > **ˌlop'sidedness** n

loquacious (lɒ'kweɪʃəs) adj characterized by or showing a tendency to talk a great deal [C17: from Latin *loquāx* from *loquī* to speak] > **lo'quaciously** adv > **loquacity** (lɒ'kwæsɪtɪ) or **lo'quaciousness** n

loquat ('ləʊkwɒt, -kwət) n **1** an ornamental evergreen rosaceous tree, *Eriobotrya japonica*, of China and Japan, having reddish woolly branches, white flowers, and small yellow edible plumlike fruits **2** the fruit of this tree ▷ Also called: **Japan plum** [C19: from Chinese (Cantonese) *lō kwat*, literally: rush orange]

lor (lɔː) interj *not standard* an exclamation of surprise or dismay [from LORD (interj)]

loran ('lɔːrən) n a radio navigation system operating over long distances. Synchronized pulses are transmitted from widely spaced radio stations to aircraft or shipping, the time of arrival of the pulses being used to determine position [C20: *lo(ng-)ra(nge) n(avigation)*]

Lorca¹ (*Spanish* 'lɔrka) n a town in SE Spain, on the Guadalentín River. Pop: 82 511 (2003 est)

Lorca² (*Spanish* 'lɔrka) n **Federico García** (feðe'riko gar'θia). 1898–1936, Spanish poet and dramatist. His poetry, such as *Romancero gitano* (1928), shows his debt to Andalusian folk poetry. His plays include the trilogy *Bodas de sangre* (1933), *Yerma* (1934), and *La Casa de Bernarda Alba* (1936)

lord (lɔːd) n **1** a person who has power or authority over others, such as a monarch or master **2** a male member of the nobility, esp in Britain **3** (in medieval Europe) a feudal superior, esp the master of a manor. See **lady** (sense 5) **4** a husband considered as head of the household (archaic except in the facetious phrase **lord and master**) **5** *astrology* a planet having a dominating influence **6** my lord a respectful form of address used to a judge, bishop, or nobleman ▷ vb **7** (tr) *now rare* to make a lord of (a person) **8** to act in a superior manner towards (esp in the phrase **lord it over**) [Old English *hlāford* bread keeper; see LOAF¹, WARD] > **'lordless** adj > **'lord,like** adj

Lord (lɔːd) n **1** a title given to God or Jesus Christ **2** *Brit* **a** a title given to men of high birth, specifically to an earl, marquess, baron, or viscount **b** a courtesy title given to the younger sons of a duke or marquess **c** the ceremonial title of certain high officials or of a bishop or archbishop: *Lord Mayor; Lord of Appeal; Law Lord; Lord Bishop of Durham* ▷ interj **3** (*sometimes not capital*) an exclamation of dismay, surprise, etc: *Good Lord!; Lord only knows!*

Lord Chancellor n *Brit government* the cabinet minister who is head of the judiciary in England and Wales and Speaker of the House of Lords

Lord Chief Justice n the judge who is second only to the Lord Chancellor in the English legal hierarchy; president of one division of the High Court of Justice

Lord High Chancellor n another name for the **Lord Chancellor**

Lord Howe Island (haʊ) n an island in the Tasman Sea, southeast of Australia: part of New South Wales. Area: 17 sq km (6 sq miles). Pop: 401 (2001)

Lord Lieutenant n **1** (in Britain) the representative of the Crown in a county **2** (formerly) the British viceroy in Ireland

lordly ('lɔːdlɪ) adj **-lier, -liest 1** haughty; arrogant; proud **2** of or befitting a lord ▷ adv **3** *archaic* in the manner of a lord > **'lordliness** n

Lord Mayor n the mayor in the City of London and in certain other important boroughs and large cities

Lord of Misrule n (formerly, in England) a person appointed master of revels at a Christmas celebration

Lord of the Flies n a name for **Beelzebub** [translation of Hebrew: see BEELZEBUB]

lordosis (lɔː'dəʊsɪs) n **1** *pathol* forward curvature of the lumbar spine: congenital or caused by trauma or disease **2** *zoology* concave arching of the back occurring in many female animals during sexual stimulation [C18: New Latin *lordōsis*, from *lordos* bent backwards] > **lordotic** (lɔː'dɒtɪk) adj

Lord President of the Council n (in Britain) the cabinet minister who presides at meetings of the Privy Council

Lord Privy Seal n (in Britain) the senior cabinet minister without official duties

Lord Protector n See **Protector**

Lord Provost n the provost of one of the five major Scottish cities (Edinburgh, Glasgow, Aberdeen, Dundee, and Perth)

Lords (lɔːdz) n the Lords short for **House of Lords**

Lord's (lɔːdz) n a cricket ground in N London; headquarters of the MCC

lords-and-ladies n (*functioning as singular*) another name for **cuckoopint**

Lord's Day n the Lord's Day the Christian Sabbath; Sunday

lordship ('lɔːdʃɪp) n the position or authority of a lord

Lordship ('lɔːdʃɪp) n (preceded by *Your* or *His*) *Brit* a title used to address or refer to a bishop, a judge of the high court, or any peer except a duke

Lord's Prayer n the Lord's Prayer the prayer taught by Jesus Christ to his disciples, as in Matthew 6:9–13, Luke 11:2–4. Also known as: **Our Father, Paternoster** (esp Latin version)

Lords Spiritual pl n the two Anglican archbishops and 24 most senior bishops of England and Wales who sit as members of the House of Lords

Lord's Supper n the Lord's Supper another term for **Holy Communion** [from I Corinthians 11:20]

Lords Temporal *pl n* the Lords Temporal (in Britain) peers other than bishops in their capacity as members of the House of Lords

lore (lɔː) *n* **1** collective knowledge or wisdom on a particular subject, esp of a traditional nature **2** knowledge or learning **3** *archaic* teaching, or something that is taught [Old English *lār*; related to *leornian* to LEARN]

Lorelei ('lɒrəˌlaɪ) *n* (in German legend) a siren, said to dwell on a rock at the edge of the Rhine south of Koblenz, who lures boatmen to destruction [C19: from German *Lurlei* name of the rock; from a poem by Clemens Brentano (1778–1842)]

Loren (*Italian* 'lɔːren) *n* **Sophia** (soˈfia), real name *Sophia Scicolone*. born 1934, Italian film actress. Her films include *Two Women* (1961) for which she won an Oscar, *The Millionairess* (1961), *Man of La Mancha* (1972), *The Cassandra Crossing* (1977), and *Prêt à Porter* (1994)

Lorentz (*Dutch* 'lɔːrənts) *n* **Hendrik Antoon** ('hɛndrɪk 'antoːn). 1853–1928, Dutch physicist: shared the Nobel prize for physics (1902) with Zeeman for their work on electromagnetic theory

Lorenz (*German* 'lɔːrɛnts) *n* **Konrad Zacharias** ('kɔnraːt tsaxaˈriːas) 1903–89, Austrian zoologist, who founded ethology. His works include *On Aggression* (1966): shared the Nobel prize for physiology or medicine 1973

lorgnette (lɔːˈnjɛt) *n* a pair of spectacles or opera glasses mounted on a handle [C19: from French, from *lorgner* to squint, from Old French *lorgne* squinting]

Lorient (*French* lɔrjɛ̃) *n* a port in W France, on the Bay of Biscay. Pop: 59 189 (1999)

lorikeet ('lɒrɪˌkiːt, ˌlɒrɪˈkiːt) *n* any of various small lories, such as *Glossopsitta versicolor* (**varied lorikeet**) or *Trichoglossus moluccanus* (**rainbow lorikeet**) [C18: from LORY + *-keet*, as in PARAKEET]

loris ('lɔːrɪs) *n, pl* -ris any of several omnivorous nocturnal slow-moving prosimian primates of the family Lorisidae, of S and SE Asia, esp *Loris tardigradus* (**slow loris**) and *Nycticebus coucang* (**slender loris**), having vestigial digits and no tails [C18: from French; of uncertain origin]

lorn (lɔːn) *adj poetic* forsaken or wretched [Old English *loren*, past participle of *-lēosan* to lose] > **ˈlornness** *n*

Lorrain (*French* lɔrɛ̃) *n* See **Claude Lorrain**

Lorraine (lɒˈreɪn; *French* lɔrɛn) *n* **1** a region and former province of E France; ceded to Germany in 1871 after the Franco-Prussian war and regained by France in 1919; rich iron-ore deposits. German name: Lothringen **2** Kingdom of Lorraine an early medieval kingdom on the Meuse, Moselle, and Rhine rivers: later a duchy **3** a former duchy in E France, once the S half of this kingdom

Lorris (*French* lɔris) *n* See **Guillaume de Lorris**

lorry ('lɒrɪ) *n, pl* -ries **1** a large motor vehicle designed to carry heavy loads, esp one with a flat platform. US and Canadian name: truck **2** off the back of a lorry *Brit informal* a phrase used humorously to imply that something has been dishonestly acquired: *it fell off the back of a lorry* **3** any of various vehicles with a flat load-carrying surface, esp one designed to run on rails [C19: perhaps related to northern English dialect *lurry* to pull, tug]

lory ('lɔːrɪ), **lowry** *or* **lowrie** ('laʊrɪ) *n, pl* -ries any of various small brightly coloured parrots of Australia and Indonesia, having a brush-tipped tongue with which to feed on nectar and pollen [C17: via Dutch from Malay *lūrī*, variant of *nūrī*]

Los Alamos (lɒs 'æləmɒs) *n* a town in the US, in New Mexico: the first atomic bomb was developed here. Pop: 18 343 (2000 est)

los Angeles (*Spanish* los 'aŋxeles) *n* See **de los Angeles**

Los Angeles (lɒs 'ændʒɪˌliːz) *n* a city in SW California, on the Pacific: the second largest city in the US, having absorbed many adjacent townships; industrial centre and port, with several universities. Pop: 3 819 951 (2003 est). Abbreviation: LA

lose (luːz) *vb* loses, losing, lost (*mainly tr*) **1** to part with or come to be without, as through theft, accident, negligence, etc **2** to fail to keep or maintain: *to lose one's balance* **3** to suffer the loss or deprivation of: *to lose a*

parent **4** to cease to have or possess **5** to fail to get or make use of: *to lose a chance* **6** (*also intr*) to fail to gain or win (a contest, game, etc): *to lose the match* **7** to fail to see, hear, perceive, or understand: *I lost the gist of his speech* **8** to waste: *to lose money gambling* **9** to wander from so as to be unable to find: *to lose one's way* **10** to cause the loss of: *his delay lost him the battle* **11** to allow to go astray or out of sight: *we lost him in the crowd* **12** (*usually passive*) to absorb or engross: *he was lost in contemplation* **13** (*usually passive*) to cause the death or destruction of: *two men were lost in the attack* **14** to outdistance or elude: *he soon lost his pursuers* **15** (*intr*) to decrease or depreciate in value or effectiveness: *poetry always loses in translation* **16** (*also intr*) (of a timepiece) to run slow (by a specified amount): *the clock loses ten minutes every day* **17** (of a physician) to fail to sustain the life of (a patient) **18** (of a woman) to fail to give birth to (a viable baby), esp as the result of a miscarriage **19** *motor racing slang* to lose control of (the car), as on a bend: *he lost it going into Woodcote* **20** lose it *slang* to lose control of oneself or one's temper [Old English *losian* to perish; related to Old English *-lēosan* as in *forlēosan* to forfeit. Compare LOOSE] > **ˈlosable** *adj* > **ˈlosableness** *n*

lose out *vb informal* **1** (*intr, adverb*) to be defeated or unsuccessful **2** lose out on to fail to secure or make use of: *we lost out on the sale*

loser ('luːzə) *n* **1** a person or thing that loses **2** a person or thing that seems destined to be taken advantage of, fail, etc: *a born loser* **3** *bridge* a card that will not take a trick

Losey ('ləʊsɪ) *n* **Joseph**. 1909–84, US film director, in Britain from 1952. His films include *The Servant* (1963), *The Go-Between* (1971), and *Don Giovanni* (1979)

losing ('luːzɪŋ) *adj* unprofitable; failing: *the business was a losing concern*

losings ('luːzɪŋz) *pl n* losses, esp money lost in gambling

loss (lɒs) *n* **1** the act or an instance of losing **2** the disadvantage or deprivation resulting from losing: *a loss of reputation* **3** the person, thing, or amount lost: *a large loss* **4** (*plural*) military personnel lost by death or capture **5** (*sometimes plural*) the amount by which the costs of a business transaction or operation exceed its revenue **6** a measure of the power lost in an electrical system expressed as the ratio of or difference between the input power and the output power **7** *insurance* **a** an occurrence of something that has been insured against, thus giving rise to a claim by a policyholder **b** the amount of the resulting claim **8** at a loss **a** uncertain what to do; bewildered **b** rendered helpless (for lack of something): *at a loss for words* **c** at less than the cost of buying, producing, or maintaining (something): *the business ran at a loss for several years* [C14: noun probably formed from *lost*, past participle of *losen* to perish, from Old English *lōsian* to be destroyed, from *los* destruction]

loss adjuster *n* *insurance* a person qualified to adjust losses incurred through fire, explosion, accident, theft, natural disaster, etc, to agree the loss and the compensation to be paid

loss leader *n* an article offered below cost in the hope that customers attracted by it will buy other goods

lost (lɒst) *adj* **1** unable to be found or recovered **2** unable to find one's way or ascertain one's whereabouts **3** confused, bewildered, or helpless: *he is lost in discussions of theory* **4** (*sometimes foll by on*) not utilized, noticed, or taken advantage of (by): *rational arguments are lost on her* **5** no longer possessed or existing because of defeat, misfortune, or the passage of time: *a lost art* **6** destroyed physically: *the lost platoon* **7** (foll by to) no longer available or open (to) **8** (foll by to) insensible or impervious (to a sense of shame, justice, etc) **9** (foll by in) engrossed (in): *he was lost in his book* **10** morally fallen: *a lost woman* **11** damned: *a lost soul* **12** get lost (*usually imperative*) *informal* go away and stay away

Lost Generation *n* (*sometimes not capitals*) **1** the large number of talented young men killed in World War I **2** the generation of writers, esp American authors such as Scott Fitzgerald and Hemingway, active after World War I

lot (lɒt) *pron* **1** (*functioning as singular or plural*; preceded by *a*) a great number or quantity: *a lot to do; a lot of people; a lot of trouble* ▷ *n* **2** a collection of objects, items, or people: *a nice lot of youngsters* **3** portion in life; destiny; fortune: *it falls to my lot to be poor* **4** any object, such as a straw or slip of paper, drawn from others at random to make a selection or choice (esp in the phrase **draw** or **cast lots**) **5** the use of lots in making a selection or choice (esp in the phrase **by lot**) **6** an assigned or apportioned share **7** an item or set of items for sale in an auction **8** *chiefly US & Canadian* an area of land: *a parking lot* **9** *US & Canadian* a piece of land with fixed boundaries **10** *chiefly US & Canadian* a film studio and the site on which it is located **11** a bad lot an unpleasant or disreputable person **12** cast in one's lot with *or* throw in one's lot with to join in with voluntarily and share the fortunes of **13** the lot the entire amount or number ▷ *adv* (preceded by *a*) *informal* **14** to a considerable extent, degree, or amount; very much: *to delay a lot* **15** a great deal of the time or often: *to sing madrigals a lot* ▷ *vb* **lots, lotting, lotted** **16** to draw lots for (something) **17** (*tr*) to divide (land, etc) into lots **18** (*tr*) another word for **allot** ▷ See also **lots** [Old English *hlot*; related to Old High German *lug* portion of land, Old Norse *hlutr* lot, share]

Lot¹ (lɒt) *n* **1** a department of S central France, in Midi-Pyrénées region. Capital: Cahors. Pop: 164 413 (2003 est). Area: 5226 sq km (2038 sq miles) **2** a river in S France, rising in the Cévennes and flowing west into the Garonne River. Length: about 483 km (300 miles)

Lot² (lɒt) *n Old Testament* Abraham's nephew: he escaped the destruction of Sodom, but his wife was changed into a pillar of salt for looking back as they fled (Genesis 19)

Lot-et-Garonne (*French* lɔtɛɡarɔn) *n* a department of SW France, in Aquitaine. Capital: Agen. Pop: 309 993 (2003 est). Area: 5385 sq km (2100 sq miles)

loth (ləʊθ) *adj* a variant spelling of **loath**

Lothair I (ləʊˈθɛə) *n* ?795–855 AD, Frankish ruler and Holy Roman Emperor (823–30, 833–34, 840–55); son of Louis I, whom he twice deposed from the throne

Lothair II *n* called *the Saxon*. ?1070–1137, German king (1125–37) and Holy Roman Emperor (1133–37). He was elected German king over the hereditary Hohenstaufen claimant

Lothario (ləʊˈθɑːrɪˌəʊ) *n*, *pl* **-os** (*sometimes not capital*) a rake, libertine, or seducer [c18: after a seducer in Nicholas Rowe's tragedy *The Fair Penitent* (1703)]

Lothian Region (ˈləʊðɪən) *n* a former local government region in SE central Scotland, formed in 1975 from East Lothian, most of Midlothian, and West Lothian; replaced in 1996 by the council areas of East Lothian, Midlothian, West Lothian, and Edinburgh

Lothians (ˈləʊðɪənz) *pl n* the Lothians three historic counties of SE central Scotland (now council areas): East Lothian, West Lothian, and Midlothian

Lothringen (ˈloːtrɪŋən) *n* the German name for **Lorraine**

lotion (ˈləʊʃən) *n* a liquid preparation having a soothing, cleansing, or antiseptic action, applied to the skin, eyes, etc [c14: via Old French from Latin *lōtiō* a washing, from *lōtus* past participle of *lavāre* to wash]

lots (lɒts) *informal* ▷ *pl n* **1** (often foll by *of*) great numbers or quantities: *lots of people; to eat lots* ▷ *adv* **2** a great deal **3** (intensifier): *the journey is lots quicker by train*

lottery (ˈlɒtərɪ) *n*, *pl* **-teries** **1** a method of raising money by selling numbered tickets and giving a proportion of the money raised to holders of numbers drawn at random **2** a similar method of raising money in which players select a small group of numbers out of a larger group printed on a ticket. If a player's selection matches some or all of the numbers drawn at random the player wins a proportion of the prize fund **3** an activity or endeavour the success of which is regarded as a matter of fate or luck [c16: from Old French *loterie*, from Middle Dutch *loterije*. See **LOT**]

lotto (ˈlɒtəʊ) *n* **1** Also called: **housey-housey** a children's game in which numbered discs, counters, etc, are drawn at random and called out, while the players cover the corresponding numbers on cards, the winner being the first to cover all the numbers, a particular row, etc. See **bingo** **2** a lottery [c18: from Italian, from Old French *lot*, from Germanic. See **LOT**]

lotus (ˈləʊtəs) *n* **1** (in Greek mythology) a fruit that induces forgetfulness and a dreamy languor in those who eat it **2** the plant bearing this fruit, thought to be the jujube, the date, or any of various other plants **3** any of several water lilies of tropical Africa and Asia, esp the white lotus (*Nymphaea lotus*), which was regarded as sacred in ancient Egypt **4** a similar plant, *Nelumbo nucifera*, which is the sacred lotus of India, China, and Tibet and also sacred in Egypt: family *Nelumbonaceae* **5** a representation of such a plant, common in Hindu, Buddhist, and ancient Egyptian carving and decorative art **6** any leguminous plant of the genus *Lotus*, of the Old World and North America, having yellow, pink, or white pealike flowers [c16: via Latin from Greek *lōtos*, from Semitic; related to Hebrew *lōt* myrrh]

lotus-eater *n Greek myth* one of a people encountered by Odysseus in North Africa who lived in indolent forgetfulness, drugged by the fruit of the legendary lotus

lotus position *n* a seated cross-legged position used in yoga, meditation, etc

loud (laʊd) *adj* **1** (of sound) relatively great in volume: *a loud shout* **2** making or able to make sounds of relatively great volume: *a loud voice* **3** clamorous, insistent, and emphatic: *loud protests* **4** (of colours, designs, etc) offensive or obtrusive to look at **5** characterized by noisy, vulgar, and offensive behaviour ▷ *adv* **6** in a loud manner **7** out loud audibly, as distinct from silently [Old English *hlud*; related to Old Swedish *hlūd*, German *laut*] > **'loudly** *adv* > **'loudness** *n*

louden (ˈlaʊdən) *vb* to make or become louder

loud-hailer *n* a portable loudspeaker having a built-in amplifier and microphone. Also called (US and Canadian): **bullhorn**

loudmouth (ˈlaʊdˌmaʊθ) *n informal* **1** a person who brags or talks too loudly **2** a person who is gossipy or tactless > **loudmouthed** (ˈlaʊdˌmaʊðd, -ˌmaʊθt) *adj*

loudspeaker (ˌlaʊdˈspiːkə) *n* a device for converting audio-frequency signals into the equivalent sound waves by means of a vibrating conical diaphragm. Sometimes shortened to: **speaker** Also called: **reproducer**

Lou Gehrig's disease (luː ˈgɛrɪɡ) *n* another name for **amyotrophic lateral sclerosis** [c20: named after *Lou Gehrig* (1903–41), US baseball player who suffered from it]

lough (lɒx, lɒk) *n* **1** an Irish word for **lake¹** **2** a long narrow bay or arm of the sea in Ireland ▷ See **loch** [c14: from Irish *loch* lake]

Loughborough (ˈlʌfbərə, -brə) *n* a town in central England, in N Leicestershire: university (1966). Pop: 55 258 (2001)

Louis (ˈluːɪs) *n* **Joe**, real name *Joseph Louis Barrow*, nicknamed *the Brown Bomber*. 1914–81, US boxer; world heavyweight champion (1937–49)

Louis I (ˈluːɪ; *French* lwi) *n* known as *Louis the Pious* or *Louis the Debonair*. 778–840 AD, king of France and Holy Roman Emperor (814–23, 830–33, 834–40): he was twice deposed by his sons

Louis II *n* **1** known as *Louis the German*. ?804–876 AD, king of Germany (843–76); son of Louis I **2** 1845–86, king of Bavaria (1864–86): noted for his extravagant castles and his patronage of Wagner. Declared insane (1886), he drowned himself **3** de Bourbon. See (Prince de) **Condé**

Louis IV *n* known as *Louis the Bavarian*. ?1287–1347, king of Germany (1314–47) and Holy Roman Emperor (1328–47)

Louis V *n* known as *Louis le Fainéant*. ?967–987 AD, last Carolingian king of France (986–87)

Louis VII *n* known as *Louis le Jeune*. c. 1120–80, king of France (1137–80). He engaged in frequent hostilities (1152–74) with Henry II of England

Louis VIII *n* known as *Coeur-de-Lion*. 1187–1226, king of France (1223–26). He was offered the English throne by opponents of King John but his invasion failed (1216)

Louis IX *n* known as *Saint Louis*. 1214–70, king of France (1226–70): led the Sixth Crusade (1248–54) and was held to ransom (1250); died at Tunis while on another crusade

Louis XI *n* 1423–83, king of France (1461–83); involved in a struggle with his vassals, esp the duke of Burgundy, in his attempt to unite France under an absolute monarchy

Louis XII n 1462–1515, king of France (1498–1515), who fought a series of unsuccessful wars in Italy

Louis XIII n 1601–43, king of France (1610–43). His mother (Marie de Médicis) was regent until 1617; after 1624 he was influenced by his chief minister Richelieu

Louis XIV n known as *le roi soleil* (the Sun King). 1638–1715, king of France (1643–1715); son of Louis XIII and Anne of Austria. Effective ruler from 1661, he established an absolute monarchy. His attempt to establish French supremacy in Europe, waging almost continual wars from 1667 to 1714, ultimately failed. But his reign is regarded as a golden age of French literature and art

Louis XV n 1710–74, king of France (1715–74); great-grandson of Louis XIV. He engaged France in a series of wars, esp the disastrous Seven Years' War (1756–63), which undermined the solvency and authority of the crown

Louis XVI n 1754–93, king of France (1774–92); grandson of Louis XV. He married Marie Antoinette in 1770 and they were guillotined during the French Revolution

Louis XVII n 1785–95, titular king of France (1793–95) during the Revolution, after the execution of his father Louis XVI; he died in prison

Louis XVIII n 1755–1824, king of France (1814–24); younger brother of Louis XVI. He became titular king after the death of Louis XVII (1795) and ascended the throne at the Bourbon restoration in 1814. He was forced to flee during the Hundred Days

Louisbourg ('lu:ɪsˌbɔːɡ) n a fortress in Canada, in Nova Scotia on SE Cape Breton Island: founded in 1713 by the French and strongly fortified (1720–40); captured by the British (1758) and demolished; reconstructed as a historic site

louis d'or (ˌluːɪ 'dɔː; *French* lwi dɔr) n, *pl* **louis d'or** (ˌluːɪz 'dɔː; *French* lwi dɔr) **1** a former French gold coin worth 20 francs **2** an old French coin minted in the reign of Louis XIII [C17: from French: golden louis, named after Louis XIII]

Louisiana (luːˌiːzɪ'ænə) n a state of the southern US, on the Gulf of Mexico: originally a French colony; bought by the US in 1803 as part of the Louisiana Purchase; chiefly low-lying. Capital: Baton Rouge. Pop: 4 496 334 (2003 est). Area: 116 368 sq km (44 930 sq miles). Abbreviations: **La** *or* (with zip code) **LA**

Louis Napoleon n the original name of **Napoleon III**

Louis of Nassau n 1538–74, a leader (1568–74) in the revolt of the Netherlands against Spain: died in battle

Louis Philippe (*French* filip) n known as the *Citizen King.* 1773–1850, king of the French (1830–48). His régime became excessively identified with the bourgeoisie and he was forced to abdicate by the revolution of 1848

Louisville ('luːɪˌvɪl) n a port in N Kentucky, on the Ohio River: site of the annual Kentucky Derby; university (1837). Pop: 248 762 (2003 est)

lounge (laʊndʒ) vb **1** (*intr*; often foll by *about* or *around*) to sit, lie, walk, or stand in a relaxed manner **2** to pass (time) lazily or idly ▷ n **3** a a communal room in a hotel, ship, theatre, etc, used for waiting or relaxing in **b** (*as modifier*): *lounge chair* **4** *chiefly Brit* a living room in a private house **5** Also called: **lounge bar, saloon bar** *Brit* a more expensive bar in a pub or hotel **6** *chiefly US & Canadian* an expensive bar, esp in a hotel **7** a sofa or couch, esp one with a headrest and no back **8** the act or an instance of lounging [C16: origin unknown]

lounger ('laʊndʒə) n **1** a comfortable sometimes adjustable couch or extending chair designed for someone to relax on **2** a loose comfortable leisure garment **3** a person who lounges

lounge suit n the customary suit of matching jacket and trousers worn by men for the normal business day

loupe (luːp) n a magnifying glass used by jewellers, horologists, etc [c20: from French (formerly an imperfect precious stone), from Old French, of obscure origin]

lour *or* **lower** (laʊə) vb (*intr*) **1** (esp of the sky, weather, etc) to be overcast, dark, and menacing **2** to scowl or frown ▷ n **3** a menacing scowl or appearance [C13 *louren*

to scowl; compare German *lauern* to lurk] > 'louring *or* 'lowering *adj* > 'louringly *or* 'loweringly *adv*

Lourdes (*French* lurd) n a town in SW France: a leading place of pilgrimage for Roman Catholics after a peasant girl, Bernadette Soubirous, had visions of the Virgin Mary in 1858. Pop: 15 203 (1999)

Lourenço Marques (ləˈrɛnsəʊ ˈmɑːk, ˈmɑːks; *Portuguese* loˈrẽsu ˈmarkɪʃ) n the former name (until 1975) of **Maputo**

lourie *or* **loerie** ('laʊrɪ) n *South African* any of several species of touraco: louries are divided into two groups, the arboreal species having a mainly green plumage and crimson wings and the species which inhabits the more open savanna areas having a plain grey plumage [from Malay *luri*]

louse (laʊs) n, *pl* **lice** (laɪs) **1** any wingless bloodsucking insect of the order *Anoplura*: includes *Pediculus capitis* (**head louse**), *Pediculus corporis* (**body louse**), and the crab louse, all of which infest man. Related adj: **pedicular 2** biting **louse** *or* **bird louse** any wingless insect of the order *Mallophaga*, such as the chicken louse: external parasites of birds and mammals with biting mouthparts **3** any of various similar but unrelated insects, such as the plant louse and book louse **4** (*pl* **louses**) *slang* an unpleasant or mean person ▷ vb (*tr*) **5** to remove lice from **6** (foll by *up*) *slang* to ruin or spoil [Old English *lūs*; related to Old High German, Old Norse *lūs*]

lousewort ('laʊsˌwɜːt) n any of various N temperate scrophulariaceous plants of the genus *Pedicularis*, having spikes of white, yellow, or mauve flowers

lousy ('laʊzɪ) *adj* **lousier, lousiest 1** *slang* very mean or unpleasant: *a lousy thing to do* **2** *slang* inferior or bad: *this is a lousy film* **3** infested with lice **4** (foll by *with*) *slang* **a** provided with an excessive amount (of): *he's lousy with money* **b** full of or teeming with > 'lousily *adv* > 'lousiness n

lout (laʊt) n a crude or oafish person; boor [c16: perhaps from Old English *lūtan* to stoop] > 'loutish *adj*

Louth (laʊθ) n a county of NE Republic of Ireland, in Leinster province on the Irish Sea: the smallest of the counties. County town: Dundalk. Pop: 101 821 (2002). Area: 821 sq km (317 sq miles)

Louvain (*French* luvɛ̃) n a town in central Belgium, in Flemish Brabant province: capital of the duchy of Brabant (11th–15th centuries) and centre of the cloth trade; university (1426). Pop: 89 777 (2004 est). Flemish name: **Leuven**

louvre *or US* **louver** ('luːvə) n **1 a** any of a set of horizontal parallel slats in a door or window, sloping outwards to throw off rain and admit air **b** Also called: **louvre boards** the slats together with the frame supporting them **2** *architect* a lantern or turret that allows smoke to escape [c14: from Old French *lovier*, of obscure origin] > 'louvred *or US* 'louvered *adj*

Louvre (*French* luvrə) n the national museum and art gallery of France, in Paris: formerly a royal palace, begun in 1546; used for its present purpose since 1793

lovable *or* **loveable** ('lʌvəbºl) *adj* attracting or deserving affection > ˌlova'bility, ˌlovea'bility *or* 'lovableness, 'loveableness n > 'lovably *or* 'loveably *adv*

lovage ('lʌvɪdʒ) n **1** a European umbelliferous plant, *Levisticum officinale*, with greenish-white flowers and aromatic fruits, which are used for flavouring food **2** Scotch lovage a similar and related plant, *Ligusticum scoticum*, of N Europe [C14 *loveache*, from Old French *luvesche*, from Late Latin *levisticum*, from Latin *ligusticum*, literally: Ligurian (plant)]

love (lʌv) vb **1** (*tr*) to have a great attachment to and affection for **2** (*tr*) to have passionate desire, longing, and feelings for **3** (*tr*) to like or desire (to do something) very much **4** (*tr*) to make love to **5** (*intr*) to be in love ▷ n **6 a** an intense emotion of affection, warmth, fondness, and regard towards a person or thing **b** (*as modifier*): *love song; love story* **7** a deep feeling of sexual attraction and desire **8** wholehearted liking for or pleasure in something **9** *Christianity* **a** God's benevolent attitude towards man **b** man's attitude of reverent devotion towards God **10** Also called: **my love** a beloved person: used esp as an endearment **11** *Brit informal* a term of address, esp but not necessarily for a person regarded as likable **12** (in tennis, squash, etc) a score of zero **13** fall in love to become in love **14** for love without payment **15** for love or money (used with a negative) in any circumstances: *I wouldn't eat a snail for love or money* **16** for the love of for the sake of **17** in love in a state of strong emotional attachment and usually sexual attraction **18** make love **a** to have sexual intercourse (with) **b** *now archaic* to engage in courtship (with) ▷ Related adj: **amatory** [Old English *lufu*; related to Old High German *luba*; compare also Latin *libēre* (originally *lubēre*) to please]

love affair *n* **1** a romantic or sexual relationship, esp a temporary one, between two people **2** a great enthusiasm or liking for something

love apple *n* an archaic name for **tomato**

lovebird ('lʌvˌbɜːd) *n* **1** any of several small African parrots of the genus *Agapornis*, often kept as cage birds **2** *informal* a lover

lovebite ('lʌvˌbaɪt) *n* a temporary red mark left on a person's skin by a partner's biting or sucking it during lovemaking

love child *n* *euphemistic* an illegitimate child; bastard

loved-up *adj* *slang* experiencing feelings of love, through or as if through taking a drug, esp the drug ecstasy

love-in-a-mist *n* an erect S European ranunculaceous plant, *Nigella damascena*, cultivated as a garden plant, having finely cut leaves and white or pale blue flowers

Lovelace ('lʌvˌleɪs) *n* **1 Countess of**, title of *Ada Augusta King*. 1815–52, English mathematician and personal assistant to Charles Babbage: daughter of Lord Byron. She wrote the first computer program **2 Richard**. 1618–58, English Cavalier poet, noted for *To Althea from Prison* (1642) and *Lucasta* (1649)

loveless ('lʌvlɪs) *adj* **1** without love: *a loveless marriage* **2** receiving or giving no love ▷ 'lovelessly *adv* ▷ 'lovelessness *n*

love-lies-bleeding *n* any of several amaranthaceous plants of the genus *Amaranthus*, esp *A. caudatus*, having drooping spikes of small red flowers

Lovell ('lʌvəl) *n* **Sir Bernard**. born 1913, English radio astronomer; founder (1951) and director of Jodrell Bank

lovelock ('lʌvˌlɒk) *n* a long lock of hair worn on the forehead

lovelorn ('lʌvˌlɔːn) *adj* miserable because of unrequited love or unhappiness in love ▷ 'love,lornness *n*

lovely ('lʌvlɪ) *adj* **-lier, -liest 1** very attractive or beautiful **2** highly pleasing or enjoyable: *a lovely time* **3** loving and attentive **4** inspiring love; lovable ▷ *n*, *pl* **-lies 5** *slang* a lovely woman ▷ 'loveliness *n*

lovemaking ('lʌvˌmeɪkɪŋ) *n* **1** sexual play and activity between lovers, esp including sexual intercourse **2** an archaic word for **courtship**

love potion *n* any drink supposed to arouse sexual love in the one who drinks it

lover ('lʌvə) *n* **1** a person, now esp a man, who has an extramarital or premarital sexual relationship with another person **2** (*often plural*) either of the two people involved in a love affair **3 a** someone who loves a specified person or thing: *a lover of music* **b** (*in combination*): *a music-lover; a cat-lover*

love seat *n* a small upholstered sofa for two people

lovesick ('lʌvˌsɪk) *adj* pining or languishing because of love ▷ 'love,sickness *n*

lovey ('lʌvɪ) *n* *Brit informal* another word for **love** (sense 11)

lovey-dovey *adj* making an excessive or ostentatious display of affection

loving ('lʌvɪŋ) *adj* feeling, showing, or indicating love and affection ▷ 'lovingly *adv* ▷ 'lovingness *n*

loving cup *n* **1** a large vessel, usually two-handled, out of which people drink in turn at a banquet **2** a similar cup awarded to the winner of a competition

low¹ (ləʊ) *adj* **1** having a relatively small distance from base to top; not tall or high: *a low hill; a low building* **2 a** situated at a relatively short distance above the ground, sea level, the horizon, or other reference position: *low cloud* **b** (*in combination*): *low-lying* **3 a** involving or containing a relatively small amount of

something: *a low supply* **b** (*in combination*): *low-pressure* **4 a** having little value or quality **b** (*in combination*): *low-grade* **5** of less than the usual or expected height, depth, or degree: *low temperature* **6 a** (of numbers) small **b** (of measurements) expressed in small numbers **7** unfavourable: *a low opinion* **8** not advanced in evolution: *a low form of plant life* **9** deep: *a low obeisance* **10** coarse or vulgar: *a low conversation* **11 a** inferior in culture or status **b** (*in combination*): *low-class* **12** in a physically or mentally depressed or weakened state **13** designed so as to reveal the wearer's neck and part of the bosom: *a low neckline* **14** with a hushed tone; quiet or soft: *a low whisper* **15** of relatively small price or monetary value: *low cost* **16** *music* relating to or characterized by a relatively low pitch **17** (of latitudes) situated not far north or south of the equator **18** having little or no money **19** abject or servile **20** *phonetics* of, relating to, or denoting a vowel whose articulation is produced by moving the back of the tongue away from the soft palate or the blade away from the hard palate, such as for the *a* in English *father*. See **high** (sense 21) **21** (of a gear) providing a relatively low forward speed for a given engine speed **22** (*usually capital*) of or relating to the Low Church ▷ *adv* **23** in a low position, level, degree, intensity, etc: *to bring someone low* **24** at a low pitch; deep: *to sing low* **25** at a low price; cheaply: *to buy low* **26** lay low **a** to cause to fall by a blow **b** to overcome, defeat or destroy **27** lie low **a** to keep or be concealed or quiet **b** to wait for a favourable opportunity ▷ *n* **28** a low position, level, or degree: *an all-time low* **29** an area of relatively low atmospheric pressure, esp a depression **30** *electronics* the voltage level in a logic circuit corresponding to logical zero [C12 *lāh*, from Old Norse *lāgr*; related to Old Frisian *lēch* low, Dutch *laag*] ▷ 'lowness *n*

low² (ləʊ) *n* **1** Also: **lowing** the sound uttered by cattle; moo ▷ *vb* **2** to make or express by a low or moo [Old English *hlōwan*; related to Dutch *loeien*, Old Saxon *hlōian*]

Low (ləʊ) *n* **Sir David**. 1891–1963, British political cartoonist, born in New Zealand: created Colonel Blimp. See **blimp²**

low-alcohol *adj* (of beer or wine) containing only a small amount of alcohol

lowan ('ləʊən) *n* *Austral* another name for **mallee fowl**

Low Archipelago *n* another name for **Tuamotu Archipelago**

lowborn (ˌləʊˈbɔːn) or **lowbred** (ˌləʊˈbrɛd) *adj* *now rare* of ignoble or common parentage; not royal or noble

lowbrow ('ləʊˌbraʊ) *disparaging* ▷ *n* **1** a person who has uncultivated or nonintellectual tastes ▷ *adj* **2** Also: **lowbrowed** of or characteristic of such a person ▷ 'low,browism *n*

Low Church *n* **1** the school of thought in the Church of England stressing evangelical beliefs and practices. See **Broad Church**, **High Church** ▷ *adj* **Low-Church 2** of or relating to this school

low comedy *n* comedy characterized by slapstick and physical action

low-context *adj* tending to communicate by electronic methods such as e-mail, rather than in person. See **high-context**

Low Countries *pl n* the lowland region of W Europe, on the North Sea: consists of Belgium, Luxembourg, and the Netherlands

low-density lipoprotein *n* a lipoprotein that is the form in which cholesterol is transported in the bloodstream to the cells and tissues of the body. High levels of low-density lipoprotein in the blood are associated with atheroma. Abbreviation: LDL

low-down *informal* ▷ *adj* **1** mean, underhand, or despicable ▷ *n* **lowdown 2** information, esp secret or true information

Löwe (German 'løːvə) *n* See **Loewe¹**

Lowell ('ləʊəl) *n* **1 Amy** (**Lawrence**). 1874–1925, US imagist poet and critic **2 James Russell**. 1819–91, US poet, essayist, and diplomat, noted for his series of poems in Yankee dialect, *Biglow Papers* (1848; 1867) **3 Robert** (**Traill Spence**). 1917–77, US poet. His volumes of verse include *Lord Weary's Castle* (1946), *Life Studies* (1959), *For the Union Dead* (1964), and a book of free translations of European poems, *Imitations* (1961)

lower¹ ('ləʊə) *adj* **1** being below one or more other things: *the lower shelf; the lower animals* **2** reduced in amount or value: *a lower price* **3** *maths* (of a limit or bound) less than or equal to one or more numbers or variables **4** (*sometimes capital*) *geology* denoting the early part or division of a period, system, formation, etc: *Lower Silurian* ▷ *vb* **5** (*tr*) to cause to become low or on a lower level; bring, put, or cause to move down **6** (*tr*) to reduce or bring down in estimation, dignity, value, etc: *to lower oneself* **7** to reduce or be reduced: *to lower one's confidence* **8** (*tr*) to make quieter: *to lower the radio* **9** (*tr*) to reduce the pitch of **10** (*tr*) *phonetics* to modify the articulation of (a vowel) by bringing the tongue further away from the roof of the mouth **11** (*intr*) to diminish or become less [C12 (comparative of LOW¹); C17 (vb)]

lower² ('laʊə) *vb* a variant spelling of **lour**

Lower Austria *n* a state of NE Austria: the largest Austrian province, containing most of the Vienna basin. Capital: Sankt Pölten. Pop: 1 552 848 (2003 est). Area: 19 170 sq km (7476 sq miles). German name: Niederösterreich

Lower California *n* a mountainous peninsula of NW Mexico, between the Pacific and the Gulf of California: administratively divided into the states of Baja California (or Baja California Norte) and Baja California Sur

Lower Canada *n* (from 1791 to 1841) the official name of the S region of the present-day province of Quebec. See **Upper Canada**

lower case *n* **1** a compositor's type case, in which the small letters are kept ▷ *adj* lower-case **2** of or relating to small letters ▷ *vb* lower-case **3** (*tr*) to print with lower-case letters

lower chamber *n* another name for **lower house**

lower class *n* **1** the social stratum having the lowest position in the social hierarchy ▷ *adj* lower-class **2** of or relating to the lower class **3** inferior or vulgar

lowerclassman (ˌləʊə'klɑːsmən) *n*, *pl* -men *US* a freshman or sophomore. Also called: underclassman

lower deck *n* **1** the deck of a ship situated immediately above the hold **2** *informal* the petty officers and seamen of a ship collectively

Lower Egypt *n* one of the two main administrative districts of Egypt: consists of the Nile Delta

lower house *n* one of the two houses of a bicameral legislature: usually the larger and more representative house. Also called: lower chamber

Lower Hutt (hʌt) *n* an industrial town in New Zealand on the S coast of North Island. Pop: 100 300 (2004 est)

Lower Lakes *pl n chiefly Canadian* Lakes Erie and Ontario

lowermost ('ləʊəˌməʊst) *adj* lowest

lower regions *pl n* the lower regions hell

Lower Saxony *n* a state of N Germany, on the North Sea and including the E Frisian Islands: a leading European producer of petroleum. Capital: Hanover. Pop: 7 993 000 (2003 est). Area: 47 408 sq km (18 489 sq miles). German name: Niedersachsen

lower world *n* **1** the earth as opposed to heaven or the spiritual world **2** another name for **hell**

lowest common denominator *n* the smallest integer or polynomial that is exactly divisible by each denominator of a set of fractions. Abbreviation: LCD Also called: least common denominator

lowest common multiple *n* the smallest number or quantity that is exactly divisible by each member of a set of numbers or quantities. Abbreviation: LCM Also called: least common multiple

Lowestoft ('ləʊstɒft) *n* a fishing port and resort in E England, in NE Suffolk on the North Sea. Pop: 68 340 (2001)

low frequency *n* a radio-frequency band or a frequency lying between 300 and 30 kilohertz. Abbreviation: LF

Low German *n* a language of N Germany, spoken esp in rural areas: more closely related to Dutch than to standard High German. Also called: Plattdeutsch Abbreviation: LG See also **German**, **High German**

low-hanging fruit *n* **1** the fruit that grows low on a tree and is therefore easy to reach **2** a course of action that

can be undertaken quickly and easily as part of a wider range of changes or solutions to a problem: *first pick the low-hanging fruit* **3** a suitable company to buy as a straightforward investment opportunity

low-impact *adj* **1** designed to cause minimal damage to the environment: *low-impact eco-tourism* **2** designed to provide exercise without being over-strenuous: *a low-impact workout*

low-key *or* **low-keyed** *adj* **1** having a low intensity or tone **2** restrained, subdued, or understated **3** (of a photograph, painting, etc) having a predominance of dark grey tones or dark colours with few highlights ▷ See **high-key**

lowland ('ləʊlənd) *n* **1** relatively low ground **2** (*often plural*) a low generally flat region ▷ *adj* **3** of or relating to a lowland or lowlands > 'lowlander *n*

Lowland ('ləʊlənd) *adj* of or relating to the Lowlands of Scotland or the dialect of English spoken there

Lowlands ('ləʊləndz) *pl n* the Lowlands a low generally flat region of central Scotland, around the Forth and Clyde valleys, separating the Southern Uplands from the Highlands > 'Lowlander *n*

Low Latin *n* any form or dialect of Latin other than the classical, such as Vulgar or Medieval Latin

low-level language *n* a computer programming language that is closer to machine language than to human language

low-level waste *n* waste material contaminated by traces of radioactivity that can be disposed of in steel drums in concrete-lined trenches but not (since 1983) in the sea. See **high-level waste**, **intermediate-level waste**

lowlife ('ləʊˌlaɪf) *n*, *pl* -lifes *slang* a member or members of the underworld

low-loader *n* a road or rail vehicle for heavy loads with a low platform for ease of access

lowly ('ləʊlɪ) *adj* -lier, -liest **1** humble or low in position, rank, status, etc **2** full of humility; meek **3** simple, unpretentious, or plain ▷ *adv* **4** in a low or lowly manner > 'lowliness *n*

Low Mass *n* a Mass that has a simplified ceremonial form and is spoken rather than sung

low-minded *adj* having a vulgar or crude mind and character > ˌlow-'mindedly *adv* > ˌlow-'mindedness *n*

low-pass filter *n electronics* a filter that transmits all frequencies below a specified value, substantially attenuating frequencies above this value

low-pitched *adj* **1** pitched low in tone **2** (of a roof) having sides with a shallow slope

low-pressure *adj* **1** having, using, or involving a pressure below normal: *a low-pressure gas* **2** relaxed or calm

low profile *n* **1** a position or attitude characterized by a deliberate avoidance of prominence or publicity ▷ *adj* low-profile **2** (of a tyre) wide in relation to its height

low-rise *adj* **1** of or relating to a building having only a few storeys ▷ *n* **2** such a building

lowry *or* **lowrie** ('laʊrɪ) *n* another name for **lory**

Lowry ('laʊrɪ) *n* **1** L(awrence) S(tephen). 1887–1976, English painter, noted for his bleak northern industrial scenes, often containing primitive or stylized figures **2** (Clarence) Malcolm. 1909–57, British novelist and writer, best known for his semiautobiographical novel *Under the Volcano* (1947)

low-spirited *adj* depressed, dejected, or miserable > ˌlow-'spiritedly *adv* > ˌlow-'spiritedness *n*

low tech *n* **1** short for **low technology 2** a style of interior design using items associated with low technology ▷ *adj* low-tech **3** of or using low technology **4** of or in the interior design style ▷ Compare **hi tech**

low technology *n* simple unsophisticated technology, often that used for centuries, that is limited to the production of basic necessities

low-tension *adj* subjected to, carrying, or capable of operating at a low voltage

low tide *n* **1** the tide when it is at its lowest level or the time at which it reaches this **2** a lowest point

lowveld ('ləʊˌfɛlt, -ˌvɛlt) *n* the lowveld another name for **bushveld**

low water *n* **1** another name for **low tide** (sense 1) **2** the state of any stretch of water at its lowest level

low-water mark *n* **1** the level reached by seawater at low tide or by other stretches of water at their lowest level **2** the lowest point or level; nadir

lox[1] (lɒks) *n* a kind of smoked salmon [c19: from Yiddish *laks*, from Middle High German *lahs* salmon]

lox[2] (lɒks) *n* short for liquid oxygen, esp when used as an oxidizer for rocket fuels

loyal ('lɔɪəl) *adj* **1** having or showing continuing allegiance **2** faithful to one's country, government, etc **3** of or expressing loyalty [c16: from Old French *loial, leial*, from Latin *lēgālis* LEGAL] > **'loyally** *adv*

loyalist ('lɔɪəlɪst) *n* a patriotic supporter of his sovereign or government > **'loyalism** *n*

Loyalist ('lɔɪəlɪst) *n* **1** (in Northern Ireland) any of the Protestants wishing to retain Ulster's link with Britain **2** (in North America) an American colonist who supported Britain during the War of American Independence **3** (in Canada) short for **United Empire Loyalist**

loyalty ('lɔɪəltɪ) *n, pl* **-ties** **1** the state or quality of being loyal **2** (*often plural*) a feeling of allegiance

loyalty card *n* a swipe card issued by a supermarket or chain store to a customer, used to record credit points awarded for money spent in the store

Loyang ('ləʊ'jæŋ) *n* a variant transliteration of the Chinese name for **Luoyang**

Loyola (lɔɪ'əʊlə) *n* See **Ignatius Loyola**

lozenge ('lɒzɪndʒ) *n* **1** Also called: **pastille, troche** *med* a medicated tablet held in the mouth until it has dissolved **2** *geometry* another name for **rhombus** **3** *heraldry* a diamond-shaped charge [c14: from Old French *losange*, of Gaulish origin; compare Vulgar Latin *lausa* flat stone] > **'lozenged** *adj*

Lozère (French lɔzɛr) *n* a department of S central France, in Languedoc-Roussillon region. Capital: Mende. Pop: 74 234 (2003 est). Area: 5180 sq km (2020 sq miles)

LP[1] *n* **1 a** a long-playing gramophone record: usually one 12 inches (30 cm) or 10 inches (25 cm) in diameter, designed to rotate at 33⅓ revolutions per minute **b** (*as modifier*): *an LP sleeve* **2** long play: a slow-recording facility on a VCR which allows twice the length of material to be recorded on a tape from that of standard play

LP[2] *abbreviation* **1** (in Britain) Lord Provost **2** Also called: **lp** low pressure

L/P *abbreviation printing* letterpress

LPG *abbreviation* liquefied petroleum gas

L-plate *n Brit* a white rectangle with an "L" sign fixed to the back and front of a motor vehicle; a red "L" sign is used to show that a driver using it is a learner who has not passed the driving test; a green "L" sign may be displayed by new drivers for up to a year after passing the driving test

Lr *the chemical symbol for* lawrencium

LSD *n* lysergic acid diethylamide; a crystalline compound prepared from lysergic acid, used in experimental medicine and taken illegally as a hallucinogenic drug. Informal name (as an illegal hallucinogen): acid

L.S.D., £.s.d. *or* **l.s.d.** *abbreviation* (in Britain, esp formerly) librae, solidi, denarii [Latin: pounds, shillings, pence]

LSE *abbreviation* London School of Economics

LSO *abbreviation* London Symphony Orchestra

Lt *abbreviation* Lieutenant

Ltd *or* **ltd** *abbreviation* (esp after the names of British business organizations) limited (liability)

LTNS *abbreviation text messaging* long time no see

LTSA *abbreviation* (in New Zealand) Land Transport Safety Authority

Lu *the chemical symbol for* lutetium

Lualaba (ˌluːə'lɑːbə) *n* a river in the SE Democratic Republic of Congo (formerly Zaïre), rising in Katanga province and flowing north as the W headstream of the River Congo. Length: about 1800 km (1100 miles)

Luanda *or* **Loanda** (lʊ'ændə) *n* the capital of Angola, a port in the west, on the Atlantic: founded in 1576, it became a centre of the slave trade to Brazil in the 17th and 18th centuries; oil refining. Pop: 2 839 000 (2005 est)

Luang Prabang (luː'æŋ prɑː'bæŋ) *n* a market town in N Laos, on the Mekong River: residence of the monarch of Laos (1946–75). Pop: 26 400 (2003 est)

luau (luː'aʊ, 'luːaʊ) *n* a feast of Hawaiian food [from Hawaiian *lū'au*]

lubber ('lʌbə) *n* **1** a big, awkward, or stupid person **2** short for **landlubber** [C14 *lobre*, probably from Scandinavian. See LOB[1]] > **'lubberly** *adj, adv* > **'lubberliness** *n*

lubber line *n* a mark on a ship's compass that designates the fore-and-aft axis of the vessel. Also called: **lubber's line**

Lubbock ('lʌbək) *n* a city in NW Texas: cotton market. Pop: 206 481 (2003 est)

Lübeck (German 'lyːbɛk) *n* a port in N Germany, in Schleswig-Holstein on the Baltic: the leading member of the Hanseatic League, and a major European commercial centre until the 15th century. Pop: 212 754 (2003 est)

Lubitsch ('luːbɪtʃ) *n* **Ernst**. 1890–1947, US film director, born in Germany; best known for such sophisticated comedies as *Forbidden Paradise* (1924) and *Ninotchka* (1939)

Lublin (Polish 'lublin) *n* an industrial city in E Poland: provisional seat of the government in 1918 and 1944. Pop: 397 000 (2005 est). Russian name: Lyublin

lubra ('luːbrə) *n Austral* an Aboriginal woman [c19: from a native Australian language]

lubricant ('luːbrɪkənt) *n* **1** a lubricating substance, such as oil ▷ *adj* **2** serving to lubricate [c19: from Latin *lūbricāns*, present participle of *lūbricāre*. See LUBRICATE]

lubricate ('luːbrɪˌkeɪt) *vb* **1** (*tr*) to cover or treat with an oily or greasy substance so as to lessen friction **2** (*tr*) to make greasy, slippery, or smooth **3** (*intr*) to act as a lubricant [c17: from Latin *lūbricāre*, from *lūbricus* slippery] > ˌlubri'cation *n* > 'lubriˌcative *adj* > 'lubriˌcator *n*

lubricity (luː'brɪsɪtɪ) *n* **1** formal or literary lewdness or salaciousness **2** *rare* smoothness or slipperiness [C15 (lewdness), C17 (slipperiness): from Old French *lubricité*, from Medieval Latin *lubricitās*, from Latin, from *lūbricus* slippery] > **lubricious** (luː'brɪʃəs) *or* **lubricous** ('luːbrɪkəs) *adj*

Lubumbashi (ˌluːbʊm'bæʃɪ) *n* a city in the S Democratic Republic of Congo (formerly Zaïre): founded in 1910 as a copper-mining centre; university (1955). Pop: 1 102 000 (2005 est)

Lucan ('luːkən) *n* Latin name *Marcus Annaeus Lucanus*. 39–65 AD, Roman poet. His epic poem *Pharsalia* describes the civil war between Caesar and Pompey

Lucania (luː'keɪnɪə) *n* the Latin name for **Basilicata**

Lucas ('luːkəs) *n* **George**. born 1944, US film director, producer, and writer of screenplays. Films include *American Graffiti* (1973) and *Star Wars* (1977) and its prequels *The Phantom Menace* (1999), *Attack of the Clones* (2002), and *Revenge of the Sith* (2005)

Lucas van Leyden ('luːkəs væn 'laɪdᵊn) *n* ?1494–1533, Dutch painter and engraver

Lucca (Italian 'lukka) *n* a city in NW Italy, in Tuscany: centre of a rich agricultural region, noted for the production of olive oil. Pop: 81 862 (2001)

luce (luːs) *n* another name for **pike**[1] [c14: from Old French *lus*, from Late Latin *lūcius* pike]

lucent ('luːsᵊnt) *adj* brilliant, shining, or translucent [c16: from Latin *lūcēns*, present participle of *lūcēre* to shine] > **'lucently** *adv*

lucerne (luː'sɜːn) *n Brit* another name for **alfalfa**

Lucerne (luː'sɜːn; French lysɛrn) *n* **1** a canton in central Switzerland, northwest of Lake Lucerne: joined the Swiss Confederacy in 1332. Pop: 352 300 (2002 est). Area: 1494 sq km (577 sq miles) ▷ German name: **Luzern 2** a city in central Switzerland, capital of Lucerne canton, on Lake Lucerne: tourist centre. Pop: 59 496 (2000) **3** Lake Lucerne a lake in central Switzerland: fed and drained chiefly by the River Reuss. Area: 115 sq km (44 sq miles). German name: **Vierwaldstättersee**

Lucian ('luːsɪən) *n* 2nd century AD, Greek writer, noted esp for his satirical *Dialogues of the Gods* and *Dialogues of the Dead*

lucid ('luːsɪd) *adj* **1** readily understood; clear **2** shining or glowing **3** *psychiatry* of or relating to a period of normality between periods of insane or irresponsible behaviour [c16: from Latin *lūcidus* full of light, from *lūx* light] > lu'cidity, 'lucidness *n* > 'lucidly *adv*

lucifer ('lu:sɪfə) *n* a friction match: originally a trade name for a match manufactured in England in the 19th century

Lucifer ('lu:sɪfə) *n* **1** the leader of the rebellion of the angels: usually identified with Satan **2** the planet Venus when it rises as the morning star [Old English, from Latin *Lūcifer*, light-bearer, from *lūx* light + *ferre* to bear]

Lucilius (lu:'sɪlɪəs) *n* **Gaius** ('gaɪəs). ?180–102 BC, Roman satirist, regarded as the originator of poetical satire

Lucina (lu:'saɪnə) *n* Roman *myth* a title or name given to Juno as goddess of childbirth [c14: from Latin *lūcīnus* bringing to the light, from *lūx* light]

luck (lʌk) *n* **1** events that are beyond control and seem subject to chance; fortune **2** success or good fortune **3** something considered to bring good luck **4** down on one's luck having little or no good luck to the point of suffering hardships **5** no such luck *informal* unfortunately not **6** try one's luck to attempt something that is uncertain [c15: from Middle Dutch *luc*; related to Middle High German *gelücke*, late Old Norse *lukka*, *lykka*]

luckless ('lʌklɪs) *adj* having no luck; unlucky > 'lucklessly *adv* > 'lucklessness *n*

Lucknow ('lʌknaʊ) *n* a city in N India, capital of Uttar Pradesh: capital of Oudh (1775–1856); the British residency was besieged (1857) during the Indian Mutiny. Pop: 2 207 340 (2001)

luck out *vb* (*intr, adverb*) to have good fortune; be lucky: *the US economy lucked out for most of the decade*

lucky ('lʌkɪ) *adj* **luckier, luckiest 1** having or bringing good fortune **2** happening by chance, esp as desired > 'luckily *adv* > 'luckiness *n*

Lucky Country *n Austral slang* a jocular name for **Australia**

lucky dip *n Brit* **1** a barrel or box filled with sawdust and small prizes for which children search **2** *informal* an undertaking of uncertain outcome

lucrative ('lu:krətɪv) *adj* producing a profit; profitable; remunerative [c15: from Old French *lucratif*; see LUCRE] > 'lucratively *adv*

lucre ('lu:kə) *n usually facetious* money or wealth (esp in the phrase **filthy lucre**) [c14: from Latin *lūcrum* gain; related to Old English *lēan* reward, German *Lohn* wages]

Lucretia (lu:'kri:ʃɪə) *n* (in Roman legend) a Roman woman who killed herself after being raped by a son of Tarquin the Proud

Lucretius (lu:'kri:ʃɪəs) *n* full name *Titus Lucretius Carus*. ?96–55 BC, Roman poet and philosopher. In his didactic poem *De rerum natura*, he expounds Epicurus' atomist theory of the universe > Lu'cretian *adj*

lucubrate ('lu:kjʊ,breɪt) *vb* (*intr*) to write or study, esp at night [c17: from Latin *lūcubrāre* to work by lamplight] > 'lucu,brator *n*

lucubration (,lu:kjʊ'breɪʃən) *n* **1** laborious study, esp at night **2** (*often plural*) a solemn literary work

Lucullus (lu:'kʌləs) *n* **Lucius Licinius** ('lu:sɪəs lɪ'sɪnɪəs). ?110–56 BC, Roman general and consul, famous for his luxurious banquets. He fought Mithradates VI (74–66) > Lu'cullan, **Lucullean** (,lu:kʌ'li:ən) *or* ,Lucul'lian *adj*

Lucy ('lu:sɪ) *n* **Saint.** died ?303 AD, a virgin martyred by Diocletian in Syracuse. Feast day: Dec 13

lud (lʌd) *n Brit* lord (in the phrase **my lud, m'lud**): used when addressing a judge in court

Lüda ('lu:'dɑ:) *or* **Lü-ta** *n* a joint name sometimes used for the two port cities of Lüshun and Dalian in NE China, in Liaoning province at the S end of the Liaodong peninsula

Luddite ('lʌdaɪt) *n* **1** *English history* any of the textile workers opposed to mechanization who rioted and organized machine-breaking between 1811 and 1816 **2** any opponent of industrial change or innovation ▷ *adj English history* **3** of or relating to the Luddites [c19: alleged to be named after Ned *Ludd*, an 18th-century Leicestershire workman, who destroyed industrial machinery]

Ludendorff (German 'lu:dəndɔrf) *n* **Erich Friedrich**

Wilhelm von ('e:rɪç 'fri:drɪç 'vɪlhɛlm fɔn). 1865–1937, German general, Hindenburg's aide in World War I

Lüdenscheid (German 'ly:dənʃaɪt) *n* a city in W Germany, in North Rhine-Westphalia: manufacturing centre for aluminium and plastics. Pop: 79 829 (2003 est)

Lüderitz (German 'ly:dərɪts) *n* a port in Namibia: diamond-mining centre. Pop (admin. constituency): 13 276 (2001)

Ludhiana (,lʊdɪ'ɑ:nə) *n* a city in N India, in the central Punjab: Punjab Agricultural University (1962). Pop: 1 395 053 (2001)

ludicrous ('lu:dɪkrəs) *adj* absurd or incongruous to the point of provoking ridicule or laughter [c17: from Latin *lūdicrus* done in sport, from *lūdus* game; related to *lūdere* to play] > 'ludicrously *adv* > 'ludicrousness *n*

Ludlow ('lʌdləʊ) *n* a market town in W central England, in Shropshire: castle (11th–16th century). Pop: 9548 (2001)

ludo ('lu:dəʊ) *n Brit* a simple board game in which players advance counters by throwing dice [c19: from Latin: I play]

Ludwigsburg (German 'lu:tvɪçsbʊrk) *n* a city in SW Germany, in Baden-Württemberg north of Stuttgart: expanded in the 18th century around the palace of the dukes of Württemberg. Pop: 87 581 (2003 est)

Ludwigshafen (German 'lu:tvɪçshɑ:fən) *n* a city in SW Germany, in the Rhineland-Palatinate, on the Rhine: chemical industry. Pop: 162 836 (2003 est)

luff (lʌf) *n* **1** nautical the leading edge of a fore-and-aft sail ▷ *vb* **2** nautical to head (a sailing vessel) into the wind so that her sails flap **3** (*intr*) *nautical* (of a sail) to flap when the wind is blowing equally on both sides **4** to move the jib of (a crane) or raise or lower the boom of (a derrick) in order to shift a load [c13 (in the sense: steering gear): from Old French *lof*, perhaps from Middle Dutch *loef* peg of a tiller; compare Old High German *laffa* palm of hand, oar blade, Russian *lapa* paw]

lug¹ (lʌg) *vb* **lugs, lugging, lugged 1** to carry or drag (something heavy) with great effort **2** (*tr*) to introduce (an irrelevant topic) into a conversation or discussion ▷ *n* **3** the act or an instance of lugging [c14: probably from Scandinavian; apparently related to Norwegian *lugge* to pull by the hair]

lug² (lʌg) *n* **1** a projecting piece by which something is connected, supported, or lifted **2** a box or basket for vegetables or fruit with a capacity of 28 to 40 pounds **3** *Scot & northern English dialect* another word for **ear 4** *slang* a man, esp a stupid or awkward one [c15 (Scots dialect) *lugge* ear, perhaps related to LUG¹ (in the sense: to pull by the ear)]

lug³ (lʌg) *n nautical* short for **lugsail**

Lugano (lʊ'gɑ:nəʊ) *n* a town in S Switzerland, on Lake Lugano: a financial centre and tourist resort. Pop: 26 560 (2000)

Lugansk (Russian lu'gansk) *n* an industrial city in E Ukraine, in the Donbass mining region: established in 1795 as an iron-founding centre. Pop: 454 000 (2005 est). Former name (1935–91): Voroshilovgrad

luge (lu:ʒ) *n* **1** a racing toboggan on which riders lie on their backs, descending feet first ▷ *vb* **2** (*intr*) to ride on a luge [c20: from French]

Luger ('lu:gə) *n trademark* a German 9 mm calibre automatic pistol [c20: named after George *Luger* (1849–1923), German gun designer]

luggage ('lʌgɪdʒ) *n* suitcases, trunks, etc, containing personal belongings for a journey; baggage [c16: perhaps from LUG¹, influenced in form by BAGGAGE]

luggage van *n Brit* a railway carriage used to transport passengers' luggage, bicycles, etc

lugger ('lʌgə) *n nautical* a small working boat rigged with a lugsail [c18: from LUGSAIL]

lughole ('lʌg,həʊl) *n Brit* an informal word for **ear¹**. See also **lug²** (sense 3)

Lugo (Spanish 'luɣo) *n* a city in NW Spain: Roman walls; Romanesque cathedral. Pop: 91 158 (2003 est)

lugsail ('lʌgsəl) *or* **lug** (lʌg) *n nautical* a four-sided sail bent and hoisted on a yard [c17: perhaps from Middle English *lugge* (now dialect) *lugge* pole, or from *lugge* ear]

lug screw *n* a small screw without a head

lugubrious (lʊˈɡuːbrɪəs) *adj* excessively mournful; doleful [c17: from Latin *lūgubris* mournful, from *lūgēre* to grieve] ▷ luˈgubriously *adv* ▷ luˈgubriousness *n*

lugworm (ˈlʌɡˌwɜːm) *n* any polychaete worm of the genus *Arenicola*, living in burrows on sandy shores and having tufted gills: much used as bait by fishermen. Sometimes shortened to: lug [c17: of uncertain origin]

Luhrmann (ˈluəmən) *n* **Baz** (**Mark Anthony**). born 1962, Australian film director and screenwriter; his films include *Strictly Ballroom* (1992), *Romeo and Juliet* (1996), and *Moulin Rouge* (2001)

Luichow Peninsula (ˈluːˈtʃaʊ) *n* a variant transliteration of the Chinese name for **Leizhou Peninsula**

Luik (lœik) *n* the Flemish name for **Liège**

Lukács (ˈluːkætʃ) *n* **Georg** (ˈɡeɪɔːk), original name *György*. 1885–1971, Hungarian Marxist philosopher and literary critic, whose works include *History and Class Consciousness* (1923), *Studies in European Realism* (1946), and *The Historical Novel* (1955)

Luke (luːk) *n New Testament* **1** **Saint Luke** a fellow worker of Paul and a physician (Colossians 4:14). Feast day: Oct 18 **2** the third Gospel, traditionally ascribed to Luke Related adj: **Lucan**

lukewarm (ˌluːkˈwɔːm) *adj* **1** (esp of water) moderately warm; tepid **2** having or expressing little enthusiasm or conviction [c14 *luke* probably from Old English *hlēow* warm; compare German *lauwarm*] ▷ ˌlukeˈwarmly *adv* ▷ ˌlukeˈwarmness *n*

Luleå (*Swedish* ˈluːlɛɔː) *n* a port in N Sweden, on the Gulf of Bothnia: industrial and shipbuilding centre; icebound in winter. Pop: 72 608 (2004 est)

lull (lʌl) *vb* **1** to soothe (a person or animal) by soft sounds or motions (esp in the phrase **lull to sleep**) **2** to calm (someone or someone's fears, suspicions, etc), esp by deception ▷ *n* **3** a short period of calm or diminished activity [c14: possibly imitative of crooning sounds; related to Middle Low German *lollen* to soothe, Middle Dutch *lollen* to talk drowsily, mumble]

lullaby (ˈlʌləˌbaɪ) *n, pl* -bies **1** a quiet song to lull a child to sleep ▷ *vb* -bies, -bying, -bied **2** (*tr*) to quiet or soothe (a child) with or as if with a lullaby [c16: perhaps a blend of LULL + GOODBYE]

Lully *n* (*French* lyli) **Jean Baptiste** (ʒɑ̃ batist), Italian name *Giovanni Battista Lulli*. 1632–87, French composer, born in Italy; founder of French opera. With Philippe Quinault as librettist, he wrote operas such as *Alceste* (1674) and *Armide* (1686); as superintendent of music at the court of Louis XIV, he wrote incidental music to comedies by Molière **2** (ˈlʌlɪ) Also called: **Lull** (*Spanish* lul) **Raymond** or **Ramón** (raˈmɔn). ?1235–1315, Spanish philosopher, mystic, and missionary. His chief works are *Ars generalis sive magna* and the Utopian novel *Blaquerna*

Luluabourg (luːˈluːəˌbʊə) *n* the former name (until 1966) of **Kananga**

lumbago (lʌmˈbeɪɡəʊ) *n* pain in the lower back; backache affecting the lumbar region [c17: from Late Latin *lumbāgo*, from Latin *lumbus* loin]

lumbar (ˈlʌmbə) *adj* of, near, or relating to the part of the body between the lowest ribs and the hipbones [c17: from New Latin *lumbāris*, from Latin *lumbus* loin]

lumbar puncture *n med* insertion of a hollow needle into the lower region of the spinal cord to withdraw cerebrospinal fluid, introduce drugs, etc

lumber[1] (ˈlʌmbə) *n* **1** *chiefly US & Canadian* **a** logs; sawn timber **b** (*as modifier*): *the lumber trade* **2** *Brit* **a** useless household articles that are stored away **b** (*as modifier*): *lumber room* ▷ *vb* **3** (*tr*) to pile together in a disorderly manner **4** (*tr*) to fill up or encumber with useless household articles **5** *chiefly US & Canadian* to convert (the trees) of (a forest) into marketable timber **6** (*tr*) *Brit informal* to burden with something unpleasant, tedious, etc [c17: perhaps from a noun use of LUMBER[2]] ▷ ˈlumberer *n* ▷ ˈlumbering *n*

lumber[2] (ˈlʌmbə) *vb* (*intr*) **1** to move awkwardly **2** an obsolete word for **rumble** [c14 *lomeren*; perhaps related to *lome* LAME[1], Swedish dialect *loma* to move ponderously] ▷ ˈlumbering *adj*

lumberjack (ˈlʌmbəˌdʒæk) *n* (esp in North America) a person whose work involves felling trees, transporting the timber, etc [c19: from LUMBER[1] + JACK[1] (man)]

lumberjacket (ˈlʌmbəˌdʒækɪt) *n* a boldly coloured, usually checked jacket in warm cloth, as worn by lumberjacks

lumberyard (ˈlʌmbəˌjɑːd) *n US & Canadian* an establishment where timber and sometimes other building materials are stored or sold. Also called (in Britain and certain other countries): timberyard

lumen (ˈluːmɪn) *n, pl* -mens *or* -mina (-mɪnə) **1** the derived SI unit of luminous flux; the flux emitted in a solid angle of 1 steradian by a point source having a uniform intensity of 1 candela. Symbol: lm **2** *anatomy* a passage, duct, or cavity in a tubular organ **3** a cavity within a plant cell enclosed by the cell walls [c19: New Latin, from Latin: light, aperture] ▷ ˈlumenal *or* ˈluminal *adj*

Lumière (*French* lymjɛr) *n* **Auguste Marie Louis Nicolas** (ogyst mari lwi nikɔla). 1862–1954, and his brother, **Louis Jean** (lwi ʒɑ̃), 1864–1948, French chemists and cinema pioneers, who invented a cinematograph and a process of colour photography

luminance (ˈluːmɪnəns) *n* **1** a state or quality of radiating or reflecting light **2** a measure (in candelas per square metre) of the brightness of a point on a surface that is radiating or reflecting light. It is the luminous intensity in a given direction of a small element of surface area divided by the orthogonal projection of this area onto a plane at right angles to the direction. Symbol: L [c19: from Latin *lūmen* light]

luminary (ˈluːmɪnərɪ) *n, pl* -naries **1** a person who enlightens or influences others **2** a famous person **3** *literary* something, such as the sun or moon, that gives off light [c15: via Old French, from Latin *lūmināre* lamp, from *lūmen* light]

luminesce (ˌluːmɪˈnɛs) *vb* (*intr*) to exhibit luminescence [back formation from LUMINESCENT]

luminescence (ˌluːmɪˈnɛsəns) *n physics* the emission of light at low temperatures by any process other than incandescence, such as phosphorescence or chemiluminescence [c19: from Latin *lūmen* light] ▷ ˌlumiˈnescent *adj*

luminous (ˈluːmɪnəs) *adj* **1** radiating or reflecting light; shining; glowing: *luminous colours* **2** (*not in technical use*) exhibiting luminescence: *luminous paint* **3** full of light; well-lit **4** (of a physical quantity in photometry) evaluated according to the visual sensation produced in an observer rather than by absolute energy measurements: *luminous flux; luminous intensity* **5** easily understood; lucid; clear **6** enlightening or wise [c15: from Latin *lūminōsus* full of light, from *lūmen* light] ▷ ˈluminously *adv* ▷ ˈluminousness *n* ▷ luminosity (ˌluːmɪˈnɒsɪtɪ) *n*

luminous flux *n* a measure of the rate of flow of luminous energy, evaluated according to its ability to produce a visual sensation. For a monochromatic light it is the radiant flux multiplied by the spectral luminous efficiency of the light. It is measured in lumens

luminous intensity *n* a measure of the amount of light that a point source radiates in a given direction. It is expressed by the luminous flux leaving the source in that direction per unit of solid angle

lumme *or* **lummy** (ˈlʌmɪ) *interj Brit* an exclamation of surprise or dismay [c19: alteration of *Lord love me*]

lummox (ˈlʌməks) *n informal* a clumsy or stupid person [c19: origin unknown]

lump[1] (lʌmp) *n* **1** a small solid mass without definite shape **2** *pathol* any small swelling or tumour **3** a collection of things; aggregate **4** *informal* an awkward, heavy, or stupid person **5** **the lump** *Brit* self-employed workers in the building trade considered collectively, esp with reference to tax and national insurance evasion **6** (*modifier*) in the form of a lump or lumps: *lump sugar* **7** **a lump in one's throat** a tight dry feeling in one's throat, usually caused by great emotion ▷ *vb* **8** (*tr; often foll by together*) to collect into a mass or group **9** (*intr*) to grow into lumps or become lumpy **10** (*tr*) to consider as a single group, often without justification **11** (*tr*) to make or cause lumps in or on **12** (*intr; often foll by along*) to move or proceed in a heavy manner [c13: probably related to early Dutch *lompe* piece, Scandinavian dialect *lump* block, Middle High German *lumpe* rag]

lump² (lʌmp) *vb* (*tr*) *informal* to tolerate or put up with; endure (in the phrase **lump it**) [c16: origin uncertain]

lumpectomy (lʌmˈpɛktəmɪ) *n, pl* -mies the surgical removal of a tumour in a breast [c20: from LUMP¹ + -ECTOMY]

lumpen (ˈlʌmpᵊn) *adj informal* stupid or unthinking [from German *Lump* vagabond, influenced in meaning by *Lumpen* rag, as in LUMPENPROLETARIAT]

lumpenproletariat (ˌlʌmpənˌprəʊlɪˈtɛərɪət) *n* (*esp* in Marxist theory) the amorphous urban social group below the proletariat, consisting of criminals, tramps, etc [German, literally: ragged proletariat]

lumpfish (ˈlʌmpˌfɪʃ) *n, pl* -fish *or* -fishes a North Atlantic scorpaenoid fish, *Cyclopterus lumpus*, having a globular body covered with tubercles, pelvic fins fused into a sucker, and an edible roe: family *Cyclopteridae*. Also called: **lumpsucker** [c16: *lump* (now obsolete) lumpfish, from Middle Dutch *lumpe*, perhaps related to LUMP¹]

lumpish (ˈlʌmpɪʃ) *adj* 1 resembling a lump 2 stupid, clumsy, or heavy ▷ **ˈlumpishly** *adv* ▷ **ˈlumpishness** *n*

lump sum *n* a relatively large sum of money, paid at one time, esp in cash

lumpy (ˈlʌmpɪ) *adj* lumpier, lumpiest 1 full of or having lumps 2 (esp of the sea) rough 3 (of a person) heavy or bulky ▷ **ˈlumpily** *adv* ▷ **ˈlumpiness** *n*

Lumumba (lʊˈmʊmbə) *n* **Patrice** (pəˈtriːs). 1925–61, Congolese statesman; first prime minister of the Democratic Republic of Congo (1960); assassinated

Luna (ˈluːnə) *n* the Roman goddess of the moon [from Latin: moon]

lunacy (ˈluːnəsɪ) *n, pl* -cies 1 (formerly) any severe mental illness 2 foolishness or a foolish act

luna moth *n* a large American saturniid moth, *Tropaea* (or *Actias*) *luna*, having light green wings with a yellow crescent-shaped marking on each forewing [c19: so named from the markings on its wings]

lunar (ˈluːnə) *adj* 1 of or relating to the moon 2 occurring on, used on, or designed to land on the surface of the moon: *lunar module* 3 relating to, caused by, or measured by the position or orbital motion of the moon [c17: from Latin *lūnāris*, from *lūna* the moon]

lunar eclipse *n* See **eclipse** (sense 1)

lunar module *n* the module used to carry two of the three astronauts on an Apollo spacecraft to the surface of the moon and back to the spacecraft

lunar month *n* See **month** (sense 6)

lunar year *n* See **year** (sense 6)

lunate (ˈluːneɪt) *adj anatomy, botany* shaped like a crescent Also: **lunated** [c18: from Latin *lūnātus* crescent-shaped, from *lūnāre*, from *lūna* moon]

lunatic (ˈluːnətɪk) *adj* Also called: (*rarely*) **lunatical** (luːˈnætɪkᵊl) 1 an archaic word for **insane** 2 foolish; eccentric; crazy ▷ *n* 3 a person who is insane [c13 (adj) via Old French from Late Latin *lūnāticus* crazy, moonstruck, from *lūna* moon]

lunatic asylum *n offens* an institution for the mentally ill

lunatic fringe *n* the members of a society or group who adopt or support views regarded as extreme or fanatical

lunch (lʌntʃ) *n* 1 a meal eaten during the middle of the day ▷ *vb* 2 (*intr*) to eat lunch 3 (*tr*) to provide or buy lunch for [c16: probably short form of LUNCHEON] ▷ **ˈluncher** *n*

luncheon (ˈlʌntʃən) *n* a lunch, esp a formal one [c16: probably variant of *nuncheon*, from Middle English *noneschench*, from *none* NOON + *schench* drink]

luncheon meat *n* a ground mixture of meat (often pork) and cereal, usually tinned

luncheon voucher *n* a voucher worth a specified amount issued to employees and redeemable at a restaurant for food. Abbreviation: **LV**

lunchroom (ˈlʌntʃˌruːm, -ˌrʊm) *n US & Canadian* a room where lunch is served or where students, employees, etc, may eat lunches they bring

Lund (lʊnd) *n* a city in SE Sweden, northeast of Malmö: founded in about 1020 by the Danish King Canute; the archbishopric for all Scandinavia in the Middle Ages; university (1668). Pop: 101 427 (2004 est)

Lundy (ˈlʌndɪ) *n* an island in SW England, in Devon, in the Bristol Channel: now a bird sanctuary. Pop: 28 (2007)

Lüneburg (German ˈlyːnəbʊrk) *n* a city in N Germany, in Lower Saxony: capital of the duchy of Brunswick-Lüneburg from 1235 to 1369; prominent Hanse town; saline springs. Pop: 70 614 (2003 est)

lunette (luːˈnɛt) *n* 1 anything that is shaped like a crescent 2 an oval or circular opening to admit light in a dome 3 a semicircular panel containing a window, mural, or sculpture 4 a type of fortification like a detached bastion 5 Also called: **lune** *RC Church* a case fitted with a bracket to hold the consecrated host [c16: from French: crescent, from *lune* moon, from Latin *lūna*]

Lunéville (French lynevil) *n* a city in NE France: scene of the signing of the **Peace of Lunéville** between France and Austria (1801). Pop: 20 200 (1999)

lung (lʌŋ) *n* 1 either one of a pair of spongy saclike respiratory organs within the thorax of higher vertebrates, which oxygenate the blood and remove its carbon dioxide 2 at the top of one's lungs in one's loudest voice; yelling [Old English *lungen*; related to Old High German *lungun* lung. Compare LIGHTS²]

lunge¹ (lʌndʒ) *n* 1 a sudden forward motion 2 *fencing* a thrust made by advancing the front foot and straightening the back leg, extending the sword arm forwards ▷ *vb* 3 to move or cause to move with a lunge 4 (*intr*) *fencing* to make a lunge [c18: shortened form of obsolete C17 *allonge*, from French *allonger* to stretch out (one's arm), from Late Latin *ēlongāre* to lengthen. Compare ELONGATE] ▷ **ˈlunger** *n*

lunge² (lʌndʒ) *n* 1 a rope used in training or exercising a horse ▷ *vb* 2 (*tr*) to exercise or train (a horse) on a lunge [c17: from Old French *longe*, shortened from *allonge*, ultimately from Latin *longus* LONG¹; related to LUNGE¹]

lungfish (ˈlʌŋˌfɪʃ) *n, pl* -fish *or* -fishes any freshwater bony fish of the subclass *Dipnoi*, having an air-breathing lung, fleshy paired fins, and an elongated body. The only living species are those of the genera *Lepidosiren* of South America, *Protopterus* of Africa, and *Neoceratodus* of Australia

Lungki or **Lung-chi** (ˈlʊŋˈkiː) *n* a former name of **Zhangzhou**

lungwort (ˈlʌŋˌwɜːt) *n* any of several Eurasian plants of the boraginaceous genus *Pulmonaria*, esp *P. officinalis*, which has spotted leaves and clusters of blue or purple flowers: formerly used to treat lung diseases

lunula (ˈluːnjʊlə) *n, pl* -nulae (-njʊliː) *or* -nules the white crescent-shaped area at the base of the human fingernail. Nontechnical name: **half-moon** [c16: from Latin: small moon, from *lūna*]

Luoyang or **Loyang** (ˈləʊˈjæŋ) *n* a city in E China, in N Henan province on the Luo River near its confluence with the Yellow River; an important Buddhist centre in the 5th and 6th centuries; a commercial and industrial centre. Pop: 1 594 000 (2005 est)

Lupercalia (ˌluːpɜːˈkeɪlɪə) *n, pl* -lia *or* -lias an ancient Roman festival of fertility, celebrated annually on Feb 15 [Latin, from *Lupercālis* belonging to *Lupercus*, a Roman god of the flocks] ▷ **ˌLuperˈcalian** *adj*

lupin or *US* **lupine** (ˈluːpɪn) *n* any leguminous plant of the genus *Lupinus*, of North America, Europe, and Africa, with large spikes of brightly coloured flowers and flattened pods [c14: from Latin *lupīnus* wolfish (see LUPINE); from the belief that the plant ravenously exhausted the soil]

lupine (ˈluːpaɪn) *adj* of, relating to, or resembling a wolf [c17: from Latin *lupīnus*, from *lupus* wolf]

lupus (ˈluːpəs) *n* any of various ulcerative skin diseases [c16: via Medieval Latin from *lupus*: wolf; said to be so called because it rapidly eats away the affected part]

lupus vulgaris (vʌlˈgeərɪs) *n* tuberculosis of the skin, esp of the face, with the formation of raised translucent nodules. Sometimes shortened to: **lupus**

lurch¹ (lɜːtʃ) *vb* (*intr*) 1 to lean or pitch suddenly to one side 2 to stagger or sway ▷ *n* 3 the act or an instance of lurching [c19: origin unknown]

lurch² (lɜːtʃ) *n* 1 **leave someone in the lurch** to desert someone in trouble 2 *cribbage* the state of a losing player with less than 30 points at the end of a game (esp in the phrase **in the lurch**) [c16: from French *lourche* a game similar to backgammon, apparently from *lourche* (adj) deceived, probably of Germanic origin]

lurch³ (lɜːtʃ) *vb* (*intr*) *archaic or dialect* to prowl or steal about suspiciously [c15: perhaps a variant of LURK]

lurcher (ˈlɜːtʃə) *n* **1** a crossbred hunting dog, usually a greyhound cross with a collie, esp one trained to hunt silently **2** *archaic* a person who prowls or lurks [c16: from LURCH³]

lure (lʊə) *vb* (*tr*) **1** (sometimes foll by *away* or *into*) to tempt or attract by the promise of some type of reward **2** *falconry* to entice (a hawk or falcon) from the air to the falconer by a lure ▷ *n* **3** a person or thing that lures **4** *angling* any of various types of brightly-coloured artificial spinning baits, usually consisting of a plastic or metal body mounted with hooks and trimmed with feathers, etc **5** *falconry* a feathered decoy to which small pieces of meat can be attached and which is equipped with a long thong [c14: from Old French *loirre* falconer's lure, from Germanic; related to Old English *lathian* to invite] ▷ ˈlurer *n*

Lurex (ˈlʊəreks) *n trademark* **1** a thin metallic thread coated with plastic **2** fabric containing such thread, which gives it a glittering appearance

lurgy (ˈlɜːgɪ) *n, pl* **-gies** *facetious* any undetermined illness [c20: origin unknown]

Luria (ˈlʊərɪə) *n* **1 Alexander Romanovich**. 1902–77, Russian psychologist, a pioneer of modern neuropsychology. His most important work concerns the psychological effects of brain tumours **2 Isaac (ben Solomon)**. 1534–72, Jewish mystic living in Egypt and Palestine: noted for his interpretation of the Cabbala

lurid (ˈlʊərɪd) *adj* **1** vivid in shocking detail; sensational **2** horrible in savagery or violence **3** pallid in colour; wan **4** glowing with an unnatural glare [c17: from Latin *lūridus* pale yellow; probably related to *lūtum* a yellow vegetable dye] ▷ ˈluridly *adv* ▷ ˈluridness *n*

Lurie (ˈlʊərɪ) *n* **Alison**. born 1926, US novelist. Her novels include *Imaginary Friends* (1967), *The War Between the Tates* (1974), *Foreign Affairs* (1985), and *The Last Resort* (1998)

lurk (lɜːk) *vb* (*intr*) **1** to move stealthily or be concealed, esp for evil purposes **2** to be present in an unobtrusive way; go unnoticed **3** to read messages posted on an electronic network without contributing messages oneself ▷ *n* **4** *Austral & NZ slang* a scheme or stratagem for success [c13: probably frequentative of LOUR; compare Middle Dutch *loeren* to lie in wait] ▷ ˈlurker *n*

lurking (ˈlɜːkɪŋ) *adj* lingering and persistent, though unsuspected or unacknowledged: *a lurking suspicion*

Lusaka (luːˈzɑːkə, -ˈsɑːkə) *n* the capital of Zambia, in the southeast at an altitude of 1280 m (4200 ft): became capital of Northern Rhodesia in 1932 and of Zambia in 1964; University of Zambia (1966). Pop: 1 450 000 (2005 est)

Lusatia (luːˈseɪʃɪə) *n* a region of central Europe, lying between the upper reaches of the Elbe and Oder Rivers: now mostly in E Germany, extending into SW Poland; inhabited chiefly by Sorbs ▷ Luˈsatian *adj, n*

luscious (ˈlʌʃəs) *adj* **1** extremely pleasurable, esp to the taste or smell **2** very attractive **3** *archaic* cloying [c15 *lucius, licius*, perhaps a shortened form of DELICIOUS] ▷ ˈlusciously *adv* ▷ ˈlusciousness *n*

lush¹ (lʌʃ) *adj* **1** (of vegetation) abounding in lavish growth **2** (esp of fruits) succulent and fleshy **3** luxurious, elaborate, or opulent [c15: probably from Old French *lasche* lax, lazy, from Latin *laxus* loose; perhaps related to Old English *læc*, Old Norse *lakr* weak, German *lasch* loose] ▷ ˈlushly *adv* ▷ ˈlushness *n*

lush² (lʌʃ) *slang* ▷ *n* **1** a heavy drinker, esp an alcoholic **2** alcoholic drink ▷ *vb* **3** *US & Canadian* to drink (alcohol) to excess [c19: origin unknown]

Lüshun (ˈluːˈʃʊn) *n* a port in NE China, in S Liaoning province, at the S end of the Liaodong peninsula; together with the city of Dalian it comprises the port complex of Lüda: jointly held by China and the Soviet Union (1945–55). Former name: Port Arthur

Lusitania (ˌluːsɪˈteɪnɪə) *n* an ancient region of the W Iberian Peninsula: a Roman province from 27 BC to the late 4th century AD: corresponds to most of present-day Portugal and the Spanish provinces of Salamanca and Cáceres

lust (lʌst) *n* **1** a strong desire for sexual gratification **2** a strong desire or drive ▷ *vb* **3** (*intr*; often foll by *after* or *for*) to have a lust (for) [Old English; related to Old High German *lust* desire, Old Norse *losti* sexual desire, Latin *lascīvus* playful, wanton, lustful. Compare LISTLESS] ▷ ˈlustful *adj* ▷ ˈlustfully *adv* ▷ ˈlustfulness *n*

lustral (ˈlʌstrəl) *adj* of or relating to a ceremony of purification [c16: from Latin *lūstrālis* adj from LUSTRUM]

lustrate (ˈlʌstreɪt) *vb* (*tr*) to purify by means of religious rituals or ceremonies [c17: from Latin *lūstrāre* to brighten] ▷ lusˈtration *n*

lustre or US **luster** (ˈlʌstə) *n* **1** reflected light; sheen; gloss **2** radiance or brilliance of light **3** great splendour of accomplishment, beauty, etc **4** a substance used to polish or put a gloss on a surface **5** a vase or chandelier from which hang cut-glass drops **6** a drop-shaped piece of cut glass or crystal used as a decoration on a chandelier, vase, etc **7** a shiny metallic surface on some pottery and porcelain **8** *mineralogy* the way in which light is reflected from the surface of a mineral. It is one of the properties by which minerals are defined ▷ *vb* **9** to make, be, or become lustrous [c16: from Old French, from Old Italian *lustro*, from Latin *lustrāre* to make bright; related to LUSTRUM] ▷ ˈlustreless or US ˈlusterless *adj* ▷ ˈlustrous *adj*

lustreware or US **lusterware** (ˈlʌstəˌwɛə) *n* pottery or porcelain ware with lustre decoration

lustrum (ˈlʌstrəm) or **lustre** *n, pl* **-trums** or **-tra** (-trə) a period of five years [c16: from Latin: ceremony of purification, from *lustrāre* to brighten, purify]

lusty (ˈlʌstɪ) *adj* **lustier, lustiest 1** having or characterized by robust health **2** strong or invigorating: *a lusty brew* ▷ ˈlustily *adv* ▷ ˈlustiness *n*

Lü-ta (ˈluːˈtɑː) *n* a variant transliteration of the Chinese name for **Lüda**

lute¹ (luːt) *n* an ancient plucked stringed instrument, consisting of a long fingerboard with frets and gut strings, and a body shaped like a sliced pear [c14: from Old French *lut*, via Old Provençal from Arabic *al 'ūd*, literally: the wood]

lute² (luːt) *n* **1** Also called: **luting** a mixture of cement and clay used to seal the joints between pipes, etc **2** *dentistry* a thin layer of cement used to fix a crown or inlay in place on a tooth ▷ *vb* **3** (*tr*) to seal (a joint or surface) with lute [c14: via Old French ultimately from Latin *lutum* clay]

lutein (ˈluːtɪɪn) *n* a xanthophyll pigment, occurring in plants, that has a light-absorbing function in photosynthesis [c20: from Latin *lūteus* yellow + -IN]

luteinizing hormone (ˈluːtɪɪˌnaɪzɪŋ) *n* a gonadotrophic hormone secreted by the anterior lobe of the pituitary gland. In female vertebrates it stimulates ovulation, and in mammals it also induces the conversion of the ruptured follicle into the corpus luteum. In male vertebrates it promotes maturation of the interstitial cells of the testes and stimulates androgen secretion [c19: from Latin *lūteum* egg yolk, from *lūteus* yellow]

lutenist (ˈluːtənɪst), **lutanist** or US and Canadian (sometimes) **lutist** (ˈluːtɪst) *n* a person who plays the lute [c17: from Medieval Latin *lūtānista*, from *lūtāna*, apparently from Old French *lut* LUTE¹]

Lutetia or **Lutetia Parisiorum** (luːˈtiːʃə pəˌrɪzɪˈɔːrəm) *n* an ancient name for **Paris³** (sense 1)

lutetium or **lutecium** (lʊˈtiːʃɪəm) *n* a silvery-white metallic element of the lanthanide series, occurring in monazite and used as a catalyst in cracking, alkylation, and polymerization. Symbol: Lu; atomic no: 71; atomic wt: 174.967; valency: 3; relative density: 9.841; melting pt: 1663°C; boiling pt: 3402°C [c19: New Latin, from Latin *Lūtētia* ancient name of Paris, home of G. Urbain (1872–1938), French chemist, who discovered it]

Luther (ˈluːθə) *n* **Martin**. 1483–1546, German leader of the Protestant Reformation. As professor of biblical theology at Wittenberg University from 1511, he began preaching the crucial doctrine of justification by faith rather than by works, and in 1517 he nailed 95 theses to the church door at Wittenberg, attacking Tetzel's sale of indulgences. He was excommunicated and outlawed by the Diet of Worms (1521) as a result of his refusal to recant, but was protected in Wartburg Castle by Frederick III of Saxony (1521–22). He translated the Bible into German (1521–34) and approved Melanchthon's Augsburg Confession (1530), defining the basic tenets of Lutheranism > 'Lutherism *n*

Lutheran ('luːθərən) *n* **1** a follower of Martin Luther (1483–1546), the German leader of the Protestant Reformation, or a member of a Lutheran Church ▷ *adj* **2** of or relating to Luther or his doctrines, the most important being justification by faith alone, consubstantiation, and the authority of the Bible **3** of or denoting any Protestant Church that follows Luther's doctrines > 'Lutheranism *n*

Luthuli *or* **Lutuli** (luːˈtuːlɪ) *n* Chief **Albert John**. 1899–1967, South African political leader. As president of the African National Congress (1952–60), he campaigned for nonviolent resistance to apartheid: Nobel peace prize 1961

Lutine bell ('luːtiːn, luːˈtiːn) *n* a bell, taken from the ship *Lutine*, kept at Lloyd's in London and rung before important announcements, esp the loss of a vessel

Luton ('luːtᵊn) *n* **1** a town in SE central England, in Luton unitary authority, S Bedfordshire: airport; motor-vehicle industries; university (1993). Pop: 185 543 (2001) **2** a unitary authority in SE central England, in Bedfordshire. Pop: 185 200 (2003 est). Area: 43 sq km (17 sq miles)

Lutosławski (*Polish* luto'slavski) *n* **Witold** ('vitɔlt). 1913–94, Polish composer, whose works frequently juxtapose aleatoric and notated writing

Lutyens ('lʌtʃəns) *n* **1** Sir **Edwin**. 1869–1944, British architect, noted for his neoclassical country houses and his planning of New Delhi, India **2** his daughter, **Elisabeth**. 1906–83, British composer

Lützen (*German* 'lytsən) *n* a town near Leipzig in E Germany, in Saxony; site of a battle (1632) in the Thirty Years' War in which the army of the Holy Roman Empire under Wallenstein was defeated by the Swedes under Gustavus Adolphus, who died in the battle

Lützow-Holm Bay ('lʊtsəʊ'həʊm) *n* an inlet of the Indian Ocean on the coast of Antarctica, between Enderby Land and Queen Maud Land

luvvie *or* **luvvy** ('lʌvɪ) *n, pl* -**vies** *facetious* a person who is involved in the acting profession or the theatre, esp one with a tendency to affectation [C20: from LOVEY]

lux¹ (lʌks) *n, pl* **lux** the derived SI unit of illumination equal to a luminous flux of 1 lumen per square metre. 1 lux is equivalent to 0.0929 foot-candle [C19: from Latin: light]

lux² (lʌks) *vb* NZ *informal* to clean with a vacuum cleaner [C20: from *Electrolux*, a vacuum-cleaner manufacturer]

Lux. *abbreviation* Luxembourg

luxate ('lʌkseɪt) *vb* (*tr*) *pathol* to put (a shoulder, knee, etc) out of joint; dislocate [C17: from Latin *luxāre* to displace, from *luxus* dislocated; related to Greek *loxos* oblique] > lux'ation *n*

luxe (lʌks, lʊks; *French* lyks) *n* See **de luxe** [C16: from French from Latin *luxus* extravagance, LUXURY]

Luxembourg ('lʌksəm,bɜːg; *French* lyksɑ̃buːr) *n* **1** a grand duchy in W Europe: it formed the Benelux customs union with the Belgium and the Netherlands in 1948 and was a founder member of the Common Market, now the European Union. Languages: French, German, and Luxemburgish. Religion: Roman Catholic majority. Currency: euro. Capital: Luxembourg. Pop: 459 000 (2004 est). Area: 2586 sq km (999 sq miles) **2** the capital of Luxembourg, on the Alzette River: an industrial centre. Pop: 77 300 (2003 est) **3** a province in SE Belgium, in the Ardennes. Capital: Arlon. Pop: 254 120 (2004 est). Area: 4416 sq km (1705 sq miles)

Luxemburg (*German* 'lʊksəmburk) *n* **Rosa** ('roːza). 1871–1919, German socialist leader, led an unsuccessful Communist revolt (1919) with Karl Liebknecht and was assassinated

Luxor ('lʌksɔː) *n* a town in S Egypt, on the River Nile: the southern part of the site of ancient Thebes; many ruins and tombs, notably the temple built by Amenhotep III

(about 1411–1375 BC). Pop: 183 000 (2005 est)

luxuriant (lʌgˈzjʊərɪənt) *adj* **1** rich and abundant; lush **2** very elaborate or ornate **3** extremely productive or fertile [C16: from Latin *luxuriāns*, present participle of *luxuriāre* to abound to excess] > lux'uriance *n* > lux'uriantly *adv*
◉ USAGE See at **luxurious**

luxuriate (lʌgˈzjʊərɪ,eɪt) *vb* (*intr*) **1** (foll by *in*) to take voluptuous pleasure; revel **2** to flourish extensively or profusely **3** to live in a sumptuous way [C17: from Latin *luxuriāre*] > lux,uri'ation *n*

luxurious (lʌgˈzjʊərɪəs) *adj* **1** characterized by luxury **2** enjoying or devoted to luxury [C14: via Old French from Latin *luxuriōsus* excessive] > lux'uriously *adv* > lux'uriousness *n*
◉ USAGE *Luxurious* is sometimes wrongly used where
◉ *luxuriant* is meant: *he had a luxuriant* (not *luxurious*)
◉ *moustache; the walls were covered with a luxuriant growth of*
◉ *wisteria*

luxury ('lʌkʃərɪ) *n, pl* -**ries 1** indulgence in and enjoyment of rich, comfortable, and sumptuous living **2** (*sometimes plural*) something that is considered an indulgence rather than a necessity **3** something pleasant and satisfying: *the luxury of independence* **4** (*modifier*) relating to, indicating, or supplying luxury [C14 (in the sense: lechery): via Old French from Latin *luxuria* excess, from *luxus* extravagance]

Luzern (luˈtsɛrn) *n* the German name for **Lucerne**

Luzon (luːˈzɒn) *n* the main and largest island of the Philippines, in the N part of the archipelago, separated from the other islands by the Sibuyan Sea: important agriculturally, producing most of the country's rice, with large forests and rich mineral resources; industrial centres at Manila and Batangas. Capital: Quezon City. Pop: 39 500 000 (2000). Area: 108 378 sq km (41 845 sq miles)

LV *abbreviation* luncheon voucher (in Britain)

Lvov (ljvof) *n* an industrial city in W Ukraine: it has belonged to Poland (1340–1772; 1919–39), Austria (1772–1918), Germany (1939–45), and the Soviet Union (1945–91); Ukrainian cultural centre, with a university (1661). Pop: 719 000 (2005 est). Ukranian name: Lviv. Polish name: Lwów. German name: Lemberg

LW *abbreviation* **1** *radio* long wave **2** low water

Lwów (lvuf) *n* the Polish name for **Lvov**

lx *symbol physics* lux

LXX *symbol* Septuagint

-ly¹ *suffix forming adjectives* **1** having the nature or qualities of: *brotherly; godly* **2** occurring at certain intervals; every: *daily; yearly* [Old English -*lic*]

-ly² *suffix forming adverbs* in a certain manner; to a certain degree: *quickly; recently; chiefly* [Old English -*lice*, from -*lic* -LY¹]

Lyallpur (,laɪəl'pʊə) *n* the former name (until 1979) of **Faisalabad**

lyase ('laɪeɪz) *n* any enzyme that catalyses the separation of two parts of a molecule by the formation of a double bond between them [C20: from Greek *lusis* a loosening + -ASE]

Lyautey (*French* ljotɛ) *n* **Louis Hubert Gonzalve** (lwi ybɛr gõzalv). 1854–1934, French marshal and colonial administrator; resident general in Morocco (1912–25)

lycanthropy (laɪˈkænθrəpɪ) *n* **1** the supposed magical transformation of a person into a wolf **2** *psychiatry* a delusion in which a person believes that he is a wolf [C16: from Greek *lukanthropía*, from *lukos* wolf + *anthrōpos* man] > lycanthropic (,laɪkən'θrɒpɪk) *adj* > lycanthrope ('laɪkən,θrəʊp, laɪ'kænθrəʊp) *n*

Lycaon (laɪˈkeɪɒn) *n Greek myth* a king of Arcadia said to have offered Zeus a plate of human flesh to learn whether the god was omniscient

Lycaonia (,laɪkeɪˈəʊnɪə) *n* an ancient region of S Asia Minor, north of the Taurus Mountains; corresponds to present-day S central Turkey

lycée *French* (lise; *English* 'liːseɪ) *n, pl* **lycées** (*French* lise; *English* 'liːseɪz) a secondary school [C19: French, from Latin: LYCEUM]

lyceum (laɪˈsɪəm) *n* (now chiefly in the names of buildings) **1** a public building for concerts, lectures, etc

2 US a cultural organization responsible for presenting concerts, lectures, etc

Lyceum (laɪˈsɪəm) *the* Lyceum *n* **1** a school and sports ground of ancient Athens: site of Aristotle's discussions with his pupils **2** Aristotelian school of philosophy [from Greek *Lukeion*, named after a temple nearby dedicated to *Apollo Lukeios*, an epithet of unknown origin]

lychee (ˌlaɪˈtʃiː) *n* a variant spelling of **litchi**

lych gate *or* **lich gate** (lɪtʃ) *n* a roofed gate to a churchyard, formerly used during funerals as a temporary shelter for the bier [C15: *lich*, from Old English *līc* corpse]

lychnis (ˈlɪknɪs) *n* any caryophyllaceous plant of the genus *Lychnis*, having red, pink, or white five-petalled flowers. See also **ragged robin** [C17: New Latin, via Latin, from Greek *lukhnis* a red flower; related to *lukhnos* lamp]

Lycia (ˈlɪsɪə) *n* an ancient region on the coast of SW Asia Minor: a Persian, Rhodian, and Roman province
> ˈLycian *adj, n*

lycopodium (ˌlaɪkəˈpəʊdɪəm) *n* any club moss of the genus *Lycopodium*, resembling moss but having vascular tissue and spore-bearing cones: family *Lycopodiaceae* [C18: New Latin, from Greek, from *lukos* wolf + *pous* foot]

Lycra (ˈlaɪkrə) *n trademark* a type of synthetic elastic fabric and fibre used for tight-fitting garments, such as swimming costumes

Lycurgus (laɪˈkɜːɡəs) *n* 9th century BC, Spartan lawgiver. He is traditionally regarded as the founder of the Spartan constitution, military institutions, and educational system

Lydda (ˈlɪdə) *n* another name for **Lod**

lyddite (ˈlɪdaɪt) *n* an explosive consisting chiefly of fused picric acid [C19: (sense 1) named after *Lydd*, a town in Kent near which the first tests were made]

Lydgate (ˈlɪdˌɡeɪt) *n* **John**. ?1370–?1450, English poet and monk. His vast output includes devotional works and translations, such as that of a French version of Boccaccio's *The Fall of Princes* (1430–38)

Lydia (ˈlɪdɪə) *n* an ancient region on the coast of W Asia Minor: a powerful kingdom in the century and a half before the Persian conquest (546 BC). Chief town: Sardis
> ˈLydian *adj, n*

lye (laɪ) *n* **1** any solution obtained by leaching, such as the caustic solution obtained by leaching wood ash **2** a concentrated solution of sodium hydroxide or potassium hydroxide [Old English *lēag*; related to Middle Dutch *lōghe*, Old Norse *laug* bath, Latin *lavāre* to wash]

Lyell (ˈlaɪəl) *n* **Sir Charles**. 1797–1875, Scottish geologist. In *Principles of Geology* (1830–33) he advanced the theory of uniformitarianism, refuting the doctrine of catastrophism

lying¹ (ˈlaɪɪŋ) *vb* the present participle and gerund of **lie¹**
lying² (ˈlaɪɪŋ) *vb* the present participle and gerund of **lie²**
lying-in *n, pl* **lyings-in a** a confinement in childbirth **b** (*as modifier*): *a lying-in hospital*

lyke-wake (ˈlaɪkˌweɪk) *n Brit* a watch held over a dead person, often with festivities [C16: perhaps from Old Norse; see LYCH GATE, WAKE¹]

Lyle (laɪl) *n* **Sandy**, full name *Alexander Walter Barr Lyle*. born 1958, Scottish professional golfer: won the British Open Championship (1985) and the US Masters (1988)

Lyly (ˈlɪlɪ) *n* **John**. ?1554–1606, English dramatist and novelist, noted for his two romances, *Euphues, or the Anatomy of Wit* (1578) and *Euphues and his England* (1580), written in an elaborate style. See also **euphuism**

Lyme disease (laɪm) *n* a disease of domestic animals and humans, caused by the spirochaete *Borrelia burgdorferi* and transmitted by ticks, and variously affecting the joints, heart, and brain [C20: named after *Lyme*, Connecticut, the town where it was first identified in humans]

Lyme Regis (laɪm ˈriːdʒɪs) *n* a resort in S England, in Dorset, on the English Channel: noted for finds of prehistoric fossils. Pop: 4406 (2001)

Lymington (ˈlɪmɪŋtən) *n* a market town in S England, in SW Hampshire, on the Solent: yachting centre and holiday resort. Pop: 14 227 (2001)

lymph (lɪmf) *n* the almost colourless fluid, containing chiefly white blood cells, that is collected from the

tissues of the body and transported in the lymphatic system [C17: from Latin *lympha* water, from earlier *limpa* influenced in form by Greek *numphē* nymph]

lymphatic (lɪmˈfætɪk) *adj* **1** of, relating to, or containing lymph **2** of or relating to the lymphatic system **3** sluggish or lacking vigour ▷ *n* **4** a lymphatic vessel [C17 (meaning: mad): from Latin *lymphāticus*. Original meaning perhaps arose from a confusion between *nymph* and LYMPH; compare Greek *numphaleptos* frenzied]

lymphatic system *n* an extensive network of capillary vessels that transports the interstitial fluid of the body as lymph to the venous blood circulation

lymphatic tissue *n* tissue, such as the lymph nodes, tonsils, spleen, and thymus, that produces lymphocytes

lymph gland *n* a former name for **lymph node**

lymph node *n* any of numerous bean-shaped masses of tissue, situated along the course of lymphatic vessels, that help to protect against infection by killing bacteria and neutralizing toxins and are the source of lymphocytes

lympho- *or before a vowel* **lymph-** *combining form* indicating lymph or the lymphatic system

lymphocyte (ˈlɪmfəʊˌsaɪt) *n* a type of white blood cell formed in lymphoid tissue > **lymphocytic** (ˌlɪmfəʊˈsɪtɪk) *adj*

lymphoid (ˈlɪmfɔɪd) *adj* of or resembling lymph, or relating to the lymphatic system

lymphoma (lɪmˈfəʊmə) *n, pl* **-mata** (-mətə) *or* **-mas** any form of cancer of the lymph nodes. Also called: **lymphosarcoma** (ˌlɪmfəʊsɑːˈkəʊmə)

Lynagh (ˈlaɪnə) *n* **Michael**. born 1963, Australian Rugby Union football player; captain of Australia 1987, 1992–95

lynch (lɪntʃ) *vb* (*tr*) (of a mob) to punish (a person) for some supposed offence by hanging without a trial [probably after Charles *Lynch* (1736–96), Virginia justice of the peace, who presided over extralegal trials of Tories during the American War of Independence] > ˈlyncher *n* > ˈlynching *n*

Lynch (lɪntʃ) *n* **1 David**. born 1946, US film director; his work includes the films *Eraserhead* (1977), *Blue Velvet* (1986), *Wild at Heart* (1990), and *Mulholland Drive* (2001) and the television series *Twin Peaks* (1990) **2 John**, known as *Jack Lynch*. 1917–99, Irish statesman; prime minister of the Republic of Ireland (1966–73; 1977–79)

lynchet (ˈlɪntʃɪt) *n* a terrace or ridge formed in prehistoric or medieval times by ploughing a hillside [Old English *hlinc* ridge]

lynch law *n* the practice of condemning and punishing a person by mob action without a proper trial

lynchpin (ˈlɪntʃˌpɪn) *n* a variant spelling of **linchpin**

Lyndsay *or* **Lindsay** (ˈlɪndzɪ) *n* **Sir David**. 1486–1554, Scottish poet and courtier, author of *Ane Pleasant Satyre of the Three Estates* (1552)

Lynn¹ (lɪn) *n* another name for **King's Lynn**. Also called: Lynn Regis (ˈriːdʒɪs)

Lynn² (lɪn) *n* **Dame Vera**, original name *Vera Margaret Lewis*. born 1917, British singer popular during World War II and known as "the forces' sweetheart". Her best-known songs are "We'll Meet Again" and "White Cliffs of Dover"

lynx (lɪŋks) *n, pl* **lynxes** *or* **lynx 1** a feline mammal, *Felis lynx* (*or canadensis*), of Europe and North America, with grey-brown mottled fur, tufted ears, and a short tail **2** the fur of this animal **3 bay lynx** another name for **bobcat 4 desert lynx** another name for **caracal** [C14: via Latin from Greek *lunx*; related to Old English *lox*, German *Luchs*] > ˈlynxˌlike *adj*

lynx-eyed *adj* having keen sight

Lyon (*French* ljɔ̃) *n* a city in SE central France, capital of Rhône department, at the confluence of the Rivers Rhône and Saône: the third largest city in France; a major industrial centre and river port. Pop: 445 452 (1999). English name: Lyons (ˈlaɪənz) Ancient name: lugdunum (lʊɡˈduːnəm)

Lyon King of Arms (ˈlaɪən) *n* the chief herald of Scotland. Also called: Lord Lyon [C14: archaic spelling of LION, referring to the figure on the royal shield]

Lyonnais (*French* ljɔnɛ) *n* a former province of E central France, on the Rivers Rhône and Saône: occupied by the present-day departments of Rhône and Loire. Chief town: Lyon

Lyonnesse (ˌlaɪəˈnɛs) *n* (in Arthurian legend) the mythical birthplace of Sir Tristram, situated in SW England and believed to have been submerged by the sea

Lyons (ˈlaɪənz) *n* **Joseph Aloysius**. 1879–1939, Australian statesman; prime minister of Australia (1931–39)

lyrate (ˈlaɪərɪt) *adj* **1** shaped like a lyre **2** (of leaves) having a large terminal lobe and smaller lateral lobes [c18: from New Latin *lyrātus*, Latin from *lyra* LYRE]

lyre (laɪə) *n* an ancient Greek stringed instrument consisting of a resonating tortoise shell to which a crossbar was attached by two projecting arms. It was plucked with a plectrum and used for accompanying songs [c13: via Old French from Latin *lyra*, from Greek *lura*]

lyrebird (ˈlaɪəˌbɜːd) *n* either of two pheasant-like Australian birds, *Menura superba* and *M. alberti*, constituting the family *Menuridae*: during courtship displays, the male spreads its tail into the shape of a lyre

lyric (ˈlɪrɪk) *adj* **1** (of poetry) **a** expressing the writer's personal feelings and thoughts **b** having the form and manner of a song **2** of or relating to such poetry **3** (of music) having songlike qualities **4** (of a singing voice) having a light quality and tone **5** intended for singing, esp (in classical Greece) to the accompaniment of the lyre ▷ *n* **6** a short poem of songlike quality **7** (*plural*) the words of a popular song ▷ Also (for senses 1–4): **lyrical** [c16: from Latin *lyricus*, from Greek *lurikos*, from *lura* LYRE] > ˈlyrically *adv* > ˈlyricalness *n*

lyrical (ˈlɪrɪkᵊl) *adj* **1** another word for **lyric** (senses 1–4) **2** enthusiastic; effusive (esp in the phrase **to wax lyrical**)

lyricism (ˈlɪrɪˌsɪzəm) *n* **1** the quality or style of lyric poetry **2** emotional or enthusiastic outpouring

lyricist (ˈlɪrɪsɪst) *n* **1** a person who writes the words for a song, opera, or musical play **2** Also called: **lyrist** a lyric poet

Lysander (laɪˈsændə) *n* died 395 BC, Spartan naval commander of the Peloponnesian War

lyse (laɪs, laɪz) *vb* to undergo or cause to undergo lysis

Lysenko (lɪˈsɛŋkəʊ; *Russian* liˈsjɛnkə) *n* **Trofim Denisovich** (traˈfim dɪˈnisəvitʃ). 1898–1976, Russian biologist and geneticist

lysergic acid diethylamide (daɪˌɛθɪlˈeɪmaɪd, -ˌiːθaɪl-) *n* See LSD

Lysias (ˈlɪsɪˌæs) *n* ?450–?380 BC, Athenian orator

Lysimachus (laɪˈsɪməkəs) *n* ?360–281 BC, Macedonian general under Alexander the Great; king of Thrace (323–281); killed in battle by Seleucus I

lysin (ˈlaɪsɪn) *n* any of a group of antibodies or other agents that cause dissolution of cells against which they are directed

Lysippus (laɪˈsɪpəs) *n* 4th century BC, Greek sculptor. He introduced a new naturalism into Greek sculpture

lysis (ˈlaɪsɪs) *n, pl* -ses (-siːz) **1** the destruction or dissolution of cells by the action of a particular lysin **2** *med* the gradual reduction in severity of the symptoms of a disease [c19: New Latin, from Greek, from *luein* to release]

-lysis *n combining form* indicating a loosening, decomposition, or breaking down: *electrolysis; paralysis* [from Greek, from *lusis* a loosening; see LYSIS]

Lysol (ˈlaɪsɒl) *n trademark* a solution containing a mixture of cresols in water, used as an antiseptic and disinfectant

-lyte *n combining form* indicating a substance that can be decomposed or broken down: *electrolyte* [from Greek *lutos* soluble, from *luein* to loose]

Lytham Saint Anne's (ˈlɪðəm sənt ˈænz) *n* a resort in NW England, in Lancashire on the Irish Sea. Pop: 41 327 (2001)

-lytic *adj combining form* indicating a loosening or dissolving: *paralytic* [from Greek, from *lusis*; see -LYSIS]

Lyttelton (ˈlɪtᵊltən) *n* **Humphrey**. born 1921, British jazz trumpeter and band leader who influenced the British revival of New Orleans jazz

Lytton (ˈlɪtᵊn) *n* **1st Baron**, title of *Edward George Earle Lytton Bulwer-Lytton*. 1803–73, British novelist, dramatist, and statesman, noted particularly for his historical romances

Lyublin (ˈljublɪn) *n* transliteration of the Russian name for **Lublin**

Mm

m¹ or **M** (ɛm) *n*, *pl* **m's**, **M's** or **Ms** **1** the 13th letter and tenth consonant of the modern English alphabet **2** a speech sound represented by this letter, usually a bilabial nasal, as in *mat*

m² *symbol for* **1** metre(s) **2** mile(s) **3** milli- **4** minute(s)

M *symbol for* **1** mach **2** medium (size) **3** mega- **4** currency mark(s) **5** million **6** (in Britain) motorway **7** *the Roman numeral for* 1000

m. *abbreviation* **1** *cricket* maiden (over) **2** male **3** mare **4** married **5** masculine

M. *abbreviation* **1** Majesty **2** (in titles) Member **3** million **4** Also: M *pl* MM or MM *French* Monsieur [French equivalent of *Mr*]

m- *prefix* indicating the use of mobile-communications technology: *m-banking*

m- *prefix* short for **meta-** (sense 4)

M'- *prefix* a variant of **Mac-**

ma (mɑː) *n* an informal word for **mother¹**

Ma (mɑː) *n* **Yo-Yo** ('jəʊjəʊ). born 1955, US cellist, born in France to Chinese parents

MA *abbreviation* **1** Massachusetts **2** Master of Arts **3** Military Academy

ma'am (mæm, mɑːm; *unstressed* məm) *n* short for **madam**

> ● USAGE **Ma'am** is used as a title of respect, especially
> ● when addressing female royalty

Maarianhamina ('mɑːriɑnhɑminɑ) *n* the Finnish name for **Mariehamn**

maas (mɑːs) *n South African* thick soured milk [from Nguni *amasi* milk]

Maas (mɑːs) *n* the Dutch name for the **Meuse**

Maastricht or **Maestricht** ('mɑːstrɪxt; *Dutch* mɑːˈstrɪxt) *n* a city in the SE Netherlands near the Belgian and German borders: capital of Limburg province, on the River Maas (Meuse); a European Community treaty (**Maastricht Treaty**) was signed here in 1992, setting out the terms for the creation of the European Union. Pop: 122 000 (2003 est)

Mab (mæb) *n* (in English and Irish folklore) a fairy queen said to create and control men's dreams

Mabuse (məˈbjuːz; *French* mabyz) *n* **Jan** (jɑn). original name *Jan Gossaert*. ?1478– ?1533, Flemish painter

mac or **mack** (mæk) *n Brit informal* short for **mackintosh** (sense 1)

Mac (mæk) *n chiefly US & Canadian* an informal term of address to a man [c20: abstracted from Mac-, prefix of Scottish surnames]

Mac-, Mc- or **M'-** *prefix* (in surnames of Scottish or Irish Gaelic origin) son of: *MacDonald; MacNeice* [from Goidelic *mac* son of; compare Welsh *mab*, Cornish *mab*]

macabre (məˈkɑːbə, -brə) *adj* gruesome; ghastly; grim [c15: from Old French *danse macabre* dance of death, probably from *macabé* relating to the Maccabees, who were associated with death because of the doctrines and prayers for the dead in II Macc. (12:43–46)]

macadam (məˈkædəm) *n* a road surface made of compressed layers of small broken stones, esp one that is bound together with tar or asphalt [c19: named after John McAdam (1756–1836), Scottish engineer, the inventor]

macadamia (ˌmækəˈdeɪmɪə) *n* **1** any tree of the Australian proteaceous genus *Macadamia*, esp *M. ternifolia*, having clusters of small white flowers and edible nutlike seeds **2** macadamia nut the seed of this tree [c19: New Latin, named after John *Macadam* (1827–1865), Australian chemist]

macadamize or **macadamise** (məˈkædəˌmaɪz) *vb* (*tr*) to construct or surface (a road) with macadam
> macˌadamiˈzation or macˌadamiˈsation *n*

Macao (məˈkaʊ) *n* a special administrative region of China, in the south of the country, across the estuary of the Zhu Jiang from Hong Kong: chief centre of European trade with China in the 18th century; attained partial autonomy in 1976; formerly (until 1999) a Portuguese overseas province under a long-term lease from China, as with Hong Kong (a UK territory until 1997); transit trade with rest of China; tourism and financial services. It retains its own currency, the pataca. Pop: 448 500 (2003 est). Area: 16 sq km (6 sq miles)

Macapá (*Portuguese* maka'pa) *n* a town in NE Brazil, capital of the federal territory of Amapá, on the Canal do Norte of the Amazon delta. Pop: 377 000 (2005 est)

Macapagal Arroyo (ˌmækəˈpeɪɡəl əˈrɔɪjəʊ) *n* **Gloria**. See **Arroyo**

macaque (mə'kɑːk) n any of various Old World monkeys of the genus *Macaca*, inhabiting wooded or rocky regions of Asia and Africa. Typically the tail is short or absent and cheek pouches are present [C17: from French, from Portuguese *macaco*, from Fiot (a W African language) *makaku*, from *kaku* monkey]

macaroni or **maccaroni** (,mækə'rəʊnɪ) n, pl -nis or -nies 1 pasta tubes made from wheat flour 2 (in 18th-century Britain) a dandy who affected foreign manners and style [C16: from Italian (Neapolitan dialect) *maccarone*, probably from Greek *makaria* food made from barley]

macaroon (,mækə'ruːn) n a kind of sweet biscuit made of ground almonds, sugar, and egg whites [C17: via French *macaron* from Italian *maccarone* MACARONI]

Macarthur (mə'kɑːθə) n **John.** 1767–1834, Australian military officer, pastoralist, and entrepreneur, born in England. He established the breeding of merino sheep in Australia and was influential in founding the Australian wool industry

MacArthur (mə'kɑːθə) n 1 **Douglas.** 1880–1964, US general. During World War II he became commanding general of US armed forces in the Pacific (1944) and accepted the surrender of Japan, the Allied occupation of which he commanded (1945–51). He was commander in chief of United Nations forces in Korea (1950–51) until dismissed by President Truman 2 **Dame Ellen.** born 1976, English yachtswoman; in 2005 she set a new world record for the fastest solo world circumnavigation

Macassar (mə'kæsə) n a variant spelling of **Makassar**

Macassar oil n an oily preparation formerly put on the hair to make it smooth and shiny [C19: so called because its ingredients were originally claimed to have come from MAKASSAR]

Macáu (mə'kau) n the Portuguese name for **Macao**

Macaulay (mə'kɔːlɪ) n 1 **Dame Rose.** 1881–1958, British novelist. Her books include *Dangerous Ages* (1921) and *The Towers of Trebizond* (1956) 2 **Thomas Babington**, 1st Baron. 1800–59, English historian, essayist, and statesman. His *History of England from the Accession of James the Second* (1848–61) is regarded as a classic of the Whig interpretation of history

macaw (mə'kɔː) n any large tropical American parrot of the genera *Ara* and *Anodorhynchus*, having a long tail and brilliant plumage [C17: from Portuguese *macau*, of unknown origin]

Macbeth (mək'bɛθ, mæk-) n died 1057, king of Scotland (1040–57): succeeded Duncan, whom he killed in battle; defeated and killed by Duncan's son Malcolm III

MacBride (mək'braɪd) n **Sean** (ʃɔːn). 1904–88, Irish statesman; minister for external affairs (1948–51); chairman of Amnesty International (1961–75); Nobel Peace Prize 1974; UN commissioner for Namibia (1974–76)

McBride (mək'braɪd) n **Willie John.** born 1940, Irish Rugby Union footballer. A forward, he played for Ireland (1962–75) and the British Lions (1962–74)

Macc. abbreviation Maccabees (books of the Apocrypha)

Maccabees ('mækə,biːz) n 1 a Jewish family of patriots who freed Judaea from Seleucid oppression (168–142 BC) 2 any of four books of Jewish history, including the last two of the Apocrypha

McCahon (mə'kɑːn) n **Colin.** 1919–87, influential New Zealand painter; noted esp for landscapes and bold abstract paintings, many featuring lettering and Christian imagery

McCall (mə'kɔːl) n **Davina (Lucy Pascale)**, born 1967, English television presenter, especially of *Big Brother* (from 2000)

McCarthy (mə'kɑːθɪ) n 1 **Cormac.** born 1933, US writer; his novels include *Suttree* (1979), *Blood Meridian* (1985), *All the Pretty Horses* (1992), *No Country for Old Men* (2005) and *The Road* (2006) 2 **Joseph R(aymond)**. 1908–57, US Republican senator, who led the (1950–54) notorious investigations of alleged Communist infiltration into the US government 3 **Mary (Therese)**. 1912–89, US novelist and critic; her works include *The Group* (1963)

McCarthyism (mə'kɑːθɪ,ɪzəm) n chiefly US 1 the practice of making unsubstantiated accusations of disloyalty or Communist leanings 2 the use of unsupported accusations for any purpose [C20: after Joseph Raymond

McCarthy (1908–57), US Republican senator, who led (1950–54) the notorious investigations of alleged Communist infiltration into the US government]
> **Mc'Carthyite** n, adj

McCartney (mə'kɑːtnɪ) n 1 Sir **Paul**. born 1942, English rock musician and songwriter; member of the Beatles (1961–70); leader of Wings (1971–81). His recordings include *Band on the Run* (1973), "Mull of Kintyre" (1977), *Flowers in the Dirt* (1989), and *Driving Rain* (2001) 2 his daughter, **Stella**. born 1971, British fashion designer.

macchiato (,mækɪ'ɑːtəʊ) n, pl -tos espresso coffee served with a dash of hot or cold milk [Italian, literally: stained]

Macclesfield ('mækᵊlz,fiːld) n a market town in NW England, in Cheshire: former centre of the silk industry; pharmaceuticals, services. Pop: 50 688 (2001)

McConnell (mə'kanᵊl) n **Jack.** born 1960, Scottish Labour politician; first minister of the Scottish Parliament (2001–07)

McCormack (mə'kɔːmæk) n **John.** 1884–1945, Irish tenor: became US citizen 1919

McCormick (mə'kɔːmɪk) n **Cyrus Hall.** 1809–84, US inventor of the reaping machine (1831)

McCoy¹ (mə'kɔɪ) n slang the genuine person or thing (esp in the phrase **the real McCoy**) [C20: perhaps after Kid *McCoy*, professional name of Norman Selby (1873–1940), American boxer, who was called "the real McCoy" to distinguish him from another boxer of that name]

McCoy² (mə'kɔɪ) n **Tony**, full name *Anthony Peter McCoy*. born 1974, Northern Irish jockey; winner of seven consecutive riders' titles in 2001–02

McCullers (mə'kʌləz) n **Carson**. 1917–67, US writer, whose novels include *The Heart is a Lonely Hunter* (1940)

MacDiarmid (mək'dʒɜːmɪd) n **Hugh**, pen name of *Christopher Murray Grieve*. 1892–1978, Scottish poet; a founder of the Scottish National Party. His poems include *A Drunk Man Looks at the Thistle* (1926)

Macdonald (mək'dɒnəld) n 1 **Flora**. 1722–90, Scottish heroine, who helped the Young Pretender to escape to Skye after his defeat at the battle of Culloden (1746) 2 Sir **John Alexander**. 1815–91, Canadian statesman, born in Scotland, who was the first prime minister of the Dominion of Canada (1867–73; 1878–91)

MacDonald (mək'dɒnəld) n **(James) Ramsay**. 1866–1937, British statesman, who led the first and second Labour Governments (1924 and 1929–31). He also led a coalition (1931–35), which the majority of the Labour Party refused to support

McDonald n Sir **Trevor**. born 1939, British television journalist, born in Trinidad; presenter of ITV's *News at Ten* (1990–99)

Macdonnell Ranges (mək'dɒnəl) pl n a mountain system of central Australia, in S central Northern Territory, extending about 160 km (100 miles) east and west of Alice Springs. Highest peak: Mount Zeil, 1531 m (5024 ft)

mace¹ (meɪs) n 1 a club, usually having a spiked metal head, used esp in the Middle Ages 2 a ceremonial staff of office carried by certain officials 3 See **macebearer** 4 an early form of billiard cue [C13: from Old French, probably from Vulgar Latin *mattea* (unattested); apparently related to Latin *mateola* mallet]

mace² (meɪs) n a spice made from the dried aril round the nutmeg seed [C14: formed as a singular from Old French *macis* (wrongly assumed to be plural), from Latin *macir* an oriental spice]

macebearer ('meɪs,bɛərə) n a person who carries a mace in processions or ceremonies

Maced. abbreviation Macedonia(n)

macedoine (,mæsɪ'dwɑːn) n 1 a hot or cold mixture of diced vegetables 2 a mixture of fruit served in a syrup or in jelly 3 any mixture; medley [C19: from French, literally: Macedonian, alluding to the mixture of nationalities in Macedonia]

Macedon ('mæsɪˌdɒn) or **Macedonia** n a region of the S Balkans, now divided among Greece, Bulgaria, and Macedonia (Former Yugoslav Republic of Macedonia). As a kingdom in the ancient world it achieved prominence under Philip II (359–336 BC) and his son Alexander the Great >‚Mace'donian *adj, n*

Macedonia (‚mæsɪ'dəʊnɪə) *n* 1 a country in SE Europe, comprising the NW half of ancient Macedon: it became part of the kingdom of Serbs, Croats, and Slovenes (subsequently Yugoslavia) in 1913; it declared independence in 1992, but Greece objected to the use of the historical name Macedonia; in 1993 it was recognized by the UN under its current official name. Official language: Macedonian. Religion: Christian majority, Muslim, nonreligious, and Jewish minorities. Currency: denar. Capital: Skopje. Pop: 2 066 000 (2004 est). Area: 25 713 sq km (10 028 sq miles) 2 an area of N Greece, comprising the regions of Macedonia Central, Macedonia West, and part of Macedonia East and Thrace. Modern Greek name: Makedhonia 3 a district of SW Bulgaria, now occupied by Blagoevgrad province. Area: 6465 sq km (2496 sq miles) >‚Mace'donian *adj, n*

Maceió (mase'jɔ) *n* a port in NE Brazil, capital of Alagôas state, on the Atlantic. Pop: 1 137 000 (2005 est)

McEnroe ('mæk°n,rəʊ) *n* John (Patrick Jr). born 1959, US tennis player: US singles champion (1979–81; 1984) and doubles champion (1979; 1981; 1989): Wimbledon singles champion (1981; 1983; 1984) and doubles champion (1979; 1981; 1983; 1984; 1992)

macerate ('mæsə,reɪt) *vb* 1 to soften or separate or be softened or separated as a result of soaking 2 to become or cause to become thin [c16: from Latin *mācerāre* to soften] >'macer,ater or'macer,ator *n* >,macer'ation *n*

McEwan (mə'kju:ən) *n* Ian (Russell). born 1948, British novelist and short-story writer. His books include *First Love, Last Rites* (1975), *The Child in Time* (1987), *The Innocent* (1990), *Amsterdam* (1998), *Atonement* (2001), and *Saturday* (2005)

McGonagall (mə'ɡɒnəɡəl) *n* William. 1830–?1902, Scottish writer of doggerel, noted for its bathos, repetitive rhymes, poor scansion, and ludicrous effect

McGrath (mə'ɡræθ) *n* Glenn (Donald). born 1970, Australian cricketer; played for Australia from 1993

MacGregor *n* Joanna (Clare). born 1959, British concert pianist and broadcaster; recordings include the "crossover" album *Play* (2001)

McGregor (mək'ɡrɛɡər) *n* Ewan. born 1971, Scottish actor; his films include *Shallow Grave* (1994), *Trainspotting* (1996), *The Phantom Menace* (1999), *Moulin Rouge* (2001), *Big Fish* (2004), and *Revenge of the Sith* (2005)

McGuffin or **MacGuffin** (mə'ɡʌfɪn) *n* an object or event in a book or a film that serves as the impetus for the plot [c20: coined (c. 1935) by Sir Alfred Joseph Hitchcock (1899–1980), English film director]

McGwire (mə'ɡwɪə) *n* Mark (David). born 1963, US baseball player

Mach[1] (mæk) *n* short for **Mach number**

Mach[2] (German max) *n* Ernst (ɛrnst). 1838–1916, Austrian physicist and philosopher. He devised the system of speed measurement using the Mach number. He also founded logical positivism, asserting that the validity of a scientific law is proved only after empirical testing

Machado (Portuguese ma'ʃadu) *n* Joaquim Maria (ʒua'kı ma'rıa). 1839–1908, Brazilian author of novels and short stories, whose novels include *Epitaph of a Small Winner* (1881) and *Dom Casmurro* (1899)

machair ('mæxər) *n* Scot (in the western Highlands of Scotland) a strip of sandy, grassy, often lime-rich land just above the high-water mark at a sandy shore: used as grazing or arable land [c17: from Scottish Gaelic]

Machaut (French maʃo) *n* Guillaume de. (ɡijɔm də) c. 1300–77, French composer and poet; a leading exponent of ars nova

Machel (mə'ʃɛl) *n* Samora (Moises) (sə'mɔːrə). 1933–86, Mozambique statesman; president of Mozambique from 1975–86

machete (mə'ʃɛtɪ, -'tʃeɪ-) or **matchet** *n* a broad heavy knife used for cutting or as a weapon, esp in parts of Central and South America [C16 *macheto*, from Spanish *machete*, from *macho* club, perhaps from Vulgar Latin *mattea* (unattested) club]

Machiavelli (,mækɪə'vɛlɪ) *n* Niccolò (nikko'lɔ). 1469–1527, Florentine statesman and political philosopher;

secretary to the war council of the Florentine republic (1498–1512). His most famous work is *Il Principe* (*The Prince*, 1532)

Machiavellian or **Machiavelian** (,mækɪə'vɛlɪən) *adj* (*sometimes not capital*) 1 of or relating to the alleged political principles of Niccolò Machiavelli (1469–1527), Florentine statesman and political philosopher; cunning, amoral, and opportunist ▷ *n* 2 a cunning, amoral, and opportunist person, esp a politician >,Machia'vellianism or ,Machia'vellism *n*

machicolate (mə'tʃɪkəʊ,leɪt) *vb* (*tr*) to construct machicolations at the top of (a wall) [c18: from Old French *machicoller*, ultimately from Provençal *machacol*, from *macar* to crush + *col* neck]

machicolation (mə,tʃɪkəʊ'leɪʃən) *n* 1 (esp in medieval castles) a projecting gallery or parapet supported on corbels having openings through which missiles could be dropped 2 any such opening

machinate ('mækɪ,neɪt, 'mæʃ-) *vb* (*usually tr*) to contrive, plan, or devise (schemes, plots, etc) [c17: from Latin *māchinārī* to plan, from *māchina* MACHINE] >'machi,nator *n*

machination (,mækɪ'neɪʃən, ,mæʃ-) *n* 1 an intrigue, plot, or scheme 2 the act of devising plots or schemes

machine (mə'ʃiːn) *n* 1 an assembly of interconnected components arranged to transmit or modify force in order to perform useful work 2 Also called: simple machine a device for altering the magnitude or direction of a force, esp a lever, screw, wedge, or pulley 3 a mechanically operated device or means of transport, such as a car, aircraft, etc 4 any mechanical or electrical device that automatically performs tasks or assists in performing tasks 5 any intricate structure or agency 6 a mechanically efficient, rigid, or obedient person 7 an organized body of people that controls activities, policies, etc ▷ *vb* 8 (*tr*) to shape, cut, or remove (excess material) from (a workpiece) using a machine tool 9 to use a machine to carry out a process on (something) [c16: via French from Latin *māchina* machine, engine, from Doric Greek *makhana* pulley; related to *makhos* device, contrivance] >ma'chinable or ma'chineable *adj*

machine code or **machine language** *n* instructions for the processing of data in a binary, octal, or hexadecimal code that can be understood and executed by a computer

machine gun *n* 1 a a rapid-firing automatic gun, usually mounted, from which small-arms ammunition is discharged b (*as modifier*): *machine-gun fire* ▷ *vb* **machine-gun -guns, -gunning, -gunned** 2 (*tr*) to shoot or fire at with a machine gun > machine gunner *n*

machine learning *n* a branch of artificial intelligence in which a computer generates rules underlying or based on raw data that has been fed into it

machinery (mə'ʃiːnərɪ) *n, pl* -eries 1 machines, machine parts, or machine systems collectively 2 a particular machine system or set of machines 3 a system similar to a machine

machine shop *n* a workshop in which machine tools are operated

machine tool *n* a power-driven machine, such as a lathe, miller, or grinder, that is used for cutting, shaping, and finishing metals or other materials >ma'chine-,tooled *adj*

machinist (mə'ʃiːnɪst) *n* 1 a person who operates machines to cut or process materials 2 a maker or repairer of machines

machismo (mæ'kɪzməʊ, -'tʃiːz-) *n* exaggerated masculine pride [Mexican Spanish, from Spanish *macho* male, from Latin *masculus* MASCULINE]

Mach number *n* (*often not capital*) the ratio of the speed of a body in a particular medium to the speed of sound in that medium. Mach number 1 corresponds to the speed of sound. Often shortened to **Mach**[1] [c19: named after Ernst Mach (1838–1916), Austrian physicist and philosopher]

macho ('mætʃəʊ) *adj* 1 denoting or exhibiting pride in characteristics believed to be typically masculine, such as physical strength, sexual appetite, etc ▷ *n, pl* machos 2 a man who displays such characteristics [c20: from Spanish: male; see MACHISMO]

Machu Picchu ('mɑːtʃuː 'piːktʃuː) n a ruined Incan city in S Peru

Macías Nguema (mə'siːəs ᵊŋ'gweɪmə) n the former name (until 1979) of **Bioko**

McIndoe ('mækɪnˌdəʊ) n Sir **Archibald Hector**. 1900–60, New Zealand plastic surgeon; noted for his pioneering work with wounded World War II airmen

McIntosh ('mækɪnˌtɒʃ) or **McIntosh red** n a Canadian variety of red-skinned eating apple [c19: named after John McIntosh (1777–c. 1845), US-born Canadian farmer on whose property the variety was first found growing wild]

mack (mæk) n Brit informal short for **mackintosh** (sense 1)

Mackay (mə'kaɪ) n a port in E Australia, in Queensland: artificial harbour. Pop: 57 649 (2001)

McKean (mə'kiːn) n Tom. born 1963, Scottish athlete: European 800 metres gold medallist (1990)

Mackellar (mə'kɛlə) n Dorothea. 1885–1968, Australian poet, who wrote "My Country", Australia's best known poem

McKellen (mə'kɛlən) n Sir Ian (Murray). born 1939, British actor, noted esp for his Shakespearean roles; films include The Lord of the Rings trilogy (2001–03)

McKenna (mə'kɛnə) n Siobhán (ʃə'vɔːn). 1923–86, Irish actress, whose notable roles included Pegeen Mike in Synge's The Playboy of the Western World and Shaw's Saint Joan

Mackenzie¹ (mə'kɛnzɪ) n a river in NW Canada, in the Northwest Territories and Nunavut, flowing northwest from Great Slave Lake to the Beaufort Sea: the longest river in Canada; navigable in summer. Length: 1770 km (1100 miles)

Mackenzie² (mə'kɛnzɪ) n 1 Sir Alexander. ?1755–1820, Scottish explorer and fur trader in Canada. He explored the Mackenzie River (1789) and was the first European to cross America north of Mexico (1793) 2 Alexander. 1822–92, Canadian statesman; first Liberal prime minister (1873–78) 3 Sir Compton. 1883–1972, English author. His works include Sinister Street (1913–14) and the comic novel Whisky Galore (1947) 4 Sir Thomas. 1854–1930, New Zealand statesman born in Scotland: prime minister of New Zealand (1912) 5 William Lyon. 1795–1861, Canadian journalist and politician, born in Scotland. He led an unsuccessful rebellion against the oligarchic Family Compact (1837)

mackerel ('mækrəl) n, pl -rel or -rels 1 a spiny-finned food fish, Scomber scombrus, occurring in northern coastal regions of the Atlantic and in the Mediterranean: family Scombridae. It has a deeply forked tail and a greenish-blue body marked with wavy dark bands on the back 2 any of various other fishes of the family Scombridae, such as Scomber colias (Spanish mackerel) and S. japonicus (Pacific mackerel) [c13: from Anglo-French, from Old French maquerel, of unknown origin]

mackerel sky n a sky patterned with cirrocumulus or small altocumulus clouds [from the similarity to the pattern on a mackerel's back]

Mackerras (mə'kɛrəs) n Charles. born 1925, Australian conductor, esp of opera; resident in England

Mackinac ('mækɪˌnɔː, -ˌnæk) n a wooded island in N Michigan, in the **Straits of Mackinac** (a channel between the lower and upper peninsulas of Michigan): an ancient Indian burial ground; state park. Length: 5 km (3 miles)

Mackinder (mə'kɪndə) n Sir Halford John. 1861–1947, British geographer noted esp for his work in political geography. His writings include Democratic Ideas and Reality (1919)

McKinley¹ (mə'kɪnlɪ) n Mount McKinley Also called: Denali a mountain in S central Alaska, in the Alaska Range: the highest peak in North America. Height: 6194 m (20 320 ft)

McKinley² (mə'kɪnlɪ) n William. 1843–1901, 25th president of the US (1897–1901). His administration was marked by high tariffs and by expansionist policies. He was assassinated

McKinnon (mə'kɪnən) n Don(ald) (Charles). born 1939, New Zealand politician; secretary-general of the Commonwealth (2000–08); deputy prime minister of New Zealand (1990–96)

mackintosh or **macintosh** ('mækɪnˌtɒʃ) n 1 a waterproof raincoat made of rubberized cloth 2 such cloth 3 any raincoat [c19: named after Charles Macintosh (1760–1843), who invented it]

Mackintosh ('mækɪnˌtɒʃ) n 1 Sir Cameron (Anthony). born 1946, British producer of musicals and theatre owner; his productions include Cats (1981), Les Misérables (1985), Miss Saigon (1987), and My Fair Lady (2001) 2 Charles Rennie. 1868–1928, Scottish architect and artist, exponent of the Art Nouveau style; designer of the Glasgow School of Art (1896)

Maclean (mə'kleɪn) n 1 Donald. 1913–83, British civil servant, who spied for the Russians: fled to the former Soviet Union (with Guy Burgess) in 1951 2 Sorley ('sɔːlɪ). 1911–96, Scottish Gaelic poet. His works include Dàin do Eimhir agus Dàin Eile (1943) and Spring Tide and Neap Tide (1977)

Macleish (mə'kliːʃ) n Archibald. 1892–1982, US poet and public official; his works include Collected Poems (1952) and J.B. (1958)

Macleod (mə'klaʊd) n John James Rickard. 1876–1935, Scottish physiologist: shared the Nobel prize for physiology or medicine (1923) with Banting for their part in discovering insulin

McLuhan (mə'kluːən) n (Herbert) Marshall. 1911–80, Canadian author of works analysing the mass media, including Understanding Media (1964) and The Medium is the Message (1967)

Macmahon (French makmaɔ̃) n Marie Edme Patrice Maurice (mari ɛdmə patris mɔris), Comte de Macmahon. 1808–93, French military commander. He commanded the troops that suppressed the Paris Commune (1871) and was elected president of the Third Republic (1873–79)

McMahon (mək'mɑːən) n Sir William. 1908–88, Australian statesman; prime minister of Australia (1971–72)

McMansion (mək'mænʃən) n informal, disparaging a large modern house considered to look mass-produced, lacking in distinguishing characteristics, and at variance with established local architecture [c20: a corruption of McDonald's, a major American fast-food enterprise noted for the ubiquity of its restaurants]

Macmillan (mək'mɪlən) n (Maurice) Harold, 1st Earl of Stockton. 1894–1986, British statesman; Conservative prime minister (1957–63)

MacMillan n 1 James (Loy). born 1959, Scottish composer and conductor; his works include two symphonies, the orchestral work Confession of Isobel Gowdie (1990), and the opera Ines de Castro (1996) 2 Sir Kenneth. 1929–92, British choreographer, dancer, and ballet director; chief choreographer for the Royal Ballet from 1970

McMillan (mək'mɪlən) n Edwin M(attison). 1907–91, US physicist; Nobel prize for chemistry 1951 (with Glenn Seaborg) for the discovery of transuranic elements

McMurdo Sound (mək'mɜːdəʊ) n an inlet of the Ross Sea in Antarctica, north of Victoria Land

McNaughten Rules or **McNaghten Rules** (mək'nɔːtᵊn) pl n (in English law) a set of rules established by the case of Regina v. McNaughten (1843) by which legal proof of insanity in the commission of a crime depends upon whether or not the accused can show either that he did not know what he was doing or that he is incapable of realizing that what he was doing was wrong

MacNeice (mək'niːs) n Louis. 1907–63, British poet, born in Northern Ireland. His works include Autumn Journal (1939) and Solstices (1961) and a translation of Agamemnon (1936)

Macon ('meɪkən) n a city in the US, in central Georgia, on the Ocmulgee River. Pop: 95 267 (2003 est)

Mâcon (French makɔ̃) n 1 a city in E central France, in the Saône valley: a centre of the wine-producing region of lower Burgundy. Pop: 34 469 (1999) 2 a red or white wine from the Mâcon area, heavier than the other burgundies

Maconchy (mə'kɒŋkɪ) n Dame Elizabeth, married name Elizabeth LeFanu. 1907–94, British composer of Irish parentage; noted esp for her chamber music, which includes 13 string quartets and *Romanza* (1980) for viola and ensemble

McPartlin (mək'pɑ:tlɪn) *n* **Antony.** born 1975, British television presenter, who appears with Declan Donnelly as Ant and Dec

Macpherson (mək'fɜːsᵊn) *n* **James.** 1736–96, Scottish poet and translator. He published supposed translations of the legendary Gaelic poet Ossian, in reality largely his own work

McPherson (mək'fɜːsən) *n* **Conor.** born 1972, Irish playwright and theatre director; his plays include *The Weir* (1997) and *Port Authority* (2001)

Macquarie (mə'kwɒrɪ) *n* **Lachlan.** 1762–1824, Australian colonial administrator; Governor of New South Wales (1809–21), noted for his reformist policies towards ex-convicts and for his record in public works such as road-building in the colony

McQueen (mə'kwiːn) *n* **1 Alexander.** born 1969, British fashion designer and master tailor. **2 Steve.** 1930–80, US film actor, noted for his portrayal of tough characters

macramé (mə'krɑːmɪ) *n* a type of ornamental work made by knotting and weaving coarse thread into a pattern [C19: via French and Italian from Turkish *makrama* towel, from Arabic *migramah* striped cloth]

Macready (mə'kriːdɪ) *n* **William Charles.** 1793–1873, English actor and theatre manager

macro ('mækrəʊ) *n, pl* **macros 1** a macro lens **2** Also called: **macro instruction** a single computer instruction that initiates a set of instructions to perform a specific task

macro- *or before a vowel* **macr-** *combining form* **1** large, long, or great in size or duration: *macroscopic* **2** (in pathology) indicating abnormal enlargement or overdevelopment [from Greek *makros* large; compare Latin *macer* MEAGRE]

macrobiotics (,mækrəʊbaɪ'ɒtɪks) *n* (*functioning as singular*) a dietary system in which foods are classified according to the principles of Yin and Yang. It advocates diets of whole grains and vegetables grown without chemical additives [C20: from MACRO- + Greek *biotos* life + -ICS] > ,macrobi'otic *adj*

macrocarpa (,mækrəʊ'kɑːpə) *n* a large coniferous tree of New Zealand, *Cupressus macrocarpa*, used for shelter belts on farms and for rough timber. Also called: Monterey cypress [C19: from New Latin, from Greek MACRO- + *karpos* fruit]

macrocephaly (,mækrəʊ'sɛfəlɪ) *n* the condition of having an abnormally large head or skull > macrocephalic (,mækrəʊsɪ'fælɪk) *or* ,macro'cephalous *adj*

macroclimate ('mækrəʊ,klaɪmɪt) *n* the prevailing climate of a large area

macrocosm ('mækrə,kɒzəm) *n* **1** a complex structure, such as the universe or society, regarded as an entirety, as opposed to microcosms, which have a similar structure and are contained within it **2** any complex entity regarded as a complete system in itself ▷ See **microcosm** [C16: via French and Latin from Greek *makros kosmos* great world] > ,macro'cosmic *adj* > ,macro'cosmically *adv*

macroeconomics (,mækrəʊ,iːkə'nɒmɪks, -,ɛk-) *n* (*functioning as singular*) the branch of economics concerned with aggregates, such as national income, consumption, and investment > ,macro,eco'nomic *adj*

macromolecule (,mækrəʊ'mɒlɪ,kjuːl) *n* any very large molecule, such as a protein or synthetic polymer

macron ('mækrɒn) *n* a diacritical mark ( ) placed over a letter, used in prosody, in the orthography of some languages, and in several types of phonetic respelling systems, to represent a long vowel [C19: from Greek *makron* something long, from *makros* long]

macroscopic (,mækrəʊ'skɒpɪk) *adj* **1** large enough to be visible to the naked eye **2** comprehensive; concerned with large units [C19: see MACRO-, -SCOPIC] > ,macro'scopically *adv*

macula ('mækjʊlə) *or* **macule** ('mækjuːl) *n, pl* **-ulae** (-jʊ,liː) *or* **-ules** *anatomy* **1** a small spot or area of distinct colour, esp the macula lutea **2** any small discoloured spot or blemish on the skin, such as a freckle [C14: from Latin] > 'macular *adj* > maculation (,mækjʊ'leɪʃən) *n*

macula lutea ('luːtɪə) *n, pl* **maculae luteae** ('luːtɪ,iː) a small yellowish oval-shaped spot, rich in cones, near the centre of the retina of the eye, where vision is especially sharp [New Latin, literally: yellow spot]

macular degeneration *n* pathological changes in the macula lutea, resulting in loss of central vision: a common cause of blindness in the elderly

mad (mæd) *adj* **madder, maddest 1** mentally deranged; insane **2** senseless; foolish: *a mad idea* **3** (often foll by *at*) *informal* angry; resentful **4** (foll by *about, on,* or *over;* often postpositive) wildly enthusiastic (about) or fond (of): *mad about football; football-mad* **5** extremely excited or confused; frantic: *a mad rush* **6** temporarily overpowered by violent reactions, emotions, etc: *mad with grief* **7** (of animals) **a** unusually ferocious: *a mad buffalo* **b** afflicted with rabies **8** like mad *informal* with great energy, enthusiasm, or haste; wildly **9** mad as a hatter crazily eccentric ▷ *vb* **mads, madding, madded 10** *archaic* to make or become mad; act or cause to act as if mad [Old English *gemǣded,* past participle of *gemǣdan* to render insane; related to *gemād* insane, and to Old High German *gimeit* silly, crazy, Old Norse *meitha* to hurt, damage]

Madag. *abbreviation* Madagascar

Madagascar (,mædə'gæskə) *n* an island republic in the Indian Ocean, off the E coast of Africa: made a French protectorate in 1895; became autonomous in 1958 and fully independent in 1960; contains unique flora and fauna. Languages: Malagasy and French. Religions: animist and Christian. Currency: franc. Capital: Antananarivo. Pop: 17 901 000 (2004 est). Area: 587 041 sq km (266 657 sq miles). Former name (1958–75): Malagasy Republic > ,Mada'gascan *n, adj*

madam ('mædəm) *n, pl* **madams** *or for sense* 1 **mesdames** ('meɪ,dæm) **1** a polite term of address for a woman, esp one considered to be of relatively high social status **2** a woman who runs a brothel **3** *Brit informal* a precocious or pompous little girl [C13: from Old French *ma dame* my lady]

madame ('mædəm; *French* madam) *n, pl* **mesdames** ('meɪ,dæm; *French* medam) a married Frenchwoman: usually used as a title equivalent to *Mrs,* and sometimes extended to older unmarried women to show respect and to women of other nationalities [C17: from French. See MADAM]

madcap ('mæd,kæp) *adj* **1** impulsive, reckless, or lively ▷ *n* **2** an impulsive, reckless, or lively person [C16: from MAD + *cap* (in the figurative sense: head)]

mad cow disease *n* an informal name for BSE

madden ('mædᵊn) *vb* to make or become mad or angry > maddening ('mædᵊnɪŋ, 'mædnɪŋ) *adj* > 'maddeningly *adv* > 'maddeningness *n*

madder ('mædə) *n* **1** any of several rubiaceous plants of the genus *Rubia,* esp the Eurasian *R. tinctoria,* which has small yellow flowers and a red fleshy root **2** the root of this plant **3** a dark reddish-purple dye formerly obtained by fermentation of this root; identical to the synthetic dye, alizarin **4** a red lake obtained from alizarin and an inorganic base; used as a pigment in inks and paints [Old English *mædere;* related to Middle Dutch *mēde,* Old Norse *mathra*]

madding ('mædɪŋ) *adj archaic* **1** acting or behaving as if mad: *the madding crowd* **2** making mad; maddening > 'maddingly *adv*

made (meɪd) *vb* **1** the past tense and past participle of **make**¹ ▷ *adj* **2** artificially produced **3** (*in combination*) produced or shaped as specified: *handmade* **4** get it made or have it made *informal* to be assured of success **5** made of money very rich

Madeira (mə'dɪərə; *Portuguese* mə'ðəirə) *n* **1** a group of volcanic islands in the N Atlantic, west of Morocco: since 1976 an autonomous region of Portugal; consists of the chief island, Madeira, Porto Santo, and the uninhabited Deserta and Selvagen Islands. Capital: Funchal. Pop: 245 012 (2001). Area: 797 sq km (311 sq miles) **2** a river in W Brazil, flowing northeast to the Amazon below Manaus. Length: 3241 km (2013 miles) **3** a rich strong fortified white wine made on Madeira

madeleine ('mædəlɪn, -,leɪn) *n* a small fancy sponge cake [C19: perhaps after *Madeleine* Paulmier, French pastry cook]

mademoiselle (ˌmædmwəˈzɛl; *French* madmwazɛl) *n, pl* **mesdemoiselles** (ˌmeɪdmwəˈzɛl; *French* medmwazɛl) **1** a young unmarried French girl or woman: usually used as a title equivalent to *Miss* **2** a French teacher or governess [c15: French, from *ma* my + *demoiselle* DAMSEL]

made-up *adj* **1** invented; fictional **2** wearing make-up **3** put together; assembled **4** (of a road) surfaced with asphalt, concrete, etc

madhouse (ˈmædˌhaʊs) *n informal* **1** a mental hospital or asylum **2** a state of uproar or confusion

Madhya Bharat (ˈmʌdjə ˈbɑːrət) *n* a former state of central India: part of Madhya Pradesh since 1956

Madhya Pradesh (ˈmʌdjə prɑːˈdɛʃ) *n* a state of central India, situated on the Deccan Plateau: rich in mineral resources, with several industrial cities: formerly the largest Indian state, it lost much of the SE to the new state of Chhattisgarh in 2000. Capital: Bhopal. Pop: 60 385 118 (2001). Area: 308 332 sq km (119 016 sq miles)

Madiba (məˈdiːbə) *n South African* a title of respect for Nelson Mandela, deriving from his Xhosa clan name

Madison¹ (ˈmædɪsᵊn) *n* a city in the US, in S central Wisconsin, on an isthmus between Lakes Mendota and Monona: the state capital. Pop: 218 432 (2003 est)

Madison² (ˈmædɪsᵊn) *n* **James.** 1751–1836, US statesman; 4th president of the US (1809–17). He helped to draft the US Constitution and Bill of Rights. His presidency was dominated by the War of 1812

Madison Avenue *n* a street in New York City: a centre of American advertising and public-relations firms and a symbol of their attitudes and methods

madly (ˈmædlɪ) *adv* **1** in an insane or foolish manner **2** with great speed and energy **3** *informal* extremely or excessively: *I love you madly*

madman (ˈmædmən) *n, pl* -men a man who is insane, esp one who behaves violently; lunatic

madness (ˈmædnɪs) *n* **1** insanity; lunacy **2** extreme anger, excitement, or foolishness **3** a nontechnical word for **rabies**

Madonna¹ (məˈdɒnə) *n* **1** *chiefly RC Church* a designation of the Virgin Mary **2** (*sometimes not capital*) a picture or statue of the Virgin Mary [c16: Italian, from *ma* my + *donna* lady]

Madonna² (məˈdɒnə) *n* full name *Madonna Louise Veronica Ciccone.* born 1958, US rock singer and film actress. Her records include "Like a Virgin" (1985), "Like a Prayer" (1989), *Ray of Light* (1998), and *Music* (2000). Her films include *Desperately Seeking Susan* (1985), and *Evita* (1996)

Madonna lily *n* a perennial widely cultivated Mediterranean lily plant, *Lilium candidum*, with white trumpet-shaped flowers

madras (ˈmædrəs, məˈdræs, -ˈdrɑːs) *n* **1** a strong fine cotton or silk fabric, usually with a woven stripe **2** a medium-hot curry: *chicken madras* [c19: so named because the material originated in the MADRAS area]

Madras (məˈdrɑːs, -ˈdræs) *n* **1** Official name: Chennai **2** the former name (until 1968) for the state of **Tamil Nadu**

madrasah, madrasa (məˈdræsə, ˈmɑːdræsə) *or* **medrese** (məˈdrɛseɪ) *n Islam* an educational institution, particularly for Islamic religious instruction [from Arabic, literally: place of learning]

Madre de Dios (*Spanish* ˈmɑːðre ðe ˈðiɔs) *n* a river in NE South America, rising in SE Peru and flowing northeast to the Beni River in N Bolivia. Length: about 965 km (600 miles)

madrepore (ˌmædrɪˈpɔː) *n* any coral of the genus *Madrepora*, many of which occur in tropical seas and form large coral reefs: order *Zoantharia* [c18: via French from Italian *madrepora* mother-stone, from *madre* mother + *-pora*, from Latin *porus* or Greek *poros* calcareous stone, stalactite] > ˌmadreˈporal *or* **madreporic** (ˌmædrɪˈpɒrɪk) ˌmadreˈporian *adj*

Madrid (məˈdrɪd) *n* the capital of Spain, situated centrally in New Castile: the highest European capital, at an altitude of about 700 m (2300 ft); a Moorish fortress in the 10th century, captured by Castile in 1083 and made capital of Spain in 1561; university (1836). Pop: 3 092 759 (2003 est)

madrigal (ˈmædrɪgᵊl) *n music* a type of 16th- or 17th-century part song for unaccompanied voices with an amatory or pastoral text [c16: from Italian, from Medieval Latin *mātricāle* primitive, apparently from Latin *mātrīcālis* of the womb, from *matrīx* womb] > ˈmadrigalˌesque *adj* > **madrigalian** (ˌmædrɪˈgeɪlɪən, -ˈgeɪ-) *adj* > ˈmadrigalist *n*

Madura (məˈdʊərə) *n* an island in Indonesia, off the NE coast of Java: extensive forests and saline springs. Capital: Pamekasan. Area: 5472 sq km (2113 sq miles) > **Madurese** (ˌmædjʊəˈriːz, ˌɪʲaduˈrese) *adj, n*

Madurai (ˈmædjʊˌraɪ) *n* a city in S India, in S Tamil Nadu: centre of Dravidian culture for over 2000 years; cotton industry. Pop: 922 913 (2001). Former name: Madura

Maeander (miːˈændə) *n* ancient name of the river: Menderes (sense 1) Also spelt: Meander

Maebashi (mɑːˈɛˈbɑːʃi) *n* a city in central Japan, on central Honshu: centre of sericulture and silk-spinning; university (1949). Pop: 283 005 (2002 est)

Maecenas (miːˈsiːnæs) *n* **1 Gaius** (ˈgaɪəs). ?70–8 BC, Roman statesman; adviser to Augustus and patron of Horace and Virgil **2** a wealthy patron of the arts

maelstrom (ˈmeɪlstrəʊm) *n* **1** a large powerful whirlpool **2** any turbulent confusion [c17: from obsolete Dutch *maelstroom*, from *malen* to grind, whirl round + *stroom* STREAM]

Maelstrom (ˈmeɪlstrəʊm) *n* a strong tidal current in a restricted channel in the Lofoten Islands off the NW coast of Norway

maenad *or* **menad** (ˈmiːnæd) *n* **1** *classical myth* a woman participant in the orgiastic rites of Dionysus; bacchante **2** a frenzied woman [c16: from Latin *Maenas*, from Greek *mainas* madwoman] > ˈmaeˈnadic *adj*

maestoso (maɪˈstəʊsəʊ) *music* ▷ *adj, adv* **1** to be performed majestically ▷ *n, pl* -sos **2** a piece or passage directed to be played in this way [c18: Italian: majestic, from Latin *māiestās* MAJESTY]

Maestricht (ˈmɑːstrɪxt; *Dutch* maːˈstrɪxt) *n* an obsolete spelling of **Maastricht**

maestro (ˈmaɪstrəʊ) *n, pl* -tri (-trɪ) *or* -tros **1** a distinguished music teacher, conductor, or musician **2** any man regarded as the master of an art: often used as a term of address [c18: Italian: master]

Maeterlinck (ˈmeɪtəˌlɪŋk; *French* mɛtɛrlɛ̃k) *n* **Comte Maurice** (mɔris). 1862–1949, Belgian poet and dramatist, noted particularly for his symbolist plays, such as *Pelléas et Mélisande* (1892), which served as the basis for an opera by Debussy, and *L'Oiseau bleu* (1909). Nobel prize for literature 1911

mae west (meɪ) *n slang* an inflatable life jacket, esp as issued to the US armed forces for emergency use [c20: after *Mae West*, 1892–1980, American actress, renowned for her generous bust]

Maewo (mɑːˈeɪwəʊ) *n* an almost uninhabited island in Vanuatu. Also called: Aurora

MAF (mæf) *n acronym for* (in New Zealand) Ministry of Agriculture and Forestry

Mafeking (ˈmæfɪˌkɪŋ) *n* the former name (until 1980) of **Mafikeng**

Mafia *or* **Maffia** (ˈmæfɪə) *n* **1** **the Mafia** an international secret organization founded in Sicily, probably in opposition to tyranny. It developed into a criminal organization and in the late 19th century was carried to the US by Italian immigrants **2** any group considered to resemble the Mafia [c19: from Sicilian dialect of Italian, literally hostility to the law, boldness, perhaps from Arabic *mahyah* bragging]

Mafikeng (ˈmæfɪˌkɛŋ) *n* a town in N South Africa: besieged by the Boers for 217 days (1899–1900) during the second Boer War: administrative headquarters of the British protectorate of Bechuanaland until 1965, although outside its borders. Pop: 23 650 (2001). Former name (until 1980): Mafeking

mafioso (ˌmæfɪˈəʊsəʊ; *Italian* mafiˈoso) *n, pl* -sos *or* -si (*Italian* -si) a person belonging to the Mafia

mag. *abbreviation* **1** magazine **2** magnitude

magainin (məˈgeɪnɪn) *n* any of a series of related substances with antibacterial properties, derived from the skins of frogs [c20: from Hebrew *magain* a shield]

Magallanes (*Spanish* maɣaˈʎanes) *n* the former name of **Punta Arenas**

magazine (ˌmæɡəˈziːn) *n* **1** a periodical paperback publication containing articles, fiction, photographs, etc **2** a metal box or drum holding several cartridges used in some kinds of automatic firearms; it is removed and replaced when empty **3** a building or compartment for storing weapons, explosives, military provisions, etc **4** a stock of ammunition **5** for a rack for automatically feeding a number of slides through a projector **6** a TV or radio programme made up of a series of short nonfiction items [c16: via French *magasin* from Italian *magazzino*, from Arabic *makhāzin*, plural of *makhzan* storehouse, from *khazana* to store away]

magdalen (ˈmæɡdəlɪn) *or* **magdalene** (ˈmæɡdəˌliːn, ˌmæɡdəˈliːnɪ) *n* **1** *literary* a reformed prostitute **2** *rare* a reformatory for prostitutes [from Mary Magdalene]

Magdalena (ˌmæɡdəˈleɪnə, -ˈliː-; *Spanish* maɣðaˈlena) *n* a river in SW Colombia, rising on the E slopes of the Andes and flowing north to the Caribbean near Barranquilla. Length: 1540 km (956 miles)

Magdalena Bay *n* an inlet of the Pacific on the coast of NW Mexico, in Lower California

Magdalene (ˈmæɡdəˌliːn, ˌmæɡdəˈliːnɪ) *n* See **Mary Magdalene**

Magdalenian (ˌmæɡdəˈliːnɪən) *adj* **1** of or relating to the latest Palaeolithic culture in Europe, which ended about 10 000 years ago ▷ *n* **2** the Magdalenian culture [c19: from French *magdalénien*, after *La Madeleine*, village in Dordogne, France, near which artefacts of the culture were found]

Magdeburg (ˈmæɡdəˌbɜːɡ; *German* ˈmakdəburk) *n* an industrial city and port in central Germany, on the River Elbe, capital of Saxony-Anhalt: a leading member of the Hanseatic League, whose local laws, the **Magdeburg Laws** were adopted by many European cities. Pop: 227 535 (2003 est)

Magellan¹ (məˈɡɛlən) *n* Strait of Magellan a strait between the mainland of S South America and Tierra del Fuego, linking the S Pacific with the S Atlantic. Length: 600 km (370 miles). Width: up to 32 km (20 miles)

Magellan² (məˈɡɛlən) *n* Ferdinand. Portuguese name *Fernão de Magalhães*. ?1480– 1521, Portuguese navigator in the service of Spain. He commanded an expedition of five ships that set out to sail to the East Indies via the West He discovered the Strait of Magellan (1520), crossed the Pacific, and reached the Philippines (1521), where he was killed by natives. One of his ships reached Spain (1522) and was therefore the first to circumnavigate the world

Magellanic Cloud (ˌmæɡɪˈlænɪk) *n* either of two small irregular galaxies, the **Large Magellanic Cloud** (Nubecula Major) and the **Small Magellanic Cloud** (Nubecula Minor), lying near the S celestial pole; they are probably satellites of the Galaxy. Distances: 163 000 light years (Large), 196 000 light years (Small)

magenta (məˈdʒɛntə) *n* **1 a** a deep purplish red that is the complementary colour of green and, with yellow and cyan, forms a set of primary colours **b** (*as adjective*): *a magenta filter* **2** another name for **fuchsin** [c19: named after *Magenta*, Italy, alluding to the blood shed in a battle there (1859)]

Maggiore (ˌmædʒɪˈɔːrɪ; *Italian* madˈdʒore) *n* Lake Maggiore a lake in N Italy and S Switzerland, in the S Lepontine Alps

maggot (ˈmæɡət) *n* **1** the soft limbless larva of dipterous insects, esp the housefly and blowfly, occurring in decaying organic matter **2** *rare* a fancy or whim [c14: from earlier *mathek*; related to Old Norse *mathkr* worm, Old English *matha*, Old High German *mado* grub]

maggoty (ˈmæɡətɪ) *adj* **1** relating to, resembling, or ridden with maggots **2** *Austral slang* annoyed, angry

Magherafelt (ˈmæhərəˌfɛlt) *n* a district of N Northern Ireland, in Co Londonderry. Pop: 40 837 (2003 est). Area: 572 sq km (221 sq miles)

Maghreb *or* **Maghrib** (ˈmʌɡrəb) *n* NW Africa, including Morocco, Algeria, Tunisia, and sometimes Libya [from Arabic, literally: the West] > **Maghrebi** *or* **ˈMaghribi** *adj, n*

magi (ˈmeɪdʒaɪ) *pl n, sing* **magus** (ˈmeɪɡəs) **1** the Zoroastrian priests of the ancient Medes and Persians **2** the three magi the wise men from the East who came to do homage to the infant Jesus (Matthew 2:1–12) and traditionally called Caspar, Melchior, and Balthazar > **magian** (ˈmeɪdʒɪən) *adj*

magic (ˈmædʒɪk) *n* **1** the art that, by use of spells, supposedly invokes supernatural powers to influence events; sorcery **2** the practice of this art **3** the practice of illusory tricks to entertain other people; conjuring **4** any mysterious or extraordinary quality or power **5** like magic very quickly ▷ *adj* Also: **magical 6** of or relating to magic: *a magic spell* **7** possessing or considered to possess mysterious powers: *a magic wand* **8** unaccountably enchanting: *magic beauty* **9** *informal* wonderful; marvellous; exciting ▷ *vb* -ics, -icking, -icked (*tr*) **10** to transform or produce by or as if by magic **11** (foll by *away*) to cause to disappear by or as if by magic [c14: via Old French *magique*, from Greek *magikē* witchcraft, from *magos* Magus] > **ˈmagical** *adj* > **ˈmagically** *adv*

magic bullet *n informal* any therapeutic agent, esp one in the early stages of development, reputed to be very effective in treating a condition, such as a malignant tumour, by specifically targeting the diseased tissue

magic eye *n* a miniature cathode-ray tube in some radio receivers, on the screen of which a pattern is displayed in order to assist tuning

magician (məˈdʒɪʃən) *n* **1** another term for **conjuror 2** a person who practises magic **3** a person who has extraordinary skill, influence, or qualities

magic lantern *n* an early type of slide projector

magic mushroom *n informal* any of various types of fungi that contain a hallucinogenic substance, esp *Psilocybe mexicana*, which contains psilocybin

magic realism *or* **magical realism** *n* a style of painting or writing that depicts images or scenes of surreal fantasy in a representational or realistic way > magic realist *or* magical realist *n*

magic square *n* a square array of rows of integers arranged so that the sum of the integers is the same when taken vertically, horizontally, or diagonally

magic wand *n* **1** a thin rod brandished by a conjuror in peforming magic tricks **2** any seemingly magical solution to a difficult problem: *there is no magic wand for us to fix it*

Maginot line (ˈmæʒɪˌnəʊ; *French* maʒino) *n* **1** a line of fortifications built by France to defend its border with Germany prior to World War II; it proved ineffective against the German invasion **2** any line of defence in which blind confidence is placed [named after André Maginot (1877–1932), French minister of war when the fortifications were begun in 1929]

magisterial (ˌmædʒɪˈstɪərɪəl) *adj* **1** commanding; authoritative **2** domineering; dictatorial **3** of or relating to a teacher or person of similar status **4** of or relating to a magistrate [c17: from Late Latin *magisteriālis*, from *magister* master] > ˌmagisˈterially *adv*

magistracy (ˈmædʒɪstrəsɪ) *or* **magistrature** (ˈmædʒɪstrəˌtjʊə) *n, pl* -cies *or* -tures **1** the office or function of a magistrate **2** magistrates collectively **3** the district under the jurisdiction of a magistrate

magistral (məˈdʒɪstrəl) *adj* **1** of, relating to, or characteristic of a master **2** *pharmacol obsolete* made up according to a special prescription [c16: from Latin *magistrālis* concerning a master, from *magister* master] > magistrality (ˌmædʒɪˈstrælɪtɪ) *n*

magistrate (ˈmædʒɪˌstreɪt, -strɪt) *n* **1** a public officer concerned with the administration of law **2** another name for **justice of the peace** [c17: from Latin *magistrātus*, from *magister* master] > ˈmagisˌtrateship *n*

magistrates' court *n* (in England) a court of summary jurisdiction held before two or more justices of the peace or a stipendiary magistrate to deal with minor crimes, certain civil actions, and preliminary hearings

Maglemosian *or* **Maglemosean** (ˌmæɡləˈməʊzɪən) *n* **1** the first Mesolithic culture of N Europe, dating from 8000 BC to about 5000 BC: important for the rare wooden objects that have been preserved, such as dugout canoes ▷ *adj* **2** designating or relating to this culture [C20: named after the site at *Maglemose*, Denmark, where the culture was first classified]

magma ('mægmə) *n*, *pl* -mas or -mata (-mətə) **1** a paste or suspension consisting of a finely divided solid dispersed in a liquid **2** hot molten rock, usually formed in the earth's upper mantle, some of which finds its way into the crust and onto the earth's surface, where it solidifies to form igneous rock [C15, from Latin: dregs (of an ointment), from Greek: salve made by kneading, from *massein* to knead] > magmatic (mæg'mætɪk) *adj*

Magna Carta or **Magna Charta** ('mægnə 'kɑːtə) *n English history* the charter granted by King John at Runnymede in 1215, recognizing the rights and privileges of the barons, church, and freemen [Medieval Latin: great charter]

Magna Graecia ('mægnə 'griːʃə) *n* (in the ancient world) S Italy, where numerous colonies were founded by Greek cities [Latin: Great Greece]

magnanimity (,mægnə'nɪmɪtɪ) *n*, *pl* -ties generosity [C14: via Old French from Latin *magnanimitās*, from *magnus* great + *animus* soul]

magnanimous (mæg'nænɪməs) *adj* generous and noble [C16: from Latin *magnanimus* great-souled] > mag'nanimously *adv*

magnate ('mægneɪt, -nɪt) *n* **1** a person of power and rank in any sphere, esp in industry **2** *history* a great nobleman [C15: back formation from earlier *magnates* from Late Latin: great men, plural of *magnās*, from Latin *magnus* great] > 'magnate,ship *n*

magnesia (mæg'niːʃə) *n* another name for **magnesium oxide** [C14: via Medieval Latin from Greek *Magnēsia*, of *Magnēs* ancient mineral-rich region] > mag'nesian or magnesic (mæg'niːsɪk) *adj*

magnesium (mæg'niːzɪəm) *n* a light silvery-white metallic element of the alkaline earth series that burns with an intense white flame, occurring principally in magnesite, dolomite, and carnallite: used in light structural alloys, flashbulbs, flares, and fireworks. Symbol: Mg; atomic no: 12; atomic wt: 24.3050; valency: 2; relative density: 1.738; melting pt: 650°C; boiling pt: 1090°C [C19: New Latin, from MAGNESIA]

magnesium oxide *n* a white tasteless substance occurring naturally as periclase: used as an antacid and laxative and in refractory materials, such as crucibles and fire bricks. Formula: MgO. Also called: magnesia

magnet ('mægnɪt) *n* **1** a body that can attract certain substances, such as iron or steel, as a result of a magnetic field; a piece of ferromagnetic substance. See also **electromagnet 2** a person or thing that exerts a great attraction [C15: via Latin from Greek *magnēs*, shortened from *ho Magnēs lithos* the Magnesian stone. See MAGNESIA]

magnetar ('mægnɪtɑː) *n* a type of neutron star that has a very intense magnetic field, over 1000 times greater than that of a pulsar [C20: from MAGNET(IC) (ST)AR, on the model of QUASAR]

magnetic (mæg'nɛtɪk) *adj* **1** of, producing, or operated by means of magnetism **2** of or concerned with a magnet **3** of or concerned with the magnetism of the earth: *the magnetic equator* **4** capable of being magnetized **5** exerting a powerful attraction: *a magnetic personality* > mag'netically *adv*

magnetic constant *n* the permeability of free space, which has the value $4\pi \times 10^{-7}$ henry per metre

magnetic declination *n* the angle that a compass needle makes with the direction of the geographical north pole at any given point on the earth's surface

magnetic dip or **magnetic inclination** *n* another name for **dip** (sense 25)

magnetic dipole moment *n* a measure of the magnetic strength of a magnet or current-carrying coil, expressed as the torque per unit magnetic-flux density produced when the magnet or coil is set with its axis perpendicular to the magnetic field

magnetic disk *n computing* another name for **disk** (sense 2)

magnetic equator *n* an imaginary line on the earth's surface, near the equator, at all points on which there is no magnetic dip

magnetic field *n* a field of force surrounding a permanent magnet or a moving charged particle, in which another permanent magnet or moving charge experiences a force

magnetic flux *n* a measure of the strength of a magnetic field over a given area perpendicular to it, equal to the product of the area and the magnetic flux density through it. Symbol: φ

magnetic mine *n* a mine designed to activate when a magnetic field such as that generated by the metal of a ship's hull is detected

magnetic needle *n* a slender magnetized rod used in certain instruments, such as the magnetic compass, for indicating the direction of a magnetic field

magnetic north *n* the direction in which a compass needle points, at an angle (the declination) from the direction of true (geographic) north

magnetic pick-up *n* a type of record player pick-up in which the stylus moves an iron core in a coil, causing a changing magnetic field that produces the current

magnetic pole *n* **1** either of two regions in a magnet where the magnetic induction is concentrated **2** either of two variable points on the earth's surface towards which a magnetic needle points, where the lines of force of the earth's magnetic field are vertical

magnetic resonance *n* the response by atoms, molecules, or nuclei subjected to a magnetic field to radio waves or other forms of energy: used in medicine for scanning. See **magnetic resonance imaging**, **magnetic resonance angiography**

magnetic resonance angiography *n* a form of magnetic resonance imaging in which either the injection of a magnetic resonance contrast agent or the movement of the blood provides information of value in diagnosis. Abbreviation: MRA

magnetic resonance imaging *n* a noninvasive medical diagnostic technique in which the absorption and transmission of high-frequency radio waves are analysed as they irradiate the hydrogen atoms in water molecules and other tissue components placed in a strong magnetic field. This computerized analysis provides a powerful aid to the diagnosis and treatment planning of many diseases, including cancer. Abbreviation: MRI

magnetic storm *n* a sudden severe disturbance of the earth's magnetic field, caused by emission of charged particles from the sun

magnetic stripe *n* (across the back of various types of cheque card, credit card, etc) a dark stripe of magnetic material consisting of several tracks onto which information may be coded and which may be read or written to electronically

magnetic tape *n* a long narrow plastic or metal strip coated or impregnated with a ferromagnetic material such as iron oxide, used to record sound or video signals or to store information in computers

magnetism ('mægnɪ,tɪzəm) *n* **1** the property of attraction displayed by magnets **2** any of a class of phenomena in which a field of force is caused by a moving electric charge **3** the branch of physics concerned with magnetic phenomena **4** powerful attraction

magnetite ('mægnɪ,taɪt) *n* a black magnetic mineral, found in igneous and metamorphic rocks and as a separate deposit. It is a source of iron. Composition: iron oxide. Formula: Fe_3O_4. Crystal structure: cubic

magnetize or **magnetise** ('mægnɪ,taɪz) *vb* (*tr*) **1** to make (a substance or object) magnetic **2** to attract strongly > ,magnet'izable or ,magnet'isable *adj* > ,magneti'zation or ,magneti'sation *n* > 'magnet,izer or 'magnet,iser *n*

magneto (mæg'niːtəʊ) *n*, *pl* -tos a small electric generator in which the magnetic field is produced by a permanent magnet, esp one for providing the spark in an internal-combustion engine [C19: short for *magnetoelectric generator*]

magneto- *combining form* indicating magnetism or magnetic properties: *magnetosphere*

magnetoelectricity (mæg,niːtəʊɪlɛk'trɪsɪtɪ) *n* electricity

produced by the action of magnetic fields
> mag,netoe'lectric or mag,netoe'lectrical adj

magnetometer (,mægnɪ'tɒmɪtə) n any instrument for measuring the intensity or direction of a magnetic field, esp the earth's field > ,magne'tometry n

magnetomotive (mæg,ni:təʊ'məʊtɪv) adj causing a magnetic flux

magnetosphere (mæg'ni:təʊ,sfɪə) n the region surrounding a planet, such as the earth, in which the behaviour of charged particles is controlled by the planet's magnetic field

magnetron ('mægnɪ,trɒn) n an electronic valve with two coaxial electrodes used with an applied magnetic field to generate high-power microwave oscillations, esp for use in radar [c20: from MAGNET + ELECTRON]

magnet school n a school that provides a focus on one subject area throughout its curriculum in order to attract, often from an early age, pupils who wish to specialize in this subject

magnific (mæg'nɪfɪk) or **magnifical** adj archaic magnificent, grandiose, or pompous [c15: via Old French from Latin magnificus great in deeds, from magnus great + facere to do] > mag'nifically adv

Magnificat (mæg'nɪfɪ,kæt) n Christianity the hymn of the Virgin Mary (Luke 1:46-55), used as a canticle [from the opening phrase in the Latin version, Magnificat anima mea Dominum (my soul doth magnify the Lord)]

magnification (,mægnɪfɪ'keɪʃən) n 1 the act of magnifying or the state of being magnified 2 the degree to which something is magnified 3 a copy, photograph, drawing, etc, of something magnified 4 a measure of the ability of a lens or other optical instrument to magnify, expressed as the ratio of the size of the image to that of the object

magnificence (mæg'nɪfɪsəns) n the quality of being magnificent [c14: via French from Latin magnificentia]

magnificent (mæg'nɪfɪsᵊnt) adj 1 splendid or impressive in appearance 2 superb or very fine 3 (esp of ideas) noble or elevated [c16: from Latin magnificentio more splendid; irregular comparative of magnificus great in deeds; see MAGNIFIC] > mag'nificently adv

magnifico (mæg'nɪfɪ,kəʊ) n, pl -coes a magnate; grandee [c16: Italian from Latin magnificus; see MAGNIFIC]

magnify ('mægnɪ,faɪ) vb -fies, -fying, -fied 1 to increase, cause to increase, or be increased in apparent size, as through the action of a lens, microscope, etc 2 to exaggerate or become exaggerated in importance: don't magnify your troubles 3 (tr) archaic to glorify [c14: via Old French from Latin magnificāre to praise] > 'magni,fiable adj

magnifying glass or **magnifier** n a convex lens used to produce an enlarged image of an object

magniloquent (mæg'nɪləkwənt) adj (of speech) lofty in style; grandiloquent [c17: from Latin magnus great + loquī to speak] > mag'niloquence n > mag'niloquently adv

Magnitogorsk (Russian məgnita'gɔrsk) n a city in central Russia, on the Ural River: founded in 1930 to exploit local magnetite ores; site of one of the world's largest metallurgical plants. Pop: 415 000 (2005 est)

magnitude ('mægnɪ,tjuːd) n 1 relative importance or significance: a problem of the first magnitude 2 relative size or extent: the magnitude of the explosion 3 maths a number assigned to a quantity, such as weight, and used as a basis of comparison for the measurement of similar quantities 4 Also called: apparent magnitude astronomy the apparent brightness of a celestial body expressed on a numerical scale on which bright stars have a low value. Values are measured by eye (visual magnitude) or more accurately by photometric or photographic methods, and range from −26.7 (the sun), through 1.5 (Sirius), down to about +30. Each integral value represents a brightness 2.512 times greater than the next highest integral value 5 Also called: earthquake magnitude geology a measure of the size of an earthquake based on the quantity of energy released: specified on the Richter scale [c14: from Latin magnitūdō size, from magnus great]

magnolia (mæg'nəʊlɪə) n 1 any tree or shrub of the magnoliaceous genus Magnolia of Asia and North America: cultivated for their white, pink, purple, or yellow showy flowers 2 the flower of any of these plants 3 a very pale pinkish-white or purplish-white colour [c18: New Latin, named after Pierre Magnol (1638–1715), French botanist]

magnox (mægnɒks) n an alloy consisting mostly of magnesium with small amounts of aluminium and other metals, used in fuel elements of nuclear reactors [c20: from mag(nesium) n(o) ox(idation)]

magnox reactor n a nuclear reactor using carbon dioxide as the coolant, graphite as the moderator, and uranium cased in magnox as the fuel

magnum ('mægnəm) n, pl -nums a wine bottle holding the equivalent of two normal bottles (approximately 52 fluid ounces) [c18: from Latin: a big thing, from magnus large]

magnum opus n a great work of art or literature, esp the greatest single work of an artist [Latin]

Magog ('meɪgɒg) n See **Gog and Magog**

magpie ('mæg,paɪ) n 1 any of various passerine birds of the genus Pica, esp P. pica, having a black-and-white plumage, long tail, and a chattering call: family Corvidae (crows, etc) 2 any of various similar birds of the Australian family Cracticidae 3 Brit a person who hoards small objects 4 a person who chatters 5 a the outmost ring but one on a target b a shot that hits this ring [c17: from Mag diminutive of Margaret, used to signify a chatterbox + PIE²]

Magritte (French magrit) n **René** (rəne). 1898–1967, Belgian surrealist painter. By juxtaposing incongruous objects, depicted with meticulous realism, his works create a bizarre and disturbing impression

maguey ('mægweɪ) n 1 any of various tropical American agave plants of the genera Agave or Furcraea, esp one that yields a fibre or is used in making an alcoholic beverage 2 the fibre from any of these plants, used esp for rope [c16: Spanish, from Taino]

magus ('meɪgəs) n, pl magi ('meɪdʒaɪ) 1 a Zoroastrian priest 2 an astrologer, sorcerer, or magician of ancient times [c14: from Latin, from Greek magos, from Old Persian magus magician]

Magus ('meɪgəs) n Simon Magus New Testament a sorcerer who tried to buy spiritual powers from the apostles (Acts 8:9-24)

Magyar ('mægjɑː) n 1 pl -yars a member of the predominant ethnic group of Hungary, also found in NW Siberia 2 the Hungarian language ▷ adj 3 of or relating to the Magyars or their language 4 sewing of or relating to a style of sleeve cut in one piece with the bodice

Magyarország ('mɒdjɔrorsaːg) n the Hungarian name for **Hungary**

Mahabharata (mə,hɑː'bɑːrətə), **Mahabharatam** or **Mahabharatum** (mə,hɑː'bɑːrətəm) n an epic Sanskrit poem of India, dealing chiefly with the struggle between two rival families. It contains many separate episodes, the most notable of which is the Bhagavad-Gita [Sanskrit, from mahā great + bhārata story]

Mahajanga (,mæhə'dʒæŋgə) n a port in NW Madagascar, on Bombetoka Bay. Pop: 147 000 (2005 est). Former name: **Majunga**

Mahalla el Kubra (mə'hɑːlə ɛl 'kuːbrə) n a city in N Egypt, on the Nile delta: one of the largest diversified textile centres in Egypt Pop: 433 000 (2005 est)

Mahanadi (mə'hɑːnədɪ) n a river in E India, rising in Chhattisgarh and flowing north, then south and east to the Bay of Bengal. Length: 885 km (550 miles)

maharajah or **maharaja** (,mɑː'rɑːdʒə) n any of various Indian princes, esp any of the rulers of the former native states [c17: Hindi, from mahā great + RAJAH]

maharani or **maharanee** (,mɑː'rɑːniː) n 1 the wife of a maharajah 2 a woman holding the rank of maharajah [c19: from Hindi, from mahā great + RANI]

Maharashtra (,mɑːhə'ræʃtrə) n a state of W central India, formed in 1960 from the Marathi-speaking S and E parts of former Bombay state: lies mainly on the Deccan plateau; mainly agricultural. Capital: Mumbai (Bombay). Pop: 96 752 247 (2001). Area: 307 690 sq km

(118 800 sq miles)

maharishi (ˌmɑːhɑːˈriːʃɪ, məˈhɑːriːʃɪ) n *Hinduism* a Hindu teacher of religious and mystical knowledge [from Hindi, from *mahā* great + *rishi* sage, saint]

mahatma (məˈhɑːtmə, -ˈhæt-) n (*sometimes capital*) 1 *Hinduism* a Brahman sage 2 *theosophy* an adept or sage [c19: from Sanskrit *mahātman*, from *mahā* great + *ātman* soul]

Mahavira (ˌmɑːhəˈvɪərə) n the title of **Vardhamana** 599–527 BC, Indian ascetic and religious teacher, regarded as the founder of Jainism

Mahayana (ˌmɑːhəˈjɑːnə) n a a liberal Buddhist school of Tibet, China, and Japan, whose adherents aim to disseminate Buddhist doctrines, seeking enlightenment not for themselves alone, but for all sentient beings b (*as modifier*): *Mahayana Buddhism* [from Sanskrit, from *mahā* great + *yāna* vehicle]

Mahdi (ˈmɑːdɪ) n 1 the title assumed by *Mohammed Ahmed*. ?1843–85, Sudanese military leader, who led a revolt against Egypt (1881) and captured Khartoum (1885) 2 *Islam* any of a number of Muslim messiahs expected to convert all mankind to Islam [Arabic *mahdīy* one who is guided, from *madā* to guide aright] > ˈMahdism n > ˈMahdist n, adj

Mahé (mɑːˈheɪ) n an island in the Indian Ocean, the chief island of the Seychelles. Capital: Victoria. Pop: 71 900 (2002 est). Area: 147 sq km (57 sq miles)

Mahfouz or **Mahfuz** (mɑːˈfuːz) n **Naguib** (nɑːˈɡiːb). 1911–2006, Egyptian novelist and writer, author of the trilogy of novels *Bain al-Kasrain* (1945–57). His novel *Children of Gebelawi* (1959) was banned by the Muslim authorities in Egypt Nobel prize for literature 1988

mahi-mahi (ˈmɑːhɪˌmɑːhɪ) n another name for: **dolphin** (sense 3) [c20: from Hawaiian, literally: strong-strong]

mah jong or **mah-jongg** (ˌmɑːˈdʒɒŋ) n a game of Chinese origin, usually played by four people, in which tiles bearing various designs are drawn and discarded until one player has an entire hand of winning combinations [from Chinese, literally: sparrows]

Mahler (ˈmɑːlə) n **Gustav** (ˈɡʊstaf). 1860–1911, Austrian composer and conductor, whose music links the romantic tradition of the 19th century with the music of the 20th century. His works include nine complete symphonies for large orchestras, the symphonic song cycle *Das Lied von der Erde* (1908), and the song cycle *Kindertotenlieder* (1902)

mahlstick (ˈmɔːlˌstɪk) n a variant spelling of **maulstick**

mahogany (məˈhɒɡənɪ) n, pl -nies 1 any of various tropical American trees of the meliaceous genus *Swietenia*, esp *S. mahogoni* and *S. macrophylla*, valued for their hard reddish-brown wood 2 any of several trees with similar wood, such as African mahogany (genus *Khaya*) and Philippine mahogany (genus *Shorea*) 3 a the wood of any of these trees: *a mahogany table* 4 a a reddish-brown colour b (*as modifier*): *mahogany skin* [c17: origin obscure]

Mahomet (məˈhɒmɪt) n same as **Mohammed**

Mahometan (məˈhɒmɪt³n) n, adj a name formerly in Western usage but never used among Muslims for the Muslim religion

mahonia (məˈhəʊnɪə) n any evergreen berberidaceous shrub of the Asian and American genus *Mahonia*, esp *M. aquifolium*: cultivated for their ornamental spiny divided leaves and clusters of small yellow flowers [c19: New Latin, named after Bernard *McMahon* (died 1816), American botanist]

Mahound (məˈhaʊnd, -ˈhuːnd) n an archaic name for: **Mohammed** [c16: from Old French *Mahun*]

mahout (məˈhaʊt) n (in India and the East Indies) an elephant driver or keeper [c17: Hindi *mahāut*, from Sanskrit *mahāmātra* of great measure, originally a title]

Mähren (ˈmɛːrən) n the German name for **Moravia¹**

mahseer (ˈmɑːsɪə) n any of various large freshwater Indian cyprinid fishes, such as *Barbus tor* [from Hindi]

Mahy (ˈmɑːhɪ) n **Margaret**. born 1936, New Zealand writer for children. Her books include *A Lion in the Meadow* (1969), *The Changeover* (1984), and *Alchemy* (2002)

Maia (ˈmaɪə) n *Greek myth* the eldest of the seven Pleiades, mother by Zeus of Hermes

maid (meɪd) n 1 *archaic or literary* a young unmarried girl; maiden 2 a a female servant b (*in combination*): *a housemaid* 3 a spinster [c12: shortened form of **MAIDEN**]

maiden (ˈmeɪd³n) n 1 *archaic or literary* a a young unmarried girl, esp when a virgin b (*as modifier*): *a maiden blush* 2 *horse racing* a a horse that has never won a race b (*as modifier*): *a maiden race* 3 *cricket* See **maiden over** 4 (*modifier*) of or relating to an older unmarried woman: *a maiden aunt* 5 (*modifier*) of or involving an initial experience or attempt: *a maiden voyage; maiden speech* 6 (*modifier*) (of a person or thing) untried; unused 7 (*modifier*) (of a place) never trodden, penetrated, or captured [Old English *mægden*; related to Old High German *magad*, Old Norse *mogr* young man, Old Irish *mug* slave] > ˈmaidenish adj > ˈmaiden-ˌlike adj

maidenhair fern or **maidenhair** (ˈmeɪd³nˌhɛə) n any fern of the cosmopolitan genus *Adiantum*, esp *A. capillis-veneris*, having delicate fan-shaped fronds with small pale-green leaflets: family *Adiantaceae* [c15: so called from the hairlike appearance of its fine fronds]

maidenhair tree n another name for **ginkgo**

maidenhead (ˈmeɪd³nˌhɛd) n 1 a nontechnical word for the: **hymen** 2 virginity; maidenhood [c13: from *maiden* + *-hed*, variant of *-HOOD*]

Maidenhead (ˈmeɪd³nˌhɛd) n a town in S England, in Windsor and Maidenhead unitary authority, Berkshire, on the River Thames. Pop: 58 848 (2001)

maidenhood (ˈmeɪd³nˌhʊd) n 1 the time during which a woman is a maiden or a virgin 2 the condition of being a maiden or virgin

maidenly (ˈmeɪd³nlɪ) adj of or befitting a maiden > ˈmaidenliness n

maiden name n a woman's surname before marriage

maiden over n *cricket* an over in which no runs are scored

maid of honour n 1 *US & Canadian* the principal unmarried attendant of a bride 2 *Brit* a small tart with an almond-flavoured filling 3 an unmarried lady attending a queen or princess

Maid of Orléans n the. another name for: **Joan of Arc**

maidservant (ˈmeɪdˌsɜːvənt) n a female servant

Maidstone (ˈmeɪdstən, -ˌstəʊn) n a town in SE England, administrative centre of Kent, on the River Medway. Pop: 89 684 (2001)

Maiduguri (ˌmaɪdʊˈɡuːrɪ) n a city in NE Nigeria, capital of Bornu State; agricultural trade centre. Pop: 828 000 (2005 est). Also called: Yerwa-Maiduguri

maihem (ˈmeɪhɛm) n a variant spelling of **mayhem**

Maikop (*Russian* maˈjkɔp) n a city in SW Russia, capital of the Adygei Republic: extensive oilfields to the southwest; mineral springs. Pop: 165 000 (2005 est)

mail¹ (meɪl) n 1 letters, packages, etc, that are transported and delivered by the post office. Also called (esp Brit): **post¹** 2 the postal system 3 a single collection or delivery of mail 4 a train, ship, or aircraft that carries mail 5 short for **electronic mail** 6 (*modifier*) of, involving, or used to convey mail: *a mail train* ▷ vb (tr) 7 *chiefly US & Canadian* to send by mail. Usual Brit word: **post¹** 8 to contact (a person) by electronic mail 9 to send (a message, document, etc) by electronic mail [c13: from Old French *male* bag, probably from Old High German *malha* wallet] > ˈmailable adj

mail² (meɪl) n 1 a type of flexible armour consisting of riveted metal rings or links 2 the hard protective shell of such animals as the turtle and lobster ▷ vb 3 (tr) to clothe or arm with mail [c14: from Old French *maille* mesh, from Latin *macula* spot]

mailbag (ˈmeɪlˌbæɡ) or **mailsack** n a large bag used for transporting or delivering mail

mailbox (ˈmeɪlˌbɒks) n 1 *chiefly US & Canadian* a a slot, usually covered with a hinged flap, through which letters, etc are delivered to a building b a private box into which letters, etc, are delivered. Also called (in Britain and certain other countries): **letter box** 2 (on a computer) the directory in which e-mail messages are stored; also used of the icon that can be clicked to provide access to e-mails

Mailer (ˈmeɪlə) n **Norman**. 1923–2007, US author. His works, which are frequently critical of modern

American society, include the war novel *The Naked and the Dead* (1948), *An American Dream* (1965), his account of the 1967 peace march on Washington *The Armies of the Night* (1968), *The Executioner's Song* (1979), and *Barbary Shore* (1998)

mailing list *n* a register of names and addresses to which advertising matter, etc, is sent by post or electronic mail

Maillol (*French* majɔl) *n* **Aristide** (aristid). 1861–1944, French sculptor, esp of monumental female nudes

maillot (mæˈjəʊ) *n* **1** tights worn for ballet, gymnastics, etc **2** a woman's swimsuit **3** a jersey [from French]

mailman ('meɪlˌmæn) *n*, *pl* -men *chiefly US & Canadian* another name for **postman**

mail merging *n computing* a software facility that can produce a large number of personalized letters by combining a file containing a list of names and addresses with one containing a single standard document

mail order *n* **1** an order for merchandise sent by post **2 a** a system of buying and selling merchandise through the post **b** (*as modifier*): *a mail-order firm*

mailshot ('meɪlˌʃɒt) *n* a circular, leaflet, or other advertising material sent by post, or the posting of such material to a large group of people at one time

maim (meɪm) *vb* (*tr*) **1** to mutilate, cripple, or disable a part of the body of (a person or animal) **2** to make defective [c14: from Old French *mahaignier* to wound, probably of Germanic origin]

mai mai ('maɪ maɪ) *n NZ* a duck-shooter's shelter; hide [probably from Australian aboriginal *mia-mia* shelter]

Maimonides (maɪˈmɒnɪˌdiːz) *n* also called **Rabbi** *Moses ben Maimon*. 1135–1204, Jewish philosopher, physician, and jurist, born in Spain. He codified Jewish law in *Mishneh Torah* (1180) > Maiˌmoniˈdean *adj, n*

main¹ (meɪn) *adj* (*prenominal*) **1** chief or principal in rank, importance, size, etc **2** sheer or utmost (esp in the phrase **by main force**) **3** *nautical* of, relating to, or denoting any gear, such as a stay or sail, belonging to the mainmast ▷ *n* **4** a principal pipe, conduit, duct, or line in a system used to distribute water, electricity, etc **5** (*plural*) **a** the main distribution network for water, gas, or electricity **b** (*as modifier*): *mains voltage* **6** the chief or most important part or consideration **7** great strength or force (now chiefly in the phrase (**with**) **might and main**) **8** *literary* the open ocean **9** *archaic* short for **Spanish Main 10** *archaic* short for **mainland 11** in the main *or* for the main on the whole; for the most part [c13: from Old English *mægen* strength]

main² (meɪn) *n* **1** a throw of the dice in dice games **2** a cockfighting contest **3** a match in archery, boxing, etc [c16: of unknown origin]

Main (meɪn; *German* main) *n* a river in central and W Germany, flowing west through Würzburg and Frankfurt to the Rhine. Length: about 515 km (320 miles)

mainbrace ('meɪnˌbreɪs) *n nautical* a brace attached to the main yard

main clause *n grammar* a clause that can stand alone as a sentence

Maine (meɪn) *n* a state of the northeastern US, on the Atlantic: chiefly hilly, with many lakes, rivers, and forests. Capital: Augusta. Pop: 1 305 728 (2003 est). Area: 86 156 sq km (33 265 sq miles). Abbreviations: Me., or (with zip code) ME

Maine-et-Loire (*French* mɛnelwar) *n* a department of W France, in Pays de la Loire region. Capital: Angers. Pop: 745 486 (2003 est). Area: 7218 sq km (2815 sq miles)

mainframe ('meɪnˌfreɪm) *n* **1 a** a high-speed general-purpose computer, usually with a large store capacity **b** (*as modifier*): *mainframe systems* **2** the central processing unit of a computer

mainland ('meɪnlənd) *n* the main part of a land mass as opposed to an island or peninsula > 'mainlander *n*

Mainland ('meɪnlənd) *n* **1** an island off N Scotland: the largest of the Shetland Islands. Chief town: Lerwick. Pop: 17 550 (2001). Area: about 583 sq km (225 sq miles) **2** Also called: **Pomona** an island off N Scotland: the largest of the Orkney Islands. Chief town: Kirkwall. Pop: 15 315 (2001). Area: 492 sq km (190 sq miles) **3** the Mainland *NZ* a South Islanders' name for **South Island**

main line *n* **1** *railways* **a** the trunk route between two points, usually fed by branch lines **b** (*as modifier*): *a main-line station* **2** *US* a main road ▷ *vb* **3** (*intr*) *slang* to inject a drug into a vein ▷ *adj* **mainline 4** having an important position, esp having responsibility for the main areas of activity > 'main,liner *n*

mainly ('meɪnlɪ) *adv* for the most part; to the greatest extent; principally

main market *n* the market for trading in the listed securities of companies on the London Stock Exchange. See **Third Market**

mainmast ('meɪnˌmɑːst) *n nautical* the chief mast of a sailing vessel with two or more masts, being the foremast of a yawl, ketch, or dandy and the second mast from the bow of most others

mainsail ('meɪnˌseɪl; *Nautical* 'meɪnsəl) *n nautical* the largest and lowermost sail on the mainmast

mainsheet ('meɪnˌʃiːt) *n nautical* the line used to control the angle of the mainsail to the wind

mainspring ('meɪnˌsprɪŋ) *n* **1** the principal power spring of a mechanism, esp in a watch or clock **2** the chief cause or motive of something

mainstay ('meɪnˌsteɪ) *n* **1** *nautical* the forestay that braces the mainmast **2** a chief support

mainstream ('meɪnˌstriːm) *n* **1 a** the main current (of a river, cultural trend, etc): *in the mainstream of modern literature* **b** (*as modifier*): *mainstream politics* ▷ *adj* **2** of or relating to the style of jazz that lies between the traditional and the modern

mainstreeting ('meɪnˌstriːtɪŋ) *n Canadian* the practice of a politician walking about the streets of a town or city to gain votes and greet supporters

maintain (meɪnˈteɪn) *vb* (*tr*) **1** to continue or retain; keep in existence **2** to keep in proper or good condition **3** to support a style of living: *the money maintained us for a month* **4** (*takes a clause as object*) to state or assert: *he maintained that Talbot was wrong* **5** to defend against contradiction; uphold: *she maintained her innocence* **6** to defend against physical attack [c13: from Old French *maintenir*, ultimately from Latin *manū tenēre* to hold in the hand] > main'tainable *adj* > main'tainer *n*

maintenance ('meɪntɪnəns) *n* **1** the act of maintaining or the state of being maintained **2** a means of support; livelihood **3** (*modifier*) of or relating to the maintaining of buildings, machinery, etc: *maintenance man* **4** *law* (formerly unlawful) the interference in a legal action by a person having no interest in it, as by providing funds to continue the action **5** *law* a provision ordered to be made by way of periodical payments or a lump sum, as after a divorce for a spouse [c14: from Old French; see MAINTAIN]

Maintenon (*French* mɛ̃tnɔ̃) *n* **Marquise de**, title of *Françoise d'Aubigné*. 1635–1719, the mistress and, from about 1685, second wife of Louis XIV

maintop ('meɪnˌtɒp) *n* a top or platform at the head of the mainmast

main-topmast *n nautical* the mast immediately above the mainmast

maintopsail (ˌmeɪnˈtɒpseɪl; *Nautical* ˌmeɪnˈtɒpsəl) *n nautical* a topsail set on the mainmast

main yard *n nautical* a yard for a square mainsail

Mainz (*German* maints) *n* a port in W Germany, capital of the Rhineland-Palatinate, at the confluence of the Main and Rhine: an archbishopric from about 780 until 1801; important in the 15th century for the development of printing (by Johann Gutenberg). Pop: 185 532 (2003 est). French name: **Mayence**

maiolica (məˈjɒlɪkə) *n* a variant of **majolica**

maisonette *or* **maisonnette** (ˌmeɪzəˈnɛt) *n* self-contained living accommodation often occupying two floors of a larger house and having its own outside entrance [c19: from French, diminutive of *maison* house]

Maistre (*French* mɛstrə) *n* **Josephe de** (ʒozɛf də). 1753–1821, French writer and diplomat, noted for his extreme reactionary views, expounded in such works as *Les Soirées de St Petersbourg* (1821)

Maitland¹ ('meɪtlənd) *n* a town in SE Australia, in E New South Wales: industrial centre of an agricultural region. Pop: 53 470 (2001)

Maitland² ('meɪtlənd) *n* Frederic William. 1850–1906, English legal historian

maître d'hôtel (ˌmɛtrə dəʊ'tɛl; *French* mɛtrə dotɛl) *n, pl* maîtres d'hôtel 1 a head waiter or steward 2 the manager or owner of a hotel [c16: from French: master of (the) hotel]

maize (meɪz) *n* 1 Also called: Indian corn a a tall annual grass, *Zea mays*, cultivated for its yellow edible grains, which develop on a spike b the grain of this plant, used for food, fodder, and as a source of oil. Usual US and Canadian name: corn¹ See also sweet corn 2 a a yellow colour b (*as modifier*): *a maize gown* [c16: from Spanish *maiz*, from Taino *mahiz*]

Maj. *abbreviation* Major

majestic (mə'dʒɛstɪk) *adj* having or displaying majesty or great dignity; grand; lofty > ma'jestically *adv*

majesty ('mædʒɪstɪ) *n* 1 great dignity of bearing; loftiness; grandeur 2 supreme power or authority [c13: from Old French, from Latin *mājestās*; related to Latin *major*, comparative of *magnus* great]

Majesty ('mædʒɪstɪ) *n, pl* -ties (preceded by *Your, His, Her,* or *Their*) a title used to address or refer to a sovereign or the wife or widow of a sovereign

majolica (mə'ʒɒlɪkə, mə'jɒl-) *or* **maiolica** *n* a type of porous pottery glazed with bright metallic oxides that was originally imported into Italy via Majorca and was extensively made in Italy during the Renaissance [c16: from Italian, from Late Latin *Mājorica* Majorca]

major ('meɪdʒə) *n* 1 *military* an officer immediately junior to a lieutenant colonel 2 a person who is superior in a group or class 3 a large or important company: *the oil majors* 4 (often preceded by *the*) *music* a major key, chord, mode, or scale 5 *US, Canadian, Austral & NZ* a the principal field of study of a student at a university, etc b a student who is studying a particular subject as his principal field: *a sociology major* 6 a person who has reached the age of legal majority 7 *logic* a major term or premise 8 a principal or important record company, film company, etc > *adj* 9 larger in extent, number, etc 10 of greater importance or priority 11 very serious or significant 12 main, chief, or principal 13 of, involving, or making up a majority 14 *music* a (of a scale or mode) having notes separated by the interval of a whole tone, except for the third and fourth degrees, and seventh and eighth degrees, which are separated by a semitone b relating to or employing notes from the major scale: *a major key* c (*postpositive*) denoting a specified key or scale as being major: *C major* d denoting a chord or triad having a major third above the root e (in jazz) denoting a major chord with a major seventh added above the root 15 *logic* constituting the major term or major premise of a syllogism 16 *chiefly US, Canadian, Austral & NZ* of or relating to a student's principal field of study at a university, etc 17 *Brit* the elder: used after a schoolboy's surname if he has one or more younger brothers in the same school: *Price major* 18 of full legal age > *vb* 19 (*intr*; usually foll by *in*) *US, Canadian, Austral & NZ* to do one's principal study (in a particular subject): *to major in English literature* 20 (*intr*; usually foll by *on*) to take or deal with as the main area of interest: *the book majors on the peasant dishes* [c15 (*adj*): from Latin, comparative of *magnus* great; c17 (*n*, in military sense): from French, short for SERGEANT MAJOR] > 'majorship *n*

Major ('meɪdʒə) *n* John. born 1943, British Conservative politician: Chancellor of the Exchequer (1989–90); prime minister (1990–97)

Majorca (mə'jɔːkə, -'dʒɔː-) *n* an island in the W Mediterranean: the largest of the Balearic Islands; tourism. Capital: Palma. Pop: 730 778 (2002 est). Area: 3639 sq km (1465 sq miles). Spanish name: **Mallorca**

major-domo (ˌmeɪdʒə'dəʊməʊ) *n, pl* -mos 1 the chief steward or butler of a great household 2 *facetious* a steward or butler [c16: from Spanish *mayordomo*, from Medieval Latin *major domūs* head of the household]

majorette (ˌmeɪdʒə'rɛt) *n* See drum majorette

major general *n* *military* an officer immediately junior to a lieutenant general > 'major-'generalship *or* 'major-'generalcy *n*

majority (mə'dʒɒrɪtɪ) *n, pl* -ties 1 the greater number or part of something 2 (in an election) the number of votes or seats by which the strongest party or candidate beats the combined opposition or the runner-up 3 the largest party or group that votes together in a legislative or deliberative assembly 4 the time of reaching or state of having reached full legal age, when a person is held competent to manage his own affairs, exercise civil rights and duties, etc 5 the rank, office, or commission of major 6 *euphemistic* the dead (esp in the phrases **join the majority, go** *or* **pass over to the majority**) 7 (*modifier*) of, involving, or being a majority: *a majority decision; a majority verdict* 8 in the majority forming or part of the greater number of something [c16: from Medieval Latin *mājoritās*, from MAJOR (*adj*)]

● USAGE The majority of can only refer to a number of
● things or people. When talking about an amount,
● *most of* should be used: *most of* (not *the majority of*) *the*
● *harvest was saved*

major league *n* *US & Canadian* a league of highest classification in baseball, football, hockey, etc

majorly ('meɪdʒəlɪ) *adv* *slang, chiefly US & Canadian* very; really; extremely: *it was majorly important for us to do that*

major orders *pl n* *RC Church* the three higher degrees of holy orders: bishop, priest, and deacon

major premise *n* *logic* the premise of a syllogism containing the predicate of its conclusion

major term *n* *logic* the predicate of the conclusion of a syllogism, also occurring as the subject or predicate in the major premise

Majunga (*French* maʒœɡa) *n* the former name of **Mahajanga**

majuscule ('mædʒə,skjuːl) *n* 1 a large letter, either capital or uncial, used in printing or writing > *adj* 2 relating to, printed, or written in such letters. See minuscule [c18: via French from Latin *mājusculus*, diminutive of *mājor* bigger, MAJOR] > majuscular (mə'dʒʌskjʊlə) *adj*

Makalu ('mʌkə,luː) *n* a massif in NE Nepal, on the border with Tibet in the Himalayas

Makarios III (mə'kɑːrɪ,ɒs) *n* original name *Mikhail Christodoulou Mouskos*. 1913–77, Cypriot archbishop, patriarch, and statesman; first president of the republic of Cyprus (1960–74; 1974–77)

Makassar, Makasar *or* **Macassar** (mə'kæsə, -'kɑː-) *n* a port in central Indonesia, on SW Sulawesi: an important native port before Portuguese (16th century) and Dutch (17th century) control; capital of the Dutch East Indies (1946–49); a major Indonesian distribution and transshipment port. Pop: 1 100 019 (2000). Former name (1971–1999): Ujung Pandang

make (meɪk) *vb* makes, making, made (*mainly tr*) 1 to bring into being by shaping, changing, or combining materials, ideas, etc; form or fashion; create 2 to draw up, establish, or form: *to make a decision; make one's will* 3 to cause to exist, bring about, or produce: *don't make a noise* 4 to cause, compel, or induce: *please make him go away* 5 to appoint or assign, as to a rank or position: *they made him chairman* 6 to constitute: *one swallow doesn't make a summer* 7 (*also intr*) to come or cause to come into a specified state or condition: *to make merry; make someone happy* 8 (*copula*) to be or become through development: *he will make a good teacher* 9 to cause or ensure the success of: *your news has made my day* 10 to amount to: *twelve inches make a foot* 11 to serve as or be suitable for: *that piece of cloth will make a coat* 12 to prepare or put into a fit condition for use: *to make a bed* 13 to be the essential element in or part of: *charm makes a good salesman* 14 to carry out, effect, or do 15 (*intr*; foll by *to, as if to,* or *as though to*) to act with the intention or with a show of doing something: *they made to go out; he made as if to hit her* 16 to use for a specified purpose: *I will make this town my base* 17 to deliver or pronounce: *to make a speech* 18 to cause to seem or represent as being 19 to earn, acquire, or win for oneself: *to make friends; make a fortune* 20 to engage in: *make love not war* 21 to traverse or cover (distance) by travelling: *we can make a hundred miles by nightfall* 22 to arrive in time for: *he didn't make the first act of the play* 23 *cards* a to win a trick with (a specified card) b to shuffle (the cards) c *bridge* to fulfil (a contract) by winning the necessary number of tricks 24 *cricket* to score (runs) **25** *electronics* to close (a circuit) permitting a flow of current **26** (*intr*) to increase in depth: *the water in the hold was making a foot a minute* **27** *informal* to gain a place or position on or in: *to make the headlines; make the first team* **28** *informal* to achieve the rank of **29** *slang* to seduce **30 make a book** to take bets on a race or other contest **31 make a day of it** to cause an activity to last a day **32 make a night of it** to cause an activity to last a night **33 make do** See **do**[1] (sense 35) **34 make eyes at** to flirt with or ogle **35 make it a** *informal* to be successful in doing something **b** (foll by *with*) *slang* to have sexual intercourse **36** make like, *slang, chiefly US & Canadian* to imitate ▷ *n* **37** brand, type, or style **38** the manner or way in which something is made **39** disposition or character; make-up **40** the act or process of making **41** the amount or number made **42** *cards* a player's turn to shuffle **43 on the make a** *informal* out for profit or conquest **b** *slang* in search of a sexual partner. See also **make out** [Old English *macian*; related to Old Frisian *makia* to construct, Dutch *maken*, German *machen* to make] ▷ 'makable *adj*

make away *vb* (*intr, adverb*) **1** to depart in haste **2 make away with a** to steal or abduct **b** to kill, destroy, or get rid of

Makeba (mə'keɪbə) *n* **Miriam**. born 1932, South African singer and political activist; banned from South Africa from 1960 to 1990

make believe *vb* **1** to pretend or enact a fantasy ▷ *n* **make-believe 2 a** a fantasy, pretence, or unreality **b** (*as modifier*): *a make-believe world*

Makedhonia (,makeðɔ'nia) *n* a transliteration of the Modern Greek name for **Macedonia** (sense 2)

make for *vb* (*intr, preposition*) **1** to head towards, esp in haste **2** to prepare to attack **3** to help to bring about

make of *vb* (*tr, preposition*) **1** to interpret as the meaning of **2** to produce or construct from: *houses made of brick* **3 make little of** *or* **make nothing of a** not to understand **b** to attribute little or no importance to **c** to gain little or no benefit from

make off *vb* **1** (*intr, adverb*) to go or run away in haste **2 make off with** to steal or abduct

make out *vb* (*adverb*) **1** (*tr*) to discern or perceive **2** (*tr*) to understand or comprehend **3** (*tr*) to write out: *he made out a cheque* **4** (*tr*) to attempt to establish or prove: *he made me out to be a liar* **5** (*intr*) to pretend: *he made out that he could cook* **6** (*intr*) to manage or fare

make over *vb* (*tr, adverb*) **1** to transfer the title or possession of (property, etc) **2** to renovate or remodel: *she made over the dress to fit her sister* ▷ *n* **makeover** ('meɪk,əʊvə) **3** a complete remodelling **4** a series of alterations, including beauty treatments and new clothes, intended to make a noticeable improvement in a person's appearance

maker ('meɪkə) *n* **1** a person who makes (something); fabricator; constructor **2** a person who executes a legal document, esp one who signs a promissory note

Maker ('meɪkə) *n* **1** a title given to **God** **2 go to meet one's Maker** *or* **meet one's Maker** to die

makeshift ('meɪkʃɪft) *adj* **1** serving as a temporary or expedient means, esp during an emergency ▷ *n* **2** something serving in this capacity

make-up *n* **1** cosmetics, such as powder, lipstick, etc, applied to the face to improve its appearance **2 a** the cosmetics, false hair, etc, used by an actor to highlight his features or adapt his appearance **b** the art or result of applying such cosmetics **3** the manner of arrangement of the parts or qualities of someone or something **4** the arrangement of type matter and illustrations on a page or in a book **5** mental or physical constitution ▷ *vb* **make up** (*adverb*) **6** (*tr*) to form or constitute: *these arguments make up the case for the defence* **7** (*tr*) to devise, construct, or compose, sometimes with the intent to deceive: *to make up a song; to make up an excuse* **8** (*tr*) to supply what is lacking or deficient in; complete: *these extra people will make up our total* **9** (*tr*) to put in order, arrange, or prepare: *to make up a bed* **10** (*intr*; foll by *for*) to compensate or atone (for) **11** to settle (differences) amicably (often in the phrase **make it up**) **12** to apply cosmetics to (the face) to enhance one's appearance or

so as to alter the appearance for a theatrical role **13** to assemble (type and illustrations) into (columns or pages) **14** (*tr*) to surface (a road) with asphalt, concrete, etc **15 make up to** *informal* **a** to make friendly overtures to **b** to flirt with

makeweight ('meɪk,weɪt) *n* **1** something put on a scale to make up a required weight **2** an unimportant person or thing added to make up a lack

Makeyevka (*Russian* maˈkjejɪfkə) *n* a city in SE Ukraine: coal-mining centre. Pop: 380 000 (2005 est)

Makhachkala (*Russian* maxətʃkaˈla) *n* a port in SW Russia, capital of the Dagestan Republic, on the Caspian Sea: fishing fleet; oil refining. Pop: 503 000 (2005 est). Former name (until 1921): **Petrovsk**

maki ('mækɪ) *n* (in Japanese cuisine) a small segment cut from a long roll of cold rice and various other ingredients wrapped in a sheet of seaweed [from Japanese, literally: roll]

making ('meɪkɪŋ) *n* **1 a** the act of a person or thing that makes or the process of being made **b** (*in combination*): *watchmaking* **2 be the making of** to cause the success of **3 in the making** in the process of becoming or being made **4** something made or the quantity of something made at one time

makings ('meɪkɪŋz) *pl n* **1** potentials, qualities, or materials: *he had the makings of a leader* **2** Also called: **rollings** *slang* the tobacco and cigarette paper used for rolling a cigarette **3** profits; earnings

Makkah *or* **Makah** ('mækə, -kɑː) *n* transliteration of the Arabic name for **Mecca**

mako[1] ('mɑːkəʊ) *n, pl* -kos any shark of the genus *Isurus*, esp *I. glaucus* of Indo-Pacific and Australian seas: family *Isuridae* [from Māori]

mako[2] ('mɑːkəʊ) *n, pl* -kos Also called: **wineberry** a small evergreen New Zealand tree, *Aristotelia serrata*: family *Elaeocarpaceae* [from Māori]

Makurdi (mə'kɜːdɪ) *n* a port in E central Nigeria, capital of Benue State on the Benue River: agricultural trade centre. Pop: 259 000 (2005 est)

Mal. *abbreviation* **1** *Bible* Malachi **2** Malay(an)

mal- *combining form* bad or badly; wrong or wrongly; imperfect or defective: *maladjusted; malfunction* [Old French, from Latin *malus* bad, *male* badly]

Malabar Coast *or* **Malabar** ('mælə,bɑː) *n* a region along the SW coast of India, extending from Goa to Cape Comorin: includes most of Kerala state

Malabo (mə'lɑːbəʊ) *n* the capital and chief port of Equatorial Guinea, on the island of Bioko in the Gulf of Guinea. Pop: 105 000 (2005 est). Former name (until 1973): **Santa Isabel**

malabsorption (,mæləb'sɔːpʃən) *n* a failure of absorption, esp by the small intestine in coeliac disease, cystic fibrosis, etc

malacca *or* **malacca cane** (mə'lækə) *n* **1** the stem of the rattan palm **2** a walking stick made from this stem

Malacca *or* **Melaka** (mə'lækə) *n* a state of SW Peninsular Malaysia: rubber plantations. Capital: Malacca. Pop: 635 791 (2000). Area: 1683 sq km (650 sq miles)

Malachi ('mælə,kaɪ) *n* *Old Testament* **1** a Hebrew prophet of the 5th century BC **2** the book containing his oracles

malachite ('mælə,kaɪt) *n* a bright green mineral, found in veins and in association with copper deposits. It is a source of copper and is used as an ornamental stone. Composition: hydrated copper carbonate. Formula: $Cu_2CO_3(OH)_2$. Crystal structure: monoclinic [C16: via Old French from Latin *molochītēs*, from Greek *molokhitis* mallow-green stone, from *molokhē* mallow]

Malachy ('mælə,kaɪ) *n* **Saint**. 1094–1148, Irish prelate; he became Archbishop of Armagh (1132) and founded (1142) the first Cistercian abbey in Ireland. Feast day: Nov 3

maladjustment (,mælə'dʒʌstmənt) *n* **1** *psychol* a failure to meet the demands of society, such as coping with problems and social relationships: usually reflected in emotional instability **2** faulty or bad adjustment ▷ ,mala'djusted *adj*

maladminister (,mæləd'mɪnɪstə) *vb* (*tr*) to administer badly, inefficiently, or dishonestly

maladministration (,mæləd,mɪnɪ'streɪʃən) *n* bad,

inefficient, or dishonest management of the affairs of an organization, such as a business or institution

maladroit (ˌmælə'drɔɪt) adj **1** showing or characterized by clumsiness; not dexterous **2** tactless and insensitive in behaviour or speech [C17: from French, from mal badly + ADROIT] > ˌmala'droitly adv > ˌmala'droitness n

malady ('mælədɪ) n, pl **-dies 1** any disease or illness **2** any unhealthy, morbid, or desperate condition [C13: from Old French, from Vulgar Latin male habitus (unattested) in poor condition, from Latin male badly + habitus, from habēre to have]

Málaga ('mæləgə; Spanish 'malaɣa) n **1** a port and resort in S Spain, in Andalusia on the Mediterranean. Pop: 547 105 (2003 est) **2** a sweet fortified dessert wine from Málaga

Malagasy (ˌmælə'gæzɪ) n **1** pl **-gasy** or **-gasies** a native or inhabitant of Madagascar **2** the official language of Madagascar belonging to the Malayo-Polynesian family > adj **3** of or relating to Madagascar, its people, or their language

Malagasy Republic n the former name (1958–75) of Madagascar

malaise (mæ'leɪz) n **1** a feeling of unease or depression **2** a mild sickness, not symptomatic of any disease or ailment **3** a complex of problems affecting a country, economy, etc: Bulgaria's economic malaise [C18: from Old French, from mal bad + aise EASE]

Malamud ('mæləməd, -mʊd) n **Bernard.** 1914–86, US novelist and short-story writer. His works include The Fixer (1966) and Dubin's Lives (1979)

malamute or **malemute** ('mælə,muːt) n an Alaskan sled dog of the spitz type, having a dense usually greyish coat [from the name of an Inuit tribe]

Malang ('mælæŋ) n a city in S Indonesia, on E Java: commercial centre. Pop: 756 982 (2000)

malapropism ('mæləprɒp,ɪzəm) n **1** the unintentional misuse of a word by confusion with one of similar sound, esp when creating a ridiculous effect, as in I am not under the affluence of alcohol **2** the habit of misusing words in this manner [C18: after Mrs Malaprop in Sheridan's play The Rivals (1775), a character who misused words, from MALAPROPOS]

malapropos (ˌmæləprə'pəʊ) adj **1** of an inappropriate or misapplied nature or kind > adv **2** in an inappropriate way or manner > n **3** something inopportune or inappropriate [C17: from French mal à propos not to the purpose]

Mälaren ('melaren) n **Lake Mälaren** a lake in S Sweden, extending 121 km (75 miles) west from Stockholm, where it joins with an inlet of the Baltic Sea (the **Saltsjön**). Area: 1140 sq km (440 sq miles)

malaria (mə'lɛərɪə) n an infectious disease characterized by recurring attacks of chills and fever, caused by the bite of an anopheles mosquito infected with any of four protozoans of the genus Plasmodium (P. vivax, P. falciparum, P. malariae, or P. ovale) [C18: from Italian mala aria bad air, from the belief that the disease was caused by the unwholesome air in swampy districts] > ma'larial, ma'larian or ma'larious adj

malarkey or **malarky** (mə'lɑːkɪ) n slang nonsense; rubbish [C20: of unknown origin]

Malatesta (Italian mala'tɛsta) n an Italian family that ruled Rimini from the 13th to the 16th century

Malathion (ˌmælə'θaɪɒn) n trademark a yellow organophosphorus insecticide used as a dust or mist for the control of house flies and garden pests. Formula: $C_{10}H_{19}O_6PS_2$ [C20: from (diethyl) MAL(EATE) + THIO- + -ON]

Malatya (ˌmɑːlɑː'tjɑː) n a city in E central Turkey: nearby is the ruined Roman and medieval city of Melitene (Old Malatya). Pop: 448 000 (2005 est)

Malawi (mə'lɑːwɪ) n **1** a republic in E central Africa: established as a British protectorate in 1891; became independent in 1964 and a republic, within the Commonwealth, in 1966; lies along the Great Rift Valley, with Lake Nyasa (Malawi) along the E border, the Nyika Plateau in the northwest, and the Shire (or Shiré) Highlands in the southeast. Official language: Chichewa; English and various other Bantu languages are also widely spoken. Religion: Christian majority,

Muslim, and animist minorities. Currency: kwacha. Capital: Lilongwe. Pop: 12 337 000 (2004 est). Area: 118 484 sq km (45 747 sq miles). Former name: Nyasaland **2 Lake Malawi** the Malawi name for (Lake) **Nyasa**

Malay (mə'leɪ) n **1** a member of a people living chiefly in Malaysia and Indonesia who are descendants of Mongoloid immigrants **2** the language of this people, belonging to the Malayo-Polynesian family > adj **3** of or relating to the Malays or their language

Malaya (mə'leɪə) n **1 States of the Federation of Malaya** part of Malaysia, in the S Malay Peninsula, constituting Peninsular Malaysia: consists of the former Federated Malay States, the former Unfederated Malay States, and the former Straits Settlements. Capital: Kuala Lumpur. Pop: 17 144 322 (2000). Area: 131 587 sq km (50 806 sq miles) **2 Federation of Malaya** a federation of the nine Malay States of the Malay Peninsula and two of the Straits Settlements (Malacca and Penang): formed in 1948: became part of the British Commonwealth in 1957 and joined Malaysia in 1963 > **Ma'layan** adj, n

Malayalam or **Malayaalam** (ˌmælɪ'ɑːləm) n a language of SW India, belonging to the Dravidian family and closely related to Tamil: the state language of Kerala

Malayali or **Malayalee** (ˌmælɪ'ɑːlɪ) n a speaker of the Malayalam language

Malay Archipelago n a group of islands in the Indian and Pacific Oceans, between SE Asia and Australia: the largest group of islands in the world; includes over 3000 Indonesian islands, about 7000 islands of the Philippines, and, sometimes, New Guinea

Malayo-Polynesian n **1** Also called: Austronesian a family of languages extending from Madagascar to the central Pacific, including Malagasy, Malay, Indonesian, Tagalog, and Polynesian > adj **2** of or relating to this family of languages

Malay Peninsula n a peninsula of SE Asia, extending south from the Isthmus of Kra in Thailand to Cape Tanjong Piai in Malaysia: consists of SW Thailand and the states of Malaya (Peninsular Malaysia)

Malaysia (mə'leɪzɪə) n a federation in SE Asia (within the Commonwealth), consisting of **Peninsular Malaysia** on the Malay Peninsula, and **East Malaysia** (Sabah and Sarawak), occupying the N part of the island of Borneo: formed in 1963 as a federation of Malaya, Sarawak, Sabah, and Singapore (the latter seceded in 1965); densely forested and mostly mountainous. Official language: Malay; English and various Chinese and Indian minority languages are also spoken. Official religion: Muslim. Currency: ringgit. Capital: Putrajaya (the transfer of government from Kuala Lumpur is taking place in stages over several years starting 1999). Pop: 24 876 000 (2004 est). Area: 333 403 sq km (128 727 sq miles) > **Ma'laysian** adj, n

Malay States pl n the former states of the Malay Peninsula that, together with Penang and Malacca, formed the Union of Malaya (1946) and the Federation of Malaya (1948). Perak, Selangor, Negri Sembilan, and Pahang were established as the Federated Malay States by the British in 1895 and Perlis, Kedah, Kelantan, and Trengannu as the Unfederated Malay States in 1909 (joined by Johore in 1914)

Malbec (mæl'bɛk) n **1** a black grape originally grown in the Bordeaux region of France and now in Argentina and Chile, used for making wine **2** a rustic mid-bodied red wine made from this grape

Malcolm ('mælkəm) n **George.** 1917–97, British harpsichordist

Malcolm III n died 1093, king of Scotland (1057–93). He became king after Macbeth

Malcolm X (ɛks) n original name Malcolm Little. 1925–65, US Black civil-rights leader: assassinated

malcontent ('mælkən,tɛnt) adj **1** disgusted or discontented > n **2** a person who is malcontent [C16: from Old French]

mal de mer French (mal də mɛr) n seasickness

Maldives ('mɔːl'diːvz) pl n **Republic of Maldives** a republic occupying an archipelago of 1087 coral islands in the Indian Ocean, southwest of Sri Lanka: came under British protection in 1887; became independent in

1965 and a republic in 1968; a member of the Commonwealth. The economy and infrastructure were severely damaged in the Indian Ocean tsunami of December 2004. Official language: Divehi. Official religion: (Sunni) Muslim. Currency: rufiyaa. Capital: Malé. Pop: 328 000 (2004 est). Area: 298 sq km (115 sq miles) > **Maldivian** (mɔːlˈdɪvɪən) *adj, n*

Maldon (ˈmɔːldən) *n* a market town in SE England, in Essex; scene of a battle (991) between the East Saxons and the victorious Danes, celebrated in *The Battle of Maldon*, an Old English poem; notable for Maldon salt, used in cookery. Pop: 20 731 (2001)

male (meɪl) *adj* **1** of, relating to, or designating the sex producing gametes (spermatozoa) that can fertilize female gametes (ova) **2** of, relating to, or characteristic of a man; masculine **3** for or composed of men or boys: *a male choir* **4** (of gametes) capable of fertilizing an egg cell in sexual reproduction **5** (of reproductive organs, such as a testis or stamen) capable of producing male gametes **6** (of flowers) bearing stamens but lacking a functional pistil **7** *electronics, mechanical engineering* having a projecting part or parts that fit into a female counterpart: *a male plug* ▷ *n* **8** a male person, animal, or plant [C14: via Old French from Latin *masculus* MASCULINE] > ˈmaleness *n*

Malé (ˈmaːleɪ) *n* the capital of the Republic of Maldives, on Malé Island in the centre of the island group. Pop: 90 000 (2005 est)

maleate (ˈmælɪˌeɪt) *n* any salt or ester of maleic acid [C19: from MALE(IC ACID) + -ATE¹]

Malebranche (French malbrɑ̃ʃ) *n* **Nicolas** (nikɔla). 1638–1715, French philosopher. Originally a follower of Descartes, he developed the philosophy of occasionalism, esp in *De la recherche de la vérité* (1674)

male chauvinism *n* the belief, held or alleged to be held by certain men, that men are inherently superior to women > **male chauvinist** *n, adj*

malediction (ˌmælɪˈdɪkʃən) *n* **1** the utterance of a curse against someone or something **2** slanderous accusation or comment [C15: from Latin *maledictiō* a reviling, from *male* ill + *dīcere* to speak] > ˌmale'dictive *or* ˌmale'dictory *adj*

malefactor (ˈmælɪˌfæktə) *n* a criminal; wrongdoer [C15: via Old French from Latin, from *malefacere* to do evil] > ˈmale'faction *n*

maleficent (məˈlɛfɪsənt) *adj* causing or capable of producing evil or mischief; harmful or baleful [C17: from Latin *maleficent-*, from *maleficus* wicked, prone to evil, from *malum* evil] > ma'lefic *adj* > ma'leficence *n*

maleic acid (məˈleɪɪk) *n* a colourless soluble crystalline substance used to synthesize other compounds. Formula: HOOCCH:CHCOOH [C19: from French *maléique*, altered form of *malique*; see MALIC ACID]

male menopause *n* a period in a man's later middle age in which he may experience an identity crisis as he feels age overtake his sexual powers

Malenkov (Russian məlɪnˈkɔf) *n* **Georgi Maksimilianovich** (gɪˈɔrgij ˌmaksjɪmɪˈljanəvjɪtʃ). 1902–88, Soviet politician; prime minister (1953–55). He was removed from the party presidium (1957) for plotting against Khrushchev; expelled from the Communist Party (1961)

Malevich (Russian ˈmalɪvitʃ) *n* **Kasimir** (kəziˈmir). 1878–1935, Russian painter. He founded the abstract art movement known as Suprematism

malevolent (məˈlɛvələnt) *adj* wishing or appearing to wish evil to others; malicious [C16: from Latin *malevolens*, from *male* ill + *volens*, present participle of *velle* to wish] > ma'levolence *n* > ma'levolently *adv*

malfeasance (mælˈfiːzəns) *n law* the doing of a wrongful or illegal act, esp by a public official. See **misfeasance, nonfeasance** [C17: from Old French *mal faisant*, from *mal* evil + *faisant* doing, from *faire* to do, from Latin *facere*] > mal'feasant *n, adj*

malformation (ˌmælfɔːˈmeɪʃən) *n* **1** the condition of being faulty or abnormal in form or shape **2** *pathol* a deformity in the shape or structure of a part, esp when congenital > mal'formed *adj*

malfunction (mælˈfʌŋkʃən) *vb* **1** (intr) to function

imperfectly or irregularly or fail to function ▷ *n* **2** failure to function or defective functioning

Malherbe (French malɛrb) *n* **François de** (frɑ̃swa də). 1555–1628, French poet and critic. He advocated the classical ideals of clarity and concision of meaning

Mali (ˈmaːli) *n* a landlocked republic in West Africa: conquered by the French by 1898 and incorporated (as French Sudan) into French West Africa; became independent in 1960; settled chiefly in the basins of the Rivers Senegal and Niger in the south. Official language: French. Religion: Muslim majority, also animist. Currency: franc. Capital: Bamako. Pop: 13 408 000 (2004 est). Area: 1 248 574 sq km (482 077 sq miles). Former name (1898–1959): French Sudan

malic acid (ˈmælɪk, ˈmeɪ-) *n* a colourless crystalline compound occurring in apples and other fruits. Formula: HOOCCH₂CH(OH)COOH [C18 *malic*, via French *malique* from Latin *mālum* apple]

malice (ˈmælɪs) *n* **1** the desire to do harm or mischief **2** evil intent **3** *law* the state of mind with which an act is committed and from which the intent to do wrong may be inferred [C13: via Old French from Latin *malitia*, from *malus* evil]

malice aforethought *n criminal law* **1** the predetermination to do an unlawful act, esp to kill or seriously injure **2** the intent with which an unlawful killing is effected, which must be proved for the crime to constitute murder

malicious (məˈlɪʃəs) *adj* **1** characterized by malice **2** motivated by wrongful, vicious, or mischievous purposes > ma'liciously *adv* > ma'liciousness *n*

malign (məˈlaɪn) *adj* **1** evil in influence, intention, or effect ▷ *vb* **2** (tr) to slander or defame [C14: via Old French from Latin *malignus* spiteful, from *malus* evil] > ma'ligner *n* > ma'lignly *adv*

malignancy (məˈlɪgnənsɪ) *n, pl* -cies **1** the state or quality of being malignant **2** *pathol* a cancerous growth

malignant (məˈlɪgnənt) *adj* **1** having or showing desire to harm others **2** tending to cause great harm; injurious **3** *pathol* (of a tumour) uncontrollable or resistant to therapy; rapidly spreading [C16: from Late Latin *malignāre* to behave spitefully, from *malignus* MALIGN] > ma'lignantly *adv*

malignity (məˈlɪgnɪtɪ) *n, pl* -ties **1** the condition or quality of being malign, malevolent, or deadly **2** (often plural) a malign or malicious act or feeling

malines (məˈliːn) *n* **1** a type of silk net used in dressmaking **2** another name for **Mechlin lace** [C19: from French *Malines* (Mechelen), where this lace was traditionally made]

Malines (malin) *n* the French name for **Mechelen**

malinger (məˈlɪŋgə) *vb* (intr) to pretend or exaggerate illness, esp to avoid work [C19: from French *malingre* sickly, perhaps from *mal* badly + Old French *haingre* feeble] > ma'lingerer *n*

Malinowski (ˌmælɪˈnɒfskɪ) *n* **Bronislaw Kasper** (brɔˈnislaf ˈkaspɛr). 1884–1942, Polish anthropologist in England and the US, who researched into the sexual behaviour of primitive people in New Guinea and Melanesia

Maliseet (ˈmælɪˌsiːt) *n* **1** a member of a Native Canadian people of New Brunswick and E Quebec **2** the Algonquian language of this people [from Micmac *malisiit* one speaking an incomprehensible language]

malkin (ˈmɔːkɪn, ˈmɔː-, ˈmæl-) *n* an archaic or dialect name for a **cat¹** [C13: diminutive of *Maud*]

mall (mæl, mɔːl) *n* **1** a shaded avenue, esp one that is open to the public **2** *US, Canadian, Austral & NZ* short for **shopping mall** [C17: after *The Mall*, in St James's Park, London. See PALL-MALL]

mallard (ˈmælɑːd) *n, pl* -lard *or* -lards a duck, *Anas platyrhynchos*, common over most of the N hemisphere, the male of which has a dark green head and reddish-brown breast: the ancestor of all domestic breeds of duck [C14: from Old French *mallart*, perhaps from *maslart* (unattested); see MALE, -ARD]

Mallarmé (French malarme) *n* **Stéphane** (stefan). 1842–98, French symbolist poet, noted for his free verse, in which he chooses words for their evocative qualities;

his works include *L'Après-midi d'un Faune* (1876), *Vers et Prose* (1893), and *Divagations* (1897)

Malle (*French* mal) *n* **Louis**. 1932–95, French film director: his films include *Le Feu follet* (1963), *Au revoir les enfants* (1987), and *Vanya on 42nd Street* (1994)

malleable ('mælɪəbəl) *adj* **1** (esp of metal) able to be worked, hammered, or shaped under pressure or blows without breaking **2** able to be influenced; pliable or tractable [c14: via Old French from Medieval Latin *malleābilis*, from Latin *malleus* hammer] > ˌmalleaˈbility *or less commonly* ˈmalleableness *n* > ˈmalleably *adv*

mallee ('mælɪ) *n* **1** any of several low shrubby eucalyptus trees that flourish in desert regions of Australia **2** **the mallee** *Austral informal* another name for the **bush¹** (sense 4) [c19: native Australian name]

mallee fowl *n* an Australian megapode, *Leipoa ocellata*, that allows its eggs to incubate naturally in a sandy mound

malleolus (mə'liːələs) *n, pl* **-li** (-ˌlaɪ) either of two rounded bony projections of the tibia and fibula on the sides of each ankle joint [c17: diminutive of Latin *malleus* hammer]

mallet ('mælɪt) *n* **1** a tool resembling a hammer but having a large head of wood, copper, lead, leather, etc, used for driving chisels, beating sheet metal, etc **2** a long stick with a head like a hammer used to strike the ball in croquet or polo [c15: from Old French *maillet* wooden hammer, diminutive of *mail* MAUL (n)]

malleus ('mælɪəs) *n, pl* **-lei** (-lɪˌaɪ) the outermost and largest of the three small bones in the middle ear of mammals. See also **incus, stapes** [c17: from Latin: hammer]

Mallorca (ma'ʎɔrka) *n* the Spanish name for **Majorca**

mallow ('mæləʊ) *n* **1** any plant of the malvaceous genus *Malva*, esp *M. sylvestris* of Europe, having purple, pink, or white flowers **2** any of various related plants, such as the marsh mallow, rose mallow, Indian mallow, and tree mallow [Old English *mealuwe*, from Latin *malva*; probably related to Greek *malakhē* mallow]

mall rat (mɔːl) *n slang, chiefly US* a youngster who spends much of his or her time in shopping malls

malm (mɑːm) *n* **1** a soft greyish limestone that crumbles easily **2** a chalky soil formed from this limestone **3** an artificial mixture of clay and chalk used to make bricks [Old English *mealm*- (in compound words); related to Old Norse *malmr* ore, Gothic *malma* sand]

Malmédy (*French* malmedi) *n* See **Eupen and Malmédy**

Malmö ('mælməʊ; *Swedish* 'malmø:) *n* a port in S Sweden, on the Sound: part of Denmark until 1658; industrial centre. Pop: 268 971 (2004 est)

malmsey ('mɑːmzɪ) *n* a sweet Madeira wine [c15: from Medieval Latin *Malmasia*, corruption of Greek *Monembasia*, Greek port from which the wine was shipped]

malnutrition (ˌmælnjuː'trɪʃən) *n* lack of adequate nutrition resulting from insufficient food, unbalanced diet, or defective assimilation

malodorous (mæl'əʊdərəs) *adj* having a bad smell

Malory ('mælərɪ) *n* Sir **Thomas**. 15th-century English author of *Le Morte d'Arthur* (?1470), a prose collection of Arthurian legends, translated from the French

Malouf ('mɑːluːf) *n* **David**. born 1934, Australian novelist, short-story writer, and poet. His novels include *An Imaginary Life* (1978), *Remembering Babylon* (1993), and *The Conversations at Curlow Creek* (1996)

Malpighi (*Italian* mal'piːgi) *n* **Marcello** (mar'tʃɛllo). 1628–94, Italian physiologist. A pioneer in microscopic anatomy, he identified the capillary system (1661) > **Malpighian** (mæl'pɪgɪən) *adj*

malpractice (mæl'præktɪs) *n* **1** immoral, illegal, or unethical professional conduct or neglect of professional duty **2** any instance of improper professional conduct

Malraux (*French* malro) *n* **André** (ɑ̃dre). 1901–76, French writer and statesman. His novels include *La Condition humaine* (1933) on the Kuomintang revolution (1927–28) and *L'Espoir* (1937) on the Spanish Civil War, in both of which events he took part. He also wrote on art, notably in *Les Voix du silence* (1951)

malt (mɔːlt) *n* **1** See **malt liquor 2** short for **malt whisky**

▷ *vb* **3** to make into or become malt **4** to make (something, esp liquor) with malt [Old English *mealt*; related to Dutch *mout*, Old Norse *malt*; see also MELT] > 'malty *adj* > 'maltiness *n*

Malta ('mɔːltə) *n* a republic occupying the islands of Malta, Gozo, and Comino, in the Mediterranean south of Sicily: governed by the Knights Hospitallers from 1530 until Napoleon's conquest in 1798; French driven out, with British help, 1800; became British dependency 1814; suffered severely in World War II; became independent in 1964 and a republic in 1974; joined the EU in 2004; a member of the Commonwealth. Official languages: Maltese and English. Official religion: Roman Catholic. Currency: euro (from January 2008 replacing the Maltese lira). Capital: Valletta. Pop: 396 000 (2004 est). Area: 316 sq km (122 sq miles)

malted milk *n* **1** a soluble powder made from dehydrated milk and malted cereals **2** a drink made from this powder

Maltese (mɔːl'tiːz) *adj* **1** of or relating to Malta, its inhabitants, or their language ▷ *n* **2** *pl* **-tese** a native or inhabitant of Malta **3** the official language of Malta, a form of Arabic with borrowings from Italian, etc

Maltese cross *n* a cross with triangular arms that taper towards the centre, sometimes having indented outer sides: formerly worn by the Knights of Malta

malt extract *n* a sticky substance obtained from an infusion of malt

Malthus ('mælθəs) *n* **Thomas Robert**. 1766–1834, English economist. He propounded his population theory in *An Essay on the Principle of Population* (1798)

Malthusian (mæl'θjuːzɪən) *adj* **1** of or relating to the theory of the English economist Thomas Robert Malthus (1766–1834) stating that increases in population tend to exceed increases in the means of subsistence and that therefore sexual restraint should be exercised ▷ *n* **2** a supporter of this theory > Mal'thusianism *n*

malting ('mɔːltɪŋ) *n* a building in which malt is made or stored. Also called: **malt house**

malt liquor *n* any alcoholic drink brewed from malt

maltose ('mɔːltəʊz) *n* a disaccharide of glucose formed by the enzymic hydrolysis of starch: used in bacteriological culture media and as a nutrient in infant feeding. Formula: $C_{12}H_{22}O_{11}$ [c19: from MALT + -OSE²]

maltreat (mæl'triːt) *vb* (*tr*) to treat badly, cruelly, or inconsiderately [c18: from French *maltraiter*] > mal'treater *n* > mal'treatment *n*

maltster ('mɔːltstə) *n* a person who makes or deals in malt

malt whisky *n* whisky made from malted barley

Maluku (mɑː'luːkuː) *n* the Indonesian name for the **Moluccas**

malvaceous (mæl'veɪʃəs) *adj* of, relating to, or belonging to the *Malvaceae*, a family of plants that includes mallow, cotton, okra, althaea, and abutilon [c17: from Latin *malvāceus*, from *malva* MALLOW]

Malvern ('mɔːlvən) *n* a town and resort in W England, in S Worcestershire on the E slopes of the **Malvern Hills**: annual dramatic festival; mineral springs. Pop: 35 588 (2001)

malversation (ˌmælvɜː'seɪʃən) *n rare* professional or public misconduct [c16: from French, from *malverser* to behave badly, from Latin *male versārī*]

Malvinas (*Spanish* mal'βinas) *pl n* **Islas Malvinas** ('izlas) the Argentine name for the **Falkland Islands**

malware ('mælwɛə) *n* a computer program designed specifically to damage or disrupt a system, such as a virus [c20: from MAL(ICIOUS) + (SOFT)WARE]

mam (mæm) *n informal or dialect* another word for **mother¹**

mama (mə'mɑː) *n old-fashioned* an informal word for **mother¹**

mamba ('mæmbə) *n* any aggressive partly arboreal tropical African venomous elapid snake of the genus *Dendroaspis*, esp *D. angusticeps* (**green** and **black mambas**) [from Zulu *im-amba*]

mambo ('mæmbəʊ) *n, pl* **-bos 1** a modern Latin American dance, resembling the rumba, derived from the ritual dance of voodoo **2** a voodoo priestess ▷ *vb*

m

-bos, -boing, -boed **3** (*intr*) to perform this dance [American Spanish, probably from Haitian Creole: voodoo priestess]

Mameluke *or* **Mamaluke** ('mæmə,lu:k) *n* **1** a member of a military class, originally of Turkish slaves, ruling in Egypt from about 1250 to 1517 and remaining powerful until crushed in 1811 **2** (in Muslim countries) a slave [c16: via French, ultimately from Arabic *mamlūk* slave, from *malaka* to possess]

Mamet ('mæmɪt) *n* **David**. born 1947, US dramatist and film director. His plays include *Sexual Perversity in Chicago* (1974), *American Buffalo* (1976), *Glengarry Glen Ross* (1983), and *Oleanna* (1992); films include *House of Games* (1987) and *Spartan* (2004)

mamilla *or* US **mammilla** (mæ'mɪlə) *n, pl* **-lae** (-li:) **1** a nipple or teat **2** any nipple-shaped part or prominence [c17: from Latin, diminutive of *mamma* breast] > 'mamillary *or* US 'mammillary *adj*

mamma ('mæmə) *n, pl* **-mae** (-miː) the milk-secreting organ of female mammals: the breast in women, the udder in cows, sheep, etc [c17: from Latin: breast] > 'mammary *adj*

mammal ('mæməl) *n* any animal of the *Mammalia*, a large class of warm-blooded vertebrates having mammary glands in the female, a thoracic diaphragm, and a four-chambered heart. The class includes the whales, carnivores, rodents, bats, primates, etc [c19: via New Latin from Latin *mamma* breast] > mammalian (mæ'meɪliən) *adj, n*

mammary gland *n* any of the milk-producing glands in mammals. In higher mammals each gland consists of a network of tubes and cavities connected to the exterior by a nipple

mammography (mæ'mɒɡrəfɪ) *n* the technique of using X-rays to examine the breast in the early detection of cancer > 'mammo,graph *or* 'mammo,gram *n*

mammon ('mæmən) *n* riches or wealth regarded as a source of evil and corruption [c14: via Late Latin from New Testament Greek *mammōnas*, from Aramaic *māmōnā* wealth] > 'mammonish *adj* > 'mammonism *n* > 'mammonist *or* 'mammonite *n*

Mammon ('mæmən) *n New Testament* the personification of riches and greed in the form of a false god

mammoth ('mæməθ) *n* **1** any large extinct elephant of the Pleistocene genus *Mammuthus* (or *Elephas*), such as *M. primigenius* (**woolly mammoth**), having a hairy coat and long curved tusks ▷ *adj* **2** of gigantic size or importance [c18: from Russian *mamot*, from Tatar *mamont*, perhaps from *mamma* earth, because of a belief that the animal made burrows]

mammy *or* **mammie** ('mæmɪ) *n, pl* **-mies** **1** a child's word for **mother**¹ **2** *chiefly Southern US* a Black woman employed as a nurse or servant to a White family

Mamoré (Spanish mamo're) *n* a river in central Bolivia, flowing north to the Beni River to form the Madeira River. Length: about 1500 km (930 miles)

man (mæn) *n, pl* **men** (mɛn) **1** an adult male human being, as distinguished from a woman **2** (*modifier*) male; masculine: *a man child* **3** *archaic* a human being regardless of sex or age, considered as a representative of mankind; a person **4** (*sometimes capital*) human beings collectively; mankind: *the development of man* **5** Also called: **modern man a** a member of any of the living races of *Homo sapiens*, characterized by erect bipedal posture, a highly developed brain, and powers of articulate speech, abstract reasoning, and imagination **b** any extinct member of the species *Homo sapiens*, such as Cro-Magnon man **6** a member of any of the extinct species of the genus *Homo*, such as Java man, Heidelberg man, and Solo man **7** an adult male human being with qualities associated with the male, such as courage or virility: *be a man* **8** manly qualities or virtues: *the man in him was outraged* **9 a** a subordinate, servant, or employee contrasted with an employer or manager **b** (*in combination*): *the number of man-days required to complete a job* **10** (*usually plural*) a member of the armed forces who does not hold commissioned, warrant, or noncommissioned rank (as in the phrase **officers and men**) **11** a member of

a group, team, etc **12** a husband, boyfriend, etc **13** an expression used parenthetically to indicate an informal relationship between speaker and hearer **14** a movable piece in various games, such as draughts **15** *South African slang* any person: used as a term of address **16** a vassal of a feudal lord **17** as **one man** with unanimous action or response **18** be **one's own man** to be independent or free **19** he's **your man** he's the person needed (for a particular task, role, job, etc) **20** man and boy from childhood **21** sort out the men from the boys *or* separate the men from the boys to separate the experienced from the inexperienced **22** to a man without exception ▷ *interj* **23** *informal* an exclamation or expletive, often indicating surprise or pleasure ▷ *vb* mans, manning, manned (*tr*) **24** to provide with sufficient people for operation, defence, etc **25** to take one's place at or near in readiness for action **26** *falconry* to induce (a hawk or falcon) to endure the presence of and handling by man, esp strangers [Old English *mann*; related to Old Frisian *man*, Old High German *man*, Dutch *man*, Icelandic *mathr*]

● **USAGE** The use of *man* to mean human beings in
● general is often considered sexist. Gender-neutral
● alternatives include *human beings*, *people* and *humankind*.
● The verb *to man* can also often be replaced by *to staff*, *to*
● *operate* and related words

Man¹ (mæn) the *n* (*sometimes not capital*) US **1** *Black slang* a White man or White men collectively, esp when in authority, in the police, or held in contempt **2** *slang* a drug peddler

Man² (mæn) *n* **Isle of Man** an island in the British Isles, in the Irish Sea between Cumbria and Northern Ireland: a UK Crown Dependency (but not part of the United Kingdom), with its own ancient parliament, the Court of Tynwald; a dependency of Norway until 1266, when for a time it came under Scottish rule; its own language, Manx, became extinct in the 19th century but has been revived to some extent. Capital: Douglas. Pop: 75 000 (2003 est). Area: 588 sq km (227 sq miles)

-man *n combining form* indicating a person who has a role, works in a place, or operates equipment as specified: *salesman; barman; cameraman*

● **USAGE** The use of words ending in *-man* is avoided as
● implying a male in job advertisements, where sexual
● discrimination is illegal, and in many other contexts
● where a term that is not gender-specific is available,
● such as *salesperson, barperson, camera operator*

mana ('mɑːnə) *n anthropol* **1** (in Polynesia, Melanesia, etc) a concept of a life force, believed to be seated in the head, and associated with high social status and ritual power **2** any power achieved by ritual means; prestige; authority [from Polynesian]

man about town *n* a fashionable sophisticate, esp one in a big city

manacle ('mænək³l) *n* **1** (*usually plural*) a shackle, handcuff, or fetter, used to secure the hands of a prisoner, convict, etc ▷ *vb* (*tr*) **2** to put manacles on **3** to confine or constrain [c14: via Old French from Latin *manicula*, diminutive of *manus* hand]

Manado (mə'nɑːdəʊ) *n* a variant of **Menado**

manage ('mænɪdʒ) *vb* (*mainly tr*) **1** (*also intr*) to be in charge (of); administer: *to manage one's affairs; to manage a shop* **2** to succeed in being able (to do something) despite obstacles; contrive **3** to have room, time, etc, for: *can you manage dinner tomorrow?* **4** to exercise control or domination over, often in a tactful or guileful manner **5** (*intr*) to contrive to carry on despite difficulties, esp financial ones **6** to wield or handle (a weapon) [c16: from Italian *maneggiare* to control, train (esp horses), ultimately from Latin *manus* hand]

manageable ('mænɪdʒəb³l) *adj* able to be managed or controlled > ,managea'bility *or less commonly* 'manageableness *n* > 'manageably *adv*

managed currency *n* a currency that is subject to governmental control with respect to the amount in circulation and the rate of exchange with other currencies

management ('mænɪdʒmənt) *n* **1** the members of the executive or administration of an organization or business **2** managers or employers collectively **3** the technique, practice, or science of managing, controlling or dealing with **4** the skilful or resourceful use of materials, time, etc **5** the specific treatment of a disease, disorder, etc

management buyout *n* the purchase of a company by its managers, usually with outside backing from a bank or other institution

management company *n* a company that manages a unit trust

manager ('mænɪdʒə) *n* **1** a person who directs or manages an organization, industry, shop, etc **2** a person who controls the business affairs of an actor, entertainer, etc **3** a person who controls the training of a sportsman or team **4** a person who has a talent for managing efficiently **5** (in Britain) a member of either House of Parliament appointed to arrange a matter in which both Houses are concerned **6** a computer program that organizes a resource, such as a set of files or a database ▷ 'manager,ship *n*

manageress (,mænɪdʒə'rɛs, 'mænɪdʒə,rɛs) *n* a woman who is in charge of a shop, department, canteen, etc

managerial (,mænɪ'dʒɪərɪəl) *adj* of or relating to a manager or to the functions, responsibilities, or position of management ▷ ,mana'gerially *adv*

manage up *vb* (*intr, adverb*) *informal* to build a successful working relationship with a superior, manager, or employer

managing ('mænɪdʒɪŋ) *adj* having administrative control or authority: *a managing director*

Managua (mə'nægwə; *Spanish* ma'naɣwa) *n* **1** the capital of Nicaragua, on the S shore of Lake Managua: chosen as capital in 1857. Pop: 1 159 000 (2005 est) **2** Lake Managua a lake in W Nicaragua: drains into Lake Nicaragua by the Tipitapa River. Length: 61 km (38 miles). Width: about 26 km (16 miles)

Manama (mə'nɑːmə) *n* the capital of Bahrain, at the N end of Bahrain Island: transit port. Pop: 142 000 (2005 est)

mana motuhake ('mɑːnə məʊtuː'hɑːkɪ) *n* NZ independence or autonomy [Māori]

mañana *Spanish* (ma'ɲana; *English* mə'njɑːnə) *n, adv* **a** tomorrow **b** some other and later time

Manassas (mə'næsəs) *n* a town in NE Virginia, west of Alexandria: site of the victory of Confederate forces in the Battles of Bull Run, or First and Second Manassas (1861; 1862), during the American Civil War. Pop: 37 166 (2003 est)

Manasseh (mə'næsɪ) *n Old Testament* **1** the elder son of Joseph (Genesis 41:51) **2** the Israelite tribe descended from him **3** the territory of this tribe, in the upper Jordan valley

man-at-arms *n, pl* men-at-arms a soldier, esp a heavily armed mounted soldier in medieval times

manatee ('mænə,tiː, ,mænə'tiː) *n* any sirenian mammal of the genus *Trichechus*, occurring in tropical coastal waters of America, the Caribbean, and Africa: family *Trichechidae*. They resemble whales and have a prehensile upper lip and a broad flattened tail [c16: via Spanish from Carib *Manattoúi*]

Manaus *or* **Manáos** (*Portuguese* mə'naus) *n* a port in N Brazil, capital of Amazonas state, on the Rio Negro 19 km (12 miles) above its confluence with the Amazon: chief commercial centre of the Amazon basin. Pop: 1 673 000 (2005 est)

man-bag *n informal* a small bag, usually with a shoulder strap, carried by a man and designed to contain personal articles [c20: in allusion to HANDBAG]

man boobs *pl n Brit informal, derogatory* overdeveloped breasts on a man, caused by excess weight or lack of exercise

Man Booker Prize *n* an annual prize for a work of Commonwealth or Irish fiction of £50,000, awarded as the **Booker Prize** from 1969–2002

Manche (*French* mɑ̃ʃ) *n* **1** a department of NW France, in Basse-Normandie region. Capital: St-Lô. Pop: 484 967 (2003 est). Area: 6412 sq km (2501 sq miles) **2** La Manche the French name for the **English Channel**

manchester ('mæntʃɪstə) *n Austral & NZ* **1** household linen or cotton goods, such as sheets and towels **2** Also called: manchester department a section of a store where such goods are sold [from MANCHESTER, England]

Manchester ('mæntʃɪstə) *n* **1** a city in NW England, in Manchester unitary authority, Greater Manchester: linked to the Mersey estuary by the **Manchester Ship Canal**: commercial, industrial, and cultural centre; formerly the centre of the cotton and textile trades; two universities. Pop: 394 269 (2001) **2** a unitary authority in NW England, in Greater Manchester. Pop: 432 500 (2003 est). Area: 116 sq km (45 sq miles)

manchineel (,mæntʃɪ'niːl) *n* a tropical American euphorbiaceous tree, *Hippomane mancinella*, having fruit and milky highly caustic poisonous sap, which causes skin blisters [c17: via French from Spanish MANZANILLA]

Manchu (mæn'tʃuː) *n* **1** *pl* -chus *or* -chu a member of a Mongoloid people of Manchuria who conquered China in the 17th century, establishing an imperial dynasty that lasted until 1912 **2** the language of this people, belonging to the Tungusic branch of the Altaic family ▷ *adj* **3** Also called: Ching Of or relating to the dynasty of the Manchus [from Manchu, literally: pure]

Manchukuo *or* **Manchoukuo** ('mæn'tʃuː'kwəʊ) *n* a former state of E Asia (1932–45), consisting of the three provinces of old Manchuria and Jehol

Manchuria (mæn'tʃʊərɪə) *n* a region of NE China, historically the home of the Manchus, rulers of China from 1644 to 1912: includes part of Inner Mongolia and the provinces of Heilongjiang, Jilin, and Liaoning. Area: about 1 300 000 sq km (502 000 sq miles) ▷ Man'churian *adj*

manciple ('mænsɪpəl) *n* a steward who buys provisions, esp in a college, Inn of Court, or monastery [c13: via Old French from Latin *mancipium* purchase, from *manceps* purchaser, from *manus* hand + *capere* to take]

Mancunian (mæn'kjuːnɪən) *n* **1** a native or inhabitant of Manchester ▷ *adj* **2** of or relating to Manchester [from Medieval Latin *Mancunium* Manchester]

-mancy *n combining form* indicating divination of a particular kind: *chiromancy* [from Old French *-mancie*, from Latin *-mantia*, from Greek *manteia* soothsaying] ▷ **-mantic** *adj combining form*

mandala ('mændələ, mæn'dɑːlə) *n Hindu & Buddhist art* any of various designs symbolizing the universe, usually circular [Sanskrit: circle]

Mandalay (,mændə'leɪ) *n* a city in central Myanmar, on the Irrawaddy River: the second largest city in the country and former capital of Burma and of Upper Burma; Buddhist religious centre. Pop: 927 000 (2005 est)

mandamus (mæn'deɪməs) *n, pl* -muses *law* formerly a writ from, now an order of, a superior court commanding an inferior tribunal, public official, corporation, etc, to carry out a public duty [c16: Latin, literally: we command, from *mandāre* to command]

mandarin ('mændərɪn) *n* **1** (in the Chinese Empire) a member of any of the nine senior grades of the bureaucracy, entered by examinations **2** a high-ranking official whose powers are extensive and thought to be outside political control **3** a person of standing and influence, as in literary or intellectual circles **4 a** a small citrus tree, *Citrus nobilis*, cultivated for its edible fruit **b** the fruit of this tree, resembling the tangerine [c16: from Portuguese *mandarim*, via Malay *menteri* from Sanskrit *mantrin* counsellor, from *mantra* counsel] ▷ 'mandarinate *n*

Mandarin Chinese *or* **Mandarin** *n* the official language of China since 1917; the form of Chinese spoken by about two thirds of the population and taught in schools throughout China

Mandarin collar *n* a high stiff round collar

mandarin duck *n* an Asian duck, *Aix galericulata*, the male of which has a brightly coloured and patterned plumage and crest

mandate *n* ('mændeɪt, -dɪt) **1** an official or authoritative instruction or command **2** *politics* the support or commission given to a government and its policies or an elected representative and his policies through an electoral victory **3** Also called: mandated territory (*often capital*) (formerly) any of the territories under the

m

trusteeship of the League of Nations administered by one of its member states **4 a** *Roman law* a contract by which one person commissions another to act for him gratuitously and the other accepts the commission **b** *contract law* a contract of bailment under which the party entrusted with goods undertakes to perform gratuitously some service in respect of such goods **c** *Scots law* a contract by which a person is engaged to act in the management of the affairs of another ▷ *vb* ('mændeɪt) (*tr*) **5** *international law* to assign (territory) to a nation under a mandate **6** to delegate authority to [c16: from Latin *mandātum* something commanded, from *mandāre* to command, perhaps from *manus* hand + *dāre* to give] > 'man,dator *n*

mandatory ('mændətərɪ, -trɪ) *adj* **1** having the nature or powers of a mandate **2** obligatory; compulsory **3** (of a state) having received a mandate over some territory ▷ *n*, *pl* **-ries 4** Also called: **mandatary** a person or state holding a mandate > 'mandatorily *adv*

Mandela (mæn'dɛlə) *n* **1 Nelson (Rolihlahla)**. born 1918, Black South African statesman: president of South Africa (1994–99). Jailed in 1962 for 5 years and, in 1964, for life, he was released in 1990 after a long international campaign; deputy president of the African National Congress (1990–91) and president (1991–97); elected president of South Africa in 1994; Nobel peace prize jointly with F. W. de Klerk in 1993 **2 (Numzano) Winnie**. born 1934, Black South African political activist: campaigned for the release of her husband Nelson Mandela; they divorced in 1996

Mandelstam *or* **Mandelshtam** ('mændəlˌʃtɑːm) *n* **1 Nadezhda (Yakovlevna)** (næ'dɛʃdə), born *Nadezhda Khazina*. 1899–1980, Soviet writer, wife of Osip Mandelstam: noted for her memoirs *Hope against Hope* (1971) and *Hope Abandoned* (1973) describing life in Stalin's Russia **2 Osip (Emilyevich)** ('ɒsiːp). 1891–?1938, Soviet poet and writer, born in Warsaw; he was persecuted by Stalin and died in a labour camp. His works include *Tristia* (1922), *Poems* (1928), and the autobiographical *Journey to Armenia* (1933)

Mandeville ('mændəvɪl) *n* **1 Bernard de**. ?1670–1733, English author, born in Holland, noted for his satire *The Fable of the Bees* (1723) **2 Sir John**. 14th century, English author of *The Travels of Sir John Mandeville*. The book claims to be an account of the author's journeys in the East but is largely a compilation from other works

mandible ('mændɪbᵊl) *n* **1** the lower jawbone in vertebrates **2** either of a pair of mouthparts in insects and other arthropods that are usually used for biting and crushing food **3** *ornithol* either the upper or the lower part of the bill, esp the lower part [c16: via Old French from Late Latin *mandibula* jaw, from *mandere* to chew] > mandibular (mæn'dɪbjʊlə) *adj* > mandibulate (mæn'dɪbjʊlɪt, -ˌleɪt) *n*, *adj*

mandolin *or* **mandoline** (ˌmændə'lɪn) *n* a plucked stringed instrument related to the lute, having four pairs of strings tuned in ascending fifths stretched over a small light body with a fretted fingerboard. It is usually played with a plectrum, long notes being sustained by the tremolo [c18: via French from Italian *mandolino*, diminutive of *mandora* lute, ultimately from Greek *pandoura* musical instrument with three strings] > ˌmando'linist *n*

mandrake ('mændreɪk) *or* **mandragora** (mæn'drægərə) *n* **1** a Eurasian solanaceous plant, *Mandragora officinarum*, with purplish flowers and a forked root. It was formerly thought to have magic powers and a narcotic was prepared from its root **2** another name for the: **May apple** [c14: probably via Middle Dutch from Latin *mandragoras* (whence Old English *mandragora*), from Greek. The form *mandrake* was probably adopted through folk etymology, because of the allegedly human appearance of the root and because *drake* (dragon) suggested magical powers]

mandrel *or* **mandril** ('mændrəl) *n* **1** a spindle on which a workpiece is supported during machining operations **2** a shaft or arbor on which a machining tool is mounted **3** the driving spindle in the headstock of a lathe [c16: perhaps related to French *mandrin* lathe]

mandrill ('mændrɪl) *n* an Old World monkey, *Mandrillus sphinx*, of W Africa. It has a short tail and brown hair, and the ridged muzzle, nose, and hindquarters are red and blue [c18: from MAN + DRILL⁴]

mane (meɪn) *n* **1** the long coarse hair that grows from the crest of the neck in such mammals as the lion and horse **2** long thick human hair [Old English *manu*; related to Old High German *mana*, Old Norse *mön*, and perhaps to Old English *mene* and Old High German *menni* necklace] > maned *adj*

manège *or* **manege** (mæ'neɪʒ) *n* **1** the art of training horses and riders **2** a riding school [c17: via French from Italian *maneggio*, from *maneggiare* to MANAGE]

manes ('mɑːneɪz; *Latin* 'mɑːnɛs) *pl n* (*sometimes capital*) (in Roman legend) **1** the spirits of the dead, often revered as minor deities **2** (*functioning as singular*) the shade of a dead person [c14: from Latin, probably: the good ones, from Old Latin *mānus* good]

Manes ('meɪniːz) *n* See **Mani**

Manet (*French* manɛ) *n* **Édouard** (edwar). 1832–83, French painter. His painting *Le Déjeuner sur l'herbe* (1863), which was condemned by the Parisian establishment, was acclaimed by the impressionists, whom he decisively influenced

maneuver (mə'nuːvə) *n*, *vb* the usual US spelling of **manoeuvre**

man Friday *n* a loyal male servant or assistant [after the native in Daniel Defoe's novel *Robinson Crusoe* (1719)]

manful ('mænfʊl) *adj* a less common word for **manly** > 'manfully *adv* > 'manfulness *n*

mangabey ('mæŋgəˌbeɪ) *n* any of several large agile arboreal Old World monkeys of the genus *Cercocebus*, of central Africa, having long limbs and tail and white upper eyelids [c18: after the name of a region in Madagascar]

Mangalore (ˌmæŋgə'lɔː) *n* a port in S India, in Karnataka on the Malabar Coast. Pop: 398 745 (2001)

manganese ('mæŋgəˌniːz) *n* a brittle greyish-white metallic element that exists in four allotropic forms, occurring principally in pyrolusite and rhodonite: used in making steel and ferromagnetic alloys. Symbol: Mn; atomic no: 25; atomic wt: 54.93805; valency: 1, 2, 3, 4, 6, or 7; relative density: 7.21–7.44; melting pt: 1246±3°C; boiling pt: 2062°C [c17: via French from Italian *manganese*, probably altered form of Medieval Latin MAGNESIA]

mange (meɪndʒ) *n* an infectious disorder mainly affecting domestic animals, characterized by itching, formation of papules and vesicles, and loss of hair: caused by parasitic mites [c14: from Old French *mangeue* itch, literally: eating, from *mangier* to eat]

mangelwurzel ('mæŋgᵊl,wɜːzᵊl) *or* **mangoldwurzel** ('mæŋgəʊld,wɜːzᵊl) *n* a Eurasian variety of the beet plant, *Beta vulgaris*, cultivated as a cattle food, having a large yellowish root [c18: from German *Mangoldwurzel*, from *Mangold* beet + *Wurzel* root]

manger ('meɪndʒə) *n* a trough or box in a stable, barn, etc, from which horses or cattle feed [c14: from Old French *maingeure* food trough, from *mangier* to eat, ultimately from Latin *mandūcāre* to chew]

mangetout ('mɑːʒ'tuː) *n* a variety of garden pea in which the pod is also edible. Also called: **sugar pea** [c20: from French; literally: eat all]

mangey ('meɪndʒɪ) *adj* **-gier**, **-giest** a variant spelling of **mangy**

mangle¹ ('mæŋgᵊl) *vb* (*tr*) **1** to mutilate, disfigure, or destroy by cutting, crushing, or tearing **2** to ruin, spoil, or mar [c14: from Norman French *mangler*, probably from Old French *mahaignier* to maim] > 'mangler *n*

mangle² ('mæŋgᵊl) *n* **1** Also called: **wringer** a machine for pressing or drying wet textiles, clothes, etc, consisting of two heavy rollers between which the cloth is passed ▷ *vb* (*tr*) **2** to press or dry in a mangle [c18: from Dutch *mangel*, ultimately from Late Latin *manganum*. See MANGONEL]

mango ('mæŋgəʊ) *n*, *pl* **-goes** *or* **-gos 1** a tropical Asian anacardiaceous evergreen tree, *Mangifera indica*, cultivated in the tropics for its fruit **2** the ovoid edible fruit of this tree, having a smooth rind and sweet juicy orange-yellow flesh [c16: via Portuguese from Malay *mangā*, from Tamil *mānkāy* from *mān* mango tree + *kāy* fruit]

mangonel ('mæŋgə,nɛl) *n history* a war engine for hurling stones [c13: via Old French from Medieval Latin *manganellus*, ultimately from Greek *manganon*]

mangrove ('mæŋgrəʊv, 'mæn-) *n* any tropical evergreen tree or shrub of the genus *Rhizophora*, having stiltlike intertwining aerial roots and growing below the highest tide levels in estuaries and along coasts, forming dense thickets: family *Rhizophoraceae* [C17 *mangrow* (changed through influence of *grove*), from Portuguese *mangue*, ultimately from Taino]

mangulate ('mæŋgjʊ,leɪt) *vb* (*tr*) *Austral slang* to bend or twist out of shape; mangle

mangy *or* **mangey** ('meɪndʒɪ) *adj* -gier, -giest **1** having or caused by mange **2** scruffy or shabby > 'manginess *n*

manhandle ('mæn,hænd²l, ,mæn'hænd²l) *vb* (*tr*) **1** to handle or push (someone) about roughly **2** to move or do by manpower rather than by machinery [c19: from MAN + HANDLE; sense 1 perhaps also influenced by Devon dialect *manangle* to mangle]

Manhattan (mæn'hæt²n, mən-) *n* **1** an island at the N end of New York Bay, between the Hudson, East, and Harlem Rivers: administratively (with adjacent islets) a borough of New York City; a major financial, commercial, and cultural centre. Pop: 1 537 195 (2000). Area: 47 sq km (22 sq miles) **2** a mixed drink consisting of four parts whisky, one part vermouth, and a dash of bitters

Manhire ('mænhɪə) *n* **Bill.** born 1946, New Zealand poet and writer. His poetry collections include *How to Take Off Your Clothes at the Picnic* (1977), *Zoetropes* (1984), and *Sunshine* (1996)

manhole ('mæn,həʊl) *n* **1** *Also called:* inspection chamber a shaft with a removable cover that leads down to a sewer or drain **2** a hole, usually with a detachable cover, through which a man can enter a boiler, tank, etc

manhood ('mænhʊd) *n* **1** the state or quality of being a man or being manly **2** men collectively **3** *Archaic* the state of being human

man-hour *n* a unit for measuring work in industry, equal to the work done by one man in one hour

manhunt ('mæn,hʌnt) *n* an organized search, usually by police, for a wanted man or fugitive

Mani ('mɑːnɪ) *n* ?216–?276 AD, Persian prophet who founded Manichaeism. Also called: Manes, Manichaeus

mania ('meɪnɪə) *n* **1** a mental disorder characterized by great excitement and occasionally violent behaviour **2** an obsessional enthusiasm or partiality [c14: via Late Latin from Greek: madness]

-mania *n combining form* indicating extreme desire or pleasure of a specified kind or an abnormal excitement aroused by something: *kleptomania; nymphomania; pyromania* [from MANIA] > -maniac *adj combining form*, *n combining form*

maniac ('meɪnɪ,æk) *n* **1** a wild disorderly person **2** a person who has a great craving or enthusiasm for something **3** *psychiatry obsolete* a person afflicted with mania [c17: from Late Latin *maniacus* belonging to madness, from Greek]

maniacal (mə'naɪək²l) *or* **maniac** ('meɪnɪæk) *adj* **1** affected with or characteristic of mania **2** characteristic of or befitting a maniac: *maniacal laughter* > ma'niacally *adv*

manic ('mænɪk) *adj* **1** characterizing, denoting, or affected by mania ▷ *n* **2** a person afflicted with mania [c19: from Greek, from MANIA]

manic-depressive *psychiatry* ▷ *adj* **1** denoting a mental disorder characterized either by an alternation between extreme euphoria and deep depression (bipolar manic-depressive disorder or syndrome) or by depression on its own or (rarely) elation on its own (unipolar disorder) ▷ *n* **2** a person afflicted with this disorder

Manichaeism *or* **Manicheism** ('mænɪkiː,ɪzəm) *n* the system of religious doctrines, including elements of Gnosticism, Zoroastrianism, Christianity, Buddhism,

etc, taught by the Persian prophet Mani (?216–?276 AD), based on a supposed primordial conflict between light and darkness or goodness and evil [c14: from Late Latin *Manichaeus*, from Late Greek *Manikhaios* of Mani] > 'Manichee *n* > Manichaean *or* Manichean (,mænɪ'kiːən) *adj*, *n*

Manichaeus *or* **Manicheus** (,mænɪ'kiːəs) *n* See Mani

manicure ('mænɪ,kjʊə) *n* **1** care of the hands and fingernails, involving shaping the nails, removing cuticles, etc ▷ *vb* **2** to care for (the hands and fingernails) in this way [c19: from French, from Latin *manus* hand + *cūra* care] > 'manicurist *n*

manifest ('mænɪ,fɛst) *adj* **1** easily noticed or perceived; obvious; plain **2** *psychoanal* of or relating to the ostensible elements of a dream: *manifest content*. See latent (sense 5) ▷ *vb* **3** (*tr*) to show plainly; reveal or display **4** (*tr*) to prove beyond doubt **5** (*intr*) (of a disembodied spirit) to appear in visible form ▷ *n* **6** a customs document containing particulars of a ship, its cargo, and its destination **7 a** a list of cargo, passengers, etc, on an aeroplane **b** a list of railway trucks or their cargo [c14: from Latin *manifestus* plain, literally: struck with the hand, from *manū* with the hand + *-festus* struck] > 'mani,festable *adj* > 'mani,festly *adv*

manifestation (,mænɪfɛ'steɪʃən) *n* **1** the act of demonstrating; display **2** the state of being manifested **3** an indication or sign **4** a public demonstration of feeling **5** the materialization of a disembodied spirit > ,mani'festative *adj*

manifesto (,mænɪ'fɛstəʊ) *n*, *pl* -tos *or* -toes a public declaration of intent, policy, aims, etc, as issued by a political party, government, or movement [c17: from Italian, from *manifestare* to MANIFEST]

manifold ('mænɪ,fəʊld) *adj formal* **1** of several different kinds; multiple **2** having many different forms, features, or elements ▷ *n* **3** something having many varied parts, forms, or features **4** a chamber or pipe with a number of inlets or outlets used to collect or distribute a fluid. In an internal-combustion engine the **inlet manifold** carries the vaporized fuel from the carburettor to the inlet ports and the **exhaust manifold** carries the exhaust gases away ▷ *vb* **5** (*tr*) to duplicate (a page, book, etc) **6** to make manifold; multiply [Old English *manigfeald*. See MANY, -FOLD] > 'mani,foldly *adv* > 'mani,foldness *n*

manikin *or* **mannikin** ('mænɪkɪn) *n* **1 a** a little man; dwarf or child **2** an anatomical model of the body or a part of the body, esp for use in medical or art instruction **3** variant spellings of **mannequin** [c17: from Dutch *manneken*, diminutive of MAN]

Manila (mə'nɪlə) *n* **1** the chief port of the Philippines, on S Luzon on Manila Bay: capital of the republic until 1948 and from 1976; seat of the Far Eastern University and the University of Santo Tomas (1611). Pop: 10 677 000 (2005 est) **2** a type of cigar made in this city **3** (*often not capital*) short for **Manila hemp**, **Manila paper**

Manila Bay *n* an almost landlocked inlet of the South China Sea in the Philippines, in W Luzon: mostly forms Manila harbour. Area: 1994 sq km (770 sq miles)

Manila hemp *or* **Manilla hemp** *n* a fibre obtained from the plant abaca, used for rope, paper, etc

Manila paper *or* **Manilla paper** *n* a strong usually brown paper made from Manila hemp or similar fibres

manilla (mə'nɪlə) *n* an early form of currency in W Africa in the pattern of a small bracelet [from Spanish: bracelet, diminutive of *mano* hand, from Latin *manus*]

man in the street *n* the typical or ordinary person, esp as a hypothetical unit in statistics

manioc ('mænɪ,ɒk) *or* **manioca** (,mænɪ'əʊkə) *n* another name for: **cassava** (sense 1) [c16: from Tupi *mandioca*; earlier form *manihot* from French, from Guarani *mandio*]

manipulate (mə'nɪpjʊ,leɪt) *vb* **1** (*tr*) to handle or use, esp with some skill, in a process or action **2** to negotiate, control, or influence (something or someone) cleverly, skilfully, or deviously **3** to falsify (a bill, accounts, etc) for one's own advantage **4** (in physiotherapy) to examine or treat manually, as in loosening a joint [c19: back formation from *manipulation*, from Latin *manipulus* handful] > manipulability (mə,nɪpjʊlə'bɪlɪtɪ) *n*

m

> ma'nipu,latable *or* ma'nipulable *adj* > ma,nipu'lation *n*
> ma'nipulative *adj* > ma'nipu,lator *n* > ma'nipulatory *adj*

Manipur (,mʌnɪ'pʊə) *n* a state in NE India: largely densely forested mountains. Capital: Imphal. Pop: 2 388 634 (2001). Area: 22 327 sq km (8621 sq miles)

Manisa ('mɑ:nɪ,sɑ:) *n* a city in W Turkey: the Byzantine seat of government (1204–1313). Pop: 237 000 (2005 est)

Manitoba (,mænɪ'təʊbə) *n* 1 a province of W Canada: consists of prairie in the southwest, with extensive forests in the north and tundra near Hudson Bay in the northeast. Capital: Winnipeg. Pop: 1 170 268 (2004 est). Area: 650 090 sq km (251 000 sq miles). Abbreviation: MB 2 Lake Manitoba a lake in W Canada, in S Manitoba: fed by the outflow from Lake Winnipegosis; drains into Lake Winnipeg. Area: 4706 sq km (1817 sq miles)
> ,Mani'toban *n*, *adj*

Manitoba maple *n* a Canadian fast-growing variety of maple

manitou, manitu ('mænɪ,tu:) *or* **manito** ('mænɪ,təʊ) *n*, *pl* -tous, -tus, -tos *or* -tou, -tu, -to (among the Algonquian Indians) a deified spirit or force [C17: from Algonquian; related to Ojibwa *manito* spirit]

Manitoulin Island (,mænɪ'tu:lɪn) *n* an island in N Lake Huron in Ontario: the largest freshwater island in the world. Length: 129 km (80 miles). Width: up to 48 km (30 miles)

Manizales (,mænɪ'zɑ:les; *Spanish* mani'θales) *n* a city in W Colombia, in the Cordillera Central of the Andes at an altitude of 2100 m (7000 ft): commercial centre of a rich coffee-growing area. Pop: 401 000 (2005 est)

man jack *n informal* a single individual (in the phrases **every man jack, no man jack**)

mankind (,mæn'kaɪnd) *n* 1 human beings collectively; humanity 2 men collectively, as opposed to womankind ● USAGE Nowadays many people object to the use of ● *mankind* to refer to all human beings and use the term ● *humankind* instead

Manley ('mænlɪ) *n* Michael Norman. 1924–97, Jamaican statesman; prime minister of Jamaica (1972–80; 1989–92)

manlike ('mæn,laɪk) *adj* resembling or befitting a man

manly ('mænlɪ) *adj* -lier, -liest 1 possessing qualities, such as vigour or courage, generally regarded as appropriate to or typical of a man; masculine 2 characteristic of or befitting a man > 'manliness *n*

man-made *adj* made or produced by man; artificial

Mann (*German* man) *n* 1 Heinrich ('haɪnrɪç). 1871–1950, German novelist: works include *Professor Unrat* (1905), which was filmed as *The Blue Angel* (1928), and *Man of Straw* (1918) 2 his brother, Thomas. 1875–1955, German novelist, in the US after 1937. His works deal mainly with the problem of the artist in bourgeois society and include the short story *Death in Venice* (1913) and the novels *Buddenbrooks* (1900), *The Magic Mountain* (1924), and *Doctor Faustus* (1947): Nobel prize for literature 1929

manna ('mænə) *n* 1 *Old Testament* the miraculous food which sustained the Israelites in the wilderness (Exodus 16:14–36) 2 any spiritual or divine nourishment 3 a windfall; an unexpected gift (esp in the phrase **manna from heaven**) 4 a sweet substance obtained from various plants, esp from an ash tree, *Fraxinus ornus* (**manna** or **flowering ash**) of S Europe, used as a mild laxative [Old English via Late Latin from Greek, from Hebrew *mān*]

Mannar (mə'nɑ:) *n* Gulf of Mannar the part of the Indian Ocean between SE India and the island of Sri Lanka: pearl fishing

manned (mænd) *adj* 1 supplied or equipped with men, esp soldiers 2 (of spacecraft, aircraft, etc) having a human crew

mannequin ('mænɪkɪn) *n* 1 a woman who wears the clothes displayed at a fashion show; model 2 a life-size dummy of the human body used to fit or display clothes [C18: via French from Dutch *manneken* MANIKIN]

manner ('mænə) *n* 1 a way of doing or being 2 a person's bearing and behaviour 3 the style or customary way of doing or accomplishing something 4 type or kind 5 mannered style, as in art; mannerism 6 in a manner of speaking in a way; so to speak 7 to the manner born

naturally fitted to a specified role or activity ▷ See also **manners** [C12: via Norman French from Old French *maniere*, from Vulgar Latin *manuāria* (unattested) a way of handling something, noun use of Latin *manuārius* belonging to the hand, from *manus* hand]

mannered ('mænəd) *adj* 1 having idiosyncrasies or mannerisms; affected 2 (*in combination*) having manners as specified: *ill-mannered*

Mannerheim ('mænə,heɪm) *n* Baron Carl Gustaf Emil. 1867–1951, Finnish soldier and statesman; president of Finland (1944–46)

mannerism ('mænə,rɪzəm) *n* 1 a distinctive and individual gesture or trait; idiosyncrasy 2 (*often capital*) a principally Italian movement in art and architecture between the High Renaissance and Baroque periods (1520–1600) that sought to represent an ideal of beauty rather than natural images of it, using characteristic distortion and exaggeration of human proportions, perspective, etc 3 adherence to a distinctive or affected manner, esp in art or literature > 'mannerist *n* > ,manner'istic *or* ,manner'istical *adj* > ,manner'istically *adv*

mannerless ('mænəlɪs) *adj* having bad manners; boorish > 'mannerlessness *n*

mannerly ('mænəlɪ) *adj* 1 well-mannered; polite; courteous ▷ *adv* 2 *now rare* with good manners; politely; courteously > 'mannerliness *n*

manners ('mænəz) *pl n* 1 social conduct 2 a socially acceptable way of behaving

Mannheim[1] ('mænhaɪm; *German* 'manhaɪm) *n* a city in SW Germany, in Baden-Württemberg at the confluence of the Rhine and Neckar: one of Europe's largest inland harbours; a cultural and musical centre. Pop: 308 353 (2003 est)

Mannheim[2] (*Hungarian* 'manhaɪm) *n* Karl (karl). 1893–1947, Hungarian sociologist, living in Britain from 1933: author of *Ideology and Utopia* (1929) and *Man and Society in an Age of Reconstruction* (1941)

mannikin ('mænɪkɪn) *n* a variant spelling of: **manikin**

Manning ('mænɪŋ) *n* 1 Henry Edward. 1808–92, British churchman. Originally an Anglican, he was converted to Roman Catholicism (1851) and made archbishop of Westminster (1865) and cardinal (1875) 2 Olivia. 1908–80, British novelist and short-story writer, best known for her novel sequence *Fortunes of War*, comprising the *Balkan Trilogy* (1960–65) and the *Levant Trilogy* (1977–80)

mannish ('mænɪʃ) *adj* 1 (of a woman) having or displaying qualities regarded as typical of a man 2 of or resembling a man > 'mannishly *adv* > 'mannishness *n*

manoeuvre *or US* **maneuver** (mə'nu:və) *n* 1 a contrived, complicated, and possibly deceptive plan or action 2 a movement or action requiring dexterity and skill 3 a **a** tactic or movement of one or a number of military or naval units **b** (*plural*) tactical exercises, usually on a large scale 4 a planned movement of an aircraft in flight 5 any change from the straight steady course of a ship ▷ *vb* 6 (*tr*) to contrive or accomplish with skill or cunning 7 (*intr*) to manipulate situations, etc, in order to gain some end 8 (*intr*) to perform a manoeuvre or manoeuvres 9 to move or deploy or be moved or deployed, as military units, etc [C15: from French, from Medieval Latin *manuopera* manual work, from Latin *manū operāre* to work with the hand] > ma'noeuvrable *or US* ma'neuverable *adj* > ma,noeuvra'bility *or US* ma,neuvera'bility *n* > ma'noeuvrer *or US* ma'neuverer *n* > ma'noeuvring *or US* ma'neuvering *n*

man of God *n* 1 a saint or prophet 2 a clergyman

man of straw *n* 1 a person of little substance 2 Also called: **straw man** *chiefly US* a person used as a cover for some dubious plan or enterprise; front man

man-of-war *or* **man o' war** *n*, *pl* **men-of-war, men o' war** 1 a warship 2 See **Portuguese man-of-war**

man-of-war bird *or* **man-o'-war bird** *n* another name for **frigate bird**

Manolete (*Spanish* mano'lete) *n* original name *Manuel Rodríguez y Sánchez*. 1917–47, Spanish bullfighter

manometer (mə'nɒmɪtə) *n* an instrument for comparing pressures; typically a glass U-tube containing mercury, in which pressure is indicated by the difference in levels in the two arms of the tube [c18: from French *manomètre*, from Greek *manos* sparse + *metron* measure] > manometric (ˌmænəʊˈmɛtrɪk) or ˌmanoˈmetrical *adj*

manor (ˈmænə) *n* **1** (in medieval Europe) the manor house of a lord and the lands attached to it **2** a manor house **3** a landed estate **4** *Brit slang* a geographical area of operation, esp of a local police force [c13: from Old French *manoir* dwelling, from *maneir* to dwell, from Latin *manēre* to remain] > manorial (məˈnɔːrɪəl) *adj*

manor house *n* (esp formerly) the house of the lord of a manor

manpower (ˈmænˌpaʊə) *n* **1** power supplied by men **2** a unit of power based on the rate at which a man can work; approximately 75 watts **3** the number of people available or required to perform a particular function

manqué *French* (mãke; *English* ˈmɒŋkeɪ) *adj* (*postpositive*) unfulfilled; potential; would-be: *the manager is an actor manqué* [c19: literally: having missed]

Manresa (*Spanish* manˈrɛsa) *n* a city in NE Spain: contains a cave used as the spiritual retreat of St Ignatius Loyola. Pop: 67 269 (2003 est)

mansard (ˈmænsɑːd, -səd) *n* Also called: mansard roof a roof having two slopes on both sides and both ends, the lower slopes being steeper than the upper [c18: from French *mansarde*, after François Mansart (1598–1666), French architect]

Mansart (*French* mãsar) *n* **1** François (frãswa). 1598–1666, French architect, who established the classical style in French architecture **2** his great-nephew, Jules Hardouin (ʒyl ardwɛ̃). 1646–1708, French architect and town planner, who completed the Palace of Versailles

manse (mæns) *n* (in certain religious denominations) the house provided for a minister [c15: from Medieval Latin *mansus* dwelling, from the past participle of Latin *manēre* to stay]

Mansell (ˈmænsəl) *n* Nigel. born 1953, English motor-racing driver: world champion in 1992

manservant (ˈmænˌsɜːvənt) *n, pl* menservants a male servant, esp a valet

Mansfield[1] (ˈmænsˌfiːld) *n* a town in central England, in W Nottinghamshire: former coal-mining and cotton-textiles industries. Pop: 69 987 (2001)

Mansfield[2] (ˈmænsˌfiːld) *n* Katherine, real name *Kathleen Mansfield Beauchamp*. 1888– 1923, British writer, born in New Zealand, noted for her short stories, such as those in *Bliss* (1920) and *The Garden Party* (1922)

Mansholt (*Dutch* ˈmɑnshɔlt) *n* Sicco Leendert (ˈsiko ˈleːndərt). 1908–95, Dutch economist and politician; vice president (1958–72) and president (1972–73) of the European Economic Community Commission. He was the author of the Mansholt Plan for the agricultural organization of the European Economic Community

mansion (ˈmænʃən) *n* **1** Also called: mansion house a large and imposing house **2** a less common word for manor house **3** *Brit* (*plural*) a block of flats [c14: via Old French from Latin *mansio* a remaining, from *mansus*; see MANSE]

Mansion House the Mansion House *n* **1** the residence of the Lord Mayor of London **2** the residence of the Lord Mayor of Dublin

man-sized *adj* **1** of a size appropriate for or convenient for a man **2** *informal* big; large

manslaughter (ˈmænˌslɔːtə) *n law* the unlawful killing of one human being by another without malice aforethought. See murder (loosely) the killing of a human being

Manson (ˈmænsən) *n* Sir Patrick. 1844–1922, British physician, who established that mosquitoes transmit certain parasites responsible for human diseases

mansuetude (ˈmænswɪˌtjuːd) *n archaic* gentleness or mildness [c14: from Latin *mansuētūdō*, from *mansuētus*, past participle of *mansuēscere* to make tame by handling, from *manus* hand + *suescēre* to train]

Mansur (manˈsʊə) *n* Abu Ja'far al- (ˈæbuː ˈdʒæfə ˈæl). 712–75 AD, 2nd caliph of the Abbasid dynasty (754–75). He founded Baghdad (762) and made it the Islamic capital

Mansûra (mænˈsʊərə) *n* See El Mansûra

manta (ˈmæntə; *Spanish* ˈmanta) *n* **1** Also called: manta ray, devilfish, devil ray any large ray (fish) of the family *Mobulidae*, having very wide winglike pectoral fins and feeding on plankton **2** a rough cotton cloth made in Spain and Spanish America **3** a piece of this used as a blanket or shawl [Spanish: cloak, from Vulgar Latin; see MANTLE. The manta ray is so called because it is caught in a trap resembling a blanket]

manteau (ˈmæntəʊ; *French* mãto) *n, pl* -teaus (-təʊz) or -teaux (*French* -to) a cloak or mantle [c17: via French from Latin *mantellum* MANTLE]

Mantegna (*Italian* manˈtɛɲɲa) *n* Andrea (anˈdrɛːa). 1431–1506, Italian painter and engraver, noted esp for his frescoes, such as those in the Ducal Palace, Mantua

mantel or *less commonly* **mantle** (ˈmæntəl) *n* **1** a wooden or stone frame around the opening of a fireplace, together with its decorative facing **2** Also called: mantel shelf a shelf above this frame [c15: from French, variant of MANTLE]

mantelet (ˈmæntəˌlɛt) or **mantlet** *n* **1** a woman's short mantle, often lace-trimmed, worn in the mid-19th century **2** a portable bulletproof screen or shelter [c14: from Old French, diminutive of *mantel* MANTLE]

mantelpiece (ˈmæntəlˌpiːs) *n* **1** Also called: mantel shelf, chimneypiece a shelf above a fireplace often forming part of the mantel **2** another word for **mantel** (sense 1)

mantic (ˈmæntɪk) *adj* **1** of or relating to divination and prophecy **2** having divining or prophetic powers [c19: from Greek *mantikos* prophetic, from *mantis* seer] > ˈmantically *adv*

-mantic *adj combining form* forming adjectives corresponding to nouns ending in **-mancy**

manticore (ˈmæntɪˌkɔː) *n* a monster with a lion's body, a scorpion's tail, and a man's head with three rows of teeth. It roamed the jungles of India and, like the Sphinx, would ask travellers a riddle and kill them when they failed to answer it [c21: from Latin *manticora*, from Greek *mantichōrās*, corruption of *martichorās*, from Persian *mardkhora* man-eater]

mantilla (mænˈtɪlə) *n* a woman's lace or silk scarf covering the shoulders and head, often worn over a comb in the hair, esp in Spain [c18: Spanish, diminutive of *manta* cloak]

Mantinea or **Mantineia** (ˌmæntɪˈneɪə) *n* (in ancient Greece) a city in E Arcadia; site of several battles

mantis (ˈmæntɪs) *n, pl* -tises or -tes (-tiːz) any carnivorous typically green insect of the family *Mantidae*, of warm and tropical regions, having a long body and large eyes and resting with the first pair of legs raised as if in prayer: order *Dictyoptera*. Also called: praying mantis [c17: New Latin, from Greek: prophet, alluding to its praying posture]

mantissa (mænˈtɪsə) *n* the fractional part of a common logarithm representing the digits of the associated number but not its magnitude: *the mantissa of 2.4771 is .4771* [c17: from Latin: something added, of Etruscan origin]

mantle (ˈmæntəl) *n* **1** *archaic* a loose wrap or cloak **2** such a garment regarded as a symbol of someone's power or authority **3** anything that covers completely or envelops **4** a small dome-shaped or cylindrical mesh impregnated with cerium or thorium nitrates, used to increase illumination in a gas or oil lamp **5** Also called: pallium *zoology* a protective layer of epidermis in molluscs that secretes a substance forming the shell **6** *ornithol* the feathers of the folded wings and back, esp when these are of a different colour from the remaining feathers **7** *geology* the part of the earth between the crust and the core, accounting for more than 82% of the earth's volume (but only 68% of its mass) and thought to be composed largely of peridotite **8** a less common spelling of **mantel** ▷ *vb* **9** (*tr*) to envelop or supply with a mantle **10** to spread over or become spread over [c13: via Old French from Latin *mantellum*, diminutive of *mantum* cloak]

Mantova (ˈmantova) *n* the Italian name for **Mantua**

mantra (ˈmæntrə, ˈmʌn-) *n* **1** *Hinduism* any of those parts of the Vedic literature which consist of the metrical psalms of praise **2** *Hinduism, Buddhism* any sacred word or syllable used as an object of concentration and embodying some aspect of spiritual power [c19: from

Sanskrit, literally: speech, instrument of thought, from *man* to think]

mantua ('mæntjʊə) *n* a loose gown of the 17th and 18th centuries, worn open in front to show the underskirt [c17: changed from MANTEAU, through the influence of MANTUA]

Mantua ('mæntjʊə) *n* a city in N Italy, in E Lombardy, surrounded by lakes: birthplace of Virgil. Pop: 47 790 (2001). Italian name: **Mantova**

manual ('mænjʊəl) *adj* 1 of or relating to a hand or hands 2 operated or done by hand 3 physical, as opposed to mental or mechanical: *manual labour* 4 by human labour rather than automatic or computer-aided means ⊳ *n* 5 a book, esp of instructions or information 6 *music* one of the keyboards played by hand on an organ 7 *military* the prescribed drill with small arms [c15: via Old French from Latin *manuālis*, from *manus* hand]
> 'manually *adv*

Manuel I (*Portuguese* ma'nwel) *n* called *the Fortunate*. 1469–1521, king of Portugal (1495–1521); his reign saw the discovery of Brazil and the beginning of Portuguese trade with India and the East

manufactory (,mænjʊ'fæktərɪ, -trɪ) *n*, *pl* **-ries** an obsolete word for: **factory** [c17: from obsolete *manufact*; see MANUFACTURE]

manufacture (,mænjʊ'fæktʃə) *vb* 1 to process or make (a product) from a raw material, esp as a large-scale operation using machinery 2 (*tr*) to invent or concoct ⊳ *n* 3 the production of goods, esp by industrial processes 4 a manufactured product 5 the creation or production of anything [c16: from obsolete *manufact* hand-made, from Late Latin *manūfactus*, from Latin *manus* hand + *facere* to make] > ,manu'facturing *n, adj*

manufacturer (,mænjʊ'fæktʃərə) *n* a person or business concern that manufactures goods or owns a factory

manuhiri (,mɑːnuː'hiːrɪ) *n* NZ 1 a visitor to a Māori marae 2 a Māori term for a non-Māori person, seen as a guest in the country [Māori]

manuka ('mɑːnuːkə) *n* a New Zealand myrtaceous tree, *Leptospermum scoparium*, with strong elastic wood and aromatic leaves. Also called: **red tea tree**

Manukau ('mɑːnuː,kaʊ) *n* a city in New Zealand, on **Manukau Harbour** (an inlet of the Tasman Sea) near Auckland on NW North Island. Pop: 326 200 (2004 est)

manumission (,mænjʊ'mɪʃən) *n* the act of freeing or the state of being freed from slavery, servitude, etc

manumit (,mænjʊ'mɪt) *vb* **-mits**, **-mitting**, **-mitted** (*tr*) to free from slavery, servitude, etc; emancipate [c15: from Latin *manūmittere* to release, from *manū* from one's hand + *ēmittere* to send away]

manure (mə'njʊə) *n* 1 animal excreta, usually with straw, used to fertilize land 2 *chiefly Brit* any material, esp chemical fertilizer, used to fertilize land ⊳ *vb* 3 (*tr*) to spread manure upon (fields or soil) [c14: from Medieval Latin *manuopera*; manual work; see MANOEUVRE]
> ma'nurer *n*

manus ('meɪnəs) *n*, *pl* **-nus** 1 *anatomy* the wrist and hand 2 the corresponding part in other vertebrates [c19: Latin: hand]

Manu Samoa ('mænʊ) *n* the international Rugby Union football team of Western Samoa

manuscript ('mænjʊ,skrɪpt) *n* 1 a book or other document written by hand 2 the original handwritten or typed version of a book, article, etc, as submitted by an author for publication 3 handwriting, as opposed to printing [c16: from Medieval Latin *manūscriptus*, from Latin *manus* hand + *scribere* to write]

Manutius (mə'njuːʃəs) *n* See **Aldus Manutius**

Manx (mæŋks) *adj* 1 of, relating to, or characteristic of the Isle of Man, its inhabitants, their language, or their dialect of English ⊳ *n* 2 a language of the Isle of Man, belonging to the N Celtic branch of the Indo-European family and closely related to Scottish Gaelic 3 (*functioning as plural*) the people of the Isle of Man [c16: earlier *Maniske*, from Scandinavian, from *Mana* Isle of Man + *-iske* -ISH]

Manx cat *n* a short-haired tailless variety of cat, believed to originate on the Isle of Man

Manxman ('mæŋksmən) *or feminine* **Manxwoman**

('mæŋkswʊmən) *n, pl* **-men** *or* **-women** a native or inhabitant of the Isle of Man

many ('mɛnɪ) *determiner* 1 (sometimes preceded by *a great* or *a good*) a a large number of: *many coaches; many times* b (*as pronoun; functioning as plural*): *many are seated already* 2 (foll by *a, an,* or *another*) each of a considerable number of: *many a man* 3 (preceded by *as, too, that,* etc) a a great number of: *as many apples as you like; too many clouds to see* b (*as pronoun; functioning as plural*): *I have as many as you* ⊳ *n* 4 **the many** the majority of mankind, esp the common people [Old English *manig*; related to Old Frisian *manich*, Middle Dutch *menech*, Old High German *manag*]

many-sided *adj* having many sides, aspects, etc
> ,many-'sidedness *n*

many-valued logic *n* the study of logical systems in which the truth-values that a proposition may have are not restricted to two, representing only truth and falsity

manzanilla (,mænzə'nɪlə) *n* a very dry pale sherry [c19: from Spanish: camomile (referring to its bouquet)]

Manzoni (*Italian* man'dzoːni) *n* **Alessandro** (ales'sandro). 1785–1873, Italian romantic novelist and poet, famous for his historical novel I *Promessi sposi* (1825–27)

Maoism ('maʊɪzəm) *n* 1 Marxism-Leninism as interpreted by Mao Tse-tung (1893–1976), the Chinese Marxist theoretician and statesman: distinguished by its theory of guerrilla warfare and its emphasis on the revolutionary potential of the peasantry 2 adherence to or reverence for Mao Tse-tung and his teachings
> 'Maoist *n, adj*

Māori ('maʊrɪ) *n* 1 *pl* **-ri** *or* **-ris** a member of the people living in New Zealand and the Cook Islands since before the arrival of European settlers. They are descended from Polynesian voyagers who migrated in successive waves from the ninth century onwards 2 the language of this people, belonging to the Malayo-Polynesian family ⊳ *adj* 3 of or relating to this people or their language

Māori bread *n* NZ bread made with fermented potato yeast

Māoriland ('maʊrɪ,lænd) *n* an obsolete name for: **New Zealand** > 'Māori,lander *n*

Māori rat *n* a small brown rat, *Rattus exulans*, native to New Zealand. Also called: **kiore**

Mao Tse-tung ('maʊ tseɪ'tʊŋ) *or* **Mao Ze Dong** *n* 1893–1976, Chinese Marxist theoretician and statesman. The son of a peasant farmer, he helped to found the Chinese Communist Party (1921) and established a soviet republic in SE China (1931–34). He led the retreat of Communist forces to NW China known as the Long March (1935–36), emerging as leader of the party. In opposing the Japanese in World War II, he united with the Kuomintang regime, which he then defeated in the ensuing civil war. He founded the People's Republic of China (1949) of which he was chairman until 1959. As party chairman until his death, he instigated the Cultural Revolution in 1966

map (mæp) *n* 1 a diagrammatic representation of the earth's surface or part of it, showing the geographical distributions, positions, etc, of natural or artificial features such as roads, towns, relief, rainfall, etc 2 a diagrammatic representation of the distribution of stars or of the surface of a celestial body 3 a maplike drawing of anything 4 *maths* another name for: **function** (sense 4) 5 a slang word for: **face** (sense 1) 6 **off the map** no longer important or in existence (esp in the phrase **wipe off the map**) 7 **put on the map** to make (a town, company, etc) well-known ⊳ *vb* **maps, mapping, mapped** (*tr*) 8 to make a map of 9 *maths* to represent or transform (a function, figure, set, etc): *the results were mapped onto a graph*. See also **map out** 10 **map onto** (*intr*) to fit in with or correspond to [c16: from Medieval Latin *mappa* (*mundi*) map (of the world), from Latin *mappa* cloth]

Map (mæp) *or* **Mapes** (mæps, 'meɪpiːz) *n* **Walter**. ?1140–?1209, Welsh ecclesiastic and satirical writer. His chief work is the miscellany *De Nugis curialium*

maple ('meɪpəl) *n* 1 any tree or shrub of the N temperate genus *Acer*, having winged seeds borne in pairs and lobed leaves: family *Aceraceae* 2 the hard close-grained wood of any of these trees, used for furniture and flooring **3** the flavour of the sap of the sugar maple ▷ See also **sugar maple** [c14: from Old English *mapel-*, as in *mapeltrēow* maple tree]

Maple Leaf *n* **the Maple Leaf** the national flag of Canada, consisting of a representation of a maple leaf in red on a white central panel with a vertical red bar on either side

maple sugar *n* *US & Canadian* sugar made from the sap of the sugar maple

maple syrup *n* a very sweet syrup made from the sap of the sugar maple

map out *vb* (*tr, adverb*) to plan or design

mapping ('mæpɪŋ) *n* *maths* another name for **function** (sense 4)

map projection *n* a means of representing or a representation of the globe or celestial sphere or part of it on a flat map, using a grid of lines of latitude and longitude

Maputo (mə'puːtəʊ) *n* the capital and chief port of Mozambique, in the south on Delagoa Bay: became capital in 1907; the nearest port to the Rand gold-mining and industrial region of South Africa. Pop: 1 316 000 (2005 est). Former name (until 1975): **Lourenço Marques**

maquette (mæ'kɛt) *n* a sculptor's small preliminary model or sketch [c20: from French, from Italian *macchietta* a little sketch, from *macchiare*, from Latin *maculāre* to stain, from *macula* spot, blemish]

maquis (maː'kiː) *n*, *pl* -**quis** (-'kiː) **1** shrubby mostly evergreen vegetation found in coastal regions of the Mediterranean: includes myrtles, heaths, arbutus, cork oak, and ilex **2** (*often capital*) **a** the French underground movement that fought against the German occupying forces in World War II **b** a member of this movement [c20: from French, from Italian *macchia* thicket, from Latin *macula* spot]

mar (maː) *vb* **mars, marring, marred** (*tr*) to cause harm to; spoil or impair [Old English *merran*; compare Old Saxon *merrian* to hinder, Old Norse *merja* to bruise] ▷ 'marrer *n*

Mar *abbreviation* March

marabou ('mærə,buː) *n* **1** a large black-and-white African carrion-eating stork, *Leptoptilos crumeniferus*, with a very short naked neck and a straight heavy bill **2** a down feather of this bird, used to trim garments [c19: from French, from Arabic *murābit* MARABOUT, so called because the stork is considered a holy bird in Islam]

marabout ('mærə,buː) *n* **1** a Muslim holy man or hermit of North Africa **2** a shrine of the grave of a marabout [c17: via French and Portuguese *marabuto*, from Arabic *murābit*]

maraca (mə'rækə) *n* a percussion instrument, usually one of a pair, consisting of a gourd or plastic shell filled with dried seeds, pebbles, etc It is used chiefly in Latin American music [c20: Brazilian Portuguese, from Tupi]

Maracaibo (,mærə'kaɪbəʊ; *Spanish* mara'kaiβo) *n* **1** a port in NW Venezuela, on the channel from Lake Maracaibo to the Gulf of Venezuela: the second largest city in the country; University of Zulia (1891); major oil centre. Pop: 2 182 000 (2005 est) **2** Lake Maracaibo a lake in NW Venezuela, linked with the Gulf of Venezuela by a dredged channel: centre of the Venezuelan and South American oil industry. Area: about 13 000 sq km (500 sq miles)

Maracanda (,mærə'kændə) *n* the ancient name for **Samarkand**

Maracay (*Spanish* mara'kai) *n* a city in N central Venezuela: developed greatly as the headquarters of Juan Vicente Gómez (1857–1935) during his dictatorship; textile industries. Pop: 1 138 000 (2005 est)

Maradona (,mærə'dɒnə) *n* **Diego Armando** (dɪ'eɪgəʊ). born 1960, Argentinian footballer

marae (mə'raɪ) *n* **1** NZ a traditional Māori tribal meeting place, originally one in the open air, now frequently a purpose-built building **2** (in Polynesia) an open-air place of worship [Māori]

Marajó (*Portuguese* mara'ʒɔ) *n* an island in N Brazil, at the mouth of the Amazon. Area: 38 610 sq km (15 444 sq miles)

Maranhão (*Portuguese* marə'ɲɐu) *n* a state of NE Brazil, on the Atlantic: forested and humid in the northwest, with high plateaus in the east and south. Capital: São Luís. Pop: 5 803 224 (2002). Area: 328 666 sq km (128 179 sq miles)

Marañón (*Spanish* mara'ɲɔn) *n* a river in NE Peru, rising in the Andes and flowing northwest into the Ucayali River, forming the Amazon. Length: about 1450 km (900 miles)

maranta (mə'ræntə) *n* any plant of the tropical American rhizomatous genus *Maranta*, some species of which are grown as pot plants for their showy leaves in variegated shades of green: family *Marantaceae* [named after Bartolomea *Maranti*, died 1571, Venetian botanist]

Maraş (mæ'ræʃ) *n* a town in S Turkey: noted formerly for the manufacture of weapons but now for carpets and embroidery. Pop: 366 000 (2005 est)

marasca (mə'ræskə) *n* a European cherry tree, *Prunus cerasus marasca*, with red acid-tasting fruit from which maraschino is made [c19: from Italian, variant of *amarasca* from *amaro*, from Latin *amārus* bitter]

maraschino (,mærə'skiːnəʊ, -'ʃiːnəʊ) *n* a liqueur made from marasca cherries and flavoured with the kernels, having a taste like bitter almonds [c18: from Italian; see MARASCA]

maraschino cherry *n* a cherry preserved in maraschino or an imitation of this liqueur, used as a garnish

marasmus (mə'ræzməs) *n* *pathol* general emaciation and wasting, esp in infants, thought to be associated with severe malnutrition or impaired utilization of nutrients [c17: from New Latin, from Greek *marasmos*, from *marainein* to waste] ▷ ma'rasmic *adj*

Marat (*French* mara) *n* **Jean Paul** (ʒɑ̃ pɔl). 1743–93, French revolutionary leader and journalist. He founded the radical newspaper *L'Ami du peuple* and was elected to the National Convention (1792). He was instrumental in overthrowing the Girondists (1793); he was stabbed to death in his bath by Charlotte Corday

marathon ('mærəθən) *n* **1** a race on foot of 26 miles 385 yards (42.195 kilometres): an event in the modern Olympics **2** **a** any long or arduous task, assignment, etc **b** (*as modifier*): *a marathon effort* [referring to the feat of the messenger who ran more than 20 miles from Marathon to Athens to bring the news of victory in 490 BC]

Marathon ('mærəθən) *n* a plain in Attica northeast of Athens: site of a victory of the Athenians and Plataeans over the Persians (490 BC)

marathoner ('mærəθənə) *n* a person who runs in a marathon

marathon group *n* (in psychotherapy) an encounter group that lasts for many hours or days

maraud (mə'rɔːd) *vb* to wander or raid in search of plunder [c18: from French *marauder* to prowl, from *maraud* vagabond] ▷ ma'rauder *n*

marauding (mə'rɔːdɪŋ) *adj* wandering or raiding in search of plunder or victims

Marbella (maː'beɪjə) *n* a coastal resort in S Spain, on the Costa del Sol. Pop: 100 000 (2004 est)

marble ('maːbʲl) *n* **1 a** a hard crystalline metamorphic rock resulting from the recrystallization of a limestone: takes a high polish and is used for building and sculpture **b** (*as modifier*): *a marble bust* **2** a block or work of art of marble **3** a small round glass or stone ball used in playing marbles ▷ *vb* **4** (*tr*) to mottle with variegated streaks in imitation of marble [c12: via Old French from Latin *marmor*, from Greek *marmaros*, related to Greek *marmairein* to gleam] ▷ 'marbled *adj*

marbles ('maːbʲlz) *n* **1** (*functioning as singular*) a game in which marbles are rolled at one another, similar to bowls **2** (*functioning as plural*) *informal* wits: *to lose one's marbles*

marbling ('maːblɪŋ) *n* **1** a mottled effect or pattern resembling marble **2** such an effect obtained by transferring floating colours from a bath of gum solution **3** the streaks of fat in lean meat

Marburg ('maːˌbɜːg; *German* 'maːrbʊrk) *n* **1** a city in W central Germany, in Hesse: famous for the religious debate between Luther and Zwingli in 1529; Europe's

first Protestant university (1527). Pop: 78 511 (2003 est)
2 the German name for **Maribor**

Marburg disease *n* a severe, sometimes fatal, viral disease of the green monkey, which may be transmitted to humans. Symptoms include fever, vomiting, and internal bleeding. Also called: green monkey disease [C20 after MARBURG, in which the first human cases were recorded]

marc (mɑːk; *French* mar) *n* **1** the remains of grapes or other fruit that have been pressed for wine-making **2** a brandy distilled from these [C17: from French, from Old French *marchier* to trample (grapes), MARCH¹]

Marc (*German* mark) *n* **Franz** (frants). 1880–1916, German expressionist painter; cofounder with Kandinsky of the *Blaue Reiter* group (1911). He is noted for his symbolic compositions of animals

marcasite ('mɑːkə,saɪt) *n* **1** a metallic pale yellow mineral consisting of iron sulphide in orthorhombic crystalline form used in jewellery. Formula: FeS₂ **2** a cut and polished form of steel or any white metal used for making jewellery [C15: from Medieval Latin *marcasīta*, from Arabic *marqashītā*, perhaps from Persian]

marcato (mɑːˈkɑːtəʊ) *music adv* with each note heavily accented [C19: from Italian: marked]

Marceau (*French* marso) *n* **Marcel** (marsɛl). 1923–2007, French mime artist

Marcel (*French* marsɛl) *n* **Gabriel** (**Honoré**) (gabriɛl). 1889–1973, French Christian existentialist philosopher and dramatist, whose philosophical works include *Being and Having* (1949) and *The Mystery of Being* (1951)

Marcellus (mɑːˈsɛləs) *n* **Marcus Claudius** ('mɑːkəs 'klɔːdɪəs). ?268–208 BC, Roman general and consul, who captured Syracuse (212) in the Second Punic War

march¹ (mɑːtʃ) *vb* **1** (*intr*) to walk or proceed with stately or regular steps, usually in a procession or military formation **2** (*tr*) to make (a person or group) proceed **3** (*tr*) to traverse or cover by marching ▷ *n* **4** the act or an instance of marching **5** a regular stride **6** a long or exhausting walk **7** advance; progression (of time, etc) **8** a distance or route covered by marching **9** a piece of music, usually in four beats to the bar, having a strongly accented rhythm **10** steal a march on to gain an advantage over, esp by a secret or underhand enterprise [C16: from Old French *marchier* to tread, probably of Germanic origin; compare Old English *mearcian* to MARK¹] > 'marcher *n*

march² (mɑːtʃ) *n* **1** Also called: marchland a frontier, border, or boundary or the land lying along it, often of disputed ownership ▷ *vb* **2** (*intr*; foll by *upon* or *with*) to share a common border (with) [C13: from Old French *marche*, from Germanic; related to MARK¹]

March¹ (mɑːtʃ) *n* the third month of the year, consisting of 31 days [from Old French, from Latin *Martius* (month) of Mars]

March² (març) *n* the German name for the **Morava** (sense 1)

Marche (*French* marʃ) *n* a former province of central France

Marches ('mɑːtʃɪz) the Marches *n* **1** the border area between England and Wales or Scotland, both characterized by continual feuding (13th–16th centuries) **2** a region of central Italy. Capital: Ancona. Pop: 1 484 601 (2003 est). Area: 9692 sq km (3780 sq miles) **3** any of various other border regions

March hare *n* a hare during its breeding season in March, noted for its wild and excitable behaviour (esp in the phrase **mad as a March hare**)

marching girl *n* (*often plural*) *Austral & NZ* one of a team of girls dressed in fancy uniform who perform marching formations

marching orders *pl n* **1** military orders, esp to infantry, giving instructions about a march, its destination, etc **2** *informal* notice of dismissal, esp from employment

marchioness ('mɑːʃənɪs, ˌmɑːʃəˈnɛs) *n* **1** the wife or widow of a marquis **2** a woman who holds the rank of marquis [C16: from Medieval Latin *marchionissa*, feminine of *marchiō* MARQUIS]

marchpane ('mɑːtʃ,peɪn) *n* an archaic word for **marzipan** (sense 1) [C15: from French]

Marciano (ˌmɑːsɪˈænəʊ, -ˈɑːnəʊ) *n* **Rocky**. original name *Rocco Francis Marchegiano* 1923–69, US heavyweight boxer; world heavyweight champion, 1952–56

Marconi (mɑːˈkəʊnɪ) *n* **Guglielmo** (guʎˈʎɛlmo). 1874–1937, Italian physicist, who developed radiotelegraphy and succeeded in transmitting signals across the Atlantic (1901): Nobel prize for physics 1909

Marco Polo ('mɑːkəʊ 'pəʊləʊ) *n* See **Polo**

Marcos ('mɑːkɒs) *n* **Ferdinand** (**Edralin**). 1917–89, Filipino statesman; president of the Philippines from 1965; deposed and exiled in 1986

Marcus Aurelius Antoninus ('mɑːkəs ɔːˈriːlɪəs ˌæntəˈnaɪnəs) *n* original name *Marcus Annius Verus*. 121–180 AD, Roman emperor (161–180) noted particularly for his *Meditations*, propounding his stoic view of life

Marcuse (mɑːˈkuːzə) *n* **Herbert**. 1898–1979, US philosopher, born in Germany. In his later works he analysed the situation of man under monopoly capitalism and the dehumanizing effects of modern technology. His works include *Eros and Civilization* (1958) and *One Dimensional Man* (1964)

Mar del Plata (*Spanish* 'mar ðel 'plata) *n* a city and resort in E Argentina, on the Atlantic: fishing port. Pop: 552 000 (2005 est)

Mardi Gras ('mɑːdɪ 'grɑː) *n* the festival of Shrove Tuesday, celebrated in some cities with great revelry [French: fat Tuesday]

Marduk ('mɑːdʊk) *n* the chief god of the Babylonian pantheon

mare¹ (mɛə) *n* the adult female of a horse or zebra [C12: from Old English, of Germanic origin; related to Old High German *mariha*, Old Norse *merr* mare]

mare² ('mɑːreɪ, -rɪ) *n, pl* maria ('mɑːrɪə) **1** (*capital when part of a name*) any of a large number of huge dry plains on the surface of the moon, visible as dark markings and once thought to be seas: *Mare Imbrium* (Sea of Showers) **2** a similar area on the surface of Mars, such as *Mare Sirenum* [from Latin: sea]

Marengo (məˈrɛŋgəʊ; *Italian* maˈrɛngo) *n* a village in NW Italy: site of a major battle in which Napoleon decisively defeated the Austrians (1800)

Marenzio (*Italian* maˈrɛntsjo) *n* **Luca** ('luːka). 1553–99, Italian composer of madrigals

mare's-nest *n* **1** a discovery imagined to be important but proving worthless **2** a disordered situation

mare's-tail *n* **1** a wisp of trailing cirrus cloud, often indicating high winds in the upper troposphere **2** an erect cosmopolitan pond plant, *Hippuris vulgaris*, with minute flowers and crowded whorls of narrow leaves: family Hippuridaceae

Margaret ('mɑːgrət) *n* **1** called the *Maid of Norway*. ?1282–90, queen of Scotland (1286–90); daughter of Eric II of Norway. Her death while sailing to England to marry the future Edward II led Edward I to declare dominion over Scotland **2** 1353–1412, queen of Sweden (1388–1412) and regent of Norway and Denmark (1380–1412), who united the three countries under her rule **3** Princess. 1930–2002, younger sister of Queen Elizabeth II of Great Britain and Northern Ireland

Margaret of Anjou *n* 1430–82, queen of England. She married the mentally unstable Henry VI of England in 1445 to confirm the truce with France during the Hundred Years' War. She became a leader of the Lancastrians in the Wars of the Roses and was defeated at Tewkesbury (1471) by Edward IV

Margaret of Navarre *n* Also called: Margaret of Angoulême 1492–1549, queen of Navarre (1544–49) by marriage to Henry II of Navarre; sister of Francis I of France. She was a poet, a patron of humanism, and author of the *Heptaméron* (1558)

Margaret of Scotland *n* **Saint**. 1045–93, queen consort of Malcolm III of Scotland. Her piety and benefactions to the church led to her canonization (1250). Feast days: June 10, Nov 16

Margaret of Valois *n* 1553–1615, daughter of Henry II of France and Catherine de' Medici; queen of Navarre (1572) by marriage to Henry of Navarre. The marriage was dissolved (1599) after his accession as Henry IV of France: noted for her *Mémoires*

margaric (mɑːˈɡærɪk) or **margaritic** adj of or resembling pearl [c19: from Greek margaron pearl]

margarine (ˌmɑːdʒəˈriːn, ˌmɑːɡə-) n a substitute for butter, prepared from vegetable and animal fats by emulsifying them with water and adding small amounts of milk, salt, vitamins, colouring matter, etc [c19: from MARGARIC]

Margarita (ˌmɑːɡəˈriːtə) n an island in the Caribbean, off the NE coast of Venezuela: pearl fishing. Capital: La Asunción

Margate (ˈmɑːɡeɪt) n a town and resort in SE England, in E Kent on the Isle of Thanet. Pop: 58 465 (2001)

marge[1] (mɑːdʒ) n Brit informal short for **margarine**

marge[2] (mɑːdʒ) n archaic a margin [c16: from French]

margin (ˈmɑːdʒɪn) or archaic **margent** (ˈmɑːdʒənt) n 1 an edge or rim, and the area immediately adjacent to it; border 2 the blank space surrounding the text on a page 3 a vertical line on a page, esp one on the left-hand side, delineating this space 4 an additional amount or one beyond the minimum necessary: a margin of error 5 chiefly Austral a payment made in addition to a basic wage, esp for special skill or responsibility 6 a bound or limit 7 the amount by which one thing differs from another 8 commerce the profit on a transaction 9 economics the minimum return below which an enterprise becomes unprofitable 10 finance collateral deposited by a client with a broker as security ▷ vb (tr) 11 to provide with a margin; border 12 finance to deposit a margin upon [c14: from Latin margō border; related to MARCH², MARK¹]

marginal (ˈmɑːdʒɪnᵊl) adj 1 of, in, on, or constituting a margin 2 close to a limit, esp a lower limit: marginal legal ability 3 not considered central or important; insignificant, minor, small 4 economics relating to goods or services produced and sold at the margin of profitability: marginal cost 5 politics chiefly Brit & NZ of or designating a constituency in which elections tend to be won by small margins: a marginal seat 6 designating agricultural land on the margin of cultivated zones ▷ noun 7 politics chiefly Brit & NZ a marginal constituency > **marginality** (ˌmɑːdʒɪˈnælɪtɪ) n > **'marginally** adv

marginalia (ˌmɑːdʒɪˈneɪlɪə) pl n notes in the margin of a book, manuscript, or letter [c19: New Latin, noun (neuter plural) from marginālis marginal]

marginalize or **marginalise** (ˈmɑːdʒɪnᵊˌlaɪz) vb (tr) to relegate to the fringes, out of the mainstream; make seem unimportant: various economic assumptions marginalize women > ˌmarginaliˈzation or ˌmarginaliˈsation n

marginate (ˈmɑːdʒɪˌneɪt) vb 1 (tr) to provide with a margin or margins ▷ adj 2 biology having a margin of a distinct colour or form [c18: from Latin margināre] > ˌmarginˈation n

Margolis (ˈmɑːɡəlɪs) n **Donald.** born 1955, US playwright; plays include The Loman Family Picnic (1989) and the Pulitzer Prize-winning Dinner with Friends (1999)

margrave (ˈmɑːˌɡreɪv) n a German nobleman ranking above a count. Margraves were originally counts appointed to govern frontier provinces, but all had become princes of the Holy Roman Empire by the 12th century [c16: from Middle Dutch markgrave, literally: count of the MARCH²] > **margravate** (ˈmɑːɡrəvɪt) or **margraviate** (mɑːˈɡreɪvɪɪt) n

margravine (ˈmɑːɡrəˌviːn) n 1 the wife or widow of a margrave 2 a woman who holds the rank of margrave [c17: from Middle Dutch, feminine of MARGRAVE]

Margrethe II (Danish marˈɡreːdə) n born 1940, queen of Denmark from 1972

marguerite (ˌmɑːɡəˈriːt) n 1 a cultivated garden plant, Chrysanthemum frutescens, whose flower heads have white or pale yellow rays around a yellow disc: family Asteraceae (composites) 2 any of various related plants with daisy-like flowers, esp C. leucanthemum [c19: from French: daisy, pearl, from Latin margarīta, from Greek margaritēs, from margaron]

maria (ˈmɑːrɪə) n the plural of **mare²**

mariachi (ˌmɑːrɪˈɑːtʃɪ) n a small ensemble of street musicians in Mexico [c20: from Mexican Spanish]

Maria de' Medici (Italian maˈriːa de ˈmɛːditʃi) n French name Marie de Médicis. 1573–1642, queen of France (1600–10) by marriage to Henry IV of France; daughter of Francesco, grand duke of Tuscany. She became regent for her son (later Louis XIII) but continued to wield power after he came of age (1614). She was finally exiled from France in 1631 after plotting to undermine Richelieu's influence at court

Mariana Islands (ˌmærɪˈɑːnə) pl n a chain of volcanic and coral islands in the W Pacific, east of the Philippines and north of New Guinea: divided politically into Guam (a US unincorporated territory) and the islands north of Guam constituting the Northern Mariana Islands (a US commonwealth territory). Area: 1018 sq km (393 sq miles). Former name (1521–1668): Ladrone Islands

Marianao (Spanish marjaˈnao) n a city in NW Cuba, adjacent to W Havana city: the chief Cuban military base. Pop: 133 016 (1989)

Mariánské Lázně (Czech ˈmarjanskɛ ˈlaːznjɛ) n a town in the W Czech Republic: a fashionable spa in the 18th and 19th centuries. Pop: 13 872 (2007 est). German name: Marienbad

Maria Theresa (məˈriːə təˈreɪzə) n 1717–80, archduchess of Austria and queen of Hungary and Bohemia (1740–80); the daughter and heiress of Emperor Charles VI of Austria; the wife of Emperor Francis I; the mother of Emperor Joseph II. In the War of the Austrian Succession (1740–48) she was confirmed in all her possessions except Silesia, which she attempted unsuccessfully to regain in the Seven Years' War (1756–63)

Maribor (ˈmærɪbɔː) n an industrial city in N Slovenia on the Drava River: a flourishing Hapsburg trading centre in the 13th century; resort. Pop: 110 668 (2002). German name: Marburg

Marie (məˈriː) n 1875–1938, queen consort of Ferdinand I of Romania. A granddaughter of Queen Victoria, she secured Romania's support for the Allies in World War I

Marie Antoinette (French mari ãtwanɛt) n 1755–93, queen of France (1774–93) by marriage to Louis XVI of France. Her opposition to reform during the Revolution contributed to the overthrow of the monarchy; guillotined

Marie Byrd Land (ˈmɑːrɪ ˈbɜːd) n the former name of **Byrd Land**

Marie de France (French mari də frɑ̃s) n 12th century AD, French poet, who probably lived in England; noted for her lais (verse narratives) based on Celtic tales

Marie Galante (French mari ɡalãt) n an island in the E Caribbean southeast of Guadeloupe, of which it is a dependency. Chief town: Grand Bourg. Pop: 12 488 (1999). Area: 155 sq km (60 sq miles)

Mariehamn (mariəˈhamn) n a city in SW Finland, chief port of the Åland Islands. Pop: 10 693 (2004 est). Finnish name: Maarianhamina

Marie Louise (French mari lwiz) n 1791–1847, empress of France (1811–15) as the second wife of Napoleon I; daughter of Francis I of Austria. On Napoleon's abdication (1815) she became Duchess of Parma

Mari El Republic (ˈmɑːrɪ) n a constituent republic of W central Russia, in the middle Volga basin. Capital: Yoshkar-Ola. Pop: 728 000 (2002). Area: 23 200 sq km (8955 sq miles)

Marienbad (ˈmærɪənˌbæd; German maˈriːənbaːt) n the German name for **Mariánské Lázně**

marigold (ˈmærɪˌɡəʊld) n 1 any of various tropical American plants of the genus Tagetes, esp T. erecta (**African marigold**) and T. patula (**French marigold**), cultivated for their yellow or orange flower heads and strongly scented foliage: family Asteraceae (composites) 2 any of various similar or related plants, such as the marsh marigold, pot marigold, bur marigold, and fig marigold [c14: from Mary (the Virgin) + GOLD]

marijuana or **marihuana** (ˌmærɪˈhwɑːnə) n 1 the dried leaves and flowers of the hemp plant, used for its euphoric effects, esp in the form of cigarettes. See also cannabis 2 another name for **hemp** (sense 1) [c19: from Mexican Spanish]

marimba (məˈrɪmbə) n a Latin American percussion instrument consisting of a set of hardwood plates placed over tuned metal resonators, played with two soft-headed sticks in each hand [c18: of West African origin]

Marin ('mɑːrɪn) *n* **John.** 1870–1953, US painter, noted esp for his watercolour landscapes and seascapes

marina (mə'riːnə) *n* an elaborate docking facility for pleasure boats [c19: via Italian and Spanish from Latin: MARINE]

marinade *n* (ˌmærɪ'neɪd) 1 a spiced liquid mixture of oil, wine, vinegar, herbs, etc, in which meat or fish is soaked before cooking 2 meat or fish soaked in this liquid ▷ *vb* ('mærɪˌneɪd) 3 a variant of **marinate** [c17: from French, from Spanish *marinada,* from *marinar* to pickle in brine, MARINATE]

marinate ('mærɪˌneɪt) *vb* to soak in marinade [c17: probably from Italian *marinato,* from *marinare* to pickle, ultimately from Latin *marīnus* MARINE] > ˌmari'nation *n*

Marinduque (ˌmɑːrɪn'duːkeɪ) *n* an island of the central Philippines, east of Mindoro: forms, with offshore islets, a province of the Philippines. Capital: Boac. Pop (Marinduque province): 217 392 (2000). Area: 960 sq km (370 sq miles)

marine (mə'riːn) *adj* (*usually prenominal*) 1 of, found in, or relating to the sea 2 of or relating to shipping, navigation, etc 3 of or relating to a body of seagoing troops: *marine corps* 4 of or relating to a government department concerned with maritime affairs 5 used or adapted for use at sea ▷ *n* 6 shipping and navigation in general 7 (*capital when part of a name*) a member of a marine corps or similar body 8 a picture of a ship, seascape, etc 9 tell it to the marines *informal* an expression of disbelief [c15: from Old French *marin,* from Latin *marīnus,* from *mare* sea]

mariner ('mærɪnə) *n* a formal or literary word for: **seaman** [c13: from Anglo-French, ultimately from Latin *marīnus* MARINE]

Marinetti (*Italian* mari'netti) *n* **Filippo Tommaso** (fi'lippo tom'maːzo). 1876–1944, Italian poet; founder of futurism (1909)

Mariolatry *or* **Maryolatry** (ˌmɛərɪ'ɒlətrɪ) *n* *derogatory* exaggerated veneration of the Virgin Mary > ˌMari'olater *or* ˌMary'olater *n* > ˌMari'olatrous *or* ˌMary'olatrous *adj*

marionette (ˌmærɪə'nɛt) *n* an articulated puppet or doll whose jointed limbs are moved by strings [c17: from French, from *Marion,* diminutive of *Marie* Mary + -ETTE]

Marist ('mɛərɪst) *RC Church n* a member of the Society of Mary, a religious congregation founded in 1824 [c19: from French *Mariste,* from *Marie* Mary (the virgin)]

Maritain (*French* maritɛ̃) *n* **Jacques** (ʒak). 1882–1973, French neo-Thomist Roman Catholic philosopher

marital ('mærɪtəl) *adj* 1 of or relating to marriage 2 of or relating to a husband [c17: from Latin *marītālis,* from *marītus* married (adj), husband (n); related to *mās* male] > 'maritally *adv*

maritime ('mærɪˌtaɪm) *adj* 1 of or relating to navigation, shipping, etc; seafaring 2 of, relating to, near, or living near the sea 3 (of a climate) having small temperature differences between summer and winter; equable [c16: from Latin *maritimus* from *mare* sea]

Maritime Alps *pl n* a range of the W Alps in SE France and NW Italy. Highest peak: Argentera, 3297 m (10 817 ft)

Maritime Command *n Canadian* the naval branch of the Canadian armed forces

Maritime Provinces *or* **Maritimes** *pl n* the Maritime Provinces another name for the Atlantic Provinces, but often excluding Newfoundland and Labrador

Maritimer ('mærɪˌtaɪmə) *n* a native or inhabitant of the Maritime Provinces of Canada

Maritsa (*Bulgarian* ma'ritsa) *n* a river in S Europe, rising in S Bulgaria and flowing east into Turkey, then south from Edirne as part of the border between Turkey and Greece to the Aegean. Length: 483 km (300 miles). Turkish name: Meriç. Greek name: Évros

Mariupol (*Russian* məri'upəlj) *n* a port in SE Ukraine, on an estuary leading to the Sea of Azov. Pop: 485 000 (2005 est). Former name (1948–91): Zhdanov

Marius ('mɛərɪəs, 'mærɪəs) *n* **Gaius** ('gaɪəs). ?155–86 BC, Roman general and consul. He defeated Jugurtha, the Cimbri, and the Teutons (107–101), but his rivalry with Sulla caused civil war (88). He was exiled but returned (87) and took Rome

Marivaux (*French* marivo) *n* **Pierre Carlet de Chamblain de** (pjɛr karlɛ də ʃɑ̃blɛ̃ də). 1688–1763, French dramatist and novelist, noted particularly for his comedies, such as *Le jeu de l'amour et du hasard* (1730) and *La Vie de Marianne* (1731–41)

marjoram ('mɑːdʒərəm) *n* 1 Also called: **sweet marjoram** an aromatic Mediterranean plant, *Origanum* (or *Marjorana*) *hortensis,* with small pale purple flowers and sweet-scented leaves, used for seasoning food and in salads: family *Lamiaceae* (labiates) 2 Also called: **wild marjoram, pot marjoram, origan** a similar and related European plant, *Origanum vulgare.* See also **oregano** [c14: via Old French *majorane,* from Medieval Latin *majorana*]

mark¹ (mɑːk) *n* 1 a visible impression, stain, etc, on a surface, such as a spot or scratch 2 a sign, symbol, or other indication that distinguishes something 3 a cross or other symbol made instead of a signature 4 a written or printed sign or symbol, as for punctuation 5 a letter, number, or percentage used to grade academic work 6 a thing that indicates position or directs; marker 7 a desired or recognized standard: *he is not up to the mark* 8 an indication of some quality, feature, or prowess 9 quality or importance; note: *a person of little mark* 10 a target or goal 11 impression or influence 12 one of the temperature settings on a gas oven: *gas mark 5* 13 (*often capital*) (in trade names) model, brand, or type 14 *slang* a suitable victim, esp for swindling 15 *nautical* one of the intervals distinctively marked on a sounding lead 16 *rugby union* an action in which a player standing inside his own 22m line catches a forward kick by an opponent and shouts "mark", entitling himself to a free kick 17 *Australian rules football* a catch of the ball from a kick of at least 10 yards, after which a free kick is taken 18 *the mark boxing* the middle of the stomach at or above the line made by the boxer's trunks 19 (in medieval England and Germany) a piece of land held in common by the free men of a community 20 make one's mark to succeed or achieve recognition 21 on your mark or on your marks a command given to runners in a race to prepare themselves at the starting line ▷ *vb* 22 to make or receive (a visible impression, trace, or stain) on (a surface) 23 (*tr*) to characterize or distinguish 24 (often foll by *off* or *out*) to set boundaries or limits (on) 25 (*tr*) to select, designate, or doom by or as if by a mark 26 (*tr*) to put identifying or designating labels, stamps, etc, on, esp to indicate price 27 (*tr*) to pay heed or attention to: *mark my words* 28 to observe; notice 29 to grade or evaluate (scholastic work) 30 *Brit sport* to stay close to (an opponent) to hamper his or her play 31 to keep (score) in some games 32 mark time a to move the feet alternately as in marching but without advancing b to act in a mechanical and routine way c to halt progress temporarily, while awaiting developments ▷ See also **markdown, mark-up** [Old English *mearc* mark; related to Old Norse *mörk* boundary land, Old High German *marha* boundary, Latin *margō* MARGIN] > 'marker *n*

mark² (mɑːk) *n* 1 See **Deutschmark, markka, Reichsmark, Ostmark** 2 a former monetary unit and coin in England and Scotland worth two thirds of a pound sterling 3 a silver coin of Germany until 1924 [Old English *marc* unit of weight of precious metal, perhaps from the marks on metal bars; apparently of Germanic origin and related to MARK¹]

Mark (mɑːk) *n New Testament* 1 one of the four Evangelists. Feast day: April 25 2 the second Gospel, traditionally ascribed to him

Mark Antony *n* See **Antony**

markdown ('mɑːkˌdaʊn) *n* 1 a price reduction ▷ *vb* mark down 2 (*tr, adverb*) to reduce in price

marked (mɑːkt) *adj* 1 obvious, evident, or noticeable 2 singled out, esp for punishment, killing, etc: *a marked man* 3 *linguistics* distinguished by a specific feature, as in phonology. For example, of the two phonemes /t/ and /d/, the /d/ is marked because it exhibits the feature of voice > **markedly** ('mɑːkɪdlɪ) *adv* > 'markedness *n*

market ('mɑːkɪt) *n* 1 a an event or occasion, usually held at regular intervals, at which people meet for the purpose of buying and selling merchandise b (as *modifier*): *market day* **2** a place, such as an open space in a town, at which a market is held **3** a shop that sells a particular merchandise: *an antique market* **4** the market business or trade in a commodity as specified: *the sugar market* **5** the trading or selling opportunities provided by a particular group of people: *the foreign market* **6** demand for a particular product or commodity **7** See **stock market** **8** See **market price, market value** **9** be in the **market for** to wish to buy or acquire **10** on the market available for purchase **11** buyer's market a market characterized by excess supply and thus favourable to buyers ▷ *vb* **-kets, -keting, -keted** **12** (*tr*) to offer or produce for sale **13** (*intr*) to buy or deal in a market [c12: from Latin *mercātus*; from *mercāri* to trade, from *merx* merchandise] > 'market**er** *n* > **marketable** ('mɑːkɪtəbªl, 'marketable) *adj* >,marketa'bility *or* 'marketableness *n* > 'market**ably** *adv*

market abuse *n* (in Britain) a statutory offence which covers insider trading and stockmarket manipulation

marketeer (,mɑːkɪ'tɪə) *n* **1** *Brit* a supporter of the European Union and of Britain's membership of it **2** a marketer

market forces *pl n* the effect of supply and demand on trading within a free market

market garden *n chiefly Brit* an establishment where fruit and vegetables are grown for sale > **market gardener** *n*

marketing ('mɑːkɪtɪŋ) *n* the provision of goods or services to meet customer or consumer needs

market maker *n* a dealer in securities on the London Stock Exchange who buys and sells as a principal and since 1986 can deal with the public as a broker

marketplace ('mɑːkɪt,pleɪs) *n* **1** a place where a public market is held **2** any centre where ideas, opinions, etc, are exchanged **3** the commercial world of buying and selling

market price *n* the prevailing price, as determined by supply and demand, at which goods, services, etc, may be bought or sold

market-test *vb* (*tr*) to put (a section of a public-sector enterprise) out to tender, often as a prelude to full-scale privatization

market town *n chiefly Brit* a town that holds a market, esp an agricultural centre in a rural area

market value *n* the amount obtainable on the open market for the sale of property, financial assets, or goods and services

Markham ('mɑːkəm) *n* Mount Markham a mountain in Antarctica, in Victoria Land. Height: 4350 m (14 272 ft)

markhor ('mɑːkɔː) *or* **markhoor** ('mɑːkʊə) *n, pl* **-khors, -khor** *or* **-khoors, -khoor** a large wild Himalayan goat, *Capra falconeri*, with a reddish-brown coat and large spiralled horns [c19: from Persian, literally: snake-eater, from *mār* snake + *-khōr* eating]

Markiewicz (mɑː'kjeɪvɪtʃ) *n* Constance, Countess, original name *Constance Gore-Booth*. 1868–1927, Irish nationalist, married to a Polish count. She fought in the Easter Rising (1916) and was sentenced to death but reprieved. The first woman elected to the British parliament (1918), she refused to take her seat

marking ('mɑːkɪŋ) *n* **1** a mark or series of marks **2** the arrangement of colours on an animal, plant, etc **3** assessment and correction of school children's or students' written work by teaching staff

markka ('mɑːkɑː, -kə) *n, pl* **-kaa** (-kɑː) the former standard monetary unit of Finland, divided into 100 penniä; replaced by the euro in 2002 [Finnish. See MARK²]

Markova (mɑː'kəʊvə) *n* Dame Alicia. real name *Lilian Alicia Marks*. (1910–2004), English ballerina

marksman ('mɑːksmən) *n, pl* **-men** **1** a person skilled in shooting **2** a serviceman selected for his skill in shooting, esp for a minor engagement > 'marksman,ship *n* > 'marks,woman *fem n*

mark-up *n* **1** a percentage or amount added to the cost of a commodity to provide the seller with a profit and to cover overheads, costs, etc **2 a** an increase in the price of a commodity **b** the amount of this increase ▷ *vb* mark up (*tr, adverb*) **3** to add a percentage for profit, overheads,

etc, to the cost of (a commodity) **4** to increase the price of

marl (mɑːl) *n* **1** a fine-grained sedimentary rock consisting of clay minerals, calcite or aragonite, and silt: used as a fertilizer ▷ *vb* **2** (*tr*) to fertilize (land) with marl [c14: via Old French, from Late Latin *margila*, diminutive of Latin *marga*] > **marlacious** (mɑː'leɪʃəs) *or* 'marly *adj*

Marlborough¹ ('mɑːlbərə, -brə, 'mɔːl-) *n* a town in S England, in Wiltshire: besieged and captured by Royalists in the Civil War (1642); site of Marlborough College, a public school founded in 1843. Pop: 7713 (2001)

Marlborough² ('mɑːlbərə, -brə, 'mɔːl-) *n* 1st Duke of. title of *John Churchill*. 1650–1722, English general; commander of British forces in the War of the Spanish Succession (1701- 14), in which he won victories at Blenheim (1704), Ramillies (1706), Oudenaarde (1708), and Malplaquet (1709)

Marley ('mɑːlɪ) *n* Bob, full name *Robert Nesta Marley*. 1945–81, Jamaican reggae singer, guitarist, and songwriter. With his group, the Wailers, his albums included *Burnin'* (1973), *Natty Dread* (1975), *Rastaman Vibration* (1976), and *Exodus* (1977)

marlin ('mɑːlɪn) *n, pl* **-lin** *or* **-lins** any of several large scombroid food and game fishes of the genera *Makaira, Istiompax*, and *Tetrapturus*, of warm and tropical seas, having a very long upper jaw: family *Istiophoridae* [c20: from MARLINESPIKE; with allusion to the shape of the beak]

marline *or* **marlin** ('mɑːlɪn) *n nautical* a light rope, usually tarred, made of two strands laid left-handed [c15: from Dutch *marlijn*, from *marren* to tie + *lijn* line]

marlinespike *or* **marlinspike** ('mɑːlɪn,spaɪk) *n nautical* a pointed metal tool used as a fid, spike, and for various other purposes

marlite ('mɑːlaɪt) *or* **marlstone** ('mɑːl,stəʊn) *n* a type of marl that contains clay and calcium carbonate and is resistant to the decomposing action of air

Marlowe ('mɑːləʊ) *n* Christopher. 1564–93, English dramatist and poet, who established blank verse as a creative form of dramatic expression. His plays include *Tamburlaine the Great* (1590), *Edward II* (?1592), and *Dr Faustus* (1604). He was stabbed to death in a tavern brawl

marmalade ('mɑːmə,leɪd) *n* a preserve made by boiling the pulp and rind of citrus fruits, esp oranges, with sugar [c16: via French from Portuguese *marmelada*, from *marmelo* quince, from Latin, from Greek *melimēlon*, from *meli* honey + *mēlon* apple]

Marmara *or* **Marmora** ('mɑːmərə) *n* Sea of Marmara a deep inland sea in NW Turkey, linked with the Black Sea by the Bosporus and with the Aegean by the Dardanelles: separates Turkey in Europe from Turkey in Asia. Area: 11 471 sq km (4429 sq miles). Ancient name: Propontis

marmite ('mɑːmaɪt) *n* a large cooking pot [from French: pot]

Marmite ('mɑːmaɪt) *n trademark Brit* a yeast and vegetable extract used as a spread, flavouring, etc

Marmolada (*Italian* marmo'la:da) *n* a mountain in NE Italy: highest peak in the Dolomites. Height: 3342 m (10 965 ft)

marmoreal (mɑː'mɔːrɪəl) *or less commonly* **marmorean** *adj* of, relating to, or resembling marble [c18: from Latin *marmoreus*, from *marmor* marble]

marmoset ('mɑːmə,zɛt) *n* **1** any small South American monkey of the genus *Callithrix* and related genera, having long hairy tails, clawed digits, and tufts of hair around the head and ears: family *Callithricidae* **2** pygmy marmoset a related form, *Cebuella pygmaea*: the smallest monkey, inhabiting tropical forests of the Amazon [c14: from Old French *marmouset* grotesque figure, of obscure origin]

marmot ('mɑːmət) *n* **1** any burrowing sciurine rodent of the genus *Marmota*, of Europe, Asia, and North America. They are heavily built, having short legs, a short furry tail, and coarse fur **2** prairie marmot another name for **prairie dog** [c17: from French *marmotte*, perhaps ultimately from Latin *mūr-* (stem of *mūs*) mouse + *montis* of the mountain]

Marne (*French* marn) *n* **1** a department of NE France, in Champagne-Ardenne region. Capital: Châlons-sur-Marne. Pop: 563 027 (2003 est). Area: 8205 sq km (3200 sq miles) **2** a river in NE France, rising on the plateau of Langres and flowing north, then west to the River Seine, north of Paris: linked by canal with the Rivers Saône, Rhine, and Aisne; scene of two unsuccessful German offensives (1914, 1918) during World War I. Length: 525 km (326 miles)

Maroc (marɔk) *n* the French name for **Morocco**

marocain (ˌmærəˌkeɪn) *n* **1** a fabric of ribbed crepe **2** a garment made from this fabric [C20: from French *maroquin* Moroccan]

maroon¹ (məˈruːn) *vb* (*tr*) **1** to leave ashore and abandon, esp on an island **2** to isolate without resources ▷ *n* **3** a descendant of a group of runaway slaves living in the remoter areas of the Caribbean or Guyana [C17 (applied to fugitive slaves): from American Spanish *cimarrón* wild, literally: dwelling on peaks, from Spanish *cima* summit]

maroon² (məˈruːn) *n* **1 a** a dark red to purplish-red colour **b** (*as adjective*): *a maroon carpet* **2** an exploding firework, esp one used as a warning signal [C18: from French, literally: chestnut, MARRON¹]

Maros (ˈmɔrɔʃ) *n* the Hungarian name for the: **Mureş**

Marprelate (ˈmɑːprelɪt) *n* **Martin**, the pen name of the anonymous author or authors of a series of satirical Puritan tracts (1588–89), attacking the bishops of the Church of England

Marq. *abbreviation* Marquis

Marquand (mɑːˈkwɒnd) *n* **J(ohn) P(hillips)**. 1893–1960, US novelist, noted for his stories featuring the Japanese detective Mr Moto and for his satirical comedies of New England life, such as *The Late George Apley* (1937)

marque (mɑːk) *n* **1** a brand of product, esp of a car **2** See **letter of marque** [from French, from *marquer* to MARK¹]

marquee (mɑːˈkiː) *n* **1** a large tent used for entertainment, exhibition, etc **2** Also called: **marquise** *chiefly US & Canadian* a canopy over the entrance to a theatre, hotel, etc [C17 (originally an officer's tent): invented singular form of MARQUISE, erroneously taken to be plural]

Marquesas Islands (mɑːˈkeɪsæs) *pl n* a group of volcanic islands in the S Pacific, in French Polynesia. Pop: 8712 (2002). Area: 1287 sq km (497 sq miles)

marquess (ˈmɑːkwɪs) *n* **1** (in the British Isles) a nobleman ranking between a duke and an earl **2** See **marquis**

marquetry *or* **marqueterie** (ˈmɑːkɪtrɪ) *n*, *pl* -quetries *or* -queteries a pattern of inlaid veneers of wood, brass, ivory, etc, fitted together to form a picture or design, used chiefly as ornamentation in furniture [C16: from Old French, from *marqueter* to inlay, from *marque* MARK¹]

Marquette (mɑːˈket) *n* **Jacques** (ʒɑk), known as *Père Marquette*. 1637–75, French Jesuit missionary and explorer, with Louis Jolliet, of the Mississippi river

Márquez (ˈmɑːkez) *n* **Gabriel García**. See (Gabriel): **García Márquez**

marquis (ˈmɑːkwɪs, mɑːˈkiː; *French* marki) *n*, *pl* -quises *or* -quis (in various countries) a nobleman ranking above a count, corresponding to a British marquess. The title of marquis is often used in place of that of marquess [C14: from Old French *marchis*, literally: count of the march, from *marche* MARCH²]

Marquis (ˈmɑːkwɪs) *n* **Don(ald Robert Perry)**. 1878–1937, US humorist; author of *archy and mehitabel* (1927)

marquise (mɑːˈkiːz; *French* markiz) *n* **1** (in various countries) another word for **marchioness 2 a** a gemstone, esp a diamond, cut in a pointed oval shape and usually faceted **b** a piece of jewellery, esp a ring, set with such a stone or with an oval cluster of stones **3** another name for **marquee** (sense 2) [C18: from French, feminine of MARQUIS]

marquisette (ˌmɑːkɪˈzet, -kwɪ-) *n* a leno-weave fabric of cotton, silk, etc [C20: from French, diminutive of MARQUISE]

Marrakech *or* **Marrakesh** (məˈrækeʃ, ˌmærəˈkeʃ) *n* a city in W central Morocco: several times capital of Morocco; tourist centre. Pop: 672 000 (2003)

marram grass (ˈmærəm) *n* any of several grasses of the genus *Ammophila*, esp *A. arenaria*, that grow on sandy shores and can withstand drying: often planted to stabilize sand dunes [C17 *marram*, from Old Norse *marálmr*, from *marr* sea + *hálmr* HAULM]

marri (ˈmærɪ) *n*, *pl* -ris a species of eucalyptus, *Eucalyptus calophylla*, of Western Australia, widely cultivated for its coloured flowers [C19: from a native Australian language]

marriage (ˈmærɪdʒ) *n* **1** the state or relationship of being husband and wife **2** the legal union or contract made by a man and woman to live as husband and wife **b** (*as modifier*): *marriage licence; marriage certificate* **3** the religious or legal ceremony formalizing this union; wedding **4** a close or intimate union, relationship, etc [C13: from Old French; see MARRY¹, -AGE]

marriageable (ˈmærɪdʒəbəl) *adj* (esp of women) suitable for marriage, usually with reference to age > ˌmarriageaˈbility *or* ˈmarriageableness *n*

marriage guidance *n* advice given to couples who have problems in their married life

married (ˈmærɪd) *adj* **1** having a husband or wife **2** joined in marriage **3** of or involving marriage or married persons **4** closely or intimately united ▷ *n* **5** (*usually plural*) a married person (esp in the phrase **young marrieds**)

Marriner (ˈmærɪnə) *n* **Sir Neville**. born 1924, British conductor and violinist; founder (1956) and director of the Academy of St Martin in the Fields, which specializes in baroque music

marron¹ (ˈmærən; *French* marɔ̃) *n* a large edible sweet chestnut [from French, of obscure origin]

marron² (ˈmærən) *n* a large freshwater crayfish of Western Australia, *Cherax tenuimanus* [from a native Australian language]

marrons glacés *French* (marɔ̃ glase) *pl n* chestnuts cooked in syrup and glazed

marrow (ˈmærəʊ) *n* **1** the fatty network of connective tissue that fills the cavities of bones **2** the vital part; essence **3** *Brit* short for **vegetable marrow** [Old English *mærg*; related to Old Frisian *merg*, Old Norse *mergr*] > ˈmarrowy *adj*

marrowbone (ˈmærəʊˌbəʊn) *n* **a** a bone containing edible marrow **b** (*as modifier*): *marrowbone jelly*

marrow fat (ˈmærəʊˌfæt) *or* **marrow pea** *n* **1** any of several varieties of pea plant that have large seeds **2** the seed of such a plant

marry¹ (ˈmærɪ) *vb* -ries, -rying, -ried **1** to take (someone as one's husband or wife) in marriage **2** (*tr*) to join or give in marriage **3** to unite or intimately **4** (*tr*; sometimes foll by *up*) to fit together or align (two things); join **5** (*tr*) *nautical* to match up (the strands of unlaid ropes before splicing [C13: from Old French *marier*, from Latin *marītāre*, from *marītus* married (man), perhaps from *mās* male]

marry² (ˈmærɪ) *interj archaic* an exclamation of surprise, anger, etc [C14: euphemistic for the Virgin *Mary*]

Marryat (ˈmærɪət) *n* **Frederick**, known as *Captain Marryat*. 1792–1848, English novelist and naval officer; author of novels of sea life, such as *Mr Midshipman Easy* (1836), and children's stories, such as *The Children of the New Forest* (1847)

marry off *vb* (*tr, adverb*) to find a husband or wife for (a person, esp one's son or daughter)

Mars¹ (mɑːz) *n* the Roman god of war, the father of Romulus and Remus

Mars² (mɑːz) *n* Also called: **the Red Planet** the fourth planet from the sun, having a reddish-orange surface with numerous dark patches and two white polar caps. It has a thin atmosphere, mainly carbon dioxide, and low surface temperatures. Spacecraft encounters have revealed a history of volcanic activity and running surface water. The planet has two tiny satellites, Phobos and Deimos. Mean distance from sun: 228 million km; period of revolution around sun: 686.98 days; period of axial rotation: 24.6225 hours; diameter and mass: 53.2 and 10.7 per cent that of earth respectively

Marsala (mɑːˈsɑːlə) *n* **1** a port in W Sicily: landing place of Garibaldi at the start of his Sicilian campaign (1860). Pop: 77 784 (2001) **2** (*sometimes not capital*) a dark sweet dessert wine made in Sicily

Marsalis (mɑː'sɑːlɪs) n **Wynton**. born 1962, US jazz and classical trumpeter

Marsanne (mɑː'sæn) n 1 a white grape grown in the N Rhône region of France and in California and Australia, used for making wine 2 a full-bodied white wine made from this grape

Marseillaise (ˌmɑːsə'leɪz; French marsɛjɛz) n the Marseillaise the French national anthem. Words and music were composed in 1792 by C. J. Rouget de Lisle as a war song for the Rhine army of revolutionary France [c18: from French (chanson) Marseillaise song of Marseille (it was first sung in Paris by the battalion of Marseille)]

marseille (mɑː'seɪl) or **marseilles** (mɑː'seɪlz) n a strong cotton fabric with a raised pattern, used for bedspreads, etc [c18: from Marseille quilting, made in Marseille]

Marseille (French marsɛj) n a port in SE France, on the Gulf of Lions: second largest city in the country and a major port; founded in about 600 BC by Greeks from Phocaea; oil refining. Pop: 798 430 (1999)

marsh (mɑːʃ) n low poorly drained land that is sometimes flooded and often lies at the edge of lakes, streams, etc. See **swamp** (sense 1) [Old English merisc; related to German Marsch, Dutch marsk; related to MERE²]

Marsh (mɑːʃ) n 1 Dame (**Edith**) **Ngaio** ('naɪəʊ). 1899–1981, New Zealand crime writer, living in Britain (from 1928). Her many detective novels include Final Curtain (1947) and Last Ditch (1977) 2 **Rodney** (**William**). born 1947, Australian cricketer. He finished his career with a world record of 355 Test match dismissals

marshal ('mɑːʃəl) n 1 (in some armies and air forces) an officer of the highest rank 2 (in England) an officer, usually a junior barrister, who accompanies a judge on circuit and performs miscellaneous secretarial duties 3 (in the US) a a Federal court officer assigned to a judicial district whose functions are similar to those of a sheriff b (in some states) the chief police or fire officer 4 an officer who organizes or conducts ceremonies, parades, etc 5 Also called: knight marshal (formerly in England) an officer of the royal family or court, esp one in charge of protocol ▷ vb -shals, -shalling, -shalled or US -shals, -shaling, -shaled (tr) 6 to arrange in order: to marshal the facts 7 to assemble and organize (troops, vehicles, etc) prior to onward movement 8 to guide or lead, esp in a ceremonious way 9 to combine (two or more coats of arms) on one shield [c13: from Old French mareschal; related to Old High German marahscalc groom, from marah horse + scalc servant] > 'marshalcy or 'marshal,ship n

Marshall ('mɑːʃəl) n 1 **Alfred** 1842–1924, English economist, author of Principles of Economics (1890) 2 **George Catlett**. 1880–1959, US general and statesman. He was chief of staff of the US army (1939–45) and, as secretary of state (1947–49), he proposed the Marshall Plan (1947), later called the European Recovery Programme: Nobel peace prize 1953 3 **John**. 1755–1835, US jurist and statesman. As chief justice of the Supreme Court (1801–35), he established the principles of US constitutional law 4 Sir **John Ross**. 1912–88, New Zealand politician; prime minister (1972)

marshalling yard n railways a place or depot where railway wagons are shunted and made up into trains and where engines, carriages, etc, are kept when not in use

Marshall Islands ('mɑːʃəl) pl n a republic, consisting of a group of 34 coral islands in the W central Pacific: formerly part of the Trust Territory of the Pacific Islands (1947–87); status of free association with the US from 1986; consists of two parallel chains, Ralik and Ratak. Official languages: Marshallese and English. Religion: Roman Catholic majority. Currency: US dollar. Capital: Delap-Uliga-Djarrit, on Majuro atoll. Pop: 53 000 (2003 est). Area: (land) 181 sq km (70 sq miles); (lagoon) 11 655 sq km (4500 sq miles)

Marshal of the Royal Air Force n a rank in the Royal Air Force comparable to that of Field Marshal in the British army

marsh fever n another name for: **malaria**

marsh gas n a hydrocarbon gas largely composed of methane formed when organic material decays in the absence of air

marshmallow (ˌmɑːʃ'mæləʊ) n 1 a sweet of a spongy texture containing gum arabic or gelatine, sugar, etc 2 a sweetened paste or confection made from the root of the marsh mallow

marsh mallow n a malvaceous plant, Althaea officinalis, that grows in salt marshes and has pale pink flowers. The roots yield a mucilage formerly used to make marshmallows

marsh marigold n a yellow-flowered ranunculaceous plant, Caltha palustris, that grows in swampy places

marshy ('mɑːʃɪ) adj marshier, marshiest of, involving, or like a marsh > 'marshiness n

Marsilius of Padua (mɑː'sɪlɪəs) n Italian name Marsiglio dei Mainardini. ?1290–?1343, Italian political philosopher, best known as the author of the Defensor pacis (1324), which upheld the power of the temporal ruler over that of the church

Marston ('mɑːstən) n **John**. ?1576–1634, English dramatist and satirist. His works include the revenge tragedies Antonio and Mellida (1602) and Antonio's Revenge (1602) and the satirical comedy The Malcontent (1604)

Marston Moor n a flat low-lying area in NE England, west of York: scene of a battle (1644) in which the Parliamentarians defeated the Royalists

marsupial (mɑː'sjuːpɪəl, -'suː-) n 1 any mammal of the order Marsupialia, in which the young are born in an immature state and continue development in the marsupium. The order occurs mainly in Australia and South and Central America and includes the opossums, bandicoots, koala, wombats, and kangaroos ▷ adj 2 of, relating to, or belonging to the Marsupialia 3 of or relating to a marsupium [c17: see MARSUPIUM]

marsupium (mɑː'sjuːpɪəm, -'suː-) n, pl -pia (-pɪə) an external pouch in most female marsupials within which the newly born offspring are suckled and complete their development [c17: New Latin, from Latin: purse, from Greek marsupion, diminutive of marsipos]

mart (mɑːt) n a market or trading centre [c15: from Middle Dutch mart MARKET]

Martaban (ˌmɑːtə'bɑːn) n Gulf of Martaban an inlet of the Bay of Bengal in Myanmar

martagon or **martagon lily** ('mɑːtəgən) n a Eurasian lily plant, Lilium martagon, cultivated for its mottled purplish-red flowers with reflexed petals [c15: from French, from Turkish martagān a type of turban]

Martel (mɑː'tɛl) n See **Charles Martel**

Martello tower or **Martello** (mɑː'tɛləʊ) n a small circular tower for coastal defence, formerly much used in Europe [c18: after Cape Mortella in Corsica, where the British navy captured a tower of this type in 1794]

marten ('mɑːtɪn) n, pl -tens or -ten 1 any of several agile arboreal musteline mammals of the genus Martes, of Europe, Asia, and North America, having bushy tails and golden brown to blackish fur. See also **pine marten** 2 the highly valued fur of these animals, esp that of M. americana ▷ See also **sable** (sense 1) [c15: from Middle Dutch martren, from Old French (peau) martrine skin of a marten, from martre, probably of Germanic origin]

Martha ('mɑːθə) n Saint Martha New Testament a sister of Mary and Lazarus, who lived at Bethany and ministered to Jesus (Luke 10:38–42). Feast day: July 29 or June 4

martial ('mɑːʃəl) adj of, relating to, or characteristic of war, soldiers, or the military life [c14: from Latin martiālis of MARS¹] > 'martialism n > 'martialist n > 'martially adv

Martial ('mɑːʃəl) n full name Marcus Valerius Martialis. ?40–?104 AD, Latin epigrammatist and poet, born in Spain

martial art n any of various philosophies of self-defence and techniques of single combat, such as judo or karate, originating in the Far East

martial law n the rule of law established and maintained by the military in the absence of civil law

Martian ('mɑːʃən) adj 1 of, occurring on, or relating to the planet Mars ▷ n 2 an inhabitant of Mars, esp in science fiction

martin ('mɑ:tɪn) *n* any of various swallows of the genera *Progne*, *Delichon*, *Riparia*, etc, having a square or slightly forked tail. See also **house martin** [c15: perhaps from St *Martin* (??316–??397 AD), bishop of Tours, because the birds were believed to migrate at the time of Martinmas]

Martin ('mɑ:tɪn) *n* **1 Archer John Porter.** 1910–2002, British biochemist; Nobel prize for chemistry 1952 (with Richard Synge; 1914–94) for developing paper chromatography (1944). He subsequently developed gas chromatography (1953) **2 Chris.** born 1977, British rock musician, lead singer of Coldplay. He is married to the US actress Gwyneth Paltrow. **3** (*French* martē) **Frank.** 1890–1974, Swiss composer. He used a modified form of the twelve-note technique in some of his works, which include *Petite Symphonie Concertante* (1946) and the oratorio *Golgotha* (1949) **4 Sir George (Henry).** born 1926, British record producer and arranger, noted for his work with the Beatles **5 John.** 1789–1854, British painter, noted for his visionary landscapes and large-scale works with biblical subjects **6 Michael (John).** born 1945, Scottish Labour politician; speaker of the House of Commons from 2000 **7 Paul (Edgar Philippe).** born 1938, Canadian Liberal politician; prime minister of Canada (2003–06) **8 Saint.** called *Saint Martin of Tours*. ?316–?397 AD, bishop of Tours (?371–?397); a patron saint of France. He furthered monasticism in Gaul. Feast day: Nov 11 or 12 **9 Steve(n).** born 1945, US film actor and comedian; his films include *The Jerk* (1979), *Roxanne* (1987), and *Bowfinger*) (1999)

Martin V *n* original name *Oddone Colonna*. 1368–1431, pope (1417–31). His election at the Council of Constance brought to an end the Great Schism

Martin du Gard (*French* martē dy gar) *n* **Roger** (rɔʒe). 1881–1958, French novelist, noted for his series of novels, *Les Thibault* (1922–40): Nobel prize for literature 1937

Martineau ('mɑ:tɪ,nəʊ) *n* **1 Harriet.** 1802–76, English author of books on political economy and of novels and children's stories **2** her brother, **James.** 1805–1900, English Unitarian theologian and minister

martinet (,mɑ:tɪ'nɛt) *n* a person who maintains strict discipline, esp in a military force [c17: from French, from the name of General *Martinet*, drillmaster under Louis XIV]

martingale ('mɑ:tɪŋ,geɪl) *n* **1** a strap from the reins to the girth of a horse preventing it from carrying its head too high **2** any gambling system in which the stakes are raised, usually doubled, after each loss **3** Also called: **martingale boom** *nautical* a chain or cable running from a jib boom to the dolphin striker, serving to counteract strain [c16: from French, of uncertain origin]

Martini¹ (*Italian* mar'ti:ni) *n* **Simone** (si'mo:ne). ?1284–1344, Sienese painter

Martini² (mɑ:'ti:nɪ) *n*, *pl* -**nis 1** *trademark* an Italian vermouth **2** a cocktail of gin and vermouth [c19 (sense 2): perhaps from the name of the inventor]

Martinique (,mɑ:tɪ'ni:k) *n* an island in the E Caribbean, in the Windward Islands of the Lesser Antilles; administratively an overseas region of France. Capital: Fort-de-France. Pop: 395 000 (2004 est). Area: 1090 sq km (420 sq miles) > ,Marti'nican *adj*,

Martinmas ('mɑ:tɪnməs) *n* the feast of St Martin on Nov 11; one of the four quarter days in Scotland

Martinů ('mɑ:tɪ,nu:; *Czech* 'martjinu:) *n* **Bohuslav** ('bɔhuslaf). 1890–1959, Czech composer

martyr ('mɑ:tə) *n* **1** a person who suffers death rather than renounce his religious beliefs **2** a person who suffers greatly or dies for a cause, belief, etc **3** a person who suffers from poor health, misfortune, etc: *he's a martyr to rheumatism* ▷ *vb* Also: 'martyr,ize *or* 'martyr,ise (*tr*) **4** to kill as a martyr **5** to make a martyr of [Old English *martir*, from Church Latin *martyr*, from Late Greek *martur-*, *martus* witness] > ,martyri'zation *or* ,martyri'sation *n* > 'martyrdom *n*

martyrology (,mɑ:tə'rɒlədʒɪ) *n*, *pl* -**gies 1** an official list of martyrs **2** *Christianity* the study of the lives of the martyrs **3** a historical account of the lives of martyrs > ,martyr'ologist *n*

marvel ('mɑ:vəl) *vb* -**vels,** -**velling,** -**velled** *or US* -**vels,** -**veling,** -**veled 1** (when *intr*, often foll by *at* or *about*; when

tr, takes a clause as object) to be filled with surprise or wonder ▷ *n* **2** something that causes wonder **3** *archaic* astonishment [c13: from Old French *merveille*, from Late Latin *mīrābilia*, from Latin *mīrābilis*, from *mīrārī* to wonder at]

Marvell ('mɑ:vəl) *n* **Andrew.** 1621–78, English poet and satirist. He is noted for his lyrical poems and verse and prose satires attacking the government after the Restoration

marvellous *or US* **marvelous** ('mɑ:vələs) *adj* **1** causing great wonder, surprise, etc; extraordinary **2** improbable or incredible **3** excellent; splendid > 'marvellously *or US* 'marvelously *adv* > 'marvellousness *or US* 'marvelousness *n*

marvel-of-Peru *n*, *pl* **marvels-of-Peru** another name for: **four-o'clock** (sense 1) [c16: first found in Peru]

Marx (mɑ:ks) *n* (karl). 1818–83, German founder of modern communism, in England from 1849. With Engels, he wrote *The Communist Manifesto* (1848). He developed his theories of the class struggle and the economics of capitalism in *Das Kapital* (1867; 1885; 1895). He was one of the founders of the International Workingmen's Association (First International) (1864)

Marx Brothers (mɑ:ks) *n* the US family of film comedians, esp **Arthur Marx**, known as **Harpo** (1888–1964), **Herbert Marx**, known as **Zeppo** (1901–79), **Julius Marx**, known as **Groucho** (1890–1977), and **Leonard Marx** known as **Chico** (1886–1961). Their films include *Animal Crackers* (1930), *Monkey Business* (1931), *Horsefeathers* (1932), *Duck Soup* (1933), and *A Day at the Races* (1937)

Marxism ('mɑ:ksɪzəm) *n* the economic and political theory and practice originated by the German political philosophers Karl Marx (1818–83) and Friedrich Engels (1820–95), that holds that actions and human institutions are economically determined, that the class struggle is the basic agency of historical change, and that capitalism will ultimately be superseded by communism > 'Marxist *n*, *adj*

Marxism-Leninism *n* the modification of Marxism by the Russian statesman and Marxist theoretician V. I. Lenin (1870–1924) stressing that imperialism is the highest form of capitalism > 'Marxist-'Leninist *n*, *adj*

Mary ('mɛərɪ) *n* **1** *New Testament* **a** Saint. Also called: the **Virgin Mary.** the mother of Jesus, believed to have conceived and borne him while still a virgin; she was married to Joseph (Matthew 1:18–25). Major feast days: Feb 2, Mar 25, May 31, Aug 15, Sept 8 **b** the sister of Martha and Lazarus (Luke 10:38–42; John 11:1–2) **2** original name *Princess Mary of Teck*. 1867–1953, queen of Great Britain and Northern Ireland (1910–36) by marriage to George V **3** *pl* **Maries** *Austral obsolete, derogatory, slang* an Aboriginal woman or girl

Mary I *n* family name *Tudor*, known as *Bloody Mary*. 1516–58, queen of England (1553–58). The daughter of Henry VIII and Catherine of Aragon, she married Philip II of Spain in 1554. She restored Roman Catholicism to England and about 300 Protestants were burnt at the stake as heretics

Mary II *n* 1662–94, queen of England, Scotland, and Ireland (1689–94), ruling jointly with her husband William III. They were offered the crown by parliament, which objected to the arbitrary rule of her father James II

Maryland ('mɛərɪ,lænd, 'mɛrɪlənd) *n* a state of the eastern US, on the Atlantic: divided into two unequal parts by Chesapeake Bay: mostly low-lying, with the Alleghenies in the northwest Capital: Annapolis. Pop: 5 508 909 (2003 est). Area: 31 864 sq km (12 303 sq miles). Abbreviations: **Md, MD**

Mary Magdalene *n* Saint Mary Magdalense *New Testament* a woman of **Magdala** ('mægdələ) in Galilee whom Jesus cured of evil spirits (Luke 8:2) and who is often identified with the sinful woman of Luke 7:36–50. In Christian tradition she is usually taken to have been a prostitute. Feast day: July 22. See also **magdalen**

Mary, Queen of Scots *n* family name *Stuart*. 1542–87, queen of Scotland (1542–67); daughter of James V of Scotland and Mary of Guise. She was married to Francis II of France (1558–60), her cousin Lord Darnley (1565–67), and the Earl of Bothwell (1567–71), who was commonly regarded as Darnley's murderer. She was forced to abdicate in favour of her son (later James VI of Scotland) and fled to England. Imprisoned by Elizabeth I until 1587, she was beheaded for plotting against the English crown

marzipan ('mɑːzɪˌpæn) *n* **1** a paste made from ground almonds, sugar, and egg whites, used to coat fruit cakes or moulded into sweets ▷ *modifier* **2** *informal* of or relating to the stratum of middle managers in a financial institution or other business: *marzipan layer job losses* [C19: via German from Italian *marzapane*. See MARCHPANE]

-mas *n combining form* indicating a Christian festival: *Christmas; Michaelmas* [from MASS]

Masaccio (Italian maˈzattʃo) *n* original name *Tommaso Guidi*. 1401–28, Florentine painter. He was the first to apply to painting the laws of perspective discovered by Brunelleschi. His chief work is the frescoes in the Brancacci chapel in the church of Sta. Maria del Carmine, Florence

Masada (məˈsɑːdə) *n* an ancient mountaintop fortress in Israel, 400 m (1300 ft) above the W shore of the Dead Sea: the last Jewish stronghold during a revolt in Judaea (66–73 AD). Besieged by the Romans for a year, almost all of the inhabitants killed themselves rather than surrender. The site is an Israeli national monument

Masai ('mɑːsaɪ, mɑːˈsaɪ, ˈmæsaɪ) *n* **1** *pl* **-sais** *or* **-sai 1** a member of a Nilotic people, formerly noted as warriors, living chiefly in Kenya and Tanzania **2** the language of this people, belonging to the Nilotic group of the Nilo-Saharan family

masala (mɑːˈsɑːlə) *n* **1** a mixture of spices ground into a paste, used in Indian cookery ▷ *adj* **2** *Hinglish* spicy; dramatic: *it was a typical masala film* [from Urdu *masalah*, from Arabic *masalih* ingredients]

Masan ('mɑːˌsɑːn) *n* a port in SE South Korea, on an inlet of the Korea Strait: first opened to foreign trade in 1899. Pop: 428 000 (2005 est)

Masaryk ('mæsərɪk; Czech 'masarik) *n* **1 Jan** (jan). 1886–1948, Czech statesman; foreign minister (1941–48). He died in mysterious circumstances after the Communists took control of the government **2** his father, **Tomáš Garrigue** ('tɔmɑːʃ 'garik). 1850–1937, Czech philosopher and statesman; a founder of Czechoslovakia (1918) and its first president (1918–35)

Masbate (mæsˈbɑːtɪ) *n* **1** an island in the central Philippines, between Negros and SE Luzon: agricultural, with resources of gold, copper, and manganese. Pop (Masbate province): 707 668 (2000). Area: 4045 sq km (1562 sq miles) **2** the capital of this island, a port in the northeast. Pop: 71 441 (2000)

masc. *abbreviation* masculine

Mascagni (Italian masˈkaɲɲi) *n* **Pietro** ('pjɛːtro). 1863–1945, Italian composer of operas, including *Cavalleria rusticana* (1890)

mascara (mæˈskɑːrə) *n* a cosmetic substance for darkening, colouring, and thickening the eyelashes, applied with a brush or rod [C20: from Spanish: mask]

Mascarene Islands (ˌmæskəˈriːn) *pl n* a group of volcanic islands in the W Indian Ocean, east of Madagascar: consists of the islands of Réunion, Mauritius, and Rodrigues. French name: Îles Mascareignes

mascarpone (ˌmæskəˈpəʊnɪ) *n* a soft Italian cream cheese [from Italian, from dialect (Lombardy) *mascherpa* ricotta]

mascon ('mæskon) *n* any of several lunar regions of high gravity [C20: from MAS(S) + CON(CENTRATION)]

mascot ('mæskət) *n* a person, animal, or thing considered to bring good luck [C19: from French *mascotte*, from Provençal *mascotto* charm, from *masco* witch]

masculine ('mæskjʊlɪn) *adj* **1** possessing qualities or characteristics considered typical of or appropriate to a man; manly **2** unwomanly **3** *grammar* denoting a gender of nouns, occurring in many inflected languages, that includes all kinds of referents as well as some male animate referents [C14: via French from Latin *masculīnus*, from *masculus* male, from *mās* a male] > 'masculinely *adv* > ˌmascu'linity *or less commonly* 'masculineness *n*

masculinize *or* **masculinise** ('mæskjʊlɪnˌaɪz) *vb* to make or become masculine, esp to cause (a woman) to show male secondary sexual characteristics as a result of taking steroids > ˌmasculini'zation *or* ˌmasculini'sation *n*

Masefield ('meɪsˌfiːld) *n* **John**. 1878–1967, English poet, novelist, and critic; poet laureate (1930–67)

maser ('meɪzə) *n* a device for amplifying microwaves, working on the same principle as a laser [C20: *m(icrowave) a(mplification by) s(timulated) e(mission of) r(adiation)*]

Maseru (məˈsɛəruː) *n* the capital of Lesotho, in the northwest near the W border with South Africa; established as capital of Basutoland in 1869. Pop: 175 000 (2005 est)

mash (mæʃ) *n* **1** a soft pulpy mass or consistency **2** *agriculture* a feed of bran, meal, or malt mixed with water and fed to horses, cattle, or poultry **3** (esp in brewing) a mixture of mashed malt grains and hot water, from which malt is extracted **4** *Brit informal* mashed potatoes **5** *Northern English dialect* a brew of tea ▷ *vb* (*tr*) **6** to beat or crush into a mash **7** to steep (malt grains) in hot water in order to extract malt, esp for making malt liquors **8** *Northern English dialect* to brew (tea) [Old English *māsc-* (in compound words); related to Middle Low German *mēsch*] > **mashed** *adj* > 'masher *n*

Masherbrum *or* **Masharbrum** ('mʌʃəˌbrum) *n* a mountain in N India, in N Kashmir in the Karakoram Range of the Himalayas. Height: 7822 m (25 660 ft)

Mashhad (mæʃˈhæd) *or* **Meshed** *n* a city in NE Iran: an important holy city of Shi'ite Muslims; carpet manufacturing. Pop: 2 147 000 (2005 est)

mashie *or* **mashy** ('mæʃɪ) *n*, *pl* **mashies** *golf* (formerly) a club, corresponding to the modern No. 5 or No. 6 iron, used for approach shots [C19: perhaps from French *massue* club, ultimately from Latin *mateola* mallet]

mashup ('mæʃʌp) *n* a piece of recorded or live music in which a producer or DJ blends together two or more tracks, often of contrasting genres [C20: from MASH blend + UP]

Masinissa *or* **Massinissa** (ˌmæsɪˈnɪsə) *n* ?238–?149 BC, king of Numidia (?210–149), who fought as an ally of Rome against Carthage in the Second Punic War

mask (mɑːsk) *n* **1** any covering for the whole or a part of the face worn for amusement, protection, disguise, etc **2** a fact, action, etc, that conceals something: *his talk was a mask for his ignorance* **3** another name for **masquerade 4** a likeness of a face or head, either sculpted or moulded, such as a death mask **5** an image of a face worn by an actor, esp in ancient Greek and Roman drama, in order to symbolize the character being portrayed **6** a variant spelling of: **masque 7** *surgery* a sterile gauze covering for the nose and mouth worn esp during operations to minimize the spread of germs **8** *sport* a protective covering for the face worn for fencing, ice hockey, etc **9** a carving in the form of a face or head, used as an ornament **10** a device placed over the nose and mouth to facilitate or prevent inhalation of a gas **11** *photog* a shield of paper, paint, etc, placed over an area of unexposed photographic surface to stop light falling on it **12** the face or head of an animal, such as a fox, or the dark coloration of the face of some animals, such as Siamese cats and certain dogs **13** *now rare* a person wearing a mask ▷ *vb* **14** to cover with or put on a mask **15** (*tr*) to conceal; disguise: *to mask an odour* **16** (*tr*) *photog* to shield a particular area of (an unexposed photographic surface) in order to prevent or reduce the action of light there [C16: from Italian *maschera*, ultimately from Arabic *maskharah* clown, from *sakhira* mockery] > **masked** *adj* > **masker** *or* **masquer** ('mɑːskə) *n*

masked ball *n* a ball at which masks are worn

masking tape *n* an adhesive tape used to mask and protect surfaces surrounding an area to be painted

masochism ('mæsəˌkɪzəm) *n* **1** *psychiatry* an abnormal condition in which pleasure, esp sexual pleasure, is derived from pain or from humiliation, domination, etc, by another person **2** a tendency to take pleasure from one's own suffering. See **sadism** [C19: named after Leopold von Sacher *Masoch* (1836–95), Austrian novelist, who described it] > 'masochist *n*, *adj* > ˌmaso'chistic *adj* > ˌmaso'chistically *adv*

mason ('meɪsᵊn) n 1 a person skilled in building with stone 2 a person who dresses stone ▷ vb 3 (tr) to construct or strengthen with masonry [c13: from Old French *masson*, of Frankish origin; perhaps related to Old English *macian* to make]

Mason ('meɪsᵊn) n short for **Freemason**

Mason-Dixon Line or **Mason and Dixon Line** ('meɪsᵊn 'dɪksən) n the state boundary between Maryland and Pennsylvania: surveyed between 1763 and 1767 by Charles Mason and Jeremiah Dixon; popularly regarded as the dividing line between North and South, esp between the free and the slave states before the American Civil War

masonic (mə'sɒnɪk) adj 1 (often capital) of, characteristic of, or relating to Freemasons or Freemasonry 2 of or relating to masons or masonry > ma'sonically adv

Masonite ('meɪsəˌnaɪt) n Austral & NZtrademark a kind of dark brown hardboard used for partitions, lining, etc

masonry ('meɪsənrɪ) n, pl -ries 1 the craft of a mason 2 work that is built by a mason; stonework or brickwork 3 (often capital) short for **Freemasonry**

Masqat ('mʌskət, -kæt) n a transliteration of the Arabic name for: **Muscat**

masque or **mask** (mɑːsk) n 1 a dramatic entertainment of the 16th to 17th centuries in England, consisting of pantomime, dancing, dialogue, and song, often performed at court 2 the words and music written for a masque 3 short for **masquerade** [c16: variant of MASK]

masquerade (ˌmæskə'reɪd) n 1 a party or other gathering to which the guests wear masks and costumes 2 the disguise worn at such a function 3 a pretence or disguise ▷ vb 4 (intr) to participate in a masquerade; disguise oneself 5 to dissemble [c16: from Spanish *mascarada*, from *mascara* MASK] > ˌmasquer'ader n

mass (mæs) n 1 a large coherent body of matter without a definite shape 2 a collection of the component parts of something 3 a large amount or number, such as a great body of people 4 the main part or majority: *the mass of the people voted against the government's policy* 5 in the mass in the main; collectively 6 the size of a body; bulk 7 physics a physical quantity expressing the amount of matter in a body. It is a measure of a body's resistance to changes in velocity (inertial mass) and also of the force experienced in a gravitational field (gravitational mass): according to the theory of relativity, inertial and gravitational masses are equal. See also **inertial mass, gravitational mass** 8 (in painting, drawing, etc) an area of unified colour, shade, or intensity, usually denoting a solid form or plane ▷ modifier 9 done or occurring on a large scale: *mass hysteria; mass radiography* 10 consisting of a mass or large number, esp of people: *a mass meeting* ▷ vb 11 to form (people or things) or (of people or things) to join together into a mass ▷ See also **masses** [c14: from Old French *masse*, from Latin *massa* that which forms a lump, from Greek *maza* barley cake; perhaps related to Greek *massein* to knead]

Mass (mæs, mɑːs) n 1 (in the Roman Catholic Church and certain Protestant Churches) the celebration of the Eucharist. See also **High Mass, Low Mass** 2 a musical setting of those parts of the Eucharistic service sung by choir or congregation [Old English *mæsse*, from Church Latin *missa*, ultimately from Latin *mittere* to send away; perhaps derived from the concluding dismissal in the Roman Mass, *Ite, missa est*, Go, it is the dismissal]

Mass. abbreviation Massachusetts

Massa (Italian 'massa) n a town in W Italy, in NW Tuscany. Pop: 66 769 (2001)

Massachusetts (ˌmæsə'tʃuːsɪts) n a state of the northeastern US, on the Atlantic: a centre of resistance to English colonial policy during the War of American Independence; consists of a coastal plain rising to mountains in the west Capital: Boston. Pop: 6 433 422 (2003 est). Area: 20 269 sq km (7826 sq miles). Abbreviations: **Mass, MA**

Massachusetts Bay n an inlet of the Atlantic on the E coast of Massachusetts

massacre ('mæsəkə) n 1 the wanton or savage killing of large numbers of people, as in battle 2 informal an overwhelming defeat, as in a game ▷ vb (tr) 3 to kill

indiscriminately or in large numbers 4 informal to defeat overwhelmingly [c16: from Old French, of unknown origin]

mass affluent pl n the large number of individuals with liquid assets of around £250,000

massage ('mæsɑːʒ, -sɑːdʒ) n 1 the act of kneading, rubbing, etc, parts of the body to promote circulation, suppleness, or relaxation ▷ vb (tr) 2 to give a massage to 3 to treat (stiffness, aches, etc) by a massage 4 to manipulate (statistics, data, etc) so that they appear to support a particular interpretation or to be better than they are; doctor 5 **massage someone's ego** to boost someone's sense of self-esteem by flattery [c19: from French, from *masser* to rub; see MASS]

massasauga (ˌmæsə'sɔːgə) n a North American venomous snake, *Sistrurus catenatus*, that has a horny rattle at the end of the tail: family *Crotalidae* (pit vipers) [c19: named after the *Missisauga* River, Ontario, Canada, where it was first found]

Massasoit ('mæsəˌsɔɪt) n died 1661, Wampanoag Indian chief, who negotiated peace with the Pilgrim Fathers (1621)

Massawa or **Massaua** (mə'sɑːwə) n a port in E central Eritrea, on the Red Sea: capital of Eritrea during Italian occupation, from 1885 until 1900. Pop: 36 700 (2004 est)

mass defect n physics the amount by which the mass of a particular nucleus is less than the total mass of its constituent particles

massé or **massé shot** ('mæsɪ) n billiards a stroke made by hitting the cue ball off centre with the cue held nearly vertically, esp so as to make the ball move in a curve around another ball before hitting the object ball [c19: from French, from *masser* to hit from above with a hammer, from *masse* sledgehammer, from Old French *mace* MACE[1]]

Masséna (French masena) n **André** (ɑ̃dre), Prince d'Essling. 1758–1817, French marshal under Napoleon I: victories at Saorgio (1794), Loano (1795), Rivoli (1797), Zürich (1799), and Caldiero (1805): defeated by Wellington in the Peninsular War (1810–11)

Massenet ('mæsəˌneɪ; French masnɛ) n **Jules Émile Frédéric** (ʒyl emil frederik). 1842–1912, French composer of operas, including *Manon* (1884), *Werther* (1892), and *Thaïs* (1894)

masses ('mæsɪz) pl n 1 **the masses** the body of common people 2 (often foll by of) informal, chiefly Brit great numbers or quantities: *masses of food*

masseur (mæ'sɜː) n a man who gives massages, esp as a profession [c19: from French *masser* to MASSAGE]

masseuse (mæ'sɜːz) n a woman who gives massages, esp as a profession

Massey ('mæsɪ) n 1 **Raymond**. 1896–1983, Canadian actor and film star. His films include *The Scarlet Pimpernel* (1934) and *East of Eden* (1955). He also appeared in the television series *Dr Kildare* (1961–65) 2 **Vincent**. 1887–1967, Canadian statesman: first Canadian governor general of Canada (1952–59) 3 **William Ferguson**. 1856–1925, New Zealand statesman, born in Ireland: prime minister of New Zealand (1912–25)

massif ('mæsiːf; French masif) n a geologically distinct mass of rock or a series of connected masses forming the peaks of a mountain range [c19: from French, noun use of *massif* MASSIVE]

Massif Central (French masif sɑ̃tral) n a mountainous plateau region of S central France, occupying about one sixth of the country: contains several extinct volcanic cones, notably Puy de Dôme, 1465 m (4806 ft). Highest point: Puy de Sancy, 1886 m (6188 ft). Area: about 85 000 sq km (33 000 sq miles)

Massine (mɑː'siːn) n **Léonide** (leɔnid). 1896–1979, US ballet dancer and choreographer, born in Russia

Massinger ('mæsɪndʒə) n **Philip**. 1583–?1640, English dramatist, noted esp for his comedy *A New Way to pay Old Debts* (1633)

Massinissa (ˌmæsɪ'nɪsə) n a variant spelling of **Masinissa**

massive ('mæsɪv) adj 1 (of objects) large in mass; bulky, heavy, and usually solid 2 impressive or imposing in quality, degree, or scope: *massive grief* 3 relatively intensive or large; considerable: *a massive dose* **4** *geology* **a** (of igneous rocks) having no stratification, cleavage, etc; homogeneous **b** (of sedimentary rocks) arranged in thick poorly defined strata **5** *mineralogy* without obvious crystalline structure [C15: from French *massif*, from *masse* MASS] ▷ 'massively *adv* ▷ 'massiveness *n*

mass-market *adj* of, for, or appealing to a large number of people; popular: *mass-market paperbacks*

mass media *pl n* the means of communication that reach large numbers of people in a short time, such as television, newspapers, magazines, and radio

mass noun *n* a noun that refers to an extended substance rather than to each of a set of isolable objects, as, for example, *water* as opposed to *lake*. In English when used indefinitely they are characteristically preceded by *some* rather than *a* or *an*; they do not have normal plural forms. See **count noun**

mass number *n* the total number of neutrons and protons in the nucleus of a particular atom

mass observation *n chiefly Brit* (*sometimes capitals*) the study of the social habits of people through observation, interviews, etc

mass-produce *vb* (*tr*) to manufacture (goods) to a standardized pattern on a large scale by means of extensive mechanization and division of labour ▷ ,mass-pro'duced *adj* ▷ ,mass-pro'ducer *n* ▷ mass production *n*

mass spectrometer *or* **mass spectroscope** *n* an analytical instrument in which ions, produced from a sample, are separated by electric or magnetic fields according to their ratios of charge to mass. A record is produced (**mass spectrum**) of the types of ion present and their relative amounts

Massys (*Flemish* 'masaɪs), **Matsys** *or* **Metsys** *n* Quentin ('kventɪn). 1466–1530, Flemish painter, based in Antwerp; noted for his portraits and scenes of everyday life

mast¹ (mɑːst) *n* **1** *nautical* any vertical spar for supporting sails, rigging, flags, etc, above the deck of a vessel or any components of such a composite spar **2** any sturdy upright pole used as a support **3** before the mast *nautical* as an apprentice seaman ▷ *vb* **4** (*tr*) *nautical* to equip with a mast or masts [Old English *mæst*; related to Middle Dutch *mast* and Latin *mālus* pole]

mast² (mɑːst) *n* the fruit of forest trees, such as beech, oak, etc, used as food for pigs [Old English *mæst*; related to Old High German *mast* food, and perhaps to MEAT]

mastaba *or* **mastabah** ('mæstəbə) *n* a mudbrick superstructure above tombs in ancient Egypt from which the pyramid developed [from Arabic: bench]

mast cell *n* a type of granular basophil cell in connective tissue that releases heparin, histamine, and serotonin during inflammation and allergic reactions [C19: from MAST², on the model of German *Mastzelle*]

mastectomy (mæ'stɛktəmɪ) *n, pl* -mies the surgical removal of a breast

master ('mɑːstə) *n* **1** the man in authority, such as the head of a household, the employer of servants, or the owner of slaves or animals **2 a** a person with exceptional skill at a certain thing **b** (*as modifier*): *a master thief* **3** (*often capital*) a great artist, esp an anonymous but influential artist **4 a** a person who has complete control of a situation **b** an abstract thing regarded as having power or influence: *they regarded fate as the master of their lives* **5 a** a workman or craftsman fully qualified to practise his trade and to train others in it **b** (*as modifier*): *master carpenter* **6 a** an original copy, stencil, tape, etc, from which duplicates are made **b** (*as modifier*): *master copy* **7** a player of a game, esp chess or bridge, who has won a specified number of tournament games **8** the principal of some colleges **9** a highly regarded teacher or leader whose religion or philosophy is accepted by followers **10** a graduate holding a master's degree **11** the chief executive officer aboard a merchant ship **12** a person presiding over a function, organization, or institution **13** *chiefly Brit* a male teacher **14** an officer of the Supreme Court of Judicature subordinate to a judge **15** the superior person or side in a contest **16** (*often capital*) the heir apparent of a Scottish viscount or baron **17** (*modifier*) overall or controlling: *master plan* **18** (*modifier*)

designating a device or mechanism that controls others: *master switch* **19** (*modifier*) main; principal: *master bedroom* ▷ *vb* (*tr*) **20** to become thoroughly proficient in **21** to overcome; defeat: *to master your emotions* **22** to rule or control as master [Old English *magister* teacher, from Latin; related to Latin *magis* more, to a greater extent]

Master ('mɑːstə) *n* **1** a title of address placed before the first name or surname of a boy **2** a respectful term of address, esp as used by disciples when addressing or referring to a religious teacher **3** an archaic equivalent of **Mr**

master aircrew *n* a warrant rank in the Royal Air Force, equal to but before a warrant officer

master-at-arms *n, pl* masters-at-arms the senior rating, of Chief Petty Officer rank, in a naval unit responsible for discipline, administration, and police duties

master builder *n* **1** a person skilled in the design and construction of buildings, esp before the foundation of the profession of architecture **2** a self-employed builder who employs labour

masterclass ('mɑːstə,klɑːs) *n* a session of tuition by an expert, esp a musician, for exceptional students, usually given in public or on television

masterful ('mɑːstəful) *adj* **1** having or showing mastery **2** fond of playing the master; imperious ▷ 'masterfully *adv* ▷ 'masterfulness *n*

● USAGE The use of *masterful* to mean masterly as in *a*
● *masterful performance*, although common, is considered
● incorrect by many people

master key *n* a key that opens all the locks of a set, the individual keys of which are not interchangeable. Also called: **pass key**

masterly ('mɑːstəlɪ) *adj* of the skill befitting a master ▷ 'masterliness *n*

mastermind ('mɑːstə,maɪnd) *vb* **1** (*tr*) to plan and direct (a complex undertaking) ▷ *n* **2** a person of great intelligence or executive talent, esp one who directs an undertaking

Master of Arts *n* a degree, usually postgraduate and in a nonscientific subject, or the holder of this degree. Abbreviation: **MA**

master of ceremonies *n* a person who presides over a public ceremony, formal dinner, or entertainment, introducing the events, performers, etc

Master of Science *n* a postgraduate degree, usually in science, or the holder of this degree. Abbreviation: **MSc**

Master of the Rolls *n* (in England) a judge of the court of appeal: the senior civil judge in the country and the Keeper of the Records at the Public Record Office

masterpiece ('mɑːstə,piːs) *or less commonly* **masterwork** ('mɑːstə,wɜːk) *n* **1** an outstanding work, achievement, or performance **2** the most outstanding piece of work of a creative artist, craftsman, etc [C17: compare Dutch *meesterstuk*, German *Meisterstück*, a sample of work submitted to a guild by a craftsman in order to qualify for the rank of master]

master plan *n* a comprehensive long-term strategy

master race *n* a race, nation, or group, such as the Germans or Nazis, as viewed by Hitler, believed to be superior to other races. German name **Herrenvolk**

Masters ('mɑːstəz) *n* Edgar Lee. 1868–1950, US poet; best known for *Spoon River Anthology* (1915)

masterstroke ('mɑːstə,strəʊk) *n* an outstanding piece of strategy, skill, talent, etc

mastery ('mɑːstərɪ) *n, pl* -teries **1** full command or understanding of a subject **2** outstanding skill; expertise **3** the power of command; control **4** victory or superiority

masthead ('mɑːst,hɛd) *n* **1** *nautical* the head of a mast **2** Also called: **flag** the name of a newspaper or periodical, its proprietors, staff, etc, printed in large type at the top of the front page ▷ *vb* (*tr*) **3** to send (a sailor) to the masthead as a punishment **4** to raise (a sail) to the masthead

mastic ('mæstɪk) *n* **1** an aromatic resin obtained from the mastic tree and used as an astringent and to make varnishes and lacquers **2** mastic tree a small Mediterranean anacardiaceous evergreen tree, *Pistacia*

m

lentiscus, that yields the resin mastic **3** any of several sticky putty-like substances used as a filler, adhesive, or seal in wood, plaster, or masonry **4** a liquor flavoured with mastic gum [c14: via Old French from Late Latin *mastichum,* from Latin, from Greek *mastikhē* resin used as chewing gum; from *mastikhan* to grind the teeth]

masticate ('mæstɪ,keɪt) *vb* **1** to chew (food) **2** to reduce (materials such as rubber) to a pulp by crushing, grinding, or kneading [c17: from Late Latin *masticāre,* from Greek *mastikhan* to grind the teeth]

masticatory ('mæstɪkətərɪ, -trɪ) *adj* **1** of, relating to, or adapted to chewing ▷ *n, pl* -tories **2** *obsolete* a medicinal substance chewed to increase the secretion of saliva

mastiff ('mæstɪf) *n* an old breed of large powerful short-haired dog, usually fawn or brindle with a dark mask [c14: from Old French, ultimately from Latin *mansuētus* tame; see MANSUETUDE]

mastitis (mæ'staɪtɪs) *n* inflammation of a breast or an udder

masto- *or before a vowel* **mast-** *combining form* indicating the breast, mammary glands, or something resembling a breast or nipple: *mastodon; mastoid* [from Greek *mastos* breast]

mastodon ('mæstə,dɒn) *n* any extinct elephant-like proboscidean mammal of the genus *Mammut* (or *Mastodon*), common in Pliocene times [c19: from New Latin, literally: breast-tooth, referring to the nipple-shaped projections on the teeth]

mastoid ('mæstɔɪd) *adj* **1** shaped like a nipple or breast **2** designating or relating to a nipple-like process of the temporal bone behind the ear ▷ *n* **3** the mastoid process **4** *informal* mastoiditis

mastoiditis (,mæstɔɪ'daɪtɪs) *n* inflammation of the mastoid process

Mastroianni ('mæstrɔɪ'jɑːnɪ) *n* **Marcello** (mɑː'tʃɛləʊ). 1924–96, Italian film actor; his films include *Le notti bianche* (1957), *La dolce vita* (1960), *Ginger and Fred* (1985), and *Prêt à Porter* (1995)

masturbate ('mæstə,beɪt) *vb* to stimulate the genital organs of (oneself or another) to achieve sexual pleasure [c19: from Latin *masturbārī,* of unknown origin; formerly thought to be derived from *manus* hand + *stuprāre* to defile] > ,mastur'bation *n* > 'mastur,bator *n* > masturbatory ('mæstə,beɪtərɪ, 'mastur,batory) *adj*

Masuria (mə'sjʊərɪə) *n* a region of NE Poland: until 1945 part of East Prussia: includes the **Masurian Lakes,** scene of Russian defeats by the Germans (1914, 1915) during World War I > Ma'surian *adj, n*

mat¹ (mæt) *n* **1** a thick flat piece of fabric used as a floor covering, a place to wipe one's shoes, etc **2** a smaller pad of material used to protect a surface from the heat, scratches, etc, of an object placed upon it **3** a large piece of thick padded material put on the floor as a surface for wrestling, judo, or gymnastic sports **4** any surface or mass that is densely interwoven or tangled: *a mat of grass and weeds* ▷ *vb* mats, matting, matted **5** to tangle or weave or become tangled or woven into a dense mass **6** (*tr*) to cover with a mat or mats [Old English *matte;* related to Old High German *matta*]

mat² (mæt) *n* **1** a border of cardboard, cloth, etc, placed around a picture to act as a frame or as a contrast between picture and frame ▷ *adj* **2** having a dull, lustreless, or roughened surface ▷ *vb* mats, matting, matted (*tr*) **3** to furnish (a picture) with a mat **4** to give (a surface) a mat finish ▷ Also (for senses 2, 4): **matt** [c17: from French, literally: dead; see CHECKMATE]

mat³ (mæt) *n printing informal* short for **matrix** (sense 4)

mat. *abbreviation* matinée

Matabeleland (,mætə'biːlɪ,lænd, -'bɛlɪ-) *n* a region of W Zimbabwe, between the Rivers Limpopo and Zambezi, comprises three provinces, Matabeleland North, Matabeleland South, and Bulawayo: rich gold deposits. Chief town: Bulawayo. Area: 181 605 sq km (70 118 sq miles)

Matadi (mə'tɑːdɪ) *n* the chief port of the Democratic Republic of Congo (formerly Zaïre), in the west at the mouth of the River Congo. Pop: 256 000 (2005 est)

matador ('mætə,dɔː) *n* **1** the principal bullfighter who is appointed to kill the bull **2** (in some card games such as

skat) one of the highest ranking cards **3** a game played with dominoes in which the dots on adjacent halves must total seven [c17: from Spanish, from *matar* to kill]

matagouri (,mætə'gʊːrɪ) *n, pl* -ris a thorny bush of New Zealand, *Discaria toumatou,* that forms thickets in open country. Also called: wild Irishman, tumatakuru [from Māori *tumatakuru*]

Mata Hari ('mɑːtə 'hɑːrɪ) *n* real name *Gertrud Margarete Zelle.* 1876–1917, Dutch dancer in France, who was executed as a German spy in World War I

matai ('mɑːtaɪ) *n, pl* -tais a coniferous evergreen tree of New Zealand, *Podocarpus spicatus,* having a bluish bark and small linear leaves arranged in two rows: timber used for flooring and weatherboards. Also called: black pine [Māori]

Matamoros (,mætə'mɔːrəs; *Spanish* mata'morɔs) *n* a port in NE Mexico, on the Río Grande: scene of bitter fighting during the US-Mexican War; centre of a cotton-growing area. Pop: 481 000 (2005 est)

Matanzas (mə'tænzəs; *Spanish* ma'tanθas) *n* a port in W central Cuba: founded in 1693 and developed into the second city of Cuba in the mid-19th century; exports chiefly sugar. Pop: 130 000 (2005 est)

Matapan ('mætə,pæn, ,mætə'pæn) *n* **Cape Matapan** a cape in S Greece, at the S central tip of the Peloponnese: the southern point of the mainland of Greece. Modern Greek name: **Taínaron**

matata (mɑː'tɑːtə:) *n, pl* matata NZ another name for: **fernbird** [Māori]

match¹ (mætʃ) *n* **1** a formal game or sports event in which people, teams, etc, compete to win **2** a person or thing able to provide competition for another: *she's met her match in talking ability* **3** a person or thing that resembles, harmonizes with, or is equivalent to another in a specified respect **4** a person or thing that is an exact copy or equal of another **5 a** a partnership between a man and a woman, as in marriage **b** an arrangement for such a partnership **6** a person regarded as a possible partner, as in marriage ▷ *vb* (*mainly tr*) **7** to fit (parts) together **8** (*also intr;* sometimes foll by *up*) to resemble, harmonize with, correspond to, or equal (one another or something else) **9** (sometimes foll by *with* or *against*) to compare in order to determine which is the superior **10** (often foll by *to* or *with*) to adapt so as to correspond with: *to match hope with reality* **11** (often foll by *with* or *against*) to arrange a competition between **12** to find a match for **13** *electronics* to connect (two circuits) so that their impedances are equal or are equalized by a coupling device, to produce a maximum transfer of energy [Old English *gemæcca* spouse; related to Old High German *gimmaha* wife, Old Norse *maki* mate] > 'matchable *adj* > 'matching *adj*

match² (mætʃ) *n* **1** a thin strip of wood or cardboard tipped with a chemical that ignites by friction when rubbed on a rough surface or a surface coated with a suitable chemical. See **safety match 2** a length of cord or wick impregnated with a chemical so that it burns slowly. It is used to fire cannons, explosives, etc [c14: from Old French *meiche,* perhaps from Latin *myxa* wick, from Greek *muxa* lamp nozzle]

matchboard ('mætʃ,bɔːd) *n* a long thin board with a tongue along one edge and a corresponding groove along the other, used with similar boards to line walls, ceilings, etc

matchbox ('mætʃ,bɒks) *n* a small box for holding matches

match-fit *adj* in good physical condition for competing in a match

matchless ('mætʃlɪs) *adj* unequalled; incomparable; peerless > 'matchlessly *adv*

matchlock ('mætʃ,lɒk) *n* **1** an obsolete type of gunlock igniting the powder by means of a slow match **2** a gun having such a lock

matchmaker ('mætʃ,meɪkə) *n* **1** a person who brings together suitable partners for marriage **2** a person who arranges competitive matches > 'match,making *n, adj*

match play *n golf* scoring according to the number of holes won and lost ▷ See **Stableford, stroke play** > match player *n*

match point n 1 sport the final point needed to win a match 2 bridge the unit used for scoring in tournaments

matchstick ('mætʃˌstɪk) n 1 the wooden part of a match ▷ adj 2 made with or as if with matchsticks 3 (esp of figures drawn with single strokes) thin and straight: matchstick men

matchwood ('mætʃˌwʊd) n 1 wood suitable for making matches 2 splinters or fragments

mate¹ (meɪt) n 1 the sexual partner of an animal 2 a marriage partner 3 a informal, chiefly Brit, Austral & NZ a friend, usually of the same sex: often used between males in direct address b (in combination) an associate, colleague, fellow sharer, etc: a classmate; a flatmate 4 one of a pair of matching items 5 nautical any officer below the master on a commercial ship 6 (in some trades) an assistant: a plumber's mate ▷ vb 7 to pair (a male and female animal) or (of animals) to pair for reproduction 8 to marry or join in marriage 9 (tr) to join as a pair; match [c14: from Middle Low German; related to Old English gemetta table-guest, from mete MEAT]

mate² (meɪt) n, vb chess See **checkmate**

maté or **mate** ('mɑːteɪ, 'mæteɪ) n 1 an evergreen tree, Ilex paraguariensis, cultivated in South America for its leaves, which contain caffeine: family Aquifoliaceae 2 a stimulating milky beverage made from the dried leaves of this tree ▷ Also called: Paraguay tea, yerba, yerba maté [c18: from American Spanish (originally referring to the vessel in which the drink was brewed), from Quechua máti gourd]

matelot, matlo or **matlow** ('mætləʊ) n slang, chiefly Brit a sailor [c20: from French]

mater ('meɪtə) n Brit public school slang, often facetious a word for: **mother¹** [c16: from Latin]

material (mə'tɪərɪəl) n 1 the substance of which a thing is made or composed; component or constituent matter 2 facts, notes, etc, that a finished work may be based on or derived from 3 cloth or fabric 4 a person who has qualities suitable for a given occupation, training, etc: that boy is not university material ▷ adj 5 of, relating to, or composed of physical substance; corporeal 6 of, relating to, or affecting economic or physical wellbeing: material ease 7 of or concerned with physical rather than spiritual interests 8 of great import or consequence: of material benefit to the workers 9 (often foll by to) relevant 10 philosophy of or relating to matter as opposed to form ▷ See also **materials** [c14: via French from Late Latin māteriālis, from Latin māteria MATTER] > ma,teri'ality n

material implication n logic the truth-functional connective that forms a compound sentence from two given sentences and assigns the value false to it only when its antecedent is true and its consequent false, without consideration of relevance; loosely corresponds to the English if ... then

materialism (mə'tɪərɪəˌlɪzəm) n 1 interest in and desire for money, possessions, etc, rather than spiritual or ethical values 2 philosophy the monist doctrine that matter is the only reality and that the mind, the emotions, etc, are merely functions of it. See **idealism** (sense 3), **dualism** (sense 2) 3 ethics the rejection of any religious or supernatural account of things > ma'terialist n, adj > ma,terial'istic adj > ma,terial'istically adv

materialize or **materialise** (mə'tɪərɪəˌlaɪz) vb 1 (intr) to become fact; actually happen 2 to invest or become invested with a physical shape or form 3 to cause (a spirit, as of a dead person) to appear in material form or (of a spirit) to appear in such form 4 (intr) to take shape; become tangible > ma,teriali'zation or ma,teriali'sation n > ma'terial,izer or ma'terial,iser n

materially (mə'tɪərɪəlɪ) adv 1 to a significant extent; considerably 2 with respect to material objects 3 philosophy with respect to substance as distinct from form

materials (mə'tɪərɪəlz) pl n the equipment necessary for a particular activity

materia medica (mə'tɪərɪə 'mɛdɪkə) n 1 the branch of medical science concerned with the study of drugs used in the treatment of disease: includes pharmacology, clinical pharmacology, and the history and physical and chemical properties of drugs 2 the drugs used in the treatment of disease [c17: from Medieval Latin: medical matter]

materiel or **matériel** (mə,tɪərɪ'ɛl) n the materials and equipment of an organization, esp a military force [c19: from French: MATERIAL]

maternal (mə'tɜːnᵊl) adj 1 of, relating to, derived from, or characteristic of a mother 2 related through the mother's side of the family: his maternal uncle [c15: from Medieval Latin māternālis, from Latin māternus, from māter mother] > ma'ternalism n > ma,ternal'istic adj > ma'ternally adv

maternity (mə'tɜːnɪtɪ) n 1 motherhood 2 the characteristics associated with motherhood; motherliness 3 (modifier) relating to pregnant women or women at the time of childbirth: a maternity ward

mateship ('meɪtʃɪp) n Austral the comradeship of friends, usually male, viewed as an institution

mate's rates pl n NZ informal preferential rates of payment offered to a friend

matey or **maty** ('meɪtɪ) Brit informal ▷ adj 1 friendly or intimate; on good terms ▷ n 2 friend or fellow: usually used in direct address > 'mateyness or 'matiness n

math (mæθ) n US & Canadian informal short for **mathematics**. Brit equivalent: **maths**

mathematical (ˌmæθə'mætɪkᵊl, ˌmæθə'mæt-) or less commonly **mathematic** adj 1 of, used in, or relating to mathematics 2 characterized by or using the precision of mathematics; exact 3 using, determined by, or in accordance with the principles of mathematics > ˌmathe'matically adv

mathematical logic n symbolic logic, esp that branch concerned with the foundations of mathematics

mathematician (ˌmæθəmə'tɪʃən, ˌmæθəmə-) n an expert or specialist in mathematics

mathematics (ˌmæθə'mætɪks, ˌmæθ'mæt-) n 1 (functioning as singular) a group of related sciences, including algebra, geometry, and calculus, concerned with the study of number, quantity, shape, and space and their interrelationships by using a specialized notation 2 (functioning as singular or plural) mathematical operations and processes involved in the solution of a problem or study of some scientific field [c14 mathematik (n), via Latin from Greek (adj), from mathēma a science, mathēmatikos, related to manthanein to learn]

maths (mæθs) n (functioning as singular) Brit informal short for **mathematics**. US and Canadian equivalent: **math**

Mathura ('mʌtʊərə, mʌ'θʊərə) n a city in N India, in W Uttar Pradesh on the Jumna River: a place of Hindu pilgrimage, revered as the birthplace of Krishna. Pop: 298 827 (2001). Former name: **Muttra**

Matilda¹ (mə'tɪldə) n Austral informal 1 a bushman's swag 2 **waltz Matilda** or **walk Matilda** to travel the road carrying one's swag [c20: from the Christian name]

Matilda² (mə'tɪldə) n known as the Empress Maud. 1102–67, only daughter of Henry I of England and wife of Geoffrey of Anjou. After her father's death (1135) she unsuccessfully waged a civil war with Stephen for the English throne; her son succeeded as Henry II

matin, mattin ('mætɪn) or **matinal** adj of or relating to matins [c14: see MATINS]

matinée ('mætɪˌneɪ) n a daytime, esp afternoon, performance of a play, concert, etc [c19: from French; see MATINS]

matinée coat or **matinée jacket** n a short coat for a baby

matins or **mattins** ('mætɪnz) n (functioning as singular or plural) 1 a chiefly RC Church the first of the seven canonical hours of prayer, originally observed at night but now often recited with lauds at daybreak b the service of morning prayer in the Church of England 2 literary a morning song, esp of birds [c13: from Old French, ultimately from Latin mātūtīnus of the morning, from Mātūta goddess of dawn]

Matisse (French matis) n **Henri** (ɑ̃ri). 1869–1954, French painter and sculptor; leader of Fauvism

matlo or **matlow** ('mætləʊ) n variant spellings of **matelot**

Matlock ('mætˌlɒk) n a town in England, on the River

Derwent, administrative centre of Derbyshire: mineral springs. Pop: 11 265 (2001)

Mato Grosso *or* **Matto Grosso** ('mætəʊ 'grɒsəʊ; *Portuguese* 'matu 'grosu) *n* **1** a high plateau of SW Brazil: forms the watershed separating the Amazon and Plata river systems **2** a state of W central Brazil: mostly on the Mato Grosso Plateau, with the Amazon basin to the north; valuable mineral resources. Capital: Cuiabá. Pop: 2 604 742 (2002). Area: 881 001 sq km (340 083 sq miles)

Mato Grosso do Sul ('du: sul) *n* a state of W central Brazil: formed in 1979 from part of Mato Grosso state. Capital: Campo Grande. Pop: 2 140 624 (2002). Area: 350 548 sq km (135 318 sq miles)

Matopo Hills (mə'təʊpə) *or* **Matopos** *pl n* the granite hills south of Bulawayo, Zimbabwe, where Cecil Rhodes chose to be buried

Matosinhos *or* **Matozinhos** (*Portuguese* mɒtu'ziɲuʃ) *n* a port in N Portugal, on the estuary of the Leça River north of Oporto: fishing industry. Pop: 167 026 (2001)

matrass *or* **mattrass** ('mætrəs) *n chem obsolete* a long-necked glass flask, used for distilling, dissolving substances, etc [c17: from French, perhaps related to Latin *mētiri* to measure]

matri- *combining form* mother or motherhood: *matriarchy* [from Latin *māter* mother]

matriarch ('meɪtrɪˌɑːk) *n* **1** a woman who dominates an organization, community, etc **2** the female head of a tribe or family, esp in a matriarchy **3** a very old or venerable woman [c17: from MATRI- + -ARCH, by false analogy with PATRIARCH] > 'matri,archal *or less commonly* 'matri,archic *adj*

matriarchy ('meɪtrɪˌɑːkɪ) *n, pl* -chies **1** a form of social organization in which a female is head of the family or society, and descent and kinship are traced through the female line **2** any society dominated by women

matric (mə'trɪk) *n Brit & South African* short for **matriculation** (sense 2)

matrices ('meɪtrɪˌsiːz, 'mæ-) *n* a plural of **matrix**

matricide ('mætrɪˌsaɪd, 'meɪ-) *n* **1** the act of killing one's own mother **2** a person who kills his mother [c16: from Latin *mātrīcīdium* (the act), *mātrīcīda* (the agent). See MATRI-, -CIDE]

matriculate (mə'trɪkjʊˌleɪt) *vb* **1** to enrol or be enrolled in an institution, esp a college or university **2** (*intr*) to attain the academic standard required for a course at such an institution [c16: from Medieval Latin *mātrīculāre* to register, from *mātrīcula*, diminutive of *matrix* list, MATRIX] > ma,tricu'lation *n*

matrilineal (ˌmætrɪ'lɪnɪəl, ˌmeɪ-) *adj* relating to descent or kinship through the female line

matrimony ('mætrɪmənɪ) *n, pl* -nies **1** the state or condition of being married **2** the ceremony or sacrament of marriage **3 a** a card game in which the king and queen together are a winning combination **b** such a combination [c14: via Norman French from Latin *mātrimōnium* wedlock, from *māter* mother] > ,matri'monial *adj* > ,matri'monially *adv*

matrix ('meɪtrɪks, 'mæ-) *n, pl* **matrices** ('meɪtrɪˌsiːz, 'mæ-) *or* **matrixes 1** a substance, situation, or environment in which something has its origin, takes form, or is enclosed **2** the intercellular substance of bone, cartilage, connective tissue, etc **3** the rock material in which fossils, pebbles, etc, are embedded **4** *printing* **a** a metal mould for casting type **b** a papier-mâché or plastic mould impressed from the forme and used for stereotyping **5** (formerly) a mould used in the production of gramophone records. It is obtained by electrodeposition onto the master **6** a bed of perforated material placed beneath a workpiece in a press or stamping machine against which the punch operates **7** *maths* a rectangular array of elements set out in rows and columns, used to facilitate the solution of problems, such as the transformation of coordinates. Usually indicated by parentheses: $\left(\begin{smallmatrix} a & b & c \\ d & e & f \end{smallmatrix}\right)$ **8** *obsolete* the womb [c16: from Latin: womb, female animal used for breeding, from *māter* mother]

matrix printer *n computing* another name for **dot-matrix printer**

matron ('meɪtrən) *n* **1** a married woman regarded as staid or dignified, esp a middle-aged woman with children **2** a woman in charge of the domestic or medical arrangements in an institution, such as a boarding school **3** *Brit* the former name for the administrative head of the nursing staff in a hospital. Official name: **nursing officer** [c14: via Old French from Latin *mātrōna*, from *māter* mother] > 'matronal *adj* > 'matron,hood *or* 'matron,ship *n* > 'matronly *adj* > 'matronliness *n*

matron of honour *n, pl* **matrons of honour** a married woman serving as chief attendant to a bride

Matsu *or* **Mazu** (mæt'su:) *n* an island group in Formosa Strait, off the SE coast of mainland China: belongs to Taiwan. Pop: 9800 (2007 est). Area: 44 sq km (17 sq miles)

Matsuo Basho ('mætsu:əʊ ba:'ʃɔ:) *n* See **Basho**

Matsuyama (ˌmætsʊ'jɑːmə) *n* a port in SW Japan, on NW Shikoku: textile and chemical industries; Ehime University (1949). Pop: 473 039 (2002 est)

Matsys (*Flemish* 'matsaɪs) *n* a variant spelling of (Quentin) **Massys**

matt *or* **matte** (mæt) *adj, n, vb* variant spellings of **mat²** (senses 2, 4)

Matt. *Bible abbreviation* Matthew

mattamore ('mætəˌmɔ:) *n* a subterranean storehouse or dwelling [c17: from French, from Arabic *matmūrā*, from *tamara* to store, bury]

matted ('mætɪd) *adj* **1** tangled into a thick mass **2** covered with or formed of matting

matter ('mætə) *n* **1** that which makes up something, esp a physical object; material **2** substance that occupies space and has mass, as distinguished from substance that is mental, spiritual, etc **3** substance of a specified type: *vegetable matter; reading matter* **4** (sometimes foll by *of* or *for*) thing; affair; concern; question: *a matter of taste; several matters to attend to; no laughing matter* **5** a quantity or amount: *a matter of a few pence* **6** the content of written or verbal material as distinct from its style or form **7** (*used with a negative*) importance; consequence **8** *philosophy* (in the writings of Aristotle and the Scholastics) that which is itself formless but can receive form and become substance **9** *philosophy* (in the Cartesian tradition) one of two basic modes of existence, the other being **mind**: matter being extended in space as well as time **10** *printing* **a** type set up, either standing or for use **b** copy to be set in type **11** a secretion or discharge, such as pus **12** *law* **a** something to be proved **b** statements or allegations to be considered by a court **13** for that matter as regards that **14** no matter **a** regardless of; irrespective of: *no matter what the excuse, you must not be late* **b** (*sentence substitute*) it is unimportant **15** the matter wrong; the trouble: *there's nothing the matter* ▷ *vb* (*intr*) **16** to be of consequence or importance **17** to form and discharge pus [C13 (n), C16 (vb): from Latin *māteria* cause, substance, esp wood, or a substance that produces something else; related to *māter* mother]

Matterhorn ('mætəˌhɔ:n) *n* a mountain on the border between Italy and Switzerland, in the Pennine Alps. Height: 4477 m (14 688 ft). French name: Mont Cervin

matter of course *n* **1** an event or result that is natural or inevitable ▷ *adj* matter-of-course (*usually postpositive*) occurring as a matter of course **3** accepting things as inevitable or natural: *a matter-of-course attitude*

matter of fact *n* **1** a fact that is undeniably true **2** *law* a statement of facts the truth of which the court must determine on the basis of the evidence before it **3** as a matter of fact actually; in fact ▷ *adj* matter-of-fact **4** unimaginative or emotionless: *he gave a matter-of-fact account of the murder*

Matthew ('mæθju:) *n New Testament* **1** Saint Matthew Also called: Levi a tax collector of Capernaum called by Christ to be one of the 12 apostles (Matthew 9:9–13; 10:3). Feast day: Sept 21 or Nov 16 **2** the first Gospel, traditionally ascribed to him

Matthew Paris *n* See **Paris²** (sense 2)

Matthews ('mæθju:z) *n* Sir **Stanley**. 1915–2002, English footballer

Matthias (mə'θaɪəs) *n* **1** 1557–1619, Holy Roman Emperor (1612–19); king of Hungary (1608–18) and Bohemia (1611–17) **2** Saint Matthias *New Testament* the disciple chosen by lot to replace Judas as one of the 12 apostles (Acts 1:15–26). Feast day: May 14 or Aug 9

Matthias I Corvinus (kɔːˈvaɪnəs) *n* ?1440–90, king of Hungary (1458–90): built up the most powerful kingdom in Central Europe. A patron of Renaissance art, he founded the Corvina library, one of the finest in Europe

matting[1] (ˈmætɪŋ) *n* **1** a coarsely woven fabric, usually made of a natural fibre such as straw or hemp and used as a floor covering, packing material, etc **2** the act or process of making mats **3** material for mats

matting[2] (ˈmætɪŋ) *n* **1** another word for: **mat**[2] (sense 1) **2** the process of producing a mat finish

mattins (ˈmætɪnz) *n* a variant spelling of **matins**

mattock (ˈmætək) *n* a type of large pick that has one end of its blade shaped like an adze, used for loosening soil, cutting roots, etc [Old English *mattuc*, of unknown origin; related to Latin *mateola* club, mallet]

mattress (ˈmætrɪs) *n* **1** a large flat pad with a strong cover, filled with straw, foam rubber, etc, and often incorporating coiled springs, used as a bed or as part of a bed **2** *Also called:* **Dutch mattress** a woven mat of brushwood, poles, etc, used to protect an embankment, dyke, etc, from scour **3** a concrete or steel raft or slab used as a foundation or footing [c13: via Old French from Italian *materasso*, from Arabic *almatrah* place where something is thrown]

maturate (ˈmætjʊˌreɪt, ˈmætjʊ-) *vb* **1** to mature or bring to maturity **2** a less common word for **suppurate** > **maturative** (məˈtjʊərətɪv, məˈtʃʊə-) *adj*

maturation (ˌmætjʊˈreɪʃən, ˌmætʃʊ-) *n* **1** the process of maturing or ripening **2** *zoology* the development of ova and spermatozoa from precursor cells in the ovary and testis, involving meiosis

mature (məˈtjʊə, -ˈtʃʊə) *adj* **1** relatively advanced physically, mentally, emotionally, etc; grown-up **2** (of plans, theories, etc) fully considered; perfected **3** due or payable: *a mature debenture* **4** *biology* **a** fully developed or differentiated: *a mature cell* **b** fully grown; adult: *a mature animal* **5** (of fruit, wine, cheese, etc) ripe or fully aged ▷ *vb* **6** to make or become mature **7** (*intr*) (of notes, bonds, etc) to become due for payment or repayment [c15: from Latin *mātūrus* early, developed] > **maˈturely** *adv* > **maˈtureness** *n*

mature student *n* a student at a college or university who has passed the usual age for formal education

maturity (məˈtjʊərɪtɪ, -ˈtʃʊə-) *n* **1** the state or quality of being mature; full development **2** *finance* **a** the date upon which a bill of exchange, bond, note, etc, becomes due for repayment **b** the state of a bill, note, etc, when due

matutinal (ˌmætjʊˈtaɪnəl) *adj* of, occurring in, or during the morning [c17: from Late Latin *mātūtīnālis*, from Latin *mātūtīnus*, from *Mātūta* goddess of the dawn]

matzo *or* **matzoh** (ˈmætsəʊ), **matza** *or* **matzah** (ˈmætsə) *n, pl* **matzos, matzohs, matzas, matzahs** *or* **matzoth** (*Hebrew* maˈtsɔt) a brittle very thin biscuit of unleavened bread, traditionally eaten during Passover [from Hebrew *matsāh*]

Maubeuge (*French* mobøʒ) *n* an industrial town in N France, near the border with Belgium. Pop: 33 546 (1999)

maudlin (ˈmɔːdlɪn) *adj* foolishly tearful or sentimental, as when drunk [c17: from Middle English *Maudelen* Mary Magdalene, typically portrayed as a tearful penitent]

Maugham (ˈmɔːm) *n* **W(illiam) Somerset.** 1874–1965, English writer. His works include the novels *Of Human Bondage* (1915) and *Cakes and Ale* (1930), short stories, and comedies

maugre *or* **mauger** (ˈmɔːɡə) *prep obsolete* in spite of [c13 (meaning: ill will): from Old French *maugre*, literally: bad pleasure]

mauger (ˈmɔːɡə) *adj Caribbean* (of persons or animals) thin or lean [from Du. *mager* thin, MEAGRE]

Maui (ˈmaʊɪ) *n* a volcanic island in S central Hawaii: the second largest of the Hawaiian Islands. Pop: 117 644 (2000). Area: 1885 sq km (728 sq miles)

maul (mɔːl) *vb* (*tr*) **1** to handle clumsily; paw **2** to batter or lacerate ▷ *n* **3** a heavy two-handed hammer suitable for driving piles, wedges, etc **4** *rugby* a loose scrum that forms around a player who is holding the ball and on

his feet [c13: from Old French *mail*, from Latin *malleus* hammer. See MALLET] > **'mauler** *n*

maulstick *or* **mahlstick** (ˈmɔːlˌstɪk) *n* a long stick used by artists to steady the hand holding the brush [c17: partial translation of Dutch *maalstok*, from obsolete *malen* to paint + *stok* STICK[1]]

Mauna Kea (ˈmaʊnə ˈkeɪɑː) *n* an extinct volcano in Hawaii, on N central Hawaii island: the highest island mountain in the world. Height: 4206 m (13 799 ft)

Mauna Loa (ˈmaʊnə ˈləʊɑː) *n* an active volcano in Hawaii, on S central Hawaii island. Height: 4171 m (13 684 ft)

maunder (ˈmɔːndə) *vb* (*intr*) to move, talk, or act aimlessly or idly [c17: perhaps from obsolete *maunder* to beg, from Latin *mendīcāre*; see MENDICANT]

maundy (ˈmɔːndɪ) *n, pl* **maundies** *Christianity* the ceremonial washing of the feet of poor persons in commemoration of Jesus' washing of his disciples' feet (John 13:4–34) re-enacted in some churches on Maundy Thursday [c13: from Old French *mandé* something commanded, from Latin *mandatum* commandment, from the words of Christ: *Mandātum novum dō vōbīs* A new commandment give I unto you]

Maundy money *n* specially minted coins distributed by the British sovereign on Maundy Thursday

Maupassant (*French* mopasɑ̃) *n* (**Henri René Albert**) **Guy de** (gi də). 1850–93, French writer, noted esp for his short stories, such as *Boule de suif* (1880), *La Maison Tellier* (1881), and *Mademoiselle Fifi* (1883). His novels include *Bel Ami* (1885) and *Pierre et Jean* (1888)

Maupertuis (*French* mopɛrtɥi) *n* **Pierre Louis Moreau de** (pjɛr lwi mɔro də). 1698–1759, French mathematician, who originated the principle of least action (or **Maupertuis principle**)

Mauretania (ˌmɒrɪˈteɪnɪə) *n* an ancient region of N Africa, corresponding approximately to the N parts of modern Algeria and Morocco > ˌ**Maure'tanian** *adj, n*

Mauriac (*French* mɔrjak) *n* **François.** 1885–1970, French novelist, noted esp for his psychological studies of the conflict between religious belief and human desire. His works include *Le désert de l'amour* (1925), *Thérèse Desqueyroux* (1927), and *Le nœud de vipères* (1932): Nobel prize for literature 1952

Maurice (ˈmɒrɪs) *n* **1** 1521–53, duke of Saxony (1541–53) and elector of Saxony (1547–53). He was instrumental in gaining recognition of Protestantism in Germany **2** known as *Maurice of Nassau.* 1567–1625, prince of Orange and count of Nassau; the son of William the Silent, after whose death he led the United Provinces of the Netherlands in their struggle for independence from Spain (achieved by 1609) **3 Frederick Denison.** 1805–72, English Anglican theologian and pioneer of Christian socialism

Mauritania (ˌmɒrɪˈteɪnɪə) *n* a republic in NW Africa, on the Atlantic: established as a French protectorate in 1903 and a colony in 1920; gained independence in 1960; lies in the Sahara; contains rich resources of iron ore. Official language: Arabic; Fulani, Soninke, Wolof, and French are also spoken. Official religion: Muslim. Currency: ouguiya. Capital: Nouakchott. Pop: 2 980 000 (2004 est). Area: 1 030 700 sq km (398 000 sq miles) > ˌ**Mauri'tanian** *adj, n*

Mauritius (məˈrɪʃəs) *n* an island and state in the Indian Ocean, east of Madagascar: originally uninhabited, it was settled by the Dutch (1638–1710) then abandoned; taken by the French in 1715 and the British in 1810; became an independent member of the Commonwealth in 1968. It is economically dependent on sugar. Official language: English; a French creole is widely spoken. Religion: Hindu majority, large Christian minority. Currency: rupee. Capital: Port Louis. Pop: 1 233 000 (2004 est). Area: 1865 sq km (720 sq miles). Former name (1715–1810): **Île-de-France** > **Mau'ritian** *adj, n*

Maurois (*French* mɔrwa) *n* **André.** pen name of *Émile Herzog.* 1885–1967, French writer, best known for his biographies, such as those of Shelley, Byron, and Proust

Maurras (*French* mora) *n* **Charles** (ʃarl). 1868–1952, French writer and political theorist, who founded (1899) the extreme right-wing group L'Action Français: sentenced (1945) to life imprisonment for supporting Pétain during World War II

Maury ('mɔːrɪ) n Matthew Fontaine. 1806–73, US pioneer hydrographer and oceanographer

mausoleum (ˌmɔːsə'lɪəm) n, pl -leums or -lea (-'lɪə) a large stately tomb [c16: via Latin from Greek mausōleion, the tomb of Mausolus, king of Caria; built at Halicarnassus in the 4th century BC]

mauve (məʊv) n 1 a any of various pale to moderate pinkish-purple or bluish-purple colours b (as adjective): a mauve flower 2 Also called: Perkin's mauve, mauveine ('məʊviːn, -vɪn) a reddish-purple aniline dye [c19: from French, from Latin malva MALLOW]

maven or **mavin** ('meɪvən) n US an expert or connoisseur [c20: from Yiddish, from Hebrew mevin understanding]

maverick ('mævərɪk) n 1 (in US and Canadian cattle-raising regions) an unbranded animal, esp a stray calf 2 a a person of independent or unorthodox views b (as modifier): a maverick politician [c19: after Samuel A. Maverick (1803–70), Texas rancher, who did not brand his cattle]

mavis ('meɪvɪs) n a popular name for the **song thrush** [c14: from Old French mauvis thrush; origin obscure]

maw (mɔː) n 1 the mouth, throat, crop, or stomach of an animal, esp of a voracious animal 2 informal the mouth or stomach of a greedy person [Old English maga; related to Middle Dutch maghe, Old Norse magi]

mawkish ('mɔːkɪʃ) adj 1 falsely sentimental, esp in a weak or maudlin way 2 nauseating or insipid in flavour, smell, etc [c17: from obsolete mawk MAGGOT + -ISH]
> 'mawkishly adv > 'mawkishness n

Mawson ('mɔːsən) n Sir Douglas. 1882–1958, Australian Antarctic explorer, born in England

max (mæks) n informal 1 the most significant, highest, furthest, or greatest thing 2 **to the max** to the ultimate extent

max. abbreviation maximum

maxi ('mæksɪ) adj 1 a (of a garment) reaching the ankle b (as noun): she wore a maxi c (in combination): a maxidress ▷ n 2 a type of large racing yacht [c20: shortened from MAXIMUM]

maxilla (mæk'sɪlə) n, pl -lae (-liː) 1 the upper jawbone in vertebrates 2 any member of one or two pairs of mouthparts in insects and other arthropods used as accessory jaws [c17: New Latin, from Latin: jaw]
> maxillar (mæk'sɪlə) or max'illary adj

maxim ('mæksɪm) n a brief expression of a general truth, principle, or rule of conduct [c15: via French from Medieval Latin, from maxima, in the phrase maxima prōpositio basic axiom (literally: greatest proposition); see MAXIMUM]

Maxim ('mæksɪm) n Sir Hiram Stevens. 1840–1916, British inventor of the first automatic machine gun (1884), born in the US

maxima ('mæksɪmə) n a plural of maximum

maximal ('mæksɪməl) adj of, relating to, or achieving a maximum; being the greatest or best possible
> 'maximally adv

Maximilian (ˌmæksɪ'mɪlɪən) n full name Ferdinand Maximilian Joseph. 1832–67, archduke of Austria and emperor of Mexico (1864–67). After the French had partially conquered Mexico, he was offered the throne but was defeated and shot by the Mexicans under Juárez

Maximilian I n 1459–1519, king of Germany (1486–1519) and Holy Roman Emperor (1493–1519)

maximin ('mæksɪˌmɪn) n 1 maths the highest of a set of minimum values 2 (in game theory, etc) the procedure of choosing the strategy that most benefits the least advantaged member of a group. See minimax [c20: from MAXI(MUM) + MIN(IMUM)]

maximize or **maximise** ('mæksɪˌmaɪz) vb (tr) to make as high or great as possible; increase to a maximum
> ˌmaximi'zation, ˌmaximi'sation or ˌmaximi'mation n
> 'maxiˌmizer or 'maxiˌmiser n

maximum ('mæksɪməm) n, pl -mums or -ma (-mə) 1 the greatest possible amount, degree, etc 2 the highest value of a variable quantity ▷ adj 3 of, being, or showing a maximum or maximums ▷ Abbreviation: max [c18:

from Latin: greatest (the neuter form used as noun), from magnus great]

Max Müller (German maks 'mylər) n See Müller (sense 1)

maxwell ('mækswəl) n the cgs unit of magnetic flux equal to the flux through one square centimetre normal to a field of one gauss. It is equivalent to 10^{-8} weber. Symbol: Mx [c20: named after James Clerk Maxwell (1831–79), Scottish physicist]

Maxwell ('mækswəl) n 1 James Clerk. 1831–79, Scottish physicist. He made major contributions to the electromagnetic theory, developing the equations (**Maxwell equations**) upon which classical theory is based. He also contributed to the kinetic theory of gases, and colour vision 2 (Ian) Robert, original name Robert Hoch. 1923–91, British publisher, born in Slovakia: founder (1949) of Pergamon Press; chairman of Mirror Group Newspapers Ltd. (1984–91); theft from his employees' pension funds and other frauds discovered after his death led to the collapse of his business

may¹ (meɪ) vb, past might (takes an infinitive without to or an implied infinitive used as an auxiliary) 1 to indicate that permission is requested by or granted to someone: he may go to the park tomorrow if he behaves himself 2 (often foll by well) to indicate possibility: the rope may break; he may well be a spy 3 to indicate ability or capacity, esp in questions: may I help you? 4 to express a strong wish: long may she reign 5 to indicate result or purpose: used only in clauses introduced by that or so that: he writes so that the average reader may understand 6 another word for **might¹** 7 to express courtesy in a question: whose child may this little girl be? 8 **be that as it may** in spite of that: a sentence connector conceding the possible truth of a previous statement and introducing an adversative clause: be that as it may, I still think he should come 9 **come what may** whatever happens 10 **that's as may be** (foll by a clause introduced by but) that may be so [Old English mæg, from magan: compare Old High German mag, Old Norse mā]

may² (meɪ) n Also called: may tree a Brit name for: hawthorn [c16: from the month of MAY, when it flowers]

May¹ (meɪ) n the fifth month of the year, consisting of 31 days [from Old French, from Latin Maius, probably from Maia, Roman goddess, identified with the Greek goddess MAIA]

May² (meɪ) n Robert McCredie. Baron. born 1936, Australian biologist and ecologist

Maya¹ ('maɪə, 'mɑːjə, 'mɑːjɑː) n the Hindu goddess of illusion, the personification of the idea that the material world is illusory > 'Mayan adj

Maya² ('maɪə) n 1 pl -ya or -yas Also called: Mayan a member of an American Indian people of Yucatan, Belize, and N Guatemala, having an ancient culture once characterized by outstanding achievements in architecture, astronomy, chronology, painting, and pottery 2 the language of this people > 'Mayan adj

Mayagüez (Spanish maja'ɣweθ) n a port in W Puerto Rico; needlework industry. Pop: 97 627 (2003 est)

Mayakovski or **Mayakovsky** (Russian məjɪ'kofskij) n Vladimir Vladimirovich (vla'dimir vla'dimirəvitʃ). 1893–1930, Russian Futurist poet and dramatist. His poems include 150 000 000 (1921) and At the Top of my Voice (1930); his plays include Vladimir Mayakovsky — a Tragedy (1913) and The Bedbug (1929)

May apple n 1 an American berberidaceous plant, Podophyllum peltatum, with edible yellowish egg-shaped fruit 2 the fruit of this plant

maybe ('meɪˌbiː) adv 1 perhaps ▷ sentence substitute 2 possibly; neither yes nor no

May beetle or **May bug** n another name for: cockchafer

Mayday ('meɪˌdeɪ) n the international radiotelephone distress signal [c20: phonetic spelling of French m'aidez help me]

May Day n the first day of May, traditionally a celebration of the coming of spring: in some countries now observed as a holiday in honour of workers

Mayence (majɑ̃s) n the French name for Mainz

Mayenne (French majɛn) n a department of NW France, in Pays de la Loire region. Capital: Laval. Pop: 290 780 (2003 est). Area: 5212 sq km (2033 sq miles)

Mayer *n* **1** (*German* 'maiər) **Julius Robert von** ('juːliʊs 'roːbɛrt fɔn). 1814–78, German physicist whose research in thermodynamics (1842) contributed to the discovery of the law of conservation of energy **2** ('meɪə) **Louis B(urt)**. 1885–1957, US film producer, born in Russia; founder and first head (1924–48) of the Metro-Goldwyn-Mayer (MGM) film company

mayest ('meɪɪst) *vb* a variant of: **mayst**

Mayfair ('meɪˌfɛə) *n* a fashionable district of west central London

mayflower ('meɪˌflaʊə) *n* **1** any of various plants that bloom in May **2** *Brit* another name for **hawthorn, cowslip, marsh marigold**

Mayflower ('meɪˌflaʊə) *n* the **Mayflower** the ship in which the Pilgrim Fathers sailed from Plymouth to Massachusetts in 1620

mayfly ('meɪˌflaɪ) *n, pl* **-flies** Also called: **dayfly** any insect of the order *Ephemeroptera* (or *Ephemerida*). The short-lived adults, found near water, have long tail appendages and large transparent wings; the larvae are aquatic

mayhap ('meɪˌhæp) *adv* an archaic word for: **perhaps** [c16: shortened from *it may hap*]

mayhem *or* **maihem** ('meɪhɛm) *n* **1** *law* the wilful and unlawful infliction of injury upon a person, esp (formerly) the injuring or removing of a limb rendering him less capable of defending himself against attack **2** any violent destruction or confusion [c15: from Anglo-French *mahem* injury, from Germanic; related to Icelandic *meitha* to hurt. See MAIM]

Mayhew ('meɪhjuː) *n* **Henry**. 1812–87, British social commentator, journalist, and writer; a founder of *Punch* (1841): best known for *London Labour and the London Poor* (1851–62)

Maying ('meɪɪŋ) *n* the traditional celebration of May Day

mayn't ('meɪənt, meɪnt) *vb contraction of* may not

Mayo[1] ('meɪəʊ) *n* a county of NW Republic of Ireland, in NW Connacht province, on the Atlantic: has many offshore islands and several large lakes. County town: Castlebar. Pop: 117 446 (2002). Area: 5397 sq km (2084 sq miles)

Mayo[2] ('meɪəʊ) *n* a family of US medical practitioners. They pioneered group practice and established (1903) the **Mayo Clinic** in Rochester, Minnesota. Foremost among them were **William Worrall Mayo** (1819–1911), his sons **William James Mayo** (1861–1939) and **Charles Horace Mayo** (1865–1939), and Charles's son, **Charles William Mayo** (1898–1968)

Mayon (maːˈjɔːn) *n* a volcano in the Philippines, on SE Luzon: Height: 2421 m (7943 ft)

mayonnaise (ˌmeɪəˈneɪz) *n* a thick creamy sauce made from egg yolks, oil, and vinegar or lemon juice, eaten with salads, eggs, etc [c19: from French, perhaps from *Mahonnais* of *Mahón*, a port in Minorca]

mayor (mɛə) *n* the chairman and civic head of a municipal corporation in many countries. Scottish equivalent: **provost** [c13: from Old French *maire*, from Latin *maior* greater. See MAJOR] > 'mayoral *adj* > 'mayorˌship *n*

mayoralty ('mɛərəltɪ) *n, pl* **-ties** the office or term of office of a mayor [c14: from Old French *mairalté*]

mayoress ('mɛərɪs) *n* **1** *chiefly Brit* the wife of a mayor **2** a female mayor

Mayotte (*French* majɔt) *n* an island in the Indian Ocean, northwest of Madagascar; administered by France. Pop (including Pamanzi): 186 026 (2004 est). Area: 374 sq km (146 sq miles)

maypole ('meɪˌpəʊl) *n* a tall pole fixed upright in an open space during May-Day celebrations, around which people dance holding streamers attached at its head

May queen *n* a girl chosen, esp for her beauty, to preside over May-Day celebrations

mayst (meɪst) *or* **mayest** *vb archaic or dialect* (used with the pronoun *thou* or its relative equivalent) a singular form of the present tense of: **may**[1]

mayweed ('meɪˌwiːd) *n* **1** Also called: **dog fennel, stinking mayweed** a widespread Eurasian weedy plant, *Anthemis cotula*, having evil-smelling leaves and daisy-like flower heads: family *Asteraceae* (composites) **2** **scentless mayweed** a similar and related plant, *Matricaria maritima*, with scentless leaves [c16: changed from Old English *mægtha* mayweed + WEED[1]]

Mazar-e-Sharif *or* **Mazar-i-Sharif** ('mæzaː iː ʒəˈriːf) *n* a city in N Afghanistan, reputed burial place of the caliph Ali; trading, agricultural, and military centre. Pop: 254 000 (2005 est)

Mazarin ('mæzərɪn; *French* mazarɛ̃) *n* **Jules** (ʒyl), original name *Giulio Mazarini*. 1602–61, French cardinal and statesman, born in Italy. He succeeded Richelieu (1642) as chief minister to Louis XIII and under the regency of Anne of Austria (1643–61), Despite the disturbances of the Fronde (1648–53), he strengthened the power of France in Europe

Mazatlán (*Spanish* maθaˈtlan) *n* a port in W Mexico, in S Sinaloa on the Pacific: situated opposite the tip of the peninsula of Lower California, for which it is the chief link with the mainland. Pop: 406 000 (2005 est)

maze (meɪz) *n* **1** a complex network of paths or passages, esp one with high hedges in a garden, designed to puzzle those walking through it **2** a similar system represented diagrammatically as a pattern of lines **3** any confusing network of streets, pathways, etc **4** a state of confusion ▷ *vb* **5** an archaic or dialect word for: **amaze** [c13: see AMAZE] > 'mazement *n* > 'mazy *adj* > 'mazily *adv* > 'maziness *n*

Mazu ('mæ'zuː) *n* the Pinyin transliteration of the Chinese name for **Matsu**

mazurka *or* **mazourka** (məˈzɜːkə) *n* **1** a Polish national dance in triple time **2** a piece of music composed for this dance [c19: from Polish: (dance) of *Mazur* (Mazovia) province in Poland]

Mazzini (*Italian* matˈtsiːni) *n* **Giuseppe** (dʒuˈzɛppe). 1805–72, Italian nationalist. In 1831, in exile, he established the Young Italy association in Marseille, which sought to unite Italy as a republic. In 1849 he was one of the triumvirate that ruled the short-lived Roman republic

Mb *computing abbreviation* megabyte

MB *abbreviation* Bachelor of Medicine

MBA *abbreviation* Master of Business Administration

Mbabane (ᵊmbaːˈbaːnɪ) *n* the capital of Swaziland, in the northwest: administrative and financial centre, with a large iron mine nearby. Pop: 71 000 (2005 est)

m-banking *n* the practice of making financial transactions or managing bank accounts using mobile phone technology [c20: M(OBILE) + BANKING]

mbaqanga (ᵊmbaːˈkæŋɡə) *n* a style of Black popular music of urban South Africa [c20: perhaps from Zulu *umbaqanga* mixture]

MBE *abbreviation* Member of the Order of the British Empire (a Brit title)

Mbeki (ᵊmˈbekɪ) *n* **Thabo** (**Mvuyelwa**) ('taːbəʊ). born 1942, South African politician: a member of the African National Congress (ANC); president of South Africa from 1999; deputy president of South Africa (1994–99)

mbira (ᵊmˈbiːrə) *n* an African musical instrument consisting of tuned metal strips attached to a resonating box, which are plucked with the thumbs. Also called: **thumb piano** [Shona]

MBO *abbreviation* management buyout

Mbujimayi (ᵊmˈbuːdʒɪˌmaɪiː) *n* a city in S Democratic Republic of Congo (formerly Zaïre): diamond mining. Pop: 821 000 (2005 est)

MC *abbreviation* **1** Master of Ceremonies **2** (in the US) Member of Congress **3** (in Britain) Military Cross

Mc- *prefix* a variant of **Mac-**
● **USAGE** For names beginning with this prefix, see
● under **Mac-**

MCC *abbreviation* (in Britain) Marylebone Cricket Club

MCG *abbreviation* (in Australia) Melbourne Cricket Ground

MCh *abbreviation* Master of Surgery [Latin *Magister Chirurgiae*]

MCP *informal abbreviation* male chauvinist pig

Md *the chemical symbol for* mendelevium

MD *abbreviation* **1** Doctor of Medicine [from Latin *Medicinae Doctor*] **2** Managing Director **3** mentally deficient **4** (in

Canada) municipal district

Md. *abbreviation* Maryland

MDF *abbreviation* medium-density fibreboard: a wood-substitute material used in interior decoration

MDMA *abbreviation* 3,4-methylenedioxymethamphetamine. Also called (informal): **ecstasy**

MDT *abbreviation* Mountain Daylight Time

me¹ (miː; *unstressed* mɪ) *pron* (*objective*) **1** refers to the speaker or writer: *that shocks me; he gave me the glass* ▷ *n* **2** *informal* the personality of the speaker or writer or something that expresses it: *the real me comes out when I'm happy* [Old English *mē* (dative); compare Dutch, German *mir*, Latin *mē* (accusative), *mihi* (dative)]

me² (miː) *n* a variant spelling of: **mi**

ME *abbreviation* **1** Marine Engineer **2** Mechanical Engineer **3** Methodist Episcopal **4** Mining Engineer **5** Middle English **6** (in titles) Most Excellent **7** myalgic encephalopathy

Me. *abbreviation* Maine

mea culpa Latin ('meɪɑː 'kʊlpɑː) an acknowledgment of guilt [literally: my fault]

mead¹ (miːd) *n* an alcoholic drink made by fermenting a solution of honey, often with spices added [Old English *meodu*; related to Old High German *metu*, Greek *methu*, Welsh *medd*]

mead² (miːd) *n* an archaic or poetic word for: **meadow** [Old English *mǣd*]

Mead¹ (miːd) *n* **Lake Mead** a reservoir in NW Arizona and SE Nevada, formed by the Hoover Dam across the Colorado River: one of the largest man-made lakes in the world. Area: 588 sq km (227 sq miles)

Mead² (miːd) *n* **Margaret**. 1901–78, US anthropologist. Her works include *Coming of Age in Samoa* (1928) and *Male and Female* (1949)

Meade (miːd) *n* **George Gordon**. 1815–72, Union general in the American Civil War. He commanded the Army of the Potomac, defeating the Confederates at Gettysburg (1863)

meadow ('mɛdəʊ) *n* **1** an area of grassland, often used for hay or for grazing of animals **2** a low-lying piece of grassland, often boggy and near a river [Old English *mǣdwe*, from *mǣd* MEAD²; related to *māwan* to MOW¹] ▷ 'meadowy *adj*

meadow grass *n* a perennial grass, *Poa pratensis*, that has erect hairless leaves and grows in meadows and similar places in N temperate regions

meadow saffron *n* another name for: **autumn crocus**

meadowsweet ('mɛdəʊˌswiːt) *n* **1** a Eurasian rosaceous plant, *Filipendula ulmaria*, with dense heads of small fragrant cream-coloured flowers **2** any of several North American rosaceous plants of the genus *Spiraea*, having pyramid-shaped sprays of small flowers

Meads (miːdz) *n* **Colin**. born 1935, New Zealand Rugby Union footballer. A forward, he played for the All Blacks (1957–71)

meagre *or US* **meager** ('miːgə) *adj* **1** deficient in amount, quality, or extent **2** thin or emaciated **3** lacking in richness or strength [C14: from Old French *maigre*,from Latin *macer* lean, poor] ▷ 'meagrely *or US* 'meagerly *adv* ▷ 'meagreness *or US* 'meagerness *n*

meal¹ (miːl) *n* **1 a** any of the regular occasions, such as breakfast, lunch, dinner, etc, when food is served and eaten **b** (*in combination*): *mealtime* **2** the food served and eaten **3 make a meal of** *informal* to perform (a task) with unnecessarily great effort [Old English *mǣl* measure, set time, meal; related to Old High German *māl* mealtime]

meal² (miːl) *n* **1** the edible part of a grain or pulse (excluding wheat) ground to a coarse powder, used chiefly as animal food **2** *Scot* oatmeal **3** *chiefly US* maize flour [Old English *melu*; compare Dutch *meel*, Old High German *melo*, Old Norse *mjöl*]

mealie *or* **mielie** ('miːlɪ) *n* South African an ear of maize [C19: from Afrikaans *milie*, from Portuguese *milho*, from Latin *milium* millet]

mealie meal *or* **mielie meal** *n* South African finely ground maize

meals on wheels *or* **meals-on-wheels** *n* (*functioning as singular*) social welfare, Brit a service, usually subsidized,

and run by a social services department or voluntary body, which delivers hot meals to elderly or housebound people who might otherwise be unable to have them

meal ticket *n* slang a person, situation, etc, providing a source of livelihood or income [from original US sense of ticket entitling holder to a meal]

mealworm ('miːlˌwɜːm) *n* the larva of various beetles of the genus *Tenebrio*, esp *T. molitor*, feeding on meal, flour, and similar stored foods: family *Tenebrionidae*

mealy ('miːlɪ) *adj* **mealier, mealiest 1** resembling meal; powdery **2** containing or consisting of meal or grain **3** sprinkled or covered with meal or similar granules **4** (esp of horses) spotted; mottled **5** pale in complexion **6** short for **mealy-mouthed** ▷ 'mealiness *n*

mealy bug *n* any plant-eating homopterous insect of the genus *Pseudococcus* and related genera, coated with a powdery waxy secretion: some species are pests of citrus fruits and greenhouse plants: family *Pseudococcidae*

mealy-mouthed *adj* hesitant or afraid to speak plainly; not outspoken [C16: from MEALY (in the sense: soft, soft-spoken)]

mean¹ (miːn) *vb* **means, meaning, meant** (*mainly tr*) **1** (*may take a clause as object or an infinitive*) to intend to convey or express **2** (*may take a clause as object or an infinitive*) intend: *she didn't mean to hurt it* **3** (*may take a clause as object*) to say or do in all seriousness: *the boss means what he says about strikes* **4** (*often passive*; *often foll by for*) to destine or design (for a certain person or purpose): *she was meant for greater things* **5** (*may take a clause as object*) to denote or connote; signify; represent **6** (*may take a clause as object*) to produce; cause: *the weather will mean long traffic delays* **7** (*may take a clause as object*) to foretell; portend: *those dark clouds mean rain* **8** to have the importance of: *money means nothing to him* **9** (*intr*) to have the intention of behaving or acting (esp in the phrases **mean well** or **mean ill**) [Old English *mǣnan*; compare Old Saxon *mēnian* to intend, Dutch *meenen*]

● USAGE In standard English, *mean* should not be
● followed by *for* when expressing intention: *I didn't*
● *mean this to happen* (not *I didn't mean for this to happen*)

mean² (miːn) *adj* **1** *chiefly Brit* miserly, ungenerous, or petty **2** despicable, ignoble, or callous: *a mean action* **3** poor or shabby: *mean clothing; a mean abode* **4** *informal, chiefly US & Canadian* bad-tempered; vicious **5** *informal* ashamed: *he felt mean about not letting the children go to the zoo* **6** *slang* excellent; skilful: *he plays a mean trombone* **7** **no mean a** of high quality: *no mean performer* **b** difficult: *no mean feat* [C12: from Old English *gemǣne* common; related to Old High German *gimeini*, Latin *communis* common, at first with no pejorative sense] ▷ 'meanly *adv* ▷ 'meanness *n*

mean³ (miːn) *n* **1** the middle point, state, or course between limits or extremes **2** moderation **3** *maths* **a** the second and third terms of a proportion, as *b* and *c* in $a/b = c/d$ **b** another name for **average** (sense 2) See also **geometric mean 4** *statistics* a statistic obtained by multiplying each possible value of a variable by its probability and then taking the sum or integral over the range of the variable ▷ *adj* **5** intermediate or medium in size, quantity, etc **6** occurring halfway between extremes or limits; average [C14: via Anglo-Norman from Old French *moien*, from Late Latin *mediānus* MEDIAN]

meander (mɪ'ændə) *vb* (*intr*) **1** to follow a winding course **2** to wander without definite aim or direction ▷ *n* **3** (*often plural*) a curve or bend, as in a river **4** (*often plural*) a winding course or movement **5** an ornamental pattern, esp as used in ancient Greek architecture [C16: from Latin *maeander*, from Greek *Maiandros* the River Maeander; see MENDERES (sense 1)] ▷ me'andering *adj*

Meander (mɪ'ændə) *n* a variant spelling of **Maeander**

mean deviation *n* statistics **1** the difference between an observed value of a variable and its mean **2** Also called: **mean deviation from the median, mean deviation from the mean, average deviation** a measure of dispersion derived by computing the mean of the absolute values of the differences between observed values of a variable and the variable's mean

meanie *or* **meany** ('miːnɪ) *n, pl* **meanies** *informal* **1** *chiefly Brit* a miserly or stingy person **2** *chiefly US* a nasty ill-tempered person

meaning ('miːnɪŋ) *n* 1 the sense or significance of a word, sentence, symbol, etc; import; semantic or lexical content 2 the purpose underlying or intended by speech, action, etc 3 the inner, symbolic, or true interpretation, value, or message 4 valid content; efficacy ▷ *adj* 5 expressive of some sense, intention, criticism, etc: *a meaning look* ▷ See also **well-meaning**

meaningful ('miːnɪŋfʊl) *adj* 1 having great meaning or validity 2 eloquent, expressive: *a meaningful silence* > 'meaningfully *adv* > 'meaningfulness *n*

meaningless ('miːnɪŋlɪs) *adj* futile or empty of meaning > 'meaninglessly *adv* > 'meaninglessness *n*

mean lethal dose *n* another term for **median lethal dose**

mean life *n physics* the average time of existence of an unstable or reactive entity, such as a nucleus, elementary particle, charge carrier, etc; lifetime. It is equal to the half-life divided by 0.693 15

means (miːnz) *n* 1 *(functioning as singular or plural)* the medium, method, or instrument used to obtain a result or achieve an end: *a means of communication* 2 *(functioning as plural)* resources or income 3 *(functioning as plural)* considerable wealth or income: *a man of means* 4 **by all means** without hesitation or doubt; certainly 5 **by no manner of means** definitely not 6 **by no means** *or* **not by any means** in no account; in no way

means test *n* a test involving the checking of a person's income to determine whether he qualifies for financial or social aid from a government

mean sun *n* an imaginary sun moving along the celestial equator at a constant rate and completing its annual course in the same time as the sun takes to move round the ecliptic at a varying rate. It is used in the measurement of mean solar time

meant (mɛnt) *vb* the past tense and past participle of **mean¹**

mean time *or* **mean solar time** *n* the time, at a particular place, measured in terms of the passage of the mean sun; the timescale is not precisely constant

meantime ('miːnˌtaɪm) *n* 1 the intervening time or period, as between events (esp in the phrase **in the meantime**) ▷ *adv* 2 another word for **meanwhile**

meanwhile ('miːnˌwaɪl) *adv* 1 during the intervening time or period 2 at the same time, esp in another place ▷ *n* 3 another word for: **meantime**

meany ('miːnɪ) *n informal* a variant spelling of **meanie**

Mearns (mɛənz) *n* the Mearns another name for **Kincardineshire**

measles ('miːzəlz) *n (functioning as singular or plural)* 1 a highly contagious viral disease common in children, characterized by fever, profuse nasal discharge of mucus, conjunctivitis, and a rash of small red spots spreading from the forehead down to the limbs. See also **German measles** 2 a disease of cattle, sheep, and pigs, caused by infestation with tapeworm larvae [c14: from Middle Low German *masele* spot on the skin; influenced by Middle English *mesel* leper, from Latin *misellus*, diminutive of *miser* wretched]

measly ('miːzlɪ) *adj* -slier, -sliest 1 *informal* meagre in quality or quantity 2 (of meat) infested with tapeworm larvae 3 having or relating to measles [c17: see MEASLES]

measurable ('mɛʒərəbᵊl, 'mɛʒrə-) *adj* able to be measured; perceptible or significant > 'measurably *adv*

measure ('mɛʒə) *n* 1 the extent, quantity, amount, or degree of something, as determined by measurement or calculation 2 a device for measuring distance, volume, etc, such as a graduated scale or container 3 a system of measurement: *give the size in metric measure* 4 a standard used in a system of measurements 5 a specific or standard amount of something: *a measure of grain; short measure; full measure* 6 a basis or standard for comparison 7 reasonable or permissible limit or bounds: *we must keep it within measure* 8 degree or extent (often in phrases such as **in some measure, in a measure**, etc): *they gave him a measure of freedom* 9 *(often plural)* a particular action intended to achieve an effect 10 a legislative bill, act, or resolution 11 *music* another word for: **bar¹** (sense 15a) 12 *prosody* poetic rhythm or cadence; metre 13 a metrical

foot 14 *poetic* a melody or tune 15 the act of measuring; measurement 16 *archaic* a dance 17 *printing* the width of a page or column of type 18 **for good measure** as an extra precaution or beyond requirements 19 **made to measure** (of clothes) made to fit an individual purchaser ▷ *vb* 20 *(tr; often foll by up)* to determine the size, amount, etc, of by measurement 21 *(intr)* to make a measurement or measurements 22 *(tr)* to estimate or determine 23 *(tr)* to function as a measurement of: *the ohm measures electrical resistance* 24 *(tr)* to bring into competition or conflict: *he measured his strength against that of his opponent* 25 *(intr)* to be as specified in extent, amount, etc: *the room measures six feet* 26 *(tr)* to travel or move over as if measuring ▷ See also **measure up** [c13: from Old French, from Latin *mēnsūra* measure, from *mēnsus*, past participle of *mētīrī* to measure]

measured ('mɛʒəd) *adj* 1 determined by measurement 2 slow, stately, or leisurely 3 carefully considered; deliberate > 'measuredly *adv*

measureless ('mɛʒəlɪs) *adj* limitless, vast, or infinite > 'measurelessly *adv*

measurement ('mɛʒəmənt) *n* 1 the act or process of measuring 2 an amount, extent, or size determined by measuring 3 a system of measures based on a particular standard

measures ('mɛʒəz) *pl n* rock strata that are characterized by a particular type of sediment or deposit: *coal measures*

measure up *vb* 1 *(adverb)* to determine the size of (something) by measurement 2 **measure up to** to fulfil (expectations, standards, etc)

measuring jug *n* a graduated jug used in cooking to measure ingredients

measuring worm *n* the larva of a geometrid moth: it has legs on its front and rear segments only and moves in a series of loops. Also called: **looper, inchworm**

meat (miːt) *n* 1 the flesh of mammals used as food, as distinguished from that of birds and fish 2 anything edible, esp flesh with the texture of meat: *crab meat* 3 food, as opposed to drink 4 the essence or gist 5 an archaic word for **meal¹** 6 **meat and drink** a source of pleasure [Old English *mete*; related to Old High German *maz* food, Old Saxon *meti*, Gothic *mats*] > 'meatless *adj*

meatball ('miːtˌbɔːl) *n* 1 minced beef, shaped into a ball before cooking 2 *US & Canadian slang* a stupid or boring person

Meath (miːð, miːθ) *n* a county of E Republic of Ireland, in Leinster province on the Irish Sea: formerly a kingdom much larger than the present county; livestock farming. County town: Trim. Pop: 134 005 (2002). Area: 2338 sq km (903 sq miles)

meatspace ('miːtˌspeɪs) *n slang* the real physical world, as contrasted with the world of cyberspace

meatus (mɪ'eɪtəs) *n*, *pl* **-tuses** *or* **-tus** *anatomy* a natural opening or channel, such as the canal leading from the outer ear to the eardrum [c17: from Latin: passage, from *meāre* to pass]

meaty ('miːtɪ) *adj* meatier, meatiest 1 of, relating to, or full of meat 2 heavily built; fleshy or brawny 3 full of import or interest: *a meaty discussion* > 'meatily *adv* > 'meatiness *n*

mebi- ('mebɪ) *prefix computing* denoting 2²⁰. Symbol: Mi [c20: from ME(GA-) + BI(NARY)]

MEC *abbreviation* (in South Africa) Member of the Executive Council

Mecca *or* **Mekka** ('mɛkə) *n* 1 a city in W Saudi Arabia, joint capital (with Riyadh) of Saudi Arabia: birthplace of Mohammed; the holiest city of Islam, containing the Kaaba. Pop: 1 529 000 (2005 est). Arabic name: Makkah 2 *(sometimes not capital)* a place that attracts many visitors: *Athens is a Mecca for tourists*

Meccano (mɪ'kɑːnəʊ) *n trademark* a construction set consisting of miniature metal or plastic parts from which mechanical models can be made

mechanic (mɪ'kænɪk) *n* a person skilled in maintaining or operating machinery, motors, etc [c14: from Latin *mēchanicus*, from Greek *mēkhanikos*, from *mēkhanē* MACHINE]

mechanical (mɪ'kænɪkᵊl) *adj* 1 made, performed, or operated by or as if by a machine or machinery: *a* *mechanical process* **2** concerned with machines or machinery **3** relating to or controlled or operated by physical forces **4** of or concerned with mechanics **5** (of a gesture, etc) automatic; lacking thought, feeling, etc **6** *philosophy* accounting for phenomena by physically determining forces ▷ me'chanicalism *n* ▷ me'chanically *adv* ▷ me'chanicalness *n*

mechanical advantage *n* the ratio of the working force exerted by a mechanism to the applied effort

mechanical drawing *n* a drawing to scale of a machine, machine component, architectural plan, etc, from which dimensions can be taken for manufacture

mechanical engineering *n* the branch of engineering concerned with the design, construction, and operation of machines and machinery

mechanical equivalent of heat *n physics* a factor for converting units of energy into heat units. It has the value 4.1868 joules per calorie

mechanician (ˌmɛkəˈnɪʃən) *or* **mechanist** *n* a person skilled in making machinery and tools; technician

mechanics (mɪˈkænɪks) *n* **1** (*functioning as singular*) the branch of science, divided into statics, dynamics, and kinematics, concerned with the equilibrium or motion of bodies in a particular frame of reference **2** (*functioning as singular*) the science of designing, constructing, and operating machines **3** the working parts of a machine **4** the technical aspects of something

mechanism (ˈmɛkəˌnɪzəm) *n* **1** a system or structure of moving parts that performs some function, esp in a machine **2** something resembling a machine in the arrangement and working of its parts **3** any form of mechanical device or any part of such a device **4** a process or technique, esp of execution: *the mechanism of novel writing* **5** *philosophy* the doctrine that human action can be explained in purely physical terms, whether mechanical or biological **6** *psychoanal* **a** the ways in which psychological forces interact and operate **b** a structure having an influence on the behaviour of a person, such as a defence mechanism

mechanistic (ˌmɛkəˈnɪstɪk) *adj* **1** *philosophy* of or relating to the theory of mechanism **2** *maths* of or relating to mechanics ▷ ˌmecha'nistically *adv* ▷ 'mechanist *n*

mechanize *or* **mechanise** (ˈmɛkəˌnaɪz) *vb* (*tr*) **1** to equip (a factory, industry, etc) with machinery **2** to make mechanical, automatic, or monotonous **3** to equip (an army, etc) with motorized or armoured vehicles ▷ ˌmechani'zation *or* ˌmechani'sation *n* ▷ 'mecha,nizer *or* 'mecha,niser *n*

mechanoreceptor (ˌmɛkənəʊrɪˈsɛptə) *n physiol* a sensory receptor, as in the skin, that is sensitive to a mechanical stimulus, such as pressure

mechanotherapy (ˌmɛkənəʊˈθɛrəpɪ) *n* the treatment of disorders or injuries by means of mechanical devices, esp devices that provide exercise for bodily parts

Mechelen (ˈmɛxələn) *n* a city in N Belgium, in Antwerp province: capital of the Netherlands from 1507 to 1530; formerly famous for lace-making; now has an important vegetable market. Pop: 76 981 (2004 est). French name: Malines. English name: Mechlin

Mechlin (ˈmɛklɪn) *n* the English name for **Mechelen**

Mechlin lace *n* bobbin lace made at Mechlin, characterized by patterns outlined by a heavier flat thread. Also called: malines

Mecklenburg (ˈmɛklənˌbɜːɡ; *German* 'meːklənburk) *n* a historic region and former state of NE Germany, along the Baltic coast; now part of Mecklenburg-West Pomerania

Mecklenburg-West Pomerania (ˌpɒməˈreɪnɪə) *n* a state of NE Germany, along the Baltic coast: consists of the former state of Mecklenburg and those parts of W Pomerania not incorporated into Poland after World War II: part of East Germany until 1990. Pop: 1 732 000 (2003 est)

meconium (mɪˈkəʊnɪəm) *n* the dark green mucoid material that forms the first faeces of a newborn infant [C17: from New Latin, from Latin: poppy juice (used also of infant's excrement because of similarity in colour), from Greek *mēkōneion*, from *mēkōn* poppy]

meconopsis (ˌmɛkəˈnɒpsɪs) *n* any plant of the mostly

Asiatic papaveraceous genus *Meconopsis*, esp *M. betonicifolia* (the Tibetan or blue poppy), grown for its showy sky-blue flowers. *M. cambrica* is the Welsh poppy [New Latin, from Greek *mēkōn* poppy + -OPSIS]

Med (mɛd) *n* the Med *informal* the Mediterranean region

MEd *abbreviation* Master of Education

med. *abbreviation* **1** medical **2** medicine **3** medium

médaillons (medaɪˈjɔ̃) *pl n* cookery small round thin pieces of meat, fish, vegetables, etc. Also called: medallions [C20: French: medallions]

medal (ˈmɛdəl) *n* **1** a small flat piece of metal bearing an inscription or image, given as an award or commemoration of some outstanding action, event, etc ▷ *vb* **-als, -alling, -alled** *or US* **-als, -aling, -aled** **2** (*tr*) to honour with a medal **3** (*intr*) *informal* (in sport) to win a medal [C16: from French *médaille*, probably from Italian *medaglia*, ultimately from Latin *metallum* METAL]

medallion (mɪˈdæljən) *n* **1** a large medal **2** an oval or circular decorative device resembling a medal, usually bearing a portrait or relief moulding, used in architecture and textile design [C17: from French, from Italian *medaglione*, from *medaglia* MEDAL]

medallist *or US* **medalist** (ˈmɛdəlɪst) *n* **1** a designer, maker, or collector of medals **2** *chiefly sport* a winner or recipient of a medal or medals

medal play *n golf* another name for **stroke play**

Medan (ˈmɛdɑːn) *n* a city in Indonesia, in NE Sumatra: seat of the University of North Sumatra (1952) and the Indonesian Islam University (1952). Pop: 1 904 273 (2000)

Medawar (ˈmɛdəwə) *n* Sir **Peter Brian**. 1915–87, English zoologist, who shared the Nobel prize for physiology or medicine (1960) with Sir Macfarlane Burnet for work on immunology

meddle (ˈmɛdəl) *vb* (*intr*) **1** (usually foll by *with*) to interfere officiously or annoyingly **2** (usually foll by *in*) to involve oneself unwarrantedly [C14: from Old French *medler*, ultimately from Latin *miscēre* to mix] ▷ 'meddler *n* ▷ 'meddling *adj*

meddlesome (ˈmɛdəlsəm) *adj* intrusive or meddling ▷ 'meddlesomely *adv* ▷ 'meddlesomeness *n*

Mede (miːd) *n* a member of an Indo-European people of West Iranian speech who established an empire in SW Asia in the 7th and 6th centuries BC ▷ 'Median *n, adj*

Medea (mɪˈdɪə) *n Greek myth* a princess of Colchis, who assisted Jason in obtaining the Golden Fleece from her father

Medellín (*Spanish* meðeˈʎin) *n* a city in W Colombia, at an altitude of 1554 m (5100 ft): the second largest city in the country, with three universities; important coffee centre, with large textile mills; dominated by drug cartels in recent years. Pop: 3 236 000 (2005 est)

media (ˈmiːdɪə) *n* **1** a plural of **medium** **2** the means of communication that reach large numbers of people, such as television, newspapers, and radio ▷ *adj* **3** of or relating to the mass media: *media hype*

● USAGE When *media* refers to the mass media, it is
● sometimes treated as a singular form, as in: *the media*
● *has shown great interest in these events*. Many people think
● this use is incorrect and that *media* should always be
● treated as a plural form: *the media have shown great*
● *interest in these events*

Media (ˈmiːdɪə) *n* an ancient country of SW Asia, south of the Caspian Sea: inhabited by the Medes; overthrew the Assyrian Empire in 612 BC in alliance with Babylonia; conquered by Cyrus the Great in 550 BC; corresponds to present-day NW Iran

mediaeval (ˌmɛdɪˈiːvəl) *adj* a variant spelling of **medieval**

media event *n* an event that is staged for or exploited by the mass media, whose attention lends it an apparent importance

medial (ˈmiːdɪəl) *adj* **1** of or situated in the middle **2** ordinary or average in size **3** *maths* relating to an average **4** another word for: **median** (senses 1, 2) [C16: from Late Latin *mediālis*, from *medius* middle] ▷ 'medially *adv*

median (ˈmiːdɪən) *adj* **1** of, relating to, situated in, or directed towards the middle **2** *statistics* of or relating to the median ▷ *n* **3** a middle point, plane, or part **4** *geometry* **a** a straight line joining one vertex of a triangle to the midpoint of the opposite side **b** a straight line joining the midpoints of the nonparallel sides of a trapezium **5** *statistics* the middle value in a frequency distribution, below and above which lie values with equal total frequencies [C16: from Latin *mediānus*, from *medius* middle] > **'medianly** *adv*

median lethal dose *or* **mean lethal dose** *n* **1** the amount of a drug or other substance that, when administered to a group of experimental animals, will kill 50 per cent of the group in a specified time **2** the amount of ionizing radiation that will kill 50 per cent of a population in a specified time

mediant ('miːdɪənt) *n music* **a** the third degree of a major or minor scale **b** (*as modifier*): *a mediant chord* [C18: from Italian *mediante*, from Late Latin *mediāre* to be in the middle]

mediastinum (ˌmiːdɪə'staɪnəm) *n, pl* **-na** (-nə) *anatomy* **1** a membrane between two parts of an organ or cavity such as the pleural tissue between the two lungs **2** the part of the thoracic cavity that lies between the lungs, containing the heart, trachea, etc [C16: from medical Latin, neuter of Medieval Latin *mediastīnus* median, from Latin: low grade of servant, from *medius* mean] > ˌmedias'tinal *adj*

mediate *vb* ('miːdɪˌeɪt) **1** (*intr; usually foll by between or in*) to intervene (between parties or in a dispute) in order to bring about agreement **2** to bring about (an agreement) between parties in a dispute **3** to resolve (differences) by mediation **4** (*intr*) to be in a middle or intermediate position **5** (*tr*) to serve as a medium for causing (a result) or transferring (objects, information, etc) ▷ *adj* ('miːdɪɪt) **6** occurring as a result of or dependent upon mediation [C16: from Late Latin *mediāre* to be in the middle] > 'mediately *adv* > 'medi,ator *n*

mediation (ˌmiːdɪ'eɪʃən) *n* the act of mediating; intercession

medic[1] ('mɛdɪk) *n informal* a doctor, medical orderly, or medical student [C17: from MEDICAL]

medic[2] ('mɛdɪk) *n* the usual US spelling of **medick**

medicable ('mɛdɪkəb°l) *adj* potentially able to be treated or cured medically

medical ('mɛdɪk°l) *adj* **1** of or relating to the science of medicine or to the treatment of patients by drugs, etc, as opposed to surgery **2** a less common word for: **medicinal** ▷ *n* **3** *informal* a medical examination [C17: from Medieval Latin *medicālis*, from Latin *medicus* physician, surgeon, from *medērī* to heal] > 'medically *adv*

medical certificate *n* **1** a document stating the result of a satisfactory medical examination **2** a doctor's certificate giving evidence of a person's unfitness for work

medical jurisprudence *n* another name for **forensic medicine**

medicament (mɪ'dɪkəmənt, 'mɛdɪ-) *n* a medicine or remedy in a specified formulation [C16: via French from Latin *medicāmentum*, from *medicāre* to cure]

medicate ('mɛdɪˌkeɪt) *vb* (*tr*) **1** to cover or impregnate (a wound, etc) with an ointment, cream, etc **2** to treat (a patient) with a medicine **3** to add a medication to (a bandage, shampoo, etc) [C17: from Latin *medicāre* to heal] > 'medicative *adj*

medication (ˌmɛdɪ'keɪʃən) *n* **1** treatment with drugs or remedies **2** a drug or remedy

Medici ('mɛdɪtʃɪ, mə'diːtʃɪ; *Italian* 'mɛːdɪtʃɪ) *n* **1** an Italian family of bankers, merchants, and rulers of Florence and Tuscany, prominent in Italian political and cultural history in the 15th, 16th, and 17th centuries, including **2 Catherine de'** (ka'triːn de). See **Catherine de' Medici 3 Cosimo I** ('kɔːzimo), known as *Cosimo the Great*. 1519–74, duke of Florence and first grand duke of Tuscany (1569–74) **4 Cosimo de'**, known as *Cosimo the Elder*. 1389–1464, Italian banker, statesman, and patron of arts, who established the political power of the family in Florence (1434) **5 Giovanni de'**, (dʒo'vanni de). See **Leo X 6 Giulio de'** ('dʒuːljo de). See **Clement VII 7 Lorenzo de'** (lo'rɛntso de), known as *Lorenzo the Magnificent*. 1449–92, Italian statesman, poet, and scholar; ruler of Florence

(1469–92) and first patron of Michelangelo **8 Maria de'** (ma'riːa de). See **Maria de' Medici** > Medicean (ˌmɛdɪ'siːən, -'tʃiː-) *adj*

medicinal (mɛ'dɪsɪn°l) *adj* **1** relating to or having therapeutic properties ▷ *n* **2** a medicinal substance > me'dicinally *adv*

medicine ('mɛdɪsɪn, 'mɛdsɪn) *n* **1** any drug or remedy for use in treating, preventing, or alleviating the symptoms of disease **2** the science of preventing, diagnosing, alleviating, or curing disease **3** any nonsurgical branch of medical science **4** the practice or profession of medicine **5** something regarded by primitive people as having magical or remedial properties **6** take one's medicine to accept a deserved punishment **7 a taste of one's own medicine** *or* **a dose of one's own medicine** an unpleasant experience in retaliation for and by similar methods to an unkind or aggressive act [C13: via Old French from Latin *medicīna* (*ars*) (art of) healing, from *medicus* doctor, from *medērī* to heal]

medicine ball *n* a heavy ball used for physical training

medicine man *n* (among certain peoples, esp North American Indians) a person believed to have supernatural powers of healing; a magician or sorcerer

medick *or US* **medic** ('mɛdɪk) *n* any small leguminous plant of the genus *Medicago*, such as black medick or sickle medick, having yellow or purple flowers and trifoliate leaves [C15: from Latin *mēdica*, from Greek *mēdikē* (*poa*) Median (grass), a type of clover]

medico ('mɛdɪˌkəʊ) *n, pl* **-cos** a doctor or medical student [C17: via Italian from Latin *medicus*]

medieval *or* **mediaeval** (ˌmɛdɪ'iːv°l) *adj* **1** of, relating to, or in the style of the Middle Ages **2** *informal* old-fashioned; primitive [C19: from New Latin *medium aevum* the middle age. See MEDIUM, AGE]

Medieval Greek *n* the Greek language from the 7th century AD to shortly after the sacking of Constantinople in 1204. Also called: Middle Greek *or* Byzantine Greek

medievalism *or* **mediaevalism** (ˌmɛdɪ'iːvəˌlɪzəm) *n* **1** the beliefs, life, or style of the Middle Ages or devotion to those **2** a belief, custom, or point of style copied or surviving from the Middle Ages

medievalist *or* **mediaevalist** (ˌmɛdɪ'iːvəlɪst) *n* a student or devotee of the Middle Ages

Medieval Latin *n* the Latin language as used throughout Europe in the Middle Ages. It had many local forms incorporating Latinized words from other languages

Medina (mɛ'diːnə) *n* a city in W Saudi Arabia: the second most holy city of Islam (after Mecca), with the tomb of Mohammed; university (1960). Pop: 1 044 000 (2005 est). Arabic name: Al Madinah. Ancient Arabic name: Yathrib

mediocre (ˌmiːdɪ'əʊkə, 'miːdɪˌəʊkə) *adj* often derogatory average or ordinary in quality [C16: via French from Latin *mediocris* moderate, literally: halfway up the mountain, from *medius* middle + *ocris* stony mountain]

mediocrity (ˌmiːdɪ'ɒkrɪtɪ, ˌmɛd-) *n, pl* **-ties 1** the state or quality of being mediocre **2** a mediocre person or thing

meditate ('mɛdɪˌteɪt) *vb* **1** (*intr; foll by on or upon*) to think about something deeply **2** (*intr*) to reflect deeply on spiritual matters, esp as a religious act **3** (*tr*) to plan, consider, or think of doing (something) [C16: from Latin *meditārī* to reflect upon] > 'meditative *adj* > 'meditatively *adv* > 'medi,tator *n*

meditation (ˌmɛdɪ'teɪʃən) *n* **1** the act of meditating; contemplation; reflection **2** contemplation of spiritual matters, esp as a religious practice

Mediterranean (ˌmɛdɪtə'reɪnɪən) *n* **1** short for the **Mediterranean Sea 2** a native or inhabitant of a Mediterranean country ▷ *adj* **3** of, relating to, situated or dwelling on or near the Mediterranean Sea **4** denoting a postulated subdivision of the Caucasoid race, characterized by slender build and dark complexion **5** *meteorol* (of a climate) characterized by hot summers and relatively warm winters when most of the annual rainfall occurs **6** (*often not capital*) obsolete situated in the middle of a landmass; inland [C16: from Latin *mediterrāneus*, from *medius* middle + *-terrāneus*, from *terra* land, earth]

Mediterranean Sea *n* a large inland sea between S Europe, N Africa, and SW Asia: linked with the Atlantic by the Strait of Gibraltar, with the Red Sea by the Suez Canal, and with the Black Sea by the Dardanelles, Sea of Marmara, and Bosporus; many ancient civilizations developed around its shores. Greatest depth: 4770 m (15 900 ft). Length: (west to east) over 3700 km (2300 miles). Greatest width: about 1368 km (850 miles). Area: (excluding the Black Sea) 2 512 300 sq km (970 000 sq miles)

medium ('miːdɪəm) *adj* **1** midway between extremes; average ▷ *n, pl* **-dia** (-dɪə) *or* **-diums 2** an intermediate or middle state, degree, or condition; mean: *the happy medium* **3** an intervening substance or agency for transmitting or producing an effect; vehicle **4** a means or agency for communicating or diffusing information, news, etc, to the public **5** a person supposedly used as a spiritual intermediary between the dead and the living **6** the substance in which specimens of animals and plants are preserved or displayed **7** *biology* Also called: culture medium a nutritive substance in which cultures of bacteria or fungi are grown **8** the substance or surroundings in which an organism naturally lives or grows **9** *art* **a** the category of a work of art, as determined by its materials and methods of production **b** the materials used in a work of art **10** any solvent in which pigments are mixed and thinned [C16: from Latin: neuter singular of *medius* middle]
● USAGE See at media¹

medium-dated *adj* (of a gilt-edged security) having between five and fifteen years to run before redemption. See **long-dated, short-dated**

medium frequency *n* a radio-frequency band or radio frequency lying between 3000 and 300 kilohertz. Abbreviation: MF

medium wave *n* **a** a radio wave with a wavelength between 100 and 1000 metres **b** (*as modifier*): *a medium-wave broadcast*

medlar ('mɛdlə) *n* **1** a small Eurasian rosaceous tree, *Mespilus germanica* **2** the fruit of this tree, which resembles the crab apple and is not edible until it has begun to decay [C14: from Old French *medlier*, from Latin *mespilum* medlar fruit, from Greek *mespilon*]

medley ('mɛdlɪ) *n* **1** a mixture of various types or elements **2** a musical composition consisting of various tunes arranged as a continuous whole **3** Also called: medley relay **a** *swimming* a race in which a different stroke is used for each length **b** *athletics* a relay race in which each leg has a different distance [C14: from Old French *medlee*, from *medler* to mix, quarrel]

Médoc (meɪ'dɒk, 'meɪdɒk; *French* medɔk) *n* **1** a district of SW France, on the left bank of the Gironde estuary: famous vineyards **2** a fine red wine from this district

medulla (mɪ'dʌlə) *n, pl* **-las** *or* **-lae** (-liː) **1** *anatomy* **a** the innermost part of an organ or structure **b** short for **medulla oblongata 2** *botany* another name for **pith** (sense 4) [C17: from Latin: marrow, pith, probably from *medius* middle] > me'dullary *or* me'dullar *adj*

medulla oblongata (ˌɒblɒŋ'gɑːtə) *n, pl* **medulla oblongatas** *or* **medullae oblongatae** (mɪ'dʌli: ˌɒblɒŋ'gɑːtiː): the lower stalklike section of the brain, continuous with the spinal cord, containing control centres for the heart and lungs [C17: New Latin: oblong-shaped medulla]

medusa (mɪ'djuːzə) *n, pl* **-sas** *or* **-sae** (-ziː) another name for **jellyfish** (sense 1) [C18: from the likeness of its tentacles to the snaky locks of Medusa] > me'dusoid *adj, n*

Medusa (mɪ'djuːzə) *n Greek myth* a mortal woman who was transformed by Athena into one of the three Gorgons. Her appearance was so hideous that those who looked directly at her were turned to stone. Perseus eventually slew her. See also **Pegasus¹** > Me'dusan *adj*

Medvedev (*Russian* mɪd'vjedɪf) *n* **Dmitry Anatolyevich** ('dmitrij ɛnɐ'tɔljɪvɪtʃ). born 1965, Russian politician; president of Russia from 2008

Medway ('mɛdˌweɪ) *n* **1** a river in SE England, flowing through Kent and the **Medway towns** (Rochester,

Chatham, and Gillingham) to the Thames estuary. Length: 110 km (70 miles) **2** a unitary authority in SE England, in Kent. Pop: 251 100 (2003 est). Area: 204 sq km (79 sq miles)

meed (miːd) *n archaic* a recompense; reward [Old English: wages; compare Old High German *mēta* pay]

meek (miːk) *adj* **1** patient, long-suffering, or submissive in disposition or nature; humble **2** spineless or spiritless; compliant [C12: related to Old Norse *mjúkr* amenable; compare Welsh *mwytho* to soften] > 'meekly *adv* > 'meekness *n*

meerkat ('mɪəˌkæt) *n* any of several South African mongooses, esp *Suricata suricatta* (**slender-tailed meerkat** or **suricate**), which has a lemur-like face and four-toed feet [C19: from Dutch: sea-cat]

meerschaum ('mɪəʃəm) *n* **1** Also called: sepiolite a white, yellowish, or pink compact earthy mineral consisting of hydrated magnesium silicate: used to make tobacco pipes and as a building stone. Formula: $Mg_2Si_3O_6(OH)_4$ **2** a tobacco pipe having a bowl made of this mineral [C18: German, literally: sea foam]

Meerut ('mɪərət) *n* an industrial city in N India, in W Uttar Pradesh: founded as a military base by the British in 1806 and scene of the first uprising (1857) of the Indian Mutiny. Pop: 1 074 229 (2001)

meet¹ (miːt) *vb* **meets, meeting, met 1** (*sometimes foll by up or (US) with*) to come together (with), either by design or by accident; encounter **2** to come into or be in conjunction or contact with (something or each other) **3** (*tr*) to come to or be at the place of arrival of: *to meet a train* **4** to make the acquaintance of or be introduced to (someone or each other) **5** to gather in the company of (someone or each other) **6** to come into the presence of (someone or each other) as opponents **7** (*tr*) to cope with effectively; satisfy: *to meet someone's demands* **8** (*tr*) to be apparent to (esp in the phrase **meet the eye**) **9** (*tr*) to return or counter: *to meet a blow with another* **10** to agree with (someone or each other): *we met him on the price he suggested* **11** (*tr; sometimes foll by with*) to experience; suffer: *he met his death in a road accident* **12** to occur together: *courage and kindliness met in him* **13** meet and greet (of a celebrity, politician, etc) to have a session of being introduced to and questioned by members of the public or journalists ▷ *n* **14** the assembly of hounds, huntsmen, etc, prior to a hunt **15** a meeting, esp a sports meeting [Old English *mētan*; related to Old Norse *mēta*, Old Saxon *mōtian*] > 'meeter *n*

meet² (miːt) *adj archaic* proper, fitting, or correct [C13: from variant of Old English *gemǣte*; related to Old High German *māza* suitability, Old Norse *mǣtr* valuable] > 'meetly *adv*

meeting ('miːtɪŋ) *n* **1** an act of coming together; encounter **2** an assembly or gathering **3** a conjunction or union **4** a sporting competition, as of athletes, or of horse racing

meeting house *n* **1** the place in which certain religious groups, esp Quakers, hold their meetings for worship **2** Also called: wharepuni NZ a large Māori tribal hall

mefloquine ('mɛfləʊˌkwiːn) *n* a synthetic drug administered orally to prevent or treat malaria [C20]

mega ('mɛgə) *adj slang* extremely good, great, or successful [C20: probably independent use of MEGA-]

mega- *combining form* **1** denoting 10^6: *megawatt*. Symbol: M **2** (in computer technology) denoting 2^{20} (1 048 576): *megabyte* **3** large or great: *megalith* [from Greek *megas* huge, powerful]

megabit ('mɛgəˌbɪt) *n computing* **1** one million bits **2** 2^{20} bits

megabuck ('mɛgəˌbʌk) *n US & Canadian slang* a million dollars

megabyte ('mɛgəˌbaɪt) *n computing* 2^{20} or 1 048 576 bytes. Abbreviation: MB

megacephaly (ˌmɛgə'sɛfəlɪ) *or* **megalocephaly** *n* the condition of having an unusually large head or cranial capacity. It can be of congenital origin or result from an abnormal overgrowth of the facial bones
> megacephalic (ˌmɛgəsɪ'fælɪk), ˌmega'cephalous, ˌmegaloce'phalic *or* ˌmegalo'cephalous *adj*

megachurch ('mɛgəˌtʃɜːtʃ) *n US* a church, usually

Protestant, with a very large congregation, typically housed in a complex offering sophisticated multimedia presentations and a range of secular facilities and services

megacity ('mɛgə,sɪtɪ) *n*, *pl* **-cities** a city with over 10 million inhabitants

megadeath ('mɛgə,dɛθ) *n* the death of a million people, esp in a nuclear war or attack

Megaera (mɪ'dʒɪərə) *n Greek myth* one of the three Furies; the others are Alecto and Tisiphone

megafauna ('mɛgə,fɔːnə) *n* the component of the fauna of a region or period that comprises the larger terrestrial animals

megaflop ('mɛgə,flɒp) *n computing* a measure of processing speed, consisting of a million floating-point operations a second [C20: from MEGA- + *flo(ating) p(oint)*]

megahertz ('mɛgə,hɜːts) *n*, *pl* **-hertz** one million hertz; one million cycles per second

megalith ('mɛgəlɪθ) *n* a stone of great size, esp one forming part of a prehistoric monument > ,mega'lithic *adj*

megalitre ('mɛgə,liːtə) *n* one million litres

megalo- *or before a vowel* **megal-** *combining form* indicating greatness, or abnormal size: *megalopolis*; *megaloblast* [from Greek *megas* great]

megalomania (,mɛgələʊ'meɪnɪə) *n* **1** a mental illness characterized by delusions of grandeur, power, wealth, etc **2** *informal* a lust or craving for power > ,megalo'maniac *adj*, *n* > megalomaniacal (,mɛgələʊmə'naɪək²l) *adj*

megalopolis (,mɛgə'lɒpəlɪs) *n* an urban complex, usually comprising several large towns [C20: MEGALO- + Greek *polis* city] > megalopolitan (,mɛgələ'pɒlɪt²n) *adj*, *n*

megalosaur ('mɛgələʊ,sɔː) *n* any very large Jurassic or Cretaceous bipedal carnivorous dinosaur of the genus *Megalosaurus*, common in Europe: suborder *Theropoda* (theropods) [C19: from New Latin *megalosaurus*, from MEGALO- + Greek *sauros* lizard]

megaphone ('mɛgə,fəʊn) *n* a funnel-shaped instrument used to amplify the voice. See also **loud-hailer** > megaphonic (,mɛgə'fɒnɪk) *adj*

megapixel ('mɛgə,pɪks²l) *n computing* one million pixels: a term used to describe the degree of resolution supplied by digital cameras, scanners, etc

megapode ('mɛgə,pəʊd) *n* any ground-living gallinaceous bird of the family *Megapodiidae*, of Australia, New Guinea, and adjacent islands. Their eggs incubate in mounds of sand, rotting vegetation, etc, by natural heat

megaproject ('mɛgə,prɒdʒɛkt) *n* a very large, expensive, or ambitious business project

Megara ('mɛgərə) *n* a town in E central Greece: an ancient trading city, founding many colonies in the 7th and 8th centuries BC. Pop: 26 562 (1991 est) (municipality): 27 252 (2001)

megathere ('mɛgə,θɪə) *n* any of various gigantic extinct American sloths of the genus *Megatherium* and related genera, common in late Cenozoic times [C19: from New Latin *megathērium*, from MEGA- + *-there*, from Greek *thērion* wild beast]

megaton ('mɛgə,tʌn) *n* **1** one million tons **2** an explosive power, esp of a nuclear weapon, equal to the power of one million tons of TNT

Me generation *n* the generation, originally in the 1970s, characterized by self-absorption; in the 1980s, characterized by material greed

Megger ('mɛgə) *n trademark* an instrument that generates a high voltage in order to test the resistance of insulation, etc

Meghalaya (,meɪgə'leɪə) *n* a state of NE India, created in 1969 from part of Assam. Capital: Shillong. Pop: 2 306 069 (2001). Area: 22 429 sq km (7800 sq miles)

Megiddo (mə'gɪdəʊ) *n* an ancient town in N Palestine, strategically located on a route linking Egypt to Mesopotamia: site of many battles, including an important Egyptian victory over rebel chieftains in 1469 or 1468 BC. See also **Armageddon**

megilp *or* **magilp** (mə'gɪlp) *n* an oil-painting medium of linseed oil mixed with mastic varnish or turpentine

[C18: of unknown origin]

megohm ('mɛg,əʊm) *n* one million ohms

megrim ('miːgrɪm) *n archaic* **1** (*often plural*) a caprice **2** a migraine [C14: see MIGRAINE]

Mehemet Ali (mɪ'hɛmɪt 'ɑːlɪ) *or* **Mohammed Ali** *n* 1769–1849, Albanian commander in the service of Turkey. He was made viceroy of Egypt (1805) and its hereditary ruler (1841), founding a dynasty that ruled until 1952

mehndi ('mɛndiː) *n* (esp in India) the practice of painting designs on the hands, feet, etc using henna [C20: from Hindi]

Mehta ('meɪtə) *n* **Zubin** ('zuːbɪn). born 1936, Indian conductor; musical director of the Israel Philharmonic orchestra from 1969

meibomian gland *n* any of the small sebaceous glands in the eyelid, beneath the conjunctiva

Meiji ('meɪdʒiː) *n* **1** *Japanese history* the reign of Emperor Mutsuhito (1867–1912), during which Japan began a rapid process of Westernization, industrialization, and expansion in foreign affairs **2** the throne name of Mutsuhito (,muːtsʊ'hiːtəʊ). 1852–1912, emperor of Japan (1867–1912) [Japanese, from Chinese *ming* enlightened + *dji* government]

Meilhac (French mɛjak) *n* **Henri** (ɑ̃ri). 1831–97, French dramatist, who collaborated with Halévy on opera libretti, esp Offenbach's *La Belle Hélène* (1865) and *La Vie parisienne* (1867)

meiny *or* **meinie** ('meɪnɪ) *n*, *pl* **meinies** *obsolete* **1** a retinue or household **2** *Scot* a crowd [C13: from Old French *mesnie*, from Vulgar Latin *mansiōnāta* (unattested), from Latin *mansiō* a lodging; see MANSION]

meiosis (maɪ'əʊsɪs) *n*, *pl* **-ses** (-,siːz) **1** a type of cell division in which a nucleus divides into four daughter nuclei, each containing half the chromosome number of the parent nucleus: occurs in all sexually reproducing organisms in which haploid gametes or spores are produced **2** *rhetoric* another word for: **litotes** [C16: via New Latin from Greek: a lessening, from *meioun* to diminish, from *meiōn* less] > meiotic (maɪ'ɒtɪk) *adj* > mei'otically *adv*

Meir (mer'ɪə) *n* **Golda** ('gəʊldə) 1898–1978, Israeli stateswoman, born in Russia; prime minister (1969–74)

Meissen (German 'maɪsən) *n* a town in E Germany, in Saxony, in Dresden district on the River Elbe: famous for its porcelain (Dresden china), first made here in 1710. Pop: 28 640 (2003 est)

-meister ('maɪstə) *n combining form* a person who excels at a particular activity: *spinmeister*; *horror-meister* [C20: from German *Meister* master]

Meistersinger ('maɪstə,sɪŋə) *n*, *pl* **-singer** *or* **-singers** a member of one of the various German guilds of workers or craftsmen organized to compose and perform poetry and music. These flourished in the 15th and 16th centuries [C19: German: master singer]

Meitner (German 'maɪtnər) *n* **Lise** ('liːzə). 1878–1968, Austrian nuclear physicist. With Hahn, she discovered protactinium (1918), and they demonstrated with F. Strassmann the fission of uranium

meitnerium ('maɪtnɪərɪəm) *n* a synthetic element produced in small quantities by high-energy ion bombardment. Symbol: Mt; atomic no: 109 [C20: named after Lise Meitner (1878–1968), Austrian nuclear physicist]

Méjico ('mɛxiko) *n* the Spanish name for **Mexico**

Mekka ('mɛkə) *n* a variant spelling of **Mecca**

Meknès (mɛk'nɛs) *n* a city in N central Morocco, in the Middle Atlas Mountains: noted for the making of carpets. Pop: 234 000 (2003)

Mekong (,miː'kɒŋ) *n* a river in SE Asia, rising in SW China in Qinghai province: flows southeast forming the border between Laos and Myanmar, and part of the border between Laos and Thailand, then continues south across Cambodia and Vietnam to the South China Sea by an extensive delta, one of the greatest rice-growing areas in Asia. Length: about 4025 km (2500 miles)

Melaka (mə'lækə) *n* another spelling of **Malacca**

melaleuca (,mɛlə'luːkə) *n* any shrub or tree of the mostly Australian myrtaceous genus *Melaleuca*, found in sandy or swampy regions [C19: New Latin, from Greek *melas* black + *leukos* white, from its black trunk and white branches]

melamine ('mɛlə,miːn) *n* **1** a colourless crystalline compound used in making synthetic resins; 2,4,6-triamino-1,3,5-triazine. Formula: $C_3H_6N_6$ **2** melamine resin or a material made from this resin [c19: from German *Melamin*, from *Melam* distillate of ammonium thiocyanate, with *-am* representing *ammonia*]

melancholia (,mɛlən'kəʊlɪə) *n* a former name for **depression** > ,melan'choli,ac *adj, n*

melancholy ('mɛlənkəlɪ) *n*, *pl* -cholies **1** a constitutional tendency to gloominess or depression **2** a sad thoughtful state of mind; pensiveness **3** *archaic* **a** a gloomy character, thought to be caused by too much black bile **b** one of the four bodily humours; black bile ▷ *adj* **4** characterized by, causing, or expressing sadness, dejection, etc [c14: via Old French from Late Latin *melancholia*, from Greek *melankholia*, from *melas* black + *kholē* bile] > ,melan'cholic *adj, n* > ,melan'cholically *adv*

Melanchthon (mə'læŋkθən; German me'lançton) *n* **Philipp** ('fiːlɪp). original surname *Schwarzerd*. 1497–1560, German Protestant reformer. His *Loci Communes* (1521) was the first systematic presentation of Protestant theology and in the Augsburg Confession (1530) he stated the faith of the Lutheran churches. He also reformed the German educational system

Melanesia (,mɛlə'niːzɪə) *n* one of the three divisions of islands in the Pacific (the others being Micronesia and Polynesia); the SW division of Oceania: includes Fiji, New Caledonia, Vanuatu, the Bismarck Archipelago, and the Louisiade, Solomon, Santa Cruz, and Loyalty Islands, which all lie northeast of Australia [c19: from Greek *melas* black + *nēsos* island; with reference to the dark skins of the inhabitants; on the model of *Polynesia*]

Melanesian (,mɛlə'niːzɪən) *adj* **1** of or relating to Melanesia, its people, or their languages ▷ *n* **2** a native or inhabitant of Melanesia: generally Negroid with frizzy hair and small stature **3** a group or branch of languages spoken in Melanesia, belonging to the Malayo-Polynesian family

melange *or* **mélange** (meɪ'lɑːnʒ) *n* a mixture; confusion [c17: from French *mêler* to mix. See MEDLEY]

melanin ('mɛlənɪn) *n* any of a group of black or dark brown pigments present in the hair, skin, and eyes of man and animals: produced in excess in certain skin diseases and in melanomas

melanism ('mɛlə,nɪzəm) *n* **1** the condition in man and animals of having dark-coloured or dark skin, feathers, etc. **Industrial melanism** is the occurrence of dark varieties of animals, esp moths, in smoke-blackened industrial regions, in which they are well camouflaged **2** another name for **melanosis** > ,mela'nistic *adj*

melano- *or before a vowel* **melan-** *combining form* black or dark: *melanin; melanism; melanocyte; melanoma* [from Greek *melas* black]

melanoma (,mɛlə'nəʊmə) *n*, *pl* -mas *or* -mata (-mətə) *pathol* a malignant tumour composed of melanocytes, occurring esp in the skin, often as a result of excessive exposure to sunlight

melanosis (,mɛlə'nəʊsɪs) *or* **melanism** ('mɛlə,nɪzəm) *n* *pathol* a skin condition characterized by excessive deposits of melanin > melanotic (,mɛlə'nɒtɪk) *adj*

Melba ('mɛlbə) *n* **1** Dame **Nellie**, stage name of *Helen Porter Mitchell*. 1861–1931, Australian operatic soprano **2** do a Melba *Austral slang* to make repeated farewell appearances

Melba toast *n* very thin crisp toast [c20: named after Dame Nellie *Melba*, stage name of Helen Porter Mitchell (1861–1931), Australian operatic soprano]

Melbourne[1] ('mɛlbən) *n* a port in SE Australia, capital of Victoria, on Port Phillip Bay: the second largest city in the country; settled in 1835 and developed rapidly with the discovery of rich goldfields in 1851; three universities. Pop: 3 160 171 (2001) > **Melburnian** (mɛl'bɜːnɪən) *n, adj*

Melbourne[2] ('mɛlbən) *n* **William Lamb**, 2nd Viscount. 1779–1848; Whig prime minister (1834; 1835–41). He was the chief political adviser to the young Queen Victoria

Melbourne Cup *n* an annual horse race run in Melbourne, since 1861

Melchior ('mɛlkɪ,ɔː) *n* **1** (in Christian tradition) one of the Magi, the others being Balthazar and Caspar **2 Lauritz** ('laʊrɪts). 1890–1973, US operatic tenor, born in Denmark

Melchizedek (mɛl'kɪzə,dɛk) *n* *Old Testament* the priest-king of Salem who blessed Abraham (Genesis 14:18-19) and was taken as a prototype of Christ's priesthood (Hebrews 7)

meld[1] (mɛld) *vb* **1** (in some card games) to declare or lay down (cards), which then score points ▷ *n* **2** the act of melding **3** a set of cards for melding [c19: from German *melden* to announce; related to Old English *meldian*]

meld[2] (mɛld) *vb* to blend or become blended; combine [c20: blend of MELT + WELD[1]]

Meleager (,mɛlɪ'eɪgə) *n* *Greek myth* one of the Argonauts, slayer of the Calydonian boar

melee *or* **mêlée** ('mɛleɪ) *n* a noisy riotous fight or brawl [c17: from French *mêlée*. See MEDLEY]

Méliès (French meljɛs) *n* **Georges** (ʒɔrʒ). 1861–1938, French pioneer film director

Melilla (Spanish melija) *n* the chief town of a Spanish enclave in Morocco, on the Mediterranean coast: founded by the Phoenicians; exports iron ore. Pop: 68 463 (2003 est)

meliorate ('miːlɪə,reɪt) *vb* a variant of **ameliorate** > meliorative ('miːlɪərətɪv) *adj, n* > ,melio'ration *n*

melisma (mɪ'lɪzmə) *n*, *pl* -mata (-mətə) *or* -mas *music* an expressive vocal phrase or passage consisting of several notes sung to one syllable [c19: from Greek: melody]

Melitopol (Russian mili'topəlj) *n* a city in SE Ukraine. Pop: 157 000 (2005 est)

Melk (mɛlk) *n* a town in N Austria, on the River Danube: noted for its baroque Benedictine abbey. Pop: 5222 (2001)

melliferous (mɪ'lɪfərəs) *or* **mellific** (mɪ'lɪfɪk) *adj* forming or producing honey [c17: from Latin *mellifer*, from *mel* honey + *ferre* to bear]

mellifluous (mɪ'lɪflʊəs) *or* **mellifluent** *adj* (of sounds or utterances) smooth or honeyed; sweet [c15: from Late Latin *mellifluus* flowing with honey, from Latin *mel* honey + *fluere* to flow] > mel'lifluously *or* mel'lifluently *adv* > mel'lifluousness *or* mel'lifluence *n*

mellow ('mɛləʊ) *adj* **1** (esp of fruits) full-flavoured; sweet; ripe **2** (esp of wines) well-matured **3** (esp of colours or sounds) soft or rich **4** kind-hearted, esp through maturity or old age **5** genial, as through the effects of alcohol **6** (of soil) soft and loamy ▷ *vb* **7** to make or become mellow; soften; mature **8** (foll by *out*) to become calm and relaxed or (esp of a drug) to have a calming or relaxing effect on (someone) [c15: perhaps from Old English *meru* soft (as through ripeness)] > 'mellowness *n*

melodeon *or* **melodion** (mɪ'ləʊdɪən) *n* *music* **1** a type of small accordion **2** a type of keyboard instrument similar to the harmonium [c19: from German, from *Melodie* melody]

melodic (mɪ'lɒdɪk) *adj* **1** of or relating to melody **2** of or relating to a part in a piece of music **3** tuneful or melodious > me'lodically *adv*

melodic minor scale *n* *music* a minor scale modified from the natural by the sharpening of the sixth and seventh when taken in ascending order and the restoration of their original pitches when taken in descending order

melodious (mɪ'ləʊdɪəs) *adj* **1** having a tune that is pleasant to the ear **2** of or relating to melody; melodic > me'lodiously *adv* > me'lodiousness *n*

melodist ('mɛlədɪst) *n* **1** a composer of melodies **2** a singer

melodize *or* **melodise** ('mɛlə,daɪz) *vb* **1** (tr) to provide with a melody **2** (tr) to make melodious **3** (intr) to sing or play melodies > 'melo,dizer *or* 'melo,diser *n*

melodrama ('mɛlə,drɑːmə) *n* **1** a play, film, etc, characterized by extravagant action and emotion **2** (formerly) a romantic drama characterized by sensational incident, music, and song **3** overdramatic emotion or behaviour [c19: from French *mélodrame*, from Greek *melos* song + *drame* DRAMA] > **melodramatist**

(ˌmɛləˈdræmətɪst) n > **melodramatic** (ˌmɛlədrəˈmætɪk) adj >ˌmelodraˈmatics pl n >ˌmelodraˈmatically adv

melody (ˈmɛlədɪ) n, pl -dies 1 music **a** a succession of notes forming a distinctive sequence; tune **b** the horizontally represented aspect of the structure of a piece of music. See **harmony** (sense 4b) **2** sounds that are pleasant because of tone or arrangement, esp words of poetry [c13: from Old French, from Late Latin melōdia, from Greek melōidia singing, from melos song + -ōidia, from aoidein to sing]

melon (ˈmɛlən) n **1** any of several varieties of two cucurbitaceous vines, cultivated for their edible fruit. See **muskmelon, watermelon 2** the fruit of any of these plants, which has a hard rind and juicy flesh [c14: via Old French from Late Latin mēlo, shortened form of mēlopepō, from Greek mēlopepōn, from mēlon apple + pepōn gourd]

Melos (ˈmiːlɒs) n an island in the SW Aegean Sea, in the Cyclades: of volcanic origin, with hot springs; centre of early Aegean civilization, where the Venus de Milo was found. Pop: 4771 (2001). Area: 132 sq km (51 sq miles). Modern Greek name: **Mílos**

Melpomene (mɛlˈpɒmɪnɪ) n Greek myth the Muse of tragedy

melt (mɛlt) vb **melts, melting, melted; melted** or **molten** (ˈməʊltən) **1** to liquefy (a solid) or (of a solid) to become liquefied, as a result of the action of heat **2** to become or make liquid; dissolve **3** (often foll by away) to disappear; fade **4** (foll by down) to melt (metal scrap) for reuse **5** (often foll by into) to blend or cause to blend gradually **6** to make or become emotional or sentimental; soften ▷ n **7** the act or process of melting **8** something melted or an amount melted [Old English meltan to digest; related to Old Norse melta to malt (beer), digest, Greek meldein to melt] >ˈmeltable adj >ˈmelter n >ˈmeltingly adv

meltdown (ˈmɛltˌdaʊn) n **1** (in a nuclear reactor) the melting of the fuel rods as a result of a defect in the cooling system, with the possible escape of radiation into the environment **2** informal a sudden disastrous failure with potential for widespread harm, as a stock-exchange crash **3** informal the process or state of irreversible breakdown or decline: *the community is slowly going into meltdown*

melting point n the temperature at which a solid turns into a liquid. It is equal to the freezing point

melting pot n **1** a pot in which metals or other substances are melted, esp in order to mix them **2** an area in which many races, ideas, etc, are mixed

melton (ˈmɛltən) n a heavy smooth woollen fabric with a short nap, used esp for overcoats. Also called: **melton cloth** [c19: from **Melton Mowbray**, Leicestershire, a former centre for making this cloth]

Melton Mowbray (ˈmɛltən ˈmaʊbrɪ) n a town in central England, in Leicestershire: pork pies and Stilton cheese. Pop: 25 554 (2001)

meltwater (ˈmɛltˌwɔːtə) n melted snow or ice

Melville (ˈmɛlvɪl) n **Herman**. 1819–91, US novelist and short-story writer. Among his works, *Moby Dick* (1851) and *Billy Budd* (written 1891, published 1924) are outstanding

Melville Island (ˈmɛlvɪl) n **1** a Canadian island in the Arctic Ocean, north of Victoria Island: in the Northwest Territories and Nunavut. Area: 41 865 sq km (16 164 sq miles) **2** an island in the Arafura Sea, off the N central coast of Australia, separated from the mainland by Clarence Strait. Area: 6216 sq km (2400 sq miles)

Melville Peninsula n a peninsula of N Canada, in Nunavut, between the Gulf of Boothia and Foxe Basin

member (ˈmɛmbə) n **1** a person who belongs to a club, political party, etc **2** any individual plant or animal in a taxonomic group **3** any part of an animal body, such as a limb **4** any part of a plant, such as a petal, root, etc **5** maths any individual object belonging to a set or logical class **6** a component part of a building or construction [c13: from Latin membrum limb, part] >ˈmemberless adj

Member (ˈmɛmbə) n (sometimes not capital) **1** short for **Member of Parliament 2** short for **Member of Congress**

3 a member of some other legislative body

Member of Congress n a member of the US Congress, esp of the House of Representatives

Member of Parliament n a member of the House of Commons or similar legislative body, as in many Commonwealth countries

membership (ˈmɛmbəʃɪp) n **1** the members of an organization collectively **2** the state of being a member

membrane (ˈmɛmbreɪn) n **1** any thin pliable sheet of material **2** a pliable sheetlike usually fibrous tissue that covers, lines, or connects plant and animal organs or cells [c16: from Latin membrāna skin covering a part of the body, from membrum **member**]

meme (miːm) n an idea or element of social behaviour passed on through generations in a culture, esp by imitation [c20: possibly from **mimic**, on the model of **gene**]

Memel (ˈmeːməl) n **1** the German name for **Klaipeda 2** the lower course of the Neman River

memento (mɪˈmɛntəʊ) n, pl -tos or -toes something that reminds one of past events; souvenir [c15: from Latin, imperative of meminisse to remember!]

memento mori (ˈmɔːriː) n an object, such as a skull, intended to remind people of the inevitability of death [c16: Latin: remember you must die]

Memling (ˈmɛmlɪŋ) or **Memlinc** (ˈmɛmlɪŋk) n **Hans** (hans). ?1430–94, Flemish painter of religious works and portraits

Memnon (ˈmɛmnɒn) n **1** Greek myth a king of Ethiopia, son of Eos: slain by Achilles in the Trojan War **2** a colossal statue of Amenhotep III at Thebes in ancient Egypt, which emitted a sound thought by the Greeks to be the voice of Memnon > **Memnonian** (mɛmˈnəʊnɪən) adj

memo (ˈmɛməʊ, ˈmiːməʊ) n, pl **memos** short for **memorandum**

memoir (ˈmɛmwɑː) n **1** a biography or historical account, esp one based on personal knowledge **2** an essay or monograph, as on a specialized topic [c16: from French, from Latin memoria **memory**] >ˈmemoirist n

memoirs (ˈmɛmwɑːz) pl n **1** a collection of reminiscences about a period, series of events, etc, written from personal experience or special sources **2** an autobiographical record **3** a collection or record, as of transactions of a society, etc

memorabilia (ˌmɛmərəˈbɪlɪə) pl n, sing -rabile (-ˈræbɪlɪ) **1** memorable events or things **2** objects connected with famous people or events [c17: from Latin, from memorābilis **memorable**]

memorable (ˈmɛmərəbəl, ˈmɛmrə-) adj worth remembering or easily remembered; noteworthy [c15: from Latin memorābilis, from memorāre to recall, from memor mindful] >ˌmemoraˈbility or ˈmemorableness n >ˈmemorably adv

memorandum (ˌmɛməˈrændəm) n, pl -dums or -da (-də) **1** a written statement, record, or communication such as within an office **2** a note of things to be remembered **3** an informal diplomatic communication, often unsigned: often summarizing the point of view of a government **4** law a short written summary of the terms of a transaction ▷ Often (esp for senses 1, 2) shortened to: **memo** [c15: from Latin: (something) to be remembered]

memorial (mɪˈmɔːrɪəl) adj **1** serving to preserve the memory of the dead or a past event **2** of or involving memory ▷ n **3** something serving as a remembrance **4** a written statement of facts submitted to a government, authority, etc, in conjunction with a petition **5** an informal diplomatic paper [c14: from Late Latin memoriāle a reminder, neuter of memoriālis belonging to remembrance] > meˈmorially adv

memorialize or **memorialise** (mɪˈmɔːrɪəˌlaɪz) vb (tr) **1** to honour or commemorate **2** to present or address a memorial to

memorize or **memorise** (ˈmɛməˌraɪz) vb (tr) to commit to memory; learn so as to remember

memory (ˈmɛmərɪ) n, pl -ries **1 a** the ability of the mind to store and recall past sensations, thoughts, knowledge, etc: *he can do it from memory* **b** the part of the brain that appears to have this function **2** the sum of everything retained by the mind **3** a particular recollection of an event, person, etc **4** the time over which recollection extends: *within his memory* **5** commemoration or remembrance: *in memory of our leader* **6** the state of being remembered, as after death **7** Also called: **RAM, main store, store** a part of a computer in which information is stored for immediate use by the central processing unit [c14: from Old French *memorie*, from Latin *memoria*, from *memor* mindful]

Memphis ('mɛmfɪs) *n* **1** a port in SW Tennessee, on the Mississippi River: the largest city in the state; a major cotton and timber market; Memphis State University (1909). Pop: 645 978 (2003 est) **2** a ruined city in N Egypt, the ancient centre of Lower Egypt, on the Nile: administrative and artistic centre, sacred to the worship of Ptah

Memphremagog (,mɛmfri:'meɪgɒg) *n* Lake Memphremagog a lake on the border between the US and Canada, in N Vermont and S Quebec. Length: about 43 km (27 miles). Width: up to 6 km (4 miles)

memsahib ('mɛm,sɑːɪb, -hɪb) *n* (formerly in India) a term of respect used of a European married woman [c19: from MA'AM + SAHIB]

men (mɛn) *n* the plural of **man**

menace ('mɛnɪs) *vb* **1** to threaten with violence, danger, etc ▷ *n* **2** *literary* a threat or the act of threatening **3** something menacing; a source of danger **4** *informal* a nuisance [c13: ultimately related to Latin *minax* threatening, from *minārī* to threaten] > 'menacer *n* > 'menacing *adj* > 'menacingly *adv*

menad ('mi:næd) *n* a variant spelling of: **maenad**

Menado (mɛ'nɑːdəʊ) *or* **Manado** *n* a port in NE Indonesia, on NE Sulawesi: founded by the Dutch in 1657. Pop: 372 887 (2000)

ménage (meɪ'nɑːʒ; *French* menaʒ) *n* the persons of a household [c17: from French, from Vulgar Latin *mansiōnāticum* (unattested) household; see MANSION]

ménage à trois *French* (menaʒ a trwa) *n*, *pl* **ménages à trois** (menaʒ a trwa) a sexual arrangement involving a married couple and the lover of one of them [literally: household of three]

menagerie (mɪ'nædʒərɪ) *n* **1** a collection of wild animals kept for exhibition **2** the place where such animals are housed [c18: from French: household management, which formerly included care of domestic animals. See MÉNAGE]

Menai Strait ('mɛnaɪ) *n* a channel of the Irish Sea between the island of Anglesey and the mainland of NW Wales: famous suspension bridge (1819–26) designed by Thomas Telford and tubular bridge (1846–50) by Robert Stephenson. Length: 24 km (15 miles). Width: up to 3 km (2 miles)

Menander (mə'nændə) *n* **1** ?160 BC–?120 BC, Greek king of the Punjab. A Buddhist convert, he reigned over much of NW India **2** ?342–?292 BC, Greek comic dramatist. The *Dyskolos* is his only complete extant comedy but others survive in adaptations by Terence and Plautus

Mencius ('mɛnʃɪəs, -ʃəs) *n* Chinese name *Mengzi* or *Meng-tze*. ?372–?289 BC, Chinese philosopher, who propounded the ethical system of Confucius

Mencken ('mɛŋkən) *n* **H(enry) L(ouis)**. 1880–1956, US journalist and literary critic, noted for *The American Language* (1919): editor of the *Smart Set* and the *American Mercury*, which he founded (1924)

mend (mɛnd) *vb* **1** (*tr*) to repair (something broken or unserviceable) **2** to improve or undergo improvement; reform (often in the phrase **mend one's ways**) **3** (*intr*) to heal or recover **4** (*intr*) (of conditions) to improve; become better ▷ *n* **5** the act of repairing **6** a mended area, esp on a garment **7** on the mend becoming better, esp in health [c12: shortened from AMEND] > 'mendable *adj* > 'mender *n*

mendacity (mɛn'dæsɪtɪ) *n*, *pl* **-ties 1** the tendency to be untruthful **2** a falsehood [c17: from Late Latin *mendācitās*, from Latin *mendāx* untruthful] > mendacious (mɛn'deɪʃəs) *adj* > men'daciously *adv*

Mendel ('mɛndəl) *n* **Gregor Johann** ('gre:gɔr jo'han). 1822–84, Austrian monk and botanist; founder of the

science of genetics. He developed his theory of organic inheritance from his experiments on the hybridization of green peas. His findings were published (1865) but remained unrecognized until 1900. See **Mendel's laws**

mendelevium (,mɛndɪ'li:vɪəm) *n* a transuranic element artificially produced by bombardment of einsteinium. Symbol: Md; atomic no: 101; half-life of most stable isotope, ^{258}Md: 60 days (approx.); valency: 2 or 3 [c20: named after Dmitri Ivanovich *Mendeleyev* (1834–1907), Russian chemist]

Mendeleyev *or* **Mendeleev** (*Russian* mɪndɪ'ljejɪf) *n* **Dmitri Ivanovich** ('dmitrij i'vanəvɪtʃ). 1834–1907, Russian chemist. He devised the original periodic table of the elements (1869)

Mendelian (mɛn'di:lɪən) *adj* of or relating to Mendel's laws

Mendel's laws ('mɛndəlz) *pl n* the principles of heredity proposed by Gregor Mendel (1822–84), the Austrian monk and botanist. The **Law of Segregation** states that each hereditary character is determined by a pair of units in the reproductive cells: the pairs separate during meiosis so that each gamete carries only one unit of each pair. The **Law of Independent Assortment** states that the separation of the units of each pair is not influenced by that of any other pair

Mendelssohn ('mɛndəlsən; *German* 'mɛndəlzoːn) *n* **1 Felix** ('fe:lɪks), full name *Jacob Ludwig Felix Mendelssohn-Bartholdy*. 1809–47, German romantic composer. His works include the overtures *A Midsummer Night's Dream* (1826) and *Fingal's Cave* (1832), five symphonies, the oratorio *Elijah* (1846), piano pieces, and songs. He was instrumental in the revival of the music of J. S. Bach in the 19th century **2** his grandfather, **Moses** ('moːzəs). 1729–86, German Jewish philosopher. His best-known work is *Jerusalem* (1783), in which he defends Judaism and appeals for religious toleration

Menderes (,mɛndə'rɛs) *n* **1** a river in SW Turkey flowing southwest, then west to the Aegean. Length: about 386 km (240 miles). Ancient name: Maeander **2** a river in NW Turkey flowing west and northwest to the Dardanelles. Length: 104 km (65 miles). Ancient name: Scamander

Mendes ('mɛndɛz) *n* **Sam(uel) (Alexander)**. born 1965, British theatre and film director, who made his name as artistic director of the Donmar Warehouse, London (1992–2002) before directing the films *American Beauty* (1999) and *The Road to Perdition* (2002). He is married to the actress Kate Winslet

Mendès-France (*French* mɛ̃dɛsfrɑ̃s) *n* **Pierre** (pjɛr). 1907–82, French statesman; prime minister (1954–55). He concluded the war in Indochina and granted independence to Tunisia

mendicant ('mɛndɪkənt) *adj* **1** begging **2** (of a member of a religious order) dependent on alms for sustenance ▷ *n* **3** a mendicant friar **4** a less common word for **beggar** [c16: from Latin *mendīcāre* to beg, from *mendīcus* beggar, from *mendus* flaw] > 'mendicancy *or* mendicity (mɛn'dɪsɪtɪ) *n*

Mendips ('mɛndɪps) *pl n* a range of limestone hills in SW England, in N Somerset: includes the Cheddar Gorge and numerous caves. Highest point: 325 m (1068 ft). Also called: Mendip Hills

Mendoza[1] (mɛn'dəʊzə; *Spanish* men'doθa) *n* a city in W central Argentina, in the foothills of the Sierra de los Paramillos: largely destroyed by an earthquake in 1861; commercial centre of an intensively cultivated irrigated region; University of Cuyo (1939). Pop: 1 072 000 (2005 est)

Mendoza[2] (*Spanish* men'doθa) *n* **Pedro de** ('peðro de). died 1537, Spanish soldier and explorer; founder of Buenos Aires (1536)

meneer (mə'nɪə) *n* a South African title of address equivalent to *sir* when used alone or *Mr* when placed before a name [Afrikaans]

Menelaus (,mɛnɪ'leɪəs) *n* *Greek myth* a king of Sparta and the brother of Agamemnon. He was the husband of Helen, whose abduction led to the Trojan War

Menelik II ('mɛnɪlɪk) *n* 1844–1913, emperor of Abyssinia (1889–1910). He defeated the Italians at Aduwa (1896),

1041 | **mental lexicon**

maintaining the independence of Abyssinia in an era of European expansion in Africa

Menes ('mi:ni:z) n the first king of the first dynasty of Egypt (?3100 BC). He is said to have united Upper and Lower Egypt and founded Memphis

menfolk ('mɛn,fəʊk) pl n men collectively, esp the men of a particular family

Mengelberg ('mɛŋgəl,bɛːg; Dutch 'mɛŋəlbɛrx) n (**Josef**) **Willem** ('wɪləm). 1871–1951, Dutch orchestral conductor, noted for his performances of the music of Mahler

Mengistu Haile Mariam (mɛn'gɪstu: 'haɪlɪ 'mɑːrɪəm) n born 1937, Ethiopian soldier and statesman; head of state from 1977 until 1991 when rebels seized power and he fled into exile

Mengzi or **Meng-tze** ('mɛŋ'tseɪ) n the Chinese name for **Mencius**

menhaden (mɛn'heɪdᵊn) n, pl -den a marine North American fish, Brevoortia tyrannus: source of fishmeal, fertilizer, and oil: family Clupeidae (herrings, etc) [c18: from Algonquian; probably related to Narragansett munnawhatteaúg fertilizer, menhaden]

menhir ('mɛnhɪə) n a single standing stone, often carved, dating from the middle Bronze Age in the British Isles and from the late Neolithic Age in W Europe [c19: from Breton men stone + hir long]

menial ('mi:nɪəl) adj 1 consisting of or occupied with work requiring little skill, esp domestic duties such as cleaning 2 of, involving, or befitting servants 3 servile ▷ n 4 a domestic servant 5 a servile person [c14: from Anglo-Norman meignial, from Old French meinie household.]

Meninga (mɪn'ɪŋgə) n **Mal.** born 1960, Australian rugby league player

meninges (mɪ'nɪndʒi:z) pl n, sing meninx ('mi:nɪŋks) the three membranes that envelop the brain and spinal cord [c17: from Greek, pl of meninx membrane] > meningeal (mɪ'nɪndʒɪəl) adj

meningitis (,mɛnɪn'dʒaɪtɪs) n inflammation of the membranes that surround the brain or spinal cord, caused by infection > meningitic (,mɛnɪn'dʒɪtɪk) adj

meningococcus (mɛ,nɪŋgəʊ'kɒkəs) n, pl -cocci (-'kɒkaɪ) the bacterium that causes cerebrospinal meningitis > me,ningo'coccal adj

meniscus (mɪ'nɪskəs) n, pl -nisci (-'nɪsaɪ) or -niscuses 1 the curved upper surface of a liquid standing in a tube, produced by the surface tension 2 a crescent-shaped lens; a concavo-convex or convexo-concave lens [c17: from New Latin, from Greek mēniskos crescent, diminutive of mēnē moon] > me'niscoid adj

Mennonite ('mɛnə,naɪt) n a member of a Protestant sect that rejects infant baptism, Church organization, and the doctrine of transubstantiation and in most cases refuses military service, public office, and the taking of oaths [c16: from German Mennonit, after Menno Simons (1496–1561), Frisian religious leader] > 'Menno,nitism n

meno ('mɛnəʊ) adv music (esp preceding a dynamic or tempo marking) to be played less quickly, less softly, etc [from Italian, from Latin minus less]

meno- combining form menstruation [from Greek mēn month]

Menon ('mɛnən) n Vengalil Krishnan Krishna ('vɛŋgəlɪl 'kriːʃnən 'kriːʃnə). 1897–1974, Indian diplomat and politician, who was a close associate of Nehru and played a key role in the Indian nationalist movement

menopause ('mɛnəʊ,pɔːz) n the period during which a woman's menstrual cycle ceases, normally occurring at an age of 45 to 50 [c19: from French, from Greek mēn month + pausis halt] > ,meno'pausal or rarely ,meno'pausic adj

menopolis (mɛ'nɒpəlɪs) n informal an area or city with a high proportion of single men [c21: from MEN + (METR)OPOLIS]

menorah (mɪ'nɔːrə; Hebrew mə'naʊrɔ) n Judaism 1 a seven-branched candelabrum used in the Temple and now an emblem of Judaism and the badge of the state of Israel 2 a candelabrum having eight branches and a shammes that is lit during the festival of Hanukkah [from Hebrew: candlestick]

Menorca (me'nɔrkə) n the Spanish name for **Minorca**

(sense 1)

menorrhagia (,mɛnɔː'reɪdʒɪə) n excessive bleeding during menstruation

menorrhoea (,mɛnə'rɪə) n normal bleeding in menstruation

Menotti (mə'nɒtɪ; Italian me'nɔtti) n **Gian Carlo** (dʒan 'karlo). 1911–2007, Italian composer, in the US from 1928. His works include the operas The Medium (1946), The Consul (1950), Amahl and the Night Visitors (1951), and Giorno di Nozze (1988)

menses ('mɛnsiːz) n, pl menses 1 another name for menstruation 2 the period of time, usually from three to five days, during which menstruation occurs 3 the matter discharged during menstruation [c16: from Latin, pl of mensis month]

Menshevik ('mɛnʃɪvɪk) or **Menshevist** n a member of the moderate wing of the Russian Social Democratic Party, advocating gradual reform to achieve socialism. See **Bolshevik** [c20: from Russian, literally: minority, from menshe less, from malo few] > 'Menshevism n

menstruate ('mɛnstrʊ,eɪt) vb (intr) to undergo menstruation [c17: from Latin menstruāre, from mensis month]

menstruation (,mɛnstrʊ'eɪʃən) n the approximately monthly discharge of blood and cellular debris from the uterus by nonpregnant women from puberty to the menopause > menstruous ('mɛnstrʊəs) or 'menstrual adj

menstruum ('mɛnstrʊəm) n, pl -struums or -strua (-strʊə) obsolete a solvent, esp one used in the preparation of a drug [c17 (meaning: solvent), c14 (menstrual discharge): from Medieval Latin, from Latin mēnstruus monthly, from mēnsis month; from an alchemical comparison between a base metal being transmuted into gold and the supposed action of the menses]

mensurable ('mɛnsjʊrəbᵊl, -ʃə-) adj a less common word for **measurable** [c17: from Late Latin mēnsūrābilis, from mēnsūra MEASURE] > ,mensura'bility n

mensural ('mɛnʃərəl) adj 1 of or involving measure 2 music of or relating to music in which notes have fixed values in relation to each other [c17: from Late Latin mēnsūrālis, from mēnsūra MEASURE]

mensuration (,mɛnʃə'reɪʃən) n 1 the study of the measurement of geometric magnitudes such as length 2 the act or process of measuring; measurement > mensurative ('mɛnʃərətɪv) adj

-ment suffix forming nouns 1 indicating state, condition, or quality: enjoyment 2 indicating the result or product of an action: embankment 3 indicating process or action: management [from French, from Latin -mentum]

mental ('mɛntᵊl) adj 1 of or involving the mind or an intellectual process 2 occurring only in the mind: mental calculations 3 affected by mental illness: a mental patient 4 concerned with care for persons with mental illness: a mental hospital 5 slang insane [c15: from Late Latin mentālis, from Latin mēns mind] > 'mentally adv

mental deficiency n psychiatry a less common term for **mental retardation**

mental handicap n a general or specific intellectual disability, resulting directly or indirectly from injury to the brain or from abnormal neurological development > mentally handicapped adj

mental healing n the healing of a disorder by mental concentration or suggestion

mental home, mental hospital or **mental institution** n a home, hospital, or institution for people who are mentally ill

mental illness n any of various disorders in which a person's thoughts, emotions, or behaviour are so abnormal as to cause suffering to himself, herself, or other people

mentalism ('mɛntᵊ,lɪzəm) n philosophy the doctrine that mind is the fundamental reality and that objects of knowledge exist only as aspects of the subject's consciousness > ,mental'istic adj

mentality (mɛn'tælɪtɪ) n, pl -ties 1 the state or quality of mental or intellectual ability 2 a way of thinking; mental inclination or character

mental lexicon n the store of words in a person's mind

mental reservation *n* a tacit withholding of full assent or an unexpressed qualification made when one is taking an oath, making a statement, etc

mental retardation *n psychiatry* the condition of having a low intelligence quotient (below 70)

menthol ('mɛnθɒl) *n* an optically active organic compound found in peppermint oil and used as an antiseptic, in inhalants, and as an analgesic. Formula: $C_{10}H_{20}O$ [C19: from German, from Latin *mentha* MINT[1]]

mentholated ('mɛnθə‚leɪtɪd) *adj* containing, treated, or impregnated with menthol

mention ('mɛnʃən) *vb* (*tr*) **1** to refer to or speak about briefly or incidentally **2** to acknowledge or honour **3** not to mention something to say nothing of (something too obvious to mention) ▷ *n* **4** a recognition or acknowledgment **5** a slight reference or allusion **6** the act of mentioning [C14: via Old French from Latin *mentiō* a calling to mind, naming, from *mēns* mind] > 'mentionable *adj*

Menton (mɛn'təʊ; *French* mātō) *n* a town and resort in SE France, on the Mediterranean: belonged to Monaco from the 14th century until 1848, then an independent republic until purchased by France in 1860. Pop: 28 812 (1999)

mentor ('mɛntɔː) *n* a wise or trusted adviser or guide [C18: from MENTOR]

Mentor ('mɛntɔː) *n* the friend whom Odysseus put in charge of his household when he left for Troy. He was the adviser of the young Telemachus

mentoring ('mɛntərɪŋ) *n* (in business) the practice of assigning a junior member of staff to the care of a more experienced person who assists him in his career

menu ('mɛnjuː) *n* **1 a** list of dishes served at a meal or that can be ordered in a restaurant **2** a list of options displayed on a visual display unit from which the operator selects an action to be carried out by positioning the cursor or by depressing the appropriate key [C19: from French *menu* small, detailed (list), from Latin *minūtus* MINUTE[2]]

Menuhin ('mɛnjʊɪn) *n* **Yehudi** (jɛ'huːdɪ), Baron. 1916–99, British violinist, born in the US

Menzies ('mɛnzɪz) *n* **Sir Robert Gordon**. 1894–1978, Australian statesman; prime minister 1939–41; 1949–66)

meow, miaou, miaow (mɪ'aʊ, mjaʊ) *or* **miaul** (mɪ'aʊl, mjaʊl) *vb* **1** (*intr*) (of a cat) to make a characteristic crying sound ▷ *interj* **2** an imitation of this sound

MEP *abbreviation* (in Britain) Member of the European Parliament

mepacrine ('mɛpəkrɪn) *n Brit* a drug, mepacrine dihydrochloride, one of the first synthetic substitutes for quinine, formerly widely used to treat malaria but now largely replaced by chloroquine. Formula: $C_{23}H_{30}ClN_3O.2HCl.2H_2O$ [C20: from ME(THYL) + PA(LUDISM + A)CR(ID)INE]

Mephistopheles (‚mɛfɪ'stɒfɪ‚liːz) *or* **Mephisto** (mə'fɪstəʊ) *n* a devil in medieval mythology and the one to whom Faust sold his soul in the Faust legend > Mephistophelean *or* Mephistophelian (‚mɛfɪstə'fiːlɪən) *adj*

mephitic (mɪ'fɪtɪk) *or* **mephitical** *adj* **1** poisonous; foul **2** foul-smelling; putrid [C17: from Late Latin *mephīticus* pestilential]

meprobamate (mə'prəʊbə‚meɪt, ‚mɛprəʊ'bæmeɪt) *n* a white bitter powder used as a hypnotic. Formula: $C_9H_{18}N_2O_4$ [ME(THYL) + PRO(PYL + CAR)BAMATE]

-mer *suffix* forming nouns *chem* denoting a substance of a particular class: *monomer; polymer* [from Greek *meros* part]

Merano (mə'rɑːnəʊ; *Italian* me'raːno) *n* a town and resort in NE Italy, in the foothills of the central Alps: capital of the Tyrol (12th–15th century); under Austrian rule until 1919. Pop: 33 656 (2001)

Merca ('mɛəkə) *n* a port in S Somalia on the Indian Ocean. Pop: 189 000 (2005 est)

mercantile ('mɜːkən‚taɪl) *adj* **1** of, relating to, or characteristic of trade or traders; commercial **2** of or relating to mercantilism [C17: from French, from Italian, from *mercante* MERCHANT]

mercantilism ('mɜːkəntɪ‚lɪzəm) *n* Also called: mercantile system *economics* a theory prevalent in

Europe during the 17th and 18th centuries asserting that the wealth of a nation depends on its possession of precious metals and therefore that the government of a nation must maximize the foreign trade surplus, and foster national commercial interests, a merchant marine, the establishment of colonies, etc > 'mercan‚tilist *n, adj*

mercaptan (mɜː'kæptæn) *n* another name (not in technical usage) for: **thiol** [C19: from German, from Medieval Latin *mercurium captans*, literally: seizing quicksilver]

Mercator (mɜː'keɪtə) *n* **Gerardus** (dʒə'rɑːdəs). Latinized name of *Gerhard Kremer*. 1512–94, Flemish cartographer and mathematician

Mercator projection (mɜː'keɪtə) *n* an orthomorphic map projection on which parallels and meridians form a rectangular grid, scale being exaggerated with increasing distance from the equator. Also called: Mercator's projection [C17: named after Gerardus *Mercator*, Latinized name of Gerhard Kremer (1512–94), Flemish cartographer and mathematician]

mercenary ('mɜːsɪnərɪ, -sɪnrɪ) *adj* **1** influenced by greed or desire for gain **2** of or relating to a mercenary or mercenaries ▷ *n, pl* -naries **3** a man hired to fight for a foreign army, etc **4** *rare* any person who works solely for pay [C16: from Latin *mercēnārius*, from *mercēs* wages]

mercer ('mɜːsə) *n Brit* a dealer in textile fabrics and fine cloth [C13: from Old French *mercier* dealer, from Vulgar Latin *merciārius* (unattested), from Latin *merx* goods, wares] > 'mercery *n*

Mercer ('mɜːsə) *n* **Johnny**, full name *John Herndon Mercer*. 1909–76, US popular songwriter and singer. His most popular songs include "Blues in the Night" (1941) and "Moon River" (1961)

mercerize *or* **mercerise** ('mɜːsə‚raɪz) *vb* (*tr*) to treat (cotton yarn) with an alkali to increase its strength and reception to dye and impart a lustrous silky appearance [C19: named after John *Mercer* (1791–1866), English maker of textiles]

merchandise *n* ('mɜːtʃən‚daɪs, -‚daɪz) **1** commercial goods; commodities ▷ *vb* ('mɜːtʃən‚daɪz) **2** to engage in the commercial purchase and sale of (goods or services); trade [C13: from Old French. See MERCHANT]

merchandising ('mɜːtʃən‚daɪzɪŋ) *n* **1** the selection and display of goods in a retail outlet **2** commercial goods, esp ones issued to exploit the popularity of a pop group, sporting event, etc

merchant ('mɜːtʃənt) *n* **1** a person engaged in the purchase and sale of commodities for profit, esp on international markets; trader **2** *chiefly US & Canadian* a person engaged in retail trade **3** (esp in historical contexts) any trader **4** *derogatory* a person dealing or involved in something undesirable: *a gossip merchant* **5** (*modifier*) **a** of the merchant navy: *a merchant sailor* **b** of or concerned with trade: *a merchant ship* ▷ *vb* **6** (*tr*) to conduct trade in; deal in [C13: from Old French, probably from Vulgar Latin *mercātāre* (unattested), from Latin *mercārī* to trade, from *merx* goods, wares]

Merchant ('mɜːtʃənt) *n* **Ismail** ('ɪzmeɪəl). 1936–2005, Indian film producer, noted for his collaboration with James Ivory on such films as *Shakespeare Wallah* (1965), *The Europeans* (1979), *A Room with a View* (1986), *The Remains of the Day* (1993), and *The Golden Bowl* (2000)

merchantable ('mɜːtʃəntəbəl) *adj* suitable for trading

merchant bank *n* (in Britain) a financial institution engaged primarily in accepting foreign bills, advising companies on flotations and takeovers, underwriting new issues, hire-purchase finance, making long-term loans to companies, and managing investment portfolios, funds, and trusts > merchant banker *n*

merchantman ('mɜːtʃəntmən) *n, pl* -men a merchant ship

merchant navy *or* **merchant marine** *n* the ships or crew engaged in a nation's commercial shipping

Mercia ('mɜːʃɪə) *n* a kingdom and earldom of central and S England during the Anglo-Saxon period that reached its height under King Offa (757–96)

Mercian ('mɜːʃɪən) *adj* **1** of or relating to Mercia or the dialect spoken there ▷ *n* **2** the dialect of Old and Middle

English spoken in the Midlands of England south of the River Humber **3** a native or inhabitant of Mercia

merciful ('mɜːsɪfʊl) *adj* showing or giving mercy; compassionate ▷ 'mercifulness *n* ▷ 'mercifully *adv*

merciless ('mɜːsɪlɪs) *adj* without mercy; pitiless, cruel, or heartless ▷ 'mercilessly *adv* ▷ 'mercilessness *n*

Merckx ('mɛrks) *n* **Eddy**. born 1945, Belgian professional cyclist: five times winner of the Tour de France, including four consecutive victories (1969–72)

Mercouri (mɜː'kuːrɪ) *n* **Melina** (mə'liːnə). 1925–94, Greek actress and politician: her films include *Never on Sunday* (1960); minister of culture (1981–85 and 1993–94)

mercurial (mɜː'kjʊərɪəl) *adj* **1** of, like, containing, or relating to mercury **2** volatile; lively: *a mercurial temperament* **3** (*sometimes capital*) of, like, or relating to the god or the planet Mercury ▷ *n* **4** *med* any salt of mercury for use as a medicine [c14: from Latin *mercuriālis*] ▷ mer'curially *adv* ▷ mer'curialness *or* mer,curi'ality *n*

mercuric (mɜː'kjʊərɪk) *adj* of or containing mercury in the divalent state; denoting a mercury(II) compound

mercuric chloride *n* a white poisonous soluble crystalline substance used as a pesticide, antiseptic, and preservative for wood. Formula: $HgCl_2$

Mercurochrome (mə'kjʊərə,krəʊm) *n* *trademark* a solution of merbromin, used as topical antibacterial agent

mercurous ('mɜːkjʊrəs) *adj* of or containing mercury in the monovalent state; denoting a mercury(I) compound. Mercurous salts contain the divalent ion Hg_2^{2+}

mercury ('mɜːkjʊrɪ) *n*, *pl* **-ries 1** Also called: **quicksilver** *or* **hydrargyrum** a heavy silvery-white toxic liquid metallic element occurring principally in cinnabar: used in thermometers, barometers, mercury-vapour lamps, and dental amalgams. Symbol: Hg; atomic no: 80; atomic wt: 200.59; valency: 1 or 2; relative density: 13.546; melting pt: −38.842°C; boiling pt: 357°C **2** any plant of the euphorbiaceous genus *Mercurialis* **3** *archaic* a messenger or courier [c14: from Latin *Mercurius* messenger of Jupiter, god of commerce; related to *merx* merchandise]

Mercury[1] ('mɜːkjʊrɪ) *n* *Roman myth* the messenger of the gods

Mercury[2] ('mɜːkjʊrɪ) *n* the second smallest planet and the nearest to the sun. Mean distance from sun: 57.9 million km; period of revolution around sun: 88 days; period of axial rotation: 59 days; diameter and mass: 38 and 5.4 per cent that of earth respectively

mercury-vapour lamp *n* a lamp in which an electric discharge through a low pressure of mercury vapour is used to produce a greenish-blue light. It is used for street lighting and is also a source of ultraviolet radiation

mercy ('mɜːsɪ) *n*, *pl* **-cies 1** compassionate treatment of or attitude towards an offender, adversary, etc, who is in one's power or care; clemency; pity **2** the power to show mercy **3** a relieving or welcome occurrence or state of affairs **4** at the mercy of in the power of [c12: from Old French, from Latin *mercēs* wages, recompense, price, from *merx* goods]

mercy flight *n* an aircraft flight to bring a seriously ill or injured person to hospital from an isolated community

mercy killing *n* another term for **euthanasia**

mere[1] (mɪə) *adj*, *superlative* **merest** being nothing more than something specified: *she is a mere child* [c15: from Latin *merus* pure, unmixed] ▷ merely ('mɪəlɪ, 'merely) *adv*

mere[2] (mɪə) *n* **1** *archaic or dialect* a lake or marsh **2** *obsolete* the sea or an inlet of it [Old English *mere* sea, lake; related to Old Saxon *meri* sea, Old Norse *marr*, Old High German *mari*; compare Latin *mare*]

mere[3] ('mɛrɪ) *n* NZ a short flat striking weapon [Māori]

-mere *n combining form* indicating a part or division [from Greek *meros* part, portion] ▷ **-meric** *adj combining form*

Meredith ('mɛrɪdɪθ) *n* **George**. 1828–1909, English novelist and poet. His works, notable for their social satire and analysis of character, include the novels *Beauchamp's Career* (1876) and *The Egoist* (1879) and the long tragic poem *Modern Love* (1862)

meretricious (,mɛrɪ'trɪʃəs) *adj* **1** superficially or garishly attractive **2** insincere **3** *archaic* of, like, or relating to a prostitute [c17: from Latin *merētrīcius*, from *merētrix* prostitute, from *merēre* to earn money] ▷ ,mere'triciously *adv* ▷ ,mere'triciousness *n*

merganser (mɜː'gænsə) *n*, *pl* **-sers** *or* **-ser** any of several typically crested large marine diving ducks of the genus *Mergus*, having a long slender hooked bill with serrated edges [c18: from New Latin, from Latin *mergus* waterfowl, from *mergere* to plunge + *anser* goose]

merge (mɜːdʒ) *vb* **1** to meet and join or cause to meet and join **2** to blend or cause to blend; fuse [c17: from Latin *mergere* to plunge] ▷ 'mergence *n*

merger ('mɜːdʒə) *n* **1** *commerce* the combination of two or more companies, either by the creation of a new organization or by absorption by one of the others **2** *law* the extinguishment of an estate, interest, contract, right, offence, etc, by its absorption into a greater one **3** the act of merging or the state of being merged

Mergui Archipelago (mɜː'gwiː) *n* a group of over 200 islands in the Andaman Sea, off the Tenasserim coast of S Myanmar: mountainous and forested

Meriç (mə'riːtʃ) *n* the Turkish name for the **Maritsa**

Mérida (*Spanish* 'meriða) *n* **1 a** a city in SE Mexico, capital of Yucatán state: founded in 1542 on the site of the ancient Mayan city of T'ho; centre of the henequen industry; university. Pop: 919 000 (2005 est) **2** a city in W Venezuela: founded in 1558 by Spanish conquistadores; University of Los Andes (1785). Pop: 319 000 (2005 est) **3** a market town in W Spain, in Extremadura, on the Guadiana River: founded in 25 BC; became the capital of Lusitania and one of the chief cities of Iberia. Pop: 52 110 (2003 est)

meridian (mə'rɪdɪən) *n* **1 a** one of the imaginary lines joining the north and south poles at right angles to the equator, designated by degrees of longitude from 0° at Greenwich to 180° **b** the great circle running through both poles **2** *astronomy* the great circle on the celestial sphere passing through the north and south celestial poles and the zenith and nadir of the observer **3** the peak; zenith: *the meridian of his achievements* **4** (in acupuncture, etc) any of the channels through which vital energy is believed to circulate round the body **5** *obsolete* noon ▷ *adj* **6** along or relating to a meridian **7** of or happening at noon **8** relating to the peak of something [c14: from Latin *merīdiānus* of midday, from *merīdiēs* midday, from *medius* MID[1] + *diēs* day]

meridional (mə'rɪdɪənᵊl) *adj* **1** along, relating to, or resembling a meridian **2** characteristic of or located in the south, esp of Europe ▷ *n* **3** an inhabitant of the south, esp of France [c14: from Late Latin *merīdiōnālis* southern; see MERIDIAN; for form, compare *septentriōnālis* SEPTENTRIONAL]

Mérimée (*French* merime) *n* **Prosper** (prɔspɛr). 1803–70, French novelist, dramatist, and short-story writer, noted particularly for his short novels *Colomba* (1840) and *Carmen* (1845), on which Bizet's opera was based

meringue (mə'ræŋ) *n* **1** stiffly beaten egg whites mixed with sugar and baked, often as a topping for pies, cakes, etc **2** a small cake or shell of this mixture, often filled with cream [c18: from French, origin obscure]

merino (mə'riːnəʊ) *n*, *pl* **-nos 1** a breed of sheep, originating in Spain, bred for their fleece **2** the long fine wool of this sheep **3** the yarn made from this wool, often mixed with cotton ▷ *adj* **4** made from merino wool [c18: from Spanish, origin uncertain]

Merionethshire (,mɛrɪ'ɒnɪθ,ʃɪə, -ʃə) *n* (until 1974) a county of N Wales, now part of Gwynedd

meristem ('mɛrɪ,stɛm) *n* a plant tissue responsible for growth, whose cells divide and differentiate to form the tissues and organs of the plant. Meristems occur within the stem (see **cambium**) and leaves and at the tips of stems and roots [c19: from Greek *meristos* divided, from *merizein* to divide, from *meris* portion] ▷ meristematic (,mɛrɪstɪ'mætɪk) *adj*

merit ('mɛrɪt) *n* **1** worth or superior quality; excellence **2** (*often plural*) a deserving or commendable quality or act **3** *Christianity* spiritual credit granted or received for good works **4** the fact or state of deserving; desert ▷ *vb* **-its**, **-iting**, **-ited 5** (*tr*) to be worthy of; deserve [c13: via Old

French from Latin *meritum* reward, desert, from *merēre* to deserve] > 'merited *adj* > 'meritless *adj*

meritocracy (ˌmɛrɪ'tɒkrəsɪ) *n*, *pl* **-cies** **1** rule by persons chosen not because of birth or wealth, but for their superior talents or intellect **2** the persons constituting such a group **3** a social system formed on such a basis > meritocratic (ˌmɛrɪtə'krætɪk) *adj*

meritorious (ˌmɛrɪ'tɔːrɪəs) *adj* praiseworthy; showing merit [C15: from Latin *meritōrius* earning money] > ˌmeri'toriously *adv* > ˌmeri'toriousness *n*

merits ('mɛrɪts) *pl n* **1** the actual and intrinsic rights and wrongs of an issue, esp in a law case, as distinct from extraneous matters and technicalities **2** on its merits on the intrinsic qualities or virtues

Merkel ('mɜːkəl) *n* **Angela.** born 1954, German politician; chair of the Christian Democratic Union from 2000; chancellor of Germany from 2005 (the first woman to hold the office)

merle or **merl** (mɜːl; *Scot* mɛrl) *n Scot* another name for the (European) **blackbird** [C15: via Old French from Latin *merula*]

Merleau-Ponty (*French* mɛrlopɔ̄ti) *n* **Maurice** (mɔrɪs). 1908–61, French phenomenological philosopher

merlin ('mɜːlɪn) *n* a small falcon, *Falco columbarius*, that has a dark plumage with a black-barred tail: used in falconry [C14: from Old French *esmerillon*, from *esmeril*, of Germanic origin]

Merlin ('mɜːlɪn) *n* (in Arthurian legend) a wizard and counsellor to King Arthur eternally imprisoned in a tree by a woman to whom he revealed his secret craft

Merlot ('mɜːləʊ) *n* (*sometimes not capital*) **1** a black grape grown in France and now throughout the wine-producing world, used, often in a blend, for making wine **2** any of various wines made from this grape [from French *merlot*, literally: young blackbird, diminutive of *merle* MERLE[1], probably alluding to the colour of the grape]

mermaid ('mɜːˌmeɪd) *n* an imaginary sea creature fabled to have a woman's head and upper body and a fish's tail [C14: from *mere* lake, inlet + MAID]

merman ('mɜːˌmæn) *n*, *pl* **-men** a male counterpart of the mermaid [C17: see MERMAID]

Meroë ('mɛrəʊˌiː) *n* an ancient city in N Sudan, on the Nile; capital of a kingdom that flourished from about 700 BC to about 350 AD

-merous *adj combining form* (in biology) having a certain number or kind of parts [from Greek *meros* part, division]

Merovingian (ˌmɛrəʊ'vɪndʒɪən) *adj* **1** of or relating to a Frankish dynasty founded by Clovis I, which ruled Gaul and W Germany from about 500 to 751 AD *⊳ n* **2** a member or supporter of this dynasty [C17: from French, from Medieval Latin *Merovingi* offspring of *Merovaeus*, Latin form of *Merowig*, traditional founder of the line]

merriment ('mɛrɪmənt) *n* gaiety, fun, or mirth

merry ('mɛrɪ) *adj* **-rier**, **-riest** **1** cheerful; jolly **2** very funny; hilarious **3** *Brit informal* slightly drunk **4** make merry to revel; be festive **5** play merry hell with *informal* to disturb greatly; disrupt [Old English *merige* agreeable] > 'merrily *adv* > 'merriness *n*

merry-andrew *n* a joker, clown, or buffoon [C17: original reference of *Andrew* unexplained]

merry-go-round *n* **1** another name for **roundabout** (sense 1) **2** a whirl of activity or events

merrymaking ('mɛrɪˌmeɪkɪŋ) *n* fun, revelry, or festivity > 'merry,maker *n*

merrythought ('mɛrɪˌθɔːt) *n Brit* a less common word for **wishbone**

Merse (mɜːs; *Scot* mɛrs) *n* **the Merse** a fertile lowland area of SE Scotland, in Scottish Borders, north of the Tweed

Merseburg (*German* 'mɛrzəburk) *n* a city in E Germany, on the Saale River, in Saxony-Anhalt: residence of the dukes of Saxe-Merseburg (1656–1738); chemical industry. Pop: 35 358 (2003 est)

Mersey ('mɜːzɪ) *n* a river in W England, rising in N Derbyshire and flowing northwest and west to the Irish Sea through a large estuary on which is situated the port of Liverpool. Length: about 112 km (70 miles)

Merseyside ('mɜːzɪˌsaɪd) *n* a metropolitan county of NW

England, administered since 1986 by the unitary authorities of Sefton, Liverpool, St Helens, Knowsley, and Wirral. Area: 652 sq km (252 sq miles)

Mersin (mɛə'siːn) *n* a port in S Turkey, on the Mediterranean: oil refinery. Pop: 603 000 (2005 est). Also called: İçel

Merthyr Tydfil ('mɜːθə 'tɪdvɪl) *n* **1** a town in SE Wales, in Merthyr Tydfil county borough: formerly an important centre for the mining industry. Pop: 30 483 (2001) **2** a county borough in SE Wales, created from part of N Mid Glamorgan in 1996. Pop: 55 400 (2003 est). Area: 111 sq km (43 sq miles)

Merton[1] ('mɜːtªn) *n* a borough in SW Greater London. Pop: 191 400 (2003 est). Area: 38 sq km (15 sq miles)

Merton[2] ('mɜːtªn) *n* **Thomas** (**Feverel**). 1915–68, US writer, monk, and mystic; noted esp for his autobiography *The Seven Storey Mountain* (1948)

mesa ('meɪsə) *n* a flat tableland with steep edges, common in the southwestern US [from Spanish: table]

mésalliance (me'zælɪəns; *French* mezaljãs) *n* marriage with a person of lower social status [C18: from French: MISALLIANCE]

Mesa Verde ('meɪsə 'vɜːd) *n* a high plateau in SW Colorado: remains of numerous prehistoric cliff dwellings, inhabited by the Pueblo Indians

mescal (me'skæl) *n* **1** Also called: peyote a spineless globe-shaped cactus, *Lophophora williamsii*, of Mexico and the southwestern US. Its button-like tubercles (**mescal buttons**) contain mescaline and are chewed by certain Indian tribes for their hallucinogenic effects **2** a colourless alcoholic spirit distilled from the fermented juice of certain agave plants [C19: from American Spanish, from Nahuatl *mexcalli* the liquor, from *metl* MAGUEY + *ixcalli* stew]

mescaline or **mescalin** ('mɛskəˌliːn, -lɪn) *n* a hallucinogenic drug derived from mescal buttons. Formula: $C_{11}H_{17}NO_3$

mesdames ('meɪˌdæm; *French* medam) *n* the plural of: **madame** and **madam** (sense 1)

mesdemoiselles (ˌmeɪdmwə'zɛl; *French* medmwazɛl) *n* the plural of **mademoiselle**

meseems (mɪ'siːmz) *vb*, *past* meseemed (*tr; takes a clause as object*) *archaic* it seems to me

mesembryanthemum (mɪzˌɛmbrɪ'ænθɪməm) *n* any plant of a South African genus (*Mesembryanthemum*) of succulent-leaved prostrate or erect plants widely grown in gardens and greenhouses: family Aizoaceae [C18: New Latin, from Greek *mesēmbria* noon + *anthemon* flower]

mesencephalon (ˌmɛsɛn'sɛfəˌlɒn) *n* the part of the brain that develops from the middle portion of the embryonic neural tube. Nontechnical name: midbrain

mesentery ('mɛsəntərɪ, 'mɛz-) *n*, *pl* **-teries** the double layer of peritoneum that is attached to the back wall of the abdominal cavity and supports most of the small intestine [C16: from New Latin *mesenterium*; see MESO- + ENTERON] > ˌmesen'teric *adj* > mesenteritis (mɛsˌɛntə'raɪtɪs) *n*

mesh (mɛʃ) *n* **1** a network; net **2** an open space between the strands of a network **3** (*often plural*) the strands surrounding these spaces **4** anything that ensnares, or holds like a net **5** the engagement of teeth on interacting gearwheels: *the gears are in mesh ⊳ vb* **6** to entangle or become entangled **7** (*intr; often foll by with*) to coordinate (with). **8** to work or cause to work in harmony [C16: probably from Dutch *maesche*; related to Old English *masc*, Old High German *masca*]

Meshach ('miːʃæk) *n Old Testament* one of Daniel's three companions who, together with Shadrach and Abednego, was miraculously saved from destruction in Nebuchadnezzar's fiery furnace (Daniel 3:12-30)

Meshed (me'ʃɛd) *n* a variant of **Mashhad**

mesial ('miːzɪəl) *adj* anatomy another word for: **medial** (sense 1) [C19: from MESO- + -IAL]

mesmerism ('mɛzməˌrɪzəm) *n psychol* **1** a hypnotic state induced by the operator's imposition of his will on that of the patient **2** an early doctrine concerning this [C19: named after F. A. *Mesmer* (1734–1815), Austrian physician] > 'mesmerist *n* > mesmeric (mɛz'mɛrɪk) *adj* > mes'merically *adv*

mesmerize or **mesmerise** ('mɛzmə‚raɪz) vb (tr) **1** a former word for: **hypnotize 2** to hold (someone) as if spellbound > ‚mesmeri'zation or ‚mesmeri'sation n > 'mesmer‚izer or 'mesmer‚iser n

mesne (miːn) adj law **1** intermediate or intervening: used esp of any assignment of property before the last: a mesne assignment **2** mesne profits rents or profits accruing during the rightful owner's exclusion from his land [c15: from legal French meien in the middle, MEAN³]

meso- or before a vowel **mes-** combining form middle or intermediate: mesomorph [from Greek misos middle]

mesoblast ('mɛsəʊ‚blæst) n another name for: **mesoderm** > ‚meso'blastic adj

mesocarp ('mɛsəʊ‚kɑːp) n the middle layer of the pericarp of a fruit, such as the flesh of a peach

mesocephalic (‚mɛsəʊsɪ'fælɪk) anatomy ▷ adj **1** having a medium-sized head, esp one with a cephalic index between 75 and 80 ▷ n **2** an individual with such a head > mesocephaly (‚mɛsəʊ'sɛfəlɪ) n

mesoderm ('mɛsəʊ‚dɜːm) n the middle germ layer of an animal embryo, giving rise to muscle, blood, bone, connective tissue, etc > ‚meso'dermal or ‚meso'dermic adj

Mesolithic (‚mɛsəʊ'lɪθɪk) n **1** the period between the Palaeolithic and the Neolithic, in Europe from about 12 000 to 3000 BC, characterized by the appearance of microliths ▷ adj **2** of or relating to the Mesolithic

Mesolonghi (‚mɛsə'lɔːŋgɪ) n a variant of: **Missolonghi**

Mesolóngion (‚mɛsə'lɒŋgɪ‚ɒn) n transliteration of the Modern Greek name for **Missolonghi**

mesomorph ('mɛsəʊ‚mɔːf) n a person with a muscular body build: said to be correlated with somatotonia

mesomorphic (‚mɛsəʊ'mɔːfɪk) or **mesomorphous** adj **1** chem existing in or concerned with an intermediate state of matter between a true liquid and a true solid **2** relating to or being a mesomorph > ‚meso'morphism n

meson ('miːzɒn) n any of a group of elementary particles, such as a pion or kaon, that usually have a rest mass between those of an electron and a proton, and an integral spin. They are responsible for the force between nucleons in the atomic nucleus [c20: from MESO- + -ON] > me'sonic or 'mesic adj

mesophyte ('mɛsəʊ‚faɪt) n any plant that grows in surroundings having an average supply of water

Mesopotamia (‚mɛsəpə'teɪmɪə) n a region of SW Asia between the lower and middle reaches of the Tigris and Euphrates rivers: site of several ancient civilizations [Latin from Greek mesopotamia (khora) (the land) between rivers] > ‚Mesopo'tamian adj, n

mesosphere ('mɛsəʊ‚sfɪə) n the atmospheric layer lying between the stratosphere and the thermosphere, characterized by a rapid decrease in temperature with height

mesotherapy (‚mɛsəʊ'θɛrəpɪ) n, pl -pies a cosmetic procedure in which minute doses of medication, vitamins, etc, are injected repeatedly into the mesodermal tissue under the skin to promote fat loss [c20: from MESO- + THERAPY]

Mesozoic (‚mɛsəʊ'zəʊɪk) adj **1** of, denoting, or relating to an era of geological time that began 250 000 000 years ago with the Triassic period and lasted about 185 000 000 years until the end of the Cretaceous period ▷ n **2** the Mesozoic the Mesozoic era

mesquite or **mesquit** (mɛ'skiːt, 'mɛskiːt) n any small leguminous tree of the genus Prosopis, esp the tropical American P. juliflora, whose sugary pods (**mesquite beans**) are used as animal fodder [c19: from Mexican Spanish, from Nahuatl mizquitl]

mess (mɛs) n **1** a state of confusion or untidiness, esp if dirty or unpleasant **2** a chaotic or troublesome state of affairs; muddle **3** informal a dirty or untidy person or thing **4** archaic a portion of food, esp soft or semiliquid food **5** a place where service personnel eat or take recreation **6** a group of people, usually servicemen, who eat together **7** the meal so taken ▷ vb **8** (tr; often foll by up) to muddle or dirty **9** (intr) to make a mess **10** (intr; often foll by with) to interfere; meddle **11** (intr; often foll by with or together) military to group together, esp for eating [c13: from Old French mes dish of food, from Late Latin missus course (at table), from Latin mittere to send

forth, set out]

mess about or **mess around** vb (adverb) **1** (intr) to occupy oneself trivially; potter **2** (when intr, often foll by with) to interfere or meddle (with) **3** (intr; sometimes foll by with) chiefly US to engage in adultery

message ('mɛsɪdʒ) n **1** a communication, usually brief, from one person or group to another **2** an implicit meaning or moral, as in a work of art **3** a formal communiqué **4** an inspired communication of a prophet or religious leader **5** a mission; errand **6** get the message informal to understand what is meant ▷ vb **7** (tr) to send as a message, esp to signal (a plan, etc) [c13: from Old French, from Vulgar Latin missāticum (unattested) something sent, from Latin missus, past participle of mittere to send]

message board n an internet discussion forum

Messager (French mɛsaʒe) n **André (Charles Prosper)** (ãdre). 1853–1929, French composer and conductor

message stick n a stick bearing carved symbols, carried by a native Australian as identification

messaging ('mɛsɪdʒɪŋ) n the practice of sending and receiving written communications by computer or mobile phone

Messalina (‚mɛsə'liːnə) n **Valeria** (və'lɪərɪə). died 48 AD, wife of the Roman emperor Claudius, notorious for her debauchery and cruelty

Messene (mɛ'siːnɪ) n an ancient Greek city in the SW Peloponnese: founded in 369 BC as the capital of Messenia

messenger ('mɛsɪndʒə) n **1** a person who takes messages from one person or group to another or others **2** a person who runs errands or is employed to run errands **3** a carrier of official dispatches; courier [c13: from Old French messagier, from MESSAGE]

messenger RNA n biochem a form of RNA, transcribed from a single strand of DNA, that carries genetic information required for protein synthesis from DNA to the ribosomes. Sometimes shortened to: **mRNA**

Messenia (mə'siːnɪə) n the southwestern area of the Peloponnese in S Greece

Messerschmitt (German 'mɛsər‚ʃmɪt) n **Willy** ('vɪli). 1898–1978, German aeronautical engineer. His military planes figured prominently in World War II, including the Me-262, the first jet fighter

mess hall n a military dining room, usually large

Messiaen (French mɛsjã) n **Olivier** (ɔlivje). 1908–92, French composer and organist. His music is distinguished by its rhythmic intricacy; he was influenced by Hindu and Greek rhythms and bird song

Messiah (mɪ'saɪə) n **1** Judaism the awaited redeemer of the Jews, to be sent by God to free them **2** Jesus Christ, when regarded in this role **3** an exceptional or hoped for liberator of a country or people [c14: from Old French Messie, ultimately from Hebrew māshīach anointed] > Mes'siah‚ship n > messianic (‚mɛsɪ'ænɪk) adj > ‚messi'anically adv > messianism (mɛ'saɪənɪzəm) n

Messier catalogue ('mɛsɪeɪ) n astronomy a catalogue of 103 nonstellar objects, such as nebulae and galaxies, prepared in 1781–86. An object is referred to by its number in this catalogue, for example the Andromeda Galaxy is referred to as M31 [c18: named after Charles Messier (1730–1817), French astronomer]

messieurs ('mɛsəz; French mesjø) n the plural of **monsieur**

Messina (mɛ'siːnə) n a port in NE Sicily, on the **Strait of Messina**: colonized by Greeks around 730 BC; under Spanish rule (1282–1676 and 1678–1713); university (1549). Pop: 252 026 (2001)

mess jacket n a waist-length jacket tapering to a point at the back, worn by officers in the mess for formal dinners

mess kit n military **1** Brit formal evening wear for officers **2** Also called: **mess gear** eating utensils used esp in the field

messmate ('mɛs‚meɪt) n a person with whom one shares meals in a mess, esp in the army

Messrs ('mɛsəz) n the plural of **Mr** [c18: abbreviation from French messieurs]

messy ('mɛsɪ) adj **messier, messiest** dirty, confused, or untidy > **'messily** *adv* > **'messiness** *n*

mestizo (mɛ'stiːzəʊ, mɪ-) *n, pl* -**zos** *or* -**zoes** a person of mixed parentage, esp the offspring of a Spanish American and an American Indian [c16: from Spanish, ultimately from Latin *miscēre* to mix] > **mestiza** (mɛ'stiːzə) *fem n*

mestranol ('mɛstrəˌnɒl, -ˌnəʊl) *n* a synthetic oestrogen used in combination with progestogens as an oral contraceptive. Formula: $C_{21}H_{26}O_2$ [c20: from M(ETHYL) + (O)ESTR(OGEN) + (*pregn*)an(*e*) ($C_{21}H_{36}$) + -OL]

Meštrović (*Serbo-Croat* 'mɛʃtrovitʃ) *n* **Ivan** ('ivan). 1883–1962, US sculptor, born in Austria: his works include portraits of Sir Thomas Beecham and Pope Pius XI

met (mɛt) *vb* the past tense and past participle of **meet**[1]

met. *abbreviation* **1** meteorological **2** meteorology

meta- *or sometimes before a vowel* **met-** *prefix* **1** indicating change, alteration, or alternation: *metabolism; metamorphosis* **2** (of an academic discipline, esp philosophy) concerned with the concepts and results of the named discipline: *metamathematics; meta-ethics* **3** occurring or situated behind or after **4** (*often in italics*) denoting that an organic compound contains a benzene ring with substituents in the 1,3-positions: *metadinitrobenzene; meta-cresol.* Abbreviation: *m-* **5** denoting an isomer, polymer, or compound related to a specified compound (often differing from similar compounds that are prefixed by *para-*): *metaldehyde* **6** denoting an oxyacid that is a lower hydrated form of the anhydride or a salt of such an acid: *metaphosphoric acid* [Greek, from *meta* with, after, between, among. Compare Old English *mid, mith* with, Old Norse *meth* with, between]

metabolic syndrome *n* a condition associated with obesity including symptoms such as glucose intolerance, insulin resistance, and raised blood pressure, which increases the risk of cardiovascular disease and diabetes

metabolism (mɪ'tæbəˌlɪzəm) *n* **1** the sum total of the chemical processes that occur in living organisms, resulting in growth, production of energy, elimination of waste material, etc **2** the sum total of the chemical processes affecting a particular substance in the body: *carbohydrate metabolism; iodine metabolism* [c19: from Greek *metabolē* change, from *metaballein* to change, from META- + *ballein* to throw] > **metabolic** (ˌmɛtə'bɒlɪk) *adj* > ˌmeta'bolically *adv*

metabolize *or* **metabolise** (mɪ'tæbəˌlaɪz) *vb* to bring about or subject to metabolism

metacarpal (ˌmɛtə'kɑːpəl) *anatomy* ▷ *adj* **1** of or relating to the metacarpus ▷ *n* **2** a metacarpal bone

metacarpus (ˌmɛtə'kɑːpəs) *n, pl* -**pi** (-paɪ) **1** the skeleton of the hand between the wrist and the fingers, consisting of five long bones **2** the corresponding bones in other vertebrates

metacentre *or US* **metacenter** ('mɛtəˌsɛntə) *n* the intersection of a vertical line through the centre of buoyancy of a floating body at equilibrium with the formerly vertical line through the centre of gravity of the body when the body is tilted > ˌmeta'centric *adj*

metacomputer (ˌmɛtəkəm'pjuːtə) *n* an interconnected and balanced set of computers that operate as a single unit > ˌmetacom'puting *n*

meta-data *pl n computing* information that is held as a description of stored data

metage ('miːtɪdʒ) *n* **1** the official measuring of weight or contents **2** a charge for this [c16: from METE[1]]

metal ('mɛtəl) *n* **1 a** any of a number of chemical elements, such as iron or copper, that are often lustrous ductile solids, have basic oxides, form positive ions, and are good conductors of heat and electricity **b** an alloy, such as brass or steel, containing one or more of these elements **2** the substance of glass in a molten state or as the finished product **3** short for **road metal 4** *informal* short for **heavy metal** (sense 1) **5** *heraldry* gold or silver **6** (*plural*) the rails of a railway ▷ *adj* **7** made of metal ▷ *vb* -**als**, -**alling**, -**alled** *or US* -**als**, -**aling**, -**aled** (*tr*) **8** to fit or cover with metal **9** to make or mend (a road) with **road metal** [c13: from Latin *metallum* mine, product of a mine,

from Greek *metallon*] > **'metalled** *adj*

metal. *or* **metall.** *abbreviation* **1** metallurgical **2** metallurgy

metalanguage ('mɛtəˌlæŋgwɪdʒ) *n* a language or system of symbols used to discuss another language or system. See **object language**

metal detector *n* a device that gives an audible or visual signal when its search head comes close to a metallic object embedded in food, buried in the ground, etc

metallic (mɪ'tælɪk) *adj* **1** of, concerned with, or consisting of metal or a metal **2** suggestive of a metal: *a metallic click; metallic lustre* **3** *chem* (of a metal element) existing in the free state rather than in combination: *metallic copper*

metallic soap *n* any one of a number of colloidal stearates, palmitates, or oleates of various metals, including aluminium, calcium, magnesium, iron, and zinc. They are used as bases for ointments, fungicides, fireproofing and waterproofing agents, and dryers for paints and varnishes

metalliferous (ˌmɛtə'lɪfərəs) *adj* containing a high concentration of metallic elements [c17: from Latin *metallifer* yielding metal, from *metallum* metal + *ferre* to bear]

metallize, metallise *or US* **metalize** ('mɛtəˌlaɪz) *vb* (*tr*) to make metallic or to coat or treat with metal > ˌmetalli'zation, ˌmetalli'sation *or US* ˌmetali'zation *n*

metallography (ˌmɛtə'lɒgrəfɪ) *n* the branch of metallurgy concerned with the composition and structure of metals and alloys > **metallographic** (mɪˌtælə'græfɪk) *adj*

metalloid *n* ('mɛtəˌlɔɪd) **1** a nonmetallic element, such as arsenic or silicon, that has some of the properties of a metal ▷ *adj* Also: **metalloidal** (ˌmɛtə'lɔɪdəl) **2** of or being a metalloid **3** resembling a metal

metallurgy (mɛ'tælədʒɪ; *US* 'mɛtəˌlɜːdʒɪ) *n* the scientific study of the extraction, refining, alloying, and fabrication of metals and of their structure and properties > ˌmetal'lurgic *or* ˌmetal'lurgical *adj* > **metallurgist** (mɛ'tælədʒɪst, 'mɛtəˌlɜːdʒɪst) *n*

metal tape *n* a magnetic recording tape coated with pure iron rather than iron oxide or chromedioxide: it gives enhanced recording quality

metalwork ('mɛtəlˌwɜːk) *n* **1** the craft of working in metal **2** work in metal or articles made from metal

metalworking ('mɛtəlˌwɜːkɪŋ) *n* the processing of metal to change its shape, size, etc, as by rolling, forging, etc, or by making metal articles > **'metalˌworker** *n*

metamere ('mɛtəˌmɪə) *n* one of the similar body segments into which earthworms, crayfish, and similar animals are divided longitudinally [c19: from META- + -MERE] > **metameral** (mɪ'tæmərəl) *adj*

metamerism (mɪ'tæməˌrɪzəm) *n* **1** Also called: **metameric segmentation** *or* **segmentation** the division of an animal into similar segments (metameres). In many vertebrates it is confined to the embryonic nervous and muscular systems **2** *chem* a type of isomerism in which molecular structures differ by the attachment of different groups to the same atom, as in $CH_3OC_3H_7$ and $C_2H_5OC_2H_5$ > **metameric** (ˌmɛtə'mɛrɪk) *adj* > ˌmeta'merically *adv*

metamict ('mɛtəˌmɪkt) *adj* of or denoting the amorphous state of a substance that has lost its crystalline structure as a result of the radioactivity of uranium or thorium within it [c19: from Danish *metamikt*, from META- + Greek *miktos* mixed] > ˌmetamicti'zation *or* ˌmetamicti'sation *n*

metamorphic (ˌmɛtə'mɔːfɪk) *or* **metamorphous** *adj* **1** relating to or resulting from metamorphosis or metamorphism **2** (of rocks) altered considerably from their original structure and mineralogy by pressure and heat

metamorphism (ˌmɛtə'mɔːfɪzəm) *n* **1** the process by which metamorphic rocks are formed **2** a variant of: **metamorphosis**

metamorphose (ˌmɛtə'mɔːfəʊz) *vb* to undergo or cause to undergo metamorphosis or metamorphism

metamorphosis (ˌmɛtə'mɔːfəsɪs) *n, pl* -**ses** (-ˌsiːz) **1** a complete change of physical form or substance **2** a complete change of character, appearance, etc **3** a person or thing that has undergone metamorphosis **4** *zoology* the rapid transformation of a larva into an adult that occurs in certain animals, for example the stage between tadpole and frog or between chrysalis and butterfly [c16: via Latin from Greek: transformation, from META- + *morphē* form]

metaphor ('mɛtəfə, -ˌfɔː) *n* a figure of speech in which a word or phrase is applied to an object or action that it does not literally denote in order to imply a resemblance, for example *he is a lion in battle.* See **simile** [c16: from Latin, from Greek *metaphora*, from *metapherein* to transfer, from META- + *pherein* to bear] > **metaphoric** (ˌmɛtə'fɒrɪk) or ˌmeta'phorical *adj* > ˌmeta'phorically *adv*

metaphrase ('mɛtəˌfreɪz) *n* **1** a literal translation ▷ *vb* (*tr*) **2** to alter or manipulate the wording of **3** to translate literally [c17: from Greek *metaphrazein* to translate]

metaphrast ('mɛtəˌfræst) *n* a person who metaphrases, esp one who changes the form of a text, as by rendering verse into prose [c17: from Medieval Greek *metaphrastēs* translator] > ˌmeta'phrastic or ˌmeta'phrastical *adj* > ˌmeta'phrastically *adv*

metaphysic (ˌmɛtə'fɪzɪk) *n* the system of first principles and assumptions underlying an enquiry or philosophical theory

metaphysical (ˌmɛtə'fɪzɪkᵊl) *adj* **1** relating to or concerned with metaphysics **2** (of a statement or theory) having the form of an empirical hypothesis, but in fact immune from empirical testing and therefore (in the view of the logical positivists) literally meaningless **3** (popularly) abstract, abstruse, or unduly theoretical **4** incorporeal; supernatural > ˌmeta'physically *adv*

Metaphysical (ˌmɛtə'fɪzɪkᵊl) *adj* **1** denoting or relating to certain 17th-century poets who combined intense feeling with ingenious thought and often used elaborate imagery and conceits. Notable among them were Donne, Herbert, and Marvell ▷ *n* **2** a poet of this group

metaphysics (ˌmɛtə'fɪzɪks) *n* (*functioning as singular*) **1** the branch of philosophy that deals with first principles, esp of being and knowing **2** the philosophical study of the nature of reality, concerned with such questions as the existence of God, the external world, etc **3** (popularly) abstract or subtle discussion or reasoning [c16: from Medieval Latin, from Greek *ta meta ta phusika* the things after the physics, from the arrangement of the subjects treated in the works of Aristotle] > **metaphysician** (ˌmɛtəfɪ'zɪʃən) or **metaphysicist** (ˌmɛtə'fɪzɪsɪst) *n*

metapsychology (ˌmɛtəsaɪ'kɒlədʒɪ) *n psychol* **1** the study of philosophical questions, such as the relation between mind and body, that go beyond the laws of experimental psychology **2** any attempt to state the general laws of psychology **3** another word for **parapsychology** > **metapsychological** (ˌmɛtəˌsaɪkə'lɒdʒɪkᵊl) *adj*

metastable (ˌmɛtə'steɪbᵊl) *physics adj* (of a body or system) having a state of apparent equilibrium although capable of changing to a more stable state > ˌmeta'sta'bility *n*

Metastasio (Italian metas'ta:zjo) *n* **Pietro** ('pjɛːtro), original name *Pietro Antonio Domenico Trapassi.* 1698–1782, Italian poet and librettist; Viennese court poet (from 1730). His works include *La clemenza di Tito* (1732)

metastasis (mɪ'tæstəsɪs) *n, pl* -**ses** (-ˌsiːz) *pathol* the spreading of a disease, esp cancer cells, from one part of the body to another [c16: via Latin from Greek: transition] > **metastatic** (ˌmɛtə'stætɪk) *adj* > ˌmeta'statically *adv*

metastasize or **metastasise** (mɪ'tæstəˌsaɪz) *vb* (*intr*) *pathol* (esp of cancer cells) to spread to a new site in the body via blood or lymph vessels

metatarsal (ˌmɛtə'tɑːsᵊl) *anatomy* ▷ *adj* **1** of or relating to the metatarsus ▷ *n* **2** any bone of the metatarsus

metatarsus (ˌmɛtə'tɑːsəs) *n, pl* -**si** (-saɪ) **1** the skeleton of the human foot between the toes and the tarsus, consisting of five long bones **2** the corresponding skeletal part in other vertebrates

metathesis (mɪ'tæθəsɪs) *n, pl* -**ses** (-ˌsiːz) the transposition of two sounds or letters in a word [c16: from Late Latin, from Greek, from *metatithenai* to transpose] > **metathetic** (ˌmɛtə'θɛtɪk) or ˌmeta'thetical *adj*

metaverse ('mɛtəˌvɜːs) *n* **1** a 3D virtual world, esp in an online role-playing game **2** the universe as portrayed in a given work of fiction [c20: from META- + (UNI)VERSE]

metazoan (ˌmɛtə'zəʊən) *n* **1** any multicellular animal of the group *Metazoa*: includes all animals except sponges ▷ *adj* Also: **metazoic 2** of, relating to, or belonging to the *Metazoa* [c19: from New Latin *Metazoa*; see META-, -ZOA]

Metchnikoff (French mɛtʃnikɔf; Russian 'mjetʃnikəf) *n* **Élie** (eli). 1845–1916, Russian bacteriologist in France. He formulated the theory of phagocytosis and shared the Nobel prize for physiology or medicine 1908

mete¹ (miːt) *vb* (*tr*) **1** (usually foll by *out*) *formal* to distribute or allot (something, often unpleasant) ▷ *vb, n* **2** *poetic, dialect* (to) measure [Old English *metan*; compare Old Saxon *metan*, Old Norse *meta*, German *messen* to measure]

mete² (miːt) *n rare* a mark, limit, or boundary (esp in the phrase **metes and bounds**) [c15: from Old French, from Latin *mēta* goal, turning post (in race)]

metempsychosis (ˌmɛtəmsaɪ'kəʊsɪs) *n, pl* -**ses** (-siːz) the migration of a soul from one body to another [c16: via Late Latin from Greek, from *metempsukhousthai*, from META- + -*em*- in + *psukhē* soul] > ˌmetemp'chosist *n*

meteor ('miːtɪə) *n* **1** a very small meteoroid that has entered the earth's atmosphere. Such objects have speeds approaching 70 kilometres per second **2** Also called: **shooting star, falling star** the bright streak of light appearing in the sky due to the incandescence of such a body heated by friction at its surface [c15: from Medieval Latin *meteōrum*, from Greek *meteōron* something aloft, from *meteōros* lofty, from *meta-* (intensifier) + *aeirein* to raise]

meteoric (ˌmiːtɪ'ɒrɪk) *adj* **1** of, formed by, or relating to meteors **2** like a meteor in brilliance, speed, or transience **3** *rare* of or relating to the weather; meteorological > ˌmete'orically *adv*

meteorism ('miːtɪəˌrɪzəm) *n med* another name for **tympanites**

meteorite ('miːtɪəˌraɪt) *n* a rocklike object consisting of the remains of a meteoroid that has fallen on earth. It may be stony (chondrite), iron, or stony iron (pallasite) > **meteoritic** (ˌmiːtɪə'rɪtɪk) *adj*

meteoroid ('miːtɪəˌrɔɪd) *n* any of the small celestial bodies that are thought to orbit the sun, possibly as the remains of comets. When they enter the earth's atmosphere, they become visible as meteors > ˌmeteor'oidal *adj*

meteorol. or **meteor.** *abbreviation* **1** meteorological **2** meteorology

meteorology (ˌmiːtɪə'rɒlədʒɪ) *n* the study of the earth's atmosphere, esp of weather-forming processes and weather forecasting [c17: from Greek *meteorologia*, from *meteōron* something aloft + -*logia* -LOGY. See METEOR] > **meteorological** (ˌmiːtɪərə'lɒdʒɪkᵊl) or ˌmeteoro'logic *adj* > ˌmeteoro'logically *adv* > ˌmeteor'ologist *n*

meteor shower *n* a transient rain of meteors, such as the Perseids, occurring at regular intervals and coming from a particular region in the sky. It is caused by the earth passing through a large number of meteoroids (a **meteor swarm**)

meter¹ ('miːtə) *n* the US spelling of **metre¹**

meter² ('miːtə) *n* the US spelling of **metre²**

meter³ ('miːtə) *n* **1** any device that measures and records the quantity of a substance, such as gas, that has passed through it during a specified period **2** See **parking meter** ▷ *vb* (*tr*) **3** to measure (a rate of flow) with a meter [c19: see METE¹]

-meter *n combining form* **1** indicating an instrument for measuring: *barometer* **2** *prosody* indicating a verse having a specified number of feet: *pentameter* [from Greek *metron* measure]

meth (mɛθ) *n informal* **1** short for **methamphetamine 2** short for **methadone**

Meth. *abbreviation* Methodist

meth- *combining form* indicating a chemical compound derived from methane or containing methyl groups

methacrylic acid (ˌmɛθəˈkrɪlɪk) *n* a colourless crystalline water-soluble substance used in the manufacture of acrylic resins; 2-methylpropenoic acid. Formula: $CH_2{:}C(CH_3)COOH$

methadone (ˈmɛθəˌdəʊn) *or* **methadon** (ˈmɛθəˌdɒn) *n* a narcotic analgesic drug similar to morphine, used to treat opiate addiction. Formula: $C_{21}H_{27}NO$ [c20: from (di)*meth*(*yl*) + A(MINO) + D(IPHENYL) + -ONE]

methamphetamine (ˌmɛθæmˈfɛtəmɪn) *n* a variety of amphetamine used for its stimulant action [c20: from METH- + AMPHETAMINE]

methanal (ˈmɛθəˌnæl) *n* the systematic name for: **formaldehyde**

methane (ˈmiːθeɪn) *n* a colourless odourless flammable gas, the simplest alkane and the main constituent of natural gas: used as a fuel. Formula: CH_4 [c19: from METH(YL) + -ANE]

methane series *n* another name for the **alkane series**. See **alkane**

methanoic acid (ˈmɛθəˌnəʊɪk) *n* the systematic name for: **formic acid**

methanol (ˈmɛθəˌnɒl) *n* a colourless volatile poisonous liquid compound used as a solvent and fuel. Formula: CH_3OH. Also called: methyl alcohol *or* wood alcohol [c20: from METHANE + -OL¹]

methaqualone (ˌmɛθəˈkweɪləʊn) *n* a nonbarbituate sedative drug used to treat stress and insomnia. Formula: $C_{16}H_{14}N_2O$

methicillin (ˌmɛθɪˈsɪlɪn) *n* a semisynthetic penicillin used to treat various infections

methinks (mɪˈθɪŋks) *vb, past* methought (*tr; takes a clause as object*) *archaic* it seems to me

metho (ˈmɛθəʊ) *n Austral* **1** an informal name for: **methylated spirits 2** a drinker of methylated spirits

method (ˈmɛθəd) *n* **1 a** a way of proceeding or doing something, esp a systematic or regular one **2** orderliness of thought, action, etc **3** (*often plural*) the techniques or arrangement of work for a particular field or subject [c16: via French from Latin *methodus,* from Greek *methodos,* literally: a going after, from *meta-* after + *hodos* way]

Method (ˈmɛθəd) *n* (*sometimes not capital*) **a** a technique of acting based on the theories of Stanislavsky, in which the actor bases his role on the inner motivation of the character he plays **b** (*as modifier*): *a Method actor*

methodical (mɪˈθɒdɪkəl) *or less commonly* **methodic** *adj* characterized by method or orderliness; systematic > me'thodically *adv*

Methodism (ˈmɛθəˌdɪzəm) *n* the system and practices of the Methodist Church, developed by the English preacher John Wesley (1703–91) and his followers

Methodist (ˈmɛθədɪst) *n* **1** a member of any of the Nonconformist denominations that derive from the system of faith and practice initiated by the English preacher John Wesley (1703–91) and his followers ▷ *adj* Also: Methodistic *or* Methodistical **2** of or relating to Methodism or the Church embodying it (the **Methodist Church**)

Methodius (mɛˈθəʊdɪəs) *n* **Saint,** with his younger brother Saint Cyril called *the Apostles of the Slavs.* 815–885 AD, Greek Christian theologian sent as a missionary to the Moravians. Feast day: Feb 14 or May 11

methodize *or* **methodise** (ˈmɛθəˌdaɪz) *vb* (*tr*) to organize according to a method; systematize > 'method,izer *or* 'method,iser *n*

methodology (ˌmɛθəˈdɒlədʒɪ) *n, pl* -gies **1** the system of methods and principles used in a particular discipline **2** the branch of philosophy concerned with the science of method and procedure > methodological (ˌmɛθədəˈlɒdʒɪkəl) *adj* > ˌmethodoˈlogically *adv* > ˌmethodˈologist *n*

methought (mɪˈθɔːt) *vb archaic* the past tense of **methinks**

meths (mɛθs) *n chiefly Brit, Austral & NZ* an informal name for **methylated spirits**

Methuselah (mɪˈθjuːzələ) *n Old Testament* a patriarch supposed to have lived 969 years (Genesis 5:21–27) who

has come to be regarded as epitomizing longevity

methyl (ˈmiːθaɪl, ˈmɛθɪl) *n* **1** (*modifier*) of, consisting of, or containing the monovalent group of atoms CH_3 **2** an organometallic compound in which methyl groups are bound directly to a metal atom [c19: from French *méthyle,* back formation from METHYLENE] > methylic (məˈθɪlɪk) *adj*

methyl acetate *n* a colourless volatile flammable liquid ester with a fragrant odour, used as a solvent, esp in paint removers. Formula: CH_3COOCH_3

methyl alcohol *n* another name for **methanol**

methylate (ˈmɛθɪˌleɪt) *vb* (*tr*) to mix with methanol

methylated spirits *or* **methylated spirit** *n* (*functioning as singular or plural*) alcohol that has been denatured by the addition of methanol and pyridine and a violet dye. Also called: metho, meths

methyl chloride *n* a colourless gas with an ether-like odour, used as a refrigerant and anaesthetic. Formula: CH_3Cl

methylene (ˈmɛθɪˌliːn) *n* (*modifier*) of, consisting of, or containing the divalent group of atoms =CH_2: *a methylene group or radical* [c19: from French *méthylène,* from Greek *methu* wine + *hulē* wood + -ENE: originally referring to a substance distilled from wood]

meticulous (mɪˈtɪkjʊləs) *adj* very precise about details, even trivial ones; painstaking [c16 (meaning: timid): from Latin *meticulōsus* fearful, from *metus* fear] > me'ticulously *adv* > me'ticulousness *n*

métier (ˈmɛtɪeɪ) *n* **1** a profession or trade, esp that to which one is well suited **2** a person's strong point or speciality [c18: from French, ultimately from Latin *ministerium* service]

me-time *n* the time a person has to himself or herself, in which to do something for his or her own enjoyment

Métis (meɪˈtiːs) *n, pl* -tis (-ˈtiːs, -ˈtiːz) **1** a person of mixed parentage **2** *Canadian* the offspring or a descendant of a French Canadian and a North American Indian [c19: from French, from Vulgar Latin *mixtīcius* (unattested) of mixed race; compare MESTIZO] > **Métisse** (meˈtiːs) *fem n*

metol (ˈmiːtɒl) *n* a colourless soluble organic substance used, in the form of its sulphate, as a photographic developer; *p*-methylaminophenol [c20: from German, an arbitrary coinage]

Metonic cycle (mɪˈtɒnɪk) *n* a cycle of nearly 235 synodic months after which the phases of the moon recur on the same days of the year [c17: named after *Meton,* 5th-century BC Athenian astronomer]

metonymy (mɪˈtɒnɪmɪ) *n, pl* -mies the substitution of a word referring to an attribute for the thing that is meant, as for example the use of the *crown* to refer to a monarch. See **synecdoche** [c16: from Late Latin from Greek: a changing of name, from *meta-* (indicating change) + *onoma* name] > metonymical (ˌmɛtəˈnɪmɪkəl) *or* ˌmetoˈnymic *adj*

metope (ˈmɛtəʊp, ˈmɛtəpɪ) *n architect* a square space between two triglyphs in a Doric frieze [c16: via Latin from Greek *metopē,* from *meta* between + *opē* one of the holes for the beam-ends]

metre¹ *or US* **meter** (ˈmiːtə) *n* **1** a metric unit of length equal to approximately 1.094 yards **2** the basic SI unit of length; the length of the path travelled by light in free space during a time interval of 1/299 792 458 of a second. In 1983 this definition replaced the previous one based on krypton-86, which in turn had replaced the definition based on the platinum-iridium metre bar kept in Paris ▷ Symbol: m^2 [c18: from French; see METRE²]

metre² *or US* **meter** (ˈmiːtə) *n* **1** *prosody* the rhythmic arrangement of syllables in verse, usually according to the number and kind of feet in a line **2** *music* another word (esp US) for: **time** (sense 22) [c14: from Latin *metrum,* from Greek *metron* measure]

metre-kilogram-second *n* See **mks units**

metric (ˈmɛtrɪk) *adj* of or relating to the metre or metric system

metrical (ˈmɛtrɪkəl) *or* **metric** (ˈmɛtrɪk) *adj* **1** of or relating to measurement **2** of or in poetic metre > 'metrically *adv*

metricate (ˈmɛtrɪˌkeɪt) *vb* to convert (a measuring

system, instrument, etc) from nonmetric to metric units > ˌmetriˈcation n

metric system n any decimal system of units based on the metre. For scientific purposes the Système International d'Unités (SI units) is used

metric ton n another name (not in technical use) for **tonne**

metro (ˈmɛtrəʊ) or **métro** (French metro) n, pl **-ros** an underground, or largely underground, railway system in certain cities, esp in Europe, such as that in Paris [c20: from French, short for chemin de fer métropolitain metropolitan railway]

metronome (ˈmɛtrəˌnəʊm) n a mechanical device which indicates the exact tempo of a piece of music by producing a clicking sound from a pendulum with an adjustable period of swing [c19: from Greek metron measure + nomos rule, law] > metronomic (ˌmɛtrəˈnɒmɪk) adj

metronymic (ˌmɛtrəˈnɪmɪk) or less commonly **matronymic** adj 1 (of a name) derived from the name of its bearer's mother or another female ancestor ▷ n 2 a metronymic name [c19: from Greek mētronumikos, from mētēr mother + onoma name]

metropolis (mɪˈtrɒpəlɪs) n, pl **-lises** 1 the main city, esp of a country or region; capital 2 a centre of activity 3 the chief see in an ecclesiastical province [c16: from Late Latin from Greek: mother city or state, from mētēr mother + polis city]

metropolitan (ˌmɛtrəˈpɒlɪtən) adj 1 of or characteristic of a metropolis 2 constituting a city and its suburbs 3 of, relating to, or designating an ecclesiastical metropolis 4 of or belonging to the home territories of a country, as opposed to overseas territories: metropolitan France ▷ n 5 a Eastern Churches the head of an ecclesiastical province, ranking between archbishop and patriarch b Church of England an archbishop c RC Church an archbishop or bishop having authority in certain matters over the dioceses in his province > ˌmetroˈpolitanism n

metropolitan county n (in England) any of the six conurbations established as administrative units in the new local government system in 1974; the metropolitan county councils were abolished in 1986

metropolitan district n any of the districts making up the metropolitan counties of England: since 1986 they have functioned as unitary authorities, forming the sole principal tier of local government. Each metropolitan district has an elected council responsible for education, social services, etc

Metropolitan Museum of Art n the principal museum in New York City: founded in 1870 and housed in its present premises in Central Park since 1880

metrorrhagia (ˌmiːtrɔːˈreɪdʒɪə, ˌmɛt-) n abnormal bleeding from the uterus [C19 NL, from Gk, mētra womb + -rraghia a breaking forth]

metrosexual (ˌmɛtrəʊˈsɛksjʊəl) informal ▷ n 1 a heterosexual man who spends a lot of time and money on his appearance and likes to shop ▷ adj 2 of or relating to metrosexuals

-metry n combining form indicating the process or science of measuring: anthropometry; geometry [from Old French -metrie, from Latin -metria, from Greek, from metron measure] > -metric adj combining form

Metsys (Flemish ˈmetsaɪs) n a variant spelling of (Quentin): Massys

Metternich (German ˈmɛtərnɪç) n **Klemens** (ˈkleːməns). 1773–1859, Austrian statesman. He became foreign minister (1809) and made a significant contribution to the Congress of Vienna (1815). From 1821 to 1848 he was both foreign minister and chancellor of Austria and is noted for his defence of autocracy in Europe

mettle (ˈmɛtəl) n 1 courage; spirit 2 inherent character 3 on one's mettle roused to putting forth one's best efforts [c16: originally variant spelling of METAL]

mettled (ˈmɛtəld) or **mettlesome** (ˈmɛtəlsəm) adj spirited, courageous, or valiant

Metz (mɛts; French mɛs) n a city in NE France on the River Moselle: a free imperial city in the 13th century; annexed by France in 1552; part of Germany (1871–1918);

centre of the Lorraine iron-mining region. Pop: 123 776 (1999)

Meung (French mœ) n See **Jean de Meung**

Meurthe-et-Moselle (French mœrtemozɛl) n a department of NE France, in Lorraine region. Capital: Nancy. Pop: 718 250 (2003 est). Area: 5280 sq km (2059 sq miles)

Meuse (mɜːz; French møz) n 1 a department of N France, in Lorraine region: heavy fighting occurred here in World War I. Capital: Bar-le-Duc. Pop: 191 728 (2003 est). Area: 6241 sq km (2434 sq miles) 2 a river in W Europe, rising in NE France and flowing north across E Belgium and the S Netherlands to join the Waal River before entering the North Sea. Length: 926 km (575 miles). Dutch name: **Maas**

MeV symbol for million electronvolts (10^6 electronvolts)

mevrou (məˈfrəʊ) n a South African title of address equivalent to Mrs when placed before a surname or madam when used alone [Afrikaans]

mew[1] (mjuː) vb 1 (intr) (esp of a cat) to make a characteristic high-pitched cry ▷ n 2 such a sound [c14: imitative]

mew[2] (mjuː) n any seagull, esp the common gull, Larus canus [Old English mǣw; compare Old Saxon mēu, Middle Dutch mēwe]

mew[3] (mjuː) n 1 a room or cage for hawks, esp while moulting ▷ vb 2 (tr, often foll by up) to confine (hawks or falcons) in a shelter, cage, etc, usually by tethering them to a perch 3 to confine, conceal [c14: from Old French mue, from muer to moult, from Latin mūtāre to change]

Mewar (mɛˈwɑː) n another name for **Udaipur** (sense 1)

mewl (mjuːl) vb 1 (intr) (esp of a baby) to cry weakly; whimper (often in the phrase **mewl and puke**) ▷ n 2 such a cry [c17: imitative]

mews (mjuːz) n (functioning as singular or plural) chiefly Brit 1 a yard or street lined by buildings originally used as stables but now often converted into dwellings 2 the buildings around a mews [c14: pl of MEW[3], originally referring to royal stables built on the site of hawks' mews at Charing Cross in London]

Mex. abbreviation 1 Mexican 2 Mexico

Mexicali (ˌmɛksɪˈkɑːlɪ; Spanish mexiˈkali) n a city in NW Mexico, capital of Baja California (Norte) state, on the border with the US adjoining Calexico, California: centre of a rich irrigated agricultural region. Pop: 840 000 (2005 est)

Mexican wave n the rippling effect produced when the spectators in successive sections of a sports stadium stand up while raising their arms and then sit down [c20: so called because it was first demonstrated at the World Cup in Mexico in 1986]

Mexico (ˈmɛksɪˌkəʊ) n 1 a republic in North America, on the Gulf of Mexico and the Pacific: early Mexican history includes the Maya, Toltec, and Aztec civilizations; conquered by the Spanish between 1519 and 1525 and achieved independence in 1821; lost Texas to the US in 1836 and California and New Mexico in 1848. It is generally mountainous with three ranges of the Sierra Madre (east, west, and south) and a large central plateau. Official language: Spanish. Religion: Roman Catholic majority. Currency: peso. Capital: Mexico City. Pop: 104 931 000 (2004 est). Area: 1 967 183 sq km (761 530 sq miles). Spanish name: **Méjico** 2 a state of Mexico, on the central plateau surrounding Mexico City, which is not administratively part of the state. Capital: Toluca. Pop: 13 096 686 (2000). Area: 21 460 sq km (8287 sq miles) 3 Gulf of Mexico an arm of the Atlantic, bordered by the US, Cuba, and Mexico: linked with the Atlantic by the Straits of Florida and with the Caribbean by the Yucatán Channel. Area: about 1 600 000 sq km (618 000 sq miles) > Mexican (ˈmɛksɪkən) adj, n

Mexico City n the capital of Mexico, on the central plateau at an altitude of 2240 m (7350 ft): founded as the Aztec capital (Tenochtitlán) in about 1300; conquered and rebuilt by the Spanish in 1521; forms, with its suburbs, the federal district of Mexico; the largest industrial complex in the country. Pop: 19 013 000 (2005 est)

m

Meyerbeer (German ˈmaiərbeːr) n **Giacomo** (ˈdʒaːkomo), real name Jakob Liebmann Beer. 1791–1864, German composer, esp of operas, such as Robert le diable (1831) and Les Huguenots (1836)

Meyerhof (German ˈmaiərhoːf) n **Otto** (**Fritz**) (ˈɔto). 1884–1951, German physiologist, noted for his work on the metabolism of muscles. He shared the Nobel prize for physiology or medicine 1922

Meyerhold (ˈmaiəhəʊlt) n **Vsevolod Emilievich**, original name Karl Theodor Kasimir. 1874–c. 1940, Russian theatre director, noted for his experimental nonrealistic productions. He was arrested in 1939 and died in custody

MEZ abbreviation Central European Time [from German Mitteleuropäische Zeit]

mezcal (mɛˈskæl) n a variant spelling of **mescal**

mezcaline (ˈmɛskəˌliːn) n a variant spelling of **mescaline**

Mézières (French mezjɛr) n a town in NE France, on the River Meuse opposite Charleville. See **Charleville-Mézières**

mezuzah (məˈzʊzə, -ˈzuː-; Hebrew məzuˈza; Yiddish məˈzuzə) n, pl **-zuzahs** or **-zuzoth** (Hebrew -zuˈzɔt) Judaism **1** a piece of parchment inscribed with biblical passages and fixed to the doorpost of the rooms of a Jewish house **2** a metal case for such a parchment, sometimes worn as an ornament [from Hebrew, literally: doorpost]

mezzanine (ˈmɛzəˌniːn, ˈmɛtsəˌniːn) n **1** Also called: mezzanine floor, entresol an intermediate storey, esp a low one between the ground and first floor of a building **2** theatre, US & Canadian the first balcony **3** theatre, Brit a room or floor beneath the stage ▷ adj **4** of or relating to an intermediate stage in a financial process: mezzanine funding [c18: from French, from Italian, diminutive of mezzano middle, from Latin mediānus MEDIAN]

mezzo (ˈmɛtsəʊ) music adv moderately; quite: mezzo forte; mezzo piano [c19: from Italian, literally: half, from Latin medius middle]

mezzo-soprano n, pl **-nos 1** a female voice intermediate between a soprano and contralto and having a range from the A below middle C to the F an eleventh above it **2** a singer with such a voice

mezzotint (ˈmɛtsəʊˌtɪnt) n **1** a method of engraving a copper plate by scraping and burnishing the roughened surface **2** a print made from a plate so treated ▷ vb **3** (tr) to engrave (a copper plate) in this fashion [c18: from Italian mezzotinto half tint]

mf music abbreviation mezzo forte [Italian: moderately loud]

MF abbreviation **1** radio medium frequency **2** Middle French

MFAT (ˈɛmfæt) n acronym for (in New Zealand) Ministry of Foreign Affairs and Trade

mfd abbreviation manufactured

mfg abbreviation manufacturing

MFH hunting abbreviation Master of Foxhounds

mfr abbreviation **1** manufacture **2** manufacturer

mg symbol for milligram

Mg the chemical symbol for magnesium

Mgr abbreviation **1** manager **2** Monseigneur **3** Monsignor

MHA abbreviation Australia Member of the House of Assembly

MHG abbreviation Middle High German

mho (məʊ) n, pl **mhos** the former name for **siemens** [c19: formed by reversing the letters of OHM (first used by Lord Kelvin)]

MHR abbreviation (in the US and Australia) Member of the House of Representatives

MHz symbol for megahertz

mi or **me** (miː) n music (in tonic sol-fa) the third degree of any major scale; mediant [c16: see GAMUT]

MI abbreviation **1** Michigan **2** Military Intelligence

mi. abbreviation mile

MI5 abbreviation Military Intelligence, section five; a former official and present-day popular name for the counterintelligence agency of the British Government

MI6 abbreviation Military Intelligence, section six; a former official and present-day popular name for the intelligence and espionage agency of the British Government

Miami (maɪˈæmɪ) n a city and resort in SE Florida, on Biscayne Bay: developed chiefly after 1896, esp with the Florida land boom of the 1920s; centre of an extensive tourist area. Pop: 376 815 (2003 est)

Miami Beach n a resort in SE Florida, on an island separated from Miami by Biscayne Bay. Pop: 89 312 (2003 est)

Miandad (mɪˈændæd) n **Javed** (ˈdʒævɪd). born 1957, Pakistani cricketer, a famous batsman; played for Pakistan 1976–94; national team coach 1999–2001

miaou or **miaow** (mɪˈaʊ, mjaʊ) vb, interj variant spellings of **meow**

miasma (mɪˈæzmə) n, pl **-mata** (-mətə) or **-mas 1** an unwholesome or foreboding atmosphere **2** pollution in the atmosphere, esp noxious vapours from decomposing organic matter [c17: New Latin, from Greek: defilement, from miainein to defile] > **miˈasmal** or **miasmatic** (ˌmaɪəzˈmætɪk) adj

Mic. Bible abbreviation Micah

mica (ˈmaɪkə) n any of a group of lustrous rock-forming minerals consisting of hydrous silicates of aluminium, potassium, etc, in monoclinic crystalline form, occurring in igneous and metamorphic rock. Because of their resistance to electricity and heat they are used as dielectrics, in heating elements, etc [c18: from Latin: grain, morsel] > **micaceous** (maɪˈkeɪʃəs) adj

Micah (ˈmaɪkə) n Old Testament **1** a Hebrew prophet of the late 8th century BC **2** the book containing his prophecies

mice (maɪs) n the plural of **mouse**

micelle, micell (mɪˈsɛl) or **micella** (mɪˈsɛlə) n chem **a** a charged aggregate of molecules of colloidal size in a solution **b** any molecular aggregate of colloidal size, such as a particle found in coal [c19: from New Latin micella, diminutive of Latin mīca crumb]

Mich. abbreviation Michigan

Michael (ˈmaɪkᵊl) n **1** 1596–1645, tsar of Russia (1613–45); founder of the Romanov dynasty **2** born 1921, king of Romania (1927–30, as part of a three-part regency; 1940–47), who relinquished the throne (1930–40) in favour of his father, Carol II. He led the coup d'état that overthrew (1944) Antonescu but was forced to abdicate (1947) by the Communists **3** Saint Michael Bible one of the archangels. Feast day: Sept 29 or Nov 8

Michaelmas (ˈmɪkᵊlməs) n Sept 29, the feast of St Michael the archangel; in England, Ireland, and Wales, one of the four quarter days

Michaelmas daisy n Brit any of various plants of the genus Aster that have small autumn-blooming purple, pink, or white flowers: family Asteraceae (composites)

Michaelmas term n the autumn term at Oxford and Cambridge Universities, the Inns of Court, and some other educational establishments

Michael VIII n surnamed Palaeologus (ˈpælɪəˌləʊgəs). 1224–82, Byzantine emperor (1259–82); founder of the Palaeologan dynasty. His reign saw the recovery of Constantinople from the Latins (1261) and the reunion (1274) of the Greek and Roman churches

Michelangelo (ˌmaɪkᵊlˈændʒɪˌləʊ) n full name Michelangelo Buonarroti. 1475–1564, Florentine sculptor, painter, architect, and poet; one of the outstanding figures of the Renaissance. Among his creations are the sculptures of David (1504) and of Moses which was commissioned for the tomb of Julius II, for whom he also painted the ceiling of the Sistine Chapel (1508–12). The Last Judgment (1533–41), also in the Sistine, includes a torturous vision of Hell and a disguised self-portrait. His other works include the design of the Laurentian Library (1523–29) and of the dome of St Peter's, Rome

Michelet (French miʃlɛ) n **Jules** (ʒyl). 1798–1874, French historian, noted esp for his Histoire de France (17 vols, 1833–67)

Michelin (French miʃəlɛ̃) n **André** (ɑ̃dre). 1853–1931, French industrialist; founder, with his brother **Édouard Michelin** (1859–1940), of the Michelin Tyre Company (1888): the first to use demountable pneumatic tyres on motor vehicles

Michelozzo (Italian mikeˈlɔttso) n full name Michelozzo di Bartolommeo. 1396–1472, Italian architect and sculptor. His most important design was the Palazzo Riccardo for the

Medici family in Florence (1444–59)

Michelson ('maɪkəlsən) *n* **Albert Abraham**. 1852–1931, US physicist, born in Germany: noted for his part in the Michelson-Morley experiment: Nobel prize for physics 1907

Michigan ('mɪʃɪgən) *n* **1** a state of the N central US, occupying two peninsulas between Lakes Superior, Huron, Michigan, and Erie: generally low-lying. Capital: Lansing. Pop: 10 079 985 (2003 est). Area: 147 156 sq km (56 817 sq miles). Abbreviations: **Mich.**, or (with zip code) **MI** **2** **Lake Michigan** a lake in the N central US between Wisconsin and Michigan: the third largest of the five Great Lakes and the only one wholly in the US; linked with Lake Huron by the Straits of Mackinac. Area: 58 000 sq km (22 400 sq miles) ▷ **Michigander** (ˌmɪʃɪ'gændə) *n* ▷ **Michigan,ite** *n, adj*

Michoacán (*Spanish* mitʃoa'kan) *n* a state of SW Mexico, on the Pacific: rich mineral resources. Capital: Morelia. Pop: 3 979 177 (2000). Area: 59 864 sq km (23 114 sq miles)

Mick (mɪk) or **Mickey** ('mɪkɪ) *n* **1** (*sometimes not capital*) *derogatory* a slang name for an Irishman or a Roman Catholic **2** *Austral* the tails side of a coin [c19: from the nickname for *Michael*]

mickey¹ or **micky** ('mɪkɪ) *n* **take the mickey** or **take the mickey out of someone** *informal* to tease someone [c20: of unknown origin]

mickey² ('mɪkɪ) *n* *Canadian* a liquor bottle of 0.375 litre capacity, flat on one side and curved on the other to fit into a pocket [c20: of unknown origin]

Mickey Finn *n* *slang* **a** a drink containing a drug to make the drinker unconscious, usually formed by the combination of chloral hydrate and alcohol. It can be poisonous **b** the drug itself [c20: of unknown origin]

Mickiewicz (*Polish* mits'kjɛvitʃ) *n* **Adam** ('adam). 1798–1855, Polish poet, whose epic *Thaddeus* (1834) is regarded as a masterpiece of Polish literature

mickle ('mɪkəl) or **muckle** ('mʌkəl) *Scot & Northern English dialect* *adj* **1** great or abundant ▷ *adv* **2** much; greatly ▷ *n* **3** a great amount, esp in the proverb, *many a little makes a mickle* **4** *Scot* a small amount, esp in the proverb, *many a mickle maks a muckle* [c13 *mikel*, from Old Norse *mikell*, replacing Old English *micel* MUCH]

micro ('maɪkrəu) *adj* **1** very small ▷ *n, pl* **-cros** **2** short for **microcomputer, microprocessor, microwave oven**

micro- or **micr-** *combining form* **1** small or minute: *microspore* **2** involving the use of a microscope: *micrography* **3** indicating a method or instrument for dealing with small quantities: *micrometer* **4** (in pathology) indicating abnormal smallness or underdevelopment: *microcephaly*; *microcyte* **5** denoting 10⁻⁶: *microsecond*. Symbol: μ [from Greek *mikros* small]

microarray (ˌmaɪkrəuə'reɪ) *n* another name for **biochip**

microbe ('maɪkrəub) *n* any microscopic organism, esp a disease-causing bacterium [c19: from French, from MICRO- + Greek *bios* life] ▷ **mi'crobial** or **mi'crobic** *adj*

microbiology (ˌmaɪkrəubaɪ'ɒlədʒɪ) *n* the branch of biology involving the study of microorganisms ▷ **microbiological** (ˌmaɪkrəuˌbaɪə'lɒdʒɪkəl) or ˌmicro,bio'logic *adj* ▷ ˌmicro,bio'logically *adv* ▷ ˌmicrobi'ologist *n*

microbrewery (ˌmaɪkrəu'bruərɪ) *n, pl* **-ries** a small, usually independent brewery that produces limited quantities of specialized beers, often sold for consumption on the premises

microcephaly (ˌmaɪkrəu'sɛfəlɪ) *n* the condition of having an abnormally small head or cranial capacity ▷ **microcephalic** (ˌmaɪkrəusɪ'fælɪk) *adj, n* ▷ ˌmicro'cephalous *adj*

microchemistry (ˌmaɪkrəu'kɛmɪstrɪ) *n* chemical experimentation with minute quantities of material ▷ ˌmicro'chemical *adj*

microchip ('maɪkrəu,tʃɪp) *n* **1** a small piece of semiconductor material carrying many integrated circuits ▷ *vb* **-chips, -chipping, -chipped** **2** (*tr*) to implant (an animal) with a microchip tag linked to a national computer network for purposes of identification

microcircuit ('maɪkrəu,sɜːkɪt) *n* a miniature electronic circuit, esp one in which a number of permanently connected components are contained in one small chip

of semiconducting material. See **integrated circuit** ▷ ˌmicro'circuitry *n*

microclimate ('maɪkrəu,klaɪmɪt) *n* *ecology* the atmospheric conditions affecting an individual or a small group of organisms, esp when they differ from the climate of the rest of the community ▷ **microclimatic** (ˌmaɪkrəuklaɪ'mætɪk) *adj* ▷ ˌmicro,clima'tology *n* ▷ **microclimatologic** (ˌmaɪkrəuˌklaɪmətə'lɒdʒɪk) or ˌmicro,climato'logical *adj* ▷ ˌmicro,clima'tologist *n*

microcomputer ('maɪkrəukəm'pjuːtə) *n* a small computer in which the central processing unit is contained in one or more silicon chips

microcosm ('maɪkrəu,kɒzəm) or **microcosmos** (ˌmaɪkrəu'kɒzmɒs) *n* **1** a miniature representation of something, esp a unit, group, or place regarded as a copy of a larger one **2** man regarded as epitomizing the universe ▷ See **macrocosm** [c15: via Medieval Latin from Greek *mikros kosmos* little world] ▷ ˌmicro'cosmic or ˌmicro'cosmical *adj*

micro-credit ('maɪkrəu,krɛdɪt) *n* the practice of lending small amounts of money on minimal security, esp to help small businesses and communities in the developing world

microdermabrasion (ˌmaɪkrəuˌdɜːmə'breɪʒən) *n* a cosmetic procedure in which rough facial skin is removed by the application of a fine abrasive spray

microdot ('maɪkrəu,dɒt) *n* **1** a microcopy about the size of a pinhead, used esp in espionage **2** a tiny tablet containing LSD

microeconomics (ˌmaɪkrəuˌiːkə'nɒmɪks, -ˌɛkə-) *n* (*functioning as singular*) the branch of economics concerned with particular commodities, firms, or individuals and the economic relationships between them ▷ ˌmicro,eco'nomic *adj*

microelectronics (ˌmaɪkrəuˌɪlɛk'trɒnɪks) *n* (*functioning as singular*) the branch of electronics concerned with microcircuits

microfibre or *US* **microfiber** ('maɪkrəu,faɪbə) *n* a very fine synthetic fibre used for textiles

microfiche ('maɪkrəu,fiːʃ) *n* a sheet of film, usually the size of a filing card, on which books, newspapers, documents, etc, can be recorded in miniaturized form [c20: from French, from MICRO- + *fiche* small card, from Old French *fichier* to fix]

microfilm ('maɪkrəu,fɪlm) *n* **1** a strip of film of standard width on which books, newspapers, documents, etc, can be recorded in miniaturized form ▷ *vb* **2** to photograph (a page, document, etc) on microfilm

microflora ('maɪkrəu,flɔːrə) *n* the community of microorganisms, including algae, fungi, and bacteria that live in or on another living organism or in a particular habitat

microgravity ('maɪkrəu,grævɪtɪ) *n* the very low apparent gravity experienced in a spacecraft in earth orbit

microhabitat (ˌmaɪkrəu'hæbɪtæt) *n* *ecology* the smallest part of the environment that supports a distinct flora and fauna, such as a fallen log in a forest

microlight or **microlite** ('maɪkrəu,laɪt) *n* a small private aircraft carrying no more than two people, with an empty weight of not more than 150 kg and a wing area not less than 10 square metres: used in pleasure flying and racing

microlith ('maɪkrəu,lɪθ) *n* *archaeol* a small Mesolithic flint tool which was made from a blade and formed part of hafted tools ▷ ˌmicro'lithic *adj*

micrometer (maɪ'krɒmɪtə) *n* **1** any of various instruments or devices for the accurate measurement of distances or angles **2** Also called: **micrometer gauge, micrometer calliper** a type of gauge for the accurate measurement of small distances, thicknesses, diameters, etc. The gap between its measuring faces is adjusted by a fine screw, the rotation of the screw giving a sensitive measure of the distance moved by the face ▷ **mi'crometry** *n* ▷ **micrometric** (ˌmaɪkrəu'mɛtrɪk) or ˌmicro'metrical *adj*

microminiaturization or **microminiaturisation** (ˌmaɪkrəuˌmɪnɪtʃəraɪ'zeɪʃən) *n* the production and

m

application of very small semiconductor components and the circuits and equipment in which they are used

micron ('maɪkrɒn) n, pl -crons or -cra (-krə) a unit of length equal to 10⁻⁶ metre. It is being replaced by the micrometre, the equivalent SI unit [C19: New Latin, from Greek *mikros* small]

Micronesia (,maɪkrəʊ'niːzɪə) n 1 one of the three divisions of islands in the Pacific (the others being Melanesia and Polynesia); the NW division of Oceania: includes the Mariana, Caroline, Marshall, and Kiribati island groups, and Nauru Island 2 **Federated States of Micronesia** an island group in the W Pacific, formerly within the United States Trust Territory of the Pacific Islands: comprises the islands of Truk, Yap, Ponape, and Kosrae: formed in 1979 when the islands became self-governing: status of free association with the US from 1982. Languages: English and Micronesian languages. Religion: Christian majority. Currency: US dollar. Capital: Palikir. Pop: 111 000 (2004 est) [C19: from MICRO- + Greek *nēsos* island; so called from the small size of many of the islands; on the model of *Polynesia*]

Micronesian (,maɪkrəʊ'niːzɪən) adj 1 of or relating to Micronesia, its inhabitants, or their languages ▷ n 2 a native or inhabitant of Micronesia, more akin to the Polynesians than the Melanesians, but having Mongoloid traces 3 a group of languages spoken in Micronesia, belonging to the Malayo-Polynesian family

microorganism (,maɪkrəʊ'ɔːgə,nɪzəm) n any organism, such as a bacterium, protozoan, or virus, of microscopic size

micropayment ('maɪkrəʊ,peɪmənt) n a system whereby a user pays a small fee to access a specific area of a website

microphone ('maɪkrə,fəʊn) n a device used in sound-reproduction systems for converting sound into electrical energy, usually by means of a ribbon or diaphragm set into motion by the sound waves. The vibrations are converted into the equivalent audio-frequency electric currents ▷ microphonic (,maɪkrə'fɒnɪk) adj

microprint ('maɪkrəʊ,prɪnt) n a microphotograph reproduced on paper and read by a magnifying device. It is used in order to reduce the size of large books, etc

microprocessor (,maɪkrəʊ'prəʊsɛsə) n computing a single integrated circuit performing the basic functions of the central processing unit in a small computer

micro-scooter n a foldable lightweight aluminium foot-propelled scooter, used by both adults and children

microscope ('maɪkrə,skəʊp) n 1 an optical instrument that uses a lens or combination of lenses to produce a magnified image of a small, close object. Modern optical microscopes have magnifications of about 1500 to 2000 2 any instrument, such as the electron microscope, for producing a magnified visual image of a small object

microscopic (,maɪkrə'skɒpɪk) or less commonly **microscopical** adj 1 not large enough to be seen with the naked eye but visible under a microscope 2 very small; minute 3 of, concerned with, or using a microscope ▷ ,micro'scopically adv

microscopy (maɪ'krɒskəpɪ) n 1 the study, design, and manufacture of microscopes 2 investigation by use of a microscope ▷ microscopist (maɪ'krɒskəpɪst) n

microsecond ('maɪkrəʊ,sɛkənd) n one millionth of a second

microsite ('maɪkrəʊ,saɪt) n a website that is intended for a specific limited purpose and is often temporary

microstate ('maɪkrəʊ,steɪt) n a very small nation that is an internationally-recognized sovereign state. Also called: mini-state

microstructure ('maɪkrəʊ,strʌktʃə) n structure on a microscopic scale, esp the structure of an alloy as observed by etching, polishing, and observation under a microscope

microsurgery (,maɪkrəʊ'sɜːdʒərɪ) n intricate surgery performed on cells, tissues, etc, using a specially designed operating microscope and miniature precision instruments

microswitch ('maɪkrəʊ,swɪtʃ) n electrical engineering a switch that operates by small movements of a lever

microtome ('maɪkrəʊ,təʊm) n an instrument used for cutting thin sections, esp of biological material, for microscopical examination ▷ microtomy (maɪ'krɒtəmɪ) n, pl -mies ▷ microtomic (,maɪkrəʊ'tɒmɪk) or ,micro'tomical adj ▷ mi'crotomist n

microwave ('maɪkrəʊ,weɪv) n 1 a electromagnetic radiation in the wavelength range 0.3 to 0.001 metres: used in radar, cooking, etc b (as modifier): microwave generator 2 short for **microwave oven** ▷ vb (tr) 3 to cook in a microwave oven

microwave background n a background of microwave electromagnetic radiation with a black-body spectrum discovered in 1965, understood to be the thermal remnant of the big bang with which the universe began

microwave detector n a device for recording the speed of a motorist

microwave oven n an oven in which food is cooked by microwaves. Often shortened to: micro, microwave

microwave spectroscopy n a type of spectroscopy in which information is obtained on the structure and chemical bonding of molecules and crystals by measurements of the wavelengths of microwaves emitted or absorbed by the sample ▷ microwave spectroscope n

micturate ('mɪktjʊ,reɪt) vb (intr) a less common word for urinate [C19: from Latin *micturīre* to desire to urinate, from *mingere* to urinate] ▷ micturition (,mɪktjʊ'rɪʃən) n

mid¹ (mɪd) adj 1 phonetics of, relating to, or denoting a vowel whose articulation lies approximately halfway between high and low, such as *e* in English *bet* ▷ n 2 an archaic word for **middle** [C12 *midre* (inflected form of *midd*, unattested); related to Old Norse *mithr*, Gothic *midjis*]

mid² or **'mid** (mɪd) prep a poetic word for **amid**

mid- combining form indicating a middle part, point, time, or position: midday; mid-April; mid-Victorian [Old English; see MIDDLE, MID¹]

midair (,mɪd'ɛə) n a some point above ground level, in the air b (as modifier): a midair collision of aircraft

Midas ('maɪdəs) n 1 Greek legend a king of Phrygia given the power by Dionysus of turning everything he touched to gold 2 the Midas touch ability to make money

mid-Atlantic adj characterized by a blend of British and American styles, elements, etc: a disc jockey's mid-Atlantic accent

midbrain ('mɪd,breɪn) n the nontechnical name for mesencephalon

midday ('mɪd'deɪ) n a the middle of the day; noon b (as modifier): a midday meal

Middelburg ('mɪdəl,bɜːg; Dutch 'mɪdəlbyrx) n a city in the SW Netherlands, capital of Zeeland province, on Walcheren Island: an important trading centre in the Middle Ages and member of the Hanseatic League; 12th-century abbey; market town. Pop: 46 000 (2003 est)

middelmannetjie (,mɪdəl'mænɪkɪ) n a continuous hump between wheel ruts on a dirt road [from Afrikaans, literally: little man in the middle]

middelskot ('mɪdəl,skɒt) n (in South Africa) an intermediate payment to a farmers' cooperative for a crop or wool clip [from Afrik. *middel* middle + *skot* payment]

midden ('mɪdən) n 1 a archaic or dialect a dunghill or pile of refuse b dialect a dustbin 2 See **kitchen midden** [C14: from Scandinavian; compare Danish *mödding* from *møg* MUCK + *dynge* pile]

middle ('mɪdəl) adj 1 equally distant from the ends or periphery of something; central 2 intermediate in status, situation, etc 3 located between the early and late parts of a series, time sequence, etc 4 not extreme, esp in size; medium 5 (esp in Greek and Sanskrit grammar) denoting a voice of verbs expressing reciprocal or reflexive action 6 (usually capital) (of a language) intermediate between the earliest and the modern forms ▷ n 7 an area or point equal in distance from the ends or periphery or in time between the early and late parts 8 an intermediate part or section, such as the waist 9 grammar the middle voice 10 logic See **middle term** 11 cricket a position on the batting creases in alignment with the middle stumps on which a batsman may take guard ▷ *vb* (*tr*) **12** to place in the middle **13** *nautical* to fold in two **14** *cricket* to hit (the ball) with the middle of the bat [Old English *middel*; compare Old Frisian *middel*, Dutch *middel*, German *mittel*]

middle age *n* the period of life between youth and old age, usually (in man) considered to occur approximately between the ages of 40 and 60 ▷ **middle-aged** *adj*

Middle Ages *n* the Middle Ages *European history* **1** (broadly) the period from the end of classical antiquity (or the deposition of the last W Roman emperor in 476 AD) to the Italian Renaissance (or the fall of Constantinople in 1453) **2** (narrowly) the period from about 1000 AD to the 15th century. See **Dark Ages**

Middle America *n* **1** the territories between the US and South America: Mexico, Central America, Panama, and the Greater and Lesser Antilles **2** the US middle class, esp those groups that are politically conservative ▷ **Middle American** *adj*, *n*

Middle Atlantic States *or* **Middle States** *pl n* the states of New York, Pennsylvania, and New Jersey

middlebrow ('mɪd²l,braʊ) *disparaging* ▷ *n* **1** a person with conventional tastes and limited cultural appreciation ▷ *adj* Also: **middlebrowed** **2** of or appealing to middlebrows

middle C *n* *music* the note graphically represented on the first ledger line below the treble staff or the first ledger line above the bass staff and corresponding in pitch to an internationally standardized fundamental frequency of 261.63 hertz

middle class *n* **1** Also called: **bourgeoisie** a social stratum that is not clearly defined but is positioned between the lower and upper classes. It consists of businessmen, professional people, etc, along with their families, and is marked by bourgeois values ▷ *adj* **middle-class** **2** of, relating to, or characteristic of the middle class

Middle Congo *n* one of the four territories of former French Equatorial Africa, in W central Africa: became an autonomous member of the French Community, as the Republic of the Congo, in 1958

middle ear *n* the sound-conducting part of the ear, containing the malleus, incus, and stapes

Middle East *n* **1** (loosely) the area around the E Mediterranean, esp Israel and the Arab countries from Turkey to North Africa and eastwards to Iran **2** (formerly) the area extending from the Tigris and Euphrates to Myanmar ▷ **Middle Eastern** *adj*

Middle England *n* a characterization of a predominantly middle-class, middle-income section of British society living mainly in suburban and rural England

Middle English *n* the English language from about 1100 to about 1450: main dialects are Kentish, Southwestern (West Saxon), East Midland (which replaced West Saxon as the chief literary form and developed into Modern English), West Midland, and Northern (from which the Scots of Lowland Scotland and other modern dialects developed)

middle game *n* *chess* the central phase between the opening and the endgame

Middle High German *n* High German from about 1200 to about 1500

Middle Low German *n* Low German from about 1200 to about 1500

middleman ('mɪd²l,mæn) *n*, *pl* -men **1** an independent trader engaged in the distribution of goods from producer to consumer **2** an intermediary

middlemost ('mɪd²l,məʊst) *adj* another word for: **midmost**

middle name *n* **1** a name between a person's first name and surname **2** a characteristic quality for which a person is known: *caution is my middle name*

middle-of-the-road *adj* **1** not extreme, esp in political views; moderate **2** of, denoting, or relating to popular music having a wide general appeal

middle passage *n* the middle passage *history* the journey across the Atlantic Ocean from the W coast of Africa to the Caribbean: the longest part of the journey

of the slave ships sailing to the Caribbean or the Americas

Middlesbrough ('mɪd²lzbrə) *n* **1** an industrial town in NE England, in Middlesbrough unitary authority, North Yorkshire: on the Tees estuary; university (1992). Pop: 142 691 (2001) **2** a unitary authority in NE England, in North Yorkshire: formerly (1974–96) part of Cleveland county. Pop: 139 000 (2003 est). Area: 54 sq km (21 sq miles)

middle school *n* (in England and Wales) a school for children aged between 8 or 9 and 12 or 13

Middlesex ('mɪd²l,sɛks) *n* a former county of SE England: became mostly part of N and W Greater London in 1965. Abbreviation: Middx

Middle States *pl n* another name for the **Middle Atlantic States**

middle term *n* *logic* the term that appears in both the major and minor premises of a syllogism, but not in the conclusion

Middleton[1] ('mɪd²ltən) *n* a town in NW England, in Rochdale Unitary Authority, Greater Manchester. Pop: 45 314 (2001)

Middleton[2] ('mɪd²ltən) *n* **1** **Kate**, real name *Catherine Elizabeth*. born 1985, English girlfriend of Prince William from 2003 **2** **Thomas**. ?1570–1627, English dramatist. His plays include the tragedies *Women beware Women* (1621) and, in collaboration with William Rowley (?1585–?1642), *The Changeling* (1622) and the political satire *A Game at Chess* (1624)

middleware ('mɪd²l,wɛə) *n* computer software that has an intermediary function between the various applications of a computer and its operating system [C20: from MIDDLE + (SOFT)WARE]

middle watch *n* *nautical* the watch between midnight and 4 a.m

middleweight ('mɪd²l,weɪt) *n* **a** a professional boxer weighing 154–160 pounds (70–72.5 kg) **b** an amateur boxer weighing 71–75 kg (157–165 pounds)

Middle West *n* another name for the **Midwest** ▷ **Middle Western** *adj* ▷ **Middle Westerner** *n*

middle youth *n* the period of life between about 30 and 50

middling ('mɪdlɪŋ) *adj* **1** mediocre in quality, size, etc; neither good nor bad, esp in health (often in the phrase **fair to middling**) ▷ *adv* **2** *informal* moderately: *middling well* [C15 (northern English and Scottish): from MID[1] + -LING[2]] ▷ '**middlingly** *adv*

Middx *abbreviation* Middlesex

middy ('mɪdɪ) *n*, *pl* -dies **1** *informal* See **midshipman** (sense 1) **2** *Austral* a middle-sized glass of beer

Mideast (,mɪd'iːst) *n* *chiefly US* another name for **Middle East**

midfield (,mɪd'fiːld) *n* *soccer* **a** the general area between the two opposing defences **b** (*as modifier*): *a midfield player*

mid-flight *adj*, *adv* **1** during a flight; whilst airborne: *a mid-flight celebration; doors opening mid-flight* ▷ *n* **2** in mid-flight during a flight; whilst airborne

Midgard ('mɪdɡɑːd), **Midgarth** ('mɪdɡɑːð) *or* **Mithgarthr** ('mɪðɡɑːðə) *n* *Norse myth* the dwelling place of mankind, formed from the body of the giant Ymir and linked by the bridge Bifrost to Asgard, home of the gods [C19: from Old Norse *mithgarthr*; see MID[1], YARD[2]]

midge (mɪdʒ) *n* **1** any fragile mosquito-like dipterous insect of the family *Chironomidae*, occurring in dancing swarms, esp near water **2** a small or diminutive person or animal [Old English *mycge*; compare Old High German *mucca*, Danish *myg*] ▷ '**midgy** *adj*

midget ('mɪdʒɪt) *n* **1** a dwarf whose skeleton and features are of normal proportions **2 a** something small of its kind **b** (*as modifier*): *a midget car* [C19: from MIDGE + -ET]

Mid Glamorgan *n* a former county of S Wales, formed in 1974 from parts of Breconshire, Glamorgan, and Monmouthshire: replaced in 1996 by the county boroughs of Bridgend, Rhondda Cynon Taff, Merthyr Tydfil, and part of Caerphilly

midgut ('mɪd,ɡʌt) *n* **1** the middle part of the digestive tract of vertebrates, including the small intestine **2** the middle part of the digestive tract of arthropods

m

mid-heavyweight *n* **a** a professional wrestler weighing 199-209 pounds (91-95 kg) **b** an amateur wrestler weighing 91-100 kg (199-220 pounds)

midi ('mɪdɪ) *adj* **a** (of a skirt, coat, etc) reaching to below the knee or midcalf **b** (*as noun*): *she wore her new midi* [C20: from MID-; on the model of MAXI and MINI]

Midi (*French* midi) *n* **1** the south of France **2** Canal du Midi a canal in S France, extending from the River Garonne at Toulouse to the Mediterranean at Sète and providing a link between the Mediterranean and Atlantic coasts: built between 1666 and 1681. Length: 181 km (150 miles)

MIDI ('mɪdɪ) *n* (*modifier*) a generally accepted specification for the external control of electronic musical instruments: *a MIDI synthesizer; a MIDI system* [C20: from m(usical) i(nstrument) d(igital) i(nterface)]

midi- *combining form* of medium or middle size, length, etc: *midibus* [C20: from MID-; on the model of MAXI and MINI]

Midian ('mɪdɪən) *n Old Testament* **1** a son of Abraham (Genesis 25:1-2) **2** a nomadic nation claiming descent from him > 'Midian,ite *n, adj* > 'Midian,itish *adj*

midinette (,mɪdɪ'nɛt; *French* midinɛt) *n, pl* -nettes (-'nɛts; *French* -nɛt) a Parisian seamstress or salesgirl in a clothes shop [C20: from French, from *midi* noon + *dinette* light meal, since the girls had time for no more than a snack at midday]

Midi-Pyrénées (*French* midipirene) *n* a region of SW France: consists of N slopes of the Pyrenees in the south, a fertile lowland area in the west crossed by the River Garonne, and the edge of the Massif Central in the north and east

midiron ('mɪd,aɪən) *n golf* a club, usually a No. 5, 6, or 7 iron, used for medium-length approach shots

midi system *n* a complete set of hi-fi sound equipment designed as a single unit that is more compact than the standard equipment

midland ('mɪdlənd) *n* **a** the central or inland part of a country **b** (*as modifier*): *a midland region*

Midlands ('mɪdləndz) *pl n* the Midlands (*functioning as plural or singular*) the central counties of England, including Warwickshire, Northamptonshire, Leicestershire, Nottinghamshire, Derbyshire, Staffordshire, the former West Midlands metropolitan county, and Worcestershire: characterized by manufacturing industries > 'Midlander *n*

midlife crisis ('mɪd,laɪf) *n* a crisis that may be experienced in middle age involving frustration, panic, and feelings of pointlessness, sometimes resulting in radical and often ill-advised changes of lifestyle

Midlothian (mɪd'ləʊðɪən) *n* a council area of SE central Scotland: the historical county of Midlothian (including Edinburgh) became part of Lothian region in 1975; separate unitary authorities were created for Midlothian and City of Edinburgh in 1996; mainly agricultural. Administrative centre: Dalkeith. Pop: 79 710 (2003 est). Area: 356 sq km (137 sq miles)

midmost ('mɪd,məʊst) *adj, adv* in the middle or midst

midnight ('mɪd,naɪt) *n* **1 a** the middle of the night; 12 o'clock at night **b** (*as modifier*): *the midnight hour* **2** burn the midnight oil to work or study late into the night

midnight sun *n* the sun visible at midnight during local summer inside the Arctic and Antarctic circles

mid-off *n cricket* the fielding position on the off side closest to the bowler

mid-on *n cricket* the fielding position on the on side closest to the bowler

midpoint ('mɪd,pɔɪnt) *n* **1** the point on a line that is at an equal distance from either end **2** a point in time halfway between the beginning and end of an event

midrib ('mɪd,rɪb) *n* the main vein of a leaf, running down the centre of the blade

midriff ('mɪdrɪf) *n* **1 a** the middle part of the human body, esp between waist and bust **b** (*as modifier*): *midriff bulge* **2** *anatomy* another name for the: **diaphragm** (sense 1) **3** the part of a woman's garment covering the midriff [Old English *midhrif*, from MID[1] + *hrif* belly]

midship ('mɪd,ʃɪp) *nautical* ⊳ *adj* **1** in, of, or relating to the middle of a vessel ⊳ *n* **2** the middle of a vessel

midshipman ('mɪd,ʃɪpmən) *n, pl* -men a probationary rank held by young naval officers under training, or an officer holding such a rank

midships ('mɪd,ʃɪps) *adv, adj nautical* See **amidships**

midst[1] (mɪdst) *n* **1** in the midst of surrounded or enveloped by; at a point during, esp a climactic one **2** in our midst among us [C14: back formation from *amiddes* AMID]

midst[2] (mɪdst) *prep poetic* See **amid**

midsummer ('mɪd'sʌmə) *n* **1 a** the middle or height of the summer **b** (*as modifier*): *a midsummer carnival* **2** another name for: **summer solstice**

Midsummer's Day *or* **Midsummer Day** *n* June 24, the feast of St John the Baptist; in England, Ireland, and Wales, one of the four quarter days. See also **summer solstice**

midterm ('mɪd'tɜːm) *n* **1 a** the middle of a term in a school, university, etc **b** (*as modifier*): *midterm exam* **2** *US politics* **a** the middle of a term of office, esp of a presidential term, when congressional and local elections are held **b** (*as modifier*): *midterm elections* **3 a** the middle of the gestation period **b** (*as modifier*): *midterm checkup*. See **term** (sense 6)

mid-Victorian *adj* **1** *Brit history* of or relating to the middle period of the reign of Queen Victoria (1837-1901) ⊳ *n* **2** a person of the mid-Victorian era

midway ('mɪd,weɪ) *adj, adv* **1** in or at the middle of the distance; halfway ⊳ *n* **2** *obsolete* a middle place, way, etc

Midway Islands *pl n* an atoll in the central Pacific, about 2100 km (1300 miles) northwest of Honolulu: annexed by the US in 1867: scene of a decisive battle (June, 1942), in which the US combined fleets destroyed Japan's carrier fleet. Pop: 30 (2004 est). Area: 5 sq km (2 sq miles)

midweek ('mɪd'wiːk) *n* **a** the middle of the week **b** (*as modifier*): *a midweek holiday*

Midwest ('mɪd'wɛst) *or* **Middle West** *n* the N central part of the US; the region consisting of the states from Ohio westwards that border on the Great Lakes, often extended to include the upper Mississippi and Missouri valleys > 'Mid'western *or* Middle Western *adj* > 'Mid'westerner *or* Middle Westerner *n*

mid-wicket *n cricket* the fielding position on the on side, approximately midway between square leg and mid-on

midwife ('mɪd,waɪf) *n, pl* -wives (-,waɪvz) a person qualified to deliver babies and to care for women before, during, and after childbirth [C14: from Old English *mid* with + *wif* woman]

midwifery ('mɪd,wɪfərɪ) *n* the art or practice of a midwife; obstetrics

midwinter ('mɪd'wɪntə) *n* **1 a** the middle or depth of the winter **b** (*as modifier*): *a midwinter festival* **2** another name for **winter solstice**

midyear ('mɪd'jɪə) *n* the middle of the year

mien (miːn) *n literary* a person's manner, bearing, or appearance, expressing personality or mood [C16: probably variant of obsolete *demean* appearance; related to French *mine* aspect]

Mieres (*Spanish* 'mjeres) *n* a city in N Spain, south of Oviedo: steel and chemical industries; iron and coal mines. Pop: 47 618 (2003 est)

Mies van der Rohe ('miːz vɑːn də 'rəʊə) *n* Ludwig. 1886-1969, US architect, born in Germany. He directed the Bauhaus (1929-33) and developed a functional style, characterized by geometrical design. His works include the Seagram building, New York (1958)

mifepristone (mɪ'fɛprɪ,stəʊn) *n* an antiprogestogenic steroid, used in the medical termination of pregnancy. Formula: $C_{29}H_{35}NO_2$ [C20: from *aminophenol* + *propyne* + *oestradiol* + -ONE]

miff (mɪf) *informal* ⊳ *vb* **1** to take offence or offend ⊳ *n* **2** a petulant mood **3** a petty quarrel [C17: perhaps an imitative expression of bad temper] > 'miffy *adj* -fier, -fiest > 'miffily *adv* > 'miffiness *n*

might[1] (maɪt) *vb* (takes an implied infinitive or an infinitive without *to*) used as an auxiliary **1** making the past tense or subjunctive mood of **may**[1]: *he might have come last night* **2** (often foll by *well*) expressing theoretical possibility: *he might well come*. In this sense *might* looks to the future and functions as a weak form of *may*. See **may¹** (sense 2) [OE *miht*]

might² (maɪt) *n* **1** power, force, or vigour, esp of a great or supreme kind **2** physical strength **3** with might and main *or* might and main See **main¹** (sense 7) [Old English *miht*; compare Old High German *maht*, Dutch *macht*]

mighty ('maɪtɪ) *adj* mightier, mightiest **1 a** having or indicating might; powerful or strong **b** (*as collective noun*; preceded by *the*): *the mighty* **2** very large; vast **3** very great in extent, importance, etc ▷ *adv* **4** *informal, chiefly US & Canadian* (intensifier): *he was mighty tired* > 'mightiness *n* > 'mightily *adv*

mignon ('miːnjɒn; *French* miɲɔ̃) *adj* small and pretty; dainty [C16: from French, from Old French *mignot* dainty] > mignonne ('mɪnjɒn; *French* miɲɔn) *fem n*

mignonette (ˌmɪnjə'nɛt) *n* **1** any of various mainly Mediterranean plants of the resedaceous genus *Reseda*, such as *R. odorata* (**garden mignonette**), that have spikes of small greenish-white flowers with prominent anthers **2** a type of fine pillow lace ▷ *adj* **3 a** of a greyish-green colour; reseda **b** (*as modifier*): *mignonette ribbons* [C18: from French, diminutive of MIGNON]

migraine ('miːɡreɪn, 'maɪ-) *n* a throbbing headache usually affecting only one side of the head and commonly accompanied by nausea and visual disturbances [C18: (earlier form, C14 *mygrame* MEGRIM): from French, from Late Latin *hēmicrānia* pain in half of the head, from Greek *hēmikrania*, from HEMI- + *kranion* CRANIUM] > 'migrainous *adj*

migrant ('maɪɡrənt) *n* **1** a person or animal that moves from one region, place, or country to another **2** an itinerant agricultural worker who travels from one district to another ▷ *adj* **3** moving from one region, place, or country to another; migratory [C17: from Latin *migrāre* to change one's abode]

migrate (maɪ'ɡreɪt) *vb* (*intr*) **1** to go from one region, country, or place of abode to settle in another, esp in a foreign country **2** (of birds, fishes, etc) to journey between different areas at specific times of the year [C17: from Latin *migrāre* to change one's abode] > mi'grator *n*

migration (maɪ'ɡreɪʃən) *n* **1** the act or an instance of migrating **2** a group of people, birds, etc, migrating in a body **3** *chem* a movement of atoms, ions, or molecules, such as the motion of ions in solution under the influence of electric fields > mi'grational *adj*

migratory ('maɪɡrətərɪ, -trɪ) *adj* **1** of, relating to, or characterized by migration **2** nomadic; itinerant

mihi ('miːhɪ) *NZ n* a Māori ceremonial greeting [Māori]

mihrab ('miːræb, -rəb) *n* *Islam* the niche in a mosque showing the direction of Mecca [from Arabic]

mikado (mɪ'kɑːdəʊ) *n, pl* -**dos** (*often capital*) *archaic* the Japanese emperor [C18: from Japanese, from *mi-* honourable + *kado* gate]

mike (maɪk) *n informal* short for **microphone**

mil (mɪl) *n* **1** a unit of length equal to one thousandth of an inch **2** a unit of angular measure, used in gunnery, equal to one sixty-four-hundredth of a circumference [C18: short for Latin *millēsimus* thousandth]

mil. *abbreviation* **1** military **2** militia

milady *or* **miladi** (mɪ'leɪdɪ) *n, pl* -**dies** (formerly) a continental title used for an English gentlewoman

Milan (mɪ'læn) *n* a city in N Italy, in central Lombardy: Italy's second largest city and chief financial and industrial centre; a centre of the Renaissance under the Visconti and Sforza families. Pop: 1 256 211 (2001). Italian name: Milano (mɪ'laːno) > ˌMila'nese *adj, n*

Milazzo (Italian mi'lattso) *n* a port in NE Sicily: founded in the 8th century BC; scene of a battle (1860), in which Garibaldi defeated the Bourbon forces. Pop: 32 108 (2001)

milch (mɪltʃ) *n* **1** (*modifier*) (esp of cattle) yielding milk **2** milch cow *informal* a source of easy income, esp a person [C13: from Old English *-milce* (in compounds); related to Old English *melcan* to milk]

mild (maɪld) *adj* **1** (of a taste, sensation, etc) not powerful or strong; bland **2** gentle or temperate in character, climate, behaviour, etc **3** not extreme; moderate **4** feeble; unassertive ▷ *n* **5** *Brit* draught beer, of darker colour than bitter and flavoured with fewer

hops [Old English *milde*; compare Old Saxon *mildi*, Old Norse *mildr*] > 'mildly *adv* > 'mildness *n*

mildew ('mɪlˌdjuː) *n* **1** any of various diseases of plants that affect mainly the leaves and are caused by parasitic fungi **2** any fungus causing this kind of disease **3** another name for **mould²** ▷ *vb* **4** to affect or become affected with mildew [Old English *mildēaw*, from mil-honey (compare Latin *mel*, Greek *mēli*) + *dēaw* DEW] > 'mil,dewy *adj*

mild steel *n* any of a class of strong tough steels that contain a low quantity of carbon (0.1–0.25 per cent)

mile (maɪl) *n* **1** Also called: **statute mile** a unit of length used in the U.K., the US, and certain other countries, equal to 1760 yards. 1 mile is equivalent to 1.609 34 kilometres **2** See **nautical mile** **3** (*often plural*) *informal* a great distance; great deal: *he missed by a mile* **4** a race extending over a mile ▷ *adv* **5** miles (intensifier): *he likes his new job miles better* [Old English *mīl*, from Latin *mīlia* (*passuum*) a thousand (paces)]

mileage *or* **milage** ('maɪlɪdʒ) *n* **1** a distance expressed in miles **2** the total number of miles that a motor vehicle has travelled **3** allowance for travelling expenses, esp as a fixed rate per mile **4** the number of miles a motor vehicle will travel on one gallon of fuel **5** *informal* use, benefit, or service provided by something **6** *informal* grounds, substance, or weight: *some mileage in the objectors' arguments*

mileometer *or* **milometer** (maɪ'lɒmɪtə) *n* a device that records the number of miles that a bicycle or motor vehicle has travelled

milepost ('maɪlˌpəʊst) *n* **1** *horse racing* a marking post on a racecourse a mile before the finishing line **2** *chiefly US & Canadian* a signpost that shows the distance in miles to or from a place

miler ('maɪlə) *n* an athlete, horse, etc, that runs or specializes in races of one mile

Miles (maɪlz) *n* **Bernard**, Baron Miles of Blackfriars. 1907–91, British actor and theatre manager. He founded the Mermaid Theatre in London, and was known as a character actor

milestone ('maɪlˌstəʊn) *n* **1** a stone pillar that shows the distance in miles to or from a place **2** a significant event in life, history, etc

Miletus (mɪ'liːtəs) *n* an ancient city on the W coast of Asia Minor: a major Ionian centre of trade and learning in the ancient world > Mi'lesian *adj, n* [via Latin from Greek *Milēsios*]

milfoil ('mɪlˌfɔɪl) *n* **1** another name for **yarrow** **2** See **water milfoil** [C13: from Old French, from Latin *milifolium*, from *mille* thousand + *folium* leaf]

Milford Haven ('mɪlfəd) *n* a port in SW Wales, in Pembrokeshire on **Milford Haven** (a large inlet of St George's Channel): major oil port. Pop: 12 830 (2001)

Milhaud (*French* mijo) *n* **Darius** (darjys). 1892–1974, French composer; member of Les Six. A notable exponent of polytonality, his large output includes operas, symphonies, ballets, string quartets, and songs

miliaria (ˌmɪlɪ'ɛərɪə) *n* an acute vesicular eruption of the skin, caused by blockage of the sweat glands [C19: from New Latin, from Latin *miliārius* MILIARY]

miliary ('mɪlɪərɪ) *adj* **1** resembling or relating to millet seeds **2** (of a disease or skin eruption) characterized by small lesions resembling millet seeds: *miliary tuberculosis* [C17: from Latin *miliārius*, from *milium* MILLET]

milieu ('miːljɜː; *French* miljø) *n, pl* -**lieux** (-ljɜː, -ljɜːz; *French* -ljø) *or* -**lieus** (miljø) surroundings, location, or setting [C19: from French, from *mi-* MID¹ + *lieu* place]

militant ('mɪlɪtənt) *adj* **1** aggressive or vigorous, esp in the support of a cause **2** warring; engaged in warfare ▷ *n* **3** a militant person [C15: from Latin *mīlitāre* to be a soldier, from *mīles* soldier] > 'militancy *or less commonly* 'militantness *n* > 'militantly *adv*

militarism (ˌmɪlɪtə'rɪzəm) *n* **1** military spirit; pursuit of military ideals **2** domination by the military in the formulation of policies, ideals, etc, esp on a political level **3** a policy of maintaining a strong military organization in aggressive preparedness for war > 'militarist *n* > ˌmilita'ristic *adj* > ˌmilita'ristically *adv*

militarize *or* **militarise** ('mɪlɪtəˌraɪz) *vb* (*tr*) **1** to convert

to military use **2** to imbue with militarism
> ˌmilitariˈzation *or* ˌmilitariˈsation *n*

military ('mɪlɪtərɪ, -trɪ) *adj* **1** of or relating to the armed
forces (esp the army), warlike matters, etc **2** of,
characteristic of, or about soldiers ▷ *n*, *pl* **-taries** *or* **-tary**
3 the military the armed services (esp the army) [c16: via
French from Latin *mīlitāris*, from *mīles* soldier]
> ˈmilitarily *adv*

military police *n* a corps within an army that performs
police and disciplinary duties > **military policeman** *n*

militate ('mɪlɪˌteɪt) *vb* (*intr*; usually foll by *against* or *for*)
(of facts, actions, etc) to have influence or effect: *the
evidence militated against his release* [c17: from Latin *mīlitātus*,
from *mīlitāre* to be a soldier]

⦿ USAGE See at **mitigate**

militia (mɪˈlɪʃə) *n* **1** a body of citizen (as opposed to
professional) soldiers **2** an organization containing men
enlisted for service in emergency only [c16: from Latin:
soldiery, from *mīles* soldier] > **miˈlitiaman** *n*

milk (mɪlk) *n* **1 a** a whitish nutritious fluid produced
and secreted by the mammary glands of mature female
mammals and used for feeding their young until
weaned **b** the milk of cows, goats, or other animals used
by man as a food or in the production of butter, cheese,
etc **2** any similar fluid in plants, such as the juice of a
coconut **3** any of various milklike pharmaceutical
preparations, such as milk of magnesia **4 cry over spilt
milk** to lament something that cannot be altered ▷ *vb*
5 to draw milk from the udder of (a cow, goat, or other
animal) **6** (*intr*) (of cows, goats, or other animals) to
yield milk **7** (*tr*) to draw off or tap in small quantities: *to
milk the petty cash* **8** (*tr*) to extract as much money, help,
etc, as possible from: *to milk a situation of its news value*
9 (*tr*) to extract venom, sap, etc, from [Old English *milc*;
compare Old Saxon *miluk*, Old High German *miluh*, Old
Norse *mjolk*] > ˈmilker *n*

milk-and-water *adj* (**milk and water** when postpositive)
weak, feeble, or insipid

milk bar *n* **1** a snack bar at which milk drinks and light
refreshments are served **2** (in Australia) a shop selling,
in addition to milk, basic provisions and other items

milk chocolate *n* chocolate that has been made with
milk, having a creamy taste

milk float *n Brit* a small motor vehicle used to deliver
milk to houses

milk leg *n* inflammation and thrombosis of the femoral
vein following childbirth, characterized by painful
swelling of the leg

milkmaid ('mɪlkˌmeɪd) *n* a girl or woman who milks
cows

milkman ('mɪlkmən) *n*, *pl* **-men** a man who delivers or
sells milk

milk of magnesia *n* a suspension of magnesium
hydroxide in water, used as an antacid and laxative

milk pudding *n chiefly Brit* a hot or cold pudding made
by boiling or baking milk with a grain, esp rice

milk round *n Brit* **1** a route along which a milkman
regularly delivers milk **2** a regular series of visits, esp as
made by recruitment officers from industry to
universities

milk run *n aeronautics informal* a routine and uneventful
flight, esp on a dangerous mission [c20: referring to the
regular and safe routine of a milkman's round]

milk shake *n* a cold frothy drink made of milk,
flavouring, and sometimes ice cream, whisked or beaten
together

milksop ('mɪlkˌsɒp) *n* a feeble or ineffectual man or
youth

milk sugar *n* another name for **lactose**

milk tooth *n* any of the first teeth to erupt; a deciduous
tooth. Also called: **baby tooth**

milkwort ('mɪlkˌwɜːt) *n* any of several plants of the
genus *Polygala*, having small blue, pink, or white flowers
with two petal-like sepals: family *Polygalaceae*. They were
formerly believed to increase milk production in cows

milky ('mɪlkɪ) *adj* **milkier, milkiest 1** resembling milk,
esp in colour or cloudiness **2** of or containing milk
3 spiritless or spineless > ˈmilkily *adv* > ˈmilkiness *n*

Milky Way the **Milky Way** *n* the diffuse band of light

stretching across the night sky that consists of millions
of faint stars, nebulae, etc, within our Galaxy [c14:
translation of Latin *via lactea*]

mill (mɪl) *n* **1** a building in which grain is crushed and
ground to make flour **2** a factory, esp one which
processes raw materials **3** any of various processing or
manufacturing machines, esp one that grinds, presses,
or rolls **4** any of various small hand mills used for
grinding pepper, salt, or coffee for domestic purposes
5 a hard roller for impressing a design, esp in a textile-
printing machine or in a machine for printing
banknotes **6** a system, institution, etc, that influences
people or things in the manner of a factory: *going through
the educational mill* **7** an unpleasant experience; ordeal
(esp in the phrases **go** or **be put through the mill**) **8** a fist
fight ▷ *vb* **9** (*tr*) to grind, press, or pulverize in or as if in
a mill **10** (*tr*) to process or produce in or with a mill **11** to
cut or roll (metal) with or as if with a milling machine
12 (*tr*) to groove or flute the edge of (a coin) **13** (*intr*; often
foll by *about* or *around*) to move about in a confused
manner **14** *archaic, slang* to fight, esp with the fists [Old
English *mylen* from Late Latin *molīna* a mill, from Latin
mola mill, millstone, from *molere* to grind] > ˈmillable *adj*
> **milled** *adj*

Mill (mɪl) *n* **1 James**. 1773–1836, Scottish philosopher,
historian, and economist. He expounded Bentham's
utilitarian philosophy in *Elements of Political Economy* (1821)
and *Analysis of the Phenomena of the Human Mind* (1829) and
also wrote a *History of British India* (1817–18) **2** his son, **John
Stuart**. 1806–73, English philosopher and economist. He
modified Bentham's utilitarian philosophy in
Utilitarianism (1861) and in his treatise *On Liberty* (1859) he
defended the rights and freedom of the individual.
Other works include *A System of Logic* (1843) and *Principles
of Political Economy* (1848)

Millais ('mɪleɪ) *n* **Sir John Everett**. 1829–96, English
painter, who was a founder of the Pre-Raphaelite
Brotherhood. His works include *The Order of Release* (1853)
and *The Blind Girl* (1856)

Millau Bridge (miyo) *n* a road bridge, the highest in the
world, crossing the River Tarn in the Massif Central in
SW France; designed by Sir Norman Foster and opened
in 2004

Millay (mɪˈleɪ) *n* **Edna St Vincent**. 1892–1950, US poet,
noted esp for her sonnets; her collections include *The
Buck in the Snow* (1928) and *Fatal Interview* (1931)

millboard ('mɪlˌbɔːd) *n* strong pasteboard, used esp in
book covers [c18: changed from *milled board*]

milldam ('mɪlˌdæm) *n* a dam built in a stream to raise
the water level sufficiently for it to turn a millwheel

millefeuille *French* (milfœj) *n Brit* a small iced cake made
of puff pastry filled with jam and cream [literally:
thousand leaves]

millefleurs ('miːlˌflɜː) *n* a design of stylized floral
patterns, used in textiles, tapestries, etc [French:
thousand flowers]

millenarian (ˌmɪlɪˈnɛərɪən) *or* **millenary** *adj* **1** of or
relating to a thousand or to a thousand years **2** of or
relating to the millennium or millenarianism ▷ *n* **3** an
adherent of millenarianism

millenarianism (ˌmɪlɪˈnɛərɪəˌnɪzəm) *n* **1** *Christianity* the
belief in a future millennium following the Second
Coming of Christ during which he will reign on earth in
peace: based on Revelation 20:1–5 **2** any belief in a future
period of ideal peace and happiness

millenary (mɪˈlɛnərɪ) *n*, *pl* **-naries 1** a sum or aggregate
of one thousand, esp one thousand years **2** another
word for a **millennium** ▷ *adj* **3** another word for
millenarian [c16: from Late Latin *millēnārius* containing a
thousand, from Latin *mille* thousand]

millennium (mɪˈlɛnɪəm) *n*, *pl* **-nia** (-nɪə) *or* **-niums 1** the
millennium *Christianity* the period of a thousand years of
Christ's awaited reign upon earth **2** a period or cycle of
one thousand years **3** a time of peace and happiness, esp
in the distant future [c17: from New Latin, from Latin
mille thousand + *annus* year; for form, compare
QUADRENNIUM] > **milˈlennial** *adj* > **milˈlennialist** *n*

Millennium Bridge *n* a pedestrian-crossing steel bridge
over the River Thames linking the City of London at St

Paul's Cathedral with the Tate Modern Gallery at Bankside: it has a span of 325 m (1056 ft)

millennium bug *n computing* any software problem arising from the change in date at the start of the 21st century

millepede ('mɪlɪˌpiːd) *or* **milleped** ('mɪlɪˌpɛd) *n* variants of millipede

millepore ('mɪlɪˌpɔː) *n* any tropical colonial coral-like medusoid hydrozoan of the order *Milleporina*, esp of the genus *Millepora*, having a calcareous skeleton [c18: from New Latin, from Latin *mille* thousand + *porus* hole]

miller ('mɪlə) *n* **1** a person who keeps, operates, or works in a mill, esp a corn mill **2** another name for **milling machine 3** a person who operates a milling machine

Miller ('mɪlə) *n* **1 Arthur.** 1915–2005, US dramatist. His plays include *Death of a Salesman* (1949), *The Crucible* (1953), *A View from the Bridge* (1955), and *Mr Peters' Connections* (1998) **2 (Alton) Glenn.** 1904–44, US composer, trombonist, and band leader. His popular compositions include "Moonlight Serenade". During World War II he was leader of the US Air Force band in Europe. He disappeared without trace on a flight between England and France **3 Henry (Valentine).** 1891–1980, US novelist, author of *Tropic of Cancer* (1934) and *Tropic of Capricorn* (1938) **4 Hugh** 1802–56, Scottish geologist and writer **5 Sir Jonathan (Wolfe).** born 1934, British doctor, actor, and theatre director. His productions include Shakespeare, Ibsen, and Chekhov as well as numerous operas. He has also presented many television medical programmes

miller's thumb *n* any of several small freshwater European fishes of the genus *Cottus*, esp *C. gobio*, having a flattened body: family *Cottidae* (bullheads, etc) [c15: from the alleged likeness of the fish's head to a thumb]

millesimal (mɪ'lɛsɪməl) *adj* **1 a** denoting a thousandth **b** (*as noun*): *a millesimal* **2** of, consisting of, or relating to a thousandth [c18: from Latin *millēsimus*]

millet ('mɪlɪt) *n* **1 a** a cereal grass, *Setaria italica*, cultivated for grain and animal fodder **2 a** an East Indian annual grass, *Panicum miliaceum*, cultivated for grain and forage, having pale round shiny seeds **b** the seed of this plant **3** any of various similar or related grasses, such as pearl millet and Indian millet [c14: via Old French from Latin *milium*; related to Greek *melinē* millet]

Millet (French milɛ) *n* **Jean François** (ʒɑ̃ frɑ̃swa). 1814–75, French painter of the Barbizon school, noted for his studies of peasants at work

Millett ('mɪlɪt) *n* **Kate.** full name *Katherine Murray Millett.* born 1934, US feminist writer and artist; books include *Sexual Politics* (1969) and *The Politics of Cruelty* (1994)

milli- *prefix* denoting 10⁻³: *millimetre* Symbol: m² [from French, from Latin *mille* thousand, this meaning being maintained in words borrowed from Latin (*millepede*)]

milliard ('mɪlɪˌɑːd, 'mɪljɑːd) *n Brit* (no longer in technical use) a thousand million. US and Canadian equivalent: **billion** [c19: from French]

millibar ('mɪlɪˌbɑː) *n* a cgs unit of atmospheric pressure equal to 10⁻³ bar, 100 newtons per square metre or 0.7500617 millimetre of mercury

Milligan ('mɪlɪgən) *n* **Spike**, real name *Terence Alan Milligan.* born 1918, British radio, stage, and film comedian and author, born in India. He appeared in *The Goon Show* (with Peter Sellers and Harry Secombe; BBC Radio, 1952–60) and his films include *Postman's Knock* (1962), *Adolf Hitler, My Part in his Downfall* (1972), *The Three Musketeers* (1974), *The Last Remake of Beau Geste* (1977), and *Yellowbeard* (1982). He was awarded an honorary knighthood in 2000

milligram *or* **milligramme** ('mɪlɪˌgræm) *n* one thousandth of a gram [c19: from French]

Millikan ('mɪlɪkən) *n* **Robert Andrews.** 1868–1953, US physicist. He measured the charge of an electron (1910), verified Einstein's equation for the photoelectric effect (1916), and studied cosmic rays; Nobel prize for physics 1923

millilitre *or US* **milliliter** ('mɪlɪˌliːtə) *n* one thousandth of a litre

millimetre *or US* **millimeter** ('mɪlɪˌmiːtə) *n* one thousandth of a metre

millimicron ('mɪlɪˌmaɪkrɒn) *n* an obsolete name for a nanometre; one millionth of a millimetre

milliner ('mɪlɪnə) *n* a person who makes or sells women's hats [c16: originally *Milaner*, a native of *Milan*, at that time famous for its fancy goods]

millinery ('mɪlɪnərɪ, -ɪnrɪ) *n* **1** hats, trimmings, etc, sold by a milliner **2** the business or shop of a milliner

milling ('mɪlɪŋ) *n* **1** the act or process of grinding, cutting, pressing, or crushing in a mill **2** the vertical grooves or fluting on the edge of a coin, etc

milling machine *n* a machine tool in which a horizontal arbor or vertical spindle rotates a cutting tool above a horizontal table, which is used to move a workpiece

million ('mɪljən) *n, pl* **-lions** *or* **-lion 1** the cardinal number that is the product of 1000 multiplied by 1000 **2** a numeral, 1 000 000, 10⁶, M, etc, representing this number **3** (*often plural*) *informal* an extremely large but unspecified number, quantity, or amount: *I have millions of things to do* ▷ *determiner* **4** (preceded by *a* or by a numeral) **a** amounting to a million: *a million light years away* **b** (*as pronoun*): *I can see a million under the microscope* [c17: via Old French from early Italian *millione*, from *mille* thousand, from Latin]

millionaire *or* **millionnaire** (ˌmɪljə'nɛə) *n* a person whose assets are worth at least a million of the standard monetary units of his country > ˌmillion'airess *or* ˌmillion'nairess *fem n*

millionth ('mɪljənθ) *n* **1 a** one of 1 000 000 approximately equal parts of something **b** (*as modifier*): *a millionth part* **2** one of 1 000 000 equal divisions of a particular scientific quantity **3** the fraction equal to one divided by 1 000 000 ▷ *adj* **4** (*usually prenominal*) **a** being the ordinal number of 1 000 000 in numbering or counting order, etc **b** (*as noun*): *the millionth to be manufactured*

millipede, millepede ('mɪlɪˌpiːd) *or* **milleped** *n* any terrestrial herbivorous arthropod of the class *Diplopoda*, having a cylindrical body made up of many segments, each of which bears two pairs of walking legs [c17: from Latin, from *mille* thousand + *pēs* foot]

millisecond ('mɪlɪˌsɛkənd) *n* one thousandth of a second

millpond ('mɪlˌpɒnd) *n* **1** a pool formed by damming a stream to provide water to turn a millwheel **2** any expanse of calm water

millrace ('mɪlˌreɪs) *or* **millrun 1** the current of water that turns a millwheel **2** the channel for this water

Mills (mɪlz) *n* **1 Hayley.** born 1946, British actress. Her films include *Pollyanna* (1960) and *The Parent Trap* (1961) **2** her father, Sir **John.** 1908–2005, British actor. His films include *This Happy Breed* (1944), *Great Expectations* (1946), and *Ryan's Daughter* (1971)

Mills bomb (mɪlz) *n* a type of high-explosive hand grenade [c20: named after Sir William *Mills* (1856–1932), English inventor]

millstone ('mɪlˌstəʊn) *n* **1** one of a pair of heavy flat disc-shaped stones that are rotated one against the other to grind grain **2** a heavy burden, such as a responsibility or obligation

millstream ('mɪlˌstriːm) *n* a stream of water used to turn a millwheel

millwheel ('mɪlˌwiːl) *n* a wheel, esp a waterwheel, that drives a mill

millwork ('mɪlˌwɜːk) *n* work done in a mill

millwright ('mɪlˌraɪt) *n* a person who designs, builds, or repairs grain mills or mill machinery

Milne (mɪln) *n* **A(lan) A(lexander).** 1882–1956, English writer, noted for his books and verse for children, including *When We Were Very Young* (1924) and *Winnie the Pooh* (1926)

milometer (maɪ'lɒmɪtə) *n* a variant spelling of **mileometer**

milord (mɪ'lɔːd) *n* (formerly) a continental title used for an English gentleman [c19: via French from English *my lord*]

Mílos ('miːlɒs) *n* transliteration of the Modern Greek name for **Melos**

Milošević (miːˈlɒsɛˌvɪtʃ) *n* **Slobodan** ('slɒbədæn). 1941–2006, Serbian politician, president of Serbia (1989–97) and of the Federal Republic of Yugoslavia

m

(1997–2000). He supported ethnic cleansing in Bosnia-Herzegovina (1992–95) and Kosovo (1998–99). He was ousted in 2000 and brought to trial (2001) for war crimes; died in prison before the trial was concluded

Miłosz ('miːlɒʃ; *Polish* 'miwoʃ) *n* **Czeslaw** ('tʃɛslɔː; 'tʃɛswaf). 1911–2004, US poet and writer, born in Lithuania, writing in Polish; author of *The Captive Mind* (1953). Nobel prize for literature 1980

Milstein ('mɪlstaɪn) *n* **Nathan**. 1904–92, US violinist, born in Ukraine

milt (mɪlt) *n* **1** the testis of a fish **2** the spermatozoa and seminal fluid produced by a fish **3** *rare* the spleen of certain animals, esp fowls and pigs ▷ *vb* **4** to fertilize (the roe of a female fish) with milt, esp artificially [Old English *milte* spleen; in the sense: fish sperm, probably from Middle Dutch *milte*] > 'milter *n*

Miltiades (mɪl'taɪəˌdiːz) *n* ?540–?489 BC, Athenian general, who defeated the Persians at Marathon (490)

Milton ('mɪltən) *n* **John**. 1608–74, English poet. His early works, notably *L'Allegro* and *Il Penseroso* (1632), the masque *Comus* (1634), and the elegy *Lycidas* (1637), show the influence of his Christian humanist education and his love of Italian Renaissance poetry. A staunch Parliamentarian and opponent of episcopacy, he published many pamphlets during the Civil War period, including *Areopagitica* (1644), which advocated freedom of the press. His greatest works were the epic poems *Paradise Lost* (1667; 1674), and *Paradise Regained* (1671) and the verse drama *Samson Agonistes* (1671)

Milton Keynes ('mɪltən 'kiːnz) *n* **1** a new town in central England, in Milton Keynes unitary authority, N Buckinghamshire: founded in 1967: electronics, clothing, machinery; seat of the Open University. Pop: 215 700 (2003 est) **2** a unitary authority in central England, in Buckinghamshire. Pop: 184 506 (2001). Area: 310 sq km (119 sq miles)

Milwaukee (mɪl'wɔːkiː) *n* a port in SE Wisconsin, on Lake Michigan: the largest city in the state; established as a trading post in the 18th century; an important industrial centre. Pop: 586 941 (2003 est) > Mil'waukeean *adj*, *n*

mim (mɪm) *adj* dialect prim, modest, or demure [c17: perhaps imitative of lip-pursing]

mime (maɪm) *n* **1** the theatrical technique of expressing an idea or mood or portraying a character entirely by gesture and bodily movement without the use of words **2** Also called: **mime artist** a performer specializing in such a technique, esp a comic actor **3** a dramatic presentation using such a technique **4** (in the classical theatre) **a** a comic performance depending for effect largely on exaggerated gesture and physical action **b** an actor in such a performance ▷ *vb* **5** to express (an idea) in actions or gestures without speech **6** (of singers or musicians) to perform as if singing (a song) or playing (a piece of music) that is actually prerecorded [Old English *mīma*, from Latin *mīmus* mimic actor, from Greek *mimos* imitator] > 'mimer *n*

MIME *computing abbreviation* multipurpose internet mail extensions

Mimeograph ('mɪmɪəˌɡrɑːf, -ˌɡræf) *n* **1** trademark an office machine for printing multiple copies of text or line drawings from an inked drum to which a cut stencil is fixed **2** a copy produced by this machine ▷ *vb* **3** to print copies from (a prepared stencil) using this machine

mimesis (mɪ'miːsɪs) *n* **1** art, literature the imitative representation of nature or human behaviour **2** biology another name for: **mimicry** (sense 2) **3** rhetoric representation of another person's alleged words in a speech [c16: from Greek, from *mimeisthai* to imitate]

mimetic (mɪ'mɛtɪk) *adj* **1** of, resembling, or relating to mimesis or imitation, as in art, etc **2** biology of or exhibiting mimicry > mi'metically *adv*

mimic ('mɪmɪk) *vb* -ics, -icking, -icked (tr) **1** to imitate (a person, a manner, etc), esp for satirical effect; ape **2** to take on the appearance of; resemble closely: *certain flies mimic wasps* **3** to copy closely or in a servile manner ▷ *n* **4** a person or an animal, such as a parrot, that is clever at mimicking **5** an animal that displays mimicry ▷ *adj* **6** of, relating to, or using mimicry; imitative

7 simulated, make-believe, or mock [c16: from Latin *mīmicus*, from Greek *mimikos*, from *mimos* MIME] > 'mimicker *n*

mimicry ('mɪmɪkrɪ) *n*, *pl* -ries **1** the act or art of copying or imitating closely; mimicking **2** the resemblance shown by one animal species, esp an insect, to another, which protects it from predators

MIMinE *abbreviation* Member of the Institute of Mining Engineers

Mimir ('miːmɪə) *n* Norse myth a giant who guarded the well of wisdom near the roots of Yggdrasil

mimosa (mɪ'məʊsə, -zə) *n* any tropical shrub or tree of the leguminous genus *Mimosa*, having ball-like clusters of yellow or pink flowers and compound leaves that are often sensitive to touch or light. See also **sensitive plant** [c18: from New Latin, probably from Latin *mīmus* MIME, because the plant's sensitivity to touch imitates the similar reaction of animals]

mimulus ('mɪmjʊləs) *n* See **monkey flower** [New Latin, from Greek *mimō* ape (from the shape of the corolla)]

min. *abbreviation* **1** minimum **2** minute(s)

Min. *abbreviation* **1** Minister **2** Ministry

Mina Hassan Tani ('miːnə hɑːˈsɑːn 'tɑːnɪ) *n* another name for: **Kénitra**

Minamoto Yoritomo ('mɪnəˌmaʊtəʊ ˌjɒrɪˈtəʊməʊ) *n* 1147–99, Japanese nobleman; the first shogun (1192–99) of the feudal era

minaret (ˌmɪnəˈrɛt, 'mɪnəˌrɛt) *n* a slender tower of a mosque having one or more balconies from which the muezzin calls the faithful to prayer [c17: from French, from Turkish, from Arabic *manārat* lamp, from *nār* fire] > ˌmina'reted *adj*

Minas Basin ('maɪnəs) *n* a bay in E Canada, in central Nova Scotia: the NE arm of the Bay of Fundy, with which it is linked by **Minas Channel**

Minas Gerais (Portuguese 'minaʒ ʒəˈraɪʒ) *n* an inland state of E Brazil: situated on the high plateau of the Brazilian Highlands; large reserves of iron ore and manganese. Capital: Belo Horizonte. Pop: 18 343 517 (2002). Area: 587 172 sq km (226 707 sq miles)

minatory ('mɪnətərɪ, -trɪ) or **minatorial** *adj* threatening or menacing [c16: from Late Latin *minātōrius*, from Latin *minārī* to threaten]

mince (mɪns) *vb* **1** (tr) to chop, grind, or cut into very small pieces **2** (tr) to soften or moderate, esp for the sake of convention or politeness: *I didn't mince my words* **3** (intr) to walk or speak in an affected dainty manner ▷ *n* **4** chiefly Brit minced meat [c14: from Old French *mincier*, from Vulgar Latin *minūtiāre* (unattested), from Late Latin *minūtia* smallness; see MINUTIAE] > mincer *n*

mincemeat ('mɪnsˌmiːt) *n* **1** a mixture of dried fruit, spices, etc, used esp for filling pies **2** minced meat **3** make mincemeat of informal to defeat completely

mince pie *n* a small round pastry tart filled with mincemeat

Minch (mɪntʃ) *n* the Minch a channel of the Atlantic divided into the **North Minch** between the mainland of Scotland and the Isle of Lewis, and the **Little Minch** between the Isle of Skye and Harris and North Uist

mincing ('mɪnsɪŋ) *adj* (of a person) affectedly elegant in gait, manner, or speech > 'mincingly *adv*

mind (maɪnd) *n* **1** the human faculty to which are ascribed thought, feeling, etc; often regarded as an immaterial part of a person **2** intelligence or the intellect, esp as opposed to feelings or wishes **3** recollection or remembrance; memory: *it comes to mind* **4** the faculty of original or creative thought; imagination: *it's all in the mind* **5** a person considered as an intellectual being: *the great minds of the past* **6** opinion or sentiment: *we are of the same mind; to change one's mind; to have a mind of one's own; to know one's mind; to speak one's mind* **7** condition, state, or manner of feeling or thought: *no peace of mind; his state of mind* **8** an inclination, desire, or purpose: *I have a mind to go* **9** attention or thoughts: *keep your mind on your work* **10** a sound mental state; sanity (esp in the phrase **out of one's mind**) **11** (in Cartesian philosophy) one of two basic modes of existence, the other being matter **12** blow someone's mind slang **a** to cause someone to have a psychedelic experience **b** to astound or surprise someone **13 give someone a piece of one's mind** to criticize or censure (someone) frankly or vehemently **14 in two minds** or **of two minds** undecided; wavering **15 make up one's mind** to decide (something or to do something) **16 on one's mind** in one's thoughts ▷ *vb* **17** (when *tr*, may take a clause as object) to take offence at: *do you mind if I smoke? I don't mind* **18** to pay attention to (something); heed; notice: *to mind one's own business* **19** (*tr*; *takes a clause as object*) to make certain; ensure: *mind you tell her* **20** (*tr*) to take care of; have charge of: *to mind the shop* **21** (when *tr*, may take a clause as object) to be cautious or careful about (something): *mind how you go; mind your step* **22** (*tr*) to obey (someone or something); heed: *mind your father!* **23** to be concerned (about); be troubled (about): *never mind your hat; never mind about your hat; never mind* **24** (*tr*; *passive*; *takes an infinitive*) to be intending or inclined (to do something): *clearly he was not minded to finish the story* **25 mind you** an expression qualifying a previous statement: *Dogs are nice. Mind you, I don't like all dogs.* Related adjective: **mental**¹ ▷ See also **mind out** [Old English *gemynd* mind; related to Old High German *gimunt* memory]

Mindanao (ˌmɪndəˈnaʊ) *n* the second largest island of the Philippines, in the S part of the archipelago: mountainous and volcanic. Chief towns: Davao, Zamboanga. Pop: 13 626 338 (2000). Area: (including offshore islands) 94 631 sq km (36 537 sq miles)

mind-bending *adj informal* **1** altering one's state of consciousness: *mind-bending drugs* **2** reaching the limit of credibility: *they offered a mind-bending salary* ▷ *n* **3** the process of brainwashing

mind-boggling *adj informal* astonishing; bewildering

minded (ˈmaɪndɪd) *adj* **1** having a mind, inclination, intention, etc, as specified: *politically minded* **2** (*in combination*): *money-minded*

minder (ˈmaɪndə) *n* **1** someone who looks after someone or something **2** short for **child minder** **3** *slang* an aide to someone in public life, esp a politician or political candidate, who keeps control of press and public relations **4** *slang* someone acting as a bodyguard, guard, or assistant, esp in the criminal underworld

mindfuck (ˈmaɪndˌfʌk) *n taboo, slang* the deliberate infliction of psychological damage

mindful (ˈmaɪndfʊl) *adj* (usually *postpositive* and foll by *of*) keeping aware; heedful: *mindful of your duties* > **ˈmindfully** *adv* > **ˈmindfulness** *n*

mind games *pl n* actions or statements intended to undermine or mislead someone else, often to gain advantage for oneself: *she started playing mind games with me*

mindless (ˈmaɪndlɪs) *adj* **1** stupid or careless **2** requiring little or no intellectual effort > **ˈmindlessly** *adv* > **ˈmindlessness** *n*

Mind Map *n trademark* a diagrammatic method of representing ideas, with related concepts arranged around a core concept [C20: created by US academic Tony Buzan (born 1942)]

mind-numbing *adj* extremely boring and uninspiring > **ˈmind-ˌnumbingly** *adv*

Mindoro (mɪnˈdɔːrəʊ) *n* a mountainous island in the central Philippines, south of Luzon. Pop: 1 062 000 (2000 est). Area: 9736 sq km (3759 sq miles)

mind out *vb* (*intr, adverb*) *Brit* to be careful or pay attention

mind-reader *n* a person seemingly able to discern the thoughts of another > **ˈmind-ˌreading** *n*

mind-set *n* the ideas and attitudes with which a person approaches a situation, esp when these are seen as being difficult to alter

mind's eye *n* the visual memory or the imagination

Mindszenty (ˈmɪndsɛntɪ) *n* **Joseph.** 1892–1975, Hungarian cardinal. He was sentenced to life imprisonment on a charge of treason (1949) but released during the 1956 Revolution

mine¹ (maɪn) *pron* **1** something or someone belonging to or associated with me: *mine is best* **2** of mine belonging to or associated with me ▷ *determiner* **3** (*preceding a vowel*) an archaic word for: *my*¹ *mine eyes; mine host* [Old English *mīn*; compare Old High German *mīn*, Old Norse *mīn*, Dutch *mijn*]

mine² (maɪn) *n* **1** a system of excavations made for the extraction of minerals, esp coal, ores, or precious stones **2** any deposit of ore or minerals **3** a lucrative source or abundant supply: *she was a mine of information* **4** a device containing an explosive designed to destroy ships, vehicles, or personnel, usually laid beneath the ground or in water **5** a tunnel or sap dug to undermine a fortification ▷ *vb* **6** to dig into (the earth) for (minerals) **7** to make (a hole, tunnel, etc) by digging or boring **8** to place explosive mines in position below the surface of (the sea or land) **9** to undermine (a fortification) by digging mines or saps **10** another word for **undermine** [C13: from Old French, probably of Celtic origin; compare Irish *mein*, Welsh *mwyn* ore, mine]

mine detector *n* an instrument designed to detect explosive mines > **mine detection** *n*

mine dump *n South African* a large mound of residue, esp from gold-mining operations

minefield (ˈmaɪnˌfiːld) *n* **1** an area of ground or water containing explosive mines **2** a subject, situation, etc, beset with hidden problems

minelayer (ˈmaɪnˌleɪə) *n* a warship or aircraft designed for the carrying and laying of mines

miner (ˈmaɪnə) *n* **1** a person who works in a mine **2** any of various insects or insect larvae that bore into and feed on plant tissues. See also **leaf miner** **3** *Austral* any of several honey-eaters of the genus *Manorina*, esp *M. melanocephala* (noisy miner), of scrub regions

mineral (ˈmɪnərəl, ˈmɪnrəl) *n* **1** any of a class of naturally occurring solid inorganic substances with a characteristic crystalline form and a homogeneous chemical composition **2** any inorganic matter **3** any substance obtained by mining, esp a metal ore **4** (*often plural*) *Brit* short for **mineral water** **5** *Brit* a soft drink containing carbonated water and flavourings ▷ *adj* **6** of, relating to, containing, or resembling minerals [C15: from Medieval Latin *minerāle* (n), from *minerālis* (adj); related to *minera* mine, ore, of uncertain origin]

mineral. *abbreviation* mineralogy or mineralogical

mineralize or **mineralise** (ˈmɪnərəˌlaɪz, ˈmɪnrə-) *vb* (*tr*) **1 a** to impregnate (organic matter, water, etc) with a mineral substance **b** to convert (such matter) into a mineral; petrify **2** (of gases, vapours, etc, in magma) to transform (a metal) into an ore > ˌmineraliˈzation or ˌmineraliˈsation *n* > **mineralizer** or **mineraliser** (ˈmɪnərəˌlaɪzə) *n*

mineralogy (ˌmɪnəˈrælədʒɪ) *n* the branch of geology concerned with the study of minerals > **mineralogical** (ˌmɪnərəˈlɒdʒɪkᵊl) or ˌmineralˈogic *adj* > ˌmineralˈogist *n*

mineral oil *n Brit* any oil of mineral origin, esp petroleum

mineral water *n* water containing dissolved mineral salts or gases, usually having medicinal properties

mineral wool *n* a fibrous material made by blowing steam or air through molten slag and used for packing and insulation

miner's right *n Austral & NZ history* a licence to prospect for minerals, esp gold [C19]

Minerva (mɪˈnɜːvə) *n* the Roman goddess of wisdom. Greek counterpart: **Athena**

minestrone (ˌmɪnɪˈstrəʊnɪ) *n* a soup made from a variety of vegetables and pasta [from Italian, from *minestrare* to serve]

minesweeper (ˈmaɪnˌswiːpə) *n* a naval vessel equipped to detect and clear mines > **ˈmineˌsweeping** *n*

Ming (mɪŋ) *n* **1** the imperial dynasty of China from 1368 to 1644 ▷ *adj* **2** of or relating to Chinese porcelain produced during the Ming dynasty, characterized by the use of brilliant colours and a fine-quality body

minging (ˈmɪŋɪŋ) *adj Brit informal* **1** ugly, disgusting, or malodorous **2** extremely poor in quality [C20: originally Scottish, of obscure origin]

mingle (ˈmɪŋgᵊl) *vb* **1** to mix or cause to mix **2** (*intr*; often foll by *with*) to come into close association [C15: from Old English *mengan* to mix; related to Middle Dutch *mengen*, Old Frisian *mengia*] > **ˈmingler** *n*

Mingus (ˈmɪŋgəs) *n* **Charles,** known as *Charlie Mingus.* 1922–79, US jazz double bassist, composer, and band leader

m

mingy ('mɪndʒɪ) *adj* -gier, -giest *Brit informal* miserly, stingy, or niggardly [C20: probably a blend of MEAN² + STINGY¹]

Minho ('miɲu) *n* the Portuguese name for the **Miño**

mini ('mɪnɪ) *adj* **1** (of a woman's dress, skirt, etc) very short; thigh-length **2** (*prenominal*) small; miniature ▷ *n*, *pl* **minis 3** something very small of its kind, esp a small car or a miniskirt

mini- *combining form* smaller or shorter than the standard size: *minibus; miniskirt* [C20: from MINIATURE and MINIMUM]

miniature ('mɪnɪtʃə) *n* **1** a model, copy, or similar representation on a very small scale **2** anything that is very small of its kind **3** a very small painting, esp a portrait, showing fine detail on ivory or vellum **4** an illuminated letter or other decoration in a manuscript **5** in miniature on a small scale ▷ *adj* **6** greatly reduced in size **7** on a small scale; minute [C16: from Italian, from Medieval Latin *miniātūra*, from *miniāre* to paint red, (in illuminating manuscripts); from MINIUM]
> 'miniaturist *n*

miniaturize *or* **miniaturise** ('mɪnɪtʃə,raɪz) *vb* (*tr*) to make or construct (something, esp electronic equipment) on a very small scale; reduce in size
> ,miniaturi'zation *or* ,miniaturi'sation *n*

minibus ('mɪnɪ,bʌs) *n* a small bus able to carry approximately ten passengers

minicab ('mɪnɪ,kæb) *n Brit* a small saloon car used as a taxi

minicomputer (,mɪnɪkəm'pju:tə) *n* a small comparatively cheap digital computer

minidisc ('mɪnɪ,dɪsk) *n* a small recordable compact disc

minidish ('mɪnɪ,dɪʃ) *n* a small parabolic aerial for reception or transmission to a communications satellite

minim ('mɪnɪm) *n* **1** a unit of fluid measure equal to one sixtieth of a drachm. It is approximately equal to one drop. Symbols: M, ♩ **2** *music* a note having the time value of half a semibreve **3** a small or insignificant person or thing **4** a downward stroke in calligraphy [C15 (in its musical meaning): from Latin *minimus* smallest]

minimal art *n* abstract painting or sculpture in which expressiveness and illusion are minimized by the use of simple geometric shapes, flat colour, and arrangements of ordinary objects > minimal artist *n*

minimalism ('mɪnɪmə,lɪzəm) *n* **1** another name for **minimal art 2** a type of music based on simple elements and avoiding elaboration or embellishment **3** design or style in which the simplest and fewest elements are used to create the maximum effect > 'minimalist *n*, *adj*

minimax ('mɪnɪ,mæks) *n* **1** *maths* the lowest of a set of maximum values **2** (in game theory, etc) the procedure of choosing the strategy that least benefits the most advantaged member of a group. See **maximin** [C20: from MINI(MUM) + MAX(IMUM)]

Mini-Me ('mɪnɪ,mi:) *n informal* **1** a person who resembles a smaller or younger version of another person **2** a person who adopts the opinions or mannerisms of a more powerful or senior person in order to win favour, achieve promotion, etc [C20: after a character in the 1999 film *Austin Powers: The Spy who Shagged Me*]

minimize *or* **minimise** ('mɪnɪ,maɪz) *vb* (*tr*) **1** to reduce to or estimate at the least possible degree or amount **2** to rank or treat at less than the true worth; belittle
> ,minimi'zation *or* ,minimi'sation *n* > 'mini,mizer *or* 'mini,miser *n*

minimum ('mɪnɪməm) *n*, *pl* -mums *or* -ma (-mə) **1** the least possible amount, degree, or quantity **2** the least amount recorded, allowed, or reached **3** (*modifier*) being the least possible, recorded, allowed, etc: *minimum age* ▷ *adj* **4** of or relating to a minimum or minimums [C17: from Latin: smallest thing, from *minimus* least]
> **minimal** ('mɪnɪməl, 'minimal) *adj* > 'minimally *adv*

minimum lending rate *n* (in Britain) the minimum rate at which the Bank of England would lend to discount houses between 1971 and 1981, after which it was replaced by the less formal base rate

minimum wage *n* the lowest wage that an employer is permitted to pay by law or union contract

mining ('maɪnɪŋ) *n* **1** the act, process, or industry of extracting coal, ores, etc, from the earth **2** *military* the process of laying mines

minion ('mɪnjən) *n* **1** a favourite or dependant, esp a servile or fawning one **2** a servile agent [C16: from French *mignon*, from Old French *mignot*, of Gaulish origin]

minipill ('mɪnɪ,pɪl) *n* a low-dose oral contraceptive containing a progestogen only

miniseries ('mɪnɪ,sɪəri:z) *n* a television programme in several parts that is shown on consecutive days or weeks for a short period

miniskirt ('mɪnɪ,skɜːt) *n* a very short skirt, originally in the 1960s one at least four inches above the knee. Often shortened to: **mini**

mini-state *n* same as **microstate**

minister ('mɪnɪstə) *n* **1** (esp in Presbyterian and some Nonconformist Churches) a member of the clergy **2** a person appointed to head a government department **3** any diplomatic agent accredited to a foreign government or head of state **4** short for **minister plenipotentiary** See envoy¹ (sense 1) **5** a diplomat ranking after an envoy extraordinary and minister plenipotentiary **6** a person who attends to the needs of others, esp in religious matters **7** a person who acts as the agent or servant of a person or thing ▷ *vb* **8** (*intr*; often foll by *to*) to attend to the needs (of); take care (of) **9** (*tr*) *archaic* to provide; supply [C13: via Old French from Latin: servant; related to *minus* less]

ministerial (,mɪnɪ'stɪərɪəl) *adj* **1** of or relating to a minister of religion or his office **2** of or relating to a government minister or ministry **3** (*often capital*) of or supporting the ministry or government against the opposition **4** *law* relating to or possessing delegated executive authority **5** acting as an agent or cause; instrumental > ,minis'terially *adv*

minister of state *n* **1** (in the British Parliament) a minister, usually below cabinet rank, appointed to assist a senior minister with heavy responsibilities **2** any government minister

Minister of the Crown *n Brit* any Government minister of cabinet rank

minister plenipotentiary *n*, *pl* ministers plenipotentiary See envoy¹ (sense 1)

ministrant ('mɪnɪstrənt) *adj* **1** ministering or serving as a minister ▷ *n* **2** a person who ministers [C17: from Latin *ministrans*, from *ministrāre* to wait upon]

ministration (,mɪnɪ'streɪʃən) *n* **1** the act or an instance of serving or giving aid **2** the act or an instance of ministering religiously [C14: from Latin *ministrātiō*, from *ministrāre* to wait upon] > ministrative ('mɪnɪstrətɪv) *adj*

ministry ('mɪnɪstrɪ) *n*, *pl* -tries **1 a** the profession or duties of a minister of religion **b** the performance of these duties **2** ministers of religion or government ministers considered collectively **3** the tenure of a minister **4 a** a government department headed by a minister **b** the buildings of such a department [C14: from Latin *ministerium* service, from *minister* servant; see MINISTER]

minium ('mɪnɪəm) *n* another name for **red lead** [C14 (meaning: vermilion): from Latin]

miniver ('mɪnɪvə) *n* white fur, used in ceremonial costumes [C13: from Old French *menu vair*, from *menu* small + *vair* variegated fur, VAIR]

mink (mɪŋk) *n*, *pl* mink *or* minks **1** any of several semiaquatic musteline mammals of the genus *Mustela*, of Europe, Asia, and North America, having slightly webbed feet **2** the highly valued fur of these animals, esp that of the American mink (*M. vison*) **3** a garment made of this, esp a woman's coat or stole [C15: from Scandinavian; compare Danish *mink*, Swedish *mänk*]

Minkowski (mɪn'kɒfskɪ) *n* **Hermann** ('hɜːmən). 1864–1909, German mathematician, born in Russia. His concept of a four-dimensional space-time continuum (1907) proved crucial for the general theory of relativity developed by Einstein

Minn. *abbreviation* Minnesota

Minna ('mɪnə) *n* a city in W central Nigeria, capital of Niger state. Pop: 278 000 (2005 est)

Minneapolis (,mɪnɪ'æpəlɪs) *n* a city in SE Minnesota, on the Mississippi River adjacent to St Paul: the largest city in the state; important centre for the grain trade. Pop: 373 188 (2003 est)

Minnelli (mɪˈnɛlɪ) *n* **Liza** (ˈlaɪzə). born 1946, US actress and singer, daughter of Judy Garland. Her films include *Charlie Bubbles* (1968), *Cabaret* (1972), *Arthur* (1981), and *Stepping Out* (1991)

minneola (ˌmɪnɪˈəʊlə) *n* a juicy citrus fruit that is a cross between a tangerine and a grapefruit [c20: perhaps from *Mineola*, Texas]

minnesinger (ˈmɪnɪˌsɪŋə) *n* one of the German lyric poets and musicians of the 12th to 14th centuries [c19: from German: love-singer]

Minnesota (ˌmɪnɪˈsəʊtə) *n* **1** a state of the N central US: chief US producer of iron ore. Capital: St Paul. Pop: 5 059 375 (2003 est). Area: 218 600 sq km (84 402 sq miles). Abbreviations: **Minn.**, *or* (with zip code) **MN 2** a river in S Minnesota, flowing southeast and northeast to the Mississippi River near St Paul. Length: 534 km (332 miles) > **Minne'sotan** *n, adj*

minnow (ˈmɪnəʊ) *n, pl* **-nows** *or* **-now 1** a small slender European freshwater cyprinid fish, *Phoxinus phoxinus* **2** a small or insignificant person [c15: related to Old English *myne* minnow; compare Old High German *muniwa* fish]

Miño (Spanish ˈmiɲo) *n* a river in SW Europe, rising in NW Spain and flowing southwest (as part of the border between Spain and Portugal) to the Atlantic. Length: 338 km (210 miles). Portuguese name: **Minho**

Minoan (mɪˈnəʊən) *adj* **1** denoting the Bronze Age culture of Crete from about 3000 BC to about 1100 BC ▷ *n* **2** a Cretan belonging to the Minoan culture [c19: named after MINOS, from the excavations at his supposed palace at Knossos]

Minogue (mɪˈnəʊg) *n* **Kylie** (ˈkaɪlɪ). born 1968, Australian singer and actress: appeared in the television series *Neighbours* from 1986; records include "I Should Be So Lucky" (1988), *Kylie Minogue* (1994), *Fever* (2001), and *X* (2007)

minor (ˈmaɪnə) *adj* **1** lesser or secondary in amount, extent, importance, or degree **2** of or relating to the minority **3** below the age of legal majority **4** *music* **a** (of a scale) having a semitone between the second and third and fifth and sixth degrees (**natural minor**) **b** (of a key) based on the minor scale **c** (*postpositive*) denoting a specified key based on the minor scale: *C minor* **d** (of an interval) reduced by a semitone from the major **e** (of a chord, esp a triad) having a minor third above the root **f** (esp in jazz) of or relating to a chord built upon a minor triad and containing a minor seventh: *a minor ninth* **5** *logic* (of a term or premise) having less generality or scope than another term or proposition **6** *US education* of or relating to an additional secondary subject taken by a student **7** (*immediately postpositive*) *Brit* the younger or junior: sometimes used after the surname of a schoolboy if he has an older brother in the same school ▷ *n* **8** a person or thing that is lesser or secondary **9** a person below the age of legal majority **10** *US & Canadian education* a subsidiary subject in which a college or university student needs fewer credits than in his or her major **11** *music* a minor key, chord, mode, or scale **12** *logic* a minor term or premise ▷ *vb* **13** (*intr*; usually foll by *in*) *US education* to take a minor [c13: from Latin: less, smaller; related to Old High German *minniro* smaller, Gothic *minniza* least, Latin *minuere* to diminish, Greek *meiōn* less]

minor axis *n* the shorter or shortest axis of an ellipse or ellipsoid

Minorca (mɪˈnɔːkə) *n* **1** an island in the W Mediterranean, northeast of Majorca: the second largest of the Balearic Islands. Chief town: Mahón. Pop: 78 796 (2002 est). Area: 702 sq km (271 sq miles). Spanish name: **Menorca 2** a breed of light domestic fowl with glossy white, black, or blue plumage > **Mi'norcan** *adj, n*

minority (maɪˈnɒrɪtɪ, mɪ-) *n, pl* **-ties 1** the smaller in number of two parts, factions, or groups **2** a group that is different racially, politically, etc, from a larger group of which it is a part **3 a** the state of being a minor **b** the period during which a person is below legal age **4** (*modifier*) relating to or being a minority: *a minority interest; a minority opinion* [c16: from Medieval Latin

minōritās, from Latin MINOR]

minor league *n US & Canadian* any professional league in baseball other than a major league

minor orders *pl n RC Church* the four lower degrees of holy orders, namely porter, exorcist, lector, and acolyte

minor premise *n logic* the premise of a syllogism containing the subject of its conclusion

minor term *n logic* the subject of the conclusion of a syllogism, also occurring as the subject or predicate in the minor premise

Minos (ˈmaɪnɒs) *n Greek myth* a king of Crete for whom Daedalus built the Labyrinth to contain the Minotaur

Minotaur (ˈmaɪnətɔː) *n Greek myth* a monster with the head of a bull and the body of a man. It was kept in the Labyrinth in Crete, feeding on human flesh, until destroyed by Theseus [c14: via Latin from Greek *Minōtauros*, from MINOS + *tauros* bull]

Minsk (mɪnsk) *n* the capital of Belarus: an industrial city and educational and cultural centre, with a university (1921). Pop: 1 709 000 (2005 est)

minster (ˈmɪnstə) *n Brit* any of certain cathedrals and large churches, usually originally connected to a monastery [Old English *mynster*, probably from Vulgar Latin *monisterium* (unattested), variant of Church Latin *monastērium* MONASTERY]

minstrel (ˈmɪnstrəl) *n* **1** a medieval wandering musician who performed songs or recited poetry with instrumental accompaniment **2** a performer in a minstrel show **3** *archaic or poetic* any poet, musician, or singer [c13: from Old French *menestral*, from Late Latin *ministeriālis* an official, from Latin MINISTER]

minstrel show *n* a theatrical entertainment consisting of songs, dances, comic turns, etc, performed by a troupe of actors wearing black face make-up

minstrelsy (ˈmɪnstrəlsɪ) *n, pl* **-sies 1** the art of a minstrel **2** the poems, music, or songs of a minstrel **3** a troupe of minstrels

mint¹ (mɪnt) *n* **1** any N temperate plant of the genus *Mentha*, having aromatic leaves and spikes of small typically mauve flowers: family *Lamiaceae* (labiates). The leaves of some species are used for seasoning and flavouring. See also **peppermint**, **spearmint 2** a sweet flavoured with mint [Old English *minte*, from Latin *mentha*, from Greek *minthē*; compare Old High German *minza*] > **'minty** *adj*

mint² (mɪnt) *n* **1** a place where money is coined by governmental authority **2** a very large amount of money ▷ *adj* **3** (of coins, postage stamps, etc) in perfect condition as issued **4 in mint condition** in perfect condition; as if new ▷ *vb* **5** to make (coins) by stamping metal **6** (*tr*) to invent (esp phrases or words) [Old English *mynet* coin, from Latin *monēta* money, mint, from the temple of Juno *Monēta*, used as a mint in ancient Rome] > **'minter** *n*

mintage (ˈmɪntɪdʒ) *n* **1** the process of minting **2** money minted **3** a fee paid for minting a coin **4** an official impression stamped on a coin

minted (ˈmɪntɪd) *adj Brit slang* wealthy

mint julep *n chiefly US* a long drink consisting of bourbon whiskey, crushed ice, sugar, and sprigs of mint

minuend (ˈmɪnjʊˌɛnd) *n* the number from which another number, the subtrahend, is to be subtracted [c18: from Latin *minuendus* (*numerus*) (the number) to be diminished]

minuet (ˌmɪnjʊˈɛt) *n* **1** a stately court dance of the 17th and 18th centuries in triple time **2** a piece of music composed for or in the rhythm of this dance, sometimes as a movement in a suite, sonata, or symphony [c17: from French *menuet* dainty (referring to the dance steps), from *menu* small]

minus (ˈmaɪnəs) *prep* **1** reduced by the subtraction of: *four minus two* (written 4 – 2) **2** *informal* deprived of; lacking: *minus the trimmings, that hat would be ordinary* ▷ *adj* **3 a** indicating or involving subtraction: *a minus sign* **b** Also called: **negative** having a value or designating a quantity less than zero: *a minus number* **4** involving a disadvantage, harm, etc: *a minus factor* **5** (*postpositive*) *education* slightly below the standard of a particular grade: *he received a B minus for his essay* **6** denoting a negative electric charge ▷ *n* **7** short for **minus sign** **8** a negative quantity **9** a disadvantage, loss, or deficit **10** *informal* something detrimental or negative ▷ Mathematical symbol: – [c15: from Latin, neuter of MINOR]

minuscule ('mɪnə,skjuːl) *n* **1** a lower-case letter **2** writing using such letters **3** a small cursive 7th-century style of lettering derived from the uncial ▷ *adj* **4** relating to, printed in, or written in small letters. See **majuscule** **5** very small **6** (of letters) lower-case [c18: from French, from Latin (*littera*) *minuscula* very small (letter), diminutive of MINOR] ▷ minuscular (mɪ'nʌskjʊlə) *adj*

minus sign *n* the symbol –, indicating subtraction or a negative quantity

minute¹ ('mɪnɪt) *n* **1** a period of time equal to 60 seconds; one sixtieth of an hour **2** Also called: **minute of arc** a unit of angular measure equal to one sixtieth of a degree. Symbol: ′ **3** any very short period of time; moment **4** a short note or memorandum **5** the distance that can be travelled in a minute: *it's only two minutes away* **6** up to the minute (**up-to-the-minute** *when prenominal*) very latest or newest ▷ *vb* (*tr*) **7** to record in minutes: *to minute a meeting* **8** to time in terms of minutes ▷ See also **minutes** [c14: from Old French from Medieval Latin *minūta*, n. use of Latin *minūtus* MINUTE²]

minute² (maɪ'njuːt) *adj* **1** very small; diminutive; tiny **2** unimportant; petty **3** precise or detailed: *a minute examination* [c15: from Latin *minūtus*, past participle of *minuere* to diminish] ▷ mi'nutely *adv* ▷ mi'nuteness *n*

minute gun ('mɪnɪt) *n* a gun fired at one-minute intervals as a sign of distress or mourning

minute hand ('mɪnɪt) *n* the pointer on a timepiece that indicates minutes, typically the longer hand of two

Minuteman ('mɪnɪt,mæn) *n, pl* -men **1** (*sometimes not capital*) (in the War of American Independence) a colonial militiaman who promised to be ready to fight at one minute's notice **2** a US three-stage intercontinental ballistic missile

minutes ('mɪnɪts) *pl n* an official record of the proceedings of a meeting, conference, convention, etc

minute steak ('mɪnɪt) *n* a small thinly-cut piece of steak that can be cooked quickly

minutiae (mɪ'njuːʃɪ,iː) *pl n, sing* -tia (-ʃɪə) small, precise, or trifling details [c18: pl of Late Latin *minūtia* smallness, from Latin *minūtus* MINUTE²]

minx (mɪŋks) *n* a bold, flirtatious, or scheming woman [c16: of unknown origin]

Minya ('mɪnjə) *n* See **El Minya**

Miocene ('maɪə,siːn) *adj* **1** of, denoting, or formed in the fourth epoch of the Tertiary period, between the Oligocene and Pliocene epochs, which lasted for 19 million years ▷ *n* **2** the Miocene this epoch or rock series [c19: from Greek *meiōn* less + -CENE]

miosis *or* **myosis** (maɪ'əʊsɪs) *n, pl* -ses (-siːz) **1** excessive contraction of the pupil of the eye, as in response to drugs **2** a variant spelling of: **meiosis** (sense 1) [c20: from Greek *muein* to shut the eyes + -OSIS] ▷ miotic *or* myotic (maɪ'ɒtɪk) *adj, n*

MIP *abbreviation* **1** monthly investment plan **2** maximum investment plan: an endowment assurance policy designed to produce maximum profits

Miquelon ('miːkə,lɒn; *French* miklɔ̃) *n* a group of islands in the French territory of **Saint Pierre and Miquelon**

Mir (mɪə) *n* the Russian (formerly Soviet) manned space station launched in February 1986 and scuttled in 2001 [c20: Russian: peace]

Mirabeau (*French* mirabo) *n* **Comte de**, title of *Honoré-Gabriel Riqueti. 1749–91, French Revolutionary politician*

mirabelle ('mɪrə,bɛl) *n* **1** a small sweet yellow-orange fruit that is a variety of greengage **2** a liqueur distilled from this [c18: from French]

miracle ('mɪrək⁰l) *n* **1** an event that is contrary to the established laws of nature and attributed to a supernatural cause **2** any amazing or wonderful event **3** a person or thing that is a marvellous example of something: *the bridge was a miracle of engineering* **4** short for **miracle play** **5** (*modifier*) being or seeming a miracle: *a miracle cure* [c12: from Latin *mīrāculum*, from *mīrārī* to

wonder at]

miracle play *n* a medieval play based on a biblical story or the life of a saint. See **mystery play**

miraculous (mɪ'rækjʊləs) *adj* **1** of, like, or caused by a miracle; marvellous **2** surprising **3** having the power to work miracles ▷ mi'raculously *adv* ▷ mi'raculousness *n*

Miraflores (,mɪrə'flɔːrəs; *Spanish* mira'flores) *n* Lake Miraflores an artificial lake in Panama, in the S Canal Zone of the Panama Canal

mirage (mɪ'rɑːʒ) *n* **1** an image of a distant object or sheet of water, often inverted or distorted, caused by atmospheric refraction by hot air **2** something illusory [c19: from French, from (*se*) *mirer* to be reflected]

Miranda (*Spanish* mi'randa) *n* **Francisco de** (fran'sisko de). 1750–1816, Venezuelan revolutionary, who planned to liberate Central and South America from Spain. A leader (1811–12) of the Venezuelan uprising, he surrendered to Spain and died in prison

mire (maɪə) *n* **1** a boggy or marshy area **2** mud, muck, or dirt ▷ *vb* **3** to sink or cause to sink in a mire **4** (*tr*) to make dirty or muddy **5** (*tr*) to involve, esp in difficulties [c14: from Old Norse *mȳrr*; related to MOSS]

mirepoix (mɪə'pwɑː) *n* a mixture of sautéed root vegetables used as a base for braising meat or for various sauces [French, probably named in honour of C. P. G. F. de Lévis, Duke of *Mirepoix*, 18th-century French general]

Miriam ('mɪrɪəm) *n* *Old Testament* the sister of Moses and Aaron. (Numbers 12:1–15). Douay name: **Mary²**

mirk (mɜːk) *n* a variant spelling of: **murk¹** ▷ 'mirky *adj* ▷ 'mirkily *adv* ▷ 'mirkiness *n*

Miró (*Spanish* mi'ro) *n* **Joan** (xwan). 1893–1983, Spanish surrealist painter

Mirren ('mɪrən) *n* **Dame Helen**, original name *Ilyena Vasilievna Mironov*, born 1945, English actor; her films include *Savage Messiah* (1972), *The Long Good Friday* (1980), *The Cook, The Thief, His Wife and Her Lover* (1989) and *The Queen* (2006), for which she won an Academy Award for Best Actress

mirror ('mɪrə) *n* **1** a surface, such as polished metal or glass coated with a metal film, that reflects light without diffusion and produces an image of an object placed in front of it **2** such a reflecting surface mounted in a frame **3** any reflecting surface **4** a thing that reflects or depicts something else: *the press is a mirror of public opinion* ▷ *vb* **5** (*tr*) to reflect, represent, or depict faithfully: *he mirrors his teacher's ideals* [c13: from Old French from *mirer* to look at, from Latin *mīrārī* to wonder at]

mirror ball *n* a large revolving ball covered with small pieces of mirror glass so that it reflects light in changing patterns: used in discos and ballrooms

mirror carp *n* a variety of the common carp (*Cyprinus carpio*) with reduced scales, giving a smooth shiny body surface

mirror image *n* **1** an image as observed in a mirror **2** an object that corresponds to another object in the same way as it would correspond to its image in a mirror

mirror writing *n* backward writing that forms a mirror image of normal writing

mirth (mɜːθ) *n* laughter, gaiety, or merriment [Old English *myrgth*; compare MERRY] ▷ 'mirthful *adj* ▷ 'mirthfulness *n* ▷ 'mirthless *adj* ▷ 'mirthlessness *n*

MIRV (mɜːv) *n acronym for* multiple independently targeted re-entry vehicle: a missile that has several warheads, each one being directed to different enemy targets

mis- *prefix* **1** wrong, bad, or erroneous; wrongly, badly, or erroneously: *misunderstanding; misfortune; misspelling; mistreat; mislead* **2** lack of: *mistrust* [Old English *mis(se)-*; related to Middle English *mes-*, from Old French *mes-*; compare Old High German *missa-*, Old Norse *mis-*]

misadventure (,mɪsəd'vɛntʃə) *n* **1** an unlucky event; misfortune **2** *law* accidental death not due to crime or negligence

misalliance (,mɪsə'laɪəns) *n* an unsuitable alliance or marriage

misanthrope ('mɪzən,θrəʊp) *or* **misanthropist** (mɪ'zænθrəpɪst) *n* a person who dislikes or distrusts other people or mankind in general [c17: from Greek

mīsanthrōpos, from _misos_ hatred + _anthrōpos_ man]
> **misanthropic** (ˌmɪzən'θrɒpɪk) _or_ **misan'thropical** _adj_
> **misanthropy** (mɪ'zænθrəpɪ) _n_

misapply (ˌmɪsə'plaɪ) _vb_ -plies, -plying, -plied (_tr_) **1** to apply wrongly or badly **2** another word for **misappropriate** > **misapplication** (ˌmɪsæplɪ'keɪʃən) _n_

misapprehend (ˌmɪsæprɪ'hend) _vb_ (_tr_) to misunderstand > ˌmisappre'hensive _adj_ > ˌmisappre'hensiveness _n_

misapprehension (ˌmɪsæprɪ'hɛnʃən) _n_ a failure to understand fully; misconception: _the misapprehension that acting was easy_

misappropriate (ˌmɪsə'prəʊprɪˌeɪt) _vb_ (_tr_) to appropriate for a wrong or dishonest use; embezzle or steal > ˌmisappropri'ation _n_

misbecome (ˌmɪsbɪ'kʌm) _vb_ -comes, -coming, -came (_tr_) to be unbecoming to or unsuitable for

misbegotten (ˌmɪsbɪ'gɒtən) _adj_ **1** unlawfully obtained: _misbegotten gains_ **2** badly conceived, planned, or designed **3** Also: **misbegot** (ˌmɪsbɪ'gɒt) _literary, dialect_ illegitimate; bastard

misbehave (ˌmɪsbɪ'heɪv) _vb_ to behave (oneself) badly > ˌmisbe'haver _n_ > **misbehaviour** (ˌmɪsbɪ'heɪvjə) _n_

misbelief (ˌmɪsbɪ'liːf) _n_ a false or unorthodox belief

misc. _abbreviation_ miscellaneous

miscalculate (ˌmɪs'kælkjʊˌleɪt) _vb_ (_tr_) to calculate wrongly > ˌmiscalcu'lation _n_

miscall (ˌmɪs'kɔːl) _vb_ (_tr_) **1** to call by the wrong name **2** _dialect_ to abuse or malign > ˌmis'caller _n_

miscarriage (mɪs'kærɪdʒ) _n_ (_also_ 'mɪskær-) **1** spontaneous expulsion of a fetus from the womb, esp prior to the 20th week of pregnancy **2** an act of mismanagement or failure: _a miscarriage of justice_ **3** _Brit_ the failure of freight to reach its destination

miscarry (mɪs'kærɪ) _vb_ -ries, -rying, -ried (_intr_) **1** to expel a fetus prematurely from the womb; abort **2** to fail **3** _Brit_ (of freight, mail, etc) to fail to reach a destination

miscast (ˌmɪs'kɑːst) _vb_ -casts, -casting, -cast (_tr_) **1** to cast badly **2** (_often passive_) **a** to cast (a role or roles) in (a play, film, etc) inappropriately: _Falstaff was certainly miscast_ **b** to assign an inappropriate role to: _he was miscast as Othello_

miscegenation (ˌmɪsɪdʒɪ'neɪʃən) _n_ interbreeding of races, esp where differences of pigmentation are involved [c19: from Latin _miscēre_ to mingle + _genus_ race]

miscellanea (ˌmɪsə'leɪnɪə) _pl n_ a collection of miscellaneous items, esp literary works [c16: from Latin: neuter pl of _miscellāneus_ MISCELLANEOUS]

miscellaneous (ˌmɪsə'leɪnɪəs) _adj_ **1** composed of or containing a variety of things; mixed; varied **2** having varied capabilities, sides, etc [c17: from Latin _miscellāneus_, from _miscellus_ mixed, from _miscēre_ to mix] > ˌmiscel'laneously _adv_ > ˌmiscel'laneousness _n_

miscellany (mɪ'sɛlənɪ; _US_ 'mɪsəˌleɪnɪ) _n_, _pl_ -nies **1** a mixed assortment of items **2** (_sometimes plural_) a miscellaneous collection of essays, poems, etc, by different authors in one volume [c16: from French _miscellanées_ (pl) MISCELLANEA] > **miscellanist** (mɪ'sɛlənɪst) _n_

mischance (mɪs'tʃɑːns) _n_ **1** bad luck **2** a stroke of bad luck

mischief ('mɪstʃɪf) _n_ **1** wayward but not malicious behaviour, usually of children, that causes trouble, irritation, etc **2** a playful inclination to behave in this way or to tease or disturb **3** injury or harm caused by a person or thing **4** a person, esp a child, who is mischievous **5** a source of trouble, difficulty, etc [c13: from Old French _meschief_ disaster, from _meschever_ to meet with calamity; from _mes-_ MIS-¹ + _chever_ to reach an end, from _chef_ end, CHIEF]

mischievous ('mɪstʃɪvəs) _adj_ **1** inclined to acts of mischief **2** teasing; slightly malicious **3** causing or intended to cause harm > 'mischievously _adv_ > 'mischievousness _n_

miscible ('mɪsɪbəl) _adj_ capable of mixing: _alcohol is miscible with water_ [c16: from Medieval Latin _miscibilis_, from Latin _miscēre_ to mix] > ˌmisci'bility _n_

misconceive (ˌmɪskən'siːv) _vb_ to have the wrong idea; fail to understand > ˌmiscon'ceiver _n_

misconception (ˌmɪskən'sɛpʃən) _n_ a false or mistaken view, opinion, or attitude

misconduct _n_ (mɪs'kɒndʌkt) **1** behaviour, such as adultery or professional negligence, that is regarded as immoral or unethical ▷ _vb_ (ˌmɪskən'dʌkt) **2** to conduct (oneself) in such a way **3** to manage (something) badly

misconstrue (ˌmɪskən'struː) _vb_ -strues, -struing, -strued (_tr_) to interpret mistakenly > ˌmiscon'struction _n_

miscreant ('mɪskrɪənt) _n_ **1** a wrongdoer or villain **2** _archaic_ an unbeliever or heretic ▷ _adj_ **3** evil or villainous **4** _archaic_ unbelieving or heretical [c14: from Old French _mescreant_ unbelieving, from _mes-_ MIS-¹ + _creant_, ultimately from Latin _credere_ to believe]

miscue (ˌmɪs'kjuː) _n_ **1** _billiards_ a faulty stroke in which the cue tip slips off the cue ball or misses it altogether **2** _informal_ a blunder or mistake ▷ _vb_ -cues, -cuing, -cued **3** (_intr_) _billiards_ to make a miscue **4** (_intr_) _theatre_ to fail to answer one's own cue or answer the cue of another

miscue analysis _n_ _Brit_ _education_ analysis of the errors a pupil makes while reading

misdate (mɪs'deɪt) _vb_ (_tr_) to date (a letter, event, etc) wrongly

misdeal (mɪs'diːl) _vb_ -deals, -dealing, -dealt **1** (_intr_) to deal out cards incorrectly ▷ _n_ **2** a faulty deal > ˌmis'dealer _n_

misdeed (ˌmɪs'diːd) _n_ an evil or illegal action

misdemean (ˌmɪsdɪ'miːn) _vb_ a rare word for **misbehave**

misdemeanour _or_ _US_ **misdemeanor** (ˌmɪsdɪ'miːnə) _n_ **1** _criminal law_ (formerly) an offence generally less heinous than a felony and which until 1967 involved a different form of trial **2** any minor offence or transgression

misdirect (ˌmɪsdɪ'rɛkt) _vb_ (_tr_) **1** to give (a person) wrong directions or instructions **2** to address (a letter, parcel, etc) wrongly > ˌmisdi'rection _n_

misdoubt (mɪs'daʊt) _vb_ an archaic word for **doubt**, **suspect**

mise en scène _French_ (miz ā sɛn) _n_ **1 a** the arrangement of properties, scenery, etc, in a play **b** the objects so arranged; stage setting **2** the environment of an event

Miseno (_Italian_ mi'zeːno) _n_ a cape in SW Italy, on the N shore of the Bay of Naples: remains of the town of Misenum, a naval base constructed by Agrippa in 31 BC

miser ('maɪzə) _n_ **1** a person who hoards money or possessions, often living miserably **2** selfish person [c16: from Latin: wretched]

miserable ('mɪzərəbəl, 'mɪzrə-) _adj_ **1** unhappy or depressed; wretched **2** causing misery, discomfort, etc: _a miserable life_ **3** contemptible: _a miserable villain_ **4** sordid or squalid: _miserable living conditions_ **5** _Scot, Austral & NZ_ mean; stingy [c16: from Old French, from Latin _miserābilis_ worthy of pity, from _miserārī_ to pity, from _miser_ wretched] > 'miserableness _n_ > 'miserably _adv_

misère (mɪ'zɛə) _n_ **1** a call in solo whist and other card games declaring a hand that will win no tricks **2** a hand that will win no tricks [c19: from French: misery]

Miserere (ˌmɪzə'rɛərɪ, -'rɪərɪ) _n_ the 51st psalm, the Latin version of which begins "Miserere mei, Deus" ("Have mercy on me, O God")

misericord _or_ **misericorde** (mɪ'zɛrɪˌkɔːd) _n_ **1** a ledge projecting from the underside of the hinged seat of a choir stall in a church, on which the occupant can support himself while standing **2** _Christianity_ **a** a relaxation of certain monastic rules for infirm or aged monks or nuns **b** a monastery where such relaxations can be enjoyed **3** a small medieval dagger used to give the death stroke to a wounded foe [c14: from Old French, from Latin _misericordia_ compassion, from _miserēre_ to pity + _cor_ heart]

miserly ('maɪzəlɪ) _adj_ of or resembling a miser; avaricious > 'miserliness _n_

misery ('mɪzərɪ) _n_, _pl_ -eries **1** intense unhappiness, discomfort, or suffering; wretchedness **2** a cause of such unhappiness, discomfort, etc **3** squalid or poverty-stricken conditions **4** _Brit informal_ a person who is habitually depressed: _he is such a misery_ [c14: via Anglo-Norman from Latin _miseria_, from _miser_ wretched]

misfeasance (mɪs'fiːzəns) _n_ _law_ the improper performance of an act that is lawful in itself. See

malfeasance, nonfeasance [C16: from Old French *mesfaisance*, from *mesfaire* to perform misdeeds]

misfile (ˌmɪsˈfaɪl) *vb* to file (papers, records, etc) wrongly

misfire (ˌmɪsˈfaɪə) *vb* (*intr*) **1** (of a firearm or its projectile) to fail to fire, explode, or ignite as or when expected **2** (of a motor engine or vehicle, etc) to fail to fire at the appropriate time, often causing a backfire **3** to fail to operate or occur as intended ▷ *n* **4** the act or an instance of misfiring

misfit *n* (ˈmɪsˌfɪt) **1** a person not suited in behaviour or attitude to a particular social environment **2** something that does not fit or fits badly ▷ *vb* (ˌmɪsˈfɪt) -fits, -fitting, -fitted (*intr*) **3** to fail to fit or be fitted

misfortune (mɪsˈfɔːtʃən) *n* **1** evil fortune; bad luck **2** an unfortunate or disastrous event; calamity

misgive (mɪsˈɡɪv) *vb* -gives, -giving, -gave, -given to make or be apprehensive or suspicious

misgiving (mɪsˈɡɪvɪŋ) *n* (*often plural*) a feeling of uncertainty, apprehension, or doubt

misguide (ˌmɪsˈɡaɪd) *vb* (*tr*) to guide or direct wrongly or badly

misguided (ˌmɪsˈɡaɪdɪd) *adj* foolish or unreasonable, esp in action or behaviour > ˌmisˈguidedly *adv*

mishandle (ˌmɪsˈhændəl) *vb* (*tr*) to handle or treat badly or inefficiently

mishap (ˈmɪshæp) *n* **1** an unfortunate accident **2** bad luck

Mishima (ˈmɪʃimə) *n* **Yukio** (juːkiəʊ). 1925–70, Japanese novelist and short-story writer, whose works reflect a preoccupation with homosexuality and death. He committed harakiri in protest at the decline of traditional Japanese values

mishit *sport n* (ˈmɪsˌhɪt) **1** a faulty shot or stroke ▷ *vb* (ˌmɪsˈhɪt) -hits, -hitting, -hit **2** to hit (a ball) with a faulty stroke

mishmash (ˈmɪʃˌmæʃ) *n* a confused collection or mixture; hotchpotch [C15: reduplication of MASH]

Mishna (ˈmɪʃnə; *Hebrew* miʃ'na) *n*, *pl* **Mishnayoth** (mɪʃnaːˈjɔt; *Hebrew* miʃna'jɔt) *Judaism* a compilation of precepts passed down as an oral tradition and collected by Judah ha-Nasi in the late second century AD. It forms the earlier part of the Talmud [C17: from Hebrew: instruction by repetition, from *shānāh* to repeat] > Mishnaic (mɪʃˈneɪɪk) *or* 'Mishnic

misinform (ˌmɪsɪnˈfɔːm) *vb* (*tr*) to give incorrect information to > misinformation (ˌmɪsɪnfəˈmeɪʃən) *n*

misinterpret (ˌmɪsɪnˈtɜːprɪt) *vb* (*tr*) to interpret badly, misleadingly, or incorrectly > ˌmisinˈterpreˈtation *n*

misjudge (ˌmɪsˈdʒʌdʒ) *vb* to judge (a person or persons) wrongly or unfairly > ˌmisˈjudger *n* > ˌmisˈjudgment *or* ˌmisˈjudgement *n*

Miskolc (*Hungarian* ˈmiʃkolts) *n* a city in NE Hungary: the second most important industrial centre in Hungary; iron and steel industries. Pop: 180 282 (2003 est)

mislay (mɪsˈleɪ) *vb* -lays, -laying, -laid (*tr*) **1** to lose (something) temporarily, esp by forgetting where it is **2** to lay (something) badly

mislead (mɪsˈliːd) *vb* -leads, -leading, -led (*tr*) **1** to give false or misleading information to **2** to lead or guide in the wrong direction > misˈleader *n* > misˈleading *adj* > misˈleadingly *adv*

mismatch (ˌmɪsˈmætʃ) *vb* **1** to match badly, esp in marriage ▷ *n* **2** a bad or inappropriate match

misnomer (ˌmɪsˈnəʊmə) *n* **1** an incorrect or unsuitable name or term for a person or thing **2** the act of referring to a person by the wrong name [C15: via Anglo-Norman from Old French *mesnommer* to misname, from Latin *nōmināre* to call by name]

miso- *or before a vowel* **mis-** *combining form* indicating hatred: *misogyny* [from Greek *misos* hatred]

misogamy (mɪˈsɒɡəmɪ, maɪ-) *n* hatred of marriage > miˈsogamist *n*

misogyny (mɪˈsɒdʒɪnɪ, maɪ-) *n* hatred of women [C17: from Greek, from MISO- + *gunē* woman] > miˈsogynist *n*, *adj* > miˌsogyˈnistic *or* miˈsogynous *adj*

misplace (ˌmɪsˈpleɪs) *vb* (*tr*) **1** to put (something) in the wrong place, esp to lose (something) temporarily by forgetting where it was placed; mislay **2** (*often passive*) to bestow (trust, confidence, affection, etc) unadvisedly

> ˌmisˈplacement *n*

misplaced modifier *n grammar* a participle intended to modify a noun but having the wrong grammatical relationship to it as for example *having left* in the sentence *Having left Europe for good, Peter's future seemed bleak indeed*

misplay (ˌmɪsˈpleɪ) *vb* **1** (*tr*) to play badly or wrongly in games or sports ▷ *n* **2** a wrong or unskilful play

misprint *n* (ˈmɪsˌprɪnt) **1** an error in printing, made through damaged type, careless reading, etc ▷ *vb* (ˌmɪsˈprɪnt) **2** (*tr*) to print (a letter) incorrectly

misprision[1] (mɪsˈprɪʒən) *n* **a** a failure to inform the proper authorities of the commission of an act of treason **b** the deliberate concealment of the commission of a felony [C15: via Anglo-French from Old French *mesprision* error, from *mesprendre* to mistake, from *mes-* MIS-[1] + *prendre* to take]

misprision[2] (mɪsˈprɪʒən) *n archaic* **1** contempt **2** failure to appreciate the value of something [C16: from MISPRIZE]

misprize *or* **misprise** (mɪsˈpraɪz) *vb* to fail to appreciate the value of; undervalue or disparage [C15: from Old French *mesprisier*, from *mes-* MIS-[1] + *prisier* to PRIZE[2]]

mispronounce (ˌmɪsprəˈnaʊns) *vb* to pronounce (a word) wrongly > mispronunciation (ˌmɪsprəˌnʌnsɪˈeɪʃən) *n*

misquote (ˌmɪsˈkwəʊt) *vb* to quote (a text, speech, etc) inaccurately > ˌmisquoˈtation *n*

misread (ˌmɪsˈriːd) *vb* -reads, -reading, -read (-ˈrɛd) (*tr*) **1** to read incorrectly **2** to misinterpret

misrepresent (ˌmɪsrɛprɪˈzɛnt) *vb* (*tr*) to represent wrongly or inaccurately > ˌmisrepresenˈtation *n* > ˌmisrepreˈsentative *adj*

misrule (ˌmɪsˈruːl) *vb* **1** (*tr*) to govern inefficiently or without humanity or justice ▷ *n* **2** inefficient or inhumane government **3** disorder

miss[1] (mɪs) *vb* **1** to fail to reach, hit, meet, find, or attain (some specified or implied aim, goal, target, etc) **2** (*tr*) to fail to attend or be present for: *to miss a train; to miss an appointment* **3** (*tr*) to fail to see, hear, understand, or perceive: *to miss a point* **4** (*tr*) to lose, overlook, or fail to take advantage of: *to miss an opportunity* **5** (*tr*) to leave out; omit: *to miss an entry in a list* **6** (*tr*) to discover or regret the loss or absence of: *he missed his watch; she missed him* **7** (*tr*) to escape or avoid (something, esp a danger), usually narrowly: *he missed death by inches* **8** miss the boat *or* miss the bus to lose an opportunity ▷ *n* **9** a failure to reach, hit, meet, find, etc **10** give something a miss *informal* to avoid (something): *give the lecture a miss; give the pudding a miss* ▷ See also **miss out** [Old English *missan* (meaning: to fail to hit); related to Old High German *missan*, Old Norse *missa*]

miss[2] (mɪs) *n informal* an unmarried woman or girl, esp a schoolgirl [C17: shortened form of MISTRESS]

Miss (mɪs) *n* a title of an unmarried woman or girl, usually used before the surname or sometimes alone in direct address [C17: shortened form of MISTRESS]

Miss. *abbreviation* Mississippi

missal (ˈmɪsəl) *n RC Church* a book containing the prayers, rites, etc, of the Masses for a complete year [C14: from Church Latin *missale* (n), from *missālis* concerning the Mass]

mis-sell *vb*, *pl* -sells, -selling, -sold to sell a financial product that is inappropriate for the needs of the customer

misshape *vb* (ˌmɪsˈʃeɪp) -shapes, -shaping, -shaped, -shaped *or* -shapen (*tr*) **1** to shape badly; deform ▷ *n* (ˈmɪsˌʃeɪp) **2** something that is badly shaped

misshapen (ˌmɪsˈʃeɪpən) *adj* badly shaped; deformed > ˌmisˈshapenness *n*

missile (ˈmɪsaɪl) *n* **1** any object or weapon that is thrown at a target or shot from an engine, gun, etc **2** a rocket-propelled weapon that flies either in a fixed trajectory (ballistic missile) or in a trajectory that can be controlled during flight (guided missile) [C17: from Latin: *missilis*, from *mittere* to send]

missilery *or* **missilry** (ˈmɪsaɪlrɪ) *n* **1** missiles collectively **2** the design, operation, or study of missiles

missing (ˈmɪsɪŋ) *adj* **1** not present; absent or lost **2** not able to be traced and not known to be dead: *nine men were missing after the attack* **3** go missing to become lost or disappear

missing link *n* **1** the missing link (*sometimes capitals*) a hypothetical extinct animal or animal group, formerly thought to be intermediate between the anthropoid apes and man **2** any missing section or part in an otherwise complete series

mission ('mɪʃən) *n* **1** a specific task or duty assigned to a person or group of people **2** a person's vocation (often in the phrase **mission in life**) **3** a group of persons representing or working for a particular country, business, etc, in a foreign country **4** a special embassy sent to a foreign country for a specific purpose **5 a** a group of people sent by a religious body, esp a Christian church, to a foreign country to do religious and social work **b** the campaign undertaken by such a group **6 a** a building or group of buildings in which missionary work is performed **b** the area assigned to a particular missionary **7** the dispatch of aircraft or spacecraft to achieve a particular task **8** a charitable centre that offers shelter, aid, or advice to the destitute or underprivileged **9** (*modifier*) of or relating to an ecclesiastical mission: *a mission station* ▷ *vb* **10** (*tr*) to direct a mission to or establish a mission in (a given region) [C16: from Latin *missiō*, from *mittere* to send]

missionary ('mɪʃənərɪ) *n, pl* -aries **1** a member of a religious mission ▷ *adj* **2** of or relating to missionaries: *missionary work* **3** resulting from a desire to convert people to one's own beliefs: *missionary zeal*

missionary position *n informal* a position for sexual intercourse in which the man lies on top of the woman and they are face to face [C20: from the belief that missionaries advocated this as the proper position to primitive peoples among whom it was unknown]

Missionary Ridge *n* a ridge in NW Georgia and SE Tennessee: site of a battle (1863) during the Civil War: Northern victory leading to the campaign in Georgia

mission creep *n* the tendency for a task, esp a military operation, to become unintentionally wider in scope than its initial objectives

mission statement *n* an official statement of the aims and objectives of a business or other organization

Mississauga (ˌmɪsə'sɔːɡə) *n* a town in SE Ontario: a SW suburb of Toronto. Pop: 612 925 (2001)

Mississippi (ˌmɪsɪ'sɪpɪ) *n* **1** a state of the southeastern US, on the Gulf of Mexico: consists of a largely forested undulating plain, with swampy regions in the northwest and on the coast, the Mississippi River forming the W border; cotton, rice, and oil. Capital: Jackson. Pop: 2 881 281 (2003 est). Area: 122 496 sq km (47 296 sq miles). Abbreviation: **Miss, MS 2** a river in the central US, rising in NW Minnesota and flowing generally south to the Gulf of Mexico through several mouths, known as the Passes: the second longest river in North America (after its tributary, the Missouri), with the third largest drainage basin in the world (after the Amazon and the Congo). Length: 3780 km (2348 miles)

Mississippian (ˌmɪsɪ'sɪpɪən) *adj* **1** of or relating to the state of Mississippi or the Mississippi River **2** (in North America) of, denoting, or formed in the lower of two subdivisions of the Carboniferous period, which lasted for 30 million years. See also **Pennsylvanian** (sense 2) ▷ *n* **3** an inhabitant or native of the state of Mississippi **4** the Mississippian the Mississippian period or rock system equivalent to the lower Carboniferous of Europe

missive ('mɪsɪv) *n* **1** a formal or official letter **2** a formal word for **letter** [C15: from Medieval Latin *missivus*, from *mittere* to send]

Missolonghi (ˌmɪsə'lɒŋɡɪ) *or* **Mesolonghi** *n* a town in W Greece, near the Gulf of Patras: famous for its defence against the Turks in 1822–23 and 1825–26 and for its association with Lord Byron, who died here in 1824. Pop (municipality): 18 354 (2001). Modern Greek name: Mesolóngion

Missouri (mɪ'zʊərɪ) *n* **1** a state of the central US: consists of rolling prairies in the north, the Ozark Mountains in the south, and part of the Mississippi flood plain in the southeast, with the Mississippi forming the E border;

chief US producer of lead and barytes. Capital: Jefferson City. Pop: 5 704 484 (2003 est). Area: 178 699 sq km (68 995 sq miles). Abbreviation: **Mo, MO 2** a river in the W and central US, rising in SW Montana: flows north, east, and southeast to join the Mississippi above St Louis; the longest river in North America; chief tributary of the Mississippi. Length: 3970 km (2466 miles) > Mi'ssourian *n, adj*

miss out *vb* **1** (*tr, adverb*) to leave out; overlook **2** (*intr, adverb; often foll by on*) to fail to experience: *by leaving early you missed out on the celebrations*

misspell (ˌmɪs'spɛl) *vb* -spells, -spelling, -spelt *or* -spelled to spell (a word or words) wrongly

misspelling (ˌmɪs'spɛlɪŋ) *n* a wrong spelling

misspend (ˌmɪs'spɛnd) *vb* -spends, -spending, -spent to spend thoughtlessly or wastefully

misstep (ˌmɪs'stɛp) *n* **1** a false step **2** an error

missus *or* **missis** ('mɪsɪz, -ɪs) *n* **1** the missus *informal* one's wife or the wife of the person addressed or referred to **2** an informal term of address for a woman [C19: spoken version of MISTRESS]

missy ('mɪsɪ) *n, pl* missies *informal* an affectionate or sometimes disparaging form of address to a young girl

mist (mɪst) *n* **1** a thin fog resulting from condensation in the air near the earth's surface **2** *meteorol* such an atmospheric condition with a horizontal visibility of 1–2 kilometres **3** a fine spray of any liquid, such as that produced by an aerosol container **4** condensed water vapour on a surface that blurs the surface **5** something that causes haziness or lack of clarity, such as a film of tears ▷ *vb* **6** to cover or be covered with or as if with mist [Old English; related to Middle Dutch, Swedish *mist*, Greek *omikhlē* fog]

mistake (mɪ'steɪk) *n* **1** an error or blunder in action, opinion, or judgment **2** a misconception or misunderstanding ▷ *vb* -takes, -taking, -took, -taken **3** (*tr*) to misunderstand; misinterpret: *she mistook his meaning* **4** (*tr*; foll by *for*) to take (for), interpret (as), or confuse (with): *she mistook his direct manner for honesty* **5** (*tr*) to choose badly or incorrectly: *he mistook his path* **6** (*intr*) to make a mistake in action, opinion, judgment, etc [C13 (meaning: to do wrong, err): from Old Norse *mistaka* to take erroneously] > mistakable *or* mistakeable (mɪ'steɪkəbᵊl) *adj* > mis'takably *or* mis'takeably *adv*

mistaken (mɪ'steɪkən) *adj* **1** (*usually predicative*) wrong in opinion, judgment, etc: *she is mistaken* **2** arising from error in judgment, opinion, etc: *a mistaken viewpoint* > mis'takenly *adv* > mis'takenness *n*

Mistassini (ˌmɪstə'siːnɪ) *n* Lake Mistassini a lake in E Canada, in N Quebec: the largest lake in the province; drains through the Rupert River into James Bay. Area: 2175 sq km (840 sq miles). Length: about 160 km (100 miles)

mister ('mɪstə) (*sometimes capital*) *n* **1** an informal form of address for a man **2** *naval* **a** the official form of address for subordinate or senior warrant officers **b** the official form of address for all officers in a merchant ship, other than the captain **c** *US navy* the official form of address used by the commanding officer to his officers, esp to the more junior **3** *Brit* the form of address for a surgeon **4** the form of address for officials holding certain positions: *mister chairman* ▷ *vb* **5** (*tr*) *informal* to call (someone) mister [C16: variant of MASTER]

Mister ('mɪstə) *n* the full form of **Mr**

Misti (*Spanish* 'misti) *n* See El Misti

mistigris ('mɪstɪɡriː) *n* **1** the joker or a blank card used as a wild card in a variety of draw poker **2** the variety of draw poker using this card [C19: from French *mistigris* jack of clubs, game in which this card was wild]

mistime (ˌmɪs'taɪm) *vb* (*tr*) to time (an action, utterance, etc) wrongly

Mistinguett (*French* mistɛ̃gɛt) *n* original name *Jeanne-Marie Bourgeois*. 1875–1956, French dancer, chanteuse, and entertainer

mistle thrush *or* **missel thrush** ('mɪsᵊl) *n* a large European thrush, *Turdus viscivorus*, with a brown back and spotted breast, noted for feeding on mistletoe berries [C18: from Old English *mistel* MISTLETOE]

mistletoe ('mɪsᵊlˌtəʊ) *n* **1** a Eurasian evergreen shrub,

Viscum album, with leathery leaves, yellowish flowers, and waxy white berries: grows as a partial parasite on various trees: used as a Christmas decoration: family *Viscaceae* **2** any of several similar and related American plants in the families *Loranthaceae* or *Viscaceae*, esp *Phoradendron flavescens* [Old English *misteltān*, from *mistel* mistletoe + *tān* twig; related to Old Norse *mistilteinn*]

mistook (mɪ'stʊk) *vb* the past tense of **mistake**

mistral ('mɪstrəl, mɪ'strɑːl) *n* a strong cold dry wind that blows through the Rhône valley and S France to the Mediterranean coast, mainly in the winter [c17: via French from Provençal, from Latin *magistrālis* MAGISTRAL, as in *magistrālis ventus* master wind]

Mistral *n* **1** (*French* mistral) **Frédéric** (frederik). 1830–1914, French Provençal poet, who led a movement to revive Provençal language and literature: shared the Nobel prize for literature 1904 **2** (*Spanish* mis'tral) **Gabriela** (ga'βrjela), pen name of *Lucila Godoy de Alcayaga*. 1889–1957, Chilean poet, educationalist, and diplomatist. Her poetry includes the collection *Desolación* (1922): Nobel prize for literature 1945

mistreat (ˌmɪs'triːt) *vb* (*tr*) to treat badly
> ˌmis'treatment *n*

mistress ('mɪstrɪs) *n* **1** a woman who has a continuing extramarital sexual relationship with a man **2** a woman in a position of authority, ownership, or control, such as the head of a household **3** a woman or female personification having control over something specified: *she was mistress of her own destiny* **4** *chiefly Brit* short for **schoolmistress** **5** an archaic or dialect word for **sweetheart** [c14: from Old French; see MASTER, -ESS]

Mistress ('mɪstrɪs) *n* an archaic or dialect title equivalent to: **Mrs**

Mistress of the Robes *n* (in Britain) a lady of high rank in charge of the Queen's wardrobe

mistrial (mɪs'traɪəl) *n* **1** a trial made void because of some error, such as a defect in procedure **2** (in the US) an inconclusive trial, as when a jury cannot agree on a verdict

mistrust (ˌmɪs'trʌst) *vb* **1** to have doubts or suspicions about (someone or something) ▷ *n* **2** distrust
> ˌmis'trustful *adj* > ˌmis'trustfully *adv*
> ˌmis'trustfulness *n*

misty ('mɪstɪ) *adj* mistier, mistiest **1** consisting of or resembling mist **2** obscured by or as if by mist **3** indistinct; blurred > 'mistily *adv* > 'mistiness *n*

misunderstand (ˌmɪsʌndə'stænd) *vb* -stands, -standing, -stood to fail to understand properly

misunderstanding (ˌmɪsʌndə'stændɪŋ) *n* **1** a failure to understand properly **2** a disagreement

misunderstood (ˌmɪsʌndə'stʊd) *adj* not properly or sympathetically understood: *a misunderstood work of art; a misunderstood adolescent*

misuse *n* (ˌmɪs'juːs) Also called: misusage **1** erroneous, improper, or unorthodox use: *misuse of words* **2** cruel or inhumane treatment ▷ *vb* (ˌmɪs'juːz) (*tr*) **3** to use wrongly **4** to treat badly or harshly [c17: from Old French *mesuser* (infinitive used as noun)] > ˌmis'user *n*

Mitchell ('mɪtʃəl) *n* **1 Joni**, original name *Roberta Joan Anderson*. born 1943, Canadian folk-rock singer and songwriter. Her albums include *Blue* (1971), *Court and Spark* (1974), *Mingus* (1979), *Turbulent Indigo* (1994), and *Shine* (2007) **2 Margaret**. 1900–49, US novelist; author of *Gone with the Wind* (1936) **3 Reginald Joseph**. 1895–1937, British aeronautical engineer; designer of the Spitfire fighter **4** Sir **Thomas Livingstone**, known as *Major Mitchell*. 1792–1855, Australian explorer born in Scotland

Mitchum ('mɪtʃəm) *n* **Robert**. 1917–97, US film actor. His many films include *Night of the Hunter* (1955) and *Farewell my Lovely* (1975)

mite[1] (maɪt) *n* any of numerous small free-living or parasitic arachnids of the order *Acarina* or *Acari* that can occur in terrestrial or aquatic habitats [Old English *mīte*; compare Old High German *mīza* gnat, Dutch *mijt*]

mite[2] (maɪt) *n* **1** a very small particle, creature, or object **2** a very small contribution or sum of money. See also **widow's mite 3** a former Flemish coin of small value **4** a mite *informal* somewhat: *he's a mite foolish* [c14: from Middle Low German, Middle Dutch *mīte*; compare MITE[1]]

Mithgarthr ('mɪð,gɑːðə) *n* a variant of **Midgard**

Mithraism ('mɪθreɪ,ɪzəm) or **Mithraicism** (mɪθ'reɪɪ,sɪzəm) *n* the ancient Persian religion of Mithras. It spread to the Roman Empire during the first three centuries AD > Mithraic (mɪθ'reɪɪk) *adj* > 'Mithraist *n*, *adj*

Mithras ('mɪθræs) or **Mithra** ('mɪθrə) *n* Persian myth the god of light, identified with the sun, who slew a primordial bull and fertilized the world with its blood

Mithridates VI or **Mithradates VI** (ˌmɪθrɪ'deɪtiːz) *n* called *the Great*. ?132–63 BC, king of Pontus (?120–63). He waged three wars against Rome (88–84; 83–81; 74–64) and was finally defeated by Pompey: committed suicide

mithridatism ('mɪθrɪdeɪ,tɪzəm) *n* immunity to large doses of poison by prior ingestion of gradually increased doses > mithridatic (ˌmɪθrɪ'dætɪk, -'deɪ-) *adj*

mitigate ('mɪtɪ,geɪt) *vb* to make or become less severe or harsh; moderate [c15: from Latin *mītigāre*, from *mītis* mild + *agere* to make] > mitigable ('mɪtɪgəbᵊl) *adj*
> ˌmiti'gation *n* > 'miti,gative or 'miti,gatory *adj*
> 'miti,gator *n*
● USAGE *Mitigate* is sometimes wrongly used where
● militate is meant: *his behaviour militates* (not *mitigates*)
● *against his chances of promotion*

Mitilíni (miti'lini) *n* transliteration of the Modern Greek name for **Mytilene** (sense 1)

mitochondrion (ˌmaɪtəʊ'kɒndrɪən) *n*, *pl* -dria (-drɪə) a small spherical or rodlike body, bounded by a double membrane, in the cytoplasm of most cells: contains enzymes responsible for energy production [c19: New Latin, from Greek *mitos* thread + *khondrion* small grain]

mitosis (maɪ'təʊsɪs, mɪ-) *n* a method of cell division, in which the nucleus divides into daughter nuclei, each containing the same number of chromosomes as the parent nucleus [c19: from New Latin, from Greek *mitos* thread] > mitotic (maɪ'tɒtɪk, mɪ-) *adj*

mitral ('maɪtrəl) *adj* **1** of or like a mitre **2** *anatomy* of or relating to the mitral valve

mitral valve *n* the valve between the left atrium and the left ventricle of the heart, consisting of two membranous flaps, that prevents regurgitation of blood into the atrium

mitre or US **miter** ('maɪtə) *n* **1** *Christianity* the liturgical headdress of a bishop or abbot, in most western churches consisting of a tall pointed cleft cap with two bands hanging down at the back **2** Also called: mitre joint a corner joint formed between two pieces of material, esp wood, by cutting bevels of equal angles at the ends of each piece **3** a bevelled surface of a mitre joint ▷ *vb* (*tr*) **4** to make a mitre joint between (two pieces of material, esp wood) **5** to confer a mitre upon: *a mitred abbot* [c14: from Old French, from Latin *mitra*, from Greek *mitra* turban]

mitre box *n* an open-ended box with sides having narrow slots to guide a saw in cutting mitre joints

mitt (mɪt) *n* **1** any of various glovelike hand coverings, such as one that does not cover the fingers **2** short for **mitten** (sense 1) **3** *baseball* a large round thickly padded leather mitten worn by the catcher **4** (*often plural*) a slang word for: **hand 5** *slang* a boxing glove [c18: shortened from MITTEN]

Mittelland Canal (*German* 'mɪtəllant) *n* a canal in Germany, linking the Rivers Rhine and Elbe. Length: 325 km (202 miles)

mitten ('mɪtᵊn) *n* **1** a glove having one section for the thumb and a single section for the other fingers. Sometimes shortened to: mitt **2** *slang* a boxing glove [c14: from Old French *mitaine*, of uncertain origin]

Mitterrand (*French* miterɑ̃) *n* **François Maurice Marie** (frɑ̃swa mɔris mari). 1916–96, French statesman; first secretary of the socialist party (1971–95); president (1981–95)

mittimus ('mɪtɪməs) *n*, *pl* -muses *law* a warrant of commitment to prison or a command to a jailer directing him to hold someone in prison [c15: from Latin: we send, the first word of such a command]

mix (mɪks) *vb* **1** (*tr*) to combine or blend (ingredients, liquids, objects, etc) together into one mass **2** (*intr*) to become or have the capacity to become combined, joined, etc: *some chemicals do not mix* **3** (*tr*) to form (something) by combining two or more constituents: *to mix cement* **4** (*tr*; often foll by *in* or *into*) to add as an additional part or element (to a mass or compound): *to mix flour into a batter* **5** (*tr*) to do at the same time; combine: *to mix study and pleasure* **6** (*tr*) to consume (drinks or foods) in close succession **7** to come or cause to come into association socially: *Pauline has never mixed well* **8** (*intr*; often foll by *with*) to go together; complement **9** (*tr*) to crossbreed (differing strains of plants or breeds of livestock), esp more or less at random **10** *music* (in sound recording) to balance and adjust (the recorded tracks) on a multitrack tape machine **11 mix it** *informal* to cause mischief or trouble, often for a person named: *she tried to mix it for John* ▷ *n* **12** the act or an instance of mixing **13** the result of mixing; mixture **14** a mixture of ingredients, esp one commercially prepared for making a cake, bread, etc **15** *music* the sound obtained by mixing **16** *informal* a state of confusion, bewilderment ▷ See also **mix-up** [c15: back formation from *mixt* mixed, via Old French from Latin *mixtus*, from *miscēre* to mix] > 'mixable *adj*

mixed (mɪkst) *adj* **1** formed or blended together by mixing **2** composed of different elements, races, sexes, etc: *a mixed school* **3** consisting of conflicting elements, thoughts, attitudes, etc > mixedness ('mɪksɪdnɪs) *n*

mixed bag *n informal* something composed of diverse elements, characteristics, people, etc

mixed blessing *n* an event, situation, etc, having both advantages and disadvantages

mixed doubles *pl n tennis* a doubles game with a man and a woman as partners on each side

mixed economy *n* an economy in which some industries are privately owned and others are publicly owned or nationalized

mixed farming *n* combined arable and livestock farming (on **mixed farms**)

mixed marriage *n* a marriage between persons of different races or religions

mixed metaphor *n* a combination of incongruous metaphors, as *when the Nazi jackboots sing their swan song*

mixed-up *adj* in a state of mental confusion; perplexed

mixer ('mɪksə) *n* **1** a person or thing that mixes **2** *informal* **a** a person considered in relation to his ability to mix socially **b** a person who creates trouble for others **3** a kitchen appliance, usually electrical, used for mixing foods, etc **4** a drink such as ginger ale, fruit juice, etc, used in preparing cocktails **5** *electronics* a device in which two or more input signals are combined to give a single output signal

mixer tap *n* a tap in which hot and cold water supplies have a joint outlet but are controlled separately

mixologist (ˌmɪk'sɒlədʒɪst) *n* **1** *humorous* a person who serves drinks, esp cocktails, at a bar **2** *music* a person skilled at mixing sounds in recording or live performance

mixture ('mɪkstʃə) *n* **1** the act of mixing or state of being mixed **2** something mixed; a result of mixing **3** *chem* a substance consisting of two or more substances mixed together without any chemical bonding between them **4** *pharmacol* a liquid medicine in which an insoluble compound is suspended in the liquid **5** *music* an organ stop that controls several ranks of pipes sounding the upper notes in a harmonic series **6** the mixture of petrol vapour and air in an internal-combustion engine [c16: from Latin *mixtūra*, from *mixtus*, past participle of *miscēre* to mix]

mix-up *n* **1** a confused condition or situation **2** *informal* a fight ▷ *vb* **mix up** (*tr*, *adverb*) **3** to make into a mixture **4** to confuse or confound: *Tom mixes John up with Bill* **5** (*often passive*) to put (someone) into a state of confusion: *I'm all mixed up* **6** (foll by *in* or *with*; usually passive) to involve (in an activity or group, esp one that is illegal): *why did you get mixed up in that drugs racket?*

Mizoguchi (ˌmiːtsəˈguːtʃi) *n* **Kenji** ('kɛndʒi). 1898–1956, Japanese film director. His films include *A Paper Doll's Whisper of Spring* (1925), *Woman of Osaka* (1940), and *Ugetsu Monogatari* (1952)

Mizoram (mɪ'zɔːrəm) *n* a state (since 1986) in NE India,

created in 1972 from the former Mizo Hills District of Assam. Capital: Aijal. Pop: 891 058 (2001). Area: about 21 081 sq km (8140 sq miles)

mizzen *or* **mizen** ('mɪz³n) *nautical* ▷ *n* **1** a sail set on a mizzenmast **2** short for **mizzenmast** ▷ *adj* **3** of or relating to any kind of gear used with a mizzenmast: *a mizzen staysail* [c15: from French *misaine*, from Italian *mezzana*, *mezzano* middle]

mizzenmast *or* **mizenmast** ('mɪz³n,mɑːst; *Nautical* 'mɪz³nməst) *n nautical* (on a vessel with three or more masts) the third mast from the bow

mizzle[1] ('mɪz³l) *vb*, *n* a dialect word for **drizzle** [c15: perhaps from Low German *miseln* to drizzle; compare Dutch dialect *miezelen* to drizzle] > 'mizzly *adj*

mizzle[2] ('mɪz³l) *vb* (*intr*) *Brit slang* to decamp [c18: of unknown origin]

mk *currency symbol for* **1** mark **2** markka

mks units *pl n* a metric system of units based on the metre, kilogram, and second as the units of length, mass, and time; it forms the basis of the SI units

mkt *abbreviation* market

ml *symbol for* **1** millilitre **2** mile

ML *abbreviation* Medieval Latin

MLA *abbreviation* **1** Member of the Legislative Assembly (of Northern Ireland) **2** Modern Language Association (of America)

Mladic (məˈladɪtʃ) *n* **Ratko** ('ratko). born 1943, Bosnian military figure, commander of the Bosnian Serb forces during the civil war of 1992–95; indicted by the U.N. for war crimes, including the massacre of 6000 Bosnian Muslims at Srebrenica (1995)

MLC *abbreviation* (in India and Australia) Member of the Legislative Council

MLitt *abbreviation* Master of Letters [Latin *Magister Litterarum*]

Mlle *n*, *pl* **Mlles** the French equivalent of **Miss** [from French *Mademoiselle*]

MLR *abbreviation* minimum lending rate

mm *symbol for* millimetre

MM *abbreviation* **1** Military Medal **2** the French equivalent of **Messrs** [from French *Messieurs*]

Mmabatho (ˌmæbˈæθəʊ) *n* the capital of the former homeland of Bophuthatswana

MMDS *abbreviation* multipoint microwave distribution system: a radio alternative to cable television

Mme *n*, *pl* **Mmes** the French equivalent of **Mrs** [from French *Madame, Mesdames*]

mmorpg *abbreviation* massive(ly) multiplayer online role-playing game: an internet-based computer game set in a virtual world, which can be played by many people at the same time, each of whom can interact with the others

MMP *abbreviation* mixed member proportional: a system of proportional representation, used in Germany and New Zealand

MMR *n* a combined vaccine against measles, mumps, and rubella, given to young children

MMS *abbreviation* multimedia messaging service: a method of transmitting graphics, video or sound files and short text messages over wireless networks, esp on mobile phones

MMus. *abbreviation* Master of Music

Mn *the chemical symbol for* manganese

MN *abbreviation* **1** (in Britain) Merchant Navy **2** Minnesota

MNA *abbreviation* (in Canada) Member of the National Assembly (of Quebec)

mnemonic (nɪ'mɒnɪk) *adj* **1** aiding or meant to aid one's memory **2** of or relating to memory or mnemonics ▷ *n* **3** something, such as a verse, to assist memory [c18: from Greek *mnēmonikos*, from *mnēmōn* mindful, from *mnasthai* to remember] > mne'monically *adv*

mnemonics (nɪ'mɒnɪks) *n* (*usually functioning as singular*) **1** the art or practice of improving or of aiding the memory **2** a system of rules to aid the memory

Mnemosyne (niː'mɒzɪˌniː, -ˌmɒs-) *n Greek myth* the goddess of memory and mother by Zeus of the Muses

mo (məʊ) *n informal* **1** *chiefly Brit* short for **moment** (sense 1) **2** *chiefly Austral* short for **moustache** (sense 1)

Mo *the chemical symbol for* molybdenum

MO *abbreviation* **1** Missouri **2** Medical Officer **3** *modus operandi*

Mo. *abbreviation* Missouri

m.o. *or* **MO** *abbreviation* **1** mail order **2** money order

-mo *suffix forming nouns* (in bookbinding) indicating book size by specifying the number of leaves formed by folding one sheet of paper: *12mo, twelvemo,* or *duodecimo; 16mo* or *sixteenmo* [abstracted from DUODECIMO]

moa ('məʊə) *n* any large flightless bird of the recently extinct order *Dinornithiformes* of New Zealand. See **ratite** [C19: from Māori]

Moab ('məʊæb) *n Old Testament* an ancient kingdom east of the Dead Sea, in what is now the SW part of Jordan: flourished mainly from the 9th to the 6th centuries BC > **Moabite** ('məʊəˌbaɪt) *adj, n*

moa hunter *n* the name given by anthropologists to the early Māori inhabitants of New Zealand

moan (məʊn) *n* **1** a low prolonged mournful sound expressive of suffering or pleading **2** any similar mournful sound, esp that made by the wind **3** a grumble or complaint ▷ *vb* **4** to utter (words) in a low mournful manner **5** (*intr*) to make a sound like a moan **6** (*usually intr*) to grumble or complain (esp in the phrase **moan and groan**) [C13: related to Old English *mǣnan* to grieve over] > **'moaner** *n* > **'moanful** *adj* > **'moaning** *n, adj*

moat (məʊt) *n* **1** a wide water-filled ditch surrounding a fortified place, such as a castle ▷ *vb* **2** (*tr*) to surround with or as if with a moat: *a moated grange* [C14: from Old French *motte* mound]

mob (mɒb) *n* **1 a** a riotous or disorderly crowd of people; rabble **b** (*as modifier*): *mob law; mob violence* **2** *often derogatory* a group or class of people, animals, or things **3** *Austral & NZ* a flock (of sheep) or a herd (of cattle, esp when droving) **4** *often derogatory* the masses **5** *slang* a gang of criminals ▷ *vb* **mobs, mobbing, mobbed** (*tr*) **6** to attack in a group resembling a mob **7** to surround, esp in order to acclaim **8** to crowd into (a building, plaza, etc) [C17: shortened from Latin *mōbile vulgus* the fickle populace; see MOBILE]

MOB *abbreviation* mobile phone

mobcap ('mɒbˌkæp) *n* a woman's large cotton cap with a pouched crown and usually a frill, worn esp during the 18th century [C18: from obsolete *mob* woman, esp a loose-living woman, + CAP]

mobe (məʊb) *n informal* a mobile phone

mobie ('məʊbɪ) *n informal* a mobile phone

mobile ('məʊbaɪl) *adj* **1** having freedom of movement; movable **2** changing quickly in expression: *a mobile face* **3** *sociol* (of individuals or social groups) moving within and between classes, occupations, and localities **4** (of military forces) able to move freely and quickly to any given area **5** *postpositive informal* having transport available: *are you mobile tonight?* ▷ *n* **6 a** a sculpture suspended in midair with delicately balanced parts that are set in motion by air currents **b** (*as modifier*): *mobile sculpture* **7** short for **mobile phone** [C15: via Old French from Latin *mōbilis*, from *movēre* to move]

Mobile ('məʊbiːl, məʊ'biːl) *n* a port in SW Alabama, on **Mobile Bay** (an inlet of the Gulf of Mexico): the state's only port and its first permanent settlement, made by French colonists in 1711. Pop: 193 464 (2003 est)

-mobile (məʊˌbiːl) *suffix forming nouns* indicating a vehicle designed for a particular person or purpose: *Popemobile*

Mobile Command *n Canadian* the Canadian army and other land forces

mobile home *n* living quarters mounted on wheels and capable of being towed by a motor vehicle

mobile phone *n* a portable telephone that works by means of a cellular radio system

mobility (məʊ'bɪlɪtɪ) *n* **1** the ability to move physically: *a knee operation has restricted his mobility; mobility is part of physical education* **2** *sociol* (of individuals or social groups) movement within or between classes and occupations **3** time that a resident of a secure unit is allowed to spend outside the unit, as preparation for an eventual return to society

mobilize *or* **mobilise** ('məʊbɪˌlaɪz) *vb* **1** to prepare for war or other emergency by organizing (national resources, the armed services, etc) **2** (*tr*) to organize for a purpose; marshal **3** (*tr*) to put into motion, circulation, or use > **'mobi,lizable** *or* **'mobi,lisable** *adj* > ,mobili'**zation** *or* ,mobili'**sation** *n*

Möbius strip ('mɜːbɪəs; German 'møːbius) *n maths* a one-sided continuous surface, formed by twisting a long narrow rectangular strip of material through 180° and joining the ends [C19: named after August *Möbius* (1790–1868), German mathematician who invented it]

moblog ('mɒbˌlɒg) *n* a chronicle, which may be shared with others, of someone's thoughts and experiences recorded in the form of mobile phone calls, text messages, and photographs [C21: MOB(ILE) + LOG¹] > **'mob,logger** *n*

MOBO ('məʊbəʊ) *n acronym for* (in Britain) Music of Black Origin: any of several awards given annually to musicians and performers of a variety of musical genres originating in Black culture

mobocracy (mɒ'bɒkrəsɪ) *n, pl* **-cies 1** rule or domination by a mob **2** the mob that rules

mobster ('mɒbstə) *n* a US slang word for: gangster

Mobutu¹ (mə'buːtuː) *n* the former name (until 1997) of Lake Albert. See **Albert¹**

Mobutu² (mə'buːtuː) *n* **Sese Seko** ('sɛsɛ 'sɛkəʊ), original name *Joseph*. 1930–97, Zaïrese statesman; president of Zaïre (now the Democratic Republic of Congo) (1970–97); accused of corruption and overthrown by rebels in 1997; died in exile

Moçambique (musəm'bikə) *n* the Portuguese name for Mozambique

moccasin ('mɒkəsɪn) *n* **1** a shoe of soft leather, esp deerskin, worn by North American Indians **2** any soft shoe resembling this **3** *NZ* a sheepshearer's footgear, usually made of sacking **4** short for **water moccasin** [C17: from Algonquian; compare Narraganset *mocussin* shoe]

moccasin flower *n* any of several North American orchids of the genus *Cypripedium* with a pink solitary flower. See also **lady's-slipper, cypripedium** (sense 1)

mocha ('mɒkə) *n* **1** a strongly flavoured dark brown coffee originally imported from Arabia **2** a flavouring made from coffee and chocolate **3** a soft glove leather with a suede finish, made from goatskin or sheepskin **4 a** a dark brown colour **b** (*as adjective*): *mocha shoes*

Mocha *or* **Mokha** ('mɒkə) *n* a port in Yemen, on the Red Sea; in the former North Yemen until 1990: formerly important for the export of Arabian coffee. Pop: 14 562 (2005 est)

mock (mɒk) *vb* **1** (when *intr*, often foll by *at*) to behave with scorn or contempt (towards); show ridicule (for) **2** (*tr*) to imitate, esp in fun; mimic **3** (*tr*) to deceive, disappoint, or delude **4** (*tr*) to defy or frustrate: *the team mocked the visitors' attempt to score* ▷ *n* **5** the act of mocking **6** a person or thing mocked **7** a counterfeit; imitation **8** (*often plural*) *informal* (in England and Wales) the school examinations taken as practice before public examinations ▷ *adj* (*prenominal*) **9** sham or counterfeit **10** serving as an imitation or substitute, esp for practice purposes: *a mock battle; mock finals* ▷ See also **mock-up** [C15: from Old French *mocquer*] > **'mockable** *adj* > **'mocker** *n* > **'mocking** *n, adj* > **'mockingly** *adv*

mockers ('mɒkəz) *pl n* **put the mockers on** *informal* to ruin the chances of success of [C20: perhaps from MOCK]

mockery ('mɒkərɪ) *n, pl* **-eries 1** ridicule, contempt, or derision **2** a derisive action or comment **3** an imitation or pretence, esp a derisive one **4** a person or thing that is mocked **5** a person, thing, or action that is inadequate or disappointing

mock-heroic *adj* **1** (of a literary work, esp a poem) imitating the style of heroic poetry in order to satirize an unheroic subject, as in Pope's *The Rape of the Lock* ▷ *n* **2** burlesque imitation of the heroic style or of a single work in this style

mockingbird ('mɒkɪŋˌbɜːd) *n* **1** *Austral* any American songbird of the family *Mimidae*, having a long tail and grey plumage: noted for their ability to mimic the song of other birds **2** a small scrub bird, *Atrichornis rufescens*, noted for its mimicry

mock orange *n* **1** Also called: **syringa** any shrub of the genus *Philadelphus*, esp *P. coronarius*, with white fragrant flowers that resemble those of the orange: family *Philadelphaceae* **2** any other shrub or tree that resembles the orange tree

mock turtle soup *n* an imitation turtle soup made from a calf's head

mock-up *n* **1** a working full-scale model of a machine, apparatus, etc, for testing, research, etc **2** a layout of printed matter ▷ *vb* **mock up 3** (*tr, adverb*) to build or make a mock-up of

mod¹ (mɒd) *n Brit* **a** a member of a group of teenagers in the mid-1960s, noted for their clothes-consciousness and opposition to the rockers **b** a member of a revived group of this type in the late 1970s and early 1980s, noted for their clothes-consciousness and opposition to the skinheads **c** (*as modifier*): *a mod haircut* [C20: from MODERNIST]

mod² (mɒd) *n* an annual Highland Gaelic meeting with musical and literary competitions [C19: from Gaelic *mòd* assembly, from Old Norse; related to MOOT]

MOD *abbreviation* (in Britain) Ministry of Defence

mod. *abbreviation* **1** moderate **2** moderato **3** modern

modal ('məʊd°l) *adj* **1** of, relating to, or characteristic of mode or manner **2** *grammar* (of a verb form or auxiliary verb) expressing a distinction of mood, such as that between possibility and actuality. The modal auxiliaries in English include *can, could, may, must, need, ought, shall, should, will,* and *would* **3** *philosophy, logic* **a** qualifying or expressing a qualification of the truth of some statement, for example, as necessary or contingent **b** relating to analogous qualifications such as that of rules as obligatory or permissive **4** *metaphysics* of or relating to the form of a thing as opposed to its attributes, substance, etc **5** *music* of or relating to a mode **6** of or relating to a statistical mode ▷ **'modally** *adv* ▷ **mo'dality** *n*

modal logic *n* **1** the logical study of such philosophical concepts as necessity, possibility, contingency, etc **2** the logical study of concepts whose formal properties resemble certain moral, epistemological, and psychological concepts

mod cons *pl n informal* modern conveniences; the usual installations of a modern house, such as hot water, heating, etc

modding ('mɒdɪŋ) *n slang* the practice of modifying a production car to alter its appearance or to increase performance

mode (məʊd) *n* **1** a manner or way of doing, acting, or existing **2** the current fashion or style **3** *music* **a** any of the various scales of notes within one octave, esp any of the twelve natural diatonic scales taken in ascending order used in plainsong, folk song, and art music until 1600 **b** (in the music of classical Greece) any of the descending diatonic scales from which the liturgical modes evolved **c** either of the two main scale systems in music since 1600: *major mode; minor mode* **4** *logic, linguistics* another name for: *mood²* (sense 2) **5** *philosophy* a complex combination of ideas the realization of which is not determined by the component ideas **6** that one of a range of values that has the highest frequency as determined statistically [C14: from Latin *modus* measure, manner]

model ('mɒd°l) *n* **1 a** a representation, usually on a smaller scale, of a device, structure, etc **b** (*as modifier*): *a model train* **2 a** a standard to be imitated **b** (*as modifier*): *a model wife* **3** a representative form, style, or pattern **4** a person who poses for a sculptor, painter, or photographer **5** a person who wears clothes to display them to prospective buyers; mannequin **6** a preparatory sculpture in clay, wax, etc, from which the finished work is copied **7** a design or style, esp one of a series of designs of a particular product ▷ *vb* **-els, -elling, -elled** *or US* **-els, -eling, -eled 8** to make a model of (something or someone) **9** to form in clay, wax, etc; mould **10** to display (clothing and accessories) as a mannequin **11** to plan or create according to a model or models [C16: from Old French *modelle*, from Italian *modello*, from Latin *modulus*, diminutive of *modus* MODE] ▷ **'modeller** *or US* **'modeler** *n*

modelling *or US* **modeling** ('mɒd°lɪŋ) *n* **1** the act or an instance of making a model **2** the practice or occupation of a person who models clothes **3** a technique in psychotherapy in which the therapist encourages the patient to model his behaviour on his own

modem ('məʊdɛm) *n computing* a device for connecting two computers by a telephone line, consisting of a modulator that converts computer signals into audio signals and a corresponding demodulator [C20: from *mo(dulator) dem(odulator)*]

Modena (Italian 'mɔːdena) *n* **1** a city in N Italy, in Emilia-Romagna: ruled by the Este family (18th–19th century); university (1678). Pop: 175 502 (2001 **2** (*sometimes not capital*) a popular variety of domestic fancy pigeon originating in Modena

moderate *adj* ('mɒdərɪt, 'mɒdrɪt) **1** not extreme or excessive; within due or reasonable limits **2** not violent; mild or temperate **3** of average quality or extent: *moderate success n* ('mɒdərɪt, 'mɒdrɪt) **4** a person who holds moderate views, esp in politics ▷ *vb* ('mɒdəˌreɪt) **5** to become or cause to become less extreme or violent **6** (when *intr*, often foll by *over*) to preside over a meeting, discussion, etc **7** *Brit & NZ* to act as an external moderator of the overall standards and marks for (some types of educational assessment) **8** *physics* to slow down (neutrons), esp by using a moderator **9** (*tr*) to monitor (the conversations in an on-line chatroom) for bad language, inappropriate content, etc [C14: from Latin *moderātus* observing moderation, from *moderārī* to restrain]

moderate breeze *n* a wind of force four on the Beaufort scale

moderation (ˌmɒdə'reɪʃən) *n* **1** the state or an instance of being moderate; mildness; balance **2** the act of moderating **3 in moderation** within moderate or reasonable limits

moderato (ˌmɒdə'rɑːtəʊ) *adv music* **1** at a moderate tempo **2** (preceded by a tempo marking) a direction indicating that the tempo specified is to be used with restraint: *allegro moderato* [C18: from Italian, from Latin *moderātus*; see MODERATE]

moderator ('mɒdəˌreɪtə) *n* **1** a person or thing that moderates **2** *Presbyterian Church* a minister appointed to preside over a Church court, synod, or general assembly **3** a presiding officer at a public or legislative assembly **4** a material, such as heavy water or graphite, used for slowing down neutrons in the cores of nuclear reactors so that they have more chance of inducing nuclear fission **5** an examiner at Oxford or Cambridge Universities in first public examinations **6** (in Britain and New Zealand) one who is responsible for consistency of standards in the grading of some educational assessments **7** a person who monitors the conversations in an on-line chatroom for bad language, inappropriate content, etc ▷ **'mode,ratorship** *n*

modern ('mɒdən) *adj* **1** of, involving, or befitting the present or a recent time; contemporary **2** of, relating to, or characteristic of contemporary styles or schools of art, literature, music, etc, esp those of an experimental kind **3** belonging or relating to the period in history from the end of the Middle Ages to the present ▷ *n* **4** a contemporary person [C16: from Old French, from Late Latin *modernus*, from *modō* (adv) just recently, from *modus* MODE] ▷ **'modernness** *or* **mo'dernity** *n*

modern apprenticeship *n* an arrangement that allows a school leaver to gain vocational qualifications while being trained in a job

Modern English *n* the English language since about 1450, esp any of the standard forms developed from the S East Midland dialect of Middle English

modernism ('mɒdəˌnɪzəm) *n* **1** modern tendencies, characteristics, thoughts, etc, or the support of these **2** something typical of contemporary life or thought **3** a 20th-century divergence in the arts from previous traditions, esp in architecture. See **International Style 4** (*capital*) *RC Church* the movement at the end of the 19th and beginning of the 20th centuries that sought to adapt doctrine to the supposed requirements of modern thought ▷ **'modernist** *n, adj* ▷ ˌmodern'istic *adj*

> ˌmodern'istically *adv*

modernize *or* **modernise** ('mɒdəˌnaɪz) *vb* **1** (*tr*) to make modern in appearance or style: *to modernize a room* **2** (*intr*) to adopt modern ways, ideas, etc > ˌmoderni'zation *or* moderni'sation *n* > 'modernˌizer *or* 'modernˌiser *n*

modern pentathlon *n* an athletic contest consisting of five different events: horse riding with jumps, fencing with electric épée, freestyle swimming, pistol shooting, and cross-country running

modest ('mɒdɪst) *adj* **1** having or expressing a humble opinion of oneself or one's accomplishments or abilities **2** reserved or shy **3** not ostentatious or pretentious **4** not extreme or excessive; moderate **5** decorous or decent [c16: via Old French from Latin *modestus* moderate, from *modus* MODE] > 'modestly *adv*

modesty ('mɒdɪstɪ) *n, pl* **-ties** the quality or condition of being modest

modicum ('mɒdɪkəm) *n* a small amount or portion [c15: from Latin: a little way, from *modicus* moderate]

modification (ˌmɒdɪfɪ'keɪʃən) *n* **1** the act of modifying or the condition of being modified **2** something modified; the result of a modification **3** a small change or adjustment **4** *grammar* the relation between a modifier and the word or phrase that it modifies > 'modifiˌcatory *or* 'modifiˌcative *adj*

modifier ('mɒdɪˌfaɪə) *n* **1** Also called: **qualifier** *grammar* a word or phrase that qualifies the sense of another word; for example, the noun *alarm* is a modifier of *clock* in *alarm clock* and the phrase *every day* is an adverbial modifier of *walks* in *he walks every day* **2** a person or thing that modifies

modify ('mɒdɪˌfaɪ) *vb* **-fies, -fying, -fied** (*mainly tr*) **1** to change the structure, character, intent, etc, of **2** to make less extreme or uncompromising **3** *grammar* (of a word or group of words) to bear the relation of modifier to (another word or group of words) **4** *linguistics* to change (a vowel) by umlaut **5** (*intr*) to be or become modified [c14: from Old French *modifier*, from Latin *modificāre* to limit, control, from *modus* measure + *facere* to make] > 'modiˌfiable *adj* > ˌmodiˌfia'bility *or* 'modiˌfiableness *n*

Modigliani (Italian modiʎ'ʎa:ni) *n* Amedeo (ame'dɛːo). 1884–1920, Italian painter and sculptor, noted esp for the elongated forms of his portraits

modish ('məʊdɪʃ) *adj* in the current fashion or style; contemporary > 'modishly *adv* > 'modishness *n*

modiste (məʊ'diːst) *n* a fashionable dressmaker or milliner [c19: from French, from *mode* fashion]

Modred ('məʊdrɪd) *or* **Mordred** ('mɔːdred) *n* (in Arthurian legend) a knight of the Round Table who rebelled against and killed his uncle King Arthur

modular ('mɒdjʊlə) *adj* of, consisting of, or resembling a module or modulus

modulate ('mɒdjʊˌleɪt) *vb* **1** (*tr*) to change the tone, pitch, or volume of **2** (*tr*) to adjust or regulate the degree of **3** *music* **a** to subject to or undergo modulation in music **b** (often foll by *to*) to make or become in tune (with a pitch, key, etc) [c16: from Latin *modulātus* in due measure, melodious, from *modulārī* to regulate, from *modus* measure] > ˌmodu'lation *n* > 'moduˌlator *n*

module ('mɒdjuːl) *n* **1** a standard unit of measure, esp one used to coordinate the dimensions of buildings and components; in classical architecture, half the diameter of a column at the base of the shaft **2** *astronautics* any of several self-contained separable units making up a spacecraft or launch vehicle, each of which has one or more specified tasks: *command module; service module* **3** *education* a short course of study, esp of a vocational or technical subject, that together with other such completed courses can count towards a particular qualification [c16: from Latin *modulus*, a diminutive of *modus* MODE]

modulus ('mɒdjʊləs) *n, pl* **-li** (-ˌlaɪ) **1** *physics* a coefficient expressing a specified property of a specified substance **2** *maths* the absolute value of a complex number. See **absolute value 3** *maths* the number by which a logarithm to one base is multiplied to give the corresponding logarithm to another base **4** *maths* an integer that can be divided exactly into the difference

between two other integers: *7 is a modulus of 25 and 11* [c16: from Latin, diminutive of *modus* measure]

modulus of elasticity *n* the ratio of the stress applied to a body or substance to the resulting strain within the elastic limit. Also called: **elastic modulus**

modus operandi ('məʊdəs ˌɒpə'rændiː, -'rændaɪ) *n, pl* **modi operandi** ('məʊdiː ˌɒpə'rændiː, 'məʊdaɪ ˌɒpə'rændaɪ) procedure; method of operating [c17: from Latin]

modus vivendi ('məʊdəs vɪ'vɛndiː, -'vɛndaɪ) *n, pl* **modi vivendi** ('məʊdiː vɪ'vɛndiː, 'məʊdaɪ vɪ'vɛndaɪ) a working arrangement between conflicting interests; practical compromise [c19: from Latin: way of living]

moer (muːr) *South African taboo, slang* ▷ *n* **1** the womb **2** a despicable person **3 the moer in** furious; enraged ▷ *vb* **4** (*tr*) to attack (someone or something) violently [from Afrikaans, literally: mother]

Moers (German mœrs) *n* a city in W Germany, in North Rhine-Westphalia: coalmining centre. Pop: 107 903 (2003 est)

Mogadishu (ˌmɒgə'diʃuː) *n* the capital and chief port of Somalia, on the Indian Ocean: founded by Arabs around the 10th century; taken by the Sultan of Zanzibar in 1871 and sold to Italy in 1905. Pop: 1 257 000 (2005 est)

Mogadon ('mɒgəˌdɒn) *n trademark* a drug of the benzodiazepine group, a brand of nitrazepam, used to treat insomnia

Mogador (ˌmɒgə'dɔː; French mɔgadɔr) *n* the former name (until 1956) of **Essaouira**

moggy ('mɒgɪ) *n, pl* **moggies** *Brit* a slang name for **cat** (sense 1) sometimes shortened to **mog** [c20: of dialect origin, originally a pet name for a cow]

Mogilev (Russian məgi'ljɔf) *or* **Mohilev** *n* an industrial city in E Belarus on the Dnieper River: passed to Russia in 1772 after Polish rule. Pop: 353 000 (2005 est)

mogul ('məʊgʌl, məʊ'gʌl) *n* **1** an important or powerful person **2** a type of steam locomotive with a wheel arrangement of two leading wheels, six driving wheels, and no trailing wheels [c18: from MOGUL]

Mogul ('məʊgʌl, məʊ'gʌl) *n* **1** a member of the Muslim dynasty of Indian emperors established by Baber in 1526 **2** a Muslim Indian, Mongol, or Mongolian ▷ *adj* **3** of or relating to the Moguls or their empire [c16: from Persian *mughul* Mongol]

mogul skiing *n* a skiing event in which skiers descend a slope which is covered in mounds of snow, making two jumps during the descent

mohair ('məʊˌhɛə) *n* **1** Also called: **angora** the long soft silky hair that makes up the outer coat of the Angora goat **2 a** a fabric made from the yarn of this hair and cotton or wool **b** (*as modifier*): *a mohair suit* [c16: variant (influenced by *hair*) of earlier *mocayare*, ultimately from Arabic *mukhayyar*, literally: choice, from *khayyara* to choose]

Moham. *abbreviation* Mohammedan

Mohammed (məʊ'hæmɪd) *n* same as **Muhammad**

Mohammed II *n* ?1430–81, Ottoman sultan of Turkey (1451–81). He captured Constantinople (1453) and conquered large areas of the Balkans

Mohammedan (məʊ'hæmɪdⁿ) *n, adj* another word, formerly common in Western usage but never used among Muslims, for: **Muslim**

Mohammedanism (məʊ'hæmɪdⁿˌnɪzəm) *n* a name, formerly common in Western usage but never used among Muslims, for the Muslim religion; Islam. See **Islam**

Mohammed Ahmed (məʊ'hæmɪd 'aːmɛd) *n* the original name of the: **Mahdi²**

Mohammed Ali *n* **1** See **Mehemet Ali 2** See **Muhammad Ali**

Mohammed Reza Pahlavi (məʊ'hæmɪd 'riːzə 'paːləvɪ) *n* See **Pahlavi¹**

Mohave Desert *n* another name for: **Mojave Desert**

Mohawk¹ ('məʊhɔːk) *n* **1** *pl* **-hawks** *or* **-hawk** a member of a North American Indian people formerly living along the Mohawk River; one of the Iroquois peoples **2** the language of this people, belonging to the Iroquoian family

Mohawk² ('məʊhɔːk) *n* a river in E central New York

State, flowing south and east to the Hudson River at Cohoes: the largest tributary of the Hudson. Length: 238 km (148 miles)

Mohenjo-Daro (məˈhɛndʒəʊˈdɑːrəʊ) *n* an excavated city in SE Pakistan, southwest of Sukkur near the River Indus: flourished during the third millennium BC

mohican (məʊˈhiːkən) *n* a punk hairstyle in which the head is shaved at the sides and the remaining strip of hair is worn stiffly erect and sometimes brightly coloured

Moholy-Nagy (məˈhəʊlɪˈnɒdʒ) *n* Laszlo (ˈlæzləʊ) or **Ladislaus** (ˈlɑːdɪsˌlaʊs). 1895–1946, US painter and teacher, born in Hungary. He worked at the Bauhaus (1923–29)

moidore (ˈmɔɪdɔː) *n* a former Portuguese gold coin [c18: from Portuguese *moeda de ouro*: money of gold]

moiety (ˈmɔɪɪtɪ) *n, pl* **-ties** *archaic* 1 a half 2 one of two parts or divisions of something [c15: from Old French *moitié*, from Latin *mediētās* middle, from *medius*]

moil (mɔɪl) *archaic or dialect* ▷ *vb* 1 to moisten or soil or become moist, soiled, etc 2 (*intr*) to toil or drudge (esp in the phrase **toil and moil**) ▷ *n* 3 toil; drudgery 4 confusion; turmoil [c14 (to moisten; later: to work hard in unpleasantly wet conditions) from Old French *moillier*, ultimately from Latin *mollis* soft] ▷ ˈ**moiler** *n*

Moirai (ˈmɔɪraɪ) *pl n, sing* **Moira** (ˈmɔɪrə) **the Moirai** the Greek goddesses of fate. See **Fates**

moire (mwɑː) *n* a fabric, usually silk, having a watered effect [c17: from French, earlier *mouaire*, from MOHAIR]

moiré (ˈmwɑːreɪ) *adj* 1 having a watered or wavelike pattern ▷ *n* 2 such a pattern, impressed on fabrics by means of engraved rollers 3 any fabric having such a pattern; moire 4 Also called: **moiré pattern** a pattern seen when two geometrical patterns, such as grids, are visually superimposed [c17: from French, from *moire* MOHAIR]

Moism (ˈməʊɪzəm) *n* the religious and ethical teaching of Mo-Zi, the Chinese religious philosopher (?470–?391 BC), and his followers, emphasizing universal love, ascetic self-discipline, and obedience to the will of Heaven

moist (mɔɪst) *adj* 1 slightly damp or wet 2 saturated with or suggestive of moisture [c14: from Old French, ultimately related to Latin *mūcidus* musty, from *mūcus* MUCUS] ▷ ˈ**moistly** *adv* ▷ ˈ**moistness** *n*

moisten (ˈmɔɪsᵊn) *vb* to make or become moist

moisture (ˈmɔɪstʃə) *n* water or other liquid diffused as vapour or condensed on or in objects

moisturize *or* **moisturise** (ˈmɔɪstʃəˌraɪz) *vb* (*tr*) to add or restore moisture to (the air, the skin, etc) ▷ ˈ**moistuˌrizer** *or* ˈ**moistuˌriser** *n*

Mojave Desert *or* **Mohave Desert** *n* a desert in S California, south of the Sierra Nevada: part of the Great Basin. Area: 38 850 sq km (15 000 sq miles)

mojo (ˈməʊdʒəʊ) *n, pl* **mojos** *or* **mojoes** *US slang* 1 a an amulet, charm, or magic spell b (*as modifier*): *ancient mojo spells* 2 the art of casting magic spells [c20: of W African origin]

moke (məʊk) *n Brit* a slang name for **donkey** (sense 1) [c19: origin obscure]

Mokha (ˈməʊkə, ˈmɒk-) *n* a variant of **Mocha**

mokopuna (ˌmɒʊkəʊˈpuːnə) *n NZ* a grandchild or young person [Māori]

Mokpo (ˌməʊkˈpəʊ) *n* a port in SW South Korea, on the Yellow Sea. Pop: 253 000 (2005 est)

mol *the chemical symbol for* mole[3]

mol. *abbreviation* 1 molecular 2 molecule

molal (ˈməʊləl) *adj chem* of or consisting of a solution containing one mole of solute per thousand grams of solvent [c20: from MOLE[3] + -AL[1]]

molar[1] (ˈməʊlə) *n* 1 any of the 12 broad-faced grinding teeth in man 2 a corresponding tooth in other mammals ▷ *adj* 3 of, relating to, or designating any of these teeth 4 used for or capable of grinding [c16: from Latin *molāris* for grinding, from *mola* millstone]

molar[2] (ˈməʊlə) *adj* 1 (of a physical quantity) per unit amount of substance: *molar volume* 2 (not recommended in technical usage) containing one mole of solute per litre of solution [c19: from Latin *mōlēs* a mass]

molasse (məˈlæs) *n* a soft sediment produced by the erosion of mountain ranges after the final phase of mountain building [c18: from French, perhaps alteration of *mollasse*, from Latin *mollis* soft]

molasses (məˈlæsɪz) *n* (*functioning as singular*) 1 the thick brown uncrystallized bitter syrup obtained from sugar during refining 2 *US & Canadian* a dark viscous syrup obtained during the refining of sugar. Also called (in Britain and certain other countries): **treacle** [c16: from Portuguese *melaço*, from Late Latin *mellāceum* must, from Latin *mel* honey]

mold (məʊld) *n, vb* the US spelling of **mould[1]**

Moldau (ˈmɔldau) *n* 1 the German name for **Moldavia** 2 the German name for the **Vltava**

Moldavia (mɒlˈdeɪvɪə) *n* 1 another name for **Moldova** 2 a former principality of E Europe, consisting of the basins of the Rivers Prut and Dniester: the E part (Bessarabia) became Moldova; the W part remains a province of Romania

moldboard (ˈməʊldˌbɔːd) *n* the US spelling of **mouldboard**

molder (ˈməʊldə) *vb, n* the US spelling of **moulder[1]**

molding (ˈməʊldɪŋ) *n* the US spelling of **moulding**

Moldova (mɒlˈdəʊvə) *n* a republic in SE Europe: comprising the E part of the former principality of Moldavia, the E part of which (Bessarabia) was ceded to the Soviet Union in 1940 and formed the Moldavian Soviet Socialist Republic until it gained independence in 1991; an agricultural region with many vineyards. Official language: Romanian. Religion: nonreligious and Christian. Currency: leu. Capital: Chişinău (Kishinev). Pop: 4 263 000 (2004 est). Area: 33 670 sq km (13 000 sq miles). Also called: **Moldavia** (mɒlˈdeɪvɪə) ▷ **Mol'dovan** *adj, n*

moldy (ˈməʊldɪ) *adj* **moldier, moldiest** the US spelling of **mouldy**

mole[1] (məʊl) *n pathol* a nontechnical name for **naevus** [Old English *māl*; related to Old High German *meil* spot]

mole[2] (məʊl) *n* 1 any small burrowing mammal, of the family *Talpidae*, of Europe, Asia, and North and Central America: order *Insectivora* (insectivores). They have velvety, typically dark fur and forearms specialized for digging 2 **golden mole** any small African burrowing molelike mammal of the family *Chrysochloridae*, having copper-coloured fur: order *Insectivora* (insectivores) 3 *informal* a spy who has infiltrated an organization and, often over a long period, become a trusted member of it [c14: from Middle Dutch *mol*, of Germanic origin; compare Middle Low German *mol*]

mole[3] (məʊl) *n* the basic SI unit of amount of substance; the amount that contains as many elementary entities as there are atoms in 0.012 kilogram of carbon-12. The entity must be specified and may be an atom, a molecule, an ion, a radical, an electron, a photon, etc [c20: from German *Mol*, short for *Molekül* MOLECULE]

mole[4] (məʊl) *n* 1 a breakwater 2 a harbour protected by a breakwater [c16: from French *môle*, from Latin *mōlēs* mass]

Molech (ˈməʊlɛk) *n Old Testament* a variant of **Moloch**

molecular (məʊˈlɛkjʊlə, mə-) *adj* of or relating to molecules ▷ **mo'lecularly** *adv*

molecular biology *n* the study of biological phenomena at the molecular level

molecular formula *n* a chemical formula indicating the numbers and types of atoms in a molecule: H_2SO_4 *is the molecular formula of sulphuric acid*

molecular genetics *n* (*functioning as singular*) the study of the molecular constitution of genes and chromosomes

molecular weight *n* the former name for **relative molecular mass**

molecule (ˈmɒlɪˌkjuːl) *n* 1 the simplest unit of a chemical compound that can exist, consisting of two or more atoms held together by chemical bonds 2 a very small particle [c18: via French from New Latin *mōlēcula*, diminutive of Latin *mōlēs* mass, MOLE[4]]

molehill (ˈməʊlˌhɪl) *n* 1 the small mound of earth thrown up by a burrowing mole 2 **make a mountain out of a molehill** to exaggerate an unimportant matter out

m

of all proportion

moleskin ('məʊl,skɪn) n **1** the dark grey dense velvety pelt of a mole, used as a fur **2** a hard-wearing cotton fabric of twill weave used for work clothes, etc **3** (modifier) made from moleskin: a moleskin waistcoat

molest (mə'lɛst) vb (tr) **1** to disturb or annoy by malevolent interference **2** to accost or attack, esp with the intention of assaulting sexually [c14: from Latin molestāre to annoy, from molestus troublesome, from mōlēs mass] > **molestation** (,məʊlɛ'steɪʃən) n > **mo'lester** n

Molière (French mɔljɛr) n real name Jean-Baptiste Poquelin. 1622–73, French dramatist, regarded as the greatest French writer of comedy. His works include Tartuffe (1664), Le Misanthrope (1666), L'Avare (1668), Le Bourgeois gentilhomme (1670), and Le Malade imaginaire (1673)

Molina (Spanish mo'lina) n See de Molina

Molise (Italian mo'li:ze) n a region of S central Italy, the second smallest of the regions: separated from **Abruzzi e Molise** in 1965. Capital: Campobasso. Pop: 321 047 (2003 est). Area: 4438 sq km (1731 sq miles)

moll (mɒl) n slang **1** the female accomplice of a gangster **2** a prostitute [c17: from Moll, familiar form of Mary]

mollify ('mɒlɪ,faɪ) vb -fies, -fying, -fied (tr) **1** to pacify; soothe **2** to lessen the harshness or severity of [c15: from Old French mollifier, via Late Latin, from Latin mollis soft + facere to make] > **'molli,fiable** adj > **,mollifi'cation** n > **'molli,fier** n

mollusc or US **mollusk** ('mɒləsk) n any invertebrate of the phylum Mollusca, having a soft unsegmented body and often a shell, secreted by a fold of skin (the mantle). The group includes the gastropods (snails, slugs, etc), bivalves (clams, mussels, etc), and cephalopods (cuttlefish, octopuses, etc) [c18: via New Latin from Latin molluscus, from mollis soft] > **molluscan** or US **molluskan** (mɒ'lʌskən) adj, n > **'mollusc-,like** or US **'mollusk-,like** adj

molly[1] ('mɒlɪ) n, pl -lies any brightly coloured tropical or subtropical American freshwater cyprinodont fish of the genus Mollienisia [c19: from New Latin Mollienisia, from Comte F. N. Mollien (1758–1850), French statesman]

molly[2] ('mɒlɪ) n, pl -lies Irish informal an effeminate, weak, or cowardly boy or man [c18: perhaps from Molly, pet name for Mary]

mollycoddle ('mɒlɪ,kɒdᵊl) vb **1** (tr) to treat with indulgent care; pamper ▷ n **2** a pampered person [c19: from MOLLY[2] + CODDLE] > **'molly,coddler** n

Molnár (Hungarian 'molna:r) n **Ferenc** ('fɛrɛnts). 1878–1952, Hungarian dramatist and novelist. His plays include Liliom (1909)

Moloch ('məʊlɒk) or **Molech** ('məʊlɛk) n Old Testament a Semitic deity to whom parents sacrificed their children

Molokai (,məʊləʊ'kɑ:ɪ) n an island in central Hawaii. Pop: 7404 (2000). Area: 676 sq km (261 sq miles)

Molopo (mə'ləʊpəʊ) n a seasonal river rising in N South Africa and flowing west and southwest to the Orange river. Length: about 1000 km (600 miles)

Molotov[1] ('mɒlə,tɒf; Russian 'mɔlətəf) n the former name (1940–62) for **Perm**

Molotov[2] ('mɒlə,tɒf; Russian 'mɔlətəf) n **Vyacheslav Mikhailovich** (vɪtʃɪ'slaf mi'xajləvɪtʃ), original surname Skriabin. 1890–1986, Soviet statesman. As commissar and later minister for foreign affairs (1939–49; 1953–56) he negotiated the nonaggression pact with Nazi Germany and attended the founding conference of the United Nations and the Potsdam conference (1945)

Molotov cocktail ('mɒlə,tɒf) n an elementary incendiary weapon, usually a bottle of petrol with a short-delay fuse or wick; petrol bomb [c20: named after Vyacheslav Mikhailovich Molotov (1890–1986), Soviet statesman]

molt (məʊlt) vb, n the usual US spelling of: **moult**

molten ('məʊltən) adj **1** liquefied; melted **2** made by having been melted: molten casts ▷ vb **3** the past participle of **melt**

Moltke (German 'mɔltkə) n **1** Count **Helmuth Johannes Ludwig von** ('hɛlmuːt jo'hanəs 'luːtvɪç fɔn). 1848–1916, German general; chief of the German general staff (1906–14) **2** his uncle Count **Helmuth Karl Bernhard von** ('hɛlmuːt karl 'bɛrnhart fɔn). 1800–91, German field

marshal; chief of the Prussian general staff (1858–88)

molto ('mɒltəʊ) adv music (preceded or followed by a musical direction, esp a tempo marking) very: allegro molto; molto adagio [from Italian, from Latin multum (adv) much]

Moluccas (məʊ'lʌkəz, mə-) or **Molucca Islands** pl n a group of islands in the Malay Archipelago, between Sulawesi (Celebes) and New Guinea. Capital: Amboina. Pop: 1 990 598 (2000). Area: about 74 505 sq km (28 766 sq miles). Indonesian name: **Maluku**. Former name: Spice Islands

mol. wt. abbreviation molecular weight

moly ('məʊlɪ) n, pl -lies **1** Greek myth a magic herb given by Hermes to Odysseus to nullify the spells of Circe **2** a liliaceous plant, Allium moly, that is native to S Europe and has yellow flowers in a dense cluster [c16: from Latin mōly, from Greek mōlu]

molybdenite (mɒ'lɪbdɪ,naɪt) n a soft grey mineral consisting of molybdenum sulphide in hexagonal crystalline form with rhenium as an impurity: the main source of molybdenum and rhenium. Formula: MoS_2

molybdenum (mɒ'lɪbdɪnəm) n a very hard ductile silvery-white metallic element occurring principally in molybdenite: used mainly in alloys, esp to harden and strengthen steels. Symbol: Mo; atomic no: 42; atomic wt: 95.94; valency: 2–6; relative density: 10.22; melting pt: 2623°C; boiling pt: 4639°C [c19: from New Latin, from Latin molybdaena galena, from Greek molubdaina, from molubdos lead]

mom (mɒm) n chiefly US & Canadian an informal word for **mother**[1]

Mombasa (mɒm'bæsə) n a port in S Kenya, on a coral island in a bay of the Indian Ocean: the chief port for Kenya, Uganda, and NE Tanzania; became British in 1887, capital of the East African Protectorate until 1907. Pop: 828 000 (2005 est)

moment ('məʊmənt) n **1** a short indefinite period of time: he'll be here in a moment **2** a specific instant or point in time: at that moment the doorbell rang **3** the moment the present point of time: at the moment it's fine **4** import, significance, or value: a man of moment **5** physics **a** a tendency to produce motion, esp rotation about a point or axis **b** the product of a physical quantity, such as force or mass, and its distance from a fixed reference point. See also **moment of inertia** [c14: from Old French, from Latin mōmentum, from movēre to move]

momentarily ('məʊməntərəlɪ, -trɪlɪ) adv **1** for an instant; temporarily **2** from moment to moment; every instant **3** US & Canadian very soon

momentary ('məʊməntərɪ, -trɪ) adj lasting for only a moment; temporary > **'momentariness** n

moment of inertia n the tendency of a body to resist angular acceleration, expressed as the sum of the products of the mass of each particle in the body and the square of its perpendicular distance from the axis of rotation

moment of truth n **1** a moment when a person or thing is put to the test **2** the point in a bullfight when the matador is about to kill the bull

momentous (məʊ'mɛntəs) adj of great significance > **mo'mentously** adv > **mo'mentousness** n

momentum (məʊ'mɛntəm) n, pl -ta (-tə) or -tums **1** physics the product of a body's mass and its velocity. Symbol: $p²$ **2** the impetus of a body resulting from its motion **3** driving power or strength [c17: from Latin: movement; see MOMENT]

momma ('mɒmə) n US & Canada another word for **mother**[1]

Mommsen (German 'mɔmzən) n **Theodor** ('te:odo:r). 1817–1903, German historian, noted esp for The History of Rome (1854–56): Nobel prize for literature 1902

Momus ('məʊməs) n, pl -muses or -mi (-maɪ) **1** Greek myth the god of blame and mockery **2** a cavilling critic

Mon. abbreviation Monday

mon- combining form a variant of: **mono-**

Monaco ('mɒnə,kəʊ, mə'nɑ:kəʊ; French mɔnako) n a principality in SW Europe, on the Mediterranean and forming an enclave in SE France: the second smallest sovereign state in the world (after the Vatican); consists of **Monaco-Ville** (the capital) on a rocky headland, **La Condamine** (a business area and port), **Monte Carlo** (the resort centre), and **Fontvieille**, a light industrial area. Language: French. Religion: Roman Catholic. Currency: euro. Pop: 34 000 (2003 est). Area: 189 hectares (476 acres) Related adj: **Monegasque** > **Monacan** ('mɒnəkən, mə'nɑ:-) *adj, n*

monad ('mɒnæd, 'məʊ-) *n* **1** *pl* **-ads** *or* **-ades** (-ə,di:z) *philosophy* any fundamental singular metaphysical entity, esp if autonomous **2** a single-celled organism, esp a flagellate protozoan **3** an atom, ion, or radical with a valency of one [c17: from Late Latin *monas*, from Greek: unit, from *monos* alone]

monadelphous (,mɒnə'dɛlfəs) *adj* **1** (of stamens) having united filaments forming a tube around the style **2** (of flowers) having monadelphous stamens [c19: from MONO- + Greek *adelphos* brother, twin + -OUS]

monadnock (mə'nædnɒk) *n* a residual hill that consists of hard rock in an otherwise eroded area [c19: named after Mount *Monadnock*, in New Hampshire]

Monaghan ('mɒnəhən) *n* **1** a county of NE Republic of Ireland, in Ulster province: many small lakes. County town: Monaghan. Pop: 52 593 (2002). Area: 1292 sq km (499 sq miles) **2** a town in NE Republic of Ireland, county town of Co Monaghan. Pop: 5717 (2002)

Mona Lisa ('məʊnə 'li:zə) *n* a portrait of a young woman painted by Leonardo da Vinci, admired for her enigmatic smile. Also called: **La Gioconda**

monandrous (mɒ'nændrəs) *adj* **1** having or preferring only one male sexual partner over a period of time **2** (of plants) having flowers with only one stamen **3** (of flowers) having only one stamen [c19: from MONO- + -ANDROUS] > **mo'nandry** *n*

Mona Passage ('məʊnə) *n* a strait between Puerto Rico and the Dominican Republic, linking the Atlantic with the Caribbean

monarch ('mɒnək) *n* **1** a sovereign head of state, esp a king, queen, or emperor, who rules usually by hereditary right **2** a supremely powerful or pre-eminent person or thing **3** Also called: **milkweed** a large migratory butterfly, *Danaus plexippus*, that has orange-and-black wings and feeds on the milkweed plant: family *Danaidae* [c15: from Late Latin *monarcha*, from Greek; see MONO-, -ARCH] > **monarchal** (mɒ'nɑ:kəl) *or* **monarchial** (mɒ'nɑ:kɪəl)

monarchy ('mɒnəkɪ) *n, pl* **-chies** **1** a form of government in which supreme authority is vested in a single and usually hereditary figure, such as a king, and whose powers can vary from those of an absolute despot to those of a figurehead **2** a country reigned over by a king, prince, or other monarch

monarda (mɒ'nɑ:də) *n* any mintlike North American plant of the genus *Monarda*: family *Lamiaceae* (labiates) [c19: from New Latin, named after N. *Monardés* (1493–1588), Spanish botanist]

monastery ('mɒnəstərɪ, -strɪ) *n, pl* **-teries** the residence of a religious community, esp of monks, living in seclusion from secular society and bound by religious vows [c15: from Church Latin *monastērium*, from Late Greek *monastērion*, from Greek *monázein* to live alone, from *monos* alone] > **monasterial** (,mɒnə'stɪərɪəl) *adj*

monastic (mə'næstɪk) *or* **monastical** *adj* **1** of or relating to monasteries or monks, nuns, etc **2** resembling this sort of life; reclusive ▷ *n* **3** a person who is committed to this way of life, esp a monk > **mo'nastically** *adv*

monasticism (mə'næstɪ,sɪzəm) *n* the monastic system, movement, or way of life

monatomic (,mɒnə'tɒmɪk) *or* **monoatomic** (,mɒnəʊə'tɒmɪk) *adj chem* **1** (of an element) having or consisting of single atoms **2** (of a compound or molecule) having only one atom or group that can be replaced in a chemical reaction **3** a less common word for **monovalent**

monaural (mɒ'nɔ:rəl) *adj* **1** relating to, having, or hearing with only one ear **2** another word for **monophonic** > **mon'aurally** *adv*

monazite ('mɒnə,zaɪt) *n* a yellow to reddish-brown mineral consisting of a phosphate of thorium, cerium, and lanthanum in monoclinic crystalline form [c19:

from German, from Greek *monazein* to live alone, so called because of its rarity]

Mönchengladbach (*German* mœnçən'glatbax) *n* a city in W Germany, in W North Rhine-Westphalia: headquarters of NATO forces in N central Europe; textile industry. Pop: 262 391 (2003 est). Former name: **München-Gladbach**

Monck (mʌŋk) *n* **George**. 1st Duke of Albemarle. 1608–70, English general. In the Civil War he was a Royalist until captured (1644) and persuaded to support the Commonwealth. After Cromwell's death he was instrumental in the restoration of Charles II (1660)

Moncton ('mɒŋktən) *n* a city in E Canada, in SE New Brunswick. Pop: 90 359 (2001)

Mondale ('mɒn,deɪl) *n* **Walter** (**Frederick**). born 1928, US Democratic politician; vice president of the US (1977–81)

Monday ('mʌndɪ) *n* the second day of the week; first day of the working week [Old English *mōnandæg* moon's day, translation of Late Latin *lūnae diēs*]

Mondrian (*Dutch* 'mɔndri:a:n) *n* **Piet** (pi:t). 1872–1944, Dutch painter, noted esp as an exponent of the abstract art movement De Stijl

monecious (mɒ'ni:ʃəs) *adj* a variant spelling of **monoecious**

Monel metal *or* **Monell metal** (mɒ'nɛl) *n trademark* any of various silvery corrosion-resistant alloys containing copper (28 per cent), nickel (67 per cent), and smaller quantities of such metals as iron, manganese, and aluminium [c20: named after A. *Monell* (died 1921), president of the International Nickel Co, New York, which introduced the alloys]

Monet (*French* mɔnɛ) *n* **Claude** (klod). 1840–1926, French landscape painter; the leading exponent of impressionism. His interest in the effect of light on colour led him to paint series of pictures of the same subject at different times of day. These include *Haystacks* (1889–93), *Rouen Cathedral* (1892–94), the *Thames* (1899–1904), and *Water Lilies* (1899–1906)

monetarism ('mʌnɪtə,rɪzəm) *n* **1** the theory that inflation is caused by an excess quantity of money in an economy **2** an economic policy based on this theory and on a belief in the efficiency of free market forces, that gives priority to achieving price stability by monetary control, balanced budgets, etc, and maintains that unemployment results from excessive real wage rates and cannot be controlled by Keynesian demand management > **'monetarist** *n, adj*

monetary ('mʌnɪtərɪ, -trɪ) *adj* **1** of or relating to money or currency **2** of or relating to monetarism: *a monetary policy* [c19: from Late Latin *monētārius*, from Latin *monēta* MONEY] > **'monetarily** *adv*

monetize *or* **monetise** ('mʌnɪ,taɪz) *vb* (*tr*) **1** to establish as the legal tender of a country **2** to give a legal value to (a coin) > **,moneti'zation** *or* **,moneti'sation** *n*

money ('mʌnɪ) *n* **1** a medium of exchange that functions as legal tender **2** the official currency, in the form of banknotes, coins, etc, issued by a government or other authority **3** a particular denomination or form of currency: *silver money* **4** *pl* **moneys** *or* **monies** *formal* **a** a pecuniary sum or income **5** an unspecified amount of paper currency or coins: *money to lend* **6** **for one's money** in one's opinion **7** **in the money** *informal* well-off; rich **8** **one's money's worth** full value for the money one has paid for something **9** **put money into** to invest money in **10** **put money on** to place a bet on ▷ *adj* **11** best, most valuable, or most eagerly anticipated: *the money shot; the money note* Related adj: **pecuniary** [c13: from Old French *moneie*, from Latin *monēta* coinage; see MINT²]

moneybags ('mʌnɪ,bægz) *n* (*functioning as singular*) *informal* a very rich person

moneychanger ('mʌnɪ,tʃeɪndʒə) *n* **1** a person engaged in the business of exchanging currencies or money **2** *chiefly US* a machine for dispensing coins

moneyed *or* **monied** ('mʌnɪd) *adj* **1** having a great deal of money; rich **2** arising from or characterized by money

money-grubbing *adj informal* seeking greedily to obtain money at every opportunity > **'money-,grubber** *n*

moneylender ('mʌnɪ,lendə) *n* a person who lends money at interest as a living > **'money,lending** *adj, n*

moneymaker ('mʌnɪˌmeɪkə) n 1 a person who is intent on accumulating money 2 a person or thing that is or might be profitable ▷ 'money,making adj, n

money of account n another name (esp US and Canadian) for: **unit of account**

money-purchase n (modifier) relating to a pension scheme in which both employer and employee make contributions to a fund that is used to buy an annuity on retirement. The amount paid as a pension depends on the size of the fund

money-spinner n informal an enterprise, idea, person, or thing that is a source of wealth

money supply n the total amount of money in a country's economy at a given time

monger ('mʌŋgə) n 1 (in combination except in archaic use) a trader or dealer: ironmonger 2 (in combination) a promoter of something unpleasant: warmonger [Old English mangere, ultimately from Latin mangō dealer; compare Old High German mangari] ▷ 'mongering n, adj

mongol ('mɒŋgəl) n a formerly used and now highly offensive name for a person affected by Down's syndrome

Mongol ('mɒŋgɒl, -gəl) n 1 a native or inhabitant of Mongolia, esp a nomad 2 the Mongolian language

Mongolia (mɒŋ'gəʊlɪə) n 1 a republic in E central Asia: made a Chinese province in 1691; became autonomous in 1911 and a republic in 1924; multiparty democracy introduced in 1990. It consists chiefly of a high plateau, with the Gobi Desert in the south, a large lake district in the northwest, and the Altai and Khangai Mountains in the west. Official language: Khalkha. Religion: nonreligious majority. Currency: tugrik. Capital: Ulan Bator. Pop: 2 630 000 (2004 est). Area: 1 565 000 sq km (604 095 sq miles). Former names: Outer Mongolia (until 1924), Mongolian People's Republic (1924-92) 2 a vast region of central Asia, inhabited chiefly by Mongols: now divided into the republic of Mongolia, Inner Mongolia (the Mongol Autonomous Region of China), and the Tuva Republic of S Russia; at its height during the 13th century under Genghis Khan

mongolian (mɒŋ'gəʊlɪən) adj (not in technical use) of, relating to, or affected by Down's syndrome

Mongolian (mɒŋ'gəʊlɪən) adj 1 of or relating to Mongolia, its people, or their language ▷ n 2 a native of Mongolia 3 the language of Mongolia

Mongolic (mɒŋ'gɒlɪk) n 1 a branch or subfamily of the Altaic family of languages, including Mongolian, Kalmuck, and Buryat 2 another word for **Mongoloid**

mongolism ('mɒŋgəˌlɪzəm) n pathol a formerly used and now highly offensive name for **Down's syndrome**

mongoloid ('mɒŋgəˌlɔɪd) old-fashioned, highly offensive ▷ adj 1 relating to or characterized by Down's syndrome ▷ n 2 a person affected by Down's syndrome

Mongoloid ('mɒŋgəˌlɔɪd) adj 1 denoting, relating to, or belonging to one of the supposed racial groups of mankind, including most of the peoples of Asia, the Inuit, and the North American Indians ▷ n 2 a member of this group

mongoose ('mɒŋˌguːs) n, pl -gooses any small predatory viverrine mammal of the genus Herpestes and related genera, occurring in Africa and from S Europe to SE Asia, typically having a long tail and brindled coat [c17: from Marathi mangūs, of Dravidian origin]

mongrel ('mʌŋgrəl) n 1 a plant or animal, esp a dog, of mixed or unknown breeding; a crossbreed or hybrid 2 highly offensive a person of mixed race 3 Austral & NZ sport toughness and physical aggression: a tall southpaw with plenty of mongrel ▷ adj 4 of mixed origin, breeding, character, etc [c15: from obsolete mong mixture; compare Old English gemong a mingling] ▷ 'mongrelism n ▷ 'mongrelly adj

'mongst (mʌŋst) prep poetic short for **amongst**

monied ('mʌnɪd) adj a less common spelling of **moneyed**

monies ('mʌnɪz) n formal a plural of **money**

moniker or **monicker** ('mɒnɪkə) n slang a person's name or nickname [c19: from Shelta munnik, altered from Irish ainm name]

monism ('mɒnɪzəm) n 1 philosophy the doctrine that the person consists of only a single substance, or that there is no crucial difference between mental and physical events or properties. See **dualism** (sense 2) 2 the attempt to explain anything in terms of one principle only [c19: from Greek monos single + -ism] ▷ 'monist n, adj

monition (məʊ'nɪʃən) n 1 a warning or caution; admonition 2 Christianity a formal notice from a bishop or ecclesiastical court requiring a person to refrain from committing a specific offence [c14: via Old French from Latin monitiō, from monēre to warn]

monitor ('mɒnɪtə) n 1 a person or piece of equipment that warns, checks, controls, or keeps a continuous record of something 2 education a a senior pupil with various supervisory duties b a pupil assisting a teacher in classroom organization, etc 3 a television screen used to display certain kinds of information in a television studio, airport, etc 4 the unit in a desk computer that contains the screen 5 a a loudspeaker used in a recording studio control room to determine quality or balance b a loudspeaker used on stage to enable musicians to hear themselves 6 any large predatory lizard of the genus Varanus and family Varanidae, inhabiting warm regions of Africa, Asia, and Australia 7 (formerly) a small heavily armoured shallow-draught warship used for coastal assault ▷ vb (tr) 8 to act as a monitor of 9 to observe or record (the activity or performance) of (an engine or other device) 10 to check (the technical quality of) (a radio or television broadcast) [c16: from Latin, from monēre to advise] ▷ monitorial (ˌmɒnɪ'tɔːrɪəl) adj ▷ 'monitress fem n

monitory ('mɒnɪtərɪ, -trɪ) adj Also: monitorial 1 warning or admonishing ▷ n, pl -ries 2 rare a letter containing a monition

monk (mʌŋk) n a male member of a religious community bound by vows of poverty, chastity, and obedience. Related adj: **monastic** [Old English munuc, from Late Latin monachus, from Late Greek: solitary (man), from Greek monos alone]

Monk (mʌŋk) n 1 Thelonious (Sphere) (θə'ləʊnɪəs). 1920–82, US jazz pianist and composer 2 a variant spelling of (George): **Monck**

monkey ('mʌŋkɪ) n 1 any of numerous long-tailed primates excluding the prosimians (lemurs, tarsiers, etc): comprise the families Cercopithecidae (Old World monkeys), Cebidae (New World monkeys), and Callithricidae (marmosets). See **Old World monkey, New World monkey** 2 any primate except man 3 a naughty or mischievous person, esp a child 4 the head of a pile-driver (**monkey engine**) or of some similar mechanical device 5 US & Canadian slang an addict's dependence on a drug (esp in the phrase **have a monkey on one's back**) 6 slang a butt of derision; someone made to look a fool (esp in the phrase **make a monkey of**) 7 slang (esp in bookmaking) £500 8 US & Canadian slang $500 9 Austral slang, archaic a sheep ▷ vb 10 (intr; usually foll by around, with, etc) to meddle, fool, or trifle 11 (tr) rare to imitate; ape [c16: perhaps from Low German; compare Middle Low German Moneke name of the ape's son in the tale of Reynard the Fox]

monkey business n informal mischievous, suspect, dishonest, or meddlesome behaviour or acts

monkey flower n any of various scrophulariaceous plants of the genus Mimulus, cultivated for their yellow or red flowers

monkey jacket n a short close-fitting jacket, esp a waist-length jacket similar to a mess jacket

monkey nut n Brit another name for a **peanut**

monkey puzzle n a South American coniferous tree, Araucaria araucana, having branches shaped like a candelabrum and stiff sharp leaves: family Araucariaceae. Also called: Chile pine [so called because monkeys allegedly have difficulty climbing them]

monkey's wedding n South African informal a combination of sunshine and light rain

monkey tricks or US **monkey shines** pl n informal mischievous behaviour or acts, such as practical jokes

monkey wrench n a wrench with adjustable jaws

monkfish ('mʌŋkˌfɪʃ) n, pl -fish or -fishes any of various anglers of the genus Lophius

monk's cloth n a heavy cotton fabric of basket weave, used mainly for bedspreads [C19: so called because a similar material was used for making monks' habits]

monkshood ('mʌŋkshʊd) n any of several poisonous N temperate plants of the ranunculaceous genus *Aconitum*, esp *A. napellus*, that have hooded blue-purple flowers

Monmouth[1] ('mɒnməθ) n a market town in E Wales, in Monmouthshire: Norman castle, where Henry V was born in 1387. Pop: 8547 (2001)

Monmouth[2] ('mɒnməθ) n **James Scott,** Duke of Monmouth. 1649–85, the illegitimate son of Charles II of England, he led a rebellion against James II in support of his own claim to the Crown; captured and beheaded

Monmouthshire ('mɒnməθˌʃɪə, -ʃə) n a county of E Wales: administratively part of England for three centuries (until 1830); mainly absorbed into the county of Gwent in 1974; reinstated with reduced boundaries in 1996: chiefly agricultural, with the Black Mountains in the N. Administrative centre: Cwmbran. Pop: 86 200 (2003 est). Area: 851 sq km (329 sq miles)

Monnet (*French* mɔnɛ) n **Jean** (ʒɑ̃). 1888–1979, French economist and public servant, regarded as founding father of the European Economic Community. He was first president (1952–55) of the European Coal and Steel Community

mono ('mɒnəʊ) adj **1** short for **monophonic** ▷ n **2** monophonic sound; monophony

mono- or before a vowel **mon-** combining form **1** one; single: *monochrome; monorail* **2** indicating that a chemical compound contains a single specified atom or group: *monoxide* [from Greek *monos*]

monoacid (ˌmɒnəʊ'æsɪd), **monacid, monoacidic** (ˌmɒnəʊə'sɪdɪk) or **monacidic** adj chem (of a base) capable of reacting with only one molecule of a monobasic acid; having only one hydroxide ion per molecule

monobasic (ˌmɒnəʊ'beɪsɪk) adj chem (of an acid, such as hydrogen chloride) having only one replaceable hydrogen atom per molecule

monocarpic (ˌmɒnəʊ'kɑːpɪk) or **monocarpous** adj botany another name for **semelparous**. Also called: hapaxanthic

monochromatic (ˌmɒnəʊkrəʊ'mætɪk) or **monochroic** (ˌmɒnəʊ'krəʊɪk) adj **1** Also called: homochromatic (of light or other electromagnetic radiation) having only one wavelength **2** physics (of moving particles) having only one kinetic energy **3** of or relating to monochromatism ▷ n **4** a person who is totally colour-blind ▷ ˌmonochro'matically adv

monochromator (ˌmɒnəʊ'krəʊmeɪtə) n physics a device that isolates a single wavelength of radiation

monochrome ('mɒnəˌkrəʊm) n **1** a black-and-white photograph or transparency **2** photog black and white **3 a** a painting, drawing, etc, done in a range of tones of a single colour **b** the technique or art of this **4** (modifier) executed in or resembling monochrome: *a monochrome print* ▷ adj **5** devoid of any distinctive or stimulating characteristics ▷ Also called (for senses 3, 4): **monotint** [C17: via Medieval Latin from Greek *monokhrōmos* of one colour] ▷ ˌmono'chromic or ˌmono'chromical adj ▷ 'monoˌchromist n

monocle ('mɒnəkᵊl) n a lens for correcting defective vision of one eye, held in position by the facial muscles [C19: from French, from Late Latin *monoculus* one-eyed, from MONO- + *oculus* eye] ▷ 'monocled adj

monocline ('mɒnəʊˌklaɪn) n a local steepening in stratified rocks with an otherwise gentle dip [C19: from MONO- + Greek *klīnein* to lean] ▷ ˌmono'clinal adj, n ▷ ˌmono'clinally adv

monoclinic (ˌmɒnəʊ'klɪnɪk) adj crystallog relating to or belonging to the crystal system characterized by three unequal axes, one pair of which are not at right angles to each other [C19: from MONO- + Greek *klīnein* to lean + -IC]

monoclinous (ˌmɒnəʊ'klaɪnəs, 'mɒnəʊˌklaɪnəs) adj (of flowering plants) having the male and female reproductive organs on the same flower. See **diclinous** [C19: from MONO- + Greek *klīnē* bed + -OUS] ▷ 'monoˌclinism n

monoclonal antibody (ˌmɒnəʊ'kləʊnᵊl) n an antibody, produced by a single clone of cells grown in culture, that is both pure and specific and is capable of proliferating indefinitely to produce unlimited quantities of identical antibodies: used in diagnosis, therapy, and biotechnology

monocoque ('mɒnəˌkɒk) n **1** a type of aircraft fuselage, car body, etc, in which all or most of the loads are taken by the skin **2** a type of racing-car, racing-cycle, or powerboat design with no separate chassis and body ▷ adj **3** of or relating to the design characteristic of a monocoque [C20: from French, from MONO- + *coque* shell]

monocotyledon (ˌmɒnəʊˌkɒtɪ'liːdᵊn) n any flowering plant of the class *Monocotyledonae*, having a single embryonic seed leaf, leaves with parallel veins, and flowers with parts in threes: includes grasses, lilies, palms, and orchids. See **dicotyledon** ▷ ˌmonoˌcoty'ledonous adj

monocracy (mɒ'nɒkrəsɪ) n, pl -cies government by one person ▷ monocrat ('mɒnəˌkræt) n ▷ ˌmono'cratic adj

monocular (mɒ'nɒkjʊlə) adj having to do with or using only one eye [C17: from Late Latin *monoculus* one-eyed] ▷ mo'nocularly adv

monoculture ('mɒnəʊˌkʌltʃə) n the continuous growing of one type of crop

monocycle ('mɒnəˌsaɪkᵊl) n another name for: **unicycle**

monocyte ('mɒnəʊˌsaɪt) n a large phagocytic leucocyte with a spherical nucleus and clear cytoplasm

monody ('mɒnədɪ) n, pl -dies **1** (in Greek tragedy) an ode sung by a single actor **2** any poem of lament for someone's death **3** music a style of composition consisting of a single vocal part, usually with accompaniment [C17: via Late Latin from Greek *monōidia*, from MONO- + *aeidein* to sing] ▷ monodic (mɒ'nɒdɪk) or mo'nodical adj ▷ 'monodist n

monoecious, monecious (mɒ'niːʃəs) or **monoicous** (mɒ'nɔɪkəs) adj **1** (of some flowering plants) having the male and female reproductive organs in separate flowers on the same plant **2** (of some animals and lower plants) hermaphrodite [C18: from New Latin *monoecia*, from MONO- + Greek *oikos* house]

monofilament (ˌmɒnə'fɪləmənt) or **monofil** ('mɒnəfɪl) n **1** synthetic thread or yarn composed of a single strand rather than twisted fibres **2** a fishing line made of monofilaments

monogamy (mɒ'nɒgəmɪ) n **1** the state or practice of having one husband or wife over a period of time **2** zoology the practice of having only one mate [C17: via French from Late Latin *monogamia*, from Greek; see MONO- + -GAMY] ▷ mo'nogamous adj

monogenesis (ˌmɒnəʊ'dʒɛnɪsɪs) or **monogeny** (mɒ'nɒdʒɪnɪ) n **1** the hypothetical descent of all organisms from a single cell or organism **2** asexual reproduction in animals **3** the direct development of an ovum into an organism resembling the adult **4** the hypothetical descent of all human beings from a single pair of ancestors

monogram ('mɒnəˌgræm) n a design of one or more letters, esp initials, embroidered on clothing, printed on stationery, etc [C17: from Late Latin *monogramma*, from Greek; see MONO-, -GRAM] ▷ monogrammatic (ˌmɒnəgrə'mætɪk) adj

monograph ('mɒnəˌgrɑːf, -ˌgræf) n **1** a paper, book, or other work concerned with a single subject or aspect of a subject ▷ vb **2** (tr) to write a monograph on ▷ **monographer** (mɒ'nɒgrəfə) or mo'nographist n ▷ ˌmono'graphic adj

monogyny (mɒ'nɒdʒɪnɪ) n the custom of having only one female sexual partner over a period of time ▷ mo'nogynist n ▷ mo'nogynous adj

monohull ('mɒnəʊˌhʌl) n a sailing vessel with a single hull

monolayer ('mɒnəʊˌleɪə) n a single layer of atoms or molecules adsorbed on a surface. Also called: **molecular film**

monolingual (ˌmɒnəʊ'lɪŋgwəl) adj knowing or expressed in only one language

monolith ('mɒnəlɪθ) n **1** a large block of stone or anything that resembles one in appearance,

m

intractability, etc **2** a statue, obelisk, column, etc, cut from one block of stone **3** a large hollow foundation piece sunk as a caisson and having a number of compartments that are filled with concrete when it has reached its correct position [C19: via French from Greek *monolithos* made from a single stone] > ˌmono'lithic *adj*

monologue ('mɒnəˌlɒg) *n* **1** a long speech made by one actor in a play, film, etc, esp when alone **2** a dramatic piece for a single performer **3** any long speech by one person, esp when interfering with conversation [C17: via French from Greek *monologos* speaking alone] > monologic (ˌmɒnə'lɒdʒɪk) *or* ˌmono'logical *adj* > monologist ('mɒnəˌlɒgɪst, mə'nɒləgɪst) *n*

monomania (ˌmɒnəʊ'meɪnɪə) *n* an excessive mental preoccupation with one thing, idea, etc > ˌmono'maniˌac *n, adj* > monomaniacal (ˌmɒnəʊmə'naɪəkᵊl) *adj*

monomark ('mɒnəmɑːk) *n Brit* a series of letters or figures to identify goods, personal articles, etc

monomer ('mɒnəmə) *n chem* a compound whose molecules can join together to form a polymer > monomeric (ˌmɒnə'mɛrɪk) *adj*

monometallism (ˌmɒnəʊ'mɛtᵊˌlɪzəm) *n* **1** the use of one metal, esp gold or silver, as the sole standard of value and currency **2** the economic policies supporting a monometallic standard > ˌmono'metallist *n*

monomial (mɒ'nəʊmɪəl) *n* **1** *maths* an expression consisting of a single term, such as 5*ax* ▷ *adj* **2** consisting of a single algebraic term [C18: MONO- + (BIN)OMIAL]

monomorphic (ˌmɒnəʊ'mɔːfɪk) *or* **monomorphous** *adj* **1** (of an individual organism) showing little or no change in structure during the entire life history **2** (of a species) existing or having parts that exist in only one form **3** (of a chemical compound) having only one crystalline form

Monongahela (məˌnɒŋgə'hiːlə) *n* a river in the northeastern US, flowing generally north to the Allegheny River at Pittsburgh, Pennsylvania, forming the Ohio River. Length: 206 km (128 miles)

mononucleosis (ˌmɒnəʊˌnjuːklɪ'əʊsɪs) *n* **1** *pathol* the presence of a large number of monocytes in the blood **2** See infectious mononucleosis

monophonic (ˌmɒnəʊ'fɒnɪk) *adj* **1** Also called: monaural (of a system of broadcasting, recording, or reproducing sound) using only one channel between source and loudspeaker **2** *music* of or relating to a style of musical composition consisting of a single melodic line

monophthong ('mɒnəfˌθɒŋ) *n* a simple or pure vowel [C17: from Greek *monophthongos*, from MONO- + *thongos* sound]

Monophysite (mɒ'nɒfɪˌsaɪt) *Christianity n* a person who holds that there is only one nature in the person of Christ, which is primarily divine with human attributes [C17: via Church Latin from Late Greek, from MONO- + *phusis* nature] > Monophysitic (ˌmɒnəʊfɪ'sɪtɪk) *adj*

monoplane ('mɒnəʊˌpleɪn) *n* an aeroplane with only one pair of wings. See biplane

monopole ('mɒnəˌpəʊl) *n physics* **1** a magnetic pole considered in isolation **2** Also called: magnetic monopole a hypothetical elementary particle postulated in certain theories of particle physics to exist as an isolated north or south magnetic pole

monopolize *or* **monopolise** (mə'nɒpəˌlaɪz) *vb* (*tr*) **1** to have, control, or make use of fully, excluding others **2** to obtain, maintain, or exploit a monopoly of (a market, commodity, etc) > moˌnopoli'zation *or* moˌnopoli'sation *n* > mo'nopoˌlizer *or* mo'nopoˌliser *n*

monopoly (mə'nɒpəlɪ) *n, pl* -lies **1** exclusive control of the market supply of a product or service **2 a** an enterprise exercising this control **b** the product or service so controlled **3** *law* the exclusive right or privilege granted to a person, company, etc, by the state to purchase, manufacture, use, or sell some commodity or to carry on trade in a specified country or area **4** exclusive control, possession, or use of something [C16: from Late Latin, from Greek *monopōlion*, from MONO- + *pōlein* to sell] > mo'nopolism *n* > mo'nopolist *n* > moˌnopo'listic *adj*

Monopoly (mə'nɒpəlɪ) *n trademark* a board game for two to six players who throw dice to advance their tokens around a board, the object being to acquire the property on which their tokens land

monorail ('mɒnəˌreɪl) *n* a single-rail railway, often elevated and with suspended cars

monorchid (mɒ'nɔːkɪd) *adj* **1** having only one testicle ▷ *n* **2** an animal or person with only one testicle

monosaccharide (ˌmɒnəʊ'sækəˌraɪd, -rɪd) *n* a simple sugar, such as glucose or fructose, that does not hydrolyse to yield other sugars

monosaturated (ˌmɒnəʊ'sætʃəˌreɪtɪd) *adj* of or relating to fats that are liquid at room temperature and derive mostly from foods such as olives, avocados, and nuts

monoski ('mɒnəʊˌskiː) *n* a wide ski on which the skier stands with both feet > 'mono,skier *n* > 'mono,skiing *n*

monosodium glutamate (ˌmɒnəʊ'səʊdɪəm) *n* a white crystalline substance, the sodium salt of glutamic acid, that has little flavour itself but enhances the flavour of proteins either by increasing the amount of saliva produced in the mouth or by stimulating the taste buds: used as a food additive, esp in Chinese foods. Formula: $NaC_5H_8O_4$. Also called: sodium glutamate Abbreviation: MSG

monospaced type ('mɒnəʊˌspeɪst) *n computing* a typeface in which the width of all letters, including the space around them, is the same

monostable (ˌmɒnəʊ'steɪbᵊl) *adj physics* (of an electronic circuit) having only one stable state but able to pass into a second state in response to an input pulse

monosyllabic (ˌmɒnəsɪ'læbɪk) *adj* **1** (of a word) containing only one syllable **2** characterized by monosyllables; curt: *a monosyllabic answer* > ˌmonosyl'labically *adv*

monosyllable ('mɒnəˌsɪləbᵊl) *n* a word of one syllable, esp one used as a sentence > ˌmono'syllaˌbism *n*

monoterpene ('mɒnəˌtɜːpiːn) *n chem* an isoprene unit, C_5H_8, forming a terpene

monotheism ('mɒnəʊθɪˌɪzəm) *n* the belief or doctrine that there is only one God > 'mono,theist *n, adj* > ˌmonothe'istic *adj* > ˌmonothe'istically *adv*

monotherapy (ˌmɒnə'θɛrəpɪ) *n, pl* -pies a medical treatment using a single drug or therapy

monotint ('mɒnəˌtɪnt) *n* another word for **monochrome** (senses 3, 4)

monotone ('mɒnəˌtəʊn) *n* **1** a single unvaried pitch level in speech, sound, etc **2** utterance, etc, without change of pitch **3** lack of variety in style, expression. etc ▷ *adj* **4** unvarying or monotonous

monotonous (mə'nɒtənəs) *adj* **1** dull and tedious, esp because of repetition **2** unvarying in pitch or cadence > mo'notonously *adv* > mo'notonousness *n*

monotony (mə'nɒtənɪ) *n, pl* -nies **1** wearisome routine; dullness **2** lack of variety in pitch or cadence

monotreme ('mɒnəʊˌtriːm) *n* any mammal of the primitive order *Monotremata*, of Australia and New Guinea: egg-laying toothless animals with a single opening (cloaca) for the passage of eggs or sperm, faeces, and urine. The group contains only the echidnas and the platypus [C19: via New Latin from MONO- + Greek *trēma* hole] > monotrematous (ˌmɒnəʊ'triːmətəs) *adj*

monotype ('mɒnəˌtaɪp) *n* **1** a single print made from a metal or glass plate on which a picture has been painted **2** *biology* a monotypic genus or species

Monotype ('mɒnəˌtaɪp) *n* **1** *trademark* any of various typesetting systems, esp originally one in which each character was cast individually from hot metal **2** type produced by such a system

monotypic (ˌmɒnəʊ'tɪpɪk) *adj* **1** (of a genus or species) consisting of only one type of animal or plant **2** of or relating to a monotype

monounsaturated (ˌmɒnəʊʌn'sætʃəˌreɪtɪd) *adj* of or relating to a class of vegetable oils, such as olive oil, the molecules of which have long chains of carbon atoms containing only one double bond. See also polyunsaturated

monovalent (ˌmɒnəʊ'veɪlənt) *adj chem* **a** having a valency of one **b** having only one valency. Also called: univalent > ˌmono'valence *or* ˌmono'valency *n*

monoxide (mɒˈnɒksaɪd) *n* an oxide that contains one oxygen atom per molecule

monozygotic (ˌmɒnəʊzaɪˈɡɒtɪk) *or* **monzygous** (ˌmɒnəʊˈzaɪɡəs) *adj* (of twins) derived from a single fertilized ovum, so identical [C20]

Monroe (mənˈrəʊ) *n* **1** James. 1758–1831, US statesman; fifth president of the US (1817–25). He promulgated the Monroe Doctrine (1823) **2** Marilyn, real name *Norma Jean Baker or Mortenson*. 1926–62, US film actress. Her films include *Niagara* (1952), *Gentlemen Prefer Blondes* (1953), and *Some Like It Hot* (1959)

Monrovia (mɒnˈrəʊvɪə) *n* the capital and chief port of Liberia, on the Atlantic: founded in 1822 as a home for freed American slaves; University of Liberia (1862). Pop: 614 000 (2005 est)

Mons (*French* mɔ̃s) *n* a town in SW Belgium, capital of Hainaut province: scene of the first battle (1914) of the British Expeditionary Force during World War I. Pop: 91 185 (2004 est). Flemish name: **Bergen**

Monseigneur *French* (mɔ̃sɛɲœʁ) *n, pl* **Messeigneurs** (mesɛɲœʁ) a title given to French bishops, prelates, and princes. Abbreviation: **Mgr** [literally: my lord]

monsieur (*French* məsjø; *English* məsˈjɜː) *n, pl* **messieurs** (*French* mesjø; *English* ˈmɛsəz) a French title of address equivalent to *sir* when used alone or *Mr* when placed before a name [literally: my lord]

Monsignor (mɒnˈsiːnjə; *Italian* monsiɲˈɲor) *n, pl* **Monsignors** *or* **Monsignori** (*Italian* monsiɲˈɲoːri) *RC Church* an ecclesiastical title attached to certain offices or distinctions usually bestowed by the Pope [C17: from Italian, from French MONSEIGNEUR]

monsoon (mɒnˈsuːn) *n* **1** a seasonal wind of S Asia that blows from the southwest in summer, bringing heavy rains, and from the northeast in winter **2** the rainy season when the SW monsoon blows, from about April to October **3** any wind that changes direction with the seasons [C16: from obsolete Dutch *monssoen*, from Portuguese *monção*, from Arabic *mawsim* season] > **monˈsoonal** *adj*

mons pubis (ˈmɒnz ˈpjuːbɪs) *n, pl* **montes pubis** (ˈmɒntiːz) the fatty cushion of flesh in human males situated over the junction of the pubic bones. See **mons veneris** [C17: New Latin: hill of the pubes]

monster (ˈmɒnstə) *n* **1** an imaginary beast, such as a centaur, usually made up of various animal or human parts **2** a person, animal, or plant with a marked structural deformity **3** a cruel, wicked, or inhuman person **4 a** a very large person, animal, or thing **b** (*as modifier*): *a monster cake* [C13: from Old French *monstre*, from Latin *monstrum* portent, from *monēre* to warn]

monstera (mɒnˈstɪərə) *n* any plant of the tropical climbing genus *Monstera*, some species of which are grown as greenhouse or pot plants for their unusual leathery perforated leaves: family *Araceae*. *M. deliciosa* is the Swiss cheese plant [New Latin, perhaps because the leaves were regarded as an aberration]

monster truck *n* a pick-up truck with extremely large tyres, often used for racing over rough terrain

monstrance (ˈmɒnstrəns) *n RC Church* a receptacle, usually of gold or silver, with a transparent container in which the consecrated Host is exposed for adoration [C16: from Medieval Latin *mōnstrantia*, from Latin *mōnstrāre* to show]

monstrosity (mɒnˈstrɒsɪtɪ) *n, pl* **-ties 1** an outrageous or ugly person or thing; monster **2** the state or quality of being monstrous

monstrous (ˈmɒnstrəs) *adj* **1** abnormal, hideous, or unnatural in size, character, etc **2** (of plants and animals) abnormal in structure **3** outrageous, atrocious, or shocking: *it is monstrous how badly he is treated* **4** huge **5** of, relating to, or resembling a monster > **ˈmonstrously** *adv* > **ˈmonstrousness** *n*

mons veneris (ˈmɒnz ˈvɛnərɪs) *n, pl* **montes veneris** (ˈmɒntiːz) the fatty cushion of flesh in human females situated over the junction of the pubic bones. See **mons pubis** [C17: New Latin: hill of Venus]

Mont. *abbreviation* Montana

montage (mɒnˈtɑːʒ; *French* mɔ̃taʒ) *n* **1** the art or process of composing pictures by the superimposition or juxtaposition of miscellaneous elements, such as other pictures or photographs **2** such a composition **3** a method of film editing involving the juxtaposition or partial superimposition of several shots to form a single image **4** a rapidly cut film sequence of this kind [C20: from French, from *monter* to MOUNT[1]]

Montagnais (ˌmɒntənˈjeɪ) *n, pl* **-gnais** (jeɪ, jeɪz) *or* **-gnaises** (jeɪz) **1** a member of an Innu people living in Labrador and eastern Quebec **2** the Algonquian language of this people [C18: from French: of the mountain, from *montagne* MOUNTAIN]

Montagu (ˈmɒntəgjuː) *n* **1** Charles. See (Earl of): **Halifax[1] 2** Lady Mary Wortley. 1689–1762, English writer, noted for her *Letters from the East* (1763)

Montaigne (*French* mɔ̃tɛɲ) *n* **Michel Eyquem de** (miʃɛl ikɛm də). 1533–92, French writer. His life's work, the *Essays* (begun in 1571), established the essay as a literary genre and record the evolution of his moral ideas

Montale (*Italian* monˈtaːle) *n* **Eugenio** (euˈdʒɛːnjo). 1896–1981, Italian poet: Nobel prize for literature 1975

Montana[1] (mɒnˈtænə) *n* a state of the western US: consists of the Great Plains in the east and the Rocky Mountains in the west Capital: Helena. Pop: 917 621 (2003 est). Area: 377 070 sq km (145 587 sq miles). Abbreviations: **Mont.**, *or* (with zip code) **MT** > **Monˈtanan** *n, adj*

Montana[2] (mɒnˈtænə) *n* **Joe.** born 1958, American football quarterback

montane (ˈmɒnteɪn) *adj* of or inhabiting mountainous regions [C19: from Latin *montānus*, from *mons* MOUNTAIN]

Montauban (*French* mɔ̃tobɑ̃) *n* a city in SW France: a stronghold in the 16th and 17th centuries, taken by Richelieu in 1629. Pop: 51 855 (1999)

Montbéliard (*French* mɔ̃beljar) *n* an industrial town in E France: former capital of the duchy of Burgundy. Pop: 27 570 (1999)

Mont Blanc (*French* mɔ̃ blɑ̃) *n* a massif in SW Europe, mainly between France and Italy: the highest mountain in the Alps; beneath it is **Mont Blanc Tunnel**, 12 km (7.5 miles) long. Highest peak (in France): 4807 m (15 771 ft)

montbretia (mɒnˈbriːʃə) *n* a widely cultivated plant of the African iridaceous genus *Crocosmia*, a cross between *C. aurea* and *C. pottsii*, with ornamental orange or yellow flowers, grown mostly as pot plants [C19: New Latin, named after A. F. E. Coquebert de *Montbret* (1780–1801), French botanist]

Montcalm (mɒntˈkɑːm; *French* mɔ̃kalm) *n* **Louis Joseph** (lwi ʒozɛf), Marquis de Montcalm de Saint-Véran. 1712–59, French general in Canada (1756); killed in Quebec by British forces under General Wolfe

Mont Cenis (*French* mɔ̃səni) *n* See (Mont): **Cenis**

Mont Cervin (mɔ̃ sɛrvɛ̃) *n* the French name for the **Matterhorn**

monte (ˈmɒntɪ) *n* a gambling card game of Spanish origin [C19: from Spanish: mountain, hence pile of cards]

Monte Carlo (ˈmɒntɪ ˈkɑːləʊ; *French* mɔ̃te karlo) *n* a town and resort forming part of the principality of Monaco, on the Riviera: famous casino and the destination of an annual car rally (the **Monte Carlo Rally**). Pop: 15 507 (2000)

Monte Cassino (ˈmɒntɪ kəˈsiːnəʊ; *Italian* ˈmonte kasˈsiːno) *n* a hill above Cassino in central Italy: site of intense battle during World War II: site of Benedictine monastery (530 AD), destroyed by Allied bombing in 1944, later restored

Monte Corno (*Italian* ˈmonte ˈkorno) *n* See (Monte): **Corno**

Montefeltro (*Italian* monteˈfeltro) *n* an Italian noble family who ruled Urbino from the 13th to the 16th century. **Federigo Montefeltro**, duke of Urbino (1422–82), was a noted patron of the arts and military leader

Montego Bay (mɒnˈtiːgəʊ) *n* a port and resort in NW Jamaica: the second largest town on the island Pop: 96 488 (2001)

Montenegro (ˌmɒntɪˈniːgrəʊ) *n* a republic in S central Europe, bordering on the Adriatic; declared a kingdom in 1910 and united with Serbia, Croatia, and other territories in 1918 to form Yugoslavia; remained united

m

with Serbia as the Federal Republic of Yugoslavia when the other Yugoslav constituent republics became independent in 1991–92; Union of Serbia and Montenegro formed in 2003 and dissolved 2006. Mainly mountainous. Language: Serbian (Montenegrin). Religion: Orthodox Christian majority. Currency: euro. Capital: Podgorica. Pop: 658 000 (2001 est). Area: 13 812 sq km (5387 sq miles) ▷ **Monte'negrin** *adj, n*

Monterey (ˌmɒntɪˈreɪ) *n* a city in W California: capital of Spain's Pacific empire from 1774 to 1825; taken by the US (1846). Pop: 29 960 (2003 est)

Monterrey (ˌmɒntəˈreɪ; *Spanish* mɔntɛˈrreɪ) *n* a city in NE Mexico, capital of Nuevo Léon state: the third largest city in Mexico; a major industrial centre, esp for metals. Pop: 1 353 000 (2005 est)

Montespan (*French* mɔ̃tɛspɑ̃) *n* **Marquise de**, title of *Françoise Athénaïs de Rochechouart*. 1641–1707, French noblewoman; mistress of Louis XIV of France

Montesquieu (*French* mɔ̃tɛskjø) *n* **Baron de la Brède et de** (barɔ̃ də la brɛd e də), title of *Charles Louis de Secondat*. 1689–1755, French political philosopher. His chief works are the satirical *Lettres persanes* (1721) and *L'Esprit des lois* (1748), a comparative analysis of various forms of government, which had a profound influence on political thought in Europe and the US

Montessori (ˌmɒntɪˈsɔːrɪ; *Italian* montesˈsɔːri) *n* **Maria** (maˈriːa). 1870–1952, Italian educational reformer, who evolved the Montessori method of teaching children

Monteux (*French* mɔ̃tø) *n* **Pierre** (pjɛr). 1875–1964, US conductor, born in France

Monteverdi (ˌmɒntɪˈvɛədɪ) *n* **Claudio** ('klaʊdɪˌəʊ). ?1567–1643, Italian composer, noted esp for his innovations in opera and for his expressive use of dissonance. His operas include *Orfeo* (1607) and *L'Incoronazione di Poppea* (1642) and he also wrote many motets and madrigals

Montevideo (ˌmɒntɪvɪˈdeɪəʊ; *Spanish* mɔnteβiˈðeo) *n* the capital and chief port of Uruguay, in the south on the Río de la Plata estuary: the largest city in the country: University of the Republic (1849); resort. Pop: 1 378 707 (1996)

Montez (mɒnˈtɛz) *n* **Lola** ('ləʊlə), original name *Marie Gilbert*. 1818–61, Irish dancer; mistress of Louis I of Bavaria (1786–1868; reigned 1825–48)

Montezuma II (ˌmɒntɪˈzuːmə) *n* 1466–1520, Aztec emperor of Mexico (?1502–20). He was overthrown and killed by the Spanish conquistador Cortés

Montfort ('mɒntfət) *n* **Simon de**, Earl of Leicester. ?1208–65, English soldier, born in Normandy. He led the baronial rebellion against Henry III and ruled England from 1264 to 1265; he was killed at Evesham

Montgolfier (*French* mɔ̃gɔlfje) *n* **Jacques Étienne** (ʒak etjɛn), 1745–99, and his brother **Joseph Michel** (ʒozɛf miʃɛl), 1740–1810, French inventors, who built (1782) and ascended in (1783) the first practical hot-air balloon

Montgomery[1] (mənt'gʌmərɪ) *n* a city in central Alabama, on the Alabama River: state capital; capital of the Confederacy (1861). Pop: 200 123 (2003 est)

Montgomery[2] (mənt'gʌmərɪ) *n* **1 Bernard Law**, 1st Viscount Montgomery of Alamein, nicknamed *Monty*. 1887–1976, British field marshal. As commander of the 8th Army in North Africa, he launched the offensive, beginning with the victory at El Alamein (1942), that drove Rommel's forces back to Tunis. He also commanded the ground forces in the invasion of Normandy (1944) and accepted Germany's surrender at Lüneburg Heath (May 7, 1945) **2 L(ucy) M(aud)**. 1874–1942, Canadian writer; her novels include *Anne of Green Gables* (1908) and its sequels.

Montgomeryshire (mənt'gʌmərɪˌʃɪə, -ˌʃə) *n* (until 1974) a county of central Wales, now part of Powys

month (mʌnθ) *n* **1** one of the twelve divisions (**calendar months**) of the calendar year **2** a period of time extending from one date to a corresponding date in the next calendar month **3** a period of four weeks or of 30 days **4** the period of time (**tropical month**) taken by the moon to return to the same longitude after one complete revolution around the earth; 27.321 58 days (approximately 27 days, 7 hours, 43 minutes, 4.5 seconds)

5 the period of time (**sidereal month**) taken by the moon to make one complete revolution around the earth, measured between two successive conjunctions with a distant star; 27.321 66 days (approximately 27 days, 7 hours, 43 minutes, 11 seconds) **6** Also called: **lunation** the period of time (**lunar** or **synodic month**) taken by the moon to make one complete revolution around the earth, measured between two successive new moons; 29.530 59 days (approximately 29 days, 12 hours, 44 minutes, 3 seconds) **7 a month of Sundays** *informal* a long unspecified period Related adjective: **mensal** [Old English *mōnath*; related to Old High German *mānōd*, Old Norse *mānathr*; compare Gothic *mena* moon]

Montherlant (*French* mɔ̃tɛrlɑ̃) *n* **Henri** (**Millon**) **de** (ɑ̃ri də). 1896–1972, French novelist and dramatist: his novels include *Les Jeunes Filles* (1935–39) and *Le Chaos et la nuit* (1963)

monthly ('mʌnθlɪ) *adj* **1** occurring, done, appearing, payable, etc, once every month **2** lasting or valid for a month ▷ *adv* **3** once a month ▷ *n, pl* **-lies 4** a book, periodical, magazine, etc, published once a month **5** *informal* a menstrual period

Montluçon (*French* mɔ̃lysɔ̃) *n* an industrial city in central France, on the Cher River. Pop: 41 362 (1999)

Montmartre (*French* mɔ̃martrə) *n* a district of N Paris, on a hill above the Seine: the highest point in the city; famous for its associations with many artists

Montparnasse (*French* mɔ̃parnas) *n* a district of S Paris, on the left bank of the Seine: noted for its cafés, frequented by artists, writers, and students

Montpelier (mɒnt'piːljə) *n* a city in N central Vermont, on the Winooski River: the state capital. Pop: 7945 (2003 est)

Montpellier (*French* mɔ̃pɛlje) *n* a city in S France, the chief town of Languedoc: its university was founded by Pope Nicholas IV in 1289; wine trade. Pop: 225 392 (1999)

Montreal (ˌmɒntrɪˈɔːl) *n* a city and major port in central Canada, in S Quebec on **Montreal Island** at the junction of the Ottawa and St Lawrence Rivers. Pop: 1 039 534 (2001). French name: **Montréal** (mɔ̃real)

Montreuil (*French* mɔ̃trœj) *n* an E suburb of Paris: formerly famous for peaches, but now industrialized. Pop: 90 674 (1999)

Montreux (*French* mɔ̃trø) *n* a town and resort in W Switzerland, in Vaud canton on Lake Geneva annual television festival. Pop: 22 454 (2000)

Montrose (mɒn'trəʊz) *n* **James Graham**, 1st Marquess and 5th Earl of Montrose. 1612–50, Scottish general, noted for his victories in Scotland for Charles I in the Civil War. He was later captured and hanged

Mont-Saint-Michel (*French* mɔ̃sɛ̃miʃɛl) *n* a rocky islet off the coast of NW France, accessible at low tide by a causeway, in the **Bay of St Michel** (an inlet of the Gulf of St Malo): Benedictine abbey (966), used as a prison from the Revolution until 1863; reoccupied by Benedictine monks since 1966. Area: 1 hectare (3 acres)

Montserrat *n* **1** (ˌmɒntsəˈræt) a volcanic island in the Caribbean, in the Leeward Islands: a UK Overseas Territory: much of the island rendered uninhabitable by volcanic eruptions in 1997. Capital: Brades (replacing Plymouth, effectively destroyed by the eruption). Pop: 4000 (2003 est). Area: 103 sq km (40 sq miles) **2** (*Spanish* mɔnsɛˈrrat) a mountain in NE Spain, northwest of Barcelona: famous Benedictine monastery. Height: 1235 m (4054 ft)

monument ('mɒnjʊmənt) *n* **1** an obelisk, statue, building, etc, erected in commemoration of a person or event or in celebration of something **2** a notable building or site, esp one preserved as public property **3** a tomb or tombstone **4** a literary or artistic work regarded as commemorative of its creator or a particular period **5** *US* a boundary marker **6** an exceptional example: *his lecture was a monument of tedium* [c13: from Latin *monumentum*, from *monēre* to remind, advise]

Monument ('mɒnjʊmənt) *n* **the Monument** a tall columnar building designed (1671) by Sir Christopher Wren to commemorate the Fire of London (1666), which destroyed a large part of the medieval city

monumental (ˌmɒnjʊ'mɛntəl) *adj* **1** like a monument,

esp in large size, endurance, or importance **2** of, relating to, or being a monument **3** *informal* (an intensifier): *monumental stupidity* > ˌmonu'mentally *adv*

Monza (*Italian* 'montsa) *n* a city in N Italy, northeast of Milan: the ancient capital of Lombardy; scene of the assassination of King Umberto I in 1900; motor-racing circuit. Pop: 120 204 (2001)

moo (muː) *vb* **1** (*intr*) (of a cow, bull, etc) to make a characteristic deep long sound; low > *interj* **2** an instance or imitation of this sound

mooch (muːtʃ) *vb slang* **1** (*intr*; often foll by *around*) to loiter or walk aimlessly **2** (*intr*) to behave in an apathetic way **3** (*intr*) to sneak or lurk; skulk **4** (*tr*) to cadge **5** (*tr*) *chiefly US & Canadian* to steal [C17: perhaps from Old French *muchier* to skulk] > 'moocher *n*

mood[1] (muːd) *n* **1** a temporary state of mind or temper: *a cheerful mood* **2** a sullen or gloomy state of mind, esp when temporary: *she's in a mood* **3** a prevailing atmosphere or feeling **4 in the mood** in a favourable state of mind (for something or to do something) [Old English *mōd* mind, feeling; compare Old Norse *mōthr* grief, wrath]

mood[2] (muːd) *n* **1** *grammar* a category of the verb or verbal inflections that expresses semantic and grammatical differences, including such forms as the indicative, subjunctive, and imperative **2** *logic* one of the possible arrangements of the syllogism, classified solely by whether the component propositions are universal or particular and affirmative or negative > Also called: **mode** [C16: from MOOD[1], influenced in meaning by MODE]

mood music *n* **1** recorded music played in the background in a place to establish a mood of relaxation, calm, etc **2** a prevailing atmosphere or feeling

moody ('muːdɪ) *adj* **moodier, moodiest** **1** sullen, sulky, or gloomy **2** temperamental or changeable > 'moodily *adv* > 'moodiness *n*

Moody ('muːdɪ) *n* **Dwight Lyman.** 1837–99, US evangelist and hymnodist, noted for his revivalist campaigns in Britain and the US with I. D. Sankey

Moog (muːg, məʊg) *n trademark music* a type of synthesizer [C20: named after Robert *Moog* (1934–2005), US engineer]

mooi (mɔɪ) *adj South African slang* pleasing; nice [Afrikaans]

mooli ('muːlɪ) *n* a type of large white radish [E African native name]

moolvie *or* **moolvi** ('muːlviː) *n* (esp in India) a Muslim doctor of the law, teacher, or learned man also used as a title of respect [C17: from Urdu, from Arabic *mawlawīy*; compare MULLAH]

moon (muːn) *n* **1** (*sometimes capital*) the natural satellite of the earth. Diameter: 3476 km; mass: 7.35 × 10²² kg; mean distance from earth: 384 400 km; periods of rotation and revolution: 27.32 days. Related adj: **lunar** **2** the face of the moon as it is seen during its revolution around the earth, esp at one of its phases: *new moon; full moon* **3** any natural satellite of a planet **4** moonlight; moonshine **5** something resembling a moon **6** a month, esp a lunar one **7 over the moon** *informal* extremely happy; ecstatic > *vb* **8** (when *tr*, often foll by *away*; when *intr*, often foll by *around*) to be idle in a listless way, as if in love, or to idle (time) away **9** (*intr*) *slang* to expose one's buttocks to passers-by [Old English *mōna*; compare Old Frisian *mōna*, Old High German *māno*] > 'moonless *adj*

Moon (muːn) *n* **William.** 1818–94, British inventor of the Moon writing system in 1847, who, himself blind, taught blind children in Brighton and printed mainly religious works from stereotyped plates of his own designing

moonbeam ('muːnˌbiːm) *n* a ray of moonlight

mooncalf ('muːnˌkɑːf) *n, pl* **-calves** (-ˌkɑːvz) **1** a born fool; dolt **2** a person who idles time away **3** *obsolete* a freak or monster

moon-faced *adj* having a round face; full-faced

moonlight ('muːnˌlaɪt) *n* **1** Also called: **moonshine** light from the sun received on earth after reflection by the moon **2** (*modifier*) illuminated by the moon: *a moonlight*

walk **3** short for **moonlight flit** > *vb* **-lights, -lighting, -lighted** (*intr*) *informal* to work at a secondary job, esp at night, and often illegitimately > 'moonˌlighter *n*

moonlight flit *n Brit informal* a hurried departure at night, esp from rented accommodation to avoid payment of rent owed. Often shortened to: **moonlight**

moonlit ('muːnlɪt) *adj* illuminated by the moon

moonquake ('muːnˌkweɪk) *n* a light tremor of the moon, detected on the moon's surface

moonscape ('muːnˌskeɪp) *n* the general surface of the moon or a representation of it

moonshine ('muːnˌʃaɪn) *n* **1** another word for: **moonlight** (sense 1) **2** *US & Canadian* illegally distilled or smuggled whisky or other spirit **3** foolish talk or thought

moonshot ('muːnˌʃɒt) *n* the launching of a spacecraft, rocket, etc, to the moon

moonstone ('muːnˌstəʊn) *n* a gem variety of orthoclase or albite that is white and translucent with bluish reflections

moonstruck ('muːnˌstrʌk) *or* **moonstricken** ('muːnˌstrɪkən) *adj* deranged or mad

moony ('muːnɪ) *adj* **moonier, mooniest** **1** *informal* dreamy or listless **2** of or like the moon

moor[1] (mʊə, mɔː) *n* a tract of unenclosed ground, usually having peaty soil covered with heather, coarse grass, bracken, and moss [Old English *mōr*; related to Old Saxon *mōr*, Old High German *muor* swamp] > 'moory *adj*

moor[2] (mʊə, mɔː) *vb* **1** to secure (a ship, boat, etc) with cables or ropes **2** (of a ship, boat, etc) to be secured in this way **3** (not in technical usage) a less common word for: **anchor** (sense 7) [C15: of Germanic origin; related to Old English *mǣrelsrāp* rope for mooring] > **moorage** ('mʊərɪdʒ, 'mɔːrɪdʒ) *n*

Moor (mʊə, mɔː) *n* a member of a Muslim people of North Africa, of mixed Arab and Berber descent. In the 8th century they were converted to Islam and established power in North Africa and Spain, where they established a civilization (756–1492) [C14: via Old French from Latin *Maurus*, from Greek *Mauros*, possibly from Berber] > 'Moorish *adj*

Moore (mʊə, mɔː) *n* **1 Bobby.** full name *Robert Frederick Moore*. 1941–93, British footballer captain of the England team that won the World Cup in 1966 **2 Dudley (Stuart John).** 1935–2002, British actor, comedian, and musician noted for his comedy partnership (1960–73) with Peter Cook and such films as 10 (1979) and *Arthur* (1981) **3 George.** 1852–1933, Irish novelist. His works include *Esther Waters* (1894) and *The Brook Kerith* (1916) **4 G(eorge) E(dward).** 1873–1958, British philosopher, noted esp for his *Principia Ethica* (1903) **5 Gerald.** 1899–1987, British pianist, noted as an accompanist esp to lieder singers **6 Henry.** 1898–1986, British sculptor. His works are characterized by monumental organic forms and include the *Madonna and Child* (1943) at St Matthew's Church, Northampton **7 Sir John.** 1761–1809, British general; commander of the British army (1808–09) in the Peninsular War: killed at Corunna **8 Marianne (Craig).** 1887–1972, US poet: her works include *Observations* (1924) and *Selected Poems* (1935) **9 Thomas.** 1779–1852, Irish poet, best known for *Irish Melodies* (1807–34)

moorhen ('mʊəˌhɛn, 'mɔː-) *n* **1** a bird, *Gallinula chloropus*, inhabiting ponds, lakes, etc, having a black plumage, red bill, and a red shield above the bill: family *Rallidae* (rails) **2** a female of the red grouse

mooring ('mʊərɪŋ, 'mɔː-) *n* **1** a place for mooring a vessel **2** a permanent anchor, dropped in the water and equipped with a floating buoy, to which vessels can moor

moorings ('mʊərɪŋz, 'mɔː-) *pl n* **1** *nautical* the ropes, anchors, etc, used in mooring a vessel **2** (*sometimes singular*) something that provides security or stability

Moorish idol *n* a tropical marine spiny-finned fish, *Zanclus canescens*, that is common around coral reefs: family *Zanclidae*. It has a deeply compressed body with yellow and black stripes, a beaklike snout, and an elongated dorsal fin

moorland ('mʊələnd, 'mɔː-) *n Brit* an area of moor

moose (muːs) *n, pl* **moose** a large North American deer, *Alces alces*, having large flattened palmate antlers: also

m

occurs in Europe and Asia where it is called an elk [C17: from Algonquian; related to Narraganset *moos*, from *moosu* he strips, alluding to the moose's habit of stripping trees]

Moose Jaw *n* a city in W Canada, in S Saskatchewan. Pop: 32 631 (2001)

moose milk *n Canadian* a mixed alcoholic drink made with ingredients such as milk and eggs and usually rum

moose pasture *n Canadian informal* land considered to be worthless, esp when lacking in extractable mineral deposits

moot (muːt) *adj* 1 subject or open to debate: *a moot point* ▷ *vb* 2 (*tr*) to suggest or bring up for debate 3 (*intr*) to plead or argue theoretical or hypothetical cases, as an academic exercise or as vocational training for law students ▷ *n* 4 a discussion or debate of a hypothetical case or point, held as an academic activity 5 (in Anglo-Saxon England) an assembly, mainly in a shire or hundred, dealing with local legal and administrative affairs [Old English *gemōt*; compare Old Saxon *mōt*, Middle High German *muoze* meeting]

moot court *n* a mock court trying hypothetical legal cases

mop (mɒp) *n* 1 an implement with a wooden handle and a head made of twists of cotton or a piece of synthetic sponge, used for polishing or washing floors, or washing dishes 2 something resembling this, such as a tangle of hair ▷ *vb* mops, mopping, mopped 3 (*tr*; often foll by *up*) to clean or soak up with or as if with a mop ▷ See also **mop up** [C15 *mappe*, from earlier *mappel*, from Medieval Latin *mappula* cloth, from Latin *mappa* napkin]

mopani *or* **mopane** (mɒˈpɑːnɪ) *n* a leguminous tree, *Colophospermum* (or *Copaifera*) *mopane*, native to southern Africa, that is highly resistant to drought and produces very hard wood [C19: from Setswana (a Bantu language) *mo-pane*]

mope (məʊp) *vb* (*intr*) 1 to be gloomy or apathetic 2 to move or act in an aimless way ▷ *n* 3 a gloomy person [C16: perhaps from obsolete *mope* fool] ▷ '**moper** *n* ▷ '**mopy** *adj*

moped ('məʊpɛd) *n Brit* a light motorcycle, not over 50cc [C20: from MOTOR + PEDAL[1], originally equipped with auxiliary pedals]

mopes (məʊps) *pl n* the mopes low spirits

mopoke ('məʊˌpəʊk) *n* 1 a small spotted owl, *Ninox novaeseelandiae*, of Australia and New Zealand. In Australia the tawny frogmouth, *Podargus strigoides*, is very often wrongly identified as the mopoke 2 *Austral & NZ slang* a slow or lugubrious person ▷ Also called: morepork [C19: imitative of the bird's cry]

moppet ('mɒpɪt) *n* a less common word for **poppet** (sense 1) [C17: from obsolete *mop* rag doll; of obscure origin]

mop up *vb* (*tr, adverb*) 1 to clean with a mop 2 *informal* to complete (a task, etc) 3 *military* to clear (remaining enemy forces) after a battle, as by killing, taking prisoner, etc

moquette (mɒˈkɛt) *n* a thick velvety fabric used for carpets, upholstery, etc [C18: from French; of uncertain origin]

MOR *abbreviation* middle-of-the-road: used esp in radio programming

Mor. *abbreviation* Morocco

Moradabad (ˌmɔːrədəˈbæd) *n* a city in N India, in N Uttar Pradesh. Pop: 641 240 (2001)

moraine (mɒˈreɪn) *n* a mass of debris, carried by glaciers and forming ridges and mounds when deposited [C18: from French, from Savoy dialect *morena*, of obscure origin] ▷ mo'rainal *or* mo'rainic *adj*

moral ('mɒrəl) *adj* 1 concerned with or relating to human behaviour, esp the distinction between good and bad or right and wrong behaviour: *moral sense* 2 adhering to conventionally accepted standards of conduct 3 based on a sense of right and wrong according to conscience: *moral courage; moral law* 4 having psychological rather than tangible effects: *moral support* 5 having the effects but not the appearance of (victory or defeat): *a moral victory; a moral defeat* 6 having a strong probability: *a moral*

certainty ▷ *n* 7 the lesson to be obtained from a fable or event 8 a concise truth; maxim 9 (*plural*) principles of behaviour in accordance with standards of right and wrong [C14: from Latin *mōrālis* relating to morals or customs, from *mōs* custom] ▷ '**morally** *adv*

morale (mɒˈrɑːl) *n* the degree of mental or moral confidence of a person or group; spirit of optimism [C18: morals, from French, n. use of MORAL (adj)]

moralist ('mɒrəlɪst) *n* 1 a person who seeks to regulate the morals of others or to imbue others with a sense of morality 2 a person who lives in accordance with moral principles ▷ ˌmoral'istic *adj* ▷ ˌmoral'istically *adv*

morality (məˈrælɪtɪ) *n, pl* -ties 1 the quality of being moral 2 conformity, or degree of conformity, to conventional standards of moral conduct 3 a system of moral principles 4 an instruction or lesson in morals 5 short for **morality play**

morality play *n* a type of drama written between the 14th and 16th centuries concerned with the conflict between personified virtues and vices

moralize *or* **moralise** ('mɒrəˌlaɪz) *vb* 1 (*intr*) to make moral pronouncements 2 (*tr*) to interpret or explain in a moral sense 3 (*tr*) to improve the morals of ▷ ˌmorali'zation *or* ˌmorali'sation *n* ▷ 'moralˌizer *or* 'moralˌiser *n*

moral majority *n* a presumed majority of people believed to be in favour of a stricter code of public morals [C20: after *Moral Majority*, a right-wing US religious organization, based on SILENT MAJORITY]

moral philosophy *n* the branch of philosophy dealing with both argument about the content of morality and meta-ethical discussion of the nature of moral judgment, language, argument, and value

Moral Rearmament *n* a worldwide movement for moral and spiritual renewal founded by Frank Buchman in 1938. Also called: Buchmanism

moral theology *n* the branch of theology dealing with ethics

Morar ('mɔːrə) *n* Loch Morar a lake in W Scotland, in the SW Highlands: the deepest in Scotland Length: 18 km (11 miles). Depth: 296 m (987 ft)

morass (məˈræs) *n* 1 a tract of swampy low-lying land 2 a disordered or muddled situation or circumstance, esp one that impedes progress [C17: from Dutch *moeras*, ultimately from Old French *marais* MARSH]

moratorium (ˌmɒrəˈtɔːrɪəm) *n, pl* -ria (-rɪə) *or* -riums 1 a legally authorized postponement of the fulfilment of an obligation 2 an agreed suspension of activity [C19: New Latin, from Late Latin *morātōrius* dilatory, from *mora* delay]

Morava (məˈrɑːvə) *n* 1 a river in central Europe, rising in the Sudeten Mountains, in the Czech Republic, and flowing south through Slovakia to the Danube: forms part of the border between the Czech Republic, Slovakia, and Austria. Length: 370 km (230 miles). German name: March 2 a river in E Serbia, formed by the confluence of the Southern Morava and the Western Morava near Stalac: flows north to the Danube. Length: 209 km (130 miles) 3 ('mɒrəvə) the Czech name for **Moravia**[1]

Moravia[1] (məˈreɪvɪə, mɒ-) *n* a region of the Czech Republic around the Morava River, bounded by the Bohemian-Moravian Highlands, the Sudeten Mountains, and the W Carpathians: became a separate Austrian crownland in 1848; part of Czechoslovakia 1918–92; valuable mineral resources. Czech name: Morava. German name: Mähren

Moravia[2] (*Italian* moˈraːvja) *n* Alberto (alˈbɛrto), pen name of *Alberto Pincherle*. 1907–90, Italian novelist and short-story writer: his works include *The Time of Indifference* (1929), *The Woman of Rome* (1949), *The Lie* (1966), and *Erotic Tales* (1985)

Moravian (məˈreɪvɪən, mɒ-) *adj* 1 of or relating to Moravia, its people, or their dialect of Czech 2 of or relating to the Moravian Church ▷ *n* 3 the Moravian dialect 4 a native or inhabitant of Moravia 5 a member of the Moravian Church ▷ Mo'ravianism *n*

moray (mɒˈreɪ) *n, pl* -rays any voracious marine coastal eel of the family *Muraenidae*, esp *Muraena helena*, marked with brilliant patterns and colours [C17: from

Portuguese *moréia*, from Latin *mūrēna*, from Greek *muraina*]

Moray¹ ('mʌrɪ) *n* a council area and historical county of NE Scotland: part of Grampian region from 1975 to 1996: mainly hilly, with the Cairngorm mountains in the S. Administrative centre: Elgin. Pop: 87 460 (2003 est). Area: 2238 sq km (874 sq miles)

Moray² *or* **Murray** ('mʌrɪ) *n* **1st Earl of**, title of *James Stuart*. ?1531–70, regent of Scotland (1567–70) following the abdication of Mary, Queen of Scots, his half-sister. He defeated Mary and Bothwell at Langside (1568); assassinated by a follower of Mary

Moray Firth *n* an inlet of the North Sea on the NE coast of Scotland. Length: about 56 km (35 miles)

morbid ('mɔːbɪd) *adj* **1** having an unusual interest in death or unpleasant events **2** gruesome **3** relating to or characterized by disease; pathologic [c17: from Latin *morbidus* sickly, from *morbus* illness] > **mor'bidity** *n* > **'morbidly** *adv* > **'morbidness** *n*

morbid anatomy *n* the branch of medical science concerned with the study of the structure of diseased organs and tissues

morbific (mɔːˈbɪfɪk) *adj* causing disease; pathogenic

Morbihan (French mɔrbiã) *n* a department of NW France, in S Brittany. Capital: Vannes. Pop: 665 540 (2003 est). Area: 7092 sq km (2766 sq miles)

mordant ('mɔːdᵊnt) *adj* **1** sarcastic or caustic **2** having the properties of a mordant **3** pungent ▷ *n* **4** a substance used before the application of a dye, possessing the ability to fix colours in textiles, leather, etc **5** an acid or other corrosive fluid used to etch lines on a printing plate [c15: from Old French: biting, from *mordre* to bite, from Latin *mordēre*] > **'mordancy** *n* > **'mordantly** *adv*

Mordecai (ˌmɔːdɪˈkaɪ, ˈmɔːdəˌkaɪ) *n Old Testament* the cousin of Esther who averted a massacre of the Jews (Esther 2–9)

mordent ('mɔːdᵊnt) *n music* a melodic ornament consisting of the rapid alternation of a note with a note one degree lower than it [c19: from German, from Italian *mordente*, from *mordere* to bite]

Mordred ('mɔːdrɛd) *n* a variant of **Modred**

Mordvinian Republic (mɔːˈdvɪnɪən) *n* a constituent republic of W central Russia, in the middle Volga basin. Capital: Saransk. Pop: 888 700 (2002). Area: 26 200 sq km (10 110 sq miles). Also called: **Mordovian Republic** (mɔːˈdəʊvɪən), **Mordovia**

more (mɔː) *determiner* **1 a** the comparative of: **much, many** *more joy than you know; more pork sausages* **b** (*as pronoun; functioning as sing or plural*): *he has more than she has; even more are dying every day* **2 a** additional; further: *no more bananas* **b** (*as pronoun; functioning as sing or plural*): *I can't take any more; more than expected* **3 more of** to a greater extent or degree: *we see more of Sue these days; more of a nuisance than it should be* ▷ *adv* **4** used to form the comparative of some adjectives and adverbs: *a more believable story; more quickly* **5** the comparative of: **much** *people listen to the radio more now* **6 more or less a** as an estimate; approximately **b** to an unspecified extent or degree: *the party was ruined, more or less* [Old English *māra*; compare Old Saxon, Old High German *mēro*, Gothic *maiza*. See also MOST]

● USAGE See at **most**

More (mɔː) *n* **1 Hannah**. 1745–1833, English writer, noted for her religious tracts, esp *The Shepherd of Salisbury Plain* **2 Sir Thomas**. 1478–1535, English statesman, humanist, and Roman Catholic Saint; Lord Chancellor to Henry VIII (1529–32). His opposition to the annulment of Henry's marriage to Catherine of Aragon and his refusal to recognize the Act of Supremacy resulted in his execution on a charge of treason. In *Utopia* (1516) he set forth his concept of the ideal state. Feast day: June 22 or July 6

Morea (mɔːˈrɪə) *n* the medieval name for the **Peloponnese**

Moreau (French mɔro) *n* **1 Gustave** (gystav) 1826–98, French symbolist painter **2 Jean Victor** (ʒã viktɔr). 1763–1813, French general in the Revolutionary and Napoleonic Wars **3 Jeanne** (ʒan). born 1928, French stage and film actress. Her films include *Jules et Jim* (1961), *Diary of a Chambermaid* (1964), and *The Proprietor* (1996)

Morecambe¹ ('mɔːkəm) *n* a port and resort in NW England, on Morecambe Bay (an inlet of the Irish Sea). Pop (with Heysham): 49 569 (2001)

Morecambe² ('mɔːkəm) *n* **Eric**, real name *John Eric Bartholomew*. 1926–84, British comedian and actor, noted esp for his comedy partnership (from 1941) with Ernie Wise (real name Ernest Wiseman, 1925–99)

moreish *or* **morish** ('mɔːrɪʃ) *adj informal* (of food) causing a desire for more

morel (mɒˈrɛl) *n* any edible saprotrophic ascomycetous fungus of the genus *Morchella*, in which the mushroom has a pitted cap: order *Pezizales* [c17: from French *morille*, probably of Germanic origin; compare Old High German *morhila*, diminutive of *morha* carrot]

Morelia (Spanish moˈrelia) *n* a city in central Mexico, capital of Michoacán state: a cultural centre during colonial times; two universities. Pop: 668 000 (2005 est). Former name (until 1828): **Valladolid**

morello (məˈrɛləʊ) *n*, *pl* **-los** a variety of small very dark sour cherry, *Prunus cerasus austera* [c17: perhaps from Medieval Latin *amārellum* diminutive of Latin *amārus* bitter, but also influenced by Italian *morello* blackish]

Morelos (Spanish moˈrelos) *n* an inland state of S central Mexico, on the S slope of the great plateau. Capital: Cuernavaca. Pop: 1 552 878 (2000 est). Area: 4988 sq km (1926 sq miles)

moreover (mɔːˈrəʊvə) *sentence connector* in addition to what has already been said; furthermore

morepork ('mɔːˌpɔːk) *n NZ* Also called: **ruru** a small spotted owl, *Ninox novaeseelandiae*, of Australia and New Zealand. Also called: (*Austral*) **mopoke**

mores ('mɔːreɪz) *pl n sociol* the customs and conventions embodying the fundamental values of a group or society [c20: from Latin, plural of *mōs* custom]

Morgan¹ *n* **1 Edwin** (**George**). born 1920, Scottish poet, noted esp for his collection *The Second Life* (1968) and his many concrete and visual poems; appointed Scottish national poet 2004 **2** (**Hywel**) **Rhodri** ('rɒdrɪ). born 1939, Welsh Labour politician; first minister of Wales from 2000

Morgan² ('mɔːgən) *n* **1 Sir Henry**. 1635–88, Welsh buccaneer, who raided Spanish colonies in the West Indies for the English **2 John Pierpont**. 1837–1913, US financier, philanthropist, and art collector **3 Thomas Hunt**. 1866–1945, US biologist. He formulated the chromosome theory of heredity. Nobel prize for physiology or medicine 1933

morganatic (ˌmɔːgəˈnætɪk) *adj* of or designating a marriage between a person of high rank and a person of low rank, by which the latter is not elevated to the higher rank and any issue have no rights to the succession of the higher party's titles, property, etc [c18: from Medieval Latin phrase *mātrimōnium ad morganāticum* marriage based on the morning-gift (a token present after consummation representing the husband's only liability); *morganātica*, ultimately from Old High German *morgan* morning; compare Old English *morgengiefu* morning-gift] > **ˌmorga'natically** *adv*

Morgan le Fay ('mɔːgən lə 'feɪ) *or* **Morgain le Fay** ('mɔːgaɪn, -gən) *n* a wicked sorceress of Arthurian legend, the half-sister of King Arthur

morgen ('mɔːgən) *n* **1** a South African unit of area, equal to about two acres or 0.8 hectare **2** a unit of area, formerly used in Prussia and Scandinavia, equal to about two thirds of an acre [c17: from Dutch: morning, a morning's ploughing]

morgue (mɔːg) *n* **1** another word for **mortuary** (sense 1) **2** *informal* a room or file containing clippings, files, etc, used for reference in a newspaper [c19: from French *la Morgue*, a Paris mortuary]

moribund ('mɒrɪˌbʌnd) *adj* **1** near death **2** stagnant; without force or vitality [c18: from Latin, from *morī* to die] > **ˌmori'bundity** *n* > **'mori,bundly** *adv*

Mörike (German 'møːrɪkə) *n* **Eduard** ('eːduart). 1804–75, German poet, noted for his lyrics, such as *On a Winter's Morning before Sunrise* and *At Midnight*

Morisco (məˈrɪskəʊ) *or* **Moresco** (məˈrɛskəʊ) *n*, *pl* **-cos** *or* **-coes 1 a** a Spanish Moor **2** a morris dance ▷ *adj* **3** Moorish [c16: from Spanish, from *Moro* MOOR]

morish ('mɔːrɪʃ) *adj* a variant spelling of: **moreish**

Morisot (*French* morizo) *n* **Berthe** (bɛrtə). 1841–95, French impressionist painter; noted for her studies of women and children

Morley¹ ('mɔːlɪ) *n* an industrial town in N England, in Leeds unitary authority, West Yorkshire. Pop: 54 051 (2001)

Morley² ('mɔːlɪ) *n* **1 Edward Williams**. 1838–1923, US chemist who collaborated with A. A. Michelson in the Michelson-Morley experiment **2 John**, Viscount Morley of Blackburn. 1838–1923, British Liberal statesman and writer; secretary of state for India (1905–10) **3 Robert**. 1908–92, British actor. His many films include *Major Barbara* (1940), *Oscar Wilde* (1960), and *The Blue Bird* (1976) **4 Thomas**. ?1557–?1603, English composer and organist, noted for his madrigals and his textbook on music, *A Plaine and Easie Introduction to Practicall Musicke* (1597)

Mormon ('mɔːmən) *n* **1** a member of the Church of Jesus Christ of Latter-day Saints, founded in 1830 at La Fayette, New York, by Joseph Smith (1805–44) **2** a prophet whose supposed revelations were recorded by Joseph Smith in the Book of Mormon ▷ *adj* **3** of or relating to the Mormons, their Church, or their beliefs > 'Mormonism *n*

morn (mɔːn) *n* a poetic word for: **morning** [Old English *morgen*; compare Old High German *morgan*, Old Norse *morginn*]

mornay ('mɔːneɪ) *adj* (*often immediately postpositive*) denoting a cheese sauce used in several dishes: *eggs mornay* [perhaps named after Philippe de *Mornay*, Seigneur du Plessis-Marly (1549–1623), French Huguenot leader]

Mornay (*French* mɔrnɛ) *n* **Philippe de** (filip də), Seigneur du Plessis-Marly. 1549–1623, French Huguenot leader. Also called: **Duplessis-Mornay**

morning ('mɔːnɪŋ) *n* **1** the first part of the day, ending at or around noon **2** sunrise; daybreak; dawn **3** the beginning or early period: *the morning of the world* **4** the morning after *informal* the aftereffects of excess, esp a hangover **5** (*modifier*) of, used, or occurring in the morning: *morning coffee* [C13 *morwening*, from MORN, formed on the model of EVENING]

morning-after pill *n* an oral contraceptive that is effective if taken some hours after intercourse

morning dress *n* formal day dress for men, comprising a morning coat, usually with grey trousers and top hat

morning-glory *n, pl* -ries any of various mainly tropical convolvulaceous plants of the genus *Ipomoea* and related genera, with trumpet-shaped blue, pink, or white flowers, which close in late afternoon

mornings ('mɔːnɪŋz) *adv informal* in the morning, esp regularly, or during every morning

morning sickness *n* nausea occurring shortly after rising: an early symptom of pregnancy

morning star *n* a planet, usually Venus, seen just before sunrise during the time that the planet is west of the sun. Also called: **daystar**

Moro¹ ('mɔːrəʊ) *n* **1** *pl* -ros *or* -ro a member of a group of predominantly Muslim peoples of the S Philippines: noted for their manufacture of weapons **2** the language of these peoples, belonging to the Malayo-Polynesian family [C19: via Spanish from Latin *Maurus* MOOR]

Moro² (*Italian* 'mɔːro) *n* **Aldo** ('aldo). 1916–78, Italian Christian Democrat statesman; prime minister of Italy (1963–68; 1974–76) and minister of foreign affairs (1965–66; 1969–72; 1973–74). He negotiated the entry of the Italian Communist Party into coalition government before being kidnapped by the Red Brigades in 1978 and murdered

morocco (mə'rɒkəʊ) *n* a fine soft leather made from goatskins, used for bookbinding, shoes, etc [C17: after MOROCCO, where it was originally made]

Morocco (mə'rɒkəʊ) *n* a kingdom in NW Africa, on the Mediterranean and the Atlantic: conquered by the Arabs in about 683, who introduced Islam; at its height under Berber dynasties (11th–13th centuries); became a French protectorate in 1912 and gained independence in 1956. It is mostly mountainous, with the Atlas Mountains in the centre and the Rif range along the Mediterranean coast, with the Sahara in the south and southeast; an important exporter of phosphates. Official language: Arabic; Berber and French are also widely spoken. Official religion: (Sunni) Muslim. Currency: dirham. Capital: Rabat. Pop: 31 064 000 (2004 est). Area: 458 730 sq km (177 117 sq miles). French name: **Maroc** > **Moroccan** (mə'rɒkən) *adj, n*

moron ('mɔːrɒn) *n* **1** a foolish or stupid person **2** a person having an intelligence quotient of between 50 and 70, able to work under supervision [C20: from Greek *mōros* foolish] > **moronic** (mɒ'rɒnɪk) *adj* > mo'ronically *adv* > 'moronism *or* mo'ronity *n*

Moroni (mə'rəʊnɪ; *French* mɔrɔni) *n* the capital of the Comoros, on the island of Njazidja (Grande Comore). Pop: 59 000 (2005 est)

morose (mə'rəʊs) *adj* ill-tempered or gloomy [C16: from Latin *mōrōsus* peevish, capricious, from *mōs* custom, will, caprice] > mo'rosely *adv* > mo'roseness *n*

-morph *n combining form* indicating shape, form, or structure of a specified kind: *ectomorph* [from Greek -*morphos*, from *morphē* shape] > -**morphic** *or* -**morphous** *adj combining form* > -**morphy** *n combining form*

morpheme ('mɔːfiːm) *n linguistics* a speech element having a meaning or grammatical function that cannot be subdivided into further such elements [C20: from French, from Greek *morphē* form, coined on the model of PHONEME; see -EME] > mor'phemic *adj* > mor'phemically *adv*

Morpheus ('mɔːfɪəs, -fjuːs) *n Greek myth* the god of sleep and dreams > 'Morphean *adj*

morphine ('mɔːfiːn) *or* **morphia** ('mɔːfɪə) *n* an alkaloid extracted from opium: used in medicine as an analgesic and sedative, although repeated use causes addiction. Formula: $C_{17}H_{19}NO_3$ [C19: from French, from MORPHEUS]

morphing ('mɔːfɪŋ) *n* a computer technique used for graphics and in films, in which one image is gradually transformed into another image without individual changes being noticeable in the process [C20: from METAMORPHOSIS]

morphogenesis (,mɔːfəʊ'dʒɛnɪsɪs) *n* **1** the development of form and structure in an organism during its growth from embryo to adult **2** the evolutionary development of form in an organism or part of an organism > **morphogenetic** (,mɔːfəʊdʒɪ'nɛtɪk) *or* ,morpho'genic *adj*

morphology (mɔː'fɒlədʒɪ) *n* **1** the branch of biology concerned with the form and structure of organisms **2** the form and structure of words in a language, esp the consistent patterns of inflection, combination, derivation and change, etc, that may be observed and classified **3** the form and structure of anything > **morphologic** (,mɔːfə'lɒdʒɪk) *or* ,morpho'logical *adj* > ,morpho'logically *adv* > mor'phologist *n*

Morphy ('mɔːfɪ) *n* **Paul**. 1837–84, US chess player, widely considered to have been the world's greatest player

Morris ('mɒrɪs) *n* **William**. 1834–96, English poet, designer, craftsman, and socialist writer. He founded the Kelmscott Press (1890)

Morris chair ('mɒrɪs) *n* an armchair with an adjustable back and large cushions [C19: named after William Morris (1834–96), English poet, designer, craftsman, and socialist writer]

morris dance ('mɒrɪs) *n* any of various old English folk dances usually performed by men (morris men) to the accompaniment of violin, concertina, etc. The dancers are adorned with bells and often represent characters from folk tales [C15 *moreys daunce* Moorish dance. See MOOR] > morris dancing *n*

Morrison ('mɒrɪsⁿn) *n* **1 Herbert Stanley**, Baron Morrison of Lambeth. 1888–1965, British Labour statesman, Home Secretary and Minister for Home Security in Churchill's War Cabinet (1942–45) **2 Jim**, full name *James Douglas Morrison*. 1943–71, US rock singer and songwriter, lead vocalist with the Doors **3 Toni**, full name *Chloe Anthony Morrison*. born 1931, US novelist, whose works include *Sula* (1974), *Song of Solomon* (1977), *Beloved* (1987), *Jazz* (1992), and *Paradise* (1998): awarded the Nobel Prize for literature in 1993 **4 Van**, full name *George Ivan Morrison*. born 1945, Northern Irish rock singer and songwriter. His albums include *Astral Weeks* (1968),

Moondance (1970), *Avalon Sunset* (1989), and *Days Like These* (1995)

morro ('mɒrəʊ; *Spanish* 'morro) *n*, *pl* **-ros** (-rəʊz; *Spanish* -ros) a rounded hill or promontory [from Spanish]

morrow ('mɒrəʊ) *n* the morrow *archaic or poetic* **1** the next day **2** the period following a specified event **3** the morning [C13 *morwe*, from Old English *morgen* morning; see **MORN**]

Mors (mɔːz) *n* the Roman god of death. Greek counterpart: Thanatos

Morse (mɔːs) *n* Samuel Finley Breese ('fɪnlɪ briːz). 1791–1872, US inventor and painter. He invented the first electric telegraph and the Morse code

morsel ('mɔːsᵊl) *n* **1** a small slice or mouthful of food **2** a small piece; bit **3** *Irish informal* a term of endearment for a child [C13: from Old French, from *mors* a bite, from Latin *morsus*, from *mordēre* to bite]

mortal ('mɔːtᵊl) *adj* **1** (of living beings, esp human beings) subject to death **2** of or involving life or the world **3** ending in or causing death; fatal: *a mortal blow* **4** deadly or unrelenting: *a mortal enemy* **5** of or like the fear of death; dire: *mortal terror* **6** great or very intense: *mortal pain* **7** possible: *there was no mortal reason to go* **8** *slang* long and tedious: *for three mortal hours* ⊳ *n* **9** a mortal being **10** *informal* a person: *a mean mortal* [C14: from Latin *mortālis*, from *mors* death] > '**mortally** *adv*

mortality (mɔːˈtælɪtɪ) *n*, *pl* **-ties** **1** the condition of being mortal **2** great loss of life, as in war or disaster **3** the number of deaths in a given period **4** mankind; humanity

mortal sin *n Christianity* a sin regarded as involving total loss of grace

mortar ('mɔːtə) *n* **1** a mixture of cement or lime or both with sand and water, used as a bond between bricks or stones or as a covering on a wall **2** a muzzle-loading cannon having a short barrel and relatively wide bore that fires low-velocity shells in high trajectories over a short range **3** a vessel, usually bowl-shaped, in which substances are pulverized with a pestle ⊳ *vb* (*tr*) **4** to join (bricks or stones) or cover (a wall) with mortar **5** to fire on with mortars [C13: from Latin *mortārium* basin in which mortar is mixed; in some senses, via Old French *mortier* substance mixed inside such a vessel]

mortarboard ('mɔːtə,bɔːd) *n* **1** a black tasselled academic cap with a flat square top covered with cloth **2** Also called: **hawk** a small square board with a handle on the underside for carrying mortar

mortgage ('mɔːgɪdʒ) *n* **1** an agreement under which a person borrows money to buy property, esp a house, and the lender may take possession of the property if the borrower fails to repay the money **2** the deed effecting such an agreement **3** the loan obtained under such an agreement: *a mortgage of £48 000* **4** a regular payment of money borrowed under such an agreement: *a mortgage of £247 per month* ⊳ *vb* (*tr*) **5** to pledge (a house or other property) as security for the repayment of a loan [C14: from Old French, literally: dead pledge, from *mort* dead + *gage* security, **GAGE**¹] > '**mortgageable** *adj*

mortgagee (,mɔːgɪˈdʒiː) *n law* the party to a mortgage who makes the loan

mortgagor ('mɔːgɪdʒə, ,mɔːgɪˈdʒɔː) or **mortgager** *n property law* a person who borrows money by mortgaging his property to the lender as security

mortician (mɔːˈtɪʃən) *n chiefly US* another word for **undertaker** [C19: from MORTUARY + *-ician*, as in *physician*]

mortification (,mɔːtɪfɪˈkeɪʃən) *n* **1** a feeling of loss of prestige or self-respect; humiliation **2** something causing this **3** *Christianity* the practice of mortifying the senses **4** another word for **gangrene**

mortify ('mɔːtɪ,faɪ) *vb* **-fies**, **-fying**, **-fied 1** (*tr*) to humiliate or cause to feel shame **2** (*tr*) *Christianity* to subdue and bring under control by self-denial, disciplinary exercises, etc **3** (*intr*) to undergo tissue death or become gangrenous [C14: via Old French from Church Latin *mortificāre* to put to death, from Latin *mors* death + *facere* to do] > '**morti,fier** *n* > '**morti,fying** *adj*

Mortimer ('mɔːtɪmə) *n* **1** Sir John (Clifford). born 1923, British barrister, playwright, and novelist, best known for the television series featuring the barrister Horace Rumpole. His novels include *Paradise Postponed* (1985) and *The Sound of Trumpets* (1998) **2** Roger de, 8th Baron of Wigmore and 1st Earl of March. 1287–1330, lover of Isabella, the wife of Edward II of England: they invaded England in 1326 and compelled the king to abdicate in favour of his son, Edward III; executed

mortise or **mortice** ('mɔːtɪs) *n* **1** a slot or recess, usually rectangular, cut into a piece of wood, stone, etc, to receive a matching projection (tenon) of another piece, or a mortise lock ⊳ *vb* (*tr*) **2** to cut a slot or recess in (a piece of wood, stone, etc) **3** to join (two pieces of wood, stone, etc) by means of a mortise and tenon [C14: from Old French *mortoise*, perhaps from Arabic *murtazza* fastened in position]

mortise lock *n* a lock set into a mortise in a door so that the mechanism of the lock is enclosed by the door

mortmain ('mɔːt,meɪn) *n law* the state or condition of lands, buildings, etc, held inalienably, as by an ecclesiastical or other corporation [C15: from Old French *mortemain*, from Medieval Latin *mortua manus* dead hand, inalienable ownership]

Morton ('mɔːtᵊn) *n* **1 4th Earl of**, title of *James Douglas*. 1516–81, regent of Scotland (1572–78) for the young James VI. He was implicated in the murders of Rizzio (1566) and Darnley (1567) and played a leading role in ousting Mary, Queen of Scots; executed **2 Jelly Roll**, real name *Ferdinand Joseph La Menthe Morton*. 1885–1941, US jazz pianist, singer, and songwriter; one of the creators of New Orleans jazz

mortuary ('mɔːtʃʊərɪ) *n*, *pl* **-aries 1** Also called: **morgue** a building where dead bodies are kept before cremation or burial ⊳ *adj* **2** of or relating to death or burial [C14 (as *n*, a funeral gift to a parish priest): via Medieval Latin *mortuārium* (*n*) from Latin *mortuārius* of the dead]

morwong ('mɔː,wɒŋ) *n* a food fish of Australasian coastal waters belonging to the *Cheilodactylidae* family [from a native Australian language]

moryah (mɒrˈjæ) *interj Irish* an exclamation of annoyance, disbelief, etc [from Irish Gaelic *Mar dhea* forsooth]

mosaic (məˈzeɪɪk) *n* **1** a design or decoration made up of small pieces of coloured glass, stone, etc **2** the process of making a mosaic **3 a** a mottled yellowing that occurs in the leaves of plants affected with any of various virus diseases **b** Also called: **mosaic disease** any of the diseases, such as **tobacco mosaic**, that produce this discoloration **4** an assembly of aerial photographs forming a composite picture of a large area on the ground [C16: via French and Italian from Medieval Latin *mōsaicus*, from Late Greek *mouseion* mosaic work, from Greek *mouseios* of the Muses, from *mousa* MUSE] > **mosaicist** (məˈzeɪɪsɪst) *n*

Mosaic (məʊˈzeɪɪk) *adj* of or relating to Moses or the laws and traditions ascribed to him

Mosaic law (məʊˈzeɪɪk) *n Old Testament* the laws of the Hebrews ascribed to Moses and contained in the Pentateuch

moschatel (,mɒskəˈtel) *n* a small N temperate plant, *Adoxa moschatellina*, with greenish-white musk-scented flowers on top of the stem, arranged as four pointing sideways at right angles to each other and one facing upwards: family *Adoxaceae*. Also called: **townhall clock, five-faced bishop** [C18: via French from Italian *moscatella*, diminutive of *moscato* MUSK]

Moscow ('mɒskəʊ) *n* the capital of Russia and of the Moscow Autonomous Region, on the Moskva River: dates from the 11th century; capital of the grand duchy of Russia from 1547 to 1712; capital of the Soviet Union 1918–91; centres on the medieval Kremlin; chief political, cultural, and industrial centre of Russia, with two universities. Pop: 10 672 000 (2005 est). Russian name: **Moskva**. Related noun: **Muscovite**

Moseley ('məʊzlɪ) *n* Henry Gwyn-Jeffreys. 1887–1915, English physicist. He showed that the wavelengths of X-rays emitted from the elements are related to their atomic numbers

Moselle (məʊˈzel) *n* **1** a department of NE France, in Lorraine region. Capital: Metz. Pop: 1 027 854 (2003 est). Area: 6253 sq km (2439 sq miles) **2** a river in W Europe, rising in NE France and flowing northwest, forming part of the border between Luxembourg and Germany, then northeast to the Rhine: many vineyards along its lower course. Length: 547 km (340 miles) **3** (*sometimes not capital*) a German white wine from the Moselle valley

Moses ('məʊzɪz) *n* **1** *Old Testament* the Hebrew prophet who led the Israelites out of Egypt to the Promised Land and gave them divinely revealed laws **2 Ed.** born 1956, US hurdler; winner of the 400 m hurdles in the 1976 and 1984 Olympic Games **3 Grandma**, real name *Anna Mary Robertson Moses*. 1860–1961, US painter of primitives, who began to paint at the age of 75

mosey ('məʊzɪ) *vb* (*intr*) *informal* (often foll by *along* or *on*) to walk in a leisurely manner; amble [C19: origin unknown]

mosh (mɒʃ) *n* **1** a type of dance, performed to loud rock music, in which people throw themselves about in a frantic and violent manner ▷ *vb* **2** (*intr*) to dance in this manner [C20: of uncertain origin]

mosher ('mɒʃə) *n* **1** someone who moshes **2** (in Britain) a young person who typically enjoys rock music and skateboarding

Moshesh (mɒ'ʃɛʃ) or **Moshoeshoe** (mɒ'ʃuʃu) *n* died 1870, African chief, who founded the Basotho nation, now Lesotho

Moskva (*Russian* mas'kva) *n* **1** transliteration of the Russian name for: **Moscow 2** a river in W central Russia, rising in the Smolensk-Moscow upland, and flowing southeast through Moscow to the Oka River: linked with the River Volga by the Moscow Canal. Length: about 500 km (310 miles)

Moslem ('mɒzləm) *n*, *pl* **-lems** or **-lem 1** an old-fashioned variant of: **Muslim** ▷ *adj* **2** an old-fashioned variant of: **Muslim** > 'Moslemism *n archaic*

Mosley ('məʊzlɪ) *n* Sir **Oswald Ernald**. 1896–1980, British politician; founder of the British Union of Fascists (1932)

mosque (mɒsk) *n* a Muslim place of worship, usually having one or more minarets and often decorated with elaborate tracery and texts from the Koran [C14: earlier *mosquee*, from Old French via Italian *moschea*, ultimately from Arabic *masjid* temple, place of prostration]

mosquito (mə'skiːtəʊ) *n*, *pl* **-toes** or **-tos** any dipterous insect of the family *Culicidae*: the females have a long proboscis adapted for piercing the skin of man and animals to suck their blood. See also **aedes, anopheles, culex** [C16: from Spanish, diminutive of *mosca* fly, from Latin *musca*]

mosquito net or **mosquito netting** *n* a fine curtain or net put in windows, around beds, etc, to keep mosquitoes out

moss (mɒs) *n* **1** any bryophyte of the phylum *Bryophyta*, typically growing in dense mats on trees, rocks, moist ground, etc **2** a clump or growth of any of these plants **3** any of various similar but unrelated plants, such as club moss, Spanish moss, Ceylon moss, rose moss, and reindeer moss **4** *Scot & Northern English* a peat bog or marsh [Old English *mos* swamp; compare Middle Dutch, Old High German *mos* bog, Old Norse *mosi*; compare also Old Norse *mýrr* MIRE] > 'moss,like *adj* > 'mossy *adj* > 'mossiness *n*

Moss (mɒs) *n* **1 Kate**. born 1974, British supermodel. **2** Sir **Stirling**. born 1929, English racing driver

moss agate *n* a variety of chalcedony with dark greenish mossy markings, used as a gemstone

mossie ('mɒsɪ) *n* another name for the **Cape sparrow** [Afrikaans]

mosso ('mɒsəʊ) *adv music* to be performed with rapidity [Italian, past participle of *muovere* to MOVE]

moss rose *n* a variety of rose, *Rosa centifolia muscosa*, that has a mossy stem and calyx and fragrant pink flowers

moss stitch *n* a knitting stitch made up of alternate plain and purl stitches

mosstrooper ('mɒs,truːpə) *n* a raider in the border country of England and Scotland in the mid-17th century [C17 *moss*, in northern English dialect sense: bog]

most (məʊst) *determiner* **1 a** a great majority of; nearly all: *most people like eggs* **b** (*as pronoun; functioning as sing or plural*): *most of them don't know; most of it is finished* **2** the

most a the superlative of: **many, much**: *you have the most money; the most apples* **b** (*as pronoun*): *the most he can afford is two pounds* **3 at most** or **at the most** at the maximum: *that girl is four at the most* **4 make the most of** to use to the best advantage: *she makes the most of her accent* ▷ *adv* **5 the most** used to form the superlative of some adjectives and adverbs **6** the superlative of **much**: *people welcome a drink most after work* **7** (*intensifier*): *a most absurd story* [Old English *māst* or *mǣst*, whence Middle English *moste*, *mēst*; compare Old Frisian *maest*, Old High German *meist*, Old Norse *mestr*]

● USAGE *More* and *most* should be distinguished when
● used in comparisons. *More* applies to cases involving
● two persons, objects, etc, *most* to cases involving three
● or more:

-most *suffix* forming the superlative degree of some adjectives and adverbs: *hindmost; uppermost* [Old English *-mest*, *-mest*, originally a superlative suffix, later mistakenly taken as derived from *mǣst* (adv) most]

Mostaganem (mə,stægə'nɛm) *n* a port in NW Algeria, on the Mediterranean Sea: exports wine, fruit, and vegetables. Pop: 133 000 (2005 est)

mostly ('məʊstlɪ) *adv* **1** almost entirely; chiefly **2** on many or most occasions; usually

Most Reverend *n* (in Britain) a courtesy title applied to Anglican and Roman Catholic archbishops

Mosul ('məʊsəl) *n* a city in N Iraq, on the River Tigris opposite the ruins of Nineveh: an important commercial centre with nearby Ayn Zalah oilfield; university. Pop: 1 236 000 (2005 est)

mot (məʊ) *n* short for **bon mot** [C16: via French from Vulgar Latin *mottum* (unattested) utterance, from Latin *muttum* a mutter, from *muttīre* to mutter]

MOT *abbreviation* **1** (in New Zealand and formerly in Britain) Ministry of Transport **2** (in Britain) MOT test: a compulsory annual test for all road vehicles over a certain age, which require a valid **MOT certificate**

mote (məʊt) *n* a tiny speck [Old English *mot*; compare Middle Dutch *mot* grit, Norwegian *mutt* speck]

motel (məʊ'tɛl) *n* a roadside hotel for motorists, usually having direct access from each room or chalet to a parking space or garage [C20: from *motor* + *hotel*]

motet (məʊ'tɛt) *n* a polyphonic choral composition used as an anthem in the Roman Catholic service [C14: from Old French, diminutive of *mot* word; see MOT]

moth (mɒθ) *n* any of numerous insects of the order *Lepidoptera* that typically have stout bodies with antennae of various shapes (but not clubbed), including large brightly coloured species, such as hawk moths, and small inconspicuous types, such as the clothes moths. See **butterfly** (sense 1) [Old English *moththe*; compare Middle Dutch *motte*, Old Norse *motti*]

mothball ('mɒθ,bɔːl) *n* **1** Also called: **camphor ball** a small ball of camphor or naphthalene used to repel clothes moths in stored clothing, blankets, etc **2 put in mothballs** to postpone work on (a project, activity, etc) ▷ *vb* (*tr*) **3** to prepare (a ship, aircraft, etc) for a long period of storage by sealing all openings with plastic to prevent corrosion **4** to take (a factory, plant, etc) out of operation but maintain it so that it can be used in the future **5** to postpone work on (a project, activity, etc)

moth-eaten *adj* **1** decayed, decrepit, or outdated **2** eaten away by or as if by moths

mother¹ ('mʌðə) *n* **1 a** a female who has given birth to offspring **b** (*as modifier*): *a mother bird* **2** (*often capital, esp as a term of address*) a person's own mother **3** a female substituting in the function of a mother **4** (*often capital*) *chiefly archaic* a term of address for an old woman **5 a** motherly qualities, such as maternal affection: *it appealed to the mother in her* **b** (*as modifier*): *mother love* **c** (*in combination*): *mothercraft* **6 a** a thing or that that creates, nurtures, protects, etc, something **b** (*as modifier*): *mother church; mother earth* **7** a title given to certain members of female religious orders **8** (*modifier*) native or innate: *mother wit* **9 be mother** to pour the tea: *I'll be mother* **10 the mother of all …** *informal* the greatest example of its kind: *the mother of all parties* ▷ *vb* (*tr*) **11** to give birth to or produce **12** to nurture, protect, etc as a mother [Old English *mōdor*; compare Old Saxon *mōdar*,

Old High German *muotar*, Latin *māter*, Greek *mētēr*]

mother² ('mʌðə) *n* a stringy slime containing various bacteria that forms on the surface of liquids undergoing acetous fermentation. It can be added to wine, cider, etc to promote vinegar formation. Also called: mother of vinegar [c16: perhaps from MOTHER¹, but compare Spanish *madre* scum, Dutch *modder* dregs, Middle Low German *modder* decaying object, *mudde* sludge]

motherboard ('mʌðə,bɔːd) *n* (in an electronic system) a printed circuit board through which signals between all other boards are routed

Mother Carey's chicken ('kɛərɪz) *n* another name for **storm petrel** [origin unknown]

Mother City *n* *South African* an informal name for **Cape Town**

mother country *n* the original country of colonists or settlers

motherfucker ('mʌðə,fʌkə) *n offensive, taboo, slang, chiefly US* a person or thing, esp an exasperating or unpleasant one. Often shortened to: mother

Mother Goose *n* the imaginary author of the collection of nursery rhymes published in 1781 in London as *Mother Goose's Melody* [c18: translated from French *Contes de ma mère l'Oye* (1697), title of a collection of tales by Charles Perrault (1628–1703), French author]

motherhood ('mʌðə,hʊd) *n* **1** the state of being a mother **2** the qualities characteristic of a mother

Mothering Sunday ('mʌðərɪŋ) *n* See **Mother's Day**

mother-in-law *n, pl* mothers-in-law the mother of one's wife or husband

motherland ('mʌðə,lænd) *n* another word for **fatherland**

mother lode *n mining* the principal lode in a system

motherly ('mʌðəlɪ) *adj* of or resembling a mother, esp in warmth, or protectiveness > 'motherliness *n*

mother-of-pearl *n* a hard iridescent substance, mostly calcium carbonate, that forms the inner layer of the shells of certain molluscs, such as the oyster. It is used to make buttons, inlay furniture, etc. Also called: nacre

mother-out-law *n informal* the mother of one's ex-husband or ex-wife

Mother's Day *n* **1** *US, Canadian, Austral & NZ* the second Sunday in May, observed as a day in honour of mothers **2** Also called: Mothering Sunday *Brit & S African* the fourth Sunday in Lent, when mothers traditionally receive presents from their children

mother ship *n* a ship providing facilities and supplies for a number of small vessels

mother superior *n, pl* mother superiors *or* mothers superior the head of a community of nuns

mother tongue *n* **1** the language first learned by a child **2** a language from which another has evolved

Motherwell ('mʌðəwəl) *n* a town in S central Scotland, the administrative centre of North Lanarkshire on the River Clyde: industrial centre. Pop: 30 311 (2001)

mother wit *n* native practical intelligence; common sense

mothproof ('mɒθ,pruːf) *adj* **1** (esp of clothes) chemically treated so as to repel clothes moths ▷ *vb* **2** (*tr*) to make (clothes, etc) mothproof

mothy ('mɒθɪ) *adj* mothier, mothiest **1** ragged; moth-eaten **2** containing moths; full of moths

motif (məʊˈtiːf) *n* **1 a** a distinctive idea, esp a theme elaborated on in a piece of music, literature, etc **2** Also called: motive a recurring form or shape in a design or pattern **3** a single added piece of decoration, such as a symbol or name on a jumper, sweatshirt, etc [c19: from French. See MOTIVE]

motile ('məʊtaɪl) *adj* capable of moving spontaneously and independently [c19: from Latin *mōtus* moved, from *movēre* to move] > motility (məʊˈtɪlɪtɪ) *n*

motion ('məʊʃən) *n* **1** the process of continual change in the physical position of an object; movement **2 a** the capacity for movement **b** a manner of movement, esp walking; gait **3** a mental impulse **4** a formal proposal to be discussed and voted on in a debate, meeting, etc **5** *law* an application made to a judge or court for an order or ruling necessary to the conduct of legal proceedings **6** *Brit* **a** the evacuation of the bowels **b** excrement

7 a part of a moving mechanism **b** the action of such a part **8** go through the motions **a** to act or perform the task (of doing something) mechanically or without sincerity **b** to mimic the action (of something) by gesture **9** in motion operational or functioning (often in the phrases set in motion, set the wheels in motion) ▷ *vb* **10** (when *tr*, *may take a clause as object or an infinitive*) to signal or direct (a person) by a movement or gesture [c15: from Latin *mōtiō* a moving, from *movēre* to move] > 'motional *adj*

Motion ('məʊʃən) *n* **Andrew.** born 1952, British poet and biographer; his collections include *Pleasure Steamers* (1978) and *Public Property* (2002): poet laureate from 1999

motion capture *n* a process by which a device can be used to capture patterns of live movement; the data is then transmitted to a computer, where simulation software displays it applied to a virtual actor

motion picture *n US & Canadian* **a** a sequence of images of moving objects photographed by a camera and providing the optical illusion of continuous movement when projected onto a screen **b** a form of entertainment, information, etc, composed of such a sequence of images and shown in a cinema, etc. Also called: film

motivate ('məʊtɪ,veɪt) *vb* (*tr*) to give incentive to > 'moti,vator *n* > ,moti'vation *n*

motivational research *n* the application of psychology to the study of consumer behaviour, esp the planning of advertising and sales campaigns. Also called: motivation research

motive ('məʊtɪv) *n* **1** the reason for a certain course of action, whether conscious or unconscious **2** a variant of motif (sense 2) ▷ *adj* **3** of or causing motion or action: *a motive force* **4** of or acting as a motive; motivating ▷ *vb* (*tr*) **5** to motivate [c14: from Old French *motif*, from Late Latin *mōtīvus* (adj) moving, from Latin *mōtus*, past participle of *movēre* to move] > 'motiveless *adj*

motive power *n* **1** any source of energy used to produce motion **2** the means of supplying power to an engine, vehicle, etc

mot juste *French* (mo ʒyst) *n, pl* mots justes (mo ʒyst) the appropriate word or expression

motley ('mɒtlɪ) *adj* **1** made up of elements of varying type, quality, etc **2** multicoloured ▷ *n* **3** a motley collection or mixture **4** the particoloured attire of a jester [c14: perhaps from *mot* speck, mote]

motocross ('məʊtə,krɒs) *n* **1** a motorcycle race across very rough ground **2** another name for: **rallycross** [c20: from MOTO(R) + CROSS(-COUNTRY)]

motor ('məʊtə) *n* **1 a** the engine, esp an internal-combustion engine, of a vehicle **b** (*as modifier*): *a motor scooter* **2** Also called: electric motor a machine that converts electrical energy into mechanical energy by means of the forces exerted on a current-carrying coil placed in a magnetic field **3** any device that converts another form of energy into mechanical energy to produce motion **4 a** *chiefly Brit* a car or other motor vehicle **b** *as modifier: motor spares* ▷ *adj* **5** producing or causing motion **6** *physiol* **a** of or relating to nerves or neurons that carry impulses that cause muscles to contract **b** of or relating to movement or to muscles that induce movement ▷ *vb* **7** (*intr*) to travel by car **8** (*tr*) *Brit* to transport by car **9** (*intr*) *informal* to move fast; make good progress [c16: from Latin *mōtor* a mover, from *movēre* to move]

motorbicycle ('məʊtə,baɪsɪkᵊl) *n* **1** a motorcycle **2** a moped

motorbike ('məʊtə,baɪk) *n* a less formal name for: **motorcycle**

motorboat ('məʊtə,bəʊt) *n* any boat powered by a motor

motorbus ('məʊtə,bʌs) *n* a bus driven by an internal-combustion engine

motorcade ('məʊtə,keɪd) *n* a parade of cars or other motor vehicles [c20: from MOTOR + CAVALCADE]

motorcar ('məʊtə,kɑː) *n* **1** a more formal word for: **car** (sense 1) **2** a self-propelled electric railway car

motorcycle ('məʊtə,saɪkᵊl) *n* **1** Also called: motorbike a two-wheeled vehicle, having a stronger frame than a bicycle, that is driven by a petrol engine, usually with a capacity of between 125 cc and 1000 cc ▷ *vb* (*intr*) **2** to ride on a motorcycle > **'motor,cyclist** *n*

motorhome ('məʊtə,həʊm) *n* a large motor vehicle with living quarters behind the driver's compartment

motorist ('məʊtərɪst) *n* a driver of a car, esp when considered as a car-owner

motorize or **motorise** ('məʊtə,raɪz) *vb* (*tr*) **1** to equip with a motor **2** to provide (military units) with motor vehicles > ,**motori'zation** or ,**motori'sation** *n*

motorman ('məʊtəmən) *n*, *pl* **-men 1** the driver of an electric train **2** the operator of a motor

motormouth ('məʊtə,maʊθ) *n slang* a garrulous person

motor scooter *n* a light motorcycle with small wheels and an enclosed engine. Often shortened to: **scooter**

motor vehicle *n* a road vehicle driven by a motor or engine, esp an internal-combustion engine

motorway ('məʊtə,weɪ) *n Brit* a main road for fast-moving traffic, having limited access, separate carriageways for vehicles travelling in opposite directions, and usually a total of four or six lanes

Motown ('məʊ,taʊn) *n trademark* music combining rhythm and blues and pop, or gospel rhythms and modern ballad harmony [C20: from *Motown Records* of Detroit; from *Mo(tor)Town*, a nickname for Detroit, Michigan, centre of the US car industry]

motte (mɒt) *n history* a natural or man-made mound on which a castle was erected [C14: see MOAT]

MOT test *n* (in Britain) See MOT (sense 2)

mottle ('mɒtəl) *vb* **1** (*tr*) to colour with streaks or blotches of different shades ▷ *n* **2** a mottled appearance, as of the surface of marble [C17: back formation from MOTLEY]

mottled ('mɒtəld) *adj* coloured with streaks or blotches of different shades

motto ('mɒtəʊ) *n*, *pl* **-toes** or **-tos 1** a short saying expressing the guiding maxim or ideal of a family, organization, etc, esp when part of a coat of arms **2** a verse or maxim contained in a paper cracker **3** a quotation prefacing a book or chapter of a book [C16: via Italian from Latin *muttum* utterance]

Mo-tzu ('məʊ'tsu:) *n* a variant transliteration of **Mo-Zi**

moue *French* (mu) *n* a disdainful or pouting look

mouflon or **moufflon** ('mu:flɒn) *n* a wild short-fleeced mountain sheep, *Ovis musimon*, of Corsica and Sardinia [C18: via French from Corsican *mufrone*, from Late Latin *mufrō*]

mouillé ('mwi:eɪ) *adj phonetics* palatalized, as in the sounds represented by Spanish *ll* or *ñ*, Italian *gl* or *gn* (pronounced as (ʎ) and (ɲ) respectively), or French *ll* (representing a (j) sound) [C19: from French, past participle of *mouiller* to moisten, from Latin *mollis* soft]

moujik ('mu:ʒɪk) *n* a variant spelling of: **muzhik**

mould¹ or US **mold** (məʊld) *n* **1** a shaped cavity used to give a definite form to fluid or plastic material **2** a frame on which something may be constructed **3** something shaped in or made on a mould **4** shape, form, design, or pattern **5** specific nature, character, or type ▷ *vb* (*tr*) **6** to make in a mould **7** to shape or form, as by using a mould **8** to influence or direct: *to mould opinion* **9** to cling to **10** *metallurgy* to make (a material such as sand) into a mould that is used in casting [C13 (*n*): changed from Old French *modle*, from Latin *modulus* a small measure, MODULE] > **'mouldable** or US **'moldable** *adj*

mould² or US **mold** (məʊld) *n* **1** a coating or discoloration caused by various saprotrophic fungi that develop in a damp atmosphere on the surface of stored food, fabrics, wallpaper, etc **2** any of the fungi that causes this growth ▷ *vb* **3** to become or cause to become covered with this growth ▷ Also called: **mildew** [C15: dialect (Northern English) *mowlde* mouldy, from the past participle of *moulen* to become mouldy, probably of Scandinavian origin; compare Old Norse *mugla* mould]

mould³ or US **mold** (məʊld) *n* loose soil, esp when rich in organic matter [Old English *molde*; related to Old High German *molta* soil, Gothic *mulde*]

mouldboard or US **moldboard** ('məʊld,bɔːd) *n* the curved blade of a plough, which turns over the furrow

moulder or US **molder** ('məʊldə) *vb* (often foll by *away*) to crumble or cause to crumble, as through decay [C16:

verbal use of MOULD³]

moulding or US **molding** ('məʊldɪŋ) *n* **1** *architect* **a** a shaped outline, esp one used on cornices, etc **b** a shaped strip made of wood, stone, etc **2** something moulded

mouldy or US **moldy** ('məʊldɪ) *adj* **mouldier, mouldiest** or US **moldier, moldiest 1** covered with mould **2** stale or musty, esp from age or lack of use **3** *slang* boring; dull > **'mouldiness** or US **'moldiness** *n*

Moulin (*French* mulɛ̃) *n* **Jean** (ʒɑ̃). 1899–1943, French lawyer and Resistance hero; Chairman of the National Council of the Resistance (1943): tortured to death by the Nazis

Moulins (*French* mulɛ̃) *n* a market town in central France, on the Allier River. Pop: 21 892 (1999)

Moulmein or **Maulmain** (maʊlˈmeɪn) *n* a port in S Myanmar, near the mouth of the Salween River: exports teak and rice. Pop: 390 000 (2005 est)

moult or US **molt** (məʊlt) *vb* **1** (of birds, mammals, reptiles, and arthropods) to shed (feathers, hair, skin, or cuticle) ▷ *n* **2** the periodic process of moulting [C14 *mouten*, from Old English *mūtian*, as in *bimūtian* to exchange for, from Latin *mūtāre* to change] > **'moulter** or US **'molter** *n*

mound (maʊnd) *n* **1** a raised mass of earth, debris, etc **2** any heap or pile: *a mound of washing* **3** a small natural hill **4** an artificial ridge of earth, stone, etc, as used for defence ▷ *vb* **5** (often foll by *up*) to gather into a mound; heap **6** (*tr*) to cover or surround with a mound: *to mound a grave* [C16: earthwork, perhaps from Old English *mund* hand, hence defence: compare Middle Dutch *mond* protection]

Mound Builder *n* a member of a group of prehistoric inhabitants of the Mississippi region who built altar-mounds, tumuli, etc

mound-builder *n* another name for **megapode**

mount¹ (maʊnt) *vb* **1** to go up (a hill, stairs, etc); climb **2** to get up on (a horse, a platform, etc) **3** (*intr*; often foll by *up*) to increase; accumulate: *excitement mounted* **4** (*tr*) to fix onto a backing, setting, or support: *to mount a photograph; to mount a slide* **5** (*tr*) to provide with a horse for riding, or to place on a horse **6** (of male animals) to climb onto (a female animal) for copulation **7** (*tr*) to prepare (a play, musical comedy, etc) for production **8** (*tr*) to plan and organize (a compaign, an exhibition, etc) **9** (*tr*) to prepare (a skeleton, dead animal, etc) for exhibition as a specimen **10** (*tr*) to place or carry (weapons) in such a position that they can be fired **11 mount guard** See **guard** (sense 19) ▷ *n* **12** a backing, setting, or support onto which something is fixed **13** the act or manner of mounting **14** a horse for riding **15** a slide used in microscopy [C16: from Old French *munter*, from Vulgar Latin *montāre* (unattested) from Latin *mons* MOUNT²] > **'mountable** *adj*

mount² (maʊnt) *n* a mountain or hill: used in literature and (when cap.) in proper names: *Mount Everest* [Old English *munt*, from Latin *mons* mountain, but influenced in Middle English by Old French *mont*]

mountain ('maʊntɪn) *n* **1 a** a natural upward projection of the earth's surface, higher and steeper than a hill and often having a rocky summit **b** (*as modifier*): *mountain people; mountain scenery* **c** (*in combination*): *a mountaintop* **2** a huge heap or mass: *a mountain of papers* **3** anything of great quantity or size **4** a surplus of a commodity, esp in the European Union: *the butter mountain* [C13: from Old French *montaigne*, from Vulgar Latin *montānea* (unattested) mountainous, from Latin *montānus*, from *mons* mountain]

mountain ash *n* **1** any of various trees of the rosaceous genus *Sorbus*, such as *S aucuparia* (**European mountain ash** or **rowan**), having clusters of small white flowers and bright red berries **2** any of several Australian eucalyptus trees, such as *Eucalyptus regnans*

mountain avens *n* See **avens** (sense 2)

mountain bike *n* a type of sturdy bicycle with at least 16 and up to 21 gears, straight handlebars, and heavy-duty tyres

mountain cat *n* any of various wild feline mammals, such as the bobcat, lynx, or puma

mountaineer (,maʊntɪˈnɪə) *n* **1** a person who climbs

mountains **2** a person living in a mountainous area ▷ *vb* **3** (*intr*) to climb mountains > ,mountain'eering *n*

mountain goat *n* any wild goat inhabiting mountainous regions

mountain laurel *n* any of various ericaceous shrubs or trees of the genus *Kalmia*, esp *K. latifolia* of E North America, which has leathery poisonous leaves and clusters of pink or white flowers. Also called: **calico bush**

mountain lion *n* another name for **puma**

mountainous ('maʊntɪnəs) *adj* **1** of or relating to mountains: *a mountainous region* **2** like a mountain, esp in size or impressiveness

mountain sickness *n* Also called: **altitude sickness** nausea, headache, and shortness of breath caused by climbing to high altitudes (usually above 12 000 ft)

Mountbatten (maʊnt'bæt³n) *n* **1** Louis (Francis Albert Victor Nicholas), 1st Earl Mountbatten of Burma 1900–79, British naval commander; great-grandson of Queen Victoria. During World War II he was supreme allied commander in SE Asia (1943–46). He was the last viceroy of India (1947) and governor general (1947–48); killed by an IRA bomb

Mount Desert Island *n* an island off the coast of Maine: lakes and granite peaks. Area: 279 sq km (108 sq miles)

mountebank ('maʊntɪ,bæŋk) *n* **1** (formerly) a person who sold quack medicines in public places **2** a charlatan; fake ▷ *vb* **3** (*intr*) to play the mountebank [c16: from Italian *montambanco* a climber on a bench, from *montare* to MOUNT² + *banco* BENCH (see also BANK¹)] > ,mounte'bankery *n*

mounted ('maʊntɪd) *adj* **1** equipped with or riding horses: *mounted police* **2** provided with a support, backing, etc

Mountie or **Mounty** ('maʊntɪ) *n*, *pl* **Mounties** *informal* a member of the Royal Canadian Mounted Police [nickname evolved from MOUNTED]

mounting ('maʊntɪŋ) *n* another word for **mount¹** (sense 12)

mounting-block *n* a block of stone formerly used to aid a person when mounting a horse

Mount Isa ('aɪzə) *n* a city in NE Australia in NW Queensland: mining of copper and other minerals. Pop: 20 525 (2001)

Mount McKinley National Park (mə'kɪnlɪ) *n* the former name of **Denali National Park and Preserve**

Mount Rainier National Park ('raɪnɪə, reɪ'nɪə, rə-) *n* a national park in W Washington, in the Cascade Range. Area: 976 sq km (377 sq miles)

mourn (mɔːn) *vb* **1** to feel or express sadness for the death or loss of (someone or something) **2** (*intr*) to observe the customs of mourning, as by wearing black [Old English *murnan*; compare Old High German *mornēn* to be troubled, Gothic *maurnan* to grieve, Greek *mermeros* worried]

mournful ('mɔːnfʊl) *adj* **1** evoking grief; sorrowful **2** gloomy; sad > 'mournfully *adv* > 'mournfulness *n*

mourning ('mɔːnɪŋ) *n* **1** the act or feelings of one who mourns; grief **2** the conventional symbols of grief, such as the wearing of black **3** the period of time during which a death is officially mourned ▷ *adj* **4** of or relating to mourning > 'mourningly *adv*

mourning band *n* a piece of black material, esp an armband, worn to indicate that the wearer is in mourning

mourning dove *n* a brown North American dove, *Zenaidura macroura*, with a plaintive song

mouse *n*, (maʊs) *pl* **mice** (maɪs) **1** any of numerous small long-tailed rodents of the families *Muridae* and *Cricetidae* that are similar to but smaller than rats. See also **fieldmouse**, **harvest mouse**, **house mouse 2** any of various related rodents, such as the jumping mouse **3** a quiet, timid, or cowardly person **4** *computing* a hand-held device used to control the cursor movement and select computing functions without keying **5** *slang* a black eye ▷ *vb* (maʊz) **6** to stalk and catch (mice) **7** (*intr*) to go about stealthily [Old English *mūs*; compare Old Saxon *mūs*, German *Maus*, Old Norse *mūs*, Latin *mūs*, Greek *mūs*] > 'mouse,like *adj*

mousemat ('maʊs,mæt) *n* a piece of material on which a computer mouse is moved

mouseover ('maʊs,əʊvə) *n* *computing* (on the page of a website) an item, esp a graphic, that changes or pops up when the pointer of a mouse moves over it

mouser ('maʊzə, 'maʊsə) *n* a cat or other animal that is used to catch mice: usually qualified

mousetrap ('maʊs,træp) *n* **1** any trap for catching mice, esp one with a spring-loaded metal bar that is released by the taking of the bait **2** *Brit informal* cheese of indifferent quality

moussaka or **mousaka** (muˈsɑːkə) *n* a dish originating in the Balkan States, consisting of meat, aubergines, and tomatoes, topped with cheese sauce [c20: from Modern Greek]

mousse (muːs) *n* **1** a light creamy dessert made with eggs, cream, fruit, etc, set with gelatine **2** a similar dish made from fish or meat **3** short for **styling mousse** [c19: from French: froth]

mousseline (*French* muslin) *n* **1** a fine fabric made of rayon or silk **2** a type of fine glass [c17: French: MUSLIN]

Moussorgsky (muˈsɔːgskɪ; *Russian* 'musərkskij) *n* a variant spelling of (Modest Petrovich) **Mussorgsky**

moustache or *US* **mustache** (məˈstɑːʃ) *n* **1** the unshaved growth of hair on the upper lip, and sometimes down the sides of the mouth **2** a similar growth of hair or bristles (in animals) or feathers (in birds) **3** a mark like a moustache [c16: via French from Italian *mostaccio*, ultimately from Doric Greek *mustax* upper lip] > mous'tached or *US* mus'tached *adj*

moustache cup *n* a cup with a partial cover to protect a drinker's moustache

Mousterian (muːˈstɪərɪən) *n* **1** a culture characterized by flint flake tools and associated with Neanderthal man, found throughout Europe, North Africa, and the Near East, dating from before 70 000–32 000 BC ▷ *adj* **2** of or relating to this culture [c20: from French *Moustérien* from archaeological finds of the same period in the cave of *Le Moustier*, Dordogne, France]

mousy or **mousey** ('maʊsɪ) *adj* **mousier**, **mousiest 1** resembling a mouse, esp in having a light brown or greyish hair colour **2** shy or ineffectual **3** infested with mice > 'mousily *adv* > 'mousiness *n*

mouth *n* (maʊθ) *pl* **mouths** (maʊðz) **1** the opening through which many animals take in food and issue vocal sounds **2** the system of organs surrounding this opening, including the lips, tongue, teeth, etc **3** the visible part of the lips on the face **4** a particular manner of speaking: *a foul mouth* **5** *informal* boastful, rude, or excessive talk: *he is all mouth* **6** the point where a river issues into a sea or lake **7** the opening of a container, such as a jar **8** the opening of or place leading into a cave, tunnel, volcano, etc **9** that part of the inner lip of a horse on which the bit acts, esp when specified as to sensitivity **10** a pout; grimace **11 down in the mouth** or **down at the mouth** in low spirits ▷ *vb* (maʊð) **12** to speak or say (something) insincerely, esp in public **13** (*tr*) to form (words) with movements of the lips but without speaking **14** (*tr*) to take (something) into the mouth or to move (something) around inside the mouth **15** (*intr*; usually foll by *at*) to make a grimace [Old English *mūth*; compare Old Norse *muthr*, Gothic *munths*, Dutch *mond*]

mouthful ('maʊθ,fʊl) *n*, *pl* **-fuls 1** as much as is held in the mouth at one time **2** a small quantity, as of food **3** a long word or phrase that is difficult to say **4** *Brit informal* an abusive response

mouth off *vb* (*intr*, *adv*) *Brit informal* to give an opinion or speak emotionally, often without much consideration

mouth organ *n* another name for **harmonica** (sense 1)

mouthpart ('maʊθ,pɑːt) *n* any of the paired appendages in arthropods that surround the mouth and are specialized for feeding

mouthpiece ('maʊθ,piːs) *n* **1** the part of a wind instrument into which the player blows **2** the part of a telephone receiver into which a person speaks **3** the part of a container forming its mouth **4** a person who acts as a spokesman, as for an organization **5** a publication, esp a periodical, expressing the official views of an organization

m

mouthwash ('maʊθ,wɒʃ) *n* a medicated aqueous solution, used for gargling and for cleansing the mouth

mouthy ('maʊðɪ) *adj* **mouthier, mouthiest** bombastic; excessively talkative

mouton ('muːtɒn) *n* sheepskin processed to resemble the fur of another animal, esp beaver or seal [from French: sheep. See MUTTON]

movable *or* **moveable** ('muːvəbəl) *adj* **1** able to be moved or rearranged; not fixed **2** (esp of religious festivals such as Easter) varying in date from year to year **3** (usually spelt **moveable**) *law* denoting or relating to personal property as opposed to realty ▷ *n* **4** (*often plural*) a movable article, esp a piece of furniture > ,mova'bility *or* 'movableness *n* > 'movably *adv*

move (muːv) *vb* **1** to go or take from one place to another; change in location or position **2** (*usually intr*) to change (one's dwelling, place of business, etc) **3** to be or cause to be in motion; stir **4** (*intr*) (of machines, etc) to work or operate **5** (*tr*) to cause (to do something); prompt **6** (*intr*) to begin to act: *move soon or we'll lose the order* **7** (*intr*) to associate oneself with a specified social circle: *to move in exalted spheres* **8** (*intr*) to make progress **9** (*tr*) to arouse affection, pity, or compassion in; touch **10** (in board games) to change the position of (a piece) or (of a piece) to change position **11** (*intr*) (of merchandise) to be disposed of by being bought **12** (when *tr, often takes a clause as object*; when *intr*, often foll by *for*) to suggest (a proposal) formally, as in debating or parliamentary procedure **13** (*intr*; usually foll by *on* or *along*) to go away or to another place; leave **14** to cause (the bowels) to evacuate or (of the bowels) to be evacuated ▷ *n* **15** the act of moving; movement **16** one of a sequence of actions, usually part of a plan; manoeuvre **17** the act of moving one's residence, place of business, etc **18** (in board games) **a** a player's turn to move his piece or take other permitted action **b** a permitted manoeuvre of a piece **19 get a move on** *informal* **a** to get started **b** to hurry up **20 on the move a** travelling from place to place **b** advancing; succeeding **c** very active; busy [c13: from Anglo-French *mover*, from Latin *movēre*]

move in *vb* (*mainly adverb*) **1** Also: (when *preposition*) **move into** (*also preposition*) to occupy or take possession of (a new residence, place of business, etc) or help (someone) to do this **2** (*intr*; often foll by *on*) *informal* to creep close (to), as in preparing to capture **3** (*intr*; often foll by *on*) *informal* to try to gain power or influence (over) or interfere (with)

movement ('muːvmənt) *n* **1 a** the act, process, or result of moving **b** an instance of moving **2** the manner of moving **3 a** a group of people with a common ideology, esp a political or religious one **b** the organized action of such a group **4** a trend or tendency in a particular sphere **5** the driving and regulating mechanism of a watch or clock **6** (*often plural*) a person's location and activities during a specific time **7 a** the evacuation of the bowels **b** the matter evacuated **8** *music* a principal self-contained section of a symphony, sonata, etc, usually having its own structure **9** tempo or pace, as in music or literature **10** *fine arts* the appearance of motion in painting, sculpture, etc **11** *prosody* the rhythmic structure of verse **12** a positional change by one or a number of military units **13** a change in the market price of a security or commodity

move on *vb* (*adverb*) **1** to move or cause (someone) to leave somewhere **2** (*intr*) to progress; evolve: *football has moved on since then* **3** (*intr*) to put a difficult experience behind one and progress mentally or emotionally

mover ('muːvə) *n* **1** *informal* a person, business, idea, etc, that is advancing or progressing **2** a person who moves a proposal, as in a debate **3** *US & Canadian* a removal firm or a person who works for one

movers and shakers *pl n informal* the people with power and influence in a particular field of activity [c20: perhaps from the line "We are the movers and shakers of the world for ever" in 'Ode' by Arthur O'Shaughnessy (1844–81), British poet]

movie ('muːvɪ) *n* **a** an informal word for: **film** (sense 1) **b** (*as modifier*): *movie ticket* [c20: from MOV(ING PICTURE) + -IE]

movieoke (,muːvɪ'əʊkɪ) *n* an entertainment in which people take it in turns, with the help of subtitles and the audience, to act out well-known scenes from movies while they are silently shown in the background [c20: from MOVIE + KARAOKE]

moving ('muːvɪŋ) *adj* **1** arousing or touching the emotions **2** changing or capable of changing position **3** causing motion > 'movingly *adv*

moving staircase *or* **moving stairway** *n* less common terms for **escalator** (sense 1)

mow (məʊ) *vb* **mows, mowing, mowed, mowed** *or* **mown** **1** to cut down (grass, crops, etc) with a hand implement or machine **2** (*tr*) to cut the growing vegetation of (a field, lawn, etc) [Old English *māwan*; related to Old High German *māen*, Middle Dutch *maeyen* to mow, Latin *metere* to reap, Welsh *medi*] > 'mower *n*

mow down *vb* (*tr, adverb*) to kill in large numbers, esp by gunfire

Mowlam ('məʊlæm) *n* **Mo**, full name *Marjorie Mowlam*. 1949–2005, British Labour politician; secretary of state for Northern Ireland (1997–99) and minister for the cabinet office (1999–2001)

mown (məʊn) *vb* a past participle of **mow**¹

Moya ('mɔɪə) *n* (**John**) **Hidalgo**. 1920–94, British architect: in partnership with Philip Powell, his designs include Skylon, Festival of Britain (1950), Wolfson College, Oxford (1974), and the Queen Elizabeth Conference Centre, Westminster (1986)

Moyle (mɔɪl) *n* a district of NE Northern Ireland, in Co Antrim. Pop: 16 302 (2003 est). Area: 494 sq km (191 sq miles)

Mozambique (,məʊzəm'biːk) *n* a republic in SE Africa: colonized by the Portuguese from 1505 onwards and a slave-trade centre until 1878; made an overseas province of Portugal in 1951; became an independent republic in 1975; became a member of the Commonwealth in 1995. Official language: Portuguese. Religion: animist majority. Currency: metical. Capital: Maputo. Pop: 19 183 000 (2004 est). Area: 812 379 sq km (313 661 sq miles). Portuguese name: *Moçambique*. Also called (until 1975): **Portuguese East Africa** > ,Mozam'bican *or* ,Mozam'biquan *adj, n*

Mozambique Channel *n* a strait between Mozambique and Madagascar. Length: about 1600 km (1000 miles). Width: 400 km (250 miles)

Mozart ('məʊtsɑːt) *n* **Wolfgang Amadeus** ('vɔlfgaŋ ama'deːʊs). 1756–91, Austrian composer. A child prodigy and prolific genius, his works include operas, such as *The Marriage of Figaro* (1786), *Don Giovanni* (1787), and *The Magic Flute* (1791), symphonies, concertos for piano, violin, clarinet, and French horn, string quartets and quintets, sonatas, songs, and Masses, such as the unfinished *Requiem* (1791) > Mo'zartean *or* Mo'zartian *adj*

Mo-Zi ('məʊ'tsiː) *or* **Mo-tzu** *n* ?470–?391 BC, Chinese religious philosopher; his teaching, expounded in the book *Mo-Zi*, emphasizes love, frugality, avoidance of aggressive war, and submission to Heaven

mozzarella (,mɒtsə'rɛlə) *n* a moist white Italian curd cheese made originally from buffalo milk [from Italian, diminutive of *mozza* a type of cheese, from *mozzare* to cut off]

mp *abbreviation* **1** melting point **2** *music* mezzo piano [Italian: moderately soft]

MP *abbreviation* **1** (in Britain and Canada) Member of Parliament **2** (in Britain) Metropolitan Police **3** Military Police **4** Mounted Police

MP3 *abbreviation* **1** MPEG-1 Audio Layer-3: tradename for software created by the Motion Picture Experts Group that enables files to be compressed quickly to 10% or less of their original size for storage on disk or hard drive or esp for transfer across the internet **2** an audio or video file created in this way

MPAA *abbreviation* Motion Picture Association of America

m-payment *n* a point-of-sale payment made through a wireless device such as a mobile phone or PDA [c20: M(OBILE) + PAYMENT]

MPEG ('em,peg) *n* *computing* a standard file format for compressing video images and audio sounds [c20: technique devised by the M(otion) P(icture) E(xperts) G(roup)]

m

mpg *abbreviation* miles per gallon

mph *abbreviation* miles per hour

MPhil *or* **MPh** *abbreviation* Master of Philosophy

MPP *abbreviation* (in Canada) Member of the Provincial Parliament (of Ontario)

Mpumalanga (m'pʌmɑːlaːŋgə) *n* a province of E South Africa; formed in 1994 (originally as Eastern Transvaal) from part of the former province of Transvaal: agriculture and service industries. Capital: Nelspruit. Pop: 3 244 306 (2004 est.). Area: 78 370 sq km (30 259 sq miles)

MPV *abbreviation* multipurpose vehicle

Mr ('mɪstə) *n*, *pl* **Messrs** ('mɛsəz) a title used before a man's name or names or before some office that he holds: *Mr Jones; Mr President* [C17: abbreviation of MISTER]

MR *abbreviation* **1** Master of the Rolls (in Britain) **2** motivation(al) research

MRA *abbreviation* **1** magnetic resonance **2** Moral Rearmament

MRC *abbreviation* (in Britain) Medical Research Council

MRI *abbreviation* magnetic resonance imaging

mRNA *abbreviation* messenger RNA

MRP *abbreviation* manufacturers' recommended price

Mrs ('mɪsɪz) *n*, *pl* **Mrs** *or* **Mesdames** a title used before the name or names of a married woman [C17: originally an abbreviation of MISTRESS]

MRSA *abbreviation* methicillin-resistant *Staphylococcus aureus*: a bacterium that enters the skin through open wounds to cause septicaemia and is extremely resistant to most antibiotics. It has been responsible for outbreaks of untreatable infections among patients in hospitals

Ms (mɪz, məs) *n* a title substituted for *Mrs* or *Miss* before a woman's name to avoid making a distinction between married and unmarried women

MS *abbreviation* **1** Master of Surgery **2** (on gravestones) memoriae sacrum [Latin: sacred to the memory of] **3** multiple sclerosis

MS. *or* **ms.** *pl* **MSS.** *or* **mss.** *abbreviation* manuscript

MSc *abbreviation* Master of Science

MSD *abbreviation* (in New Zealand) Ministry of Social Development

MS-DOS (ɛm'ɛs'dɒs) *n* *trademark* *computing* a type of disk operating system [C20: from *M(icro)s(oft)*, the company that developed it, + DOS]

MSG *abbreviation* monosodium glutamate

Msgr *abbreviation* Monsignor

MSP *abbreviation* Member of the Scottish Parliament

MST *abbreviation* Mountain Standard Time

Mt *or* **mt** *abbreviation* **1** mount: *Mt Everest* **2** Also called: **mtn** mountain

MT *abbreviation* Montana

mtDNA *abbreviation* mitochondrial deoxyribonucleic acid

MTech *abbreviation* Master of Technology

mtg *abbreviation* meeting

MTV *abbreviation* music television: a US music channel that operates 24 hours a day

mu (mjuː) *n* the 12th letter in the Greek alphabet (M, μ), a consonant, transliterated as *m*

Mu'awiyah I (ˌmuːəˈwiːjə) *n* ?602–680 AD, first caliph (661–80) of the Omayyad dynasty of Damascus; regarded as having secularized the caliphate

Mubarak (muˈbaːrək) *n* (**Muhammad**) **Hosni** ('hʊsnɪ). born 1928, Egyptian statesman; president of Egypt from 1981

much (mʌtʃ) *determiner* **1 a** (*usually used with a negative*) a great quantity or degree of: *there isn't much honey left* **b** (*as pronoun*): *much has been learned from this* **2** a bit much *informal* rather excessive **3** make much of **a** (*used with a negative*) to make sense of: *he couldn't make much of her babble* **b** to give importance to: *she made much of this fact* **c** to pay flattering attention to: *the reporters made much of the film star* **4** not much of not to any appreciable degree or extent: *he's not much of an actor really* **5** not up to much *informal* of a low standard: *this beer is not up to much* ▷ *adv* **6** considerably: *they're much better now* **7** practically; nearly (*esp in the phrase* **much the same**) **8** (*usually used with a negative*) often; a great deal: *it doesn't happen much in this country* **9** much as *or* as much as even though; although:

much as I'd like to, I can't come ▷ See also **more**, **most** [Old English *mycel*; related to Old English *micel* great, Old Saxon *mikil*, Gothic *mikils*; compare also Latin *magnus*, Greek *megas*]

muchness ('mʌtʃnɪs) *n* **1** *archaic or informal* magnitude **2** much of a muchness *Brit* very similar

mucid ('mjuːsɪd) *adj* *rare* mouldy, musty, or slimy [C17: from Latin *mūcidus*, from *mucēre* to be mouldy] > **mu'cidity**, **'mucidness** *n*

mucilage ('mjuːsɪlɪdʒ) *n* **1** a sticky preparation, such as gum or glue, used as an adhesive **2** a complex glutinous carbohydrate secreted by certain plants [C14: via Old French from Late Latin *mūcilāgo* mouldy juice; see MUCID] > **mucilaginous** (ˌmjuːsɪˈlædʒɪnəs) *adj*

muck (mʌk) *n* **1** farmyard dung or decaying vegetable matter **2** Also called: **muck soil** an organic soil rich in humus and used as a fertilizer **3** dirt or filth **4** *slang*, *chiefly Brit* rubbish **5** make a muck of *slang*, *chiefly Brit* to ruin or spoil ▷ *vb* (*tr*) **6** to spread manure upon (fields, gardens, etc) **7** to soil or pollute **8** (*often foll by out*) to clear muck from [C13: probably of Scandinavian origin; compare Old Norse *myki* dung, Norwegian *myk*] > **'mucky** *adj* > **'muckily** *adv* > **'muckiness** *n*

muck about *vb* *Brit slang* **1** (*intr*) to waste time; misbehave **2** (when *intr*, foll by *with*) to interfere with, annoy, or waste the time of

mucker ('mʌkə) *n* *Brit slang* **a** a friend; mate **b** a coarse person > **'muckerish** *adj*

muck in *vb* (*intr*, *adverb*) *Brit slang* to share something, such as duties, work, etc (with other people)

muckrake ('mʌkˌreɪk) *vb* (*intr*) to seek out and expose scandal, esp concerning public figures > **'muck,raker** *n* > **'muck,raking** *n*

mucksweat ('mʌkˌswɛt) *n* *Brit informal* profuse sweat or a state of profuse sweating

muckymuck ('mʌkɪˌmʌk) *n* *Canadian informal* a person who is or looks very important [from Chinook jargon; see HIGH-MUCK-A-MUCK]

mucous ('mjuːkəs) *or* **mucose** ('mjuːkəus, -kəuz) *adj* of, resembling, or secreting mucus [C17: from Latin *mūcōsus* slimy, from MUCUS] > **mucosity** (mjuːˈkɒsɪtɪ) *n*

● USAGE The noun *mucus* is often misspelled *mucous*. ● *Mucous* can only be correctly used as an adjective

mucous membrane *n* a mucus-secreting membrane that lines body cavities or passages that are open to the external environment

mucus ('mjuːkəs) *n* the slimy protective secretion of the mucous membranes, consisting mainly of mucin [C17: from Latin: nasal secretions; compare *mungere* to blow the nose; related to Greek *muxa* mucus, *muktēr* nose]

● USAGE See at **mucous**

mud (mʌd) *n* **1** a fine-grained soft wet deposit that occurs on the ground after rain, at the bottom of ponds, lakes, etc **2** *informal* slander or defamation **3** clear as mud *informal* not at all clear **4** here's mud in your eye *informal* a humorous drinking toast **5** someone's name is mud *informal* someone is disgraced **6** throw mud at *or* sling mud at *informal* to slander; vilify ▷ *vb* **muds**, **mudding**, **mudded** **7** (*tr*) to soil or cover with mud [C14: probably from Middle Low German *mudde*; compare Middle High German *mot* swamp, mud, Swedish *modd* slush]

mud bath *n* **1** a medicinal bath in heated mud **2** a dirty or muddy occasion, state, etc

mud crab *n* a large edible crab, *Scylla serrata*, of Australian mangrove regions

muddle ('mʌdᵊl) *vb* (*tr*) **1** (*often foll by up*) to mix up (objects, items, etc); jumble **2** to confuse **3** *US* to mix or stir (alcoholic drinks, etc) ▷ *n* **4** a state of physical or mental confusion [C16: perhaps from Middle Dutch *moddelen* to make muddy] > **'muddled** *adj* > **'muddling** *adj*, *n* > **'muddler** *n*

muddleheaded (ˌmʌdᵊlˈhɛdɪd) *adj* mentally confused or vague > **ˌmuddle'headedness** *n*

muddle through *vb* (*intr*, *adverb*) *chiefly Brit* to succeed in some undertaking in spite of lack of organization

muddy ('mʌdɪ) *adj* **-dier**, **-diest** **1** covered or filled with mud **2** not clear or bright: *muddy colours* **3** cloudy: *a muddy liquid* **4** (esp of thoughts) confused or vague ▷ *vb* **-dies**,

m

-dying, -died **5** to become or cause to become muddy
▷ **'muddily** *adv* ▷ **'muddiness** *n*

mudeye ('mʌdaɪ) *n Austral* the larva of the dragonfly,
commonly used as a fishing bait

mudfish ('mʌd,fɪʃ) *n, pl* **-fish** *or* **-fishes** any of various
fishes, such as the bowfin and cichlids, that live at or
frequent the muddy bottoms of rivers, lakes, etc

mud flat *n* a tract of low muddy land, esp near an
estuary, that is covered at high tide and exposed at low
tide

mudflow ('mʌd,fləʊ) *n geology* a flow of soil or fine-
grained sediment mixed with water down a steep
unstable slope

mudguard ('mʌd,gɑːd) *n* a curved part of a motorcycle,
bicycle, etc, attached above the wheels to reduce the
amount of water or mud thrown up by them. US and
Canadian name: **fender**

mud hen *n* any of various birds that frequent marshes
or similar places, esp the coots, rails, etc

mudlark ('mʌd,lɑːk) *n* **1** *slang, now rare* a street urchin
2 (formerly) one who made a living by picking up odds
and ends in the mud of tidal rivers **3** *Austral slang* a
racehorse that runs well on a wet or muddy course

mud map *n Austral informal* a map drawn on the ground
with a stick, or any other roughly drawn map

mudpack ('mʌd,pæk) *n* a cosmetic astringent paste
containing fuller's earth, used to improve the
complexion

mud puppy *n* any aquatic North American salamander
of the genus *Necturus*, esp *N. maculosus*, having red
feathery external gills and other persistent larval
features: family *Proteidae*

mudskipper ('mʌd,skɪpə) *n* any of various gobies of the
genus *Periophthalmus* and related genera that occur in
tropical coastal regions of Africa and Asia and can move
on land by means of their strong pectoral fins

mudslinging ('mʌd,slɪŋɪŋ) *n* casting malicious slurs on
an opponent, esp in politics ▷ **'mud,slinger** *n*

mudstone ('mʌd,stəʊn) *n* a dark grey clay rock similar
to shale but with the lamination less well developed

mud turtle *n* any of various small turtles of the genus
Kinosternon and related genera that inhabit muddy rivers
in North and Central America: family *Kinosternidae*

muesli ('mjuːzlɪ) *n* a mixture of rolled oats, nuts, fruit,
etc, eaten with milk [Swiss German, from German *Mus*
mush, purée + *-li*, diminutive suffix]

muesli bar *n* a snack made of compressed muesli
ingredients

muezzin (muːˈɛzɪn) *n Islam* the official of a mosque who
calls the faithful to prayer five times a day from the
minaret [c16: changed from Arabic *mu'adhdhin*]

muff[1] (mʌf) *n* an open-ended cylinder of fur or cloth
into which the hands are placed for warmth [c16:
probably from Dutch *mof*, ultimately from French *mouffle*
MUFFLE[1]]

muff[2] (mʌf) *vb* **1** to perform (an action) awkwardly **2** (*tr*)
to bungle (a shot, catch, etc) in a game ▷ *n* **3** any
unskilful play in a game, esp a dropped catch **4** any
clumsy or bungled action **5** a bungler [c19: of uncertain
origin]

muffin ('mʌfɪn) *n* **1** *Brit* a thick round baked yeast roll,
usually toasted and served with butter **2** *US & Canadian* a
small cup-shaped sweet bread roll, usually eaten hot
with butter [c18: perhaps from Low German *muffen*,
cakes]

muffle[1] ('mʌfʰl) *vb* (*tr*) **1** (often foll by *up*) to wrap up (the
head) in a scarf, cloak, etc, for warmth **2** to deaden
(a sound or noise), esp by wrapping **3** to prevent (the
expression of something) by (someone) ▷ *n* **4** something
that muffles **5** a kiln with an inner chamber for firing
porcelain, enamel, etc, at a low temperature [c15:
probably from Old French; compare Old French *moufle*
mitten, *emmouflé* wrapped up]

muffle[2] ('mʌfʰl) *n* the fleshy hairless part of the upper
lip and nose in ruminants and some rodents [c17: from
French *mufle*, of unknown origin]

muffler ('mʌflə) *n* **1** a thick scarf, collar, etc **2** *US &
Canadian* any device designed to reduce noise, esp the
tubular device containing baffle plates in the exhaust

system of a motor vehicle. Also called (in Britain and
certain other countries): **silencer**

mufti[1] ('mʌftɪ) *n, pl* **-tis 1** a Muslim legal expert and
adviser on the law of the Koran **2** (in the former
Ottoman empire) the leader of the religious community
[c16: from Arabic *muftī*, from *aftā* to give a (legal)
decision]

mufti[2] ('mʌftɪ) *n, pl* **-tis** civilian dress, esp as worn by a
person who normally wears a military uniform [c19:
perhaps from MUFTI[1]]

Mufulira (,muːfuːˈlɪərə) *n* a mining town in the Copper
Belt of Zambia. Pop: 220 000 (2005 est)

mug[1] (mʌg) *n* **1** a drinking vessel with a handle, usually
cylindrical and made of earthenware **2** Also called:
mugful the quantity held by a mug or its contents [c16:
probably from Scandinavian; compare Swedish *mugg*]

mug[2] (mʌg) *n* **1** *slang* a person's face or mouth: *get your
ugly mug out of here!* **2** *Brit slang* a gullible person, esp one
who is swindled easily **3** a mug's game a worthless
activity ▷ *vb* **mugs, mugging, mugged 4** (*tr*) *informal* to
attack or rob (someone) violently [c18: perhaps from
MUG[1], since drinking vessels were sometimes modelled
into the likeness of a face] > **'mugger** *n*

Mugabe (muˈgɑːbɪ) *n* **Robert**. born 1925, Zimbabwean
politician; leader of one wing of the Patriotic Front
against the government of Ian Smith of Rhodesia, and
of the Zanu party; prime minister (1980–87); president
from 1988

muggins ('mʌgɪnz) *n* **1** *Brit slang* **a** a simpleton; silly
person **b** a title used humorously to refer to oneself **2** a
card game [c19: probably from the surname *Muggins*]

muggy ('mʌgɪ) *adj* **-gier, -giest** (of weather, air, etc)
unpleasantly warm and humid [c18: dialect *mug* drizzle,
probably from Scandinavian; compare Old Norse *mugga*
mist] > **'mugginess** *n*

Mughal ('muːgɑːl) *n* a variant spelling of **Mogul**

mug shot *n informal* a photograph of a person's face, esp
one resembling a police-file picture

Muhammad (mʊˈhæməd) *n* ?570–632 AD, the prophet
believed by Muslims to be the channel for the final
unfolding of God's revelation to mankind: popularly
regarded as the founder of Islam. He began to teach in
Mecca in 610 but persecution forced him to flee with his
followers to Medina in 622. After several battles, he
conquered Mecca (630), establishing the principles of
Islam (embodied in the Koran) over all Arabia

Muhammad Ali, Muhammed Ali *or* **Mohammed Ali**
('ɑːlɪ, ɑːˈliː, ˈælɪ) *n* original name *Cassius (Marcellus) Clay*.
born 1942, US boxer, who was world heavyweight
champion three times (1964–67; 1974–78; 1978)

Muhammadan *or* **Muhammedan** (mʊˈhæmədᵊn) *n, adj
rare, archaic* another word (not in Muslim use) for **Muslim**

Mühlhausen (myːlˈhauzən) *n* the German name for
Mulhouse

Muir (mjʊə) *n* **Edwin**. 1887–1959, Scottish poet, novelist,
and critic

Muir Glacier (mjʊə) *n* a glacier in SE Alaska, in the St
Elias Mountains, flowing southeast from Mount
Fairweather. Area: about 900 sq km (350 sq miles)

mujaheddin, mujahedeen *or* **mujahideen**
('muːdʒəhəˈdiːn) *pl n* the mujaheddin (*sometimes capital*)
(in Afghanistan and Iran) fundamentalist Muslim
guerrillas; in Afghanistan in 1992 the mujaheddin
overthrew the government but were unable to agree on
a constitution due to factional conflict and in 1996
Taliban forces seized power [c20: from Arabic *mujāhidīn*
fighters, ultimately from JIHAD]

Mukden ('mʊkdən) *n* a former name of **Shenyang**

mukluk ('mʌklʌk) *n* a soft boot, usually of sealskin,
worn by the Inuit [from Inuktitut *muklok* large seal]

muktuk ('mʌktʌk) *n Canadian* the thin outer skin of the
beluga, used as food [from Inuktitut]

mulatto (mjuːˈlætəʊ) *n, pl* **-tos** *or* **-toes 1** a person having
one Black and one White parent ▷ *adj* **2** of a light brown
colour [c16: from Spanish *mulato* young mule, variant of
mulo MULE[1]]

mulberry ('mʌlbərɪ, -brɪ) *n, pl* **-ries 1** any moraceous tree
of the temperate genus *Morus*, having edible blackberry-
like fruit, such as *M. alba* (**white mulberry**), the leaves of

which are used to feed silkworms 2 the fruit of any of these trees 3 any of several similar or related trees, such as the paper mulberry and Indian mulberry 4 a a dark purple colour b (as adjective): a mulberry dress [C14: from Latin mōrum, from Greek moron; related to Old English mōrberie; compare Dutch moerbezie, Old High German mūrberi]

mulch (mʌltʃ) n 1 half-rotten vegetable matter, peat, etc, used to prevent soil erosion or enrich the soil ▷ vb 2 (tr) to cover (the surface of land) with mulch [C17: from obsolete mulch soft; related to Old English mylisc mellow; compare dialect German molsch soft, Latin mollis soft]

Mulciber (ˈmʌlsɪbə) n another name for: Vulcan¹

mulct (mʌlkt) vb (tr) 1 to cheat or defraud 2 to fine (a person) ▷ n 3 a fine or penalty [C15: via French from Latin multa a fine]

Muldoon (mʌlˈduːn) n Sir **Robert David**. 1921–92, New Zealand statesman; prime minister of New Zealand (1975–84)

mule¹ (mjuːl) n 1 the sterile offspring of a male donkey and a female horse, used as a beast of burden 2 any hybrid animal: a mule canary 3 Also called: **spinning mule** a machine invented by Samuel Crompton that spins cotton into yarn and winds the yarn on spindles 4 informal an obstinate or stubborn person [C13: from Old French mul, from Latin mūlus ass, mule]

mule² (mjuːl) n a backless shoe or slipper [C16: from Old French mulleus a magistrate's shoe]

muleta (mjuːˈletə) n the small cape attached to a stick used by the matador during the final stages of a bullfight [Spanish: small mule, crutch, from mula MULE¹]

muleteer (ˌmjuːlɪˈtɪə) n a person who drives mules

mulga (ˈmʌlgə) n Austral 1 any of various Australian acacia shrubs, esp Acacia aneura, which grows in the central desert regions and has leaflike leafstalks 2 scrub comprised of a dense growth of acacia 3 the outback; bush [from a native Australian language]

Mulhacén (Spanish mulaˈθen) n a mountain in S Spain, in the Sierra Nevada: the highest peak in Spain Height: 3478 m (11 410 ft)

Mülheim an der Ruhr (German ˈmyːlhaim an der ˈruːr) or **Mülheim** n an industrial city in W Germany, in North Rhine-Westphalia on the River Ruhr: river port. Pop: 170 745 (2003 est)

Mulhouse (French myluz) n a city in E France, on the Rhône-Rhine canal: under German rule (1871–1918); textiles. Pop: 110 359 (1999). German name: **Mühlhausen**

muliebrity (ˌmjuːlɪˈɛbrɪtɪ) n 1 the condition of being a woman 2 femininity [C16: via Late Latin from Latin muliēbris womanly, from mulier woman]

mulish (ˈmjuːlɪʃ) adj stubborn; obstinate; headstrong > ˈmulishly adv > ˈmulishness n

mull¹ (mʌl) vb (tr; often foll by over) to study or ponder [C19: probably from MUDDLE]

mull² (mʌl) vb (tr) to heat (wine, ale, etc) with sugar and spices to make a hot drink > ˈmulled adj [C17: of unknown origin]

mull³ (mʌl) n a light muslin fabric of soft texture [C18: earlier mulmull, from Hindi malmal]

mull⁴ (mʌl) n Scot a promontory [C14: related to Gaelic maol, Icelandic múli]

Mull (mʌl) n a mountainous island off the west coast of Scotland, in the Inner Hebrides, separated from the mainland by the **Sound of Mull**. Chief town: Tobermory. Pop: 2667 (2001). Area: 909 sq km (351 sq miles)

mullah or **mulla** (ˈmʌlə, ˈmulə) n (formerly) a Muslim scholar, teacher, or religious leader: also used as a title of respect [C17: from Turkish molla, Persian and Hindi mulla, from Arabic mawlā master]

mullein or **mullen** (ˈmʌlɪn) n any of various European herbaceous plants of the scrophulariaceous genus Verbascum, such as V. thapsus (common mullein or Aaron's rod), typically having tall spikes of yellow flowers and broad hairy leaves. See also **Aaron's rod** [C15: from Old French moleine, probably from Old French mol soft, from Latin mollis]

muller (ˈmʌlə) n a flat heavy implement of stone or iron used to grind material against a slab of stone [C15: probably from mullen to grind to powder; compare Old

English myl dust]

Muller (ˈmʌlə) n **Hermann Joseph**. 1890–1967, US geneticist, noted for his work on the transmutation of genes by X-rays: Nobel prize for physiology or medicine 1946

Müller (German ˈmylər) n 1 **Friedrich Max** (ˈfriːdrɪç maks). 1823–1900, British Sanskrit scholar born in Germany 2 **Johann** (joˈhan). See **Regiomontanus** 3 **Johannes Peter** (joˈhanəs ˈpeːtər). 1801–58, German physiologist, anatomist, and experimental psychologist 4 **Paul Hermann** (paul ˈhɛrman). 1899–1965, Swiss chemist. He synthesized DDT (1939) and discovered its use as an insecticide: Nobel prize for physiology or medicine 1948

mullet¹ (ˈmʌlɪt) n any of various teleost food fishes belonging to the families Mugilidae (grey mullet) or Mullidae (red mullet) [C15: via Old French from Latin mullus, from Greek mullos]

mullet² (ˈmʌlɪt) n a hairstyle in which the hair is short at the top and long at the back [C20: origin unknown]

Mulligan (ˈmʌlɪgən) n **Gerry**, full name Gerald Joseph Mulligan. 1927–96, US jazz saxophonist, who pioneered the cool jazz style of the 1950s

mulligatawny (ˌmʌlɪgəˈtɔːnɪ) n a curry-flavoured soup of Anglo-Indian origin, made with meat stock [C18: from Tamil milakutanni, from milaku pepper + tanni water]

Mulliken (ˈmʌlɪkən) n **Robert Sanderson**. 1896–1986, US physicist and chemist, who won the Nobel prize for chemistry (1966) for his work on bonding and the electronic structure of molecules

Mullingar (ˌmʌlɪnˈgɑː) n a town in N central Republic of Ireland, the county town of Co Westmeath; site of cathedral; cattle raised. Pop: 15 621 (2002)

mullion (ˈmʌlɪən) n 1 a vertical member between the casements or panes of a window or the panels of a screen ▷ vb 2 (tr) to furnish (a window, screen, etc) with mullions [C16: variant of Middle English munial, from Old French moinel, of unknown origin]

mullock (ˈmʌlək) n 1 Austral waste material from a mine 2 poke mullock at Austral informal to ridicule [C14: related to Old English myl dust, Old Norse mylja to crush; see MULLER]

mulloway (ˈmʌləˌweɪ) n a large Australian marine sciaenid fish, Sciaena antarctica, valued for sport and food [C19: of unknown origin]

Mulroney (mʌlˈrəʊnɪ) n (Martin) **Brian**. born 1939, Canadian lawyer, businessman, and statesman; Conservative prime minister (1984–93)

Multan (ˌmʊlˈtɑːn) n a city in central Pakistan, near the Chenab River. Pop: 1 459 000 (2005 est)

multangular (mʌlˈtæŋgjʊlə) or **multiangular** adj having many angles

multi- combining form 1 many or much: multiflorous; multimillion 2 more than one: multiparous; multistorey [from Latin multus much, many]

multicultural (ˌmʌltɪˈkʌltʃərəl) adj consisting of, relating to, or designed for the cultures of several different races > ˌmultiˈculturaˌlism n > ˌmultiˈculturaˌlist adj, n

multifactorial (ˌmʌltɪfækˈtɔːrɪəl) adj involving or including a number of elements or factors

multifarious (ˌmʌltɪˈfɛərɪəs) adj having many parts of great variety [C16: from Late Latin multifārius manifold, from Latin multifāriam on many sides] > ˌmultiˈfariously adv > ˌmultiˈfariousness n

multiflora rose (ˌmʌltɪˈflɔːrə) n an Asian climbing shrubby rose, Rosa multiflora, having clusters of small fragrant flowers: the source of many cultivated roses

multiform (ˈmʌltɪˌfɔːm) adj having many forms or kinds

multigym (ˈmʌltɪˌdʒɪm) n an exercise apparatus incorporating a variety of weights, used for toning the muscles

multilateral (ˌmʌltɪˈlætərəl, -ˈlætrəl) adj 1 of or involving more than two nations or parties: a multilateral pact 2 having many sides > ˌmultiˈlaterally adv

multilingual (ˌmʌltɪˈlɪŋgwəl) adj 1 able to speak more than two languages 2 written or expressed in more than two languages

multimedia (ˌmʌltɪˈmiːdɪə) adj 1 of or relating to the use of a combination of media 2 computing of or relating to

m

any of various systems which can manipulate data in a variety of forms, such as sound, graphics, or text

multimillionaire (ˌmʌltɪˌmɪljəˈnɛə) n a person with a fortune of several million pounds, dollars, etc

multinational (ˌmʌltɪˈnæʃənˀl) adj 1 (of a large business company) operating in several countries ▷ n 2 such a company

multipack (ˈmʌltɪˌpæk) n a form of packaging of foodstuffs, etc, that contains several units and is offered at a price below that of the equivalent number of units

multiparous (mʌlˈtɪpərəs) adj (of certain species of mammal) producing many offspring at one birth [c17: from New Latin multiparus]

multipartite (ˌmʌltɪˈpɑːtaɪt) adj 1 divided into many parts or sections 2 government a less common word for: multilateral

multiparty (ˌmʌltɪˈpɑːtɪ) adj of or relating to a state, political system, etc, in which more than one political party is permitted: multiparty democracy

multiplayer (ˈmʌltɪˌpleɪə) n a mode of play involving more than one player at one time in a computer or video game

multiple (ˈmʌltɪpˀl) adj 1 having or involving more than one part, individual, etc 2 electronics, US & Canadian (of a circuit) having a number of conductors in parallel ▷ n 3 the product of a given number or polynomial and any other one: 6 is a multiple of 2 4 short for **multiple store** [c17: via French from Late Latin multiplus, from Latin MULTIPLEX] > ˈmultiply adv

multiple-choice adj having a number of possible given answers out of which the correct one must be chosen

multiple personality n psychiatry a mental disorder in which an individual's personality appears to have become separated into two or more distinct personalities, each with its own complex organization. Nontechnical name: **split personality**

multiple sclerosis n a chronic progressive disease of the central nervous system characterized by loss of some of the myelin sheath surrounding certain nerve fibres and resulting in speech and visual disorders, tremor, muscular incoordination, partial paralysis, etc

multiple store n one of several retail enterprises under the same ownership and management. Also called: **multiple shop**

multiplex (ˈmʌltɪˌplɛks) n 1 telecomm a the use of a common communications channel for sending two or more messages or signals. In **frequency-division multiplex** the frequency band transmitted by the common channel is split into narrower bands each of which constitutes a distinct channel. In **time-division multiplex** different channels are established by intermittent connections to the common channel b (as modifier): a multiplex transmitter 2 a a purpose-built complex containing a number of cinemas and usually a restaurant or bar b (as modifier): a multiplex cinema ▷ adj 3 a less common word for: **multiple** ▷ vb 4 to send (messages or signals) or (of messages or signals) be sent by multiplex [c16: from Latin: having many folds, from MULTI- + plicāre to fold]

multiplexer or **multiplexor** (ˈmʌltɪˌplɛksə) n computing a device that enables the simultaneous transmission of several messages or signals over one communications channel

multiplicand (ˌmʌltɪplɪˈkænd) n a number to be multiplied by another number, the multiplier. See also **multiplier** [c16: from Latin multiplicandus, gerund of multiplicāre to MULTIPLY]

multiplication (ˌmʌltɪplɪˈkeɪʃən) n 1 an arithmetical operation, defined initially in terms of repeated addition, usually written $a \times b$, $a.b$, or ab, by which the product of two quantities is calculated: to multiply a by positive integral b is to add a to itself b times. Multiplication by fractions can then be defined in the light of the associative and commutative properties; multiplication by $1/n$ is equivalent to multiplication by 1 followed by division by n: for example $0.3 \times 0.7 = 0.3 \times 7/10 = (0.3 \times 7)/10 = 2.1/10 = 0.21$ 2 the act of multiplying or state of being multiplied 3 the act or process in animals, plants, or people of reproducing or

breeding > ˌmultipliˈcational adj

multiplication sign n the symbol ×, placed between numbers to be multiplied, as in $3 \times 4 \times 5 = 60$

multiplication table n one of a group of tables giving the results of multiplying two numbers together

multiplicity (ˌmʌltɪˈplɪsɪtɪ) n, pl -ties 1 a large number or great variety 2 the state of being multiple

multiplier (ˈmʌltɪˌplaɪə) n 1 a person or thing that multiplies 2 the number by which another number, the multiplicand, is multiplied. See also **multiplicand** 3 physics any device or instrument, such as a photomultiplier, for increasing an effect 4 economics the ratio of the total change in income (resulting from successive rounds of spending) to an initial autonomous change in expenditure

multiply (ˈmʌltɪˌplaɪ) vb -plies, -plying, -plied 1 to increase or cause to increase in number, quantity, or degree 2 (tr) to combine (two numbers or quantities) by multiplication 3 (intr) to increase in number by reproduction [c13: from Old French multiplier, from Latin multiplicāre to multiply, from multus much, many + plicāre to fold] > ˈmulti,pliable or ˈmulti,plicable adj

multiprocessor (ˌmʌltɪˈprəʊsɛsə) n computing a number of central processing units linked together to enable parallel processing to take place

multipurpose vehicle n a large car, similar to a van, designed to carry up to eight passengers. Abbreviation: MPV

multi-skilled adj possessing or trained in more than one skill or area of expertise

multi-skilling n the practice of training employees to do a number of different tasks

multistage (ˈmʌltɪˌsteɪdʒ) adj 1 (of a rocket or missile) having several stages, each of which can be jettisoned after it has burnt out 2 (of a turbine, compressor, or supercharger) having more than one rotor 3 (of any process or device) having more than one stage

multistorey (ˌmʌltɪˈstɔːrɪ) adj 1 (of a building) having many storeys ▷ n 2 a multistorey car park

multitasking (ˈmʌltɪˌtɑːskɪŋ) n 1 computing the execution of various diverse tasks simultaneously 2 the carrying out of two or more tasks at the same time by one person

multitrack (ˈmʌltɪˌtræk) adj (in sound recording) using tape containing two or more tracks, usually four to twenty-four

multitude (ˈmʌltɪˌtjuːd) n 1 a large gathering of people 2 the multitude the common people 3 a large number 4 the state or quality of being numerous [c14: via Old French from Latin multitūdō]

multitudinous (ˌmʌltɪˈtjuːdɪnəs) adj 1 very numerous 2 rare great in extent, variety, etc 3 poetic crowded > ˌmultiˈtudinously adv > ˌmultiˈtudinousness n

multi-user adj (of a computer) capable of being used by several people at once

multivalent (ˌmʌltɪˈveɪlənt) adj another word for polyvalent > ˌmultiˈvalency n

multiverse (ˈmʌltɪˌvɜːs) n astronomy the aggregate of all existing matter, of which the universe is but a tiny fragment

mum[1] (mʌm) n chiefly Brit an informal word for mother[1] [c19: a child's word]

mum[2] (mʌm) adj 1 keeping information to oneself; silent ▷ n 2 mum's the word silence or secrecy is to be observed [c14: suggestive of closed lips]

mum[3] or **mumm** (mʌm) vb mums, mumming, mummed (intr) to act in a mummer's play [c16: verbal use of MUM[2]]

Mumbai (mʊmˈbaɪ) n a port in W India, capital of Maharashtra state, on the Arabian Sea: ceded by Portugal to England in 1661 and of major importance in British India; commercial and industrial centre, esp for cotton. Pop:11 914 398 (2001). Former English name: **Bombay**

mumble (ˈmʌmbˀl) vb 1 to utter indistinctly, as with the mouth partly closed; mutter 2 rare to chew (food) ineffectually or with difficulty ▷ n 3 an indistinct or low utterance or sound [c14 momelen, from MUM[2]] > ˈmumbler n > ˈmumbling adj > ˈmumblingly adv

mumbo jumbo (ˈmʌmbəʊ) n, pl mumbo jumbos 1 foolish religious reverence, ritual, or incantation 2 meaningless or unnecessarily complicated language

3 an object of superstitious awe or reverence [c18: probably from Mandingo *mama dyumbo*, name of a tribal god]

mu meson (mju:) *n* a former name for: **muon**

Mumford ('mʌmfəd) *n* **Lewis.** 1895–1990, US sociologist, whose works are chiefly concerned with the relationship between man and his environment. They include *The City in History* (1962) and *Roots of Contemporary Architecture* (1972)

mummer ('mʌmə) *n* **1** one of a group of masked performers in folk play or mime **2** *humorous or derogatory* an actor [c15: from Old French *momeur*, from *momer* to mime; related to *momon* mask]

Mummerset ('mʌməsɪt, -ˌsɛt) *n* an imitation West Country accent used in drama [c20: from MUMMER + (SOMER)SET]

mummery ('mʌmərɪ) *n, pl* **-meries 1** a performance by mummers **2** hypocritical or ostentatious ceremony

mummify ('mʌmɪˌfaɪ) *vb* **-fies, -fying, -fied 1** (*tr*) to preserve the body of (a human or animal) as a mummy **2** (*intr*) to dry up; shrivel > ˌmummifiˈcation *n*

mummy¹ ('mʌmɪ) *n, pl* **-mies 1** an embalmed or preserved body, esp as prepared for burial in ancient Egypt **2** a mass of pulp **3** a dark brown pigment [c14: from Old French *momie*, from Medieval Latin *mumia*, from Arabic *mūmiyah* asphalt, from Persian *mūm* wax]

mummy² ('mʌmɪ) *n, pl* **-mies** *chiefly Brit* a child's word for: **mother¹** [c19: variant of MUM¹]

mump¹ (mʌmp) *vb* (*intr*) *archaic* to be silent [c16 (to grimace, sulk, be silent): of imitative origin, alluding to the shape of the mouth when mumbling or chewing]

mump² (mʌmp) *vb* (*intr*) *archaic* to beg [c17: perhaps from Dutch *mompen* to cheat]

mumps (mʌmps) *n* (*functioning as singular or plural*) an acute contagious viral disease of the parotid salivary glands, characterized by swelling of the affected parts, fever, and pain beneath the ear: usually affects children [c16: from MUMP¹ (to grimace)] > 'mumpish *adj*

mumsy ('mʌmzɪ) *adj* **-sier, -siest** out of fashion; homely or drab

munch (mʌntʃ) *vb* to chew (food) steadily, esp with a crunching noise [c14 *monche*, of imitative origin; compare CRUNCH]

Munch (muŋk) *n* **Edvard** ('ɛdvard). 1863–1944, Norwegian painter and engraver, whose works, often on the theme of death, include *The Scream* (1893); a major influence on the expressionists, esp on *die Brücke*

München ('mynçən) *n* the German name for **Munich**

München-Gladbach (mynçən'glatbax) *n* the former name of: **Mönchengladbach**

mundane (mʌnˈdeɪn, mʌnˈdeɪn) *adj* **1** everyday, ordinary, or banal **2** relating to the world or worldly matters [c15: from French *mondain*, via Late Latin, from Latin *mundus* world] > 'mundanely *adv* > mun'danity *or* 'mundaneness *n*

mung (mʌŋ) *vb* (*tr*) *computing slang* to process (computer data) [c20: *m*(ash) *u*(ntil) *n*(o) *g*(ood)]

mung bean (mʌŋ) *n* **1** an E Asian bean plant, *Phaseolus aureus*, grown for forage and as the source of bean sprouts used in oriental cookery **2** the seed of this plant [c20 *mung*, changed from *mungo*, from Tamil *mūngu*, ultimately from Sanskrit *mudga*]

Munich ('mju:nɪk) *n* a city in S Germany, capital of the state of Bavaria, on the Isar River: became capital of Bavaria in 1508; headquarters of the Nazi movement in the 1920s; a major financial, commercial, and manufacturing centre. Pop: 1 247 873 (2003 est). German name: **München**

municipal (mju:ˈnɪsɪpˀl) *adj* of or relating to a town, city, or borough or its local government [c16: from Latin *mūnicipium* a free town, from *mūniceps* citizen from *mūnia* responsibilities + *capere* to take] > mu'nicipally *adv*

municipality (mju:ˌnɪsɪˈpælɪtɪ) *n, pl* **-ties 1** a city, town, or district enjoying some degree of local self-government **2** the governing body of such a unit

municipalize *or* **municipalise** (mju:ˈnɪsɪpəˌlaɪz) *vb* (*tr*) **1** to bring under municipal ownership or control **2** to make a municipality of > muˌnicipaliˈzation *or* muˌnicipaliˈsation *n*

munificent (mju:ˈnɪfɪsənt) *adj* **1** (of a person) very generous; bountiful **2** (of a gift) generous; liberal [c16: back formation from Latin *mūnificentia* liberality, from *mūnificus*, from *mūnus* gift + *facere* to make] > mu'nificence *or* mu'nificentness *adv*

muniments ('mju:nɪmənts) *pl n* *law* the title deeds and other documentary evidence relating to the title to land

munition (mju:ˈnɪʃən) *vb* (*tr*) to supply with munitions [c16: via French from Latin *mūnītiō* fortification, from *mūnīre* to fortify. See AMMUNITION]

munitions (mju:ˈnɪʃənz) *pl n* (*sometimes singular*) military equipment and stores, esp ammunition

Munnings ('mʌnɪŋz) *n* **Sir Alfred.** 1878–1959, British painter, best known for his horse paintings

Munro¹ (mʌnˈrəʊ) *n, pl* **Munros** *mountaineering* any separate mountain peak over 3000 feet high: originally used of Scotland only but now sometimes extended to other parts of the British Isles [c20: named after Hugh Thomas Munro (1856–1919), who published a list of these in 1891]

Munro² (mʌnˈrəʊ) *n* **1** **Alice**, original name *Alice Laidlaw*. born 1931, Canadian short-story writer; her books include *Lives of Girls and Women* (1971), *The Moons of Jupiter* (1982), and *The Love of a Good Woman* (1999) **2** **H(ector)** H(ugh), pen name Saki. 1870–1916, Scottish author, born in Burma (now Myanmar), noted for his collections of satirical short stories, such as *Reginald* (1904) and *Beasts and Superbeasts* (1914)

Munster ('mʌnstə) *n* a province of SW Republic of Ireland: the largest of the four provinces and historically a kingdom; consists of the counties of Clare, Cork, Kerry, Limerick, Tipperary, and Waterford. Capital: Cork. Pop: 1 100 614 (2002). Area: 24 125 sq km (9315 sq miles)

Münster (German 'mynstər) *n* a city in NW Germany, in North Rhine-Westphalia on the Dortmund-Ems Canal: one of the treaties comprising the Peace of Westphalia (1648) was signed here; became capital of Prussian Westphalia in 1815. Pop: 269 579 (2003 est)

Münsterberg ('munstəˌbɜːg) *n* **Hugo.** 1863–1916, German psychologist, in the US from 1897, noted for his pioneering work in applied psychology

munted ('mʌntɪd) *adj* *NZ sl* **1** (of an object) destroyed or ruined **2** (of a person) abnormal or peculiar [c20 from ?]

muntjac *or* **muntjak** ('mʌntˌdʒæk) *n* any small Asian deer of the genus *Muntiacus*, typically having a chestnut-brown coat, small antlers, and a barklike cry [c18: probably changed from Javanese *mindjangan* deer]

Müntzer ('muntzə; German 'myntzər) *n* **Thomas.** c. 1490–1525, German radical religious and political reformer; executed for organizing the Peasants' War (1524–25)

muon ('mju:ɒn) *n* a positive or negative elementary particle with a mass 207 times that of an electron and spin ½. It was originally called the mu meson but is now classified as a lepton [c20: short for MU MESON] > muonic (mju:'ɒnɪk) *adj*

muppet ('mʌpɪt) *n* *slang* a stupid person [c20: from the name for the puppets used in the television programme *The Muppet Show*]

mural ('mjʊərəl) *n* **1** a large painting or picture on a wall ▷ *adj* **2** of or relating to a wall [c15: from Latin *mūrālis*, from *mūrus* wall] > 'muralist *n*

Muralitharan (ˌmɜːrəˈlɪθərən) *n* **Muttiah** (məˈtaɪə). born 1972, Sri Lankan cricketer, a famous spin bowler; has played for Sri Lanka since 1992

Murasaki Shikibu (ˌmʊərɑːˈsɑːkiː ˈʃiːkiːˌbuː) *n* 11th-century Japanese court lady, author of *The Tale of Genji*, perhaps the world's first novel

Murat (French myra) *n* **Joachim** (ʒɔaʃɛ̃). 1767-1815, French marshal, during the Napoleonic Wars; king of Naples (1808–15)

Murchison ('mɜːtʃɪsˀn) *n* **Sir Roderick Impey.** 1792–1871, Scottish geologist: played a major role in establishing parts of the geological time scale, esp the Silurian, Permian, and Devonian periods

Murcia (Spanish 'murθja) *n* **1** a region and ancient kingdom of SE Spain, on the Mediterranean: taken by the Moors in the 8th century; an independent Muslim kingdom in the 11th and 12th centuries **2** a city in SE

Spain, capital of Murcia province: trading centre for a rich agricultural region; silk industry; university (1915). Pop: 391 146 (2003 est)

murder ('mɜːdə) n **1** the unlawful premeditated killing of one human being by another. See **manslaughter 2** *informal* something dangerous, difficult, or unpleasant: *driving around London is murder* **3 cry blue murder** *informal* to make an outcry **4 get away with murder** *informal* to escape censure; do as one pleases ▷ vb (*mainly tr*) **5** (*also intr*) to kill (someone) unlawfully with premeditation or during the commission of a crime **6** to kill brutally **7** *informal* to destroy; ruin **8** *informal* to defeat completely; beat decisively: *the home team murdered their opponents* [Old English *morthor*; related to Old English *morth*, Old Norse *morth*, Latin *mors* death; compare French *meurtre*] > 'murderer n > 'murderess *fem* n

murderous ('mɜːdərəs) adj **1** intending, capable of, or guilty of murder **2** *informal* very dangerous, difficult, or unpleasant: *a murderous road* > 'murderously adv > 'murderousness n

Murdoch ('mɜːdɒk) n **1** Dame (**Jean**) **Iris**. 1919–99, British writer. Her books include *The Bell* (1958), *A Severed Head* (1961), *The Sea, The Sea* (1978), which won the Booker Prize, *The Philosopher's Pupil* (1983), and *Existentialists and Mystics* (1997) **2** (**Keith**) **Rupert**. born 1931, US publisher and media entrepreneur, born in Australia; chairman of News International Ltd (including Times Newspapers Ltd), 20th Century-Fox, and HarperCollins

Mureş ('muəreʃ) n a river in SE central Europe, rising in central Romania in the Carpathian Mountains and flowing west to the Tisza River at Szeged, Hungary. Length: 885 km (550 miles). Hungarian name: **Maros**

murex ('mjuəreks) n, pl **murices** ('mjuərɪˌsiːz) any of various spiny-shelled marine gastropods of the genus *Murex* and related genera; formerly used as a source of the dye Tyrian purple [c16: from Latin *mūrex* purple fish; related to Greek *muax* sea mussel]

muriatic acid (ˌmjuərɪ'ætɪk) n a former name for **hydrochloric acid** [c17: from Latin *muriāticus* pickled, from *muria* brine]

Murillo (mjuə'rɪləu; *Spanish* mu'riʎo) n **Bartolomé Esteban** (bartolo'me es'teβan). 1618–82, Spanish painter, esp of religious subjects and beggar children

murk or **mirk** (mɜːk) n **1** gloomy darkness ▷ adj **2** an archaic variant of **murky** [c13: probably from Old Norse *myrkr* darkness; compare Old English *mirce* dark]

murky or **mirky** ('mɜːkɪ) adj **murkier**, **murkiest** or **mirkier**, **mirkiest 1** gloomy or dark **2** cloudy or impenetrable as with smoke or fog > 'murkily or 'mirkily adv > 'murkiness or 'mirkiness n

Murman Coast ('muəmən) or **Murmansk Coast** n a coastal region of NW Russia, in the north of the Kola Peninsula within the Arctic Circle, but ice-free

Murmansk (*Russian* 'murmənsk) n a port in NW Russia, on the Kola Inlet of the Barents Sea: founded in 1915; the world's largest town north of the Arctic Circle, with a large fishing fleet. Pop: 316 000 (2005 est)

murmur ('mɜːmə) n **1** a continuous low indistinct sound, as of distant voices **2** an indistinct utterance: *a murmur of satisfaction* **3** a complaint; grumble: *he made no murmur at my suggestion* **4** *med* any abnormal soft blowing sound heard within the body, usually over the chest ▷ vb **-murs**, **-muring**, **-mured 5** to utter (something) in a murmur **6** (*intr*) to complain in a murmur [c14: as n, from Latin *murmur*; vb via Old French *murmurer* from Latin *murmurāre* to rumble] > 'murmurer n > 'murmuring n, adj > 'murmurously adj

murphy ('mɜːfɪ) n, pl **-phies** a dialect or informal word for: **potato** [c19: from the common Irish surname *Murphy*]

Murphy ('mɜːfɪ) n **1 Alex**. born 1939, British rugby league player and coach **2 Eddie**, full name *Edward Regan Murphy*. born 1951, US film actor and comedian. His films include *48 Hours* (1982), *Beverly Hills Cop* (1984), *Coming to America* (1988), and *Dr Dolittle* (1998) **3 William Parry**. 1892–1987, US physician: with G. R. Minot, he discovered the liver treatment for anaemia and they shared, with G. H. Whipple, the Nobel prize for physiology or medicine in 1934

Murphy-O'Connor ('mɜːfɪəu'kɒnə) n **Cormac**. born 1932, British cardinal, Archbishop of Westminster from 2000

murrain ('mʌrɪn) n *archaic* **1** any plaguelike disease in cattle **2** a plague [c14: from Old French *morine*, from *morir* to die, from Latin *morī*]

Murray[1] ('mʌrɪ) n a river in SE Australia, rising in New South Wales and flowing northwest into SE South Australia, then south into the sea at Encounter Bay: the main river of Australia, important for irrigation and power. Length: 2590 km (1609 miles)

Murray[2] ('mʌrɪ) n **1** 1st Earl of. See (1st Earl of): **Moray**[1] **2** Sir (**George**) **Gilbert** (**Aimé**). 1866–1957, British classical scholar, born in Australia: noted for his verse translations of Greek dramatists, esp Euripides **3** Sir **James Augustus Henry**. 1837–1915, Scottish lexicographer; one of the original editors (1879–1915) of what became the *Oxford English Dictionary* **4 Les**, full name *Leslie Allan Murray*. born 1938, Australian poet; his collections include *The Weatherboard Cathedral* (1969), *The Daylight Moon* (1987), *Subhuman Redneck Poems* (1996), and *The Biplane Houses* (2007) **5** Murray of Epping Forest, Baron, title of *Lionel Murray*, known as *Len*. 1922–2004, British trades union leader; general secretary of the Trades Union Congress (1973–84)

Murray cod n a large Australian freshwater fish, *Maccullochella peeli*, chiefly of the Murray and Darling rivers

Murrumbidgee (ˌmʌrəm'bɪdʒɪ) n a river in SE Australia, rising in S New South Wales and flowing north and west to the Murray River: important for irrigation. Length: 1690 km (1050 miles)

murther ('mɜːðə) n, vb an archaic word for **murder** > 'murtherer n

mus. *abbreviation* **1** music **2** museum

MusB or **MusBac** *abbreviation* Bachelor of Music

muscadel or **muscadelle** (ˌmʌskə'dɛl) n another name for **muscatel**

muscadine ('mʌskədɪn, -ˌdaɪn) n **1** a woody climbing vitaceous plant, *Vitis rotundifolia*, of the southeastern US **2** Also called: **scuppernong**, **bullace grape** the thick-skinned musk-scented purple grape produced by this plant: used to make wine [c16: from MUSCADEL]

muscae volitantes ('mʌsiː vɒlɪ'tæntiːz) pl n *pathol* moving black specks or threads seen before the eyes, caused by opaque fragments floating in the vitreous humour or a defect in the lens [c18: New Latin: flying flies]

muscat ('mʌskət, -kæt) n **1** any of various grapevines that produce sweet white grapes used for making wine or raisins **2** another name for **muscatel** (sense 1) [c16: via Old French from Provençal *muscat*, from *musc* MUSK]

Muscat ('mʌskət, -kæt) n the capital of the Sultanate of Oman, a port on the Gulf of Oman: a Portuguese port from the early 16th century; controlled by Persia (1650–1741). Pop: 689 000 (2005 est). Arabic name: **Masqaṭ**

Muscat and Oman n the former name (until 1970) of (the Sultanate of) **Oman**

muscatel (ˌmʌskə'tɛl), **muscadel** or **muscadelle** n **1** Also called: **muscat** a rich sweet wine made from muscat grapes **2** the grape or raisin from a muscat vine [c14: from Old French *muscadel*, from Old Provençal, from *moscadel*, from *muscat* musky. See MUSK]

muscle ('mʌsəl) n **1** a tissue composed of bundles of elongated cells capable of contraction and relaxation to produce movement in an organ or part **2** an organ composed of muscle tissue **3** strength or force ▷ vb **4** (*intr*; often foll by *in*, *on*, etc) *informal* to force one's way (in) [c16: from medical Latin *musculus* little mouse, from the imagined resemblance of some muscles to mice, from Latin *mūs* mouse] > 'muscly adj

muscle-bound adj **1** having overdeveloped and inelastic muscles **2** lacking flexibility

muscleman ('mʌsəlˌmæn) n, pl **-men 1** a man with highly developed muscles **2** a henchman employed by a gangster to intimidate or use violence upon victims

Muscovite ('mʌskəˌvaɪt) n **1** a native or inhabitant of Moscow ▷ adj **2** an archaic word for **Russian**

Muscovy ('mʌskəvɪ) n **1** a Russian principality (13th to

16th centuries), of which Moscow was the capital **2** an archaic name for **Russia, Moscow**

Muscovy duck or **musk duck** n a large crested widely domesticated South American duck, *Cairina moschata*, having a greenish-black plumage with white markings and a large red caruncle on the bill [C17: originally *musk duck*, a name later mistakenly associated with Muscovy]

muscular ('mʌskjʊlə) adj **1** having well-developed muscles; brawny **2** of, relating to, or consisting of muscle [C17: from New Latin *muscularis*, from *musculus* MUSCLE] > **muscularity** (ˌmʌskjʊ'lærɪtɪ) n > 'muscularly adv

muscular dystrophy n a genetic disease characterized by progressive deterioration and wasting of muscle fibres, causing difficulty in walking

musculature ('mʌskjʊlətʃə) n **1** the arrangement of muscles in an organ or part **2** the total muscular system of an organism

musculoskeletal (ˌmʌskjʊləʊ'skɛlɪt²l) adj of or relating to the skeleton and musculature taken together

MusD or **MusDoc** abbreviation Doctor of Music

muse¹ (mjuːz) vb **1** (when intr, often foll by on or about) to reflect (about) or ponder (on), usually in silence **2** (intr) to gaze thoughtfully ▷ n **3** archaic a state of abstraction [C14: from Old French *muser*, perhaps from *mus* snout, from Medieval Latin *mūsus*]

muse² (mjuːz) n a goddess that inspires a creative artist, esp a poet [C14: from Old French, from Latin *Mūsa*, from Greek *Mousa* a Muse]

Muse (mjuːz) n *Greek myth* any of nine sister goddesses, each of whom was regarded as the protectress of a different art or science. Daughters of Zeus and Mnemosyne, the nine are Calliope, Clio, Erato, Euterpe, Melpomene, Polyhymnia, Terpsichore, Thalia, and Urania

musette (mjuː'zɛt; French myzɛt) n **1** a type of bagpipe with a bellows popular in France during the 17th and 18th centuries **2** a dance, with a drone bass originally played by a musette [C14: from Old French, diminutive of *muse* bagpipe]

museum (mjuː'zɪəm) n a place or building where objects of historical, artistic, or scientific interest are exhibited, preserved, or studied [C17: via Latin from Greek *Mouseion* home of the Muses, from *Mousa* MUSE]

museum piece n **1** an object of sufficient age or interest to be kept in a museum **2** informal a person or thing regarded as antiquated or decrepit

Museveni (ˌmʊsə'veɪnɪ) n Yoweri. born 1944, Ugandan politician; president of Uganda from 1986

Musgrave ('mʌzɡreɪv) n Thea. born 1928, Scottish composer, noted esp for her operas

mush¹ (mʌʃ) n **1** a soft pulpy mass or consistency **2** US a thick porridge made from corn meal **3** informal cloying sentimentality ▷ vb **4** (tr) to reduce (a substance) to a soft pulpy mass [C17: from obsolete *moose* porridge; probably related to MASH; compare Old English *mōs* food]

mush² (mʌʃ) Canadian ▷ interj **1** an order to dogs in a sled team to start up or go faster ▷ vb **2** to travel by or drive a dog sled ▷ n **3** a journey with a dogsled [C19: perhaps from French *marchez* or *marchons*, imperatives of *marcher* to advance]

Musharraf (mə'ʃærəf) n Pervez ('pɛrveɪz). born 1943, Pakistani general and politician; became military leader of Pakistan following a coup in 2001; president from 2002

mushroom ('mʌʃruːm, -rʊm) n **1 a** the fleshy spore-producing body of any of various basidiomycetous fungi, typically consisting of a cap (pileus) at the end of a stem arising from an underground mycelium. Some species, such as the field mushroom, are edible. See **toadstool b** (as modifier): *mushroom soup* **2 a** something resembling a mushroom in shape or rapid growth **b** (as modifier): *mushroom expansion* ▷ vb (intr) **3** to grow rapidly: *demand mushroomed overnight* **4** to assume a mushroom-like shape [C15: from Old French *mousseron*, from Late Latin *mussiriō*, of obscure origin]

mushroom cloud n the large mushroom-shaped cloud of dust, debris, etc produced by a nuclear explosion

mushy ('mʌʃɪ) adj mushier, mushiest **1** soft and pulpy

2 informal excessively sentimental or emotional > 'mushily adv > 'mushiness n

music ('mjuːzɪk) n **1** an art form consisting of sequences of sounds in time, esp tones of definite pitch organized melodically, harmonically, rhythmically and according to tone colour **2** the sounds so produced, esp by singing or musical instruments **3** written or printed music, such as a score or set of parts **4** any sequence of sounds perceived as pleasing or harmonious **5 face the music** informal to confront the consequences of one's actions [C13: via Old French from Latin *mūsica*, from Greek *mousikē (tekhnē)* (art) belonging to the Muses, from *Mousa* MUSE]

musical ('mjuːzɪk²l) adj **1** of, relating to, or used in music **2** harmonious; melodious: *musical laughter* **3** talented in or fond of music **4** involving or set to music ▷ n **5** Also called: **musical comedy** a light romantic play or film having dialogue interspersed with songs and dances > 'musically adv > 'musicalness or ˌmusi'cality n

musical chairs n (functioning as singular) **1** a party game in which players walk around chairs while music is played, there being one fewer chair than players. Whenever the music stops, the player who fails to find a chair is eliminated **2** any situation involving a number of people in a series of interrelated changes

musical ride n Canadian a display by riders on horseback of manoeuvres to music, esp by members of the Royal Canadian Mounted Police

music box or **musical box** n a mechanical instrument that plays tunes by means of pins on a revolving cylinder striking the tuned teeth of a comblike metal plate, contained in a box

music centre n a single hi-fi unit containing e.g. a turntable, amplifier, radio, cassette player, and compact disc player

music drama n **1** an opera in which the musical and dramatic elements are of equal importance and strongly interfused **2** the genre of such operas [C19: translation of German *Musikdrama*, coined by Wagner to describe his later operas]

music hall n chiefly Brit **1** a variety entertainment consisting of songs, comic turns, etc. US and Canadian name: **vaudeville 2** a theatre at which such entertainments are staged

musician (mjuː'zɪʃən) n a person who plays or composes music, esp as a profession > **mu'sicianly** adj > **musi'cianship** n

musicology (ˌmjuːzɪ'kɒlədʒɪ) n the scholarly study of music > **musicological** (ˌmjuːzɪkə'lɒdʒɪk²l) adj > ˌmusi'cologist n

music paper n paper ruled or printed with a stave for writing music

Musil (German 'muːzɪl) n Robert ('roːbɛrt). 1880–1942, Austrian novelist, whose novel *The Man Without Qualities* (1930–42) is an ironic examination of contemporary ills

musique concrète French (myzik kɔkrɛt) n another term for **concrete music**

musk (mʌsk) n **1** a strong-smelling glandular secretion of the male musk deer, used in perfumery **2** a similar substance produced by certain other animals, such as the civet and otter, or manufactured synthetically **3** any of several scrophulariaceous plants of the genus *Mimulus*, esp the North American *M. moschatus*, which has yellow flowers and was formerly cultivated for its musky scent **4** the smell of musk or a similar heady smell **5** (modifier) containing or resembling musk: *musk oil; a musk flavour* [C14: from Late Latin *muscus*, from Greek *moskhos*, from Persian *mushk*, probably from Sanskrit *mushkā* scrotum (from the appearance of the musk deer's musk bag), diminutive of *mūsh* MOUSE]

musk deer n a small central Asian mountain deer, *Moschus moschiferus*. The male has long tusklike canine teeth and secretes musk

musk duck n **1** another name for **Muscovy duck 2** a duck, *Biziura lobata*, inhabiting swamps, lakes, and streams in Australia. The male has a leathery pouch beneath the bill and emits a musky odour

muskeg ('mʌsˌkɛɡ) n chiefly Canadian **1** undrained boggy land characterized by sphagnum moss vegetation **2** a bog or swamp of this nature [C19: from Algonquian: grassy swamp]

muskellunge ('mʌskə,lʌndʒ), **maskalonge** ('mæskə,lɒndʒ) *or* **maskanonge** ('mæskə,nɒndʒ) *n*, *pl* -lunges, -longes, -nonges *or* -lunge, -longe, -nonge a large North American freshwater game fish, *Esox masquinongy*: family Esocidae (pikes, etc). Often (informal) shortened to: **musky¹** [C18 *maskinunga*, of Algonquian origin; compare Ojibwa *mashkinonge* big pike]

musket ('mʌskɪt) *n* a long-barrelled muzzle-loading shoulder gun used between the 16th and 18th centuries by infantry soldiers [C16: from French *mousquet*, from Italian *moschetto* arrow, earlier: sparrow hawk, from *moscha* a fly, from Latin *musca*]

musketeer (,mʌskɪ'tɪə) *n* (formerly) a soldier armed with a musket

musketry ('mʌskɪtrɪ) *n* **1** muskets or musketeers collectively **2** the technique of using small arms

Muskie ('mʌskɪ) *n* Edmund (Sixtus). 1914–96, US Democratic politician: Governor of Maine (1955–59): senator for Maine (1959–80): Secretary of State (1980–81)

muskmelon ('mʌsk,mɛlən) *n* **1** any of several varieties of the melon *Cucumis melo*, such as the cantaloupe and honeydew **2** the fruit of any of these melons, having ribbed or warty rind and sweet yellow, white, or green flesh with a musky aroma

musk ox *n* a large bovid mammal, *Ovibos moschatus*, which has a dark shaggy coat, short legs, and widely spaced downward-curving horns and emits a musky smell: now confined to the tundras of Canada and Greenland

muskrat ('mʌsk,ræt) *n*, *pl* -rats *or* -rat **1** a North American beaver-like amphibious rodent, *Ondatra zibethica*, closely related to but larger than the voles: family Cricetidae **2** the brown fur of this animal ▷ Also called: musquash [C17: by folk etymology, from the same source as MUSQUASH]

musk rose *n* a prickly shrubby Mediterranean rose, *Rosa moschata*, cultivated for its white musk-scented flowers

musky ('mʌskɪ) *adj* muskier, muskiest resembling the smell of musk; having a heady or pungent sweet aroma > 'muskiness *n*

Muslim ('muzlɪm, 'mʌz-) *or* **Moslem** *n*, *pl* -lims *or* -lim **1** a follower of the religion of Islam ▷ *adj* **2** of or relating to Islam, its doctrines, culture, etc [C17: from Arabic, literally: one who surrenders] > 'Muslimism *or* 'Moslemism *n* old-fashioned, dismissive

muslin ('mʌzlɪn) *n* a fine plain-weave cotton fabric [C17: from French *mousseline*, from Italian *mussolina*, from Arabic *mawṣiliy* of Mosul, from *Mawṣil* Mosul, Iraq, where it was first produced]

muso ('mju:zəʊ) *n*, *pl* musos slang **1** Brit derogatory a musician, esp a pop musician, regarded as being overconcerned with technique rather than musical content or expression **2** Austral any musician, esp a professional one

musquash ('mʌskwɒʃ) *n* another name for muskrat, used esp to refer to its fur [C17: from Algonquian: compare Natick *musquash*, Abnaki *muskwessu*]

muss (mʌs) US & Canadian informal ▷ *vb* **1** (tr; often foll by *up*) to make untidy; rumple ▷ *n* **2** a state of disorder; muddle [C19: probably a blend of MESS + FUSS] > 'mussy *adj*

mussel ('mʌsəl) *n* **1** any of various marine bivalves of the genus *Mytilus* and related genera, esp *M. edulis* (edible mussel), having a dark slightly elongated shell and living attached to rocks, etc **2** any of various freshwater bivalves of the genera *Anodonta*, *Unio*, etc, attached to rocks, sand, etc having a flattened oval shell (a source of mother-of-pearl). The zebra mussel, *Dreissena polymorpha*, can be a serious nuisance in water mains [Old English *muscle*, from Vulgar Latin *muscula* (unattested), from Latin *musculus*, diminutive of *mūs* mouse]

musselcracker ('mʌsəl,krækə) *n* South African a large variety of sea bream, *Sparodon durbanensis*, that feeds on shellfish and is a popular food and game fish

Musset (French mysɛ) *n* Alfred de (alfred də). 1810–57, French romantic poet and dramatist: his works include the play *Lorenzaccio* (1834) and the lyrics *Les Nuits* (1835–37),

tracing his love affair with George Sand

Mussolini (,mʊsə'li:nɪ; *Italian* musso'li:ni) *n* Benito (be'ni:to) known as *il Duce*. 1883–1945, Italian Fascist dictator. After the Fascist march on Rome, he was appointed prime minister by King Victor Emmanuel III (1922) and assumed dictatorial powers. He annexed Abyssinia and allied Italy with Germany (1936), entering World War II in 1940. He was forced to resign following the Allied invasion of Sicily (1943) and was eventually shot by Italian partisans

Mussorgsky *or* **Moussorgsky** (mʊ'sɔ:gskɪ; *Russian* 'musərkskij) *n* Modest Petrovich (ma'dɛst pɪ'trɔvitʃ). 1839–81, Russian composer. He translated inflections of speech into melody in such works as the song cycle *Songs and Dances of Death* (1875–77) and the opera *Boris Godunov* (1874). His other works include *Pictures at an Exhibition* (1874) for piano

Mussulman *or* **Mussalman** ('mʌsəlmən) *n*, *pl* -mans an archaic word for **Muslim** [C16: from Persian *Musulmān* (pl) from Arabic *Muslimūn*, pl of MUSLIM]

must¹ (mʌst; *unstressed* məst, məs) *vb* (takes an infinitive without *to* or an implied infinitive) **1** used as an auxiliary to express obligation or compulsion: *you must pay your dues*. In this sense, *must* does not form a negative. If used with a negative infinitive it indicates obligatory prohibition **2** used as an auxiliary to indicate necessity: *I must go to the bank tomorrow* **3** used as an auxiliary to indicate the probable correctness of a statement: *he must be there by now* **4** used as an auxiliary to indicate inevitability: *all good things must come to an end* **5** used as an auxiliary to express resolution **a** on the part of the speaker when used with I or we: *I must finish this* **b** on the part of another or others as imputed to them by the speaker, when used with *you, he, she, they*, etc: *let him get drunk if he must* **6** (used emphatically) used as an auxiliary to express conviction or certainty on the part of the speaker: *he must have reached the town by now, surely; you must be joking* **7** (foll by *away*) used with an implied verb of motion to express compelling haste: *I must away* ▷ *n* **8** an essential or necessary thing: *strong shoes are a must for hill walking* [Old English *mōste* past tense of *mōtan* to be allowed, be obliged; related to Old Saxon *mōtan*, Old High German *muozan*, German *müssen*]

must² (mʌst) *n* the newly pressed juice of grapes or other fruit ready for fermentation [Old English, from Latin *mustum* new wine, must, from *mustus* (adj) newborn]

must³ (mʌst) *n* mustiness or mould [C17: back formation from MUSTY]

must- *combining form* indicating that something is highly recommended or desirable: *a must-see film; this season's must-haves*

mustache (mə'stɑ:ʃ) *n* the US spelling of moustache

mustachio (mə'stɑ:ʃɪ,əʊ) *n*, *pl* -chios (*often plural when considered as two halves*) often humorous a moustache, esp when bushy or elaborately shaped [C16: from Spanish *mostacho* and Italian *mostaccio*]

mustachioed (mə'stɑ:ʃɪ,əʊd) *adj* often humorous having a moustache, esp when bushy or elaborately shaped

Mustafa Kemal ('mʊstəfə kə'mɑ:l) *n* See Atatürk

mustang ('mʌstæŋ) *n* a small breed of horse, often wild or half wild, found in the southwestern US [C19: from Mexican Spanish *mestengo*, from *mesta* a group of stray animals]

mustard ('mʌstəd) *n* **1** any of several Eurasian plants of the genus *Brassica*, esp black mustard and white mustard, having yellow or white flowers and slender pods and cultivated for their pungent seeds: family Brassicaceae (crucifers) **2** a paste made from the powdered seeds of any of these plants and used as a condiment **3 a** a brownish-yellow colour **b** (*as adjective*): *a mustard carpet* **4** slang, chiefly US zest or enthusiasm [C13: from Old French *moustarde*, from Latin *mustum* MUST², since the original condiment was made by adding must]

mustard and cress *n* seedlings of white mustard and garden cress, used in salads

mustard gas *n* an oily liquid vesicant compound used in chemical warfare. Its vapour causes blindness and burns. Formula: $(ClCH_2CH_2)_2S$

mustard plaster n med a mixture of powdered black mustard seeds and an adhesive applied to the skin for its relaxing, stimulating, or counterirritant effects

musteline ('mʌstɪˌlaɪn, -lɪn) adj of, relating to, or belonging to the *Mustelidae*, a family of typically predatory mammals including weasels, ferrets, minks, polecats, badgers, skunks, and otters: order *Carnivora* (carnivores) [c17: from Latin *mustēlīnus*, from *mustēla* weasel, from *mūs* mouse + -*tēla*, of unknown origin]

muster ('mʌstə) vb 1 to call together (numbers of men) for duty, inspection, etc, or (of men) to assemble in this way 2 US a **muster in** to enlist into military service b **muster out** to discharge from military service 3 (tr; sometimes foll by *up*) to summon or gather: *to muster one's arguments; to muster up courage* ▷ n 4 an assembly of military personnel for duty, inspection, etc 5 a collection, assembly, or gathering 6 *Austral & NZ* the rounding up of livestock 7 **pass muster** to be acceptable [c14: from old French *moustrer*, from Latin *monstrāre* to show, from *monstrum* portent, omen]

musth or **must** (mʌst) n (often preceded by *in*) a state of frenzied sexual excitement in the males of certain large mammals, esp elephants, associated with discharge from a gland between the ear and eye [c19: from Urdu *mast*, from Persian: drunk]

must-have n 1 an essential possession: *the mobile phone is now a must-have for children* ▷ adj 2 essential: *a must-have fashion accessory*

musty ('mʌstɪ) adj -tier, -tiest 1 smelling or tasting old, stale, or mouldy 2 old-fashioned, dull, or hackneyed: *musty ideas* [c16: perhaps a variant of obsolete *moisty*, influenced by MUST³] > 'mustily adv > 'mustiness n

mutable ('mjuːtəb³l) adj able to or tending to change [c14: from Latin *mūtābilis* fickle, from *mūtāre* to change] > ˌmutaˈbility or less commonly 'mutableness n > 'mutably adv

mutagen ('mjuːtədʒən) n a substance or agent that can induce genetic mutation [c20: from MUTATION + -GEN] > mutagenic (ˌmjuːtəˈdʒɛnɪk) adj

mutagenesis (ˌmjuːtəˈdʒɛnɪsɪs) n *genetics* the generation, usually intentional, of mutations [c20: from MUTATION + -CENESIS]

mutant ('mjuːtᵊnt) n 1 Also called: **mutation** an animal, organism, or gene that has undergone mutation ▷ adj 2 of, relating to, undergoing, or resulting from change or mutation [c20: from Latin *mutāre* to change]

Mutare (muːˈtɑːrɪ) n a city in E Zimbabwe, near the Mozambique border: rail and trade centre in a mining and tobacco-growing region. Pop: 160 000 (2005 est). Former name (until 1982): **Umtali**

mutate (mjuːˈteɪt) vb to undergo or cause to undergo mutation [c19: from Latin *mūtātus* changed, from *mūtāre* to change]

mutation (mjuːˈteɪʃən) n 1 the act or process of mutating; change; alteration 2 a change or alteration 3 a change in the chromosomes or genes of a cell. When this change occurs in the gametes the structure and development of the resultant offspring may be affected 4 another word for: **mutant** (sense 1) 5 a physical characteristic of an individual resulting from this type of chromosomal change 6 *phonetics* a (in Germanic languages) another name for: **umlaut** b (in Celtic languages) a phonetic change in certain initial consonants caused by a preceding word > muˈtational adj > muˈtationally adv

mutatis mutandis Latin (muːˈtɑːtɪs muːˈtændɪs) the necessary changes having been made

mutch (mʌtʃ) n a close-fitting linen cap formerly worn by women and children in Scotland [c15: from Middle Dutch *mutse* cap, from Medieval Latin *almucia* ALMUCE]

mute (mjuːt) adj 1 not giving out sound or speech; silent 2 unable to speak; dumb 3 unspoken or unexpressed 4 *law* (of a person arraigned on indictment) refusing to answer a charge 5 *phonetics* another word for: **plosive** 6 (of a letter in a word) silent ▷ n 7 a person who is unable to speak 8 *law* a person who refuses to plead when arraigned on indictment for an offence 9 any of various devices used to soften the tone of stringed or brass instruments 10 *phonetics* a plosive consonant; stop 11 a silent letter 12 an actor in a dumb show 13 a hired mourner at a funeral ▷ vb (tr) 14 to reduce the volume of (a musical instrument) by means of a mute, soft pedal, etc 15 to subdue the strength of (a colour, tone, lighting, etc) [c14 *muwet* from Old French *mu*, from Latin *mūtus* silent] > 'mutely adv > 'muteness n

- ● USAGE Using this word to refer to people without
- ● speech is considered outdated and offensive and
- ● should be avoided. The phrase *profoundly deaf* is a
- ● suitable alternative in many contexts.

muted ('mjuːtɪd) adj 1 (of a sound or colour) softened 2 (of an emotion or action) subdued or restrained 3 (of a musical instrument) being played while fitted with a mute

mute swan n a Eurasian swan, *Cygnus olor*, with a pure white plumage, an orange-red bill with a black base, and a curved neck

mutha ('mʌðə) n *offensive, taboo, slang, chiefly US* short for **motherfucker** [c20: from a pronunciation of *mother*]

muti ('mʊtɪ) n *South African informal* medicine, esp herbal medicine [from Zulu *umuthi* tree, medicine]

Muti ('mʊtɪ) n **Riccardo** (rɪˈkɑːdəʊ). born 1941, Italian conductor: musical director of Philharmonia Orchestra, London (1979–82), Philadelphia Orchestra (1980–92), and La Scala, Milan (1986–2005)

mutilate ('mjuːtɪˌleɪt) vb (tr) 1 to deprive of a limb, essential part, etc; maim; dismember 2 to mar, expurgate, or damage (a text, book, etc) [c16: from Latin *mutilāre* to cut off; related to *mutilus* maimed] > ˌmutiˈlation n > 'mutiˌlative adj > 'mutiˌlator n

mutineer (ˌmjuːtɪˈnɪə) n a person who mutinies

mutinous ('mjuːtɪnəs) adj 1 openly rebellious or disobedient 2 characteristic or indicative of mutiny > 'mutinously adv > 'mutinousness n

mutiny ('mjuːtɪnɪ) n, pl -nies 1 open rebellion against constituted authority, esp by seamen or soldiers against their officers ▷ vb -nies, -nying, -nied 2 (intr) to engage in mutiny [c16: from obsolete *mutine*, from Old French *mutin* rebellious, from *meute* mutiny, ultimately from Latin *movēre* to move]

mutism ('mjuːtɪzəm) n 1 the state of being mute 2 *psychiatry* a a refusal to speak although the mechanism of speech is not damaged b the lack of development of speech, due usually to early deafness

Mutsuhito (ˌmuːtsʊˈhiːtəʊ) n See **Meiji**

mutt (mʌt) n *slang* 1 an inept, ignorant, or stupid person 2 a mongrel dog; cur [c20: shortened from MUTTONHEAD]

mutter ('mʌtə) vb 1 to utter (something) in a low and indistinct tone 2 (intr) to grumble or complain 3 (intr) to make a low continuous murmuring sound ▷ n 4 a muttered sound or complaint [c14 *moteren*; related to Norwegian (dialect) *mutra*, Old High German *mutilōn*; compare Old English *mōtian* to speak] > 'muttering n, adj

Mutter ('mʊtə) n **Anne-Sophie**. born 1963, German violinist

mutton ('mʌtᵊn) n 1 the flesh of sheep, esp of mature sheep, used as food 2 **mutton dressed as lamb** an older woman dressed up to look young [c13 *moton* sheep, from Old French, from Medieval Latin *multō*, of Celtic origin; the term was adopted in printing to distinguish the pronunciation of *em quad* from *en quad*] > 'muttony adj

muttonbird ('mʌtᵊnˌbɜːd) n 1 *Austral* any of several shearwaters, having a dark plumage with greyish underparts, esp the sooty shearwater (*Puffinus griseus*) of New Zealand, which is collected for food by Māoris. It inhabits the Pacific Ocean and in summer nests in Australia and New Zealand 2 any of various petrels esp the short tailed shearwater, *Puffinus tenuirostris*, which inhabits the Pacific Ocean and in summer nests in S Australia [c19: so named because their cooked flesh is claimed to taste like mutton]

mutton chop n a piece of mutton from the loin

muttonchops ('mʌtᵊnˌtʃɒps) pl n side whiskers trimmed in the shape of chops, widening out from the temples

muttonhead ('mʌtᵊnˌhɛd) n *slang* a stupid or ignorant person; fool > 'muttonˌheaded adj

Muttra ('mʌtrə) n the former name of **Mathura**

mutual ('mjuːtʃʊəl) adj 1 experienced or expressed by each of two or more people or groups about the other;

reciprocal: *mutual distrust* **2** common to or shared by both or all of two or more parties: *a mutual friend; mutual interests* **3** denoting an insurance company, etc, in which the policyholders share the profits and expenses and there are no shareholders [C15: from Old French *mutuel*, from Latin *mūtuus* reciprocal (originally: borrowed); related to *mūtāre* to change] > **mutuality** (ˌmjuːtjʊˈælɪtɪ) *or* **'mutualness** *n* > **'mutually** *adv*

● **USAGE** The use of *mutual* to mean *common to or shared by*
● *two or more parties* was formerly considered incorrect,
● but is now acceptable. Tautologous use of *mutual*
● should be avoided: *cooperation* (not *mutual cooperation*)
● *between the two countries*

mutual induction *n* the production of an electromotive force in a circuit by a current change in a second circuit magnetically linked to the first

mutual insurance *n* a system of insurance by which all policyholders become company members under contract to pay premiums into a common fund out of which claims are paid. See also **mutual** (sense 3)

mutuel ('mjuːtjʊəl) *n* short for **pari-mutuel**

muu-muu ('muːˌmuː) *n* a loose brightly-coloured dress worn by women in Hawaii [from Hawaiian]

Muybridge ('maɪbrɪdʒ) *n* **Eadweard** ('ɛdwəd), original name *Edward James Muggeridge*. 1830–1904, US photographer, born in England; noted for his high-speed photographic studies of animals and people in motion

Muzak ('mjuːzæk) *n* trademark recorded light music played in shops, restaurants, factories, etc, to entertain, increase sales or production, etc

muzhik, moujik *or* **mujik** ('muːʒɪk) *n* a Russian peasant, esp under the tsars [C16: from Russian: peasant]

Muzorewa (ˌmuzəˈreɪwə) *n* **Abel (Tendekayi)** ('eɪbˀl) born 1925, Zimbabwean Methodist bishop and politician; president of the African National Council (1971–85). He was one of the negotiators of an internal settlement (1978–79); prime minister of Rhodesia (1979)

muzzle ('mʌzˀl) *n* **1** the projecting part of the face, usually the jaws and nose, of animals such as the dog and horse **2** a guard or strap fitted over an animal's nose and jaws to prevent it biting or eating **3** the front end of a gun barrel ▷ *vb* (*tr*) **4** to prevent from being heard or noticed **5** to put a muzzle on (an animal) [C15 *mosel*, from Old French *musel*, diminutive of *muse* snout, from Medieval Latin *mūsus*, of unknown origin] > **'muzzler** *n*

muzzle-loader *n* a firearm receiving its ammunition through the muzzle > **'muzzle-ˌloading** *adj*

muzzle velocity *n* the velocity of a projectile as it leaves a firearm's muzzle

muzzy ('mʌzɪ) *adj* **-zier, -ziest 1** blurred, indistinct, or hazy **2** confused, muddled, or befuddled [C18: origin obscure] > **'muzzily** *adv* > **'muzziness** *n*

MVO *abbreviation* (in Britain) Member of the Royal Victorian Order

MVP *abbreviation* (in the US and Australia) most valuable player: the man or woman judged to be the outstanding player in a sport during a particular season or championship

MW *symbol for* **1** megawatt ▷ *abbreviation* **2** *radio* medium wave

Mweru ('mwɛəruː) *n* a lake in central Africa, on the border between Zambia and the Democratic Republic of Congo (formerly Zaïre). Area: 4196 sq km (1620 sq miles)

Mx *physics symbol for* maxwell

my (maɪ) *determiner* **1** of, belonging to, or associated with the speaker or writer (me): *my own ideas; do you mind my smoking?* **2** used in various forms of address: *my lord; my dear boy* ▷ *interj* **3** an exclamation of surprise, awe, etc: *my, how you've grown!* [C12 *mī*, variant of Old English *mīn* when preceding a word beginning with a consonant]

myalgia (maɪˈældʒɪə) *n* pain in a muscle or a group of muscles [C19: from MYO- + -ALGIA]

myalgic encephalopathy (maɪˈældʒɪk ɛnˌsɛfəlˈɒpfɪ) *n* a condition characterized by painful muscles, extreme fatigue, and general debility, sometimes occuring as a sequel to viral illness. Also called **chronic fatigue syndrome** Abbreviation: **ME**

myalism ('maɪəˌlɪzəm) *n* a kind of witchcraft, similar to

obi, practised esp in the Caribbean [C19: from *myal*, probably of West African origin]

myall ('maɪəl) *n* **1** any of several Australian acacias, esp *Acacia pendula*, having hard scented wood used for fences **2** a native Australian living independently of society [C19: from a native Australian name]

Myanmar *or* **Myanma** ('maɪænmɑː, 'mjænmɑː) *n* a republic in SE Asia, on the Bay of Bengal and the Andaman Sea: unified from small states in 1752; annexed by Britain (1823–85) and made a province of India in 1886; became independent in 1948. It is generally mountainous, with the basins of the Chindwin and Irrawaddy Rivers in the central part and the Irrawaddy delta in the south. Official language: Burmese. Religion: Buddhist majority. Currency: kyat. Capital: Yangon. Pop: 50 101 000 (2004 est). Area: 676 577 sq km (261 228 sq miles). Former official name (until 1989, though still widely used): **Burma**

mycelium (maɪˈsiːlɪəm) *n, pl* **-lia** (-lɪə) the vegetative body of fungi: a mass of branching filaments (hyphae) that spread throughout the nutrient substratum [C19 (literally: nail of fungus): from MYCO- + Greek *hēlos* nail] > **my'celial** *adj*

Mycenae (maɪˈsiːniː) *n* an ancient Greek city in the NE Peloponnesus on the plain of Argos

Mycenaean (ˌmaɪsɪˈniːən) *adj* **1** of or relating to ancient Mycenae or its inhabitants **2** of or relating to the Aegean civilization of Mycenae (1400 to 1100BC)

-mycete *combining form* indicating a fungus: *ascomycete* [from New Latin *-mycetes*, from Greek *mukētes*, plural of *mukēs* fungus]

-mycin *n combining form* indicating an antibiotic compound derived from a fungus: *streptomycin* [from Greek *mukēs* fungus + -IN]

myco- *or before a vowel* **myc-** *combining form* indicating fungus: *mycology* [from Greek *mukēs* fungus]

mycology (maɪˈkɒlədʒɪ) *n* the branch of biology concerned with the study of fungi > **mycological** (ˌmaɪkəˈlɒdʒɪkˀl) *or* **ˌmyco'logic** *adj* > **my'cologist** *n*

mycoplasma (ˌmaɪkəʊˈplæzmə) *n* any prokaryotic microorganism of the genus *Mycoplasma*, some species of which cause disease (**mycoplasmosis**) in animals and humans

mycorrhiza *or* **mycorhiza** (ˌmaɪkəˈraɪzə) *n, pl* **-zae** (-ziː) *or* **-zas** an association of a fungus and a plant in which the fungus lives within or on the outside of the plant's roots forming a symbiotic or parasitic relationship [C19: from MYCO- + Greek *rhiza* root] > **ˌmycor'rhizal** *or* **ˌmyco'rhizal** *adj*

mycosis (maɪˈkəʊsɪs) *n* any infection or disease caused by fungus > **mycotic** (maɪˈkɒtɪk) *adj*

mycotoxin (ˌmaɪkəˈtɒksɪn) *n* any of various toxic substances produced by fungi some of which may affect food and others of which are alleged to have been used in warfare > **ˌmycotox'ology** *n*

mycotrophic (ˌmaɪkəʊˈtrɒfɪk) *adj botany* (of a plant) symbiotic with a fungus, esp a mycorrhizal fungus

myelin ('maɪɪlɪn) *or* **myeline** ('maɪɪˌliːn) *n* a white tissue forming an insulating sheath (**myelin sheath**) around certain nerve fibres. Damage to the myelin sheath causes neurological disease

myelitis (ˌmaɪɪˈlaɪtɪs) *n* inflammation of the spinal cord or of the bone marrow

myeloma (ˌmaɪɪˈləʊmə) *n, pl* **-mas** *or* **-mata** (-mətə) a usually malignant tumour of the bone marrow or composed of cells normally found in bone marrow

Myers ('maɪəz) *n* **L(eopold) H(amilton)**. 1881–1944, British novelist, best known for his novel sequence *The Near and the Far* (1929–40)

Mykonos ('mɪkənɒs, -əʊs, 'miːkə-) *n* a Greek island in the S Aegean Sea, one of the Cyclades: a popular tourist resort with many churches. Pop: 9306 (2001)

My Lai (ˌmaɪ ˈlaɪ, 'miː) *n* a village in S Vietnam where in 1968 US troops massacred over 400 civilians

mynah *or* **myna** ('maɪnə) *n* any of various tropical Asian starlings of the genera *Acridotheres, Gracula*, etc, esp *G. religiosa* (see **hill mynah**), some of which can mimic human speech [C18: from Hindi *mainā*, from Sanskrit *madanā*]

Mynheer (məˈnɪə) n a Dutch title of address equivalent to *Sir* when used alone or to *Mr* when placed before a name [c17: from Dutch *mijnheer*, my lord]

myo- or before a vowel **my-** combining form muscle: *myocardium* [from Greek *mus* MUSCLE]

myocardium (ˌmaɪəʊˈkɑːdɪəm) n, pl -**dia** (-dɪə) the muscular tissue of the heart [c19: from *myo-* + *cardium*, from Greek *kardia* heart]

myology (maɪˈɒlədʒɪ) n the branch of medical science concerned with the structure and diseases of muscles

myope (ˈmaɪəʊp) n any person afflicted with myopia [c18: via French from Greek *muōps*; see MYOPIA]

myopia (maɪˈəʊpɪə) n inability to see distant objects clearly because the images are focused in front of the retina; short-sightedness [c18: via New Latin from Greek *muōps* short-sighted, from *mūein* to close (the eyes), blink + *ōps* eye] > **myopic** (maɪˈɒpɪk) adj > **myˈopically** adv

myosin (ˈmaɪəsɪn) n the chief protein of muscle that interacts with actin to form actomyosin during muscle contraction; it is also present in many other cell types [c19: from MYO- + -OSE[2] + -IN]

myosotis (ˌmaɪəˈsəʊtɪs) or **myosote** (ˈmaɪəˌsəʊt) n any plant of the boraginaceous genus *Myosotis*. See **forget-me-not** [c18: New Latin from Greek *muosōtis* mouse-ear (referring to its furry leaves), from *muos*, genitive of *mus* mouse + -*ōt*-, stem of *ous* ear]

myriad (ˈmɪrɪəd) adj **1** innumerable ▷ n **2** (also used in plural) a large indefinite number **3** archaic ten thousand [c16: via Late Latin from Greek *murias* ten thousand]

myriapod (ˈmɪrɪˌpɒd) n **1** any terrestrial arthropod of the group *Myriapoda*, having a long segmented body and many walking limbs: includes the centipedes and millipedes ▷ adj **2** of, relating to, or belonging to the *Myriapoda* [c19: from New Latin *Myriapoda*. See MYRIAD, -POD]

Myrmidon (ˈmɜːmɪˌdɒn, -dᵊn) n, pl **Myrmidons** or **Myrmidones** (mɜːˈmɪdᵊˌniːz) **1** Greek myth one of a race of people whom Zeus made from a nest of ants. They settled in Thessaly and were led against Troy by Achilles **2** (often not capital) a follower or henchman

myrobalan (maɪˈrɒbələn, mɪ-) n **1** the dried plumlike fruit of various tropical trees of the genus *Terminalia*, used in dyeing, tanning, ink, and medicine **2** a dye extracted from this fruit [c16: via Latin from Greek *murobalanos*, from *muron* ointment + *balanos* acorn]

Myron (ˈmaɪərən) n 5th century BC, Greek sculptor. He worked mainly in bronze and introduced a greater variety of pose into Greek sculpture, as in his *Discobolus*

myrrh (mɜː) n **1** any of several burseraceous trees and shrubs of the African and S Asian genus *Commiphora*, esp *C. myrrha*, that exude an aromatic resin **2** the resin obtained from such a plant, used in perfume, incense, and medicine [Old English *myrre*, via Latin from Greek *murrha*, ultimately from Akkadian *murrū*; compare Hebrew *mōr*, Arabic *murr*]

myrtle (ˈmɜːtᵊl) n any evergreen shrub or tree of the myrtaceous genus *Myrtus*, esp *M. communis*, a S European shrub with pink or white flowers and aromatic blue-black berries [c16: from Medieval Latin *myrtilla*, from Latin *myrtus*, from Greek *murtos*]

mySAP (ˈmaɪˌsæp) n trademark a Web-integrated software application used by businesses to plan and control product distribution, human resources, budgets, etc

myself (maɪˈsɛlf) pron **1 a** the reflexive form of *I* or *me* **b** (intensifier): *I myself know of no answer* **2** (preceded by a copula) my usual self: *I'm not myself today* **3** not standard used instead of *I* or *me* in compound noun phrases: *John and myself are voting together*

Mysia (ˈmɪsɪə) n an ancient region in the NW corner of Asia Minor > **ˈMysian** adj, n

Mysore (maɪˈsɔː) n **1** a city in S India, in S Karnataka state: former capital of the state of Mysore; manufacturing and trading centre; university (1916). Pop: 742 261 (2001) **2** the former name (until 1973) of **Karnataka**

mysterious (mɪˈstɪərɪəs) adj **1** characterized by or indicative of mystery **2** puzzling, curious, or enigmatic > **mysˈteriously** adv > **mysˈteriousness** n

mystery[1] (ˈmɪstərɪ, -trɪ) n, pl -**teries 1** an unexplained or inexplicable event, phenomenon, etc **2** a person or thing that arouses curiosity or suspense because of an unknown, obscure, or enigmatic quality **3** the state or quality of being obscure, inexplicable, or enigmatic **4** a story, film, etc, which arouses suspense and curiosity because of facts concealed **5** Christianity any truth that is divinely revealed but otherwise unknowable **6** Christianity a sacramental rite, such as the Eucharist, or (when plural) the consecrated elements of the Eucharist **7** (often plural) any of various rites of certain ancient Mediterranean religions **8** short for **mystery play** [c14: via Latin from Greek *mustērion* secret rites. See MYSTIC]

mystery[2] (ˈmɪstərɪ) n, pl -**teries** archaic **1** a trade, occupation, or craft **2** a guild of craftsmen [c14: from Medieval Latin *mistērium*, from Latin *ministerium* occupation, from *minister* official]

mystery play n (in the Middle Ages) a type of drama based on the life of Christ. See **miracle play**

mystery tour n an excursion to an unspecified destination

mystic (ˈmɪstɪk) n **1** a person who achieves mystical experience or an apprehension of divine mysteries ▷ adj **2** another word for **mystical** [c14: via Latin from Greek *mustikos*, from *mustēs* mystery initiate; related to *muein* to initiate into sacred rites]

mystical (ˈmɪstɪkᵊl) adj **1** relating to or characteristic of mysticism **2** Christianity having a divine or sacred significance that surpasses natural human apprehension **3** having occult or metaphysical significance, nature, or force > **ˈmystically** adv

mysticism (ˈmɪstɪˌsɪzəm) n **1** belief in or experience of a reality surpassing normal human understanding or experience, esp a reality perceived as essential to the nature of life **2** a system of contemplative prayer and spirituality aimed at achieving direct intuitive experience of the divine **3** obscure or confused belief or thought

mystify (ˈmɪstɪˌfaɪ) vb -**fies**, -**fying**, -**fied** (tr) **1** to confuse, bewilder, or puzzle **2** to make mysterious or obscure [c19: from French *mystifier*, from *mystère* MYSTERY[1] or *mystique* MYSTIC] > ˌmystifiˈcation n > ˈmystiˌfying adj

mystique (mɪˈstiːk) n an aura of mystery, power, and awe that surrounds a person or thing [c20: from French (adj): MYSTIC]

myth (mɪθ) n **1 a** a story about superhuman beings of an earlier age taken by preliterate society to be a true account, usually of how natural phenomena, social customs, etc, came into existence **b** another word for **mythology** (senses 1, 3) **2** a person or thing whose existence is fictional or unproven [c19: via Late Latin from Greek *muthos* fable, word]

myth. abbreviation **1** mythological **2** mythology

mythical (ˈmɪθɪkᵊl) or **mythic** (ˈmɪθɪk) adj **1** of or relating to myth **2** imaginary or fictitious > ˈmythically adv

mythicize or **mythicise** (ˈmɪθɪˌsaɪz) vb (tr) to make into or treat as a myth > ˈmythicist, ˈmythiˌcizer or ˈmythiˌciser n

mytho- combining form myth

mythologize or **mythologise** (mɪˈθɒləˌdʒaɪz) vb **1** to tell, study, or explain (myths) **2** (intr) to create or make up myths **3** (tr) to convert into a myth > myˈthologer, myˈtholoˌgizer or myˈtholoˌgiser n

mythology (mɪˈθɒlədʒɪ) n, pl -**gies 1** a body of myths, esp one associated with a particular culture, institution, person, etc **2** a body of stories about a person, institution, etc **3** myths collectively **4** the study or collecting of myths > **mythological** (ˌmɪθəˈlɒdʒɪkᵊl) adj > myˈthologist n

mythomania (ˌmɪθəʊˈmeɪnɪə) n psychiatry the tendency to lie, exaggerate, or relate incredible imaginary adventures as if they had really happened, occurring in some mental disorders > **mythomaniac** (ˌmɪθəʊˈmeɪnɪˌæk) n, adj

mythopoeia (ˌmɪθəʊˈpiːə) or **mythopoesis** (ˌmɪθəpəʊˈiːsɪs) n the composition or making of myths [c19: from Greek, from *muthopoiein*, from *muthos* myth + *poiein* to make]

m

mythos ('maɪθɒs, 'mɪθɒs) *n, pl* **-thoi** (-θɔɪ) **1** the complex of beliefs, values, attitudes, etc, characteristic of a specific group or society **2** another word for **myth, mythology**

Mytilene (ˌmɪtɪ'liːnɪ) *n* **1** a port on the Greek island of Lesbos: Roman remains; Byzantine fortress. Pop: (municipality): 37 881 (2001). Modern Greek name: Mitilíni **2** a former name for **Lesbos**

myxo ('mɪksəʊ) *n Austral slang* short for **myxomatosis**

myxo- *or before a vowel* **myx-** *combining form* mucus or slime: *myxomycete* [from Greek *muxa* slime, mucus]

myxoedema *or US* **myxedema** (ˌmɪksɪ'diːmə) *n* a disease resulting from underactivity of the thyroid gland characterized by puffy eyes, face, and hands and mental sluggishness. See also **cretinism**

myxoma (mɪk'səʊmə) *n, pl* **-mas** *or* **-mata** (-mətə) a tumour composed of mucous connective tissue, usually situated in subcutaneous tissue > **myxomatous** (mɪk'sɒmətəs) *adj*

myxomatosis (ˌmɪksəmə'təʊsɪs) *n* an infectious and usually fatal viral disease of rabbits characterized by swelling of the mucous membranes and formation of skin tumours; transmitted by flea bites

myxomycete (ˌmɪksəʊmaɪ'siːt) *n* a slime mould, esp a slime mould of the phylum *Myxomycota* (division *Myxomycetes* in traditional classifications) > ˌmyxomy'cetous *adj*

myxovirus ('mɪksəʊˌvaɪərəs) *n* any of a group of viruses that cause influenza, mumps, and certain other diseases

Mzansi (əm'zʌnsɪ) *n South African* a low-cost national banking account [C21 from Xhosa, literally: South]

m

Nn

n¹ or **N** (ɛn) n, pl **n's**, **N's** or **Ns** **1** the 14th letter and 11th consonant of the modern English alphabet **2** a speech sound represented by this letter, usually an alveolar nasal, as in *nail*

n² symbol for **1** neutron **2** optics index of refraction **3** nano-

n³ (ɛn) determiner an indefinite number (of): *there are n objects in a box*

N symbol for **1** Also called: **kt** chess knight **2** newton(s) **3** chem nitrogen **4** North **5** noun

n. abbreviation **1** neuter **2** new **3** nominative **4** noun

Na the chemical symbol for sodium [Latin *natrium*]

NA abbreviation North America

NAAFI or **Naafi** ('næfɪ) n **1** acronym Navy, Army, and Air Force Institutes: an organization providing canteens, shops, etc, for British military personnel at home or overseas **2** a canteen, shop, etc, run by this organization

naartjie ('nɑːtʃɪ) n South African a tangerine [Afrikaans]

nab (næb) vb **nabs**, **nabbing**, **nabbed** (tr) informal **1** to arrest **2** to seize suddenly; snatch [c17: perhaps of Scandinavian origin; compare Danish *nappe*, Swedish *nappa* to snatch. See KIDNAP]

nabla ('næblə) n maths another name for **del** [c19: from Greek *nabla* stringed instrument, because it is shaped like a harp]

Nablus ('nɑːbləs) n a town in the West Bank: near the site of ancient Shechem. Pop: 136 000 (2005 est)

nabob ('neɪbɒb) n **1** informal a rich, powerful, or important man **2** (formerly) a European who made a fortune in the Orient, esp in India **3** another name for a **nawab** [c17: from Portuguese *nababo*, from Hindi *nawwāb*; see NAWAB]

Nabokov (nə'bɒkɒf, 'næbə,kɒf) n **Vladimir Vladimirovich** (vla'dimir vla'dimirəvitʃ). 1899–1977, US novelist, born in Russia. His works include *Lolita* (1955), *Pnin* (1957), *Pale Fire* (1962), and *Ada* (1969) > **Nabokovian** (,næbə'kəʊvɪən) adj

Naboth ('neɪbɒθ) n Old Testament an inhabitant of Jezreel, murdered by King Ahab at the instigation of his wife Jezebel for refusing to sell his vineyard (I Kings 21)

nacelle (nə'sɛl) n a streamlined enclosure on an aircraft, not part of the fuselage, to accommodate an engine, passengers, crew, etc [c20: from French: small boat, from Late Latin *nāvicella*, a diminutive of Latin *nāvis* ship]

nacho ('nɑːtʃəʊ) n, pl **nachos** Mexican cookery a snack consisting of a piece of tortilla topped with cheese, hot peppers, etc, and grilled

NACODS ('neɪkɒdz) n acronym for National Association of Colliery Overmen, Deputies, and Shotfirers

nacre ('neɪkə) n the technical name for **mother-of-pearl** [c16: via French from Old Italian *naccara*, from Arabic *naqqārah* shell, drum] > **'nacred** adj

nacreous ('neɪkrɪəs) adj relating to or consisting of mother-of-pearl

NACRO or **Nacro** ('nækrəʊ) n acronym for National Association for the Care and Resettlement of Offenders

Nadar (French nadar) n real name *Gaspard Félix Tournachon*. 1820–1910, French photographer, writer, and caricaturist: noted for his portrait photographs of artists and writers and for taking the first aerial photographs (1858)

Nader ('neɪdə) n **Ralph**. born 1934, US lawyer and campaigner for consumer rights and the environment: a candidate for president in 1996, 2000, and 2004

nadir ('neɪdɪə, 'næ-) n **1** the point on the celestial sphere directly below an observer and diametrically opposite the zenith **2** the lowest or deepest point; depths [c14: from Old French, from Arabic *nazīr as-samt*, literally: opposite the zenith]

nadors ('nɑː,dɔːz) n South African a thirst brought on by excessive consumption of alcohol [from Afrikaans *na* after + *dors* thirst]

nae (neɪ) or **na** (nɑː) determiner a Scot word for **no¹** or **not**

naevus or US **nevus** ('niːvəs) n, pl **-vi** (-vaɪ) any congenital growth or pigmented blemish on the skin; birthmark or mole [c19: from Latin; related to (g)natus born, produced by nature] > **'naevoid** or US **'nevoid** adj

naff (næf) adj Brit slang inferior; in poor taste [c19: perhaps back slang for *fan*, short for FANNY] > **'naffness** n

naff off sentence substitute Brit slang a forceful expression of dismissal or contempt

NAFTA ('næftə) n acronym for North American Free Trade Agreement

nag¹ (næg) vb **nags**, **nagging**, **nagged** **1** to scold or annoy constantly **2** (when intr, often foll by at) to be a constant source of discomfort or worry (to) ▷ *n* **3** a person, esp a woman, who nags [C19: of Scandinavian origin; compare Swedish *nagga* to GNAW, irritate, German *nagen*] > **'nagger** *n*

nag² (næg) *n* **1** *often derogatory* a horse **2** a small riding horse [C14: of Germanic origin; related to NEIGH]

Nagaland ('nɑːɡəˌlænd) *n* a state of NE India: formed in 1962 from parts of Assam and the North-East Frontier Agency; inhabited chiefly by Naga tribes; consists of almost inaccessible forested hills and mountains (the **Naga Hills**); shifting cultivation predominates. Capital: Kohima. Pop: 1 988 636 (2001). Area: 16 579 sq km (6401 sq miles)

nagana (nəˈɡɑːnə) *n* a disease of all domesticated animals of central and southern Africa, caused by parasitic protozoa of the genus *Trypanosoma* transmitted by tsetse flies [from Zulu *u-nakane*]

Nagano (nəˈɡɑːnəʊ) *n* a city in central Japan, on central Honshu: Buddhist shrine; two universities. Pop: 359 045 (2002 est)

Nagarjuna (ˌnæɡɑːˈdʒuːnə) *n* c. 150–c. 250 AD, Indian Buddhist monk, founder of the Madhyamika (Middle Path) school of Mahayana Buddhism: noted for his philosophical writings

Nagasaki (ˌnɑːɡəˈsɑːkɪ) *n* a port in SW Japan, on W Kyushu: almost completely destroyed in 1945 by the second atomic bomb dropped on Japan by the US; shipbuilding industry. Pop: 419 901 (2002 est)

Nagorno-Karabakh Autonomous Region (nəˈɡɔːnəʊkærəˈbɑːk) *n* an administrative division in S Azerbaijan. In 1990–94 Armenian claims to the region led to violent unrest and fighting between national forces. Capital: Stepanakert. Pop: 143 000 (2000 est). Area: 4400 sq km (1700 sq miles)

Nagoya ('nɑːɡəʊjə) *n* a city in central Japan, on S Honshu on Ise Bay: a major industrial centre. Pop: 2 109 681 (2002 est)

Nagpur (næɡˈpʊə) *n* a city in central India, in NE Maharashtra state: became capital of the kingdom of Nagpur (1743); capital of the Central Provinces (later Madhya Pradesh) from 1861 to 1956. Pop: 2 051 320 (2001)

Nagy (*Hungarian* nɒdʒ) *n* **Imre** ('imrɛ). 1896–1958, Hungarian statesman; prime minister (1953–55; 1956). He was removed from office and later executed when Soviet forces suppressed the revolution of 1956; reburied with honours in 1989

Nagyszeben ('nɒdʒsɛˌbɛn) *n* the Hungarian name for Sibiu

Nagyvárad ('nɒdʒvɑːrɒd) *n* the Hungarian name for Oradea

Nah. *abbreviation Bible* Nahum

Naha ('nɑːhə) *n* a port in S Japan, on the SW coast of Okinawa Island: chief city of the Ryukyu Islands. Pop: 303 146 (2002 est)

NAHT (in Britain) *abbreviation* National Association of Head Teachers

Nahuatl ('nɑːwɑːtˀl, nɑːˈwɑːtˀl) *n* **1** (*pl* **-tl** or **-tls**) a member of one of a group of Central American and Mexican Indian peoples including the Aztecs **2** the language of these peoples, belonging to the Uto-Aztecan family

Nahum ('neɪhəm) *n Old Testament* **1** a Hebrew prophet of the 7th century BC **2** the book containing his oracles

naiad ('naɪæd) *n, pl* **-ads** or **-ades** (-əˌdiːz) **1** *Greek myth* a nymph dwelling in a lake, river, spring, or fountain **2** the aquatic larva of the dragonfly, mayfly, and related insects **3** Also called: **water nymph** any monocotyledonous submerged aquatic plant of the genus *Naias* (or *Najas*), having narrow leaves and small flowers: family *Naiadaceae* (or *Najadaceae*) [C17: via Latin from Greek *nāias* water nymph; related to *ndein* to flow]

naïf (nɑːˈiːf) *adj, n* a less common word for **naive**

nail (neɪl) *n* **1** a fastening device usually made from round or oval wire, having a point at one end and a head at the other **2** anything resembling such a fastening device, esp in function or shape **3** the horny plate covering part of the dorsal surface of the fingers or toes. Related adj: **ungual 4** the claw of a mammal, bird, or reptile **5** a unit of length, formerly used for measuring

cloth, equal to two and a quarter inches **6 hit the nail on the head** to do or say something correct or telling **7 on the nail** (of payments) at once (esp in the phrase **pay on the nail**) ▷ *vb* (*tr*) **8** to attach with or as if with nails **9** *informal* to arrest or seize **10** *informal* to hit or bring down, as with a shot **11** *informal* to expose or detect (a lie or liar) **12** to fix or focus (one's eyes, attention, etc) on an object **13** to stud with nails [Old English *nægl*; related to Old High German *nagal* nail, Latin *unguis* fingernail, claw, Greek *onux*] > **'nailer** *n*

nail-biting *n* **1** the act or habit of biting one's fingernails **2 a** anxiety or tension **b** (*as modifier*): *nail-biting suspense*

nail bomb *n* an explosive device containing nails, used by terrorists to cause serious injuries in crowded situations

nailbrush ('neɪlˌbrʌʃ) *n* a small stiff-bristled brush for cleaning the fingernails

nailed-on *adj slang* certain, definite; guaranteed to be successful

nailfile ('neɪlˌfaɪl) *n* a small file, chiefly either of metal or of board coated with emery, used to trim the nails

nail polish, nail varnish or US **nail enamel** *n* a quick-drying lacquer applied to colour the nails or make them shiny or esp both

nail set or **nail punch** *n* a punch for driving the head of a nail below or flush with the surrounding surface

nainsook ('neɪnsʊk, 'næn-) *n* a light soft plain-weave cotton fabric, used esp for babies' wear [C19: from Hindi *nainsukh*, literally: delight to the eye, from *nain* eye + *sukh* delight, from Sanskrit *sukha*]

Naipaul ('naɪpɔːl) *n* **Sir V(idiadhar) S(urajprasad)**. born 1932, Trinidadian novelist of Indian descent, living in Britain. His works include *A House for Mr Biswas* (1961), *In a Free State* (1971), which won the Booker Prize, *A Bend in the River* (1979), *The Enigma of Arrival* (1987), and *Beyond Belief* (1998): Nobel prize for literature 2001

naira ('naɪrə) *n* the standard monetary unit of Nigeria, divided into 100 kobo [C20: altered from NIGERIA]

Nairnshire ('nɛənˌʃɪə, -ʃə) *n* (until 1975) a county of NE Scotland, now part of Highland

Nairobi (naɪˈrəʊbɪ) *n* the capital of Kenya, in the southwest at an altitude of 1650 m (5500 ft): founded in 1899; became capital in 1905; commercial and industrial centre; the **Nairobi National Park** (a game reserve) is nearby. Pop: 2 818 000 (2005 est)

Naismith ('neɪsmɪə) *n* **James**. 1861–1939, Canadian sportsman and coach; inventor of basketball

naive, naïve (nɑːˈiːv, naɪˈiːv) or **naïf** *adj* **1** having or expressing innocence and credulity; ingenuous **2** lacking developed powers of analysis, reasoning, or criticism: *a naive argument* **3** another word for **primitive** (sense 5) ▷ *n* **4** *rare* a person who is naive, esp in artistic style. See **primitive** (sense 9) [C17: from French, feminine of *naïf*, from Old French *naif* native, spontaneous, from Latin *nātīvus* NATIVE, from *nasci* to be born] > **na'ively, na'ïvely** or **na'ïfly** *adv* > **na'iveness, na'ïveness** or **na'ïfness** *n*

naivety (naɪˈiːvtɪ), **naiveté** or **naïveté** (ˌnɑːiːvˈteɪ) *n, pl* **-ties** or **-tés 1** the state or quality of being naive; ingenuousness; simplicity **2** a naive act or statement

Najaf ('nædʒæf) *n* a holy city in central Iraq, near the River Euphrates; burial place of the Caliph Ali and a centre of the Shiite faith. Pop: 639 000 (2005 est)

naked ('neɪkɪd) *adj* **1** having the body completely unclothed; undressed **2** having no covering; bare; exposed: *a naked flame* **3** with no qualification or concealment; stark; plain: *the naked facts* **4** unaided by any optical instrument, such as a telescope or microscope (esp in the phrase **the naked eye**) **5** (usually foll by *of*) stripped or destitute: *naked of weapons* **6** (of animals) lacking hair, feathers, scales, etc **7** *law* **a** unsupported by authority or financial or other consideration: *a naked contract* **b** lacking some essential condition to render valid; incomplete [Old English *nacod*; related to Old High German *nackot* (German *nackt*), Old Norse *noktr*, Latin *nudus*] > **'nakedly** *adv*

naked ladies *n* (*functioning as singular*) another name for **autumn crocus**

naked lady *n* a leafless pink orchid found in Australia and New Zealand

Nakhichevan (*Russian* nəxitʃɪ'vanj) *n* a city in W Azerbaijan, capital of the Nakhichevan Autonomous Republic: an ancient trading town; ceded to Russia in 1828. Pop: 66 800 (1994)

Nakhichevan Autonomous Republic (nə,kɪtʃɛ'vɑːn) *n* a region belonging to Azerbaijan, from which it is separated by part of Armenia; annexed by Russia in 1828; unilaterally declared secession from the Soviet Union in 1990. Capital: Nakhichevan. Pop: 363 000 (2000 est). Area: 5500 sq km (2120 sq miles)

Nakuru (nə'kuːruː) *n* a town in W Kenya, on Lake Nakuru: commercial centre of an agricultural region. Pop: 264 000 (2005 est)

Nalchik (*Russian* 'naljtʃik) *n* a city in SW Russia, capital of the Kabardino-Balkar Republic, in a valley of the Greater Caucasus: health resort. Pop: 283 000 (2005 est)

naltrexone (næl'trɛksəʊn) *n* a narcotic antagonist, similar to morphine, used chiefly in the treatment of heroin addiction [c20: from *N-al(lylnor)ox(ymorph)one*, + the arbitrary insertion of *-trex-*]

Nam *or* '**Nam** (næm) *n chiefly US informal* Vietnam

Namangan (*Russian* nəman'gan) *n* a city in E Uzbekistan. Pop: 471 000 (2005 est)

Namaqualand (nə'mɑːkwə,lænd) *n* a semiarid coastal region of SW Africa, extending from near Windhoek, Namibia, into W South Africa: divided by the Orange River into **Little Namaqualand** in South Africa, and **Great Namaqualand** in Namibia; rich mineral resources. Area: 47 961 sq km (18 518 sq miles). Also called: **Namaland** ('nɑːmə,lænd)

namaste (,nʌməs'teɪ) *interj* a salutation used in India [c21: via Hindi from Sanskrit, from *namas* salutation, bow + *te* to you]

namby-pamby (,næmbɪ'pæmbɪ) *adj* **1** sentimental or prim in a weak insipid way **2** clinging, feeble, or spineless ▷ *n*, *pl* **-bies** **3** a person who is namby-pamby [c18: a nickname of Ambrose Phillips (died 1749), whose pastoral verse was ridiculed for being insipid]

Nam Co ('nɑːm 'kɔː) *or* **Nam Tso** *n* a salt lake in SW China, in SE Tibet at an altitude of 4629 m (15 186 ft). Area: about 1800 sq km (700 sq miles). Also called: **Tengri Nor**

name (neɪm) *n* **1** a word or term by which a person or thing is commonly and distinctively known **2** mere outward appearance or form as opposed to fact (esp in the phrase **in name**): *he was a ruler in name only* **3** a word, title, or phrase descriptive of character, usually abusive or derogatory: *to call a person names* **4** reputation, esp, if unspecified, good reputation: *he's made quite a name for himself* **5 a** a famous person or thing: *a name in the advertising world* **b** *chiefly US & Canadian* (*as modifier*): *a name product* **6** a member of Lloyd's who provides part of the capital of a syndicate and shares in its profits or losses but does not arrange its business **7 in the name of a** for the sake of **b** by the sanction or authority of **8 name of the game a** anything that is essential, significant, or important **b** expected or normal conditions, circumstances, etc: *in gambling, losing money's the name of the game* **9 to one's name** belonging to one: *I haven't a penny to my name* ▷ *vb* (*tr*) **10** to give a name to; call by a name **11** to refer to by name; cite: *he named three French poets* **12** to determine, fix, or specify: *they have named a date for the meeting* **13** to appoint to or cite for a particular title, honour, or duty; nominate: *he was named Journalist of the Year* **14** to ban (an MP) from the House of Commons by mentioning him formally by name as being guilty of disorderly conduct **15 name and shame** to reveal the identity of a person or organization guilty of illegal or unacceptable behaviour in order to embarrass them into not repeating the offence **16 name names** to cite people, esp in order to blame or accuse them **17 name the day** to choose the day for one's wedding [Old English *nama*, related to Latin *nomen*, Greek *noma*, Old High German *namo*, German *Namen*] ▷ '**namable** *or* '**nameable** *adj*

name-calling *n* verbal abuse, esp as a crude form of argument

namecheck ('neɪm,tʃɛk) *vb* (*tr*) **1** to mention (someone) specifically by name ▷ *n* **2** a specific mention of

someone's name, for example on a radio programme

name day *n* **1** *RC Church* the feast day of a saint whose name one bears **2** another name for **ticket day**

name-dropping *n informal* the practice of referring frequently to famous or fashionable people, esp as though they were intimate friends, in order to impress others

nameless ('neɪmlɪs) *adj* **1** without a name; anonymous **2** incapable of being named; indescribable: *a nameless horror seized him* **3** too unpleasant or disturbing to be mentioned: *nameless atrocities* ▷ '**namelessness** *n*

namely ('neɪmlɪ) *adv* that is to say

Namen ('nɑːmə) *n* the Flemish name for **Namur**

nameplate ('neɪm,pleɪt) *n* a small panel on or next to the door of a room or building, bearing the occupant's name and profession

namesake ('neɪm,seɪk) *n* a person or thing named after another [c17: probably a shortening of the phrase describing people connected *for the name's sake*]

nametape ('neɪm,teɪp) *n* a narrow cloth tape bearing the owner's name and attached to an article

Namhoi ('nɑː'm'hɔɪ) *n* another name for **Foshan**

Namibe (næ'miːb) *n* a port in SW Angola: fishing industry. Pop: 132 900 (2004 est)

Namibia (nɑː'mɪbɪə, nə-) *n* a country in southern Africa bordering on South Africa: annexed by Germany in 1884 and mandated by the League of Nations to South Africa in 1920. The mandate was terminated by the UN in 1966 but this was ignored by South Africa, as was the 1971 ruling by the International Court of Justice that the territory be surrendered. Independence was achieved in 1990 and Namibia became a member of the Commonwealth; Walvis Bay remained a South African enclave until 1994 when it was returned to Namibia. Official language: English; Afrikaans and German also spoken. Religion: mostly animist, with some Christians. Currency: dollar. Capital: Windhoek. Pop: 2 011 000 (2004 est). Area: 823 207 sq km (317 887 sq miles). Also called: **South West Africa** ▷ **Na'mibian** *adj, n*

Namier ('neɪmɪə) *n* Sir **Lewis Bernstein**, original name *Ludwik Bernsztajn vel Niemirowski*. 1888–1960, British historian, born in Poland: noted esp for his studies of 18th-century British politics

Nam Tso ('nɑːm 'tsɔː) *n* a variant transliteration of the Chinese name for **Nam Co**

Namur (næ'mʊə; *French* namyr) *n* **1** a province of S Belgium. Capital: Namur. Pop: 452 856 (2004 est). Area: 3660 sq km (1413 sq miles) **2** a town in S Belgium, capital of Namur province: strategically situated on a promontory between the Sambre and Meuse Rivers, besieged and captured many times. Pop: 106 213 (2004 est) ▷ Flemish name: **Namen**

nan (næn), **nana** *or* **nanna** ('nænə) *n* a child's words for **grandmother** [see NANNY; compare Greek *nanna* aunt, Medieval Latin *nonna* old woman]

nana ('nɑːnə) *n* **1** *slang* a fool **2** *Austral slang* the head **3 do one's nana** *Austral slang* to become very angry **4 off one's nana** *Austral slang* mad; insane [c19: probably from BANANA]

Nanaimo bar (nə'naɪməʊ) *n* *Canadian* a chocolate-coated sweet with a filling made from butter and icing sugar [c20: named after *Nanaimo*, a city on Vancouver Island]

Nanak ('nɑːnək) *n* 1469–1538, Indian religious leader; founder and first guru of Sikhism

nana nap *n informal* a short sleep, esp taken by an elderly person [c21: from NAN]

Nana Sahib ('nænə 'sɑːhɪb) *n* real name *Dandhu Panth*. ?1825–?1860, Indian nationalist, who led the uprising at Cawnpore during the Indian Mutiny

nan bread *or* **naan** (nɑːn) *n* (in Indian cookery) a slightly leavened bread in a large flat leaf shape [from Hindi]

Nanchang *or* **Nan-ch'ang** ('næn'tʃæŋ) *n* a walled city in SE China, capital of Jiangxi province, on the Kan River: largest city in the Poyang basin. Pop: 1 742 000 (2005 est)

Nancy ('nænsɪ; *French* nɑ̃si) *n* a city in NE France: became the capital of the dukes of Lorraine in the 12th century, becoming French in 1766; administrative and financial centre. Pop: 103 605 (1999)

Nanda Devi ('nʌndə 'diːvɪ) *n* a mountain in N India, in Uttarakhand in the Himalayas. Height: 7817 m (25 645 ft)

NAND circuit *or* **NAND gate** (nænd) *n electronics* a computer logic circuit having two or more input wires and one output wire that has an output signal if one or more of the input signals are at a low voltage. See **OR circuit** [C20: from *not* + AND; see NOT CIRCUIT, AND CIRCUIT]

nandrolone ('nændrə,ləʊn) *n* an anabolic steroid present in the body in small amounts but also produced by metabolism of other steroids, sometimes taken as performance-enhancing drugs by athletes and bodybuilders

nang (næŋ) *adj Brit youth slang* excellent; cool [C21: of uncertain origin]

Nanga Parbat ('nʌŋgə 'pɑːbʌt) *n* a mountain in N India, in NW Kashmir in the W Himalayas. Height: 8126 m (26 660 ft)

Nanhai ('nɑːn'haɪ) *n* the Chinese name for the **South China Sea**

Nanjing ('næn'dʒɪŋ), **Nanking** ('næn'kɪŋ) *or* **Nan-ching** *n* a port in E central China, capital of Jiangsu province, on the Yangtze River: capital of the Chinese empire and a literary centre from the 14th to 17th centuries; capital of Nationalist China (1928–37); site of a massacre of about 300 000 civilians by the invading Japanese army in 1937; university (1928). Pop: 2 806 000 (2005 est)

nankeen (næn'kiːn) *or* **nankin** ('nænkɪn) *n* **1** a hard-wearing buff-coloured cotton fabric **2 a** a pale greyish-yellow colour **b** (*as adjective*): *a nankeen carpet* [C18: named after *Nanking*, China, where it originated]

Nanning *or* **Nan-ning** ('næn'nɪŋ) *n* a port in S China, capital of Guanxi, on the Xiang River: rail links with Vietnam. Pop: 1 395 000 (2005 est)

nanny ('nænɪ) *n, pl* **-nies 1** a nurse or nursemaid for children **2 a** any person or thing regarded as treating people like children, esp by being patronizing or overprotective **b** (*as modifier*): *the nanny state* **3** a child's word for **grandmother** ▷ *vb* **nannies, nannying, nannied 4** (*intr*) to nurse or look after someone else's children **5** (*tr*) to be overprotective towards [C19: child's name for a nurse]

nannygai ('nænɪ,gaɪ) *n, pl* -**gais** an edible sea fish, *Centroberyx affinis*, of Australia which is red in colour and has large prominent eyes. Also called: **red fish** [C19: from a native Australian language]

nanny goat *n* a female goat

nano- *combining form* denoting 10^{-9}: *nanosecond*. Symbol: n² [from Latin *nānus* dwarf, from Greek *nanos*]

nanobe ('nænəʊb) *n* a microbe that measures between 50 and 100 nanometres across and is smaller than the smallest known bacterium

nanogram *or* **nanogramme** ('nænəʊ,græm) *n* one billionth (10^{-9}) of a gram. Symbol: ng

nanoparticle ('nænəʊ,pɑːtɪkᵊl) *n* a particle with dimensions less than 100 nanometres

nanophysics ('nænəʊ,fɪzɪks) *n* the physics of structures and artefacts with dimensions in the nanometre range or of phenomena occurring in nanaseconds

nanosecond ('nænəʊ,sɛkənd) *n* one thousand-millionth of a second

nanotechnology (,nænəʊtɛk'nɒlədʒɪ) *n* a branch of technology dealing with the manufacture of objects with dimensions of less than 100 nanometres and the manipulation of individual molecules and atoms

Nansen ('nænsən) *n* **Fridtjof** ('frɪdjɔf). 1861–1930, Norwegian arctic explorer, statesman, and scientist. He crossed Greenland (1888–89) and attempted to reach the North Pole (1893–96), attaining a record 86° 14′ N (1895). He was the League of Nations' high commissioner for refugees (1920–22): Nobel peace prize 1922

Nansen bottle ('nænsən) *n* an instrument used by oceanographers for obtaining samples of sea water from a desired depth [C19: named after Fridtjof *Nansen* (1861–1930), Norwegian arctic explorer, statesman, and scientist]

Nan Shan (næn 'ʃæn) *pl n* a mountain range in N central China, mainly in Qinghai province, with peaks over 6000 m (20 000 ft)

Nanterre (nɑ̃tɛr) *n* a town in N France, on the Seine: an industrial suburb of Paris. Pop: 84 281 (1999)

Nantes (French nɑ̃t) *n* a port in W France, at the head of the Loire estuary: scene of the signing of the Edict of Nantes and of the Noyades (drownings) during the French Revolution; extensive shipyards, and large metallurgical and food processing industries. Pop: 270 251 (1999)

Nantong *or* **Nantung** ('næn'tʌŋ) *n* a city in E China, in Jiangsu province on the Yangtze estuary. Pop: 898 000 (2005 est)

Nantucket (næn'tʌkɪt) *n* an island off SE Massachusetts: formerly a centre of the whaling industry; now a resort. Length: nearly 24 km (15 miles). Width: 5 km (3 miles). Pop (county and town): 10 724 (2003 est)

Naoise ('niːʃə) *n Irish myth* the husband of Deirdre, killed by his uncle Conchobar. See also **Deirdre**

Naomi ('neɪəmɪ) *n Old Testament* the mother-in-law of Ruth (Ruth 1:2)

nap¹ (næp) *vb* **naps, napping, napped** (*intr*) **1** to sleep for a short while; doze **2** to be unaware or inattentive; be off guard (esp in the phrase **catch someone napping**) ▷ *n* **3** a short light sleep; doze [Old English *hnappian*; related to Middle High German *napfen*]

nap² (næp) *n* **1** the raised fibres of velvet or similar cloth **2** any similar downy coating **3** *Austral informal* blankets, bedding ▷ *vb* **naps, napping, napped 4** (*tr*) to raise the nap of (cloth, esp velvet) by brushing or similar treatment [C15: probably from Middle Dutch *noppe*; related to Old English *hnoppian* to pluck]

nap³ (næp) *n* **1** Also called: **napoleon** a card game similar to whist, usually played for stakes **2** a call in this card game, undertaking to win all five tricks **3** *horse racing* a tipster's choice for an almost certain winner **4 nap hand** a position in which there is a very good chance of success if a risk is taken ▷ *vb* **naps, napping, napped 5** (*tr*) *horse racing* to name (a horse) as likely to win a race [C19: short for NAPOLEON, the original name of the card game]

napalm ('neɪpɑːm, 'næ-) *n* **1** a thick and highly incendiary liquid, usually consisting of petrol gelled with aluminium soaps, used in firebombs, flame-throwers, etc ▷ *vb* **2** (*tr*) to attack with napalm [C20: from NA(PHTHENE) + PALM(ITATE)]

nape (neɪp) *n* the back of the neck [C13: of unknown origin]

napery ('neɪpərɪ) *n rare* household linen, esp table linen [C14: from Old French *naperie*, from *nape* tablecloth, from Latin *mappa*. See NAPKIN]

Naphtali ('næftə,laɪ) *n Old Testament* **1** Jacob's sixth son, whose mother was Rachel's handmaid (Genesis 30:7–8) **2** the tribe descended from him **3** the territory of this tribe, between the Sea of Galilee and the mountains of central Galilee

naphtha ('næfθə, 'næp-) *n* a distillation product from coal tar boiling in the approximate range 80–170°C and containing aromatic hydrocarbons [C16: via Latin from Greek, of Iranian origin; related to Persian *neft* naphtha]

naphthalene, naphthaline ('næfθə,liːn, 'næp-) *or* **naphthalin** ('næfθəlɪn, 'næp-) *n* a white crystalline volatile solid with a characteristic penetrating odour: an aromatic hydrocarbon used in mothballs and in the manufacture of dyes, explosives, etc Formula: $C_{10}H_8$ [C19: from NAPHTHA + ALCOHOL + -ENE] ▷ **naphthalic** ('næfθəlɪk, næp-) *adj*

naphthene ('næfθiːn, 'næp-) *n* any of a class of cycloalkanes, mainly derivatives of cyclopentane, found in petroleum [C20: from NAPHTHA + -ENE]

naphthol ('næfθɒl, 'næp-) *n* a white crystalline solid having two isomeric forms, **alpha-naphthol**, used in dyes, and **beta-naphthol**, used in dyes and as an antioxidant. Formula: $C_{10}H_7OH$ [C19: from NAPHTHA + -OL¹]

Napier¹ ('neɪpɪə) *n* a port in New Zealand, on E North Island on Hawke Bay: wool trade centre. Pop: 56 100 (2004 est)

Napier² ('neɪpɪə) *n* **1** Sir **Charles James.** 1782–1853, British general and colonial administrator: conquered Sind (1843): governor of Sind (1843–47) **2 John**. 1550–1617, Scottish mathematician: invented logarithms and pioneered the decimal notation used today **3 Robert (Cornelis)**, 1st Baron Napier of Magdala. 1810–90, British field marshal, who commanded in India during the Sikh Wars (1845, 1848–49) and the Indian Mutiny (1857–59). He captured Magdala (1868) while rescuing British diplomats from Ethiopia

Napierian logarithm (nəˈpɪərɪən, neɪ-) *n* another name for **natural logarithm**

Napier's bones (ˈneɪpɪəz) *pl n* a set of graduated rods formerly used for multiplication and division [C17: based on a method invented by John *Napier* (1550–1617), Scottish mathematician]

napkin (ˈnæpkɪn) *n* **1** Also called: **table napkin** a usually square piece of cloth or paper used while eating to protect the clothes, wipe the mouth, etc; serviette **2** *rare* a similar piece of cloth used for example as a handkerchief or headscarf **3** a more formal name for **nappy¹ 4** a less common term for **sanitary towel** [C15: from Old French, from *nape* tablecloth, from Latin *mappa* small cloth, towel; see MAP]

Naples (ˈneɪpᵊlz) *n* **1** a port in SW Italy, capital of Campania region, on the Bay of Naples: the third largest city in the country; founded by Greeks in the 6th century BC; incorporated into the Kingdom of the Two Sicilies in 1140 and its capital (1282–1503); university (1224). Pop: 1 004 500 (2001). Italian name **Napoli**. Related adj: **Neapolitan 2 Bay of Naples** an inlet of the Tyrrhenian Sea in the SW coast of Italy

napoleon (nəˈpəʊlɪən) *n* **1** a former French gold coin worth 20 francs bearing a portrait of either Napoleon I (1769–1821), Emperor of the French (1804–15), or Napoleon III (1808–73), Emperor of the French (1852–70) **2** *cards* the full name for **nap³** (sense 1) [C19: from French *napoléon*, after *Napoleon* I]

Napoleon I (nəˈpəʊlɪən) *n* full name *Napoleon Bonaparte*. 1769–1821, Emperor of the French (1804–15). He came to power as the result of a coup in 1799 and established an extensive European empire. A brilliant general, he defeated every European coalition against him until, irreparably weakened by the Peninsular War and the Russian campaign (1812), his armies were defeated at Leipzig (1813). He went into exile but escaped and ruled as emperor during the Hundred Days. He was finally defeated at Waterloo (1815). As an administrator, his achievements were of lasting significance and include the *Code Napoléon*, which remains the basis of French law

Napoleon II *n* Duke of Reichstadt. 1811–32, son of Napoleon Bonaparte and Marie Louise. He was known as the *King of Rome* during the first French empire and was entitled Napoleon II by Bonapartists after Napoleon I's death (1821)

Napoleon III *n* full name *Charles Louis Napoleon Bonaparte*, known as *Louis-Napoleon*. 1808–73, Emperor of the French (1852–70); nephew of Napoleon I. He led two abortive Bonapartist risings (1836; 1840) and was elected president of the Second Republic (1848), establishing the Second Empire in 1852. Originally successful in foreign affairs, he was deposed after the disastrous Franco-Prussian War

Napoleonic (nə,pəʊlɪˈɒnɪk) *adj* relating to or characteristic of Napoleon I (1769–1821), Emperor of the French (1804–15), or his era

Napoli (ˈnɑːpoli) *n* the Italian name for **Naples**

nappe (næp) *n* **1** a large sheet or mass of rock, commonly a recumbent fold, that has been thrust from its original position by earth movements **2** the sheet of water that flows over a dam or weir **3** *geometry* either of the two parts into which a **cone** (sense 2) is divided by the vertex [C20: from French: tablecloth]

nappy¹ (ˈnæpɪ) *n*, *pl* **-pies** *Brit* a piece of soft material, esp towelling or a disposable material, wrapped around a baby in order to absorb its excrement. Also called: **napkin** US and Canadian name: **diaper** [C20: changed from NAPKIN]

nappy² (ˈnæpɪ) *adj* **-pier, -piest 1** having a nap; downy; fuzzy **2** (of alcoholic drink, esp beer) **a** having a head;

frothy **b** strong or heady

nappy rash *n Brit* (in babies) any irritation to the skin around the genitals, anus, or buttocks, usually caused by contact with urine or excrement. Formal name: **napkin rash** US and Canadian name: **diaper rash**

Nara (ˈnɑːrə) *n* a city in central Japan, on S Honshu: the first permanent capital of Japan (710–784). Pop: 364 411 (2002 est)

Narayan (nəˈraɪjən) *n* **R(asipuram) K(rishnaswamy)**. 1906–2001, Indian novelist writing in English. His books include *Swami and Friends* (1938), *The Man-Eater of Malgudi* (1961), *Under the Banyan Tree* (1985), and *Grandmother's Tale* (1993)

Narayanganj (nəˈrɑːjən,gʌndʒ) *n* a city in central Bangladesh, on the Ganges delta just southeast of Dhaka. Pop: 241 393 (2001)

Narbada (nəˈbʌdə) *n* another name for the **Narmada**

Narbonne (French narbɔn) *n* a city in S France: capital of the Roman province of **Gallia Narbonensis**; harbour silted up in the 14th century. Pop: 46 510 (1999)

narc (nɑːk) *n US slang* a narcotics agent

narcissism (ˈnɑːsɪˌsɪzəm) or **narcism** (ˈnɑːˌsɪzəm) *n* **1** an exceptional interest in or admiration for oneself, esp one's physical appearance **2** sexual satisfaction derived from contemplation of one's own physical or mental endowments [C19: from NARCISSUS] > **ˈnarcissist** *n* > ˌnarcisˈsistic *adj*

narcissus (nɑːˈsɪsəs) *n*, *pl* **-cissuses** or **-cissi** (-ˈsɪsaɪ, -ˈsɪsiː) any amaryllidaceous plant of the Eurasian genus *Narcissus*, esp *N. poeticus*, whose yellow, orange, or white flowers have a crown surrounded by spreading segments [C16: via Latin from Greek *nárkissos*, perhaps from *narkē* numbness, because of narcotic properties attributed to species of the plant]

Narcissus (nɑːˈsɪsəs) *n Greek myth* a beautiful youth who fell in love with his reflection in a pool and pined away, becoming the flower that bears his name

narco- *or sometimes before a vowel* **narc-** *combining form* **1** indicating numbness or torpor: *narcolepsy* **2** connected with or derived from illicit drug production: *narcoeconomies* [from Greek *narkē* numbness]

narcoanalysis (ˌnɑːkəʊəˈnælɪsɪs) *n* psychoanalysis of a patient in a trance induced by a narcotic drug

narcolepsy (ˈnɑːkəˌlɛpsɪ) *n pathol* a rare condition characterized by sudden and uncontrollable episodes of deep sleep > **narcoˈleptic** *adj*

narcosis (nɑːˈkəʊsɪs) *n* unconsciousness induced by narcotics or general anaesthetics

narcotic (nɑːˈkɒtɪk) *n* **1** any of a group of drugs, such as heroin, morphine, and pethidine, that produce numbness and stupor. They are used medicinally to relieve pain but are sometimes also taken for their pleasant effects; prolonged use may cause addiction **2** anything that relieves pain or induces sleep, mental numbness, etc **3** any illegal drug ▷ *adj* **4** of, relating to, or designating narcotics **5** of or relating to narcotics addicts or users [C14: via Medieval Latin from Greek *narkōtikós*, from *narkoûn* to render numb, from *narkē* numbness] > **narˈcotically** *adv*

narcotism (ˈnɑːkəˌtɪzəm) *n* stupor or addiction induced by narcotic drugs

narcotize or **narcotise** (ˈnɑːkəˌtaɪz) *vb* (*tr*) to place under the influence of a narcotic drug > ˌnarcotiˈzation or ˌnarcotiˈsation *n*

nard (nɑːd) *n* **1** another name for **spikenard** (senses 1, 2) **2** any of several plants, such as certain valerians, whose aromatic roots were formerly used in medicine [C14: via Latin from Greek *nárdos*, perhaps ultimately from Sanskrit *nalada* Indian spikenard, perhaps via Semitic (Hebrew *nēr'd*, Arabic *nārdīn*)]

nardoo (nɑːˈduː) *n* **1** another name of certain cloverlike ferns of the genus *Marsilea*, which grow in swampy areas **2** the spores of such a plant, used as food in Australia [C19: from a native Australian language]

nares (ˈnɛəriːz) *pl n*, *sing* **naris** (ˈnɛərɪs) *anatomy* the nostrils [C17: from Latin; related to Old English *nasu*, Latin *nāsus* nose]

narghile, nargile or **nargileh** (ˈnɑːɡɪlɪ, -ˌleɪ) *n* another name for **hookah** [C19: from French *narguilé*, from Persian *nārgīleh* a pipe having a bowl made of coconut shell, from *nārgīl* coconut]

nark (nɑːk) *slang* ▷ *n* **1** *Brit, Austral & NZ* an informer or spy, esp one working for the police (**copper's nark**) **2** *Brit* a person who complains irritatingly ▷ *vb* **3** *Brit, Austral & NZ* to annoy, upset, or irritate: *he was narked by her indifference* **4** (*intr*) *Brit, Austral & NZ* to inform or spy, esp for the police **5** (*intr*) *Brit* to complain irritatingly [C19: probably from Romany *nāk* nose]

narky ('nɑːkɪ) *adj* narkier, narkiest *slang* irritable, complaining, or sarcastic

Narmada (nəˈmʌdə) *or* **Narbada** *n* a river in central India, rising in Madhya Pradesh and flowing generally west to the Gulf of Cambay in a wide estuary: the second most sacred river in India. Length: 1290 km (801 miles)

Narraganset *or* **Narragansett** (ˌnærəˈgænsɪt) *n* **1** (*pl* **-set, -sets** *or* **-sett, -setts**) a member of a North American Indian people formerly living in Rhode Island **2** the language of this people, belonging to the Algonquian family

Narragansett Bay *n* an inlet of the Atlantic in SE Rhode Island: contains several islands, including Rhode Island, Prudence Island, and Conanicut Island

narrate (nəˈreɪt) *vb* **1** to tell (a story); relate **2** to speak in accompaniment of (a film, television programme, etc) [C17: from Latin *narrāre* to recount, from *gnārus* knowing] > **narˈratable** *adj*

narration (nəˈreɪʃən) *n* **1** the act or process of narrating **2** a narrated account or story; narrative

narrative ('nærətɪv) *n* **1** an account, report, or story, as of events, experiences, etc **2** **the narrative** the part of a literary work that relates events **3** the process or technique of narrating ▷ *adj* **4** telling a story: *a narrative poem* **5** of or relating to narration: *narrative art*

narrator (nəˈreɪtə) *n* **1** a person who tells a story or gives an account of something **2** a person who speaks in accompaniment of a film, television programme, etc

narrow ('nærəʊ) *adj* **1** small in breadth, esp in comparison to length **2** limited in range or extent **3** limited in outlook; lacking breadth of vision **4** limited in means or resources; meagre **5** barely adequate or successful (esp in the phrase **a narrow escape**) **6** painstakingly thorough; minute: *a narrow scrutiny* **7** *finance* denoting an assessment of liquidity as including notes and coin in circulation with the public, banks' till money, and banks' balances: *narrow money*. See **broad** (sense 12) **8** *phonetics* another word for **tense**¹ (sense 4) ▷ *vb* **9** to make or become narrow; limit; restrict ▷ *n* **10** a narrow place, esp a pass or strait ▷ See also **narrows** [Old English *nearu*; related to Old Saxon *naru*] > **ˈnarrowly** *adv* > **ˈnarrowness** *n*

narrowband ('nærəʊˌbænd) *n* a limited-capacity transmission channel such as that used for transmitting telephone calls and faxes

narrow boat *n* a long narrow bargelike boat with a beam of 2.1 m (7 ft) or less, used on canals

narrow gauge *n* **1** a railway track with a smaller distance between the lines than the standard gauge of 56½ in ▷ *adj* **narrow-gauge** *or* **narrow-gauged** **2** of, relating to, or denoting a railway with a narrow gauge

narrow-minded *adj* having a biased or illiberal viewpoint; bigoted, intolerant, or prejudiced > **ˌnarrowˈmindedness** *n*

narrows ('nærəʊz) *pl n* a narrow part of a strait, river, current, etc

narthex ('nɑːθɛks) *n* **1** a portico at the west end of a basilica or church, esp one that is at right angles to the nave **2** a rectangular entrance hall between the porch and nave of a church [C17: via Latin from Medieval Greek: enclosed porch, enclosure (earlier: box), from Greek *narthēx* giant fennel, the stems of which were used to make boxes]

Narva (*Russian* 'narvə) *n* a port in Estonia on the Narva River near the Gulf of Finland: developed around a Danish fortress in the 13th century; textile centre. Pop: 66 712 (2007 est)

Narvik ('nɑːvɪk; *Norwegian* 'narvik) *n* a port in N Norway: scene of two naval battles in 1940; exports iron ore from Kiruna and Gällivare (Sweden). Pop: 18 542 (2004 est)

narwhal, narwal ('nɑːwəl) *or* **narwhale** ('nɑːˌweɪl) *n* an arctic toothed whale, *Monodon monoceros*, having a black-spotted whitish skin and, in the male, a long spiral tusk: family Monodontidae [C17: of Scandinavian origin; compare Danish, Norwegian *narhval*, from Old Norse *nāhvalr*, from *nār* corpse + *hvalr* whale, from its white colour, supposed to resemble a human corpse]

nary ('neərɪ) *adv dialect* not; never: *nary a man was left* [C19: variant of *ne'er a* never a]

NASA ('næsə) *n* (in the US) *acronym for* National Aeronautics and Space Administration

nasal ('neɪzʰl) *adj* **1** of or relating to the nose **2** *phonetics* pronounced with the soft palate lowered allowing air to escape via the nasal cavity instead of or as well as through the mouth ▷ *n* **3** a nasal speech sound, such as English *m*, *n*, or *ng* [C17: from French from Late Latin *nāsālis*, from Latin *nāsus* nose] > **nasality** (neɪˈzælɪtɪ) *n* > **ˈnasally** *adv*

nasalize *or* **nasalise** ('neɪzʰˌlaɪz) *vb* (*tr*) to pronounce nasally > **ˌnasaliˈzation** *or* **ˌnasaliˈsation** *n*

nascent ('næsʰnt, 'neɪ-) *adj* starting to grow or develop; being born [C17: from Latin *nascēns* present participle of *nāscī* to be born] > **ˈnascence** *or* **ˈnascency** *n*

NASDAQ ('næzdæk) *n* (in the US) *acronym for* National Association of Securities Dealers Automated Quotations System

Naseby ('neɪzbɪ) *n* a village in Northamptonshire: site of a major Parliamentarian victory (1645) in the Civil War, when Cromwell routed Prince Rupert's force

Nash (næʃ) *n* **1** **John**. 1752–1835, English town planner and architect. He designed Regent's Park, Regent Street, and the Marble Arch in London **2** **Ogden**. 1902–71, US humorous poet **3** **Paul**. 1889–1946, English painter, noted esp as a war artist in both World Wars and for his landscapes **4** **Richard**, known as *Beau Nash*. 1674–1762, English dandy **5** See (Thomas) **Nashe 6** Sir **Walter**. 1882–1968, New Zealand Labour statesman, born in England: prime minister of New Zealand (1957–60)

Nashe *or* **Nash** (næʃ) *n* **Thomas**. 1567–1601, English pamphleteer, satirist, and novelist, author of the first picaresque novel in English, *The Unfortunate Traveller, or the Life of Jack Wilton* (1594)

Nashville ('næʃvɪl) *n* a city in central Tennessee, the state capital, on the Cumberland River: an industrial and commercial centre, noted for its recording industry. Pop (including Davidson): 544 765 (2003 est)

Nasik ('nɑːsɪk) *n* a city in W India, in Maharashtra: a centre for Hindu pilgrims. Pop: 1 076 967 (2001)

Nasiriyah (ˌnæzɪˈriːə) *n* a city in S Iraq, on the River Euphrates; agricultural and trading centre. Pop: 425 000 (2005 est)

Naskapi (nəˈskæpɪ) *n* a member of an Innu people living in Quebec [from Cree]

Nasmyth ('neɪsmɪθ) *n* **James**. 1808–90, British engineer; inventor of the steam hammer (1839)

naso- *combining form* nose: *nasopharynx* [from Latin *nāsus* nose]

nasogastric (ˌneɪzəʊˈgæstrɪk) *adj anatomy* of or relating to the nose and stomach: *a nasogastric tube*

Nassau *n* **1** (*German* 'nasaʊ) a region of W central Germany: formerly a duchy (1816–66), from which a branch of the House of Orange arose (represented by the present rulers of the Netherlands and Luxembourg); annexed to the Prussian province of Hesse-Nassau in 1866; corresponds to present-day W Hesse and NE Rhineland-Palatinate states **2** ('næsɔː) the capital and chief port of the Bahamas, on the NE coast of New Providence Island: resort. Pop: 229 000 (2005 est)

nassella tussock (nəˈsɛlə) *n* a type of tussock grass, originally of South America, now regarded as a noxious weed in New Zealand

Nassella Tussock Board *n NZ* one of many local statutory organizations set up in different regions of New Zealand to eradicate the invasive nassella tussock weed

Nasser ('nɑːsə, 'næsə) *n* **Gamal Abdel** (gəˈmɑːl ˈæbdɛl). 1918–70, Egyptian soldier and statesman; president of Egypt (1956–70). He was one of the leaders of the coup that deposed King Farouk (1952) and became premier

(1954). His nationalization of the Suez Canal (1956) led to an international crisis, and during his presidency Egypt was twice defeated by Israel (1956; 1967)

Nastase (nə'stæsi) n Ilie ('iːliː). born 1946, Romanian tennis player

nastic movement ('næstɪk) n a response of plant parts that is independent of the direction of the external stimulus, such as the opening of buds caused by an alteration in light intensity [C19 nastic, from Greek nastos close-packed, from nassein to press down]

nasturtium (nə'stɜːʃəm) n any of various plants of the genus Tropaeolum, esp T. major, having round leaves and yellow, red, or orange trumpet-shaped spurred flowers: family Tropaeolaceae [C17: from Latin: kind of cress, from nāsus nose + tortus twisted, from torquēre to twist, distort; so called because the pungent smell causes one to wrinkle one's nose]

nasty ('nɑːstɪ) adj -tier, -tiest 1 unpleasant, offensive, or repugnant 2 (of an experience, condition, etc) unpleasant, dangerous, or painful: a nasty wound 3 spiteful, abusive, or ill-natured 4 obscene or indecent ▷ n, pl -ties 5 an offensive or unpleasant person or thing: a video nasty [C14: origin obscure; probably related to Swedish dialect nasket and Dutch nestig dirty] > 'nastily adv > 'nastiness n

NAS/UWT abbreviation (in Britain) National Association of Schoolmasters/Union of Women Teachers

nat. abbreviation 1 national 2 natural

natal ('neɪtᵊl) adj of or relating to birth [C14: from Latin nātālis of one's birth, from nātus, from nascī to be born]

Natal (nə'tæl) n 1 a former province of E South Africa, between the Drakensberg and the Indian Ocean: set up as a republic by the Boers in 1838; became a British colony in 1843; joined South Africa in 1910; replaced by KwaZulu-Natal in 1994. Capital: Pietermaritzburg 2 (Portuguese na'tal) a port in NE Brazil, capital of Rio Grande do Norte state, near the mouth of the Potengi River. Pop: 1 049 000 (2005 est)

natant ('neɪtᵊnt) adj (of aquatic plants) floating on the water [C18: from Latin natāns, present participle of natāre to swim]

natation (nə'teɪʃən) n formal or a literary word for swimming [C16: from Latin natātiō a swimming, from natāre to swim]

natatory (nə'teɪtərɪ) or **natatorial** (ˌnætə'tɔːrɪəl, ˌneɪtə'tɔːrɪəl) adj of or relating to swimming [C18: from Late Latin natātōrius, from natāre to swim]

natch (nætʃ) sentence substitute informal short for **naturally** (sense 3)

nates ('neɪtiːz) pl n, sing -tis (-tɪs) a technical word for the **buttocks** [C17: from Latin; compare Greek nōton back, nosthi buttocks]

NATFHE abbreviation National Association of Teachers in Further and Higher Education

Nathan ('neɪθən) n Old Testament a prophet at David's court (II Samuel 7:1–17; 12:1–15)

Nathanael (nə'θænjəl) n New Testament a Galilean who is perhaps to be identified with Bartholomew among the apostles (John 1:45–51; 21:1)

natheless ('neɪθlɪs) or **nathless** ('næθlɪs) archaic sentence connector another word for **nonetheless** [Old English nāthylǣs, from nā never + thȳ for that + lǣs less]

nation ('neɪʃən) n 1 an aggregation of people or peoples of one or more cultures, races, etc, organized into a single state: the Australian nation 2 a community of persons not constituting a state but bound by common descent, language, history, etc: the French-Canadian nation [C13: via Old French from Latin nātiō birth, tribe, from nascī to be born] > 'nation,hood n

national ('næʃᵊnᵊl) adj 1 of, involving, or relating to a nation as a whole 2 of, relating to, or characteristic of a particular nation: the national dress of Poland ▷ n 3 a citizen or subject 4 a national newspaper > 'nationally adv

national anthem n a patriotic hymn or other song adopted by a nation for use on public or state occasions

national assistance n (in Britain) formerly a weekly allowance paid to certain people by the state to bring their incomes up to minimum levels established by law

national bank n 1 (in the US) a commercial bank

incorporated under a Federal charter and legally required to be a member of the Federal Reserve System 2 a bank owned and operated by a government

National Curriculum n (in England and Wales) the curriculum of subjects taught in state schools progressively from 1989. There are ten foundation subjects: English, maths, and science (the core subjects); art, design and technology, geography, history, music, physical education, and a foreign language. Pupils are assessed according to specified attainment targets throughout each of four key stages. Schools must also provide religious education and from 1999 lessons in citizenship. Abbreviation: NC

national debt n the total outstanding borrowings of a nation's central government

National Economic Development Council n an advisory body on general economic policy in Britain, composed of representatives of government, management, and trade unions: established in 1962; abolished in 1992. Abbreviation: NEDC

National Enterprise Board n a public corporation established in 1975 to help the economy of the UK. In 1981 it merged with the National Research and Development Council to form the British Technology Group. Abbreviation: NEB

National Front n (in Britain) a small political party of the right with racist and other extremist policies

National Gallery n a major art gallery in London, in Trafalgar Square. Founded in 1824, it contains the largest collection of paintings in Britain

national grid n 1 Brit a network of high-voltage power lines connecting major power stations 2 a grid of metric coordinates used by the Ordnance Survey in Britain and Ireland and in New Zealand by the New Zealand Lands and Survey Department and printed on their maps

National Guard n 1 (sometimes not capitals) the armed force, first commanded by Lafayette, that was established in France in 1789 and existed intermittently until 1871 2 (in the US) a state military force that can be called into federal service by the president

National Health Service n (in Britain) the system of national medical services since 1948, financed mainly by taxation. Abbreviation: NHS

national hunt n Brit (often capitals) a the racing of horses on racecourses with jumps b (as modifier): a National Hunt jockey

national income n economics the total of all incomes accruing over a specified period to residents of a country and consisting of wages, salaries, profits, rent, and interest

national insurance n (in Britain) state insurance based on weekly contributions from employees and employers and providing payments to the unemployed, the sick, the retired, etc, as well as medical services

nationalism ('næʃənəˌlɪzəm, 'næʃnə-) n 1 a sentiment based on common cultural characteristics that binds a population and often produces a policy of national independence or separatism 2 loyalty or devotion to one's country; patriotism 3 exaggerated, passionate, or fanatical devotion to a national community > 'nationalist n, adj > ˌnational'istic adj

nationality (ˌnæʃə'nælɪtɪ) n, pl -ties 1 the state or fact of being a citizen of a particular nation 2 a body of people sharing common descent, history, language, etc; a nation 3 a national group: 30 different nationalities are found in this city 4 national character or quality 5 the state or fact of being a nation; national status

nationalize or **nationalise** ('næʃənəˌlaɪz, 'næʃnə-) vb (tr) 1 to put (an industry, resources, etc) under state control or ownership 2 to make national in scope, character, or status 3 a less common word for **naturalize** > ˌnationali'zation or ˌnationali'sation n

national park n an area of countryside for public use designated by a national government as being of notable scenic, environmental, or historical importance

National Park n a mountainous volcanic region in New Zealand, in the central North Island: ski resort

National Party n 1 (in New Zealand) the more conservative of the two main political parties 2 (in

Australia) a political party drawing its main support from rural areas **3** (in South Africa) a political party composed mainly of centre-to-right-wing Afrikaners, which ruled from 1948 until the country's first multiracial elections in 1994: renamed the **New National Party** (NNP) in 1999

National Savings Bank n (in Britain) a government savings bank, run through the post office, esp for small savers

national service n compulsory military service

National Socialism n German history the doctrines and practices of the Nazis, involving the supremacy of the Austrian-born German dictator Adolf Hitler (1889–1945) as Führer (1934–45), anti-Semitism, state control of the economy, and national expansion > **National Socialist** n, adj

national superannuation n NZ a means-related pension paid to elderly people

National Tests pl n (sometimes not capitals) Brit education externally devised assessments in the core subjects of English, mathematics and science that school students in England and Wales sit at the end of Key Stages 1 to 3. Often referred to as: SATs

National Theatre n the former name of the **Royal National Theatre**

National Trust n **1** (in Britain) an organization concerned with the preservation of historic buildings and monuments and areas of the countryside of great beauty in England, Wales, and Northern Ireland. It was founded in 1895 and incorporated by act of parliament in 1907. The **National Trust for Scotland** was founded in 1931 **2** (in Australia) a similar organization in each of the states

nation-building n South African the advocacy of national solidarity in South Africa in the post-apartheid era

nationwide ('neɪʃən,waɪd) adj covering or available to the whole of a nation; national

native ('neɪtɪv) adj **1** relating or belonging to a person or thing by virtue of conditions existing at the time of birth: my native city **2** inherent, natural, or innate: a native strength **3** born in a specified place: a native German **4** (when postpositive, foll by to) originating in a specific place or area: kangaroos are native to Australia **5** characteristic of or relating to the indigenous inhabitants of a country or area: the native art of the New Guinea Highlands **6** (of chemical elements, esp metals) found naturally in the elemental form **7** unadulterated by civilization, artifice, or adornment; natural **8** archaic related by birth or race **9** go native (of a settler) to adopt the lifestyle of the local population, esp when it appears less civilized ▷ n **10** (usually foll by of) a person born in a particular place: a native of Geneva **11** (usually foll by of) a species originating in a particular place or area **12** a member of an indigenous people of a country or area, esp a non-White people, as opposed to colonial settlers and immigrants [C14: from Latin nātīvus innate, natural, from nascī to be born] > 'natively adv > 'nativeness n

Native American n a member of the indigenous peoples of North America

native bear n an Austral. name for **koala**

native-born adj born in the country or area indicated

native cat n Austral any of various Australian catlike carnivorous marsupials of the genus Dasyurus

native companion n Austral another name for the **brolga** [C19: so called because the birds were observed in pairs]

native dog n Austral a dingo

Native States pl n the former 562 semi-independent states of India, ruled by Indians but subject to varying degrees of British authority: merged with provinces by 1948; largest states were Hyderabad, Gwalior, Baroda, Mysore, Cochin, Jammu and Kashmir, Travancore, Sikkim, and Indore. Also called: **Indian States and Agencies**

nativity (nə'tɪvɪtɪ) n, pl -ties birth or origin, esp in relation to the circumstances surrounding it [C14: via Old French from Late Latin nātīvitas birth: see NATIVE]

Nativity (nə'tɪvɪtɪ) n **1** the birth of Jesus Christ **2** the feast of Christmas as a commemoration of this **3 a** an

artistic representation of the circumstances of the birth of Christ **b** (as modifier): a Nativity play

NATO or **Nato** ('neɪtəʊ) n acronym for North Atlantic Treaty Organization, an international organization composed of the US, Canada, Britain, and a number of European countries: established by the **North Atlantic Treaty** (1949) for purposes of collective security. In 1994 it launched the partnerships for peace initiative, in order to forge alliances with former Warsaw Pact countries; in 1997 a treaty of cooperation with Russia was signed and in 1999 Hungary, Poland, and the Czech Republic became full NATO members

natron ('neɪtrən) n a whitish or yellow mineral that consists of hydrated sodium carbonate and occurs in saline deposits and salt lakes. Formula: $Na_2CO_3.10H_2O$ [C17: via French and Spanish from Arabic natrūn, from Greek nitron]

natter ('nætə) chiefly Brit ▷ vb **1** (intr) to talk idly and at length; chatter or gossip ▷ n **2** prolonged idle chatter or gossip [C19: changed from gnatter to grumble, of imitative origin; compare Low German gnatteren]

natterjack ('nætə,dʒæk) n a European toad, Bufo calamita, of sandy regions, having a greyish-brown body marked with reddish warty processes: family Bufonidae [C18: of unknown origin]

natty ('nætɪ) adj -tier, -tiest informal smart in appearance or dress; spruce; dapper [C18: perhaps from obsolete netty, from net NEAT¹; compare Old French net trim] > 'nattily adv > 'nattiness n

natural ('nætʃrəl, -tʃərəl) adj **1** of, existing in, or produced by nature: natural science; natural cliffs **2** in accordance with human nature **3** as is normal or to be expected; ordinary or logical: the natural course of events **4** not acquired; innate: a natural gift for sport **5** being so through innate qualities: a natural leader **6** not supernatural or strange: natural phenomena **7** not constrained or affected; genuine or spontaneous **8** following or resembling nature or life; lifelike: she looked more natural without her make-up **9** not affected by man or civilization; uncultivated; wild: in the natural state this animal is not ferocious **10** being or made from organic material; not synthetic: a natural fibre like cotton **11** illegitimate; born out of wedlock **12** not adopted but rather related by blood: her natural parents **13** music **a** not sharp or flat **b** (postpositive) denoting a note that is neither sharp nor flat **c** (of a key or scale) containing no sharps or flats **14** based on the principles and findings of human reason and what is to be learned of God from nature rather than on revelation: natural religion ▷ n **15** informal a person or thing regarded as certain to qualify for success, selection, etc: the horse was a natural for first place **16** music **a** Also called (US): **cancel** an accidental cancelling a previous sharp or flat. Usual symbol: ♮ **b** a note affected by this accidental **17** obsolete an imbecile; idiot > 'naturalness n

natural childbirth n a method of childbirth characterized by the absence of anaesthetics, in which the expectant mother is given special breathing and relaxing exercises

natural gas n a gaseous mixture consisting mainly of methane trapped below ground; used extensively as a fuel

natural history n **1** the study of animals and plants in the wild state **2** the sum of these phenomena in a given place or at a given time > natural historian n

natural immunity n immunity with which an individual is born, which has a genetic basis

naturalism ('nætʃrə,lɪzəm, -tʃərə-) n **1** a movement, esp in art and literature, advocating detailed realistic and factual description, esp that in 19th-century France in the writings of the novelists Emile Zola (1840–1902), Gustave Flaubert (1821–80), etc **2** the belief that all religious truth is based not on revelation but rather on the study of natural causes and processes **3** philosophy **a** scientific account of the world in terms of causes and natural forces that rejects all spiritual, supernatural, or teleological explanations **4** action or thought caused by natural desires and instincts

naturalist ('nætʃrəlɪst, -tʃərəl-) n **1** a person who is expert or interested in botany or zoology, esp in the field **2** a person who advocates or practises naturalism, esp in art or literature

naturalistic (ˌnætʃrəˈlɪstɪk, -tʃərə-) *adj* **1** of, imitating, or reproducing nature in effect or characteristics **2** of or characteristic of naturalism, esp in art or literature **3** of or relating to naturalists > ˌnaturalˈistically *adv*

naturalize *or* **naturalise** (ˈnætʃrəˌlaɪz, -tʃərə-) *vb* **1** (*tr*) to give citizenship to (a person of foreign birth) **2** to be or cause to be adopted in another place, as a word, custom, etc **3** (*tr*) to introduce (a plant or animal from another region) and cause it to adapt to local conditions **4** (*intr*) (of a plant or animal) to adapt successfully to a foreign environment and spread there **5** (*tr*) to make natural or more lifelike > ˌnaturaliˈzation *or* ˌnaturaliˈsation *n*

natural language *n* a language that has evolved naturally as a means of communication among people

natural logarithm *n* a logarithm to the base e. Usually written logₑ or ln. Also called: **Napierian logarithm**

naturally (ˈnætʃrəlɪ, -tʃərə-) *adv* **1** in a natural or normal way **2** through nature; inherently; instinctively ▷ *adv, sentence substitute* **3** of course; surely

natural number *n* any of the numbers 0,1,2,3,4,... that can be used to count the members of a set; the nonnegative integers

natural philosophy *n* (now only used in Scottish universities) physical science, esp physics > **natural philosopher** *n*

natural resources *pl n* naturally occurring materials such as coal, fertile land, etc, that can be used by man

natural science *n* the sciences collectively that are involved in the study of the physical world and its phenomena, including biology, physics, chemistry, and geology, but excluding social sciences, abstract or theoretical sciences, such as mathematics, and applied sciences

natural selection *n* a process resulting in the survival of those individuals from a population of animals or plants that are best adapted to the prevailing environmental conditions. The survivors tend to produce more offspring than those less well adapted, so that the characteristics of the population change over time, thus accounting for the process of evolution

natural theology *n* the attempt to derive theological truth, and esp the existence of God, from empirical facts by reasoned argument. Compare **revealed religion**

nature (ˈneɪtʃə) *n* **1** the fundamental qualities of a person or thing; identity or essential character **2** (*often capital, esp when personified*) the whole system of the existence, arrangement, forces, and events of all physical life that are not controlled by man **3** all natural phenomena and plant and animal life, as distinct from man and his creations **4** a wild primitive state untouched by man or civilization **5** natural unspoilt scenery or countryside **6** disposition or temperament **7** tendencies, desires, or instincts governing behaviour **8** the normal biological needs or requirements of the body **9** sort; kind; character **10 against nature** unnatural or immoral **11 by nature** essentially or innately **12 call of nature** *informal, euphemistic, or humorous* the need to urinate or defecate **13 from nature** using natural models in drawing, painting, etc **14 in (of) the nature of** essentially the same as; by way of [c13: via Old French from Latin *nātūra*, from *nātus*, past participle of *nascī* to be born]

nature reserve *n* an area of land that is protected and managed in order to preserve a particular type of habitat and its flora and fauna which are often rare or endangered

nature study *n* the study of the natural world, esp animals and plants, by direct observation at an elementary level

nature trail *n* a path through countryside designed and usually signposted to draw attention to natural features of interest

naturism (ˈneɪtʃəˌrɪzəm) *n* another name for **nudism** > ˈnaturist *n, adj*

naturopathy (ˌneɪtʃəˈrɒpəθɪ) *n* a method of treating disorders, involving the use of herbs and other naturally

grown foods, sunlight, fresh air, etc. Also called: **nature cure** > **naturopath** (ˈneɪtʃərəˌpæθ) *n* > ˌnaturoˈpathic *adj*

Naucratis (ˈnɔːkrətɪs) *n* an ancient Greek city in N Egypt, in the Nile delta: founded in the 7th century BC

naught (nɔːt) *n* **1** *archaic or literary* nothing or nothingness; ruin or failure **2** a variant spelling (esp US) of **nought 3 set at naught** to have disregard or scorn for; disdain ▷ *adv* **4** *archaic, or literary* not at all: *it matters naught* ▷ *adj* **5** *obsolete* worthless, ruined, or wicked [Old English *nāwiht*, from *nā* NO¹ + *wiht* thing, person; see WIGHT¹, WHIT]

naughty (ˈnɔːtɪ) *adj* **-tier, -tiest 1** (esp of children or their behaviour) mischievous or disobedient; bad **2** mildly indecent; titillating [c14 (originally: needy, of poor quality): from NAUGHT] > ˈnaughtily *adv* > ˈnaughtiness *n*

nauplius (ˈnɔːplɪəs) *n, pl* **-plii** (-plɪˌaɪ) the larva of many crustaceans, having a rounded unsegmented body with three pairs of limbs [c19: from Latin: type of shellfish, from Greek *Nauplios*, one of the sons of Poseidon]

Nauru (naːˈuːruː) *n* an island republic in the SW Pacific, west of Kiribati: administered jointly by Australia, New Zealand, and Britain as a UN trust territory before becoming independent in 1968; a member of the Commonwealth (formerly a special member not represented at all meetings, until 1999). The economy is based on export of phosphates. Languages: Nauruan (a Malayo-Polynesian language) and English. Religion: Christian. Currency: Australian dollar. Capital: Yaren. Pop: 13 000 (2003 est). Area: 2130 hectares (5263 acres). Former name: **Pleasant Island** > Na'uruan *adj, n*

nausea (ˈnɔːzɪə, -sɪə) *n* **1** the sensation that precedes vomiting **2** a feeling of disgust or revulsion [c16: via Latin from Greek: seasickness, from *naus* ship]

nauseate (ˈnɔːzɪˌeɪt, -sɪ-) *vb* **1** (*tr*) to arouse feelings of disgust or revulsion in **2** to feel or cause to feel sick > ˈnauseˌating *adj* > ˈnauseˌatingly *adv*

nauseous (ˈnɔːzɪəs, -sɪəs) *adj* **1** causing nausea **2** distasteful to the mind or senses; repulsive > ˈnauseously *adv* > ˈnauseousness *n*

Nausicaä (nɔːˈsɪkɪə) *n Greek myth* a daughter of Alcinous, king of the Phaeacians, who assisted the shipwrecked Odysseus after discovering him on a beach

-naut *n combining form* indicating a person engaged in the navigation of a vehicle, esp one used for scientific investigation: *astronaut*

nautch *or* **nauch** (nɔːtʃ) *n* an intricate traditional Indian dance performed by professional dancing girls [c18: from Hindi *nāc*, from Sanskrit *nrtya*, from *nrtyati* he acts or dances]

nautical (ˈnɔːtɪkᵊl) *adj* of, relating to, or involving ships, navigation, or sailors [c16: from Latin *nauticus*, from Greek *nautikos*, from *naus* ship] > ˈnautically *adv*

nautical mile *n* **1** Also called: **international nautical mile, air mile** a unit of length, used esp in navigation, equivalent to the average length of a minute of latitude, and corresponding to a latitude of 45°, i.e. 1852 m (6076.12 ft) **2** a former British unit of length equal to 1853.18 m (6080 ft), which was replaced by the international nautical mile in 1970. Former name: **geographical mile** Compare **sea mile**

nautilus (ˈnɔːtɪləs) *n, pl* **-luses** *or* **-li** (-ˌlaɪ) **1** any cephalopod mollusc of the genus *Nautilus*, esp the pearly nautilus **2** short for **paper nautilus** [c17: via Latin from Greek *nautilos* sailor, from *naus* ship]

NAV *abbreviation* net asset value

Navaho *or* **Navajo** (ˈnævəˌhəʊ, ˈnɑː-) *n* **1** (*pl* **-ho, -hos, -hoes** *or* **-jo, -jos, -joes**) a member of a North American Indian people of Arizona, New Mexico, and Utah **2** the language of this people, belonging to the Athapascan group of the Na-Dene phylum [c18: from Spanish *Navajó* pueblo, from Tena *Navahu* large planted field]

naval (ˈneɪvᵊl) *adj* **1** of, relating to, characteristic of, or having a navy **2** of or relating to ships; nautical [c16: from Latin *nāvālis*, from *nāvis* ship; related to Greek *naus*, Old Norse *nōr* ship, Sanskrit *nau*]

naval architecture *n* the designing of ships > **naval architect** *n*

Navaratri (nævəˈrɑːtrɪ) *n* an annual Hindu festival

celebrated over nine days in September-October. Observed throughout India, it commemorates the slaying of demons by Rama and the goddess Durga; in some places it is dedicated to all female deities. Also called: **Durga Puja** [from Sanskrit *navaratri* nine nights]

navarin ('nævərɪn; *French* navaṙẽ) *n* a stew of mutton or lamb with root vegetables [from French]

Navarino (nava'riːno) *n* **1** the Italian name for **Pylos 2** a sea battle (Oct 20, 1827) in which the defeat of the Turkish-Egyptian fleet by a combined British, French, and Russian fleet decided Greek independence

Navarre (nə'vɑː) *n* a former kingdom of SW Europe: established in the 9th century by the Basques; the parts south of the Pyrenees joined Spain in 1515 and the N parts passed to France in 1589. Capital: Pamplona. Spanish name: **Navarra** (nɑ'βarra)

nave¹ (neɪv) *n* the central space in a church, extending from the narthex to the chancel and often flanked by aisles [c17: via Medieval Latin from Latin *nāvis* ship, from the similarity of shape]

nave² (neɪv) *n* the central block or hub of a wheel [Old English *nafu, nafa*; related to Old High German *naba*]

navel ('neɪv³l) *n* **1** the scar in the centre of the abdomen, usually forming a slight depression, where the umbilical cord was attached. Technical name: **umbilicus**. Related adj: **umbilical 2** a central part, location, or point; middle [Old English *nafela*; related to Old Frisian *navla*, Old High German *nabulo* (German *Nabel*), Latin *umbilīcus*]

navel orange *n* a sweet orange that is usually seedless and has at its apex a navel-like depression enclosing an underdeveloped secondary fruit

navelwort ('neɪv³l,wɜːt) *n* another name for **pennywort** (sense 1)

navicular *anatomy* ▷ *adj* (nə'vɪkjʊlə) **1** shaped like a boat ▷ *n also* **naviculare** (nə,vɪkjʊ'lɑːrɪ) **2** a small boat-shaped bone of the wrist or foot [c16: from Late Latin *nāviculāris*, from Latin *nāvicula*, diminutive of *nāvis* ship]

navigable ('nævɪgəb³l) *adj* **1** wide, deep, or safe enough to be sailed on or through: *a navigable channel* **2** capable of being steered or controlled: *a navigable raft* ▷ ,naviga'bility *or* 'navigableness *n* ▷ 'navigably *adv*

navigate ('nævɪ,geɪt) *vb* **1** to plan, direct, or plot the path or position of (a ship, an aircraft, etc) **2** (*tr*) to travel over, through, or on (water, air, or land) in a boat, aircraft, etc **3** *informal* to direct (oneself, one's way, etc) carefully or safely: *he navigated his way to the bar* **4** (*intr*) (of a passenger in a motor vehicle) to give directions to the driver; point out the route [c16: from Latin *nāvigāre* to sail, from *nāvis* ship + *agere* to drive]

navigation (,nævɪ'geɪʃən) *n* **1** the skill or process of plotting a route and directing a ship, aircraft, etc, along it **2** the act or practice of navigating: *dredging made navigation of the river possible* ▷ ,navi'gational *adj*

navigator ('nævɪ,geɪtə) *n* **1** a person who is skilled in or performs navigation, esp on a ship or aircraft **2** (*esp formerly*) a person who explores by ship **3** an instrument or device for assisting a pilot to navigate an aircraft

Návpaktos (*Greek* 'nafpaktos) *n* the Greek name for Lepanto

Navratilova (næ,vrætɪ'ləʊvə) *n* **Martina.** born 1956, Czech-born US tennis player: Wimbledon champion 1978, 1979, 1982–87, 1990; world champion 1980 and 1984

navvy ('nævɪ) *n, pl* -**vies** *Brit informal* a labourer on a building site, excavations, etc [c19: shortened from *navigator*, builder of a **NAVIGATION** (sense 4)]

navy ('neɪvɪ) *n, pl* -**vies 1** the warships and auxiliary vessels of a nation or ruler **2 the navy** (*often capital*) the branch of a country's armed services comprising such ships, their crews, and all their supporting services and equipment **3** short for **navy blue 4** *archaic or literary* a fleet of ships [c14: via Old French from Vulgar Latin *nāvia* (unattested), from Latin *nāvis* ship]

navy blue *n* **a** a dark greyish-blue colour **b** (*as adjective*): *a navy-blue suit* [c19: from the colour of the British naval uniform]

Navy List *n* (in Britain) an official list of all serving commissioned officers of the Royal Navy and reserve officers liable for recall

navy yard *n* a naval shipyard, esp in the US

nawab (nə'wɑːb) *n* (formerly) a Muslim ruling prince or powerful landowner in India [c18: from Hindi *nawwāb*, from Arabic *nuwwāb*, plural of *na'ib* viceroy, governor]

Naxos ('næksɒs) *n* a Greek island in the S Aegean, the largest of the Cyclades: ancient centre of the worship of Dionysius. Pop: 18 188 (2001). Area: 438 sq km (169 sq miles)

nay (neɪ) *sentence substitute* **1** a word for **no¹**: archaic or dialectal except in voting by voice ▷ *n* **2** a person who votes in the negative ▷ *adv* **3** (*sentence modifier*) *archaic* an emphatic form of **no¹** [c12: from Old Norse *nei*, from *ne* not + *ei* ever, **AY¹**]

Nayarit (*Spanish* naja'rit) *n* a state of W Mexico, on the Pacific: includes the offshore Tres Marías Islands. Capital: Tepic. Pop: 919 739 (2000). Area: 27 621 sq km (10 772 sq miles)

Nay Pyi Taw *or* **Naypyidaw** ('neɪ 'pji: 'taʊ) *n* the official capital of Myanmar (Burma), built in the centre of the country near Pyinmana in 2005–2006, and superseding Yangon (Rangoon) for main government functions. Pop: officially approaching 1 000 000 in 2007

Nazarene (,næzə'riːn, 'næz-) *n also*: **Nazarite 1** an early name for a **Christian** (Acts 24:5) or (when preceded by *the*) for Jesus Christ (?4 BC–?29 AD), the founder of Christianity **2** a member of one of several groups of Jewish-Christians found principally in Syria ▷ *adj* **3** of or relating to Nazareth or the Nazarenes

Nazareth ('næzərɪθ) *n* a town in N Israel, in Lower Galilee: the home of Jesus in his youth. Pop: 62 700 (2003 est)

Nazarite *or* **Nazirite** ('næzə,raɪt) *n* a religious ascetic of ancient Israel [c16: from Latin *Nazaraeus*, from Hebrew *nāzīr*, from *nāzar* to consecrate + -ITE¹]

Naze (neɪz) *n* **the Naze 1** a flat marshy headland in SE England, in Essex on the North Sea coast **2** another name for **Lindesnes**

Nazi ('nɑːtsɪ) *n, pl* **Nazis 1** a member of the fascist National Socialist German Workers' Party, which was founded in 1919 and seized political control in Germany in 1933 under the Austrian-born German dictator Adolf Hitler (1889–1945) ▷ *adj* **2** of, characteristic of, or relating to the Nazis [c20: from German, phonetic spelling of the first two syllables of *Nationalsozialist* National Socialist] ▷ 'Naz,ism *or* 'Nazi,ism *n*

Nb *the chemical symbol for* niobium

NB¹ *abbreviation* New Brunswick

NB², N.B., nb *or* **n.b.** *abbreviation* nota bene [Latin: note well]

NBA *abbreviation* **1** (in the US) National Basketball Association **2** (the former) Net Book Agreement

NC *or* **N.C.** *abbreviation* **1** North Carolina **2** *Brit education* National Curriculum

NCC (in Britain) *abbreviation* (the former) Nature Conservancy Council

NCEA (in New Zealand) *abbreviation* National Certificate of Educational Attainment

NCIS (in Britain) *abbreviation* National Criminal Intelligence Service

NCO *abbreviation* noncommissioned officer

nd *abbreviation* no date

Nd *the chemical symbol for* neodymium

ND, N.D. *or* **N. Dak.** *abbreviation* North Dakota

Ndjamena *or* **N'djamena** (ᵊndʒɑː'meɪnə) *n* the capital of Chad, in the southwest, at the confluence of the Shari and Logone Rivers: trading centre for livestock. Pop: 866 000 (2005 est). Former name (until 1973): **Fort Lamy**

Ndola (ᵊn'dəʊlə) *n* a city in N Zambia: copper, cobalt, and sugar refineries. Pop: 478 000 (2005 est)

N'Dour (ᵊn'dʊə) *n* **Youssou** ('jusu). born 1959, Senegalese singer and musician, whose work has popularized African music in the West; recordings include *Nelson Mandela* (1986), *Eyes Open* (1992), and *Nothing's in Vain* (2002)

NDP *abbreviation* **1** net domestic product **2** (in Canada) New Democratic Party

NDT *abbreviation* nondestructive testing

Ne *the chemical symbol for* neon

NE¹ 1 *symbol for* northeast(ern) **2** *abbreviation* Nebraska

NE² or **N.E.** *abbreviation* New England

ne- *combining form* a variant of **neo-**, esp used before a vowel: *Nearctic*

Neagh (neɪ) *n* **Lough Neagh** a lake in Northern Ireland, in SW Co Antrim: the largest lake in the British Isles. Area: 388 sq km (150 sq miles)

Neanderthal man (nɪˈændəˌtɑːl) *n* a type of primitive man, *Homo neanderthalensis*, or *H. sapiens neanderthalensis*, occurring throughout much of Europe in late Palaeolithic times: it is thought that they did not interbreed with other early humans and are not the ancestors of modern humans [C19: from the anthropological findings (1857) in the Neandertal, a valley near Düsseldorf, Germany]

neap (niːp) *adj* **1** of, relating to, or constituting a neap tide ▷ *n* **2** short for **neap tide** [Old English, as in *nēpflōd* neap tide, of uncertain origin]

Neapolitan (ˌnɪəˈpɒlɪtᵊn) *n* **1** a native or inhabitant of Naples ▷ *adj* **2** of or relating to Naples [C15: from Latin *Neāpolītānus*, ultimately from Greek *Neapolis* new town]

Neapolitan ice cream *n* ice cream, usually in brick form, with several layers of different colours and flavours

neap tide *n* either of the two tides that occur at the first or last quarter of the moon when the tide-generating forces of the sun and moon oppose each other and produce the smallest rise and fall in tidal level. Compare **spring tide** (sense 1)

near (nɪə) *prep* **1** at or to a place or time not far away from; close to ▷ *adv* **2** at or to a place or time not far away; close by **3** short for **nearly**: *I was damn near killed* ▷ *adj* **4** at or in a place not far away **5** (*postpositive*) not far away in time; imminent: *departure time was near* **6** (*prenominal*) only just successful or only just failing: *a near escape* **7** (*postpositive*) *informal* miserly, mean **8** (*prenominal*) closely connected or intimate: *a near relation* ▷ *vb* **9** to come or draw close (to) ▷ *n* **10** Also called: **nearside** the left side of a horse, team of animals, vehicle, etc **b** (*as modifier*): *the near foreleg* [Old English *nēar* (adv), comparative of *nēah* close, NIGH; related to Old Frisian *niār*, Old Norse *nēr*, Old High German *nāhōr*] ▷ **'nearness** *n*

nearby (ˈnɪəˌbaɪ) *adj* not far away; close at hand

Nearctic (nɪˈɑːktɪk) *adj* of or denoting a zoogeographical region consisting of North America, north of the tropic of Cancer, and Greenland

Near East *n* **1** another term for the **Middle East** **2** (formerly) the Balkan States and the area of the Ottoman Empire

near gale *n meteorol* a wind of force seven on the Beaufort scale or from 32–38 mph

nearly (ˈnɪəlɪ) *adv* **1** not quite; almost; practically **2** **not nearly** nowhere near; not at all: *not nearly enough money* **3** closely: *the person most nearly concerned*

near miss *n* **1** a bomb, shell, etc, that does not exactly hit the target **2** any attempt or shot that just fails to be successful **3** an incident in which two vehicles narrowly avoid collision

near point *n optics* the nearest point to the eye at which an object remains in focus

nearside (ˈnɪəˌsaɪd) *n* **1** **the nearside** *chiefly Brit* **a** a side of a vehicle normally nearer the kerb (in Britain, the left side) **b** (*as modifier*): *the nearside door* **2** **a** the left side of an animal, team of horses, etc **b** (*as modifier*): *the nearside flank*

near-sighted (ˌnɪəˈsaɪtɪd) *adj* relating to or suffering from myopia ▷ **ˌnear-'sightedly** *adv*

near thing *n informal* an event or action whose outcome is nearly a failure, success, disaster, etc

neat¹ (niːt) *adj* **1** clean, tidy, and orderly **2** liking or insisting on order and cleanliness; fastidious **3** smoothly or competently done; efficient: *a neat job* **4** pat or slick: *his excuse was suspiciously neat* **5** (of alcoholic drinks) without added water, lemonade, etc; undiluted **6** *slang, chiefly US & Canadian* good; pleasing; admirable [C16: from Old French *net*, from Latin *nitidus* clean, shining, from *nitēre* to shine; related to Middle Irish *niam* beauty, brightness, Old Persian *naiba-* beautiful] ▷ **'neatly** *adv* ▷ **'neatness** *n*

neat² (niːt) *n, pl* **neat** *archaic* or *dialect* a domestic bovine animal [Old English *neat*]

neaten (ˈniːtᵊn) *vb* (*tr*) to make neat; tidy

neath or **'neath** (niːθ) *prep archaic* short for **beneath**

Neath Port Talbot (niːθ ˈpɔːt ˈtɔːlbət, ˈtæl-) *n* a county borough in S Wales, created from part of West Glamorgan in 1996. Administrative centre: Port Talbot. Pop: 135 300 (2003 est). Area: 439 sq km (169 sq miles)

neat's-foot oil *n* a yellow fixed oil obtained by boiling the feet and shinbones of cattle and used esp to dress leather

neb (nɛb) *n archaic* or *dialect* **1** *chiefly Scot & northern English* the peak of a cap **2** the beak of a bird or the nose or snout of an animal **3** the projecting part or end of anything [Old English *nebb*; related to Old Norse *nef*, Old High German *snabul* (German *Schnabel*)]

NEB *abbreviation* **1** New English Bible **2** (the former) National Enterprise Board

Nebo (ˈniːbəʊ) *n* **Mount Nebo** a mountain in Jordan, northeast of the Dead Sea: the highest point of a ridge known as Pisgah, from which Moses viewed the Promised Land just before his death (Deuteronomy 34:1). Height: 802 m (2631 ft)

Nebr. *abbreviation* Nebraska

Nebraska (nɪˈbræskə) *n* a state of the western US: consists of an undulating plain. Capital: Lincoln. Pop: 1 739 291 (2003 est). Area: 197 974 sq km (76 483 sq miles). Abbreviations: **Nebr.**, **NE** > **Ne'braskan** *adj, n*

Nebuchadnezzar (ˌnɛbjʊkədˈnɛzə) or **Nebuchadrezzar** *n Old Testament* a king of Babylon, 605–562 BC, who conquered and destroyed Jerusalem and exiled the Jews to Babylon (II Kings 24–25)

nebula (ˈnɛbjʊlə) *n, pl* **-lae** (-ˌliː) or **-las 1** *astronomy* a diffuse cloud of particles and gases (mainly hydrogen) that is visible either as a hazy patch of light (either an **emission** or a **reflection nebula**) or an irregular dark region against a brighter background (**dark nebula**) **2** *pathol* opacity of the cornea [C17: from Latin: mist, cloud; related to Greek *nephélē* cloud, Old High German *nebul* cloud, Old Norse *njól* night] > **'nebular** *adj*

nebular hypothesis *n* the theory that the solar system evolved from the gravitational collapse of nebular matter

nebulize or **nebulise** (ˈnɛbjʊˌlaɪz) *vb* (*tr*) to convert (a liquid) into a mist or fine spray; atomize > ˌnebuli'zation or ˌnebuli'sation *n*

nebulizer or **nebuliser** (ˈnɛbjʊˌlaɪzə) *n* a device for converting a drug in liquid form into a mist or fine spray which is inhaled through a mask to provide medication for the respiratory system. Also called: **inhalator**

nebulosity (ˌnɛbjʊˈlɒsɪtɪ) *n, pl* **-ties 1** the state or quality of being nebulous **2** *astronomy* a nebula

nebulous (ˈnɛbjʊləs) *adj* **1** lacking definite form, shape, or content; vague or amorphous: *nebulous reasons* **2** of, characteristic of, or resembling a nebula **3** *rare* misty or hazy > **'nebulousness** *n*

NEC *abbreviation* National Executive Committee

necessaries (ˈnɛsɪsərɪz) *pl n* (*sometimes singular*) what is needed; essential items: *the necessaries of life*

necessarily (ˈnɛsɪsərɪlɪ, ˌnɛsɪˈsɛrɪlɪ) *adv* **1** as an inevitable or natural consequence **2** as a certainty: *he won't necessarily come*

necessary (ˈnɛsɪsərɪ) *adj* **1** needed to achieve a certain desired effect or result; required **2** resulting from necessity; inevitable: *the necessary consequences of your action* **3** *logic* **a** (of a statement, formula, etc) true under all interpretations or in all possible circumstances **b** (of a proposition) determined to be true by its meaning, so that its denial would be self-contradictory **c** (of a condition) entailed by the truth of some statement or the obtaining of some state of affairs. See **sufficient** (sense 2) **4** *rare* compelled, as by necessity or law; not free ▷ *n* **5** **the necessary** *informal* the money required for a particular purpose **6** **do the necessary** *informal* to do something that is necessary in a particular situation ▷ See also **necessaries** [C14: from Latin *necessārius* indispensable, from *necesse* unavoidable]

necessitarianism (nɪˌsɛsɪˈtɛərɪəˌnɪzəm) or **necessarianism** (ˌnɛsɪˈsɛərɪəˌnɪzəm) *n philosophy* another word for **determinism** Compare **libertarian** > ne,cessi'tarian or ,neces'sarian n, adj

necessitate (nɪ'sɛsɪˌteɪt) vb (tr) **1** to cause as an unavoidable and necessary result **2** (usually passive) to compel or require (someone to do something)

necessitous (nɪ'sɛsɪtəs) adj very needy; destitute; poverty-stricken

necessity (nɪ'sɛsɪtɪ) n, pl -ties **1** (sometimes plural) something needed for a desired result; prerequisite: necessities of life **2** a condition or set of circumstances, such as physical laws or social rules, that inevitably requires a certain result: it is a matter of necessity to wear formal clothes when meeting the Queen **3** the state or quality of being obligatory or unavoidable **4** urgent requirement, as in an emergency or misfortune: in time of necessity we must all work together **5** poverty or want **6** rare compulsion through laws of nature; fate **7** logic the property of being necessary **8** of necessity inevitably; necessarily

neck (nɛk) n **1** the part of an organism connecting the head with the rest of the body **2** the part of a garment around or nearest the neck **3** something resembling a neck in shape or position: the neck of a bottle **4** anatomy a constricted portion of an organ or part, such as the cervix of the uterus **5** a narrow or elongated projecting strip of land; a peninsula or isthmus **6** a strait or channel **7** the part of a violin, cello, etc, that extends from the body to the tuning pegs and supports the fingerboard **8** a solid block of lava from the opening of an extinct volcano, exposed after erosion of the surrounding rock **9** the length of a horse's head and neck taken as an approximate distance by which one horse beats another in a race: to win by a neck **10** informal impudence; audacity **11** architect the narrow band at the top of the shaft of a column between the necking and the capital, esp as used in the Tuscan order **12** get it in the neck informal to be reprimanded or punished severely **13** neck and neck absolutely level or even in a race or competition **14** neck of the woods informal an area or locality: a quiet neck of the woods **15** informal **a** save one's neck to escape from a difficult or dangerous situation **b** save someone's neck to help someone else escape from such a situation **16** stick one's neck out informal to risk criticism, ridicule, failure, etc, by speaking one's mind ▷ vb **17** (intr) informal to kiss, embrace, or fondle someone or one another passionately [Old English hnecca; related to Old High German hnack, Old Irish cnocc hill]

Neckar ('nɛkɑː) n a river in SW Germany, rising in the Black Forest and flowing generally north into the Rhine at Mannheim. Length: 394 km (245 miles)

neckband ('nɛkˌbænd) n a band around the neck of a garment as finishing, decoration, or a base for a collar

neckcloth ('nɛkˌklɒθ) n a large ornamental usually white cravat worn formerly by men

Necker ('nɛkə; French nɛkɛr) n Jacques (ʒak). 1732–1804, French financier and statesman, born in Switzerland; finance minister of France (1777–81; 1788–90). He attempted to reform the fiscal system and in 1789 he recommended summoning the States General. His subsequent dismissal was one of the causes of the storming of the Bastille (1789)

neckerchief ('nɛkətˌʃɪf, -ˌtʃiːf) n a piece of ornamental cloth, often square, worn around the neck [c14: from NECK + KERCHIEF]

necking ('nɛkɪŋ) n informal the activity of kissing and embracing passionately

necklace ('nɛklɪs) n **1** a chain, band, or cord, often bearing beads, pearls, jewels, etc, worn around the neck as an ornament, esp by women **2** (in South Africa) a tyre soaked in petrol, placed round a person's neck, and set on fire in order to burn the person to death ▷ vb **3** (tr) South African to kill (someone) by placing a burning tyre round his or her neck

neckline ('nɛkˌlaɪn) n the shape or position of the upper edge of a dress, blouse, etc

necktie ('nɛkˌtaɪ) n the US name for **tie** (sense 10)

neckwear ('nɛkˌwɛə) n articles of clothing, such as ties, scarves, etc, worn around the neck

necro- or before a vowel **necr-** combining form indicating death, a dead body, or dead tissue: necrology; necrophagous; necrosis [from Greek nekros corpse]

necrobiosis (ˌnɛkrəʊbaɪ'əʊsɪs) n physiol the normal degeneration and death of cells

necrolatry (nɛ'krɒlətrɪ) n the worship of the dead

necrology (nɛ'krɒlədʒɪ) n, pl -gies **1** a list of people recently dead **2** a less common word for **obituary** > necrological (ˌnɛkrə'lɒdʒɪkᵊl) adj

necromancy ('nɛkrəʊˌmænsɪ) n **1** the art or practice of supposedly conjuring up the dead, esp in order to obtain from them knowledge of the future **2** black magic; sorcery [c13: (as in sense 1) ultimately from Greek nekromanteia, from nekros corpse; (as in sense 2) from Medieval Latin nigromantia, from Latin niger black, which replaced necro- through folk etymology] > 'necroˌmancer n > ˌnecro'mantic adj

necrophilia (ˌnɛkrəʊ'fɪlɪə) n sexual attraction for or sexual intercourse with dead bodies. Also called: necromania, necrophilism > ˌnecro'philiˌac or necrophile ('nɛkrəʊˌfaɪl) n > ˌnecro'philic adj

necropolis (nɛ'krɒpəlɪs) n, pl -lises or -leis (-ˌleɪs) a burial site or cemetery [c19: Greek, from nekros dead + polis city]

necropsy ('nɛkrɒpsɪ) or **necroscopy** (nɛ'krɒskəpɪ) n, pl -sies or -pies another name for **autopsy** [c19: from Greek nekros dead body + opsis sight]

necrosis (nɛ'krəʊsɪs) n **1** the death of one or more cells in the body, usually within a localized area, as from an interruption of the blood supply to that part **2** death of plant tissue due to disease, frost, etc [c17: New Latin from Greek nekrōsis, from nekroun to kill, from nekros corpse] > necrotic (nɛ'krɒtɪk) adj

nectar ('nɛktə) n **1** a sugary fluid produced in the nectaries of plants and collected by bees and other animals **2** classical myth the drink of the gods. Compare **ambrosia** (sense 1) **3** any delicious drink, esp a sweet one [c16: via Latin from Greek néktar, perhaps nek- death (related to nekros corpse) + -tar, related to Sanskrit tarati he overcomes; compare Latin nex death and trans across] > nectareous (nɛk'tɛərɪəs) or 'nectarous adj

nectarine ('nɛktərɪn) n **1** a variety of peach tree, Prunus persica nectarina **2** the fruit of this tree, which has a smooth skin [c17: apparently from NECTAR]

nectary ('nɛktərɪ) n, pl -ries any of various glandular structures secreting nectar that occur in the flowers, leaves, stipules, etc, of a plant [c18: from New Latin nectarium, from NECTAR]

ned (nɛd) n Scot slang, derogatory a young working-class male who dresses in casual sports clothes [c20: a shortened form of Edward]

neddy ('nɛdɪ) n, pl -dies a child's word for a **donkey** [c18: from Ned, pet form of Edward]

Nederland ('neːdərlɑnt) n the Dutch name for the **Netherlands**

née or **nee** (neɪ) adj indicating the maiden name of a married woman: Mrs Bloggs née Blandish [c19: from French: past participle (fem) of naître to be born, from Latin nascī]

need (niːd) vb **1** (tr) to be in want of: to need money **2** (tr) to require or be required of necessity (to be or do something); be obliged: to need to do more work **3** (takes an infinitive without to) used as an auxiliary in negative and interrogative sentences to express necessity or obligation and does not add -s when used with he, she, it, and singular nouns: need he go? **4** (intr) archaic to be essential or necessary to: there needs no reason for this ▷ n **5** the fact or an instance of feeling the lack of something: he has need of a new coat **6** a requirement: the need for vengeance **7** necessity or obligation resulting from some situation: no need to be frightened **8** distress or extremity: a friend in need **9** extreme poverty or destitution; penury ▷ See also **needs** [Old English nēad, nied; related to Old Frisian nēd, Old Saxon nōd, Old High German nōt]

needful ('niːdfʊl) adj **1** necessary; needed; required **2** archaic needy; poverty-stricken ▷ n **3** the needful informal money or funds > 'needfulness n

needle ('niːdᵊl) n **1** a pointed slender piece of metal, usually steel, with a hole or eye in it through which thread is passed for sewing **2** a somewhat larger rod with a point at one or each end, used in knitting **3** a similar instrument with a hook at one end for crocheting **4 a** another name for **stylus** (sense 3) **b** a small thin pointed device, esp one made of stainless steel, used to transmit the vibrations from a gramophone record to the pick-up **5** *med* the long hollow pointed part of a hypodermic syringe, which is inserted into the body **6** *surgery* a pointed steel instrument, often curved, for suturing, puncturing, or ligating **7** a long narrow stiff leaf, esp of a conifer, in which water loss is greatly reduced: *pine needles* **8** any slender sharp spine, such as the spine of a sea urchin **9** any slender pointer for indicating the reading on the scale of a measuring instrument **10** short for **magnetic needle 11** a sharp pointed metal instrument used in engraving and etching **12** anything long and pointed, such as an obelisk **13** *informal* **a** anger or intense rivalry, esp in a sporting encounter **b** (*as modifier*): *a needle match* **14 get** *or* **have the needle** *Brit informal* to feel dislike, distaste, nervousness, or annoyance (for): *she got the needle after he had refused her invitation* ▷ *vb* **15** (*tr*) *informal* to goad or provoke, as by constant criticism **16** (*tr*) to sew, embroider, or prick (fabric) with a needle [Old English *nǣdl*; related to Gothic *nēthla*, German *Nadel*]

needlecord ('niːdᵊlˌkɔːd) *n* a corduroy fabric with narrow ribs

needlepoint ('niːdᵊlˌpɔɪnt) *n* **1** embroidery done on canvas with the same stitch throughout so as to resemble tapestry **2** another name for **point lace**

needless ('niːdlɪs) *adj* not required or desired; unnecessary > **'needlessly** *adv* > **'needlessness** *n*

needlestick ('niːdᵊlˌstɪk) *adj* (of an injury) caused by accidentally pricking the skin with a hypodermic needle

needle time *n* the limited time allocated by a radio channel to the broadcasting of music from records

needlewoman ('niːdᵊlˌwʊmən) *n*, *pl* -**women** a woman who does needlework; seamstress

needlework ('niːdᵊlˌwɜːk) *n* work done with a needle, esp sewing and embroidery

needs (niːdz) *adv* **1** (preceded or foll by *must*) of necessity: *we must needs go; we will go, if needs must* ▷ *pl n* **2** what is required; necessities: *the needs of the third world; his needs are modest*

needy ('niːdɪ) *adj* **needier, neediest a** in need of practical or emotional support; distressed **b** (*as collective noun; preceded by the*): *the needy*

Néel *French* (neel) *n* **Louis** (lwi). 1904–2000, French physicist, noted for his research on magnetism; shared the Nobel prize for physics in 1970

neep (niːp) *n Brit* a dialect name for a **turnip** [Old English *nǣp*, from Latin *nāpus* turnip]

ne'er (nɛə) *adv* a poetic contraction of **never**

ne'er-do-well *n* **1** an improvident, irresponsible, or lazy person ▷ *adj* **2** useless; worthless: *your ne'er-do-well schemes*

NEET (niːt) *n* (in Britain) ▷ *acronym for* not in employment, education, or training: a person so described

nefarious (nɪ'fɛərɪəs) *adj* evil; wicked; sinful [c17: from Latin *nefārius*, from *nefās* unlawful deed, from *nē* not + *fās* divine law] > **ne'fariously** *adv* > **ne'fariousness** *n*

Nefertiti (ˌnɛfə'tiːtɪ) *or* **Nofretete** *n* 14th century BC, Egyptian queen; wife of Akhenaton

neg. *abbreviation* negative(ly)

negate (nɪ'geɪt) *vb* (*tr*) **1** to make ineffective or void; nullify; invalidate **2** to deny or contradict [c17: from Latin *negāre*, from *neg-*, variant of *nec* not + *aio* I say] > **ne'gator** *or* **ne'gater** *n*

negation (nɪ'geɪʃən) *n* **1** the opposite or absence of something **2** a negative thing or condition **3** the act or an instance of negating

negative ('nɛgətɪv) *adj* **1** expressing or meaning a refusal or denial: *a negative answer* **2** lacking positive or affirmative qualities, such as enthusiasm, interest, or optimism **3** showing or tending towards opposition or resistance **4** measured in a direction opposite to that regarded as positive **5** *biology* indicating movement or growth away from a particular stimulus: *negative geotropism* **6** *med* (of the results of a diagnostic test)

indicating absence of the disease or condition for which the test was made **7** another word for **minus** (senses 3b, 4) **8** *physics* **a** (of an electric charge) having the same polarity as the charge of an electron **b** (of a body, system, ion, etc) having a negative electric charge; having an excess of electrons **9** short for **electronegative 10** of or relating to a photographic negative **11** *logic* (of a categorial proposition) denying the satisfaction by the subject of the predicate, as in *some men are irrational; no pigs have wings* ▷ *n* **12** a statement or act of denial, refusal, or negation **13** a negative person or thing **14** *photog* a piece of photographic film or a plate, previously exposed and developed, showing an image that, in black-and-white photography, has a reversal of tones. In colour photography the image is in complementary colours to the subject so that blue sky appears yellow, green grass appears purple, etc **15** *physics* a negative object, such as a terminal or a plate in a voltaic cell **16** a sentence or other linguistic element with a negative meaning, as the English word *not* **17** a quantity less than zero or a quantity to be subtracted **18** *logic* a negative proposition **19 in the negative** indicating denial or refusal ▷ *vb* (*tr*) **20** to deny or nullify; negate **21** to show to be false; disprove **22** to refuse consent to or approval of: *the proposal was negatived* > **'negatively** *adv* > **'negativeness** *or* ˌnega'tivity *n*

negative equity *n* the state of holding a property the value of which is less than the amount of mortgage still unpaid

negative feedback *n* See **feedback**

negative resistance *n* a characteristic of certain electronic components in which an increase in the applied voltage increases the resistance, producing a proportional decrease in current

negative sign *n* the symbol (–) used to indicate a negative quantity or a subtraction; minus sign

negativism ('nɛgətɪˌvɪzəm) *n* **1** a tendency to be or a state of being unconstructively critical **2** any sceptical or derisive system of thought > **'negativist** *n, adj*

Negev ('nɛgɛv) *or* **Negeb** ('nɛgɛb) *n* the S part of Israel, on the Gulf of Aqaba: a triangular-shaped semidesert region, with large areas under irrigation; scene of fighting between Israeli and Egyptian forces in 1948. Chief town: Beersheba. Area: 12 820 sq km (4950 sq miles)

neglect (nɪ'glɛkt) *vb* (*tr*) **1** to fail to give due care, attention, or time to: *to neglect a child* **2** to fail (to do something) through thoughtlessness or carelessness: *he neglected to tell her* **3** to ignore or disregard: *she neglected his frantic signals* ▷ *n* **4** lack of due care or attention; negligence: *the child starved through neglect* **5** the act or an instance of neglecting or the state of being neglected [c16: from Latin *neglegere* to neglect, from *nec* not + *legere* to select]

neglectful (nɪ'glɛktfʊl) *adj* (when *postpositive*, foll by *of*) not giving due care and attention (to); careless; heedless

negligee *or* **negligée** ('nɛglɪˌʒeɪ) *n* **1** a woman's light dressing gown, esp one that is lace-trimmed **2** a thin and revealing woman's nightdress **3** any informal attire [c18: from French *négligée*, past participle (fem) of *négliger* to NEGLECT]

negligence ('nɛglɪdʒəns) *n* **1** the state or quality of being negligent **2** a negligent act **3** *law* a civil wrong whereby a person or party is in breach of a legal duty of care to another which results in loss or injury to the claimant

negligent ('nɛglɪdʒənt) *adj* **1** habitually neglecting duties, responsibilities, etc; lacking attention, care, or concern; neglectful **2** careless or nonchalant > **'negligently** *adv*

negligible ('nɛglɪdʒəbᵊl) *adj* so small, unimportant, etc, as to be not worth considering; insignificant > **'negligibly** *adv*

negotiable (nɪ'gəʊʃəbᵊl) *adj* **1** able to be negotiated **2** (of a bill of exchange, promissory note, etc) legally transferable in title from one party to another > neˌgotia'bility *n*

negotiable instrument *n* a legal document, such as a cheque or bill of exchange, that is freely negotiable

negotiate (nɪ'gəʊʃɪˌeɪt) *vb* **1** to work or talk (with others) to achieve (a transaction, an agreement, etc) **2** (*tr*) to succeed in passing through, around, or over: *to negotiate a mountain pass* **3** (*tr*) *finance* **a** to transfer (a negotiable commercial paper) by endorsement to another in return for value received **b** to sell (financial assets) **c** to arrange for (a loan) [C16: from Latin *negōtiārī* to do business, from *negōtium* business, from *nec* not + *ōtium* leisure] > ne'goti,ator *n* > ne,goti'ation *n*

Negress ('ni:grɪs) *n* a female Black person

Negrillo (nɪ'grɪləʊ) *n, pl* **-los** *or* **-loes** a member of a dwarfish Negroid race of central and southern Africa [C19: from Spanish, diminutive of *negro* black]

Negri Sembilan ('nɛgrɪ sɛm'bi:lən) *n* a state of S Peninsular Malaysia: mostly mountainous, with large areas under paddy and rubber. Capital: Seremban. Pop: 859 924 (2000). Area: 6643 sq km (2565 sq miles)

Negrito (nɪ'gri:təʊ) *n, pl* **-tos** *or* **-toes** a member of any of various dwarfish Negroid peoples of SE Asia and Melanesia [C19: from Spanish, diminutive of *negro* black]

negritude ('ni:grɪ,tju:d, 'nɛg-) *n* **1** the fact of being a Negro **2** awareness and cultivation of the Negro heritage, values, and culture [C20: from French, from *nègre* NEGRO[1]]

Negro[1] ('ni:grəʊ) *old-fashioned or offensive* ▷ *n, pl* **-groes 1** a member of any of the dark-skinned indigenous peoples of Africa and their descendants elsewhere ▷ *adj* **2** relating to or characteristic of Negroes [C16: from Spanish or Portuguese: black, from Latin *niger* black] > 'Negro,ism *n*

Negro[2] ('neɪgrəʊ, 'nɛg-) *Río Negro n* **1** a river in NW South America, rising in E Colombia (as the Guainía) and flowing east, then south as part of the border between Colombia and Venezuela, entering Brazil and continuing southeast to join the Amazon at Manáus. Length: about 2250 km (1400 miles) **2** a river in S central Argentina, formed by the confluence of the Neuquén and Limay Rivers and flowing east and southeast to the Atlantic. Length: about 1014 km (630 miles) **3** a river in central Uruguay, rising in S Brazil and flowing southwest into the Uruguay River. Length: about 467 km (290 miles)

Negroid ('ni:grɔɪd) *adj* **1** denoting, relating to, or belonging to a darker-complexioned supposed racial group of mankind. This group includes the indigenous peoples of Africa south of the Sahara, their descendants elsewhere, and some Melanesian peoples ▷ *n* **2** a member of this racial group

Negropont ('nɛgrəʊ,pɒnt) *n* **1** the former English name for **Euboea 2** the medieval English name for **Chalcis**

Negros ('neɪgrəʊs; *Spanish* 'neɣrɒs) *n* an island of the central Philippines, one of the Visayan Islands. Capital: Bacolod. Pop: 3 700 000 (2000 est). Area: 12 704 sq km (4904 sq miles)

negus ('ni:gəs) *n, pl* **-guses** a hot drink of port and lemon juice, usually spiced and sweetened [C18: named after Col. Francis *Negus* (died 1732), its English inventor]

Negus ('ni:gəs) *n, pl* **-guses** a title of the emperor of Ethiopia [from Amharic: king]

Neh. *abbreviation Bible* Nehemiah

Nehemiah (,ni:ɪ'maɪə) *n Old Testament* **1** a Jewish official at the court of Artaxerxes, king of Persia, who in 444 BC became a leader in the rebuilding of Jerusalem after the Babylonian captivity **2** the book recounting the acts of Nehemiah

Nehru ('nɛəru:) *n* **1 Jawaharlal** (dʒəwəhə'lɑ:l). 1889–1964, Indian statesman and nationalist leader. He spent several periods in prison for his nationalist activities and practised a policy of noncooperation with Britain during World War II. He was the first prime minister of the republic of India (1947–64) **2** his father, **Motilal** (məʊti'lɑ:l), known as *Pandit Nehru*. 1861–1931, Indian nationalist, lawyer, and journalist; first president of the reconstructed Indian National Congress

neigh (neɪ) *n* **1** the high-pitched cry of a horse; whinny ▷ *vb* **2** (*intr*) to make a neigh or a similar noise [Old English *hnǣgan*; related to Old Saxon *hnēgian*]

neighbour *or US* **neighbor** ('neɪbə) *n* **1** a person who lives near or next to another **2 a** a person or thing near or next to another **b** (*as modifier*): *neighbour states* ▷ *vb*

3 (when *intr*, often foll by *on*) to be or live close (to a person or thing) [Old English *nēahbūr*, from *nēah* NIGH + *būr*, *gebūr* dweller; see BOOR] > 'neighbouring *or US* 'neighboring *adj*

neighbourhood *or US* **neighborhood** ('neɪbə,hʊd) *n* **1** the immediate environment; surroundings; vicinity **2** a district where people live **3** the people in a particular area; neighbours **4** *maths* the set of all points whose distance from a given point is less than a specified value **5** (*modifier*) of or for a neighbourhood: *a neighbourhood community worker* **6** in the neighbourhood of approximately (a given number)

neighbourhood watch *n* a scheme under which members of a community agree together to take responsibility for keeping an eye on each other's property, as a way of preventing crime

neighbourly *or US* **neighborly** ('neɪbəlɪ) *adj* kind, friendly, or sociable, as befits a neighbour > 'neighbourliness *or US* 'neighborliness *n*

Neill (ni:l) *n* **1 A(lexander) S(utherland)**. 1883–1973, Scottish educationalist and writer, who put his progressive educational theories into practice at Summerhill school (founded 1921) **2 Sam.** born 1947, New Zealand film and television actor; his work includes the television series *Reilly, Ace of Spies*, and the films *My Brilliant Career* (1979), *Dead Calm* (1989), and *Jurassic Park* (1993)

Neisse ('naɪsə) *n* **1** Also called: **Glatzer Neisse** ('glɑːtsə) a river in SW Poland, rising on the northern Czech border, and flowing northeast to join the Oder near Brzeg. Length: about 193 km (120 miles) **2** Also called: **Lusatian Neisse** a river in E Europe, rising near Liberec in the Czech Republic and flowing north to join the Oder: forms part of the German-Polish border. Length: 225 km (140 miles)

neither ('naɪðə, 'ni:ðə) *determiner* **1 a** not one nor the other (of two); not either **b** (*as pronoun*): *neither can win* ▷ *conj* **2** (*coordinating*) **a** (used preceding alternatives joined by *nor*) not: *neither John nor Mary nor Joe went* **b** another word for **nor** (sense 2) ▷ *adv* **3** (*sentence modifier*) *not standard* another word for **either** (sense 4) [C13 (literally, *ne either* not either): changed from Old English *nāwther*, from *nāhwæther*, from *nā* not + *hwæther* which of two; see WHETHER]

● USAGE A verb following a compound subject that uses
● *neither...* should be in the singular if both subjects are
● in the singular: *neither Jack nor John has done the work*

Nejd (nɛʒd, neɪd) *n* a region of central Saudi Arabia: formerly an independent sultanate of Arabia; united with Hejaz to form the kingdom of Saudi Arabia (1932)

Nekrasov (*Russian* nɪ'krasəf) *n* **Nikolai Alekseyevich** (nika'laj alık'sjejıvıtʃ). 1821–77, Russian poet, who wrote chiefly about the sufferings of the peasantry

nekton ('nɛktɒn) *n* the population of free-swimming animals that inhabits the middle depths of a sea or lake [C19: via German from Greek *nēkton* a swimming thing, from *nēkhein* to swim]

nelly ('nɛlɪ) *n* **not on your nelly** (*sentence substitute*) *Brit slang* not under any circumstances; certainly not

nelson ('nɛlsən) *n* any wrestling hold in which a wrestler places his arm or arms under his opponent's arm or arms from behind and exerts pressure with his palms on the back of his opponent's neck [C19: from a proper name]

Nelson[1] ('nɛlsən) *n* **1** a town in NW England, in E Lancashire: textile industry. Pop: 28 998 (2001) **2** a port in New Zealand, on N South Island on Tasman Bay. Pop: 45 300 (2004 est) **3 River Nelson** a river in central Canada, in N central Manitoba, flowing from Lake Winnipeg northeast to Hudson Bay. Length: about 650 km (400 miles)

Nelson[2] ('nɛlsən) *n* **1 Horatio,** Viscount Nelson. 1758–1805, British naval commander during the Revolutionary and Napoleonic Wars. He became rear admiral in 1797 after the battle of Cape St Vincent and in 1798 almost destroyed the French fleet at the battle of the Nile. He was killed at Trafalgar (1805) after defeating Villeneuve's fleet **2 Willie.** born 1933, US country singer and songwriter

Nelspruit ('nɛls,prɔɪt) *n* a city in NE South Africa, the capital of Mpumalanga province on the Crocodile River: trading and agricultural centre, esp for fruit, with a growing tourist trade. Pop: 21 541 (2001)

Neman *or* **Nyeman** (*Russian* 'njɛmən) *n* a river in NE Europe, rising in Belarus and flowing northwest through Lithuania to the Baltic. Length: 937 km (582 miles). Polish name: **Niemen**

nematic (nɪ'mætɪk) *adj chem* (of a substance) existing in or having a mesomorphic state in which a linear orientation of the molecules causes anisotropic properties [C20: NEMAT(O)- (referring to the threadlike chains of molecules in liquid) + -IC]

nemato- *or before a vowel* **nemat-** *combining form* indicating a threadlike form: *nematocyst* [from Greek *nēma* thread]

nematocyst ('nɛmətə,sɪst, nɪ'mætə-) *n* a structure in coelenterates, such as jellyfish, consisting of a capsule containing a hollow coiled thread that can be everted to sting or paralyse prey and enemies

nematode ('nɛmə,təʊd) *n* any unsegmented worm of the phylum (or class) *Nematoda*, having a tough outer cuticle. The group includes free-living forms and disease-causing parasites, such as the hookworm and filaria. Also called: **nematode worm, roundworm**

Nembutal ('nɛmbjʊ,tɑːl) *n* a trademark for pentobarbital sodium

Nemea (nɪ'miːə) *n* (in ancient Greece) a valley in N Argolis in the NE Peloponnese; site of the **Nemean Games,** a Panhellenic festival and athletic competition held every other year ▷ **Ne'mean** *adj*

Nemean lion (nɪ'miːən) *n Greek myth* an enormous lion that was strangled by Hercules as his first labour

nemertean (nɪ'mɜːtɪən) *or* **nemertine** ('nɛmə,taɪn) *n* 1 Also called: **ribbon worm** any soft flattened ribbon-like marine worm of the phylum (or class) *Nemertea* (or *Nemertina*), having an eversible threadlike proboscis ▷ *adj* 2 of, relating to, or belonging to the *Nemertea* [C19: via New Latin from Greek *Nēmertēs* a NEREID]

nemesia (nɪ'miːʒə) *n* any plant of the southern African scrophulariaceous genus *Nemesia*: cultivated for their brightly coloured (often reddish) flowers [C19: New Latin, from Greek *nemesion*, name of a plant resembling this]

Nemesis ('nɛmɪsɪs) *n*, *pl* **-ses** (-,siːz) 1 *Greek myth* the goddess of retribution and vengeance 2 (*sometimes not capital*) any agency of retribution and vengeance [C16: via Latin from Greek: righteous wrath, from *némein* to distribute what is due]

nemophila (nə'mɒfɪlə) *n* any of a genus, *Nemophila*, of low-growing hairy annual plants, esp *N. menziesii*, grown for its blue or white flowers: family *Hydrophyllaceae* [New Latin, from Greek *nemos* a grove + *philein* to love]

neo- *or sometimes before a vowel* **ne-** *combining form* 1 (*sometimes capital*) new, recent, or a new or modern form or development: *neoclassicism; neocolonialism* 2 (*usually capital*) the most recent subdivision of a geological period: *Neogene* [from Greek *neos* new]

neoclassical (,niːəʊ'klæsɪkəl) *or* **neoclassic** *adj* 1 of, relating to , or in the style of neoclassicism in art, architecture, etc 2 of, relating to , or in the style of neoclassicism in music

neoclassicism (,niːəʊ'klæsɪ,sɪzəm) *n* 1 a late 18th- and early 19th-century style in architecture, decorative art, and fine art, based on the imitation of surviving classical models and types 2 *music* a movement of the 1920s, involving Hindemith, Stravinsky, etc, that sought to avoid the emotionalism of late romantic music by reviving the use of counterpoint, forms such as the classical suite, and small instrumental ensembles

neocolonialism (,niːəʊkə'ləʊnɪə,lɪzəm) *n* (in the modern world) political control by an outside power of a country that is in theory sovereign and independent, esp through the domination of its economy ▷ ,**neoco'lonial** *adj* ▷ ,**neoco'lonialist** *n*

neo-con (,niːəʊ'kɒn) *n US informal* **a** a neo-conservative **b** (*as modifier*): *a neo-con think tank*

neo-conservatism *n* (in the US) a right-wing tendency that originated amongst supporters of the political left

and has become characterized by its support of hawkish foreign policies ▷ ,**neo-con'servative** *adj*, *n*

Neo-Darwinism (,niːəʊ'dɑːwɪn,ɪzəm) *n* the modern version of the Darwinian theory of evolution, which incorporates the principles of genetics to explain how inheritable variations can arise by mutation

neodymium (,niːəʊ'dɪmɪəm) *n* a toxic silvery-white metallic element of the lanthanide series, occurring principally in monazite: used in colouring glass. Symbol: Nd; atomic no: 60; atomic wt: 144.24; valency: 3; relative density: 6.80 and 7.00 (depending on allotrope); melting pt: 1024°C; boiling pt: 3127°C [C19: New Latin; see NEO- + DIDYMIUM]

neogothic (,niːəʊ'gɒθɪk) *n* another name for **Gothic Revival**

Neolithic (,niːəʊ'lɪθɪk) *n* 1 the cultural period that lasted in SW Asia from about 9000 to 6000 BC and in Europe from about 4000 to 2400 BC and was characterized by primitive crop growing and stock rearing and the use of polished stone and flint tools and weapons ▷ *adj* 2 relating to this period

neologism (nɪ'ɒlə,dʒɪzəm) *or* **neology** *n*, *pl* **-gisms** *or* **-gies** 1 a newly coined word, or a phrase or familiar word used in a new sense 2 the practice of using or introducing neologisms [C18: via French from NEO- + -logism, from Greek *logos* word, saying] ▷ **ne'ologist** *n*

neologize *or* **neologise** (nɪ'ɒlə,dʒaɪz) *vb* (*intr*) to invent or use neologisms

neomycin (,niːəʊ'maɪsɪn) *n* an antibiotic obtained from the bacterium *Streptomyces fradiae*, administered locally in the treatment of skin and eye infections or orally for bowel infections. Formula: $C_{12}H_{26}N_4O_6$ [C20: from NEO- + Greek *mukēs* fungus + -IN]

neon ('niːɒn) *n* 1 a colourless odourless rare gaseous element, an inert gas occurring in trace amounts in the atmosphere: used in illuminated signs and lights. Symbol: Ne; atomic no: 10; atomic wt: 20.1797; valency: 0; density: 0.899 90 kg/m³; melting pt: -248.59°C; boiling pt: -246.08°C 2 (*modifier*) of or illuminated by neon or neon lamps: *neon sign* [C19: via New Latin from Greek *neon* new]

neonatal (,niːəʊ'neɪtªl) *adj* of or relating to newborn children, esp in the first week of life and up to four weeks old ▷ '**neo,nate** *n*

neophyte ('niːəʊ,faɪt) *n* 1 a person newly converted to a religious faith 2 *RC Church* a novice in a religious order 3 a novice or beginner [C16: via Church Latin from New Testament Greek *neophutos* recently planted, from *neos* new + *phuton* a plant]

neoplasm ('niːəʊ,plæzəm) *n pathol* any abnormal new growth of tissue; tumour

Neo-Platonism *or* **Neoplatonism** (,niːəʊ'pleɪtə,nɪzəm) *n* a philosophical system which was first developed in the 3rd century AD as a synthesis of Platonic, Pythagorean, and Aristotelian elements, and which, although originally opposed to Christianity, later incorporated it. It dominated European thought until the 13th century and re-emerged during the Renaissance ▷ **Neo-Platonic** (,niːəʊplə'tɒnɪk) *adj* ▷ **Neo-'Platonist** *n*, *adj*

neoprene ('niːəʊ,priːn) *n* a synthetic rubber obtained by the polymerization of chloroprene. It is resistant to oil and ageing and is used in waterproof products, such as diving suits, paints, and adhesives [C20: from NEO- + PR(OPYL) + -ENE]

Neoptolemus (,niːɒp'tɒləməs) *n Greek myth* a son of Achilles and slayer of King Priam of Troy. Also called: **Pyrrhus**

neoteny (nɪ'ɒtənɪ) *n* the persistence of larval or fetal features in the adult form of an animal. For example, the adult axolotl, a salamander, retains larval external gills [C19: from New Latin *neotenia*, from Greek NEO- + *teinein* to stretch]

neoteric (,niːəʊ'tɛrɪk) *rare* ▷ *adj* 1 belonging to a new fashion or trend; modern ▷ *n* 2 a new writer or philosopher [C16: via Late Latin from Greek *neōterikos* young, fresh, from *neoteros* younger, more recent, from *neos* new, recent]

NEPAD ('niːpæd) *n acronym for* New Partnership for African Development: an economic development organization set up by the African union in 2001

Nepal (nɪˈpɔːl) *n* a kingdom in S Asia: the world's only Hindu kingdom; united in 1768 by the Gurkhas; consists of swampy jungle in the south and great massifs, valleys, and gorges of the Himalayas over the rest of the country, with many peaks over 8000 m (26 000 ft) (notably Everest and Kangchenjunga). A multiparty democracy was instituted in 1990. Official language: Nepali. Official religion: Hinduism; Mahayana Buddhist minority. Currency: rupee. Capital: Katmandu. Pop: 25 724 000 (2004 est). Area: 147 181 sq km (56 815 sq miles) > **Nepalese** (ˌnɛpəˈliːz) *adj, n*

Nepali (nɪˈpɔːlɪ) *n* **1** the official language of Nepal, also spoken in Sikkim and parts of India. It forms the E group of Pahari and belongs to the Indic branch of Indo-European **2** (*pl* **-pali** *or* **-palis**) a native or inhabitant of Nepal; a Nepalese ▷ *adj* **3** of or relating to Nepal, its inhabitants, or their language; Nepalese

nepenthe (nɪˈpɛnθɪ) *n* a drug, or the plant providing it, that ancient writers referred to as a means of forgetting grief or trouble [c16: via Latin from Greek *nēpenthes* sedative made from a herb, from *nē*- not + *penthos* grief]

nepeta (ˈnɛpətə) *n* See **catmint** [Latin: catmint]

nephew (ˈnɛvjuː, ˈnɛf-) *n* a son of one's sister or brother [c13: from Old French *neveu*, from Latin *nepōs*; related to Old English *nefa*, Old High German *nevo* relative]

nephology (nɪˈfɒlədʒɪ) *n* the study of clouds

nephridium (nɪˈfrɪdɪəm) *n, pl* **-ia** (-ɪə) a simple excretory organ of many invertebrates, consisting of a tube through which waste products pass to the exterior [c19: New Latin: little kidney]

nephrite (ˈnɛfraɪt) *n* a tough fibrous amphibole mineral: a variety of jade consisting of calcium magnesium silicate in monoclinic crystalline form. Formula: $Ca_2Mg_5Si_8O_{22}(OH)_2$. Also called: **kidney stone** [c18: via German *Nephrit* from Greek *nephrós* kidney, so called because it was thought to be beneficial in kidney disorders]

nephritic (nɪˈfrɪtɪk) *adj* **1** of or relating to the kidneys **2** relating to or affected with nephritis

nephritis (nɪˈfraɪtɪs) *n* inflammation of a kidney

nephro- *or before a vowel* **nephr-** *combining form* kidney or kidneys: *nephrotomy* [from Greek *nephros*]

nephrology (nɪˈfrɒlədʒɪ) *n* the branch of medicine concerned with diseases of the kidney > **neˈphrologist** *n*

nephron (ˈnɛfrɒn) *n* any of the minute urine-secreting tubules that form the functional unit of the kidneys

nephroscope (ˈnɛfrəˌskəʊp) *n* a tubular medical instrument inserted through an incision in the skin to enable examination of a kidney > **nephroscopy** (nɪˈfrɒskəpɪ) *n*

ne plus ultra *Latin* (ˈneɪ ˈplʊs ˈʊltraː) *n* the extreme or perfect point or state [literally: not more beyond (that is, go no further), allegedly a warning to sailors inscribed on the Pillars of Hercules at Gibraltar]

Nepos (ˈniːpɒs) *n* **Cornelius**. ?100–?25 bc, Roman historian and biographer; author of *De Viris illustribus*

nepotism (ˈnɛpəˌtɪzəm) *n* favouritism shown to relatives or close friends by those with power or influence [c17: from Italian *nepotismo*, from *nepote* NEPHEW, from the former papal practice of granting special favours to nephews or other relatives] > **nepotist** *n*

Neptune[1] (ˈnɛptjuːn) *n* the Roman god of the sea. Greek counterpart: Poseidon

Neptune[2] (ˈnɛptjuːn) *n* the eighth planet from the sun, having eight satellites, the largest being Triton and Nereid, and a faint planar system of rings or ring fragments. Mean distance from sun: 4497 million km; period of revolution around sun: 164.8 years; period of rotation: 14 to 16 hours; diameter and mass: 4.0 and 17.2 times that of earth respectively

neptunium (nɛpˈtjuːnɪəm) *n* a silvery metallic transuranic element synthesized in the production of plutonium and occurring in trace amounts in uranium ores. Symbol: Np; atomic no: 93; half-life of most stable isotope, ^{237}Np: 2.14×10^6 years; valency: 3, 4, 5, or 6; relative density: 20.25; melting pt: 639±1°C; boiling pt: 3902°C (est) [c20: from NEPTUNE[2], the planet beyond Uranus, because neptunium is the element beyond

uranium in the periodic table]

NERC *abbreviation* Natural Environment Research Council

nerd *or* **nurd** (nɜːd) *n slang* **1** a boring or unpopular person, esp one obsessed with something specified: *a computer nerd* **2** a stupid and feeble person > **nerdish** *or* **'nurdish** *adj* > **'nerdy** *or* **'nurdy** *adj*

Nereid (ˈnɪərɪɪd) *n, pl* **Nereides** (nəˈriːəˌdiːz) *Greek myth* any of the 50 sea nymphs who were the daughters of the sea god Nereus [c17: via Latin from Greek *Nērēid*, from NEREUS; compare Latin *nāre* to swim]

Nereus (ˈnɪərɪˌuːs) *n Greek myth* a sea god who lived in the depths of the sea with his wife Doris and their daughters the Nereides

Neri (ˈnɪərɪ) *n* **Saint Philip**. Italian name *Filippo de' Neri*. 1515–95, Italian priest; founder of the Congregation of the Oratory (1564). Feast day: May 26

nerine (nəˈriːnɪ) *n* any plant of the bulbous S African genus *Nerine*, related to the amaryllis; several species are grown as garden or pot plants for their beautiful pink, orange, red, or white flowers. *N. sarniensis* is the pink-flowered Guernsey lily: family *Amaryllidaceae* [Latin, from Greek *nērēis* a sea nymph]

Nernst (German nɛrnst) *n* **Walther Hermann** (ˈvaltər ˈhɛrman). 1864–1941, German physical chemist who formulated the third law of thermodynamics: Nobel prize for chemistry 1920

Nero (ˈnɪərəʊ) *n* full name *Nero Claudius Caesar Drusus Germanicus*; original name *Lucius Domitius Ahenobarbus*. 37–68 AD, Roman emperor (54–68). He became notorious for his despotism and cruelty, and was alleged to have started the fire (64) that destroyed a large part of Rome

neroli oil *or* **neroli** (ˈnɪərəlɪ) *n* a brown oil distilled from the flowers of various orange trees, esp the Seville orange: used in perfumery [c17: named after Anne Marie de la Tremoïlle of *Neroli*, French-born Italian princess believed to have discovered it]

Neruda (Spanish neˈruða) *n* **Pablo** (ˈpaβlo), real name *Neftalí Ricardo Reyes*. 1904–73, Chilean poet. His works include *Veinte poemas de amor y una canción desesperada* (1924) and *Canto general* (1950), an epic history of the Americas: Nobel prize for literature 1971

Nerva (ˈnɜːvə) *n* full name *Marcus Cocceius Nerva*. ?30–98 AD, Roman emperor (96–98), who introduced some degree of freedom after the repressive reign of Domitian. He adopted Trajan as his son and successor

Nerval (French nɛrval) *n* **Gérard de** (ʒerar də), real name *Gérard Labrunie*. 1808–55, French poet, noted esp for the sonnets of mysticism, myth, and private passion in *Les Chimères* (1854)

nervate (ˈnɜːveɪt) *adj* (of leaves) having veins

nervation (nɜːˈveɪʃən) *or* **nervature** (ˈnɜːvətʃə) *n* a less common word for **venation**

nerve (nɜːv) *n* **1** any of the cordlike bundles of fibres that conduct sensory or motor impulses between the brain or spinal cord and another part of the body **2** courage, bravery, or steadfastness **3 lose one's nerve** to become timid, esp failing to perform some audacious act **4** *informal* boldness or effrontery; impudence **5** muscle or sinew (often in the phrase **strain every nerve**) **6** any of the veins of an insect's wing ▷ *vb* (*tr*) **7** to give courage to (oneself); steel (oneself) **8** to provide with nerve or nerves ▷ See also **nerves** [c16: from Latin *nervus*; related to Greek *neuron*; compare Sanskrit *snāvan* sinew]

nerve block *n* induction of anaesthesia in a specific part of the body by injecting a local anaesthetic close to the sensory nerves that supply it

nerve cell *n* another name for **neurone**

nerve centre *n* **1** a group of nerve cells associated with a specific function **2** a principal source of control over any complex activity

nerve fibre *n* a threadlike extension of a nerve cell; axon

nerve gas *n* (esp in chemical warfare) any of various poisonous gases that have a paralysing effect on the central nervous system that can be fatal

nerve impulse *n* the electrical wave transmitted along a nerve fibre, usually following stimulation of the nerve-cell body

nerveless ('nɜːvlɪs) *adj* 1 calm and collected 2 listless or feeble >'**nervelessly** *adv*

nerve-racking *or* **nerve-wracking** *adj* very distressing, exhausting, or harrowing

nerves (nɜːvz) *pl n informal* 1 the imagined source of emotional control: *my nerves won't stand it* 2 anxiety, tension, or imbalance: *she's all nerves* 3 get on one's nerves to irritate, annoy, or upset one

Nervi (*Italian* 'nɛrvi) *n* **Pier Luigi** (pjɛːr luˈiːdʒi). 1891–1979, Italian engineer and architect; noted for his pioneering use of reinforced concrete as a decorative material. He codesigned the UNESCO building in Paris (1953)

nervine ('nɜːviːn) *adj* 1 having a soothing or calming effect upon the nerves ▷ *n* 2 *obsolete* a nervine drug or agent [c17: from New Latin *nervīnus*, from Latin *nervus* NERVE]

nervous ('nɜːvəs) *adj* 1 very excitable or sensitive; highly strung 2 (often foll by *of*) apprehensive or worried 3 of, relating to, or containing nerves; neural: *nervous tissue* 4 affecting the nerves or nervous tissue: *a nervous disease* 5 *archaic* active, vigorous, or forceful >'**nervously** *adv* >'**nervousness** *n*

nervous breakdown *n* any mental illness not primarily of organic origin, in which the patient ceases to function properly, often accompanied by severely impaired concentration, anxiety, insomnia, and lack of self-esteem; used esp of episodes of depression

nervous system *n* the sensory and control apparatus of all multicellular animals above the level of sponges, consisting of a network of nerve cells

nervure ('nɜːvjʊə) *n* 1 *entomol* any of the stiff chitinous rods that form the supporting framework of an insect's wing; vein 2 *botany* any of the veins or ribs of a leaf [c19: from French; see NERVE, -URE]

nervy ('nɜːvɪ) *adj* nervier, nerviest 1 *Brit informal* tense or apprehensive 2 having or needing bravery or endurance 3 *US & Canadian informal* brash or cheeky 4 *archaic* muscular; sinewy

Nesbit ('nɛzbɪt) *n* **E**(dith). 1858–1924, British writer of children's books, including *The Phoenix and the Carpet* (1904) and *The Railway Children* (1906)

nescience ('nɛsɪəns) *n* a formal or literary word for ignorance [c17: from Late Latin *nescientia*, from Latin *nescīre* to be ignorant of, from *ne* not + *scīre* to know; compare SCIENCE] >'**nescient** *adj*

ness (nɛs) *n archaic* a promontory or headland [Old English *næs* headland; related to Old Norse *nes*, Old English *nasu* NOSE]

Ness (nɛs) *n* Loch Ness a lake in NW Scotland, in the Great Glen: said to be inhabited by an aquatic monster. Length: 36 km (22.5 miles). Depth: 229 m (754 ft)

-ness *suffix forming nouns chiefly from adjectives and participles* indicating state, condition, or quality, or an instance of one of these: *greatness; selfishness; meaninglessness; a kindness* [Old English *-nes*, of Germanic origin; related to Gothic *-nassus*]

Nesselrode ('nɛsəlˌrəʊd; *Russian* nɪsɪlˈrɔdə) *n* Count **Karl Robert**. 1780–1862, Russian diplomat: as foreign minister (1822–56), he negotiated the Treaty of Paris after the Crimean War (1856)

Nessus ('nɛsəs) *n Greek myth* a centaur that killed Hercules. A garment dipped in its blood fatally poisoned Hercules, who had been given it by Deianira who thought it was a love charm

nest (nɛst) *n* 1 a place or structure in which birds, fishes, insects, reptiles, mice, etc, lay eggs or give birth to young 2 a number of animals of the same species and their young occupying a common habitat: *an ants' nest* 3 a place fostering something undesirable: *a nest of thievery* 4 a cosy or secluded place 5 a set of things, usually of graduated sizes, designed to fit together: *a nest of tables* ▷ *vb* 6 (*intr*) to make or inhabit a nest 7 (*intr*) to hunt for birds' nests 8 (*tr*) to place in a nest [Old English; related to Latin *nīdus* (nest) and to BENEATH, SIT]

nest egg *n* 1 a fund of money kept in reserve; savings 2 a natural or artificial egg left in a nest to induce hens to lay their eggs in it

nestle ('nɛsəl) *vb* 1 (*intr*; often foll by *up* or *down*) to snuggle, settle, or cuddle closely 2 (*intr*) to be in a

sheltered or protected position; lie snugly 3 (*tr*) to shelter or place snugly or partly concealed, as in a nest [Old English *nestlian*. See NEST]

nestling ('nɛstlɪŋ, 'nɛslɪŋ) *n* **a** a young bird not yet fledged **b** (*as modifier*): *a nestling thrush* [c14: from NEST + -LING¹]

Nestor ('nɛstɔː) *n Greek myth* the oldest and wisest of the Greeks in the Trojan War

Nestorius (nɛˈstɔːrɪəs) *n* died ?451 AD, Syrian churchman: patriarch of Constantinople (428–431); deposed for heresy by the Council of Ephesus

net¹ (nɛt) *n* 1 an openwork fabric of string, rope, wire, etc; mesh 2 a device made of, used to protect or enclose things or to trap animals 3 a thin light mesh fabric of cotton, nylon, or other fibre, used for curtains, dresses, etc 4 a plan, strategy, etc, intended to trap or ensnare: *the murderer slipped through the police net* 5 sport **a** a strip of net that divides the playing area into two equal parts **b** a shot that hits the net, whether or not it goes over 6 the goal in soccer, hockey, etc 7 (*often plural*) *cricket* **a** a pitch surrounded by netting, used for practice **b** a practice session in a net 8 *informal* short for **internet** 9 another word for **network** (sense 2) ▷ *vb* **nets**, **netting**, **netted** 10 (*tr*) to catch with or as if with a net; ensnare 11 (*tr*) to shelter or surround with a net 12 to make a net out of (rope, string, etc) 13 (*intr*) to hit a shot into the net [Old English *net*; related to Gothic *nati*, Dutch *net*]

net² *or* **nett** (nɛt) *adj* 1 remaining after all deductions, as for taxes, expenses, losses, etc: *net profit*. Compare **gross** (sense 2) 2 (of weight) after deducting tare 3 ultimate; final; conclusive (esp in the phrase **net result**) ▷ *n* 4 net income, profits, weight, etc ▷ *vb* **nets**, **netting**, **netted** 5 (*tr*) to yield or earn as clear profit [c14: clean, neat, from French *net* NEAT¹; related to Dutch *net*, German *nett*]

Netaji ('neɪtɑːdʒɪ) *n* the title for (Subhash Chandra) **Bose** [Hindi, from *neta* leader + -JI]

Netanyahu (nɛtˈənˈjɑːhuː) *n* **Benjamin** ('bɪnjæˌmiːn). born 1949, Israeli politician: leader of the Likud party (1993–99); prime minister (1996–99)

net asset value *n* the total value of the assets of an organization less its liabilities and capital charges. Abbreviation: NAV

netball ('nɛtˌbɔːl) *n* a team game similar to basketball, played mainly by women

Net Book Agreement *n* a former agreement between UK publishers and booksellers that until 1995 prohibited booksellers from undercutting the price of books sold in bookshops. Abbreviation: NBA

net domestic product *n economics* the gross domestic product minus an allowance for the depreciation of capital goods. Abbreviation: NDP

Neth. *abbreviation* Netherlands

nether ('nɛðə) *adj* placed or situated below, beneath, or underground: *nether regions; a nether lip* [Old English *niothera*, *nithera*, literally: further down, from *nither* down. Related to Old Irish *nitaram*, German *nieder*]

Netherlands ('nɛðələndz) *the* **Netherlands** *n* (*functioning as singular or plural*) 1 Also called: **Holland** a kingdom in NW Europe, on the North Sea: declared independence from Spain in 1581 as the United Provinces; became a major maritime and commercial power in the 17th century, gaining many overseas possessions; it formed the Benelux customs union with the Belgium and Luxembourg in 1948 and was a founder member of the Common Market, now the European Union. It is mostly flat and low-lying, with about 40 per cent of the land being below sea level, much of it on polders protected by dykes. Official language: Dutch. Religion: Christian majority, Protestant and Roman Catholic, large nonreligious minority. Currency: euro. Capital: Amsterdam, with the seat of government at The Hague. Pop: 16 227 000 (2004 est). Area: 41 526 sq km (16 033 sq miles). Dutch name: **Nederland** 2 the kingdom of the Netherlands together with the Flemish-speaking part of Belgium, esp as ruled by Spain and Austria before 1581; the Low Countries > **Netherlander** ('nɛðəˌlændə) *n*

Netherlands Antilles *pl n* the Netherlands Antilles two groups of islands in the Caribbean, in the Lesser Antilles: overseas division of the Netherlands, consisting of the S group of Curaçao, Aruba, and Bonaire, and the N group of Saint Eustatius, Saba, and the S part of Saint Martin; economy based on refining oil from Venezuela. Capital: Willemstad (on Curaçao). Pop: 222 000 (2004 est). Area: 996 sq km (390 sq miles). Former name **Curaçao**

Netherlands East Indies *pl n* the Netherlands East Indies a former name (1798–1945) for **Indonesia**

Netherlands Guiana *n* a former name for **Surinam**

Netherlands West Indies *pl n* the Netherlands West Indies a former name for the **Netherlands Antilles**

nethermost ('nɛðə,məʊst) *adj* farthest down; lowest

nether world *n* **1** the world after death; the underworld **2** hell **3** a criminal underworld

netiquette ('nɛtɪ,kɛt) *n* the informal code of behaviour on the internet [C20: from NET(WORK) + (ET)IQUETTE]

netizen ('nɛtɪzᵊn) *n informal* a person who regularly uses the internet [C20: from (INTER)NET + (CIT)IZEN]

net national product *n* gross national product minus an allowance for the depreciation of capital goods. Abbreviation: **NNP**

net present value *n accounting* an assessment of the long-term profitability of a project made by adding together all the revenue it can be expected to achieve over its whole life and deducting all the costs involved, discounting both future costs and revenue at an appropriate rate. Abbreviation: **NPV**

net profit *n* gross profit minus all operating costs not included in the calculation of gross profit, esp wages, overheads, and depreciation

net realizable value *n* the net value of an asset if it were to be sold, taking into account the cost of making the sale and of bringing the asset into a saleable state. Abbreviation: **NRV**

Netrebko (nə'trɛbkəʊ) *n* **Anna.** born 1971, Russian operatic soprano

netsuke ('nɛtsʊkɪ) *n* (in Japan) a carved toggle, esp of wood or ivory, originally used to tether a medicine box, purse, etc, worn dangling from the waist [C19: from Japanese]

nett (nɛt) *adj, n, vb* a variant spelling of **net²**

netting ('nɛtɪŋ) *n* any netted fabric or structure

nettle ('nɛtᵊl) *n* **1** any weedy plant of the temperate urticaceous genus *Urtica*, such as *U. dioica* (**stinging nettle**), having serrated leaves with stinging hairs and greenish flowers **2** any of various other urticaceous plants with stinging hairs or spines **3** any of various plants that resemble urticaceous nettles, such as the dead-nettle, hemp nettle, and horse nettle **4** grasp the nettle to attempt or approach something with boldness and courage ▷ *vb* **5** to bother; irritate **6** to sting as a nettle does [Old English *netele*; related to Old High German *nazza* (German *Nessel*)]

nettle rash *n* a nontechnical name for **urticaria**

network ('nɛt,wɜːk) *n* **1** an interconnected group or system: *a network of shops* **2** Also called: **net** a system of intersecting lines, roads, veins, etc **3** another name for **net¹** (sense 1) **4** *radio, television* a group of broadcasting stations that all transmit the same programme simultaneously **5** *electronics* a system of interconnected components or circuits **6** *computing* a system of interconnected computer systems, terminals, and other equipment allowing information to be exchanged ▷ *vb* **7** (tr) *radio, television* to broadcast on stations throughout the country **8** *computing* (of computers, terminals, etc) to connect or be connected **9** (intr) to form business contacts through informal social meetings

Neubrandenburg (German nɔy'brandənburk) *n* a city in NE Germany, in Mecklenburg-West Pomerania: 14th-century city walls. Pop: 69 157 (2003 est)

Neuchâtel (French nøʃatɛl) *n* **1** a canton in the Jura Mountains of W Switzerland. Capital: Neuchâtel. Pop: 167 000 (2002 est). Area: 798 sq km (308 sq miles) **2** a town in W Switzerland, capital of Neuchâtel canton, on Lake Neuchâtel: until 1848 the seat of the last hereditary rulers in Switzerland. Pop: 32 914 (2000) **3** Lake Neuchâtel a lake in W Switzerland: the largest lake wholly in Switzerland. Area: 216 sq km (83 sq miles)

Neuilly-sur-Seine (French nœjisyrsɛn) *n* a town in N France, on the Seine: a suburb of NW Paris. Pop: 59 848 (1999)

Neumann *n* **1** (German 'nɔyman) Johann Balthasar (jo'han 'baltazar). 1687–1753, German rococo architect. His masterpiece is the church of Vierzehnheiligen in Bavaria **2** ('njuːmən) See (John) **von Neumann**

neume *or* **neum** (njuːm) *n music* one of a series of notational symbols used before the 14th century [C15: from Medieval Latin *neuma* group of notes sung on one breath, from Greek *pneuma* breath]

Neumünster (German nɔy'mynstər) *n* a town in N Germany, in Schleswig-Holstein: manufacturing of textiles and machinery. Pop: 78 951 (2003 est)

neural ('njʊərəl) *adj* of or relating to a nerve or the nervous system > **'neurally** *adv*

neural chip *n* another name for **neurochip**

neural computer *n* another name for **neurocomputer**

neuralgia (njʊ'rældʒɪə) *n* severe spasmodic pain caused by damage to or malfunctioning of a nerve and often following the course of the nerve > **neu'ralgic** *adj*

neural tube *n* the structure in mammalian embryos that develops into the brain and spinal cord. Incomplete development results in **neural-tube defects**, such as spina bifida, in a newborn baby

neurasthenia (,njʊərəs'θiːnɪə) *n* an obsolete technical term for a neurosis characterized by extreme lassitude and inability to cope with any but the most trivial tasks

neuritis (njʊ'raɪtɪs) *n* inflammation of a nerve or nerves, often accompanied by pain and loss of function in the affected part > **neuritic** (njʊ'rɪtɪk) *adj*

neuro- *or before a vowel* **neur-** *combining form* indicating a nerve or the nervous system: *neuroblast; neurology* [from Greek *neuron* nerve; related to Latin *nervus*]

neurobiology (,njʊərəʊbaɪ'ɒlədʒɪ) *n* the study of the anatomy, physiology, and biochemistry of the nervous system > **,neurobi'ologist** *n*

neuroblastoma (,njʊərəʊblæs'təʊmə) *n, pl* **-mata** *or* **-mas** *pathol* a malignant tumour that derives from neuroblasts, occurring mainly in the adrenal gland

neurochip ('njʊərəʊ,tʃɪp) *n computing* a semiconductor chip designed for use in an electronic neural network. Also called: **neural chip**

neurocognitive (,njʊərə'kɒgnɪtɪv) *adj* of or relating to cognitive functions associated with particular areas of the brain

neurocomputer ('njʊərəʊkəm,pjuːtə) *n* a type of computer designed to mimic the action of the human brain by use of an electronic neural network. Also called: **neural computer**

neuroendocrine (,njʊərəʊ'ɛndəʊ,kraɪn) *adj* of, relating to, or denoting the dual control of certain body functions by both nervous and hormonal stimulation: *neuroendocrine system*

neuroglia (njʊ'rɒglɪə) *n* another name for **glia**

neurohormone ('njʊərəʊ,hɔːməʊn) *n* a hormone, such as noradrenaline, oxytocin, or vasopressin, that is produced by specialized nervous tissue rather than by endocrine glands

neurolemma (,njʊərəʊ'lɛmə) *n* the thin membrane that forms a sheath around nerve fibres [C19: New Latin, from NEURO- + Greek *eilēma* covering]

neurology (njʊ'rɒlədʒɪ) *n* the study of the anatomy, physiology, and diseases of the nervous system > **neurological** (,njʊərə'lɒdʒɪkᵊl) *adj*

neuromarketing ('njʊərəʊ,mɑː'kɪtɪŋ) *n* the process of researching the brain patterns of consumers to reveal their responses to particular advertisements and products before developing new advertising campaigns and branding techniques

neuromuscular (,njʊərəʊ'mʌskjʊlə) *adj* of, relating to, or affecting nerves and muscles

neurone ('njʊərəʊn) *or* **neuron** ('njʊərɒn) *n* a cell specialized to conduct nerve impulses: consists of a cell body, axon, and dendrites. Also called: **nerve cell** > **neu'ronal** *adj* > **neuronic** (njʊ'rɒnɪk) *adj*

neuropathology (,njʊərəʊpə'θɒlədʒɪ) *n* the study of diseases of the nervous system

neuropathy (njʊ'rɒpəθɪ) *n* disease of the nervous system > **neuropathic** (,njʊərəʊ'pæθɪk) *adj*

> ˌneuro'pathically *adv*

neurophysiology (ˌnjʊərəʊˌfɪzɪ'blədʒɪ) *n* the study of the functions of the nervous system
> **neurophysiological** (ˌnjʊərəʊˌfɪzɪə'lɒdʒɪkəl) *adj*

neuropterous (njʊ'rɒptərəs) or **neuropteran** *adj* of, relating to, or belonging to the *Neuroptera*, an order of insects having two pairs of large much-veined wings and biting mouthparts: includes the lacewings and antlions [c18: from New Latin *Neuroptera*; see NEURO-, -PTEROUS]

neuroscience ('njʊərəʊˌsaɪəns) *n* the study of the anatomy, physiology, biochemistry, and pharmacology of the nervous system > 'neuroˌscientist *n*

neurosis (njʊ'rəʊsɪs) *n, pl* **-ses** (-siːz) a relatively mild mental disorder, characterized by symptoms such as hysteria, anxiety, depression, or obsessive behaviour

neurosurgery (ˌnjʊərəʊ'sɜːdʒərɪ) *n* the branch of surgery concerned with the nervous system
> ˌneuro'surgical *adj*

neurotic (njʊ'rɒtɪk) *adj* 1 of, relating to, or afflicted by neurosis ▷ *n* 2 a person who is afflicted with a neurosis or who tends to be emotionally unstable or unusually anxious > neu'rotically *adv* > neu'roti,cism *n*

neurotomy (njʊ'rɒtəmɪ) *n, pl* **-mies** the surgical cutting of a nerve, esp to relieve intractable pain

neurotransmitter (ˌnjʊərəʊtrænz'mɪtə) *n* a chemical by which a nerve cell communicates with another nerve cell or with a muscle

Neusatz ('nɔyzats) *n* the German name for **Novi Sad**

Neuss (*German* nɔys) *n* an industrial city in W Germany, in North Rhine-Westphalia west of Düsseldorf: founded as a Roman fortress in the 1st century AD. Pop: 152 050 (2003 est)

Neustria ('njuːstrɪə) *n* the western part of the kingdom of the Merovingian Franks formed in 561 AD in what is now N France > 'Neustrian *adj*

neuter ('njuːtə) *adj* 1 *grammar* **a** denoting or belonging to a gender of nouns which for the most part have inanimate referents or do not specify the sex of their referents **b** (*as noun*): German "Mädchen" (meaning "girl") is a neuter 2 (of animals and plants) having nonfunctional, underdeveloped, or absent reproductive organs 3 sexless or giving no indication of sex ▷ *n* 4 a sexually underdeveloped female insect, such as a worker bee 5 a castrated animal, esp a domestic animal ▷ *vb* 6 (*tr*) to castrate or spay (an animal) [c14: from Latin, from *ne* not + *uter* either (of two)]

neutral ('njuːtrəl) *adj* 1 not siding with any party to a war or dispute 2 of, belonging to, or appropriate to a neutral party, country, etc 3 (of a colour such as white or black) having no hue; achromatic 4 (of a colour) dull, but harmonizing with most other colours 5 a less common term for **neuter** (sense 2) 6 *chem* neither acidic nor alkaline 7 *physics* having zero charge or potential 8 *phonetics* (of a vowel) articulated with the tongue relaxed in mid-central position and the lips midway between spread and rounded: *the word "about" begins with a neutral vowel* ▷ *n* 9 a neutral person, nation, etc 10 a citizen of a neutral state 11 the position of the controls of a gearbox that leaves the transmission disengaged [c16: from Latin *neutrālis*; see NEUTER] > 'neutrally *adv*

neutralism ('njuːtrəˌlɪzəm) *n* (in international affairs) the policy, practice, or attitude of neutrality, noninvolvement, or nonalignment with power blocs > 'neutralist *n, adj*

neutrality (njuː'trælɪtɪ) *n* 1 the state or character of being neutral, esp in a dispute, contest, etc 2 the condition of being chemically or electrically neutral

neutralize or **neutralise** ('njuːtrəˌlaɪz) *vb* (*mainly tr*) 1 (*also intr*) to render or become ineffective or neutral by counteracting, mixing, etc; nullify 2 (*also intr*) to make or become electrically or chemically neutral 3 to exclude (a country) from the sphere of warfare or alliances by international agreement: *the great powers neutralized Belgium in the 19th century* > ˌneutrali'zation or ˌneutrali'sation *n* > 'neutralˌizer or 'neutralˌiser *n*

neutretto (njuː'trɛtəʊ) *n, pl* **-tos** *physics* 1 the neutrino associated with the muon 2 (formerly) any of various hypothetical neutral particles [c20: from NEUTR(INO) +

diminutive suffix *-etto*]

neutrino (njuː'triːnəʊ) *n, pl* **-nos** *physics* a stable leptonic neutral elementary particle with very small or possibly zero rest mass and spin $\frac{1}{2}$ that travels at the speed of light. Three types exist, associated with the electron, the muon, and the tau particle [c20: from Italian, diminutive of *neutrone* NEUTRON]

neutron ('njuːtron) *n* *physics* a neutral elementary particle with a rest mass of $1.674\ 92716 \times 10^{-27}$ kilogram and spin $\frac{1}{2}$; classified as a baryon. In the nucleus of an atom it is stable but when free it decays [c20: from NEUTRAL, on the model of ELECTRON]

neutron bomb *n* a type of nuclear weapon designed to provide a high yield of neutrons but to cause little blast or long-lived radioactive contamination. The neutrons destroy all life in the target area, which theoretically can be entered relatively soon after the attack

neutron gun *n* *physics* a device used for producing a beam of fast neutrons

neutron number *n* the number of neutrons in the nucleus of an atom. Symbol: *N*

neutron star *n* a star that has collapsed under its own gravity to a diameter of about 10 to 15 km. It is composed mostly of neutrons, has a mass of between 1.4 and about 3 times that of the sun, and a density in excess of 10^{17} kilograms per cubic metre

Nev. *abbreviation* Nevada

Neva ('niːvə; *Russian* nɪ'va) *n* a river in NW Russia, flowing west to the Gulf of Finland by the delta on which Saint Petersburg stands. Length: 74 km (46 miles)

Nevada (nɪ'vɑːdə) *n* a state of the western US: lies almost wholly within the Great Basin, a vast desert plateau; noted for production of gold and copper. Capital: Carson City. Pop: 2 241 154 (2003 est). Area: 284 612 sq km (109 889 sq miles). Abbreviations: **Nev.**, (with zip code) **NV** > Ne'vadan *n*

névé ('nevɛɪ) *n* a mass of porous ice, formed from snow, that has not yet become frozen into glacier ice. Also called: **firn** [c19: from Swiss French *névé* glacier, from Late Latin *nivātus* snow-cooled, from *nix* snow]

never ('nɛvə) *adv, sentence substitute* 1 at no time; not ever 2 certainly not; by no means; in no case ▷ *interj* 3 Also: **well I never!** surely not! [Old English *nǣfre*, from *ne* not + *ǣfre* EVER]

● USAGE In informal speech and writing, *never* can be
● used instead of *not* with the simple past tenses of
● certain verbs for emphasis (*I never said that; I never*
● *realized how clever he was*), but this usage should be
● avoided in serious writing

nevermore (ˌnɛvə'mɔː) *adv* *literary* never again

never-never *informal* ▷ *n* 1 the hire-purchase system of buying 2 *Austral* remote desert country, as that of W Queensland and central Australia ▷ *adj* 3 imaginary; idyllic (esp in the phrase **never-never land**)

Nevers (*French* nəvɛr) *n* a city in central France: capital of the former duchy of Nivernais; engineering industry. Pop: 40 932 (1999)

nevertheless (ˌnɛvəðə'lɛs) *sentence connector* in spite of that; however; yet

Nevis *n* 1 ('niːvɪs, 'nɛvɪs) an island in the Caribbean, part of St Kitts-Nevis; the volcanic cone of **Nevis Peak**, which rises to 1002 m (3287 ft), lies in the centre of the island. Capital: Charlestown. Pop: 11 181 (2001. Area: 129 sq km (50 sq miles) 2 ('nɛvɪs) See Ben Nevis

Nevski ('nɛfskɪ; *Russian* 'njɛfskij) *n* See **Alexander Nevski**

new (njuː) *adj* 1 **a** recently made or brought into being **b** (*as collective noun*; preceded by *the*): *the new* 2 of a kind never before existing; novel: *a new concept in marketing* 3 having existed before but only recently discovered: *a new comet* 4 markedly different from what was before: *the new liberalism* 5 (often foll by *to* or *at*) recently introduced (to); inexperienced (in) or unaccustomed (to): *new to this neighbourhood* 6 (*capital in names or titles*) more or most recent of two or more things with the same name: *the New Testament* 7 (*prenominal*) fresh; additional: *I'll send some new troops* 8 (often foll by *to*) unknown; novel: *this is new to me* 9 (of a cycle) beginning or occurring again: *a new year* 10 (*prenominal*) (of crops) harvested early 11 changed, esp for the better: *she returned* *a new woman from her holiday* **12** up-to-date; fashionable **13** the new the new vogue: *comedy is the new rock'n'roll* ▷ *adv* (usually in combination) **14** recently, freshly: *new-laid eggs* **15** anew; again ▷ See also **news** [Old English *nīowe*; related to Gothic *niujis*, Old Norse *naujas*, Latin *novus*] > 'newness *n*

New Age *n* **1 a** a philosophy, originating in the late 1980s, characterized by a belief in alternative medicine, astrology, spiritualism, etc **b** (*as modifier*): *New Age therapies* **2** short for **New Age music**

New Age music *or* **New Age** *n* a type of gentle melodic popular music originating in the US in the late 1980s, which takes in elements of jazz, folk, and classical music and is played largely on synthesizers and acoustic instruments

New Amsterdam *n* the Dutch settlement established on Manhattan (1624–26); capital of New Netherlands; captured by the English and renamed New York in 1664

Newark ('njuːək) *n* **1** a town in N central England, in Nottinghamshire. Pop: 35 454 (2001) **2** a port in NE New Jersey, just west of New York City, on Newark Bay and the Passaic River: the largest city in the state; founded in 1666 by Puritans from Connecticut; industrial and commercial centre. Pop: 277 911 (2003 est)

New Australia *n* the colony on socialist principles founded by William Lane in Paraguay in 1893

New Australian *n* an immigrant to Australia, esp one whose native tongue is not English

New Bedford *n* a port and resort in SE Massachusetts, near Buzzards Bay: settled by Plymouth colonists in 1652; a leading whaling port (18th–19th centuries). Pop: 94 112 (2003 est)

newbie ('njuːbɪ) *n slang* a newcomer, esp in computing or on the internet [C20: origin unknown; possibly from *new boy*]

newborn ('njuːˌbɔːn) *adj* **1** recently or just born **2** (of hope, faith, etc) reborn

New Britain *n* an island in the S Pacific, northeast of New Guinea: the largest island of the Bismarck Archipelago; part of Papua New Guinea; mountainous, with several active volcanoes. Capital: Rabaul. Pop: 161 737 (2000). Area: 36 519 sq km (14 100 sq miles)

New Brunswick *n* a province of SE Canada on the Gulf of St Lawrence and the Bay of Fundy: extensively forested. Capital: Fredericton. Pop: 751 384 (2004 est). Area: 72 092 sq km (27 835 sq miles). Abbreviation: NB > New Brunswicker ('brʌnzwɪkə) *n*

new brutalism *n* another name for **brutalism**

Newbury ('njuːbərɪ) *n* a market town in West Berkshire unitary authority, S England: scene of a Parliamentarian victory (1643) and a Royalist victory (1644) during the Civil War; telecommunications, racecourse. Pop: 32 675 (2001)

New Caledonia *n* an island in the SW Pacific, east of Australia: forms, with its dependencies, a French Overseas Country; discovered by Captain Cook in 1774; rich mineral resources. Capital: Nouméa. Pop: 232 000 (2004 est). Area: 19 103 sq km (7374 miles). French name: Nouvelle-Calédonie

New Canadian *n Canad* a recent immigrant to Canada

New Castile *n* a region and former province of central Spain. Chief town: Toledo

Newcastle ('njuːˌkɑːsᵊl) *n* a port in SE Australia, in E New South Wales near the mouth of the Hunter River: important industrial centre, with extensive steel, metalworking, engineering, shipbuilding, and chemical industries. It suffered Australia's first recorded fatal earthquake, in 1989. Pop: 279 975 (2001)

Newcastle ('njuːˌkɑːsᵊl) *n* **Duke of,** the title of *Thomas Pelham Holles.* 1693–1768, English Whig prime minister (1754–56; 1757–62): brother of Henry Pelham

Newcastle-under-Lyme *n* a town in W central England, in Staffordshire. Pop: 74 427 (2001). Often shortened to: **Newcastle**

Newcastle upon Tyne *n* **1** a port in NE England in Newcastle upon Tyne unitary authority, Tyne and Wear, near the mouth of the River Tyne opposite Gateshead: Roman remains; engineering industries, including ship repairs; two universities (1937, 1992). Pop: 189 863 (2001).

Often shortened to: **Newcastle 2** a unitary authority in NE England, in Tyne and Wear. Pop: 266 600 (2003 est). Area: 112 sq km (43 sq miles)

new chum *n* **1** *Austral & NZ archaic, informal* a recent British immigrant **2** *Austral* a novice in any activity

Newcomb ('njuːkəm) *n* **Simon.** 1835–1909, US astronomer, noted for his tables of celestial bodies and astronomical constants

Newcombe ('njuːkəm) *n* **John** (**David**). born 1944, Australian tennis player; winner of seven Grand Slam singles titles (1967–74)

Newcomen ('njuːˌkʌmən) *n* **Thomas.** 1663–1729, English engineer who invented a steam engine, which James Watt later modified and developed

newcomer ('njuːˌkʌmə) *n* a person who has recently arrived or started to participate in something

New Country *n* a style of country music that emerged in the late 1980s characterized by a more contemporary sound and down-to-earth rather than sentimental lyrics

New Delhi *n* See **Delhi**

new economy *n* the postindustrial world economy based on internet trading and advanced technology

newel ('njuːəl) *n* **1** the central pillar of a winding staircase, esp one that is made of stone **2** See **newel post** [C14: from Old French *nouel* knob, from Medieval Latin *nōdellus*, diminutive of *nōdus* NODE]

newel post *n* the post at the top or bottom of a flight of stairs that supports the handrail. Sometimes shortened to: **newel**

New England *n* **1** the NE part of the US, consisting of the states of Maine, New Hampshire, Vermont, Massachusetts, Rhode Island, and Connecticut: settled originally chiefly by Puritans in the mid-17th century **2** a region in SE Australia, in the northern tablelands of New South Wales > ˌNew 'Englander *n*

New England Range *n* a mountain range in SE Australia, in NE New South Wales: part of the Great Dividing Range. Highest peak: Ben Lomond, 1520 m (4986 ft)

New English Bible *n* a new Modern English version of the Bible and Apocrypha, published in full in 1970

newfangled ('njuːˈfæŋɡld) *adj* newly come into existence or fashion, esp excessively modern [C14 *newefangel* liking new things, from *new* + *-fangel,* from Old English *fōn* to take]

New Forest *n* a region of woodland and heath in S England, in SW Hampshire: a hunting ground of the West Saxon kings; tourist area, noted for its ponies; made into a national park in 2005. Area: 336 sq km (130 sq miles)

new-found *adj* newly or recently discovered: *new-found confidence*

Newfoundland ('njuːfəndlənd, -fənlənd, -ˌlænd, njuːˈfaʊndlənd) *n* **1** an island of E Canada, separated from the mainland by the Strait of Belle Isle: with the Coast of Labrador forms the province of Newfoundland and Labrador; consists of a rugged plateau with the Long Range Mountains in the west Area: 110 681 sq km (42 734 sq miles) **2** the former name for **Newfoundland and Labrador 3** a very large heavy breed of dog similar to a Saint Bernard with a flat coarse usually black coat > New'foundlander *n*

Newfoundland and Labrador *n* a province of E Canada, consisting of the island of Newfoundland and the Coast of Labrador: usually known as Newfoundland until its official long form was adopted as the main name in 2001. Capital: St John's. Pop: 517 027 (2004 est). Area: 404 519 sq km (156 185 sq miles)

Newfoundland Standard Time *n* one of the standard times used in Canada, three and a half hours behind Greenwich Mean Time

New France *n* the former French colonies and possessions in North America, most of which were lost to England and Spain by 1763: often restricted to French possessions in Canada

Newgate ('njuːɡɪt, -ˌɡeɪt) *n* a famous London prison, in use from the Middle Ages: demolished in 1902

New Georgia *n* **1** a group of islands in the SW Pacific, in the Solomon Islands **2** the largest island in this group. Area: about 1300 sq km (500 sq miles)

New Granada n 1 a former Spanish presidency and later viceroyalty in South America. At its greatest extent it consisted of present-day Panama, Colombia, Venezuela, and Ecuador **2** the name of Colombia when it formed, with Panama, part of Great Colombia (1819–30)

New Guinea n 1 an island in the W Pacific, north of Australia: divided politically into Papua (formerly Irian Jaya, a province of Indonesia) in the west and Papua New Guinea in the east. There is a central chain of mountains and a lowland area of swamps in the south and along the Sepik River in the north. Area: 775 213 sq km (299 310 sq miles) **2** Trust Territory of New Guinea (until 1975) an administrative division of the former Territory of Papua and New Guinea, consisting of the NE part of the island of New Guinea together with the Bismarck Archipelago; now part of Papua New Guinea

Newham ('njuːəm) n a borough of E Greater London, on the River Thames: established in 1965. Pop: 250 600 (2003 est). Area: 36 sq km (14 sq miles)

New Hampshire n a state of the northeastern US: generally hilly. Capital: Concord. Pop: 1 287 687 (2003 est). Area: 23 379 sq km (9027 sq miles). Abbreviations: N.H., (with zip code) NH

New Harmony n a village in SW Indiana, on the Wabash River: scene of two experimental cooperative communities, the first founded in 1815 by George Rapp, a German religious leader, and the second by Robert Owen in 1825

Newhaven ('njuːˌheɪvᵊn) n a ferry port and resort on the S coast of England, in East Sussex. Pop: 12 276 (2001)

New Haven n an industrial city and port in S Connecticut, on Long Island Sound: settled in 1638 by English Puritans, who established it as a colony in 1643; seat of Yale University (1701). Pop: 124 512 (2003 est)

New Hebrides pl n the former name (until 1980) of Vanuatu

Ne Win ('neɪ 'wɪn) n U (uː). 1911–2002, Burmese statesman and general; prime minister (1958–60), head of the military government (1962–74), and president (1974–81)

New Ireland n an island in the S Pacific, in the Bismarck Archipelago, separated from New Britain by St George's Channel: part of Papua New Guinea. Chief town and port: Kavieng. Pop (province): 118 148 (2000). Area (including adjacent islands): 9850 sq km (3800 sq miles)

newish ('njuːɪʃ) adj fairly new

new issue n stock exchange an issue of shares being offered to the public for the first time

New Jersey n a state of the eastern US, on the Atlantic and Delaware Bay: mostly low-lying, with a heavy industrial area in the northeast and many coastal resorts. Capital: Trenton. Pop: 8 638 396 (2003 est). Area: 19 479 sq km (7521 sq miles). Abbreviation: NJ

New Jerusalem n Christianity heaven regarded as the prototype of the earthly Jerusalem; the heavenly city

New Journalism n a style of journalism originating in the US in the 1960s, which uses techniques borrowed from fiction to portray a situation or event as vividly as possible

Newlands ('njuːləndz) n John Alexander. 1838–98, British chemist: classified the elements in order of their atomic weight, noticing similarities in every eighth and thus discovering his law of octaves

New Latin n the form of Latin used since the Renaissance, esp for scientific nomenclature

New Look n the New Look a fashion in women's clothes introduced in 1947, characterized by long full skirts

newly ('njuːlɪ) adv 1 recently; lately or just **2** again; afresh; anew: newly raised hopes **3** in a new manner; differently: a newly arranged room hairdo

newlywed ('njuːlɪˌwɛd) n (often plural) a recently married person

Newman ('njuːmən) n 1 **Barnet**. 1905–70, US painter, a founder of Abstract Expressionism: his paintings include the series Stations of the Cross (1965–66) **2** John

Henry. 1801–90, British theologian and writer. Originally an Anglican minister, he was a prominent figure in the Oxford Movement. He became a Roman Catholic (1845) and a priest (1847) and was made a cardinal (1879). His writings include the spiritual autobiography, Apologia pro vita sua (1864), a treatise on the nature of belief, The Grammar of Assent (1870), and hymns **3** Paul. born 1925, US film actor and director, who appeared in such films as Hud (1963), Butch Cassidy and the Sundance Kid (1969), The Sting (1973), The Verdict (1982), The Color of Money (1986), Nobody's Fool (1994), and Road to Perdition (2002)

New Man n the New Man a type of modern man who allows the caring side of his nature to show by being supportive and by sharing child care and housework

Newmarket ('njuːˌmɑːkɪt) n a town in SE England, in W Suffolk: a famous horse-racing centre since the reign of James I. Pop: 16 947 (2001)

new maths n (functioning as singular) Brit an approach to mathematics in which the basic principles of set theory are introduced at an elementary level

new media n a the internet and other postindustrial forms of telecommunication **b** (as modifier): the new-media industry

New Mexico n a state of the southwestern US: has high semiarid plateaus and mountains, crossed by the Rio Grande and the Pecos River; large Spanish-American and Indian populations; contains over two-thirds of US uranium reserves. Capital: Santa Fé. Pop: 1 874 614 (2003 est). Area: 314 451 sq km (121 412 sq miles). Abbreviation: NM > New Mexican adj, n

new moon n the moon when it appears as a narrow waxing crescent

New National Party n See National Party (sense 3)

New Netherland ('nɛðələnd) n a Dutch North American colony of the early 17th century, centred on the Hudson valley. Captured by the English in 1664, it was divided into New York and New Jersey

New Orleans ('ɔːliːənz, -lənz, ɔːˈliːnz) n a port in SE Louisiana, on the Mississippi River about 172 km (107 miles) from the sea: the largest city in the state and the second most important port in the US; founded by the French in 1718; belonged to Spain (1763–1803). It is largely below sea level, built around the Vieux Carré (French quarter); famous for its annual Mardi Gras festival and for its part in the history of jazz; a major commercial, industrial, and transportation centre. Pop: 469 032 (2003 est)

New Plymouth n a port in New Zealand, on W North Island: founded in 1841. Pop: 69 200 (2004 est)

Newport ('njuːˌpɔːt) n 1 a city and port in SE Wales, in Newport county borough on the River Usk: electronics. Pop: 116 143 (2001) **2** a county borough in SE Wales, created from part of Gwent in 1996. Pop: 139 300 (2003 est). Area: 190 sq km (73 sq miles) **3** a port in SE Rhode Island: founded in 1639, it became one of the richest towns of colonial America; centre of a large number of US naval establishments. Pop: 26 136 (2003 est) **4** a town in S England, administrative centre of the Isle of Wight. Pop: 22 957 (2001)

Newport News n (functioning as singular) a port in SE Virginia, at the mouth of the James River: an industrial centre, with one of the world's largest shipyards. Pop: 181 647 (2003 est)

New Providence n an island in the Atlantic, in the Bahamas. Chief town: Nassau. Pop: 210 832 (2000). Area: 150 sq km (58 sq miles)

New Quebec n a region of E Canada, formerly the Ungava district of Northwest Territories (1895–1912), extending from the line of the Eastmain and Hamilton Rivers north between Hudson Bay and Labrador: absorbed by Quebec in 1912: contains extensive iron deposits. Area: about 777 000 sq km (300 000 sq miles)

New Romney n a market town in SE England, in Kent on Romney Marsh: of early importance as one of the Cinque Ports, but is now over 1.6 km (1 mile) inland. Pop: 9406 (2001). Former name (until 1563): Romney

Newry ('njʊərɪ) n a city and port in Northern Ireland, in Newry and Mourne district, Co Down. Pop: 27 433 (2001)

Newry and Mourne (mɔːn) n a district of SE Northern Ireland, in Co Down. Pop: 89 644 (2003 est). Area: 909 sq km (351 sq miles)

news (njuːz) n (functioning as singular) 1 current events; important or interesting recent happenings 2 information about such events, as in the mass media 3 **the news** a presentation, such as a radio broadcast, of information of this type 4 interesting or important information not previously known or realized 5 a person, fashion, etc, widely reported in the mass media: she is no longer news in the film world [C15: from Middle English newes, plural of newe new (adj) on model of Old French noveles or Medieval Latin nova new things] > '**newless** adj

news agency n an organization that collects news reports for newspapers, periodicals, etc. Also called: **press agency**

newsagent ('njuːz,eɪdʒənt) or US **newsdealer** ('njuːz,diːlə) n a shopkeeper who sells newspapers, stationery, etc

newscast ('njuːz,kɑːst) n a radio or television broadcast of the news [C20: from NEWS + (BROAD)CAST] > '**news,caster** n

news conference n another name for **press conference**

newsflash ('njuːz,flæʃ) n a brief item of important news, often interrupting a radio or television programme

newsgroup ('njuːz,gruːp) n computing a forum where subscribers exchange information about a specific subject by electronic mail

New Siberian Islands pl n an archipelago in the Arctic Ocean, off the N mainland of Russia, in the Sakha Republic. Area: about 37 555 sq km (14 500 sq miles)

newsletter ('njuːz,letə) n 1 Also called: **news-sheet** a printed periodical bulletin circulated to members of a group 2 history a written or printed account of the news

newsmonger ('njuːz,mʌŋɡə) n old-fashioned a gossip

New South n Austral informal See **New South Wales**

New South Wales n a state of SE Australia: originally contained over half the continent, but was reduced by the formation of other states (1825–1911); consists of a narrow coastal plain, separated from extensive inland plains by the Great Dividing Range; the most populous state; mineral resources. Capital: Sydney. Pop: 6 716 277 (2003 est). Area: 801 428 sq km (309 433 sq miles)

newspaper ('njuːz,peɪpə) n 1 a a weekly or daily publication consisting of folded sheets and containing articles on the news, features, reviews, and advertisements. Often shortened to: **paper** b (as modifier): a newspaper article 2 a less common name for **newsprint**

newspaperman ('njuːz,peɪpə,mæn) n, pl -men 1 a man who works for a newspaper as a reporter or editor 2 the male owner or proprietor of a newspaper 3 a man who sells newspapers in the street

newspeak ('njuː,spiːk) n the language of bureaucrats and politicians, regarded as deliberately ambiguous and misleading [C20: from 1984, a novel by George Orwell]

newsprint ('njuːz,prɪnt) n an inexpensive wood-pulp paper used for newspapers

newsreader ('njuːz,riːdə) n a news announcer on radio or television

newsreel ('njuːz,riːl) n a short film with a commentary presenting current events

newsroom ('njuːz,ruːm, -,rʊm) n a room in a newspaper office or television or radio station, where news is received and prepared for publication or broadcasting

newsstand ('njuːz,stænd) n a portable stand or stall in the street, from which newspapers are sold

new start n an employee who has just joined a company or organization

New Style n the present method of reckoning dates using the Gregorian calendar

news vendor n a person who sells newspapers

newsworthy ('njuːz,wɜːðɪ) adj sufficiently interesting to be reported in a news bulletin

newsy ('njuːzɪ) adj newsier, newsiest full of news, esp gossip or personal news

newt (njuːt) n any of various small semiaquatic urodele amphibians, such as Triturus vulgaris (**common newt**) of

Europe, having a long slender body and tail and short feeble legs [C15: from a newt, a mistaken division of an ewt; ewt, from Old English eveta EFT]

New Testament n the collection of writings consisting of the Gospels, Acts of the Apostles, Pauline and other Epistles, and the book of Revelation, composed soon after Christ's death and added to the Jewish writings of the Old Testament to make up the Christian Bible

newton ('njuːtən) n the derived SI unit of force that imparts an acceleration of 1 metre per second per second to a mass of 1 kilogram; equivalent to 10^5 dynes or 7.233 poundals. Symbol: N [C20: named after Sir Isaac NEWTON]

Newton ('njuːtən) n Sir **Isaac**. 1642–1727, English mathematician, physicist, astronomer, and philosopher, noted particularly for his law of gravitation, his three laws of motion, his theory that light is composed of corpuscles, and his development of calculus independently of Leibnitz. His works include Principia Mathematica (1687) and Opticks (1704) > Newtonian (njuːˈtəʊnɪən) adj

Newtonian telescope n a type of astronomical reflecting telescope in which light is reflected from a large concave mirror, onto a plane mirror, and through a hole in the side of the body of the telescope to form an image

Newton's law of gravitation n the principle that two particles attract each other with forces directly proportional to the product of their masses divided by the square of the distance between them

Newton's laws of motion pl n three laws of mechanics describing the motion of a body. **The first law** states that a body remains at rest or in uniform motion in a straight line unless acted upon by a force. **The second law** states that a body's rate of change of momentum is proportional to the force causing it. **The third law** states that when a force acts on a body due to another body then an equal and opposite force acts simultaneously on that body

Newtown ('njuː,taʊn) n a new town in central Wales, in Powys. Pop: 10 358 (2001)

new town n (in Britain) a town that has been planned as a complete unit and built with government sponsorship, esp to accommodate overspill population

Newtownabbey (,njuːtən'æbɪ) n 1 a town in Northern Ireland, in Newtownabbey district, Co Antrim on Belfast Lough: the third largest town in Northern Ireland, formed in 1958 by the amalgamation of seven villages; light industrial centre, esp for textiles. Pop: 62 056 (2001) 2 a district of E Northern Ireland, in Co Antrim. Pop: 80 285 (2003 est). Area: 151 sq km (58 sq miles)

Newtown St Boswells ('sənt 'bɒzwəlz) n a village in SE Scotland, administrative centre of Scottish Borders: agricultural centre. Pop: 1199 (2001)

New Urbanism n an international movement concerned with tackling the problems associated with urban sprawl and car dependency > New Urbanist n

new-variant Creutzfeldt-Jakob disease or **variant Creutzfeldt-Jakob disease** n a form of Creutzfeldt-Jakob disease thought to be transmitted by eating beef or beef products infected with BSE. Abbreviations: nvCJD, vCJD

new wave n a movement in art, film-making, politics, etc, that consciously breaks with traditional ideas

New Windsor n the official name of **Windsor**[1] (sense 1)

New World n **the New World** the Americas; the western hemisphere

New World monkey n any monkey of the family Cebidae, of Central and South America, having widely separated nostrils: many are arboreal and have a prehensile tail

New Year n the first day or days of the year in various calendars, usually celebrated as a holiday

New Year's Day n Jan 1, celebrated as a holiday in many countries

New Year's Eve n the evening of Dec 31, often celebrated with parties. See also **Hogmanay**

New York n 1 Also called: **New York City** a city in SE New York State, at the mouth of the Hudson River: the largest city and chief port of the US; settled by the Dutch as New Amsterdam in 1624 and captured by the British in 1664, when it was named New York; consists of five boroughs (Manhattan, the Bronx, Queens, Brooklyn, and Richmond) and many islands, with its commercial and financial centre in Manhattan; the country's leading commercial and industrial city. Pop: 8 085 742 (2003 est). Abbreviation: **NYC 2** a state of the northeastern US: consists chiefly of a plateau with the Finger Lakes in the centre, the Adirondack Mountains in the northeast, the Catskill Mountains in the southeast, and Niagara Falls in the west. Capital: Albany. Pop: 19 190 115 (2003 est). Area: 123 882 sq km (47 831 sq miles). Abbreviation: **NY** > ˌNew ˈYorker *n*

New York Bay *n* an inlet of the Atlantic at the mouth of the Hudson River: forms the harbour of the port of New York

New York minute *n chiefly US & Canadian informal* a very short period of time; instant [C20: from the supposedly fast pace of life in New York]

New York State Barge Canal *n* a system of inland waterways in New York State, connecting the Hudson River with Lakes Erie and Ontario and, via Lake Champlain, with the St Lawrence. Length: 845 km (525 miles)

New Zealand ('zi:lənd) *n* an independent dominion within the Commonwealth, occupying two main islands (the North Island and the South Island), Stewart Island, the Chatham Islands, and a number of minor islands in the SE Pacific: original Māori inhabitants ceded sovereignty to the British government in 1840; became a dominion in 1907; a major world exporter of dairy products, wool, and meat. Official languages: English and Māori. Religion: Christian majority, nonreligious and Māori minorities. Currency: New Zealand dollar. Capital: Wellington. Pop: 3 905 000 (2004 est). Area: 270 534 sq km (104 454 sq miles) > ˌNew ˈZealander *n*

Nexø (*Danish* 'nɛgsøːˌ) *n* **Martin Andersen** ('marten). 1869–1954, Danish novelist. His chief works are the novels *Pelle the Conqueror* (1906–10), which deals with the labour movement, and *Ditte, Daughter of Man* (1917–21)

next (nɛkst) *adj* **1** immediately following: *the next patient to be examined; do it next week* **2** immediately adjoining: *the next room* **3** closest to in degree: *the tallest boy next to James; the next-best thing* **4** the next (Sunday) but one the (Sunday) after the next ▷ *adv* **5** at a time or on an occasion immediately to follow: *the patient to be examined next; next, he started to unscrew the telephone receiver* **6** next to **a** adjacent to; at or on one side of: *the house next to ours* **b** following in degree: *next to your mother, who do you love most?* **c** almost: *next to impossible* ▷ *prep* **7** *archaic* next to [Old English *nēhst*, superlative of *nēah* NIGH; compare NEAR, NEIGHBOUR]

next door *adj, adv* (**next-door** when prenominal) at, in, or to the adjacent house, flat, building, etc

next of kin *n* a person's closest relative or relatives

nexus ('nɛksəs) *n, pl* **nexus 1** a means of connection between members of a group or things in a series; link; bond **2** a connected group or series [C17: from Latin: a binding together, from *nectere* to bind]

Ney (neɪ; *French* nɛ) *n* **Michel** (miʃɛl), Duc d'Elchingen. 1769–1815, French marshal, who earned the epithet *Bravest of the Brave* at the battle of Borodino (1812) in the Napoleonic Wars. He rallied to Napoleon on his return from Elba and was executed for treason (1815)

Nez Percé ('nɛz 'pɜːs; *French* ne 'pɜːs) *n* **1** (*pl* **Nez Percés** ('pɜːsɪz; *French* pɛrse) *or* **Nez Percé**) a member of a North American Indian people of the Pacific coast, a tribe of the Sahaptin **2** the Sahaptin language of this people [French, literally: pierced nose]

NF (in Britain) *abbreviation* National Front

NFB (in Canada) *abbreviation* National Film Board

NFU (in Britain) *abbreviation* National Farmers' Union

NG *abbreviation* **1** (in the US) National Guard **2** New Guinea **3** Also: **ng** no good

ngai (ᵊŋˈɡaːiː) *prefix NZ* clan or tribe: used before the names of certain Māori tribes: *Ngai Tahu* [Māori]

ngaio ('naɪəʊ) *n, pl* **ngaios** a small New Zealand tree,

Myoporum laetum, yielding useful timber: family *Myoporaceae* [from Māori]

Ngaliema Mountain (ᵊŋɡɑːˈljeɪmə) *n* the Congolese name for (Mount) **Stanley**

ngati ('naːtiː) *n, pl* **ngati** *NZ* (occurring as part of the name of a tribe) tribe or clan [Māori]

Nguyen Kao Ky (ᵊŋˈɡuːjen 'kaʊ 'kiː) *n* See **Ky**

Nha Trang ('njaː 'træŋ) *n* a port in SE Vietnam, on the South China Sea: nearby temples of the Cham civilization; fishing industry. Pop: 382 000 (2005 est)

NHI (in Britain) *abbreviation* National Health Insurance

NHL (in Canada) *abbreviation* National Hockey League

NHS (in Britain) *abbreviation* National Health Service

Ni *the chemical symbol for* nickel

NI *abbreviation* **1** (in Britain) national insurance **2** Northern Ireland **3** *NZ* North Island

niacin ('naɪəsɪn) *n* another name for **nicotinic acid** [C20: from NI(COTINIC) AC(ID) + -IN]

Niagara (naɪˈægrə, -ˈægərə) *n* a river in NE North America, on the border between W New York State and Ontario, Canada, flowing from Lake Erie to Lake Ontario. Length: 45 km (28 miles)

Niagara Falls *n* **1** (*functioning as plural*) the falls of the Niagara River, on the border between the US and Canada between Lake Erie and Lake Ontario: divided by Goat Island into the American Falls, 50 m (167 ft) high and approximately 300 m (985 ft) wide, and the Horseshoe or Canadian Falls, 47 m (158 ft) high and by some estimates well over 800 m (2625 ft) wide **2** (*functioning as singular*) a city in W New York State, situated at the falls of the Niagara River. Pop: 78 815 (2001) **3** (*functioning as singular*) a city in S Canada, in SE Ontario on the Niagara River just below the falls: linked to the city of Niagara Falls in the US by three bridges. Pop: 78 815 (2001)

Niamey (njaˈmeɪ) *n* the capital of Niger, in the southwest on the River Niger: became capital in 1926; airport and land route centre. Pop: 997 000 (2005 est)

Niarchos (nɪˈɑːkɒs) *n* **Stavros Spyro** ('stævrɒs 'spɪərəʊ). 1909–96, Greek shipowner. He pioneered the use of supertankers in the 1950s

nib (nɪb) *n* **1** the writing point of a pen, esp an insertable tapered metal part with a split tip **2** a point, tip, or beak **3** (*plural*) crushed cocoa beans ▷ *vb* **nibs, nibbing, nibbed** (*tr*) **4** to provide with a nib **5** to prepare or sharpen the nib of [C16 (in the sense: beak): origin obscure; compare Northern German *nibbe* tip. See NEB, NIBBLE]

nibble ('nɪbᵊl) *vb* (when *intr*, often foll by *at*) **1** (esp of animals, such as mice) to take small repeated bites (of) **2** to take dainty or tentative bites: *to nibble at a cake* **3** to bite (at) gently or caressingly ▷ *n* **4** a small mouthful **5** an instance or the act of nibbling **6** (*plural*) *informal* small items of food, esp savouries, usually served with drinks [C15: related to Low German *nibbelen*. Compare NIB, NEB] > 'nibbler *n*

Nibelung ('niːbəˌlʊŋ) *n, pl* **-lungs** *or* **-lungen** (-ˌlʊŋən) *German myth* **1** any of the race of dwarfs who possessed a treasure hoard stolen by Siegfried **2** one of Siegfried's companions or followers **3** (in the *Nibelungenlied*) a member of the family of Gunther, king of Burgundy

niblick ('nɪblɪk) *n golf* (formerly) a club, a No. 9 iron, giving a great deal of lift [C19: of unknown origin]

nibs (nɪbz) *n* **his nibs** (*functioning as singular*) *slang* a mock title used of someone in authority [C19: of unknown origin]

NIC *abbreviation* newly industrialized country

nicad ('naɪˌkæd) *n* a rechargeable dry-cell battery with a nickel anode and a cadmium cathode [C20: NI(CKEL) + CAD(MIUM)]

Nicaea (naɪˈsiːə) *n* an ancient city in NW Asia Minor, in Bithynia: site of the **first council of Nicaea** (325 AD), which composed the Nicene Creed. Modern Turkish name: Iznik > **Nicene** ('naɪsiːn) *or* Ni'caean *adj*

NICAM ('naɪkæm) *n acronym for* near-instantaneous companding system: a technique for coding audio signals into digital form

Nicaragua (ˌnɪkəˈrægjʊə, -gwə; *Spanish* nikaˈraɣwa) *n* **1** a republic in Central America, on the Caribbean and the Pacific: colonized by the Spanish from the 1520s; gained independence in 1821 and was annexed by Mexico, becoming a republic in 1838. Official language: Spanish. Religion: Roman Catholic majority. Currency: córdoba. Capital: Managua. Pop: 5 596 000 (2004 est). Area: 131 812 sq km (50 893 sq miles) **2 Lake Nicaragua** a lake in SW Nicaragua, separated from the Pacific by an isthmus 19 km (12 miles) wide: the largest lake in Central America. Area: 8264 sq km (3191 sq miles) ▷ **Nicaraguan** (ˌnɪkəˈrægjʊən, -gwən) *adj, n*

niccolite (ˈnɪkəˌlaɪt) *n* a copper-coloured mineral consisting of nickel arsenide in hexagonal crystalline form, occurring associated with copper and silver ores: a source of nickel. Formula: NiAs [C19: from New Latin *niccolum* NICKEL + -ITE[1]]

nice (naɪs) *adj* **1** pleasant or commendable: *a nice day* **2** kind or friendly: *a nice gesture of help* **3** good or satisfactory: *they made a nice job of it* **4** subtle, delicate, or discriminating: *a nice point in the argument* **5** precise; skilful: *a nice fit* **6** *now rare* fastidious; respectable: *he was not too nice about his methods* **7** *obsolete* **a** foolish or ignorant **b** delicate **c** shy; modest **d** wanton [C13 (originally: foolish): from Old French *nice* simple, silly, from Latin *nescius* ignorant, from *nescīre* to be ignorant; see NESCIENCE] ▷ **ˈnicely** *adv* ▷ **ˈniceness** *n* ▷ **ˈnicish** *adj*

Nice (*French* nis) *n* a city in SE France, on the Mediterranean: a leading resort of the French Riviera; founded by Phocaeans from Marseille in about the 3rd century BC Pop: 342 738 (1999)

NICE (naɪs) *n* (in Britain) *acronym for* National Institute for Clinical Excellence: a body established in 1999 to provide authoritative guidance on current best practice in medicine and to promote high-quality cost-effective medical treatment in the NHS

nice-looking *adj informal* attractive in appearance; pretty or handsome

nicety (ˈnaɪsɪtɪ) *n, pl* **-ties** **1** a subtle point of delicacy or distinction: *a nicety of etiquette* **2** (*usually plural*) a refinement or delicacy: *the niceties of first-class travel* **3** subtlety, delicacy, or precision **4 to a nicety** with precision

nicey-nicey (ˌnaɪsɪˈnaɪsɪ) *adj, adv informal* trying to be pleasant, but in a way that suggests artifice or exaggeration; ingratiating(ly)

niche (nɪtʃ, niːʃ) *n* **1** a recess in a wall, esp one that contains a statue **2** a position particularly suitable for the person occupying it: *he found his niche in politics* **3** (*modifier*) relating to or aimed at a small specialized group or market **4** *ecology* the role of a plant or animal within its community and habitat, which determines its activities, relationships with other organisms, etc ▷ *vb* **5** (*tr*) to place (a statue) in a niche; ensconce (oneself) [C17: from French, from Old French *nichier* to nest, from Vulgar Latin *nīdicāre* (unattested) to build a nest, from Latin *nīdus* NEST]

niche market *n* a demand for a very specialized product or commodity

Nicholas (ˈnɪkələs) *n* **Saint**. 4th-century AD bishop of Myra, in Asia Minor; patron saint of Russia and of children, sailors, merchants, and pawnbrokers. Feast day: Dec 6. See also Santa Claus

Nicholas I *n* **1 Saint**, called *the Great*. died 867 AD, Italian ecclesiastic; pope (858–867). He championed papal supremacy. Feast day: Nov 13 **2** 1796–1855, tsar of Russia (1825–55). He gained notoriety for his autocracy and his emphasis on military discipline and bureaucracy

Nicholas II *n* 1868–1918, tsar of Russia (1894–1917). After the disastrous Russo-Japanese War (1904–05), he was forced to summon a representative assembly, but his continued autocracy and incompetence precipitated the Russian Revolution (1917): he abdicated and was shot

Nicholas V *n* original name *Tommaso Parentucelli*. 1397–1455, Italian ecclesiastic; pope (1447–55). He helped to found the Vatican Library

Nicholas of Cusa (ˈkjuːzə) *n* 1401–64, German cardinal, philosopher, and mathematician: anticipated Copernicus in asserting that the earth revolves around the sun

Nichols (ˈnɪkəlz) *n* **Peter** (**Richard**). born 1927, British dramatist, whose works include *A Day in the Death of Joe*

Egg (1967), the musical *Privates on Parade* (1977), and *Blue Murder* (1995)

Nicholson (ˈnɪkəlsən) *n* **1 Ben**. 1894–1982, English painter, noted esp for his abstract geometrical works **2 Jack**. born 1937, US film actor. His films include *Easy Rider* (1969), *One Flew Over the Cuckoo's Nest* (1974), *Terms of Endearment* (1983), *Batman* (1989), *As Good As It Gets* (1998), and *About Schmidt* (2002) **3 John**. 1821–57, British general and administrator, born in Ireland: deputy commissioner in the Punjab (1851–56), where he became the object of hero-worship among the natives and kept the Punjab loyal during the Indian Mutiny: played a major role in the capture of Delhi

Nichrome (ˈnaɪkrəʊm) *n trademark* any of various alloys containing nickel, iron, and chromium, with smaller amounts of other components. It is used in electrical heating elements, furnaces, etc

Nicias (ˈnɪsɪəs) *n* died 414 BC, Athenian statesman and general. He ended the first part of the Peloponnesian War by making peace with Sparta (421)

nick (nɪk) *n* **1** a small notch or indentation on an edge or surface **2 in good nick** *informal* in good condition **3 in the nick of time** at the last possible moment; at the critical moment ▷ *vb* **4** (*tr*) to chip or cut **5** (*tr*) *slang, chiefly Brit* **a** to steal **b** to take into legal custody; arrest **6** (*intr; often foll by off*) *informal* to move or depart rapidly **7** to divide and reset (certain of the tail muscles of a horse) to give the tail a high carriage **8** (*tr*) to guess, catch, etc, exactly **9 nick someone for** *US & Canadian slang* to defraud someone to the extent of [C15: perhaps changed from C14 *nocke* NOCK]

nickel (ˈnɪkəl) *n* **1** a malleable ductile silvery-white metallic element that is strong and corrosion-resistant, occurring principally in pentlandite and niccolite: used in alloys, esp in toughening steel, in electroplating, and as a catalyst in organic synthesis. Symbol: Ni; atomic no: 28; atomic wt: 58.6934; valency: 0, 1, 2, or 3; relative density: 8.902; melting pt: 1455°C; boiling pt: 2914°C **2** a US and Canadian coin and monetary unit worth five cents ▷ *vb* **-els, -elling, -elled** *or US* **-els, -eling, -eled 3** (*tr*) to plate with nickel [C18: shortened form of German *Kupfernickel* NICCOLITE, literally: copper demon, so called by miners because it was mistakenly thought to contain copper]

nickelodeon (ˌnɪkəˈləʊdɪən) *n US* **1** an early form of jukebox **2** (formerly) a cinema charging five cents for admission [C20: from NICKEL + (MEL)ODEON]

nickel plate *n* a thin layer of nickel deposited on a surface, usually by electrolysis

nickel silver *n* any of various white alloys containing copper (46–63 per cent), zinc (18–36 per cent), and nickel (6–30 per cent): used in making tableware, etc. Also called: German silver, pakthong

nickel steel *n engineering* steel containing between 0.5 and 6.0 per cent nickel to increase its strength

nicker[1] (ˈnɪkə) *vb* (*intr*) **1** (of a horse) to neigh softly **2** to laugh quietly; snigger [C18: perhaps from NEIGH]

nicker[2] (ˈnɪkə) *n, pl* **-er** *Brit slang* a pound sterling [C20: of unknown origin]

Nicklaus (ˈnɪklaʊs) *n* **Jack**. born 1940, US professional golfer: won the British Open Championship (1966; 1970; 1978) and the US Open Championship (1962; 1967; 1972; 1980)

nick-nack (ˈnɪkˌnæk) *n* a variant spelling of **knick-knack**

nickname (ˈnɪkˌneɪm) *n* **1** a familiar, pet, or derisory name given to a person, animal, or place **2** a shortened or familiar form of a person's name: *Joe is a nickname for Joseph* ▷ *vb* **3** (*tr*) to call by a nickname; give a nickname to [C15 *a nekename*, mistaken division of *an ekename* an additional name, from *eke* addition + NAME]

Nicobar Islands (ˈnɪkəˌbɑː) *pl n* a group of 19 islands in the Indian Ocean, south of the Andaman Islands, with which they form a territory of India. Area: 1645 sq km (635 sq miles)

Nicodemus (ˌnɪkəˈdiːməs) *n New Testament* a Pharisee and a member of the Sanhedrin, who supported Jesus against the other Pharisees (John 8:50–52)

Nicolai (*German* nikoˈlaɪ) *n* **Carl Otto Ehrenfried** (karl ˈɔto ˈeːrənfriːt). 1810–49, German composer: noted for his opera *The Merry Wives of Windsor* (1849)

Nicol prism ('nɪkᵊl) *n* a device composed of two prisms of Iceland spar or calcite cut at specified angles and cemented together with Canada balsam. It is used for producing plane-polarized light [c19: named after William *Nicol* (?1768–1851), Scottish physicist, its inventor]

Nicolson ('nɪkəlsən) *n* Sir **Harold** (**George**). 1886–1968, British diplomat, politician, and author: married to Vita Sackville-West

Nicosia (ˌnɪkə'siːə, -'sɪə) *n* the capital of Cyprus, in the central part on the Pedieos River: capital since the 10th century. Pop (Greek and Turkish): 211 000 (2005 est). Greek name: **Levkosia**. Turkish name: **Lefkoşa**

nicotiana (nɪˌkəʊʃɪ'ɑːnə, -'eɪnə) *n* any solanaceous plant of the American and Australian genus *Nicotiana*, such as tobacco, having white, yellow, or purple fragrant flowers [c16: see NICOTINE]

nicotinamide (ˌnɪkə'tɪnəˌmaɪd, -'tiːn-) *n* the amide of nicotinic acid: a component of the vitamin B complex and essential in the diet for the prevention of pellagra. Formula: $C_6H_6ON_2$

nicotine ('nɪkəˌtiːn) *n* a colourless oily acrid toxic liquid that turns yellowish-brown in air and light: the principal alkaloid in tobacco, used as an agricultural insecticide. Formula: $C_{10}H_{14}N_2$ [c19: from French, from New Latin *herba nicotiana* Nicot's plant, named after J. *Nicot* (1530–1600), French diplomat who introduced tobacco into France] > 'nico,tined *adj* > nicotinic (ˌnɪkə'tɪnɪk) *adj*

nicotinic acid *n* a vitamin of the B complex that occurs in milk, liver, yeast, etc Lack of it in the diet leads to the disease pellagra. Formula: $(C_5H_4N)COOH$

nicotinism ('nɪkətiːˌnɪzəm) *n pathol* a toxic condition of the body or a bodily organ or part caused by nicotine

Nictheroy (*Portuguese* nite'rɔi) *n* another name for **Niterói**

nictitate ('nɪktɪˌteɪt) *or* **nictate** ('nɪkteɪt) *vb* technical words for **blink** (sense 1) [c19: from Medieval Latin *nictitāre* to wink repeatedly, from Latin *nictāre* to wink, from *nicere* to beckon] > ˌnicti'tation *or* nic'tation *n*

nictitating membrane ('nɪktɪˌteɪtɪŋ) *n* (in reptiles, birds, and some mammals) a thin fold of skin beneath the eyelid that can be drawn across the eye

NICU *abbreviation* neonatal intensive care unit

Nidaros (*Norwegian* 'niːdaːrɔːs) *n* the former name (1930–31) of **Trondheim**

NIDDM *abbreviation* noninsulin-dependent diabetes mellitus, a form of diabetes in which insulin production is inadequate or the body becomes resistant to insulin

nidicolous (nɪ'dɪkələs) *adj* (of young birds) remaining in the nest for some time after hatching [c19: from Latin *nīdus* nest + *colere* to inhabit]

nidifugous (nɪ'dɪfjʊgəs) *adj* (of young birds) leaving the nest very soon after hatching [c19: from Latin *nīdus* nest + *fugere* to flee]

nidify ('nɪdɪˌfaɪ) *or* **nidificate** ('nɪdɪfɪˌkeɪt) *vb* -fies, -fying, -fied *or* -cates, -cating, -cated (*intr*) (of a bird) to make or build a nest [c17: from Latin *nīdificāre*, from *nīdus* a nest + *facere* to make] > ˌnidifi'cation *n*

Niebuhr ('niːbʊə) *n* 1 **Barthold Georg** ('baːtɔlt 'geːɔrk). 1776–1831, German historian, noted for his critical approach to sources, esp in *History of Rome* (1811–32) 2 **Reinhold** ('raɪnˌhəʊld). 1892–1971, US Protestant theologian. His works include *Moral Man and Immoral Society* (1932) and *The Nature and Destiny of Man* (1941–43)

niece (niːs) *n* a daughter of one's sister or brother [c13: from Old French: niece, granddaughter, ultimately from Latin *neptis* granddaughter]

Niederösterreich ('niːdərøˌstəraɪç) *n* the German name for **Lower Austria**

Niedersachsen ('niːdərˌzaksən) *n* the German name for **Lower Saxony**

niello (nɪ'ɛləʊ) *n, pl* -li (-lɪ) *or* -los 1 a black compound of sulphur and silver, lead, or copper used to incise a design on a metal surface 2 the process of decorating surfaces with niello 3 a surface or object decorated with niello [c19: from Italian from Latin *nigellus* blackish, from *niger* black]

Nielsen ('niːlsən; *Danish* 'nelsən) *n* **Carl** (**August**) (karl). 1865–1931, Danish composer. His works include six symphonies and the opera *Masquerade* (1906)

Niemen ('njɛmɛn) *n* the Polish name for the **Neman**

Niemeyer ('niːˌmaɪə) *n* **Oscar**. born 1907, Brazilian architect. His work includes many buildings in Brasília, esp the president's palace (1959) and the cathedral (1964)

Niemöller (*German* 'niːˌmœlər) *n* **Martin** ('martiːn). 1892–1984, German Protestant theologian, who was imprisoned (1938–45) for his opposition to Hitler

Niepce (*French* njɛps) *n* **Joseph-Nicéphore** (jozɛfnisefor). 1765–1833, French inventor. He produced the first photographic image (1816)

Nietzsche ('niːtʃə) *n* **Friedrich Wilhelm** ('friːdrɪç 'vɪlhɛlm). 1844–1900, German philosopher, poet, and critic, noted esp for his concept of the superman and his rejection of traditional Christian values. His chief works are *The Birth of Tragedy* (1872), *Thus Spake Zarathustra* (1883–91), and *Beyond Good and Evil* (1886) > Nietzschean ('niːtʃɪən) *n, adj* > 'Nietzscheˌism *or* 'Nietzscheˌism *n*

Nièvre (*French* njɛvrə) *n* a department of central France, in Burgundy region. Capital: Nevers. Pop: 222 298 (2003 est). Area: 6888 sq km (2686 sq miles)

niff (nɪf) *Brit slang* ▷ *n* 1 a bad smell ▷ *vb* (*intr*) 2 to smell badly; stink [c20: perhaps from SNIFF] > 'niffy *adj*

Niflheim ('nɪvᵊl,heɪm) *n* *Norse myth* the abode of the dead [Old Norse, literally: mist home]

nifty ('nɪftɪ) *adj* -tier, -tiest *informal* 1 pleasing, apt, or stylish 2 quick, agile [c19: of uncertain origin] > 'niftily *adv* > 'niftiness *n*

nigella (naɪ'dʒɛlə) *n* another name for **love-in-a-mist** [New Latin, diminutive of Latin *niger* black, from the colour of the seeds]

Niger *n* 1 (niː'ʒɛə, 'naɪdʒə) a landlocked republic in West Africa: important since earliest times for its trans-Saharan trade routes; made a French colony in 1922 and became fully independent in 1960; exports peanuts and livestock. Official language: French. Religion: Muslim majority. Currency: franc. Capital: Niamey. Pop: 12 415 000 (2004 est). Area: 1 267 000 sq km (489 000 sq miles) 2 ('naɪdʒə) a river in West Africa, rising in S Guinea and flowing in a great northward curve through Mali, then southwest through Niger and Nigeria to the Gulf of Guinea: the third longest river in Africa, with the largest delta, covering an area of 36 260 sq km (14 000 sq miles). Length: 4184 km (2600 miles) 3 ('naɪdʒə) a state of W central Nigeria. Capital: Minna. Pop: 3 950 249 (2006). Area: 76 363 sq km (29 476 sq miles) > Ni'gerien *adj, n*

Nigeria (naɪ'dʒɪərɪə) *n* a republic in West Africa, on the Gulf of Guinea: Lagos annexed by the British in 1861; protectorates of Northern and Southern Nigeria formed in 1900 and united as a colony in 1914; gained independence as a member of the Commonwealth in 1960 (membership suspended from 1995 to 1999 following human rights violations); Eastern Region seceded as the Republic of Biafra for the duration of the severe civil war (1967–70); ruled by military governments from 1966. It consists of a belt of tropical rain forest in the south, with semidesert in the extreme north and highlands in the east; the main export is petroleum. Official language: English; Hausa, Ibo, and Yoruba are the chief regional languages. Religion: animist, Muslim, and Christian. Currency: naira. Capital: Abuja. Pop: 127 117 000 (2004 est). Area: 923 773 sq km (356 669 sq miles) > Ni'gerian *adj, n*

niggard ('nɪgəd) *n* 1 a stingy person ▷ *adj* 2 *archaic* miserly [c14: perhaps of Scandinavian origin; related to Swedish dialect *nygg* and Old English *hnēaw* stingy]

niggardly ('nɪgədlɪ) *adj* 1 stingy or ungenerous 2 meagre: *a niggardly salary* ▷ *adv* 3 stingily; grudgingly > 'niggardliness *n*

nigger ('nɪgə) *n taboo* 1 a a derogatory name for a Black person b (*as modifier*): *nigger minstrels* 2 derogatory a member of any dark-skinned race 3 nigger in the woodpile *old-fashioned, offensive* a hidden snag or hindrance [c18: from C16 dialect *neeger*, from French *nègre*, from Spanish NEGRO[1]]

niggle ('nɪgᵊl) *vb* 1 (*intr*) to find fault continually 2 (*intr*) to be preoccupied with details; fuss **3** (tr) to irritate; worry ▷ n **4** a slight or trivial objection or complaint **5** a slight feeling as of misgiving, uncertainty, etc [C16: from Scandinavian; related to Norwegian *nigla*. Compare NIGGARD] ▷ **'niggler** n ▷ **'niggly** adj

niggling ('nɪglɪŋ) adj **1** petty **2** fussy **3** irritating **4** requiring painstaking work **5** persistently troubling: *a niggling back pain*

nigh (naɪ) adj, adv, prep an archaic, poetic, or dialect word for **near** [Old English *nēah, nēh*; related to German *nah*, Old Frisian *nei*. Compare NEAR, NEXT]

night (naɪt) n **1** the period of darkness each 24 hours between sunset and sunrise, as distinct from day **2** (*modifier*) of, occurring, working, etc, at night: *a night nurse* **3** the occurrence of this period considered as a unit: *four nights later they left* **4** the period between sunset and retiring to bed; evening **5** the time between bedtime and morning **6** the weather conditions of the night: *a clear night* **7** the activity or experience of a person during a night **8** (*sometimes capital*) any evening designated for a special observance or function **9** nightfall or dusk **10** a state or period of gloom, ignorance, etc **11 make a night of it** to go out and celebrate for most of the night ▷ Related adj: **nocturnal** [Old English *niht*; compare Dutch *nacht*, Latin *nox*, Greek *nux*]

night blindness n *pathol* a nontechnical term for **nyctalopia** ▷ **'night,blind** adj

nightcap ('naɪt,kæp) n **1** a bedtime drink, esp an alcoholic or hot one **2** a soft cap formerly worn in bed

nightclothes ('naɪt,kləʊðz) pl n clothes worn in bed

nightclub ('naɪt,klʌb) n a place of entertainment open until late at night, formerly offering food, drink, a floor show, etc, but now usually playing loud amplified music for dancing

nightdress ('naɪt,drɛs) n *Brit* a loose dress worn in bed by women. Also called: **nightgown, nightie**

nightfall ('naɪt,fɔːl) n the approach of darkness; dusk

night fighter n an interceptor aircraft used for operations at night

nightgown ('naɪt,gaʊn) n **1** another name for **nightdress 2** a man's nightshirt

nighthawk ('naɪt,hɔːk) n **1** Also called: **bullbat, mosquito hawk** any American nightjar of the genus *Chordeiles* and related genera, having a dark plumage and, in the male, white patches on the wings and tail **2** *informal* another name for **night owl**

nightie or **nighty** ('naɪtɪ) n, pl **nighties** *informal* short for **nightdress**

nightingale ('naɪtɪŋ,geɪl) n a brownish European songbird, *Luscinia megarhynchos*, with a broad reddish-brown tail: well known for its musical song, usually heard at night [Old English *nihtegale*, literally: night-singer, from *night* + *galan* to sing]

Nightingale ('naɪtɪŋ,geɪl) n **Florence**, known as *the Lady with the Lamp*. 1820–1910, English nurse, famous for her work during the Crimean War. She helped to raise the status and quality of the nursing profession and founded a training school for nurses in London (1860)

nightjar ('naɪt,dʒɑː) n any nocturnal bird of the family *Caprimulgidae*, esp *Caprimulgus europaeus* (**European nightjar**): order *Caprimulgiformes*. They have a cryptic plumage and large eyes and feed on insects [C17: NIGHT + JAR², so called from its discordant cry]

night latch n a door lock that is operated by means of a knob on the inside and a key on the outside

nightlife ('naɪt,laɪf) n social life or entertainment taking place in the late evening or night, as in nightclubs

night-light n a dim light burning at night, esp for children

nightlong ('naɪt,lɒŋ) adj, adv throughout the night

nightly ('naɪtlɪ) adj **1** happening or relating to each night **2** happening at night ▷ adv **3** at night or each night

nightmare ('naɪt,mɛə) n **1** a terrifying or deeply distressing dream **2** a an event or condition resembling a terrifying dream **b** (*as modifier*): *a nightmare drive* **3** a thing that is feared **4** (formerly) an evil spirit supposed to harass or suffocate sleeping people [C13 (meaning: incubus; C16: bad dream): from NIGHT + Old English *mare, mære* evil spirit, from Germanic; compare Old Norse *mara* incubus, Polish *zmora*, French *cauchemar* nightmare] ▷ **'night,marish** adj

night owl or **night hawk** n *informal* a person who is or prefers to be up and about late at night

nights (naɪts) adv *informal* at night, esp regularly: *he works nights*

night safe n a safe built into the outside wall of a bank, in which customers can deposit money at times when the bank is closed

night school n an educational institution that holds classes in the evening for those who are not free during the day

nightshade ('naɪt,ʃeɪd) n any of various solanaceous plants, such as deadly nightshade, woody nightshade, and black nightshade [Old English *nihtscada*, apparently NIGHT + SHADE, referring to the poisonous or soporific qualities of these plants]

night shift n **1** a group of workers who work a shift during the night in an industry or occupation where a day shift or a back shift are also worked **2** the period worked

nightshirt ('naɪt,ʃɜːt) n a loose knee-length or longer shirtlike garment worn in bed by men

nightspot ('naɪt,spɒt) n an informal word for **nightclub**

night-time n the time from sunset to sunrise; night as distinct from day

night watch n **1** a watch or guard kept at night, esp for security **2** the period of time the watch is kept **3** a person who keeps such a watch; night watchman

night watchman n **1** Also called: **night watch** a person who keeps guard at night on a factory, public building, etc **2** *cricket* a batsman sent in to bat to play out time when a wicket has fallen near the end of a day's play

nightwear ('naɪt,wɛə) n apparel worn in bed or before retiring to bed; pyjamas, nightdress, dressing gown, etc

nigiri (niːˈgiːriː) n (in Japanese cuisine) a small oval block of cold rice topped with wasabi and a thin slice of fish, prawn, etc, and sometimes held together by a thin band of seaweed [from Japanese, literally: grasp, as the rice is shaped by hand]

nigrescent (naɪˈɡrɛsᵊnt) adj blackish; dark [C18: from Latin *nigrescere* to grow black, from *niger* black; see NEGRO¹] ▷ **ni'grescence** n

nihil *Latin* ('naɪhɪl, 'nɪːhɪl) n nil; nothing

nihilism ('naɪɪ,lɪzəm) n **1** a complete denial of all established authority and institutions **2** *philosophy* an extreme form of scepticism that systematically rejects all values, belief in existence, the possibility of communication, etc **3** a revolutionary doctrine of destruction for its own sake **4** the practice or promulgation of terrorism [C19: from Latin *nihil* nothing + -ISM, on the model of German *Nihilismus*] ▷ **'nihilist** n, adj ▷ **,nihil'istic** adj ▷ **nihility** (naɪˈhɪlɪtɪ) n

nihil obstat ('ɒbstæt) the phrase used by a Roman Catholic censor to declare publication inoffensive to faith or morals [Latin, literally: nothing hinders]

Nihon ('niː'hɒn) n transliteration of a Japanese name for **Japan**

Niigata ('niː,ɡɑːtə) n a port in central Japan, on NW Honshu at the mouth of the Shinano River: the chief port on the Sea of Japan. Pop: 514 678 (2002 est)

Nijinsky (nɪˈdʒɪnskɪ) n **Waslaw** or **Vaslav** (vats'laf). 1890–1950, Russian ballet dancer and choreographer, who was associated with Diaghilev. His creations include settings of Stravinsky's *Petrushka* and *The Rite of Spring*

Nijmegen ('naɪ,meɪɡən; Dutch 'nɛimeːxə) n an industrial town in the E Netherlands, in Gelderland province on the Waal River: the oldest town in the country; scene of the signing (1678) of the peace treaty between Louis XIV, the Netherlands, Spain, and the Holy Roman Empire. Pop: 156 000 (2003 est). German name: **Nimwegen**

-nik suffix forming nouns denoting a person associated with a specified state, belief, or quality: *beatnik; refusenik* [C20: from Russian *-nik*, as in SPUTNIK, and influenced by Yiddish *-nik* (agent suffix)]

Nikaria (nɪˈkɛərɪə, naɪ-) n another name for **Icaria**

Nike ('naɪkiː) *n Greek myth* the winged goddess of victory. Roman counterpart: **Victoria** [from Greek: victory]

Nikkei Stock Average ('nɪkeɪ) *n* an index of prices on the Tokyo Stock Exchange [c20: from *Nik(on) Kei(zai Shimbun)*, a Japanese newspaper group]

Nikko ('niːkəʊ) *n* a town in central Japan, on NE Honshu: a major pilgrimage centre, with a 4th-century Shinto shrine, a Buddhist temple (767), and the shrines and mausoleums of the Tokugawa shoguns. Pop: 17 527 (2002 est)

Nikolainkaupunki (*Finnish* ˌnikəlain'kaʊpʊŋki) *n* the former name of **Vaasa**

Nikolayev (*Russian* nika'lajif) *n* a city in S Ukraine on the Southern Bug about 64 km (40 miles) from the Black Sea: founded as a naval base in 1788; one of the leading Black Sea ports. Pop: 518 000 (2005 est). Former name: **Vernoleninsk**

nil (nɪl) *n* another word for nothing: used esp in the scoring of certain games [c19: from Latin]

Nile (naɪl) *n* a river in Africa, rising in S central Burundi in its remotest headstream, the **Luvironza**: flows into Lake Victoria and leaves the lake as the **Victoria Nile**, flowing to Lake Albert, which is drained by the **Albert Nile**, becoming the White Nile on the border between Uganda and the Sudan; joined by its chief tributary, the **Blue Nile** (which rises near Lake Tana, Ethiopia) at Khartoum, and flows north to its delta on the Mediterranean; the longest river in the world. Length: (from the source of the Luvironza to the Mediterranean) 6741 km (4187 miles)

Nile green *n* **a** a pale bluish-green colour **b** (*as adjective*): *a Nile-green dress*

nilgai ('nɪlɡaɪ), **nilghau** *or* **nylghau** ('nɪlɡɔː) *n, pl* **-gai**, **-gais** *or* **-ghau**, **-ghaus** a large Indian antelope, *Boselaphus tragocamelus*. The male is blue-grey with white markings and has small horns; the female is brownish and has no horns [c19: from Hindi *nīlgāw* blue bull, from Sanskrit *nīla* dark blue + *go* bull]

Nilgiri Hills ('nɪlɡɪrɪ) *or* **Nilgiris** *pl n* a plateau in S India, in Tamil Nadu. Average height: 2000 m (6500 ft), reaching 2635 m (8647 ft) in Doda Betta

Nilotic (naɪ'lɒtɪk) *adj* **1** of or relating to the Nile **2** of, relating to, or belonging to a tall Negroid pastoral people inhabiting the S Sudan, parts of Kenya and Uganda, and neighbouring countries **3** relating to or belonging to the group of languages spoken by the Nilotic peoples [c17: via Latin from Greek *Neilotikós*, from *Neilos* the **Nile**]

Nilsson (*Swedish* 'nilsɔn) *n* **Birgit** ('birgit). 1918–2006, Swedish operatic soprano

nimble ('nɪmbᵊl) *adj* **1** agile, quick, and neat in movement **2** alert; acute [Old English *næmel* quick to grasp, and *numol* quick at seizing, both from *niman* to take] > **'nimbleness** *n* > **'nimbly** *adv*

nimbostratus (ˌnɪmbəʊ'streɪtəs, -'strɑːtəs) *n, pl* **-ti** (-taɪ) a dark-coloured rain-bearing stratus cloud

nimbus ('nɪmbəs) *n, pl* **-bi** (-baɪ) *or* **-buses 1 a** a dark grey rain-bearing cloud **b** (*in combination*): *cumulonimbus clouds* **2 a** an emanation of light surrounding a saint or deity **b** a representation of this emanation **3** a surrounding aura or atmosphere [c17: from Latin: cloud, radiance]

NIMBY ('nɪmbɪ) *n acronym for* not in my back yard: a person who objects to the occurrence of something if it will affect him or her or take place in his or her locality

Nîmes (*French* nim) *n* a city in S France: Roman remains including an amphitheatre and the Pont du Gard aqueduct. Pop: 133 424 (1999)

Nimitz ('nɪmɪts) *n* **Chester William**. 1885–1966, US admiral; commander in chief of the US Pacific fleet in World War II (1941–45)

Nimrod ('nɪmrɒd) *n* **1** *Old Testament* a hunter, who was famous for his prowess (Genesis 10:8–9) **2** a person who is dedicated to or skilled in hunting

Nimrud (nɪm'ruːd) *n* an ancient city in Assyria, near the present-day city of Mosul (Iraq): founded in about 1250 BC and destroyed by the Medes in 612 BC; excavated by Sir Austen Henry Layard

Nimwegen ('nɪmveːɡən) *n* the German name for **Nijmegen**

Nimzowitsch ('nɪmzəˌvɪtʃ) *n* **Aaron Isayevich** (ɪ'zaɪɛvɪtʃ)

1886–1935, Latvian chess player and theorist; influential in enunciating the principles of the hypermodern school, of which he was the main instigator

nincompoop ('nɪnkəmˌpuːp, 'nɪŋ-) *n* a stupid person; fool; idiot [c17: of unknown origin]

nine (naɪn) *n* **1** the cardinal number that is the sum of one and eight **2** a numeral, 9, IX, etc, representing this number **3** something representing, represented by, or consisting of nine units, such as a playing card with nine symbols on it **4** Also called: **nine o'clock** nine hours after noon or midnight: *the play starts at nine* **5** dressed (up) to the nines *informal* elaborately dressed **6 999** (in Britain) the telephone number of the emergency services **7 nine to five** normal office hours: *he works nine to five; a nine-to-five job* ▷ *determiner* **8 a** amounting to nine: *nine days* **b** (*as pronoun*): *nine of the ten are ready* [Old English *nigon*; related to Gothic *niun*, Latin *novem*]

nine-days wonder *n* something that arouses great interest, but only for a short period

nine-eleven, 9-11 *or* **9/11** *n* the 11th of September 2001, the day on which the twin towers of the World Trade Center in New York were flown into and destroyed by aeroplanes hijacked by Islamic fundamentalists. Also called: **September eleven** [c21: from the US custom of expressing dates in figures, the day of the month following the number of the month]

ninefold ('naɪnˌfəʊld) *adj* **1** equal to or having nine times as many or as much **2** composed of nine parts ▷ *adv* **3** by or up to nine times as many or as much

ninepins ('naɪnˌpɪnz) *n* **1** (*functioning as singular*) another name for **skittles 2** (*singular*) one of the pins used in this game

nineteen (ˌnaɪn'tiːn) *n* **1** the cardinal number that is the sum of ten and nine and is a prime number **2** a numeral, 19, XIX, etc, representing this number **3** something represented by, representing, or consisting of 19 units **4** talk nineteen to the dozen to talk incessantly ▷ *determiner* **5 a** amounting to nineteen: *nineteen pictures* **b** (*as pronoun*): *only nineteen voted* [Old English *nigontīne*]

nineteenth (ˌnaɪn'tiːnθ) *adj* **1** (*usually prenominal*) **a** coming after the eighteenth in numbering or counting order, position, time, etc, being the ordinal number of nineteen. Often written: 19th **b** (*as noun*): *the nineteenth was rainy* ▷ *n* **2 a** one of 19 approximately equal parts of something **b** (*as modifier*): *a nineteenth part* **3** the fraction that is equal to one divided by 19 (1/19)

nineteenth hole *n golf slang* the bar in a golf clubhouse [c20: from its being the next objective after a standard 18-hole round]

ninetieth ('naɪntɪɪθ) *adj* **1** (*usually prenominal*) **a** being the ordinal number of ninety in numbering or counting order, position, time, etc Often written: 90th **b** (*as noun*): *the ninetieth in succession* ▷ *n* **2 a** one of 90 approximately equal parts of something **b** (*as modifier*): *a ninetieth part* **3** the fraction that is one divided by 90 (1/90)

ninety ('naɪntɪ) *n, pl* **-ties 1** the cardinal number that is the product of ten and nine **2** a numeral, 90, XC, etc, representing this number **3** something represented by, representing, or consisting of 90 units ▷ *determiner* **4 a** amounting to ninety: *ninety times out of a hundred* **b** (*as pronoun*): *at least ninety are thought to be missing* [Old English *nigontig*]

Nineveh ('nɪnɪvə) *n* the ancient capital of Assyria, on the River Tigris opposite the present-day city of Mosul (N Iraq): at its height in the 8th and 7th centuries BC; destroyed in 612 BC by the Medes and Babylonians > **Ninevite** ('nɪnɪˌvaɪt) *n*

Ningbo *or* **Ningpo** ('nɪŋ'pəʊ) *n* a port in E China, in NE Zhejiang, on the Yung River, about 20 km (12 miles) from its mouth at Hangzhou Bay: one of the first sites of European settlement in China. Pop: 1 188 000 (2005 est)

Ningsia *or* **Ninghsia** ('nɪŋ'ʃjɑː) *n* **1** a former province of NW China: mostly included in Inner Mongolia in 1954, with the smaller part constituted as the Ningxia Hui AR in 1958 **2** the former name of **Yinchuan**

Ningxia Hui Autonomous Region ('nɪŋ'ʃjɑː 'huːɪ) *n* an administrative division of NW China, south of Inner

Mongolia. Capital: Yinchuan. Pop: 5 800 000 (2003 est). Area: 66 400 sq km (25 896 sq miles)

Ninian ('nɪnɪən) *n* **Saint.** ?360–?432 AD, the first known apostle of Scotland; built a stone church (*candida casa*) at Whithorn on his native Solway; preached to the Picts. Feast day: Sept 16

ninja ('nɪndʒə) *n, pl* -**ja** *or* -**jas** (*sometimes capital*) a person skilled in **ninjutsu**, a Japanese martial art characterized by stealthy movement and camouflage [Japanese]

ninny ('nɪnɪ) *n, pl* -**nies** a dull-witted person [c16: perhaps from *an innocent* simpleton]

ninth (naɪnθ) *adj* **1** (*usually prenominal*) **a** coming after the eighth in counting order, position, time, etc; being the ordinal number of *nine*. Often written: 9th **b** (*as noun*): *he came on the ninth; ninth in line* ▷ *n* **2 a** one of nine equal or nearly equal parts of an object, quantity, measurement, etc **b** (*as modifier*): *a ninth part* **3** the fraction equal to one divided by nine (1/9) **4** *music* **a** an interval of one octave plus a second **b** one of two notes constituting such an interval ▷ *adv* **5** Also called: **ninthly** after the eighth person, position, event, etc [Old English *nigotha*; related to Old High German *niunto*, Old Norse *nīundi*]

Ninus ('naɪnəs) *n* a king of Assyria and the legendary founder of Nineveh, husband of Semiramis

Niobe ('naɪəbɪ) *n Greek myth* a daughter of Tantalus, whose children were slain after she boasted of them: although turned into stone, she continued to weep ▷ **Niobean** (naɪˈəʊbɪən) *adj*

niobium (naɪˈəʊbɪəm) *n* a ductile white superconductive metallic element that occurs principally in columbite and tantalite: used in steel alloys. Symbol: Nb; atomic no: 41; atomic wt: 92.90638; valency: 2, 3, or 5; relative density: 8.57; melting pt: 2469±10°C; boiling pt: 4744°C [c19: from New Latin, from NIOBE (daughter of Tantalus), so named because it occurred in TANTALITE]

nip¹ (nɪp) *vb* **nips, nipping, nipped** (*mainly tr*) **1** to catch or tightly compress, as between a finger and the thumb; pinch **2** (often foll by *off*) to remove by clipping, biting, etc **3** (when *intr*, often foll by *at*) to give a small sharp bite (to): *the dog nipped at his heels* **4** (esp of the cold) to affect with a stinging sensation **5** to harm through cold: *the frost nipped the young plants* **6** to check or destroy the growth of (esp in the phrase **nip in the bud**) **7** *slang* to steal **8** (*intr*; foll by *along, up, out*, etc) *Brit informal* to hurry; dart **9** *slang, chiefly US & Canadian* to snatch ▷ *n* **10** the act of nipping; a pinch, snip, etc **11 a** a frosty or chilly quality **b** severe frost or cold: *the first nip of winter* **12** *archaic* a taunting remark **13** **nip and tuck a** *chiefly US & Canadian* neck and neck **b** *informal* plastic surgery performed for cosmetic reasons **14** **put the nips in** *Austral & NZ slang* to exert pressure on someone, esp in order to extort money [c14: of Scandinavian origin; compare Old Norse *hnippa* to prod]

nip² (nɪp) *n* **1** a small drink of spirits; dram **2** *chiefly Brit* a measure of spirits usually equal to one sixth of a gill ▷ *vb* **nips, nipping, nipped 3** to drink (spirits), esp habitually in small amounts [c18: shortened from *nipperkin* a vessel holding a half-pint or less, of uncertain origin; compare Dutch *nippen* to sip]

Nipigon ('nɪpɪgɒn) *n* **Lake Nipigon** a lake in central Canada, in NW Ontario, draining into Lake Superior via the **Nipigon River**. Area: 4843 sq km (1870 sq miles)

Nipissing ('nɪpɪsɪŋ) *n* **Lake Nipissing** a lake in central Canada, in E Ontario between the Ottawa River and Georgian Bay. Area: 855 sq km (330 sq miles)

nipper ('nɪpə) *n* **1** a person or thing that nips **2** the large pincer-like claw of a lobster, crab, or similar crustacean **3** *informal* a small child **4** *Austral* a type of small prawn used as bait

nippers ('nɪpəz) *pl n* an instrument or tool, such as a pair of pliers, for snipping, pinching, or squeezing

nipple ('nɪpəl) *n* **1** Also called: **mamilla, papilla, teat** the small conical projection in the centre of the areola of each breast, which in women contains the outlet of the milk ducts **2** something resembling a nipple in shape or function **3** Also called: **grease nipple** a small drilled bush, usually screwed into a bearing, through which grease is introduced [c16: from earlier *neble, nible*, perhaps from NEB, NIB]

nipplewort ('nɪpəl,wɜːt) *n* an annual Eurasian plant, *Lapsana communis*, with pointed oval leaves and small yellow flower heads: family *Asteraceae* (composites)

Nippon ('nɪpɒn) *n* transliteration of a Japanese name for **Japan** ▷ **Nipponese** (,nɪpəˈniːz) *adj, n*

Nippur (nɪˈpʊə) *n* an ancient Sumerian and Babylonian city, the excavated site of which is in SE Iraq: an important religious centre, abandoned in the 12th or 13th century

nippy ('nɪpɪ) *adj* -**pier**, -**piest 1** (of weather) chilly, keen, or frosty **2** *Brit informal* **a** quick; nimble; active **b** (of a motor vehicle) small and relatively powerful **3** (of a dog) inclined to bite ▷ **'nippily** *adv*

Nirenberg ('naɪrən,bɜːg) *n* **Marshall Warren.** born 1927, US biochemist; shared the Nobel prize for physiology or medicine (1968) for his role in deciphering the genetic code

NIREX ('naɪrɛks) *n acronym for* Nuclear Industry Radioactive Waste Executive

nirvana (nɪəˈvɑːnə, nɜː-) *n Buddhism, Hinduism* final release from the cycle of reincarnation attained by extinction of all desires and individual existence, culminating (in Buddhism) in absolute blessedness, or (in Hinduism) in absorption into Brahman [c19: from Sanskrit: extinction, literally: a blowing out, from *nir-* out + *vāti* it blows]

Niš *or* **Nish** (niːʃ) *n* an industrial town in Serbia, in the SE: situated on routes between central Europe and the Aegean. Pop: 203 670 (2002)

Nisei ('niːseɪ) *n* a native-born citizen of the United States or Canada whose parents were Japanese immigrants [Japanese, literally: second generation]

Nishapur (,niːʃɑːˈpʊə) *n* a town in NE Iran, at an altitude of 1195 m (3920 ft): birthplace and burial place of Omar Khayyám. Pop: 208 000 (2005 est)

Nishinomiya (,niːʃɪˈnɒmɪjə) *n* an industrial city in central Japan, on S Honshu, northwest of Osaka. Pop: 436 877 (2002 est)

nisi ('naɪsaɪ) *adj* (*postpositive*) *law* (of a court order) coming into effect on a specified date unless cause is shown within a certain period why it should not: *a decree nisi* [c19: from Latin: unless, if not]

Nissen hut ('nɪsən) *n* a military shelter of semicircular cross section, made of corrugated steel sheet [c20: named after Lt Col. Peter *Nissen* (1871–1930), British mining engineer, its inventor]

nit¹ (nɪt) *n* **1** the egg of a louse, usually adhering to human hair **2** the larva of a louse or similar insect [Old English *hnitu*; related to Dutch *neet*, Old High German *hniz*]

nit² (nɪt) *n* a unit of luminance equal to 1 candela per square metre [c20: from Latin *nitor* brightness]

nit³ (nɪt) *n informal, chiefly Brit* short for **nitwit**

nit⁴ (nɪt) *n* a unit of information equal to 1.44 bits. Also called: **nepit** [c20: from N(*apierian dig*)it]

nit⁵ (nɪt) *n* **keep nit** *Austral informal* to keep watch, esp during illegal activity [c19: from NIX¹]

Niterói (*Portuguese* niteˈrɔi) *n* a port in SE Brazil, on Guanabara Bay opposite Rio de Janeiro: contains Brazil's chief shipyards. Pop: 458 465 (2000). Also called: **Nictheroy**

nit-pick *vb* (*intr*) *informal* to raise petty objections or concern oneself with insignificant details

nit-picking *informal* ▷ *n* **1** a concern with insignificant details, esp with the intention of finding fault ▷ *adj* **2** showing such a concern; fussy [c20: from NIT¹ + PICK¹] ▷ **'nit-,picker** *n*

nitrate ('naɪtreɪt) *n* **1** any salt or ester of nitric acid, such as sodium nitrate, NaNO₃ **2** a fertilizer consisting of or containing nitrate salts ▷ *vb* **3** (*tr*) to treat with nitric acid or a nitrate **4** to convert or be converted into a nitrate ▷ **ni'tration** *n*

nitre *or US* **niter** ('naɪtə) *n* another name for **potassium nitrate** *or* **sodium nitrate** [c14: via Old French from Latin *nitrum*, from Greek *nitron* NATRON]

nitric ('naɪtrɪk) *adj* of or containing nitrogen, esp in the pentavalent state

nitric acid *n* a colourless or yellowish fuming corrosive liquid usually used in aqueous solution. It is an oxidizing agent and a strong monobasic acid: important in the manufacture of fertilizers, explosives, and many other chemicals. Formula: HNO_3. Former name: **aqua fortis**

nitric oxide *n* a colourless slightly soluble gas forming red fumes of nitrogen dioxide in air. Formula: NO. Systematic name: **nitrogen monoxide**

nitride ('naɪtraɪd) *n* a compound of nitrogen with a more electropositive element, for example magnesium nitride, Mg_3N_2

nitrification (ˌnaɪtrɪfɪ'keɪʃən) *n* **1** the oxidation of the ammonium compounds in dead organic material into nitrites and nitrates by soil nitrobacteria, making nitrogen available to plants **2** the addition of a nitro group to an organic compound

nitrify ('naɪtrɪˌfaɪ) *vb* **-fies, -fying, -fied** (*tr*) **1** to treat or cause to react with nitrogen or a nitrogen compound **2** to treat (soil) with nitrates **3** (of nitrobacteria) to convert (ammonium compounds) into nitrates by oxidation

nitrite ('naɪtraɪt) *n* any salt or ester of nitrous acid

nitro- *or before a vowel* **nitr-** *combining form* **1** indicating that a chemical compound contains a nitro group, $-NO_2$: *nitrobenzene* **2** indicating that a chemical compound is a nitrate ester: *nitrocellulose* [from Greek *nitron* NATRON]

nitrobacteria (ˌnaɪtrəʊbæk'tɪərɪə) *pl n, sing* **-terium** (-'tɪərɪəm) soil bacteria of the order *Pseudomonadales* that are involved in nitrification, including species of *Nitrosomonas* and *Nitrobacter*

nitrobenzene (ˌnaɪtrəʊ'bɛnziːn) *n* a yellow oily toxic water-insoluble liquid compound, used as a solvent and in the manufacture of aniline. Formula: $C_6H_5NO_2$

nitrocellulose (ˌnaɪtrəʊ'sɛljʊˌləʊs) *n* another name (not in chemical usage) for **cellulose nitrate**

nitrogen ('naɪtrədʒən) *n* a colourless odourless relatively unreactive gaseous element that forms 78 per cent (by volume) of the air, occurs in many compounds, and is an essential constituent of proteins and nucleic acids: used in the manufacture of ammonia and other chemicals and as a refrigerant. Symbol: N; atomic no: 7; atomic wt: 14.00674; valency: 3 or 5; density: $1/2506$ kg/m³; melting pt: –210.00°C; boiling pt: –195.8°C

nitrogen cycle *n* the natural circulation of nitrogen by living organisms. Nitrates in the soil, derived from dead organic matter by bacterial action, are absorbed and synthesized into complex organic compounds by plants and reduced to nitrates again when the plants and the animals feeding on them die and decay

nitrogen dioxide *n* a red-brown poisonous irritating gas that, at ordinary temperatures, exists in equilibrium with dinitrogen tetroxide. It is an intermediate in the manufacture of nitric acid, a nitrating agent, and also an oxidizer for rocket fuels. Formula: NO_2

nitrogen fixation *n* **1** the conversion of atmospheric nitrogen into nitrogen compounds by certain bacteria, such as *Rhizobium* in the root nodules of legumes **2** a process, such as the Haber process, in which atmospheric nitrogen is converted into a nitrogen compound, used esp for the manufacture of fertilizer

nitrogenize *or* **nitrogenise** (naɪ'trɒdʒɪˌnaɪz) *vb* to combine or treat with nitrogen or a nitrogen compound > niˌtrogeniˈzation *or* niˌtrogeniˈsation *n*

nitrogen monoxide *n* the systematic name for **nitric oxide**

nitrogen mustard *n* any of a class of organic compounds resembling mustard gas in their molecular structure. General formula: $RN(CH_2CH_2Cl)_2$, where R is an organic group: important in the treatment of cancer

nitrogenous (naɪ'trɒdʒɪnəs) *adj* containing nitrogen or a nitrogen compound: *a nitrogenous fertilizer*

nitroglycerine (ˌnaɪtrəʊ'glɪsəˌriːn) *or* **nitroglycerin** (ˌnaɪtrəʊ'glɪsərɪn) *n* a pale yellow viscous explosive liquid substance made from glycerol and nitric and sulphuric acids and used in explosives and in medicine as a vasodilator. Formula: $CH_2NO_3CHNO_3CH_2NO_3$. Also called: **trinitroglycerine**

nitromethane (ˌnaɪtrəʊ'miːθeɪn) *n* an oily colourless liquid obtained from methane and used as a solvent and rocket fuel and in the manufacture of synthetic resins.

Formula: CH_3NO_2

nitrous ('naɪtrəs) *adj* of, derived from, or containing nitrogen, esp in a low valency state [C17: from Latin *nitrōsus* full of natron]

nitrous acid *n* a weak monobasic acid known only in solution and in the form of nitrite salts. Formula: HNO_2

nitrous oxide *n* a colourless nonflammable slightly soluble gas with a sweet smell: used as an anaesthetic in dentistry and surgery. Formula: N_2O. Also called: **laughing gas**

nitty ('nɪtɪ) *adj* **-tier, -tiest** infested with nits

nitty-gritty ('nɪtɪ'grɪtɪ) *n* **the nitty-gritty** *informal* the basic facts of a matter, situation, etc [C20: perhaps rhyming compound formed from GRIT]

nitwit ('nɪtˌwɪt) *n* *informal* a foolish person [C20: perhaps from NIT¹ + WIT¹]

Niue ('njuːeɪ) *n* an island in the S Pacific, between Tonga and the Cook Islands: annexed by New Zealand (1901); achieved full internal self-government in 1974. Chief town and port: Alofi. Pop: 2000 (2003 est). Area: 260 sq km (100 sq miles). Also called: **Savage Island** > **Niuean** (njuː'ɪən) *adj, n*

Niven ('nɪvən) *n* **David.** 1909–83, British film actor and author. His films include *The Prisoner of Zenda* (1937), *Around the World in 80 Days* (1956), *Casino Royale* (1967), and *Paper Tiger* (1975). He wrote the autobiographical *The Moon's a Balloon* (1972) and *Bring on the Empty Horses* (1975)

Nivernais (*French* nivɛrnɛ) *n* a former province of central France, around Nevers

nix¹ (nɪks) *US & Canadian informal* ▷ *sentence substitute* **1** another word for **no¹** (sense 1) ▷ *n* **2** a rejection or refusal **3** nothing at all [C18: from German, colloquial form of *nichts* nothing]

nix² (nɪks) *n* *German myth* a male water sprite, usually unfriendly to humans [C19: from German *Nixe* nymph or water spirit, from Old High German *nihhus*; related to Old English *nicor* sea monster]

Nixon ('nɪksən) *n* **Richard M(ilhous).** 1913–94, US Republican politician; 37th president from 1969 until he resigned over the Watergate scandal in 1974

Nizam (nɪ'zɑːm) *n* the title of the ruler of Hyderabad, India, from 1724 to 1948

Nizam al-Mulk (æl'mʊlk) *n* title of *Abu Ali Hasan Ibn Ali*. ?1018–92, Persian statesman; vizier of Persia (1063–92) for the Seljuk sultans: assassinated

Nizhni Novgorod (*Russian* 'niʒnij 'nɒvgərət) *n* a city and port in central Russia, at the confluence of the Volga and Oka Rivers: situated on the Volga route from the Baltic to central Asia; birthplace of Maxim Gorki. Pop: 1 288 000 (2005 est). Former name (1932–91): **Gorki**

Nizhni Tagil (*Russian* 'niʒnij ta'gil) *n* a city in central Russia, on the E slopes of the Ural Mountains: a major metallurgical centre. Pop: 382 000 (2005 est

NJ *or* **N.J.** *abbreviation* New Jersey

Njord (njɔːd) *or* **Njorth** (njɔːθ) *n* *Norse myth* the god of the sea, fishing, and prosperity

Nkomo (ᵊŋ'kəʊməʊ) *n* **Joshua.** 1917–99, Zimbabwean politician; coleader, with Robert Mugabe, of the Patriotic Front (1976–80) against the government of Ian Smith in Rhodesia; minister (1980–82; 1988–99) and vice-president (1990–96).

nkosi (ᵊŋ'kɔːsɪ) *n* *South African* a term of address to a superior; master; chief [Nguni *inkosi* chief, lord]

Nkosi Sikelel' iAfrica (ŋ'kɔsɪ ˌsɪke'lɛlɪ ˌafrɪ'ka) *n* the unofficial anthem of the Black people of South Africa, officially recognized as a national anthem (along with parts of 'Die Stem' and an English verse) in 1991 [from Xhosa, Lord Bless Africa]

Nkrumah (ᵊŋ'kruːmə) *n* **Kwame** ('kwaːmɪ). 1909–72, Ghanaian statesman, prime minister (1957-60) and president (1960-66). He led demands for self-government in the 1950s, achieving Ghanaian independence in 1957. He was overthrown by a military coup (1966)

NM *or* **N. Mex.** *abbreviation* New Mexico

NMR *abbreviation* nuclear magnetic resonance

NNE *symbol for* north-northeast

NNP *abbreviation* **1** net national product **2** (in South Africa) New National Party

n

NNW *symbol for* north-northwest

no¹ (nəʊ) *sentence substitute* **1** used to express denial, disagreement, refusal, disapproval, disbelief, or acknowledgment of negative statements ▷ *n, pl* **noes** or **nos 2** an answer or vote of no **3** (*often plural*) a person who votes in the negative **4 the noes have it** there is a majority of votes in the negative **5 not take no for an answer** to continue in a course of action despite refusals [Old English *nā*, from *ne* not, no + *ā* ever; see AY¹]

no² (nəʊ) *determiner* **1** not any, not a, or not one: *there's no money left; no card in the file* **2** not by a long way; not at all: *she's no youngster* **3** (foll by comparative adjectives and adverbs) not: *no less than forty men; no more quickly than before* [Old English *nā*, changed from *nān* NONE¹]

No¹ or **Noh** (nəʊ) *n, pl* **No** or **Noh** the stylized classic drama of Japan, developed in the 15th century or earlier, using music, dancing, chanting, elaborate costumes, and themes from religious stories or myths [from Japanese *nō* talent, from Chinese *neng*]

No² (nəʊ) *n* **Lake No** a lake in the S central Sudan, where the Bahr el Jebel (White Nile) is joined by the Bahr el Ghazal. Area: about 103 sq km (40 sq miles)

No³ the chemical symbol for nobelium

No. *abbreviation* **1** north(ern) **2** Also: **no.** (*pl* **Nos.** or **nos.**) number [from French *numéro*]

n.o. *abbreviation cricket* not out

no' (no, nəʊ) *adv Scot* not

no-account *adj* **1** worthless; good-for-nothing ▷ *n* **2** a worthless person

Noah (ˈnəʊə) *n Old Testament* a Hebrew patriarch, who saved himself, his family, and specimens of each species of animal and bird from the Flood by building a ship (**Noah's Ark**) in which they all survived (Genesis 6–8)

nob¹ (nɒb) *n cribbage* **1** the jack of the suit turned up **2** one for his nob the call made with this jack, scoring one point [c19: of uncertain origin]

nob² (nɒb) *n slang, chiefly Brit* a person of social distinction [c19: of uncertain origin]

no-ball *n* **1** *cricket* an illegal ball, as for overstepping the crease, throwing, etc, for which the batting side scores a run, and from which the batsman can be out only by being run out **2** *rounders* an illegal ball, esp one bowled too high or too low ▷ *sentence substitute* **3** *cricket, rounders* a call by the umpire indicating a no-ball ▷ *vb* **4** (*tr*) *cricket* (of an umpire) **a** to suborn (a bowler, esp a juror) by threats, bribery, etc **4** to steal; filch **5** to get hold of; grab **6** to kidnap [c19: back formation from *nobbler*, from false division of *an hobbler* (one who hobbles horses) as *a nobbler*] > **nobbler** *n*

nobble (ˈnɒbəl) *vb* (*tr*) *Brit slang* **1** to disable (a racehorse), esp with drugs **2** to win over or outwit (a person) by underhand means **3** to suborn (a person, esp a juror) by threats, bribery, etc **4** to steal; filch **5** to get hold of; grab **6** to kidnap [c19: back formation from *nobbler*, from false division of *an hobbler* (one who hobbles horses) as *a nobbler*] > **nobbler** *n*

Nobel (nəʊˈbɛl) *n* **Alfred Bernhard** (ˈalfreːd ˈbæːrnhard). 1833–96, Swedish chemist and philanthropist, noted for his invention of dynamite (1866) and his bequest founding the Nobel prizes

nobelium (nəʊˈbiːlɪəm) *n* a transuranic element produced artificially from curium. Symbol: No; atomic no: 102; half-life of most stable isotope, ²⁵⁵No: 180 seconds (approx.); valency: 2 or 3 [c20: New Latin, named after *Nobel* Institute, Stockholm, where it was discovered]

Nobel prize (nəʊˈbɛl) *n* a prize for outstanding contributions to chemistry, physics, physiology or medicine, literature, economics, and peace that may be awarded annually. It was established in 1901; the prize for economics being added in 1969. The recipients are chosen by an international committee centred in Sweden, except for the peace prize which is awarded in Oslo by a committee of the Norwegian parliament

Nobile (*Italian* nobile) *n* **Umberto.** 1885–1978, Italian aeronautical engineer and aviator. He flew his *Norge* airship over the North Pole (1926) with Amundsen and his *Italia* airship over the Pole in 1928, crashing on the return

nobility (nəʊˈbɪlɪtɪ) *n, pl* **-ties 1** a socially or politically privileged class whose titles are conferred by descent or by royal decree **2** the state or quality of being morally or

spiritually good; dignity: *the nobility of his mind* **3** (in the British Isles) the class of people holding the title of dukes, marquesses, earls, viscounts, or barons and their feminine equivalents collectively; peerage

noble (ˈnəʊbəl) *adj* **1** of or relating to a hereditary class with special social or political status, often derived from a feudal period **2** of or characterized by high moral qualities; magnanimous: *a noble deed* **3** having dignity or eminence; illustrious **4** grand or imposing; magnificent: *a noble avenue of trees* **5** of superior quality or kind; excellent: *a noble strain of horses* **6** *chem* **a** (of certain elements) chemically unreactive **b** (of certain metals, esp copper, silver, and gold) resisting oxidation ▷ *n* **7** a person belonging to a privileged social or political class whose status is usually indicated by a title conferred by sovereign authority or descent **8** (in the British Isles) a person holding the title of duke, marquess, earl, viscount, or baron, or a feminine equivalent **9** a former Brit gold coin having the value of one third of a pound [c13: via Old French from Latin *nōbilis*, originally, capable of being known, hence well-known, noble, from *noscere* to know] > **ˈnobleness** *n* > **ˈnobly** *adv*

nobleman (ˈnəʊbəlmən) *n, pl* **-men** a man of noble rank, title, or status; peer; aristocrat

noble savage *n* (in romanticism) an idealized view of primitive man

noblesse oblige (nəʊˈblɛs əʊˈbliːʒ; *French* nɔblɛs ɔbliʒ) *n often ironic* the supposed obligation of nobility to be honourable and generous [French, literally: nobility obliges]

noblewoman (ˈnəʊbəlwʊmən) *n, pl* **-women** a woman of noble rank, title, or status; peer; aristocrat

nobody (ˈnəʊbədɪ) *pron* **1** no person; no-one ▷ *n, pl* **-bodies 2** an insignificant person
● USAGE See at **everyone**

Nobunaga (ˈnɒbuːˌnɑːɡə) *n* See **Oda Nobunaga**

nock (nɒk) *n* **1** a notch on an arrow that fits on the bowstring **2** either of the grooves at each end of a bow that hold the bowstring ▷ *vb* (*tr*) **3** to fit (an arrow) on a bowstring **4** to put a groove or notch in (a bow or arrow) [c14: related to Swedish *nock* tip]

no-claims bonus *n* a reduction on an insurance premium, esp one covering a motor vehicle, if no claims have been made within a specified period. Also called: **no-claim bonus**

noctambulism (nɒkˈtæmbjʊˌlɪzəm) or **noctambulation** (nɒkˌtæmbjʊˈleɪʃən) *n* another word for **somnambulism** [c19: from Latin *nox* night + *ambulāre* to walk]

noctilucent (ˌnɒktɪˈluːsənt) *adj* shining at night, usu. of very high altitude clouds observable in the summer twilight sky

noctuid (ˈnɒktjʊɪd) *n* any nocturnal moth of the family *Noctuidae*: includes the underwings and antler moth [c19: via New Latin from Latin *noctua* night owl, from *nox* night]

noctule (ˈnɒktjuːl) *n* any of several large Old World insectivorous bats of the genus *Nyctalus*, esp *N. noctula*: family *Vespertilionidae* [c18: probably from Late Latin *noctula* night owl, from Latin *noctua* night owl]

nocturnal (nɒkˈtɜːnəl) *adj* **1** of, used during, occurring in, or relating to the night **2** (of animals) active at night **3** (of plants) having flowers that open at night and close by day [c15: from Late Latin *nocturnālis*, from Latin *nox* night] > **ˌnoctur'nality** *n* > **noc'turnally** *adv*

nocturne (ˈnɒktɜːn) *n* **1** a short, lyrical piece of music, esp one for the piano **2** a painting or tone poem of a night scene

nod (nɒd) *vb* **nods, nodding, nodded 1** to lower and raise (the head) briefly, as to indicate agreement, invitation, etc **2** (*tr*) to express or indicate by nodding: *she nodded approval* **3** (*tr*) to bring or direct by nodding: *she nodded me towards the manager's office* **4** (*intr*) (of flowers, trees, etc) to sway or bend forwards and back **5** (*intr*) to let the head fall forward through drowsiness; be almost asleep **6** (*intr*) to be momentarily inattentive or careless: *even Homer sometimes nods* **7 nodding acquaintance** a slight, casual, or superficial knowledge (of a subject or a person) ▷ *n* **8** a quick down-and-up movement of the head, as in assent, command, etc **9** a short sleep; nap.

See **land of Nod** ▷ See also **nod off** [C14 *nodde*, of obscure origin] > 'nodding*adj, n*

noddle¹ ('nɒdəl) *n informal, chiefly Brit* the head or brains: *use your noddle!* [c15: origin obscure]

noddle² ('nɒdəl) *vb informal, chiefly Brit* to nod (the head), as through drowsiness [c18: from NOD]

noddy¹ ('nɒdɪ) *n, pl* **-dies 1** any of several tropical terns of the genus *Anous*, esp *A. stolidus* (**common noddy**), typically having a dark plumage **2** a fool or dunce [c16: perhaps noun use of obsolete *noddy* foolish, drowsy, perhaps from NOD (vb); the bird is so called because it allows itself to be caught by hand]

noddy² ('nɒdɪ) *n, pl* **-dies** (*usually plural*) *television* film footage of an interviewer's reactions to comments made by an interviewee, used in editing the interview after it has been recorded [c20: from NOD]

node (nəʊd) *n* **1** a knot, swelling, or knob **2** the point on a plant stem from which the leaves or lateral branches grow **3** *physics* a point at which the amplitude of one of the two kinds of displacement in a standing wave has zero or minimum value. Generally the other kind of displacement has its maximum value at this point **4** Also called: **crunode** *maths* a point at which two branches of a curve intersect, each branch having a distinct tangent **5** *maths, linguistics* one of the objects of which a graph or a tree consists; vertex **6** *astronomy* either of the two points at which the orbit of a body intersects the plane of the ecliptic. When the body moves from the south to the north side of the ecliptic it passes the **ascending node** and from the north to the south side it passes the **descending node 7** *anatomy* any natural bulge or swelling of a structure or part, such as those that occur along the course of a lymphatic vessel (**lymph node**) **8** *computing* an interconnection point on a computer network [c16: from Latin *nōdus* knot]

nod off *vb (intr, adverb) informal* to fall asleep

nodule ('nɒdjuːl) *n* **1** a small knot, lump, or node **2** Also called: **root nodule** any of the knoblike outgrowths on the roots of clover and many other legumes: contain bacteria involved in nitrogen fixation **3** *anatomy* any small node or knoblike protuberance **4** a small rounded lump of rock or mineral substance, esp in a matrix of different rock material [c17: from Latin *nōdulus*, from *nōdus* knot] > 'nodular, 'nodulose*or* 'nodulous*adj*

Noel*or* **Noël** (nəʊ'ɛl) *n* **1** (esp in carols) another word for **Christmas 2** (*often not capital) rare* a Christmas carol [c19: from French, from Latin *nātālis* a birthday; see NATAL]

noetic (nəʊ'ɛtɪk) *adj* of or relating to the mind, esp to its rational and intellectual faculties [c17: from Greek *noētikos*, from *noein* to think, from *nous* the mind]

Nofretete (ˌnɒfrɛ'tiːtɪ) *n* same as **Nefertiti**

nog*or* **nogg** (nɒg) *n* **1** Also called: **flip** a drink, esp an alcoholic one, containing beaten egg **2** *East Anglian dialect* strong local beer [C17 (originally: a strong beer): of obscure origin]

noggin ('nɒgɪn) *n* **1** a small quantity of spirits, usually 1 gill **2** a small mug or cup **3** an informal word for **head** (sense 1) [c17: of obscure origin]

no-go area *n* a district in a town that is barricaded off, usually by a paramilitary organization, within which the police, army, etc, can only enter by force

Noguchi (nɔː'guːtʃɪ) *n* **Hideyo** ('hiːdɛˌjɔː). 1876–1928, Japanese bacteriologist, active in the US. He made important discoveries in the treatment of syphilis

Noh (nəʊ) *n* a variant spelling of **No¹**

noir (nwɑː) *adj* (of a film) showing characteristics of a *film noir*, in plot or style

noise (nɔɪz) *n* **1** a sound, esp one that is loud or disturbing **2** loud shouting; clamour; din **3** any undesired electrical disturbance in a circuit, degrading the useful information in a signal. See also **signal-to-noise ratio 4** undesired or irrelevant elements in a visual image: *removing noise from pictures* **5** talk or interest: *noise about strikes* **6** (*plural*) conventional comments or sounds conveying a reaction, attitude, feeling, etc: *she made sympathetic noises* **7** make a noise to talk a great deal or complain **8** make noises about *informal* to give indications of one's intentions: *the government is making noises about new social security arrangements* **9** noises off

theatre sounds made offstage intended for the ears of the audience: used as a stage direction ▷ *vb* **10** (*tr;* usually foll by *abroad* or *about*) to spread (news, gossip, etc) **11** (*intr*) *rare* to talk loudly or at length **12** (*intr*) *rare* to make a din or outcry; be noisy [c13: from Old French, from Latin: NAUSEA]

noiseless ('nɔɪzlɪs) *adj* making little or no sound; silent > 'noiselessly*adv* > 'noiselessness*n*

noise pollution *n* annoying or harmful noise in an environment

noisette (nwɑː'zɛt) *adj* **1** flavoured or made with hazelnuts ▷ *n* **2** a small round boneless slice of lamb from the fillet or leg **3** a chocolate made with hazelnuts [from French: hazelnut]

noisome ('nɔɪsəm) *adj* **1** (esp of smells) offensive **2** harmful or noxious [c14: from obsolete *noy*, variant of ANNOY + -SOME¹] > 'noisomely*adv* > 'noisomeness*n*

noisy ('nɔɪzɪ) *adj* **noisier, noisiest 1** making a loud or constant noise **2** full of or characterized by noise > 'noisily*adv* > 'noisiness*n*

Nolan ('nəʊlən) *n* **1** **Michael Patrick**, Baron. 1928–2007, British judge; chairman of the Committee on Standards in Public Life (1994–97) **2** Sir **Sidney**. 1917–92, Australian painter, whose works explore themes in Australian folklore

Nolde (German 'nɔldə) *n* **Emil** ('eːmiːl). 1867–1956, German painter and engraver, noted particularly for his violent use of colour and the primitive masklike quality of his figures

nolens volens *Latin* ('nəʊlɛnz 'vəʊlɛnz) *adv* whether willing or unwilling

Nollekens ('nɒləkɪnz) *n* **Joseph**. 1737–1823, British neoclassical sculptor of portrait busts, tombs, and mythological subjects

nolle prosequi ('nɒlɪ 'prɒsɪˌkwaɪ) *n law* an entry made on the court record when the plaintiff in a civil suit or prosecutor in a criminal prosecution undertakes not to continue the action or prosecution. See **non prosequitur** [Latin: do not pursue (prosecute)]

nomad ('nəʊmæd) *n* **1** a member of a people or tribe who move from place to place to find pasture and food **2** a person who continually moves from place to place; wanderer [c16: via French from Latin *nomas* wandering shepherd, from Greek; related to *nemein* to feed, pasture] > 'nomadism*n* > no'madic*adj* > no'madically*adv*

no-man's-land *n* **1** land between boundaries, esp an unoccupied zone between opposing forces **2** an unowned or unclaimed piece of land **3** an ambiguous area of activity or thought

no-mark *n Brit slang* an insignificant or worthless person [c20: from 'someone who makes *no mark*']

nom de guerre ('nɒm də 'gɛə) *n, pl* **noms de guerre** ('nɒm də 'gɛə) an assumed name; pseudonym [French, literally: war name]

nom de plume ('nɒm də 'pluːm) *n, pl* **noms de plume** ('nɒm də 'pluːm) another term for **pen name**

nomenclator ('nəʊmɛnˌkleɪtə) *n* a person who invents or assigns names, as in scientific classification [c16: from Latin, from *nōmen* name + *calāre* to call]

nomenclature (nəʊ'mɛnklətʃə; US 'nəʊmənˌkleɪtʃər) *n* the terminology used in a particular science, art, activity, etc [c17: from Latin *nōmenclātūra* list of names; see NOMENCLATOR]

nominal ('nɒmɪnəl) *adj* **1** in name only; theoretical: *the nominal leader* **2** minimal in comparison with real worth or what is expected; token: *a nominal fee* **3** of, relating to, constituting, bearing, or giving a name **4** *grammar* of or relating to a noun or noun phrase ▷ *n* **5** *grammar* a nominal element; a noun, noun phrase, or syntactically similar structure **6** *bell-ringing* the harmonic an octave above the strike tone of a bell [c15: from Latin *nōminālis* of a name, from *nōmen* name] > 'nominally*adv*

nominalism ('nɒmɪnəˌlɪzəm) *n* the philosophical theory that the variety of objects to which a single general word, such as *dog*, applies have nothing in common but the name > 'nominalist*n, adj*

nominal value *n* another name for **par value**

nominate *vb* ('nɒmɪˌneɪt) (*mainly tr*) **1** to propose as a candidate, esp for an elective office **2** to appoint to an office or position **3** to name (someone) to act on one's behalf, esp to conceal one's identity **4** (*intr*) *Austral* to stand as a candidate in an election **5** *archaic* to name, entitle, or designate ▷ *adj* ('nɒmɪnɪt) **6** *rare* having a particular name [c16: from Latin *nōmināre* to call by name, from *nōmen* name] > 'nomi,nator *n* > ,nomi'nation *n*

nominative ('nɒmɪnətɪv, 'nɒmnə-) *adj* **1** *grammar* denoting a case of nouns and pronouns in inflected languages that is used esp to identify the subject of a finite verb **2** appointed rather than elected to a position, office, etc **3** bearing the name of a person ▷ *n* **4** *grammar* **a** the nominative case **b** a word or speech element in the nominative case [c14: from Latin *nōminātīvus* belonging to naming, from *nōmen* name] > nominatival (,nɒmɪnə'taɪvᵊl, ,nɒmnə-) *adj*

nominee (,nɒmɪ'ni:) *n* **1** a person who is nominated to an office or as a candidate **2 a** a person or organization named to act on behalf of someone else, esp to conceal the identity of the nominator **b** (*as modifier*): *nominee shareholder* [c17: from NOMINATE + -EE]

nomogram ('nɒmə,græm, 'nəʊmə-) *or* **nomograph** *n* **1** an arrangement of two linear or logarithmic scales such that an intersecting straight line enables intermediate values or values on a third scale to be read off **2** any graphic representation of numerical relationships [c20: from Greek *nomos* law + -GRAM, on the model of French *nomogramme*]

-nomy *n combining form* indicating a science or the laws governing a certain field of knowledge: *agronomy; economy* [from Greek -*nomia* law; related to *nemein* to distribute, control] > -nomic *adj combining form*

non- *prefix* **1** indicating negation: *nonexistent* **2** indicating refusal or failure: *noncooperation* **3** indicating exclusion from a specified class of persons or things: *nonfiction* **4** indicating lack or absence, esp of a quality associated with what is specified: *nonobjective; nonevent* [from Latin *nōn* not]

nonaddictive (,nɒnə'dɪktɪv) *adj* not of, relating to, or causing addiction

nonage ('nəʊnɪdʒ) *n* **1** *law* the state of being under any of various ages at which a person may legally enter into certain transactions, such as the making of binding contracts, marrying, etc **2** any period of immaturity

nonagenarian (,nəʊnədʒɪ'nɛərɪən) *n* **1** a person who is from 90 to 99 years old ▷ *adj* **2** of, relating to, or denoting a nonagenarian [c19: from Latin *nōnāgēnārius*, from *nōnāginta* ninety]

nonaggression (,nɒnə'grɛʃən) *n* **a** restraint of aggression, esp between states **b** (*as modifier*): *a nonaggression pact*

nonagon ('nɒnə,gɒn) *n* a polygon having nine sides. Also called: **enneagon** > **nonagonal** (nɒn'ægənᵊl) *adj*

nonalcoholic (,nɒnælkə'hɒlɪk) *adj* not containing alcohol: *nonalcoholic drinks*

nonaligned (,nɒnə'laɪnd) *adj* (of states) not part of a major alliance or power bloc, esp not allied to the US, China, or formerly the Soviet Union > ,nona'lignment *n*

nonce (nɒns) *n* the present time or occasion (now only in the phrase **for the nonce**) [c12: from the phrase *for the nonce*, a mistaken division of *for then anes*, literally: for the once, from *then* dative singular of *the* + *anes* ONCE]

nonce word *n* a word coined for a single occasion

nonchalant ('nɒnʃələnt) *adj* casually unconcerned or indifferent; uninvolved [c18: from French, from *nonchaloir* to lack warmth, from NON- + *chaloir*, from Latin *calēre* to be warm] > 'nonchalance *n*

non-com ('nɒn,kɒm) *n US* short for **noncommissioned officer**

noncombatant (nɒn'kɒmbətənt) *n* **1** a civilian in time of war **2** a member of the armed forces whose duties do not include fighting, such as a chaplain or surgeon

noncommissioned officer (,nɒnkə'mɪʃənd) *n* (in the armed forces) a person, such as a sergeant or corporal, who is appointed from the ranks as a subordinate officer

noncommittal (,nɒnkə'mɪtᵊl) *adj* not involving or revealing commitment to any particular opinion or course of action

non compos mentis *Latin* ('nɒn 'kɒmpəs 'mɛntɪs) *adj* mentally incapable of managing one's own affairs; of unsound mind [Latin: not in control of one's mind]

nonconformist (,nɒnkən'fɔ:mɪst) *n* **1** a person who does not conform to generally accepted patterns of behaviour or thought ▷ *adj* **2** of or characterized by behaviour that does not conform to generally accepted patterns > ,noncon'formism *n*

Nonconformist (,nɒnkən'fɔ:mɪst) *n* **1** a member of a Protestant denomination that dissents from an Established Church, esp the Church of England ▷ *adj* **2** of, relating to, or denoting Nonconformists > ,Noncon'formity *or* ,Noncon'formism *n*

noncontributory (,nɒnkən'trɪbjʊtərɪ, -trɪ) *adj* **1 a** denoting an insurance or pension scheme for employees, the premiums which are paid entirely by the employer **b** (of a state benefit) not dependent on national insurance contributions **2** not providing contribution; noncontributing

nondenominational (,nɒndɪ,nɒmɪ'neɪʃənᵊl) *adj* not of or related to any religious denomination

nondescript ('nɒndɪ,skrɪpt) *adj* **1** lacking distinct or individual characteristics; having no outstanding features ▷ *n* **2** a nondescript person or thing [c17: from NON- + Latin *dēscriptus*, past participle of *dēscrībere* to copy, DESCRIBE]

non-dom (,nɒn'dɒm) *n infirmal* a nondomiciled person

nondomiciled (nɒn'dɒmɪ,saɪld) *adj* of, relating to, or denoting a person who is not domiciled in his country of origin

none¹ (nʌn) *pron* **1** not any of a particular class: *none of my letters has arrived* **2** no-one; nobody: *there was none to tell the tale* **3** no part (of a whole); not any (of): *none of it looks edible* **4** **none other** no other person: *none other than the Queen herself* **5** **none the** (foll by a comparative adjective) in no degree: *she was none the worse for her ordeal* **6** **none too** not very: *he was none too pleased with his car* [Old English *nān*, literally: not one]

none² (nəʊn) *n* another word for **nones**

nonentity (nɒn'ɛntɪtɪ) *n, pl* **-ties 1** an insignificant person or thing **2** a nonexistent thing **3** the state of not existing; nonexistence

nones (nəʊnz) *n* (*functioning as singular or plural*) **1** (in the Roman calendar) the ninth day before the ides of each month: the seventh day of March, May, July, and October, and the fifth of each other month **2** *chiefly RC Church* the fifth of the seven canonical hours of the divine office, originally fixed at the ninth hour of the day, about 3 p.m. [Old English *nōn*, from Latin *nōna hora* ninth hour, from *nōnus* ninth]

nonesuch *or* **nonsuch** ('nʌn,sʌtʃ) *n archaic* a matchless person or thing; nonpareil

nonet (nɒ'nɛt) *n* **1** a piece of music composed for a group of nine instruments **2** an instrumental group of nine players [c19: from Italian *nonetto*, from *nono* ninth, from Latin *nōnus*]

nonetheless (,nʌnðə'lɛs) *sentence connector* despite that; however; nevertheless

non-Euclidean geometry *n* the branch of modern geometry in which certain axioms of Euclidean geometry are restated. It introduces fundamental changes into the concept of space

nonevent (,nɒnɪ'vɛnt) *n* a disappointing or insignificant occurrence, esp one predicted to be important

nonexecutive director (,nɒnɪg'zɛkjʊtɪv) *n* a director of a commercial company who is not a full-time member of the company but is brought in to advise the other directors

nonexistent (,nɒnɪg'zɪstənt) *adj* **1** not having being or existence **2** not present under specified conditions or in a specified place > ,nonex'istence *n*

nonfeasance (nɒn'fi:zᵊns) *n law* a failure to act when under an obligation to do so. Compare **malfeasance**, **misfeasance** [c16: from NON- + *feasance* (obsolete) performing or doing, from French *faisance*, from *faire* to do, from Latin *facere*]

nonferrous (nɒn'fɛrəs) *adj* **1** denoting any metal other than iron **2** not containing iron

nonflammable (nɒnˈflæməbəl) *adj* incapable of burning or not easily set on fire; not flammable

nong (nɒŋ) *n Austral slang* a stupid or incompetent person [C19: perhaps alteration of obsolete English dialect *nigmenog* silly fellow, of unknown origin]

non-Hodgkin's lymphoma (-ˈhɒdʒkɪnz) *n* any form of lymphoma other than Hodgkin's disease

noni (ˈnəʊnɪ) *n* a tree, *Morinda citrifolia*, native to SE Asia and the Pacific islands, juice from the fruit of which is marketed as a health supplement [Hawaiian]

nonillion (nəʊˈnɪljən) *n* **1** (in Britain, France, and Germany) the number represented as one followed by 54 zeros (10⁵⁴) **2** (in the US and Canada) the number represented as one followed by 30 zeros (10³⁰). Brit word: quintillion[C17: from French, from Latin *nōnus* ninth, on the model of MILLION]

nonintervention (ˌnɒnɪntəˈvɛnʃən) *n* refusal to intervene, esp the abstention by a state from intervening in the affairs of other states or in its own internal disputes

noninvasive (ˌnɒnɪnˈveɪsɪv) *adj* (of medical treatment) not involving the making of a relatively large incision in the body or the insertion of instruments, etc, into the patient

nonjudgmental or **nonjudgemental** (ˌnɒndʒʌdʒˈmɛntəl) *adj* of, relating to, or denoting an attitude, approach, etc, that is open and not incorporating a judgment one way or the other

nonjuror (nɒnˈdʒʊərə) *n* a person who refuses to take an oath, as of allegiance

Nonjuror (nɒnˈdʒʊərə) *n* any of a group of clergy in England and Scotland who declined to take the oath of allegiance to William and Mary in 1689

nonlinear (nɒnˈlɪnɪə) *adj* not of, in, along, or relating to a line

nonmetal (nɒnˈmɛtəl) *n* any of a number of chemical elements that form negative ions, have acidic oxides, and are generally poor conductors of heat and electricity

nonmetallic (ˌnɒnmɪˈtælɪk) *adj* **1** not of metal **2** of, concerned with, or being a nonmetal

nonmoral (nɒnˈmɒrəl) *adj* not involving or related to morality or ethics; neither moral nor immoral

Nono (Italian ˈnɔːnɔ) *n* **Luigi** (luˈiːdʒi). 1924–90, Italian composer of 12-tone music

nonobjective (ˌnɒnəbˈdʒɛktɪv) *adj* of or designating an art movement in which things are depicted in an abstract or purely formalized way, not as they appear in reality

no-nonsense (ˌnəʊˈnɒnsəns) *adj* sensible, practical, straightforward; without nonsense of any kind: *a businesslike no-nonsense approach; a severe no-nonsense look*

nonpareil (ˈnɒnpərəl, ˌnɒnpəˈreɪl) *n* **1** a person or thing that is unsurpassed or unmatched; peerless example **2** (formerly) a size of printers' type equal to 6 point **3** *US* a small bead of coloured sugar used to decorate cakes, biscuits, etc **4** *chiefly US* a flat round piece of chocolate covered with this sugar ▷ *adj* **5** having no match or equal; peerless [C15: from French, from NON- + *pareil* similar]

nonpersistent (ˌnɒnpəˈsɪstənt) *adj* (of pesticides) breaking down rapidly after application; not persisting in the environment

non-person *n* a person regarded as nonexistent or unimportant; a nonentity

nonplus (nɒnˈplʌs) *vb* -plusses, -plussing, -plussed or US -pluses, -plusing, -plused **1** (*tr*) to put at a loss; confound ▷ *n, pl* -pluses **2** a state of utter perplexity prohibiting action or speech [C16: from Latin *nōn plūs* no further (that is, nothing further can be said or done)]

nonprofessional (ˌnɒnprəˈfɛʃənəl) *adj* **1** not of, relating to, suitable for, or engaged in a profession **2** not undertaken or performed for gain or by people who are paid

non-profit-making *adj* not yielding a profit, esp because organized or established for some other reason: *a non-profit-making organization*

nonproliferation (ˌnɒnprəˌlɪfərˈeɪʃən) *n* **a** limitation of the production or spread of something, esp nuclear or chemical weapons **b** (*as modifier*): *a nonproliferation treaty*

non-pros (ˌnɒnˈprɒs) *n* **1** short for **non prosequitur** ▷ *vb* -prosses, -prossing, -prossed **2** (*tr*) to enter a judgment of non prosequitur against (a plaintiff)

non prosequitur (ˈnɒn prəʊˈsɛkwɪtə) *n law* (formerly) a judgment in favour of a defendant when the plaintiff failed to take the necessary steps in an action within the time allowed. See **nolle prosequi** [Latin, literally: he does not prosecute]

nonracial (nɒnˈreɪʃəl) *adj* not related to racial factors or discrimination

nonrepresentational (ˌnɒnrɛprɪzɛnˈteɪʃənəl) *adj art* another word for **abstract** (sense 4)

nonresident (nɒnˈrɛzɪdənt) *n* **1** a person who is not residing in the place implied or specified **2** a British person employed abroad on a contract for a minimum of one year, who is exempt from UK income tax provided that he does not spend more than 90 days in the UK during that tax year ▷ *adj* **3** not residing in the place specified > non'residence or non'residency *n*

nonresistant (ˌnɒnrɪˈzɪstənt) *adj* **1** incapable of resisting something, such as a disease; susceptible **2** *history* (esp in 17th-century England) practising passive obedience to royal authority even when its commands were unjust

nonrestrictive (ˌnɒnrɪˈstrɪktɪv) *adj* **1** not restrictive or limiting **2** *grammar* denoting a relative clause that is not restrictive. Compare **restrictive** (sense 2)

non-secure *adj computing* of or relating to a channel of communication, esp on the internet, that is not restricted to authorized users and is not therefore guaranteed to be private and confidential

nonsense (ˈnɒnsəns) *n* **1** something that has or makes no sense; unintelligible language; drivel **2** conduct or action that is absurd **3** foolish or evasive behaviour or manners: *she'll stand no nonsense* **4** See **no-nonsense** **5** things of little or no value or importance; trash ▷ *interj* **6** an exclamation of disagreement > nonsensical (nɒnˈsɛnsɪkəl) *adj* > non'sensically *adv* > non'sensicalness or non,sensi'cality *n*

nonsense verse *n* verse in which the sense is nonexistent or absurd, such as that of Edward Lear

non sequitur (ˈnɒn ˈsɛkwɪtə) *n* **1** a statement having little or no relevance to what preceded it **2** *logic* a conclusion that does not follow from the premises [Latin, literally: it does not follow]

nonsmoker (nɒnˈsməʊkə) *n* **1** a person who does not smoke **2** a train compartment in which smoking is forbidden > non'smoking *adj*

nonspecific urethritis (nɒnspəˌsɪfɪk) *n* inflammation of the urethra as a result of a venereal infection that cannot be traced to a specific cause. Abbreviation: NSU

nonstandard (nɒnˈstændəd) *adj* **1** denoting or characterized by idiom, vocabulary, etc, that is not regarded as correct and acceptable by educated native speakers of a language; not standard **2** deviating from a given standard

nonstarter (nɒnˈstɑːtə) *n* **1** a horse that fails to run in a race for which it has been entered **2** a person or thing that is useless, has little chance of success, etc

nonstick (ˈnɒnˈstɪk) *adj* (of saucepans, frying pans, etc) coated with a substance such as polytetrafluoroethylene (PTFE) that prevents food sticking to them

nonstop (ˈnɒnˈstɒp) *adj, adv* done without pause or interruption: *a nonstop flight*

nonsuch (ˈnʌnˌsʌtʃ) *n* a variant spelling of **nonesuch**

nonsuit (nɒnˈsuːt, -ˈsjuːt) *law* ▷ *n* **1** an order of a judge dismissing a suit when the plaintiff fails to show he has a good cause of action or fails to produce any evidence ▷ *vb* **2** (*tr*) to order the dismissal of the suit of (a person)

nontechnical (nɒnˈtɛknɪkəl) *adj* not relating to, characteristic of, or skilled in a particular field of activity and its terminology

non troppo (ˈnɒn ˈtrɒpəʊ) *adv music* (preceded by a musical direction, esp a tempo marking) not to be observed too strictly (esp in the phrases **allegro ma non troppo, adagio ma non troppo**)

non-U (nɒnˈjuː) *adj Brit informal* (esp of language) not characteristic of or used by the upper class

nonunion (nɒnˈjuːnjən) *adj* **1** not belonging or related to a trade union: *nonunion workers* **2** not favouring or employing union labour: *a nonunion shop* **3** not produced by union labour

nonvoter (nɒnˈvəʊtə) *n* **1** a person who does not vote **2** a person not eligible to vote

nonvoting (nɒnˈvəʊtɪŋ) *adj* **1** of or relating to a nonvoter **2** *finance* (of shares) not entitling the holder to vote at company meetings

noodle¹ (ˈnuːdᵊl) *n* (*often plural*) a ribbon-like strip of pasta: noodles are often served in soup or with a sauce [c18: from German *Nudel*, origin obscure]

noodle² (ˈnuːdᵊl) *n* **1** *US & Canadian* a slang word for **head** (sense 1) **2** a simpleton [c18: perhaps a blend of NODDLE¹ and NOODLE¹]

noodling (ˈnuːdlɪŋ) *n slang* aimless musical improvisation

nook (nʊk) *n* **1** a corner or narrow recess, as in a room **2** a secluded or sheltered place; retreat [c13: origin obscure; perhaps related to Norwegian dialect *nok* hook]

nooky *or* **nookie** (ˈnʊkɪ) *n slang* sexual intercourse [c20: of uncertain origin; perhaps from NOOK]

noon (nuːn) *n* **1 a** the middle of the day; 12 o'clock in the daytime or the time or point at which the sun crosses the local meridian **b** (*as modifier*): *the noon sun* **2** *poetic* the highest, brightest, or most important part; culmination [Old English *nōn*, from Latin *nōna* (*hōra*) ninth hour (originally 3 p.m., the ninth hour from sunrise)]

noonday (ˈnuːnˌdeɪ) *n* the middle of the day; noon

no-one *or* **no one** *pron* no person; nobody
● USAGE See at **everyone**

noontime (ˈnuːnˌtaɪm) *or* **noontide** *n* the middle of the day; noon

Noordbrabant (noːrdˈbraːbɑnt) *n* the Dutch name for **North Brabant**

Noordholland (noːrtˈhɔlɑnt) *n* the Dutch name for **North Holland**

noose (nuːs) *n* **1** a loop in the end of a rope or cord, such as a lasso, snare, or hangman's halter, usually tied with a slipknot **2** something that restrains, binds, or traps **3** put one's head in a noose to bring about one's own downfall ▷ *vb* (*tr*) **4** to secure or catch in or as if in a noose **5** to make a noose of or in [c15: perhaps from Provençal *nous*, from Latin *nōdus* NODE]

no-par *adj* (of securities) without a par value

nor (nɔː; *unstressed* nə) *conj* (*coordinating*), *prep* **1** (used to join alternatives the first of which is preceded by *neither*) and not: *neither measles nor mumps* **2** (foll by an auxiliary verb or *have*, *do*, or *be* used as main verbs) (and) not...either: *they weren't talented — nor were they particularly funny* **3** *dialect* than: *better nor me* **4** *poetic* neither: *nor wind nor rain* [c13: contraction of Old English *nōther*, from *nāhwæther* NEITHER]

noradrenaline (ˌnɒrəˈdrɛnəlɪn, -liːn) *or* **noradrenalin** *n* a hormone secreted by the adrenal medulla, increasing blood pressure and heart rate, and by the endings of sympathetic nerves, when it acts as a neurotransmitter both centrally and peripherally. Formula: $C_8H_{11}NO_3$. US name: norepinephrine

NOR circuit *or* **NOR gate** (nɔː) *n computing* a logic circuit having two or more input wires and one output wire that has a high-voltage output signal only if all input signals are at a low voltage. Compare **AND circuit** [c20: from NOR, so named because the action performed is similar to the operation of the conjunction *nor* in logic]

Nord (*French* nɔr) *n* a department of N France, in Nord-Pas-de-Calais region. Capital: Lille. Pop: 2 561 800 (2003 est). Area: 5774 sq km (2252 sq miles)

Nordau (*German* ˈnɔrdau) *n* **Max Simon** (maks ˈziːmɔn), original name *Max Simon Südfeld*. 1849–1923, German author, born in Hungary; a leader of the Zionist movement

Nordenskjöld (*Swedish* ˈnuːrdənʃœld) *n* Baron **Nils Adolf Erik** (nils ˈɑːdɔlf ˈeːrik). 1832–1901, Swedish Arctic explorer and geologist, born in Finland. He was the first to navigate the Northeast Passage (1878–79)

Nordenskjöld Sea (*Swedish* ˈnuːrdənʃœld) *n* the former name of the **Laptev Sea** [named after N.A.E. NORDENSKJÖRD]

nordic (ˈnɔːdɪk) *adj skiing* of or relating to competitions in cross-country racing and ski-jumping. Compare **alpine** (sense 4)

Nordic (ˈnɔːdɪk) *adj* of, relating to, or belonging to a subdivision of the Caucasoid race typified by the tall blond blue-eyed long-headed inhabitants of N Britain, Scandinavia, N Germany, and the Netherlands **2** (of recreational walking) incorporating the use of poles that resemble ski poles to aid movement [c19: from French *nordique*, from *nord* NORTH]

Nordkyn Cape (*Norwegian* ˈnuːrçyːn) *n* a cape in N Norway: the northernmost point of the European mainland

Nord-Pas-de-Calais (*French* nɔrpadəkalɛ) *n* a region of N France, on the Straits of Dover (the **Pas de Calais**): coal-mining, textile, and metallurgical industries

Nordrhein-Westfalen (ˈnɔrtrainvɛstˈfaːlən) *n* the German name for **North Rhine-Westphalia**

norepinephrine (ˌnɔːrɛpɪˈnɛfrɪn, -riːn) *n* the US name for **noradrenaline**

Norfolk (ˈnɔːfək) *n* **1** a county of E England, on the North Sea and the Wash: low-lying, with large areas of fens in the west and the Broads in the east; rich agriculturally. Administrative centre: Norwich. Pop: 810 700 (2003 est). Area: 5368 sq km (2072 sq miles) **2** a port in SE Virginia, on the Elizabeth River and Hampton Roads: headquarters of the US Atlantic fleet; shipbuilding. Pop: 241 727 (2003 est)

Norfolk Island *n* an island in the S Pacific, between New Caledonia and N New Zealand: an Australian external territory; discovered by Captain Cook in 1774; a penal settlement in early years. Capital: Kingston. Pop: 2114 (2007). Area: 36 sq km (14 sq miles)

Norfolk jacket *n* a man's single-breasted belted jacket with one or two chest pockets and a box pleat down the back [c19: worn in NORFOLK for duck shooting]

Norge (ˈnɔrɡə) *n* the Norwegian name for **Norway**

noria (ˈnɔːrɪə) *n* a water wheel with buckets attached to its rim for raising water from a stream into irrigation canals: common in Spain and the Orient [c18: via Spanish from Arabic *nā'ūra*, from *na'ara* to creak]

Noricum (ˈnɒrɪkəm) *n* an Alpine kingdom of the Celts, south of the Danube: comprises present-day central Austria and parts of Bavaria; a Roman province from about 16 BC

nork (nɔːk) *n* (*usually plural*) *Austral slang* a female breast [c20: of unknown origin]

norm (nɔːm) *n* **1** an average level of achievement or performance, as of a group or person **2** a standard of achievement or behaviour that is required, desired, or designated as normal [c19: from Latin *norma* carpenter's rule, square]

normal (ˈnɔːmᵊl) *adj* **1** usual; regular; common; typical: *the normal way of doing it; the normal level* **2** constituting a standard: *if we take this as normal* **3** *psychol* **a** being within certain limits of intelligence, educational success or ability, etc **b** conforming to the conventions of one's group **4** *biology, med* (of laboratory animals) maintained in a natural state for purposes of comparison with animals treated with drugs, etc **5** *chem* (of a solution) containing a number of grams equal to the equivalent weight of the solute in each litre of solvent. Symbol: *N* **6** *chem* denoting a straight-chain hydrocarbon: *a normal alkane*. Prefix: **n-**, e.g. *n*-octane **7** *geometry* another word for **perpendicular** (sense 1) ▷ *n* **8** the usual, average, or typical state, degree, form, etc **9** anything that is normal **10** *geometry* a line or plane perpendicular to another line or plane or to the tangent of a curved line or plane at the point of contact [c16: from Latin *normālis* conforming to the carpenter's square, from *norma* NORM] ▷ **normality** (nɔːˈmælɪtɪ) *or esp US* **normalcy** *n*

normal curve *n statistics* a symmetrical bell-shaped curve representing the probability density function of a normal distribution. The area of a vertical section of the curve represents the probability that the random variable lies between the values which delimit the section

normal distribution *n statistics* a continuous distribution of a random variable with its mean, median, and mode equal, the probability density function of which is given by $(exp-[(x-\mu)^2/2\sigma^2]/\sigma\sqrt(2\pi))$ where μ is the mean and σ² the variance. Also called: **Gaussian distribution**

normalize or **normalise** ('nɔːməˌlaɪz) vb (tr) **1** to bring or make into the normal state **2** to bring into conformity with a standard **3** to heat (steel) above a critical temperature and allow it to cool in air to relieve internal stresses; anneal ▷ ˌnormaliˈzation or ˌnormaliˈsation n

normally ('nɔːməlɪ) adv **1** as a rule; usually; ordinarily **2** in a normal manner

normal time n sport the standard length of time allowed for a match before any extra time, such as injury time, is added

Norman[1] ('nɔːmən) n **1** (in the Middle Ages) a member of the people of Normandy descended from the 10th-century Scandinavian conquerors of the country and the native French **2** a native or inhabitant of Normandy **3** another name for **Norman French** ▷ adj **4** of, relating to, or characteristic of the Normans, esp the Norman kings of England, the Norman people living in England, or their dialect of French **5** of, relating to, or characteristic of Normandy or its inhabitants **6** denoting, relating to, or having the style of Romanesque architecture used in Britain from the Norman Conquest until the 12th century. It is characterized by the rounded arch, the groin vault, massive masonry walls, etc

Norman[2] ('nɔːmən) n **1 Greg.** born 1955, Australian golfer **2 Jessye** ('dʒɛsɪ). born 1945, US Black soprano

Norman Conquest n the invasion and settlement of England by the Normans, following the Battle of Hastings (1066)

Normandy ('nɔːməndɪ) n a former province of N France, on the English Channel: settled by Vikings under Rollo in the 10th century; scene of the Allied landings in 1944. Chief town: Rouen

Norman French n the medieval Norman and English dialect of Old French

normative ('nɔːmətɪv) adj **1** implying, creating, or prescribing a norm or standard, as in language: *normative grammar* **2** expressing value judgments or prescriptions as contrasted with stating facts

Norn[1] (nɔːn) n Norse myth any of the three virgin goddesses of fate, who predestine the lives of the gods and men [c18: Old Norse]

Norn[2] (nɔːn) n the medieval Norse language of the Orkneys, Shetlands, and parts of N Scotland. It was extinct by 1750 [c17: from Old Norse norréna Norwegian, from northr north]

Norodom Sihanouk (ˌnɒrəˈdɒm ˈsiːəˌnʊk) n See Sihanouk

norovirus ('nɔːrəʊˌvaɪrəs) n a virus which is a common cause of gastroenteritis [c20: from *Norwalk*, Ohio, site of an outbreak in 1968]

Norrington ('nɒrɪŋtən) n Sir **Roger** (**Arthur Carver**). born 1934, British conductor; noted for period performances of early music

Norrköping (Swedish 'nɔrtçøˌpiŋ) n a port in SE Sweden, near the Baltic. Pop: 124 378 (2004 est)

Norse (nɔːs) adj **1** of, relating to, or characteristic of ancient and medieval Scandinavia or its inhabitants **2** of, relating to, or characteristic of Norway ▷ n **3** the N group of Germanic languages, spoken in Scandinavia; Scandinavian **b** any one of these languages, esp in their ancient or medieval forms **4 the Norse** (*functioning as plural*) **a** the Norwegians **b** the Vikings

Norseman ('nɔːsmən) n, pl -men another name for a **Viking**

north (nɔːθ) n **1** one of the four cardinal points of the compass, at 0° or 360°, that is 90° from east and west and 180° from south **2** the direction along a meridian towards the North Pole **3** the direction in which a compass needle points; magnetic north **4 the North** (*often capital*) any area lying in or towards the north **5** cards (*usually capital*) the player or position at the table corresponding to north on the compass ▷ adj **6** situated in, moving towards, or facing the north **7** (esp of the wind) from the north ▷ adv **8** in, to, or towards the

north [Old English; related to Old Norse *northr*, Dutch *noord*, Old High German *nord*]

North[1] (nɔːθ) **the North** n **1** the northern area of England, generally regarded as reaching approximately the southern boundaries of Yorkshire and Lancashire **2** (in the US) the area approximately north of Maryland and the Ohio River, esp those states north of the Mason-Dixon Line that were known as the Free States during the Civil War **3** the northern part of North America, esp the area consisting of Alaska, the Yukon, the Northwest Territories, and Nunavut; the North Country **4** the countries of the world that are economically and technically advanced ▷ adj **5** of or denoting the northern part of a specified country, area, etc

North[2] (nɔːθ) n **1 Frederick**, 2nd Earl of Guildford, called **Lord North**. 1732– 92, British statesman; prime minister (1770–82), dominated by George III. He was held responsible for the loss of the American colonies **2 Sir Thomas**. ?1535–?1601, English translator of Plutarch's *Lives* (1579), which was the chief source of Shakespeare's Roman plays

North Africa n the part of Africa between the Mediterranean and the Sahara: consists chiefly of Morocco, Algeria, Tunisia, Libya, and N Egypt ▷ **North African** adj, n

Northallerton (nɔːˈθælətᵊn) n a market town in N England, administrative centre of North Yorkshire. Pop: 15 517 (2001)

North America n the third largest continent, linked with South America by the Isthmus of Panama and bordering on the Arctic Ocean, the N Pacific, the N Atlantic, the Gulf of Mexico, and the Caribbean. It consists generally of a great mountain system (the Western Cordillera) extending along the entire W coast, actively volcanic in the extreme north and south, with the Great Plains to the east and the Appalachians still further east, separated from the Canadian Shield by an arc of large lakes (Great Bear, Great Slave, Winnipeg, Superior, Michigan, Huron, Erie, Ontario); reaches its greatest height of 6194 m (20 320 ft) in Mount McKinley, Alaska, and its lowest point of 85 m (280 ft) below sea level in Death Valley, California, and ranges from snowfields, tundra, and taiga in the north to deserts in the southwest and tropical forests in the extreme south. Pop: 332 156 000 (2005 est). Area: over 24 000 000 sq km (9 500 000 sq miles) ▷ **North American** adj, n

North American Free Trade Agreement n an international trade agreement between the United States, Canada, and Mexico. Abbreviation: **NAFTA**

Northampton (nɔːˈθæmptən, nɔːˈθhæmp-) n **1** a town in central England, administrative centre of Northamptonshire, on the River Nene: footwear and engineering industries. Pop: 189 474 (2001) **2** short for **Northamptonshire**

Northamptonshire (nɔːˈθæmptənˌʃɪə, -ʃə, nɔːˈθhæmp-) n a county of central England: agriculture, food processing, engineering, and footwear industries. Administrative centre: Northampton. Pop: 642 700 (2003 est). Area: 2367 sq km (914 sq miles). Abbreviation: **Northants**

Northants (nɔːˈθænts) abbreviation Northamptonshire

North Atlantic Drift or **North Atlantic Current** n the warm ocean current flowing northeast, under the influence of prevailing winds, from the Gulf of Mexico towards NW Europe and warming its climate. Also called: **Gulf Stream**

North Atlantic Treaty Organization n the full name of **NATO**

North Ayrshire ('ɛəʃɪə, -ʃə) n a council area of W central Scotland, on the Firth of Clyde: comprises the N part of the historical county of Ayrshire, including the Isle of Arran; formerly part of Strathclyde Region (1975–96): chiefly agricultural, with fishing and tourism. Administrative centre: Irvine. Pop: 136 030 (2003 est). Area: 884 sq km (341 sq miles)

North Borneo n the former name (until 1963) of **Sabah**

northbound ('nɔːθˌbaʊnd) adj going or leading towards the north

North Brabant n a province of the S Netherlands:

n

formed part of the medieval duchy of Brabant. Capital: 's Hertogenbosch. Pop: 2 400 000 (2003 est). Area: 4965 sq km (1917 sq miles). Dutch name: Noordbrabant

north by east n one point on the compass east of north, 11° 15′ clockwise from north

north by west n one point on the compass west of north, 348° 45′ clockwise from north

North Cape n 1 a cape on N Magerøy Island, in the Arctic Ocean off the N coast of Norway 2 a cape on N North Island, New Zealand

North Carolina n a state of the southeastern US, on the Atlantic: consists of a coastal plain rising to the Piedmont Plateau and the Appalachian Mountains in the west Capital: Raleigh. Pop: 8 407 248 (2003 est). Area: 126 387 sq km (48 798 sq miles). Abbreviation: NC> **North Carolinian** (ˌkærəˈlɪnɪən) adj, n

North Channel n a strait between NE Ireland and SW Scotland, linking the North Atlantic with the Irish Sea

Northcliffe (ˈnɔːθklɪf) n **Viscount.** title of *Alfred Charles William Harmsworth.* 1865- -1922, British newspaper proprietor. With his brother, 1st Viscount Rothermere, he built up a vast chain of newspapers. He founded the *Daily Mail* (1896), the *Daily Mirror* (1903), and acquired *The Times* (1908)

North Country n the North Country another name for: **North¹** (sense 1)

Northd abbreviation Northumberland

North Dakota n a state of the western US: mostly undulating prairies and plains, rising from the Red River valley in the east to the Missouri plateau in the west, with the infertile Bad Lands in the extreme west Capital: Bismarck. Pop: 633 837 (2003 est). Area: 183 019 sq km (70 664 sq miles). Abbreviation: ND> **North Dakotan**adj, n

North Down n a district of E Northern Ireland, in Co Down. Pop: 77 110 (2003 est). Area: 82 sq km (32 sq miles)

northeast (ˌnɔːθˈiːst; Nautical ˌnɔːrˈiːst) n 1 the point of the compass or direction midway between north and east, 45° clockwise from north 2 the northeast (often capital) any area lying in or towards this direction ▷ adj also **northeastern** 3 (sometimes capital) of or denoting the northeastern part of a specified country, area, etc: northeast Lincolnshire 4 situated in, proceeding towards, or facing the northeast 5 (esp of the wind) from the northeast ▷ adv 6 in, to, towards, or (esp of the wind) from the northeast > ˌnorthˈeasternmostadj

Northeast (ˌnɔːθˈiːst) n the Northeast the northeastern part of England, esp Northumberland, Durham, and the Tyneside area

northeast by east n one point on the compass east of northeast, 56° 15′ clockwise from north

northeast by north n one point on the compass north of northeast, 33° 45′ clockwise from north

northeaster (ˌnɔːθˈiːstə; Nautical ˌnɔːrˈiːstə) n a strong wind or storm from the northeast

northeasterly (ˌnɔːθˈiːstəlɪ; Nautical ˌnɔːrˈiːstəlɪ) adj, adv 1 in, towards, or (esp of a wind) from the northeast ▷ n, pl -lies 2 a wind or storm from the northeast

North East Frontier Agency n the former name (until 1972) of **Arunachal Pradesh**

North East Lincolnshire (ˈlɪŋkənˌʃɪə, -ʃə) n a unitary authority in E England, in Lincolnshire: formerly (1974-96) part of the county of Humberside. Pop: 157 400 (2003 est). Area: 192 sq km (74 sq miles)

Northeast Passage n a shipping route along the Arctic coasts of Europe and Asia, between the Atlantic and Pacific: first navigated by Nordenskjöld (1878-79)

northeastward (ˌnɔːθˈiːstwəd; Nautical ˌnɔːrˈiːstwəd) adj 1 towards or (esp of a wind) from the northeast ▷ n 2 a direction towards or area in the northeast > ˌnorthˈeastwardlyadj, adv

norther (ˈnɔːðə) n chiefly Southern US a wind or storm from the north

northerly (ˈnɔːðəlɪ) adj 1 of, relating to, or situated in the north ▷ adv, adj 2 towards or in the direction of the north 3 from the north: a northerly wind ▷ n, pl -lies 4 a wind from the north > ˈnortherlinessn

northern (ˈnɔːðən) adj 1 situated in or towards the north 2 directed or proceeding towards the north 3 (esp of

winds) proceeding from the north 4 (sometimes capital) of, relating to, or characteristic of the north or North

Northern Cape n the largest but least populated province in South Africa, in the NW part of the country; created in 1994 from part of Cape Province: agriculture, mining (esp diamonds). Capital: Kimberley. Pop: 899 349 (2004 est). Area: 139 703 sq km (361 830 sq miles)

Northern Dvina n See **Dvina** (sense 1)

Northerner (ˈnɔːðənə) n (sometimes not capital) a native or inhabitant of the north of any specified region, esp England or the US

northern hemisphere n (often capitals) that half of the globe lying north of the equator

Northern Ireland n that part of the United Kingdom occupying the NE part of Ireland: separated from the rest of Ireland, which became independent in law in 1920; it remained part of the United Kingdom, with a separate Parliament (Stormont), inaugurated in 1921, and limited self-government: scene of severe conflict between Catholics and Protestants, including terrorist bombing from 1969: direct administration from Westminster from 1972: assembly and powersharing executive established in 1998-99 following the Good Friday Agreement of 1998, suspended in 2002, and reinstated 2007. Capital: Belfast. Pop: 1 702 628 (2003 est). Area: 14 121 sq km (5452 sq miles)

Northern Isles pl n Orkney and Shetland

northern lights pl n another name for **aurora borealis**

Northern Mariana Islands (ˌmærɪˈɑːnə) n a US commonwealth territory in the N Pacific, formerly part of the Trust Territory of the Pacific Islands (1947-87). Capital: Saipan island (Capitol Hill). Pop: 84 000 (2007 est). Area: 477 sq km (184 sq miles)

northernmost (ˈnɔːðənˌməʊst) adj situated or occurring farthest north

Northern Province n the former name for **Limpopo** (sense 1)

Northern Rhodesia n the former name (until 1964) of **Zambia**

Northern Territories pl n a former British protectorate in W Africa, established in 1897; attached to the Gold Coast in 1901; now constitutes the Northern Region of Ghana (since 1957)

Northern Territory n an administrative division of N central Australia, on the Timor and Arafura Seas: the Arunta Desert lies in the east, the Macdonnell Ranges in the south, and Arnhem Land in the north (containing Australia's largest Aboriginal reservation)); the Ashmore and Cartier Islands constitute a separate Australian External Territory. Capital: Darwin. Pop: 198 700 (2003 est). Area: 1 347 525 sq km (520 280 sq miles)

North Holland n a province of the NW Netherlands, on the peninsula between the North Sea and IJsselmeer: includes the West Frisian Island of Texel. Capital: Haarlem. Pop: 2 573 000 (2003 est). Area: 2663 sq km (1029 sq miles). Dutch name: Noordholland

northing (ˈnɔːθɪŋ, -ðɪŋ) n 1 navigation movement or distance covered in a northerly direction, esp as expressed in the resulting difference in latitude 2 astronomy a north or positive declination

North Island n the northernmost of the two main islands of New Zealand. Pop: 3 087 200 (2004 est). Area: 114 729 sq km (44 297 sq miles)

North Korea n a republic in NE Asia, on the Sea of Japan (East Sea) and the Yellow Sea: established in 1948 as a people's republic; mostly rugged and mountainous, with fertile lowlands in the west Language: Korean. Currency: won. Capital: Pyongyang. Pop: 22 776 000 (2004 est). Area: 122 313 sq km (47 225 sq miles). Official name: Democratic People's Republic of KoreaKorean name: Chosŏn

North Korean adj 1 of or relating to North Korea or its inhabitants ▷ n 2 a native or inhabitant of North Korea

North Lanarkshire (ˈlænəkˌʃɪə, -ʃə) n a council area of central Scotland: consists mainly of the NE part of the historical county of Lanarkshire; formerly (1974-96) part of Strathclyde Region: engineering and metalworking industries. Administrative centre: Motherwell. Pop: 321 820 (2003 est). Area: 1771 sq km (684 sq miles)

Northland ('nɔːθlənd) *n* **1** the peninsula containing Norway and Sweden **2** (in Canada) the far north
> 'Northlander *n*

North Lincolnshire ('lɪŋkənʃɪə, -ʃə) *n* a unitary authority of NE England, in Lincolnshire: formerly (1975–96) part of the county of Humberside. Pop: 155 000 (2003 est). Area: 1497 sq km (578 sq miles)

Northman ('nɔːθmən) *n, pl* -men another name for a **Viking**

north-northeast *n* **1** the point on the compass or the direction midway between north and northeast, 22° 30′ clockwise from north ▷ *adj, adv* **2** in, from, or towards this direction

north-northwest *n* the point on the compass or the direction midway between northwest and north, 337° 30′ clockwise from north

north of 60 *n Canadian* the area of Canada lying north of 60 degrees N

North Ossetian Republic (ə'siːʃən) *n* a constituent republic of S Russia, on the N slopes of the central Caucasus Mountains. Capital: Vladikavkaz. Pop: 709 900 (2002). Area: about 8000 sq km (3088 sq miles). Also called: **North Ossetia, Alania**

North Pole *n* **1** the northernmost point on the earth's axis, at a latitude of 90°N **2** Also called: **north celestial pole** *astronomy* the point of intersection of the earth's extended axis and the northern half of the celestial sphere, lying about 1° from Polaris **3** (*usually not capitals*) the pole of a freely suspended magnet, which is attracted to the earth's magnetic North Pole

North Rhine-Westphalia *n* a state of W Germany: formed in 1946 by the amalgamation of the Prussian province of Westphalia with the N part of the Prussian Rhine province and later with the state of Lippe; part of West Germany until 1990: highly industrialized. Capital: Düsseldorf. Pop: 18 080 000 (2003 est). Area: 34 039 sq km (13 142 sq miles). German name: **Nordrhein-Westfalen**

North Riding *n* (until 1974) an administrative division of Yorkshire, now constituting most of North Yorkshire

North Saskatchewan *n* a river in W Canada, rising in W Alberta and flowing northeast, east, and southeast to join the South Saskatchewan River and form the Saskatchewan River. Length: 1223 km (760 miles)

North Sea *n* an arm of the Atlantic between Great Britain and the N European mainland. Area: about 569 800 sq km (220 000 sq miles). Former name: **German Ocean**

North-Sea gas *n* (in Britain) natural gas obtained from deposits below the North Sea

North Somerset ('sʌmə,set) *n* a unitary authority of SW England, in Somerset: formerly (1974–96) part of the county of Avon. Pop: 191 400 (2003 est). Area: 375 sq km (145 sq miles)

North Star *n* the North Star another name for **Polaris** (sense 1)

North Tyneside ('taɪnsaɪd) *n* a unitary authority of NE England, in Tyne and Wear. Pop: 190 800 (2003 est). Area: 84 sq km (32 sq miles)

Northumberland[1] (nɔː'θʌmbələnd) *n* the northernmost county of England, on the North Sea: hilly in the north (the Cheviots) and west (the Pennines), with many Roman remains, notably Hadrian's Wall; shipbuilding, coal mining. Administrative centre: Morpeth. Pop: 309 200 (2003 est). Area: 5032 sq km (1943 sq miles). Abbreviation: **Northd**

Northumberland[2] (nɔː'θʌmbələnd) *n* **1st Duke of,** title of *John Dudley.* 1502–53, English statesman and soldier, who governed England (1549–53) during the minority of Edward VI. His attempt (1553) to gain the throne for his daughter-in-law, Lady Jane Grey, led to his execution

Northumbria (nɔː'θʌmbrɪə) *n* **1** (in Anglo-Saxon Britain) a region that stretched from the Humber to the Firth of Forth: formed in the 7th century AD, it became an important intellectual centre; a separate kingdom until 876 AD **2** an area of NE England roughly corresponding to the Anglo-Saxon region of Northumbria
> North'umbrian *adj, n*

North Vietnam *n* a region of N Vietnam, on the Gulf of Tonkin: an independent Communist state from 1954 until 1976. Area: 164 061 sq km (63 344 sq miles)

northward ('nɔːθwəd; *Nautical* 'nɔːðəd) *adj* **1** moving, facing, or situated towards the north ▷ *n* **2** the northward part, direction, etc; the north ▷ *adv* **3** a variant of **northwards**

northwards ('nɔːθwədz) *or* **northward** *adv* towards the north

northwest (,nɔːθ'west; *Nautical* ,nɔː'west) *n* **1** the point of the compass or direction midway between north and west, clockwise 315° from north **2** the northwest (*often capital*) any area lying in or towards this direction ▷ *adj* also **northwestern 3** (*sometimes capital*) of or denoting the northwestern part of a specified country, area, etc: *northwest Greenland* ▷ *adj, adv* **4** in, to, towards, or (esp of the wind) from the northwest
> ,north'westernmost *adj*

Northwest (,nɔːθ'west) *n* the Northwest the northwestern part of England, esp Lancashire and the Lake District

North West *n* a province in N South Africa, created in 1994 from the NE part of Cape Province and part of Transvaal: agriculture and service industries. Capital: Mafikeng. Pop: 3 807 469 (2004 est). Area: 116 320 sq km (44 911 sq miles)

northwest by north *n* one point on the compass north of northwest, 326° 15′ clockwise from north

northwest by west *n* one point on the compass south of northwest, 303° 45′ clockwise from north

northwester (,nɔːθ'westə; *Nautical* ,nɔː'westə) *n* a strong wind or storm from the northwest

northwesterly (,nɔːθ'westəlɪ; *Nautical* ,nɔː'westəlɪ) *adj, adv* **1** in, towards, or (esp of a wind) from the northwest ▷ *n, pl* -lies **2** a wind or storm from the northwest

North-West Frontier Province *n* a province in N Pakistan between Afghanistan and Jammu and Kashmir: part of British India from 1901 until 1947; of strategic importance, esp for the Khyber Pass. Capital: Peshawar. Pop: 20 170 000 (2003 est). Area: 74 522 sq km (28 773 sq miles)

Northwest Passage *n* the passage by sea from the Atlantic to the Pacific along the N coast of America: attempted for over 300 years by Europeans seeking a short route to the Far East, before being successfully navigated by Amundsen (1903–06)

Northwest Territories *pl n* a territory of NW Canada including part of Victoria Island and several other islands of the Arctic; comprised over a third of Canada's total area until Nunavut became a separate territory in 1999: rich mineral resources. Pop: 42 810 (2004 est). Area: 2 082 910 sq km (804 003 sq miles). Abbreviation: **NWT**

Northwest Territory *n* See **Old Northwest**

northwestward (,nɔːθ'westwəd; *Nautical* ,nɔː'westwəd) *adj* **1** towards or (esp of a wind) from the northwest ▷ *n* **2** a direction towards or area in the northwest
> ,north'westwardly *adj, adv*

Northwich ('nɔːθwɪtʃ) *n* a town in NW England, in Cheshire: salt and chemical industries. Pop: 39 568 (2001)

North Yemen *n* a former republic in SW Arabia, on the Red Sea; now part of Yemen: declared a republic in 1962: united with South Yemen in 1990. See also **Yemen, South Yemen**

North Yorkshire *n* a county in N England, formed in 1974 from most of the North Riding of Yorkshire and parts of the East and West Ridings: the geographical and ceremonial county includes the unitary authorities of Middlesbrough, Redcar and Cleveland, and part of Stockton on Tees (all within Cleveland until 1996), and York (created in 1997). Administrative centre: Northallerton. Pop (excluding unitary authorities): 576 100 (2003 est). Area (excluding unitary authorities): 8037 sq km (3102 sq miles)

Norton ('nɔːtn) *n* **Graham,** real name *Graham Walker.* born 1963, Irish comedian noted for his camp humour

Norw. *abbreviation* **1** Norway **2** Norwegian

Norway ('nɔː,weɪ) *n* a kingdom in NW Europe, occupying the W part of the Scandinavian peninsula: first united in the Viking age (800–1050); under the rule of Denmark (1523–1814) and Sweden (1814–1905); became an independent monarchy in 1905. Its coastline is deeply indented by fjords and fringed with islands, rising inland to plateaus and mountains. Norway has a large fishing fleet and its merchant navy is among the world's largest Official language: Norwegian. Official religion: Evangelical Lutheran. Currency: krone. Capital: Oslo. Pop: 4 552 000 (2004 est). Area: 323 878 sq km (125 050 sq miles). Norwegian name: **Norge**

Norway lobster *n* a European lobster, *Nephrops norvegicus*, fished for food

Norway maple *n* a large Eurasian maple tree, *Acer platanoides*, with broad five-lobed pale green leaves

Norway spruce *n* a European spruce tree, *Picea abies*, planted for timber and ornament, having drooping branches and dark green needle-like leaves

Norwegian (nɔː'wiːdʒən) *adj* 1 of, relating to, or characteristic of Norway, its language, or its people ▷ *n* 2 any of the various North Germanic languages of Norway 3 a native, citizen, or inhabitant of Norway

Norwegian Sea *n* part of the Arctic Ocean between Greenland and Norway

Norwich ('nɒrɪdʒ) *n* a city in E England, administrative centre of Norfolk: cathedral (founded 1096); University of East Anglia (1963): traditionally a centre of the footwear industry, now has engineering, financial services. Pop: 174 047 (2001)

Nos.or **nos.** *abbreviation* numbers

nose (nəʊz) *n* 1 the organ of smell and entrance to the respiratory tract, consisting of a prominent structure divided into two hair-lined air passages by a median septum. Related adj: **nasal** 2 the sense of smell itself: in hounds and other animals, the ability to follow trails by scent (esp in the phrases **a good nose, a bad nose**) 3 another word for **bouquet** (sense 2) 4 instinctive skill or facility, esp in discovering things (sometimes in the phrase **follow one's nose**): *he had a nose for good news stories* 5 any part regarded as resembling a nose in form or function, such as a nozzle or spout 6 the forward part of a vehicle, aircraft, etc, esp the front end of an aircraft 7 narrow margin of victory (in the phrase **(win) by a nose**) 8 **cut off one's nose to spite one's face** to carry out a vengeful action that hurts oneself more than another 9 **get up someone's nose** *informal* to annoy or irritate someone 10 **keep one's nose clean** to stay out of trouble; behave properly 11 **lead someone by the nose** to make someone do unquestioningly all one wishes; dominate someone 12 **look down one's nose at** *informal* to be contemptuous or disdainful of 13 **nose to tail** (of vehicles) moving or standing very close behind one another 14 **on the nose** *slang* **a** (in horse-race betting) to win only: *I bet twenty pounds on the nose on that horse* **b** *chiefly US & Canadian* precisely; exactly **c** *Austral* bad or bad-smelling 15 **pay through the nose** *informal* to pay an exorbitant price 16 **put someone's nose out of joint** *informal* to thwart or offend someone, esp by supplanting him or gaining something he regards as his 17 **rub someone's nose in it** *informal* to remind someone unkindly of his failing or error 18 **turn up one's nose (at)** *informal* to behave disdainfully towards 19 **with one's nose in the air** haughtily ▷ *vb* 20 (tr) (esp of horses, dogs, etc) to rub, touch, or sniff with the nose; nuzzle 21 to smell or sniff (wine, etc) 22 (intr; usually foll by *after* or *for*) to search (for) by or as if by scent 23 to move or cause to move forwards slowly and carefully: *the car nosed along the cliff top; we nosed the car into the garage* 24 (intr; foll by *into, around, about*, etc) to pry or snoop (into) or meddle (in) [Old English *nosu*; related to Old Frisian *nose*, Norwegian *nosa* to smell and *nus* smell] ▷ **'noseless** *adj* ▷ **'nose,like** *adj*

nosebag ('nəʊz,bæg) *n* a bag, fastened around the head of a horse and covering the nose, in which feed is placed

noseband ('nəʊz,bænd) *n* the detachable part of a horse's bridle that goes around the nose

nosebleed ('nəʊz,bliːd) *n* bleeding from the nose, as the result of injury, etc

nose cone *n* the conical forward section of a missile, spacecraft, etc, designed to withstand high temperatures, esp during re-entry into the earth's atmosphere

nose dive *n* 1 a sudden plunge with the nose or front pointing downwards, esp of an aircraft 2 *informal* a sudden drop or sharp decline: *prices took a nose dive* ▷ *vb* **nose-dive** 3 to perform or cause to perform a nose dive

nose flute *n* (esp in the South Sea Islands) a type of flute blown through the nose

nosegay ('nəʊz,geɪ) *n* a small bunch of flowers; posy [C15: from NOSE + archaic *gay* a toy]

nose job *n slang* a surgical remodelling of the nose for cosmetic reasons

nosepiece ('nəʊz,piːs) *n* 1 Also called: **nasal** a piece of armour, esp part of a helmet, that serves to protect the nose 2 the connecting part of a pair of spectacles that rests on the nose; bridge 3 the part of a microscope to which one or more objective lenses are attached 4 a less common word for **noseband**

nose rag *n slang* a handkerchief

nose ring *n* a ring fixed through the nose, as for leading a bull

nose wheel *n* a wheel fitted to the forward end of a vehicle, esp the landing wheel under the nose of an aircraft

nosey ('nəʊzɪ) *adj* a variant spelling of **nosy**

nosh (nɒʃ) *slang* ▷ *n* 1 food or a meal ▷ *vb* 2 to eat [C20: from Yiddish; compare German *naschen* to nibble]

no-show *n* a person who fails to take up a reserved seat, place, etc, without having cancelled it

nosh-up *n Brit slang* a large and satisfying meal

no-side *n rugby* the end of a match, signalled by the referee's whistle

noso-or before a vowel **nos-** *combining form* disease: *nosology* [from Greek *nosos*]

nosocomial (,nɒsə'kəʊmɪəl) *adj med* originating in hospital [C19: New Latin *nosocomialis*, via Late Latin from Greek, from *nosokomos* one that tends the sick, from *nosos* (see NOSO-) + *komein* to tend]

nosology (nɒ'sɒlədʒɪ) *n* the branch of medicine concerned with the classification of diseases > **nosological** (,nɒsə'lɒdʒɪkᵊl) *adj*

nostalgia (nɒ'stældʒə, -dʒɪə) *n* 1 a yearning for the return of past circumstances, events, etc 2 the evocation of this emotion, as in a book, film, etc 3 longing for home or family; homesickness [C18: New Latin (translation of German *Heimweh* homesickness), from Greek *nostos* a return home + -ALGIA] > **nos'talgic** *adj, n*

nostoc ('nɒstɒk) *n* any cyanobacterium of the genus *Nostoc*, occurring in moist places as rounded colonies consisting of coiled filaments in a gelatinous substance [C17: New Latin, coined by Paracelsus]

Nostradamus (,nɒstrə'dɑːməs) *n* Latinized name of *Michel de Notredame*. 1503–66, French physician and astrologer; author of a book of prophecies in rhymed quatrains, *Centuries* (1555)

nostril ('nɒstrɪl) *n* either of the two external openings of the nose [Old English *nosthyrl*, from *nosu* NOSE + *thyrel* hole]

nostro account ('nɒstrəʊ) *n* a bank account conducted by a British bank with a foreign bank, usually in the foreign currency. Compare **vostro account**

nostrum ('nɒstrəm) *n* 1 a patent or quack medicine 2 a favourite remedy, as for political or social problems [C17: from Latin: our own (make), from *noster* our]

nosyor **nosey** ('nəʊzɪ) *adj* **nosier, nosiest** *informal* prying or inquisitive > **'nosily** *adv* > **'nosiness** *n*

nosy parker *n informal* a prying person [C20: apparently arbitrary use of surname *Parker*]

not (nɒt) *adv* 1 **a** used to negate the sentence, phrase, or word that it modifies: *I will not stand for it* **b** (in combination): *they cannot go* 2 **not that** (conjunction) which is not to say or suppose that: *I expect to lose the game — not that I mind* ▷ *sentence substitute* 3 used to indicate denial, negation, or refusal: *certainly not* [C14 *not*, variant of *nought* nothing, from Old English *nāwiht*, from *nā* no + *wiht* creature, thing. See NAUGHT, NOUGHT]

nota bene Latin ('nəʊtə 'biːnɪ) note well; take note. Abbreviation: NB

notability (,nəʊtə'bɪlɪtɪ) *n, pl* **-ties** 1 the state or quality of being notable 2 a distinguished person; notable

notable ('nəʊtəbᵊl) *adj* 1 worthy of being noted or

remembered; remarkable; distinguished ▷ *n* **2** a notable person [c14: via Old French from Latin *notābilis*, from *notāre* to NOTE] > '**notably** *adv*

notaire (nɒʊˈtɛə) *n* (in France) a public official authorized by the state to attest and certify certain legal documents, oversee property transactions, etc [French]

notarize *or* **notarise** ('nəʊtəˌraɪz) *vb* (*tr*) to attest to or authenticate (a document, contract, etc), as a notary

notary ('nəʊtərɪ) *n*, *pl* **-ries** **1** a notary public **2** (*formerly*) a clerk licensed to prepare legal documents **3** *archaic* a clerk or secretary [c14: from Latin *notārius* clerk, from *nota* a mark, note] > **notarial** (nəʊˈtɛərɪəl) *adj* > '**notaryship** *n*

notary public *n*, *pl* **notaries public** a public official, usually a solicitor, who is legally authorized to administer oaths, attest and certify certain documents, etc

notation (nəʊˈteɪʃən) *n* **1** any series of signs or symbols used to represent quantities or elements in a specialized system, such as music or mathematics **2** the act or process of notating **3** a note or record [c16: from Latin *notātiō* a marking, from *notāre* to NOTE] > **no'tational** *adj*

notch (nɒtʃ) *n* **1** a V-shaped cut or indentation; nick **2** a cut or nick made in a tally stick or similar object **3** *US & Canadian* a narrow pass or gorge **4** *informal* a step or level (esp in the phrase **a notch above**) ▷ *vb* (*tr*) **5** to cut or make a notch in **6** to record with or as if with a notch **7** (usually foll by *up*) *informal* to score or achieve: *the team notched up its fourth win* [c16: from incorrect division of *an otch* (as *a notch*), from Old French *oche* notch, from Latin *obsecāre* to cut off, from *secāre* to cut]

NOT circuit *or* **NOT gate** (nɒt) *n* *computing* a logic circuit that has a high-voltage output signal if the input signal is low, and vice versa: used extensively in computers. Also called: **inverter**, **negator** [c20: so named because the action performed on electrical signals is similar to the operation of *not* in logical constructions]

note (nəʊt) *n* **1** a brief summary or record in writing, esp a jotting for future reference **2** a brief letter, usually of an informal nature **3** a formal written communication, esp from one government to another **4** a short written statement giving any kind of information **5** a critical comment, explanatory statement, or reference in the text of a book, often preceded by a number **6** short for **banknote** **7** a characteristic element or atmosphere: *a note of sarcasm* **8** a distinctive vocal sound, as of a species of bird or animal **9** any of a series of graphic signs representing a musical sound whose pitch is indicated by position on the stave and whose duration is indicated by the sign's shape **10** Also called (esp US and Canadian): **tone** a musical sound of definite fundamental frequency or pitch **11** a key on a piano, organ, etc **12** a sound, as from a musical instrument, used as a signal or warning: *the note to retreat was sounded* **13** short for **promissory note** **14** *archaic or poetic* a tune or melody **15** **of note** **a** distinguished or famous **b** worth noticing or paying attention to; important: *nothing of note* **16** **strike the right note** to behave appropriately **17** **strike a false note** to behave inappropriately **18** **take note** (often foll by *of*) to observe carefully; pay close attention (to) ▷ *vb* (*tr*; *may take a clause as object*) **19** to notice; perceive **20** to pay close attention to; observe: *they noted every movement* **21** to make a written note or memorandum of: *she noted the date in her diary* **22** to make particular mention of; remark upon: *I note that you do not wear shoes* **23** to write down (music, a melody, etc) in notes **24** to take (an unpaid or dishonoured bill of exchange) to a notary public to re-present the bill and if it is still unaccepted or unpaid to note the circumstances in a register. See **protest** (sense 9) **25** a less common word for **annotate** [c13: via Old French from Latin *nota* sign, indication] > '**noteless** *adj*

notebook ('nəʊtˌbʊk) *n* a book for recording notes or memoranda

notebook computer *n* a portable computer smaller than a laptop model, often approximately the size of a sheet of A4 paper

notecase ('nəʊtˌkeɪs) *n* a less common word for **wallet** (sense 1)

noted ('nəʊtɪd) *adj* **1** distinguished; celebrated; famous

---

2 of special note or significance; noticeable > '**notedly** *adv*

notelet ('nəʊtlɪt) *n* a folded card with a printed design on the front, for writing a short informal letter

notepaper ('nəʊtˌpeɪpə) *n* paper for writing letters; writing paper

noteworthy ('nəʊtˌwɜːðɪ) *adj* worthy of notice; notable > '**note,worthiness** *n*

nothing ('nʌθɪŋ) *pron* **1** (*indefinite*) no thing; not anything, as of an implied or specified class of things: *I can give you nothing* **2** no part or share: *to have nothing to do with this crime* **3** a matter of no importance or significance: *it doesn't matter, it's nothing* **4** indicating the absence of anything perceptible; nothingness **5** indicating the absence of meaning, value, worth, etc: *to amount to nothing* **6** zero quantity; nought **7** **be nothing to** **a** not to concern or be significant to (someone) **b** to be not nearly as good as **8** **have** *or* **be nothing to do with** to have no connection with **9** **nothing but** not something other than; only **10** **nothing doing** *informal* an expression of dismissal, disapproval, lack of compliance with a request, etc **11** **nothing if not** at the very least; certainly **12** **nothing less than** *or* **nothing short of** downright **13** **there's nothing to it** it is very simple, easy, etc **14** **think nothing of** **a** to regard as routine, easy, or natural **b** to have no compunction or hesitation about **c** to have a very low opinion of ▷ *adv* **15** in no way; not at all: *he looked nothing like his brother* ▷ *n* **16** *informal* a person or thing of no importance or significance **17** **sweet nothings** words of endearment or affection [Old English *nāthing*, *nān thing*, from *nān* NONE[1] + THING[1]]

nothingness ('nʌθɪŋnɪs) *n* **1** the state or condition of being nothing; nonexistence **2** absence of consciousness or life **3** complete insignificance or worthlessness **4** something that is worthless or insignificant

notice ('nəʊtɪs) *n* **1** the act of perceiving; observation; attention: *to escape notice* **2** **take notice** to pay attention; attend **3** **take no notice of** to ignore or disregard **4** information about a future event; warning; announcement **5** a displayed placard or announcement giving information **6** advance notification of intention to end an arrangement, contract, etc, as of renting or employment (esp in the phrase **give notice**) **7** **at short notice** with notification only a little in advance **8** *chiefly Brit* dismissal from employment **9** favourable, interested, or polite attention: *she was beneath his notice* **10** a theatrical or literary review: *the play received very good notices* ▷ *vb* (*tr*) **11** to become conscious or aware of; perceive; note **12** to point out or remark upon **13** to pay polite or interested attention to **14** to recognize or acknowledge (an acquaintance) [c15: via Old French from Latin *notitia* fame, from *nōtus* known, celebrated]

noticeable ('nəʊtɪsəb°l) *adj* easily seen or detected; perceptible > '**noticeably** *adv*

notice board *n* *Brit* a board on which notices, advertisements, bulletins, etc, are displayed. US and Canadian name: **bulletin board**

notifiable ('nəʊtɪˌfaɪəb°l) *adj* **1** denoting certain infectious diseases of humans, such as smallpox and tuberculosis, outbreaks of which must be reported to the public health authorities **2** denoting certain infectious diseases of animals, such as BSE, foot-and-mouth disease, and rabies, outbreaks of which must be reported to the appropriate veterinary authority

notification (ˌnəʊtɪfɪˈkeɪʃən) *n* **1** the act of notifying **2** a formal announcement **3** something that notifies; a notice

notify ('nəʊtɪˌfaɪ) *vb* **-fies**, **-fying**, **-fied** (*tr*) **1** to inform; tell **2** *chiefly Brit* to draw attention to; make known; announce [c14: from Old French *notifier*, from Latin *notificāre* to make known, from *nōtus* known + *facere* to make] > '**noti,fier** *n*

notion ('nəʊʃən) *n* **1** a vague idea; impression **2** an idea, concept, or opinion **3** an inclination or whim ▷ See also **notions** [c16: from Latin *nōtiō* a becoming acquainted (with), examination (of), from *noscere* to know]

notional ('nəʊʃən°l) *adj* **1** relating to, expressing, or consisting of notions or ideas **2** not evident in reality; hypothetical or imaginary: *a notional tax credit* **3** characteristic of a notion or concept, esp in being speculative or imaginary; abstract **4** *grammar* **a** (of a word) having lexical meaning **b** another word for **semantic** > 'notionally *adv*

notions ('nəʊʃənz) *pl n chiefly US & Canadian* pins, cotton, ribbon, and similar wares used for sewing; haberdashery

notochord ('nəʊtə,kɔːd) *n* a fibrous longitudinal rod in all embryo and some adult chordate animals, immediately above the gut, that supports the body. It is replaced in adult vertebrates by the vertebral column

notorious (nəʊ'tɔːrɪəs) *adj* **1** well-known for some bad or unfavourable quality, deed, etc; infamous **2** *rare* generally known or widely acknowledged [c16: from Medieval Latin *notōrius* well-known, from *nōtus* known, from *noscere* to know] > notoriety (,nəʊtə'raɪɪtɪ) *or* no'toriousness *n* > no'toriously *adv*

notornis (nəʊ'tɔːnɪs) *n* a rare flightless rail of the genus *Notornis*, of New Zealand [c19: New Latin, from Greek *notos* south + *ornis* bird]

not proven ('prəʊvᵊn) *adj* (*postpositive*) a third verdict available to Scottish courts, returned when there is evidence against the defendant but insufficient to convict

Notre Dame ('nəʊtrə 'dɑːm, 'nɒtrə; *French* nɔtrə dam) *n* the early Gothic cathedral of Paris, on the Île de la Cité: built between 1163 and 1257

no-trump *bridge* ▷ *n also* **no-trumps 1** a bid or contract to play without trumps ▷ *adj also* **no-trumper 2** (of a hand) of balanced distribution suitable for playing without trumps

Nottingham ('nɒtɪŋəm) *n* **1** a city in N central England, administrative centre of Nottinghamshire, on the River Trent: scene of the outbreak of the Civil War (1642); famous for its associations with the Robin Hood legend; two universities. Pop: 249 584 (2001) **2** a unitary authority in N central England, in Nottinghamshire. Pop: 273 900 (2003 est). Area: 78 sq km (30 sq miles)

Nottinghamshire ('nɒtɪŋəm,ʃɪə, -ʃə) *n* an inland county of central England: generally low-lying, with part of the S Pennines and the remnant of Sherwood Forest in the east. Nottingham became an independent unitary authority in 1998. Administrative centre: Nottingham. Pop (excluding Nottingham): 755 400 (2003 est). Area (excluding Nottingham): 2086 sq km (805 sq miles). Abbreviation: **Notts**

Nottm *abbreviation* Nottingham

Notts (nɒts) *abbreviation* Nottinghamshire

Notus ('nəʊtəs) *n classical myth* a personification of the south or southwest wind

notwithstanding (,nɒtwɪθ'stændɪŋ, -wɪð-) *prep* **1** (*often immediately postpositive*) in spite of; despite ▷ *conj* **2** (*subordinating*) despite the fact that; although ▷ *sentence connector* **3** in spite of that; nevertheless [c14: NOT + *withstanding*, from Old English *withstandan*, on the model of Medieval Latin *non obstante*, Old French *non obstant*]

Nouakchott (*French* nwakʃɔt) *n* the capital of Mauritania, near the Atlantic coast: replaced St Louis as capital in 1957; situated on important caravan routes. Pop: 559 000 (2002 est)

nougat ('nuːgɑː, 'nʌgət) *n* a hard chewy pink or white sweet containing chopped nuts, cherries, etc [c19: via French from Provençal *nogat*, from *noga* nut, from Latin *nux* nut]

nought (nɔːt) *n also* naught, ought, aught **1** the digit 0; zero: used esp in counting or numbering ▷ *n, adj, adv* **2** a variant spelling of **naught** [Old English *nōwiht*, from *ne* not, no + *ōwiht* something; see WHIT]

noughties ('nɔːtɪz) *pl n informal* the years from 2000 to 2009

noughts and crosses *n* (*functioning as singular*) a game in which two players, one using a nought, "O", the other a cross, "X", alternately mark one square out of nine formed by two pairs of crossed lines, the winner being the first to get three of his symbols in a row. US and Canadian terms: tick-tack-toe, (US) crisscross

Nouméa (nuː'meɪə; *French* numea) *n* the capital and

chief port of the French Overseas Territory of New Caledonia. Pop: 146 000 (2005 est)

noun (naʊn) *n* **a** a word or group of words that refers to a person, place, or thing or any syntactically similar word **b** (*as modifier*): *a noun phrase.* Abbreviation: **N, n.** Related adj: **nominal** [c14: via Anglo-French from Latin *nōmen* NAME] > 'nounal *adj*

nourish ('nʌrɪʃ) *vb* (*tr*) **1** to provide with the materials necessary for life and growth **2** to support or encourage (an idea, feeling, etc); foster: *to nourish resentment* [c14: from Old French *norir*, from Latin *nūtrīre* to feed, care for] > 'nourisher *n* > 'nourishing *adj*

nourishment ('nʌrɪʃmənt) *n* **1** the act or state of nourishing **2** a substance that nourishes; food; nutriment

nous (naʊs) *n* **1** *metaphysics* mind or reason, esp when regarded as the principle governing all things **2** *Brit slang* common sense; intelligence [c17: from Greek, literally: mind]

nouveau *or before a plural noun* **nouveaux** ('nuːvəʊ) *adj* (*prenominal*) *facetious or derogatory* having recently become the thing specified: *a nouveau hippy* [c20: French, literally: new; on the model of NOUVEAU RICHE]

nouveau riche (,nuːvəʊ 'riːʃ) *n, pl* **nouveaux riches** (,nuːvəʊ 'riːʃ; *French* nuvo riʃ) (*often plural* and preceded by *the*) a person who has acquired wealth recently and is regarded as vulgarly ostentatious or lacking in social graces [French, literally: new rich]

Nouvelle-Calédonie (nuvɛlkaledɔni) *n* the French name for **New Caledonia**

nouvelle cuisine ('nuːvɛl kwiː'ziːn) *n* a style of preparing and presenting food, often raw or only lightly cooked, with light sauces, and unusual combinations of flavours and garnishes [c20: French, literally: new cookery]

Nov *abbreviation* November

nova ('nəʊvə) *n, pl* -vae (-viː) *or* -vas a variable star that undergoes a cataclysmic eruption, observed as a sudden large increase in brightness with a subsequent decline over months or years; it is a close binary system with one component a white dwarf [c19: New Latin *nova* (*stella*) new (star), from Latin *novus* new]

Novalis (*German* no'vaːlɪs) *n* real name *Friedrich von Hardenberg*. 1772–1801, German romantic poet. His works include the mystical *Hymnen an die Nacht* (1797; published 1800) and *Geistliche Lieder* (1799)

Nova Lisboa (*Portuguese* 'nɔvə liʒ'βoə) *n* the former name (1928–73) of **Huambo**

Novara (*Italian* no'vaːra) *n* a city in NW Italy, in NE Piedmont: scene of the Austrian defeat of the Piedmontese in 1849. Pop: 100 910 (2001)

Nova Scotia ('nəʊvə 'skəʊʃə) *n* **1** a peninsula in E Canada, between the Gulf of St Lawrence and the Bay of Fundy **2** a province of E Canada, consisting of the Nova Scotia peninsula and Cape Breton Island: first settled by the French as Acadia. Capital: Halifax. Pop: 936 960 (2004 est). Area: 52 841 sq km (20 402 sq miles) ▷ Abbreviation: NS > 'Nova 'Scotian *n, adj*

Nova Scotia duck tolling retriever *n* a Canadian variety of retriever

Novaya Zemlya (*Russian* 'nɔvəjə zɪm'lja) *n* an archipelago in the Arctic Ocean, off the NE coast of Russia: consists of two large islands and many islets. Area: about 81 279 sq km (31 382 sq miles)

novel¹ ('nɒvᵊl) *n* **1** an extended work in prose, either fictitious or partly so, dealing with character, action, thought, etc, esp in the form of a story **2** the novel the literary genre represented by novels [c15: from Old French *novelle*, from Latin *novella* (*narrātiō*) new (story); see NOVEL²]

novel² ('nɒvᵊl) *adj* of a kind not seen before; fresh; new; original [c15: from Latin *novellus* new, diminutive of *novus* new]

novelette (,nɒvə'lɛt) *n* **1** an extended prose narrative story or short novel **2** a novel that is regarded as being slight, trivial, or sentimental **3** a short piece of lyrical music, esp one for the piano

novelettish (,nɒvə'lɛtɪʃ) *adj* characteristic of a novelette; trite or sentimental

novelist ('nɒvəlɪst) *n* a writer of novels

novelistic (ˌnɒvəˈlɪstɪk) *adj* of or characteristic of novels, esp in style or method of treatment: *his novelistic account annoyed other historians*

novella (nəʊˈvɛlə) *n, pl* **-las** *or* **-le** (-leɪ) **1** (formerly) a short narrative tale, esp a popular story having a moral or satirical point, such as those in Boccaccio's *Decameron* **2** a short novel; novelette [c20: from Italian; see NOVEL¹]

Novello (nəˈvɛləʊ) *n* **Ivor,** real name *Ivor Novello Davies.* 1893–1951, Welsh actor, composer, songwriter, and dramatist

novelty ('nɒvəltɪ) *n, pl* **-ties 1 a** the quality of being new and fresh and interesting **b** (*as modifier*): *novelty value* **2** a new or unusual experience or occurrence **3** (*often plural*) a small usually cheap new toy, ornament, or trinket [c14: from Old French *novelté*; see NOVEL²]

November (nəʊˈvɛmbə) *n* the eleventh month of the year, consisting of 30 days [c13: via Old French from Latin: ninth month, from *novem* nine]

novena (nəʊˈviːnə) *n, pl* **-nas** *or* **-nae** (-niː) *RC Church* a devotion consisting of prayers or services on nine consecutive days [c19: from Medieval Latin, from Latin *novem* nine]

Novgorod (Russian 'nɒvɡərət) *n* a city in NW Russia, on the Volkhov River; became a principality in 862 under Rurik, an event regarded as the founding of the Russian state; a major trading centre in the Middle Ages; destroyed by Ivan the Terrible in 1570. Pop: 215 000 (2005 est)

novice ('nɒvɪs) *n* **1 a** a person who is new to or inexperienced in a certain task, situation, etc; beginner; tyro **b** (*as modifier*): *novice driver* **2** a probationer in a religious order **3** a racehorse, esp a steeplechaser or hurdler, that has not won a specified number of races [c14: via Old French from Latin *novīcius*, from *novus* new]

Novi Sad (Serbian 'nɒvi: 'sa:d) *n* a port in Serbia, in the NE on the River Danube: founded in 1690 as the seat of the Serbian patriarch; university (1960). Pop: 234 151 (2002). German name: **Neusatz**

novitiate *or* **noviciate** (nəʊˈvɪʃɪɪt, -ˌeɪt) *n* **1** the state of being a novice, esp in a religious order, or the period for which this lasts **2** the part of a religious house where the novices live [c17: from French *noviciat*, from Latin *novīcius* NOVICE]

Novocaine ('nəʊvəˌkeɪn) *n* a trademark for **procaine hydrochloride.** See **procaine**

Novokuznetsk (Russian nɒvəkuz'njɛtsk) *n* a city in S central Russia: iron and steel works. Pop: 542 000 (2005 est). Former name (1932–61): **Stalinsk**

Novosibirsk (Russian nəvəsi'birsk) *n* a city in W central Russia, on the River Ob: the largest town in Siberia; developed with the coming of the Trans-Siberian railway in 1893; important industrial centre. Pop: 1 425 000 (2005 est)

now (naʊ) *adv* **1** at or for the present time or moment **2** at this exact moment; immediately **3** in these times; nowadays **4** given the present circumstances: *now we'll have to stay to the end* **5** (preceded by *just*) very recently: *he left just now* **6** (often preceded by *just*) very soon: *he is leaving just now* **7** (**every**) **now and again** *or* **then** occasionally; on and off **8 now now!** (*interjection*) an exclamation used to rebuke or pacify someone ▷ *conj* **9** (*subordinating*; often foll by *that*) seeing that; since it has become the case that: *now you're in charge, things will be better* ▷ *sentence connector* **10 a** used as a transitional particle or hesitation word: *now, I can't really say* **b** used for emphasis: *now listen to this* **c** used at the end of a command, esp in dismissal: *run along, now* ▷ *n* **11** the present moment or time: *now is the time to go* ▷ *adj* **12** *informal* of the moment; fashionable: *the now look is street fashion* [Old English *nū*; compare Old Saxon *nū*, German *nun*, Latin *nunc*, Greek *nu*]

nowadays ('naʊəˌdeɪz) *adv* in these times [c14: from NOW + *adays* from Old English *a* on + *dæges* genitive of DAY]

noway ('nəʊˌweɪ) *adv* **1** in no manner; not at all; nowise ▷ *sentence substitute* **no way 2** used to make an emphatic refusal, denial, etc

Nowel *or* **Nowell** (nəʊˈɛl) *n* archaic spellings of **Noel**

nowhere ('nəʊˌwɛə) *adv* **1** in, at, or to no place; not anywhere **2 get nowhere (fast)** *informal* to fail completely to make any progress **3 nowhere near** far from; not nearly ▷ *n* **4** a nonexistent or insignificant place **5 middle of nowhere** a completely isolated, featureless, or insignificant place

no-win *adj* offering no possibility of a favourable outcome (esp in the phrase **a no-win situation**)

nowise ('nəʊˌwaɪz) *adv* another word for **noway**

now-now *adv* *South African informal* right away; immediately: *I'll do it now-now!*

nowt (naʊt) *n* *Northern English* a dialect word for **nothing** [from NAUGHT]

Nox (nɒks) *n* the Roman goddess of the night

noxious ('nɒkʃəs) *adj* poisonous or harmful [c17: from Latin *noxius* harmful, from *noxa* injury] > **'noxiously** *adv* > **'noxiousness** *n*

Noyon (French nwajɔ̃) *n* a town in N France: scene of the coronations of Charlemagne (768) and Hugh Capet (987); birthplace of John Calvin. Pop: 14 471 (1999)

nozzle ('nɒzᵊl) *n* a projecting pipe or spout from which fluid is discharged [c17 *nosle, nosel*, diminutive of NOSE]

Np 1 *symbol for* neper **2** *the chemical symbol for* neptunium

NP *or* **np** *abbreviation* Notary Public

NPA *abbreviation* Newspaper Publishers' Association

NPD *abbreviation commerce* new product development

NPL *abbreviation* National Physical Laboratory

NPV *abbreviation* **1** net present value **2** no par value

NRC *abbreviation* (in Canada) National Research Council

NRI *abbreviation* (in India) Non-Resident Indian: an Indian citizen or person of Indian origin living abroad

NRL *abbreviation* (in Australia) National Rugby League

NRMA *abbreviation* (in Australia) National Roads and Motorists Association

NRN *abbreviation text messaging* no reply necessary

NRT *abbreviation* nicotine replacement therapy: a type of treatment designed to help people give up smoking in which gradually decreasing doses of nicotine are administered through patches on the skin etc to avoid the effects of sudden withdrawal from the drug

NRV *abbreviation* net realizable value

NS *abbreviation* **1** New Style (method of reckoning dates) **2** (esp in postal addresses) Nova Scotia **3** nuclear ship

NSAID *abbreviation* nonsteroidal anti-inflammatory drug: any of a class of drugs, including aspirin and ibuprofen, used for reducing inflammation and pain in rheumatic diseases. Possible adverse effects include gastric ulceration

NSB *abbreviation* National Savings Bank

NSG *abbreviation Brit education* nonstatutory guidelines: practical nonmandatory advice and information on the implementation of the National Curriculum

NSPCC *abbreviation* National Society for the Prevention of Cruelty to Children

NSU *abbreviation* nonspecific urethritis

NSW *abbreviation* New South Wales

NT 1 National Trust **2** New Testament **3** Northern Territory (of Australia) **4** (esp in postal addresses) Nunavut **5** no-trump

-n't *contraction of* not: used as an enclitic after *be* and *have* when they function as main verbs and after auxiliary verbs or verbs operating syntactically as auxiliaries: *can't; don't; shouldn't; needn't; daren't; isn't*

nth (ɛnθ) *adj* **1** *maths* of or representing an unspecified ordinal number, usually the greatest in a series of values: *the nth power* **2** *informal* being the last, most recent, or most extreme of a long series: *for the nth time, eat your lunch!* **3 to the nth degree** *informal* to the utmost extreme; as much as possible

NTO (in Britain) *abbreviation* National Training Organization

NTP *abbreviation* normal temperature and pressure: standard conditions of 0°C temperature and 101.325 kPa (760 mmHg) pressure. Also: **STP**

nt. wt. *or* **nt wt** *abbreviation* net weight

n-type *adj* **1** (of a semiconductor) having more conduction electrons than mobile holes **2** associated with or resulting from the movement of electrons in a semiconductor

n

nu (njuː) *n* the 13th letter in the Greek alphabet (N, ν), a consonant, transliterated as *n* [from Greek, of Semitic origin]

Nu (njuː) *n* **U** (uː), original name *Thakin Nu.* 1907–95, Burmese statesman and writer; prime minister (1948–56, 1957–58, 1960–62). He attempted to establish parliamentary democracy, but was ousted (1962) by Ne Win

nuance (njuːˈɑːns, ˈnjuːɑːns) *n* a subtle difference in colour, meaning, tone, etc; a shade or graduation [c18: from French, from *nuer* to show light and shade, ultimately from Latin *nūbēs* a cloud]

nub (nʌb) *n* **1** a small lump or protuberance **2** a small piece or chunk **3** the point or gist: *the nub of a story* [c16: variant of *knub*, from Middle Low German *knubbe* KNOB] > **'nubbly** *or* **'nubby** *adj*

nubble (ˈnʌbᵊl) *n* a small lump [c19: diminutive of NUB]

Nubia (ˈnjuːbɪə) *n* an ancient region of NE Africa, on the Nile, extending from Aswan to Khartoum

Nubian (ˈnjuːbɪən) *n* **1** a native or inhabitant of Nubia, an ancient region of NE Africa **2** the language spoken by the people of Nubia ▷ *adj* **3** of or relating to Nubia or its inhabitants **4** *informal* of or relating to Black culture

Nubian Desert *n* a desert in the NE Sudan, between the Nile valley and the Red Sea: mainly a sandstone plateau

nubile (ˈnjuːbaɪl) *adj* (of a girl or woman) **1** ready or suitable for marriage by virtue of age or maturity **2** sexually attractive [c17: from Latin *nūbilis*, from *nūbere* to marry] > **nubility** (njuːˈbɪlɪtɪ) *n*

Nubuck (ˈnjuːˌbʌk) *n* (*sometimes not capital*) leather that has been rubbed on the flesh side of the skin to give it a fine velvet-like finish

nucha (ˈnjuːkə) *n, pl* **-chae** (-kiː) *zoology, anatomy* the back or nape of the neck [c14: from Medieval Latin, from Arabic *nukhā'* spinal marrow] > **'nuchal** *adj*

nuclear (ˈnjuːklɪə) *adj* **1** of, concerned with, or involving the nucleus of an atom: *nuclear fission* **2** *biology* of, relating to, or contained within the nucleus of a cell: *a nuclear membrane* **3** of, relating to, forming, or resembling any other kind of nucleus **4** of, concerned with, or operated by energy from fission or fusion of atomic nuclei: *a nuclear weapon* **5** involving, concerned with, or possessing nuclear weapons: *nuclear war; a nuclear strike*

nuclear bomb *n* a bomb whose force is due to uncontrolled nuclear fusion or nuclear fission

nuclear chemistry *n* the branch of chemistry concerned with nuclear reactions

nuclear energy *n* energy released during a nuclear reaction as a result of fission or fusion. Also called: atomic energy

nuclear family *n sociol, anthropol* a primary social unit consisting of parents and their offspring

nuclear fission *n* the splitting of an atomic nucleus into approximately equal parts, either spontaneously or as a result of the impact of a particle usually with an associated release of energy. Sometimes shortened to fission. Compare **nuclear fusion**

nuclear fuel *n* a fuel that provides nuclear energy, used in nuclear power stations, nuclear submarines, etc

nuclear fusion *n* a reaction in which two nuclei combine to form a nucleus with the release of energy. Sometimes shortened to **fusion**

nuclear magnetic resonance *n* a technique for determining the magnetic moments of nuclei by subjecting a substance to high-frequency radiation and a large magnetic field. The technique is used as a method of determining structure. Abbreviation: **NMR**

nuclear medicine *n* the branch of medicine concerned with the use of radionuclides in the diagnosis and treatment of disease

nuclear physics *n* (*functioning as singular*) the branch of physics concerned with the structure and behaviour of the nucleus and the particles of which it consists

nuclear power *n* power, esp electrical or motive, produced by a nuclear reactor. Also called: **atomic power**

nuclear reaction *n* a process in which the structure and energy content of an atomic nucleus is changed by interaction with another nucleus or particle

nuclear reactor *n* a device in which a nuclear reaction

is maintained and controlled for the production of nuclear energy. Sometimes shortened to **reactor**

nuclear waste *n* another name for **radioactive waste**

nuclear winter *n* a period of extremely low temperatures and little light that has been suggested would occur as a result of a nuclear war

nuclease (ˈnjuːklɪˌeɪz) *n* any of a group of enzymes that hydrolyse nucleic acids to simple nucleotides

nucleate *adj* (ˈnjuːklɪɪt, -ˌeɪt) **1** having a nucleus ▷ *vb* (ˈnjuːklɪˌeɪt) (*intr*) **2** to form a nucleus

nuclei (ˈnjuːklɪˌaɪ) *n* a plural of **nucleus**

nucleic acid (njuːˈkliːɪk, -ˈkleɪ-) *n biochem* any of a group of complex compounds with a high molecular weight that are vital constituents of all living cells. See also **RNA, DNA**

nucleo- *or before a vowel* **nucle-** *combining form* **1** nucleus or nuclear **2** nucleic acid [from Latin *nucleus* kernel, from *nux* nut]

nucleolus (ˌnjuːklɪˈəʊləs) *n, pl* **-li** (-laɪ) a small rounded body within a resting nucleus that contains RNA and proteins and is involved in the production of ribosomes. Also called: **'nucleˌole** [c19: from Latin, diminutive of NUCLEUS] > **ˌnucleˈolar, 'nucleoˌlate** *or* **'nucleoˌlated** *adj*

nucleon (ˈnjuːklɪˌɒn) *n* a proton or neutron, esp one present in an atomic nucleus [c20: from NUCLE(US) + -ON]

nucleonics (ˌnjuːklɪˈɒnɪks) *n* (*functioning as singular*) the branch of physics concerned with the applications of nuclear energy > **ˌnucleˈonic** *adj* > **ˌnucleˈonically** *adv*

nucleon number *n* another name for **mass number**

nucleoside (ˈnjuːklɪəˌsaɪd) *n biochem* a compound containing a purine or pyrimidine base linked to a sugar (usually ribose or deoxyribose) [c20: from NUCLEO- + -OSE² + -IDE]

nucleotide (ˈnjuːklɪəˌtaɪd) *n biochem* a compound consisting of a nucleoside linked to phosphoric acid. Nucleic acids are made up of long chains (polynucleotides) of such compounds [c20: from NUCLEO- + *t* (added for ease of pronunciation) + -IDE]

nucleus (ˈnjuːklɪəs) *n, pl* **-clei** (-klɪˌaɪ) *or* **-cleuses 1** a central or fundamental part or thing around which others are grouped; core **2** a centre of growth or development; basis; kernel: *the nucleus of an idea* **3** *biology* (in the cells of eukaryotes) a large compartment, bounded by a double membrane, that contains the chromosomes and associated molecules and controls the characteristics and growth of the cell **4** *astronomy* the central portion in the head of a comet, consisting of small solid particles of ice and frozen gases, which vaporize on approaching the sun to form the coma and tail **5** *physics* the positively charged dense region at the centre of an atom, composed of protons and neutrons, about which electrons orbit **6** *chem* a fundamental group of atoms in a molecule serving as the base structure for related compounds and remaining unchanged during most chemical reactions [c18: from Latin: kernel, from *nux* nut]

nuclide (ˈnjuːklaɪd) *n* a species of atom characterized by its atomic number and its mass number [c20: from NUCLEO- + -ide, from Greek *eidos* shape]

nude (njuːd) *adj* **1** completely unclothed; undressed **2** having no covering; bare; exposed **3** *law* **a** lacking some essential legal requirement, esp supporting evidence **b** (of a contract, agreement, etc) made without consideration and void unless under seal ▷ *n* **4** the state of being naked (esp in the phrase **in the nude**) **5** a naked figure, esp in painting, sculpture, etc [c16: from Latin *nūdus*] > **'nudely** *adv*

nudge (nʌdʒ) *vb* (*tr*) **1** to push or poke (someone) gently, esp with the elbow, to get attention; jog **2** to push slowly or lightly: *as I drove out, I just nudged the gatepost* **3** to give (someone) a gentle reminder or encouragement ▷ *n* **4** a gentle poke or push **5** a gentle reminder [c17: perhaps from Scandinavian; compare Icelandic *nugga* to push] > **'nudger** *n*

nudi- *combining form* naked or bare: *nudibranch* [from Latin *nūdus*]

nudibranch (ˈnjuːdɪˌbræŋk) *n* any marine gastropod of the order *Nudibranchia*, characterized by a shell-less, often beautifully coloured, body bearing external gills and other appendages. Also called: **sea slug** [C19: from NUDI- + *branchia*, from Latin *branchia* gills]

nudism ('nju:dɪzəm) *n* the practice of nudity, esp for reasons of health, religion, etc ▷ '**nudist** *n, adj*

nudity ('nju:dɪtɪ) *n, pl* **-ties** the state or fact of being nude; nakedness

Nuevo Laredo (*Spanish* 'nweβo la'reðo) *n* a city and port of entry in NE Mexico, in Tamaulipas state on the Rio Grande opposite Laredo, Texas: oil industries. Pop: 353 000 (2005 est)

Nuevo León ('nweivəu ler'əʊn, nu:'eɪ-; *Spanish* 'nweβo le'ɔn) *n* a state of NE Mexico: the first centre of heavy industry in Latin America. Capital: Monterrey. Pop: 3 826 240 (2000). Area: 64 555 sq km (24 925 sq miles)

Nuffield ('nʌfiːld) *n* **William Richard Morris**, 1st Viscount Nuffield. 1877–1963, English motorcar manufacturer and philanthropist. He endowed Nuffield College at Oxford (1937) and the Nuffield Foundation (1943), a charitable trust for the furtherance of medicine and education

nugatory ('nju:gətərɪ, -trɪ) *adj* **1** of little value; trifling **2** not valid: *a nugatory law* [C17: from Latin *nūgātōrius*, from *nūgārī* to jest, from *nūgae* trifles]

nugget ('nʌgɪt) *n* **1** a small piece or lump, esp of gold in its natural state **2** something small but valuable or excellent [C19: origin unknown]

Nugget ('nʌgɪt) *NZ* ▷ *n* **1** *trademark* shoe polish ▷ *vb* **2** (*tr; sometimes not capital*) *informal* to shine (shoes)

nuggety ('nʌgɪtɪ) *adj* **1** of or resembling a nugget **2** *Austral & NZ informal* (of a person) thickset; stocky

nuisance ('nju:səns) *n* **1 a** a person or thing that causes annoyance or bother **b** (*as modifier*): *nuisance calls* **2** *law* something unauthorized that is obnoxious or injurious to the community at large (**public nuisance**) or to an individual, esp in relation to his ownership or occupation of property (**private nuisance**) **3 nuisance value** the usefulness of a person's or thing's capacity to cause difficulties or irritation [C15: via Old French from *nuire* to injure, from Latin *nocēre*]

NUJ (in Britain) *abbreviation* National Union of Journalists

Nu Jiang ('nu: 'dʒjæŋ) *n* the Chinese name for the Salween

nuke (nju:k) *slang* ▷ *vb* **1** (*tr*) to attack or destroy with nuclear weapons ▷ *n* **2** a nuclear bomb

Nuku'alofa (,nu:ku:ə'lɔ:fə) *n* the capital of Tonga, a port on the N coast of Tongatapu Island. Pop: 36 000 (2005 est)

Nukus (*Russian* nu'kus) *n* a city in Uzbekistan, capital of the Kara-Kalpak Autonomous Republic, on the Amu Darya River. Pop: 325 000 (2005 est)

null (nʌl) *adj* **1** without legal force; invalid; (esp in the phrase **null and void**) **2** without value or consequence; useless **3** lacking distinction; characterless **4** nonexistent; amounting to nothing **5** *maths* **a** quantitatively zero **b** relating to zero **c** (of a set) having no members **6** *physics* involving measurement in which an instrument has a zero reading, as with a Wheatstone bridge [C16: from Latin *nullus* none, from *ne* not + *ullus* any]

nullah ('nʌlɑ:) *n* a stream or drain [C18: from Hindi *nālā*]

Nullarbor Plain ('nʌləˌbɔ:) *n* a vast low plateau of S Australia: extends north from the Great Australian Bight to the Great Victoria Desert; has no surface water or trees. Area: 260 000 sq km (100 000 sq miles)

null hypothesis *n statistics* the residual hypothesis if the alternative hypothesis tested against it fails to achieve a predetermined significance level

nullify ('nʌlɪˌfaɪ) *vb* **-fies, -fying, -fied** (*tr*) **1** to render legally void or of no effect **2** to render ineffective or useless; cancel out [C16: from Late Latin *nullificāre* to despise, from Latin *nullus* of no account + *facere* to make] ▷ ˌnulli'fi'cation *n*

nullity ('nʌlɪtɪ) *n, pl* **-ties 1** the state of being null **2** a null or legally invalid act or instrument **3** something null, ineffective, characterless, etc [C16: from Medieval Latin *nullitās*, from Latin *nullus* no, not any]

NUM (in Britain and South Africa) *abbreviation* National Union of Mineworkers

Num. *abbreviation Bible* Numbers

Numantia (nju:'mæntɪə) *n* an ancient city in N Spain: a centre of Celtic resistance to Rome in N Spain: captured by Scipio the Younger in 133 BC ▷ Nu'mantian *adj, n*

Numa Pompilius ('nju:mə pɒm'pɪlɪəs) *n* the legendary second king of Rome (?715–?673 BC), said to have instituted religious rites

numb (nʌm) *adj* **1** deprived of feeling through cold, shock, etc **2** unable to move; paralysed ▷ *vb* **3** (*tr*) to make numb; deaden, shock, or paralyse [C15 *nomen*, literally: taken (with paralysis), from Old English *niman* to take; related to Old Norse *nema*, Old High German *niman*] ▷ '**numbly** *adv* ▷ '**numbness** *n*

numbat ('nʌmˌbæt) *n* a small Australian marsupial, *Myrmecobius fasciatus*, having a long snout and tongue and strong claws for hunting and feeding on termites: family *Dasyuridae*. Also called: **banded anteater** [C20: from a native Australian language]

number ('nʌmbə) *n* **1** a concept of quantity that is or can be derived from a single unit, the sum of a collection of units, or zero. Every number occupies a unique position in a sequence, enabling it to be used in counting. It can be assigned to one or more sets that can be arranged in a hierarchical classification: every number is a *complex number*; a complex number is either an *imaginary number* or a *real number*, and the latter can be a *rational number* or an *irrational number*; a rational number is either an *integer* or a *fraction*, while an irrational number can be a *transcendental number* or an *algebraic number*. See also **cardinal number, ordinal number 2** the symbol used to represent a number; numeral **3** a numeral or string of numerals used to identify a person or thing, esp in numerical order: *a telephone number* **4** the person or thing so identified or designated: *she was number seven in the race* **5** the sum or quantity of equal or similar units or things: *a large number of people* **6** one of a series, as of a magazine or periodical; issue **7 a** a self-contained piece of pop or jazz music **b** a self-contained part of an opera or other musical score, esp one for the stage **8** a group or band of people, esp an exclusive group: *he was one of our number* **9** *slang* a person, esp a woman: *who's that nice little number?* **10** *informal* an admired article, esp an item of clothing for a woman: *that little number is by Dior* **11** a grammatical category for the variation in form of nouns, pronouns, and any words agreeing with them, depending on how many persons or things are referred to, esp as singular or plural in number and in some languages dual or trial **12** any number of several or many **13** by numbers *military* (of a drill procedure, etc) performed step by step, each move being made on the call of a number **14** get *or* have someone's number *informal* to discover someone's true character or intentions **15** one's number is up *Brit informal* one is finished; one is ruined or about to die **16** without *or* beyond number of too great a quantity to be counted; innumerable ▷ *vb* (*mainly tr*) **17** to assign a number to **18** to add up to; total **19** (*also intr*) to list (items) one by one; enumerate **20** (*also intr*) to put or be put into a group, category, etc: *they were numbered among the worst hit* **21** to limit the number of: *his days were numbered* [C13: from Old French *nombre*, from Latin *numerus*]

number crunching *n computing* the large-scale processing of numerical data

numbered account *n banking* an account identified only by a number, esp one in a Swiss bank that could contain funds illegally obtained

numberless ('nʌmbəlɪs) *adj* **1** too many to be counted; countless **2** not containing or consisting of numbers ▷ '**numberlessly** *adv*

number one *n* **1** the first in a series or sequence **2** an informal phrase for **oneself, myself, etc**: *to look after number one* **3** *informal* the most important person; leader, chief: *he's number one in the organization* **4** *informal* the bestselling pop record in any one week ▷ *adj* **5** first in importance, urgency, quality, etc: *number one priority*

numberplate ('nʌmbəˌpleɪt) *n* a plate mounted on the front and back of a motor vehicle bearing the registration number. Usual US term: **license plate**, (Canadian) **licence plate**

numbers game *or* **numbers racket** *n US* an illegal

lottery in which money is wagered on a certain combination of digits appearing at the beginning of a series of numbers published in a newspaper, as in share prices or sports results

Number Ten n 10 Downing Street, the British prime minister's official London residence

number theory n the study of integers, their properties, and the relationship between integers

numbfish ('nʌm,fɪʃ) n, pl -fish or -fishes any of several electric rays, such as Narcine tasmaniensis (**Australian numbfish**) [C18: so called because it numbs its victims]

numbles ('nʌmbᵊlz) pl n archaic the heart, lungs, liver, etc, of an deer or other animal, cooked for food [C14: from Old French nombles, plural of nomble thigh muscle of a deer, changed from Latin lumbulus a little loin, from lumbus loin; see HUMBLE PIE]

numbskull or **numskull** ('nʌm,skʌl) n a stupid person; dolt; blockhead [C18: from NUMB + SKULL]

numen ('nju:mɛn) n, pl -mina (-mɪnə) 1 (esp in ancient Roman religion) a deity or spirit presiding over a thing or place 2 a guiding principle, force, or spirit [C17: from Latin: a nod (indicating a command), divine power; compare nuere to nod]

numerable ('nju:mərəbᵊl) adj able to be numbered or counted > 'numerably adv

numeracy ('nju:mərəsɪ) n the ability to use numbers, esp in arithmetical operations

numeral ('nju:mərəl) n 1 a symbol or group of symbols used to express a number: for example, 6 (Arabic), VI (Roman), 110 (binary) ▷ adj 2 of, consisting of, or denoting a number [C16: from Late Latin numerālis belonging to number, from Latin numerus number]

numerate adj ('nju:mərɪt) 1 able to use numbers, esp in arithmetical operations ▷ vb ('nju:mə,reɪt) (tr) 2 to read (a numerical expression) 3 a less common word for **enumerate** [C18 (vb): from Latin numerus number + -ATE¹, by analogy with literate]

numeration (,nju:mə'reɪʃən) n 1 the act or process of writing, reading, or naming numbers 2 a system of numbering or counting > 'numerative adj

numerator ('nju:mə,reɪtə) n 1 maths the dividend of a fraction: the numerator of ⅞ is 7. Compare **denominator** 2 a person or thing that numbers; enumerator

numerical (nju:'mɛrɪkᵊl) or **numeric** adj 1 of, relating to, or denoting a number or numbers 2 measured or expressed in numbers: numerical value > nu'merically adv

numerology (,nju:mə'rɒlədʒɪ) n the study of numbers, such as the figures in a birth date, and of their supposed influence on human affairs > numerological (,nju:mərə'lɒdʒɪkᵊl) adj

numerous ('nju:mərəs) adj 1 being many 2 consisting of many units or parts: a numerous collection > 'numerously adv > 'numerousness n

Numidia (nju:'mɪdɪə) n an ancient country of N Africa, corresponding roughly to present-day Algeria: flourished until its invasion by Vandals in 429; chief towns were Cirta and Hippo Regius > Nu'midian adj, n

numinous ('nju:mɪnəs) adj 1 denoting, being, or relating to a numen; divine 2 arousing spiritual or religious emotions 3 mysterious or awe-inspiring [C17: from Latin numin-, NUMEN + -OUS]

numismatics (,nju:mɪz'mætɪks) n (functioning as singular) the study or collection of coins, medals, etc. Also called: numismatology [C18: from French numismatique, from Latin nomisma, from Greek: piece of currency, from nomizein to have in use, from nōmos use] > ,numis'matic adj > ,numis'matically adv

nummulite ('nʌmjʊ,laɪt) n any of various large fossil protozoans of the family Nummulitidae, common in Tertiary times: phylum Foraminifera (foraminifers) [C19: from New Latin Nummulites genus name, from Latin nummulus, from nummus coin]

numpty ('nʌmptɪ) n, pl -ties Scot informal a stupid person [C20: of unknown origin]

numskull ('nʌm,skʌl) n a variant spelling of **numbskull**

nun (nʌn) n a female member of a religious order [Old English nunne, from Church Latin nonna, from Late Latin: form of address used for an elderly woman] > 'nunlike adj > 'nunhood n

Nunavut ('nu:nə,vu:t) n a territory of NW Canada, formed in 1999 from part of the Northwest Territories as a semiautonomous region for the Inuit; includes Baffin Island and Ellesmere Island. Capital: Iqaluit. Pop: 29 644 (2004 est). Area: 2 093 190 sq km (808 185 sq miles)

nun buoy (nʌn) n nautical a buoy, conical at the top, marking the right side of a channel leading into a harbour: green in British waters but red in US waters [C18: from obsolete nun a child's spinning top + BUOY]

Nunc Dimittis ('nʌŋk dɪ'mɪtɪs, 'nʊŋk) n 1 the Latin name for the Canticle of Simeon (Luke 2:29–32) 2 a musical setting of this [from the opening words (Vulgate): now let depart]

nunciature ('nʌnsɪətʃə) n the office or term of office of a nuncio [C17: from Italian nunziatura; see NUNCIO]

nuncio ('nʌnsɪ,əʊ, -sɪ-) n, pl -cios RC Church a diplomatic representative of the Holy See, ranking above an internuncio and esp having ambassadorial status [C16: via Italian from Latin nuntius messenger]

Nuneaton (nʌn'i:tᵊn) n a town in central England, in Warwickshire. Pop: 70 721 (2001)

Nunn (nʌn) n Sir **Trevor** (**Robert**). born 1940, British theatre director; artistic director (1968–86) and chief executive (1968–86) of the Royal Shakespeare Company; artistic director of the Royal National Theatre (1997–2003). His productions include Nicholas Nickleby (1980), Cats (1981), and Les Misérables (1985)

nunnery ('nʌnərɪ) n, pl -neries the convent or religious house of a community of nuns

nuptial ('nʌpʃəl, -tʃəl) adj 1 relating to marriage; conjugal: nuptial vows 2 zoology of or relating to mating: the nuptial flight of a queen bee [C15: from Latin nuptiālis, from nuptiae marriage, from nubere to marry] > 'nuptially adv

nuptials ('nʌpʃəlz, -tʃəlz) pl n (sometimes singular) a marriage ceremony; wedding

nurd (nɜ:d) n a variant spelling of **nerd**

Nuremberg ('njʊərəm,bɜ:g) n a city in S Germany, in N Bavaria: scene of annual Nazi rallies (1933–38), the anti-Semitic Nuremberg decrees (1935), and the trials of Nazi leaders for their war crimes (1945–46); important metalworking and electrical industries. Pop: 493 553 (2003 est). German name: Nürnberg

Nureyev ('njʊərɪ,ɛf, njʊ'reɪ-) n **Rudolf**. 1938–93, Austrian ballet dancer, born in the Soviet Union: he lived in England (1961–83) and France (1983–89). He became an Austrian citizen in 1982

Nurhachi (,nʊə'hɑ:tʃɪ) n 1559–1626, Manchurian leader, who unified the Manchurian state and began (1618) the Manchurian conquest of China

Nuri ('nʊərɪ) n 1 pl -ris or -ri Also called: Kafir a member of an Indo-European people of Nuristan and neighbouring parts of Pakistan 2 Also called: Kafiri the Indo-Iranian language of this people

Nuri as-Said ('nju:rɪ æssaɪ'i:d) n 1888–1958, Iraqi soldier and statesman: prime minister of Iraq 14 times between 1930 and 1958: he died during a military coup

Nuristan (,nʊərɪ'stɑ:n) n a region of E Afghanistan: consists mainly of high mountains (including part of the Hindu Kush), steep narrow valleys, and forests. Area: about 13 000 sq km (5000 sq miles). Former name: Kafiristan

Nurmi ('nɜ:mɪ; Finnish 'nurmi) n **Paavo** ('pɑ:vɔ), known as The Flying Finn. 1897– 1973, Finnish runner, winner of the 1500, 5000, and 10 000 metres' races at the 1924 Olympic Games in Paris

Nürnberg ('nyrnbɛrk) n the German name for **Nuremberg**

nurse (nɜ:s) n 1 a person who tends the sick, injured, or infirm 2 short for **nursemaid** 3 a woman employed to breast-feed another woman's child; wet nurse 4 a worker in a colony of social insects that takes care of the larvae ▷ vb (mainly tr) 5 (also intr) to tend (the sick) 6 (also intr) to feed (a baby) at the breast; suckle 7 to try to cure (an ailment) 8 to clasp carefully or fondly: she nursed the crying child in her arms 9 (also intr) (of a baby) to suckle at the breast (of) 10 to attend to carefully; foster, cherish: he nursed the magazine through its first year; having a very small majority he nursed the constituency diligently 11 to harbour; preserve: to nurse a grudge 12 billiards to keep (the balls) together for a series of cannons [C16: from earlier *norice*, Old French *nourice*, from Late Latin *nūtrīcia* nurse, from Latin *nūtrīcius* nourishing, from *nūtrīre* to nourish]

nursemaid ('nɜːsˌmeɪd) *or* **nurserymaid** ('nɜːsrɪˌmeɪd) *n* a woman or girl employed to look after someone else's children. Often shortened to **nurse**

nurse practitioner *n* a nurse who has specialized advanced skills in diagnosis, psychosocial assessment, and patient management and is permitted to prescribe certain drugs

nursery ('nɜːsrɪ) *n, pl* -ries 1 a room in a house set apart for use by children 2 a place where plants, young trees, etc, are grown commercially 3 an establishment providing residential or day care for babies and very young children; crèche 4 anywhere serving to foster or nourish new ideas, etc 5 Also called: **nursery cannon billiards** a a series of cannons with the three balls adjacent to a cushion, esp near a corner pocket b a cannon in such a series

nurseryman ('nɜːsrɪmən) *n, pl* -men a person who owns or works in a nursery in which plants are grown

nursery rhyme *n* a short traditional verse or song for children, such as *Little Jack Horner*

nursery school *n* a school for young children, usually from three to five years old

nursery slopes *pl n* gentle slopes used by beginners in skiing

nursery stakes *pl n* a race for two-year-old horses

nurse shark *n* any of various sharks of the family *Orectolobidae*, such as *Ginglymostoma cirratum* of the Atlantic Ocean, having an external groove on each side of the head between the mouth and nostril [C15 *nusse fisshe* (later influenced in spelling by NURSE), perhaps from division of obsolete *an huss* shark, dogfish (of uncertain origin) as *a nuss*]

nursing ('nɜːsɪŋ) *n* a the practice or profession of caring for the sick and injured b (*as modifier*): *a nursing home*

nursing home *n* a private hospital or residence staffed and equipped to care for aged or infirm persons

nursing officer *n* (in Britain) the official name for **matron** (sense 3)

nursling *or* **nurseling** ('nɜːslɪŋ) *n* a child or young animal that is being suckled, nursed, or fostered

nurture ('nɜːtʃə) *n* 1 the act or process of promoting the development, etc, of a child 2 something that nourishes ▷ *vb* (*tr*) 3 to feed or support 4 to educate or train [C14: from Old French *norriture*, from Latin *nutrīre* to nourish] > **'nurturer** *n*

NUS (in Britain) *abbreviation* National Union of Students

Nusa Tenggara ('nuːsə tɛŋ'gɑːrə) *n* an island chain east of Java, mostly in Indonesia: the main islands are Bali, Lombok, Sumbawa, Sumba, Flores, Alor, and Timor. Pop: 11 112 702 (2000). Area: 73 144 sq km (28 241 sq miles). English name: **Lesser Sunda Islands**

nut (nʌt) *n* 1 a dry one-seeded indehiscent fruit that usually possesses a woody wall 2 (*not in technical use*) any similar fruit, such as the walnut, having a hard shell and an edible kernel 3 the edible kernel of such a fruit 4 *slang* an eccentric person 5 a slang word for **head** (sense 1) 6 **do one's nut** *Brit slang* to be extremely angry; go into a rage 7 **off one's nut** *slang* mad, crazy, or foolish 8 a person or thing that presents difficulties (esp in the phrase **a tough** *or* **hard nut to crack**) 9 a small square or hexagonal block, usu. metal, with a threaded hole through the middle for screwing on the end of a bolt 10 Also called (US and Canadian): **frog** *music* a the ledge or ridge at the upper end of the fingerboard of a violin, cello, etc, over which the strings pass to the tuning pegs b the end of a violin bow that is held by the player 11 a small usually gingery biscuit 12 *Brit* a small piece of coal ▷ *vb* nuts, nutting, nutted 13 (*intr*) to gather nuts ▷ See also **nuts** [Old English *hnutu*; related to Old Norse *hnot*, Old High German *hnuz* (German *Nuss*)]

NUT (in Britain) *abbreviation* National Union of Teachers

nutant ('njuːtᵊnt) *adj botany* having the apex hanging down [C18: from Latin *nūtāre* to nod]

nutation (njuː'teɪʃən) *n* 1 *astronomy* a periodic variation in the precession of the earth's axis causing the earth's poles to oscillate about their mean position 2 Also

called: **circumnutation** the spiral growth of a shoot, tendril, or similar plant organ, caused by variation in the growth rate in different parts 3 the act or an instance of nodding the head [C17: from Latin *nutātiō*, from *nūtāre* to nod]

nutbrown ('nʌt'braʊn) *adj* of a brownish colour, esp a reddish-brown

nutcase ('nʌtˌkeɪs) *n slang* an insane or very foolish person

nutcracker ('nʌtˌkrækə) *n* 1 (*often plural*) a device for cracking the shells of nuts 2 either of two birds, *Nucifraga caryocatactes* of the Old World or *N. columbianus* (**Clark's nutcracker**) of North America, having speckled plumage and feeding on nuts, seeds, etc: family *Corvidae* (crows)

nutgall ('nʌtˌgɔːl) *n* a nut-shaped gall caused by gall wasps on the oak and other trees

nuthatch ('nʌtˌhætʃ) *n* any songbird of the family *Sittidae*, esp *Sitta europaea*, having strong feet and bill, and feeding on insects, seeds, and nuts [C14 *notehache*, from *note* nut + *hache* hatchet, from the bird's habit of splitting nuts; see NUT, HACK[1]]

nuthouse ('nʌtˌhaʊs) *n slang* a mental hospital or asylum

nutmeg ('nʌtmɛg) *n* 1 an East Indian evergreen tree, *Myristica fragrans*, cultivated in the tropics for its hard aromatic seed: family *Myristicaceae*. See also **mace**[2] 2 the seed of this tree, used as a spice 3 a greyish-brown colour ▷ *vb* -megs, -megging, -megged (*tr*) 4 *Brit sport informal* to kick or hit the ball between the legs of (an opposing player) [C13: from Old French *nois muguede*, from Old Provençal *noz muscada* musk-scented nut, from Latin *nux* NUT + *muscus* MUSK]

nutraceutical (ˌnjuːtrə'sjuːtɪkᵊl) *n* another name for **functional food**

nutria ('njuːtrɪə) *n* another name for the **coypu**, used esp to refer to its fur [C19: from Spanish: otter, variant of *lutria*, ultimately from Latin *lūtra* otter]

nutrient ('njuːtrɪənt) *n* 1 any of the mineral substances that are absorbed by the roots of plants for nourishment 2 any substance that nourishes an organism ▷ *adj* 3 providing or contributing to nourishment [C17: from Latin *nūtrīre* to nourish]

nutriment ('njuːtrɪmənt) *n* any material providing nourishment [C16: from Latin *nūtrīmentum*, from *nūtrīre* to nourish] > **nutrimental** (ˌnjuːtrɪ'mɛntᵊl) *adj*

nutrition (njuː'trɪʃən) *n* 1 a process in animals and plants involving the intake of nutrient materials and their subsequent assimilation into the tissues 2 the act or process of nourishing 3 the study of nutrition, esp in humans [C16: from Late Latin *nūtrītiō*, from *nūtrīre* to nourish] > **nu'tritional** *or less commonly* **nutritionary** **nu'tritionary** *adj* > **nu'tritionist** *n*

nutritious (njuː'trɪʃəs) *adj* nourishing, sometimes to a high degree [C17: from Latin *nūtrīcius* nourishing, from *nūtrix* a NURSE] > **nu'tritiously** *adv* > **nu'tritiousness** *n*

nutritive ('njuːtrɪtɪv) *adj* 1 providing nourishment 2 of, concerning, or promoting nutrition ▷ *n* 3 a nutritious food

nuts (nʌts) *adj* 1 a slang word for **insane** 2 (foll by *about* or *on*) *slang* extremely fond (of) or enthusiastic (about) ▷ *interj* 3 *slang* an expression of disappointment, contempt, refusal, or defiance

nuts and bolts *pl n informal* the essential or practical details

nutshell ('nʌtˌʃɛl) *n* 1 the shell around the kernel of a nut 2 **in a nutshell** in essence; briefly

nutter ('nʌtə) *n Brit slang* a mad or eccentric person

nutty ('nʌtɪ) *adj* -tier, -tiest 1 containing or abounding in nuts 2 resembling nuts, esp in taste 3 a slang word for **insane** 4 (foll by *over* or *about*) *informal* extremely fond (of) or enthusiastic (about) > **'nuttiness** *n*

Nuuk (nuːk) *n* the capital of Greenland, in the southwest: the oldest Danish settlement in Greenland, founded in 1721. Pop: 14 350 (2004 est). Danish name (official name until 1979): **Godthaab**

Nuxalk (nuː'xɒlk) *n* a member of a Salishan Native Canadian people of British Columbia [from Salish]

nux vomica ('nʌks 'vɒmɪkə) *n* 1 an Indian spiny

loganiaceous tree, *Strychnos nux-vomica*, with orange-red berries containing poisonous seeds **2** any of the seeds of this tree, which contain strychnine and other poisonous alkaloids **3** a medicine manufactured from the seeds of this tree, formerly used as a heart stimulant [c16: from Medieval Latin: vomiting nut]

nuzzle ('nʌzᵊl) *vb* **1** to push or rub gently against the nose or snout **2** (*intr*) to nestle; lie close **3** (*tr*) to dig out with the snout [c15 *nosele*, from NOSE (n)]

NV *abbreviation* Nevada

nvCJD *abbreviation* new-variant Creutzfeld-Jakob disease

NVQ (in Britain) *abbreviation* national vocational qualification: a qualification that rewards competence in a specified type of employment

NW *symbol for* northwest(ern)

NWT *abbreviation* Northwest Territories (of Canada)

NY or **N.Y.** *abbreviation* New York (city or state)

nyala ('njɑːlə) *n, pl* **-la** or **-las** **1** a spiral-horned southern African antelope, *Tragelaphus angasi*, with a fringe of white hairs along the length of the back and neck **2** mountain nyala a similar and related Ethiopian animal, *T. buxtoni*, lacking the white crest [from Zulu]

Nyasa or **Nyassa** (nɪ'æsə, naɪ'æsə) *n* Lake Nyasa a lake in central Africa at the S end of the Great Rift Valley: the third largest lake in Africa, drained by the Shire River into the Zambezi. Area: about 28 500 sq km (11 000 sq miles)

Nyasaland (nɪ'æsə,lænd, naɪ'æsə-) *n* the former name (until 1964) of **Malawi**

NYC *abbreviation* New York City

nyctalopia (,nɪktə'ləʊpɪə) *n* inability to see normally in dim light. Nontechnical name: night blindness [c17: via Late Latin from Greek *nuktálōps*, from *nux* night + *alaos* blind + *ōps* eye]

nyctitropism (nɪk'tɪtrə,pɪzəm) *n* a tendency of some plant parts to assume positions at night that are different from their daytime positions [c19: *nyct-*, from Greek *nukt-*, *nux* night + -TROPISM]

nye (naɪ) *n* a flock of pheasants. Also called: **nide, eye** [c15: from Old French *ni*, from Latin *nīdus* nest]

Nyeman (*Russian* 'njɛmən) *n* a variant spelling of **Neman**

Nyerere (njə'rɛrɪ, nɪ-) *n* **Julius Kambarage** (kæm'bɑːrɑːgə). 1922–99, Tanzanian statesman; president (1964–85). He became prime minister of Tanganyika in 1961 and president in 1962, negotiating the union of Tanganyika and Zanzibar to form Tanzania (1964)

Nyíregyháza (*Hungarian* 'nji:rɛtjhɑːzɔ) *n* a market town in NE Hungary. Pop: 116 899 (2003 est)

Nykøbing (*Danish* 'nykø:beŋ) *n* a port in Denmark, on the W coast of Falster Island. Pop: 16 784 (2004 est)

nylon ('naɪlɒn) *n* **1** a class of synthetic polyamide materials made by copolymerizing dicarboxylic acids with diamines. They can be moulded into a variety of articles, such as combs and machine parts. Nylon monofilaments are used for bristles, etc, and nylon fibres can be spun into yarn **2** yarn or cloth made of nylon, used for clothing, stockings, etc [c20: originally a trademark]

NYLON ('naɪlɒn) *n informal* a high-earning business executive who enjoys a transatlantic lifestyle, living part of the year in New York City and part in London [c20: from N(*ew*) Y(*ork*) + Lon(*don*)]

nylons ('naɪlɒnz) *pl n* stockings made of nylon or other man-made material

Nyman ('naɪmən) *n* **Michael**. born 1944, British composer; works include the opera *The Man Who Mistook His Wife For a Hat* (1986) and scores for films, including *The Piano* (1992) and several films by Peter Greenaway

nymph (nɪmf) *n* **1** *myth* a spirit of nature envisaged as a beautiful maiden **2** *chiefly poetic* a beautiful young woman **3** the immature form of some insects, such as the dragonfly and mayfly, and certain arthropods. Nymphs resemble the adult, apart from having underdeveloped reproductive organs and (in the case of insects) wings, and develop into the adult without a pupal stage [c14: via Old French from Latin, from Greek *numphē* nymph; related to Latin *nūbere* to marry] > 'nymphal or 'nymphean *adj* > 'nymphlike *adj*

nympha ('nɪmfə) *n, pl* **-phae** (-fiː) *anatomy* either one of the labia minora [c17: from Latin: bride, NYMPH]

nymphet ('nɪmfɪt) *n* a young girl who is sexually precocious and desirable [c17 (meaning: a young nymph): diminutive of NYMPH]

nympho ('nɪmfəʊ) *n, pl* **-phos** *informal* a nymphomaniac

nympholepsy ('nɪmfə,lɛpsɪ) *n, pl* **-sies** a state of violent emotion, esp when associated with a desire for something one cannot have [c18: from NYMPHOLEPT, on the model of *epilepsy*] [c19: from Greek *numpholēptos* caught by nymphs, from *numphē* nymph + *lambanein* to seize] > ,nympho'leptic *adj* > 'nympho,lept *n*

nymphomania (,nɪmfə'meɪnɪə) *n* a neurotic condition in women in which the symptoms are a compulsion to have sexual intercourse with as many men as possible and an inability to have lasting relationships with them [c18: New Latin, from Greek *numphē* nymph + -MANIA] > ,nympho'maniac *n, adj* > nymphomaniacal (,nɪmfəʊmə'naɪəkᵊl) *adj*

Nysa ('nɪsə) *n* the Polish name for the **Neisse** (sense 1)

NYSE *abbreviation* New York Stock Exchange

nystagmus (nɪ'stægməs) *n* involuntary movement of the eye comprising a smooth drift followed by a flick back, occurring in several situations, for example after the body has been rotated or in disorders of the cerebellum [c19: New Latin, from Greek *nustagmos*]

NZ *international car registration for* New Zealand

NZEF *abbreviation* New Zealand Expeditionary Force, the New Zealand army that served throughout World War I. **2** NZEF is used to refer to the Second New Zealand Expeditionary Force, in World War II

Oo

o *or* **O** (əʊ) *n, pl* **o's, O's** *or* **Os 1** the 15th letter and fourth vowel of the modern English alphabet **2** any of several speech sounds represented by this letter, in English as in *code, pot, cow, move,* or *form* **3** another name for **nought**

O¹ *symbol for* **1** *chem* oxygen **2** a human blood type of the ABO group

O² (əʊ) *interj* **1** a variant spelling of **oh 2** an exclamation introducing an invocation, entreaty, wish, etc: *O God!; O for the wings of a dove!*

o' (ə) *prep informal or archaic* shortened form of **of:** *a cup o' tea*

O'- *prefix* (in surnames of Irish Gaelic origin) descendant of: *O'Corrigan* [from Irish Gaelic *ó, ua* descendant]

-o *suffix* forming informal and slang variants and abbreviations, esp of nouns: *wino; lie doggo; Jacko* [probably special use of OH]

-o- *connective vowel* used to connect elements in a compound word: *chromosome; filmography.* See **-i-** [from Greek, stem vowel of many nouns and adjectives in combination]

oaf (əʊf) *n* a stupid or loutish person [c17: variant of Old English *ælf* ELF] > **'oafish** *adj* > **'oafishness** *n*

Oahu (əʊ'ɑːhuː) *n* an island in central Hawaii: the third largest of the Hawaiian Islands. Chief town: Honolulu. Pop: 876 151 (2000). Area: 1574 sq km (608 sq miles)

oak (əʊk) *n* **1** any deciduous or evergreen tree or shrub of the fagaceous genus *Quercus,* having acorns as fruits and lobed leaves **2 a** the wood of any of these trees, used esp as building timber and for making furniture **b** (*as modifier*): *an oak table* **3** any of various trees that resemble the oak, such as the poison oak, silky oak, and Jerusalem oak **4** the leaves of an oak tree, worn as a garland [Old English *āc;* related to Old Norse *eik,* Old High German *eih,* Latin *aesculus*]

oak apple *or* **oak gall** *n* any of various brownish round galls on oak trees, containing the larva of certain wasps

oaked (əʊkt) *adj* relating to wine that is stored for a time in oak barrels prior to bottling

oaken ('əʊkən) *adj* made of the wood of the oak

Oakham ('əʊkəm) *n* a market town in E central England, the administrative centre of Rutland. Pop: 9620 (2001)

Oakland ('əʊklənd) *n* a port and industrial centre in W California, on San Francisco Bay; damaged by earthquake in 1989. Pop: 398 844 (2003 est)

Oakley ('əʊklı) *n* **Annie,** real name *Phoebe Anne Oakley Mozee.* 1860–1926, US markswoman

Oaks (əʊks) *n* (*functioning as singular*) **the Oaks** a horse race for fillies held annually at Epsom since 1779: one of the classics of English flat racing [named after an estate near Epsom]

oakum ('əʊkəm) *n* loose fibre obtained by unravelling old rope, used esp for caulking seams in wooden ships [Old English *ācuma,* variant of *ācumba,* literally: off-combings, from *ā-* off + *-cumba,* from *cemban* to COMB]

Oakville ('əʊkvɪl) *n* a city in SE Canada, in SE Ontario on Lake Ontario southwest of Toronto: motor-vehicle industry. Pop: 144 738 (2001)

O & M *abbreviation* organization and method (in studies of working methods)

OAP (in Britain) *abbreviation* **1** old age pension **2** old age pensioner

oar (ɔː) *n* **1 a** long shaft of wood for propelling a boat by rowing, having a broad blade that is dipped into and pulled against the water. Oars were also used for steering certain kinds of ancient sailing boats **2** short for **oarsman 3 put one's oar in** to interfere or interrupt ▷ *vb* **4** to row or propel with or as if with oars [Old English *ār,* of Germanic origin; related to Old Norse *ār*] > **'oarless** *adj* > **'oar,like** *adj*

oarfish ('ɔː,fɪʃ) *n, pl* **-fish** *or* **-fishes** a very long ribbonfish, *Regalecus glesne,* with long slender ventral fins [c19: referring to the flattened oarlike body]

oarlock ('ɔː,lɒk) *n US & Canadian* a swivelling device attached to the gunwale of a boat that holds an oar in place and acts as a fulcrum during rowing. Also called: rowlock

oarsman ('ɔːzmən) *n, pl* **-men** a man who rows, esp one who rows in a racing boat > **'oarsman,ship** *n*

OAS *abbreviation* **1** Organization of American States **2** Organisation de l'armée secrète; an organization of European settlers in Algeria who opposed Algerian independence by acts of terrorism (1961–63)

oasis (əʊ'eɪsɪs) *n, pl* **-ses** (-siːz) **1** a fertile patch in a desert occurring where the water table approaches or reaches the ground surface **2** a place of peace, safety, or happiness in the midst of trouble or difficulty [C17: via Latin from Greek, probably of Egyptian origin]

oast (əʊst) *n chiefly Brit* **1** a kiln for drying hops **2** Also called: **oast house** a building containing such kilns, usually having a conical or pyramidal roof [Old English āst; related to Old Norse *eisa* fire]

Oastler ('əʊstlə) *n* **Richard**. 1789–1861, British social reformer; he campaigned against child labour and helped achieve the ten-hour day (1847)

oat (əʊt) *n* **1** an erect annual grass, *Avena sativa*, grown in temperate regions for its edible seed **2** (*usually plural*) the seeds or fruits of this grass **3** any of various other grasses of the genus *Avena*, such as the wild oat **4** *poetic* a flute made from an oat straw **5 feel one's oats** *US & Canadian informal* **a** to feel exuberant **b** to feel self-important **6 sow one's (wild) oats** to indulge in adventure or promiscuity during youth [Old English *āte*, of obscure origin]

oatcake ('əʊt,keɪk) *n* a brittle unleavened oatmeal biscuit

oaten ('əʊtᵊn) *adj* made of oats or oat straw

Oates (əʊts) *n* **1** Captain **Lawrence Edward Grace**. 1880–1912, English explorer. He died on Scott's second Antarctic expedition **2** **Titus**. ('taɪtəs). 1649–1705, English conspirator. He fabricated the Popish Plot (1678), a supposed Catholic conspiracy to kill Charles II, burn London, and massacre Protestants. His perjury caused the execution of many innocent Catholics

oath (əʊθ) *n*, *pl* **oaths** (əʊðz) **1** a solemn pronouncement to affirm the truth of a statement or to pledge a person to some course of action, often involving a sacred being or object as witness **2** the form of such a pronouncement **3** an irreverent or blasphemous expression, esp one involving the name of a deity; curse **4 on, upon** *or* **under oath a** under the obligation of an oath **b** *law* having sworn to tell the truth, usually with one's hand on the Bible **5 take an oath** to declare formally with an oath or pledge, esp before giving evidence [Old English *āth*; related to Old Saxon, Old Frisian *ēth*, Old High German *eid*]

oatmeal ('əʊt,miːl) *n* **1** meal ground from oats, used for making porridge, oatcakes, etc **2 a** a greyish-yellow colour **b** (*as adjective*): *an oatmeal coat*

OAU *abbreviation* the former Organization of African Unity (now called the **African Union**)

Oaxaca (wə'hɑːkə; *Spanish* oa'xaka) *n* **1** a state of S Mexico, on the Pacific: includes most of the Isthmus of Tehuantepec; inhabited chiefly by Indians. Capital: Oaxaca de Juárez. Pop: 3 432 180 (2000). Area: 95 363 sq km (36 820 sq miles) **2** a city in S Mexico, capital of Oaxaca state: founded in 1486 by the Aztecs and conquered by Spain in 1521. Pop: 483 000 (2005 est)

Ob (*Russian* ɔpj) *n* a river in N central Russia, formed at Bisk by the confluence of the Biya and Katun Rivers and flowing generally north to the **Gulf of Ob** (an inlet of the Arctic Ocean): one of the largest rivers in the world, with a drainage basin of about 2 930 000 sq km (1 131 000 sq miles). Length: 3682 km (2287 miles)

OB *Brit abbreviation* **1** Old Boy **2** outside broadcast

ob. *abbreviation* **1** (on tombstones) obiit **2** obiter **3** oboe [(for sense 1) Latin: he (or she) died; (for sense 2) Latin: incidentally; in passing]

ob- *prefix* inverse or inversely: *obovate* [from Old French, from Latin *ob*. In compound words of Latin origin, *ob-* (and *oc-, of-, op-*) indicates: to, towards (*object*); against (*oppose*); away from (*obsolete*); before (*obstetric*); down, over (*obtect*); for the sake of (*obsecrate*); and is used as an intensifier (*oblong*)]

Obad. *Bible abbreviation* Obadiah

Obadiah (,əʊbə'daɪə) *n Old Testament* **1** a Hebrew prophet **2** the book containing his oracles, chiefly directed against Edom ▷ Douay spelling: **Abdias** (æb'daɪəs)

Oban ('əʊbᵊn) *n* a small port and resort in W Scotland, in Argyll and Bute on the Firth of Lorne. Pop: 8120 (2001)

Obasanjo (,ɒbə'sændʒeʊ) *n* **Olusegun** (ɒlʊ'seɪgʌn). born 1937, Nigerian politician and general; head of the military government (1976–79); president (1999–2007)

obbligato *or* **obligato** (,ɒblɪ'gɑːtəʊ) *music* ▷ *adj* **1** not to be omitted in performance ▷ *n*, *pl* **-tos** *or* **-ti** (-tiː) **2** an essential part in a score: *with oboe obbligato* [C18: from Italian, from *obbligare* to **OBLIGE**]

obconic (ɒb'kɒnɪk) *or* **obconical** *adj botany* (of a fruit or similar part) shaped like a cone and attached at the pointed end

obcordate (ɒb'kɔːdeɪt) *adj botany* heart-shaped and attached at the pointed end: *obcordate leaves*

obdurate ('ɒbdjʊrɪt) *adj* **1** not easily moved by feelings or supplication; hardhearted **2** impervious to persuasion, esp to moral persuasion [C15: from Latin *obdūrāre* to make hard, from *ob-* (intensive) + *dūrus* hard; compare **ENDURE**] ▷ **'obduracy** *or* **'obdurateness** *n* ▷ **'obdurately** *adv*

OBE *abbreviation* Officer of the Order of the British Empire (a Brit title)

obeah ('əʊbɪə) *n* another word for **obi²**

obedience (ə'biːdɪəns) *n* **1** the condition or quality of being obedient **2** the act or an instance of obeying; dutiful or submissive behaviour **3** the authority vested in a Church or similar body **4** the collective group of persons submitting to this authority

obedient (ə'biːdɪənt) *adj* obeying or willing to obey [C13: from Old French, from Latin *oboediens*, present participle of *oboedīre* to **OBEY**] ▷ **o'bediently** *adv*

obeisance (əʊ'beɪsəns, əʊ'biː-) *n* **1** an attitude of deference or homage **2** a gesture expressing obeisance [C14: from Old French *obéissant*, present participle of *obéir* to **OBEY**] ▷ **o'beisant** *adj*

obelisk ('ɒbɪlɪsk) *n* **1** a stone pillar having a square or rectangular cross section and sides that taper towards a pyramidal top, often used as a monument in ancient Egypt **2** *printing* another name for **dagger** (sense 2) [C16: via Latin from Greek *obeliskos* a little spit, from *obelos* spit] ▷ **,obe'liscal** *adj* ▷ **,obe'liskoid** *adj*

obelus ('ɒbɪləs) *n*, *pl* **-li** (-,laɪ) **1** a mark (— or ÷) used in editions of ancient documents to indicate spurious words or passages **2** another name for **dagger** (sense 2) [C14: via Late Latin from Greek *obelos* spit]

Oberammergau (*German* oːbər'amərgaʊ) *n* a village in S Germany, in Bavaria in the foothills of the Alps: famous for its Passion Play, performed by the villagers every ten years (except during the World Wars) since 1634, in thanksgiving for the end of the Black Death. Pop: 5363 (2003 est)

Oberhausen (*German* 'oːbərhauzən) *n* an industrial city in W Germany, in North Rhine-Westphalia on the Rhine-Herne Canal: site of the first ironworks in the Ruhr. Pop: 220 033 (2003 est)

Oberland ('əʊbə,lænd) *n* the lower parts of the Bernese Alps in central Switzerland, mostly in S Bern canton

Oberon ('əʊbə,rɒn) *n* (in medieval folklore) the king of the fairies, husband of Titania

Oberösterreich ('oːbər,ø:stəraɪç) *n* the German name for **Upper Austria**

obese (əʊ'biːs) *adj* excessively fat or fleshy; corpulent [C17: from Latin *obēsus*, from *ob-* (intensive) + *edere* to eat] ▷ **o'besity** *or* **o'beseness** *n*

obesogenic (əʊ'biːsə,dʒɛnɪk) *adj med* causing obesity: *an obesogenic environment*

obey (ə'beɪ) *vb* **1** to carry out (instructions or orders); comply with (demands) **2** to behave or act in accordance with (one's feelings, whims, etc) [C13: from Old French *obéir*, from Latin *oboedīre*, from *ob-* to, towards + *audīre* to hear] ▷ **o'beyer** *n*

obfuscate ('ɒbfʌs,keɪt) *vb* (*tr*) **1** to obscure or darken **2** to perplex or bewilder [C16: from Latin *ob-* (intensive) + *fuscāre* to blacken, from *fuscus* dark] ▷ **,obfus'catory** *adj* ▷ **obfuscation** (,ɒbfʌs'keɪʃən) *n*

obi¹ ('əʊbɪ) *n*, *pl* **obis** *or* **obi** a broad sash tied in a large flat bow at the back, worn by Japanese women and children as part of the national costume [C19: from Japanese]

obi² ('əʊbɪ) *or* **obeah** *n*, *pl* **obis** *or* **obeahs 1** a kind of witchcraft originating in Africa and practised by some West Indians **2** a charm or amulet used in this [of West African origin; compare Edo *obi* poison] ▷ **'obiism** *n*

obit ('ɒbɪt, 'əʊbɪt) *n informal* **1** short for **obituary 2** a memorial service

obiter dictum (ˈɒbɪtə ˈdɪktəm, ˈəʊ-) n, pl **obiter dicta** (ˈdɪktə) 1 law an observation by a judge on some point of law not directly in issue in the case before him and thus neither requiring his decision nor serving as a precedent, but nevertheless of persuasive authority 2 any comment, remark, or observation made in passing [Latin: something said in passing]

obituary (əˈbɪtjʊərɪ) n, pl -aries a published announcement of a death, often accompanied by a short biography of the dead person [c18: from Medieval Latin obituārius, from Latin obīre to fall, from ob- down + īre to go] > o'bituarist n

obj. abbreviation 1 grammar object(ive) 2 objection

object¹ (ˈɒbdʒɪkt) n 1 a tangible and visible thing 2 a person or thing seen as a focus or target for feelings, thought, etc 3 an aim, purpose, or objective 4 informal a ridiculous or pitiable person, spectacle, etc 5 philosophy that towards which cognition is directed, as contrasted with the thinking subject; anything regarded as external to the mind, esp in the external world 6 grammar a noun, pronoun, or noun phrase whose referent is the recipient of the action of a verb. See also **direct object, indirect object** 7 grammar a noun, pronoun, or noun phrase that is governed by a preposition 8 no object not a hindrance or obstacle: money is no object 9 computing a self-contained identifiable component of a software system or design [c14: from Late Latin objectus something thrown before (the mind), from Latin obicere; see OBJECT²]

object² (əbˈdʒɛkt) vb 1 (tr; takes a clause as object) to state as an objection 2 (intr; often foll by to) to raise or state an objection (to); present an argument (against) [c15: from Latin obicere, from ob- against + jacere to throw] > ob'jector n

object glass n optics another name for **objective** (sense 10)

objectify (əbˈdʒɛktɪˌfaɪ) vb -fies, -fying, -fied (tr) to represent concretely; present as an object > ˌobjectifiˈcation n

objection (əbˈdʒɛkʃən) n 1 an expression, statement, or feeling of opposition or dislike 2 a cause for such an expression, statement, or feeling 3 the act of objecting

objectionable (əbˈdʒɛkʃənəb°l) adj unpleasant, offensive, or repugnant > objectionaˈbility or ob'jectionableness n > ob'jectionably adv

objective (əbˈdʒɛktɪv) adj 1 existing independently of perception or an individual's conceptions 2 undistorted by emotion or personal bias 3 of or relating to actual and external phenomena as opposed to thoughts, feelings, etc 4 med (of disease symptoms) perceptible to persons other than the individual affected 5 grammar denoting a case of nouns and pronouns, esp in languages having only two cases, that is used to identify the direct object of a finite verb or preposition and for various other purposes. In English the objective case of pronouns is also used in many elliptical constructions (as in Poor me! Who, him?), as the subject of a gerund (as in It was me helping him), informally as a predicate complement (as in It's me), and in nonstandard use as part of a compound subject (as in Him, Larry, and me went fishing). See also **accusative** 6 of, or relating to a goal or aim ▷ n 7 the object of one's endeavours; goal; aim 8 an actual phenomenon; reality 9 grammar the objective case 10 Also called: **object glass** optics the lens or combination of lenses nearest to the object in an optical instrument ▷ Compare **subjective** > objectival (ˌɒbdʒɛkˈtaɪvəl) adj > ob'jectively adv > ˌobjec'tivity or less commonly ob'jectiveness n

objectivism (əbˈdʒɛktɪˌvɪzəm) n 1 the tendency to stress what is objective 2 philosophy the philosophical doctrine that reality is objective, and that sense data correspond with it > ob'jectivist n, adj > ˌobjectiv'istic adj

object language n a language described by or being investigated by another language. Compare **metalanguage**

object lesson n a convincing demonstration of some principle or ideal

object linking and embedding n See OLE

object program n a computer program translated from the equivalent source program into machine language by the compiler or assembler

object relations theory n a form of psychoanalytic theory postulating that people relate to others in order to develop themselves

objet d'art French (ɔbʒɛ dar) n, pl **objets d'art** (ɔbʒɛ dar) a small object considered to be of artistic worth [literally: object of art]

objurgate (ˈɒbdʒəˌgeɪt) vb (tr) to scold or reprimand [c17: from Latin objurgāre, from ob- against + jurgāre to scold] > ˌobjur'gation n > 'objur,gator n > objurgatory (ɒbˈdʒɜːgətərɪ, -trɪ) adj

oblate¹ (ˈɒbleɪt) adj having an equatorial diameter of greater length than the polar diameter: the earth is an oblate sphere. Compare **prolate** [c18: from New Latin oblātus lengthened, from Latin ob- towards + lātus, past participle of ferre to bring]

oblate² (ˈɒbleɪt) n a person dedicated to a monastic or religious life [c19: from French oblat, from Medieval Latin oblātus, from Latin offerre to OFFER]

oblation (ɒˈbleɪʃən) n Christianity 1 the offering of the bread and wine of the Eucharist to God 2 any offering made for religious or charitable purposes [c15: from Church Latin oblātiō; see OBLATE²] > oblatory (ˈɒblətərɪ, -trɪ) or ob'lational adj

obligate (ˈɒblɪˌgeɪt) vb 1 to compel, constrain, or oblige morally or legally 2 (in the US) to bind (property, funds, etc) as security ▷ adj 3 compelled, bound, or restricted 4 biology able to exist under only one set of environmental conditions [c16: from Latin obligāre to OBLIGE] > 'obligable adj > ob'ligative adj > 'obli,gator n

obligation (ˌɒblɪˈgeɪʃən) n 1 a moral or legal requirement; duty 2 the act of obligating or the state of being obligated 3 law a a written contract containing a penalty b an instrument acknowledging indebtedness to secure the repayment of money borrowed 4 a person or thing to which one is bound morally or legally 5 a service or favour for which one is indebted

obligato (ˌɒblɪˈgɑːtəʊ) adj, n music a variant spelling of **obbligato**

obligatory (ɒˈblɪgətərɪ, -trɪ) adj 1 required to be done, obtained, possessed, etc 2 of the nature of or constituting an obligation > ob'ligatorily adv

oblige (əˈblaɪdʒ) vb 1 (tr; often passive) to bind or constrain (someone to do something) by legal, moral, or physical means 2 (tr; usually passive) to make indebted or grateful (to someone) by doing a favour or service 3 to do a service or favour to (someone): she obliged the guest with a song [c13: from Old French obliger, from Latin obligāre, from ob- to, towards + ligāre to bind] > o'bliger n

obligee (ˌɒblɪˈdʒiː) n a person in whose favour an obligation, contract, or bond is created; creditor

obliging (əˈblaɪdʒɪŋ) adj ready to do favours; agreeable; kindly > o'bligingly adv > o'bligingness n

obligor (ˌɒblɪˈgɔː) n a person who binds himself by contract to perform some obligation; debtor

oblique (əˈbliːk) adj 1 at an angle; slanting; sloping 2 geometry a (of lines, planes, etc) neither perpendicular nor parallel to one another or to another line, plane, etc b not related to or containing a right angle 3 indirect or evasive 4 grammar denoting any case of nouns, pronouns, etc, other than the nominative and vocative 5 biology having asymmetrical sides or planes: an oblique leaf ▷ n 6 something oblique, esp a line 7 another name for **solidus** (sense 1) ▷ vb (intr) 8 to take or have an oblique direction 9 (of a military formation) to move forward at an angle [c15: from Old French, from Latin oblīquus, of obscure origin] > o'bliquely adv > o'bliqueness n > obliquity (əˈblɪkwɪtɪ) n > o'bliquitous adj

oblique angle n an angle that is not a right angle or any multiple of a right angle

obliterate (əˈblɪtəˌreɪt) vb (tr) to destroy every trace of; wipe out completely [c16: from Latin oblitterāre to erase, from ob- out + littera letter] > o,blite'ration n > o'bliterative adj > o'bliter,ator n

oblivion (əˈblɪvɪən) n 1 the condition of being forgotten or disregarded 2 law an intentional overlooking, esp of political offences; amnesty; pardon [c14: via Old French from Latin oblīviō forgetfulness, from oblīviscī to forget]

oblivious (əˈblɪvɪəs) *adj* (foll by *to* or *of*) unaware or forgetful ▷ ob'liviously *adv* ▷ ob'liviousness *n*
● **USAGE** It was formerly considered incorrect to use
● *oblivious* to mean *unaware*, but this use is now
● acceptable

oblong ('ɒb,lɒŋ) *adj* 1 having an elongated, esp rectangular, shape ▷ *n* 2 a figure or object having this shape [c15: from Latin *oblongus*, from *ob*- (intensive) + *longus* LONG¹]

obloquy ('ɒbləkwɪ) *n, pl* -quies 1 defamatory or censorious statements, esp when directed against one person 2 disgrace brought about by public abuse [c15: from Latin *obloquium* contradiction, from *ob*- against + *loquī* to speak]

obnoxious (əbˈnɒkʃəs) *adj* 1 extremely unpleasant 2 *obsolete* exposed to harm, injury, etc [c16: from Latin *obnoxius*, from *ob*- to + *noxa* injury, from *nocēre* to harm] ▷ ob'noxiously *adv* ▷ ob'noxiousness *n*

oboe ('əʊbəʊ) *n* 1 a woodwind instrument of the family that includes the bassoon and cor anglais, consisting of a conical tube fitted with a mouthpiece having a double reed. It has a penetrating nasal tone. Range: about two octaves plus a sixth upwards from B flat below middle C 2 a person who plays this instrument in an orchestra ▷ Archaic form: **hautboy** [c18: via Italian *oboe*, phonetic approximation to French *haut bois*, literally: high wood (referring to its pitch)] ▷ 'oboist *n*

oboe d'amore (dɑːˈmɔːreɪ) *n* a type of oboe pitched a minor third lower than the oboe itself. It is used chiefly in the performance of baroque music [Italian: oboe of love]

Obote (ɒˈbəʊteɪ, -tɪ) *n* (**Apollo**) **Milton**. 1924–2005, Ugandan politician; prime minister of Uganda (1962–66) and president (1966–71; 1980–85). He was deposed by Amin in 1971 and remained in exile until 1980; deposed again in 1985 by the Acholi army

O'Brien (əˈbraɪən) *n* 1 **Conor Cruise**. born 1917, Irish diplomat and writer. As an Irish Labour MP he served in the coalition government of 1973–77, becoming a senator (1977–79). He edited the *Observer* (1978–81) 2 **Edna**. born 1936, Irish novelist. Her books include *The Country Girls* (1960), *Johnny I Hardly Knew You* (1977), and *In the Forest* (2002) 3 **Flann**, real name Brian O'Nolan. 1911–66, Irish novelist and journalist. His novels include *At Swim-Two-Birds* (1939) and the posthumously published *The Third Policeman* (1967). As Myles na Gopaleen he wrote a satirical column for the *Irish Times* 4 **Kerry**. born 1945. Australian journalist and broadcaster

obs *abbreviation* obsolete

obscene (əbˈsiːn) *adj* 1 offensive or outrageous to accepted standards of decency or modesty 2 *law* (of publications) having a tendency to deprave or corrupt 3 disgusting; repellent [c16: from Latin *obscēnus* inauspicious, perhaps related to *caenum* filth] ▷ ob'scenely *adv*

obscenity (əbˈsɛnɪtɪ) *n, pl* -ties 1 the state or quality of being obscene 2 an obscene act, statement, word, etc

obscurant (əbˈskjʊərənt) *n* an opposer of reform and enlightenment ▷ **obscurantism** (,ɒbˈsjʊˈræntɪzəm) *n* ▷ ,obscu'rantist *n, adj*

obscure (əbˈskjʊə) *adj* 1 unclear or abstruse 2 indistinct, vague, or indefinite 3 inconspicuous or unimportant 4 hidden, secret, or remote 5 (of a vowel) reduced to or transformed into a neutral vowel (ə) 6 gloomy, dark, clouded, or dim ▷ *vb* (*tr*) 7 to make unclear, vague, or hidden 8 to cover or cloud over 9 *phonetics* to pronounce (a vowel) with articulation that causes it to become a neutral sound represented by (ə) [c14: via Old French from Latin *obscūrus* dark] ▷ **obscuration** (,ɒbskjʊˈreɪʃən) *n* ▷ ob'scurely *adv* ▷ ob'scureness *n*

obscurity (əbˈskjʊərɪtɪ) *n, pl* -ties 1 the state or quality of being obscure 2 an obscure person or thing

obsequies ('ɒbsɪkwɪz) *pl n, sing* -quy funeral rites [c14: via Anglo-Norman from Medieval Latin *obsequiae* (influenced by Latin *exsequiae*), from *obsequium* compliance]

obsequious (əbˈsiːkwɪəs) *adj* 1 obedient or attentive in an ingratiating or servile manner 2 *now rare* submissive or compliant [c15: from Latin *obsequiōsus* compliant, from

obsequium compliance, from *obsequi* to follow, from *ob*- to + *sequi* to follow] ▷ ob'sequiously *adv* ▷ ob'sequiousness *n*

observance (əbˈzɜːvəns) *n* 1 recognition of or compliance with a law, custom, practice, etc 2 a ritual, ceremony, or practice, esp of a religion 3 observation or attention 4 the degree of strictness of a religious order or community in following its rule 5 *archaic* respectful or deferential attention

observant (əbˈzɜːvənt) *adj* 1 paying close attention to detail; watchful or heedful 2 adhering strictly to rituals, ceremonies, laws, etc ▷ ob'servantly *adv*

observation (,ɒbzəˈveɪʃən) *n* 1 the act of observing or the state of being observed 2 a comment or remark 3 detailed examination of phenomena prior to analysis, diagnosis, or interpretation: *the patient was under observation* 4 the facts learned from observing 5 *navigation* **a** a sight taken with an instrument to determine the position of an observer relative to that of a given heavenly body **b** the data so taken ▷ ,obser'vational *adj* ▷ ,obser'vationally *adv*

observatory (əbˈzɜːvətərɪ, -trɪ) *n, pl* -ries 1 an institution or building specially designed and equipped for observing meteorological and astronomical phenomena 2 any building or structure providing an extensive view of its surroundings

observe (əbˈzɜːv) *vb* 1 (*tr; may take a clause as object*) to see; perceive; notice: *we have observed that you steal* 2 (when *tr, may take a clause as object*) to watch (something) carefully; pay attention to (something) 3 to make observations of (something), esp scientific ones 4 (when *intr*, usually foll by *on* or *upon*; when *tr, may take a clause as object*) to make a comment or remark: *the speaker observed that times had changed* 5 (*tr*) to abide by, keep, or follow (a custom, tradition, law, holiday, etc) [c14: via Old French from Latin *observāre*, from *ob*- to + *servāre* to watch] ▷ ob'servable *adj* ▷ ob'server *n*

obsess (əbˈsɛs) *vb* 1 (*tr; when passive, foll by with* or *by*) to preoccupy completely; haunt 2 (*intr; usually foll by on* or *over*) to worry neurotically or obsessively; brood [c16: from Latin *obsessus* besieged, past participle of *obsidēre*, from *ob*- in front of + *sedēre* to sit]

obsession (əbˈsɛʃən) *n* 1 *psychiatry* a persistent idea or impulse that continually forces its way into consciousness, often associated with anxiety and mental illness 2 a persistent preoccupation, idea, or feeling 3 the act of obsessing or the state of being obsessed ▷ ob'sessional *adj* ▷ ob'sessionally *adv*

obsessive (əbˈsɛsɪv) *adj* 1 *psychiatry* motivated by a persistent overriding idea or impulse, often associated with anxiety and mental illness 2 continually preoccupied with a particular activity, person, or thing ▷ *n* 3 *psychiatry* a person subject to obsession 4 a person who is continually preoccupied with a particular activity, person, or thing ▷ ob'sessively *adv* ▷ ob'sessiveness *n*

obsessive-compulsive disorder *n psychiatry* an anxiety disorder in which patients are driven to repeat the same act, such as washing their hands, over and over again, usually for many hours

obsidian (ɒbˈsɪdɪən) *n* a dark volcanic glass formed by very rapid solidification of lava. Also called: **Iceland agate** [c17: from Latin *obsidiānus*, erroneous transcription of *obsiānus (lapis)* (stone of) *Obsius*, the name (in Pliny) of the discoverer of a stone resembling obsidian]

obsolesce (,ɒbsəˈlɛs) *vb* (*intr*) to become obsolete

obsolescent (,ɒbsəˈlɛsᵊnt) *adj* becoming obsolete or out of date [c18: from Latin *obsolescere*; see OBSOLETE] ▷ ,obso'lescence *n*

obsolete ('ɒbsəliːt, ,ɒbsəˈliːt) *adj* 1 out of use or practice; not current 2 out of date; unfashionable or outmoded 3 *biology* (of parts, organs, etc) vestigial; rudimentary [c16: from Latin *obsolētus* worn out, past participle of *obsolēre* (unattested), from *ob*- opposite to + *solēre* to be used] ▷ 'obso,letely *adv* ▷ 'obso,leteness *n*

obstacle ('ɒbstəkᵊl) *n* 1 a person or thing that opposes or hinders something 2 *Brit* a fence or hedge used in showjumping [c14: via Old French from Latin *obstāculum*, from *obstāre*, from *ob*- against + *stāre* to stand]

obstacle race *n* a race in which competitors have to

negotiate various obstacles

obstetric (ɒb'stɛtrɪk) *or* **obstetrical** *adj* of or relating to childbirth or obstetrics [c18: via New Latin from Latin *obstetrīcius*, from *obstetrix* a midwife, literally: woman who stands opposite, from *obstāre* to stand in front of; see OBSTACLE] > ob'stetrically *adv*

obstetrician (ˌɒbstɪ'trɪʃən) *n* a physician who specializes in obstetrics

obstetrics (ɒb'stɛtrɪks) *n* (*functioning as singular*) the branch of medicine concerned with childbirth and the treatment of women before and after childbirth

obstinacy ('ɒbstɪnəsɪ) *n, pl* -cies 1 the state or quality of being obstinate 2 an obstinate act, attitude, etc

obstinate ('ɒbstɪnɪt) *adj* 1 adhering fixedly to a particular opinion, attitude, course of action, etc 2 self-willed or headstrong 3 difficult to subdue or alleviate; persistent: *an obstinate fever* [c14: from Latin *obstinātus*, past participle of *obstināre* to persist in, from *ob*- (intensive) + *stin*-, variant of *stare* to stand] > 'obstinately *adv*

obstreperous (əb'strɛpərəs) *adj* noisy or rough, esp in resisting restraint or control [c16: from Latin, from *obstrepere*, from *ob*- against + *strepere* to roar] > ob'streperously *adv* > ob'streperousness *n*

obstruct (əb'strʌkt) *vb* (*tr*) 1 to block (a road, passageway, etc) with an obstacle 2 to make (progress or activity) difficult 3 to impede or block a clear view of [c17: Latin *obstructus* built against, past participle of *obstruere*, from *ob*- against + *struere* to build] > ob'structor *n* > ob'structive *adj, n* > ob'structively *adv* > ob'structiveness *n*

obstruction (əb'strʌkʃən) *n* 1 a person or thing that obstructs 2 the act or an instance of obstructing 3 delay of business, esp in a legislature by means of procedural devices 4 *sport* the act of unfairly impeding an opposing player > ob'structional *adj*

obstructionist (əb'strʌkʃənɪst) *n* a person who deliberately obstructs business, esp in a legislature > ob'structionism *n*

obtain (əb'teɪn) *vb* 1 (*tr*) to gain possession of; acquire; get 2 (*intr*) to be customary, valid, or accepted: *a new law obtains in this case* [c15: via Old French from Latin *obtinēre* to take hold of, from *ob*- (intensive) + *tenēre* to hold] > ob'tainable *adj* > ob,taina'bility *n* > ob'tainer *n* > ob'tainment *n*

obtrude (əb'tru:d) *vb* 1 to push (oneself, one's opinions, etc) on others in an unwelcome way 2 (*tr*) to push out or forward [c16: from Latin *obtrūdere*, from *ob*- against + *trūdere* to push forward] > ob'truder *n* > obtrusion (əb'tru:ʒən) *n*

obtrusive (əb'tru:sɪv) *adj* 1 obtruding or tending to obtrude 2 sticking out; protruding; noticeable > ob'trusively *adv* > ob'trusiveness *n*

obtund (ɒb'tʌnd) *vb* (*tr*) *rare* to deaden or dull [c14: from Latin *obtundere* to beat against, from *ob*- against + *tundere* to belabour] > ob'tundent *adj, n*

obtuse (əb'tju:s) *adj* 1 mentally slow or emotionally insensitive 2 *maths* (of an angle) lying between 90° and 180° 3 not sharp or pointed 4 indistinctly felt, heard, etc; dull: *obtuse pain* 5 (of a leaf or similar flat part) having a rounded or blunt tip [c16: from Latin *obtūsus* dulled, past participle of *obtundere* to beat down; see OBTUND] > ob'tusely *adv* > ob'tuseness *n*

obverse ('ɒbvɜ:s) *adj* 1 facing or turned towards the observer 2 forming or serving as a counterpart 3 (of certain plant leaves) narrower at the base than at the top ▷ *n* 4 a counterpart or complement 5 the side of a coin that bears the main design or device 6 *logic* a categorial proposition derived from another by replacing the original predicate by its negation and changing the proposition from affirmative to negative or vice versa, as *no sum is correct* from *every sum is incorrect* [c17: from Latin *obversus* turned towards, past participle of *obvertere*, from *ob*- to + *vertere* to turn] > ob'versely *adv*

obvert (ɒb'vɜ:t) *vb* (*tr*) 1 *logic* to deduce the obverse of (a proposition) 2 *rare* to turn so as to show the main or other side [c17: from Latin *obvertere* to turn towards; see OBVERSE] > ob'version *n*

obviate ('ɒbvɪˌeɪt) *vb* (*tr*) to avoid or prevent (a need or

difficulty) [c16: from Late Latin *obviātus* prevented, past participle of *obviāre*; see OBVIOUS] > ˌobvi'ation *n*

● USAGE Only things that have not yet occurred can be
● *obviated*. For example, one can *obviate* a possible future
● difficulty, but not one that already exists

obvious ('ɒbvɪəs) *adj* 1 easy to see or understand; evident 2 exhibiting motives, feelings, intentions, etc, clearly or without subtlety 3 naive or unsubtle: *the play was rather obvious* [c16: from Latin *obvius*, from *obviam* in the way, from *ob*- against + *via* way] > 'obviousness *n*

obviously ('ɒbvɪəslɪ) *adv* 1 in a way that is easy to see or understand; evidently 2 without subtlety 3 (*sentence modifier*) it is obvious that; clearly: *obviously not everyone wants a bank account*

OC *abbreviation* Officer Commanding

o/c *abbreviation* overcharge

O Canada *n* the Canadian national anthem

ocarina (ˌɒkə'ri:nə) *n* an egg-shaped wind instrument with a protruding mouthpiece and six to eight finger holes, producing an almost pure tone [c19: from Italian: little goose, from *oca* goose, ultimately from Latin *avis* bird]

O'Casey (əʊ'keɪsɪ) *n* Sean (ʃɔ:n). 1880–1964, Irish dramatist. His plays include *Juno and the Paycock* (1924) and *The Plough and the Stars* (1926), which are realistic pictures of Dublin slum life

Occam ('ɒkəm) *n* a variant spelling of (William of) Ockham

Occam's razor *n* a variant spelling of **Ockham's razor**

occasion (ə'keɪʒən) *n* 1 (sometimes foll by *of*) the time of a particular happening or event 2 (sometimes foll by *for*) a reason or cause (to do or be something); grounds 3 an opportunity (to do something); chance 4 a special event, time, or celebration: *the party was quite an occasion* 5 on occasion every so often 6 rise to the occasion to have the courage, wit, etc, to meet the special demands of a situation 7 take occasion to avail oneself of an opportunity (to do something) ▷ *vb* 8 (*tr*) to bring about, esp incidentally or by chance [c14: from Latin *occāsiō* a falling down, from *occidere*, from *ob*- down + *cadere* to fall]

occasional (ə'keɪʒənəl) *adj* 1 taking place from time to time; not frequent or regular 2 of, for, or happening on special occasions 3 serving as an occasion (for something)

occasionally (ə'keɪʒənəlɪ) *adv* from time to time

occasional table *n* a small table with no regular use

occident ('ɒksɪdənt) *n* a literary or formal word for **west** See **orient** [c14: via Old French from Latin *occidere* to fall, go down (with reference to the setting sun); see OCCASION]

Occident ('ɒksɪdənt) *n* the Occident 1 the countries of Europe and America 2 the western hemisphere > Occidental (ˌɒksɪ'dəntəl) *adj, n*

occidental (ˌɒksɪ'dɛntəl) *adj* a literary or formal word for **western**

occipital (ɒk'sɪpɪtəl) *adj* 1 of or relating to the back of the head or skull ▷ *n* 2 short for **occipital bone**

occipital bone *n* the saucer-shaped bone that forms the back part of the skull and part of its base

occipital lobe *n* the posterior portion of each cerebral hemisphere, concerned with the interpretation of visual sensory impulses

occiput ('ɒksɪˌpʌt, -pət) *n, pl* occiputs *or* occipita (ɒk'sɪpɪtə) the back part of the head or skull [c14: from Latin, from *ob*- at the back of + *caput* head]

occlude (ə'klu:d) *vb* 1 (*tr*) to block or stop up (a passage or opening); obstruct 2 (*tr*) to prevent the passage of 3 (*tr*) *chem* (of a solid) to incorporate (a substance) by absorption or adsorption 4 *meteorol* to form or cause to form an occluded front 5 *dentistry* to produce or cause to produce occlusion, as in chewing [c16: from Latin *occlūdere*, from *ob*- (intensive) + *claudere* to close] > oc'cludent *adj*

occluded front *n* *meteorol* the line or plane occurring where the cold front of a depression has overtaken the warm front, raising the warm sector from ground level. Also called: **occlusion**

occlusion (ə'klu:ʒən) *n* 1 the act or process of occluding or the state of being occluded 2 *meteorol* another term for **occluded front** 3 *dentistry* the normal position of the teeth when the jaws are closed ▷ o'cclusive *adj, n*

occult *adj* (ɒ'kʌlt, 'ɒkʌlt) 1 a of or characteristic of magical, mystical, or supernatural arts, phenomena, or influences b (*as noun*): *the occult* 2 beyond ordinary human understanding 3 secret or esoteric ▷ *vb* (ɒ'kʌlt) 4 *astronomy* (of a celestial body) to hide (another celestial body) from view by occultation or (of a celestial body) to become hidden by occultation 5 to hide or become hidden or shut off from view 6 (*intr*) (of lights, esp in lighthouses) to shut off at regular intervals [c16: from Latin *occultus*, past participle of *occulere*, from *ob-* over, up + *-culere*, related to *celāre* to conceal] ▷ oc'cultness *n* ▷ 'occul,tism *n* ▷ 'occultist *n, adj*

occultation (,ɒkʌl'teɪʃən) *n* the temporary disappearance of one celestial body as it moves out of sight behind another body

occupancy ('ɒkjʊpənsɪ) *n, pl* **-cies** 1 the act of occupying; possession of a property 2 *law* the possession and use of property by or without agreement and without any claim to ownership 3 *law* the act of taking possession of unowned property, esp land, with the intent of thus acquiring ownership 4 the condition or fact of being an occupant, esp a tenant 5 the period of time during which one is an occupant, esp of property

occupant ('ɒkjʊpənt) *n* 1 a person, thing, etc, holding a position or place 2 *law* a person who has possession of something, esp an estate, house, etc; tenant 3 *law* a person who acquires by occupancy the title to something previously without an owner

occupation (,ɒkjʊ'peɪʃən) *n* 1 a person's regular work or profession; job or principal activity 2 any activity on which time is spent by a person 3 the act of occupying or the state of being occupied 4 the control of a country by a foreign military power 5 the period of time that a nation, place, or position is occupied 6 (*modifier*) for the use of the occupier of a particular property: *occupation road; occupation bridge* ▷ ,occu'pational *adj* ▷ ,occu'pationally *adv*

occupational psychology *n psychol* the study of human behaviour at work, including ergonomics, selection procedures, and the effects of stress

occupational therapy *n med* treatment of people with physical, emotional, or social problems, using purposeful activity to help them overcome or learn to deal with their problems

occupation groupings *pl n* a system of classifying people according to occupation, based originally on information obtained by government census and subsequently developed by market research. The classifications are used by the advertising industry to identify potential markets. The groups are **A, B, C1, C2, D,** and **E**

occupier ('ɒkjʊ,paɪə) *n* 1 *Brit* a person who is in possession or occupation of a house or land 2 a person or thing that occupies

occupy ('ɒkjʊ,paɪ) *vb* **-pies, -pying, -pied** (*tr*) 1 to live or be established in (a house, flat, office, etc) 2 (*often passive*) to keep (a person) busy or engrossed; engage the attention of 3 (*often passive*) to take up (a certain amount of time or space) 4 to take and hold possession of, esp as a demonstration: *students occupied the college buildings* 5 to fill or hold (a position or rank) [c14: from Old French *occuper*, from Latin *occupāre* to seize hold of, from *ob-* (intensive) + *capere* to take]

occur (ə'kɜː) *vb* **-curs, -curring, -curred** (*intr*) 1 to happen; take place; come about 2 to be found or be present; exist 3 (foll by *to*) to be realized or thought of (by); suggest itself (to) [c16: from Latin *occurrere* to run up to, from *ob-* to + *currere* to run]

● **USAGE** It is usually regarded as incorrect to talk of pre-
● arranged events *occurring* or *happening*: *the wedding took*
● *place* (not *occurred* or *happened*) *in the afternoon*

occurrence (ə'kʌrəns) *n* 1 something that occurs; a happening; event 2 the act or an instance of occurring: *a crime of frequent occurrence*

OCD *abbreviation* obsessive-compulsive disorder

ocean ('əʊʃən) *n* 1 a very large stretch of sea, esp one of the five oceans of the world, the Atlantic, Pacific,

Indian, Arctic, and Antarctic 2 the body of salt water covering approximately 70 per cent of the earth's surface 3 a huge quantity or expanse: *an ocean of replies* 4 *literary* the sea [c13: via Old French from Latin *ōceanus*, from Greek *ōkeanos* OCEANUS]

oceanarium (,əʊʃə'nɛərɪəm) *n, pl* **-iums** or **-ia** (-ɪə) a large saltwater aquarium for marine life

ocean-going *adj* (of a ship, boat, etc) suited for travel on the open ocean

Oceania (,əʊʃɪ'ɑːnɪə) *n* the islands of the central and S Pacific, including Melanesia, Micronesia, and Polynesia: sometimes also including Australasia and the Malay Archipelago ▷ Oceanian *adj, n*

oceanic (,əʊʃɪ'ænɪk) *adj* 1 of or relating to the ocean 2 living in the depths of the ocean beyond the continental shelf at a depth exceeding 200 metres: *oceanic fauna* 3 huge or overwhelming

Oceanid (əʊ'sɪənɪd) *n, pl* **Oceanids** or **Oceanides** (,əʊsɪ'ænɪ,diːz) *Greek myth* any of the ocean nymphs born of Oceanus and Tethys

oceanography (,əʊʃə'nɒgrəfɪ, ,əʊʃɪə-) *n* the branch of science dealing with the physical, chemical, geological, and biological features of the oceans and ocean basins ▷ ,ocean'ographer *n* ▷ oceanographic (,əʊʃənə'græfɪk, ,əʊʃɪə-) or ,oceano'graphical *adj*

oceanology (,əʊʃə'nɒlədʒɪ, ,əʊʃɪə-) *n* the study of the sea, esp of its economic geography

Oceanus (əʊ'sɪənəs) *n Greek myth* a Titan, divinity of the stream believed to flow around the earth

ocellus (ɒ'sɛləs) *n, pl* **-li** (-laɪ) 1 the simple eye of insects and some other invertebrates, consisting basically of light-sensitive cells 2 any eyelike marking in animals, such as the eyespot on the tail feather of a peacock [c19: via New Latin from Latin: small eye, from *oculus* eye] ▷ o'cellar *adj* ▷ ocellate ('ɒsɪ,leɪt) ocellated ('ɒsɪ,leɪtɪd) *adj* ▷ ,ocel'lation *n*

ocelot ('ɒsɪ,lɒt, 'əʊ-) *n* a feline mammal, *Felis pardalis*, inhabiting the forests of Central and South America and having a dark-spotted buff-brown coat [c18: via French from Nahuatl *ocelotl* jaguar]

och (ɒx) *interj* *Scot & Irish* an expression of surprise, contempt, annoyance, impatience, or disagreement

oche ('ɒkɪ) *n darts* the mark or ridge on the floor behind which a player must stand to throw [of unknown origin; perhaps connected with obsolete *oche* to chop off, from Old French *ocher* to cut a notch in]

ochlocracy (ɒk'lɒkrəsɪ) *n, pl* **-cies** rule by the mob; mobocracy [c16: via French, from Greek *okhlokratia*, from *okhlos* mob + *kratos* power] ▷ ochlocrat ('ɒklə,kræt) *n* ▷ ochlocratic (,ɒklə'krætɪk) *adj*

ochone (ɒ'xəʊn) *interj* *Scot & Irish* an expression of sorrow or regret [from Gaelic *ochóin*]

ochre or *US* **ocher** ('əʊkə) *n* 1 any of various natural earths containing ferric oxide, silica, and alumina: used as yellow or red pigments 2 a a moderate yellow-orange to orange colour b (*as adjective*): *an ochre dress* ▷ *vb* 3 (*tr*) to colour with ochre [c15: from Old French *ocre*, from Latin *ōchra*, from Greek *ōkhra*, from *ōkhros* pale yellow] ▷ ochreous ('əʊkrɪəs, 'əʊkərəs), 'ochrous, ochry ('əʊkərɪ, 'əʊkrɪ) or *US* 'ocherous, 'ochery *adj*

-ock *suffix forming nouns* indicating smallness: *hillock* [Old English *-oc, -uc*]

Ockeghem or **Okeghem** ('ɒkə,gɛm; *Dutch* 'ɔkəxəm) *n* **Johannes** (joː'hɑnəs), **Jean d'** (ʒɑ̃ d), or **Jan van** (jɑn vɑn). ?1430–?95, Flemish composer. Also called: Ockenheim ('ɒkən,haɪm)

ocker ('ɒkə) *Austral slang* ▷ *n* 1 (*often capital*) an uncultivated or boorish Australian ▷ *adj, adv* 2 typical of such a person [c20: of uncertain origin]

Ockham or **Occam** ('ɒkəm) *n* **William of.** died ?1349, English nominalist philosopher, who contested the temporal power of the papacy and ended the conflict between nominalism and realism. See **Ockham's razor**

Ockham's razor or **Occam's razor** ('ɒkəmz) *n* a maxim, attributed to William of Ockham, stating that in explaining something assumptions must not be needlessly multiplied. Also called: **the principle of economy**

o'clock (ə'klɒk) *adv* 1 used after a number from one to twelve to indicate the hour of the day or night **2** used after a number to indicate direction or position relative to the observer, twelve o'clock being directly ahead or overhead and other positions being obtained by comparisons with a clock face [c18: abbreviation for *of the clock*]

O'Connell (əʊˈkɒnʲl) *n* Daniel. 1775–1847, Irish nationalist leader and orator, whose election to the British House of Commons (1828) forced the acceptance of Catholic emancipation (1829)

O'Connor (əʊˈkɒnə) *n* **1 Feargus**. 1794–1855, Irish politician and journalist, a leader of the Chartist movement **2 (Mary) Flannery**. 1925–64, US novelist and short-story writer, author of *Wise Blood* (1952) and *The Violent Bear it Away* (1960) **3 Frank**, real name *Michael O'Donovan*. 1903–66, Irish short- story writer and critic **4 Thomas Power**, known as *Tay Pay*. 1848–1929, Irish journalist and nationalist leader

OCR *abbreviation* optical character reader *or* recognition

Oct *abbreviation* October

oct- *combining form* a variant of **octo-** before a vowel

octa- *combining form* a variant of **octo-**

octad (ˈɒktæd) *n* **1** a group or series of eight **2** *chem* an element or group with a valency of eight [c19: from Greek *oktās*, from *oktō* eight] > **oc'tadic** *adj*

octagon (ˈɒktəgən) *or less commonly* **octangle** (ˈɒktæŋɡʲl) *n* a polygon having eight sides [c17: via Latin from Greek *oktagōnos*, having eight angles] > **octagonal** (ɒkˈtægənʲl) *adj*

octahedron (ˌɒktəˈhiːdrən) *n, pl* **-drons** *or* **-dra** (-drə) a solid figure having eight plane faces

octal notation *or* **octal** (ˈɒktəl) *n* a number system having a base 8: often used in computing, one octal digit being equivalent to a group of three bits

octane (ˈɒkteɪn) *n* a liquid alkane hydrocarbon found in petroleum and existing in 18 isomeric forms, esp the isomer *n*-octane. Formula: C_8H_{18}

octane number *or* **octane rating** *n* a measure of the quality of a petrol expressed as the percentage of isooctane in a mixture of isooctane and *n*-heptane that gives a fuel with the same antiknock qualities as the given petrol

octant (ˈɒktənt) *n* **1** *maths* **a** any of the eight parts into which the three planes containing the Cartesian coordinate axes divide space **b** an eighth part of a circle **2** *astronomy* the position of a celestial body when it is at an angular distance of 45° from another body **3** an instrument used for measuring angles, similar to a sextant but having a graduated arc of 45° [c17: from Latin *octans* half quadrant, from *octo* eight]

octavalent (ˌɒktəˈveɪlənt) *adj* *chem* having a valency of eight

octave (ˈɒktɪv) *n* **1 a** the interval between two musical notes one of which has twice the pitch of the other and lies eight notes away from it counting inclusively along the diatonic scale **b** one of these two notes, esp the one of higher pitch **c** (*as modifier*): *an octave leap* **2** *prosody* a rhythmic group of eight lines of verse **3** (ˈɒkteɪv) **a** a feast day and the seven days following **b** the final day of this period **4** the eighth of eight basic intervals in fencing **5** any set or series of eight ▷ *adj* **6** consisting of eight parts [c14: (originally: eighth day) via Old French from Medieval Latin *octāva diēs* eighth day (after a festival), from Latin *octo* eight]

Octavia (ɒkˈteɪvɪə) *n* died 11 BC, wife of Mark Antony; sister of Augustus

Octavian (ɒkˈteɪvɪən) *n* the name of **Augustus** before he became emperor (27 BC).

octavo (ɒkˈteɪvəʊ) *n, pl* **-vos 1** Also called: **eightvo** a book size resulting from folding a sheet of paper of a specified size to form eight leaves: *demi-octavo*. Often written 8vo, 8° **2** a book of this size [c16: from New Latin phrase *in octavo* in an eighth (of a whole sheet)]

octennial (ɒkˈtɛnɪəl) *adj* **1** occurring every eight years **2** lasting for eight years [c17: from Latin *octennium* eight years, from *octo* eight + *annus* year] > **oc'tennially** *adv*

octet (ɒkˈtɛt) *n* **1** any group of eight, esp eight singers or musicians **2** a piece of music composed for such a group **3** *prosody* another word for **octave** (sense 2) **4** *chem* a

group of eight electrons forming a stable shell in an atom [c19: from Latin *octo* eight, on the model of DUET]

octillion (ɒkˈtɪljən) *n* **1** (in Britain and Germany) the number represented as one followed by 48 zeros (10^{48}) **2** (in the US, Canada, and France) the number represented as one followed by 27 zeros (10^{27}) [c17: from French, on the model of MILLION] > **oc'tillionth** *adj*

octo-, **octa-** *or before a vowel* **oct-** *combining form* eight: *octosyllabic*; *octangion* [from Latin *octo*, Greek *oktō*]

October (ɒkˈtəʊbə) *n* the tenth month of the year, consisting of 31 days [Old English, from Latin, from *octo* eight, since it was the eighth month in Roman reckoning]

Octobrist (ɒkˈtəʊbrɪst) *n* a member of a Russian political party favouring the constitutional reforms granted in a manifesto issued by Nicholas II in Oct 1905

octocentenary (ˌɒktəʊsɛnˈtiːnərɪ) *n, pl* **-naries** an eight-hundredth anniversary

octogenarian (ˌɒktəʊdʒɪˈnɛərɪən) *n, pl* **-narians 1** a person who is from 80 to 89 years old ▷ *adj* **2** of or relating to an octogenarian [c19: from Latin *octōgēnārius* containing eighty, from *octōgēnī* eighty each]

octopus (ˈɒktəpəs) *n, pl* **-puses 1** any cephalopod mollusc of the genera *Octopus*, *Eledone*, etc, having a soft oval body with eight long suckered tentacles and occurring at the sea bottom: order *Octopoda* (octopods) **2** a powerful influential organization with far-reaching effects, esp harmful ones [c18: via New Latin from Greek *oktōpous* having eight feet]

octoroon *or* **octaroon** (ˌɒktəˈruːn) *n* a person having one quadroon and one White parent and therefore having one-eighth Black blood. ▷ Compare **quadroon** [c19: OCTO- + -*roon* as in QUADROON]

octosyllable (ˈɒktəˌsɪləbʲl) *n* **1** a line of verse composed of eight syllables **2** a word of eight syllables > **octosyllabic** (ˌɒktəsɪˈlæbɪk) *adj*

octroi (ˈɒktrwɑː) *n* **1** (in some European countries, esp France) a duty on various goods brought into certain towns or cities **2** the place where such a duty is collected **3** the officers responsible for its collection [c17: from French *octroyer* to concede, from Medieval Latin *auctorizāre* to AUTHORIZE]

octuple (ˈɒktjʊpʲl) *n* **1** a quantity or number eight times as great as another ▷ *adj* **2** eight times as much or as many **3** consisting of eight parts ▷ *vb* **4** (*tr*) to multiply by eight [c17: from Latin *octuplus*, from *octo* eight + -*plus* as in *duplus* double]

ocular (ˈɒkjʊlə) *adj* **1** of or relating to the eye ▷ *n* **2** another name for **eyepiece** [c16: from Latin *oculāris* from *oculus* eye] > **'ocularly** *adv*

ocularist (ˈɒkjʊlərɪst) *n* a person who makes artificial eyes

oculate (ˈɒkjʊˌleɪt) *adj* *zoology* **1** possessing eyes **2** relating to or resembling eyes: *oculate markings*

oculist (ˈɒkjʊlɪst) *n* *med* a former term for **ophthalmologist** [c17: via French from Latin *oculus* eye]

od (ɒd, əʊd), **odyl** *or* **odyle** (ˈɒdɪl) *n* *archaic* a hypothetical force formerly thought to be responsible for many natural phenomena, such as magnetism, light, and hypnotism [c19: coined arbitrarily by Baron Karl von Reichenbach (1788–1869), German scientist] > **'odic** *adj*

OD[1] (ˌəʊˈdiː) *informal n* **1** an overdose of a drug ▷ *vb* **OD's**, **OD'ing**, **OD'd 2** (*intr*) to take an overdose of a drug [c20: from *o*(*ver*)*d*(*ose*)]

OD[2] *abbreviation* **1** Officer of the Day **2** ordnance datum **3** outside diameter **4** Also: **o.d.** military olive drab **5** Also: **O/D** banking **a** on demand **b** overdrawn

odalisque *or* **odalisk** (ˈəʊdəlɪsk) *n* a female slave or concubine [c17: via French, changed from Turkish *ōdalik*, from *ōdah* room + -*lik* n suffix]

Oda Nobunaga (ˈəʊdə ˌnɒbjuːˈnɑːɡə) *n* 1534–82, Japanese general and feudal leader, who unified much of Japan under his control: assassinated

odd (ɒd) *adj* **1** unusual or peculiar in appearance, character, etc **2** occasional, incidental, or random: *odd jobs* **3** leftover or additional: *odd bits of wool* **4 a** not divisible by two **b** represented or indicated by a number that is not divisible by two: *graphs are on odd pages*.

Compare **even**[1] (sense 7) **5** being part of a matched pair or set when the other or others are missing: *an odd sock; odd volumes* **6** (*in combination*) used to designate an indefinite quantity more than the quantity specified in round numbers: *fifty-odd pounds* **7** out-of-the-way or secluded: *odd corners* **8 odd man out** a person or thing excluded from others forming a group, unit, etc ▷ *n* **9** *golf* **a** one stroke more than the score of one's opponent **b** an advantage or handicap of one stroke added to or taken away from a player's score **10** a thing or person that is odd in sequence or number ▷ See also **odds** [C14: *odde*: from Old Norse *oddi* point, angle, triangle, third or odd number. Compare Old Norse *oddr* point, spot, place; Old English *ord* point, beginning] > '**oddly** *adv* > '**oddness** *n*

oddball ('ɒd,bɔ:l) *informal* ▷ *n* **1** Also called: **odd bod, odd fish** a strange or eccentric person ▷ *adj* **2** strange or peculiar

Oddfellow ('ɒd,fɛləʊ) *n* a member of the **Independent Order of Oddfellows**, a secret benevolent and fraternal association founded in England in the 18th century

oddity ('ɒdɪtɪ) *n, pl* **-ties 1** an odd person or thing **2** an odd quality or characteristic **3** the condition of being odd

odd-jobman *or* **odd-jobber** *n, pl* **-men** *or* **-bers** a person who does casual work, esp domestic repairs

odd-man rush *n ice hockey* an attacking move when the defence is outnumbered by the opposing team

oddment ('ɒdmənt) *n* (*often plural*) an odd piece or thing; leftover

odds (ɒdz) *pl n* **1** (foll by *on* or *against*) the probability, expressed as a ratio, that a certain event will take place: *the odds against the outsider are a hundred to one* **2** the amount, expressed as a ratio, by which the wager of one better is greater than that of another: *he was offering odds of five to one* **3** the likelihood that a certain state of affairs will be found to be so: *the odds are that he is drunk* **4** an equalizing allowance, esp one given to a weaker side in a contest **5** *Brit* a significant difference (esp in the phrase **it makes no odds**) **6 at odds** on bad terms **7 give** *or* **lay odds** to offer a bet with favourable odds **8 take odds** to accept such a bet **9 over the odds** a more than is expected, necessary, etc **b** unfair or excessive **10 what's the odds?** *Brit informal* what difference does it make?

odds and ends *pl n* miscellaneous items or articles

odds-on *adj* **1** (of a chance, horse, etc) rated at even money or less to win **2** regarded as more or most likely to win, succeed, happen, etc

ode (əʊd) *n* **1** a lyric poem, typically addressed to a particular subject, with lines of varying lengths and complex rhythms **2** (formerly) a poem meant to be sung [C16: via French from Late Latin *ōda*, from Greek *ōidē*, from *aeidein* to sing]

-ode[1] *n combining form* denoting resemblance: *nematode* [from Greek *-ōdēs*, from *eidos* shape, form]

-ode[2] *n combining form* denoting a path or way: *electrode* [from Greek *-odos*, from *hodos* a way]

Odense (*Danish* 'o:dənsə) *n* a port in S Denmark, on Funen Island: cathedral founded by King Canute in the 11th century. Pop: 145 554 (2004 est)

Oder ('əʊdə) *n* a river in central Europe, rising in the NE Czech Republic and flowing north and west, forming part of the border between Germany and Poland, to the Baltic. Length: 913 km (567 miles). Czech and Polish name: **Odra**

Oder-Neisse Line ('əʊdə'naɪsə) *n* the present-day boundary between Germany and Poland along the Rivers Oder and Neisse. Established in 1945, it originally separated the Soviet Zone of Germany from the regions under Polish administration

Odessa (əʊ'dɛsə; *Russian* a'djesə) *n* a port in S Ukraine on the Black Sea: the chief Russian grain port in the 19th century; university (1865); industrial centre and important naval base. Pop: 1 010 000 (2005 est)

Odets (əʊ'dɛts) *n* Clifford. 1906–63, US dramatist; founder member of the Group Theatre. His plays include *Waiting for Lefty* (1935) and *Golden Boy* (1937)

odeum ('əʊdɪəm) *n, pl* **odea** ('əʊdɪə) (esp in ancient

Greece and Rome) a building for musical performances. Also called: **odeon** [C17: from Latin, from Greek *ōideion*, from *ōidē* ODE]

Odin ('əʊdɪn) *or* **Othin** ('əʊðɪn) *n Norse myth* the supreme creator god; the divinity of wisdom, culture, war, and the dead. Germanic counterpart: Wotan, Woden

odious ('əʊdɪəs) *adj* offensive; repugnant [C17: from Latin; see ODIUM] > '**odiousness** *n*

odium ('əʊdɪəm) *n* **1** the dislike accorded to a hated person or thing **2** hatred; repugnance [C17: from Latin; related to *ōdī* I hate, Greek *odussasthai* to be angry]

Odoacer (,ɒdə'eɪsə) *or* **Odovacar** (,əʊdə'va:kə) *n* ?434–493 AD, barbarian ruler of Italy (476–493); assassinated by Theodoric

odometer (ɒ'dɒmɪtə, əʊ-) *n US & Canadian* a device that records the number of miles that a bicycle or motor vehicle has travelled. Also called: **mileometer** [C18 *hodometer*, from Greek *hodos* way + -METER] > o'**dometry** *n*

-odont *adj and n combining form* having teeth of a certain type; -toothed: *acrodont* [from Greek *odōn* tooth]

odonto- *or before a vowel* **odont-** *combining form* indicating a tooth or teeth: *odontology* [from Greek *odōn* tooth]

odontoglossum (ɒ,dɒntə'glɒsəm) *n* any epiphytic orchid of the tropical American genus *Odontoglossum*, having clusters of brightly coloured flowers

odontology (,ɒdɒn'tɒlədʒɪ) *n* the branch of science concerned with the anatomy, development, and diseases of teeth and related structures > **odontological** (ɒ,dɒntə'lɒdʒɪkəl) *adj* > ,**odon'tologist** *n*

odoriferous (,əʊdə'rɪfərəs) *adj* having or emitting an odour, esp a fragrant one > ,**odor'iferously** *adv* > ,**odor'iferousness** *n*

odoriphore (əʊ'dɒrɪ,fɔ:) *n chem* the group of atoms in an odorous molecule responsible for its odour

odorous ('əʊdərəs) *adj* having or emitting a characteristic smell or odour > '**odorously** *adv* > '**odorousness** *n*

odour *or US* **odor** ('əʊdə) *n* **1** the property of a substance that gives it a characteristic scent or smell **2** a pervasive quality about something: *an odour of dishonesty* **3** repute or regard (in the phrases **in good odour, in bad odour**) [C13: from Old French *odur*, from Latin *odor*; related to Latin *olēre* to smell, Greek *ōzein*] > '**odourless** *or US* '**odorless** *adj*

Odovacar (,əʊdə'va:kə) *n* same as **Odoacer**

Odra ('ɒdra) *n* the Czech and Polish name for the **Oder**

Odysseus (ə'di:sɪəs) *n Greek myth* one of the foremost of the Greek heroes at the siege of Troy, noted for his courage and ingenuity. His return to his kingdom of Ithaca was fraught with adventures in which he lost all his companions and he was acknowledged by his wife Penelope only after killing her suitors. Roman name: Ulysses

Odyssey ('ɒdɪsɪ) *n* **1** a Greek epic poem, attributed to Homer (c. 800 BC), describing the ten-year homeward wanderings of Odysseus after the fall of Troy **2** (*often not capital*) any long eventful journey > **Odyssean** (,ɒdɪ'si:ən) *adj*

Oe *symbol for* oersted

Oë ('aʊɪ) *n* Kenzaburo (kɛnzə'bʊraʊ). born 1932, Japanese novelist and writer; his books include *The Catch* (1958), *A Personal Matter* (1964), and *Silent Cry* (1989): Nobel prize for literature 1994

OE *abbreviation* Old English (language)

OECD *abbreviation* Organization for Economic Cooperation and Development; an association of 21 nations to promote growth and trade, set up in 1961 to supersede the OEEC

OECS *abbreviation* Organisation of Eastern Caribbean States

OED *abbreviation* Oxford English Dictionary

oedema *or* **edema** (ɪ'di:mə) *n, pl* **-mata** (-mətə) **1** *pathol* an excessive accumulation of serous fluid in the intercellular spaces of tissue **2** *plant pathol* an abnormal swelling in a plant caused by a large mass of parenchyma or an accumulation of water in the tissues [C16: via New Latin from Greek *oidēma*, from *oidein* to swell] > **oedematous, edematous** (ɪ'dɛmətəs) *or* oe'**dema,tose, e'dema,tose** *adj*

Oedipus ('i:dɪpəs) n Greek myth the son of Laius and Jocasta, the king and queen of Thebes, who killed his father, being unaware of his identity, and unwittingly married his mother, by whom he had four children. When the truth was revealed, he put out his eyes and Jocasta killed herself

Oedipus complex n psychoanal a group of emotions, usually unconscious, involving the desire of a child, esp a male child, to possess sexually the parent of the opposite sex while excluding the parent of the same sex >'oedipal or,oedi'pean adj

OEEC abbreviation Organization for European Economic Cooperation; an organization of European nations set up in 1948 to allocate postwar US aid and to stimulate trade and cooperation. It was superseded by the OECD in 1961

Oehlenschläger or**Öhlenschläger** (Danish 'øːlənslɛːgər) n **Adam Gottlob** ('adam 'gɔtlɔp). 1779–1850, Danish romantic poet and dramatist

OEM abbreviation original equipment manufacturer: a computer company whose products are made by customizing basic parts supplied by others

oenology or**renology** (i:'nɒlədʒɪ) n the study of wine [c19: from Greek oinos wine + -LOGY] >oenological or enological (,i:nə'lɒdʒɪkəl) adj >oe'nologist ore'nologist n

Oenone (i:'nəʊnɪ) n Greek myth a nymph of Mount Ida, whose lover Paris left her for Helen

oenothera (,i:nə'θɪərə) n any plant of the large taxonomically complicated American genus Oenothera, typically having yellow flowers that open in the evening: family Onagraceae. See **evening primrose**

o'er (ɔː, əʊə) prep, adv a poetic contraction of over

oersted ('ɜːstɛd) n the cgs unit of magnetic field strength; the field strength that would cause a unit magnetic pole to experience a force of 1 dyne in a free space. It is equivalent to 79.58 amperes per metre. Symbol: Oe [c20: named after H. C. Oersted (1777–1851), Danish physicist, who discovered electromagnetism]

oesophagus or US**esophagus** (i:'sɒfəgəs) n, pl-gi (-ˌgaɪ) the part of the alimentary canal between the pharynx and the stomach; gullet [c16: via New Latin from Greek oisophagos, from oisein, future infinitive of pherein to carry + -phagos, from phagein to eat] >oesophageal or US esophageal (i:,sɒfə'dʒiːəl) adj

oestradiol (,i:strə'daɪɒl, ,ɛstrə-) or US**estradiol** n the most potent oestrogenic hormone secreted by the mammalian ovary: synthesized and used to treat oestrogen deficiency and cancer of the breast. Formula: $C_{18}H_{24}O_2$ [c20: from New Latin, from OESTRIN + DI-^{1} + -OL^1]

oestrin ('i:strɪn, 'ɛstrɪn) or US**estrin** n an obsolete term for **oestrogen** [c20: from OESTR(US) + -IN]

oestrogen ('i:strədʒən, 'ɛstrə-) or US**estrogen** n any of several steroid hormones, that are secreted chiefly by the ovaries and placenta, that induce oestrus, stimulate changes in the female reproductive organs during the oestrous cycle, and promote development of female secondary sexual characteristics [c20: from OESTRUS + -GEN] >oestrogenic (,i:strə'dʒɛnɪk, ,ɛstrə-) or US estrogenic (,ɛstrə'dʒɛnɪk, ,i:strə-) adj >,oestro'genically or US,estro'genically adv

oestrous cycle ('i:strəs, 'ɛstrəs) n a hormonally controlled cycle of activity of the reproductive organs in many female mammals. The follicular stage (growth of the Graafian follicles, thickening of the lining of the uterus, secretion of oestrogen, and ovulation, is succeeded by the luteal phase (formation of the corpus luteum and secretion of progesterone), followed by regression and a return to the first stage

oestrus ('i:strəs, 'ɛstrəs), US**estrus** or**estrum** ('i:strəm, 'ɛstrəm) n a regularly occurring period of sexual receptivity in most female mammals, except humans, during which ovulation occurs and copulation can take place; heat [c17: from Latin oestrus gadfly, hence frenzy, from Greek oistros] >'oestrous, 'oestral or US'estrous, 'estral adj

oeuvre French (œvrə) n **1** a work of art, literature, music, etc **2** the total output of a writer, painter, etc [ultimately from Latin opera, plural of opus work]

of (ɒv; unstressed əv) prep **1** used with a verbal noun or gerund to link it with a following noun that is either the subject or the object of the verb embedded in the gerund: the breathing of a fine swimmer (subject); the breathing of clean air (object) **2** used to indicate possession, origin, or association: the house of my sister; to die of hunger **3** used after words or phrases expressing quantities: a pint of milk **4** constituted by, containing, or characterized by: a family of idiots; a rod of iron; a man of some depth **5** used to indicate separation, as in time or space: within a mile of the town; within ten minutes of the beginning of the concert **6** used to mark apposition: the city of Naples; a speech on the subject of archaeology **7** about; concerning: speak to me of love **8** used in passive constructions to indicate the agent: he was beloved of all **9** informal used to indicate a day or part of a period of time when some activity habitually occurs: I go to the pub of an evening **10** US before the hour of: a quarter of nine [Old English (as prep and adv); related to Old Norse af, Old High German aba, Latin ab, Greek apo]

● USAGE See at **off**

OF abbreviation Old French (language)

Ofcom ('ɒfkɒm) n acronym for Office of Communications: a government body regulating the telecommunications industries; a super-regulator merging the Radio Authority, Independent Television Commission, and Oftel (in Britain)

off (ɒf) prep **1** used to indicate actions in which contact is absent or rendered absent, as between an object and a surface: to lift a cup off the table **2** used to indicate the removal of something that is or has been appended to or in association with something else: to take the tax off potatoes **3** out of alignment with: we are off course **4** situated near to or leading away from: just off the High Street **5** not inclined towards: I'm off work; I've gone off you ▷ adv **6** (particle) so as to be deactivated or disengaged: turn off the radio **7** (particle) **a** so as to get rid of: sleep off a hangover **b** so as to be removed from, esp as a reduction: he took ten per cent off **8** spent away from work or other duties: take the afternoon off **9 a** on a trip, journey, or race: I saw her off at the station **b** (particle) so as to be completely absent, used up, or exhausted: this stuff kills off all vermin **10** out from the shore or land: the ship stood off **11 a** out of contact; at a distance: the ship was 10 miles off **b** out of the present location: the girl ran off **12** away in the future: August is less than a week off **13** (particle) so as to be no longer taking place: the match has been rained off **14** (particle) removed from contact with something, as clothing from the body: the girl took all her clothes off **15** offstage: noises off **16** off and on or on and off occasionally; intermittently: he comes here off and on **17** off with (interjection) a command, often peremptory, or an exhortation to remove or cut off (something specified): off with his head; off with that coat, my dear ▷ adj **18** not on; no longer operative: the off position on the dial **19** (postpositive) not or no longer taking place; cancelled or postponed: the meeting is off **20** in a specified condition regarding money, provisions, etc: well off; how are you off for bread? **21** unsatisfactory or disappointing: his performance was rather off; an off year for good tennis **22** (postpositive) in a condition as specified: I'd be better off without this job **23** (postpositive) no longer on the menu; not being served at the moment: sorry, love, haddock is off **24** (postpositive) (of food or drink) having gone bad, sour, etc: this milk is off ▷ n **25** cricket **a** the part of the field on that side of the pitch to which the batsman presents his bat when taking strike: thus for a right-hander, off is on the right-hand side **b** (in combination) a fielding position in this part of the field: mid-off **c** (as modifier): the off stump [originally variant of OF; fully distinguished from it in the 17th century]

● USAGE In standard English, off is not followed by of: he stepped off (not off of) the platform

Offa ('ɒfə) n died 796 AD, king of Mercia (757–796), who constructed an earthwork (**Offa's Dyke**) between Wales and Mercia

OFFA ('ɒfə) n acronym for Orthopaedic Foundation for Animals

offal ('ɒfəl) n **1** the edible internal parts of an animal, such as the heart, liver, and tongue **2** dead or decomposing organic matter **3** refuse; rubbish [c14:

from OFF + FALL, referring to parts fallen or cut off; compare German *Abfall* rubbish]

Offaly ('ɒfəlɪ) *n* an inland county of E central Republic of Ireland, in Leinster province: formerly an ancient kingdom, which also included parts of Tipperary, Leix, and Kildare. County town: Tullamore. Pop: 63 663 (2002). Area: 2000 sq km (770 sq miles)

off-balance sheet reserve *n accounting* a sum of money or an asset that should appear on a company's balance but does not; hidden reserve

offbeat ('ɒf,biːt) *n* **1** *music* any of the normally unaccented beats in a bar, such as the second and fourth beats in a bar of four-four time. They are stressed in most rock and some jazz and dance music, such as the bossa nova ▷ *adj* **2 a** unusual, unconventional, or eccentric **b** (*as noun*): *he liked the offbeat in fashion*

off break *n cricket* a bowled ball that spins from off to leg on pitching

off-Broadway *adj* **1** designating the kind of experimental, low-budget, or noncommercial productions associated with theatre outside the Broadway area in New York **2** (of theatres) not located on Broadway

off colour *adj* (**off-colour** *when prenominal*) **1** *chiefly Brit* slightly ill; unwell **2** indecent or indelicate; risqué

offcut ('ɒf,kʌt) *n* a piece of paper, plywood, fabric, etc, remaining after the main pieces have been cut; remnant

Offenbach[1] (*German* 'ɔfənbax) *n* a city in central Germany, on the River Main in Hesse opposite Frankfurt am Main: leather-goods industry. Pop: 119 208 (2003 est)

Offenbach[2] ('ɒfən,bɑːk; *French* ɔfɛnbak) *n* **Jacques** (ʒak). 1819–80, German-born French composer of many operettas, including *Orpheus in the Underworld* (1858), and of the opera *The Tales of Hoffmann* (1881)

offence *or US* **offense** (ə'fɛns) *n* **1** a violation or breach of a law, custom, rule, etc **2** any moral wrong or crime **3** annoyance, displeasure, or resentment **4** **give offence (to)** to cause annoyance or displeasure to someone **5** a source of annoyance, displeasure, or anger **6** attack; assault **7** *archaic* injury or harm

offend (ə'fɛnd) *vb* **1** to hurt the feelings, sense of dignity, etc, of (a person) **2** (*tr*) to be disagreeable to; disgust: *the smell offended him* **3** (*intr except in archaic uses*) to break (a law or laws in general) [C14: via Old French *offendre* to strike against, from Latin *offendere*, from *ob-* against + *fendere* to strike] ▷ **offender** *n* ▷ **offending** *adj*

offensive (ə'fɛnsɪv) *adj* **1** unpleasant or disgusting, as to the senses **2** causing anger or annoyance; insulting **3** for the purpose of attack rather than defence ▷ *n* **4** **the offensive** an attitude or position of aggression **5** an assault, attack, or military initiative, esp a strategic one ▷ **offensively** *adv* ▷ **offensiveness** *n*

offer ('ɒfə) *vb* **1** to present or proffer (something, someone, oneself, etc) for acceptance or rejection **2** (*tr*) to present as part of a requirement: *she offered English as a second subject* **3** (*tr*) to provide or make accessible: *this stream offers the best fishing* **4** (*intr*) to present itself: *if an opportunity should offer* **5** (*tr*) to show or express willingness or the intention (to do something) **6** (*tr*) to put forward (a proposal, opinion, etc) for consideration **7** (*tr*) to present for sale **8** (*tr*) to propose as payment; bid or tender **9** (*when tr, often foll by up*) to present (a prayer, sacrifice, etc) as or during an act of worship **10** (*tr*) to show readiness for: *to offer battle* **11** (*intr*) *archaic* to make a proposal of marriage ▷ *n* **12** something, such as a proposal or bid, that is offered **13** the act of offering or the condition of being offered **14** a proposal of marriage **15 on offer** for sale at a reduced price [Old English, from Latin *offerre* to present, from *ob-* to + *ferre* to bring]

offer document *n* a document sent by a person or firm making a takeover bid to the shareholders of the target company, giving details of the offer that has been made and, usually, reasons for accepting it

offering ('ɒfərɪŋ) *n* **1** something that is offered **2** a contribution to the funds of a religious organization **3** a sacrifice, as of an animal, to a deity

offertory ('ɒfətərɪ) *n, pl* **-tories** **1** the oblation of the bread and wine at the Eucharist **2** the offerings of the

worshippers at this service **3** the prayers said or sung while the worshippers' offerings are being received [C14: from Church Latin *offertōrium* place appointed for offerings, from Latin *offerre* to OFFER]

offhand (,ɒf'hænd) *adj also* **offhanded**, *adv* **1** without care, thought, or consideration; sometimes, brusque or ungracious: *an offhand manner* **2** without preparation or warning; impromptu ▷ **offhandedly** *adv* ▷ **offhandedness** *n*

Offiah (ɒ'faɪə) *n* **Martin.** born 1965, English Rugby League football player

office ('ɒfɪs) *n* **1 a** a room or set of rooms in which business, professional duties, clerical work, etc, are carried out **b** (*as modifier*): *office furniture; an office boy* **2** (*often plural*) the building or buildings in which the work of an organization, such as a business or government department, is carried out **3** a commercial or professional business: *the architect's office approved the plans* **4** the group of persons working in an office: *it was a happy office until she came* **5** (*capital when part of a name*) (in Britain) a department of the national government: *the Home Office* **6** (*capital when part of a name*) (in the US) **a** a governmental agency, esp of the Federal government **b** a subdivision of such an agency or of a department: *Office of Science and Technology* **7 a** a position of trust, responsibility, or duty, esp in a government or organization: *the office of president; to seek office* **b** (*in combination*): *an office-holder* **8** duty or function: *the office of an administrator* **9** (*often plural*) a minor task or service: *domestic offices* **10** (*often plural*) an action performed for another, usually a beneficial action: *through his good offices* **11** a place where tickets, information, etc, can be obtained: *a ticket office* **12** *Christianity* **a** (*often plural*) a ceremony or service, prescribed by ecclesiastical authorities, esp one for the dead **b** *RC Church* the official daily service **c** short for **divine office** **13** (*plural*) the parts of a house or estate where work is done, goods are stored, etc **14** (*usually plural*) *Brit euphemistic* a lavatory (esp in the phrase **usual offices**) **15 in office** (of a government) in power **16 out of office** (of a government) out of power **17 the office** *slang* a hint or signal [C13: via Old French from Latin *officium* service, duty, from *opus* work, service + *facere* to do]

office block *n* a large building designed to provide office accommodation

office boy *n* a former name for **office junior**

office junior *n* a young person, esp a school-leaver, employed in an office for running errands and doing other minor jobs

officer ('ɒfɪsə) *n* **1** a person in the armed services who holds a position of responsibility, authority, and duty, esp one who holds a commission **2** See **police officer** **3** (on a non-naval ship) any person including the captain and mate, who holds a position of authority and responsibility: *radio officer; engineer officer* **4** a person appointed or elected to a position of responsibility or authority in a government, society, etc **5** a government official: *a customs officer* **6** (in the Order of the British Empire) a member of the grade below commander ▷ *vb* (*tr*) **7** to furnish with officers **8** to act as an officer over (some section, group, organization, etc)

officer of the day *n* a military officer whose duty is to take charge of the security of the unit or camp for a day. Also called: **orderly officer**

official (ə'fɪʃəl) *adj* **1** of or relating to an office, its administration, or its duration **2** sanctioned by, recognized by, or derived from authority: *an official statement* **3** having a formal ceremonial character: *an official dinner* ▷ *n* **4** a person who holds a position in an organization, government department, etc, esp a subordinate position

officialdom (ə'fɪʃəldəm) *n* **1** the outlook or behaviour of officials, esp those rigidly adhering to regulations; bureaucracy **2** officials or bureaucrats collectively

officialese (ə,fɪʃə'liːz) *n* language characteristic of official documents, esp when verbose or pedantic

officially (ə'fɪʃəlɪ) *adv* **1** in a formal or authoritative manner: *the Queen officially opened the dome* **2** in a way that is formally acknowledged but is not necessarily the case: *officially on the dole but actually holding a job*

Official Receiver *n* an officer appointed by the Department of Trade and Industry to receive the income and manage the estate of a bankrupt pending the appointment of a trustee in bankruptcy. See also **receiver** (sense 2)

Official Referee *n law* (in England) a circuit judge attached to the High Court who is empowered to try certain cases, esp where a detailed examination of accounts or other documents is involved

officiant (ə'fɪʃɪənt) *n* a person who presides and officiates at a religious ceremony

officiate (ə'fɪʃɪˌeɪt) *vb* (*intr*) 1 to hold the position, responsibility, or function of an official 2 to conduct a religious or other ceremony [C17: from Medieval Latin *officiāre*, from Latin *officium*; see OFFICE] >of‚fici'ation *n* >of'fici‚ator *n*

officious (ə'fɪʃəs) *adj* 1 unnecessarily or obtrusively ready to offer advice or services 2 *diplomacy* informal or unofficial [C16: from Latin *officiōsus* kindly, from *officium* service; see OFFICE] >of'ficiously *adv* >of'ficiousness *n*

offing ('ɒfɪŋ) *n* 1 the part of the sea that can be seen from the shore 2 **in the offing** likely to occur soon

offish ('ɒfɪʃ) *adj informal* aloof or distant in manner >'offishly *adv* >'offishness *n*

off key *adj, adv* (**off-key** *when prenominal*) 1 *music* **a** not in the correct key **b** out of tune 2 out of keeping; discordant

off label *adj, adv* (**off-label** *when prenominal*) (of a prescription drug) relating to use, or being used, in ways for which it has not been approved

off-licence *n Brit* 1 a shop, or a counter in a pub or hotel, where alcoholic drinks are sold for consumption elsewhere. US equivalents: package store, liquor store 2 a licence permitting such sales

off limits *adj* (**off-limits** *when prenominal*) 1 not to be entered; out of bounds ▷ *adv* 2 in or into an area forbidden by regulations

offline ('ɒfˌlaɪn) *or* **off-line** *adj* 1 of, relating to, or concerned with a part of a computer system not connected to the central processing unit but controlled by a computer storage device. ▷ Compare **online** 2 disconnected from a computer; switched off ▷ *adv* 3 while not connected to a computer or the internet

off-load *vb* (*tr*) to get rid of (something unpleasant or burdensome), as by delegation to another

off message *adj* (**off-message** *when prenominal*) not adhering to or reflecting the official line of a political party, government, or other organization

off-peak *adj* of or relating to services as used outside periods of intensive use or electricity supplied at cheaper rates during the night

off-piste *adj* of or relating to skiing on virgin snow off the regular runs

off plan *adj* (**off-plan** *when prenominal*) (of a new building) considered with reference to its plans, before it has been built

off-putting *adj Brit informal* disconcerting or disturbing

off-ramp *n* a short steep one-way road by which traffic can leave a motorway or highway

off-road *adj* (of a motor vehicle) designed or built for use away from public roads, esp on rough terrain

off-roader *n* 1 a motor vehicle designed for use away from public roads, esp on rough terrain 2 an owner or driver of an off-road vehicle

off-roading *n* the sport or activity of driving vehicles over rough terrain

off-sales *pl n Brit* sales of alcoholic drink for consumption off the premises by a pub or an off-licence attached to a pub

off season *adj* (**off-season** *when prenominal*) 1 denoting or occurring during a period of little activity in a trade or business ▷ *n* 2 such a period ▷ *adv* 3 in an off-season period

offset *n* ('ɒfˌsɛt) 1 something that counterbalances or compensates for something else 2 **a** a printing method in which the impression is made onto an intermediate surface, such as a rubber blanket, which transfers it to the paper **b** (*modifier*) relating to, involving, or printed by

offset: *offset letterpress; offset lithography* 3 another name for **set-off** 4 *botany* a short runner in certain plants, such as the houseleek, that produces roots and shoots at the tip 5 a ridge projecting from a range of hills or mountains 6 a narrow horizontal or sloping surface formed where a wall is reduced in thickness towards the top 7 *surveying* a measurement of distance to a point at right angles to a survey line ▷ *vb* (ˌɒf'sɛt) -sets, -setting, -set 8 (*tr*) to counterbalance or compensate for 9 (*tr*) to print (pictures, text, etc) using the offset process 10 (*tr*) to construct an offset in (a wall) 11 (*intr*) to project or develop as an offset

offshoot ('ɒfˌʃuːt) *n* 1 a shoot or branch growing from the main stem of a plant 2 something that develops or derives from a principal source or origin

offshore (ˌɒf'ʃɔː) *adj, adv* 1 from, away from, or at some distance from the shore 2 *NZ* overseas; abroad ▷ *adj* 3 sited or conducted at sea as opposed to on land: *offshore industries* 4 based or operating abroad in places where the tax system is more advantageous than that of the home country: *offshore banking; offshore fund*

offshoring ('ɒfˌʃɔːrɪŋ) *n* the practice of moving a company's operating base to a foreign country where labour costs are cheaper

offside ('ɒf'saɪd) *adj, adv* 1 *sport* (in football, hockey, etc) in a position illegally ahead of the ball or puck when it is played, usually when within one's opponents' half or the attacking zone ▷ *n* 2 **the offside** *chiefly Brit* **a** the side of a vehicle nearest the centre of the road (in Britain, the right side) **b** (*as modifier*): *the offside passenger door*

offsider (ˌɒf'saɪdə) *n Austral & NZ* a partner or assistant

offspring ('ɒfˌsprɪŋ) *n* 1 the immediate descendant or descendants of a person, animal, etc; progeny 2 a product, outcome, or result

offstage ('ɒf'steɪdʒ) *adj, adv* out of the view of the audience; off the stage

off-the-peg *adj* (of clothing) ready to wear; not produced especially for the person buying

off the shelf *adv* 1 from stock and readily available: *you can have this model off the shelf* ▷ *adj* (**off-the-shelf** *when prenominal*) 2 of or relating to a product that is readily available: *an off-the-shelf model* 3 of or denoting a company that has been registered with the Registrar of Companies for the sole purpose of being sold

off-the-wall *adj* (**off the wall** *when postpositive*) *slang* new or unexpected in an unconventional or eccentric way: *an off-the-wall approach to humour* [C20: possibly from the use of the phrase in handball and squash to describe a shot that is unexpected]

off-white *n* 1 a colour, such as cream or bone, consisting of white mixed with a tinge of grey or with a pale hue ▷ *adj* 2 of such a colour: *an off-white coat*

Ofgem ('ɒfˌdʒɛm) *n* (in Britain) *acronym for* Office of Gas and Electricity Markets: a government body formed in 1999 by the merger of the separate regulatory bodies for gas and electricity; its functions are to promote competition and protect consumers' interests

Ofili (ɒ'fiːlɪ) *n* **Chris(topher)**. born 1968, British painter, noted esp for his brightly coloured collages using elephant dung: Turner Prize 1998

O'Flaherty (əʊ'flæhətɪ) *n* **Liam** ('lɪəm). 1897–1984, Irish novelist and short-story writer. His novels include *The Informer* (1925) and *Famine* (1937)

OFS *abbreviation* (Orange) Free State

oft (ɒft) *adv* short for **often** (archaic or poetic except in combinations such as **opt-repeated** and **oft-recurring**) [Old English *oft*; related to Old High German *ofto*]

OFT (in Britain) *abbreviation* Office of Fair Trading

often ('ɒfᵊn, 'ɒftᵊn) *adv* 1 frequently or repeatedly; much of the time 2 **as often as not** quite frequently 3 **every so often** at intervals 4 **more often than not** in more than half the instances ▷ *adj* 5 *archaic* repeated; frequent [C14: variant of OFT before vowels and *h*]

Ogaden (ˌɒgə'dɛn) *n* **the Ogaden** a region of SE Ethiopia, bordering on Somalia: consists of a desert plateau, inhabited by Somali nomads; a secessionist movement, supported by Somalia, has existed within the region since the early 1960s and led to bitter fighting between Ethiopia and Somalia (1977–78)

Ogasawara Gunto (ˌɒɡəsəˈwɑːrə ˈɡʌntəʊ) n transliteration of the Japanese name for the **Bonin Islands**

Ogbomosho (ˌɒɡbəˈməʊʃəʊ) n a city in SW Nigeria: the third largest town in Nigeria; trading centre for an agricultural region. Pop: 959 000 (2005 est)

Ogden (ˈɒɡdən) n C(harles) K(ay). 1889–1957, English linguist, who, with I. A. Richards, devised Basic English

Ogdon (ˈɒɡdən) n John (Andrew Howard). 1937–89, British pianist and composer

ogee (ˈəʊdʒiː) n architect 1 Also called: **talon** a moulding having a cross section in the form of a letter S 2 short for **ogee arch** [C15: probably variant of OGIVE]

ogee arch n architect a pointed arch having an S-shaped curve on both sides. Sometimes shortened to: **ogee**

Ogen melon (ˈəʊɡɛn) n a variety of small melon having a green skin and sweet pale green flesh [C20: named after a kibbutz in Israel where it was first developed]

ogham or **ogam** (ˈɒɡəm, ɔːm) n an ancient alphabetical writing system used by the Celts in Britain and Ireland, consisting of straight lines drawn or carved perpendicular to or at an angle to another long straight line [C17: from Old Irish *ogom*, of uncertain origin but associated with the name *Ogma*, legendary inventor of this alphabet]

ogive (ˈəʊdʒaɪv, əʊˈdʒaɪv) n 1 a diagonal rib or groin of a Gothic vault 2 another name for **lancet arch** [C17: from Old French, of uncertain origin] > o'gival adj

ogle (ˈəʊɡ³l) vb 1 to look at (someone) amorously or lustfully 2 (tr) to stare or gape at ▷ n 3 a flirtatious or lewd look [C17: probably from Low German *oegeln*, from *oegen* to look at] > 'ogler n

Oglethorpe (ˈəʊɡ³lˌθɔːp) n James Edward. 1696–1785, English general and colonial administrator; founder of the colony of Georgia (1733)

Ogooué or **Ogowe** (ɒˈɡəʊweɪ) n a river in W central Africa, rising in SW Congo-Brazzaville and flowing generally northwest and north through Gabon to the Atlantic. Length: about 970 km (683 miles)

Ogopogo (ˌəʊɡəʊˈpəʊɡəʊ) n an aquatic monster said to live in Okanagan Lake in British Columbia, Canada [apparently an arbitrary coinage]

O grade n (formerly, in Scotland) 1 a the basic level of the Scottish Certificate of Education, now replaced by Standard Grade b (as modifier): O grade history 2 a pass in a particular subject at O grade: she has ten O grades

ogre (ˈəʊɡə) n 1 (in folklore) a giant, usually given to eating human flesh 2 any monstrous or cruel person [C18: from French, perhaps from Latin *Orcus* god of the infernal regions] > 'ogreish adj > 'ogress fem n

Ogun (əʊˈɡʊn) n a state of SW Nigeria. Capital: Abeokuta. Pop: 3 728 098 (2006). Area: 16 762 sq km (6472 sq miles)

oh (əʊ) interj an exclamation expressive of surprise, pain, pleasure, etc

OH abbreviation Ohio

O. Henry (əʊ ˈhɛnrɪ) n pen name of William Sidney Porter. 1862–1910, US short-story writer. His collections of stories, characterized by his use of caricature and surprising endings, include Cabbages and Kings (1904) and The Four Million (1906)

OHG abbreviation Old High German

O'Higgins (əʊˈhɪɡɪnz; Spanish oˈiɣins) n 1 Ambrosio (æmˈbrəʊzɪˌəʊ). ?1720–1801, Irish soldier, who became viceroy of Chile (1789–96) and of Peru (1796–1801) 2 his son, Bernardo (bɛrˈnarðo). 1778–1842, Chilean revolutionary. He was one of the leaders in the struggle for independence from Spain and was Chile's first president (1817–23)

Ohio (əʊˈhaɪəʊ) n 1 a state of the central US, in the Midwest on Lake Erie: consists of prairies in the W and the Allegheny plateau in the E, the Ohio River forming the S and most of the E borders. Capital: Columbus. Pop: 11 435 798 (2003 est). Area: 107 044 sq km (41 330 sq miles). Abbreviation and zip code: OH 2 a river in the eastern US, formed by the confluence of the Allegheny and Monongahela Rivers at Pittsburgh: flows generally W and SW to join the Mississippi at Cairo, Illinois, as its chief E tributary. Length: 1570 km (975 miles)

Öhlenschläger (Danish ˈøːlənslɛːɣər) n a variant spelling of **Oehlenschläger**

ohm (əʊm) n the derived SI unit of electrical resistance; the resistance between two points on a conductor when a constant potential difference of 1 volt between them produces a current of 1 ampere. Symbol: Ω [C19: named after Georg Simon OHM]

Ohm (əʊm) n Georg Simon (ˈɡeːɔrk ˈziːmɔn). 1787–1854, German physicist, who formulated the law named after him

ohmmeter (ˈəʊmˌmiːtə) n an instrument for measuring electrical resistance

OHMS abbreviation (in Britain and the dominions of the Commonwealth) On Her (or His) Majesty's Service

Ohm's law (əʊmz) n the principle that the electric current passing through a conductor is directly proportional to the potential difference across it, provided that the temperature remains constant. The constant of proportionality is the resistance of the conductor [C19: named after Georg Simon OHM]

oho (əʊˈhəʊ) interj an exclamation expressing surprise, exultation, or derision

oi¹ (ɔɪ) Brit ▷ interj 1 a cry used to attract attention, esp in an aggressive way ▷ adj 2 of or relating to a form of punk rock popular esp among skinheads in the late 1970s and 1980s

oi² (ɒɪ) n, pl oi NZ another name for **grey-faced petrel** [Māori]

-oid suffix forming adjectives and associated nouns indicating likeness, resemblance, or similarity: anthropoid [from Greek *-oeidēs* resembling, form of, from *eidos* form]

-oidea suffix forming plural proper nouns forming the names of zoological classes or superfamilies: Crinoidea; Canoidea [from New Latin, from Latin *-oīdēs* -OID]

oil (ɔɪl) n 1 any of a number of viscous liquids with a smooth sticky feel. They are usually flammable, insoluble in water, soluble in organic solvents, and are obtained from plants and animals, from mineral deposits, and by synthesis. They are used as lubricants, fuels, perfumes, foodstuffs, and raw materials for chemicals. See also **essential oil** 2 another name for **petroleum** b (as modifier): an oil engine; an oil rig 3 a Also called: **lubricating oil** any of a number of substances usually derived from petroleum and used for lubrication b (in combination): an oilcan; an oilstone c (as modifier): an oil pump 4 Also called: **fuel oil** a petroleum product used as a fuel in domestic heating, industrial furnaces, marine engines, etc 5 Brit a paraffin, esp when used as a domestic fuel b (as modifier): an oil lamp; an oil stove 6 any substance of a consistency resembling that of oil: oil of vitriol 7 the solvent, usually linseed oil, with which pigments are mixed to make artists' paints 8 a (often plural) oil colour or paint b (as modifier): an oil painting 9 an oil painting 10 the good (dinkum) oil Austral & NZ slang facts or news 11 strike oil a to discover petroleum while drilling for it b informal to become very rich or successful ▷ vb (tr) 12 to lubricate, smear, polish, etc, with oil or an oily substance 13 informal to bribe (esp in the phrase oil someone's palm) 14 oil the wheels to make things run smoothly [C12: from Old French *oile*, from Latin *oleum* (olive) oil, from *olea* olive tree, from Greek *elaia* OLIVE] > 'oil-ˌoily adj

oil cake n stock feed consisting of compressed cubes made from the residue of the crushed seeds of oil-bearing crops such as linseed

oilcan (ˈɔɪlˌkæn) n a container with a long nozzle for applying lubricating oil to machinery

oilcloth (ˈɔɪlˌklɒθ) n 1 waterproof material made by treating one side of a cotton fabric with a drying oil, or a synthetic resin 2 another name for **linoleum**

oil drum n a metal drum used to contain or transport oil

oilfield (ˈɔɪlˌfiːld) n an area containing reserves of petroleum, esp one that is already being exploited

oilfired (ˈɔɪlˌfaɪəd) adj (of central heating) using oil as fuel

oilgas (ˈɔɪlˌɡæs) n a gaseous mixture of hydrocarbons used as a fuel, obtained by the destructive distillation of mineral oils

oilman (ˈɔɪlmən) n, pl -men 1 a person who owns or

operates oil wells **2** a person who makes or sells oil

oil of cloves *n* another name for **clove oil**

oil of vitriol *n* another name for **sulphuric acid**

oil paint *or* **oil colour** *n* paint made of pigment ground in oil, usually linseed oil, used for oil painting

oil painting *n* **1** a picture painted with oil paints **2** the art or process of painting with oil paints **3** *he's no oil painting informal* he is not good-looking

oil palm *n* a tropical African palm tree, *Elaeis guineensis*, the fruits of which yield palm oil

oil rig *n* See **rig**¹ (sense 6)

Oil Rivers *pl n* the delta of the Niger River in S Nigeria

oil sand *n* a sandstone impregnated with hydrocarbons, esp such deposits in Alberta, Canada

oil-seed rape *n* another name for **rape**²

oil shale *n* a fine-grained shale containing oil, which can be extracted by heating

oilskin ('ɔɪl,skɪn) *n* **1 a** a cotton fabric treated with oil and pigment to make it waterproof **b** (*as modifier*): *an oilskin hat* **2** (*often plural*) a protective outer garment of this fabric

oil slick *n* a mass of floating oil covering an area of water, esp oil that has leaked or been discharged from a ship

oilstone ('ɔɪl,stəʊn) *n* a stone with a fine grain lubricated with oil and used for sharpening cutting tools. See also **whetstone**

oil well *n* a boring into the earth or sea bed for the extraction of petroleum

oily ('ɔɪlɪ) *adj* **oilier, oiliest 1** soaked in or smeared with oil or grease **2** consisting of, containing, or resembling oil **3** flatteringly servile or obsequious > **'oilily** *adv* > **'oiliness** *n*

oink (ɔɪŋk) *interj* an imitation or representation of the grunt of a pig

ointment ('ɔɪntmənt) *n* **1** a fatty or oily medicated formulation applied to the skin to heal or protect **2** a similar substance used as a cosmetic [C14: from Old French *oignement*, from Latin *unguentum* UNGUENT]

Oireachtas ('ɛrəkθəs; *Gaelic* 'ɛrəxtəs) *n* the parliament of the Republic of Ireland, consisting of the president, the Dáil Éireann, and the Seanad Éireann [Irish: assembly, from Old Irish *airech* nobleman]

Oise (*French* waz) *n* **1** a department of N France, in Picardy region. Capital: Beauvais. Pop: 776 999 (2003 est). Area: 5887 sq km (2296 sq miles) **2** a river in N France, rising in Belgium, in the Ardennes, and flowing southwest to join the Seine at Conflans. Length: 302 km (188 miles)

Oistrakh ('ɔɪstraːk; *Russian* 'ɔjstrəx) *n* **1** David (da'vit). 1908–74, Russian violinist **2** his son, **Igor** ('igərj). born 1931, Russian violinist

Oita ('ɔɪtə) *n* an industrial city in SW Japan, on NE Kyushu: dominated most of Kyushu in the 16th century. Pop: 437 699 (2002 est)

Ojibwa (əʊ'dʒɪbwə) *n* **1** (*pl* **-was** *or* **-wa**) a member of a North American Indian people living in a region west of Lake Superior **2** the language of this people, belonging to the Algonquian family

OK *abbreviation* Oklahoma

O.K. (,əʊ'keɪ) *informal* ▷ *sentence substitute* **1** an expression of approval, agreement, etc ▷ *adj, adv* (*usually postpositive*) **2** in good or satisfactory condition **3** permissible: *is it O.K. if I go home now?* **4** acceptable but not outstanding: *the party was O.K.* ▷ *vb* **O.K.s, O.K.ing** (,əʊ'keɪɪŋ), **O.K.ed** (,əʊ'keɪd) **5** (*tr*) to approve or endorse ▷ *n, pl* **O.K.s 6** approval or agreement ▷ Also: **OK, o.k., okay** [C19: perhaps from *o*(*ll*) *k*(*orrect*), jocular alteration of *all correct*]

Okanagan (,əʊkə'nɑːgən) *n* **1** a river in North America that flows south from Okanagan Lake in Canada into the Columbia River in NE Washington, US Length: about 483 km (300 miles) **2** Also called: **Okanogan, Okinagan** a member of a North American Indian people living in the Okanagan River valley in British Columbia and Washington **3** Also called: **Okanogan, Okinagan** the language of this people, belonging to the Salish family

Okanagan Lake *n* a lake in SW Canada, in S British Columbia: drained by the Okanagan River into the Columbia River. Length: about 111 km (69 miles). Width: from 3.2–6.4 km (2–4 miles)

okapi (əʊ'kɑːpɪ) *n, pl* **-pis** *or* **-pi** a ruminant mammal, *Okapia johnstoni*, of the forests of central Africa, having a reddish-brown coat with horizontal white stripes on the legs and small horns: family *Giraffidae* [C20: from a Central African word]

Okavango *or* **Okovango** (,əʊkə'vɑːŋgəʊ) *n* a river in SW central Africa, rising in central Angola and flowing southeast, then east as part of the border between Angola and Namibia, then southeast across the Caprivi Strip into Botswana to form a great marsh known as the **Okavango Basin, Delta** *or* **Swamp**. Length: about 1600 km (1000 miles)

okay (,əʊ'keɪ) *sentence substitute, adj, vb, n* a variant of **O.K.**

Okayama (,ɒkə'jɑːmə) *n* a city in SW Japan, on W Honshu on the Inland Sea. Pop: 621 809 (2002 est)

oke (əʊk) *n South African* an informal word for **man** [from Afrikaans]

Okeechobee (,əʊkɪ'tʃəʊbɪ) *n* **Lake Okeechobee** a lake in S Florida, in the Everglades: second largest freshwater lake wholly within the US Area: 1813 sq km (700 sq miles)

O'Keeffe (əʊ'kiːf) *n* **Georgia.** 1887–1986, US painter, best known for her semiabstract still lifes, esp of flowers: married the photographer Alfred Stieglitz

Okefenokee Swamp (,əʊkɪfɪ'nəʊkɪ) *n* a swamp in the US, in SE Georgia and N Florida: protected flora and fauna. Area: 1554 sq km (600 sq miles)

Okeghem ('ɒkə,gɛm; *Dutch* 'ɔkəxəm) *n* a variant spelling of **Ockeghem**

Okhotsk ('əʊkɒtsk; *Russian* a'ɔxtsk) *n* **Sea of Okhotsk** part of the NW Pacific, surrounded by the Kamchatka Peninsula, the Kurile Islands, Sakhalin Island, and the E coast of Siberia. Area: 1 589 840 sq km (613 838 sq miles)

Okinawa (,əʊkɪ'nɑːwə) *n* a coral island of SW Japan, the largest of the Ryukyu Islands in the N Pacific: scene of heavy fighting in World War II; administered by the US (1945–72); agricultural. Chief town: Naha. Pop: 1 318 218 (2000). Area: 1176 sq km (454 sq miles)

Okla. *abbreviation* Oklahoma

Oklahoma (,əʊklə'həʊmə) *n* a state in the S central US: consists of plains in the west, rising to mountains in the southwest and east; important for oil. Capital: Oklahoma City. Pop: 3 511 532 (2003 est). Area: 181 185 sq km (69 956 sq miles). Abbreviation: **Okla., OK** > ,Okla'homan *n, adj*

Oklahoma City *n* a city in central Oklahoma: the state capital and a major agricultural and industrial centre. Pop: 523 303 (2003 est)

okra ('əʊkrə) *n* **1** Also called: **ladies' fingers** an annual malvaceous plant, *Hibiscus esculentus*, of the Old World tropics, with yellow-and-red flowers and edible oblong sticky green pods **2** the pod of this plant, eaten in soups, stews, etc. See also **gumbo** (sense 1) [C18: of W African origin]

Okri ('ɒkrɪ) *n* **Ben.** born 1959, Nigerian writer; his books include the Booker-prizewinning *The Famished Road* (1991), *Dangerous Love* (1996), and *In Arcadia* (2002)

-ol¹ *suffix forming nouns* denoting an organic chemical compound containing a hydroxyl group, esp alcohols and phenols: *ethanol; quinol* [from ALCOHOL]

-ol² *n combining form* (*not used systematically*) a variant of **-ole**¹

Olaf I ('əʊləf) *or* **Olav I** ('əʊləv) *n* known as *Olaf Tryggvesson.* ?965–?1000 AD, king of Norway (995–?1000). He began the conversion of Norway to Christianity

Olaf II *or* **Olav II** *n* **Saint.** 995–1030 AD, king of Norway (1015–28), who worked to complete the conversion of Norway to Christianity; deposed by Canute; patron saint of Norway. Feast day: July 29

Olaf V *or* **Olav V** *n* 1903–91, king of Norway 1957–91; son of Haakon VII

Öland (*Swedish* 'øːland) *n* an island in the Baltic Sea, separated from the mainland of SE Sweden by Kalmar Sound: the second largest Swedish island. Chief town: Borgholm. Pop: 24 628 (2004 est). Area: 1347 sq km (520 sq miles)

old (əʊld) *adj* **1** having lived or existed for a relatively long time: *an old man; an old tradition; old wine; an old house; an old country* **2 a** of or relating to advanced years or a long life: *old age* **b** (*as collective noun; preceded by the*): *the old* **c** old and young people of all ages **3** decrepit or senile **4** worn with age or use: *old clothes; an old car* **5 a** (*postpositive*) having lived or existed for a specified period: *a child who is six years old* **b** (*in combination*): *a six-year-old child* **c** (*as noun in combination*): *a six-year-old* **6** (*capital when part of a name or title*) earlier or earliest of two or more things with the same name: *the old edition; the Old Testament; old Norwich* **7** (*capital when part of a name*) designating the form of a language in which the earliest known records are written: *Old English* **8** (*prenominal*) familiar through long acquaintance or repetition: *an old friend; an old excuse* **9** practised; hardened: *old in cunning* **10** (*prenominal; often preceded by good*) cherished; dear: used as a term of affection or familiarity: *good old George* **11** *informal* (with any of several nouns) used as a familiar form of address to a person: *old thing; old bean; old stick; old fellow* **12** skilled through long experience (esp in the phrase **an old hand**) **13** out-of-date; unfashionable **14** remote or distant in origin or time of origin: *an old culture* **15** (*prenominal*) former; previous: *my old house was small* **16 a** (*prenominal*) established for a relatively long time: *an old member* **b** (*in combination*): *old-established* **17** sensible, wise, or mature: *old beyond one's years* **18** (*intensifier*) (esp in phrases such as **a good old time, any old thing, any old how**, etc) **19** (of crops) harvested late **20 good old days** an earlier period of time regarded as better than the present **21 little old** *informal* indicating affection, esp humorous affection: *my little old wife* **22 the old one** (or *gentleman*) *informal* a jocular name for **Satan** ▷ *n* **23** an earlier or past time (esp in the phrase **of old**): *in days of old* [Old English *eald*; related to Old Saxon *ald*, Old High German, German *alt*, Latin *altus* high] >'**oldish** *adj* >'**oldness** *n*

old age pension *n* a former name for the state **retirement pension** >**old age pensioner** *n*

Old Bailey *n* the chief court exercising criminal jurisdiction in London; the Central Criminal Court of England

Old Bill *n* (*functioning as plural; preceded by the*) *Brit slang* policemen collectively or in general [C20: of uncertain origin: perhaps derived from the World War I cartoon of a soldier with a drooping moustache]

old boy *n* **1** (*sometimes capitals*) *Brit* a male ex-pupil of a school **2** *informal, chiefly Brit* **a** a familiar name used to refer to a man **b** an old man

old boy network *n Brit informal* the appointment to power of former pupils of the same small group of public schools or universities

Old Castile *n* a region of N Spain, on the Bay of Biscay: formerly a province. Spanish name: **Castilla la Vieja**

Oldcastle ('əʊld,kɑːsᵊl) *n* Sir **John**, Baron Cobham. ?1378–1417, Lollard leader. In 1411 he led an English army in France but in 1413 he was condemned as a heretic and later hanged and burnt. He is thought to have been a model for Shakespeare's character Falstaff in *Henry IV*

Old Contemptibles *pl n* the British expeditionary force to France in 1914 [so named from the Kaiser's alleged reference to them as a "contemptible little army"]

old country *n* the country of origin of an immigrant or an immigrant's ancestors

Old Dart *n* the Old Dart *Austral slang* England [C19: of unknown origin]

Old Delhi *n* See **Delhi**

olden ('əʊldᵊn) *adj* an archaic or poetic word for **old**: *in olden days; in olden times*

Oldenbarneveldt (,ɒldən'bɑːnə,vɛlt) *n* **Johan van.** 1547–1619, Dutch statesman, regarded as a founder of Dutch independence; the leading figure (from 1586) in the United Provinces of the Netherlands: executed by Maurice of Nassau

Oldenburg¹ ('əʊldᵊn,bɜːg; *German* 'ɔldənburk) *n* **1** a city in NW Germany, in Lower Saxony: former capital of Oldenburg state. Pop: 158 340 (2003 est) **2** a former state of NW Germany: became part of Lower Saxony in 1946

Oldenburg² ('əʊldᵊn,bɜːg) *n* **Claes** (klɔːs). born 1929, US pop sculptor and artist, born in Sweden

Old English *n* **1** Also called: **Anglo-Saxon** the English language from the time of the earliest settlements in the fifth century AD to about 1100. The main dialects were West Saxon (the chief literary form), Kentish, and Anglian. Abbreviation: **OE** **2** *printing* a Gothic typeface commonly used in England up until the 18th century

Old English sheepdog *n* a breed of large bobtailed sheepdog with a profuse shaggy coat

older ('əʊldə) *adj* **1** the comparative of **old** **2** Also (of people, esp members of the same family): **elder** having lived or existed longer; of greater age

old-fashioned *adj* **1** belonging to, characteristic of, or favoured by former times; outdated: *old-fashioned ideas* **2** favouring or adopting the dress, manners, fashions, etc, of a former time **3** *Scot & northern English dialect* old for one's age: *an old-fashioned child* ▷ *n* **4** a cocktail containing spirit, bitters, fruit, etc

Oldfield ('əʊld,fiːld) *n* **Bruce.** born 1950, British fashion designer

Old French *n* the French language in its earliest forms, from about the 9th century up to about 1400. Abbreviation: **OF**

old girl *n* **1** (*sometimes capitals*) *Brit* a female ex-pupil of a school **2** *informal, chiefly Brit* **a** a familiar name used to refer to a woman **b** an old woman

Old Glory *n* a nickname for the flag of the United States of America

old gold *n* **a** a dark yellow colour, sometimes with a brownish tinge **b** (*as adjective*): *an old-gold carpet*

old guard *n* **1** a group that works for a long-established or old-fashioned cause or principle **2** the conservative element in a political party or other group [C19: from OLD GUARD]

Oldham ('əʊldəm) *n* **1** a town in NW England, in Oldham unitary authority, Greater Manchester. Pop: 103 544 (2001) **2** a unitary authority in NW England, in Greater Manchester. Pop: 218 100 (2003 est). Area: 141 sq km (54 sq miles)

old hat *adj* (*postpositive*) old-fashioned or trite

Old High German *n* a group of West Germanic dialects that eventually developed into modern German; High German up to about 1200: spoken in the Middle Ages on the upper Rhine, in Bavaria, Alsace, and elsewhere, including Alemannic, Bavarian, Langobardic, and Upper Franconian. Abbreviation: **OHG**

oldie ('əʊldɪ) *n informal* **1** an old person or thing **2** *Austral* a parent: *children and their oldies*

Old Irish *n* the Celtic language of Ireland up to about 900 AD, introduced to Scotland by Irish settlers about 500 AD

old lady *n* an informal term for **mother**¹ or **wife** (sense 1)

Old Latin *n* the Latin language before the classical period, up to about 100 BC

old-line party *n Canadian* either the Liberal Party or the Conservative Party

Old Low German *n* the Saxon and Low Franconian dialects of German up to about 1200; the old form of modern Low German and Dutch. Abbreviation: **OLG**

old maid *n* **1** a woman regarded as unlikely ever to marry; spinster **2** *informal* a prim, fastidious, or excessively cautious person **3** a card game using a pack from which one card has been removed, in which players try to avoid holding the unpaired card at the end of the game >,old-'maidish *adj*

old man *n* **1** an informal term for **father** or **husband** (sense 1) **2** (*sometimes capitals*) *informal* a man in command, such as an employer, foreman, or captain of a ship **3** *sometimes facetious* an affectionate term used in addressing a man **4** *Christianity* the unregenerate aspect of human nature

old man's beard *n* any of various plants having a white feathery appearance, esp traveller's joy and Spanish moss

old master *n* **1** one of the great European painters of the period 1500 to 1800 **2** a painting by one of these

old moon *n* a phase of the moon lying between last quarter and new moon, when it appears as a waning crescent

Old Nick *n informal* a jocular name for **Satan**

Old Norse *n* the language or group of dialects of medieval Scandinavia and Iceland from about 700 to about 1350, forming the North Germanic branch of the Indo-European family of languages. Abbreviation: **ON**

Old Northwest *n* (in the early US) the land between the Great Lakes, the Mississippi, and the Ohio River. Awarded to the US in 1783, it was organized into the Northwest Territory in 1787 and now forms the states of Ohio, Indiana, Illinois, Wisconsin, Michigan, and part of Minnesota. See also **Northwest Territory**

Old Pretender *n* See (James Francis Edward) **Stuart**

Old Prussian *n* the former language of the non-German Prussians, belonging to the Baltic branch of the Indo-European family: extinct by 1700

old rose *n* **a** a greyish-pink colour **b** (*as adjective*): *old-rose gloves*

Old Saxon *n* the Saxon dialect of Low German up to about 1200, from which modern Low German is derived. Abbreviation: **OS**

old school *n* **1** *chiefly Brit* a school formerly attended by a person **2** a group of people favouring traditional ideas or conservative practices

old school tie *n* **1** *Brit* a distinctive tie that indicates which school the wearer attended **2** the attitudes, loyalties, values, etc, associated with British public schools

Old South *n* the American South before the Civil War

oldster ('əʊldstə) *n* *informal* an older person

old style *n* *printing* a type style reviving the characteristics of old face

Old Style *n* the former method of reckoning dates using the Julian calendar. ▷ Compare **New Style**

Old Testament *n* the collection of books comprising the sacred Scriptures of the Hebrews and essentially recording the history of the Hebrew people as the chosen people of God; the first part of the Christian Bible

old-time *adj* (*prenominal*) of or relating to a former time; old-fashioned: *old-time dancing*

old-timer *n* **1** a person who has been in a certain place, occupation, etc, for a long time **2** *US* an old man

Olduvai Gorge ('ɒldʊˌvaɪ) *n* a gorge in N Tanzania, north of the Ngorongoro Crater: fossil evidence of early man and other closely related species, together with artefacts

old wives' tale *n* a belief, usually superstitious or erroneous, passed on by word of mouth as a piece of traditional wisdom

old woman *n* **1** an informal term for **mother** *or* **wife** (sense 1) **2** a timid, fussy, or cautious person ▷ ˌold-ˈwomanish *adj*

Old World *n* that part of the world that was known before the discovery of the Americas, comprising Europe, Asia, and Africa; the eastern hemisphere

old-world *adj* of or characteristic of former times, esp, in Europe, quaint or traditional

Old World monkey *n* any monkey of the family *Cercopithecidae*, including macaques, baboons, and mandrills. They are more closely related to anthropoid apes than are the New World monkeys, having nostrils that are close together and nonprehensile tails

OLE *computing abbreviation* object linking and embedding: a system for linking and embedding data, images, and programs from different sources

-ole¹ *or* **-ol** *n combining form* **1** denoting an organic unsaturated compound containing a 5-membered ring: *thiazole* **2** denoting an aromatic organic ether: *anisole* [from Latin *oleum* oil, from Greek *elaion*, from *elaia* olive]

-ole² *suffix of nouns* indicating something small: *arteriole* [from Latin *-olus*, diminutive suffix]

oleaceous (ˌəʊlɪˈeɪʃəs) *adj* of, relating to, or belonging to the *Oleaceae*, a family of trees and shrubs, including the ash, jasmine, privet, lilac, and olive [C19: via New Latin from Latin *olea* OLIVE; see also OIL]

oleaginous (ˌəʊlɪˈædʒɪnəs) *adj* **1** resembling or having the properties of oil **2** containing or producing oil [C17: from Latin *oleāginus*, from *olea* OLIVE; see also OIL]

oleander (ˌəʊlɪˈændə) *n* a poisonous evergreen Mediterranean apocynaceous shrub or tree, *Nerium oleander*, with fragrant white, pink, or purple flowers. Also called: **rosebay** [C16: from Medieval Latin, variant of *arodandrum*, perhaps from Latin RHODODENDRON]

olearia (ˌɒlɪˈɛərɪə) *n* *Austral* another word for **daisy bush**

oleate ('əʊlɪˌeɪt) *n* any salt or ester of oleic acid, containing the ion $C_{17}H_{33}COO^-$ or the group $C_{17}H_{33}COO-$: common components of natural fats

OLED *abbreviation* organic light-emitting diode

oleic acid (əʊˈliːɪk) *n* a colourless oily liquid unsaturated acid occurring, as the glyceride, in almost all natural fats used in making soaps, ointments, cosmetics, and lubricating oils. Formula: $CH_3(CH_2)_7CH:CH(CH_2)_7COOH$ [C19 *oleic*, from Latin *oleum* oil + -IC]

olein ('əʊlɪɪn) *n* another name for **triolein** [C19: from French *oléine*, from Latin *oleum* oil + -IN]

oleo- *combining form* oil: *oleomargarine* [from Latin *oleum* OIL]

oleomargarine (ˌəʊlɪəʊˌmɑːdʒəˈriːn) *or* **oleomargarin** (ˌəʊlɪəʊˈmɑːdʒərɪn) *n* other names (esp US) for **margarine**

oleoresin (ˌəʊlɪəʊˈrɛzɪn) *n* **1** a semisolid mixture of a resin and essential oil, obtained from certain plants **2** *pharmacol* a liquid preparation of resins and oils, obtained by extraction from plants ▷ ˌoleoˈresinous *adj*

oleum ('əʊlɪəm) *n*, *pl* **olea** ('əʊlɪə) *or* **oleums** another name for **fuming sulphuric acid** [from Latin: oil, referring to its oily consistency]

O level *n* (formerly, in Britain) **1 a** the basic level of the General Certificate of Education, now replaced by GCSE **b** (*as modifier*): *O level maths* **2** a pass in a particular subject at O level: *he has eight O levels* Formal name: **Ordinary level**

olfaction (ɒlˈfækʃən) *n* **1** the sense of smell **2** the act or function of smelling

olfactory (ɒlˈfæktərɪ, -trɪ) *adj* **1** of or relating to the sense of smell ▷ *n*, *pl* **-ries 2** (*usually plural*) an organ or nerve concerned with the sense of smell [C17: from Latin *olfactus*, past participle of *olfacere*, from *olere* to smell + *facere* to make]

OLG *abbreviation* Old Low German

oligarch ('ɒlɪˌgɑːk) *n* a member of an oligarchy

oligarchy ('ɒlɪˌgɑːkɪ) *n*, *pl* **-chies 1** government by a small group of people **2** a state or organization so governed **3** a small body of individuals ruling such a state **4** *chiefly US* a small clique of private citizens who exert a strong influence on government [C16: via Medieval Latin from Greek *oligarkhia*, from *olígos* few + -ARCHY] ▷ ˌoliˈgarchic *or* ˌoliˈgarchical *adj*

oligo- *or before a vowel* **olig-** *combining form* indicating a few or little: *oligopoly* [from Greek *olígos* little, few]

Oligocene ('ɒlɪgəʊˌsiːn, ɒ'lɪg-) *adj* **1** of, denoting, or formed in the third epoch of the Tertiary period, which lasted for 10 000 000 years ▷ *n* **2** the Oligocene the Oligocene epoch or rock series [C19: OLIGO- + -CENE]

oligochaete ('ɒlɪgəʊˌkiːt) *n* **1** any freshwater or terrestrial annelid worm of the class *Oligochaeta*, having bristles (chaetae) borne singly along the length of the body: includes the earthworms ▷ *adj* **2** of, relating to, or belonging to the class *Oligochaeta* [C19: from New Latin; see OLIGO-, CHAETA]

oligopoly (ˌɒlɪˈgɒpəlɪ) *n*, *pl* **-lies** *economics* a market situation in which control over the supply of a commodity is held by a small number of producers each of whom is able to influence prices and thus directly affect the position of competitors [C20: from OLIGO- + Greek *pōlein* to sell, on the model of MONOPOLY] ▷ ˌoliˌgopoˈlistic *adj*

oligosaccharide (ˌɒlɪgəʊˈsækəˌraɪd, -rɪd) *n* any one of a class of carbohydrates consisting of a few monosaccharide units linked together. See **polysaccharide**

oligospermia (ˌɒlɪgəʊˈspɜːmɪə) *n* the condition of having less than the normal number of spermatozoa in the semen: a cause of infertility in men

oligotrophic (ˌɒlɪgəʊˈtrɒfɪk) *adj* (of lakes and similar habitats) poor in nutrients and plant life and rich in oxygen [C20: from OLIGO- + Greek *trophein* to nourish + -IC] ▷ **oligotrophy** (ˌɒlɪˈgɒtrəfɪ) *n*

Ólimbos ('ɔlɪmbɔs) *n* transliteration of the Modern

Greek name for (Mount) **Olympus** (sense 1)

olio ('əʊlɪˌəʊ) *n*, *pl* **olios** **1** a dish of many different ingredients **2** a miscellany or potpourri [c17: from Spanish *olla* stew, from Latin: jar]

Oliphant ('ɒlɪfənt) *n* Sir **Mark Laurence Elwin**. 1901–2000, British nuclear physicist, born in Australia

olivaceous (ˌɒlɪ'veɪʃəs) *adj* of an olive colour

Olivares (ˌəʊlɪ'vɑːreɪs) *n* **Conde-Duque de**, title of *Gaspar de Guzmán y Pimental*. 1587–1645, Spanish statesman: court favourite and prime minister (1621–43) of Philip IV. His attempts to establish Hapsburg domination of Europe ended in failure

olive ('ɒlɪv) *n* **1** an evergreen oleaceous tree, *Olea europaea*, of the Mediterranean region but cultivated elsewhere, having white fragrant flowers, and edible shiny black fruits **2** the fruit of this plant, eaten as a relish and used as a source of olive oil **3** the wood of the olive tree, used for ornamental work **4** any of various trees or shrubs resembling the olive **5 a** a yellow-olive colour **b** (*as adjective*): *an olive coat* ▷ *adj* **6** of, relating to, or made of the olive tree, its wood, or its fruit [c13: via Old French from Latin *oliva*, related to Greek *elaia* olive tree; compare Greek *elaion* oil]

olive branch *n* **1** a branch of an olive tree used to symbolize peace **2** any offering of peace or conciliation

olive crown *n* (*esp* in ancient Greece and Rome) a garland of olive leaves awarded as a token of victory

olive drab *n* *US* **1 a** a dull but fairly strong greyish-olive colour **b** (*as adjective*): *an olive-drab jacket* **2** cloth or clothes in this colour, esp the uniform of the US Army

olive green *n* **a** a colour that is greener, stronger, and brighter than olive; deep yellowish-green **b** (*as adjective*): *an olive-green coat*

olive oil *n* a pale yellow oil pressed from ripe olive fruits and used in cooking, medicines, soaps, etc

Oliver ('ɒlɪvə) *n* **1** one of Charlemagne's 12 paladins. See also **Roland 2 Isaac**. ?1556–1617, English portrait miniaturist, born in France: he studied under Hilliard and worked at James I's court **3** **Jamie** (**Trevor**). born 1975, British chef and presenter of television cookery programmes **4** **Joseph**, known as *King Oliver*. 1885–1938, US pioneer jazz cornetist

Olives ('ɒlɪvz) *n* **Mount of Olives** a hill to the east of Jerusalem: in New Testament times the village Bethany (Mark 11:11) was on its eastern slope and Gethsemane on its western one

Olivier (ə'lɪvɪˌeɪ) *n* **Laurence** (**Kerr**), Baron Olivier of Brighton. 1907–89, English stage, film, and television actor and director: director of the National Theatre Company (1961–73): films include the Shakespeare adaptations *Henry V* (1944), *Hamlet* (1948), and *Richard III* (1956)

olivine ('ɒlɪˌviːn, ˌɒlɪ'viːn) *n* an olive-green mineral of the olivine group, found in igneous and metamorphic rocks. The clear-green variety (peridot) is used as a gemstone. Composition: magnesium iron silicate. Formula: $(MgFe)_2SiO_4$. Crystal structure: orthorhombic. Also called: **chrysolite** [c18: from German, named after its colour]

olla ('ɒlə; *Spanish* 'oʎa) *n* **1** a cooking pot **2** short for **olla podrida** [Spanish, from Latin *olla*, variant of *aulla* pot]

olla podrida (pɒ'driːdə; *Spanish* po'ðriða) *n* **1** a Spanish dish, consisting of a stew with beans, sausages, etc **2** an assortment; miscellany [literally: rotten pot]

Olmec ('ɒlmɛk) *n*, *pl* **-mecs** *or* **-mec** **1** a member of an ancient Central American Indian people who inhabited the southern Gulf Coast of Mexico and flourished between about 1200 and 400 BC ▷ *adj* **2** of or relating to these people or their civilization or culture

Olmütz ('ɔlmyts) *n* the German name for **Olomouc**

ology ('ɒlədʒɪ) *n*, *pl* **-gies** *informal* a science or other branch of knowledge [c19: abstracted from words with this ending, such as *theology, biology*, etc; see **-LOGY**]

Olomouc (*Czech* 'ɒləmɒʊts) *n* a city in the Czech Republic, in North Moravia on the Morava River: capital of Moravia until 1640; university (1576). Pop: 102 000 (2005 est). German name: **Olmütz**

oloroso (ˌɒlə'rəʊsəʊ) *n* a full-bodied golden-coloured sweet sherry [from Spanish: fragrant]

Olsen ('əʊlsⁿn) *n* **Mary-Kate** and **Ashley** ('æʃlɪ). born 1986, US twin juvenile act who became famous sharing a role in the sitcom *Full House* (1987–95); now known for their videos, CDs, and numerous branded products

Olsztyn (*Polish* 'ɔlʃtin) *n* a town in NE Poland: founded in 1334 by the Teutonic Knights; communications centre. Pop: 176 000 (2005 est)

Olympia (ə'lɪmpɪə) *n* **1** a plain in Greece, in the NW Peloponnese: in ancient times a major sanctuary of Zeus and site of the original Olympic Games **2** a port in W Washington, the state capital, on Puget Sound. Pop: 43 963 (2003 est)

Olympiad (ə'lɪmpɪˌæd) *n* **1** a staging of the modern Olympic Games **2** the four-year period between consecutive celebrations of the Olympic Games; a unit of ancient Greek chronology dating back to 776 BC **3** an international contest in chess, bridge, etc

Olympian (ə'lɪmpɪən) *adj* **1** of or relating to Mount Olympus or to the classical Greek gods **2** majestic or godlike in manner or bearing **3** of or relating to ancient Olympia or its inhabitants ▷ *n* **4** a god of Olympus **5** an inhabitant or native of ancient Olympia **6** *chiefly US* a competitor in the Olympic Games

Olympic (ə'lɪmpɪk) *adj* **1** of or relating to the Olympic Games **2** of or relating to ancient Olympia

Olympic Games *n* (*functioning as singular or plural*) **1** the greatest Panhellenic festival, held every fourth year in honour of Zeus at ancient Olympia. From 472 BC, it consisted of five days of games, sacrifices, and festivities **2** Also called: **the Olympics** the modern revival of these games, consisting of international athletic and sporting contests held every four years in a selected country since their inception in Athens in 1896

Olympic Mountains *pl n* a mountain range in NW Washington: part of the Coast Range. Highest peak: Mount Olympus, 2427 m (7965 ft)

Olympic Peninsula *n* a large peninsula of W Washington

Olympus (əʊ'lɪmpəs) *n* **1** **Mount Olympus** a mountain in NE Greece: the highest mountain in Greece, believed in Greek mythology to be the dwelling place of the greater gods. Height: 2911 m (9550 ft). Modern Greek name: **Ólimbos 2 Mount Olympus** a mountain in NW Washington: highest peak of the Olympic Mountains. Height: 2427 m (7965 ft) **3** a poetic word for **heaven**

Olynthus (əʊ'lɪnθəs) *n* an ancient city in N Greece: the centre of Chalcidice

OM *abbreviation* Order of Merit (a Brit title)

-oma *n combining form* indicating a tumour: *carcinoma* [from Greek *-ōma*]

Omagh (əʊ'mɑː, 'əʊmə) *n* **1** a market town in Northern Ireland. Pop: 19 910 (2001) **2** a district of W Northern Ireland, in Co Tyrone. Pop: 49 560 (2003 est). Area: 1130 sq km (436 sq miles)

Omaha ('əʊməˌhɑː) *n* a city in E Nebraska, on the Missouri River opposite Council Bluffs, Iowa: the largest city in the state; the country's largest livestock market and meat-packing centre. Pop: 404 267 (2003 est)

Oman (əʊ'mɑːn) *n* a sultanate in SE Arabia, on the **Gulf of Oman** and the Arabian Sea: the most powerful state in Arabia in the 19th century, ruling Zanzibar, much of the Persian coast, and part of Pakistan. Official language: Arabic. Official religion: Muslim. Currency: rial. Capital: Muscat. Pop: 2 935 000 (2004 est). Area: about 306 000 sq km (118 150 sq miles). Former name (until 1970): **Muscat and Oman** ▷ **O'mani** *n*, *adj*

Omar ('əʊmɑː) *or* **Umar** *n* died 644 AD, the second caliph of Islam (634–44). During his reign Islamic armies conquered Syria and Mesopotamia: murdered

Omar Khayyám ('əʊmɑː kaɪ'ɑːm) *n* ?1050–?1123, Persian poet, mathematician, and astronomer, noted for the *Rubáiyát*, a collection of quatrains, popularized in the West by Edward Fitzgerald's version (1859)

omasum (əʊ'meɪsəm) *n*, *pl* **-sa** (-sə) another name for **psalterium** [c18: from Latin: bullock's tripe]

Omayyad *or* **Ommiad** (əʊ'maɪæd) *n*, *pl* **-yads**, **-yades** (-əˌdiːz) *or* **-ads**, **-ades** (-əˌdiːz) **1** a caliph of the dynasty ruling (661–750 AD) from its capital at Damascus **2** an emir (756–929 AD) or caliph (929–1031 AD) of the Omayyad dynasty in Spain

ombre or US **omber** ('ɒmbə) n an 18th-century card game [C17: from Spanish hombre man, referring to the player who attempts to win the stakes]

ombudsman ('ɒmbʊdzmən) n, pl-men (in Britain) an official, without power of sanction or mechanism of appeal, who investigates complaints of maladministration by members of the public against national or local government or its servants. Formal names: **Parliamentary Commissioner, Financial Ombudsman** [C20: from Swedish: commissioner]

Omdurman (ˌɒmdɜːˈmɑːn) n a city in the central Sudan, on the White Nile, opposite Khartoum, with which it forms the country's largest city; scene of the **Battle of Omdurman** (1898), in which the Mahdi's successor was defeated by Lord Kitchener's forces. Pop: recent estimates vary between 1 000 000 and 3 000 000

-ome n combining form denoting a mass or part of a specified kind: rhizome [variant of -OMA]

omega ('əʊmɪɡə) n 1 the 24th and last letter of the Greek alphabet (Ω, ω), a long vowel, transliterated as o or ō 2 the ending or last of a series [C16: from Greek ō mega big o; see MEGA-, OMICRON]

omega-3 fatty acid n an unsaturated fatty acid that occurs naturally in fish oil and is valuable in reducing blood-cholesterol levels

omega minus n an unstable negatively charged elementary particle, classified as a baryon, that has a mass 3273 times that of the electron

omelette or esp US **omelet** ('ɒmlɪt) n a savoury or sweet dish of beaten eggs cooked in fat [C17: from French omelette, changed from alumette, from alumelle sword blade, changed by mistaken division from la lemelle, from Latin (see LAMELLA); apparently from the flat shape of the omelette]

omen ('əʊmən) n 1 a phenomenon or occurrence regarded as a sign of future happiness or disaster 2 prophetic significance ▷ vb 3 (tr) to portend [C16: from Latin]

omentum (əʊˈmɛntəm) n, pl-ta (-tə) anatomy a double fold of peritoneum connecting the stomach with other abdominal organs [C16: from Latin: membrane, esp a caul, of obscure origin]

omertà Italian (omer'ta) n a conspiracy of silence

omicron ('ɒmɪkrɒn, 'ɒmɪkrɒn) n the 15th letter in the Greek alphabet (O, o), a short vowel, transliterated as o [from Greek ō mikron small o; see MICRO-, OMEGA]

ominous ('ɒmɪnəs) adj 1 foreboding evil 2 serving as or having significance as an omen [C16: from Latin ōminōsus, from OMEN] > 'ominously adv > 'ominousness n

omission (əʊˈmɪʃən) n 1 something that has been omitted or neglected 2 the act of omitting or the state of having been omitted [C14: from Latin omissiō, from omittere to OMIT] > o'missive adj

omit (əʊˈmɪt) vb omits, omitting, omitted (tr) 1 to neglect to do or include 2 to fail (to do something) [C15: from Latin omittere, from ob- away + mittere to send] > omissible (əʊˈmɪsɪbᵊl) adj > o'mitter n

Ommiad (əʊˈmaɪæd) n, pl-ads, -ades (-əˌdiːz) a variant spelling of **Omayyad**

omni- combining form all or everywhere: omnipresent [from Latin omnis all]

omnibus ('ɒmnɪˌbʌs, -bəs) n, pl-buses 1 a less common word for **bus** (sense 1) 2 Also called: **omnibus volume** a collection of works by one author or several works on a similar topic, reprinted in one volume 3 Also called: **omnibus edition** a television or radio programme consisting of two or more programmes broadcast earlier in the week ▷ adj 4 (prenominal) of, dealing with, or providing for many different things or cases [C19: from Latin, literally: for all, from omnis all]

omnicompetent (ˌɒmnɪˈkɒmpɪtənt) adj able to judge or deal with all matters > ˌomni'competence n

omnidirectional (ˌɒmnɪdɪˈrɛkʃənᵊl, -daɪ-) adj (of an antenna) capable of transmitting and receiving radio signals equally in any direction in the horizontal plane

omnifarious (ˌɒmnɪˈfɛərɪəs) adj of many or all varieties or forms [C17: from Late Latin omnifārius, from Latin omnis all + -farius doing, related to facere to do] > ˌomni'fariously

adv > ˌomni'fariousness n

omnific (ɒmˈnɪfɪk) or **omnificent** (ɒmˈnɪfɪsᵊnt) adj rare creating all things [C17: via Medieval Latin from Latin omni- + -ficus, from facere to do] > om'nificence n

omnipotent (ɒmˈnɪpətənt) adj 1 having very great or unlimited power ▷ n 2 the Omnipotent an epithet for God [C14: via Old French from Latin omnipotens all-powerful, from OMNI- + potens, from posse to be able] > om'nipotence n > om'nipotently adv

omnipresent (ˌɒmnɪˈprɛzᵊnt) adj (esp of a deity) present in all places at the same time > ˌomni'presence n

omniscient (ɒmˈnɪsɪənt) adj 1 having infinite knowledge or understanding 2 having very great or seemingly unlimited knowledge [C17: from Medieval Latin omnisciens, from Latin OMNI- + scīre to know] > om'niscience n > om'nisciently adv

omnium-gatherum ('ɒmnɪəmˈɡæðərəm) n often facetious a miscellaneous collection; assortment [C16: from Latin omnium of all, from omnis all + Latinized form of English gather]

omnivorous (ɒmˈnɪvərəs) adj 1 eating food of both animal and vegetable origin, or any type of food indiscriminately 2 taking in or assimilating everything, esp with the mind [C17: from Latin omnivorus all-devouring, from OMNI- + vorāre to eat greedily] > om'nivorously adv > om'nivorousness n

OMOV or **omov** ('əʊmɒv) n acronym for one member one vote: a voting system in which each voter has one vote to cast

Omphale ('ɒmfəˌliː) n Greek myth a queen of Lydia, whom Hercules was required to serve as a slave to atone for the murder of Iphitus

omphalos ('ɒmfəˌlɒs) n 1 (in the ancient world) a sacred conical object, esp a stone. The most famous omphalos at Delphi was assumed to mark the centre of the earth 2 the central point 3 literary another word for **navel** [Greek: navel]

Omsk (ɒmsk) n a city in W central Russia, at the confluence of the Irtysh and Om Rivers: a major industrial centre, with pipelines from the second Baku oilfield. Pop: 1 132 000 (2005 est)

Omuta ('əʊmuːˌtɑː) n a city in SW Japan, on W Kyushu on Ariake Bay: former coal-mining centre; chemical industries and manufacturing. Pop: 139 345 (2002 est)

on (ɒn) prep 1 in contact or connection with the surface of; at the upper surface of: an apple on the ground; a mark on the table cloth 2 attached to: a puppet on a string 3 carried with: I've no money on me 4 in the immediate vicinity of; close to or along the side of: a house on the sea; this verges on the ridiculous! 5 within the time limits of a day or date: he arrived on Thursday 6 being performed upon or relayed through the medium of: what's on the television? 7 at the occasion of: on his retirement 8 used to indicate support, subsistence, contingency, etc: he lives on bread; it depends on what you want 9 a regularly taking (a drug): she's on the pill b addicted to: he's on heroin 10 by means of (something considered as a mode of transport) (esp in such phrases as on foot, on wheels, on horseback, etc) 11 in the process or course of: on a journey; on strike 12 concerned with or relating to: a tax on potatoes; a programme on archaeology 13 used to indicate the basis, grounds, or cause, of a statement or action: I have it on good authority 14 against: used to indicate opposition: they marched on the city at dawn 15 used to indicate a meeting or encounter: he crept up on her 16 (used with an adjective preceded by the) indicating the manner or way in which an action is carried out: on the sly; on the cheap 17 informal a staked or wagered as a bet: ten pounds on that horse b charged to: the drinks are on me ▷ adv (often used as a particle) 18 in the position or state required for the commencement or sustained continuation, as of a mechanical operation: the radio's been on all night 19 attached to, surrounding, or placed in contact with something 20 in a manner indicating continuity, persistence, concentration, etc: don't keep on about it; the play went on all afternoon 21 in a direction towards something, esp forwards; so as to make progress: we drove on towards London; march on! 22 **on and off** or **off and on** intermittently; from time to time 23 **on and on** without ceasing; continually ▷ adj

24 functioning; operating: *turn the switch to the on position* **25** (*postpositive*) *informal* **a** performing, as on stage: *I'm on in five minutes* **b** definitely taking place: *the match is on for Friday; their marriage is still on* **c** tolerable, practicable, acceptable, etc: *your plan just isn't on* **26 on at** *informal* nagging: *she was always on at her husband* **27** *cricket* (of a bowler) bowling ▷ *n* **28** *cricket* **a** (*modifier*) relating to or denoting the leg side of a cricket field or pitch: *the on side; an on drive* **b** (*in combination*) used to designate certain fielding positions on the leg side: *long-on; mid-on* [Old English *an, on*; related to Old Saxon *an*, Old High German, Gothic *ana*]

On (ɒn) *n* the ancient Egyptian and biblical name for **Heliopolis**

ON *abbreviation* **1** Old Norse **2** (esp in postal addresses) Ontario

-on *suffix forming nouns* **1** indicating a chemical substance: *interferon; parathion* **2** (in physics) indicating an elementary particle or quantum: *electron; photon* **3** (in chemistry) indicating an inert gas: *neon; radon* **4** (in biochemistry) a molecular unit: *codon; operon* [from ION]

onager ('ɒnədʒə) *n, pl* **-gri** (-ˌɡraɪ) *or* **-gers** **1** a Persian variety of the wild ass, *Equus hemionus* **2** an ancient war engine for hurling stones [c14: from Late Latin: military engine for stone throwing, from Latin: wild ass, from Greek *onagros*, from *onos* ass + *agros* field]

onanism ('əʊnəˌnɪzəm) *n* another name for **masturbation** *or* **coitus interruptus** [c18: after *Onan*, son of Judah; see Genesis 38:9] > '**onanist** *n, adj* > ˌonan'istic *adj*

Onassis (əʊ'næsɪs) *n* **Aristotle** (**Socrates**). 1906–75, Argentinian (formerly Greek) shipowner, born in Turkey. In 1968 he married **Jacqueline**, 1929–94, the widow of US President John F. Kennedy

once (wʌns) *adv* **1** one time; on one occasion or in one case **2** at some past time; formerly: *I could speak French once* **3** by one step or degree (of relationship): *a cousin once removed* **4** (in conditional clauses, negatives, etc) ever; at all: *if you once forget it* **5** multiplied by one **6 once and away a** conclusively **b** occasionally **7 once and for all** conclusively; for the last time **8 once in a while** occasionally; now and then **9 once or twice** *or* **once and again** a few times **10 once upon a time** used to begin fairy tales and children's stories ▷ *conj* **11** (*subordinating*) as soon as; if ever or whenever ▷ *n* **12** one occasion or case: *you may do it, this once* **13 all at once a** suddenly or without warning **b** simultaneously **14 at once a** immediately **b** simultaneously **15 for once** this time, if (or but) at no other time [C12 *ones, ānes*, adverbial genitive of *on, ān* ONE]

once-over *n informal* **1 a** a quick examination or appraisal **2** a quick but comprehensive piece of work **3** a violent beating or thrashing (esp in the phrase **give** (**a person** or **thing**) **the** (or **a**) **once-over**)

oncer ('wʌnsə) *n slang* **1** *Brit* (formerly) a one-pound note **2** *Austral* a person elected to Parliament who can only expect to serve one term **3** *NZ* something that happens on only one occasion [c20: from ONCE]

oncogene ('ɒŋkəʊˌdʒiːn) *n* any of several genes, first identified in viruses but present in all cells, that when abnormally activated can cause cancer [c20 from Gk *onkos* mass, tumour + GENE]

oncology (ɒŋ'kɒlədʒɪ) *n* the branch of medicine concerned with the study, classification, and treatment of tumours > on'cologist *n*

oncoming ('ɒnˌkʌmɪŋ) *adj* **1** coming nearer in space or time; approaching ▷ *n* **2** the approach or onset: *the oncoming of winter*

oncost ('ɒnˌkɒst) *n Brit* **1** another word for **overhead** (sense 5) **2** (*sometimes plural*) another word for **overheads**

Ondaatje (ɒn'daːtʃe) *n* **Michael**. born 1943, Sri Lankan-born Canadian writer: his works include the poetry collection *There's a Trick with a Knife I'm Learning to Do* (1979), the Booker-prizewinning novel *The English Patient* (1992, filmed 1997), *Anil's Ghost* (2000), and *Divisadero* (2007)

on dit *French* (ɔ̃ di) *n, pl* **on dits** (ɔ̃ di) a rumour; piece of gossip [literally: it is said, they say]

Ondo ('ɒndəʊ) *n* a state of SW Nigeria, on the Bight of Benin. Capital: Akure. Pop: 3 441 024 (2004). Area: 15 500 sq km (5985 sq miles)

one (wʌn) *determiner* **1 a** single; lone; not two or more **b** (*as pronoun*): *one is enough for now; one at a time* **c** (in combination): *one-eyed; one-legged* **2 a** distinct from all others; only; unique: *one girl in a million* **b** (*as pronoun*): *one of a kind* **3 a** a specified (person, item, etc) as distinct from another or others of its kind: *raise one hand and then the other* **b** (*as pronoun*): *which one is correct?* **4** a certain, indefinite, or unspecified (time); some: *one day you'll be sorry* **5** *informal* an emphatic word for a² or an¹: *it was one hell of a fight* **6** a certain (person): *one Miss Jones was named* **7 in one** *or* **all in one** combined; united **8 all one a** all the same **b** of no consequence: *it's all one to me* **9 at one** (often foll by **with**) in a state of agreement or harmony **10 be made one** (of a man and a woman) to become married **11 many a one** many people **12 neither one thing nor the other** indefinite, undecided, or mixed **13 never a one** none **14 one and all** everyone, without exception **15 one by one** one at a time; individually **16 one or two** a few **17 one way and another** on balance **18 one with another** on average ▷ *pron* **19** an indefinite person regarded as typical of every person: *one can't say any more than that* **20** any indefinite person: used as the subject of a sentence to form an alternative grammatical construction to that of the passive voice: *one can catch fine trout in this stream* **21** *archaic* an unspecified person: *one came to him* ▷ *n* **22** the smallest whole number and the first cardinal number; unity **23** a numeral (1, I, i, etc) representing this number **24** *inf* a joke or story (esp in **the one about**) **25** something representing, represented by, or consisting of one unit **26** Also called: **one o'clock** one hour after noon or midnight **27** a blow or setback (esp in the phrase **one in the eye for**) **28 the Holy One** *or* **the One above** God **29 the Evil One** Satan; the devil ▷ Related prefixes: **mono-, uni-** [Old English *ān*, related to Old French *ān, ēn*, Old High German *ein*, Old Norse *einn*, Latin *unus*, Greek *oinē* ace]

-one *suffix forming nouns* indicating that a chemical compound is a ketone: *acetone* [arbitrarily from Greek *-ōnē*, feminine patronymic suffix, but perhaps influenced by *-one* in OZONE]

one another *pron* the reflexive form of plural pronouns when the action, attribution, etc, is reciprocal: *they kissed one another; knowing one another*. Also: **each other**

one-armed bandit *n* a fruit machine operated by pulling down a lever at one side

Onega (*Russian* a'njega) *n* a lake in NW Russia, mostly in the Karelian Republic: the second largest lake in Europe. Area: 9891 sq km (3819 sq miles)

one-horse *adj* **1** drawn by or using one horse **2** (*prenominal*) *informal* small or obscure: *a one-horse town*

Oneida (əʊ'naɪdə) *n, pl* **-das** *or* **-da 1 Lake Oneida** a lake in central New York State: part of the New York State Barge Canal system. Length: about 35 km (22 miles). Greatest width: 9 km (6 miles) **2 the Oneida** (*functioning as plural*) a North American Indian people formerly living east of Lake Ontario; one of the Iroquois peoples **3** a member of this people **4** the language of this people, belonging to the Iroquoian family [from Iroquois *onēyóte*', literally: standing stone]

O'Neill (əʊ'niːl) *n* **Eugene** (**Gladstone**). 1888–1953, US dramatist. His works, which are notable for their emotional power and psychological analysis, include *Desire under the Elms* (1924), *Strange Interlude* (1928), *Mourning becomes Elektra* (1931), *Long Day's Journey into Night* (1941), and *The Iceman Cometh* (1946): Nobel prize for literature 1936

one-liner *n informal* a short joke or witty remark or riposte

one-man *adj* consisting of or done by or for one man: *a one-man band; a one-man show*

oneness ('wʌnnɪs) *n* **1** the state or quality of being one; singleness **2** the state of being united; agreement **3** uniqueness **4** sameness

one-night stand *n* **1** a performance given only once at any one place **2** *informal* a sexual encounter lasting only one evening or night

one-off *n Brit* **a** something that is carried out or made only once **b** (*as modifier*): *a one-off job* [See OFF (sense 15)]

one-on-one *adj* denoting a relationship or encounter in which someone is involved with only one other person

one-parent family *n* a household consisting of at least one dependent child and the mother or father, the other parent being dead or permanently absent

one-piece *adj* 1 (of a garment, esp a bathing costume) made in one piece ▷ *n* 2 a garment, esp a bathing costume, made in one piece

onerous (ˈɒnərəs, ˈəʊ-) *adj* 1 laborious or oppressive 2 *law* (of a contract, lease, etc) having or involving burdens or obligations that counterbalance or outweigh the advantages [c14: from Latin *onerōsus* burdensome, from *onus* load] >'**onerously** *adv* >'**onerousness** *n*

oneself (wʌnˈsɛlf) *pron* 1 a the reflexive form of **one** (senses 19, 20) b (intensifier): *one doesn't do that oneself* 2 (preceded by a copula) one's normal or usual self: *one doesn't feel oneself after such an experience*

one-sided *adj* 1 considering or favouring only one side of a matter, problem, etc 2 having all the advantage on one side 3 larger or more developed on one side 4 having, existing on, or occurring on one side only >'one-'**sidedly** *adv* >'one-'**sidedness** *n*

one-size-fits-all *adj* relating to policies or approaches that are standard and not tailored to individual needs

one-step *n* an early 20th-century ballroom dance with long quick steps, the precursor of the foxtrot

one-stop *adj* having or providing a range of related services or goods in one place: *a one-stop shop*

One Thousand Guineas *n* See **Thousand Guineas**

one-time *adj* (*prenominal*) at some time in the past; former

one-to-one *adj* 1 (of two or more things) corresponding exactly 2 denoting a relationship or encounter in which someone is involved with only one other person: *one-to-one tuition* 3 *maths* characterized by or involving the pairing of each member of one set with only one member of another set, without remainder

one-track *adj* 1 *informal* obsessed with one idea, subject, etc 2 having or consisting of a single track

one-trick pony *n* *informal*, *chiefly US* a person or thing considered as being limited to only one single talent, capability, quality, etc

one-up *adj* *informal* having or having scored an advantage or lead over someone or something >'one'-**upmanship** *n*

one-way *adj* 1 moving or allowing travel in one direction only: *one-way traffic* 2 entailing no reciprocal obligation, action, etc: *a one-way agreement*

ongoing (ˈɒnˌɡəʊɪŋ) *adj* 1 actually in progress: *ongoing projects* 2 continually moving forward; developing 3 remaining in existence; continuing

onion (ˈʌnjən) *n* 1 an alliaceous plant, *Allium cepa*, having greenish-white flowers: cultivated for its rounded edible bulb 2 the bulb of this plant, consisting of concentric layers of white succulent leaf bases with a pungent odour and taste 3 *know one's onions Brit slang* to be fully acquainted with a subject [c14: via Anglo-Norman from Old French *oignon*, from Latin *unio* onion, related to UNION] >'**oniony** *adj*

Onions (ˈʌnjənz) *n* **Charles Talbut.** 1873–1965, English lexicographer; an editor of the *Oxford English Dictionary*

onionskin (ˈʌnjənˌskɪn) *n* a glazed translucent paper

Onitsha (əˈnɪtʃə) *n* a port in S Nigeria, in Anambra State on the Niger River: industrial centre. Pop: 565 000 (2005 est)

online *or* **on-line** (ˈɒnˌlaɪn) *adj* 1 of, relating to, or concerned with a peripheral device that is directly connected to and controlled by the central processing unit of a computer 2 of or relating to the internet: *online shopping* 3 occurring as part of, or involving, a continuous sequence of operations, such as a production line ▷ *adv* 4 while connected to a computer or the internet ▷ Compare **offline**

onlooker (ˈɒnˌlʊkə) *n* a person who observes without taking part >'on,**looking** *adj*

only (ˈəʊnlɪ) *adj* (*prenominal*) 1 the only being single or very few in number: *the only men left in town were too old to bear arms* 2 (of a child) having no siblings 3 unique by virtue of being superior to anything else; peerless 4 one

and only a (*adjective*) incomparable; unique b (*as noun*) the object of all one's love: *you are my one and only* ▷ *adv* 5 without anyone or anything else being included; alone: *you have one choice only; only a genius can do that* 6 merely or just: *it's only Henry* 7 no more or no greater than: *we met only an hour ago* 8 used in conditional clauses introduced by *if* to emphasize the impossibility of the condition ever being fulfilled: *if I had only known, this would never have happened* 9 not earlier than; not...until: *I only found out yesterday* 10 *if only* an expression used to introduce a wish, esp one felt to be unrealizable 11 *only if* never...except when 12 *only too* a (intensifier): *he was only too pleased to help* b most regrettably (esp in the phrase *only too true*) ▷ *sentence connector* 13 but; however: used to introduce an exception or condition: *play outside: only don't go into the street* [Old English *ānlīc*, from *ān* ONE + *-līc* -LY²]

● USAGE In informal English, *only* is often used as a
● sentence connector: *I would have phoned you, only I didn't*
● *know your number.* This use should be avoided in formal
● writing: *I would have phoned you if I'd known your number.* In
● formal speech and writing, *only* is placed directly
● before the word or words that it modifies: *she could*
● *interview only three applicants in the morning.* In all but the
● most formal contexts, however, it is generally
● regarded as acceptable to put *only* before the verb: *she*
● *could only interview three applicants in the morning.* Care
● must be taken not to create ambiguity, esp in written
● English, in which intonation will not, as it does in
● speech, help to show to which item in the sentence
● *only* applies. A sentence such as *she only drinks tea in the*
● *afternoon* is capable of two interpretations and is
● therefore better rephrased either as *she drinks only tea in*
● *the afternoon* (i.e. no other drink) or *she drinks tea only in*
● *the afternoon* (i.e. at no other time)

on message *adj* (**on-message** *when prenominal*) adhering to or reflecting the official line of a political party, government, or other organization

o.n.o. *abbreviation* (in advertisements in Britain, Australia, and New Zealand) or near(est) offer

onomastics (ˌɒnəˈmæstɪks) *n* (*functioning as singular*) the study of proper names, esp of their origins

onomatopoeia (ˌɒnəˌmætəˈpiːə) *n* 1 the formation of words whose sound is imitative of the sound of the noise or action designated, such as *hiss*, *buzz*, and *bang* 2 the use of such words for poetic or rhetorical effect [c16: via Late Latin from Greek *onoma* name + *poiein* to make] >,ono'mato'**poeic** *or* **onomatopoetic** (ˌɒnəˌmætəpəʊˈɛtɪk) *adj* >,ono,mato'**poeically** *or* ,ono,matopo'**etically** *adv*

Onondaga (ˌɒnənˈdɑːɡə) *n* 1 Lake Onondaga a salt lake in central New York State. Area: about 13 sq km (5 sq miles) 2 (*pl* -gas *or* -ga) a member of a North American Indian Iroquois people formerly living between Lake Champlain and the St Lawrence River 3 the language of this people, belonging to the Iroquoian family [from Iroquois *onótáge'*, literally: on the top of the hill (the name of their principal village)]

on-ramp *n* 1 a ramp that provides access to the specified part of a road system: *an interstate highway on-ramp* 2 a method of accessing a service or facility: *an important on-ramp to the on-line world*

onrush (ˈɒnˌrʌʃ) *n* a forceful forward rush or flow

ONS (in Britain) *abbreviation* Office for National Statistics

onset (ˈɒnˌsɛt) *n* 1 an attack; assault 2 a start; beginning

onshore (ˈɒnˈʃɔː) *adj*, *adv* 1 towards the land: *an onshore gale* 2 on land; not at sea

onside (ˌɒnˈsaɪd) *adj*, *adv* 1 *sport* (of a player) in a legal position, as when behind the ball or with a required number of opponents between oneself and the opposing team's goal line ▷ *adj* 2 taking one's part or side; working towards the same goal (esp in the phrase **get someone onside**). ▷ Compare **offside**

onslaught (ˈɒnˌslɔːt) *n* a violent attack [c17: from Middle Dutch *aenslag*, from *aan* ON + *slag* a blow, related to SLAY]

Ont. *abbreviation* Ontario

Ontario (ɒnˈtɛərɪəʊ) *n* 1 a province of central Canada: lies mostly on the Canadian Shield and contains the fertile plain of the lower Great Lakes and the St

Lawrence River, one of the world's leading industrial areas; the second largest and the most populous province. Capital: Toronto. Pop: 12 392 721 (2004 est). Area: 891 198 sq km (344 092 sq miles). Abbreviations: Ont. or ON **2 Lake Ontario** a lake between the US and Canada, bordering on New York State and Ontario province: the smallest of the Great Lakes; linked with Lake Erie by the Niagara River and Welland Canal; drained by the St Lawrence. Area: 19 684 sq km (7600 sq miles) > **Ontarian** (ɒnˈtɛərɪən) or **Ontarioan** (ɒnˈtɛərɪˌəʊən) n, adj

onto or **on to** ('ɒntʊ; unstressed 'ɒntə) prep **1** to a position that is on: step onto the train as it passes **2** having become aware of (something illicit or secret): the police are onto us **3** into contact with: get onto the factory

● USAGE Onto is now generally accepted as a word in its
● own right. On to is still used, however, where on is
● considered to be part of the verb: he moved on to a
● different town as contrasted with he jumped onto the stage

onto- combining form existence or being: ontogeny; ontology [from Late Greek, from ōn (stem ont-) being, present participle of einai to be]

ontogeny (ɒnˈtɒdʒənɪ) or **ontogenesis** (ˌɒntəˈdʒɛnɪsɪs) n the entire sequence of events involved in the development of an individual organism. ▷ Compare **phylogeny** > ontogenic (ˌɒntəˈdʒɛnɪk) or ˌontoge'netic adj > ˌonto'genically or ˌontoge'netically adv

ontology (ɒnˈtɒlədʒɪ) n **1** philosophy the branch of metaphysics that deals with the nature of being **2** logic the set of entities presupposed by a theory > ontological (ˌɒntəˈlɒdʒɪkᵊl) adj > ˌonto'logically adv

onus ('əʊnəs) n, pl onuses a responsibility, task, or burden [c17: from Latin: burden]

onward ('ɒnwəd) adj **1** directed or moving forwards, onwards, etc ▷ adv **2** a variant of **onwards**

onwards ('ɒnwədz) or **onward** adv at or towards a point or position ahead, in advance, etc

onychophoran (ˌɒnɪˈkɒfərən) n any wormlike terrestrial invertebrate of the phylum Onychophora, having a segmented body, short unjointed limbs, and breathing by means of tracheae: intermediate in structure and evolutionary development between annelids and arthropods [from New Latin Onychophora, from Greek onukh- nail, claw + -PHORE]

-onym n combining form indicating a name or word: acronym; pseudonym [from Greek -onumon, from onuma, Doric variant of onoma name]

onyx ('ɒnɪks) n **1** a variety of chalcedony with alternating black and white parallel bands, used as a gemstone. Formula: SiO_2 **2** a compact variety of calcite used as an ornamental stone; onyx marble. Formula: $CaCO_3$ [c13: from Latin from Greek: fingernail (so called from its veined appearance)]

ONZ abbreviation Order of New Zealand (a NZ title)

oo- or **oö-** combining form egg or ovum: oosperm [from Greek ōion egg EGG[1]]

oocyte ('əʊəˌsaɪt) n an immature female germ cell that gives rise to an ovum after two meiotic divisions

oodles ('uːdᵊlz) pl n informal great quantities: oodles of money [c20: of uncertain origin]

oogamy (əʊˈɒgəmɪ) n sexual reproduction involving a small motile male gamete and a large much less motile female gamete: occurs in all higher animals and some plants > o'ogamous adj

Ookpik ('uːkpɪk) n Canadian trademark a sealskin doll resembling an owl, first made in 1963 by an Inuit and used abroad as a symbol of Canadian handicrafts [from Inuktitut ukpik a snowy owl]

oolite ('əʊəˌlaɪt) n any sedimentary rock, esp limestone, consisting of tiny spherical concentric grains within a fine matrix [c18: from French from New Latin oolitēs, literally: egg stone; probably a translation of German Rogenstein roe stone] > oolitic (ˌəʊəˈlɪtɪk) adj

oolith ('əʊəˌlɪθ) n any of the tiny spherical grains of sedimentary rock of which oolite is composed

oology (əʊˈɒlədʒɪ) n the branch of ornithology concerned with the study of birds' eggs > oological (ˌəʊəˈlɒdʒɪkᵊl) adj > o'ologist n

oolong ('uːˌlɒŋ) n a kind of dark tea, grown in China, that is partly fermented before being dried [c19: from Chinese wu lung, from wu black + lung dragon]

oom ('uːəm) n South African a title of respect used to address an elderly man [Afrikaans: literally, uncle]

oomiak or **oomiac** ('uːmɪˌæk) n other words for **umiak**

oompah ('uːmˌpɑː) n a representation of the sound made by a deep brass instrument, esp in military band music

oomph (ʊmf) n informal **1** enthusiasm, vigour, or energy **2** sex appeal [c20: perhaps imitative of the bellow of a mating bull]

oophorectomy (ˌəʊəfəˈrɛktəmɪ) n, pl -mies surgical removal of an ovary or ovarian tumour. Also called: ovariectomy See **ovariotomy** [c19: from New Latin ōophoron ovary, from Greek ōion egg + phoros bearing, + -ECTOMY]

oops (ʊps, uːps) interj an exclamation of surprise or of apology as when someone drops something or makes a mistake

Oort (ɔːt) n Jan Hendrick. 1900–92, Dutch astronomer, who confirmed (1927) and developed the theory of galactic rotation. He was the first to propose (1950) the existence of a mass of comets orbiting the sun far beyond the orbit of Pluto (the **Oort cloud**)

Oostende (oːstˈɛndə) n the Flemish name for **Ostend**

ooze[1] (uːz) vb **1** (intr) to flow or leak out slowly, as through pores or very small holes **2** to exude or emit (moisture, gas, etc) **3** (tr) to overflow with: to ooze charm **4** (intr; often foll by away) to disappear or escape gradually ▷ n **5** a slow flowing or leaking **6** an infusion of vegetable matter, such as sumach or oak bark, used in tanning [Old English wōs juice]

ooze[2] (uːz) n **1** a soft thin mud found at the bottom of lakes and rivers **2** a fine-grained calcareous or siliceous marine deposit consisting of the hard parts of planktonic organisms **3** muddy ground, esp of bogs [Old English wāse mud; related to Old French wāse, Old Norse veisa]

oozy[1] ('uːzɪ) adj oozier, ooziest moist or dripping

oozy[2] ('uːzɪ) adj oozier, ooziest of, resembling, or containing mud; slimy > 'oozily adv > 'ooziness n

OP abbreviation **1** Ordo Praedicatorum (the Dominicans) **2** organophosphate [(for sense 1) Latin: Order of Preachers]

op. abbreviation **1** operation **2** opus **3** operator

o.p. or **O.P.** abbreviation out of print

opacity (əʊˈpæsɪtɪ) n, pl -ties **1** the state or quality of being opaque **2** the degree to which something is opaque **3** an opaque object or substance **4** obscurity of meaning; unintelligibility

opah ('əʊpə) n a large soft-finned deep-sea teleost fish, Lampris regius (or luna), of the Atlantic and Pacific Oceans and the Mediterranean Sea, having a deep, brilliantly coloured body: family Lampridae. Also called: moonfish, kingfish [c18: of West African origin]

opal ('əʊpᵊl) n an amorphous, usually iridescent, mineral that can be of almost any colour, found in igneous rocks and around hot springs. It is used as a gemstone. Composition: hydrated silica. Formula: $SiO_2.nH_2O$ [c16: from Latin opalus, from Greek opallios, from Sanskrit upala precious stone] > 'opal-ˌlike adj

opalescent (ˌəʊpəˈlɛsᵊnt) adj having or emitting an iridescence like that of an opal > ˌopal'escence n > ˌopale'sce vb

opal glass n glass that is opalescent or white, made by the addition of fluorides

opaline ('əʊpəˌlaɪn) adj **1** opalescent ▷ n **2** an opaque or semiopaque whitish glass

opaque (əʊˈpeɪk) adj **1** not transmitting light; not transparent or translucent **2** not reflecting light; lacking lustre or shine; dull **3** hard to understand; unintelligible **4** unintelligent; dense ▷ n **5** photog an opaque pigment used to block out particular areas on a negative ▷ vb opaques, opaquing, opaqued (tr) **6** to make opaque **7** photog to block out particular areas, such as blemishes, on (a negative), using an opaque [c15: from Latin opācus shady] > o'paquely adv > o'paqueness n

op art (ɒp) n a style of abstract art chiefly concerned with the exploitation of optical effects such as the illusion of movement [c20 *op*, short for *optical*]

op. cit. *abbreviation* (in textual annotations) opere citato [Latin: in the work cited]

ope ('əʊp) *vb, adj* an archaic or poetic word for **open**

OPEC ('əʊ,pɛk) *n acronym for* Organization of Petroleum-Exporting Countries: an organization formed in 1961 to administer a common policy for the sale of petroleum. Its members are Algeria, Angola, Indonesia, Iran, Iraq, Kuwait, Libya, Nigeria, Qatar, Saudi Arabia, the United Arab Emirates, and Venezuela. Ecuador and Gabon were members but withdrew in 1992 and 1995 respectively

op-ed ('ɒp,ɛd) *n* **a** a page of a newspaper where varying opinions are expressed by columnists, commentators, etc **b** (*as modifier*): *an op-ed column in the New York Times* [c20: from *op(posite) ed(itorial page)*]

open ('əʊpⁿn) *adj* **1** not closed or barred **2** affording free passage, access, view, etc; not blocked or obstructed **3** not sealed, fastened, or wrapped **4** having the interior part accessible: *an open drawer* **5** extended, expanded, or unfolded: *an open newspaper; an open flower* **6** ready for business **7** able to be obtained; available: *the position advertised last week is no longer open* **8** unobstructed by buildings, trees, etc: *open countryside* **9** free to all to join, enter, use, visit, etc: *an open competition* **10** unengaged or unoccupied: *the doctor has an hour open for you to call* **11** See **open season 12** not decided or finalized: *an open question* **13** ready to entertain new ideas; not biased or prejudiced: *an open mind* **14** extended or eager to receive (esp in the phrase **with open arms**) **15** exposed to view; blatant: *open disregard of the law* **16** liable or susceptible: *you will leave yourself open to attack if you speak* **17** (of climate or seasons) free from frost; mild **18** free from navigational hazards, such as ice, sunken ships, etc **19** having large or numerous spacing or apertures: *open ranks* **20** full of small openings or gaps; porous: *an open texture* **21** *music* **a** (of a violin or guitar string) not stopped with the finger **b** (of a pipe, such as an organ pipe) not closed at either end **c** (of a note) played on such a string or pipe **22** *commerce* **a** in operation; active: *an open account* **b** unrestricted; unlimited: *open credit; open insurance cover* **23** See **open cheque 24** (of a return ticket) not specifying a date for travel **25** *sport* (of a goal, court, etc) unguarded or relatively unprotected **26** (of a wound) exposed to the air **27** (esp of the large intestine) free from obstruction **28** undefended and of no military significance: *an open city* **29** *phonetics* **a** denoting a vowel pronounced with the lips relatively wide apart **b** denoting a syllable that does not end in a consonant, as in *pa* **30** *maths* (of a set) containing points whose neighbourhood consists of other points of the same set: *points inside a circle are an open set* **31** *computing* (of software or a computer system) designed to an internationally agreed standard in order to allow communication between computers, irrespective of size, maufacturer, etc ▷ *vb* **32** to move or cause to move from a closed or fastened position: *to open a window* **33** (when *intr,* foll by *on* or *onto*) to render, be, or become accessible or unobstructed: *to open a road; to open a parcel; the door opens into the hall* **34** (*intr*) to come into or appear in view: *the lake opened before us* **35** to extend or unfold or cause to extend or unfold: *to open a newspaper* **36** to disclose or uncover or be disclosed or uncovered: *to open one's heart* **37** to cause (the mind) to become receptive or (of the mind) to become receptive **38** to operate or cause to operate: *to open a shop* **39** (when *intr,* sometimes foll by *out*) to make or become less compact or dense in structure: *to open ranks* **40** to set or be set in action; start: *to open a discussion; to open the batting* **41** (*tr*) to arrange for (a bank account, savings account, etc) usually by making an initial deposit **42** to turn to a specified point in (a book, magazine, etc): *open at page one* **43** *law* to make the opening statement in (a case before a court of law) **44** (*intr*) *cards* to bet, bid, or lead first on a hand ▷ *n* **45 the open** any wide or unobstructed space or expanse, esp of land or water **46** See **open air 47** *sport* **a** competition which anyone may enter **48** **bring into the open** to make evident or public **49** **come into the open** to become evident or public ▷ See also **open up** [Old English; related to Old French *open, epen,* Old Saxon *opan,* Old High German *offan*] > **'openable** *adj* > **'openly** *adv*

> **'openness** *n* > **'opener** *n*

open air *n* **a** the place or space where the air is unenclosed; the outdoors **b** (*as modifier*): *an open-air concert*

open-and-shut *adj* easily decided or solved; obvious: *an open-and-shut case*

opencast mining ('əʊpən,kɑːst) *n Brit* mining by excavating from the surface. Also called: (*esp US*) **strip mining,** (*Austral. and NZ*) **open-cut mining** [c18: from OPEN + archaic *cast* ditch or cutting]

open chain *n* a chain of atoms in a molecule that is not joined at its ends into the form of a ring

open cheque *n* an uncrossed cheque that can be cashed at the drawee bank

open circuit *n* an incomplete electrical circuit in which no current flows

Open College *n* **the Open College** (in Britain) a college of art founded in 1987 for mature students studying foundation courses in arts and crafts by television programmes, written materials, and tutorials

open day *n* an occasion on which an institution, such as a school, is open for inspection by the public

open door *n* **1** a policy or practice by which a nation grants opportunities for trade to all other nations equally **2** free and unrestricted admission ▷ *adj* **open-door 3** open to all; accessible

open-ended *adj* **1** without definite limits, as of duration or amount: *an open-ended contract* **2** denoting a question, esp one on a questionnaire, that cannot be answered "yes", "no", or "don't know"

open-eyed *adj* **1** with the eyes wide open, as in amazement **2** watchful; alert

open-faced *adj* **1** having an ingenuous expression **2** (of a watch) having no lid or cover other than the glass

open-handed *adj* generous; liberal > ,open-'handedly *adv* > ,open-'handedness *n*

open-hearted *adj* **1** kindly and warm **2** disclosing intentions and thoughts clearly; candid > ,open-'heartedness *n*

open-hearth furnace *n* (esp formerly) a steel-making reverbatory furnace in which pig iron and scrap are contained in a shallow hearth and heated by producer gas

open-heart surgery *n* surgical repair of the heart during which the blood circulation is often maintained mechanically

open house *n* **1** Also called (in Britain and certain other countries): **at-home** *US & Canadian* an occasion on which an institution, such as a school, is open for inspection by the public. **2 keep open house** to be always ready to provide hospitality

opening ('əʊpənɪŋ) *n* **1** the act of making or becoming open **2** a vacant or unobstructed space, one that will serve as a passageway; gap **3** *chiefly US* a tract in a forest in which trees are scattered or absent **4** the first part or stage of something **5 a** the first performance of something, esp a theatrical production **b** (*as modifier*): *the opening night* **6** a specific or formal sequence of moves at the start of any of certain games, esp chess or draughts **7** an opportunity or chance, esp for employment or promotion in a business concern **8** *law* the preliminary statement made by counsel to the court or jury before adducing evidence in support of his case

opening time *n Brit* the time at which public houses can legally start selling alcoholic drinks

open-jaw *n* (*modifier*) relating to a ticket that allows a traveller to arrive in one place and depart from another

open learning *n* a system of further education on a flexible part-time basis

open letter *n* a letter, esp one of protest, addressed to a person but also made public, as through the press

open market *n* **a** a market in which prices are determined by supply and demand, there are no barriers to entry, and trading is not restricted to a specific area **b** (*as modifier*): *open-market value*

open marriage *n* a marriage in which the partners are free to pursue their own social and sexual lives

open-minded *adj* having a mind receptive to new ideas, arguments, etc; unprejudiced > ,open-'mindedness *n*

open-mouthed *adj* **1** having an open mouth, esp in

surprise **2** greedy or ravenous **3** clamorous or vociferous

open-plan *adj* having no or few dividing walls between areas: *an open-plan office floor*

open position *n commerce* a situation in which a dealer in commodities, securities, or currencies has either unsold stock or uncovered sales

open prison *n* a penal establishment in which the prisoners are trusted to serve their sentences and so do not need to be locked up, thus extending the range of work and occupation they can safely undertake

open punctuation *n* punctuation characterized by sparing use of stops, esp of the comma. ▷ Compare **close punctuation**

open question *n* **1** a matter which is undecided **2** a question that cannot be answered with a yes or no but requires a developed answer

open-reel *adj* another term for **reel-to-reel**

open season *n* a specified period of time in the year when it is legal to hunt or kill game or fish protected at other times by law

open secret *n* something that is supposed to be secret but is widely known

open sesame *n* a very successful means of achieving a result [from the magical words used by Ali Baba in *The Arabian Nights' Entertainments* to open the door of the robbers' den]

open shop *n* an establishment in which persons are hired and employed irrespective of their membership or nonmembership of a trade union

open side *n rugby* **1 a** the side of the scrum on which the majority of the backs are ranged (*as modifier*): *an open-side flanker* **2** openside a flanker who plays on the open side of the scrum

open slather *n* See **slather** (sense 2)

open source *n* **a** intellectual property, esp computer source code, that is made freely available to the general public by its creators **b** (*as modifier*): *open source software*

open system *n computing* an operating system that is not specific to a particular supplier, but conforms to more widely compatible standards

Open University *n* the Open University (in Britain) a university founded in 1969 for mature students studying by television and radio lectures, correspondence courses, local counselling, and summer schools

open up *vb* (*adverb*) **1** (*intr*) to start firing a gun or guns **2** (*intr*) to speak freely or without restraint **3** (*intr*) *informal* (of a motor vehicle) to accelerate **4** (*tr*) to render accessible: *the motorway opened up the remoter areas* **5** to make or become more exciting or lively: *the game opened up after half-time*

open verdict *n* a finding by a coroner's jury of death without stating the cause

openwork (ˈəʊp°nˌwɜːk) *n* ornamental work, as of metal or embroidery, having a pattern of openings or holes

opera[1] (ˈɒpərə, ˈɒprə) *n* **1** an extended dramatic work in which music constitutes a dominating feature, either consisting of separate recitatives, arias, and choruses, or having a continuous musical structure **2** the branch of music or drama represented by such works **3** the score, libretto, etc, of an opera **4** a theatre where opera is performed [c17: via Italian from Latin: work, a work, plural of *opus* work]

opera[2] (ˈɒpərə) *n* a plural of **opus**

operable (ˈɒpərəb°l, ˈɒprə-) *adj* **1** capable of being treated by a surgical operation **2** capable of being operated **3** capable of being put into practice > ˌoperaˈbility *n* > ˈoperably *adv*

opéra bouffe (ˈɒpərə ˈbuːf; *French* ɔpera buf) *n, pl* opéras bouffes (*French* ɔpera buf) a type of light or satirical opera common in France during the 19th century [from French: comic opera]

opera buffa (ˈbuːfə; *Italian* ˈɒpera ˈbuffa) *n, pl* opera buffas *or* opere buffe (*Italian* ˈɒpere ˈbuffe) comic opera, esp that originating in Italy during the 18th century [from Italian: comic opera]

opéra comique (kɒˈmiːk; *French* ɔpera kɔmik) *n, pl* opéras comiques (*French* ɔpera kɔmik) a type of opera, not necessarily comic, current in France during the 19th century and characterized by spoken dialogue. It

originated in satirical parodies of grand opera

opera glasses *pl n* small low-powered binoculars used by audiences in theatres and opera houses

opera hat *n* a collapsible top hat operated by a spring

opera house *n* a theatre designed for opera

operand (ˈɒpəˌrænd) *n* a quantity or function upon which a mathematical or logical operation is performed [c19: from Latin *operandum* (something) to be worked upon, from *operārī* to work]

operant (ˈɒpərənt) *adj* **1** producing effects; operating ▷ *n* **2** a person or thing that operates **3** *psychol* any response by an organism that is not directly caused by a stimulus

opera seria (ˈsɪərɪə; *Italian* ˈɒpera ˈseːrja) *n, pl* opere serie (*Italian* ˈɒpere ˈseːrje) a type of opera current in 18th-century Italy based on a serious plot, esp a mythological tale [from Italian: serious opera]

operate (ˈɒpəˌreɪt) *vb* **1** to function or cause to function **2** (*tr*) to control the functioning of **3** to manage, direct, run, or pursue (a business, system, etc) **4** (*intr*) to perform a surgical operation (upon a person or animal) **5** (*intr*) to produce a desired or intended effect **6** (*tr*; usually foll by *on*) to treat or process in a particular or specific way **7** (*intr*) to conduct military or naval operations **8** (*intr*) to deal in securities on a stock exchange [c17: from Latin *operārī* to work]

operatic (ˌɒpəˈrætɪk) *adj* **1** of or relating to opera **2** histrionic or exaggerated > ˌoperˈatically *adv*

operating budget *n accounting* a forecast of the sales revenue, production costs, overheads, cash flow, etc, of an organization, used to monitor its trading activities, usually for one year

operating system *n* the set of software that controls the overall operation of a computer system, typically by performing such tasks as memory allocation, job scheduling, and input/output control

operating theatre *n* a room in which surgical operations are performed

operation (ˌɒpəˈreɪʃən) *n* **1** the act, process, or manner of operating **2** the state of being in effect, in action, or operative (esp in the phrases **in** *or* **into operation**) **3** a process, method, or series of acts, esp of a practical or mechanical nature **4** *surgery* any manipulation of the body or one of its organs or parts to repair damage, arrest the progress of a disease, remove foreign matter, etc **5 a** a military or naval action, such as a campaign, manoeuvre, etc **b** (*capital and prenominal when part of a name*) Operation Crossbow **6** *maths* any procedure, such as addition, multiplication, involution, or differentiation, in which one or more numbers or quantities are operated upon according to specific rules **7** a commercial or financial transaction

operational (ˌɒpəˈreɪʃən°l) *adj* **1** of or relating to an operation or operations **2** in working order and ready for use **3** *military* capable of, needed in, or actually involved in operations > ˌoperˈationally *adv*

operationalism (ˌɒpəˈreɪʃənəˌlɪzəm) *or* **operationism** (ˌɒpəˈreɪʃəˌnɪzəm) *n philosophy* the theory that scientific terms are defined by the experimental operations which determine their applicability > ˌoperˌationalˈistic *adj*

operations research *n* the analysis of problems in business and industry involving the construction of models and the application of linear programming, critical path analysis, and other quantitative techniques. Also called: **operational research**

operative (ˈɒpərətɪv) *adj* **1** in force, effect, or operation **2** exerting force or influence **3** producing a desired effect; significant: *the operative word* **4** of or relating to a surgical procedure ▷ *n* **5** a worker, esp one with a special skill **6** *US* a private detective > ˈoperatively *adv* > ˈoperativeness *or* ˌoperaˈtivity *n*

operator (ˈɒpəˌreɪtə) *n* **1** a person who operates a machine, instrument, etc, esp a person who makes connections on a telephone switchboard or at an exchange **2** a person who owns or operates an industrial or commercial establishment **3** a speculator, esp one who operates on currency or stock markets **4** *informal* a person who manipulates affairs and other people **5** *maths* any symbol, term, letter, etc, used to indicate or express a specific operation or process, such as Δ (the differential operator)

operculum (əʊˈpɜːkjʊləm) *n, pl* **-la** (-lə) *or* **-lums 1** *zoology* **a** the hard bony flap covering the gill slits in fishes **b** the bony plate in certain gastropods covering the opening of the shell when the body is withdrawn **2** *botany* the covering of the spore-bearing capsule of a moss **3** *biology* any other covering or lid in various organisms [c18: via New Latin from Latin: lid, from *operīre* to cover] > o'**percular** *or* **operculate** (əʊˈpɜːkjʊlɪt, -ˌleɪt) *adj*

operetta (ˌɒpəˈrɛtə) *n* a type of comic or light-hearted opera [c18: from Italian: a small OPERA¹] > ˌoper'**ettist** *n*

ophicleide (ˈɒfɪˌklaɪd) *n music* an obsolete keyed wind instrument of bass pitch [c19: from French *ophicléide*, from Greek *ophis* snake + *kleis* key]

ophidian (əʊˈfɪdɪən) *adj* **1** snakelike **2** of, relating to, or belonging to the *Ophidia*, a suborder of reptiles that comprises the snakes ▷ *n* **3** any reptile of the suborder *Ophidia*; a snake [c19: from New Latin *Ophidia* name of suborder, from Greek *ophidion*, from *ophis* snake]

Ophir (ˈəʊfə) *n Bible* a region, probably situated on the SW coast of Arabia on the Red Sea, renowned, esp in King Solomon's reign, for its gold and precious stones (I Kings 9:28; 10:10)

ophthalmia (ɒfˈθælmɪə) *n* inflammation of the eye, often including the conjunctiva [c16: via Late Latin from Greek, from *ophthalmos* eye; see OPTIC]

ophthalmic (ɒfˈθælmɪk) *adj* of or relating to the eye

ophthalmic optician *n* See **optician**

ophthalmo- *or before a vowel* **ophthalm-** *combining form* indicating the eye or the eyeball [from Greek *ophthalmos* EYE¹]

ophthalmology (ˌɒfθælˈmɒlədʒɪ) *n* the branch of medicine concerned with the eye and its diseases > **ophthalmological** *adj* > ˌophthal'**mologist** (ˌɒfθælˈmɒlədʒɪst) *n*

ophthalmoscope (ɒfˈθælməˌskəʊp) *n* an instrument for examining the interior of the eye > **ophthalmoscopic** (ɒfˌθælməˈskɒpɪk) *adj*

Ophüls (ˈɔːfəls; *German* ˈɔphyls) *n* **Max** (maks). 1902–57, German film director, whose films include *Liebelei* (1932), *La Signora di tutti* (1934), *La Ronde* (1950), *Le Plaisir* (1952), and *Lola Montes* (1955)

-opia *n combining form* indicating a visual defect or condition: *myopia* [from Greek, from *ōps* eye] > **-opic** *adj combining form*

opiate *n* (ˈəʊpɪɪt) **1** any of various narcotic drugs, such as morphine and heroin, that act on opioid receptors **2** any other narcotic or sedative drug **3** something that soothes, deadens, or induces sleep ▷ *adj* (ˈəʊpɪɪt) **4** containing or consisting of opium **5** inducing relaxation; soporific ▷ *vb* (ˈəʊpɪˌeɪt) (*tr*) *rare* **6** to treat with an opiate **7** to dull or deaden [c16: from Medieval Latin *opiātus*; from Latin *opium* poppy juice, OPIUM]

opine (əʊˈpaɪn) *vb* (when *tr, usually takes a clause as object*) to hold or express an opinion: *he opined that it was all a sad mistake* [c16: from Latin *opīnārī*]

opinion (əˈpɪnjən) *n* **1** judgment or belief not founded on certainty or proof **2** the prevailing or popular feeling or view: *public opinion* **3** evaluation, impression, or estimation of the value or worth of a person or thing **4** an evaluation or judgment given by an expert: *a medical opinion* **5** the advice given by a barrister or counsel on a case submitted to him or her for a view on the legal points involved **6 a matter of opinion** a point open to question **7 be of the opinion that** to believe that [c13: via Old French from Latin *opīniō* belief, from *opīnārī* to think; see OPINE]

opinionated (əˈpɪnjəˌneɪtɪd) *adj* holding obstinately and unreasonably to one's own opinions; dogmatic > o'**pinion**ˌatedly *adv* > o'**pinion**ˌatedness *n*

opinionative (əˈpɪnjənətɪv) *adj rare* **1** of or relating to opinion **2** another word for **opinionated** > o'**pinionatively** *adv* > o'**pinionativeness** *n*

opinion poll *n* another term for a **poll** (sense 3)

opioid (ˈəʊpɪˌɔɪd) *n* any of a group of substances that resemble morphine in their physiological or pharmacological effects, esp in their pain-relieving properties

opium (ˈəʊpɪəm) *n* **1** the dried juice extracted from the unripe seed capsules of the opium poppy that contains alkaloids such as morphine and codeine: used in medicine as an analgesic **2** something having a tranquillizing or stupefying effect [c14: from Latin: poppy juice, from Greek *opion*, diminutive of *opos* juice of a plant]

opium poppy *n* a poppy, *Papaver somniferum*, of SW Asia, with greyish-green leaves and typically white or reddish flowers: widely cultivated as a source of opium

Oporto (əˈpɔːtəʊ) *n* a port in NW Portugal, near the mouth of the Douro River: the second largest city in Portugal, famous for port wine (begun in 1678). Pop: 263 131 (2001). Portuguese name: **Porto**

opossum (əˈpɒsəm) *n, pl* **-sums** *or* **-sum 1** any thick-furred marsupial, esp *Didelphis marsupialis* (**common opossum**), of the family *Didelphidae* of S North, Central, and South America, having an elongated snout and a hairless prehensile tail **2** any of various similar animals, esp the phalanger, *Trichosurus vulpecula*, of the New Zealand bush. Also called (Austral. and NZ): **possum** [c17: from Algonquian *aposoum*; related to Delaware *apássum*, literally: white beast]

Oppenheimer (ˈɒpənˌhaɪmə) *n* **J(ulius) Robert.** 1904–67, US nuclear physicist. He was director of the Los Alamos laboratory (1943–45), which produced the first atomic bomb. He opposed the development of the hydrogen bomb (1949) and in 1953 was alleged to be a security risk. He was later exonerated

opponent (əˈpəʊnənt) *n* **1** a person who opposes another in a contest, battle, etc **2** *anatomy* an opponent muscle ▷ *adj* **3** opposite, as in position **4** *anatomy* (of a muscle) bringing two parts into opposition **5** opposing; contrary [c16: from Latin *oppōnere* to oppose, from *ob-* against + *pōnere* to place] > op'**ponency** *n*

opportune (ˈɒpəˌtjuːn) *adj* **1** occurring at a time that is suitable or advantageous **2** fit or suitable for a particular purpose or occurrence [c15: via Old French from Latin *opportūnus*, from *ob-* to + *portus* harbour (originally: coming to the harbour, obtaining timely protection)] > ˈoppor,**tunely** *adv* > ˈoppor,**tuneness** *n*

opportunist (ˌɒpəˈtjuːnɪst) *n* **1** a person who adapts his actions, responses, etc, to take advantage of opportunities, circumstances, etc ▷ *adj* **2** taking advantage of opportunities and circumstances in this way > ˌoppor'**tunism** *n*

opportunistic (ˌɒpətjuˈnɪstɪk) *adj* **1** of or characterized by opportunism **2** *med* (of an infection) caused by any microorganism that is harmless to a healthy person but debilitates a person whose immune system has been weakened by disease or drug treatment

opportunity (ˌɒpəˈtjuːnɪtɪ) *n, pl* **-ties 1** a favourable, appropriate, or advantageous combination of circumstances **2** a chance or prospect

opportunity shop *n Austral & NZ* a shop selling second-hand goods for charitable funds. Also called: **op-shop**

opposable (əˈpəʊzəbəl) *adj* **1** capable of being opposed **2** Also called: **apposable** (of the thumb of primates, esp man) capable of being moved into a position facing the other digits so as to be able to touch the ends of each **3** capable of being placed opposite something else > op'**posably** *adv* > opˌposa'**bility** *n*

oppose (əˈpəʊz) *vb* **1** (*tr*) to fight against, counter, or resist strongly **2** (*tr*) to be hostile or antagonistic to; be against **3** (*tr*) to place or set in opposition; contrast or counterbalance **4** (*tr*) to place opposite or facing **5** (*intr*) to be or act in opposition [c14: via Old French from Latin *oppōnere*, from *ob-* against + *pōnere* to place] > op'**poser** *n* > op'**posing** *adj* > **oppositive** (əˈpɒzɪtɪv) *adj*

opposite (ˈɒpəzɪt, -sɪt) *adj* **1** situated or being on the other side or at each side of something between **2** facing or going in contrary directions: *opposite ways* **3** diametrically different in character, tendency, belief, etc: *opposite views* **4** *botany* **a** (of leaves, flowers, etc) arranged in pairs on either side of the stem **b** (of parts of a flower) arranged opposite the middle of another part **5** *maths* **a** (of two vertices or sides in an even-sided polygon) separated by the same number of vertices or sides in both a clockwise and anticlockwise direction

b (of a side in a triangle) facing a specified angle ▷ *n* **6** a person or thing that is opposite; antithesis ▷ *prep* **7** Also called: **opposite to** facing; corresponding to (something on the other side of a division) **8** as a co-star with: *she played opposite Olivier in "Hamlet"* ▷ *adv* **9** on opposite sides: *she lives opposite* >'**oppositely** *adv* >'**oppositeness** *n*

opposite number *n* a person holding an equivalent and corresponding position on another side or situation

opposition (ˌɒpəˈzɪʃən) *n* **1** the act of opposing or the state of being opposed **2** hostility, unfriendliness, or antagonism **3** a person or group antagonistic or opposite in aims to another **4** **a** **the opposition** a political party or group opposed to the ruling party or government **b** (*capital as part of a name, esp in Britain and other Commonwealth countries*): *Her Majesty's Loyal Opposition* **c** **in opposition** (of a political party) opposing the government **5** a position facing or opposite another **6** something that acts as an obstacle to some course or progress **7** *astronomy* the position of an outer planet or the moon when it is in line or nearly in line with the earth as seen from the sun and is approximately at its nearest to the earth **8** *astrology* an exact aspect of 180° between two planets, etc, an orb of 8° being allowed **9** *logic* **a** the relation between propositions having the same subject and predicate but differing in quality, quantity, or both, as with *all men are wicked; no men are wicked; some men are not wicked* **b** **square of opposition** a diagram representing these relations with the contradictory propositions at diagonally opposite corners >ˌoppo'**sitional** *adj* >ˌoppo'**sitionist** *n* >ˌoppo'**sitionless** *adj*

oppress (əˈprɛs) *vb* (*tr*) **1** to subjugate by cruelty, force, etc **2** to afflict or torment **3** to lie heavy on (the mind, imagination, etc) [c14: via Old French from Medieval Latin *oppressāre*, from Latin *opprimere*, from *ob-* against + *premere* to press] >op'**pressingly** *adv* >op'**pressor** *n*

oppression (əˈprɛʃən) *n* **1** the act of subjugating by cruelty, force, etc or the state of being subjugated in this way **2** the condition of being afflicted or tormented **3** the condition of having something lying heavily on one's mind, imagination, etc

oppressive (əˈprɛsɪv) *adj* **1** cruel, harsh, or tyrannical **2** heavy, constricting, or depressing >op'**pressively** *adv* >op'**pressiveness** *n*

opprobrious (əˈprəʊbrɪəs) *adj* **1** expressing scorn, disgrace, or contempt **2** shameful or infamous >op'**probriously** *adv* >op'**probriousness** *n*

opprobrium (əˈprəʊbrɪəm) *n* **1** the state of being abused or scornfully criticized **2** reproach or censure **3** a cause of disgrace or ignominy [c17: from Latin *ob-* against + *probrum* a shameful act]

oppugn (əˈpjuːn) *vb* (*tr*) to call into question; dispute [c15: from Latin *oppugnāre*, from *ob-* against + *pugnāre* to fight, from *pugnus* clenched fist; see PUGNACIOUS] >op'**pugner** *n*

OPRA ('ɒprə) *n* (in Britain) *acronym for* Occupational Pensions Regulatory Authority

Ops (ɒps) *n* the Roman goddess of abundance and fertility, wife of Saturn. Greek counterpart: Rhea

op-shop *n* *Austral & NZ informal* short for **opportunity shop**

opsin ('ɒpsɪn) *n* the protein that together with retinene makes up the purple visual pigment rhodopsin [c20: back formation from RHODOPSIN]

-opsis *n combining form* indicating a specified appearance or resemblance: *meconopsis* [from Greek *opsis* sight]

opsonin ('ɒpsənɪn) *n* a constituent of blood serum that renders invading bacteria more susceptible to ingestion by phagocytes in the serum [c20: from Greek *opsōnion* victuals] >**opsonic** (ɒpˈsɒnɪk) *adj*

opt (ɒpt) *vb* (when *intr*, foll by *for*) to show preference (for) or choose (to do something). See also **opt in**, **opt out** [c19: from French *opter*, from Latin *optāre* to choose]

optative ('ɒptətɪv) *adj* **1** indicating or expressing choice, preference, or wish **2** *grammar* denoting a mood of verbs in Greek, Sanskrit, etc, expressing a wish ▷ *n* **3** *grammar* **a** the optative mood **b** a verb in this mood [c16: via French *optatif*, from Late Latin *optātīvus*, from Latin *optāre* to desire]

optic ('ɒptɪk) *adj* **1** of or relating to the eye or vision **2** a less common word for **optical** ▷ *n* **3** an informal word for **eye**[1] [c16: from Medieval Latin *opticus*, from Greek *optikos*, from *optos* visible, seen; related to *ōps* eye]

Optic ('ɒptɪk) *n* *Brit trademark* a device attached to an inverted bottle for dispensing measured quantities of liquid, such as whisky, gin, etc

optical ('ɒptɪkᵊl) *adj* **1** of, relating to, producing, or involving light **2** of or relating to the eye or to the sense of sight; optic **3** (esp of a lens) aiding vision or correcting a visual disorder >'**optically** *adv*

optical activity *n* the ability of substances that are optical isomers to rotate the plane of polarization of a transmitted beam of plane-polarized light

optical character reader *n* a computer peripheral device enabling letters, numbers, or other characters usually printed on paper to be optically scanned and input to a storage device, such as magnetic tape. The device uses the process of **optical character recognition**. Abbreviation (for both *reader* and *recognition*): OCR

optical crown *n* an optical glass of low dispersion and relatively low refractive index. It is used in the construction of lenses

optical disc *n* *computing* an inflexible disc on which information is stored in digital form by laser technology. Also called: **video disc**

optical fibre *n* a communications cable consisting of a thin glass fibre in a protective sheath. Light transmitted along the fibre may be modulated with vision, sound, or data signals. See also **fibre optics**

optical flint *n* an optical glass of high dispersion and high refractive index containing lead oxide. They are used in the manufacture of lenses, artificial gems, and cut glass

optical glass *n* any of several types of clear homogeneous glass of known refractive index used in the construction of lenses, etc

optical isomerism *n* isomerism of chemical compounds in which the two isomers differ only in that their molecules are mirror images of each other >**optical isomer** *n*

optical mouse *n* *computing* a type of computer mouse that uses light-emitting and -sensing devices to detect where it is

optical scanner *n* a computer peripheral device enabling printed material, including characters and diagrams, to be scanned and converted into a form that can be stored in a computer. See also **optical character reader**

optician (ɒpˈtɪʃən) *n* **a** Also called: **optometrist** a general name used to refer to an ophthalmic optician, a person qualified to examine the eyes and prescribe and supply spectacles and contact lenses **b** a general name used to refer to a dispensing optician, a person who supplies and fits spectacle frames but is not qualified to prescribe lenses ▷ Compare **ophthalmologist**

optics ('ɒptɪks) *n* (*functioning as singular*) the branch of science concerned with vision and the generation, nature, propagation, and behaviour of electromagnetic light

optimal ('ɒptɪməl) *adj* another word for **optimum** (sense 2)

optimism ('ɒptɪˌmɪzəm) *n* **1** the tendency to expect the best and see the best in all things **2** hopefulness; confidence **3** the doctrine of the ultimate triumph of good over evil **4** the philosophical doctrine that this is the best of all possible worlds ▷ Compare **pessimism** [c18: from French *optimisme*, from Latin *optimus* best, superlative of *bonus* good] >'**optimist** *n* >ˌopti'**mistic** or ˌopti'**mistical** *adj* >ˌopti'**mistically** *adv*

optimize *or* **optimise** ('ɒptɪˌmaɪz) *vb* **1** (*tr*) to take the full advantage of **2** (*tr*) to plan or carry out (an economic activity) with maximum efficiency **3** (*intr*) to be optimistic **4** (*tr*) to write or modify (a computer program) to achieve maximum efficiency in storage capacity, time, cost, etc >ˌoptimi'**zation** *or* ˌoptimi'**sation** *n*

optimum ('ɒptɪməm) *n, pl* **-ma** (-mə) *or* **-mums 1** a condition, degree, amount or compromise that produces the best possible result ▷ *adj* **2** most favourable or advantageous; best: *optimum conditions* [C19: from Latin: the best (thing), from *optimus* best; see OPTIMISM]

optimum population *n economics* a population that is sufficiently large to provide an adequate workforce with minimal unemployment

opt in *v* (*intr, adverb*) to choose to be involved in or part of a scheme, etc

option ('ɒpʃən) *n* **1** the act or an instance of choosing or deciding **2** the power or liberty to choose **3** an exclusive opportunity, usually for a limited period, to buy something at a future date: *he has a six-month option on the Canadian rights to this book* **4** *commerce* the right to buy (**call option**) or sell (**put option**) a fixed quantity of a commodity, security, foreign exchange, etc, at a fixed price at a specified date in the future. See also **traded option 5** something chosen; choice **6 keep** *or* **leave one's options open** not to commit oneself **7** See **soft option** ▷ *vb* **8** (*tr*) to obtain or grant an option on [C17: from Latin *optiō* free choice, from *optāre* to choose]

optional ('ɒpʃənᵊl) *adj* possible but not compulsory; left to personal choice > **'optionally** *adv*

option money *n commerce* the price paid for buying an option

optometrist (ɒp'tɒmɪtrɪst) *n* a person who is qualified to examine the eyes and prescribe and supply spectacles and contact lenses. Also called (*esp Brit*): **ophthalmic optician**

optometry (ɒp'tɒmɪtrɪ) *n* the science or practice of testing visual acuity and prescribing corrective lenses > **optometric** (,ɒptə'mɛtrɪk) *adj*

optophone ('ɒptə,fəʊn) *n* a device for blind people that converts printed words into sounds

opt out *vb* **1** (*intr, adverb; often foll by of*) to choose not to be involved (in) or part (of) ▷ *n* **opt-out 2** the act of opting out, esp of local-authority administration: *opt-outs by hospitals and schools*

opulent ('ɒpjʊlənt) *adj* **1** having or indicating wealth **2** abundant or plentiful [C17: from Latin *opulens*, from *opēs* (pl) wealth] > **opulence** *or less commonly* **opulency** *n* > **'opulently** *adv*

opuntia (ɒ'pʌnʃɪə) *n* any cactus of the genus *Opuntia*, esp prickly bear, having fleshy branched stems and green, red, or yellow flowers [C17: New Latin, from Latin *Opuntia* (*herba*) the Opuntian (plant), from *Opus*, ancient town of Locris, Greece]

opus ('əʊpəs, 'ɒp-) *n, pl* **opuses** *or* **opera** ('ɒpərə) **1** an artistic composition, esp a musical work **2** (*often capital*) (usually followed by a number) a musical composition by a particular composer, generally catalogued in order of publication: *Beethoven's opus 61 is his violin concerto.* Abbreviation: **op** [C18: from Latin: a work; compare Sanskrit *apas* work]

Opus Dei ('əʊpəs 'deɪɪ) *n* **1** another name for **divine office 2** an international Roman Catholic organization of lay people and priests founded in Spain in 1928 by Josemaria Escrivá de Balaguer (1902–75), with the aim of spreading Christian principles

or¹ (ɔː; *unstressed* ə) *conj* (*coordinating*) **1** used to join alternatives **2** used to join rephrasings of the same thing: *to serve in the army, or rather to fight in the army; twelve, or a dozen* **3** used to join two alternatives when the first is preceded by *either* or *whether*: *whether it rains or not we'll be there; either yes or no* **4** one or two a few **5** a poetic word for **either** or **whether** as the first element in correlatives, with *or* also preceding the second alternative [C13: contraction of *other*, used to introduce an alternative, changed (through influence of EITHER) from Old English *oththe*; compare Old High German *odar* (German *oder*)]

or² (ɔː) *adj* (*usually postpositive*) *heraldry* of the metal gold [C16: via French from Latin *aurum* gold]

OR *abbreviation* **1** operations research **2** Oregon **3** *military* other ranks

-or¹ *suffix forming nouns from verbs* a person or thing that does what is expressed by the verb: *actor; conductor; generator; sailor* [via Old French *-eur, -eor,* from Latin *-or* or *-ātor*]

-or² *suffix forming nouns* **1** indicating state, condition, or

activity: *terror; error* **2** the US spelling of **-our**

ora ('ɔːrə) *n* the plural of **os²**

ORAC ('ɔːræk) *n acronym for* Oxygen Radical Absorbance Capacity: a measure of the ability of a substance, esp the blood, to absorb free radicals, used in determining the antioxidant effects of foods

orache *or esp US* **orach** ('ɒrɪtʃ) *n* any of several herbaceous plants or small shrubs of the chenopodiaceous genus *Atriplex*, esp *A. hortensis* (**garden orache**), which is cultivated as a vegetable. They have typically greyish-green lobed leaves and inconspicuous flowers [C15: from Old French *arache*, from Latin *atriplex*, from Greek *atraphaxus*, of obscure origin]

oracle ('ɒrəkᵊl) *n* **1** a prophecy, often obscure or allegorical, revealed through the medium of a priest or priestess at the shrine of a god **2** a shrine at which an oracular god is consulted **3** an agency through which a prophecy is transmitted **4** any person or thing believed to indicate future action with infallible authority [C14: via Old French from Latin *ōrāculum*, from *ōrāre* to request]

oracular (ɒ'rækjʊlə) *adj* **1** of or relating to an oracle **2** wise and prophetic **3** mysterious or ambiguous > **o'racularly** *adv*

oracy ('ɔːrəsɪ) *n* the capacity to express oneself in and understand spoken speech [C20: from Latin *or-, os* mouth, by analogy with *literacy*]

Oradea (Romanian o'radea) *n* an industrial city in NW Romania, in Transylvania: ceded by Hungary (1919). Pop: 182 000 (2005 est.). German name: **Grosswardein.** Hungarian name: **Nagyvárad**

oral ('ɔːrəl, 'ɒrəl) *adj* **1** spoken or verbal **2** relating to, affecting, or for use in the mouth: *an oral thermometer* **3** denoting a drug to be taken by mouth: *an oral contraceptive* **4** of, relating to, or using spoken words **5** *psychoanal* relating to a stage of psychosexual development during which the child's interest is concentrated on the mouth ▷ *n* **6** an examination in which the questions and answers are spoken rather than written [C17: from Late Latin *ōrālis*, from Latin *ōs* face] > **'orally** *adv*

oral history *n* the memories of living people about events or social conditions which they experienced in their earlier lives taped and preserved as historical evidence

oral hygiene *n* another name for **dental hygiene**

orality (ɔː'rælɪtɪ) *n* **1** the quality of being oral **2** a tendency to favour the spoken rather than the written form of language

oral society *n* a society that has not developed literacy

Oran (ɔ'ræn, ə'rɑːn; *French* ɔrã) *n* a port in NW Algeria: the second largest city in the country; scene of the destruction by the British of most of the French fleet in the harbour in 1940 to prevent its capture by the Germans. Pop: 744 000 (2005 est)

orange ('ɒrɪndʒ) *n* **1** any of several citrus trees, esp *Citrus sinensis* (**sweet orange**) and the Seville orange, cultivated in warm regions for their round edible fruit **2 a** the fruit of any of these trees, having a yellowish-red bitter rind and segmented juicy flesh **b** (*as modifier*): *orange peel* **3** the hard wood of any of these trees **4** any of a group of colours, such as that of the skin of an orange, that lie between red and yellow in the visible spectrum in the approximate wavelength range 620–585 nanometres **5** a dye or pigment producing these colours **6** orange cloth or clothing: *dressed in orange* **7** any of several trees or herbaceous plants that resemble the orange, such as mock orange ▷ *adj* **8** of the colour orange [C14: via Old French from Old Provençal *auranja*, from Arabic *nāranj*, from Persian *nārang*, from Sanskrit *nāranga*, probably of Dravidian origin]

Orange¹ ('ɒrɪndʒ) *n* **1** a princely family of Europe. Its possessions, originally centred in S France, passed in 1544 to the count of Nassau, who became William I of Orange and helped to found the United Provinces of the Netherlands. Since 1815 it has been the name of the reigning house of the Netherlands. It was the ruling house of Great Britain and Ireland under William III and Mary (1689–94) and under William III as sole monarch (1694–1702) **2** (*modifier*) of or relating to the Orangemen

3 (*modifier*) of or relating to the royal dynasty of Orange

Orange² *n* **1** (ˈɒrɪndʒ) a river in S Africa, rising in NE Lesotho and flowing generally west across the South African plateau to the Atlantic: the longest river in South Africa. Length: 2093 km (1300 miles) **2** (*French* ɔrɑ̃ʒ) a town in SE France: a small principality in the Middle Ages, the descendants of which formed the House of Orange. Pop: 27 989 (1999)

orangeade (ˌɒrɪndʒˈeɪd) *n* an effervescent or still orange-flavoured drink

orange blossom *n* the flowers of the orange tree, traditionally worn by brides

Orange Free State *n* a former province of central South Africa, between the Orange and Vaal rivers: settled by Boers in 1836 after the Great Trek; annexed by Britain in 1848; became a province of South Africa in 1910; replaced in 1994 by the new province of Free State; economy based on agriculture and mineral resources (esp gold and uranium). Capital: Bloemfontein

Orangeman (ˈɒrɪndʒmən) *n*, *pl* **-men** a member of a society founded in Ireland (1795) to uphold the Protestant religion, the Protestant dynasty, and the Protestant constitution. **Orange Lodges** have since spread to many parts of the former British Empire [c18: after William, prince of *Orange* (king of England as William III)]

Orangeman's Day *n* the 12th of July, celebrated by Protestants in Northern Ireland to commemorate the anniversary of the Battle of the Boyne (1690)

orange pekoe *n* a superior grade of black tea made from the small leaves at the tips of the plant stems and growing in India and Sri Lanka

orange roughy (ˈrʌfɪ) *n*, *pl* **orange roughies** a marine food fish, *Hoplostethus atlanticus*, of S Pacific waters

orangery (ˈɒrɪndʒərɪ, -dʒrɪ) *n*, *pl* **-eries** a building, such as a greenhouse, in which orange trees are grown

orange stick *n* a small stick used to clean the fingernails and cuticles, having one pointed and one rounded end

orangewood (ˈɒrɪndʒˌwʊd) *n* **a** the hard fine-grained yellowish wood of the orange tree **b** (*as modifier*): *an orangewood table*

orang-utan (ˌɔːˌræŋuːˈtæn, ˌɔːˈræŋuːˈtæn) *or* **orang-utang** (ˌɔːˌræŋuːˈtæŋ, ˌɔːˈræŋuːˈtæŋ) *n* a large anthropoid ape, *Pongo pygmaeus*, of the forests of Sumatra and Borneo, with shaggy reddish-brown hair and strong arms [c17: from Malay *orang hutan*, from *ōrang* man + *hūtan* forest]

orate (ɔːˈreɪt) *vb* (*intr*) **1** to make or give an oration **2** to speak pompously and lengthily

oration (ɔːˈreɪʃən) *n* **1** a formal public declaration or speech **2** any rhetorical, lengthy, or pompous speech [c14: from Latin *ōrātiō* speech, harangue, from *ōrāre* to plead, pray]

orator (ˈɒrətə) *n* **1** a public speaker, esp one versed in rhetoric **2** a person given to lengthy or pompous speeches **3** *obsolete* the claimant in a cause of action in chancery

oratorio (ˌɒrəˈtɔːrɪəʊ) *n*, *pl* **-rios** a dramatic but unstaged musical composition for soloists, chorus, and orchestra, based on a religious theme [c18: from Italian, literally: ORATORY², referring to the Church of the Oratory at Rome where musical services were held]

oratory¹ (ˈɒrətərɪ, -trɪ) *n* **1** the art of public speaking **2** rhetorical skill or style [c16: from Latin (*ars*) *ōrātōria* (the art of) public speaking] > ˌoraˈtorical *adj* > ˌoraˈtorically *adv*

oratory² (ˈɒrətərɪ, -trɪ) *n*, *pl* **-ries** a small room or secluded place, set apart for private prayer [c14: from Anglo-Norman, from Church Latin *ōrātōrium* place of prayer, from *ōrāre* to plead, pray]

orb (ɔːb) *n* **1** (in royal regalia) an ornamental sphere surmounted by a cross, representing the power of a sovereign **2** a sphere; globe **3** *poetic* another word for **eye¹** **4** *obsolete or poetic* **a** a celestial body, esp the earth or sun **b** the orbit of a celestial body ▷ *vb* **5** to make or become circular or spherical **6** (*tr*) an archaic word for encircle [c16: from Latin *orbis* circle, disc]

orbicular (ɔːˈbɪkjʊlə), **orbiculate** *or* **orbiculated** *adj* **1** circular or spherical **2** (of a leaf or similar flat part)

circular or nearly circular > **orbicularity** (ɔːˌbɪkjʊˈlærɪtɪ) *n* > **orˈbicularly** *adv*

Orbison (ˈɔːbɪsən) *n* **Roy** (**Kelton**). 1936–89, US pop singer and songwriter. His records include the singles "Only the Lonely" (1960) and "Oh Pretty Woman" (1964) and the album *Mystery Girl* (1989)

orbit (ˈɔːbɪt) *n* **1** *astronomy* the curved path, usually elliptical, followed by a planet, satellite, comet, etc, in its motion around another celestial body under the influence of gravitation **2** a range or field of action or influence; sphere **3** *anatomy* the bony cavity containing the eyeball **4** *zoology* **a** the skin surrounding the eye of a bird **b** the hollow in which lies the eye or eyestalk of an insect or other arthropod **5** *physics* the path of an electron in its motion around the nucleus of an atom ▷ *vb* **6** to move around (a body) in a curved path, usually circular or elliptical **7** (*tr*) to send (a satellite, spacecraft, etc) into orbit **8** (*intr*) to move in or as if in an orbit [c16: from Latin *orbita* course, from *orbis* circle, ORB]

orbital (ˈɔːbɪtᵊl) *adj* **1** of or denoting an orbit **2** (of a motorway or major road circuit) circling a large city ▷ *n* **3** a region surrounding an atomic nucleus in which the probability distribution of the electrons is given by a wave function **4** an orbital road > **ˈorbitally** *adv*

orbital velocity *n* the velocity required by a spacecraft, satellite, etc, to enter and maintain a given orbit

orc (ɔːk) *n* any of various whales, such as the killer and grampus [c16: via Latin *orca*, perhaps from Greek *orux* whale]

Orcadian (ɔːˈkeɪdɪən) *n* **1** a native or inhabitant of Orkney ▷ *adj* **2** of or relating to Orkney [from Latin *Orcades* the Orkney Islands]

Orcagna (Italian orˈkaɲa) *n* **Andrea** (anˈdrɛːa), original name *Andrea di Cione*. ?1308–68, Florentine painter, sculptor, and architect

orchard (ˈɔːtʃəd) *n* **1** an area of land devoted to the cultivation of fruit trees **2** a collection of fruit trees especially cultivated [Old English *orceard*, *ortigeard*, from *ort-*, from Latin *hortus* garden + *geard* YARD²]

orchestra (ˈɔːkɪstrə) *n* **1** a large group of musicians, esp one whose members play a variety of different instruments **2** a group of musicians, each playing the same type of instrument **3** Also called: **orchestra pit** the space reserved for musicians in a theatre, immediately in front of or under the stage **4** *chiefly US & Canadian* the stalls in a theatre **5** (in the ancient Greek theatre) the semicircular space in front of the stage [c17: via Latin from Greek: the space in the theatre reserved for the chorus, from *orkheisthai* to dance] > **orchestral** (ɔːˈkɛstrəl) *adj* > **orˈchestrally** *adv*

orchestrate (ˈɔːkɪˌstreɪt) *vb* (*tr*) **1** to score or arrange (a piece of music) for orchestra **2** to arrange, organize, or build up for special or maximum effect > ˌorchesˈtration *n* > **ˈorchesˌtrator** *n*

orchid (ˈɔːkɪd) *n* any terrestrial or epiphytic plant of the family *Orchidaceae*, often having flowers of unusual shapes and beautiful colours, specialized for pollination by certain insects [c19: from New Latin *Orchideae*; see ORCHIS]

orchidectomy (ˌɔːkɪˈdɛktəmɪ) *n*, *pl* **-mies** the surgical removal of one or both testes [c19: from Greek *orkhis* testicle + -ECTOMY]

orchil (ˈɔːkɪl, -tʃɪl) *or* **archil** *n* **1** any of various lichens, esp any of the genera *Roccella*, *Dendrographa*, and *Lecanora* **2** Also called: **cudbear** a purplish dye obtained by treating these lichens with aqueous ammonia: contains orcinol, orcein, and litmus [c15: from Old French *orcheil*, of uncertain origin]

orchis (ˈɔːkɪs) *n* **1** any terrestrial orchid of the N temperate genus *Orchis*, having fleshy tubers and spikes of typically pink flowers **2** any of various temperate or tropical orchids of the genus *Habenaria*, such as the fringed orchis [c16: via Latin from Greek *orkhis* testicle; so called from the shape of its roots]

orcinol (ˈɔːsɪˌnɒl) *or* **orcin** (ˈɔːsɪn) *n* a colourless crystalline water-soluble solid that occurs in many lichens and from which the dyes found in litmus are derived. Formula: $CH_3C_6H_3(OH)_2$ [c20: from New Latin *orcina*, from Italian *orcello* ORCHIL]

OR circuit or **gate** (ɔː) n computing a logic circuit having two or more input wires and one output wire that gives a high-voltage output signal if one or more input signals are at a high voltage: used extensively as a basic circuit in computers [C20: so named from its similarity to the function of or in logical constructions]

Orcus (ˈɔːkəs) n another name for **Dis** (sense 1)

Orczy (ˈɔːtsɪ) n Baroness **Emmuska** (ˈɛmuʃkə). 1865–1947, British novelist, born in Hungary; author of The Scarlet Pimpernel (1905)

Ord (ɔːd) n a river in NE Western Australia, rising on the Kimberley Plateau and flowing generally north to the Timor Sea: subject of a major irrigation scheme. Length: about 500 km (300 miles)

ordain (ɔːˈdeɪn) vb (tr) **1** to consecrate (someone) as a priest; confer holy orders upon **2** (may take a clause as object) to decree, appoint, or predestine irrevocably **3** (may take a clause as object) to order, establish, or enact with authority **4** obsolete to select for an office [C13: from Anglo-Norman ordeiner, from Late Latin ordināre, from Latin ordo ORDER] > or'dainer n > or'dainment n

ordeal (ɔːˈdiːl) n **1** a severe or trying experience **2** history a method of trial in which the guilt or innocence of an accused person was determined by subjecting him to physical danger, esp by fire or water. The outcome was regarded as an indication of divine judgment [Old English ordāl, ordēl; related to Old Frisian ordēl, Old High German urteili (German Urteil) verdict. See DEAL[1], DOLE[1]]

order (ˈɔːdə) n **1** a state in which all components or elements are arranged logically, comprehensibly, or naturally **2** an arrangement or disposition of things in succession; sequence: alphabetical order **3** an established or customary method or state, esp of society **4** a peaceful or harmonious condition of society: order reigned in the streets **5** (often plural) a class, rank, or hierarchy: the lower orders **6** biology any of the taxonomic groups into which a class is divided and which contains one or more families. Carnivora, Primates, and Rodentia are three orders of the class Mammalia **7** an instruction that must be obeyed; command **8 a** a commission or instruction to produce or supply something in return for payment **b** the commodity produced or supplied **c** (as modifier): order form **9** a procedure followed by an assembly, meeting, etc **10** (capital when part of a name) a body of people united in a particular aim or purpose **11** Also called: **religious order** (usually capital) a group of persons who bind themselves by vows in order to devote themselves to the pursuit of religious aims **12** history a society of knights constituted as a fraternity, such as the Knights Templars **13 a** a group of people holding a specific honour for service or merit, conferred on them by a sovereign or state **b** the insignia of such a group **14 a** any of the five major classical styles of architecture classified by the style of columns and entablatures used **b** any style of architecture **15** Christianity **a** the sacrament by which bishops, priests, etc, have their offices conferred upon them **b** any of the degrees into which the ministry is divided **c** the office of an ordained Christian minister **16** maths **a** the number of times a function must be differentiated to obtain a given derivative **b** the order of the highest derivative in a differential equation **c** the number of rows or columns in a determinant or square matrix **d** the number of members of a finite group **17** the order military the dress, equipment, or formation directed for a particular purpose or undertaking: drill order; battle order **18** a tall order something difficult, demanding, or exacting **19** in order **a** properly arranged **b** appropriate or fitting **20** in order to (preposition; foll by an infinitive) so that it is possible to: to eat in order to live **21** in order that (conjunction) with the purpose that; so that **22** keep order to maintain or enforce order **23** of or in the order of having an approximately specified size or quantity **24** on order having been ordered or commissioned but not having been delivered **25** out of order **a** not in sequence **b** not working **c** not following the rules or customary procedure **26** to order **a** according to a buyer's specifications **b** on request or demand > vb **27** (tr) to give a command to (a person or animal to do or

be something) **28** to request (something) to be supplied or made, esp in return for payment **29** (tr) to instruct or command to move, go, etc (to a specified place): they ordered her into the house **30** (tr; may take a clause as object) to authorize; prescribe: the doctor ordered a strict diet **31** (tr) to arrange, regulate, or dispose (articles) in their proper places **32** (of fate or the gods) to will; ordain > interj **33** an exclamation demanding that orderly behaviour be restored [C13: from Old French ordre, from Latin ordō] > 'orderer n

order-driven adj denoting an electronic market system, esp for stock exchanges, in which prices are determined by the publication of orders to buy or sell. ▷ Compare **quote-driven**

order in council n (in Britain and various other Commonwealth countries) a decree of the Cabinet, usually made under the authority of a statute: in theory a decree of the sovereign and Privy Council

orderly (ˈɔːdəlɪ) adj **1** in order, properly arranged, or tidy **2** obeying or appreciating method, system, and arrangement **3** military of or relating to orders: an orderly book ▷ n, pl -lies **4** med a male hospital attendant **5** military a junior rank detailed to carry orders or perform minor tasks for a more senior officer > 'orderliness n

orderly room n military a room in the barracks of a battalion or company used for general administrative purposes

Order of Australia n an order awarded to Australians for outstanding achievement or for service to Australia or to humanity at large; established in 1975

Order of Canada n an order awarded to Canadians for outstanding achievement; established in 1967

order of magnitude n the approximate size of something, esp measured in powers of 10

Order of Merit n Brit an order conferred on civilians and servicemen for eminence in any field

order of the day n **1** the general directive of a commander in chief or the specific instructions of a commanding officer **2** informal the prescribed or only thing offered or available **3** (in Parliament and similar legislatures) any item of public business ordered to be considered on a specific day **4** an agenda or programme

Order of the Garter n the highest order of English knighthood, open to women since 1987. It consists of the sovereign, 24 knight companions, and extra members created by statute. Also called: **the Garter**

order paper n a list indicating the order in which business is to be conducted, esp in Parliament

orders (ˈɔːdəz) pl n **1** short for **holy orders 2** in (holy) orders ordained **3** take (holy) orders to become ordained **4** short for **major orders** or **minor orders**

ordinal (ˈɔːdɪnəl) adj **1** denoting a certain position in a sequence of numbers **2** of, relating to, or characteristic of an order in biological classification ▷ n **3** short for **ordinal number 4** a book containing the forms of services for the ordination of ministers **5** RC Church a service book [C14 (in the sense: orderly): from Late Latin ordinalis denoting order or place in a series, from Latin ordō ORDER]

ordinal number n a number denoting relative position in a sequence, such as first, second, third. Sometimes shortened to: **ordinal**

ordinance (ˈɔːdɪnəns) n an authoritative regulation, decree, law, or practice [C14: from Old French ordenance, from Latin ordināre to set in order]

ordinarily (ˈɔːdᵊnrɪlɪ, ˌɔːdᵊˈnɛrɪlɪ) adv in ordinary, normal, or usual practice; usually; normally

ordinary (ˈɔːdᵊnrɪ) adj **1** of common or established type or occurrence **2** familiar, everyday, or unexceptional **3** uninteresting or commonplace **4** having regular or ex officio jurisdiction: an ordinary judge **5** maths (of a differential equation) containing two variables only and derivatives of one of the variables with respect to the other ▷ n, pl -naries **6** a common or average situation, amount, or degree (esp in the phrase **out of the ordinary**) **7** a normal or commonplace person or thing **8** civil law a judge who exercises jurisdiction in his own right **9** (usually capital) an ecclesiastic, esp a bishop, holding an office to which certain jurisdictional powers are attached **10** *RC Church* **a** the parts of the Mass that do not vary from day to day **b** a prescribed form of divine service, esp the Mass **11** the US name for **penny-farthing** **12** *heraldry* any of several conventional figures, such as the bend, the fesse, and the cross, commonly charged upon shields **13** *history* a clergyman who visited condemned prisoners before their death **14** *Brit obsolete* **a** a meal provided regularly at a fixed price **b** the inn providing such meals **15** in ordinary *Brit* (used esp in titles) in regular service or attendance: *physician in ordinary to the sovereign* [c16 (adj) and c13 (some n senses): ultimately from Latin *ordinārius* orderly, from *ordō* order]

Ordinary level *n* (in Britain) the formal name for **O level**

ordinary rating *n* a rank in the Royal Navy comparable to that of a private in the army

ordinary seaman *n* a seaman of the lowest rank, being insufficiently experienced to be an able-bodied seaman

ordinary shares *pl n Brit* shares representing part of the capital issued by a company and entitling their holders to a dividend that varies according to the prosperity of the company, to vote at all meetings of members, and to a claim on the net assets of the company, after the holders of preference shares have been paid. US equivalent: **common stock** ▷ Compare **preference shares**

ordinate ('ɔːdɪnɪt) *n* the vertical or y-coordinate of a point in a two-dimensional system of Cartesian coordinates. ▷ Compare **abscissa** [c16: from New Latin phrase (*linea*) *ordināte* (*applicāta*) (line applied) in an orderly manner, from *ordināre* to arrange in order]

ordination (,ɔːdɪ'neɪʃən) *n* **1 a** the act of conferring holy orders **b** the reception of holy orders **2** the condition of being ordained or regulated **3** an arrangement or order

ordnance ('ɔːdnəns) *n* **1** cannon or artillery **2** military supplies; munitions **3** the ordnance a department of an army or government dealing with military supplies [c14: variant of ORDINANCE]

ordnance datum *n* mean sea level calculated from observation taken at Newlyn, Cornwall, and used as the official basis for height calculation on British maps. Abbreviation: OD

Ordnance Survey *n* the official map-making body of the British or Irish government

Ordovician (,ɔːdəʊ'vɪʃɪən) *adj* **1** of, denoting, or formed in the second period of the Palaeozoic era, between the Cambrian and Silurian periods, which lasted for 45 000 000 years during which marine invertebrates flourished ▷ *n* **2** the Ordovician the Ordovician period or rock system [c19: from Latin *Ordovices* ancient Celtic tribe in N Wales]

ordure ('ɔːdjʊə) *n* excrement; dung [c14: via Old French, from *ord* dirty, from Latin *horridus* shaggy]

Ordzhonikidze *or* **Orjonikidze** (*Russian* ardʒəni'kidzɪ) *n* the former name (1954–91) of **Vladikavkaz**

ore (ɔː) *n* any naturally occurring mineral or aggregate of minerals from which economically important constituents, esp metals, can be extracted [Old English *ār, ōra*; related to Gothic *aiz*, Latin *aes*, Dutch *oer*]

öre (ˈøːrə) *n*, *pl* **öre** a Scandinavian monetary unit worth one hundredth of a Swedish krona or (**øre**) one hundredth of a Danish and Norwegian krone

oread ('ɔːrɪˌæd) *n Greek myth* a mountain nymph [c16: via Latin from Greek *Oreias*, from *oros* mountain]

Örebro (*Swedish* œːrəˈbruː) *n* a town in S Sweden: one of Sweden's oldest towns; scene of the election of Jean Bernadotte as heir to the throne in 1810. Pop: 126 940 (2004 est)

orecchiette *or* **orecchietti** (,ɒrəkɪ'ɛtɪ) *pl n* small ear-shaped pasta pieces [c21: from Italian, literally: little ears]

Oreg. *abbreviation* Oregon

oregano (,ɒrɪ'gɑːnəʊ) *n* **1** a Mediterranean variety of wild marjoram (*Origanum vulgare*), with pungent leaves **2** the dried powdered leaves of this plant, used to season food [c18: American Spanish, from Spanish, from Latin *orīganum*, from Greek *origanon* an aromatic herb, perhaps marjoram]

Oregon ('ɒrɪgən) *n* a state of the northwestern US, on

the Pacific: consists of the Coast and Cascade Ranges in the west and a plateau in the east; important timber production. Capital: Salem. Pop: 3 559 596 (2003 est). Area: 251 418 sq km (97 073 sq miles). Abbreviation: Oreg., OR

Oregon trail *n* an early pioneering route across the central US, from Independence, W Missouri, to the Columbia River country of N Oregon: used chiefly between 1804 and 1860. Length: about 3220 km (2000 miles)

Orel *or* **Oryol** (*Russian* aˈrjɔl) *n* a city in W Russia; founded in 1564 but damaged during World War II. Pop: 333 000 (2005 est)

Ore Mountains (ɔː) *pl n* another name for the **Erzgebirge**

Orenburg ('ɒrən,bɜːg; *Russian* arɪn'burk) *n* a city in W Russia, on the Ural River. Pop: 550 000 (2005 est). Former name (1938–57): Chkalov

Orense (*Spanish* o'rense) *n* a city in NW Spain, in Galicia on the Miño River: warm springs. Pop: 109 475 (2003 est)

Oresme (*French* ɔrɛm) *n* **Nicole d'** (nikɔl). ?1320–82, French economist, mathematician, and cleric: bishop of Lisieux (1378–82)

Orestes (ɒ'rɛstiːz) *n Greek myth* the son of Agamemnon and Clytemnestra, who killed his mother and her lover Aegisthus in revenge for their murder of his father

Øresund (œːrəˈsund) *n* the Danish name for the **Sound**

orf (ɔːf) *n vet science* an infectious disease of sheep and sometimes goats and cattle, characterized by scabby pustular lesions on the muzzle and lips; caused by a paramyxovirus. Technical name: **contagious pustular dermatitis** Also called: (*Austral*) scabby mouth

orfe (ɔːf) *n* a small slender European cyprinoid fish, *Idus idus*, occurring in two colour varieties, namely the **silver orfe** and the **golden orfe**, popular aquarium fishes [c17: from German; related to Latin *orphus*, Greek *orphos* the sea perch]

Orff (ɔːf) *n* **Carl** (karl). 1895–1982, German composer. His works include the secular oratorio *Carmina Burana* (1937) and the opera *Antigone* (1949)

org *an internet domain name for* an organization, usually a nonprofit-making organization

organ ('ɔːgən) *n* **1 a** Also called: **pipe organ** a large complex musical keyboard instrument in which sound is produced by means of a number of pipes arranged in sets or stops, supplied with air from a bellows. The largest instruments possess three or more manuals and one pedal keyboard and have the greatest range of any instrument **b** (*as modifier*): *organ pipe; organ stop; organ loft* **2** any instrument, such as a harmonium, in which sound is produced in this way **3** a fully differentiated structural and functional unit, such as a kidney or a root, in an animal or plant **4** an agency or medium of communication, esp a periodical issued by a specialist group or party **5** an instrument with which something is done or accomplished **6** a euphemistic word for **penis** [c13: from Old French *organe*, from Latin *organum* implement, from Greek *organon* tool; compare Greek *ergein* to work]

organdie *or esp US* **organdy** ('ɔːgəndɪ, ɔː'gæn-) *n*, *pl* **-dies** a fine and slightly stiff cotton fabric used esp for dresses [c19: from French *organdi*, of unknown origin]

organelle (,ɔːgə'nɛl) *n* a structural and functional unit, such as a mitochondrion, in a cell or unicellular organism [c20: from New Latin *organella*, from Latin *organum*: see ORGAN]

organ-grinder *n* a street musician playing a hand organ for money

organic (ɔː'gænɪk) *adj* **1** of, relating to, derived from, or characteristic of living plants and animals **2** of or relating to animal or plant constituents or products having a carbon basis **3** of or relating to one or more organs of an animal or plant **4** of, relating to, or belonging to the class of chemical compounds that are formed from carbon: *an organic compound* **5** constitutional in the structure of something; fundamental; integral **6** of or characterized by the coordination of integral parts; organized **7** of or relating to the essential constitutional laws regulating the government of a state: *organic law* **8** of, relating to, or grown with the use of fertilizers or pesticides deriving from animal or vegetable matter, rather than from chemicals ▷ *n* **9** any substance, such as a fertilizer or pesticide, that is derived from animal or vegetable matter > or'ganically *adv*

organic chemistry *n* the branch of chemistry concerned with the compounds of carbon: originally confined to compounds produced by living organisms but now extended to include man-made substances based on carbon, such as plastics

organic light-emitting diode *n* a cell that emits light when voltage is applied: used as a display device replacing LCD technology in hand-held devices such as mobile phones because it is brighter, thinner, faster,and cheaper. Abbreviation: OLED

organism ('ɔːɡəˌnɪzəm) *n* **1** any living biological entity, such as an animal, plant, fungus, or bacterium **2** anything resembling a living creature in structure, behaviour, etc > ˌorgan'ismal *or* ˌorgan'ismic *adj* > ˌorgan'ismally *adv*

organist ('ɔːɡənɪst) *n* a person who plays the organ

organization *or* **organisation** (ˌɔːɡənaɪ'zeɪʃən) *n* **1** the act of organizing or the state of being organized **2** an organized structure or whole **3** a business or administrative concern united and constructed for a particular end **4** a body of administrative officials, as of a political party, a government department, etc **5** order or system; method > ˌorgani'zational *or* ˌorgani'sational *adj*

organizational psychology *n* the study of the structure of an organization and of the ways in which the people in it interact, usually undertaken in order to improve the organization

organize *or* **organise** ('ɔːɡəˌnaɪz) *vb* **1** to form (parts or elements of something) into a structured whole; coordinate **2** (*tr*) to arrange methodically or in order **3** (*tr*) to provide with an organic structure **4** (*tr*) to enlist (the workers) of (a factory, concern, or industry) in a trade union **5** (*intr*) to join or form an organization or trade union **6** (*tr*) *informal* to put (oneself) in an alert and responsible frame of mind [c15: from Medieval Latin *organizare*, from Latin *organum* ORGAN]

organizer *or* **organiser** ('ɔːɡəˌnaɪzə) *n* **1** a person who organizes or is capable of organizing **2** a container with a number of compartments for storage: *hanging organizers to keep your clothes smart* **3** *embryol* any part of an embryo or any substance produced by it that induces specialization of undifferentiated cells

organometallic (ˌɔːɡænəʊmɪ'tælɪk) *adj* of, concerned with, or being an organic compound with one or more metal atoms in its molecules

organon ('ɔːɡəˌnɒn) *or* **organum** *n*, *pl* **organa** ('ɔːɡənə), **-nons** *or* **-na**, **-nums** *Epistemology* **1** a system of logical or scientific rules, esp that of Aristotle **2** *archaic* a sense organ, regarded as an instrument for acquiring knowledge [c16: from Greek: implement; see ORGAN]

organophosphate (ˌɔːɡænəʊ'fɒsfeɪt) *n* any of a group of organic compounds containing phosphate groups and used as a pesticide

organotin (ˌɔːɡænəʊ'tɪn) *adj* of, concerned with, or being an organic compound with one or more tin atoms in its molecules: used as a pesticide, hitherto considered to decompose safely, now found to be toxic in the food chain

organza (ɔː'ɡænzə) *n* a thin stiff fabric of silk, cotton, nylon, rayon, etc [c20: perhaps related to ORGANZINE]

organzine ('ɔːɡənˌziːn, ɔː'ɡænziːn) *n* **1** a strong thread made of twisted strands of raw silk **2** fabric made of such threads [c17: from French *organsin*, from Italian *organzino*, probably from *Urgench*, a town in Uzbekistan where the fabric was originally produced]

orgasm ('ɔːɡæzəm) *n* **1** the most intense point during sexual excitement, characterized by extremely pleasurable sensations and in the male accompanied by ejaculation of semen **2** *rare* intense or violent excitement [c17: from New Latin *orgasmus*, from Greek *orgasmos*, from *organ* to mature, swell] > or'gasmic *or* or'gastic *adj*

orgeat ('ɔːʒɑː; *French* ɔrʒa) *n* a drink made from barley or almonds, and orange flower water [c18: via French, from *orge* barley, from Latin *hordeum*]

orgy ('ɔːdʒɪ) *n*, *pl* **-gies 1** a wild gathering marked by promiscuous sexual activity, excessive drinking, etc **2** an act of immoderate or frenzied indulgence **3** (*often plural*) secret religious rites of Dionysus, Bacchus, etc, marked by drinking, dancing, and songs [c16: from French *orgies*, from Latin *orgia*, from Greek: nocturnal festival] > ˌorgi'astic *adj*

oribi ('ɒrɪbɪ) *n*, *pl* **-bi** *or* **-bis** a small African antelope, *Ourebia ourebi*, of grasslands and bush south of the Sahara, with fawn-coloured coat and, in the male, ridged spikelike horns [c18: from Afrikaans, probably from Khoikhoi *arab*]

oriel window ('ɔːrɪəl) *n* a bay window, esp one that is supported by one or more brackets or corbels [c14: from Old French *oriol* gallery, perhaps from Medieval Latin *auleolum* niche]

orient ('ɔːrɪənt) **1** *poetic* another word for **east**. Compare **occident 2** *archaic* the eastern sky or the dawn **3 a** the iridescent lustre of a pearl **b** (*as modifier*): *orient pearls* **4** a pearl of high quality ▷ *adj* ('ɔːrɪənt) **5** *archaic* (of the sun, stars, etc) rising ▷ *vb* ('ɔːrɪˌɛnt) **6** to adjust or align (oneself or something else) according to surroundings or circumstances **7** (*tr*) to position, align, or set (a map, surveying instrument, etc) with reference to the points of the compass or other specific directions **8** (*tr*) to set or build (a church) in an easterly direction [c18: via French from Latin *oriēns* rising (sun), from *orīrī* to rise]

Orient ('ɔːrɪənt) **the Orient** *n* **1** the countries east of the Mediterranean **2** the eastern hemisphere

oriental (ˌɔːrɪ'ɛntəl) *adj* another word for **eastern**. Compare **occidental**

Oriental (ˌɔːrɪ'ɛntəl) *adj* **1** (*sometimes not capital*) of or relating to the Orient **2** of or denoting a zoogeographical region consisting of southeastern Asia from India to Borneo, Java, and the Philippines ▷ *n* **3** (*sometimes not capital*) an inhabitant, esp a native, of the Orient

Orientalism (ˌɔːrɪ'ɛntəˌlɪzəm) *n* **1** knowledge of or devotion to the Orient **2** an Oriental quality, style, or trait > Ori'entalist *n* > ˌOri'ental'istic *adj*

orientate ('ɔːrɪənˌteɪt) *vb* a variant of **orient**

orientation (ˌɔːrɪɛn'teɪʃən) *n* **1** the act or process of orienting or the state of being oriented **2** position or positioning with relation to the points of the compass or other specific directions **3** the adjustment or alignment of oneself or one's ideas to surroundings or circumstances **4** Also called: **orientation course** *chiefly US & Canadian* **a** a course, programme, lecture, etc, introducing a new situation or environment **b** (*as modifier*): *an orientation talk* **5** *psychol* the knowledge of one's own temporal, social, and practical circumstances in life **6** basic beliefs or preferences **7** the siting of a church on an east-west axis, usually with the altar at the E end > ˌorien'tational *adj*

-oriented *suffix* forming adjectives designed for, directed towards, motivated by, or concerned with: *sports-oriented*

orienteer (ˌɔːrɪən'tɪə) *vb* (*intr*) **1** to take part in orienteering ▷ *n* **2** a person who takes part in orienteering

orienteering (ˌɔːrɪən'tɪərɪŋ) *n* a sport in which contestants race on foot over a course consisting of checkpoints found with the aid of a map and a compass [c20: from Swedish *orientering*; compare ORIENT]

orifice ('ɒrɪfɪs) *n* *chiefly technical* an opening or mouth into a cavity; vent; aperture [c16: via French from Late Latin *ōrificium*, from Latin *ōs* mouth + *facere* to make]

oriflamme ('ɒrɪˌflæm) *n* a scarlet flag, originally of the abbey of St Denis in N France, adopted as the national banner of France in the Middle Ages [c15: via Old French, from Latin *aurum* gold + *flamma* flame]

orig. *abbreviation* **1** origin **2** original(ly)

origami (ˌɒrɪ'ɡɑːmɪ) *n* the art or process, originally Japanese, of paper folding [from Japanese, from *ori* a folding + *kami* paper]

origan ('ɒrɪɡən) *n* another name for **marjoram** (sense 2)

[c16: from Latin *orīganum*, from Greek *origanon* an aromatic herb, perhaps marjoram; compare OREGANO]

origanum (əˈrɪɡənəm) *n* any plant of the herbaceous aromatic Mediterranean genus *Origanum*: family *Lamiaceae*. See **oregano** [New Latin, from Greek *origanon* wild marjoram]

Origen (ˈɒrɪˌdʒɛn) *n* ?185–?254 AD, Christian theologian, born in Alexandria. His writings include *Hexapla*, a synopsis of the Old Testament, *Contra Celsum*, a defence of Christianity, and *De principiis*, a statement of Christian theology

origin (ˈɒrɪdʒɪn) *n* **1** a primary source; derivation **2** the beginning of something; first stage or part **3** (*often plural*) ancestry or parentage; birth; extraction **4** *anatomy* **a** the end of a muscle, opposite its point of insertion **b** the beginning of a nerve or blood vessel or the site where it first starts to branch out **5** *maths* **a** the point of intersection of coordinate axes or planes **b** the point whose coordinates are all zero **6** *commerce* the country from which a commodity or product originates: *shipment from origin* [c16: from French *origine*, from Latin *orīgō* beginning, birth, from *orīrī* to rise, spring from]

original (əˈrɪdʒɪnⁿl) *adj* **1** of or relating to an origin or beginning **2** fresh and unusual; novel **3** able to think of or carry out new ideas or concepts **4** being that from which a copy, translation, etc, is made ▷ *n* **5** the first and genuine form of something, from which others are derived **6** a person or thing used as a model in art or literature **7** a person whose way of thinking is unusual or creative **8** the first form or occurrence of something

originality (əˌrɪdʒɪˈnælɪtɪ) *n, pl* **-ties 1** the quality or condition of being original **2** the ability to create or innovate

originally (əˈrɪdʒɪnəlɪ) *adv* **1** in the first place **2** in an original way **3** with reference to the origin or beginning

original sin *n* a state of sin held to be innate in mankind as the descendants of Adam

originate (əˈrɪdʒɪˌneɪt) *vb* **1** to come or bring into being **2** (*intr*) *US & Canadian* (of a bus, train, etc) to begin its journey at a specified point > ˌoriˈgiˈnation *n* > oˈrigiˌnator *n*

O-ring *n* a rubber ring used in machinery as a seal against oil, air, etc

Orinoco (ˌɒrɪˈnəʊkəʊ) *n* a river in N South America, rising in S Venezuela and flowing west, then north as part of the border between Colombia and Venezuela, then east to the Atlantic by a great delta: the third largest river system in South America, draining an area of 945 000 sq km (365 000 sq miles); reaches a width of 22 km (14 miles) during the rainy season. Length: about 2575 km (1600 miles)

oriole (ˈɔːrɪˌəʊl) *n* **1** any songbird of the mainly tropical Old World family *Oriolidae*, such as *Oriolus oriolus* (**golden oriole**), having a long pointed bill and a mostly yellow-and-black plumage **2** any American songbird of the family *Icteridae*, esp those of the genus *Icterus*, such as the Baltimore oriole, with a typical male plumage of black with either orange or yellow [c18: from Medieval Latin *oryolus*, from Latin *aureolus*, diminutive of *aureus*, from *aurum* gold]

Orion[1] (əˈraɪən) *n Greek myth* a Boeotian giant famed as a great hunter, who figures in several tales

Orion[2] (əˈraɪən) *n, Latin genitive* Orionis (ˌɔːrɪˈəʊnɪs) a conspicuous constellation near Canis Major containing two first magnitude stars (Betelgeuse and Rigel) and a distant bright emission nebula (the **Orion Nebula**) associated with a system of giant molecular clouds and star formation

orison (ˈɒrɪzⁿn) *n literary* another word for **prayer**[1] [c12: from Old French *oreison*, from Late Latin *ōrātiō*, from Latin: speech, from *ōrāre* to speak]

Orissa (ɒˈrɪsə) *n* a state of E India, on the Bay of Bengal: part of the province of Bihar and Orissa (1912–36); enlarged by the addition of 25 native states in 1949. Capital: Bhubaneswar. Pop: 36 706 920 (2001). Area: 155 707 sq km (60 119 sq miles)

Oriya (ɒˈriːə) *n* **1** (*pl* **-ya**) a member of a people of India living chiefly in Orissa and neighbouring states **2** the state language of Orissa, belonging to the Indic branch

of the Indo-European family

Orizaba (ˌɒrɪˈzɑːbə; *Spanish* oriˈθaβa) *n* **1** a city and resort in SE Mexico, in Veracruz state. Pop: 327 000 (2005 est) **2** Pico de Orizaba the Spanish name for **Citlaltépetl**

Orjonikidze (*Russian* ardʒəniˈkidzi) *n* a variant spelling of **Ordzhonikidze**

Orkney (ˈɔːknɪ), **Orkneys** (ˈɔːknɪz) *or* **Orkney Islands** *pl n* a group of over 70 islands off the N coast of Scotland, separated from the mainland by the Pentland Firth: constitutes an island authority of Scotland; low-lying and treeless; many important prehistoric remains. Administrative centre: Kirkwall. Pop: 19 310 (2003 est). Area: 974 sq km (376 sq miles) Related word: **Orcadian**

Orkneyman (ˈɔːknɪmən) *n, pl* **-men** a native or inhabitant of Orkney > ˈOrkneyˌwoman *n*

Orlando (ɔːˈlændəʊ) *n* a city in the US, in Florida: site of Walt Disney World. Pop: 199 336 (2003 est)

Orléans[1] (ɔːˈlɪənz; *French* ɔrleã) *n* a city in N central France, on the River Loire: famous for its deliverance by Joan of Arc from the long English siege in 1429; university (1305); an important rail and road junction. Pop: 113 126 (1999)

Orléans[2] (*French* ɔrleã) *n* **1 Charles** (ʃarl), Duc d'Orléans. 1394–1465, French poet; noted for the poems written during his imprisonment in England; father of Louis XII **2 Louis Philippe Joseph** (lwi filip ʒozɛf), Duc d'Orléans, known as *Philippe Égalité* (after 1792). 1747–93, French nobleman, who supported the French Revolution and voted for the death of his cousin, Louis XVI, but was executed after his son, the future king Louis-Philippe, defected to the Austrians

Orlon (ˈɔːlɒn) *n trademark* a crease-resistant acrylic fibre or fabric used for clothing, furnishings, etc

orlop *or* **orlop deck** (ˈɔːlɒp) *n nautical* (in a vessel with four or more decks) the lowest deck [c15: from Dutch *overloopen* to run over, spill. See OVER, LEAP]

Orlov (ˈɔːlɒf) *n* Count **Grigori Grigorievich.** 1734–83, Russian soldier and a lover of Catherine II. He led (with his brother, Count **Aleksey Grigorievich Orlov**, 1737–1808) the coup that brought Catherine to power

Orly (ˈɔːliː; *French* ɔrli) *n* a suburb of SE Paris, France, with an international airport

Ormandy (ˈɔːməndɪ) *n* Eugene. 1899–1985, US conductor, born in Hungary

Ormazd *or* **Ormuzd** (ˈɔːməzd) *n Zoroastrianism* the creative deity, embodiment of good and opponent of Ahriman. Also called: Ahura Mazda [from Persian, from Avestan *Ahura-Mazda*, from *ahura* spirit + *mazdā* wise]

ormer (ˈɔːmə) *n* **1** Also called: sea-ear an edible marine gastropod mollusc, *Haliotis tuberculata*, that has an ear-shaped shell perforated with holes and occurs near the Channel Islands **2** any other abalone [c17: from French (Guernsey dialect), apparently from Latin *auris* ear + *mare* sea]

ormolu (ˈɔːməˌluː) *n* **1 a** a gold-coloured alloy of copper, tin, or zinc used to decorate furniture, mouldings, etc **b** (*as modifier*) **2** gold prepared to be used for gilding [c18: from French *or moulu* ground gold]

Ormonde (ˈɔːmənd) *n* **1st Duke of**, title of James Butler. 1610–88, Anglo-Irish general; commander (1641–50) of the royalist forces in Ireland; Lord Lieutenant of Ireland (1661–69; 1677–84)

Ormuz (ˈɔːmʌz) *n* a variant spelling of **Hormuz**

ornament *n* (ˈɔːnəmənt) **1** anything that enhances the appearance of a person or thing **2** decorations collectively: *she was totally without ornament* **3** a small decorative object **4** something regarded as a source of pride or beauty **5** *music* any of several decorations, such as the trill, mordent, etc, occurring chiefly as improvised embellishments in baroque music ▷ *vb* (ˈɔːnəˌmɛnt) (*tr*) **6** to decorate with or as if with ornaments **7** to serve as an ornament to [c14: from Latin *ornāmentum*, from *ornāre* to adorn] > ˌornamenˈtation *n*

ornamental (ˌɔːnəˈmɛntⁿl) *adj* **1** of value as an ornament; decorative **2** (of a plant) used to decorate houses, gardens, etc ▷ *n* **3** a plant cultivated for show or decoration > ˌornaˈmentally *adv*

ornate (ɔːˈneɪt) *adj* **1** heavily or elaborately decorated **2** (of style in writing) overembellished; flowery [c15:

from Latin *ornāre* to decorate] > or'nately *adv*
> or'nateness *n*

Orne (French ɔrn) *n* a department of NW France, in Basse-Normandie. Capital: Alençon. Pop: 291 274 (2003 est). Area: 6144 sq km (2396 sq miles)

ornery ('ɔːnərɪ) *adj US & Canadian dialect or informal* 1 stubborn or vile-tempered 2 low; treacherous: *an ornery trick* 3 ordinary [C19: alteration of ORDINARY]
> 'orneriness *n*

ornitho- *or before a vowel* **ornith-** *combining form* bird or birds: *ornithology; ornithomancy; ornithopter; ornithoscopy; ornithosis* [from Greek *ornis*, *ornith-* bird]

ornithology (ˌɔːnɪˈθɒlədʒɪ) *n* the study of birds, including their physiology, classification, ecology, and behaviour > **ornithological** (ˌɔːnɪθəˈlɒdʒɪkəl) *adj*
> ˌornithoˈlogically *adv* > ˌorniˈthologist *n*

ornithorhynchus (ˌɔːnɪθəʊˈrɪŋkəs) *n* the technical name for **duck-billed platypus** [C19: New Latin, from ORNITHO- + Greek *rhunkhos* bill]

oro-¹ *combining form* mountain: *orogeny; orography* [from Greek *oros*]

oro-² *combining form* oral; mouth: *oromaxillary* [from Latin, from *ōs*]

orogeny (ɒˈrɒdʒɪnɪ) *or* **orogenesis** (ˌɒrəʊˈdʒɛnɪsɪs) *n* the formation of mountain ranges by intense upward displacement of the earth's crust, usually associated with folding, thrust faulting, and other compressional processes > **oro'genic** (ˌɒrəʊˈdʒɛnɪk) *or* **orogenetic** (ˌɒrəʊdʒɪˈnɛtɪk) *adj*

Orontes (ɒˈrɒntiːz) *n* a river in SW Asia, rising in Lebanon and flowing north through Syria into Turkey, where it turns west to the Mediterranean. Length: 571 km (355 miles). Arabic name: 'Asi

orotund ('ɒrəʊˌtʌnd) *adj* 1 (of the voice) resonant; booming 2 (of speech or writing) bombastic; pompous [C18: from Latin phrase *ore rotundo* with rounded mouth]

Orozco (Spanish oˈrɔθko) *n* **José Clemente** (xoˈse kleˈmente). 1883–1949, Mexican painter, noted for his monumental humanistic murals

orphan ('ɔːfən) *n* 1 a a child, one or (more commonly) both of whose parents are dead b (*as modifier*): *an orphan child* ▷ *vb* 2 (*tr*) to deprive of one or both parents [C15: from Late Latin *orphanus*, from Greek *orphanos*; compare Latin *orbus* bereaved]

orphanage ('ɔːfənɪdʒ) *n* 1 an institution for orphans and abandoned children 2 the state of being an orphan

Orphean ('ɔːfɪən) *adj* 1 of or relating to Orpheus 2 melodious or enchanting

Orpheus ('ɔːfɪəs, -fjuːs) *n* Greek myth a poet and lyre-player credited with the authorship of the poems forming the basis of Orphism. He married Eurydice and sought her in Hades after her death. He failed to win her back and was killed by a band of bacchantes

Orphic ('ɔːfɪk) *adj* 1 of or relating to Orpheus or Orphism 2 (*sometimes not capital*) mystical or occult > **'Orphically** *adv*

Orphism ('ɔːfɪzəm) *n* a mystery religion of ancient Greece, widespread from the 6th century BC onwards, combining pre-Hellenic beliefs, the Thracian cult of (Dionysius) Zagreus, etc > **Or'phistic** *adj*

orpiment ('ɔːpɪmənt) *n* a yellow mineral consisting of arsenic trisulphide in monoclinic crystalline form occurring in association with realgar: it is an ore of arsenic. Formula: As_2S_3 [C14: via Old French from Latin *auripigmentum* gold pigment]

orpine ('ɔːpaɪn) *or* **orpin** ('ɔːpɪn) *n* a succulent perennial N temperate crassulaceous plant, *Sedum telephium*, with toothed leaves and heads of small purplish-white flowers [C14: from Old French, apparently from ORPIMENT (perhaps referring to the yellow flowers of a related species)]

Orpington ('ɔːpɪŋtən) *n* a district of SE London, part of the Greater London borough of Bromley from 1965

Orr (ɔː) *n* **Robert Gordon**, known as *Bobby*. born 1948, Canadian ice-hockey player

orrery ('ɒrərɪ) *n*, *pl* **-ries** a mechanical model of the solar system in which the planets can be moved at the correct relative velocities around the sun [C18: originally made for Charles Boyle, Earl of *Orrery*]

orris¹ *or* **orrice** ('ɒrɪs) *n* 1 any of various irises, esp *Iris*

florentina, that have fragrant rhizomes 2 Also called: 'orrisroot the rhizome of such a plant, prepared and used as perfume [C16: variant of IRIS]

orris² ('ɒrɪs) *n* a kind of lace made of gold or silver, used esp in the 18th century [from Old French *orfreis*, from Latin *auriphrygium* Phrygian gold]

Orsini (Italian orˈsiːni) *n* an Italian aristocratic family that was prominent in Rome from the 12th to the 18th century

Orsk (Russian ɔrsk) *n* a city in W Russia, on the Ural River: a major railway and industrial centre, with an oil refinery linked by pipeline with the Emba field (on the Caspian). Pop: 247 000 (2005 est)

Ortega (ɔːˈteɪɡə) *n* **Daniel**, full surname *Ortega Saavedra*. born 1945, Nicaraguan politician and former resistance leader; president of Nicaragua (1985–90) and from 2007

Ortegal (Spanish orteˈɣal) *n* **Cape Ortegal** a cape in NW Spain, projecting into the Bay of Biscay

Ortega y Gasset (Spanish orˈteɣa i ɡaˈsɛt) *n* **José** (xoˈse). 1883–1955, Spanish essayist and philosopher. His best-known work is *The Revolt of the Masses* (1930)

orthicon ('ɔːθɪˌkɒn) *n* a television camera tube in which an optical image produces a corresponding electrical charge pattern on a mosaic surface that is scanned from behind by an electron beam. The resulting discharge of the mosaic provides the output signal current. See also **image orthicon** [C20: from ORTHO- + ICON(OSCOPE)]

ortho- *or before a vowel* **orth-** *combining form* 1 straight or upright: *orthotropous* 2 perpendicular or at right angles: *orthoclastic* 3 correct or right: *orthodontics; orthodox; orthography; orthoptics* 4 (*often in italics*) denoting an organic compound containing a benzene ring with substituents attached to adjacent carbon atoms (the 1,2- positions) 5 denoting an oxyacid regarded as the highest hydrated form of the anhydride or a salt of such an acid: *orthophosphoric acid* 6 denoting a diatomic substance in which the spins of the two atoms are parallel: *orthohydrogen* [from Greek *orthos* straight, right, upright]

orthochromatic (ˌɔːθəʊkrəʊˈmætɪk) *adj* photog of or relating to an emulsion giving a rendering of relative light intensities of different colours that corresponds approximately to the colour sensitivity of the eye, esp one that is insensitive to red light. See **panchromatic**

orthoclase ('ɔːθəʊˌkleɪs, -ˌkleɪz) *n* a white to pale yellow, red, or green mineral of the feldspar group, found in igneous, sedimentary, and metamorphic rocks. It is used in the manufacture of glass and ceramics. Composition: potassium aluminium silicate. Formula: $KAlSi_3O_8$. Crystal structure: monoclinic

orthodontics (ˌɔːθəʊˈdɒntɪks) *or* **orthodontia** (ˌɔːθəʊˈdɒntɪə) *n* (*functioning as singular*) the branch of dentistry concerned with preventing or correcting irregularities of the teeth > ˌortho'dontic *adj*
> ˌortho'dontist *n*

orthodox ('ɔːθəˌdɒks) *adj* 1 conforming with established or accepted standards, as in religion, behaviour, or attitudes 2 conforming to the Christian faith as established by the early Church [C16: via Church Latin from Greek *orthodoxos*, from *orthos* correct + *doxa* belief]
> 'ortho,doxly *adv* > 'ortho,doxy *n*

Orthodox ('ɔːθəˌdɒks) *adj* 1 of or relating to the Orthodox Church of the East 2 (*sometimes not capital*) of or relating to Orthodox Judaism

Orthodox Church *n* 1 Also called: **Byzantine Church, Eastern Orthodox Church, Greek Orthodox Church** the collective body of those Eastern Churches that were separated from the western Church in the 11th century and are in communion with the Greek patriarch of Constantinople 2 any of these Churches

Orthodox Judaism *n* the form of Judaism characterized by allegiance to the traditional interpretation and to strict observance of the Mosaic Law as interpreted in the Talmud, etc, and regarded as divinely revealed

orthoepy ('ɔːθəʊˌɛpɪ) *n* the study of correct or standard pronunciation [C17: from Greek *orthoepeia*, from ORTHO- straight + *epos* word] > **ortho'epic** *adj*
> ˌortho'epically *adv*

orthogenesis (ˌɔːθəʊˈdʒɛnɪsɪs) *n* 1 biology a evolution of a group of organisms predetermined to occur in a

particular direction **b** the theory that proposes such a development **2** the theory that there is a series of stages through which all cultures pass in the same order
> orthogenetic (ˌɔːθəʊdʒɪˈnɛtɪk) *adj*
> ˌorthoge'netically *adv*

orthogonal (ɔːˈθɒɡənᵊl) *adj* relating to, consisting of, or involving right angles; perpendicular
> or'thogonally *adv*

orthographic (ˌɔːθəʊˈɡræfɪk) *or* **orthographical** *adj* of or relating to orthography > ˌortho'graphically *adv*

orthography (ɔːˈθɒɡrəfɪ) *n, pl* **-phies** **1** a writing system **2 a** spelling considered to be correct **b** the principles underlying spelling **3** the study of spelling
> or'thographer *or* or'thographist *n*

orthopaedics *or US* **orthopedics** (ˌɔːθəʊˈpiːdɪks) *n* (*functioning as singular*) **1** the branch of surgery concerned with disorders of the spine and joints and the repair of deformities of these parts **2** dental orthopaedics another name for: **orthodontics** > ˌortho'paedist *or US* ˌortho'pedist *n* > ˌortho'paedic *or* (*US*) ˌortho'pedic *adj*

orthopteran (ɔːˈθɒptərəs) *n, pl* **-terans** **1** *Also:* orthopteron, *pl* **-tera** (-tərə) any orthopterous insect ▷ *adj* **2** another word for **orthopterous**

orthopterous (ɔːˈθɒptərəs) *or* **orthopteran** *adj* of, relating to, or belonging to the *Orthoptera*, a large order of insects, including crickets, locusts, and grasshoppers, having leathery forewings and membranous hind wings, hind legs adapted for leaping, and organs of stridulation

orthoptic (ɔːˈθɒptɪk) *adj* relating to normal binocular vision

orthoptics (ɔːˈθɒptɪks) *n* (*functioning as singular*) the science or practice of correcting defective vision, as by exercises to strengthen weak eye muscles > or'thoptist *n*

orthorhombic (ˌɔːθəʊˈrɒmbɪk) *adj crystallog* relating to the crystal system characterized by three mutually perpendicular unequal axes

Ortles (*Italian* ˈɔrtles) *pl n* a range of the Alps in N Italy. Highest peak: 3899 m (12 792 ft). *Also called:* Ortler (ˈɔːtlə)

ortolan (ˈɔːtələn) *n* **1** *Also called:* ortolan bunting a brownish Old World bunting, *Emberiza hortulana*, regarded as a delicacy **2** any of various other small birds eaten as delicacies, esp the bobolink [C17: via French from Latin *hortulānus*, from *hortulus*, diminutive of *hortus* garden]

Orton (ˈɔːtᵊn) *n* Joe (**Kingsley**). 1933–67, British dramatist, noted for his black comedies: these include *Entertaining Mr Sloane* (1964), *Loot* (1966), and *What the Butler Saw* (1969)

Oruro (*Spanish* oˈruro) *n* a city in W Bolivia: a former silver-mining centre; university (1892); tin, copper, and tungsten. Pop: 206 000 (2005 est)

Orvieto (*Italian* orˈvjeːto) *n* **1** a market town in central Italy, in Umbria: Etruscan remains. Pop: 20 705 (2001) **2** a light white wine from this region

Orwell (ˈɔːwəl, -wɛl) *n* George, real name *Eric Arthur Blair*. 1903–50, English novelist and essayist, born in India. He is notable for his social criticism, as in *The Road to Wigan Pier* (1932); his account of his experiences of the Spanish Civil War *Homage to Catalonia* (1938); and his satirical novels *Animal Farm* (1945), an allegory on the Russian Revolution, and *1984* (1949), in which he depicts an authoritarian state of the future > **Orwellian** (ɔːˈwɛlɪən) *adj*

-ory¹ *suffix forming nouns* **1** indicating a place for: *observatory* **2** something having a specified use: *directory* [via Old French *-orie*, from Latin *-ōrium*, *-ōria*]

-ory² *suffix forming adjectives* of or relating to; characterized by; having the effect of: *contributory; promissory* [via Old French *-orie*, from Latin *-ōrius*]

oryx (ˈɒrɪks) *n, pl* **-yxes** *or* **-yx** any large African antelope of the genus *Oryx*, typically having long straight nearly upright horns [C14: via Latin from Greek *orux* stonemason's axe, used also of the pointed horns of an antelope]

os¹ (ɒs) *n, pl* **ossa** (ˈɒsə) *anatomy* the technical name for **bone** [C16: from Latin: bone; compare Greek *osteon*]

os² (ɒs) *n, pl* **ora** (ˈɔːrə) *anatomy, zoology* a mouth or

mouthlike part or opening [C18: from Latin]

Os *the chemical symbol for* osmium

OS *abbreviation* **1** Old Style (method of reckoning dates) **2** Ordinary Seaman **3** (in Britain) Ordnance Survey **4** outsize **5** Old Saxon (language)

Osage orange (əʊˈseɪdʒ, ˈəʊseɪdʒ) *n* **1** a North American moraceous tree, *Maclura pomifera*, grown for hedges and ornament **2** the warty orange-like fruit of this plant

Osaka (əʊˈsɑːkə) *n* a port in S Japan, on S Honshu on Osaka Bay (an inlet of the Pacific): the third largest city in Japan (the chief commercial city during feudal times); university (1931); an industrial and commercial centre. Pop: 2 484 326 (2002 est)

Osborne (ˈɒzbən, -ˌbɔːn) *n* John (**James**). 1929–94, British dramatist. His plays include *Look Back in Anger* (1956), containing the prototype of the angry young man, Jimmy Porter, *The Entertainer* (1957), and *Inadmissible Evidence* (1964)

Oscar (ˈɒskə) *n* any of several small gold statuettes awarded annually in the United States by the Academy of Motion Picture Arts and Sciences for outstanding achievements in films. Official name: **Academy Award** [C20: sense 1 said to have been named after a remark made by an official on first seeing the statuette, that it reminded her of her uncle Oscar]

Oscar II *n* 1829–1907, king of Sweden (1872–1907) and of Norway (1872–1905)

oscillate (ˈɒsɪˌleɪt) *vb* **1** (*intr*) to move or swing from side to side regularly **2** (*intr*) to waver between opinions, courses of action, etc **3** *physics* to undergo or produce or cause to undergo or produce oscillation [C18: from Latin *oscillāre* to swing, from *oscillum* a swing]

oscillating universe theory *n* the theory that the universe is oscillating between periods of expansion and collapse

oscillation (ˌɒsɪˈleɪʃən) *n* **1** *physics, statistics* **a** a regular fluctuation in value, position, or state about a mean value, such as the variation in an alternating current or the regular swinging of a pendulum **b** a single cycle of such a fluctuation **2** the act or process of oscillating > **oscillatory** (ˈɒsɪlətərɪ, -trɪ) *adj*

oscillator (ˈɒsɪˌleɪtə) *n* **1** a circuit or instrument for producing an alternating current or voltage of a required frequency **2** any instrument for producing oscillations **3** a person or thing that oscillates

oscillogram (ɒˈsɪləˌɡræm) *n* the recording obtained from an oscillograph or the trace on an oscilloscope screen

oscillograph (ɒˈsɪləˌɡrɑːf, -ˌɡræf) *n* a device for producing a graphical record of the variation of an oscillating quantity, such as an electric current > **oscillographic** (ɒˌsɪləˈɡræfɪk) *adj* > **oscillography** (ˌɒsɪˈlɒɡrəfɪ) *n*

oscilloscope (ɒˈsɪləˌskəʊp) *n* an instrument for producing a representation of a quantity that rapidly changes with time on the screen of a cathode-ray tube. The changes are converted into electric signals, which are applied to plates in the cathode-ray tube. Changes in the magnitude of the potential across the plates deflect the electron beam and thus produce a trace on the screen

oscine (ˈɒsaɪn, ˈɒsɪn) *adj* of, relating to, or belonging to the *Oscines*, a suborder of passerine birds that includes most of the songbirds [C17: via New Latin from Latin *oscen* singing bird]

oscitancy (ˈɒsɪtənsɪ) *or* **oscitance** *n, pl* **-tancies** *or* **-tances** **1** the state of being drowsy, lazy, or inattentive **2** the act of yawning ▷ *Also called:* **oscitation** [C17: from Latin *oscitāre* to gape, yawn] > **oscitant** *adj*

oscular (ˈɒskjʊlə) *adj* **1** *zoology* of or relating to an osculum **2** of or relating to the mouth or to kissing

osculate (ˈɒskjʊˌleɪt) *vb* **1** *usually humorous* to kiss **2** (*intr*) (of an organism or group of organisms) to be intermediate between two taxonomic groups **3** *geometry* to touch in osculation [C17: from Latin *ōsculārī* to kiss; see OSCULUM]

osculation (ˌɒskjʊˈleɪʃən) *n* **1** *Also called:* tacnode *maths* a point at which two branches of a curve have a common tangent, each branch extending in both directions of the tangent **2** *rare* the act or an instance of kissing > **osculatory** ('ɒskjʊlətərɪ, -trɪ) *adj*

osculum ('ɒskjʊləm) *n, pl* **-la** (-lə) *zoology* a mouthlike aperture, esp the opening in a sponge out of which water passes [c17: from Latin: a kiss, little mouth, diminutive of *ōs* mouth]

-ose[1] *suffix forming adjectives* possessing; resembling: *verbose; grandiose* [from Latin *-ōsus; see* -ous]

-ose[2] *suffix forming nouns* **1** indicating a carbohydrate, esp a sugar: *lactose* **2** indicating a decomposition product of protein: *albumose* [from GLUCOSE]

Oshawa ('ɒʃəwə) *n* a city in central Canada, in SE Ontario on Lake Ontario: motor-vehicle industry. Pop: 139 051 (2001)

Oshogbo (ə'ʃɒgbəʊ) *n* a city in SW Nigeria: trade centre. Pop: 629 000 (2005 est)

Oshun (əʊ'ʃʌn) *or* **Osun** *n* a state of SW Nigeria. Capital: Oshogbo. Pop: 3 423 535 (2006). Area: 9251 sq km (3570 sq miles)

osier ('əʊzɪə) *n* **1** any of various willow trees, esp *Salix viminalis*, whose flexible branches or twigs are used for making baskets, etc **2** a twig or branch from such a tree **3** any of several North American dogwoods, esp the red osier [c14: from Old French, probably from Medieval Latin *ausèria*, perhaps of Gaulish origin; compare Breton *aoz*]

Osijek (Croatian 'ɒsijɛk) *n* a town in NE Croatia on the Drava River: under Turkish rule from 1526 to 1687. Pop: 85 000 (2005 est)

Osiris (əʊ'saɪrɪs) *n* an ancient Egyptian god, ruler of the underworld and judge of the dead > **O'sirian** *adj*

-osis *suffix forming nouns* **1** indicating a process or state: *metamorphosis* **2** indicating a diseased condition: *tuberculosis*. See **-iasis** **3** indicating the formation or development of something: *fibrosis* [from Greek, suffix used to form nouns from verbs with infinitives in *-oein* or *-oun*]

Osler ('ɒzlə) *n* **Sir William**. 1849–1919, Canadian physician, pioneer of residency in medical training

Oslo ('ɒzləʊ; *Norwegian* 'uslu) *n* the capital and chief port of Norway, in the southeast at the head of **Oslo Fjord** (an inlet of the Skagerrak): founded in about 1050; university (1811); a major commercial and industrial centre, producing about a quarter of Norway's total output. Pop: 521 886 (2004 est). Former names: Christiania (1624–1877), Kristiania (1877–1924)

Osman I ('ɒzmən, ɒz'mɑːn) *or* **Othman I** *n* 1259–1326, Turkish sultan; founder of the Ottoman Empire

Osmanli (ɒz'mænlɪ) *adj* **1** of or relating to the Ottoman Empire ▷ *n* **2** *pl* **-lis** (formerly) a subject of the Ottoman Empire [c19: from Turkish, from Osman I (1259–1326), Turkish sultan]

osmiridium (ˌɒzmɪ'rɪdɪəm) *n* a very hard corrosion-resistant white or grey natural alloy of osmium and iridium in variable proportions, often containing smaller amounts of platinum, ruthenium, and rhodium: used esp in pen nibs [c19: from OSM(IUM) + IRIDIUM]

osmium ('ɒzmɪəm) *n* a very hard brittle bluish-white metal occurring with platinum and alloyed with iridium in osmiridium: used to produce platinum alloys, mainly for pen tips and instrument pivots, as a catalyst, and in electric-light filaments. Symbol: Os; atomic no: 76; atomic wt: 190.2; valency: 0 to 8; relative density: 22.57; melting pt: 3033±30°C; boiling pt: 5012±100°C [c19: from Greek *osmē* smell, so called from its penetrating odour]

osmoregulation (ˌɒzməʊˌrɛgjʊ'leɪʃən) *n zoology* the adjustment of the osmotic pressure of a cell or organism in relation to the surrounding fluid

osmose ('ɒzməʊs, -məʊz, 'ɒs-) *vb* to undergo or cause to undergo osmosis [c19 (n): abstracted from the earlier terms *endosmose* and *exosmose*; related to Greek *ōsmos* push]

osmosis (ɒz'məʊsɪs, ɒs-) *n* **1** the passage of a solvent through a semipermeable membrane from a less concentrated to a more concentrated solution until both solutions are of the same concentration **2** diffusion through any membrane or porous barrier, as in dialysis **3** gradual or unconscious assimilation or adoption, as of

ideas [c19: Latinized form from OSMOSE (n), from Greek *ōsmos* push, thrust] > **osmotic** (ɒz'mɒtɪk, ɒs-) *adj* > **os'motically** *adv*

osmotic pressure *n* the pressure necessary to prevent osmosis into a given solution when the solution is separated from the pure solvent by a semipermeable membrane

osmunda (ɒz'mʌndə) *or* **osmund** ('ɒzmənd) *n* any fern of the genus *Osmunda*, such as the royal fern, having large spreading fronds: family *Osmundaceae* [c13: from Old French *osmonde*, of unknown origin]

Osnabrück (German ɔsna'bryk) *n* an industrial city in NW Germany, in Lower Saxony: a member of the Hanseatic League in the Middle Ages; one of the treaties comprising the Peace of Westphalia (1648) was signed here. Pop: 165 517 (2003 est)

osprey ('ɒsprɪ, -preɪ) *n* **1** a large broad-winged fish-eating diurnal bird of prey, *Pandion haliaetus*, with a dark back and whitish head and underparts: family *Pandioridae*. Often called (US and Canadian): **fish hawk** **2** any of the feathers of various other birds, used esp as trimming for hats [c15: from Old French *ospres*, apparently from Latin *ossifraga*, literally: bone-breaker, from *os* bone + *frangere* to break]

Ossa ('ɒsə) *n* a mountain in NE Greece, in E Thessaly: famous in mythology for the attempt of the twin giants, Otus and Ephialtes, to reach heaven by piling Ossa on Olympus and Pelion on Ossa. Height: 1978 m (6489 ft)

ossein ('ɒsɪɪn) *n* a protein that forms the organic matrix of bone, constituting about 40 per cent of its matter [c19: from Latin *osseus* bony, from *os* bone]

osseous ('ɒsɪəs) *adj* consisting of or containing bone, bony [c17: from Latin *osseus*, from *os* bone] > **'osseously** *adv*

Ossetia (ɒ'siːtjə, ɒ'sɛtjə) *n* a region of central Asia, in the Caucasus: consists administratively of the North Ossetian Republic in Russia and South Ossetia (formerly an Autonomous Region) in Georgia > **Ossetic** (ɒ'sɛtɪk) *or* **Ossetian** (ɒ'siːʃən) *adj, n*

Ossian ('ɒsɪən) *n* a legendary Irish hero and bard of the 3rd century AD. See also **Macpherson** > **Ossianic** ('ɒsɪ'ænɪk) *adj*

Ossietzky (ˌɒsɪ'ɛtskɪ) *n* **Carl von** (karl fɔn). 1889–1938, German pacifist leader. He was imprisoned for revealing Germany's secret rearmament (1931–32) and again under Hitler (1933–36): Nobel peace prize 1935

ossify ('ɒsɪˌfaɪ) *vb* **-fies, -fying, -fied** **1** to convert or be converted into bone **2** (*intr*) (of habits, attitudes, etc) to become inflexible [c18: from French *ossifier*, from Latin *os* bone + *facere* to make] > **'ossiˌfier** *n* > **ˌossifi'cation** *n*

ossuary ('ɒsjʊərɪ) *n, pl* **-aries** any container for the burial of human bones, such as an urn or vault [c17: from Late Latin *ossuārium*, from Latin *os* bone]

osteal ('ɒstɪəl) *adj* **1** of or relating to bone or to the skeleton **2** composed of bone; osseous [c19: from Greek *osteon* bone]

osteitis (ˌɒstɪ'aɪtɪs) *n* inflammation of a bone > **osteitic** (ˌɒstɪ'ɪtɪk)

Ostend (ɒs'tɛnd) *n* a port and resort in NW Belgium, in West Flanders on the North Sea. Pop: 68 273 (2004 est). French name: **Ostende** (ɔstɑ̃d) Flemish name: **Oostende**

ostensible (ɒ'stɛnsɪb²l) *adj* **1** apparent; seeming **2** pretended [c18: via French from Medieval Latin *ostensibilis*, from Latin *ostendere* to show, from *ob-* before + *tendere* to extend] > **os,tensi'bility** *n* > **os'tensibly** *adv*

ostensive (ɒ'stɛnsɪv) *adj* **1** obviously or manifestly demonstrative **2** a less common word for **ostensible** **3** *philosophy* (of a definition) given by demonstrative means, esp by pointing [c17: from Late Latin *ostentīvus*, from Latin *ostendere* to show; see OSTENSIBLE] > **os'tensively** *adv*

ostentation (ˌɒstɛn'teɪʃən) *n* pretentious, showy, or vulgar display > **ˌosten'tatious** *adj* > **ˌosten'tatiously** *adv*

osteo- *or before a vowel* **oste-** *combining form* indicating bone or bones: *osteopathy* [from Greek *osteon*]

osteoarthritis (ˌɒstɪəʊɑː'θraɪtɪs) *n* chronic inflammation of the joints, esp those that bear weight, with pain and stiffness > **osteoarthritic** (ˌɒstɪəʊɑː'θrɪtɪk) *adj, n*

osteology (ˌɒstɪˈɒlədʒɪ) n the study of the structure and function of bones > **osteological** (ˌɒstɪəˈlɒdʒɪkəl) adj > ˌosteoˈlogically adv > ˌosteˈologist n

osteoma (ˌɒstɪˈəʊmə) n, pl -mata (-mətə) or -mas a benign tumour composed of bone or bonelike tissue

osteomalacia (ˌɒstɪəʊməˈleɪʃɪə) n a disease in adults characterized by softening of the bones, resulting from a deficiency of vitamin D and of calcium and phosphorus [C19: from New Latin, from OSTEO- + Greek malakia softness] > ˌosteomaˈlacial or osteomalacic (ˌɒstɪəʊməˈlæsɪk) adj

osteomyelitis (ˌɒstɪəʊˌmaɪɪˈlaɪtɪs) n inflammation of bone marrow, caused by infection

osteopathy (ˌɒstɪˈɒpəθɪ) n a system of healing based on the manipulation of bones or other parts of the body > **osteopathic** (ˌɒstɪəˈpæθɪk) adj > ˌosteoˈpathically adv > ˈosteoˌpath or less commonly ˌosteˈopathist n

osteoplasty (ˈɒstɪəˌplæstɪ) n, pl -ties the branch of surgery concerned with bone repair or bone grafting

osteoporosis (ˌɒstɪəʊpɔːˈrəʊsɪs) n porosity and brittleness of the bones due to loss of calcium from the bone matrix [C19: from OSTEO- + PORE² + -OSIS] > **osteoporotic** (ˌɒstɪəʊpɔːˈrɒtɪk) adj

Österreich (ˈøːstəraɪç) n the German name for **Austria**

Ostia (ˈɒstɪə) n an ancient town in W central Italy, originally at the mouth of the Tiber but now about 6 km (4 miles) inland: served as the port of ancient Rome; ruins excavated since 1854

ostinato (ˌɒstɪˈnɑːtəʊ) n **a** a continuously reiterated musical phrase **b** (as modifier): an ostinato passage [Italian: from Latin obstinātus OBSTINATE]

ostler or **hostler** (ˈɒslə) n archaic a stableman, esp one at an inn [C15: variant of hostler, from HOSTEL]

Ostmark (ˈɒstˌmɑːk; German ˈɔstmark) n (formerly) the standard monetary unit of East Germany, divided into 100 pfennigs [German, literally: east mark]

Ostpreussen (ˈɔstprɔysən) n the German name for **East Prussia**

ostracize or **ostracise** (ˈɒstrəˌsaɪz) vb (tr) **1** to exclude or banish (a person) from a particular group, society, etc **2** (in ancient Greece) to punish by temporary exile [C17: from Greek ostrakizein to select someone for banishment by voting on potsherds; see OSTRACON] > **ostracism** n > ˌostraˈcizable or ˌostraˈcisable adj > ˈostraˌcizer or ˈostraˌciser n

ostracon (ˈɒstrəˌkɒn) n (in ancient Greece) a potsherd used for ostracizing [from Greek]

Ostrava (Czech ˈɔstrava) n an industrial city in the E Czech Republic, on the River Oder: the chief coal-mining area in the Czech Republic, in Upper Silesia. Pop: 316 000 (2005 est)

ostrich (ˈɒstrɪtʃ) n, pl -triches or -trich **1** a fast-running flightless African bird, Struthio camelus, that is the largest living bird, with stout two-toed feet and dark feathers, except on the naked head, neck, and legs: order Struthioniformes **2** American ostrich another name for rhea **3** a person who refuses to recognize the truth, reality, etc: a reference to the ostrich's supposed habit of burying its head in the sand [C13: from Old French ostrice, from Latin avis bird + Late Latin struthio ostrich, from Greek strouthion]

Ostrovsky (ɒsˈtrɒfskɪ) n Aleksandr Nikolayevich. 1823–86, Russian dramatist, noted for his satirical comedies about the bourgeoisie. His plays include The Bankrupt (1849) and The Storm (1859), a tragedy

Ostwald (German ˈɔstvalt) n Wilhelm (ˈvɪlhelm). 1853–1932, German chemist, noted for his pioneering work in catalysis. He also invented a process for making nitric acid from ammonia and developed a new theory of colour: Nobel prize for chemistry 1909

Osun (əʊˈsʌn) n a variant spelling of **Oshun**

Oswald (ˈɒzwəld) n **1** Lee Harvey. 1939–63, presumed assassin (1963) of US president John F. Kennedy; murdered by Jack Ruby two days later **2** Saint. ?605–41 AD, king of Northumbria (634–41); with St Aidan he restored Christianity to the region. He was killed in battle by Penda of Mercia. Feast day: Aug 5

Oświęcim (Polish ɔʃˈfjɛntʃim) n the Polish name for **Auschwitz**

OT abbreviation **1** occupational therapy **2** Old Testament **3** overtime

Otago (ɒˈtɑːgəʊ) n a council region of New Zealand, formerly a province, founded by Scottish settlers in the south of South Island. The University of Otago (1869) in Dunedin is the oldest university in New Zealand. Chief town: Dunedin. Pop: 195 000 (2004 est)

otalgia (əʊˈtældʒɪə, -dʒə) n the technical name for **earache**

OTC abbreviation **1** (in Britain) Officers' Training Corps **2** over-the-counter

OTE abbreviation on-target earnings: referring to the salary a salesperson should be able to achieve

other (ˈʌðə) determiner **1 a** (when used before a singular noun, usually preceded by the) the remaining (one or ones in a group of which one or some have been specified): I'll read the other sections of the paper later **b** the other (as pronoun; functioning as sing): one walks while the other rides **2** (a) different (one or ones from that or those already specified or understood): he found some other house; no other man but you; other days were happier **3** additional; further: there are no other possibilities **4** (preceded by every) alternate; two: it buzzes every other minute **5** other than **a** apart from; besides: a lady other than his wife **b** different from: he couldn't be other than what he is **6** no other archaic nothing else: I can do no other **7** or other (preceded by a phrase or word with some) used to add vagueness to the preceding pronoun, noun, noun phrase, or adverb: some dog or other bit him; he's somewhere or other **8** other things being equal conditions being the same or unchanged **9** the other day a few days ago **10** the other thing an unexpressed alternative ▷ pron **11** another: show me one other **12** (plural) additional or further ones **13** (plural) other people or things **14** the others the remaining ones (of a group) ▷ adv **15** (usually used with a negative and foll by than) otherwise; differently: they couldn't behave other than they do [Old English ōther; related to Old Saxon āthar, ōthar, Old High German andar] > **otherness** n

other-directed adj guided by values derived from external influences

other ranks pl n (rarely used in singular) chiefly Brit (in the armed forces) all those who do not hold a commissioned rank

otherwise (ˈʌðəˌwaɪz) sentence connector **1** or else; if not, then: go home — otherwise your mother will worry ▷ adv **2** differently: I wouldn't have thought otherwise **3** in other respects: an otherwise hopeless situation ▷ adj **4** (predicative) of an unexpected nature; different: the facts are otherwise ▷ pron **5** something different in outcome: success or otherwise [C14: from Old English on ōthre wīsan in other manner]

other world n the spirit world or afterlife

otherworldly (ˌʌðəˈwɜːldlɪ) adj **1** of or relating to the spiritual or imaginative world **2** impractical or unworldly > ˌotherˈworldliness n

Othin (ˈəʊðɪn) n a variant of **Odin**

Othman (ˈɒθmən, ɒθˈmɑːn) adj, n a variant of **Ottoman**

Othman I n same as **Osman I**

Otho I (ˈəʊθəʊ) n same as **Otto I**

otic (ˈəʊtɪk, ˈɒtɪk) adj of or relating to the ear [C17: from Greek ōtikos, from ous ear]

-otic suffix forming adjectives **1** relating to or affected by: sclerotic **2** causing: narcotic [from Greek -ōtikos]

otiose (ˈəʊtɪˌəʊs, -ˌəʊz) adj **1** serving no useful purpose: otiose language **2** rare indolent; lazy [C18: from Latin ōtiōsus leisured, from ōtium leisure] > **otiosity** (ˌəʊtɪˈɒsɪtɪ) or ˈotiˌoseness n

otitis (əʊˈtaɪtɪs) n inflammation of the ear, esp the middle ear (**otitis media**), with pain, impaired hearing, etc, or the outer ear (**otitis externa**), with inflammation between the ear drum and the external opening

oto- or before a vowel **ot-** combining form indicating the ear: otitis, otolith [from Greek ous, ōt- ear]

otolaryngology (ˌəʊtəʊˌlærɪŋˈɡɒlədʒɪ) n the branch of medicine concerned with the ear, nose, and throat and their diseases. Sometimes called otorhinolaryngology > otolaryngological (ˌəʊtəʊləˌrɪŋɡəˈlɒdʒɪkəl) adj > ˌotoˌlarynˈgologist n

otolith (ˈəʊtəʊˌlɪθ) n any of the granules of calcium

carbonate in the inner ear of vertebrates. Movement of otoliths, caused by a change in position of the animal, stimulates sensory hair cells, which convey the information to the brain > ˌoto'lithic *adj*

otology (əʊ'tɒlədʒɪ) *n* the branch of medicine concerned with the ear > otological (ˌəʊtə'lɒdʒɪkᵊl) *adj* > o'tologist *n*

O'Toole (əʊ'tuːl) *n* (**Seamus**) **Peter**. born 1932, British actor, born in Ireland. His films include *Lawrence of Arabia* (1962), *The Lion in Winter* (1968), *High Spirits* (1988), and *Fairytale* (1998); stage appearances include *Jeffrey Bernard is Unwell* (1989)

otorrhoea (ˌəʊtə'rɪə) *n pathol* a discharge from the ears

otoscope ('əʊtəˌskəʊp) *n* another name for **auriscope** > otoscopic (ˌəʊtəʊ'skɒpɪk) *adj*

Otranto (Italian 'ɔːtranto) *n* a small port in SE Italy, in Apulia on the **Strait of Otranto**: the most easterly town in Italy; dates back to Greek times and was an important Roman port; its ruined castle was the setting of Horace Walpole's *Castle of Otranto*. Pop: 5282 (2001)

OTT *slang abbreviation* over the top. See **top¹** (sense 16)

ottava rima (əʊ'taːvə 'riːmə) *n prosody* a stanza form consisting of eight iambic pentameter lines, rhyming a b a b a b c c [Italian: eighth rhyme]

Ottawa ('ɒtəwə) *n* **1** the capital of Canada, in E Ontario on the Ottawa River: name changed from Bytown to Ottawa in 1854. Pop: 774 072 (2001) **2** a river in central Canada, rising in W Quebec and flowing west, then southeast to join the St Lawrence River as its chief tributary at Montreal; forms the border between Quebec and Ontario for most of its length. Length: 1120 km (696 miles)

otter ('ɒtə) *n, pl* -ters *or* -ter **1** any freshwater carnivorous musteline mammal of the subfamily *Lutrinae*, esp *Lutra lutra* (**Eurasian otter**), typically having smooth fur, a streamlined body, and webbed feet **2** the fur of any of these animals **3** Also called: otter board a type of fishing tackle consisting of a weighted board to which hooked and baited lines are attached ▷ *vb* **4** to fish using an otter [Old English *otor*; related to Old Norse *otr*, Old High German *ottar*, Greek *hudra*, Sanskrit *udra*]

Otterburn ('ɒtəˌbɜːn) *n* a village in NE England, in central Northumberland: scene of a battle (1388) in which the Scots, led by the earl of Douglas, defeated the English, led by Hotspur

otter hound *n* a dog used for otter hunting, esp one of a breed, now rare, that stands about 60 cm (24 in.) high and has a harsh thick coat, often greyish with tan markings

Otto (German 'ɔto) *n* **Rudolf** ('ruːdɔlf). 1869–1937, German theologian: his best-known work is *The Idea of the Holy* (1923)

Otto I ('ɒtəʊ) *or* **Otho I** *n* called *the Great*. 912–73 AD, king of Germany (936–73); Holy Roman Emperor (962–73)

Otto IV *n* ?1175–1218. German king and Holy Roman Emperor (1198–1215): invaded S Italy (1210) but was later (1214) defeated by France and deposed

ottoman ('ɒtəmən) *n, pl* -mans **1 a** a low padded seat, usually armless, sometimes in the form of a chest **b** a cushioned footstool **2** a corded fabric [c17: from French *ottomane*, feminine of OTTOMAN]

Ottoman ('ɒtəmən) *or* **Othman** *adj* **1** history of or relating to the Ottomans or the Ottoman Empire **2** denoting or relating to the Turkish language ▷ *n, pl* -mans **3** a member of a Turkish people who invaded the Near East in the late 13th century [c17: from French, via Medieval Latin, from Arabic *Othmāni* Turkish, from Turkish *Othman* Osman I (1259–1326), founder of the Ottoman Empire]

Ottoman Empire *n* the former Turkish empire in Europe, Asia, and Africa, which lasted from the late 13th century until the end of World War I. Also called: Turkish Empire

Otway ('ɒtweɪ) *n* **Thomas**. 1652–85, English dramatist, noted for *The Orphan* (1680) and *Venice Preserv'd* (1682)

ou (əʊ) *n South African slang* a man, bloke, or chap [Afrikaans]

OU *abbreviation* **1** the Open University **2** Oxford University

Ouachita *or* **Washita** ('wɒʃɪˌtɔː) *n* a river in the S central US, rising in the **Ouachita Mountains** and flowing east, south, and southeast into the Red River in E Louisiana. Length: 974 km (605 miles)

Ouagadougou (ˌwɑːɡə'duːɡuː) *n* the capital of Burkina Faso, on the central plateau: terminus of the railway from Abidjan (Côte d'Ivoire). Pop: 870 000 (2005 est)

ouananiche (ˌwɑːnə'niːʃ) *n* a landlocked variety of the Atlantic salmon, *Salmo salar*, found in lakes in SE Canada [from Canadian French, from Montagnais *wananish*, diminutive of *wanans* salmon]

oubaas ('əʊˌbɑːs) *n South African* a person who is senior in years or rank [Afrikaans]

Oubangui (uː'bɑːŋɡiː, juː'bæŋɡɪ) *n* the French name for Ubangi

oubliette (ˌuːblɪ'ɛt) *n* a dungeon the only entrance to which is through the top [c19: from French, from *oublier* to forget]

ouch (aʊtʃ) *interj* an exclamation of sharp sudden pain

Oudh (aʊd) *n* **1** a region of N India, in central Uttar Pradesh: annexed by Britain in 1856 and a centre of the Indian Mutiny (1857–58); joined with Agra in 1877, becoming the United Provinces of Agra and Oudh in 1902, which were renamed Uttar Pradesh in 1950 **2** another name for Ayodhya

Oudry (French udri) *n* **Jean-Baptiste** (ʒɑ̃batist). 1686–1755, French rococo painter and tapestry designer

Ouessant (wɛsɑ̃) *n* the French name for Ushant

ought¹ (ɔːt) *vb* (foll by to; takes an infinitive or implied infinitive) used as an auxiliary **1** to indicate duty or obligation: *you ought to pay your dues* **2** to express prudent expediency: *you ought to be more careful with your money* **3** (usually with reference to future time) to express probability or expectation: *you ought to finish this work by Friday* **4** to express a desire or wish on the part of the speaker: *you ought to come next week* [Old English *āhte*, past tense of *āgan* to OWE; related to Gothic *aihta*]
● USAGE In correct English, *ought* is not used with *did* or *had*. I ought not to do it, not I didn't ought to do it; I ought not to have done it, not I hadn't ought to have done it

ought² (ɔːt) *pron, adv* a variant spelling of **aught¹**

ought³ (ɔːt) *n* a less common word for **nought** (sense 1) [c19: mistaken division of *a nought* as *an ought*; see NOUGHT]

Ouida ('wiːdə) *n* real name *Marie Louise de la Ramée*. 1839–1908, British popular novelist, best known for *Under Two Flags* (1867)

Ouija board ('wiːdʒə) *n trademark* a board on which are marked the letters of the alphabet. Answers to questions are spelt out by a pointer or glass held by the fingertips of the participants, and are supposedly formed by spiritual forces [c19: from French *oui* yes + German *ja* yes]

Oujda (uːdʒ'dɑː) *n* a city in NE Morocco, near the border with Algeria: frontier post. Pop: 454 000 (2003)

Oulu ('oːluː) *n* an industrial city and port in W Finland, on the Gulf of Bothnia: university (1959). Pop: 125 928 (2003 est). Swedish name: Uleåborg

ouma ('əʊmɑː) *n South African* **1** grandmother, esp in titular use with surname **2** *slang* any elderly woman [Afrikaans]

ounce¹ (aʊns) *n* **1** a unit of weight equal to one sixteenth of a pound (avoirdupois); 1 ounce is equal to 437.5 grains or 28.349 grams. Abbreviation: oz **2** a unit of weight equal to one twelfth of a Troy or Apothecaries' pound; 1 ounce is equal to 480 grains or 31.103 grams **3** short for **fluid ounce 4** a small portion or amount [c14: from Old French *unce*, from Latin *uncia* a twelfth; from *ūnus* one]

ounce² (aʊns) *n* another name for **snow leopard** [c18: from Old French *once*, by mistaken division of *lonce* as if *l'once*, from Latin LYNX]

our (aʊə) *determiner* **1** of, belonging to, or associated in some way with us: *our best vodka; our parents are good to us* **2** belonging to or associated with all people or people in general: *our nearest planet is Venus* **3** a formal word for *my* used by editors or other writers, and monarchs [Old English *ūre* (genitive plural), from us; related to Old French, Old Saxon *ūser*, Old High German *unsēr*, Gothic *unsara*]

-our *suffix forming nouns* indicating state, condition, or activity: *behaviour; labour* [in Old French *-eur*, from Latin *-or*, noun suffix]

Our Father *n* another name for the **Lord's Prayer**, taken from its opening words

ours (aʊəz) *pron* 1 something or someone belonging to or associated with us: *ours have blue tags* 2 of ours belonging to or associated with us

ourself (aʊə'sɛlf) *pron archaic* a variant of **myself**, formerly used by monarchs or editors in formal contexts

ourselves (aʊə'sɛlvz) *pron* 1 a the reflexive form of *we* or *us* b (intensifier): *we ourselves will finish it* 2 (*preceded by a copula*) our usual selves: *we are ourselves when we're together* 3 *not standard* used instead of *we* or *us* in compound noun phrases: *other people and ourselves*

-ous *suffix forming adjectives* 1 having, full of, or characterized by: *dangerous; spacious; languorous* 2 (in chemistry) indicating that an element is chemically combined in the lower of two possible valency states: *ferrous; stannous*. Compare **-ic** (sense 2) [from Old French, from Latin *-ōsus* or *-us*, Greek *-os*, adj suffixes]

Ouse (uːz) *n* 1 Also called: **Great Ouse** a river in E England, rising in Northamptonshire and flowing northeast to the Wash near King's Lynn; for the last 56 km (35 miles) follows mainly artificial channels. Length: 257 km (160 miles) 2 a river in NE England, in Yorkshire, formed by the confluence of the Swale and Ure Rivers: flows southeast to the Humber. Length: 92 km (57 miles) 3 a river in S England, rising in Sussex and flowing south to the English Channel. Length: 48 km (30 miles)

ousel ('uːzᵊl) *n* a variant spelling of **ouzel**

oust (aʊst) *vb* (*tr*) 1 to force out of a position or place; supplant or expel 2 *property law* to deprive (a person) of the possession of land [c16: from Anglo-Norman *ouster*, from Latin *obstāre* to withstand, from *ob-* against + *stāre* to stand]

ouster ('aʊstə) *n property law* the act of dispossessing of freehold property; eviction; ejection

out (aʊt) *adv* 1 (*often used as a particle*) at or to a point beyond the limits of some location; outside: *get out at once* 2 (*particle*) out of consciousness: *she passed out at the sight of blood* 3 (*particle*) used to indicate a burst of activity as indicated by the verb: *fever broke out* 4 (*particle*) used to indicate obliteration of an object: *the graffiti were painted out* 5 (*particle*) used to indicate an approximate drawing or description: *sketch out; chalk out* 6 public; revealed: *the secret is out* 7 on sale or on view to the public: *the book is being brought out next May* 8 (of a young woman) in or into polite society: *Lucinda had a fabulous party when she came out* 9 (of the sun, stars, etc) visible 10 (of a jury) withdrawn to consider a verdict in private 11 (*particle*) used to indicate exhaustion or extinction: *the sugar's run out; put the light out* 12 (*particle*) used to indicate a goal or object achieved at the end of the action specified by the verb: *he worked it out; let's fight it out, then!* 13 (*preceded by a superlative*) existing: *the friendliest dog in town* 14 an expression in signalling, radio, etc, to indicate the end of a transmission 15 out of a at or to a point outside: *out of his reach* b away from; not in: *stepping out of line; out of focus* c because of, motivated by: *doing it out of jealousy* d from (a material or source): *made out of plastic* e not or no longer having any of (a substance, material, etc): *we're out of sugar* ▷ *adj* (*postpositive*) 16 not or not any longer worth considering: *that plan is out because of the weather* 17 not allowed: *smoking on duty is out* 18 (*also prenominal*) not in vogue; unfashionable: *that sort of dress is out these days* 19 (of a fire or light) no longer burning or providing illumination 20 not working: *the radio's out* 21 not in; not at home 22 desirous of or intent on (something or doing something): *I'm out for as much money as I can get* 23 Also called: **out on strike** on strike 24 (in several games and sports) denoting the state in which a player is caused to discontinue active participation, esp in some specified role 25 used up; exhausted: *our supplies are completely out* 26 worn into holes: *this sweater is out at the elbows* 27 inaccurate, deficient, or discrepant: *out by six pence* 28 not in office or authority 29 completed or concluded,

as of time: *before the year is out* 30 in flower: *the roses are out now* 31 *informal* not concealing one's homosexuality ▷ *prep* 32 out of; out through: *he ran out the door* ▷ *interj* 33 a an exclamation, usually peremptory, of dismissal, reproach, etc b (in wireless telegraphy) an expression used to signal that the speaker is signing off 34 out with it a command to make something known immediately, without missing any details ▷ *n* 35 *chiefly US* a method of escape from a place, difficult situation, punishment, etc 36 *baseball* an instance of the putting out of a batter; putout ▷ *vb* 37 (*tr*) to put or throw out 38 (*intr*) to be made known or effective despite efforts to the contrary (esp in the phrase **will out**): *the truth will out* 39 (*tr*) *informal* (of homosexuals) to expose (a public figure) as being a fellow homosexual 40 (*tr*) *informal* to expose something secret, embarrassing, or unknown about (a person): *he was eventually outed as a talented goal scorer* [Old English *ūt*; related to Old Saxon, Old Norse *ūt*, Old High German *ūz*, German *aus*]

● **USAGE** The use of *out* as a preposition, though
● common in American English, is regarded as
● incorrect in British English: *he climbed out of* (not *out*) *a*
● *window; he went out through the door*

out- *prefix* 1 excelling or surpassing in a particular action: *outlast; outlive* 2 indicating an external location or situation away from the centre: *outpost; outpatient* 3 indicating emergence, an issuing forth, etc: *outcrop; outgrowth* 4 indicating the result of an action: *outcome*

outage ('aʊtɪdʒ) *n* 1 a quantity of goods missing or lost after storage or shipment 2 a period of power failure, machine stoppage, etc

out and away *adv* by far

out-and-out *adj* (*prenominal*) thoroughgoing; complete

outback ('aʊt,bæk) *n* a the remote bush country of Australia b (*as modifier*): *outback life*

outbalance (,aʊt'bæləns) *vb* (*tr*) another word for **outweigh**

outboard ('aʊt,bɔːd) *adj* 1 (of a boat's engine) portable, with its own propeller, and designed to be attached externally to the stern 2 in a position away from, or further away from, the centre line of a vessel or aircraft, esp outside the hull or fuselage ▷ *adv* 3 away from the centre line of a vessel or aircraft, esp outside the hull or fuselage ▷ *n* 4 an outboard motor

outbound ('aʊt,baʊnd) *adj* going out; outward bound

outbrave (,aʊt'breɪv) *vb* (*tr*) 1 to surpass in bravery 2 to confront defiantly

outbreak ('aʊt,breɪk) *n* a sudden, violent, or spontaneous occurrence, esp of disease or strife

outbuilding ('aʊt,bɪldɪŋ) *n* a building subordinate to but separate from a main building; outhouse

outburst ('aʊt,bɜːst) *n* 1 a sudden and violent expression of emotion 2 an explosion or eruption

outcast ('aʊt,kɑːst) *n* 1 a person who is rejected or excluded from a social group 2 a vagabond or wanderer 3 anything thrown out or rejected ▷ *adj* 4 rejected, abandoned, or discarded; cast out

outcaste ('aʊt,kɑːst) *n* 1 a person who has been expelled from a caste 2 a person having no caste ▷ *vb* 3 (*tr*) to cause (someone) to lose his caste

outclass (,aʊt'klɑːs) *vb* (*tr*) 1 to surpass in class, quality, etc 2 to defeat easily

outcome ('aʊt,kʌm) *n* something that follows from an action, dispute, situation, etc; result; consequence

outcrop *n* ('aʊt,krɒp) 1 part of a rock formation or mineral vein that appears at the surface of the earth 2 an emergence; appearance ▷ *vb* (,aʊt'krɒp) -crops, -cropping, -cropped (*intr*) 3 (of rock strata, mineral veins, etc) to protrude through the surface of the earth

outcry *n* ('aʊt,kraɪ) *pl* -cries 1 a widespread or vehement protest 2 clamour; uproar 3 *commerce* a method of trading in which dealers shout out bids and offers at a prearranged meeting: *sale by open outcry* ▷ *vb* (,aʊt'kraɪ) -cries, -crying, -cried 4 (*tr*) to cry louder or make more noise than (someone or something)

outdated (,aʊt'deɪtɪd) *adj* old-fashioned or obsolete

outdo (,aʊt'duː) *vb* -does, -doing, -did, -done (*tr*) to surpass or exceed in performance or execution

outdoor ('aʊt,dɔː) *adj* (*prenominal*) taking place, existing, or intended for use in the open air: *outdoor games; outdoor* *clothes*. Also called: out-of-door

outdoors (ˌaʊtˈdɔːz) *adv* 1 Also called: out-of-doors in the open air; outside ▷ *n* 2 the world outside or far away from human habitation

outer ('aʊtə) *adj* (*prenominal*) 1 being or located on the outside; external 2 further from the middle or central part ▷ *n* 3 *archery* a the white outermost ring on a target b a shot that hits this ring 4 *Austral* the unsheltered part of the spectator area at a sports ground 5 on the outer *Austral & NZ informal* excluded or neglected

outer bar *n* (in England) a collective name for junior barristers who plead from outside the bar of the court

outercourse ('aʊtəˌkɔːs) *n* sexual activity between partners that does not include actual penetration [C20 OUTER + INTERCOURSE]

Outer Hebrides *pl n* See **Hebrides**

Outer Mongolia *n* the former name (until 1924) of the republic of **Mongolia**

outermost ('aʊtəˌməʊst) *adj* furthest from the centre or middle; outmost

outer space *n* (*not in technical usage*) any region of space beyond the atmosphere of the earth

outfall ('aʊtˌfɔːl) *n* the end of a river, sewer, drain, etc, from which it discharges

outfield ('aʊtˌfiːld) *n* 1 *cricket* the area of the field relatively far from the pitch; the deep. ▷ Compare **infield** (sense 1) 2 *baseball* a the area of the playing field beyond the lines connecting first, second, and third bases b the positions of the left fielder, centre fielder, and right fielder taken collectively 3 *agriculture* farmland most distant from the farmstead > 'out,fielder *n*

outfit ('aʊtˌfɪt) *n* 1 a set of articles or equipment for a particular task, occupation, etc 2 a set of clothes, esp a carefully selected one 3 *informal* any group or association regarded as a cohesive unit, such as a military company, business house, etc ▷ *vb* -fits, -fitting, -fitted 4 to furnish or be furnished with an outfit, equipment, etc > 'out,fitter *n*

outflank (ˌaʊtˈflæŋk) *vb* (*tr*) 1 to go around the flank of (an opposing army) 2 to get the better of

outflow ('aʊtˌfləʊ) *n* 1 anything that flows out, such as liquid, money, ideas, etc 2 the amount that flows out 3 the act or process of flowing out

outfox (ˌaʊtˈfɒks) *vb* (*tr*) to surpass in guile or cunning

outgeneral (ˌaʊtˈdʒɛnərəl) *vb* -als, -alling, -alled *or US* -als, -aling, -aled (*tr*) to surpass in generalship

outgo *vb* (ˌaʊtˈgəʊ) -goes, -going, -went, -gone 1 (*tr*) to exceed or outstrip ▷ *n* ('aʊtˌgəʊ) 2 cost; outgoings; outlay 3 something that goes out; outflow

outgoing ('aʊtˌgəʊɪŋ) *adj* 1 departing; leaving 2 leaving or retiring from office 3 friendly and sociable ▷ *n* 4 the act of going out

outgoings ('aʊtˌgəʊɪŋz) *pl n* expenditure

outgrow (ˌaʊtˈgrəʊ) *vb* -grows, -growing, -grew, -grown (*tr*) 1 to grow too large for (clothes, shoes, etc) 2 to lose (a habit, idea, reputation, etc) in the course of development or time 3 to grow larger or faster than

outgrowth ('aʊtˌgrəʊθ) *n* 1 a thing growing out of a main body 2 a development, result, or consequence 3 the act of growing out

outgun (ˌaʊtˈgʌn) *vb* -guns, -gunning, -gunned (*tr*) 1 to surpass in fire power 2 to surpass in shooting 3 *informal* to surpass or excel

out-half *n* *rugby* another term for **stand-off half**. Also called: outside half

outhouse ('aʊtˌhaʊs) *n* a building near to, but separate from, a main building; outbuilding

outing ('aʊtɪŋ) *n* 1 a short outward and return journey; trip; excursion 2 *informal* the naming by homosexuals of other prominent homosexuals, often against their will

outjockey (ˌaʊtˈdʒɒkɪ) *vb* (*tr*) to outwit by deception

outlandish (aʊtˈlændɪʃ) *adj* 1 grotesquely unconventional in appearance, habits, etc 2 *archaic* foreign > out'landishly *adv* > out'landishness *n*

outlast ('aʊtˌlɑːst) *vb* (*tr*) to last longer than

outlaw ('aʊtˌlɔː) *n* 1 (formerly) a person excluded from the law and deprived of its protection 2 any fugitive from the law, esp a habitual transgressor ▷ *vb* (*tr*) 3 to put (a person) outside the law and deprive of its

protection 4 to ban > 'out,lawry *n*

outlay *n* ('aʊtˌleɪ) 1 an expenditure of money, effort, etc ▷ *vb* (ˌaʊtˈleɪ) -lays, -laying, -laid 2 (*tr*) to spend (money)

outlet ('aʊtlɛt, -lɪt) *n* 1 an opening or vent permitting escape or release 2 a a market for a product or service b a commercial establishment retailing the goods of a particular producer or wholesaler 3 a channel that drains a body of water 4 a point in a wiring system from which current can be taken to supply electrical devices

outlier ('aʊtˌlaɪə) *n* 1 an outcrop of rocks that is entirely surrounded by older rocks 2 a person, thing, or part situated away from a main or related body 3 a person who lives away from his place of work, duty, etc

outline ('aʊtˌlaɪn) *n* 1 a preliminary or schematic plan, draft, account, etc 2 (*usually plural*) the important features of an argument, theory, work, etc 3 the line by which an object or figure is or appears to be bounded 4 a a drawing or manner of drawing consisting only of external lines b (*as modifier*): *an outline map* ▷ *vb* (*tr*) 5 to draw or display the outline of 6 to give the main features or general idea of

outline font *n* *computing* a font format that makes use of fillable geometric outlines of letters and symbols, allowing fonts to be scaled up or down while still retaining their intended shape. Also called: vector font ▷ Compare **bitmap font**

outlive (ˌaʊtˈlɪv) *vb* (*tr*) 1 to live longer than (someone) 2 to live beyond (a date or period): *he outlived the century* 3 to live through (an experience)

outlook ('aʊtˌlʊk) *n* 1 a mental attitude or point of view 2 the probable or expected condition or outcome of something: *the weather outlook* 3 the view from a place 4 view or prospect 5 the act or state of looking out

outlying ('aʊtˌlaɪɪŋ) *adj* distant or remote from the main body or centre, as of a town or region

outmanoeuvre *or US* **outmaneuver** (ˌaʊtməˈnuːvə) *vb* (*tr*) to secure a strategic advantage over by skilful manoeuvre

outmoded (ˌaʊtˈməʊdɪd) *adj* no longer fashionable or widely accepted > ˌout'modedly *adv* > ˌout'modedness *n*

outmost ('aʊtˌməʊst) *adj* another word for **outermost**

outnumber (ˌaʊtˈnʌmbə) *vb* (*tr*) to exceed in number

out of bounds *adj, adv* (*postpositive*) 1 (often foll by *to*) not to be entered (by); barred (to) 2 outside specified or prescribed limits

out of date *adj, adv* (**out-of-date** *when prenominal*) no longer valid, current, or fashionable; outmoded

out-of-door *adj* (*prenominal*) another term for **outdoor**

out-of-doors *adv, adj* (*postpositive*) in the open air; outside. Also called: outdoors

out of pocket *adj* (**out-of-pocket** *when prenominal*) 1 (*postpositive*) having lost money, as in a commercial enterprise 2 without money to spend 3 (*prenominal*) (of expenses) unbudgeted and paid for in cash

out-of-the-way *adj* (*prenominal*) 1 distant from more populous areas 2 uncommon or unusual

outpatient ('aʊtˌpeɪʃənt) *n* a nonresident hospital patient. ▷ Compare **inpatient**

outperform (ˌaʊtpəˈfɔːm) *vb* (*tr*) to perform better than (someone or something)

outplacement ('aʊtˌpleɪsmənt) *n* a service that offers counselling and careers advice, esp to redundant executives, which is paid for by their previous employer

outpoint (ˌaʊtˈpɔɪnt) *vb* (*tr*) to score more points than

outport ('aʊtˌpɔːt) *n* 1 *chiefly Brit* a subsidiary port built in deeper water than the original port 2 *Canadian* one of the many isolated fishing villages located in the bays and other indentations of the Newfoundland coast

outpost ('aʊtˌpəʊst) *n* *military* a a position stationed at a distance from the area occupied by a major formation b the troops assigned to such a position 2 an outlying settlement or position

outpour *n* ('aʊtˌpɔː) 1 the act of flowing or pouring out 2 something that pours out ▷ *vb* (ˌaʊtˈpɔː) 3 to pour or cause to pour out freely or rapidly

outpouring ('aʊtˌpɔːrɪŋ) *n* 1 a passionate or exaggerated outburst; effusion 2 another word for **outpour** (sense 1)

output ('aʊtˌpʊt) *n* 1 the act of production or manufacture 2 Also called: **outturn** the amount produced, as in a given period: *a high weekly output* **3** the material produced, manufactured, yielded, etc **4** *electronics* **a** the power, voltage, or current delivered by a circuit or component **b** the point at which the signal is delivered **5** the power, energy, or work produced by an engine or a system **6** *computing* **a** the information produced by a computer **b** the operations and devices involved in producing this information **7** *(modifier)* of or relating to electronic, computer, or other output: *output signal; output device; output tax* ▷ *vb* -puts, -putting, -put *or* -putted *(tr)* **8** *computing* to cause (data) to be emitted as output

outrage ('aʊt,reɪdʒ) *n* **1** a wantonly vicious or cruel act **2** a gross violation of decency, morality, honour, etc **3** profound indignation, anger, or hurt, caused by such an act ▷ *vb* *(tr)* **4** to cause profound indignation, anger, or resentment in **5** to offend grossly (feelings, decency, human dignity, etc) **6** to commit an act of wanton viciousness, cruelty, or indecency on **7** a euphemistic word for **rape**! [C13 (meaning: excess): via French from *outré* beyond, from Latin *ultrā*]

outrageous (aʊt'reɪdʒəs) *adj* **1** being or having the nature of an outrage **2** grossly offensive to decency, authority, etc **3** violent or unrestrained in behaviour or temperament **4** extravagant or immoderate > **out'rageously** *adv* > **out'rageousness** *n*

Outram ('uːtrəm) *n* Sir **James**. 1803–63, British soldier and administrator in India; he participated in the relief of Lucknow (1857) during the Indian Mutiny

outrank (,aʊt'ræŋk) *vb* *(tr)* **1** to be of higher rank than **2** to take priority over

outré ('uːtreɪ) *adj* deviating from what is usual or proper [C18: from French past participle of *outrer* to pass beyond]

outride (,aʊt'raɪd) *vb* -rides, -riding, -rode, -ridden *(tr)* **1** to outdo by riding faster, farther, or better than **2** (of a vessel) to ride out (a storm)

outrider ('aʊt,raɪdə) *n* **1** a person who goes in advance to investigate, discover a way, etc; scout **2** a person who rides in front of or beside a carriage, esp as an attendant or guard **3** *US* a mounted herdsman

outrigger ('aʊt,rɪgə) *n* **1** a framework for supporting a pontoon outside and parallel to the hull of a boat to provide stability **2** a boat equipped with such a framework, esp one of the canoes of the South Pacific **3** any projecting framework attached to a boat, aircraft, building, etc, to act as a support **4** *rowing* another name for **rigger** (sense 2) [C18: from OUT- + RIG¹ + -ER¹; perhaps influenced by archaic *outligger* outlier]

outright *adj* *(prenominal)* ('aʊt,raɪt) **1** without qualifications or limitations: *outright ownership* **2** complete; total **3** straightforward; direct ▷ *adv* (,aʊt'raɪt) **4** without restrictions **5** without reservation or concealment: *ask outright* **6** instantly: *he was killed outright*

outrush ('aʊt,rʌʃ) *n* a flowing or rushing out

outset ('aʊt,sɛt) *n* a start; beginning (esp in the phrase **from** (*or* **at**) **the outset**)

outside *prep* (,aʊt'saɪd) **1** (sometimes foll by *of*) on or to the exterior of: *outside the house* **2** beyond the limits of **3** apart from; other than: *no-one knows outside you and me* ▷ *adj* ('aʊt,saɪd) **4** *(prenominal)* situated on the exterior: *an outside lavatory* **5** remote; unlikely **6** not a member of **7** the greatest possible or probable (prices, odds, etc) **8** (of a road lane, esp in a dual carriageway or motorway) situated nearer or nearest to the central reservation, for use by faster or overtaking vehicles ▷ *adv* (,aʊt'saɪd) **9** outside a specified thing or place; out of doors **10** *slang* not in prison ▷ *n* ('aʊt,saɪd) **11** the external side or surface **12** the external appearance or aspect **13** (of a path, pavement, etc) the side nearest the road or away from a wall or building **14** *sport* an outside player, as in football **15** *(plural)* the outer sheets of a ream of paper **16** *Canadian* (in the north) the settled parts of Canada **17** at the outside *informal* at the most or at the greatest extent: *two days at the outside*
  ● USAGE The use of *outside of* and *inside of*, although fairly
  ● common, is generally thought to be incorrect or non-
  ● standard: *she waits outside* (not *outside of*) *the school*

outside broadcast *n radio, television* a broadcast not

made from a studio

outside director *n* a director of a company who is not employed by that company but is often employed by a holding or associated company

outside half *n rugby* another term for **stand-off half**. Also called: **out-half**

outsider (,aʊt'saɪdə) *n* **1** a person or thing excluded from or not a member of a set, group, etc **2** a contestant, esp a horse, thought unlikely to win in a race **3** *Canadian* (in the north) a person who does not live in the Arctic regions

outsize ('aʊt,saɪz) *adj* **1** Also called: **outsized** very large or larger than normal ▷ *n* **2** something outsize, such as a garment or person **3** *(modifier)* relating to or dealing in outsize clothes: *an outsize shop*

outskirts ('aʊt,skɜːts) *pl n* *(sometimes singular)* outlying or bordering areas, districts, etc, as of a city

outsmart (,aʊt'smɑːt) *vb* *(tr)* *informal* to get the better of; outwit

outsource (,aʊt'sɔːs) *vb* *(tr)* (of a manufacturer) **1** to subcontract (work) to another company **2** to buy in (components for a product) rather than manufacture them

outspan *South African* ▷ *n* ('aʊt,spæn) **1** an area on a farm kept available for travellers to rest and refresh animals **2** the act of unharnessing or unyoking ▷ *vb* (,aʊt'spæn) -spans, -spanning, -spanned **3** *(tr)* to unharness or unyoke (animals) **4** *(intr)* to relax [C19: partial translation of Afrikaans *uitspan*, from *uit* out + *spannen* to stretch]

outspoken (,aʊt'spəʊkən) *adj* **1** candid or bold in speech **2** said or expressed with candour or boldness

outspread *vb* (,aʊt'sprɛd) -spreads, -spreading, -spread **1** to spread out or cause to spread out ▷ *adj* ('aʊt,sprɛd) **2** spread or stretched out **3** scattered or diffused widely ▷ *n* ('aʊt,sprɛd) **4** a spreading out

outstanding (,aʊt'stændɪŋ) *adj* **1** superior; excellent; distinguished **2** prominent, remarkable, or striking **3** still in existence; unsettled, unpaid, or unresolved **4** (of shares, bonds, etc) issued and sold **5** projecting or jutting upwards or outwards > ,out'standingly *adv*

outstation ('aʊt,steɪʃən) *n* a station or post in a remote region

outstay (,aʊt'steɪ) *vb* *(tr)* **1** to stay longer than **2** to stay beyond (a limit) **3** outstay one's welcome See **overstay** (sense 2)

outstretch (,aʊt'strɛtʃ) *vb* *(tr)* **1** to extend or expand; stretch out **2** to stretch or extend beyond

outstrip (,aʊt'strɪp) *vb* -strips, -stripping, -stripped *(tr)* **1** to surpass in a sphere of activity, competition, etc **2** to be or grow greater than **3** to go faster than and leave behind

outtake ('aʊt,teɪk) *n* an unreleased take from a recording session, film, or television programme

out there *adj slang* (**out-there** when prenominal) unconventional or eccentric: *he blends sublime pop moments with some real out-there stuff*

out-tray *n* (in an office) a tray for outgoing correspondence, documents, etc

outturn ('aʊt,tɜːn) *n* another word for **output** (sense 2)

outvote (,aʊt'vəʊt) *vb* *(tr)* to defeat by a majority of votes

outward ('aʊtwəd) *adj* **1** of or relating to what is apparent or superficial **2** of or relating to the outside of the body **3** belonging or relating to the external, as opposed to the mental, spiritual, or inherent **4** of, relating to, or directed towards the outside or exterior **5** the outward man **a** the body as opposed to the soul **b** *facetious* clothing ▷ *adv* **6** (of a ship) away from port **7** a variant of **outwards** ▷ *n* **8** the outward part; exterior > 'outwardness *n*

Outward Bound *n* trademark (in Britain) a scheme to provide adventure training for young people

outwardly ('aʊtwədlɪ) *adv* **1** in outward appearance **2** with reference to the outside or outer surface; externally

outwards ('aʊtwədz) *or* **outward** *adv* towards the outside; out

outwear (,aʊt'wɛə) *vb* -wears, -wearing, -wore, -worn *(tr)* **1** to use up or destroy by wearing **2** to last or wear longer than **3** to outlive, outgrow, or develop beyond **4** to deplete or exhaust in strength, determination, etc

outweigh (ˌaʊtˈweɪ) vb (tr) **1** to prevail over; overcome **2** to be more important or significant than

outwit (ˌaʊtˈwɪt) vb -wits, -witting, -witted (tr) to get the better of by cunning or ingenuity

outwith (ˈaʊtˈwɪθ) prep Scot outside; beyond

outwork n (ˈaʊtˌwɜːk) **1** (often plural) defences which lie outside main defensive works **2** work performed away from the factory, office, etc, by which it has been commissioned ▷ vb (ˌaʊtˈwɜːk) -works, -working, -worked or -wrought (tr) **3** to work better, harder, etc, than **4** to work out to completion > 'out,worker n

ouzel or **ousel** (ˈuːzəl) n **1** short for **ring ouzel** or **water ouzel** (see **dipper**) **2** an archaic name for the (European) blackbird [Old English ōsle, related to Old High German amsala (German Amsel), Latin merula MERLE]

ouzo (ˈuːzəʊ) n a strong aniseed-flavoured spirit from Greece [Modern Greek ouzon, of obscure origin]

ova (ˈəʊvə) n the plural of **ovum**

oval (ˈəʊvəl) adj **1** having the shape of an ellipse or ellipsoid ▷ n **2** anything that is oval in shape, such as a sports ground [c16: from Medieval Latin ōvālis, from Latin ōvum egg] > 'ovally adv > 'ovalness or ovality (əʊˈvælɪtɪ) n

Oval (ˈəʊvəl) n the Oval a cricket ground in south London, in the borough of Lambeth

Oval Office n the Oval Office **1** the private office of the president of the US, a large oval room in the White House **2** the US presidency

ovariectomy (əʊˌvɛərɪˈɛktəmɪ) n, pl -mies surgery another name for **oophorectomy**

ovary (ˈəʊvərɪ) n, pl -ries **1** either of the two female reproductive organs, which produce ova and secrete oestrogen hormones **2** the corresponding organ in vertebrate and invertebrate animals **3** botany the hollow basal region of a carpel containing one or more ovules. In some plants the carpels are united to form a single compound ovary [c17: from New Latin ōvārium, from Latin ōvum egg] > ovarian (əʊˈvɛərɪən) adj

ovate (ˈəʊveɪt) adj **1** shaped like an egg **2** (esp of a leaf) shaped like the longitudinal section of an egg, with the broader end at the base [c18: from Latin ōvātus egg-shaped; see ovum] > 'ovately adv

ovation (əʊˈveɪʃən) n **1** an enthusiastic reception, esp one of prolonged applause: a standing ovation **2** a victory procession less glorious than a triumph awarded to a Roman general [c16: from Latin ovātiō rejoicing, from ovāre to exult] > o'vational adj

oven (ˈʌvən) n **1** an enclosed heated compartment or receptacle for baking or roasting food **2** a similar device, usually lined with a refractory material, used for drying substances, firing ceramics, heat-treating, etc ▷ vb **3** (tr) to cook in an oven [Old English ofen; related to Old High German ofan, Old Norse ofn] > 'oven-,like adj

ovenable (ˈʌvənəbəl) adj (of food) suitable for cooking in an oven

ovenbird (ˈʌvənˌbɜːd) n **1** any of numerous small brownish South American passerine birds of the family Furnariidae that build oven-shaped clay nests **2** a common North American warbler, Seiurus aurocapillus, that has an olive-brown striped plumage with an orange crown and builds a cup-shaped nest on the ground

oven-ready adj (of various foods) bought already prepared so that they are ready to be cooked in the oven

ovenware (ˈʌvənˌwɛə) n heat-resistant dishes in which food can be both cooked and served

over (ˈəʊvə) prep **1** directly above; on the top of; via the top or upper surface of: over one's head **2** on or to the other side of: over the river **3** during; through, or throughout (a period of time): to travel over England **5** throughout the whole extent of: over the racecourse **6** above; in preference to: I like that over everything else **7** by the agency of (an instrument of telecommunication): we heard it over the radio **8** more than: over a century ago **9** on the subject of; about: an argument over nothing **10** while occupied in: discussing business over golf **11** having recovered from the effects of:

she's not over that last love affair yet **12** over and above added to; in addition to ▷ adv **13** in a state, condition, situation, or position that is or has been placed or put over something: to climb over **14** (particle) so as to cause to fall: knocking over a policeman **15** at or to a point across intervening space, water, etc **16** throughout a whole area: the world over **17** (particle) from beginning to end, usually cursorily **18** throughout a period of time: stay over for this week **19** (esp in signalling and radio) it is now your turn to speak, act, etc **20** more than is expected or usual: not over well **21** over again once more **22** over against **a** opposite to **b** contrasting with **23** over and over (often foll by again) repeatedly ▷ adj **24** (postpositive) finished; no longer in progress ▷ adv, adj **25** remaining; surplus (often in the phrase **left over**) ▷ n **26** cricket **a** a series of six balls bowled by a bowler from the same end of the pitch **b** the play during this [Old English ofer; related to Old High German ubir, obar, Old Norse yfir, Latin super, Greek huper]

over- prefix **1** excessive or excessively; beyond an agreed or desirable limit: overcharge; overdue; oversimplify **2** indicating superior rank: overseer **3** indicating location or movement above: overhang **4** indicating movement downwards: overthrow

overact (ˌəʊvərˈækt) vb to act or behave in an exaggerated manner, as in a theatrical production. Also called: **overplay**

overage (ˌəʊvərˈeɪdʒ) adj beyond a specified age

overall adj (ˈəʊvərˌɔːl) (prenominal) **1** from one end to the other **2** including or covering everything: the overall cost ▷ adv (ˌəʊvərˈɔːl) **3** in general; on the whole ▷ n (ˈəʊvərˌɔːl) **4** Brit a protective work garment usually worn over ordinary clothes **5** (plural) hard-wearing work trousers with a bib and shoulder straps or jacket attached

overarch (ˌəʊvərˈɑːtʃ) vb (tr) to form an arch over

overarching (ˌəʊvərˈɑːtʃɪŋ) adj overall; all-encompassing: an overarching concept

overarm (ˈəʊvərˌɑːm) sport ▷ adj **1** bowled, thrown, or performed with the arm raised above the shoulder ▷ adv **2** with the arm raised above the shoulder

overawe (ˌəʊvərˈɔː) vb (tr) to subdue, restrain, or overcome by affecting with a feeling of awe

overbalance vb (ˌəʊvəˈbæləns) **1** to lose or cause to lose balance **2** (tr) another word for **outweigh** ▷ n (ˈəʊvəˌbæləns) **3** excess of weight, value, etc

overbear (ˌəʊvəˈbɛə) vb -bears, -bearing, -bore, -borne **1** (tr) to dominate or overcome **2** (tr) to press or bear down with weight or physical force **3** to produce or bear (fruit, progeny, etc) excessively

overbearing (ˌəʊvəˈbɛərɪŋ) adj **1** domineering or dictatorial in manner or action **2** of particular or overriding importance or significance > ˌover'bearingly adv

overblown (ˌəʊvəˈbləʊn) adj **1** overdone or excessive **2** bombastic; turgid: overblown prose **3** (of flowers, such as the rose) past the stage of full bloom

overboard (ˌəʊvəˈbɔːd) adv **1** from on board a vessel into the water **2** go overboard informal **a** to be extremely enthusiastic **b** to go to extremes **3** throw overboard to reject or abandon

overbook (ˌəʊvəˈbuːk) vb (tr) to make more reservations than there are places, tickets, hotel rooms, etc, available

overbuild (ˌəʊvəˈbɪld) vb -builds, -building, -built (tr) **1** to build over or on top of **2** to erect too many buildings in (an area) **3** to build too large or elaborately

overburden vb (ˌəʊvəˈbɜːdən) **1** (tr) to load with excessive weight, work, etc ▷ n (ˈəʊvəˌbɜːdən) **2** an excessive burden or load **3** geology the sedimentary rock material that covers coal seams, mineral veins, etc > ˌover'burdensome adj

overcast adj (ˈəʊvəˌkɑːst) **1** covered over or obscured, esp by clouds **2** meteorol (of the sky) more than 95 per cent cloud-covered **3** gloomy or melancholy **4** sewn over by overcasting ▷ vb (ˌəʊvəˈkɑːst) **5** to sew (an edge, as of a hem) with long stitches passing successively over the edge ▷ n (ˈəʊvəˌkɑːst) **6** meteorol the state of the sky when more than 95 per cent of it is cloud-covered

overcharge vb (ˌəʊvəˈtʃɑːdʒ) **1** to charge too much **2** (tr) to fill or load beyond capacity **3** *literary* another word for **exaggerate** ▷ *n* (ˌəʊvəˈtʃɑːdʒ) **4** an excessive price or charge **5** an excessive load

overclocking (ˌəʊvəˈklɒkɪŋ) *n* the practice of modifying a computer (esp with a cooling system) to allow its processors to run at greater speeds than the manufacturer intended > ˌover'clocker *n* > ˌover'clock *vb*

overcloud (ˌəʊvəˈklaʊd) *vb* **1** to make or become covered with clouds **2** to make or become dark or dim

overcoat (ˈəʊvəˌkəʊt) *n* a warm heavy coat worn over the outer clothes in cold weather

overcome (ˌəʊvəˈkʌm) *vb* **-comes, -coming, -came, -come 1** (*tr*) to get the better of in a conflict **2** (*tr; often passive*) to render incapable or powerless by laughter, sorrow, exhaustion, etc **3** (*tr*) to surmount (obstacles, objections, etc) **4** (*intr*) to be victorious

overcrop (ˌəʊvəˈkrɒp) *vb* **-crops, -cropping, -cropped** (*tr*) to exhaust (land) by excessive cultivation

overdo (ˌəʊvəˈduː) *vb* **-does, -doing, -did, -done** (*tr*) **1** to take or carry too far; do to excess **2** to exaggerate, overelaborate, or overplay **3** to cook or bake too long **4 overdo it** *or* **things** to overtax one's strength, capacity, etc

overdose *n* (ˈəʊvəˌdəʊs) **1** (esp of drugs) an excessive dose ▷ *vb* (ˌəʊvəˈdəʊs) **2** to take an excessive dose or give an excessive dose to > ˌover'dosage *n*

overdraft (ˈəʊvəˌdrɑːft) *n* **1** a draft or withdrawal of money in excess of the credit balance on a bank or building-society cheque account **2** the amount of money drawn or withdrawn thus

overdraw (ˌəʊvəˈdrɔː) *vb* **-draws, -drawing, -drew, -drawn 1** to draw on (a bank account) in excess of the credit balance **2** (*tr*) to exaggerate in describing or telling

overdress *vb* (ˌəʊvəˈdrɛs) **1** to dress (oneself or another) too elaborately or finely ▷ *n* (ˈəʊvəˌdrɛs) **2** a dress that may be worn over a jumper, blouse, etc

overdrive *n* (ˈəʊvəˌdraɪv) **1** a very high gear in a motor vehicle used at high speeds to reduce wear and save fuel ▷ *vb* (ˌəʊvəˈdraɪv) **-drives, -driving, -drove, -driven 2** (*tr*) to drive too hard or too far; overwork or overuse

overdub (in multitrack recording) ▷ *vb* (ˌəʊvəˈdʌb) **-dubs, -dubbing, -dubbed 1** to add (new sound) on a spare track or tracks ▷ *n* (ˈəʊvəˌdʌb) **2** the addition of new sound to a recording; the blending of various layers of sound in one recording

overdue (ˌəʊvəˈdjuː) *adj* past the time specified, required, or preferred for arrival, occurrence, payment, etc

overegg (ˌəʊvərˈɛg) *vb* (*tr*) to exaggerate (a feature of something) to the point of unreasonableness (esp in the phrase **overegg the pudding**)

overestimate *vb* (ˌəʊvərˈɛstɪˌmeɪt) **1** (*tr*) to value or estimate too highly ▷ *n* (ˌəʊvərˈɛstɪmɪt) **2** an estimate that is too high > ˌover,esti'mation *n*

overexpose (ˌəʊvərɪksˈpəʊz) *vb* (*tr*) **1** to expose too much or for too long **2** *photog* to expose (a film, plate, or paper) for too long a period or with too bright a light > ˌoverex'posure *n*

overflow *vb* (ˌəʊvəˈfləʊ) **-flows, -flowing, -flowed** *or formerly* **-flown 1** to flow or run over (a limit, brim, bank, etc) **2** to fill or be filled beyond capacity so as to spill or run over **3** (*intr; usually foll by with*) to be filled with happiness, tears, etc **4** (*tr*) to spread or cover over; flood or inundate ▷ *n* (ˈəʊvəˌfləʊ) **5** overflowing matter, esp liquid **6** any outlet that enables surplus liquid to be discharged or drained off, esp one just below the top of a tank or cistern **7** the amount by which a limit, capacity, etc, is exceeded

overfold (ˈəʊvəˌfəʊld) *n* *geology* a fold in which one or both limbs have been inclined more than 90° from their original orientation

overfunding (ˈəʊvəˌfʌndɪŋ) *n* (in Britain) a government policy in which it sells more of its securities than would be required to finance public spending, with the object of absorbing surplus funds to curb inflation

overgrow (ˌəʊvəˈgrəʊ) *vb* **-grows, -growing, -grew, -grown 1** (*tr*) to grow over or across (an area, path, lawn, etc) **2** (*tr*) to choke or supplant by a stronger growth

3 (*tr*) to grow too large for **4** (*intr*) to grow beyond normal size > 'over,growth *n*

overhand (ˈəʊvəˌhænd) *adj* **1** thrown or performed with the hand raised above the shoulder **2** sewn with thread passing over two edges in one direction ▷ *adv* **3** with the hand above the shoulder; overarm **4** with shallow stitches passing over two edges ▷ *vb* **5** to sew (two edges) overhand

overhang *vb* (ˌəʊvəˈhæŋ) **-hangs, -hanging, -hung 1** to project or extend beyond (a surface, building, etc) **2** (*tr*) to hang or be suspended over **3** (*tr*) to menace, threaten, or dominate ▷ *n* (ˈəʊvəˌhæŋ) **4** a formation, object, part of a structure, etc, that extends beyond or hangs over something, such as an outcrop of rock overhanging a mountain face **5** the amount or extent of projection

overhaul *vb* (ˌəʊvəˈhɔːl) (*tr*) **1** to examine carefully for faults, necessary repairs, etc **2** to make repairs or adjustments to (a car, machine, etc) **3** to overtake ▷ *n* (ˈəʊvəˌhɔːl) **4** a thorough examination and repair

overhead *adj* (ˈəʊvəˌhɛd) **1** situated or operating above head height or some other reference level **2** (*prenominal*) inclusive: *the overhead price included meals* ▷ *adv* (ˌəʊvəˈhɛd) **3** over or above head height, esp in the sky ▷ *n* (ˈəʊvəˌhɛd) **4 a** a stroke in racket games played from above head height **b** (*as modifier*): *an overhead smash* **5** (*modifier*) of, concerned with, or resulting from overheads: *overhead costs* ▷ See also **overheads**

overhead camshaft *n* a type of camshaft situated above the cylinder head in an internal-combustion engine. It is usually driven by a chain or a toothed belt from the crankshaft and the cams bear directly onto the valve stems or rocker arms

overhead projector *n* a projector that throws an enlarged image of a transparency onto a surface above and behind the person using it. Alterations and additions can be made to the material on the transparency while the projector is in use

overheads (ˈəʊvəˌhɛdz) *pl n* business expenses, such as rent, that are not directly attributable to any department or product and can therefore be assigned only arbitrarily

overhead-valve engine *n* a type of internal-combustion engine in which the inlet and exhaust valves are in the cylinder head above the pistons. US name: **valve-in-head engine**

overhear (ˌəʊvəˈhɪə) *vb* **-hears, -hearing, -heard** (*tr*) to hear (a person, remark, etc) without the knowledge of the speaker

overheat (ˌəʊvəˈhiːt) *vb* **1** to make or become excessively hot **2** (*tr; often passive*) to make very agitated, irritated, etc **3** (*intr*) (of an economy) to tend towards inflation, often as a result of excessive growth in demand **4** (*tr*) to cause (an economy) to tend towards inflation ▷ *n* **5** the condition of being overheated

Overijssel (*Dutch* oːvərˈɛisəl) *n* a province of the E Netherlands: generally low-lying. Capital: Zwolle. Pop: 1 101 000 (2003 est). Area: 3929 sq km (1517 sq miles)

overjoy (ˌəʊvəˈdʒɔɪ) *vb* (*tr*) to give great delight to

overjoyed (ˌəʊvəˈdʒɔɪd) *adj* delighted; excessively happy

overkill (ˈəʊvəˌkɪl) *n* **1** the capability to deploy more weapons, esp nuclear weapons, than is necessary to ensure military advantage **2** any capacity or treatment that is greater than that required or appropriate

overland (ˈəʊvəˌlænd) *adj, adv* (*prenominal*) **1** over or across land ▷ *vb* **2** *Austral history* to drive (cattle or sheep) overland > 'over,lander *n*

overlap *vb* (ˌəʊvəˈlæp) **-laps, -lapping, -lapped 1** (of two things) to extend or lie partly over (each other) **2** to cover and extend beyond something **3** (*intr*) to coincide partly in time, subject, etc ▷ *n* (ˈəʊvəˌlæp) **4** a part that overlaps or is overlapped **5** the amount, length, etc, overlapping **6** *geology* the horizontal extension of the upper beds in a series of rock strata beyond the lower beds, usually caused by submergence of the land

overlay *vb* (ˌəʊvəˈleɪ) **-lays, -laying, -laid** (*tr*) **1** to lay or place something over or upon (something else) **2** (often foll by *with*) to cover, overspread, or conceal (with) **3** (foll by *with*) to cover (a surface) with an applied decoration: *ebony overlaid with silver* **4** to achieve the correct printing pressure all over (a forme or plate) by adding to the appropriate areas of the packing ▷ *n* (ˈəʊvəˌleɪ) **5** something that is laid over something else; covering **6** an applied decoration or layer, as of gold leaf **7** a transparent sheet giving extra details to a map or diagram over which it is designed to be placed **8** *printing* material, such as paper, used to overlay a forme or plate

overleaf (ˌəʊvəˈliːf) *adv* on the other side of the page

overlie (ˌəʊvəˈlaɪ) *vb* -lies, -lying, -lay, -lain(*tr*) **1** to lie or rest upon. Compare **overlay 2** to kill (a baby or newborn animal) by lying upon it

overlong (ˌəʊvəˈlɒŋ) *adj, adv* too or excessively long

overlook *vb* (ˌəʊvəˈlʊk) (*tr*) **1** to fail to notice or take into account **2** to disregard deliberately or indulgently **3** to afford a view of from above: *the house overlooks the bay* **4** to rise above **5** to look at carefully **6** to bewitch or cast the evil eye upon (someone) ▷ *n* (ˈəʊvəˌlʊk) *US* **7** a high place affording a view **8** an act of overlooking

overlord (ˈəʊvəˌlɔːd) *n* a supreme lord or master > ˈover,lordshipn

overly (ˈəʊvəlɪ) *adv* too; excessively

overman *vb* (ˌəʊvəˈmæn) -mans, -manning, -manned **1** (*tr*) to supply with an excessive number of men ▷ *n* (ˈəʊvəˌmæn), *pl* -men **2** a man who oversees others **3** the Nietzschean superman

overmaster (ˌəʊvəˈmɑːstə) *vb* (*tr*) to overpower

overmatch *chiefly US* ▷ *vb*, (ˌəʊvəˈmætʃ) (*tr*) **1** to be more than a match for **2** to match with a superior opponent ▷ *n* (ˈəʊvəˌmætʃ) **3** a person superior in ability **4** a match in which one contestant is superior

overmuch (ˌəʊvəˈmʌtʃ) *adv, adj* **1** too much; very much ▷ *n* **2** an excessive amount

overnice (ˌəʊvəˈnaɪs) *adj* too fastidious, precise, etc

overnight *adv* (ˌəʊvəˈnaɪt) **1** for the duration of the night **2** in or as if in the course of one night; suddenly: *the situation changed overnight* ▷ *adj* (ˈəʊvəˌnaɪt) (*usually prenominal*) **3** done in, occurring in, or lasting the night: *an overnight stop* **4** staying for one night **5** for use during a single night **6** occurring in or as if in the course of one night; sudden: *an overnight victory*

overpass *n* (ˈəʊvəˌpɑːs) **1** another name for **flyover** (sense 1) ▷ *vb* (ˌəʊvəˈpɑːs) -passes, -passing, -passed(*tr*) *now rare* **2** to pass over, through, or across **3** to exceed **4** to ignore

overplay (ˌəʊvəˈpleɪ) *vb* **1** (*tr*) to exaggerate the importance of **2** **overplay one's hand** to overestimate the worth or strength of one's position

overpower (ˌəʊvəˈpaʊə) *vb* (*tr*) **1** to conquer or subdue by superior force **2** to have such a strong effect on as to make helpless or ineffective **3** to supply with more power than necessary > ˌoverˈpoweringadj

overpriced (ˌəʊvəˈpraɪst) *adj* charging or charged at too high a price

overprint *vb* (ˌəʊvəˈprɪnt) **1** (*tr*) to print (additional matter or another colour) on a sheet of paper ▷ *n* (ˈəʊvəˌprɪnt) **2** additional matter or another colour printed onto a previously printed sheet **3** additional matter, other than a change in face value, applied to a finished postage stamp by printing, stamping, etc

overqualified (ˌəʊvəˈkwɒlɪˌfaɪd) *adj* having more managerial experience or academic qualifications than required for a particular job

overrate (ˌəʊvəˈreɪt) *vb* (*tr*) to assess too highly

overreach (ˌəʊvəˈriːtʃ) *vb* **1** (*tr*) to defeat or thwart (oneself) by attempting to do or gain too much **2** (*tr*) to aim for but miss by going too far or attempting too much **3** to get the better of (a person) by trickery **4** (*tr*) to reach or extend beyond or over **5** (*intr*) to reach or go too far **6** (*intr*) (of a horse) to strike the back of a forefoot with the edge of the opposite hind foot

overreact (ˌəʊvərɪˈækt) *vb* (*intr*) to react excessively to something > ˌoverreˈactionn

override (ˌəʊvəˈraɪd) *vb* -rides, -riding, -rode, -ridden(*tr*) **1** to set aside or disregard with superior authority or power **2** to supersede or annul **3** to dominate or vanquish by or as if by trampling down **4** to take manual control of (a system that is usually under automatic control) **5** to extend or pass over, esp to overlap **6** to ride (a horse) too hard **7** to ride over or across ▷ *n* **8** a device or system that can override an automatic control

overrider (ˈəʊvəˌraɪdə) *n* either of two metal or rubber attachments fitted to the bumper of a motor vehicle to prevent the bumpers interlocking with those of another vehicle

overriding (ˌəʊvəˈraɪdɪŋ) *adj* taking precedence

overrule (ˌəʊvəˈruːl) *vb* (*tr*) **1** to disallow the arguments of (a person) by the use of authority **2** to rule or decide against (an argument, decision, etc) **3** to prevail over, dominate, or influence **4** to exercise rule over

overrun *vb* (ˌəʊvəˈrʌn) -runs, -running, -ran, -run **1** (*tr*) to swarm or spread over rapidly **2** to run over (something); overflow **3** to extend or run beyond a limit **4** (*intr*) (of an engine) to run with a closed throttle at a speed dictated by that of the vehicle it drives, as on a decline **5** (*tr*) to print (a book, journal, etc) in a greater quantity than ordered **6** (*tr*) *printing* to transfer (set type and other matter) from one column, line, or page, to another **7** (*tr*) *archaic* to run faster than ▷ *n* (ˈəʊvəˌrʌn) **8** the act or an instance of overrunning **9** the amount or extent of overrunning **10** the number of copies of a publication in excess of the quantity ordered

overseas *adv* (ˌəʊvəˈsiːz) **1** beyond the sea; abroad ▷ *adj* (ˈəʊvəˈsiːz) **2** of, to, in, from, or situated in countries beyond the sea **3** Also called: **oversea** (ˌəʊvəˈsiː) of or relating to passage over the sea ▷ *n* (ˌəʊvəˈsiːz) **4** (*functioning as singular*) *informal* a foreign country or foreign countries collectively

oversee (ˌəʊvəˈsiː) *vb* -sees, -seeing, -saw, -seen(*tr*) **1** to watch over and direct; supervise **2** to watch secretly or accidentally

overseer (ˈəʊvəˌsiːə) *n* **1** a person who oversees others, esp workmen **2** *Brit history* short for **overseer of the poor**; a minor official of a parish attached to the workhouse or poorhouse

oversell (ˌəʊvəˈsɛl) *vb* -sells, -selling, -sold **1** (*tr*) to sell more of (a commodity) than can be supplied **2** to use excessively aggressive methods in selling (commodities) **3** (*tr*) to exaggerate the merits of

overset (ˌəʊvəˈsɛt) *vb* -sets, -setting, -set(*tr*) **1** to disturb or upset **2** *printing* to set (type or copy) in excess of the space available

oversew (ˈəʊvəˌsəʊ, ˌəʊvəˈsəʊ) *vb* -sews, -sewing, -sewed, -sewnto sew (two edges) with close stitches that pass over them both

oversexed (ˌəʊvəˈsɛkst) *adj* having an excessive preoccupation with or need for sexual activity

overshadow (ˌəʊvəˈʃædəʊ) *vb* (*tr*) **1** to render insignificant or less important in comparison **2** to cast a shadow or gloom over

overshoe (ˈəʊvəˌʃuː) *n* a protective shoe worn over an ordinary shoe

overshoot (ˌəʊvəˈʃuːt) *vb* -shoots, -shooting, -shot **1** to shoot or go beyond (a mark or target) **2** to cause (an aircraft) to fly or taxi too far along (a runway) during landing or taking off, or (of an aircraft) to fly or taxi too far along a runway **3** (*tr*) to pass swiftly over or down over, as water over a wheel ▷ *n* **4** an act or instance of overshooting **5** the extent of such overshooting

overshot (ˈəʊvəˌʃɒt) *adj* **1** having or designating an upper jaw that projects beyond the lower jaw, esp when considered as an abnormality **2** (of a water wheel) driven by a flow of water that passes over the wheel rather than under it

oversight (ˈəʊvəˌsaɪt) *n* **1** an omission or mistake, esp one made through failure to notice something **2** supervision

oversize *adj* (ˌəʊvəˈsaɪz) **1** Also called: **oversized** larger than the usual size ▷ *n* (ˈəʊvəˌsaɪz) **2** a size larger than the usual or proper size **3** something that is oversize

overskirt (ˈəʊvəˌskɜːt) *n* an outer skirt, esp one that reveals a decorative underskirt

overspend *vb* (ˌəʊvəˈspɛnd) -spends, -spending, -spent **1** to spend in excess of (one's desires or what one can afford or is allocated) **2** (*tr; usually passive*) to wear out; exhaust ▷ *n* (ˈəʊvəˌspɛnd) **3** the amount by which someone or something is overspent

overspill *n* (ˈəʊvəˌspɪl) **1 a** something that spills over or is in excess **b** (*as modifier*): *overspill population* ▷ *vb* (ˌəʊvəˈspɪl)

-spills, -spilling, -spilt *or* -spilled **2** (*intr*) to overflow

overstate (ˌəʊvəˈsteɪt) *vb* (*tr*) to state too strongly; exaggerate or overemphasize > ˈover.statement *n*

overstay (ˌəʊvəˈsteɪ) *vb* (*tr*) **1** to stay beyond the time, limit, or duration of **2** overstay *or* outstay one's welcome to stay (at a party, on a visit, etc), longer than pleases the host or hostess

overstayer (ˈəʊvəˌsteɪə) *n* a person who illegally remains in a country after the period of the permitted visit has ended

overstep (ˌəʊvəˈstɛp) *vb* -steps, -stepping, -stepped (*tr*) to go beyond (a certain or proper limit)

overstrung (ˌəʊvəˈstrʌŋ) *adj* **1** too highly strung; tense **2** (of a piano) having two sets of strings crossing each other at an oblique angle

overstuff (ˌəʊvəˈstʌf) *vb* (*tr*) **1** to force too much into **2** to cover (furniture) entirely with upholstery

oversubscribe (ˌəʊvəsəbˈskraɪb) *vb* (*tr; often passive*) to subscribe or apply for in excess of available supply > ˌoversubˈscription *n*

overt (ˈəʊvɜːt, əʊˈvɜːt) *adj* **1** open to view; observable **2** *law* open; deliberate. Criminal intent may be inferred from an overt act [C14: via Old French, from *ovrir* to open, from Latin *aperīre*] > ˈovertly *adv*

overtake (ˌəʊvəˈteɪk) *vb* -takes, -taking, -took, -taken **1** *chiefly Brit* to move past (another vehicle or person) travelling in the same direction **2** (*tr*) to pass or do better than, after catching up with **3** (*tr*) to come upon suddenly or unexpectedly: *night overtook him* **4** (*tr*) to catch up with; draw level with

overtax (ˌəʊvəˈtæks) *vb* (*tr*) **1** to tax too heavily **2** to impose too great a strain on

over-the-counter *adj* **1 a** (of securities) not listed or quoted on a stock exchange **b** (of a security market) dealing in such securities **c** (of security transactions) conducted through a broker's office directly between purchaser and seller and not on a stock exchange **2** (of medicinal drugs) able to be sold without a prescription. Abbreviation: OTC ▷ Compare **POM**

overthink (ˌəʊvəˈθɪŋk) *vb* -thinks, -thinking, -thought to spend more time thinking about something than is necessary or productive

overthrow *vb* (ˌəʊvəˈθrəʊ) -throws, -throwing, -threw, -thrown **1** (*tr*) to effect the downfall or destruction of (a ruler, institution, etc), esp by force **2** (*tr*) to throw or turn over **3** (*tr*) to throw (something, esp a ball) too far ▷ *n* (ˈəʊvəˌθrəʊ) **4** downfall; destruction **5** *cricket* **a** a ball thrown back too far by a fielder **b** a run scored because of this

overthrust (ˈəʊvəˌθrʌst) *n* *geology* a reverse fault in which the rocks on the upper surface of a fault plane have moved over the rocks on the lower surface

overtime *n* (ˈəʊvəˌtaɪm) **1 a** work at a regular job done in addition to regular working hours **b** (*as modifier*): *overtime pay* **2** the rate of pay established for such work **3** time in excess of a set period **4** *US & Canadian sport* extra time ▷ *adv* (ˈəʊvəˌtaɪm) **5** beyond the regular or stipulated time ▷ *vb* (ˌəʊvəˈtaɪm) **6** (*tr*) to exceed the required time for (a photographic exposure)

overtone (ˈəʊvəˌtəʊn) *n* **1** (*often plural*) additional meaning or nuance: *overtones of despair* **2** *music, acoustics* any of the tones, with the exception of the fundamental, that constitute a musical sound and contribute to its quality, each having a frequency that is a multiple of the fundamental frequency

overture (ˈəʊvəˌtjʊə) *n* **1** *music* **a** a piece of orchestral music containing contrasting sections that is played at the beginning of an opera or oratorio, often containing the main musical themes of the work **b** Also called: concert overture a one-movement orchestral piece, usually having a descriptive or evocative title **2** (*often plural*) a proposal, act, or gesture initiating a relationship, negotiation, etc **3** something that introduces what follows ▷ *vb* (*tr*) **4** to make or present an overture to **5** to introduce with an overture [C14: via Old French, from Late Latin *apertūra* opening, from Latin *aperīre* to open; see OVERT]

overturn *vb* (ˌəʊvəˈtɜːn) **1** to turn or cause to turn from an upright or normal position **2** (*tr*) to overthrow or

destroy **3** (*tr*) to invalidate; reverse: *the bill was passed in the Commons but overturned in the Lords* ▷ *n* (ˈəʊvəˌtɜːn) **4** the act of overturning or the state of being overturned

over-use *vb* (ˌəʊvəˈjuːz) (*tr*) **1** to use excessively ▷ *n* (ˌəʊvəˈjuːs) **2** excessive use

overview (ˈəʊvəˌvjuː) *n* a general survey

overweening (ˌəʊvəˈwiːnɪŋ) *adj* **1** (of a person) excessively arrogant or presumptuous **2** (of opinions, appetites, etc) excessive; immoderate [C14: OVER- + *weening*, from Old English *wēnan*: see WEEN] > ˌover'weeningness *n*

overweight *adj* (ˌəʊvəˈweɪt) **1** weighing more than is usual, allowed, or healthy ▷ *n* (ˈəʊvəˌweɪt) **2** extra or excess weight ▷ *vb* (ˌəʊvəˈweɪt) **3** to give too much emphasis or consideration to **4** to add too much weight to **5** to weigh down

overwhelm (ˌəʊvəˈwɛlm) *vb* (*tr*) **1** to overpower the thoughts, emotions, or senses of **2** to overcome with irresistible force **3** to cover over or bury completely **4** to weigh or rest upon overpoweringly

overwhelming (ˌəʊvəˈwɛlmɪŋ) *adj* overpowering in effect, number, or force > ˌover'whelmingly *adv*

overwind (ˌəʊvəˈwaɪnd) *vb* -winds, -winding, -wound (*tr*) to wind (a watch) beyond the proper limit

overwork *vb* (ˌəʊvəˈwɜːk) (*mainly tr*) **1** (*also intr*) to work or cause to work too hard or too long **2** to use too much: *to overwork an excuse* **3** to decorate the surface of ▷ *n* (ˈəʊvəˌwɜːk) **4** excessive or excessively tiring work

overwrite (ˌəʊvəˈraɪt) *vb* -writes, -writing, -wrote, -written **1** to write (something) in an excessively ornate or prolix style **2** to write too much about (someone or something) **3** to write on top of (other writing) **4** to record on a storage medium, such as a magnetic disk, thus destroying what was originally recorded there

overwrought (ˌəʊvəˈrɔːt) *adj* **1** full of nervous tension; agitated **2** too elaborate; fussy: *an overwrought style* **3** (*often postpositive* and foll by *with*) with the surface decorated or adorned

Ovett (ˈəʊvɛt) *n* Steve. born 1955, British middle-distance runner: winner of the 800 metres in the 1980 Olympic Games

ovi- *or* **ovo-** *combining form* egg or ovum: *oviform; ovotestis* [from Latin *ōvum*]

Ovid (ˈɒvɪd) *n* Latin name *Publius Ovidius Naso*. 43 BC–?17 AD, Roman poet. His verse includes poems on love, *Ars Amatoria*, on myths, *Metamorphoses*, and on his sufferings in exile, *Tristia* > Ovidian (ɒˈvɪdɪən) *adj*

oviduct (ˈɒvɪˌdʌkt, ˈəʊ-) *n* the tube through which ova are conveyed from an ovary. Also called (in mammals): Fallopian tube > oviducal (ˌɒvɪˈdjuːkᵊl, ˌəʊ-) *or* ˌovi'ductal *adj*

Oviedo (Spanish oˈβjeðo) *n* a city in NW Spain: capital of Asturias from 810 until 1002; centre of a coal- and iron-mining area. Pop: 207 699 (2003 est)

oviform (ˈəʊvɪˌfɔːm) *adj* biology shaped like an egg

ovine (ˈəʊvaɪn) *adj* of, relating to, or resembling a sheep [C19: from Late Latin *ovīnus*, from Latin *ovis* sheep]

oviparous (əʊˈvɪpərəs) *adj* (of fishes, reptiles, birds, etc) producing eggs that hatch outside the body of the mother. ▷ Compare **ovoviviparous, viviparous** (sense 1) > **oviparity** (ˌɒvɪˈpærɪtɪ) *n* > o'viparously *adv*

ovipositor (ˌɒvɪˈpɒzɪtə) *n* **1** the egg-laying organ of most female insects, consisting of a pair of specialized appendages at the end of the abdomen **2** a similar organ in certain female fishes, formed by an extension of the edges of the genital opening [C19: OVI- + *positus*, past participle of Latin *pōnere* to place] > ovi'posit *vb*

ovoid (ˈəʊvɔɪd) *adj* **1** egg-shaped ▷ *n* **2** something that is ovoid

ovoviviparous (ˌəʊvəʊvaɪˈvɪpərəs) *adj* (of certain reptiles, fishes, etc) producing eggs that hatch within the body of the mother. Compare **oviparous, viviparous** (sense 1) > ovoviviparity (ˌəʊvəʊˌvaɪvɪˈpærɪtɪ) *n*

ovulate (ˈɒvjʊˌleɪt) *vb* (*intr*) to produce or discharge eggs from an ovary [C19: from OVULE] > ˌovu'lation *n*

ovulation method *n* another name for **Billings method**

ovule (ˈɒvjuːl) *n* **1** a small body in seed-bearing plants that consists of the integument(s), nucellus, and embryosac (containing the egg cell) and develops into the seed after fertilization **2** *zoology* an immature ovum [c19: via French from Medieval Latin *ōvulum* a little egg, from Latin *ōvum* egg] > 'ovular*adj*

ovum ('əʊvəm) *n, pl* **ova** ('əʊvə) an unfertilized female gamete; egg cell [from Latin: egg]

ow (aʊ) *interj* an exclamation of pain

owe (əʊ) *vb* (*mainly tr*) **1** to be under an obligation to pay (someone) to the amount of **2** (*intr*) to be in debt: *he still owes for his house* **3** (often foll by *to*) to have as a result (of) **4** to feel the need or obligation to do, give, etc **5** to hold or maintain in the mind or heart esp in the phrase **owe a grudge** [Old English *āgan* to have (c12: to have to); related to Old Saxon *ēgan*, Old High German *eigan*]

Owen ('əʊɪn) *n* **1** David (**Anthony Llewellyn**), Baron. born 1938, British politician: Labour foreign secretary (1977–79); cofounder of the Social Democratic Party (1981) and its leader (1983–87): leader (1988–92) of the section of the Social Democratic Party that did not merge with the Liberal Party in 1988; peace envoy to Bosnia-Herzegovina (1992–94) **2** Michael (**James**). born 1979, English footballer; plays for Newcastle United (from 2005) and England (from 1997) **3** Sir Richard. 1804–92, English comparative anatomist and palaeontologist **4** Robert. 1771–1858, Welsh industrialist and social reformer. He formed a model industrial community at New Lanark, Scotland, and pioneered cooperative societies. His books include *New View of Society* (1813) **5** Wilfred. 1893–1918, English poet of World War I, who was killed in action

Owen gun *n* a type of simple recoil-operated 9 mm sub-machine-gun first used by Australian forces in World War II [named after E. E. *Owen* (1915–49), its Australian inventor]

Owens ('əʊɪnz) *n* Jesse, real name *John Cleveland Owens*. 1913–80, US Black athlete: won four gold medals at the Berlin Olympics (1936)

Owen Stanley Range *n* a mountain range in SE New Guinea. Highest peak: Mount Victoria, 4073 m (13 363 ft)

Owerri (ə'wɛrɪ) *n* a market town in S Nigeria, capital of Imo state. Pop (local government areas): 401 873 (2006)

owing ('əʊɪŋ) *adj* **1** (*postpositive*) owed; due **2** owing to (*preposition*) because of or on account of

owl (aʊl) *n* **1** any nocturnal bird of prey of the order *Strigiformes*, having large front-facing eyes, a small hooked bill, soft feathers, and a short neck **2** any of various breeds of owl-like fancy domestic pigeon (esp the **African owl, Chinese owl,** and **English owl**) **3** a person who looks or behaves like an owl, esp in having a solemn manner [Old English *ūle*; related to Dutch *uil*, Old High German *ūwila*, Old Norse *ugla*] > 'owl-,like*adj* > 'owlish*adj*

owlet ('aʊlɪt) *n* a young or nestling owl

own (əʊn) *determiner* (*preceded by a possessive*) **1 a** (*intensifier*): *John's own idea; your own mother* **b** (*as pronoun*): *I'll use my own* **2** on behalf of oneself or in relation to oneself: *he is his own worst enemy* **3** come into one's own **a** to become fulfilled: *she really came into her own when she got divorced* **b** to receive what is due to one **4** hold one's own to maintain one's situation or position, esp in spite of opposition or difficulty **5** on one's own **a** without help **b** by oneself; alone ▷ *vb* **6** (*tr*) to have as one's possession **7** (when *intr*, often foll by *up, to,* or *up to*) to confess or admit; acknowledge **8** (*tr; takes a clause as object*) *now rare* to concede: *I own that you are right* [Old English *āgen*, originally past participle of *āgan* to have; related to Old Saxon *ēgan*, Old Norse *eiginn*. See also owe]

own brand *n* **a** an item packaged and marketed under the brand name of a particular retailer, usually a large supermarket chain, rather than that of the manufacturer **b** (*as modifier*): *own-brand products.* ▷ Also called: **own label**

owner ('əʊnə) *n* a person who owns; legal possessor

owner-occupier *n* *Brit* a person who owns or is in the process of buying the house or flat he lives in

ownership ('əʊnəʃɪp) *n* **1** the state or fact of being an owner **2** legal right of possession; proprietorship

own goal *n* **1** *soccer* a goal scored by a player accidentally playing the ball into his or her own team's net **2** *informal* any action that results in disadvantage to the person who took it or to a party, group, etc with which that

person is associated

ox (ɒks) *n, pl* **oxen** ('ɒksən) **1** an adult castrated male of any domesticated species of cattle, esp *Bos taurus,* used for draught work and meat **2** any bovine mammal, esp any of the domestic cattle [Old English *oxa*; related to Old Saxon, Old High German *ohso*, Old Norse *oxi*]

oxalic acid (ɒk'sælɪk) *n* a colourless poisonous crystalline dicarboxylic acid found in many plants: used as a bleach and a cleansing agent for metals. Formula: $(COOH)_2$ [c18: from French *oxalique*, from Latin *oxalis* garden sorrel; see oxalis]

oxalis ('ɒksəlɪs, ɒk'sælɪs) *n* any plant of the genus *Oxalis,* having clover-like leaves which contain oxalic acid and white, pink, red, or yellow flowers: family *Oxalidaceae.* See also **wood sorrel** [c18: via Latin from Greek: sorrel, sour wine, from *oxus* acid, sharp]

oxblood ('ɒks,blʌd) *or* **oxblood red** *adj* of a dark reddish-brown colour

oxbow ('ɒks,bəʊ) *n* **1** a U-shaped piece of wood fitted under and around the neck of a harnessed ox and attached to the yoke **2** Also called: **oxbow lake, cutoff** a small curved lake lying on the flood plain of a river and constituting the remnant of a former meander

Oxbridge ('ɒks,brɪdʒ) *n* **a** the British universities of Oxford and Cambridge, esp considered as ancient and prestigious academic institutions, bastions of privilege and superiority, etc **b** (*as modifier*): *Oxbridge graduates*

oxen ('ɒksən) *n* the plural of **ox**

Oxenstierna *or* **Oxenstjerna** (*Swedish* 'uksənfæːrna) *n* Count Axel (aksəl). 1583–1654, Swedish statesman. He was chancellor (1612–54) and successfully directed Swedish foreign policy for most of the Thirty Years' War

oxeye ('ɒks,aɪ) *n* **1** any Eurasian plant of the genus *Buphthalmum,* having daisy-like flower heads with yellow rays and dark centres: family *Asteraceae* (composites) **2** any of various North American plants of the related genus *Heliopsis,* having daisy-like flowers **3** **oxeye daisy**a type of hardy perennial chrysanthemum

ox-eyed *adj* having large round eyes, like those of an ox

OXFAMor **Oxfam** ('ɒksfæm) *n acronym for* Oxford Committee for Famine Relief

Oxford[1] ('ɒksfəd) *n* **1** a city in S England, administrative centre of Oxfordshire, at the confluence of the Rivers Thames and Cherwell: Royalist headquarters during the Civil War; seat of Oxford University, consisting of 40 separate colleges, the oldest being University College (1249), and Oxford Brookes University (1993); motor-vehicle industry. Pop: 143 016 (2001). Related word: **Oxonian** **2** Also called: **Oxford Down** a breed of sheep with middle-length wool and a dark brown face and legs **3** a type of stout laced shoe with a low heel **4** a lightweight fabric of plain or twill weave used esp for men's shirts

Oxford[2] ('ɒksfəd) *n* 1st Earl of. title of (Robert) **Harley**

Oxford bags *pl n* trousers with very wide baggy legs, originally popular in the 1920s

Oxford blue *n* **1 a** a dark blue colour **b** (*as adjective*): *an Oxford-blue scarf* **2** a person who has been awarded a blue from Oxford University

Oxford Movement *n* a movement within the Church of England that began at Oxford in 1833 and was led by Pusey, Newman, and Keble. It affirmed the continuity of the Church with early Christianity and strove to restore the High-Church ideals of the 17th century. Its views were publicized in a series of tracts (**Tracts for the Times**) 1833–41. The teaching and practices of the Movement are maintained in the High-Church tradition within the Church of England. Also called: **Tractarianism**

Oxfordshire ('ɒksfəd,ʃɪə, -ʃə) *n* an inland county of S central England: situated mostly in the basin of the Upper Thames, with the Cotswolds in the west and the Chilterns in the southeast. Administrative centre: Oxford. Pop: 615 200 (2003 est). Area: 2608 sq km (1007 sq miles). Abbreviation: **Oxon**

oxidant ('ɒksɪdənt) *n* a substance that acts or is used as an oxidizing agent

oxidation (,ɒksɪ'deɪʃən) *n* **a** the act or process of oxidizing **b** (*as modifier*): *an oxidation state; an oxidation*

O

potential > ˌoxiˈdational *adj* > ˈoxiˌdative *adj* > ˈoxiˌdate *vb*

oxidation-reduction *n* **a** a reversible chemical process usually involving the transfer of electrons, in which one reaction is an oxidation and the reverse reaction is a reduction **b** Also: **redox** (*as modifier*): *an oxidation-reduction reaction*

oxide (ˈɒksaɪd) *n* **1** any compound of oxygen with another element **2** any organic compound in which an oxygen atom is bound to two alkyl or aryl groups; an ether or epoxide [C18: from French, from *ox(ygène)* + *(ac)ide*; see OXYGEN, ACID]

oxidize *or* **oxidise** (ˈɒksɪˌdaɪz) *vb* **1** to undergo or cause to undergo a chemical reaction with oxygen, as in formation of an oxide **2** to form or cause to form a layer of metal oxide, as in rusting **3** to lose or cause to lose hydrogen atoms **4** to undergo or cause to undergo a decrease in the number of electrons > ˌoxidiˈzation *or* ˌoxidiˈsation *n*

oxidizing agent *n* *chem* a substance that oxidizes another substance, being itself reduced in the process. Common oxidizing agents are oxygen, hydrogen peroxide, and ferric salts

oxlip (ˈɒksˌlɪp) *n* **1** Also called: **paigle** a primulaceous Eurasian woodland plant, *Primula elatior*, with small drooping pale yellow flowers **2** Also called: **false oxlip** a similar and related plant that is a natural hybrid between the cowslip and primrose [Old English *oxanslyppe*, literally: ox's slippery dropping; see SLIP³, compare COWSLIP]

oxo acid (ˈɒksəʊ) *n* another name for **oxyacid**

Oxon *abbreviation* Oxfordshire [from Latin *Oxonia*]

Oxon. (ˈɒksən) *abbreviation* (in degree titles) of Oxford [from Latin *Oxoniensis*]

Oxonian (ɒkˈsəʊnɪən) *adj* **1** of or relating to Oxford or Oxford University ▷ *n* **2** a member of Oxford University **3** an inhabitant or native of Oxford

oxpecker (ˈɒksˌpɛkə) *n* either of two African starlings, *Buphagus africanus* or *B. erythrorhynchus*, having flattened bills with which they obtain food from the hides of cattle. Also called: **tick-bird**

oxtail (ˈɒksˌteɪl) *n* the skinned tail of an ox, used esp in soups and stews

oxter (ˈɒkstə) *n* *Scot, Irish & Northern English dialect* the armpit [C16: from Old English *oxta*; related to Old High German *Ahsala*, Latin *axilla*]

oxtongue (ˈɒksˌtʌŋ) *n* **1** any of various Eurasian plants of the genus *Picris*, having oblong bristly leaves and clusters of dandelion-like flowers: family *Asteraceae* (composites) **2** any of various other plants having bristly tongue-shaped leaves, such as alkanet **3** the tongue of an ox, braised or boiled as food

Oxus (ˈɒksəs) *n* the ancient name for the **Amu Darya**

oxy-¹ *combining form* denoting something sharp; acute: *oxytone* [from Greek, from *oxus*]

oxy-² *combining form* containing or using oxygen: *oxyacetylene*

oxyacetylene (ˌɒksɪəˈsɛtɪˌliːn) *n* **a** a mixture of oxygen and acetylene; used in a blowpipe for cutting or welding metals at high temperatures **b** (*as modifier*): *an oxyacetylene burner*

oxyacid (ˌɒksɪˈæsɪd) *n* any acid that contains oxygen. Also called: **oxo acid**

oxygen (ˈɒksɪdʒən) *n* **a** a colourless odourless highly reactive gaseous element: the most abundant element in the earth's crust (49.2 per cent). It is essential for aerobic respiration and almost all combustion and is widely used in industry. Symbol: O; atomic no: 8; atomic wt: 15.9994; valency: 2; density: 1.429 kg/m³; melting pt: –218.79°C; boiling pt: –182.97°C **b** (*as modifier*): *an oxygen mask* > **oxygenic** (ˌɒksɪˈdʒɛnɪk) *or* **oxygenous** (ɒkˈsɪdʒɪnəs) *adj*

oxygenate (ˈɒksɪdʒɪˌneɪt), **oxygenize** *or* **oxygenise** (ˈɒksɪdʒɪˌnaɪz) *vb* to enrich or be enriched with oxygen: *to oxygenate blood* > ˌoxygenˈation *n* > ˈoxygeˌnizer *or* ˈoxygeˌniser *n*

oxygen tent *n* *med* a transparent enclosure covering a bedridden patient, into which oxygen is released to help maintain respiration

oxyhaemoglobin *or US* **oxyhemoglobin**

(ˌɒksɪˌhiːməʊˈgləʊbɪn, -ˌhɛm-) *n* *biochem* the bright red product formed when oxygen from the lungs combines with haemoglobin in the blood

oxyhydrogen (ˌɒksɪˈhaɪdrədʒən) *n* **a** a mixture of hydrogen and oxygen used to provide an intense flame for welding **b** (*as modifier*): *an oxyhydrogen blowpipe*

oxymoron (ˌɒksɪˈmɔːrɒn) *n, pl* **-mora** (-ˈmɔːrə) *rhetoric* an epigrammatic effect, by which contradictory terms are used in conjunction: *living death; fiend angelical* [C17: via New Latin from Greek *oxumōron*, from *oxus* sharp + *mōros* stupid]

oxytetracycline (ˌɒksɪˌtɛtrəˈsaɪklɪn) *n* a broad-spectrum antibiotic, obtained from the bacterium *Streptomyces rimosus*, used in treating various infections. Formula: $C_{22}H_{24}N_2O_9$

oyer and terminer (ˈɔɪə; ˈtɜːmɪnə) *n* **1** *English law* (formerly) a commission issued to judges to try cases on assize. It became obsolete with the abolition of assizes and the setting up of crown courts in 1972 **2** the court in which such a hearing was held [C15: from Anglo-Norman, from *oyer* to hear + *terminer* to judge]

oyez *or* **oyes** (əʊˈjɛs, -ˈjɛz) *interj* **1** a cry, usually uttered three times, by a public crier or court official for silence and attention before making a proclamation ▷ *n* **2** such a cry [C15: via Anglo-Norman from Old French *oiez* hear!]

-oyl *suffix of nouns* (in chemistry) indicating an acyl group or radical: *ethanoyl; methanoyl* [C20: from O(XYGEN) + -YL]

Oyo (ˈəʊjəʊ) *n* a state of SW Nigeria. Capital: Ibadan. Pop: 5 591 589 (2006). Area: 28 454 sq km (10 986 sq miles)

oyster (ˈɔɪstə) *n* **1 a** any edible marine bivalve mollusc of the genus *Ostrea*, having a rough irregularly shaped shell and occurring on the sea bed, mostly in coastal waters **b** (*as modifier*): *oyster farm; oyster knife* **2** any of various similar and related molluscs, such as the pearl oyster and the **saddle oyster** (*Anomia ephippium*) **3** the oyster-shaped piece of dark meat in the hollow of the pelvic bone of a fowl **4** something from which advantage, delight, profit, etc, may be derived: *the world is his oyster* **5** *informal* a very uncommunicative person ▷ *vb* **6** (*intr*) to dredge for, gather, or raise oysters [C14 *oistre*, from Old French *uistre*, from Latin *ostrea*, from Greek *ostreon*; related to Greek *osteon* bone, *ostrakon* shell]

oyster bed *n* a place, esp on the sea bed, where oysters breed and grow naturally or are cultivated for food or pearls. Also called: **oyster bank, oyster park**

oystercatcher (ˈɔɪstəˌkætʃə) *n* any shore bird of the genus *Haematopus* and family *Haematopodidae*, having a black or black-and-white plumage and a long stout laterally compressed red bill

oyster crab *n* any of several small soft-bodied crabs of the genus *Pinnotheres*, esp *P. ostreum*, that live as commensals in the mantles of oysters

oyster plant *n* another name for **salsify** (sense 1) and **sea lungwort** (see **lungwort** sense 2)

oz *or* **oz.** *abbreviation* ounce [from Italian *onza*]

Oz (ɒz) *n* *Austral slang* Australia

Özal (əʊˈzaːl) *n* Turgut (ˈtɜːgʊt). 1927–93, Turkish statesman: prime minister of Turkey (1983–89); president (1989–93)

Ozalid (ˈɒzəlɪd) *n* **1** *trademark* a method of duplicating typematter, illustrations, etc, when printed on translucent paper. It is used for proofing **2** a reproduction produced by this method [C20: formed by reversing DIAZO and inserting *l*]

Ozark Mountains (ˈəʊzɑːk) *or* **Ozarks** (ˈəʊzɑːks) *pl n* an eroded plateau in S Missouri, N Arkansas, and NE Oklahoma. Area: about 130 000 sq km (50 000 sq miles). Also called: **Ozark Plateau**

Ozero Baykal (*Russian* ˈɒzjɪrə bʌjˈkɑl) *n* the Russian name for (Lake) **Baikal**

ozocerite *or* **ozokerite** (əʊˈzəʊkəˌraɪt) *n* a brown or greyish wax that occurs associated with petroleum and is used for making candles and wax paper [C19: from German *Ozokerit*, from Greek *ozein* to smell + *kēros* beeswax]

ozone (ˈəʊzəʊn, əʊˈzəʊn) *n* **1** a colourless gas with a chlorine-like odour, formed by an electric discharge in oxygen: a strong oxidizing agent, used in bleaching, sterilizing water, purifying air, etc Formula: O_3; density:

2.14 kg/m³; melting pt: –192°C; boiling pt: –110.51°C

2 *informal* clean bracing air, as found at the seaside [C19: from German *Ozon*, from Greek: smell] > ozonic (əʊˈzɒnɪk) *or* 'ozonous *adj*

ozone-friendly *adj* not harmful to the ozone layer; using substances that do not produce gases harmful to the ozone layer: *an ozone-friendly refrigerator*

ozone layer *n* the region of the stratosphere with the highest concentration of ozone molecules, which by absorbing high-energy solar ultraviolet radiation protects organisms on earth. Also called: ozonosphere

ozonize *or* **ozonise** (ˈəʊzəʊˌnaɪz) *vb* (*tr*) **1** to convert (oxygen) into ozone **2** to treat (a substance) with ozone > ˌozoniˈzation *or* ˌozoniˈsation *n* > 'ozoˌnizer *or* 'ozoˌniser *n*

ozonosphere (əʊˈzəʊnəˌsfɪə, -ˈzɒnə-) *n* another name for **ozone layer**

Pp

p¹ or **P** (pi:) *n, pl* **p's, P's** or **Ps 1** the 16th letter and 12th consonant of the modern English alphabet **2** a speech sound represented by this letter, usually a voiceless bilabial stop, as in *pig* **3** mind one's p's and q's to be careful to behave correctly and use polite or suitable language

p² *symbol for* **1** (in Britain) penny *or* pence **2** *music* piano: an instruction to play quietly **3** pico- **4** *physics* **a** momentum **b** proton **c** pressure

P *symbol for* **1** *chem* phosphorus **2** *physics* **a** pressure **b** power **c** parity **d** poise **3** (on road signs) parking **4** *chess* pawn **5** *currency* **a** (the former) peseta **b** peso **c** pataca ▷ *abbreviation* **6** pharmacy only: used to label medicines that can be obtained without a prescription, but only at a shop at which there is a pharmacist

p. *abbreviation* **1** *pl* **pp** page **2** part **3** participle **4** past **5** per **6** post [Latin: after] **7** pro [Latin: in favour of; for]

p- *prefix* short for **para-¹** (sense 6)

P45 *n* (in Britain) **1** a severance form issued by the Inland Revenue via an employer to a person leaving employment **2** get one's P45 *informal* to be dismissed from one's employment

pa¹ (pɑ:) *n* an informal word for **father**

pa² or **pah** (pɑ:) *n* NZ **1** a Māori village or settlement **2** *history* a Māori defensive position and settlement on a hilltop [Māori]

Pa *the chemical symbol for* **1** protactinium ▷ *symbol for* **2** pascal

PA *abbreviation* **1** personal assistant **2** *military* Post Adjutant **3** power of attorney **4** press agent **5** Press Association **6** *banking* private account **7** public-address system **8** publicity agent **9** Publishers Association **10** purchasing agent **11** *insurance* particular average

Pa. *abbreviation* Pennsylvania

p.a. *abbreviation* per annum [Latin: yearly]

Pablum ('pɑ:bləm) *n trademark* a cereal food for infants, developed in Canada

Pabst (*German* pɑ:pst) *n* **G(eorge) W(ilhelm)**. 1885–1967, German film director, whose films include *Joyless Street* (1925), *Pandora's Box* (1929), and *The Last Act* (1954)

pabulum ('pæbjʊləm) *n rare* **1** food **2** food for thought, esp when bland or dull [c17: from Latin, from *pascere* to feed]

PABX *abbreviation* (in Britain) private automatic branch exchange. See also **PBX**

PAC *abbreviation* Pan-Africanist Congress

Pac. *abbreviation* Pacific

paca ('pɑ:kə, 'pækə) *n* a large burrowing hystricomorph rodent, *Cuniculus paca*, of Central and South America, having white-spotted brown fur and a large head: family *Dasyproctidae* [c17: from Spanish, from Tupi]

pace¹ (peɪs) *n* **1 a** a single step in walking **b** the distance covered by a step **2** a measure of length equal to the average length of a stride, approximately 3 feet **3** speed of movement, esp of walking or running **4** rate or style of proceeding at some activity: *to live at a fast pace* **5** manner or action of stepping, walking, etc; gait **6** any of the manners in which a horse or other quadruped walks or runs, the three principal paces being the walk, trot, and canter (or gallop) **7** a manner of moving, natural to the camel and sometimes developed in the horse, in which the two legs on the same side of the body are moved and put down at the same time **8** keep pace with to proceed at the same speed as **9** put someone through his paces to test the ability of someone **10** set the pace to determine the rate at which a group runs or walks or proceeds at some other activity ▷ *vb* **11** (tr) to set or determine the pace for, as in a race **12** (often foll by *about, up and down,* etc) to walk with regular slow or fast paces, as in boredom, agitation, etc: *to pace the room* **13** (tr; often foll by *out*) to measure by paces: *to pace out the distance* **14** (intr) to walk with slow regular strides **15** (intr) (of a horse) to move at the pace (the specially developed gait) [c13: via Old French from Latin *passūs* step, from *pandere* to spread, unfold, extend (the legs as in walking)]

pace² *Latin* ('peɪsɪ; *English* 'pɑ:kɛ) *prep* with due deference to: used to acknowledge politely someone who disagrees with the speaker or writer [c19: from Latin, from *pāx* peace]

PACE (peɪs) *n acronym for* (in England and Wales) Police and Criminal Evidence Act

pace bowler *n cricket* a bowler who characteristically delivers the ball rapidly

pacemaker ('peɪsˌmeɪkə) n 1 a person, horse, vehicle, etc, used in a race or speed trial to set the pace 2 a person, an organization, etc, regarded as being the leader in a particular field of activity 3 Also called: **cardiac pacemaker** a small area of specialized tissue within the wall of the right atrium of the heart whose spontaneous electrical activity initiates and controls the beat of the heart 4 Also called: **artificial pacemaker** an electronic device for use in certain cases of heart disease to assume the functions of the natural cardiac pacemaker

pacer ('peɪsə) n 1 a horse trained to move at a special gait, esp for racing 2 another word for **pacemaker** (sense 1)

pacesetter ('peɪsˌsɛtə) n another word for **pacemaker** (senses 1, 2)

paceway ('peɪsˌweɪ) n Austral a racecourse for trotting and pacing

Pachelbel (German 'pɑxəlbɛl) n **Johann** ('johan). 1653–1706, German organist and composer, noted esp for his popular *Canon in D Major*

pachinko (pə'tʃɪŋkəʊ) n a Japanese game similar to pinball [c20: possibly from Japanese *pachin*, imitative of the sound of a ball being fired by a trigger]

pachisi (pə'tʃiːzɪ, pɑː-) n an Indian game somewhat resembling backgammon, played on a cruciform board using six cowries as dice [c18: from Hindi *pacīsī*, from *pacīs* twenty-five (the highest score possible in one throw)]

Pachomius (pə'kəʊmɪəs) n **Saint.** ?290–346 AD, Egyptian hermit; founder of the first Christian monastery (318). Feast day: May 14 or 15

Pachuca (Spanish pa'tʃuka) n a city in central Mexico, capital of Hidalgo state, in the Sierra Madre Oriental: silver mines; university (1961). Pop: 333 000 (2005 est)

pachyderm ('pækɪˌdɜːm) n any very large thick-skinned mammal, such as an elephant, rhinoceros, or hippopotamus [c19: from French *pachyderme*, from Greek *pakhudermos* thick-skinned, from *pakhus* thick + *derma* skin] > ˌpachy'dermatous adj

pacific (pə'sɪfɪk) adj 1 tending or conducive to peace; conciliatory 2 not aggressive; opposed to the use of force 3 free from conflict; peaceful [c16: from Old French *pacifique*, from Latin *pācificus*, from *pāx* peace + *facere* to make] > pa'cifically adv

Pacific (pə'sɪfɪk) n 1 **the Pacific** short for **Pacific Ocean** ▷ adj 2 of or relating to the Pacific Ocean or its islands

Pacific Islands pl n a former Trust Territory; an island group in the W Pacific Ocean, mandated to Japan after World War I and assigned to the US by the United Nations in 1947: comprised 2141 islands (96 inhabited) of the Caroline, Marshall, and Mariana groups (excluding Guam). In 1978 the Northern Marianas became a commonwealth in union with the US. The three remaining entities consisting of the Marshall Islands, the Republic of Palau (or Belau), and the Federated States of Micronesia became self-governing during the period 1979–80. In 1982 they signed agreements of free association with the US. Land area: about 1800 sq km (700 sq miles), scattered over about 7 500 000 sq km (3 000 000 sq miles) of ocean

Pacific Northwest n the region of North America lying north of the Columbia River and west of the Rockies

Pacific Ocean n the world's largest and deepest ocean, lying between Asia and Australia and North and South America: almost landlocked in the north, linked with the Arctic Ocean only by the Bering Strait, and extending to Antarctica in the south; has exceptionally deep trenches, and a large number of volcanic and coral islands. Area: about 165 760 000 sq km (64 000 000 sq miles). Average depth: 4215 m (14 050 ft). Greatest depth: Challenger Deep (in the Marianas Trench), 11 033 m (37 073 ft). Greatest width: (between Panama and Mindanao, Philippines) 17 066 km (10 600 miles)

Pacific rim n the regions, countries, etc, that lie on the western shores of the Pacific Ocean, esp in the context of their developing manufacturing capacity and consumer markets

Pacific Rose n a large variety of eating apple from New Zealand, with sweet flesh

pacifier ('pæsɪˌfaɪə) n 1 a person or thing that pacifies 2 US & Canadian a baby's dummy or teething ring

pacifism ('pæsɪˌfɪzəm) n 1 the belief that violence of any kind is unjustifiable and that one should not participate in war 2 the belief that international disputes can be settled by arbitration rather than war > 'pacifist n, adj

pacify ('pæsɪˌfaɪ) vb -fies, -fying, -fied (tr) 1 to calm the anger or agitation of; mollify 2 to restore to peace or order, esp by the threat or use of force [c15: from Old French *pacifier*; see PACIFIC] > ˌpaci'fiable adj > pacification (ˌpæsɪfɪ'keɪʃən) n

Pacino (pə'tʃiːnəʊ) n **Al**, full name *Alfredo James Pacino* born 1940, US film actor; his films include *The Godfather* (1972), *Dog Day Afternoon* (1975), *Scent of a Woman* (1992), for which he won an Oscar, and *Insomnia* (2002)

pack[1] (pæk) n 1 a a bundle or load, esp one carried on the back b (as modifier): *a pack animal* 2 a collected amount of anything 3 a complete set of similar things, esp a set of 52 playing cards 4 a group of animals of the same kind, esp hunting animals: *a pack of hounds* 5 any group or band that associates together, esp for criminal purposes 6 *rugby* the forwards of a team or both teams collectively, as in a scrum or in rucking 7 the basic organizational unit of Cub Scouts and Brownie Guides 8 short for **pack ice** 9 the quantity of something, such as food, packaged for preservation 10 *med* a sheet or blanket, either damp or dry, for wrapping about the body, esp for its soothing effect 11 short for **backpack, rucksack** 12 a parachute folded and ready for use 13 *computing* another name for **deck** (sense 5) 14 **go to the pack** Austral & NZ informal to fall into a lower state or condition ▷ vb 15 to place or arrange (articles) in (a container), such as clothes in a suitcase 16 (tr) to roll up into a bundle 17 (when passive, often foll by out) to press tightly together; cram: *the audience packed into the foyer; the hall was packed out* 18 to form (snow, ice, etc) into a hard compact mass or (of snow, ice, etc) to become compacted 19 (tr) to press in or cover tightly 20 (tr) to load (a horse, donkey, etc) with a burden 21 (often foll by off or away) to send away or go away, esp hastily 22 (tr) to seal (a joint) by inserting a layer of compressible material between the faces 23 (tr) *med* to treat with a pack 24 (tr) *slang* to be capable of inflicting (a blow): *he packs a mean punch* 25 (tr) US informal to carry or wear habitually: *he packs a gun* 26 (tr; often foll by *into, to*, etc) US, Canadian & NZ to carry (goods), esp on the back 27 **send packing** informal to dismiss peremptorily ▷ See also **pack in, pack up** [c13: related to Middle Low German *pak*, of obscure origin] > 'packable adj

pack[2] (pæk) vb (tr) to fill (a legislative body, committee, etc) with one's own supporters: *to pack a jury* [c16: perhaps changed from PACT]

package ('pækɪdʒ) n 1 any wrapped or boxed object or group of objects 2 a a proposition, offer, or thing for sale in which separate items are offered together as a single or inclusive unit b (as modifier): *a package holiday; a package deal* 3 the act or process of packing or packaging 4 *computing* a set of programs designed for a specific type of problem in statistics, production control, etc, making it unnecessary for a separate program to be written for each problem 5 US & Canadian ▷ vb (tr) 6 to wrap in or put into a package 7 to design and produce a package for (retail goods) 8 to group (separate items) together as a single unit 9 to compile (complete books) for a publisher to market

package store n US a store where alcoholic drinks are sold for consumption elsewhere. Canadian name (also sometimes used in the US): **liquor store**

packaging ('pækɪdʒɪŋ) n 1 the box or wrapping in which a product is offered for sale 2 the presentation of a person, product, television programme, etc, to the public in a way designed to build up a favourable image

pack drill n a military punishment by which the offender is made to march about carrying a full pack of equipment

packer ('pækə) n 1 a person or company whose business is to pack goods, esp food: *a meat packer* 2 a person or machine that packs

packet ('pækɪt) n 1 a small or medium-sized container of cardboard, paper, etc, often together with its contents: *a packet of biscuits*. Usual US and Canadian word: package, pack 2 a small package; parcel 3 Also called: packet boat a boat that transports mail, passengers, goods, etc, on a fixed short route 4 *slang* a large sum of money: *to cost a packet* 5 *computing* a unit into which a larger piece of data is broken down for more efficient transmission ▷ *vb* 6 (*tr*) to wrap up in a packet or as a packet [C16: from Old French *pacquet*, from *pacquer* to pack, from Old Dutch *pak* a pack]

packhorse ('pæk,hɔːs) n a horse used to transport goods, equipment, etc

pack ice n a large area of floating ice, usually occurring in polar seas, consisting of separate pieces that have become massed together

pack in *vb* (*tr, adverb*) *Brit & NZ informal* to stop doing (something) (esp in the phrase **pack it in**)

packing ('pækɪŋ) n 1 a material used to cushion packed goods b (*as modifier*): *a packing needle* 2 the packaging of foodstuffs 3 any substance or material used to make watertight or gastight joints, esp in a stuffing box

pack rat n any rat of the genus *Neotoma*, of W North America, having a long tail that is furry in some species: family *Cricetidae*

packsaddle ('pæk,sædªl) n a saddle hung with packs, equipment, etc, used on a pack animal

packthread ('pæk,θred) n a strong twine for sewing or tying up packages

pack up *vb* (*adverb*) 1 to put (things) away in a proper or suitable place 2 *informal* to give up (an attempt) or stop doing (something) 3 (*intr*) (of an engine, machine, etc) to fail to operate; break down

pact (pækt) n an agreement or compact between two or more parties, nations, etc, for mutual advantage [C15: from Old French *pacte*, from Latin *pactum*, from *pacīscī* to agree]

pad¹ (pæd) n 1 a thick piece of soft material used to make something comfortable, give it shape, or protect it 2 Also called: stamp pad, ink pad a block of firm absorbent material soaked with ink for transferring to a rubber stamp 3 Also called: notepad, writing pad a number of sheets of paper fastened together along one edge 4 a flat piece of stiff material used to back a piece of blotting paper 5 a the fleshy cushion-like underpart of the foot of a cat, dog, etc b any of the parts constituting such a structure 6 any of various level surfaces or flat-topped structures, such as a launch pad 7 the large flat floating leaf of the water lily 8 *slang* a person's residence ▷ *vb* pads, padding, padded (*tr*) 9 to line, stuff, or fill out with soft material, esp in order to protect or give shape to 10 (often foll by *out*) to inflate with irrelevant or false information: *to pad out a story* [C16: origin uncertain; compare Low German *pad* sole of the foot]

pad² (pæd) *vb* pads, padding, padded 1 (*intr*; often foll by *along, up*, etc) to walk with a soft or muffled tread 2 (when *intr*, often foll by *around*) to travel (a route) on foot, esp at a slow pace; tramp: *to pad around the country* ▷ n 3 a dull soft sound, esp of footsteps [C16: perhaps from Middle Dutch *paden*, from *pad* PATH]

Padang ('pɑːdɑːŋ) n a port in W Indonesia, in W Sumatra at the foot of the **Padang Highlands** on the Indian Ocean. Pop: 713 242 (2000)

padded cell n a room, esp one in a mental hospital, with padded surfaces in which violent inmates are placed

padding ('pædɪŋ) n 1 any soft material used to pad clothes, furniture, etc 2 superfluous material put into a speech or written work to pad it out; waffle 3 inflated or false entries in a financial account, esp an expense account

paddle¹ ('pædªl) n 1 a short light oar with a flat blade at one or both ends, used without a rowlock to propel a canoe or small boat 2 Also called: **float** a blade of a water wheel or paddle wheel 3 a period of paddling: *to go for a paddle upstream* 4 a a paddle wheel used to propel a boat b (*as modifier*): *a paddle steamer* 5 any of various instruments shaped like a paddle and used for beating,

mixing, etc 6 a table-tennis bat 7 the flattened limb of a seal, turtle, or similar aquatic animal, specialized for swimming ▷ *vb* 8 to propel (a canoe, small boat, etc) with a paddle 9 **paddle one's own canoe a** to be self-sufficient **b** to mind one's own business 10 (*tr*) to stir or mix with or as if with a paddle 11 to row (a boat) steadily, esp (of a racing crew) to row firmly but not at full pressure 12 (*intr*) to swim with short rapid strokes, like a dog 13 (*tr*) *US & Canadian informal* to spank [C15: of unknown origin] > 'paddlern

paddle² ('pædªl) *vb* (*mainly intr*) 1 to walk or play barefoot in shallow water, mud, etc 2 to dabble the fingers, hands, or feet in water 3 to walk unsteadily, like a baby 4 (*tr*) *archaic* to fondle with the fingers ▷ n 5 the act of paddling in water [C16: of uncertain origin] > 'paddlern

paddle wheel n a large wheel fitted with paddles, turned by an engine to propel a vessel on the water

paddock ('pædək) n 1 a small enclosed field, often for grazing or training horses, usually near a house or stable 2 (in horse racing) the enclosure in which horses are paraded and mounted before a race, together with the accompanying rooms 3 *Austral & NZ* any area of fenced land [C17: variant of dialect *parrock*, from Old English *pearruc* enclosure, of Germanic origin. See PARK]

paddy¹ ('pædɪ) n, pl -dies 1 Also called: paddy field a field planted with rice 2 rice as a growing crop or when harvested but not yet milled [from Malay *pādī*]

paddy² ('pædɪ) n, pl -dies*Brit informal* a fit of temper [C19: from PADDY]

Paddy ('pædɪ) n, pl -dies (*sometimes not capital*) an informal, often derogatory, name for an Irishman [from *Patrick*]

pademelonor **paddymelon** ('pædɪ,mɛlən) n a small wallaby of the genus *Thylogale*, of coastal scrubby regions of Australia [C19: from a native Australian name]

Paderborn (German pɑ:dər'bɔrn) n a market town in NW Germany, in North Rhine-Westphalia: scene of the meeting between Charlemagne and Pope Leo III (799 AD) that led to the foundation of the Holy Roman Empire. Pop: 141 800 (2003 est)

Paderewski (Polish padɛ'rɛfski) n **Ignace Jan** (iɲas jan). 1860–1941, Polish pianist, composer, and statesman; prime minister (1919)

padkos ('pad,kɒs) pl n *South African* snacks and provisions for a journey [Afrikaans, literally: road food]

padlock ('pæd,lɒk) n 1 a detachable lock having a hinged or sliding shackle, which can be used to secure a door, lid, etc, by passing the shackle through rings or staples ▷ *vb* 2 (*tr*) to fasten with or as if with a padlock [C15 *pad*, of obscure origin]

Padova ('pɑːdova) n the Italian name for **Padua**

padre ('pɑːdrɪ) n *informal* (*sometimes capital*) 1 father: used to address or refer to a clergyman, esp a priest 2 a chaplain to the armed forces [via Spanish or Italian from Latin *pater* father]

padsaw ('pæd,sɔː) n a small narrow saw used for cutting curves [C19: from PAD¹ (in the sense: a handle that can be fitted to various tools) + SAW¹]

Padua ('pædʒʊə, 'pædjʊə) n a city in NE Italy, in Veneto: important in Roman and Renaissance times; university (1222); botanical garden (1545). Pop: 204 870 (2001). Italian name: **Padova**

Padus ('peɪdəs) n the Latin name for the **Po**²

paeanor *sometimes US* **pean** ('piːən) n 1 a hymn sung in ancient Greece in invocation of or thanksgiving to a deity 2 any song of praise 3 enthusiastic praise: *the film received a paean from the critics* [C16: via Latin from Greek *paiān* hymn to Apollo, from his title *Paiān*, denoting the physician of the gods]

paediatricianor *chiefly US* **pediatrician** (,piːdɪə'trɪʃən) n a medical practitioner who specializes in paediatrics

paediatricsor *chiefly US* **pediatrics** (,piːdɪ'ætrɪks) n (*functioning as singular*) the branch of medical science concerned with children and their diseases > ,paedi'atricor (*chiefly US*) ,pedi'atricadj

paedo-,*before a vowel* **paed-**,*esp US* **pedo-**or *esp US* **ped-** *combining form* indicating a child or children [from Greek *pais, paid-* child]

paedomorphosis (,piːdə'mɔːfəsɪs) n the resemblance of

adult animals to the young of their ancestors: seen in the evolution of modern man, who shows resemblances to the young stages of australopithecines

paedophilia *or esp US* **pedophilia** (ˌpiːdəʊˈfɪlɪə) *n* the condition of being sexually attracted to children
> ˌpaedoˈphiliˌac *or* (*esp US*) ˌpedoˈphiliˌac *n, adj*
> **paedophile** *or* (*esp US*) **pedophile** (ˈpiːdəʊˌfaɪl) *n*

paella (paɪˈɛlə; *Spanish* paˈeʎa) *n, pl* -**las** (-ləz; *Spanish* -ʎas) **1** a Spanish dish made from rice, shellfish, chicken, and vegetables **2** the large flat frying pan in which a paella is cooked [from Catalan, from Old French *paelle*, from Latin *patella* small pan]

paeony (ˈpiːənɪ) *n, pl* -**nies** a variant spelling of **peony**

Paestum (ˈpɛstəm) *n* an ancient Greek colony on the coast of Lucania in S Italy

Páez (*Spanish* ˈpaes) *n* **José Antonio** (xoˈse anˈtonjo). 1790–1873, Venezuelan revolutionary leader; first president (1831–46) of independent Venezuela

PAGAD *abbreviation South African* People Against Gangsterism and Drugs, a vigilante organization formed in the Western Cape around 1995 and subsequently associated with Islamic fundamentalism

pagan (ˈpeɪɡən) *n* **1** a member of a group professing a polytheistic religion or any religion other than Christianity, Judaism, or Islam **2** a person without any religion; heathen ▷ *adj* **3** of or relating to pagans or their faith or worship **4** heathen; irreligious [c14: from Church Latin *pāgānus* civilian (hence, not a soldier of Christ), from Latin: countryman, villager, from *pāgus* village] > ˈ**pagandom** *n* > ˈ**paganish** *adj* > ˈ**paganism** *n*

Paganini (*Italian* pagaˈniːni) *n* **Niccolò** (nikkoˈlɔ). 1782–1840, Italian violinist and composer

paganize *or* **paganise** (ˈpeɪɡəˌnaɪz) *vb* to become pagan, render pagan, or convert to paganism

page[1] (peɪdʒ) *n* **1** *pl* **pp** one side of one of the leaves of a book, newspaper, letter, etc or the written or printed matter it bears **2** such a leaf considered as a unit **3** a screenful of information from a website, teletext service, etc, displayed on a television monitor or visual display unit **4** an episode, phase, or period: *a glorious page in the revolution* ▷ *vb* **5** another word for **paginate** [c15: via Old French from Latin *pāgina*]

page[2] (peɪdʒ) *n* **1** a boy employed to run errands, carry messages, etc, for the guests in a hotel, club, etc **2** a youth in attendance at official functions or ceremonies, esp weddings **3** *medieval history* **a** a boy in training for knighthood in personal attendance on a knight **b** a youth in the personal service of a person of rank, esp in a royal household ▷ *vb* (*tr*) **4** to call out the name of (a person), esp by a loudspeaker system, so as to give him a message **5** to call (a person) by an electronic device, such as a pager **6** to act as a page or to attend as a page [c13: via Old French from Italian *paggio*, probably from Greek *paidion* boy, from *pais* child]

Page (peɪdʒ) *n* **1** Sir **Earle** (**Christmas Grafton**). 1880–1961, Australian statesman; co-leader, with S. M. Bruce, of the federal government of Australia (1923–29) **2** Sir **Frederick Handley**. 1885–1962, English pioneer in the design and manufacture of aircraft

pageant (ˈpædʒənt) *n* **1** an elaborate colourful parade or display portraying scenes from history, esp one involving rich costume **2** any magnificent or showy display, procession, etc [c14: from Medieval Latin *pāgina* scene of a play, from Latin: PAGE[1]]

pageantry (ˈpædʒəntrɪ) *n, pl* -**ries** **1** spectacular display or ceremony **2** *archaic* pageants collectively

pageboy (ˈpeɪdʒˌbɔɪ) *n* **1** a smooth medium-length hairstyle with the ends of the hair curled under and a long fringe falling onto the forehead from the crown **2** a less common word for **page**[2] (sense 1)

pager (ˈpeɪdʒə) *n* a small electronic device, capable of receiving short messages; usually carried by people who need to be contacted urgently (e.g. doctors)

page-turner *n* an exciting novel, such as a thriller, with a fast-moving story

pageview (ˈpeɪdʒˌvjuː) *n computing* an electronic page of information displayed in response to a user's request, such as one page of a website

paginate (ˈpædʒɪˌneɪt) *vb* (*tr*) to number the pages of (a

book, manuscript, etc) in sequence. See **foliate**
> ˌpagiˈnation *n*

Paglia (ˈpæɡlɪə) *n* **Camille**. born 1947, US writer and academic, noted for provocative cultural studies such as *Sexual Personae* (1990) and *Vamps and Tramps* (1995)

Pagnol (*French* panjol) *n* **Marcel** (**Paul**) (marsɛl). 1895–1974, French dramatist, film director, and novelist, noted for his depiction of Provençal life in such films as *Manon des Sources* (1952; remade 1986)

pagoda (pəˈɡəʊdə) *n* an Indian or Far Eastern temple, esp a tower, usually pyramidal and having many storeys [c17: from Portuguese *pagode*, ultimately from Sanskrit *bhagavatī* divine]

pagoda tree *n* a Chinese leguminous tree, *Sophora japonica*, with ornamental white flowers and dark green foliage

Pago Pago (ˈpɑːŋɡəʊ ˈpɑːŋɡəʊ) *n* a port in American Samoa, on SE Tutuila Island. Pop: 4278 (2000). Former name: **Pango Pango**

Pahang (pəˈhʌŋ) *n* a state of Peninsular Malaysia, on the South China Sea: the largest Malayan state; mountainous and heavily forested. Capital: Kuantan. Pop: 1 288 376 (2000). Area: 35 965 sq km (13 886 sq miles)

Pahlavi[1] (ˈpɑːləvɪ) *or* **Pehlevi** *n* the Middle Persian language, esp as used in classical Zoroastrian and Manichean literature [c18: from Persian *pahlavī*, from Old Persian *Parthava* PARTHIA]

Pahlavi[2] (ˈpɑːləvɪ) *n* **1** **Mohammed Reza** (ˈriːzə). 1919–80, shah of Iran (1941–79); forced into exile (1979) during civil unrest following which an Islamic republic was established led by the Ayatollah Khomeini **2** his father, **Reza**. 1877–1944, shah of Iran (1925–41). Originally an army officer, he gained power by a coup d'état (1921) and was chosen shah by the National Assembly. He reorganized the army and did much to modernize Iran

Pahsien (ˈpɑːʃjɛn) *n* a former name for **Chongqing**

paid (peɪd) *vb* **1** the past tense and past participle of **pay**[1] **2** put paid to *chiefly Brit & NZ* to end or destroy: *breaking his leg put paid to his hopes of running in the Olympics*

paid-up *adj* **1** having paid the due, full, or required fee to be a member of an organization, club, political party, etc **2** denoting a security in which all the instalments have been paid; fully paid: *a paid-up share* **3** denoting all the money that a company has received from its shareholders: *the paid-up capital* **4** denoting an endowment assurance policy on which the payment of premiums has stopped and the surrender value has been used to purchase a new single-premium policy

Paignton (ˈpeɪntən) *n* a town and resort in SW England, in Devon: administratively part of Torbay since 1968

pail (peɪl) *n* **1** a bucket, esp one made of wood or metal **2** Also called: **pailful** the quantity that fills a pail [Old English *pægel*; compare Catalan *paella* frying pan, PAELLA]

paillasse (ˈpælɪˌæs, ˌpælɪˈæs) *n* a variant spelling (esp US) of **palliasse**

pain (peɪn) *n* **1** the sensation of acute physical hurt or discomfort caused by injury, illness, etc **2** emotional suffering or mental distress **3 on pain of** subject to the penalty of **4** Also called: **pain in the neck**, (*taboo*) **pain in the arse** *informal* a person or thing that is a nuisance ▷ *vb* (*tr*) **5** to cause (a person) distress, hurt, grief, anxiety, etc **6** *informal* to annoy; irritate ▷ See also **pains** [c13: from Old French *peine*, from Latin *poena* punishment, grief, from Greek *poinē* penalty] > ˈ**painless** *adj* > ˈ**painlessly** *adv* > ˈ**painlessness** *n*

Paine (peɪn) *n* **Thomas**. 1737–1809, American political pamphleteer, born in England. His works include the pamphlets *Common Sense* (1776) and *Crisis* (1776–83), supporting the American colonists' fight for independence; *The Rights of Man* (1791–92), a justification of the French Revolution; and *The Age of Reason* (1794–96), a defence of deism

pained (peɪnd) *adj* having or expressing pain or distress, esp mental or emotional distress

painful (ˈpeɪnfʊl) *adj* **1** causing pain; distressing: *a painful duty* **2** affected with pain **3** tedious or difficult **4** *informal* extremely bad > ˈ**painfully** *adv* > ˈ**painfulness** *n*

painkiller (ˈpeɪnˌkɪlə) *n* **1** an analgesic drug or agent **2** anything that relieves pain

pains (peɪnz) *pl n* **1** care, trouble, or effort (esp in the phrases **take pains, be at pains to**) **2** painful sensations experienced during contractions in childbirth; labour pains

painstaking ('peɪnz,teɪkɪŋ) *adj* extremely careful, esp as to fine detail: *painstaking research* ⊳ '**pains,takingness** *n*

paint (peɪnt) *n* **1** a substance used for decorating or protecting a surface, esp a mixture consisting of a solid pigment suspended in a liquid, that when applied to a surface dries to form a hard coating **2** a dry film of paint on a surface **3** the solid pigment of a paint before it is suspended in liquid **4** *informal* face make-up, such as rouge **5** short for **greasepaint** ⊳ *vb* **6** to make (a picture) of (a figure, landscape, etc) with paint applied to a surface such as canvas **7** to coat (a surface) with paint, as in decorating **8** (*tr*) to apply (liquid) onto (a surface): *her mother painted the cut with antiseptic* **9** (*tr*) to apply make-up onto (the face, lips, etc) **10** (*tr*) to describe vividly in words **11 paint the town red** *informal* to celebrate uninhibitedly; go on a spree [c13: from Old French *peint* painted, from *peindre* to paint, from Latin *pingere* to paint, adorn] ⊳ '**painty** *adj*

paintball game ('peɪnt,bɔːl) *n* a game in which teams of players simulate a military skirmish, shooting each other with paint pellets that explode on impact, marking the players who have been shot

paintbox ('peɪnt,bɒks) *n* a box containing a tray of dry watercolour paints

paintbrush ('peɪnt,brʌʃ) *n* a brush used to apply paint

paint-by-numbers *adj* formulaic; showing no original thought or creativity [c20: from children's painting books in which the colours to be used are identified by numbers on the design to be painted]

Painted Desert *n* a section of the high plateau country of N central Arizona, along the N side of the Little Colorado River Valley: brilliant-coloured rocks; occupied largely by Navaho and Hopi Indians. Area: about 20 000 sq km (7500 sq miles)

painted lady *n* a migratory nymphalid butterfly, *Vanessa cardui*, with pale brownish-red mottled wings

painter¹ ('peɪntə) *n* **1** a person who paints surfaces as a trade **2** an artist who paints pictures

painter² ('peɪntə) *n* a line attached to the bow of a boat for tying it up [c15: probably from Old French *penteur* strong rope]

painting ('peɪntɪŋ) *n* **1** the art or process of applying paints to a surface such as canvas, to make a picture or other artistic composition **2** a composition or picture made in this way **3** the act of applying paint to a surface with a brush

paint stripper *or* **paint remover** *n* a liquid, often caustic, used to remove paint from a surface

paintwork ('peɪnt,wɜːk) *n* a surface, such as wood or a car body, that is painted

pair (pɛə) *n*, *pl* **pairs** *or functioning as singular or plural* **pair 1** two identical or similar things matched for use together: *a pair of socks* **2** two persons, animals, things, etc, used or grouped together: *a pair of horses; a pair of scoundrels* **3** an object considered to be two identical or similar things joined together: *a pair of trousers* **4** two people joined in love or marriage **5** a male and a female animal of the same species, esp such animals kept for breeding purposes **6** *parliamentary procedure* **a** two opposed members who both agree not to vote on a specified motion or for a specific period of time **b** the agreement so made **7** two playing cards of the same rank or denomination **8** one member of a matching pair: *I can't find the pair to this glove* ⊳ *vb* **9** (often foll by *off*) to arrange or fall into groups of twos **10** to group or be grouped in matching pairs **11** to join or be joined in marriage; mate or couple **12** (when *tr, usually passive*) *parliamentary procedure* to form or cause to form a pair [c13: from Old French *paire*, from Latin *paria* equal (things), from *pār* equal]

● USAGE Like other collective nouns, *pair* takes a
● singular or a plural verb according to whether it is
● seen as a unit or as a collection of two things: *the pair*
● *are said to dislike each other; a pair of good shoes is essential*

paisley ('peɪzlɪ) *n* **1** a pattern of small curving shapes with intricate detailing, usually printed in bright colours **2** a soft fine wool fabric traditionally printed with this pattern **3** a garment made of this fabric, esp a shawl popular in the late 19th century **4** (*modifier*) of or decorated with this pattern: *a paisley scarf* [c19: named after PAISLEY]

Paisley¹ ('peɪzlɪ) *n* an industrial town in SW Scotland, the administrative centre of Renfrewshire: one of the world's chief centres for the manufacture of thread, linen, and gauze in the 19th century. Pop: 74 170 (2001)

Paisley² ('peɪzlɪ) *n* **1 Bob.** 1919–96, English footballer and manager **2 Rev. Ian (Richard Kyle)**. born 1926, Northern Ireland politician and Presbyterian minister; cofounder (1972) and leader of the Ulster Democratic Unionist Party, First Minister of Northern Ireland from 2007 to 2008

pajamas (pə'dʒɑːməz) *pl n* the US spelling of **pyjamas**

Pakeha ('pɑːkɪ,hɑː) *n* (in New Zealand) a person who is not of Māori ancestry, esp a White person [from Māori]

Paki ('pækɪ) *Brit slang, offensive* ⊳ *n*, *pl* **Pakis 1** a Pakistani or person of Pakistani descent ⊳ *adj* **2** Pakistani or of Pakistani descent

Pakistan (,pɑːkɪ'stɑːn) *n* **1** a republic in S Asia, on the Arabian Sea: the Union of Pakistan, formed in 1947, comprised West and East Pakistan; East Pakistan gained independence as Bangladesh in 1971 and West Pakistan became Pakistan; a member of the Commonwealth from 1947, it withdrew from 1972 until 1989; contains the fertile plains of the Indus valley rising to mountains in the north and west Official language: Urdu. Official religion: Muslim. Currency: rupee. Capital: Islamabad. Pop: 157 315 000 (2004 est). Area: 801 508 sq km (309 463 sq miles) **2** a former republic in S Asia consisting of the provinces of West Pakistan and East Pakistan (now Bangladesh), 1500 km (900 miles) apart: formed in 1947 from the predominantly Muslim parts of India ⊳ ,**Paki'stani** *n, adj*

pakora (pə'kɔːrə) *n* an Indian dish consisting of pieces of vegetable, chicken, etc, dipped in a spiced batter and deep-fried: served with a piquant sauce [c20: from Hindi]

pal (pæl) *informal* ⊳ *n* **1** a close friend; comrade ⊳ *vb* **pals, palling, palled 2** (*intr*; usually foll by *with* or *about*) to associate as friends [c17: from English Gypsy: brother, ultimately from Sanskrit *bhrātar* BROTHER]

PAL (pæl) *n acronym for* phase alternation line: a colour-television broadcasting system used generally in Europe

Pal. *abbreviation* Palestine

palace ('pælɪs) *n* (*capital when part of a name*) **1** the official residence of a reigning monarch or member of a royal family **2** the official residence of various high-ranking church dignitaries or members of the nobility, as of an archbishop **3** a large and richly furnished building resembling a royal palace [c13: from Old French *palais*, from Latin *Palātium* PALATINE², the site of the palace of the emperors]

Palacio Valdés (*Spanish* pa'laθjo bal'des) *n* **Armando** (ar'mando). 1853–1938, Spanish novelist and critic

paladin ('pælədɪn) *n* **1** one of the legendary twelve peers of Charlemagne's court **2** a knightly champion [c16: via French from Italian *paladino*, from Latin *palātīnus* imperial official, from *Palātium* PALATINE²]

palaeo-, *before a vowel* **palae-**, *esp US* **paleo-** *or esp US* **pale-** *combining form* old, ancient, or prehistoric: *palaeography* [from Greek *palaios* old]

palaeobotany (,pælɪəʊ'bɒtənɪ) *n* the study of fossil plants ⊳ ,**palaeo'botanist** *n*

Palaeocene ('pælɪəʊ,siːn) *adj* **1** of, denoting, or formed in the first epoch of the Tertiary period, which lasted for 10 million years ⊳ *n* **2 the Palaeocene** the Palaeocene epoch or rock series [c19: from French from *paléo-* PALAEO- + Greek *kainos* new, recent]

palaeoclimatology (,pælɪəʊ,klaɪmə'tɒlədʒɪ) *n* the study of climates of the geological past ⊳ ,**palaeo,clima'tologist** *n*

palaeoecology (,pælɪəʊɪ'kɒlədʒɪ) *n* the study of fossil animals and plants in order to deduce their ecology and the environmental conditions in which they lived ⊳ ,**palaeo,eco'logical** *adj* ⊳ ,**palaeoe'cologist** *n*

palaeography (ˌpælɪˈɒɡrəfɪ) n 1 the study of the handwritings of the past, and often the manuscripts as well, so that they may be dated, read, etc, and may serve as historical and literary sources 2 a handwriting of the past > palae'ographer n > palaeographic (ˌpælɪəʊˈɡræfɪk) or ˌpalaeo'graphical adj

Palaeolithic (ˌpælɪəʊˈlɪθɪk) n 1 the period of the emergence of primitive man and the manufacture of unpolished chipped stone tools, about 2.5 million to 3 million years ago until about 12 000 BC. ▷ adj 2 (sometimes not capital) of or relating to this period

palaeomagnetism (ˌpælɪəʊˈmæɡnɪˌtɪzəm) n the study of the fossil magnetism in rocks, used to determine the past configurations of the continents and to investigate the past shape and magnitude of the earth's magnetic field

palaeontology (ˌpælɪɒnˈtɒlədʒɪ) n the study of fossils to determine the structure and evolution of extinct animals and plants and the age and conditions of deposition of the rock strata in which they are found [C19: from PALAEO- + ONTO- + -LOGY] > palaeontological (ˌpælɪˌɒntəˈlɒdʒɪkᵊl) adj > ˌpalaeon'tologist n

Palaeozoic (ˌpælɪəʊˈzəʊɪk) adj 1 of, denoting, or relating to an era of geological time that began 600 million years ago with the Cambrian period and lasted about 375 million years until the end of the Permian period ▷ n 2 the Palaeozoic the Palaeozoic era [C19: from PALAEO- + Greek zōē life + -IC]

Palagi (paːˈlaŋi) n, pl -gi NZ a Samoan name for European [from Samoan papālagi]

palanquin or **palankeen** (ˌpælənˈkiːn) n a covered litter, formerly used in the Orient, carried on the shoulders of four men [C16: from Portuguese palanquim, from Prakrit pallanka, from Sanskrit paryanka couch]

palatable (ˈpælətəbᵊl) adj 1 pleasant to taste 2 acceptable or satisfactory > ˌpalata'bility or 'palatableness n > 'palatably adv

palatal (ˈpælətᵊl) adj 1 Also called: palatine of or relating to the palate 2 phonetics of, relating to, or denoting a speech sound articulated with the blade of the tongue touching the hard palate ▷ n 3 Also called: palatine the bony plate that forms the palate 4 phonetics a palatal speech sound, such as the semivowel (j) > 'palatally adv

palatalize or **palatalise** (ˈpælətəˌlaɪz) vb (tr) to pronounce (a speech sound) with the blade of the tongue touching the palate > ˌpalatali'zation or ˌpalatali'sation n

palate (ˈpælɪt) n 1 the roof of the mouth, separating the oral and nasal cavities. See hard palate, soft palate 2 the sense of taste: she had no palate for the wine 3 relish or enjoyment [C14: from Latin palātum, perhaps of Etruscan origin]

palatial (pəˈleɪʃəl) adj of, resembling, or suitable for a palace; sumptuous > pa'latially adv

palatinate (pəˈlætɪnɪt) n a territory ruled by a palatine prince or noble or count palatine

Palatinate (pəˈlætɪnɪt) n 1 the Palatinate either of two territories in SW Germany, once ruled by the counts palatine. Upper Palatinate is now in Bavaria; Lower or Rhine Palatinate is now in Rhineland-Palatinate, Baden-Württemberg, and Hesse. German name: Pfalz 2 a native or inhabitant of the Palatinate

palatine¹ (ˈpæləˌtaɪn) adj 1 (of an individual) possessing royal prerogatives in a territory 2 of, belonging to, characteristic of, or relating to a count palatine, county palatine, palatinate, or palatine 3 of or relating to a palace ▷ n 4 feudal history the lord of a palatinate 5 any of various important officials at the late Roman, Merovingian, or Carolingian courts [C15: via French from Latin palātīnus belonging to the palace, from palātium; see PALACE]

palatine² (ˈpæləˌtaɪn) adj 1 of or relating to the palate ▷ n 2 either of two bones forming the hard palate [C17: from French palatin, from Latin palātum palate]

Palatine (ˈpæləˌtaɪn) n 1 one of the Seven Hills of Rome: traditionally the site of the first settlement of Rome ▷ adj 2 of, relating to, or designating this hill

Palau (paːˈlaʊ) or **Belau** n Republic of Palau a republic comprising a group of islands in the W Pacific, in the W Caroline Islands; administratively part of the UN Trust Territory of the Pacific Islands 1947–87; entered into an agreement of free association with the US (1980); became fully independent in 1994. Chief island: Babelthuap. Capital: Melekeok, on Babelthuap (functions moved from Koror in 2006). Pop: 20 000 (2003 est). Area: 476 sq km (184 sq miles). Former name: Pelew Islands

palaver (pəˈlɑːvə) n 1 tedious or time-consuming business, esp when of a formal nature: all the palaver of filling in forms 2 loud and confused talk and activity; hubbub 3 (often used humorously) a conference 4 now rare talk intended to flatter or persuade ▷ vb 5 (intr) (often used humorously) to have a conference 6 (intr) to talk loudly and confusedly 7 (tr) to flatter or cajole [C18: from Portuguese palavra talk, from Latin parabola PARABLE]

Palawan (Spanish paˈlavan) n an island of the SW Philippines between the South China Sea and the Sulu Sea: the westernmost island in the country; mountainous and forested. Capital: Puerto Princesa. Pop (Palawan province): 755 412 (2000). Area: 11 785 sq km (4550 sq miles)

palazzo pants (pəˈlætsəʊ) pl n women's trousers with very wide legs [C20: palazzo from Italian, literally: PALACE]

pale¹ (peɪl) adj 1 lacking brightness of colour; whitish: pale morning light 2 (of a colour) whitish; produced by a relatively small quantity of colouring agent 3 dim or wan: the pale stars 4 feeble: a pale effort ▷ vb 5 to make or become pale or paler; blanch 6 (intr; often foll by before) to lose superiority or importance (in comparison to): her beauty paled before that of her hostess [C13: from Old French palle, from Latin pallidus pale, from pallēre to look wan] > 'palely adv > 'paleness n

pale² (peɪl) n 1 a wooden post or strip used as an upright member in a fence 2 an enclosing barrier, esp a fence made of pales 3 an area enclosed by a pale 4 heraldry an ordinary consisting of a vertical stripe, usually in the centre of a shield 5 beyond the pale outside the limits of social convention [C14: from Old French pal, from Latin pālus stake; compare POLE¹]

paleface (ˈpeɪlˌfeɪs) n a derogatory term for a White person, said to have been used by North American Indians

Palembang (paːˈlɛmbaːŋ) n a port in W Indonesia, in S Sumatra; oil refineries; university (1955). Pop: 1 451 419 (2000)

Palencia (Spanish paˈlenθia) n a city in N central Spain: earliest university in Spain (1208); seat of Castilian kings (12th–13th centuries); communications centre. Pop: 81 378 (2003 est)

Palenque (Spanish paˈlenke) n the site of an ancient Mayan city in S Mexico famous for its architectural ruins

paleo- or before a vowel **pale-** combining form variants (esp US) of palaeo-

Palermo (pəˈlɛəməʊ, -ˈlɜː-; Italian paˈlɛrmo) n the capital of Sicily, on the NW coast: founded by the Phoenicians in the 8th century BC Pop: 686 722 (2001)

Palestine (ˈpælɪˌstaɪn) n 1 Also called: the Holy Land, Canaan the area between the Jordan River and the Mediterranean Sea in which most of the biblical narrative is located 2 the province of the Roman Empire in this region 3 the former British mandatory territory created by the League of Nations in 1922 (but effective from 1920), and including all of the present territories of Israel and Jordan between whom it was partitioned by the UN in 1948

Palestine Liberation Organization n an organization founded in 1964 with the aim of creating a state for Palestinians; it recognized the state of Israel in 1993 and Israel granted Palestinians autonomy in the Gaza Strip and West Bank. Abbreviation: PLO

Palestinian (ˌpælɪˈstɪnɪən) adj 1 of or relating to Palestine ▷ n 2 a native or inhabitant of the former British mandate, or their descendants, esp such Arabs now living in the Palestinian Administered Territories, Jordan, Lebanon, or Israel, or as refugees from Israeli-occupied territory

Palestinian Administered Territories *n* the Gaza Strip and the West Bank in Israel: these areas were granted autonomous status under the control of the Palestinian National Authority following the 1993 peace agreement between Israel and the Palestine Liberation Organization. Also called: **Palestinian Autonomous Areas**

Palestinian National Authority *n* the authority formed in 1994 to govern the Palestinian Administered Territories: it controls policy on health, education, social welfare, direct taxation, tourism, and culture and manages elections to the Palestinian Council Abbreviation: **PNA**

Palestrina (ˌpælɛˈstriːnə) *n* Giovanni Pierluigi da (dʒoˈvanni pierˈluiːdʒi da). ?1525–94, Italian composer and master of counterpoint. His works, nearly all for unaccompanied choir and religious in nature, include the *Missa Papae Marcelli* (1555)

palette (ˈpælɪt) *n* **1** Also called: **pallet** a flat piece of wood, plastic, etc, used by artists as a surface on which to mix their paints **2** the range of colours characteristic of a particular artist, painting, or school of painting: *a restricted palette* **3** the available range of colours or patterns that can be displayed by a computer on a visual display unit [C17: from French, diminutive of *pale* shovel, from Latin *pala* spade]

palette knife *or* **pallet knife** *n* a round-ended spatula with a thin flexible blade used esp by artists for mixing, applying, and scraping off paint, esp oil paint

Paley (ˈpeɪlɪ) *n* William. 1743–1805, English theologian and utilitarian philosopher. His chief works are *The Principles of Moral and Political Philosophy* (1785), *Horae Paulinae* (1790), *A View of the Evidences of Christianity* (1794), and *Natural Theology* (1802)

palfrey (ˈpɔːlfrɪ) *n* archaic a light saddle horse, esp ridden by women [C12: from Old French *palefrei*, from Medieval Latin *palafredus*, from Late Latin *paraverēdus*, from Greek *para* beside + Latin *verēdus* light fleet horse, of Celtic origin]

Palgrave (ˈpɔːlɡreɪv, ˈpæl-) *n* Francis Turner. 1824–97, British critic and poet, editor of the poetry anthology *The Golden Treasury* (1861)

Pali (ˈpɑːlɪ) *n* an ancient language of India derived from Sanskrit; the language of the Buddhist scriptures [C19: from Sanskrit *pāli-bhāsa*, from *pāli* canon + *bhāsa* language, of Dravidian origin]

palimony (ˈpælɪmənɪ) *n* US alimony awarded to a nonmarried partner after the break-up of a long-term relationship [C20: from a blend of *pal* + *alimony*]

palimpsest (ˈpælɪmpˌsɛst) *n* **1** a manuscript on which two or more successive texts have been written, each one being erased to make room for the next ▷ *adj* **2** (of a text) written on a palimpsest **3** (of a document) used as a palimpsest [C17: from Latin *palimpsestus* parchment cleaned for reuse, from Greek *palimpsēstos*, from *palin* again + *psēstos* rubbed smooth, from *psēn* to scrape]

palindrome (ˈpælɪnˌdrəʊm) *n* a word or phrase the letters of which, when taken in reverse order, give the same word or phrase, such as *able was I ere I saw Elba* [C17: from Greek *palindromos* running back again, from *palin* again + -DROME] ▷ **palindromic** (ˌpælɪnˈdrɒmɪk) *adj*

paling (ˈpeɪlɪŋ) *n* **1** a fence made of pales **2** pales collectively **3** a single pale **4** the act of erecting pales

palisade (ˌpælɪˈseɪd) *n* **1** a strong fence made of stakes driven into the ground, esp for defence **2** one of the stakes used in such a fence ▷ *vb* **3** (*tr*) to enclose with a palisade [C17: via French, from Old Provençal *palissada*, ultimately from Latin *pālus* stake; see PALE², POLE¹]

Palissy (French palisi) *n* Bernard (bɛrnar). 1510–89, French Huguenot potter and writer on natural history, noted for his rustic glazed earthenware: died in the Bastille

Palk Strait (pɔːk, pɔːlk) *n* a channel between SE India and N Ceylon. Width: about 64 km (40 miles)

pall¹ (pɔːl) *n* **1** a cloth covering, usually black, spread over a coffin or tomb **2** a coffin, esp during the funeral ceremony **3** a dark heavy covering; shroud: *the clouds formed a pall over the sky* **4** a depressing or oppressive atmosphere: *her bereavement cast a pall on the party* **5** heraldry an ordinary consisting of a Y-shaped bearing **6** *Christianity* a small square linen cloth with which the chalice is covered at the Eucharist ▷ *vb* **7** (*tr*) to cover or depress with a pall [Old English *pæll*, from Latin: PALLIUM]

pall² (pɔːl) *vb* **1** (*intr*; often foll by *on*) to become or appear boring, insipid, or tiresome (to): *history classes palled on me* **2** to cloy or satiate, or become cloyed or satiated [C14: variant of APPAL]

Palladian (pəˈleɪdɪən) *adj* denoting, relating to, or having the neoclassical style of architecture created by Palladio [C18: after Andrea PALLADIO] ▷ **Palˈladianˌism** *n*

Palladio (Italian palˈladio) *n* **Andrea** (anˈdrɛːa). 1508–80, Italian architect who revived and developed classical architecture, esp the ancient Roman ideals of symmetrical planning and harmonic proportions. His treatise *Four Books on Architecture* (1570) and his designs for villas and palaces profoundly influenced 18th-century domestic architecture in England and the US

palladium¹ (pəˈleɪdɪəm) *n* a ductile malleable silvery-white element of the platinum metal group occurring principally in nickel-bearing ores: used as a hydrogenation catalyst and, alloyed with gold, in jewellery. Symbol: Pd; atomic no: 46; atomic wt: 106.42; valency: 2, 3, or 4; relative density: 1202; melting pt: 1555°C; boiling pt: 2964°C [C19: named after the asteroid PALLAS, at the time (1803) a recent discovery]

palladium² (pəˈleɪdɪəm) *n* something believed to ensure protection; safeguard [C17: after the PALLADIUM]

Palladium (pəˈleɪdɪəm) *n* a statue of Pallas Athena, esp the one upon which the safety of Troy depended

Pallas (ˈpæləs) *n* astronomy the second largest asteroid (diameter 520 km), revolving around the sun in a period of 4.62 years

Pallas Athena *or* **Pallas** *n* another name for **Athena**

pallbearer (ˈpɔːlˌbɛərə) *n* a person who carries or escorts the coffin at a funeral

pallet¹ (ˈpælɪt) *n* a straw-filled mattress or bed [C14: from Anglo-Norman *paillet*, from Old French *paille* straw, from Latin *palea* straw]

pallet² (ˈpælɪt) *n* **1** an instrument with a handle and a flat, sometimes flexible, blade used by potters for shaping **2** a standard-sized platform of box section open at two ends on which goods may be stacked. The open ends allow the entry of the forks of a lifting truck so that the palletized load can be raised and moved about easily **3** *horology* the locking lever that engages and disengages alternate end pawls with the escape wheel to give impulses to the balance **4** a variant spelling of **palette** (sense 1) **5** *music* a flap valve of wood faced with leather that opens to allow air from the wind chest to enter an organ pipe, causing it to sound [C16: from Old French *palette* a little shovel, from *pale* spade, from Latin *pala* spade]

palletize *or* **palletise** (ˈpælɪˌtaɪz) *vb* (*tr*) to stack or transport on a pallet or pallets ▷ **ˌpalletiˈzation** *or* **ˌpalletiˈsation** *n*

palliasse *or esp US* **paillasse** (ˈpælɪˌæs, ˌpælɪˈæs) *n* a straw-filled mattress; pallet [C18: from French *paillasse*, from Italian *pagliaccio*, ultimately from Latin *palea* PALLET¹]

palliate (ˈpælɪˌeɪt) *vb* (*tr*) **1** to lessen the severity of (pain, disease, etc) without curing or removing; alleviate; mitigate **2** to cause (an offence) to seem less serious by concealing evidence; extenuate [C16: from Late Latin *palliāre* to cover up, from Latin *pallium* a cloak, PALLIUM] ▷ **ˌpalliˈation** *n*

palliative (ˈpælɪətɪv) *adj* **1** serving to palliate; relieving without curing ▷ *n* **2** something that palliates, such as a sedative drug or agent ▷ **ˈpalliatively** *adv*

pallid (ˈpælɪd) *adj* **1** lacking colour or brightness; wan: *a pallid complexion* **2** lacking vigour; vapid: *a pallid performance* [C17: from Latin *pallidus*, from *pallēre* to be PALE¹] ▷ **ˈpallidly** *adv* ▷ **ˈpallidness** *or* **palˈlidity** *n*

pallium (ˈpælɪəm) *n*, *pl* **-lia** (-lɪə) *or* **-liums** **1** a garment worn by men in ancient Greece or Rome, made by draping a large rectangular cloth about the body **2** *chiefly RC Church* a woollen vestment consisting of a band encircling the shoulders with two lappets hanging from it front and back: worn by the pope, all archbishops, and (as a mark of special honour) some bishops **3** Also called: **mantle** *anatomy* the cerebral cortex and contiguous white matter **4** *zoology* another name for: **mantle** (sense 5) [C16: from Latin: cloak; related to Latin *palla* mantle]

pall-mall ('pæl'mæl) *n obsolete* **1** a game in which a ball is driven by a mallet along an alley and through an iron ring **2** the alley itself [C17: from obsolete French, from Italian *pallamaglio*, from *palla* ball + *maglio* mallet]

Pall Mall ('pæl 'mæl) *n* a street in central London, noted for its many clubs

pallor ('pælə) *n* a pale condition, esp when unnatural: *fear gave his face a deathly pallor* [C17: from Latin: whiteness (of the skin), from *pallēre* to be PALE[1]]

pally ('pælɪ) *adj* **-lier, -liest** *informal* on friendly or familiar terms

palm[1] (pɑːm) *n* **1** the inner part of the hand from the wrist to the base of the fingers **2** a linear measure based on the breadth or length of a hand, equal to three to four inches or seven to ten inches respectively **3** the part of a glove that covers the palm **4 a** the side of the blade of an oar that faces away from the direction of a boat's movement during a stroke **b** the face of the fluke of an anchor **5** a flattened or expanded part of the antlers of certain deer **6 in the palm of one's hand** at one's mercy or command ▷ *vb* (*tr*) **7** to conceal in or about the hand, as in sleight-of-hand tricks ▷ See also **palm off** [C14 *paume*, via Old French from Latin *palma*; compare Old English *folm* palm of the hand, Greek *palamē*] > **palmar** ('pælmə) *adj*

palm[2] (pɑːm) *n* **1** any treelike plant of the tropical and subtropical monocotyledonous family *Arecaceae* (formerly *Palmae* or *Palmaceae*), usually having a straight unbranched trunk crowned with large pinnate or palmate leaves **2** a leaf or branch of any of these trees, a symbol of victory, success, etc **3** merit or victory **4** an emblem or insignia representing a leaf or branch worn on certain military decorations [Old English, from Latin *palma*, from the likeness of its spreading fronds to a hand; see PALM[1]] > **palmaceous** (pæl'meɪʃəs) *adj*

Palma[1] (Spanish 'palma) *n* the capital of the Balearic Islands, on the SW coast of Majorca: tourist centre. Pop: 367 277 (2003 est). Official name: **Palma de Mallorca**

Palma[2] (Italian 'palma) *n* **Jacopo** (ja'kopo), known as **Palma Vecchio**, original name *Jacopo Negretti*. ?1480–1528, Venetian painter, noted esp for his portraits of women

palmate ('pælmeit, -mɪt) *or* **palmated** *adj* **1** shaped like an open hand: *palmate antlers* **2** *botany* having more than three lobes or segments that spread out from a common point: *palmate leaves* **3** (of the feet of most water birds) having three toes connected by a web [C18: from Latin *palmatus*, from *palma* palm; see PALM[2]]

Palm Beach *n* a town in SE Florida, on an island between Lake Worth (a lagoon) and the Atlantic: major resort and tourist centre. Pop: 9759 (2003 est)

Palme (Swedish 'palmə) *n* (Sven) **Olof** (Joachim) ('uːlof). 1927–86, Swedish Social Democratic statesman; prime minister (1969–76, 1982–86); assassinated

palmer ('pɑːmə) *n* **1** (in Medieval Europe) a pilgrim bearing a palm branch as a sign of his visit to the Holy Land **2** (in Medieval Europe) any pilgrim [C13: from Old French *palmier*, from Medieval Latin *palmārius*, from Latin *palma* palm]

Palmer ('pɑːmə) *n* **1 Arnold.** born 1929, US professional golfer: won the US Open Championship (1960) and the British Open Championship (1961; 1962) **2 Samuel.** 1805–81, English painter of visionary landscapes, influenced by William Blake

Palmer Archipelago *n* a group of islands between South America and Antarctica: part of the British Antarctic Territory (formerly the British colony of the Falkland Islands and Dependencies). (Claims are suspended under the Antarctic Treaty). Former name: **Antarctic Archipelago**

Palmer Land *n* the S part of the Antarctic Peninsula

Palmer Peninsula *n* the former name (until 1964) for the **Antarctic Peninsula**

Palmerston[1] ('pɑːməstən) *n* the former name

(1869–1911) of **Darwin**[1]

Palmerston[2] ('pɑːməstən) *n* **Henry John Temple,** 3rd Viscount Palmerston. 1784–1865, British statesman; foreign secretary (1830–34; 1835–41; 1846–51); prime minister (1855–58; 1859–65). His talent was for foreign affairs, in which he earned a reputation as a British nationalist and for high-handedness and gunboat diplomacy

Palmerston North *n* a city in New Zealand, in the S North Island on the Manawatu River. Pop: 78 100 (2004 est)

Palmer-Tomkinson ('pɑːmə'tɒmkɪnsən) *n* **Tara.** born 1971, British socialite, television personality, and journalist

palmette (pæl'mɛt) *n archaeol* an ornament or design resembling the palm leaf [C19: from French: a little PALM[2]]

palmetto (pæl'mɛtəʊ) *n*, *pl* **-tos** *or* **-toes 1** any of several small chiefly tropical fan palms, esp any of the genus *Sabal*, of the southeastern US **2** any of various other fan palms such as chiromancy of the genera *Serenoa*, *Thrinax*, and *Chamaerops* [C16: from Spanish *palmito* a little PALM[2]]

Palmira (Spanish pal'mira) *n* a city in W Colombia: agricultural centre. Pop: 253 000 (2005 est)

palmistry ('pɑːmɪstrɪ) *n* the process or art of interpreting character, telling fortunes, etc, by the configuration of lines, marks, and bumps on a person's hand. Also called: **chiromancy** [C15 *pawmestry*, from *paume* PALM[1]; the second element is unexplained] > **palmist** *n*

palmitate ('pælmɪˌteɪt) *n* any salt or ester of palmitic acid

palmitic acid (pæl'mɪtɪk) *n* a white crystalline solid that is a saturated fatty acid: used in the manufacture of soap and candles. Formula: $(C_{15}H_{31})COOH$. Systematic name: **hexadecanoic acid** [C19: from French *palmitique*; see PALM[2], -ITE[2], -IC]

palm off *vb* (*tr, adverb*; often foll by **on**) **1** to offer, sell, or spend fraudulently: *to palm off a counterfeit coin* **2** to divert in order to be rid of: *I palmed the unwelcome visitor off on John*

palm oil *n* a yellow butter-like oil obtained from the fruit of the oil palm, used as an edible fat and in soap

Palm Springs *n* a city in the US, in California: a popular tourist resort. Pop: 45 228 (2003 est)

Palm Sunday *n* the Sunday before Easter commemorating Christ's triumphal entry into Jerusalem

palmtop computer ('pɑːmˌtɒp) *n* a computer that has a small screen and compressed keyboard and is small enough to be held in the hand, often used as a personal organizer

palmy ('pɑːmɪ) *adj* **palmier, palmiest 1** prosperous, flourishing, or luxurious: *a palmy life* **2** covered with, relating to, or resembling palms

palmyra (pæl'maɪrə) *n* a tall tropical Asian palm, *Borassus flabellifer*, with large fan-shaped leaves used for thatching and weaving; grown also for its edible seedlings [C17: from Portuguese *palmeira* palm tree (see PALM[2]); perhaps influenced by PALMYRA, city in Syria]

Palmyra (pæl'maɪrə) *n* **1** an ancient city in central Syria: said to have been built by Solomon. Biblical name: **Tadmor 2** an island in the central Pacific, in the Line Islands: under US administration

Palo Alto *n* **1** ('pæləʊ 'æltəʊ) a city in W California, southeast of San Francisco: founded in 1891 as the seat of Stanford University. Pop: 57 233 (2003 est) **2** (Spanish 'palo 'alto) a battlefield in E Mexico, northwest of Monterrey, where the first battle (1846) of the Mexican War took place, in which the Mexicans under General Mariano Arista were defeated by the Americans under General Zachary Taylor

palo cortado ('pæləʊ kɔr'tadəʊ) *n* a rich, dry sherry [Spanish, literally: crossed stick (referring to the classification system in which butts of palo cortado are marked with a vertical line and one or more horizontal lines)]

Palomar ('pæləˌmɑː:) *n* **Mount Palomar** a mountain in S California, northeast of San Diego: site of **Mount Palomar Observatory**, which has a large (200-inch) reflecting telescope. Height: 1871 m (6140 ft)

P

palomino (ˌpæləˈmiːnəʊ) *n, pl* -**nos** a golden horse with a cream or white mane and tail [American Spanish, from Spanish: dovelike, from Latin *palumbīnus*, from *palumbēs* ring dove]

Palos (Spanish ˈpalɔs) *n* a village and former port in SW Spain: starting point of Columbus' voyage of discovery to America (1492)

palp (pælp) *or* **palpus** (ˈpælpəs) *n, pl* palps *or* palpi (ˈpælpaɪ) **1** either of a pair of sensory appendages that arise from the mouthparts of crustaceans and insects **2** either of a pair of tactile organs arising from the head or anterior end of certain annelids and molluscs [C19: from French, from Latin *palpus* a touching]

palpable (ˈpælpəbᵊl) *adj* **1** (*usually prenominal*) easily perceived by the senses or the mind; obvious: *the excuse was a palpable lie* **2** capable of being touched; tangible **3** *med* capable of being discerned by the sense of touch [C14: from Late Latin *palpābilis* that may be touched, from Latin *palpāre* to stroke, touch] > ˌpalpaˈbility *or* ˈpalpableness *n* > ˈpalpably *adv*

palpate (ˈpælpeɪt) *vb* (*tr*) *med* to examine (an area of the body) by the sense of touch and pressure [C19: from Latin *palpāre* to stroke] > palˈpation *n*

palpebral (ˈpælpɪbrəl) *adj* of or relating to the eyelid [C19: from Late Latin *palpebrālis*, from Latin *palpebra* eyelid; probably related to *palpāre* to stroke]

palpitate (ˈpælpɪˌteɪt) *vb* (*intr*) **1** (of the heart) to beat with abnormal rapidity **2** to flutter or tremble [C17: from Latin *palpitāre* to throb, from *palpāre* to stroke] > ˈpalpitant *adj* > ˌpalpiˈtation *n*

palsy (ˈpɔːlzɪ) *pathol* ⊳ *n, pl* -**sies 1** paralysis, esp of a specified type: *cerebral palsy* ⊳ *vb* -**sies, -sying, -sied** (*tr*) **2** to paralyse [C13 *palesi*, from Old French *paralisie*, from Latin PARALYSIS] > ˈpalsied *adj*

palter (ˈpɔːltə) *vb* (*intr*) **1** to act or talk insincerely **2** to haggle [C16: of unknown origin]

Paltrow (ˈpɒltrəʊ) *n* Gwyneth (Kate). born 1973, US film actress; her films include *Emma* (1996), *Sliding Doors* (1998), *Shakespeare in Love* (1998), and *Sylvia* (2003)

paltry (ˈpɔːltrɪ) *adj* -**trier, -triest 1** insignificant; meagre **2** worthless or petty [C16: from Low Germanic *palter, paltrig* ragged] > ˈpaltrily *adv* > ˈpaltriness *n*

paludal (pəˈljuːdᵊl, ˈpæljʊdᵊl) *adj rare* **1** of, relating to, or produced by marshes **2** malarial [C19: from Latin *palus* marsh; related to Sanskrit *palvala* pond]

paludism (ˈpæljʊˌdɪzəm) *n pathol* a rare word for **malaria** [C19: from Latin *palus* marsh]

palynology (ˌpælɪˈnɒlədʒɪ) *n* the study of living and fossil pollen grains and plant spores [C20: from Greek *palunein* to scatter + -LOGY] > palynological (ˌpælɪnəˈlɒdʒɪkᵊl) *adj* > ˌpalyˈnologist *n*

Pamirs (pəˈmɪəz) *pl n* the Pamirs a mountainous area of central Asia, mainly in Tajikistan and partly in Kyrgyzstan, extending into China and Afghanistan: consists of a complex of high ranges, from which the Tian Shan projects to the north, the Kunlun and Karakoram to the east, and the Hindu Kush to the west; Ismoil Somoni (formerly Communism Peak) is situated in the Tajik Pamirs. Highest peak: Kongur Shan, 7719 m (25 326 ft)

Pamlico Sound (ˈpæmlɪkəʊ) *n* an inlet of the Atlantic between the E coast of North Carolina and its chain of offshore islands. Length: 130 km (80 miles)

pampas (ˈpæmpəz) *n* (*functioning as singular or more often plural*) **a** the extensive grassy plains of temperate South America, esp in Argentina **b** (*as modifier*): *pampas dwellers* [C18: from American Spanish *pampa* (sing), from Quechua *bamba* plain] > pampean (ˈpæmpɪən, pæmˈpiːən) *adj*

pampas grass (ˈpæmpəs, -pəz) *n* any of various large grasses of the South American genus *Cortaderia* and related genera, widely cultivated for their large feathery silver-coloured flower branches

Pampeluna (ˌpæmpəˈluːnə) *n* the former name of Pamplona

pamper (ˈpæmpə) *vb* (*tr*) **1** to treat with affectionate and usually excessive indulgence; coddle; spoil **2** *archaic* to feed to excess [C14: of Germanic origin; compare German dialect *pampfen* to gorge oneself] > ˈpamperer *n*

pamphlet (ˈpæmflɪt) *n* **1** a brief publication generally having a paper cover; booklet **2** a brief treatise, often on a subject of current interest, published in pamphlet form [C14 *pamflet*, from Anglo-Latin *panfletus*, from Medieval Latin *Pamphilus* title of a popular 12th-century amatory poem from Greek *Pamphilos* masculine proper name]

pamphleteer (ˌpæmflɪˈtɪə) *n* **1** a person who writes or issues pamphlets, esp of a controversial nature ⊳ *vb* **2** (*intr*) to write or issue pamphlets

Pamphylia (pæmˈfɪlɪə) *n* an area on the S coast of ancient Asia Minor

Pamplona (pæmˈpləʊnə; Spanish pamˈplona) *n* a city in N Spain in the foothills of the Pyrenees: capital of the kingdom of Navarre from the 11th century until 1841. Pop: 190 937 (2003 est). Former name: Pampeluna

Pamuk (ˈpæmək) *n* Orhan. born 1952, Turkish novelist and writer; author of *The Black Book* (1990), *My Name is Red* (1998), *Snow* (2002) and *Istanbul: Memories of a City* (2003). Nobel prize for literature 2006

pan¹ (pæn) *n* **1 a** a wide metal vessel used in cooking **b** (*in combination*): *saucepan* **2** Also called: panful the amount such a vessel will hold **3** any of various similar vessels used esp in industry, as for boiling liquids **4** a dish used by prospectors, esp gold prospectors, for separating a valuable mineral from the gravel or earth containing it by washing and agitating **5** either of the two dishlike receptacles on a balance **6** Also called: lavatory pan *Brit* the bowl of a lavatory **7 a** a natural or artificial depression in the ground where salt can be obtained by the evaporation of brine **b** a natural depression containing water or mud **8** See **hardpan**, **brainpan 9** a small cavity containing priming powder in the locks of old guns **10** a hard substratum of soil ⊳ *vb* pans, panning, panned **11** (when *tr*, often foll by *off* or *out*) to wash (gravel) in a pan to separate particles of (valuable minerals) from it **12** (*intr*, often foll by *out*) (of gravel) to yield valuable minerals by this process **13** (*tr*) *informal* to criticize harshly: *the critics panned his new play* ⊳ See also **pan out** [Old English *panne*; related to Old Saxon, Old Norse *panna*, Old High German *pfanna*]

pan² (pæn) *vb* pans, panning, panned **1** to move (a film camera) or (of a film camera) to be moved so as to follow a moving object or obtain a panoramic effect ⊳ *n* **2** the act of panning [C20: shortened from *panoramic*]

Pan (pæn) *n* Greek myth the god of fields, woods, shepherds, and flocks, represented as a man with a goat's legs, horns, and ears Related adjs: **Pandean**, **Panic**.

Pan. *abbreviation* Panama

pan- *combining form* **1** all or every: *panchromatic* **2** including or relating to all parts or members: *Pan-African; pantheistic* [from Greek *pan*, neuter of *pas* all]

panacea (ˌpænəˈsɪə) *n* a remedy for all diseases or ills [C16: via Latin from Greek *panakeia* healing everything, from *pan* all + *akēs* remedy] > ˌpanaˈcean *adj*

panache (pəˈnæʃ, -ˈnɑːʃ) *n* **1** a dashing manner; style; swagger: *he rides with panache* **2** a feathered plume on a helmet [C16: via French from Old Italian *pennacchio*, from Late Latin *pinnāculum* feather, from Latin *pinna* feather; compare Latin *pinnāculum* PINNACLE]

panada (pəˈnɑːdə) *n* a mixture of flour, water, etc, or of breadcrumbs soaked in milk, used as a thickening [C16: from Spanish, from *pan* bread, from Latin *pānis*]

Pan-Africanist Congress *n* a South African political party, founded as a liberation movement in 1959. Abbreviation: PAC

Panaji (pɑːˈnɑːdʒiː) *n* a variant of Panjim

Panama (ˌpænəˈmɑː, ˈpænəˌmɑː) *n* **1** a republic in Central America, occupying the Isthmus of Panama: gained independence from Spain in 1821 and joined Greater Colombia; became independent in 1903, with the immediate area around the canal forming the Canal Zone under US jurisdiction; Panama assumed sovereignty over the Canal Zone in 1979 and full control in 1999. Official language: Spanish; English is also widely spoken. Religion: Roman Catholic majority. Currency: balboa. Capital: Panama City. Pop: 3 178 000 (2004 est). Area: 75 650 sq km (29 201 sq miles) **2** Isthmus of Panama an isthmus linking North and South

America, between the Pacific and the Caribbean. Length: 676 km (420 miles). Width (at its narrowest point): 50 km (31 miles). Former name: **Darien 3 Gulf of Panama** a wide inlet of the Pacific in Panama > **Panamanian** (ˌpænəˈmeɪnɪən) *adj, n*

Panama Canal *n* a canal across the Isthmus of Panama, linking the Atlantic and Pacific Oceans: extends from Colón on the Caribbean Sea southeast to Balboa on the Gulf of Panama; built by the US (1904–14), after an unsuccessful previous attempt (1880–89) by the French under de Lesseps. Length: 64 km (40 miles)

Panama Canal Zone *n* See **Canal Zone**

Panama City *n* the capital of Panama, near the Pacific entrance of the Panama Canal: developed rapidly with the building of the Panama Canal; seat of the University of Panama (1935). Pop: 950 000 (2005 est)

Panama hat *n* (*sometimes not capital*) a hat made of the plaited leaves of the jipijapa plant of Central and South America. Often shortened to: **Panama**

Pan-American *adj* of, relating to, or concerning North, South, and Central America collectively or the advocacy of political or economic unity among American countries > **'Pan-A'merican,ism** *n*

panatella (ˌpænəˈtɛlə) *n* a long slender cigar [American Spanish *panetela* long slim biscuit, from Italian *panatella* small loaf, from *pane* bread, from Latin *pānis*]

Panay (pɑːˈnaɪ) *n* an island in the central Philippines, the westernmost of the Visayan Islands. Pop: 3 500 000 (2000). Area: 12 300 sq km (4750 sq miles)

pancake (ˈpænˌkeɪk) *n* 1 a thin flat cake made from batter and fried on both sides, often served rolled and filled with a sweet or savoury mixture 2 Also called: **pancake landing** an aircraft landing made by levelling out a few feet from the ground and then dropping onto it ▷ *vb* 3 to cause (an aircraft) to make a pancake landing or (of an aircraft) to make a pancake landing

Pancake Day *n* another name for **Shrove Tuesday**

panchromatic (ˌpænkrəʊˈmætɪk) *adj photog* (of an emulsion or film) made sensitive to all colours by the addition of suitable dyes to the emulsion > **panchromatism** (pænˈkrəʊməˌtɪzəm) *n*

pancosmism (pænˈkɒzˌmɪzəm) *n* the philosophical doctrine that the material universe is all that exists [c19: see PAN-, COSMOS, -ISM]

pancreas (ˈpænkrɪəs) *n* a large elongated glandular organ, situated behind the stomach, that secretes insulin and pancreatic juice [c16: via New Latin from Greek *pankreas*, from PAN- + *kreas* flesh] > **pancreatic** (ˌpænkrɪˈætɪk) *adj*

pancreatic juice *n* the clear alkaline secretion of the pancreas that is released into the duodenum and contains several digestive enzymes

pancreatin (ˈpænkrɪətɪn) *n* the powdered extract of the pancreas of certain animals, such as the pig, used in medicine as an aid to digestion by virtue of the enzymes it contains

panda (ˈpændə) *n* 1 Also called: **giant panda** a large black-and-white herbivorous bearlike mammal, *Ailuropoda melanoleuca*, related to the raccoons and inhabiting the high mountain bamboo forests of China: family *Procyonidae* 2 **lesser panda** *or* **red panda** a closely related smaller animal resembling a raccoon, *Ailurus fulgens*, of the mountain forests of S Asia, having a reddish-brown coat and ringed tail [c19: via French from a native Nepalese word]

panda car *n* *Brit* a police patrol car, esp a blue and white one [c20: so called because it was originally white with black or blue markings, supposedly resembling the markings of the giant panda]

pandanus (pænˈdeɪnəs) *n, pl* -**nuses** any of various Old World tropical palmlike plants of the genus *Pandanus*, having large aerial prop roots and leaves that yield a fibre used for making mats, etc: family *Pandanaceae* [c19: via New Latin from Malay *pandan*]

Pandarus (ˈpændərəs) *n* 1 *Greek myth* the leader of the Lycians, allies of the Trojans in their war with the Greeks. He broke the truce by shooting Menelaus with an arrow and was killed in the ensuing battle by Diomedes 2 (in medieval legend) the procurer of

Cressida on behalf of Troilus

Pandean (pænˈdiːən) *adj* of or relating to the god Pan

pandect (ˈpændɛkt) *n* 1 a treatise covering all aspects of a particular subject 2 (*often plural*) the complete body of laws of a country; legal code [c16: via Late Latin from Greek *pandektēs* containing everything, from PAN- + *dektēs* receiver, from *dekhesthai* to receive]

pandemic (pænˈdɛmɪk) *adj* 1 (of a disease) affecting persons over a wide geographical area; extensively epidemic ▷ *n* 2 a pandemic disease [c17: from Late Latin *pandēmus*, from Greek *pandēmos* general, from PAN- + *demos* the people]

pandemonium (ˌpændɪˈməʊnɪəm) *n* 1 wild confusion; uproar 2 a place of uproar and chaos [c17: coined by Milton to designate the capital of hell in *Paradise Lost*, from PAN- + Greek *daimōn* DEMON]

pander (ˈpændə) *vb* 1 (*intr*; foll by *to*) to give gratification (to weaknesses or desires) 2 (archaic when *tr*) to act as a go-between in a sexual intrigue (for) ▷ *n* Also: **panderer** 3 a person who caters for vulgar desires, esp in order to make money 4 a person who procures a sexual partner for another; pimp [c16 (n): from *Pandare* PANDARUS]

pandit (ˈpʌndɪt; *spelling pron* ˈpændɪt) *n Hinduism* a variant of **pundit** (sense 3)

Pandit (ˈpʌndɪt) *n* **Vijaya Lakshmi** (vɪˈjaɪə ˈlɑːkʃmɪ). 1900–90, Indian politician and diplomat; sister of Jawaharlal Nehru

P & L *abbreviation* profit and loss

P & O *abbreviation* the Peninsular and Oriental Steam Navigation Company

Pandora (pænˈdɔːrə) *or* **Pandore** (pænˈdɔː, ˈpændɔː) *n Greek myth* the first woman, made out of earth as the gods' revenge on man for obtaining fire from Prometheus. Given a box (**Pandora's box**) that she was forbidden to open, she disobeyed out of curiosity and released from it all the ills that beset man, leaving only hope within [from Greek, literally: all-gifted]

p & p *Brit abbreviation* postage and packing

pane (peɪn) *n* 1 a sheet of glass in a window or door 2 a panel of a window, door, wall, etc 3 a flat section or face, as of a cut diamond [c13: from Old French *pan* portion, from Latin *pannus* rag]

paneer (pəˈnɪə) *n* a soft white cheese, used in Indian cookery [c20: from Hindi *panīr* cheese]

panegyric (ˌpænɪˈdʒɪrɪk) *n* a formal public commendation; eulogy [c17: via French and Latin from Greek, from *panēguris* public gathering, from PAN- + *aguris* assembly] > **pane'gyrical** *adj* > **pane'gyrically** *adv* > **pane'gyrist** *n*

panel (ˈpænəl) *n* 1 a flat section of a wall, door, etc 2 any distinct section or component of something formed from a sheet of material, esp of a car body, the spine of a book, etc 3 a piece of material inserted in a skirt, dress, etc 4 **a** a group of persons selected to act as a team in a quiz, to judge a contest, to discuss a topic before an audience, etc **b** (*as modifier*): *a panel game* 5 *law* **a** a list of persons summoned for jury service **b** the persons on a specific jury 6 *Scots law* a person indicted or accused of crime after appearing in court 7 **a** a thin board used as a surface or backing for an oil painting **b** a painting done on such a surface 8 any picture with a length much greater than its breadth 9 See **instrument panel** 10 (formerly, in Britain) **a** a list of patients insured under the National Health Insurance Scheme **b** a list of medical practitioners within a given area available for consultation by these patients ▷ *vb* -**els**, -**elling**, -**elled** *or* US -**els**, -**eling**, -**eled** (*tr*) 11 to furnish or decorate with panels 12 *law* **a** to empanel (a jury) **b** (in Scotland) to bring (a person) to trial; indict [c13: from Old French: portion, from *pan* piece of cloth, from Latin *pannus*; see PANE¹]

panel beater *n* a person who beats out the bodywork of motor vehicles

panelling *or* US **paneling** (ˈpænəlɪŋ) *n* 1 panels collectively, as on a wall or ceiling 2 material used for making panels

panellist *or* US **panelist** (ˈpænəlɪst) *n* a member of a panel, esp on a radio or television programme

panel pin *n* a light slender nail with a narrow head

panel saw *n* a saw with a long narrow blade for cutting thin wood

panel van *n* **1** *Austral* a small van with two rear doors, esp one having windows and seats in the rear **2** *NZ* a small enclosed delivery van

Pan-European *adj* of or relating to all European countries or the advocacy of political or economic unity among European countries

pang (pæŋ) *n* a sudden brief sharp feeling, as of loneliness, physical pain, or hunger [c16: variant of earlier *prange*, of Germanic origin]

panga ('pæŋɡə) *n* a broad heavy knife of E Africa, used as a tool or weapon [from a native E African word]

Pang-fou ('pæŋ'fu:) *n* a variant transliteration of the Chinese name for **Bengbu**

pangolin (pæŋ'ɡəʊlɪn) *n* any mammal of the order *Pholidota* found in tropical Africa, S Asia, and Indonesia, having a body covered with overlapping horny scales and a long snout specialized for feeding on ants and termites. Also called: **scaly anteater** [c18: from Malay *peng-gōling*, from *gōling* to roll over; from its ability to roll into a ball]

Pango Pango ('pɑ:ŋɡəʊ 'pɑ:ŋɡəʊ) *n* the former name of Pago Pago

Pan Gu ('pæn'ɡu:) *or* **P'an Ku** *n* 32–92 AD, Chinese historian and court official, noted for his history of the Han dynasty: died in prison

panhandle¹ ('pæn,hændəl) *n* (*sometimes capital*) (in the US) a narrow strip of land that projects from one state into another

panhandle² ('pæn,hændəl) *vb* *US & Canadian informal* to accost and beg from (passers-by), esp on the street [c19: probably a back formation from *panhandler* a person who begs with a pan] > 'pan,handler *n*

Panhellenic (,pænhɛ'lɛnɪk) *adj* of or relating to all the Greeks, all Greece, or Panhellenism

panic ('pænɪk) *n* **1** a sudden overwhelming feeling of terror or anxiety, esp one affecting a whole group of people **2** (*modifier*) of or resulting from such terror: *panic measures* ▷ *vb* **-ics, -icking, -icked 3** to feel or cause to feel panic [c17: from French *panique*, from New Latin *pānicus*, from Greek *panikos* emanating from Pan, considered as the source of irrational fear] > 'panicky *adj*

Panic ('pænɪk) *adj* of or relating to the god Pan

panic attack *n* an episode of acute and disabling anxiety associated with such physical symptoms as hyperventilation and sweating

panic button *n* a button or switch that operates any of various safety devices, for use in an emergency

panic disorder *n* *psychiatry* a condition in which a person experiences recurrent panic attacks

panic grass *n* any of various grasses of the genus *Panicum*, such as millet, grown in warm and tropical regions for fodder and grain [C15 *panic*, from Latin *pānicum*, probably a back formation from *pānicula* PANICLE]

panicle ('pænɪkəl) *n* a compound raceme, occurring esp in grasses [c16: from Latin *pānicula* tuft, diminutive of *panus* thread, ultimately from Greek *penos* web; related to *penion* bobbin] > 'panicled *adj* > paniculate (pə'nɪkjʊ,leɪt, -lɪt) *or* pa'niculated *adj* > pa'nicu,lately *adv*

panic room *n* a secure room with a separate telephone line within a house, to which a person can flee if someone breaks in

panic-stricken *or* **panic-struck** *adj* affected by panic

panini (pæ'ni:ni:) *n*, *pl* -ni *or* -nis a type of Italian bread, usually served grilled with a variety of fillings [c20: from Italian, pl of *panino* a bread roll]

panjandrum (pæn'dʒændrəm) *n* a pompous self-important official or person of rank [c18: after a character, the *Grand Panjandrum*, in a nonsense work (1755) by Samuel Foote, English playwright and actor]

Panjim ('pɑ:n,ʒɪm) *or* **Panaji** *n* the capital of the Indian state of Goa (formerly capital of the union territory of Goa, Daman, and Diu until 1987): a port on the Arabian Sea on the coast of Goa. Pop: 58 785 (2001)

Pankhurst ('pæŋkhɜːst) *n* **1** Dame **Christabel**. 1880–1958, English suffragette **2** her mother, **Emmeline**. 1858–1928, English suffragette leader, who founded the militant

Women's Social and Political Union (1903) **3** Sylvia, daughter of Emmeline Pankhurst. 1882–1960, English suffragette and pacifist

pan loaf *n* *Irish & Scot dialect* a loaf of bread with a light crust all the way round. Often shortened to: **pan**

Panmunjom ('pɑ:n'mʊn'dʒɒm) *n* a village in the demilitarized zone of Korea: site of truce talks leading to the end of the Korean War (1950–53)

pannage ('pænɪdʒ) *n* *archaic* **1** pasturage for pigs, esp in a forest **2** payment for this **3** acorns, beech mast, etc, on which pigs feed [c13: from Old French *pasnage*, ultimately from Latin *pastion-, pastiō* feeding, from *pascere* to feed]

pannier ('pænɪə) *n* **1** a large basket, esp one of a pair slung over a beast of burden **2** one of a pair of bags slung either side of the back wheel of a motorcycle, bicycle, etc **3** (esp in the 18th century) **a** a hooped framework to distend a woman's skirt **b** one of two puffed-out loops of material worn drawn back onto the hips to reveal the underskirt [c13: from Old French *panier*, from Latin *pānārium* basket for bread, from *pānis* bread]

pannikin ('pænɪkɪn) *n* *chiefly Brit* a small metal cup or pan [c19: from PAN¹ + -KIN]

pannikin boss *n* *Austral informal* a person in charge of a few fellow workers

Pannonia (pə'nəʊnɪə) *n* a region of the ancient world south and west of the Danube: made a Roman province in 6 AD

panoply ('pænəplɪ) *n*, *pl* -plies **1** a complete or magnificent array **2** the entire equipment of a warrior [c17: via French from Greek *panoplia* complete armour, from PAN- + *hopla* armour, pl of *hoplon* tool] > 'panoplied *adj*

panoptic (pæn'ɒptɪk) *or* **panoptical** *adj* taking in all parts, aspects, etc, in a single view; all-embracing: *a panoptic survey* [c19: from Greek *panoptēs* seeing everything, from PAN- + *optos* visible]

panorama (,pænə'rɑ:mə) *n* **1** an extensive unbroken view, as of a landscape, in all directions **2** a wide or comprehensive survey **3** a large extended picture or series of pictures of a scene, unrolled before spectators a part at a time so as to appear continuous **4** another name for **cyclorama** [c18: from PAN- + Greek *horāma* view] > panoramic (,pænə'ræmɪk) *adj* > ,pano'ramically *adv*

pan out *vb* (*intr, adverb*) *informal* to work out; turn out; result

panpipes ('pæn,paɪps) *pl n* (*often singular; often capital*) a number of reeds or whistles of graduated lengths bound together to form a musical wind instrument. Also called: **pipes of Pan, syrinx**

pansy ('pænzɪ) *n*, *pl* -sies **1** any violaceous garden plant that is a variety of *Viola tricolor*, having flowers with rounded velvety petals, white, yellow, or purple in colour. See also **wild pansy 2** *slang, offensive* an effeminate or homosexual man or boy [c15: from Old French *pensée* thought, from *penser* to think, from Latin *pensāre*]

pant (pænt) *vb* **1** to breathe with noisy deep gasps, as when out of breath from exertion or excitement **2** to say (something) while breathing thus **3** (*intr, often foll by for*) to have a frantic desire (for); yearn **4** (*intr*) to pulsate; throb rapidly ▷ *n* **5** the act or an instance of panting **6** a short deep gasping noise; puff [c15: from Old French *pantaisier*, from Greek *phantasioun* to have visions, from *phantasia* FANTASY]

pantalets *or* **pantalettes** (,pæntə'lɛts) *pl n* **1** long drawers, usually trimmed with ruffles, extending below the skirts: worn during the early and mid 19th century **2** a pair of ruffles for the ends of such drawers [c19: diminutive of PANTALOONS]

pantaloon (,pæntə'lu:n) *n* *theatre* **1** (in pantomime) an absurd old man, the butt of the clown's tricks **2** (*usually capital*) (in commedia dell'arte) a lecherous old merchant dressed in pantaloons [c16: from French *Pantalon*, from Italian *Pantalone*, local nickname for a Venetian, probably from *San Pantaleone*, a fourth-century Venetian saint]

pantaloons (,pæntə'lu:nz) *pl n* **1 a** *history* men's tight-fitting trousers, esp those fastening under the instep worn in the late 18th and early 19th centuries **b** children's trousers resembling these **2** *informal or facetious* any trousers, esp baggy ones

pantechnicon (pæn'tɛknɪkən) *n Brit* **1** a large van, esp one used for furniture removals **2** a warehouse where furniture is stored [C19: from PAN- + Greek *tekhnikon* relating to the arts, from *tekhnē* art; originally the name of a London bazaar, the building later being used as a furniture warehouse]

Pantelleria (*Italian* pantelle'ri:a) *n* an Italian island in the Mediterranean, between Sicily and Tunisia: of volcanic origin; used by the Romans as a place of banishment. Pop: 7679 (2004 est.). Area: 83 sq km (32 sq miles)

pantheism ('pænθɪ,ɪzəm) *n* **1** the doctrine that God is the transcendent reality of which man, nature, and the material universe are manifestations **2** any doctrine that regards God as identical with the material universe or the forces of nature **3** readiness to worship all or a large number of gods >'**pantheist** *n* >,**panthe'istic**, ,**panthe'istical** *adj* >,**panthe'istically** *adv*

pantheon (pæn'θi:ən, 'pænθɪən) *n* **1** (esp in ancient Greece or Rome) a temple to all the gods **2** all the gods collectively of a religion **3** a monument or building commemorating a nation's dead heroes [C14: via Latin from Greek *Pantheion*, from PAN- + -*theios* divine, from *theos* god]

Pantheon (pæn'θi:ən, 'pænθɪən) *n* a circular temple in Rome dedicated to all the gods, built by Agrippa in 27 BC, rebuilt by Hadrian 120–24 AD, and used since 609 AD as a Christian church

panther ('pænθə) *n, pl* -**thers** *or* -**ther** **1** another name for the leopard, esp the black variety, which is known as the **black panther** **2** *US & Canadian* any of various related animals, esp the puma [C14: from Old French *pantère*, from Latin *panthēra*, from Greek *panthēr*; perhaps related to Sanskrit *pundarīka* tiger]

panties ('pæntɪz) *pl n* a pair of women's or children's underpants

pantihose ('pæntɪ,həυz) *pl n* chiefly *US* a variant spelling of **pantyhose**

pantile ('pæn,taɪl) *n* a roofing tile, with an S-shaped cross section, laid so that the downward curve of one tile overlaps the upward curve of the adjoining tile [C17: from PAN[1] + TILE]

pantisocracy (,pæntɪ'sɒkrəsɪ) *n* a community, social group, etc, in which all have rule and everyone is equal [C18: coined by Robert Southey (1774–1843), English poet): from Greek, from PANTO- + *isos* equal + -CRACY]

panto ('pæntəυ) *n, pl* -**tos** *Brit informal* short for **pantomime** (sense 1)

panto- *or before a vowel* **pant-** *combining form* all: *pantisocracy; pantofle; pantograph; pantomime* [from Greek *pant-, pas*]

pantograph ('pæntə,grɑːf) *n* **1** an instrument consisting of pivoted levers for copying drawings, maps, etc, to any desired scale **2** a sliding type of current collector, esp a diamond-shaped frame mounted on a train roof in contact with an overhead wire **3** a device consisting of a parallelogram of jointed rods used to suspend a studio lamp so that its height can be adjusted >**pantographic** (,pæntə'græfɪk) *adj*

pantomime ('pæntə,maɪm) *n* **1** (in Britain) a kind of play performed at Christmas time characterized by farce, music, lavish sets, stock roles, and topical jokes **2** a theatrical entertainment in which words are replaced by gestures and bodily actions **3** action without words as a means of expression **4** *informal, chiefly Brit* a confused or farcical situation ▷ *vb* **5** another word for **mime** (sense 5) [C17: via Latin from Greek *pantomīmos*; see PANTO-, MIME] >**pantomimic** (,pæntə'mɪmɪk) *adj*

pantothenic acid (,pæntə'θɛnɪk) *n* an oily acid that is a vitamin of the B complex: occurs widely in animal and vegetable foods and is essential for cell growth. Formula: $C_9H_{17}NO_5$ [C20: from Greek *pantothen* from every side]

pantry ('pæntrɪ) *n, pl* -**tries** a small room or cupboard in which provisions, cooking utensils, etc, are kept; larder

[C13: via Anglo-Norman, from Old French *paneterie* store for bread, ultimately from Latin *pānis* bread]

pants (pænts) *pl n* **1** *Brit* an undergarment reaching from the waist to the thighs or knees **2** *Also called:* **trousers** a garment shaped to cover the body from the waist to the ankles or knees with separate tube-shaped sections for both legs **3 scare the pants off** *informal* to scare extremely ▷ *adj* **4** *Brit slang* inferior [C19: shortened from *pantaloons*; see PANTALOON]

panty girdle ('pæntɪ) *n* a foundation garment with a crotch, often of lighter material than a girdle

pantyhose ('pæntɪ,həυz) *n US, Canadian & NZ* a one-piece clinging garment covering the body from the waist to the feet, worn by women in place of stockings. Also called: **pantihose**, (*esp Brit*) **tights** [C20: from PANTIES + HOSE[2]]

Panufnik (pæ'nu:fnɪk) *n* Sir **Andrzej** (ændrei). 1914–91, British composer and conductor, born in Poland. His works include nine symphonies, the cantata *Winter Solstice* (1972), Polish folk-song settings, and ballet music

panzer ('pænzə; *German* 'pantsər) *n* **1** (*modifier*) of, relating to, or characteristic of the fast mechanized armoured units employed by the German army in World War II: *a panzer attack* **2** a vehicle belonging to a panzer unit, esp a tank **3** (*plural*) armoured troops [C20: from German, from Middle High German, from Old French *panciere* coat of mail, from Latin *pantex* PAUNCH]

panzerotto (,pæntsə'rɒtəυ) *n Canadian* a baked turnover with a folded, sealed pocket containing tomato, cheese, and sometimes other fillings [C20: of Italian origin, from *panza* belly]

Pão de Açúcar (p[ẽ]ʃ[ə]un di a'sukar) *n* the Portuguese name for the: **Sugar Loaf Mountain**

Paolozzi (paυ'lɒtsɪ) *n* Sir **Eduardo** (**Luigi**). 1924–2005, British sculptor and designer, noted esp for his semiabstract metal figures

Paoting *or* **Pao-ting** ('paυ'tɪŋ) *n* a variant transliteration of the Chinese name for **Baoding**

Paotow ('paυ'taυ) *n* a variant transliteration of the Chinese name for **Baotou**

pap[1] (pæp) *n* **1** any soft or semiliquid food, such as bread softened with milk, esp for babies or invalids; mash **2** *South African* porridge made from maize **3** worthless or oversimplified ideas; drivel [C15: from Middle Low German *pappe*, via Medieval Latin *pappāre* to eat; compare Dutch *pap*, Italian *pappa*]

pap[2] (pæp) *n* **1** *Scot & northern English dialect* a nipple or teat **2** something resembling a breast or nipple, such as (formerly) one of a pair of rounded hilltops [C12: of Scandinavian origin, imitative of a sucking sound; compare Latin *papilla* nipple, Sanskrit *pippalaka*]

pap[3] (pæp) *vb* -**ps**, -**ping**, -**ped** (*tr*) (of the paparazzi) to follow and photograph (a famous person) [C20: from PAPARAZZO]

papa (pə'pɑː) *n old-fashioned* an informal word for **father** (sense 1) [C17: from French, a children's word for father; compare Late Latin *pāpa*, Greek *pappa*]

papacy ('peɪpəsɪ) *n, pl* -**cies** **1** the office or term of office of a pope **2** the system of government in the Roman Catholic Church that has the pope as its head [C14: from Medieval Latin *pāpātia*, from *pāpa* POPE[1]]

Papadopoulos (,pæpə'dɒpələs; *Greek* papa'ðopulɔs) *n* **1 Georgios**. 1919–99, Greek army officer and statesman; prime minister (1967–73) and president (1973) in Greece's military government **2 Tassos Nikolaou**. born 1934, Cypriot politician: president of Cyprus from 2003

papain (pə'peɪɪn, -'paɪɪn) *n* a proteolytic enzyme occurring in the unripe fruit of the papaya tree, *Carica papaya*: used as a meat tenderizer and in medicine as an aid to protein digestion [C19: from PAPAYA]

papal ('peɪp[ə]l) *adj* of or relating to the pope or the papacy >'**papally** *adv*

Papal States *pl n* the temporal domain of the popes in central Italy from 756 AD until the unification of Italy in 1870. Also called: **States of the Church**

Papandreou (,pæpən'dreɪu:; *Greek* papan'ðreu) *n* **Andreas** (**George**) (an'dreas). 1919–96, Greek economist and socialist politician; prime minister (1981–89; 1993–96)

paparazzo (ˌpæpəˈrætsəʊ) *n, pl* -razzi (-ˈrætsiː) a freelance photographer who specializes in candid camera shots of famous people and often invades their privacy to obtain such photographs [c20: from Italian]

papaveraceous (pəˌpeɪvəˈreɪʃəs) *adj* of, relating to, or belonging to the *Papaveraceae*, a family of plants having large showy flowers and a cylindrical seed capsule with pores beneath the lid: includes the poppies and greater celandine [c19: from New Latin, from Latin *papāver* POPPY]

papaverine (pəˈpeɪvəˌriːn, -rɪn) *n* a white crystalline almost insoluble alkaloid found in opium and used as an antispasmodic to treat coronary spasms and certain types of colic. Formula: $C_{20}H_{21}NO_4$ [c19: from Latin *papāver* POPPY]

papaw (pəˈpɔː) *or* **pawpaw** *n* **1** another name for **papaya 2** Also called: **custard apple a** a bush or small tree, *Asimina triloba*, of central North America, having small fleshy edible fruit: family *Annonaceae* **b** the fruit of this tree [c16: from Spanish PAPAYA]

papaya (pəˈpaɪə) *n* **1** a Caribbean evergreen tree, *Carica papaya*, with a crown of large dissected leaves and large green hanging fruit: family *Caricaceae* **2** the fruit of this tree, having a yellow sweet edible pulp and small black seeds ▷ Also called: papaw, pawpaw [c15 *papaye*, from Spanish *papaya*, from an American Indian language; compare Carib *ababai*]

Papeete (ˌpɑːpɪˈiːtɪ) *n* the capital of French Polynesia, on the NW coast of Tahiti: one of the largest towns in the S Pacific. Pop: 130 000 (2005 est)

Papen (German ˈpɑːpən) *n* **Franz von** (frants fɔn). 1879–1969, German statesman; chancellor (1932) and vice chancellor (1933–34) under Hitler, whom he was instrumental in bringing to power

paper (ˈpeɪpə) *n* **1** a substance made from cellulose fibres derived from rags, wood, etc, often with other additives, and formed into flat thin sheets suitable for writing on, decorating walls, wrapping, etc **2** a single piece of such material, esp if written or printed on **3** (*usually plural*) documents for establishing the identity of the bearer; credentials **4** Also called: ship's papers (*plural*) official documents relating to the ownership, cargo, etc, of a ship **5** (*plural*) collected diaries, letters, etc **6** See **wallpaper 7** *government* See **white paper, green paper 8** a lecture or short published treatise on a specific subject **9** a short essay, as by a student **10 a** a set of written examination questions **b** the student's answers **11** *commerce* See **commercial paper 12** *theatre slang* a free ticket **13** on paper in theory, as opposed to fact ▷ *adj* **14** made of paper: *paper cups do not last long* **15** thin like paper: *paper walls* **16** (*prenominal*) existing only as recorded on paper but not yet in practice: *paper profits; paper expenditure* **17** taking place in writing: *paper battles* ▷ *vb* **18** to cover (walls) with wallpaper **19** (*tr*) to cover or furnish with paper **20** (*tr*) *theatre slang* to fill (a performance) by giving away free tickets (esp in the phrase **paper the house**) ▷ See also **paper over** [c14: from Latin PAPYRUS] > ˈpaperer *n* > ˈpapery *adj* > ˈpaperiness *n*

paperback (ˈpeɪpəˌbæk) *n* **1** a book or edition with covers made of flexible card, sold relatively cheaply. See **hardback**. Also called: paperbound *adj* **soft-cover 2** of or denoting a paperback or publication of paperbacks ▷ *vb* (*tr*) **3** to publish in paperback > ˈpaperˌbacker *n*

paperbark (ˈpeɪpəˌbɑːk) *n* **1** any of several Australian myrtaceous trees of the genus *Melaleuca*, esp *M. quinquenervia*, of swampy regions, having spear-shaped leaves and papery bark that can be peeled off in thin layers **2** the papery bark of any of these trees

paperboy (ˈpeɪpəˌbɔɪ) *n* a boy employed to deliver newspapers, magazines, etc > ˈpaperˌgirl *fem n*

paper chase *n* a former type of cross-country run in which a runner laid a trail of paper for others to follow

paperclip (ˈpeɪpəˌklɪp) *n* a clip for holding sheets of paper together, esp one made of bent wire

paper-cutter *n* a machine for cutting paper, usually a blade mounted over a table on which paper can be aligned

paperhanger (ˈpeɪpəˌhæŋə) *n* a person who hangs wallpaper as an occupation

paperknife (ˈpeɪpəˌnaɪf) *n, pl* -knives a knife with a comparatively blunt blade, esp one of wood, bone, etc, for opening sealed envelopes

paper money *n* paper currency issued by the government or the central bank as legal tender and which circulates as a substitute for specie

paper mulberry *n* a small moraceous E Asian tree, *Broussonetia papyrifera*, the inner bark of which was formerly used for making paper in Japan. See also **tapa**

paper nautilus *n* any cephalopod mollusc of the genus *Argonauta*, esp *A. argo*, of warm and tropical seas, having a papery external spiral shell: order *Octopoda* (octopods). Also called: argonaut

paper over *vb* (*tr, adverb*) to conceal (something controversial or unpleasant)

paper tape *n* a strip of paper for recording information in the form of rows of either six or eight holes, some or all of which are punched to produce a combination used as a discrete code symbol, formerly used in computers, telex machines, etc. US equivalent: perforated tape

paper tiger *n* a nation, institution, etc, that appears powerful but is in fact weak or insignificant [c20: translation of a Chinese phrase first applied to the US]

paperweight (ˈpeɪpəˌweɪt) *n* a small heavy object placed on loose papers to prevent them from scattering

paperwork (ˈpeɪpəˌwɜːk) *n* clerical work, such as the completion of forms or the writing of reports or letters

Paphian (ˈpeɪfɪən) *adj* **1** of or relating to Paphos **2** of or relating to Aphrodite **3** *literary* of sexual love

Paphlagonia (ˌpæfləˈɡəʊnɪə) *n* an ancient country and Roman province in N Asia Minor, on the Black Sea

Paphos[1] (ˈpafɒs) *n* a town in SW Cyprus, near the sites of two ancient cities: famous as the centre of Aphrodite worship and traditionally the place at which she landed after her birth among the waves. Pop: 53 060 (2001)

Paphos[2] (ˈpeɪfɒs) *or* **Paphus** (ˈpeɪfəs) *n Greek myth* the son of Pygmalion and Galatea, who succeeded his father on the throne of Cyprus

papier-mâché (ˌpæpjeɪˈmæʃeɪ; *French* papjemaʃe) *n* **1** a hard strong substance suitable for painting on, made of paper pulp or layers of paper mixed with paste, size, etc, and moulded when moist ▷ *adj* **2** made of papier-mâché [c18: from French, literally: chewed paper]

papilla (pəˈpɪlə) *n, pl* -lae (-liː) **1** the small projection of tissue at the base of a hair, tooth, or feather **2** any other similar protuberance [c18: from Latin: nipple; related to Latin *papula* pimple] > paˈpillary *or* ˈpapillate *adj*

papilloma (ˌpæpɪˈləʊmə) *n, pl* -mata (-mətə) *or* -mas *pathol* a benign tumour derived from epithelial tissue and forming a rounded or lobulated mass [c19: from PAPILLA + -OMA]

papillon (ˈpæpɪˌlɒn) *n* a breed of toy spaniel with large ears [French: butterfly, from Latin *pāpiliō*]

papillote (ˈpæpɪˌləʊt) *n* **1** a paper frill around cutlets, etc **2** en papillote (*French* ã papijɔt) (of food) cooked in oiled greaseproof paper or foil [c18: from French PAPILLON]

papist (ˈpeɪpɪst) *n, adj* (*often capital*) *usually disparaging* another term for **Roman Catholic** [c16: from French *papiste*, from Church Latin *pāpa* POPE[1]] > paˈpistical *or* paˈpistic *adj* > ˈpapistry *n*

papoose *or* **pappoose** (pəˈpuːs) *n* **1** an American Indian baby or child **2** a pouchlike bag used for carrying a baby, worn on the back [c17: from Algonquian *papoos*]

pappus (ˈpæpəs) *n, pl* pappi (ˈpæpaɪ) a ring of fine feathery hairs surrounding the fruit in composite plants, such as the thistle; aids dispersal of the fruits by the wind [c18: via New Latin, from Greek *pappos* grandfather, old man, old man's beard, hence: pappus, down] > ˈpappose *or* ˈpappous *adj*

Pappus of Alexandria (ˈpæpəs) *n* 3rd century BC, Greek mathematician, whose eight-volume *Synagoge* is a valuable source of information about Greek mathematics

paprika (ˈpæprɪkə, pæˈpriː-) *n* **1** a mild powdered seasoning made from a sweet variety of red pepper **2** the fruit or plant from which this seasoning is obtained [c19: via Hungarian from Serbian, from *papar* PEPPER]

Pap test *or* **Pap smear** (pæp) *n med* **1** another name for **cervical smear 2** a similar test for precancerous cells in other organs ▷ Also called: **Papanicolaou smear** [C20: named after George *Papanicolaou* (1883–1962), US anatomist, who devised it]

Papua ('pæpjʊə) n **1 Territory of Papua** a former territory of Australia, consisting of SE New Guinea and adjacent islands: now part of Papua New Guinea **2 Gulf of Papua** an inlet of the Coral Sea in the SE coast of New Guinea > **'Papuan** adj, n

Papua New Guinea n a country in the SW Pacific; consists of the E half of New Guinea, the Bismarck Archipelago, the W Solomon Islands, Trobriand Islands, D'Entrecasteaux Islands, Woodlark Island, and the Louisiade Archipelago; administered by Australia from 1949 until 1975, when it became an independent member of the Commonwealth. Official language: English; Tok Pisin (English Creole) and Motu are widely spoken. Religion: Christian majority. Currency: kina. Capital: Port Moresby. Pop: 5 836 000 (2004 est). Area: 461 693 sq km (178 260 sq miles)

papule ('pæpju:l) *or* **papula** ('pæpjʊlə) n, *pl* **-ules** *or* **-ulae** (-jʊ‚li:) *pathol* a small solid usually round elevation of the skin [C19: from Latin *papula* pustule, pimple] > **'papular** adj

papyrology (‚pæpɪ'rɒlədʒɪ) n the study of ancient papyri > ‚papy'rologist n

papyrus (pə'paɪrəs) n, *pl* **-ri** (-raɪ) *or* **-ruses 1** a tall aquatic cyperaceous plant, *Cyperus papyrus*, of S Europe and N and central Africa with small green-stalked flowers arranged like umbrella spokes around the stem top **2** a kind of paper made from the stem pith of this plant, used by the ancient Egyptians, Greeks, and Romans **3** an ancient document written on this paper [C14: via Latin from Greek *papūros* reed used in making paper]

par (pɑː) n **1** an accepted level or standard, such as an average (esp in the phrase **up to par**) **2** a state of equality (esp in the phrase **on a par with**) **3** *finance* the established value of the unit of one national currency in terms of the unit of another where both are based on the same metal standard **4** *commerce* **a** See **par value b** the condition of equality between the current market value of a share, bond, etc, and its face value (the **nominal par**). This equality is indicated by **at par**, while **above** (or **below**) **par** indicates that the market value is above (or below) face value **5** *golf* an estimated standard score for a hole or course that a good player should make: *par for the course was 72* **6 below par** *or* **under par** not feeling or performing as well as normal **7 par for the course** an expected or normal occurrence or situation ▷ *adj* **8** average or normal **9** (*usually prenominal*) *commerce* of or relating to par: *par value* [C17: from Latin *pār* equal, on a level; see PEER¹]

par. *abbreviation* **1** paragraph **2** parenthesis **3** parish

Par. *abbreviation* Paraguay

para ('pærə) n *informal* **1 a** a soldier in an airborne unit **b** an airborne unit **2** a paragraph

Pará (Portuguese pa'ra) n **1** a state of N Brazil, on the Atlantic: mostly dense tropical rainforest Capital: Belém. Pop: 6 453 683 (2002). Area: 1 248 042 sq km (474 896 sq miles) **2** another name for **Belém 3** an estuary in N Brazil into which flow the Tocantins River and a branch of the Amazon. Length: about 320 km (200 miles)

para-¹ *or before a vowel* **par-** *prefix* **1** beside; near: *parameter; parathyroid* **2** beyond: *parapsychology* **3** resembling: *paramnesia* **4** defective; abnormal: *paraesthesia* **5** subsidiary to: *paraphysis* **6** (*usually in italics*) denoting that an organic compound contains a benzene ring with substituents attached to atoms that are directly opposite across the ring (the 1,4- positions) **7** denoting an isomer, polymer, or compound related to a specified compound: *paraldehyde; paracasein* **8** denoting the form of a diatomic substance in which the spins of the two constituent atoms are antiparallel: *parahydrogen* [from Greek *para* (prep) alongside, beyond]

para-² *combining form* indicating an object that acts as a protection against something: *parachute; parasol* [via French from Italian *para-*, from *parare* to defend, shield against, ultimately from Latin *parāre* to prepare]

para-aminobenzoic acid n *biochem* an acid present in yeast and liver: used in the manufacture of dyes and pharmaceuticals. Formula: $C_6H_4(NH_2)COOH$

parabasis (pə'ræbəsɪs) n, *pl* **-ses** (-‚si:z) (in classical Greek comedy) an address from the chorus to the audience [C19: from Greek, from *parabanein* to step forward]

paraben ('pærə‚ben) n any ester of parahydroxybenzoic acid, some of which are used in cosmetics and pharmaceuticals and have been found in breast cancer tumours

parabiosis (‚pærəbaɪ'əʊsɪs) n **1** the natural union of two individuals, such as Siamese twins, so that they share a common circulation of the blood **2** a similar union induced for experimental or therapeutic purposes [C20: from PARA-¹ + Greek *biōsis* manner of life, from *bios* life] > **parabiotic** (‚pærəbaɪ'ɒtɪk) adj

parable ('pærəb°l) n **1** a short story that uses familiar events to illustrate a religious or ethical point **2** any of the stories of this kind told by Jesus Christ [C14: from Old French *parabole*, from Latin *parabola* comparison, from Greek *parabolē* analogy, from *paraballein* to throw alongside, from PARA-¹ + *ballein* to throw]

parabola (pə'ræbələ) n a conic section formed by the intersection of a cone by a plane parallel to its side. Standard equation: $y^2 = 4ax$, where $2a$ is the distance between focus and directrix [C16: via New Latin from Greek *parabolē* a setting alongside; see PARABLE]

parabolic¹ (‚pærə'bɒlɪk) adj **1** of, relating to, or shaped like a parabola **2** shaped like a paraboloid: *a parabolic mirror*

parabolic² (‚pærə'bɒlɪk) *or* **parabolical** adj of or resembling a parable > ‚para'bolically adv

parabolic aerial n a formal name for **dish aerial**

paraboloid (pə'ræbə‚lɔɪd) n a geometric surface whose sections parallel to two coordinate planes are parabolic and whose sections parallel to the third plane are either elliptical or hyperbolic. Equations $x^2/a^2 \pm y^2/b^2 = 2cz$ > pa‚rabo'loidal adj

Paracelsus (‚pærə'selsəs) n **Philippus Aureolus** ('fɪlɪpəs ‚ɔːrɪ'əʊlə), real name *Theophrastus Bombastus von Hohenheim*. 1493–1541, Swiss physician and alchemist, who pioneered the use of specific treatment, based on observation and experience, to remedy particular diseases

paracetamol (‚pærə'si:tə‚mɒl, -'setə-) n a mild analgesic and antipyretic drug used as an alternative to aspirin [C20: from *para-acetamidophenol*]

parachronism (pə'rækrə‚nɪzəm) n an error in dating, esp by giving too late a date. See **prochronism** [C17: from PARA-¹ + -*chronism*, as in ANACHRONISM]

parachute ('pærə‚ʃuːt) n **1** a device used to retard the fall of a man or object from an aircraft, consisting of a large fabric canopy connected to a harness ▷ *vb* **2** (of troops, supplies, etc) to land or cause to land by parachute from an aircraft [C18: from French, from PARA-² + *chute* fall] > 'para‚chutist n

Paraclete ('pærə‚kli:t) n *Christianity* the Holy Ghost as comforter or advocate [C15: via Old French from Church Latin *Paraclētus*, from Late Greek *Paraklētos* advocate, from Greek *parakalein* to summon as a helper, from PARA-¹ + *kalein* to call]

parade (pə'reɪd) n **1** an ordered, esp ceremonial, march, assembly, or procession, as of troops being reviewed: *on parade* **2** Also called: **parade ground** a place where military formations regularly assemble **3** a visible show or display: *to make a parade of one's grief* **4** a public promenade or street of shops **5** a successive display of things or people **6** the interior area of a fortification **7** a parry in fencing **8 rain on someone's parade** to hinder someone's enjoyment; upset someone's plans **9 on parade a** on display **b** showing oneself off ▷ *vb* **10** (when *intr*, often foll by *through* or *along*) to walk or march, esp in a procession (through): *to parade the streets* **11** (*tr*) to exhibit or flaunt: *he was parading his medals* **12** (*tr*) to cause to assemble in formation, as for a military parade **13** (*intr*) to walk about in a public place [C17: from French: a making ready, a setting out, a boasting display; compare Italian *parata*, Spanish *parada*, all ultimately from Latin *parāre* to prepare] > pa'**rader** *n*

paradiddle ('pærə,dɪd°l) *n* a group of four drum beats produced by using alternate sticks in the pattern right-left-right-right or left-right-left-left [C20: of imitative origin]

paradigm ('pærə,daɪm) *n* **1** *grammar* the set of all the inflected forms of a word or a systematic arrangement displaying these forms **2** a pattern or model **3** (in the philosophy of science) a very general conception of the nature of scientific endeavour within which a given enquiry is undertaken [C15: via French and Latin from Greek *paradeigma* pattern, from *paradeiknunai* to compare, from PARA-¹ + *deiknunai* to show] > **paradigmatic** (,pærədɪg'mætɪk) *adj*

paradigm shift *n* a radical change in underlying beliefs or theory [C20: coined by T.S. Kuhn (1922–96), US philosopher of science]

paradisal (,pærə'daɪs°l), **paradisiacal** (,pærədɪ'saɪək°l) *or* **paradisiac** (,pærə'dɪsɪ,æk) *adj* of, relating to, or resembling paradise

paradise ('pærə,daɪs) *n* **1** heaven as the ultimate abode or state of the righteous **2** *Islam* the sensual garden of delights that the Koran promises the faithful after death **3** Also called: **limbo** (according to some theologians) the intermediate abode or state of the just prior to the Resurrection of Jesus, as in Luke 23:43 **4** any place or condition that fulfils all one's desires or aspirations **5** a park in which foreign animals are kept [Old English, from Church Latin *paradīsus*, from Greek *paradeisos* garden, of Persian origin; compare Avestan *pairidaēza* enclosed area, from *pairi-* around + *daēza* wall]

paradise duck *n* a large duck, *Casarca variegata*, of New Zealand, having a brightly coloured plumage

paradox ('pærə,dɒks) *n* **1** a seemingly absurd or self-contradictory statement that is or may be true: *religious truths are often expressed in paradox* **2** a self-contradictory proposition, such as *I always tell lies* **3** a person or thing exhibiting apparently contradictory characteristics **4** an opinion that conflicts with common belief [C16: from Late Latin *paradoxum*, from Greek *paradoxos* opposed to existing notions, from PARA-¹ + *doxa* opinion] > ,para'**doxical** *adj* > ,para'**doxically** *adv*

paradoxical sleep *n* *physiol* sleep that appears to be deep but that is characterized by a brain wave pattern similar to that of wakefulness, rapid eye movements, and heavier breathing

paraffin ('pærəfɪn) *or less commonly* **paraffine** ('pærə,fi:n) *n* **1** Also called: **paraffin oil**, (*esp US and Canadian*) **kerosene** a liquid mixture consisting mainly of alkane hydrocarbons with boiling points in the range 150°–300°C, used as an aircraft fuel, in domestic heaters, and as a solvent **2** another name for **alkane 3** See **paraffin wax 4** See **liquid paraffin** ▷ *vb* (*tr*) **5** to treat with paraffin or paraffin wax [C19: from German, from Latin *parum* too little + *affinis* adjacent; so called from its chemical inertia]

paraffin wax *n* a white insoluble odourless waxlike solid consisting mainly of alkane hydrocarbons with melting points in the range 50°–60°C, used in candles, waterproof paper, and as a sealing agent. Also called: **paraffin**

paragliding ('pærə,glaɪdɪŋ) *n* the sport of cross-country gliding using a specially designed parachute shaped like flexible wings.

paragon ('pærəgən) *n* a model of excellence; pattern: *a paragon of virtue* [C16: via French from Old Italian *paragone* comparison, from Medieval Greek *parakonē* whetstone, from Greek *parakonan* to sharpen against, from PARA-¹ + *akonan* to sharpen, from *akonē* whetstone]

paragraph ('pærə,grɑːf, -,græf) *n* **1** (in a piece of writing) one of a series of subsections each usually devoted to one idea and each usually marked by the beginning of a new line, indentation, increased interlinear space, etc **2** *printing* the character ¶, used as a reference mark or to indicate the beginning of a new paragraph **3** a short article in a newspaper ▷ *vb* (*tr*) **4** to form into paragraphs **5** to express or report in a paragraph [C16: from Medieval Latin *paragraphus*, from Greek *paragraphos* line drawing attention to part of a text, from *paragraphein*

to write beside, from PARA-¹ + *graphein* to write] > **paragraphic** (,pærə'græfɪk) *or* ,para'**graphical** *adj* > ,para'**graphically** *adv*

paragraphia (,pærə'grɑːfɪə) *n* *psychiatry* the habitual writing of a different word or letter from the one intended, often the result of a mental disorder or brain injury [C20: from New Latin; see PARA-¹, -GRAPH]

Paraguay ('pærə,gwaɪ) *n* **1** an inland republic in South America: colonized by the Spanish from 1537, gaining independence in 1811; lost 142 500 sq km (55 000 sq miles) of territory and over half its population after its defeat in the war against Argentina, Brazil, and Uruguay (1865–70). It is divided by the Paraguay River into a sparsely inhabited semiarid region (Chaco) in the west, and a central region of wooded hills, tropical forests, and rich grasslands, rising to the Paraná plateau in the east. Official languages: Spanish and Guarani. Religion: Roman Catholic majority. Currency: guarani. Capital: Asunción. Pop: 6 018 000 (2004 est). Area: 406 750 sq km (157 047 sq miles) **2** a river in South America flowing south through Brazil and Paraguay to the Paraná River. Length: about 2400 km (1500 miles) > ,**Para'guayan** *adj, n*

Paraguay tea *n* another name for **maté**

parahydrogen (,pærə'haɪdrədʒən) *n* *chem* the form of molecular hydrogen (constituting about 25 per cent of the total at normal temperatures) in which the nuclei of the two atoms in each molecule spin in opposite directions

Paraíba (Portuguese para'iba) *n* **1** a state of NE Brazil, on the Atlantic: consists of a coastal strip, with hills and plains inland; irrigated agriculture. Capital: João Pessoa. Pop: 3 494 893 (2002). Area: 56 371 sq km (21 765 sq miles) **2** Also called: **Paraíba do Sul** ('du: sul) a river in SE Brazil, flowing southwest and then northeast to the Atlantic near Campos. Length: 1060 km (660 miles) **3** Also called: **Paraíba do Norte** ('du: 'nɔrtə) a river in NE Brazil, in Paraíba state, flowing northwest and east to the Atlantic. Length: 386 km (240 miles) **4** the former name (until 1930) of **João Pessoa**

parakeet *or* **parrakeet** ('pærə,kiːt) *n* any of numerous small usually brightly coloured long-tailed parrots, such as *Psittacula krameri* (**ring-necked parakeet**), of Africa [C16: from Spanish *periquito* and Old French *paroquet* parrot, of uncertain origin]

paraldehyde (pə'rældɪ,haɪd) *n* a colourless liquid substance that is a cyclic trimer of acetaldehyde: used in making dyestuffs and as a hypnotic and anticonvulsant drug. Formula: $(C_2H_4O)_3$

paralipsis (,pærə'lɪpsɪs) *or* **paraleipsis** (,pærə'laɪpsɪs) *n*, *pl* **-ses** (-siːz) a rhetorical device in which an idea is emphasized by the pretence that it is too obvious to discuss, as in *there are many drawbacks to your plan, not to mention the cost* [C16: via Late Latin from Greek: neglect, from *paraleipein* to leave aside, from PARA-¹ + *leipein* to leave]

parallax ('pærə,læks) *n* **1** an apparent change in the position of an object resulting from a change in position of the observer **2** *astronomy* the angle subtended at a celestial body, esp a star, by the radius of the earth's orbit. **Annual** or **heliocentric parallax** is the apparent displacement of a nearby star resulting from its observation from the earth. **Diurnal** or **geocentric parallax** results from the observation of a planet, the sun, or the moon from the surface of the earth [C17: via French from New Latin *parallaxis*, from Greek: change, from *parallassein* to change, from PARA-¹ + *allassein* to alter] > **parallactic** (,pærə'læktɪk) *adj*

parallel ('pærə,lɛl) *adj* (when *postpositive*, usually foll by *to*) **1** separated by an equal distance at every point; never touching or intersecting: *parallel walls* **2** corresponding; similar: *parallel situations* **3** *music* Also called: **consecutive** (of two or more parts or melodies) moving in similar motion but keeping the same interval apart throughout: *parallel fifths* **b** denoting successive chords in which the individual notes move in parallel motion **4** *grammar* denoting syntactic constructions in which the constituents of one construction correspond to those of the other **5** *computing* operating on several items of

information, instructions, etc, simultaneously ▷ *n*
6 *maths* one of a set of parallel lines, planes, etc **7** an
exact likeness **8** a comparison **9** Also called: **parallel of
latitude** any of the imaginary lines around the earth
parallel to the equator, designated by degrees of latitude
ranging from 0° at the equator to 90° at the poles **10** (*as
modifier*): *a parallel circuit*. See **series** (sense 6) ▷ *vb* **-lels,
-leling, -leled** (*tr*) **11** to make parallel **12** to supply a
parallel to **13** to be a parallel to or correspond with: *your
experience parallels mine* [c16: via French and Latin from
Greek *parallēlos* alongside one another, from PARA-¹ +
allēlos one another]

parallel bars *pl n gymnastics* **a** (*functioning as plural*) a pair
of wooden bars on uprights, sometimes at different
heights, for various exercises **b** (*functioning as singular*) an
event in a gymnastic competition in which competitors
exercise on such bars

parallelepiped, parallelopiped (ˌpærəˌlɛləˈpaɪpɛd) *or*
parallelepipedon (ˌpærəˌlɛləˈpaɪpɪdən) *n* a geometric
solid whose six faces are parallelograms [c16: from
Greek *parallēlos* PARALLEL + *epipedon*
plane surface, from EPI- + *pedon* ground]

parallel importing *n* the importing of certain goods,
esp pharmaceutical drugs, by dealers who undersell
local manufacturers

paralleling (ˈpærəˌlɛlɪŋ) *n* a form of trading in which
companies buy highly priced goods in a market in
which the prices are low in order to be able to sell them
in a market in which the prices are higher

parallelism (ˈpærəlɛˌlɪzəm) *n* **1** the state of being parallel
2 *grammar* the repetition of a syntactic construction in
successive sentences for rhetorical effect

parallelogram (ˌpærəˈlɛləˌgræm) *n* a quadrilateral
whose opposite sides are parallel and equal in length.
See also **rhombus, rectangle, trapezium, trapezoid** [c16:
via French from Late Latin, from Greek *parallēlogrammon*,
from *parallēlos* PARALLEL + *grammē* line, related to *graphein*
to write]

parallelogram rule *n maths, physics* a rule for finding
the resultant of two vectors by constructing a
parallelogram with two adjacent sides representing the
magnitudes and directions of the vectors, the diagonal
through the point of intersection of the vectors
representing their resultant

parallel port *n computing* (on a computer) a socket that
can be used for connecting devices that send and receive
data at more than one bit at a time; often used for
connecting printers

parallel processing *n* the performance by a computer
system of two or more simultaneous operations

parallel ruler *n engineering* a drawing instrument in
which two parallel edges are connected so that they
remain parallel, although the distance between them
can be varied

paralogism (pəˈræləˌdʒɪzəm) *n* **1** *logic, psychol* an
argument that is unintentionally invalid. See **sophism**
2 any invalid argument or conclusion [c16: via Late Latin
from Greek *paralogismos*, from *paralogizesthai* to argue
fallaciously, from PARA-¹ + *-logizesthai*, ultimately from
logos word] ▷ **paˈralogist** *n*

Paralympian (ˌpærəˈlɪmpɪən) *n* a competitor in the
Paralympics

Paralympics (ˌpærəˈlɪmpɪks) *pl n* **the Paralympics** a
sporting event, modelled on the Olympic Games, held
solely for disabled competitors [c20: PARALLEL +
OLYMPICS]

paralyse *or US* **paralyze** (ˈpærəˌlaɪz) *vb* (*tr*) **1** *pathol* to
affect with paralysis **2** *med* to render (a part of the body)
insensitive to pain, touch, etc, esp by injection of an
anaesthetic **3** to make immobile; transfix [c19: from
French *paralyser*, from *paralysie* PARALYSIS] ▷ ˌparaly'sation
or US ˌparaly'zation *n* ▷ 'para,lyser *or US* 'para,lyzer *n*

paralysis (pəˈrælɪsɪs) *n, pl* **-ses** (-ˌsiːz) **1** *pathol*
a impairment or loss of voluntary muscle function or of
sensation (**sensory paralysis**) in a part or area of the
body, usually caused by a lesion or disorder of the
muscles or the nerves supplying them **b** a disease
characterized by such impairment or loss; palsy
2 cessation or impairment of activity: *paralysis of industry*

by strikes [c16: via Latin from Greek *paralusis*; see PARA-¹,
-LYSIS]

paralytic (ˌpærəˈlɪtɪk) *adj* **1** of, relating to, or of the
nature of paralysis **2** afflicted with or subject to
paralysis **3** *Brit informal* very drunk ▷ *n* **4** a person
afflicted with paralysis

paramagnetism (ˌpærəˈmægnɪˌtɪzəm) *n physics* the
phenomenon exhibited by substances that have a
relative permeability slightly greater than unity and a
positive susceptibility. The effect is due to the
alignment of unpaired spins of electrons in atoms of the
material ▷ **paramagnetic** (ˌpærəmægˈnɛtɪk) *adj*

Paramaribo (ˌpærəˈmærɪˌbəʊ; *Dutch* paːraˈmaːriːboː) *n*
the capital and chief port of Surinam, 27 km (17 miles)
from the Atlantic on the Surinam River: the only large
town in the country. Pop: 261 000 (2005 est)

paramatta *or* **parramatta** (ˌpærəˈmætə) *n* a
lightweight twill-weave fabric of wool formerly with
silk or cotton, used for dresses, etc, now used esp for
rubber-proofed garments [c19: named after *Parramatta*,
New South Wales, Australia, where it was originally
produced]

paramecium (ˌpærəˈmiːsɪəm) *n, pl* **-cia** (-sɪə) any
freshwater protozoan of the genus *Paramecium*, having an
oval body covered with cilia and a ventral ciliated groove
for feeding: phylum *Ciliophora* (ciliates) [c18: New Latin,
from Greek *paramēkēs* elongated, from PARA-¹ + *mēkos*
length]

paramedic (ˌpærəˈmedɪk) *or* **paramedical** *n* **1** a person,
such as a laboratory technician, who supplements the
work of the medical profession **2** a member of an
ambulance crew trained in a number of life-saving
skills, including infusion and cardiac care

parameter (pəˈræmɪtə) *n informal* any constant or
limiting factor: *a designer must work within the parameters of
budget and practicality* [c17: from New Latin; see PARA-¹,
-METER] ▷ **parametric** (ˌpærəˈmɛtrɪk) *or* ˌpara'metrical *adj*

parametric amplifier *n* a type of high-frequency
amplifier in which energy from a pumping oscillator is
transferred to the input signal through a circuit with a
varying parameter, usually a varying reactance

paramilitary (ˌpærəˈmɪlɪtəri, -trɪ) *adj* **1** denoting or
relating to a group of personnel with military structure
functioning either as a civil force or in support of
military forces **2** denoting or relating to a force with
military structure conducting armed operations against
a ruling or occupying power

paramount (ˈpærəˌmaʊnt) *adj* of the greatest
importance or significance; pre-eminent [c16: via
Anglo-Norman from Old French *paramont*, from *par* by +
-*amont* above, from Latin *ad montem* to the mountain]
▷ 'para,mountcy *n* ▷ 'para,mountly *adv*

paramour (ˈpærəˌmʊə) *n* **1** *now usually derogatory* a lover,
esp an adulterous woman **2** an archaic word for **beloved**
(sense 2) [c13: from Old French, literally: through love]

Paraná *n* **1** (paraˈna) a state of S Brazil, on the Atlantic:
consists of a coastal plain and a large rolling plateau
with extensive forests. Capital: Curitiba. Pop: 9 798 006
(2002). Area: 199 555 sq km (77 048 sq miles) **2** (paraˈna) a
city in E Argentina, on the Paraná River opposite Santa
Fe: capital of Argentina (1853–1862). Pop: 305 000 (2005
est) **3** (*Portuguese* paraˈna; *Spanish* paraˈna) a river in
central South America, formed in S Brazil by the
confluence of the Rio Grande and the Paranaíba River
and flowing generally south to the Atlantic through the
Río de la Plata estuary. Length: 2900 km (1800 miles)

parang (ˈpɑːræŋ) *n* a short stout straight-edged knife
used by the Dyaks of Borneo [c19: from Malay]

paranoia (ˌpærəˈnɔɪə) *n* **1** a mental disorder
characterized by any of several types of delusions, in
which the personality otherwise remains relatively
intact **2** *informal* intense fear or suspicion, esp when
unfounded [c19: via New Latin from Greek: frenzy, from
paranoos distraught, from PARA-¹ + *noos* mind] ▷ **paranoiac**
(ˌpærəˈnɔɪɪk) *or* **paranoic** (ˌpærəˈnəʊɪk) *adj, n* ▷ 'para,noid
adj, n

paranormal (ˌpærəˈnɔːməl) *adj* **1** beyond normal
explanation ▷ *n* **2 the paranormal** paranormal
happenings generally

parapente ('pærə,pɛntɪ) n **1** another name for paraskiing **2** the form of parachute used in this sport

parapet ('pærəpɪt, -,pɛt) n **1** a low wall or railing along the edge of a balcony, roof, etc **2** Also called: breastwork a rampart, mound of sandbags, bank, etc, in front of a trench, giving protection from fire from the front [c16: from Italian parapetto, literally: chest-high wall, from PARA-² + petto, from Latin pectus breast]

paraph ('pæræf) n a flourish after a signature, originally to prevent forgery [c14: via French from Medieval Latin paraphus, variant of paragraphus PARAGRAPH]

paraphernalia (,pærəfə'neɪlɪə) pl n (sometimes functioning as singular) **1** miscellaneous articles or equipment **2** law (formerly) articles of personal property given to a married woman by her husband before or during marriage and regarded in law as her possessions over which she has some measure of control [c17: via Medieval Latin from Latin parapherna personal property of a married woman, apart from her dowry, from Greek, from PARA-¹ + phernē dowry, from pherein to carry]

paraphrase ('pærə,freɪz) n **1** an expression of a statement or text in other words, esp in order to clarify ▷ vb **2** to put (something) into other words; restate (something) [c16: via French from Latin paraphrasis, from Greek, from paraphrazein to recount] > paraphrastic (,pærə'fræstɪk) adj

paraplegia (,pærə'pli:dʒə) n pathol paralysis of the lower half of the body, usually as the result of disease or injury of the spine [c17: via New Latin from Greek: a blow on one side, from PARA-¹ + plēssein to strike] > ,para'plegic adj, n

parapraxis (,pærə'præksɪs) n psychoanal a minor error in action, such as slips of the tongue, supposedly the result of repressed impulses [c20: from PARA-¹ + Greek praxis a doing, deed]

parapsychology (,pærəsaɪ'kɒlədʒɪ) n the study of mental phenomena, such as telepathy, which are beyond the scope of normal physical explanation > parapsychological (,pærəsaɪkə'lɒdʒɪk^əl) adj > ,parapsy'chologist n

Paraquat ('pærə,kwɒt) n trademark a yellow extremely poisonous soluble solid used in solution as a weedkiller

parascending ('pærə,sɛndɪŋ) n a sport in which a participant wears a parachute and becomes airborne by being towed by a vehicle into the wind and then descends by parachute

paraselene (,pærəsɪ'li:nɪ) n, pl -nae (-ni:) meteorol a bright image of the moon on a lunar halo. Also called: mock moon [c17: New Latin, from PARA-¹ + Greek selēnē moon]

parasite ('pærə,saɪt) n **1** an animal or plant that lives in or on another (the host) from which it obtains nourishment. The host does not benefit from the association and is often harmed by it **2** a person who habitually lives at the expense of others; sponger [c16: via Latin from Greek parasitos one who lives at another's expense, from PARA-¹ + sitos grain] > parasitic (,pærə'sɪtɪk) or ,para'sitical adj > ,para'sitically adv

parasitize or **parasitise** ('pærəsɪ,taɪz, -saɪ-) vb (tr) **1** to infest or infect with parasites **2** to live on (another organism) as a parasite

parasitoid ('pærəsɪ,tɔːd) n zoology an animal, esp an insect, that is parasitic during the larval stage of its life cycle but becomes free-living when adult

parasitology (,pærəsaɪ'tɒlədʒɪ) n the branch of biology that is concerned with the study of parasites > parasitological (,pærəsaɪt^ə'lɒdʒɪk^əl) adj > ,parasit'ologist n

paraskiing ('pærə,ski:ɪŋ) n the sport of jumping off high mountains wearing skis and a light parachute composed of inflatable paper fabric tubes that form a semirigid wing. Also called: parapente

parasol ('pærə,sɒl) n an umbrella used for protection against the sun; sunshade [c17: via French from Italian parasole, from PARA-² + sole sun, from Latin sōl]

parasuicide (,pærə'su:ɪ,saɪd) n the deliberate infliction of injury on oneself or the taking of a drug overdose as an attempt at suicide which may not be intended to be successful

parasympathetic (,pærə,sɪmpə'θɛtɪk) adj anatomy, physiol of or relating to the division of the autonomic nervous system that acts in opposition to the sympathetic system by slowing the heartbeat, constricting the bronchi of the lungs, stimulating the smooth muscles of the digestive tract, etc. See sympathetic (sense 4)

parasynthesis (,pærə'sɪnθɪsɪs) n formation of words by means of compounding a phrase and adding an affix, as for example light-headed, which is light + head with the affix -ed > parasynthetic (,pærəsɪn'θɛtɪk) adj

parataxis (,pærə'tæksɪs) n the juxtaposition of clauses in a sentence without the use of a conjunction, as for example None of my friends stayed — they all left early [c19: New Latin from Greek, from paratassein, literally: to arrange side by side, from PARA-¹ + tassein to arrange] > paratactic (,pærə'tæktɪk) adj

parathion (,pærə'θaɪɒn) n a slightly water-soluble toxic oil, odourless and colourless when pure, used as an insecticide. Formula: $C_{10}H_{14}NO_5PS$ [c20: from PARA-¹ + THIO- + -ON]

parathyroid gland n any one of the small egg-shaped endocrine glands situated near or embedded within the thyroid gland: they secrete parathyroid hormone

paratroops ('pærə,tru:ps) pl n troops trained and equipped to be dropped by parachute into a battle area. Also called: paratroopers, parachute troops

paratyphoid fever n pathol a disease resembling but less severe than typhoid fever, characterized by chills, headache, nausea, vomiting, and diarrhoea, caused by bacteria of the genus Salmonella

paravane ('pærə,veɪn) n a torpedo-shaped device towed from the bow of a vessel so that the cables will cut the anchors of any moored mines [c20: from PARA-² + VANE]

par avion French (par avjɔ̃) adv by aeroplane: used in labelling paper mail sent by air

parazoan (,pærə'zəʊən) n, pl -zoa (-'zəʊə) any multicellular invertebrate of the group Parazoa, which consists of the sponges (phylum Porifera) [c19: from parazoa, formed on the model of protozoa and metazoa, from PARA-¹ + Greek zōon animal]

parboil ('pɑː,bɔɪl) vb (tr) **1** to boil until partially cooked, often before further cooking **2** to subject to uncomfortable heat [c15: from Old French parboillir, from Late Latin perbullīre to boil thoroughly (see PER-, BOIL²); modern meaning due to confusion of par- with part]

parbuckle ('pɑː,bʌk^əl) n **1** a rope sling for lifting or lowering a heavy cylindrical object, such as a cask or tree trunk ▷ vb **2** (tr) to raise or lower (an object) with such a sling [c17 parbunkel: of uncertain origin]

Parcae ('pɑːsiː) pl n, sing Parca ('pɑːkə) the Parcae the Roman goddesses of fate

parcel ('pɑːs^əl) n **1** something wrapped up; package **2** a group of people or things having some common characteristic **3** a quantity of some commodity offered for sale; lot **4** a distinct portion of land ▷ vb -cels, -celling, -celled or US -cels, -celing, -celed (tr) **5** (often foll by up) to make a parcel of; wrap up **6** (often foll by out) to divide (up) into portions [c14: from Old French parcelle, from Latin particula PARTICLE]

parcener ('pɑːsɪnə) n a person who takes an equal share with another or others; coheir. Also called: coparcener [c13: from Old French parçonier, from parçon distribution, from Latin partītiō a sharing, from partīre to divide]

parch (pɑːtʃ) vb **1** to deprive or be deprived of water; dry up: the sun parches the fields **2** (tr; usually passive) to make very thirsty **3** (tr) to roast (corn, etc) lightly [c14: of obscure origin]

Parcheesi (pɑː'tʃiːzɪ) n trademark a modern board game derived from the ancient game of pachisi

parchment ('pɑːtʃmənt) n **1** the skin of certain animals, such as sheep, treated to form a durable material, as for bookbinding, or (esp formerly) manuscripts **2** a manuscript, bookbinding, etc, made of or resembling this material **3** Also called: parchment paper a type of stiff yellowish paper resembling parchment [c13: from Old French parchemin, via Latin from Greek pergamēnē, from Pergamēnos of Pergamum (where parchment was made); the form of Old French parchemin was influenced by parche leather, from Latin Parthica (pellis) Parthian (leather)] ▷ **'parchmenty** *adj*

pard (pɑːd) *n archaic* a leopard or panther [C13: via Old French from Latin *pardus,* from Greek *pardos*]

pardon ('pɑːd³n) *vb* (*tr*) **1** to excuse or forgive (a person) for (an offence, mistake, etc): *to pardon someone; to pardon a fault* ▷ *n* **2** forgiveness; allowance **3 a** release from punishment for an offence **b** the warrant granting such release **4** a Roman Catholic indulgence ▷ *sentence substitute* **5** Also: **pardon me, I beg your pardon** a sorry; excuse me **b** what did you say? [C13: from Old French, from Medieval Latin *perdōnum,* from *perdōnāre* to forgive freely, from Latin *per* (intensive) + *dōnāre* to grant] ▷ **'pardonable** *adj* ▷ **'pardonably** *adv*

pardoner ('pɑːd³nə) *n* (before the Reformation) a person licensed to sell ecclesiastical indulgences

Pardubice (Czech 'pardubitsɛ) *n* a city in the central Czech Republic, on the Elbe River: 13th-century cathedral; oil refinery. Pop: 88 559 (2007 est)

pare (pɛə) *vb* (*tr*) **1** to peel or cut (the outer layer) from (something) **2** to cut the edges from (the nails); trim **3** to decrease bit by bit [C13: from Old French *parer* to adorn, from Latin *parāre* to make ready] ▷ **'parer** *n*

Paré (French pare) *n* **Ambroise** (ābrwaz). 1510–90, French surgeon. He reintroduced ligature of arteries following amputation instead of cauterization

paregoric (ˌpærə'gɒrɪk) *n* a medicine containing opium, benzoic acid, camphor (English paregoric) or ammonia (Scottish paregoric), and anise oil, formerly widely used to relieve diarrhoea and coughing in children [C17 (meaning: relieving pain): via Late Latin from Greek *parēgorikos* soothing, from *parēgoros* relating to soothing speech, from PARA-¹ (beside, alongside of) + *-ēgor-,* from *agoreuein* to speak in assembly, from *agora* assembly]

pareira (pə'rɛərə) *n* the root of a South American menispermaceous climbing plant, *Chondrodendron tomentosum,* used as a diuretic, tonic, and as a source of curare [C18: from Portuguese *pareira brava,* literally: wild vine]

parenchyma (pə'rɛŋkɪmə) *n* **1** unspecialized plant tissue consisting of simple thin-walled cells with intervening air spaces: constitutes the greater part of fruits, stems, roots, etc **2** animal tissue that constitutes the essential or specialized part of an organ as distinct from the blood vessels, connective tissue, etc, associated with it [C17: via New Latin from Greek *parenkhuma* something poured in beside, from PARA-¹ + *enkhuma* infusion] ▷ **parenchymatous** (ˌpærɛŋ'kɪmətəs) *adj*

parent ('pɛərənt) *n* **1** a father or mother **2** a person acting as a father or mother; guardian **3** *rare* an ancestor **4** a source or cause **5** an organism or organization that has produced one or more organisms or organizations similar to itself **6** *physics, chem* a precursor, such as a nucleus or compound, of a derived entity [C15: via Old French from Latin *parens* parent, from *parere* to bring forth] ▷ **'parenthood** *n* ▷ **pa'rental** *adj*

parentage ('pɛərəntɪdʒ) *n* **1** ancestry **2** derivation from a particular origin

parent company *n* a company that owns more than half the shares of another company

parenteral (pæ'rɛntərəl) *adj med* **1** (esp of the route by which a drug is administered) by means other than through the digestive tract, esp by injection **2** designating a drug to be injected [C20: from PARA-¹ + ENTERO-² + -AL¹]

parenthesis (pə'rɛnθɪsɪs) *n, pl* **-ses** (-ˌsiːz) **1** a phrase, often explanatory or qualifying, inserted into a passage with which it is not grammatically connected, and marked off by brackets, dashes, etc **2** Also called: **bracket** either of a pair of characters, (), used to enclose such a phrase or as a sign of aggregation in mathematical or logical expressions **3** an intervening occurrence; interlude; interval **4 in parenthesis** inserted as a parenthesis [C16: via Late Latin from Greek: something placed in besides, from *parentithenai,* from PARA-¹ + EN-² + *tithenai* to put] ▷ **paren'thetic** (ˌpærən'θɛtɪk) or **,paren'thetical** *adj* ▷ **,paren'thetically** *adv*

parenthesize or **parenthesise** (pə'rɛnθɪˌsaɪz) *vb* (*tr*) **1** to place in parentheses **2** to insert as a parenthesis **3** to intersperse (a speech, writing, etc) with parentheses

parenting ('pɛərəntɪŋ) *n* the care and upbringing of a child

parent teacher association *n* a social group of the parents of children at a school and their teachers formed in order to foster better understanding between them and to organize activities on behalf of the school

parergon (pə'rɛəgɒn) *n, pl* **-ga** (-gə) work that is not one's main employment [C17: from Latin, from Greek, from PARA-¹ + *ergon* work]

paresis (pə'riːsɪs, 'pærɪsɪs) *n, pl* **-ses** (-ˌsiːz) *pathol* incomplete or slight paralysis of motor functions [C17: via New Latin from Greek: a relaxation, from *parienai* to let go, from PARA-¹ + *hienai* to release] ▷ **paretic** (pə'rɛtɪk) *adj*

Pareto (Italian pa'rɛːto) *n* **1** **Vilfredo** (vil'freːdo). 1848–1923, Italian sociologist and economist. He anticipated Fascist principles of government in his *Mind and Society* (1916) **2** (*modifier*) denoting a law, mathematical formula, etc, originally used by Pareto to express the frequency distribution of incomes in a society

par excellence French (par ɛksɛlɑ̃s; English pɑːr 'ɛksələns) *adv* to a degree of excellence; beyond comparison [literally: by (way of) excellence]

parfait (pɑː'feɪ) *n* a rich frozen dessert made from eggs and cream with ice cream, fruit, etc [from French: PERFECT]

parget ('pɑːdʒɪt) *n* **1** Also called: **pargeting a** plaster, mortar, etc, used to line chimney flues or cover walls **b** plasterwork that has incised ornamental patterns ▷ *vb* (*tr*) **2** to cover or decorate with parget [C14: from Old French *pargeter* to throw over, from *par* PER- + *geter,* from Medieval Latin *jactāre* to throw]

parhelic circle *n meteorol* a luminous band at the same altitude as the sun, parallel to the horizon, caused by reflection of the sun's rays by ice crystals in the atmosphere

parhelion (pɑː'hiːlɪən) *n, pl* **-lia** (-lɪə) one of several bright spots on the parhelic circle or solar halo, caused by the diffraction of light by ice crystals in the atmosphere, esp around sunset. Also called: **mock sun** [C17: via Latin from Greek *parēlion,* from PARA-¹ (beside) + *hēlios* sun] ▷ **parhelic** (pɑː'hiːlɪk, -'hɛlɪk) or **parheliacal** (ˌpɑːhɪ'laɪək³l) *adj*

pariah (pə'raɪə, 'pærɪə) *n* **1** a social outcast **2** (formerly) a member of a low caste in South India [C17: from Tamil *paraiyan* drummer, from *parai* drum; so called because members of the caste were the drummers at festivals]

pariah dog *n* another term for **pye-dog**

Paricutín (Spanish pariku'tin) *n* a volcano in W central Mexico, in Michoacán state, formed in 1943 after a week of earth tremors; grew to a height of 2500 m (8200 ft) in a year and buried the village of Paricutín

parietal (pə'raɪɪt³l) *adj* **1** *anatomy, biology* of, relating to, or forming the walls or part of the walls of a bodily cavity or similar structure: *the parietal bones of the skull* **2** of or relating to the side of the skull **3** (of plant ovaries) having ovules attached to the walls **4** *US* living or having authority within a college ▷ *n* **5** a parietal bone [C16: from Late Latin *parietālis,* from Latin *pariēs* wall]

parietal lobe *n* the portion of each cerebral hemisphere concerned with the perception and interpretation of sensations of touch, temperature, and taste and with muscular movements

pari-mutuel (ˌpærɪ'mjuːtjʊəl) *n, pl* **pari-mutuels** or **paris-mutuels** (ˌpærɪ'mjuːtjʊəlz) **a** a system of betting in which those who have bet on the winners of a race share in the total amount wagered less a percentage for the management **b** (*as modifier*): *the pari-mutuel machine* [C19: from French, literally: mutual wager]

paring ('pɛərɪŋ) *n* (often plural) something pared or cut off

pari passu Latin (ˌpærɪ 'pæsuː, 'pɑːrɪ) *adv* usually *legal* with equal speed or progress; equally: often used to refer to the right of creditors to receive assets from the same source without one taking precedence

Paris¹ ('pærɪs; French pari) *n* **1** the capital of France, in the north on the River Seine: constitutes a department; dates from the 3rd century BC, becoming capital of France in 987; centre of the French Revolution; centres around its original site on an island in the Seine, the **Île**

de la Cité, containing Notre Dame; university (1150). Pop: 2 125 246 (1999). Ancient name: Lutetia **2 Treaty of Paris a** a treaty of 1783 between the US, Britain, France, and Spain, ending the War of American Independence **b** a treaty of 1763 signed by Britain, France, and Spain that ended their involvement in the Seven Years' War **c** a treaty of 1898 between Spain and the US bringing to an end the Spanish-American War [via French and Old French, from Late Latin (*Lūtētia*) *Parisiōrum* (marshes) of the *Parisii*, a tribe of Celtic Gaul] > **Pa'risian** *adj, n*

Paris² ('pærɪs) *n* **1** *Greek myth* a prince of Troy, whose abduction of Helen from her husband Menelaus started the Trojan War **2 Matthew.** ?1200–59, English chronicler, whose principal work is the *Chronica Majora*

Paris Club *n* an informal group of representatives from IMF member nations whose governments or central banks have lent money to governments of other countries

Paris Commune *n* *French history* the council established in Paris in the spring of 1871 in opposition to the National Assembly and esp to the peace negotiated with Prussia following the Franco-Prussian War. Troops of the Assembly crushed the Commune with great bloodshed

Paris green *n* an emerald-green poisonous insoluble substance used as a pigment and insecticide. It is a double salt of copper arsenite and copper acetate. Formula: $3Cu(AsO_2)_2.Cu(C_2H_3O_2)_2$

parish ('pærɪʃ) *n* **1** a subdivision of a diocese, having its own church and a clergyman. Related adj: **parochial** **2** the churchgoers of such a subdivision **3** (in England and, formerly, Wales) the smallest unit of local government in rural areas **4** (in Louisiana) a unit of local government corresponding to a county in other states of the US **5** the people living in a parish **6 on the parish** *history* receiving parochial relief [c13: from Old French *paroisse*, from Church Latin *parochia*, from Late Greek *paroikia*, from *paroikos* Christian, sojourner, from Greek: neighbour, from PARA-¹ (beside) + *oikos* house]

parish clerk *n* an official designated to carry out various duties, either for a church parish or a parish council

parish council *n* (in England and, formerly, Wales) the administrative body of a parish. See **parish** (sense 3)

parishioner (pə'rɪʃənə) *n* a member of a particular parish

parish pump *adj* of only local interest; parochial

parish register *n* a book in which the births, baptisms, marriages, and deaths in a parish are recorded

parity ('pærɪtɪ) *n, pl* **-ties** **1** equality of rank, pay, etc **2** close or exact analogy or equivalence **3** *finance* **a** the amount of a foreign currency equivalent at the established exchange rate to a specific sum of domestic currency **b** a similar equivalence between different forms of the same national currency, esp the gold equivalent of a unit of gold-standard currency **4** equality between prices of commodities or securities in two separate markets **5** *physics* **a** a property of a physical system characterized by the behaviour of the sign of its wave function when all spatial coordinates are reversed in direction. The wave function either remains unchanged (**even parity**) or changes in sign (**odd parity**) **b** a quantum number describing this property, equal to +1 for even parity systems and –1 for odd parity systems. Symbol: *P* **6** *maths* a relationship between two integers. If both are odd or both even they have the same parity; if one is odd and one even they have different parity **7** (in the US) a system of government support for farm products [c16: from Late Latin *pāritās*; see PAR]

parity check *n* a check made of computer data to ensure that the total number of bits of value 1 (or 0) in each unit of information remains odd or even after transfer between a peripheral device and the memory or vice versa

park (pɑːk) *n* **1** a large area of land preserved in a natural state for recreational use by the public **2** a piece of open land in a town with public amenities **3** a large area of land forming a private estate **4** an area designed and landscaped to accommodate a range of related

enterprises, businesses, research establishments, etc: *science park* **5** *US & Canadian* a playing field or sports stadium **6 the park** *Brit informal* a soccer pitch **7** a gear selector position on the automatic transmission of a motor vehicle that acts as a parking brake **8** the area in which the equipment and supplies of a military formation are assembled ▷ *vb* **9** to stop and leave (a vehicle) temporarily **10** to manoeuvre (a motor vehicle) into a space for it to be left: *try to park without hitting the kerb* **11** *stock exchange* to register (securities) in the name of another or of nominees in order to conceal their real ownership **12** (*tr*) *informal* to leave or put somewhere: *park yourself in front of the fire* **13** (*intr*) *military* to arrange equipment in a park **14** (*tr*) to enclose in or as a park [c13: from Old French *parc*, from Medieval Latin *parricus* enclosure, from Germanic; compare Old High German *pfarrih* pen, Old English *pearruc* PADDOCK] > **'park,like** *adj*

Park (pɑːk) *n* **1 Mungo** ('mʌŋgəʊ). 1771–1806, Scottish explorer. He led two expeditions (1795–97; 1805–06) to trace the course of the Niger in Africa. He was drowned during the second expedition **2 Nick,** full name *Nicholas Wulstan Park.* born 1958, British animator and film director; his films include *A Grand Day Out* (1992), which introduced the characters Wallace and Gromit, and the feature-length *Chicken Run* (2000) **3 Chung Hee.** ('tʃʊŋ 'hiː). 1917–79, South Korean politician; president of the Republic of Korea (1963–79); assassinated

parka ('pɑːkə) *n* a warm hip-length weatherproof coat with a hood, originally worn by the Inuit [c19: from Aleutian: skin]

parkade ('pɑːkeɪd) *n* *Canadian* a building used as a car park [c20: from PARK + (ARC)ADE]

Parker ('pɑːkə) *n* **1 Sir Alan (William).** born 1944, British film director and screenwriter; his films include *Midnight Express* (1978), *Mississippi Burning* (1988), *The Commitments* (1991), and *Angela's Ashes* (2000); chairman of the British Film Institute (1998–99) and of the Film Council from 1999 **2 Charlie.** nickname *Bird* or *Yardbird.* 1920–55, US jazz alto saxophonist and composer; the leading exponent of early bop **3 Dorothy (Rothschild).** 1893–1967, US writer, noted esp for the ironical humour of her short stories **4 Matthew.** 1504–75, English prelate. As archbishop of Canterbury (1559–75), he supervised Elizabeth I's religious settlement

Parker Bowles ('pɑːkə bəʊlz) *n* **Camilla** (née *Shand*). born 1947, became the second wife of Prince Charles in 2005; created Duchess of Cornwall

Parkes (pɑːks) *n* **Sir Henry.** 1815–96, Australian journalist and politician born in England, five times premier of New South Wales, advocate of free trade and Federation, and a founder of the public education system

parkin ('pɑːkɪn) *or* **perkin** *n* (in Britain and New Zealand) a moist spicy ginger cake usually containing oatmeal [c19: of unknown origin]

parking lot *n* *US & Canadian* an area or building reserved for parking cars

parking meter *n* a timing device, usually coin-operated, that indicates how long a vehicle may be left parked

parking orbit *n* an orbit around the earth or moon in which a spacecraft can be placed temporarily in order to prepare for the next step in its programme

parking ticket *n* a summons served for a parking offence

Parkinson's disease ('pɑːkɪnsənz) *n* a progressive chronic disorder of the central nervous system characterized by impaired muscular coordination and tremor. Often shortened to: **Parkinson's.** Also called: Parkinsonism [c19: named after James *Parkinson* (1755–1824), British surgeon, who first described it]

Parkinson's law *n* the notion, expressed facetiously as a law of economics, that work expands to fill the time available for its completion [c20: named after C. N. *Parkinson* (1909–93), British historian and writer, who formulated it]

park keeper *n* (in Britain) an official employed by a local authority to patrol and supervise a public park

parkland ('pɑːk,lænd) *n* grassland with scattered trees

parky ('pɑːkɪ) *adj* **parkier, parkiest** *(usually postpositive) Brit informal* (of the weather) chilly; cold [C19: perhaps from PERKY]

parlance ('pɑːləns) *n* a particular manner of speaking, esp when specialized; idiom: *political parlance* [C16: from Old French, from *parler* to talk, via Medieval Latin from Late Latin *parabola* speech, PARABLE; compare PARLEY]

parlando (pɑːˈlændəʊ) *adj, adv music* to be performed as though speaking [Italian: speaking, from *parlare* to speak]

parley ('pɑːlɪ) *n* **1** a discussion, esp between enemies under a truce to decide terms of surrender, etc ▷ *vb* **2** (*intr*) to discuss, esp with an enemy under a truce [C16: from French, from *parler* to talk, via Medieval Latin *parabolāre*, from Late Latin *parabola* speech, PARABLE]

parliament ('pɑːləmənt) *n* **1** an assembly of the representatives of a political nation or people, often the supreme legislative authority **2** any legislative or deliberative assembly, conference, etc [C13: from Anglo-Latin *parliamentum*, from Old French *parlement*, from *parler* to speak; see PARLEY]

Parliament ('pɑːləmənt) *n* **1** the highest legislative authority in Britain, consisting of the House of Commons, which exercises effective power, the House of Lords, and the sovereign **2** a similar legislature in another country **3** any of the assemblies of such a body created by a general election and royal summons and dissolved before the next election

parliamentarian (,pɑːləmɛnˈtɛərɪən) *n* **1** an expert in parliamentary procedures, etc ▷ *adj* **2** of or relating to a parliament or parliaments

parliamentary (,pɑːləˈmɛntərɪ, -trɪ) *adj* (*sometimes capital*) **1** proceeding from a parliament or Parliament: *a parliamentary decree* **2** conforming to or derived from the procedures of a parliament or Parliament: *parliamentary conduct* **3** having a parliament or Parliament

Parliamentary Commissioner *or in full* **Parliamentary Commissioner for Administration** *n* (in Britain) the official name for **ombudsman** (sense 1)

parliamentary private secretary *n* (in Britain) a backbencher in Parliament who assists a minister, esp in liaison with backbenchers. Abbreviation: **PPS**

parliamentary secretary *n* (in Britain) a Member of Parliament appointed, usually as a junior minister, to assist a Minister of the Crown with departmental responsibilities

parlour *or US* **parlor** ('pɑːlə) *n* **1** *old-fashioned* a living room, esp one kept tidy for the reception of visitors **2** a reception room in a priest's house, convent, etc **3** a small room for guests away from the public rooms in an inn, club, etc **4** *chiefly US, Canadian & NZ* a room or shop equipped as a place of business: *a billiard parlor* **5** *Caribbean* a small shop, esp one selling cakes and nonalcoholic drinks **6** Also called: **milking parlour** a building equipped for the milking of cows [C13: from Anglo-Norman *parlur*, from Old French *parleur* room in convent for receiving guests, from *parler* to speak; see PARLEY]

parlous ('pɑːləs) *adj* **1** *archaic or humorous* or difficult **2** cunning ▷ *adv* **3** extremely [C14 *perlous*, variant of PERILOUS] > **'parlously** *adv* > **'parlousness** *n*

Parma *n* **1** (*Italian* 'parma) a city in N Italy, in Emilia-Romagna: capital of the duchy of Parma and Piacenza from 1545 until it became part of Italy in 1860; important food industry (esp Parmesan cheese). Pop: 163 457 (2001). **2** ('pɑːmə) a city in NE Ohio, south of Cleveland. Pop: 83 861 (2003 est)

Parma ham *n* cured ham from Italy

Parmenides (pɑːˈmɛnɪˌdiːz) *n* 5th century BC, Greek Eleatic philosopher, born in Italy. He held that the universe is single and unchanging and denied the existence of change and motion. His doctrines are expounded in his poem *On Nature*, of which only fragments are extant

Parmesan cheese *n* a hard dry cheese made from skimmed milk, used grated, esp on pasta dishes and soups

Parmigianino (*Italian* parmidʒaˈniːno) *n* real name *Girolamo Francesco Maria Mazzola*. 1503–40, Italian painter, one of the originators of mannerism. Also called:

Parmigiano (parmiˈdʒano)

Parnaíba *or* **Parnahiba** (*Portuguese* parnaˈiba) *n* a river in NE Brazil, rising in the Serra das Mangabeiras and flowing generally northeast, to the Atlantic. Length: about 1450 km (900 miles)

Parnassus (pɑːˈnæsəs) *n* **1 Mount Parnassus** a mountain in central Greece, in NW Boeotia: in ancient times sacred to Dionysus, Apollo, and the Muses, with the Castalian Spring and Delphi on its slopes. Height: 2457 m (8061 ft). Modern Greek name: **Liákoura 2 a** the world of poetry **b** a centre of poetic or other creative activity **3** a collection of verse or belles-lettres > **Parnassian** *adj*

Parnell ('pɑːnəl, pɑːˈnɛl) *n* **Charles Stewart.** 1846–91, Irish nationalist, who led the Irish Home Rule movement in Parliament (1880–90) with a calculated policy of obstruction. Although Gladstone was converted to Home Rule (1886), Parnell's career was ruined by the scandal over his adultery with Mrs O'Shea > **'Parnel,lism** *n* > **'Parnellite** *n, adj*

parochial (pəˈrəʊkɪəl) *adj* **1** narrow in outlook or scope; provincial **2** of or relating to a parish or parishes [C14: via Old French from Church Latin *parochiālis*; see PARISH] > **pa'rochial,ism** *n* > **pa'rochially** *adv*

parody ('pærədɪ) *n, pl* **-dies 1** a musical, literary, or other composition that mimics the style of another composer, author, etc, in a humorous or satirical way **2** something so badly done as to seem an intentional mockery; travesty ▷ *vb* **-dies, -dying, -died 3** (*tr*) to make a parody of [C16: via Latin from Greek *paroidiā* satirical poem, from PARA-¹ + *ōidē* song] > **parodic** (pəˈrɒdɪk) *or* **pa'rodical** *adj* > **'parodist** *n*

parol ('pærəl, pəˈrəʊl) *law* ▷ *n* **1** an oral statement; word of mouth (now only in the phrase **by parol**) ▷ *adj* **2 a** (of a contract, lease, etc) made orally or in writing but not under seal **b** expressed or given by word of mouth: *parol evidence* [C15: from Old French *parole* speech; see PAROLE]

parole (pəˈrəʊl) *n* **1 a** the freeing of a prisoner before his sentence has expired, on the condition that he is of good behaviour **b** the duration of such conditional release **2 a** promise given by a prisoner, as to be of good behaviour if granted liberty or partial liberty **3** *linguistics* language as manifested in the individual speech acts of particular speakers **4 on parole** conditionally released from detention ▷ *vb* (*tr*) **5** to place (a person) on parole [C17: from Old French, from the phrase *parole d'honneur* word of honour; *parole* from Late Latin *parabola* speech] > **parolee** (pəˌrəʊˈliː) *n*

paronomasia (,pærənəʊˈmeɪzɪə) *n* *rhetoric* a play on words, esp a pun [C16: via Latin from Greek: a play on words, from *paronomazein* to make a change in naming, from PARA-¹ (beside) + *onomazein* to name, from *onoma* a name]

Páros ('pærɒs) *n* a Greek island in the S Aegean Sea, in the Cyclades: site of the discovery (1627) of the Parian Chronicle, a marble tablet outlining Greek history from before 1000 BC to about 354 BC (now at Oxford University). Pop: 12 853 (2001). Area: 166 sq km (64 sq miles)

parotid (pəˈrɒtɪd) *adj* **1** relating to or situated near the parotid gland ▷ *n* **2** See **parotid gland** [C17: via French, via Latin from Greek *parōtis*, from PARA-¹ (near) + *-ōtis*, from *ous* ear]

parotid gland *n* a large salivary gland, in man situated in front of and below each ear

parotitis (,pærəˈtaɪtɪs) *or* **parotiditis** (pə,rɒtɪˈdaɪtɪs) *n* inflammation of the parotid gland. See also **mumps**

-parous *adj combining form* giving birth to: *oviparous* [from Latin *-parus*, from *parere* to bring forth]

parousia (pəˈruːsɪə) *n* *Christianity* another term for the **Second Coming** [C19: from Greek: presence]

paroxysm ('pærək,sɪzəm) *n* **1** an uncontrollable outburst: *a paroxysm of giggling* **2** *pathol* **a** a sudden attack or recurrence of a disease **b** any fit or convulsion [C17: via French from Medieval Latin *paroxysmus* annoyance, from Greek *paroxusmos*, from *paroxunein* to goad, from PARA-¹ (intensifier) + *oxunein* to sharpen, from *oxus* sharp] > **,parox'ysmal** *or* **,parox'ysmic** *adj*

parquet ('pɑːkeɪ, -kɪ) *n* **1** a floor covering of pieces of hardwood fitted in a decorative pattern; parquetry **2** Also called: **parquet floor** a floor so covered **3** US the stalls of a theatre ▷ *vb* (*tr*) **4** to cover (a floor) with parquet [c19: from Old French: small enclosure, from *parc* enclosure; see PARK]

parquetry ('pɑːkɪtrɪ) *n* a geometric pattern of inlaid pieces of wood, often of different kinds, esp as used to cover a floor or to ornament furniture

parr (pɑː) *n, pl* **parrs** *or* **parr** a salmon up to two years of age, with dark spots and transverse bands [c18: of unknown origin]

Parr (pɑː) *n* **Catherine.** 1512–48, sixth wife of Henry VIII of England

parrakeet ('pærəˌkiːt) *n* a variant spelling of **parakeet**

parramatta (ˌpærə'mætə) *n* a variant spelling of **paramatta**

parricide ('pærɪˌsaɪd) *n* **1** the act of killing either of one's parents **2** a person who kills his parent [c16: from Latin *parricīdium* murder of a parent or relative, and from *parricīda* one who murders a relative, from *parri-* (element related to Greek *pēos* kinsman) + *-cīdium, -cīda* -CIDE] > ˌparri'cidal *adj*

parrot ('pærət) *n* **1** any bird of the tropical and subtropical order *Psittaciformes*, having a short hooked bill, compact body, bright plumage, and an ability to mimic sounds **2** a person who repeats or imitates the words or actions of another unintelligently **3 sick as a parrot** *usually facetious* extremely disappointed ▷ *vb* -rots, -roting, -roted **4** (*tr*) to repeat or imitate mechanically without understanding [c16: probably from French *paroquet*; see PARAKEET] > 'parrotry *n*

parrot-fashion *adv informal* without regard for meaning; by rote: *she learned it parrot-fashion*

parrot fever *or* **parrot disease** *n* another name for **psittacosis**

parrotfish ('pærətˌfɪʃ) *n, pl* **-fish** *or* **-fishes 1** any brightly coloured tropical marine percoid fish of the family *Scaridae*, having parrot-like jaws **2** *Austral* any of various brightly coloured marine fish of the family *Labridae*

parry ('pærɪ) *vb* **-ries, -rying, -ried 1** to ward off (an attack) by blocking or deflecting, as in fencing **2** (*tr*) to evade (questions), esp adroitly ▷ *n, pl* **-ries 3** an act of parrying, esp (in fencing) using a stroke or circular motion of the blade **4** a skilful evasion, as of a question [c17: from French *parer* to ward off, from Latin *parāre* to prepare]

Parry ('pærɪ) *n* **1** Sir (**Charles**) **Hubert** (**Hastings**). 1848–1918, English composer, noted esp for his choral works **2** Sir **William Edward.** 1790–1855, English arctic explorer, who searched for the Northwest Passage (1819–25) and attempted to reach the North Pole (1827)

parse (pɑːz) *vb grammar* to assign constituent structure to (a sentence or the words in a sentence) [c16: from Latin *pars* (*ōrātiōnis*) part (of speech)]

parsec ('pɑːˌsɛk) *n* a unit of astronomical distance equal to the distance from earth at which stellar parallax would be 1 second of arc; equivalent to 3.0857×10^{16} m or 3.262 light years [c20: from PARALLAX + SECOND²]

Parsee *or* **Parsi** ('pɑːsiː) *n* an adherent of a monotheistic religion of Zoroastrian origin, the practitioners of which were driven out of Persia by the Muslims in the eighth century AD. It is now found chiefly in western India [c17: from Persian *Pārsī* a Persian, from Old Persian *Pārsa* PERSIA] > 'Parseeˌism *n*

parser ('pɑːzə) *n computing* a program or part of a program that interprets input to a computer by recognizing key words or analysing sentence structure

Parsifal ('pɑːsɪf°l, -ˌfɑːl) *or* **Parzival** *n German myth* the hero of a medieval cycle of legends about the Holy Grail. English eqivalent: **Percival**

parsimony ('pɑːsɪmənɪ) *n* extreme care or reluctance in spending; frugality; niggardliness [c15: from Latin *parcimōnia*, from *parcere* to spare] > **parsimonious** (ˌpɑːsɪ'məʊnɪəs) *adj* > ˌparsi'moniously *adv*

parsley ('pɑːslɪ) *n* **1 a** S European umbelliferous plant, *Petroselinum crispum*, widely cultivated for its curled aromatic leaves, which are used in cooking **2** any of various similar and related plants, such as fool's-parsley, stone parsley, and cow parsley [c14 *persely*, from Old

English *petersilie* + Old French *persil, peresil*, both ultimately from Latin *petroselīnum* rock parsley, from Greek *petroselinon*, from *petra* rock + *selinon* parsley]

parsnip ('pɑːsnɪp) *n* **1** a strong-scented umbelliferous plant, *Pastinaca sativa*, cultivated for its long whitish root **2** the root of this plant, eaten as a vegetable **3** any of several similar plants, esp the cow parsnip [c14: from Old French *pasnaie*, from Latin *pastināca*, from *pastināre* to dig, from *pastinum* two-pronged tool for digging; also influenced by Middle English *nepe* TURNIP]

parson ('pɑːs°n) *n* **1** a parish priest in the Church of England, formerly applied only to those who held ecclesiastical benefices **2** any clergyman [c13: from Medieval Latin *persōna* parish priest, representative of the parish, from Latin: personage; see PERSON]

parsonage ('pɑːs°nɪdʒ) *n* the residence of a parson who is not a rector or vicar, as provided by the parish

parson bird *n* another name for **tui** [c19: so called because of its dark plumage with white neck feathers]

Parsons ('pɑːsənz) *n* **1** Sir **Charles Algernon.** 1854–1931, English engineer, who developed the steam turbine **2 Gram**, real name *Cecil Connor*. 1946–73 US country-rock singer and songwriter; founder of the Flying Burrito Brothers (1968–70), he later released the solo albums *G.P.* (1973) and *Grievous Angel* (1974) **3 Talcott.** 1902–79, US sociologist, author of *The Structure of Social Action* (1937) and *The Social System* (1951)

parson's nose *n* the fatty extreme end portion of the tail of a fowl when cooked. Also called: **pope's nose**

part (pɑːt) *n* **1** a piece or portion of a whole **2** an integral constituent of something: *dancing is part of what we teach* **3** an amount less than the whole; bit: *they only recovered part of the money* **4** one of several equal or nearly equal divisions: *mix two parts flour to one part water* **5** an actor's role in a play **6** a person's proper role or duty: *everyone must do his part* **7** (*often plural*) area: *you're well known in these parts* **8** anatomy any portion of a larger structure **9** a component that can be replaced in a machine, engine, etc: *spare parts* **10** US, *Candadian & Austral*. the line of scalp showing when sections of hair are combed in opposite directions. British equivalent: **parting 11** *music* one of a number of separate melodic lines making up the texture of music **12** for the most part generally **13 in part** to some degree; partly **14 of many parts** having many different abilities **15 on the part of** on behalf of **16 part and parcel** an essential ingredient **17 play a part a** to pretend to be what one is not **b** (foll by *in*) to have something to do (with); be instrumental (in): *to play a part in the king's downfall* **18 take in good part** to respond to (teasing) with good humour **19 take part in** to participate in **20 take someone's part** to support someone in an argument ▷ *vb* **21** to divide or separate from one another; take or come apart: *to part the curtains; the seams parted when I washed the dress* **22** to go away or cause to go away from one another; stop or cause to stop seeing each other: *the couple parted amicably* **23** (*intr; foll by from*) to leave; say goodbye (to) **24** (*intr; foll by with*) to relinquish, esp reluctantly: *I couldn't part with my teddy bear* **25** (*tr; foll by from*) to cause to relinquish, esp reluctantly: *he's not easily parted from his cash* **26** (*intr*) to split; separate: *the path parts here* **27** (*tr*) to arrange (the hair) in such a way that a line of scalp is left showing **28** (*intr*) a euphemism for **die¹** (sense 1) **29** (*intr*) *archaic* to depart ▷ *adv* **30** to some extent; partly ▷ See also **parts** [c13: via Old French from Latin *partīre* to divide, from *pars* a part]

part. *abbreviation* **1** participle **2** particular

partake (pɑː'teɪk) *vb* **-takes, -taking, -took, -taken** (*mainly intr*) **1** (foll by *in*) to have a share; participate: *to partake in the excitement* **2** (foll by *of*) to take or receive a portion, esp of food or drink: *each partook of the food offered to him* **3** (foll by *of*) to suggest or have some of the quality (of): *music partaking of sadness* **4** (*tr*) *archaic* to share in [c16: back formation from *partaker*, earlier *part taker*, based on Latin *particeps* participant; see PART, TAKE] > par'taker *n*

● USAGE *Partake of* is sometimes wrongly used as if it
● were a synonym of *eat* or *drink*. Correctly, one can only
● *partake of* food or drink which is available for several
● people to share

parterre (pɑː'tɛə) *n* **1** a formally patterned flower garden

2 *Brit & Irish* the pit in a theatre [C17: from French, from *par* along + *terre* ground]

parthenogenesis (ˌpɑːθɪnəʊˈdʒɛnɪsɪs) *n* a type of reproduction, occurring in some insects and flowers, in which the unfertilized ovum develops directly into a new individual [C19: from Greek *parthenos* virgin + *genesis* birth] > **parthenogenetic** (ˌpɑːθɪˌnəʊdʒɪˈnɛtɪk) *adj*

Parthenon (ˈpɑːθəˌnɒn, -nən) *n* the temple on the Acropolis in Athens built in the 5th century BC and regarded as the finest example of the Greek Doric order

Parthenopaeus (ˌpɑːθənəʊˈpiːəs) *n Greek myth* one of the Seven against Thebes, son of Atalanta

Parthenope (pɑːˈθɛnəpɪ) *n Greek myth* a siren, who drowned herself when Odysseus evaded the lure of the sirens' singing. Her body was said to have been cast ashore at what became Naples

Parthia (ˈpɑːθɪə) *n* a country in ancient Asia, southeast of the Caspian Sea, that expanded into a great empire dominating SW Asia in the 2nd century BC It was destroyed by the Sassanids in the 3rd century AD

Parthian shot *n* another term for **parting shot** [alluding to the custom of Parthian archers who shot their arrows backwards while retreating]

partial (ˈpɑːʃəl) *adj* **1** relating to only a part; not general or complete: *a partial eclipse* **2** biased: *a partial judge* **3** (*postpositive*; foll by *to*) having a particular liking (for) **4** *maths* designating or relating to an operation in which only one of a set of independent variables is considered at a time ▷ *n* **5** Also called: **partial tone** *music, acoustics* any of the component tones of a single musical sound, including both those that belong to the harmonic series of the sound and those that do not **6** *maths* a partial derivative [C15: from Old French *parcial*, from Late Latin *partiālis* incomplete, from Latin *pars* PART] > ˈpartially *adv* > ˈpartialness *n*

● USAGE See at **partly**

partial derivative *n* the derivative of a function of two or more variables with respect to one of the variables, the other or others being considered constant. Written ∂f/∂x

partiality (ˌpɑːʃɪˈælɪtɪ) *n, pl* -ties **1** favourable prejudice or bias **2** (usually foll by *for*) liking or fondness **3** the state or condition of being partial

partible (ˈpɑːtəbəl) *adj* (esp of property or an inheritance) divisible; separable [C16: from Late Latin *partibilis*, from *part-, pars* PART]

participate (pɑːˈtɪsɪˌpeɪt) *vb* (*intr*; often foll by *in*) to take part, be or become actively involved, or share (in) [C16: from Latin *participāre*, from *pars* PART + *capere* to take] > par**ˈticipant** *adj, n* > par**ˌtici*ˈpation*** *n* > par**ˈtici*ˌpator*** *n* > par**ˈticipatory** *adj*

participle (ˈpɑːtɪsɪpəl, pɑːˈtɪsɪpəl) *n* a nonfinite form of verbs, in English and other languages, used adjectivally and in the formation of certain compound tenses. See also **present participle, past participle** [C14: via Old French from Latin *participium*, from *particeps* partaker, from *pars* PART + *capere* to take] > **participial** (ˌpɑːtɪˈsɪpɪəl) *adj, n* > ˌparti**ˈcipially** *adv*

particle (ˈpɑːtɪkəl) *n* **1** an extremely small piece of matter; speck **2** a very tiny amount; iota: *it doesn't make a particle of difference* **3** a function word, esp (in certain languages) a word belonging to an uninflected class having suprasegmental or grammatical function **4** a common affix, such as *re-, un-,* or *-ness* **5** *physics* a body with finite mass that can be treated as having negligible size, and internal structure **6** See **elementary particle 7** *RC Church* a small piece broken off from the Host at Mass **8** *archaic* a section or clause of a document [C14: from Latin *particula* a small part, from *pars* PART]

particle accelerator *n* a machine for accelerating charged elementary particles to very high energies, used for research in nuclear physics

particle physics *n* the study of fundamental particles and their properties. Also called: **high-energy physics**

parti-coloured *or* **party-coloured** (ˈpɑːtɪˌkʌləd) *adj* having different colours in different parts; variegated [C16 *parti*, from (obsolete) *party* of more than one colour, from Old French: striped, from Latin *partīre* to divide]

particular (pəˈtɪkjʊlə) *adj* **1** (*prenominal*) of or belonging to a single or specific person, thing, category, etc; specific; special: *the particular demands of the job; no particular reason* **2** (*prenominal*) exceptional or marked: *a matter of particular importance* **3** (*prenominal*) relating to or providing specific details or circumstances: *a particular account* **4** exacting or difficult to please, esp in details; fussy **5** (of the solution of a differential equation) obtained by giving specific values to the arbitrary constants in a general equation **6** *logic* (of a proposition) affirming or denying something about only some members of a class of objects, as in *some men are not wicked*. See **universal** (sense 10) ▷ *n* **7** a separate distinct item that helps to form a generalization: opposed to *general* **8** (*often plural*) an item of information; detail: *complete in every particular* **9** **in particular** especially, particularly, or exactly [C14: from Old French *particuler*, from Late Latin *particulāris* concerning a part, from Latin *particula* PARTICLE v]

particular average *n insurance* partial damage to or loss of a ship or its cargo affecting only the shipowner or one cargo owner. Abbreviation: **PA** See **general average**

particularism (pəˈtɪkjʊləˌrɪzəm) *n* **1** exclusive attachment to the interests of one group, class, sect, etc, esp at the expense of the community as a whole **2** the principle of permitting each state or minority in a federation the right to further its own interests or retain its own laws, traditions, etc **3** *theol* the doctrine that divine grace is restricted to the elect > par**ˈticularist** *n, adj*

particularity (pəˌtɪkjʊˈlærɪtɪ) *n, pl* -ties **1** (*often plural*) a specific circumstance: *the particularities of the affair* **2** great attentiveness to detail; fastidiousness **3** the quality of being precise: *a description of great particularity* **4** the state or quality of being particular as opposed to general; individuality

particularize *or* **particularise** (pəˈtɪkjʊləˌraɪz) *vb* **1** to treat in detail; give details (about) **2** (*intr*) to go into detail > par**ˌticulari*ˈzation*** *or* par**ˌticulari*ˈsation*** *n*

particularly (pəˈtɪkjʊləlɪ) *adv* **1** very much; exceptionally: *I wasn't particularly successful* **2** in particular; specifically: *pensioners, particularly the less well-off*

particulate (pɑːˈtɪkjʊlɪt, -ˌleɪt) *n* **1** a substance consisting of separate particles ▷ *adj* **2** of or made up of separate particles

parting (ˈpɑːtɪŋ) *n* **1** *Brit* the line of scalp showing when sections of hair are combed in opposite directions. US, Canadian, and Austral. equivalent: **part 2** the act of separating or the state of being separated **3 a** a departure or leave-taking, esp one causing a final separation **b** (*as modifier*): *a parting embrace* **4** a place or line of separation or division **5** *chem* a division of a crystal along a plane that is not a cleavage plane **6** a euphemism for **death** ▷ *adj* (*prenominal*) **7** *literary* departing: *the parting day* **8** serving to divide or separate

parting shot *n* a hostile remark or gesture delivered while departing. Also called: **Parthian shot**

partisan *or* **partizan** (ˌpɑːtɪˈzæn, ˈpɑːtɪˌzæn) *n* **1** an adherent or devotee of a cause, party, etc **2 a** a member of an armed resistance group within occupied territory, esp in Italy or the Balkans in World War II **b** (*as modifier*): *partisan forces* ▷ *adj* **3** of, relating to, or characteristic of a partisan **4** relating to or excessively devoted to one party, faction, etc; one-sided [C16: via French, from Old Italian *partigiano*, from *parte* faction, from Latin *pars* PART] > ˌparti**ˈsanship** *or* ˌparti**ˈzanship** *n*

partita (pɑːˈtiːtə) *n, pl* -te (-teɪ) *or* -tas *music* a type of suite [Italian: divided (piece), from Latin *partīre* to divide]

partite (ˈpɑːtaɪt) *adj* **1** (*in combination*) composed of or divided into a specified number of parts: *bipartite* **2** (esp of plant leaves) divided almost to the base to form two or more parts [C16: from Latin *partīre* to divide]

partition (pɑːˈtɪʃən) *n* **1** a division into parts; separation **2** something that separates, such as a thin screen dividing a room in two **3** a part or share **4** a division of a country into two or more separate nations **5** *property law* a division of property, esp realty, among joint owners ▷ *vb* (*tr*) **6** (often foll by *off*) to separate or apportion into sections: *to partition a room off with a large screen* [C15: via Old French from Latin *partītiō*, from *partīre* to divide]

partitive (ˈpɑːtɪtɪv) *adj* **1** *grammar* indicating that a noun involved in a construction refers only to a part or fraction of what it otherwise refers to. The phrase *some of the butter* is a partitive construction; in some inflected languages it would be translated by the genitive case of the noun **2** serving to separate or divide into parts ▷ *n* **3** *grammar* a partitive linguistic element or feature [c16: from Medieval Latin *partitīvus* serving to divide, from Latin *partīre* to divide] > **'partitively** *adv*

partly ('pɑːtlɪ) *adv* to some extent; not completely
● USAGE *Partly* and *partially* are to some extent
● interchangeable, but *partly* should be used when
● referring to a part or parts of something: *the building is*
● *partly* (not *partially*) *of stone,* while *partially* is preferred
● for the meaning *to some extent: his mother is partially* (not
● *partly*) *sighted*

partner ('pɑːtnə) *n* **1** an ally or companion: *a partner in crime* **2** a member of a partnership **3** one of a pair of dancers or players on the same side in a game: *my bridge partner* **4** either member of a couple in a relationship ▷ *vb* **5** to be or cause to be a partner (of) [c14: variant (influenced by PART) of PARCENER]

partnership ('pɑːtnəʃɪp) *n* **1 a** a contractual relationship between two or more persons carrying on a joint business venture with a view to profit, each incurring liability for losses and the right to share in the profits **b** the deed creating such a relationship **c** the persons associated in such a relationship **2** the state or condition of being a partner

part of speech *n* a class of words sharing important syntactic or semantic features; a group of words in a language that may occur in similar positions or fulfil similar functions in a sentence. The chief parts of speech in English are noun, pronoun, adjective, determiner, adverb, verb, preposition, conjunction, and interjection

parton ('pɑːtɒn) *n* *physics* a hypothetical elementary particle postulated as a constituent of neutrons and protons [from PART + -ON]

Parton ('pɑːtən) *n* Dolly. born 1946, US country and pop singer and songwriter

partook (pɑːˈtʊk) *vb* the past tense of **partake**

partridge ('pɑːtrɪdʒ) *n*, *pl* **-tridges** or **-tridge** any of various small Old World gallinaceous game birds of the genera *Perdix, Alectoris,* etc, esp *P. perdix* (**common** or **European partridge**): family *Phasianidae* (pheasants) [c13: from Old French *perdriz,* from Latin *perdix,* from Greek]

Partridge ('pɑːtrɪdʒ) *n* Eric (**Honeywood**). 1894–1979, British lexicographer, born in New Zealand; author of works on English usage, idiom, slang, and etymology

parts (pɑːts) *pl n* **1** personal abilities or talents: *a man of many parts* **2** short for **private parts**

Parts of Holland *n* See Holland¹ (sense 3)

Parts of Kesteven *n* See (Parts of) **Kesteven**

Parts of Lindsey *n* See (Parts of) **Lindsey**

part song *n* **1** a song composed in harmonized parts **2** (*in more technical usage*) a piece of homophonic choral music in which the topmost part carries the melody

part-time *adj* **1** for less than the entire time appropriate to an activity: *a part-time job; a part-time waitress* ▷ *adv* **part time 2** on a part-time basis: *he works part time* ▷ See **fulltime** > **,part-'timer** *n*

parturient (pɑːˈtjʊərɪənt) *adj* **1** of or relating to childbirth **2** giving birth **3** producing or about to produce a new idea, etc [c16: via Latin *parturīre,* from *parere* to bring forth] > **par'turiency** *n*

parturition (,pɑːtjʊˈrɪʃən) *n* the act or process of giving birth [c17: from Late Latin *parturītiō,* from *parturīre* to be in labour]

part work *n* *Brit* a series of magazines issued as at weekly or monthly intervals, which are designed to be bound together to form a complete course or book

party ('pɑːtɪ) *n*, *pl* **-ties 1 a** a social gathering for pleasure, often held as a celebration **b** (*as modifier*): *party spirit* **c** (*in combination*): *partygoer* **2** a group of people associated in some activity: *a rescue party* **3 a** (*often capital*) a group of people organized together to further a common political aim, such as the election of its candidates to public office **b** (*as modifier*): *party politics* **4** a person, esp one who participates in some activity such

as entering into a contract **5** the person or persons taking part in legal proceedings, such as plaintiff or prosecutor: *a party to the action* **6** *informal, humorous* a person **7** **to come to the party** to take part or become involved ▷ *vb* **-ties, -tying, -tied** (*intr*) **8** *informal* to celebrate; revel ▷ *adj* **9** *heraldry* (of a shield) divided vertically into two colours, metals, or furs [c13: from Old French *partie* part, faction, from Latin *partīre* to divide; see PART]

party line *n* **1** a telephone line serving two or more subscribers **2** the policies or dogma of a political party, to which all members are expected to subscribe

party list *n* (*modifier*) of or relating to a system of voting in which people vote for a party rather than for a candidate. Parties are assigned the number of seats which reflects their share of the vote. See **proportional representation**

party pooper ('puːpə) *n* *informal* a person whose behaviour or personality spoils other people's enjoyment [c20: originally US]

party popper *n* a small plastic cylinder which, when a string is pulled, makes a small bang and fires thin paper streamers into the air

party wall *n* *property law* a wall separating two properties or pieces of land and over which each of the adjoining owners has certain rights

Parumov ('pærəmɒv) Georgi. born 1957, Bulgarian politician, president of Bulgaria from 2002

par value *n* the value imprinted on the face of a share certificate or bond and used to assess dividend, capital ownership, or interest

parvenu ('pɑːvə,njuː) *n* **1** a person, esp a man, who, having risen socially or economically, is considered to be an upstart or to lack the appropriate refinement for his or her new position ▷ *adj* **2** of or characteristic of a parvenu [c19: from French, from *parvenir* to attain, from Latin *pervenīre,* from *per* through + *venīre* to come]

parvovirus ('pɑːvəʊ,vaɪrəs) *n* any of a group of viruses characterized by their very small size, each of which is specific to a particular species, as for example canine parvovirus [c20: New Latin from Latin *parvus* little + VIRUS]

Parzival (German 'partsifal) *n* a variant of **Parsifal**

pas (pɑː; *French* pɑ) *n*, *pl* **pas** (pɑːz; *French* pɑ) a dance step or movement, esp in ballet [c18: French, literally: step]

PAS *abbreviation* physician-assisted suicide: a practice in which a terminally-ill person requests a medical practitioner to administer a lethal dose of medication

Pasadena (,pæsəˈdiːnə) *n* a city in SW California, east of Los Angeles. Pop: 144 413 (2003 est)

Pasay ('pɑːsaɪ) *n* a city in the Philippines, on central Luzon just south of Manila, on Manila Bay. Pop: 364 000 (2005 est). Also called: **Rizal**

pascal ('pæskᵊl) *n* the derived SI unit of pressure; the pressure exerted on an area of 1 square metre by a force of 1 newton; equivalent to 10 dynes per square centimetre or 1.45×10^{-4} pound per square inch. Symbol: **Pa** [c20: named after Blaise Pascal (1623–62), French philosopher, mathematician, and physicist]

Pascal (French paskal) *n* Blaise (blɛz). 1623–62, French philosopher, mathematician, and physicist. As a scientist, he made important contributions to hydraulics and the study of atmospheric pressure and, with Fermat, developed the theory of probability. His chief philosophical works are *Lettres provinciales* (1656–57), written in defence of Jansenism and against the Jesuits, and *Pensées* (1670), fragments of a Christian apologia

Pascal's triangle *n* a triangle consisting of rows of numbers; the apex is 1 and each row starts and ends with 1, other numbers being obtained by adding together the two numbers on either side in the row above: used to calculate probabilities [c17: named after Blaise Pascal (1623–62), French philosopher, mathematician, and physicist]

paschal ('pæskᵊl) *adj* **1** of or relating to Passover **2** of or relating to Easter

Paschal Lamb *n* **1** (*sometimes not capitals*) *Old Testament* the lamb killed and eaten on the first day of the Passover **2** Christ regarded as this sacrifice

pas de basque (ˌpɑː də ˈbɑːsk; *French* pɑ də bask) *n, pl* **pas de basque** a dance step performed usually on the spot, consisting of one long and two short movements during which the weight is transferred from one foot to the other: used esp in reels and jigs [from French, literally: Basque step]

Pas-de-Calais (*French* pɑdkalɛ) *n* a department of N France, in Nord-Pas-de-Calais region, on the Straits of Dover (the **Pas de Calais**): the part of France closest to the British Isles. Capital: Arras. Pop: 1 451 307 (2003 est.). Area: 6752 sq km (2633 sq miles)

pas de deux (*French* pɑddø) *n, pl* **pas de deux** *ballet* a sequence for two dancers [French: step for two]

pash (pæʃ) *n slang* infatuation [C20: from PASSION]

pasha *or* **pacha** (ˈpɑːʃə, ˈpæʃə) *n* (formerly) a provincial governor or other high official of the Ottoman Empire or the modern Egyptian kingdom: placed after a name when used as a title [C17: from Turkish *paşa*]

pashm (ˈpæʃəm) *n* the underfur of various Tibetan animals, esp goats, used for cashmere shawls [from Persian, literally: wool]

pashmina (pæʃˈmiːnə) *n* a scarf or shawl made of pashm [from Persian *pashmina*; see PASHM]

Pashto, Pushto (ˈpʌʃtəʊ) *or* **Pushtu** *n* **1** a language of Afghanistan and NW Pakistan, belonging to the East Iranian branch of the Indo-European family: since 1936 the official language of Afghanistan **2** *pl* **-to** *or* **-tos, -tu** *or* **-tus** a speaker of the Pashto language; a Pathan ▷ *adj* **3** denoting or relating to this language or a speaker of it

Pašić (pɑːˈʃitʃ) *n* Nicola. 1845-1926, Serbian statesman; prime minister of Serbia (1891-92; 1904-05; 1906-08; 1909-11; 1912-18) and of the Kingdom of Serbs, Croats, and Slovenes (1921-24; 1924-26)

Pasionaria (*Spanish* pasjoˈnarja) *n* **La** (la), real name *Dolores Ibarruri*. 1895-1989, Spanish Communist leader, who lived in exile in the Soviet Union (1939-75)

Pasiphaë (pəˈsɪfiːiː) *n Greek myth* the wife of Minos and mother (by a bull) of the Minotaur

Pasmore (ˈpæsˌmɔː) *n* **Victor**. 1908-98, British artist. Originally a figurative painter, he devoted himself to abstract paintings and reliefs after 1947

paso doble (ˈpæsəʊ ˈdəʊbleɪ; *Spanish* ˈpaso ˈdoβle) *n, pl* **paso dobles** *or* **pasos dobles** (*Spanish* ˈpasos ˈdoβles) **1** a modern ballroom dance in fast duple time **2** a piece of music composed for or in the rhythm of this dance [Spanish: double step]

Pasolini (*Italian* pazoˈlini) *n* Pier Paolo (pjɛr ˈpɑːolo). 1922-75, Italian film director. His films include *The Gospel according to St Matthew* (1964), *Oedipus Rex* (1967), *Theorem* (1968), *Pigsty* (1969) and *Decameron* (1970)

pas op (ˈpɑːs ˌɒp) *interj South African* beware [Afrikaans]

pasqueflower (ˈpɑːskˌflaʊə, ˈpæsk-) *n* **1** a purple-flowered herbaceous ranunculaceous plant, *Anemone pulsatilla* (or *Pulsatilla vulgaris*), of N and Central Europe and W Asia **2** any of several related North American plants, such as *A. patens* [C16: from French *passefleur*, from *passer* to excel + *fleur* flower; changed to *pasqueflower* Easter flower, because it blooms at Easter]

pasquinade (ˌpæskwɪˈneɪd) *or* **pasquil** (ˈpæskwɪl) *n* an abusive lampoon or satire, esp one posted in a public place [C17: from Italian *Pasquino* name given to an ancient Roman statue disinterred in 1501, which was annually posted with satirical verses]

pass (pɑːs) *vb* **1** to go onwards or move by or past (a person, thing, etc) **2** to run, extend, or lead through, over, or across (a place): *the route passes through the city* **3** to go through or cause to go through (an obstacle or barrier): *to pass a needle through cloth* **4** to move or cause to move onwards or over: *he passed his hand over her face* **5** (*tr*) to go beyond or exceed: *this victory passes all expectation* **6** to gain or cause to gain an adequate or required mark, grade, or rating in (an examination, course, etc): *the examiner passed them all* **7** (often foll by *away* or *by*) to elapse or allow to elapse: *we passed the time talking* **8** (*intr*) to take place or happen: *what passed at the meeting?* **9** to speak or exchange or be spoken or exchanged: *angry words passed between them* **10** to spread or cause to spread: *we passed the news round the class* **11** to transfer or exchange or be transferred or exchanged: *the bomb passed from hand to hand*

12 (*intr*) to undergo change or transition: *to pass from joy to despair* **13** (when *tr*, often foll by *down*) to transfer or be transferred by inheritance: *the house passed to the younger son* **14** to agree to or sanction or to be agreed to or receive the sanction of a legislative body, person of authority, etc: *the assembly passed 10 resolutions* **15** (*tr*) (of a legislative measure) to undergo (a procedural stage) and be agreed: *the bill passed the committee stage* **16** (when *tr*, often foll by *on* or *upon*) to pronounce or deliver (judgment, findings, etc): *the court passed sentence* **17** to go or allow to go without comment or censure: *the intended insult passed unnoticed* **18** (*intr*) to opt not to exercise a right, as by not answering a question or not making a bid or a play in card games **19** *physiol* to discharge (urine, faeces, etc) from the body **20** **pass water** to urinate **21** (*intr*) to come to an end or disappear: *his anger soon passed* **22** (*intr*; usually foll by *as* or *for*) to be likely to be mistaken for or accepted as (someone or something else): *you could easily pass for your sister* **23** *sport* to hit, kick, or throw (the ball) to another player **24** **bring to pass** *archaic* to cause to happen **25** **come to pass** to happen ▷ *n* **26** the act of passing **27** a route through a range of mountains where the summit is lower or where there is a gap between peaks **28** a permit, licence, or authorization to do something without restriction **29 a** a document allowing entry to and exit from a military installation **b** a document authorizing leave of absence **30** *Brit* **a** the passing of a college or university examination to a satisfactory standard but not as high as honours **b** (*as modifier*): *a pass degree* **31** a dive, sweep, or bombing or landing run by an aircraft **32** a motion of the hand or of a wand as a prelude to or part of a conjuring trick **33** *informal* an attempt, in words or action, to invite sexual intimacy (esp in the phrase **make a pass at**) **34** a state of affairs or condition, esp a bad or difficult one (esp in the phrase **a pretty pass**) **35** *sport* the transfer of a ball from one player to another **36** *fencing* a thrust or lunge with a sword **37** *bridge* the act of passing (making no bid) ▷ *interj* **38** *bridge* a call indicating that a player has no bid to make ▷ See also **pass off, pass out, pass over** etc [C13: from Old French *passer* to pass, surpass, from Latin *passūs* step, PACE¹]

pass. *abbreviation* passive

passable (ˈpɑːsəbªl) *adj* **1** adequate, fair, or acceptable: *a passable speech* **2** (of an obstacle) capable of being passed or crossed **3** (of currency) valid for general circulation **4** (of a proposed law) able to be ratified or enacted > ˈpassableness *n*

passacaglia (ˌpæsəˈkɑːljə) *n* **1** an old Spanish dance in slow triple time **2** a slow instrumental piece characterized by a series of variations on a particular theme played over a repeated bass part. See also **chaconne** (sense 1) [C17: earlier *passacalle*, from Spanish *pasacalle* street dance, from *paso* step + *calle* street; the ending *-alle* was changed to *-aglia* to suggest an Italian origin]

passage (ˈpæsɪdʒ) *n* **1** a channel, opening, etc, through or by which a person or thing may pass **2** *music* a section or division of a piece, movement, etc **3** a way, as in a hall or lobby **4** a section of a written work, speech, etc, esp one of moderate length **5** a journey, esp by ship: *the outward passage took a week* **6** the act or process of passing from one place, condition, etc, to another: *passage of a gas through a liquid* **7** the permission, right, or freedom to pass: *to be denied passage through a country* **8** the enactment of a law or resolution by a legislative or deliberative body **9** an evacuation of the bowels **10** *rare* an exchange or interchange, as of blows, words, etc (esp in the phrase **passage of arms**) [C13: from Old French from *passer* to PASS]

passageway (ˈpæsɪdʒˌweɪ) *n* a way, esp one in or between buildings; passage

Passamaquoddy Bay (ˌpæsəməˈkwɒdɪ) *n* an inlet of the Bay of Fundy between New Brunswick (Canada) and Maine (US) at the mouth of the St Croix River

pass band *n* the band of frequencies that is transmitted with maximum efficiency through a circuit, filter, etc

passbook (ˈpɑːsˌbʊk) *n* **1** a book for keeping a record of withdrawals from and payments into a building society

2 another name for **bankbook 3** (formerly in South Africa) an official document serving to identify the bearer, his race, his residence, and his employment

Passchendaele ('pæʃən,deɪl) *n* a village in NW Belgium, in West Flanders province: the scene of heavy fighting during the third battle of Ypres in World War I during which 245 000 British troops were lost

passé ('pɑːseɪ, 'pɑseɪ; *French* pɑse) *adj* **1** out-of-date: *passé ideas* **2** past the prime; faded: *a passé society beauty* [c18: from French, past participle of *passer* to PASS]

passenger ('pæsɪndʒə) *n* **1 a** a person travelling in a car, train, boat, etc, not driven by him **b** (*as modifier*): *a passenger seat* **2** *chiefly Brit* a member of a group or team who is a burden on the others through not participating fully in the work [c14: from Old French *passager* passing, from PASSAGE¹]

passenger pigeon *n* a gregarious North American pigeon, *Ectopistes migratorius*: became extinct at the beginning of the 20th century

passe-partout (,pæspɑː'tuː; *French* pɑspɑrtu) *n* **1** a mounting for a picture in which strips of strong gummed paper are used to bind together the glass, picture, and backing **2** the gummed paper used for this **3** a mat, often decorated, on which a picture is mounted **4** something that secures entry everywhere, esp a master key [c17: from French, literally: pass everywhere]

passepied (pɑːs'pjeɪ) *n*, *pl* **-pieds** (-'pjeɪ) **1** a lively minuet of Breton origin, in triple time, popular in the 17th century **2** a piece of music composed for or in the rhythm of this dance [c17: from French: pass the foot]

passer-by *n*, *pl* **passers-by** a person that is passing or going by, esp on foot

passerine ('pæsə,raɪn, -,riːn) *adj* **1** of, relating to, or belonging to the *Passeriformes*, an order of birds characterized by the perching habit: includes the larks, finches, crows, thrushes, starlings, etc ▷ *n* **2** any bird belonging to the order *Passeriformes* [c18: from Latin *passer* sparrow]

passim *Latin* ('pæsɪm) *adv* here and there; throughout: used to indicate that what is referred to; occurs frequently in the work cited

passing ('pɑːsɪŋ) *adj* **1** transitory or momentary: *a passing fancy* **2** cursory or casual in action or manner: *a passing reference* ▷ *adv*, *adj* **3** *archaic* to an extreme degree: *the events were passing strange* ▷ *n* **4** a place where or means by which one may pass, cross, ford, etc **5** a euphemism for **death 6** **in passing** by the way; incidentally: *he mentioned your visit in passing*

passing bell *n* a bell rung to announce a death or a funeral. Also called: **death bell** *or* **death knell**

passing note *or US* **passing tone** *n music* a nonharmonic note through which a melody passes from one harmonic note to the next

passion ('pæʃən) *n* **1** ardent love or affection **2** intense sexual love **3** a strong affection or enthusiasm for an object, concept, etc: *a passion for poetry* **4** any strongly felt emotion, such as love, hate, envy, etc **5** a state or outburst of extreme anger: *he flew into a passion* **6** the object of an intense desire, ardent affection, or enthusiasm **7** an outburst expressing intense emotion: *he burst into a paroxysm of sobs* **8** the sufferings and death of a Christian martyr [c12: via French from Church Latin *passiō* suffering, from Latin *patī* to suffer]
> 'passionless *adj*

Passion ('pæʃən) *n* **1** the sufferings of Christ from the Last Supper to his death on the cross **2** any of the four Gospel accounts of this **3** a musical setting of this: *the St Matthew Passion*

passionate ('pæʃənɪt) *adj* **1** manifesting or exhibiting intense sexual feeling or desire: *a passionate lover* **2** capable of, revealing, or characterized by intense emotion **3** easily roused to anger; quick-tempered
> 'passionately *adv*

passionflower ('pæʃən,flaʊə) *n* any passifloraceous plant of the tropical American genus *Passiflora*, cultivated for their red, yellow, greenish, or purple showy flowers: some species have edible fruit [c17: so called from the alleged resemblance between parts of the flower and the instruments of Christ's crucifixion]

passion fruit *n* the edible fruit of any of various passionflowers, esp granadilla

Passion play *n* a play depicting the Passion of Christ

passive ('pæsɪv) *adj* **1** not active or not participating perceptibly in an activity, organization, etc **2** unresisting and receptive to external forces; submissive **3** affected or acted upon by an external object or force **4** *grammar* denoting a voice of verbs in sentences in which the grammatical subject is not the logical subject but rather the recipient of the action described by the verb, as *was broken* in the sentence *The glass was broken by a boy* **5** *chem* (of a substance, esp a metal) apparently chemically unreactive, usually as a result of the formation of a thin protective layer that prevents further reaction **6** *electronics, telecomm* **a** containing no source of power and therefore capable only of attenuating a signal: *a passive network* **b** not capable of amplifying a signal or controlling a function: *a passive communications satellite* **7** *finance* (of a bond, share, debt, etc) yielding no interest ▷ *n* **8** *grammar* **a** the passive voice **b** a passive verb [c14: from Latin *passīvus* susceptible of suffering, from *patī* to undergo]
> 'passively *adv* > pas'sivity *or* 'passiveness *n*

passive-aggressive *adj psychoanal* of or relating to a personality that harbours aggressive emotions while behaving in a calm or detached manner

passive euthanasia *n* a form of euthanasia in which medical treatment that will keep a dying patient alive for a time is withdrawn

passive resistance *n* resistance to a government, law, etc, made without violence, as by fasting, demonstrating peacefully, or refusing to cooperate

passive smoking *n* the inhalation of smoke from other people's cigarettes by a nonsmoker > **passive smoker** *n*

passkey ('pɑːs,kiː) *n* **1** any of various keys, esp a latchkey **2** another term for **master key, skeleton key**

pass law *n* (formerly, in South Africa) a law restricting the movement of Black Africans, esp from rural to urban areas

pass off *vb* (*adverb*) **1** to be or cause to be accepted or circulated in a false character or identity: *he passed the fake diamonds off as real* **2** (*intr*) to come to a gradual end; disappear: *eventually the pain passed off* **3** to emit (a substance) as a gas or vapour, or (of a substance) to be emitted in this way **4** (*intr*) to take place: *the meeting passed off without disturbance* **5** (*tr*) to set aside or disregard: *I managed to pass off his insult*

pass out *vb* (*adverb*) **1** (*intr*) *informal* to become unconscious; faint **2** (*intr*) *Brit* (esp of an officer cadet) to qualify for a military commission; complete a course of training satisfactorily: *General Smith passed out from Sandhurst in 1933* **3** (*tr*) to distribute

pass over *vb* **1** (*tr*, *adverb*) to take no notice of; disregard: *they passed me over in the last round of promotions* **2** (*intr*, *preposition*) to disregard (something bad or embarrassing)

Passover ('pɑːs,əʊvə) *n* **1** Also called: **Pesach, Pesah, Feast of the Unleavened Bread** an eight-day Jewish festival beginning on Nisan 15 and celebrated in commemoration of the passing over or sparing of the Israelites in Egypt, when God smote the firstborn of the Egyptians (Exodus 12). Related adj: **paschal 2** another term for the **Paschal Lamb** [c16: from *pass over*, translation of Hebrew *pesah*, from *pāsah* to pass over]

passport ('pɑːspɔːt) *n* **1** an official document issued by a government, identifying an individual, granting him permission to travel abroad, and requesting the protection of other governments for him **2** a licence granted by a state to a foreigner, allowing the passage of his person or goods through the country **3** a quality, asset, etc, that gains a person admission or acceptance [c15: from French *passeport*, from *passer* to PASS + PORT¹]

pass up *vb* (*tr*, *adverb*) *informal* to let go by; ignore: *I won't pass up this opportunity*

password ('pɑːs,wɜːd) *n* **1** a secret word, phrase, etc, that ensures admission or acceptance by proving identity, membership, etc **2** an action, quality, etc, that gains admission or acceptance **3** a sequence of characters used to gain access to a computer system

Passy (*French* pasi) *n* **Frédéric** (frederik). 1822–1912,

French politician and economist, who campaigned for international arbitration to prevent war: shared the first Nobel peace prize 1901

past (pɑːst) *adj* **1** completed, finished, and no longer in existence: *past happiness* **2** denoting or belonging to all or a segment of the time that has elapsed at the present moment: *the past history of the world* **3** denoting a specific unit of time that immediately precedes the present one: *the past month* **4** (*prenominal*) denoting a person who has held and relinquished an office or position; former: *a past president* **5** *grammar* denoting any of various tenses of verbs that are used in describing actions, events, or states that have been begun or completed at the time of utterance. See **aorist**, **imperfect** (sense 3), **perfect** (sense 8) ▷ *n* **6** the past the period of time or a segment of it that has elapsed: *forget the past* **7** the history, experience, or background of a nation, person, etc: *a soldier with a distinguished past* **8** an earlier period of someone's life, esp one that contains events kept secret or regarded as disreputable **9** *grammar* **a** a past tense **b** a verb in a past tense ▷ *adv* **10** at a specified or unspecified time before the present; ago: *three years past* **11** on or onwards: *I greeted him but he just walked past* ▷ *prep* **12** beyond in time: *it's past midnight* **13** beyond in place or position: *the library is past the church* **14** moving beyond; in a direction that passes: *he walked past me* **15** beyond or above the reach, limit, or scope of: *his foolishness is past comprehension* **16** beyond or above in number or amount: *to count past ten* **17** past it *informal* unable to perform the tasks one could do when one was younger **18** not put it past someone to consider someone capable of (the action specified) [c14: from *passed*, past participle of PASS]

● **USAGE** The past participle of *pass* is sometimes
● wrongly spelt *past: the time for recriminations has passed*
● (not *past*)

pasta ('pæstə) *n* any of several variously shaped edible preparations made from a flour and water dough, such as spaghetti [Italian, from Late Latin: PASTE¹]

paste (peɪst) *n* **1** a mixture or material of a soft or malleable consistency, such as toothpaste **2** an adhesive made from water and flour or starch, used esp for joining pieces of paper **3** a preparation of food, such as meat, that has been powdered to a creamy mass, for spreading on bread, crackers, etc **4** any of various sweet doughy confections: *almond paste* **5** dough, esp when prepared with shortening, as for making pastry **6 a** Also called: **strass** a hard shiny glass used for making imitation gems **b** an imitation gem made of this glass **7** the combined ingredients of porcelain. See also **hard paste**, **soft paste** ▷ *vb* (*tr*) **8** (often foll by *on* or *onto*) to attach by or as if by using paste: *he pasted posters onto the wall* **9** (usually foll by *with*) to cover (a surface) with paper, usually attached with an adhesive: *he pasted the wall with posters* [c14: via Old French from Late Latin *pasta* dough, from Greek *pastē* barley porridge, from *pastos*, from *passein* to sprinkle]

pasteboard ('peɪst,bɔːd) *n* **1** a stiff board formed from layers of paper or pulp pasted together, esp as used in bookbinding ▷ *adj* **2** flimsy; insubstantial

pastel ('pæstˀl, pæ'stɛl) *n* **1 a** a substance made of ground pigment bound with gum, used for making sticks for drawing **b** a crayon of this **c** a drawing done in such crayons **2** the medium or technique of pastel drawing **3** a pale delicate colour ▷ *adj* **4** (of a colour) pale; delicate: *pastel blue* [c17: via French from Italian *pastello*, from Late Latin *pastellus* woad compounded into a paste, diminutive of *pasta* PASTE¹] > **'pastelist** or **'pastellist** *n*

pastern ('pæstən) *n* the part of a horse's foot between the fetlock and the hoof [c14: from Old French *pasturon*, from *pasture* a hobble, from Latin *pāstōrius* of a shepherd, from PAST]

Pasternak ('pæstə,næk; *Russian* pəstɪr'nak) *n* **Boris Leonidovich** (ba'ris lɪa'nidəvitʃ). 1890–1960, Russian lyric poet, novelist, and translator, noted particularly for his novel of the Russian Revolution, *Dr. Zhivago* (1957). He was awarded the Nobel prize for literature in 1958, but was forced to decline it

paste-up *n printing* **1** an assembly of typeset matter, illustrations, etc, pasted on a sheet of paper or board and used as a guide or layout in the production of a publication **2** a sheet of paper or board on which are pasted artwork, typeset matter, etc, for photographing prior to making a printing plate

Pasteur (*French* pastœr) *n* **Louis** (lwi). 1822–95, French chemist and bacteriologist. His discovery that the fermentation of milk and alcohol was caused by microorganisms resulted in the process of pasteurization. He also devised methods of immunization against anthrax and rabies and pioneered stereochemistry

pasteurism ('pæstə,rɪzəm, -stjə-, 'pɑː-) *n med* a method of securing immunity from rabies in a person who has been bitten by a rabid animal, by daily injections of progressively more virulent suspensions of the infected spinal cord of a rabbit that died of rabies. Also called: **Pasteur treatment**

pasteurization or **pasteurisation** (,pæstəraɪ'zeɪʃən, -stjə-, ,pɑː-) *n* the process of heating beverages, such as milk, beer, wine, or cider, or solid foods, such as cheese or crab meat, to destroy harmful or undesirable microorganisms or to limit the rate of fermentation by the application of controlled heat

pasteurize or **pasteurise** ('pæstə,raɪz, -stjə-, 'pɑː-) *vb* (*tr*) **1** to subject (milk, beer, etc) to pasteurization **2** *rare* to subject (a patient) to pasteurism > **pasteurizer** or **pasteuriser** ('pæstə,raɪzə, -stjə-, 'pɑː-) *n*

pastiche (pæ'stiːʃ) or **pasticcio** ('pæ'stɪtʃəʊ) *n* **1** a work of art that mixes styles, materials, etc **2** a work of art that imitates the style of another artist or period [c19: French *pastiche*, Italian *pasticcio*, literally: piecrust (hence, something blended), from Late Latin *pasta* PASTE]

pastille or **pastil** ('pæstɪl) *n* **1** a small flavoured or medicated lozenge for chewing **2** an aromatic substance burnt to fumigate the air [c17: via French from Latin *pastillus* small loaf, from *pānis* bread]

pastime ('pɑːs,taɪm) *n* an activity or entertainment which makes time pass pleasantly [c15: from PASS + TIME, on the model of French *passe-temps*]

past master *n* **1** a person with talent for, or experience in, a particular activity: *a past master of tact* **2** a person who has held the office of master in a Freemasons' lodge, guild, etc

Pasto (*Spanish* 'pasto) *n* a city in SE Colombia, at an altitude of 2590 m (8500 ft). Pop: 404 000 (2005 est)

pastor ('pɑːstə) *n* **1** a clergyman or priest in charge of a congregation **2** a person who exercises spiritual guidance over a number of people **3** an archaic word for **shepherd** (sense 1) **4** Also called: **rosy pastor** a S Asian starling, *Sturnus roseus*, having glossy black head and wings and a pale pink body [c14: from Latin: shepherd, from *pascere* to feed] > **'pastor,ship** *n*

pastoral ('pɑːstərəl) *adj* **1** of, characterized by, or depicting rural life, scenery, etc **2** (of a literary work) dealing with an idealized form of rural existence in a conventional way **3** (of land) used for pasture **4** denoting or relating to the branch of theology dealing with the duties of a clergyman or priest to his congregation **5** of or relating to a clergyman or priest in charge of a congregation or his duties as such **6** of or relating to a teacher's responsibility for the personal, as the distinct from the educational, development of pupils **7** of or relating to shepherds, their work, etc ▷ *n* **8** a literary work or picture portraying rural life, esp the lives of shepherds in an idealizing way. See also **eclogue 9** *music* a variant of **pastorale 10** *Christianity* **a** a letter from a clergyman to the people under his charge **b** the letter of a bishop to the clergy or people of his diocese **c** Also called: **pastoral staff** the crosier or staff carried by a bishop as a symbol of his pastoral responsibilities [c15: from PASTOR] > **'pastoral,ism** *n* > **'pastorally** *adv*

pastorale (,pæstə'rɑːl) *n, pl* **-rales** *music* **1** a composition evocative of rural life, characterized by moderate compound duple or quadruple time and sometimes a droning accompaniment **2** a musical play based on a rustic story, popular during the 16th century [c18: Italian, from Latin: PASTORAL]

pastoralist (ˈpɑːstərəlɪst) *n Austral* a grazier or land-holder raising sheep, cattle, etc, on a large scale

pastorate (ˈpɑːstərɪt) *n* **1** the office or term of office of a pastor **2** a body of pastors; pastors collectively

past participle *n* a participial form of verbs used to modify a noun that is logically the object of a verb, also used in certain compound tenses and passive forms of the verb in English and other languages

past perfect *grammar* ▷ *adj* **1** denoting a tense of verbs used in relating past events where the action had already occurred at the time of the action of a main verb that is itself in a past tense. In English this is a compound tense formed with *had* plus the past participle ▷ *n* **2 a** the past perfect tense **b** a verb in this tense

pastrami (pəˈstrɑːmɪ) *n* highly seasoned smoked beef, esp prepared from a shoulder cut [from Yiddish, from Romanian *pastramă,* from *păstra* to preserve]

pastry (ˈpeɪstrɪ) *n, pl* **-tries 1** a dough of flour, water, shortening, and sometimes other ingredients **2** baked foods, such as tarts, made with this dough **3** an individual cake or pastry pie [c16: from PASTE]

pasturage (ˈpɑːstʃərɪdʒ) *n* **1** the right to graze or the business of grazing cattle **2** another word for **pasture**

pasture (ˈpɑːstʃə) *n* **1** land covered with grass or herbage and grazed by or suitable for grazing by livestock **2** a specific tract of such land ▷ *vb* **3** (*tr*) to cause (livestock) to graze or (of livestock) to graze (a pasture) [c13: via Old French from Late Latin *pāstūra,* from *pascere* to feed]

pasty¹ (ˈpeɪstɪ) *adj* **pastier, pastiest 1** of or like the colour, texture, etc, of paste **2** (esp of the complexion) pale or unhealthy-looking > ˈ**pastily** *adv* > ˈ**pastiness** *n*

pasty² (ˈpæstɪ) *n, pl* **pasties** a round of pastry folded over a filling of meat, vegetables, etc: *Cornish pasty* [c13: from Old French *pastée,* from Late Latin *pasta* dough]

PA system *n* See **public-address system**

pat¹ (pæt) *vb* **pats, patting, patted 1** to hit (something) lightly with the palm of the hand or some other flat surface: *to pat a ball* **2** to slap (a person or animal) gently, esp on the back, as an expression of affection, congratulation, etc **3** (*tr*) to shape, smooth, etc, with a flat instrument or the palm **4** (*intr*) to walk or run with light footsteps **5 pat someone on the back** *informal* to congratulate or encourage someone ▷ *n* **6** a light blow with something flat **7** a gentle slap **8** a small mass of something: *a pat of butter* **9** the sound made by a light stroke or light footsteps **10 pat on the back** *informal* a gesture or word indicating approval or encouragement [c14: perhaps imitative]

pat² (pæt) *adv* **1** Also: **off pat** exactly or fluently memorized or mastered: *he recited it pat* **2** opportunely or aptly **3 stand pat a** *chiefly US & Canadian* to refuse to abandon a belief, decision, etc **b** (in poker, etc) to play without adding new cards to the hand dealt ▷ *adj* **4** exactly right for the occasion; apt: *a pat reply* **5** too exactly fitting; glib: *a pat answer to a difficult problem* **6** exactly right: *a pat hand in poker* [c17: perhaps adverbial use ("with a light stroke") of PAT¹]

pat³ (pæt) *n* **on one's pat** *Austral informal* alone; on one's own [c20: rhyming slang, from *Pat Malone*]

patagium (pəˈteɪdʒɪəm) *n, pl* **-gia** (-dʒɪə) **1** a web of skin between the neck, limbs, and tail in bats and gliding mammals that functions as a wing **2** a membranous fold of skin connecting margins of a bird's wing to the shoulder [c19: New Latin from Greek *patageion* gold border on a tunic]

Patagonia (ˌpætəˈɡəʊnɪə) *n* **1** the southernmost region of South America, in Argentina and Chile extending from the Andes to the Atlantic. Area: about 777 000 sq km (300 000 sq miles) **2** an arid tableland in the southernmost part of Argentina, rising towards the Andes in the west

Patagonian toothfish (ˈtuːθˌfɪʃ) *n* a large food fish, *Dissostichus eleginoides,* found in the cold deep waters of the southern Atlantic and Indian oceans. Also called: **Chilean sea bass**

patch (pætʃ) *n* **1 a** a piece of material used to mend a garment or to make patchwork, a sewn-on pocket, etc **b** (*as modifier*): *a patch pocket* **2** a small piece, area, expanse,

etc **3 a** a small plot of land **b** its produce: *a patch of cabbages* **4** *med* **a** a protective covering for an injured eye **b** any protective dressing **5** an imitation beauty spot, esp one made of black or coloured silk, worn by both sexes, esp in the 18th century **6** Also called: **flash** *US* an identifying piece of fabric worn on the shoulder of a uniform, on a vehicle, etc **7** a small contrasting section or stretch: *a patch of cloud in the blue sky* **8** a scrap; remnant **9** a bad patch a difficult or troubled time **10 not a patch on** *informal* not nearly as good as ▷ *vb* (*tr*) **11** to mend or supply (a garment, etc) with a patch or patches **12** to put together or produce with patches **13** (of material) to serve as a patch to **14** (often foll by *up*) to mend hurriedly or in a makeshift way **15** (often foll by *up*) to make (up) or settle (a quarrel) **16** to connect (electric circuits) together temporarily by means of a patch board **17** (usually foll by *through*) to connect (a telephone call) by means of a patch board **18** *computing* to correct or improve (a program) by adding a small set of instructions [c16 *pacche,* perhaps from French *pieche* PIECE] > ˈ**patcher** *n*

patch board or **patch panel** *n* a device with a large number of sockets into which electrical plugs can be inserted to form many different temporary circuits: used in telephone exchanges, computer systems, etc. Also called: **plugboard**

patchouli, pachouli or **patchouly** (ˈpætʃʊlɪ, pəˈtʃuːlɪ) *n* **1** any of several Asiatic trees of the genus *Pogostemon,* the leaves of which yield a heavy fragrant oil: family *Lamiaceae* (labiates) **2** the perfume made from this oil [c19: from Tamil *paccilai,* from *paccu* green + *ilai* leaf]

patch pocket *n* a pocket on the outside of a garment

patch test *n med* a test to detect an allergic reaction by applying small amounts of a suspected substance to the skin and then examining the area for signs of irritation

patchwork (ˈpætʃˌwɜːk) *n* **1** needlework done by sewing pieces of different materials together **2** something, such as a theory, made up of various parts

patchy (ˈpætʃɪ) *adj* **patchier, patchiest 1** irregular in quality, occurrence, intensity, etc: *a patchy essay* **2** having or forming patches > ˈ**patchily** *adv* > ˈ**patchiness** *n*

pate (peɪt) *n* the head, esp with reference to baldness or (in facetious use) intelligence [c14: of unknown origin]

pâté (ˈpæteɪ; *French* pɑte) *n* **1** a spread of very finely minced liver, poultry, etc, served usually as an hors d'oeuvre **2** a savoury pie of meat or fish [from French: PASTE]

pâté de foie gras (pɑte də fwɑ ɡrɑ) *n, pl* **pâtés de foie gras** (pɑte də fwɑ ɡrɑ) a smooth rich paste made from the liver of a specially fattened goose, considered a great delicacy [French: pâté of fat liver]

patella (pəˈtɛlə) *n, pl* **-lae** (-liː) *anatomy* a small flat triangular bone in front of and protecting the knee joint. Nontechnical name: **kneecap** [c17: from Latin, from *patina* shallow pan] > **paˈtellar** *adj*

paten (ˈpætən), **patin** or **patine** (ˈpætɪn) *n* a plate, usually made of silver or gold, esp the plate on which the bread is placed in the Eucharist [c13: from Old French *patene,* from Medieval Latin, from Latin *patina* pan]

patency (ˈpeɪtənsɪ) *n* the condition of being obvious

Patenier *n* Joachim. See (Joachim) **Patinir**

patent (ˈpætənt, ˈpeɪtənt) *n* **1 a** a government grant to an inventor assuring him the sole right to make, use, and sell his invention for a limited period **b** a document conveying such a grant **2** an invention, privilege, etc, protected by a patent **3 a** an official document granting a right **b** any right granted by such a document ▷ *adj* **4** open or available for inspection (esp in the phrases **letters patent, patent writ**) **5** (ˈpeɪtənt) obvious: *their scorn was patent to everyone* **6** concerning protection, appointment, etc, of or by a patent or patents **7** proprietary **8** (esp of a bodily passage or duct) being open or unobstructed ▷ *vb* (*tr*) **9** to obtain a patent for **10** (in the US) to grant (public land or mineral rights) by a patent **11** *metallurgy* to heat (a metal) above a transformation temperature and cool it at a rate that allows cold working [c14: via Old French from Latin *patēre* to lie open; n use, short for *letters patent,* from

Medieval Latin *litterae patentes* letters lying open (to public inspection)] > 'patentable *adj* > ,patenta'bility *n*

patent leather *n* leather or imitation leather processed with lacquer to give a hard glossy surface

patently ('peɪt³ntlɪ) *adv* obviously

patent medicine *n* a medicine protected by a patent and available without a doctor's prescription

Patent Office ('pæt³nt) *n* a government department that issues patents

Patent Rolls *pl n* (in Britain) the register of patents issued

pater ('peɪtə) *n* *Brit chiefly facetious* a public school slang word for **father** [from Latin]

Pater ('peɪtə) *n* **Walter (Horatio)**. 1839–94, English essayist and critic, noted for his prose style and his advocation of the "love of art for its own sake". His works include the philosophical romance *Marius the Epicurean* (1885), *Studies in the History of the Renaissance* (1873), and *Imaginary Portraits* (1887)

paterfamilias (,peɪtəfə'mɪlɪˌæs) *n, pl* **patresfamilias** (,pɑ:treɪzfə'mɪlɪˌæs) **1** the male head of a household **2** *Roman law* **a** the head of a household having authority over its members **b** the parental or other authority of another person [Latin: father of the family]

paternal (pə'tɜ:n³l) *adj* **1** relating to or characteristic of a father, esp in showing affection, encouragement, etc; fatherly **2** (*prenominal*) related through the father: *his paternal grandfather* **3** inherited or derived from the male parent [C17: from Late Latin *paternālis*, from Latin *pater* father] > pa'ternally *adv*

paternalism (pə'tɜ:nəˌlɪzəm) *n* the attitude or policy of a government or other authority that manages the affairs of a country, company, community, etc, in the manner of a father, esp in usurping individual responsibility and the liberty of choice > pa'ternalist *n, adj* > pa,ternal'istic *adj* > pa,ternal'istically *adv*

paternity (pə'tɜ:nɪtɪ) *n* **1 a** the fact or state of being a father **b** (*as modifier*): *a paternity suit was filed against the man* **2** descent or derivation from a father **3** authorship or origin: *the paternity of the theory is disputed* [C15: from Late Latin *paternitās*, from Latin *pater* father]

paternoster (,pætə'nɒstə) *n* **1** *RC Church* the beads at the ends of each decade of the rosary marking the points at which the Paternoster is recited **2** *Also called:* **paternoster line** a type of fishing tackle in which short lines and hooks are attached at intervals to the main line **3** a type of lift in which platforms are attached to continuous chains. The lift does not stop at each floor but passengers enter while it is moving [Latin, literally: our father (from the opening of the Lord's Prayer)]

Paternoster (,pætə'nɒstə) *n* (*sometimes not capital*) *RC Church* **1** the Lord's Prayer, esp in Latin **2** the recital of this as an act of devotion [see PATERNOSTER]

Paterson[1] ('pætəs³n) *n* a city in NE New Jersey: settled by the Dutch in the late 17th century. Pop: 150 782 (2003 est)

Paterson[2] ('pætəs³n) *n* **1 Andrew Barton**, known as *Banjo Paterson*. 1864–1941, Australian poet. His works include "Waltzing Matilda" and "The Man from Snowy River" **2 William**. 1658–1719, Scottish merchant and banker: founded the Bank of England (1694)

Paterson's curse *n Austral.* a purple-flowered noxious plant, *Echium plantagineum*, a close relative of viper's bugloss, naturalized in Australia and NZ where its harmfulness to livestock has prompted attempts to limit its spread. *Also called:* **Salvation Jane** *See* **viper's bugloss**

path (pɑ:θ) *n, pl* **paths** (pɑ:ðz) **1** a road or way, esp a narrow trodden track **2** a surfaced walk, as through a garden **3** the course or direction in which something moves: *the path of a whirlwind* **4** a course of conduct: *the path of virtue* **5** *computing* the directions for reaching a particular file or directory, as traced hierarchically through each of the parent directories usually from the root; the file or directory and all parent directories are separated from one another in the path by slashes [Old English *pæth*; related to Old High German, German *Pfad*] > 'pathless *adj*

path. (pæθ) *abbreviation* **1** pathological **2** pathology

-path *n combining form* **1** denoting a person suffering from a specified disease or disorder: *neuropath* **2** denoting a practitioner of a particular method of treatment: *osteopath* [back formation from -PATHY]

Pathan (pə'tɑ:n) *n* a member of the Pashto-speaking people of Afghanistan, NW Pakistan, and elsewhere, most of whom are Muslim in religion [C17: from Hindi]

pathetic (pə'θɛtɪk) *adj* **1** evoking or expressing pity, sympathy, etc **2** distressingly inadequate: *the old man sat huddled in front of a pathetic fire* **3** *Brit informal* ludicrously or contemptibly uninteresting or worthless: *the standard of goalkeeping in amateur football today is pathetic* **4** *obsolete* of or affecting the feelings [C16: from French *pathétique*, via Late Latin from Greek *pathetikos* sensitive, from *pathos* suffering; see PATHOS] > pa'thetically *adv*

pathetic fallacy *n* (in literature) the presentation of inanimate objects in nature as possessing human feelings

pathfinder ('pɑ:θˌfaɪndə) *n* **1** a person who makes or finds a way, esp through unexplored areas or fields of knowledge **2** an aircraft or parachutist who indicates a target area by dropping flares, etc **3** a radar device used for navigation or homing onto a target

pathfinder prospectus *n* a prospectus regarding the flotation of a new company that contains only sufficient details to test the market reaction

pathname ('pɑ:θˌneɪm) *n computing* the name of a file or directory together with its position in relation to other directories traced back in a line to the root; the names of the file and each of the parent directories are separated from one another by slashes

patho- or before a vowel **path-** combining form disease: *pathology* [from Greek *pathos* suffering; see PATHOS]

pathogen ('pæθəˌdʒɛn) or **pathogene** ('pæθəˌdʒiːn) *n* any agent that can cause disease > **pathogenic** (,pæθə'dʒɛnɪk) *adj*

pathogenesis (,pæθə'dʒɛnɪsɪs) or **pathogeny** (pə'θɒdʒɪnɪ) *n* the origin, development, and resultant effects of a disease > **pathogenetic** (,pæθəʊdʒɪ'nɛtɪk) *adj*

pathological (,pæθə'lɒdʒɪk³l) or *less commonly* **pathologic** *adj* **1** of or relating to pathology **2** relating to, involving, or caused by disease **3** *informal* compulsively motivated: *a pathological liar* > ,patho'logically *adv*

pathologize or **pathologise** (pə'θɒlə[dg]aɪz) *vb* (*tr*) to represent (something) as a disease: *this pathologizing of parenthood*

pathology (pə'θɒlədʒɪ) *n, pl* **-gies** **1** the branch of medicine concerned with the cause, origin, and nature of disease, including the changes occurring as a result of disease **2** the manifestations of disease, esp changes occurring in tissues or organs > pa'thologist *n*

pathos ('peɪθɒs) *n* **1** the quality or power, esp in literature or speech, of arousing feelings of pity, sorrow, etc **2** a feeling of sympathy or pity [C17: from Greek: suffering; related to *penthos* sorrow]

pathway ('pɑ:θˌweɪ) *n* **1** another word for **path** (senses 1, 2) **2** *biochem* a chain of reactions associated with a particular metabolic process

-pathy *n combining form* **1** indicating feeling, sensitivity, or perception: *telepathy* **2** indicating disease or a morbid condition: *psychopathy* **3** indicating a method of treating disease: *osteopathy* [from Greek *patheia* suffering; see PATHOS] > -pathic *adj combining form*

Patiala (,pʌtɪ'ɑ:lə) *n* a city in N India, in E Punjab: seat of the Punjabi University (1962). Pop: 302 870 (2001)

patience ('peɪʃəns) *n* **1** tolerant and even-tempered perseverance **2** the capacity for calmly enduring pain, trying situations, etc **3** *chiefly Brit* any of various card games for one player only, in which the cards may be laid out in various combinations as the player tries to use up the whole pack. US equivalent: **solitaire** [C13: via Old French from Latin *patientia* endurance, from *patī* to suffer]

patient ('peɪʃənt) *adj* **1** enduring trying circumstances with even temper **2** tolerant; understanding **3** capable of accepting delay with equanimity **4** persevering or diligent: *a patient worker* ▷ *n* **5** a person who is receiving medical care [C14: see PATIENCE] > 'patiently *adv*

patina[1] ('pætɪnə) *n, pl* **-nas** **1** a film of oxide formed on the surface of a metal, esp the green oxidation of bronze or copper **2** any fine layer on a surface: *a patina of frost* **3** the sheen on a surface that is caused by much handling [c18: from Italian: coating, from Latin: PATINA²]

patina² ('pætɪnə) *n, pl* -nae (-ˌniː) a broad shallow dish used in ancient Rome [from Latin, from Greek *patanē* platter]

Patinir or **Patenier** (ˌpɑːtɪˈnɪə) *n* **Joachim** ('jəʊəkɪm). ?1485–1524, Flemish painter, noted esp for the landscapes in his paintings on religious themes

patio ('pætɪˌəʊ) *n, pl* -os **1** an open inner courtyard, esp one in a Spanish or Spanish-American house **2** an area adjoining a house, esp one that is paved and used for outdoor activities [c19: from Spanish: courtyard]

patisserie (pəˈtiːsərɪ) *n* **1** a shop where fancy pastries are sold **2** such pastries [c18: French, from *pâtissier* pastry cook, ultimately from Late Latin *pasta* PASTE]

Patmore ('pætmɔː) *n* **Coventry (Kersey Dighton)**. 1823–96, English poet. His works, celebrating both conjugal and divine love, include *The Angel in the House* (1854–62) and *The Unknown Eros* (1877)

Patmos ('pætmɒs) *n* a Greek island in the Aegean, in the NW Dodecanese: St John's place of exile (about 95 AD), where he wrote the Apocalypse. Pop: 2984 (2001). Area: 34 sq km (13 sq miles)

Patna ('pætnə) *n* a city in NE India, capital of Bihar state, on the River Ganges: founded in the 5th century BC; university (1917); centre of a rice-growing region. Pop: 1 376 950 (2001)

Patna rice *n* a variety of long-grain rice, used for savoury dishes

patois ('pætwɑː; *French* patwa) *n, pl* patois ('pætwɑːz; *French* patwa) **1** an unwritten regional dialect of a language, esp of French, usually considered substandard **2** the jargon of particular group [c17: from Old French: rustic speech, perhaps from *patoier* to handle awkwardly, from *patte* paw]

Paton ('peɪtən) *n* **Alan (Stewart)**. 1903–88, South African writer, noted esp for his novel dealing with racism and apartheid in South Africa, *Cry, the Beloved Country* (1965)

pat. pend. *abbreviation* patent pending

Patras (pəˈtræs, 'pætrəs) *n* a port in W Greece, in the NW Peloponnese on the **Gulf of Patras** (an inlet of the Ionian Sea): one of the richest cities in Greece until the 3rd century BC; under Turkish rule from 1458 to 1687 and from 1715 until the War of Greek Independence, which began here in 1821. Pop: 193 000 (2005 est). Modern Greek name: **Pátrai** ('patrɛ)

patri- *combining form* father: *patricide; patrilocal* [from Latin *pater*, Greek *patēr* FATHER]

patrial ('peɪtrɪəl) *n* (in Britain formerly) a person having by statute the right of abode in the United Kingdom, and so not subject to immigration control [c20: from Latin *patria* native land]

patriarch ('peɪtrɪˌɑːk) *n* **1** the male head of a tribe or family **2** a very old or venerable man **3** *Old Testament* any of a number of persons regarded as the fathers of the human race, divided into the antediluvian patriarchs, from Adam to Noah, and the postdiluvian, from Noah to Abraham **4** *Old Testament* any of the three ancestors of the Hebrew people: Abraham, Isaac, or Jacob **5** *Old Testament* any of Jacob's twelve sons, regarded as the ancestors of the twelve tribes of Israel **6** *early Christian Church* the bishop of one of several principal sees, esp those of Rome, Antioch, and Alexandria **7** *Eastern Orthodox Church* the bishops of the four ancient principal sees of Constantinople, Antioch, Alexandria, and Jerusalem, and also of Russia, Romania, and Serbia, the bishop of Constantinople (the **ecumenical Patriarch**) being highest in dignity among these **8** *RC Church* **a** a title given to the pope **b** a title given to a number of bishops, esp of the Uniat Churches, indicating their rank as immediately below that of the pope **9** the oldest or most venerable member of a group, community, etc **10** a person regarded as the founder of a community, tradition, etc [c12: via Old French from Church Latin *patriarcha*] > ˌpatri'archal *adj*

patriarchate ('peɪtrɪˌɑːkɪt) *n* the office, jurisdiction,

province, or residence of a patriarch

patriarchy ('peɪtrɪˌɑːkɪ) *n, pl* -chies **1** a form of social organization in which a male is the head of the family and descent, kinship, and title are traced through the male line **2** any society governed by such a system

patriate ('pætrɪˌeɪt, 'peɪtrɪˌeɪt) *vb* (*tr*) to bring under the authority of an autonomous country, for example as in the transfer of the Canadian constitution from UK to Canadian responsibility > ˌpatri'ation *n*

patrician (pəˈtrɪʃən) *n* **1** a member of the hereditary aristocracy of ancient Rome. In the early republic the patricians held almost all the higher offices **2** (in medieval Europe) a member of the upper class in numerous Italian republics and German free cities **3** an aristocrat **4** a person of refined conduct, tastes, etc ▷ *adj* **5** (esp in ancient Rome) of, relating to, or composed of patricians **6** aristocratic [c15: from Old French *patricien*, from Latin *patricius* noble, from *pater* father]

patricide ('pætrɪˌsaɪd) *n* **1** the act of killing one's father **2** a person who kills his father > ˌpatri'cidal *adj*

Patrick ('pætrɪk) *n* **Saint**. 5th century AD, Christian missionary in Ireland, probably born in Britain; patron saint of Ireland. Feast day: March 17

patrilineal (ˌpætrɪˈlɪnɪəl) or **patrilinear** *adj* tracing descent, kinship, or title through the male line

patrimony ('pætrɪmənɪ) *n, pl* -nies **1** an inheritance from one's father or other ancestor **2** the endowment of a church [c14 *patrimoyne*, from Old French, from Latin *patrimonium* paternal inheritance] > **patrimonial** (ˌpætrɪˈməʊnɪəl) *adj*

patriot ('peɪtrɪət, 'pæt-) *n* a person who vigorously supports his country and its way of life [c16: via French from Late Latin *patriōta*, from Greek *patriōtēs*, from *patris* native land; related to Greek *patēr* father; compare Latin *pater* father, *patria* fatherland] > **patriotic** (ˌpætrɪˈɒtɪk) *adj* > ˌpatri'otically *adv*

Patriot ('peɪtrɪət) *n* a US surface-to-air missile system with multiple launch stations and the capability to track multiple targets by radar

patriotism ('pætrɪəˌtɪzəm) *n* devotion to one's own country and concern for its defence

patristic (pəˈtrɪstɪk) or **patristical** *adj* of or relating to the Fathers of the Church, their writings, or the study of these > pa'tristics *n* (*functioning as singular*)

Patroclus (pəˈtrɒkləs) *n* *Greek myth* a friend of Achilles, killed in the Trojan War by Hector. His death made Achilles return to the fight after his quarrel with Agamemnon

patrol (pəˈtrəʊl) *n* **1** the action of going through or around a town, neighbourhood, etc, at regular intervals for purposes of security or observation **2** a person or group that carries out such an action **3** a military detachment with the mission of security, gathering information, or combat with enemy forces **4** a division of a troop of Scouts or Guides ▷ *vb* -trols, -trolling, -trolled **5** to engage in a patrol of (a place) [c17: from French *patrouiller*, from *patouiller* to flounder in mud, from *patte* paw] > pa'troller *n*

patrol car *n* a police car with a radio telephone used for patrolling streets and motorways

patrology (pəˈtrɒlədʒɪ) *n* **1** the study of the writings of the Fathers of the Church **2** a collection of such writings [c17: from Greek *patr-*, *patēr* father + -LOGY] > pa'trologist *n*

patrol wagon *n* US, Austral. & NZ a police van for transporting prisoners. Also called: (*Informal*) **paddy wagon** or (US) **police wagon**

patron¹ ('peɪtrən) *n* **1** a person, esp a man, who sponsors or aids artists, charities, etc; protector or benefactor **2** a customer of a shop, hotel, etc, esp a regular one **3** See **patron saint** [c14: via Old French from Latin *patrōnus* protector, from *pater* father]

patron² *French* (patrɔ̃) *n* a man, who owns or manages a hotel, restaurant, or bar

patronage ('pætrənɪdʒ) *n* **1 a** the support given or custom brought by a patron or patroness **b** the position of a patron **2** (in politics) **a** the practice of making appointments to office, granting contracts, etc **b** the favours so distributed **3 a** a condescending manner

b any kindness done in a condescending way

patronize *or* **patronise** ('pætrə,naɪz) *vb* **1** to behave or treat in a condescending way **2** (*tr*) to act as a patron or patroness by sponsoring or bringing trade to > 'patron,izer *or* 'patron,iser *n*

patronizing *or* **patronising** ('pætrə,naɪzɪŋ) *adj* having a superior manner; condescending > 'patron,izingly *or* 'patron,isingly *adv*

patron saint *n* a saint regarded as the particular guardian of a country, church, trade, person, etc

patronymic (,pætrə'nɪmɪk) *adj* **1** (of a name) derived from the name of its bearer's father or ancestor. In Western cultures, many surnames are patronymic in origin, as for example Irish names beginning with O' and English names ending with *-son*; in other cultures, such as Russian, a special patronymic name is used in addition to the surname ▷ *n* **2** a patronymic name [c17: via Late Latin from Greek *patronumikos*, from *patēr* father + *onoma* NAME]

patroon (pə'truːn) *n* (in the US) a Dutch land-holder in New Netherland and New York with manorial rights in the colonial era [c18: from Dutch: PATRON¹]

patsy ('pætsɪ) *n, pl* **-sies** *slang, chiefly US & Canadian* **1** a person who is easily cheated, victimized, etc **2** a scapegoat [c20: of unknown origin]

patten ('pætᵊn) *n* a wooden clog or sandal on a raised wooden platform or metal ring [c14: from Old French *patin*, probably from *patte* paw]

patter¹ ('pætə) *vb* **1** (*intr*) to walk or move with quick soft steps **2** to strike with or make a quick succession of light tapping sounds ▷ *n* **3** a quick succession of light tapping sounds, as of feet: *the patter of mice* [c17: from PAT¹]

patter² ('pætə) *n* **1** the glib rapid speech of comedians, salesmen, etc **2** quick idle talk; chatter **3** the jargon of a particular group; lingo ▷ *vb* **4** (*intr*) to speak glibly and rapidly **5** to repeat (prayers) in a mechanical or perfunctory manner [c14: from Latin *pater* in *Pater Noster* Our Father]

pattern ('pætᵊn) *n* **1** an arrangement of repeated or corresponding parts, decorative motifs, etc **2** a decorative design: *a paisley pattern* **3** a style: *various patterns of cutlery* **4** a plan or diagram used as a guide in making something: *a paper pattern for a dress* **5** a standard way of moving, acting, etc: *traffic patterns* **6** a model worthy of imitation: *a pattern of kindness* **7** a representative sample **8** a wooden or metal shape or model used in a foundry to make a mould ▷ *vb* (*tr*) **9** (often foll by *after* or *on*) to model **10** to arrange as or decorate with a pattern [c14: from *patron*, from Medieval Latin *patrōnus* example, from Latin PATRON¹]

Patti ('pætɪ) *n* **Adelina** (ade'liːna). 1843–1919, Italian operatic coloratura soprano, born in Spain

Patton ('pætᵊn) *n* **George Smith.** 1885–1945, US general, who successfully developed tank warfare as an extension of cavalry tactics in World War II: captured Palermo, Sicily (1942) and much of France (1944)

patty ('pætɪ) *n, pl* **-ties** **1** a small flattened cake of minced food **2** a small pie [c18: from French PÂTÉ]

patu ('pɑːtuː) *n, pl* **patus** a short Māori club, now used ceremonially [Māori]

patulous ('pætjʊləs) *adj botany* spreading widely or expanded: *patulous branches* [c17: from Latin *patulus* open, from *patēre* to lie open]

Pau (French po) *n* a city in SW France: residence of the French kings of Navarre; tourist centre for the Pyrenees. Pop: 78 732 (1999)

paua ('pɑːʊa) *n* an edible abalone, *Haliotis iris*, of New Zealand, having an iridescent shell used esp for jewellery [from Māori]

paucity ('pɔːsɪtɪ) *n* **1** smallness of quantity; insufficiency; dearth **2** smallness of number; fewness [c15: from Latin *paucitās* scarcity, from *paucus* few]

Paul (pɔːl) *n* **1 Saint.** Also called: **Paul the Apostle, Saul of Tarsus.** original name *Saul.* died ?67 AD, one of the first Christian missionaries to the Gentiles, who died a martyr in Rome. Until his revelatory conversion he had assisted in persecuting the Christians. He wrote many of the Epistles in the New Testament. Feast day: June 29.

Related adj: **Pauline 2 Jean.** See Jean Paul **3 Les,** real name *Lester Polfuss.* born 1915, US guitarist: creator of the solid-body electric guitar and pioneer in multitrack recording

Paul I *n* **1** 1754–1801, tsar of Russia (1796–1801); son of Catherine II; assassinated **2** 1901–64, king of the Hellenes (1947–64); son of Constantine I

Paul III *n* original name *Alessandro Farnese.* 1468–1549, Italian ecclesiastic; pope (1534–49). He excommunicated Henry VIII of England (1538) and inaugurated the Counter-Reformation by approving the establishment of the Jesuits (1540), instituting the Inquisition in Italy, and convening the Council of Trent (1545)

Paul VI *n* original name *Giovanni Battista Montini.* 1897–1978, Italian ecclesiastic; pope (1963–1978)

Pauli exclusion principle *n physics* the principle that two identical fermions cannot occupy the same quantum state in a body such as an atom. Sometimes shortened to **exclusion principle** [c20: from Wolfgang *Pauli* (1900–58), US physicist born in Austria]

Pauline ('pɔːlaɪn) *adj* relating to Saint Paul (died ?67 AD), the Christian missionary, martyr, and writer of many of the epistles in the New Testament, or to his doctrines

Paul Jones *n* an old-time dance in which partners are exchanged [c19: named after John Paul Jones (1747–92), Scots-born US naval commander]

paulownia (pɔː'ləʊnɪə) *n* any scrophulariaceous tree of the Japanese genus *Paulownia*, esp *P. tomentosa*, having large heart-shaped leaves and clusters of purplish or white flowers [c19: New Latin, named after Anna *Paulovna*, daughter of Paul I of Russia]

Pauli ('pɔːlɪ, 'paʊlɪ) *n* **Wolfgang** ('vɒlf,gæn). 1900–58, US physicist, born in Austria. He formulated the exclusion principle (1924) and postulated the existence of the neutrino (1931), later confirmed by Fermi: Nobel prize for physics 1945

Pauling ('pɔːlɪŋ) *n* **Linus Carl** ('laɪnəs). 1901–94, US chemist, noted particularly for his work on the nature of the chemical bond and his opposition to nuclear tests: Nobel prize for chemistry 1954; Nobel peace prize 1962

Paulinus (pɔː'laɪnəs) *n* **Saint.** died 644 AD, Roman missionary to England; first bishop of York and archbishop of Rochester. Feast day: Oct 10

Paulinus of Nola ('nəʊlə) *n* **Saint.** ?353–431 AD, Roman consul and Christian poet; bishop of Nola (409–431). Feast day: June 22

Paumotu Archipelago (paʊ'məʊtuː) *n* another name for the **Tuamotu Archipelago**

paunch (pɔːntʃ) *n* **1** the belly or abdomen, esp when protruding **2** another name for **rumen** ▷ *vb* (*tr*) **3** to stab in the stomach; disembowel [c14: from Anglo-Norman *paunche*, from Old French *pance*, from Latin *pantices* (pl) bowels]

paunchy ('pɔːntʃɪ) *adj* **-ier, -iest** having a protruding belly or abdomen > 'paunchiness *n*

pauper ('pɔːpə) *n* **1** a person who is extremely poor **2** (formerly) a destitute person supported by public charity [c16: from Latin: poor] > 'pauper,ism *n*

pauperize *or* **pauperise** ('pɔːpə,raɪz) *vb* (*tr*) to make a pauper of; impoverish

Pausanias (pɔː'seɪnɪəs) *n* 2nd century AD, Greek geographer and historian. His *Description of Greece* gives a valuable account of the topography of ancient Greece

pause (pɔːz) *vb* (*intr*) **1** to cease an action temporarily; stop **2** to hesitate; delay: *she replied without pausing* ▷ *n* **3** a temporary stop or rest, esp in speech or action; short break **4** *prosody* another word for **caesura 5** Also called: fermata *music* a continuation of a note or rest beyond its normal length **6** give pause to to cause to hesitate [c15: from Latin *pausa* pause, from Greek *pausis*, from *pauein* to halt]

pav (pæv) *n Austral & NZ informal* short for **pavlova**

pavane *or* **pavan** (pə'vɑːn, -'væn, 'pævᵊn) *n* **1** a slow and stately dance of the 16th and 17th centuries **2** a piece of music composed for or in the rhythm of this dance, usually characterized by a slow stately triple time [c16: *pavan*, via French from Spanish *pavana*, from Old Italian *padovana* Paduan (dance), from *Padova* Padua]

Pavarotti (Italian pava'rɔti) *n* **Luciano** 1935–2007, Italian operatic tenor, specializing in works by Verdi and Puccini

pave (peɪv) *vb* (*tr*) **1** to cover (a road, path, etc) with a firm surface suitable for travel, as with paving stones or concrete **2** to serve as the material for a pavement or other hard layer: *bricks paved the causeway* **3** (often foll by *with*) to cover with a hard layer (of): *shelves paved with marble* **4** to prepare or make easier (esp in the phrase **pave the way**): *to pave the way for future development* [c14: from Old French *paver*, from Latin *pavīre* to ram down] > **'paver** *n*

pavement ('peɪvmənt) *n* **1** a hard-surfaced path for pedestrians alongside and a little higher than a road. US and Canadian word: **sidewalk 2** the material used in paving [c13: from Latin *pavīmentum* a hard floor, from *pavīre* to beat hard]

Pavese (*Italian* pa'veːse) *n* **Cesare** ('tʃeːzare). 1908–50, Italian writer and translator. His works include collections of poems, such as *Verrà la morte e avrà i tuoi occhi* (1953), short stories, such as the collection *Notte di festa* (1953), and the novel *La Luna e i falò* (1950)

Pavia ('paːvɪə) *n* a town in N Italy, in Lombardy: noted for its Roman and medieval remains, including the tomb of St Augustine. Pop: 71 214 (2001)

pavilion (pə'vɪljən) *n* **1** *Brit* a building at a sports ground, esp a cricket pitch, in which players change **2** a summerhouse or other decorative shelter **3** a building or temporary structure, esp one that is open and ornamental, for housing exhibitions **4** a large ornate tent, esp one with a peaked top, as used by medieval armies **5** one of a set of buildings that together form a hospital or other large institution ▷ *vb* (*tr*) *literary* **6** to place or set in or as if in a pavilion: *pavilioned in splendour* **7** to provide with a pavilion or pavilions [c13: from Old French *pavillon* canopied structure, from Latin *pāpiliō* butterfly, tent]

paving ('peɪvɪŋ) *n* **1** a paved surface; pavement **2** material used for a pavement, such as paving stones, bricks, or asphalt

Pavlodar (*Russian* pəvla'dar) *n* a port in NE Kazakhstan on the Irtysh River: major industrial centre with an oil refinery. Pop: 303 000 (2005 est)

Pavlov ('pævlɒv; *Russian* 'pavləf) *n* **Ivan Petrovich** (i'van pɪ'trovɪtʃ). 1849–1936, Russian physiologist. His study of conditioned reflexes in dogs influenced behaviourism. He also made important contributions to the study of digestion: Nobel prize for physiology or medicine 1904

pavlova (pæv'ləʊvə) *n* a meringue cake topped with whipped cream and fruit [c20: named after Anna PAVLOVA]

Pavlova (pæv'ləʊvə; *Russian* 'pavləvə) *n* **Anna** ('annə). 1885–1931, Russian ballerina

paw (pɔː) *n* **1** any of the feet of a four-legged mammal, bearing claws or nails **2** *informal* a hand, esp one that is large, clumsy, etc ▷ *vb* **3** to scrape or contaminate with the paws or feet **4** (*tr*) *informal* to touch or caress in a clumsy, rough, or overfamiliar manner; maul [c13: via Old French from Germanic; related to Middle Dutch *pōte*, German *Pfote*]

pawky ('pɔːkɪ) *adj* **pawkier, pawkiest** *Scot* having or characterized by a dry wit [c17: from Scottish *pawk* trick, of unknown origin] > **'pawkily** *adv* > **'pawkiness** *n*

pawl (pɔːl) *n* a pivoted lever shaped to engage with a ratchet wheel to prevent motion in a particular direction [c17: perhaps from Dutch *pal* pawl]

pawn¹ (pɔːn) *vb* (*tr*) **1** to deposit (an article) as security for the repayment of a loan, esp from a pawnbroker **2** to stake: *to pawn one's honour* ▷ *n* **3** an article deposited as security **4** the condition of being so deposited (esp in the phrase **in pawn**) **5** a person or thing that is held as a security, esp a hostage **6** the act of pawning [c15: from Old French *pan* security, from Latin *pannus* cloth, apparently because clothing was often left as a surety; compare Middle Flemish *paen* pawn, German *Pfand* pledge] > **'pawnage** *n*

pawn² (pɔːn) *n* **1** a chessman of the lowest theoretical value, limited to forward moves of one square at a time with the option of two squares on its initial move: it captures with a diagonal move only **2** a person, group,

etc, manipulated by another [c14: from Anglo-Norman *poun*, from Old French *pehon*, from Medieval Latin *pedō* infantryman, from Latin *pēs* foot]

pawnbroker ('pɔːn,brəʊkə) *n* a dealer licensed to lend money at a specified rate of interest on the security of movable personal property, which can be sold if the loan is not repaid within a specified period > **'pawn,broking** *n*

pawnshop ('pɔːn,ʃɒp) *n* the premises of a pawnbroker

pawn ticket *n* a receipt for goods pawned

pawpaw ('pɔː,pɔː) *n* a variant of papaw, papaya

pax (pæks) *n* **1** *chiefly RC Church* **a** a greeting signifying Christian love transmitted from one to another of those assisting at the Eucharist; kiss of peace **b** a small metal or ivory plate, often with a representation of the Crucifixion, formerly used to convey the kiss of peace from the celebrant at Mass to those attending it, who kissed the plate in turn ▷ *interj* **2** *Brit school slang* a call signalling an end to hostilities or claiming immunity from the rules of a game: usually accompanied by a crossing of the fingers [Latin: peace]

Pax (pæks) *n* the Roman goddess of peace [Latin: peace]

PAX *abbreviation* private automatic exchange

Paxman ('pæksmən) *n* **Jeremy** (**Dickson**). born 1950, British journalist, broadcaster, and author, noted esp for his political interviews

Paxton ('pækstən) *n* **Sir Joseph**. 1801–65, English architect, who designed Crystal Palace (1851), the first large structure of prefabricated glass and iron parts

pay¹ (peɪ) *vb* **pays, paying, paid 1** to discharge (a debt, obligation, etc) by giving or doing something: *he paid his creditors* **2** (when *intr*, often foll by *for*) to give (money) to (a person) in return for goods or services: *they pay their workers well; they pay by the hour* **3** to give or afford (a person) a profit or benefit: *it pays one to be honest* **4** (*tr*) to give or bestow (a compliment, regards, attention, etc) **5** (*tr*) to make (a visit or call) **6** (*intr*; often foll by *for*) to give compensation or make amends **7** (*tr*) to yield a return of: *the shares pay 15 per cent* **8** *Austral informal* to acknowledge or accept (something) as true, just, etc **9 pay one's way a** to contribute one's share of expenses **b** to remain solvent without outside help ▷ *n* **10** a money given in return for work or services; a salary or wage **b** (*as modifier*): *a pay slip; pay claim* **11** paid employment (esp in the phrase **in the pay of**) **12** (*modifier*) requiring the insertion of money or discs before or during use: *a pay phone; a pay toilet* **13** (*modifier*) rich enough in minerals to be profitably mined or worked: *pay gravel* ▷ See also **pay back, pay for, pay off, pay out, pay up** [c12: from Old French *payer*, from Latin *pācāre* to appease (a creditor), from *pāx* PEACE]

pay² (peɪ) *vb* **pays, paying, payed** (*tr*) *nautical* to caulk (the seams of a wooden vessel) with pitch or tar [c17: from Old French *peier*, from Latin *picāre*, from *pix* pitch]

payable ('peɪəbᵊl) *adj* **1** (often foll by *on*) to be paid: *payable on the third of each month* **2** that is capable of being paid **3** capable of being profitable **4** (of a debt) imposing an obligation on the debtor to pay, esp at once

pay-and-display *adj* denoting a car-parking system in which a motorist buys a permit to park for a specified period from a coin-operated machine and displays the permit on or near the windscreen of his or her car so that it can be seen by a parking attendant

pay back *vb* (*tr, adverb*) **1** to retaliate against: *to pay someone back for an insult* **2** to give or do (something equivalent) in return for a favour, insult, etc **3** to repay (a loan) ▷ *n* **payback 4 a** the return on an investment **b** Also called: **payback period** the time taken for a project to cover its outlay **5 a** something done in order to gain revenge **b** (*as modifier*): *payback killings*

pay bed *n* an informal name for **private pay bed**

payday ('peɪ,deɪ) *n* the day on which wages or salaries are paid

pay dirt *n* **1** a deposit rich enough in minerals to be worth mining **2 strike pay dirt** *or* **hit pay dirt** *informal* to achieve one's objective

PAYE *abbreviation* (in Britain and New Zealand) pay as you earn; a system by which income tax levied on wage and salary earners is paid by employers directly to the government

payee (peɪˈiː) *n* the person to whom a cheque, money order, etc, is made out

payer (ˈpeɪə) *n* **1** a person who pays **2** the person named in a commercial paper as responsible for its payment on redemption

pay for *vb* (*preposition*) **1** to make payment (of) for **2** (*intr*) to suffer or be punished, as for a mistake, wrong decision, etc

paying guest *n* a euphemism for **lodger** Abbreviation: **PG**

payload (ˈpeɪˌləʊd) *n* **1** that part of a cargo earning revenue **2 a** the passengers, cargo, or bombs carried by an aircraft **b** the equipment carried by a rocket, satellite, or spacecraft **3** the explosive power of a warhead, bomb, etc, carried by a missile or aircraft

paymaster (ˈpeɪˌmɑːstə) *n* an official of a government, business, etc, responsible for the payment of wages and salaries

payment (ˈpeɪmənt) *n* **1** the act of paying **2** a sum of money paid **3** something given in return; punishment or reward

paynim (ˈpeɪnɪm) *n* *archaic* **1** a heathen or pagan **2** a Muslim [c13: from Old French *paienime*, from Late Latin *pāgānismus* paganism, from *pāgānus* PAGAN]

pay off *vb* **1** (*tr, adverb*) to pay all that is due in wages, etc, and discharge from employment **2** (*tr, adverb*) to pay the complete amount of (a debt, bill, etc) **3** (*intr, adverb*) to turn out to be profitable, effective, etc: *the gamble paid off* **4** (*tr, adverb or intr, preposition*) to take revenge on (a person) or for (a wrong done): *to pay someone off for an insult* **5** (*tr, adverb*) *informal* to give a bribe to ▷ *n* **payoff** **6** the final settlement, esp in retribution **7** *informal* the climax, consequence, or outcome of events, a story, etc, esp when unexpected or improbable **8** the final payment of a debt, salary, etc **9** the time of such a payment **10** *informal* a bribe

payola (peɪˈəʊlə) *n* *informal, chiefly US* **1** a bribe given to secure special treatment, esp to a disc jockey to promote a commercial product **2** the practice of paying or receiving such bribes [c20: from PAY¹ + *-ola*, as in *Pianola*]

pay out *vb* (*adverb*) **1** to distribute (money); disburse **2** (*tr*) to release (a rope) gradually, hand over hand ▷ *n* **payout 3** a sum of money paid out

pay-per-view *n* **a** a system of television broadcasting by which subscribers pay for each programme they wish to receive **b** (*as modifier*): *a pay-per-view channel*

payphone (ˈpeɪˌfəʊn) *n* a public telephone operated by coins or a phonecard

payroll (ˈpeɪˌrəʊl) *n* **1** a list of employees, specifying the salary or wage of each **2 a** the total of these amounts or the actual money equivalent **b** (*as modifier*): *a payroll tax*

Paysandú (*Spanish* paisanˈdu) *n* a port in W Uruguay, on the Uruguay River: the third largest city in the country. Pop: 73 272 (2004)

Pays de la Loire (*French* pei də la lwar) *n* a region of W France, on the Bay of Biscay: generally low-lying, drained by the River Loire and its tributaries; agricultural

payt *abbreviation* payment

Payton (ˈpeɪtᵊn) *n* **Walter**. 1954–99, American footballer and sports administrator

pay up *vb* (*adverb*) to pay (money) promptly, in full, or on demand

Paz (*Spanish* pas) *n* **Octavio** (ɔkˈtaβjo). 1914–98, Mexican poet and essayist. His poems include the cycle *Piedra de Sol* (1957) and *Blanco* (1967). Nobel prize for literature 1990

Pb *the chemical symbol for* lead [from New Latin *plumbum*]

PB *abbreviation* athletics personal best

PBS *abbreviation* US Public Broadcasting Service

PBX *abbreviation* (in Britain) private branch exchange; a telephone system that handles the internal and external calls of a building, firm, etc

pc *abbreviation* **1** per cent **2** postcard **3** *obsolete* (in prescriptions) post cibum [Latin: after meals]

PC *abbreviation* **1** personal computer **2** Parish Council(lor) **3** (in Britain and Canada) Police Constable **4** politically correct **5** (in Britain and Canada) Privy Council(lor) **6** (in Canada) Progressive Conservative

PCB *abbreviation* polychlorinated biphenyl

PCC *abbreviation* (in Britain) Press Complaints Commission

PCP *n* Also called: *informal* **angel dust** phenylcyclohexylpiperidine (phencyclidine); a depressant drug used illegally as a hallucinogen

PCR *abbreviation* polymerase chain reaction: a technique for rapidly producing many copies of a fragment of DNA for diagnostic or research purposes

PCV *abbreviation* (in Britain) passenger carrying vehicle

pd *abbreviation* **1** paid **2** Also called: **PD** per diem **3** potential difference

Pd *the chemical symbol for* palladium

PDA *abbreviation* personal digital assistant

PDF *computing abbreviation* portable document format: a format in which documents may be viewed

PDR *abbreviation* price-dividend ratio

P-D ratio *n* short for **price-dividend ratio**

PDSA *abbreviation* (in Britain) People's Dispensary for Sick Animals

PDT *abbreviation* (in the US and Canada) Pacific Daylight Time

PE *abbreviation* **1** physical education **2** potential energy **3** Presiding Elder **4** Also called: **p.e** printer's error **5** *statistics* probable error **6** Protestant Episcopal

pea (piː) *n* **1** an annual climbing leguminous plant, *Pisum sativum*, with small white flowers and long green pods containing edible green seeds: cultivated in temperate regions **2** the seed of this plant, eaten as a vegetable **3** any of several other leguminous plants, such as the sweet pea, chickpea, and cowpea [c17: from PEASE (incorrectly assumed to be a plural)]

Peabody (ˈpiːˌbɒdɪ) *n* **George**. 1795–1869, US merchant, banker, and philanthropist in the US and England

peace (piːs) *n* **1 a** the state existing during the absence of war **b** (*as modifier*): *peace negotiations* **2** (*modifier*) denoting a person or thing symbolizing support for international peace: *peace women* **3** (*often capital*) a treaty marking the end of a war **4** a state of harmony between people or groups; freedom from strife **5** law and order within a state; absence of violence or other disturbance: *a breach of the peace* **6** absence of mental anxiety (often in the phrase **peace of mind**) **7** a state of stillness, silence, or serenity **8 at peace a** in a state of harmony or friendship **b** in a state of serenity **c** dead: *the old lady is at peace now* **9 hold one's peace** or **keep one's peace** to keep silent **10 keep the peace** to maintain or refrain from disturbing law and order ▷ *vb* **11** (*intr*) *except as an imperative obsolete* to be or become silent or still [c12: from Old French *pais*, from Latin *pāx*]

peaceable (ˈpiːsəbᵊl) *adj* **1** inclined towards peace **2** tranquil; calm > **ˈpeaceableness** *n* > **ˈpeaceably** *adv*

Peace Corps *n* an agency of the US government that sends American volunteers to developing countries, where they work on educational and other projects: established in 1961

peace dividend *n* additional money available to a government from cuts in defence expenditure because of the end of a period of hostilities

peaceful (ˈpiːsfʊl) *adj* **1** not in a state of war or disagreement **2** tranquil; calm **3** not involving violence: *peaceful picketing* **4** of, relating to, or in accord with a time of peace **5** inclined towards peace > **ˈpeacefully** *adv* > **ˈpeacefulness** *n*

peacekeeping (ˈpiːsˌkiːpɪŋ) *n* **a** the maintenance of peace, esp the prevention of further fighting between hostile forces in an area **b** (*as modifier*): *a UN peacekeeping force*

peacemaker (ˈpiːsˌmeɪkə) *n* a person who establishes peace, esp between others > **ˈpeaceˌmaking** *n*

peace offering *n* **1** something given to an adversary in the hope of procuring or maintaining peace **2** *Judaism* a sacrificial meal shared between the offerer and Jehovah to intensify the union between them

peace pipe *n* a long decorated pipe smoked by North American Indians on ceremonial occasions, esp as a token of peace. Also called: **calumet, pipe of peace**

Peace River *n* a river in W Canada, rising in British Columbia as the Finlay River and flowing northeast into the Slave River. Length: 1715 km (1065 miles)

peace sign *n* a gesture made with the palm of the hand outwards and the index and middle fingers raised in a V

peacetime ('piːsˌtaɪm) *n* **a** a period without war; time of peace **b** (*as modifier*): *a peacetime agreement*

peach[1] (piːtʃ) *n* **1** a small rosaceous tree, *Prunus persica*, with pink flowers and rounded edible fruit: cultivated in temperate regions **2** the soft juicy fruit of this tree, which has a downy reddish-yellow skin, yellowish-orange sweet flesh, and a single stone **3 a** a pinkish-yellow to orange colour **b** (*as adjective*): *a peach dress* **4** *informal* a person or thing that is especially pleasing [C14 *peche*, from Old French, from Medieval Latin *persica*, from Latin *Persicum mālum* Persian apple]

peach[2] (piːtʃ) *vb* (*intr except in obsolete uses*) *slang* to inform against an accomplice [c15: variant of earlier *apeche*, from French, from Late Latin *impedicāre* to entangle; see IMPEACH]

peach brandy *n* (*esp in S. Africa*) a brandy made from fermented peaches

peach Melba *n* a dessert made of halved peaches, vanilla ice cream, and Melba sauce [C20: named after Dame Nellie *Melba*, stage name of *Helen Porter Mitchell* (1861–1931), Australian operatic soprano]

peachy ('piːtʃɪ) *adj* **peachier, peachiest 1** of or like a peach, esp in colour or texture **2** *informal* excellent; fine > **'peachiness** *n*

peacock ('piːˌkɒk) *n, pl* **-cocks** *or* **-cock 1** a male peafowl, having a crested head and a very large fanlike tail marked with blue and green eyelike spots **2** another name for **peafowl 3** a vain strutting person ▷ *vb* **4** to display (oneself) proudly [C14 *pecok, pe-* from Old English *pāwa* (from Latin *pāvō* peacock) + COCK[1]] > **'pea,cockish** *adj* > **'pea,hen** *fem n*

Peacock ('piːˌkɒk) *n* **Thomas Love.** 1785–1866, English novelist and poet, noted for his satirical romances, including *Headlong Hall* (1816) and *Nightmare Abbey* (1818)

peacock blue *n* **a** a greenish-blue colour **b** (*as adjective*): *a peacock-blue car*

peafowl ('piːˌfaʊl) *n, pl* **-fowls** *or* **-fowl** either of two large pheasants, *Pavo cristatus* (**blue peafowl**) of India and Ceylon and *P. muticus* (**green peafowl**) of SE Asia. The males (peacocks) have a characteristic bright plumage

pea green *n* **a** a yellowish-green colour **b** (*as adjective*): *a pea-green teapot*

pea jacket *or* **peacoat** ('piːˌkəʊt) *n* a sailor's short heavy double-breasted overcoat of navy wool [c18: from Dutch *pijjekker*, from *pij* coat of coarse cloth + *jekker* jacket]

peak (piːk) *n* **1** a pointed end, edge, or projection: *the peak of a roof* **2** the pointed summit of a mountain **3** a mountain with a pointed summit **4** the point of greatest development, strength, etc: *the peak of his career* **5 a** a sharp increase in a physical quantity followed by a sharp decrease: *a voltage peak* **b** the maximum value of this quantity **c** (*as modifier*): *peak voltage* **6** Also called: **visor** a projecting piece on the front of some caps **7** *nautical* **a** the extreme forward (**forepeak**) or aft (**afterpeak**) part of the hull **b** (*of a fore-and-aft quadrilateral sail*) the after uppermost corner **c** the after end of a gaff ▷ *vb* **8** (*tr*) *nautical* to set (a gaff) or tilt (oars) vertically **9** to form or reach or cause to form or reach a peak or maximum ▷ *adj* **10** of or relating to a period of highest use or demand, as for watching television, commuting, etc: *peak viewing hours; peak time* [c16: perhaps from PIKE[2], influenced by BEAK[1]; compare Spanish *pico*, French *pic*, Middle Low German *pēk*] > **'peaky** *or* **'peakish** *adj*

Peak District *n* a region of N central England, mainly in N Derbyshire at the S end of the Pennines: consists of moors in the north and a central limestone plateau; many caves. Highest point: 727 m (2088 ft)

Peake (piːk) *n* **Mervyn.** 1911–68, English novelist, poet, and illustrator. In his trilogy *Gormenghast* (1946–59), he creates, with vivid imagination, a grotesque Gothic world

peaked (piːkt) *adj* having a peak; pointed

peak load *n* the maximum load on an electrical power-supply system

peal (piːl) *n* **1** a loud prolonged usually reverberating sound, as of bells, thunder, or laughter **2** *bell-ringing* a series of changes rung in accordance with specific rules, consisting of not fewer than 5000 permutations in a ring of eight bells **3** (*not in technical usage*) the set of bells in a belfry ▷ *vb* **4** (*intr*) to sound with a peal or peals **5** (*tr*) to give forth loudly and sonorously **6** (*tr*) to ring (bells) in peals [C14 *pele*, variant of *apele* APPEAL]

peanut ('piːˌnʌt) *n* **a** a leguminous plant, *Arachis hypogaea*, of tropical America: widely cultivated for its edible seeds. The seed pods are forced underground where they ripen **b** Also called: **goober, goober pea,** (*Brit*) **groundnut,** (*Brit*) **monkey nut** the edible nutlike seed of this plant, used for food and as a source of oil ▷ See also **peanuts**

peanut butter *n* a brownish oily paste made from peanuts

peanuts ('piːˌnʌts) *n* *slang* a trifling amount of money

pear (pɛə) *n* **1** a widely cultivated rosaceous tree, *Pyrus communis*, having white flowers and edible fruits **2** the sweet gritty-textured juicy fruit of this tree, which has a globular base and tapers towards the apex **3** the wood of this tree, used for making furniture **4 go pear-shaped** *informal* to go wrong: *the plan started to go pear-shaped* [Old English *pere*, ultimately from Latin *pirum*]

pearl[1] (pɜːl) *n* **1** a hard smooth lustrous typically rounded structure occurring on the inner surface of the shell of a clam or oyster: consists of calcium carbonate secreted in layers around an invading particle such as a sand grain; much valued as a gem **2** any artificial gem resembling this **3** See **mother-of-pearl 4** a person or thing that is like a pearl, esp in beauty or value **5** a pale greyish-white colour, often with a bluish tinge ▷ *adj* **6** of, made of, or set with pearl or mother-of-pearl **7** having the shape or colour of a pearl ▷ *vb* **8** (*tr*) to set with or as if with pearls **9** to shape into or assume a pearl-like form or colour **10** (*intr*) to dive or search for pearls [c14: from Old French, from Vulgar Latin *pernula* (unattested), from Latin *perna* sea mussel]

pearl[2] (pɜːl) *n, vb* a variant spelling of **purl**[1] (senses 2, 3, 5)

pearl ash *n* the granular crystalline form of potassium carbonate

pearl barley *n* barley ground into small round grains, used in cooking, esp in soups and stews

Pearl Harbor *n* an almost landlocked inlet of the Pacific on the S coast of the island of Oahu, Hawaii: site of a US naval base attacked by the Japanese in 1941, resulting in the US entry into World War II

Pearl River *n* **1** a river in central Mississippi, flowing southwest and south to the Gulf of Mexico. Length: 789 km (490 miles) **2** the English name for the **Zhu Jiang**

pearly ('pɜːlɪ) *adj* **pearlier, pearliest 1** resembling a pearl, esp in lustre **2** decorated with pearls or mother-of-pearl ▷ *n, pl* **pearlies** (*in Britain*) **3** a London costermonger who wears on ceremonial occasions a traditional dress of dark clothes covered with pearl buttons **4** (*plural*) the clothes or the buttons themselves > **'pearliness** *n*

Pearly Gates *pl n* *informal* the entrance to heaven

pearly king *n* the male London costermonger whose ceremonial clothes display the most lavish collection of pearl buttons

pearly nautilus *n* any of several cephalopod molluscs of the genus *Nautilus*, esp *N. pompilius*, of warm and tropical seas, having a partitioned pale pearly external shell with brown stripes. Also called: **chambered nautilus**

pearmain ('pɛəˌmeɪn) *n* any of several varieties of apple having a red skin [c15: from Old French *permain* a type of pear, perhaps from Latin *Parmēnsis* of Parma]

Pears (pɪəz) *n* **Sir Peter.** 1910–86, British tenor, associated esp with the works of Benjamin Britten

Pearse (pɪəs) *n* **Patrick (Henry),** Irish name *Pádraic.* 1879–1916, Irish nationalist, who planned and led the Easter Rising (1916): executed by the British

Pearson ('pɪəsən) *n* **1 Karl.** 1857–1936, British mathematician, noted for his work in statistics, esp as applied to biological problems **2 Lester B(owles).** 1897–1972, Canadian Liberal statesman; prime minister (1963–68): Nobel peace prize 1957 for helping to resolve the Suez crisis (1956)

peart (pɪət) *adj* *archaic or dialect* lively; spirited; brisk [c15:

variant of PERT] > 'peartly *adv*

Peary ('pɪərɪ) *n* **Robert Edwin**. 1856–1920, US arctic explorer, generally regarded as the first man to reach the North Pole (1909)

peasant ('pɛz⁰nt) *n* **1** a member of a class of low social status that depends on either cottage industry or agricultural labour as a means of subsistence **2** *informal* a person who lives in the country; rustic **3** *informal* an uncouth or uncultured person [c15: from Anglo-French, from Old French *paisant*, from *pais* country, from Latin *pāgus* rural area; see PAGAN]

peasantry ('pɛz⁰ntrɪ) *n* peasants as a class

pease (piːz) *n*, *pl* pease an archaic or dialect word for **pea** [Old English *peose*, via Late Latin from Latin *pisa* peas, pl of *pisum*, from Greek *pison*]

peasecod or **peascod** ('piːz,kɒd) *n* *archaic* the pod of a pea plant [c14: from PEASE + COD²]

pease pudding *n* (esp in Britain) a dish of split peas that have been soaked and boiled served with ham or pork

peashooter ('piːˌʃuːtə) *n* a tube through which pellets such as dried peas are blown, used as a toy weapon

peasouper (ˌpiːˈsuːpə) *n* **1** *informal, chiefly Brit* dense dirty yellowish fog **2** *Canadian* a disparaging name for a **French Canadian**

peat (piːt) *n* **a** a compact brownish deposit of partially decomposed vegetable matter saturated with water: found in uplands and bogs in temperate and cold regions and used as a fuel (when dried) and as a fertilizer **b** (*as modifier*): *peat bog* [c14: from Anglo-Latin *peta*, perhaps from Celtic; compare Welsh *peth* thing] > 'peaty *adj*

peat moss *n* any of various mosses, esp sphagnum, that grow in wet places in dense masses and decay to form peat. See also **sphagnum**

pebble ('pɛb⁰l) *n* **1** a small smooth rounded stone, esp one worn by the action of water **2 a** a transparent colourless variety of rock crystal, used for making certain lenses **b** such a lens **3** (*modifier*) *informal* (of a lens or of spectacles) thick, with a high degree of magnification or distortion **4 a** a grainy irregular surface, esp on leather **b** leather having such a surface ▷ *vb* (*tr*) **5** to pave, cover, or pelt with pebbles **6** to impart a grainy surface to (leather) [Old English *papolstān*, from *papol-* (perhaps of imitative origin) + *stān* stone] > 'pebbly *adj*

pebble dash *n* *Brit* a finish for external walls consisting of small stones embedded in plaster

pebi- ('pɛbɪ) *prefix computing* denoting 2⁵⁰: *pebibyte* [c20: from PE(TA-) + (K)BI(NARY)]

pec (pɛk) *n* (*usually plural*) *informal* short for **pectoral muscle**

pecan (pɪˈkæn, 'piːkən) *n* **1** a hickory tree, *Carya pecan* (or *C. illinoensis*), of the southern US, having deeply furrowed bark and edible nuts **2** the smooth oval nut of this tree, which has a sweet oily kernel [c18: from Algonquian *paccan*; related to Ojibwa *pagân* nut with a hard shell, Cree *pakan*]

peccable ('pɛkəb⁰l) *adj* liable to sin; susceptible to temptation [c17: via French from Medieval Latin *peccābilis*, from Latin *peccāre* to sin]

peccadillo (ˌpɛkəˈdɪləʊ) *n*, *pl* -loes or -los a petty sin or trifling fault [c16: from Spanish *pecadillo*, from *pecado* sin, from Latin *peccātum*, from *peccāre* to transgress]

peccant ('pɛkənt) *adj rare* **1** guilty of an offence; corrupt **2** violating or disregarding a rule; faulty **3** producing disease; morbid [c17: from Latin *peccans*, from *peccāre* to sin] > 'peccancy *n*

peccary ('pɛkərɪ) *n*, *pl* -ries or -ry either of two piglike artiodactyl mammals, *Tayassu tajacu* (**collared peccary**) or *T. albirostris* (**white-lipped peccary**) of forests of southern North America, Central and South America: family *Tayassuidae* [c17: from Carib]

Pechenga ('pɛtʃɪŋɡə) *n* a region of NW Russia, a former territory of N Finland, ceded by Soviet Russia to Finland in 1920 and taken back in 1944. Former name: **Petsamo** (1920–1944)

Pechora (*Russian* pɪˈtʃɔrə) *n* a river in N Russia, rising in the Ural Mountains and flowing north in a great arc to

the **Pechora Sea** (the SE part of the Barents Sea). Length: 1814 km (1127 miles)

peck¹ (pɛk) *n* **1** a unit of dry measure equal to 8 quarts or one quarter of a bushel **2** a container used for measuring this quantity **3** a large quantity or number [c13: from Anglo-Norman, of uncertain origin]

peck² (pɛk) *vb* **1** (when *intr*, sometimes foll by *at*) to strike with the beak or with a pointed instrument **2** (*tr*; sometimes foll by *out*) to dig (a hole) by pecking **3** (*tr*) (of birds) to pick up (corn, worms, etc) by pecking **4** (*intr*; often foll by *at*) to nibble or pick (at one's food) **5** *informal* to kiss (a person) quickly and lightly **6** (*intr*; foll by *at*) to nag ▷ *n* **7** a quick light blow, esp from a bird's beak **8** a mark made by such a blow **9** *informal* a quick light kiss [c14: of uncertain origin; compare PICK¹, Middle Low German *pekken* to jab with the beak]

Peck (pɛk) *n* **Gregory**. 1916–2003, US film actor; his films include *Keys of the Kingdom* (1944), *The Gunfighter* (1950), *The Big Country* (1958), *To Kill a Mockingbird* (1963), *The Omen* (1976), and *Other People's Money* (1991)

pecker ('pɛkə) *n Brit slang* spirits (esp in the phrase **keep one's pecker up**)

pecking order *n* **1** Also called: **peck order** a natural hierarchy in a group of gregarious birds, such as domestic fowl **2** any hierarchical order, as among people in a particular group

Peckinpah ('pɛkɪnˌpɑː) *n* **Sam(uel David)**. 1926–84, US film director, esp of Westerns, such as *The Wild Bunch* (1969). Among his other films are *Straw Dogs* (1971), *Bring me the Head of Alfredo Garcia* (1974), and *Cross of Iron* (1977)

peckish ('pɛkɪʃ) *adj informal, chiefly Brit* feeling slightly hungry; having an appetite [c18: from PECK²]

Pecos ('peɪkəs; *Spanish* 'pekɔs) *n* a river in the southwestern US, rising in N central New Mexico and flowing southeast to the Rio Grande. Length: about 1180 km (735 miles)

Pécs (*Hungarian* peːtʃ) *n* an industrial city in SW Hungary: university (1367). Pop: 158 942 (2003 est)

pecten ('pɛktɪn) *n*, *pl* -tens or -tines (-tɪˌniːz) **1** a comblike structure in the eye of birds and reptiles, consisting of a network of blood vessels projecting inwards from the retina, which it is thought to supply with oxygen **2** any other comblike part or organ [c18: from Latin: a comb, from *pectere*, related to Greek *pekein* to comb]

pectin ('pɛktɪn) *n biochem* any of the acidic hemicelluloses that occur in ripe fruit and vegetables: used in the manufacture of jams because of their ability to solidify to a gel when heated in a sugar solution (may be referred to on food labels as **E440(a)**) [c19: from Greek *pēktos* congealed, from *pegnuein* to set] > 'pectic or 'pectinous *adj*

pectoral ('pɛktərəl) *adj* **1** of or relating to the chest, breast, or thorax: *pectoral fins* **2** worn on the breast or chest: *a pectoral medallion* ▷ *n* **3** a pectoral organ or part, esp a muscle or fin **4** a medicine or remedy for disorders of the chest or lungs **5** anything worn on the chest or breast for decoration or protection [c15: from Latin *pectorālis*, from *pectus* breast] > 'pectorally *adv*

pectoral fin *n* either of a pair of fins, situated just behind the head in fishes, that help to control the direction of movement during locomotion

pectoral muscle *n* either of two large chest muscles (**pectoralis major** and **pectoralis minor**), that assist in movements of the shoulder and upper arm

peculate ('pɛkjʊˌleɪt) *vb* to appropriate or embezzle (public money) [c18: from Latin *pecūlārī*, from *pecūlium* private property (originally, cattle); see PECULIAR] > ˌpecuˈlation *n* > 'pecuˌlator *n*

peculiar (pɪˈkjuːlɪə) *adj* **1** strange or unusual; odd: *a peculiar individual; a peculiar idea* **2** distinct from others; special **3** (*postpositive*; foll by *to*) belonging characteristically or exclusively (to): *peculiar to North America* [c15: from Latin *pecūliāris* concerning private property, from *pecūlium*, literally: property in cattle, from *pecus* cattle] > pe'culiarly *adv*

peculiarity (pɪˌkjuːlɪˈærɪtɪ) *n*, *pl* -ties **1** a strange or unusual habit or characteristic **2** a distinguishing trait, etc that is characteristic of a particular person;

idiosyncrasy **3** the state or quality of being peculiar

pecuniary (prɪˈkjuːnɪərɪ) *adj* **1** consisting of or relating to money **2** *law* (of an offence) involving a monetary penalty [c16: from Latin *pecūniāris*, from *pecūnia* money] > pe'cuniarily *adv*

pecuniary advantage *n law* financial advantage that is dishonestly obtained by deception and that constitutes a criminal offence

-ped *or* **-pede** *n combining form* foot or feet: *quadruped; centipede* [from Latin *pēs*, *ped-* foot]

pedagogue *or sometimes US* **pedagog** (ˈpɛdəˌgɒg) *n* **1** a teacher or educator **2** a pedantic or dogmatic teacher [c14: from Latin *paedagōgus*, from Greek *paidagōgos* slave who looked after his master's son, from *pais* boy + *agōgos* leader] > ˌpeda'gogic *or* ˌpeda'gogical *adj* > ˌpeda'gogically *adv*

pedagogy (ˈpɛdəˌgɒgɪ, -ˌgɒdʒɪ, -ˌgəʊdʒɪ) *n* the principles, practice, or profession of teaching

pedal¹ (ˈpɛdəl) *n* **1 a** any foot-operated lever or other device, esp one of the two levers that drive the chain wheel of a bicycle, the foot brake, clutch control, or accelerator of a car, one of the levers on an organ controlling deep bass notes, or one of the levers on a piano used to create a muted effect or sustain tone **b** (*as modifier*): *a pedal cycle; a pianist's pedal technique* ▷ *vb* **-als, -alling, -alled** *or US* **-als, -aling, -aled** **2** to propel (a bicycle, boat, etc) by operating the pedals **3** (*intr*) to operate the pedals of an organ, piano, etc, esp in a certain way **4** to work (pedals of any kind) [c17: from Latin *pedālis*; see PEDAL²]

pedal² (ˈpiːdəl) *adj* of or relating to the foot or feet [c17: from Latin *pedālis*, from *pēs* foot]

pedal point (ˈpɛdəl) *n music* a sustained bass note, over which the other parts move bringing about changing harmonies. Often shortened to: **pedal**

pedal steel guitar *n* a floor-mounted, multineck, lap steel guitar with each set of strings tuned to a different open chord and foot pedals to raise or lower the pitch

pedant (ˈpɛdənt) *n* **1** a person who relies too much on academic learning or who is concerned chiefly with insignificant detail **2** *archaic* a schoolmaster or teacher [c16: via Old French from Italian *pedante* teacher; perhaps related to Latin *paedagōgus* PEDAGOGUE]

pedantic (prɪˈdæntɪk) *adj* of, relating to, or characterized by pedantry > pe'dantically *adv*

pedantry (ˈpɛdəntrɪ) *n, pl* **-ries** the habit or an instance of being a pedant, esp in the display of useless knowledge or minute observance of petty rules or details

pedate (ˈpɛdeɪt) *adj* **1** (of a plant leaf) divided into several lobes arising at a common point, the lobes often being stalked and the lateral lobes sometimes divided into smaller lobes **2** *zoology* having or resembling a foot: *a pedate appendage* [c18: from Latin *pedātus* equipped with feet, from *pēs* foot]

peddle (ˈpɛdəl) *vb* **1** to go from place to place selling (goods, esp small articles) **2** (*tr*) to sell (illegal drugs, esp narcotics) **3** (*tr*) to advocate (ideas) persistently or importunately: *to peddle a new philosophy* [c16: back formation from PEDLAR]

peddler (ˈpɛdlə) *n* **1** a person who sells illegal drugs, esp narcotics **2** the usual US spelling of **pedlar**

pederast *or sometimes* **paederast** (ˈpɛdəˌræst) *n* a man who practises pederasty

pederasty *or sometimes* **paederasty** (ˈpɛdəˌræstɪ) *n* homosexual relations between men and boys [c17: from New Latin *paederastia*, from Greek, from *pais* boy + *erastēs* lover, from *eran* to love] > ˌpeder'astic *or sometimes* ˌpaeder'astic *adj*

pedestal (ˈpɛdɪstəl) *n* **1** a base that supports a column, statue, etc, as used in classical architecture **2** a position of eminence or supposed superiority (esp in the phrases **place, put,** *or* **set on a pedestal**) [c16: from French *piédestal*, from Old Italian *piedestallo*, from *pie* foot + *di* of + *stallo* a stall]

pedestrian (prɪˈdɛstrɪən) *n* **1 a** a person travelling on foot; walker **b** (*as modifier*): *a pedestrian precinct* ▷ *adj* **2** dull; commonplace: *a pedestrian style of writing* [c18: from Latin *pedester*, from *pēs* foot]

pedestrian crossing *n Brit* a path across a road marked as a crossing for pedestrians

pedestrianize *or* **pedestrianise** (prɪˈdɛstrɪəˌnaɪz) *vb* (*tr*) to convert (a street) into an area for the use of pedestrians only, by excluding all motor vehicles > peˌdestriani'zation *or* peˌdestriani'sation *n*

pedi- *combining form* indicating the foot: *pedicure* [from Latin *pēs*, *ped-* foot]

pedicab (ˈpɛdɪˌkæb) *n* a pedal-operated tricycle, available for hire, with an attached seat for one or two passengers

pedicel (ˈpɛdɪˌsɛl) *n* **1** the stalk bearing a single flower of an inflorescence **2** Also called: **peduncle** *biology* any short stalk bearing an organ or organism [c17: from New Latin *pedicellus*, from Latin *pedīculus*, from *pēs* foot] > **pedicellate** (prɪˈdɪsɪˌleɪt) *adj*

pedicle (ˈpɛdɪkəl) *n biology* any small stalk; pedicel; peduncle [c17: from Latin *pedīculus* small foot; see PEDICEL]

pedicular (prɪˈdɪkjʊlə) *adj* **1** relating to, infested with, or caused by lice **2** *biology* of or relating to a stem, stalk, or pedicle [c17: from Latin *pedīculāris*, from *pedīculus*, diminutive of *pedis* louse]

pediculosis (prɪˌdɪkjʊˈləʊsɪs) *n pathol* the state of being infested with lice [c19: via New Latin from Latin *pedīculus* louse; see PEDICULAR] > **pediculous** (prɪˈdɪkjʊləs) *adj*

pedicure (ˈpɛdɪˌkjʊə) *n* professional treatment of the feet, either by a medical expert or a cosmetician [c19: via French from Latin *pēs* foot + *curāre* to care for]

pedigree (ˈpɛdɪˌgriː) *n* **1 a** the line of descent of a purebred animal **b** (*as modifier*): *a pedigree bull* **2** a document recording this **3** a genealogical table, esp one indicating pure ancestry [c15: from Old French *pie de grue* crane's foot, alluding to the spreading lines used in a genealogical chart] > 'pediˌgreed *adj*

pediment (ˈpɛdɪmənt) *n* a low-pitched gable, esp one that is triangular, as used in classical architecture [c16: from obsolete *periment*, perhaps workman's corruption of PYRAMID] > ˌpedi'mental *adj*

pedipalp (ˈpɛdɪˌpælp) *n* either member of the second pair of head appendages of arachnids: specialized for feeding, locomotion, etc [c19: from New Latin *pedipalpi*, from Latin *pēs* foot + *palpus* palp]

pedlar, *esp US* **peddler** *or esp US* **pedler** (ˈpɛdlə) *n* a person who peddles; hawker [c14: changed from *peder*, from *ped*, peddle basket, of obscure origin]

pedo- *or before a vowel* **ped-** *combining form* variants (esp US) of **paedo-**

pedology (prɪˈdɒlədʒɪ) *n* the study of the formation, characteristics, and distribution of soils

pedometer (prɪˈdɒmɪtə) *n* a device containing a pivoted weight that records the number of steps taken in walking and hence the distance travelled

Pedro I (ˈpɛdrəʊ) *n* 1798–1834, first emperor of Brazil (1822–31); son of John VI of Portugal: declared Brazilian independence (1822)

Pedro II *n* 1825–91, last emperor of Brazil (1831–89); son of Pedro I. He was deposed when Brazil became a republic (1889)

peduncle (prɪˈdʌŋkəl) *n* **1** the stalk of a plant bearing an inflorescence or solitary flower **2** *anatomy* a stalklike structure, esp a large bundle of nerve fibres within the brain **3** *biology* another name for **pedicel** (sense 2) [c18: from New Latin *pedunculus*, from Latin *pedīculus* little foot; see PEDICLE] > pe'duncled *or* peduncular (prɪˈdʌŋkjʊlə) *adj*

pee (piː) *informal* ▷ *vb* **pees, peeing, peed** **1** (*intr*) to urinate ▷ *n* **2** urine **3** the act of urinating [c18: a euphemism for PISS, based on the initial letter]

Peebles (ˈpiːbəlz) *n* a town in SE Scotland, in Scottish Borders. Pop: 8065 (2001)

Peeblesshire (ˈpiːbəlzˌʃɪə, -ʃə) *n* (until 1975) a county of SE Scotland, now part of Scottish Borders. Also called: **Tweeddale**

peek (piːk) *vb* **1** (*intr*) to glance quickly or furtively; peep ▷ *n* **2** a quick or furtive glance [c14: *pike*, related to Middle Dutch *kiken* to peek]

peekaboo (ˈpiːkəˌbuː) *n* **1** a game for young children, in which one person hides his face and suddenly reveals it and cries "peekaboo." ▷ *adj* **2** (of a garment) made of fabric that is almost transparent or patterned with small holes [C16: from PEEK + BOO]

peel¹ (piːl) *vb* **1** (*tr*) to remove (the skin, rind, outer covering, etc) of (a fruit, egg, etc) **2** (*intr*) (of paint, etc) to be removed from a surface, esp through weathering **3** (*intr*) (of a surface) to lose its outer covering of paint, etc esp through weathering **4** (*intr*) (of a person or part of the body) to shed skin in flakes or (of skin) to be shed in flakes, esp as a result of sunburn ▷ *n* **5** the skin or rind of a fruit, etc ▷ See also **peel off** [Old English *pilian* to strip off the outer layer, from Latin *pilāre* to make bald, from *pilus* a hair]

peel² (piːl) *n* a long-handled shovel used by bakers for moving bread, in an oven [C14 *pele*, from Old French, from Latin *pāla* spade, from *pangere* to drive in; see PALETTE]

peel³ (piːl) *n* (in Britain) a fortified tower of the 16th century on the borders between England and Scotland, built to withstand raids [C14 (fence made of stakes): from Old French *piel* stake, from Latin *pālus*; see PALE², PALING]

Peel (piːl) *n* **1** **John**, real name *John Robert Parker Ravenscroft*. 1939–2004, British broadcaster; presented his influential Radio 1 music programme (1967–2004) and Radio 4's *Home Truths* (1998–2004) **2 Sir Robert**. 1788–1850, British statesman; Conservative prime minister (1834–35; 1841–46). As Home Secretary (1828–30) he founded the Metropolitan Police and in his second ministry carried through a series of free-trade budgets culminating in the repeal of the Corn Laws (1846), which split the Tory party ▷ '**Peelite** *n*

Peele (piːl) *n* **George**. ?1556–?96, English dramatist and poet. His works include the pastoral drama *The Arraignment of Paris* (1584) and the comedy *The Old Wives' Tale* (1595)

peeler¹ ('piːlə) *n* **1** a special knife or mechanical device for peeling vegetables, fruit, etc: *a potato peeler* **2** US slang a striptease dancer

peeler² ('piːlə) *n* Brit dated, slang another word for **policeman** [C19: from the founder of the police force, Sir Robert Peel (1788–1850), British Conservative statesman]

peeling ('piːlɪŋ) *n* a strip of skin, rind, bark, etc, that has been peeled off: *a potato peeling*

peel off *vb* (*adverb*) **1** to remove or be removed by peeling **2** (*intr*) *slang* to undress **3** (*intr*) (of an aircraft) to turn away as by banking, and leave a formation

peen (piːn) *n* **1** the end of a hammer head opposite the striking face, often rounded or wedge-shaped ▷ *vb* **2** (*tr*) to strike with the peen of a hammer or with a stream of metal shot in order to bend or shape (a sheet of metal) [C17: variant of *pane*, perhaps from French *panne*, ultimately from Latin *pinna* point]

Peenemünde (,piːnə'mʊndə) *n* a village in N Germany, in Mecklenburg-West Pomerania on the Baltic coast: site of a German rocket-development centre in World War II

peep¹ (piːp) *vb* (*intr*) **1** to peer furtively or secretly, as through a small aperture or from a hidden place **2** to appear partially or briefly: *the sun peeped through the clouds* ▷ *n* **3** a quick or furtive look **4** the first appearance: *the peep of dawn* [C15: variant of PEEK]

peep² (piːp) *vb* (*intr*) **1** (esp of young birds) to utter shrill small noises **2** to speak in a thin shrill voice ▷ *n* **3** a peeping sound [C15: of imitative origin]

peeper ('piːpə) *n* **1** a person who peeps **2** (*often plural*) a slang word for **eye¹** (sense 1)

peephole ('piːp,həʊl) *n* a small aperture, such as one in the door of a flat for observing callers before opening

Peeping Tom *n* a man who furtively observes women undressing; voyeur [C19: after the tailor who, according to legend, peeped at Lady Godiva when she rode naked through Coventry]

peepshow ('piːp,ʃəʊ) *n* **1** Also called: **raree show** a small box with a peephole through which a series of pictures, esp of erotic poses, can be seen **2** a booth from which a viewer can see a live nude model for a fee

peepul ('piːp°l) *or* **pipal** *n* an Indian moraceous tree, *Ficus religiosa*, resembling the banyan: regarded as sacred by Buddhists. Also called: **bo tree** [C18: from Hindi *pīpal*, from Sanskrit *pippala*]

peer¹ (pɪə) *n* **1** a member of a nobility; nobleman **2** a person who holds any of the five grades of the British nobility: duke, marquess, earl, viscount, and baron. See also **life peer** **3** a person who is an equal in social standing, rank, age, etc [C14 (in sense 3): from Old French *per*, from Latin *pār* equal]

peer² (pɪə) *vb* (*intr*) **1** to look intently with or as if with difficulty: *to peer into the distance* **2** to appear partially or dimly: *the sun peered through the fog* [C16: from Flemish *pieren* to look with narrowed eyes]

peerage ('pɪərɪdʒ) *n* **1** the whole body of peers; aristocracy **2** the position, rank, or title of a peer **3** (esp in the British Isles) a book listing the peers and giving genealogical and other information about them

peeress ('pɪərɪs) *n* **1** the wife or widow of a peer **2** a woman holding the rank of a peer in her own right

peer group *n* a social group composed of individuals of approximately the same age

peerless ('pɪəlɪs) *adj* having no equals; matchless

peer review *n* the evaluation by fellow specialists of research that someone has done in order to assess its suitability for publication or further development ▷ ,peer-re'viewed *adj*

peer-to-peer *adj* (of a computer network) designed so that computers can send information directly to one another without passing through a centralized server. Abbreviation: P2P

peeve (piːv) *informal* ▷ *vb* **1** (*tr*) to irritate; vex; annoy ▷ *n* **2** something that irritates; vexation [C20: back formation from PEEVISH] ▷ peeved *adj*

peevish ('piːvɪʃ) *adj* fretful or irritable [C14: of unknown origin] ▷ 'peevishly *adv* ▷ 'peevishness *n*

peewee ('piːwiː) *n* **1** a variant (esp Scot) of **peewit** **2** Austral **3** Canadian **a** an age level of 12 to 13 in amateur sport, esp ice hockey **b** (*as modifier*): *peewee hockey*

peewit ('piːwɪt) *n* another name for **lapwing** [C16: imitative of its call]

peg (pɛg) *n* **1** a small cylindrical pin or dowel, sometimes slightly tapered, used to join two parts together **2** a pin pushed or driven into a surface: used to mark scores, define limits, support coats, etc **3** *music* any of several pins passing through the head (**peg box**) of a stringed instrument, which can be turned so as to tune strings wound around them **4** Also called: **clothes peg** Brit a split or hinged pin for fastening wet clothes to a line to dry. US and Canadian equivalent: **clothespin** **5** Brit a small drink of wine or spirits, esp of brandy or whisky and soda **6** an opportunity or pretext for doing something: *a peg on which to hang a theory* **7** *informal* a level of self-esteem, importance, etc (esp in the phrases **bring** or **take down a peg**) **8** *informal* See **peg leg** **9** off the peg chiefly Brit (of clothes) ready to wear, as opposed to tailor-made ▷ *vb* pegs, pegging, pegged **10** (*tr*) to knock or insert a peg into or pierce with a peg **11** (*tr*; sometimes foll by *down*) to secure with pegs: *to peg a tent* **12** (*tr*) to mark (a score) with pegs, as in some card games **13** (*tr*) *informal* to aim and throw (missiles) at a target **14** (*intr*; foll by *away, along*, etc) chiefly Brit to work steadily: *he pegged away at his job for years* **15** (*tr*) to stabilize (the price of a commodity, an exchange rate, etc) by legislation or market operations [C15: from Low Germanic *pegge*]

Pegasus ('pɛgəsəs) *n* Greek myth an immortal winged horse, which sprang from the blood of the slain Medusa and enabled Bellerophon to achieve many great deeds as his rider

pegboard ('pɛg,bɔːd) *n* **1** a board having a pattern of holes into which small pegs can be fitted, used for playing certain games or keeping a score **2** another name for **solitaire** (sense 1) **3** hardboard perforated by a pattern of holes in which articles may be pegged or hung, as for display

peg leg *n* *informal* **1** an artificial leg, esp one made of wood **2** a person with an artificial leg

pegmatite ('pɛgmə,taɪt) *n* any of a class of exceptionally coarse-grained intrusive igneous rocks consisting chiefly of quartz and feldspar: often occurring as dykes among igneous rocks of finer grain [C19: from Greek *pegma* something joined together]

P

peg out vb (adverb) **1** (intr) informal to collapse or die
2 (intr) cribbage to score the point that wins the game
3 (tr) to mark or secure with pegs: to peg out one's claims to a
piece of land
peg top n a child's spinning top, usually made of wood
with a metal centre pin
peg-top adj (of skirts, trousers, etc) wide at the hips
then tapering off towards the ankle
Pegu (pɛˈguː) n a city in S Myanmar: capital of a united
Burma (16th century). Pop: 307 000 (2005 est)
Péguy (French pegi) n **Charles** (ʃarl). 1873–1914, French
poet and essayist, whose works include Le Mystère de la
charité de Jeanne d'Arc (1910); founder of the journal Cahiers
de la quinzaine (1900–14): killed in World War I
Pei (peɪ) n I(eoh) M(ing). born 1917, US architect, born in
China. His buildings include the E wing of the National
Museum of Art, Washington DC (1978), a glass and steel
pyramid at the Louvre, Paris (1989), and the Rock and
Roll Hall of Fame, Cleveland, USA (1995)
PEI abbreviation Prince Edward Island
peignoir (ˈpeɪnwɑː) n a woman's dressing gown or
negligee [c19: from French, from peigner to comb, since
the garment was worn while the hair was combed]
Peipus (ˈpaɪpəs) n a lake in W Russia, on the boundary
with Estonia: drains into the Gulf of Finland. Area: 3512
sq km (1356 sq miles). Russian name: Chudskoye Ozero
Peiraeus (paɪˈriːəs, pɪˈreɪ-) n a variant spelling of Piraeus
Peirce (pɪəs) n **Charles Sanders**. 1839–1914, US logician,
philosopher, and mathematician; pioneer of
pragmatism
pejoration (ˌpiːdʒəˈreɪʃən) n **1** linguistics semantic change
whereby a word acquires unfavourable connotations
2 the process of worsening; deterioration
pejorative (prˈdʒɒrətɪv, ˈpiːdʒər-) adj **1** (of words,
expressions, etc) having an unpleasant or disparaging
connotation ▷ n **2** a pejorative word, expression, etc [c19:
from French péjoratif, from Late Latin pējōrātus, past
participle of pējōrāre to make worse, from Latin pēior
worse] > peˈjoratively adv
pekan (ˈpɛkən) n another name for **fisher** (sense 2) [c18:
from Canadian French pékan, of Algonquian origin;
compare Abnaki pékané]
peke (piːk) n informal a Pekingese dog
Peking (ˈpiːkɪŋ) n the former English name of **Beijing**
Pekingese (ˌpiːkɪŋˈiːz) or **Pekinese** (ˌpiːkəˈniːz) n **1** pl -ese
a small breed of pet dog with a profuse straight coat,
curled plumed tail, and short wrinkled muzzle **2** the
dialect of Mandarin Chinese spoken in Beijing (formerly
Peking), the pronunciation of which serves as a
standard for the language **3** pl -ese a native or
inhabitant of Beijing (formerly Peking) ▷ adj **4** of or
relating to Beijing (formerly Peking) or its inhabitants
Peking man n an early type of man, Homo erectus,
remains of which, of the Lower Palaeolithic age, were
found in a cave near Peking (now Beijing), China, in
1927
pekoe (ˈpiːkəʊ) n a high-quality tea made from the
downy tips of the young buds of the tea plant [c18: from
Chinese (Amoy) peh ho, from peh white + ho down]
pelage (ˈpɛlɪdʒ) n the coat of a mammal, consisting of
hair, wool, fur, etc [c19: via French from Old French pel
animal's coat, from Latin pilus hair]
Pelagian Islands (pɛˈleɪdʒɪən) pl n a group of Italian
islands (Lampedusa, Linosa, and Lampione) in the
Mediterranean, between Tunisia and Malta. Pop: 6066
(2004 est). Area: about 27 sq km (11 sq miles). Italian
name: Isole Pelagie
Pelagianism (pɛˈleɪdʒɪəˌnɪzəm) n Christianity a heretical
doctrine, first formulated by the British monk PELAGIUS,
that rejected the concept of original sin and maintained
that the individual takes the initial steps towards
salvation by his own efforts and not by the help of
divine grace
pelagic (pɛˈlædʒɪk) adj **1** of or relating to the open sea:
pelagic whaling **2** (of marine life) living or occurring in the
upper waters of open sea [c17: from Latin pelagicus, from
pelagus, from Greek pelagos sea]
Pelagius (pɛˈleɪdʒɪəs) n ?360–?420 AD, British monk, who
originated the body of doctrines known as Pelagianism

and was condemned for heresy (417) > Peˈlagian adj, n.
See also **Pelagianism**
pelargonium (ˌpɛlɑːˈɡəʊnɪəm) n any plant of the chiefly
southern African geraniaceous genus Pelargonium, having
circular or lobed leaves and red, pink, or white aromatic
flowers: includes many cultivated geraniums [c19: via
New Latin from Greek pelargos stork, on the model of
GERANIUM; from the likeness of the seed vessels to a
stork's bill]
Pelé (ˈpɛleɪ) n real name Edson Arantes do Nascimento. born
1940, Brazilian footballer. He was awarded an honorary
knighthood in 1997
Pelée (pɛˈleɪ) n **Mount Pelée** a volcano in the Caribbean,
in N Martinique: erupted in 1902, killing every person
but one in the town of Saint-Pierre. Height: 1463 m
(4800 ft)
Peleus (ˈpɛlɪəs, ˈpiːlɪəs) n Greek myth a king of the
Myrmidons; father of Achilles
Pelew Islands (pɪˈluː) pl n a former name of (the
Republic of) **Palau**
pelf (pɛlf) n contemptuous money or wealth, esp if
dishonestly acquired; lucre [c14: from Old French pelfre
booty; related to Latin pilāre to despoil]
pelham (ˈpɛləm) n a horse's bit for a double bridle, less
severe than a curb but more severe than a snaffle
[probably from the proper name Pelham]
Pelham (ˈpɛləm) n **Henry**. 1696–1754, British statesman:
prime minister (1743–54); brother of Thomas Pelham
Holles, 1st Duke of Newcastle
Pelham Holles (ˈpɛləm ˈhɒlɪs) n **Thomas**. See (1st Duke
of) **Newcastle¹**
Pelias (ˈpiːlɪˌæs) n Greek myth a son of Poseidon and Tyro.
He feared his nephew Jason and sent him to recover the
Golden Fleece, hoping he would not return
pelican (ˈpɛlɪkən) n any aquatic bird of the tropical and
warm water family Pelecanidae, such as P. onocrotalus
(**white pelican**): order Pelecaniformes. They have a long
straight flattened bill, with a distensible pouch for
engulfing fish [Old English pellican, from Late Latin
pelicānus, from Greek pelekān; perhaps related to Greek
pelekus axe, perhaps from the shape of the bird's bill;
compare Greek pelekas woodpecker]
pelican crossing n a type of road crossing marked by
black-and-white stripes or by two rows of metal studs
and consisting of a pedestrian-operated traffic-light
system [c20: from pe(destrian) li(ght) con(trolled) crossing,
with -con adapted to -can of pelican]
Pelion (ˈpiːlɪən) n a mountain in NE Greece, in E
Thessaly. In Greek mythology it was the home of the
centaurs. Height: 1548 m (5079 ft)
pelisse (pɛˈliːs) n **1** a fur-trimmed cloak **2** a high-waisted
loose coat, usually fur-trimmed, worn esp by women in
the early 19th century [c18: via Old French from
Medieval Latin pellicia cloak, from Latin pellis skin]
Pella (ˈpɛlə) n an ancient city in N Greece: the capital of
Macedonia under Philip II
pellagra (pəˈleɪɡrə, -ˈlæ-) n pathol a disease caused by a
dietary deficiency of nicotinic acid, characterized by
burning or itching often followed by scaling of the skin,
inflammation of the mouth, diarrhoea, mental
impairment, etc [c19: via Italian from pelle skin + -agra,
from Greek agra paroxysm] > pelˈlagrous adj
pellet (ˈpɛlɪt) n **1** a small round ball, esp of compressed
matter **2 a** an imitation bullet used in toy guns **b** a
piece of small shot **3** a stone ball formerly used as a
catapult or cannon missile **4** Also called: **cast, casting**
ornithol a mass of undigested food, including bones, fur,
feathers, etc, that is regurgitated by certain birds, esp
birds of prey **5** a small pill ▷ vb (tr) **6** to strike with
pellets **7** to make or form into pellets [c14: from Old
French pelote, from Vulgar Latin pilota (unattested), from
Latin pila ball]
Pelletier (French pɛltje) n **Pierre Joseph** (pjɛr ʒɔzɛf).
1788–1842, French chemist, who isolated quinine,
chlorophyll, and other chemical substances
pellitory (ˈpɛlɪtərɪ, -trɪ) n, pl -ries **1** any of various
urticaceous plants of the S and W European genus
Parietaria, esp P. diffusa (**pellitory-of-the-wall** or **wall
pellitory**), that grow in crevices and have long narrow

leaves and small pink flowers **2 pellitory of Spain** a small Mediterranean plant, *Anacyclus pyrethrum*, the root of which contains an oil formerly used to relieve toothache: family *Asteraceae* (composites) [C16 *peletre*, from Old French *piretre*, from Latin *pyrethrum*, from Greek *purethron*, from *pur* fire, from the hot pungent taste of the root]

pell-mell ('pɛl'mɛl) *adv* **1** in a confused headlong rush: *the hounds ran pell-mell into the yard* **2** in a disorderly manner: *the things were piled pell-mell in the room* ▷ *adj* **3** disordered; tumultuous: *a pell-mell rush for the exit* ▷ *n* **4** disorder; confusion [C16: from Old French *pesle-mesle*, jingle based on *mesler* to MEDDLE]

pellucid (pɛ'lu:sɪd) *adj* **1** transparent or translucent **2** extremely clear in style and meaning; limpid [C17: from Latin *pellūcidus*, variant of *perlūcidus*, from *perlūcēre* to shine through, from *per* through + *lūcēre* to shine] > **pel'lucidly** *adv* > **,pellu'cidity** *or* **pel'lucidness** *n*

pelmet ('pɛlmɪt) *n* an ornamental drapery or board fixed above a window to conceal the curtain rail [C19: probably from French *palmette* palm-leaf decoration on cornice moulding; see PALMETTE]

Peloponnese (,pɛləpə'ni:s) *n* **the Peloponnese** the S peninsula of Greece, joined to central Greece by the Isthmus of Corinth: chief cities in ancient times were Sparta and Corinth, now Patras. Pop: 503 300 (2001). Area: 21 439 sq km (8361 sq miles). Medieval name: **Morea** Modern Greek name: **Peloponnesos**

Pelops ('pi:lɒps) *n Greek myth* the son of Tantalus, who as a child was killed by his father and served up as a meal for the gods

pelota (pə'lɒtə) *n* any of various games played in Spain, Spanish America, SW France, etc, by two players who use a basket strapped to their wrists or a wooden racket to propel a ball against a specially marked wall [C19: from Spanish: ball, from Old French *pelote*; see PELLET]

Pelotas (*Portuguese* pe'lɔtas) *n* a port in S Brazil, in Rio Grande do Sul on the Canal de São Gonçalo. Pop: 323 000 (2005 est)

peloton ('pɛlə,tɒn) *n cycle racing* the main field of riders in a road race [C20: French, literally: pack]

pelt¹ (pɛlt) *vb* **1** (*tr*) to throw (missiles) at (a person) **2** (*tr*) to hurl (insults) at (a person) **3** (*intr*; foll by *along*, *over*, etc) to move rapidly; hurry **4** (*intr*; often foll by *down*) to rain heavily ▷ *n* **5** a blow **6** speed (esp in the phrase **at full pelt**) [C15: of uncertain origin, perhaps from PELLET]

pelt² (pɛlt) *n* **1** the skin of a fur-bearing animal, such as a mink, esp when it has been removed from the carcass **2** the hide of an animal, stripped of hair and ready for tanning [C15: perhaps back formation from PELTRY]

peltast ('pɛltæst) *n* (in ancient Greece) a lightly armed foot soldier [C17: from Latin *peltasta*, from Greek *peltastēs* soldier equipped with a *pelta*, a small leather shield]

peltate ('pɛlteɪt) *adj* (of leaves) having the stalk attached to the centre of the lower surface [C18: from Latin *peltātus* equipped with a *pelta*, a small shield; see PELTAST]

peltry ('pɛltrɪ) *n, pl* -**ries** the pelts of animals collectively [C15: from Old French *peleterie* collection of pelts, from Latin *pilus* hair]

pelvic fin *n* either of a pair of fins attached to the pelvic girdle of fishes that help to control the direction of movement during locomotion

pelvic inflammatory disease *n* inflammation of a woman's womb, Fallopian tubes, or ovaries as a result of infection with one of a group of bacteria. Abbreviation: **PID**

pelvimetry (pɛl'vɪmɪtrɪ) *n obstetrics* measurement of the dimensions of the female pelvis

pelvis ('pɛlvɪs) *n, pl* -**vises** *or* -**ves** (-vi:z) **1** the large funnel-shaped structure at the lower end of the trunk of most vertebrates: in man it is formed by the hipbones and sacrum **2** the bones that form this structure **3** any anatomical cavity or structure shaped like a funnel or cup [C17: from Latin: basin, laver] > **pelvic** *adj*

Pemba ('pɛmbə) *n* an island in the Indian Ocean, off the E coast of Africa north of Zanzibar: part of Tanzania; produces about half the world's cloves. Chief town: Chake Chake. Pop: 362 166 (2002). Area: 984 sq km (380 sq miles)

Pembroke ('pɛmbrʊk) *n* **1** a town in SW Wales, in

Pembrokeshire on Milford Haven: 11th-century castle where Henry VII was born. Pop (with Pembroke Dock): 15 890 (2001) **2** the smaller variety of corgi, usually having a short tail

Pembrokeshire ('pɛmbrʊkʃɪə, -ʃə) *n* a county of SW Wales, on the Irish Sea and the Bristol Channel: formerly (1974–96) part of Dyfed: a hilly peninsula with a deeply indented coast: tourism, agriculture, oil refining. Administrative centre: Haverfordwest Pop: 116 300 (2003 est). Area: 1589 sq km (614 sq miles)

pemmican *or* **pemican** ('pɛmɪkən) *n* a small pressed cake of shredded dried meat, pounded into paste with fat and berries or dried fruits, used originally by American Indians and now chiefly for emergency rations [C19: from Cree *pimikân*, from *pimii* fat, grease]

pemphigus ('pɛmfɪgəs, pɛm'faɪ-) *n pathol* any of a group of blistering skin diseases, esp a potentially fatal form (**pemphigus vulgaris**) characterized by large blisters on the skin, mucous membranes of the mouth, genitals, intestines, etc, which eventually rupture and form painful denuded areas from which critical amounts of bodily protein, fluid, and blood may be lost [C18: via New Latin from Greek *pemphix* bubble]

pen¹ (pɛn) *n* **1** an implement for writing or drawing using ink, formerly consisting of a sharpened and split quill, and now of a metal nib attached to a holder. See also **ballpoint, fountain pen 2** the writing end of such an implement; nib **3** style of writing **4 the pen** writing as an occupation ▷ *vb* **pens, penning, penned 5** (*tr*) to write or compose [Old English *pinne*, from Late Latin *penna* (quill) pen, from Latin: feather]

pen² (pɛn) *n* **1** an enclosure in which domestic animals are kept **2** any place of confinement **3** a dock for servicing submarines, esp one having a bombproof roof ▷ *vb* **pens, penning, penned** *or* **pent 4** (*tr*) to enclose or keep in a pen [Old English *penn*, perhaps related to PIN]

pen³ (pɛn) *n US & Canadian informal* short for **penitentiary** (sense 1)

pen⁴ (pɛn) *n* a female swan [C16: of unknown origin]

PEN (pɛn) *n acronym for* International Association of Poets, Playwrights, Editors, Essayists, and Novelists

Pen. *abbreviation* Peninsula

penal ('pi:nəl) *adj* **1** of, relating to, constituting, or prescribing punishment **2** used or designated as a place of punishment: *a penal institution* [C15: from Late Latin *poenālis* concerning punishment, from *poena* penalty] > **'penally** *adv*

penal code *n* the codified body of the laws in any legal system that relate to crime and its punishment

penalize *or* **penalise** ('pi:nə,laɪz) *vb* (*tr*) **1** to impose a penalty on (someone), as for breaking a law or rule **2** to inflict a handicap or disadvantage on **3** *sport* to award a free stroke, point, or penalty against (a player or team) **4** to declare (an act) legally punishable; make subject to a penalty > **,penali'zation** *or* **,penali'sation** *n*

penalty ('pɛnəltɪ) *n, pl* -**ties 1** a legal or official punishment, such as a term of imprisonment **2** some other form of punishment, such as a fine or forfeit for not fulfilling a contract **3** loss, suffering, or other unfortunate result of one's own action, error, etc **4** *sport, games* a handicap awarded against a player or team for illegal play, such as a free shot at goal by the opposing team, loss of points, etc [C16: from Medieval Latin *poenālitās* penalty; see PENAL]

penalty area *n soccer* a rectangular area in front of the goal, within which the goalkeeper may handle the ball and within which a penalty is awarded for a foul by the defending team

penalty box *n* **1** *soccer* another name for **penalty area 2** *ice hockey* a bench for players serving time penalties

penalty corner *n hockey* a free hit from the goal line taken by the attacking side. Also called: **short corner**

penalty point *n* **1** *Brit* an endorsement on a driving licence due to a motoring offence: *he also got eight penalty points on his licence* **2** a point awarded against a sports team or competitor for an infringement of the rules

penalty rates *pl n Austral & NZ* rates of pay, such as double time, paid to employees working outside normal working hours

penalty shoot-out n 1 soccer a method of deciding the winner of a drawn match, in which players from each team attempt to score with a penalty kick 2 a similar method of resolving a tie in hockey, ice hockey, polo, etc

penance ('pɛnəns) n 1 voluntary self-punishment to atone for a sin, crime, etc 2 a feeling of regret for one's wrongdoings 3 Christianity a a punishment usually consisting of prayer, fasting, etc, undertaken voluntarily as an expression of penitence for sin b a punishment of this kind imposed by church authority as a condition of absolution ▷ vb 4 (tr) (of ecclesiastical authorities) to impose a penance upon (a sinner) [c13: via Old French from Latin paenitentia repentance; related to Latin poena penalty]

Penang (pɪ'næŋ) n 1 Also called: **Pulau Pinang** a state of Peninsular Malaysia: consists of the island of Penang and the province Wellesley on the mainland, which first united administratively in 1798 as a British colony. Capital: George Town. Pop: 1 313 449 (2000). Area: 1030 sq km (398 sq miles) 2 a forested island off the NW coast of Malaya, in the Strait of Malacca. Area: 293 sq km (113 sq miles). Former name (until about 1867): **Prince of Wales Island** 3 another name for **George Town**

penates (pə'nɑːtiːz) pl n See **lares and penates** [Latin]

pence (pɛns) n a plural of **penny**
  ● USAGE Since the decimalization of British currency
  ● and the introduction of the abbreviation **p**, as in 10p,
  ● 85p, etc, the abbreviation has tended to replace pence in
  ● speech, as in 4p (,fɔː'piː), 12p (,twɛlv'piː), etc

penchant ('pɒŋʃɒŋ) n a strong inclination or liking; bent or taste [c17: from French, from pencher to incline, from Latin pendēre to be suspended]

Penchi ('pɛn'tʃiː) n a variant transliteration of the Chinese name for **Benxi**

pencil ('pɛnsəl) n 1 a thin cylindrical instrument used for writing, drawing, etc, consisting of a rod of graphite or other marking substance, usually either encased in wood and sharpened or held in a mechanical metal device 2 something similar in shape or function: a styptic pencil; an eyebrow pencil 3 a narrow set of lines or rays, such as light rays, diverging from or converging to a point 4 rare an artist's individual style or technique in drawing ▷ vb -cils, -cilling, -cilled or US -cils, -ciling, -ciled (tr) 5 to draw, colour, or write with a pencil 6 to mark with a pencil [c14: from Old French pincel, from Latin pēnicillus painter's brush, from pēniculus a little tail, from pēnis tail] > 'penciller or US 'penciler n

pend (pɛnd) vb (intr) to await judgment or settlement [c15: from Latin pendēre to hang; related to Latin pendere to suspend]

Penda ('pɛndə) n died 655 AD, king of Mercia (?634–55)

pendant ('pɛndənt) n 1 a an ornament that hangs from a piece of jewellery b a necklace with such an ornament 2 a hanging light, esp a chandelier 3 a carved ornament that is suspended from a ceiling or roof ▷ adj 4 a variant spelling of **pendent** [c14: from Old French, from pendre to hang, from Latin pendēre to hang down; related to Latin pendere to hang, pondus weight, Greek span to pull]

pendent ('pɛndənt) adj 1 dangling 2 jutting 3 (of a grammatical construction) incomplete: a pendent nominative is a construction having no verb 4 a less common word for **pending** (senses 2, 3) ▷ n 5 a variant spelling of **pendant** [c15: from Old French pendant, from pendre to hang; see PENDANT] > 'pendency n

pendentive (pɛn'dɛntɪv) n any of four triangular sections of vaulting with concave sides, positioned at a corner of a rectangular space to support a circular or polygonal dome [c18: from French pendentif, from Latin pendens hanging, from pendere to hang]

Penderecki (Polish pɛndɛ'rɛtski) n Krzysztof ('kʃiʃtɔf). born 1933, Polish composer, noted for his highly individual orchestration. His works include Threnody for the Victims of Hiroshima for strings (1960), Stabat Mater (1962), Polish Requiem (1983–84), and the opera Ubu Rex (1991)

pending ('pɛndɪŋ) prep 1 while waiting for or anticipating ▷ adj (postpositive) 2 not yet decided, confirmed, or finished 3 imminent: these developments have been pending for some time

pendragon (pɛn'drægən) n a supreme war chief or leader of the ancient Britons [Welsh, literally: head dragon]

pen drive n computing another name for **key drive**

pendulous ('pɛndjʊləs) adj hanging downwards, esp so as to swing from side to side [c17: from Latin pendulus, from pendēre to hang down] > 'pendulously adv > 'pendulousness n

pendulum ('pɛndjʊləm) n 1 a body mounted so that it can swing freely under the influence of gravity. It is either a bob hung on a light thread (**simple pendulum**) or a more complex structure (**compound pendulum**) 2 such a device used to regulate a clockwork mechanism 3 something that changes its position, attitude, etc fairly regularly: the pendulum of public opinion [c17: from Latin pendulus PENDULOUS]

pene- or before a vowel **pen-** prefix almost: peneplain [from Latin paene]

Penelope (pə'nɛləpɪ) n Greek myth the wife of Odysseus, who remained true to him during his long absence despite the importunities of many suitors

peneplain or **peneplane** ('piːnɪ,pleɪn, ,piːnɪ'pleɪn) n a relatively flat land surface produced by a long period of erosion [c19: from PENE- + PLAIN[1]]

penetrant ('pɛnɪtrənt) adj 1 sharp; penetrating ▷ n 2 chem a substance that lowers the surface tension of a liquid and thus causes it to penetrate or be absorbed more easily 3 a person or thing that penetrates

penetrate ('pɛnɪ,treɪt) vb 1 to find or force a way into or through (something); pierce; enter 2 to diffuse through (a substance); permeate 3 (tr) to see through: their eyes could not penetrate the fog 4 (tr) (of a man) to insert the penis into the vagina of (a woman) 5 (tr) to grasp the meaning of (a principle, etc) 6 (intr) to be understood: his face lit up as the new idea penetrated [c16: from Latin penetrāre; related to penitus inner, and penus the interior of a house] > ,penetra'bility n > 'pene,trator n

penetrating ('pɛnɪ,treɪtɪŋ) adj tending to or able to penetrate: a penetrating mind; a penetrating voice > 'pene,tratingly adv

penetration (,pɛnɪ'treɪʃən) n 1 the act or an instance of penetrating 2 the ability or power to penetrate 3 keen insight or perception 4 military an offensive manoeuvre that breaks through an enemy's defensive position 5 Also called: **market penetration** the proportion of the total number of potential purchasers of a product or service who either are aware of its existence or actually buy it

Peneus (pɪ'niːəs) n the ancient name for the **Salambria**

pen friend n another name for **pen pal**

Penghu or **P'eng-hu** ('pɛŋ'huː) n transliteration of the Chinese name for the **Pescadores**

Pengpu ('pɛŋ'puː) n a variant transliteration of the Chinese name for **Bengbu**

penguin ('pɛŋgwɪn) n any flightless marine bird, such as Aptenodytes patagonica (king penguin) and Pygoscelis adeliae (Adélie penguin), of the order Sphenisciformes of cool southern, esp Antarctic, regions: they have wings modified as flippers, webbed feet, and feathers lacking barbs [c16: perhaps from Welsh pen gwyn, from pen head + gwyn white]

penicillin (,pɛnɪ'sɪlɪn) n any of a group of antibiotics with powerful bactericidal action, used to treat many types of infections, including pneumonia, gonorrhoea, and infections caused by streptococci and staphylococci: originally obtained from the fungus Penicillium, esp P. notatum. Formula: R-C$_9$H$_{11}$N$_2$O$_4$S where R is one of several side chains [c20: from PENICILLIUM]

penicillium (,pɛnɪ'sɪlɪəm) n, pl -cilliums or -cillia (-'sɪlɪə) any ascomycetous saprotrophic fungus of the genus Penicillium, which commonly grow as a green or blue mould on stale food: some species are used in cheese-making and others as a source of penicillin [c19: New Latin, from Latin pēnicillus tuft of hairs; named from the tufted appearance of the sporangia of this fungus]

penillion or **pennillion** (pɪ'nɪlɪən) pl n, sing **penill** (pɪ'nɪl) the Welsh art or practice of singing poetry in counterpoint to a traditional melody played on the harp [from Welsh: verses, plural of penill verse, stanza]

peninsula (pɪ'nɪnsjʊlə) n a narrow strip of land

projecting into a sea or lake from the mainland [c16: from Latin, literally: almost an island, from *paene* PENE- + *insula* island] > **pen'insular** *adj*
● **USAGE** The noun *peninsula* is sometimes confused with
● the adjective *peninsular: the Iberian peninsula* (not
● *peninsular*)

Peninsula *n* the Peninsula short for the **Iberian Peninsula**

penis ('piːnɪs) *n, pl* **-nises** *or* **-nes** (-niːz) the male organ of copulation in higher vertebrates, also used for urine excretion in many mammals [c17: from Latin] > **penile** ('piːnaɪl) *adj*

penitent ('pɛnɪtənt) *adj* **1** feeling regret for one's sins; repentant ▷ *n* **2** a person who is penitent **3** *Christianity* **a** a person who repents his sins and seeks forgiveness for them **b** *RC Church* a person who confesses his sins to a priest and submits to a penance imposed by him [c14: from Church Latin *paenitēns* regretting, from *paenitēre* to repent, of obscure origin] > **'penitence** *n* > **'penitently** *adv*

penitential (ˌpɛnɪ'tɛnʃəl) *adj* **1** of, showing, or constituting penance ▷ *n* **2** *chiefly RC Church* a book or compilation of instructions for confessors **3** a less common word for **penitent** (senses 2, 3) > **ˌpeni'tentially** *adv*

penitentiary (ˌpɛnɪ'tɛnʃərɪ) *n, pl* **-ries** **1** (in the US and Canada) a state or federal prison: in Canada, esp a federal prison for offenders convicted of serious crimes. Sometimes shortened to **pen**[1] **2** *RC Church* **a** a cardinal who presides over a tribunal that decides all matters affecting the sacrament of penance **b** this tribunal itself ▷ *adj* **3** another word for **penitential** (sense 1) **4** *US & Canadian* (of an offence) punishable by imprisonment in a penitentiary [c15 (meaning also: an officer dealing with penances): from Medieval Latin *poenitēntiārius*, from Latin *paenitēns* PENITENT]

Penki ('pɛntʃɪ) *n* a variant transliteration of the Chinese name for **Benxi**

penknife ('pɛnˌnaɪf) *n, pl* **-knives** a small knife with one or more blades that fold into the handle; pocketknife [c15: so called because it was originally used for making and repairing quill pens]

penman ('pɛnmən) *n, pl* **-men** **1** a person skilled in handwriting **2** a person who writes by hand in a specified way: *a bad penman* **3** an author

penmanship ('pɛnmənʃɪp) *n* style or technique of writing by hand

Penn (pɛn) *n* **1** Irving. born 1917, US photographer, noted for his portraits and his innovations in colour photography **2** William. 1644–1718, English Quaker and founder of Pennsylvania

Penn. *or* **Penna** *abbreviation* Pennsylvania

penna ('pɛnə) *n, pl* **-nae** (-niː) *ornithol* any large feather that has a vane and forms part of the main plumage of a bird [Latin: feather]

pen name *n* an author's pseudonym. Also called: **nom de plume**

pennant ('pɛnənt) *n* **1** a type of pennon, esp one flown from vessels as identification or for signalling **2** *chiefly US, Canadian & Austral* **a** a flag serving as an emblem of championship in certain sports **b** (*as modifier*): *pennant cricket* [c17: probably a blend of PENDANT and PENNON]

pennate ('pɛneɪt) *or* **pennated** *adj biology* **1** having feathers, wings, or winglike structures **2** another word for **pinnate** [c19: from Latin *pennātus*, from *penna* wing]

penne ('pɛnɪ) *n* pasta in the form of short tubes [c20: Italian, literally: quills]

Penney ('pɛnɪ) *n* **William George**, Baron Penney of East Hendred. 1909–91, British mathematician. He worked on the first atomic bomb and became chairman of the UK Atomic Energy Authority (1964–67)

penni ('pɛnɪ) *n, pl* **-niä** (-nɪə) *or* **-nis** a former Finnish monetary unit worth one hundredth of a markka [Finnish, from Low German *pennig* PENNY]

penniless ('pɛnɪlɪs) *adj* very poor; almost totally without money > **'pennilessly** *adv* > **'pennilessness** *n*

Pennine Alps ('pɛnaɪn) *pl n* a range of the Alps between Switzerland and Italy. Highest peak: Monte Rosa, 4634 m (15 204 ft)

Pennines ('pɛnaɪnz) *pl n* a system of hills in England, extending from the Cheviot Hills in the north to the River Trent in the south: forms the watershed for the main rivers of N England. Highest peak: Cross Fell, 893 m (2930 ft). Also called: **the Pennine Chain**

Pennine Way *n* a long-distance footpath extending from Edale, Derbyshire, for 402 km (250 miles) to Kirk Yetholm, Scottish Borders

pennon ('pɛnən) *n* **1 a** a long flag, often tapering and rounded, divided, or pointed at the end, originally a knight's personal flag **2** a small tapering or triangular flag borne on a ship or boat **3** a poetic word for **wing** [c14: via Old French ultimately from Latin *penna* feather]

Pennsylvania (ˌpɛnsɪl'veɪnɪə) *n* a state of the northeastern US: almost wholly in the Appalachians, with the Allegheny Plateau to the west and a plain in the southeast; the second most important US state for manufacturing. Capital: Harrisburg. Pop: 12 365 455 (2003 est). Area: 116 462 sq km (44 956 sq miles). Abbreviations: **Pa, Penn, PA**

Pennsylvania Dutch *n* **1** Also called: **Pennsylvania German** a dialect of German spoken in E Pennsylvania **2 the Pennsylvania Dutch** (*functioning as plural*) a group of German-speaking people in E Pennsylvania, descended from 18th-century settlers from SW Germany and Switzerland

Pennsylvanian (ˌpɛnsɪl'veɪnɪən) *adj* **1** of the state of Pennsylvania **2** (in North America) of, denoting, or formed in the upper of two divisions of the Carboniferous period, which lasted 30 million years, during which coal measures were formed ▷ *n* **3** an inhabitant or native of the state of Pennsylvania **4 the Pennsylvanian** the Pennsylvanian period or rock system, equivalent to the Upper Carboniferous of Europe

penny ('pɛnɪ) *n, pl* **pennies** *or* **pence** (pɛns) **1** (in Britain) a bronze coin having a value equal to one hundredth of a pound **2** (in Britain before 1971) a bronze or copper coin having a value equal to one twelfth of a shilling or one two-hundred-and-fortieth of a pound **3** a former monetary unit of the Republic of Ireland worth one hundredth of a pound **4** *pl* **pennies** (in the US and Canada) a cent **5** a coin of similar value, as used in several other countries **6** (*used with a negative*) *informal, chiefly Brit* the least amount of money: *I don't have a penny* **7 a pretty penny** *informal* a considerable sum of money **8 spend a penny** *Brit informal* to urinate **9 the penny dropped** *informal, chiefly Brit* the explanation of something was finally realized [Old English *penig, pening*; related to Old Saxon *penni(n)g*, Old High German *pfeni(n)c*, German *Pfennig*]

penny arcade *n chiefly US* a public place with various coin-operated machines for entertainment; amusement arcade

Penny Black *n* the first adhesive postage stamp, issued in Britain in 1840; an imperforate stamp bearing the profile of Queen Victoria on a dark background

penny-dreadful *n, pl* **-fuls** *Brit informal* a cheap, often lurid or sensational book or magazine

penny-farthing *n Brit* an early type of bicycle with a large front wheel and a small rear wheel, the pedals being attached to the front wheel [c20: so called because of the similarity between the relative sizes of the wheels and the relative sizes of the (old) penny and farthing coins]

penny-pinching *adj informal* excessively careful with money > **'penny-ˌpincher** *n*

pennyroyal (ˌpɛnɪ'rɔɪəl) *n* **1 a** a Eurasian plant, *Mentha pulegium*, with hairy leaves and small mauve flowers, that yields an aromatic oil used in medicine: family *Lamiaceae* (labiates) **2** Also called: **mock pennyroyal** a similar and related plant, *Hedeoma pulegioides*, of E North America [c16: variant of Anglo-Norman *puliol real*, from Old French *pouliol* (from Latin *pūleium* pennyroyal) + *real* ROYAL]

penny shares *pl n stock exchange* securities with a low market price, esp less than 20p, enabling small investors to purchase a large number for a relatively small outlay

pennyweight ('pɛnɪˌweɪt) *n* a unit of weight equal to 24 grains or one twentieth of an ounce (Troy)

penny whistle *n* a type of flageolet with six finger holes, esp a cheap one made of metal. Also called: tin whistle

penny-wise *adj* **1** greatly concerned with saving small sums of money **2** penny-wise and pound-foolish careful about trifles but wasteful in large ventures

pennywort ('pɛnɪ,wɜːt) *n* Also called: navelwort a crassulaceous Eurasian rock plant, *Umbilicus rupestris* (or *Cotyledon umbilicus*), with whitish-green tubular leaves and rounded leaves **2** a marsh plant, *Hydrocotyle vulgaris*, of Europe and North Africa, having circular leaves and greenish-pink flowers: family *Hydrocotylaceae* **3** any of various other plants with rounded penny-like leaves

pennyworth ('pɛnɪ,wɜːθ) *n* **1** the amount that can be bought for a penny **2** a small amount: *he hasn't got a pennyworth of sense*

penology (piː'nɒlədʒɪ) *n* **1** the branch of the social sciences concerned with the punishment of crime **2** the science of prison management [c19: from Greek *poinē* punishment] > penological (,piːnə'lɒdʒɪkəl) *adj* > pe'nologist *n*

pen pal *n* a person with whom one regularly exchanges letters, often a person in another country whom one has not met. Also called: pen friend

penpusher ('pɛn,pʊʃə) *n* a person who writes a lot, esp a clerk involved with boring paperwork > 'pen,pushing *adj, n*

Penrith (pɛn'rɪθ) *n* a market town in NW England, in Cumbria. Pop: 14 471 (2001)

Penrose ('pɛnrəʊz) *n* Sir **Roger**. born 1931, British mathematician and theoretical physicist, noted for his investigation of black holes

pension[1] ('pɛnʃən) *n* **1** a regular payment made by the state to people over a certain age to enable them to subsist without having to work **2** a regular payment made by an employer to former employees after they retire **3** a regular payment made to a retired person as the result of his or her contributions to a personal pension scheme **4** any regular payment made on charitable grounds, by way of patronage, or in recognition of merit, service, etc: *a pension paid to a disabled soldier* ▷ *vb* **5** (*tr*) to grant a pension to [c14: via Old French from Latin *pēnsiō* a payment, from *pendere* to pay] > 'pensionable *adj* > 'pensionless *adj* > 'pensioner *n*

pension[2] *French* (pãsjɔ̃) *n* (in France and some other countries) a relatively cheap boarding house [c17: French; extended meaning of *pension* grant; see PENSION[1]]

pensioneer trustee (,pɛnʃə'nɪə) *n* (in Britain) a person authorized by the Inland Revenue to oversee the management of a pension fund

pension off *vb* (*tr, adverb*) **1** to cause to retire from a post and pay a pension to **2** to discard, because old and worn: *to pension off submarines*

pensive ('pɛnsɪv) *adj* **1** deeply or seriously thoughtful, often with a tinge of sadness **2** expressing or suggesting pensiveness [c14: from Old French *pensif*, from *penser* to think, from Latin *pensāre* to consider; compare PENSION[1]] > 'pensively *adv* > 'pensiveness *n*

penstemon (pɛn'stiːmən) *n* a variant (esp US) of pentstemon

penstock ('pɛn,stɒk) *n* **1** a conduit that supplies water to a hydroelectric power plant **2** a channel bringing water from the head gates to a water wheel **3** a sluice for controlling water flow [c17: from PEN[2] + STOCK]

pent (pɛnt) *vb* a past tense and past participle of pen[2]

penta- combining form five: pentagon; pentameter; pentaprism [from Greek *pente* five]

pentacle ('pɛntəkəl) *n* another name for pentagram [c16: from Italian *pentacolo* something having five corners; see PENTA-]

pentad ('pɛntæd) *n* **1** a group or series of five **2** the number or sum of five **3** a period of five years **4** *chem* a pentavalent element, atom, or radical **5** *meteorol* a period of five days [c17: from Greek *pentas* group of five]

pentadactyl (,pɛntə'dæktɪl) *adj* (of the limbs of amphibians, reptiles, birds, and mammals) consisting of an upper arm or thigh, a forearm or shank, and a

hand or foot bearing five digits

pentagon ('pɛntə,gɒn) *n* a polygon having five sides > pentagonal (pɛn'tægənəl) *adj*

Pentagon ('pɛntə,gɒn) *n* **1** the five-sided building in Arlington, Virginia, that houses the headquarters of the US Department of Defense **2** the military leadership of the US

pentagram ('pɛntə,græm) *n* **1** a star-shaped figure formed by extending the sides of a regular pentagon to meet at five points **2** such a figure used as a magical or symbolic figure by the Pythagoreans, black magicians, etc ▷ Also called: pentacle, pentangle

pentahedron (,pɛntə'hiːdrən) *n, pl* -drons *or* -dra (-drə) a solid figure having five plane faces. See also polyhedron > ,penta'hedral *adj*

pentamerous (pɛn'tæmərəs) *adj* consisting of five parts, esp (of flowers) having the petals, sepals, and other parts arranged in groups of five

pentameter (pɛn'tæmɪtə) *n* **1** a verse line consisting of five metrical feet **2** (in classical prosody) a verse line consisting of two dactyls, one stressed syllable, two dactyls, and a final stressed syllable ▷ *adj* **3** designating a verse line consisting of five metrical feet

pentamidine (pɛn'tæmɪ,diːn, -dɪn) *n* a drug used to treat protozoal infections, esp pneumonia caused by *Pneumocystis carinii* in patients with AIDS

pentane ('pɛnteɪn) *n* an alkane hydrocarbon having three isomers, esp the isomer with a straight chain of carbon atoms (*n*-pentane) which is a colourless flammable liquid used as a solvent. Formula: C_5H_{12}

pentangle ('pɛn,tæŋgəl) *n* another name for pentagram

pentanoic acid (,pɛntə'nəʊɪk) *n* a colourless liquid carboxylic acid with an unpleasant odour, used in making perfumes, flavourings, and pharmaceuticals. Formula: $CH_3(CH_2)_3COOH$. Also called: valeric acid [from PENTANE]

pentaquark ('pɛntə,kwɑːk) *n* *physics* a postulated subatomic particle consisting of four quarks and one antiquark, thought not to exist in actuality [c21]

Pentateuch ('pɛntə,tjuːk) *n* the first five books of the Old Testament regarded as a unity [c16: from Church Latin *pentateuchus*, from Greek PENTA- + *teukhos* tool (in Late Greek: scroll)] > ,Penta'teuchal *adj*

pentathlon (pɛn'tæθlən) *n* an athletic contest consisting of five different events, based on a competition in the ancient Greek Olympics [c18: from Greek *pentathlon*, from PENTA- + *athlon* contest]

pentatomic (,pɛntə'tɒmɪk) *adj* *chem* having five atoms in the molecule

pentatonic scale (,pɛntə'tɒnɪk) *n* *music* any of several scales consisting of five notes, the most commonly encountered one being composed of the first, second, third, fifth, and sixth degrees of the major diatonic scale

pentavalent (,pɛntə'veɪlənt) *adj* *chem* having a valency of five. Also called: quinquevalent

pentazocine (pɛn'tæzəʊ,siːn) *n* a powerful synthetic drug used in medical practice as a narcotic analgesic

Pentecost ('pɛntɪ,kɒst) *n* **1** a Christian festival occurring on Whit Sunday commemorating the descent of the Holy Ghost on the apostles **2** Also called: Feast of Weeks, Shavuot *Judaism* the harvest festival celebrated fifty days after the second day of Passover on the sixth and seventh days of Sivan, and commemorating the giving the Torah on Mount Sinai [Old English, from Church Latin *pentēcostē*, from Greek *pentēkostē* fiftieth]

Pentecostal (,pɛntɪ'kɒstəl) *adj* **1** (*usually prenominal*) of or relating to any of various Christian groups that emphasize the charismatic aspects of Christianity and adopt a fundamental attitude to the Bible **2** of or relating to Pentecost or the influence of the Holy Ghost ▷ *n* **3** a member of a Pentecostal Church > ,Pente'costalist *n, adj*

Pentelikon (pɛn'tɛlɪkɒn) *n* a mountain in SE Greece, near Athens: famous for its white marble, worked regularly from the 6th century BC, from which the chief buildings and sculptures in Athens are made. Height: 1109 m (3638 ft)

Penthesileia *or* **Penthesilea** (,pɛnθəsɪ'leɪə) *n* *Greek myth*

the daughter of Ares and queen of the Amazons, whom she led to the aid of Troy. She was slain by Achilles

Pentheus ('pɛnθɪəs) n Greek myth the grandson of Cadmus and his successor as king of Thebes, who resisted the introduction of the cult of Dionysus. In revenge the god drove him mad and he was torn to pieces by a group of bacchantes, one of whom was his mother

penthouse ('pɛnt,haʊs) n 1 a flat or maisonette built onto the top floor or roof of a block of flats 2 a construction on the roof of a building, esp one used to house machinery 3 a shed built against a building, esp one that has a sloping roof [C14 pentis (later penthouse, by folk etymology), from Old French apentis, from Late Latin appendicium appendage, from Latin appendere to hang from; see APPENDIX]

Pentland Firth ('pɛntlənd) n a channel between the mainland of N Scotland and the Orkney Islands: notorious for rough seas. Length: 32 km (20 miles). Width: up to 13 km (8 miles)

pentobarbital sodium (,pɛntə'bɑːbɪ,təʊn) n a barbiturate drug used in medicine as a sedative and hypnotic. Formula: $C_{11}H_{17}N_2O_3Na$

pentode ('pɛntəʊd) n 1 an electronic valve having five electrodes: a cathode, anode, and three grids 2 (modifier) (of a transistor) having three terminals at the base or gate [C20: from PENTA- + Greek hodos way]

Pentothal sodium ('pɛntə,θæl) n a trademark for **thiopental sodium**

pentstemon (pɛnt'stiːmən) or esp US **penstemon** n any scrophulariaceous plant of the North American genus Penstemon (or Pentstemon), having white, pink, red, blue, or purple flowers with five stamens, one of which is bearded and sterile [C18: New Latin, from PENTA- + Greek stēmōn thread (here: stamen)]

pent-up adj (pent up when postpositive) not released; repressed: pent-up emotions

pentyl acetate n a colourless combustible liquid used as a solvent for paints, in the extraction of penicillin, in photographic film, and as a flavouring. Formula: $CH_3COOC_5H_{11}$. Also called: **amyl acetate**

penult ('pɛnʌlt, pɪ'nʌlt) or **penultima** (pɪ'nʌltɪmə) n the last syllable but one in a word [C16: Latin paenultima syllaba, from paene ultima almost the last]

penultimate (pɪ'nʌltɪmɪt) adj 1 next to the last ▷ n 2 anything that is next to the last, esp a penult [C17: from Latin paene almost + ULTIMATE, on the model of Latin paenultimus]

penumbra (pɪ'nʌmbrə) n, pl -brae (-briː) or -bras 1 a fringe region of half shadow resulting from the partial obstruction of light by an opaque object 2 astronomy the lighter and outer region of a sunspot 3 painting the point or area in which light and shade blend ▷ See umbra [C17: via New Latin from Latin paene almost + umbra shadow] > pe'numbral or pe'numbrous adj

penurious (pɪ'njʊərɪəs) adj 1 niggardly with money 2 lacking money or means > pe'nuriously adv > pe'nuriousness n

penury ('pɛnjʊrɪ) n 1 extreme poverty 2 extreme scarcity [C15: from Latin pēnūria dearth, of obscure origin]

Penza (Russian 'pjɛnzə) n a city in W Russia: manufacturing centre. Pop: 514 000 (2005 est)

Penzance (pɛn'zæns) n a town in SW England, in SW Cornwall: the westernmost town in England; resort and fishing port. Pop: 20 255 (2001)

Penzias ('pɛntsɪəs, 'pɛnz-) n Arno Allan. born 1933, US astrophysicist, who shared the Nobel prize for physics (1978) with Robert W. Wilson for their discovery of cosmic microwave background radiation

peon[1] ('piːən, 'piːɒn) n 1 a Spanish-American farm labourer or unskilled worker 2 (formerly in Spanish America) a debtor compelled to work off his debts 3 any very poor person [C19: from Spanish peón peasant, from Medieval Latin pedō man who goes on foot, from Latin pēs foot; compare Old French paon PAWN[2]]

peon[2] (pjuːn, 'piːən, 'piːɒn) n (in India, Sri Lanka, etc, esp formerly) 1 a messenger or attendant, esp in an office 2 a native policeman 3 a foot soldier [C17: from Portuguese peão orderly; see PEON[1]]

peony or **paeony** ('piːənɪ) n, pl -nies 1 any of various ranunculaceous shrubs and plants of the genus Paeonia, of Eurasia and North America, having large pink, red, white, or yellow flowers 2 the flower of any of these plants [Old English peonie, from Latin paeōnia, from Greek paiōnia; related to paiōnios healing, from paiōn physician]

people ('piːpəl) n (usually functioning as plural) 1 persons collectively or in general 2 a group of persons considered together: blind people 3 pl peoples the persons living in a country and sharing the same nationality: the French people 4 one's family: he took her home to meet his people 5 persons loyal to someone powerful: the king's people accompanied him in exile 6 the people a the mass of persons without special distinction, privileges, etc b the body of persons in a country, esp those entitled to vote ▷ vb 7 (tr) to provide with or as if with people or inhabitants [C13: from Old French pople, from Latin populus; see POPULACE]

people carrier n another name for **multipurpose vehicle**

people mover n 1 any of various automated forms of transport for large numbers of passengers over short distances, such as a moving pavement, driverless cars, etc 2 another name for **multipurpose vehicle**

people's democracy n (in Communist ideology) a country or form of government in transition from bourgeois democracy to socialism. In this stage there is more than one class, the largest being the proletariat, led by the Communist Party, which is therefore the dominant power

people's front n a less common term for **popular front**

people skills pl n the ability to deal with, influence, and communicate with other people

Peoria (pɪ'ɔːrɪə) n a port in N central Illinois, on the Illinois River. Pop: 112 907 (2003 est)

pep (pɛp) n 1 high spirits, energy, or vitality ▷ vb peps, pepping, pepped 2 (tr; usually foll by up) to liven by imbuing with new vigour [C20: short for PEPPER]

PEP (pɛp) n acronym for 1 personal equity plan: a method of saving in the U.K. with certain tax advantages, in which investments up to a fixed annual value can be purchased: replaced by the ISA in 1999 but arrangements for existing PEPs remain unchanged ▷ abbreviation 2 political and economic planning

peperomia (pɛpə'rəʊmɪə) n any plant of the large genus Peperomia from tropical and subtropical America with slightly fleshy ornamental leaves, some of which are grown as pot plants: family Piperaceae [New Latin, from Greek peperi pepper + homoios similar + -IA]

Pepin the Short ('pɛpɪn) n died 768 AD, king of the Franks (751–768); son of Charles Martel and father of Charlemagne. He deposed the Merovingian king (751) and founded the Carolingian dynasty

peplum ('pɛpləm) n, pl -lums or -la (-lə) a flared ruffle attached to the waist of a jacket, bodice, etc [C17: from Latin: full upper garment, from Greek peplos shawl]

pepo ('piːpəʊ) n, pl -pos the fruit of any of various cucurbitaceous plants, such as the melon, squash, cucumber, and pumpkin, having a firm rind, fleshy watery pulp, and numerous seeds [C19: from Latin: pumpkin, from Greek pepōn edible gourd, from peptein to ripen]

pepper ('pɛpə) n 1 a woody climbing plant, Piper nigrum, of the East Indies, having small black berry-like fruits: family Piperaceae 2 the dried fruit of this plant, which is ground to produce a sharp hot condiment. See also **black pepper, white pepper** 3 any of various other plants of the genus Piper 4 Also called: **capsicum** any of various tropical plants of the solanaceous genus Capsicum, esp C. frutescens, the fruits of which are used as a vegetable and a condiment. See also **sweet pepper, red pepper, cayenne pepper** 5 the fruit of any of these capsicums, which has a mild or pungent taste 6 the condiment made from the fruits of any of these plants ▷ vb 7 to season with pepper 8 to sprinkle liberally; dot: his prose was peppered with alliteration 9 to pelt with small missiles [Old English piper, from Latin, from Greek peperi; compare French poivre, Old Norse piparr]

pepper-and-salt adj 1 (of cloth) marked with a fine mixture of black and white 2 (of hair) streaked with grey: *a pepper-and-salt moustache*

peppercorn ('pɛpə,kɔːn) *n* **1** the small dried berry of the pepper plant (*Piper nigrum*) **2** something trifling

peppercorn rent *n* a rent that is very low or nominal

pepper mill *n* a small hand mill used to grind peppercorns

peppermint ('pɛpə,mɪnt) *n* **1** a temperate mint plant, *Mentha piperita*, with purple or white flowers: cultivated for its downy leaves, which yield a pungent oil **2** the oil from this plant, which is used as a flavouring **3** a sweet flavoured with peppermint

pepperoni (,pɛpə'rəʊnɪ) *n* a highly seasoned dry sausage of pork and beef spiced with pepper, used esp on pizza [C20: from Italian *peperoni,* plural of *peperone* cayenne pepper]

pepper pot *n* **1** a small container with perforations in the top for sprinkling pepper **2** a Caribbean stew of meat, rice, vegetables, etc, highly seasoned with cassareep

pepper spray *n* a defence spray agent derived from hot cayenne peppers, which causes temporary blindness and breathing difficulty, sometimes used to control riots

pepper tree *n* Also called: **mastic tree** any of several evergreen anacardiaceous trees of the chiefly South American genus *Schinus,* esp *S. molle,* having yellowish-white flowers and bright red ornamental fruits

peppery ('pɛpərɪ) *adj* **1** flavoured with or tasting of pepper **2** quick-tempered; irritable **3** full of bite and sharpness: *a peppery speech* > **'pepperiness** *n*

pep pill *n informal* a tablet containing a stimulant drug

peppy ('pɛpɪ) *adj* **-pier, -piest** *informal* full of vitality; bouncy or energetic > **'peppily** *adv* > **'peppiness** *n*

pepsin or **pepsine** ('pɛpsɪn) *n* a proteolytic enzyme produced in the stomach in the inactive form pepsinogen, which, when activated by acid, splits proteins into peptones [C19: via German from Greek *pepsis,* from *peptein* to digest]

pep talk *n informal* an enthusiastic talk designed to increase confidence, production, cooperation, etc

peptic ('pɛptɪk) *adj* **1** of, relating to, or promoting digestion **2** of, relating to, or caused by pepsin or the action of the digestive juices [C17: from Greek *peptikos* capable of digesting, from *pepsis* digestion, from *peptein* to digest]

peptic ulcer *n pathol* an ulcer of the mucous membrane lining those parts of the alimentary tract exposed to digestive juices. It can occur in the oesophagus, the stomach, the duodenum, the jejunum, or in parts of the ileum

peptide ('pɛptaɪd) *n* any of a group of compounds consisting of two or more amino acids linked by chemical bonding between their respective carboxyl and amino groups

peptide bond *n biochem* a chemical amide linkage, –NH-CO–, formed by the condensation of the amino group of one amino acid with the carboxyl group of another

peptone ('pɛptəʊn) *n biochem* any of a group of compounds that form an intermediary group in the digestion of proteins to amino acids [C19: from German *Pepton,* from Greek *pepton* something digested, from *peptein* to digest] > **peptonic** (pɛp'tɒnɪk) *adj*

Pepys (piːps) *n* Samuel. 1633–1703, English diarist and naval administrator. His diary, which covers the period 1660–69, is a vivid account of London life through such disasters as the Great Plague, the Fire of London, and the intrusion of the Dutch fleet up the Thames

per (pɜː; *unstressed* pə) *determiner* **1** for every: *three pence per pound* ▷ *prep* **2** (esp in some Latin phrases) by; through **3** as per according to: *as per specifications* **4** as per usual *informal* as usual [C15: from Latin: by, for each]

per- *prefix* **1** through: *pervade* **2** throughout: *perennial* **3** away, beyond: *perfidy* **4** (intensifier): *pervervid* **5** indicating that a chemical compound contains a high proportion of a specified element: *peroxide; perchloride* **6** indicating that a chemical element is in a higher than usual state of oxidation: *permanganate; perchlorate* [from Latin *per* through]

Pera ('pɪərə) *n* the former name of **Beyoğlu**

peracid (pɜːr'æsɪd) *n* an acid, such as perchloric acid, in which the element forming the acid radical exhibits its highest valency

peradventure (pərəd'vɛntʃə, ,pɜːr-) *archaic* ▷ *adv* **1** by chance; perhaps ▷ *n* **2** chance, uncertainty, or doubt [C13: from Old French *par aventure* by chance]

Peraea or **Perea** (pə'riːə) *n* a region of ancient Palestine, east of the River Jordan and the Dead Sea

Perak ('pɛərə, 'pɪərə, pɪ'ræk) *n* a state of NW Peninsular Malaysia, on the Strait of Malacca: tin mining. Capital: Ipoh. Pop: 2 051 236 (2000). Area: 21 005 sq km (8110 sq miles)

perambulate (pə'ræmbjʊ,leɪt) *vb* **1** to walk about (a place) **2** (*tr*) to walk round in order to inspect [C16: from Latin *perambulāre* to traverse, from *per* through + *ambulāre* to walk] > **per,ambu'lation** *n* > **perambulatory** (pə'ræmbjʊlətərɪ, -trɪ) *adj*

perambulator (pə'ræmbjʊ,leɪtə) *n* a formal word for **pram**[1]

per annum (pər 'ænəm) *adv* every year or by the year

P/E ratio *abbreviation* price-earnings ratio

percale (pə'keɪl, -'kɑːl) *n* a close-textured woven cotton fabric, plain or printed, used esp for sheets [C17: via French from Persian *pargālah* piece of cloth]

per capita (pə 'kæpɪtə) *adj, adv* of or for each person [Latin, literally: according to heads]

perceive (pə'siːv) *vb* **1** to become aware of (something) through the senses, esp the sight; recognize or observe **2** (*tr; may take a clause as object*) to come to comprehend; grasp [C13: from Old French *perçoivre,* from Latin *percipere* seize entirely, from PER- (thoroughly) + *capere* to grasp] > **per'ceivable** *adj* > **per'ceivably** *adv*

per cent (pə 'sɛnt) *adv* **1** Also called: **per centum** in or for every hundred. Symbol: % ▷ *n* Also: **per'cent** **2** a percentage or proportion **3** (*often plural*) securities yielding a rate of interest as specified: *he bought three percents* [C16: from Medieval Latin *per centum* out of every hundred]

percentage (pə'sɛntɪdʒ) *n* **1** proportion or rate per hundred parts **2** *commerce* the interest, tax, commission, or allowance on a hundred items **3** any proportion in relation to the whole **4** *informal* profit or advantage

percentile (pə'sɛntaɪl) *n* one of 99 actual or notional values of a variable dividing its distribution into 100 groups with equal frequencies; the 90th percentile is the value of a variable such that 90% of the relevant population is below that value. Also called: **centile**

percept ('pɜːsɛpt) *n* **1** a concept that depends on recognition by the senses, such as sight, of some external object or phenomenon **2** an object or phenomenon that is perceived [C19: from Latin *perceptum,* from *percipere* to PERCEIVE]

perceptible (pə'sɛptəb³l) *adj* able to be perceived; noticeable or recognizable > **per,cepti'bility** *n* > **per'ceptibly** *adv*

perception (pə'sɛpʃən) *n* **1** the act or the effect of perceiving **2** insight or intuition gained by perceiving **3** the ability or capacity to perceive **4** way of perceiving; awareness or consciousness; view: *advertising affects the customer's perception of a product* **5** the process by which an organism detects and interprets information from the external world by means of the sensory receptors [C15: from Latin *perceptiō* comprehension; see PERCEIVE] > **per'ceptional** *adj* > **per'ceptual** *adj* > **per'ceptually** *adv*

perceptive (pə'sɛptɪv) *adj* **1** quick at perceiving; observant **2** perceptual **3** able to perceive > **per'ceptively** *adv* > **per'ceptiveness** or **,percep'tivity** *n*

Perceval ('pɜːsɪv³l) *n* Spencer. 1762–1812, British statesman; prime minister (1809–12); assassinated

perch[1] (pɜːtʃ) *n* **1** a pole, branch, or other resting place above ground on which a bird roosts or alights **2** a similar resting place for a person or thing **3** another name for **rod** (sense 7) ▷ *vb* **4** (usually foll by *on*) to alight, rest, or cause to rest on or as if on a perch: *the bird perched on the branch; the cap was perched on his head* [C13 *perche* stake, from Old French, from Latin *pertica* long stake]

perch[2] (pɜːtʃ) *n, pl* **perch** or **perches** **1** any freshwater spiny-finned teleost fish of the family *Percidae,* esp those of the genus *Perca,* such as *P. fluviatilis* of Europe and *P.*

flavescens (**yellow perch**) of North America: valued as food and game fishes **2** any of various similar or related fishes. Related adj: **percoid** [C13: from Old French *perche*, from Latin *perca*, from Greek *perkē*; compare Greek *perkos* spotted]

perchance (pə'tʃɑːns) *adv archaic or poetic* **1** perhaps; possibly **2** by chance; accidentally [C14: from Anglo-French *par chance*; see PER, CHANCE]

Percheron ('pɜːʃəˌrɒn) *n* a compact heavy breed of carthorse, grey or black in colour [C19: from French, from *le Perche*, region of NW France where the breed originated]

perchloric acid (pə'klɔːrɪk) *n* a colourless syrupy oxyacid of chlorine containing a greater proportion of oxygen than chloric acid. It is a powerful oxidizing agent and is used as a laboratory reagent. Formula: $HClO_4$

percipient (pə'sɪpɪənt) *adj* **1** able to perceive **2** perceptive ▷ *n* **3** a person or thing that perceives [C17: from Latin *percipiens* observing, from *percipere* to grasp; see PERCEIVE] > **per'cipience***n* > **per'cipiently***adv*

Percivalor **Perceval** ('pɜːsɪvªl) *n* (in Arthurian legend) a knight in King Arthur's court. German equivalent: **Parzival**

percolate *vb* ('pɜːkəˌleɪt) **1** to cause (a liquid) to pass through a fine mesh, porous substance, etc, or (of a liquid) to pass through a fine mesh, porous substance, etc; trickle: *rain percolated through the roof* **2** to permeate; penetrate gradually: *water percolated the road* **3** to make (coffee) or (of coffee) to be made in a percolator ▷ *n* ('pɜːkəlɪt, -ˌleɪt) **4** a product of percolation [C17: from Latin *percolāre*, from PER + *cōlāre* to strain, from *cōlum* a strainer; see COLANDER] > **percolable** ('pɜːkələbªl) *adj* > ˌperco'lation*n*

percolator ('pɜːkəˌleɪtə) *n* a kind of coffeepot in which boiling water is forced up through a tube and filters down through the coffee grounds into a container

per contra ('pɜː 'kɒntrə) *adv* on the contrary [from Latin]

percuss (pə'kʌs) *vb* (*tr*) **1** to strike sharply, rapidly, or suddenly **2** *med* to tap on (a body surface) with the fingertips or a special hammer to aid diagnosis or for therapeutic purposes [C16: from Latin *percutere*, from *per*-through + *quatere* to shake] > **per'cussion***n*

percussion (pə'kʌʃən) *n* **1** the act, an instance, or an effect of percussing **2** *music* the family of instruments in which sound arises from the striking of materials with sticks, hammers, or the hands **3** *music* instruments of this family constituting a section of an orchestra, band, etc **4** *med* the act of percussing a body surface **5** the act of exploding a percussion cap [C16: from Latin *percussiō*, from *percutere* to hit; see PERCUSS] > **per'cussive***adj* > **per'cussively***adv* > **per'cussiveness***n*

percussion cap *n* a detonator consisting of a paper or thin metal cap containing material that explodes when struck and formerly used in certain firearms

percussion instrument *n* any of various musical instruments that produce a sound when their resonating surfaces are struck directly, as with a stick or mallet, or by leverage action. They may be of definite pitch (as a kettledrum or xylophone), indefinite pitch (as a gong or rattle), or a mixture of both (as various drums)

percussionist (pə'kʌʃənɪst) *n* *music* a person who plays any of several percussion instruments, esp in an orchestra

percutaneous (ˌpɜːkjʊ'teɪnɪəs) *adj* *med* effected through the skin, as in the absorption of an ointment

Percy ('pɜːsɪ) *n* **1** Sir **Henry**, known as *Harry Hotspur*. 1364–1403, English rebel, who was killed leading an army against Henry IV **2 Thomas**. 1729–1811, English bishop and antiquary. His *Reliques of Ancient English Poetry* (1765) stimulated the interest of Romantic writers in old English and Scottish ballads

Perdido (*Spanish* per'ðiðo) *n* Monte Perdido ('mɔnte) a mountain in NE Spain, in the central Pyrenees. Height: 3352 m (10 997 ft). French name **Perdu**

per diem ('pɜː 'daɪɛm, 'diːɛm) *adv* **1** every day or by the day ▷ *n* **2** an allowance for daily expenses, usually those incurred while working [from Latin]

perdition (pə'dɪʃən) *n* **1** *Christianity* **a** final and irrevocable spiritual ruin **b** this state as one that the wicked are said to be destined to endure for ever **2** another word for **hell 3** *archaic* utter disaster, ruin, or destruction [C14: from Late Latin *perditiō* ruin, from Latin *perdere* to lose, from PER- (away) + *dāre* to give]

Perdu (pɛrdy) *n* Mont Perduthe French name for (Monte) **Perdido**

perdurable (pə'djʊərəbªl) *adj rare* extremely durable [C13: from Late Latin *perdūrābilis*, from Latin *per*-(intensive) + *dūrābilis* long-lasting, from *dūrus* hard]

père French (pɛr; English pɛə) *n* an addition to a French surname to specify the father rather than the son of the same name: *Dumas père*

Perea (pə'riːə) *n* a variant spelling of **Peraea**

Père David's deer *n* a large grey deer, *Elaphurus davidianus*, surviving only in captivity as descendants of a herd preserved in the Imperial hunting park near Beijing [C20: named after Father A. *David* (died 1900), French missionary]

peregrinate ('pɛrɪgrɪˌneɪt) *vb* **1** (*intr*) to travel or wander about from place to place; voyage **2** (*tr*) to travel through (a place) [C16: from Latin, from *peregrīnārī* to travel; see PEREGRINE] > 'peregriˌnator*n* > ˌperegri'nation*n*

peregrine ('pɛrɪgrɪn) *adj archaic* **1** coming from abroad **2** travelling or migratory; wandering [C14: from Latin *peregrīnus* foreign, from *pereger* being abroad, from *per* through + *ager* land (that is, beyond one's own land)]

peregrine falcon *n* a falcon, *Falco peregrinus*, occurring in most parts of the world, having a dark plumage on the back and wings and lighter underparts

Pereira (*Spanish* pe'reira) *n* a town in W central Colombia: cattle trading and coffee processing. Pop: 656 000 (2005 est)

Perelman ('pɛrəlmən, 'pɜːl-) *n* S(**idney**) J(**oseph**). 1904–79, US humorous writer. After scriptwriting for the Marx Brothers, he published many collections of articles, including *Crazy Like a Fox* (1944) and *Eastward, Ha!* (1977)

peremptory (pə'rɛmptərɪ) *adj* **1** urgent or commanding: *a peremptory ring on the bell* **2** not able to be remitted or debated; decisive **3** positive or assured in speech, manner, etc; dogmatic **4** *law* **a** admitting of no denial or contradiction; precluding debate **b** obligatory rather than permissive [C16: from Anglo-Norman *peremptorie*, from Latin *peremptōrius* decisive, from *perimere* to take away completely, from PER- (intensive) + *emere* to take] > **per'emptorily***adv* > **per'emptoriness***n*

perennial (pə'rɛnɪəl) *adj* **1** lasting throughout the year or through many years **2** everlasting; perpetual ▷ *n* **3** a woody or herbaceous plant that can continue its growth for at least two years [C17: from Latin *perennis* continual, from *per* through + *annus* year] > **per'ennially***adv*

Peres ('pɛrɛs) *n* **Shimon** (ʃiː'məʊn). born 1923, Israeli statesman, born in Poland: prime minister (1984–86; 1995–96); president from 2007; Nobel peace prize 1994 jointly with Yasser Arafat and Yitzhak Rabin

perestroika (ˌpɛrə'strɔɪkə) *n* the policy of reconstructing the economy, etc, of the former Soviet Union under the leadership of Mikhail Gorbachov [C20: Russian, literally: reconstruction]

Pérez de Cuéllar ('pɛrɛs də 'kweɪjɑː) *n* **Javier** ('hæviɛr). born 1920, Peruvian diplomat and UN secretary-general (1982–91)

Pérez Galdós ('pɛrɛs gɑːl'dɒs) *n* **Benito**. 1843–1920, Spanish novelist. His works include the *Episodios nacionales* (1873–1912), a series of historical novels, and *Fortunata y Jacinta* (1886–87)

Perez-Reverte ('pɛrɛz rə'vɛːteɪ) *n* **Arturo**. born 1952, Spanish novelist and writer; his books include *The Fencing Master* (1988), *The Dumas Club* (1993), *The Queen of the South* (2002) and the historical 'Captain Alatriste' series, beginning with *Captain Alatriste* (1996)

perfect *adj* ('pɜːfɪkt) **1** having all essential elements **2** unblemished; faultless: *a perfect gemstone* **3** correct or precise: *perfect timing* **4** utter or absolute: *a perfect stranger* **5** excellent in all respects: *a perfect day* **6** *maths* exactly divisible into equal integral or rational roots: *36 is a perfect square* **7** *botany* **a** (of flowers) having functional stamens and pistils **b** (of plants) having all parts present **8** *grammar* denoting a tense of verbs used in describing an action that has been completed by the subject. In English this is a compound tense, formed with *have* or *has* plus the past participle **9** *music* **a** of or relating to the intervals of the unison, fourth, fifth, and octave **b** Also called: **full, final** (of a cadence) ending on the tonic chord, giving a feeling of conclusion ▷ *n* ('pɜːfɪkt) **10** *grammar* **a** the perfect tense **b** a verb in this tense ▷ *vb* (pə'fɛkt) (*tr*) **11** to make perfect; improve to one's satisfaction: *he is in Paris to perfect his French* **12** to make fully accomplished [c13: from Latin *perfectus*, from *perficere* to perform, from *per* through + *facere* to do]

● **USAGE** For most of its meanings, the adjective *perfect*
● describes an absolute state, i.e. one that cannot be
● qualified; thus something is either *perfect* or *not perfect*,
● and cannot be *more perfect* or *less perfect*. However when
● *perfect* means excellent in all respects, a comparative
● can be used with it without absurdity: *the next day the*
● *weather was even more perfect*

perfect gas *n* another name for **ideal gas**
perfectible (pə'fɛktəb°l) *adj* capable of becoming or being made perfect > per,fecti'bility *n*
perfection (pə'fɛkʃən) *n* **1** the act of perfecting or the state or quality of being perfect **2** the highest degree of a quality, etc: *the perfection of faithfulness* **3** an embodiment of perfection [c13: from Latin *perfectiō* a completing, from *perficere* to finish]
perfectionism (pə'fɛkʃə,nɪzəm) *n* **1** *philosophy* the doctrine that man can attain perfection in this life **2** the demand for the highest standard of excellence > per'fectionist *n, adj*
perfective (pə'fɛktɪv) *adj* **1** tending to perfect **2** *grammar* denoting an aspect of verbs in some languages, including English, used to express that the action or event described by the verb is or was completed: *I lived in London for ten years* is perfective; *I have lived in London for ten years* is imperfective, since the implication is that I still live in London
perfectly ('pɜːfɪktlɪ) *adv* **1** completely, utterly, or absolutely **2** in a perfect way; extremely well
perfect number *n* an integer, such as 28, that is equal to the sum of all its possible factors, excluding itself
perfect participle *n* another name for **past participle**
perfect pitch *n* another name (not in technical usage) for **absolute pitch** (sense 1)
pervervid (pɜː'fɜːvɪd) *adj literary* extremely ardent, enthusiastic, or zealous [c19: from New Latin *perfervidus*, from Latin *per-* (intensive) + *fervidus* FERVID]
perfidious (pə'fɪdɪəs) *adj* guilty, treacherous, or faithless; deceitful > per'fidiously *adv* > per'fidiousness *n* > 'perfidy *n* [c16: from Latin *perfidia*, from *perfidus* faithless, from *per* beyond + *fidēs* faith]
perfoliate (pə'fəʊlɪɪt, -,eɪt) *adj* (of a leaf) having a base that completely encloses the stem, so that the stem appears to pass through it [c17: from New Latin *perfoliātus*, from Latin *per-* through + *folium* leaf] > per,foli'ation *n*
perforate *vb* ('pɜːfə,reɪt) **1** to make a hole or holes in (something); penetrate **2** (*tr*) to punch rows of holes between (stamps, coupons, etc) for ease of separation ▷ *adj* ('pɜːfərɪt) **3** *biology* pierced by small holes: *perforate shells* **4** *philately* another word for **perforated** (sense 2) [c16: from Latin *perforāre*, from *per-* through + *forāre* to pierce] > **perforable** ('pɜːfərəb°l) *adj* > 'perforative or 'perforatory *adj* > 'perfo,rator *n*
perforated ('pɜːfə,reɪtɪd) *adj* **1** pierced with one or more holes **2** (esp of stamps) having perforations
perforation (,pɜːfə'reɪʃən) *n* **1** the act of perforating or the state of being perforated **2** a hole or holes made in something **3 a** a method of making individual stamps, coupons, etc, easily separable by punching holes along their margins **b** the holes punched in this way
perforce (pə'fɔːs) *adv* by necessity; unavoidably [c14: from Old French *par force*; see PER, FORCE[1]]
perform (pə'fɔːm) *vb* **1** to carry out or do (an action) **2** (*tr*) to fulfil or comply with: *to perform someone's request* **3** to present or enact (a play, concert, etc) before or otherwise entertain an audience: *the group performed Hamlet* [c14: from Anglo-Norman *perfourmer* (influenced by *forme*

FORM), from Old French *parfournir*, from *par-* PER- + *fournir* to provide; see FURNISH] > per'formable *adj* > per'former *n*
performance (pə'fɔːməns) *n* **1** the act, process, or art of performing **2** an artistic or dramatic production: *last night's performance was terrible* **3** manner or quality of functioning: *a machine's performance* **4** *informal* mode of conduct or behaviour, esp when distasteful or irregular: *what did you mean by that performance at the restaurant?* **5** *informal* any tiresome procedure: *what a performance dressing the children to play in the snow!*
performance art *n* a theatrical presentation that incorporates various art forms, such as dance, sculpture, music, etc
performance indicator *n* a quantitative or qualitative measurement, or any other criterion, by which the performance, efficiency, achievement, etc of a person or organization can be assessed, often by comparison with an agreed standard or target
performative (pə'fɔːmətɪv) *adj linguistics, philosophy* **1 a** denoting an utterance that constitutes some act, esp the act described by the verb. For example, *I confess that I was there* is itself a confession, and so is performative in the narrower sense, while *I'd like you to meet ...* (effecting an introduction) is performative only in the looser sense **b** (*as noun*): *that sentence is a performative* **2 a** denoting a verb that may be used as the main verb in such an utterance **b** (*as noun*): *"promise" is a performative*
performing arts *pl n* the arts that are primarily performed before an audience, such as dance and drama
perfume *n* ('pɜːfjuːm) **1** a mixture of alcohol and fragrant essential oils extracted from flowers, spices, etc, or made synthetically, used esp to impart a pleasant long-lasting scent to the body, stationery, etc **2** a scent or odour, esp a fragrant one ▷ *vb* (pə'fjuːm) **3** (*tr*) to impart a perfume to [c16: from French *parfum*, probably from Old Provençal *perfum*, from *perfumar* to make scented, from *per* through (from Latin) + *fumar* to smoke, from Latin *fumāre* to smoke]
perfumer (pə'fjuːmə) or **perfumier** (pə'fjuːmjeɪ) *n* a person who makes or sells perfume
perfumery (pə'fjuːmərɪ) *n, pl* -eries **1** a place where perfumes are sold **2** a factory where perfumes are made **3** the process of making perfumes **4** perfumes in general
perfunctory (pə'fʌŋktərɪ) *adj* **1** done superficially, only as a matter of routine; careless or cursory **2** dull or indifferent [c16: from Late Latin *perfunctōrius* negligent, from *perfunctus* dispatched, from *perfungī* to fulfil; see FUNCTION] > per'functorily *adv* > per'functoriness *n*
perfuse (pə'fjuːz) *vb* (*tr*) **1** to suffuse or permeate (a liquid, colour, etc) through or over (something) **2** *surgery* to pass (a fluid) through organ tissue to ensure adequate exchange of oxygen and carbon monoxide [c16: from Latin *perfūsus* wetted, from *perfundere* to pour over, from PER- + *fundere* to pour] > per'fused *adj* > per'fusion *n* > per'fusionist *n* > per'fusive *adj*
Pergamum ('pɜːgəməm) *n* an ancient city in NW Asia Minor, in Mysia: capital of a major Hellenistic monarchy of the same name that later became a Roman province
pergola ('pɜːgələ) *n* a horizontal trellis or framework, supported on posts, that carries climbing plants and may form a covered walk [c17: via Italian from Latin *pergula* projection from a roof, from *pergere* to go forward]
Pergolesi (Italian pergo'leːsi) *n* **Giovanni Battista** (dʒoˈvanni batˈtista). 1710–36, Italian composer: his works include the operetta *La Serva padrona* (1733) and the *Stabat Mater* (1736) for women's voices
perhaps (pə'hæps; *informal* præps) *adv* **1 a** possibly; maybe **b** (*as sentence modifier*): *he'll arrive tomorrow, perhaps; perhaps you'll see him tomorrow* ▷ *sentence substitute* **2** it may happen, be so, etc; maybe [C16 *perhappes*, from *per* by + *happes* chance, HAP[1]]
peri ('pɪərɪ) *n, pl* -ris **1** (in Persian folklore) one of a race of beautiful supernatural beings **2** any beautiful fairy-like creature [c18: from Persian: fairy, from Avestan *pairikā* witch]
peri- *prefix* **1** enclosing, encircling, or around: *pericardium; pericarp; perigon* **2** near or adjacent: *perihelion* [from Greek

peri around, near, about]

perianth ('pɛrɪˌænθ) *n* the outer part of a flower, consisting of the calyx and corolla [c18: from French *périanthe*, from New Latin, from PERI- + Greek *anthos* flower]

periapt ('pɛrɪˌæpt) *n rare* a charm or amulet [c16: via French from Greek *periapton*, from PERI- + *haptos* clasped, from *haptein* to fasten]

pericarditis (ˌpɛrɪkaˈdaɪtɪs) *n* inflammation of the pericardium

pericardium (ˌpɛrɪˈkaːdɪəm) *n, pl* **-dia** (-dɪə) the membranous sac enclosing the heart [c16: via New Latin from Greek *perikardion*, from PERI- + *kardia* heart] > ˌperi'cardial *or* ˌperi'cardiac *adj*

pericarp ('pɛrɪˌkaːp) *n* the part of a fruit enclosing the seeds that develops from the wall of the ovary [c18: via French from New Latin *pericarpium*] > ˌperi'carpial *or* ˌperi'carpic *adj*

perichondrium (ˌpɛrɪˈkɒndrɪəm) *n, pl* **-dria** (-drɪə) the white fibrous membrane that covers the surface of cartilage [c18: New Latin, from PERI- + Greek *chondros* cartilage]

periclase ('pɛrɪˌkleɪs) *n* a mineral consisting of magnesium oxide in the form of isometric crystals or grains: occurs in metamorphosed limestone [c19: from New Latin *periclasia*, from Greek *peri* very + *klasis* a breaking, referring to its perfect cleavage]

Pericles ('pɛrɪˌkliːz) *n* ?495–429 BC, Athenian statesman and leader of the popular party, who contributed greatly to Athens' political and cultural supremacy in Greece. In power from about 460 BC, he was responsible for the construction of the Parthenon. He conducted the Peloponnesian War (431–404 BC) successfully until his death

pericline ('pɛrɪˌklaɪn) *n* **1** a white translucent variety of albite in the form of elongated crystals **2** Also called: **dome** a dome-shaped formation of stratified rock with its slopes following the direction of folding [c19: from Greek *periklinēs* sloping on all sides, from PERI- + *klinein* to lean] > ˌperi'clinal *adj*

pericranium (ˌpɛrɪˈkreɪnɪəm) *n, pl* **-nia** (-nɪə) the fibrous membrane covering the external surface of the skull [c16: New Latin, from Greek *perikranion*]

peridot ('pɛrɪˌdɒt) *n* a pale green transparent variety of the olivine chrysolite, used as a gemstone [c14: from Old French *peritot*, of unknown origin]

perigee ('pɛrɪˌdʒiː) *n* the point in its orbit around the earth when the moon or an artificial satellite is nearest the earth [c16: via French from Greek *perigeion*, from PERI- + *gea* earth] > ˌperi'gean *or* ˌperi'geal *adj*

periglacial (ˌpɛrɪˈgleɪʃəl) *adj* relating to a region bordering a glacier: *periglacial climate*

Périgueux ('pɛrɪˌgɜː; *French* perigø) *n* a town in SW France, capital of the Dordogne: noted for its Roman remains, medieval cathedral, and pâté de foie gras. Pop: 30 193 (1999)

perihelion (ˌpɛrɪˈhiːlɪən) *n, pl* **-lia** (-lɪə) the point in its orbit when a planet or comet is nearest the sun [c17: from New Latin *perihēlium*, from PERI- + Greek *hēlios* sun]

peril ('pɛrɪl) *n* exposure to risk or harm; danger or jeopardy [c13: via Old French from Latin *periculum*]

perilous ('pɛrɪləs) *adj* very hazardous or dangerous: *a perilous journey* > 'perilously *adv* > 'perilousness *n*

perilune ('pɛrɪˌluːn) *n* the point in a lunar orbit when a spacecraft launched from the moon is nearest the moon [c20: from PERI- + *-lune*, from Latin *lūna* moon]

perimenopause (ˌpɛrɪˈmɛnəˌpɔːz) *n* the period leading up to the menopause during which some of the symptoms associated with menopause may be experienced > ˌperiˌmeno'pausal *adj*

perimeter (pəˈrɪmɪtə) *n* **1** *maths* **a** the curve or line enclosing a plane area **b** the length of this curve or line **2 a** any boundary around something, such as a field **b** (*as modifier*): *a perimeter fence; a perimeter patrol* **3** a medical instrument for measuring the limits of the field of vision [c16: from French *périmètre*, from Latin *perimetros*; see PERI-, -METER] > perimetric (ˌpɛrɪˈmɛtrɪk) *or* ˌperi'metrical *adj*

perinatal (ˌpɛrɪˈneɪtəl) *adj* of, relating to, or occurring in the period from about three months before to one month after birth

perineum (ˌpɛrɪˈniːəm) *n, pl* **-nea** (-ˈniːə) **1** the region of the body between the anus and the genital organs, including some of the underlying structures **2** the nearly diamond-shaped surface of the human trunk between the thighs [c17: from New Latin, from Greek *perinaion*, from PERI- + *inein* to empty out] > ˌperi'neal *adj*

period ('pɪərɪəd) *n* **1 a** a portion of time of indefinable length: *he spent a period away from home* **2 a** a portion of time specified in some way: *the Arthurian period; Picasso's blue period* **b** (*as modifier*): *period costume* **3** a nontechnical name for an occurrence of menstruation **4** *geology* a unit of geological time during which a system of rocks is formed: *the Jurassic period* **5** a division of time, esp of the academic day **6** *physics, maths* the time taken to complete one cycle of a regularly recurring phenomenon; the reciprocal of frequency. Symbol: *T* **7** *astronomy* the time interval between two successive maxima or minima of light variation of a variable star **8** *chem* one of the horizontal rows of elements in the periodic table. Each period starts with an alkali metal and ends with a rare gas. See **group** (sense 10) **9** *rare* a completion or end [c14 *peryod*, from Latin *periodus*, from Greek *periodos* circuit, from PERI- + *hodos* way]

period drama *n* a drama set in a particular historical period

periodic (ˌpɪərɪˈɒdɪk) *adj* **1** happening or recurring at intervals; intermittent **2** of, relating to, or resembling a period **3** having or occurring in repeated periods or cycles > ˌperi'odically *adv* > **periodicity** (ˌpɪərɪəˈdɪsɪtɪ) *n*

periodical (ˌpɪərɪˈɒdɪkəl) *n* **1** a publication issued at regular intervals, usually monthly or weekly ▷ *adj* **2** of or relating to such publications **3** published at regular intervals **4** periodic or occasional

periodic function (ˌpɪərɪˈɒdɪk) *n maths* a function, such as sin *x*, whose value is repeated at constant intervals

periodic law (ˌpɪərɪˈɒdɪk) *n* Also called: **Mendeleev's law** the principle that the chemical properties of the elements are periodic functions of their atomic weights or, more accurately, of their atomic numbers

periodic sentence (ˌpɪərɪˈɒdɪk) *n rhetoric* a sentence in which the completion of the main clause is left to the end, thus creating an effect of suspense

periodic table (ˌpɪərɪˈɒdɪk) *n* a table of the elements, arranged in order of increasing atomic number, based on the periodic law. Elements having similar chemical properties and electronic structures appear in vertical columns (groups)

periodontal (ˌpɛrɪəˈdɒntəl) *adj* of, denoting, or affecting the gums and other tissues surrounding the teeth: *periodontal disease*

periodontics (ˌpɛrɪəˈdɒntɪks) *n* (*functioning as singular*) the branch of dentistry concerned with diseases affecting the tissues and structures that surround teeth. Also called: **periodontology** [c19: from PERI- + *-odontics*, from Greek *odōn* tooth] > ˌperio'dontic *adj* > ˌperio'dontically *adv*

periosteum (ˌpɛrɪˈɒstɪəm) *n, pl* **-tea** (-tɪə) a thick fibrous two-layered membrane covering the surface of bones [c16: New Latin, from Greek *periosteon*, from PERI- + *osteon* bone] > ˌperi'osteal *adj*

peripatetic (ˌpɛrɪpəˈtɛtɪk) *adj* **1** itinerant **2** *Brit* employed in two or more educational establishments and travelling from one to another: *a peripatetic football coach* ▷ *n* **3** a peripatetic person [c16: from Latin *peripatēticus*, from Greek *peripatētikos*, from *peripatein* to pace to and fro] > ˌperipa'tetically *adv*

Peripatetic (ˌpɛrɪpəˈtɛtɪk) *adj* **1** of or relating to the teachings of the Greek philosopher Aristotle (384–322 BC), who used to teach philosophy while walking about the Lyceum in ancient Athens ▷ *n* **2** a student of Aristotelianism

peripeteia, peripetia (ˌpɛrɪpɪˈtaɪə, -ˈtɪə) *or* **peripety** (pəˈrɪpətɪ) *n* (esp in drama) an abrupt turn of events or reversal of circumstances [c16: from Greek, from PERI- + *piptein* to fall (to change suddenly, literally: to fall around)]

peripheral (pəˈrɪfərəl) *adj* **1** not relating to the most important part of something; incidental, minor, or superficial **2** of, relating to, or of the nature of a periphery **3** *anatomy* of, relating to, or situated near the surface of the body: *a peripheral nerve* ▷ **pe'ripherally** *adv*

peripheral device *or* **peripheral unit** *n* *computing* any device, such as a disk, printer, modem, or screen, concerned with input/output, storage, etc. Often shortened to: **peripheral**

periphery (pə'rɪfərɪ) *n, pl* **-eries 1** the outermost boundary of an area **2** the outside surface of something [c16: from Late Latin *peripheria*, from Greek, from PERI- + *pherein* to bear]

periphrasis (pə'rɪfrəsɪs) *n, pl* **-rases** (-rə,siːz) **1** a roundabout way of expressing something; circumlocution **2** an expression of this kind [c16: via Latin from Greek, from PERI- + *phrazein* to declare]

perisarc ('pɛrɪ,saːk) *n* the outer chitinous layer secreted by colonial hydrozoan coelenterates, such as species of *Obelia* [c19: from PERI- + -*sarc*, from Greek *sarx* flesh]

periscope ('pɛrɪ,skəʊp) *n* any of a number of optical instruments that enable the user to view objects that are not in the direct line of vision, such as one in a submarine for looking above the surface of the water. They have a system of mirrors or prisms to reflect the light and often contain focusing lenses [c19: from Greek *periskopein* to look around; see PERI-, -SCOPE] ▷ ,peri'scopic *adj*

perish ('pɛrɪʃ) *vb* (*intr*) **1** to be destroyed or die, esp in an untimely way **2** (*tr* sometimes followed by *with* or *from*) to cause to suffer: *we were perished with cold* **3** to rot: *leather perishes if exposed to bad weather* ▷ **4 do a perish** *Austral informal* to die or come near to dying of thirst or starvation [c13: from Old French *périr*, from Latin *perīre* to pass away entirely, from PER- (away) + *īre* to go]

perishable ('pɛrɪʃəb³l) *adj* **1** liable to rot or wither ▷ *n* **2** (*often plural*) a perishable article, esp food ▷ ,perisha'bility *or* 'perishableness *n*

perishing ('pɛrɪʃɪŋ) *adj* **1** *informal* (of weather, etc) extremely cold **2** *slang* (intensifier qualifying something undesirable): *it's a perishing nuisance!* ▷ 'perishingly *adv*

perisperm ('pɛrɪ,spɜːm) *n* the nutritive tissue surrounding the embryo in certain seeds, and developing from the nucellus of the ovule

perissodactyl (pə,rɪsəʊ'dæktɪl) *or* **perissodactyle** (pə,rɪsəʊ'dæktaɪl) *n* **1** any placental mammal of the order *Perissodactyla*, having hooves with an odd number of toes: includes horses, tapirs, and rhinoceroses ▷ *adj* **2** of, relating to, or belonging to the *Perissodactyla* [c19: from New Latin *perissodactylus*, from Greek *perissos* uneven + *daktulos* digit]

peristalsis (,pɛrɪ'stælsɪs) *n, pl* **-ses** (-siːz) *physiol* the succession of waves of involuntary muscular contraction of various bodily tubes, esp of the alimentary tract, where it effects transport of food and waste products [c19: from New Latin, from PERI- + Greek *stalsis* compression, from *stellein* to press together] ▷ ,peri'staltic *adj*

peristome ('pɛrɪ,stəʊm) *n* **1** a fringe of pointed teeth surrounding the opening of a moss capsule **2** any of various parts surrounding the mouth of invertebrates, such as echinoderms and earthworms, and of protozoans [c18: from New Latin *peristoma*, from PERI- + Greek *stoma* mouth]

peristyle ('pɛrɪ,staɪl) *n* **1** a colonnade that surrounds a court or building **2** an area that is surrounded by a colonnade [c17: via French from Latin *peristylum*, from Greek *peristulon*, from PERI- + *stulos* column]

peritoneal dialysis a technique of dialysis used when haemodialysis is inappropriate; it makes use of the peritoneum as an autogenous semipermeable membrane

peritoneum (,pɛrɪtə'niːəm) *n, pl* **-nea** (-'niːə) *or* **-neums** a thin translucent serous sac that lines the walls of the abdominal cavity and covers most of the viscera [c16: via Late Latin from Greek *peritonaion*, from *peritonos* stretched around, from PERI- + *tenein* to stretch] ▷ ,perito'neal *adj*

peritonitis (,pɛrɪtə'naɪtɪs) *n* inflammation of the peritoneum

periwig ('pɛrɪ,wɪg) *n* a wig, such as a peruke [c16 *perwyke*,

changed from French *perruque* wig, PERUKE]

periwinkle¹ ('pɛrɪ,wɪŋk³l) *n* any of various edible marine gastropods of the genus *Littorina*, esp *L. littorea*, having a spirally coiled shell. Often shortened to: **winkle** [c16: of unknown origin]

periwinkle² ('pɛrɪ,wɪŋk³l) *n* any of several Eurasian apocynaceous evergreen plants of the genus *Vinca*, such as *V. minor* (**lesser periwinkle**) and *V. major* (**greater periwinkle**), having trailing stems and blue flowers [c14 *pervenke*, from Old English *perwince*, from Late Latin *pervinca*]

perjure ('pɜːdʒə) *vb* (*tr*) *criminal law* to render (oneself) guilty of perjury [c15: from Old French *parjurer*, from Latin *perjūrāre*, from PER- + *jūrāre* to make an oath, from *jūs* law] ▷ 'perjurer *n*

perjured ('pɜːdʒəd) *adj* *criminal law* **1 a** having sworn falsely **b** having committed perjury **2** involving or characterized by perjury: *perjured evidence*

perjury ('pɜːdʒərɪ) *n, pl* **-juries** *criminal law* the offence committed by a witness in judicial proceedings who, having been lawfully sworn or having affirmed, wilfully gives false evidence [c14: from Anglo-French *parjurie*, from Latin *perjūrium* a false oath; see PERJURE] ▷ perjurious (pɜː'dʒʊərɪəs) *adj*

perk¹ (pɜːk) *adj* **1** pert; brisk; lively ▷ *vb* **2** See **perk up** [c16: see PERK UP]

perk² (pɜːk) *vb* *informal* **1** (*intr*) (of coffee) to percolate **2** (*tr*) to percolate (coffee)

perk³ (pɜːk) *n* *Brit informal* short for **perquisite**

perk up *vb* (*adverb*) **1** to make or become more cheerful, hopeful, or lively **2** to rise or cause to rise briskly: *the dog's ears perked up* **3** (*tr*) to make smarter in appearance: *she perked up her outfit with a bright scarf* **4** (*intr*) *Austral slang* to vomit [c14 *perk*, perhaps from Norman French *perquer*; see PERCH¹]

perky ('pɜːkɪ) *adj* **perkier, perkiest 1** jaunty; lively **2** confident; spirited ▷ 'perkily *adv* 'perkiness *n*

Perl (pɜːl) *n* a computer language that is used for text manipulation, esp on the World Wide Web [c20: from p(*ractical*) e(*xtraction and*) r(*eport*) l(*anguage*)]

perlemoen ('pɛələ,mʊn) *n* *South African* another name for **abalone** [from Afrikaans, from Dutch *paarlemoer* mother of pearl]

Perlis ('pɛəlɪs, 'pɜː-) *n* a state of NW Peninsular Malaysia, on the Andaman Sea: a dependency of Thailand until 1909. Capital: Kangar. Pop: 204 450 (2000). Area: 810 sq km (313 sq miles)

perlite *or* **pearlite** ('pɜːlaɪt) *n* a variety of obsidian consisting of masses of small pearly globules: used as a filler, insulator, and soil conditioner [c19: from French, from *perle* PEARL¹]

Perlman ('pɜːlmən) *n* **Itzhak** ('ɪtzæk). born 1945, Israeli violinist; polio victim

perm¹ (pɜːm) *n* **1 a** hairstyle produced by treatment with heat, chemicals, etc which gives long-lasting waves, curls, or other shaping. Also called (*esp formerly*) **permanent wave** ▷ *vb* **2** (*tr*) to give a perm to (hair)

perm² (pɜːm) *n* short for **permutation** (sense 4)

Perm (*Russian* pjermj) *n* a port in W Russia, on the Kama River: oil refinery; university (1916). Pop: 984 000 (2005 est). Former name (1940–62): **Molotov**

perma- *prefix* *informal* indicating a fixed state: *a permatan; perma-grin*

permafrost ('pɜːmə,frɒst) *n* ground that is permanently frozen, often to great depths, the surface sometimes thawing in the summer [c20: from PERMA(NENT) + FROST]

permalloy (pɜːm'ælɔɪ) *n* any of various alloys containing iron and nickel (45–80 per cent) and sometimes smaller amounts of chromium and molybdenum [c20: from PERM(EABILITY) + ALLOY]

permanence ('pɜːmənəns) *n* the state or quality of being permanent

permanency ('pɜːmənənsɪ) *n, pl* **-cies 1** a person or thing that is permanent **2** another word for **permanence**

permanent ('pɜːmənənt) *adj* **1** existing or intended to exist for an indefinite period: *a permanent structure* **2** not expected to change for an indefinite time; not temporary: *a permanent condition* [c15: from Latin *permanens* continuing, from *permanēre* to stay to the end, from *per-* through + *manēre* to remain]

permanent health insurance *n* a form of insurance that provides up to 75 per cent of a person's salary, until retirement, in case of prolonged illness or disability

permanent magnet *n* a magnet, often of steel, that retains its magnetization after the magnetic field producing it has been removed

permanent press *n* a chemical treatment for clothing that makes the fabric crease-resistant and sometimes provides a garment with a permanent crease or pleats

permanent resident *n Canadian* an immigrant who has been given official residential status, often prior to being granted citizenship

permanent wave *n* another name (esp formerly) for **perm**¹ (sense 1)

permanent way *n chiefly Brit* the track of a railway, including the ballast, sleepers, rails, etc

permanganate (pə'mæŋɡəˌneɪt, -nɪt) *n* a salt of permanganic acid

permanganic acid (ˌpɜːmænˈɡænɪk) *n* a monobasic acid known only in solution and in the form of permanganate salts. Formula: $HMnO_4$

permeability (ˌpɜːmɪəˈbɪlɪtɪ) *n* 1 the state or quality of being permeable 2 a measure of the response of a medium to a magnetic field, expressed as the ratio of the magnetic flux density in the medium to the field strength; measured in henries per metre. Symbol: μ

permeable ('pɜːmɪəbᵊl) *adj* capable of being permeated, esp by liquids [c15: from Late Latin *permeābilis*, from Latin *permeāre* to pervade; see PERMEATE] > **'permeableness** *n* > **'permeably** *adv*

permeance ('pɜːmɪəns) *n* 1 the act of permeating 2 the reciprocal of the reluctance of a magnetic circuit. Symbol: Λ > **'permeant** *adj, n*

permeate ('pɜːmɪˌeɪt) *vb* 1 to penetrate or pervade (a substance, area, etc): *a lovely smell permeated the room* 2 to pass through or cause to pass through by osmosis or diffusion: *to permeate a membrane* [c17: from Latin *permeāre*, from *per-* through + *meāre* to pass] > **ˌperme'ation** *n* > **'permeative** *adj*

Permian ('pɜːmɪən) *adj* 1 of, denoting, or formed in the last period of the Palaeozoic era, between the Carboniferous and Triassic periods, which lasted for 60 000 000 years ▷ *n* 2 the Permian the Permian period or rock system [c19: after PERM, Russia]

permissible (pə'mɪsəbᵊl) *adj* permitted; allowable > **perˌmissi'bility** *n* > **per'missibly** *adv*

permission (pə'mɪʃən) *n* authorization to do something

permissive (pə'mɪsɪv) *adj* 1 tolerant; lenient: *permissive parents* 2 indulgent in matters of sex: *a permissive society* 3 granting permission > **per'missively** *adv* > **per'missiveness** *n*

permit *vb* (pə'mɪt) **-mits, -mitting, -mitted** 1 (*tr*) to grant permission to do something: *you are permitted to smoke* 2 (*tr*) to consent to or tolerate: *she will not permit him to come* 3 (when *intr*, often foll by *of*; when *tr*, often foll by an infinitive) to allow the possibility (of): *the passage permits of two interpretations; his work permits him to relax nowadays* ▷ *n* ('pɜːmɪt) 4 an official certificate or document granting authorization; licence 5 permission, esp written permission [c15: from Latin *permittere*, from *per-* through + *mittere* to send] > **per'mitter** *n*

permittivity (ˌpɜːmɪˈtɪvɪtɪ) *n, pl* **-ties** a measure of the response of a substance to an electric field, expressed as the ratio of its electric displacement to the applied field strength; measured in farads per metre

permutate ('pɜːmjuˌteɪt) *vb* to alter the sequence or arrangement (of); treat by permutation: *endlessly permutating three basic designs*

permutation (ˌpɜːmjʊˈteɪʃən) *n* 1 *maths* **a** an ordered arrangement of the numbers, terms, etc, of a set into specified groups: *the permutations of a, b, and c, taken two at a time, are ab, ba, ac, ca, bc, cb* **b** a group formed in this way. The number of permutations of *n* objects taken *r* at a time is $n!/(n-r)!$. Symbol: **nPr** See **combination** (sense 6) 2 a combination of items made by reordering 3 an alteration; transformation 4 a fixed combination for

selections of results on football pools. Usually shortened to: **perm** [c14: from Latin *permūtātiō*, from *permūtāre* to change thoroughly; see MUTATION] > **ˌpermu'tational** *adj*

permute (pə'mjuːt) *vb* (*tr*) 1 to change the sequence of 2 *maths* to subject to permutation [c14: from Latin *permūtāre*, from PER- + *mūtāre* to change, alter]

Pernambuco (ˌpɜːnəmˈbjuːkəʊ; *Portuguese* pernəm'buku) *n* 1 a state of NE Brazil, on the Atlantic: consists of a humid coastal plain rising to a high inland plateau. Capital: Recife. Pop: 8 084 667 (2002). Area: 98 280 sq km (37 946 sq miles) 2 the former name of **Recife**

pernicious (pə'nɪʃəs) *adj* 1 wicked or malicious: *pernicious lies* 2 causing grave harm; deadly [c16: from Latin *perniciōsus*, from *perniciēs* ruin, from PER- (intensive) + *nex* death] > **per'niciously** *adv* > **per'niciousness** *n*

pernicious anaemia *n* a form of anaemia characterized by lesions of the spinal cord, weakness, sore tongue, numbness in the arms and legs, diarrhoea, etc: associated with inadequate absorption of vitamin B_{12}

pernickety (pə'nɪkɪtɪ) *or US* **persnickety** *adj informal* 1 excessively precise and attentive to detail; fussy 2 (of a task) requiring close attention; exacting [c19: originally Scottish, of unknown origin]

Pernik (*Bulgarian* 'pernik) *n* an industrial town in W Bulgaria, on the Struma River. Pop: 84 000 (2005 est). Former name (1949–62): Dimitrovo

Perón (*Spanish* pe'rɔn) *n* 1 Juan Domingo (xwan do'mɪŋgo). 1895–1974, Argentine soldier and statesman; dictator (1946–55). He was deposed in 1955, remaining in exile until 1973, when he was elected president (1973–74) 2 his third wife, **María Estella** (ma'ria es'teʎa), known as *Isabel*. born 1931, president of Argentina (1974–76); deposed 3 (**María**) **Eva** (**Duarte**) **de Perón** ('eβa), known as *Evita*. Second wife of Juan Domingo Perón. 1919–52, Argentine film actress: active in politics and social welfare (1946–52) > **Pe'ronist** *n, adj*

peroneal (ˌpɛrəˈniːəl) *adj anatomy* of or relating to the fibula or the outer side of the leg [c19: from New Latin *peronē* fibula, from Greek: fibula]

perorate ('pɛrəˌreɪt) *vb* (*intr*) 1 to speak at length, esp in a formal manner 2 to conclude a speech or sum up, esp with a formal recapitulation

peroration (ˌpɛrəˈreɪʃən) *n rhetoric* the conclusion of a speech or discourse, in which points made previously are summed up or recapitulated, esp with greater emphasis [c15: from Latin *perōrātiō*, from *perōrāre*, from PER- (thoroughly) + *orāre* to speak]

perovskite (pe'rɒvskaɪt) *n* a yellow, brown, or greyish-black mineral form of calcium titanate with some rare-earth elements, which is used in certain high-temperature ceramic superconductors [c19: named after Count Lev Alekseevich Perovski (1792–1856), Russian statesman]

peroxide (pə'rɒksaɪd) *n* 1 short for hydrogen peroxide, esp when used for bleaching hair 2 any of a class of metallic oxides, such as sodium peroxide, Na_2O_2, that contain the divalent ion $^-O-O^-$ 3 (*not in technical usage*) any of certain dioxides, such as manganese peroxide, MnO_2, that resemble peroxides in their formula but do not contain the $^-O-O^-$ ion 4 any of a class of organic compounds whose molecules contain two oxygen atoms bound together. They tend to be explosive 5 (*modifier*) of, relating to, bleached with, or resembling peroxide ▷ *vb* 6 (*tr*) to bleach (the hair) with peroxide

perp (pɜːp) *n US & Canad informal* a person who has committed a crime [c20: from PERPETRATE]

perpendicular (ˌpɜːpənˈdɪkjʊlə) *adj* 1 Also called: **normal** at right angles to a horizontal plane 2 denoting, relating to, or having the style of Gothic architecture used in England during the 14th and 15th centuries, characterized by tracery having vertical lines, a four-centred arch, and fan vaulting 3 upright; vertical ▷ *n* 4 *geometry* a line or plane perpendicular to another 5 any instrument used for indicating the vertical line through a given point [c14: from Latin *perpendiculāris*, from *perpendiculum* a plumb line, from *per-* through + *pendēre* to hang] > **perpendicularity** (ˌpɜːpənˌdɪkjʊˈlærɪtɪ) *n* > **ˌperpen'dicularly** *adv*

perpetrate ('pɜːpɪˌtreɪt) *vb* (*tr*) to perform or be

responsible for (a deception, crime, etc) [c16: from Latin *perpetrāre*, from *per-* (thoroughly) + *patrāre* to perform, perhaps from *pater* father, leader in the performance of sacred rites] > ˌperpe'tration *n* > 'perpeˌtrator *n*
● USAGE *Perpetrate* and *perpetuate* are sometimes
● confused: *he must answer for the crimes he has perpetrated*
● (not *perpetuated*); *the book helped to perpetuate* (not
● *perpetrate*) *some of the myths surrounding his early life*

perpetual (pə'pɛtjʊəl) *adj* **1** (*usually prenominal*) eternal; permanent **2** (*usually prenominal*) seemingly ceaseless because often repeated: *your perpetual complaints* [c14: via Old French from Latin *perpetuālis* universal, from *perpes* continuous, from *per-* (thoroughly) + *petere* to go towards] > per'petually *adv*

perpetual debenture *n* a bond or debenture that can either never be redeemed or cannot be redeemed on demand

perpetual motion *n* Also called: **perpetual motion of the first kind** motion of a hypothetical mechanism that continues indefinitely without any external source of energy. It is impossible in practice because of friction

perpetuate (pə'pɛtjʊˌeɪt) *vb* (*tr*) to cause to continue or prevail: *to perpetuate misconceptions* [c16: from Latin *perpetuāre* to continue without interruption, from *perpetuus* PERPETUAL] > perˌpetu'ation *n*
● USAGE See at **perpetrate**

perpetuity (ˌpɜːpɪ'tjuːɪtɪ) *n*, *pl* **-ties 1** eternity **2** the state or quality of being perpetual **3** *property law* a limitation preventing the absolute disposal of an estate for longer than the period allowed by law **4** an annuity with no maturity date and payable indefinitely **5** in perpetuity for ever [c15: from Old French *perpetuite*, from Latin *perpetuitās* continuity; see PERPETUAL]

Perpignan (*French* pɛrpiɲã) *n* a town in S France: historic capital of Roussillon. Pop: 105 115 (1999)

perplex (pə'plɛks) *vb* (*tr*) **1** to puzzle; bewilder; confuse **2** to complicate: *to perplex an issue* [c15: from obsolete *perplex* (adj) intricate, from Latin *perplexus* entangled, from *per-* (thoroughly) + *plectere* to entwine]

perplexity (pə'plɛksɪtɪ) *n*, *pl* **-ties 1** the state of being perplexed **2** the state of being intricate or complicated **3** something that perplexes

per pro ('pɜː 'prəʊ) *prep* by delegation to; through the agency of: used when signing documents on behalf of someone else [Latin: abbreviation of *per prōcūrātiōnem*]
● USAGE See at **pp²**

perp walk *n* US *informal* an arranged public appearance of a recently arrested criminal for the benefit of the media

perquisite ('pɜːkwɪzɪt) *n* **1** an incidental benefit gained from a certain type of employment, such as the use of a company car **2** a customary benefit received in addition to a regular income **3** a customary tip **4** something expected or regarded as an exclusive right ▷ Often (informal) shortened to: **perk** [c15: from Medieval Latin *perquīsītum* an acquired possession, from Latin *perquīrere* to seek earnestly for something, from *per-* (thoroughly) + *quaerere* to ask for, seek]

Perrault (*French* pɛro) *n* **Charles** (ʃarl). 1628–1703, French author, noted for his *Contes de ma mère l'oye* (1697), which contains the fairy tales *Little Red Riding Hood, Cinderella,* and *The Sleeping Beauty*

Perrier water or **Perrier** ('pɛriei) *n* trademark a sparkling mineral water from the south of France [c20: named after a spring *Source Perrier,* at Vergèze, France]

Perrin (*French* pɛrɛ̃) *n* **Jean Baptiste** (ʒã batist). 1870–1942, French physicist. His researches on the distribution and diffusion of particles in colloids (1911) gave evidence for the physical reality of molecules, confirmed the explanation of Brownian movement in terms of kinetic theory, and determined the magnitude of the Avogadro constant. He also studied cathode rays: Nobel prize for physics 1926

perron ('pɛrən) *n* an external flight of steps, esp one at the front entrance of a building [c14: from Old French, from *pierre* stone, from Latin *petra*]

perry ('pɛrɪ) *n*, *pl* **-ries** alcoholic drink made of pears, similar in taste to cider [C14 *pereye*, from Old French *peré*, ultimately from Latin *pirum* pear]

Perry ('pɛrɪ) *n* **1** **Fred(erick John)**. 1909–95, English tennis and table-tennis player; world singles table-tennis champion (1929); Wimbledon singles champion (1934–36) **2** **Grayson**. born 1960, British potter. A transvestite, he won the Turner Prize (2003). **3** **Matthew Calbraith**. 1794–1858, US naval officer, who led a naval expedition to Japan that obtained a treaty (1854) opening up Japan to western trade **4** his brother, **Oliver Hazard**. 1785–1819, US naval officer. His defeat of a British squadron on Lake Erie (1813) was the turning point in the War of 1812, leading to the recapture of Detroit

perse (pɜːs) *n* **a** a dark greyish-blue colour **b** (*as adjective*): *perse cloth* [c14: from Old French, from Medieval Latin *persus,* perhaps changed from Latin *Persicus* Persian]

per se (pɜː 'seɪ) *adv* by or in itself; intrinsically [Latin]

Perse (pɜːs; *French* pɛrs) *n* **Saint-John** ('sɪndʒən), real name *Alexis Saint- Léger.* 1887–1975, French poet, born in Guadeloupe. His works include *Anabase* (1922) and *Chronique* (1960). Nobel prize for literature 1960

persecute ('pɜːsɪˌkjuːt) *vb* (*tr*) **1** to oppress, harass, or maltreat, esp because of race, religion, etc **2** to bother persistently [c15: from Old French *persecuter,* back formation from *persecuteur,* from Late Latin *persecūtor* pursuer, from *persequī* to take vengeance upon] > 'perseˌcutive *adj* > 'perseˌcutor *n*

persecution (ˌpɜːsɪ'kjuːʃən) *n* the act of persecuting or the state of being persecuted

persecution complex *n* *psychol* an acute irrational fear that other people are plotting one's downfall and that they are responsible for one's failures

Persephone (pə'sɛfənɪ) *n* *Greek myth* a daughter of Zeus and Demeter, abducted by Hades and made his wife and queen of the underworld, but allowed part of each year to leave it. Roman counterpart: *Proserpina*

Persepolis (pə'sɛpəlɪs) *n* the capital of ancient Persia in the Persian Empire and under the Seleucids: founded by Darius; sacked by Alexander the Great in 330 BC

Perseus ('pɜːsɪəs) *n* *Greek myth* a son of Zeus and Danaë, who with Athena's help slew the Gorgon Medusa and rescued Andromeda from a sea monster

perseverance (ˌpɜːsɪ'vɪərəns) *n* **1** continued steady belief or efforts, withstanding discouragement or difficulty; persistence **2** *Christianity* persistence in remaining in a state of grace until death

perseveration (pɜːˌsɛvə'reɪʃən) *n* *psychol* the tendency for an impression, idea, or feeling to dissipate only slowly and to recur during unrelated experiences

persevere (ˌpɜːsɪ'vɪə) *vb* (*intr*; often foll by *in*) to show perseverance [c14: from Old French *perseverer,* from Latin *perseverāre,* from *perseverus* very strict; see SEVERE]

Pershing¹ ('pɜːʃɪŋ) *n* **John Joseph**, nickname *Black Jack.* 1860–1948, US general. He was commander in chief of the American Expeditionary Force in Europe (1917–19)

Pershing² ('pɜːʃɪŋ) *n* a US ballistic missile capable of carrying a nuclear or conventional warhead [c20: after John Joseph Pershing (1860–1948), US general]

Persia ('pɜːʃə) *n* **1** the former name (until 1935) of **Iran 2** another name for **Persian Empire**

Persian ('pɜːʃən) *adj* **1** of or relating to ancient Persia or modern Iran, their inhabitants, or their languages ▷ *n* **2** a native, citizen, or inhabitant of modern Iran; an Iranian **3** the language of Iran or Persia in any of its ancient or modern forms, belonging to the West Iranian branch of the Indo-European family

Persian carpet or **Persian rug** *n* a carpet or rug made in Persia or other countries of the Near East by knotting silk or wool yarn by hand onto a woven backing, characterized by rich colours and flowing or geometric designs

Persian cat *n* a long-haired variety of domestic cat with a stocky body, round face, short nose, and short thick legs

Persian Empire *n* the S Asian empire established by Cyrus the Great in the 6th century BC and overthrown by Alexander the Great in the 4th century BC. At its height it extended from India to Europe

Persian Gulf *n* a shallow arm of the Arabian Sea between SW Iran and Arabia: linked with the Arabian Sea by the Strait of Hormuz and the Gulf of Oman;

important for the oilfields on its shores. Area: 233 000 sq km (90 000 sq miles)

Persian lamb *n* **1** a black loosely curled fur obtained from the skin of the karakul lamb **2** a karakul lamb

persiennes (ˌpɜːsɪˈɛnz) *pl n* outside window shutters having louvres to keep out the sun while maintaining ventilation [C19: from French, from *persien* Persian]

persiflage (ˈpɜːsɪˌflɑːʒ) *n* light frivolous conversation, style, or treatment; friendly teasing [C18: via French, from *persifler* to tease, from *per-* (intensive) + *siffler* to whistle, from Latin *sībilāre* to whistle]

persimmon (pɜːˈsɪmən) *n* **1** any of several tropical trees of the genus *Diospyros*, typically having hard wood and large orange-red fruit: family *Ebenaceae* **2** the sweet fruit of any of these trees, which is edible when completely ripe [C17: of Algonquian origin; related to Delaware *pasīmēnan* dried fruit]

Persis (ˈpɜːsɪs) *n* an ancient region of SW Iran: homeland of the Achaemenid dynasty

persist (pəˈsɪst) *vb* (*intr*) **1** (often foll by *in*) to continue steadfastly or obstinately despite opposition or difficulty **2** to continue to exist or occur without interruption: *the rain persisted throughout the night* [C16: from Latin *persistere*, from *per-* (intensive) + *sistere* to stand steadfast, from *stāre* to stand] > **per'sister** *n*

persistence (pəˈsɪstəns) *or* **persistency** *n* **1** the quality of persisting; tenacity **2** the act of persisting; continued effort or existence **3** the continuance of an effect after the cause of it has stopped

persistent (pəˈsɪstənt) *adj* **1** showing persistence **2** incessantly repeated; unrelenting: *your persistent questioning* **3** (of plant parts) remaining attached to the plant after the normal time of withering **4** *zoology* (of parts normally present only in young stages) present in the adult **5** (of a chemical, esp when used as an insecticide) slow to break down; not easily degradable > **per'sistently** *adv*

persistent organic pollutant *n* a toxin resulting from a manufacturing process, which remains in the environment for many years. Abbreviation: **POP**

persistent vegetative state *n med* an irreversible condition, resulting from brain damage, characterized by lack of consciousness, thought, and feeling, although reflex activities (such as breathing) continue. Abbreviation: **PVS**

person (ˈpɜːsən) *n, pl* **persons 1** an individual human being **2** the body of a human being, sometimes including his or her clothing: *guns hidden on his person* **3** a grammatical category into which pronouns and forms of verbs are subdivided depending on whether they refer to the speaker, the person addressed, or some other individual, thing, etc **4** a human being or a corporation recognized in law as having certain rights and obligations [C13: from Old French *persone*, from Latin *persōna* mask, perhaps from Etruscan *phersu* mask]

-person *suffix forming nouns* sometimes used instead of *-man* and *-woman* or *-lady*: *chairperson*; *salesperson*

● USAGE See at **-man**

persona (pɜːˈsəʊnə) *n, pl* **-nae** (-niː) **1** (*often plural*) a character in a play, novel, etc **2** (in Jungian psychology) the mechanism that conceals a person's true thoughts and feelings, esp in his adaptation to the outside world [Latin: mask]

personable (ˈpɜːsənəbəl) *adj* pleasant in appearance and personality > **'personableness** *n* > **'personably** *adv*

personage (ˈpɜːsənɪdʒ) *n* **1** an important or distinguished person **2** another word for **person** (sense 1) **3** *rare* a figure in literature, history, etc

persona grata Latin (pɜːˈsəʊnə ˈɡrɑːtə) *n, pl* **personae gratae** (pɜːˈsəʊniː ˈɡrɑːtiː) an acceptable person, esp a diplomat acceptable to the government of the country to which he or she is sent

personal (ˈpɜːsənəl) *adj* **1** of or relating to the private aspects of a person's life: *personal letters; a personal question* **2** (*prenominal*) of or relating to a person's body, its care, or its appearance: *personal hygiene; great personal beauty* **3** belonging to or intended for a particular person and no-one else: *as a personal favour; for your personal use* **4** (*prenominal*) undertaken by an individual himself: *a*

personal appearance by a celebrity **5** referring to, concerning, or involving a person's individual personality, intimate affairs, etc, esp in an offensive way: *personal remarks; don't be so personal* **6** having the attributes of an individual conscious being: *a personal God* **7** of or arising from the personality **8** of, relating to, or denoting grammatical person **9** *law* of or relating to movable property, such as money

personal care *n* help given to elderly or infirm people with essential everyday activities such as washing, dressing, and meals

personal column *n* a newspaper column containing personal messages, advertisements by charities, requests for friendship, holiday companions, etc

personal computer *n* a small inexpensive computer used in word processing, playing computer games, etc

personal digital assistant *n* a palmtop computer for storing information. Abbreviation: **PDA**

personal equity plan *n* the full name for **PEP**

personality (ˌpɜːsəˈnælɪtɪ) *n, pl* **-ties 1** *psychol* the sum total of all the behavioural and mental characteristics by means of which an individual is recognized as being unique **2** the distinctive character of a person that makes him socially attractive: *a salesman needs a lot of personality* **3** a well-known person in a certain field, such as sport or entertainment **4** a remarkable person: *the old fellow is a real personality* **5** (*often plural*) a personal remark

personalize *or* **personalise** (ˈpɜːsənəˌlaɪz) *vb* (*tr*) **1** to endow with personal or individual qualities or characteristics **2** to mark (stationery, clothing, etc) with a person's initials, name, etc **3** to take (a remark, etc) personally **4** another word for **personify** > ˌpersonali'zation *or* ˌpersonali'sation *n*

personally (ˈpɜːsənəlɪ) *adv* **1** without the help or intervention of others: *I'll attend to it personally* **2** (*sentence modifier*) in one's own opinion or as regards oneself: *personally, I hate onions* **3** as if referring to oneself: *to take the insults personally* **4** as a person: *we like him personally, but professionally he's incompetent*

personal organizer *n* **1** a diary that stores personal records, appointments, notes, etc **2** a pocket-sized electronic device that performs the same functions

personal pronoun *n* a pronoun having a definite person or thing as an antecedent and functioning grammatically in the same way as the noun that it replaces. In English, the personal pronouns include *I, you, he, she, it, we,* and *they,* and are inflected for case

personal property *n law* movable property, such as furniture or money. See **real property**. Also called: **personalty**

personal shopper *n* a person employed, esp by a shop, to accompany and advise customers on shopping trips or to select items for them

personal stereo *n* a very small audio cassette player designed to be worn attached to a belt and used with lightweight headphones

personal stylist *n* a person employed by a rich or famous client to offer advice on clothes, hairstyles, and other aspects of personal appearance

persona non grata Latin (pɜːˈsəʊnə nɒn ˈɡrɑːtə) *n, pl* **personae non gratae** (pɜːˈsəʊniː nɒn ˈɡrɑːtiː) **1** an unacceptable or unwelcome person **2** a diplomatic or consular officer who is not acceptable to the government or sovereign to whom he or she is accredited

personate (ˈpɜːsəˌneɪt) *vb* (*tr*) **1** to act the part of (a character in a play); portray **2** *criminal law* to assume the identity of (another person) with intent to deceive > ˌperson'ation *n* > 'personative *adj* > 'personˌator *n*

personhood (ˈpɜːsənˌhʊd) *n chiefly US* the condition of being a person who is an individual with inalienable rights, esp under the 14th Amendment of the Constitution of the United States

personification (pɜːˌsɒnɪfɪˈkeɪʃən) *n* **1** the attribution of human characteristics to things, abstract ideas, etc, as for literary or artistic effect **2** the representation of an abstract quality or idea in the form of a person, creature, etc, as in art and literature **3** a person or thing that personifies **4** a person or thing regarded as an

embodiment of a quality: *he is the personification of optimism*
personify (pɜːˈsɒnɪˌfaɪ) *vb* **-fies, -fying, -fied** (*tr*) **1** to attribute human characteristics to (a thing or abstraction) **2** to represent (an abstract quality) in human or animal form **3** (of a person or thing) to represent (an abstract quality), as in art or literature **4** to be the embodiment of > per'soni,fier*n*
personned *adj* another word for **manned**
personnel (ˌpɜːsəˈnɛl) *n* **1** the people employed in an organization or for a service or undertaking **2 a** Also called: **human resources** the office or department that interviews, appoints, or keeps records of employees **b** (*as modifier*): *a personnel officer* [C19: from French, ultimately from Late Latin *persōnālis* personal (adj); see PERSON]
person of colour *n* a person who is not white
perspective (pəˈspɛktɪv) *n* **1 a** a way of regarding situations, facts, etc, and judging their relative importance **2** the proper or accurate point of view or the ability to see it; objectivity: *try to get some perspective on your troubles* **3** the theory or art of suggesting three dimensions on a two-dimensional surface, in order to recreate the appearance and spatial relationships that objects or a scene in recession present to the eye **4** the appearance of objects, buildings, etc, relative to each other, as determined by their distance from the viewer, or the effects of this distance on their appearance [C14: from Medieval Latin *perspectīva ars* the science of optics, from Latin *perspicere* to inspect carefully, from *per-* (intensive) + *specere* to behold] > per'spectively*adv*
Perspex (ˈpɜːspɛks) *n trademark* any of various clear acrylic resins, used chiefly as a substitute for glass
perspicacious (ˌpɜːspɪˈkeɪʃəs) *adj* acutely perceptive or discerning [C17: from Latin *perspicax*, from *perspicere* to look at closely; see PERSPECTIVE] > ,perspi'caciously*adv* > perspicacity (ˌpɜːspɪˈkæsɪtɪ) *or* ,perspi'caciousness*n*
perspicuous (pəˈspɪkjʊəs) *adj* (of speech or writing) easily understood; lucid [C15: from Latin *perspicuus* transparent, from *perspicere* to explore thoroughly; see PERSPECTIVE] > per'spicuously*adv* > per'spicuousness*n*
perspiration (ˌpɜːspəˈreɪʃən) *n* **1** the act or process of insensibly eliminating fluid through the pores of the skin, which evaporates immediately **2** the sensible elimination of fluid through the pores of the skin, which is visible as droplets through the pores of the skin **3** the salty fluid secreted through the pores of the skin; sweat
perspire (pəˈspaɪə) *vb* to secrete or exude (perspiration) through the pores of the skin [C17: from Latin *perspīrāre* to blow, from *per-* (through) + *spīrāre* to breathe; compare INSPIRE] > per'spiringly*adv*
persuade (pəˈsweɪd) *vb* (*tr; may take a clause as object or an infinitive*) **1** to induce, urge, or prevail upon successfully: *he finally persuaded them to buy it* **2** to cause to believe; convince: *even with the evidence, the police were not persuaded* [C16: from Latin *persuādēre*, from *per-* (intensive) + *suādēre* to urge, advise] > per'suadable *or* per'suasible*adj* > per,suada'bility *or* per,suasi'bility*n* > per'suader*n*
persuasion (pəˈsweɪʒən) *n* **1** the act of persuading or of trying to persuade **2** the power to persuade **3** the state of being persuaded; strong belief **4** an established creed or belief, esp a religious one **5** a sect, party, or faction [C14: from Latin *persuāsiō*; see PERSUADE]
persuasive (pəˈsweɪsɪv) *adj* having the power or ability to persuade; tending to persuade: *a persuasive salesman* > per'suasively*adv* > per'suasiveness*n*
pert (pɜːt) *adj* **1** saucy, impudent, or forward **2** jaunty: *a pert little hat* **3** *obsolete* clever or brisk [C13: variant of earlier *apert*, from Latin *apertus* open, from *aperīre* to open; influenced by Old French *aspert*, from Latin *expertus* EXPERT] > 'pertly*adv* > 'pertness*n*
pertain (pəˈteɪn) *vb* (*intr; often foll by to*) **1** to have reference, relation, or relevance: *issues pertaining to women* **2** to be appropriate: *the product pertains to real user needs* **3** to belong (to) or be a part (of); be an adjunct, attribute, or accessory (of) [C14: from Latin *pertinēre*, from *per-* (intensive) + *tenēre* to hold]
Perth (pɜːθ) *n* **1** a town in central Scotland, in Perth and Kinross on the River Tay: capital of Scotland from the 12th century until the assassination of James I there in 1437. Pop: 43 450 (2001) **2** a city in SW Australia, capital

of Western Australia, on the Swan River: major industrial centre; University of Western Australia (1911). Pop: 1 176 542 (2001)
Perth and Kinross (kɪnˈrɒs) *n* a council area of N central Scotland, corresponding mainly to the historical counties of Perthshire and Kinross-shire: part of Tayside Region from 1975 until 1996: chiefly mountainous, with agriculture, tourism, and forestry. Administrative centre: Perth. Pop: 135 990 (2003 est). Area: 5321 sq km (2019 sq miles)
Perthshire (ˈpɜːθʃɪə, -ʃə) *n* (until 1975) a county of central Scotland, now part of Perth and Kinross council area
pertinacious (ˌpɜːtɪˈneɪʃəs) *adj* **1** doggedly resolute in purpose or belief; unyielding **2** stubbornly persistent [C17: from Latin *pertināx*, from *per-* (intensive) + *tenāx* clinging, from *tenēre* to hold] > ,perti'naciously*adv* > pertinacity (ˌpɜːtɪˈnæsɪtɪ) *or* ,perti'naciousness*n*
pertinent (ˈpɜːtɪnənt) *adj* relating to the matter at hand; relevant [C14: from Latin *pertinēns*, from *pertinēre* to PERTAIN] > 'pertinence*n* > 'pertinently*adv*
perturb (pəˈtɜːb) *vb* (*tr, often passive*) **1** to disturb the composure of; trouble **2** to throw into disorder **3** *physics, astronomy* to cause (a planet, electron, etc) to undergo a perturbation [C14: from Old French *pertourber*, from Latin *perturbāre* to confuse, from *per-* (intensive) + *turbāre* to agitate, from *turba* confusion] > per'turbable*adj* > per'turbing*adj*
perturbation (ˌpɜːtəˈbeɪʃən) *n* **1** the act of perturbing or the state of being perturbed **2** a cause of disturbance or upset **3** *physics* a secondary influence on a system that modifies simple behaviour, such as the effect of the other electrons on one electron in an atom **4** *astronomy* a small continuous deviation in the inclination and eccentricity of the orbit of a planet or comet, due to the attraction of neighbouring planets
pertussis (pəˈtʌsɪs) *n* the technical name for: **whooping cough** [C18: New Latin, from Latin *per-* (intensive) + *tussis* cough] > per'tussal*adj*
Peru (pəˈruː) *n* a republic in W South America, on the Pacific: the centre of the great Inca Empire when conquered by the Spanish in 1532; gained independence in 1824 by defeating Spanish forces with armies led by San Martín and Bolívar; consists of a coastal desert, rising to the Andes; an important exporter of minerals and a major fishing nation. Official languages: Spanish, Quechua, and Aymara. Official religion: Roman Catholic. Currency: nuevo sol. Capital: Lima. Pop: 27 567 000 (2004 est). Area: 1 285 215 sq km (496 222 sq miles) > Peruvian (pəˈruːvɪən) *adj, n*
Peru Current *n* another name for the Humboldt Current
Perugia (pəˈruːdʒə; *Italian* peˈruːdʒa) *n* a city in central Italy, in Umbria: centre of the Umbrian school of painting (15th century); university (1308); Etruscan and Roman remains. Pop: 149 125 (2001) **1** Lake Perugia another name for (Lake) **Trasimene**
Perugino (*Italian* peruˈdʒino) *n* **Il** (il), real name *Pietro Vannucci*. 1446–1523, Italian painter; master of Raphael. His works include the fresco *Christ giving the Keys to Peter* in the Sistine Chapel, Rome
peruke (pəˈruːk) *n* a type of wig for men, fashionable in the 17th and 18th centuries. Also called: **periwig** [C16: from French *perruque*, from Italian *perrucca* wig, of obscure origin]
peruse (pəˈruːz) *vb* (*tr*) **1** to read or examine with care; study **2** to browse or read through in a leisurely way [C15 (meaning: to use up): from PER- (intensive) + USE] > pe'rusal*n* > pe'ruser*n*
Perutz (ˈpɛrʊts) *n* **Max Ferdinand**. 1914–2002, British biochemist, born in Austria. With J. C. Kendrew, he worked on the structure of haemoglobin and shared the Nobel prize for chemistry 1962
Peruzzi (*Italian* peˈruttsi) *n* **Baldassare Tommaso** (baldasˈsaːre tomˈmaːzo). 1481–1536, Italian architect and painter of the High Renaissance. The design of the Palazzo Massimo, Rome, is attributed to him
perv (pɜːv) *slang* ▷ *n* **1** a pervert ▷ *vb* Also: **perve** (*intr*) **2** *Austral* to give a person an erotic look
pervade (pɜːˈveɪd) *vb* (*tr*) to spread through or

throughout, esp subtly or gradually; permeate [c17: from Latin *pervādere*, from *per-* through + *vādere* to go] >**pervasion** (pɜːˈveɪʒən) *n*

pervasive (pɜːˈveɪsɪv) *adj* pervading or tending to pervade [c18: from Latin *pervāsus*, past participle of *pervādere* to PERVADE] >**per'vasively** *adv* >**per'vasiveness** *n*

perverse (pəˈvɜːs) *adj* **1** deliberately deviating from what is regarded as normal, good, or proper **2** persistently holding to what is wrong **3** wayward or contrary; obstinate; cantankerous [c14: from Old French *pervers*, from Latin *perversus* turned the wrong way] >**per'versely** *adv* >**per'verseness** *n*

perversion (pəˈvɜːʃən) *n* **1** any abnormal means of obtaining sexual satisfaction **2** the act of perverting or the state of being perverted **3** a perverted form or usage

pervert *vb* (pəˈvɜːt) (*tr*) **1** to use wrongly or badly **2** to interpret wrongly or badly; distort **3** to lead into deviant or perverted beliefs or behaviour; corrupt **4** to debase ▷ *n* (ˈpɜːvɜːt) **5** a person who practises sexual perversion [c14: from Old French *pervertir*, from Latin *pervertere* to turn the wrong way, from *per-* (indicating deviation) + *vertere* to turn] >**per'verted** *adj* >**per'vertedly** *adv* >**per'vertedness** *n* >**per'verter** *n* >**per'vertible** *adj*

pervious (ˈpɜːvɪəs) *adj* **1** able to be penetrated; permeable **2** receptive to new ideas; open-minded [c17: from Latin *pervius*, from *per-* (through) + *via* a way] >**perviously** *adv* >**perviousness** *n*

pes (peɪz, piːz) *n*, *pl* **pedes** (ˈpɛdiːz) the technical name for the human: foot [c19: New Latin: foot]

PES *abbreviation* Party of European Socialists: the Socialist, Democratic, and Labour parties of the European Union, founded in 1992

Pesaro (*Italian* ˈpeːzaro) *n* a port and resort in E central Italy, in the Marches on the Adriatic. Pop: 91 086 (2001)

Pescadores (ˌpɛskəˈdɔːrɪz) *pl n* a group of 64 islands in Formosa Strait, separated from Taiwan (to which it belongs) by the **Pescadores Channel**. Pop: 91 950 (2007 est). Area: 127 sq km (49 sq miles). Chinese name: **Penghu**

Pescara (*Italian* pesˈkaːra) *n* a city and resort in E central Italy, on the Adriatic. Pop: 116 286 (2001)

peseta (pəˈseɪtə; *Spanish* peˈseta) *n* the former standard monetary unit of Spain and Andorra, divided into 100 céntimos; replaced by the euro in 2002 [c19: from Spanish, diminutive of PESO]

Peshawar (pəˈʃɔːə) *n* a city in N Pakistan, at the E end of the Khyber Pass: one of the oldest cities in Pakistan and capital of the ancient kingdom of Gandhara; university (1950). Pop: 1 255 000 (2005 est)

pesky (ˈpɛskɪ) *adj* **peskier, peskiest** *informal, chiefly US & Canadian* troublesome: *pesky flies* [c19: probably changed from ˈpesty; see PEST] >**peskily** *adv* >**peskiness** *n*

peso (ˈpeɪsəʊ; *Spanish* ˈpeso) *n*, *pl* **-sos** (-səʊz; *Spanish* -sos) **1** the standard monetary unit, comprising 100 centavos, of Argentina, Chile, Colombia, Cuba, the Dominican Republic, Mexico, and the Philippines; formerly also of Guinea-Bissau, where it was replaced by the CFA franc **2** the standard monetary unit of Uruguay, divided into 100 centesimos **3** another name for **piece of eight** [c16: from Spanish: weight, from Latin *pēnsum* something weighed out, from *pendere* to weigh]

pessary (ˈpɛsərɪ) *n*, *pl* **-ries** *med* **1** a device for inserting into the vagina, either as a support for the uterus or (**diaphragm pessary**) to deliver a drug, such as a contraceptive **2** a medicated vaginal suppository [c14: from Late Latin *pessārium*, from Latin *pessum*, from Greek *pessos* plug]

pessimism (ˈpɛsɪˌmɪzəm) *n* **1** the tendency to expect the worst and see the worst in all things **2** the doctrine of the ultimate triumph of evil over good **3** the doctrine that this world is corrupt and that man's sojourn in it is a preparation for some other existence [c18: from Latin *pessimus* worst, from *malus* bad] >**pessimist** *n* >**ˌpessi'mistic** *or less commonly* **ˌpessi'mistical** *adj* >**ˌpessi'mistically** *adv*

Pessoa (pɛˈsəʊə) *n* **Fernando**. 1888–1935, Portuguese poet, who ascribed much of his work to three imaginary poets, Alvaro de Campos, Alberto Caeiro, and Ricardo Reis

pest (pɛst) *n* **1** a person or thing that annoys, esp by imposing itself when it is not wanted; nuisance **2 a** any organism that damages crops, injures or irritates livestock or man, or reduces the fertility of land **b** (*as modifier*): *pest control* **3** *rare* an epidemic disease or pestilence [c16: from Latin *pestis* plague, of obscure origin]

Pestalozzi (ˌpɛstəˈlɒtsɪ) *n* **Johann Heinrich** (joˈhan ˈhainriç). 1746–1827, Swiss educational reformer. His emphasis on learning by observation exerted a wide influence on elementary education

pester (ˈpɛstə) *vb* (*tr*) to annoy or nag continually [c16: from Old French *empestrer* to hobble (a horse), from Vulgar Latin *impāstōriāre* (unattested) to use a hobble, from *pāstōria* (unattested) a hobble, from Latin *pāstōrius* relating to a herdsman, from *pastor* herdsman] >**pesterer** *n* >**pesteringly** *adv*

pesticide (ˈpɛstɪˌsaɪd) *n* a chemical used for killing pests, esp insects and rodents >**ˌpesti'cidal** *adj*

pestiferous (pɛˈstɪfərəs) *adj* **1** *informal* troublesome; irritating **2** breeding, carrying, or spreading infectious disease **3** corrupting; pernicious [c16: from Latin *pestifer*, from *pestis* contagious disease, PEST + *ferre* to bring] >**pes'tiferously** *adv* >**pes'tiferousness** *n*

pestilence (ˈpɛstɪləns) *n* **1 a** any epidemic outbreak of a deadly and highly infectious disease, such as the plague **b** such a disease **2** an evil influence or idea

pestilent (ˈpɛstɪlənt) *adj* **1** annoying; irritating **2** highly destructive morally or physically; pernicious **3** infected with or likely to cause epidemic or infectious disease [c15: from Latin *pestilens* unwholesome, from *pestis* plague] >**pestilently** *adv*

pestilential (ˌpɛstɪˈlɛnʃəl) *adj* **1** dangerous or troublesome; harmful or annoying **2** of, causing, or resembling pestilence >**ˌpesti'lentially** *adv*

pestle (ˈpɛsəl) *n* **1** a club-shaped instrument for mixing or grinding substances in a mortar **2** a tool for pounding or stamping ▷ *vb* **3** to pound (a substance or object) with or as if with a pestle [c14: from Old French *pestel*, from Latin *pistillum*; related to *pinsāre* to crush]

pesto (ˈpɛstəʊ) *n* a sauce for pasta, consisting of basil leaves, pine nuts, garlic, oil, and Parmesan cheese, all crushed together [Italian, shortened form of *pestato*, past participle of *pestare* to pound, crush]

pet¹ (pet) *n* **1** a tame animal kept in a household for companionship, amusement, etc **2** a person who is fondly indulged; favourite: *teacher's pet* ▷ *adj* **3** kept as a pet: *a pet dog* **4** of or for pet animals: *pet food* **5** particularly cherished; favourite: *a pet theory; a pet hatred* **6** familiar or affectionate: *a pet name* **7 pet day** *Scot & Irish* a single fine day during a period of bad weather ▷ *vb* **pets, petting, petted 8** (*tr*) to treat (a person, animal, etc) as a pet; pamper **9** (*tr*) to pat or fondle (an animal, child, etc) **10** (*intr*) *informal* (of two people) to caress each other in an erotic manner, as during lovemaking (often in the phrase **heavy petting**) [c16: origin unknown] >**petter** *n*

pet² (pet) *n* **1** a fit of sulkiness, esp at what is felt to be a slight; pique ▷ *vb* **pets, petting, petted 2** (*intr*) to take offence; sulk [c16: of uncertain origin]

PET *abbreviation* **1** positron emission tomography ▷ *n* *acronym for* **2** potentially exempt transfer: a procedure in the UK whereby gifting property and cash is tax-free, provided that the donor lives for at least seven years after the gift is made

Pet. *Bible abbreviation* Peter

peta- *prefix* denoting 10¹⁵: *petametres* Symbol: **P** [c20: so named because it is the SI prefix after TERA-; on the model of PENTA-, the prefix after TETRA-]

petabyte (ˈpɛtəˌbaɪt) *n* *computing* 10¹⁵ or 2⁵⁰ bytes

Pétain (*French* petɛ̃) *n* **Henri Philippe Omer** (ãri filip ɔmɛr). 1856–1951, French marshal, noted for his victory at Verdun (1916) in World War I and his leadership of the pro-Nazi government of unoccupied France at Vichy (1940–44); imprisoned for treason (1945)

petal (ˈpɛtəl) *n* any of the separate parts of the corolla of a flower: often brightly coloured [c18: from New Latin *petalum*, from Greek *petalon* leaf; related to *petannunai* to lie open] >**petaline** *adj* >**petal-ˌlike** *adj* >**petalled** *adj*

-petal *adj combining form* seeking: *centripetal* [from New Latin *-petus*, from Latin *petere* to seek]

petard (pɪ'tɑːd) *n* **1** (formerly) a device containing explosives used to breach a wall, doors, etc **2 hoist with one's own petard** being the victim of one's own schemes **3** a type of explosive firework [c16: from French: firework, from *péter* to break wind, from Latin *pēdere*]

petaurist (pə'tɔːrɪst) *n* another name for **flying phalanger** [c20: from Latin *petaurista* tightrope walker]

petcock ('pɛt,kɒk) *n* a small valve for checking the water level in a steam boiler or draining condensed steam from the cylinder of a steam engine [c19: from PET¹ or perhaps French *pet*, from *péter* to break wind + COCK¹]

petechia (pɪ'tiːkɪə) *n*, *pl* -chiae (-kɪ,iː) a minute discoloured spot on the surface of the skin or mucous membrane, caused by an underlying ruptured blood vessel [c18: via New Latin from Italian *petecchia* freckle, of obscure origin] > **pe'techial** *adj*

peter¹ ('piːtə) *vb* (*intr*; foll by *out* or *away*) to fall (off) in volume, intensity, etc, and finally cease [c19: of unknown origin]

peter² ('piːtə) *n* *slang* **1** a safe, till, or cash box **2** a prison cell [c20: meaning a case): from the name *Peter*]

Peter¹ ('piːtə) *n* *New Testament* **1** Saint.. Also called: **Simon Peter**. died ?67 AD, a fisherman of Bethsaida, who became leader of the apostles and is regarded by Roman Catholics as the first pope; probably martyred at Rome. Feast day: June 29 or Jan 18 **2** either of two epistles traditionally ascribed to Peter (in full **The First Epistle** and **The Second Epistle of Peter**)

Peter² ('piːtə) *n* *New Testament* either of the two epistles traditionally ascribed to the apostle Peter (in full **The First Epistle** and **The Second Epistle of Peter**)

Peter I *n* known as *Peter the Great*. 1672–1725, tsar of Russia (1682–1725), who assumed sole power in 1689. He introduced many reforms in government, technology, and the western European ideas. He also acquired new territories for Russia in the Baltic and founded the new capital of St Petersburg (1703)

Peter III *n* 1728–62, grandson of Peter I and tsar of Russia (1762): deposed in a coup d'état led by his wife (later Catherine II); assassinated

Peterborough ('piːtəbərə, -brə) *n* **1** a city in central England, in Peterborough unitary authority, N Cambridgeshire on the River Nene: industrial centre; under development as a new town since 1968. Pop: 136 292 (2001) **2** a unitary authority in central England, in Cambridgeshire. Pop: 158 800 (2003 est). Area: 402 sq km (155 sq miles) **3** Soke of Peterborough a former administrative unit of E central England, generally considered part of Northamptonshire or Huntingdonshire: absorbed into Cambridgeshire in 1974 **4** a city in SE Canada, in SE Ontario: manufacturing centre. Pop: 73 303 (2001) **5** a traditional type of wooden canoe formerly made in Peterborough, SE Ontario

Peterlee ('piːtə,liː) *n* a new town in Co Durham, founded in 1948. Pop: 29 936 (2001)

peterman ('piːtəmən) *n*, *pl* -men *slang* a burglar skilled in safe-breaking [c19: from PETER³]

Petermann Peak ('piːtəmən) *n* a mountain in E Greenland. Height: 2932 m (9645 ft)

Peter Pan *n* a youthful, boyish, or immature man [c20: after the main character in *Peter Pan* (1904), a play by J. M. Barrie]

Peter Principle *n* **the Peter Principle** the theory, usually taken facetiously, that all members in a hierarchy rise to their own level of incompetence [c20: from the book *The Peter Principle* (1969) by Dr. Lawrence J. *Peter* and Raymond Hull, in which the theory was originally propounded]

Petersburg ('piːtəz,bɜːg) *n* a city in SE Virginia, on the Appomattox River: scene of prolonged fighting (1864–65) during the final months of the American Civil War. Pop: 33 091 (2003 est)

petersham ('piːtəfəm) *n* **1** a thick corded ribbon used to stiffen belts, button bands, etc **2** a heavy woollen fabric used esp for coats **3** a kind of overcoat made of such fabric [c19: named after Viscount *Petersham* (died 1851), English army officer]

Peterson ('piːtəsᵊn) *n* **Oscar (Emmanuel)**. 1925–2007, Canadian jazz pianist and singer, who led his own trio from the early 1950s

Peter's pence *or* **Peter pence** *n* **1** an annual tax, originally of one penny, formerly levied for the maintenance of the Papal See: abolished by Henry VIII in 1534 **2** a voluntary contribution made by Roman Catholics in many countries for the same purpose [c13: referring to St PETER, considered as the first pope]

Peters' projection *n* a form of modified world map projection that attempts to reflect accurately the relative surface areas of landmasses, an approach which gives greater prominence (than do standard representations) to equatorial countries [c20: named after Arno *Peters*, German historian]

Peter the Hermit *n* ?1050–1115, French monk and preacher of the First Crusade

pethidine ('pɛθɪ,diːn) *n* a white crystalline water-soluble drug used as an analgesic. Formula: $C_{15}H_{21}NO_2.HCl$ [c20: perhaps a blend of PIPERIDINE + ETHYL]

petiole ('pɛtɪ,əʊl) *n* **1** the stalk by which a leaf is attached to the rest of the plant **2** *zoology* a slender stalk or stem, such as the connection between the thorax and abdomen of ants [c18: via French from Latin *petiolus* little foot, from *pēs* foot]

Petipa (French pətipa) *n* **Marius**. 1819–1910, French ballet dancer and choreographer of the Russian imperial ballet: collaborated with Tchaikovsky on *The Sleeping Beauty* (1890)

petit ('pɛtɪ) *adj* (*prenominal*) *chiefly law* of little or lesser importance; small [c14: from Old French: little, of obscure origin]

Petit (French pəti) *n* **Roland** (rɔlã). born 1924, French ballet dancer and choreographer. His innovative ballets include *Carmen* (1949), *Kraanerg* (1969), and *The Blue Angel* (1985); he also choreographed films, such as *Anything Goes* (1956) and *Black Tights* (1960)

petit bourgeois ('pɛtɪ 'bʊəʒwɑː; French pəti burʒwa) *n*, *pl* **petits bourgeois** ('pɛtɪ 'bʊəʒwɑːz; French pəti burʒwa) **1** Also called: **petite bourgeoisie, petty bourgeoisie** the section of the middle class with the lowest social status, generally composed of shopkeepers, lower clerical staff, etc **2** a member of this stratum ▷ *adj* **3** of, relating to, or characteristic of the petit bourgeois, esp indicating a sense of self-righteousness and a high degree of conformity to established standards of behaviour

petite (pə'tiːt) *adj* (of a woman) small, delicate, and dainty [c18: from French, feminine of *petit* small]

petit four ('pɛtɪ 'fɔː; French pəti fur) *n*, *pl* **petits fours** ('pɛtɪ 'fɔːz; French pəti fur) any of various very small rich sweet cakes and biscuits, usually decorated with fancy icing, marzipan, etc [French, literally: little oven]

petition (pɪ'tɪʃən) *n* **1** a written document signed by a large number of people demanding some form of action from a government or other authority **2** any formal request to a higher authority or deity; entreaty **3** *law* a formal application in writing made to a court asking for some specific judicial action: *a petition for divorce* **4** the action of petitioning ▷ *vb* **5** (*tr*) to address or present a petition to (a person in authority, government, etc): *to petition Parliament* **6** (*intr*; foll by *for*) to seek by petition [c14: from Latin *petītiō*, from *petere* to seek] > **pe'titionary** *adj*

petitioner (pɪ'tɪʃənə) *n* **1** a person who presents a petition **2** *chiefly Brit* the plaintiff in a divorce suit

petitio principii (pɪ'tɪʃɪ,əʊ prɪn'kɪpɪ,aɪ) *n* *logic* a form of fallacious reasoning in which the conclusion has been assumed in the premises; begging the question [c16: Latin, translation of Greek *to en arkhei aiteisthai* an assumption at the beginning]

petit jury *n* a jury of 12 persons empanelled to determine the facts of a case and decide the issue pursuant to the direction of the court on points of law. Also called: **petty jury** > **petit juror** *n*

petit larceny *n* (formerly in England) the stealing of property valued at 12 pence or under. Abolished 1827. Also called: **petty larceny** See **grand larceny**

petit mal ('pɛtɪ 'mæl; French pəti mal) *n* a mild form of epilepsy characterized by periods of impairment or loss of consciousness for up to 30 seconds. See **grand mal** [C19: French: little illness]

petit point ('pɛtɪ 'pɔɪnt; *French* pəti pwɛ̃) *n* **1** Also called: **tent stitch** a small diagonal needlepoint stitch used for fine detail **2** work done with such stitches, esp fine tapestry [French: small point]

Petőfi (*Hungarian* 'pɛtøːfi) *n* **Sándor** ('ʃaːndor). 1823–49, Hungarian lyric poet and patriot

Petra ('pɛtrə, 'piːtrə) *n* an ancient city in the south of present-day Jordan; capital of the Nabataean kingdom

Petrarch ('pɛtrɑːk) *n* Italian name *Francesco Petrarca*. 1304–74, Italian lyric poet and scholar, who greatly influenced the values of the Renaissance. His collection of poems *Canzoniere*, inspired by his ideal love for Laura, was written in the Tuscan dialect. He also wrote much in Latin, esp the epic poem *Africa* (1341) and the *Secretum* (1342), a spiritual self-analysis ▷ **Pe'trarchan** *adj*

Petrarchan sonnet *n* a sonnet form associated with the poet Petrarch, having an octave rhyming a b b a a b b a and a sestet rhyming either c d e c d e or c d c d c d

petrel ('pɛtrəl) *n* any oceanic bird of the order *Procellariiformes*, having a hooked bill and tubular nostrils: includes albatrosses, storm petrels, and shearwaters [C17: variant of earlier *pitteral*, associated by folk etymology with St *Peter*, because the bird appears to walk on water]

Petri dish ('pɛtrɪ) *n* a shallow circular flat-bottomed dish, often with a fitting cover, used in laboratories, esp for producing cultures of microorganisms [C19: named after J. R. *Petri* (1852–1921), German bacteriologist]

Petrie ('pɛtrɪ) *n* Sir (**William Matthew**) **Flinders**. 1853–1942, British Egyptologist and archaeologist

petrifaction (,pɛtrɪ'fækʃən) *or* **petrification** (,pɛtrɪfɪ'keɪʃən) *n* **1** the act or process of forming petrified organic material **2** the state of being petrified

Petrified Forest *n* a national park in E Arizona, containing petrified coniferous trees about 170 000 000 years old

petrify ('pɛtrɪ,faɪ) *vb* **-fies, -fying, -fied** **1** (*tr; often passive*) to convert (organic material, esp plant material) into a fossilized form by impregnation with dissolved minerals so that the original appearance is preserved **2** to make or become dull, unresponsive, insensitive, etc; deaden **3** (*tr; often passive*) to stun or daze with horror, fear, etc [C16: from French *pétrifier*, ultimately from Greek *petra* stone, rock] ▷ **'petri,fier** *n*

petro- *or before a vowel* **petr-** *combining form* **1** indicating stone or rock: *petrology* **2** indicating petroleum, its products, etc: *petrochemical* **3** of or relating to a petroleum-producing country: *petrostate* [from Greek *petra* rock or *petros* stone]

petrochemical (,pɛtrəʊ'kɛmɪkᵊl) *n* **1** any substance, such as acetone or ethanol, obtained from petroleum or natural gas ▷ *adj* **2** of, concerned with, or obtained from petrochemicals or related to petrochemistry

petrochemistry (,pɛtrəʊ'kɛmɪstrɪ) *n* **1** the chemistry of petroleum and its derivatives **2** the branch of chemistry concerned with the chemical composition of rocks

petrodollar ('pɛtrəʊ,dɒlə) *n* money, paid in dollars, earned by a country for the exporting of petroleum

petroglyph ('pɛtrə,glɪf) *n* a drawing or carving on rock, esp a prehistoric one [C19: via French from Greek *petra* stone + *gluphē* carving]

Petrograd ('pɛtrəʊ,græd; *Russian* pɪtra'grat) *n* a former name (1914–24) of **Saint Petersburg**

petrography (pɛ'trɒɡrəfɪ) *n* the branch of petrology concerned with the description and classification of rocks ▷ **pe'trographer** *n* ▷ **petrographic** (,pɛtrə'græfɪk) *or* ,**petro'graphical** *adj*

petrol ('pɛtrəl) *n* any one of various volatile flammable liquid mixtures of hydrocarbons, mainly hexane, heptane, and octane, obtained from petroleum and used as a solvent and a fuel for internal-combustion engines. Usually petrol also contains additives such as antiknock compounds and corrosion inhibitors. US and Canadian name: **gasoline** [C16: via French from Medieval Latin PETROLEUM]

petrolatum (,pɛtrə'leɪtəm) *n* a translucent gelatinous

substance obtained from petroleum; used as a lubricant and in medicine as an ointment base and protective dressing. Also called: **mineral jelly, petroleum jelly** [C19: from PETROL + Latin *-atum* -ATE¹]

petrol bomb *n* **1** a home-made incendiary device, consisting of a bottle filled with petrol and stoppered with a wick, that is thrown by hand; a Molotov cocktail ▷ *vb* **petrol-bomb** (*tr*) **2** to attack with petrol bombs

petrol engine *n* an internal-combustion engine that uses petrol as fuel

petroleum (pə'trəʊlɪəm) *n* a dark-coloured thick flammable crude oil occurring in sedimentary rocks around the Persian Gulf, in parts of North and South America, and below the North Sea, consisting mainly of hydrocarbons. Fractional distillation separates the crude oil into petrol, paraffin, diesel oil, lubricating oil, etc Fuel oil, paraffin wax, asphalt, and carbon black are extracted from the residue [C16: from Medieval Latin, from Latin *petra* stone + *oleum* oil]

petroleum jelly *n* another name for **petrolatum**

petrology (pɛ'trɒlədʒɪ) *n, pl* -**gies** the study of the composition, origin, structure, and formation of rocks. Abbreviation: **petrol** ▷ **petrological** (,pɛtrə'lɒdʒɪkᵊl) *adj* ▷ **pe'trologist** *n*

petrol station *n* Brit another term for **filling station**

Petronius (pɪ'trəʊnɪəs) *n* **Gaius** ('gaɪəs), known as *Petronius Arbiter*. died 66 AD, Roman satirist, supposed author of the *Satyricon*, a picaresque account of the licentiousness of contemporary society

Petropavlovsk (*Russian* pɪtra'pavləfsk) *n* a city in N Kazakhstan on the Ishim River. Pop: 190 000 (2005 est)

Petrópolis (*Portuguese* pe'trɒpulis) *n* a city in SE Brazil, north of Rio de Janeiro: resort. Pop: 280 000 (2005 est)

Petrosian (pɪ'trəʊʒən) *n* **Tigran** (tig'ran). 1929–84, Soviet chess player; world champion (1963–69)

petrous ('pɛtrəs, 'piː-) *adj anatomy* denoting the dense part of the temporal bone that surrounds the inner ear [C16: from Latin *petrōsus* full of rocks]

Petrovsk (*Russian* pɪ'trɒfsk) *n* the former name (until 1921) of **Makhachkala**

Petrozavodsk (*Russian* pɪtrəza'vɒtsk) *n* a city in NW Russia, capital of the Karelian Autonomous Republic, on Lake Onega: developed around ironworks established by Peter the Great in 1703; university (1940). Pop: 265 000 (2005 est)

Petsamo (*Finnish* 'pɛtsamɔ) *n* the former name (1920–1944) for **Pechenga**

petticoat ('pɛtɪ,kəʊt) *n* a woman's light undergarment in the form of an underskirt or including a bodice supported by shoulder straps **1** *informal* **a** a humorous or mildly disparaging name for a woman **b** (*as modifier*): *petticoat politics* [C15: see PETTY, COAT]

pettifogger ('pɛtɪ,fɒɡə) *n* **1** a lawyer of inferior status who conducts unimportant cases, esp one who is unscrupulous or resorts to trickery **2** any person who quibbles or fusses over details [C16: from PETTY + *fogger*, of uncertain origin, perhaps from *Fugger*, name of a family (C15–16) of German financiers] ▷ **'petti,foggery** *n*

pettifogging ('pɛtɪ,fɒɡɪŋ) *adj* **1** petty: *pettifogging details* **2** mean; quibbling: *pettifogging lawyers*

pettish ('pɛtɪʃ) *adj* peevish; petulant [C16: from PET²] ▷ **'pettishly** *adv* ▷ **'pettishness** *n*

petty ('pɛtɪ) *adj* -**tier, -tiest** **1** trivial; trifling; inessential: *petty details* **2** of a narrow-minded, mean, or small-natured disposition or character: *petty spite* **3** minor or subordinate in rank: *petty officialdom* **4** *law* of lesser importance [C14: from Old French PETIT] ▷ **'pettily** *adv* ▷ **'pettiness** *n*

petty cash *n* a small cash fund kept on a firm's premises for the payment of minor incidental expenses

petty jury *n* a variant spelling of **petit jury** ▷ **petty juror** *n*

petty larceny *n* a variant spelling of **petit larceny**

petty officer *n* a noncommissioned officer in a naval service, comparable in rank to a sergeant in an army or marine corps

petty sessions *n* (*functioning as singular or plural*) another term for **magistrates' court**

petulant ('pɛtjʊlənt) *adj* irritable, impatient, or sullen in a peevish or capricious way [C16: via Old French from Latin *petulāns* bold, from *petulāre* (unattested) to attack playfully, from *petere* to assail] > **'petulance** or **'petulancy** *n* > **'petulantly** *adv*

petunia (pɪ'tjuːnɪə) *n* any solanaceous plant of the tropical American genus *Petunia*: cultivated for their white, pink, blue, or purple funnel-shaped flowers [C19: via New Latin from obsolete French *petun* variety of tobacco, from Tupi *petyn*]

petuntse or **petuntze** (pɪ'tʌntsɪ, -'tʊn-) *n* a fusible feldspathic mineral used in hard-paste porcelain; china stone [C18: from Chinese (Beijing) *pe tun tzu*, from *pe* white + *tun* heap + *tzu* offspring]

Pevsner ('pɛvznə) *n* 1 Antoine (ãtwan). 1886–1962, French constructivist sculptor and painter, born in Russia; brother of Naum Gabo 2 Sir Nikolaus ('nɪkəlaʊs). 1902–83, British architectural historian, born in Germany: his series *Buildings of England* (1951–74) describes every structure of account in the country

pew (pjuː) *n* 1 (in a church) **a** one of several long benchlike seats with backs, used by the congregation **b** an enclosed compartment reserved for the use of a family or other small group 2 *Brit informal* a seat (esp in the phrase **take a pew**) [C14 *pywe*, from Old French *puye*, from Latin *podium* a balcony, from Greek *podion* supporting structure, from *pous* foot]

pewit ('piːwɪt) *n* another name for **lapwing** [C13: imitative of the bird's cry]

pewter ('pjuːtə) *n* 1 **a** any of various alloys containing tin (80–90 per cent), lead (10–20 per cent), and sometimes small amounts of other metals, such as copper and antimony **b** (*as modifier*): *pewter ware; a pewter tankard* 2 plate or kitchen utensils made from pewter [C14: from Old French *peaultre*, of obscure origin; related to Old Provençal *peltre* pewter] > **'pewterer** *n*

peyote (peɪ'əʊtɪ, pɪ-) *n* another name for **mescal** (sense 1) [Mexican Spanish, from Nahuatl *peyotl*]

pF *symbol for* picofarad

pf. *abbreviation* 1 perfect 2 Also called: **pfg** pfennig 3 preferred

Pfalz (pfalts) *n* the German name for the **Palatinate**

pfennig ('fɛnɪɡ; *German* 'pfɛnɪç) *n*, *pl* **-nigs** or **-nige** (*German* -nɪɡə) a former German monetary unit worth one hundredth of a Deutschmark [German: PENNY]

PFI *abbreviation* (in Britain) Private Finance Initiative

Pforzheim (*German* 'pfɔrtshaim) *n* a city in SW Germany, in W Baden-Württemberg: centre of the German watch and jewellery industry. Pop: 119 046 (2003 est)

PG *symbol for* a film certified for viewing by anyone, but which contains scenes that may be unsuitable for children, for whom parental guidance is necessary [C20: from abbreviation of *parental guidance*]

pg. *abbreviation* page

Pg. *abbreviation* 1 Portugal 2 Portuguese

PGR *abbreviation* psychogalvanic response

pH *n* potential of hydrogen; a measure of the acidity or alkalinity of a solution equal to the common logarithm of the reciprocal of the concentration of hydrogen ions in moles per cubic decimetre of solution. Pure water has a pH of 7, acid solutions have a pH less than 7, and alkaline solutions a pH greater than 7

phacelia (fə'siːlɪə) *n* any plant of the mostly annual American genus *Phacelia*, esp *P. campanularia*, grown for its large, deep blue bellflowers: family *Hydrophyllaceae* [New Latin, from Greek *phakelos* cluster (from the habit of the flowers) +-IA]

Phaeacian (fiː'eɪʃən) *n Greek myth* one of a race of people inhabiting the island of Scheria visited by Odysseus on his way home from the Trojan War

Phaedra ('fiːdrə) *n Greek myth* the wife of Theseus, who falsely accused her stepson Hippolytus of raping her and then hanged herself because he spurned her amorous advances

Phaedrus ('fiːdrəs) *n* ?15 BC–?50 AD, Roman author of five books of Latin verse fables, based chiefly on Aesop

Phaëthon ('feɪəθɒn) *n Greek myth* the son of Helios (the sun god) who borrowed his father's chariot and nearly set the earth on fire by approaching too close to it. Zeus

averted the catastrophe by striking him down with a thunderbolt

phaeton ('feɪt³n) *n* a light four-wheeled horse-drawn carriage with or without a top, usually having two seats [C18: from PHAËTON]

phage (feɪdʒ) *n* short for **bacteriophage**

-phage *n combining form* indicating something that eats or consumes something specified: *bacteriophage* [from Greek *-phagos*; see PHAGO-] > **-phagous** *adj combining form*

phago- or before a vowel **phag-** combining form eating, consuming, or destroying: *phagocyte* [from Greek *phagein* to consume]

phagocyte ('fæɡə,saɪt) *n* an amoeboid cell or protozoan that engulfs particles, such as food substances or invading microorganisms > **phagocytic** (,fæɡə'sɪtɪk) *adj*

phagocytosis (,fæɡəsaɪ'təʊsɪs) *n* the process by which a cell, such as a white blood cell, ingests microorganisms, other cells, and foreign particles

-phagy or **-phagia** *n combining form* indicating an eating or devouring: *anthropophagy* [from Greek *-phagia*; see PHAGO-]

phalange ('fælændʒ) *n*, *pl* **phalanges** (fæ'lændʒiːz) *anatomy* another name for **phalanx** (sense 4) [C16: via French, ultimately from Greek PHALANX]

phalangeal (fə'lændʒɪəl) *adj anatomy* of or relating to a phalanx or phalanges

phalanger (fə'lændʒə) *n* any of various Australasian arboreal marsupials, such as *Trichosurus vulpecula* (**brush-tailed phalanger**), having dense fur and a long tail: family *Phalangeridae*. Also called (Austral. and NZ): **possum, flying phalanger** [C18: via New Latin from Greek *phalaggion* spider's web, referring to its webbed hind toes]

phalanx ('fælæŋks) *n*, *pl* **phalanxes** or **phalanges** (fæ'lændʒiːz) 1 an ancient Greek and Macedonian battle formation of hoplites presenting long spears from behind a wall of overlapping shields 2 any closely ranked unit or mass of people: *the police formed a phalanx to protect the embassy* 3 a number of people united for a common purpose 4 *anatomy* any of the bones of the fingers or toes 5 *botany* a bundle of stamens, joined together by their stalks (filaments) [C16: via Latin from Greek: infantry formation in close ranks, bone of finger or toe]

phalarope ('fælə,rəʊp) *n* any aquatic shore bird of the family *Phalaropidae*, such as *Phalaropus fulicarius* (**grey phalarope**), of northern oceans and lakes, having a long slender bill and lobed toes: order *Charadriiformes* [C18: via French from New Latin *Phalaropus*, from Greek *phalaris* coot +*pous* foot]

phallic ('fælɪk) *adj* 1 of, relating to, or resembling a phallus: *a phallic symbol* 2 *psychoanal* relating to a stage of psychosexual development during which a male child's interest is concentrated on the genital organs 3 of or relating to phallicism

phallicism ('fælɪ,sɪzəm) or **phallism** *n* the worship or veneration of the phallus

phallus ('fæləs) *n*, *pl* **-luses** or **-li** (-laɪ) 1 another word for **penis** 2 an image of the penis, esp as a religious symbol of reproductive power [C17: via Late Latin from Greek *phallos*]

-phane *n combining form* indicating something resembling a specified substance: *cellophane* [from Greek *phainein* to shine, (in passive) appear]

phanerogam ('fænərəʊ,ɡæm) *n* any plant of the former major division *Phanerogamae*, which included all seed-bearing plants. now called: **spermatophyte** [C19: from New Latin *phanerogamus*, from Greek *phaneros* visible +*gamos* marriage] > **,phanero'gamic** or **phanerogamous** (,fænə'rɒɡəməs) *adj*

phantasm ('fæntæzəm) *n* 1 a phantom 2 an illusory perception of an object, person, etc [C13: from Old French *fantasme*, from Latin *phantasma*, from Greek; related to Greek *phantazein* to cause to be seen, from *phainein* to show] > **phan'tasmal** or **phan'tasmic** *adj*

phantasmagoria (,fæntæzmə'ɡɔːrɪə) or **phantasmagory** (fæn'tæzməɡərɪ) *n* 1 *psychol* a shifting medley of real or imagined figures, as in a dream 2 *films* a sequence of pictures made to vary in size rapidly while remaining in focus **3** *rare* a shifting scene composed of different elements [C19: probably from French *fantasmagorie* production of phantasms, from PHANTASM + *-agorie*, perhaps from Greek *ageirein* to gather together] > **phantasmagoric** (ˌfæntæzməˈɡɒrɪk) or **ˌphantasmaˈgorical** *adj*

phantasy (ˈfæntəsɪ) *n*, *pl* **-sies** an archaic spelling of **fantasy**

phantom (ˈfæntəm) *n* **1 a** an apparition or spectre **b** (*as modifier*): *a phantom army marching through the sky* **2** the visible representation of something abstract, esp as appearing in a dream or hallucination: *phantoms of evil haunted his sleep* **3** something apparently unpleasant or horrific that has no material form [C13: from Old French *fantosme*, from Latin *phantasma* PHANTASM]

phantom limb *n* the illusion that a limb still exists following its amputation, sometimes with pain (**phantom limb pain**)

phantom pregnancy *n* the occurrence of signs of pregnancy, such as enlarged abdomen and absence of menstruation, when no embryo is present, due to hormonal imbalance. Also called: **false pregnancy**

-phany *n combining form* indicating a manifestation: *theophany* [from Greek *-phania*, from *phainein* to show; see -PHANE] > **-phanous** *adj combining form*

phar., Phar., pharm. or **Pharm.** *abbreviation* **1** pharmaceutical **2** pharmacist **3** pharmacopoeia **4** pharmacy

Pharaoh (ˈfɛərəʊ) *n* the title of the ancient Egyptian kings [Old English *Pharaon*, via Latin, Greek, and Hebrew ultimately from Egyptian *pr-'o* great house] > **Pharaonic** (ˌfɛəˈrɒnɪk) *adj*

Pharisaic (ˌfærɪˈseɪɪk) or **Pharisaical** *adj* **1** *Judaism* of, relating to, or characteristic of the Pharisees or Pharisaism **2** (*often not capital*) righteously hypocritical > **ˌPhariˈsaically** *adv*

Pharisaism (ˈfærɪseɪˌɪzəm) or **Phariseeism** (ˈfærɪsiːˌɪzəm) *n* **1** *Judaism* the tenets and customs of the Pharisees **2** (*often not capital*) observance of the external forms of religion without genuine belief; hypocrisy

Pharisee (ˈfærɪˌsiː) *n* **1** *Judaism* a member of an ancient Jewish sect that was opposed to the Sadducees, teaching strict observance of Jewish tradition as interpreted rabbinically and believing in life after death and in the coming of theMessiah **2** (*often not capital*) a self-righteous or hypocritical person [Old English *Farīsēus*, ultimately from Aramaic *perīshāiyā*, pl of *perīsh* separated]

pharma (ˈfɑːmə) *n* pharmaceutical companies when considered together as an industry

pharmaceutical (ˌfɑːməˈsjuːtɪkəl) or *less commonly* **pharmaceutic** *adj* of or relating to drugs or pharmacy [C17: from Late Latin *pharmaceuticus*, from Greek *pharmakeus* purveyor of drugs; see PHARMACY] > **ˌpharmaˈceutically** *adv*

pharmaceutics (ˌfɑːməˈsjuːtɪks) *n* **1** (*functioning assingular*) another term for **pharmacy** (sense 1) **2** (*functioning asplural*) pharmaceutical remedies

pharmacist (ˈfɑːməsɪst) or *less commonly* **pharmaceutist** (ˌfɑːməˈsjuːtɪst) *n* a person qualified to prepare and dispense drugs

pharmaco- *combining form* indicating drugs: *pharmacology; pharmacopoeia* [from Greek *pharmakon* drug, potion]

pharmacogenomics (ˌfɑːməkəʊdʒɪˈnɒmɪks) *n* (*functioning assingular*) the study of human genetic variability in relation to drug action and its application to medical treatment > **ˌpharmacogeˈnomic** *adj*

pharmacognosy (ˌfɑːməˈkɒɡnəsɪ) *n* the branch of pharmacology concerned with crude drugs of plant and animal origin [C19: from PHARMACO- + gnosy, from Greek *gnosis*knowledge] > **ˌpharmaˈcognosist** *n*

pharmacology (ˌfɑːməˈkɒlədʒɪ) *n* the science of drugs, including their characteristics and uses > **pharmacological** (ˌfɑːməkəˈlɒdʒɪkəl) *adj* > **ˌpharmacoˈlogically** *adv* > **ˌpharmaˈcologist** *n*

pharmacopoeia or *sometimes US* **pharmacopeia** (ˌfɑːməkəˈpiːə) *n* an authoritative book containing a list of medicinal drugs with their uses, preparation, dosages, formulas, etc [C17: via New Latin from Greek *pharmakopoiia* art of preparing drugs, from PHARMACO- +

-poiia, from *poiein* to make] > **ˌpharmacoˈpoeial** or **ˌpharmacoˈpoeic** *adj*

pharmacy (ˈfɑːməsɪ) *n*, *pl* **-cies** **1** Also called: **pharmaceutics** the practice or art of preparing and dispensing drugs **2** a dispensary [C14: from Medieval Latin *pharmacia*, from Greek *pharmakeia* making of drugs, from *pharmakon* drug]

pharming[1] (ˈfɑːmɪŋ) *n* the practice of rearing or growing genetically-modified animals or plants in order to develop pharmaceutical products [C20: blend of PHARMACEUTICAL + FARMING]

pharming[2] (ˈfɑːmɪŋ) *n* the practice of redirecting computer users from legitimate websites to fraudulent ones for the purposes of extracting confidential data [C21: from *farming* in the sense of cultivating and harvesting; computer-hacker slang often replaces f with *ph*]

Pharos (ˈfɛərɒs) *n* a large Hellenistic lighthouse built on an island off Alexandria in Egypt in about 280 BC and destroyed by an earthquake in the 14th century: usually included among the Seven Wonders of the World

Pharsalus (fɑːˈseɪləs) *n* an ancient town in Thessaly in N Greece. Several major battles were fought nearby, including Caesar's victory over Pompey (48BC)

pharyngeal (ˌfærɪnˈdʒiːəl) or **pharyngal** (fəˈrɪŋɡəl) *adj* **1** of, relating to, or situated in or near the pharynx **2** *phonetics* pronounced or supplemented in pronunciation with an articulation in or constriction of the pharynx [C19: from New Latin *pharyngeus*; see PHARYNX]

pharyngitis (ˌfærɪnˈdʒaɪtɪs) *n* inflammation of the pharynx

pharynx (ˈfærɪŋks) *n*, *pl* **pharynges** (fæˈrɪndʒiːz) or **pharynxes** the part of the alimentary canal between the mouth and the oesophagus [C17: via New Latin from Greek *pharunx* throat; related to Greek *pharanx* chasm]

phascogale (ˈfæskəɡeɪl, ˌfæsˈkɑːɡəlɪ) *n* *Austral* another name for **tuan**[2]

phase (feɪz) *n* **1** any distinct or characteristic period or stage in a sequence of events or chain of development: *there were two phases to the resolution; his immaturity was a passing phase* **2** *astronomy* one of the recurring shapes of the portion of the moon or an inferior planet illuminated by the sun **3** *physics* the fraction of a cycle of a periodic quantity that has been completed at a specific reference time, expressed as an angle **4** *physics* a particular stage in a periodic process or phenomenon **5 in phase** (of two waveforms) reaching corresponding phases at the same time **6 out of phase** (of two waveforms) not in phase **7** *chem* a distinct state of matter characterized by homogeneous composition and properties and the possession of a clearly defined boundary **8** *zoology* a variation in the normal form of an animal, esp a colour variation, brought about by seasonal or geographical change ▷ *vb* (*tr*) **9** (*often passive*) to execute, arrange, or introduce gradually or in stages: *a phased withdrawal* **10** (sometimes foll by *with*) to cause (a part, process, etc) to function or coincide with (another part, process, etc): *he tried to phase the intake and output of the machine; he phased the intake with the output* **11** *chiefly US* to arrange (processes, goods, etc) to be supplied or executed when required [C19: from New Latin *phases*, pl of *phasis*, from Greek: aspect; related to Greek *phainein* to show] > **ˈphasic** or **ˈphaseal** *adj*

phase in *vb* (*tr, adverb*) to introduce in a gradual or cautious manner: *the legislation will be phased in over two years*

phase modulation *n* a type of modulation, used in communication systems, in which the phase of a radio carrier wave is varied by an amount proportional to the instantaneous amplitude of the modulating signal

phase out *vb* **1** (*tr, adverb*) to discontinue or withdraw gradually ▷ *n* **phase-out 2** the action or an instance of phasing out: *a phase-out of conventional forces*

phase rule *n* the principle that in any system in equilibrium the number of degrees of freedom is equal to the number of components less the number of phases plus two. See also **degree of freedom**

-phasia *n combining form* indicating speech disorder of a

specified kind: *aphasia* [from Greek, from *phanai* to speak]
> **-phasic** *adj combining form*, *n combining form*

phat (fæt) *adj slang* terrific; superb [c20: from Black slang, a corruption of FAT]

phatic ('fætɪk) *adj* (of speech, esp of conversational phrases) used to establish social contact and to express sociability rather than specific meaning [c20: from Greek *phat(os)* spoken + -IC]

PhD *abbreviation* Doctor of Philosophy. Also called: **DPhil**

pheasant ('fɛzənt) *n* **1** any of various long-tailed gallinaceous birds of the family *Phasianidae*, esp *Phasianus colchicus* (**ring-necked pheasant**), having a brightly-coloured plumage in the male: native to Asia but introduced elsewhere **2** any of various other gallinaceous birds of the family *Phasianidae*, including the quails and partridges **3** *US & Canadian* any of several other gallinaceous birds, esp the ruffed grouse [c13: from Old French *fesan*, from Latin *phāsiānus*, from Greek *phasianos ornis* Phasian bird, named after the River *Phasis*, in Colchis]

Phebe ('fi:bɪ) *n* a variant spelling of **Phoebe**[1]

Pheidippides *or* **Phidippides** (faɪ'dɪpɪ,di:z) *n* 5th century BC Athenian athlete, who ran to Sparta to seek help against the Persians before the Battle of Marathon (490 BC)

phellem ('fɛləm) *n botany* the technical name for **cork** (sense 4) [c20: from Greek *phellos* cork + PHLOEM]

phenacetin (fɪ'næsɪtɪn) *n* a white crystalline solid formerly used in medicine to relieve pain and fever. Because of its kidney toxicity it has been superseded by paracetamol. Formula:$CH_3CONHC_6H_4OC_2H_5$. Also called: **acetophenetidin** [c19: from PHENETIDINE + ACETYL + -IN]

phenetidine (fɪ'nɛtɪ,di:n, -dɪn) *n* a liquid amine that is a derivative of phenetole, existing in three isomeric forms: used in the manufacture of dyestuffs. Formula:$H_2NC_6H_4OC_2H_5$ [c19: from PHENETOLE + -ID[3] + -INE[2]]

phenix ('fi:nɪks) *n* a US spelling of **phoenix**

pheno- *or before a vowel* **phen-** *combining form* showing or manifesting: *phenotype* **1** indicating that a molecule contains benzene rings: *phenobarbital* [from Greek *phaino-* shining, from *phainein* to show; its use in a chemical sense is exemplified in *phenol*, so called because originally prepared from illuminating gas]

phenobarbital (,fi:nəʊ'ba:bɪt°l) *n* a white crystalline derivative of barbituric acid used as a sedative for treating insomnia and as an anticonvulsant in epilepsy. Formula: $C_{12}H_{12}N_2O_3$

phenocryst ('fi:nə,krɪst, 'fɛn-) *n* any of several large crystals that are embedded in a mass of smaller crystals in igneous rocks such as porphyry [c19: from PHENO-(shining) + CRYSTAL]

phenol ('fi:nɒl) *n* **1** Also called: **carbolic acid** a white crystalline soluble poisonous acidic derivative of benzene, used as an antiseptic and disinfectant and in the manufacture of resins,nylon, dyes, explosives, and pharmaceuticals; hydroxybenzene. Formula:C_6H_5OH **2** *chem* any of a class of weakly acidic organic compounds whose molecules contain one or more hydroxyl groups bound directly to a carbon atom in anaromatic ring

phenolic resin *n* any one of a class of resins derived from phenol, used in paints, adhesives, and as thermosetting plastics

phenology (fɪ'nɒlədʒɪ) *n* the study of recurring phenomena, such as animal migration, esp as influenced by climatic conditions [c19: from PHENO(MENON) + -LOGY] > **phenological** (,fi:nə'lɒdʒɪk°l) *adj* > **phe'nologist** *n*

phenolphthalein (,fi:nɒl'θeɪli:n, -lɪɪn, -'θæl-) *n* a colourless crystalline compound used in medicine as a laxative and in chemistry as an indicator. Formula:$C_{20}H_{14}O_4$

phenomena (fɪ'nɒmɪnə) *n* a plural of **phenomenon**

phenomenal (fɪ'nɒmɪn°l) *adj* **1** of or relating to a phenomenon **2** extraordinary; outstanding; remarkable: *a phenomenal achievement* **3** *philosophy* known or perceived by the senses rather than the mind > **phe'nomenally** *adv*

phenomenalism (fɪ'nɒmɪnə,lɪzəm) *n philosophy* the doctrine that statements about physical objects and the external world can be analysed in terms of possible or actual experiences, andthat entities, such as physical objects, are only mental constructions out of phenomenal appearances > **phe'nomenalist** *n*, *adj*

phenomenology (fɪ,nɒmɪ'nɒlədʒɪ) *n philosophy* **1** the movement founded by Husserl that concentrates on the detailed description of conscious experience, without recourse to explanation, metaphysical assumptions, and traditional philosophical questions **2** the science of phenomena as opposed to the science of being > **phenomenological** (fɪ,nɒmɪnə'lɒdʒɪk°l) *adj*

phenomenon (fɪ'nɒmɪnən) *n*, *pl* **-ena** (-ɪnə) *or* **-enons 1** anything that can be perceived as an occurrence or fact by the senses **2** any remarkable occurrence or person **3** *philosophy* **a** the object of perception, experience, etc **b** (in the writings of Kant) a thing as it appears and is interpreted in perception and reflection, as distinguished from its real nature as a thing-in-itself [c16: via Late Latin from Greek *phainomenon*, from *phainesthai* toappear, from *phainein* to show]

● USAGE Although *phenomena* is often treated as if it
● were singular, correct usage is to employ *phenomenon*
● with a singular construction and *phenomena* with a
● plural: *that is an interesting phenomenon* (not *phenomena*);
● *several new phenomena were recorded in his notes*

phenothiazine (,fi:nəʊ'θaɪəzi:n) *n* **1** a colourless to light yellow insoluble crystallinecompound used as an anthelmintic for livestock and in insecticides. Formula: $C_{12}H_9NS$ **2** any of several drugs derived from phenothiazine and used as strong tranquillizers and in the treatment of schizophrenia

phenotype ('fi:nəʊ,taɪp) *n* the physical and biochemical characteristics of an organism as determined by the interaction of its genetic constitution and the environment > **phenotypic** (,fi:nəʊ'tɪpɪk) *or* ,**pheno'typical** *adj* > ,**pheno'typically** *adv*

phenyl ('fi:naɪl, 'fɛnɪl) *n* (*modifier*) of, containing, or consisting of the monovalent groupC_6H_5, derived from benzene: *a phenyl group or radical*

phenylalanine (,fi:naɪl'ælə,ni:n, ,fɛnɪl-) *n* an aromatic essential amino acid; a component of proteins

phenylbutazone (,fi:naɪl'bju:tə,zəʊn) *n* an anti-inflammatory drug used in the treatment of rheumatic diseases; it has been largely superseded by other NSAIDs [c20: from (*dioxodi*)*phenylbut*(*ylpyr*)*azo*(*lidi*)*ne*]

phenylethylamine (,fi:naɪl,ɛθɪl,ə'mi:n, ,fɛnɪl-) *n* an amine that occurs naturally as a neurotransmitter in the brain, has properties similar to those of amphetamine, is an antidepressant, and is found in chocolate. Formula: $C_8H_{11}N$

phenylketonuria (,fi:naɪl,ki:tə'njʊərɪə) *n* a congenital metabolic disorder characterized by the abnormal accumulation of phenylalanine in the body fluids, resulting in various degrees of mental deficiency [c20: New Latin; see PHENYL, KETONE, -URIA]

pheromone ('fɛrə,məʊn) *n* a chemical substance, secreted externally by certain animals, such as insects, affecting the behaviour or physiology of other animals of the same species [c20: *phero-*, from Greek *pherein* to bear +(HOR)MONE]

phew (fju:) *interj* an exclamation of relief, surprise, disbelief, weariness, etc

phi (faɪ) *n*, *pl* **phis** the 21st letter in the Greek alphabet (Φ, φ), a consonant, transliterated as *ph* or *f*

phial ('faɪəl) *n* a small bottle for liquids; vial [c14: from Old French *fiole*, from Latin *phiola* saucer, from Greek *phialē* wide shallow vessel]

Phi Beta Kappa ('faɪ 'beɪtə 'kæpə, 'bi:tə) *n* (in the US) **1** a national honorary society, founded in 1776, membership of which is based on high academic ability **2** a member of this society [from the initials of the Greek motto *philosophia biou kubernētēs* philosophy the guide of life]

Phidias ('fɪdɪ,æs) *n* 5th century BC, Greek sculptor, regarded as one of the greatest of sculptors. He executed the sculptures of the Parthenon and the colossal statue of Zeus at Olympia, one of the Seven Wonders of the World: neither survives in the original > **'Phidian** *adj*

P

Phidippides (faɪˈdɪpɪˌdiːz) n a variant spelling of **Pheidippides**

phil. abbreviation 1 philosophy 2 philharmonic

Phil. abbreviation 1 Philippians 2 Philippines 3 Philharmonic

Philadelphia (ˌfɪləˈdɛlfɪə) n a city and port in SE Pennsylvania, at the confluence of the Delaware and Schuylkill Rivers: the fourth largest city in the US; founded by Quakers in 1682; cultural and financial centre of the American colonies and the federal capital (1790–1800); scene of the Continental Congresses (1774–83) and the signing of the Declaration of Independence (1776). Pop: 1 479 339 (2003est)

philadelphus (ˌfɪləˈdɛlfəs) n any shrub of the N temperate genus *Philadelphus,* cultivated for their strongly scented showy flowers: family *Hydrangeaceae.* See also **mock orange** (sense 1) [C19: New Latin, from Greek *philadelphon* mock orange, literally: loving one's brother]

Philae (ˈfaɪliː) n an island in Upper Egypt, in the Nile north of the Aswan Dam: of religious importance in ancient times; almost submerged since the raising of the level of the dam

philander (fɪˈlændə) vb (intr; often follby with) (of a man) to flirt with women [C17: from Greek *philandros* fond of men, from *philos* loving +*anēr* man; used as a name for a lover in literary works] > phi'landerer n

philanthropic (ˌfɪlənˈθrɒpɪk) or **philanthropical** adj showing concern for humanity, esp by performing charitable actions, donating money, etc > ˌphilan'thropically adv

philanthropy (fɪˈlænθrəpɪ) n, pl -pies 1 the practice of performing charitable or benevolent actions 2 love of mankind in general [C17: from Late Latin *philanthrōpia,* from Greek: love of mankind, from *philos* loving + *anthrōpos* man] > phi'lanthropist or philanthrope (ˈfɪlənˌθrəʊp) n

philately (fɪˈlætəlɪ) n the collection and study of postage stamps and all related material concerned with postal history [C19: from French *philatélie,* from PHILO- + Greek *ateleia* exemption from charges (here referring to stamps), from A-[1] +*telos* tax, payment] > philatelic (ˌfɪləˈtɛlɪk) adj > ˌphila'telically adv > phi'latelist n

Philby (ˈfɪlbɪ) n 1 **Harold Adrian Russell,** known as **Kim.** 1912–88, English double agent; defected to the Soviet Union (1963) 2 his father, **H(arry) Saint John (Bridger).** 1885–1960, British explorer, civil servant, and Arabist

-phile or **-phil** n combining form indicating a person or thing having a fondness or preference for something specified: *bibliophile; Francophile* [from Greek *philos* loving]

Philem. Bible abbreviation Philemon

Philemon[1] (faɪˈliːmɒn) n New Testament 1 a Christian of Colossae whose escaped slave came to meet Paul 2 the book (in full **The Epistle of Paul the Apostle to Philemon**), asking Philemon to forgive the slave

Philemon[2] (faɪˈliːmɒn) n Greek myth a poor Phrygian, who with his wife Baucis offered hospitality to the disguised Zeus and Hermes

philharmonic (ˌfɪlhɑːˈmɒnɪk, ˌfɪlə-) adj 1 fond of music 2 (capital when part of a name) denoting an orchestra, choir, society, etc, devoted to the performance, appreciation, and study of music ▷ n 3 (capital when part of a name) a specific philharmonic choir, orchestra, orsociety [C18: from French *philharmonique,* from Italian *filarmonico* music-loving; see PHILO-, HARMONY]

philhellene (fɪlˈhɛliːn) or **philhellenist** (fɪlˈhɛlɪnɪst) n 1 a lover of Greece and Greek culture 2 European history a supporter of the cause of Greek national independence > philhellenic (ˌfɪlhɛˈliːnɪk) adj

-philia n combining form 1 indicating a tendency towards: *haemophilia* 2 indicating an abnormal liking for: *necrophilia* [from Greek *philos* loving] > -philiac n combining form > -philous or -philic adj combining form

philibeg (ˈfɪlɪˌbɛg) n a variant spelling of filibeg

Philip (ˈfɪlɪp) n 1 New Testament a Also called: Philip the Evangelist one of the seven deacons appointed by the early Church b Also called: Philip the Tetrarch one of the sons of Herod the Great, who was ruler of part of former Judaea (4 BC–34 AD) (Luke 3:1) 2 King, American

Indian name *Metacomet.* died 1676, American Indian chief, the son of Massasoit. He waged King Philip's War against the colonists of New England (1675–76) and was killed in battle 3 **Prince.** another name for the (Duke of) Edinburgh[1]

Philip I n 1 known as *Philip the Handsome.* 1478–1506, king of Castile (1506); father of Emperor Charles V and founder of the Hapsburg dynasty in Spain 2 title of Philip II of Spain as king of Portugal

Philip II n 1 382–336 BC, king of Macedonia (359–336); the father of Alexander the Great 2 known as *Philip Augustus.* 1165–1223, Capetian king of France (1180–1223); set out on the Third Crusade with Richard I of England (1190) 3 1527–98, king of Spain (1556–98) and, as Philip I, king of Portugal (1580–98); the husband of Mary I of England (1554–58). He championed the Counter-Reformation, sending the Armada against England (1588)

Philip IV n known as *Philip the Fair.* 1268–1314, king of France (1285–1314): he challenged the power of the papacy, obtaining the elevation of Clement V as pope residing at Avignon (the beginning of the Babylonian captivity of the papacy)

Philippeville (ˈfɪlɪpˌvɪl) n the former name of **Skikda**

Philippi (fɪˈlɪpaɪ, ˈfɪlɪ-) n an ancient city in NE Macedonia: scene of the victory of Antony and Octavian over Brutus and Cassius (42 BC) > Phi'lippian adj, n

philippic (fɪˈlɪpɪk) n a bitter or impassioned speech of denunciation; invective

Philippine (ˈfɪlɪˌpiːn) adj another word for **Filipino** (sense 3)

Philippines (ˈfɪlɪˌpiːnz, ˌfɪlɪˈpiːnz) n Republic of the Philippines (functioning assingular) a republic in SE Asia, occupying an archipelago of about 7100 islands (including Luzon, Mindanao, Samar, and Negros): became a Spanish colony in 1571 but ceded to the US in 1898 after the Spanish-American War; gained independence in 1946. The islands are generally mountainous and volcanic. Official languages: Filipino, based on Tagalog, and English. Religion: Roman Catholic majority. Currency: peso. Capital: Manila. Pop: 81 408 000 (2004 est). Area: 300 076 sq km (115 860 sq miles) Related word: **Filipino**

Philippine Sea n part of the NW Pacific Ocean, east and north of the Philippines

Philippopolis (ˌfɪlɪˈpɒpəlɪs) n transliteration of the Greek name for **Plovdiv**

Philip V n 1683–1746, king of Spain (1700–46) and founder of the Bourbon dynasty in Spain. His accession began the War of Spanish Succession (1701–13)

Philip VI n 1293–1350, first Valois king of France (1328–50). Edward III of England claimed his throne, which with other disputes led to the beginning of the Hundred Years' War (1337)

Philip the Bold n 1342–1404, duke of Burgundy (1363–1404), noted for his courage at Poitiers (1356) in the Hundred Years' War: regent of France for his nephew Charles VI (1368–88, 1392–1404)

Philip the Good n 1396–1467, duke of Burgundy (1419–67), under whose rule Burgundy was one of the most powerful states in Europe

Philip the Magnanimous n 1504–67, German prince; landgrave of Hesse (1509–67). He helped to crush (1525) the Peasants' Revolt and formed (1531) the League of Schmalkaden, an alliance of German Protestant rulers

Philistia (fɪˈlɪstɪə) n an ancient country on the coast of SW Palestine > Phi'listian adj

Philistine (ˈfɪlɪˌstaɪn) n 1 a person who is unreceptive to or hostile towards culture, the arts, etc; a smug boorish person 2 a member of the non-Semitic people who inhabited ancient Philistia ▷ adj 3 (sometimes not capital) boorishly uncultured 4 of or relating to the ancient Philistines > Philistinism (ˈfɪlɪstɪˌnɪzəm) n

Phillip (ˈfɪlɪp) n Arthur. 1738–1814, English naval commander; captain general of the First Fleet, which carried convicts from Portsmouth to Sydney Cove, Australia, where he founded New South Wales

Phillips (ˈfɪlɪps) n Captain **Mark.** born 1948, English three-day-event horseman; married to Anne, the Princess Royal, divorced 1992

phillumenist (fɪ'lju:mənɪst, -'lu:-) *n* a person who collects matchbox labels [C20: from PHILO- + Latin *lumen* light + -IST]

philo- *or before a vowel* **phil-** *combining form* indicating a love of: *philology; philanthropic* [from Greek *philos* loving]

Philoctetes (,fɪlɒk'ti:ti:z, fɪ'lɒktɪ,ti:z) *n Greek myth* a hero of the Trojan War, in which he killed Paris with the bow and poisoned arrows given to him by Hercules

philodendron (,fɪlə'dɛndrən) *n*, *pl*-drons *or*-dra (-drə) any aroid evergreen climbing plant of the tropical American genus *Philodendron*: cultivated as house plants [C19: New Latin from Greek: lover of trees]

philogyny (fɪ'lɒdʒɪnɪ) *n rare* fondness for women [C17: from Greek *philogunia*, from PHILO- + *gunē* woman] >**phi'logynist** *n*

Philo Judaeus ('faɪləʊ dʒu:'di:əs) *n* ?20 BC–?50 AD, Jewish philosopher, born in Alexandria. He sought to reconcile Judaism with Greek philosophy

philology (fɪ'lɒlədʒɪ) *n* **1** comparative and historical linguistics **2** the scientific analysis of written records and literary texts **3** (no longer in scholarly use) the study of literature in general [C17: from Latin *philologia*, from Greek: love of language] >**philological** (,fɪlə'lɒdʒɪkᵊl) *adj* >,**philo'logically** *adv* >**phi'lologist** *or less commonly* **phi'loLoger** *n*

philomel ('fɪlə,mɛl) *or* **philomela** (,fɪləʊ'mi:lə) *n* poetic names for a **nightingale** [C14 *philomene*, via Medieval Latin from Latin *philomēla*, from Greek]

Philomela (,fɪləʊ'mi:lə) *n Greek myth* an Athenian princess, who was raped and had her tongue cut out by her brother-in-law Tereus, and subsequently was transformed into a nightingale. See **Procne**

philoprogenitive (,fɪləʊprəʊ'dʒenɪtɪv) *adj rare* **1** fond of children **2** producing many offspring

philos. *abbreviation* **1** philosopher **2** philosophical

philosopher (fɪ'lɒsəfə) *n* **1** a student, teacher, or devotee of philosophy **2** a person of philosophical temperament, esp one who is patient, wise, and stoical **3** (formerly) an alchemist or devotee of occult science

philosopher's stone *n* a stone or substance thought by alchemists to be capable of transmuting base metals into gold

philosophical (,fɪlə'sɒfɪkᵊl) *or* **philosophic** *adj* **1** of or relating to philosophy or philosophers **2** reasonable, wise, or learned **3** calm and stoical, esp in the face of difficulties or disappointments >,**philo'sophically** *adv*

philosophical analysis *n* a philosophical method in which language and experience are analysed in an attempt to provide new insights into various philosophical problems

philosophize *or* **philosophise** (fɪ'lɒsə,faɪz) *vb* **1** (*intr*) to make philosophical pronouncements and speculations **2** (*tr*) to explain philosophically >**phi'loso,phizer** *or* **phi'loso,phiser** *n*

philosophy (fɪ'lɒsəfɪ) *n*, *pl*-phies **1** the academic discipline concerned with making explicit the nature and significance of ordinary and scientific beliefs and investigating the intelligibility of concepts by means of rational argument concerning their presuppositions, implications, and interrelationships; in particular, the rational investigation of the nature and structure of reality (metaphysics), the resources and limits of knowledge (epistemology), the principles and import of moral judgment(ethics), and the relationship between language and reality (semantics) **2** the particular doctrines relating to these issues of some specific individual or school: *the philosophy of Descartes* **3** the critical study of the basic principles and concepts of a discipline: *the philosophy of law* **4** any system of belief, values, or tenets **5** a personal outlook or viewpoint **6** serenity of temper [C13: from Old French *filosofie*, from Latin *philosophia*, from Greek, from *philosophos* lover of wisdom]

-philous *or* **-philic** *adj combining form* indicating love of or fondness for: *heliophilous* [from Latin *-philus*, from Greek *-philos*; see -PHILE]

philtre *or US* **philter** ('fɪltə) *n* a drink supposed to arouse love, desire, etc [C16: from Latin *philtrum*, from Greek *philtron* love potion, from *philos* loving]

phimosis (faɪ'məʊsɪs) *n* abnormal tightness of the foreskin, preventing its being retracted over the tip of the penis [C17: via New Latin from Greek: a muzzling, from *phimos* a muzzle]

phishing ('fɪʃɪŋ) *n* the practice of using fraudulent e-mails and copies of legitimate websites to extract financial data from computer users for purposes of identity theft [C21: from *fishing* in the sense of catching the unwary by offering bait; computer-hacker slang often replaces *f* with *ph*]

phiz (fɪz) *n slang, chiefly Brit* the face or a facial expression. Also called: **phizog** ('fɪzɒg, fɪ'zɒg) [C17: colloquial shortening of PHYSIOGNOMY]

Phiz (fɪz) *n* real name *Hablot Knight Browne*. 1815–82, English painter, noted for his illustrations for Dickens' novels

phlebitis (flɪ'baɪtɪs) *n* inflammation of a vein [C19: via New Latin from Greek; see PHLEBO-, -ITIS] >**phlebitic** (flɪ'bɪtɪk) *adj*

phlebo- *or before a vowel* **phleb-** *combining form* indicating a vein: *phlebotomy* [from Greek *phleps*, *phleb-* vein]

phlebotomy (flɪ'bɒtəmɪ) *n*, *pl*-mies surgical incision into a vein [C14: via Old French *flebothomie*, from Late Latin *phlebotomia*, from Greek]

Phlegethon ('flɛgɪ,θɒn) *n Greek myth* a river of fire in Hades [C14: from Greek, literally: blazing, from *phlegethein* to flame, blaze]

phlegm (flɛm) *n* **1** the viscid mucus secreted by the walls of the respiratory tract **2** *archaic* one of the four bodily humours **3** apathy; stolidity; indifference **4** self-possession; imperturbability; coolness [C14: from Old French *fleume*, from Late Latin *phlegma*, from Greek: inflammation, from *phlegein* to burn] >**'phlegmy** *adj*

phlegmatic (flɛg'mætɪk) *or* **phlegmatical** *adj* **1** having a stolid or unemotional disposition **2** not easily excited >**phleg'matically** *adv*

phloem ('fləʊɛm) *n* tissue in higher plants that conducts synthesized food substances to all parts of the plant [C19: via German from Greek *phloos* bark]

phlogiston (flɒ'dʒɪstɒn, -tən) *n chem* a hypothetical substance formerly thought to be present in all combustible materials and to be released during burning [C18: via New Latin from Greek, from *phlogizein* to set alight; related to *phlegein* to burn]

phlox (flɒks) *n*, *pl* **phlox** *or* **phloxes** any polemoniaceous plant of the chiefly North American genus *Phlox*: cultivated for their clusters of white, red, or purple flowers [C18: via Latin from Greek: a plant of glowing colour, literally: flame]

phlyctena *or* **phlyctaena** (flɪk'ti:nə) *n*, *pl*-nae (-ni:) *pathol* a small blister, vesicle, or pustule [C17: via New Latin from Greek *phluktaina*, from *phluzein* toswell]

Phnom Penh *or* **Pnom Penh** (,pnɒm 'pɛn) *n* the capital of Cambodia, a port in the south at the confluence of the Mekong and Tonle Sap Rivers: capital of the country since 1865; university (1960). Pop: 1 174 000 (2005 est)

pho (fəʊ) *n* a Vietnamese noodle soup [C20: from Vietnamese, perhaps from French *feu* fire]

-phobe *n combining form* indicating a person or thing that fears or hates: *Germanophobe; xenophobe* [from Greek *-phobos* fearing] >**-phobic** *adj combining form*

phobia ('fəʊbɪə) *n psychiatry* an abnormal intense and irrational fear of a given situation, organism, or object [C19: from Greek *phobos* fear]

-phobia *n combining form* indicating an extreme abnormal fear of or aversion to: *acrophobia; claustrophobia* [via Latin from Greek, from *phobos* fear] >**-phobic** *adj combining form*

Phocaea (fəʊ'si:ə) *n* an ancient port in Asia Minor, the northernmost of Ionian cities on the W coast of Asia Minor: an important maritime state (about 1000–600BC)

Phocis ('fəʊsɪs) *n* an ancient district of central Greece, on the Gulf ofCorinth: site of the Delphic oracle

phocomelia (,fəʊkəʊ'mi:lɪə) *or* **phocomely** (fəʊ'kɒməlɪ) *n* a congenital deformity resulting from prenatal interference with the development of the fetal limbs, characterized esp by short stubby hands or feet attached close to the body [C19: via New Latin from Greek *phōkē* a seal + *melos* a limb]

phoebe ('fi:bɪ) *n* any of several greyish-brown North

American flycatchers of the genus *Sayornis*, such as *S. phoebe* (**easternphoebe**) [c19: imitative of the bird's call]

Phoebe *or* **Phebe** ('fi:bɪ) *n* **1** *classical myth* a Titaness, who later became identified with Artemis (Diana) as goddess of the moon **2** *poetic* a personification of the moon

Phoebus ('fi:bəs) *n* **1** Also called: **Phoebus Apollo** *Greek myth* Apollo as the sun god **2** *poetic* a personification of the sun [c14: via Latin from Greek *Phoibos* bright; related to *phaoslight*]

Phoenicia (fə'nɪʃɪə, -'ni:-) *n* an ancient maritime country extending from the Mediterranean Sea to the Lebanon Mountains, now occupied by the coastal regions of Lebanon and parts of Syria and Israel: consisted of a group of city-states, at their height between about 1200 and 1000 BC, that were leading traders of the ancient world

Phoenician (fə'ni:ʃən, -'nɪʃɪən) *n* **1** a member of an ancient Semitic people of NW Syria who dominated the trade of the ancient world in the first millennium BC and founded colonies throughout the Mediterranean **2** the extinct language of this people, belonging to the Canaanitic branch of the Semitic subfamily of the Afro-Asiatic family ▷ *adj* **3** of or relating to Phoenicia, the Phoenicians, or their language

phoenix *or US* **phenix** ('fi:nɪks) *n* **1** a legendary Arabian bird said to set fire to itself and rise anew from the ashes every 500 years **2** a person or thing of surpassing beauty or quality [Old English *fenix*, via Latin from Greek *phoinix*; identical in form with Greek *Phoinix* Phoenician, purple]

Phoenix ('fi:nɪks) *n* a city in central Arizona, capital city of the state, on the Salt River. Pop: 1 388 416 (2003 est)

Phoenix Islands *pl n* a group of eight coral islands in the central Pacific: administratively part of Kiribati. Area: 28 sq km (11 sq miles)

Phomvihane ('pɒmvɪhɑ:n) *n* **Kaysone** ('kaɪsɒn). 1920–92, Laotian Communist statesman; prime minister of Laos (1975–91); president (1991–92)

phon (fɒn) *n* a unit of loudness that measures the intensity of a sound by the number of decibels it is above a reference tone having a frequency of 1000 hertz and a root-mean-square sound pressure of 20×10^{-6} pascal [c20: via German from Greek *phōnē* sound, voice]

phonate (fəʊ'neɪt) *vb* (*intr*) to articulate speech sounds, esp to cause the vocal cords to vibrate in the execution of a voiced speech sound [c19: from Greek *phōnē* voice] ▷ **pho'nation** *n*

phone[1] (fəʊn) *n, vb* short for **telephone**

phone[2] (fəʊn) *n phonetics* a single uncomplicated speech sound [c19: from Greek *phōnē* sound, voice]

-phone *combining form* **1** (*forming nouns*) indicating voice, sound, or a device giving off sound: *microphone; telephone* **2** (*forming nouns andadjectives*) (a person) speaking a particular language: *Francophone* [from Greek *phōnē* voice, sound] ▷ **-phonic** *adj combining form*

phonecam ('fəʊn,kam) *n* a digital camera incorporated in a mobile phone

phonecard ('fəʊn,kɑ:d) *n* a card for use in a cardphone that operates for the number or duration of calls paid for in the purchase price of the card

phone-in *n* **a** a radio or television programme in which listeners' orviewers' questions, comments, etc, are telephoned to the studio and broadcast live **b** (*as modifier*): *a phone-in discussion*

phone-jack *vb* (*tr*) to steal the mobile phone from (a person) [c21: PHONE[1] + (HI)JACK] ▷ **'phone-jacker** *n*

phoneme ('fəʊni:m) *n linguistics* one of the set of speech sounds in any given language that serve to distinguish one word from another. A phoneme may consist of several phonetically distinct articulations, which are regarded as identical by native speakers, since one articulation may be substituted for another without any change of meaning. Thus /p/ and /b/ are separate phonemes in English because they distinguish such words as *pet* and *bet*, whereas the light and dark /l/sounds in *little* are not separate phonemes since they may be transposed without changing meaning [c20: via French from Greek *phōnēma* sound, speech]

phonemics (fə'ni:mɪks) *n* (*functioning assingular*) that aspect of linguistics concerned with the classification, analysis, interrelation, and environmental changes of the phonemes of a language ▷ **pho'nemicist** *n*

phonetic (fə'nɛtɪk) *adj* **1** of or relating to phonetics **2** denoting any perceptible distinction between one speech sound and another, irrespective of whether the sounds are phonemes or allophones **3** conforming to pronunciation: *phonetic spelling* [c19: from New Latin *phōnēticus*, from Greek *phōnētikos*, from*phōnein* to make sounds, speak] ▷ **pho'netically** *adv*

phonetician (,fəʊnɪ'tɪʃən) *n* a person skilled in phonetics or one who employs phonetics in his work

phonetics (fə'nɛtɪks) *n* (*functioning assingular*) the science concerned with the study of speech processes, including the production, perception, and analysis of speech sounds from both anacoustic and a physiological point of view. This science, though capable of being applied to language studies, technically excludes linguistic considerations

phonetist ('fəʊnɪtɪst) *n* **1** another name for **phonetician** **2** a person who advocates or uses a system of phonetic spelling

phoney *or esp US* **phony** ('fəʊnɪ) *informal* ▷ *adj* **-nier, -niest** **1** not genuine; fake **2** (of a person) insincere or pretentious ▷ *n, pl* **-neys** *or* **-nies** **3** an insincere or pretentious person **4** something that is not genuine; a fake [c20: origin uncertain] ▷ **'phoneyness** *or esp US* **'phoniness** *n*

phonics ('fɒnɪks) *n* (*functioning assingular*) **1** an obsolete name for **acoustics** (sense 1) **2** a method of teaching people to read by training them to associate letters with their phonetic values ▷ **'phonic** *adj* ▷ **'phonically** *adv*

phono- *or before a vowel* **phon-** *combining form* indicating a sound or voice: *phonograph; phonology* [from Greek *phōnē* sound, voice]

phonogram ('fəʊnə,græm) *n* any written symbol standing for a sound, syllable,morpheme, or word ▷ **,phono'gramic** *or* **,phono'grammic** *adj*

phonograph ('fəʊnə,grɑ:f, -,græf) *n* **1** an early form of gramophone capable of recording and reproducing sound on wax cylinders **2** Also called: **gramophone, record player** *US & Canadian* a device for reproducing the sounds stored on a record: now usually applied to the nearly obsolete type that uses a clockwork motor and acoustic horn

phonographic (,fəʊnə'græfɪk) *adj* **1** of or relating to phonography **2** of or relating to the recording of music

phonography (fəʊ'nɒgrəfɪ) *n* **1** a writing system that represents sounds by individual symbols **2** the employment of such a writing system

phonology (fə'nɒlədʒɪ) *n, pl* **-gies** **1** the study of the sound system of a language or of languages in general **2** such a sound system ▷ **phonological** (,fəʊnə'lɒdʒɪkəl, ,fɒn-) *adj* ▷ **,phono'logically** *adv* ▷ **pho'nologist** *n*

phonon ('fəʊnɒn) *n physics* a quantum of vibrational energy in the acoustic vibrations of a crystal lattice [c20: from PHONO- + -ON]

-phony *n combining form* indicating a specified type of sound: *cacophony; euphony* [from Greek *-phōnia*, from *phōnē* sound] ▷ **-phonic** *adj combining form*

phooey ('fu:ɪ) *interj informal* an exclamation of scorn, contempt, disbelief, etc [c20: probably variant of PHEW]

-phore *n combining form* indicating a person or thing that bears or produces: *gonophore; semaphore* [from New Latin *-phorus*, from Greek *-phoros* bearing, from *pherein* to bear] ▷ **-phorous** *adj combining form*

-phoresis *n combining form* indicating a transmission: *electrophoresis* [from Greek *phorēsis* being carried, from *pherein* to bear]

phormium ('fɔ:mɪəm) *n* any plant of the New Zealand bulbous genus *Phormium*, with leathery evergreen leaves and red or yellow flowers in panicles [New Latin, from Greek *phormos* a basket (from a use for the fibres)]

phosgene ('fɒzdʒi:n) *n* a colourless easily liquefied poisonous gas, carbonyl chloride, with an odour resembling that of new-mown hay: used in chemical warfare as a lethal choking agent and in the manufacture of pesticides, dyes, and polyurethane

P

resins. Formula: COCl₂ [C19: from Greek *phôs* light + *-gene*, variant of -GEN]

phosphate ('fɒsfeɪt) *n* **1** any salt or ester of any phosphoric acid, esp a salt of orthophosphoric acid **2** (*often plural*) any of several chemical fertilizers containing phosphorous compounds [C18: from French *phosphat*; see PHOSPHORUS,-ATE¹] > **phosphatic** (fɒsˈfætɪk) *adj*

phosphatide ('fɒsfəˌtaɪd) *n* another name for **phospholipid**

phosphatidylcholine (ˌfɒsfətɪdaɪlˈkəʊliːn) *n* the systematic name for **lecithin**

phosphene ('fɒsfiːn) *n* the sensation of light caused by pressure on the eyelid of a closed eye or by other mechanical or electrical interference with the visual system [C19: from Greek *phôs* light + *phainein* to show]

phosphide ('fɒsfaɪd) *n* any compound of phosphorus with another element, esp a more electropositive element

phosphine ('fɒsfiːn) *n* a colourless flammable gas that is slightly soluble in water and has a strong fishy odour: used as a pesticide. Formula:PH₃

phosphite ('fɒsfaɪt) *n* any salt or ester of phosphorous acid

phospho- *or before a vowel* **phosph-** *combining form* containing phosphorus: *phosphocreatine* [from French, from *phosphore* PHOSPHORUS]

phospholipid (ˌfɒsfəˈlɪpɪd) *n* any of a group of compounds composed of fatty acids, phosphoric acid, and a nitrogenous base: important constituents of all membranes. Also called: **phosphatide**

phosphonic acid (fɒsˈfɒnɪk) *n* the systematic name for **phosphorous acid**

phosphor ('fɒsfə) *n* a substance, such as the coating on a cathode-ray tube,capable of emitting light when irradiated with particles or electromagnetic radiation [C17: from French, ultimately from Greek *phôsphoros* PHOSPHORUS]

phosphorate ('fɒsfəˌreɪt) *vb* to treat or combine with phosphorus

phosphor bronze *n* any of various hard corrosion-resistant alloys containing copper, tin (2–8 per cent), and phosphorus (0.1–0.4 per cent): used in gears, bearings, cylinder casings, etc

phosphoresce (ˌfɒsfəˈrɛs) *vb* (*intr*) to exhibit phosphorescence

phosphorescence (ˌfɒsfəˈrɛsəns) *n* **1** *physics* a fluorescence that persists after the bombarding radiation producing it has stopped **2** the light emitted in phosphorescence **3** the emission of light during a chemical reaction, such as bioluminescence, in which insufficient heat is evolved to cause fluorescence. See **fluorescence** > ˌphosphoˈrescent *adj*

phosphoric (fɒsˈfɒrɪk) *adj* of or containing phosphorus in the pentavalent state

phosphoric acid *n* **1** Also called: **orthophosphoric acid** a colourless solid tribasic acid used in the manufacture of fertilizers and soap. Formula: H₃PO₄ **2** any oxyacid of phosphorus produced by reaction between phosphorus pentoxide and water

phosphorous ('fɒsfərəs) *adj* of or containing phosphorus in the trivalent state

phosphorous acid *n* **1** Also called: **orthophosphorous acid** a white or yellowish hygroscopic crystalline dibasic acid. Formula: H₃PO₃. Systematic name **phosphoric acid 2** any oxyacid of phosphorus containing less oxygen than the corresponding phosphoric acid

phosphorus ('fɒsfərəs) *n* **1** an allotropic nonmetallic element occurring in phosphates and living matter. Ordinary phosphorus is a toxic flammable phosphorescent whitesolid; the red form is less reactive and nontoxic: used in matches, pesticides, and alloys. The radioisotope **phosphorus-32** (**radiophosphorus**), with a half-life of 14.3 days, is used in radiotherapy and as a tracer. Symbol: P; atomic no: 15; atomic wt: 30.973 762; valency: 3 or 5; relative density: 1.82 (white), 2.20 (red); melting pt: 44.1°C (white); boiling pt: 280°C (white) **2** a less common name for a **phosphor** [C17: via

Latin from Greek *phôsphoros* light-bringing, from *phôs* light +*pherein* to bring]

Phosphorus ('fɒsfərəs) *n* a morning star, esp Venus

phossy jaw ('fɒsɪ) *n* a gangrenous condition of the lower jawbone caused by prolonged exposure to phosphorus fumes [C19: *phossy*, colloquial shortening of PHOSPHORUS]

phot (fɒt, fəʊt) *n* a unit of illumination equal to one lumen per square centimetre. 1 phot is equal to 10 000 lux [C20: from Greek *phôs* light]

photic ('fəʊtɪk) *adj* **1** of or concerned with light **2** Also called: **photobathic** designating the zone of the sea where photosynthesis takes place [C19: from PHOTO- + -IC]

photo ('fəʊtəʊ) *n, pl* -**tos** short for **photograph** (sense 1)

photo- *combining form* **1** of, relating to, or produced by light: *photosynthesis* **2** indicating a photographic process: *photolithography* [from Greek *phôs, phôt-* light]

photo call *n* a time arranged for photographers, esp press photographers, to take pictures of a celebrity, the cast of a play, etc, usually for publicity purposes

photocell ('fəʊtəʊˌsɛl) *n* a device in which the photoelectric or photovoltaic effector photoconductivity is used to produce a current or voltage when exposed to light or other electromagnetic radiation. They are used in exposure meters, burglar alarms, etc. Also called: **photoelectric cell, electric eye**

photochemistry (ˌfəʊtəʊˈkɛmɪstrɪ) *n* the branch of chemistry concerned with the chemical effects of light and other electromagnetic radiations

photochromic (ˌfəʊtəʊˈkrəʊmɪk) *adj* (of glass) changing colour with the intensity of incident light, used, for example, in sunglasses that darken as the sunlight becomes brighter

photocomposition (ˌfəʊtəʊˌkɒmpəˈzɪʃən) *n* printing typesetting by exposing type characters onto photographic film or photosensitive paper in order to make printing plates. Also called: **photosetting, phototypesetting**

photoconductivity (ˌfəʊtəʊˌkɒndʌkˈtɪvɪtɪ) *n* the change in the electrical conductivity of certain substances, such as selenium, as a result of the absorption of electromagnetic radiation > **photoconductive** (ˌfəʊtəʊkənˈdʌktɪv) *adj* > ˌphotoconˈductor *n*

photocopier ('fəʊtəʊˌkɒpɪə) *n* an instrument using light-sensitive photographic materials to reproduce written, printed, or graphic work

photocopy ('fəʊtəʊˌkɒpɪ) *n, pl* -**copies 1** a photographic reproduction of written, printed, or graphic work ▷ *vb* -**copies, -copying, -copied 2** to reproduce (written, printed, or graphic work) on photographic material

photodegradable (ˌfəʊtəʊdɪˈɡreɪdəbˀl) *adj* (of plastic) capable of being decomposed by prolonged exposure to light

photoelectric (ˌfəʊtəʊɪˈlɛktrɪk) *or* **photoelectrical** *adj* of or concerned with electric or electronic effects caused by light or other electromagnetic radiation > **photoelectricity** (ˌfəʊtəʊɪlɛkˈtrɪsɪtɪ) *n*

photoelectric cell *n* another name for **photocell**

photoelectric effect *n* **1** the ejection of electrons from a solid by an incident beam of sufficiently energetic electromagnetic radiation **2** any phenomenon involving electricity and electromagnetic radiation, such as photoemission

photoelectron (ˌfəʊtəʊɪˈlɛktrɒn) *n* an electron ejected from an atom, molecule, or solid by an incident photon

photoemission (ˌfəʊtəʊɪˈmɪʃən) *n* the emission of electrons due to the impact of electromagnetic radiation, esp as a result of the photoelectric effect

photoengraving (ˌfəʊtəʊɪnˈɡreɪvɪŋ) *n* **1** a photomechanical process for producing letterpress printing plates **2** a plate made by this process **3** a print made from such a plate > ˌphotoenˈgrave *vb* > ˌphotoenˈgraver *n*

photo finish *n* **1** a finish of a race in which contestants are so close that a photograph is needed to decide the result **2** any race or competition in which the winners or placed contestants are separated by a very small margin

P

Photofit ('fəʊtəʊ,fɪt) *n trademark* **a** a method of combining photographs of facial features,hair, etc, into a composite picture of a face: formerly used by the police to trace suspects from witnesses' descriptions **b** (*as modifier*): *a Photofit picture*

photoflash ('fəʊtəʊ,flæʃ) *n* another name for **flashbulb**

photoflood ('fəʊtəʊ,flʌd) *n* a highly incandescent tungsten lamp used as an artificial light source for indoor photography, television, etc. The brightness is obtained by operating with higher than normal current

photog. *abbreviation* **1** photograph **2** photographer **3** photographic **4** photography

photogenic (,fəʊtəʊ'dʒɛnɪk) *adj* **1** (esp of a person) having features, colouring, and a general facial appearance that look attractive in photographs **2** *biology* producing or emitting light > ,photo'genically *adv*

photogram ('fəʊtə,græm) *n* **1** a picture, usually abstract, produced on a photographic material without the use of a camera, as by placing an object on the material and exposing to light **2** *obsolete* a photograph, often of the more artistic kind rather than a mechanical record

photogrammetry (,fəʊtəʊ'græmɪtrɪ) *n* the process of making measurements from photographs, used esp in the construction of maps from aerial photographs and also in military intelligence, medical and industrial research, etc

photograph ('fəʊtə,grɑːf, -,græf) *n* **1** an image of an object, person, scene, etc, in the form of a print or slide recorded by a camera on photosensitive material. Often shortened to **photo** ▷ *vb* **2** to take a photograph of (an object, person, scene, etc) > pho'tographer *n*

photographic (,fəʊtə'græfɪk) *adj* **1** of or relating to photography **2** like a photograph in accuracy or detail **3** (of a person's memory) able to retain facts, appearances, etc, in precise detail, often after only a very short view of or exposure to them > ,photo'graphically *adv*

photography (fə'tɒgrəfɪ) *n* **1** the process of recording images on sensitized material by the action of light, X-rays, etc, and the chemical processing of this material to produce a print, slide, or cine film **2** the art, practice, or occupation of taking and printing photographs, making cine films, etc

photogravure (,fəʊtəʊgrə'vjʊə) *n* **1** any of various methods in which an intaglio plate for printing is produced by the use of photography **2** matter printed from such a plate [C19: from PHOTO- + French *gravure* engraving]

photojournalism (,fəʊtəʊ'dʒɜːnᵊ,lɪzəm) *n* journalism in which photographs are the predominant feature > ,photo'journalist *n*

photokinesis (,fəʊtəʊkɪ'niːsɪs, -kaɪ-) *n biology* the movement of an organism in response to the stimulus of light

photolithography (,fəʊtəʊlɪ'θɒgrəfɪ) *n* **1** a lithographic printing process using photographically made plates **2** *electronics* a process used in the manufacture of semiconductor devices, thin-film circuits, optical devices, and printed circuits in which a particular pattern is transferred from a photograph onto a substrate, producing a pattern that acts as a mask during an etching or diffusion process > ,photoli'thographer *n*

photoluminescence (,fəʊtəʊ,luːmɪ'nɛsᵊns) *n* luminescence resulting from the absorption of light or infrared or ultraviolet radiation

photolysis (fəʊ'tɒlɪsɪs) *n* chemical decomposition caused by light or other electromagnetic radiation > photolytic (,fəʊtəʊ'lɪtɪk) *adj*

photomechanical (,fəʊtəʊmɪ'kænɪkᵊl) *adj* of or relating to any of various methods by which printing plates are made using photography > ,photome'chanically *adv*

photometer (fəʊ'tɒmɪtə) *n* an instrument used in photometry, usually one that compares the illumination produced by a particular light source with that produced by a standard source

photometry (fəʊ'tɒmɪtrɪ) *n* **1** the measurement of the intensity of light **2** the branch of physics concerned with such measurements > pho'tometrist *n*

photomicrograph (,fəʊtəʊ'maɪkrə,grɑːf, -,græf) *n* a photograph of a microscope image > ,photomi'crography *n*

photomontage (,fəʊtəʊmɒn'tɑːʒ) *n* **1** the technique of producing a composite picture by combining several photographs: used esp in advertising **2** the composite picture so produced

photomultiplier (,fəʊtəʊ'mʌltɪ,plaɪə) *n* a device sensitive to electromagnetic radiation, consisting of a photocathode, from which electrons are released by incident photons, and an electron multiplier, which amplifies and produces a detectable pulse of current

photon ('fəʊtɒn) *n* a quantum of electromagnetic radiation, regarded as a particle with zero rest mass and charge, unit spin, and energy equal to the product of the frequency of the radiation and the Planck constant

photo-offset *n printing* an offset process in which the plates are produced photomechanically

photo opportunity *n* an opportunity, either preplanned or accidental, for the press to photograph a politician, celebrity, or event

photoperiod (,fəʊtəʊ'pɪərɪəd) *n* the period of daylight in every 24 hours, esp in relation to its effects on plants and animals

photoperiodism (,fəʊtəʊ'pɪərɪə,dɪzəm) *n* the response of plants and animals by behaviour, growth,etc, to photoperiods

photophobia (,fəʊtəʊ'fəʊbɪə) *n* **1** *pathol* abnormal sensitivity of the eyes to light, esp as the result of inflammation **2** *psychiatry* abnormal fear of or aversion to sunlight or well-lit places > ,photo'phobic *adj*

photopolymer (,fəʊtəʊ'pɒlɪmə) *n* a polymeric material that is sensitive to light: used in printing plates, microfilms, etc

photoreceptor (,fəʊtəʊrɪ'sɛptə) *n zoology, physiol* a light-sensitive cell or organ that conveys impulses through the sensory neuron connected to it

photorefractive keratectomy (,fəʊtəʊrɪ'fræktɪv ,kɛrə'tɛktəmɪ) *n* laser eye surgery that involves scraping away the protective cells of the cornea before reshaping its surface to improve vision. Abbreviation: PRK

photosensitive (,fəʊtəʊ'sɛnsɪtɪv) *adj* sensitive to electromagnetic radiation, esp light > ,photo,sensi'tivity *n* > photosensitize or photosensitise (,fəʊtəʊ'sɛnsɪ,taɪz) *vb*

photoset ('fəʊtəʊ,sɛt) *vb* -sets, -setting, -set (*tr*) to set (type matter) by photosetting > 'photo,setter *n*

photoshoot ('fəʊtəʊ,ʃuːt) *n* a session in which a photographer takes pictures of someone for publication

Photoshop ('fəʊtəʊ,ʃɒp) *vb* -shops, -shopping, -shopped (*tr*) to alter (a digital photograph or other image), using an image editing application, especially Adobe Photoshop

photosphere ('fəʊtəʊ,sfɪə) *n* the visible surface of the sun, several hundred kilometres thick > photospheric (,fəʊtəʊ'sfɛrɪk) *adj*

photostat ('fəʊtəʊ,stæt) *n* **1** a machine or process used to make quick positive or negative photographic copies of written, printed, or graphic matter **2** any copy made by such a machine ▷ *vb* -stats, -statting or -stating, -statted or -stated **3** to make a photostat copy (of)

photosynthesis (,fəʊtəʊ'sɪnθɪsɪs) *n* (in plants) the synthesis of organic compounds from carbon dioxide and water (with the release of oxygen) using light energy absorbed by chlorophyll > photosynthetic (,fəʊtəʊsɪn'θɛtɪk) *adj* > ,photosyn'thetically *adv*

phototaxis (,fəʊtəʊ'tæksɪs) or **phototaxy** *n* the movement of an entire organism in response to light

phototropism (,fəʊtəʊ'trəʊpɪzəm) *n* the growth response of plant parts to the stimulus of light, producing a bending towards the light source > ,photo'tropic *adj*

photovoltaic effect *n* the effect observed when electromagnetic radiation falls on a thin film of one solid deposited on the surface of a dissimilar solid producing a difference in potential between the two materials

phrasal verb *n* (in English grammar) a phrase that consists of a verb plus an adverbial or prepositional particle, esp one the meaning of which cannot be deduced by analysis of the meaning of the constituents: *"take in" meaning "deceive" is a phrasal verb*

phrase (freɪz) *n* **1** a group of words forming an immediate syntactic constituent of a clause. See **clause** (sense 1) **2** *music* a small group of notes forming a coherent unit of melody ▷ *vb* (*tr*) **3** *music* to divide (a melodic line, part, etc) into musical phrases, esp in performance **4** to express orally or in a phrase [c16: from Latin *phrasis*, from Greek: speech, from *phrazein* to declare,tell]

phrase book *n* a book containing frequently used expressions and their equivalents in a foreign language, esp for the use of tourists

phrase marker *n* *linguistics* a representation, esp one in the form of a tree diagram,of the constituent structure of a sentence

phraseogram ('freɪzɪəˌgræm) *n* a symbol representing a phrase, as in shorthand

phraseology (ˌfreɪzɪ'ɒlədʒɪ) *n*, *pl* -**gies** **1** the manner in which words or phrases are used **2** a set of phrases used by a particular group of people > **phraseological** (ˌfreɪzɪə'lɒdʒɪkəl) *adj*

phrasing ('freɪzɪŋ) *n* **1** the way in which something is expressed, esp in writing; wording **2** *music* the division of a melodic line, part, etc, into musical phrases

phreaking ('fri:kɪŋ) *n* the act of gaining unauthorized access to telecommunication systems, esp to obtain free calls [c20: blend of FREAKING + PHONE]

phrenetic (frɪ'nɛtɪk) *adj* an obsolete spelling of **frenetic** > **phre'netically** *adv*

phrenic ('frɛnɪk) *adj* **1 a** of or relating to the diaphragm **b** (*as noun*): *the phrenic* **2** *obsolete* of or relating to the mind [c18: from New Latin *phrenicus*, from Greek *phrēn* mind, diaphragm]

phrenology (frɪ'nɒlədʒɪ) *n* (formerly) the branch of science concerned with localization of function in the human brain, esp determination of the strength of the faculties by the shape and size of the skull overlying the parts of the brain thought to be responsible for them > **phrenological** (ˌfrɛnə'lɒdʒɪkəl) *adj* > **phre'nologist** *n*

Phrixus ('frɪksəs) *n* *Greek myth* the son of Athamas and Nephele who escaped the wrath of his father's mistress, Ino, by flying to Colchis on a winged ram with a golden fleece. See also **Helle, Golden Fleece**

Phrygia ('frɪdʒɪə) *n* an ancient country of W central Asia Minor

Phrygian ('frɪdʒɪən) *adj* **1** of or relating to ancient Phrygia, its inhabitants, or their extinct language **2** *music* of or relating to an authentic mode represented by the natural diatonic scale from E to E ▷ *n* **3** a native or inhabitant of ancient Phrygia **4** an ancient language of Phrygia, belonging to the Thraco-Phrygian branch of the Indo-European family: recorded in a few inscriptions

Phrygian cap *n* a conical cap of soft material worn during ancient times that became a symbol of liberty during the French Revolution

Phryne ('fraɪnɪ) *n* real name *Muesarete*. 4th century BC, Greek courtesan; lover of Praxiteles and model for Apelles' painting *Aphrodite Rising from the Waves*

phthalate ('θælɪt, 'fθæl-) *n* a salt or ester of phthalic acid. Esters are commonly used as plasticizers in PVC; when ingested they can cause kidney and liver damage

phthalein ('θeɪliːn, -lɪɪn, 'θæl-, 'fθæl-) *n* any of a class of organic compounds obtained by the reaction of phthalic anhydride with a phenol and used in dyes [c19: from *phthal-*, shortened form of NAPHTHALENE +-IN]

phthalic acid ('θælɪk, 'fθæl-) *n* a soluble colourless crystalline acid used in the synthesis of dyes and perfumes; 1,2-benzenedicarboxylic acid. Formula:$C_6H_4(COOH)_2$ [c19 *phthalic*, from *phthal-* (see PHTHALEIN) +-IC]

phthisis ('θaɪsɪs, 'fθaɪ-, 'taɪ-) *n* any disease that causes wasting of the body, esp pulmonary tuberculosis [c16: via Latin from Greek: a wasting away, from *phthinein* to waste away]

Phuket (ˌpuː'kɛt) *n* **1** an island and province of S Thailand, in the Andaman Sea: mainly flat; suffered

badly in the Indian Ocean tsunami of December 2004. Area: 534sq km (206 sq miles) **2** the chief town of the island of Phuket; a popular tourist resort

phut (fʌt) *informal* ▷ *n* **1** a representation of a muffled explosive sound ▷ *adv* **2 go phut** to break down or collapse [c19: of imitative origin]

phycomycete (ˌfaɪkəʊ'maɪsiːt) *n* any of a primitive group of fungi, formerly included in the class *Phycomycetes* but now classified in different phyla: includes certain mildews and moulds

Phyfe or **Fife** (faɪf) *n* Duncan. ?1768–1854, US cabinet-maker, born in Scotland

phyla ('faɪlə) *n* the plural of **phylum**

phylactery (fɪ'læktərɪ) *n*, *pl* -**teries** **1** Also called: **Tefillah** *Judaism* (*usually plural*) either of the pair of blackened square cases containing parchments inscribed with biblical passages, bound by leather thongs to the head and left arm, and worn by Jewish men during weekday morning prayers **2** a reminder or aid to remembering **3** *archaic* an amulet or charm [c14: from Late Latin *phylactērium*, from Greek *phulaktērion* outpost,from *phulax* a guard]

phyletic (faɪ'lɛtɪk) or **phylogenetic** (ˌfaɪləʊdʒɪ'nɛtɪk) *adj* of or relating to the evolution of a species or group of organisms [c19: from Greek *phuletikos* tribal]

-phyll or **-phyl** *n* *combining form* leaf: *chlorophyll* [from Greek *phullon*]

phyllo- or *before a vowel* **phyll-** *combining form* leaf: *phyllopod* [from Greek *phullon* leaf]

phyllode ('fɪləʊd) *n* a flattened leafstalk that resembles and functions as a leaf [c19: from New Latin *phyllodium*, from Greek *phullōdēs* leaflike]

phylloquinone (ˌfɪləʊkwɪ'nəʊn) *n* a viscous fat-soluble liquid occurring in plants: essential for the production of prothrombin, required in blood clotting. Formula:$C_{31}H_{46}O_2$. Also called: **vitamin K₁**

phyllotaxis (ˌfɪlə'tæksɪs) or **phyllotaxy** *n*, *pl* -**taxes** (-'tæksiːz) or -**taxies** **1** the arrangement of the leaves on a stem **2** the study of this arrangement in different plants > ˌ**phyllo'tactic** *adj*

-phyllous *adj combining form* having leaves of a specified number or type: *monophyllous* [from Greek *-phullos* of a leaf]

phylloxera (ˌfɪlɒk'sɪərə, fɪ'lɒksərə) *n*, *pl* -**rae** (-riː) or -**ras** any homopterous insect of the genus *Phylloxera*,such as *P. vitifolia* (or *Viteus vitifolii*) (**vine phylloxera**), typically feeding on plant juices, esp of vines: family *Phylloxeridae* [c19: from New Latin PHYLLO- + Greek *xēros* dry]

phylo- or *before a vowel* **phyl-** *combining form* tribe; race; phylum: *phylogeny* [from Greek *phulon* race]

phylogeny (faɪ'lɒdʒɪnɪ) or **phylogenesis** (ˌfaɪləʊ'dʒɛnɪsɪs) *n*, *pl* -**nies** or -**geneses** (-'dʒɛnɪˌsiːz) *biology* the sequence of events involved in the evolution of a species, genus, etc. See **ontogeny** [c19: from PHYLO- + -GENY] > **phylogenic** (ˌfaɪləʊ'dʒɛnɪk) or **phylogenetic** (ˌfaɪləʊdʒɪ'nɛtɪk) *adj*

phylum ('faɪləm) *n*, *pl* -**la** (-lə) **1** a major taxonomic division of living organisms that contains one or more classes. An example is the phylum *Arthropoda* (insects, crustaceans, arachnids, etc, and myriapods) **2** any analogous group, such as a group of related language families or linguistic stocks [c19: New Latin, from Greek *phulon* race]

phys. *abbreviation* **1** physical **2** physician **3** physics **4** physiological **5** physiology

physalis (faɪ'seɪlɪs) *n* See **Chinese lantern** [New Latin, from Greek *physallis* a bladder (from the form of the calyx)]

physic ('fɪzɪk) *n* **1** *rare* a medicine or drug, esp a cathartic or purge **2** *archaic* the art or skill of healing ▷ *vb* -**ics**, -**icking**, -**icked** **3** (*tr*) *archaic* to treat (a patient) with medicine [c13: from Old French *fisique*, via Latin, from Greek *phusikē*, from *phusis* nature]

physical ('fɪzɪkəl) *adj* **1** of or relating to the body, as distinguished from the mind or spirit **2** of, relating to, or resembling material things or nature: *the physical universe* **3** involving or requiring bodily contact: *rugby is a physical sport* **4** of or concerned with matter and energy **5** of or relating to physics **6** perceptible to the senses;

apparent: *a physical manifestation* ▷ See also **physicals**
> **'physically** *adv*

physical anthropology *n* the branch of anthropology dealing with the genetic aspectof human development and its physical variations

physical chemistry *n* the branch of chemistry concerned with the way in which the physical properties of substances depend on and influence their chemical structure, properties, and reactions

physical education *n* training and practice in sports, gymnastics, etc, as in schools and colleges. Abbreviation: **PE**

physical geography *n* the branch of geography that deals with the natural features of the earth's surface

physical jerks *pl n Brit informal* See **jerk¹** (sense 6)

physicals ('fɪzɪkəlz) *pl n commerce* commodities that can be purchased and used, as opposed to those bought and sold in a futures market. Also called: **actuals**

physical science *n* any of the sciences concerned with nonliving matter, energy, and the physical properties of the universe, such as physics, chemistry, astronomy, and geology

physical therapy *n* another term for **physiotherapy**

physician (fɪ'zɪʃən) *n* **1** a person legally qualified to practise medicine, esp one specializing in areas of treatment other than surgery; doctor of medicine **2** *archaic* any person who treats diseases; healer [c13: from Old French *fisicien*, from *fisique*PHYSIC]

physicist ('fɪzɪsɪst) *n* a person versed in or studying physics

physics ('fɪzɪks) *n (functioning assingular)* **1** the branch of science concerned with the properties of matter and energy and the relationships between them. It is based on mathematics and traditionally includes mechanics, optics, electricity and magnetism, acoustics, and heat. Modern physics, based on quantum theory, includes atomic, nuclear, particle, and solid-state studies. It can also embrace applied fields such as geophysics and meteorology **2** physical properties of behaviour: *the physics of the electron* **3** *archaic* natural science or natural philosophy [c16: from Latin *physica*, translation of Greek *ta phusika* natural things, from *phusis* nature]

physio ('fɪzɪəʊ) *n informal* short for **physiotherapy**

physio- *or before a vowel* **phys-** *combining form* **1** of or relating to nature or natural functions: *physiology* **2** physical: *physiotherapy* [from Greek *phusio*, from *phusis* nature, from *phuein* to make grow]

physiocrat ('fɪzɪəʊ,kræt) *n* a follower of Quesnay's doctrines of government, believing that the inherent natural order governing society was based on land and its natural products as the only true form of wealth [c18: from French *physiocrate*; see PHYSIO-, -CRAT] > **physiocracy** (,fɪzɪ'ɒkrəsɪ) *n*

physiognomy (,fɪzɪ'ɒnəmɪ) *n* **1** a person's features or characteristic expression considered as an indication of personality **2** the art or practice of judging character from facial features **3** the outward appearance of something, esp the physical characteristics of a geographical region [c14: from Old French *phisonomie*, via Medieval Latin, from Late Greek*phusiognōmia*, erroneous for Greek *phusiognōmonia*, from *phusis*nature + *gnōmōn* judge] > **physiognomic** (,fɪzɪə'nɒmɪk) *or* **physiog'nomical** *adj* > **physiog'nomically** *adv* > **physi'ognomist** *n*

physiography (,fɪzɪ'ɒgrəfɪ) *n* another name for **geomorphology**, **physical geography** > **physi'ographer** *n* > **physiographic** (,fɪzɪə'græfɪk) *or* **physio'graphical** *adj*

physiol. *abbreviation* **1** physiological **2** physiology

physiology (,fɪzɪ'ɒlədʒɪ) *n* **1** the branch of science concerned with the functioning of organisms **2** the processes and functions of all or part of an organism [c16: from Latin *physiologia*, from Greek] > **physi'ologist** *n* > **,physio'logical** *adj* > **,physio'logically** *adv*

physiotherapy (,fɪzɪəʊ'θɛrəpɪ) *n* the therapeutic use of physical agents or means, such as massage, exercises, etc > **,physio'therapist** *n*

physique (fɪ'ziːk) *n* the general appearance of the body with regard to size,shape, muscular development, etc [c19: via French, from *physique* (adj) natural, from Latin *physicus* physical]

-phyte *n combining form* indicating a plant of a specified type or habitat: *lithophyte; thallophyte* [from Greek *phuton* plant] > **-phytic** *adj combining form*

phyto- *or before a vowel* **phyt-** *combining form* indicating a plant or vegetation: *phytogenesis* [from Greek *phuton* plant, from *phuein* to make grow]

phytochemical (,faɪtəʊ'kɛmɪkəl) *adj* **1** of or relating to phytochemistry or phytochemicals ▷ *n* **2** a chemical that occurs naturally in a plant

phytochemistry (,faɪtəʊ'kɛmɪstrɪ) *n* the branch of chemistry concerned with plants, their chemical composition and processes > **,phyto'chemist** *n*

phytochrome ('faɪtəʊ,krəʊm) *n botany* a blue-green pigment existing in two interchangeable forms, present in most plants, that mediates many light-dependent processes, including photoperiodism and the greening of leaves

phytogenesis (,faɪtəʊ'dʒɛnɪsɪs) *or* **phytogeny** (faɪ'tɒdʒənɪ) *n* the branch of botany concerned with the origin and evolution of plants

phyton ('faɪtɒn) *n* a unit of plant structure, usually considered as the smallest part of the plant that is capable of growth when detached from the parent plant [c20: from Greek. See -PHYTE]

phytopathology (,faɪtəʊpə'θɒlədʒɪ) *n* the branch of botany concerned with diseases of plants

phytosanitary (,faɪtəʊ'sænɪtərɪ) *adj* of or relating to the health of plants

phytotherapy (,faɪtəʊ'θɛrəpɪ) *n* the use of plants and plant products for medicinal purposes

phytotoxin (,faɪtə'tɒksɪn) *n* a toxin, such as strychnine, that is produced by a plant > **,phyto'toxic** *adj*

pi¹ (paɪ) *n, pl pis* **1** the 16th letter in the Greek alphabet (Π, π), a consonant, transliterated as *p* **2** *maths* a transcendental number, fundamental to mathematics, that is the ratio of the circumference of a circle to its diameter. Approximate value: 3.141 592...; symbol: π [c18 (mathematical use): representing the first letter of Greek *periphereia* PERIPHERY]

pi² *or* **pie** (paɪ) *n, pl pies* **1** a jumbled pile of printer's type **2** a jumbled mixture ▷ *vb* **pies, piing, pied** *or* **pies, pieing, pied** (*tr*) **3** to spill and mix (set type) indiscriminately **4** to mix up [c17: of uncertain origin]

pi³ (paɪ) *adj Brit slang* short for **pious** (senses 2, 3)

PI *abbreviation* **1** Philippine Islands **2** private investigator

Piacenza (Italian pja'tʃɛntsa) *n* a town in N Italy, in Emilia-Romagna on the River Po. Pop: 95 594 (2001)

piacevole (pi:æʃ'eɪvəʊleɪ) *adj* **1** making expiation for a sacrilege **2** requiring expiation [c17: from Latin *piāculum* propitiatory sacrifice, from *piāre* to appease]

piacular (paɪ'ækjʊlə) *adj* **1** making expiation for a sacrilege **2** requiring expiation [c17: from Latin *piāculum* propitiatory sacrifice, from *piāre* to appease]

Piaf (French pjaf) *n* Edith (edit), real name *Edith Giovanna Gassion*, known as *the Little Sparrow*, 1915–63, French singer

piaffe (pɪ'æf) *n dressage* a passage done on the spot [c18: from French, from *piaffer* to strut]

Piaget (French pjaʒe) *n* Jean (ʒɑ̃). 1896–1980, Swiss psychologist, noted for his work on the development of the cognitive functions in children

pia mater ('paɪə 'meɪtə) *n* the innermost of the three membranes (meninges) that cover the brain and spinal cord. See **meninges** [c16: from Medieval Latin, literally: pious mother, intended to translate Arabic *umm raqīqah* tender mother]

pianism ('piːə,nɪzəm) *n* technique, skill, or artistry in playing the piano > **pia'nistic** *adj*

pianissimo (pɪə'nɪsɪ,məʊ) *adj, adv music* (to be performed) very quietly. Symbol: *pp²* [c18: from Italian, superlative of *piano* soft]

pianist ('pɪənɪst) *n* a person who plays the piano

piano¹ (pɪ'ænəʊ) *n, pl -anos* a musical stringed instrument resembling a harp set in a vertical or horizontal frame, played by depressing keys that cause hammers to strike the strings and produce audible vibrations [c19: short for PIANOFORTE]

piano² ('pjɑːnəʊ) *adj, adv music* (to be performed) softly [c17: from Italian, from Latin *plānus* flat; see PLAIN¹]

Piano (Italian pj'ɑno) *n* **Renzo**. born 1937, Italian architect; buildings include the Pompidou Centre, Paris (1977; with Richard Rogers) and the Potsdamer Platz redevelopment, Berlin (1998)

piano accordion *n* an accordion in which the right hand plays a piano-like keyboard. See accordion > piano accordionist *n*

pianoforte (pɪˈænəʊˈfɔːtɪ) *n* the full name for: **piano**[1] [C18: from Italian, originally (*gravecembalo col*) *piano e forte* (harpsichord with) soft and loud; see PIANO[2], FORTE[2]]

Pianola (pɪəˈnəʊlə) *n trademark* a type of mechanical piano in which the keys are depressed by air pressure from bellows, this air flow being regulated by perforations in a paper roll

piano roll *n* a perforated roll of paper actuating the playing mechanism of a Pianola

piastre *or* **piaster** (pɪˈæstə) *n* 1 (formerly) the standard monetary unit of South Vietnam, divided into 100 cents 2 a fractional monetary unit of Egypt, Lebanon, and Syria worth one hundredth of a pound; formerly also used in the Sudan [C17: from French *piastre*, from Italian *piastra d'argento* silver plate; related to Italian *piastro* PLASTER]

Piauí (*Portuguese* pjaˈui) *n* a state of NE Brazil, on the Atlantic: rises to a semiarid plateau, with the more humid Paranaíba valley in the west Capital: Teresina. Pop: 2 898 223 (2002). Area: 250 934 sq km (96 886 sq miles)

Piave (*Italian* ˈpjaːve) *n* a river in NE Italy, rising near the border with Austria and flowing south and southeast to the Adriatic: the main line of Italian defence during World War I. Length: 220 km (137 miles)

piazza (pɪˈætsə, -ˈædzə; *Italian* ˈpjattsa) *n* 1 a large open square in an Italian town 2 *chiefly Brit* a covered passageway or gallery [C16: from Italian: marketplace, from Latin *platēa* courtyard, from Greek *plateia*; see PLACE]

pic (pɪk) *n*, *pl* **pics** *or* **pix** *informal* a photograph, picture, or illustration [C20: shortened from PICTURE]

pica[1] (ˈpaɪkə) *n* 1 Also called: **em, pica em** a printer's unit of measurement, equal to 12 points or 0.166 ins 2 a typewriter type size having 10 characters to the inch [C15: from Anglo-Latin *pīca* list of ecclesiastical regulations, apparently from Latin *pīca* magpie, with reference to its habit of making collections of miscellaneous items; the connection between the original sense (ecclesiastical list) and the typography meanings is obscure]

pica[2] (ˈpaɪkə) *n pathol* an abnormal craving to ingest substances such as clay, dirt, or hair, sometimes occurring during pregnancy, in persons with chlorosis, etc [C16: from medical Latin, from Latin: magpie, being an allusion to its omnivorous feeding habits]

Picabia (pɪˈkɑːbɪə; *French* pikabja) *n* **Francis**. 1879–1953, French painter, designer, and writer, associated with the cubist, Dadaist, and surrealist movements

picador (ˈpɪkəˌdɔː) *n bullfighting* a horseman who pricks the bull with a lance in the early stages of a fight to goad and weaken it [C18: from Spanish, literally: pricker, from *picar* to prick; see PIQUE[1]]

Picard (*French* pikar) *n* **Jean** (ʒɑ̃). 1620–82, French astronomer. He was the first to make a precise measurement of a longitude line, enabling him to estimate the earth's radius

Picardy (ˈpɪkədɪ) *n* a region of N France: mostly low-lying; scene of heavy fighting in World War I. French name: **Picardie** (pikardi)

picaresque (ˌpɪkəˈrɛsk) *adj* of or relating to a type of fiction in which the hero, a rogue, goes through a series of episodic adventures. It originated in Spain in the 16th century [C19: via French from Spanish *picaresco*, from *pícaro* a rogue]

picaroon *or* **pickaroon** (ˌpɪkəˈruːn) *n archaic* an adventurer or rogue [C17: from Spanish *picarón*, from *pícaro*]

Picasso (pɪˈkæsəʊ) *n* **Pablo** (ˈpæbləʊ). 1881–1973, Spanish painter and sculptor, resident in France: a highly influential figure in 20th-century art and a founder, with Braque, of cubism. A prolific artist, his works include *The Dwarf Dancer* (1901), belonging to his blue period; the first cubist painting *Les Demoiselles d'Avignon*

(1907); *Three Dancers* (1925), which appeared in the first surrealist exhibition; and *Guernica* (1937), inspired by an event in the Spanish Civil War

picayune (ˌpɪkɪˈjuːn) *adj* Also: **picayunish** *US & Canadian informal* 1 of small value or importance 2 mean; petty ▷ *n* 3 *US* any coin of little value, esp a five-cent piece [C19: from French *picaillon* coin from Piedmont, from Provençal *picaioun*, of unknown origin]

Piccadilly (ˌpɪkəˈdɪlɪ) *n* one of the main streets of London, running from Piccadilly Circus to Hyde Park Corner

piccalilli (ˈpɪkəˌlɪlɪ) *n* a pickle of mixed vegetables, esp onions, cauliflower, and cucumber, in a mustard sauce [C18 *piccalillo*, perhaps a coinage based on PICKLE]

piccanin (ˈpɪkəˌnɪn, ˌpɪkəˈnɪn) *n South African offensive* a Black African child [variant of PICCANINNY]

piccaninny *or esp US* **pickaninny** (ˌpɪkəˈnɪnɪ) *n*, *pl* **-nies** *offensive* a small Black or Aboriginal child [C17: perhaps from Portuguese *pequenino* tiny one, from *pequeno* small]

Piccard (*French* pikar) *n* 1 **Auguste** (ogyst). 1884–1962, Swiss physicist, whose study of cosmic rays led to his pioneer balloon ascents in the stratosphere (1931–32) 2 his twin brother, **Jean Félix** (ʒɑ̃ feliks). 1884–1963, US chemist and aeronautical engineer, born in Switzerland, noted for his balloon ascent into the stratosphere (1934)

piccolo (ˈpɪkəˌləʊ) *n*, *pl* **-los** a woodwind instrument, the smallest member of the flute family, lying an octave above that of the flute [C19: from Italian: small; compare English PETTY, French *petit*]

pick[1] (pɪk) *vb* 1 to choose (something) deliberately or carefully, from or as if from a group or number; select 2 to pluck or gather (fruit, berries, or crops) from (a tree, bush, field, etc) 3 (*tr*) to remove loose particles from (the teeth, the nose, etc) 4 (esp of birds) to nibble or gather (corn, etc) 5 (when *intr*, foll by *at*) to nibble (at) fussily or without appetite 6 to separate (strands, fibres, etc), as in weaving 7 (*tr*) to provoke (an argument, fight, etc) deliberately 8 (*tr*) to steal (money or valuables) from (a person's pocket) 9 (*tr*) to open (a lock) with an instrument other than a key 10 to pluck the strings of (a guitar, banjo, etc) 11 (*tr*) to make (one's way) carefully on foot: *they picked their way through the rubble* 12 **pick and choose** to select fastidiously, fussily, etc 13 **pick someone's brains** to obtain information or ideas from someone ▷ *n* 14 freedom or right of selection (esp in the phrase **take one's pick**) 15 a person, thing, etc, that is chosen first or preferred: *the pick of the bunch* 16 the act of picking 17 the amount of a crop picked at one period or from one area ▷ See also **pick at, pick off** etc [C15: from earlier *piken* to pick, influenced by French *piquer* to pierce; compare Middle Low German *picken*, Dutch *pikken*]

pick[2] (pɪk) *n* 1 a tool with a handle carrying a long steel head curved and tapering to a point at one or both ends, used for loosening soil, breaking rocks, etc 2 any of various tools used for picking, such as an ice pick or toothpick 3 a plectrum ▷ *vb* 4 (*tr*) to pierce, dig, or break up (a hard surface) with a pick 5 (*tr*) to form (a hole) in this way [C14: perhaps variant of PIKE[2]] > **picker** *n*

pickaback (ˈpɪkəˌbæk) *n*, *adv*, *adj*, *vb* another word for **piggyback**

pick at *vb* (*intr*, *preposition*) to make criticisms of in a niggling or petty manner

pickaxe *or US* **pickax** (ˈpɪkˌæks) *n* 1 a large pick or mattock ▷ *vb* 2 to use a pickaxe on (earth, rocks, etc) [C15: from earlier *pikois* (but influenced also by AXE), from Old French *picois*, from *pic* PICK[2]; compare also PIQUE[1]]

pickerel (ˈpɪkərəl, ˈpɪkrəl) *n*, *pl* **-el** *or* **-els** any of several North American freshwater game fishes, such as *Esox americanus* and *E. niger*: family Esocidae (pikes, walleye, etc) [C14: a small pike; diminutive of PIKE[1]]

Pickering (ˈpɪkərɪŋ) *n* 1 **Edward Charles**. 1846–1919, US astronomer, who invented the meridian photometer 2 his brother, **William Henry**. 1858–1938, US astronomer, who discovered Phoebe, the ninth satellite of Saturn, and predicted (1919) the existence and position of Pluto

picket (ˈpɪkɪt) *n* 1 a pointed stake, post, or peg that is driven into the ground to support a fence, provide a marker for surveying, etc 2 an individual or group that stands outside an establishment to make a protest, to dissuade or prevent employees or clients from entering, etc **3** Also called: **picquet** a small detachment of troops or warships positioned towards the enemy to give early warning of attack ▷ *vb* **4** to post or serve as pickets at (a factory, embassy, etc): *let's go and picket the shop* **5** to guard (a main body or place) by using or acting as a picket **6** (*tr*) to fasten (a horse or other animal) to a picket **7** (*tr*) to fence (an area, boundary, etc) with pickets [c18: from French *piquet*, from Old French *piquer* to prick; see PIKE²] ▷ **'picketer** *n*

picket fence *n* a fence consisting of pickets supported at close regular intervals by being driven into the ground, by interlacing with strong wire, or by nailing to horizontal timbers fixed to posts in the ground

picket line *n* a line of people acting as pickets

Pickford ('pɪkfəd) *n* **Mary**, real name *Gladys Mary Smith*. 1893–1979, US actress in silent films, born in Canada

pickings ('pɪkɪŋz) *pl n* (*sometimes singular*) money, profits, etc, acquired easily or by more or less dishonest means; spoils

pickle ('pɪkᵊl) *n* **1** (*often plural*) vegetables, such as cauliflowers, onions, etc, preserved in vinegar, brine, etc **2** any food preserved in this way **3** a liquid or marinade, such as spiced vinegar, for preserving vegetables, meat, fish, etc **4** *chiefly US & Canadian* a cucumber that has been preserved and flavoured in a pickling solution, such as brine or vinegar **5** *informal* an awkward or difficult situation: *to be in a pickle* **6** *Brit informal* a mischievous child ▷ *vb* (*tr*) **7** to preserve in a pickling liquid **8** to immerse (a metallic object) in a liquid, such as an acid, to remove surface scale [c14: perhaps from Middle Dutch *pekel*; related to German *Pökel* brine] ▷ **'pickler** *n*

pickled ('pɪkᵊld) *adj* **1** preserved in a pickling liquid **2** *informal* intoxicated; drunk

picklock ('pɪk,lɒk) *n* **1** a person who picks locks, esp one who gains unlawful access to premises by this means **2** an instrument for picking locks

pick-me-up *n informal* a tonic or restorative, esp a special drink taken as a stimulant

pick off *vb* (*tr, adverb*) to aim at and shoot one by one

pick on *vb* (*tr, preposition*) to select (someone) for something unpleasant, esp in order to bully, blame, or cause to perform a distasteful task

pick out *vb* (*tr, adverb*) **1** to select for use or special consideration, illustration, etc, as from a group **2** to distinguish (an object from its surroundings), as in painting: *she picked out the woodwork in white* **3** to perceive or recognize (a person or thing previously obscured): *we picked out his face among the crowd* **4** to distinguish (sense or meaning) from or as if from a mass of detail or complication **5** to play (a tune) tentatively, by or as if by ear

pickpocket ('pɪk,pɒkɪt) *n* a person who steals from the pockets or handbags of others in public places

pick-up *n* **1** Also called: **pick-up truck** a small truck with an open body and low sides, used for light deliveries **2** *informal, chiefly US* an ability to accelerate rapidly: *this car has good pick-up* **3** *informal* a casual acquaintance, usually one made with sexual intentions **4** *informal* **a** a stop to collect passengers, goods, etc **b** the people or things collected **5** *informal* an improvement **6** *slang* a pick-me-up ▷ *adj* **7** *US & Canadian* organized, arranged, or assembled hastily and without planning: *a pick-up band; pick-up games* ▷ *vb* **pick up** (*adverb*) **8** (*tr*) to gather up in the hand or hands **9** (*tr*) to acquire, obtain, or purchase casually, incidentally, etc **10** (*tr*) to catch (a disease): *she picked up a bad cold during the weekend* **11** (*intr*) to improve in health, condition, activity, etc: *the market began to pick up* **12** (*reflexive*) to raise (oneself) after a fall or setback **13** (*tr*) to notice or sense: *she picked up a change in his attitude* **14** (*tr*) to resume where one left off; return to: *we'll pick up after lunch; they picked up the discussion* **15** (*tr*) to learn gradually or as one goes along **16** (*tr*) to take responsibility for paying (a bill): *he picked up the bill for dinner* **17** (*tr*) *informal* to reprimand: *he picked her up on her table manners* **18** (*tr*) to collect or give a lift to (passengers, hitchhikers, goods, etc) **19** (*tr*) *informal* to become acquainted with, esp with a view to having sexual relations **20** (*tr*) *informal* to arrest

21 (*tr*) to receive (electrical signals, a radio signal, sounds, etc), as for transmission or amplification

Pickwickian (pɪk'wɪkɪən) *adj* **1** of, relating to, or resembling Mr Pickwick in *The Pickwick Papers*, a novel by English novelist Charles Dickens (1812–70), esp in being naive or benevolent **2** (of the use or meaning of a word, etc) odd or unusual

picky ('pɪkɪ) *adj* **pickier, pickiest** *informal* fussy; finicky; choosy ▷ **'pickily** *adv* ▷ **'pickiness** *n*

picnic ('pɪknɪk) *n* **1** a trip or excursion to the country, seaside, etc, on which people bring food to be eaten in the open air **2 a** any informal meal eaten outside **b** (*as modifier*): *a picnic lunch* **3** *informal, chiefly Austral* a troublesome situation or experience **4** no picnic *informal* a hard or disagreeable task ▷ *vb* **-nics, -nicking, -nicked 5** (*intr*) to eat a picnic [c18: from French *piquenique*, of unknown origin] ▷ **'picnicker** *n*

picnic races *pl n Austral* horse races for amateur riders held in rural areas

pico- *prefix* denoting 10^{-12}: *picofarad* Symbol: p² [from Spanish *pico* small quantity, odd number, peak]

Pico de Aneto (*Spanish* 'piko de a'neto) *n* See **Aneto**

Pico della Mirandola (*Italian* 'piːko ,della mi'randola) *n* Count **Giovanni** (dʒo'vanni). 1463–94, Italian Platonist philosopher. His attempt to reconcile the ideas of classical, Christian, and Arabic writers in a collection of 900 theses, prefaced by his *Oration on the Dignity of Man* (1486), was condemned by the pope

Pico de Teide (*Spanish* 'piko de 'teiðe) *n* See **Teide**

picot ('piːkəʊ) *n* any of a pattern of small loops, as on lace [c19: from French: small point, from *pic* point]

picotee (,pɪkə'tiː) *n* a type of carnation having pale petals edged with a darker colour, usually red [c18: from French *picoté* marked with points, from PICOT]

picric acid ('pɪkrɪk) *n* a toxic sparingly soluble crystalline yellow acid used as a dye, antiseptic, and explosive. Formula: $C_6H_2OH(NO_2)_3$

Pict (pɪkt) *n* a member of any of the peoples who lived in Britain north of the Forth and Clyde in the first to the fourth centuries AD: later applied chiefly to the inhabitants of NE Scotland. Throughout Roman times the Picts carried out border raids [Old English *Peohtas*; later forms from Late Latin *Pictī* painted men, from *pingere* to paint] ▷ **'Pictish** *n, adj*

pictograph ('pɪktə,grɑːf, -,græf) *n* **1** a picture or symbol standing for a word or group of words, as in written Chinese **2** a chart on which symbols are used to represent values, such as population levels or consumption [c19: from Latin *pictus*, from *pingere* to paint] ▷ **pictographic** (,pɪktə'græfɪk) *adj* ▷ **pictography** (pɪk'tɒgrəfɪ) *n*

pictorial (pɪk'tɔːrɪəl) *adj* **1** relating to, consisting of, or expressed by pictures **2** (of books, newspapers, etc) containing pictures **3** (of language, style, etc) suggesting a picture; vivid; graphic ▷ *n* **4** a magazine, newspaper, etc, containing many pictures [c17: from Late Latin *pictōrius*, from Latin *pictor* painter, from *pingere* to paint] ▷ **pic'torially** *adv*

picture ('pɪktʃə) *n* **1 a** a visual representation of something, such as a person or scene, produced on a surface, as in a photograph, painting, etc **b** (*as modifier*): *picture gallery; picture postcard* **2** a mental image or impression: *a clear picture of events* **3** a verbal description, esp one that is vivid **4** a situation considered as an observable scene: *the political picture* **5** a person or thing that bears a close resemblance to another: *he was the picture of his father* **6** a person, scene, etc, considered as typifying a particular state or quality: *the picture of despair* **7** a complete image on a television screen, comprising two interlaced fields **8 a** a motion picture; film **b** (*as modifier*): *picture theatre* **9 the pictures** *chiefly Brit & Austral* a cinema or film show **10** another name for **tableau vivant 11 in the picture** informed about a given situation ▷ *vb* (*tr*) **12** to visualize or imagine **13** to describe or depict, esp vividly **14** (*often passive*) to put in a picture or make a picture of: *they were pictured sitting on the rocks* [c15: from Latin *pictūra* painting, from *pingere* to paint]

picture card *n* another name for **court card**

picture hat n a decorated hat with a very wide brim, esp as worn by women in paintings by Gainsborough and Reynolds

picture house n chiefly Brit an old-fashioned name for **cinema** (sense 1a)

picture messaging n 1 the practice of sending and receiving photographs by mobile phone 2 the practice of communicating by mobile phone using graphics or pictures rather than text

picture moulding n 1 the edge around a framed picture 2 Also called: **picture rail** the moulding or rail near the top of a wall from which pictures can be hung

picture palace n Brit an old-fashioned name for **cinema** (sense 1a)

picture phone n a mobile phone that can take, send, and receive photographs

picturesque (,pɪktʃə'rɛsk) adj 1 visually pleasing, esp in being striking or vivid: a picturesque view 2 (of language) graphic; vivid [c18: from French pittoresque (but also influenced by PICTURE), from Italian pittoresco, from pittore painter, from Latin pictor] ▷ ,pictur'esquely adv ▷ ,pictur'esqueness n

picture tube n another name for **television tube**

picture window n a large window having a single pane of glass, usually placed so that it overlooks a view

picture writing n 1 any writing system that uses pictographs 2 a system of artistic expression and communication using pictures or symbolic figures

PID abbreviation pelvic inflammatory disease

piddle ('pɪdəl) vb 1 (intr) informal to urinate 2 (when tr, often foll by away) to spend (one's time) aimlessly; fritter [c16: origin unknown] ▷ **piddler** n

piddling ('pɪdlɪŋ) adj informal petty; trifling; trivial ▷ **piddlingly** adv

piddock ('pɪdək) n any marine bivalve of the family Pholadidae, boring into rock, clay, or wood by means of sawlike shell valves [c19: origin uncertain]

pidgin ('pɪdʒɪn) n a language made up of elements of two or more other languages and used for contacts, esp trading contacts, between the speakers of other languages. Unlike creoles, pidgins do not constitute the mother tongue of any speech community [c19: perhaps from Chinese pronunciation of English business]

pidgin English n a pidgin in which one of the languages involved is English

pie[1] (paɪ) n 1 a baked food consisting of a sweet or savoury filling in a pastry-lined dish, often covered with a pastry crust 2 **pie in the sky** illusory hope or promise of some future good; false optimism [c14: of obscure origin]

pie[2] (paɪ) n an archaic or dialect name for **magpie** [c13: via Old French from Latin pīca magpie; related to Latin pīcus woodpecker]

pie[3] (paɪ) n, vb printing a variant spelling of **pi**[2]

piebald ('paɪ,bɔːld) adj 1 marked or spotted in two different colours, esp black and white ▷ n 2 a black-and-white pied horse [c16: PIE[2] + BALD; see also PIED]

pie cart n NZ a mobile van selling warmed-up food and drinks

piece (piːs) n 1 an amount or portion forming a separate mass or structure; bit: a piece of wood 2 a small part, item, or amount forming part of a whole, esp when broken off or separated: a piece of bread 3 a length by which a commodity is sold, esp cloth, wallpaper, etc 4 an instance or occurrence: a piece of luck 5 an example or specimen of a style or type, such as an article of furniture: a beautiful piece of Dresden china 6 informal an opinion or point of view: to state one's piece 7 a literary, musical, or artistic composition 8 a coin having a value as specified: fifty-pence piece 9 a small object, often individually shaped and designed, used in playing certain games, esp board games: chess pieces 10 a firearm or cannon 11 any chessman other than a pawn 12 Scot & English dialect a packed lunch taken to work, school, etc 13 **go to pieces a** (of a person) to lose control of oneself; have a breakdown **b** (of a building, organization, etc) to disintegrate 14 **nasty piece of work** Brit informal a cruel or mean person 15 **of a piece** of the same kind; alike ▷ vb (tr) 16 (often foll by together) to fit or assemble piece by

piece 17 (often foll by up) to patch or make up (a garment) by adding pieces [c13 pece, from Old French, of Gaulish origin; compare Breton pez piece, Welsh peth portion]

pièce de résistance French (pjɛs də rezistãs) n 1 the principal or most outstanding item in a series or creative artist's work 2 the main dish of a meal [lit: piece of resistance]

piece goods pl n goods, esp fabrics, made in standard widths and lengths. Also called: **yard goods**

piecemeal ('piːs,miːl) adv 1 by degrees; bit by bit; gradually 2 in or into pieces or piece from piece ▷ adj 3 fragmentary or unsystematic: a piecemeal approach [c13 pecemele, from PIECE + -mele, from Old English mælum quantity taken at one time]

piece of eight n, pl **pieces of eight** a former Spanish coin worth eight reals; peso

piecework ('piːs,wɜːk) n work paid for according to the quantity produced

pie chart n a circular graph divided into sectors proportional to the magnitudes of the quantities represented

piecrust table ('paɪ,krʌst) n a round table, ornamented with carved moulding suggestive of a pie crust

pied (paɪd) adj having markings of two or more colours [c14: from PIE[2]; an allusion to the magpie's black-and-white colouring]

pied-à-terre (,pjeɪtɑː'tɛə) n, pl **pieds-à-terre** (,pjeɪtɑː'tɛə) a flat, house, or other lodging for secondary or occasional use [French, literally: foot on (the) ground]

piedmont ('piːdmɒnt) adj (prenominal) (of glaciers, plains, etc) formed or situated at the foot of a mountain or mountain range [from Italian piémonte mountain foot]

Piedmont ('piːdmɒnt) n 1 a region of NW Italy: consists of the upper Po Valley; mainly agricultural. Chief town: Turin. Pop: 4 231 334 (2003 est). Area: 25 399 sq km (9807 sq miles). Italian name: **Piemonte** 2 a low plateau of the eastern US, between the coastal plain and the Appalachian Mountains

Pied Piper n 1 Also called: **the Pied Piper of Hamelin** (in German legend) a piper who rid the town of Hamelin of rats by luring them away with his music and then, when he was not paid for his services, lured away its children 2 (sometimes not capitals) a person who entices others to follow him

pied wagtail n a British songbird, Motacilla alba yarrellii, with a black throat and back, long black tail, and white underparts and face: family Motacillidae (wagtails and pipits)

pie-eyed adj a slang term for **drunk** (sense 1)

Piemonte (Italian pje'monte) n the Italian name for **Piedmont** (sense 1)

Pienaar (pɪə'nɑː) n (Jacobus) Francois: born 1967, South African Rugby Union footballer; captain of the South African team that won the Rugby World Cup in 1995

pier (pɪə) n 1 a structure with a deck that is built out over water, and used as a landing place, promenade, etc 2 a pillar that bears heavy loads, esp one of rectangular cross section 3 the part of a wall between two adjacent openings 4 another name for **buttress** (sense 1) [c12 per, from Anglo-Latin pera pier supporting a bridge]

pierce (pɪəs) vb (mainly tr) 1 to thrust into or penetrate sharply or violently 2 to force (a way, route, etc) through (something) 3 (of light) to shine through or penetrate (darkness) 4 (also intr) to discover or realize (something) suddenly or (of an idea) to become suddenly apparent 5 (of sounds or cries) to sound sharply through (the silence) 6 to move or affect (a person's emotions, bodily feelings, etc) deeply or sharply 7 (intr) to penetrate or be capable of penetrating: piercing cold [c13 percen, from Old French percer, ultimately from Latin pertundere, from per through + tundere to strike]

Pierce (pɪəs) n **Franklin**. 1804–69, US statesman; 14th president of the US (1853–57)

piercing ('pɪəsɪŋ) adj 1 (of a sound) sharp and shrill 2 (of eyes or a look) intense and penetrating 3 (of cold or wind) intense or biting ▷ n 4 the art or practice of piercing body parts for the insertion of jewellery 5 an instance of the piercing of a body part ▷ **piercingly** adv

pier glass *n* a tall narrow mirror, usually one of a pair or set, designed to hang on the wall between windows, usually above a pier table

Pieria (paɪˈɪərɪə) *n* a region of ancient Macedonia, west of the Gulf of Salonika: site of the Pierian Spring

Pierian Spring *n* a sacred fountain in Pieria, in Greece, fabled to inspire those who drank from it

Pierides (paɪˈɪərɪˌdiːz) *pl n* *Greek myth* **1** the Muses. See **Muse 2** nine maidens of Thessaly, who were defeated in a singing contest by the Muses and turned into magpies for their effrontery

pieris (ˈpaɪərɪs) *n* any plant of a genus, *Pieris*, of American and Asiatic shrubs, esp *P. formosa forrestii*, grown for the bright red colour of its young foliage: family *Ericaceae* [New Latin, from Greek *Pierides*, a name for the Muses]

Piero della Francesca (Italian ˈpjɛːro ˌdella franˈtʃeska) *n* ?1420–92, Italian painter, noted particularly for his frescoes of the *Legend of the True Cross* in San Francesco, Arezzo

Piero di Cosimo (Italian ˈpjɛːro di ˈkɔːzimo) *n* 1462–1521, Italian painter, noted for his mythological works

Pierre (pɪə) *n* a city in central South Dakota, capital of the state, on the Missouri River. Pop: 13 502 (2003 est)

Pierrot (ˈpɪərəʊ; *French* pjɛro) *n* **1 a** male character from French pantomime with a whitened face, white costume, and pointed hat **2** (*usually not capital*) a clown or masquerader so made up

pier table *n* a side table designed to stand against a wall between windows

pietà (pɪɛˈtɑː) *n* a sculpture, painting, or drawing of the dead Christ, supported by the Virgin Mary [Italian: pity, from Latin *pietās* PIETY]

Pietermaritzburg (ˌpiːtəˈmærɪtsˌbɜːɡ) *n* a city in E South Africa, the capital of KwaZulu-Natal: founded in 1839 by the Boers: gateway to Natal's mountain resorts. Pop: 223 519 (2001)

pietism (ˈpaɪɪˌtɪzəm) *n* a less common word for **piety** > ˈpietist *n* > ˌpieˈtistic *or* ˌpieˈtistical *adj*

piet-my-vrou (ˈpiːtˌmeɪˈfrəʊ) *n* *South African* a cuckoo, *Notococcyx solitarius*, having a red breast [from Afrikaans *piet* Peter + *my* my + *vrou* wife: onomatopoeic, based on the bird's three clear notes]

Pietro da Cortona (Italian ˈpjɛːro da korˈtoːna) *n* real name *Pietro Berrettini*. 1596–1669, Italian baroque painter and architect

piety (ˈpaɪɪtɪ) *n, pl* **-ties 1** dutiful devotion to God and observance of religious principles **2** the quality or characteristic of being pious **3** *now rare* devotion and obedience to parents or superiors [C13 *piete*, from Old French, from Latin *pietās* piety, dutifulness, from *pius* PIOUS]

piezoelectric effect *or* **piezoelectricity** (paɪˌiːzəʊɪlɛkˈtrɪsɪtɪ) *n* *physics* **a** the production of electricity or electric polarity by applying a mechanical stress to certain crystals **b** the converse effect in which stress is produced in a crystal as a result of an applied potential difference > piˌezoeˈlectrically *adv*

piffling (ˈpɪflɪŋ) *adj* worthless, trivial

pig (pɪɡ) *n* **1** any artiodactyl mammal of the African and Eurasian family *Suidae*, esp *Sus scrofa* (**domestic pig**), typically having a long head with a movable snout, a thick bristle-covered skin, and, in wild species, long curved tusks **2** a domesticated pig weighing more than 120 pounds (54 kg). Related adj: **porcine 3** *informal* a dirty, greedy, or bad-mannered person **4** the meat of swine; pork **5** *derogatory* a slang word for **policeman 6 a** a mass of metal, such as iron, copper, or lead, cast into a simple shape for ease of storing or transportation **b** a mould in which such a mass of metal is formed **7** *Brit informal* something that is difficult or unpleasant **8** an automated device propelled through a duct or pipeline to clear impediments or check for faults, leaks, etc **9** a pig in a poke something bought or received without prior sight or knowledge **10** make a pig of oneself *informal* to overindulge oneself **11** on the pig's back *Irish & NZ* successful; established: *he's on the pig's back now* ▷ *vb* **pigs, pigging, pigged 12** (*intr*) (of a sow) to give birth **13** Also called: **pig it** (*intr*) *informal* to live in

squalor **14** Also: **pig out** (*tr*) *informal* to devour (food) greedily [C13 *pigge*, of obscure origin]

pigeon (ˈpɪdʒɪn) *n* *Brit informal* concern or responsibility (often in the phrase **it's his, her,** etc, **pigeon**) [C19: altered from PIDGIN]

pigeon breast *n* a deformity of the chest characterized by an abnormal protrusion of the breastbone, caused by rickets or by obstructed breathing during infancy

pigeonhole (ˈpɪdʒɪnˌhəʊl) *n* **1 a** small compartment for papers, letters, etc, as in a bureau **2** a hole or recess in a dovecote for pigeons to nest in **3** *informal* a category or classification ▷ *vb* (*tr*) **4** to put aside or defer **5** to classify or categorize, esp in a rigid manner

pigeon-toed *adj* having the toes turned inwards

pigface (ˈpɪɡˌfeɪs) *n* *Austral* a creeping succulent plant of the genus *Carpobrotus*, having bright-coloured flowers and red fruits and often grown for ornament: family *Aizoaceae*

piggery (ˈpɪɡərɪ) *n, pl* **-geries 1** a place where pigs are kept and reared **2** great greediness; piggishness

piggish (ˈpɪɡɪʃ) *adj* **1** like a pig, esp in appetite or manners **2** *informal, chiefly Brit* obstinate or mean > ˈpiggishly *adv* > ˈpiggishness *n*

Piggott (ˈpɪɡət) *n* **Lester (Keith)**. born 1935, English flat-racing jockey: he won the Derby nine times

piggy (ˈpɪɡɪ) *n, pl* **-gies 1** a child's word for a pig, esp a piglet **2** piggy in the middle **a** a children's game in which one player attempts to retrieve a ball thrown over him or her by at least two other players **b** a situation in which a person or group is caught up in a disagreement between other people or groups

piggyback (ˈpɪɡɪˌbæk) *or* **pickaback** *n* **1** a ride on the back and shoulders of another person **2** a system whereby a vehicle, aircraft, etc, is transported for part of its journey on another vehicle, such as a flat railway wagon, another aircraft, etc ▷ *adv* **3** on the back and shoulders of another person **4** on or as an addition to something else ▷ *adj* **5** of or for a piggyback: *a piggyback ride; piggyback lorry trains* **6** of or relating to a type of heart transplant in which the transplanted heart functions in conjunction with the patient's own heart

piggy bank *n* a child's coin bank shaped like a pig with a slot for coins

pig-headed *adj* stupidly stubborn > ˌpig-ˈheadedly *adv* > ˌpig-ˈheadedness *n*

pig iron *n* crude iron produced in a blast furnace and poured into moulds in preparation for making wrought iron, steels, alloys, etc

Pig Island *n* *NZ informal* New Zealand

pig-jump *vb* (*intr*) (of a horse) to jump from all four legs

piglet (ˈpɪɡlɪt) *n* a young pig

pigmeat (ˈpɪɡˌmiːt) *n* a less common name for **pork** or **ham**¹

pigment (ˈpɪɡmənt) *n* **1** a substance occurring in plant or animal tissue and producing a characteristic colour, such as chlorophyll in green plants and haemoglobin in red blood **2** any substance used to impart colour **3** a powder that is mixed with a liquid to give a paint, ink, etc [C14: from Latin *pigmentum*, from *pingere* to paint] > ˈpigmentary *adj*

pigmentation (ˌpɪɡmənˈteɪʃən) *n* **1** coloration in plants, animals, or man caused by the presence of pigments **2** the deposition of pigment in animals, plants, or man

Pigmy (ˈpɪɡmɪ) *n, pl* **-mies** a variant spelling of **Pygmy**

pignut (ˈpɪɡˌnʌt) *n* **1** Also called: **hognut a** the bitter nut of any of several North American hickory trees, esp *Carya glabra* (**brown hickory**) **b** any of the trees bearing such a nut **2** another name for **earthnut**

Pigouvian tax (pɪˈɡuːvɪən) *n* a tax levied to counter an economic negative externality, for example taxing producers of industrial pollution in order to encourage pollution control [C20: named after Arthur Pigou (1877-1959), English economist]

pig-root *vb* (*intr*) *Austral & NZ* another term for: **pig-jump**

pigs (pɪɡz) *interj* *Austral slang* an expression of derision or disagreement. Also: **pig's arse, pig's bum**

Pigs (pɪɡz) *n* Bay of Pigs See **Bay of Pigs**

pigskin (ˈpɪɡˌskɪn) *n* **1** the skin of the domestic pig **2** leather made of this skin **3** *US & Canadian informal* a football ▷ *adj* **4** made of pigskin

pigsticking ('pɪg,stɪkɪŋ) *n* the sport of hunting wild boar ▷ **'pig,sticker** *n*

pigsty ('pɪg,staɪ) *or US and Canadian* **pigpen** *n, pl* -sties **1** a pen for pigs; sty **2** *Brit* a dirty or untidy place

pigswill ('pɪg,swɪl) *n* waste food or other edible matter fed to pigs. Also called: pig's wash

pigtail ('pɪg,teɪl) *n* **1 a** a bunch of hair or one of two bunches on either side of the face, worn loose or plaited **2** a twisted roll of tobacco ▷ **'pig,tailed** *adj*

pika ('paɪkə) *n* any burrowing lagomorph mammal of the family *Ochotonidae* of mountainous regions of North America and Asia, having short rounded ears, a rounded body, and rudimentary tail. Also called: cony [C19: from Tungusic *piika*]

pikau ('piːkaʊ) *n* NZ a pack, knapsack, or rucksack [Māori]

pike¹ (paɪk) *n, pl* pike *or* pikes **1** any of several large predatory freshwater teleost fishes of the genus *Esox*, esp *E. lucius* (**northern pike**), having a broad flat snout, strong teeth, and an elongated body covered with small scales: family *Esocidae* **2** any of various similar fishes [C14: short for *pikefish*, from Old English *pīc* point, with reference to the shape of its jaw]

pike² (paɪk) *n* **1 a** a medieval weapon consisting of an iron or steel spearhead joined to a long pole, the pikestaff **2** a point or spike ▷ *vb* **3** (*tr*) to stab or pierce using a pike [Old English *pīc* point, of obscure origin] ▷ **'pikeman** *n*

pike³ (paɪk) *n* short for **turnpike** (sense 1)

pike⁴ (paɪk) *n* Northern English dialect a pointed or conical hill [Old English *pīc*, of obscure origin]

pike⁵ (paɪk) *or* **piked** (paɪkt) *adj* (of the body position of a diver) bent at the hips but with the legs straight [C20: of obscure origin]

pikelet ('paɪklɪt) *n* a dialect word for a **crumpet** (sense 1) [C18: from Welsh *bara pyglyd* pitchy bread]

pikeperch ('paɪk,pɜːtʃ) *n, pl* -perch *or* -perches any of various pikelike freshwater teleost fishes of the genera *Stizostedion* (or *Lucioperca*), such as *S. lucioperca* of Europe: family *Percidae* (perches)

piker ('paɪkə) *n* slang **1** Austral a wild bullock **2** Austral & NZ a useless person; failure **3** US, Austral & NZ a lazy person; shirker **4** a mean person [C19: perhaps related to PIKE³]

Pikes Peak *n* a mountain in central Colorado, in the Rockies. Height: 4300 m (14 109 ft)

pikestaff ('paɪk,stɑːf) *n* the wooden handle of a pike

pikey ('paɪkɪ) *n* Brit slang, derogatory **1** a gypsy or vagrant **2** a member of the underclass [perhaps from TURNPIKE]

pilaster (pɪˈlæstə) *n* a shallow rectangular column attached to the face of a wall [C16: from French *pilastre*, from Latin *pīla* pillar] ▷ **pi'lastered** *adj*

Pilate ('paɪlət) *n* **Pontius** ('pɒnʃəs, 'pɒntɪəs). Roman procurator of Judaea (?26–?36 AD), who ordered the crucifixion of Jesus, allegedly against his better judgment

Pilatus (German piˈlaːtʊs) *n* a mountain in central Switzerland, in Unterwalden canton: derives its name from the legend that the body of Pontius Pilate lay in a former lake on the mountain. Height: 2122 m (6962 ft)

pilau (pɪˈlaʊ), **pilaf**, **pilaff**, ('pɪlæf) **pilao**, (pɪˈlaʊ) **pilaw** (pɪˈlɔː) *or* **pulao** (puˈlaʊ) *n* a dish originating from the East, consisting of rice flavoured with spices and cooked in stock, to which meat, poultry, or fish may be added [C17: from Turkish *pilāw*, from Persian]

pilchard ('pɪltʃəd) *n* **1** a European food fish, *Sardina* (or *Clupea*) *pilchardus*, with a rounded body covered with large scales: family *Clupeidae* (herrings) **2** a related fish, *Sardinops neopilchardus*, of S Australian waters [C16: *pylcher*, of obscure origin]

Pilcomayo (Spanish pilkoˈmajo) *n* a river in S central South America, rising in W central Bolivia and flowing southeast, forming the border between Argentina and Paraguay, to the Paraguay River at Asunción. Length: about 1600 km (1000 miles)

pile¹ (paɪl) *n* **1** a collection of objects laid on top of one another or of other material stacked vertically; heap; mound **2** *informal* a large amount of money (esp in the phrase **make a pile**) **3** (*often plural*) *informal* a large

amount: *a pile of work* **4** a less common word for **pyre** **5** a large building or group of buildings **6** short for **voltaic pile** **7** physics a structure of uranium and a moderator used for producing atomic energy; nuclear reactor **8** metallurgy an arrangement of wrought-iron bars that are to be heated and worked into a single bar **9** the point of an arrow ▷ *vb* **10** (often foll by *up*) to collect or be collected into or as if into a pile: *snow piled up in the drive* **11** (*intr*; foll by *in, into, off, out*, etc) to move in a group, esp in a hurried or disorganized manner: *to pile off the bus* **12 pile arms** to prop a number of rifles together, muzzles together and upwards, butts forming the base **13 pile it on** *informal* to exaggerate ▷ See also **pile up** [C15: via Old French from Latin *pīla* stone pier]

pile² (paɪl) *n* **1** a long column of timber, concrete, or steel that is driven into the ground to provide a foundation for a vertical load (a **bearing pile**) or a group of such columns to resist a horizontal load from earth or water pressure (a **sheet pile**) **2** heraldry an ordinary shaped like a wedge, usually displayed point-downwards ▷ *vb* (*tr*) **3** to drive (piles) into the ground **4** to provide or support (a structure) with piles [Old English *pīl*, from Latin *pīlum*]

pile³ (paɪl) *n* **1** textiles **a** the yarns in a fabric that stand up or out from the weave, as in carpeting, velvet, flannel, etc **b** one of these yarns **2** soft fine hair, fur, wool, etc [C15: from Anglo-Norman *pyle*, from Latin *pilus* hair]

pileate ('paɪlɪɪt, -,eɪt, 'pɪl-) *or* **pileated** ('paɪlɪ,eɪtɪd, 'pɪl-) *adj* **1** (of birds) having a crest **2** botany having a pileus [C18: from Latin *pīleātus* wearing a felt cap, from PILEUS]

pile-driver *n* **1** a machine that drives piles into the ground either by repeatedly allowing a heavy weight to fall on the head of the pile or by using a steam hammer **2** *informal* a forceful punch or kick

pileous ('paɪlɪəs, 'pɪl-) *adj* biology **1** hairy **2** of or relating to hair [C19: ultimately from Latin *pilus* a hair]

piles (paɪlz) *pl n* a nontechnical name for **haemorrhoids** [C15: from Latin *pilae* balls (referring to the appearance of external piles)]

pileum ('paɪlɪəm, 'pɪl-) *n, pl* -lea (-lɪə) the top of a bird's head from the base of the bill to the occiput [C19: New Latin, from PILEUS]

pile up *vb* (*adverb*) **1** to gather or be gathered in a pile; accumulate **2** *informal* to crash or cause to crash ▷ *n* pile-up **3** *informal* a multiple collision of vehicles

pileus ('paɪlɪəs, 'pɪl-) *n, pl* -lei (-lɪ,aɪ) the upper cap-shaped part of a mushroom or similar spore-producing body [C18 (botanical use): New Latin, from Latin: felt cap]

pilewort ('paɪl,wɜːt) *n* any of several plants, such as lesser celandine, thought to be effective in treating piles

pilfer ('pɪlfə) *vb* to steal (minor items), esp in small quantities [C14 *pylfre* (n) from Old French *pelfre* booty; see PELF] ▷ **'pilferer** *n* ▷ **'pilfering** *n*

pilgrim ('pɪlgrɪm) *n* **1** a person who undertakes a journey to a sacred place as an act of religious devotion **2** any wayfarer [C12: from Provençal *pelegrin*, from Latin *peregrīnus* foreign, from *per* through + *ager* field, land; see PEREGRINE]

pilgrimage ('pɪlgrɪmɪdʒ) *n* **1** a journey to a shrine or other sacred place **2** a journey or long search made for exalted or sentimental reasons ▷ *vb* **3** (*intr*) to make a pilgrimage

Pilgrim Fathers *or* **Pilgrims** *pl n* the **Pilgrim Fathers** the English Puritans who sailed on the Mayflower to New England, where they founded Plymouth Colony in SE Massachusetts (1620)

piliferous (paɪˈlɪfərəs) *adj* **1** (esp of plants or their parts) bearing or ending in a hair or hairs **2** designating the outer layer of root epidermis, which bears the root hairs [C19: from Latin *pilus* hair + -FEROUS. Compare PILE³]

piling ('paɪlɪŋ) *n* **1** the act of driving piles **2** a number of piles **3** a structure formed of piles

pill¹ (pɪl) *n* **1** a small spherical or ovoid mass of a medicinal substance, intended to be swallowed whole **2 the pill** (*sometimes capital*) *informal* an oral contraceptive **3** something unpleasant that must be endured (esp in the phrase **bitter pill to swallow**) **4** *slang* a ball or disc **5** a small ball of matted fibres that forms on the surface of a fabric through rubbing **6** *slang* an unpleasant or boring person ▷ *vb* **7** (*tr*) to give pills to **8** (*tr*) to make pills of **9** (*intr*) **a** to form into small balls **b** (of a fabric) to form small balls of fibre on its surface through rubbing **10** (*tr*) *slang* to blackball [c15: from Middle Flemish *pille*, from Latin *pilula* a little ball, from *pila* ball]

pill² (pɪl) *vb* **1** *archaic or dialect* to peel or skin (something) **2** *archaic* to pillage or plunder (a place) **3** *obsolete* to make or become bald [Old English *pilian*, from Latin *pilāre* to strip]

pillage ('pɪlɪdʒ) *vb* **1** to rob (a town, village, etc) of (booty or spoils), esp during a war ▷ *n* **2** the act of pillaging **3** something obtained by pillaging; booty [c14: via Old French from *piller* to despoil, probably from *peille* rag, from Latin *pīleus* felt cap] > **'pillager** *n*

pillar ('pɪlə) *n* **1** an upright structure of stone, brick, metal, etc, that supports a superstructure or is used for ornamentation **2** something resembling this in shape or function: *a pillar of stones; a pillar of smoke* **3** a tall, slender, usually sheer rock column, forming a separate top **4** a prominent supporter: *a pillar of the Church* **5** from **pillar to post** from one place to another ▷ *vb* **6** (*tr*) to support with or as if with pillars [c13: from Old French *pilier*, from Latin *pīla*; see PILE¹]

pillar box *n* (in Britain) a red pillar-shaped public letter box situated on a pavement

Pillars of Hercules *pl n* the two promontories at the E end of the Strait of Gibraltar: the Rock of Gibraltar on the European side and the Jebel Musa on the African side; according to legend, formed by Hercules

pillbox ('pɪl,bɒks) *n* **1** a box for pills **2** a small enclosed fortified emplacement, usually made of reinforced concrete **3** a small round hat, now worn esp by women

pillion ('pɪljən) *n* **1** a seat or place behind the rider of a motorcycle, scooter, horse, etc ▷ *adv* **2** on a pillion: *to ride pillion* [c16: from Gaelic; compare Scottish *pillean*, Irish *pillín* couch; related to Latin *pellis* skin]

pilliwinks ('pɪlɪ,wɪŋks) *pl n* a medieval instrument of torture for the fingers and thumbs [c14: of uncertain origin]

pillock ('pɪlək) *n* *Brit slang* a stupid or annoying person [c14: from Scandinavian dialect *pillicock* penis]

pillory ('pɪlərɪ) *n*, *pl* **-ries 1** a wooden framework into which offenders were formerly locked by the neck and wrists and exposed to public abuse and ridicule **2** exposure to public scorn or abuse ▷ *vb* **-ries, -rying, -ried** (*tr*) **3** to expose to public scorn or ridicule **4** to punish by putting in a pillory [c13: from Anglo-Latin *pillorium*, from Old French *pilori*, of uncertain origin; related to Provençal *espillori*]

pillow ('pɪləʊ) *n* **1** a cloth case stuffed with feathers, foam rubber, etc, used to support the head, esp during sleep **2** Also called: **cushion** a padded cushion or board on which pillow lace is made **3** anything like a pillow in shape or function ▷ *vb* (*tr*) **4** to rest (one's head) on or as if on a pillow **5** to serve as a pillow for [Old English *pylwe*, from Latin *pulvīnus* cushion; compare German *Pfühl*]

pillowcase ('pɪləʊ,keɪs) *or* **pillowslip** ('pɪləʊ,slɪp) *n* a removable washable cover of cotton, linen, nylon, etc, for a pillow

pillow fight *n* a mock fight in which participants thump each other with pillows

pillow lace *n* lace made by winding thread around bobbins on a padded cushion or board. See **point lace**

pillow talk *n* intimate conversation in bed

Pílos ('pilɒs) *n* transliteration of the Modern Greek name for **Pylos**

pilose ('paɪləʊz) *or* **pilous** *adj* *biology* covered with fine soft hairs: *pilose leaves* [c18: from Latin *pilōsus*, from *pilus* hair] > **pilosity** (paɪ'lɒsɪtɪ) *n*

pilot ('paɪlət) *n* **1 a** a person who is qualified to operate an aircraft or spacecraft in flight **b** (*as modifier*): *pilot error* **2 a** a person who is qualified to steer or guide a ship into or out of a port, river mouth, etc **b** (*as modifier*): *a pilot ship* **3** a person who steers a ship **4** a person who acts as a leader or guide **5** *machinery* a guide, often consisting of a tongue or dowel, used to assist in joining two mating parts together **6** *machinery* a plug gauge for measuring

an internal diameter **7** an experimental programme on radio or television **8** (*modifier*) used in or serving as a test or trial: *a pilot project* **9** (*modifier*) serving as a guide: *a pilot beacon* ▷ *vb* (*tr*) **10** to act as pilot of **11** to control the course of **12** to guide or lead (a project, people, etc) [c16: from French *pilote*, from Medieval Latin *pilotus*, ultimately from Greek *pēdon* oar; related to Greek *pous* foot]

pilotage ('paɪlətɪdʒ) *n* **1** the act of piloting an aircraft or ship **2** a pilot's fee **3** the navigation of an aircraft by the observation of ground features and use of charts

pilot balloon *n* a meteorological balloon used to observe air currents

pilot fish *n* **1** a small carangid fish, *Naucrates ductor*, of tropical and subtropical seas, marked with dark vertical bands: often accompanies sharks and other large fishes **2** any of various similar or related fishes

pilot house *n* *nautical* an enclosed structure on the bridge of a vessel from which it can be navigated; wheelhouse

pilot lamp *n* a small light in an electric circuit or device that lights up when the circuit is closed or when certain conditions prevail

pilot light *n* **1** a small auxiliary flame that ignites the main burner of a gas appliance when the control valve opens **2** a small electric light used as an indicator

pilot officer *n* the most junior commissioned rank in the British Royal Air Force and in certain other air forces

pilot study *n* a small-scale experiment or set of observations undertaken to decide how and whether to launch a full-scale project

Pils (pɪlz, pɪls) *n* a type of lager-like beer [c20: abbrev. of PILSNER]

Pilsen ('pɪlzən) *n* the German name for **Plzeň**

Pilsner ('pɪlznə) *or* **Pilsener** *n* a type of pale beer with a strong flavour of hops [named after PILSEN, where it was originally brewed]

Piłsudski (*Polish* piw'sutski) *n* **Józef** ('juzɛf). 1867–1935, Polish nationalist leader and statesman; president (1918–21) and premier (1926–28; 1930)

pilule ('pɪljuːl) *n* a small pill [c16: via French from Latin *pilula* little ball, from *pila* ball] > **pilular** *adj*

pimento (pɪ'mɛntəʊ) *n*, *pl* **-tos** another name for **allspice**, **pimiento** [c17: from Spanish *pimiento* pepper plant, from Medieval Latin *pigmenta* spiced drink, from Latin *pigmentum* PIGMENT]

pimentón (,piː'mɛn'tɒn) *n* smoked chilli powder [from Spanish]

pi meson *n* another name for **pion**

pimiento (pɪ'mjɛntəʊ, -'mɛn-) *n*, *pl* **-tos** a Spanish pepper, *Capsicum annuum*, with a red fruit used raw in salads, cooked as a vegetable, and as a stuffing for green olives. Also called: **pimento** [variant of PIMENTO]

pimp¹ (pɪmp) *n* **1** a man who solicits for a prostitute or brothel and lives off the earnings **2** a man who procures sexual gratification for another; procurer; pander ▷ *vb* **3** (*intr*) to act as a pimp [c17: of unknown origin]

pimp² (pɪmp) *slang, chiefly Austral & NZ* ▷ *n* **1** a spy or informer ▷ *vb* **2** (*intr*; often foll by *on*) to inform (on) [of unknown origin]

pimpernel ('pɪmpə,nɛl, -nᵊl) *n* **1** any of several plants of the primulaceous genus *Anagallis*, such as the scarlet pimpernel, typically having small star-shaped flowers **2** any of several similar and related plants, such as *Lysimachia nemorum* (**yellow pimpernel**) [c15: from Old French *pimpernelle*, ultimately from Latin *piper* PEPPER; compare Old English *pipeneale*]

pimple ('pɪmpᵊl) *n* a small round usually inflamed swelling of the skin [c14: related to Old English *pipilian* to break out in spots; compare Latin *papula* pimple] > **pimpled** *adj* > **'pimply** *adj* > **'pimpliness** *n*

pimp up *or* **pimp out** *vb* (*tr, adverb*) to make (someone or something, esp a car) more extravagantly decorated, as with flashy accessories, etc [c20: from the extravagant clothing and vehicles popularly associated with *pimps*] > **pimped-up** *or* **pimped-out** *adj*

pin (pɪn) *n* **1** a short stiff straight piece of wire pointed at one end and either rounded or having a flattened head at the other: used mainly for fastening pieces of cloth, paper, etc, esp temporarily **2** short for **cotter pin, hairpin, panel pin, rolling pin, safety pin 3** an ornamental brooch, esp a narrow one **4** a badge worn fastened to the clothing by a pin **5** something of little or no importance (esp in the phrases **not care** or **give a pin (for)**) **6** a peg or dowel **7** anything resembling a pin in shape, function, etc **8** (in various bowling games) a usually club-shaped wooden object set up in groups as a target **9** Also called: **cotter pin, safety pin** a clip on a hand grenade that prevents its detonation until removed or released **10** *nautical* **a** See **belaying pin b** the sliding closure for a shackle **11** *music* a metal tuning peg on a piano, the end of which is inserted into a detachable key by means of which it is turned **12** *surgery* a metal rod, esp of stainless steel, for holding together adjacent ends of fractured bones during healing **13** *chess* a position in which a piece is pinned against a more valuable piece or the king **14** *golf* the flagpole marking the hole on a green ▷ *vb* **pins, pinning, pinned** (*tr*) **15** to attach, hold, or fasten with or as if with a pin or pins **16** to transfix with a pin, spear, etc **17** (foll by *on*) *informal* to place (the blame for something): *he pinned the charge on his accomplice* **18** *chess* to cause (an enemy piece) to be effectively immobilized by attacking it with a queen, rook, or bishop so that moving it would reveal a check or expose a more valuable piece to capture ▷ See also **pin down** [Old English *pinn*; related to Old High German *pfinn*, Old Norse *pinni* nail]

PIN (pɪn) *n acronym for* personal identification number: a number used by a holder of a cash card or credit card used in EFTPOS

pinaceous (paɪˈneɪʃəs) *adj* of, relating to, or belonging to the *Pinaceae*, a family of conifers with needle-like leaves: includes pine, spruce, fir, larch, and cedar [c19: via New Latin from Latin *pīnus* a pine]

pinafore (ˈpɪnəˌfɔː) *n* **1** *chiefly Brit* an apron, esp one with a bib **2** *chiefly Brit* a sleeveless dress worn over a blouse or sweater **3** *chiefly US* an overdress buttoning at the back [c18: from PIN + AFORE]

Pinar del Río (*Spanish* piˈnar ðɛl ˈrrio) *n* a city in W Cuba: tobacco industry. Pop: 158 000 (2005 est)

pinaster (paɪˈnæstə, pɪ-) *n* a Mediterranean pine tree, *Pinus pinaster*, with paired needles and prickly cones. Also called: **maritime pinaster, cluster pinaster** [c16: from Latin: wild pine, from *pīnus* pine]

pinball (ˈpɪnˌbɔːl) *n* **a** a game in which the player shoots a small ball through several hazards on a table, electrically operated machine, etc **b** (*as modifier*): *a pinball machine*

pince-nez (ˈpænsˌneɪ, ˈpɪns-; *French* pɛ̃sne) *n, pl* **pince-nez** eyeglasses that are held in place only by means of a clip over the bridge of the nose [c19: French, literally: pinch-nose]

pincers (ˈpɪnsəz) *pl n* **1** Also called: **pair of pincers** a gripping tool consisting of two hinged arms with handles at one end and, at the other, curved bevelled jaws that close on the workpiece: used esp for extracting nails **2** the pair or pairs of jointed grasping appendages in lobsters and certain other arthropods [c14: from Old French *pinceour*, from Old French *pincier* to PINCH]

pinch (pɪntʃ) *vb* **1** to press (something, esp flesh) tightly between two surfaces, esp between a finger and the thumb **2** to confine, squeeze, or painfully press (toes, fingers, etc) because of lack of space: *these shoes pinch* **3** (*tr*) to cause stinging pain to: *the cold pinched his face* **4** (*tr*) to make thin or drawn-looking, as from grief, lack of food, etc **5** (usually foll by *on*) to provide (oneself or another person) with meagre allowances, amounts, etc **6** pinch pennies to live frugally because of meanness or to economize **7** (usually foll by *off, out,* or *back*) to remove the tips of (buds, shoots, etc) to correct or encourage growth **8** (*tr*) *informal* to steal or take without asking **9** (*tr*) *informal* to arrest ▷ *n* **10** a squeeze or sustained nip **11** the quantity of a substance, such as salt, that can be taken between a thumb and finger **12** a very small quantity **13** at a pinch if absolutely necessary [c16: probably from Old Norman French *pinchier* (unattested); related to Old French *pincier* to pinch; compare Late Latin *punctiāre* to prick]

pinchbeck (ˈpɪntʃˌbɛk) *n* **1** an alloy of copper and zinc, used as imitation gold **2** a spurious or cheap imitation; sham ▷ *adj* **3** made of pinchbeck **4** sham, spurious, or cheap [c18 (the alloy), c19 (something spurious): after Christopher *Pinchbeck* (?1670–1732), English watchmaker who invented it]

pinchpenny (ˈpɪntʃˌpɛnɪ) *adj* **1** niggardly; miserly ▷ *n, pl* **-nies 2** a miserly person; niggard

Pinckney (ˈpɪŋknɪ) *n* **1 Charles.** 1757–1824, US statesman, who was a leading member of the convention that framed the US Constitution (1787) **2** his cousin, **Charles Cotesworth.** 1746–1825, US soldier, statesman, and diplomat, who also served at the Constitutional Convention **3** his brother, **Thomas.** 1750–1828, US soldier and politician. He was US minister to Britain (1792–96) and special envoy to Spain (1795–96)

Pincus (ˈpɪŋkəs) *n* **Gregory Goodwin.** 1903–67, US physiologist, whose work on steroid hormones led to the development of the first contraceptive pill

pincushion (ˈpɪnˌkʊʃən) *n* a small well-padded cushion in which pins are stuck ready for use

Pindar (ˈpɪndə) *n* ?518–?438 BC, Greek lyric poet, noted for his *Epinikia*, odes commemorating victories in the Greek games

pin down *vb* (*tr, adverb*) **1** to force (someone) to make a decision or carry out a promise **2** to define clearly: *he had a vague suspicion that he couldn't quite pin down* **3** to confine to a place: *the fallen tree pinned him down*

Pindus (ˈpɪndəs) *n* a mountain range in central Greece between Epirus and Thessaly. Highest peak: Mount Smólikas, 2633 m (8639 ft). Modern Greek name: **Píndhos** (ˈpinðɔs)

pine¹ (paɪn) *n* **1** any evergreen resinous coniferous tree of the genus *Pinus*, of the N hemisphere, with long needle-shaped leaves and brown cones: family *Pinaceae* **2** the wood of any of these trees [Old English *pīn*, from Latin *pīnus* pine]

pine² (paɪn) *vb* **1** (*intr*; often foll by *for* or an infinitive) to feel great longing or desire; yearn **2** (*intr*; often foll by *away*) to become ill, feeble, or thin through worry, longing, etc [Old English *pīnian* to torture, from *pīn* pain, from Medieval Latin *pēna*, from Latin *poena* PAIN]

Pine (paɪn) *n* **Courtney.** born 1964, British jazz saxophonist

pineal eye *n* an outgrowth of the pineal gland that forms an eyelike structure on the top of the head in certain cold-blooded vertebrates

pineal gland or **pineal body** *n* a pea-sized organ in the brain, situated beneath the posterior part of the corpus callosum, that secretes melatonin into the bloodstream

pineapple (ˈpaɪnˌæpᵊl) *n* **1** a tropical American bromeliaceous plant, *Ananas comosus*, cultivated in the tropics for its large fleshy edible fruit **2** the fruit of this plant, consisting of an inflorescence clustered around a fleshy axis and surmounted by a tuft of leaves **3** *military slang* a hand grenade [c14 *pinappel* pine cone; c17: applied to the fruit because of its appearance]

pine cone *n* the seed-producing structure of a pine tree. See **cone** (sense 3a)

pine marten *n* a marten, *Martes martes*, of N European and Asian coniferous woods, having dark brown fur with a creamy-yellow patch on the throat

pinene (ˈpaɪniːn) *n* either of two isomeric terpenes, found in many essential oils and constituting the main part of oil of turpentine. The commonest structural isomer (α-pinene) is used in the manufacture of camphor, solvents, plastics, and insecticides. Formula: $C_{10}H_{16}$ [c20: from PINE¹ + -ENE]

pine nut or **pine kernel** *n* the edible seed of certain pine trees

Pinero (pɪˈnɪərəʊ) *n* Sir **Arthur Wing.** 1855–1934, English dramatist. His works include the farce *Dandy Dick* (1887) and the problem play *The Second Mrs Tanqueray* (1893)

Pines (paɪnz) *n* Isle of Pines the former name of the (Isle of) Youth

pine tar *n* a brown or black semisolid or viscous substance, produced by the destructive distillation of pine wood, used in roofing compositions, paints, medicines, etc

pinfeather ('pɪnˌfɛðə) n ornithol a feather emerging from the skin and still enclosed in its horny sheath

pinfold ('pɪnˌfəʊld) n 1 a pound for stray cattle ▷ vb 2 (tr) to gather or confine in or as if in a pinfold [Old English pundfald, from POUND³ + FOLD²]

ping (pɪŋ) n 1 a short high-pitched resonant sound, as of a bullet striking metal or a sonar echo 2 computing a system for testing whether internet systems are responding and how long in milliseconds it takes them to respond ▷ vb 3 (intr) to make such a noise 4 (tr) computing to send a test message to (a computer or server) in order to check whether it is responding or how long it takes it to respond [C19: of imitative origin]

pinger ('pɪŋə) n a device that makes a pinging sound, esp one that can be preset to ring at a particular time

Ping-Pong ('pɪŋˌpɒŋ) n trademark another name for **table tennis**. Also called: **ping pong**

pinhead ('pɪnˌhɛd) n 1 the head of a pin 2 something very small 3 informal a stupid or contemptible person > 'pin,headed adj > 'pin,headedness n

pinhole ('pɪnˌhəʊl) n a small hole made with or as if with a pin

pinion¹ ('pɪnjən) n 1 chiefly poetic a bird's wing 2 the part of a bird's wing including the flight feathers ▷ vb (tr) 3 to hold or bind the (arms) of (a person) so as to restrain or immobilize him 4 to confine or shackle 5 to make (a bird) incapable of flight by removing that part of (the wing) from which the flight feathers grow [C15: from Old French pignon wing, from Latin pinna wing]

pinion² ('pɪnjən) n a cogwheel that engages with a larger wheel or rack, which it drives or by which it is driven [C17: from French pignon cogwheel, from Old French peigne comb, from Latin pecten comb; see PECTEN]

Piniós (pi'njɔs) n transliteration of the Modern Greek name for the **Salambria**

pink¹ (pɪŋk) n 1 any of a group of colours with a reddish hue that are of low to moderate saturation and can usually reflect or transmit a large amount of light; a pale reddish tint 2 pink cloth or clothing: dressed in pink 3 any of various Old World plants of the caryophyllaceous genus Dianthus, such as D. plumarius (**garden pink**), cultivated for their fragrant flowers. See also **carnation** (sense 1) 4 any of various plants of other genera, such as the moss pink 5 the flower of any of these plants 6 the highest or best degree, condition, etc (esp in the phrases **in the pink of health, in the pink**) 7 a a huntsman's scarlet coat b a huntsman who wears a scarlet coat ▷ adj 8 of the colour pink 9 Brit informal left-wing 10 informal of or relating to homosexuals or homosexuality: the pink vote 11 (of a huntsman's coat) scarlet or red ▷ vb 12 (intr) another word for **knock** (sense 7) [C16 (THE FLOWER), C18 (THE COLOUR): PERHAPS A SHORTENING OF PINKEYE] > 'pinkish adj > 'pinkness n > 'pinky adj

pink² (pɪŋk) vb (tr) 1 to prick lightly with a sword or rapier 2 to decorate (leather, cloth, etc) with a perforated or punched pattern 3 to cut with pinking shears [C14: perhaps of Low German origin; compare Low German pinken to peck]

pink³ (pɪŋk) n a sailing vessel with a narrow overhanging transom [C15: from Middle Dutch pinke, of obscure origin]

Pinkerton ('pɪŋkətən) n **Allan**. 1819–84, US private detective, born in Scotland. He founded the first detective agency in the US (1850) and organized an intelligence system for the Federal States of America (1861)

pinkeye ('pɪŋkˌaɪ) n 1 Also called: **acute conjunctivitis** an acute contagious inflammation of the conjunctiva of the eye, characterized by redness, discharge, etc: usually caused by bacterial infection 2 Also called: **infectious keratitis** a similar condition affecting the cornea of horses and cattle [C16: partial translation of obsolete Dutch pinck oogen small eyes]

Pink Floyd (pɪŋk flɔɪd) n British rock group, formed in 1966: originally comprised Syd Barrett (1946–2006), Roger Waters (born 1944), Rick Wright (born 1945), and Nick Mason (born 1945); Barrett was replaced by Dave Gilmour (born 1944) in 1968 and Waters left in 1986.

Recordings include The Piper at the Gates of Dawn (1967), Dark Side of the Moon (1973), Wish You Were Here (1975), and The Division Bell (1994)

pinkie or **pinky** ('pɪŋkɪ) n, pl -ies Scot, US & Canadian the little finger [C19: from Dutch pinkje, diminutive of PINK¹; compare PINKEYE]

pinking shears pl n scissors with a serrated edge on one or both blades, producing a wavy edge to material cut, thus preventing fraying

pink salmon n 1 any salmon having pale pink flesh, esp Oncorhynchus gorbuscha, of the Pacific Ocean 2 the flesh of such a fish

pin money n 1 an allowance by a husband to his wife for personal expenditure 2 money saved or earned to be used for incidental expenses

pinna ('pɪnə) n, pl -nae (-niː) or -nas 1 any leaflet of a pinnate compound leaf 2 zoology a feather, wing, fin, or similarly shaped part 3 another name for **auricle** (sense 2) [C18: via New Latin from Latin: wing, feather, fin]

pinnace ('pɪnɪs) n any of various kinds of ship's tender [C16: from French pinace, apparently from Old Spanish pinaza, literally: something made of pine, ultimately from Latin pīnus pine]

pinnacle ('pɪnəkᵊl) n 1 the highest point or level, esp of fame, success, etc 2 a towering peak, as of a mountain 3 a slender upright structure in the form of a cone, pyramid, or spire on the top of a buttress, gable, or tower ▷ vb (tr) 4 to set on or as if on a pinnacle 5 to furnish with a pinnacle or pinnacles 6 to crown with a pinnacle [C14: via Old French from Late Latin pinnāculum a peak, from Latin pinna wing]

pinnate ('pɪneɪt, 'pɪnɪt) or **pinnated** adj 1 like a feather in appearance 2 (of compound leaves) having the leaflets growing opposite each other in pairs on either side of the stem [C18: from Latin pinnātus, from pinna feather] > 'pinnately adv > pin'nation n

pinniped ('pɪnɪˌpɛd) or **pinnipedian** (ˌpɪnɪ'piːdɪən) adj 1 of, relating to, or belonging to the Pinnipedia, an order of aquatic placental mammals having a streamlined body and limbs specialized as flippers: includes seals, sea lions, and the walrus ▷ n 2 any pinniped animal [C19: from New Latin pinnipēs, from Latin pinna feather, fin + pēs foot]

pinnule ('pɪnjuːl) n, pl pinnules or pinnulae ('pɪnjuˌliː) 1 any of the lobes of a leaflet of a pinnate compound leaf, which is itself pinnately divided 2 zoology any feather-like part, such as any of the arms of a sea lily [C16: from Latin pinnula, diminutive of pinna feather] > 'pinnular adj

pinny ('pɪnɪ) n, pl -nies a child's or informal name for **pinafore** (sense 1)

Pinochet ('piːnəˌʃeɪ) or **Pinochet Ugarte** ('piːnəˌʃeɪ u'ɡɑːteɪ) n **Augusto** (au'ɣusto). 1915-2006, Chilean general and statesman; president of Chile (1974–90) following his overthrow of Allende (1973): charged (2001) with murder and kidnapping but found unfit to stand trial

pinochle, penuchle, penuckle or **pinocle** ('piːnʌkᵊl) n 1 a card game for two to four players similar to bezique 2 the combination of queen of spades and jack of diamonds in this game [C19: of unknown origin]

Pinotage ('pɪnətɑːʒ) n 1 a red grape variety of South Africa, a cross between the Pinot Noir and the Hermitage 2 any of the red wines made from this grape

Pinot Grigio ('piːnəʊ 'ɡriːdʒəʊ) n 1 a variety of grape, grown in Italy for wine-making 2 any of the white Italian wines made from this grape [Italian grigio grey]

Pinot Noir ('piːnəʊ nwɑː) n 1 a variety of black grape, grown esp for wine-making 2 any of the red wines made from this grape [French]

PIN pad n a small keypad at a point of sale on which someone making a purchase using a credit or debit card types his or her PIN to confirm the purchase

pinpoint ('pɪnˌpɔɪnt) vb (tr) 1 to locate or identify exactly: to pinpoint a problem; to pinpoint a place on a map ▷ n 2 an insignificant or trifling thing 3 the point of a pin 4 (modifier) exact: a pinpoint aim

pinprick ('pɪnˌprɪk) n 1 a slight puncture made by or as if by a pin 2 a small irritation ▷ vb 3 (tr) to puncture with or as if with a pin

pins and needles *n* (*functioning as singular*) *informal* **1** a tingling sensation in the fingers, toes, legs, etc, caused by the return of normal blood circulation after its temporary impairment **2 on pins and needles** in a state of anxious suspense or nervous anticipation

Pinsent ('pɪn,sent) *n* Sir **Matthew** (**Clive**). born 1970, British oarsman; won four gold medals in rowing events at consecutive Olympic Games (1992, 1996, 2000, 2004)

Pinsk (*Russian* pinsk) *n* a city in SW Belarus: capital of a principality (13th–14th centuries). Pop: 134 000 (2005 est)

pinstripe ('pɪn,straɪp) *n* (in textiles) a very narrow stripe in fabric or the fabric itself, used esp for men's suits

pint (paɪnt) *n* **1** a unit of liquid measure of capacity equal to one eighth of a gallon. 1 Brit pint is equal to 0.568 litre, 1 US pint to 0.473 litre **2** a unit of dry measure of capacity equal to one half of a quart. 1 US dry pint is equal to one sixty-fourth of a US bushel or 0.5506 litre **3** a measure having such a capacity **4** *Brit informal* **a** a pint of beer **b** a drink of beer: *he's gone out for a pint* [c14: from Old French *pinte*, of uncertain origin; perhaps from Medieval Latin *pincta* marks used in measuring liquids, ultimately from Latin *pingere* to paint; compare Middle Low German, Middle Dutch *pinte*]

pinta¹ ('pɪntə) *n* a tropical infectious skin disease caused by the bacterium *Treponema carateum* and characterized by the formation of papules and loss of pigmentation in circumscribed areas. Also called: **mal de pinto** [c19: from American Spanish, from Spanish: spot, ultimately from Latin *pictus* painted, from *pingere* to paint]

pinta² ('paɪntə) *n informal* a pint of milk [c20: phonetic rendering of *pint of*]

pintail ('pɪn,teɪl) *n*, *pl* **-tails** *or* **-tail** a greyish-brown duck, *Anas acuta*, with slender pointed wings and a pointed tail

Pinter ('pɪntə) *n* **Harold**. born 1930, English dramatist. His plays, such as *The Caretaker* (1959), *The Homecoming* (1964), *No Man's Land* (1974), *Moonlight* (1993), and *Celebration* (2000), are noted for their equivocal and halting dialogue: Nobel prize for literature 2005 > ,Pinter'esque *adj*

pintle ('pɪntªl) *n* **1** a pin or bolt forming the pivot of a hinge **2** the link bolt, hook, or pin on a vehicle's towing bracket **3** the needle or plunger of the injection valve of an oil engine [Old English *pintel* penis]

pinto ('pɪntəʊ) *US & Canadian* ⊳ *adj* **1** marked with patches of white; piebald ⊳ *n*, *pl* **-tos 2** a pinto horse [c19: from American Spanish (originally: painted, spotted), ultimately from Latin *pingere* to paint]

pint-size *or* **pint-sized** *adj informal* very small; tiny

pin tuck *n* a narrow ornamental fold used esp on shirt fronts and dress bodices

Pinturicchio (*Italian* pintu'rikkjo) *or* **Pintoricchio** (*Italian* pinto'rikkjo) *n* real name *Bernardino di Betto*. ?1454–1513, Italian painter of the Umbrian school

pin-up *n* **1** *informal* **a** a picture of a sexually attractive person, esp when partially or totally undressed **b** (*as modifier*): *a pin-up magazine* **2** *slang* a person who has appeared in such a picture **3** a photograph of a famous personality

pinwheel ('pɪn,wiːl) *n* another name for **Catherine wheel** (sense 1)

pinworm ('pɪn,wɜːm) *n* a parasitic nematode worm, *Enterobius vermicularis*, infecting the colon, rectum, and anus of humans: family *Oxyuridae*. Also called: **threadworm**

piny ('paɪnɪ) *adj* **pinier, piniest** of, resembling, or covered with pine trees

Pinyin ('pɪn'jɪn) *n* a system of romanized spelling developed in China in 1958: used to transliterate Chinese characters into the Roman alphabet

Pinzón (*Spanish* pin'θɔn) *n* **1 Martín Alonzo** (mar'tin a'lonθo). ?1440–93, Spanish navigator, who commanded the *Pinta* on Columbus' first expedition (1492–93), which he abandoned in a vain attempt to be the first to arrive back in Spain **2** his brother, **Vicente Yáñez** (bi'θente 'jaɲɛθ). ?1460–?1524, Spanish navigator, who commanded the *Niña* on Columbus' first expedition (1492–93)

pion ('paɪɒn) *or* **pi meson** *n physics* a meson having a positive or negative charge and a rest mass 273.13 times

that of the electron, or no charge and a rest mass 264.14 times that of the electron [c20: from Greek letter PI¹ + ON]

pioneer (,paɪə'nɪə) *n* **1 a** a colonist, explorer, or settler of a new land, region, etc **b** (*as modifier*): *a pioneer wagon* **2** an innovator or developer of something new **3** *military* a member of an infantry group that digs entrenchments, makes roads, etc **4** *ecology* the first species of plant or animal to colonize an area of bare ground ⊳ *vb* **5** to be a pioneer (in or of) **6** (*tr*) to initiate, prepare, or open up: *to pioneer a medical programme* [c16: from Old French *paonier* infantryman, from *paon* PAWN²; see also PEON¹]

pious ('paɪəs) *adj* **1** having or expressing reverence for a god or gods; religious; devout **2** marked by reverence **3** marked by false reverence; sanctimonious **4** sacred; not secular **5** *archaic* having or expressing devotion for one's parents or others [c17: from Latin *pius*, related to *piāre* to expiate] > 'piously *adv* > 'piousness *n*

Piozzi ('pjɔːtsɪ) *n* **Hester Lynch**. See (Hester Lynch) **Thrale**

pip¹ (pɪp) *n* **1** the seed of a fleshy fruit, such as an apple or pear **2** any of the segments marking the surface of a pineapple **3** a rootstock or flower of the lily of the valley or certain other plants [c18: short for PIPPIN]

pip² (pɪp) *n* **1** a short high-pitched sound, a sequence of which can act as a time signal, esp on radio **2** a radar blip **3 a** a spot or single device, such as a spade, diamond, heart, or club on a playing card **b** any of the spots on dice or dominoes **4** Also called: **star** *informal* the emblem worn on the shoulder by junior officers in the British Army, indicating their rank ⊳ *vb* **pips, pipping, pipped 5** (of a young bird) **a** (*intr*) to chirp; peep **b** to pierce (the shell of its egg) while hatching **6** (*intr*) to make a short high-pitched sound [c16 (in the sense: spot or speck); c17 (vb); c20 (in the sense: short high-pitched sound): of obscure, probably imitative origin; senses 1 and 5 are probably related to PEEP²]

pip³ (pɪp) *n* **1** a contagious disease of poultry characterized by the secretion of thick mucus in the mouth and throat **2** *facetious, slang* a minor human ailment **3** *Brit, Austral, NZ & S African slang* a bad temper or depression (esp in the phrase **give (someone) the pip**) **4 get the pip** *or* **have the pip** *NZ informal* to sulk ⊳ *vb* **pips, pipping, pipped 5** *Brit slang* to cause to be annoyed or depressed [c15: from Middle Dutch *pippe*, ultimately from Latin *pituita* phlegm; see PITUITARY]

pip⁴ (pɪp) *vb* **pips, pipping, pipped** (*tr*) *Brit slang* **1** to wound or kill, esp with a gun **2** to defeat (a person), esp when his success seems certain (often in the phrase **pip at the post**) **3** to blackball or ostracize [c19 (originally in the sense: to blackball): probably from PIP²]

pipal ('paɪpªl) *n* a variant of **peepul**

pipe¹ (paɪp) *n* **1** a long tube of metal, plastic, etc, used to convey water, oil, gas, etc **2** a long tube or case **3 a** an object made in any of various shapes and sizes, consisting of a small bowl with an attached tubular stem, in which tobacco or other substances are smoked **b** (*as modifier*): *a pipe bowl* **4** Also called: **pipeful** the amount of tobacco that fills the bowl of a pipe **5** *zoology, botany* any of various hollow organs, such as the respiratory passage of certain animals **6 a** any musical instrument whose sound production results from the vibration of an air column in a simple tube **b** any of the tubular devices on an organ, in which air is made to vibrate either directly, as in a flue pipe, or by means of a reed **7** an obsolete three-holed wind instrument, held in the left hand while played and accompanied by the tabor. See **tabor 8 the pipes** See **bagpipes 9** a shrill voice or sound, as of a bird **10 a** a boatswain's pipe **b** the sound it makes **11** (*plural*) *informal* the respiratory tract or vocal cords **12** *metallurgy* a conical hole in the head of an ingot, made by escaping gas as the metal cools **13** a cylindrical vein of rich ore, such as one of the vertical diamond-bearing veins at Kimberley, South Africa **14** Also called: **volcanic pipe** a vertical cylindrical passage in a volcano through which molten lava is forced during eruption **15** *US slang* something easy to do, esp a simple course in college **16 put that in your pipe and smoke it** *informal* accept that fact if you can ⊳ *vb* **17** to play (music) on a pipe **18** (*tr*) to summon or lead by a pipe: *to pipe the dancers* **19** to utter (something) shrilly **20 a** to signal orders to (the crew) by a boatswain's pipe **b** (*tr*) to signal the arrival or departure of: *to pipe the admiral aboard* **21** (*tr*) to convey (water, gas, etc) by a pipe or pipes **22** (*tr*) to provide with pipes **23** (*tr*) to trim (an article, esp of clothing) with piping **24** (*tr*) to force (cream, icing, etc) through a shaped nozzle to decorate food ▷ See also **pipe down, pipe up** [Old English *pīpe* (n), *pīpian* (vb), ultimately from Latin *pīpāre* to chirp]

pipe² (paɪp) *n* **1** a large cask for wine, oil, etc **2** a measure of capacity for wine equal to four barrels. 1 pipe is equal to 126 US gallons or 105 Brit gallons **3** a cask holding this quantity with its contents [c14: via Old French (in the sense: tube, tubular vessel), ultimately from Latin *pīpāre* to chirp; compare PIPE¹]

pipe bomb *n* a small explosive device hidden in a pipe or drain, detonated by means of a timer

pipeclay ('paɪpˌkleɪ) *n* **1** a fine white pure clay, used in the manufacture of tobacco pipes and pottery and for whitening leather and similar materials ▷ *vb* **2** (*tr*) to whiten with pipeclay

pipe cleaner *n* a short length of thin wires twisted so as to hold tiny tufts of yarn: used to clean the stem of a tobacco pipe

piped music *n* light popular music prerecorded and played through amplifiers in a shop, restaurant, factory, etc, as background music. See also **Muzak**

pipe down *vb* (*intr, adverb*) *informal* to stop talking, making noise, etc

pipe dream *n* a fanciful or impossible plan or hope [alluding to dreams produced by smoking an opium pipe]

pipefish ('paɪpˌfɪʃ) *n, pl* -**fish** *or* -**fishes** any of various teleost fishes of the genera *Nerophis, Syngnathus*, etc, having a long tubelike snout and an elongated body covered with bony plates: family *Syngnathidae*. Also called: **needlefish**

pipefitting ('paɪpˌfɪtɪŋ) *n* **1 a** the act or process of bending, cutting to length, and joining pipes **b** the branch of plumbing involving this **2** the threaded gland nuts, unions, adaptors, etc, used for joining pipes > '**pipeˌfitter** *n*

pipeline ('paɪpˌlaɪn) *n* **1** a long pipe, esp underground, used to transport oil, natural gas, etc, over long distances **2** a medium of communication, esp a private one **3** in the pipeline in the process of being completed, delivered, or produced ▷ *vb* (*tr*) **4** to convey by pipeline **5** to supply with a pipeline

pipe major *n* the noncommissioned officer, generally of warrant officer's rank, who is responsible for the training, duty, and discipline of a military or civilian pipe band

pipe organ *n* another name for **organ** (sense 1) See **reed organ**

piper ('paɪpə) *n* **1** a person who plays a pipe or bagpipes **2 pay the piper and call the tune** to bear the cost of an undertaking and control it

Piper ('paɪpə) *n* **John.** 1903–92, British artist. An official war artist in World War II, he is known esp for his watercolours of bombed churches and his stained glass in Coventry Cathedral

piperidine (pɪ'perɪˌdiːn, -dɪn) *n* a colourless liquid heterocyclic compound with a peppery ammoniacal odour: used in making rubbers and curing epoxy resins. Formula: $C_5H_{11}N$

piperine ('pɪpəˌraɪn, -rɪn) *n* a crystalline insoluble alkaloid that is the active ingredient of pepper, used as a flavouring and as an insecticide. Formula: $C_{17}H_{19}NO_3$ [c19: from Latin *piper* PEPPER]

piperonal ('pɪpərəʊˌnæl) *n* a white fragrant aldehyde used in flavourings, perfumery, and suntan lotions. Formula: $C_8H_6O_3$. Also called: **heliotropin**

pipette (pɪ'pet) *n* **1** a calibrated glass tube drawn to a fine bore at one end, filled by sucking liquid into the bulb, and used to transfer or measure known volumes of liquid ▷ *vb* **2** (*tr*) to transfer or measure out (a liquid) using a pipette [c19: via French: little pipe, from *pipe* PIPE¹]

pipe up *vb* (*intr, adverb*) **1** to commence singing or playing

a musical instrument: *the band piped up* **2** to speak up, esp in a shrill voice

pipi ('pɪpiː) *n, pl* **pipi** *or* **pipis** any of various shellfishes, esp *Plebidonax deltoides* of Australia or *Mesodesma novae-zelandiae* of New Zealand [Māori]

piping ('paɪpɪŋ) *n* **1** pipes collectively, esp pipes formed into a connected system, as in the plumbing of a house **2** a cord of icing, whipped cream, etc, often used to decorate desserts and cakes **3** a thin strip of covered cord or material, used to edge hems, etc **4** the sound of a pipe or a set of bagpipes **5** the art or technique of playing a pipe or bagpipes **6** a shrill voice or sound, esp a whistling sound ▷ *adj* **7** making a shrill sound **8** *archaic* relating to the pipe (associated with peace), as opposed to martial instruments, such as the fife or trumpet ▷ *adv* **9 piping hot** extremely hot

pipistrelle (ˌpɪpɪ'strel) *n* any of numerous small brownish insectivorous bats of the genus *Pipistrellus*, occurring in most parts of the world: family *Vespertilionidae* [c18: via French from Italian *pipistrello*, from Latin *vespertīliō* a bat, from *vesper* evening, because of its nocturnal habits]

pipit ('pɪpɪt) *n* any of various songbirds of the genus *Anthus* and related genera, having brownish speckled plumage and a long tail: family *Motacillidae*. Also called: **titlark** [c18: probably of imitative origin]

pipkin ('pɪpkɪn) *n* a small metal or earthenware vessel [c16: perhaps a diminutive of PIPE²; see -KIN]

pippin ('pɪpɪn) *n* **1** any of several varieties of eating apple with a rounded oblate shape **2** the seed of any of these fruits [c13: from Old French *pepin*, of uncertain origin]

pipsissewa (pɪp'sɪsəwə) *n* any of several ericaceous plants of the Asian and American genus *Chimaphila*, having jagged evergreen leaves and white or pinkish flowers. Also called: **wintergreen** [c19: from Cree *pipisisikweu*, literally: it breaks it into pieces, so called because it was believed to be efficacious in treating bladder stones]

pipsqueak ('pɪpˌskwiːk) *n informal* a person or thing that is insignificant or contemptible [c20: from PIP² + SQUEAK]

piquant ('piːkənt, -kɑːnt) *adj* **1** having an agreeably pungent or tart taste **2** lively or stimulating to the mind [c16: from French (literally: prickling), from *piquer* to prick, goad; see PIQUE¹] > '**piquancy** *or less commonly* '**piquantness** *n* > '**piquantly** *adv*

pique¹ (piːk) *n* **1** a feeling of resentment or irritation, as from having one's pride wounded ▷ *vb* **piques, piquing, piqued** (*tr*) **2** to cause to feel resentment or irritation **3** to excite or arouse **4** (foll by *on* or *upon*) to pride or congratulate (oneself) [c16: from French, from *piquer* to prick, sting; see PICK¹]

pique² (piːk) *piquet* ▷ *n* **1** a score of 30 points made by a player from a combination of cards held before play begins and from play while his opponent's score is nil ▷ *vb* **2** to score a pique (against) [c17: from French *pic*, of uncertain origin]

piqué ('piːkeɪ) *n* a close-textured fabric of cotton, silk, or spun rayon woven with lengthwise ribs [c19: from French *piqué* pricked, from *piquer* to prick]

piquet (pɪ'ket, -'keɪ) *n* a card game for two people playing with a reduced pack and scoring points for card combinations and tricks won [c17: from French, of unknown origin; compare PIQUE²]

piracy ('paɪrəsɪ) *n, pl* -**cies 1** *Brit* robbery on the seas within admiralty jurisdiction **2** a felony, such as robbery or hijacking, committed aboard a ship or aircraft **3** the unauthorized use or appropriation of patented or copyrighted material, ideas, etc [c16: from Anglo-Latin *pirātia*, from Late Greek *peirāteia*; see PIRATE]

Piraeus *or* **Peiraeus** (paɪ'riːəs, pɪ'reɪ-) *n* a port in SE Greece, adjoining Athens: the country's chief port; founded in the 5th century BC as the port of Athens. Pop (municipality): 181 933 (2001). Modern Greek name: **Piraiévs** (ˌpɪrɛ'ɛfs)

piragua (pɪ'rɑːgwə, -'ræg-) *n* another word for **pirogue** [c17: via Spanish from Carib: dugout canoe]

Pirandello (*Italian* piran'dɛllo) *n* **Luigi** (lu'iːdʒi). 1867–1936, Italian short-story writer, novelist, and dramatist. His plays include *Right you are (If you think so)* (1917), *Six Characters in Search of an Author* (1921), and *Henry IV* (1922): Nobel prize for literature 1934

Piranesi (*Italian* pira'ne:si) *n* **Giambattista** (dʒambat'tista). 1720–78, Italian etcher and architect: etchings include *Imaginary Prisons* and *Views of Rome*

piranha *or* **piraña** (pɪ'rɑːnjə) *n* any of various small freshwater voracious fishes of the genus *Serrasalmus* and related genera, of tropical America, having strong jaws and sharp teeth: family *Characidae* (characins) [c19: via Portuguese from Tupi: fish with teeth, from *pirá* fish + *sainha* tooth]

pirate ('paɪrɪt) *n* **1** a person who commits piracy **2 a** a vessel used by pirates **b** (*as modifier*): *a pirate ship* **3** a person who illicitly uses or appropriates someone else's literary, artistic, or other work **4 a** a person or group of people who broadcast illegally **b** (*as modifier*): *a pirate radio station* ▷ *vb* **5** (*tr*) to use, appropriate, or reproduce (artistic work, ideas, etc) illicitly [c15: from Latin *pīrāta*, from Greek *peirātēs* one who attacks, from *peira* an attempt, attack] ▷ **piratical** (paɪ'rætɪk³l) *or* **pi'ratic** *adj* ▷ **pi'ratically** *adv*

piri-piri (ˌpɪrɪ'pɪrɪ) *n* a hot sauce, of Portuguese colonial origin, made from red chilli peppers [from a Bantu language: literally: pepper]

Pirithoüs (paɪ'rɪθəʊəs) *n* *Greek myth* a prince of the Lapiths, who accomplished many great deeds with his friend Theseus

pirogue (pɪ'rəʊg) *or* **piragua** *n* any of various kinds of dugout canoes [c17: via French from Spanish PIRAGUA]

pirouette (ˌpɪrʊ'ɛt) *n* **1** a body spin, esp in dancing, on the toes or the ball of the foot ▷ *vb* **2** (*intr*) to perform a pirouette [c18: from French, from Old French *pirouet* spinning top; related to Italian *pirolo* little peg]

Pisa ('piːzə; *Italian* 'piːsa) *n* a city in Tuscany, NW Italy, near the mouth of the River Arno: flourishing maritime republic (11th–12th centuries), contains a university (1343), a cathedral (1063), and the Leaning Tower (begun in 1174 and about 5 m (17 ft) from perpendicular); tourism. Pop: 89 694 (2001)

Pisanello (*Italian* pisa'nɛllo) *n* **Antonio** (an'tɔ:njo). ?1395–?1455, Italian painter and medallist; a major exponent of the International Gothic style. He is best known for his portrait medals and drawings of animals

Pisano (*Italian* pi'saːno) *n* **1 Andrea** (an'drea), real name *Andrea de Pontedera*. ?1290–1348, Italian sculptor and architect, noted for his bronze reliefs on the door of the baptistry in Florence **2 Giovanni** (dʒo'vanni). ?1250–?1320, Italian sculptor, who successfully integrated classical and Gothic elements in his sculptures, esp in his pulpit in St Andrea, Pistoia **3** his father, **Nicola** (ni'kɔːla). ?1220–?84, Italian sculptor, who pioneered the classical style and is often regarded as a precursor of the Italian Renaissance: noted esp for his pulpit in the baptistry of Pisa Cathedral

piscatorial (ˌpɪskə'tɔːrɪəl) *or* **piscatory** ('pɪskətərɪ, -trɪ) *adj* **1** of or relating to fish, fishing, or fishermen **2** devoted to fishing [c19: from Latin *piscātōrius*, from *piscātor* fisherman] ▷ **pisca'torially** *adv*

Pisces ('paɪsiːz, 'pɪ-) *n*, *Latin genitive* **Piscium** ('paɪsɪəm) **1** *astronomy* a faint extensive zodiacal constellation lying between Aquarius and Aries on the ecliptic **2** *astrology* Also called: **the Fishes** the twelfth sign of the zodiac, symbol ♓, having a mutable water classification and ruled by the planets Jupiter and Neptune. The sun is in this sign between about Feb 19 and March 20 **3 a** a taxonomic group that comprises all fishes. See **fish** (sense 1) **b** a taxonomic group that comprises the bony fishes only. See **teleost** [c14: Latin: the fishes]

pisci- *combining form* fish: *pisciculture* [from Latin *piscis*]

pisciculture ('pɪsɪˌkʌltʃə) *n* the rearing and breeding of fish under controlled conditions ▷ **ˌpisci'cultural** *adj* ▷ **ˌpisci'culturist** *n, adj*

piscina (pɪ'siːnə) *n*, *pl* **-nae** (-niː) *or* **-nas** *RC Church* a stone basin, with a drain, in a church or sacristy where water used at Mass is poured away [c16: from Latin: fish pond, from *piscis* a fish]

piscine ('pɪsaɪn) *adj* of, relating to, or resembling a fish

piscivorous (pɪ'sɪvərəs) *adj* feeding on fish

Pisgah ('pɪzgə) *n* Mount Pisgah *Old Testament* the mountain slopes to the northeast of the Dead Sea, from one of which, Mount Nebo, Moses viewed Canaan

pish (pʃ, pɪʃ) *interj* **1** an exclamation of impatience or contempt ▷ *vb* **2** to make this exclamation at (someone or something)

Pishpek (pɪʃ'pɛk) *n* a variant transliteration of the Kyrgyz name for **Bishkek**

pisiform ('pɪsɪˌfɔːm) *adj* **1** *zoology, botany* resembling a pea ▷ *n* **2** a small pealike bone on the ulnar side of the carpus [c18: via New Latin from Latin *pīsum* pea + *forma* shape]

Pisistratus (paɪ'sɪstrətəs) *n* ?600–527 BC, tyrant of Athens: he established himself in firm control of the city following his defeat of his aristocratic rivals at Pallene (546)

pismire ('pɪsˌmaɪə) *n* an archaic or dialect word for an **ant** [c14: literally: urinating ant, from the odour of formic acid characteristic of an ant hill]: from PISS + obsolete *mire* ant, of Scandinavian origin; compare Old Norse *maurr*, Middle Low German *mīre* ant]

piss (pɪs) *slang* ▷ *vb* **1** (*intr*) to urinate **2** (*tr*) to discharge as or in one's urine: *to piss blood* ▷ *n* **3** an act of urinating **4** urine **5** take the piss to tease or make fun of someone or something [c13: from Old French *pisser*, probably of imitative origin]

pissant ('pɪsænt) *US informal* ▷ *n* **1** an insignificant or contemptible person ▷ *adj* **2** insignificant or contemptible [c17: from PISS + ANT]

Pissarro (pɪ'saːrəʊ; *French* pisaro) *n* **Camille** (kamij). 1830–1903, French impressionist painter, esp of landscapes

piss artist *n* *slang* **1** a boastful or incompetent person **2** a person who drinks heavily and gets drunk frequently

pissed (pɪst) *adj* **1** *Brit, Austral & NZ slang* intoxicated; drunk **2** *US slang* annoyed, irritated, or disappointed

piss off *vb* (*adverb*) *slang* **1** (*tr; often passive*) to annoy, irritate, or disappoint **2** (*intr*) *chiefly Brit* to go away; depart, often used to dismiss a person

piss-poor *adj* *slang* of a contemptibly low standard or quality; pathetic

piss-take *n* *informal* something that is done to tease or make fun of someone or something; a parody or lampoon

piss-up *n* *slang, chiefly Brit* a drinking session

pistachio (pɪ'staːʃɪˌəʊ) *n*, *pl* **-os** **1** an anacardiaceous tree, *Pistacia vera*, of the Mediterranean region and W Asia, with small hard-shelled nuts **2** Also called: **pistachio nut** the nut of this tree, having an edible green kernel **3** the sweet flavour of the pistachio nut, used esp in ice creams ▷ *adj* **4** of a yellowish-green colour [c16: via Italian and Latin from Greek *pistakion* pistachio nut, from *pistakē* pistachio tree, from Persian *pistah*]

piste (piːst) *n* a trail, slope, or course for skiing [c18: via Old French from Old Italian *pista*, from *pistare* to tread down]

pistil ('pɪstɪl) *n* the female reproductive part of a flower, consisting of one or more separate or fused carpels; gynoecium [c18: from Latin *pistillum* PESTLE]

pistillate ('pɪstɪlɪt, -ˌleɪt) *adj* (of plants) **1** having pistils but no anthers **2** having or producing pistils

Pistoia (*Italian* pis'tɔːja) *n* a city in N Italy, in N Tuscany: scene of the defeat and death of Catiline in 62 BC Pop: 84 274 (2001)

pistol ('pɪst³l) *n* **1** a short-barrelled handgun **2 hold a pistol to a person's head** to threaten a person in order to force him to do what one wants ▷ *vb* **-tols, -tolling, -tolled** *or US* **-tols, -toling, -toled 3** (*tr*) to shoot with a pistol [c16: from French *pistole*, from German, from Czech *píšt'ala* pistol, pipe; related to Russian *pischal* shepherd's pipes]

pistole (pɪ'stəʊl) *n* any of various gold coins of varying value, formerly used in Europe [c16: from Old French, shortened from *pistolet*, literally: little PISTOL]

pistol grip *n* **a** a handle shaped like the butt of a pistol **b** (*as modifier*): *a pistol-grip camera*

pistol-whip *vb* **-whips, -whipping, -whipped** (*tr*) to beat or strike with a pistol barrel

piston ('pɪstən) *n* a disc or cylindrical part that slides to and fro in a hollow cylinder. In an internal-combustion engine it is forced to move by the expanding gases in the cylinder head and is attached by a pivoted connecting rod to a crankshaft or flywheel, thus converting reciprocating motion into rotation [c18: via French from Old Italian *pistone*, from *pistare* to pound, grind, from Latin *pīnsere* to crush, beat]

piston ring *n* a split ring, usually made of cast iron, that fits into a groove on the rim of a piston to provide a spring-loaded seal against the cylinder wall

piston rod *n* 1 the rod that connects the piston of a reciprocating steam engine to the crosshead 2 a less common name for a **connecting rod**

pit¹ (pɪt) *n* 1 a large, usually deep opening in the ground 2 a a mine or excavation with a shaft, esp for coal b the shaft in a mine c (*as modifier*): *pit pony; pit prop* 3 a concealed danger or difficulty 4 **the pit** hell 5 Also called: **orchestra pit** the area that is occupied by the orchestra in a theatre, located in front of the stage 6 an enclosure for fighting animals or birds, esp gamecocks 7 *anatomy* a a small natural depression on the surface of a body, organ, structure, or part; fossa b the floor of any natural bodily cavity: *the pit of the stomach* 8 *pathol* a small indented scar at the site of a former pustule; pockmark 9 a working area at the side of a motor-racing track for servicing or refuelling vehicles 10 a section on the floor of a commodity exchange devoted to a special line of trading 11 the ground floor of the auditorium of a theatre 12 another word for **pitfall** (sense 2) ▷ *vb* **pits, pitting, pitted** 13 (*tr*; often foll by *against*) to match in opposition, esp as antagonists 14 to mark or become marked with pits 15 (*tr*) to place or bury in a pit ▷ See also **pits** [Old English *pytt*, from Latin *puteus*; compare Old French *pet*, Old High German *pfuzzi*]

pit² (pɪt) *chiefly US & Canadian* ▷ *n* 1 the stone of a cherry, plum, etc ▷ *vb* **pits, pitting, pitted** 2 (*tr*) to extract the stone from a (fruit) [c19: from Dutch: kernel; compare PITH]

pitapat (ˌpɪtəˈpæt) *adv* 1 with quick light taps or beats ▷ *vb* **-pats, -patting, -patted** 2 (*intr*) to make quick light taps or beats ▷ *n* 3 such taps or beats

pit bull terrier *n* a dog resembling the Staffordshire bull terrier but somewhat larger: developed for dog-fighting; it is not recognized by kennel clubs and is regarded as dangerous. It is not allowed in some countries, including the UK

Pitcairn Island (pɪtˈkɛən, ˈpɪtkɛən) *n* an island in the S Pacific: forms with the islands of Ducie, Henderson and Oeno (all uninhabited) a UK Overseas Territory; Pitcairn itself was uninhabited until the landing in 1790 of the mutineers of H.M.S. *Bounty* and their Tahitian companions. Capital: Adamstown. Pop: 47 (2004 est.). Area: 4.6 sq km (1.75 sq miles)

pitch¹ (pɪtʃ) *vb* 1 to hurl or throw (something); cast; fling 2 (*usually tr*) to set up (a camp, tent, etc) 3 (*tr*) to aim or fix (something) at a particular level, position, style, etc: *if you advertise privately you may pitch the price too low* 4 (*tr*) to aim to sell a (product) to a specified market or on a specified basis 5 (*intr*) to slope downwards 6 (*intr*) to fall forwards or downwards 7 (*intr*) (of a vessel) to dip and raise its bow and stern alternately 8 *cricket* to bowl (a ball) so that it bounces on a certain part of the wicket, or (of a ball) to bounce on a certain part of the wicket 9 (*intr*) (of a missile, aircraft, etc) to deviate from a stable flight attitude by movement of the longitudinal axis about the lateral axis 10 (*tr*) (in golf) to hit (a ball) steeply into the air, esp with backspin to minimize roll 11 (*tr*) *music* a to sing or play accurately (a note, interval, etc) b (*usually passive*) (of a wind instrument) to specify or indicate its basic key or harmonic series by its size, manufacture, etc 12 *baseball* a (*tr*) to throw (a baseball) to a batter b (*intr*) to act as pitcher in a baseball game ▷ *n* 13 the degree of elevation or depression 14 a the angle of descent of a downward slope b such a slope 15 the extreme height or depth 16 *mountaineering* a section of a route between two belay points, sometimes equal to the full length of the rope but often shorter 17 the degree of slope of a roof, esp when expressed as a ratio of height to span 18 the distance between corresponding points on

adjacent members of a body of regular form, esp the distance between teeth on a gearwheel or between threads on a screw thread 19 the pitching motion of a ship, missile, etc 20 the distance a propeller advances in one revolution, assuming no slip 21 *music* an absolute frequency assigned to a specific note, fixing the relative frequencies of all other notes. The fundamental frequencies of the notes A–G, in accordance with the frequency A = 440 hertz, were internationally standardized and accepted in 1939 22 *cricket* the rectangular area between the stumps, 22 yards long and 10 feet wide; the wicket 23 the act or manner of pitching a ball, as in cricket 24 *chiefly Brit* a vendor's station, esp on a pavement 25 *slang* a persuasive sales talk, esp one routinely repeated 26 *chiefly Brit* (in many sports) the field of play 27 Also called: **pitch shot** *golf* an approach shot in which the ball is struck in a high arc 28 **queer someone's pitch** *Brit informal* to upset someone's plans ▷ See also **pitch in, pitch into** [c13 *picchen*; possibly related to PICK¹]

pitch² (pɪtʃ) *n* 1 any of various heavy dark viscid substances obtained as a residue from the distillation of tars 2 any of various similar substances, such as asphalt, occurring as natural deposits 3 crude turpentine obtained as sap from pine trees ▷ *vb* 4 (*tr*) to apply pitch to (something) [Old English *pic*, from Latin *pix*]

pitch accent *n* (in languages such as Ancient Greek or modern Swedish) an accent in which emphatic syllables are pronounced on a higher musical pitch relative to other syllables. Also called: **tonic accent**

pitch-black *adj* 1 extremely dark; unlit: *the room was pitch-black* 2 of a deep black colour

pitchblende (ˈpɪtʃˌblɛnd) *n* a blackish mineral that is a type of uraninite and occurs in veins, frequently associated with silver: the principal source of uranium and radium. Formula: UO_2 [c18: partial translation of German *Pechblende*, from *Pech* PITCH² (from its black colour) + BLENDE]

pitch-dark *adj* extremely or completely dark

pitched battle *n* 1 a battle ensuing from the deliberate choice of time and place, engaging all the planned resources for lifting, turning, or tossing 2 any fierce encounter, esp one with large numbers

pitcher¹ (ˈpɪtʃə) *n* a large jug, usually rounded with a narrow neck and often of earthenware, used mainly for holding water [c13: from Old French *pichier*, from Medieval Latin *picārium*, variant of *bicārium* BEAKER]

pitcher² (ˈpɪtʃə) *n* *baseball* the player on the fielding team who pitches the ball to the batter

pitcher plant *n* any of various insectivorous plants of the genera *Sarracenia, Darlingtonia, Nepenthes,* and *Cephalotus,* having leaves modified to form pitcher-like organs that attract and trap insects, which are then digested

pitchfork (ˈpɪtʃˌfɔːk) *n* 1 a long-handled fork with two or three long curved tines for lifting, turning, or tossing hay ▷ *vb* (*tr*) 2 to use a pitchfork on (something) 3 to thrust (someone) unwillingly into a position

pitch in *vb* (*intr, adverb*) 1 to cooperate or contribute 2 to begin energetically

pitch into *vb* (*intr, preposition*) *informal* 1 to assail physically or verbally 2 to get on with doing (something)

pitch pine *n* 1 any of various coniferous trees of the genus *Pinus,* esp *P. rigida,* of North America, having red-brown bark and long lustrous light brown cones: valued as a source of turpentine and pitch 2 the wood of any of these trees

pitch pipe *n* a small pipe, esp one having a reed like a harmonica, that sounds a note or notes of standard frequency. It is used for establishing the correct starting note for unaccompanied singing

pitchy (ˈpɪtʃɪ) *adj* **pitchier, pitchiest** 1 full of or covered with pitch 2 resembling pitch ▷ **pitchiness** *n*

piteous (ˈpɪtɪəs) *adj* exciting or deserving pity ▷ **piteously** *adv* ▷ **piteousness** *n*

pitfall (ˈpɪtˌfɔːl) *n* 1 an unsuspected difficulty or danger 2 a trap in the form of a concealed pit, designed to catch men or wild animals [Old English *pytt* PIT¹ + *fealle* trap]

pith (pɪθ) *n* **1** the soft fibrous tissue lining the inside of the rind in fruits such as the orange and grapefruit **2** the essential or important part, point, etc **3** weight; substance **4** Also called: medulla *botany* the central core of unspecialized cells surrounded by conducting tissue in stems **5** the soft central part of a bone, feather, etc ▷ *vb* (*tr*) **6** to kill (animals) by severing the spinal cord **7** to remove the pith from (a plant) [Old English *pitha*; compare Middle Low German *pedik*, Middle Dutch *pitt(e)*]

pithead ('pɪt,hɛd) *n* the top of a mine shaft and the buildings, hoisting gear, etc, situated around it

pithecanthropus (,pɪθɪkæn'θrəʊpəs, -'kænθrə-) *n*, *pl* -pi (-,paɪ) any primitive apelike man of the former genus *Pithecanthropus*, now included in the genus *Homo*. See **Java man** [C19: New Latin, from Greek *pithēkos* ape + *anthrōpos* man]

pith helmet *n* a lightweight hat made of pith that protects the wearer from the sun. Also called: topee, topi

pithos ('pɪθɒs, 'paɪ-) *n*, *pl* -thoi (-θɔɪ) a large ceramic container for oil or grain [from Greek]

pithy ('pɪθɪ) *adj* pithier, pithiest **1** terse and full of meaning or substance **2** of, resembling, or full of pith ▷ 'pithily *adv* ▷ 'pithiness *n*

pitiable ('pɪtɪəbəl) *adj* exciting or deserving pity or contempt ▷ 'pitiableness *n* ▷ 'pitiably *adv*

pitiful ('pɪtɪfʊl) *adj* **1** arousing or deserving pity **2** arousing or deserving contempt **3** *archaic* full of pity or compassion ▷ 'pitifully *adv* ▷ 'pitifulness *n*

pitiless ('pɪtɪlɪs) *adj* having or showing little or no pity or mercy ▷ 'pitilessly *adv* ▷ 'pitilessness *n*

pitman ('pɪtmən) *n*, *pl* -men *chiefly Scot & northern English* a person who works down a mine, esp a coal miner

Pitman ('pɪtmən) *n* Sir **Isaac**. 1813–97, English inventor of a system of phonetic shorthand (1837)

piton ('piːtɒn; *French* pitɔ̃) *n* *mountaineering* a metal spike that may be driven into a crevice of rock or into ice and used to secure a rope [C20: from French: ringbolt]

pits (pɪts) *pl n* the pits *slang* the worst possible person, place, or thing [C20: perhaps shortened from *armpits*]

pit stop *n* **1** *motor racing* a brief stop made at a pit by a racing car for repairs, refuelling, etc **2** *informal* any stop made during a car journey for refreshment, rest, or refuelling

Pitt (pɪt) *n* **1** **William Bradley**, known as **Brad**, born 1963, US actor; his films include *Thelma and Louise* (1991), *Interview with the Vampire* (1994), *Fight Club* (1999), and *Babel* (2006) **2** **William**, known as **Pitt the Elder**, 1st Earl of Chatham. 1708–78, British statesman. He was first minister (1756–57; 1757–61; 1766–68) and achieved British victory in the Seven Years' War (1756–63) **3** his son **William**, known as **Pitt the Younger**. 1759–1806, British statesman. As prime minister (1783–1801; 1804–06), he carried through important fiscal and tariff reforms. From 1793, his attention was focused on the wars with revolutionary and Napoleonic France

pitta bread *or* **pitta** ('pɪtə) *n* a flat rounded slightly leavened bread, originally from the Middle East, with a hollow inside like a pocket, which can be filled with food [from Modern Greek: a cake]

pittance ('pɪtⁿns) *n* a small amount or portion, esp a meagre allowance of money: *working long hours for a pittance* [C16: from Old French *pietance* ration, ultimately from Latin *pietās* duty]

pitter-patter ('pɪtə,pætə) *n* **1** the sound of light rapid taps or pats, as of raindrops ▷ *vb* **2** (*intr*) to make such a sound ▷ *adv* **3** with such a sound

Pitt-Rivers ('pɪt'rɪvəz) *n* **Augustus Henry Lane Fox**. 1827–1900, British archaeologist; first inspector of ancient monuments (1882): assembled a major anthropological collection of tools and weapons (now in the **Pitt-Rivers Museum**, Oxford)

Pittsburgh ('pɪtsbɜːg) *n* a port in SW Pennsylvania, at the confluence of the Allegheny and Monongahela Rivers, which form the Ohio River: settled around Fort Pitt in 1758; developed rapidly with the discovery of iron deposits and one of the world's richest coalfields; the largest river port in the US and an important industrial centre, formerly with large steel mills. Pop: 325 337 (2003 est)

pituitary (pɪ'tjuːɪtərɪ, -trɪ) *n*, *pl* -taries **1** See **pituitary gland** ▷ *adj* **2** of or relating to the pituitary gland [C17: from Late Latin *pītuītārius* slimy, from *pītuīta* phlegm]

pituitary gland *or* **pituitary body** *n* the master endocrine gland, attached by a stalk to the base of the brain. Its two lobes (the adenohypophysis and neurohypophysis) secrete hormones affecting skeletal growth, development of the sex glands, and the functioning of the other endocrine glands

pit viper *n* any venomous snake of the New World family *Crotalidae*, having a heat-sensitive organ in a pit on each side of the head: includes the rattlesnakes

pity ('pɪtɪ) *n*, *pl* pities **1** sympathy or sorrow felt for the sufferings of another **2** have pity on *or* take pity on to have sympathy or show mercy for **3** something that causes regret or pity **4** an unfortunate chance: *what a pity you can't come* ▷ *vb* pities, pitying, pitied **5** (*tr*) to feel pity for [C13: from Old French *pité*, from Latin *pietās* duty] ▷ 'pitying *adj* ▷ 'pityingly *adv*

pityriasis (,pɪtə'raɪəsɪs) *n* any of a group of skin diseases characterized by the shedding of dry flakes of skin [C17: via New Latin from Greek *pituriasis* scurfiness, from *pituron* bran]

più (pju:) *adv* *music* (in combination) more (quickly, softly, etc): *più allegro; più mosso; più lento* [Italian, from Latin *plus* more]

piupiu ('piːuːˌpiːuː) *n* a skirt made from the leaves of the New Zealand flax, worn by Māoris on ceremonial occasions [Māori]

Piura (*Spanish* 'pjura) *n* a city in NW Peru: the oldest colonial city in Peru, founded by Pizarro in 1532; commercial centre of an agricultural district. Pop: 357 000 (2005 est)

Pius II ('paɪəs) *n* pen name *Aeneas Silvius*, original name *Enea Silvio de' Piccolomini*. 1405–64, Italian ecclesiastic, humanist, poet, and historian; pope (1458–64)

Pius IV *n* original name *Giovanni Angelo de' Medici*. 1499–1565, pope (1559–65). He reconvened the Council of Trent (1562), confirming its final decrees

Pius V *n* Saint. original name *Michele Ghislieri*. 1504–72, Italian ecclesiastic; pope (1566–72). He attempted to enforce the reforms decreed by the Council of Trent, excommunicated Elizabeth I of England (1570), and organized the alliance that defeated the Turks at Lepanto (1571). Feast day: 30 April

Pius VI *n* original name *Giovanni Angelico Braschi*. 1717–99, Italian ecclesiastic; pope (1775–99). He opposed French attempts to limit papal authority and denounced (1791) the French Revolution: he died a prisoner of the French in the Revolutionary Wars

Pius VII *n* original name *Luigi Barnaba Chiaramonti*. 1740–1823, Italian ecclesiastic; pope (1800–23). He concluded a concordat with Napoleon (1801) and consecrated him as emperor of France (1804), but resisted his annexation of the Papal States (1809)

Pius IX *n* original name *Giovanni Maria Mastai-Ferretti*. 1792–1878, Italian ecclesiastic; pope (1846–78). He refused to recognize the incorporation of Rome and the Papal States in the kingdom of Italy, confining himself to the Vatican after 1870. He decreed the dogma of the Immaculate Conception (1854) and convened the Vatican Council, which laid down the doctrine of papal infallibility (1870)

Pius X *n* Saint. original name *Giuseppe Sarto*. 1835–1914, Italian ecclesiastic; pope (1903–14). He condemned Modernism (1907) and initiated a new codification of canon law. Feast day: Aug 21

Pius XI *n* original name *Achille Ratti*. 1857–1939, Italian ecclesiastic; pope (1922–39). He signed the Lateran Treaty (1929), by which the Vatican City was recognized as an independent state. His encyclicals condemned Nazism and Communism

Pius XII *n* original name *Eugenio Pacelli*. 1876–1958, Italian ecclesiastic; pope (1939–58): his attitude towards Nazi German anti-Semitism has been a matter of controversy

pivot ('pɪvət) *n* **1** a short shaft or pin supporting something that turns; fulcrum **2** the end of a shaft or arbor that terminates in a bearing **3** a person or thing upon which progress, success, etc, depends **4** the person or position from which a military formation takes its reference, as when altering position ▷ *vb* **5** (*tr*) to mount on or provide with a pivot or pivots **6** (*intr*) to turn on or as if on a pivot [c17: from Old French; perhaps related to Old Provençal *pua* tooth of a comb]

pivotal ('pɪvətəl) *adj* **1** of, involving, or acting as a pivot **2** of crucial importance

pix¹ (pɪks) *pl n informal* photographs; prints

pix² (pɪks) *n* a less common spelling of **pyx**

pixel ('pɪksəl) *n* any of a number of very small picture elements that make up a picture, as on a visual display unit [c20: from *pix* pictures + *el(ement)*]

pixie *or* **pixy** ('pɪksɪ) *n, pl* **pixies** (in folklore) a fairy or elf [c17: of obscure origin]

pixilated *or* **pixillated** ('pɪksɪ,leɪtɪd) *adj chiefly US* **1** eccentric or whimsical **2** *slang* drunk [c20: from PIXIE + *-lated*, as in *stimulated, titillated*, etc]

Pizarro (pɪˈzɑːrəʊ; *Spanish* piˈθarrɔ) *n* **Francisco** (franˈθisko). ?1475–1541, Spanish conqueror of Peru. He landed in Peru (1532), murdered the Inca King Atahualpa (1533), and founded Lima as the new capital of Peru (1535). He was murdered by his own followers

pizza ('piːtsə) *n* a dish of Italian origin consisting of a baked disc of dough covered with cheese and tomatoes, usually with the addition of mushrooms, anchovies, sausage, or ham [c20: from Italian, perhaps from Vulgar Latin *picea* (unattested), from Latin *piceus* relating to PITCH²; perhaps related to Modern Greek *pitta* cake]

pizzazz *or* **pizazz** (pəˈzæz) *n informal* an attractive combination of energy and style; sparkle, vitality, glamour [c20: origin obscure]

pizzeria (ˌpiːtsəˈriːə) *n* a place where pizzas are made, sold, or eaten [c20: from Italian, from PIZZA + *-eria* -ERY]

pizzicato (ˌpɪtsɪˈkɑːtəʊ) *music* ▷ *adj, adv* **1** (in music for the violin family) to be plucked with the finger ▷ *n* **2** the style or technique of playing a normally bowed stringed instrument in this manner [c19: from Italian: pinched, from *pizzicare* to twist, twang]

pizzle ('pɪzəl) *n archaic or dialect* the penis of an animal, esp a bull [c16: of Germanic origin; compare Low German *pēsel*, Flemish *pēzel*, Middle Dutch *pēze* sinew]

pk *pl* **pks** *abbreviation* **1** pack **2** park **3** peak

pkg. *pl* **pkgs** *abbreviation* package

pl *abbreviation* **1** place **2** plate **3** plural

Pl. *abbreviation* (in street names) Place

PLA *abbreviation* Port of London Authority

plaas (plɑːs) *n South African* a farm [Afrikaans]

placable ('plækəbəl) *adj* easily placated or appeased [c15: via Old French from Latin *plācābilis*, from *plācāre* to appease; related to *placēre* to please] > ˌplacaˈbility *or* ˈplacableness *n*

placard ('plækɑːd) *n* **1** a printed or written notice for public display; poster **2** a small plaque or card ▷ *vb* (*tr*) **3** to post placards on or in **4** to publicize or advertise by placards **5** to display as a placard [c15: from Old French *plaquart*, from *plaquier* to plate, lay flat; see PLAQUE]

placate (pləˈkeɪt) *vb* (*tr*) to pacify or appease [c17: from Latin *plācāre*; see PLACABLE] > plaˈcation *n* > placatory (pləˈkeɪtərɪ, ˈplækətərɪ, -trɪ) *or* (*less commonly*) placative (pləˈkeɪtɪv, ˈplækətɪv) *adj*

place (pleɪs) *n* **1** a particular point or part of space or of a surface, esp that occupied by a person or thing **2** a geographical point, such as a town, city, etc **3** a position or rank in a sequence or order **4** an open square lined with houses of a similar type in a city or town **5** space or room **6** a house or living quarters **7** a country house with grounds **8** any building or area set aside for a specific purpose **9** a passage in a book, play, film, etc: *to lose one's place* **10** suitable, appropriate, or customary surroundings (esp in the phrases **out of place, in place**) **11** right, prerogative, or duty: *it is your place to give a speech* **12** appointment, position, or job: *a place at college* **13** position, condition, or state: *if I were in your place* **14 a** a space or seat, as at a dining table **b** (*as modifier*): *place mat* **15** *maths* the relative position of a digit in a number **16** any of the best times in a race **17** *horse racing* **a** *Brit* the first, second, or third position at the finish **b** *US &*

Canadian the first or usually the second position at the finish **c** (*as modifier*): *a place bet* **18** all over the place in disorder or disarray **19** give place to someone to make room for or be superseded by someone **20** go places *informal* **a** to travel **b** to become successful **21** in place of **a** instead of; in lieu of: *go in place of my sister* **b** in exchange for: *he gave her it in place of her ring* **22** know one's place to be aware of one's inferior position **23** put someone in his place to humble someone who is arrogant, conceited, forward, etc **24** take one's place to take up one's usual or specified position **25** take the place of to be a substitute for **26** take place to happen or occur ▷ *vb* (*mainly tr*) **27** to put or set in a particular or appropriate place **28** to find or indicate the place of **29** to identify or classify by linking with an appropriate context: *to place a face* **30** to regard or view as being: *to place prosperity above sincerity* **31** to make (an order, a bet, etc) **32** to find a home or job for (someone) **33** to appoint to an office or position **34** (*often foll by with*) to put under the care (of) **35** to direct or aim carefully **36** (*passive*) *Brit* to cause (a racehorse, greyhound, athlete, etc) to arrive in first, second, third, or sometimes fourth place **37** (*intr*) *US & Canadian* (of a racehorse, greyhound, etc) to finish among the first three in a contest, esp in second position **38** to invest (funds) **39** to insert (an advertisement) in a newspaper, journal, etc [c13: via Old French from Latin *platēa* courtyard, from Greek *plateia*, from *platus* broad; compare French *plat* flat]

Place (pleɪs) *n* **Francis.** 1771–1854, British radical, who campaigned for the repeal (1824) of the Combination Acts, which forbade the forming of trade unions, and for parliamentary reform

placebo (pləˈsiːbəʊ) *n, pl* **-bos** *or* **-boes** **1** *med* an inactive substance or other sham form of therapy administered to a patient usually to compare its effects with those of a real drug or treatment, but sometimes for the psychological benefit to the patient through his believing he is receiving treatment **2** something said or done to please or humour another **3** *RC Church* a traditional name for the vespers of the office for the dead [C13 (in the ecclesiastical sense): from Latin *Placebo Domino* I shall please the Lord (from the opening of the office for the dead); C19 (in the medical sense)]

placebo effect *n med* a positive therapeutic effect claimed by a patient after receiving a placebo believed by him to be an active drug

place card *n* a card placed on a dinner table before a seat, as at a formal dinner, indicating who is to sit there

place kick *football* ▷ *n* **1** a kick in which the ball is placed in position before it is kicked ▷ *vb* **place-kick** **2** to kick (a ball) using a place kick

placement ('pleɪsmənt) *n* **1** the act of placing or the state of being placed **2** arrangement or position **3** the process or business of finding employment

placenta (pləˈsɛntə) *n, pl* **-tas** *or* **-tae** (-tiː) **1** the vascular organ formed in the uterus during pregnancy, consisting of both maternal and embryonic tissues and providing oxygen and nutrients for the fetus and transfer of waste products from the fetal to the maternal blood circulation **2** *botany* the part of the ovary of flowering plants to which the ovules are attached [c17: via Latin from Greek *plakoeis* flat cake, from *plax* flat]

placer ('plæsə) *n* **a** surface sediment containing particles of gold or some other valuable mineral **b** (*in combination*): *placer-mining* [c19: from American Spanish: deposit, from Spanish *plaza* PLACE]

place setting *n* the set of items of cutlery, crockery, and glassware laid for one person at a dining table

placet ('pleɪsɛt) *n* a vote or expression of assent by saying the word *placet* [c16: from Latin, literally: it pleases]

placid ('plæsɪd) *adj* having a calm appearance or nature [c17: from Latin *placidus* peaceful; related to *placēre* to please] > placidity (pləˈsɪdɪtɪ) *or* ˈplacidness *n* > ˈplacidly *adv*

placing ('pleɪsɪŋ) *n stock exchange* a method of issuing securities to the public using an intermediary, such as a stockbroking firm

placket ('plækɪt) *n dressmaking* **1** a piece of cloth sewn in under a closure with buttons, hooks and eyes, zips, etc **2** the closure itself [c16: perhaps from Middle Dutch *plackaet* breastplate, from Medieval Latin *placca* metal plate]

placoid ('plækɔɪd) *adj* **1** platelike or flattened **2** (of the scales of sharks and other elasmobranchs) toothlike; composed of dentine with an enamel tip and basal pulp cavity [c19: from Greek *plac-*, *plax* flat]

plafond (plə'fɒn; *French* plafɔ̃) *n* a ceiling, esp one having ornamentation [c17: from French, literally: ceiling, maximum, from *plat* flat + *fond* bottom, from Latin *fundus* bottom]

plagal ('pleɪɡ³l) *adj* **1** (of a cadence) progressing from the subdominant to the tonic chord, as in the *Amen* of a hymn **2** (of a mode) commencing upon the dominant of an authentic mode, but sharing the same final as the authentic mode. Plagal modes are designated by the prefix *Hypo-* before the name of their authentic counterparts ▷ See **authentic** (sense 5) [c16: from Medieval Latin *plagālis*, from *plaga*, perhaps from Greek *plagos* side]

plage (plɑːʒ) *n astronomy* a bright patch in the sun's chromosphere [French, literally: beach, strand]

plagiarism ('pleɪdʒə,rɪzəm) *n* **1** the act of plagiarizing **2** something plagiarized ▷ 'plagiarist *n* ▷ ˌplagia'ristic *adj*

plagiarize *or* **plagiarise** ('pleɪdʒə,raɪz) *vb* to appropriate (ideas, passages, etc) from (another work or author) ▷ 'plagiaˌrizer *or* 'plagiaˌriser *n*

plagioclase ('pleɪdʒɪəʊ,kleɪz) *n* a series of feldspar minerals consisting of a mixture of sodium and calcium aluminium silicates in triclinic crystalline form: includes albite, oligoclase, and labradorite ▷ plagioclastic (ˌpleɪdʒɪəʊ'klæstɪk) *adj*

plague (pleɪɡ) *n* **1** any widespread and usually highly contagious disease with a high fatality rate **2** an infectious disease of rodents, esp rats, transmitted to man by the bite of the rat flea (*Xenopsylla cheopis*) **3** See **bubonic plague 4** something that afflicts or harasses **5** *informal* an annoyance or nuisance **6** a pestilence, affliction, or calamity on a large scale, esp when regarded as sent by God ▷ *vb* plagues, plaguing, plagued (tr) **7** to afflict or harass **8** to bring down a plague upon **9** *informal* to annoy [c14: from Late Latin *plāga* pestilence, from Latin: a blow; related to Greek *plēgē* a stroke, Latin *plangere* to strike]

plaguy *or* **plaguey** ('pleɪɡɪ) *archaic, informal* ▷ *adj* **1** disagreeable or vexing ▷ *adv* **2** disagreeably or annoyingly ▷ 'plaguily *adv*

plaice (pleɪs) *n, pl* plaice *or* plaices **1** a European flatfish, *Pleuronectes platessa*, having an oval brown body marked with red or orange spots and valued as a food fish: family Pleuronectidae **2** *US & Canadian* any of various other fishes of the family Pleuronectidae, esp *Hippoglossoides platessoides* [c13: from Old French *plaïz*, from Late Latin *platessa* flatfish, from Greek *platus* flat]

plaid (plæd, pleɪd) *n* **1** a long piece of cloth of a tartan pattern, worn over the shoulder as part of Highland costume **2 a** a crisscross weave or cloth **b** (*as modifier*): *a plaid scarf* [c16: from Scottish Gaelic *plaide*, of obscure origin]

Plaid Cymru (ˌplaɪd 'kʌmrɪ) *n* the Welsh nationalist party [c20: Welsh, literally: party of Wales]

plain¹ (pleɪn) *adj* **1** flat or smooth; level **2** not complicated; clear: *the plain truth* **3** not difficult; simple or easy: *a plain task* **4** honest or straightforward **5** lowly, esp in social rank or education **6** without adornment or show: *a plain coat* **7** (of fabric) without pattern or of simple untwilled weave **8** not mixed; **9** not attractive; simple: *plain vodka* **10** *knitting* of or done in plain ▷ *n* **11** a level or almost level tract of country, esp an extensive treeless region **12** a simple stitch in knitting made by putting the right needle into a loop on the left needle, passing the wool round the right needle, and pulling it through the loop, thus forming a new loop ▷ *adv* **13** (*intensifier*): *just plain tired* [c13: from Old French: simple, from Latin *plānus* level, distinct, clear] ▷ 'plainly *adv* ▷ 'plainness *n*

plain² (pleɪn) *vb* a dialect or poetic word for **complain** [c14 *pleignen*, from Old French *plaindre* to lament, from

Latin *plangere* to beat]

plainchant ('pleɪn,tʃɑːnt) *n* another name for **plainsong** [c18: from French, rendering Medieval Latin *cantus plānus*; see PLAIN¹]

plain chocolate *n* chocolate with a slightly bitter flavour and dark colour

plain clothes *pl n* **a** ordinary clothes, as distinguished from uniform, as worn by a police detective on duty **b** (*as modifier*): *a plain-clothes policeman*

plain flour *n* flour to which no raising agent has been added

plain sailing *n* **1** *informal* smooth or easy progress **2** *nautical* sailing in a body of water that is unobstructed; clear sailing

plainsman ('pleɪnzmən) *n, pl* -men a person who lives in a plains region, esp in the Great Plains of North America

Plains of Abraham *n* (*functioning as singular*) a field in E Canada between Quebec City and the St Lawrence River: site of an important British victory (1759) in the Seven Years' War, which cost the French their possession of Canada

plainsong ('pleɪn,sɒŋ) *n* the style of unison unaccompanied vocal music used in the medieval Church, esp in Gregorian chant [c16: translation of Medieval Latin *cantus plānus*]

plain-spoken *adj* candid; frank; blunt

plaint (pleɪnt) *n* **1** *archaic* a complaint or lamentation **2** *law* a statement in writing of grounds of complaint made to a court of law and asking for redress of the grievance [c13: from Old French *plainte*, from Latin *planctus* lamentation, from *plangere* to beat]

plaintiff ('pleɪntɪf) *n* (formerly) a person who brings a civil action in a court of law [c14: from legal French *plaintif*, from Old French *plaintif* (adj) complaining, from *plainte* PLAINT]

plaintive ('pleɪntɪv) *adj* expressing melancholy; mournful [c14: from Old French *plaintif* grieving, from *plainte* PLAINT] ▷ 'plaintively *adv* ▷ 'plaintiveness *n*

plait (plæt) *n* **1** a length of hair, ribbon, etc, that has been plaited **2** a rare spelling of **pleat** ▷ *vb* **3** (tr) to intertwine (strands or strips) in a pattern [c15 *pleyt*, from Old French *pleit*, from Latin *plicāre* to fold; see PLY²]

plan (plæn) *n* **1** a detailed scheme, method, etc, for attaining an objective **2** (*sometimes plural*) a proposed, usually tentative idea for doing something **3** a drawing to scale of a horizontal section through a building taken at a given level; a view from above an object or an area in orthographic projection **4** an outline, sketch, etc ▷ *vb* plans, planning, planned **5** to form a plan (for) or make plans (for) **6** (tr) to make a plan of (a building) **7** (tr; *takes a clause as object or an infinitive*) to have in mind as a purpose; intend [c18: via French from Latin *plānus* flat; compare PLANE¹, PLAIN¹]

planar ('pleɪnə) *adj* **1** of or relating to a plane **2** lying in one plane; flat [c19: from Late Latin *plānāris* on level ground, from Latin *plānus* flat]

planarian (plə'nɛərɪən) *n* any free-living turbellarian flatworm of the mostly aquatic suborder Tricladida, having a three-branched intestine [c19: from New Latin *Plānāria* type genus, from Late Latin *plānārius* level, flat; see PLANE¹]

planar process *n* a method of producing diffused junctions in semiconductor devices. A pattern of holes is etched into an oxide layer formed on a silicon substrate, into which impurities are diffused through the holes

planchet ('plɑːntʃɪt) *n* a piece of metal ready to be stamped as a coin, medal, etc; flan [c17: from French: little board, from *planche* PLANK¹]

planchette (plɑːn'ʃet) *n* a heart-shaped board on wheels, on which messages are written under supposed spirit guidance [c19: from French: little board, from *planche* PLANK¹]

Planck (plæŋk; *German* plaŋk) *n* Max (**Karl Ernst Ludwig**) (maks). 1858–1947, German physicist who first formulated the quantum theory (1900): Nobel prize for physics 1918

Planck constant *or* **Planck's constant** *n* a fundamental constant equal to the energy of any quantum of radiation divided by its frequency. It has a value of 6.62606876 × 10⁻³⁴ joule seconds [C20: after Max PLANCK]

plane¹ (pleɪn) *n* **1** *maths* a flat surface in which a straight line joining any two of its points lies entirely on that surface **2** a flat or level surface **3** a level of existence, performance, attainment, etc **4 a** short for **aeroplane b** a wing or supporting surface of an aircraft or hydroplane ▷ *adj* **5** level or flat **6** *maths* (of a curve, figure, etc) lying entirely in one plane ▷ *vb* (*intr*) **7** to fly without moving wings or using engines; glide **8** (of a boat) to rise partly and skim over the water when moving quickly [C17: from Latin *plānum* level surface]

plane² (pleɪn) *n* **1** a tool with an adjustable sharpened steel blade set obliquely in a wooden or iron body, for levelling or smoothing timber surfaces, cutting mouldings or grooves, etc **2** a flat tool, usually metal, for smoothing the surface of clay or plaster in a mould ▷ *vb* (*tr*) **3** to level, smooth, or cut (timber, wooden articles, etc) using a plane or similar tool **4** (often foll by *off*) to remove using a plane [C14: via Old French from Late Latin *plāna* plane, from *plānāre* to level]

plane³ (pleɪn) *n* See **plane tree**

plane geometry *n* the study of the properties of and relationships between plane curves, figures, etc

plane polarization *n* a type of polarization in which the electric vector of waves of light or other electromagnetic radiation is restricted to vibration in a single plane

planet ('plænɪt) *n* **1** Also called: **major planet** any of the eight celestial bodies, Mercury, Venus, Earth, Mars, Jupiter, Saturn, Uranus, and Neptune, that revolve around the sun in elliptical orbits and are illuminated by light from the sun **2** Also called: **extrasolar planet** any other celestial body revolving around a star, illuminated by light from that star **3** *astrology* any of the planets of the solar system, excluding the earth but including the sun and moon, each thought to rule one or sometimes two signs of the zodiac [C12: via Old French from Late Latin *planēta*, from Greek *planētēs* wanderer, from *planaein* to wander]

plane table *n* a surveying instrument consisting of a drawing board mounted on adjustable legs, and used in the field for plotting measurements directly

planetarium (,plænɪ'tɛərɪəm) *n*, *pl* -**iums** *or* -**ia** (-ɪə) **1** an instrument for simulating the apparent motions of the sun, moon, and planets against a background of stars by projecting images of these bodies onto the inside of a domed ceiling **2** a building in which such an instrument is housed **3** a model of the solar system, sometimes mechanized to show the relative motions of the planets

planetary ('plænɪtərɪ, -trɪ) *adj* **1** of or relating to a planet **2** mundane; terrestrial **3** wandering or erratic **4** (of a gear, esp an epicyclic gear) having an axis that rotates around that of another gear

planetesimal hypothesis (,plænɪ'tɛsɪməl) *n* the discredited theory that the close passage of a star to the sun caused many small bodies (**planetesimals**) to be drawn from the sun, eventually coalescing to form the planets [C20: *planetesimal*, from PLANET + INFINITESIMAL]

planetoid ('plænɪ,tɔɪd) *n* another name for **asteroid** (sense 1) > ,plane'toidal *adj*

plane tree *or* **plane** *n* any tree of the genus *Platanus*, having ball-shaped heads of fruits and leaves with pointed lobes: family *Platanaceae*. The hybrid *P. × acerifolia* (**London plane**) is frequently planted in towns [C14 *plane*, from Old French, from Latin *platanus*, from Greek *platanos*, from *platos* wide, referring to the leaves]

planet Zog *n Brit informal* a place or situation that is far removed from reality or what is currently happening: *those of you who've been on planet Zog for the last ten years*

plangent ('plændʒənt) *adj* **1** having a loud deep sound **2** resonant and mournful in sound [C19: from Latin *plangere* to beat (esp the breast, in grief); see PLAIN²]

planimeter (plæ'nɪmɪtə) *n* a mechanical integrating instrument for measuring the area of an irregular plane figure, such as the area under a curve, by moving a point attached to an arm around the perimeter of the figure

planish ('plænɪʃ) *vb* (*tr*) to give a final finish to (metal) by hammering or rolling to produce a smooth surface [C16: from Old French *planir* to smooth out, from Latin *plānus* flat, PLAIN¹]

planisphere ('plænɪ,sfɪə) *n* a projection or representation of all or part of a sphere on a plane surface, such as a polar projection of the celestial sphere onto a chart [C14: from Medieval Latin *plānisphaerium*, from Latin *plānus* flat + Greek *sphaira* globe]

plank (plæŋk) *n* **1** a stout length of sawn timber **2** something that supports or sustains **3** one of the policies in a political party's programme **4 walk the plank** to be forced by pirates to walk to one's death off the end of a plank jutting out over the water from the side of a ship **5** *Brit slang* a stupid person; idiot ▷ *vb* (*tr*) **6** to cover or provide (an area) with planks [C13: from Old Norman French *planke*, from Late Latin *planca* board, from *plancus* flat-footed; probably related to Greek *plax* flat surface]

planking ('plæŋkɪŋ) *n* a number of planks

plankton ('plæŋktən) *n* the organisms inhabiting the surface layer of a sea or lake, consisting of small drifting plants and animals, such as diatoms [C19: via German from Greek *planktos* wandering, from *plazesthai* to roam]

planned economy *n* another name for **command economy**

planned obsolescence *n* the policy of deliberately limiting the life of a product in order to encourage the purchaser to replace it. Also called: **built-in obsolescence**

planner ('plænə) *n* **1** a person who makes plans, esp for the development of a town, building, etc **2** a chart for recording future appointments, tasks, goals, etc

planning permission *n* (in Britain) formal permission that must be obtained from a local authority before development or a change of use of land or buildings

plano- *or sometimes before a vowel* **plan-** *combining form* indicating flatness or planeness: *plano-concave* [from Latin *plānus* flat, level]

plano-concave (,pleɪnəʊ'kɒnkeɪv) *adj* (of a lens) having one side concave and the other side plane

plano-convex (,pleɪnəʊ'kɒnveks) *adj* (of a lens) having one side convex and the other side plane

plant¹ (plɑːnt) *n* **1** any living organism that typically synthesizes its food from inorganic substances, possesses cellulose cell walls, responds slowly and often permanently to a stimulus, lacks specialized sense organs and nervous system, and has no powers of locomotion **2** such an organism that is green, terrestrial, and smaller than a shrub or tree; a herb **3** a cutting, seedling, or similar structure, esp when ready for transplantation **4** *informal* a thing positioned secretly for discovery by another, esp in order to incriminate an innocent person **5** *billiards, snooker* a position in which the cue ball can be made to strike an intermediate which then pockets another ball ▷ *vb* (*tr*) **6** (often foll by *out*) to set (seeds, crops, etc) into (ground) to grow **7** to place firmly in position **8** to establish; found **9** to implant in the mind **10** *slang* to deliver (a blow) **11** *informal* to position or hide, esp in order to deceive or observe **12** to place (young fish, oysters, spawn, etc) in (a lake, river, etc) to stock the water [Old English, from Latin *planta* a shoot, cutting] > 'plantable *adj* > 'plant,like *adj*

plant² (plɑːnt) *n* **1 a** the land, buildings, and equipment used in carrying on an industrial, business, or other undertaking or service **b** (*as modifier*): *plant costs* **2** a factory or workshop **3** mobile mechanical equipment for construction, road-making, etc [C20: special use of PLANT¹]

Plantagenet (plæn'tædʒɪnɪt) *n* a line of English kings, ruling from the ascent of Henry II (1154) to the death of Richard III (1485) [C12: from Old French, literally: sprig of broom, with reference to the crest of the Angevin kings, from Latin *planta* sprig + *genista* broom]

plantain¹ ('plæntɪn) *n* any of various N temperate plants of the genus *Plantago*, esp *P. major* (**great plantain**), which has a rosette of broad leaves and a slender spike of small greenish flowers: family *Plantaginaceae*. See also **ribwort** [C14 *plauntein*, from Old French *plantein*, from Latin *plantāgō,* from *planta* sole of the foot]

plantain² ('plæntɪn) *n* a large tropical musaceous plant, *Musa paradisiaca* [c16: from Spanish *platano* plantain, PLANE TREE]

plantain lily *n* any of several Asian plants of the liliaceous genus *Hosta,* having broad ribbed leaves and clusters of white, blue, or lilac flowers

plantar ('plæntə) *adj* of, relating to, or occurring on the sole of the foot or a corresponding part [c18: from Latin *plantāris,* from *planta* sole of the foot]

plantation (plæn'teɪʃən) *n* **1** an estate, esp in tropical countries, where cash crops such as rubber, oil palm, etc, are grown on a large scale **2** a group of cultivated trees or plants **3** (formerly) a colony or group of settlers

planter ('plɑːntə) *n* **1** the owner or manager of a plantation **2** a machine designed for rapid, uniform, and efficient planting of seeds in the ground **3** a colonizer or settler **4** a decorative pot or stand for house plants

plantigrade ('plæntɪ,greɪd) *adj* **1** walking with the entire sole of the foot touching the ground, as, for example, man and bears ▷ *n* **2** a plantigrade animal [c19: via French from New Latin *plantigradus,* from Latin *planta* sole of the foot + *gradus* a step]

plant louse *n* another name for an **aphid**

plaque (plæk, plɑːk) *n* **1** an ornamental or commemorative inscribed tablet or plate of porcelain, wood, etc **2** a small flat brooch or badge, as of a club, etc **3** *pathol* any small abnormal patch on or within the body, such as the typical lesion of psoriasis **4** short for **dental plaque** [c19: from French, from *plaquier* to plate, from Middle Dutch *placken* to beat (metal) into a thin plate]

plash (plæʃ) *vb, n* a less common word for **splash** [Old English *plæsc,* probably imitative; compare Dutch *plas*] > 'plashy *adj*

-plasia *or* **-plasy** *n combining form* indicating growth, development, or change [from New Latin, from Greek *plasis* a moulding, from *plassein* to mould]

plasm ('plæzəm) *n* **1** protoplasm of a specified type: *germ plasm* **2** a variant of **plasma**

-plasm *n combining form* (in biology) indicating the material forming cells: *protoplasm; cytoplasm* [from Greek *plasma* something moulded; see PLASMA] > -plasmic *adj combining form*

plasma ('plæzmə) *or* **plasm** *n* **1** the clear yellowish fluid portion of blood or lymph in which the red blood cells, white blood cells, and platelets are suspended **2** a former name for **protoplasm, cytoplasm 3** *physics* a hot ionized material consisting of nuclei and electrons. It is sometimes regarded as a fourth state of matter and is the material present in the sun, most stars, and fusion reactors **4** a green slightly translucent variety of chalcedony, used as a gemstone [c18: from Late Latin: something moulded, from Greek, from *plassein* to mould] > plasmatic (plæz'mætɪk) *or* 'plasmic *adj*

plasma screen *n* a type of flat screen on a television or visual display unit in which the image is created by electric current passing through many gas-filled cells

plasma torch *n* an electrical device for converting a gas into a plasma, used for melting metal

plasmid ('plæzmɪd) *n* a small circle of bacterial DNA that is independent of the main bacterial chromosome. Plasmids often contain genes for drug resistances and can be transmitted between bacteria of the same and different species: used in genetic engineering [c20: from PLASM + -ID¹]

plasmodium (plæz'məʊdɪəm) *n, pl* -dia (-dɪə) **1** an amoeboid mass of protoplasm, containing many nuclei: a stage in the life cycle of certain organisms, esp the nonreproductive stage of the slime moulds **2** any parasitic sporozoan protozoan of the genus *Plasmodium,* such as *P. falciparum* and *P. vivax,* which cause malaria [c19: New Latin; see PLASMA, -ODE¹] > plas'modial *adj*

plasmolysis (plæz'mɒlɪsɪs) *n* the shrinkage of protoplasm away from the cell walls that occurs as a result of excessive water loss, esp in plant cells

Plassey ('plæsɪ) *n* a village in NE India, in W Bengal: scene of Clive's victory (1757) over Siraj-ud-daula, which established British supremacy over India

-plast *n combining form* indicating an organized living cell or particle of living matter: *protoplast* [from Greek *plastos* formed, from *plassein* to form]

plaster ('plɑːstə) *n* **1** a mixture of lime, sand, and water, sometimes stiffened with hair or other fibres, that is applied to the surface of a wall or ceiling as a soft paste that hardens when dry **2** *Brit, Austral & NZ* an adhesive strip of material, usually medicated, for dressing a cut, wound, etc **3** short for **mustard plaster, plaster of Paris** ▷ *vb* **4** to coat (a wall, ceiling, etc) with plaster **5** (*tr*) to apply like plaster **6** (*tr*) to cause to lie flat or to adhere **7** (*tr*) to apply a plaster cast to **8** (*tr*) *slang* to strike or defeat with great force [Old English, from Medieval Latin *plastrum* medicinal salve, building plaster, via Latin from Greek *emplastron* curative dressing, from EM- + *plassein* to form] > 'plasterer *n*

plasterboard ('plɑːstə,bɔːd) *n* a thin rigid board, in the form of a layer of plaster compressed between two layers of fibreboard, used to form or cover walls

plastered ('plɑːstəd) *adj slang* intoxicated; drunk

plaster of Paris *n* **1** a white powder that sets to a hard solid when mixed with water, used for making sculptures and casts, as an additive for lime plasters, and for making casts for setting broken limbs. It is usually the hemihydrate of calcium sulphate, $2CaSO_4.H_2O$ **2** the hard plaster produced when this powder is mixed with water: usually a hydrated form of calcium sulphate [c15: from Medieval Latin *plastrum parisiense,* originally made from the gypsum of *Paris*]

plastic ('plæstɪk, 'plɑː-) *n* **1** any one of a large number of synthetic usually organic materials that have a polymeric structure and can be moulded when soft and then set, esp such a material in a finished state containing plasticizer, stabilizer, filler, pigments, etc Plastics are classified as thermosetting (such as Bakelite) or thermoplastic (such as PVC) and are used in the manufacture of many articles and in coatings, artificial fibres, etc ▷ *adj* **2** made of plastic **3** easily influenced; impressionable **4** capable of being moulded or formed **5** *fine arts* **a** of or relating to moulding or modelling: *the plastic arts* **b** produced or apparently produced by moulding: *the plastic draperies of Giotto's figures* **6** having the power to form or influence: *the plastic forces of the imagination* **7** *biology* of or relating to any formative process; able to change, develop, or grow: *plastic tissues* **8** *slang* superficially attractive yet unoriginal or artificial: *plastic food* [c17: from Latin *plasticus* relating to moulding, from Greek *plastikos,* from *plassein* to form] > 'plastically *adv*

-plastic *adj combining form* growing or forming [from Greek *plastikos;* see PLASTIC]

plastic bomb *n* a bomb consisting of a putty-like explosive charge fitted with a detonator and timing device

plastic bullet *n* a solid PVC cylinder, 10 cm long and 38 mm in diameter, fired by police or military forces to regain control in riots. Also called: *formal baton round*

plastic explosive *n* an adhesive jelly-like explosive substance

Plasticine ('plæstɪ,siːn) *n trademark* a soft coloured material used, esp by children, for modelling

plasticize *or* **plasticise** ('plæstɪ,saɪz) *vb* to make or become plastic, as by the addition of a plasticizer > ,plastici'zation *or* ,plastici'sation *n*

plasticizer *or* **plasticiser** ('plæstɪ,saɪzə) *n* any of a number of substances added to materials in order to modify their physical properties. Their uses include softening and improving the flexibility of plastics and preventing dried paint coatings from becoming too brittle

plastic money *n* credit cards, used instead of cash [c20: from the cards being made of plastic]

plastic surgery *n* the branch of surgery concerned with therapeutic or cosmetic repair or re-formation of missing, injured, or malformed tissues or parts > **plastic surgeon** *n*

plastid ('plæstɪd) *n* any of various small particles in the cytoplasm of the cells of plants and some animals that contain pigments, starch, oil, protein, etc [C19: via German from Greek *plastēs* sculptor, from *plassein* to form]

plastron ('plæstrən) *n* the bony plate forming the ventral part of the shell of a tortoise or turtle [C16: via French from Italian *piastrone*, from *piastra* breastplate, from Latin *emplastrum* PLASTER] > 'plastral *adj*

-plasty *n combining form* indicating plastic surgery involving a bodily part, tissue, or a specified process: *rhinoplasty; neoplasty* [from Greek *-plastia*; see -PLAST]

plat¹ (plæt) *n* a small area of ground; plot [C16 (also occurring in Middle English in place names): originally variant of PLOT²]

plat² (plæt) *n, vb* plats, platting, platted *dialect* a variant spelling of **plait** [C16: variant of PLAIT]

Plata (Spanish 'plata) *n* Río de la Plata ('rio de la) an estuary on the SE coast of South America, between Argentina and Uruguay, formed by the Uruguay and Paraná Rivers. Length: 275 km (171 miles). Width: (at its mouth) 225 km (140 miles). Also known as: La Plata

Plataea (pla'ti:ə) *n* an ancient city in S Boeotia, traditionally an ally of Athens: scene of the defeat of a great Persian army by the Greeks in 479 BC

platan ('plætᵊn) *n* another name for **plane tree** [C14: from Latin *platanus*, from Greek *platanos*; see PLANE TREE]

plat du jour ('plɑː də 'ʒʊə; *French* pla dy ʒur) *n, pl* plats du jour ('plɑːz də 'ʒʊə; *French* pla dy ʒur) the specially prepared or recommended dish of the day on a restaurant's menu [French, literally: dish of the day]

plate (pleɪt) *n* **1 a** a shallow usually circular dish made of porcelain, earthenware, glass, etc, on which food is served or from which food is eaten **b** (*as modifier*): *a plate rack* **2** Also called: **plateful** the contents of a plate or the amount a plate will hold **b** *Austral & NZ* a plate of cakes, sandwiches, etc, brought by a guest to a party: *everyone was asked to bring a plate* **3** an entire course of a meal: *a cold plate* **4** any shallow or flat receptacle, esp for receiving a collection in church **5** flat metal of uniform thickness obtained by rolling, usually having a thickness greater than about three millimetres **6** a thin coating of metal usually on another metal, as produced by electrodeposition, chemical action, etc **7** metal or metalware that has been coated in this way, esp with gold or silver: *Sheffield plate* **8** dishes, cutlery, etc, made of gold or silver **9** a sheet of metal, plastic, rubber, etc, having a printing surface produced by a process such as stereotyping, moulding, or photographic deposition **10** a print taken from such a sheet or from a woodcut, esp when appearing in a book **11** a thin flat sheet of a substance, such as metal or glass **12** armour made of overlapping or articulated pieces of thin metal **13** *photog* a sheet of glass, or sometimes metal, coated with photographic emulsion on which an image can be formed by exposure to light **14** an orthodontic device, esp one used for straightening children's teeth **15** an informal word for **denture** (sense 1) **16** *anatomy* any flat platelike structure or part **17 a** a cup or trophy awarded to the winner of a sporting contest, esp a horse race **b** a race or contest for such a prize **18** any of the rigid layers of the earth's lithosphere of which there are believed to be at least 15 **19** *electronics chiefly US* the anode in an electronic valve **20** a horizontal timber joist that supports rafters or studs **21** a light horseshoe for flat racing **22** Also called: **Communion plate** *RC Church* a flat plate held under the chin of a communicant in order to catch any fragments of the consecrated Host **23** on a plate in such a way as to be acquired without further trouble: *he was handed the job on a plate* **24** on one's plate waiting to be done or dealt with ▷ *vb* (*tr*) **25** to coat (a surface, usually metal) with a thin layer of other metal by electrolysis, chemical reaction, etc **26** to cover with metal plates, as for protection **27** *printing* to make a stereotype or electrotype from (type or another plate) **28** to form (metal) into plate, esp by rolling [C13: from Old French: thin metal sheet, something flat, from Vulgar Latin *plattus* (unattested); related to Greek *platus* flat]

Plate (pleɪt) *n* River Plate the English name for the (Río de la) **Plata**

plateau ('plætəʊ) *n, pl* -eaus *or* -eaux (-əʊz) **1** a wide

mainly level area of elevated land **2** a relatively long period of stability; levelling off: *the rising prices reached a plateau* ▷ *vb* (*intr*) **3** to remain at a stable level for a relatively long period [C18: from French, from Old French *platel* something flat, from *plat* flat; see PLATE]

Plateau ('plætəʊ) *n* a state of central Nigeria, formed in 1976 from part of Benue-Plateau State: tin mining. Capital: Jos. Pop: 3 178 712 (2006). Area: 30 913 sq km (11 936 sq miles)

plated ('pleɪtɪd) *adj* **a** coated with a layer of metal **b** (*in combination*): *gold-plated*

plate glass *n* glass formed into a thin sheet by rolling, used for windows

platelayer ('pleɪt,leɪə) *n Brit* a workman who lays and maintains railway track. US and Canadian name: **trackman**

platelet ('pleɪtlɪt) *n* a minute cell occurring in the blood of vertebrates and involved in clotting of the blood [C19: a small PLATE]

platen ('plætᵊn) *n* **1** a flat plate in a printing press that presses the paper against the type **2** the roller on a typewriter, against which the keys strike [C15: from Old French *platine*, from *plat* flat; see PLATE]

plater ('pleɪtə) *n* **1** a person or thing that plates **2** *horse racing* a mediocre horse entered chiefly for minor races

plate tectonics *n* (*functioning as singular*) *geology* the study of the structure of the earth's crust and mantle with reference to the theory that the earth's lithosphere is divided into large rigid blocks (**plates**) that are floating on semifluid rock and are thus able to interact with each other at their boundaries, and to the associated theories of continental drift and seafloor spreading

plate up *vb* (*adverb*) to put food on a plate, ready for serving

platform ('plætfɔːm) *n* **1** a raised floor or other horizontal surface, such as a stage for speakers **2** a raised area at a railway station, from which passengers have access to the trains **3** See **drilling platform** **4** the declared principles, aims, etc, of a political party, an organization, or an individual **5 a** the thick raised sole of some high-heeled shoes **b** (*as modifier*): *platform shoes* **6** a vehicle or level place on which weapons are mounted and fired **7** a specific type of computer hardware or computer operating system [C16: from French *plateforme*, from *plat* flat + *forme* form, layout]

platform ticket *n* a ticket for admission to railway platforms but not for travel

Plath (plæθ) *n* **Sylvia**. 1932–63, US poet living in England. She wrote two volumes of verse, *The Colossus* (1960) and *Ariel* (1965), and a novel, *The Bell Jar* (1963): she was married to Ted Hughes

platina ('plætɪnə, plə'ti:nə) *n* an alloy of platinum and several other metals, including palladium, osmium, and iridium [C18: from Spanish: silvery element, from *plata* silver, from Provençal: silver plate]

plating ('pleɪtɪŋ) *n* **1** a coating or layer of material, esp metal **2** a layer or covering of metal plates

Platini (French platini) *n* **Michel**. born 1955, French football player and sports administrator

platiniridium (,plætɪnɪ'rɪdɪəm) *n* any alloy of platinum and iridium: used in jewellery, electrical contacts, and hypodermic needles

platinize *or* **platinise** ('plætɪ,naɪz) *vb* (*tr*) to coat with platinum > ,platini'zation *or* ,platini'sation *n*

platinum ('plætɪnəm) *n* a ductile malleable silvery-white metallic element, very resistant to heat and chemicals. It occurs free and in association with other platinum metals, esp in osmiridium: used in jewellery, laboratory apparatus, electrical contacts, dentistry, electroplating, and as a catalyst. Symbol: Pt; atomic no: 78; atomic wt: 195.08; valency: 1–4; relative density: 21.45; melting pt: 1769°C; boiling pt: 3827±100°C [C19: New Latin, from PLATINA, on the model of other metals with the suffix *-um*]

platinum black *n chem* a black powder consisting of very finely divided platinum metal. It is used as a catalyst, esp in hydrogenation reactions

platinum-blond *or feminine* **platinum-blonde** *adj* **1** (of hair) of a pale silver-blond colour **2 a** having hair of this colour **b** (*as noun*): *she was a platinum blonde*

platinum disc *n* **a** (in Britain) an album certified to have sold 300 000 copies or a single certified to have sold 600 000 copies **b** (in the US) an album or single certified to have sold one million copies

platinum metal *n* any of the group of precious metallic elements consisting of ruthenium, rhodium, palladium, osmium, iridium, and platinum

platitude (ˈplætɪˌtjuːd) *n* **1** a trite, dull, or obvious remark or statement; a commonplace **2** staleness or insipidity of thought or language; triteness [C19: from French, literally: flatness, from *plat* flat]
> ˌplatiˈtudinous *adj*

platitudinize *or* **platitudinise** (ˌplætɪˈtjuːdɪˌnaɪz) *vb* (*intr*) to speak or write in platitudes

Plato (ˈpleɪtəʊ) *n* ?427–?347 BC, Greek philosopher: with his teacher Socrates and his pupil Aristotle, he is regarded as the initiator of western philosophy. His influential theory of ideas, which makes a distinction between objects of sense perception and the universal ideas or forms of which they are an expression, is formulated in such dialogues as *Phaedo*, *Symposium*, and *The Republic*. Other works include *The Apology* and *Laws*

Platonic (pləˈtɒnɪk) *adj* **1** of or relating to Plato or his teachings **2** (*often not capital*) free from physical desire: *Platonic love* > Plaˈtonically *adv*

Platonic solid *n* any of the five possible regular polyhedra: cube, tetrahedron, octahedron, icosahedron, and dodecahedron [C17: named after PLATO, who was the first to list them]

Platonism (ˈpleɪtəˌnɪzəm) *n* the teachings of Plato (BC) and his followers, esp the philosophical theory that the meanings of general words are real existing abstract entities (Forms) and that particular objects have properties in common by virtue of their relationship with these Forms > ˈPlatonist *n*

platoon (pləˈtuːn) *n* **1** *military* a subunit of a company usually comprising three sections of ten to twelve men: commanded by a lieutenant **2** a group or unit of people, esp one sharing a common activity, characteristic, etc [C17: from French *peloton* little ball, group of men, from *pelote* ball; see PELLET]

Plattdeutsch (*German* ˈplatdɔytʃ) *n* another name for **Low German** [literally: flat (that is, low) German]

Platte (plæt) *n* a river system of the central US, formed by the confluence of the **North Platte** and **South Platte** at North Platte, Nebraska: flows generally east to the Missouri River. Length: 499 km (310 miles)

platteland (ˈplatəˌlant) *n* the platteland (in South Africa) the country districts or rural areas [C20: from Afrikaans, from Dutch *plat* flat + *land* country]

platter (ˈplætə) *n* **1** a large shallow usually oval dish or plate, used for serving food **2** a course of a meal, usually consisting of several different foods served on the same plate: *a seafood platter* [C14: from Anglo-Norman *plater*, from *plat* dish, from Old French *plat* flat; see PLATE]

platy- *combining form* indicating something flat: *platyhelminth* [from Greek *platus* flat]

platypus (ˈplætɪpəs) *n*, *pl* -puses See **duck-billed platypus** [C18: from PLATY- + -*pus*, from Greek *pous* foot]

platyrrhine (ˈplætɪˌraɪn) *or* **platyrrhinian** (ˌplætɪˈrɪnɪən) *adj* **1** (esp of New World monkeys) having widely separated nostrils opening to the side of the face **2** (of humans) having an unusually short wide nose [C19: from New Latin *platyrrhinus*, from PLATY- + -*rrhinus*, from Greek *rhis* nose]

plaudit (ˈplɔːdɪt) *n* (*usually plural*) **1** an expression of enthusiastic approval or approbation **2** a round of applause [C17: shortened from earlier *plauditē*, from Latin: applaud!, from *plaudere* to APPLAUD]

Plauen (*German* ˈplauən) *n* a city in E central Germany, in Saxony: textile centre. Pop: 70 070 (2003 est)

plausible (ˈplɔːzəbəl) *adj* **1** apparently reasonable, valid, truthful, etc: *a plausible excuse* **2** apparently trustworthy or believable: *a plausible speaker* [C16: from Latin *plausibilis* worthy of applause, from *plaudere* to APPLAUD]
> ˌplausiˈbility *or* ˈplausibleness *n* > ˈplausibly *adv*

Plautus (ˈplɔːtəs) *n* Titus Maccius (ˈtaɪtəs ˈmæksɪəs). ?254–?184 BC, Roman comic dramatist. His 21 extant

works, adapted from Greek plays, esp those by Menander, include *Menaechmi* (the basis of Shakespeare's *The Comedy of Errors*), *Miles Gloriosus*, *Rudens*, and *Captivi*

play (pleɪ) *vb* **1** to occupy oneself in (a sport or diversion); amuse oneself in (a game) **2** (*tr*) to contend against (an opponent) in a sport or game: *Ed played Tony at chess and lost* **3** to fulfil or cause to fulfil (a particular role) in a team game: *he plays defence; he plays in the defence* **4** (*intr*; often foll by *about* or *around*) to behave carelessly, esp in a way that is unconsciously cruel or hurtful; trifle or dally (with): *to play about with a young girl's affections* **5** (when *intr*, often foll by *at*) to perform or act the part (of) in or as in a dramatic production; assume or simulate the role (of) **6** to act out or perform (a dramatic production) **7** (*intr*) to be received: *How will these policies play in Middle England?* **8** to have the ability to perform on (a musical instrument): *David plays the harp* **9** to perform (on a musical instrument) as specified: *he plays out of tune* **10** (*tr*) **a** to reproduce (a tune, melody, piece of music, note, etc) on an instrument **b** to perform works by (a specific composer): *to play Brahms* **11** to discharge or cause to discharge: *he played the water from the hose onto the garden* **12** to operate, esp to cause (a record player, radio, etc) to emit sound or (of a record player, radio, etc) to emit (sound) **13** to move or cause to move freely, quickly, or irregularly: *lights played on the scenery* **14** (*tr*) *stock exchange* to speculate or operate aggressively for gain in (a market) **15** (*tr*) *angling* to attempt to tire (a hooked fish) by alternately letting out and reeling in line and by using the rod's flexibility **16** to put (a card, counter, piece, etc) into play **17** to gamble (money) on a game **18 play fair** *or* **play fair with someone** to prove oneself fair in one's dealings **19 play false** *or* **play fair with someone** to prove oneself unfair in one's dealings **20 play for time** to act so as to delay the outcome of some activity so as to gain time to one's own advantage **21 play into the hands of** to act directly to the advantage of (an opponent) ▷ *n* **22** a dramatic composition written for performance by actors on a stage, on television, etc; drama **23** the performance of a dramatic composition **24 a** games, exercise, or other activity undertaken for pleasure, diversion, etc, esp by children **b** (*in combination*): *playroom* **25** manner of action, conduct, or playing: *fair play* **26** the playing or conduct of a game or the period during which a game is in progress: *rain stopped play* **27** *US & Canadian* a move or manoeuvre in a game: *a brilliant play* **28** the situation of a ball that is within the defined area and being played according to the rules (in the phrases **in play**, **out of play**) **29** the act of playing for stakes; gambling **30** action, activity, or operation: *the play of the imagination* **31** freedom of or scope or space for movement: *too much play in the rope* **32** light, free, or rapidly shifting motion: *the play of light on the water* **33** fun, jest, or joking: *I only did it in play* **34 call into play** to bring into operation **35 make a play for** *informal* to make an obvious attempt to gain ▷ See also **play along**, **playback**, **play down** etc [Old English *plega* (n), *plegan* (vb); related to Middle Dutch *pleyen*] > ˈplayable *adj*

play-act *vb* **1** (*intr*) to pretend or make believe **2** (*intr*) to behave in an overdramatic or affected manner **3** to act in or as in (a play) > ˈplay-ˌacting *n* > ˈplay-ˌactor *n*

play along *vb* (*adverb*) **1** (*intr*; usually foll by *with*) to cooperate (with), esp as a temporary measure **2** (*tr*) to manipulate as if in a game, esp for one's own advantage: *he played the widow along until he gave him her money*

playback (ˈpleɪˌbæk) *n* **1** the act or process of reproducing a recording, esp on magnetic tape **2** the part of a tape recorder serving to reproduce or used for reproducing recorded material ▷ *vb* **play back** (*adverb*) **3** to reproduce (recorded material) on (a magnetic tape) by means of a tape recorder

playbill (ˈpleɪˌbɪl) *n* **1** a poster or bill advertising a play **2** the programme of a play

playboy (ˈpleɪˌbɔɪ) *n* a man, esp one of private means, who devotes himself to the pleasures of nightclubs, expensive holiday resorts, female company, etc

play-centre *n* NZ a regular meeting of small children arranged by their parents or a welfare agency to give them an opportunity of supervised creative play. Also called (esp in Britain): playgroup

play down vb (tr, adverb) to make little or light of; minimize the importance of

player ('pleɪə) n 1 a person who participates in or is skilled at some game or sport 2 a person who plays a game or sport professionally 3 a person who plays a musical instrument 4 an actor 5 informal a participant, esp a powerful one, in a particular field of activity: a leading city player

Player ('pleɪə) n **Gary** ('gæɪ). born 1935, South African professional golfer: won the British Open Championship (1959; 1968; 1974) and the US Open Championship (1965)

player piano n a mechanical piano; Pianola

playful ('pleɪfʊl) adj 1 full of high spirits and fun: a playful kitten 2 good-natured and humorous: a playful remark > 'playfully adv

playgoer ('pleɪˌɡəʊə) n a person who goes to theatre performances, esp frequently

playground ('pleɪˌɡraʊnd) n 1 an outdoor area for children's play, esp one having swings, slides, etc, or adjoining a school 2 a place or region particularly popular as a sports or holiday resort

playgroup ('pleɪˌɡruːp) n a regular meeting of small children arranged by their parents or a welfare agency to give them an opportunity of supervised creative play

playhouse ('pleɪˌhaʊs) n 1 a theatre where live dramatic performances are given 2 a toy house, small room, etc, for children to play in

playing card n one of a pack of 52 rectangular stiff cards, used for playing a variety of games, each card having one or more symbols of the same kind (diamonds, hearts, clubs, or spades) on the face, but an identical design on the reverse

playing field n chiefly Brit a field or open space used for sport

playlet ('pleɪlɪt) n a short play

playlist ('pleɪˌlɪst) n 1 a list of records chosen for playing, as on a radio station 2 a list of tracks to be played in a particular order on an MP3 player or CD player ▷ vb 3 (tr) to put (a song or record) on a playlist

play-lunch n NZ a schoolchild's mid-morning snack

playmaker ('pleɪˌmeɪkə) n sport a player whose role is to create scoring opportunities for his or her team-mates

playmate ('pleɪˌmeɪt) or **playfellow** n a friend or partner in play or recreation

play off vb (adverb) 1 (tr; usually foll by against) to deal with or manipulate as if in playing a game: to play one person off against another 2 (intr) to take part in a play-off ▷ n play-off 3 sport an extra contest to decide the winner when two or more competitors are tied 4 chiefly US & Canadian a contest or series of games to determine a championship, as between the winners of two competitions

play on vb (intr) 1 (adverb) to continue to play 2 Also called: play upon (preposition) to exploit or impose upon (the feelings or weakness of another) to one's own advantage

play on words n another term for pun¹ (sense 1)

playpen ('pleɪˌpen) n a small enclosure, usually portable, in which a young child can be left to play in safety

playschool ('pleɪˌskuːl) n an informal nursery group taking preschool children in half-day sessions

PlayStation ('pleɪˌsteɪʃən) n trademark a video games console

play-the-ball n rugby league a method for bringing the ball back into play after a tackle, in which the tackled player is allowed to stand up and kick or heel the ball behind him or her to a team-mate

plaything ('pleɪˌθɪŋ) n 1 a toy 2 a person regarded or treated as a toy

playtime ('pleɪˌtaɪm) n a time for play or recreation, esp the school break

play up vb (adverb) 1 (tr) to emphasize or highlight: to play up one's best features 2 Brit informal to behave irritatingly (towards) 3 (intr) Brit informal (of a machine, car, etc) to function erratically: the car is playing up again 4 Brit informal

to hurt; give (one) pain or trouble: my back's playing me up again 5 play up to a to support (another actor) in a performance b to try to gain favour with by flattery

playwright ('pleɪˌraɪt) n a person who writes plays

plaza ('plɑːzə; Spanish 'plaθa) n 1 an open space or square, esp in Spain or a Spanish-speaking country 2 chiefly US & Canadian a modern complex of shops, buildings, and parking areas [c17: from Spanish, from Latin platēa courtyard, from Greek plateia; see PLACE]

plc or **PLC** abbreviation public limited company

plea (pliː) n 1 an earnest entreaty or request 2 a law something alleged or pleaded by or on behalf of a party to legal proceedings in support of his claim or defence b criminal law the answer made by an accused to the charge: a plea of guilty c (in Scotland and formerly in England) a suit or action at law 3 an excuse, justification, or pretext: he gave the plea of a previous engagement [c13: from Anglo-Norman plai, from Old French plaid lawsuit, from Medieval Latin placitum court order (literally: what is pleasing), from Latin placēre to please]

plea bargaining n law an agreement between the prosecution and defence, sometimes including the judge, in which the accused agrees to plead guilty to a lesser charge in return for more serious charges being dropped

plead (pliːd) vb pleads, pleading, pleaded, plead (plɛd) or esp Scot & US pled (plɛd) 1 (when intr, often foll by with) to appeal earnestly or humbly (to) 2 (tr; may take a clause as object) to give as an excuse; offer in justification or extenuation: to plead ignorance; he pleaded that he was insane 3 law to declare oneself to be (guilty or not guilty) in answer to the charge 4 law to advocate (a case) in a court of law 5 (intr) law a to file pleadings b to address a court as an advocate [c13: from Old French plaidier, from Medieval Latin placitāre to have a lawsuit, from Latin placēre to please; see PLEA] > 'pleadable adj > 'pleader n

pleadings ('pliːdɪŋz) pl n law (formerly) the formal written statements presented alternately by the claimant and defendant in a lawsuit setting out the respective matters relied upon

pleasance ('plɛzəns) n 1 a secluded part of a garden laid out with trees, walks, etc 2 archaic enjoyment or pleasure [C14 plesance, from Old French plaisance, from plaisant pleasant, from plaisir to PLEASE]

pleasant ('plɛzənt) adj 1 giving or affording pleasure; enjoyable 2 having pleasing or agreeable manners, appearance, habits, etc 3 obsolete merry and lively [c14: from Old French plaisant, from plaisir to PLEASE] > 'pleasantly adv

Pleasant Island n the former name of **Nauru**

pleasantry ('plɛzəntrɪ) n, pl -ries 1 (often plural) an agreeable or amusing remark, often one made in order to be polite: they exchanged pleasantries 2 an agreeably humorous manner or style [c17: from French plaisanterie, from plaisant PLEASANT]

please (pliːz) vb 1 to give satisfaction, pleasure, or contentment to (a person); make or cause (a person) to be glad 2 to be the will of or have the will (to): if it pleases you; the court pleases 3 if you please if you will or wish, sometimes used in ironic exclamation 4 pleased with happy because of 5 please oneself to do as one likes ▷ adv 6 (sentence modifier) used in making polite requests and in pleading, asking for a favour, etc 7 yes please a polite formula for accepting an offer, invitation, etc [C14 plese, from Old French plaisir, from Latin placēre to please, satisfy] > pleased adj > pleasedly ('pliːzɪdlɪ) adv

Pleasence ('plɛzəns) n **Donald**. 1919–95, British actor. His films include Dr Crippen (1962) and Cul de Sac (1966)

pleasing ('pliːzɪŋ) adj giving pleasure; likable or gratifying > 'pleasingly adv

pleasurable ('plɛʒərəbəl) adj enjoyable, agreeable, or gratifying > 'pleasurably adv

pleasure ('plɛʒə) n 1 an agreeable or enjoyable sensation or emotion: the pleasure of hearing good music 2 something that gives or affords enjoyment or delight: his garden was his only pleasure 3 a amusement, recreation, or enjoyment b (as modifier): a pleasure boat; pleasure ground 4 euphemistic sexual gratification or enjoyment: he took his pleasure of her

P

5 a person's preference or choice ▷ *vb* **6** (when *intr*, often foll by *in*) to give pleasure to or take pleasure (in) [C14 *plesir*, from Old French; related to Old French *plaisir* to PLEASE]

pleat (pliːt) *n* **1** any of various types of fold formed by doubling back fabric and pressing, stitching, or steaming into place ▷ *vb* **2** (*tr*) to arrange (material, part of a garment, etc) in pleats [C16: variant of PLAIT]

pleb (plɛb) *n* **1** short for **plebeian** **2** *Brit informal*, *often derogatory* a common vulgar person

plebeian (pləˈbiːən) *adj* **1** of, relating to, or characteristic of the common people, esp those of Rome **2** lacking refinement; vulgar: *plebeian tastes* ▷ *n* **3** one of the common people, esp one of the Roman plebs **4** a person who is coarse or lacking in discernment [C16: from Latin *plēbēius* belonging to the people, from *plēbs* the common people of ancient Rome] ▷ pleˈbeianˌism *n*

plebiscite (ˈplɛbɪˌsaɪt, -sɪt) *n* **1** a direct vote by the electorate of a state, region, etc, on some question of usually national importance, such as union with another state or acceptance of a government programme **2** any expression or determination of public opinion on some matter ▷ See also **referendum** [C16: from Old French *plébiscite*, from Latin *plēbiscītum* decree of the people, from *plēbs* the populace + *scītum*, from *scīscere* to decree, approve, from *scīre* to know] ▷ plebiscitary (pləˈbɪsɪtərɪ) *adj*

plectrum (ˈplɛktrəm) *n*, *pl* **-trums** *or* **-tra** (-trə) any implement for plucking a string, such as a small piece of plastic, wood, etc, used to strum a guitar, or the quill that plucks the string of a harpsichord [C17: from Latin *plēctrum* quill, plectrum, from Greek *plektron*, from *plessein* to strike]

pled (plɛd) *vb* *Scot law*, *US* a past tense and past participle of **plead**

pledge (plɛdʒ) *n* **1** a formal or solemn promise or agreement, esp to do or refrain from doing something **2 a** collateral for the payment of a debt or the performance of an obligation **b** the condition of being collateral (esp in the phrase **in pledge**) **3** a sign, token, or indication: *the gift is a pledge of their sincerity* **4** an assurance of support or goodwill, conveyed by drinking to a person, cause, etc; toast: *we drank a pledge to their success* **5** a person who binds himself, as by becoming bail or surety for another **6 sign the pledge** *or* **take the pledge** to make a vow to abstain from alcoholic drink ▷ *vb* **7** to promise formally or solemnly **8** (*tr*) to bind or secure by or as if by a pledge: *they were pledged to secrecy* **9** to give, deposit, or offer (one's word, freedom, property, etc) as a guarantee, as for the repayment of a loan **10** to drink a toast to (a person, cause, etc) [C14: from Old French *plege*, from Late Latin *plebium* gage, security, from *plebīre* to pledge, of Germanic origin; compare Old High German *pflegan* to look after, care for] ▷ ˈpledgable *adj* ▷ pledgor, pledgeor (plɛdʒˈɔː) *or* pledger (ˈplɛdʒə) *n*

pledgee (plɛdʒˈiː) *n* **1** a person to whom a pledge is given **2** a person to whom property is delivered as a pledge

pledget (ˈplɛdʒɪt) *n* a small flattened pad of wool, cotton, etc, esp for use as a pressure bandage to be applied to wounds or sores [C16: of unknown origin]

-plegia *n combining form* indicating a specified type of paralysis: *paraplegia* [from Greek, from *plēgē* stroke, from *plēssein* to strike] ▷ **-plegic** *adj combining form*, *n combining form*

pleiad (ˈplaɪəd) *n* a brilliant or talented group, esp one with seven members [C16: originally French *Pléiade*, name given by Pierre de Ronsard (1524–85) to himself and six other poets after a group of Alexandrian Greek poets who were called this after the PLEIADES]

Pleiades (ˈplaɪəˌdiːz) *pl n* *Greek myth* the seven daughters of Atlas, placed as stars in the sky either to save them from the pursuit of Orion or, in another account, after they had killed themselves for grief over the death of their half-sisters the Hyades

Pleiocene (ˈplaɪəʊˌsiːn) *adj*, *n* a variant spelling of **Pliocene**

Pleistocene (ˈplaɪstəˌsiːn) *adj* **1** of, denoting, or formed in the first epoch of the Quaternary period, which

lasted for about 1 600 000 years. It was characterized by extensive glaciations of the N hemisphere and the evolutionary development of man ▷ *n* **2** the Pleistocene the Pleistocene epoch or rock series [C19: from Greek *pleistos* most + *kainos* recent]

Plekhanov (Russian plʲɪrˈɡanəf) *n* Georgi Valentinovich (ˈgjɪɔrgjɪ valɪnˈtjinəvjtʃ). 1857–1918, Russian revolutionary; founder of Russian Marxism and leader of the Russian Social Democratic Workers' Party

plenary (ˈpliːnərɪ, ˈplɛn-) *adj* **1** full, unqualified, or complete: *plenary powers*; *plenary indulgence* **2** (of assemblies, councils, etc) attended by all the members [C15: from Late Latin *plēnārius*, from Latin *plēnus* full; related to Middle English *plener*; see PLENUM] ▷ ˈplenarily *adv*

plenipotentiary (ˌplɛnɪpəˈtɛnʃərɪ) *adj* **1** (esp of a diplomatic envoy) invested with or possessing full power or authority **2** conferring full power or authority **3** (of power or authority) full; absolute ▷ *n*, *pl* **-aries** **4** a person invested with full authority to transact business, esp a diplomat authorized to represent a country. See also **envoy¹** (sense 1) [C17: from Medieval Latin *plēnipotentiārius*, from Latin *plēnus* full + *potentia* POWER]

plenitude (ˈplɛnɪˌtjuːd) *n* **1** abundance; copiousness **2** the condition of being full or complete [C15: via Old French from Latin *plēnitūdō*, from *plēnus* full]

plenteous (ˈplɛntɪəs) *adj* **1** ample; abundant: *a plenteous supply of food* **2** producing or yielding abundantly: *a plenteous grape harvest* [C13 *plenteus*, from Old French *plentivous*, from *plentif* abundant, from *plenté* PLENTY] ▷ ˈplenteously *adv* ▷ ˈplenteousness *n*

plentiful (ˈplɛntɪfʊl) *adj* **1** ample; abundant **2** having or yielding an abundance: *a plentiful year* ▷ ˈplentifully *adv* ▷ ˈplentifulness *n*

plenty (ˈplɛntɪ) *n*, *pl* **-ties** **1** (often foll by *of*) a great number, amount, or quantity; lots: *plenty of time*; *there are plenty of cars on display here* **2** generous or ample supplies of wealth, produce, or resources: *the age of plenty* **3** in plenty existing in abundance: *food in plenty* ▷ *determiner* **4 a** very many; ample: *plenty of people believe in ghosts* **b** (as pronoun): *there's plenty more*; *that's plenty, thanks* ▷ *adv* **5** *informal* more than adequately; abundantly: *the water's plenty hot enough* [C13: from Old French *plenté*, from Late Latin *plēnitās* fullness, from Latin *plēnus* full]

Plenty (ˈplɛntɪ) *n* **Bay of Plenty** a large bay of the Pacific on the NE coast of the North Island, New Zealand

plenum (ˈpliːnəm) *n*, *pl* **-nums** *or* **-na** (-nə) **1** an enclosure containing gas at a higher pressure than the surrounding environment **2** a fully attended meeting or assembly, esp of a legislative body **3** (esp in the philosophy of the Stoics) space regarded as filled with matter [C17: from Latin: space filled by matter, from *plēnus* full]

pleo- *combining form* a variant of: **plio-** *pleochroism*; *pleomorphism*

pleochroism (plɪˈɒkrəʊˌɪzəm) *n* a property of certain crystals of absorbing light to an extent that depends on the orientation of the electric vector of the light with respect to the optic axes of the crystal. The effect occurs in uniaxial crystals (**dichroism**) and esp in biaxial crystals (**trichroism**) [C19: PLEO- + -*chroism*, from Greek *khrōs* skin colour] ▷ pleochroic (ˌplɪəˈkrəʊɪk) *adj*

pleomorphism (ˌpliːəˈmɔːˌfɪzəm) *or* **pleomorphy** (ˈpliːəˌmɔːfɪ) *n* **1** the occurrence of more than one different form in the life cycle of a plant or animal **2** the occurrence of more than one different form of crystal of one chemical compound; polymorphism ▷ ˌpleoˈmorphic *adj*

pleonasm (ˈpliːəˌnæzəm) *n* *rhetoric* **1** the use of more words than necessary or an instance of this, such as *a tiny little child* **2** a word or phrase that is superfluous [C16: from Latin *pleonasmus*, from Greek *pleonasmos* excess, from *pleonazein* to be redundant] ▷ ˌpleoˈnastic *adj*

plesiosaur (ˈpliːsɪəˌsɔː) *n* any of various extinct marine reptiles of the order *Sauropterygia*, esp any of the suborder *Plesiosauria*, of Jurassic and Cretaceous times, having a long neck, short tail, and paddle-like limbs [C19: from New Latin *plēsiosaurus*, from Greek *plēsios* near + *sauros* a lizard]

P

plethora ('plɛθərə) *n* **1** superfluity or excess; overabundance **2** *pathol obsolete* a condition caused by dilation of superficial blood vessels, characterized esp by a reddish face [c16: via Medieval Latin from Greek *plēthōrē* fullness, from *plēthein* to grow full] > plethoric (plɛ'θɒrɪk) *adj*

pleura ('plʊərə) *n*, *pl* **pleurae** ('plʊəri:) the thin transparent serous membrane enveloping the lungs and lining the walls of the thoracic cavity [c17: via Medieval Latin from Greek: side, rib] > 'pleural *adj*

pleurisy ('plʊərɪsɪ) *n* inflammation of the pleura, characterized by pain that is aggravated by deep breathing or coughing [c14: from Old French *pleurisie*, from Late Latin *pleurisis*, from Greek *pleuritis*, from *pleura* side] > pleuritic (plʊ'rɪtɪk) *adj*, *n*

pleuro- *or before a vowel* **pleur-** *combining form* **1** of or relating to the side **2** indicating the pleura [from Greek *pleura* side]

pleuropneumonia (,plʊərəʊnjuː'məʊnɪə) *n* the combined disorder of pleurisy and pneumonia

Pleven (*Bulgarian* 'plɛvɛn) *or* **Plevna** (*Bulgarian* 'plɛvna) *n* a town in N Bulgaria: taken by Russia from the Turks in 1877 after a siege of 143 days. Pop: 102 000 (2005 est)

Plexiglas ('plɛksɪ,glɑːs) *n trademark US* a transparent plastic, polymethylmethacrylate, used for combs, plastic sheeting, etc

plexor ('plɛksə) *or* **plessor** *n med* a small hammer with a rubber head for use in percussion of the chest and testing reflexes [c19: from Greek *plēxis* a stroke, from *plēssein* to strike]

plexus ('plɛksəs) *n*, *pl* **-uses** *or* **-us** **1** any complex network of nerves, blood vessels, or lymphatic vessels **2** an intricate network or arrangement [c17: New Latin, from Latin *plectere* to braid, PLAIT]

pliable ('plaɪəb³l) *adj* easily moulded, bent, influenced, or altered > ,plia'bility *n* > 'pliableness *n* > 'pliably *adv*

pliant ('plaɪənt) *adj* **1** easily bent; supple: *a pliant young tree* **2** yielding readily to influence; compliant [c14: from Old French, from *plier* to fold, bend; see PLY²] > 'pliancy *or* 'pliantness *n* > 'pliantly *adv*

plicate ('plaɪkeɪt) *or* **plicated** *adj* having or arranged in parallel folds or ridges; pleated: *a plicate leaf*; *plicate rock strata* [c18: from Latin *plicātus* folded, from *plicāre* to fold] > plication (plaɪ'keɪʃən) *or* plicature ('plɪkətʃə) *n*

plié ('pliːeɪ) *n* a classic ballet practice posture with back erect and knees bent [French: bent, from *plier* to bend]

plier ('plaɪə) *n* a person who plies a trade

pliers ('plaɪəz) *pl n* a gripping tool consisting of two hinged arms with usually serrated jaws that close on the workpiece [c16: from PLY¹]

plight¹ (plaɪt) *n* a condition of extreme hardship, danger, etc [C14 *plit*, from Old French *pleit* fold, PLAIT; probably influenced by Old English *pliht* peril, PLIGHT²]

plight² (plaɪt) *vb* (*tr*) **1** to promise formally or pledge (allegiance, support, etc) **2** plight one's troth to make a promise of marriage **3** *archaic or dialect* a solemn promise, esp of engagement; pledge [Old English *pliht* peril; related to Old High German, German *Pflicht* duty] > 'plighter *n*

plimsoll *or* **plimsole** ('plɪmsəl) *n Brit* a light rubber-soled canvas shoe worn for various sports. Also called: gym shoe, sandshoe [c20: so called because of the resemblance of the rubber sole to a Plimsoll line]

Plimsoll line ('plɪmsəl) *n* another name for **load line** [c19: named after Samuel *Plimsoll* (1824–98), MP, who advocated its adoption]

plinth (plɪnθ) *n* **1** Also called: **socle** the rectangular slab or block that forms the lowest part of the base of a column, statue, pedestal, or pier **2** Also called: **plinth course** the lowest part of the wall of a building that appears above ground level, esp one that is formed of a course of stone or brick **3** a flat block on either side of a doorframe, where the architrave meets the skirting [c17: from Latin *plinthus*, from Greek *plinthos* brick, shaped stone]

Pliny ('plɪnɪ) *n* **1** known as *Pliny the Elder*. Latin name *Gaius Plinius Secundus*. 23–79 AD, Roman writer, the author of the encyclopedic *Natural History* (77) **2** his nephew, known as *Pliny the Younger*. Latin name *Gaius Plinius Caecilius Secundus*.

?62–?113 AD, Roman writer and administrator, noted for his letters

plio-, pleo- *or* **pleio-** *combining form* greater in size, extent, degree, etc; more: *Pliocene* [from Greek *pleiōn* more, from *polus* much, many]

Pliocene *or* **Pleiocene** ('plaɪəʊ,siːn) *adj* **1** of, denoting, or formed in the last epoch of the Tertiary period, which lasted for three million years, during which many modern mammals appeared ▷ *n* **2** the Pliocene the Pliocene epoch or rock series [c19: PLIO- + -*cene*, from Greek *kainos* recent]

plissé ('pliːseɪ, 'plɪs-) *n* **1** fabric with a wrinkled finish, achieved by treatment involving caustic soda: *cotton plissé* **2** such a finish on a fabric [French *plissé* pleated, from *plisser* to pleat; see PLY²]

PLO *abbreviation* Palestine Liberation Organization

Płock (pwɒtsk) *n* a town in central Poland, on the River Vistula: several Polish kings are buried in the cathedral: oil refining, petrochemical works. Pop: 130 000 (2005 est)

plod (plɒd) *vb* **plods, plodding, plodded** **1** to make (one's way) or walk along (a path, road, etc) with heavy usually slow steps **2** (*intr*) to work slowly and perseveringly ▷ *n* **3** the act of plodding **4** *Brit slang* a policeman [c16: of imitative origin] > 'plodding *adj* > 'ploddingly *adv* > 'plodder *n*

Ploești (*Romanian* plo'jeʃtj) *n* a city in SE central Romania: centre of the Romanian petroleum industry. Pop: 204 000 (2005 est)

-ploid *adj combining form*, *n combining form* indicating a specific multiple of a single set of chromosomes: *diploid* [from Greek -*pl*(*oos*) -fold + -OID] > -ploidy *n combining form*

Plomer ('pluːmə) *n* **William** (**Charles Franklyn**). 1903–73, British poet, novelist, and short-story writer, born in South Africa. His novels include *Turbott Wolfe* (1926) and *The Case is Altered* (1932)

plonk¹ (plɒŋk) *vb* **1** (often foll by *down*) to drop or be dropped, esp heavily or suddenly: *he plonked the money on the table* ▷ *n* **2** the act or sound of plonking

plonk² (plɒŋk) *n Brit, Austral & NZ informal* alcoholic drink, usually wine, esp of inferior quality [c20: perhaps from French *blanc* white, as in *vin blanc* white wine]

plonker ('plɒŋkə) *n slang* a stupid person [c20: from PLONK¹]

plop (plɒp) *n* **1** the characteristic sound made by an object dropping into water without a splash ▷ *vb* **plops, plopping, plopped** **2** to fall or cause to fall with the sound of a plop: *the stone plopped into the water* ▷ *interj* **3** an exclamation imitative of this sound: *to go plop* [c19: imitative of the sound]

plosion ('pləʊʒən) *n phonetics* the sound of an abrupt break or closure, esp the audible release of a stop. Also called: **explosion**

plosive ('pləʊsɪv) *phonetics* ▷ *adj* **1** articulated with or accompanied by plosion ▷ *n* **2** a plosive consonant; stop [c20: from French, from *explosif* EXPLOSIVE]

plot¹ (plɒt) *n* **1** a secret plan to achieve some purpose, esp one that is illegal or underhand **2** the story or plan of a play, novel, etc **3** *military* a graphic representation of an individual or tactical setting that pinpoints an artillery target **4** *chiefly US* a diagram or plan, esp a surveyor's map **5** lose the plot *informal* to lose one's ability or judgment in a given situation ▷ *vb* **plots, plotting, plotted** **6** to plan secretly (something illegal, revolutionary, etc); conspire **7** (*tr*) to mark (a course, as of a ship or aircraft) on a map **8** (*tr*) to make a plan or map of **9 a** to locate and mark (one or more points) on a graph by means of coordinates **b** to draw (a curve) through these points **10** (*tr*) to construct the plot of (a literary work) [c16: from PLOT², influenced in use by COMPLOT] > 'plotter *n*

plot² (plɒt) *n* a small piece of land: *a vegetable plot* [Old English: piece of land, plan of an area]

Plotinus (plɒ'taɪnəs) *n* ?205–?270 AD, Roman Neo-Platonist philosopher, born in Egypt

plough *or esp US* **plow** (plaʊ) *n* **1** an agricultural implement with sharp blades, attached to a horse, tractor, etc, for cutting or turning over the earth **2** any of various similar implements, such as a device for clearing snow **3** (in agriculture) ploughed land **4** put one's hand to the plough to begin or undertake a task ▷ *vb* **5** to till (the soil) with a plough **6** to make (furrows or grooves) in (something) with or as if with a plough **7** (when *intr*, usually foll by *through*) to move (through something) in the manner of a plough **8** (*intr*; foll by *through*) to work at slowly or perseveringly **9** (*intr*; foll by *into* or *through*) (of a vehicle) to run uncontrollably into something in its path **10** (*intr*) *Brit slang* to fail an examination [Old English *plōg* plough land; related to Old Norse *plogr*, Old High German *pfluoc*] > 'plougher or *esp US* 'plower *n*

Plough (plaʊ) *n* the Plough the group of the seven brightest stars in the constellation Ursa Major. Also known as: **Charles's Wain**. Usual US name: **the Big Dipper**

plough back *vb* (*tr*, *adverb*) to reinvest (the profits of a business) in the same business

ploughman or *esp US* **plowman** ('plaʊmən) *n*, *pl* -men a man who ploughs, esp using horses

ploughman's lunch *n* a snack lunch, served esp in a pub, consisting of bread and cheese with pickle

ploughshare or *esp US* **plowshare** ('plaʊˌʃɛə) *n* the horizontal pointed cutting blade of a mouldboard plough

Plovdiv (*Bulgarian* 'plɔvdif) *n* a city in S Bulgaria on the Maritsa River: the second largest town in Bulgaria; conquered by Philip II of Macedonia in 341 BC; capital of Roman Thracia; commercial centre of a rich agricultural region. Pop: 339 000 (2005 est.). Greek name: Philippopolis

plover ('plʌvə) *n* **1** any shore bird of the family *Charadriidae*, typically having a round head, straight bill, and large pointed wings: order *Charadriiformes* **2** green plover another name for **lapwing** [C14: from Old French *plovier* rainbird, from Latin *pluvia* rain]

plow (plaʊ) *n*, *vb* the usual US spelling of **plough**

Plowright ('plaʊˌraɪt) *n* Dame **Joan**. born 1929, British actress, married to Laurence Olivier (1961–89)

ploy (plɔɪ) *n* **1** a manoeuvre or tactic in a game, conversation, etc; stratagem; gambit **2** any business, job, hobby, etc, with which one is occupied: *angling is his latest ploy* **3** *chiefly Brit* a frolic, escapade, or practical joke [C18: originally Scot and northern English, perhaps from obsolete *n* sense of EMPLOY meaning an occupation]

PLP *abbreviation* (in Britain) Parliamentary Labour Party

PLR *abbreviation* Public Lending Right

PLU *text messaging abbreviation* people like us

pluck (plʌk) *vb* **1** (*tr*) to pull off (feathers, fruit, etc) from (a fowl, tree, etc) **2** (when *intr*, foll by *at*) to pull or tug **3** (*tr*; foll by *off*, *away*, etc) *archaic* to pull (something) forcibly or violently (from something or someone) **4** (*tr*) to sound the strings of (a musical instrument) with the fingers, a plectrum, etc **5** (*tr*) *slang* to fleece or swindle ▷ *n* **6** courage, usually in the face of difficulties or hardship **7** a sudden pull or tug **8** the heart, liver, and lungs, esp of an animal used for food [Old English *pluccian*, *plyccan*; related to German *pflücken*] > 'plucker *n*

pluck up *vb* (*tr*, *adverb*) **1** to pull out; uproot **2** to muster (courage, one's spirits, etc)

plucky ('plʌkɪ) *adj* pluckier, pluckiest having or showing courage in the face of difficulties, danger, etc > 'pluckily *adv* > 'pluckiness *n*

plug (plʌg) *n* **1** a piece of wood, cork, or other material, often cylindrical in shape, used to stop up holes and gaps or as a wedge for taking a screw or nail **2** a device having one or more pins to which an electric cable is attached: used to make an electrical connection when inserted into a socket **3** Also called: **volcanic plug** a mass of solidified magma filling the neck of an extinct volcano **4** See **sparking plug** **5 a** a cake of pressed or twisted tobacco, esp for chewing **b** a small piece of such a cake **6** *informal* a recommendation or other favourable mention of a product, show, etc, as on television, on radio, or in newspapers ▷ *vb* plugs, plugging, plugged **7** (*tr*) to stop up or secure (a hole, gap, etc) with or as if with a plug **8** (*tr*) to insert or use (something) as a plug: *to plug a finger into one's ear* **9** (*tr*) *informal* to make favourable and often-repeated mentions of (a song,

product, show, etc), esp on television, on radio, or in newspapers **10** (*tr*) *slang* to shoot with a gun: *he plugged six rabbits* **11** (*tr*) *slang* to punch or strike **12** (*intr*; foll by *along*, *away*, etc) *informal* to work steadily or persistently [C17: from Middle Dutch *plugge*; related to Middle Low German *plugge*, German *Pflock*] > 'plugger *n*

plug and play or **plug'n'play** *n* **1** *computing* a feature of hardware that enables computers to automatically detect and configure hardware devices without the need for intervention ▷ *adj* plug-and-play **2** capable of detecting the addition of a new input or output device and automatically activating the appropriate control software ▷ Abbreviation: PnP

plugged-in *adj* *slang* up-to-date; abreast of the times

plughole ('plʌgˌhəʊl) *n* a hole, esp in a bath, basin, or sink, through which waste water drains and which can be closed with a plug

plug in *vb* **1** (*tr*, *adverb*) to connect (an electrical appliance) with a power source by means of an electrical plug ▷ *n* **plug-in 2** a device that can be connected by means of a plug **3** *computing* a module or piece of software that can be added to a system to provide extra functions or features, esp software that enhances the capabilities of a web browser **4** *computing* (*as modifier*): *plug-in memory cards*

plug-ugly *adj* **1** *informal* extremely ugly ▷ *n*, *pl* -lies **2** *US slang* a city tough; ruffian [C19: origin obscure; originally applied to ruffians in New York who attempted to exert political pressure]

plum (plʌm) *n* **1** a small rosaceous tree, *Prunus domestica*, with white flowers and an edible oval fruit that is purple, yellow, or green and contains an oval stone **2** the fruit of this tree **3** a raisin, as used in a cake or pudding **4 a** a dark reddish-purple colour **b** (*as adjective*): *a plum carpet* **5** *informal* **a** something of a superior or desirable kind, such as a financial bonus **b** (*as modifier*): *a plum job* [Old English *plūme*; related to Latin *prunum*, German *Pflaume*]

plumage ('pluːmɪdʒ) *n* the layer of feathers covering the body of a bird [C15: from Old French, from *plume* feather, from Latin *plūma* down]

plumate ('pluːmeɪt, -mɪt) or **plumose** *adj* zoology, botany **1** of, relating to, or possessing one or more feathers or plumes **2** resembling a plume; covered with small hairs: *a plumate seed* [C19: from Latin *plumātus* covered with feathers; see PLUME]

plumb (plʌm) *n* **1** a weight, usually of lead, suspended at the end of a line and used to determine water depth or verticality **2** the perpendicular position of a line suspended plumb line (esp in the phrases **out of plumb**, **off plumb**) ▷ *adv* Also: **plum 3** in a vertical or perpendicular line **4** *informal*, *chiefly US* (intensifier): *plumb stupid* **5** *informal* exactly; precisely (also in the phrase **plumb on**) ▷ *vb* **6** (*tr*, often foll by *up*) to test the alignment of or adjust to the vertical with a plumb line **7** (*tr*) to undergo or experience (the worst extremes of misery, sadness, etc): *to plumb the depths of despair* **8** (*tr*) to understand or master (something obscure): *to plumb a mystery* **9** to connect or join (a device such as a tap) to a water pipe or drainage system [C13: from Old French *plomb* (unattested) lead line, from Old French *plon* lead, from Latin *plumbum* lead] > 'plumbable *adj*

plumbago (plʌmˈbeɪgəʊ) *n*, *pl* -gos **1** any plumbaginaceous plant of the genus *Plumbago*, of warm regions, having clusters of blue, white, or red flowers **2** another name for **graphite** [C17: from Latin: lead ore, leadwort, translation of Greek *polubdaina* lead ore, from *polubdos* lead]

plumber ('plʌmə) *n* a person who installs and repairs pipes, fixtures, etc, for water, drainage, and gas [C14: from Old French *plommier* worker in lead, from Late Latin *plumbārius*, from Latin *plumbum* lead]

plumbing ('plʌmɪŋ) *n* **1** Also called: **plumbery** the trade or work of a plumber **2** the pipes, fixtures, etc, used in a water, drainage, or gas installation **3** the act or procedure of using a plumb to gauge depth, a vertical, etc

plumbism ('plʌmˌbɪzəm) *n* chronic lead poisoning [C19: from Latin *plumbum* lead]

plumb line *n* a string with a metal weight at one end that, when suspended, points directly towards the earth's centre of gravity and so is used to determine verticality, the depth of water, etc

plumb rule *n* a plumb line attached to a narrow board, used by builders, surveyors, etc

plume (pluːm) *n* **1** a feather, esp one that is large or ornamental **2** a feather or cluster of feathers worn esp formerly as a badge or ornament in a headband, hat, etc **3** *biology* any feathery part, such as the structure on certain fruits and seeds that aids dispersal by wind **4** something that resembles a plume: *a plume of smoke* **5** a token or decoration of honour; prize ▷ *vb* (*tr*) **6** to adorn or decorate with feathers or plumes **7** (of a bird) to clean or preen (itself or its feathers) **8** (foll by *on* or *upon*) to pride or congratulate (oneself) [c14: from Old French, from Latin *plūma* downy feather]

plummet (ˈplʌmɪt) *vb* -mets, -meting, -meted **1** (*intr*) to drop down; plunge ▷ *n* **2** a lead plumb used by anglers to determine the depth of water [c14: from Old French *plommet* ball of lead, from *plomb* lead, from Latin *plumbum*]

plummy (ˈplʌmɪ) *adj* -mier, -miest **1** of, full of, or resembling plums **2** *Brit informal* (of speech) having a deep tone and a refined and somewhat drawling articulation **3** *Brit informal* choice; desirable

plumose (ˈpluːməʊs, -məʊz) *adj* another word for **plumate** [c17: from Latin *plūmōsus* feathery]

plump¹ (plʌmp) *adj* **1** well filled out or rounded; fleshy or chubby: *a plump turkey* **2** bulging, as with contents; full: *a plump wallet* ▷ *vb* **3** (often foll by *up* or *out*) to make or become plump: *to plump up a pillow* [c15 (meaning: dull, rude), c16 (in current senses): perhaps from Middle Dutch *plomp* dull, blunt] > ˈplumply *adv* > ˈplumpness *n*

plump² (plʌmp) *vb* **1** (often foll by *down*, *into*, etc) to drop or fall suddenly and heavily **2** (*intr*; foll by *for*) to give support (to) or make a choice (of) one out of a group or number ▷ *n* **3** a heavy abrupt fall or the sound of this ▷ *adv* **4** suddenly or heavily **5** straight down; directly: *the helicopter landed plump in the middle of the field* ▷ *adj, adv* **6** in a blunt, direct, or decisive manner [c14: probably of imitative origin; compare Middle Low German *plumpen*, Middle Dutch *plompen*]

plum pudding *n* (in Britain) a dark brown rich boiled or steamed pudding made with flour, suet, sugar, and dried fruit

plumule (ˈpluːmjuːl) *n* **1** the embryonic shoot of seed-bearing plants **2** a down feather of young birds that persists in some adults [c18: from Late Latin *plūmula* a little feather]

plumy (ˈpluːmɪ) *adj* plumier, plumiest **1** plumelike; feathery **2** consisting of, covered with, or adorned with feathers

plunder (ˈplʌndə) *vb* **1** to steal (valuables, goods, sacred items, etc) from (a town, church, etc) by force, esp in time of war; loot **2** (*tr*) to rob or steal (choice or desirable things) from (a place): *to plunder an orchard* ▷ *n* **3** anything taken by plundering or theft; booty **4** the act of plundering; pillage [c17: probably from Dutch *plunderen* (originally: to plunder household goods); compare Middle High German *plunder* bedding, household goods] > ˈplunderer *n*

plunge (plʌndʒ) *vb* **1** (usually foll by *into*) to thrust or throw (something, oneself, etc): *they plunged into the sea* **2** to throw or be thrown into a certain state or condition: *the room was plunged into darkness* **3** (usually foll by *into*) to involve or become involved deeply (in) **4** (*intr*) to move or dash violently or with great speed or impetuosity **5** (*intr*) to descend very suddenly or steeply: *the ship plunged in heavy seas; a plunging neckline* **6** (*intr*) *informal* to speculate or gamble recklessly, for high stakes, etc ▷ *n* **7** a leap or dive as into water **8** *informal* a swim; dip **9** a pitching or tossing motion **10** take the plunge *informal* to resolve to do something dangerous or irrevocable [c14: from Old French *plongier*, from Vulgar Latin *plumbicāre* (unattested) to sound with a plummet, from Latin *plumbum* lead]

plunger (ˈplʌndʒə) *n* **1** a rubber suction cup fixed to the end of a rod, used to clear blocked drains **2** a device or part of a machine that has a plunging or thrusting motion; piston **3** *informal* a reckless gambler

plunk (plʌŋk) *vb* **1** to pluck (the strings) of (a banjo, harp, etc) or (of such an instrument) to give forth a sound when plucked **2** (often foll by *down*) to drop or be dropped, esp heavily or suddenly ▷ *n* **3** the act or sound of plunking [c20: imitative]

Plunket *or* **Plunkett** (ˈplʌŋkət) *n* **Saint Oliver**. 1629–81, Irish Roman Catholic churchman and martyr; wrongly executed as a supposed conspirator in the Popish Plot (1678). Feast day: July 11

pluperfect (pluːˈpɜːfɪkt) *adj, n grammar* another term for **past perfect** [c16: from the Latin phrase *plūs quam perfectum* more than perfect]

plural (ˈplʊərəl) *adj* **1** containing, involving, or composed of more than one person, thing, item, etc **2** denoting a word indicating that more than one referent is being referred to or described ▷ *n* **3** *grammar* **a** the plural number **b** a plural form [c14: from Old French *plurel*, from Late Latin *plūrālis* concerning many, from Latin *plūs* more] > ˈplurally *adv*

pluralism (ˈplʊərəˌlɪzəm) *n* **1** the holding by a single person of more than one ecclesiastical benefice or office **2** *sociol* a theory of society as several autonomous but interdependent groups which either share power or continuously compete for power **3** the existence in a society of groups having distinctive ethnic origin, cultural forms, religions, etc **4** *philosophy* **a** the metaphysical doctrine that reality consists of more than two basic types of substance. See **monism** (sense 1) **dualism** (sense 2) **b** the metaphysical doctrine that reality consists of independent entities rather than one unchanging whole > ˈpluralist *n, adj* > ˌpluralˈistic *adj*

plurality (plʊəˈrælɪtɪ) *n, pl* -ties **1** the state of being plural or numerous **2** *maths* a number greater than one **3** *US & Canadian* British equivalent: relative majority **4** a large number **5** the greater number; majority **6** another word for **pluralism** (sense 1)

pluralize *or* **pluralise** (ˈplʊərəˌlaɪz) *vb* **1** (*intr*) to hold more than one ecclesiastical benefice or office at the same time **2** to make or become plural

pluri- *combining form* denoting several [from Latin *plur-*, plus more, plures several]

pluripotent (ˌplʊərɪˈpəʊtənt) *adj biology* capable of differentiating into different types of body cell

plus (plʌs) *prep* **1** increased by the addition of: *four plus two* (written 4 + 2) **2** with or with the addition of: *a good job, plus a new car* ▷ *adj* **3** Also called: positive (prenominal) indicating or involving addition: *a plus sign* **4** another word for **positive** (sense 7) **5** on the positive part of a scale or coordinate axis: *a value of +x* **6** indicating the positive side of an electrical circuit **7** involving positive advantage or good: *a plus factor* **8** (postpositive) *informal* having a value above that which is stated or expected: *she had charm plus* **9** (postpositive) slightly above a specified standard on a particular grade or percentage: *he received a B+ rating on his essay* ▷ *n* **10** short for **plus sign** **11** a positive quantity **12** *informal* something positive or to the good **13** a gain, surplus, or advantage ▷ Mathematical symbol: + [c17: from Latin: more; compare Greek *pleiōn*, Old Norse *fleiri* more, German *viel* much]

● **USAGE** *Plus*, *together with*, and *along with* do not create
● compound subjects in the way that *and* does: the
● number of the verb depends on that of the subject to
● which *plus*, *together with*, or *along with* is added: *this task,*
● *plus all the others, was* (not *were*) *undertaken by the*
● *government; the doctor, together with the nurses, was* (not
● *were*) *waiting for the patient*

plus fours *pl n* men's baggy knickerbockers reaching below the knee, now only worn for hunting, golf, etc [c20: so called because the trousers are made with four inches of material to hang over at the knee]

plush (plʌʃ) *n* **1** a fabric with a cut pile that is longer and softer than velvet ▷ *adj* **2** Also called: plushy *informal* lavishly appointed; rich; costly [c16: from French *pluche*, from Old French *peluchier* to pluck, ultimately from Latin *pilus* a hair, PILE³] > ˈplushly *adv*

plus sign *n* the symbol +, indicating addition or positive quantity

plus size *n* **a** a clothing size designed for people who are above the average size **b** (*as modifier*): *plus-size underwear*

Plutarch ('pluːtɑːk) n ?46–?120 AD, Greek biographer and philosopher, noted for his *Parallel Lives* of distinguished Greeks and Romans

Pluto¹ ('pluːtəʊ) n *classical myth* the god of the underworld; Hades > Plu'tonian *adj*

Pluto² ('pluːtəʊ) n the second-largest dwarf planet in the solar system, located in the Kuiper belt; discovered in 1930 by Clyde Tombaugh (1906–97); classified as a planet until 2006, when it was reclassified as a dwarf planet. It has a diameter of 2390 km [Latin, from Greek *Ploutōn*, literally: the rich one]

plutocracy (pluːˈtɒkrəsɪ) n, pl -cies **1** the rule or control of society by the wealthy **2** a state or government characterized by the rule of the wealthy **3** a class that exercises power by virtue of its wealth [c17: from Greek *ploutokratia* government by the rich, from *ploutos* wealth + -*kratia* rule, power] > plutocratic (ˌpluːtəˈkrætɪk) *adj* > ˌpluto'cratically *adv*

plutocrat ('pluːtəˌkræt) n a member of a plutocracy

pluton ('pluːtɒn) n any mass of igneous rock that has solidified below the surface of the earth [c20: back formation from PLUTONIC]

plutonic (pluːˈtɒnɪk) *adj* (of igneous rocks) derived from magma that has cooled and solidified below the surface of the earth [c20: named after PLUTO¹]

plutonium (pluːˈtəʊnɪəm) n a highly toxic metallic transuranic element. It occurs in trace amounts in uranium ores and is produced in a nuclear reactor by neutron bombardment of uranium-238. The most stable and important isotope, **plutonium-239**, readily undergoes fission and is used as a reactor fuel in nuclear power stations and in nuclear weapons. Symbol: Pu; atomic no: 94; half-life of ^{239}Pu: 24 360 years; valency: 3, 4, 5, or 6; relative density (alpha modification): 19.84; melting pt: 640°C; boiling pt: 3230°C [c20: named after the dwarf planet *Pluto* because Pluto lies beyond Neptune and plutonium was discovered soon after NEPTUNIUM]

Plutus ('pluːtəs) n the Greek god of wealth [from Greek *ploutos* wealth]

pluvial ('pluːvɪəl) *adj* **1** of, characterized by, or due to the action of rain; rainy ▷ n **2** a climate characterized by persistent heavy rainfall, esp one occurring in unglaciated regions during the Pleistocene epoch [c17: from Latin *pluviālis* rainy, from *pluvia* rain]

pluviometer (ˌpluːvɪˈɒmɪtə) n an obsolete word for **rain gauge** > pluviometric (ˌpluːvɪəˈmɛtrɪk) *adj* > ˌpluvio'metrically *adv*

ply¹ (plaɪ) vb plies, plying, plied (*mainly tr*) **1** to carry on, pursue, or work at (a job, trade, etc) **2** to manipulate or wield (a tool) **3** to sell (goods, wares, etc), esp at a regular place **4** (usually foll by *with*) to provide (with) or subject (to) repeatedly or persistently: *he plied us with drink the whole evening; to ply a horse with a whip; he plied the speaker with questions* **5** (*intr*) to perform or work steadily or diligently **6** (*also intr*) (esp of a ship) to travel regularly along (a route) or in (an area): *to ply between Dover and Calais; to ply the trade routes* [c14 *plye*, short for *aplye* to APPLY]

ply² (plaɪ) n, pl plies **1 a** a layer, fold, or thickness, as of cloth, wood, yarn, etc **b** (*in combination*): *four-ply* **2** a thin sheet of wood glued to other similar sheets to form plywood **3** one of the strands twisted together to make rope, yarn, etc [c15: from Old French *pli* fold, from *plier* to fold, from Latin *plicāre*]

Plymouth ('plɪməθ) n **1** a port in SW England, in Plymouth unitary authority, SW Devon, on **Plymouth Sound** (an inlet of the English Channel): Britain's chief port in Elizabethan times; the last port visited by the Pilgrim Fathers in the *Mayflower* before sailing to America; naval base; university (1992). Pop: 243 795 (2001) **2** a unitary authority in SW England, in Devon. Pop: 241 500 (2003 est). Area: 76 sq km (30 sq miles) **3** a city in SE Massachusetts, on **Plymouth Bay**: the first permanent European settlement in New England; founded by the Pilgrim Fathers. Pop: 54 109 (2003 est) **4** the former capital of Montserrat, in the Caribbean; largely destroyed by volcanic eruption in 1997

Plymouth Brethren *pl n* a religious sect founded *c.* 1827,

strongly Puritanical in outlook and prohibiting many secular occupations for its members. It combines elements of Calvinism, Pietism, and millenarianism, and has no organized ministry

plyometrics (ˌplaɪəʊˈmɛtrɪks) *pl n* (*functioning as singular*) a system of exercise in which the muscles are repeatedly stretched and suddenly contracted [c20: from Greek *plio* more + METRIC] > ˌplyo'metric *adj*

plywood ('plaɪˌwʊd) n a structural board consisting of an odd number of thin layers of wood glued together under pressure, with the grain of one layer at right angles to the grain of the adjoining layer

Plzeň (*Czech* 'plzɛnj) n an industrial city in the Czech Republic. Pop: 163 000 (2005 est). German name: **Pilsen**

pm *abbreviation* premium

Pm *the chemical symbol for* promethium

PM *abbreviation* **1** Prime Minister **2** Past Master (of a fraternity) **3** Paymaster **4** Postmaster **5** *military* Provost Marshal

p.m., P.M., pm *or* **PM** *abbreviation* **1** (indicating the time period from midday to midnight) post meridiem [Latin: after noon] **2** post-mortem (examination)

PMC *abbreviation* private military company: a commercial organization whose employees are paid to carry out military or security duties in cooperation with or in the place of regular military formations

PMG *abbreviation* **1** Paymaster General **2** Postmaster General

PMQs *abbreviation* (in the UK) Prime Minister's questions

PMS *abbreviation* premenstrual syndrome

PMT *abbreviation* premenstrual tension

PNdB *abbreviation* perceived noise decibel

pneuma ('njuːmə) n *philosophy* a person's vital spirit, soul, or creative energy. See **psyche** [c19: from Greek: breath, spirit, wind; related to *pnein* to blow, breathe]

pneumatic (njʊˈmætɪk) *adj* **1** of or concerned with air, gases, or wind **2** (of a machine or device) operated by compressed air or by a vacuum **3** containing compressed air: *a pneumatic tyre* **4** (of the bones of birds) containing air spaces which reduce their weight as an adaptation to flying ▷ n **5** a pneumatic tyre [c17: from Late Latin *pneumaticus* of air or wind, from Greek *pneumatikos* of air or breath, from PNEUMA] > pneu'matically *adv*

pneumatics (njʊˈmætɪks) n (*functioning as singular*) the branch of physics concerned with the mechanical properties of gases, esp air

pneumatology (ˌnjuːməˈtɒlədʒɪ) n **1** the branch of theology concerned with the Holy Ghost and other spiritual beings **2** an obsolete name for **psychology** (sense 1)

pneumatophore (njuːˈmætəʊˌfɔː) n **1** a specialized root of certain swamp plants, such as the mangrove, that branches upwards, rising above ground, and undergoes gaseous exchange with the atmosphere **2** a polyp in coelenterates of the order *Siphonophora*, such as the Portuguese man-of-war, that is specialized as a float

pneumo-, pneumono-, *before a vowel* **pneum-** *or* *before a vowel* **pneumon-** *combining form* of or related to a lung or the lungs; respiratory: *pneumoconiosis; pneumogastric* [from Greek *pneumōn* lung or *pneuma* breath]

pneumococcus (ˌnjuːməʊˈkɒkəs) n, pl -cocci (-ˈkɒkaɪ) a spherical bacterium that occurs in the respiratory tract, esp the Gram-positive *Diplococcus pneumoniae*, which causes pneumonia

pneumoconiosis (ˌnjuːməʊˌkəʊnɪˈəʊsɪs) *or* **pneumonoconiosis** (ˌnjuːmənəʊˌkəʊnɪˈəʊsɪs) n any disease of the lungs or bronchi caused by the inhalation of metallic or mineral particles: characterized by inflammation, cough, and fibrosis [c19: shortened from *pneumonoconiosis*, from PNEUMO- + -*coniosis*, from Greek *konis* dust]

pneumoencephalogram (ˌnjuːməʊɛnˈsɛfələˌgræm) n See **encephalogram**

pneumogastric (ˌnjuːməʊˈgæstrɪk) *adj anatomy* **1** of or relating to the lungs and stomach **2** a former term for **vagus**

pneumonectomy (ˌnjuːməʊˈnɛktəmɪ) *or* **pneumectomy** (njuːˈmɛktəmɪ) n, pl -mies the surgical removal of a lung or part of a lung [c20: from Greek *pneumōn* lung + -ECTOMY]

pneumonia (njuːˈməʊnɪə) *n* inflammation of one or both lungs, in which the air sacs (alveoli) become filled with liquid, which renders them useless for breathing. It is usually caused by bacterial (esp pneumococcal) or viral infection [C17: New Latin from Greek from *pneumōn* lung]

pneumothorax (ˌnjuːməʊˈθɔːræks) *n* the abnormal presence of air between the lung and the wall of the chest (pleural cavity), resulting in collapse of the lung

PNI *abbreviation* psychoneuroimmunology

p-n junction *n electronics* a boundary between a p-type and n-type semiconductor that functions as a rectifier and is used in diodes and junction transistors

Pnom Penh (ˈnɒm ˈpɛn) *n* a variant spelling of **Phnom Penh**

PnP *abbreviation* plug 'n' play

po (pəʊ) *n, pl* **pos** *Brit* an informal word for **chamber pot** [C19: from POT[1]]

Po[1] the chemical symbol for polonium

Po[2] (pəʊ) *n* a river in N Italy, rising in the Cottian Alps and flowing northeast to Turin, then east to the Adriatic: the longest river in Italy. Length: 652 km (405 miles). Latin name: Padus

PO *abbreviation* **1** Post Office **2** Personnel Officer **3** petty officer **4** Pilot Officer **5** Also called: p.o. postal order

poach[1] (pəʊtʃ) *vb* **1** to catch (game, fish, etc) illegally by trespassing on private property **2** to encroach on or usurp (another person's rights, duties, etc) or steal (an idea, employee, etc) **3** *tennis, badminton* to take or play (shots that should belong to one's partner) **4** to break up (land) into wet muddy patches, as by riding over it, or (of land) to become broken up in this way [C17: from Old French *pocher*, of Germanic origin; compare Middle Dutch *poken* to prod; see POKE[1]] > **'poacher** *n*

poach[2] (pəʊtʃ) *vb* to simmer (eggs, fish, etc) very gently in water, milk, stock, etc [C15: from Old French *pochier* to enclose in a bag (as the yolks are enclosed by the whites); compare POKE[2]]

Pocahontas (ˌpɒkəˈhɒntəs) *n* original name *Matoaka*; married name *Rebecca Rolfe*. ?1595–1617, American Indian, who allegedly saved the colonist Captain John Smith from being killed

pochard (ˈpəʊtʃəd) *n, pl* **-chards** or **-chard** any of various diving ducks of the genera *Aythya* and *Netta*, esp *A. ferina* of Europe, the male of which has a grey-and-black body and a reddish head [C16: of unknown origin]

pock (pɒk) *n* **1** any pustule resulting from an eruptive disease, esp from smallpox **2** another word for **pockmark** (sense 1) [Old English *pocc*; related to Middle Dutch *pocke*, perhaps to Latin *bucca* cheek] > **'pocky** *adj*

pocket (ˈpɒkɪt) *n* **1** a small bag or pouch in a garment for carrying small articles, money, etc **2** any bag or pouch or anything resembling this **3** a cavity or hollow in the earth, etc, such as one containing gold or other ore **4** a small enclosed or isolated area: *a pocket of resistance* **5** *billiards, snooker* any of the six holes with pouches or nets let into the corners and sides of a billiard table **6** *South African* a bag or sack of vegetables or fruit **7** in one's pocket under one's control **8** out of pocket having made a loss, as after a transaction **9** line one's pockets to make money, esp by dishonesty when in a position of trust ⊳ *vb* **-ets**, **-eting**, **-eted** (*tr*) **10** to put into one's pocket **11** to take surreptitiously or unlawfully; steal **12** to conceal or keep back (feelings): *he pocketed his pride and accepted help* **13** *billiards, snooker* to drive (a ball) into a pocket [C15: from Anglo-Norman *poket* a little bag, from *poque* bag, from Middle Dutch *poke* POKE[2], bag; related to French *poche* pocket] > **'pocketless** *adj*

pocket battleship *n* a small heavily armoured and armed battle cruiser specially built to conform with treaty limitations on tonnage and armament, esp any of those built by Germany in the 1930s

pocket billiards *n* (*functioning as singular*) *billiards* any game played on a table in which the object is to pocket the balls, esp snooker and pool

pocketbook (ˈpɒkɪtˌbʊk) *n US & Canadian* a small bag or case for money, papers, etc, carried by a handle or in the pocket

pocket borough *n* (before the Reform Act of 1832) an English borough constituency controlled by one person or family who owned the land

pocket drive or **keyring drive** *n computing* a small portable memory device that can be plugged into the USB port of many different types of computer

pocketful (ˈpɒkɪtfʊl) *n, pl* **-fuls** as much as a pocket will hold

pocketknife (ˈpɒkɪtˌnaɪf) *n, pl* **-knives** a small knife with one or more blades that fold into the handle; penknife

pocket money *n* **1** *Brit* a small weekly sum of money given to children by parents as an allowance **2** money for day-to-day spending, incidental expenses, etc

pockmark (ˈpɒkˌmɑːk) *n* **1** Also called: **pock** a pitted scar left on the skin after the healing of a smallpox or similar pustule **2** any pitting of a surface that resembles or suggests such scars ⊳ *vb* **3** (*tr*) to scar or pit (a surface) with pockmarks

poco (ˈpəʊkəʊ; *Italian* ˈpɔːko) or **un poco** *adj, adv music* (in combination) a little; to a small degree [from Italian: little, from Latin *paucus* few, scanty]

poco a poco *adv* (in combination) *music* little by little: *poco a poco rall* [Italian]

pod (pɒd) *n* **1 a** the fruit of any leguminous plant, consisting of a long two-valved case that contains seeds and splits along both sides when ripe **b** the seedcase as distinct from the seeds **2** any similar fruit **3 a** a streamlined structure attached by a pylon to an aircraft and used to house a jet engine (**podded engine**), fuel tank, armament, etc ⊳ *vb* **pods**, **podding**, **podded 4** (*tr*) to remove the pod or shell from (peas, beans, etc) [C17: perhaps back formation from earlier *podware* bagged vegetables, probably from *pod*, variant of COD[2] + WARE[1]]

-pod or **-pode** *n combining form* indicating a certain type or number of feet: *arthropod; tripod* [from Greek *-podos* footed, from *pous* foot]

podagra (pəˈdæɡrə) *n* gout of the foot or big toe [C15: via Latin from Greek, from *pous* foot + *agra* a trap]

podcast (ˈpɒdˌkɑːst) *n* **1** an audio file similar to a radio broadcast, which can be downloaded and listened to on a computer, iPod, etc ⊳ *vb* **-casts**, **-casting**, **-cast** or **-casted 2** (*intr*) to create such files and make them available for downloading **3** (*tr*) to make (music, interviews, etc) available using this format > **'pod,caster** *n* > **'pod,casting** *n*

poddy (ˈpɒdɪ) *n, pl* **-dies** *Austral* a handfed calf or lamb [perhaps from *poddy* (adj) fat]

podge (pɒdʒ) or **pudge** (pʌdʒ) *n informal* a short chubby person

Podgorica or **Podgoritsa** (*Russian* ˈpɒdɡɒˌriːtsa) *n* the capital of Montenegro: under Turkish rule (1474–1878). Pop: 230 000 (2005 est). Former name (1946–92): Titograd

podgy (ˈpɒdʒɪ) *adj* **podgier, podgiest** short and fat; chubby > **'podgily** *adv* > **'podginess** *n*

podiatry (pəˈdaɪətrɪ) *n* another word for **chiropody** [C20: from Greek *pous* foot] > **podiatric** (ˌpəʊdɪˈætrɪk) *adj* > **po'diatrist** *n*

podium (ˈpəʊdɪəm) *n, pl* **-diums** or **-dia** (-dɪə) **1** a small raised platform used by lecturers, orchestra conductors, etc; dais **2** a plinth that supports a colonnade or wall **3** a low wall surrounding the arena of an ancient amphitheatre **4** *zoology* any footlike organ, such as the tube foot of a starfish [C18: from Latin: platform, balcony, from Greek *podion* little foot, from *pous* foot]

-podium *n combining form* a part resembling a foot: *pseudopodium* [from New Latin: footlike; see PODIUM]

Podolsk (*Russian* paˈdɔljsk) *n* an industrial city in W Russia, near Moscow. Pop: 177 000 (2005 est)

podophyllin or **podophylin resin** (ˌpɒdəʊˈfɪlɪn) *n* a bitter yellow resin obtained from the dried underground stems of the May apple and mandrake: used to treat warts and formerly as a cathartic [C19: from New Latin *Podophyllum* genus of herbs including the May apple, from *podo-*, from Greek *pous* foot + *phullon* leaf]

-podous *adj combining form* having feet of a certain kind or number: *cephalopodous*

pod person *n, pl* **pod people** *informal* a person who behaves in a strange esp mechanical way, as if not fully human [C20: from the science-fiction film *Invasion of the*

Body Snatchers (1956; remade 1978) in which individual humans are replaced by alien replicas grown in giant pods]

podzol ('pɒdzɒl) *or* **podsol** ('pɒdsɒl) *n* a type of soil characteristic of coniferous forest regions having a greyish-white colour in its upper leached layers [c20: from Russian: ash ground, from *pod* ground + *zola* ashes]

Poe (pəʊ) *n* **Edgar Allan**. 1809–49, US short-story writer, poet, and critic. Most of his short stories, such as *The Fall of the House of Usher* (1839) and the *Tales of the Grotesque and Arabesque* (1840), are about death, decay, and madness. *The Murders in the Rue Morgue* (1841) is regarded as the first modern detective story

poem ('pəʊɪm) *n* **1** a composition in verse, usually characterized by concentrated and heightened language in which words are chosen for their sound and suggestive power as well as for their sense, and using such techniques as metre, rhyme, and alliteration **2** a literary composition that is not in verse but exhibits the intensity of imagination and language common to it: *a prose poem* **3** anything resembling a poem in beauty, effect, etc [c16: from Latin *poēma*, from Greek, variant of *poiēma* something composed, created, from *poiein* to make]

poep (pʊp) *n* *South African slang* **1** an emission of intestinal gas from the anus **2** a mean or despicable person [Afrikaans]

poesy ('pəʊɪzɪ) *n*, *pl* **-sies 1** an archaic word for **poetry 2** *poetic* the art of writing poetry [c14: via Old French from Latin *poēsis*, from Greek, from *poiēsis* poetic art, creativity, from *poiein* to make]

poet ('pəʊɪt) *or sometimes when feminine* **poetess** *n* **1** a person who writes poetry **2** a person with great imagination and creativity [c13: from Latin *poēta*, from Greek *poiētēs* maker, poet, from *poiein* to make]

poetaster (,pəʊɪ'tæstə, -'teɪ-) *n* a writer of inferior verse [c16: from Medieval Latin; see POET, -ASTER]

poetic (pəʊ'etɪk) *or* **poetical** *adj* **1** characteristic of poetry, as in being elevated, sublime, etc **2** characteristic of a poet **3** recounted in verse > **po'etically** *adv*

poeticize (pəʊ'etɪ,saɪz), **poetize,** (,pəʊɪ,taɪz) **poeticise** *or* **poetise** *vb* **1** (*tr*) to put into poetry or make poetic **2** (*intr*) to speak or write poetically

poetic justice *n* fitting retribution; just deserts

poetic licence *n* justifiable departure from conventional rules of form, fact, logic, etc, as in poetry

poetics (pəʊ'etɪks) *n* (*usually functioning as singular*) **1** the principles and forms of poetry or the study of these, esp as a form of literary criticism **2** a treatise on poetry

poet laureate *n*, *pl* **poets laureate** *Brit* the poet appointed as court poet of Britain who is given a post as an officer of the Royal Household. The first was Ben Jonson in 1616

poetry ('pəʊɪtrɪ) *n* **1** literature in metrical form; verse **2** the art or craft of writing verse **3** poetic qualities, spirit, or feeling in anything **4** anything resembling poetry in rhythm, beauty, etc [c14: from Medieval Latin *poētria*, from Latin *poēta* POET]

po-faced *adj* (of a person) wearing a disapproving stern expression [c20: possibly from PO + POKER-FACED]

pogey *or* **pogy** ('pəʊgɪ) *n*, *pl* **pogeys** *or* **pogies** *Canadian slang* **1** financial or other relief given to the unemployed by the government; dole **2** unemployment insurance **3 a** the office distributing relief to the unemployed **b** (*as modifier*): *pogey clothes* [c20: from earlier *pogie* workhouse, of unknown origin]

pogo stick *n* a stout pole with a handle at the top, steps for the feet and a spring at the bottom, so that the user can spring up, down, and along on it [c20: of uncertain origin]

pogrom ('pɒgrəm) *n* an organized persecution or extermination of an ethnic group, esp of Jews [c20: via Yiddish from Russian: destruction, from *po-* like + *grom* thunder]

Pohai (,pəʊ'haɪ) *n* a variant transliteration of the Chinese name for **Bohai**

pohutukawa (pə,hu:tə'ka:wə) *n* a myrtaceous New Zealand tree, *Metrosideros excelsa*, with red flowers and

hard red wood [from Māori]

poi (pɔɪ) *n* *NZ* a ball of woven flax swung rhythmically in poi dances [Māori]

poi dance *n* *NZ* a women's formation dance that involves singing and manipulating a poi

-poiesis *n combining form* indicating the act of making or producing something specified: *haematopoiesis* [from Greek, from *poiēsis* a making; see POESY] > -poietic *adj combining form*

poignant ('pɔɪnjənt, -nənt) *adj* **1** sharply distressing or painful to the feelings **2** to the point; cutting or piercing: *poignant wit* **3** keen or pertinent in mental appeal: *a poignant subject* **4** pungent in smell [c14: from Old French, from Latin *pungens* pricking, from *pungere* to sting, pierce, grieve] > **'poignancy** *or* **'poignance** *n* > **'poignantly** *adv*

poikilothermic (,pɔɪkɪləʊ'θɜːmɪk) *or* **poikilothermal** (,pɔɪkɪləʊ'θɜːməl) *adj* (of all animals except birds and mammals) having a body temperature that varies with the temperature of the surroundings [c19: from Greek *poikilos* various + THERMAL]

Poincaré (*French* pwɛkare) *n* **1 Jules Henri** (ʒyl ãri). 1854–1912, French mathematician, physicist, and philosopher. He made important contributions to the theory of functions and to astronomy and electromagnetic theory **2** his cousin, **Raymond** (rɛmõ). 1860–1934, French statesman; premier of France (1912–13; 1922–24; 1926–29); president (1913–20)

poinciana (,pɔɪnsɪ'ɑːnə) *n* any tree of the tropical leguminous genera *Caesalpinia* (formerly *Poinciana*) having large orange or red flowers [c17: New Latin, named after M. de Poinci, 17th-century governor of the French Antilles]

poind (pɪnd) *vb* (*tr*) *Scots law* **1** to take (property of a debtor) in execution or by way of distress; distrain **2** to impound (stray cattle, etc) [c15: from Scots, variant of Old English *pyndan* to impound]

poinsettia (pɔɪn'setɪə) *n* a euphorbiaceous shrub, *Euphorbia* (or *Poinsettia*) *pulcherrima*, of Mexico and Central America, widely cultivated for its showy scarlet bracts, which resemble petals [c19: New Latin, from the name of J. P. Poinsett (1799–1851), US Minister to Mexico, who introduced it to the US]

point (pɔɪnt) *n* **1** a dot or tiny mark **2** a location, spot, or position **3** any dot or mark used in writing or printing, such as a decimal point or a full stop **4** the sharp tapered end of a pin, knife, etc **5** *maths* **a** a geometric element having no dimensions and whose position in space is located by means of its coordinates **b** a location: *point of inflection* **6** a promontory, usually smaller than a cape **7** a specific condition or degree **8** a moment: *at that point he left the room* **9** an important or fundamental reason, aim, etc: *the point of this exercise is to train new teachers* **10** an essential element or thesis in an argument: *you've made your point; I take your point* **11** a suggestion or tip **12** a detail or item **13** an important or outstanding characteristic, physical attribute, etc: *he has his good points* **14** a distinctive characteristic or quality of an animal, esp one used as a standard in judging livestock **15** (*often plural*) any of the extremities, such as the tail, ears, or feet, of a domestic animal **16** *ballet* (*often plural*) the tip of the toes **17** a single unit for measuring or counting, as in the scoring of a game **18** *printing* a unit of measurement equal to one twelfth of a pica, or approximately 0.01384 inch. There are approximately 72 points to the inch **19** *finance* a unit of value used to quote security and commodity prices and their fluctuations **20** *navigation* **a** one of the 32 marks on the circumference of a compass card indicating direction **b** the angle of 11°15′ between two adjacent marks **21** *cricket* a fielding position at right angles to the batsman on the off side and relatively near the pitch **22** either of the two electrical contacts that make or break the current flow in the distributor of an internal-combustion engine **23** *Brit* (*often plural*) a junction of railway tracks in which a pair of rails can be moved so that a train can be directed onto either of two lines. US and Canadian equivalent: **switch 24** (*often plural*) a piece of ribbon, cord, etc, with metal tags at the end: used during the 16th and 17th centuries to fasten clothing **25** *Brit* short for **power point 26** the position of the body of a pointer or setter when it discovers game **27** *boxing* a mark awarded for a scoring blow, knockdown, etc **28** any diacritic used in a writing system, esp in a phonetic transcription, to indicate modifications of vowels or consonants **29** *jewellery* a unit of weight equal to 0.01 carat **30** the act of pointing **31** beside the point not pertinent; irrelevant **32** case in point a specific, appropriate, or relevant instance or example **33** make a point of **a** to make (something) one's regular habit **b** to do (something) because one thinks it important **34** not to put too fine a point on it to speak plainly and bluntly **35** on the point of or at the point of at the moment immediately before a specified condition, action, etc, is expected to begin: *on the point of leaving the room* **36** score points off to gain an advantage at someone else's expense **37** to the point pertinent; relevant **38** up to a point not completely ▷ *vb* **39** (usually foll by *at* or *to*) to indicate the location or direction of by or as by extending (a finger or other pointed object) towards it: *he pointed to the front door; don't point that gun at me* **40** (*intr*; usually foll by *at* or *to*) to indicate or identify a specific person or thing among several: *he pointed at the bottle he wanted; all evidence pointed to Donald as the murderer* **41** (*tr*) to direct or cause to go or face in a specific direction or towards a place or goal: *point me in the right direction* **42** (*tr*) to sharpen or taper **43** (*intr*) (of gun dogs) to indicate the place where game is lying by standing rigidly with the muzzle turned in its direction **44** (*tr*) to finish or repair the joints of (brickwork, masonry, etc) with mortar or cement **45** (*tr*) *music* to mark (a psalm text) with vertical lines to indicate the points at which the music changes during chanting **46** (*tr*) *phonetics* to provide (a letter or letters) with diacritics **47** (*tr*) to provide (a Hebrew or similar text) with vowel points ▷ See also **point off, point out, point up** [c13: from Old French: spot, from Latin *punctum* a point, from *pungere* to pierce; also influenced by Old French *pointe* pointed end, from Latin *pungere*]

point after *n* *American football* a score given for a successful kick between the goalposts and above the crossbar, following a touchdown

point-and-click *adj* *computing* of or relating to the way a computer mouse can be used to select and operate functions from a computer screen: *a bright and cheerful point-and-click interface*

point-and-shoot *adj* of or relating to a camera in which the lens aperture and shutter speed are automatically adjusted

point-blank *adj* **1 a** aimed or fired at a target so close that it is unnecessary to make allowance for the drop in the course of the projectile **b** permitting such aim or fire without loss of accuracy: *at point-blank range* **2** plain or blunt: *a point-blank question* ▷ *adv* **3** directly or straight **4** plainly or bluntly [c16: from POINT + BLANK (in the sense: centre spot of an archery target)]

point duty *n* **1** the stationing of a policeman or traffic warden at a road junction to control and direct traffic **2** the position at the head of a military patrol, regarded as being the most dangerous

pointe (pɔ̃t) *n* *ballet* the tip of the toe (esp in the phrase **on pointes**) [from French: point]

Pointe-à-Pitre (French pwɛtapitrə) *n* the chief port of Guadeloupe, on SW Grande-Terre Island in the Caribbean. Pop: 20 948 (1999)

pointed ('pɔɪntɪd) *adj* **1** having a point **2** cutting or incisive: *a pointed wit* **3** obviously directed at or intended for a particular person or aspect: *pointed criticism* **4** emphasized or made conspicuous: *pointed ignorance* **5** (of an arch or style of architecture employing such an arch) Gothic **6** *music* (of a psalm text) marked to show changes in chanting **7** (of Hebrew text) with vowel points marked ▷ '**pointedly** *adv*

Pointe-Noire (French pwɛtnwar) *n* a port in S Congo-Brazzaville, on the Atlantic: the country's chief port and former capital (1950–58). Pop: 638 000 (2005 est)

pointer ('pɔɪntə) *n* **1** a person or thing that points **2** an indicator on a measuring instrument **3** a long rod or

cane used by a lecturer to point to parts of a map, blackboard, etc **4** one of a breed of large swift smooth-coated dogs, usually white with black, liver, or lemon markings: when on shooting expeditions it points to the bird with its nose, body, and tail in a straight line **5** a helpful piece of information or advice

pointillism ('pwæntɪˌlɪzəm, -tiːˌɪzəm, 'pɔɪn-) *n* the technique of painting elaborated from impressionism, in which dots of unmixed colour are juxtaposed on a white ground so that from a distance they fuse in the viewer's eye into appropriate intermediate tones [c19: from French, from *pointiller* to mark with tiny dots, from *pointille* little point, from Italian *puntiglio*, from *punto* POINT] ▷ '**pointillist** *n, adj*

pointing ('pɔɪntɪŋ) *n* the act or process of repairing or finishing joints in brickwork, masonry, etc, with mortar

point lace *n* lace made by a needle with buttonhole stitch on a paper pattern. Also called: **needlepoint** See **pillow lace**

pointless ('pɔɪntlɪs) *adj* **1** without a point **2** without meaning, relevance, or force **3** *sport* without a point scored ▷ '**pointlessly** *adv*

point off *vb* (*tr, adverb*) to mark off from the right-hand side (a number of decimal places) in a whole number to create a mixed decimal: *point off three decimal places in 12345 and you get 12.345*

point of honour *n, pl* points of honour a circumstance, event, etc, that involves the defence of one's principles, social honour, etc

point of no return *n* **1** a point at which an irreversible commitment must be made to an action, progression, etc **2** a point in a journey at which, if one continues, supplies will be insufficient for a return to the starting place

point of order *n, pl* points of order a question raised in a meeting or deliberative assembly by a member as to whether the rules governing procedures are being breached

point of sale *n* (in retail distribution) the place at which a sale is made. Abbreviation: **POS**

point of view *n, pl* points of view **1** a position from which someone or something is observed **2** a mental viewpoint or attitude

point out *vb* (*tr, adverb*) to indicate or specify

pointsman ('pɔɪntsˌmæn, -mən) *n, pl* -men **1** a person who operates railway points **2** a policeman or traffic warden on point duty

point source *n* *optics* a source of light or other radiation that can be considered to have negligible dimensions

points system *n* *Brit* a system used to assess applicants' eligibility for local authority housing, based on (points awarded for) such factors as the length of time the applicant has lived in the area, how many children are in the family, etc

point-to-point *n* *Brit* a steeplechase organized by a recognized hunt or other body, usually restricted to amateurs riding horses that have been regularly used in hunting

point up *vb* (*tr, adverb*) to emphasize, esp by identifying: *he pointed up the difficulties we would encounter*

pointy ('pɔɪntɪ) *adj* pointier, pointiest having a sharp point or points; pointed

pointy-head *n* *chiefly US disparaging, informal* an intellectual ▷ '**pointy-ˌheaded** *adj*

poise¹ (pɔɪz) *n* **1** composure or dignity of manner **2** physical balance or assurance in movement or bearing **3** the state of being balanced or stable; equilibrium; stability **4** the position of hovering ▷ *vb* **5** to be or cause to be balanced or suspended **6** (*tr*) to hold, as in readiness: *to poise a lance* [c16: from Old French *pois* weight, from Latin *pēnsum*, from *pendere* to weigh]

poise² (pwaːz, pɔɪz) *n* the cgs unit of viscosity; the viscosity of a fluid in which a tangential force of 1 dyne per square centimetre maintains a difference in velocity of 1 centimetre per second between two parallel planes 1 centimetre apart. It is equivalent to 0.1 newton second per square metre. Symbol: **P** [c20: named after Jean Louis Marie *Poiseuille* (1799–1869), French physician]

poised (pɔɪzd) *adj* **1** self-possessed; dignified; exhibiting composure **2** balanced and prepared for action

poison ('pɔɪzᵊn) n **1** any substance that can impair function, cause structural damage, or otherwise injure the body **2** something that destroys, corrupts, etc **3** a substance that retards a chemical reaction or destroys or inhibits the activity of a catalyst **4** a substance that absorbs neutrons in a nuclear reactor and thus slows down the reaction. It may be added deliberately or formed during fission ▷ vb (tr) **5** to give poison to (a person or animal) esp with intent to kill **6** to add poison to **7** to taint or infect with or as if with poison **8** (foll by *against*) to turn (a person's mind) against: *he poisoned her mind against me* **9** to retard or stop (a chemical or nuclear reaction) by the action of a poison [c13: from Old French *puison* potion, from Latin *pōtiō* a drink, esp a poisonous one, from *pōtāre* to drink] > 'poisoner n

poison ivy n any of several North American anacardiaceous shrubs or vines of the genus *Rhus* (or *Toxicodendron*), esp *R. radicans*, which has small green flowers and whitish berries that cause an itching rash on contact

poisonous ('pɔɪzənəs) adj **1** having the effects or qualities of a poison **2** capable of killing or inflicting injury; venomous **3** corruptive or malicious > 'poisonously adv > 'poisonousness n

poison-pen letter n a letter written in malice, usually anonymously, and intended to abuse, frighten, or insult the recipient

poison pill n *finance* a tactic used by a company fearing an unwelcome takeover bid, in which the value of the company is automatically reduced, as by the sale of an issue of shares having an option unfavourable to the bidders, if the bid is successful

poison sumach n an anacardiaceous swamp shrub, *Rhus* (or *Toxicodendron*) *vernix* of the southeastern US, that has greenish-white berries and causes an itching rash on contact with the skin

Poisson (French pwasɔ̃) n **Siméon Denis** (simeɔ̃ dəni). 1781–1840, French mathematician, noted for his application of mathematical theory to physics, esp electricity and magnetism

Poisson distribution ('pwɑ:sᵊn) n *statistics* a distribution that represents the number of events occurring randomly in a fixed time at an average rate λ; symbol $P_0(\lambda)$. For large n and small p with $np = \lambda$ it approximates to the binomial distribution $Bi(n,p)$ [c19: named after Siméon Denis Poisson]

Poitiers (French pwatje) n a city in S central France: capital of the former province of Poitou until 1790; scene of the battle (1356) in which the English under the Black Prince defeated the French; university (1432). Pop: 83 448 (1999)

Poitou (French pwatu) n a former province of W central France, on the Atlantic. Chief town: Poitiers

Poitou-Charentes (French pwatuʃarɑ̃t) n a region of W central France, on the Bay of Biscay: mainly low-lying

poke¹ (pəʊk) vb **1** (tr) to jab or prod, as with the elbow, the finger, a stick, etc **2** (tr) to make (a hole, opening, etc) by or as by poking **3** (when intr, often foll by at) to thrust (at) **4** (tr) informal to hit with the fist; punch **5** (usually foll by in, out, out of, through, etc) to protrude or cause to protrude: *don't poke your arm out of the window* **6** (tr) to stir (a fire, pot, etc) by poking **7** (intr) to meddle or intrude **8** (intr; often foll by about or around) to search or pry **9** poke one's nose into ▷ n **10** a jab or prod **11** informal a blow with one's fist; punch [c14: from Low German and Middle Dutch *poken* to thrust, prod, strike]

poke² (pəʊk) n **1** dialect a pocket or bag **2** a pig in a poke See pig (sense 9) [c13: from Old Northern French *poque*, of Germanic origin; related to Old English *pocca* bag, Old Norse *poki* pouch, Middle Dutch *poke* bag; compare poach²]

poke³ (pəʊk) n **1** Also called: poke bonnet a woman's bonnet with a brim that projects at the front, popular in the 18th and 19th centuries **2** the brim itself [c18: from poke¹ (in the sense: to thrust out, project)]

poker¹ ('pəʊkə) n a metal rod, usually with a handle, for stirring a fire

poker² ('pəʊkə) n a card game of bluff and skill in which

bets are made on the hands dealt, the highest-ranking hand (containing the most valuable combinations of sequences and sets of cards) winning the pool [c19: probably from French *poque* similar card game]

poker face n informal a face without expression, as that of a poker player attempting to conceal the value of his cards

poker-faced adj informal having a deliberately expressionless face

poker machine n Austral & NZ a fruit machine

pokerwork ('pəʊkə,wɜ:k) n the art of decorating wood or leather by burning a design with a heated metal point; pyrography

pokeweed ('pəʊk,wi:d), **pokeberry** or **pokeroot** n a tall North American plant, *Phytolacca americana*, that has small white flowers, juicy purple berries, and a poisonous purple root used medicinally: family Phytolaccaceae [c18: poke, shortened from Algonquian *puccoon* plant used in dyeing, from *pak* blood]

pokie or **pokey** ('pəʊkɪ) n Austral & NZ informal short for **poker machine**

poky or **pokey** ('pəʊkɪ) adj pokier, pokiest **1** informal (esp of rooms) small and cramped **2** without speed or energy; slow [c19: from poke¹ (in slang sense: to confine)] > 'pokily adv > 'pokiness n

Pol. abbreviation **1** Poland **2** Polish

Pola ('pɔ:la) n the Italian name for **Pula**

Poland ('pəʊlənd) n a republic in central Europe, on the Baltic: first united in the 10th century; dissolved after the third partition effected by Austria, Russia, and Prussia in 1795; re-established independence in 1918; invaded by Germany in 1939; ruled by a Communist government from 1947 to 1989, when a multiparty system was introduced; joined the EU in 2004. It consists chiefly of a low undulating plain in the north, rising to a low plateau in the south, with the Sudeten and Carpathian Mountains along the S border. Official language: Polish. Religion: Roman Catholic majority. Currency: złoty. Capital: Warsaw. Pop: 38 551 000 (2004 est). Area: 311 730 sq km (120 359 sq miles). Polish name: Polska

Polanski (pə'lænskɪ) n **Roman.** born 1933, Polish film director with a taste for the macabre, as in *Repulsion* (1965) and *Rosemary's Baby* (1968): later films include *Tess* (1980), *Death and the Maiden* (1995), and *The Pianist* (2002)

polar ('pəʊlə) adj **1** situated at or near, coming from, or relating to either of the earth's poles or the area inside the Arctic or Antarctic Circles: *polar regions* **2** having or relating to a pole or poles **3** pivotal or guiding in the manner of the Pole Star **4** directly opposite, as in tendency or character **5** chem Also called: heteropolar (of a molecule or compound) being or having a molecule in which there is an uneven distribution of electrons and thus a permanent dipole moment: *water has polar molecules*

polar bear n a white carnivorous bear, *Thalarctos maritimus*, of coastal regions of the North Pole

polar circle n a term for either the **Arctic Circle** or **Antarctic Circle**

polar coordinates pl n a pair of coordinates for locating a point in a plane by means of the length of a radius vector, r, which pivots about the origin to establish the angle, θ, that the position of the point makes with a fixed line. Usually written (r, θ)

polar distance n the angular distance of a star, planet, etc, from the celestial pole; the complement of the declination

polar front n meteorol a front dividing cold polar air from warmer temperate or tropical air

Polari (pə'lɑ:rɪ) n an English slang that is derived from the Lingua Franca of Mediterranean ports; brought to England by sailors from the 16th century onwards. A few words survive, esp in male homosexual slang [c19: from Italian *parlare* to speak]

polarimeter (,pəʊlə'rɪmɪtə) n an instrument for measuring the amount of polarization of light > polarimetric (,pəʊlərɪ'mɛtrɪk) adj

Polaris (pə'lɑ:rɪs) n **1** Also called: the Pole Star, the North Star the brightest star in the constellation Ursa Minor, situated slightly less than 1° from the north celestial pole. It is a Cepheid variable, with a period of four days. Visual magnitude: 2.08–2.17; spectral type: F8Ib **2** a type of US two-stage intermediate-range ballistic missile, usually fired by a submerged submarine [shortened from Medieval Latin *stella polaris* polar star]

polariscope (pəʊˈlærɪˌskəʊp) *n* an instrument for detecting polarized light or for observing objects under polarized light, esp for detecting strain in transparent materials

polarity (pəʊˈlærɪtɪ) *n*, *pl* -ties **1** the condition of having poles **2** the condition of a body or system in which it has opposing physical properties at different points, esp magnetic poles or electric charge **3** the particular state of a part of a body or system that has polarity: *an electrode with positive polarity* **4** the state of having or expressing two directly opposite tendencies, opinions, etc

polarization *or* **polarisation** (ˌpəʊləraɪˈzeɪʃən) *n* **1** the condition of having or giving polarity **2** *physics* the process or phenomenon in which the waves of light or other electromagnetic radiation are restricted to certain directions of vibration, usually specified in terms of the electric field vector

polarize *or* **polarise** (ˈpəʊləˌraɪz) *vb* **1** to acquire or cause to acquire polarity **2** to acquire or cause to acquire polarization **3** to cause people to adopt extreme opposing positions: *to polarize opinion*

polar lights *pl n* the aurora borealis in the N hemisphere or the aurora australis in the S hemisphere

polarography (ˌpəʊləˈrɒɡrəfɪ) *n* a technique for analysing and studying ions in solution by using an electrolytic cell with a very small cathode and obtaining a graph (**polarogram**) of the current against the potential to determine the concentration and nature of the ions. Because the cathode is small, polarization occurs and each type of anion is discharged at a different potential. The apparatus (**polarograph**) usually employs a dropping-mercury cathode

Polaroid (ˈpəʊləˌrɔɪd) *trademark n* **1** a type of plastic sheet that can polarize a transmitted beam of normal light because it is composed of long parallel molecules. It only transmits plane-polarized light if these molecules are parallel to the plane of polarization and, since reflected light is partly polarized, it is often used in sunglasses to eliminate glare **2** Polaroid Land Camera any of several types of camera yielding a finished print by means of a special developing and processing technique that occurs inside the camera and takes only a few seconds to complete **3** (*plural*) sunglasses with lenses made from Polaroid plastic

polder (ˈpəʊldə, ˈpɒl-) *n* a stretch of land reclaimed from the sea or a lake, esp in the Netherlands [C17: from Middle Dutch *polre*]

pole¹ (pəʊl) *n* **1 a** long slender usually round piece of wood, metal, or other material **2** the piece of timber on each side of which a pair of carriage horses are hitched **3** another name for **rod** (sense 7) **4** up the pole *Brit, Austral & NZ informal* **a** slightly mad **b** mistaken; on the wrong track ▷ *vb* **5** (*tr*) to strike or push with a pole **6** (*tr*) **a** to set out (an area of land or garden) with poles **b** to support (a crop, such as hops or beans) on poles **7** to punt (a boat) [Old English *pāl*, from Latin *pālus* a stake, prop; see PALE²]

pole² (pəʊl) *n* **1** either of the two antipodal points where the earth's axis of rotation meets the earth's surface. See also **North Pole**, **South Pole 2** *physics* either of the two regions at the extremities of a magnet to which the lines of force converge or from which they diverge **3** *biology* either end of the axis of a cell, spore, ovum, or similar body **4** either of two mutually exclusive or opposite actions, opinions, etc **5** poles apart *or* poles asunder having widely divergent opinions, tastes, etc [C14: from Latin *polus* end of an axis, from Greek *polos* pivot, axis, pole; related to Greek *kuklos* circle]

Pole¹ (pəʊl) *n* a native, inhabitant, or citizen of Poland or a speaker of Polish

Pole² (pəʊl) *n* **Reginald**. 1500–58, English cardinal; last Roman Catholic archbishop of Canterbury (1556–58)

poleaxe *or US* **poleax** (ˈpəʊlˌæks) *n* **1** another term for

battle-axe (sense 1) ▷ *vb* **2** (*tr*) to hit or fell with or as if with a poleaxe [C14 *pollax* battle-axe, from POLL + AXE]

polecat (ˈpəʊlˌkæt) *n*, *pl* -cats *or* -cat **1** a dark brown musteline mammal, *Mustela putorius*, of woodlands of Europe, Asia, and N Africa, that is closely related to but larger than the weasel and gives off an unpleasant smell **2** *US* a nontechnical name for **skunk** (sense 1) [C14 *polcat*, perhaps from Old French *pol* cock, from Latin *pullus*, + CAT¹; from its habit of preying on poultry]

pole dancing *n* a form of entertainment in which a scantily dressed woman dances erotically, turning on and posing against a vertically fixed pole on a stage > pole dancer *n*

polemic (pəˈlɛmɪk) *adj* Also: po'lemical **1** of or involving dispute or controversy ▷ *n* **2** an argument or controversy, esp over a doctrine, belief, etc **3** a person engaged in such an argument or controversy [C17: from Medieval Latin *polemicus*, from Greek *polemikos* relating to war, from *polemos* war] > po'lemically *adv* > polemicist (pəˈlɛmɪsɪst) *n*

polemics (pəˈlɛmɪks) *n* (*functioning as singular*) the art or practice of dispute or argument, as in attacking or defending a doctrine or belief

pole position *n* **1** (in motor racing) the starting position on the inside of the front row, generally considered the best one **2** an advantageous starting position

pole star *n* a guiding principle, rule, standard, etc

Pole Star *n* the Pole Star the star closest to the N celestial pole at any particular time. At present this is Polaris, but it will eventually be replaced by some other star owing to precession of the earth's axis

pole vault *n* **1** the pole vault a field event in which competitors attempt to clear a high bar with the aid of an extremely flexible long pole ▷ *vb* **pole-vault 2** (*intr*) to perform a pole vault or compete in the pole vault > 'pole-ˌvaulter *n*

poley (ˈpəʊlɪ) *adj Austral* (of cattle) hornless or polled

Poliakoff (ˌpɒlɪˈɑːkɒf) *n* **Stephen**. born 1952, British playwright and film director; work includes the stage plays *Breaking the Silence* (1984) and *Blinded by the Sun* (1996) and the television serials *The Lost Prince* (2003) and *Friends and Crocodiles* (2005)

police (pəˈliːs) *n* **1** the police the organized civil force of a state, concerned with maintenance of law and order, the detection and prevention of crime, etc **2** (*functioning as plural*) the members of such a force collectively **3** any organized body with a similar function: *security police* ▷ *vb* (*tr*) **4** to regulate, control, or keep in order by means of a police or similar force **5** to observe or record the activity or enforcement of: *a committee was set up to police the new agreement on picketing* [C16: via French from Latin *politīa* administration, government; see POLITY]

police dog *n* a dog, often an Alsatian, trained to help the police, as in tracking

policeman (pəˈliːsmən) *or feminine* **policewoman** *n, pl* -men *or* -women a member of a police force, esp one holding the rank of constable

police officer *n* a member of a police force, esp a constable; policeman

police procedural *n* a novel, film, or television drama that deals realistically with police work

police state *n* a state or country in which a repressive government maintains control through the police

police station *n* the office or headquarters of the police force of a district

policy¹ (ˈpɒlɪsɪ) *n, pl* -cies **1** a plan of action adopted or pursued by an individual, government, party, business, etc **2** wisdom, prudence, shrewdness, or sagacity **3** *Scot*(often plural) the improved grounds surrounding a country house [C14: from Old French *policie*, from Latin *politīa* administration, POLITY]

policy² (ˈpɒlɪsɪ) *n, pl* -cies a document containing a contract of insurance [C16: from Old French *police* certificate, from Old Italian *polizza*, from Latin *apodixis* proof, from Greek *apodeixis* demonstration, proof]

Polignac (French pɔliɲak) *n* **Prince de**, title of *Auguste Jules Armand Marie de Polignac*. 1780–1847, French statesman; prime minister (1829–30) to Charles X: his extreme royalist and ultramontane policies provoked the 1830 revolution and cost Charles X the throne

polio ('pəʊlɪəʊ) n short for **poliomyelitis**

poliomyelitis (,pəʊlɪəʊ,maɪə'laɪtɪs) n an acute infectious viral disease, esp affecting children. In its paralytic form (**acute anterior poliomyelitis**) the brain and spinal cord are involved, causing weakness, paralysis, and wasting of muscle. Also called: infantile paralysis [C19: New Latin, from Greek *polios* grey + *muelos* marrow]

polish ('pɒlɪʃ) vb 1 to make or become smooth and shiny by rubbing, esp with wax or an abrasive 2 (tr) to make perfect or complete 3 to make or become elegant or refined ▷ n 4 a finish or gloss 5 the act of polishing or the condition of having been polished 6 a substance used to produce a smooth and shiny, often protective surface 7 elegance or refinement, esp in style, manner, etc [C13 polis, from Old French *polir*, from Latin *polīre* to polish] > 'polisher n

Polish ('pəʊlɪʃ) adj 1 of, relating to, or characteristic of Poland, its people, or their language ▷ n 2 the official language of Poland, belonging to the West Slavonic branch of the Indo-European family

Polish Corridor n the strip of land through E Pomerania providing Poland with access to the sea (1919–39), given to her in 1919 in the Treaty of Versailles, and separating East Prussia from the rest of Germany. It is now part of Poland

polished ('pɒlɪʃt) adj 1 accomplished: *a polished actor* 2 impeccably or professionally done: *a polished performance* 3 (of rice) having had the outer husk removed by milling

polish off vb (tr, adverb) informal 1 to finish or process completely 2 to dispose of or kill; eliminate

polish up vb (adverb) 1 to make or become smooth and shiny by polishing 2 (when intr, foll by on) to study or practise until adept at; improve: *polish up your spelling; he's polishing up on his German*

Politburo ('pɒlɪt,bjʊərəʊ) n 1 the executive and policy-making committee of a Communist Party 2 the supreme policy-making authority in most Communist countries [C20: from Russian: contraction of *Politicheskoe Buro* political bureau]

polite (pə'laɪt) adj 1 showing regard for others, in manners, speech, behaviour, etc; courteous 2 cultivated or refined: *polite society* 3 elegant or polished: *polite letters* [C15: from Latin *polītus* polished; see POLISH] > po'litely adv > po'liteness n

politesse (,pɒlɪ'tes) n formal or genteel politeness [C18: via French from Italian *politezza*, ultimately from Latin *polīre* to POLISH]

Politian (pəʊ'lɪʃən, pɒ-) n Italian name *Angelo Polliziano*; original name *Angelo Ambrogini*. 1454–94, Florentine humanist and poet

politic ('pɒlɪtɪk) adj 1 artful or shrewd; ingenious 2 crafty or unscrupulous; cunning 3 an archaic word for **political** ▷ See also **body politic** [C15: from Old French *politique*, from Latin *polīticus* concerning civil administration, from Greek *politikos*, from *politēs* citizen, from *polis* city] > 'politicly adv

political (pə'lɪtɪkᵊl) adj 1 of or relating to the state, government, the body politic, public administration, policy-making, etc 2 a of, involved in, or relating to government policy-making as distinguished from administration or law b of or relating to the civil aspects of government as distinguished from the military 3 of, dealing with, or relating to politics: *a political person* 4 of, characteristic of, or relating to the parties and the partisan aspects of politics 5 organized or ordered with respect to government: *a political unit* > po'litically adv

political economy n the former name for **economics** (sense 1)

politically correct adj demonstrating progressive ideals, esp by avoiding vocabulary that is considered offensive, discriminatory, or judgmental, esp concerning race and gender. Abbreviation: PC > political correctness n

political prisoner n someone imprisoned for holding, expressing, or acting in accord with particular political beliefs

political science n (esp as an academic subject) the study of the state, government, and politics: one of the social sciences > political scientist n

politician (,pɒlɪ'tɪʃən) n 1 a person actively engaged in politics, esp a full-time professional member of a deliberative assembly 2 a person who is experienced or skilled in the art or science of politics, government, or administration; statesman 3 disparaging, chiefly US a person who engages in politics out of a wish for personal gain, as realized by holding a public office

politicize or **politicise** (pə'lɪtɪ,saɪz) vb 1 (tr) to render political in tone, interest, or awareness 2 (intr) to participate in political discussion or activity > po,litici'zation or po,litici'sation n

politicking ('pɒlɪ,tɪkɪŋ) n political activity, esp seeking votes

politico (pə'lɪtɪ,kəʊ) n, pl -cos an informal word for a **politician** (senses 1, 3) [C17: from Italian or Spanish]

politics ('pɒlɪtɪks) n 1 (functioning as singular) the practice or study of the art and science of forming, directing, and administrating states and other political units; the art and science of government; political science 2 (functioning as singular) the complex or aggregate of relationships of people in society, esp those relationships involving authority or power 3 (functioning as plural) political activities or affairs: *party politics* 4 (functioning as singular) the business or profession of politics 5 (functioning as singular or plural) any activity concerned with the acquisition of power, gaining one's own ends, etc: *company politics are frequently vicious* 6 (functioning as plural) opinions, principles, sympathies, etc, with respect to politics: *his conservative politics*

polity ('pɒlɪtɪ) n, pl -ties 1 a form of government or organization of a state, church, society, etc; constitution 2 a politically organized society, state, city, etc 3 the management of public or civil affairs 4 political organization [C16: from Latin *polītia*, from Greek *politeia* citizenship, civil administration, from *politēs* citizen, from *polis* city]

Polk (pəʊk) n **James Knox**. 1795–1849, US statesman; 11th president of the US (1845–49). During his administration, Texas and territory now included in New Mexico, Texas and territory now included in New Mexico, Colorado, Utah, Nevada, Arizona, Oregon, and California were added to the Union

polka ('pɒlkə) n, pl -kas 1 a 19th-century Bohemian dance with three steps and a hop, in fast duple time 2 a piece of music composed for or in the rhythm of this dance ▷ vb -kas, -kaing, -kaed 3 (intr) to dance a polka [C19: via French from Czech *pulka* half-step, from *pul* half]

polka dot n one of a pattern of small circular regularly spaced spots on a fabric [C19: of uncertain origin]

poll (pəʊl) n 1 the casting, recording, or counting of votes in an election; a voting 2 the result or quantity of such a voting: *a heavy poll* 3 Also called: opinion poll a a canvassing of a representative sample of a large group of people on some question in order to determine the general opinion of the group b the results or record of such a canvassing 4 any counting or enumeration 5 the occipital or back part of the head of an animal ▷ vb (mainly tr) 6 to receive (a vote or quantity of votes): *he polled 10 000 votes* 7 to receive, take, or record the votes of: *he polled the whole town* 8 to canvass (a person, group, area, etc) as part of a survey of opinion 9 (sometimes intr) to cast (a vote) in an election 10 to clip or shear 11 to remove or cut short the horns of (cattle) [C13 (in the sense: a human head) and C17 (in the modern sense: a counting of heads, votes): from Middle Low German *polle* hair of the head, head, top of a tree; compare Swedish *pull* crown of the head]

pollack or **pollock** ('pɒlək) n, pl -lacks, -lack or -locks, -lock a gadoid food fish, *Pollachius pollachius*, that has a dark green back and a projecting lower jaw and occurs in northern seas, esp the North Atlantic Ocean [C17: from earlier Scottish *podlok*, of obscure origin]

Pollack ('pɒlək) n **Sydney**. born 1934, US film director. His films include *Tootsie* (1982), *Out of Africa* (1986), and *The Firm* (1993)

Pollaiuolo (Italian pollaj'wɔːlo) n 1 **Antonio** (an'tɔːnjo), ?1432–98, Florentine painter, sculptor, goldsmith, and engraver: his paintings include the *Martyrdom of St*

Sebastian **2** his brother **Piero** ('pjɛːro). ?1443–96, Florentine painter and sculptor

pollan ('pɒlən) *n* any of several varieties of the whitefish *Coregonus pollan* that occur in lakes in Northern Ireland [c18: probably from Irish *poll* lake]

pollard ('pɒləd) *n* **1** an animal, such as a sheep or deer, that has either shed its horns or antlers or has had them removed **2** a tree that has had its top cut off to encourage the formation of a crown of branches ▷ *vb* **3** (*tr*) to convert into a pollard; poll [c16: hornless animal; see POLL]

pollen ('pɒlən) *n* a fine powdery substance produced by the anthers of seed-bearing plants, consisting of numerous fine grains containing the male gametes [c16: from Latin: powder; compare Greek *palē* pollen] > **pollinic** (pə'lɪnɪk) *adj*

Pollen ('pɒlən) *n* **Daniel**. 1813–96, New Zealand statesman, born in Ireland: prime minister of New Zealand (1876)

pollen analysis *n* another name for **palynology**

pollen count *n* a measure of the pollen present in the air over a 24-hour period, often published to enable sufferers from hay fever to predict the severity of their attacks

pollex ('pɒlɛks) *n*, *pl* **-lices** (-lɪˌsiːz) the first digit of the forelimb of amphibians, reptiles, birds, and mammals, such as the thumb of man and other primates [c19: from Latin: thumb, big toe] > **pollical** ('pɒlɪkᵊl) *adj*

pollinate ('pɒlɪˌneɪt) *vb* (*tr*) to transfer pollen from the anthers to the stigma of (a flower) > ˌpolli'nation *n* > 'polliˌnator *n*

polling booth *n* a semienclosed space in which a voter stands to mark a ballot paper during an election

polling station *n* a building, such as a school, designated as the place to which voters go during an election to cast their votes

polliwog *or* **pollywog** ('pɒlɪˌwɒg) *n Brit dialect, US & Canadian* another name for **tadpole** [c15 *polwygle*; see POLL, WIGGLE]

Pollock ('pɒlək) *n* **1** Sir **Frederick**. 1845–1937, English legal scholar: with Maitland, he wrote *History of English Law before the Time of Edward I* (1895) **2** **Jackson**. 1912–56, US abstract expressionist painter; chief exponent of action painting in the US

pollster ('pəʊlstə) *n* a person who conducts opinion polls

poll tax *n* **1** a tax levied per head of adult population **2** an informal name for (the former) **community charge**

pollutant (pə'luːtᵊnt) *n* a substance that pollutes, esp a chemical or similar substance that is produced as a waste product of an industrial process

pollute (pə'luːt) *vb* (*tr*) **1** to contaminate, as with poisonous or harmful substances **2** to make morally corrupt or impure; sully **3** to desecrate or defile [C14 *polute*, from Latin *polluere* to defile] > pol'luter *n*

pollution (pə'luːʃən) *n* **1** the act of polluting or the state of being polluted **2** harmful or poisonous substances introduced into an environment

Pollux ('pɒləks) *n classical myth* See **Castor and Pollux**

Pollyanna (ˌpɒlɪ'ænə) *n* a person who is constantly or excessively optimistic [c20: after the chief character in *Pollyanna* (1913), a novel by Eleanor Porter (1868–1920), US writer]

polo ('pəʊləʊ) *n* **1** a game similar to hockey played on horseback using long-handled mallets (**polo sticks**) and a wooden ball **2** short for **water polo 3** Also called: polo neck **a** a collar on a garment, worn rolled over to fit closely round the neck **b** a garment, esp a sweater, with such a collar [c19: from Balti (dialect of Kashmir): ball, from Tibetan *pulu*]

Polo ('pəʊləʊ) *n* **Marco** ('mɑːkəʊ). 1254–1324, Venetian merchant, famous for his account of his travels in Asia. After travelling overland to China (1271–75), he spent 17 years serving Kublai Khan before returning to Venice by sea (1292–95)

Polokwane (ˌpɒlə'kwɑːnɪ) *n* a town in NE South Africa, the capital of Limpopo province: commercial and agricultural centre. Pop: 90 398 (2001)

polonaise (ˌpɒlə'neɪz) *n* **1** a ceremonial marchlike dance

in three-four time from Poland **2** a piece of music composed for or in the rhythm of this dance **3** a woman's costume with a tight bodice and an overskirt drawn back to show a decorative underskirt [c18: from French *danse polonaise* Polish dance]

polonium (pə'ləʊnɪəm) *n* a very rare radioactive element that occurs in trace amounts in uranium ores. The isotope **polonium-210** is produced artificially and is used as a lightweight power source in satellites and to eliminate static electricity in certain industries. Symbol: Po; atomic no: 84; half-life of most stable isotope, ^{209}Po: 103 years; valency: –2, 0, 2, 4, or 6; relative density (alpha modification): 9.32; melting pt: 254°C; boiling pt: 962°C [c19: New Latin, from Medieval Latin *Polōnia* Poland; named in honour of the Polish nationality of its discoverer, Marie Curie]

polony (pə'ləʊnɪ) *n*, *pl* **-nies** *Brit* another name for **bologna sausage** [c16: perhaps from BOLOGNA]

polo shirt *n* a knitted cotton short-sleeved shirt with a collar and three-button opening at the neck

Pol Pot ('pɒl 'pɒt) *n* original name *Kompong Thom*. 1925–98, Cambodian Communist statesman; prime minister of Kampuchea (1976; 1977–79); his policies led to the deaths of thousands in labour camps before he was overthrown by Vietnamese forces; in 1997 his former supporters in the Khmer Rouge captured him and claimed to have tried and sentenced him to life imprisonment

Polska ('pɒlska) *n* the Polish name for **Poland**

Poltava (*Russian* pal'tavə) *n* a city in E Ukraine: scene of the victory (1709) of the Russians under Peter the Great over the Swedes under Charles XII; centre of an agricultural region. Pop: 319 000 (2005 est)

poltergeist ('pɒltəˌgaɪst) *n* a spirit believed to manifest its presence by rappings and other noises and also by acts of mischief, such as throwing furniture about [c19: from German, from *poltern* to be noisy + *Geist* GHOST]

poltroon (pɒl'truːn) *n* an abject or contemptible coward [c16: from Old French *poultron*, from Old Italian *poltrone* lazy good-for-nothing, apparently from *poltrīre* to lie indolently in bed, from *poltro* bed]

poly ('pɒlɪ) *n*, *pl* **polys 1** *informal* short for **polytechnic** ▷ *adj* **2** *informal* short for **polyester**

poly- *combining form* **1** more than one; many or much: *polyhedron* **2** having an excessive or abnormal number or amount [from Greek *polus* much, many; related to Old English *fela* many]

polyamide (ˌpɒlɪ'æmaɪd, -mɪd) *n* any one of a class of synthetic polymeric materials containing recurring -CONH- groups. See also **nylon**

polyandry ('pɒlɪˌændrɪ) *n* **1** the practice or condition of being married to more than one husband at the same time **2** the practice in animals of a female mating with more than one male during one breeding season **3** the condition in flowers of having a large indefinite number of stamens [c18: from Greek *poluandria*, from POLY- + *-andria* from *anēr* man] > ˌpoly'androus *adj*

polyanthus (ˌpɒlɪ'ænθəs) *n*, *pl* **-thuses** any of several hybrid garden primroses, esp *Primula polyantha*, which has brightly coloured flowers [c18: New Latin, Greek: having many flowers]

polyatomic (ˌpɒlɪə'tɒmɪk) *adj* (of a molecule) containing more than two atoms

poly bag ('pɒlɪ) *n Brit informal* a polythene bag, esp one used to store or protect food or household articles

polybasic (ˌpɒlɪ'beɪsɪk) *adj* (of an acid) having two or more replaceable hydrogen atoms per molecule

Polybius (pəʊ'lɪbɪəs) *n* ?205–?123 BC, Greek historian. Under the patronage of Scipio the Younger, he wrote in 40 books a history of Rome from 264 BC to 146 BC

polycarboxylate (ˌpɒlɪ'kɑːbɒkˌsɪleɪt) *n* a salt or ester of a polycarboxylic acid. Polycarboxylate esters are used in certain detergents

polycarboxylic acid (ˌpɒlɪkɑː'bɒkˌsɪlɪk) *n* a type of carboxylic acid containing two or more carboxyl groups

Polycarp ('pɒlɪˌkɑːp) *n* **Saint**. ?69–?155 AD, Christian martyr and bishop of Smyrna, noted for his letter to the church at Philippi. Feast day: Feb 23

polycarpic (ˌpɒlɪ'kɑːpɪk) *or* **polycarpous** *adj* (of a plant) able to produce flowers and fruit several times in successive years or seasons ▷ 'poly,carpy n

polycentrism (,pɒlɪ'sɛntrɪzəm) n (formerly) the fact, principle, or advocacy of the existence of more than one guiding or predominant ideological or political centre in a political system, alliance, etc, in the Communist world

polychaete ('pɒlɪ,kiːt) n 1 any marine annelid worm of the class *Polychaeta*, having a distinct head and paired fleshy appendages (parapodia) that bear bristles (chaetae or setae) and are used in swimming: includes the lugworms, ragworms, and sea mice ▷ adj Also: polychaetous 2 of, relating to, or belonging to the class *Polychaeta* [c19: from New Latin, from Greek *polukhaitēs*: having much hair; see CHAETA]

polychromatic (,pɒlɪkrəʊ'mætɪk), **polychromic** (,pɒlɪ'krəʊmɪk) or **polychromous** adj 1 having various or changing colours 2 (of light or other electromagnetic radiation) containing radiation with more than one wavelength ▷ polychromatism (,pɒlɪ'krəʊmə,tɪzəm) n

polyclinic (,pɒlɪ'klɪnɪk) n a hospital or clinic able to treat a wide variety of diseases: general hospital

Polyclitus, Polycleitus (,pɒlɪ'klaɪtəs) or **Polycletus** (,pɒlɪ'kliːtəs) n 5th-century BC Greek sculptor, noted particularly for his idealized bronze sculptures of the male nude, such as the *Doryphoros*

polycotton ('pɒlɪkɒtᵊn) n a fabric made from a mixture of polyester and cotton

polycotyledon (,pɒlɪ,kɒtɪ'liːdᵊn) n any of various plants, esp gymnosperms, that have or appear to have more than two cotyledons ▷ ,poly,coty'ledonous adj

Polycrates (pə'lɪkrə,tiːz) n died ?522 BC, Greek tyrant of Samos, who was crucified by a Persian satrap

polycyclic (,pɒlɪ'saɪklɪk) adj 1 (of a molecule or compound) containing or having molecules that contain two or more closed rings of atoms 2 biology having two or more rings or whorls: *polycyclic shells; a polycyclic stele* ▷ n 3 a polycyclic compound

polycystic (,pɒlɪ'sɪstɪk) adj med containing many cysts: *a polycystic ovary*

polycystic ovary syndrome n a hormonal disorder in which the Graafian follicles in the ovary fail to develop completely so that they are unable to ovulate, remaining as multiple cysts that distend the ovary. The results can include reduced fertility, obesity, and hirsutism

polydactyl (,pɒlɪ'dæktɪl) adj Also: polydactylous 1 (of man and other vertebrates) having more than the normal number of digits ▷ n 2 a human or other vertebrate having more than the normal number of digits [c19: via French from Greek *poludactulos* many-toed; see DACTYL]

Polydeuces (,pɒlɪ'djuːsiːz) n the Greek name of **Pollux**. See **Castor and Pollux**

polyester (,pɒlɪ'ɛstə) n any of a large class of synthetic materials that are polymers containing recurring -COO- groups: used as plastics, textile fibres, and adhesives

polyethene (,pɒlɪ'ɛθiːn) n the systematic name for polythene

polyethylene (,pɒlɪ'ɛθɪ,liːn) n another name for polythene

polygamy (pə'lɪgəmɪ) n 1 the practice of having more than one wife or husband at the same time 2 a the condition of having male, female, and hermaphrodite flowers on the same plant b the condition of having these different types of flower on separate plants of the same species 3 the practice in male animals of having more than one mate during one breeding season [c16: via French from Greek *polugamia* from POLY- + -GAMY] ▷ po'lygamist n ▷ po'lygamous adj ▷ po'lygamously adv

polygene ('pɒlɪ,dʒiːn) n any of a group of genes that each produce a small quantitative effect on a particular characteristic of the phenotype, such as height

polygenesis (,pɒlɪ'dʒɛnɪsɪs) n 1 biology evolution of a polyphyletic organism or group 2 the hypothetical descent of the different races of man from different ultimate ancestors ▷ polygenetic (,pɒlɪdʒɪ'nɛtɪk) adj

polygenic (,pɒlɪ'dʒɛnɪk) adj of, relating to, or controlled by polygenes: *polygenic inheritance*

polyglot ('pɒlɪ,glɒt) adj 1 having a command of many languages 2 written in, composed of, or containing many languages ▷ n 3 a person with a command of many languages 4 a book, esp a Bible, containing several versions of the same text written in various languages 5 a mixture or confusion of languages [c17: from Greek *poluglōttos* literally: many-tongued, from POLY- + glōtta tongue]

Polygnotus (,pɒlɪg'nəʊtəs) n 5th century BC, Greek painter: associated with Cimon in rebuilding Athens

polygon ('pɒlɪ,gɒn) n a closed plane figure bounded by three or more straight sides that meet in pairs in the same number of vertices, and do not intersect other than at these vertices. The sum of the interior angles is $(n-2) \times 180°$ for n sides; the sum of the exterior angles is 360°. A **regular polygon** has all its sides and angles equal. Specific polygons are named according to the number of sides, such as triangle, pentagon, etc [c16: via Latin from Greek *polugōnon* figure with many angles] ▷ polygonal (pə'lɪgᵊnᵊl) adj ▷ po'lygonally adv

polygonum (pə'lɪgənəm) n any polygonaceous plant of the genus *Polygonum*, having stems with knotlike joints and spikes of small white, green, or pink flowers [c18: New Latin, from Greek *polugonon* knotgrass, from *polu*- POLY- + -gonon, from *gonu* knee]

polygraph ('pɒlɪ,grɑːf, -,græf) n 1 an instrument for the simultaneous electrical or mechanical recording of several involuntary physiological activities, including blood pressure, skin resistivity, pulse rate, respiration, and sweating, used esp as a would-be lie detector 2 a device for producing copies of written, printed, or drawn matter [c18: from Greek *polugraphos* writing copiously]

polygyny (pə'lɪdʒɪnɪ) n 1 the practice or condition of being married to more than one wife at the same time 2 the practice in animals of a male mating with more than one female during one breeding season 3 the condition in flowers of having many carpels [c18: from POLY- + -gyny, from Greek *gunē* a woman] ▷ po'lygynous adj

polyhedron (,pɒlɪ'hiːdrən) n, pl -drons or -dra (-drə) a solid figure consisting of four or more plane faces (all polygons), pairs of which meet along an edge, three or more edges meeting at a vertex. In a **regular polyhedron** all the faces are identical regular polygons making equal angles with each other. Specific polyhedrons are named according to the number of faces, such as tetrahedron, icosahedron, etc [c16: from Greek *poluedron*, from POLY- + *hedron* side, base] ▷ ,poly'hedral adj

Polyhymnia (,pɒlɪ'hɪmnɪə) n Greek myth the Muse of singing, mime, and sacred dance [Latin, from Greek *Polumnia* full of songs; see POLY-, HYMN]

polymath ('pɒlɪ,mæθ) n a person of great and varied learning [c17: from Greek *polumathēs* having much knowledge] ▷ polymathy (pə'lɪməθɪ) n

polymer ('pɒlɪmə) n a naturally occurring or synthetic compound, such as starch or Perspex, that has large molecules made up of many relatively simple repeated units ▷ polymerism (pə'lɪmə,rɪzəm, 'pɒlɪmə-) n

polymerase (pə'lɪməreɪz) n any enzyme that catalyses the synthesis of a polymer, esp the synthesis of DNA or RNA

polymeric (,pɒlɪ'mɛrɪk) adj of, concerned with, or being a polymer: *a polymeric compound* [c19: from Greek *polumerēs* having many parts]

polymerization or **polymerisation** (pə,lɪməraɪ'zeɪʃən, ,pɒlɪməraɪ-) n the act or process of forming a polymer or copolymer, esp a chemical reaction in which a polymer is formed

polymerize or **polymerise** ('pɒlɪmə,raɪz, pə'lɪmə-) vb to react or cause to react to form a polymer

polymerous (pə'lɪmərəs) adj biology having or being composed of many parts

polymorph ('pɒlɪ,mɔːf) n 1 a species of animal or plant that exhibits polymorphism 2 any of the crystalline forms of a chemical compound that exhibits polymorphism [c19: from Greek *polumorphos* having many forms]

polymorphic function n computing a function in a computer program that can deal with a number of different types of data

polymorphism (ˌpɒlɪˈmɔːfɪzəm) n 1 biology the occurrence of more than one form of individual in a single species within an interbreeding population 2 the existence or formation of different types of crystal of the same chemical compound

polymorphous (ˌpɒlɪˈmɔːfəs) or **polymorphic** adj 1 having, taking, or passing through many different forms or stages 2 (of a substance) exhibiting polymorphism

Polynesia (ˌpɒlɪˈniːʒə, -ʒɪə) n one of the three divisions of islands in the Pacific, the others being Melanesia and Micronesia: includes Samoa, Society, Marquesas, Mangareva, Tuamotu, Cook, and Tubuai Islands, and Tonga [c18: via French from POLY- + Greek nēsos island]

Polynesian (ˌpɒlɪˈniːʒən, -ʒɪən) adj 1 of or relating to Polynesia, its people, or any of their languages ▷ n 2 a member of the people that inhabit Polynesia, generally of Caucasoid features with light skin and wavy hair 3 a branch of the Malayo-Polynesian family of languages, including Māori and Hawaiian and a number of other closely related languages of the S and central Pacific

polyneuritis (ˌpɒlɪnjʊˈraɪtɪs) n inflammation of many nerves at the same time

Polynices (ˌpɒlɪˈnaɪsiːz) n Greek myth a son of Oedipus and Jocasta, for whom the Seven Against Thebes sought to regain Thebes. He and his brother Eteocles killed each other in single combat before its walls

polynomial (ˌpɒlɪˈnəʊmɪəl) adj 1 of, consisting of, or referring to two or more names or terms ▷ n 2 a a mathematical expression consisting of a sum of terms each of which is the product of a constant and one or more variables raised to a positive or zero integral power. For one variable, x, the general form is given by: $a_0 x^n + a_1 x^{n-1} + \ldots + a_{n-1} x + a_n$, where a_0, a_1, etc, are real numbers b Also called: **multinomial** any mathematical expression consisting of the sum of a number of terms 3 biology a taxonomic name consisting of more than two terms, such as Parus major minor in which minor designates the subspecies

polynucleotide (ˌpɒlɪˈnjuːklɪəˌtaɪd) n biochem a molecular chain of nucleotides chemically bonded by a series of ester linkages between the phosphoryl group of one nucleotide and the hydroxyl group of the sugar in the adjacent nucleotide. Nucleic acids consist of long chains of polynucleotides

polynya (ˈpɒlənˌjɑː) n a stretch of open water surrounded by ice, esp near the mouths of large rivers, in arctic seas [c19: from Russian, from poly open, hollowed-out]

polyp (ˈpɒlɪp) n 1 zoology one of the two forms of individual that occur in coelenterates. It usually has a hollow cylindrical body with a ring of tentacles around the mouth 2 Also called: **polypus** pathol a small vascularized growth arising from the surface of a mucous membrane, having a rounded base or a stalklike projection [c16 polip, from French polype nasal polyp, from Latin pōlypus sea animal, nasal polyp, from Greek polupous having many feet] > ˈpolypous or ˈpolypoid adj

polypeptide (ˌpɒlɪˈpeptaɪd) n any of a group of natural or synthetic polymers made up of amino acids chemically linked together; this class includes the proteins

polypetalous (ˌpɒlɪˈpɛtələs) adj (of flowers) having many distinct or separate petals

polyphagia (ˌpɒlɪˈfeɪdʒə) n 1 an abnormal desire to consume excessive amounts of food, esp as the result of a neurological disorder 2 the habit of certain animals, esp certain insects, of feeding on many different types of food [c17: New Latin, from Greek, from poluphagos eating much; see POLY-, -PHAGY] > polyphagous (pəˈlɪfəgəs) adj

polyphase (ˈpɒlɪˌfeɪz) adj 1 Also called: **multiphase** (of an electrical system, circuit, or device) having, generating, or using two or more alternating voltages of the same frequency, the phases of which are cyclically displaced by fractions of a period 2 having more than one phase

Polyphemus (ˌpɒlɪˈfiːməs) n Greek myth a cyclops who imprisoned Odysseus and his companions in his cave. To effect his escape, Odysseus blinded him

polyphone (ˈpɒlɪˌfəʊn) n a letter or character having more than one phonetic value, such as English c, pronounced (k) before a, o, or u or (s) before e or i

polyphonic (ˌpɒlɪˈfɒnɪk) adj 1 music composed of relatively independent melodic lines or parts; contrapuntal 2 many-voiced 3 phonetics of, relating to, or denoting a polyphone > ˌpoly'phonically adv

polyphony (pəˈlɪfənɪ) n, pl -nies 1 polyphonic style of composition or a piece of music utilizing it 2 the use of polyphones in a writing system [c19: from Greek poluphōnia diversity of tones, from POLY- + phōnē speech, sound] > po'lyphonous adj

polypill (ˈpɒlɪˌpɪl) n a proposed medication intended to reduce the likelihood of heart attacks and strokes, containing doses of different drugs to lower blood cholesterol, control blood pressure, and reduce the clotting tendency of the blood

polyploid (ˈpɒlɪˌplɔɪd) adj (of cells, organisms, etc) having more than twice the basic (haploid) number of chromosomes > ˌpoly'ploidal or ˌpoly'ploidic adj > ˈpoly,ploidy n

polypod (ˈpɒlɪˌpɒd) Also called: **polypodous** (pəˈlɪpədəs) adj 1 (esp of insect larvae) having many legs or similar appendages n 2 an animal of this type

polypody (ˈpɒlɪˌpəʊdɪ) n, pl -dies any of various ferns of the genus Polypodium, esp P. vulgare, having deeply divided leaves and round naked sori: family Polypodiaceae [c15: from Latin polypodium, from Greek, from POLY- + pous foot]

polypropylene (ˌpɒlɪˈprəʊpɪˌliːn) n any of various tough flexible synthetic thermoplastic materials made by polymerizing propylene and used for making moulded articles, laminates, bottles, pipes, and fibres for ropes, bristles, upholstery, and carpets

polypus (ˈpɒlɪpəs) n, pl -pi (-paɪ) pathol another word for: **polyp** (sense 2) [c16: via Latin from Greek: POLYP]

polysaccharide (ˌpɒlɪˈsækəˌraɪd, -rɪd) or **polysaccharose** (ˌpɒlɪˈsækəˌrəʊz, -ˌrəʊs) n any one of a class of carbohydrates whose molecules contain linked monosaccharide units: includes starch, inulin, and cellulose. General formula: $(C_6H_{10}O_5)_n$. See also **oligosaccharide**

polysemy (pəˈlɪsɪmɪ, pəˈlɪsəmɪ) n the existence of several meanings in a single word [c20: from New Latin polysēmia, from Greek polusēmos having many meanings, from POLY- + sēma a sign] > ˌpoly'semous adj

polysomic (ˌpɒlɪˈsəʊmɪk) adj of, relating to, or designating a basically diploid chromosome complement, in which some but not all the chromosomes are represented more than twice [c20: from POLY- + -SOME³ + -IC]

polystyrene (ˌpɒlɪˈstaɪriːn) n a synthetic thermoplastic material obtained by polymerizing styrene; used as a white rigid foam (**expanded polystyrene**) for insulating and packing and as a glasslike material in light fittings and water tanks

polysyllable (ˈpɒlɪˌsɪləbᵊl) n a word consisting of more than two syllables > polysyllabic (ˌpɒlɪsɪˈlæbɪk) adj

polysyndeton (ˌpɒlɪˈsɪndɪtən) n rhetoric the use of several conjunctions in close succession, esp where some might be omitted, as in he ran and jumped and laughed for joy [c16: POLY- + -syndeton, from Greek sundetos bound together]

polytechnic (ˌpɒlɪˈtɛknɪk) n 1 Brit a college offering advanced full- and part-time courses, esp vocational courses, in many fields at and below degree standard ▷ adj 2 of or relating to technical instruction and training [c19: via French from Greek polutekhnos skilled in many arts. See TECHNIC]

polytetrafluoroethylene (ˌpɒlɪˌtetrəˌflʊərəʊˈɛθɪˌliːn) n a white thermoplastic material with a waxy texture, made by polymerizing tetrafluoroethylene. It is nonflammable, resists chemical action and radiation, and has a high electrical resistance and an extremely low coefficient of friction. It is used for making gaskets, hoses, insulators, bearings, and for coating metal surfaces in chemical plants and in nonstick cooking vessels. Also called (trademark): **Teflon**

P

polytheism ('pɒlɪθiː,ɪzəm, ,pɒlɪ'θiːɪzəm) *n* the worship of or belief in more than one god ▷ ,polythe'istic *adj* ▷ ,polythe'istically *adv*

polythene ('pɒlɪ,θiːn) *n* any one of various light thermoplastic materials made from ethylene with properties depending on the molecular weight of the polymer. The common forms are a waxy flexible plastic (**low-density polythene**) and a tougher rigid more crystalline form (**high-density polythene**). Polythene is used for packaging, moulded articles, pipes and tubing, insulation, textiles, and coatings on metal. Systematic name: **polyethene** Also called: polyethylene

polytonality (,pɒlɪtəʊ'nælɪtɪ) *or* **polytonalism** *n music* the simultaneous use of more than two different keys or tonalities ▷ ,poly'tonal *adj* ▷ ,poly'tonally *adv*

polytunnel ('pɒlɪ,tʌnəl) *n* a large tunnel made of polythene and used as a greenhouse

polyunsaturated (,pɒlɪʌn'sætʃə,reɪtɪd) *adj* of or relating to a class of animal and vegetable fats, the molecules of which consist of long carbon chains with many double bonds. Polyunsaturated compounds are less likely to be converted into cholesterol in the body. They are widely used in margarines and in the manufacture of paints and varnishes. See also **monounsaturated**

polyurethane (,pɒlɪ'jʊərə,θeɪn) *or* **polyurethan** (,pɒlɪ'jʊərə,θæn) *n* a class of synthetic materials made by copolymerizing an isocyanate and a polyhydric alcohol and commonly used as a foam (**polyurethane foam**) for insulation and packing, as fibres and hard inert coatings, and in a flexible form (**polyurethane rubber**) for diaphragms and seals

polyvalent (,pɒlɪ'veɪlənt, pə'lɪvələnt) *adj* 1 *chem* having more than one valency 2 (of a vaccine) **a** effective against several strains of the same disease-producing microorganism, antigen, or toxin **b** produced from cultures containing several strains of the same microorganism ▷ ,poly'valency *n*

polyvinyl (,pɒlɪ'vaɪnɪl, -'vaɪnᵊl) *n* (*modifier*) designating a plastic or resin formed by polymerization of a vinyl derivative

polyvinyl acetate *n* a colourless odourless tasteless resin used in emulsion paints, adhesives, sealers, a substitute for chicle in chewing gum, and for sealing porous surfaces

polyvinyl chloride *n* the full name of **PVC**

polyvinyl resin *n* any of a class of thermoplastic resins that are made by polymerizing or copolymerizing a vinyl compound. The commonest type is PVC

Polyxena (pɒ'lɪksɪnə) *n Greek myth* a daughter of King Priam of Troy, who was sacrificed on the command of Achilles' ghost

polyzoan (,pɒlɪ'zəʊən) *n, adj* another word for **bryozoan** [c19: from New Latin, *Polyzoa* class name, from POLY- + -zoan, from Greek *zoion* an animal]

pom (pɒm) *n slang, Austral & NZ* short for **pommy**

POM *abbreviation* prescription-only medicine *or* medication. See OTC

pomace ('pʌmɪs) *n* 1 the pulpy residue of apples or similar fruit after crushing, as in cider-making 2 any pulpy substance left after crushing, mashing, etc [c16: from Medieval Latin *pōmācium* cider, from Latin *pōmum* apple]

pomaceous (pɒ'meɪʃəs) *adj* of, relating to, or bearing pomes, such as the apple, pear, and quince trees [c18: from New Latin *pōmāceus*, from Latin *pōmum* apple]

pomade (pə'mɑːd, -'meɪd) *n* 1 a perfumed oil or ointment put on the hair, as to make it smooth and shiny ▷ *vb* 2 (*tr*) to put pomade on ▷ Also called: pomatum (pə'meɪtəm) [c16: from French *pommade*, from Italian *pomato* (originally made partly from apples), from Latin *pōmum* apple]

pomander (pəʊ'mændə) *n* 1 a mixture of aromatic substances in a sachet or an orange, formerly carried as scent or as a protection against disease 2 a container for such a mixture [c15: from Old French *pome d'ambre*, from Medieval Latin *pōmum ambrae* apple of amber]

Pombal (Portuguese pom'bal) *n* **Marquês de** (mərkeʃ 'də:). title of *Sebastião José de Carvalho e Mello*. 1699–1782, Portuguese statesman, who dominated Portuguese

government from 1750 to 1777 and instituted many administrative and economic reforms

pome (pəʊm) *n* the fleshy fruit of the apple and related plants, consisting of an enlarged receptacle enclosing the ovary and seeds [c15: from Old French, from Late Latin *pōma* apple, pl (assumed to be sing) of Latin *pōmum* apple]

pomegranate ('pɒmɪ,grænɪt, 'pɒm,grænɪt) *n* 1 an Asian shrub or small tree, *Punica granatum*, cultivated in semitropical regions for its edible fruit: family *Punicaceae* 2 the many-chambered globular fruit of this tree, which has tough reddish rind, juicy red pulp, and many seeds [c14: from Old French *pome grenate*, from Latin *pōmum* apple + *grenate*, from Latin *grānātum*, from *grānātus* full of seeds]

pomelo ('pɒmɪ,ləʊ) *n, pl* -los 1 the fruit of this tree 2 *chiefly US* another name for **grapefruit** ▷ Also called: shaddock [c19: from Dutch *pompelmoes*, perhaps from *pompoen* big + Portuguese *limão* a lemon]

Pomerania (,pɒmə'reɪnɪə) *n* a region of N central Europe, extending along the S coast of the Baltic Sea from Stralsund to the Vistula River: now chiefly in Poland, with a small area in NE Germany. German name: Pommern. Polish name: Pomorze

Pomeranian (,pɒmə'reɪnɪən) *adj* 1 of or relating to Pomerania or its inhabitants ▷ *n* 2 a breed of toy dog of the spitz type with a long thick straight coat

pomfret ('pʌmfrɪt, 'pɒm-) *or* **pomfret-cake** *n* a small black rounded confection of liquorice. Also called: Pontefract cake [c19: from *Pomfret*, earlier form of PONTEFRACT, where the cake was originally made]

pomiculture ('pɒmɪ,kʌltʃə) *n* the cultivation of fruit [c19: from Latin *pōmum* apple, fruit + CULTURE]

pommel ('pʌməl, 'pɒm-) *n* 1 the raised part on the front of a saddle 2 a knob at the top of a sword or similar weapon ▷ *vb* -mels, -melling, -melled *or US* -mels, -meling, -meled 3 a less common word for **pummel** [c14: from Old French *pomel* knob, from Vulgar Latin *pōmellum* (unattested) little apple, from Latin *pōmum* apple]

Pommern ('pɒmərn) *n* the German name for **Pomerania**

pommy ('pɒmɪ) *n, pl* -mies (*sometimes capital*) *slang* a mildly offensive word used by Australians and New Zealanders for an English person. Sometimes shortened to: pom [c20: of uncertain origin. Among a number of explanations are: (1) based on a blend of IMMIGRANT and POMEGRANATE (alluding to the red cheeks of English immigrants); (2) from the abbreviation POME, Prisoner of Mother England (referring to convicts)]

pomology (pɒ'mɒlədʒɪ) *n* the branch of horticulture that is concerned with the study and cultivation of fruit [c19: from New Latin *pōmologia*, from Latin *pōmum* apple, fruit] ▷ pomological (,pɒmə'lɒdʒɪkᵊl) *adj*

Pomona¹ (pə'məʊnə) *n* (in Orkney) another name for **Mainland**

Pomona² (pə'məʊnə) *n* the Roman goddess of fruit trees

Pomorze (pɔ'mɔːʒɛ) *n* the Polish name for **Pomerania**

pomp (pɒmp) *n* 1 stately or magnificent display; ceremonial splendour 2 vain display, esp of dignity or importance 3 *obsolete* a procession or pageant [c14: from Old French *pompe*, from Latin *pompa* procession, from Greek *pompē*; related to Greek *pompein* to send]

pompadour ('pɒmpə,dʊə) *n* an early 18th-century hairstyle for women, having the front hair arranged over a pad to give it greater height and bulk [c18: named after its originator Jeanne Antoinette Poisson, the Marquise de POMPADOUR]

Pompadour (French pɔ̃padur) *n* **Marquise de,** title of *Jeanne Antoinette Poisson*. 1721–64, mistress of Louis XV of France (1745–64), whom she greatly influenced

pompano ('pɒmpə,nəʊ) *n, pl* -no *or* -nos 1 any of several deep-bodied carangid food fishes of the genus *Trachinotus*, esp *T. carolinus*, of American coastal regions of the Atlantic 2 a spiny-finned food fish, *Palometa simillima*, of North American coastal regions of the Pacific: family *Stromateidae* (butterfish, etc) [c19: from Spanish *pámpano* type of fish, of uncertain origin]

Pompeii (pɒm'peɪiː) *n* an ancient city in Italy, southeast of Naples: buried by an eruption of Vesuvius (79 AD); excavation of the site, which is extremely well preserved, began in 1748

Pompey¹ ('pɒmpɪ) n an informal name for **Portsmouth**

Pompey² ('pɒmpɪ) n called *Pompey the Great*; Latin name *Gnaeus Pompeius Magnus*. 106–48 BC, Roman general and statesman; a member with Caesar and Crassus of the first triumvirate (60). He later quarrelled with Caesar, who defeated him at Pharsalus (48). He fled to Egypt and was murdered

Pompidou (French pɔ̃pidu) n **Georges** (ʒɔrʒ). 1911–74, French statesman; president of France (1969–74)

pompom ('pɒmpɒm) or **pompon** n 1 a ball of tufted silk, wool, feathers, etc, worn on a hat for decoration 2 a the small globelike flower head of certain cultivated varieties of dahlia and chrysanthemum b (as modifier): *pompom dahlia* [c18: from French, from Old French pompe knot of ribbons, of uncertain origin]

pom-pom ('pɒmpɒm) n an automatic rapid-firing, small-calibre cannon, esp a type of anti-aircraft cannon used in World War II. Also called: **pompom** [c19: of imitative origin]

pompous ('pɒmpəs) adj 1 exaggeratedly or ostentatiously dignified or self-important 2 ostentatiously lofty in style: *a pompous speech* 3 rare characterized by ceremonial pomp or splendour > **'pompously** adv > **'pompousness** n > **pomposity** (pɒm'pɒsɪtɪ) n

'pon (pɒn) poetic or archaic ▷ prep 1 upon ▷ contraction of 2 upon

ponce (pɒns) derogatory, slang, chiefly Brit ▷ n 1 a man given to ostentatious or effeminate display in manners, speech, dress, etc 2 another word for **pimp¹** ▷ vb 3 (intr; often foll by around or about) to act like a ponce [c19: from Polari, from Spanish pu(n)to male prostitute or French pront prostitute]

Ponce (Spanish 'pɔnθe) n a port in S Puerto Rico, on the Caribbean: the second largest town on the island; settled in the 16th century. Pop: 185 930 (2003 est)

Ponce de León ('pɒns də 'liːən; Spanish 'pɔnθe ðe le'ɔn) n **Juan** (xwan). ?1460–1521, Spanish explorer. He settled (1509) and governed (1510–12) Puerto Rico and discovered (1513) Florida

poncho ('pɒntʃəʊ) n, pl -chos a cloak of a kind originally worn in South America, made of a rectangular or circular piece of cloth, esp wool, with a hole in the middle to put the head through [c18: from American Spanish, from Araucanian pantho woollen material]

pond (pɒnd) n a pool of still water, often artificially created [c13 ponde enclosure; related to POUND³]

ponder ('pɒndə) vb (when intr, sometimes foll by on or over) to give thorough or deep consideration (to); meditate (upon) [c14: from Old French ponderer, from Latin ponderāre to weigh, consider, from pondus weight; related to pendere to weigh]

ponderous ('pɒndərəs) adj 1 (esp of movement) lacking ease or lightness; awkward, lumbering, or graceless 2 dull or laborious: *a ponderous oration* [c14: from Latin ponderōsus of great weight, from pondus weight]

pond hockey n Canadian ice hockey played on a frozen pond

Pondicherry (,pɒndɪ'tʃɛrɪ) n the former official name (until 2006) for **Puducherry**

pond lily n another name for **water lily**

pondok ('pɒndɒk) or **pondokkie** (pɒn'dɒkɪ) n (in southern Africa) a crudely made house built of tin sheet, reeds, etc [c20: from Malay pondók leaf house]

Pondoland ('pɒndəʊ,lænd) n an area in SE central South Africa: inhabited chiefly by the Pondo people

pond scum n a greenish layer floating on the surface of stagnant waters, consisting of various freshwater algae

pondweed ('pɒnd,wiːd) n 1 any of various water plants of the genus Potamogeton, which grow in ponds and slow streams: family Potamogetonaceae 2 Also called: **waterweed** Brit any of various unrelated water plants, such as Canadian pondweed, mare's-tail, and water milfoil, that have thin or much divided leaves

pone¹ (pəʊn) n Southern US Also called: **pone bread, corn pone** bread made of maize [c17: from Algonquian; compare Delaware apán baked]

pone² (pəʊn, 'pəʊnɪ) n cards the player to the right of

the dealer, or the nondealer in two-handed games [c19: from Latin: put!, that is, play, from ponere to put]

pong (pɒŋ) Brit informal ▷ n 1 a disagreeable or offensive smell; stink ▷ vb 2 (intr) to give off an unpleasant smell; stink [c20: perhaps from Romany pan to stink] > **'pongy** adj

ponga ('pɒŋə) n a tall tree fern, Cyathea dealbata, of New Zealand, with large feathery leaves [Māori]

pongee (pɒn'dʒiː, 'pɒndʒiː) n 1 a thin plain-weave silk fabric from China or India, left in its natural colour 2 a cotton or rayon fabric similar to or in imitation of this, but not necessarily in the natural colour [c18: from Mandarin Chinese (Peking) pen-chī woven at home, on one's own loom, from pen own + chi loom]

pongid ('pɒŋgɪd, 'pɒndʒɪd) n 1 any primate of the family Pongidae, which includes the gibbons and the great apes ▷ adj 2 of, relating to, or belonging to the family Pongidae [from New Latin Pongo type genus, from Kongo mpongi ape]

pongo ('pɒŋgəʊ) n, pl -gos an anthropoid ape, esp an orang-utan or (formerly) a gorilla [c17: from Kongo mpongo]

poniard ('pɒnjəd) n 1 a small dagger with a slender blade ▷ vb 2 (tr) to stab with a poniard [c16: from Old French poignard dagger, from poing fist, from Latin pugnus; related to Latin pugnāre to fight]

pons Varolii (və'rəʊlɪ,aɪ) n, pl pontes Varolii ('pɒntiːz) a broad white band of connecting nerve fibres that bridges the hemispheres of the cerebellum in mammals [c16: New Latin, literally: bridge of Varoli, after Costanzo Varoli (?1543–75), Italian anatomist]

Ponta Delgada (Portuguese 'pɔntɐ ðel'ɡaðɐ) n a port in the E Azores, on S São Miguel Island: chief commercial centre of the archipelago. Pop: 65 853 (2001)

Pontchartrain ('pɒntʃə,treɪn) n **Lake Pontchartrain** a shallow lagoon in SE Louisiana, linked with the Gulf of Mexico by a narrow channel, the **Rigolets**: resort and fishing centre. Area: 1620 sq km (625 sq miles)

Pontefract ('pɒntɪ,frækt) n an industrial town in N England, in Wakefield unitary authority, West Yorkshire: castle (1069), in which Richard II was imprisoned and murdered (1400). Pop: 28 250 (2001)

Pontevedra (Spanish pɔnte'βeðra) n a port in NW Spain: takes its name from a 12-arched Roman bridge, the Pons Vetus. Pop: 77 993 (2003 est)

Pontiac ('pɒntɪ,æk) n died 1769, chief of the Ottawa Indians, who led a rebellion against the British (1763–66)

Pontianak (,pɒntɪ'ɑːnæk) n a port in Indonesia, on W coast of Borneo almost exactly on the equator. Pop: 464 534 (2000)

Pontic ('pɒntɪk) adj denoting or relating to the Black Sea [c15: from Latin Ponticus, from Greek, from Pontos PONTUS]

pontifex ('pɒntɪ,fɛks) n, pl pontifices (pɒn'tɪfɪ,siːz) (in ancient Rome) any of the senior members of the Pontifical College, presided over by the **Pontifex Maximus** [c16: from Latin, perhaps from Etruscan but influenced by folk etymology as if meaning literally: bridge-maker, from pons bridge + -fex from facere to make]

pontiff ('pɒntɪf) n a former title of the pagan high priest at Rome, later used of popes and occasionally of other bishops, and now confined exclusively to the pope [c17: from French pontife, from Latin PONTIFEX]

pontifical (pɒn'tɪfɪkᵊl) adj 1 of, relating to, or characteristic of a pontiff, the pope, or a bishop 2 having an excessively authoritative manner; pompous ▷ n 3 RC Church, Church of England a book containing the prayers and ritual instructions for ceremonies restricted to a bishop > **pon'tifically** adv

pontificals (pɒn'tɪfɪkᵊlz) pl n chiefly RC Church the insignia and special vestments worn by a bishop, esp when celebrating High Mass

pontificate vb (pɒn'tɪfɪ,keɪt) (intr) 1 to speak or behave in a pompous or dogmatic manner 2 to serve or officiate as a pontiff, esp in celebrating a Pontifical Mass ▷ n (pɒn'tɪfɪkɪt) 3 the office or term of office of a pontiff, now usually the pope

Pontine Marshes ('pɒntaɪn) pl n an area of W Italy, southeast of Rome: formerly malarial swamps, drained in 1932–34 after numerous attempts since 160 BC had failed. Italian name: Agro Pontino ('a:gro pon'ti:no)

Ponting ('pɒntɪŋ) n **Ricky** (**Thomas**). born 1974, Australian cricketer; a batsman, he played for Australia (from 1995), captaining the side from 2004

Pontius Pilate ('pɒnʃəs, 'pɒntɪəs 'paɪlət) n See **Pilate**

pontoon¹ (pɒn'tu:n) n **1 a** a watertight float or vessel used where buoyancy is required in water, as in supporting a bridge, in salvage work, or where a temporary or mobile structure is required in military operations **b** (as modifier): a pontoon bridge **2** nautical a float, often inflatable, for raising a vessel in the water [c17: from French ponton, from Latin pontō punt, floating bridge, from pōns bridge]

pontoon² (pɒn'tu:n) n Also called: (esp US) twenty-one, vingt-et-un a gambling game in which players try to obtain card combinations worth 21 points [c20: probably an alteration of French vingt-et-un, literally: twenty-one]

Pontoppidan (Danish pont'topidan) n **Henrik**. 1857–1943, Danish novelist and short-story writer, author of the novel sequences The Promised Land (1891–95), Lykke-Per (1898–1904), and The Empire of Death (1912–16). Nobel prize for literature 1917

Pontormo (Italian pon'tormo) n **Jacopo da** ('ja:kopo da). original name Jacopo Carrucci. 1494–1556, Italian mannerist painter

Pontus ('pɒntəs) n an ancient region of NE Asia Minor, on the Black Sea: became a kingdom in the 4th century BC; at its height under Mithridates VI (about 115–63 BC), when it controlled all Asia Minor; defeated by the Romans in the mid-1st century BC

Pontus Euxinus (ju:k'saɪnəs) n the Latin name of the **Black Sea**

Pontypool (,pɒntɪ'pu:l) n an industrial town in E Wales, in Torfaen county borough: famous for lacquered ironware in the 18th century. Pop: 35 447 (2001)

Pontypridd (,pɒntɪ'pri:ð) n an industrial town in S Wales, in Rhondda Cynon Taff county borough. Pop: 29 781 (2001)

pony ('pəʊnɪ) n, pl **ponies 1** any of various breeds of small horse, usually under 14.2 hands **2** a small drinking glass, esp for liqueurs **3** anything small of its kind **4** Brit slang a sum of £25, esp in bookmaking **5** Also called: trot US slang a literal translation used by students, often illicitly, in preparation for foreign language lessons or examinations; crib [c17: from Scottish powney, perhaps from obsolete French poulenet a little colt, from poulain colt, from Latin pullus young animal, foal]

ponytail ('pəʊnɪ,teɪl) n a hairstyle in which the hair is pulled tightly into a band or ribbon at the back of the head into a loose hanging fall

pony trekking n the act of riding ponies cross-country, esp as a pastime

ponzu ('pɒn,zu:) n a type of Japanese dipping sauce made from orange juice, sake, sugar, soy sauce, and red pepper [c21: from Japanese]

poo (pu:) interj, n, vb another spelling of **pooh**

pooch (pu:tʃ) n a slang word for **dog** (sense 1) [of unknown origin]

poodle ('pu:dəl) n **1** a breed of dog, with varieties of different sizes, having curly hair, which is often clipped from ribs to tail for showing: originally bred to hunt waterfowl **2** a person who is servile; lackey [c19: from German Pudel, short for Pudelhund, from pudeln to splash + Hund dog; the dogs were formerly trained as water dogs; see PUDDLE, HOUND¹]

poof (puf, pu:f) or **poove** n Brit derogatory, slang a male homosexual [c20: from French pouffe puff] > **'poofy** adj

poofter ('puftə, 'pu:f-) n derogatory, slang **1** a man who is considered effeminate or homosexual **2** NZ a contemptible person [c20: expanded form of POOF]

pooh (pu:) interj **1** an exclamation of disdain, contempt, or disgust ▷ n **2** a childish word for **faeces** ▷ vb **3** a childish word for **defecate**

Pooh-Bah ('pu:'ba:) n a pompous self-important official holding several offices at once and fulfilling none of them [c19: after the character, the Lord-High-Everything-Else, in The Mikado (1885), a light opera by Gilbert and Sullivan]

pooh-pooh ('pu:'pu:) vb (tr) to express disdain or scorn for; dismiss or belittle

pool¹ (pu:l) n **1** a small body of still water, usually fresh; small pond **2** a small isolated collection of liquid spilt or poured on a surface; puddle: a pool of blood **3** a deep part of a stream or river where the water runs very slowly **4** an underground accumulation of oil or gas, usually forming a reservoir in porous sedimentary rock **5** See **swimming pool** [Old English pōl; related to Old Frisian pōl, German Pfuhl]

pool² (pu:l) n **1** any communal combination of resources, funds, etc: a typing pool **2** the combined stakes of the betters in many gambling sports or games; kitty **3** commerce a group of producers who conspire to establish and maintain output levels and high prices, each member of the group being allocated a maximum quota; price ring **4** finance chiefly US a joint fund organized by security-holders for speculative or manipulative purposes on financial markets **5** any of various billiard games in which the object is to pot all the balls with the cue ball, esp that played with 15 coloured and numbered balls; pocket billiards ▷ vb (tr) **6** to combine (investments, money, interests, etc) into a common fund, as for a joint enterprise **7** commerce to organize a pool of (enterprises) [c17: from French poule, literally: hen used to signify stakes in a card game, from Medieval Latin pulla hen, from Latin pullus young animal]

Poole (pu:l) n **1** a port and resort in S England, in Poole unitary authority, Dorset, on **Poole Harbour**; seat of Bournemouth University (1992). Pop: 144 800 (2001) **2** a unitary authority in S England, in Dorset. Pop: 137 500 (2003 est). Area: 37 sq km (14 sq miles)

Pool Malebo ('pu:l mə'li:bəʊ) n the Congolese name for **Stanley Pool**

pools (pu:lz) pl n Brit an organized nationwide principally postal gambling pool betting on the result of football matches. Also called: **football pools** [c20: from POOL² (in the sense: a gambling kitty)]

Poona or **Pune** ('pu:nə) n a city in W India, in W Maharashtra: under British rule served as the seasonal capital of the Bombay Presidency. Pop: 2 540 069 (2001)

poontang ('pu:ntæŋ) n taboo, slang **1** the female pudenda **2** a woman considered as a sexual object **3** sexual intercourse [possibly from F: putain prostitute]

poop¹ (pu:p) nautical ▷ n **1** a raised structure at the stern of a vessel, esp a sailing ship ▷ vb **2** (tr) (of a wave or sea) to break over the stern of (a vessel) **3** (intr) (of a vessel) to ship a wave or sea over the stern, esp repeatedly [c15: from Old French pupe, from Latin puppis poop, ship's stern]

poop² (pu:p) vb US & Canadian slang **1** (tr; usually passive) to cause to become exhausted; tire: he was pooped after the race **2** (intr; usually foll by out) to give up or fail, esp through tiredness: he pooped out of the race [c14 poupen to blow, make a sudden sound, perhaps of imitative origin]

poop³ (pu:p) informal ▷ vb (intr) **1** to defecate ▷ n **2** faeces; excrement [perhaps related to POOP²]

pooper-scooper n a device used to remove dogs' excrement from public areas [c20: POOP³ + -ER¹ + SCOOPER]

Poopó (Spanish poo'po) n **Lake Poopó** a lake in SW Bolivia, at an altitude of 3688 m (12 100 ft): fed by the Desaguadero River. Area: 2540 sq km (980 sq miles)

poor (pʊə, pɔ:) adj **1** lacking financial or other means of subsistence; needy **2** characterized by or indicating poverty: the country had a poor economy **3** deficient in amount; scanty or inadequate: a poor salary **4** (when postpositive, usually foll by in) badly supplied (with resources, materials, etc): a region poor in wild flowers **5** lacking in quality; inferior **6** (prenominal) deserving of pity; unlucky: poor John is ill again [c13: from Old French povre, from Latin pauper; see PAUPER, POVERTY] > **'poorness** n

poor box n a box, esp one in a church, used for the collection of alms or money for the poor

poorhouse ('pʊə,haʊs, 'pɔ:-) n (formerly) a publicly maintained institution offering accommodation to the poor

poor law *n English history* a law providing for the relief or support of the poor from public, esp parish, funds

poorly ('pʊəlɪ, 'pɔ:-) *adv* **1** in a poor way or manner; badly ▷ *adj* **2** (*usually postpositive*) *informal* in poor health; rather ill

poort (pʊət) *n* (in South Africa) a steep narrow mountain pass, usually following a river or stream [c19: from Afrikaans, from Dutch: gateway; see PORT⁴]

poor White *n often offensive* **a** a poverty-stricken and underprivileged White person, esp in the southern US and South Africa **b** (*as modifier*): *poor White trash*

pop¹ (pʊp) *vb* **pops, popping, popped 1** to make or cause to make a light sharp explosive sound **2** to burst open or cause to burst open with such a sound **3** (*intr; often foll by in, out, etc*) *informal* to come (to) or go (from) rapidly or suddenly; to pay a brief or unexpected visit (to) **4** (*intr*) (*esp of the eyes*) to protrude: *her eyes popped with amazement* **5** to shoot or fire at (a target) with a firearm **6** (*tr*) to place or put with a sudden movement: *she popped some tablets into her mouth* **7** (*tr*) *slang* to take (a drug) in pill form or as an injection **8 pop the question** *informal* to propose marriage ▷ *n* **9** a light sharp explosive sound; crack **10** a flavoured nonalcoholic carbonated beverage ▷ *adv* **11** with a popping sound ▷ See also **pop off** [c14: of imitative origin]

pop² (pʊp) *n* **1 a** music of general appeal, esp among young people, that originated as a distinctive genre in the 1950s. It is generally characterized by a strong rhythmic element and the use of electrical amplification **b** (*as modifier*): *pop music; a pop record; a pop group* **2** *informal* a piece of popular or light classical music ▷ *adj* **3** *informal* short for **popular**

pop³ (pʊp) *n* **1** an informal word for **father 2** *informal* a name used in addressing an old or middle-aged man

POP *abbreviation* **1** point of presence: a device that enables access to the internet **2** *internet* post office protocol: a protocol which brings e-mail to and from a mail server **3** Post Office Preferred (size of envelopes, etc) **4** persistent organic pollutant

pop. *abbreviation* **1** popular **2** popularly **3** population

pop art *n* a movement in modern art that imitates the methods, styles, and themes of popular culture and mass media, such as comic strips, advertising, and science fiction

popcorn ('pʊp,kɔːn) *n* **1** a variety of maize having hard pointed kernels that puff up when heated **2** the puffed edible kernels of this plant [c19: so called because of the noise the grains make when they swell up and burst on heating]

pope (pəʊp) *n* **1** (*often capital*) the bishop of Rome as head of the Roman Catholic Church. Related adj: **papal 2** *Eastern Orthodox Churches* **a** a title sometimes given to a parish priest **b** a title sometimes given to the Greek Orthodox patriarch of Alexandria [Old English *papa*, from Church Latin: bishop, esp of Rome, from Late Greek *papas* father-in-God, from Greek *pappas* father]

Pope (pəʊp) *n* **Alexander.** 1688–1744, English poet, regarded as the most brilliant satirist of the Augustan period, esp with his *Imitations of Horace* (1733–38). His technical virtuosity is most evident in *The Rape of the Lock* (1712–14). Other works include *The Dunciad* (1728; 1742), the *Moral Essays* (1731–35), and *An Essay on Man* (1733–34)

popera ('pʊpərə, 'pɒprə) *n* music drawing on opera or classical music and aiming for popular appeal [c20: from POP² (sense 1) + OPERA]

popery ('pəʊpərɪ) *n* a derogatory name for **Roman Catholicism**

popeyed ('pʊp,aɪd) *adj* **1** having bulging prominent eyes **2** staring in astonishment; amazed

popgun ('pʊp,gʌn) *n* a toy gun that fires a pellet or cork by means of compressed air and makes a popping sound

popinjay ('pʊpɪn,dʒeɪ) *n* **1** a conceited, foppish, or excessively talkative person **2** an archaic word for **parrot 3** the figure of a parrot used as a target [c13 *papeniai*, from Old French *papegay* a parrot, from Spanish *papagayo*, from Arabic *babaghā*]

popish ('pəʊpɪʃ) *adj derogatory* belonging to or characteristic of Roman Catholicism

poplar ('pʊplə) *n* **1** any tree of the salicaceous genus *Populus*, of N temperate regions, having triangular leaves, flowers borne in catkins, and light soft wood **2** any of various trees resembling the true poplars, such as the tulip tree [c14: from Old French *poplier*, from *pouple*, from Latin *pōpulus*]

poplin ('pʊplɪn) *n* a strong fabric, usually of cotton, in plain weave with fine ribbing, used for dresses, children's wear, etc [c18: from French *papeline*, perhaps from *Poperinge*, a centre of textile manufacture in Flanders]

popliteal (pʊp'lɪtɪəl, ,pʊplɪ'ti:əl) *adj* of, relating to, or near the part of the leg behind the knee [c18: from New Latin *popliteus* the muscle behind the knee joint, from Latin *poples* the ham of the knee]

Popocatépetl (,pʊpə'kætəpetəl, -,kætɪ'petəl; *Spanish* popoka'tepetl) *n* a volcano in SE central Mexico, southeast of Mexico City. Height: 5452 m (17 887 ft)

pop off *vb* (*intr, adverb*) *informal* **1** to depart suddenly or unexpectedly **2** to die, esp suddenly or unexpectedly

Popov (*Russian* pa'pɔf) *n* **1 2 Oleg** (**Konstantinovich**). born 1930, Russian clown, a member of the Moscow Circus

poppadom *or* **poppadum** ('pʊpədəm) *n* a thin round crisp Indian bread, fried or roasted and served with curry, etc [from Hindi]

popper ('pʊpə) *n* **1** a person or thing that pops **2** *Brit* an informal name for **press stud 3** *chiefly US & Canadian* a container for cooking popcorn in **4** *slang* an amyl nitrite capsule, which is crushed and its contents inhaled by drug users as a stimulant

Popper ('pʊpə) *n* **Sir Karl.** 1902–94, British philosopher, born in Vienna. In *The Logic of Scientific Discovery* (1934), he proposes that knowledge cannot be absolutely confirmed, but rather that science progresses by the experimental refutation of the current theory and its consequent replacement by a new theory, equally provisional but covering more of the known data. *The Open Society and its Enemies* (1945) is a critique of dogmatic political philosophies, such as Marxism. Other works are *The Poverty of Historicism* (1957), *Conjectures and Refutations* (1963), and *Objective Knowledge* (1972) ▷ **Popperian** (pɒ'pɪərɪən) *n, adj*

poppet ('pʊpɪt) *n* **1** a term of affection for a small child or sweetheart **2** Also called: **poppet valve** a mushroom-shaped valve that is lifted from its seating against a spring by applying an axial force to its stem: commonly used as an exhaust or inlet valve in an internal-combustion engine **3** *nautical* a temporary supporting brace for a vessel hauled on land or in a dry dock [c14: early variant of PUPPET]

popping crease *n cricket* a line four feet in front of and parallel with the bowling crease, at or behind which the batsman stands [c18: from POP¹ (in the obsolete or dialect sense: to hit) + CREASE¹]

popple ('pʊpəl) *vb* (*intr*) **1** (of boiling water or a choppy sea) to heave or toss; bubble **2** (*often foll by along*) (of a stream or river) to move with an irregular tumbling motion [c14: of imitative origin; compare Middle Dutch *popelen* to bubble, throb]

poppy¹ ('pʊpɪ) *n, pl* **-pies 1** any of numerous papaveraceous plants of the temperate genus *Papaver*, having red, orange, or white flowers and a milky sap **2** any of several similar or related plants, such as the California poppy, prickly poppy, horned poppy, and Welsh poppy **3** *obsolete* any of the drugs, such as opium, that are obtained from these plants **4 a** a strong red to reddish-orange colour **b** (*as adjective*): *a poppy dress* **5** an artificial red poppy flower worn to mark Remembrance Sunday [Old English *popæg*, ultimately from Latin *papāver*]

poppy² ('pʊpɪ) *adj* **-pier, -piest** of or relating to pop music

poppycock ('pʊpɪ,kɒk) *n informal* senseless chatter; nonsense [c19: from Dutch dialect *pappekak*, literally: soft excrement, from *pap* soft + *kak* dung; see PAP¹]

Poppy Day *n* an informal name for **Remembrance Sunday**

poppyhead ('pʊpɪ,hɛd) *n* **1** the hard dry seed-containing capsule of a poppy. See also **capsule** (sense 3a) **2** a carved ornament, esp one used on the top of the end of a pew or bench in Gothic church architecture

poppy seed *n* the small grey seeds of one type of poppy flower, used esp on loaves and as a cake filling

popsy ('pɒpsɪ) *n, pl* -sies *old-fashioned, Brit slang* an attractive young woman [c19: diminutive formed from *pop*, shortened from POPPET; originally a nursery term]

populace ('pɒpjʊləs) *n* (*sometimes functioning as plural*) **1** the inhabitants of an area **2** the common people; masses [c16: via French from Italian *popolaccio* the common herd, from *popolo* people, from Latin *populus*]

popular ('pɒpjʊlə) *adj* **1** appealing to the general public; widely favoured or admired **2** favoured by an individual or limited group: *I'm not very popular with her* **3** connected with, representing, or prevailing among the general public; common: *popular discontent* **4** appealing to or comprehensible to the layman: *a popular lecture on physics* ▷ *n* **5** (*usually plural*) cheap newspapers with mass circulation; the popular press [c15: from Latin *populāris* belonging to the people, democratic, from *populus* people] > popularity (,pɒpjʊ'lærɪtɪ) *n* > 'popularly *adv*

popular front *n* (*often capital*) any of the left-wing groups or parties that were organized from 1935 onwards to oppose the spread of fascism

popularize *or* **popularise** ('pɒpjʊlə,raɪz) *vb* (*tr*) **1** to make popular; make attractive to the general public **2** to make or cause to become more easily understandable or acceptable > ,populari'zation *or* ,populari'sation *n* > 'popular,izer *or* 'popular,iser *n*

populate ('pɒpjʊ,leɪt) *vb* (*tr*) **1** (*often passive*) to live in; inhabit **2** to provide a population for; colonize or people [c16: from Medieval Latin *populāre* to provide with inhabitants, from Latin *populus* people]

population (,pɒpjʊ'leɪʃən) *n* **1** (*sometimes functioning as plural*) all the persons inhabiting a country, city, or other specified place **2** the number of such inhabitants **3** (*sometimes functioning as plural*) all the people of a particular race or class in a specific area: *the Chinese population of San Francisco* **4** the act or process of providing a place with inhabitants; colonization **5** *ecology* a group of individuals of the same species inhabiting a given area **6** *astronomy* either of two main groups of stars classified according to age and location. **Population I** consists of younger metal-rich hot white stars, many occurring in galactic clusters and forming the arms of spiral galaxies. Stars of **population II** are older, the brightest being red giants, and are found in the centre of spiral and elliptical galaxies in globular clusters **7** Also called: universe *statistics* the entire finite or infinite aggregate of individuals or items from which samples are drawn

population explosion *n* a rapid increase in the size of a population caused by such factors as a sudden decline in infant mortality or an increase in life expectancy

population pyramid *n* a pyramid-shaped diagram illustrating the age distribution of a population: the youngest are represented by a rectangle at the base, the oldest by one at the apex

populism ('pɒpjʊ,lɪzəm) *n* a political strategy based on a calculated appeal to the interests or prejudices of ordinary people

populist ('pɒpjʊlɪst) *adj* **1** appealing to the interests or prejudices of ordinary people ▷ *n* **2** a person, esp a politician, who appeals to the interests or prejudices of ordinary people

Populist ('pɒpjʊlɪst) *n* **1** *US history* a member of the People's Party, formed largely by agrarian interests to contest the 1892 presidential election. The movement gradually dissolved after the 1904 election ▷ *adj* Also: Populistic **2** of, characteristic of, or relating to the People's Party, the Populists, or any individual or movement with similar aims > 'Populism *n*

populous ('pɒpjʊləs) *adj* containing many inhabitants; abundantly populated [c15: from Late Latin *populōsus*] > 'populously *adv* > 'populousness *n*

pop-up *adj* **1** (of an appliance) characterized by or having a mechanism that pops up: *a pop-up toaster* **2** (of a book) having pages that rise when opened to simulate a three-dimensional form **3** *computing* (of a menu on a computer screen, etc) suddenly appearing when an option is selected ▷ *vb* pop up **4** (*intr, adverb*) to appear suddenly from below ▷ *n* **5** *computing* something that appears over or above the open window on a computer screen

porangi ('pɔːræŋɪ) *adj* NZ *informal* crazy; mad [Māori]

porbeagle ('pɔː,biːgʲl) *n* any of several voracious sharks of the genus *Lamna*, esp *L. nasus*, of northern seas: family *Isuridae*. Also called: mackerel shark [c18: from Cornish *porgh-bugel*, of obscure origin]

porcelain ('pɔːslɪn, -leɪn, 'pɔːsə-) *n* **1 a** a more or less translucent ceramic material, the principal ingredients being kaolin and petuntse (hard paste) or other clays, ground glassy substances, soapstone, bone ash, etc **2** an object made of this or such objects collectively **3** (*modifier*) of, relating to, or made from this material: *a porcelain cup* [c16: from French *porcelaine*, from Italian *porcellana* cowrie shell, porcelain (from its shell-like finish), literally: relating to a sow (from the resemblance between a cowrie shell and a sow's vulva), from *porcella* little sow, from *porca* sow, from Latin; see PORK] > porcellaneous (,pɔːsə'leɪnɪəs) *adj*

porch (pɔːtʃ) *n* **1** a low structure projecting from the doorway of a house and forming a covered entrance **2** US & Canadian an exterior roofed gallery, often partly enclosed; veranda [c13: from French *porche*, from Latin *porticus* portico]

porcine ('pɔːsaɪn) *adj* of, connected with, or characteristic of pigs [c17: from Latin *porcīnus*, from *porcus* pig]

porcino (pɔː'tʃiːnəʊ) *n, pl* porcini (pɔː'tʃiːnɪ) an edible saprotrophic basidiomycetous woodland fungus, *Boletus edulis*, with a brown shining cap covering white spore-bearing tubes and having a rich nutty flavour: family *Boletineae*. Also called: cep [Italian, from Latin *porcīnus*, from *porcus* pig]

porcupine ('pɔːkjʊ,paɪn) *n* any of various large hystricomorph rodents of the families *Hystricidae*, of Africa, Indonesia, S Europe, and S Asia, and *Erethizontidae*, of the New World. All species have a body covering of protective spines or quills [c14 *porc despyne* pig with spines, from Old French *porc espin*; see PORK, SPINE] > 'porcu,pinish *adj* > 'porcu,piny *adj*

porcupine fish *n* any of various plectognath fishes of the genus *Diodon* and related genera, of temperate and tropical seas, having a body that is covered with sharp spines and can be inflated into a globe: family *Diodontidae*. Also called: globefish

porcupine grass *n* Austral another name for **spinifex** (sense 2)

porcupine provisions *pl n* *finance* provisions, such as poison pills or staggered directorships, made in the bylaws of a company to deter takeover bids. Also called: shark repellents

pore[1] (pɔː) *vb* (*intr*) **1** (foll by *over*) to make a close intent examination or study (of a book, map, etc): *he pored over the documents for several hours* **2** (foll by *over, on,* or *upon*) to think deeply (about) **3** (foll by *over, on,* or *upon*) *rare* to look earnestly or intently (at); gaze fixedly (upon) [c13 *pouren*; perhaps related to PEER[2]]
● USAGE See at **pour**

pore[2] (pɔː) *n* **1** *anatomy, zoology* any small opening in the skin or outer surface of an animal **2** *botany* any small aperture, esp that of a stoma through which water vapour and gases pass **3** any other small hole, such as a space in a rock, soil, etc [c14: from Late Latin *porus*, from Greek *poros* passage, pore]

porgy ('pɔːgɪ) *n, pl* -gy *or* -gies Also called: pogy any of various sparid fishes, many of which occur in American Atlantic waters [c18: from Spanish *pargo*, from Latin *phager* type of fish, from Greek *phagros* sea bream]

Pori (Finnish 'pɔrɪ) *n* a port in SW Finland, on the Gulf of Bothnia. Pop: 76 189 (2003 est). Swedish name: **Björneborg**

poriferan (pɔː'rɪfərən) *n* any invertebrate of the phylum *Porifera*, which comprises the sponges [c19: from New Latin *porifer* bearing pores]

Porirua (,pɒrɪ'ruːə) *n* a city in New Zealand, on the North Island just north of Wellington. Pop: 50 600 (2004 est)

pork (pɔːk) *n* the flesh of pigs used as food [c13: from Old French *porc*, from Latin *porcus* pig]

porker ('pɔːkə) *n* a pig, esp a young one weighing between 40 and 67 kg, fattened to provide meat such as pork chops

pork pie *n* 1 a pie filled with minced seasoned pork 2 See porky²

porkpie hat ('pɔːk,paɪ) *n* a hat with a round flat crown and a brim that can be turned up or down

porky¹ ('pɔːkɪ) *adj* porkier, porkiest 1 belonging to or characteristic of pork 2 *informal* fat; obese

porky² ('pɔːkɪ) *n, pl* porkies *Brit slang* a lie. Also called: pork pie [from rhyming slang *pork pie* lie]

porn (pɔːn) *or* **porno** ('pɔːnəʊ) *n, adj informal* short for pornography

pornography (pɔː'nɒgrəfɪ) *n* 1 writings, pictures, films, etc, designed to stimulate sexual excitement 2 the production of such material ▷ Sometimes (informal) shortened to: **porn** [c19: from Greek *pornographos* writing of harlots, from *pornē* a harlot + *graphein* to write] > por'nographer *n* > pornographic (,pɔːnə'græfɪk) *adj* > ,porno'graphically *adv*

poromeric (,pɔːrə'mɛrɪk) *adj* 1 (of a plastic) permeable to water vapour ▷ *n* 2 a substance having this characteristic, esp one based on polyurethane and used in place of leather in making shoe uppers [c20: from PORO(SITY) + (POLY)MER + -IC]

porosity (pɔː'rɒsɪtɪ) *n, pl* -ties 1 the state or condition of being porous 2 *geology* the ratio of the volume of space to the total volume of a rock [c14: from Medieval Latin *porōsitās*, from Late Latin *porus* PORE²]

porous ('pɔːrəs) *adj* 1 permeable to water, air, or other fluids 2 *biology, geology* having pores; poriferous 3 easy to cross or penetrate: *the porous border into Thailand; the most porous defence in the league* [c14: from Medieval Latin *porōsus*, from Late Latin *porus* PORE²] > 'porously *adv* > 'porousness *n*

porphyria (pɔː'fɪrɪə) *n* a hereditary disease of body metabolism, producing symptoms including abdominal pain, mental confusion, and photosensitivity [c19: from New Latin, from *porphyrin* a purple substance excreted by patients suffering from this condition, from Greek *porphura* purple]

porphyry ('pɔːfɪrɪ) *n, pl* -ries 1 any igneous rock with large crystals embedded in a finer groundmass of minerals 2 *obsolete* a reddish-purple rock consisting of large crystals of feldspar in a finer groundmass of feldspar, hornblende, etc [c14 *porfurie*, from Late Latin *porphyrītēs*, from Greek *porphurītēs* (*lithos*) purple (stone), from *porphuros* purple]

Porphyry ('pɔːfɪrɪ) *n* original name *Malchus*. 232–305 AD, Greek Neo-Platonist philosopher, born in Syria; disciple and biographer of Plotinus

porpoise ('pɔːpəs) *n, pl* -poises *or* -poise 1 any of various small cetacean mammals of the genus *Phocaena* and related genera, having a blunt snout and many teeth: family *Delphinidae* (or *Phocaenidae*) 2 (*not in technical use*) any of various related cetaceans, esp the dolphin [c14: from French *pourpois*, from Medieval Latin *porcopiscus* (from Latin *porcus* pig + *piscis* fish), replacing Latin *porcus marīnus* sea pig]

porridge ('pɒrɪdʒ) *n* 1 a dish made from oatmeal or another cereal, cooked in water or milk to a thick consistency 2 *slang* a term in prison (esp in the phrase **do porridge**) [c16: variant (influenced by Middle English *porray*) pottage) of POTTAGE]

porringer ('pɒrɪndʒə) *n* a small dish, often with a handle, for soup, porridge, etc [c16: changed from Middle English *potinger, poteger*, from Old French *potager*, from *potage* soup, contents of a pot; see POTTAGE]

Porsena ('pɔːsɪnə) *or* **Porsenna** ('pɔː'sɛnə) *n* **Lars** (lɑːz). 6th century BC, a legendary Etruscan king, alleged to have besieged Rome in a vain attempt to reinstate Tarquinius Superbus on the throne

Porson ('pɔːsᵊn) *n* **Richard**. 1759–1808, English classical scholar, noted for his editions of Aeschylus and Euripides

port¹ (pɔːt) *n* 1 a town or place alongside navigable water with facilities for the loading and unloading of ships 2 See **port of entry** [Old English, from Latin *portus* harbour, port]

port² (pɔːt) *n* 1 Also called (formerly): **larboard a** the left side of an aircraft or vessel when facing the nose or bow **b** (*as modifier*). See **starboard** (sense 1) ▷ *vb* 2 to turn or be turned towards the port [c17: origin uncertain]

port³ (pɔːt) *n* a sweet fortified dessert wine [c17: after *Oporto*, Portugal, from where it came originally]

port⁴ (pɔːt) *n* 1 *nautical* **a** an opening in the side of a ship, fitted with a watertight door, for access to the holds **b** See **porthole** (sense 1) 2 a small opening in a wall, armoured vehicle, etc, for firing through 3 an aperture, as one controlled by a valve, by which fluid enters or leaves the cylinder head of an engine, compressor, etc 4 *electronics* a logic circuit for the input and ouput of data 5 *chiefly Scot* a gate or portal in a town or fortress [Old English, from Latin *porta* gate]

port⁵ (pɔːt) *military vb* (*tr*) to carry (a rifle, etc) in a position diagonally across the body with the muzzle near the left shoulder [c14: from Old French, from *porter* to carry, from Latin *portāre*]

port⁶ (pɔːt) *n Austral* (esp in Queensland) a suitcase or school case [c20: shortened from PORTMANTEAU]

Port. *abbreviation* 1 Portugal 2 Portuguese

portable ('pɔːtəbᵊl) *adj* 1 able to be carried or moved easily, esp by hand 2 (of software, files, etc) able to be transferred from one type of computer system to another ▷ *n* 3 an article designed to be readily carried by hand, such as a television, typewriter, etc [c14: from Late Latin *portābilis*, from Latin *portāre* to carry] > ,porta'bility *n* > 'portably *adv*

Port Adelaide *n* the chief port of South Australia, near Adelaide on St Vincent Gulf. Pop: 33 145 (2006)

Portadown (,pɔːtə'daun) *n* a town in S Northern Ireland, in the district of Armagh. Pop: 25 958 (2001)

portage ('pɔːtɪdʒ; *French* pɔrtaʒ) *n* 1 the act of carrying; transport 2 the cost of carrying or transporting 3 the act or process of transporting boats, supplies, etc, overland between navigable waterways 4 the route overland used for such transport ▷ *vb* 5 to transport (boats, supplies, etc) overland between navigable waterways [c15: from French, from Old French *porter* to carry]

Portakabin ('pɔːtə,kæbɪn) *n* trademark a portable building quickly set up for use as a temporary office, etc

portal ('pɔːtᵊl) *n* 1 an entrance, gateway, or doorway, esp one that is large and impressive 2 *computing* an internet site providing links to other sites ▷ *adj* 3 *anatomy* **a** of or relating to a portal vein: *hepatic portal system* **b** of or relating to a porta [c14: via Old French from Medieval Latin *portāle*, from Latin *porta* gate, entrance]

portal vein *n* any vein connecting two capillary networks, esp in the liver (**hepatic portal vein**)

portamento (,pɔːtə'mɛntəʊ) *n, pl* -ti (-tɪ) *music* a smooth slide from one note to another in which intervening notes are not separately discernible [c18: from Italian: a carrying, from Latin *portāre* to carry]

Port Arthur *n* 1 a former penal settlement (1833–70) in Australia, on the S coast of the Tasman Peninsula, Tasmania 2 the former name of **Lüshun**

portative ('pɔːtətɪv) *adj* 1 a less common word for **portable** 2 concerned with the act of carrying [c14: from French, from Latin *portāre* to carry]

Port-au-Prince ('pɔːtəʊ'prɪns; *French* pɔrtoprɛ̃s) *n* the capital and chief port of Haiti, in the south on the Gulf of Gonaïves: founded in 1749 by the French; university (1944). Pop: 2 090 000 (2005 est)

Port Blair (blɛə) *n* the capital of the Indian Union Territory of the Andaman and Nicobar Islands, a port on the SE coast of South Andaman Island: a former penal colony. Pop: 100 186 (2001)

portcullis (pɔːt'kʌlɪs) *n* an iron or wooden grating suspended vertically in grooves in the gateway of a castle or fortified town and able to be lowered so as to bar the entrance [c14 *port colice*, from Old French *porte coleïce* sliding gate, from *porte* door, entrance + *coleïce*, from *couler* to slide, flow, from Late Latin *cōlāre* to filter]

Porte (pɔːt) *n* Also called: **Sublime Porte** the court or government of the Ottoman Empire [c17: shortened from French *Sublime Porte* High Gate, rendering the

Turkish title *Babi Ali*, the imperial gate, which was regarded as the seat of government]

porte-cochere (ˌpɔːtkɒˈʃɛə) *n* **1** a large covered entrance for vehicles leading into a courtyard **2** a large roof projecting over a drive to shelter travellers entering or leaving vehicles [C17: from French: carriage entrance, from *porte* gateway + *coche* coach]

Port Elizabeth *n* a port in S South Africa, on Algoa Bay: motor-vehicle manufacture, fruit canning; resort. Pop: 237 502 (2001)

portend (pɔːˈtɛnd) *vb* (*tr*) to give warning of; predict or foreshadow [C15: from Latin *portendere* to indicate, foretell; related to *prōtendere* to stretch out]

portent (ˈpɔːtɛnt) *n* **1** a sign or indication of a future event, esp a momentous or calamitous one; omen **2** momentous or ominous significance: *a cry of dire portent* **3** a miraculous occurrence; marvel [C16: from Latin *portentum* sign, omen, from *portendere* to PORTEND]

portentous (pɔːˈtɛntəs) *adj* **1** of momentous or ominous significance **2** miraculous, amazing, or awe-inspiring; prodigious **3** self-important or pompous

porter¹ (ˈpɔːtə) *n* **1** a person employed to carry luggage, parcels, supplies, etc, esp at a railway station or hotel **2** (in hospitals) a person employed to move patients from place to place **3** *US & Canadian* a railway employee who waits on passengers, esp in a sleeper [C14: from Old French *portour*, from Late Latin *portātor*, from Latin *portāre* to carry]

porter² (ˈpɔːtə) *n* **1** *chiefly Brit* a person in charge of a gate or door; doorman or gatekeeper **2** a person employed by a university or college as a caretaker and doorkeeper who also answers enquiries **3** a person in charge of the maintenance of a building, esp a block of flats [C13: from Old French *portier*, from Late Latin *portārius* doorkeeper, from Latin *porta* door]

porter³ (ˈpɔːtə) *n* *Brit* a dark sweet ale brewed from black malt [C18: shortened from *porter's ale*, apparently because it was a favourite beverage of porters]

Porter (ˈpɔːtə) *n* **1 Cole.** 1893–1964, US composer and lyricist of musical comedies. His most popular songs include *Night and Day* and *Let's do It* **2 George,** Baron Porter of Luddenham. 1920–2002, British chemist, who shared a Nobel prize for chemistry in 1967 for his work on flash photolysis **3 Katherine Anne.** 1890–1980, US short-story writer and novelist. Her best-known collections of stories are *Flowering Judas* (1930) and *Pale Horse, Pale Rider* (1939) **4 Peter.** born 1929, Australian poet, living in Britain **5 Rodney Robert.** 1917–85, British biochemist: shared the Nobel prize for physiology or medicine 1972 for determining the structure of an antibody **6 William Sidney.** original name of **O. Henry**

porterhouse (ˈpɔːtəˌhaʊs) *n* **1** Also called: porterhouse steak a thick choice steak of beef cut from the middle ribs or sirloin **2** (formerly) a place in which porter, beer, etc, and sometimes chops and steaks, were served [C19 (sense 1): said to be named after a porterhouse or chophouse in New York]

portfire (ˈpɔːtˌfaɪə) *n* (formerly) a slow-burning fuse used for firing rockets and fireworks and, in mining, for igniting explosives [C17: from French *porte-feu*, from *porter* to carry + *feu* fire]

portfolio (pɔːtˈfəʊlɪəʊ) *n*, *pl* **-os 1** a flat case, esp of leather, used for carrying maps, drawings, etc **2** the contents of such a case, such as drawings, paintings, or photographs, that demonstrate recent work **3** such a case used for carrying ministerial or state papers **4** the responsibilities or role of the head of a government department: *the portfolio for foreign affairs* **5** Minister without portfolio a cabinet minister who is not responsible for any government department **6** the complete investments held by an individual investor or by a financial organization [C18: from Italian *portafoglio*, from *portāre* to carry + *foglio* leaf, paper, from Latin *folium* leaf]

Port-Gentil (*French* pɔrʒãti) *n* the chief port of Gabon, in the west near the mouth of the Ogooué River: oil refinery. Pop: 80 841 (1993)

Port Harcourt (ˈhɑːkət, -kɔːt) *n* a port in S Nigeria, capital of Rivers state on the Niger delta: the nation's

second largest port; industrial centre. Pop: 942 000 (2005 est)

porthole (ˈpɔːtˌhəʊl) *n* **1** a small aperture in the side of a vessel to admit light and air, usually fitted with a watertight glass or metal cover, or both. Sometimes shortened to **port¹ 2** an opening in a wall or parapet through which a gun can be fired; embrasure

portico (ˈpɔːtɪkəʊ) *n, pl* **-coes** *or* **-cos 1** a covered entrance to a building; porch **2** a covered walkway in the form of a roof supported by columns or pillars, esp one built on to the exterior of a building [C17: via Italian from Latin *porticus* PORCH]

portière (ˌpɔːtɪˈɛə; *French* pɔrtjɛr) *n* a curtain hung in a doorway [C19: via French from Medieval Latin *portāria*, from Latin *porta* door] > **porti'èred** *adj*

Porţile de Fier (pɔrˈtsiːlɛ dɛ ˈfjɛr) *n* the Romanian name for the **Iron Gate**

portion (ˈpɔːʃən) *n* **1** a part of a whole; fraction **2** a part allotted or belonging to a person or group **3** an amount of food served to one person; helping **4** *law* **a** a share of property, esp one coming to a child from the estate of his parents **b** dowry **5** a person's lot or destiny ⊳ *vb* (*tr*) **6** to divide up; share out **7** to give a share to (a person); assign or allocate [C13: via Old French from Latin *portiō* portion, allocation; related to *pars* PART] > **'portionless** *adj*

Port Jackson *n* an inlet of the Pacific on the coast of SE Australia, forming a fine natural harbour: site of the city of Sydney, spanned by Sydney Harbour Bridge

Port Jackson willow *or* **Port Jackson wattle** *n* an Australian acacia tree, *Acacia cyanophylla*, introduced in the 19th century into South Africa, where it is now regarded as a pest

Portland¹ (ˈpɔːtlənd) *n* **1 Isle of Portland** a rugged limestone peninsula in SW England, in Dorset, connected to the mainland by a narrow isthmus and by Chesil Bank: the lighthouse of **Portland Bill** lies at the S tip; famous for the quarrying of **Portland stone,** a fine building material **2** an inland port in NW Oregon, on the Willamette River: the largest city in the state; shipbuilding and chemical industries. Pop: 538 544 (2003 est) **3** a port in SW Maine, on Casco Bay: the largest city in the state; settled by the English in 1632, destroyed successively by French, Indian, and British attacks, and rebuilt; capital of Maine (1820–32). Pop: 63 635 (2003 est)

Portland² (ˈpɔːtlənd) *n* **3rd Duke of.** title of *William Henry Cavendish Bentinck.* 1738–1809, British statesman; prime minister (1783; 1807–09); father of Lord William Cavendish Bentinck

Portland cement *n* a cement that hardens under water and is made by heating a slurry of clay and crushed chalk or limestone to clinker in a kiln [C19: named after the Isle of PORTLAND, because its colour resembles that of the stone quarried there]

Portlaoise (ˌpɔːtˈliːʃə) *n* a town in central Republic of Ireland, county town of Laois: site of a top-security prison. Pop: 12 127 (2002)

Port Louis (ˈluːɪs, ˈluːɪ) *n* the capital and chief port of Mauritius, on the NW coast on the Indian Ocean. Pop: 146 876 (2002 est)

portly (ˈpɔːtlɪ) *adj* **-lier, -liest 1** stout or corpulent **2** *archaic* stately; impressive [C16: from PORT⁵ (in the sense: deportment, bearing)] > **'portliness** *n*

Port Lyautey (ljəʊˈteɪ) *n* the former name (1932–56) of **Kénitra**

portmanteau (pɔːtˈmæntəʊ) *n, pl* **-teaus** *or* **-teaux** (-təʊz) **1** (formerly) a large travelling case made of stiff leather, esp one hinged at the back so as to open out into two compartments **2** (*modifier*) embodying several uses or qualities: *the heroine is a portmanteau figure of all the virtues* [C16: from French: cloak carrier, from *porter* to carry + *manteau* cloak, MANTLE]

portmanteau word *n* another name for **blend** (sense 7) [C19: from the idea that two meanings are packed into one word]

Port Moresby (ˈmɔːzbɪ) *n* the capital and chief port of Papua New Guinea, on the SE coast on the Gulf of Papua: important Allied base in World War II. Pop: 290 000 (2005 est)

P

Portnet ('pɔːtnɛt) *n South African* the South African Port Authority

Port Nicholson ('nɪkəlsən) *n* **1** the first British settlement in New Zealand, established on Wellington Harbour in 1840: grew into Wellington **2** the former name for Wellington Harbour [c19: named after Capt John *Nicholson*, Australian naval officer]

Porto ('portu) *n* the Portuguese name for **Oporto**

Porto Alegre (*Portuguese* 'portu a'lɛgri) *n* a port in S Brazil, capital of the Rio Grande do Sul state: the country's chief inland port; the chief commercial centre of S Brazil, with two universities (1936 and 1948). Pop: 3 795 000 (2005 est)

Portobelo (ˌpɔːtəʊ'bɛləʊ) *n* a small port in Panama, on the Caribbean northeast of Colón: the most important port in South America in colonial times; declined with the opening of the Panama Canal. Pop: 3300 (1997)

port of call *n* **1** any port where a ship stops, excluding its home port **2** any place visited on a traveller's itinerary

port of entry *n law* an airport, harbour, etc, where customs officials are stationed to supervise the entry into and exit from a country of persons and merchandise

Port of Spain *n* the capital and chief port of Trinidad and Tobago, on the W coast of Trinidad. Pop: 56 000 (2005 est)

Porto Novo ('pɔːtəʊ 'nəʊvəʊ) *n* the capital of Benin, in the southwest on a coastal lagoon: formerly a centre of Portuguese settlement and the slave trade. Pop: 253 000 (2005 est)

Porto Rico ('pɔːtə 'riːkəʊ) *n* the former name (until 1932) of **Puerto Rico**

Porto Velho (*Portuguese* 'portu 'vɛʎu) *n* a city in W Brazil, capital of the federal territory of Rondônia on the Madeira River. Pop: 301 000 (2005 est)

Port Phillip Bay *or* **Port Phillip** ('fɪlɪp) *n* a bay in SE Australia, which forms the harbour of Melbourne

portrait ('pɔːtrɪt, -treɪt) *n* **1** a painting, drawing, sculpture, photograph, or other likeness of an individual, esp of the face **2** a verbal description or picture, esp of a person's character ▷ *adj* **3** *printing* (of a publication or an illustration in a publication) of greater height than width. See **landscape** (sense 5a)

portraiture ('pɔːtrɪtʃə) *n* **1** the practice or art of making portraits **2 a** another term for **portrait** (sense 1) **b** portraits collectively **3** a verbal description

portray (pɔː'treɪ) *vb* (*tr*) **1** to represent in a painting, drawing, sculpture, etc; make a portrait of **2** to make a verbal picture of; depict in words **3** to play the part of (a character) in a play or film [c14: from Old French *portraire* to depict, from Latin *prōtrahere* to drag forth, bring to light, from PRO-¹ + *trahere* to drag] ▷ **por'trayal** *n* ▷ **por'trayer** *n*

Port Royal *n* **1** a fortified town in SE Jamaica, at the entrance to Kingston harbour: capital of Jamaica in colonial times **2** the former name (until 1710) of **Annapolis Royal 3** (*French* pɔr rwajal) an educational institution about 27 km (17 miles) west of Paris that flourished from 1638 to 1704, when it was suppressed by papal bull as it had become a centre of Jansenism. Its teachers were noted esp for their work on linguistics: their *Grammaire générale et raisonnée* exercised much influence

Port Said ('saːiːd, saɪd) *n* a port in NE Egypt, at the N end of the Suez Canal: founded in 1859 when the Suez Canal was begun; became the largest coaling station in the world and later an oil-bunkering port; damaged in the Arab-Israeli wars of 1967 and 1973. Pop: 546 000 (2005 est)

Port-Salut ('pɔː sə'luː; *French* pɔrsaly) *n* a mild semihard whole-milk cheese of a round flat shape. Also called: Port du Salut [c19: named after the Trappist monastery at *Port du Salut* in NW France where it was first made]

Portsmouth ('pɔːtsməθ) *n* **1** Also called: *informal* Pompey a port in S England, in Portsmouth unitary authority, Hampshire, on the English Channel: Britain's chief naval base; university (1992). Pop: 187 056 (2001) **2** a unitary authority in S England, in Hampshire. Pop:

188 700 (2003 est). Area: 37 sq km (14 sq miles) **3** a port in SE Virginia, on the Elizabeth River: naval base; shipyards. Pop: 99 617 (2003 est)

Port Sudan *n* the chief port of the Sudan, in the NE on the Red Sea. Pop: 499 000 (2005 est)

Port Talbot ('tɔːlbət, 'tæl-) *n* a port in SE Wales, in Neath Port Talbot county borough on Swansea Bay: established as a coal port in the mid-19th century; large steelworks; ore terminal. Pop: 35 633 (2001)

Portugal ('pɔːtjʊgᵊl) *n* a republic in SW Europe, on the Atlantic: became an independent monarchy in 1139 and expelled the Moors in 1249 after more than four centuries of Muslim rule; became a republic in 1910; under the dictatorship of Salazar from 1932 until 1968, when he was succeeded by Dr Caetano, who was overthrown by a junta in 1974; constitutional government restored in 1976. Portugal is a member of the European Union. Official language: Portuguese. Religion: Roman Catholic majority. Currency: euro. Capital: Lisbon. Pop: 10 072 000 (2004 est). Area: 91 831 sq km (35 456 sq miles)

Portuguese (ˌpɔːtjʊ'giːz) *n* **1** the official language of Portugal, its overseas territories, and Brazil: the native language of approximately 110 million people. It belongs to the Romance group of the Indo-European family and is derived from the Galician dialect of Vulgar Latin **2** *pl* -guese a native, citizen, or inhabitant of Portugal ▷ *adj* **3** relating to, denoting, or characteristic of Portugal, its inhabitants, or their language

Portuguese East Africa *n* a former name (until 1975) of **Mozambique**

Portuguese Guinea *n* the former name (until 1974) of **Guinea-Bissau**

Portuguese India *n* a former Portuguese overseas province on the W coast of India, consisting of Goa, Daman, and Diu: established between 1505 and 1510; annexed by India in 1961

Portuguese man-of-war *n* any of several large complex colonial hydrozoans of the genus *Physalia*, esp *P. physalis*, having an aerial float and long stinging tentacles: order Siphonophora. Sometimes shortened to: man-of-war

Portuguese Timor *n* a former name for **East Timor**

Portuguese West Africa *n* a former name (until 1975) of **Angola**

portulaca (ˌpɔːtjʊ'lækə, -'leɪkə) *n* any portulacaceous plant of the genus *Portulaca*, such as rose moss and purslane, of tropical and subtropical America, having yellow, pink, or purple showy flowers [c16: from Latin: PURSLANE]

POS *abbreviation* point of sale

pose¹ (pəʊz) *vb* **1** to assume or cause to assume a physical attitude, as for a photograph or painting **2** (*intr*; often foll by *as*) to pretend to be or present oneself (as something one is not) **3** (*intr*) to affect an attitude or play a part in order to impress others **4** (*tr*) to put forward, ask, or assert: *to pose a question* ▷ *n* **5** a physical attitude, esp one deliberately adopted for or represented by an artist or photographer **6** a mode of behaviour that is adopted for effect [c14: from Old French *poser* to set in place, from Late Latin *pausāre* to cease, put down (influenced by Latin *pōnere* to place)]

pose² (pəʊz) *vb* (*tr*) *rare* to puzzle or baffle [c16: from obsolete *appose*, from Latin *appōnere* to put to, set against; see OPPOSE]

Poseidon (pɒ'saɪdᵊn) *n Greek myth* the god of the sea and of earthquakes; brother of Zeus, Hades, and Hera. He is generally depicted in art wielding a trident. Roman counterpart: Neptune

Posen ('pəʊzən) *n* the German name for **Poznań**

poser¹ ('pəʊzə) *n* **1** a person who poses **2** *informal* a person who likes to be seen in trendsetting clothes in fashionable bars, discos, etc

poser² ('pəʊzə) *n* a baffling or insoluble question

poseur (pəʊ'zɜː) *n* a person who strikes an attitude or assumes a pose in order to impress others [c19: from French, from *poser* to POSE¹]

posh (pɒʃ) *informal, chiefly Brit adj* **1** smart, elegant, or fashionable; exclusive **2** upper-class or genteel [c19: often said to be an acronym of the phrase *port out,*

P

starboard home, the most desirable location for a cabin in British ships sailing to and from the East, being the north-facing or shaded side; but more likely to be a development of obsolete slang posh a dandy]

posit ('pɒzɪt) vb (tr) **1** to assume or put forward as fact or the factual basis for an argument; postulate **2** to put in position [c17: from Latin pōnere to place, position]

position (pə'zɪʃən) n **1** the place, situation, or location of a person or thing: he took up a position to the rear **2** the appropriate or customary location: the telescope is in position for use **3** the manner in which a person or thing is placed; arrangement **4** military an area or point occupied for tactical reasons **5** mental attitude; point of view; stand: what's your position on this issue? **6** social status or standing, esp high social standing **7** a post of employment; job **8** the act of positing a fact or viewpoint **9** something posited, such as an idea, proposition, etc **10** sport the part of a field or playing area where a player is placed or where he generally operates **11** music the vertical spacing or layout of the written notes in a chord. Chords arranged with the three upper voices close together are in **close position**. Chords whose notes are evenly or widely distributed are in **open position 12** (in classical prosody) the situation in which a short vowel may be regarded as long, that is, when it occurs before two or more consonants **13** finance the market commitment of a dealer in securities, currencies, or commodities: a long position; a short position **14** in a position (foll by an infinitive) able (to) ▷ vb (tr) **15** to put in the proper or appropriate place; locate **16** sport to place (oneself or another player) in a particular part of the field or playing area **17** to put (someone or something) in a position (esp in relation to others) that confers a strategic advantage: he's trying to position himself for a leadership bid **18** marketing to promote (a product or service) by tailoring it to the needs of a specific market or by clearly differentiating it from its competitors (e.g. in terms of price or quality) [c15: from Late Latin positiō a positioning, affirmation, from pōnere to place, lay down] > po'sitional adj

positional notation n the method of denoting numbers by the use of a finite number of digits, each digit having its value multiplied by its place value, as in $936 = (9 \times 100) + (3 \times 10) + 6$

position audit n commerce a systematic assessment of the current strengths and weaknesses of an organization as a prerequisite for future strategic planning

positive ('pɒzɪtɪv) adj **1** characterized by or expressing certainty or affirmation: a positive answer **2** composed of or possessing actual or specific qualities; real: a positive benefit **3** tending to emphasize what is good or laudable; constructive: he takes a very positive attitude when correcting pupils' mistakes **4** tending towards progress or improvement; moving in a beneficial direction **5** philosophy constructive rather than sceptical **6** (prenominal) informal (intensifier): a positive delight **7** maths having a value greater than zero: a positive number **8** maths **a** measured in a direction opposite to that regarded as negative **b** having the same magnitude as but opposite sense to an equivalent negative quantity **9** grammar denoting the usual form of an adjective as opposed to its comparative or superlative form **10** physics **a** (of an electric charge) having an opposite polarity to the charge of an electron and the same polarity as the charge of a proton **b** (of a body, system, ion, etc) having a positive electric charge; having a deficiency of electrons **11** short for **electropositive 12** med (of the results of an examination or test) indicating the existence or presence of a suspected disorder or pathogenic organism **13** economics of or denoting an analysis that is free of ethical, political, or value judgments ▷ n **14** something that is positive **15** maths a quantity greater than zero **16** photog a print or slide showing a photographic image whose colours or tones correspond to those of the original subject **17** grammar the positive degree of an adjective or adverb **18** a positive object, such as a terminal or plate in a voltaic cell [c13: from Late Latin positīvus positive, agreed on an

arbitrary basis, from pōnere to place] > 'positiveness or ,posi'tivity n

positive discrimination or **positive action** n the provision of special opportunities in employment, training, etc for a disadvantaged group, such as women, ethnic minorities, etc

positive feedback n See **feedback** (sense 1)

positively ('pɒzɪtɪvlɪ) adv **1** in a positive manner **2** (intensifier): he disliked her: in fact, he positively hated her

positive vetting n the checking of a person's background, political affiliation, etc, to assess his suitability for a position that may involve national security

positivism ('pɒzɪtɪ,vɪzəm) n **1** a strong form of empiricism, esp as established in the philosophical system of Auguste Comte, the French mathematician and philosopher (1798–1857), that rejects metaphysics and theology as seeking knowledge beyond the scope of experience, and holds that experimental investigation and observation are the only sources of substantial knowledge. See also **logical positivism 2** the quality of being definite, certain, etc > 'positivist n, adj

positron ('pɒzɪ,trɒn) n physics the antiparticle of the electron, having the same mass but an equal and opposite charge. It is produced in certain decay processes and in pair production, annihilation occurring when it collides with an electron [c20: from posi(tive + elec)tron]

positron emission tomography n a technique for assessing brain activity and function by recording the emission of positrons from radioactively labelled substances, such as glucose or dopamine

positronium (,pɒzɪ'trəʊnɪəm) n physics a short-lived entity consisting of a positron and an electron bound together. It decays by annihilation to produce two or three photons [c20: from POSITRON + -IUM]

posology (pə'sɒlədʒɪ) n the branch of medicine concerned with the determination of appropriate doses of drugs or agents [c19: from French posologie, from Greek posos how much]

poss. abbreviation **1** possession **2** possessive **3** possible **4** possibly

posse ('pɒsɪ) n **1** Also called: posse comitatus US the able-bodied men of a district assembled together and forming a group upon whom the sheriff may call for assistance in maintaining law and order **2** law possibility (esp in the phrase in posse) **3** slang a Jamaican street gang in the US **4** informal a group of friends or associates [c16: from Medieval Latin (n): power, strength, from Latin (vb): to be able, have power]

posse comitatus (,kɒmɪ'tɑːtəs) n the formal legal term for **posse** (sense 1) [Medieval Latin: strength (manpower) of the county]

possess (pə'zɛs) vb (tr) **1** to have as one's property; own **2** to have as a quality, faculty, characteristic, etc: to possess good eyesight **3** to have knowledge or mastery of: to possess a little French **4** to gain control over or dominate: whatever possessed you to act so foolishly? **5** (foll by of) to cause to be the owner or possessor: I am possessed of the necessary information **6** to have sexual intercourse with **7** now rare to keep control over or maintain (oneself or one's feelings) in a certain state or condition: possess yourself in patience until I tell you the news [c15: from Old French possesser, from Latin possidēre to own, occupy; related to Latin sedēre to sit] > pos'sessor n

possessed (pə'zɛst) adj **1** (foll by of) owning or having **2** (usually postpositive) under the influence of a powerful force, such as a spirit or strong emotion **3** a less common word for **self-possessed**

possession (pə'zɛʃən) n **1** the act of possessing or state of being possessed: in possession of the crown **2** anything that is owned or possessed **3** (plural) wealth or property **4** the state of being controlled or dominated by or as if by evil spirits **5** the physical control or occupancy of land, property, etc, whether or not accompanied by ownership: to take possession of a house **6** a territory subject to a foreign state or to a sovereign prince: colonial possessions **7** sport control of the ball, puck, etc, as exercised by a player or team

possessive (pəˈzɛsɪv) *adj* **1** of or relating to possession or ownership **2** having or showing an excessive desire to possess, control, or dominate: *a possessive mother* **3** *grammar* **a** another word for **genitive** (sense 1) **b** denoting an inflected form of a noun or pronoun used to convey the idea of possession, association, etc, as *my* or *Harry's* ▷ *n* **4** *grammar* **a** the possessive case **b** a word or speech element in the possessive case > pos'sessively *adv* > pos'sessiveness *n*

posset (ˈpɒsɪt) *n* a drink of hot milk curdled with ale, beer, etc, flavoured with spices, formerly used as a remedy for colds [C15 *poshoote*, of unknown origin]

possibility (ˌpɒsɪˈbɪlɪtɪ) *n, pl* **-ties 1** the state or condition of being possible **2** anything that is possible **3** a competitor, candidate, etc, who has a moderately good chance of winning, being chosen, etc **4** (*often plural*) a future prospect or potential: *my new house has great possibilities*

possible (ˈpɒsɪbˀl) *adj* **1** capable of existing, taking place, or proving true without contravention of any natural law **2** capable of being achieved: *it is not possible to finish in three weeks* **3** having potential or capabilities for favourable use or development: *the idea is a possible money-spinner* **4** that may or may not happen or have happened; feasible but less than probable: *it is possible that man will live on Mars* **5** *logic* (of a statement, formula, etc) capable of being true under some interpretation, or in some circumstances. Usual symbol: *Mp* or ◇*p*, where *p* is the given expression ▷ *n* **6** another word for **possibility** (sense 3) [C14: from Latin *possibilis* that may be, from *posse* to be able, have power]

● **USAGE** Although it is very common to talk about
● something being *very possible* or *more possible*, these uses
● are generally thought to be incorrect, since *possible*
● describes an absolute state, and therefore something
● can only be *possible* or *not possible*: it is very likely (not *very*
● *possible*) that he will resign; it has now become easier (not *more*
● *possible*) to obtain an entry visa

possibly (ˈpɒsɪblɪ) *sentence substitute, adv* **1 a** perhaps or maybe **b** (*as sentence modifier*): *possibly he'll come* ▷ *adv* **2** by any chance; at all: *he can't possibly come*

possum (ˈpɒsəm) *n* **1** an informal name for **opossum** (sense 1) **2** *Also called:* **phalanger** *Austral. & NZ* any of various Australasian arboreal marsupials, such as *Trichosurus vulpecula* (**brush-tailed phalanger**), having dense fur and a long tail: family *Phalangeridae* **3 play possum** to pretend to be dead, ignorant, asleep, etc, in order to deceive an opponent

post¹ (pəʊst) *n* **1** a length of wood, metal, etc, fixed upright in the ground to serve as a support, marker, point of attachment, etc **2** *horse racing* **a** either of two upright poles marking the beginning (**starting post**) and end (**winning post**) of a racecourse **b** the finish of a horse race ▷ *vb* (*tr*) **3** (sometimes foll by *up*) to fasten or put up (a notice) in a public place **4** to announce by means of or as if by means of a poster: *to post banns* **5** to publish (a name) on a list [Old English, from Latin *postis*; related to Old High German *first* ridgepole, Greek *pastas* colonnade]

post² (pəʊst) *n* **1** a position to which a person is appointed or elected; appointment; job **2** a position or station to which a person, such as a sentry, is assigned for duty **3** a permanent military establishment **4** *Brit* either of two military bugle calls (**first post** and **last post**) ordering or giving notice of the time to retire for the night **5** See **trading post** (sense 1) ▷ *vb* **6** (*tr*) to assign to or station at a particular place or position **7** *chiefly Brit* to transfer to a different unit or ship on taking up a new appointment, etc [C16: from French *poste*, from Italian *posto*, ultimately from Latin *pōnere* to place]

post³ (pəʊst) *n* **1** *chiefly Brit* letters, packages, etc, that are transported and delivered by the Post Office; mail **2** *chiefly Brit* a single collection or delivery of mail **3** *Brit* an official system of mail delivery **4** (formerly) any of a series of stations furnishing relays of men and horses to deliver mail over a fixed route **5** a rider who carried mail between such stations **6** *Brit* short for **post office 7** any of various book sizes, esp 5¼ by 8¼ inches (**post octavo**) and 8¼ by 10¼ inches (**post quarto**) **8** by return of post

Brit by the next mail in the opposite direction ▷ *vb* **9** (*tr*) *chiefly Brit* to send by post. US and Canadian word: **mail 10** (*tr*) *book-keeping* **a** to enter (an item) in a ledger **b** (*often foll by up*) to compile or enter all paper items in (a ledger) **11** (*tr*) to inform of the latest news (esp in the phrase **keep someone posted**) **12** (*intr*) (formerly) to travel with relays of post horses **13** *archaic* to travel or dispatch with speed; hasten ▷ *adv* **14** with speed; rapidly **15** by means of post horses [C16: via French from Italian *poste*, from Latin *posita* something placed, from *pōnere* to put, place]

post- *prefix* **1** after in time or sequence; following; subsequent: *postgraduate* **2** behind; posterior to: *postorbital* [from Latin, from *post* after, behind]

postage (ˈpəʊstɪdʒ) *n* **a** the charge for delivering a piece of mail **b** (*as modifier*): *postage charges*

postage meter *n chiefly US & Canadian* a postal franking machine. Also called: **postal meter**

postage stamp *n* **1** a printed paper label with a gummed back for attaching to mail as an official indication that the required postage has been paid **2** a mark directly printed or embossed on an envelope, postcard, etc, serving the same function

postal (ˈpəʊstˀl) *adj* of or relating to a Post Office or to the mail-delivery service > 'postally *adv*

postal code *n Canadian* a code of letters and digits used as part of a postal address to aid the sorting of mail

postal note *n Austral & NZ* the usual name for **postal order**

postal order *n* a written order for the payment of a sum of money, to a named payee, obtainable and payable at a post office

postbag (ˈpəʊstˌbæg) *n* **1** *chiefly Brit* another name for **mailbag 2** the mail received by a magazine, radio programme, public figure, etc

postbox (ˈpəʊstˌbɒks) *n chiefly Brit* a box into which mail is put for collection by the postal service. Also called: letter box

postcard (ˈpəʊstˌkɑːd) *n* a card, often bearing a photograph, picture, etc, on one side, (**picture postcard**), for sending a message by post without an envelope

post chaise *n* a closed four-wheeled horse-drawn coach used as a rapid means for transporting mail and passengers in the 18th and 19th centuries [C18: from POST³ + CHAISE]

postcode (ˈpəʊstˌkəʊd) *n Brit & Austral* a code of letters and digits used as part of a postal address to aid the sorting of mail. Also called: **postal code** US equivalent: **zip code**

postcode discrimination *n* discrimination on the basis of the area where someone lives, with relation to employment, credit rating, etc

postcode lottery *n Brit* a situation in which the standard of medical care, education, etc, received by the public varies from area to area, depending on the funding policies of various health boards, local authorities, etc

postcode prescribing *n Brit* the practice of prescribing more or less expensive and effective medical treatments to patients depending on where they live in a country, and which treatments their health board is willing and able to provide

post-consumer *adj* **a** (of a consumer item) having been discarded for disposal or recovery **b** having been recycled

postdate (pəʊstˈdeɪt) *vb* (*tr*) **1** to write a future date on (a document), as on a cheque to prevent it being paid until then **2** to assign a date to (an event, period, etc) that is later than its previously assigned date of occurrence **3** to be or occur at a later date than

postdoctoral (pəʊstˈdɒktərəl) *adj* of, relating to, or designating studies, research, or professional work above the level of a doctorate

poster (ˈpəʊstə) *n* **1** a large printed picture, used for decoration **2** a placard or bill posted in a public place as an advertisement

poster boy *or* **poster girl** *n* **1** a person who appears on a poster **2** a person who typifies or represents a particular characteristic, cause, opinion, etc: *a poster girl for late* *motherhood* ▷ Also called: **poster child**

poste restante ('pəʊst rɪ'stænt; *French* pɔst rɛstɑ̃t) *n* **1** (not in the US and Canada) an address on mail indicating that it should be kept at a specified post office until collected by the addressee **2** the mail-delivery service or post-office department that handles mail having this address. US and Canadian equivalent: **general delivery** [French, literally: mail remaining]

posterior (pɒ'stɪərɪə) *adj* **1** situated at the back of or behind something **2** coming after or following another in a series **3** coming after in time ▷ *n* **4** the buttocks; rump [c16: from Latin: latter, from *posterus* coming next, from *post* after] ▷ **pos'teriorly** *adv*

posterity (pɒ'stɛrɪtɪ) *n* **1** future or succeeding generations **2** all of one's descendants [c14: from French *postérité*, from Latin *posteritās* future generations, from *posterus* coming after, from *post* after]

postern ('pɒstən) *n* a back door or gate, esp one that is for private use [c13: from Old French *posterne*, from Late Latin *posterula* (*jānua*) a back (entrance), from *posterus* coming behind; see POSTERIOR, POSTERITY]

poster paint or **poster colour** *n* a gum-based opaque watercolour paint used for writing posters, etc

postfeminist (pəʊst'fɛmɪnɪst) *adj* **1** resulting from or including the beliefs and ideas of feminism **2** differing from or showing moderation of these beliefs and ideas ▷ *n* **3** a person who believes in or advocates any of the ideas that have developed from the feminist movement

post-Fordism (,pəʊst'fɔ:dɪzəm) *n* the idea that modern industrial production has moved away from mass production in huge factories, as pioneered by Henry Ford, the US car manufacturer (1863–1947), towards specialized markets based on small flexible manufacturing units > **,post-'Fordist** *adj*

post-free *adv, adj* **1** *Brit* with the postage prepaid; **post-paid** **2** free of postal charge

postglacial (pəʊst'ɡleɪsɪəl) *adj* formed or occurring after a glacial period, esp after the Pleistocene epoch

postgraduate (pəʊst'ɡrædjʊɪt) *n* **1** a student who has obtained a degree from a university, etc, and is pursuing studies for a more advanced qualification **2** (*modifier*) of or relating to such a student or to his studies ▷ Also (US and Canadian): **graduate**

posthaste ('pəʊst'heɪst) *adv* **1** with great haste; as fast as possible ▷ *n* **2** *archaic* great haste

post horn *n* a simple valveless natural horn consisting of a long tube of brass or copper, either straight or coiled; formerly often used to announce the arrival of a mailcoach

post horse *n* (formerly) a horse kept at an inn or post house for use by postriders or for hire to travellers

post house *n* (formerly) a house or inn where horses were kept for postriders or for hire to travellers

posthumous ('pɒstjʊməs) *adj* **1** happening or continuing after one's death **2** (of a book, etc) published after the author's death **3** (of a child) born after the father's death [c17: from Latin *postumus* the last, but modified as though from Latin *post* after + *humus* earth, that is, after the burial] > **'posthumously** *adv*

posthypnotic suggestion (,pəʊsthɪp'nɒtɪk) *n* a suggestion made to the subject while in a hypnotic trance, to be acted upon at some time after emerging from the trance

postiche (pɒ'stiːʃ) *adj* **1** (of architectural ornament) inappropriately applied; sham **2** false or artificial; spurious ▷ *n* **3** another term for **hairpiece** (sense 2) **4** anything that is false; sham or pretence [c19: from French, from Italian *apposticcio* (n), from Late Latin *appositīcius* (adj); see APPOSITE]

postilion or **postillion** (pɒ'stɪljən) *n* a person who rides the near horse of the leaders in order to guide a team of horses drawing a coach [c16: from French *postillon*, from Italian *postiglione*, from *posta* POST³]

postimpressionism (,pəʊstɪm'prɛʃə,nɪzəm) *n* a movement in painting in France at the end of the 19th century, begun by Paul Cézanne (1839–1906) and exemplified by Paul Gauguin (1848–1903), Vincent Van Gogh (1853–90), and Henri Matisse (1869–1954), which rejected the naturalism and momentary effects of impressionism but adapted its use of pure colour to paint subjects with greater subjective emotion > ,**postim'pressionist** *n, adj*

postindustrial (,pəʊstɪn'dʌstrɪəl) *adj* characteristic of, relating to, or denoting work or a society that is no longer based on heavy industry

posting ('pəʊstɪŋ) *n* **1** an appointment to a position or post, usually in another town or country **2** an electronic mail message sent to a bulletin board, website, etc, and intended for access by every user

postliminy ('pəʊst'lɪmɪnɪ) or **postliminium** (,pəʊstlɪ'mɪnɪəm) *n, pl* -**inies** or -**inia** (-ɪnɪə) *international law* the right by which persons and property seized in war are restored to their former status on recovery [c19: (in this sense): from Latin *postlīminium* a return behind one's threshold, from *līmen* threshold]

postlude ('pəʊstluːd) *n music* a final or concluding piece or movement [c19: from POST- + -*lude*, from Latin *lūdus* game; compare PRELUDE]

postman ('pəʊstmən) or *feminine* **postwoman** *n, pl* -**men** or -**women** a person who carries and delivers mail as a profession

postman's knock *n* a children's party game in which a kiss is exchanged for a pretend letter

postmark ('pəʊst,mɑːk) *n* **1** any mark stamped on mail by postal officials, such as a simple obliteration, date mark, or indication of route ▷ *vb* **2** (*tr*) to put such a mark on mail

postmaster ('pəʊst,mɑːstə) *n* **1** Also (feminine): **postmistress** an official in charge of a local post office **2** the person responsible for managing the electronic mail at a site

postmaster general *n, pl* **postmasters general** the executive head of the postal service in certain countries

postmeridian (,pəʊstmə'rɪdɪən) *adj* after noon; in the afternoon or evening [c17: from Latin *postmerīdiānus* in the afternoon; see POST-, MERIDIAN]

post meridiem ('pəʊst mə'rɪdɪəm) the full form of **p.m.** [c17: Latin: after noon]

post mill *n* a windmill built round a central post on which the whole mill can be turned so that the sails catch the wind

postmillennialism (,pəʊstmɪ'lɛnɪə,lɪzəm) *n* the doctrine or belief that the Second Coming of Christ will be preceded by the millennium > ,**postmil'lennialist** *n*

postmortem (pəʊst'mɔːtəm) *adj* **1** (*prenominal*) occurring after death ▷ *n* **2** analysis or study of a recently completed event: *a postmortem on a game of chess* **3** See **postmortem examination** [c18: from Latin, literally: after death]

postmortem examination *n* dissection and examination of a dead body to determine the cause of death. Also called: **autopsy**, **necropsy**

postnatal (pəʊst'neɪtᵊl) *adj* existing or taking place after giving birth

Postnet ('pəʊstnɛt) *n South African* an official postal service in South Africa

post-obit (pəʊst'əʊbɪt, -'ɒbɪt) *chiefly law* ▷ *n* **1** Also called: **post-obit bond** a bond given by a borrower, payable after the death of a specified person, esp one given to a moneylender by an expectant heir promising to repay when his interest falls into possession ▷ *adj* **2** taking effect after death [c18: from Latin *post obitum* after death]

post office *n* a building or room where postage stamps are sold and other postal business is conducted

Post Office *n* a government department or authority in many countries responsible for postal services and often telecommunications

post office box *n* a private numbered place in a post office, in which letters received are kept until called for

postoperative (pəʊst'ɒpərətɪv, -'ɒprətɪv) *adj* of, relating to, or occurring in the period following a surgical operation

post-paid *adv, adj* with the postage prepaid

postpone (pəʊst'pəʊn, pə'spəʊn) *vb* (*tr*) **1** to put off or delay until a future time **2** to put behind in order of importance; defer [c16: from Latin *postpōnere* to put after, neglect, from POST- + *ponere* to place] > **post'ponement** *n*

postpositive (pəʊst'pɒzɪtɪv) *adj* **1** (of an adjective or other modifier) placed after the word modified, either immediately after, as in *two men abreast,* or as part of a complement, as in *those men are bad* ▷ *n* **2** a postpositive modifier

postprandial (pəʊst'prændıəl) *adj* of or relating to the period immediately after lunch or dinner

postscript ('pəʊs,skrıpt, 'pəʊst-) *n* **1** a message added at the end of a letter, after the signature **2** any supplement, as to a document or book [C16: from Late Latin *postscribere* to write after, from POST- + *scribere* to write]

poststructuralism (pəʊst'strʌktʃərə,lɪzəm) *n* an approach to literature that, proceeding from the tenets of structuralism, maintains that, as words have no absolute meaning, any text is open to an unlimited range of interpretations > post'structuralist *n, adj*

post-traumatic stress disorder *n* a psychological condition, characterized by anxiety, withdrawal, and a proneness to physical illness, that may follow a traumatic experience. Abbreviation: **PTSD**

postulant ('pɒstjʊlənt) *n* a person who makes a request or application, esp a candidate for admission to a religious order [C18: from Latin *postulāns* asking, from *postulāre* to ask, demand] > 'postulancy *or* 'postulant,ship *n*

postulate *vb* ('pɒstjʊ,leɪt) (*tr; may take a clause as object*) **1** to assume to be true or existent; take for granted **2** to ask, demand, or claim **3** to nominate (a person) to a post or office subject to approval by a higher authority ▷ *n* ('pɒstjʊlɪt) **4** something taken as self-evident or assumed as the basis of an argument **5** a necessary condition or prerequisite **6** a fundamental principle **7** *logic, maths* an unproved and indemonstrable statement that should be taken for granted: used as an initial premise or underlying hypothesis in a process of reasoning [C16: from Latin *postulāre* to ask for, require; related to *pōscere* to request] > ,postu'lation *n*

postulator ('pɒstjʊ,leɪtə) *n RC Church* a person, usually a priest, deputed to prepare and present a plea for the beatification or canonization of some deceased person

posture ('pɒstʃə) *n* **1** a position or attitude of the limbs or body **2** a characteristic manner of bearing the body; carriage: *to have good posture* **3** the disposition of the parts of a visible object **4** a mental attitude or frame of mind **5** a state, situation, or condition **6** a false or affected attitude; pose ▷ *vb* **7** to assume or cause to assume a bodily position or attitude **8** (*intr*) to assume an affected or unnatural bodily or mental posture; pose [C17: via French from Italian *postura,* from Latin *positūra,* from *pōnere* to place] > 'postural *adj* > 'posturer *n*

postviral syndrome (,pəʊst'vaɪrəl) *n* Abbreviation: **PVS**

post-war *adj* happening or existing after a war: *the early post-war years*

posy ('pəʊzı) *n, pl* -sies **1** a small bunch of flowers or a single flower; nosegay **2** *archaic* a brief motto or inscription, esp one on a trinket or a ring [C16: variant of POESY]

pot¹ (pɒt) *n* **1** a container made of earthenware, glass, or similar material; usually round and deep, often having a handle and lid, used for cooking and other domestic purposes **2** short for **flowerpot, teapot 3** the amount that a pot will hold; potful **4** a chamber pot, esp a small one designed for a baby or toddler **5** a handmade piece of pottery **6** a large mug or tankard, as for beer **7** *Austral* any of various measures used for serving beer **8** *informal* a cup or trophy, esp of silver, awarded as a prize in a competition **9** the money or stakes in the pool in gambling games, esp poker **10** (*often plural*) *informal* a large amount, esp of money **11** See **potbelly 12** go to pot to go to ruin; deteriorate ▷ *vb* **pots, potting, potted** (*mainly tr*) **13** to put or preserve (goods, meat, etc) in a pot **14** to shoot (game) for food rather than for sport **15** (*also intr*) to shoot casually or without careful aim at (an animal, etc) **16** (*also intr*) to shape clay as a potter **17** *billiards, snooker* to pocket (a ball) **18** *informal* to capture or win; secure [Late Old English *pott,* from Medieval Latin *pottus* (unattested), perhaps from Latin *pōtus* a drink; compare Middle Low German *pot,* Old Norse *pottr*]

pot² (pɒt) *n slang* cannabis used as a drug in any form,

such as leaves (marijuana or hemp) or resin (hashish) [C20: perhaps shortened from Mexican Indian *potiguaya*]

potable ('pəʊtəb³l) *adj* **1** a less common word for **drinkable** ▷ *n* **2** something fit to drink; a beverage [C16: from Late Latin *pōtābilis* drinkable, from Latin *pōtāre* to drink] > ,pota'bility *n*

potae ('pɒtaɪ) *n NZ* a hat [Māori]

potage French (pɒtaʒ; *English* pəʊ'tɑːʒ) *n* any thick soup [C16: from Old French; see POTTAGE]

potamic (pə'tæmɪk) *adj* of or relating to rivers [C19: from Greek *potamos* river]

potash ('pɒtæʃ) *n* **1** another name for potassium carbonate, esp the form obtained by leaching wood ash **2** another name for **potassium hydroxide 3** potassium chemically combined in certain compounds: *chloride of potash* [C17 *pot ashes,* translation of obsolete Dutch *potaschen;* so called because originally obtained by evaporating the lye of wood ashes in pots]

potassium (pə'tæsɪəm) *n* a light silvery element of the alkali metal group that is highly reactive and rapidly oxidizes in air; occurs principally in carnallite and sylvite. It is used when alloyed with sodium as a cooling medium in nuclear reactors and its compounds are widely used, esp in fertilizers. Symbol: K; atomic no: 19; atomic wt: 39.0983; valency: 1; relative density: 0.862; melting pt: 63.71°C; boiling pt: 759°C [C19: New Latin *potassa* potash] > po'tassic *adj*

potassium-argon dating *n* a technique for determining the age of minerals based on the occurrence in natural potassium of a small fixed amount of radioisotope ^{40}K that decays to the stable argon isotope ^{40}Ar with a half-life of 1.28×10^9 years. Measurement of the ratio of these isotopes thus gives the age of the mineral

potassium bromide *n* a white crystalline soluble substance with a bitter saline taste used in making photographic papers and plates and in medicine as a sedative. Formula: KBr

potassium carbonate *n* a white odourless substance used in making glass and soft soap and as an alkaline cleansing agent. Formula: K_2CO_3

potassium chlorate *n* a white crystalline soluble substance used in fireworks, matches, and explosives, and as a disinfectant and bleaching agent. Formula: $KClO_3$

potassium cyanide *n* a white poisonous granular soluble solid substance used in photography and in extracting gold from its ores. Formula: KCN

potassium hydrogen tartrate *n* a colourless or white soluble crystalline salt used in baking powders, soldering fluxes, and laxatives. Formula: $KHC_4H_4O_6$. Also called (not in technical usage): **cream of tartar**

potassium hydroxide *n* a white deliquescent alkaline solid used in the manufacture of soap, liquid shampoos, and detergents. Formula: KOH

potassium nitrate *n* a colourless or white crystalline compound used in gunpowders, pyrotechnics, fertilizers, and as a preservative for foods, esp as a curing salt for ham, sausages, etc (**E252**). Formula: KNO_3. Also called: **saltpetre, nitre**

potassium permanganate *n* a dark purple poisonous odourless soluble crystalline solid, used as a bleach, disinfectant, and antiseptic. Formula: $KMnO_4$

potation (pəʊ'teɪʃən) *n* **1** the act of drinking **2** a drink or draught, esp of alcoholic drink [C15: from Latin *pōtātiō* a drinking, from *pōtāre* to drink]

potato (pə'teɪtəʊ) *n, pl* -toes **1** Also called: **Irish potato, white potato a** a solanaceous plant, *Solanum tuberosum,* of South America: widely cultivated for its edible tubers **b** the starchy oval tuber of this plant, which has a brown or red skin and is cooked and eaten as a vegetable **2** any of various similar plants, esp the sweet potato [C16: from Spanish *patata* white potato, from Taino *batata* sweet potato]

potato beetle *n* another name for the **Colorado beetle**

potato chip *n* **1** (*usually plural*) another name for **chip** (sense 4) **2** (*usually plural*) *US & Canadian* a very thin slice of potato fried and eaten cold as a snack. Also called (in Britain and certain other countries): **crisp**

potato crisp *n* (*usually plural*) another name for **crisp** (sense 10)

potbelly ('pɒt,bɛlɪ) *n, pl* -lies 1 a protruding or distended belly 2 a person having such a belly

potboiler ('pɒt,bɔɪlə) *n* *informal* a literary or artistic work of little merit produced quickly in order to make money

pot-bound *adj* (of a pot plant) having grown to fill all the available root space and therefore lacking room for continued growth

potboy ('pɒt,bɔɪ) *or* **potman** ('pɒtmən) *n, pl* -boys *or* -men *chiefly Brit* (esp formerly) a youth or man employed at a public house to serve beer, etc

potch (pɒtʃ) *n* *chiefly Austral slang* inferior quality opal used in jewellery for mounting precious opals [c20: of uncertain origin]

poteen *or* **poitín** (pɒ'tiːn) *n* (in Ireland) illicit spirit, often distilled from potatoes [c19: from Irish *poitín* little pot, from *pota* pot]

Potemkin *or* **Potyomkin** (pɒ'tɛmkɪn; *Russian* pa'tjɔmkɪn) *n* 1 **Grigori Aleksandrovich** (grɪ'gɔrɪj alɪk'sandrəvɪtʃ). 1739–91, Russian soldier and statesman; lover of Catherine II, whose favourite he remained until his death 2 apparently impressive but actually sham or artificial: *North Korea's Potemkin hospital* [c20: after the Russian statesman Grigori Aleksandrovich *Potemkin* (1739–91), who is reputed to have erected sham villages along the route of the Empress Catherine II's 1787 tour of the Crimea]

potent ('pəʊtᵊnt) *adj* 1 possessing great strength; powerful 2 (of arguments, etc) persuasive or forceful 3 influential or authoritative 4 tending to produce violent physical or chemical effects: *a potent poison* 5 (of a male) capable of having sexual intercourse [c15: from Latin *potēns* able, from *posse* to be able] > 'potently *adv* > 'potency *or* 'potence *n* [c16: from Latin *potentia* power, from *posse* to be able]

potentate ('pəʊtᵊn,teɪt) *n* a person who possesses great power or authority, esp a ruler or monarch [c14: from Late Latin *potentātus* ruler, from Latin: rule, command, from *potens* powerful, from *posse* to be able]

potential (pə'tɛnʃəl) *adj* 1 a possible but not yet actual b (*prenominal*) capable of being or becoming but not yet in existence; latent 2 *grammar* (of a verb or form of a verb) expressing possibility, as English *may* and *might* 3 an archaic word for **potent**¹ ▷ *n* 4 latent but unrealized ability or capacity: *Jones has great potential as a sales manager* 5 *grammar* a potential verb or verb form 6 short for **electric potential** [c14: from Old French *potencial*, from Late Latin *potentiālis*, from Latin *potentia* power] > po'tentially *adv*

potential difference *n* the difference in electric potential between two points in an electric field; the work that has to be done in transferring unit positive charge from one point to the other, measured in volts. Symbol: U, ΔV *or* Δφ Abbreviation: pd

potential energy *n* the energy of a body or system as a result of its position in an electric, magnetic, or gravitational field. It is measured in joules (SI units), electronvolts, ergs, etc. Symbol: Ep, V, U *or* φ Abbreviation: PE

potentiality (pə,tɛnʃɪ'ælɪtɪ) *n, pl* -ties 1 latent or inherent capacity or ability for growth, fulfilment, etc 2 a person or thing that possesses such a capacity

potentiate (pə'tɛnʃɪ,eɪt) *vb* (*tr*) 1 to cause to be potent 2 *med* to increase (the individual action or effectiveness) of two drugs by administering them in combination with each other

potentilla (,pəʊtᵊn'tɪlə) *n* any rosaceous plant or shrub of the N temperate genus *Potentilla*, having five-petalled flowers [c16: New Latin, from Medieval Latin: garden valerian, from Latin *potēns* powerful, from **POTENT**]

potentiometer (pə,tɛnʃɪ'ɒmɪtə) *n* 1 an instrument for determining a potential difference or electromotive force by measuring the fraction of it that balances a standard electromotive force 2 a device with three terminals, two of which are connected to a resistance wire and the third to a brush moving along the wire, so that a variable potential can be tapped off: used in electronic circuits, esp as a volume control ▷ Sometimes shortened to: **pot** > po,tenti'ometry *n*

potful ('pɒtfʊl) *n* the amount held by a pot

pother ('pɒðə) *n* 1 a commotion, fuss, or disturbance 2 a choking cloud of smoke, dust, etc ▷ *vb* 3 to make or be troubled or upset [c16: of unknown origin]

potherb ('pɒt,hɜːb) *n* any plant having leaves, flowers, stems, etc, that are used in cooking for seasoning and flavouring or are eaten as a vegetable

pothole ('pɒt,həʊl) *n* 1 *geography* a a deep hole in limestone areas resulting from action by running water. See also **sinkhole** (sense 1) b a circular hole in the bed of a river produced by abrasion 2 a deep hole, esp one produced in a road surface by wear or weathering

potholing ('pɒt,həʊlɪŋ) *n* *Brit* a sport in which participants explore underground caves > 'pot,holer *n*

pothook ('pɒt,hʊk) *n* 1 a curved or S-shaped hook used for suspending a pot over a fire 2 a long hook used for lifting hot pots, lids, etc 3 an S-shaped mark, often made by children when learning to write

pothouse ('pɒt,haʊs) *n* *Brit* (formerly) a small tavern or pub

pothunter ('pɒt,hʌntə) *n* 1 a person who hunts for food or for profit without regard to the rules of sport 2 *informal* a person who enters competitions for the sole purpose of winning prizes

potion ('pəʊʃən) *n* 1 a drink, esp of medicine, poison, or some supposedly magic beverage 2 a rare word for **beverage** [c13: via Old French from Latin *pōtiō* a drink, especially a poisonous one, from *pōtāre* to drink]

Potiphar ('pɒtɪfə) *n* *Old Testament* one of Pharaoh's officers, who bought Joseph as a slave (Genesis 37:36)

potlatch ('pɒt,lætʃ) *n* *anthropol* a competitive ceremonial activity among certain North American Indians, esp the Kwakiutl, involving a lavish distribution of gifts and the destruction of property to emphasize the wealth and status of the chief or clan [c19: from Chinook, from Nootka *patshatl* a giving, present]

pot luck *n* *informal* 1 a whatever food happens to be available without special preparation b (*as modifier*) 2 whatever is available (esp in the phrase **take pot luck**)

pot marigold *n* a Central European and Mediterranean plant, *Calendula officinalis*, grown for its rayed orange-and-yellow showy flowers, the petals of which were formerly used to colour food: family *Asteraceae* (composites)

Potomac (pə'təʊmək) *n* a river in the E central US, rising in the Appalachian Mountains of West Virginia: flows northeast, then generally southeast to Chesapeake Bay. Length (from the confluence of headstreams): 462 km (287 miles)

potometer (pə'tɒmɪtə) *n* an apparatus that measures the rate of water uptake by a plant or plant part [from Latin *pōtāre* to drink + -**METER**]

potoroo (,pɒtə'ruː) *n* another name for **kangaroo rat** [from a native Australian language]

Potosí (*Spanish* poto'si) *n* a city in S Bolivia, at an altitude of 4066 m (13 340 ft): one of the highest cities in the world; developed with the discovery of local silver in 1545; tin mining; university (1571). Pop: 144 000 (2005 est)

potpourri (,pəʊ'pʊərɪ) *n, pl* -ris 1 a collection of mixed flower petals dried and preserved in a pot to scent the air 2 a collection of unrelated or disparate items; miscellany 3 a medley of popular tunes 4 a stew of meat and vegetables [c18: from French, literally: rotten pot, translation of Spanish *olla podrida* miscellany]

pot roast *n* meat, esp beef, that is browned and cooked slowly in a covered pot with very little water, often with vegetables added

Potsdam ('pɒtsdæm; *German* 'pɔtsdam) *n* a city in Germany, the capital of Brandenburg on the Havel River: residence of Prussian kings and German emperors and scene of the **Potsdam Conference** of 1945, at which the main Allied powers agreed on a plan to occupy Germany at the end of the Second World War. Pop: 144 979 (2003 est)

potsherd ('pɒt,ʃɜːd) *or* **potshard** ('pɒt,ʃɑːd) *n* a broken fragment of pottery [c14: from **POT**¹ + *schoord* piece of broken crockery; see **SHARD**]

pot shot *n* 1 a chance shot taken casually, hastily, or without careful aim **2** a shot fired to kill game in disregard of the rules of sport **3** a shot fired at quarry within easy range, often from an ambush

pot still *n* a type of still used in distilling whisky in which heat is applied directly to the pot in which the wash is contained

pottage ('pɒtɪdʒ) *n* a thick meat or vegetable soup [c13: from Old French *potage* contents of a pot, from *pot* POT¹]

potted ('pɒtɪd) *adj* **1** placed or grown in a pot **2** cooked or preserved in a pot: *potted shrimps* **3** *informal* summarized or abridged: *a potted version of a novel*

potter¹ ('pɒtə) *n* a person who makes pottery

potter² ('pɒtə) *or esp US and Canadian* **putter** *chiefly Brit vb* **1** (*intr*; often foll by *about* or *around*) to busy oneself in a desultory though agreeable manner **2** (*intr*; often foll by *along* or *about*) to move with little energy or direction: *to potter about town* **3** (*tr*; usually foll by *away*) to waste (time): *to potter the day away* ▷ *n* **4** the act of pottering [c16 (in the sense: to poke repeatedly): from Old English *potian* to thrust; see PUT] > 'potterer *or esp US & Canadian* 'putterer

Potter ('pɒtə) *n* **1** (**Helen**) Beatrix. 1866–1943, British author and illustrator of children's animal stories, such as *The Tale of Peter Rabbit* (1902) **2** Dennis (**Christopher George**). 1935–94, British dramatist. His TV plays include *Pennies from Heaven* (1978), *The Singing Detective* (1986), and *Blackeyes* (1989) **3** Paulus. 1625–54, Dutch painter, esp of animals **4** Stephen. 1900–70, British humorist and critic. Among his best-known works are *Gamesmanship* (1947) and *One-Upmanship* (1952), on the art of achieving superiority over others

Potteries ('pɒtərɪz) *pl n* the Potteries (*sometimes functioning as singular*) a region of W central England, in Staffordshire, in which the china and earthenware industries are concentrated

potter's field *n* **1** US a cemetery where the poor or unidentified are buried at the public expense **2** *New Testament* the land bought by the Sanhedrin with the money paid for the betrayal of Jesus (which Judas had returned to them) to be used as a burial place for strangers and the friendless poor (Acts 1:19; Matthew 27:7)

potter's wheel *n* a device with a horizontal rotating disc, on which clay is shaped into pots, bowls, etc, by hand

pottery ('pɒtərɪ) *n, pl* -teries **1** articles, vessels, etc, made from earthenware and dried and baked in a kiln **2** a place where such articles are made **3** the craft or business of making such articles Related adjective: **fictile** [c15: from Old French *poterie*, from *potier* potter, from *pot* POT¹]

potting shed ('pɒtɪŋ) *n* a building in which plants are set in flowerpots and in which empty pots, potting compost, etc, are stored

pottle ('pɒtᵊl) *n* **1** *archaic* a liquid measure equal to half a gallon **2** NZ a plastic or cardboard container for foods such as yoghurt, fruit salad, or cottage cheese [c14: *potel*, from Old French: a small POT¹]

potto ('pɒtəʊ) *n, pl* -tos **1** a short-tailed prosimian primate, *Perodicticus potto*, having vertebral spines protruding through the skin in the neck region, native to tropical forests in West and Central Africa: family *Lorisidae* **2** another name for **kinkajou** [c18: of West African origin; compare Wolof *pata* type of tail-less monkey]

Pott's disease (pɒts) *n* a disease of the spine, usually caused by tubercular infection and characterized by weakening and gradual disintegration of the vertebrae and the intervertebral discs [c18: named after Percivall Pott (1714–88), English surgeon]

Pott's fracture *n* a fracture of the lower part of the fibula, usually with dislocation of the ankle [c18: see POTT'S DISEASE]

potty¹ ('pɒtɪ) *adj* -tier, -tiest *Brit informal* **1** foolish or slightly crazy **2** trivial or insignificant **3** (foll by *about* or *on*) very keen (about) [c19: perhaps from POT¹] > 'pottiness *n*

potty² ('pɒtɪ) *n, pl* -ties a child's word for **chamber pot**

POTUS ('pəʊtəs) *n* acronym for *informal* (in the US)

President of the United States

Potyomkin (*Russian* pa'tjɔmkɪn) *n* a variant spelling of **Potemkin**

pouch (paʊtʃ) *n* **1** a small flexible baglike container: *a tobacco pouch* **2** a saclike structure in any of various animals, such as the abdominal receptacle marsupium in marsupials or the cheek fold in rodents **3** *anatomy* any sac, pocket, or pouchlike cavity or space in an organ or part **4** another word for **mailbag** **5** a Scot word for **pocket** ▷ *vb* **6** (*tr*) to place in or as if in a pouch **7** to arrange or become arranged in a pouchlike form **8** (*tr*) (of certain birds and fishes) to swallow [c14: from Old Norman French *pouche*, from Old French *poche* bag; see POKE²] > 'pouchy *adj*

pouf *or* **pouffe** (puːf) *n* **1** a large solid cushion, usually cylindrical or cubic in shape, used as a seat **2 a** a woman's hair style, fashionable esp in the 18th century, in which the hair is piled up in rolled puffs **b** a pad set in the hair to make such puffs **3** (puf, puːf) *Brit derogatory, slang* less common spellings of **poof** [c19: from French; see PUFF]

poulard *or* **poularde** ('puːlɑːd) *n* a hen that has been spayed for fattening. See **capon** [c18: from Old French *pollarde*, from *polle* hen; see PULLET]

Poulenc (*French* pulɛ̃:k) *n* **Francis** (frãsis). 1899–1963, French composer; a member of Les Six. His works include the operas *Les Mamelles de Tirésias* (1947) and *Dialogues des Carmélites* (1957), and the ballet *Les Biches* (1924)

poult (pəʊlt) *n* the young of a gallinaceous bird, esp of domestic fowl [c15: syncopated variant of *poulet* PULLET]

poulterer ('pəʊltərə) *n Brit* another word for **poultryman** [c17: from obsolete *poulter*, from Old French *pouletier*, from *poulet* PULLET]

poultice ('pəʊltɪs) *n* **1** Also called: **cataplasm** *med* a local moist and often heated application for the skin consisting of substances such as kaolin, linseed, or mustard, used to improve the circulation, treat inflamed areas, etc **2** *Austral slang* a large sum of money, esp a debt [c16: from earlier *pultes*, from Latin *puls* a thick porridge]

poultry ('pəʊltrɪ) *n* domestic fowls collectively [c14: from Old French *pouletrie*, from *pouletier* poultry-dealer]

poultryman ('pəʊltrɪmən) *or* **poulterer** *n, pl* -trymen *or* -terers **1** Also called: **chicken farmer** a person who rears domestic fowls, esp chickens, for their eggs or meat **2** a dealer in poultry, esp one who sells the dressed carcasses

pounce¹ (paʊns) *vb* **1** (*intr*; often foll by *on* or *upon*) to spring or swoop, as in capturing prey ▷ *n* **2** the act of pouncing; a spring or swoop **3** the claw of a bird of prey [c17: apparently from Middle English *punson* pointed tool; see PUNCHEON²] > 'pouncer *n*

pounce² (paʊns) *n* **1 a** a very fine resinous powder, esp of cuttlefish bone, formerly used to dry ink or sprinkled over parchment or unsized writing paper to stop the ink from running **2** a fine powder, esp of charcoal, that is tapped through perforations in paper corresponding to the main lines of a design in order to transfer the design to another surface **3** (*as modifier*): *a pounce box* ▷ *vb* **4** to dust (paper) with pounce **5** to transfer (a design) by means of pounce [c18: from Old French *ponce*, from Latin *pūmex* PUMICE] > 'pouncer *n*

pouncet box ('paʊnsɪt) *n* a box with a perforated top used for containing perfume [c16 *pouncet*, perhaps alteration of *pounced* punched, perforated; see POUNCE¹]

pound¹ (paʊnd) *vb* **1** (when *intr*, often foll by *on* or *at*) to strike heavily and often **2** (*tr*) to beat to a pulp; pulverize **3** (*tr*) to instil by constant drilling: *to pound Latin into him* **4** (*tr*; foll by *out*) to produce, as by typing heavily **5** to walk (the pavement, street, etc) repeatedly: *he pounded the pavement looking for a job* **6** (*intr*) to throb heavily ▷ *n* **7** a heavy blow; thump **8** the act of pounding [Old English *pūnian*; related to Dutch *puin* rubble] > 'pounder *n*

pound² (paʊnd) *n* **1** an avoirdupois unit of weight that is divided into 16 ounces and is equal to 0.453 592 kilograms. Abbreviation: **lb¹ 2** a troy unit of weight divided into 12 ounces equal to 0.373 242 kilograms **3 a** the standard monetary unit of the United Kingdom, the Channel Islands, the Isle of Man, and various UK overseas territories, divided into 100 pence **b** (*as modifier*): *a pound coin* **4** the standard monetary unit of the following countries **a** Cyprus: divided into 100 cents **b** Egypt: divided into 100 piastres **c** Syria: divided into 100 piastres **5** Also called: **pound Scots** a former Scottish monetary unit originally worth an English pound but later declining in value to 1 shilling 8 pence **6** Also called: **punt** the former standard monetary unit of the Republic of Ireland, divided into 100 pence; replaced by the euro in 2002 [Old English *pund,* from Latin *pondō* pound; related to German *Pfund* pound, Latin *pondus* weight]

pound³ (paʊnd) *n* **1** an enclosure, esp one maintained by a public authority, for keeping officially removed vehicles or distrained goods or animals, esp stray dogs **2** a place where people are confined **3 a** a trap for animals **b** a trap or keepnet for fish ▷ *vb* **4** (*tr*) to confine in or as if in a pound; impound, imprison, or restrain [C14: from Late Old English *pund-* as in *pundfeald* PINFOLD]

Pound (paʊnd) *n* **Ezra (Loomis).** 1885–1972, US poet, translator, and critic, living in Europe. Indicted for treason by the US government (1945) for pro-Fascist broadcasts during World War II, he was committed to a mental hospital until 1958. He was a founder of imagism and championed the early work of such writers as T. S. Eliot, Joyce, and Hemingway. His life work, the *Cantos* (1925–70), is an unfinished sequence of poems, which incorporates mythological and historical materials in several languages as well as political, economic, and autobiographical elements

poundage (ˈpaʊndɪdʒ) *n* **1** a tax, charge, or other payment of so much per pound of weight **2** a tax, charge, or other payment of so much per pound sterling **3** a weight expressed in pounds

poundal (ˈpaʊndəl) *n* the fps unit of force; the force that imparts an acceleration of 1 foot per second per second to a mass of 1 pound. 1 poundal is equivalent to 0.1382 newton or 1.382×10^4 dynes [C19: from POUND² + QUINTAL]

pound cost averaging *n* stock exchange a method of accumulating capital by investing a fixed sum in a particular security at regular intervals, in order to achieve an average purchase price below the arithmetic average of the market prices on the purchase dates

-pounder (ˈpaʊndə) *n* (*in combination*) **1** something weighing a specified number of pounds: *a 200-pounder* **2** something worth a specified number of pounds: *a ten-pounder* **3** a gun that discharges a shell weighing a specified number of pounds: *a two-pounder*

pound sterling *n* See pound² (sense 3)

pour (pɔː) *vb* **1** to flow or cause to flow in a stream **2** (*tr*) to issue, emit, etc, in a profuse way **3** Also called: **pour with rain** (*intr*; often foll by *down*) to rain heavily: *it's pouring down outside* **4** (*intr*) to move together in large numbers; swarm **5** (*intr*) to serve tea, coffee, etc: *shall I pour?* **6** it never rains but it pours events, esp unfortunate ones, come together or occur in rapid succession **7 pour cold water on** *informal* to be unenthusiastic about or discourage **8 pour oil on troubled waters** to try to calm a quarrel, etc ▷ *n* **9** a pouring; downpour [C13: of unknown origin] ▷ ˈpourer *n*

⊛ **USAGE** The verbs *pour* and *pore* are sometimes
⊛ confused: *she poured cream over her strudel; she pored* (not
⊛ *poured*) *over the manuscript*

pourboire *French* (purbwar) *n* a tip; gratuity [literally: for drinking]

poussin (*French* pusē) *n* a young chicken reared for eating [from French]

Poussin (*French* pusē) *n* **Nicolas** (nikɔla). 1594–1665, French painter, regarded as a leader of French classical painting. He is best known for the austere historical and biblical paintings and landscapes of his later years

pout¹ (paʊt) *vb* **1** to thrust out (the lips), as when sullen, or (of the lips) to be thrust out **2** (*intr*) to swell out; protrude **3** (*tr*) to utter with a pout ▷ *n* **4** (*sometimes* **the pouts**) a fit of sullenness **5** the act or state of pouting [C14: of uncertain origin; compare Swedish dialect *puta* inflated, Danish *pude* PILLOW] ▷ ˈpoutingly *adv*

▷ ˈpouty *adj*

pout² (paʊt) *n, pl* **pout** *or* **pouts** **1** short for **eelpout 2** any of various gadoid food fishes, esp the bib (also called **whiting pout**) **3** any of certain other stout-bodied fishes [Old English *-pūte* as in *ǣlepūte* eelpout; related to Dutch *puit* frog]

pouter (ˈpaʊtə) *n* **1** a person or thing that pouts **2** a breed of domestic pigeon with a large crop capable of being greatly puffed out

poutine (puːˈtiːn) *n* Canadian a dish of chipped potatoes topped with curd cheese and a tomato-based sauce [from Canadian French]

poverty (ˈpɒvətɪ) *n* **1** the condition of being without adequate food, money, etc **2** scarcity or dearth: *a poverty of wit* **3** a lack of elements conducive to fertility in land or soil [C12: from Old French *poverté,* from Latin *paupertās* restricted means, from *pauper* POOR]

poverty-stricken *adj* suffering from extreme poverty

poverty trap *n* the situation of being unable to escape poverty because of being dependent on state benefits, which are reduced by the same amount as any extra income gained

pow (paʊ) *interj* an exclamation imitative of a collision, explosion, etc

POW *abbreviation* prisoner of war

powan (ˈpaʊən) *n* a freshwater whitefish, *Coregonus clupeoides,* occurring in some Scottish lakes [C17: Scottish variant of POLLAN]

powder (ˈpaʊdə) *n* **1** a solid substance in the form of tiny loose particles **2** any of various preparations in this form, such as gunpowder, face powder, or soap powder **3** fresh loose snow, esp when considered as skiing terrain **4 take a powder** US & Canadian slang to run away or disappear ▷ *vb* **5** to turn into powder; pulverize **6** (*tr*) to cover or sprinkle with or as if with powder [C13: from Old French *poldre,* from Latin *pulvis* dust] ▷ ˈpowderer *n* ▷ ˈpowdery *adj*

powder blue *n* **a** a dusty pale blue colour **b** (*as adjective*)

powder burn *n* a superficial burn of the skin caused by a momentary intense explosion, esp of gunpowder

powder flask *n* a small flask or case formerly used to carry gunpowder

powder horn *n* a powder flask consisting of the hollow horn of an animal

powder keg *n* **1** a small barrel used to hold gunpowder **2** *informal* a potential source or scene of violence, disaster, etc

powder metallurgy *n* the science and technology of producing solid metal components from metal powder by compaction and sintering

powder monkey *n* (formerly) a boy who carried powder from the magazine to the guns on warships

powder puff *n* a soft pad or ball of fluffy material used for applying cosmetic powder to the skin

powder room *n* *euphemistic* a lavatory for women in a restaurant, department store, etc

powdery mildew *n* a plant disease characterized by a superficial white powdery growth on stems and leaves, caused by parasitic ascomycetous fungi of the family *Erysiphaceae:* affects the rose, aster, apple, vine, oak, etc

Powell (ˈpaʊəl) *n* **1** (ˈpəʊəl) **Anthony (Dymoke)** (ˈdɪmək). 1905–2000, British novelist, best known for his sequence of novels under the general title *A Dance to the Music of Time* (1951–75) **2 Cecil Frank.** 1903–69, British physicist, who was awarded the Nobel prize for physics in 1950 for his discovery of the pi-meson **3 Colin (Luther)** (ˈcəʊlɪn). born 1937, US politician and general; Republican secretary of state (2001–05) **4 Earl,** known as **Bud Powell.** 1924–1966, US modern-jazz pianist **5 (John) Enoch.** 1912–98, British politician. An outspoken opponent of Commonwealth immigration into Britain and of British membership of the Common Market (now the European Union), in 1974 he resigned from the Conservative Party, returning to Parliament as a United Ulster Unionist Council member (1974–87) **6 Michael.** 1905–90, British film writer, producer, and director, best known for his collaboration (1942–57) with Emeric Pressburger. Films include *The Life and Death of Colonel Blimp* (1943), *A Matter of Life and Death* (1946), *The Red Shoes* (1948), *The Tales of*

Hoffman (1951), and *Peeping Tom* (1960)

power ('paʊə) n 1 ability or capacity to do something 2 (*often plural*) a specific ability, capacity, or faculty 3 political, financial, social, etc, force or influence 4 control or dominion or a position of control, dominion, or authority 5 a state or other political entity with political, industrial, or military strength 6 a person who exercises control, influence, or authority: *he's a power in the state* 7 a prerogative, privilege, or liberty 8 a legal authority to act, esp in a specified capacity, for another b the document conferring such authority 9 a a military force b military potential 10 *maths* a the value of a number or quantity raised to some exponent b another name for **exponent** (sense 4) 11 *statistics* the probability of rejecting the null hypothesis in a test when it is false. The power of a test of a given null depends on the particular alternative hypothesis against which it is tested 12 *physics, engineering* a measure of the rate of doing work expressed as the work done per unit time. It is measured in watts, horsepower, etc. Symbol: P 13 a the rate at which electrical energy is fed into or taken from a device or system. It is expressed, in a direct-current circuit, as the product of current and voltage and, in an alternating-current circuit, as the product of the effective values of the current and voltage and the cosine of the phase angle between them. It is measured in watts b (*as modifier*): *a power amplifier* 14 the ability to perform work 15 a mechanical energy as opposed to manual labour b (*as modifier*): *a power mower* 16 a particular form of energy: *nuclear power* 17 a a measure of the ability of a lens or optical system to magnify an object, equal to the reciprocal of the focal length. It is measured in dioptres b another word for **magnification** 18 *informal* a large amount or quantity: *a power of good* 19 (*plural*) the sixth of the nine orders into which the angels are traditionally divided in medieval angelology 20 in one's power (*often foll by an infinitive*) able or allowed (to) 21 in someone's power under the control or sway of someone 22 the powers that be the established authority or administration ▷ *vb* (*tr*) 23 to give or provide power to 24 to fit (a machine) with a motor or engine 25 (*intr*) *slang* to travel with great speed or force [C13: from Anglo-Norman *poer*, from Vulgar Latin *potēre* (unattested), from Latin *posse* to be able]

power amplifier n *electronics* an amplifier that is usually the final amplification stage in a device and is designed to give the required power output

power-assisted *adj* (of the steering or brakes in a motor vehicle) helped by mechanical power

powerboat ('paʊə,bəʊt) n a boat propelled by an inboard or outboard motor

powerboating ('paʊə,bəʊtɪŋ) n the sport of driving powerboats in racing competitions

power broker n a person with power and influence, esp one who operates behind the scenes

power cut n a temporary interruption or reduction in the supply of electrical power to a particular area. Sometimes shortened to: **cut**

power dive n 1 a steep dive by an aircraft with its engines at high power ▷ *vb* **power-dive** 2 to cause (an aircraft) to perform a power dive or (of an aircraft) to perform a power dive

power dressing n a style of dressing in severely tailored suits, adopted by some women executives to project an image of efficiency

powerful ('paʊəfʊl) *adj* 1 having great power, force, potency, or effect 2 extremely effective or efficient in action: *a powerful drug; a powerful lens* 3 *dialect* large or great: *a powerful amount of trouble* ▷ *adv* 4 *dialect* extremely; very: *he ran powerful fast* > '**powerfully** *adv* > '**powerfulness** n

powerhouse ('paʊə,haʊs) n 1 an electrical generating station or plant 2 *informal* a forceful or powerful person or thing

powerless ('paʊəlɪs) *adj* without power or authority > '**powerlessly** *adv* > '**powerlessness** n

powerlifting ('paʊə,lɪftɪŋ) n a form of weightlifting in which contestants compete in the dead lift, squat, and bench press > '**power,lifter** n

power lunch n a high-powered business meeting conducted over lunch

power of attorney n 1 legal authority to act for another person in certain specified matters 2 the document conferring such authority ▷ Also called: **letter of attorney**

power pack n a device for converting the current from a supply into direct or alternating current at the voltage required by a particular electrical or electronic device

power plant n 1 the complex, including machinery, associated equipment, and the structure housing it, that is used in the generation of power, esp electrical power 2 the equipment supplying power to a particular machine or for a particular operation or process

power play n 1 behaviour or tactics intended to magnify a person's influence or power 2 the use of brute strength or force of numbers in order to achieve an objective

power point n an electrical socket mounted on or recessed into a wall

power-sharing n a political arrangement in which opposing groups in a society participate in government

power station n an electrical generating station

power steering n a form of steering used on vehicles, where the torque applied to the steering wheel is augmented by engine power. Also called: **power-assisted steering**

power structure n the structure or distribution of power and authority in a community

power walking n walking at a brisk pace while pumping the arms as part of an aerobic exercise routine

power yoga n a form of yoga involving aerobic exercises and constant strenuous movement

Powhatan (,paʊhə'tæn, paʊ'hætən) n American Indian name *Wahunsonacock*. died 1618, American Indian chief of a confederacy of tribes; father of Pocahontas

powhiri (,pəʊ'fiːrɪ) n NZ a Māori ceremony of welcome, esp to a marae [Māori]

powwow ('paʊ,waʊ) n 1 a talk, conference, or meeting 2 a magical ceremony of certain North American Indians, usually accompanied by feasting and dancing 3 (among certain North American Indians) a medicine man 4 a meeting of or negotiation with North American Indians ▷ *vb* 5 (*intr*) to hold a powwow [C17: from Algonquian; related to Natick *pauwau* one who practises magic, Narraganset *powwaw*]

Powys[1] ('paʊɪs) n a county in E Wales, formed in 1974 from most of Breconshire, Montgomeryshire, and Radnorshire. Administrative centre: Llandrindod Wells. Pop: 129 300 (2003 est). Area: 5077 sq km (1960 sq miles)

Powys[2] ('pəʊɪs) n 1 **John Cowper** ('kuːpə). 1872–1963, British novelist, essayist, and poet, who spent much of his life in the US His novels include *Wolf Solent* (1929), *A Glastonbury Romance* (1932), and *Owen Glendower* (1940) 2 his brother, **Llewelyn**. 1884–1939, British essayist and journalist 3 his brother, **T(heodore) F(rancis)**. 1875–1953, British novelist and short-story writer, noted for such religious fables as *Mr Weston's Good Wine* (1927) and *Unclay* (1931)

pox (pɒks) n 1 any disease characterized by the formation of pustules on the skin that often leave pockmarks when healed 2 the pox an informal name for **syphilis** 3 a pox on someone (*interjection*) *archaic* an expression of intense disgust or aversion for someone [C15: changed from *pocks*, plural of POCK]

Poznań (*Polish* 'pɔznajn) n a city in W Poland, on the Warta River: the centre of Polish resistance to German rule (1815–1918, 1939–45). Pop: 661 000 (2005 est). German name: Posen

Pozsony ('pɔʒɒnj) n the Hungarian name for **Bratislava**

pozzuolana (,pɒtswə'lɑːnə) *or* **pozzolana** (,pɒtsə'lɑːnə) n 1 a type of porous volcanic ash used in making hydraulic cements 2 any of various artificial substitutes for this ash used in cements ▷ Also called: **puzzolana** [C18: from Italian: of POZZUOLI]

Pozzuoli (*Italian* pot'tswɔːli) n a port in SW Italy, in Campania on the **Gulf of Pozzuoli** (an inlet of the Bay of Naples): in a region of great volcanic activity; founded in the 6th century BC by the Greeks. Pop: 78 754 (2001)

pp[1] *abbreviation* **1** past participle **2** (in formal correspondence) per pro [Latin *per procurationem*: by delegation to] **3** privately printed ▷ *symbol for* **4** *music* pianissimo: an instruction to play very quietly
● **USAGE** In formal correspondence, when Brenda Smith
● is signing on behalf of Peter Jones, she should write
● *Peter Jones pp* (or *per pro*) *Brenda Smith*, not the other way
● about

pp[2] *or* **PP** *abbreviation* **1** parcel post **2** prepaid **3** post-paid **4** (in prescriptions) post prandium [Latin: after a meal]

PP *abbreviation* **1** Parish Priest **2** past President

pp. *abbreviation* pages

P2P *abbreviation* peer-to-peer

ppd *abbreviation* **1** post-paid **2** prepaid

PPE *abbreviation* **1** philosophy, politics, and economics: a university course **2** personal protective equipment: clothing and equipment used to ensure personal safety in the workplace

ppm *abbreviation* **1** *chem* parts per million **2** Also called: PPM peak programme meter

PPP *abbreviation* **1** purchasing power parity: a rate of exchange between two currencies that gives them equal purchasing powers in their own economies **2** private-public partnership: an agreement in which a private company commits skills or capital to a public-sector project for a financial return

ppr *or* **p.pr.** *abbreviation* present participle

PPS *abbreviation* **1** parliamentary private secretary **2** Also called: pps post postscriptum [(for sense 2) Latin: after postscript; additional postscript]

PQ *abbreviation* (in Canada) **1** (esp in postal addresses) Province of Quebec **2** Parti Québécois

PQE *or* **Pqe** *abbreviation* post-qualification experience

pr *abbreviation* **1** *pl* prs pair **2** paper **3** (in prescriptions) per rectum [Latin: through the rectum; to be inserted into the anus] **4** power

Pr *the chemical symbol for* praseodymium

PR *abbreviation* **1** proportional representation **2** public relations **3** Puerto Rico

Pr. *abbreviation* **1** Priest **2** Prince

practicable ('præktıkəb°l) *adj* **1** capable of being done; feasible **2** usable [c17: from French *praticable*, from *pratiquer* to practise; see PRACTICAL] > ,practica'bility *or* 'practicableness *n* > 'practicably *adv*
● **USAGE** See at **practical**

practical ('præktɪk°l) *adj* **1** of, involving, or concerned with experience or actual use; not theoretical **2** of or concerned with ordinary affairs, work, etc **3** adapted or adaptable for use **4** of, involving, or trained by practice **5** being such for all useful or general purposes; virtual ▷ *n* **6** an examination in the practical skills of a subject: *a science practical* [c17: from earlier *practic*, from French *pratique*, via Late Latin from Greek *praktikos*, from *prassein* to experience, negotiate, perform] > ,practi'cality *or* 'practicalness *n*
● **USAGE** A distinction is usually made between *practical*
● and *practicable*. *Practical* refers to a person, idea, project,
● etc, as being more concerned with or relevant to
● practice than theory: *he is a very practical person; the idea*
● *had no practical application*. Practicable refers to a project
● or idea as being capable of being done or put into
● effect: *the plan was expensive, yet practicable*

practical joke *n* a prank or trick usually intended to make the victim appear foolish > practical joker *n*

practically ('præktɪkəlı, -klı) *adv* **1** virtually; almost: *it has rained practically every day* **2** in actuality rather than in theory: *what can we do practically to help?*

practice ('præktɪs) *n* **1** a usual or customary action or proceeding: *it was his practice to rise at six; he made a practice of stealing stamps* **2** repetition or exercise of an activity in order to achieve mastery and fluency **3** the condition of having mastery of a skill or activity through repetition (esp in the phrases **in practice, out of practice**) **4** the exercise of a profession: *he set up practice as a lawyer* **5** the act of doing something: *he put his plans into practice* **6** the established method of conducting proceedings in a court of law ▷ *vb* **7** the US spelling of **practise** [c16: from Medieval Latin *practicāre* to practise, from Greek *praktikē* practical science, practical work, from *prattein* to do, act]

practise *or* US **practice** ('præktɪs) *vb* **1** to do or cause to do repeatedly in order to gain skill **2** (*tr*) to do (something) habitually or frequently: *they practise ritual murder* **3** to observe or pursue (something, such as a religion): *to practise Christianity* **4** to work at (a profession, job, etc): *he practises medicine* **5** (foll by *on* or *upon*) to take advantage of (someone, someone's credulity, etc) [c15: see PRACTICE]

practised *or* US **practiced** ('præktɪst) *adj* **1** expert; skilled; proficient **2** acquired or perfected by practice

practitioner (præk'tɪʃənə) *n* **1** a person who practises a profession or art **2** *Christian Science* a person authorized to practise spiritual healing [c16: from *practician*, from Old French *praticien*, from *pratiquer* to PRACTISE]

Prader-Willi syndrome (,prɑ:də'vɪlɪ) *n* a congenital condition characterized by obsessive eating, obesity, mental retardation, and small genitalia [c20: after Andrea *Prader* (1919–2001) and Heinrich *Willi* (1900–71), Swiss paediatricians]

Prado ('prɑ:dəʊ) *n* an art gallery in Madrid housing an important collection of Spanish paintings

prae- *prefix* an archaic variant of **pre-**

praedial *or* **predial** ('pri:dɪəl) *adj* **1** of or relating to land, farming, etc **2** attached to or occupying land [c16: from Medieval Latin *praediālis*, from Latin *praedium* farm, estate] > ,praedi'ality *or* ,predi'ality *n*

praesidium (prɪ'sɪdɪəm) *n* a variant spelling of presidium

praetor *or* **pretor** ('pri:tə, -tɔ:) *n* (in ancient Rome) any of several senior magistrates ranking just below the consuls [c15: from Latin: one who leads the way, probably from *praeīre*, from *prae-* before + *īre* to go] > prae'torial *or* pre'torial *adj* > 'praetorship *or* 'pretorship *n*

Praetorius (German prɛ'to:riʊs) *n* **Michael** ('mɪçaeːl). 1571–1621, German composer and musicologist, noted esp for his description of contemporary musical practices and instruments, *Syntagma musicum* (1615–19)

pragmatic (præg'mætɪk) *adj* **1** advocating behaviour that is dictated more by practical consequences than by theory or dogma **2** *philosophy* of or relating to pragmatism **3** involving everyday or practical business **4** of or concerned with the affairs of a state or community **5** *rare* interfering or meddlesome; officious [c17: from Late Latin *prāgmaticus*, from Greek *prāgmatikos* from *pragma* act, from *prattein* to do] > prag,mati'cality *n* > prag'matically *adv*

pragmatic sanction *n* an edict, decree, or ordinance issued with the force of fundamental law by a sovereign

pragmatism ('prægmə,tɪzəm) *n* **1** action or policy dictated by consideration of the immediate practical consequences rather than by theory or dogma **2** *philosophy* **a** the doctrine that the content of a concept consists only in its practical applicability **b** the doctrine that truth consists not in correspondence with the facts but in successful coherence with experience > 'pragmatist *n*, *adj* > ,pragma'tistic *adj*

Prague (prɑ:g) *n* the capital and largest city of the Czech Republic, on the Vltava River: a rich commercial centre during the Middle Ages; site of Charles University (1348) and a technical university (1707); scene of defenestrations (1419 and 1618) that contributed to the outbreak of the Hussite Wars and the Thirty Years' War respectively. Pop: 1 164 000 (2005 est). Czech name: Praha

Praha ('praha) *n* the Czech name for **Prague**

prairie ('prɛərɪ) *n* (*often plural*) a treeless grassy plain of the central US and S Canada. See **pampas, steppe, savanna** [c18: from French, from Old French *prairie*, from Latin *prātum* meadow]

prairie chicken, prairie fowl, prairie grouse *or* **prairie hen** *n* either of two mottled brown-and-white grouse, *Tympanuchus cupido* or *T. pallidicinctus*, of North America

prairie crocus *n Canadian* a spring flower of the buttercup family

prairie dog *n* any of several gregarious sciurine rodents of the genus *Cynomys*, such as *C. ludovicianus*, that live in large complex burrows in the prairies of North America. Also called: **prairie marmot**

prairie-dogging *n informal* (in an open-plan office) the practice of looking over the top of one's partition in order to discover the source of or reason for a commotion [C20: after the actions of a PRAIRIE DOG, which stands on its hind legs to get a better view of something]

prairie oyster *n* **1** a drink consisting of raw unbeaten egg, vinegar or Worcester sauce (**Worcester oyster**), salt, and pepper: a supposed cure for a hangover **2** the testicles of a bull calf cooked and eaten

Prairie Provinces *pl n* the Canadian provinces of Manitoba, Saskatchewan, and Alberta, which lie in the N Great Plains region of North America: the chief wheat and petroleum producing area of Canada

prairie schooner *n chiefly US* a horse-drawn covered wagon similar to but smaller than a Conestoga wagon, used in the 19th century to cross the prairies of North America

prairie wolf *n* another name for **coyote** (sense 1)

praise (preɪz) *n* **1** the act of expressing commendation, admiration, etc **2** the extolling of a deity or the rendering of homage and gratitude to a deity **3 sing someone's praises** to commend someone highly ▷ *vb* (*tr*) **4** to express commendation, admiration, etc, for **5** to proclaim or describe the glorious attributes of (a deity) with homage and thanksgiving [C13: from Old French *preisier*, from Late Latin *pretiāre* to esteem highly, from Latin *pretium* prize; compare PRIZE², PRECIOUS] > 'praiser *n*

praiseworthy ('preɪz,wɜːðɪ) *adj* deserving of praise; commendable > 'praise,worthily *adv* > 'praise,worthiness *n*

Prakrit ('prɑːkrɪt) *n* any of the vernacular Indic languages as distinguished from Sanskrit: spoken from about 300 BC to the Middle Ages [C18: from Sanskrit *prākrta* original, from *pra-* before + *kr* to do, make + *-ta* indicating a participle] > Pra'kritic *adj*

praline ('prɑːliːn) *n* **1** a confection of nuts with caramelized sugar, used in desserts and as a filling for chocolates **2** Also called: **sugared almond** a sweet consisting of an almond encased in sugar [C18: from French, named after César de Choiseul, comte de Plessis-Praslin (1598–1675), French field marshal whose chef first concocted it]

pralltriller ('prɑːl,trɪlə) *n* an ornament used in 18th-century music consisting of an inverted mordent with an added initial upper note [German: bouncing trill]

pram¹ (præm) *n Brit* a cot-like four-wheeled carriage for a baby. US and Canadian term: **baby carriage** [C19: shortened and altered from PERAMBULATOR]

pram² (prɑːm) *n nautical* a light tender with a flat bottom and a bow formed from the ends of the side and bottom planks meeting in a small raised transom [C16: from Middle Dutch *prame*; related to Old Frisian *prām*]

prance (prɑːns) *vb* **1** (*intr*) to swagger or strut **2** (*intr*) to caper, gambol, or dance about **3** (*intr*) (of a horse) to move with high lively springing steps **4** (*tr*) to cause to prance ▷ *n* **5** the act or an instance of prancing [C14 *prauncen*; perhaps related to German *prangen* to be in full splendour; compare Danish (dialect) *pransk* lively, spirited, used of a horse] > 'prancer *n* > 'prancingly *adv*

prandial ('prændɪəl) *adj facetious* of or relating to a meal [C19: from Latin *prandium* meal, luncheon]

Prandtl (German 'prantəl) *n* **Ludwig** ('luːtvɪç). 1875–1953, German physicist, who made important contributions to aerodynamics and aeronautics

prang (præŋ) *chiefly Brit slang* ▷ *n* **1** an accident or crash in an aircraft, car, etc **2** an aircraft bombing raid ▷ *vb* **3** to crash or damage (an aircraft, car, etc) **4** to damage (a town, etc) by bombing [C20: possibly imitative of an explosion; perhaps related to Malay *perang* war, fighting]

prank¹ (præŋk) *n* a mischievous trick or joke, esp one in which something is done rather than said [C16: of unknown origin] > 'prankish *adj*

prank² (præŋk) *vb* **1** (*tr*) to dress or decorate showily or gaudily **2** (*intr*) to make an ostentatious display [C16: from Middle Dutch *pronken*; related to German *Prunk* splendour, *prangen* to be in full splendour]

Prasad (prə'sɑːd) *n* **Rajendra** (rɑː'dʒendrə). 1884–1963, Indian statesman and journalist; first president of the Republic of India (1950–62)

prase (preɪz) *n* a light green translucent variety of chalcedony [C14: from French, from Latin *prasius* a leek-green stone, from Greek *prasios*, from *prason* a leek]

praseodymium (,preɪzɪəʊ'dɪmɪəm) *n* a malleable ductile silvery-white element of the lanthanide series of metals. It occurs principally in monazite and bastnaesite and is used with other rare earths in carbon-arc lights and as a pigment in glass. Symbol: Pr; atomic no: 59; atomic wt: 140.90765; valency: 3; relative density: 6.773; melting pt: 931°C; boiling pt: 3520°C [C20: New Latin, from Greek *prasios* of a leek-green colour + DIDYMIUM]

prat (præt) *n slang* an incompetent or ineffectual person: often used as a term of abuse [C20: probably special use of C16 *prat* buttocks, of unknown origin]

Pratchett ('prætʃɪt) *n* **Terence** (**David John**), known as *Terry*. born 1948, British writer, noted for his comic fantasy novels in the *Discworld* series

prate (preɪt) *vb* **1** (*intr*) to talk idly and at length; chatter **2** (*tr*) to utter in an idle or empty way ▷ *n* **3** idle or trivial talk; prattle; chatter [C15: of Germanic origin; compare Middle Dutch *prāten*, Icelandic and Norwegian *prata*, Danish *prate*] > 'prater *n* > 'pratingly *adv*

pratfall ('præt,fɔːl) *n US & Canadian slang* a fall upon one's buttocks [C20: from C16 *prat* buttocks (of unknown origin) + FALL]

pratincole ('prætɪŋ,kəʊl, 'preɪ-) *n* any of various swallow-like shore birds of the southern Old World genus *Glareola* and related genera, esp *G. pratincola*, having long pointed wings, short legs, and a short bill: family *Glareolidae*, order *Charadriiformes* [C18: from New Latin *pratincola* field-dwelling, from Latin *prātum* meadow + *incola* inhabitant]

Prato (Italian 'prɑːto) *n* a walled city in central Italy, in Tuscany: woollen industry. Pop: 172 499 (2001)

prattle ('prætəl) *vb* **1** (*intr*) to talk in a foolish or childish way; babble **2** (*tr*) to utter in a foolish or childish way ▷ *n* **3** foolish or childish talk [C16: from Middle Low German *pratelen* to chatter; see PRATE] > 'prattler *n*

prau (praʊ) *n* another word for **proa**

prawn (prɔːn) *n* **1** any of various small edible marine decapod crustaceans of the genera *Palaemon*, *Penaeus*, etc, having a slender flattened body with a long tail and two pairs of pincers **2 come the raw prawn** *Austral informal* to attempt deception [C15: of obscure origin]

prawn-sandwich *adj Informal* characterizing or belonging to the type of spectator at a football match who is motivated to attend more by the corporate hospitality available than a true devotion to a particular club: *the prawn-sandwich brigade*

praxis ('præksɪs) *n, pl* **praxises** *or* **praxes** ('præksiːz) **1** the practice and practical side of a profession or field of study, as opposed to the theory **2** a practical exercise **3** accepted practice or custom [C16: via Medieval Latin from Greek: deed, action, from *prassein* to do]

Praxiteles (præk'sɪtɪ,liːz) *n* 4th-century BC Greek sculptor: his works include statues of Hermes at Olympia, which survives, and of Aphrodite at Cnidus

pray (preɪ) *vb* **1** (when *intr*, often foll by *for*; when *tr*, *usually takes a clause as object*) to utter prayers (to God or other object of worship): *we prayed to God for the sick child* **2** (when *tr*, *usually takes a clause as object or an infinitive*) to make an earnest entreaty (to or for); beg or implore: *she prayed to be allowed to go; leave, I pray you* ▷ *interj* **3** *archaic* I beg you; please: *pray, leave me alone* [C13: from Old French *preier*, from Latin *precārī* to implore, from *prex* an entreaty; related to Old English *frignan*, Old High German *frāgēn* to ask, Old Norse *fregna* to enquire]

prayer¹ (preə) *n* **1** a personal communication or petition addressed to a deity, esp in the form of supplication, adoration, praise, contrition, or thanksgiving **2** a similar personal communication that does not involve adoration, addressed to beings venerated as being closely associated with a deity, such as angels or saints **3** the practice of praying: *prayer is our solution to human problems* **4** (*often plural*) a form of devotion, either public or private, spent mainly or wholly praying: *morning prayers* **5** (*capital when part of a recognized name*) a form of words used in praying: *the Lord's Prayer* **6** an object or benefit prayed for **7** an earnest request, petition, or entreaty [C13 *preiere*, from Old French, from Medieval Latin *precāria*, from Latin *precārius* obtained by begging, from *prex* prayer]

prayer² ('preɪə) *n* a person who prays > 'prayerful *adj* > 'prayerfully *adv* > 'prayerfulness *n*

prayer book (preə) *n ecclesiast* a book containing the prayers used at church services or recommended for private devotions

prayer rug (preə) *n* the small carpet on which a Muslim kneels and prostrates himself while saying his prayers. Also called: prayer mat

prayer wheel (preə) *n Buddhism* (esp in Tibet) a wheel or cylinder inscribed with or containing prayers, each revolution of which is counted as an uttered prayer, so that such prayers can be repeated by turning it

praying mantis *or* **praying mantid** *n* another name for mantis

PRB *abbreviation* (after the signatures of Pre-Raphaelite painters) Pre-Raphaelite Brotherhood

PRC *abbreviation* People's Republic of China

pre- *prefix* before in time, rank, order, position, etc: *predate*; *pre-eminent*; *premeditation*; *prefrontal*; *preschool* [from Latin *prae-*, from *prae* before, beforehand, in front]

preach (priːtʃ) *vb* **1** to make known (religious truth) or give religious or moral instruction or exhortation in (sermons) **2** to advocate (a virtue, action, etc), esp in a moralizing way [C13: from Old French *prechier*, from Church Latin *praedicāre*, from Latin: to proclaim in public; see PREDICATE]

preacher ('priːtʃə) *n* **1** a person who has the calling and function of preaching the Christian Gospel, esp a Protestant clergyman **2** a person who preaches

preachify ('priːtʃɪˌfaɪ) *vb* -fies, -fying, -fied (*intr*) *informal* to preach or moralize in a tedious manner > 'preachi,fying *n*

preachment ('priːtʃmənt) *n* **1** the act of preaching **2** a tedious or pompous sermon or discourse

preachy ('priːtʃɪ) *adj* preachier, preachiest *informal* inclined to or marked by preaching

preacquisition profit (ˌpriːækwɪ'zɪʃən) *n* the retained profit of a company earned before a takeover and therefore not eligible for distribution as a dividend to the shareholders of the acquiring company

preamble (priː'æmbəl) *n* **1** a preliminary or introductory statement, esp attached to a statute or constitution setting forth its purpose **2** a preliminary or introductory conference, event, fact, etc [C14: from Old French *préambule*, from Late Latin *praeambulum* walking before, from Latin *prae-* before + *ambulāre* to walk]

preamplifier (priː'æmplɪˌfaɪə) *n* an electronic amplifier used to improve the signal-to-noise ratio of an electronic device. It boosts a low-level signal to an intermediate level before it is transmitted to the main amplifier

prebend ('prɛbənd) *n* **1** the stipend assigned by a cathedral or collegiate church to a canon or member of the chapter **2** the land, tithe, or other source of such a stipend **3** a less common word for **prebendary 4** *Church of England* the office, formerly with an endowment, of a prebendary [C15: from Old French *prébende*, from Medieval Latin *praebenda* pension, stipend, from Latin *praebēre* to offer, supply, from *prae* forth + *habēre* to have, offer] > prebendal (prɪ'bɛndəl) *adj*

prebendary ('prɛbəndərɪ, -drɪ) *n, pl* -daries **1** a canon or member of the chapter of a cathedral or collegiate church who holds a prebend **2** *Church of England* an honorary canon with the title of prebendary

prebiotic (ˌpriːbaɪ'ɒtɪk) *adj* occurring or existing before the emergence of life

prebiotics (ˌpriːbaɪ'ɒtɪks) *n* natural substances in some foods that encourage the growth of healthy bacteria in the gut

Precambrian *or* **Pre-Cambrian** (priː'kæmbrɪən) *adj* **1** of, denoting, or formed in the earliest geological era, which lasted for about 4 000 000 000 years before the Cambrian period ▷ *n* **2** the Precambrian the Precambrian era

precancel (priː'kænsəl) *vb* -cels, -celling, -celled *or US*

-cels, -celing, -celed (*tr*) to cancel (postage stamps) before placing them on mail

precancerous *adj* (esp of cells) displaying characteristics that may develop into cancer

precarious (prɪ'kɛərɪəs) *adj* **1** liable to failure or catastrophe; insecure; perilous **2** *archaic* dependent on another's will [C17: from Latin *precārius* obtained by begging (hence, dependent on another's will), from *prex* PRAYER¹] > pre'cariously *adv* > pre'cariousness *n*

precast ('priːˌkɑːst) *adj* (esp of concrete when employed as a structural element in building) cast in a particular form before being used

precaution (prɪ'kɔːʃən) *n* **1** an action taken to avoid a dangerous or undesirable event **2** caution practised beforehand; circumspection [C17: from French, from Late Latin *praecautiō*, from Latin *praecavēre* to guard against, from *prae* before + *cavēre* to beware] > pre'cautionary *or* pre'cautional *adj*

precautionary principle *n* the precept that an action should not be taken if the consequences are uncertain and potentially dangerous

precede (prɪ'siːd) *vb* **1** to go or be before (someone or something) in time, place, rank, etc **2** (*tr*) to preface or introduce [C14: via Old French from Latin *praecēdere* to go before, from *prae* before + *cēdere* to move]

precedence ('prɛsɪdəns) *or* **precedency** *n* **1** the act of preceding or the condition of being precedent **2** the ceremonial order or priority to be observed by persons of different stations on formal occasions: *the officers are seated according to precedence* **3** a right to preferential treatment: *I take precedence over you*

precedent *n* ('prɛsɪdənt) **1** *law* a judicial decision that serves as an authority for deciding a later case **2** an example or instance used to justify later similar occurrences ▷ *adj* (prɪ'siːdᵊnt, 'prɛsɪdənt) **3** preceding

precedented ('prɛsɪˌdɛntɪd) *adj* (of a decision, etc) supported by having a precedent

precedential (ˌprɛsɪ'dɛnʃəl) *adj* **1** of, involving, or serving as a precedent **2** having precedence

preceding (prɪ'siːdɪŋ) *adj* (*prenominal*) going or coming before; former

precentor (prɪ'sɛntə) *n* **1** a cleric who directs the choral services in a cathedral **2** a person who leads a congregation or choir in the sung parts of church services [C17: from Late Latin *praecentor* leader of the music, from *prae* before + *canere* to sing] > precentorial (ˌpriːsɛn'tɔːrɪəl) *adj* > pre'centor,ship *n*

precept ('priːsɛpt) *n* **1** a rule or principle for action **2** a guide or rule for morals; maxim **3** a direction, esp for a technical operation **4** *law* **a** a writ or warrant **b** (in England) an order to collect money under a rate [C14: from Latin *praeceptum* maxim, injunction, from *praecipere* to admonish, from *prae* before + *capere* to take] > pre'ceptive *adj* > pre'ceptively *adv*

preceptor (prɪ'sɛptə) *n rare* a tutor or instructor > preceptorial (ˌpriːsɛp'tɔːrɪəl) *or* pre'ceptoral *adj* > pre'ceptress *fem n*

precession (prɪ'sɛʃən) *n* **1** the act of preceding **2** See **precession of the equinoxes 3** the motion of a spinning body, such as a top, gyroscope, or planet, in which it wobbles so that the axis of rotation sweeps out a cone [C16: from Late Latin *praecessiō* a going in advance, from Latin *praecēdere* to PRECEDE] > pre'cessional *adj* > pre'cessionally *adv*

precession of the equinoxes *n* the slightly earlier occurrence of the equinoxes each year due to the slow continuous westward shift of the equinoctial points along the ecliptic by 50 seconds of arc per year. It is caused by the precession of the earth's axis around the ecliptic pole, with a period of 25 800 years

precinct ('priːsɪŋkt) *n* **1 a** an enclosed area or building marked by a fixed boundary such as a wall **b** such a boundary **2** an area in a town, often closed to traffic, that is designed or reserved for a particular purpose: *a shopping precinct; pedestrian precinct* **3** *US* **a** a district of a city for administrative or police purposes **b** the precinct responsible for such a district [C15: from Medieval Latin *praecinctum* (something) surrounded, from Latin *praecingere* to gird around, from *prae* before, around +

cingere to gird]

precincts ('priːsɪŋkts) *pl n* the surrounding region or area

preciosity (ˌprɛʃɪˈɒsɪtɪ) *n*, *pl* -ties fastidiousness or affectation, esp in speech or manners

precious ('prɛʃəs) *adj* **1** beloved; dear; cherished **2** very costly or valuable **3** very fastidious or affected, as in speech, manners, etc **4** *informal* worthless: *you and your precious ideas!* ▷ *adv* **5** *informal* (intensifier): *there's precious little time* [c13: from Old French *precios*, from Latin *pretiōsus* valuable, from *pretium* price, value] > 'preciously *adv* > 'preciousness *n*

precious metal *n* any of the metals gold, silver, or platinum

precious stone *n* any of certain rare minerals, such as diamond, ruby, sapphire, emerald, or opal, that are highly valued as gemstones

precipice ('prɛsɪpɪs) *n* **a** the steep sheer face of a cliff or crag **b** the cliff or crag itself [c16: from Latin *praecipitium* steep place, from *praeceps* headlong] > 'precipiced *adj*

precipitant (prɪˈsɪpɪtənt) *adj* **1** hasty or impulsive; rash **2** rushing or falling rapidly or without heed **3** abrupt or sudden ▷ *n* **4** *chem* a substance or agent that causes a precipitate to form > pre'cipitance *or* pre'cipitancy *n*

precipitate (prɪˈsɪpɪˌteɪt) **1** (*tr*) to cause to happen too soon or sooner than expected; bring on **2** to throw or fall from or as from a height **3** to cause (moisture) to condense and fall as snow, rain, etc, or (of moisture, rain, etc) to condense and fall thus **4** *chem* to undergo or cause to undergo a process in which a dissolved substance separates from solution as a fine suspension of solid particles ▷ *adj* (prɪˈsɪpɪtɪt) **5** rushing ahead **6** done rashly or with undue haste **7** sudden and brief ▷ *n* (prɪˈsɪpɪtɪt) **8** *chem* a precipitated solid in its suspended form or after settling or filtering [c16: from Latin *praecipitāre* to throw down headlong, from *praeceps* headlong, steep, from *prae* before, in front + *caput* head] > pre'cipitable *adj* > pre,cipita'bility *n* > pre'cipitately *adv* > pre'cipi,tator *n*

precipitation (prɪˌsɪpɪˈteɪʃən) *n* **1** *meteorol* **a** rain, snow, sleet, dew, etc, formed by condensation of water vapour in the atmosphere **b** the deposition of these on the earth's surface **2** the production or formation of a chemical precipitate **3** the act of precipitating or the state of being precipitated **4** rash or undue haste

precipitous (prɪˈsɪpɪtəs) *adj* **1** resembling a precipice or characterized by precipices **2** very steep **3** hasty or precipitate > pre'cipitously *adv* > pre'cipitousness *n*

 • USAGE The use of *precipitous* to mean *hasty* is thought
 • by some people to be incorrect

precis *or* **précis** ('preɪsiː) *n*, *pl* precis *or* précis ('preɪsiːz) **1** a summary of the essentials of a text; abstract ▷ *vb* **2** (*tr*) to make a precis of [c18: from French: PRECISE]

precise (prɪˈsaɪs) *adj* **1** strictly correct in amount or value: *a precise sum* **2** designating a certain thing and no other; particular: *this precise location* **3** using or operating with total accuracy: *precise instruments* **4** strict in observance of rules, standards, etc: *a precise mind* [c16: from French *précis*, from Latin *praecīdere* to curtail, from *prae* before + *caedere* to cut] > pre'ciseness *n*

precisely (prɪˈsaɪslɪ) *adv* **1** in a precise manner ▷ *sentence substitute* **2** exactly: used to confirm a statement by someone else

precision (prɪˈsɪʒən) *n* **1** the quality of being precise; accuracy **2** (modifier) characterized by or having a high degree of exactness: *precision grinding; a precision instrument* [c17: from Latin *praecīsiō* a cutting off; see PRECISE] > pre'cisionism *n* > pre'cisionist *n*

preclude (prɪˈkluːd) *vb* (*tr*) **1** to exclude or debar **2** to make impossible, esp beforehand [c17: from Latin *praeclūdere* to shut up, from *prae* in front, before + *claudere* to close] > preclusion (prɪˈkluːʒən) *n* > preclusive (prɪˈkluːsɪv) *adj*

precocial (prɪˈkəʊʃəl) *adj* **1** (of the young of some species of birds after hatching) covered with down, having open eyes, and capable of leaving the nest within a few days of hatching ▷ *n* **2** a precocial bird ▷ See **altricial** [c19: see PRECOCIOUS]

precocious (prɪˈkəʊʃəs) *adj* **1** ahead in development,

such as the mental development of a child **2** *botany* (of plants, fruit, etc) flowering or ripening early [c17: from Latin *praecox* early maturing, from *prae* early + *coquere* to ripen] > pre'cociously *adv*

precognition (ˌpriːkɒɡˈnɪʃən) *n* *psychol* the alleged ability to foresee future events [c17: from Late Latin *praecognitiō* foreknowledge, from *praecognoscere* to foresee, from *prae* before + *cognoscere* to know, ascertain] > precognitive (priːˈkɒɡnɪtɪv) *adj*

preconceive (ˌpriːkənˈsiːv) *vb* (*tr*) to form an idea of beforehand; conceive of ahead in time

preconception (ˌpriːkənˈsɛpʃən) *n* **1** an idea or opinion formed beforehand **2** a bias; prejudice

precondition (ˌpriːkənˈdɪʃən) *n* **1** a necessary or required condition; prerequisite ▷ *vb* **2** (*tr*) *psychol* to present successively two stimuli to (an organism) without reinforcement so that they become associated; if a response is then conditioned to the second stimulus on its own, the same response will be evoked by the first stimulus

preconize *or* **preconise** ('priːkəˌnaɪz) *vb* (*tr*) **1** to announce or commend publicly **2** (of the pope) to approve the appointment of (a nominee) to one of the higher dignities in the Roman Catholic Church [c15: from Medieval Latin *praecōnizāre* to make an announcement, from Latin *praecō* herald] > ˌpreconi'zation *or* ˌpreconi'sation *n*

precursor (prɪˈkɜːsə) *n* **1** a person or thing that precedes and shows or announces someone or something to come; harbinger **2** a predecessor or forerunner **3** a chemical substance that gives rise to another more important substance [c16: from Latin *praecursor* one who runs in front, from *praecurrere*, from *prae* in front + *currere* to run]

precursory (prɪˈkɜːsərɪ) *or* **precursive** *adj* **1** serving as a precursor **2** preliminary or introductory

pred. *abbreviation* predicate

predacious *or* **predaceous** (prɪˈdeɪʃəs) *adj* (of animals) habitually hunting and killing other animals for food [c18: from Latin *praeda* plunder; compare PREDATORY] > pre'daciousness, pre'daceousness *or* predacity (prɪˈdæsɪtɪ) *n*

predate (priːˈdeɪt) *vb* (*tr*) **1** to affix a date to (a document, paper, etc) that is earlier than the actual date **2** to assign a date to (an event, period, etc) that is earlier than the actual or previously assigned date of occurrence **3** to be or occur at an earlier date than; precede in time

predation (prɪˈdeɪʃən) *n* a relationship between two species of animal in a community, in which one (the predator) hunts, kills, and eats the other (the prey)

predator ('prɛdətə) *n* **1** any carnivorous animal **2** a predatory person or thing

predatory ('prɛdətərɪ, -trɪ) *adj* **1** *zoology* another word for **predacious** (sense 1) **2** of, involving, or characterized by plundering, robbing, etc [c16: from Latin *praedātōrius* rapacious, from *praedārī* to pillage, from *praeda* booty] > 'predatorily *adv* > 'predatoriness *n*

predecease (ˌpriːdɪˈsiːs) *vb* to die before (some other person)

predecessor ('priːdɪˌsɛsə) *n* **1** a person who precedes another, as in an office **2** something that precedes something else **3** an ancestor; forefather [c14: via Old French from Late Latin *praedēcessor*, from *prae* before + *dēcēdere* to go away, from *dē* away + *cēdere* to go]

predella (prɪˈdɛlə; *Italian* preˈdɛlla) *n*, *pl* -le (-liː; *Italian* -le) **1** a painting or sculpture or a series of small paintings or sculptures in a long narrow strip forming the lower edge of an altarpiece or the face of an altar step or platform **2** a platform in a church upon which the altar stands [c19: from Italian: stool, step, probably from Old High German *bret* board]

predestinarian (ˌpriːdɛstɪˈnɛərɪən) *theol* ▷ *n* **1** a person who believes in divine predestination ▷ *adj* **2** of or relating to predestination or characterizing those who believe in it

predestinate *vb* (priːˈdɛstɪˌneɪt) **1** (*tr*) another word for **predestine** ▷ *adj* (priːˈdɛstɪnɪt, -ˌneɪt) **2** predestined or foreordained

predestination (priːˌdɛstɪˈneɪʃən) *n* **1** *theol* **a** the act of

God foreordaining every event from eternity **b** the doctrine or belief, esp associated with Calvin, that the final salvation of some of mankind is foreordained from eternity by God **2** the act of predestining or the state of being predestined

predestine (priːˈdɛstɪn) *or* **predestinate** *vb* (*tr*) **1** to foreordain; determine beforehand **2** *theol* (of God) to decree from eternity (any event, esp the final salvation of individuals) [C14: from Latin *praedestināre* to resolve beforehand, from *destināre* to determine, DESTINE]

predetermine (ˌpriːdɪˈtɜːmɪn) *vb* (*tr*) **1** to determine beforehand **2** to influence or incline towards an opinion beforehand; bias ▷ ˌprede,termiˈnation *n* ▷ ˌpredeˈterminative *adj*

predicable (ˈprɛdɪkəbᵊl) *adj* **1** capable of being predicated or asserted ▷ *n* **2** a quality, attribute, etc, that can be predicated **3** *logic obsolete* one of the five Aristotelian classes of predicates (**the five heads of predicables**), namely genus, species, difference, property, and relation [C16: from Latin *praedicābilis*, from *praedicāre* to assert publicly; see PREDICATE, PREACH] ▷ ˌpredicaˈbility *or* ˈpredicableness *n*

predicament (prɪˈdɪkəmənt) *n* **1** a perplexing, embarrassing, or difficult situation **2** (ˈprɛdɪkəmənt) *logic obsolete* one of Aristotle's ten categories of being [C14: from Late Latin *praedicāmentum* what is predicated, from *praedicāre* to announce, assert; see PREDICATE]

predicant (ˈprɛdɪkənt) *adj* **1** of or relating to preaching ▷ *n* **2** a member of a religious order founded for preaching, esp a Dominican [C17: from Latin *praedicāns* preaching, from *praedicāre* to say publicly; see PREDICATE]

predicate *vb* (ˈprɛdɪˌkeɪt) (*mainly tr*) **1** (*also intr; when tr, may take a clause as object*) to proclaim, declare, or affirm **2** to imply or connote **3** (foll by *on or upon*) to base or found (a proposition, argument, etc) **4** *logic* to assert or affirm (a property, characteristic, or condition) of the subject of a proposition ▷ *n* (ˈprɛdɪkɪt) **5** *grammar* the part of a sentence in which something is asserted or denied of the subject of a sentence; one of the two major components of a sentence, the other being the subject **6** *logic* an expression that is derived from a sentence by the deletion of a name ▷ *adj* (ˈprɛdɪkɪt) **7** of or relating to something that has been predicated [C16: from Latin *praedicāre* to assert publicly, from *prae* in front, in public + *dīcere* to say] ▷ ˌprediˈcation *n*

predicate calculus *n* the system of symbolic logic concerned not only with relations between propositions as wholes but also with the representation by symbols of individuals and predicates in propositions and with quantification over individuals. See also **propositional calculus**

predicative (prɪˈdɪkətɪv) *adj grammar* relating to or occurring within the predicate of a sentence: *a predicative adjective*. See **attributive** ▷ preˈdicatively *adv*

predict (prɪˈdɪkt) *vb* (*tr; may take a clause as object*) to state or make a declaration about in advance, esp on a reasoned basis; foretell [C17: from Latin *praedīcere* to mention beforehand, from *prae* before + *dīcere* to say] ▷ preˈdictable *adj* ▷ preˌdictaˈbility *or* preˈdictableness *n* ▷ preˈdictably *adv* ▷ preˈdictive *adj* ▷ preˈdictively *adv*

prediction (prɪˈdɪkʃən) *n* **1** the act of predicting **2** something predicted; a forecast, prophecy, etc

predigest (ˌpriːdaɪˈdʒɛst, -dɪ-) *vb* (*tr*) to treat (food) artificially to aid subsequent digestion in the body ▷ ˌprediˈgestion *n*

predikant *or* **predicant** (ˌprɛdɪˈkænt) *n* a minister in the Dutch Reformed Church, esp in South Africa [from Dutch, from Old French *predicant*, from Late Latin *praedicans* preaching, from *praedicāre* to PREACH]

predilection (ˌpriːdɪˈlɛkʃən) *n* a predisposition, preference, or bias [C18: from French *prédilection*, from Medieval Latin *praedīligere* to prefer, from Latin *prae* before + *dīligere* to love]

predispose (ˌpriːdɪˈspəʊz) *vb* (*tr*)(often foll by *to* or *towards*) to incline or make (someone) susceptible to something beforehand ▷ ˌpredisˈposal *n* ▷ ˌpredispoˈsition *n*

prednisolone (prɛdˈnɪsəˌləʊn) *n* a steroid drug derived from prednisone and having the same uses as cortisone

[C20: altered from PREDNISONE]

prednisone (ˈprɛdnɪˌsəʊn) *n* a steroid drug derived from cortisone and having the same uses [C20: perhaps from PRE(GNANT) + -D(IE)N(E) + (CORT)ISONE]

predominant (prɪˈdɒmɪnənt) *adj* **1** having superiority in power, influence, etc, over others **2** prevailing; prominent ▷ preˈdominance *or* preˈdominancy *n* ▷ preˈdominantly *adv*

predominate *vb* (prɪˈdɒmɪˌneɪt) **1** (*intr*; often foll by *over*) to have power, influence, or control **2** (*intr*) to prevail or preponderate ▷ *adj* (prɪˈdɒmɪnɪt) **3** another word for **predominant** [C16: from Medieval Latin *praedominārī*, from Latin *prae* before + *dominārī* to bear rule, domineer] ▷ preˈdominately *adv* ▷ preˌdomiˈnation *n*

pre-eclampsia (ˌpriːɪˈklæmpsɪə) *n pathol* a toxic condition of pregnancy characterized by high blood pressure, protein in the urine, abnormal weight gain, and oedema

pre-embryo (priːˈɛmbrɪəʊ) *n* the structure formed after fertilization of an ovum but before differentiation of embryonic tissue

pre-eminent (prɪˈɛmɪnənt) *adj* extremely eminent or distinguished; outstanding ▷ pre-ˈeminence *n* ▷ pre-ˈeminently *adv*

pre-empt (prɪˈɛmpt) *vb* **1** (*tr*) to acquire in advance of or to the exclusion of others; appropriate **2** (*tr*) *chiefly US* to occupy (public land) in order to acquire a prior right to purchase **3** (*intr*) *bridge* to make a high opening bid, often on a weak hand, to shut out opposition bidding ▷ pre-ˈemptor *n*

pre-emption (prɪˈɛmpʃən) *n* **1** *law* the purchase of or right to purchase property in advance of or in preference to others **2** *international law* the right of a government to intercept and seize for its own purposes goods or property of the subjects of another state while in transit, esp in time of war [C16: from Medieval Latin *praeemptiō*, from *praeemere* to buy beforehand, from *emere* to buy]

pre-emptive (prɪˈɛmptɪv) *adj* **1** of, involving, or capable of pre-emption **2** *bridge* (of a high bid) made to shut out opposition bidding **3** *military* designed to reduce or destroy an enemy's attacking strength before it can use it: *a pre-emptive strike*

preen (priːn) *vb* **1** (of birds) to maintain (feathers) in a healthy condition by arrangement, cleaning, and other contact with the bill **2** to dress or array (oneself) carefully; primp **3** (usually foll by *on*) to pride or congratulate (oneself) [C14 *preinen*, probably from *prunen*, influenced by *prenen* to prick, pin; suggestive of the pricking movement of the bird's beak] ▷ ˈpreener *n*

pre-exist *adj* occuring or existing previously ▷ ˌpre-exˈistence *n*

pref. *abbreviation* **1** preface **2** preference **3** preferred **4** prefix

prefab (ˈpriːˌfæb) *n* a building that is prefabricated, esp a small house

prefabricate (priːˈfæbrɪˌkeɪt) *vb* (*tr*) to manufacture sections of (a building), esp in a factory, so that they can be easily transported to and rapidly assembled on a building site ▷ preˌfabriˈcation *n*

preface (ˈprɛfɪs) *n* **1** a statement written as an introduction to a literary or other work, typically explaining its scope, intention, method, etc; foreword **2** anything introductory ▷ *vb* (*tr*) **3** to furnish with a preface **4** to serve as a preface to [C14: from Medieval Latin *praefātia*, from Latin *praefātiō* a saying beforehand, from *praefārī* to utter in advance, from *prae* before + *fārī* to say] ▷ ˈprefacer *n*

prefatory (ˈprɛfətərɪ, -trɪ) *or* **prefatorial** (ˌprɛfəˈtɔːrɪəl) *adj* of, involving, or serving as a preface; introductory [C17: from Latin *praefārī* to say in advance; see PREFACE]

prefect (ˈpriːfɛkt) *n* **1** (in France, Italy, etc) the chief administrative officer in a department **2** (in France, etc) the head of a police force **3** *Brit* a schoolchild appointed to a position of limited power over his fellows **4** (in ancient Rome) any of several magistrates or military commanders **5** *RC Church* one of two senior masters in a Jesuit school or college (the **prefect of studies** and the **prefect of discipline** or **first prefect**) [C14: from Latin

praefectus one put in charge, from *praeficere* to place in authority over, from *prae* before + *facere* to do, make] ▷ **prefectoral** (ˌpriːfɛkˈtɔːrɪəl) *adj*

prefecture (ˈpriːfɛkˌtjʊə) *n* **1** the office, position, or area of authority of a prefect **2** the official residence of a prefect in France, Italy, etc

prefer (prɪˈfɜː) *vb* **-fers**, **-ferring**, **-ferred 1** (*when tr, may take a clause as object or an infinitive*) to like better or value more highly: *I prefer to stand* **2** (*esp of the police*) to put (charges) before a court, judge, magistrate, etc, for consideration and judgment **3** (*tr, often passive*) to advance in rank over another or others; promote [C14: from Latin *praeferre* to carry in front, prefer, from *prae* in front + *ferre* to bear]
  ● USAGE Normally, *to* is used after *prefer* and *preferable*,
  ● not *than*: *I prefer Brahms to Tchaikovsky; a small income is*
  ● *preferable to no income at all.* However, *than* or *rather than*
  ● should be used to link infinitives: *I prefer to walk than/*
  ● *rather than to catch the train*

preferable (ˈprɛfərəbəl, ˈprɛfrəbəl) *adj* preferred or more desirable ▷ **ˈpreferably** *adv*
  ● USAGE Since *preferable* already means *more desirable*, one
  ● should not say something is *more preferable* or *most*
  ● *preferable*

preference (ˈprɛfərəns, ˈprɛfrəns) *n* **1** the act of preferring **2** something or someone preferred **3** *commerce* the granting of favour or precedence to particular foreign countries, as by levying differential tariffs

preference shares *pl n Brit & Austral* shares representing part of the capital issued by a company and entitling their holders to priority with respect to both net profit and net assets. Preference shares usually carry a definite rate of dividend that is generally lower than that declared on ordinary shares. US and Canadian name: **preferred stock**. See **ordinary shares, preferred ordinary shares**

preferential (ˌprɛfəˈrɛnʃəl) *adj* **1** showing or resulting from preference **2** giving, receiving, or originating from preference in international trade ▷ ˌprefer**ˈentially** *adv*

preferment (prɪˈfɜːmənt) *n* **1** the act of promoting or advancing to a higher position, office, etc **2** the state of being preferred for promotion or social advancement **3** the act of preferring

preferred ordinary shares *pl n Brit* shares issued by a company that rank between preference shares and ordinary shares in the payment of dividends. See **preference shares**

prefigure (priːˈfɪɡə) *vb* (*tr*) **1** to represent or suggest in advance **2** to imagine or consider beforehand ▷ ˌpreˈfigurement *n* ▷ ˌprefiguˈration *n* ▷ preˈfigurative *adj* ▷ preˈfiguratively *adv* ▷ preˈfigurativeness *n*

prefix *n* (ˈpriːfɪks) **1** *grammar* an affix that precedes the stem to which it is attached, as for example *un-* in *unhappy*. See **suffix** (sense 1) **2** something coming or placed before ▷ *vb* (priːˈfɪks, ˈpriːfɪks) (*tr*) **3** to put or place before **4** *grammar* to add (a morpheme) as a prefix to the beginning of a word ▷ prefixion (priːˈfɪkʃən) *n*

prefrontal (priːˈfrʌntəl) *adj* situated in, involving, or relating to the foremost part of the frontal lobe of the brain

preglacial (priːˈɡleɪsɪəl) *adj* formed or occurring before a glacial period, esp before the Pleistocene epoch

pregnable (ˈprɛɡnəbəl) *adj* capable of being assailed or captured [C15 *prenable*, from Old French *prendre* to take, from Latin *prehendere* to lay hold of, catch]

pregnancy (ˈprɛɡnənsɪ) *n, pl* **-cies 1** the state or condition of being pregnant **2** the period from conception to childbirth

pregnant (ˈprɛɡnənt) *adj* **1** carrying a fetus or fetuses within the womb **2** full of meaning or significance **3** inventive or imaginative **4** prolific or fruitful [C16: from Latin *praegnāns* with child, from *prae* before + *(g)nascī* to be born] ▷ ˈpregnantly *adv*

prehensile (prɪˈhɛnsaɪl) *adj* adapted for grasping, esp by wrapping around a support: *a prehensile tail* [C18: from French *préhensile*, from Latin *prehendere* to grasp] ▷ prehensility (ˌpriːhɛnˈsɪlɪtɪ) *n*

prehension (prɪˈhɛnʃən) *n* **1** the act of grasping **2** apprehension by the senses or the mind

prehistoric (ˌpriːhɪˈstɒrɪk) *or* **prehistorical** *adj* of or relating to man's development before the appearance of the written word ▷ ˌprehisˈtorically *adv* ▷ preˈhistory *n* ▷ prehistorian (ˌpriːhɪˈstɔːrɪən) *n*

pre-ignition (ˌpriːɪɡˈnɪʃən) *n* ignition of all or part of the explosive charge in an internal-combustion engine before the exact instant necessary for correct operation

prejudge (priːˈdʒʌdʒ) *vb* (*tr*) to judge beforehand, esp without sufficient evidence

prejudice (ˈprɛdʒʊdɪs) *n* **1** an opinion formed beforehand, esp an unfavourable one based on inadequate facts **2** the act or condition of holding such opinions **3** intolerance of or dislike for people of a specific race, religion, etc **4** disadvantage or injury resulting from prejudice **5** to the prejudice of to the detriment of **6** without prejudice *law* without dismissing or detracting from an existing right or claim ▷ *vb* (*tr*) **7** to cause to be prejudiced **8** to disadvantage or injure by prejudice [C13: from Old French *préjudice*, from Latin *praejūdicium* a preceding judgment, disadvantage, from *prae* before + *jūdicium* trial, sentence, from *jūdex* a judge]

prejudicial (ˌprɛdʒʊˈdɪʃəl) *adj* causing prejudice; detrimental or damaging ▷ ˌprejuˈdicially *adv*

prelacy (ˈprɛləsɪ) *n, pl* **-cies 1** Also called: **prelature** (ˈprɛlɪtʃə) **a** the office or status of a prelate **b** prelates collectively **2** Also called: **prelatism** (ˈprɛləˌtɪzəm) *often derogatory* government of the Church by prelates

prelapsarian (ˌpriːlæpˈsɛərɪən) *adj* characteristic of or relating to the human state or time before the Fall: *prelapsarian innocence*

prelate (ˈprɛlɪt) *n* a Church dignitary of high rank, such as a cardinal, bishop, or abbot [C13: from Old French *prélat*, from Church Latin *praelātus*, from Latin *praeferre* to hold in special esteem, PREFER] ▷ prelatic (prɪˈlætɪk) *or* preˈlatical *adj*

preliminaries (prɪˈlɪmɪnərɪz) *pl n* the full word for **prelims**

preliminary (prɪˈlɪmɪnərɪ) *adj* **1** (*usually prenominal*) occurring before or in preparation; introductory ▷ *n, pl* **-naries 2** a preliminary event or occurrence **3** an eliminating contest held before the main competition [C17: from New Latin *praelīmināris*, from Latin *prae* before + *līmen* threshold] ▷ preˈliminarily *adv*

prelims (ˈpriːlɪmz, prəˈlɪmz) *pl n* **1** Also called: **front matter** the pages of a book, such as the title page and contents, before the main text **2** the first public examinations taken for the bachelor's degree in some universities **3** (*in Scotland*) the school examinations taken as practice before public examinations [C19: a contraction of PRELIMINARIES]

preloved (ˈpriːˌlʌvd) *adj Austral informal* previously owned or used; second-hand

prelude (ˈprɛljuːd) *n* **1 a** a piece of music that precedes a fugue, or forms the first movement of a suite, or an introduction to an act in an opera, etc **b** (*esp for piano*) a self-contained piece of music **2** something serving as an introduction or preceding event, occurrence, etc ▷ *vb* **3** to serve as a prelude to (something) **4** (*tr*) to introduce by a prelude [C16: (n) from Medieval Latin *praelūdium*, from *prae* before + *-lūdium* entertainment, from Latin *lūdus* play; (vb) from Late Latin *praelūdere* to play beforehand, rehearse, from *lūdere* to play] ▷ preˈludial *adj*

premarital (priːˈmærɪtəl) *adj* (*esp of sexual relations*) occurring before marriage

premature (ˌprɛməˈtjʊə, ˈprɛməˌtjʊə) *adj* **1** occurring or existing before the normal or expected time **2** impulsive or hasty: *a premature judgment* **3** (*of an infant*) weighing less than 2500 g (5½ lbs) and usually born before the end of the full period of gestation [C16: from Latin *praemātūrus*, very early, from *prae* in advance + *mātūrus* ripe] ▷ ˌpremaˈturely *adv*

premedical (priːˈmɛdɪkəl) *adj* **1** of or relating to a course of study prerequisite for entering medical school **2** of or relating to a person engaged in such a course of study

premedication (ˌpriːmɛdɪˈkeɪʃən) *n surgery* any drugs administered to sedate and otherwise prepare a patient for general anaesthesia

premeditate (prɪˈmɛdɪˌteɪt) *vb* to plan or consider

P

(something, such as a violent crime) beforehand ▷ pre'medi,tator *n*

premeditation (prɪ,mɛdɪ'teɪʃən) *n* **1** *law* prior resolve to do some act or to commit a crime **2** the act of premeditating

premenstrual syndrome *or* **premenstrual tension** *n* a group of symptoms, including nervous tension and fluid retention, any of which may be experienced as a result of hormonal changes in the days before a menstrual period starts. Abbreviations: **PMS, PMT**

premier ('prɛmjə) *n* **1** another name for **prime minister 2** any of the heads of governments of the Canadian provinces and the Australian states **3** (*plural*) *Austral* the winners of a premiership ▷ *adj* (*prenominal*) **4** first in importance, rank, etc **5** first in occurrence; earliest [c15: from Old French: first, from Latin *prīmārius* principal, from *prīmus* first]

premiere ('prɛmɪ,ɛə, 'prɛmɪə) *n* **1** the first public performance of a film, play, opera, etc **2** the leading lady in a theatre company ▷ *vb* **3** to give or be the first public performance of [c19: from French, feminine of *premier* first]

premiership ('prɛmjəʃɪp) *n* **1** the office of premier **2 a** a championship competition held among a number of sporting clubs **b** a victory in such a championship

premillennialism (,priːmɪ'lɛnɪə,lɪzəm) *n* the doctrine or belief that the millennium will be preceded by the Second Coming of Christ ▷ ,premil'lennialist *n* ▷ ,premille'narian *n, adj*

Preminger ('prɛmɪndʒə) *n* Otto (Ludwig). 1906–86, US film director, born in Austria. His films include *Carmen Jones* (1954) and *Anatomy of a Murder* (1959)

premise *n* ('prɛmɪs) **1** Also called: **premiss** *logic* a statement that is assumed to be true for the purpose of an argument from which a conclusion is drawn ▷ *vb* (prɪ'maɪz, 'prɛmɪs) **2** (when *tr, may take a clause as object*) to state or assume (a proposition) as a premise in an argument, theory, etc [c14: from Old French *prémisse*, from Medieval Latin *praemissa* sent on before, from Latin *praemittere* to dispatch in advance, from *prae* before + *mittere* to send]

premises ('prɛmɪsɪz) *pl n* **1** a piece of land together with its buildings, esp considered as a place of business **2** *law* (in a deed, etc) the matters referred to previously; the aforesaid; the foregoing

premium ('priːmɪəm) *n* **1** an amount paid in addition to a standard rate, price, wage, etc; bonus **2** the amount paid or payable, usually in regular instalments, for an insurance policy **3** the amount above nominal or par value at which something sells **4** an offer of something free or at a specially reduced price as an inducement to buy a commodity or service **5** a prize given to the winner of a competition; award **6** *US* an amount sometimes charged for a loan of money in addition to the interest **7** great value or regard: *to put a premium on someone's services* **8** a fee, now rarely required, for instruction or apprenticeship in a profession or trade **9 at a premium a** in great demand or of high value, usually because of scarcity **b** above par [c17: from Latin *praemium* prize, booty, reward]

Premium Savings Bonds *pl n* (in Britain) bonds issued by the Treasury since 1956 for purchase by the public. No interest is paid but there is a monthly draw for cash prizes of various sums. Also called: **premium bonds**

premolar (pri:'məʊlə) *adj* **1** situated before a molar tooth ▷ *n* **2** any one of eight bicuspid teeth in the human adult, two situated on each side of both jaws between the first molar and the canine

premonition (,prɛmə'nɪʃən) *n* **1** an intuition of a future, usually unwelcome, occurrence; foreboding **2** an early warning of a future event; forewarning [c16: from Late Latin *praemonitiō*, from Latin *praemonēre* to admonish beforehand, from *prae* before + *monēre* to warn, advise] ▷ premonitory (prɪ'mɒnɪtərɪ, -trɪ) *adj*

Premonstratensian (,pri:mɒnstrə'tɛnsɪən) *n* **a** a member of a religious order founded at Prémontré in N France in 1120 by St Norbert (about 1080–1134) **b** (*as modifier*): *a Premonstratensian canon* [c17: from Medieval Latin (*locus*) *praemonstrātus* the place foreshown, because

it was said to have been prophetically pointed out by St Norbert]

prenatal (pri:'neɪtəl) *adj* **1** occurring or present before birth; during pregnancy ▷ *n* **2** *informal* a prenatal examination ▷ Also called: **antenatal**

prenominal (pri:'nɒmɪnəl) *adj* placed before a noun, esp (of an adjective or sense of an adjective) used only before a noun

prentice ('prɛntɪs) *n* an archaic word for **apprentice**

prenup ('pri:ˌnʌp) *n Informal* a prenuptial agreement

prenuptial agreement *n* a contract made between a man and woman before they marry, agreeing on the distribution of their assets in the event of divorce

preoccupation (pri:,ɒkjʊ'peɪʃən) *or* **preoccupancy** (pri:'ɒkjʊpənsɪ) *n* **1** the state of being preoccupied, esp mentally **2** something that holds the attention or preoccupies the mind

preoccupied (pri:'ɒkjʊ,paɪd) *adj* **1** engrossed or absorbed in something, esp one's own thoughts **2** already or previously occupied

preoccupy (pri:'ɒkjʊ,paɪ) *vb* -pies, -pying, -pied (*tr*) **1** to engross the thoughts or mind of **2** to occupy before or in advance of another [c16: from Latin *praeoccupāre* to capture in advance, from *prae* before + *occupāre* to seize, take possession of]

preordain (,pri:ɔː'deɪn) *vb* (*tr*) to ordain, decree, or appoint beforehand

prep (prɛp) *n* **1** *informal* short for **preparation** (sense 5) *or* (chiefly *US*) **preparatory school** ▷ *vb* preps, prepping, prepped **2** (*tr*) to prepare (a patient) for a medical operation or procedure

prep. *abbreviation* **1** preparation **2** preparatory **3** preposition

preparation (,prɛpə'reɪʃən) *n* **1** the act or process of preparing **2** the state of being prepared; readiness **3** (*often plural*) a measure done in order to prepare for something; provision: *to make preparations for something* **4** something that is prepared, esp a medicinal formulation **5** (esp in a boarding school) **a** homework **b** the period reserved for this. Usually shortened to: **prep 6** *music* **a** the anticipation of a dissonance so that the note producing it in one chord is first heard in the preceding chord as a consonance **b** a note so employed

preparative (prɪ'pærətɪv) *adj* **1** serving to prepare; preparatory ▷ *n* **2** something that prepares ▷ pre'paratively *adv*

preparatory (prɪ'pærətərɪ, -trɪ) *adj* **1** serving to prepare **2** introductory or preliminary **3** occupied in preparation **4 preparatory to** as a preparation to; before: *a drink preparatory to eating* ▷ pre'paratorily *adv*

preparatory school *n* **1** (in Britain) a private school, usually single-sex and for children between the ages of 6 and 13, generally preparing pupils for public school **2** (in the US) a private secondary school preparing pupils for college ▷ Often shortened to: **prep school**

prepare (prɪ'pɛə) *vb* **1** to make ready or suitable in advance for a particular purpose or for some use, event, etc: *to prepare a meal; to prepare to go* **2** to put together using parts or ingredients; compose or construct **3** (*tr*) to equip or outfit, as for an expedition **4** (*tr*) *music* to soften the impact of (a dissonant note) by the use of preparation **5 be prepared** (*foll by an infinitive*) to be willing and able (to do something): *I'm not prepared to reveal these figures* [c15: from Latin *praeparāre*, from *prae* before + *parāre* to make ready] ▷ pre'parer *n*

preparedness (prɪ'pɛərɪdnɪs) *n* the state of being prepared or ready, esp militarily ready for war

prepay (pri:'peɪ) *vb* -pays, -paying, -paid (*tr*) to pay for in advance ▷ pre'payable *adj*

prepense (prɪ'pɛns) *adj* (*postpositive*) (usually in legal contexts) arranged in advance; premeditated (esp in the phrase **malice prepense**) [c18: from Anglo-Norman *purpensé*, from Old French *purpenser* to consider in advance, from *penser* to think, from Latin *pēnsāre* to weigh, consider]

preponderance (prɪ'pɒndərəns) *or* **preponderancy** (prɪ'pɒndərənsɪ) *n* the quality of being greater in weight, force, influence, etc: *the overwhelming preponderance of right-handed people*

preponderant (prɪ'pɒndərənt) *adj* greater in weight, force, influence, etc > pre'ponderantly *adv*

preponderate (prɪ'pɒndə,reɪt) *vb* (*intr*) **1** (often foll by *over*) to be more powerful, important, numerous, etc (than) **2** to be of greater weight than something else [C17: from Late Latin *praeponderāre* to be of greater weight, from *pondus* weight] > pre,ponder'ation *n*

preposition (,prepə'zɪʃən) *n* a word or group of words used before a noun or pronoun to relate it grammatically or semantically to some other constituent of a sentence [C14: from Latin *praepositiō* a putting before, from *pōnere* to place] > ,prepo'sitional *adj* > ,prepo'sitionally *adv*

● USAGE The practice of ending a sentence with a
● preposition (*Venice is a place I should like to go to*) was
● formerly regarded as incorrect, but is now acceptable
● and is the preferred form in many contexts

prepossess (,pri:pə'zɛs) *vb* (*tr*) **1** to preoccupy or engross mentally **2** to influence in advance for or against a person or thing; prejudice; bias **3** to make a favourable impression on beforehand > prepossession (,pri:pə'zɛʃən) *n*

prepossessing (,pri:pə'zɛsɪŋ) *adj* creating a favourable impression; attractive

preposterous (prɪ'pɒstərəs) *adj* contrary to nature, reason, or sense; absurd; ridiculous [C16: from Latin *praeposterus* reversed, from *prae* in front, before + *posterus* following] > pre'posterously *adv* > pre'posterousness *n*

prepotency (prɪ'pəʊtᵊnsɪ) *n* **1** *genetics* the ability of one parent to transmit more characteristics to its offspring than the other parent **2** *botany* the ability of pollen from one source to bring about fertilization more readily than that from other sources [C15: from Latin *praepotens* very powerful, from *posse* to be able] > pre'potent *adj* > pre'potently *adv*

preppy ('prɛpɪ) *informal* ▷ *adj* **1** characteristic of or denoting a fashion style of neat, understated, and often expensive clothes; young but classic: suggesting that the wearer is well off, upper class, and conservative ▷ *n, pl* -pies **2** a person exhibiting such style [C20: originally US, from *preppy* a person who attends or has attended a preparatory school before college]

prep school *n informal* See **preparatory school**

prepuce ('pri:pju:s) *n* **1** the retractable fold of skin covering the tip of the penis. Nontechnical name: **foreskin 2** a similar fold of skin covering the tip of the clitoris [C14: from Latin *praepūtium*]

prequel ('pri:kwəl) *n* a film or book about an earlier stage of a story or a character's life, released because the later part of it has already been successful [C20: from PRE- + (*se*)*quel*]

Pre-Raphaelite (,pri:'ræfəlaɪt) *n* **1** a member of the **Pre-Raphaelite Brotherhood**, an association of British painters and writers including Dante Gabriel Rossetti (1828–82), Holman Hunt (1827–1910), and Sir John Everett Millais (1829–96), founded in 1848 to combat the shallow conventionalism of academic painting and revive the fidelity to nature and the vivid realistic colour that they considered typical of Italian painting before Raphael (1483–1520) ▷ *adj* **2** of, in the manner of, or relating to Pre-Raphaelite painting and painters > ,Pre-'Raphael,itism *n*

prerequisite (pri:'rɛkwɪzɪt) *adj* **1** required as a prior condition ▷ *n* **2** something required as a prior condition

prerogative (prɪ'rɒgətɪv) *n* **1** an exclusive privilege or right exercised by a person or group of people holding a particular office or hereditary rank **2** any privilege or right **3** a power, privilege, or immunity restricted to a sovereign or sovereign government ▷ *adj* **4** having or able to exercise a prerogative [C14: from Latin *praerogātīva* privilege, earlier: group with the right to vote first, from *prae* before + *rogāre* to ask, beg for]

Pres. *abbreviation* President

presage *n* ('prɛsɪdʒ) **1** an intimation or warning of something about to happen; portent; omen **2** a sense of what is about to happen; foreboding ▷ *vb* ('prɛsɪdʒ, prɪ'seɪdʒ) **3** (*tr*) to have a presentiment of **4** (*tr*) to give a forewarning of; portend [C14: from Latin *praesāgium* presentiment, from *praesāgīre* to perceive beforehand,

from *sāgīre* to perceive acutely] > pre'sageful *adj* > pre'sager *n*

presale ('pri:seɪl) *n* the practice of arranging the sale of a product before it is available > pre'sell *vb* (*tr*)

presbyopia (,prɛzbɪ'əʊpɪə) *n* a progressively diminishing ability of the eye to focus, noticeable from middle to old age, caused by loss of elasticity of the crystalline lens [C18: New Latin, from Greek *presbus* old man + *ōps* eye] > presbyopic (,prɛzbɪ'ɒpɪk) *adj*

presbyter ('prɛzbɪtə) *n* **1 a** an elder of a congregation in the early Christian Church **b** (in some Churches having episcopal politics) an official who is subordinate to a bishop and has administrative, teaching, and sacerdotal functions **2** (in some hierarchical Churches) another name for **priest** [C16: from Late Latin, from Greek *presbuteros* an older man, from *presbus* old man]

presbyterial (,prɛzbɪ'tɪərɪəl) *adj* of or relating to a presbyter or presbytery. Also: **presbyteral** (prɛz'bɪtərəl) > ,presby'terially *adv*

presbyterian (,prɛzbɪ'tɪərɪən) *adj* **1** of, relating to, or designating Church government by presbyters or lay elders ▷ *n* **2** an upholder of this type of Church government > ,presby'terianism *n*

Presbyterian (,prɛzbɪ'tɪərɪən) *adj* **1** of or relating to any of various Protestant Churches governed by presbyters or lay elders and adhering to various modified forms of Calvinism ▷ *n* **2** a member of a Presbyterian Church > ,Presby'terianism *n*

presbytery ('prɛzbɪtərɪ, -trɪ) *n, pl* -teries **1** *Presbyterian Church* **a** a local Church court composed of ministers and elders **b** the congregations or churches within the jurisdiction of any such court **2** the part of a cathedral or church east of the choir, in which the main altar is situated; sanctuary **3** presbyters or elders collectively **4** *RC Church* the residence of a parish priest [C15: from Old French *presbiterie*, from Church Latin *presbyterium*, from Greek *presbyterion*; see PRESBYTER]

prescience ('prɛsɪəns) *n* knowledge of events before they take place; foreknowledge [C14: from Latin *praescīre* to foreknow, from *prae* before + *scīre* to know] > 'prescient *adj*

Prescott ('prɛskət) *n* **1 John Leslie**. born 1938, British politician: deputy leader of the Labour Party (1994–2007); deputy prime minister (1997–2007); secretary of state for the environment, transport, and the regions (1997–2001); minister for local government and the regions (2002–07) **2 William Hickling** ('hɪklɪŋ). 1796–1859, US historian, noted for his work on the history of Spain and her colonies

prescribe (prɪ'skraɪb) *vb* **1** to lay down as a rule or directive **2** *med* to recommend or order the use of (a drug or other remedy) [C16: from Latin *praescrībere* to write previously, from *prae* before + *scrībere* to write] > pre'scriber *n*

prescript ('pri:skrɪpt) *n* something laid down or prescribed [C16: from Latin *praescrīptum* something written down beforehand, from *praescrībere* to PRESCRIBE]

prescription (prɪ'skrɪpʃən) *n* **1 a** written instructions from a physician, dentist, etc, to a pharmacist stating the form, dosage strength, etc, of a drug to be issued to a specific patient **b** the drug or remedy prescribed **2 a** written instructions from an optician specifying the lenses needed to correct defects of vision **b** (*as modifier*): *prescription glasses* **3** the act of prescribing **4** something that is prescribed **5** a long established custom or a claim based on one **6** *law* **a** the uninterrupted possession of property over a stated period of time, after which a right or title is acquired (**positive prescription**) **b** the barring of adverse claims to property, etc, after a specified period of time has elapsed, allowing the possessor to acquire title (**negative prescription**) [C14: from legal Latin *praescriptiō* an order, prescription; see PRESCRIBE]

prescriptive (prɪ'skrɪptɪv) *adj* **1** making or giving directions, rules, or injunctions **2** sanctioned by long-standing usage or custom **3** derived from or based upon legal prescription: *a prescriptive title* > pre'scriptiveness *n*

preseason ('pri:,si:zᵊn) *n* **a** the period immediately before the official season for a particular sport begins

b (*as modifier*): *a series of preseason friendly matches*
presence ('prɛzəns) *n* **1** the state or fact of being present
2 the immediate proximity of a person or thing
3 personal appearance or bearing, esp of a dignified
nature **4** an imposing or dignified personality **5** an
invisible spirit felt to be nearby **6** *electronics* a recording
control that boosts mid-range frequencies **7** *obsolete*
assembly or company [c14: via Old French from Latin
praesentia a being before, from *praeesse* to be before, from
prae before + *esse* to be]
presence chamber *n* the room in which a great person,
such as a monarch, receives guests, assemblies, etc
presence of mind *n* the ability to remain calm and act
constructively during times of crisis
presenile dementia (pri:'si:naɪl) *n* a form of dementia,
of unknown cause, starting before a person is old
present[1] ('prɛzªnt) *adj* **1** (*prenominal*) in existence at the
moment in time at which an utterance is spoken or
written **2** (*postpositive*) being in a specified place, thing,
etc: *the murderer is present in this room* **3** (*prenominal*) now in
consideration or under discussion: *the present topic; the
present author* **4** *grammar* denoting a tense of verbs used
when the action or event described is occurring at the
time of utterance or when the speaker does not wish to
make any explicit temporal reference **5** *archaic* readily
available; instant: *present help is at hand* ⊳ *n* **6** *grammar*
a the present tense **b** a verb in this tense **7 for the
present** for the time being; temporarily ⊳ See also
presents [c13: from Latin *praesens*, from *praeesse* to be in
front of, from *prae-* before, in front + *esse* to be]
present[2] *vb* (prɪ'zɛnt) (*mainly tr*) **1** to introduce (a person)
to another, esp to someone of higher rank **2** to
introduce to the public: *to present a play* **3** to introduce
and compere (a radio or television show) **4** to show;
exhibit: *he presented a brave face to the world* **5** to bring or
suggest to the mind: *to present a problem* **6** to give or
award: *to present a prize* **7** to endow with or as if with a
gift or award: *to present a university with a foundation
scholarship* **8** to offer formally: *to present one's compliments*
9 to offer or hand over for action or settlement: *to present
a bill* **10** to represent or depict in a particular manner: *the
actor presented Hamlet as a very young man* **11** to salute
someone with (one's weapon) (usually in the phrase
present arms) **12** to aim or point (a weapon) **13** to
nominate (a clergyman) to a bishop for institution to a
benefice in his diocese **14** to lay (a charge, etc) before a
court, magistrate, etc, for consideration or trial **15** to
bring a formal charge or accusation against (a person);
indict **16** (*intr*) *med* to seek treatment for a particular
symptom or problem: *she presented with postnatal depression*
17 (*intr*) *informal* to produce a favourable, etc impression:
*she presents well in public; he presents as harmless but has
poisoned his family* **18 present oneself** to appear, esp at a
specific time and place ⊳ *n* ('prɛzªnt) **19** anything that is
presented; a gift [c13: from Old French *presenter*, from
Latin *praesentāre* to exhibit, offer, from *praesens* PRESENT[1]]
presentable (prɪ'zɛntəbªl) *adj* **1** fit to be presented or
introduced to other people **2** fit to be displayed or
offered > pre'sentableness or pre‚senta'bility *n*
> pre'sentably *adv*
presentation (‚prɛzən'teɪʃən) *n* **1** the act of presenting or
state of being presented **2** the manner of presenting,
esp the organization of visual details to create an overall
impression **3** a verbal report presented with illustrative
material, such as slides, graphs, etc: *a presentation on the
company results* **4** a an offering or bestowal, as of a gift
b (*as modifier*): *a presentation copy of a book* **5** a performance
or representation, as of a play **6** the formal introduction
of a person, as into society or at court; debut **7** the act or
right of nominating a clergyman to a benefice
> ‚presen'tational *adj*
presentationism (‚prɛzən'teɪʃə‚nɪzəm) *n* *philosophy* the
theory that objects are identical with our perceptions of
them. See **representationalism** > ‚presen'tationist *n, adj*
presentative (prɪ'zɛntətɪv) *adj* **1** *philosophy* able to be
known or perceived immediately **2** subject to or
conferring the right of ecclesiastical presentation
present-day *n* (*modifier*) of the modern day; current: *I
don't like present-day fashions*

presenteeism (‚prɛzən'ti:ɪzəm) *n* the practice of
persistently working longer hours and taking fewer
holidays than the terms of one's employment demand,
esp as a result of fear of losing one's job [c20: a play on
ABSENTEEISM]
presenter (prɪ'zɛntə) *n* **1** a person who presents
something or someone **2** *radio, television* a person who
introduces a show, links items, interviews guests, etc;
compere
presentient (prɪ'sɛnʃənt, -'zɛn-, pri:-) *adj* characterized
by or experiencing a presentiment [c19: from Latin
praesentiens present participle of *praesentire*, from *prae-* PRE-
+ *sentire* to feel]
presentiment (prɪ'zɛntɪmənt) *n* a sense of something
about to happen; premonition [c18: from obsolete
French, from *pressentir* to sense beforehand; see PRE-,
SENTIMENT]
presently ('prɛzəntlɪ) *adv* **1** in a short while; soon **2** at
the moment **3** an archaic word for **immediately**
presentment (prɪ'zɛntmənt) *n* **1** the act of presenting or
state of being presented; presentation **2** something
presented, such as a picture, play, etc **3** *law chiefly US* a
statement on oath by a grand jury of something within
their own knowledge or observation, esp the
commission of an offence when the indictment has
been laid before them **4** *commerce* the presenting of a
bill of exchange, promissory note, etc
present participle *n* a participial form of verbs used
adjectivally when the action it describes is
contemporaneous with that of the main verb of a
sentence and also used in the formation of certain
compound tenses. In English this form ends in *-ing*
present perfect *adj, n* *grammar* another term for **perfect**
(senses 8, 10)
presents ('prɛzənts) *pl n* *law* used in a deed or document
to refer to itself: *know all men by these presents*
preservative (prɪ'zɜ:vətɪv) *n* **1** something that preserves
or tends to preserve, esp a chemical added to foods to
inhibit decomposition ⊳ *adj* **2** tending or intended to
preserve
preserve (prɪ'zɜ:v) *vb* (*mainly tr*) **1** to keep safe from
danger or harm; protect **2** to protect from decay or
dissolution; maintain: *to preserve old buildings* **3** to
maintain possession of; keep up: *to preserve a façade of
indifference* **4** to prevent from decomposition or chemical
change **5** to prepare (food), as by freezing, drying, or
salting, so that it will resist decomposition **6** to make
preserves of (fruit, etc) **7** to rear and protect (game) in
restricted places for hunting or fishing **8** (*intr*) to
maintain protection and favourable conditions for game
in preserves ⊳ *n* **9** something that preserves or is
preserved **10** a special area or domain: *archaeology is the
preserve of specialists* **11** (*usually plural*) fruit, etc, prepared by
cooking with sugar **12** areas where game is reared for
private hunting or fishing [c14: via Old French, from
Late Latin *praeservāre* literally: to keep safe in advance,
from Latin *prae-* before + *servāre* to keep safe]
> pre'servable *adj* > preservation (‚prɛzə'veɪʃən) *n*
> pre'server *n*
preset (prɪ'sɛt) *vb* **-sets, -setting, -set** (*tr*) **1** to set (a
timing device) so that something begins to operate at
the time specified ⊳ *n* **2** *electronics* a control, such as a
variable resistor, that is not as accessible as the main
controls and is used to set initial conditions
preshrunk (pri:'ʃrʌŋk) *adj* (of fabrics, garments, etc)
having undergone a shrinking process during
manufacture so that further shrinkage will not occur
preside (prɪ'zaɪd) *vb* (*intr*) **1** to sit in or hold a position of
authority, as over a meeting **2** to exercise authority;
control [c17: via French from Latin *praesidēre* to
superintend, from *prae* before + *sedēre* to sit]
presidency ('prɛzɪdənsɪ) *n, pl* **-cies a** the office, dignity,
or term of a president **b** (*often capital*) the office of
president of a republic, esp the office of the President of
the US
president ('prɛzɪdənt) *n* **1** (*often capital*) the chief
executive or head of state of a republic, esp of the US
2 (in the US) the chief executive officer of a company,
corporation, etc **3** a person who presides over an

assembly, meeting, etc **4** the chief executive officer of certain establishments of higher education [c14: via Old French from Late Latin *praesidens* ruler; see PRESIDE] ▷ **presidential** (ˌprɛzɪˈdɛnʃəl) *adj* ▷ ˌpresiˈdentially *adv* ▷ ˈpresidentˌship *n*

presidium *or* **praesidium** (prɪˈsɪdɪəm) *n, pl* **-iums** *or* **-ia** (-ɪə) **1** (*often capital*) (in Communist countries) a permanent committee of a larger body, such as a legislature, that acts for it when it is in recess **2** a collective presidency, esp of a nongovernmental organization [c20: from Russian *prezidium*, from Latin *praesidium*, from *praesidēre* to superintend; see PRESIDE]

Presley (ˈprɛzlɪ) *n* **Elvis** (**Aaron** *or* **Aron**). 1935–77, US rock and roll singer. His recordings include "That's all Right (Mama)" (1954), "Heartbreak Hotel" (1956), "Hound Dog" (1956), numbers from the films *Loving You* and *Jailhouse Rock* (both 1957), and "Suspicious Minds" (1970)

press¹ (prɛs) *vb* **1** to apply or exert weight, force, or steady pressure on: *he pressed the button on the camera* **2** (*tr*) to squeeze or compress so as to alter in shape or form **3** to apply heat or pressure to (clothing) so as to smooth out or mark with creases; iron **4** to make (objects) from soft material by pressing with a mould, form, etc, esp to make gramophone records from plastic **5** (*tr*) to hold tightly or clasp, as in an embrace **6** (*tr*) to extract or force out (juice) by pressure (from) **7** (*tr*) to force, constrain, or compel **8** to importune or entreat (a person) insistently; urge: *they pressed for an answer* **9** to harass or cause harassment **10** (*tr*) to plead or put forward strongly or importunately: *to press a claim* **11** (*intr*) to be urgent **12** (*tr; usually passive*) to have little of: *we're hard pressed for time* **13** (when *intr*, often foll by *on* or *forward*) to hasten or advance or cause to hasten or advance in a forceful manner **14** (*intr*) to crowd; throng; push **15** (*tr*) *archaic* to trouble or oppress ▷ *n* **16** any machine that exerts pressure to form, shape, or cut materials or to extract liquids, compress solids, or hold components together while an adhesive joint is formed **17** See **printing press 18** the art or process of printing **19** to press *or* to the press to be printed: *when is this book going to press?* **20** the press **a** news media and agencies collectively, esp newspapers **b** (*as modifier*): *a press matter; press relations* **21** the opinions and reviews in the newspapers, etc: *the play received a poor press* **22** the act of pressing or state of being pressed **23** the act of crowding, thronging, or pushing together **24** a closely packed throng of people; crowd; multitude **25** a cupboard, esp a large one used for storing clothes or linen **26** a wood or metal clamp or vice to prevent tennis rackets, etc, from warping when not in use **27** *weightlifting* a lift in which the weight is raised to shoulder level and then above the head [c14 *pressen*, from Old French *presser*, from Latin *pressāre*, from *premere* to press]

press² (prɛs) *vb* (*tr*) **1** to recruit (men) by forcible measures for military service **2** to use for a purpose other than intended, (esp in the phrase **press into service**) ▷ *n* **3** recruitment into military service by forcible measures, as by a press gang [c16: back formation from *prest* to recruit soldiers; see PREST²; also influenced by PRESS¹]

press agent *n* a person employed to obtain favourable publicity, such as notices in newspapers, for an organization, actor, etc

press box *n* an area reserved for reporters, as in a sports stadium

Pressburg (ˈprɛsbʊrk) *n* the German name for **Bratislava**

Pressburger (ˈprɛsˌbɜːɡə) *n* **Emeric** (ˈɛmərɪk). 1902–88, Hungarian film writer and producer, living in Britain: best known for his collaboration (1942–57) with Michael Powell. Films include *The Life and Death of Colonel Blimp* (1943), *I Know Where I'm Going* (1945), and *A Matter of Life and Death* (1946)

press conference *n* an interview for press and television reporters given by a politician, film star, etc

press fit *n* *engineering* a type of fit for mating parts, usually tighter than a sliding fit, used when the parts do not have to move relative to each other

press gallery *n* an area set apart for newspaper

reporters, esp in a legislative assembly

press gang *n* **1** (formerly) a detachment of men used to press civilians for service in the navy or army ▷ *vb* **press-gang** (*tr*) **2** to force (a person) to join the navy or army by a press gang **3** to induce (a person) to perform a duty by forceful persuasion

pressing (ˈprɛsɪŋ) *adj* **1** demanding immediate attention **2** persistent or importunate ▷ *n* **3** a large specified number of gramophone records produced at one time from a master record **4** *football* the tactic of trying to stay very close to the opposition when they are in possession of the ball ▷ ˈpressingly *adv*

pressman (ˈprɛsmən, -ˌmæn) *n, pl* **-men 1** a person who works for the press **2** a person who operates a printing press

press of sail *n* *nautical* the most sail a vessel can carry under given conditions. Also called: press of canvas

press release *n* an official announcement or account of a news item circulated to the press

pressroom (ˈprɛsˌruːm, -ˌrʊm) *n* the room in a printing establishment that houses the printing presses

press stud *n* a fastening device consisting of one part with a projecting knob that snaps into a hole on another like part, used esp in closures in clothing. Also called: snap fastener

press-up *n* an exercise in which the body is alternately raised from and lowered to the floor by the arms only, the trunk being kept straight with the toes and hands resting on the floor. Also called (US and Canadian): push-up

pressure (ˈprɛʃə) *n* **1** the state of pressing or being pressed **2** the exertion of force by one body on the surface of another **3** a moral force that compels: *to bring pressure to bear* **4** an urgent claim or demand or series of urgent claims or demands: *to work under pressure* **5** a burdensome condition that is hard to bear: *the pressure of grief* **6** the normal force applied to a unit area of a surface, usually measured in pascals (newtons per square metre), millibars, torr, or atmospheres **7** short for **atmospheric pressure, blood pressure** ▷ *vb* **8** (*tr*) to constrain or compel, as by the application of moral force **9** another word for **pressurize** [c14: from Late Latin *pressūra* a pressing, from Latin *premere* to press]

pressure cooker *n* a strong hermetically sealed pot in which food may be cooked quickly under pressure at a temperature above the normal boiling point of water ▷ pressure-cook *vb*

pressure group *n* a group of people who seek to exert pressure on legislators, public opinion, etc, in order to promote their own ideas or welfare

pressure point *n* any of several points on the body above an artery that, when firmly pressed, will control bleeding from the artery at a point farther away from the heart

pressure suit *n* an inflatable suit worn by a person flying at high altitudes or in space, to provide protection from low pressure

pressure ulcer *or* **pressure sore** *n* another term for **bedsore**

pressurize *or* **pressurise** (ˈprɛʃəˌraɪz) *vb* (*tr*) **1** to increase the pressure in (an enclosure, such as an aircraft cabin) in order to maintain approximately atmospheric pressure when the external pressure is low **2** to increase pressure on (a fluid) **3** to make insistent demands of (someone); coerce ▷ ˌpressuriˈzation *or* ˌpressuriˈsation *n*

pressurized-water reactor *n* a nuclear reactor using water as coolant and moderator at a pressure that is too high to allow boiling to take place inside the reactor. The fuel is enriched uranium oxide cased in zirconium

presswork (ˈprɛsˌwɜːk) *n* **1** the operation of a printing press **2** the matter printed by a printing press

prest¹ (prɛst) *adj obsolete* prepared for action or use; ready [c13: via Old French from Late Latin *praestus* ready to hand; see PRESTO]

prest² (prɛst) *n obsolete* **a** a loan of money **b** wages paid in advance [c16: originally, loan money offered as an inducement to recruits, from Old French: advance pay in the army, from *prester* to lend, from Latin *praestāre* to provide, from *prae* before + *stāre* to stand]

P

Prester John ('prɛstə) n a legendary Christian priest and king, believed in the Middle Ages to have ruled in the Far East, but identified in the 14th century with the king of Ethiopia [C14 *Prestre Johan*, from Medieval Latin *presbyter Iohannes* Priest John]

prestidigitation (,prɛstɪ,dɪdʒɪ'teɪʃən) n another name for **sleight of hand** [C19: from French: quick-fingeredness, from Latin *praestigiae* feats of juggling, tricks, probably influenced by French *preste* nimble, and Latin *digitus* finger; see PRESTIGE]

prestige (prɛ'stiːʒ) n 1 high status or reputation achieved through success, influence, wealth, etc; renown 2 a the power to influence or impress; glamour b (*modifier*) *a prestige car* [C17: via French from Latin *praestigiae* feats of juggling, tricks; apparently related to Latin *praestringere* to bind tightly, blindfold, from *prae* before + *stringere* to draw tight, bind] > pre'stigious *adj* > pres'tigiously *adv* > pres'tigiousness n

prestige pricing n *marketing* the practice of giving a product a high price to convey the idea that it must be of high quality or status

prestissimo (prɛ'stɪsɪ,məʊ) *music* ▷ *adj, adv* 1 to be played as fast as possible ▷ n, pl -mos 2 a piece or passage directed to be played in this way [C18: from Italian: very quickly, from *presto* fast]

presto ('prɛstəʊ) *adj, adv* 1 *music* to be played very fast ▷ *adv* 2 immediately, suddenly, or at once (esp in the phrase **hey presto**) ▷ n, pl -tos 3 *music* a movement or passage directed to be played very quickly [C16: from Italian: fast, from Late Latin *praestus* (adj) ready to hand, Latin *praestō* (adv) present]

Preston ('prɛstən) n a city in NW England, administrative centre of Lancashire, on the River Ribble: developed as a weaving centre (17th–18th centuries); university (1992). Pop: 184 836 (2001)

Prestonpans (,prɛstən'pænz) n a small town and resort in SE Scotland, in East Lothian on the Firth of Forth: scene of the battle (1745) in which the Jacobite army of Prince Charles Edward defeated government forces under Sir John Cope. Pop: 7153 (2001)

prestressed concrete n concrete that contains steel wires, cables, etc, that are prestressed within their elastic limit to counteract the stresses that will occur under load

Prestwich ('prɛstwɪtʃ) n a town in NW England, in Bury unitary authority, Greater Manchester. Pop: 31 693 (2001)

Prestwick ('prɛstwɪk) n a town in SW Scotland, in South Ayrshire on the Firth of Clyde; international airport, golf course: tourism. Pop: 14 934 (2001)

presumably (prɪ'zjuːməblɪ) *adv* (*sentence modifier*) one presumes or supposes that: *presumably he won't see you, if you're leaving tomorrow*

presume (prɪ'zjuːm) *vb* 1 (when *tr, often takes a clause as object*) to take (something) for granted; assume 2 (when *tr, often foll by an infinitive*) to take upon oneself (to do something) without warrant or permission; dare: *do you presume to copy my work?* 3 (*intr; foll by on or upon*) to rely or depend: *don't presume on his agreement* 4 *law* to take as proved until contrary evidence is produced [C14: via Old French from Latin *praesūmere* to take in advance, from *prae* before + *sūmere* to take; see ASSUME] > pre'sumedly (prɪ'zjuːmɪdlɪ) *adv* > pre'suming *adj*

presumption (prɪ'zʌmpʃən) n 1 the act of presuming 2 bold or insolent behaviour or manners 3 a belief or assumption based on reasonable evidence 4 a ground or basis on which to presume 5 *law* an inference of the truth of a fact from other facts proved, admitted, or judicially noticed [C13: via Old French from Latin *praesūmptiō* a using in advance, anticipation, from *praesūmere* to take beforehand; see PRESUME]

presumptive (prɪ'zʌmptɪv) *adj* 1 based on presumption or probability 2 affording reasonable ground for belief > pre'sumptively *adv*

presumptuous (prɪ'zʌmptjʊəs) *adj* characterized by presumption or tending to presume; bold; forward > pre'sumptuously *adv* > pre'sumptuousness n

presuppose (,priːsə'pəʊz) *vb* (*tr*) 1 to take for granted; assume 2 to require or imply as a necessary prior condition > presupposition (,priːsʌpə'zɪʃən) n

preteen (priː'tiːn) n a boy or girl approaching his or her teens

pretence *or US* **pretense** (prɪ'tɛns) n 1 the act of pretending 2 a false display; affectation 3 a claim, esp a false one, to a right, title, or distinction 4 make-believe or feigning 5 a false claim or allegation; pretext

pretend (prɪ'tɛnd) *vb* 1 (when *tr, usually takes a clause as object or an infinitive*) to claim or allege (something untrue) 2 (*tr; may take a clause as object or an infinitive*) to make believe, as in a play: *you pretend to be Ophelia* 3 (*intr; foll by to*) to present a claim, esp a dubious one: *to pretend to the throne* 4 (*intr; foll by to*) *obsolete* to aspire as a candidate or suitor (for) ▷ *adj* 5 fanciful; make-believe; simulated [C14: from Latin *praetendere* to stretch forth, feign, from *prae* in front + *tendere* to stretch]

pretender (prɪ'tɛndə) n 1 a person who pretends or makes false allegations 2 a person who mounts a claim, as to a throne or title

pretension (prɪ'tɛnʃən) n 1 (*often plural*) a false or unsupportable claim, esp to merit, worth, or importance 2 a specious or unfounded allegation; pretext 3 the state or quality of being pretentious

pretentious (prɪ'tɛnʃəs) *adj* 1 making claim to distinction or importance, esp undeservedly 2 having or creating a deceptive outer appearance of great worth; ostentatious > pre'tentiously *adv* > pre'tentiousness n

preter- *prefix* beyond, more than, or exceeding: *preternatural* [from Latin *praeter-*, from *praeter*]

preterite *or US* **preterit** ('prɛtərɪt) *grammar* ▷ n 1 a tense of verbs used to relate past action, formed in English by inflection of the verb, as *jumped, swam* 2 a verb in this tense ▷ *adj* 3 denoting this tense [C14: from Late Latin *praeteritum* (*tempus*) past (time, tense), from Latin *praeterīre* to go by, from PRETER- + *īre* to go]

preterm (,priː'tɜːm) *adj* 1 (of a baby) born prematurely ▷ *adv* 2 prematurely

pretermit (,priːtə'mɪt) *vb* -mits, -mitting, -mitted (*tr*) *rare* 1 to overlook intentionally; disregard 2 to fail to do; neglect; omit [C16: from Latin *praetermittere* to let pass, from PRETER- + *mittere* to send, release]

preternatural (,priːtə'nætʃrəl) *adj* 1 beyond what is ordinarily found in nature; abnormal 2 another word for **supernatural** [C16: from Medieval Latin *praeternātūrālis*, from Latin *praeter natūram* beyond the scope of nature] > ,preter'naturally *adv*

pretext ('priːtɛkst) n 1 a fictitious reason given in order to conceal the real one 2 a specious excuse; pretence [C16: from Latin *praetextum* disguise, from *praetexere* to weave in front, disguise; see TEXTURE]

pretor ('priːtə) n a variant spelling of **praetor**

Pretoria (prɪ'tɔːrɪə) n a city in N South Africa, the administrative capital of South Africa; formerly capital of Transvaal province: two universities (1873, 1930); large steelworks. Pop: 525 384 (2001)

Pretorius (prɪ'tɔːrɪəs) n 1 **Andries Wilhelmus Jacobus** ('ɑndriːs wɪl'hɛlmys jaː'koːbys). 1799–1853, a Boer leader in the Great Trek (1838) to escape British sovereignty; he also led an expedition to the Transvaal (1848). The town Pretoria was named after him 2 his son, **Marthinus Wessels** (mar'tiːnys 'wɛsəls). 1819–1901, first president of the South African Republic (1857–71) and of the Orange Free State (1859–63)

prettify ('prɪtɪ,faɪ) *vb* -fies, -fying, -fied (*tr*) to make pretty, esp in a trivial fashion; embellish > ,prettifi'cation n > 'pretti,fier n

pretty ('prɪtɪ) *adj* -tier, -tiest 1 pleasing or appealing in a delicate or graceful way 2 dainty, neat, or charming 3 commendable; good of its kind: *he replied with a pretty wit* 4 *informal, often ironic* excellent, grand, or fine: *here's a pretty mess!* 5 *informal* lacking in masculinity; effeminate; foppish 6 *Scot* vigorous or brave 7 **sitting pretty** *informal* well placed or established financially, socially, etc ▷ n, pl -ties 8 a pretty person or thing ▷ *adv* 9 *informal* fairly or moderately; somewhat 10 *informal* quite or very ▷ *vb* -ties, -tying, -tied 11 (*tr; often foll by up*) to make pretty; adorn [Old English *prættig* clever; related to Middle Low German *prattich* obstinate, Dutch *prettig* glad, Old Norse *prettugr* cunning] > 'prettily *adv* > 'prettiness n

pretty-pretty *adj informal* excessively or ostentatiously pretty: *a pretty-pretty village*

pretzel ('prɛtsəl) *n* a brittle savoury biscuit, in the form of a knot or stick, glazed and salted on the outside, eaten esp in Germany and the US [C19: from German, from Old High German *brezitella*; perhaps related to Medieval Latin *bracellus* bracelet, from Latin *bracchium* arm]

Preussen ('prɔysən) *n* the German name for **Prussia**

prevail (prɪ'veɪl) *vb* (*intr*) 1 (often foll by *over* or *against*) to prove superior; gain mastery: *skill will prevail* 2 to be or appear as the most important feature; be prevalent 3 to exist widely; be in force 4 (often foll by *on* or *upon*) to succeed in persuading or inducing [C14: from Latin *praevalēre* to be superior in strength, from *prae* beyond + *valēre* to be strong] > pre'vailer *n*

prevailing (prɪ'veɪlɪŋ) *adj* 1 generally accepted; widespread: *the prevailing opinion* 2 most frequent or conspicuous; predominant: *the prevailing wind is from the north* > pre'vailingly *adv*

prevalent ('prɛvələnt) *adj* 1 widespread or current 2 superior in force or power; predominant [C16 (in the sense: powerful): from Latin *praevalens* very strong, from *praevalēre*: see PREVAIL] > 'prevalence *or* 'prevalentness *n* > 'prevalently *adv*

prevaricate (prɪ'værɪˌkeɪt) *vb* (*intr*) to speak or act falsely or evasively with intent to deceive [C16: from Latin *praevāricārī* to walk crookedly, from *prae* beyond + *vāricare* to straddle the legs; compare Latin *vārus* bent] > preˌvari'cation *n* > pre'variˌcator *n*

prevent (prɪ'vɛnt) *vb* 1 (*tr*) to keep from happening, esp by taking precautionary action 2 (*tr*; often foll by *from*) to keep (someone from doing something); hinder; impede 3 (*intr*) to interpose or act as a hindrance 4 (*tr*) *archaic* to anticipate or precede [C15: from Latin *praevenīre*, from *prae* before + *venīre* to come] > pre'ventable *or* pre'ventible *adj* > pre'ventably *or* pre'ventibly *adv*

prevention (prɪ'vɛnʃən) *n* 1 the act of preventing 2 a hindrance, obstacle, or impediment

preventive (prɪ'vɛntɪv) *adj* 1 tending or intended to prevent or hinder 2 *med* tending to prevent disease; prophylactic 3 (in Britain) of, relating to, or belonging to the customs and excise service or the coastguard ▷ *n* 4 something that serves to prevent or hinder 5 *med* any drug or agent that tends to prevent or protect against disease > pre'ventively *adv*

Prévert (*French* prevɛr) *n* **Jacques** (ʒak). 1900–77, Parisian poet, satirist, and writer of film scripts, noted esp for his song poems. He was a member of the surrealist group from 1925 to 1929

preview *or US* **prevue** ('priːˌvjuː) *n* 1 an advance or preliminary view or sight 2 an advance showing before public presentation of a film, art exhibition, etc, usually before an invited audience of celebrities and journalists ▷ *vb* 3 (*tr*) to view in advance

Previn ('prɛvɪn) *n* **André** ('ɒndreɪ). born 1929, US orchestral conductor, born in Germany; living in Britain

previous ('priːvɪəs) *adj* 1 (*prenominal*) existing or coming before something else in time or position; prior 2 (*postpositive*) *informal* taking place or done too soon; premature 3 previous to before; prior to [C17: from Latin *praevius* leading the way, from *prae* before + *via* way] > 'previously *adv* > 'previousness *n*

previous question *n* 1 (in the House of Commons) a motion to drop the present topic under debate, put in order to prevent a vote 2 (in the House of Lords and US legislative bodies) a motion to vote on a bill or other question without delay

previse (prɪ'vaɪz) *vb* (*tr*) *rare* 1 to predict or foresee 2 to notify in advance [C16: from Latin *praevidēre* to foresee, from *prae* before + *vidēre* to see]

prevision (prɪ'vɪʒən) *n* *rare* 1 the act or power of foreseeing; prescience 2 a prophetic vision or prophecy

Prévost d'Exiles (*French* prevo dɛgzil) *n* **Antoine François** (ãtwan frãswa), known as *Abbé Prévost*. 1697–1763, French novelist, noted for his romance *Manon Lescaut* (1731), which served as the basis for operas by Puccini and Massenet

prey (preɪ) *n* 1 an animal hunted or captured by another for food 2 a person or thing that becomes the victim of a

hostile person, influence, etc 3 beast of prey an animal that preys on others for food 4 bird of prey a bird that preys on others for food 5 an archaic word for **booty**[1] ▷ *vb* (*intr*; often foll by *on* or *upon*) 6 to hunt or seize food by killing other animals 7 to make a victim (of others), as by profiting at their expense 8 to exert a depressing or obsessive effect (on the mind, spirits, etc); weigh heavily (upon) [C13: from Old French *preie*, from Latin *praeda* booty; see PREDATORY] > 'preyer *n*

Priam ('praɪəm) *n* *Greek myth* the last king of Troy, killed at its fall. He was father by Hecuba of Hector, Paris, and Cassandra

priapic (praɪ'æpɪk, -'eɪ-) *or* **priapean** (ˌpraɪə'piːən) *adj* 1 (*sometimes capital*) of or relating to Priapus 2 a less common word for **phallic**

priapism ('praɪəˌpɪzəm) *n* *pathol* prolonged painful erection of the penis, caused by neurological disorders, obstruction of the penile blood vessels, etc [C17: from Late Latin *priāpismus*, ultimately from Greek PRIAPUS]

Priapus (praɪ'eɪpəs) *n* 1 (in classical antiquity) the god of the male procreative power and of gardens and vineyards 2 (*often not capital*) a representation of the penis

Pribilof Islands ('prɪbɪləf) *pl n* a group of islands in the Bering Sea, off SW Alaska, belonging to the US: the breeding ground of the northern fur seal. Area: about 168 sq km (65 sq miles). Also called: **Fur Seal Islands**

price (praɪs) *n* 1 the sum in money or goods for which anything is or may be bought or sold 2 the cost at which anything is obtained 3 the cost of bribing a person 4 a sum of money offered or given as a reward for a capture or killing 5 value or worth, esp high worth 6 *gambling* another word for **odds** 7 at any price whatever the price or cost 8 at a price at a high price 9 what price something? what are the chances of something happening now? ▷ *vb* (*tr*) 10 to fix or establish the price of 11 to ascertain or discover the price of 12 price out of the market to charge so highly for as to prevent the sale, hire, etc, of [C13 *pris*, from Old French, from Latin *pretium* price, value, wage] > 'pricer *n*

price control *n* the establishment and maintenance of maximum price levels for basic goods and services by a government, esp during periods of war or inflation

price-dividend ratio *n* the ratio of the price of a share on a stock exchange to the dividends per share paid in the previous year, used as a measure of a company's potential as an investment. Abbreviations: P-D ratio, PDR

price-earnings ratio *n* the ratio of the price of a share on a stock exchange to the earnings per share, used as a measure of a company's future profitability. Abbreviation: P/E ratio

price-fixing *n* 1 the setting of prices by agreement among producers and distributors 2 another name for **price control, resale price maintenance**

price leadership *n* *marketing* the setting of the price of a product or service by a dominant firm at a level that competitors can match, in order to avoid a price war

priceless ('praɪslɪs) *adj* 1 of inestimable worth; beyond valuation; invaluable 2 *informal* extremely amusing or ridiculous > 'pricelessly *adv* > 'pricelessness *n*

price ring *n* a group of traders formed to maintain the prices of their goods

prices and incomes policy *n* voluntary or statutory regulation of the level of increases in prices and incomes

price-sensitive *adj* likely to affect the price of property, esp shares and securities: *price-sensitive information*

pricey *or* **pricy** ('praɪsɪ) *adj* **pricier, priciest** an informal word for **expensive**

prick (prɪk) *vb* (*mainly tr*) 1 a to make (a small hole) in (something) by piercing lightly with a sharp point b to wound in this manner 2 (*intr*) to cause or have a piercing or stinging sensation 3 to cause to feel a sharp emotional pain: *knowledge of such poverty pricked his conscience* 4 to puncture or pierce 5 to mark, delineate, or outline by dots or punctures 6 (*also intr*; usually foll by *up*) to rise or raise erect; point: *the dog pricked his ears up at his master's call* 7 (usually foll by *out* or *off*) to transplant (seedlings) into a larger container **8** *archaic* to rouse or impel; urge on **9 prick up one's ears** to start to listen attentively; become interested ▷ *n* **10** the act of pricking or the condition or sensation of being pricked **11** a mark made by a sharp point; puncture **12** a sharp emotional pain resembling the physical pain caused by being pricked: *a prick of conscience* **13** a taboo slang word for **penis 14** *slang, derogatory* an obnoxious or despicable man **15** an instrument or weapon with a sharp point, such as a thorn, goad, bee sting, etc **16** the footprint or track of an animal, esp a hare **17 kick against the pricks** to hurt oneself by struggling against something in vain [Old English *prica* point, puncture; related to Dutch *prik*, Icelandic *prik* short stick, Swedish *prick* point, stick]

pricket ('prɪkɪt) *n* **1** a male deer in the second year of life having unbranched antlers **2** a sharp metal spike on which to stick a candle [C14 *priket*, from *prik* PRICK]

prickle ('prɪkᵊl) *n* **1** *botany* a pointed process arising from the outer layer of a stem, leaf, etc, and containing no woody or conducting tissue. See **thorn** (sense 1) **2** a pricking or stinging sensation ▷ *vb* **3** to feel or cause to feel a stinging sensation **4** (*tr*) to prick, as with a thorn [Old English *pricel*; related to Middle Low German *prekel*, German *Prickel*]

prickly ('prɪklɪ) *adj* **-lier, -liest 1** having or covered with prickles **2** stinging or tingling **3** bad-tempered or irritable **4** full of difficulties; knotty: *a prickly problem* > '**prickliness** *n*

prickly heat *n* a nontechnical name for **miliaria**

prickly pear *n* **1** any of various tropical cacti of the genus *Opuntia*, having flattened or cylindrical spiny joints and oval fruit that is edible in some species **2** the fruit of any of these plants

pride (praɪd) *n* **1** a feeling of honour and self-respect; a sense of personal worth **2** excessive self-esteem; conceit **3** a source of pride **4** satisfaction or pleasure taken in one's own or another's success, achievements, etc (esp in the phrase **take (a) pride in**) **5** the better or most superior part of something; flower **6** the most flourishing time **7** a group (of lions) **8** the mettle of a horse; courage; spirit **9** *archaic* display, pomp, or splendour **10 pride of place** the most important position ▷ *vb* **11** (*tr*; foll by *on* or *upon*) to take pride in (oneself) for [Old English *prȳda*; related to Latin *prodesse* to be useful, Old Norse *prūthr* stately; see PROUD] > '**prideful** *adj* > '**pridefully** *adv*

Pride (praɪd) *n* **Thomas.** died 1658, English soldier on the Parliamentary side during the Civil War. He expelled members of the Long Parliament hostile to the army (**Pride's Purge,** 1648) and signed Charles I's death warrant

prie-dieu (priː'djɜː) *n* a piece of furniture consisting of a low surface for kneeling upon and a narrow front surmounted by a rest for the elbows or for books, for use when praying [C18: from French, from *prier* to pray + *Dieu* God]

prier *or* **pryer** ('praɪə) *n* a person who pries

priest (priːst) *or feminine* **priestess** *n* **1** *Christianity* a person ordained to act as a mediator between God and man in administering the sacraments, preaching, blessing, guiding, etc **2** (in episcopal Churches) a minister in the second grade of the hierarchy of holy orders, ranking below a bishop but above a deacon **3** a minister of any religion **4** (in some non-Christian religions) an official who offers sacrifice on behalf of the people and performs other religious ceremonies ▷ *vb* (*tr*) **5** to make a priest; ordain [Old English *prēost*, apparently from PRESBYTER; related to Old High German *prēster*, Old French *prestre*] > '**priest,like** *adj* > '**priest,hood** *n* > '**priestly** *adj* > '**priestliness** *n*

priestcraft ('priːst,krɑːft) *n* **1** the art and skills involved in the work of a priest **2** *derogatory* the influence of priests upon politics or the use by them of secular power

priest-hole *or* **priest's hole** *n* a secret chamber in certain houses in England, built as a hiding place for Roman Catholic priests when they were proscribed in the 16th and 17th centuries

Priestley ('priːstlɪ) *n* **1 J(ohn) B(oynton).** 1894–1984, English author. His works include the novels *The Good*

Companions (1929) and *Angel Pavement* (1930) and the play *An Inspector Calls* (1946) **2 Joseph.** 1733–1804, English chemist, political theorist, and clergyman, in the US from 1794. He discovered oxygen (1774) independently of Scheele and isolated and described many other gases

prig¹ (prɪg) *n* a person who is smugly self-righteous and narrow-minded [C18: of unknown origin] > '**priggery** *or* '**priggishness** *n* > '**priggish** *adj* > '**priggishly** *adv*

prig² (prɪg) *Brit slang, archaic* ▷ *vb* **prigs, prigging, prigged 1** another word for **steal** ▷ *n* **2** another word for **thief** [C16: of unknown origin]

Prigogine (*French* prigoʒin) *n* Viscount **Ilya** (ilja). 1917–2003, Belgian chemist, born in Russia: Nobel prize for chemistry 1977 for his work on nonequilibrium thermodynamics

prim (prɪm) *adj* **primmer, primmest 1** affectedly proper, precise, or formal ▷ *vb* **prims, primming, primmed 2** (*tr*) to make prim **3** to purse (the mouth) primly or (of the mouth) to be so pursed [C18: of unknown origin] > '**primly** *adv* > '**primness** *n*

prima ballerina ('priːmə) *n* a leading female ballet dancer [from Italian, literally: first ballerina]

primacy ('praɪməsɪ) *n, pl* **-cies 1** the state of being first in rank, grade, etc **2** *Christianity* the office, rank, or jurisdiction of a primate or senior bishop or (in the Roman Catholic Church) the pope

prima donna ('priːmə 'dɒnə) *n, pl* **prima donnas 1** a female operatic star; diva **2** *informal* a temperamental person [C19: from Italian: first lady]

prima facie ('praɪmə 'feɪʃɪ) *at* first sight; as it seems at first [C15: from Latin, from *prīmus* first + *faciēs* FACE]

prima-facie evidence *n law* evidence that is sufficient to establish a fact or to raise a presumption of the truth of a fact unless controverted

primal ('praɪməl) *adj* **1** first or original **2** chief or most important [C17: from Medieval Latin *prīmālis*, from Latin *prīmus* first]

primaquine ('praɪmə,kwiːn) *n* a synthetic drug used in the treatment of malaria. Formula: $C_{15}H_{21}N_3O$ [C20: from *prima-*, from Latin *prīmus* first + QUIN(OLIN)E]

primarily ('praɪmərəlɪ) *adv* **1** principally; chiefly; mainly **2** at first; originally

primary ('praɪmərɪ) *adj* **1** first in importance, degree, rank, etc **2** first in position or time, as in a series **3** fundamental; basic **4** being the first stage; elementary **5** (*prenominal*) of or relating to the education of children up to the age of 11 **6** (of the flight feathers of a bird's wing) growing from the manus **7 a** being the part of an electric circuit, such as a transformer or induction coil, in which a changing current induces a current in a neighbouring circuit: *a primary coil* **b** (of a current) flowing in such a circuit **8 a** (of a product) consisting of a natural raw material; unmanufactured **b** (of production or industry) involving the extraction or winning of such products. Agriculture, fishing, forestry, hunting, and mining are primary industries **9** *linguistics* (of Latin, Greek, or Sanskrit tenses) referring to present or future time **10** *geology* relating to magmas that have not experienced fractional crystallization or crystal contamination ▷ *n, pl* **-ries 11** a person or thing that is first in rank, occurrence, etc **12** (in the US) a preliminary election in which the voters of a state or region choose a party's convention delegates, nominees for office, etc. Full name: **primary election 13** See **primary colour 14** any of the flight feathers growing from the manus of a bird's wing **15** a primary coil, winding, inductance, or current in an electric circuit **16** *astronomy* a celestial body around which one or more specified secondary bodies orbit: *the sun is the primary of the earth* [C15: from Latin *prīmārius* of the first rank, principal, from *prīmus* first]

primary accent *or* **primary stress** *n linguistics* the strongest accent in a word or breath group, as that on the first syllable of *agriculture*

primary cell *n* an electric cell that generates an electromotive force by the direct and usually irreversible conversion of chemical energy into electrical energy. It cannot be recharged efficiently by an electric current. Also called: **voltaic cell**

primary colour *n* **1** Also called: **additive primary** any of three spectral colours (usually red, green, and blue) that can be mixed to match any other colour, including white light but excluding black **2** Also called: **subtractive primary** any one of the spectral colours cyan, magenta, or yellow that can be subtracted from white light to match any other colour. An equal mixture of the three produces a black pigment **3** Also called: **psychological primary** any one of the colours red, yellow, green, or blue. All other colours look like a mixture of two or more of these colours and they play a unique role in the processing of colour by the visual system

primary school n **1** (in Britain) a school for children below the age of 11. It is usually divided into an infant and a junior section **2** (in the US and Canada) a school equivalent to the first three or four grades of elementary school, sometimes including a kindergarten

primate¹ ('praɪmeɪt) n **1** any placental mammal of the order *Primates*, typically having flexible hands and feet with opposable first digits, good eyesight, and, in the higher apes, a highly developed brain: includes lemurs, lorises, monkeys, apes, and man ▷ *adj* **2** of, relating to, or belonging to the order *Primates* [c18: from New Latin *primates*, plural of *prīmās* principal, from *prīmus* first] > **primatial** (praɪ'meɪʃəl) *adj*

primate² ('praɪmeɪt) n **1** another name for **archbishop** **2 Primate of all England** the Archbishop of Canterbury **3 Primate of England** the Archbishop of York [c13: from Old French, from Latin *prīmās* principal, from *prīmus* first]

prime (praɪm) *adj* **1** (*prenominal*) first in quality or value; first-rate **2** (*prenominal*) fundamental; original **3** (*prenominal*) first in importance, authority, etc; chief **4** *maths* **a** having no factors except itself or one: $x^2 + x + 3$ *is a prime polynomial* **b** (foll by *to*) having no common factors (with): *20 is prime to 21* **5** *finance* having the best credit rating: *prime investments* ▷ n **6** the time when a thing is at its best **7** a period of power, vigour, etc, usually following youth (esp in the phrase **the prime of life**) **8** *maths* short for **prime number** **9** *chiefly RC Church* the second of the seven canonical hours of the divine office, originally fixed for the first hour of the day, at sunrise **10** the first of eight basic positions from which a parry or attack can be made in fencing ▷ *vb* **11** to prepare (something); make ready **12** (*tr*) to apply a primer, such as paint or size, to (a surface) **13** (*tr*) to fill (a pump) with its working fluid before starting, in order to improve the sealing of the pump elements and to expel air from it before starting **14** (*tr*) to increase the quantity of fuel in the float chamber of (a carburettor) in order to facilitate the starting of an engine **15** (*tr*) to insert a primer into (a gun, mine, charge, etc) preparatory to detonation or firing **16** (*tr*) to provide with facts, information, etc, beforehand; brief [(*adj*) C14: from Latin *prīmus* first; (n) C13: from Latin *prīma (hora)* the first (hour); (vb) C16: of uncertain origin, probably connected with n] > **primeness** n

prime cost n the portion of the cost of a commodity that varies directly with the amount of it produced, principally comprising materials and labour. Also called: **variable cost**

prime meridian n the 0° meridian from which the other meridians or lines of longitude are calculated, usually taken to pass through Greenwich

prime minister n **1** the head of a parliamentary government **2** the chief minister of a sovereign or a state

prime mover n **1** the original or primary force behind an idea, enterprise, etc **2 a** the source of power, such as fuel, wind, electricity, etc, for a machine **b** the means of extracting power from such a source, such as a steam engine, electric motor, etc

prime number n an integer that cannot be factorized into other integers but is only divisible by itself or 1, such as 2, 3, 5, 7, and 11

primer¹ ('praɪmə) n an introductory text, such as a school textbook [c14: via Anglo-Norman from Medieval Latin *prīmārius (liber)* a first (book), from Latin *prīmārius* **PRIMARY**]

primer² ('praɪmə) n **1** a person or thing that primes **2** a

device, such as a tube containing explosive, for detonating the main charge in a gun, mine, etc **3** a substance, such as paint, applied to a surface as a base, sealer, etc [c15: see **PRIME** (vb)]

prime rate n the lowest commercial interest rate charged by a bank at a particular time

prime time n the peak viewing time on television, for which advertising rates are the highest

primeval *or* **primaeval** (praɪ'mi:vəl) *adj* of or belonging to the first age or ages, esp of the world [c17: from Latin *prīmaevus* youthful, from *prīmus* first + *aevum* age] > **pri'mevally** *or* **pri'maevally** *adv*

priming ('praɪmɪŋ) n **1** something used to prime **2** a substance, used to ignite an explosive charge

primitive ('prɪmɪtɪv) *adj* **1** of or belonging to the first or beginning; original **2** characteristic of an early state, esp in being crude or uncivilized: *a primitive dwelling* **3** *anthropol* denoting or relating to a preliterate and nonindustrial social system **4** *biology* of, relating to, or resembling an early stage in the evolutionary development of a particular group of organisms: *primitive amphibians* **5** showing the characteristics of primitive painters; untrained, childlike, or naive **6** *obsolete* of, relating to, or denoting rocks formed in or before the Palaeozoic era **7** *obsolete* denoting a word from which another word is derived, as for example *hope*, from which *hopeless* is derived **8** *Protestant theol* of, relating to, or associated with a minority group that breaks away from a sect, denomination, or Church in order to return to what is regarded as the original simplicity of the Gospels ▷ n **9** a primitive person or thing **10 a** an artist whose work does not conform to traditional, academic, or avant-garde standards of Western painting, such as a painter from an African or Oceanic civilization **b** a painter of the pre-Renaissance era in European painting **c** a painter of any era whose work appears childlike or untrained. Also called (for senses 11a, 11c): **naive** **11 a** a work by such an artist **12** a word or concept from which another word or concept is derived **13** *maths* a curve, function, or other form from which another is derived [c14: from Latin *prīmitīvus* earliest of its kind, primitive, from *prīmus* first] > **'primitively** *adv* > **'primitiveness** n

primitivism ('prɪmɪtɪˌvɪzəm) n **1** the condition of being primitive **2** the notion that the value of primitive cultures is superior to that of the modern world > **'primitivist** n, *adj*

Primitivo (ˌprɪmɪ'ti:vəʊ) n, pl **-vos** **1** a black grape grown in the Puglia region of Italy, used for making wine **2** a strong red wine made from this grape [c21: from Italian, literally: primitive, probably because the grape tends to ripen earlier than other grapes]

primo ('pri:məʊ) n, pl **-mos** *or* **-mi** (-mɪ) **1** *music* the upper or right-hand part in a piano duet **2** Also called: **primo tempo** at the same speed as at the beginning of the piece [Italian: first, from Latin *prīmus*]

Primo de Rivera (*Spanish* 'primo de ri'βera) n **1 José Antonio** (xo'se an'tonjo). 1903–36, Spanish politician; founded Falangism **2** his father, **Miguel** (mi'ɣɛl). 1870–1930, Spanish general; dictator of Spain (1923–30)

primogenitor (ˌpraɪməʊ'dʒɛnɪtə) n **1** a forefather; ancestor **2** an earliest parent or ancestor, as of a race [c17: alteration of **PROGENITOR** after **PRIMOGENITURE**]

primogeniture (ˌpraɪməʊ'dʒɛnɪtʃə) n **1** the state of being a first-born **2** *law* the right of an eldest son to succeed to the estate of his ancestor to the exclusion of all others [c17: from Medieval Latin *prīmōgenitūra* birth of a first child, from Latin *prīmō* at first + Late Latin *genitūra* a birth] > **primogenitary** (ˌpraɪməʊ'dʒɛnɪtərɪ, -trɪ) *adj*

primordial (praɪ'mɔ:dɪəl) *adj* **1** existing at or from the beginning; earliest; primeval **2** constituting an origin; fundamental **3** *biology* of or relating to an early stage of development [c14: from Late Latin *prīmōrdiālis* original, from Latin *prīmus* first + *ōrdīrī* to begin] > **pri'mordially** *adv*

primp (prɪmp) *vb* to dress (oneself), esp in fine clothes; prink [c19: probably from **PRINK**]

primrose ('prɪmˌrəʊz) n **1** any of various temperate primulaceous plants of the genus *Primula*, esp *P. vulgaris* of Europe, which has pale yellow flowers **2** short for **evening primrose** **3** Also called: **primrose yellow** a light to moderate yellow, sometimes with a greenish tinge ▷ *adj* **4** of, relating to, or abounding in primroses **5** of the colour primrose [C15: from Old French *primerose*, from Medieval Latin *prima rosa* first rose]

primrose path *n* the primrose path a pleasurable way of life

primula ('primjʊlə) *n* any primulaceous plant of the N temperate genus *Primula*, having white, yellow, pink, or purple funnel-shaped flowers with five spreading petals: includes the primrose, oxlip, cowslip, and polyanthus [C18: New Latin, from Medieval Latin *prīmula* (*vēris*) little first one (of the spring)]

primum mobile *Latin* ('praɪmʊm 'məʊbɪlɪ) *n* **1** a prime mover **2** *astronomy* the outermost empty sphere in the Ptolemaic system that was thought to revolve around the earth from east to west in 24 hours carrying with it the inner spheres of the planets, sun, moon, and fixed stars [C15: from Medieval Latin: first moving (thing)]

Primus ('praɪməs) *n* *trademark* a portable paraffin cooking stove, used esp by campers. Also called: **Primus stove**

prince (prɪns) *n* **1** (in Britain) a son of the sovereign or of one of the sovereign's sons **2** a nonreigning male member of a sovereign family **3** the monarch of a small territory, such as Monaco, usually called a principality, that was at some time subordinate to an emperor or king **4** any sovereign; monarch **5** a nobleman in various countries, such as Italy and Germany **6** an outstanding member of a specified group: *a merchant prince* [C13: via Old French from Latin *princeps* first man, ruler, chief] ▷ 'prince,like *adj* ▷ 'princedom *n*

Prince (prɪns) *n* full name *Prince Rogers Nelson*. born 1958, US rock singer, songwriter, record producer, and multi-instrumentalist. His albums include *Dirty Mind* (1981), *Purple Rain* (1984), *Parade* (1986), and *Emancipation* (1996); in 2007 he released his latest album *Planet Earth* as a free gift with a British newspaper

prince consort *n* the husband of a female sovereign, who is himself a prince

Prince Edward Island *n* an island in the Gulf of St Lawrence that constitutes the smallest Canadian province. Capital: Charlottetown. Pop: 137 864 (2004 est). Area: 5656 sq km (2184 sq miles). Abbrevs: **PE, PEI** ▷ **Prince Edward Islander** *n*

princeling ('prɪnslɪŋ) *n* **1** Also called: **princekin** a young prince **2** Also called: **princelet** the ruler of an insignificant territory; petty or minor prince

princely ('prɪnslɪ) *adj* **-lier, -liest 1** generous or lavish **2** of, belonging to, or characteristic of a prince ▷ *adv* **3** in a princely manner ▷ 'princeliness *n*

Prince of Darkness *n* another name for **Satan**

Prince of Peace *n* *Bible* the future Messiah (Isaiah 9:6): held by Christians to be Christ

Prince of Wales[1] *n* the eldest son and heir apparent of the British sovereign

Prince of Wales[2] *n* Cape Prince of Wales a cape in W Alaska, on the Bering Strait opposite the coast of the extreme northeast of Russia: the westernmost point of North America

Prince of Wales Island *n* **1** an island in N Canada, in Nunavut. Area: about 36 000 sq km (14 000 sq miles) **2** an island in SE Alaska, the largest island in the Alexander Archipelago. Area: about 4000 sq km (1500 sq miles) **3** an island in NE Australia, in N Queensland in the Torres Strait **4** the former name (until about 1867) of the island of **Penang**

prince regent *n* a prince who acts as regent during the minority, disability, or absence of the legal sovereign

Prince Regent *n* George IV as regent of Great Britain and Ireland during the insanity of his father (1811–20)

Prince Rupert ('ruːpət) *n* a port in W Canada, on the coast of British Columbia: one of the W termini of the Canadian National transcontinental railway. Pop: 14 643 (2001)

prince's feather *n* **1** an amaranthaceous garden plant, *Amaranthus hybridus hypochondriacus*, with upright spikes of bristly brownish-red flowers **2** a tall tropical polygonaceous plant, *Polygonum orientale*, with ovate leaves and hanging spikes of pink flowers

princess (prɪn'sɛs) *n* **1** (in Britain) a daughter of the sovereign or of one of the sovereign's sons **2** a nonreigning female member of a sovereign family **3** the wife and consort of a prince **4** any very attractive or outstanding woman **5** Also called: **princess dress, princess line** a style of dress with a fitted bodice and an A-line skirt that is shaped by seams from shoulder to hem without a seam at the waistline

princess royal *n* the eldest daughter of a British or (formerly) a Prussian sovereign: a title not always conferred

Princeton ('prɪnstən) *n* a town in central New Jersey: settled by Quakers in 1696; an important educational centre, seat of Princeton University (founded at Elizabeth in 1747 and moved here in 1756); scene of the battle (1777) during the War of American Independence in which Washington's troops defeated the British on the university campus. Pop: 13 577 (2003 est)

principal ('prɪnsɪp³l) *adj* (*prenominal*) **1** first in importance, rank, value, etc; chief **2** denoting or relating to capital or property as opposed to interest, etc ▷ *n* **3** a person who is first in importance or directs some event, action, organization, etc **4** (in Britain) a civil servant of an executive grade who is in charge of a section **5** *law* **a** a person who engages another to act as his agent **b** an active participant in a crime **c** the person primarily liable to fulfil an obligation **6** the head of a school or other educational institution **7** *finance* **a** capital or property, as contrasted with the income derived from it **b** the original amount of a debt on which interest is calculated **8** a main roof truss or rafter **9** *music* **a** the chief instrumentalist in a section of the orchestra **b** either of two types of open diapason organ stops, one of four-foot length and pitch and the other of eight-foot length and pitch [C13: via Old French from Latin *principālis* chief, from *princeps* chief man, **PRINCE**] ▷ 'principalship *n* ▷ 'principally *adv*

principal boy *n* the leading male role in a pantomime, played by a woman

principality (,prɪnsɪ'pælɪtɪ) *n*, *pl* **-ties 1** a territory ruled by a prince **2** the dignity or authority of a prince [C14 (in the sense: pre-eminence): via Old French from Latin *principālis* **PRINCIPAL**]

principal nursing officer *n* a grade of nurse concerned with administration in the British National Health Service

principal parts *pl n grammar* the main inflected forms of a verb, from which all other inflections may be deduced. In English they are generally considered to consist of the third person present singular, present participle, past tense, and past participle

principate ('prɪnsɪ,peɪt) *n* **1** a state ruled by a prince **2** a form of rule in the early Roman Empire in which some republican forms survived

principle ('prɪnsɪp³l) *n* **1** a standard or rule of personal conduct: *a man of principle* **2** (*often plural*) a set of such moral rules: *he'd stoop to anything; he has no principles* **3** a fundamental or general truth or law **4** the essence of something **5** a source or fundamental cause; origin **6** a rule or law concerning a natural phenomenon or the behaviour of a system: *the principle of the conservation of mass* **7** *chem* a constituent of a substance that gives the substance its characteristics and behaviour **8** in principle in theory or essence **9** on principle because of or in demonstration of a principle [C14: from Latin *principium* beginning, basic tenet]

● **USAGE** *Principle* and *principal* are often confused: the ● *principal* (not *principle*) *reason for his departure; the plan was* ● *approved in principle* (not *in principal*)

principled ('prɪnsɪp³ld) *adj* **a** having high moral principles **b** (*in combination*): *high-principled*

prink (prɪŋk) *vb* **1** to dress (oneself, etc) finely; deck out **2** (*intr*) to preen oneself [C16: probably changed from **PRANK**[2] (to adorn, decorate)]

print (prɪnt) *vb* **1** to reproduce (text, pictures, etc), esp in large numbers, by applying ink to paper or other material by one of various processes **2** to produce or reproduce (a manuscript, a book, data, etc) in print, as for publication **3** to write (letters, etc) in the style of printed matter **4** to mark or indent (a surface) by pressing (something) onto it **5** to produce a photographic print from (a negative) **6** (*tr*) to implant or fix in the mind or memory **7** (*tr*) to make (a mark or indentation) by applying pressure ▷ *n* **8** printed matter such as newsprint **9** a printed publication such as a newspaper or book **10** in print **a** in printed or published form **b** (of a book, etc) offered for sale by the publisher **11** out of print no longer available from a publisher **12** a design or picture printed from an engraved plate, wood block, or other medium **13** printed text, esp with regard to the typeface used: *small print* **14** a positive photographic image in colour or black and white produced, usually on paper, from a negative image on film. See **slide** (sense 12) **15 a** a fabric with a printed design **b** (*as modifier*): *a print dress* **16 a** a mark or indentation made by pressing something onto a surface **b** a stamp, die, etc, that makes such an impression **c** the surface subjected to such an impression **17** See **fingerprint** ▷ See also **print out** [C13 *priente*, from Old French: something printed, from *preindre* to make an impression, from Latin *premere* to press] > 'printable *adj*

printer ('prɪntə) *n* **1** a person or business engaged in printing **2** a machine or device that prints **3** *computing* an output device for printing results on paper

printer's devil *n* an apprentice or errand boy in a printing establishment

printing ('prɪntɪŋ) *n* **1** the process, business, or art of producing printed matter **2** printed text **3** Also called: **impression** all the copies of a book or other publication printed at one time **4** a form of writing in which letters resemble printed letters

printing press *n* any of various machines used for printing

printmaker ('prɪnt,meɪkə) *n* a person who makes print, esp a craftsman or artist in this field

print out *vb* (*tr, adverb*) **1** (of a computer output device, such as a line printer) to produce (printed information) **print-out** *or* **printout** *n* **2** such printed information

print shop *n* a place in which printing is carried out

prion ('priːɒn) *n* a protein in the brain, an abnormal form of which is thought to be the transmissable agent responsible for certain spongiform encephalopathies, such as BSE, scrapie, Creutzfeldt-Jakob disease, and kuru [C20: altered from *pro(teinaceous) in(fectious particle)*]

prior¹ ('praɪə) *adj* **1** (*prenominal*) previous; preceding **2** prior to before; until [C18: from Latin: previous]

prior² ('praɪə) *n* **1** the superior of a house and community in certain religious orders **2** the deputy head of a monastery or abbey, ranking immediately below the abbot [C11: from Late Latin: head, from Latin (adj): previous, from Old Latin *pri* before] > 'priorate *n* > 'prioress *n*

Prior ('praɪə) *n* **Matthew.** 1664–1721, English poet and diplomat, noted for his epigrammatic occasional verse

priority (praɪ'ɒrɪtɪ) *n, pl* **-ties 1** the condition of being prior; antecedence; precedence **2** the right of precedence over others **3** something given specified attention: *my first priority*

priory ('praɪərɪ) *n, pl* **-ories** a religious house governed by a prior, sometimes being subordinate to an abbey [C13: from Medieval Latin *priōria*; see PRIOR²]

Pripet ('priːpɪt) *n* a river in E Europe, rising in NW Ukraine and flowing northeast into Belarus across the **Pripet Marshes** (the largest swamp in Europe), then east into the Dnieper River. Length: about 800 km (500 miles)

Priscian ('prɪʃɪən) *n* Latin name *Priscianus Caesariensis.* 6th century AD, Latin grammarian

prise *or* **prize** (praɪz) *vb* (*tr*) **1** to force open by levering **2** to extract or obtain with difficulty: *they had to prise the news out of him* [C17: from Old French *prise* a taking, from *prendre* to take, from Latin *prehendere*; see PRIZE¹]

prism ('prɪzəm) *n* **1** a transparent polygonal solid, often having triangular ends and rectangular sides, for dispersing light into a spectrum or for reflecting and deviating light. They are used in spectroscopes, binoculars, periscopes, etc **2** *maths* a polyhedron having parallel, polygonal, and congruent bases and sides that

are parallelograms [C16: from Medieval Latin *prisma*, from Greek: something shaped by sawing, from *prizein* to saw]

prismatic (prɪz'mætɪk) *adj* **1** concerned with, containing, or produced by a prism **2** exhibiting bright spectral colours: *prismatic light* **3** *crystallog* another word for **orthorhombic** > pris'matically *adv*

prison ('prɪzən) *n* **1** a public building used to house convicted criminals and accused persons remanded in custody and awaiting trial **2** any place of confinement or seeming confinement [C12: from Old French *prisun*, from Latin *prēnsiō* a capturing, from *prehendere* to lay hold of]

prisoner ('prɪzənə) *n* **1** a person deprived of liberty and kept in prison or some other form of custody as a punishment for a crime, while awaiting trial, or for some other reason **2** a person confined by any of various restraints: *we are all prisoners of time* **3** take someone prisoner to capture and hold someone as a prisoner, esp as a prisoner of war

prisoner of war *n* a person, esp a serviceman, captured by an enemy in time of war. Abbreviation: **POW**

prisoner's base *n* a children's game involving two teams, members of which chase and capture each other to increase the number of children in their own base

prissy ('prɪsɪ) *adj* **-sier, -siest** fussy and prim, esp in a prudish way [C20: probably from PRIM + SISSY] > 'prissily *adv* > 'prissiness *n*

Priština (Serbian 'priːʃtina) *n* the capital of Kosovo: under Turkish control until 1912; severely damaged in the Kosovo conflict of 1999; nearby is the 14th-century Gračanica monastery. Pop: 261 000 (2005 est)

pristine ('prɪstaɪn, -tiːn) *adj* **1** of or involving the earliest period, state, etc; original **2** pure; uncorrupted **3** fresh, clean, and unspoiled: *his pristine new car* [C15: from Latin *pristinus* primitive; related to *prīmus* first, PRIME]
● USAGE The use of *pristine* to mean *fresh, clean, and*
● *unspoiled* is considered by some people to be incorrect

Pritchett ('prɪtʃɪt) *n* Sir V(ictor) S(awdon). 1900–97, British short-story writer, novelist, essayist, and autobiographer; his works include *Mr Beluncle* (1951) and *A Careless Widow* (1989)

prithee ('prɪðɪ) *interj archaic* pray thee; please [C16: shortened from *I pray thee*]

privacy ('praɪvəsɪ, 'prɪvəsɪ) *n* **1** the condition of being private or withdrawn; seclusion **2** the condition of being secret; secrecy

private ('praɪvɪt) *adj* **1** not widely or publicly known: *they had private reasons for the decision* **2** confidential; secret: *a private conversation* **3** not for general or public use: *a private bathroom* **4** (*prenominal*) individual; special: *my own private recipe* **5** (*prenominal*) having no public office, rank, etc: *a private man* **6** (*prenominal*) denoting a soldier of the lowest military rank **7** (of a place) retired; sequestered; not overlooked **8** in private in secret; confidentially ▷ *n* **9** a soldier of the lowest rank, sometimes separated into qualification grades, in many armies and marine corps [C14: from Latin *prīvātus* belonging to one individual, withdrawn from public life, from *prīvāre* to deprive, bereave] > 'privately *adv*

private bill *n* a bill presented to Parliament or Congress on behalf of a private individual, corporation, etc

private company *n* a limited company that does not issue shares for public subscription and whose owners do not enjoy an unrestricted right to transfer their shareholdings. See **public company**

private detective *n* an individual privately employed to investigate a crime, keep watch on a suspected person, or make other inquiries. Also called: **private investigator**

private enterprise *n* economic activity undertaken by private individuals or organizations under private ownership

privateer (,praɪvə'tɪə) *n* **1** an armed, privately owned vessel commissioned by a government for war service, esp the capture of enemy merchant ships **2** Also called: **privateersman** a commander or member of the crew of a privateer ▷ *vb* **3** a competitor, esp in motor racing, who is privately financed rather than sponsored by a manufacturer **4** (*intr*) to serve as a privateer

private eye *n informal* a private detective

Private Finance Initiative *n* (in Britain) a government scheme to encourage private investment in public projects. Abbreviation: **PFI**

private health insurance *n* insurance against the need for medical treatment as a private patient

private hotel *n* **1** a residential hotel or boarding house in which the proprietor has the right to refuse to accept a person as a guest, esp a person arriving by chance **2** *Austral & NZ* a hotel not having a licence to sell alcoholic liquor

private income *n* an income from sources other than employment, such as investment. Also called: **private means**

private life *n* the social or family life or personal relationships of an individual, esp of a person in the public eye, such as a politician or celebrity

private member *n* a member of a legislative assembly, such as the House of Commons, not having an appointment in the government

private member's bill *n* a public bill introduced in the House of Commons or the legislative assemblies of Canada, Australia, or New Zealand by a private member

private parts *or* **privates** ('praɪvɪts) *pl n* euphemistic terms for **genitals**

private patient *n Brit* a patient receiving medical treatment not paid for by the National Health Service

private pay bed *n* (in Britain) a bed in a National Health Service hospital, reserved for private patients who pay a consultant acting privately for treatment and who are charged by the health service for use of hospital facilities

private practice *n Brit* medical practice that is not part of the National Health Service

private school *n* a school under the financial and managerial control of a private body or charitable trust, accepting mostly fee-paying pupils

private secretary *n* **1** a secretary entrusted with the personal and confidential matters of a business executive **2** a civil servant who acts as aide to a minister or senior government official

private sector *n* the part of a country's economy that consists of privately owned enterprises

privation (praɪ'veɪʃən) *n* **1** loss or lack of the necessities of life, such as food and shelter **2** hardship resulting from this **3** the state of being deprived [C14: from Latin *prīvātiō* deprivation]

privative ('prɪvətɪv) *adj* **1** causing privation **2** expressing lack or negation, as for example the English suffix *-less* and prefix *un-* [C16: from Latin *prīvātīvus* indicating loss, negative] > **'privatively** *adv*

privatize *or* **privatise** ('praɪvɪ,taɪz) *vb* (*tr*) to transfer (the production of goods or services) from the public sector of an economy into private ownership and operation > **,privati'zation** *or* **,privati'sation** *n*

privet ('prɪvɪt) *n* **a** any oleaceous shrub of the genus *Ligustrum*, esp *L. vulgare* or *L. ovalifolium*, having oval dark green leaves, white flowers, and purplish-black berries **b** (*as modifier*): *a privet hedge* [C16: of unknown origin]

privilege ('prɪvɪlɪdʒ) *n* **1** a benefit, immunity, etc, granted under certain conditions **2** the advantages and immunities enjoyed by a small usually powerful group or class, esp to the disadvantage of others: *one of the obstacles to social harmony is privilege* **3** *US stock exchange* a speculative contract permitting its purchaser to make optional purchases or sales of securities at a specified time over a limited period of time ▷ *vb* (*tr*) **4** to bestow a privilege or privileges upon **5** (foll by *from*) to free or exempt [C12: from Old French *privilège*, from Latin *prīvilēgium* law relevant to rights of an individual, from *prīvus* an individual + *lēx* law]

privileged ('prɪvɪlɪdʒd) *adj* **1** enjoying or granted as a privilege or privileges **2** *law* **a** not actionable as a libel or slander **b** (of a communication, document, etc) that a witness cannot be compelled to divulge

privity ('prɪvɪtɪ) *n*, *pl* **-ties 1** a legally recognized relationship existing between two parties, such as that between lessor and lessee and between the parties to a contract: *privity of estate*; *privity of contract* **2** secret knowledge that is shared [C13: from Old French *priveté*]

privy ('prɪvɪ) *adj* privier, priviest **1** (postpositive; foll by *to*) participating in the knowledge of something secret **2** *archaic* secret, hidden, etc ▷ *n*, *pl* **privies 3** a lavatory, esp an outside one **4** *law* a person in privity with another. See **privity** (sense 1) [C13: from Old French *privé* something private, from Latin *prīvātus* PRIVATE]

privy council *n* **1** the council of state of a monarch or noble, esp formerly **2** (in Canada) a ceremonial body of advisers of the governor general, the chief of them being the Federal cabinet ministers **3** *archaic* a private or secret council

Privy Council *n* the private council of the British sovereign, consisting of all current and former ministers of the Crown and other distinguished subjects, all of whom are appointed for life > **Privy Counsellor** *n*

privy purse *n* (*often capitals*) **1** (in Britain) an allowance voted by Parliament for the private expenses of the monarch: part of the civil list **2** an official of the royal household responsible for dealing with the monarch's private expenses. Full name: **Keeper of the Privy Purse**

privy seal *n* (*often capitals*) (in Britain) a seal affixed to certain documents issued by royal authority: of less rank and importance than the great seal

Prix Goncourt (*French* pri gɔ̃kur) *n* an annual prize for a work of French fiction [C20: after the Académie *Goncourt*, which awards the prizes, founded by the will of Edmond Goncourt (1822–96), French writer]

prize¹ (praɪz) *n* **1 a** a reward or honour for victory or for having won a contest, competition, etc **b** (*as modifier*): *prize jockey*; *prize essay* **2** something given to the winner of any game of chance, lottery, etc **3** something striven for **4** any valuable property captured in time of war, esp a vessel [C14: from Old French *prise* a capture, from Latin *prehendere* to seize; influenced also by Middle English *prise* reward; see PRICE]

prize² (praɪz) *vb* (*tr*) to esteem greatly; value highly [C15: *prise*, from Old French *preisier* to PRAISE]

prize court *n law* a court having jurisdiction to determine how property captured at sea in wartime is to be distributed

prizefight ('praɪz,faɪt) *n* a boxing match for a prize or purse, esp one of the fights popular in the 18th and 19th centuries > **'prize,fighter** *n* > **'prize,fighting** *n*

prize ring *n* **1** the enclosed area or ring used by prizefighters **2** the prize ring the sport of prizefighting

PRK *abbreviation* photorefractive keratectomy

pro¹ (prəʊ) *adv* **1** in favour of a motion, issue, course of action, etc ▷ *prep* **2** in favour of ▷ *n*, *pl* **pros 3** (*usually plural*) an argument or vote in favour of a proposal or motion. See also **pros and cons** [from Latin *prō* (prep) in favour of]

pro² (prəʊ) *n*, *pl* **pros 1** *informal* short for **professional** ▷ *adj* **2** *informal* short for **professional** [C19: by shortening]

PRO *abbreviation* **1** Public Records Office **2** public relations officer

pro-¹ *prefix* **1** in favour of; supporting: *pro-Chinese* **2** acting as a substitute for: *proconsul*; *pronoun* [from Latin *prō* (adv and prep). In compound words borrowed from Latin, *prō-* indicates: forward, out (*project*); forward and down (*prostrate*); away from a place (*prodigal*); onward in time or space (*proceed*); extension outwards (*propagate*); before in time or place (*provide*, *protect*); on behalf of (*procure*); acting as a substitute for (*pronominal*); and sometimes intensive force (*promiscuous*)]

pro-² *prefix* before in time or position; anterior; forward: *prophase*; *procephalic*; *prognathous* [from Greek *pro* (prep) before (in time, position, rank, etc)]

proa ('prəʊə) *or* **prau** *n* any of several kinds of canoe-like boats used in the South Pacific, esp one equipped with an outrigger and sails [C16: from Malay *parāhū* a boat]

proactive (prəʊ'æktɪv) *adj* **1** tending to initiate change rather than reacting to events **2** *psychol* of or denoting a mental process that affects a subsequent process [C20: from PRO-² + (RE)ACTIVE]

pro-am ('prəʊ'æm) *adj* **1** (of a golf tournament, snooker tournament, etc) involving both professional and amateur players ▷ *n* **2** a sporting tournament involving both professional and amateur players

probability (ˌprɒbəˈbɪlɪtɪ) *n, pl* **-ties 1** the condition of being probable **2** an event or other thing that is probable **3** *statistics* a measure or estimate of the degree of confidence one may have in the occurrence of an event, measured on a scale from zero (impossibility) to one (certainty). It may be defined as the proportion of favourable outcomes to the total number of possibilities if these are indifferent (**mathematical probability**), or the proportion observed in a sample (**empirical probability**), or the limit of this as the sample size tends to infinity (**relative frequency**), or by more subjective criteria (**subjective probability**)

probable (ˈprɒbəbəl) *adj* **1** likely to be or to happen but not necessarily so **2** most likely: *the probable cause of the accident* ▷ *n* **3** a person who is probably to be chosen for a team, event, etc [c14: via Old French from Latin *probābilis* that may be proved, from *probāre* to prove]

probably (ˈprɒbəblɪ) *adv* **1** (*sentence modifier; not used with a negative or in a question*) in all likelihood or probability: *I'll probably see you tomorrow* ▷ *sentence substitute* **2** I believe such a thing or situation may be the case

proband (ˈprəʊbænd) *n* another name (esp US) for: **propositus** (sense 1) [c20: from Latin *probandus*, gerundive of *probāre* to test]

probang (ˈprəʊbæŋ) *n surgery* a long flexible rod, often with a small sponge at one end, for inserting into the oesophagus, as to apply medication [c17: variant, apparently by association with PROBE, of *provang*, name coined by W. Rumsey (1584–1660), Welsh judge, its inventor; of unknown origin]

probate (ˈprəʊbɪt, -beɪt) *n* **1** the act or process of officially proving the authenticity and validity of a will **2** the official certificate stating a will to be genuine and conferring on the executors power to administer the estate **3** (*modifier*) of, relating to, or concerned with probate: *probate value; a probate court* ▷ *vb* **4** (*tr*) *chiefly US & Canadian* to establish officially the authenticity and validity of (a will) [c15: from Latin *probāre* to inspect]

probation (prəˈbeɪʃən) *n* **1** a system of dealing with offenders by placing them under the supervision of a probation officer **2** on probation **a** under the supervision of a probation officer **b** undergoing a test period **3** a trial period, as for a teacher, religious novitiate, etc ▷ pro'bational *or* pro'bationary *adj*

probationer (prəˈbeɪʃənə) *n* a person on probation

probation officer *n* an officer of a court who supervises offenders placed on probation and assists and befriends them

probe (prəʊb) *vb* **1** (*tr*) to search into or question closely **2** to examine (something) with or as if with a probe ▷ *n* **3** something that probes, examines, or tests **4** *surgery* a slender and usually flexible instrument for exploring a wound, sinus, etc **5** a thorough inquiry, such as one by a newspaper into corrupt practices **6** *electronics* a lead connecting to or containing a measuring or monitoring circuit used for testing **7** any of various devices that provide a coupling link, esp a flexible tube extended from an aircraft to link it with another so that it can refuel **8** See **space probe** [c16: from Medieval Latin *proba* investigation, from Latin *probāre* to test] ▷ 'probeable *adj* ▷ 'prober *n*

probiotic (ˌprəʊbaɪˈɒtɪk) *n* **1** a harmless bacterium that helps to protect the body from harmful bacteria **2** a substance that encourages the growth of natural healthy bacteria in the gut ▷ *adj* **3** of or relating to probiotics: *probiotic yogurt* [c20: from PRO-¹ + (ANTI)BIOTIC]

probity (ˈprəʊbɪtɪ) *n* confirmed integrity; uprightness [c16: from Latin *probitās* honesty, from *probus* virtuous]

problem (ˈprɒbləm) *n* **1 a** any thing, matter, person, etc, that is difficult to deal with, solve, or overcome **b** (*as modifier*): *a problem child* **2** a puzzle, question, etc, set for solution **3** *maths* a statement requiring a solution usually by means of one or more operations or geometric constructions **4** (*modifier*) designating a literary work that deals with difficult moral questions: *a problem play* [c14: from Late Latin *problēma*, from Greek:

something put forward; related to *proballein* to throw forwards, from PRO-² + *ballein* to throw]

problematic (ˌprɒbləˈmætɪk) *or* **problematical** *adj* **1** having the nature or appearance of a problem; questionable **2** *logic obsolete* (of a proposition) asserting that a property may or may not hold ▷ ˌproblem'atically *adv*

pro bono publico *Latin* (ˈprəʊ ˈbəʊnəʊ ˈpʊblɪkəʊ) for the public good

proboscidean *or* **proboscidian** (ˌprəʊbəˈsɪdɪən) *adj* **1** of, relating to, or belonging to the *Proboscidea*, an order of massive herbivorous placental mammals having tusks and a long trunk: contains the elephants ▷ *n* **2** any proboscidean animal

proboscis (prəʊˈbɒsɪs) *n, pl* **-cises** *or* **-cides** (-sɪˌdiːz) **1** a long flexible prehensile trunk or snout, as of an elephant **2** the elongated mouthparts of certain insects, adapted for piercing or sucking food **3** any similar part or organ **4** *informal, facetious* a person's nose, esp if large [c17: via Latin from Greek *proboskis* trunk of an elephant, from *boskein* to feed]

procaine (ˈprəʊkeɪn, prəʊˈkeɪn) *n* a colourless or white crystalline water-soluble substance used, as the hydrochloride, as a local anaesthetic; 2-diethylaminoethyl-4-amino benzoate. Formula: $NH_2C_6H_4COOC_2H_4N(C_2H_5)_2$ [c20: from PRO-¹ + (CO)CAINE]

procathedral (ˌprəʊkəˈθiːdrəl) *n* a church serving as a cathedral

procedure (prəˈsiːdʒə) *n* **1** a way of acting or progressing in a course of action, esp an established method **2** the established mode or form of conducting the business of a legislature, the enforcement of a legal right, etc **3** *computing* another name for **subroutine** ▷ pro'cedural *adj* ▷ pro'cedurally *adv*

proceed (prəˈsiːd) *vb* (*intr*) **1** (often foll by *to*) to advance or carry on, esp after stopping **2** (often foll by *with*) to undertake and continue (something or to do something): *he proceeded with his reading* **3** (often foll by *against*) to institute or carry on a legal action **4** to emerge or originate; arise: *evil proceeds from the heart* [c14: from Latin *prōcēdere* to advance, from PRO-¹ + *cēdere* to go] ▷ pro'ceeder *n*

proceeding (prəˈsiːdɪŋ) *n* **1** an act or course of action **2 a** the institution of a legal action **b** any step taken in a legal action **3** (*plural*) the minutes of the meetings of a club, society, etc **4** (*plural*) legal action; litigation **5** (*plural*) the events of an occasion, meeting, etc

proceeds (ˈprəʊsiːdz) *pl n* **1** the profit or return derived from a commercial transaction, investment, etc **2** the result, esp the revenue or total sum, accruing from some undertaking or course of action, as in commerce

process¹ (ˈprəʊses) *n* **1** a series of actions that produce a change or development: *the process of digestion* **2** a method of doing or producing something **3** the course of time **4 a** a summons, writ, etc, commanding a person to appear in court **b** the whole proceedings in an action at law **5** a natural outgrowth or projection of a part, organ, or organism **6** (*modifier*) relating to the general preparation of a printing forme or plate by the use, at some stage, of photography ▷ *vb* (*tr*) **7** to subject to a routine procedure; handle **8** to treat or prepare by a special method, esp to treat (food) in order to preserve it: *to process cheese* **9 a** to institute legal proceedings against **b** to serve a process on **10** *photog* **a** to develop, rinse, fix, wash, and dry (exposed film, etc) **b** to produce final prints or slides from (undeveloped film) **11** *computing* to perform mathematical and logical operations on (data) according to programmed instructions in order to obtain the required information [c14: from Old French *procès*, from Latin *prōcessus* an advancing, from *prōcēdere* to PROCEED]

process² (prəˈses) *vb* (*intr*) to proceed in or as if in a procession [c19: back formation from PROCESSION]

procession (prəˈseʃən) *n* **1** the act of proceeding in a regular formation **2** a group of people or things moving forwards in an orderly, regular, or ceremonial manner **3** *Christianity* the emanation of the Holy Spirit ▷ *vb* **4** (*intr*) *rare* to go in procession [c12: via Old French from Latin *prōcessiō* a marching forwards]

processional (prəˈsɛʃənəl) *adj* **1** of, relating to, or suitable for a procession ▷ *n* **2** *Christianity* **a** a book containing the prayers, hymns, litanies, and liturgy prescribed for processions **b** a hymn, litany, etc, used in a procession

processor (ˈprəʊsɛsə) *n* **1** *computing* another name for **central processing unit 2** a person or thing that carries out a process

process-server *n* a sheriff's officer who serves legal documents such as writs for appearance in court

procès-verbal *French* (prɔsɛvɛrbal) *n, pl* -*baux* (-bo) a written record of an official proceeding; minutes [C17: from French: see PROCESS¹, VERBAL]

pro-choice *adj* (of an organization, pressure group, etc) supporting the right of a woman to have an abortion. See **pro-life**

prochronism (ˈprəʊkrəˌnɪzəm) *n* an error in dating that places an event earlier than it actually occurred [C17: from PRO-² + Greek *khronos* time + -ISM, by analogy with ANACHRONISM]

proclaim (prəˈkleɪm) *vb* (*tr*) **1** (*may take a clause as object*) to announce publicly **2** to praise or extol [C14: from Latin *prōclāmāre* to shout aloud] > proˈclaimer *n* > proclamation (ˌprɒkləˈmeɪʃən) *n* > proclamatory (prəˈklæmətərɪ, -trɪ) *adj*

proclitic (prəʊˈklɪtɪk) *adj* **1 a** relating to or denoting a monosyllabic word or form having no stress or accent and pronounced as a prefix of the following word, as in English 't for *it* in '*twas* **b** (in classical Greek) relating to or denoting a word that throws its accent onto the following word ▷ *n* **2** a proclitic word or form [C19: from New Latin *proclīticus*, from Greek *proklinein* to lean forwards; formed on the model of ENCLITIC]

proclivity (prəˈklɪvɪtɪ) *n, pl* -ties a tendency or inclination [C16: from Latin *prōclīvitās*, from *prōclīvis* steep, from PRO-¹ + *clīvus* a slope]

Proclus (ˈprəʊkləs, ˈprɒk-) *n* ?410–485 AD, Greek Neo-Platonist philosopher

Procne (ˈprɒknɪ) *n Greek myth* a princess of Athens, who punished her husband for raping her sister Philomela by feeding him the flesh of their son. She was changed at her death into a swallow. See **Philomela**

proconsul (prəʊˈkɒnsəl) *n* **1** an administrator or governor of a colony, occupied territory, or other dependency **2** (in ancient Rome) the governor of a senatorial province [C14: from Latin, from *prō consule* (someone acting) for the consul. See PRO-², CONSUL] > proconsular (prəʊˈkɒnsjʊlə) *adj*

Procopius (prəʊˈkəʊpɪəs) *n* ?490–?562 AD, Byzantine historian, noted for his account of the wars of Justinian I against the Persians, Vandals, and Ostrogoths

procrastinate (prəʊˈkræstɪˌneɪt, prə-) *vb* (*usually intr*) to put off or defer (an action) until a later time; delay [C16: from Latin *prōcrāstināre* to postpone until tomorrow, from PRO-¹ + *crās* tomorrow] > proˌcrastiˈnation *n* > proˈcrastiˌnator *n*

procreate (ˈprəʊkrɪˌeɪt) *vb* **1** to beget or engender (offspring) **2** (*tr*) to bring into being [C16: from Latin *prōcreāre*, from PRO-¹ + *creāre* to create] > ˈprocreant or ˈprocreˌative *adj* > ˌprocreˈation *n* > ˈprocreˌator *n*

Procrustean (prəʊˈkrʌstɪən) *adj* tending or designed to produce conformity by violent or ruthless methods

Procrustes (prəʊˈkrʌstiːz) *n Greek myth* a robber, who put travellers in his bed, stretching or lopping off their limbs so that they fitted it [C16: from Greek *Prokroustēs* the stretcher, from *prokrouein* to extend by hammering out]

proctology (prɒkˈtɒlədʒɪ) *n* the branch of medical science concerned with the rectum

proctor (ˈprɒktə) *n* **1 a** a member of the teaching staff of any of certain universities having the duties of enforcing discipline **2** (formerly) an agent, esp one engaged to conduct another's case in a court **3** *Church of England* one of the elected representatives of the clergy in Convocation and the General Synod [C14: syncopated variant of PROCURATOR] > proctorial (prɒkˈtɔːrɪəl) *adj*

procumbent (prəʊˈkʌmbənt) *adj* Also called: **prostrate 1** (of stems) growing along the ground **2** leaning forwards or lying on the face [C17: from Latin *prōcumbere* to fall

forwards; compare INCUMBENT]

procurator (ˈprɒkjʊˌreɪtə) *n* **1** (in ancient Rome) a civil official of the emperor's administration, often employed as the governor of a minor province or as a financial agent **2** *rare* a person engaged and authorized by another to manage his affairs [C13: from Latin: a manager, from *prōcūrāre* to attend to] > procuracy (ˈprɒkjʊrəsɪ) *or* ˈprocuˌratorship *n* > procuratorial (ˌprɒkjʊrəˈtɔːrɪəl) *adj*

procurator fiscal *n* (in Scotland) a legal officer who performs the functions of public prosecutor and coroner

procure (prəˈkjʊə) *vb* **1** (*tr*) to obtain or acquire; secure **2** to obtain (women or girls) to act as prostitutes [C13: from Latin *prōcūrāre* to look after, from PRO-¹ + *cūrāre* to care for] > proˈcurable *adj* > proˈcurement *n*

procurer (prəˈkjʊərə) *n* a person who procures, esp one who procures women or girls as prostitutes

prod (prɒd) *vb* prods, prodding, prodded **1** to poke or jab with or as if with a pointed object **2** (*tr*) to rouse or urge to action ▷ *n* **3** the act or an instance of prodding **4** a sharp or pointed object **5** a stimulus or reminder [C16: of uncertain origin] > ˈprodder *n*

prod. *abbreviation* **1** produce **2** produced **3** product

Prodi (ˈprɒdɪ) *n* **Romano** (rəˈmɑːnəʊ). born 1939, Italian politician; prime minister (1996–98) and from 2006; president of the European Commission (1999–2004)

prodigal (ˈprɒdɪɡ³l) *adj* **1** recklessly wasteful or extravagant, as in disposing of goods or money **2** lavish in giving or yielding: *prodigal of compliments* ▷ *n* **3** a person who spends lavishly or squanders money [C16: from Medieval Latin *prōdigālis* wasteful, from Latin *prōdigus* lavish, from *prōdigere* to squander, from PRO-¹ + *agere* to drive] > ˌprodiˈgality *n* > ˈprodigally *adv*

prodigious (prəˈdɪdʒəs) *adj* **1** vast in size, extent, power, etc **2** wonderful or amazing [C16: from Latin *prōdigiōsus* marvellous, from *prōdigium*, see PRODIGY] > proˈdigiously *adv* > proˈdigiousness *n*

prodigy (ˈprɒdɪdʒɪ) *n, pl* -gies **1** a person, esp a child, of unusual or marvellous talents **2** anything that is a cause of wonder and amazement **3** something monstrous or abnormal [C16: from Latin *prōdigium* an unnatural happening, from PRO-¹ + -*igium*, probably from *āio* I say]

prodrug (ˈprəʊˌdrʌg) *n* a compound that is itself biologically inactive but is metabolized in the body to produce an active therapeutic drug

produce *vb* (prəˈdjuːs) **1** to bring (something) into existence; yield **2** to bring forth (a product) by mental or physical effort; make: *she produced a delicious dinner for us* **3** (*tr*) to give birth to **4** (*tr*) to present to view: *to produce evidence* **5** to bring before the public: *he produced two plays and a film last year* **6** (*tr*) *geometry* to extend (a line) ▷ *n* (ˈprɒdjuːs) **7** anything that is produced; product [C15: from Latin *prōdūcere* to bring forward, from PRO-¹ + *dūcere* to lead] > proˈducible *adj* > proˌduciˈbility *n*

producer (prəˈdjuːsə) *n* **1** a person or thing that produces **2** *Brit* a person responsible for the artistic direction of a play, including interpretation of the script, preparation of the actors, and overall design **3** *US & Canadian* a person who organizes the stage production of a play, including the finance, management, etc **4** the person who takes overall administrative responsibility for a film or television programme. See **director** (sense 4) **5** the person who supervises the arrangement, recording, and mixing of a record **6** *economics* a person or business enterprise that generates goods or services for sale. See **consumer** (sense 1) **7** *chem* an apparatus or plant for making producer gas

producer gas *n* a mixture of carbon monoxide and nitrogen produced by passing air over hot coke, used mainly as a fuel

product (ˈprɒdʌkt) *n* **1** something produced by effort, or some mechanical or industrial process **2** the result of some natural process **3** a result or consequence [C15: from Latin *prōductum* (something) produced, from *prōdūcere* to bring forth]

product differentiation *n commerce* the real or illusory distinction between competing products in a market

production (prəˈdʌkʃən) *n* **1** the act of producing

2 anything that is produced; product **3** the amount produced or the rate at which it is produced **4** *economics* the creation or manufacture for sale of goods and services with exchange value **5** any work created as a result of literary or artistic effort **6** the organization and presentation of a film, play, opera, etc **7** (*modifier*) manufactured by a mass-production process: *a production model of a car* > pro'ductional *adj*

production line *n* a factory system in which parts or components of the end product are transported by a conveyor through a number of different sites at each of which a manual or machine operation is performed on them without interrupting the flow of production

productive (prə'dʌktɪv) *adj* **1** producing or having the power to produce; fertile **2** yielding favourable or effective results **3** *economics* **a** producing or capable of producing goods and services that have monetary or exchange value **b** of or relating to such production: *the productive processes of an industry* **4** (*postpositive*; foll by *of*) resulting in: *productive of good results* > pro'ductively *adv* > pro'ductiveness *n*

productivity (ˌprɒdʌk'tɪvɪtɪ) *n* **1** the output of an industrial concern in relation to the materials, labour, etc, it employs **2** the state of being productive

product liability *n* the liability to the public of a manufacturer or trader for selling a faulty product

product life cycle *n marketing* the four stages (introduction, growth, maturity, and decline) into one of which the sales of a product fall during its market life

product line *n marketing* a group of related products marketed by the same company

product placement *n* the practice of a company paying for its product to be placed in a prominent position in a film or television programme as a form of advertising

proem ('prəʊɛm) *n* an introduction or preface, such as to a work of literature [C14: from Latin *prooemium* introduction, from Greek *prooimion*, from PRO-² + *hoimē* song] > proemial (prəʊ'iːmɪəl) *adj*

proenzyme (prəʊ'ɛnzaɪm) *n* the inactive form of an enzyme; zymogen

Prof. *abbreviation* Professor

profane (prə'feɪn) *adj* **1** having or indicating contempt, irreverence, or disrespect for a divinity or something sacred **2** not designed or used for religious purposes; secular **3** not initiated into the inner mysteries or sacred rites **4** vulgar, coarse, or blasphemous: *profane language* ▷ *vb* (*tr*) **5** to treat or use (something sacred) with irreverence **6** to put to an unworthy or improper use [C15: from Latin *profānus* outside the temple, from PRO-¹ + *fānum* temple] > profanation (ˌprɒfə'neɪʃən) *n* > pro'fanely *adv* > pro'faneness *n*

profanity (prə'fænɪtɪ) *n*, *pl* **-ties 1** the state or quality of being profane **2** vulgar or irreverent action, speech, etc

profess (prə'fɛs) *vb* **1** to affirm or announce (something, such as faith); acknowledge: *to profess ignorance; to profess a belief in God* **2** (*tr*) to claim (something, such as a feeling or skill, or to be or do something), often insincerely or falsely: *to profess to be a skilled driver* **3** to receive or be received into a religious order, as by taking vows [C14: from Latin *profitērī* to confess openly, from PRO-¹ + *fatērī* to confess]

professed (prə'fɛst) *adj* (*prenominal*) **1** avowed or acknowledged **2** alleged or pretended **3** professing to be qualified as: *a professed philosopher* **4** having taken vows of a religious order > professedly (prə'fɛsɪdlɪ) *adv*

profession (prə'fɛʃən) *n* **1** an occupation requiring special training in the liberal arts or sciences, esp one of the three learned professions, law, theology, or medicine **2** the body of people in such an occupation **3** the act of professing; avowal; declaration **4** Also called: profession of faith a declaration of faith in a religion, esp as made on entering the Church of that religion or an order belonging to it [C13: from Medieval Latin *professiō* the taking of vows upon entering a religious order, from Latin: public acknowledgment; see PROFESS]

professional (prə'fɛʃənəl) *adj* **1** of, relating to, suitable for, or engaged in as a profession **2** engaging in an activity for gain or as a means of livelihood **3 a** extremely competent in a job, etc **b** (of a piece of work or anything performed) produced with competence or skill **4** undertaken or performed for gain or by people who are paid ▷ *n* **5** a person who belongs to or engages in one of the professions **6** a person who engages for his livelihood in some activity also pursued by amateurs **7** a person who engages in an activity with great competence **8** an expert player of a game who gives instruction, esp to members of a club by whom he is hired > pro'fessionally *adv* > pro'fessionalism *n* > pro'fessiona,lism *n*

professional foul *n football* a deliberate foul committed as a last-ditch tactic to prevent an opponent from scoring

professor (prə'fɛsə) *n* **1** the principal lecturer or teacher in a field of learning at a university or college; a holder of a university chair **2** *chiefly US & Canadian* any teacher in a university or college **3** a person who professes his opinions, beliefs, etc [C14: from Medieval Latin: one who has made his profession in a religious order, from Latin: a public teacher; see PROFESS] > professorial (ˌprɒfɪ'sɔːrɪəl) *adj* > ,profes'sorially *adv* > professoriate (ˌprɒfɪ'sɔːrɪɪt) *or* professorate (prə'fɛsərɪt) *n*

proffer ('prɒfə) *vb* **1** (*tr*) to offer for acceptance; tender ▷ *n* **2** the act of proffering [C13: from Old French *proffrir*, from PRO-¹ + *offrir* to offer]

proficient (prə'fɪʃənt) *adj* **1** having great facility (in an art, occupation, etc); skilled ▷ *n* **2** an archaic word for an expert [C16: from Latin *prōficere* to make progress, from PRO-¹ + *facere* to make] > pro'ficiency *n* > pro'ficiently *adv*

profile ('prəʊfaɪl) *n* **1** a side view, outline, or representation of an object, esp of a human face or head **2** a short biographical sketch of a subject **3** a graph, table, or list of scores representing the extent to which a person, field, or object exhibits various tested characteristics or tendencies: *a population profile* **4** a vertical section of soil from the ground surface to the parent rock showing the different horizons **5 a** a vertical section of part of the earth's crust showing the layers of rock **b** a representation of such a section **6** the outline of the shape of a river valley either from source to mouth (**long profile**) or at right angles to the flow of the river (**cross profile**) ▷ *vb* (*tr*) **7** to draw, write, or make a profile of **8** to cut out a shape from a blank (as of steel) with a cutter [C17: from Italian *profilo*, from *profilare* to sketch lightly, from PRO-¹ + Latin *fīlum* thread] > profilist ('prəʊfɪlɪst) *n*

profile component *n Brit education* attainment targets in different subjects brought together for the general assessment of a pupil

profiling ('prəʊˌfaɪlɪŋ) *n* the practice of categorizing people and predicting their behaviour according to particular characteristics such as race or age: *racial profiling*

profit ('prɒfɪt) *n* **1** (*often plural*) excess of revenues over outlays and expenses in a business enterprise over a given period of time, usually a year **2** the monetary gain derived from a transaction **3** income derived from property or an investment, as contrasted with capital gains **4** *economics* **a** the income or reward accruing to a successful entrepreneur and held to be the motivating factor of all economic activity in a capitalist economy **b** (*as modifier*): *the profit motive* **5** a gain, benefit, or advantage ▷ *vb* **6** to gain or cause to gain profit [C14: from Latin *prōfectus* advance, from *prōficere* to make progress; see PROFICIENT] > 'profitless *adj*

profitable ('prɒfɪtəbəl) *adj* affording gain, benefit, or profit > 'profitably *adv* > ,profita'bility *n*

profit and loss *n book-keeping* an account compiled at the end of a financial year showing that year's revenue and expense items and indicating gross and net profit or loss

profit centre *n* a unit or department of a company that is responsible for its costs and its profits

profiteer (ˌprɒfɪ'tɪə) *n* **1** a person who makes excessive profits, esp by charging exorbitant prices for goods in short supply ▷ *vb* **2** (*intr*) to make excessive profits

profiterole (ˌprɒfɪtə'rəʊl, 'prɒfɪtəˌrəʊl, prə'fɪtəˌrəʊl) *n* a small case of choux pastry with a sweet or savoury filling [C16: from French, literally: a small profit, (related to the gifts, etc, given to a servant), from *profiter* to PROFIT]

profit-sharing *n* a system in which a portion of the net profit of a business is distributed to its employees, usually in proportion to their wages or their length of service

profit taking *n* selling commodities, securities, etc, at a profit after a rise in market values or before an expected fall in values

profit warning *n* a public announcement made by a company to shareholders and others warning that profits for a stated period will be much lower than had been expected

profligate ('prɒflɪɡɪt) *adj* 1 shamelessly immoral or debauched 2 wildly extravagant or wasteful ▷ *n* 3 a profligate person [c16: from Latin *prōflīgātus* corrupt, from *prōflīgāre* to overthrow, from PRO-¹ + *flīgere* to beat] > **profligacy** ('prɒflɪɡəsɪ) *n* > **'profligately** *adv*

pro forma ('prəʊ 'fɔːmə) *adj* 1 prescribing a set form or procedure ▷ *adv* 2 performed in a set manner [Latin: for form's sake]

profound (prə'faʊnd) *adj* 1 penetrating deeply into subjects or ideas: *a profound mind* 2 showing or requiring great knowledge or understanding: *a profound treatise* 3 situated at or extending to a great depth 4 reaching to or stemming from the depths of one's nature: *profound regret* 5 intense or absolute: *profound silence* 6 thoroughgoing; extensive: *profound changes* ▷ *n* 7 archaic or literary a great depth; abyss [c14: from Old French *profund*, from Latin *profundus* deep, from PRO-¹ + *fundus* bottom] > **pro'foundly** *adv* > **profoundness** or **profundity** (prə'fʌndɪtɪ) *n*

Profumo (prə'fjuːməʊ) *n* John (**Dennis**). 1915–2006 British Conservative politician; secretary of state for war (1960–63). He resigned after a scandal that threatened the government of Harold Macmillan

profuse (prə'fjuːs) *adj* 1 plentiful, copious, or abundant: *profuse compliments* 2 (often foll by *in*) free or generous in the giving (of): *profuse in thanks* [c15: from Latin *profundere* to pour lavishly] > **pro'fusely** *adv* > **pro'fuseness** or **pro'fusion** *n*

progenitive (prəʊ'dʒɛnɪtɪv) *adj* capable of bearing offspring > **pro'genitiveness** *n*

progenitor (prəʊ'dʒɛnɪtə) *n* 1 a direct ancestor 2 an originator or founder of a future development; precursor [c14: from Latin: ancestor, from PRO-¹ + *genitor* parent, from *gignere* to beget]

progeny ('prɒdʒɪnɪ) *n*, *pl* -nies 1 the immediate descendant or descendants of a person, animal, etc 2 a result or outcome [c13: from Latin *prōgeniēs* lineage; see PROGENITOR]

progesterone (prəʊ'dʒɛstəˌrəʊn) *n* a steroid hormone, secreted mainly by the corpus luteum in the ovary, that prepares and maintains the uterus for pregnancy. Formula: $C_{21}H_{30}O_2$ [c20: from PRO-¹ + GE(STATION) + STER(OL) + -ONE]

progestogen (prəʊ'dʒɛstədʒən) or **progestin** (prə'dʒɛstɪn) *n* any of a group of steroid hormones that have progesterone-like activity, used in oral contraceptives and in treating gynaecological disorders [c20: from PROGEST(ERONE) + -O- + -GEN]

prognathous (prɒɡ'neɪθəs) or **prognathic** (prɒɡ'næθɪk) *adj* having a projecting lower jaw [c19: from PRO-² + Greek *gnathos* jaw]

prognosis (prɒɡ'nəʊsɪs) *n*, *pl* -noses (-'nəʊsiːz) 1 *med* a prediction of the course or outcome of a disease or disorder 2 any forecast or prediction [c17: via Latin from Greek: knowledge beforehand]

prognostic (prɒɡ'nɒstɪk) *adj* 1 of, relating to, or serving as a prognosis 2 foretelling or predicting ▷ *n* 3 *med* any symptom or sign used in making a prognosis 4 a sign or forecast of some future occurrence [c15: from Old French *pronostique*, from Latin *prognōsticum*, from Greek *prognōstikon*, from *progignōskein* to know in advance]

prognosticate (prɒɡ'nɒstɪˌkeɪt) *vb* 1 to foretell (future events) according to present signs or indications; prophesy 2 (*tr*) to foreshadow or portend [c16: from Medieval Latin *prognōsticāre* to predict] > **progˌnostiˈcation** *n* > **progˈnosticative** *adj*

> **progˈnostiˌcator** *n*

program or *sometimes* **programme** ('prəʊɡræm) *n* 1 a sequence of coded instructions fed into a computer, enabling it to perform specified logical and arithmetical operations on data ▷ *vb* -grams, -gramming, -grammed or -grammes, -gramming, -grammed 2 (*tr*) to feed a program into (a computer) 3 (*tr*) to arrange (data) into a suitable form so that it can be processed by a computer 4 (*intr*) to write a program > 'programmer *n*

programmable or **programable** (prəʊ'ɡræməbᵊl) *adj* (esp of a device or operation) capable of being programmed for automatic operation or computer processing

programme or US **program** ('prəʊɡræm) *n* 1 a written or printed list of the events, performers, etc, in a public performance 2 a performance or series of performances, often presented at a scheduled time, esp on radio or television 3 a specially arranged selection of things to be done: *what's the programme for this afternoon?* 4 a plan, schedule, or procedure 5 a syllabus or curriculum ▷ *vb* -grammes, -gramming, -grammed or US -grams, -graming, -gramed 6 to design or schedule (something) as a programme ▷ *n*, *vb* 7 *computing* a variant spelling of **program** [c17: from Late Latin *programma*, from Greek: written public notice, from PRO-² + *graphein* to write] > ˌprograˈmmatic *adj*

programmed learning *n* a teaching method in which the material to be learnt is broken down into easily understandable parts on which the pupil is able to test himself

programme music *n* music that is intended to depict or evoke a scene or idea

programme of study *n* Brit *education* the prescribed syllabus that pupils must be taught at each key stage in the National Curriculum

programming language *n* a simple language system designed to facilitate the writing of computer programs

program statement *n* a single instruction in a computer program

program trading *n* trading on international stock exchanges using a computer program to exploit differences between stock index futures and actual share prices on world equity markets

progress *n* ('prəʊɡrɛs) 1 movement forwards, esp towards a place or objective 2 satisfactory development, growth, or advance: *she is making progress in maths* 3 advance towards completion, maturity, or perfection: *the steady onward march of progress* 4 (*modifier*) of or relating to progress 5 *biology* increasing complexity, adaptation, etc, during the development of an individual or evolution of a group 6 *Brit* a stately royal journey 7 in progress taking place; under way ▷ *vb* (prə'ɡrɛs) 8 (*intr*) to move forwards or onwards, as towards a place or objective [c15: from Latin *prōgressus* a going forwards, from *prōgredī* to advance, from PRO-¹ + *gradī* to step]

progression (prə'ɡrɛʃən) *n* 1 the act of progressing; advancement 2 the act or an instance of moving from one thing or unit in a sequence to the next 3 *maths* a sequence of numbers in which each term differs from the succeeding term by a constant relation. See also **arithmetic progression, geometric progression, harmonic progression** 4 *music* movement, esp of a logical kind, from one note to the next (**melodic progression**) or from one chord to the next (**harmonic progression**) > pro'gressional *adj*

progressive (prə'ɡrɛsɪv) *adj* 1 of or relating to progress 2 proceeding or progressing by steps or degrees 3 (*often capital*) favouring or promoting political or social reform through government action, or even revolution, to improve the lot of the majority: *a progressive policy* 4 denoting or relating to an educational system that allows flexibility in learning procedures, based on activities determined by the needs and capacities of the individual child, the aim of which is to integrate academic with social development 5 (esp of a disease) advancing in severity, complexity, or extent 6 (of a dance, card game, etc) involving a regular change of partners after one figure, one game, etc 7 denoting an aspect of verbs in some languages, including English, used to express prolonged or continuous activity as opposed to momentary or habitual activity: *a progressive aspect of the verb "to walk" is "is walking."* ▷ *n* **8** a person who advocates progress, as in education, politics, etc **9 a** the progressive aspect of a verb **b** a verb in this aspect > pro'**gressively** *adv* > pro'**gressiveness** *n* > pro'**gressivism** *n* > pro'**gressivist** *n*

progress payment *n* an instalment of a larger payment made to a contractor for work carried out up to a specified stage of the job

prohibit (prə'hɪbɪt) *vb* (*tr*) **1** to forbid by law or other authority **2** to hinder or prevent [C15: from Latin *prohibēre* to prevent, from PRO-¹ + *habēre* to hold] > pro'**hibiter** *or* pro'**hibitor** *n*

prohibition (,prəʊɪ'bɪʃən) *n* **1** the act of prohibiting or state of being prohibited **2** an order or decree that prohibits **3** (*sometimes capital*) (esp in the US) a policy of legally forbidding the manufacture, transportation, sale, or consumption of alcoholic beverages except for medicinal or scientific purposes **4** *law* an order of a superior court (in Britain the High Court) forbidding an inferior court to determine a matter outside its jurisdiction > ,prohi'**bitionary** *adj*

Prohibition (,prəʊɪ'bɪʃən) *n* the period (1920–33) when the manufacture, sale, and transportation of intoxicating liquors was banned by constitutional amendment in the US > ,Prohi'**bitionist** *n*

prohibitive (prə'hɪbɪtɪv) *or less commonly* **prohibitory** (prə'hɪbɪtərɪ, -trɪ) *adj* **1** prohibiting or tending to prohibit **2** (esp of prices) tending to or designed to discourage sale or purchase > pro'**hibitively** *adv* > pro'**hibitiveness** *n*

project *n* ('prɒdʒɛkt) **1** a proposal, scheme, or design **2 a** a task requiring considerable and concerted effort, such as one by students **b** the subject of such a task ▷ *vb* (prə'dʒɛkt) **3** (*tr*) to propose or plan **4** (*tr*) to predict; estimate; extrapolate: *we can project future needs on the basis of the current birth rate* **5** (*tr*) to throw or cast forwards **6** to jut or cause to jut out **7** (*tr*) to send forth or transport in the imagination: *to project oneself into the future* **8** (*tr*) to cause (an image) to appear on a surface **9** to cause (one's voice) to be heard clearly at a distance **10** *psychol* **a** (*intr*) (esp of a child) to believe that others share one's subjective mental life **b** to impute to others (one's hidden desires and impulses), esp as a means of defending oneself **11** (*tr*) *geometry* to draw a projection of **12** (*intr*) to communicate effectively, esp to a large gathering [C14: from Latin *prōicere* to throw down, from PRO-¹ + *iacere* to throw]

projectile (prə'dʒɛktaɪl) *n* **1** an object or body thrown forwards **2** any self-propelling missile, esp one powered by a rocket or the rocket itself **3** any object that can be fired from a gun, such as a bullet or shell ▷ *adj* **4** capable of being or designed to be hurled forwards **5** projecting or thrusting forwards **6** *zoology* another word for **protrusile** [C17: from New Latin *prōjectilis* jutting forwards]

projection (prə'dʒɛkʃən) *n* **1** the act of projecting or the state of being projected **2** an object or part that juts out **3** See **map projection** **4** the representation of a line, figure, or solid on a given plane as it would be seen from a particular direction or in accordance with an accepted set of rules **5** a scheme or plan **6** a prediction based on known evidence and observations **7 a** the process of showing film on a screen **b** the image or images shown **8** *psychol* **a** the belief, esp in children, that others share one's subjective mental life **b** the process of projecting one's own hidden desires and impulses > pro'**jectional** *adj*

projectionist (prə'dʒɛkʃənɪst) *n* a person responsible for the operation of film projection machines

projective geometry *n* the branch of geometry concerned with the properties of solids that are invariant under projection and section

projector (prə'dʒɛktə) *n* **1** an optical instrument that projects an enlarged image of individual slides onto a screen or wall. Full name: **slide projector 2** an optical instrument in which a strip of film is wound past a lens at a fixed speed so that the frames can be viewed as a continuously moving sequence on a screen or wall. Full name: film *or* cine projector **3** a device for projecting a light beam **4** a person who devises projects

prokaryote *or* **procaryote** (prəʊ'kærɪɒt) *n* any organism having cells in each of which the genetic material is in a single DNA chain, not enclosed in a nucleus. Bacteria and archaeans are prokaryotes. See **eukaryote** [from PRO-² + KARYO- + -*ote* as in *zygote*] > prokaryotic *or* procaryotic (prəʊ,kærɪ'ɒtɪk) *adj*

Prokofiev (prə'kɒfɪ,ɛf; *Russian* pra'kɔfjɪf) *n* **Sergei Sergeyevich** (sɪr'gjej sɪr'gjejɪvɪtʃ). 1891–1953, Soviet composer. His compositions include the orchestral fairy tale *Peter and the Wolf* (1936), the opera *The Love for Three Oranges* (1921), and seven symphonies

Prokopyevsk (*Russian* pra'kɔpjɪfsk) *n* a city in S Russia: the chief coal-mining centre of the Kuznetsk Basin. Pop: 216 000 (2005 est)

prolactin (prəʊ'læktɪn) *n* a gonadotrophic hormone secreted by the anterior lobe of the pituitary gland. In mammals it stimulates the secretion of progesterone by the corpus luteum and initiates and maintains lactation

prolapse ('prəʊlæps, prəʊ'læps) *pathol* ▷ *n* **1** Also called: prolapsus (prəʊ'læpsəs) the sinking or falling down of an organ or part, esp the womb ▷ *vb* (*intr*) **2** (of an organ, etc) to sink from its normal position [C17: from Latin *prōlābi* to slide along, from PRO-¹ + *lābī* to slip]

prolate ('prəʊleɪt) *adj* having a polar diameter of greater length than the equatorial diameter. See **oblate¹** [C17: from Latin *prōferre* to enlarge] > '**prolately** *adv*

prole (prəʊl) *n, adj* derogatory, slang, chiefly Brit short for **proletarian**

prolegomenon (,prəʊlɛ'gɒmɪnən) *n, pl* -na (-nə) (*often plural*) a preliminary discussion, esp a formal critical introduction to a lengthy text [C17: from Greek, from *prolegein*, from PRO-² + *legein* to say] > ,prole'**gomenal** *adj*

prolepsis (prəʊ'lɛpsɪs) *n, pl* -ses (-siːz) **1** a rhetorical device by which objections are anticipated and answered in advance **2** use of a word after a verb in anticipation of its becoming applicable through the action of the verb, as *flat* in *hammer it flat* [C16: via Late Latin from Greek: anticipation, from *prolambanein* to anticipate, from PRO-² + *lambanein* to take] > pro'**leptic** *adj*

proletarian (,prəʊlɪ'tɛərɪən) *or less commonly* **proletary** ('prəʊlɪtərɪ, -trɪ) *adj* **1** of, relating, or belonging to the proletariat ▷ *n, pl* -tarians *or* -taries **2** a member of the proletariat [C17: from Latin *prōlētārius* one whose only contribution to the state was his offspring, from *prōlēs* offspring] > ,prole'**tarianism** *n*

proletariat (,prəʊlɪ'tɛərɪət) *n* **1** all wage-earners collectively **2** the lower or working class **3** (in Marxist theory) the class of wage-earners, esp industrial workers, in a capitalist society, whose only possession of significant material value is their labour **4** (in ancient Rome) the lowest class of citizens, who had no property [C19: via French from Latin *prōlētārius* PROLETARIAN]

pro-life *adj* (of an organization, pressure group, etc) supporting the right to life of the unborn; against abortion, experiments on embryos, etc > ,pro-'**lifer** *n*

proliferate (prə'lɪfə,reɪt) *vb* **1** to grow or reproduce (new parts, cells, etc) rapidly **2** to grow or increase or cause to grow or increase rapidly [C19: from Medieval Latin *prōlifer* having offspring, from Latin *prōlēs* offspring + *ferre* to bear] > pro'**liferative** *adj* > pro,life'**ation** *n*

prolific (prə'lɪfɪk) *adj* **1** producing fruit, offspring, etc, in abundance **2** producing constant or successful results **3** (often foll by *in* or *of*) rich or fruitful [C17: from Medieval Latin *prōlificus*, from Latin *prōlēs* offspring] > pro'**lifically** *adv* > pro'**lificness** *or* pro'**lificacy** *n*

prolix ('prəʊlɪks, prəʊ'lɪks) *adj* **1** (of a speech, book, etc) so long as to be boring; verbose **2** indulging in prolix speech or writing; long-winded [C15: from Latin *prōlixus* stretched out widely, from PRO-¹ + *līquī* to flow] > pro'**lixity** *or less commonly* pro'**lixness** > pro'**lixly** *adv*

prolocutor (prəʊ'lɒkjʊtə) *n* a chairman, esp of the lower house of clergy in a convocation of the Anglican Church [C15: from Latin: advocate, from PRO-¹ + *loquī* to speak] > pro'**locutor,ship** *n*

PROLOG *or* **Prolog** ('prəʊlɒg) *n* a computer programming language based on mathematical logic

P

[C20: from *pro(gramming in) log(ic)*]

prologue *or often US* **prolog** ('prəʊlɒg) *n* **1 a** the prefatory lines introducing a play or speech **b** the actor speaking these lines **2** a preliminary act or event **3** (in early opera) **a** an introductory scene in which a narrator summarizes the main action of the work **b** a brief independent play preceding the opera, esp one in honour of a patron ▷ *vb* **-logues, -loguing, -logued** *or US* **-logs, -loging, -loged 4** (*tr*) to introduce or preface with or as if with a prologue [C13: from Latin *prologus*, from Greek *prologos*, from PRO-² + *logos* discourse]

prolong (prə'lɒŋ) *vb* (*tr*) to lengthen in duration or space; extend [C15: from Late Latin *prōlongāre* to extend, from Latin PRO-¹ + *longus* long] > **prolongation** (,prəʊlɒŋ'geɪʃən) *n*

prolusion (prə'lu:ʒən) *n* **1** a preliminary written exercise **2** an introductory essay, sometimes of a slight or tentative nature [C17: from Latin *prōlūsiō* preliminary exercise, from *prōlūdere* to practise beforehand, from PRO-¹ + *lūdere* to play] > **prolusory** (prə'lu:zərɪ) *adj*

prom (prɒm) *n* **1** *Brit* short for **promenade concert 2** *US & Canadian informal*

PROM (prɒm) *n acronym computing* programmable read only memory

promenade (,prɒmə'nɑ:d) *n* **1** *chiefly Brit* a public walk, esp at a seaside resort **2** a leisurely walk, esp one in a public place for pleasure or display **3** a marchlike step in dancing **4** a marching sequence in a square or country dance ▷ *vb* **5** to take a promenade in or through (a place) **6** (*intr*) *dancing* to perform a promenade **7** (*tr*) to display or exhibit (someone or oneself) on or as if on a promenade [C16: from French, from *promener* to lead out for a walk, from Late Latin *prōmināre* to drive (cattle) along, from PRO-¹ + *mināre* to drive, probably from *minārī* to threaten] > ,**prome'nader** *n*

promenade concert *n* a concert at which some of the audience stand rather than sit

promenade deck *n* an upper covered deck of a passenger ship for the use of the passengers

promethazine (prəʊ'mɛθə,zi:n) *n* an antihistamine drug used to treat allergies and to prevent vomiting, esp in motion sickness [C20: from PRO(PYL) + (*di*)*meth*(*ylamine*) + (PHENOTHI)AZINE]

Promethean (prə'mi:θɪən) *adj* **1** of or relating to Prometheus **2** creative, original, or life-enhancing

Prometheus (prə'mi:θɪəs) *n Greek myth* a Titan, who stole fire from Olympus to give to mankind and in punishment was chained to a rock, where an eagle tore at his liver until Hercules freed him

promethium (prə'mi:θɪəm) *n* a radioactive element of the lanthanide series artificially produced by the fission of uranium. Symbol: Pm; atomic no: 61; half-life of most stable isotope, ^{145}Pm: 17.7 years; valency: 3; melting pt: 1042°C; boiling pt: 2460°C (approx.) [C20: New Latin from PROMETHEUS]

prominence ('prɒmɪnəns) *n* **1** the state or quality of being prominent **2** something that is prominent, such as a protuberance **3** relative importance or consequence **4** *astronomy* an eruption of incandescent gas from the sun's surface that can reach an altitude of several hundred thousand kilometres. Prominences are visible during a total eclipse. When viewed in front of the brighter solar disc, they are called filaments

prominent ('prɒmɪnənt) *adj* **1** jutting or projecting outwards **2** standing out from its surroundings; noticeable **3** widely known; eminent [C16: from Latin *prōminēre* to jut out, from PRO-¹ + *ēminēre* to project] > '**prominently** *adv*

promiscuous (prə'mɪskjʊəs) *adj* **1** indulging in casual and indiscriminate sexual relationships **2** consisting of a number of dissimilar parts or elements mingled in a confused or indiscriminate manner **3** indiscriminate in selection **4** casual or heedless [C17: from Latin *prōmiscuus* indiscriminate, from PRO-¹ + *miscēre* to mix] > pro'**miscuously** *adv* > pro'**miscuousness** *n* > ,promi'**scuity** *n*

promise ('prɒmɪs) *vb* **1** (often foll by *to*; when *tr, may take a clause as object or an infinitive*) to give an assurance of (something to someone); undertake (to do something) in the future: *I promise that I will come* **2** (*tr*) to undertake to give (something to someone): *he promised me a car for my birthday* **3** (when *tr, takes an infinitive*) to cause one to expect that in the future one is likely (to be or do something): *she promises to be a fine soprano* **4** (*usually passive*) to engage to be married; betroth: *I'm promised to Bill* **5** (*tr*) to assure (someone) of the authenticity or inevitability of something (often in the parenthetic phrase **I promise you,** used to emphasize a statement): *there'll be trouble, I promise you* ▷ *n* **6** an undertaking or assurance given by one person to another agreeing or guaranteeing to do or give something, or not to do or give something, in the future **7** indication of forthcoming excellence or goodness: *a writer showing considerable promise* **8** the thing of which an assurance is given [C14: from Latin *prōmissum* a promise, from *prōmittere* to send forth] > '**promiser** *n* > ,promi'**see** *n* > **promisor** (,prɒmɪ'sɔ:, 'prɒmɪ,sɔ:) *n*

Promised Land *n* **1** *Old Testament* the land of Canaan, promised by God to Abraham and his descendants as their heritage (Genesis 12:7) **2** heaven, esp when considered as the goal towards which Christians journey in their earthly lives **3** any longed-for place where one expects to find greater happiness or fulfilment

promising ('prɒmɪsɪŋ) *adj* showing promise of favourable development or future success > '**promisingly** *adv*

promissory ('prɒmɪsərɪ) *adj* **1** containing, relating to, or having the nature of a promise **2** *insurance* stipulating how the provisions of an insurance contract will be fulfilled after it has been signed

promissory note *n chiefly US commerce* a document, usually negotiable, containing a signed promise to pay a stated sum of money to a specified person at a designated date or on demand. Also called: **note, note of hand**

promo ('prəʊməʊ) *n, pl* **-mos a** *informal* something that is used to promote a product, esp a videotape film used to promote a pop record **b** (*as modifier*): *a promo video* [C20: shortened from *promotion*]

promontory ('prɒməntərɪ, -trɪ) *n, pl* **-ries 1** a high point of land, esp of rocky coast, that juts out into the sea **2** *anatomy* any of various projecting structures [C16: from Latin *prōmunturium* headland; related to *prōminēre*; see PROMINENT]

promote (prə'məʊt) *vb* (*tr*) **1** to further or encourage the progress or existence of **2** to raise to a higher rank, status, degree, etc **3** to advance (a pupil or student) to a higher course, class, etc **4** to urge the adoption of; work for: *to promote reform* **5** to encourage the sale of (a product) by advertising or securing financial support [C14: from Latin *prōmovēre* to push onwards, from PRO-¹ + *movēre* to move] > pro'**motion** *n* > pro'**motional** *adj*

promoter (prə'məʊtə) *n* **1** a person or thing that promotes **2** a person who helps to organize, develop, or finance an undertaking **3** a person who organizes and finances a sporting event, esp a boxing match

prompt (prɒmpt) *adj* **1** performed or executed without delay **2** quick or ready to act or respond ▷ *adv* **3** *informal* punctually ▷ *vb* **4** (*tr*) to urge (someone to do something) **5** to remind (an actor, singer, etc) of lines forgotten during a performance **6** (*tr*) to refresh the memory of **7** (*tr*) to give rise to by suggestion: *his affairs will prompt discussion* ▷ *n* **8** *commerce* **a** the time limit allowed for payment of the debt incurred by purchasing goods or services on credit **b** the contract specifying this time limit **c** Also called: **prompt note** a memorandum sent to a purchaser to remind him of the time limit and the sum due [C15: from Latin *promptus* evident, from *prōmere* to produce, from PRO-¹ + *emere* to buy] > '**promptly** *adv* > '**promptness** *n*

prompter ('prɒmptə) *n* **1** a person offstage who reminds the actors of forgotten lines or cues **2** a person, thing, etc, that prompts

promptitude ('prɒmptɪ,tju:d) *n* the quality of being prompt; punctuality

prompt side *n theatre* the side of the stage where the prompter is, usually to the actor's left in Britain and to his right in the United States

promulgate ('prɒməl,geɪt) *vb* (*tr*) **1** to put into effect (a

law, decree, etc), esp by formal proclamation **2** to
announce or declare officially **3** to make widespread
[c16: from Latin *prōmulgāre* to bring to public knowledge;
probably related to *provulgāre* to publicize, from PRO-¹ +
vulgāre to make common, from *vulgus* the common
people] > ˌpromul'gation *n* > 'promul,gator *n*

pron. *abbreviation* **1** pronominal **2** pronoun **3** pronounced
4 pronunciation

pronate (prəʊ'neɪt) *vb* (*tr*) to turn (a limb, hand, or foot)
so that the palm or sole is directed downwards [c19:
from Late Latin *prōnāre* to bend forwards, bow]
> pro'nation *n* > pro'nator *n*

prone (prəʊn) *adj* **1** lying flat or face downwards;
prostrate **2** sloping or tending downwards **3** having an
inclination to do something [c14: from Latin *prōnus* bent
forward, from PRO-¹] > 'pronely *adv* > 'proneness *n*

-prone *adj combining form* liable or disposed to suffer:
accident-prone

prong (prɒŋ) *n* **1 a** a sharply pointed end of an
instrument, such as on a fork **2** any pointed projecting
part ▷ *vb* **3** (*tr*) to prick or spear with or as if with a prong
[c15: related to Middle Low German *prange* a stake, Gothic
anaprangan to afflict] > pronged *adj*

pronghorn ('prɒŋˌhɔːn) *n* a ruminant mammal,
Antilocapra americana, inhabiting rocky deserts of North
America and having small branched horns: family
Antilocapridae. Also called: American antelope

pronominal (prəʊ'nɒmɪnᵊl) *adj* relating to or playing
the part of a pronoun [c17: from Late Latin *prōnōminālis*,
from *prōnōmen* a PRONOUN] > pro'nominally *adv*

pronoun ('prəʊˌnaʊn) *n* one of a class of words that
serves to replace a noun phrase that has already been or
is about to be mentioned in the sentence or context [c16:
from Latin *prōnōmen*, from PRO-¹ + *nōmen* noun]

pronounce (prə'naʊns) *vb* **1** to utter or articulate (a
sound or sequence of sounds) **2** (*tr*) to utter or articulate
(sounds or words) in the correct way **3** (*tr; may take a
clause as object*) to proclaim officially and solemnly: *I now
pronounce you man and wife* **4** (when *tr, may take a clause as
object*) to declare as one's judgment: *to pronounce the death
sentence upon someone* [c14: from Latin *prōnuntiāre* to
announce, from PRO-¹ + *nuntiāre* to announce]
> pro'nounceable *adj* > pro'nouncer *n*

pronounced (prə'naʊnst) *adj* **1** strongly marked or
indicated **2** (of a sound) articulated with vibration of
the vocal cords; voiced > pronouncedly
(prə'naʊnsɪdlɪ) *adv*

pronouncement (prə'naʊnsmənt) *n* **1** an official or
authoritative statement or announcement **2** the act of
pronouncing, declaring, or uttering formally

pronto ('prɒntəʊ) *adv informal* at once; promptly [c20:
from Spanish: quick, from Latin *promptus* PROMPT]

pronunciation (prəˌnʌnsɪ'eɪʃən) *n* **1** the act, instance, or
manner of pronouncing sounds **2** the supposedly
correct manner of pronouncing sounds in a given
language **3** a phonetic transcription of a word

proof (pruːf) *n* **1** any evidence that establishes or helps
to establish the truth, validity, quality, etc, of
something **2** *law* the whole body of evidence upon
which the verdict of a court is based **3** *maths, logic* a
sequence of steps or statements that establishes the
truth of a proposition **4** the act of testing the truth of
something (esp in the phrase **put to the proof**) **5** *Scots
law* trial before a judge without a jury **6** *printing* a trial
impression made from composed type, or a print-out
(from a laser printer, etc) for the correction of errors
7 (in engraving, etc) a print made by an artist or under
his supervision for his own satisfaction before he hands
the plate over to a professional printer **8** *photog* a trial
print from a negative **9 a** the alcoholic strength of proof
spirit **b** the strength of a beverage or other alcoholic
liquor as measured on a scale in which the strength of
proof spirit is 100 degrees ▷ *adj* **10** (*usually postpositive;
foll by against*) able to resist; impervious to: *the roof is proof
against rain* **11** having the alcoholic strength of proof
spirit **12** of proved strength or impenetrability: *proof
armour* ▷ *vb* **13** (*tr*) to take a proof from (type matter, a
plate, etc) **14** to proofread (text) or inspect (a print, etc),
as for approval **15** to render (something) proof, esp to

waterproof [c13: from Old French *preuve* a test, from Late
Latin *proba*, from Latin *probāre* to test]

-proof *adj, vb combining form* secure against (damage by);
(make) impervious to: *waterproof; mothproof; childproof*
[from PROOF (adj)]

proofread ('pruːfˌriːd) *vb* -reads, -reading, -read (-ˌrɛd)
to read (copy or printer's proofs) to detect and mark
errors to be corrected > 'proof,reader *n*

proof spirit *n* (in Britain and Canada) a mixture of
alcohol and water or an alcoholic beverage that contains
49.28 per cent of alcohol by weight, 57.1 per cent by
volume at 51°F: up until 1980 used as a standard of
alcoholic liquids

prop¹ (prɒp) *vb* props, propping, propped (when *tr*, often
foll by *up*) **1** (*tr*) to support with a rigid object, such as a
stick **2** (*tr*; usually also foll by *against*) to place or lean
3 (*tr*) to sustain or support ▷ *n* **4** something that gives
rigid support, such as a stick **5** *rugby* either of the
forwards at either end of the front row of a scrum [c15:
related to Middle Dutch *proppe* vine prop; compare Old
High German *pfropfo* shoot, German *Pfropfen* stopper]

prop² (prɒp) *n* short for **property** (sense 8)

prop³ (prɒp) *n* an informal word for **propeller**

propaedeutic (ˌprəʊpɪ'djuːtɪk) *n* **1** (*often plural*)
preparatory instruction basic to further study of an art
or science ▷ *adj* Also: propaedeutical **2** of, relating to, or
providing such instruction [c19: from Greek *propaideuein*
to teach in advance, from PRO-² + *paideuein* to rear]

propaganda (ˌprɒpə'gændə) *n* **1** the organized
dissemination of information, allegations, etc, to assist
or damage the cause of a government, movement, etc
2 such information, allegations, etc [c18: from Italian,
use of *propāgandā* in the New Latin title *Sacra Congregatio de
Propaganda Fide* Sacred Congregation for Propagating the
Faith] > ˌpropa'gandism *n* > ˌpropa'gandist *n, adj*

Propaganda (ˌprɒpə'gændə) *n RC Church* a congregation
responsible for directing the work of the foreign
missions and the training of priests for these

propagandize or **propagandise** (ˌprɒpə'gændaɪz) *vb*
(*intr*) to spread or organize propaganda

propagate ('prɒpəˌgeɪt) *vb* **1** *biology* to reproduce or cause
to reproduce; breed **2** (*tr*) to promulgate; disseminate
3 *physics* to move through, cause to move through, or
transmit, esp in the form of a wave: *to propagate sound*
4 (*tr*) to transmit (characteristics) from one generation
to the next [c16: from Latin *propāgāre* to increase (plants)
by cuttings, from *propāgēs* a cutting, from *pangere* to
fasten] > ˌpropa'gation *n* > ˌpropa'gational *adj*
> 'propagative *adj* > propagator ('prɒpəˌgeɪtə,
'propaˌgator) *n*

propane ('prəʊpeɪn) *n* a colourless flammable gaseous
alkane found in petroleum and used as a fuel. Formula:
$CH_3CH_2CH_3$ [c19: from PROPIONIC ACID + -ANE]

propanedioic acid (ˌprəʊpeɪndaɪ'əʊɪk) *n* a colourless
crystalline compound occurring in sugar beet. Formula:
$C_3H_4O_4.CH_2(COOH)_2$. Also called: malonic acid [c20: from
PROPANE + DI-¹ + -O- + -IC]

propanoic acid (ˌprəʊpə'nəʊɪk) *n* a colourless liquid
carboxylic acid used in inhibiting the growth of moulds
in bread. Formula: CH_3CH_2COOH. Former name:
propionic acid [c20: from PROPANE + -O- + -IC]

pro patria Latin ('prəʊ 'pætrɪˌɑː) for one's country

propel (prə'pɛl) *vb* -pels, -pelling, -pelled (*tr*) to impel,
drive, or cause to move forwards [c15: from Latin
prōpellere to drive onwards, from PRO-¹ + *pellere* to drive]
> propellant or propellent (prə'pɛlənt) *n*

propeller (prə'pɛlə) *n* **1** a device having blades radiating
from a central hub that is rotated to produce thrust to
propel a ship, aircraft, etc **2** a person or thing that
propels

propelling pencil *n* a pencil consisting of a metal or
plastic case containing a replaceable lead. As the point
is worn away the lead can be extended, usually by
turning part of the case

propend (prəʊ'pɛnd) *vb* (*intr*) *obsolete* to be inclined or
disposed [c16: from Latin *prōpendēre* to hang forwards]

propene ('prəʊpiːn) *n* a colourless gaseous hydrocarbon
of the alkene series obtained by cracking petroleum:
used in synthesizing many organic compounds.

Formula: CH₃CH:CH₂. Also called: propylene

propensity (prə'pɛnsɪtɪ) *n, pl* **-ties** **1** a natural tendency or disposition **2** *obsolete* partiality [c16: from Latin *prōpensus* inclined to, from *prōpendēre* to PROPEND]

proper ('prɒpə) *adj* **1** (*usually prenominal*) appropriate or suited for some purpose: *in its proper place* **2** correct in behaviour or conduct **3** excessively correct in conduct; vigorously moral **4** up to a required or regular standard **5** (*immediately postpositive*) (of an object, quality, etc) referred to or named specifically so as to exclude anything not directly connected with it: *his claim is connected with the deed proper* **6** (*postpositive; foll by to*) belonging to or characteristic of a person or thing **7** (*prenominal*) *Brit informal* (*intensifier*): *I felt a proper fool* **8** (*usually postpositive*) (of heraldic colours) considered correct for the natural colour of the object or emblem depicted: *three martlets proper* **9** *archaic* pleasant or good ⊳ *adv* **10** good and proper *informal* thoroughly ⊳ *n* **11** the parts of the Mass that vary according to the particular day or feast on which the Mass is celebrated [c13: via Old French from Latin *prōprius* special] > 'properly *adv* > 'properness *n*

proper fraction *n* a fraction in which the numerator has a lower absolute value than the denominator, as ½ or x/(3 + x²)

proper motion *n* the very small continuous change in the direction of motion of a star relative to the sun. It is determined from its radial and tangential motion

proper noun *or* **proper name** *n* the name of a person, place, or object, as for example *Iceland, Patrick,* or *Uranus.* See **common noun**

propertied ('prɒpətɪd) *adj* owning land or property

Propertius (prə'pɜːʃɪəs, -ʃəs) *n* **Sextus** ('sɛkstəs). ?50–?15 BC, Roman elegiac poet

property ('prɒpətɪ) *n, pl* **-ties** **1** something of value, either tangible, such as land, or intangible, such as patents, copyrights, etc **2** *law* the right to possess, use, and dispose of anything **3** possessions collectively or the fact of owning possessions of value **4 a** a piece of land or real estate, esp used for agricultural purposes **b** (*as modifier*): *property rights* **5** *chiefly Austral* a ranch or station, esp a small one **6** a quality, attribute, or distinctive feature of anything, esp a characteristic attribute such as the density or strength of a material **7** *logic obsolete* **8** any movable object used on the set of a stage play or film. Usually shortened to: **prop¹** [c13: from Old French *propriété,* from Latin *proprietās* something personal, from *proprius* one's own]

property bond *n* a bond issued by a life-assurance company, the premiums for which are invested in a property-owning fund

property centre *n* a service for buying and selling property, including conveyancing, provided by a group of local solicitors

property man *n* a member of the stage crew in charge of the stage properties

prophecy ('prɒfɪsɪ) *n, pl* **-cies** **1 a** a message of divine truth revealing God's will **b** the act of uttering such a message **2** a prediction or guess **3** the function, activity, or charismatic endowment of a prophet or prophets [c13: ultimately from Greek *prophētēs* PROPHET]

prophesy ('prɒfɪˌsaɪ) *vb* **-sies, -sying, -sied** **1** to reveal or foretell (something, esp a future event) by or as if by divine inspiration **2** (*intr*) *archaic* to give instruction in religious subjects [c14 *prophecien,* from PROPHECY] > 'prophe,siable *adj* > 'prophe,sier *n*

prophet ('prɒfɪt) *n* **1** a person who supposedly speaks by divine inspiration, esp one through whom a divinity expresses his will **2** a person who predicts the future: *a prophet of doom* **3** a spokesman for a movement, doctrine, etc [c13: from Old French *prophète,* from Latin *prophēta,* from Greek *prophētēs* one who declares the divine will, from PRO-² + *phanai* to speak] > 'prophetess *fem n*

Prophet ('prɒfɪt) *n* **the Prophet 1** the principal designation of Mohammed as the founder of Islam **2** a name for Joseph Smith as founder of the Mormon Church

prophetic (prə'fɛtɪk) *adj* **1** of or relating to a prophet or prophecy **2** containing or of the nature of a prophecy;

predictive > pro'phetically *adv*

prophylactic (ˌprɒfɪ'læktɪk) *adj* **1** protecting from or preventing disease **2** protective or preventive ⊳ *n* **3** a prophylactic drug or device, esp a condom [c16: via French from Greek *prophulaktikos,* from *prophulassein* to guard by taking advance measures, from PRO-² + *phulax* a guard]

prophylaxis (ˌprɒfɪ'læksɪs) *n* the prevention of disease or control of its possible spread

propinquity (prə'pɪŋkwɪtɪ) *n* **1** nearness in place or time **2** nearness in relationship [c14: from Latin *propinquitās* closeness, from *propinquus* near, from *prope* near by]

propionic acid (ˌprəʊpɪ'ɒnɪk) *n* the former name for **propanoic acid** [c19: from Greek *pro-* first + *pionic* from *piōn* fat, because it is first in order of the fatty acids]

propitiate (prə'pɪʃɪˌeɪt) *vb* (*tr*) **1** to appease or make well disposed; conciliate [c17: from Latin *propitiāre* to appease, from *propitius* gracious] > pro'pitiable *adj* > pro,piti'ation *n* > pro'pitiative *adj* > pro'piti,ator *n*

propitious (prə'pɪʃəs) *adj* **1** favourable; auguring well **2** gracious or favourably inclined [c15: from Latin *propitius* well disposed, from *prope* close to] > pro'pitiously *adv* > pro'pitiousness *n*

propjet ('prɒpˌdʒɛt) *n* another name for **turboprop**

propolis ('prɒpəlɪs) *n* a greenish-brown resinous aromatic substance collected by bees from the buds of trees for use in the construction of hives. Also called: bee glue, hive dross [c17: via Latin from Greek: suburb, bee glue, from *pro-* before + *polis* city]

proponent (prə'pəʊnənt) *n* a person who argues in favour of something [c16: from Latin *prōpōnere* to PROPOSE]

Propontis (prə'pɒntɪs) *n* the ancient name for (the Sea of) **Marmara**

proportion (prə'pɔːʃən) *n* **1** the correct or desirable relationship between parts of a whole; balance or symmetry **2** a part considered with respect to the whole **3** (*plural*) dimensions or size: *a building of vast proportions* **4** a share, part, or quota **5** *maths* a relationship that maintains a constant ratio between two variable quantities: *x increases in direct proportion to y* **6** *maths* a relationship between four numbers or quantities in which the ratio of the first pair equals the ratio of the second pair ⊳ *vb* (*tr*) **7** to adjust in relative amount, size, etc **8** to cause to be harmonious in relationship of parts [c14: from Latin *prōportiō* (a translation of Greek *analogia*), from phrase *prō portiōne,* literally: for (its, his, one's) PORTION] > pro'portionable *adj* > pro'portionably *adv* > pro'portionment *n*

proportional (prə'pɔːʃənˀl) *adj* **1** of, involving, or being in proportion ⊳ *n* **2** *maths* an unknown term in a proportion: *in a/b = c/x, x is the fourth proportional* > pro,portion'ality *n* > pro'portionally *adv*

proportional font *n* *computing* a font type in which the width of letters and symbols varies depending on the letter or symbol

proportional representation *n* representation of parties in an elective body in proportion to the votes they win. Abbreviation: PR Compare **first-past-the-post** See also **Additional Member System, Alternative Vote, party list, Single Transferable Vote**

proportionate *adj* (prə'pɔːʃənɪt) **1** being in proper proportion ⊳ *vb* (prə'pɔːʃəˌneɪt) **2** (*tr*) to make proportionate > pro'portionately *adv*

proposal (prə'pəʊzˀl) *n* **1** the act of proposing **2** something proposed, as a plan **3** an offer, esp of marriage

propose (prə'pəʊz) *vb* **1** (when *tr, may take a clause as object*) to put forward (a plan, motion, etc) for consideration or action **2** (*tr*) to nominate, as for a position **3** (*tr*) to plan or intend (to do something): *I propose to leave town now* **4** (*tr*) to announce the drinking of (a toast) to (the health of someone, etc) **5** (*intr; often foll by to*) to make an offer of marriage (to someone) [c14: from Old French *proposer,* from Latin *prōpōnere* to display, from PRO-¹ + *pōnere* to place] > pro'posable *adj* > pro'poser *n*

proposition (ˌprɒpə'zɪʃən) *n* **1** a proposal or topic presented for consideration **2** *philosophy* the content of a sentence that affirms or denies something and is capable of being true or false **3** *maths* a statement or theorem, usually containing its proof **4** *informal* a person or matter to be dealt with: *he's a difficult proposition* **5** an invitation to engage in sexual intercourse ▷ *vb* **6** (*tr*) to propose a plan, deal, etc, to, esp to engage in sexual intercourse [C14 *proposicioun*, from Latin *prōpositiō* a setting forth; see PROPOSE] > ˌpropoˈsitional *adj*

propositional calculus *n* the system of symbolic logic concerned only with the relations between propositions as wholes, taking no account of their internal structure. See **predicate calculus**

propositus (prəˈpɒzitəs) *or feminine* **proposita** (prəˈpɒzitə) *n, pl* -ti (-ˌtaɪ) *or feminine* -tae (-tiː) *med* the first patient to be investigated in a family study, to whom all relationships are referred. Also called (esp US): proband [from New Latin, from Latin *prōpōnere* to set forth; see PROPOUND]

propound (prəˈpaʊnd) *vb* (*tr*) **1** to suggest or put forward for consideration **2** *English law* to produce (a will or similar instrument) to the proper court or authority in order for its validity to be established [C16 *propone*, from Latin *prōpōnere* to set forth, from PRO-¹ + *pōnere* to place] > proˈpounder *n*

propranolol (prəʊˈprænəˌlɒl) *n* a drug used in the treatment of angina pectoris, arrhythmia, hypertension, and some forms of tremor. Formula: $C_{16}H_{21}NO_2$ [C20: from PRO(PYL) + *pr(op)*anol (from PROPANE + -OL) + -OL]

proprietary (prəˈpraɪɪtərɪ, -trɪ) *adj* **1** of, relating to, or belonging to property or proprietors **2** privately owned and controlled **3** *med* of or denoting a drug or agent manufactured and distributed under a trade name. See **ethical** (sense 3) ▷ *n, pl* -taries **4** *med* a proprietary drug or agent **5** a proprietor or proprietors collectively **6** **a** right to property **b** property owned **7** Also called: lord proprietary (in Colonial America) an owner, governor, or grantee of a proprietary colony [C15: from Late Latin *proprietārius* an owner, from *proprius* one's own] > proˈprietarily *adv*

proprietary name *n* a name that is a trademark

proprietor (prəˈpraɪətə) *n* **1** an owner of an unincorporated business enterprise **2** a person enjoying exclusive right of ownership to some property > proprietorial (prəˌpraɪəˈtɔːrɪəl) *adj* > proˈprietress *or* proˈprietrix *fem n*

propriety (prəˈpraɪɪtɪ) *n, pl* -ties **1** the quality or state of being appropriate or fitting **2** conformity to the prevailing standard of behaviour, speech, etc **3** the proprieties (*plural*) the standards of behaviour considered correct by polite society [C15: from Old French *propriété*, from Latin *proprietās* a peculiarity, from *proprius* one's own]

proprioceptor (ˌprəʊprɪəˈsɛptə) *n* *physiol* any receptor (as in the gut, blood vessels, muscles, etc) that supplies information about the state of the body [C20: from *proprio-*, from Latin *proprius* one's own + RECEPTOR] > ˌproprioˈceptive *adj*

proptosis (prɒpˈtəʊsɪs) *n, pl* -ses (-siːz) *pathol* the forward displacement of an organ or part, such as the eyeball [C17: via Late Latin from Greek, from *propiptein* to fall forwards]

propulsion (prəˈpʌlʃən) *n* **1** the act of propelling or the state of being propelled **2** a propelling force [C15: from Latin *prōpellere* to PROPEL] > propulsive (prəˈpʌlsɪv) *or* proˈpulsory *adj*

propyl (ˈprəʊpɪl) *n* (*modifier*) of, consisting of, or containing the monovalent group of atoms C_3H_7- [C19: from PROP(IONIC ACID) + -YL]

propylaeum (ˌprɒpɪˈliːəm) *or* **propylon** (ˈprɒpɪˌlɒn) *n, pl* -laea (-ˈliːə) *or* -lons, -la a portico, esp one that forms the entrance to a temple [C18: via Latin from Greek *propulaion* before the gate, from PRO-² + *pulē* gate]

propylene (ˈprəʊpɪˌliːn) *n* another name for **propene** [C19: from PROPYL + -ENE]

propylene glycol *n* a colourless viscous hydroscopic sweet-tasting compound used as an antifreeze and brake fluid. Formula: $CH_3CH(OH)CH_2OH$

pro rata (ˈprəʊ ˈrɑːtə) in proportion [Medieval Latin]

prorate (prəʊˈreɪt, ˈprəʊreɪt) *vb chiefly US & Canadian* to

divide, assess, or distribute (something) proportionally [C19: from PRO RATA] > proˈratable *adj* > proˈration *n*

prorogue (prəˈrəʊg) *vb* to discontinue the meetings of (a legislative body) without dissolving it [C15: from Latin *prorogāre* literally: to ask publicly, from *prō-* in public + *rogāre* to ask] > prorogation (ˌprəʊrəˈgeɪʃən) *n*

prosaic (prəʊˈzeɪɪk) *adj* **1** lacking imagination **2** having the characteristics of prose [C16: from Late Latin *prōsaicus*, from Latin *prōsa* PROSE] > proˈsaically *adv*

pros and cons *pl n* the various arguments in favour of and against a motion, course of action, etc [C16: from Latin *prō* for + *con*, from *contrā* against]

proscenium (prəˈsiːnɪəm) *n, pl* -nia (-nɪə) *or* -niums **1** the arch or opening separating the stage from the auditorium together with the area immediately in front of the arch **2** (in ancient theatres) the stage itself [C17: via Latin from Greek *proskēnion*, from *pro-* before + *skēnē* scene]

prosciutto (prəʊˈʃuːtəʊ; *Italian* proˈʃutto) *n* cured ham from Italy: usually served as an hors d'oeuvre [Italian, literally: dried beforehand, from *pro-* PRE- + *asciutto* dried]

proscribe (prəʊˈskraɪb) *vb* (*tr*) **1** to condemn or prohibit **2** to outlaw; banish; exile [C16: from Latin *prōscrībere* to put up a written public notice, from *prō-* in public + *scrībere* to write] > proˈscriber *n* > proˈscription *n* > proˈscriptive *adj* > proˈscriptively *adv* > proˈscriptiveness *n*

prose (prəʊz) *n* **1** spoken or written language as in ordinary usage, distinguished from poetry by its lack of a marked metrical structure **2** a passage set for translation into a foreign language **3** commonplace or dull discourse, expression, etc **4** (*modifier*) written in prose **5** (*modifier*) matter-of-fact ▷ *vb* **6** to write or say (something) in prose **7** (*intr*) to speak or write in a tedious style [C14: via Old French from Latin phrase *prōsa ōrātiō* straightforward speech, from *prorsus* prosaic, from *prōvertere* to turn forwards, from PRO-¹ + *vertere* to turn] > ˈproseˌlike *adj*

prosecute (ˈprɒsɪˌkjuːt) *vb* **1** (*tr*) to bring a criminal action against (a person) for some offence **2** (*intr*) **a** to seek redress by legal proceedings **b** to institute or conduct a prosecution **3** (*tr*) to engage in or practise (a profession or trade) **4** (*tr*) to continue to do (a task, etc) [C15: from Latin *prōsequī* to follow, from *prō-* forward + *sequī* to follow] > ˈproseˌcutable *adj*

prosecution (ˌprɒsɪˈkjuːʃən) *n* **1** the act of prosecuting or the state of being prosecuted **2 a** the institution and conduct of legal proceedings against a person **b** the proceedings brought in the name of the Crown to put an accused on trial **3** the lawyers acting for the Crown to put the case against a person **4** the following up or carrying on of something begun, esp with a view to its accomplishment or completion

prosecutor (ˈprɒsɪˌkjuːtə) *n* a person who institutes or conducts legal proceedings, esp in a criminal court

proselyte (ˈprɒsɪˌlaɪt) *n* **1** a person newly converted to a religious faith or sect; a convert, esp a gentile converted to Judaism ▷ *vb* **2** a less common word for **proselytize** [C14: from Church Latin *prosēlytus*, from Greek *prosēlutos* recent arrival, convert, from *proserchesthai* to draw near] > proselytism (ˈprɒsɪlɪˌtɪzəm) *n* > proselytic (ˌprɒsɪˈlɪtɪk) *adj*

proselytize *or* **proselytise** (ˈprɒsɪlɪˌtaɪz) *vb* to convert (someone) from one religious faith to another > ˈproselytˌizer *or* ˈproselytˌiser *n*

prosencephalon (ˌprɒsɛnˈsɛfəlɒn) *n, pl* -la (-lə) the part of the brain that develops from the anterior portion of the neural tube. Nontechnical name: forebrain [C19: from New Latin, from Greek *prosō* forward + *enkephalos* brain]

prosenchyma (prɒsˈɛŋkɪmə) *n* a plant tissue consisting of long narrow cells with pointed ends: occurs in conducting tissue [C19: from New Latin, from Greek *pros-* towards + *enkhuma* infusion; compare PARENCHYMA]

Proserpina (prəʊˈsɜːpɪnə) *n* the Roman goddess of the underworld. Greek counterpart: Persephone

prosimian (prəʊˈsɪmɪən) *n* **1** any primate of the primitive suborder *Prosimii*, including lemurs, lorises, and tarsiers ▷ *adj* **2** of, relating to, or belonging to the

Prosimii [C19: via New Latin from PRO-² + Latin *sīmia* ape]

prosit *German* ('prəʊzɪt) *interj* good health! cheers! [German, from Latin, literally: may it prove beneficial]

prosody ('prɒsədɪ) *n* **1** the study of poetic metre and of the art of versification, including rhyme, stanzaic forms, and the quantity and stress of syllables **2** a system of versification **3** the patterns of stress and intonation in a language [C15: from Latin *prosōdia* accent of a syllable, from Greek *prosōidia* song set to music, from *pros* towards + *ōidē*, from *aoidē* song; see ODE] > **prosodic** (prə'sɒdɪk) *adj* > **'prosodist** *n*

prosopopoeia *or* **prosopopeia** (ˌprɒsəpə'piːə) *n* **1** *rhetoric* another word for **personification 2** a figure of speech that represents an imaginary, absent, or dead person speaking or acting [C16: via Latin from Greek *prosōpopoiia* dramatization, from *prosōpon* face + *poiein* to make]

prospect *n* ('prɒspɛkt) **1** (*sometimes plural*) a probability or chance for future success, esp as based on present work or aptitude **2** a view or scene, esp one offering an extended outlook **3** a prospective buyer, project, etc **4** a survey or observation **5** *mining* **a** a known or likely deposit of ore **b** the location of a deposit of ore **c** the yield of mineral obtained from a sample of ore ▷ *vb* (prə'spɛkt) **6** (when *intr*, often foll by *for*) to explore (a region) for gold or other valuable minerals **7** (*tr*) to work (a mine) to discover its profitability **8** (*intr*; often foll by *for*) to search (for) [C15: from Latin *prōspectus* distant view, from *prōspicere* to look into the distance, from *prō-* forward + *specere* to look]

prospective (prə'spɛktɪv) *adj* **1** looking towards the future **2** (*prenominal*) anticipated or likely > **pro'spectively** *adv*

prospector (prə'spɛktə) *n* a person who searches for the natural occurrence of gold, petroleum, etc

prospectus (prə'spɛktəs) *n, pl* **-tuses 1** a formal statement giving details of a forthcoming event, such as the publication of a book or an issue of shares **2** a pamphlet or brochure giving details of courses, as at a college or school [C18: Latin, literally: distant view; see PROSPECT]

prosper ('prɒspə) *vb* (*usually intr*) to thrive, succeed, etc, or cause to thrive, succeed, etc in a healthy way [C15: from Latin *prosperāre* to succeed, from *prosperus* fortunate, from PRO-¹ + *spēs* hope]

prosperity (prɒ'spɛrɪtɪ) *n* the condition of prospering; success or wealth

prosperous ('prɒspərəs) *adj* **1** flourishing; prospering **2** rich; affluent; wealthy > **'prosperously** *adv*

Prost (*French* prɒst) *n* **Alain** (alɛ̃). born 1955, French motor-racing driver: world champion 1985, 1986, 1989, and 1993

prostaglandin (ˌprɒstə'ɡlændɪn) *n* any of a group of potent hormone-like compounds composed of essential fatty acids and found in all mammalian tissues, esp human semen. Prostaglandins stimulate the muscles of the uterus and affect the blood vessels; they are used to induce abortion or birth [C20: from *prosta(te) gland + -IN*; it was originally believed to be secreted by the prostate gland]

prostate ('prɒsteɪt) *n* **1** Also called: **prostate gland** a gland in male mammals that surrounds the neck of the bladder and urethra and secretes a liquid constituent of the semen ▷ *adj* **2** Also called: **prostatic** (prɒ'stætɪk) of or relating to the prostate gland. See also **PSA** [C17: via Medieval Latin from Greek *prostatēs* something standing in front (of the bladder), from *pro-* in front + *histanai* to cause to stand]

prosthesis ('prɒsθɪsɪs, prɒs'θiːsɪs) *n, pl* **-ses** (-ˌsiːz) **1** *surgery* **a** the replacement of a missing bodily part with an artificial substitute **b** an artificial part such as a limb, eye, or tooth **2** *linguistics* another word for **prothesis** [C16: via Late Latin from Greek: an addition, from *prostithenai* to add, from *pros-* towards + *tithenai* to place] > **prosthetic** (prɒs'θɛtɪk) *adj* > **pros'thetically** *adv*

prosthetics (prɒs'θɛtɪks) *n* (*functioning as singular*) the branch of surgery concerned with prosthesis

prostitute ('prɒstɪˌtjuːt) *n* **1** a woman who engages in sexual intercourse for money **2** a man who engages in such activity, esp in homosexual practices **3** a person

who offers his talent or work for unworthy purposes ▷ *vb* (*tr*) **4** to offer (oneself or another) in sexual intercourse for money **5** to offer (a person, esp oneself, or a person's talent) for unworthy purposes [C16: from Latin *prōstituere* to expose to prostitution, from *prō-* in public + *statuere* to cause to stand] > **ˌprosti'tution** *n* > **'prostiˌtutor** *n*

prostrate *adj* ('prɒstreɪt) **1** lying with the face downwards, as in submission **2** exhausted physically or emotionally **3** helpless or defenceless **4** (of a plant) growing closely along the ground ▷ *vb* (prɒ'streɪt) (*tr*) **5** to bow or cast (oneself) down, as in submission **6** to lay or throw down flat, as on the ground **7** to make helpless or defenceless **8** to make exhausted [C14: from Latin *prōsternere* to throw to the ground, from *prō-* before + *sternere* to lay low] > **pros'tration** *n*

prostyle ('prəʊstaɪl) *adj* **1** (of a building) having a row of columns in front, esp as in the portico of a Greek temple ▷ *n* **2** a prostyle building, portico, etc [C17: from Latin *prostȳlos*, from Greek: with pillars in front, from PRO-² + *stulos* pillar]

prosumer (prə'sjuːmə) *n* an amateur user of electronic equipment that is of a standard suitable for professional use [C21: PROFESSIONAL + CONSUMER]

prosy ('prəʊzɪ) *adj* **prosier, prosiest 1** of the nature of or similar to prose **2** dull, tedious, or long-winded > **'prosily** *adv* > **'prosiness** *n*

Prot. *abbreviation* Protestant

protactinium (ˌprəʊtæk'tɪnɪəm) *n* a toxic radioactive metallic element that occurs in uranium ores and is produced by neutron irradiation of thorium. Symbol: Pa; atomic no: 91; half-life of the most stable isotope, ^{231}Pa: 32 500 years; valency: 4 or 5; relative density: 15.37 (calc.); melting pt: 1572°C

protagonist (prəʊ'tæɡənɪst) *n* **1** the principal character in a play, story, etc **2** a supporter, esp when important or respected, of a cause, political party, etc [C17: from Greek *prōtagōnistēs*, from *prōtos* first + *agōnistēs* actor] > **pro'tagonism** *n*

Protagoras (prəʊ'tæɡəˌræs) *n* ?485–?411 BC, Greek philosopher and sophist, famous for his dictum "Man is the measure of all things."

protasis ('prɒtəsɪs) *n, pl* **-ses** (-siːz) **1** *logic, grammar* the antecedent of a conditional statement, such as *it rains* in *if it rains the game will be cancelled*. See **apodosis 2** (in classical drama) the introductory part of a play [C17: via Latin from Greek: a proposal, from *pro-* before + *teinein* to extend]

protea ('prəʊtɪə) *n* any shrub or small tree of the genus *Protea*, of tropical and southern Africa, having flowers with coloured bracts arranged in showy heads: family Proteaceae [C20: from New Latin, from PROTEUS, referring to the large number of different forms of the plant]

protean (prəʊ'tiːən, 'prəʊtɪən) *adj* readily taking on various shapes or forms; variable [C16: from PROTEUS]

Proteas ('prəʊtɪəz) *pl n* the Proteas *South African* the international cricket team of South Africa

protease ('prəʊtɪˌeɪs) *n* any enzyme involved in proteolysis [C20: from PROTEIN + -ASE]

protease inhibitor *n* any one of a class of antiviral drugs that impair the growth and replication of HIV by inhibiting the action of protease produced by the virus: used in the treatment of AIDS

protect (prə'tɛkt) *vb* (*tr*) **1** to defend from trouble, harm, attack, etc **2** *economics* to assist (domestic industries) by the imposition of protective tariffs on imports **3** *commerce* to provide funds in advance to guarantee payment of (a note, draft, etc) [C16: from Latin *prōtegere* to cover before, from PRO-¹ + *tegere* to cover]

protectant (prə'tɛktənt) *n* a chemical substance that affords protection, as against frost, rust, insects, etc

protection (prə'tɛkʃən) *n* **1** the act of protecting or the condition of being protected **2** something that protects **3 a** the imposition of duties or quotas on imports, designed for the protection of domestic industries against overseas competition, expansion of domestic employment, etc **b** Also called: **protectionism** the system, policy, or theory of such restrictions **4** *informal* **a** Also called: **protection money** money demanded by gangsters for freedom from molestation **b** freedom

from molestation purchased in this way
> pro'tection,ism n > pro'tectionist n, adj

protective (prə'tɛktɪv) adj 1 giving or capable of giving protection 2 economics of, relating to, or intended for protection of domestic industries ▷ n 3 something that protects 4 a condom > pro'tectively adv
> pro'tectiveness n

protective coloration n the coloration of an animal that enables it to blend with its surroundings and therefore escape the attention of predators

protector (prə'tɛktə) n 1 a person or thing that protects 2 history a person who exercised royal authority during the minority, absence, or incapacity of the monarch > pro'tectress fem n

Protector (prə'tɛktə) n short for Lord Protector, the title borne by Oliver Cromwell (1653–58) and by Richard Cromwell (1658–59) as heads of state during the period known as the **Protectorate**

protectorate (prə'tɛktərɪt) n 1 a territory largely controlled by but not annexed to a stronger state 2 the office or period of office of a protector

protégé or feminine **protégée** ('prəʊtɪ,ʒeɪ) n a person who is protected and aided by the patronage of another person [c18: from French protéger to PROTECT]

protein ('prəʊtiːn) n any of a large group of nitrogenous compounds of high molecular weight that are essential constituents of all living organisms. They consist of one or more chains of amino acids linked by peptide bonds and are folded into a specific three-dimensional shape maintained by further chemical bonding [c19: via German from Greek prōteios primary, from protos first + -IN] > ,protein'aceous, pro'teinic or pro'teinous adj

pro tempore Latin ('prəʊ 'tɛmpərɪ) adv, adj for the time being

proteolysis (,prəʊtɪ'ɒlɪsɪs) n the hydrolysis of proteins into simpler compounds by the action of enzymes: occurs esp during digestion [c19: from New Latin, from proteo- (from PROTEIN) + -LYSIS] > proteolytic (,prəʊtɪə'lɪtɪk) adj

proteomics (,prəʊtɪ'ɒmɪks) n (functioning as singular) the branch of biochemistry concerned with the structure and analysis of the proteins occurring in living organisms

protest n ('prəʊtɛst) 1 a public, often organized, dissent or manifestation of such dissent b (as modifier): a protest march 2 a declaration or objection that is formal or solemn 3 a formal notarial statement drawn up on behalf of a creditor and declaring that the debtor has dishonoured a bill of exchange or promissory note 4 the act of protesting ▷ vb (prə'tɛst) 5 (when intr, foll by against, at, about, etc; when tr, may take a clause as object) to make a strong objection (to something, esp a supposed injustice or offence) 6 (when tr, may take a clause as object) to assert or affirm in a formal or solemn manner 7 (when tr, may take a clause as object) to put up arguments against; disagree; complain; object: "I'm okay," she protested; he protested that it was not his turn to wash up 8 (tr) chiefly US to object forcefully to: leaflets protesting Dr King's murder 9 (tr) to declare formally that (a bill of exchange or promissory note) has been dishonoured [c14: from Latin prōtestārī to make a formal declaration, from prō- before + testārī to assert] > pro'testant adj, n > pro'tester or pro'testor n > pro'testingly adv

Protestant ('prɒtɪstənt) n a an adherent of Protestantism b (as modifier): the Protestant Church

Protestantism ('prɒtɪstən,tɪzəm) n the religion or religious system of any of the Churches of Western Christendom that are separated from the Roman Catholic Church and adhere substantially to principles established by Luther, Calvin, etc, in the Reformation

protestation (,prəʊtɛs'teɪʃən) n 1 the act of protesting 2 a strong declaration

Proteus ('prəʊtɪəs) n Greek myth a prophetic sea god capable of changing his shape at will

prothalamion (,prəʊθə'leɪmɪən) or **prothalamium** n, pl -mia (-mɪə) a song or poem in celebration of a marriage [c16: from Greek pro- before + thalamos marriage; coined by Edmund Spenser, on the model of EPITHALAMION]

prothallus (prəʊ'θæləs) or **prothallium** (prəʊ'θælɪəm) n,

pl -li (-laɪ) or -lia (-lɪə) botany the small flat free-living gametophyte that bears the reproductive organs of ferns, horsetails, and club mosses. It is either a green disc on the soil surface or it is colourless and subterranean [c19: from New Latin, from pro- before + Greek thallus a young shoot]

prothesis ('prɒθɪsɪs) n a process in the development of a language by which a phoneme or syllable is prefixed to a word to facilitate pronunciation: Latin "scala" gives Spanish "escala" by prothesis [c16: via Late Latin from Greek: a setting out in public, from pro- forth + thesis a placing] > prothetic (prə'θɛtɪk) adj > pro'thetically adv

prothrombin (prəʊ'θrɒmbɪn) n biochem a zymogen found in blood that gives rise to thrombin on activation

protist ('prəʊtɪst) n (in some classification systems) any organism belonging to the kingdom Protista, originally including bacteria, protozoans, algae, and fungi, regarded as distinct from plants and animals. It was later restricted to protozoans, unicellular algae, and simple fungi. See also **protoctist** [c19: from New Latin Protista most primitive organisms, from Greek prōtistos the very first, from prōtos first]

protium ('prəʊtɪəm) n the most common isotope of hydrogen, having a mass number of 1 [c20: New Latin, from PROTO- + -IUM]

proto- or sometimes before a vowel **prot-** combining form 1 indicating the first in time, order, or rank: protomartyr 2 primitive, ancestral, or original: prototype 3 indicating the first in a series of chemical compounds: protoxide [from Greek prōtos first, from pro before; see PRO-²]

protocol ('prəʊtə,kɒl) n 1 the formal etiquette and code of behaviour, precedence, and procedure for state and diplomatic ceremonies 2 a memorandum or record of an agreement, esp one reached in international negotiations, a meeting, etc 3 (chiefly US) a a record of data or observations on a particular experiment or proceeding b an annexe appended to a treaty to deal with subsidiary matters or to render the treaty more lucid 4 an amendment to a treaty or convention 5 computing the set form in which data must be presented for handling by a particular computer configuration, esp in the transmission of information between different computer systems [c16: from Medieval Latin prōtocollum, from Late Greek prōtokollon sheet glued to the front of a manuscript, from PROTO- + kolla glue]

protoctist (prəʊ'tɒktɪst) n (in modern biological classifications) any unicellular or simple multicellular organism belonging to the kingdom Protoctista, which includes protozoans, algae, and slime moulds [c19: from New Latin protoctista, perhaps from Greek prototokos first born]

protohuman (,prəʊtəʊ'hjuːmən) n 1 any of various prehistoric primates that resembled modern man ▷ adj 2 of or relating to any of these primates

Proto-Indo-European n the prehistoric unrecorded language that was the ancestor of all Indo-European languages

protomartyr (,prəʊtəʊ'mɑːtə) n 1 St Stephen as the first Christian martyr 2 the first martyr to lay down his life in any cause

proton ('prəʊtɒn) n a stable, positively charged elementary particle, found in atomic nuclei in numbers equal to the atomic number of the element. It is a baryon with a charge of $1.602176462 \times 10^{-19}$ coulomb, a rest mass of $1.672\,62159 \times 10^{-27}$ kilogram, and spin $\frac{1}{2}$ [c20: from Greek prōtos first]

protoplasm ('prəʊtə,plæzəm) n biology the living contents of a cell, differentiated into cytoplasm and nucleoplasm [c19: from New Latin, from PROTO- + Greek plasma form] > ,proto'plasmic adj

prototype ('prəʊtə,taɪp) n 1 one of the first units manufactured of a product, which is tested so that the design can be changed if necessary before the product is manufactured commercially 2 a person or thing that serves as an example of a type 3 biology the ancestral or primitive form of a species or other group; an archetype > ,proto'typal, prototypic (,prəʊtə'tɪpɪk) or ,proto'typical adj

protozoan (ˌprəʊtəˈzəʊən) *n, pl* -**zoa** (-ˈzəʊə) *or* -**zoans** 1 Also called: **protozoon** (ˌprəʊtəˈzəʊɒn) *pl* -**zoa** any of various minute unicellular organisms formerly regarded as invertebrates of the phylum *Protozoa* but now usually classified in certain phyla of protoctists. Protozoans include flagellates, ciliates, sporozoans, amoebas, and foraminifers ▷ *adj* Also: **protozoic** 2 of or relating to protozoans [C19: via New Latin from Greek PROTO- + *zoion* animal]

protract (prəˈtrækt) *vb* (*tr*) 1 to lengthen or extend (a speech, etc); prolong in time 2 (of a muscle) to draw, thrust, or extend (a part, etc) forwards 3 to plot or draw using a protractor and scale [C16: from Latin *prōtrahere* to prolong, from PRO-¹ + *trahere* to drag] > **proˈtraction** *n*

protracted (prəˈtræktɪd) *adj* extended or lengthened in time; prolonged > **proˈtractedly** *adv* > **proˈtractedness** *n*

protractile (prəˈtræktaɪl) *or less commonly* **protractible** *adj* able to be extended or protruded: *protractile muscle*

protractor (prəˈtræktə) *n* 1 an instrument for measuring or drawing angles on paper, usually a flat semicircular transparent plastic sheet graduated in degrees 2 *anatomy* a former term for **extensor**

protrude (prəˈtruːd) *vb* 1 to thrust or cause to thrust forwards or outwards 2 to project or cause to project from or as if from a surface [C17: from Latin, from PRO-² + *trudere* to thrust] > **proˈtrusion** *n* > **proˈtrusive** *adj* > **proˈtrusively** *adv* > **proˈtrusiveness** *n*

protrusile (prəˈtruːsaɪl) *adj zoology* capable of being thrust forwards: *protrusile jaws*

protuberant (prəˈtjuːbərənt) *adj* swelling out from the surrounding surface; bulging [C17: from Late Latin *prōtūberāre* to swell, from PRO-¹ + *tūber* swelling] > **proˈtuberance** *or* **proˈtuberancy** *n* > **proˈtuberantly** *adv*

proud (praʊd) *adj* 1 (foll by *of*, an infinitive, or a clause) pleased or satisfied, as with oneself, one's possessions, achievements, etc, or with another person, his or her achievements, qualities, etc 2 feeling honoured or gratified by or as if by some distinction 3 having an inordinately high opinion of oneself; arrogant or haughty 4 characterized by or proceeding from a sense of pride: *a proud moment* 5 having a proper sense of self-respect 6 stately or distinguished 7 bold or fearless 8 (of a surface, edge, etc) projecting or protruding from the surrounding area 9 (of animals) restive or excited, esp sexually; on heat ▷ *adv* 10 **do someone proud** a to entertain someone on a grand scale: *they did us proud at the hotel* b to honour or distinguish a person: *his honesty did him proud* [Late Old English *prūd*, from Old French *prud, prod* brave, from Late Latin *prōde* useful, from Latin *prōdesse* to be of value, from *prōd-*, variant of *prō-* for + *esse* to be] > **ˈproudly** *adv* > **ˈproudness** *n*

proud flesh *n* a non-technical name for **granulation tissue** [C14: from PROUD (in the sense: swollen, protruding)]

Proudhon (French prudɔ̃) *n* **Pierre Joseph** (pjɛr ʒɔzɛf). 1809–65, French socialist, whose pamphlet *What is Property?* (1840) declared that property is theft

Proust (French prust) *n* 1 **Joseph Louis** (ʒɔzɛf lwi). 1754–1826, French chemist, who formulated the law of constant proportions 2 **Marcel** (marsɛl). 1871–1922, French novelist whose long novel *À la recherche du temps perdu* (1913–27) deals with the relationship of the narrator to themes such as art, time, memory, and society

Prout (praʊt) *n* 1 **Ebenezer**. 1835–1909, English musicologist and composer, noted for his editions of works by Handel and J. S. Bach 2 **William**. 1785–1850, English chemist, noted for his modification of the atomic theory

Prov. *abbreviation* 1 *Bible* Proverbs 2 Province 3 Provost

prove (pruːv) *vb* **proves, proving, proved, proved** *or* **proven** (mainly *tr*) 1 (may take a clause as object or an infinitive) to establish or demonstrate the truth or validity of; verify, esp by using an established sequence of procedures or statements 2 to establish the quality of, esp by experiment or scientific analysis 3 *law* to establish the validity and genuineness of (a will) 4 to show (oneself) able or courageous 5 (*copula*) to be found or shown (to be): *this has proved useless; he proved to be invaluable* 6 (*intr*) (of dough) to rise in a warm place before

baking [C12: from Old French *prover*, from Latin *probāre* to test, from *probus* honest] > **ˈprovable** *adj* > ˌprovaˈbility *n* > **ˈprovably** *adv*

proven (ˈpruːvən) *vb* 1 a past participle of **prove** 2 See **not proven** ▷ *adj* 3 tried; tested: *a proven method*

provenance (ˈprɒvɪnəns) *or chiefly US* **provenience** (prəʊˈviːnɪəns) *n* a place of origin, esp that of a work of art or archaeological specimen [C19: from French, from *provenir*, from Latin *prōvenīre* to originate, from *venīre* to come]

Provençal (ˌprɒvɒnˈsɑːl; *French* prɔvãsal) *adj* 1 relating to, denoting, or characteristic of Provence, its inhabitants, their dialect of French, or their Romance language ▷ *n* 2 a language of Provence, closely related to Catalan, French, and Italian, belonging to the Romance group of the Indo-European family. It was important in the Middle Ages as a literary language, and attempts have been made since the 19th century to revive its literary status 3 a native or inhabitant of Provence

Provence (*French* prɔvãs) *n* a former province of SE France, on the Mediterranean, and the River Rhône: forms part of the administrative region of Provence-Alpes-Côte d'Azur

provender (ˈprɒvɪndə) *n* 1 any dry feed or fodder for domestic livestock 2 food in general [C14: from Old French *provendre*, from Late Latin *praebenda* grant, from Latin *praebēre* to proffer; influenced also by Latin *prōvidēre* to look after]

proverb (ˈprɒvɜːb) *n* 1 a short, memorable, and often highly condensed saying embodying, esp with bold imagery, some commonplace fact or experience 2 a person or thing exemplary in respect of a characteristic: *Antarctica is a proverb for extreme cold* 3 *ecclesiast* a wise saying or admonition providing guidance [C14: via Old French from Latin *prōverbium*, from *verbum* word]

proverbial (prəˈvɜːbɪəl) *adj* 1 (*prenominal*) commonly or traditionally referred to, esp as being an example of some peculiarity, characteristic, etc 2 of, connected with, embodied in, or resembling a proverb > **proˈverbially** *adv*

provide (prəˈvaɪd) *vb* (mainly *tr*) 1 to put at the disposal of; furnish or supply 2 to afford; yield: *this meeting provides an opportunity to talk* 3 (*intr*, often foll by *for* or *against*) to take careful precautions (over): *he provided against financial ruin by wise investment* 4 (*intr*, foll by *for*) to supply means of support (to), esp financially: *he provides for his family* 5 to confer and induct into ecclesiastical offices [C15: from Latin *prōvidēre* to provide for, from *prō-* beforehand + *vidēre* to see] > **proˈvider** *n*

providence (ˈprɒvɪdəns) *n* 1 a *Christianity* God's foreseeing protection and care of his creatures b such protection and care as manifest by some other force 2 a supposed manifestation of such care and guidance 3 the foresight or care exercised by a person in the management of his affairs or resources

Providence¹ (ˈprɒvɪdəns) *n Christianity* God, esp as showing foreseeing care and protection of his creatures [C14: via French from Latin *prōvidentia*, from *prōvidēre* to provide; see PROVIDE, -ENCE]

Providence² (ˈprɒvɪdəns) *n* a port in NE Rhode Island, capital of the state, at the head of Narragansett Bay: founded by Roger Williams in 1636. Pop: 176 365 (2003 est)

provident (ˈprɒvɪdənt) *adj* 1 providing for future needs 2 exercising foresight in the management of one's affairs or resources 3 characterized by or proceeding from foresight [C15: from Latin *prōvidēns* foreseeing, from *prōvidēre* to PROVIDE] > **ˈprovidently** *adv*

providential (ˌprɒvɪˈdɛnʃəl) *adj* relating to, characteristic of, or presumed to proceed from or as if from divine providence > ˌproviˈdentially *adv*

provident society *n* another name for **friendly society**

providing (prəˈvaɪdɪŋ) *or* **provided** *conj* (subordinating; sometimes foll by *that*) on the condition or understanding (that): *I'll play, providing you pay me*

province (ˈprɒvɪns) *n* 1 a territory governed as a unit of a country or empire 2 **the provinces** (*plural*) those parts of a country lying outside the capital and other large cities and regarded as outside the mainstream of sophisticated culture **3** an area or branch of learning, activity, etc **4** the field or extent of a person's activities or office **5** RC Church, Church of England an ecclesiastical territory, usually consisting of several dioceses, and having an archbishop or metropolitan at its head **6** a major administrative and territorial subdivision of a religious order **7** history a region of the Roman Empire outside Italy ruled by a governor from Rome [C14: from Old French, from Latin *prōvincia* conquered territory]

Provincetown ('prɒvɪnsˌtaʊn) n a village in SE Massachusetts, at the tip of Cape Cod: scene of the first landing place of the Pilgrims (1620) and of the signing of the Mayflower Compact (1620). Pop: 3472 (2003 est)

provincewide ('prɒvɪnsˌwaɪd) Canadian ▷ adj **1** covering or available to the whole of a province: *a provincewide referendum* ▷ adv **2** throughout a province: *an advertising campaign to go provincewide*

provincial (prə'vɪnʃəl) adj **1** of or connected with a province **2** characteristic of or connected with the provinces; local **3** having attitudes and opinions supposedly common to people living in the provinces; rustic or unsophisticated; limited **4** NZ denoting a football team representing a province, one of the historical administrative areas of New Zealand ▷ n **5** a person lacking the sophistications of city life; rustic or narrow-minded individual **6** a person coming from or resident in a province or the provinces **7** the head of an ecclesiastical province **8** the head of a major territorial subdivision of a religious order > provinciality (prəˌvɪnʃɪ'ælɪtɪ) n > pro'vincially adv

provincialism (prə'vɪnʃəˌlɪzəm) n **1** narrowness of mind or outlook; lack of sophistication **2** a word or attitude characteristic of a provincial **3** attention to the affairs of one's province rather than the whole nation **4** the state or quality of being provincial

provincial police n (in Canada) the police force of a province, esp Ontario or Quebec

provirus ('prəʊˌvaɪrəs) n the inactive form of a virus in a host cell

provision (prə'vɪʒən) n **1** the act of supplying or providing food, etc **2** something that is supplied or provided **3** preparations made beforehand (esp in the phrase **make provision for**) **4** (plural) food and other necessities, esp for an expedition **5** a demand, condition, or stipulation formally incorporated in a document; proviso **6** the conferring of and induction into ecclesiastical offices ▷ vb **7** (tr) to supply with provisions [C14: from Latin *prōvīsiō* a providing; see PROVIDE] > pro'visioner n

provisional (prə'vɪʒənᵊl) or less commonly **provisionary** (prə'vɪʒənərɪ) adj subject to later alteration; temporary or conditional: *a provisional decision* > pro'visionally adv

Provisional (prə'vɪʒənᵊl) adj **1** of, designating, or relating to the unofficial factions of the IRA and Sinn Féin that became increasingly dominant following a split in 1969. The Provisional movement remained committed to a policy of terrorism until its ceasefires of the mid-1990s ▷ n **2** Also called: Provo a member of the Provisional IRA or Sinn Féin

proviso (prə'vaɪzəʊ) n, pl -sos or -soes **1** a clause in a document or contract that embodies a condition or stipulation **2** a condition or stipulation [C15: from Medieval Latin phrase *prōvīsō quod* it being provided that, from Latin *prōvīsus* provided]

provisory (prə'vaɪzərɪ) adj **1** containing a proviso; conditional **2** another word for **provisional 3** making provision > pro'visorily adv

Provo ('prəʊvəʊ) n, pl -vos another name for a **Provisional** (sense 2)

provocateur (prəˌvɒkə'tɜː) n a person who deliberately behaves controversially in order to provoke argument or other strong reactions

provocation (ˌprɒvə'keɪʃən) n **1** the act of provoking or inciting **2** something that causes indignation, anger, etc

provocative (prə'vɒkətɪv) adj acting as a stimulus or incitement, esp to anger or sexual desire; provoking: *a provocative look; a provocative remark* > pro'vocatively adv

provoke (prə'vəʊk) vb (tr) **1** to anger or infuriate **2** to

cause to act or behave in a certain manner; incite or stimulate **3** to promote (certain feelings, esp anger, indignation, etc) in a person [C15: from Latin *prōvocāre* to call forth, from *vocāre* to call] > pro'voking adj > pro'vokingly adv

provost ('prɒvəst) n **1** the head of certain university colleges or schools **2** (in Scotland) the chairman and civic head of certain district councils or (formerly) of a burgh council. See **convener** (sense 2) **3** Church of England the senior dignitary of one of the more recent cathedral foundations **4** RC Church **a** the head of a cathedral chapter in England and some other countries **b** (formerly) the member of a monastic community second in authority under the abbot **5** (in medieval times) an overseer, steward, or bailiff in a manor [Old English *profost*, from Medieval Latin *prōpositus* placed at the head (of), from Latin *praepōnere* to place first, from *prae-* before + *pōnere* to put]

provost marshal (prə'vəʊ) n the officer in charge of military police and thus responsible for military discipline in a large camp, area, or city

prow (praʊ) n the bow of a vessel [C16: from Old French *proue*, from Latin *prora*, from Greek *prōra*; related to Latin *pro* in front]

prowess ('praʊɪs) n **1** outstanding or superior skill or ability **2** bravery or fearlessness, esp in battle [C13: from Old French *proesce*, from *prou* good; see PROUD]

prowl (praʊl) vb **1** (when intr, often foll by *around* or *about*) to move stealthily around (a place) as if in search of prey or plunder ▷ n **2** the act of prowling **3** on the prowl **a** moving around stealthily **b** zealously pursuing members of the opposite sex [C14 *prollen*, of unknown origin] > 'prowler n

prox. abbreviation proximo (next month)

proximal ('prɒksɪməl) adj anatomy situated close to the centre, median line, or point of attachment or origin > 'proximally adv

proximate ('prɒksɪmɪt) adj **1** next or nearest in space or time **2** very near; close **3** immediately preceding or following in a series **4** a less common word for **approximate** [C16: from Late Latin *proximāre* to draw near, from Latin *proximus* next, from *prope* near] > 'proximately adv

proximity (prɒk'sɪmɪtɪ) n **1** nearness in space or time **2** nearness or closeness in a series [C15: from Latin *proximitās* closeness; see PROXIMATE]

proximo ('prɒksɪməʊ) adv in or during the next or coming month (esp abbreviated in formal correspondence): *a letter of the seventh proximo* See **instant, ultimo** [C19: from Latin: in or on the next, from *proximus* next]

proxy ('prɒksɪ) n, pl proxies **1** a person authorized to act on behalf of someone else; agent: *to vote by proxy* **2** the authority, esp in the form of a document, given to a person to act on behalf of someone else **3** computing short for **proxy server** [C15: *prokesye*, contraction of *procuracy*, from Latin *prōcūrātiō* procuration; see PROCURE]

proxy server n computing a computer that acts as an intermediary between a client machine and a server, caching information to save access time

Prozac ('prəʊzæk) n trademark fluoxetine; a drug that prolongs the action of serotonin in the brain; used as an antidepressant

PRP abbreviation **1** performance-related pay **2** profit-related pay

PRT abbreviation petroleum revenue tax

prude (pruːd) n a person who affects or shows an excessively modest, prim, or proper attitude, esp regarding sex [C18: from French, from *prudefemme*, from Old French *prode femme* respectable woman; see PROUD] > 'prudish adj > 'prudishly adv > 'prudishness or 'prudery n

prudence ('pruːdəns) n **1** caution in practical affairs; discretion or circumspection **2** care taken in the management of one's resources **3** consideration for one's own interests **4** the condition or quality of being prudent

prudent ('pruːdᵊnt) adj **1** discreet or cautious in managing one's activities; circumspect **2** practical and careful in providing for the future **3** exercising good judgment or common sense [c14: from Latin *prūdēns* far-sighted, contraction of *prōvidens* acting with foresight; see PROVIDENT] > 'prudently *adv*

prudential (pru:'dɛnʃəl) *adj* 1 characterized by or resulting from prudence 2 exercising prudence or sound judgment > pru'dentially *adv*

Prudentius (pru:'dɛnʃəs) *n* **Aurelius Clemens** (ɔː'riːlɪəs 'klɛmɛnz). 348–410 AD, Latin Christian poet, born in Spain. His works include the allegory *Psychomachia*

Prud'hon (*French* prydɔ̃) *n* **Pierre Paul** (pjɛr pɔl). 1758–1823, French painter, noted for the romantic and mysterious aura of his portraits

pruinose ('pruːɪˌnəʊs, -ˌnəʊz) *adj botany* coated with a powdery or waxy bloom [c19: from Latin *pruīnōsus* frost-covered, from *pruīna* hoarfrost]

prune[1] (pruːn) *n* 1 a purplish-black partially dried fruit of any of several varieties of plum tree 2 *slang, chiefly Brit* a dull, uninteresting, or foolish person [c14: from Old French *prune*, from Latin *prūnum* plum, from Greek *prounon*]

prune[2] (pruːn) *vb* 1 to remove (dead or superfluous twigs, branches, etc) from (a tree, shrub, etc), esp by cutting off 2 to remove (anything undesirable or superfluous) from (a book, etc) [c15: from Old French *proignier* to clip, probably from *provigner* to prune vines, from *provain* layer (of a plant), from Latin *propāgo* a cutting] > 'prunable *adj* > 'pruner *n*

prunella (pruː'nɛlə), **prunelle** (pruː'nɛl) *or* **prunello** (pruː'nɛləʊ) *n* a strong fabric, esp a twill-weave worsted, used for gowns and the uppers of some shoes [c17: perhaps from PRUNELLE, with reference to the colour of the cloth]

prunelle (pruː'nɛl) *n* a green French liqueur made from sloes [c18: from French: a little plum, from *prune* PRUNE[1]]

pruning hook *n* a tool with a curved steel blade terminating in a hook, used for pruning

prurient ('prʊərɪənt) *adj* 1 unusually or morbidly interested in sexual thoughts or activities 2 exciting or encouraging lustfulness; erotic [c17: from Latin *prūrīre* to itch, to lust after] > 'prurience *n* > 'pruriently *adv*

prurigo (prʊə'raɪgəʊ) *n* a chronic inflammatory disease of the skin characterized by the formation of papules and intense itching [c19: from Latin: an itch] > **pruriginous** (prʊə'rɪdʒɪnəs) *adj*

pruritus (prʊə'raɪtəs) *n pathol* any intense sensation of itching [c17: from Latin: an itching; see PRURIENT] > **pruritic** (prʊə'rɪtɪk) *adj*

Prussia ('prʌʃə) *n* a former German state in N and central Germany, extending from France and the Low Countries to the Baltic Sea and Poland: developed as the chief military power of the Continent, leading the North German Confederation from 1867–71, when the German Empire was established; dissolved in 1947 and divided between East and West Germany, Poland, and the former Soviet Union. Area: (in 1939) 294 081 sq km (113 545 sq miles). German name: **Preussen**

Prussian ('prʌʃən) *adj* 1 of, relating to, or characteristic of Prussia or its people, esp of the Junkers and their formal military tradition ▷ *n* 2 a German native or inhabitant of Prussia 3 see **Old Prussian**

Prussian blue *n* 1 any of a number of blue pigments containing ferrocyanide or ferricyanide complexes 2 a the blue or deep greenish-blue colour of this pigment b (*as adjective*): *a Prussian-blue carpet*

prussic acid ('prʌsɪk) *n* the weakly acidic extremely poisonous aqueous solution of hydrogen cyanide [c18: from French *acide prussique* Prussian acid, so called because obtained from Prussian blue]

Prut (*Russian* prut) *n* a river in E Europe, rising in SW Ukraine and flowing generally southeast, forming part of the border between Romania and Moldova, to join the River Danube. Length: 853 km (530 miles)

PRW *text messaging abbreviation* parents are watching

pry[1] (praɪ) *vb* **pries**, **prying**, **pried** 1 (*intr*; often foll by *into*) to make an impertinent or uninvited inquiry (about a private matter, topic, etc) ▷ *n, pl* **pries** 2 the act of prying 3 a person who pries [c14: of unknown origin]

pry[2] (praɪ) *vb* **pries**, **prying**, **pried** *US & Canadian* to extract or obtain with difficulty: *they had to pry the news*

out of him Equivalent term (in Britain and other countries): prise [c14: of unknown origin]

pryer ('praɪə) *n* a variant spelling of **prier**

Prynne (prɪn) *n* **William**. 1600–69, English Puritan leader and pamphleteer, whose ears were cut off in punishment for his attacks on Laud

Przemyśl (*Polish* 'pʃɛmɪʃl) *n* a city in SE Poland, near the border with Ukraine on the San River: a fortress in the early Middle Ages; belonged to Austria (1722–1918). Pop: 66 968 (2007 est)

Przewalski's horse (ˌpɜːʒə'vælskɪz) *n* a wild horse, *Equus przewalskii*, of W Mongolia, having an erect mane and no forelock: extinct in the wild, only a few survive in captivity [c19: named after the Russian explorer Nikolai Mikhailovich Przewalski (1839–88), who discovered it]

PS *abbreviation* 1 Passenger Steamer 2 Police Sergeant 3 Also called: ps postscript 4 private secretary 5 prompt side

Ps. *or* **Psa.** *Bible abbreviation* Psalm

PSA *abbreviation* prostatic specific antigen: an enzyme secreted by the prostate gland, increased levels of which are found in the blood of patients with cancer of the prostate

psalm (sɑːm) *n* 1 (*often capital*) any of the 150 sacred songs, lyric poems, and prayers that together constitute a book (Psalms) of the Old Testament 2 a musical setting of one of these poems 3 any sacred song or hymn [Old English, from Late Latin *psalmus*, from Greek *psalmos* song accompanied on the harp, from *psallein* to play (the harp)] > '**psalmic** *adj*

psalmist ('sɑːmɪst) *n* the composer of a psalm or psalms, esp (when *capital* and preceded by *the*) David, traditionally regarded as the author of The Book of Psalms

psalmody ('sɑːmədɪ, 'sæl-) *n, pl* **-dies** 1 the act of singing psalms or hymns 2 the art or practice of the setting to music or singing of psalms [c14: via Late Latin from Greek *psalmōidia* singing accompanied by a harp, from *psalmos* (see PSALM) + *ōidē* ODE] > '**psalmodist** *n* > **psalmodic** (sɑː'mɒdɪk, sæl-) *adj*

Psalter ('sɔːltə) *n* 1 another name for Psalms, esp in the version in the Book of Common Prayer 2 a translation, musical, or metrical version of the Psalms 3 a devotional or liturgical book containing a version of Psalms, often with a musical setting [Old English *psaltere*, from Late Latin *psaltērium*, from Greek *psaltērion* stringed instrument, from *psallein* to play a stringed instrument]

psalterium (sɔːl'tɪərɪəm) *n, pl* **-teria** (-'tɪərɪə) the third compartment of the stomach of ruminants, between the reticulum and abomasum. Also called: omasum [c19: from Latin *psaltērium* PSALTER; from the similarity of its folds to the pages of a book]

psaltery ('sɔːltərɪ) *n, pl* **-teries** *music* an ancient stringed instrument similar to the lyre, but having a trapezoidal sounding board over which the strings are stretched [Old English: see PSALTER]

p's and q's *pl n* behaviour within social conventions; manners (esp in the phrase *to mind one's p's and q's*) [altered from *p(lea)se* and *(than)k-you's*]

PSBR *abbreviation* (in Britain) public sector borrowing requirement: the excess of government expenditure over receipts (mainly from taxation) that has to be financed by borrowing from the banks or the public

psephology (sɛ'fɒlədʒɪ) *n* the statistical and sociological study of elections [c20: from Greek *psephos* pebble, vote + -LOGY, from the ancient Greeks' custom of voting with pebbles] > **psephological** (ˌsɛfə'lɒdʒɪkəl) *adj* > ˌpsepho'logically *adv* > pse'phologist *n*

pseud (sjuːd) *n* 1 *informal* a false, artificial, or pretentious person ▷ *adj* 2 another word for **pseudo**

Pseudepigrapha (ˌsjuːdɪ'pɪgrəfə) *pl n* various Jewish writings from the first century BC to the first century AD that claim to have been divinely revealed but which have been excluded from the Greek canon of the Old Testament [c17: from Greek *pseudepigraphos* falsely entitled, from PSEUDO- + *epigraphein* to inscribe] > **Pseudepigraphic** (ˌsjuːdɛpɪ'græfɪk), ˌPseudepi'graphical *or* ˌPseude'pigraphous *adj*

pseudo ('sju:dəʊ) *adj informal* not genuine; pretended

pseudo- *or sometimes before a vowel* **pseud-** *combining form* **1** false, pretending, or unauthentic: *pseudo-intellectual* **2** having a close resemblance to: *pseudopodium* [from Greek *pseudēs* false, from *pseudein* to lie]

pseudocarp ('sju:dəʊˌkɑ:p) *n* a fruit, such as the strawberry or apple, that includes parts other than the ripened ovary > ˌpseudo'carpous *adj*

Pseudo-Dionysius (ˌsju:dəʊˌdaɪə'nɪsɪəs) *n* the name given to the unidentified author (c. 500 AD) of important theological works formerly attributed to Dionysius the Areopagite. See also **Dionysius the Areopagite**

pseudoephedrine (ˌsju:dəʊ'ɛfɪˌdri:n, -ˌdrɪn) *n* a drug similar in action to ephedrine, used extensively as a decongestant

pseudomorph ('sju:dəʊˌmɔ:f) *n* a mineral that has an uncharacteristic crystalline form as a result of assuming the shape of another mineral that it has replaced > ˌpseudo'morphic *or* ˌpseudo'morphous *adj* > ˌpseudo'morphism *n*

pseudonym ('sju:dəˌnɪm) *n* a fictitious name adopted, esp by an author [C19: via French from Greek *pseudōnumon*] > ˌpseudo'nymity *n* > pseu'donymous *adj* > pseu'donymously *adv*

pseudopodium (ˌsju:dəʊ'pəʊdɪəm) *n*, *pl* **-dia** (-dɪə) a temporary projection from the cell of an amoeboid protozoan, leucocyte, etc, used for feeding and locomotion

pseudovector (ˌsju:dəʊ'vɛktə) *n maths* a variable quantity, such as angular momentum, that has magnitude and orientation with respect to an axis. The components are even functions of the coordinates

psf *abbreviation* pounds per square foot

pshaw (pʃɔ:) *interj becoming rare* an exclamation of disgust, impatience, disbelief, etc

psi¹ *abbreviation* pounds per square inch

psi² (psaɪ) *n* **1** the 23rd letter of the Greek alphabet (Ψ, ψ), a composite consonant, transliterated as *ps* **2** paranormal or psychic phenomena collectively

psilocybin (ˌsɪlə'saɪbɪn, ˌsaɪlə-) *n* a crystalline phosphate ester that is the active principle of the hallucinogenic fungus *Psilocybe mexicana*. Formula: $C_{12}H_{17}N_2O_4P$ [C20: from New Latin *Psilocybe* (from Greek *psilos* bare + *kubē* head) + -IN]

psi particle *n* See J/psi particle

psittacine ('sɪtəˌsaɪn, -sɪn) *adj* of, relating to, or resembling a parrot [C19: from Late Latin *psittacīnus*, from Latin *psittacus* a parrot]

psittacosis (ˌsɪtə'kəʊsɪs) *n* a disease of parrots, caused by the obligate intracellular parasite *Chlamydia psittaci*, that can be transmitted to man, in whom it produces inflammation of the lungs and pneumonia. Also called: parrot fever [C19: from New Latin, from Latin *psittacus* a parrot, from Greek *psittakos*; see -OSIS]

Pskov (*Russian* pskɔf) *n* **1** a city in NW Russia, on the Velikaya River: one of the oldest Russian cities, at its height in the 13th and 14th centuries. Pop: 203 000 (2005 est) **2** Lake Pskov the S part of Lake Peipus in NW Russia, linked to the main part by a channel 24 km (15 miles) long. Area: about 1000 sq km (400 sq miles)

PSNI *abbreviation* Police Service of Northern Ireland, established in 2000

psoas ('səʊəs) *n* either of two muscles of the loins that aid in flexing and rotating the thigh [C17: from New Latin, from Greek *psoai* (pl)]

psoriasis (sə'raɪəsɪs) *n* a skin disease characterized by the formation of reddish spots and patches covered with silvery scales: tends to run in families [C17: via New Latin from Greek: itching disease, from *psōra* itch] > psoriatic (ˌsɔːrɪ'ætɪk) *adj*

psst (pst) *interj* an exclamation of beckoning, esp one made surreptitiously

PST *abbreviation* (in the US and Canada) Pacific Standard Time

PSV *abbreviation* (in Britain) public service vehicle (now called passenger carrying vehicle)

psych *or* **psyche** (saɪk) *vb* (*tr*) *informal* to subject (someone) to psychoanalysis. See also **psych out, psych**

up [C20: shortened from PSYCHOANALYSE]

psyche ('saɪkɪ) *n* the human mind or soul [C17: from Latin, from Greek *psukhē* breath, soul; related to Greek *psukhein* to breathe]

Psyche ('saɪkɪ) *n Greek myth* a beautiful girl loved by Eros (Cupid), who became the personification of the soul

psychedelic *or* **psychodelic** (ˌsaɪkɪ'dɛlɪk) *adj* **1** relating to or denoting new or altered perceptions or sensory experiences, as through the use of hallucinogenic drugs **2** denoting any of the drugs, esp LSD, that produce these effects **3** *informal* (of painting, fabric design, etc) having the vivid colours and complex patterns popularly associated with the visual effects of psychedelic states [C20: from PSYCHE + Greek *delos* visible] > ˌpsyche'delically *or* ˌpsycho'delically *adv*

psychiatry (saɪ'kaɪətrɪ) *n* the branch of medicine concerned with the diagnosis and treatment of mental disorders > psy'chiatrist *n* > ˌpsychi'atric *or* ˌpsychi'atrical *adj* > ˌpsychi'atrically *adv*

psychic ('saɪkɪk) *adj* **1 a** outside the possibilities defined by natural laws, as mental telepathy **b** (of a person) sensitive to forces not recognized by natural laws **2** mental as opposed to physical; psychogenic **3** *bridge* (of a bid) based on less strength than would normally be required to make the bid ▷ *n* **4** a person who is sensitive to parapsychological forces or influences [C19: from Greek *psukhikos* of the soul or life] > 'psychical *adj* > 'psychically *adv*

psycho ('saɪkəʊ) *n*, *pl* **-chos** an informal and offensive word for **psychopath** *or* **psychopathic**

psycho- *or sometimes before a vowel* **psych-** *combining form* indicating the mind or psychological or mental processes: *psychology; psychogenesis; psychosomatic* [from Greek *psukhē* spirit, breath]

psychoactive (ˌsaɪkəʊ'æktɪv) *adj* capable of affecting mental activity

psychoanalyse *or US* **psychoanalyze** (ˌsaɪkəʊ'ænəˌlaɪz) *vb* (*tr*) to examine or treat (a person) by psychoanalysis

psychoanalysis (ˌsaɪkəʊə'nælɪsɪs) *n* a method of studying the mind and treating mental and emotional disorders based on revealing and investigating the role of the unconscious mind > psychoanalyst (ˌsaɪkəʊ'ænəlɪst) *n* > psychoanalytic (ˌsaɪkəʊˌænə'lɪtɪk) *or* ˌpsycho,ana'lytical *adj* > ˌpsycho,ana'lytically *adv*

psychobiology (ˌsaɪkəʊbaɪ'ɒlədʒɪ) *n psychol* the attempt to understand the psychology of organisms in terms of their biological functions and structures > psychobiological (ˌsaɪkəʊˌbaɪə'lɒdʒɪk³l) *adj* > ˌpsychobi'ologist *n*

psychochemical (ˌsaɪkəʊ'kemɪk³l) *n* **1** any of various chemical compounds whose primary effect is the alteration of the normal state of consciousness ▷ *adj* **2** of or relating to such chemical compounds

psychodrama ('saɪkəʊˌdrɑːmə) *n* **1** *psychiatry* a form of group therapy in which individuals act out, before an audience, situations from their past **2** a film, television drama, etc, in which the psychological development of the characters is emphasized

psychodynamics (ˌsaɪkəʊdaɪ'næmɪks) *n* (*functioning as singular*) *psychol* the study of interacting motives and emotions > ˌpsychody'namic *adj*

psychogenic (ˌsaɪkəʊ'dʒenɪk) *adj psychol* (esp of disorders or symptoms) of mental, rather than organic, origin > ˌpsycho'genically *adv*

psychokinesis (ˌsaɪkəʊkɪ'niːsɪs, -kaɪ-) *n* (in parapsychology) alteration of the state of an object by mental influence alone, without any physical intervention [C20: from PSYCHO- + Greek *kinēsis* motion]

psycholinguistics (ˌsaɪkəʊlɪŋ'gwɪstɪks) *n* (*functioning as singular*) the psychology of language, including language acquisition by children, the mental processes underlying adult comprehension and production of speech, language disorders, etc > ˌpsycho'linguist *n*

psychological (ˌsaɪkə'lɒdʒɪk³l) *adj* **1** of or relating to psychology **2** of or relating to the mind or mental activity **3** having no real or objective basis; arising in the mind: *his backaches are all psychological* **4** affecting the mind > ˌpsycho'logically *adv*

psychological moment *n* the most appropriate time

for producing a desired effect

psychological operations *pl n* another term for **psychological warfare**

psychological warfare *n* the military application of psychology, esp to propaganda and attempts to influence the morale of enemy and friendly groups in time of war

psychologize *or* **psychologise** (saɪˈkɒləˌdʒaɪz) *vb* (*intr*) 1 to make interpretations of behaviour and mental processes 2 to carry out investigation in the field of psychology

psychology (saɪˈkɒlədʒɪ) *n*, *pl* -gies 1 the scientific study of all forms of human and animal behaviour, sometimes concerned with the methods through which behaviour can be modified 2 *informal* the mental make-up or structure of an individual that causes him or her to think or act in the way he or she does > psyˈchologist *n*

psychometrics (ˌsaɪkəʊˈmɛtrɪks) *n* (*functioning as singular*) 1 the branch of psychology concerned with the design and use of psychological tests 2 the application of statistical and mathematical techniques to psychological testing

psychometry (saɪˈkɒmɪtrɪ) *n psychol* 1 measurement and testing of mental states and processes 2 (in parapsychology) the supposed ability to deduce facts about objects related to them by touching objects related to them > psychometric (ˌsaɪkəʊˈmɛtrɪk) *or* psychometrical *adj* > ˌpsychoˈmetrically *adv*

psychomotor (ˌsaɪkəʊˈməʊtə) *adj* of, relating to, or characterizing movements of the body associated with mental activity

psychoneuroimmunology (ˌsaɪkəʊˌnjʊərəʊˌɪmjʊˈnɒlədʒɪ) *n* the study of the effects of psychological factors on the immune system. Abbreviation: PNI

psychoneurosis (ˌsaɪkəʊnjʊˈrəʊsɪs) *n*, *pl* -roses (-ˈrəʊsiːz) another word for **neurosis**

psychopath (ˈsaɪkəʊˌpæθ) *n* a person afflicted with a personality disorder characterized by a tendency to commit antisocial and sometimes violent acts and a failure to feel guilt for such acts. Also called: sociopath > ˌpsychoˈpathic *adj* > ˌpsychoˈpathically *adv*

psychopathology (ˌsaɪkəʊpəˈθɒlədʒɪ) *n* the scientific study of mental disorders > psychopathological (ˌsaɪkəʊˌpæθəˈlɒdʒɪkᵊl) *adj*

psychopathy (saɪˈkɒpəθɪ) *n psychiatry* any mental disorder or disease

psychopharmacology (ˌsaɪkəʊˌfɑːməˈkɒlədʒɪ) *n* the study of drugs that affect the mind

psychophysics (ˌsaɪkəʊˈfɪzɪks) *n* (*functioning as singular*) the branch of psychology concerned with the relationship between physical stimuli and the effects they produce in the mind > ˌpsychoˈphysical *adj*

psychophysiology (ˌsaɪkəʊˌfɪzɪˈɒlədʒɪ) *n* the branch of psychology concerned with the physiological basis of mental processes > psychophysiological (ˌsaɪkəʊˌfɪzɪəˈlɒdʒɪkᵊl) *adj*

psychosexual (ˌsaɪkəʊˈsɛksjʊəl) *adj* of or relating to the mental aspects of sex, such as sexual fantasies > ˌpsychoˈsexually *adv*

psychosis (saɪˈkəʊsɪs) *n*, *pl* -choses (-ˈkəʊsiːz) any form of severe mental disorder in which the individual's contact with reality becomes highly distorted [c19: New Latin, from PSYCHO- + -OSIS]

psychosocial (ˌsaɪkəʊˈsəʊʃəl) *adj* of or relating to processes or factors that are both social and psychological in origin

psychosomatic (ˌsaɪkəʊsəˈmætɪk) *adj* of or relating to disorders, such as stomach ulcers, thought to be caused or aggravated by psychological factors such as stress

psychosurgery (ˌsaɪkəʊˈsɜːdʒərɪ) *n* any surgical procedure on the brain, such as a frontal lobotomy, to relieve serious mental disorders > psychosurgical (ˌsaɪkəʊˈsɜːdʒɪkᵊl) *adj*

psychotherapy (ˌsaɪkəʊˈθɛrəpɪ) *or less commonly* **psychotherapeutics** (ˌsaɪkəʊˌθɛrəˈpjuːtɪks) *n* the treatment of nervous disorders by psychological methods > ˌpsychoˌtheraˈpeutic *adj*

> ˌpsychoˌtheraˈpeutically *adv* > ˌpsychoˈtherapist *n*

psychotic (saɪˈkɒtɪk) *psychiatry* ▷ *adj* 1 of, relating to, or characterized by psychosis ▷ *n* 2 a person experiencing psychosis > psyˈchotically *adv*

● **USAGE** It is preferable to talk about *a person experiencing*
● *psychosis* rather than *a psychotic*, which reduces a
● person's individuality

psychotomimetic (saɪˌkɒtəʊmɪˈmɛtɪk) *adj* (of drugs such as LSD and mescaline) capable of inducing psychotic symptoms

psych out *vb* (*mainly tr, adverb*) *informal* 1 to guess correctly the intentions of (another); outguess 2 to analyse or solve (a problem, etc) psychologically 3 to intimidate or frighten

psychrometer (saɪˈkrɒmɪtə) *n* a type of hygrometer consisting of two thermometers, one of which has a dry bulb and the other a bulb that is kept moist and ventilated. The difference between the readings of the thermometers gives an indication of atmospheric humidity

psych up *vb* (*tr, adverb*) *informal* to get (oneself or another) into a state of psychological readiness for an action, performance, etc

psyops (ˈsaɪˌɒps) *pl n* short for **psychological operations**

pt *abbreviation* 1 part 2 patient 3 payment 4 point 5 port 6 pro tempore

Pt *abbreviation* (in place names) 1 Point 2 Port ▷ *the chemical symbol for* 3 platinum

PT *abbreviation* 1 physical therapy 2 physical training 3 postal telegraph

pt. *abbreviation* pint

PTA *abbreviation* Parent-Teacher Association

Ptah (ptɑː, tɑː) *n* (in ancient Egypt) a major god worshipped as the creative power, esp at Memphis

ptarmigan (ˈtɑːmɪgən) *n*, *pl* -gans *or* -gan any of several arctic and subarctic grouse of the genus *Lagopus*, esp *L. mutus*, which has a white winter plumage [c16: changed (perhaps influenced by Greek *pteron* wing) from Scottish Gaelic *tarmachan*, diminutive of *tarmach*, of obscure origin]

Pte *military abbreviation* private

pteridology (ˌtɛrɪˈdɒlədʒɪ) *n* the branch of botany concerned with the study of ferns and related plants [c19: from *pterido-*, from Greek *pteris* fern + -LOGY] > pteridological (ˌtɛrɪdəʊˈlɒdʒɪkᵊl) *adj*

pteridophyte (ˈtɛrɪdəʊˌfaɪt) *n* (in traditional classification) any plant of the division *Pteridophyta*, reproducing by spores and having vascular tissue, roots, stems, and leaves: includes the ferns, horsetails, and club mosses. In modern classifications these plants are placed in separate phyla [c19: from *pterido-*, from Greek *pteris* fern + -PHYTE]

ptero- *combining form* wing, feather, or a part resembling a wing: *pterodactyl* [from Greek *pteron* wing, feather]

pterodactyl (ˌtɛrəˈdæktɪl) *n* any extinct flying reptile of the genus *Pterodactylus* and related genera, having membranous wings supported on an elongated fourth digit [c19: from PTERO- + Greek *daktulos* finger]

pteropod (ˈtɛrəˌpɒd) *n* any small marine gastropod mollusc of the group or order *Pteropoda*, in which the foot is expanded into two winglike lobes for swimming and the shell is absent or thin-walled. Also called: sea butterfly

pterosaur (ˈtɛrəˌsɔː) *n* any extinct flying reptile of the order *Pterosauria*, of Jurassic and Cretaceous times: included the pterodactyls

-pterous *or* **-pteran** *adj combining form* indicating a specified number or type of wings: *dipterous* [from Greek *-pteros*, from *pteron* wing]

pterygoid process (ˈtɛrɪˌgɔɪd) *n anatomy* either of two long bony plates extending downwards from each side of the sphenoid bone within the skull [c18 *pterygoid*, from Greek *pterugoeidēs*, from *pterux* wing; see -OID]

ptisan (tɪˈzæn) *n* 1 grape juice drained off without pressure 2 a variant spelling of **tisane** [c14: from Old French *tisane*, from Latin *ptisana*, from Greek *ptisanē* barley groats]

PTN *abbreviation* public telephone network: the telephone network provided in Britain by British Telecom

PTO or **pto** abbreviation please turn over

Ptolemaic (ˌtɒlɪˈmeɪɪk) adj **1** of or relating to the 2nd century AD Greek astronomer, mathematician and geographer Ptolemy or to his conception of the universe **2** of or relating to the Macedonian dynasty that ruled Egypt from the death of Alexander the Great (323 BC) to the death of Cleopatra (30 BC)

Ptolemaic system n the theory of planetary motion developed by Ptolemy from the hypotheses of earlier philosophers, stating that the earth lay at the centre of the universe with the sun, the moon, and the known planets revolving around it in complicated orbits. Beyond the largest of these orbits lay a sphere of fixed stars

Ptolemy (ˈtɒlɪmɪ) n Latin name Claudius Ptolemaeus. 2nd century AD, Greek astronomer, mathematician, and geographer. His Geography was the standard geographical textbook until the discoveries of the 15th century. His system of astronomy (see **Ptolemaic system**), as expounded in the Almagest, remained undisputed until the Copernican system was evolved

Ptolemy I n called Ptolemy Soter. ?367–283 BC, king of Egypt (323–285 BC), a general of Alexander the Great, who obtained Egypt on Alexander's death and founded the Ptolemaic dynasty: his capital Alexandria became the centre of Greek culture

Ptolemy II n called Philadelphus. 309–246 BC, the son of Ptolemy I; king of Egypt (285–246). Under his rule the power, prosperity, and culture of Egypt was at its height

ptomaine or **ptomain** (ˈtəʊmeɪn) n any of a group of amines, such as cadaverine or putrescine, formed by decaying organic matter [c19: from Italian ptomaina, from Greek ptoma corpse, from piptein to fall]

ptomaine poisoning n a popular term for **food poisoning** [c19: because ptomaines were once erroneously thought to be a cause of food poisoning]

ptosis (ˈtəʊsɪs) n, pl ptoses (ˈtəʊsiːz) prolapse or drooping of a part, esp the eyelid [c18: from Greek: a falling] > ptotic (ˈtɒtɪk) adj

PTSD abbreviation post-traumatic stress disorder

Pty Austral, NZ & South African abbreviation proprietary: used to denote a private limited company

ptyalin (ˈtaɪəlɪn) n biochem an amylase secreted in the saliva of man and other animals [c19: from Greek ptualon saliva, from ptuein to spit]

p-type adj **1** (of a semiconductor) having a density of mobile holes in excess of that of conduction electrons **2** associated with or resulting from the movement of holes in a semiconductor: p-type conductivity

Pu the chemical symbol for plutonium

pub (pʌb) n **1** chiefly Brit a building with a bar and one or more public rooms licensed for the sale and consumption of alcoholic drink, often also providing light meals. Formal name: public house **2** Austral & NZ a hotel ▷ vb pubs, pubbing, pubbed **3** (intr) informal to visit a pub or pubs (esp in the phrase **go pubbing**)

pub. abbreviation **1** public **2** publication **3** published **4** publisher **5** publishing

pub-crawl informal, chiefly Brit ▷ n **1** a drinking tour of a number of pubs or bars ▷ vb **2** (intr) to make such a tour

puberty (ˈpjuːbətɪ) n the period at the beginning of adolescence when the sex glands become functional and the secondary sexual characteristics emerge. Also called: pubescence [c14: from Latin pūbertās maturity, from pūber adult] > **pubertal** adj

pubes n (ˈpjuːbiːz) pl pubes (ˈpjuːbiːz) **1** the region above the external genital organs, covered with hair from the time of puberty **2** the pubic bones **3** the plural of **pubis** ▷ pl n (ˈpjuːbz) **4** informal pubic hair [from Latin]

pubescent (pjuːˈbesᵊnt) adj **1** arriving or having arrived at puberty **2** (of certain plants and animals or their parts) covered with a layer of fine short hairs or down [c17: from Latin pūbēscere to reach manhood, from pūber adult] > pu'bescence n

pubic (ˈpjuːbɪk) adj of or relating to the pubes or pubis: pubic hair

pubis (ˈpjuːbɪs) n, pl -bes (-biːz) one of the three sections of the hipbone that forms part of the pelvis [c16: shortened from New Latin os pūbis bone of the PUBES]

public (ˈpʌblɪk) adj **1** of, relating to, or concerning the people as a whole **2** open or accessible to all: public gardens **3** performed or made openly or in the view of all: public proclamation **4** (prenominal) well-known or familiar to people in general: a public figure **5** (usually prenominal) maintained at the expense of, serving, or for the use of a community: a public library **6** open, acknowledged, or notorious: a public scandal **7** go public (of a private company) to issue shares for subscription by the public ▷ n **8** the community or people in general **9** a part or section of the community grouped because of a common interest, activity, etc: the racing public [c15: from Latin pūblicus, changed from pōplicus of the people, from populus people]

public-address system n a system of one or more microphones, amplifiers, and loudspeakers for increasing the sound level of speech or music, used in auditoriums, public gatherings, etc. Sometimes shortened to: PA system

publican (ˈpʌblɪkən) n **1** (in Britain) a person who keeps a public house **2** (in ancient Rome) a public contractor, esp one who farmed the taxes of a province [c12: from Old French publicain, from Latin pūblicānus tax gatherer, from pūblicum public revenues]

publication (ˌpʌblɪˈkeɪʃən) n **1** the act or process of publishing a printed work **2** any printed work offered for sale or distribution **3** the act or an instance of making information public [c14: via Old French from Latin pūblicātiō confiscation of an individual's property, from pūblicāre to seize and assign to public use]

public bar n Brit a bar in a public house usually serving drinks at a cheaper price than in the saloon bar

public company n a limited company whose shares may be purchased by the public and traded freely on the open market and whose share capital is not less than a statutory minimum; public limited company. See **private company**

public convenience n a public lavatory, esp one in a public place

public corporation n (in Britain) an organization established to run a nationalized industry or state-owned enterprise. The chairman and board members are appointed by a government minister, and the government has overall control

public domain n **1** the status of a published work or invention upon which the copyright or patent has expired or which has not been patented or subject to copyright. It may thus be freely used by the public **2** in the public domain able to be discussed and examined freely by the general public

public enemy n a notorious person, such as a criminal, who is regarded as a menace to the public

public goods pl n services such as national defence, law enforcement, and road building, that are for the benefit of, and available to, all members of the public

public house n **1** Brit the formal name for **pub** **2** US & Canadian an inn, tavern, or small hotel

public-interest group n the usual US and Canadian name for **pressure group**

publicist (ˈpʌblɪsɪst) n **1** a person who publicizes something, esp a press or publicity agent **2** a journalist **3** rare a person learned in public or international law

publicity (pʌˈblɪsɪtɪ) n **1 a** the technique or process of attracting public attention to people, products, etc, as by the use of the mass media **b** (as modifier): a publicity agent **2** public interest resulting from information supplied by such a technique or process **3** information used to draw public attention to people, products, etc **4** the state of being public [c18: via French from Medieval Latin pūblicitās; see PUBLIC]

publicize or **publicise** (ˈpʌblɪˌsaɪz) vb (tr) to bring to public notice; advertise

Public Lending Right n the right of authors to receive payment when their books are borrowed from public libraries

public-liability insurance n (in Britain) a form of insurance, typically taken out by business owners, that pays compensation to a member of the public suffering injury or damage as a result of the policyholder or his

P

employees failing to take reasonable care

public limited company *n* another name for **public company** Abbreviation: **plc** *or* **PLC**

publicly ('pʌblɪklɪ) *adv* **1** in a public manner; without concealment; openly **2** in the name or with the consent of the public

public nuisance *n* **1** *law* an illegal act causing harm to members of a particular community rather than to any individual **2** *informal* a person who is generally considered objectionable

public opinion *n* the attitude of the public, esp as a factor in determining the actions of government

public prosecutor *n* *law* an official in charge of prosecuting important cases

Public Record Office *n* an institution in which official records are stored and kept available for inspection by the public

public relations *n* (*functioning as singular or plural*) **1 a** the practice of creating, promoting, or maintaining goodwill and a favourable image among the public towards an institution, public body, etc **b** (*as modifier*): *the public relations industry* **2** the condition of the relationship between an organization and the public **3** the professional staff employed to create, promote, or maintain a favourable relationship between an organization and the public ▷ Abbreviation: **PR**

public school *n* **1** (in England and Wales) a private independent fee-paying secondary school **2** (in the US) any school that is part of a free local educational system **3** in certin Canadian provinces, a public elementray school as distinguished from a separate school

public sector *n* the part of an economy that consists of state-owned institutions, including nationalized industries and services provided by local authorities

public servant *n* **1** an elected or appointed holder of a public office **2** *Austral. & NZ* a member of the public service. British equivalent: civil servant

public service *n* *Austral & NZ* the service responsible for the public administration of the government of a country. It excludes the legislative, judicial, and military branches. Members of the public service have no official political allegiance and are not generally affected by changes of governments. British equivalent: civil service

public-spirited *adj* having or showing active interest in public welfare or the good of the community

public utility *n* an enterprise concerned with the provision to the public of essentials, such as electricity or water

public works *pl n* engineering projects and other constructions, financed and undertaken by a government for the community

publish ('pʌblɪʃ) *vb* **1** to produce and issue (printed or electronic matter) for distribution and sale **2** (*intr*) to have one's written work issued for publication **3** (*tr*) to announce formally or in public **4** (*tr*) to communicate (defamatory matter) to someone other than the person defamed: *to publish a libel* [c14: from Old French *puplier*, from Latin *pūblicāre* to make **PUBLIC**] > **'publishable** *adj*

publisher ('pʌblɪʃə) *n* **1** a company or person engaged in publishing periodicals, books, music, etc **2** *US & Canadian* the proprietor of a newspaper or his representative

Puccini (puˈtʃiːnɪ) *n* **Giacomo** ('dʒaːkomo). 1858–1924, Italian operatic composer, noted for the dramatic realism of his operas, which include *Manon Lescaut* (1893), *La Bohème* (1896), *Tosca* (1900), and *Madame Butterfly* (1904)

puce (pjuːs) *n* a colour varying from deep red to dark purplish-brown [c18: shortened from French *couleur puce* flea colour, from Latin *pūlex* flea]

puck[1] (pʌk) *n* **1** a small disc of hard rubber used in ice hockey **2** a stroke at the ball in hurling **3** *Irish slang* a sharp blow ▷ *vb* **4** to strike (the ball) in hurling **5** *Irish slang* to strike hard; punch [c19: of unknown origin]

puck[2] (pʌk) *n* (*often capital*) a mischievous or evil spirit [Old English *pūca*, of obscure origin] > **'puckish** *adj*

pucka ('pʌkə) *adj* a less common spelling of **pukka**

pucker ('pʌkə) *vb* **1** to gather or contract (a soft surface such as the skin of the face) into wrinkles or folds, or (of such a surface) to be so gathered or contracted ▷ *n* **2** a wrinkle, crease, or irregular fold [c16: perhaps related to **POKE**[2], from the creasing into baglike wrinkles]

pudding ('pʊdɪŋ) *n* **1** a sweetened usually cooked dessert made in many forms and of various ingredients, such as flour, milk, and eggs, with fruit, etc **2** a savoury dish, usually soft and consisting partially of pastry or batter: *steak-and-kidney pudding* **3** the dessert course in a meal **4** a sausage-like mass of seasoned minced meat, oatmeal, etc, stuffed into a prepared skin or bag and boiled [c13 *poding*; compare Old English *puduc* a wart, Low German *puddek* sausage] > **'puddingy** *adj*

pudding stone *n* a conglomerate rock in which there is a difference in colour or composition between the pebbles and the matrix

puddle ('pʌdˀl) *n* **1** a small pool of water, esp of rain **2** a small pool of any liquid **3** a worked mixture of wet clay and sand that is impervious to water and is used to line a pond or canal ▷ *vb* **4** (*tr*) to make (clay, etc) into puddle **5** (*tr*) to subject (iron) to puddling [c14 *podel*, diminutive of Old English *pudd* ditch, of obscure origin] > **'puddler** *n* > **'puddly** *adj*

puddling ('pʌdlɪŋ) *n* a process for converting pig iron into wrought iron by heating it with ferric oxide in a furnace to oxidize the carbon

pudency ('pjuːdˀnsɪ) *n* modesty, shame, or prudishness [c17: from Late Latin *pudentia*, from Latin *pudēre* to feel shame]

pudendum (pjuːˈdɛndəm) *n*, *pl* **-da** (-də) (*often plural*) the human external genital organs collectively, esp of a female [c17: from Late Latin, from Latin *pudenda* the shameful (parts), from *pudēre* to be ashamed] > pu'dendal *or* pudic ('pjuːdɪk) *adj*

pudgy ('pʌdʒɪ) *adj* pudgier, pudgiest a variant spelling (esp US) of **podgy** [c19: of uncertain origin; compare earlier *pudsy* plump, perhaps from Scottish *pud* stomach, plump child] > **'pudgily** *adv* > **'pudginess** *n*

Pudovkin (Russian puˈdɔfkjin) *n* **Vsevolod** ('fsjevələt). 1893–1953, Russian film director; noted for his silent films, such as *Mother* (1926) and *Storm over Asia* (1928)

Pudsey ('pʌdzɪ) *n* a town in N England, in Leeds unitary authority, West Yorkshire. Pop: 32 391 (2001)

Puducherry (ˌpuːduːˈtʃɛrɪ) *n* **1 a** a Union Territory of SE India: transferred from French to Indian administration in 1954 and made a Union Territory in 1962. Capital: Puducherry. Pop: 973 829 (2001 est). Area: 479 sq km (185 sq miles) **2** a port in SE India, capital of the Union Territory of Puducherry (Pondicherry), on the Coromandel Coast. Pop: 220 749 (2001) ▷ Former official name (until 2006): Pondicherry

Puebla (Spanish ˈpweβla) *n* **1** an inland state of S central Mexico, situated on the Anáhuac Plateau. Capital: Puebla. Pop: 5 070 346 (2000 est). Area: 33 919 sq km (13 096 sq miles) **2** a city in S Mexico, capital of Puebla state: founded in 1532; university (1537). Pop: 1 880 000 (2005 est)

pueblo ('pwɛbləu; Spanish 'pweβlo) *n*, *pl* **-los** (-ləuz; Spanish **-los**) **1** a communal village, built by certain Indians of the southwestern US and parts of Latin America, consisting of one or more flat-roofed stone or adobe houses **2** (in Spanish America) a village or town [c19: from Spanish: people, from Latin *populus*]

Pueblo[1] ('pwɛbləu) *n*, *pl* **-lo** *or* **-los** a member of any of the North American Indian peoples who live in pueblos, including the Tanoans, Zuñi, and Hopi

Pueblo[2] ('pwɛbləu) *n* a city in Colorado: a centre of the steel industry. Pop: 103 648 (2001 est)

puerile ('pjuəraɪl) *adj* **1** exhibiting silliness; immature; trivial **2** of or characteristic of a child [c17: from Latin *puerīlis* childish, from *puer* a boy] > **'puerilely** *adv* > **puerility** (pjuəˈrɪlɪtɪ) *n*

puerperal (pjuːˈɜːpərəl) *adj* of, relating to, or occurring during the puerperium [c18: from New Latin *puerperālis* relating to childbirth; see **PUERPERIUM**]

puerperal fever *n* a serious, formerly widespread, form of blood poisoning caused by infection contracted during childbirth

puerperal psychosis *n* a mental disorder sometimes

occurring in women after childbirth, characterized by deep depression, delusions of the child's death, and homicidal feelings towards the child

puerperium (pjʊəˈpɪərɪəm) *n* the period following childbirth, lasting approximately six weeks, during which the uterus returns to its normal size and shape [c17: from Latin: childbirth, from *puerperus* relating to a woman in labour, from *puer* boy + *parere* to bear]

Puerto Rico ('pwɜːtəʊ 'riːkəʊ, 'pweə-) *n* an autonomous commonwealth (in association with the US) occupying the smallest and easternmost of the Greater Antilles in the Caribbean: one of the most densely populated areas in the world; ceded by Spain to the US in 1899. Currency: US dollar. Capital: San Juan. Pop: 3 897 000 (2004 est). Area: 9104 sq km (3515 sq miles). Former name (until 1932): Porto Rico Abbreviation: PR > **Puerto Rican** ('pwɜːtəʊ 'riːkən, 'pweə-) *adj, n*

Pufendorf (*German* 'puːfəndɔrf) *n* **Samuel von** ('zamuəl fon). 1632–94, German jurist and philosopher, who lived in Sweden and Denmark. His *De Jure naturae et gentium* (1672) was an important contribution to the philosophy of natural and international law

puff (pʌf) *n* **1** a short quick draught, gust, or emission, as of wind, smoke, air, etc, esp a forceful one **2** the amount of wind, smoke, etc, released in a puff **3** the sound made by or associated with a puff **4** an instance of inhaling and expelling the breath as in smoking **5** a light aerated pastry usually filled with cream, jam, etc **6** a powder puff **7** exaggerated praise, as of a book, product, etc, esp through an advertisement **8** a piece of clothing fabric gathered up so as to bulge in the centre while being held together at the edges **9** a loose piece of hair wound into a cylindrical roll, usually over a pad, and pinned in place in a coiffure **10** one's breath (esp in the phrase **out of puff**) **11** *derogatory, slang* a male homosexual ▷ *vb* **12** to blow or breathe or cause to blow or breathe in short quick draughts or blasts **13** (*tr*; often foll by *out*; usually passive) to cause to be out of breath **14** to take puffs or draws at (a cigarette, cigar, or pipe) **15** to move with or by the emission of puffs: *the steam train puffed up the incline* **16** (often foll by *up, out*, etc) to swell, as with air, pride, etc **17** (*tr*) to praise with exaggerated empty words, often in advertising **18** (*tr*) to apply (cosmetic powder) from a powder puff to (the face) [Old English *pyffan*; related to Dutch German *puffen*, Swiss *pfuffen*, Norwegian *puffa*, all of imitative origin] > **'puffy** *adj* > **'puffily** *adv* > **'puffiness** *n*

puff adder *n* **1** a large venomous African viper, *Bitis arietans*, that is yellowish-grey with brown markings and inflates its body when alarmed **2** another name for **hognose snake**

puffball ('pʌfˌbɔːl) *n* any of various basidiomycetous saprotrophic fungi of the genera *Calvatia* and *Lycoperdon*, having a round fruiting body that discharges a cloud of brown spores when mature

puffer ('pʌfə) *n* **1** a person or thing that puffs **2** Also called: **globefish** any marine plectognath fish of the family *Tetraodontidae*, having an elongated spiny body that can be inflated to form a globe

puffin ('pʌfɪn) *n* any of various northern diving birds of the family *Alcidae* (auks, etc), esp *Fratercula arctica* (**common** or **Atlantic puffin**), having a black-and-white plumage and a brightly coloured vertically flattened bill: order *Charadriiformes* [c14: perhaps of Cornish origin]

puff pastry or *US* **puff paste** *n* a dough rolled in thin layers incorporating fat to make a rich flaky pastry for pies, rich pastries, etc

puff-puff *n* Brit a children's name for a steam locomotive or railway train

pug[1] (pʌg) *n* Also called: **carlin** a small compact breed of dog with a smooth coat, lightly curled tail, and a short wrinkled nose [c16: of uncertain origin] > **'puggish** *adj*

pug[2] (pʌg) *vb* **pugs, pugging, pugged** (*tr*) **1** to mix or knead (clay) with water to form a malleable mass or paste, often in a **pug mill 2** to fill or stop with clay or a similar substance [c19: of uncertain origin]

pug[3] (pʌg) *n* a slang name for **boxer** (sense 1) [c20: shortened from PUGILIST]

Pugachov ('pʊgətʃɒf) *n* **Yemelyan Ivanovich**. 1726–75,

Russian Cossack rebel, leader of a major revolt against the government of Catherine II: executed

Puget (*French* pyʒɛ) *n* **Pierre** (pjɛr). 1620–94, French Baroque sculptor, best known for his *Milo of Crotona* (c. 1680)

Puget Sound ('pjuːdʒɪt) *n* an inlet of the Pacific in NW Washington. Length: about 130 km (80 miles)

pugging ('pʌgɪŋ) *n* material such as clay, mortar, sawdust, sand, etc, inserted between wooden flooring and ceiling to reduce the transmission of sound. Also called: **pug**

puggree, pugree ('pʌgrɪ) or **puggaree, pugaree** ('pʌgərɪ) *n* **1** the usual Indian word for **turban 2** a scarf, usually pleated, around the crown of some hats, esp sun helmets [c17: from Hindi *pagrī*, from Sanskrit *parikara*]

pugilism ('pjuːdʒɪˌlɪzəm) *n* the art, practice, or profession of fighting with the fists; boxing [c18: from Latin *pugil* a boxer; related to *pugnus* fist, *pugna* a fight] > **'pugilist** *n* > ˌpugi'listic *adj* > ˌpugi'listically *adv*

Pugin ('pjuːdʒɪn) *n* **Augustus** (**Welby Northmore**). 1812–52, British architect; a leader of the Gothic Revival. He collaborated with Sir Charles Barry on the Palace of Westminster (begun 1836)

Puglia ('puːʎʎa) *n* the Italian name for **Apulia**

pugnacious (pʌgˈneɪʃəs) *adj* readily disposed to fight; belligerent [c17: from Latin *pugnāx*] > **pug'naciously** *adv* > **pugnacity** (pʌgˈnæsɪtɪ) or **pug'naciousness** *n*

pug nose *n* a short stubby upturned nose [c18: from PUG[1]] > **'pug-ˌnosed** *adj*

Pugwash conferences ('pʌgˌwɒʃ) *pl n* international peace conferences of scientists held regularly to discuss world problems: Nobel peace prize 1995 awarded to Joseph Rotblat, one of the founders of the conferences, secretary-general (1957–73), and president from 1988 [c20: from *Pugwash*, Nova Scotia, where the first conference was held]

puisne ('pjuːnɪ) *adj* (esp of a subordinate judge) of lower rank [c16: from Anglo-French, from Old French *puisné* born later, from *puis* at a later date, from Latin *posteā* afterwards + *né* born, from *naistre* to be born, from Latin *nascī*]

puissance ('pjuːɪsᵊns, 'pwiːsɑːns) *n* **1** a competition in showjumping that tests a horse's ability to jump a limited number of large obstacles **2** *archaic or poetic* power [c15: from Old French; see PUISSANT]

puissant ('pjuːɪsᵊnt) *adj* *archaic or poetic* powerful [c15: from Old French, ultimately from Latin *potēns* mighty, from *posse* to have power] > **'puissantly** *adv*

puke (pjuːk) *slang* ▷ *vb* **1** to vomit ▷ *n* **2** the act of vomiting **3** the matter vomited [c16: probably of imitative origin; compare German *spucken* to spit]

pukeko ('pʊkəkəʊ) *n, pl* **-kos** a wading bird, *Porphyrio melanotus*, of New Zealand, with a brightly coloured plumage [Māori]

pukka or **pucka** ('pʌkə) *adj* (esp in India) properly or perfectly done, constructed, etc [c17: from Hindi *pakkā* firm, from Sanskrit *pakva*]

puku ('puːkuː) *n* NZ the belly or stomach [Māori]

Pula (*Croatian* 'puːla) *n* a port in NW Croatia at the S tip of the Istrian Peninsula: made a Roman military base in 178 BC; became the main Austro-Hungarian naval station and passed to Italy in 1919, to Yugoslavia in 1947, and is now in independent Croatia. Pop: 67 000 (2007 est). Italian name: **Pola**

Pulau Pinang ('pʊlaʊ pɪ'næŋ) *n* another name for **Penang**

pulchritude ('pʌlkrɪˌtjuːd) *n* *formal or literary* physical beauty [c15: from Latin *pulchritūdō*, from *pulcher* beautiful] > ˌpulchri'tudinous *adj*

Pulci (*Italian* 'pultʃi) *n* **Luigi** ('lwiːdʒi). 1432–84, Italian poet. His masterpiece is the comic epic poem *Morgante* (1483)

pule (pjuːl) *vb* (*intr*) to cry plaintively; whimper [c16: perhaps of imitative origin] > **'puler** *n*

Pulitzer ('pʊlɪtsə) *n* **Joseph**. 1847–1911, US newspaper publisher, born in Hungary. He established the Pulitzer prizes

Pulitzer prize ('pʊlɪtsə) *n* one of a group of prizes established by Joseph Pulitzer and awarded yearly since

1917 for excellence in American journalism, literature, and music

pull (pʊl) *vb* (*mainly tr*) **1** (*also intr*) to exert force on (an object) so as to draw it towards the source of the force **2** to exert force on so as to remove; extract: *to pull a tooth* **3** to strip of feathers, hair, etc; pluck **4** to draw the entrails from (a fowl) **5** to rend or tear **6** to strain (a muscle, ligament, or tendon) injuriously **7** (usually foll by *off*) *informal* to perform or bring about: *to pull off a million-pound deal* **8** (often foll by *on*) *informal* to draw out (a weapon) for use: *he pulled a knife on his attacker* **9** *informal* to attract: *the pop group pulled a crowd* **10** (*also intr*) *slang* to attract (a sexual partner) **11** (*intr*; usually foll by *on* or *at*) to drink or inhale deeply: *to pull at one's pipe; pull on a bottle of beer* **12** to put on or make (a grimace): *to pull a face* **13** (*also intr*; foll by *away, out, over*, etc) to move (a vehicle) or (of a vehicle) to be moved in a specified manner **14** to withdraw or remove: *the board decided to pull their support* **15** *sport* to hit (a ball) so that it veers away from the direction in which the player intended to hit it (to the left for a right-handed player) **16** *cricket* to hit (a ball pitched straight or on the off side) to the leg side **17** *hurling* to strike (a fast-moving ball) in the same direction as it is already moving **18** (*also intr*) to row (a boat) or take a stroke of (an oar) in rowing **19** (of a rider) to restrain (a horse), esp to prevent it from winning a race **20** (*intr*) (of a horse) to resist strongly the attempts of a rider to rein in or check it **21 pull a fast one** *slang* to play a sly trick **22 pull apart** *or* **pull to pieces** to criticize harshly **23 pull one's punches** **a** *informal* to restrain the force of one's criticisms or actions **b** *boxing* to restrain the force of one's blows, esp when deliberately losing after being bribed, etc ▷ *n* **24** an act or an instance of pulling or being pulled **25** the force or effort used in pulling: *the pull of the moon affects the tides on earth* **26** the act or an instance of taking in drink or smoke **27** something used for pulling, such as a knob or handle **28** *informal* special advantage or influence: *his uncle is chairman of the company, so he has quite a lot of pull* **29** *informal* the power to attract attention or support **30** a period of rowing **31** a single stroke of an oar in rowing **32** the act of pulling the ball in golf, cricket, etc **33** the act of checking or reining in a horse ▷ See also **pull down, pull in**, etc [Old English *pullian*; related to Icelandic *pūla* to beat] > 'puller *n*

pull down *vb* (*tr, adverb*) to destroy or demolish: *the old houses were pulled down*

pullet ('pʊlɪt) *n* a young hen of the domestic fowl, less than one year old [c14: from Old French *poulet* chicken, from Latin *pullus* a young animal or bird]

pulley ('pʊlɪ) *n* **1** a wheel with a grooved rim in which a rope, chain, or belt can run in order to change the direction or point of application of a force applied to the rope, etc **2** a number of such wheels pivoted in parallel in a block, used to raise heavy loads **3** a wheel with a flat, convex, or grooved rim mounted on a shaft and driven by or driving a belt passing around it [C14 *poley*, from Old French *polie*, from Vulgar Latin *polidium* (unattested), apparently from Late Greek *polidion* (unattested) a little pole, from Greek *polos* axis]

pull in *vb* (*adverb*) **1** (*intr*; often foll by *to*) to reach a destination: *the train pulled in at the station* **2** Also called: **pull over** (*intr*) (of a motor vehicle, driver, etc) **a** to draw in to the side of the road in order to stop or to allow another vehicle to pass **b** to stop (at a café, lay-by, etc) **3** (*tr*) to draw or attract: *his appearance will pull in the crowds* **4** (*tr*) *slang* to arrest **5** (*tr*) to earn or gain (money) ▷ *n* **pull-in 6** *Brit* a roadside café, esp for lorry drivers

Pullman[1] ('pʊlmən) *n*, *pl* **-mans** a luxurious railway coach, esp a sleeping car. Also called: **Pullman car** [c19: named after George M. *Pullman* (1831–97), the US inventor who first manufactured such coaches]

Pullman[2] ('pʊlmən) *n* **Philip**. born 1946, British author. Writing primarily for older children, he is best known for the fantasy trilogy *His Dark Materials* (1997–2000)

pull off *vb* (*tr*) **1** to remove (clothing) forcefully **2** (*adverb*) to succeed in performing (a difficult feat)

pull out *vb* (*adverb*) **1** (*tr*) to extract **2** (*intr*) to depart: *the train pulled out of the station* **3** *military* to withdraw or escape or be withdrawn or rescued, as from a difficult situation **4** (*intr*) (of a motor vehicle, driver, etc) **a** to draw away from the side of the road **b** to draw out from behind another vehicle to overtake **5** (*intr*) to abandon a position or situation, esp a dangerous or embarrassing one **6** (foll by *of*) to level out or cause to level out (from a dive) ▷ *n* **pull-out 7** an extra leaf of a book that folds out **8** a removable section of a magazine, etc

pullover ('pʊlˌəʊvə) *n* a garment, esp a sweater, that is pulled on over the head

pull over *vb* **1** (*intr*) (of a motor vehicle, driver, etc) to halt at the side of the road **2** (*tr*) (of a police officer) to instruct (the driver of a motor vehicle) to halt at the side of the road

pull through *vb* Also called: **pull round** to survive or recover or cause to survive or recover, esp after a serious illness or crisis

pull together *vb* **1** (*intr, adverb*) to cooperate or work harmoniously **2 pull oneself together** *informal* to regain one's self-control or composure

pullulate ('pʌljʊˌleɪt) *vb* (*intr*) **1** (of animals, etc) to breed rapidly or abundantly; teem; swarm **2** (of plants or plant parts) to sprout, bud, or germinate [c17: from Latin *pullulāre* to sprout, from *pullulus* a baby animal, from *pullus* young animal] > ˌpulluˈlation *n*

pull up *vb* (*adverb*) **1** (*tr*) to remove by the roots **2** (often foll by *with* or *on*) to move level (with) or ahead (of) or cause to move level (with) or ahead (of), esp in a race **3** to stop **4** (*tr*) to rebuke ▷ *n* **pull-up 5** an exercise in which the body is raised up by the arms pulling on a horizontal bar fixed above the head **6** *Brit old-fashioned* a roadside café

pulmonary ('pʌlmənərɪ, -mənrɪ, 'pʊl-) *adj* **1** of, or relating to or affecting the lungs **2** having lungs or lunglike organs [c18: from Latin *pulmōnārius*, from *pulmō* a lung; related to Greek *pleumōn* a lung]

pulmonary artery *n* either of the two arteries that convey oxygen-depleted blood from the heart to the lungs

pulmonary vein *n* any one of the four veins that convey oxygen-rich blood from the lungs to the heart

pulp (pʌlp) *n* **1** soft or fleshy plant tissue, such as the succulent part of a fleshy fruit **2** a moist mixture of cellulose fibres, as obtained from wood, from which paper is made **3 a** a magazine or book containing trite or sensational material, and usually printed on cheap rough paper **b** (*as modifier*): *a pulp novel* **4** *dentistry* the soft innermost part of a tooth, containing nerves and blood vessels **5** any soft soggy mass or substance **6** mining pulverized ore, esp when mixed with water ▷ *vb* **7** to reduce (a material or solid substance) to pulp or (of a material or solid substance) to be reduced to pulp **8** (*tr*) to remove the pulp from (fruit) [c16: from Latin *pulpa*] > 'pʌlpɪ *adj* > 'pulpily *adv* > 'pulpiness *n*

pulpit ('pʊlpɪt) *n* **1** a raised platform, usually surrounded by a barrier, set up in churches as the appointed place for preaching, leading in prayer, etc **2** a medium for expressing an opinion, such as a column in a newspaper **3 the pulpit a** the preaching of the Christian message **b** the clergy or their message and influence [c14: from Latin *pulpitum* a platform]

pulpwood ('pʌlpˌwʊd) *n* pine, spruce, or any other soft wood used to make paper

pulque ('pʊlkɪ; *Spanish* 'pulke) *n* a light alcoholic drink from Mexico made from the juice of various agave plants, esp the maguey [c17: from Mexican Spanish, apparently from Nahuatl, from *puliuhqui* decomposed, since it will only keep for a day]

pulsar ('pʌlˌsɑː) *n* any of a number of very small extremely dense objects first observed in 1967, which rotate very rapidly and emit very regular pulses of polarized radiation, esp radio waves. They are thought to be neutron stars formed following supernova explosions [c20: from *puls(ating st)ar*, on the model of QUASAR]

pulsate (pʌlˈseɪt) *vb* (*intr*) **1** to expand and contract with a rhythmic beat; throb **2** *physics* to vary in intensity, magnitude, size, etc **3** to quiver or vibrate [c18: from Latin *pulsāre* to push] > **pulsative** ('pʌlsətɪv) *adj*

> pul'sation *n* > pul'sator *n* > pulsatory ('pʌlsətərɪ, -trɪ) *adj*

pulsatilla (ˌpʌlsə'tɪlə) *n* another name for: **pasqueflower** [c16: from Medieval Latin, from *pulsāta* beaten (by the wind)]

pulsating star *n* a type of variable star, the variation in brightness resulting from expansion and subsequent contraction of the star

pulse¹ (pʌls) *n* **1** *physiol* **a** the rhythmic contraction and expansion of an artery at each beat of the heart, often discernible to the touch at points such as the wrists **b** a single pulsation of the heart or arteries **2** *physics, electronics* **a** a transient sharp change in voltage, current, or some other quantity normally constant in a system **b** one of a series of such transient disturbances, usually recurring at regular intervals and having a characteristic geometric shape **3** **a** a recurrent rhythmic series of beats, waves, vibrations, etc **b** any single beat, wave, etc, in such a series **4** bustle, vitality, or excitement: *the pulse of a city* **5** keep one's finger on the pulse to be well-informed about current events ▷ *vb* **6** (*intr*) to beat, throb, or vibrate **7** (*tr*) to provide an electronic pulse to operate (a slide projector) [c14 *pous*, from Latin *pulsus* a beating, from *pellere* to beat] > 'pulseless *adj*

pulse² (pʌls) *n* **1** the edible seeds of any of several leguminous plants, such as peas, beans, and lentils **2** the plant producing any of these seeds [c13 *pols*, from Old French, from Latin *puls* pottage of pulse]

pulsejet ('pʌls,dʒɛt) *n* a type of ramjet engine in which air is admitted through movable vanes that are closed by the pressure resulting from each intermittent explosion of the fuel in the combustion chamber, thus causing a pulsating thrust. Also called: pulsejet engine, pulsojet ('pʌlsəʊ,dʒɛt)

pulse modulation *n* *electronics* a type of modulation in which a train of pulses is used as the carrier wave, one or more of its parameters, such as amplitude, being modulated or modified in order to carry information

pulsimeter (pʌl'sɪmɪtə) *n* *med* an instrument for measuring the strength and rate of the pulse

pulverize *or* **pulverise** ('pʌlvə,raɪz) *vb* **1** to reduce (a substance) to fine particles, as by crushing or grinding, or (of a substance) to be so reduced **2** (*tr*) to destroy completely; defeat or injure seriously [c16: from Late Latin *pulverizare* or French *pulvériser*, from Latin *pulverum*, from *pulvis* dust] > 'pulver,izable *or* 'pulver,isable *adj* > ,pulveri'zation *or* ,pulveri'sation *n* > 'pulver,izer *or* 'pulver,iser *n*

pulverulent (pʌl'vɛrʊlənt) *adj* consisting of, covered with, or crumbling to dust or fine particles [c17: from Latin *pulverulentus*, from *pulvis* dust]

puma ('pjuːmə) *n* a large American feline mammal, *Felis concolor*, that resembles a lion, having a plain greyish-brown coat and long tail. Also called: cougar, mountain lion [c18: via Spanish from Quechuan]

pumice ('pʌmɪs) *n* **1** Also called: pumice stone a light porous acid volcanic rock having the composition of rhyolite, used for scouring and, in powdered form, as an abrasive and for polishing ▷ *vb* **2** (*tr*) to rub or polish with pumice [c15 *pomys*, from Old French *pomis*, from Latin *pūmex*] > pumiceous (pjuː'mɪʃəs) *adj*

pummel ('pʌməl) *vb* -mels, -melling, -melled *or US* -mels, -meling, -meled (*tr*) to strike repeatedly with or as if with the fists. Also (less commonly): pommel [c16: see POMMEL]

pump¹ (pʌmp) *n* **1** any device for compressing, driving, raising, or reducing the pressure of a fluid, esp by means of a piston or set of rotating impellers **2** *biology* a mechanism for the active transport of ions, such as protons, calcium ions, and sodium ions, across cell membranes: *a sodium pump* ▷ *vb* **3** (when *tr*, usually foll by *from, out, into, away*, etc) to raise or drive (air, liquid, etc, esp into or from something) with a pump or similar device **4** (*tr*; usually foll by *in* or *into*) to supply in large amounts: *to pump capital into a project* **5** (*tr*) to deliver (shots, bullets, etc) repeatedly with great force **6** to operate (something, esp a handle or lever) in the manner of a pump or (of something) to work in this

way: *to pump the pedals of a bicycle* **7** (*tr*) to obtain (information) from (a person) by persistent questioning **8** (*intr*; usually foll by *from* or *out of*) (of liquids) to flow freely in large spurts: *oil pumped from the fissure* [c15: from Middle Dutch *pumpe* pipe, probably from Spanish *bomba*, of imitative origin]

pump² (pʌmp) *n* **1** a low-cut low-heeled shoe without fastenings, worn esp for dancing **2** a type of shoe with a rubber sole, used in games such as tennis; plimsoll [c16: of unknown origin]

pump-and-dump *n* the practice of buying shares, generating favourable publicity about them, especially on the internet, then selling them when the price accordingly rises

pumpernickel ('pʌmpə,nɪk²l) *n* a slightly sour black bread, originating in Germany, made of coarse rye flour [c18: from German, of uncertain origin]

pumpkin ('pʌmpkɪn) *n* **1** any of several creeping cucurbitaceous plants of the genus *Cucurbita*, esp *C. pepo* of North America and *C. maxima* of Europe **2** the large round fruit of any of these plants, which has a thick orange rind, pulpy flesh, and numerous seeds **3** (*often capital*) *chiefly US* a term of endearment [c17: from earlier *pumpion*, from French *pompon*, from Latin *pepo*, from Greek *pepōn*, from *pepōn* ripe, from *peptein* to ripen]

pump priming *n* **1** the act or process of introducing fluid into a pump to improve the sealing of the pump parts on starting and to expel air from it **2** *US* government expenditure designed to stimulate economic activity in stagnant or depressed areas **3** another term for **deficit financing**

pun¹ (pʌn) *n* **1** the use of words or phrases to exploit ambiguities and innuendoes in their meaning, usually for humorous effect; a play on words. An example is: *"Ben Battle was a soldier bold, And used to war's alarms: But a cannonball took off his legs, So he laid down his arms."* (Thomas Hood) ▷ *vb* puns, punning, punned **2** (*intr*) to make puns [c17: possibly from Italian *puntiglio* point of detail, wordplay; see PUNCTILIO]

pun² (pʌn) *vb* puns, punning, punned (*tr*) *Brit* to pack (earth, rubble, etc) by pounding [c16: dialectal variant of POUND¹]

puna *Spanish* ('puna) *n* **1** a high cold dry plateau, esp in the Andes **2** another name for **mountain sickness** [c17: from American Spanish, from Quechuan]

Punakha *or* **Punaka** ('puːnəkə) *n* a town in W central Bhutan: a former capital of the country

punch¹ (pʌntʃ) *vb* **1** to strike blows (at), esp with a clenched fist **2** *Western US* to herd or drive (cattle), esp for a living **3** (*tr*) to poke or prod with a stick or similar object ▷ *n* **4** a blow with the fist **5** *informal* telling force, point, or vigour: *his arguments lacked punch* [c15: perhaps a variant of POUNCE²] > 'puncher *n*

punch² (pʌntʃ) *n* **1** a tool or machine for piercing holes in a material **2** a tool or machine used for stamping a design on something or shaping it by impact **3** the solid die of a punching machine for cutting, stamping, or shaping material **4** *computing* a device, such as a card punch or tape punch, used for making holes in a card or paper tape ▷ *vb* **5** (*tr*) to pierce, cut, stamp, shape, or drive with a punch [c14: shortened from *puncheon*, from Old French *ponçon*; see PUNCHEON²]

punch³ (pʌntʃ) *n* any mixed drink containing fruit juice and, usually, alcoholic liquor, generally hot and spiced [c17: perhaps from Hindi *pānch*, from Sanskrit *pañca* five; the beverage originally included five ingredients]

Punch (pʌntʃ) *n* the main character in the traditional children's puppet show **Punch and Judy**

punchbag ('pʌntʃ,bæg) *n* Also called (US and Canadian): punching bag a suspended stuffed bag that is punched for exercise, esp boxing training

punchball ('pʌntʃ,bɔːl) *n* **1** a stuffed or inflated ball, supported by a flexible rod, that is punched for exercise, esp boxing training **2** *US* a game resembling baseball in which a light ball is struck with the fist

punchbowl ('pʌntʃ,bəʊl) *n* **1** a large bowl for serving punch, lemonade, etc, usually with a ladle and often having small drinking glasses hooked around the rim **2** *Brit* a bowl-shaped depression in the land

punch-drunk *adj* **1** demonstrating or characteristic of the behaviour of a person who has suffered repeated blows to the head, esp a professional boxer **2** dazed; stupefied

punched card *or esp US* **punch card** *n* (formerly) a card on which data can be coded in the form of punched holes. In computing, there were usually 80 columns and 12 rows, each column containing a pattern of holes representing one character

punched tape *or sometimes US* **perforated tape** *n* other terms for **paper tape**

puncheon[1] ('pʌntʃən) *n* a large cask of variable capacity, usually between 70 and 120 gallons [C15 *poncion*, from Old French *ponchon*, of uncertain origin]

puncheon[2] ('pʌntʃən) *n* **1** a short wooden post that is used as a vertical strut **2** a less common name for **punch**[2] (sense 1) [C14 *ponson*, from Old French *ponçon*, from Latin *punctiō* a puncture, from *pungere* to prick]

Punchinello (ˌpʌntʃɪ'nɛləʊ) *n, pl* **-los** *or* **-loes** **1** a type of clown from Italian burlesque or puppet shows, the prototype of Punch **2** (*sometimes not capital*) any grotesque or absurd character [C17: from earlier *Polichinello*, from Italian (Neapolitan dialect) *Polecenella*, from Italian *pulcino* chicken, ultimately from Latin *pullus* young animal]

punch line *n* the culminating part of a joke, funny story, etc, that gives it its humorous or dramatic point

punch-up *n Brit informal* a fight, brawl, or violent argument

punchy ('pʌntʃɪ) *adj* **punchier, punchiest** **1** an informal word for **punch-drunk** **2** *informal* incisive or forceful > 'punchily *adv* > 'punchiness *n*

punctate ('pʌŋkteɪt) *adj* having or marked with minute spots, holes, ordepressions [C18: from New Latin *punctātus*, from Latin *punctum* a point] > punc'tation *n*

punctilio (pʌŋk'tɪlɪˌəʊ) *n, pl* **-os** **1** strict attention to minute points of etiquette **2** a petty formality or fine point of etiquette [C16: from Italian *puntiglio* small point, from *punto* point, from Latin *punctum* point]

punctilious (pʌŋk'tɪlɪəs) *adj* **1** paying scrupulous attention to correctness in etiquette **2** attentive to detail > punc'tiliously *adv* > punc'tiliousness *n*

punctual ('pʌŋktjʊəl) *adj* **1** arriving or taking place at an arranged time;prompt **2** (of a person) having the characteristic of always keeping to arranged times, as for appointments, meetings, etc **3** *obsolete* precise; exact; apposite **4** *maths* consisting of or confined to a point in space [C14: from Medieval Latin *punctuālis* concerning detail, from Latin *punctum* point] > ˌpunctu'ality *n* > 'punctually *adv*

punctuate ('pʌŋktjʊˌeɪt) *vb* (*mainly tr*) **1** (*also intr*) to insert punctuation marks into (a written text) **2** to interrupt or insert at frequent intervals: *a meeting punctuated by heckling* **3** to give emphasis to [C17: from Medieval Latin *punctuāre* to prick, from Latin *punctum* aprick, from *pungere* to puncture]

punctuation (ˌpʌŋktjʊ'eɪʃən) *n* **1** the use of symbols not belonging to the alphabet of a writing system to indicate aspects of the intonation and meaning not otherwise conveyed in the written language **2** the symbols used for this purpose

punctuation mark *n* any of the signs used in punctuation, such as a comma or question mark

puncture ('pʌŋktʃə) *n* **1** a small hole made by a sharp object **2** a perforation and loss of pressure in a pneumatic tyre, made by sharp stones, glass, etc **3** the act of puncturing or perforating ▷ *vb* **4** (*tr*) to pierce (a hole) in (something) with a sharp object **5** to cause (something pressurized, esp a tyre) to lose pressure by piercing, or (of a tyre, etc) to be pierced and collapse in this way **6** (*tr*) to depreciate (a person's self-esteem, pomposity, etc) [C14: from Latin *punctūra*, from *pungere* to prick]

pundit ('pʌndɪt) *n* **1** an expert **2** (formerly) a learned person **3** Also called: **pandit** a Brahman learned in Sanskrit and, esp in Hindu religion, philosophy or law [C17: from Hindi *pandit*, from Sanskrit *pandita* learned man, from *pandita* learned]

punditry ('pʌndɪtrɪ) *n* the expressing of expert opinions

Pune ('puːnə) *n* another name for **Poona**

punga ('pʌŋə) *n* a variant spelling of **ponga**

pungent ('pʌndʒənt) *adj* **1** having an acrid smell or sharp bitter flavour **2** (of wit, satire, etc) biting; caustic **3** *biology* ending in a sharp point [C16: from Latin *pungens* piercing, from *pungere* to prick] > 'pungency *n* > 'pungently *adv*

Punic ('pjuːnɪk) *adj* **1** of or relating to ancient Carthage or the Carthaginians ▷ *n* **2** the language of the ancient Carthaginians; a late form of Phoenician [C15: from Latin *Pūnicus*, variant of *Poenicus* Carthaginian, from Greek *Phoinix*]

punish ('pʌnɪʃ) *vb* **1** to force (someone) to undergo a penalty or sanction, such as imprisonment, fines, death, etc, for some crime or misdemeanour **2** (*tr*) to inflict punishment for (some crime, etc) **3** (*tr*) to use or treat harshly or roughly, esp as by overexertion: *to punish a horse* **4** (*tr*) *informal* to consume (some commodity) in large quantities: *to punish the bottle* [C14 *punisse*, from Old French *punir*, from Latin *pūnīre* to punish, from *poena* penalty] > 'punisher *n* > 'punishing *adj* > 'punishable *adj* > ˌpunisha'bility *n*

punishment ('pʌnɪʃmənt) *n* **1** a penalty or sanction given for any crime oroffence **2** the act of punishing or state of being punished **3** *informal* rough treatment

punitive ('pjuːnɪtɪv) *adj* relating to, involving, or with the intention of inflicting punishment: *a punitive expedition* [C17: from Medieval Latin *pūnītīvus* concerning punishment, from Latin *pūnīre* to punish] > 'punitively *adv*

Punjab (pʌn'dʒɑːb, 'pʌndʒɑːb) *n* **1** (formerly) a province in NW British India: divided between India and Pakistan in 1947 **2** a state of NW India: reorganized in 1966 as a Punjabi-speaking state, a large part forming the new state of Haryana; mainly agricultural. Capital: Chandigarh. Pop: 24 289 296 (2001). Area: 50 255 sq km(19 403 sq miles) **3** a province of W Pakistan: created in 1947. Capital: Lahore. Pop: 82 710 000 (2003 est). Area: 205 344 sq km (127 595 sq miles)

Punjabi *or* **Panjabi** (pʌn'dʒɑːbɪ) *n* **1** a member of the chief people of the Punjab **2** the state language of the Punjab, belonging to the Indic branch of the Indo-European family ▷ *adj* **3** of or relating to the Punjab, its people, or their language

Punjab States *pl n* (formerly) a group of states in NW India, amalgamated in 1956 with Punjab state

punk[1] (pʌŋk) *n* **1** a youth movement of the late 1970s, characterized by anti-Establishment slogans and outrageous clothes and hairstyles **2** an inferior, rotten, or worthless person or thing **3** worthless articles collectively **4** *obsolete* a young male homosexual; catamite **5** *obsolete* a prostitute ▷ *adj* **6** inferior, rotten, or worthless [C16: via Polari from Spanish *pu(n)ta* prostitute, *pu(n)to* male prostitute]

punk[2] (pʌŋk) *n* dried decayed wood that smoulders when ignited: used as tinder [C18: of uncertain origin]

punka *or* **punkah** ('pʌŋkə) *n* a fan made of a palm leaf or leaves [C17: from Hindi *pankhā*, from Sanskrit *paksaka* fan, from *paksa* wing]

punk rock *n* a fast abrasive style of rock music of the late 1970s, characterized by aggressive or offensive lyrics and performance > **punk rocker** *n*

punnet ('pʌnɪt) *n chiefly Brit* a small basket for fruit, such as strawberries [C19: perhaps diminutive of dialect *pun* POUND[2]]

punster ('pʌnstə) *n* a person who is fond of making puns, esp one who makes a tedious habit of this

punt[1] (pʌnt) *n* **1** an open flat-bottomed boat with square ends, propelled by a pole ▷ *vb* **2** to propel (a boat, esp a punt) by pushing with a pole on the bottom of a river, etc [Old English *punt* shallow boat, from Latin *pontō* punt, PONTOON[1]]

punt[2] (pʌnt) *n* **1** a kick in certain sports, such as rugby, in which the ball is released and kicked before it hits the ground **2** any long high kick ▷ *vb* **3** to kick (a ball, etc) using a punt [C19: perhaps a variant of English dialect *bunt* to push, perhaps a nasalized variant of BUTT[3]]

punt[3] (pʌnt) *chiefly Brit* ▷ *vb* **1** (*intr*) to gamble; bet ▷ *n* **2** a gamble or bet, esp against the bank, as in roulette, or on horses **3** Also called: **punter** a person who bets **4** take a **punt** at *Austral & NZ informal* to have an attempt or try at (something) [C18: from French *ponter* to punt, from *ponte* bet laid against the banker, from Spanish *punto* point, from Latin *punctum*]

punt⁴ (pʌnt) *n* (formerly) the Irish pound [Irish Gaelic: pound]

Punta Arenas (*Spanish* 'punta a'renas) *n* a port in S Chile, on the Strait of Magellan: the southernmost city in the world. Pop: 118 000 (2005 est). Former name: Magallanes

punter¹ ('pʌntə) *n* a person who punts a boat

punter² ('pʌntə) *n* a person who kicks a ball

punter³ ('pʌntə) *n* **1** a person who places a bet **2** *slang* a prostitute's client **3** *slang* a victim of a con man

puny ('pju:nɪ) *adj* **-nier**, **-niest 1** having a small physique or weakly constitution **2** paltry; insignificant [C16: from Old French *puisne* PUISNE] > 'puniness *n*

pup (pʌp) *n* **1 a** a young dog, esp when under one year of age; puppy **b** the young of various other animals, such as the seal **2** in pup (of a bitch) pregnant **3** *informal, chiefly Brit contemptuous* a conceited young man (esp in the phrase **young pup**) **4** sell someone a pup to swindle someone by selling him something worthless ⊳ *vb* pups, pupping, pupped **5** (of dogs, seals, etc) to give birth to (young) [C18: back formation from PUPPY]

pupa ('pju:pə) *n, pl* **-pae** (-pi:) *or* **-pas** an insect at the immobile nonfeeding stage of development between larva and adult, when many internal changes occur [C19: via New Latin, from Latin: a doll, puppet] > 'pupal *adj*

pupate (pju:'peɪt) *vb* (*intr*) (of an insect larva) to develop into a pupa > pu'pation *n*

pupil¹ ('pju:pˀl) *n* **1 a** a student who is taught by a teacher, esp a youngstudent **2** *civil law, Scots law* a boy under 14 or a girl under 12 who is in the care of a guardian [C14: from Latin *pupillus* an orphan, from *pūpus* a child] > pupillage *or* (*US*) pupilage ('pju:pɪlɪdʒ) *n* > pupillary *or* pupilary ('pju:pɪlərɪ) *adj*

pupil² ('pju:pˀl) *n* the dark circular aperture at the centre of the iris of the eye, through which light enters [C16: from Latin *pūpilla*, diminutive of *pūpa* girl, puppet; from the tiny reflections in the eye] > pupillary *or* pupilary ('pju:pɪlərɪ) *adj*

pupiparous (pju:'pɪpərəs) *adj* (of certain dipterous flies) producing young that have already reached the pupa stage at the time of hatching [C19: from New Latin *pupiparus*, from PUPA + *parere* to bring forth]

puppet ('pʌpɪt) *n* **1 a** a small doll or figure of a person or animal moved by strings attached to its limbs or by the hand inserted in its cloth body **b** (*as modifier*): *a puppet theatre* **2 a** a person, group, state, etc, that appears independent but is in fact controlled by another **b** (*as modifier*): *a puppet government* [C16 *popet*, perhaps from Old French *poupette* little doll, ultimately from Latin *pūpa* girl, doll]

puppeteer (ˌpʌpɪ'tɪə) *n* a person who manipulates puppets

puppetry ('pʌpɪtrɪ) *n* **1** the art of making and manipulating puppets and presenting puppet shows **2** unconvincing or specious presentation

puppy ('pʌpɪ) *n, pl* **-pies 1** a young dog; pup **2** *informal, contemptuous* a brash or conceited young man; pup [C15 *popi*, from Old French *popée* doll; compare PUPPET] > 'puppy,hood *n* > 'puppyish *adj*

puppy fat *n* fatty tissue that develops in childhood or adolescence and usually disappears by maturity

puppy love *n* another term for **calf love**

Purana (pʊ'rɑ:nə) *n* any of a class of Sanskrit writings not included in the Vedas, characteristically recounting the birth and deeds of Hindu gods and the creation, destruction, or recreation of the universe [C17: from Sanskrit: ancient, from *purā* formerly]

Purbeck marble *or* **Purbeck stone** ('pɜ:bɛk) *n* a fossil-rich limestone that takes a high polish: used for building, etc [C15: named after *Purbeck*, Dorset, where it is quarried]

purblind ('pɜ:ˌblaɪnd) *adj* **1** partly or nearly blind

2 lacking in insight or understanding; obtuse [C13: see PURE, BLIND; compare PARBOIL]

Purcell ('pɜ:sˀl) *n* **1 Edward Mills.** 1912–97, US physicist, noted for his work on the magnetic moments of atomic nuclei: shared the Nobel prize for physics (1952) **2 Henry.** ?1659–95, English composer, noted chiefly for his rhythmic and harmonic subtlety in setting words. His works include the opera *Dido and Aeneas* (1689), music for the theatrical pieces *King Arthur* (1691) and *The Fairy Queen* (1692), several choral odes, fantasias, sonatas, and church music

purchase ('pɜ:tʃɪs) *vb* (*tr*) **1** to obtain (goods, etc) by payment **2** to obtain by effort, sacrifice, etc: *to purchase one's freedom* **3** to draw, haul, or lift (a load) with the aid of mechanical apparatus ⊳ *n* **4** something that is purchased, esp an article bought with money **5** the act of buying **6** acquisition of an estate by any lawful means other than inheritance **7** a rough measure of the mechanical advantage achieved by a lever **8** a firm foothold, grasp, etc, as for climbing or levering something [C13: from Old French *porchacier* to strive to obtain, from *por-* for +*chacier* to CHASE¹] > 'purchaser *n* > 'purchasable *adj* > ˌpurchasa'bility *n*

purchase tax *n Brit* a tax levied on nonessential consumer goods and added to selling prices by retailers

purdah *or* **purda** ('pɜ:də) *n* **1** the custom in some Muslim and Hindu communities of keeping women in seclusion, with clothing that conceals them completely when they go out **2** a screen in a Hindu house used to keep the women out of view [C19: from Hindi *parda* veil, from Persian *pardah*]

pure (pjʊə) *adj* **1** not mixed with any extraneous or dissimilar materials,elements, etc **2** free from tainting or polluting matter; clean; wholesome: *pure water* **3** free from moral taint or defilement: *pure love* **4** (prenominal) (intensifier): *pure stupidity; a pure coincidence* **5** (of a subject, etc) studied in its theoretical aspects rather than for its practical applications: *pure mathematics; pure science* **6** (of a vowel) pronounced with more or less unvarying quality without any glide; monophthongal **7** (of a consonant) not accompanied by another consonant **8** of supposedly unmixed racial descent **9** *genetics, biology* breeding true for one or more characteristics; homozygous [C13: from Old French *pur*, from Latin *pūrus* unstained] > 'pureness *n* > 'purely *adv*

purebred *adj* ('pjʊə'brɛd) **1** denoting a pure strain obtained through many generations of controlled breeding for desirable traits ⊳ *n* ('pjʊəˌbrɛd) **2** a purebred animal

purée ('pjʊəreɪ) *n* **1** a smooth thick pulp of cooked and sieved fruit, vegetables, meat, or fish ⊳ *vb* **-rées**, **-réeing**, **-réed 2** (*tr*) to make (cooked foods) into a purée [C19: from French *purer* to PURIFY]

pure laine (pjʊə 'lɛn) *n* (in Quebec) a person belonging to a long-established family of French descent [French, literally: pure wool]

purfle ('pɜ:fˀl) *n* Also: **purfling 1** a ruffled or curved ornamental band, as on clothing, furniture, etc ⊳ *vb* **2** (*tr*) to decorate with such a band or bands [C14: from Old French *purfiler* to decorate with a border, from *filer* to spin, from *fil* thread, from Latin *filum*]

purgation (pɜ:'geɪʃən) *n* the act of purging or state of being purged; purification

purgative ('pɜ:gətɪv) *med* ⊳ *n* **1** a drug or agent for purging the bowels ⊳ *adj* **2** causing evacuation of the bowels; cathartic > 'purgatively *adv*

purgatory ('pɜ:gətərɪ, -trɪ) *n* **1** *chiefly RC Church* a state or place in which the souls of those who have died in a state of grace are believed to undergo a limited amount of suffering to expiate their venial sins and become purified of the remaining effects of mortal sin **2** a place or condition of suffering or torment, esp one that is temporary [C13: from Old French *purgatoire*, from Medieval Latin *pūrgātōrium*, literally: place of cleansing, from Latin *pūrgāre* to PURGE] > ˌpurga'torial *adj* > ˌpurga'torially *adv*

purge (pɜ:dʒ) *vb* **1** (*tr*) to rid (something) of (impure or undesirable elements) **2** (*tr*) to rid (a state, political party, etc) of (dissident or troublesome people) **3** (*tr*) **a** to empty (the bowels) by evacuation of faeces **b** to cause (a person) to evacuate his bowels **4 a** to clear (a person) of a charge **b** to free (oneself) of guilt, as by atonement **5** (*intr*) to be cleansed or purified ▷ *n* **6** the act or process of purging **7** the elimination of opponents or dissidents from a state, political party, etc **8** a purgative drug or agent; cathartic [c14: from Old French *purger,* from Latin *pūrgāre* to purify]

purificator ('pjʊərɪfɪˌkeɪtə) *n Christianity* a small white linen cloth used to wipe the chalice and paten and also the lips and fingers of the celebrant at the Eucharist

purify ('pjʊərɪˌfaɪ) *vb* **-fies, -fying, -fied 1** to free (something) of extraneous, contaminating, or debasing matter **2** (*tr*) to free (a person, etc) from sin or guilt **3** (*tr*) to make clean, as in a ritual, esp the churching of women after childbirth [c14: from Old French *purifier,* from Late Latin *pūrificāre* to cleanse, from *pūrus* pure + *facere* to make] > ˌpurifiˈcation *n* > purificatory ('pjʊərɪfɪˌkeɪtərɪ) *adj* > ˈpuriˌfier *n*

Purim ('pʊərɪm; *Hebrew* puːˈriːm) *n* a Jewish holiday celebrated on Adar 14, in February or March, and in Adar Sheni in leap years, to commemorate the deliverance of the Jews from the massacre planned for them by Haman (Esther 9) [Hebrew *pūrīm,* plural of *pūr* lot; from the casting of lots by Haman]

purine ('pjʊəriːn) *or* **purin** ('pjʊərɪn) *n* **1** a colourless crystalline solid that can be prepared from uric acid. Formula: $C_5H_4N_4$ **2** *Also called:* purine base any of a number of nitrogenous bases, such as guanine and adenine, that are derivatives of purine and constituents of nucleic acids and certain coenzymes [c19: from German *Purin*; see PURE, URIC, -INE²]

puriri (puːˈriːriː) *n, pl* **-ris** a forest tree, *Vitex lucens,* of New Zealand, having red berries and glossy green leaves and yielding a durable dark brown timber

purism ('pjʊəˌrɪzəm) *n* insistence on traditional canons of correctness of form or purity of style or content, esp in language, art, or music > purist *adj, n* > puˈristic *adj*

puritan ('pjʊərɪt³n) *n* **1** a person who adheres to strict moral or religious principles, esp one opposed to luxury and sensual enjoyment ▷ *adj* **2** characteristic of a puritan [c16: from Late Latin *pūritās* PURITY] > ˈpuritanˌism *n*

Puritan ('pjʊərɪt³n) (in the late 16th and 17th centuries) *n* **1** any of the more extreme English Protestants, most of whom were Calvinists, who wished to purify the Church of England of most of its ceremony and other aspects that they deemed to be Catholic ▷ *adj* **2** of, characteristic of, or relating to the Puritans > ˈPuritanˌism *n*

puritanical (ˌpjʊərɪˈtænɪk³l) *adj* **1** *usually disparaging* strict in moral or religious outlook, esp in shunning sensual pleasures **2** (*sometimes capital*) of or relating to a puritan or the Puritans > ˌpuriˈtanically *adv*

purity ('pjʊərɪtɪ) *n* the state or quality of being pure

purl¹ (pɜːl) *n* **1** *Also called:* purl stitch a knitting stitch made by doing a plain stitch backwards **2** a decorative border, as of lace **3** gold or silver wire thread ▷ *vb* **4** to knit (a row or garment) in purl stitch **5** to edge (something) with a purl ▷ *Also for senses 2, 3,5*: pearl [c16: from dialect *pirl* to twist into a cord]

purl² (pɜːl) *vb* **1** (*intr*) (of a stream, etc) to flow with a gentle curling or rippling movement and a murmuring sound ▷ *n* **2** a curling movement of water; eddy **3** a murmuring sound, as of a shallow stream [c16: related to Norwegian *purla* to bubble]

purler¹ ('pɜːlə) *n informal* a headlong or spectacular fall (esp in the phrase **come a purler**)

purler² ('pɜːlə) *n Austral slang* something outstanding in its class [of unknown origin]

purlieu ('pɜːljuː) *n* **1** *English history* land on the edge of a forest that was once included within the bounds of the royal forest but was later separated although still subject to some of the forest laws, esp regarding hunting **2** (*usually plural*) a neighbouring area; outskirts **3** (*often plural*) a place one frequents; haunt [c15 *purlewe,* from Anglo-French *puralé* a going through (influenced also by Old French *lieu* place), from Old French *puraler* to traverse, from *pur* through + *aler* to go]

purlin *or* **purline** ('pɜːlɪn) *n* a horizontal beam that provides intermediate support for the common rafters of a roof construction [c15: of uncertain origin]

purloin (pɜːˈlɔɪn) *vb* to take (something) dishonestly; steal [c15: from Old French *porloigner* to put at a distance, from *por-* for + *loin* distant, from Latin *longus* long] > purˈloiner *n*

purple ('pɜːp³l) *n* **1** a colour between red and blue **2** a dye or pigment producing such a colour **3** cloth of this colour, often used to symbolize royalty or nobility **4 the purple** high rank; nobility **5 a** the official robe of a cardinal **b** the rank, office, or authority of a cardinal as signified by this ▷ *adj* **6** of the colour purple **7** (of writing) excessively elaborate or full of imagery: *purple prose* [Old English, from Latin *purpura* purple dye, from Greek *porphura* the purple fish (*Murex*)] > ˈpurpleness *n* > ˈpurplish *adj* > ˈpurply *adj*

purple heart *n* **1** any of several tropical American leguminous trees of the genus *Peltogyne* **2** *informal, chiefly Brit* a heart-shaped purple tablet consisting mainly of amphetamine

Purple Heart *n* a decoration awarded to members of the US Armed Forces for a wound incurred in action

purple patch *n* **1** *Also called:* purple passage a section in a piece of writing characterized by rich, fanciful, or ornate language **2** *slang* a period of success, good fortune, etc

purport *vb* (pɜːˈpɔːt) (*tr*) **1** to claim (to be a certain thing, etc) by manner or appearance, esp falsely **2** (esp of speech or writing) to signify or imply ▷ *n* ('pɜːpɔːt) **3** meaning; significance **4** purpose; object; intention [c15: from Anglo-French: contents, from Old French *porporter* to convey, from *por-* forth + *porter* to carry, from Latin *portāre*]

purpose ('pɜːpəs) *n* **1** the reason for which anything is done, created, or exists **2** a fixed design, outcome, or idea that is the object of an action or other effort **3** fixed intention in doing something; determination: *a man of purpose* **4** practical advantage or use: *to work to good purpose* **5** that which is relevant or under consideration (esp in the phrase **to** or **from the purpose**) **6** *archaic* purport **7 on purpose** intentionally ▷ *vb* (*tr*) **8** to intend or determine to do (something) [c13: from Old French *porpos,* from *porposer* to plan, from Latin *prōpōnere* to PROPOSE]

purpose-built *adj* made to serve a specific purpose

purposeful ('pɜːpəsfʊl) *adj* **1** having a definite purpose in view **2** fixed in one's purpose; determined > ˈpurposefully *adv* > ˈpurposefulness *n*

● **USAGE** *Purposefully* is sometimes wrongly used where *purposely* is meant: *he had purposely* (not *purposefully*) *left the door unlocked*

purposely ('pɜːpəslɪ) *adv* for a definite reason; on purpose

● **USAGE** See at **purposeful**

purposive ('pɜːpəsɪv) *adj* **1** relating to, having, or indicating conscious intention **2** serving a purpose; useful > ˈpurposively *adv* > ˈpurposiveness *n*

purpura ('pɜːpjʊrə) *n pathol* any of several blood diseases causing purplish spots or patches on the skin due to subcutaneous bleeding [c18: via Latin from Greek *porphura* a shellfish yielding purple dye]

purr (pɜː) *vb* **1** (*intr*) (esp of cats) to make a low vibrant sound, usually considered as expressing pleasure, etc **2** (*tr*) to express (pleasure, etc) by this sound ▷ *n* **3** a purring sound [c17: of imitative origin; compare French *ronronner* to purr, German *schnurren,* Dutch *snorren*]

purse (pɜːs) *n* **1** a small bag or pouch, often made of soft leather, for carrying money, esp coins **2** *US & Canadian* a woman's handbag **3** anything resembling a small bag or pouch in form or function **4** wealth; funds **5** a sum of money that is offered, esp as a prize ▷ *vb* **6** (*tr*) to contract (the mouth, lips, etc) into a small rounded shape [Old English *purs,* probably from Late Latin *bursa* bag, ultimately from Greek: leather]

purser ('pɜːsə) *n* an officer aboard a passenger ship, merchant ship, or aircraft who keeps the accounts and attends to the welfare of the passengers

purse seine *n* a large net towed, usually by two boats, that encloses a school of fish and is then closed at the bottom by means of a line resembling the string formerly used to draw shut the neck of a money pouch or purse

purse strings *pl n* control of finance or expenditure (esp in such phrases as **hold** or **control the purse strings**)

purslane ('pɜːslɪn, -leɪn) *n* a weedy portulacaceous plant, *Portulaca oleracea*, with small yellow flowers and fleshy leaves, which are used in salads and as a potherb [C14 *purcelane*, from Old French *porcelaine*, from Late Latin *porcillāgō*, from Latin *porcillāca*, variant of *portulāca*]

pursuance (pə'sjuːəns) *n* the carrying out or pursuing of an action, plan,etc

pursuant (pə'sjuːənt) *adj* 1 (*usuallypostpositive*; often foll by *to*) *chiefly law* in agreement or conformity 2 *archaic* pursuing [C17: related to Middle English *poursuivant* following after, from Old French; see PURSUE] > **pur'suantly** *adv*

pursue (pə'sjuː) *vb* -sues, -suing, -sued (*mainly tr*) 1 (*also intr*) to follow (a fugitive, etc) in order to capture or overtake 2 (esp of something bad or unlucky) to follow closely or accompany: *ill health pursued her* 3 to seek or strive to attain (some object, desire,etc) 4 to follow the precepts of (a plan, policy, etc) 5 to apply oneself to (one's studies, hobbies, etc) 6 to follow persistently or seek to become acquainted with 7 to continue to discuss or argue (a point, subject, etc) [C13: from Anglo-Norman *pursiwer*, from Old French *poursivre*, from Latin *prōsequī* to follow after] > **pur'suer** *n*

pursuit (pə'sjuːt) *n* 1 **a** the act of pursuing, chasing, or striving after **b** (*as modifier*): *a pursuit plane* 2 an occupation, hobby, or pastime 3 (in cycling) a race in which the riders set off at intervals along the track and attempt to overtake each other [C14: from Old French *poursiute*, from *poursivre* to prosecute, PURSUE]

pursuivant ('pɜːsɪvənt) *n* 1 the lowest rank of heraldic officer 2 *history* a state or royal messenger 3 *history* a follower or attendant [C14: from Old French, from *poursivre* to PURSUE]

purulent ('pjʊərʊlənt) *adj* of, relating to, or containing pus [C16: from Latin *pūrulentus*, from PUS] > **'purulence** or **'purulency** *n*

Purús (*Spanish* pu'rus ; *Portuguese* pu'ruʃ) *n* a river in NW central South America, rising in SE Peru and flowing northeast to the Amazon. Length: about 3200 km (2000 miles)

purvey (pə'veɪ) *vb* (*tr*) 1 to sell or provide (commodities, esp foodstuffs) on a large scale 2 to publish or make available (lies, scandal,etc) [C13: from Old French *porveeir*, from Latin *prōvidēre* to PROVIDE] > **pur'veyor** *n*

purveyance (pə'veɪəns) *n* 1 *history* the collection or requisition of provisions for a sovereign 2 *rare* the act of purveying

purview ('pɜːvjuː) *n* 1 the scope of operation or concern of something 2 the breadth or range of outlook or understanding 3 *law* the body of a statute, containing the enacting clauses [C15: from Anglo-Norman *purveu*, from *porveeir* to furnish; see PURVEY]

pus (pʌs) *n* the yellow or greenish fluid product of inflammation, composed largely of dead leucocytes, exuded plasma, and liquefied tissue cells [C16: from Latin *pūs*; related to Greek *puon* pus]

Pusan ('puː'sæn) *n* a port in SE South Korea, on the Korea Strait: the second largest city and chief port of the country; industrial centre; two universities.Pop: 3 527 000 (2005 est)

Pusey ('pjuːzɪ) *n* **Edward Bouverie** ('buːvərɪ). 1800–82, British ecclesiastic; a leader with Keble and Newman of the Oxford Movement

push (pʊʃ) *vb* 1 (when *tr*, often foll by *off, away*, etc) to apply steady force to (something) in order to move it 2 to thrust (one's way) through something, such as a crowd, by force 3 (*tr*) to encourage or urge (a person) to some action, decision, etc 4 (when *intr*, often foll by *for*) to be an advocate or promoter (of): *to push for acceptance of one's theories* 5 (*tr*) to use one's influence to help (a person): *to push one's own candidate* 6 to bear upon (oneself or another person) in order to achieve more effort, better results, etc 7 *sport* to hit (a ball) with a stiff pushing

stroke 8 (*tr*) *informal* to sell (narcotic drugs) illegally ▷ *n* 9 the act of pushing; thrust 10 a part or device that is pressed to operate some mechanism 11 *informal* a special effort or attempt to advance, as of an army in a war 12 *Austral slang* a group or gang, esp one considered to be a clique 13 *sport* a stiff pushing stroke 14 at a push *informal* with difficulty; only just 15 the push *informal, chiefly Brit* dismissal, esp from employment ▷ See also **push in, push off**, etc [C13: from Old French *pousser*, from Latin *pulsāre*, from *pellere* to drive]

push-bike *n Brit* an informal name for **bicycle**

push button *n* 1 an electrical switch operated by pressing a button, which closes or opens a circuit 2 push-button (*modifier*) **a** operated by a push button: *a push-button radio* **b** initiated as simply as by pressing a button: *push-button warfare*

pushcart ('pʊʃ,kɑːt) *n chiefly US & Canadian* a handcart, typically having two wheels and a canvas roof,used esp by street vendors. Also called: **barrow**

pushchair ('pʊʃ,tʃeə) *n* a usually collapsible chair-shaped carriage in which a small child may be wheeled. Also called: **baby buggy, buggy** US and Canadian word: **stroller**. Austral. words: **pusher, stroller**

pushed (pʊʃt) *adj* (often foll by *for*) *informal* short (of) or in need of (time, money, etc)

pusher ('pʊʃə) *n* 1 *informal* a person who sells illegal drugs, esp narcotics such as heroin and morphine 2 *informal* an actively or aggressively ambitious person 3 a person or thing that pushes 4 *Austral* the usual name for **pushchair**

push in *vb* (*intr, adverb*) to force one's way into a group of people, queue,etc

pushing ('pʊʃɪŋ) *adj* 1 enterprising, resourceful, or aggressively ambitious 2 impertinently self-assertive ▷ *adv* 3 almost or nearly (a certain age, speed, etc): *pushing fifty* > **'pushingly** *adv*

Pushkin[1] ('pʊʃkɪn) *n* a town in NW Russia: site of the imperial summer residence and Catherine the Great's palace. Pop: 84 628 (2002)

Pushkin[2] ('pʊʃkɪn) *n* **Aleksander Sergeyevich** (alɪk'sandr sɪr'gjejɪvɪtʃ). 1799–1837, Russian poet, novelist, and dramatist. His works include the romantic verse tale *The Prisoner of the Caucasus* (1822), the verse novel *Eugene Onegin* (1833), the tragedy *Boris Godunov* (1825), and the novel *The Captain's Daughter* (1836)

push money *n* a cash inducement provided by a manufacturer or distributor for a retailer or his staff, to reward successful selling

push off *vb* (*adverb*) 1 Also: **push out** to move into open water, as by being cast off from a mooring 2 (*intr*) *informal* to go away; leave

pushover ('pʊʃ,əʊvə) *n informal* 1 something that is easily achieved or accomplished 2 a person, team, etc, that is easily taken advantage of or defeated

push-pull *n* (*modifier*) using two similar electronic devices, such as matched valves, made to operate 180° out of phase with each other. The outputs are combined to produce a signal that replicates the input waveform: *a push-pull amplifier*

push-start *vb* (*tr*) 1 to start (a motor vehicle) by pushing it while it is in gear, thus turning the engine ▷ *n* 2 the act or process of starting a vehicle in this way

push through *vb* (*tr*) to compel to accept: *the bill was pushed through Parliament*

Pushto ('pʌʃtəʊ) or **Pushtu** ('pʌʃtuː) *n, adj* variant spellings of **Pashto**

push-up *n US & Canadian* an exercise in which the body is alternately raised from and lowered to the floor by the arms only, the trunk being kept straight with the toes and hands resting on the floor. Also called (in Britain and certain other countries): **press-up**

pushy ('pʊʃɪ) *adj* **pushier, pushiest** *informal* 1 offensively assertive or forceful 2 aggressively or ruthlessly ambitious > **'pushily** *adv* > **'pushiness** *n*

pusillanimous (,pjuːsɪ'lænɪməs) *adj* characterized by a lack of courage or determination [C16: from Late Latin *pusillanimis* from Latin *pusillus* weak + *animus* courage] > **pusillanimity** (,pjuːsɪlə'nɪmɪtɪ) *n* > **,pusil'lanimously** *adv*

Puskas ('puskəs) *n* **Ferenc** ('fɛrɛnk). 1927–2006, Hungarian footballer; played for Hungary (1945–56) and Real Madrid (1958–66)

puss (pus) *n* **1** an informal name for a **cat**¹ **2** *slang* a girl or woman **3** an informal name for a **hare** [C16: related to Middle Low German *pūs*, Dutch *poes*, Lithuanian *puz*]

pussy¹ ('pusɪ) *n*, *pl* **pussies 1** Also called: **puss, pussycat** ('pusɪˌkæt) an informal name for a **cat**¹ **2** a furry catkin, esp that of the pussy willow **3** *taboo*, *slang* the female pudenda **4** *taboo*, *slang*, *chiefly US* an ineffectual or timid person [C18: from PUSS]

pussy² ('pʌsɪ) *adj* **-sier, -siest** containing pus

pussycat ('pusɪˌkæt) *n* **1** an informal or child's name for a **cat**¹ (sense 1) **2** *Brit informal* an endearing or gentle person

pussyfoot ('pusɪˌfut) *informal vb* (*intr*) **1** to move about stealthily or warily like a cat **2** to avoid committing oneself

pussy willow ('pusɪ) *n* a willow tree that produces silvery silky catkins, esp *Salix caprea* or *S. cinerea* in Britain or *S. discolor* in North America

pustulant ('pʌstjʊlənt) *adj* **1** causing the formation of pustules ▷ *n* **2** an agent causing such formation

pustulate *vb* ('pʌstjʊˌleɪt) **1** to form or cause to form into pustules ▷ *adj* ('pʌstjʊlɪt, -ˌleɪt) **2** covered with pustules > ˌpustu'lation *n*

pustule ('pʌstjuːl) *n* **1** a small inflamed elevated area of skin containing pus **2** any small distinct spot resembling a pimple or blister [C14: from Latin *pustula* a blister, variant of *pūsula*; compare Greek *phusallis* bladder, *phusa* bellows] > pustular ('pʌstjʊlə) *adj*

put (put) *vb* **puts, putting, put** (*mainly tr*) **1** to cause to be (in a position or place): *to put a book on the table* **2** to cause to be (in a state, relation, etc): *to put one's things in order* **3** (foll by *to*) to cause (a person) to experience the endurance or suffering (of): *to put to death; to put to the sword* **4** to set or commit (to an action, task, or duty), esp by force: *he put him to work* **5** to render, transform, or translate: *to put into English* **6** to set (words) in a musical form (esp in the phrase **put to music**) **7** (foll by *at*) to estimate: *he put the distance at fifty miles* **8** (foll by *to*) to utilize (for the purpose of): *he put his knowledge to good use* **9** (foll by *to*) to couple a female animal (with a male) for the purpose of breeding: *the farmer put his heifer to the bull* **10** to state; express: *to put it bluntly* **11** to set or make (an end or limit): *he put an end to the proceedings* **12** to present for consideration in anticipation of an answer or vote; propose: *he put the question to the committee; I put it to you that one day you will all die* **13** to invest (money) in: *he put five thousand pounds into the project* **14** to impart: *to put zest into a party* **15** to throw or cast **16** not know where to put oneself to feel awkward or embarrassed **17** stay put to refuse to leave; keep one's position ▷ *n* **18** a throw or cast, esp in putting the shot **19** Also called: **put option** *stock exchange* an option to sell a stated amount of securities at a specified price during a specified limited period ▷ See also **put about, put across**, etc [C12 *puten* to push; related to Old English *potian* to push, Norwegian *pota*, Icelandic *pota* to poke]

put about *vb* (*adverb*) **1** *nautical* to change course or cause to change course **2** (*tr*) to make widely known **3** (*tr*; *usually passive*) to disconcert or disturb

put across *vb* (*tr*) **1** (*adverb*) to communicate in a comprehensible way: *he couldn't put things across very well* **2** **put one across** *informal* to get (someone) to accept or believe a claim, excuse, etc, by deception: *they put one across their teacher*

put aside *vb* (*tr*, *adverb*) **1** to move (an object, etc) to one side, esp in rejection **2** to store up; save: *to put money aside for a rainy day* **3** to ignore or disregard: *let us put aside our differences*

putative ('pjuːtətɪv) *adj* **1** (*prenominal*) commonly regarded as being: *the putative father* **2** (*prenominal*) considered to exist or have existed; inferred [C15: from Late Latin *putātīvus* supposed, from *putāre* to consider] > 'putatively *adv*

put away *vb* (*tr*, *adverb*) **1** to return (something) to the correct or proper place **2** to save: *to put away money for the future* **3** to lock up in a prison, mental institution, etc:

they put him away for twenty years **4** to eat or drink, esp in large amounts

put back *vb* (*tr*, *adverb*) **1** to return to its former place **2** to move to a later time or date: *the wedding was put back a fortnight* **3** to delay or impede the progress of: *the strike put back production severely*

put by *vb* (*tr*, *adverb*) to set aside (money, goods, etc) to be kept for the future; store; save

put down *vb* (*tr*, *adverb*) **1** to make a written record of **2** to repress: *to put down a rebellion* **3** to consider; account: *they put him down for an ignoramus* **4** to attribute: *I put the mistake down to his inexperience* **5** to put to death, because of old age or illness **6** to table on the agenda: *the MPs put down a motion on the increase in crime* **7** to dismiss, reject, or humiliate ▷ *n* **put-down 8** a cruelly crushing remark

put forth *vb* (*tr*, *adverb*) *formal* **1** to present; propose **2** (of a plant) to produce or bear (leaves, branches, shoots, etc)

put forward *vb* (*tr*, *adverb*) **1** to propose; suggest **2** to offer the name of; nominate

put in *vb* (*adverb*) **1** (*intr*) *nautical* to bring a vessel into port, esp for a brief stay **2** (often foll by *for*) to apply or cause to apply (for a job, in a competition, etc) **3** (*tr*) to submit: *he put in his claims form* **4** to intervene with (a remark) during a conversation **5** (*tr*) to devote (time, effort, etc) to a task: *he put in three hours overtime last night* **6** (*tr*) to establish or appoint: *he put in a manager* **7** (*tr*) *cricket* to cause (a team, esp the opposing one) to bat: *England won the toss and put the visitors in to bat*

Putin ('pjutɪn) *n* **Vladimir** (**Vladimirovich**). born 1952, Russian statesman; president of Russia (2000–08); prime minister from 2008

Putnam ('pʌtnəm) *n* **1 Israel.** 1718–90, American general in the War of Independence **2** his cousin **Rufus.** 1738–1824, American soldier in the War of Independence; surveyor general of the US (1796–1803)

put off *vb* **1** (*tr*, *adverb*) to postpone or delay: *they have put off the dance until tomorrow* **2** (*tr*, *adverb*) to evade (a person) by postponement or delay: *they tried to put him off, but he came anyway* **3** (*tr*, *adverb*) to confuse; disconcert: *he was put off by her appearance* **4** (*tr*, *preposition*) to cause to lose interest in or enjoyment of: *the accident put him off driving*

put on *vb* (*tr*, *mainly adverb*) **1** to clothe oneself in **2** (*usually passive*) to adopt (an attitude or feeling) insincerely: *his misery was just put on* **3** to present or stage (a play, show, etc) **4** to increase or add: *she put on weight; the batsman put on fifty runs before lunch* **5** to cause (an electrical device) to function **6** (*also preposition*) to wager (money) on a horse race, game, etc **7** (*also preposition*) to impose as a burden or levy: *to put a tax on cars* **8** *cricket* to cause (a bowler) to bowl

put out *vb* (*tr*, *adverb*) **1** (*often passive*) **a** to annoy; anger **b** to confound or disturb; confuse **2** to extinguish or douse (a fire, light, etc) **3** to poke forward: *to put out one's tongue* **4** to be or present a source of inconvenience or annoyance to (a person): *I hope I'm not putting you out* **5** to issue or publish; broadcast: *the authorities put out a leaflet* **6** to render unconscious **7** to dislocate: *he put out his shoulder in the accident* **8** to pass, give out (work to be done) at different premises **9** to lend (money) at interest **10** *cricket* to dismiss (a player or team)

put over *vb* (*tr*, *adverb*) **1** *informal* to communicate (facts, information, etc) comprehensibly **2** *chiefly US* to postpone; defer **3** **put one over on** or **put a fast one over on** *informal* to get (someone) to accept or believe a claim, excuse, etc, by deception: *he put one over on his boss*

put-put ('pʌtˌpʌt) *informal* ▷ *n* **1** a light chugging or popping sound, as made by a petrol engine ▷ *vb* **-puts, -putting, -putted 2** (*intr*) to make or travel along with such a sound

putrefy ('pjuːtrɪˌfaɪ) *vb* **-fies, -fying, -fied** (of organic matter) to decompose or rot with an offensive smell [C15: from Old French *putrefier* + Latin *putrefacere*, from *puter* rotten + *facere* to make] > putrefaction (ˌpjuːtrɪˈfækʃən) *n* > ˌputreˈfactive or ˌputreˈfacient (ˌpjuːtrɪˈfeɪʃənt) *adj*

putrescent (pjuːˈtrɛsᵊnt) *adj* **1** becoming putrid; rotting **2** characterized by or undergoing putrefaction [C18: from Latin *putrescere* to become rotten] > puˈtrescence *n*

putrid ('pjuːtrɪd) *adj* **1** (of organic matter) in a state of decomposition, usually giving off a foul smell: *putrid* *meat* **2** morally corrupt or worthless **3** sickening; foul: *a putrid smell* **4** *informal* deficient in quality or value: *a putrid film* [C16: from Latin *putridus* rotten, from *putrēre* to be rotten] ▷ pu'tridity *or* 'putridness *n* ▷ 'putridly *adv*

putsch (pʊtʃ) *n* a violent and sudden uprising; political revolt, esp a coup d'état [C20: from German: from Swiss German: a push, of imitative origin]

putt (pʌt) *golf* ▷ *n* **1** a stroke on the green with a putter to roll the ball into or near the hole ▷ *vb* **2** to strike (the ball) in this way [C16: of Scottish origin; related to PUT]

puttee *or* **putty** ('pʌtɪ) *n, pl* -tees *or* -ties (*usually plural*) a strip of cloth worn wound around the legs from the ankle to the knee, esp as part of a military uniform in World War I [C19: from Hindi *pattī*, from Sanskrit *pattikā*, from *patta* cloth]

putter¹ ('pʌtə) *n golf* **1** a club for putting, usually having a solid metal head **2** a golfer who putts

putter² ('pʌtə) *US & Canadian* ▷ *vb* **1** (*intr*; often foll by *about* or *around*) to busy oneself in a desultory though agreeable manner **2** (*intr*; often foll by *along* or *about*) to move with little energy or direction **3** (*tr*; usually foll by *away*) to waste (time) ▷ *n* **4** the act of puttering ▷ Equivalent term (in Britain and certain other countries): potter [C16 (in the sense: to poke repeatedly): from Old English *potian* to thrust; see PUT]

putter³ ('pʊtə) *n* **1** a person who puts: *the putter of a question* **2** a person who puts the shot

put through *vb* (*tr, mainly adverb*) **1** to carry out to a conclusion: *he put through his plan* **2** (*also preposition*) to organize the processing of: *she put through his application to join the organization* **3** to connect by telephone **4** to make (a telephone call)

putting green ('pʌtɪŋ) *n* **1** (on a golf course) the area of closely mown grass at the end of a fairway where the hole is **2** an area of smooth grass with several holes for putting games

Puttnam ('pʌtnəm) *n* **David**, Baron. born 1941, British film producer. Films include *Chariots of Fire* (1981), *The Killing Fields* (1984), *Memphis Belle* (1990), and *My Life So Far* (1999)

putto ('pʊtəʊ) *n, pl* -ti (-tɪ) a representation of a small boy, a cherub or cupid, esp in baroque painting or sculpture [from Italian, from Latin *putus* boy]

putty ('pʌtɪ) *n, pl* -ties **1** a stiff paste made of whiting and linseed oil that is used to fix glass panes into frames and to fill cracks or holes in woodwork,etc **2** any substance with a similar consistency, function, or appearance **3** a mixture of lime and water with sand or plaster of Paris used on plaster as a finishing coat **4** (*as modifier*): *a putty knife* **5** a person who is easily influenced or persuaded: *he's putty in her hands* **6** a colour varying from a greyish-yellow to a greyish-brown or brownish-grey **b** (*as adjective*) ▷ *vb* -ties, -tying, -tied **7** (*tr*) to fix, fill, or coat with putty [C17: from French *potée* a potful]

Putumayo (*Spanish* putu'majo) *n* a river in NW South America, rising in S Colombia and flowing southeast as most of the border between Colombia and Peru, entering the Amazon in Brazil: scene of the Putumayo rubber scandal (1910–11) during the rubber boom, in which many Indians were enslaved and killed by rubber exploiters. Length: 1578 km (980 miles). Brazilian name: **Içá**

put up *vb* (*adverb, mainly tr*) **1** to build; erect: *to put up a statue* **2** to accommodate or be accommodated at: *can you put me up for tonight?* **3** to increase (prices) **4** to submit or present (a plan, case, etc) **5** to offer: *to put a house up for sale* **6** to provide or supply; give: *to put up a good fight* **7** to provide (money) for; invest in: *they put up five thousand for the new project* **8** to preserve or can (jam, etc) **9** to pile up (long hair) on the head in any of several styles **10** (*also intr*) to nominate or be nominated as a candidate, esp for a political or society post: *he put his wife up as secretary; he put up for president* **11** *archaic* to return (a weapon) to its holder, as a sword to its sheath **12** put up to **a** to inform or instruct (a person) about (tasks, duties,etc) **b** to urge or goad (a person) on to; incite to **13** put up with *informal* to endure; tolerate ▷ *adj* put-up **14** dishonestly or craftily prearranged or conceived (esp in the phrase **put-up job**)

put upon *vb* (*intr,preposition, usually passive*) **1** to presume on (a person's generosity, good nature, etc); take advantage of: *he's always being put upon* **2** to impose hardship on; maltreat

putz (pʌts) *n US slang* a despicable or stupid person [from Yiddish *puts* ornament]

Puvis de Chavannes (*French* pyvis də ʃavan) *n* **Pierre Cécile** (pjɛr sesil). 1824–98, French mural painter

Puy de Dôme (pwi də dom) *n* **1** a department of central France in Auvergne region. Capital: Clermont-Ferrand. Pop: 609 817 (2003 est). Area: 8016 sq km (3094 sq miles) **2** a mountain in central France, in the Auvergne Mountains: a volcanic plug. Height: 1485 m (4872 ft)

Puy de Sancy (*French* pwi də sɑ̃si) *n* a mountain in S central France: highest peak of the Monts Dore. Height: 1886 m (6188 ft)

Pu-yi ('puː'jiː) *n* **Henry**. 1906–67, last emperor of China as Xuan-Tong (1908–12); emperor of the Japanese puppet state of Manchukuo as Kang-de (1934–45)

puzzle ('pʌz³l) *vb* **1** to perplex or be perplexed **2** (*intr*; foll by *over*) to attempt the solution (of); ponder (about): *he puzzled over her absence* **3** (*tr*; usually foll by *out*) to solve by mental effort: *he puzzled out the meaning of the inscription* ▷ *n* **4** a person or thing that puzzles **5** a problem that cannot be easily or readily solved **6** the state or condition of being puzzled **7** a toy, game, or question presenting a problem that requires skill or ingenuity for its solution [C16: of unknown origin] ▷ 'puzzling *adj* ▷ 'puzzlement *n*

PVC *abbreviation* polyvinyl chloride; a synthetic thermoplastic material made by polymerizing vinyl chloride. The properties depend on the added plasticizer.The flexible forms are used in hosepipes, insulation, shoes, garments, etc. Rigid PVC is used for moulded articles

PVR *abbreviation* personal(ized) video recorder: a device for recording and replaying television programmes and films etc that uses a hard disk rather than videocassettes or DVDs and has various computer functions

PVS *abbreviation* **1** persistent vegetative state **2** postviral syndrome

Pvt. *military abbreviation* private

PW *abbreviation* policewoman

PWA *abbreviation* person with AIDS

PWR *abbreviation* pressurized-water reactor

pyaemia *or* **pyemia** (paɪ'iːmɪə) *n* blood poisoning characterized by pus-forming microorganisms in the blood [C19: from New Latin, from Greek *puon* pus + *haima* blood] ▷ py'aemic *or* py'emic *adj*

Pydna ('pɪdnə) *n* a town in ancient Macedonia: site of a major Roman victory over the Macedonians, resulting in the downfall of their kingdom (168BC)

pye-dog, pie-dog *or* **pi-dog** *n* an ownerless half-wild Asian dog [C19: Anglo-Indian *pye*, *paë*, from Hindi *pāhī* outsider]

pyelitis (ˌpaɪə'laɪtɪs) *n* inflammation of the pelvis of the kidney ▷ pyelitic (ˌpaɪə'lɪtɪk) *adj*

Pygmalion (pɪg'meɪlɪən) *n Greek myth* a king of Cyprus, who fell in love with the statue of a woman he had sculpted and which his prayers brought to life as Galatea

pygmy *or* **pigmy** ('pɪgmɪ) *n, pl* -mies **1** an abnormally undersized person **2** something that is a very small example of its type **3** a person of little importance or significance **4** (*modifier*) of very small stature or size [C14: *pigmeis* the Pygmies, from Latin *Pygmaeus* a Pygmy, from Greek *pugmaios* undersized, from *pugmē* fist] ▷ pygmaean *or* pygmean (pɪg'miːən) *adj*

Pygmy *or* **Pigmy** ('pɪgmɪ) *n, pl* -mies a member of one of the dwarf peoples of Equatorial Africa,noted for their hunting and forest culture

pyinkado (pjɪŋ'kɑːdəʊ) *n* **1** a leguminous tree, *Xylia xylocarpa* (or *dolabriformis*), native to India and Myanmar **2** the heavy durable timber of this tree, used for construction [C19: from Burmese]

pyjamas *or US* **pajamas** (pə'dʒɑːməz) *pl n* **1** loose-fitting nightclothes comprising a jacket or top and trousers **2** full loose-fitting ankle-length trousers worn by either sex in various Eastern countries [C19: from Hindi, from

Persian *pāē* leg + *jāmah* clothing, garment]

pyknic ('pɪknɪk) *adj* (of a physical type) characterized by a broad squat fleshy physique with a large chest and abdomen [C20: from Greek *puknos* thick]

pylon ('paɪlən) *n* **1** a large vertical steel tower-like structure supporting high-tension electrical cables **2** a post or tower for guiding pilots or marking a turning. point in a race **3** a streamlined aircraft structure for attaching an engine pod, external fuel tank, etc, to the main body of the aircraft **4** a monumental gateway, such as one at the entrance to an ancient Egyptian temple [C19: from Greek *pulōn* a gateway]

pylorus (paɪ'lɔːrəs) *n*, *pl* -ri (-raɪ) the small circular opening at the base of the stomach through which partially digested food (chyme) passes to the duodenum [C17: via Late Latin from Greek *pulōrus* gatekeeper, from *pulē* gate + *ouros* guardian]

Pylos ('paɪlɒs) *n* a port in SW Greece, in the SW Peloponnese; scene of a defeat of the Spartans by the Athenians (425 BC) during the Peloponnesian War and of the Battle of Navarino. Italian name: Navarino Modern Greek name: Pílos

Pym (pɪm) *n* **1** Barbara (**Mary Crampton**). 1913–80, British novelist, noted for such comedies of middle-class English life as *Excellent Women* (1952), *A Glass of Blessings* (1958), and *The Sweet Dove Died* (1978) **2** John. ?1584–1643, leading English parliamentarian during the events leading to the Civil War. He took a prominent part in the impeachment of Buckingham (1626) and of Strafford and Laud (1640)

Pynchon ('pɪntʃən) *n* Thomas. born 1937, US novelist, author of *V* (1963), *The Crying of Lot 49* (1967), *Gravity's Rainbow* (1973), *Mason and Dixon* (1997), and *Against the Day* (2006)

pyo- or before a vowel **py-** *combining form* denoting pus: *pyosis* [from Greek *puon*]

Pyongyang or **P'yŏng-yang** ('pjɒŋ'jæŋ) *n* the capital of North Korea, in the southwest on the Taedong River: industrial centre; university (1946). Pop: 3 284 000 (2005est)

pyorrhoea or *esp US* **pyorrhea** (ˌpaɪə'rɪə) *n* inflammation of the gums characterized by the discharge of pus and loosening of the teeth; periodontal disease > ˌpyor'rhoeal, ˌpyor'rhoeic or *esp US* ˌpyor'rheal or ˌpyor'rheic *adj*

pyracantha (ˌpaɪrə'kænθə) *n* any rosaceous shrub of the genus *Pyracantha*, esp the firethorn, widely cultivated for ornament [C17: from Greek *purakantha* name of a shrub, from PYRO- + *akantha* thorn]

pyramid ('pɪrəmɪd) *n* **1** a huge masonry construction that has a square base and, as in the case of the ancient Egyptian royal tombs, four sloping triangular sides **2** an object, formation, or structure resembling such a construction **3** *maths* a solid having a polygonal base and triangular sides that meet in a common vertex **4** *crystallog* a crystal form in which three planes intersect all three axes of the crystal **5** *finance* a group of enterprises containing a series of holding companies structured so that the top holding company controls the entire group with a relatively small proportion of the total capital invested **6** (*plural*) a game similar to billiards with fifteen coloured balls ▷ *vb* **7** to build up or be arranged in the form of a pyramid **8** *finance* to form (companies) into a pyramid [C16 (earlier *pyramis*): from Latin *pyramis*, from Greek *puramis*, probably from Egyptian] > pyramidal (pɪ'ræmɪdᵊl), ˌpyra'midical or ˌpyra'midic *adj* > py'ramidally or ˌpyra'midically *adv*

pyramid selling *n* a practice adopted by some manufacturers of advertising for distributors and selling them batches of goods. The first distributors then advertise for more distributors who are sold subdivisions of the original batches at an increased price. This process continues until the final distributors are left with a stock that is unsaleable except at a loss

Pyramus and Thisbe ('pɪrəməs, 'θɪzbɪ) *n* (in Greek legend) two lovers of Babylon: Pyramus, wrongly supposing Thisbe to be dead, killed himself and she, encountering him in his death throes, did the same

pyre (paɪə) *n* a heap or pile of wood or other combustible material, esp one used for cremating a corpse [C17: from Latin *pyra*, from Greek *pura* hearth, from *pur* fire]

Pyrenees (ˌpɪrə'niːz) *pl n* a mountain range between France and Spain, extending from the Bay of Biscay to the Mediterranean. Highest peak: Pico de Aneto, 3404 m (11 168ft)

Pyrénées-Atlantiques (*French* pirenez-atlãtik) or **Pyrénées** *n* a department of SW France in Aquitaine region. Capital: Pau. Pop: 614 174 (2003 est). Area: 7712 sq km (3008 sq miles). Former name: Basses-Pyrénées

Pyrénées-Orientales (*French* pirenezɔrjãtal) *n* a department of S France, in Languedoc-Roussillon region. Capital: Perpignan. Pop: 411 447 (2003 est). Area: 4144 sq km (1616 sqmiles)

pyrethrin (paɪ'riːθrɪn) *n* Also called: pyrethrin I an oily water-insoluble compound used as an insecticide. Formula: $C_{21}H_{28}O_3$ [C19: from PYRETHRUM + -IN]

pyrethrum (paɪ'riːθrəm) *n* **1** any of several cultivated Eurasian chrysanthemums, such as *Chrysanthemum coccineum* and *C. roseum*, with white, pink, red, or purple flowers **2** any insecticide prepared from the dried flowers of any of these plants, esp *C. roseum* [C16: via Latin from Greek *purethron* feverfew, probably from *puretos* fever; see PYRETIC]

pyretic (paɪ'rɛtɪk) *adj pathol* of, relating to, or characterized by fever [C18: from New Latin *pyreticus*, from Greek *puretos* fever, from *pur* fire]

Pyrex ('paɪrɛks) *n trademark* **a** any of a variety of borosilicate glasses that have low coefficients of expansion, making them suitable for heat-resistant glassware used in cookery and chemical apparatus **b** (*as modifier*): *a Pyrex dish*

pyrexia (paɪ'rɛksɪə) *n* a technical name for **fever** [C18: from New Latin, from Greek *purexis*, from *puressein* to be feverish, from *pur* fire] > py'rexial or py'rexic *adj*

pyridine ('pɪrɪˌdiːn) *n* a colourless hygroscopic liquid with a characteristic odour. It is a basic heterocyclic compound containing one nitrogen atom and five carbon atoms in its molecules and is used as a solvent and in preparing other organic chemicals. Formula: C_5H_5N [C19: from PYRO- + -ID + -INE²]

pyridoxine (ˌpɪrɪ'dɒksiːn) *n biochem* a derivative of pyridine that is a precursor of the compounds pyridoxal and pyridoxamine. Also called: vitamin B_6 [C20: from PYRID (INE) + OX(YGEN) + -INE²]

pyrimidine (paɪ'rɪmɪˌdiːn) *n* **1** a liquid or crystalline organic compound with a penetrating odour; 1,3-diazine. It is a weakly basic soluble heterocyclic compound and can be prepared from barbituric acid. Formula: $C_4H_4N_2$ **2** Also called: pyrimidine base any of a number of similar compounds having a basic structure that is derived from pyrimidine, including cytosine, thymine, and uracil, which are constituents of nucleic acids [C20: variant of PYRIDINE]

pyrite ('paɪraɪt) *n* a yellow mineral, found in igneous and metamorphic rocks and in veins. It is a source of sulphur and is used in the manufacture of sulphuric acid. Composition: iron sulphide. Formula: FeS_2. Crystal structure: cubic. Also called: iron pyrites, pyrites [C16: from Latin *pyrites* flint, from Greek *puritēs* (*lithos*) fire(stone), that is, capable of withstanding or striking fire, from *pur* fire] > pyritic (paɪ'rɪtɪk) or py'ritous *adj*

pyrites (paɪ'raɪtiːz; *in combination* 'paɪraɪts) *n*, *pl* -tes **1** another name for **pyrite 2** any of a number of other disulphides of metals, esp of copper and tin

pyro- or before a vowel **pyr-** *combining form* **1** denoting fire, heat, or high temperature: *pyromania*; *pyrometer* **2** *chem* denoting a new substance obtained by heating another: *pyroboric acid is obtained by heating boric acid* **3** *mineralogy* **a** having a property that changes upon the application of heat **b** having a flame-coloured appearance: *pyroxylin* [from Gk *pur* fire]

pyroelectricity (ˌpaɪrəʊɪlɛk'trɪsɪtɪ, -ˌiːlɛk-) *n* the development of opposite charges at the ends of the axis of certain hemihedral crystals, such as tourmaline, as a result of a change in temperature

pyrogallol (ˌpaɪrəʊ'gælɒl) *n* a white lustrous crystalline soluble phenol with weakly acidic properties; 1,2,3-trihydroxybenzene: used as a photographic developer and for absorbing oxygen. Formula: $C_6H_3(OH)_3$ [C20: from PYRO- + GALL(IC)^2 +-OL^1]

pyrogenic (ˌpaɪrəʊˈdʒɛnɪk) or **pyrogenous** (paɪˈrɒdʒɪnəs) adj **1** produced by or producing heat **2** pathol causing or resulting from fever **3** geology less common words for **igneous**

pyrography (paɪˈrɒɡrəfɪ) n, pl -phies **1** the art or process of burning designs on wood or leather with heated tools or a flame **2** a design made by this process > py'rographer n > pyrographic (ˌpaɪrəʊˈɡræfɪk) adj

pyroligneous (ˌpaɪrəʊˈlɪɡnɪəs) or **pyrolignic** adj (of a substance) produced by the action of heat on wood, esp by destructive distillation [C18: from French pyroligneux, from PYRO- + ligneus LIGNEOUS]

pyrolysis (paɪˈrɒlɪsɪs) n **1** the application of heat to chemical compounds in order to cause decomposition **2** chemical decomposition of compounds caused by high temperatures > pyrolytic (ˌpaɪrəʊˈlɪtɪk) adj

pyromania (ˌpaɪrəʊˈmeɪnɪə) n psychiatry the uncontrollable impulse and practice of setting things on fire > ˌpyro'mani,ac n

pyrometer (paɪˈrɒmɪtə) n an instrument for measuring high temperatures, esp by measuring the brightness (**optical pyrometer**) or total quantity (**radiationpyrometer**) of the radiation produced by the source. Other types include the resistance thermometer and the thermocouple > pyrometric (ˌpaɪrəʊˈmɛtrɪk) adj > ˌpyro'metrically adv > py'rometry n

pyrope ('paɪrəʊp) n a deep yellowish-red garnet that consists of magnesium aluminium silicate and is used as a gemstone. Formula:$Mg_3Al_2(SiO_4)_3$ [C14 (used loosely of a red gem; modern sense C19): from Old French pirope,from Latin pyrōpus bronze, from Greek purōpus fiery-eyed, from pur fire + ōps eye]

pyrophoric (ˌpaɪrəʊˈfɒrɪk) adj **1** (of a chemical) igniting spontaneously on contact with air **2** (of an alloy) producing sparks when struck or scraped: lighter flints are made of pyrophoric alloy [C19: from New Latin pyrophorus, from Greek purophoros fire-bearing, from pur fire + pherein to bear]

pyrosis (paɪˈrəʊsɪs) n pathol a technical name for **heartburn** [C18: from New Latin, from Greek: a burning, from puroun to burn, from pur fire]

pyrostat ('paɪrəʊ,stæt) n **1** a device that activates an alarm or extinguisher in the event of a fire **2** a thermostat for use at high temperatures > ˌpyro'static adj

pyrotechnics (ˌpaɪrəʊˈtɛknɪks) n **1** (functioning as singular) the art or craft of making fireworks **2** (functioning as singular or plural) a firework display **3** (functioning as singular or plural) brilliance of display, as in the performance of music > ˌpyro'technic or ˌpyro'technical adj

pyroxene (paɪˈrɒksiːn) n any of a group of silicate minerals having the general formula $ABSi_2O_6$, where A is usually calcium, sodium,magnesium, or iron, and B is usually magnesium, iron, chromium, manganese, or aluminium. Pyroxenes occur in basic igneous rocks and some metamorphic rocks, and have colours ranging from white to dark green or black. They may be monoclinic (clinopyroxenes) or orthorhombic (orthopyroxenes) in crystal structure. Examples are augite (the most important pyroxene), diopside, enstatite, hypersthene, and jadeite [C19: from PYRO- + -xene from Greek xenos foreign, because it was mistakenly thought to have originated elsewhere when found in igneous rocks]

pyroxylin (paɪˈrɒksɪlɪn) n a yellow substance obtained by nitrating cellulose with a mixture of nitric and sulphuric acids; guncotton: used to make collodion, plastics, lacquers, and adhesives [C19: from PYRO- + XYL(O)- + -IN]

pyrrhic ('pɪrɪk) prosody ▷ n **1** a metrical foot of two short or unstressed syllables ▷ adj **2** (of poetry) composed in pyrrhics [C16: via Latin, from Greek purrhikhē,

traditionally said to be named after its inventor Purrhikhos]

Pyrrhic victory n a victory in which the victor's losses are as great as those of the defeated. Also called: Cadmean victory [named after Pyrrhus (319–272 BC), king of Epirus (306–272), who defeated the Romans at Asculum in 279 BC but suffered heavy losses]

Pyrrho ('pɪrəʊ) n ?365–?275 BC, Greek philosopher; founder of scepticism. He maintained that true wisdom and happiness lie in suspension of judgment, since certain knowledge is impossible to attain > 'Pyrrhonism n > 'Pyrrhonist n, adj

Pyrrhus ('pɪrəs) n **1** 319–272 BC, king of Epirus (306–272). He invaded Italy but was ultimately defeated by the Romans (275 BC) **2** another name for **Neoptolemus** > 'Pyrrhic adj

pyruvic acid (paɪˈruːvɪk) n a colourless pleasant-smelling liquid formed as an intermediate in the metabolism of proteins and carbohydrates, helping to release energy to the body; 2-oxopropanoic acid. Formula: $CH_3COCOOH$ [C19: pyruvic from PYRO- + Latin ūva grape]

Pythagoras (paɪˈθæɡərəs) n ?580–?500 BC, Greek philosopher and mathematician. He founded a religious brotherhood, which followed a life of strict asceticism and greatly influenced the development of mathematics and its application to music and astronomy

Pythagoras' theorem n the theorem that in a right-angled triangle the square of the length of the hypotenuse equals the sum of the squares of the other two sides

Pythagorean (paɪˌθæɡəˈriːən) adj **1** of or relating to Pythagoras, the Greek philosopher and mathematician (?580–?500 BC) ▷ n **2** a follower of Pythagoras

Pytheas ('pɪθɪəs) n 4th century BC, Greek navigator. He was the first Greek to visit and describe the coasts of Spain, France, and the British Isles and may have reached Iceland

Pythia ('pɪθɪə) n Greek myth the priestess of Apollo at Delphi, who transmitted the oracles

Pythian ('pɪθɪən) adj Also: Pythic **1** of or relating to Delphi or its oracle ▷ n **2** the priestess of Apollo at the oracle of Delphi [C16: via Latin Pÿthius from Greek Puthios of Delphi]

python ('paɪθən) n any large nonvenomous snake of the family Pythonidae of Africa, S Asia, and Australia, such as Pythonreticulatus (**reticulated python**). They can reach a length of more than 20 feet and stalk their prey by constriction [C16: New Latin, after PYTHON] > pythonic (paɪˈθɒnɪk) adj

Python ('paɪθən) n Greek myth a dragon, killed by Apollo at Delphi

pythoness ('paɪθə,nɛs) n a woman, such as Apollo's priestess at Delphi, believed to be possessed by an oracular spirit [C14 phitonesse, ultimately from Greek Puthōn PYTHON]

pyuria (paɪˈjʊərɪə) n pathol any condition characterized by the presence of pus in the urine [C19: from New Latin, from Greek puon pus + ouron urine]

pyx or less commonly **pix** (pɪks) n **1** Also called: pyx chest the chest in which coins from the British mint are placed to be tested for weight, etc **2** Christianity any receptacle in which the Eucharistic Host is kept [C14: from Latin pyxis small box, from Greek, from puxos boxtree]

pyxidium (pɪkˈsɪdɪəm) or **pyxis** ('pɪksɪs) n, pl -ia (-ɪə) or pyxides ('pɪksɪ,diːz) the dry fruit of such plants as the plantain: a capsule whose upper part falls off when mature so that the seeds are released [C19: via New Latin from Greek puxidion a little box, from puxis box]

pyxis ('pɪksɪs) n, pl pyxides ('pɪksɪ,diːz) **1** a small box used by the ancient Greeks and Romans to hold medicines, etc **2** another name for **pyxidium** [C14: via Latin from Greek: box]

q¹ or Q (kjuː) *n*, *pl* **q's**, **Q's or Qs 1** the 17th letter and 13th consonant of the modern English alphabet **2** a speech sound represented by this letter, in English usually a voiceless velar stop, as in *unique* and *quick*

q² *symbol for* quintal

Q *symbol for* **1** *chess* queen **2** question **3** *physics* heat

q. *abbreviation* **1** quart **2** quarter **3** quarterly

Q. *abbreviation* **1** quartermaster **2** (*pl* **Qq**, **qq**) Also: **q** quarto **3** Queen **4** question

qabalah (kəˈbɑːlə) *n* a variant spelling of **kabbalah** > qabalism (ˈkæbəˌlɪzəm) *n* > qabalist *n* ˌqabaˈlistic *adj*

Qabis (ˈkɑːbɪs) *n* the Arabic name for **Gabès**

Qaboos bin Said (kəˈbuːs bɪn ˈsaɪd) *n* born 1940, Sultan of Oman from 1970

Qaddafi (gəˈdɑːfɪ) *n* **Moamar al** (ˈməʊəˌmɑːˌæl). See (Moamar al) **Gaddafi**

qadi (ˈkɑːdɪ, ˈkeɪdɪ) *n*, *pl* **-dis** a variant spelling of **cadi**

Qairwan (kaɪəˈwɑːn) *n* a variant of **Kairouan**

QANTAS (ˈkwɒntəs) *n* the Australian national airline [acronym of Queensland and Northern Territory Aerial Services, its original name: founded 1920]

Qaraghandy (*Kazakh* kɑrɑɣɑnˈdɪ) *n* a variant transliteration of the Kazakh name for **Karaganda**

QARANC *abbreviation* Queen Alexandra's Royal Army Nursing Corps

Qatar or Katar (kæˈtɑː) *n* a state in E Arabia, occupying a peninsula in the Persian Gulf: under Persian rule until the 19th century; became a British protectorate in 1916; declared independence in 1971; exports petroleum and natural gas. Official language: Arabic. Official religion: (Sunni) Muslim. Currency: riyal. Capital: Doha. Pop: 619 000 (2004 est). Area: about 11 000 sq km (4250 sq miles) > Qatari or Katari (kæˈtɑːrɪ) *adj*, *n*

Qattara Depression (kəˈtɑːrə) *n* an arid basin in the Sahara, in NW Egypt, impassable to vehicles. Area: about 18 000 sq km (7000 sq miles). Lowest point: 133 m (435 ft) below sea level

qawwali (kəˈvɑːlɪ) *n* an Islamic religious song, esp in Asia

QB *abbreviation* Queen's Bench

QC *abbreviation* **1** Queen's Counsel **2** (esp in postal addresses) Quebec

QED *abbreviation* **1** quod erat demonstrandum [Latin: which was to be shown or proved] **2** quantum electrodynamics

Qeshm (ˈkeʃəm) or **Qishm** *n* **1** the largest island in the Persian Gulf: part of Iran. Area: 1336 sq km (516 sq miles) **2** the chief town of this island

Q factor *n* **1** a measure of the relationship between stored energy and rate of energy dissipation in certain electrical components, devices, etc, thus indicating their efficiency **2** Also called: **Q value** the heat released in a nuclear reaction, usually expressed in millions of electronvolts for each individual reaction. Symbol: Q [C20: short for *quality factor*]

Q fever *n* an acute disease characterized by fever and pneumonia, transmitted to man by the rickettsia *Coxiella burnetii* [C20: from *q(uery) fever* (the cause being unknown when it was named)]

qi (tʃiː) *n* a variant of **chi²**

Qian Long (ˈtʃɪˈæn ˈlɒŋ) or **Ch'ien-lung** *n* original name *Hong-li*. 1711–99, Chinese emperor of the Qing dynasty. He expanded the Chinese empire and was a patron of the arts

Qingdao (ˈtʃɪŋˈdaʊ), **Tsingtao or Chingtao** *n* a port in E China, in E Shandong province on Jiazhou Bay, developed as a naval base and fort in 1891. Shandong university (1926). Pop: 2 431 000 (2005 est)

Qinghai, Tsinghai or **Chinghai** (ˈtʃɪŋˈhaɪ) *n* **1** a province of NW China: consists largely of mountains and high plateaus. Capital: Xining. Pop: 5 340 000 (2003 est). Area: 721 000 sq km (278 400 sq miles) **2** the Pinyin transliteration of the Chinese name for **Koko Nor**

Qiqihar, Chichihaerh, Ch'i-ch'i-haerh or **Tsitsihar** (ˈtʃiːˌtʃiːˈhɑː) *n* a city in NE China, in Heilongjiang province on the Nonni River. Pop: 1 452 000 (2005 est)

Qishm (ˈkɪʃəm) *n* a variant of **Qeshm**

Qld or **QLD** *abbreviation* Queensland

QM *abbreviation* Quartermaster

QMG *abbreviation* Quartermaster General

QMV *abbreviation* Qualified Majority Voting

Qom (kɒm), **Qum** or **Kum** *n* a city in NW central Iran: a place of pilgrimage for Shiite Muslims. Pop: 1 045 000 (2005 est)

qr. *pl* **qrs** *abbreviation* **1** quarter **2** quarterly **3** quire

Q-ship *n* a merchant ship with concealed guns, used to decoy enemy ships into the range of its weapons [named from *q(uery)*]

QSM *abbreviation* (in New Zealand) Queen's Service Medal

QSO *abbreviation* **1** *astronomy* quasi-stellar object **2** (in New Zealand) Queen's Service Order

qt *pl* **qt** *or* **qts** *abbreviation* quart

q.t. *informal abbreviation* **1** quiet **2** on the q.t. secretly

QTS *abbreviation* (in Britain) Qualified Teacher Status

qua (kweɪ, kwɑ:) *prep* in the capacity of; by virtue of being [c17: from Latin, ablative singular (feminine) of *qui* who]

quack[1] (kwæk) *vb* (*intr*) **1** (of a duck) to utter a harsh guttural sound **2** to make a noise like a duck ▷ *n* **3** the harsh guttural sound made by a duck [c17: of imitative origin; related to Dutch *kwakken*, German *quacken*]

quack[2] (kwæk) *n* **1 a** an unqualified person who claims medical knowledge or other skills **b** (*as modifier*): *a quack doctor* **2** *Brit, Austral & NZ informal* a doctor; physician or surgeon ▷ *vb* **3** (*intr*) to act in the manner of a quack [c17: short for QUACKSALVER] > 'quackish *adj*

quackery ('kwækərɪ) *n*, *pl* **-eries** the activities or methods of a quack

quack grass *n* another name for **couch grass** [c19: a variant of QUICK GRASS]

quacksalver ('kwæk,sælvə) *n* an archaic word for **quack**[2] [c16: from Dutch, from *quack*, apparently: to hawk + *salf* SALVE[1]]

quad[1] (kwɒd) *n* short for **quadrangle** (sense 2)

quad[2] (kwɒd) *n* *printing* a block of type metal used for spacing

quad[3] (kwɒd) *n* short for **quadruplet** (sense 1)

quad[4] (kwɒd) *adj, n* short for **quadraphonics**

quad bike *or* **quad** *n* a vehicle like a motorcycle with four large wheels, designed for off-road uses

Quadragesima (,kwɒdrə'dʒɛsɪmə) *n* Also called: **Quadragesima Sunday** the first Sunday in Lent [c16: from Medieval Latin *quadrāgēsima dies* the fortieth day]

Quadragesimal (,kwɒdrə'dʒɛsɪməl) *adj* of, relating to, or characteristic of Lent or the season of Lent

quadrangle ('kwɒd,ræŋɡ^əl) *n* **1** *geometry* a plane figure consisting of four points connected by four lines. In a **complete quadrangle**, six lines connect all pairs of points **2** a rectangular courtyard, esp one having buildings on all four sides **3** the building surrounding such a courtyard [c15: from Late Latin *quadrangulum* figure having four corners] > quadrangular (kwɒ'dræŋɡjʊlə) *adj*

quadrant ('kwɒdrənt) *n* **1** *geometry* **a** a quarter of the circumference of a circle **b** the area enclosed by two perpendicular radii of a circle and its circumference **c** any of the four sections into which a plane is divided by two coordinate axes **2** a piece of a mechanism in the form of a quarter circle, esp one used as a cam or a gear sector **3** an instrument formerly used in astronomy and navigation for measuring the altitudes of stars, consisting of a graduated arc of 90° and a sighting mechanism attached to a movable arm [c14: from Latin *quadrāns* a quarter] > quadrantal (kwɒ'drænt^əl) *adj*

quadraphonics *or* **quadrophonics** (,kwɒdrə'fɒnɪks) *n* (*functioning as singular*) a system of sound recording and reproduction that uses four independent loudspeakers to give directional sources of sound. The speakers are fed by four separate amplified signals > ,quadra'phonic *or* ,quadro'phonic *adj*

quadrat ('kwɒdrət) *n* *ecology* an area of vegetation, often one square metre, marked out for study of the plants in the surrounding area [c14 (meaning "a square"): variant of QUADRATE]

quadrate *n* ('kwɒdrɪt, -reɪt) **1** a cube, square, or a square or cubelike object **2** one of a pair of bones of the upper jaw of fishes, amphibians, reptiles, and birds that articulates with the lower jaw. In mammals it forms the incus ▷ *adj* ('kwɒdrɪt, -reɪt) **3** of or relating to this bone **4** square or rectangular ▷ *vb* (kwɒ'dreɪt) **5** (*tr*) to make square or rectangular **6** (often foll by *with*) to conform or cause to conform [c14: from Latin *quadrāre* to make square]

quadratic (kwɒ'drætɪk) *maths* ▷ *n* **1** Also called: **quadratic equation** an equation containing one or more terms in which the variable is raised to the power of two, but no terms in which it is raised to a higher power ▷ *adj* **2** of or relating to the second power

quadrature ('kwɒdrətʃə) *n* **1** *maths* the process of determining a square having an area equal to that of a given figure or surface **2** the process of making square or dividing into squares **3** *astronomy* a configuration in which two celestial bodies, usually the sun and the moon or a planet, form an angle of 90° with a third body, usually the earth **4** *electronics* the relationship between two waves that are 90° out of phase

quadrella (kwɒ'drɛlə) *n* *Austral* four nominated horseraces in which the punter bets on selecting the four winners

quadrennial (kwɒ'drɛnɪəl) *adj* **1** occurring every four years **2** relating to or lasting four years ▷ *n* **3** a period of four years > quad'rennially *adv*

quadrennium (kwɒ'drɛnɪəm) *n*, *pl* **-niums** *or* **-nia** (-nɪə) a period of four years [c17: from Latin *quadriennium*, from QUADRI- + *annus* year]

quadri- *or before a vowel* **quadr-** *combining form* four: *quadrilateral; quadrilingual; quadrisyllabic* [from Latin; compare *quattuor* four]

quadric ('kwɒdrɪk) *maths* ▷ *adj* **1** having or characterized by an equation of the second degree, usually in two or three variables **2** of the second degree ▷ *n* **3** a quadric curve, surface, or function

quadriceps ('kwɒdrɪ,sɛps) *n*, *pl* **-cepses** (-,sɛpsɪz) *or* **-ceps** *anatomy* a large four-part muscle of the front of the thigh, which extends the leg [c19: New Latin, from QUADRI- + -*ceps* as in BICEPS]

quadrifid ('kwɒdrɪfɪd) *adj* *botany* divided into four lobes or other parts: *quadrifid leaves*

quadrilateral (,kwɒdrɪ'lætərəl) *adj* **1** having or formed by four sides ▷ *n* **2** Also called: **tetragon** a polygon having four sides. A **complete quadrilateral** consists of four lines and their six points of intersection

quadrille[1] (kwɒ'drɪl, kwə-) *n* **1** a square dance of five or more figures for four or more couples **2** a piece of music for such a dance, alternating between simple duple and compound duple time [c18: via French from Spanish *cuadrilla*, diminutive of *cuadro* square, from Latin *quadra*]

quadrille[2] (kwɒ'drɪl, kwə-) *n* an old card game for four players [c18: from French, from Spanish *cuartillo*, from *cuarto* fourth, from Latin *quartus*, influenced by QUADRILLE[1]]

quadrillion (kwɒ'drɪljən) *n* **1** (in Britain) the number represented as one followed by 24 zeros (10^{24}). US and Canadian word: **septillion** **2** (in the US and Canada) the number represented as one followed by 15 zeros (10^{15}) ▷ *determiner* **3** (preceded by *a* or a numeral) amounting to this number: *a quadrillion atoms* [c17: from French *quadrillon*, from QUADRI- + -*illion*, on the model of *million*] > quad'rillionth *adj*

quadrinomial (,kwɒdrɪ'nəʊmɪəl) *n* an algebraic expression containing four terms

quadriplegia (,kwɒdrɪ'pli:dʒɪə, -dʒə) *n* *pathol* paralysis of all four limbs, usually as the result of injury to the spine. Also called: **tetraplegia** [c20: from QUADRI- + Greek *plēgē* a blow, from *plēssein* to strike] > ,quadri'plegic *adj, n*

quadrivalent (,kwɒdrɪ'veɪlənt) *adj* *chem* another word for **tetravalent** > ,quadri'valency *or* ,quadri'valence *n*

quadrivium (kwɒ'drɪvɪəm) *n*, *pl* **-ia** (-ɪə) (in medieval learning) the higher division of the seven liberal arts, consisting of arithmetic, geometry, astronomy, and music [from Medieval Latin, from Latin: crossroads, meeting of four ways, from QUADRI- + *via* way] > qua'drivial *adj*

quadroon (kwɒ'dru:n) *n* the offspring of a Mulatto and a White person; a person who is one-quarter Black [c18: from Spanish *cuarterón*, from *cuarto* quarter, from Latin *quartus*]

quadrumanous (kwɒ'dru:mənəs) *adj* (of monkeys and apes) having all four feet specialized for use as hands [c18: from New Latin *quadrumanus*, from QUADRI- + Latin *manus* hand]

q

quadruped ('kwɒdrʊ,pɛd) n 1 an animal, esp a mammal, that has all four limbs specialized for walking ▷ adj 2 having four feet [c17: from Latin *quadrupēs*, from *quadru-* (see QUADRI-) + *pēs* foot] > quadrupedal (kwɒ'dru:pɪd³l, ,kwɒdrʊ'pɛd³l) adj

quadruple ('kwɒdrʊp³l, kwɒ'dru:p³l) vb 1 to multiply by four or increase fourfold ▷ adj 2 four times as much or as many; fourfold 3 consisting of four parts ▷ n 4 a quantity or number four times as great as another [c16: via Old French from Latin *quadruplus*, from *quadru-* (see QUADRI-) + *-plus* -fold] > 'quadruply adv

quadruplet ('kwɒdrʊplɪt, kwɒ'dru:plɪt) n 1 one of four offspring born at one birth 2 a group or set of four similar things 3 *music* a group of four notes to be played in a time value of three

quadruple time n musical time in which there are four beats in each bar

quadruplicate adj (kwɒ'dru:plɪkɪt, -,keɪt) 1 fourfold or quadruple ▷ vb (kwɒ'dru:plɪ,keɪt) 2 to multiply or be multiplied by four ▷ n (kwɒ'dru:plɪkɪt, -,keɪt) 3 a group or set of four things [c17: from Latin *quadruplicāre* to increase fourfold]

quaestor ('kwi:stə, -tɔ:) or sometimes US **questor** ('kwɛstə) n any of several magistrates of ancient Rome, usually a financial administrator [c14: from Latin, from *quaerere* to inquire] > quaestorial (kwɛ'stɔ:rɪəl) adj

quaff (kwɒf, kwɑ:f) vb to drink heartily or in one draught [c16: perhaps of imitative origin; compare Middle Low German *quassen* to eat or drink excessively] > 'quaffer n

quag (kwæg, kwɒg) n another word for **quagmire** [c16: perhaps related to QUAKE; compare Middle Low German *quabbe*]

quagga ('kwægə) n, pl -gas or -ga a recently extinct member of the horse family (*Equidae*), *Equus quagga*, of southern Africa: it had a sandy brown colouring with zebra-like stripes on the head and shoulders [c18: from obsolete Afrikaans, from Khoikhoi *qǔagga*; compare Xhosa *i-qwara* something striped]

quaggy ('kwægɪ, 'kwɒgɪ) adj -gier, -giest 1 resembling a marsh or quagmire; boggy 2 yielding, soft, or flabby

quagmire ('kwæg,maɪə, 'kwɒg-) n 1 a soft wet area of land that gives way under the feet; bog 2 an awkward, complex, or embarrassing situation [c16: from QUAG + MIRE]

quahog ('kwɑ:,hɒg) n an edible clam, *Venus* (or *Mercenaria*) *mercenaria*, native to the Atlantic coast of North America, having a large heavy rounded shell [c18: from Narraganset, short for *poquauhock*, from *pohkeni* dark + *hogki* shell]

quaich or **quaigh** (kwex, kweɪx) n, pl quaichs or quaighs *Scot* a small shallow drinking cup, usually with two handles [from Scottish Gaelic *cuach* cup]

Quai d'Orsay (French ke dɔrse) n the quay along the S bank of the Seine, Paris, where the French foreign office is situated

quail¹ (kweɪl) n, pl quails or quail any small Old World gallinaceous game bird of the genus *Coturnix* and related genera, having a rounded body and small tail: family *Phasianidae* (pheasants) [c14: from Old French *quaille*, from Medieval Latin *quaccula*, probably of imitative origin]

quail² (kweɪl) vb (intr) to shrink back with fear; cower [c15: perhaps from Old French *quailler*, from Latin *coāgulāre* to curdle]

quaint (kweɪnt) adj 1 attractively unusual, esp in an old-fashioned style 2 odd, peculiar, or inappropriate [c13 (in the sense: clever): from Old French *cointe*, from Latin *cognitus* known, from *cognoscere* to ascertain] > 'quaintly adv > 'quaintness n

quair (kwer, kweə) n *Scot* a book [a variant of QUIRE]

quake (kweɪk) vb (intr) 1 to shake or tremble with or as with fear 2 to convulse or quiver, as from instability ▷ n 3 the act or an instance of quaking 4 *informal* short for **earthquake** [Old English *cwacian*; related to Old English *cweccan* to shake, Old Irish *bocaim*, German *wackeln*]

Quaker ('kweɪkə) n 1 a member of the Religious Society of Friends, a Christian sect founded by the English religious leader George Fox (1624–91) about 1650, whose central belief is the doctrine of the Inner Light. Quakers reject sacraments, ritual, and formal ministry, hold meetings at which any member may speak, and have promoted many causes for social reform ▷ adj 2 of, relating to, or designating the Religious Society of Friends or its religious beliefs or practices [c17: originally a derogatory nickname, alluding either to their alleged ecstatic fits, or to George Fox's injunction to "*quake* at the word of the Lord"] > 'Quakeress fem n > 'Quakerish adj > 'Quakerism n

quaking ('kweɪkɪŋ) adj unstable or unsafe to walk on, as a bog or quicksand

quaking grass n any grass of the genus *Briza*, of N temperate regions and South America, having delicate flower branches that shake in the wind

quaky ('kweɪkɪ) adj quakier, quakiest inclined to quake; shaky; tremulous > 'quakily adv > 'quakiness n

qualification (,kwɒlɪfɪ'keɪʃən) n 1 an official record of achievement awarded on the successful completion of a course of training or passing of an exam 2 an ability, quality, or attribute, esp one that fits a person to perform a particular job or task 3 a condition that modifies or limits; restriction 4 the act of qualifying or state of being qualified

qualified ('kwɒlɪ,faɪd) adj 1 having the abilities, qualities, attributes, etc, necessary to perform a particular job or task 2 limited, modified, or restricted; not absolute

Qualified Majority Voting n a voting system, used by the EU Council of Ministers, enabling certain resolutions to be passed without unanimity. Abbreviation: QMV

qualify ('kwɒlɪ,faɪ) vb -fies, -fying, -fied 1 to provide or be provided with the abilities or attributes necessary for a task, office, duty, etc: *his degree qualifies him for the job; he qualifies for the job, but would he do it well?* 2 (tr) to make less strong, harsh, or violent; moderate or restrict 3 (tr) to modify or change the strength or flavour of 4 (tr) *grammar* another word for **modify** (sense 3) 5 (tr) to attribute a quality to; characterize 6 (intr) to progress to the final stages of a competition, as by winning preliminary contests [c16: from Old French *qualifier*, from Medieval Latin *quālificāre* to characterize, from Latin *quālis* of what kind + *facere* to make] > 'quali,fiable adj > 'quali,fier n

qualitative ('kwɒlɪtətɪv, -,teɪ-) adj involving or relating to distinctions based on quality or qualities > 'qualitatively adv

qualitative analysis n See **analysis** (sense 4)

quality ('kwɒlɪtɪ) n, pl -ties 1 a distinguishing characteristic, property, or attribute 2 the basic character or nature of something 3 a trait or feature of personality 4 degree or standard of excellence, esp a high standard 5 (formerly) high social status or the distinction associated with it 6 musical tone colour; timbre 7 *logic* the characteristic of a proposition that is dependent on whether it is affirmative or negative 8 *phonetics* the distinctive character of a vowel, determined by the configuration of the mouth, tongue, etc, when it is articulated and distinguished from the pitch and stress with which it is uttered 9 (modifier) having or showing excellence or superiority: *a quality product* [c13: from Old French *qualité*, from Latin *quālitās* state, nature, from *quālis* of what sort]

quality control n control of the relative quality of a manufactured product, usually by statistical sampling techniques

qualm (kwɑ:m) n 1 a sudden feeling of sickness or nausea 2 a pang or sudden feeling of doubt, esp concerning moral conduct; scruple 3 a sudden sensation of misgiving or unease [Old English *cwealm* death or plague; related to Old High German *qualm* despair, Dutch *kwalm* smoke, stench] > 'qualmish adj

quandary ('kwɒndrɪ, -dərɪ) n, pl -ries a situation or circumstance that presents problems difficult to solve; predicament; dilemma [c16: of uncertain origin; perhaps related to Latin *quandō* when]

quandong, quandang ('kwɒn,dɒŋ) or **quantong** ('kwɒn,tɒŋ) n 1 Also called: native peach a a small Australian santalaceous tree, *Eucarya acuminata* (or

Fusanus acuminatus) **b** the edible fruit or nut of this tree, used in preserves **2** silver quandong **a** an Australian tree, *Elaeocarpus grandis*: family *Elaeocarpaceae* **b** the pale easily worked timber of this tree [from a native Australian language]

quango ('kwæŋɡəʊ) *n, pl* -gos a semipublic government-financed administrative body whose members are appointed by the government [C20: from *qu(asi-)a(utonomous) n(on)g(overnmental) o(rganization)*]

quangocracy (kwæŋ'ɡɒkrəsɪ) *n, pl* -cies **1** the control or influence ascribed to quangos **2** quangos collectively

quant¹ (kwɒnt) *n* **1** a long pole for propelling a boat, esp a punt, by pushing on the bottom of a river or lake ▷ *vb* **2** to propel (a boat) with a quant [C15: probably from Latin *contus* a pole, from Greek *kontos*]

quant² (kwɒnt) *n informal* a highly paid computer specialist with a degree in a quantitative science, employed by a financial house to predict the future price movements of securities, commodities, currencies, etc [C20: from QUANTITATIVE]

Quant (kwɒnt) *n* **Mary.** born 1934, British fashion designer, whose Chelsea Look of miniskirts and geometrically patterned fabrics dominated London fashion in the 1960s

quanta ('kwɒntə) *n* the plural of **quantum**

quantifier ('kwɒntɪˌfaɪə) *n* **1** *logic* any other symbol with an analogous interpretation: *the existential quantifier,* (∃x), *corresponds to the words "there is something, x, such that ..."* **2** *grammar* a word or phrase in a natural language having this role, such as *some, all,* or *many* in English

quantify ('kwɒntɪˌfaɪ) *vb* -fies, -fying, -fied (*tr*) **1** to discover or express the quantity of **2** *logic* to specify the quantity of (a term) by using a quantifier, such as *all, some,* or *no* [C19: from Medieval Latin *quantificāre,* from Latin *quantus* how much + *facere* to make] ▷ 'quanti,fiable *adj* ▷ quantification (ˌkwɒntɪfɪˈkeɪʃən) *n*

quantitative ('kwɒntɪtətɪv, -ˌteɪ-) *or* **quantitive** *adj* **1** involving or relating to considerations of amount or size **2** capable of being measured **3** *prosody* denoting or relating to a metrical system, such as that in Latin and Greek verse, that is based on the relative length rather than stress of syllables ▷ 'quantitatively *or* 'quantitively *adv*

quantitative analysis *n* See **analysis** (sense 4)

quantity ('kwɒntɪtɪ) *n, pl* -ties **1 a** a specified or definite amount, weight, number, etc **b** (*as modifier*): *a quantity estimate* **2** the aspect or property of anything that can be measured, weighed, counted, etc **3** a large or considerable amount **4** *maths* an entity having a magnitude that may be denoted by a numerical expression **5** *physics* a specified magnitude or amount; the product of a number and a unit **6** *logic* the characteristic of a proposition dependent on whether it is a universal or particular statement, considering all or only part of a class **7** *prosody* the relative duration of a syllable or the vowel in it [C14: from Old French *quantité,* from Latin *quantitās* extent, amount, from *quantus* how much]

● USAGE The use of a plural noun after *quantity of* as in *a* ● *large quantity of bananas* was formerly considered ● incorrect, but is now acceptable

quantity surveyor *n* a person who estimates the cost of the materials and labour necessary for a construction job

quantize *or* **quantise** ('kwɒntaɪz) *vb* (*tr*) **1** *physics* to restrict (a physical quantity) to one of a set of values characterized by quantum numbers **2** *maths* to limit (a variable) to values that are integral multiples of a basic unit ▷ ˌquanti'zation *or* ˌquanti'sation *n*

quantum ('kwɒntəm) *n, pl* -ta (-tə) **1** *physics* **a** the smallest quantity of some physical property, such as energy, that a system can possess according to the quantum theory **b** a particle with such a unit of energy **2** amount or quantity, esp a specific amount **3** (*modifier*) loosely, sudden, spectacular, or vitally important: *a quantum improvement* [C17: from Latin *quantus* (adj) how much]

quantum computer *n* a type of computer which uses the ability of quantum systems to be in many different states at once, thus allowing it to perform many different computations simultaneously

quantum electrodynamics *n physics* a relativistic quantum mechanical theory concerned with electromagnetic interactions. Abbreviation: QED

quantum mechanics *n* (*functioning as singular*) the branch of mechanics, based on the quantum theory used for interpreting the behaviour of elementary particles and atoms, which do not obey Newtonian mechanics

quantum meruit Latin ('meru:ɪt) as much as he has earned: denoting a payment for goods or services in partial fulfilment of a contract or for those supplied when no price has been agreed

quantum number *n physics* one of a set of integers or half-integers characterizing the energy states of a particle or system of particles. A function of the number multiplied by a fixed quantity gives the observed value of some specified physical quantity possessed by the system

quantum teleportation *n physics* a process by which a change in the quantum state of one subatomic particle in an entangled pair occurs instantly in its twin, wherever it may be

quantum theory *n* a theory concerning the behaviour of physical systems based on Planck's idea that they can only possess certain properties, such as energy and angular momentum, in discrete amounts (quanta). The theory later developed in several equivalent mathematical forms based on De Broglie's theory and on the Heisenberg uncertainty principle

quaquaversal (ˌkwɑːkwəˈvɜːsəl) *adj geology* directed outwards in all directions from a common centre [C18: from Latin *quāquā* in every direction + *versus* towards]

quarantine ('kwɒrənˌtiːn) *n* **1** a period of isolation or detention, esp of persons or animals arriving from abroad, to prevent the spread of disease, usually consisting of the maximum known incubation period of the suspected disease **2** the place or area where such detention is enforced **3** any period or state of enforced isolation ▷ *vb* **4** (*tr*) to isolate in or as if in quarantine [C17: from Italian *quarantina* period of forty days, from *quaranta* forty, from Latin *quadrāgintā*]

quarantine flag *n nautical* the yellow signal flag for the letter Q, flown alone from a vessel to indicate that there is no disease aboard and to request pratique or, with a second signal flag, to indicate that there is disease aboard. Also called: **yellow flag, yellow jack**

quark¹ (kwɑːk) *n physics* any of a set of six hypothetical elementary particles together with their antiparticles thought to be fundamental units of all baryons and mesons but unable to exist in isolation. The magnitude of their charge is either two thirds or one third of that of the electron [C20: coined by James Joyce (1882–1941), Irish novelist and short-story writer, in the novel *Finnegans Wake,* and given special application in physics]

quark² (kwɑːk) *n* a type of low-fat soft cheese [from German]

Quarles (kwɔːlz, kwɑːlz) *n* **Francis.** 1592–1644, English poet

quarrel¹ ('kwɒrəl) *n* **1** an angry disagreement; argument **2** a cause of disagreement or dispute; grievance ▷ *vb* -rels, -relling, -relled *or US* -rels, -reling, -reled (*intr*; often foll by *with*) **3** to engage in a disagreement or dispute; argue **4** to find fault; complain [C14: from Old French *querele,* from Latin *querēlla* complaint, from *querī* to complain] ▷ 'quarreller *or US* 'quarreler *n*

quarrel² ('kwɒrəl) *n* **1** an arrow having a four-edged head, fired from a crossbow **2** a small square or diamond-shaped pane of glass, usually one of many in a fixed or casement window and framed with lead [C13: from Old French *quarrel* pane, from Medieval Latin *quadrellus,* diminutive of Latin *quadrus* square]

quarrelsome ('kwɒrəlsəm) *adj* inclined to quarrel or disagree; belligerent

quarrian *or* **quarrion** ('kwɒrɪən) *n* a cockatiel, *Leptolophus hollandicus,* of scrub and woodland regions of inland Australia, that feeds on seeds and grasses [C20: probably from a native Australian language]

quarry¹ ('kwɒrɪ) *n, pl* -ries **1** an open surface excavation for the extraction of building stone, slate, marble, etc, by drilling, blasting, or cutting **2** a copious source of something, esp information ▷ *vb* -ries, -rying, -ried **3** to extract (stone, slate, etc) from or as if from a quarry **4** (*tr*) to excavate a quarry in **5** to obtain (something, esp information) diligently and laboriously [c15: from Old French *quarriere*, from *quarre* (unattested) square-shaped stone, from Latin *quadrāre* to make square]

quarry² ('kwɒrɪ) *n*, *pl* -ries **1** an animal, bird, or fish that is hunted, esp by other animals; prey **2** anything pursued or hunted [c14 *quirre* entrails offered to the hounds, from Old French *cuirée* what is placed on the hide, from *cuir* hide, from Latin *corium* leather; probably also influenced by Old French *coree* entrails, from Latin *cor* heart]

quarryman ('kwɒrɪmən) *n*, *pl* -men a man who works in or manages a quarry

quarry tile *n* a square or diamond-shaped unglazed floor tile

quart (kwɔːt) *n* **1** a unit of liquid measure equal to a quarter of a gallon or two pints. 1 US quart (0.946 litre) is equal to 0.8326 UK quart. 1 UK quart (1.136 litres) is equal to 1.2009 US quarts **2** a unit of dry measure equal to 2 pints or one eighth of a peck [c14: from Old French *quarte*, from Latin *quartus* fourth]

quartan ('kwɔːtᵊn) *adj* (esp of a malarial fever) occurring every third day [c13: from Latin *febris quartāna* fever occurring every fourth day, reckoned inclusively]

quarte French (kart) *n* the fourth of eight basic positions from which a parry or attack can be made in fencing [c18: from French, fem of *quart* a quarter]

quarter ('kwɔːtə) *n* **1** one of four equal or nearly equal parts of an object, quantity, amount, etc **2** Also called: **fourth** the fraction equal to one divided by four (1/4) **3** *US & Canadian* a quarter of a dollar; 25-cent piece **4** a unit of weight equal to a quarter of a hundredweight. 1 US quarter is equal to 25 pounds; 1 Brit quarter is equal to 28 pounds **5** short for **quarter-hour 6** a fourth part of a year; three months **7** *astronomy* **a** one fourth of the moon's period of revolution around the earth **b** either of two phases of the moon, **first quarter** or **last quarter** when half of the lighted surface is visible from the earth **8** *informal* a unit of weight equal to a quarter of a pound or 4 ounces **9** *Brit* a unit of capacity for grain, etc, usually equal to 8 UK bushels **10** *sport* one of the four periods into which certain games are divided **11** *nautical* the part of a vessel's side towards the stern, usually aft of the aftermost mast **12** a region or district of a town or city: *the Spanish quarter* **13** a region, direction, or point of the compass **14** (*sometimes plural*) an unspecified person or group of people: *to get word from the highest quarter* **15** mercy or pity, as shown to a defeated opponent (esp in the phrases **ask for** or **give quarter**) **16** any of the four limbs, including the adjacent parts, of the carcass of a quadruped or bird **17** *heraldry* one of four more or less equal quadrants into which a shield may be divided ▷ *vb* **18** (*tr*) to divide into four equal or nearly equal parts **19** (*tr*) to divide into any number of parts **20** (*tr*) (esp formerly) to dismember (a human body) **21** to billet or be billeted in lodgings, esp (of military personnel) in civilian lodgings **22** (*intr*) (of gun dogs or hounds) to range over an area of ground in search of game or the scent of quarry **23** (*intr*) *nautical* (of the wind) to blow onto a vessel's quarter **24** (*tr*) *heraldry* **a** to divide (a shield) into four separate bearings with a cross **b** to place (one set of arms) in diagonally opposite quarters to another ▷ *adj* **25** being or consisting of one of four equal parts ▷ See also **quarters** [c13: from Old French *quartier*, from Latin *quartārius* a fourth part, from *quartus* fourth]

quarterback ('kwɔːtəˌbæk) *n US & Canadian* a player in American or Canadian football, positioned usually behind the centre, who directs attacking play

quarter-bound *adj* (of a book) having a binding consisting of two types of material, the better type being used on the spine

quarter day *n* any of four days in the year when certain payments become due. In England, Wales, and Northern Ireland these are Lady Day, Midsummer's Day, Michaelmas, and Christmas. In Scotland they are Candlemas, Whit Sunday, Lammas, and Martinmas

quarterdeck ('kwɔːtəˌdɛk) *n nautical* the after part of the weather deck of a ship, traditionally the deck on a naval vessel for official or ceremonial use

quartered ('kwɔːtəd) *adj* **1** *heraldry* (of a shield) divided into four sections, each having contrasting arms or having two sets of arms, each repeated in diagonally opposite corners **2** (of a log) sawn into four equal parts along two diameters at right angles to each other; quartersawn

quarterfinal ('kwɔːtəˌfaɪnᵊl) *n* the round before the semifinal in a competition

quarter-hour *n* **1** a period of 15 minutes **2** any of the points on the face of a timepiece that mark 15 minutes before or after the hour, and sometimes 30 minutes after

quartering ('kwɔːtərɪŋ) *n* **1** *military* the allocation of accommodation to service personnel **2** *heraldry* **a** the marshalling of several coats of arms on one shield, usually representing intermarriages **b** any coat of arms marshalled in this way

quarterlife crisis ('kwɔːtəˌlaɪf) *n* a crisis that may be experienced in one's twenties, involving anxiety over the direction and quality of one's life

quarterlight ('kwɔːtəˌlaɪt) *n Brit* a small pivoted window in the door of a car for ventilation

quarterly ('kwɔːtəlɪ) *adj* **1** occurring, done, paid, etc, at intervals of three months **2** of, relating to, or consisting of a quarter ▷ *n*, *pl* -lies **3** a periodical issued every three months ▷ *adv* **4** once every three months

quartermaster ('kwɔːtəˌmɑːstə) *n* **1** an officer responsible for accommodation, food, and equipment in a military unit **2** a rating in the navy, usually a petty officer, with particular responsibility for steering a ship and other navigational duties

quarter-miler *n* an athlete who specializes in running the quarter mile or the 400 metres

quartern ('kwɔːtən) *n* **1** a fourth part of certain weights or measures, such as a peck or a pound **2** Also called: **quartern loaf** *Brit* **a** a type of loaf 4 inches square, used esp for making sandwiches **b** any loaf weighing 1600 g when baked [c13: from Old French *quarteron*, from *quart* a quarter]

quarter note *n US & Canadian music* a note having the time value of a quarter of a semibreve. Also called: crotchet

quarter plate *n* a photographic plate measuring $3\frac{1}{4} \times 4\frac{1}{4}$ inches (8.3 × 10.8 cm)

quarters ('kwɔːtəz) *pl n* **1** housing or accommodation, esp as provided for military personnel and their families **2** the stations assigned to military personnel, esp to each crew member of a warship: *general quarters*

quarter sessions *n* (*functioning as singular or plural*) (in England and Wales, formerly) a criminal court held four times a year before justices of the peace or a recorder, empowered to try all but the most serious offences and to hear appeals from petty sessions. Replaced in 1972 by crown courts

quarterstaff ('kwɔːtəˌstɑːf) *n*, *pl* -staves (-ˌsteɪvz, -ˌstɑːvz) a stout iron-tipped wooden staff about 6ft long, formerly used in England as a weapon [c16: of uncertain origin]

quarter tone *n music* a quarter of a whole tone; a pitch interval corresponding to 50 cents measured on the well-tempered scale

quartet *or* **quartette** (kwɔːˈtɛt) *n* **1** a group of four singers or instrumentalists or a piece of music composed for such a group **2** any group of four [c18: from Italian *quartetto*, diminutive of *quarto* fourth]

quartic ('kwɔːtɪk) *adj*, *n* another word for **biquadratic** [c19: from Latin *quartus* fourth]

quartile ('kwɔːtaɪl) *n* **1** *statistics* one of three actual or notional values of a variable dividing its distribution into four groups with equal frequencies ▷ *adj* **2** *statistics* denoting or relating to a quartile **3** *astrology* denoting an aspect of two heavenly bodies when their longitudes differ by 90° [c16: from Medieval Latin *quartīlis*, from Latin *quartus* fourth]

quarto ('kwɔːtəʊ) *n*, *pl* -tos a book size resulting from folding a sheet of paper, usually crown or demy, into four leaves or eight pages, each one quarter the size of the sheet [c16: from New Latin phrase *in quartō* in quarter]

quartz (kwɔːts) *n* a colourless mineral often tinted by impurities, found in igneous, sedimentary, and metamorphic rocks. It is used in the manufacture of glass, abrasives, and cement, and also as a gemstone; the violet-purple variety is amethyst, the brown variety is cairngorm, the yellow variety is citrine, and the pink variety is rose quartz. Composition: silicon dioxide. Formula: SiO_2. Crystal structure: hexagonal [c18: from German *Quarz*, of Slavic origin]

quartz clock *or* **watch** *n* a clock or watch that is operated by the vibrations of a quartz crystal controlled by a microcircuit

quartz crystal *n* a thin plate or rod cut in certain directions from a piece of piezoelectric quartz and accurately ground so that it vibrates at a particular frequency

quartz glass *n* a colourless glass composed of almost pure silica, resistant to very high temperatures and transparent to near-ultraviolet radiation

quartz-iodine lamp *or* **quartz lamp** *n* a type of tungsten-halogen lamp containing small amounts of iodine and having a quartz envelope, operating at high temperature and producing an intense light for use in car headlamps, etc

quartzite (ˈkwɔːtsaɪt) *n* 1 a very hard metamorphic rock consisting of a mosaic of intergrown quartz crystals 2 a white or grey sandstone composed of quartz

quasar (ˈkweɪzɑː, -sɑː) *n* any of a class of extragalactic objects that emit an immense amount of energy in the form of light, infrared radiation, etc, from a compact source. They are extremely distant and their energy generation is thought to involve a supermassive black hole located in the centre of a galaxy [c20: *quas(i-stell)ar (object)*]

quash (kwɒʃ) *vb* (*tr*) 1 to subdue forcefully and completely; put down; suppress 2 to annul or make void (a law, decision, etc) 3 to reject (an indictment, writ, etc) as invalid [c14: from Old French *quasser*, from Latin *quassāre* to shake]

quasi- *combining form* 1 almost but not really; seemingly: *a quasi-religious cult* 2 resembling but not actually being; so-called: *a quasi-scholar* [from L., lit: as if]

Quasimodo (Italian kwaˈziːmodo) *n* **Salvatore** (salvaˈtoːre). 1901–68, Italian poet, whose early work expresses symbolist ideas and techniques. His later work is more concerned with political and social issues: Nobel prize for literature 1959

quasi-stellar object *n* a member of any of several classes of astronomical bodies, including **quasars** (strong radio sources) and **quasi-stellar galaxies** (no traceable radio emission), both of which have exceptionally large red shifts. Abbreviation: QSO

quassia (ˈkwɒʃə) *n* 1 any tree of the tropical American simaroubaceous genus *Quassia*, having bitter bark and wood 2 the bark and wood of *Quassia amara* and of a related tree, *Picrasma excelsa*, used in furniture making [c18: from New Latin, named after Graman *Quassi*, a slave who discovered (1730) the medicinal value of the root]

quatercentenary (ˌkwætəsɛnˈtiːnərɪ) *n, pl* -naries a 400th anniversary or the year or celebration marking it [c19: from Latin *quater* four times + CENTENARY] > **quatercentennial** (ˌkwætəsɛnˈtɛnɪəl) *adj, n*

quaternary (kwəˈtɜːnərɪ) *adj* 1 consisting of fours or by fours 2 fourth in a series 3 *chem* containing or being an atom bound to four other atoms or groups ▷ *n, pl* -naries 4 the number four or a set of four [c15: from Latin *quaternārius* each containing four, from *quaternī* by fours, distributive of *quattuor* four]

Quaternary (kwəˈtɜːnərɪ) *adj* 1 of, denoting, or formed in the most recent period of geological time, which succeeded the Tertiary period nearly two million years ago ▷ *n* 2 **the Quaternary** the Quaternary period or rock system, divided into Pleistocene and Holocene (Recent) epochs or series

quaternion (kwəˈtɜːnɪən) *n* 1 *maths* a generalized complex number consisting of four components, $x = x_0 + x_1 i + x_2 j + x_3 k$, where $x, x_0 ... x_3$ are real numbers and $i^2 = j^2 = k^2 = -1$, $ij = -ji = k$, etc 2 another word for **quaternary** (sense 4) [c14: from Late Latin *quaterniōn*, from Latin *quaternī* four at a time]

Quathlamba (kwaːˈtlɑːmbaː) *n* the Sotho name for the **Drakensberg**

quatrain (ˈkwɒtreɪn) *n* a stanza or poem of four lines, esp one having alternate rhymes [c16: from French, from *quatre* four, from Latin *quattuor*]

Quatre Bras (French katrə bra) *n* a village in Belgium near Brussels; site of a battle in June 1815 where Wellington defeated the French under Marshal Ney, immediately preceding the battle of Waterloo

quatrefoil (ˈkætrəˌfoɪl) *n* 1 a leaf composed of four leaflets 2 *architect* a carved ornament having four foils arranged about a common centre, esp one used in tracery [c15: from Old French, from *quatre* four + *-foil* leaflet; compare TREFOIL]

quattrocento (ˌkwætrəʊˈtʃɛntəʊ; Italian kwattroˈtʃɛnto) *n* the 15th century, esp in reference to Renaissance Italian art and literature [Italian, shortened from *milquattrocento* 1400]

quaver (ˈkweɪvə) *vb* 1 to say or sing (something) with a trembling voice 2 (*intr*) (esp of the voice) to quiver, tremble, or shake 3 (*intr*) *rare* to sing or play quavers or ornamental trills ▷ *n* 4 *music* a note having the time value of an eighth of a semibreve. Usual US and Canadian name: eighth note 5 a tremulous sound or note (in the sense: to vibrate, QUIVER[1]): from *quaven* to tremble, of Germanic origin; compare Low German *quabbeln* to tremble] > **ˈquavering** *adj* > **ˈquaveringly** *adv*

quay (kiː) *n* a wharf, typically one built parallel to the shoreline [c14 *keye*, from Old French *kai*, of Celtic origin; compare Cornish *kē* hedge, fence, Old Breton *cai* fence]

quayage (ˈkiːɪdʒ) *n* 1 a system of quays 2 a charge for the use of a quay

Quayle (kweɪl) *n* Sir (**John**) **Anthony**. 1913–89, British actor and theatrical producer: director (1948–56) of the Shakespeare Memorial Theatre

quayside (ˈkiːˌsaɪd) *n* the edge of a quay along the water

qubit (ˈkjuːbɪt) *n* *computing* a quantum bit [c20: from QU(ANTUM) + BIT[4]]

Que. abbreviation Quebec

quean (kwiːn) *n* 1 *archaic* **a** a boisterous, impudent, or disreputable woman **b** a prostitute; whore 2 *Scot* a young unmarried woman or girl [Old English *cwene*; related to Old Saxon, Old High German *quena*, Gothic *qino*, Old Norse *kona*, Greek *gunē* woman. Compare QUEEN]

queasy (ˈkwiːzɪ) *adj* -sier, -siest 1 having the feeling that one is about to vomit; nauseous 2 feeling or causing uneasiness: *a queasy conscience* [c15: of uncertain origin] > **ˈqueasily** *adv* > **ˈqueasiness** *n*

Quebec (kwɪˈbɛk, kə-, kɛ-) *n* 1 a province of E Canada: the largest Canadian province; a French colony from 1608 to 1763, when it passed to Britain; lying mostly on the Canadian Shield, it has vast areas of forest and extensive tundra and is populated mostly in the plain around the St Lawrence River. Capital: Quebec. Pop: 7 542 760 (2004 est). Area: 1 540 680 sq km (594 860 sq miles). Abbreviation: PQ 2 a port in E Canada, capital of the province of Quebec, situated on the St Lawrence River: founded in 1608 by Champlain; scene of the battle of the Plains of Abraham (1759), by which the British won Canada from the French. Pop: 169 076 (2001) 3 *communications* a code word for the letter *q* > Que'becker or Que'becer *n*

Québécois (French kebekwa) *n, pl* -cois (-kwa) a native or inhabitant of the province of Quebec, esp a French-speaking one

quebracho (keɪˈbrɑːtʃəʊ; Spanish keˈβratʃo) *n, pl* -chos (-tʃəʊz; Spanish -tʃos) 1 either of two anacardiaceous South American trees, *Schinopsis lorentzii* or *S. balansae*, having a tannin-rich hard wood used in tanning and dyeing 2 an apocynaceous South American tree, *Aspidosperma quebrachoblanco*, whose bark yields alkaloids used in medicine and tanning 3 the wood or bark of any of these trees [c19: from American Spanish, from quiebracha, from *quebrar* to break (from Latin *crepāre* to rattle) + *hacha* axe (from French *hache*)]

Quechua, Kechua ('kɛtʃwə) *or* **Quichua** *n* **1** (*pl* -uas *or* -ua) a member of any of a group of South American Indian peoples of the Andes, including the Incas **2** the language or family of languages spoken by these peoples, possibly distantly related to the Tupï-Guarani family ▷ 'Quechuan, 'Kechuan *or* 'Quichuan *adj, n*

queen (kwi:n) *n* **1 a** female sovereign who is the official ruler or head of state **2** the wife or widow of a king **3** a woman or a thing personified as a woman considered the best or most important of her kind: *a beauty queen; the queen of ocean liners* **4** *slang* an effeminate male homosexual **5** the only fertile female in a colony of social insects, such as bees, ants, and termites, from the eggs of which the entire colony develops **6** an adult female cat **7** one of four playing cards in a pack, one for each suit, bearing the picture of a queen **8** a chess piece, theoretically the most powerful piece, able to move in a straight line in any direction or diagonally, over any number of squares ▷ *vb* **9** *chess* to promote (a pawn) to a queen when it reaches the eighth rank **10** (*tr*) to crown as queen **11** (*intr*) to reign as queen **12 queen it** (often foll by *over*) *informal* to behave in an overbearing manner [Old English *cwēn*; related to Old Saxon *quān* wife, Old Norse *kvæn*, Gothic *qēns* wife]

Queen (kwi:n) *n* **1** Ellery ('ɛlərɪ). pseudonym of *Frederic Dannay* (1905–82) and *Manfred B. Lee* (1905–71), US co-authors of detective novels featuring a sleuth also called Ellery Queen

Queen-Anne *n* **1** a style of furniture popular in England about 1700–20 and in America about 1720–70, characterized by the use of unencumbered curves, walnut veneer, and the cabriole leg ▷ *adj* **2** in or of this style **3** denoting or relating to a style of architecture popular in England during the early 18th century, characterized by red-brick construction with classical ornamentation

Queen Anne's lace *n* another name for **cow parsley**

queen bee *n* **1** the fertile female bee in a hive **2** *informal* a woman in a position of dominance or ascendancy over her peers or associates

Queenborough in Sheppey ('kwi:nbərə, 'ʃɛpɪ) *n* a town in SE England, in Kent: formed in 1968 by the amalgamation of Queenborough, Sheerness, and Sheppey. Pop: 3471 (2001)

Queen Charlotte Islands *pl n* a group of about 150 islands off the W coast of Canada: part of British Columbia. Pop: about 6000 (latest est). Area: 9596 sq km (3705 sq miles)

queen consort *n* the wife of a reigning king

queen dowager *n* the widow of a king

Queen Elizabeth Islands *pl n* a group of islands off the N coast of Canada: the northernmost islands of the Canadian Arctic archipelago, lying N of latitude 74°N; part of Nunavut. Area: about 390 000 sq km (150 000 sq miles)

queenly ('kwi:nlɪ) *adj* -lier, -liest resembling or appropriate to a queen

Queen Mab (mæb) *n* (in British folklore) a bewitching fairy who rules over men's dreams

Queen Maud Land (mɔːd) *n* the large section of Antarctica between Coats Land and Enderby Land: claimed by Norway in 1939. (Claims are suspended under the Antarctic Treaty of 1959)

Queen Maud Range *n* a mountain range in Antarctica, in S Ross Dependency, extending for about 800 km (500 miles)

queen mother *n* the widow of a former king who is also the mother of the reigning sovereign

queen olive *n* a variety of olive having large fleshy fruit suitable for pickling, esp one from around Seville in Spain

queen post *n* one of a pair of vertical posts that connect the tie beam of a truss to the principal rafters. Compare **king post**

Queens (kwi:nz) *n* a borough of E New York City, on Long Island. Pop: 2 225 486 (2003 est)

Queen's Award *n* either of two awards instituted by royal warrant (1976) for a sustained increase in export earnings by a British firm (**Queen's Award for Export Achievement**) or for an advance in technology (**Queen's Award for Technological Achievement**)

Queen's Bench Division *n* (in England when the sovereign is female) one of the divisions of the High Court of Justice. Also called (when the sovereign is male): King's Bench

Queensberry rules ('kwi:nzbərɪ, -brɪ) *pl n* **1** the code of rules followed in modern boxing, requiring the use of padded gloves, rounds of three minutes, and restrictions on the types of blows allowed **2** *informal* gentlemanly or polite conduct, esp in a dispute [c19: named after the ninth Marquess of *Queensberry*, who originated the rules in 1869]

Queen's Counsel *n* (in England when the sovereign is female) a barrister or advocate appointed Counsel to the Crown on the recommendation of the Lord Chancellor, entitled to sit within the bar of the court and to wear a silk gown

Queen's County *n* the former name of **Laois**

queen's English *n* (when the British sovereign is female) standard Southern British English

queen's evidence *n English law* (when the sovereign is female) evidence given for the Crown against his or her former associates in crime by an accomplice (esp in the phrase **turn queen's evidence**). US equivalent: state's evidence

Queen's Guide *n* (in Britain and the Commonwealth when the sovereign is female) a Guide who has passed the highest tests of proficiency

queen's highway *n* **1** (in Britain when the sovereign is female) any public road or right of way **2** (in Canada) a main road maintained by the provincial government

queen-size *or* **queen-sized** *adj* (of a bed, etc) larger or longer than normal size but smaller or shorter than king-size

Queensland ('kwi:nz,lænd, -lənd) *n* a state of NE Australia: fringed on the Pacific side by the Great Barrier Reef; the Great Dividing Range lies in the east, separating the coastal lowlands from the dry Great Artesian Basin in the south. Capital: Brisbane. Pop: 3 840 111 (2003 est). Area: 1 727 500 sq km (667 000 sq miles) ▷ Queenslander ('kwi:nz,lændə, -ləndə) *n*

Queensland nut *n* another name for **macadamia**

Queen's Scout *n* (in Britain and the Commonwealth when the sovereign is female) a Scout who has passed the highest tests of endurance, proficiency, and skill. US equivalent: Eagle Scout

queer (kwɪə) *adj* **1** differing from the normal or usual in a way regarded as odd or strange **2** suspicious, dubious, or shady **3** faint, giddy, or queasy **4** *informal, highly offensive* homosexual **5** *informal* odd or unbalanced mentally; eccentric or slightly mad **6** *slang* worthless or counterfeit ▷ *n* **7** *informal, highly offensive* a homosexual, usually a male ▷ *vb* (*tr*) *informal* **8** to spoil or thwart (esp in the phrase **queer someone's pitch**) **9** to put in a difficult or dangerous position [c16: perhaps from German *quer* oblique, ultimately from Old High German *twērh*] ▷ 'queerly *adv* > 'queerness *n*

● **USAGE** Although the term *queer* meaning homosexual
● is still considered highly offensive when used by non-
● homosexuals, it is often used by homosexuals
● themselves as a positive term, as in *queer politics, queer*
● *cinema*

queer fish *n Brit informal* an eccentric or odd person

queer street *n* (sometimes capitals) *informal* a difficult situation, such as debt or bankruptcy (in the phrase **in queer street**)

quell (kwɛl) *vb* (*tr*) **1** to suppress or beat down (rebellion, disorder, etc); subdue **2** to overcome or allay [Old English *cwellan* to kill; related to Old Saxon *quellian*, Old High German *quellen*, Old Norse *kvelja* to torment] ▷ 'queller *n*

Quelpart ('kwɛl,pɑːt) *n* a former name of **Cheju**

Quemoy (kɛ'mɔɪ) *n* an island in Formosa Strait, off the SE coast of China: administratively part of Taiwan. Pop (with associated islets): 80 000 (latest est). Area: 130 sq km (50 sq miles)

quench (kwɛntʃ) *vb* (*tr*) **1** to satisfy (one's thirst, desires, etc); slake **2** to put out (a fire, flame, etc); extinguish **3** to put down or quell; suppress **4** to cool (hot metal) by plunging it into cold water [Old English *ācwencan* to extinguish; related to Old Frisian *quinka* to vanish] > **'quenchable** *adj* > **'quencher** *n*

Queneau (*French* kəno) *n* **Raymond** (rɛmɔ̃). 1903–76. French writer, influenced in the 1920s by surrealism. His novels include *Zazie dans le métro* (1959)

quenelle (kə'nɛl) *n* a finely sieved mixture of cooked meat or fish, shaped into various forms and cooked in stock or fried as croquettes [C19: from French, from German *Knödel* dumpling, from Old High German *knodo* knot]

Quercia (*Italian* 'kwɛrtʃa) *n* **Jacopo della**. See **Jacopo della Quercia**

Querétaro (*Spanish* ke'retaro) *n* **1** an inland state of central Mexico: economy based on agriculture and mining. Capital: Querétaro. Pop: 1 402 010 (2000). Area: 11 769 sq km (4544 sq miles) **2** a city in central Mexico, capital of Querétaro state: scene of the signing (1848) of the treaty ending the US-Mexican War and of the execution of Emperor Maximilian (1867). Pop: 913 000 (2005 est)

querist ('kwɪərɪst) *n* a person who makes inquiries or queries; questioner

quern (kwɜːn) *n* a stone hand mill for grinding corn [Old English *cweorn*; related to Old Frisian *quern*, Old High German *kurn*, Old Norse *kverna*, Gothic *quairnus* millstone]

quernstone ('kwɜːn,stəun) *n* **1** another name for **millstone** (sense 1) **2** one of the two small circular stones used in a quern

querulous ('kwɛrʊləs, 'kwɛrjʊ-) *adj* **1** inclined to make whining or peevish complaints **2** characterized by or proceeding from a complaining fretful attitude or disposition [C15: from Latin *querulus* from *querī* to complain] > **'querulously** *adv* > **'querulousness** *n*

query ('kwɪərɪ) *n*, *pl* **-ries 1** a question, esp one expressing doubt, uncertainty, or an objection **2** a less common name for **question mark** ▷ *vb* **-ries, -rying, -ried** (*tr*) **3** to express uncertainty, doubt, or an objection concerning (something) **4** to express as a query **5** *US* to put a question to (a person); ask [C17: from earlier *quere*, from Latin *quaere* ask!, from *quaerere* to seek, inquire]

query language *n computing* the instructions and procedures used to retrieve information from a database

quesadilla (,keɪsə'diːljə, -'diːjə) *n* a toasted tortilla filled with cheese and sometimes other ingredients [C21: from Spanish, diminutive of *queso* cheese]

Quesnay (*French* kɛnɛ) *n* **François** (frɑ̃swa). 1694–1774, French political economist, encyclopedist, and physician. He propounded the theory championed by the physiocrats in his *Tableau économique* (1758)

quest (kwɛst) *n* **1** the act or an instance of looking for or seeking; search **2** (in medieval romance) an expedition by a knight or company of knights to accomplish some prescribed task, such as finding the Holy Grail **3** the object of a search; goal or target ▷ *vb* (*mainly intr*) **4** (foll by *for* or *after*) to go in search (of) **5** (of gun dogs or hounds) to search for game **6** (*also tr*) *archaic* to go in search of (a thing); seek or pursue [C14: from Old French *queste*, from Latin *quaesita* sought, from *quaerere* to seek] > **'quester** *n* > **'questingly** *adv*

question ('kwɛstʃən) *n* **1** a form of words addressed to a person in order to elicit information or evoke a response; interrogative sentence **2** a point at issue: *it's only a question of time until she dies; the question is how long they can keep up the pressure* **3** a difficulty or uncertainty; doubtful point **4 a** an act of asking **b** an investigation into some problem or difficulty **5** a motion presented for debate by a deliberative body **6** put the question to require members of a deliberative assembly to vote on a motion presented **7** *law* a matter submitted to a court or other tribunal for judicial or quasi-judicial decision **8** beyond (all) question beyond (any) dispute or doubt **9** call in or into question **a** to make (something) the subject of disagreement **b** to cast doubt upon the validity, truth, etc, of (something) **10** in question under discussion: *this is the man in question* **11** out of the question beyond

consideration; unthinkable or impossible ▷ *vb* (*mainly tr*) **12** to put a question or questions to (a person); interrogate **13** to make (something) the subject of dispute or disagreement **14** to express uncertainty about the validity, truth, etc, of (something); doubt [C13: via Old French from Latin *quaestiō*, from *quaerere* to seek] > **'questioner** *n*

questionable ('kwɛstʃənəbᵊl) *adj* **1** (esp of a person's morality or honesty) admitting of some doubt; dubious **2** of disputable value or authority > **'questionableness** or ˌquestiona'bility *n* > **'questionably** *adv*

questioning ('kwɛstʃənɪŋ) *adj* **1** proceeding from or characterized by a feeling of doubt or uncertainty **2** enthusiastic or eager for philosophical or other investigations; intellectually stimulated: *an alert and questioning mind* > **'questioningly** *adv*

questionless ('kwɛstʃənlɪs) *adj* **1** blindly adhering, as to a principle or course of action; unquestioning **2** a less common word for **unquestionable** > **'questionlessly** *adv*

question mark *n* **1** the punctuation mark ?, used at the end of questions and in other contexts where doubt or ignorance is implied **2** this mark used for any other purpose, as to draw attention to a possible mistake, as in a chess commentary

question master *n Brit* the chairman of a quiz or panel game

questionnaire (,kwɛstʃə'nɛə, ,kɛs-) *n* a set of questions on a form, submitted to a number of people in order to collect statistical information [C20: from French, from *questionner* to ask questions]

question time *n* (in parliamentary bodies of the British type) a period of time set aside each day for members to question government ministers

Quetta ('kwɛtə) *n* a city in W central Pakistan, at an altitude of 1650 m (5500 ft): a summer resort, military station, and trading centre. Pop: 744 000 (2005 est)

quetzal ('kɛtsəl) or **quezal** (kɛ'saːl) *n*, *pl* **-zals** or **-zales** (-'saːlɛs) **1** Also called: resplendent trogon a crested bird, *Pharomachrus mocinno*, of Central and N South America, which has a brilliant green, red, and white plumage and, in the male, long tail feathers: family *Trogonidae*, order *Trogoniformes* (trogons) **2** the standard monetary unit of Guatemala, divided into 100 centavos [via American Spanish from Nahuatl *quetzalli* brightly coloured tail feather]

Quetzalcoatl (,kɛtsəlkəu'ætᵊl) *n* a god of the Aztecs and Toltecs, represented as a feathered serpent

queue (kjuː) *chiefly Brit* ▷ *n* **1** a line of people, vehicles, etc, waiting for something **2** *computing* a list in which entries are deleted from one end and inserted at the other **3** a pigtail ▷ *vb* **queues, queuing** or **queueing, queued 4** (*intr*; often foll by *up*) to form or remain in a line while waiting **5** *computing* to arrange (a number of programs) in a predetermined order for accessing by a computer ▷ *US and Canadian word*: line [C16 (in the sense: tail); C18 (in the sense: pigtail): via French from Latin *cauda* tail]

queue-jump *vb* (*intr*) **1** to take a place in a queue ahead of those already queuing; push in **2** to obtain prior consideration or some other advantage out of turn or unfairly > **queue-jumper** *n*

Quevedo y Villegas (kɛ'veɪðəui: vɪl'jeɪgæs) *n* **Francisco Gómez de**. 1580–1645, Spanish poet and writer, noted for his satires and the picaresque novel *La historia de la vida del Buscón* (1626)

Quezon City ('keɪzɒn) *n* a city in the Philippines, on central Luzon adjoining Manila: capital of the Philippines from 1948 to 1976; seat of the University of the Philippines (1908). Pop: 2 173 831 (2000)

Quezon y Molina ('keɪzɒn iː mɒ'liːnɑ; *Spanish* ke'θon i mo'lina) *n* **Manuel Luis** (ma'nwɛl lwis). 1878–1944, Philippine statesman: first president of the Philippines (from 1935) and head of the government in exile after the Japanese conquest of the islands in World War II

quibble ('kwɪbᵊl) *vb* (*intr*) **1** to make trivial objections; prevaricate **2** *archaic* to play on words; pun ▷ *n* **3** a trivial objection or equivocation, esp one used to avoid an issue **4** *archaic* a pun [C17: probably from obsolete *quib*, perhaps from Latin *quibus* (from *quī* who, which), as used in legal

documents, with reference to their obscure phraseology]
> 'quibbler *n* > 'quibbling *adj, n*

Quiberon (*French* kibrɔ̃) *n* a peninsula of NW France, on the S coast of Brittany: a naval battle was fought off its coast in 1759 during the Seven Years' War, in which the British defeated the French

quiche (kiːʃ) *n* an open savoury tart with a rich custard filling to which bacon, onion, cheese, etc, are added [*French*, from German *Kuchen* cake]

quick (kwɪk) *adj* **1** (of an action, movement, etc) performed or occurring during a comparatively short time: *a quick move* **2** lasting a comparatively short time; brief **3** accomplishing something in a time that is shorter than normal: *a quick worker* **4** characterized by rapidity of movement; swift or fast **5** immediate or prompt **6** (*postpositive*) eager or ready to perform (an action): *quick to criticize* **7** responsive to stimulation; perceptive or alert; lively **8** eager or enthusiastic for learning **9** easily excited or aroused **10** skilfully swift or nimble in one's movements or actions; deft: *quick fingers* **11** *archaic* **a** alive; living **b** (*as noun*) living people (esp in the phrase **the quick and the dead**) **12** quick with child *archaic* pregnant, esp being in an advanced state of pregnancy, when the movements of the fetus can be felt ▷ *n* **13** any area of living flesh that is highly sensitive to pain or touch, esp that under a toenail or fingernail or around a healing wound **14** the vital or most important part (of a thing) **15** cut someone to the quick to hurt someone's feelings deeply; offend gravely ▷ *adv informal* **16** in a rapid or speedy manner; swiftly **17** soon: *I hope he comes quick* **18** a command requiring the hearer to perform an action immediately or in as short a time as possible [Old English *cwicu* living; related to Old Saxon *quik*, Old High German *queck*, Old Norse *kvikr* alive, Latin *vīvus* alive, Greek *bios* life] > 'quickly *adv* > 'quickness *n*

quick-change artist *n* an actor or entertainer who undertakes several rapid changes of costume during his performance

quicken ('kwɪkən) *vb* **1** to make or become faster; accelerate **2** to impart to or receive vigour, enthusiasm, etc; stimulate or be stimulated: *science quickens man's imagination* **3** to make or become alive; revive **4 a** (of an unborn fetus) to begin to show signs of life **b** (of a pregnant woman) to reach the stage of pregnancy at which movements of the fetus can be felt

quick-freeze *vb* -freezes, -freezing, -froze, -frozen (*tr*) to preserve (food) by subjecting it to rapid refrigeration at temperatures of 0°C or lower

quickie ('kwɪkɪ) *n informal* **1** Also called (esp Brit): **quick one** a speedily consumed alcoholic drink **2 a** anything made, done, produced, or consumed rapidly or in haste **b** (*as modifier*): *a quickie divorce; a quickie ceremony*

quicklime ('kwɪk,laɪm) *n* another name for **calcium oxide** [c15: from QUICK (in the archaic sense: living) + LIME¹]

quick march *n* **1** a march at quick time or the order to proceed at such a pace ▷ *interj* **2** a command to commence such a march

quicksand ('kwɪk,sænd) *n* a deep mass of loose wet sand that submerges anything on top of it

quickset ('kwɪk,sɛt) *chiefly Brit* ▷ *n* **1 a** a plant or cutting, esp of hawthorn, set so as to form a hedge **b** such plants or cuttings collectively **2** a hedge composed of such plants ▷ *adj* **3** composed of such plants [c15: from *quick* in the archaic sense live, growing + *set* to plant, set in the ground]

quicksilver ('kwɪk,sɪlvə) *n* **1** another name for **mercury** (sense 1) ▷ *adj* **2** rapid or unpredictable in movement or change [Old English, from *cwicu* alive (see QUICK) + *seolfor* silver]

quickstep ('kwɪk,stɛp) *n* **1** a modern ballroom dance in rapid quadruple time **2** a piece of music composed for or in the rhythm of this dance ▷ *vb* -steps, -stepping, -stepped **3** (*intr*) to perform this dance

quick-tempered *adj* readily roused to anger; irascible

quickthorn ('kwɪk,θɔːn) *n* hawthorn, esp when planted as a hedge [c17: probably from *quick* in the sense "fast-growing": compare QUICKSET]

quick time *n military* the normal marching rate of 120 paces to the minute

quick-witted *adj* having a keenly alert mind, esp as used to avert danger, make effective reply, etc > ,quick-'wittedly *adv* > ,quick-'wittedness *n*

quid¹ (kwɪd) *n* a piece of tobacco, suitable for chewing [Old English *cwidu* chewing resin; related to Old High German *quiti* glue, Old Norse *kvātha* resin; see CUD]

quid² (kwɪd) *n, pl* quid *Brit slang* **1** one pound sterling **2** quids in in a very favourable or advantageous position [c17: of obscure origin]

quidditch ('kwɪdɪtʃ) *n* an imaginary game in which players fly on broomsticks [c20: coined by the British novelist J.K. Rowling (born 1965) in the novel *Harry Potter and the Philosopher's Stone*]

quiddity ('kwɪdɪtɪ) *n, pl* -ties **1** *philosophy* the essential nature of something **2** a petty or trifling distinction; quibble [c16: from Medieval Latin *quidditās*, from Latin *quid* what]

quidnunc ('kwɪd,nʌŋk) *n* a person eager to learn news and scandal; gossipmonger [c18: from Latin, literally: what now]

quid pro quo ('kwɪd prəʊ 'kwəʊ) *n, pl* quid pro quos **1** a reciprocal exchange **2** something given in compensation, esp an advantage or object given in exchange for another [c16: from Latin: something for something]

quiescent (kwɪ'ɛsᵊnt) *adj* quiet, inactive, or dormant [c17: from Latin *quiescere* to rest] > qui'escence or qui'escency *n* > qui'escently *adv*

quiet ('kwaɪət) *adj* **1** characterized by an absence or near absence of noise **2** characterized by an absence of turbulent motion or disturbance; peaceful, calm, or tranquil: *a quiet glade; the sea is quiet tonight* **3** free from activities, distractions, worries, etc; untroubled: *a quiet life; a quiet day at work* **4** marked by an absence of work, orders, etc; not busy: *the factory is very quiet at the moment* **5** private; not public; secret: *a quiet word with someone* **6** free from anger, impatience, or other extreme emotion **7** free from pretentiousness or vain display; modest or reserved: *quiet humour* **8** *astronomy* (of the sun) exhibiting a very low number of sunspots, solar flares, and other surface phenomena; inactive ▷ *n* **9** the state of being silent, peaceful, or untroubled **10** on the quiet without other people knowing; secretly ▷ *vb* **11** a less common word for **quieten** [c14: from Latin *quiētus*, past participle of *quiēscere* to rest, from *quiēs* repose, rest] > 'quietness *n*

quieten ('kwaɪətᵊn) *vb chiefly Brit* **1** (often foll by *down*) to make or become calm, silent, etc; pacify or become peaceful **2** (*tr*) to allay (fear, doubts, etc)

quietism ('kwaɪə,tɪzəm) *n* **1** a form of religious mysticism originating in Spain in the late 17th century, requiring withdrawal of the spirit from all human effort and complete passivity to God's will **2** a state of passivity and calmness of mind towards external events > 'quietist *n, adj*

quietly ('kwaɪətlɪ) *adv* **1** in a quiet manner **2** just quietly *Austral* between you and me; confidentially

quietude ('kwaɪə,tjuːd) *n* the state or condition of being quiet, peaceful, calm, or tranquil

quietus (kwaɪ'iːtəs, -'eɪtəs) *n, pl* -tuses **1** anything that serves to quash, eliminate, or kill **2** a release from life; death **3** the discharge or settlement of debts, duties, etc [c16: from Latin *quiētus est*, literally: he is at rest, QUIET]

quiff (kwɪf) *n Brit* a prominent tuft of hair, esp one brushed up above the forehead [c19: of unknown origin]

quill (kwɪl) *n* **1 a** any of the large stiff feathers of the wing or tail of a bird **b** the hollow central part of a bird's feather; calamus **2** a bird's feather made into a pen for writing **3** any of the stiff hollow spines of a porcupine or hedgehog **4** a device, formerly usually made from a crow quill, for plucking a harpsichord string **5** a small roll of bark, esp one of dried cinnamon **6** (in weaving) a bobbin or spindle **7** a fluted fold, as in a ruff ▷ *vb* (*tr*) **8** to wind (thread, yarn, etc) onto a spool or bobbin **9** to make or press fluted folds in (a ruff) [c15 (in the sense: hollow reed or pipe): of uncertain origin; compare Middle Low German *quiele* quill]

Quiller-Couch (,kwɪlə'kuːtʃ) *n* Sir Arthur (Thomas), known as Q. 1863–1944, British critic and novelist, who

q

edited the *Oxford Book of English Verse* (1900)

Quilmes (*Spanish* 'kilmes) *n* a city in E Argentina: a resort and suburb of Buenos Aires. Pop: 518 788 (2001)

quilt (kwɪlt) *n* **1** a thick warm cover for a bed, consisting of a soft filling sewn between two layers of material, usually with crisscross seams **2** a bedspread or counterpane **3** anything quilted or resembling a quilt ▷ *vb* (*tr*) **4** to stitch together (two pieces of fabric) with (a thick padding or lining) between them **5** to create (a garment, covering, etc) in this way **6** to pad with material [c13: from Old French *coilte* mattress, from Latin *culcita* stuffed item of bedding] > 'quilter *n*

quilting ('kwɪltɪŋ) *n* **1** material used for making a quilt **2** the act or process of making a quilt **3** quilted work

Quimper (*French* kɛ̃pɛr) *n* a city in NW France: capital of Finistère department. Pop: 63 238 (1999)

quin (kwɪn) *n Brit* short for **quintuplet** (sense 2) US and Canadian word: **quint**

quinary ('kwaɪnərɪ) *adj* **1** consisting of fives or by fives **2** fifth in a series **3** (of a number system) having a base of five [c17: from Latin *quīnārius* containing five, from *quīnī* five each]

quince (kwɪns) *n* **1** a small widely cultivated Asian rosaceous tree, *Cydonia oblonga*, with pinkish-white flowers and edible pear-shaped fruits **2** the acid-tasting fruit of this tree, much used in preserves **3 Japanese** or **flowering quince**. another name for **japonica** [c14 *quince* plural of *quyn* quince, from Old French *coin*, from Latin *cotōneum*, from Greek *kudōnion* quince, Cydonian (apple)]

quincentenary (ˌkwɪnsɛn'tiːnərɪ) *n*, *pl* -naries a 500th anniversary or the year or celebration marking it [c19: irregularly from Latin *quinque* five + CENTENARY] > quincentennial (ˌkwɪnsɛn'tɛnɪəl) *adj*, *n*

quincunx ('kwɪnkʌŋks) *n* a group of five objects arranged in the shape of a rectangle with one at each of the four corners and the fifth in the centre [c17: from Latin: five twelfths, from *quinque* five + *uncia* twelfth; in ancient Rome, this was a coin worth five twelfths of an AS² and marked with five spots] > quincuncial (kwɪn'kʌnʃəl) *adj* > quin'cuncially *adv*

Quine (kwaɪn) *n* **Willard van Orman**. 1908–2000, US philosopher. His works include *Word and Object* (1960), *Philosophy of Logic* (1970), *The Roots of Reference* (1973), and *The Logic of Sequences* (1990)

quinella (kwɪ'nɛlə) *n Austral & NZ* a form of betting on a horse race in which the punter bets on selecting the first and second place-winners in any order [from American Spanish *quiniela* a game of chance]

Qui Nhong ('kwiː 'njɒŋ) *n* a port in SE Vietnam, on the South China Sea. Pop: 163 385 (1992 est)

quinidine ('kwɪnɪˌdiːn) *n* a crystalline alkaloid drug that is an optically active diastereoisomer of quinine: used to treat heart arrhythmias. Formula: $C_{20}H_{24}N_2O_2$

quinine (kwɪ'niːn; *US* 'kwaɪnaɪn) *n* a bitter crystalline alkaloid extracted from cinchona bark, the salts of which are used as a tonic, antipyretic, analgesic, etc, and in malaria therapy. Formula: $C_{20}H_{24}N_2O_2$ [c19: from Spanish *quina* cinchona bark, from Quechua *kina* bark]

Quinn (kwɪn) *n* **Anthony**. 1915–2001, US film actor, born in Mexico: noted esp for his performances in *La Strada* (1954) and *Zorba the Greek* (1964)

quinoa ('kiːnəʊə, kwɪ'nəʊə) *n* a grain high in nutrients traditionally grown as a staple food high in the Andes [Spanish]

quinol ('kwɪnɒl) *n* another name for **hydroquinone**

quinoline ('kwɪnəˌliːn, -lɪn) *n* an oily colourless insoluble basic heterocyclic compound synthesized by heating aniline, nitrobenzene, glycerol, and sulphuric acid: used as a food preservative and in the manufacture of dyes and antiseptics. Formula: C_9H_7N

quinquagenarian (ˌkwɪŋkwədʒɪ'nɛərɪən) *n* **1** a person between 50 and 59 years old ▷ *adj* **2** being between 50 and 59 years old **3** of or relating to a quinquagenarian [c16: from Latin *quīnquāgēnārius* containing fifty, from *quīnquāgēnī* fifty each]

Quinquagesima (ˌkwɪŋkwə'dʒɛsɪmə) *n* the Sunday preceding Ash Wednesday, the beginning of Lent. Also called: **Quinquagesima Sunday** [c14: via Medieval Latin from Latin *quīnquāgēsima diēs* fiftieth day]

quinque- *combining form* five: *quinquevalent* [from Latin *quinque*]

quinquecentenary (ˌkwɪŋkwɪsɛn'tiːnərɪ) *n*, *pl* -naries another name for **quincentenary**

quinquennial (kwɪn'kwɛnɪəl) *adj* **1** occurring once every five years or over a period of five years ▷ *n* **2** a fifth anniversary > quin'quennially *adv*

quinquennium (kwɪn'kwɛnɪəm) *n*, *pl* -nia (-nɪə) a period or cycle of five years [c17: from Latin *quinque* five + *annus* year]

quinquereme (ˌkwɪŋkwɪ'riːm) *n* an ancient Roman galley with five banks of oars on each side [c16: from Latin *quinquerēmis*, from QUINQUE- + *rēmus* oar]

quinquevalent (ˌkwɪŋkwɪ'veɪlənt, kwɪn'kwɛvələnt) *adj chem* another word for **pentavalent** > ˌquinque'valency or quinquevalence (ˌkwɪŋkwɪ'veɪləns, kwɪn'kwɛvələns) *n*

quinsy ('kwɪnzɪ) *n* inflammation of the tonsils and surrounding tissues with the formation of abscesses [c14: via Old French and Medieval Latin from Greek *kunankhē*, from *kuōn* dog + *ankhein* to strangle]

quint¹ (kwɪnt) *n* **1** an organ stop sounding a note a fifth higher than that normally produced by the key depressed **2** (kɪnt) *piquet* a sequence of five cards in the same suit [c17: from French *quinte*, from Latin *quintus* fifth]

quint² (kwɪnt) *n US & Canadian* short for **quintuplets**. Also called (in Britain and certain other countries): **quin**

quintain ('kwɪntɪn) *n* (esp in medieval Europe) a post or target set up for tilting exercises for mounted knights or foot soldiers [c14: from Old French *quintaine*, from Latin: street in a Roman camp between the fifth and sixth maniples, from *quintus* fifth]

quintal ('kwɪnt³l) *n* **1** a unit of weight equal to 100 pounds **2** a unit of weight equal to 100 kilograms [c15: via Old French from Arabic *qintār*, possibly from Latin *centēnārius* consisting of a hundred]

quintan ('kwɪntən) *adj* (of a fever) occurring every fourth day [c17: from Latin *febris quintāna* fever occurring every fifth day, reckoned inclusively]

Quintana Roo (*Spanish* kin'tana 'rɔɔ) *n* a state of SE Mexico, on the E Yucatán Peninsula: hot, humid, forested, and inhabited chiefly by Maya Indians. Capital: Chetumal. Pop: 287 000 (2005 est). Area: 50 350 sq km (19 463 sq miles)

quinte *French* (kɛ̃t) *n* the fifth of eight basic positions from which a parry or attack can be made in fencing [c18: French, from Latin *quinta*, fem of *quintus* fifth, from *quinque* five]

quintessence (kwɪn'tɛsəns) *n* **1** the most typical representation of a quality, state, etc **2** an extract of a substance containing its principle in its most concentrated form **3** (in ancient and medieval philosophy) ether, the fifth and highest essence or element after earth, water, air, and fire, which was thought to be the constituent matter of the heavenly bodies and latent in all things [c15: via French from Medieval Latin *quinta essentia* the fifth essence, translation of Greek *pemptē ousia*] > quintessential (ˌkwɪntɪ'sɛnʃəl) *adj* > ˌquintes'sentially *adv*

quintet or **quintette** (kwɪn'tɛt) *n* **1** a group of five singers or instrumentalists or a piece of music composed for such a group **2** any group of five [c19: from Italian *quintetto*, from *quinto* fifth]

Quintilian (kwɪn'tɪljən) *n* Latin name *Marcus Fabius Quintilianus*. ?35–?96 AD, Roman rhetorician and teacher

quintillion (kwɪn'tɪljən) *n*, *pl* -lions or -lion **1** (in Britain, France, and Germany) the number represented as one followed by 30 zeros (10³⁰). US and Canadian word: **nonillion 2** (in the US and Canada) the number represented as one followed by 18 zeros (10¹⁸). Former Brit word: trillion [c17: from Latin *quintus* fifth + -*illion*, as in MILLION] > quin'tillionth *adj*

quintuple ('kwɪntjʊp³l, kwɪn'tjuːp³l) *vb* **1** to multiply by five ▷ *adj* **2** five times as much or as many; fivefold **3** consisting of five parts ▷ *n* **4** a quantity or number five times as great as another [c16: from French, from Latin *quintus*, on the model of QUADRUPLE]

quintuplet ('kwɪntjʊplɪt, kwɪn'tjuːplɪt) *n* **1** a group or set of five similar things **2** one of five offspring born at one birth **3** *music* a group of five notes to be played in a time value of three, four, or some other value

quintuplicate *adj* (kwɪn'tjuːplɪkɪt) **1** fivefold or quintuple ▷ *vb* (kwɪn'tjuːplɪˌkeɪt) **2** to multiply or be multiplied by five ▷ *n* (kwɪn'tjuːplɪkɪt) **3** a group or set of five things

quip (kwɪp) *n* **1** a sarcastic or cutting remark; gibe **2** a witty or clever saying **3** *archaic* another word for **quibble** ▷ *vb* quips, quipping, quipped **4** (*intr*) to make a quip [c16: from earlier *quippy*, probably from Latin *quippe* indeed, to be sure]

quire (kwaɪə) *n* **1** a set of 24 or 25 sheets of paper; a twentieth of a ream **2** four sheets of paper folded once to form a section of 16 pages **3** a set of all the sheets in a book [c15 *quayer*, from Old French *quaier*, from Latin *quaternī* four at a time, from *quater* four times]

Quirinal ('kwɪrɪnəl) *n* one of the seven hills on which ancient Rome was built

Quirinus (kwɪ'raɪnəs) *n Roman myth* a god of war, who came to be identified with the deified Romulus

quirk (kwɜːk) *n* **1** an individual peculiarity of character; mannerism or foible **2** an unexpected twist or turn: *a quirk of fate* **3** a continuous groove in an architectural moulding **4** a flourish, as in handwriting [c16: of unknown origin] > 'quirky *adj* > 'quirkiness *n*

quirt (kwɜːt) *US & South African* ▷ *n* **1** a whip with a leather thong at one end ▷ *vb* (*tr*) **2** to strike with a quirt [c19: from Spanish *cuerda* CORD]

quisling ('kwɪzlɪŋ) *n* a traitor who aids an occupying enemy force; collaborator [c20: after Major Vidkun *Quisling* (1887–1945), Norwegian collaborator with the Nazis]

quit (kwɪt) *vb* quits, quitting, quitted *or chiefly US* quit **1** (*tr*) to depart from; leave **2** to resign; give up (a job) **3** (*intr*) (of a tenant) to give up occupancy of premises and leave them **4** to desist or cease from (something or doing something); break off **5** (*tr*) to pay off (a debt); discharge or settle **6** (*tr*) *archaic* to conduct or acquit (oneself); comport (oneself) ▷ *adj* **7** (*usually predicative*; foll by *of*) free (from); released (from) [c13: from Old French *quitter*, from Latin *quiētus* QUIET; see QUIETUS]

quitch grass (kwɪtʃ) *n* another name for **couch grass**. Sometimes shortened to: **quitch** [Old English *cwice*; perhaps related to *cwicu* living, QUICK (with the implication that the grass cannot be killed); compare Dutch *kweek*, Norwegian *kvike*, German *Queckengras*]

quitclaim ('kwɪtˌkleɪm) *law* ▷ *n* **1** a formal renunciation of any claim against a person or of a right to land ▷ *vb* **2** (*tr*) to renounce (a claim) formally [c14: from Anglo-French *quiteclame*, from *quite* QUIT + *clamer* to declare (from Latin *clamāre* to shout)]

quite (kwaɪt) *adv* **1** to the greatest extent; completely or absolutely: *you're quite right; quite the opposite* **2** (*not used with a negative*) to a noticeable or partial extent; somewhat: *she's quite pretty* **3** in actuality; truly **4** quite a (*not used with a negative*) of an exceptional, considerable, or noticeable kind: *quite a girl; quite a long walk* **5** quite something a remarkable or noteworthy thing or person ▷ *sentence substitute* **6** Also: quite so an expression used to indicate agreement or assent [c14: adverbial use of *quite* (adj) QUIT]

◉ USAGE See at **very**

Quito ('kiːtəʊ; *Spanish* 'kito) *n* the capital of Ecuador, in the north at an altitude of 2850 m (9350 ft), just south of the equator: the oldest capital in South America, existing many centuries before the Incan conquest in 1487; a cultural centre since the beginning of Spanish rule (1534); two universities. Pop: 1 514 000 (2005 est)

quitrent ('kwɪtˌrent) *n* (formerly) a rent payable by a freeholder or copyholder to his lord that released him from liability to perform services

quits (kwɪts) *adj* (*postpositive*) *informal* **1** on an equal footing; even **2** call it quits to agree to end a dispute, contest, etc, agreeing that honours are even

quittance ('kwɪtəns) *n* **1** release from debt or other obligation **2** a receipt or other document certifying this [c13: from Old French, from *quitter* to release from obligation; see QUIT]

quitter ('kwɪtə) *n* a person who gives up easily;

defeatist, deserter, or shirker

quiver¹ ('kwɪvə) *vb* **1** (*intr*) to shake with a rapid tremulous movement; tremble ▷ *n* **2** the state, process, or noise of shaking or trembling [c15: from obsolete *cwiver* quick, nimble; compare QUAVER] > 'quivering *adj* > 'quivery *adj*

quiver² ('kwɪvə) *n* a case for arrows [c13: from Old French *cuivre*; related to Old English *cocer*, Old Saxon *kokari*, Old High German *kohhari*, Medieval Latin *cucurum*]

qui vive (ˌkiː 'viːv) *n* on the qui vive on the alert; attentive [c18: from French, literally: long live who?, sentry's challenge (equivalent to "To whose party do you belong?" or "Whose side do you support?")]

Quixote ('kwɪksət; *Spanish* ki'xote) *n* See **Don Quixote**

quixotic (kwɪk'sɒtɪk) *adj* preoccupied with an unrealistically optimistic or chivalrous approach to life; impractically idealistic [c18: after DON QUIXOTE] > quix'otically *adv*

quiz (kwɪz) *n, pl* quizzes **1 a** an entertainment in which the general or specific knowledge of the players is tested by a series of questions, esp as a radio or television programme **b** (*as modifier*): *a quiz programme* **2** any set of quick questions designed to test knowledge **3** an investigation by close questioning; interrogation **4** *obsolete* a practical joke; hoax **5** *obsolete* a puzzling or eccentric individual **6** *obsolete* a person who habitually looks quizzically at others, esp through a small monocle ▷ *vb* quizzes, quizzing, quizzed (*tr*) **7** to investigate by close questioning; interrogate **8** *US & Canadian informal* to test or examine the knowledge of (a student or class) **9** (*tr*) *obsolete* to look quizzically at, esp through a small monocle [c18: of unknown origin] > 'quizzer *n*

quizzical ('kwɪzɪkəl) *adj* questioning and mocking or supercilious > 'quizzically *adv*

Qum (kʊm) *n* a variant of **Qom**

Qumran ('kʊmrɑːn) *n* See **Khirbet Qumran**

Qungur ('kʊŋɡʊə) *n* a variant transliteration of the Chinese name for **Kongur Shan**

quod (kwɒd) *n chiefly Brit* a slang word for **jail** [c18: of uncertain origin; perhaps changed from *quad*, short for *quadrangle*]

quod erat demonstrandum (*Latin* 'kwɒd 'ɛræt ˌdɛmən'strændʊm) (at the conclusion of a proof, esp of a theorem in Euclidean geometry) which was to be proved. Abbreviation: QED

quodlibet ('kwɒdlɪˌbɛt) *n* **1** a light piece of music based on two or more popular tunes **2** a subtle argument, esp one prepared as an exercise on a theological topic [c14: from Latin, from *quod* what + *libet* pleases, that is, whatever you like]

quoin, coign *or* **coigne** (kwɔɪn, kɔɪn) *n* **1** an external corner of a wall **2** Also called: cornerstone a stone forming the external corner of a wall **3** another name for **keystone** (sense 1) **4** *printing* a metal or wooden wedge or an expanding mechanical device used to lock type up in a chase **5** a wedge used for any of various other purposes, such as (formerly) to adjust elevation in muzzle-loading cannon [c16: variant of COIN (corner)]

quoit (kɔɪt) *n* a ring of iron, plastic, rope, etc, used in the game of quoits [c15: of unknown origin]

quoits (kɔɪts) *pl n* (*usually functioning as singular*) a game in which quoits are tossed at a stake in the ground in attempts to encircle it

quokka ('kwɒkə) *n* a small wallaby, *Setonix brachyurus*, of Western Australia, occurring mostly on offshore islands [from a native Australian language]

quoll (kwɒl) *n Austral* another name for **native cat** [c18: from a native Australian language]

quondam ('kwɒndæm) *adj* (*prenominal*) of an earlier time; former [c16: from Latin adv: formerly]

quorate ('kwɔːˌreɪt) *adj Brit* constituting or having a quorum

Quorn (kwɔːn) *n trademark* a vegetable protein developed from a type of fungus and used in cooking as a meat substitute

quorum ('kwɔːrəm) *n* a minimum number of members in an assembly, society, board of directors, etc, required to be present before any valid business can be transacted [c15: from Latin, literally: of whom, occurring in Latin commissions in the formula *quorum vos...duos* (etc) *volumus* of whom we wish that you be...two]

quota ('kwəʊtə) *n* **1** the proportional share or part of a whole that is due from, due to, or allocated to a person or group **2** a prescribed number or quantity, as of items to be manufactured, imported, or exported, immigrants admitted to a country, or students admitted to a college [C17: from Latin *quota pars* how big a share?, from *quotus* of what number]

quotable ('kwəʊtəbᵊl) *adj* apt or suitable for quotation ▷ ˌquota'bility *n*

quota sampling *n* *marketing* a method of conducting marketing research in which the sample is selected according to a quota-system based on such factors as age, sex, social class, etc

quotation (kwəʊ'teɪʃən) *n* **1** a phrase or passage from a book, poem, play, etc, remembered and spoken, esp to illustrate succinctly or support a point or an argument **2** the act or habit of quoting from books, plays, poems, etc **3** *commerce* a statement of the current market price of a security or commodity **4** an estimate of costs submitted by a contractor to a prospective client; tender **5** *printing* a large block of type metal that is less than type-high and is used to fill up spaces in type pages

quotation mark *n* either of the punctuation marks used to begin or end a quotation, respectively " and " or ' and ' in English printing and writing. When double marks are used, single marks indicate a quotation within a quotation, and vice versa. Also called: **inverted comma**

quote (kwəʊt) *vb* **1** to recite a quotation (from a book, play, poem, etc), esp as a means of illustrating or supporting a statement **2** (*tr*) to put quotation marks round (a word, phrase, etc) **3** *stock exchange* to state (a current market price) of (a security or commodity) ▷ *n* **4** (*often plural*) an informal word for **quotation mark** ▷ *interj* **5** an expression used parenthetically to indicate that the words that follow it form a quotation [C14: from Medieval Latin *quotāre* to assign reference numbers to passages, from Latin *quot* how many]

quoted company *n* a company whose shares are quoted on a stock exchange

quote-driven *adj* denoting an electronic market system, esp for stock exchanges, in which prices are determined by quotations made by market makers or dealers. Compare **order-driven**

quote-unquote *interj* an expression used before or part before and part after a quotation to identify it as such, and sometimes to dissociate the writer or speaker from it

quoth (kwəʊθ) *vb archaic* (used with all pronouns except *thou* and *you*, and with nouns) another word for **said¹** (sense 2) [Old English *cwæth*, third person singular of *cwethan* to say; related to Old Frisian *quetha* to say, Old Saxon, Old High German *quethan*; see BEQUEATH]

quotha ('kwəʊθə) *interj archaic* an expression of mild sarcasm, used in picking up a word or phrase used by someone else [C16: from *quoth a* quoth he]

quotidian (kwəʊ'tɪdɪən) *adj* **1** (esp of attacks of malarial fever) recurring daily **2** everyday; commonplace ▷ *n* **3** a malarial fever characterized by attacks that recur daily [C14: from Latin *quotīdiānus*, variant of *cottīdiānus* daily]

quotient ('kwəʊʃənt) *n* **1 a** the result of the division of one number or quantity by another **b** the integral part of the result of division **2** a ratio of two numbers or quantities to be divided [C15: from Latin *quotiens* how often]

quo vadis ('kwəʊ 'vɑːdɪs) where are you going? [Latin: from the Vulgate version of John 16:5]

quo warranto ('kwəʊ wɒ'ræntəʊ) *n law* a proceeding initiated to determine or (formerly) a writ demanding by what authority a person claims an office, franchise, or privilege [from Medieval Latin: by what warrant]

Qu Qiu Bai ('tʃuː 'tʃjuː 'beɪ) *or* **Ch'ü Ch'iu-pai** *n* 1889–1935, Chinese communist leader who was also an important literary figure: executed by the Nationalist forces in Shanghai

Qur'an (kʊ'rɑːn, -'ræn) *n* a variant of **Koran**

qv *abbreviation* (denoting a cross reference) quod vide [New Latin: which (word, item, etc) see]

qwerty *or* **QWERTY keyboard** ('kwɜːtɪ) *n* the standard English language typewriter keyboard layout with the characters q, w, e, r, t, and y positioned on the top row of alphabetic characters at the left side of the keyboard

Rr

r or **R** (ɑː) *n*, *pl* **r's**, **R's** or **Rs** **1** the 18th letter and 14th consonant of the modern English alphabet **2** a speech sound represented by this letter, in English usually an alveolar semivowel, as in *red* **3** See **three Rs**

R *symbol for* **1** *chem* radical **2** *currency* **a** rand **b** rupee **3** Réaumur temperature (scale) **4** *physics, electronics* resistance **5** roentgen or röntgen **6** *chess* rook **7** Royal **8** *chem* gas constant **9** (in the US and Australia) **a** restricted exhibition (used to describe a category of film certified as unsuitable for viewing by anyone under the age of 18) **b** (*as modifier*): *an R film*

r. *abbreviation* **1** rare **2** recto **3** Also: **r** rod (unit of length) **4** ruled **5** *cricket, baseball* run(s)

R.¹ *abbreviation* **1** rabbi **2** rector **3** Regina [Latin: Queen] **4** Republican **5** response (in Christian liturgy) **6** Rex [Latin: King] **7** River **8** Royal

R.² or **r.** *abbreviation* **1** registered (trademark) **2** right **3** river **4** rouble

Ra¹ *the chemical symbol for* radium

Ra² (rɑː) or **Re** *n* the ancient Egyptian sun god, depicted as a man with a hawk's head surmounted by a solar disc and serpent

RA *abbreviation* **1** rear admiral **2** *astronomy* right ascension **3** (in Britain) Royal Academician *or* Academy **4** (in Britain) Royal Artillery

RAAF *abbreviation* Royal Australian Air Force

Rabat (rəˈbɑːt) *n* the capital of Morocco, in the northwest on the Atlantic coast, served by the port of Salé: became a military centre in the 12th century and a Corsair republic in the 17th century. Pop: 673 000 (2003)

Rabaul (rɑːˈbaʊl) *n* a port in Papua New Guinea, on NE New Britain Island, in the Bismarck Archipelago: capital of the Territory of New Guinea until 1941; almost surrounded by volcanoes. Pop: 17 855 (2001 est)

Rabbath Ammon (ˈræbəθ ˈæmən) *n Old Testament* the ancient royal city of the Ammonites, on the site of modern Amman

rabbet (ˈræbɪt) or **rebate** *n* **1** a recess, groove, or step, usually of rectangular section, cut into a surface or along the edge of a piece of timber to receive a mating piece ▷ *vb* (*tr*) **2** to cut or form a rabbet in (timber) **3** to join (pieces of timber) using a rabbet [c15: from Old French *rabattre* to beat down]

rabbi (ˈræbaɪ) *n*, *pl* **-bis** the religious leader of a congregation; the minister of a synagogue [Hebrew, from *rabh* master + *-ī* my]

rabbinate (ˈræbɪnɪt) *n* **1** the position, function, or tenure of office of a rabbi **2** rabbis collectively

rabbinic (rəˈbɪnɪk) or **rabbinical** *adj* of or relating to the rabbis, their teachings, writings, views, language, etc ▷ **rabˈbinically** *adv*

Rabbinic (rəˈbɪnɪk) *n* the form of the Hebrew language used by the rabbis of the Middle Ages

rabbit (ˈræbɪt) *n*, *pl* **-bits** or **-bit** **1** any of various common gregarious burrowing leporid mammals, esp *Oryctolagus cuniculus* of Europe and North Africa and the cottontail of America. They are closely related and similar to hares but are smaller and have shorter ears **2** the fur of such an animal **3** *Brit informal* a novice or poor performer at a game or sport ▷ *vb* **4** (*intr*) to hunt or shoot rabbits **5** (*intr*; often foll by *on* or *away*) *Brit informal* to talk inconsequentially; chatter [c14: perhaps from Walloon *robett*, diminutive of Flemish *robbe* rabbit, of obscure origin: c20 in sense 5, from rhyming slang *rabbit and pork* talk]

rabbit fever *n pathol* another name for **tularaemia**

rabbit punch *n* a sharp blow to the back of the neck that can cause loss of consciousness or even death. Austral name: **rabbit killer**

rabble (ˈræbəl) *n* **1** a disorderly crowd; mob **2** **the rabble** *contemptuous* the common people [c14 (in the sense: a pack of animals): of uncertain origin; perhaps related to Middle Dutch *rabbelen* to chatter, rattle]

rabble-rouser *n* a person who manipulates the passions of the mob; demagogue ▷ **ˈrabble-ˌrousing** *adj, n*

Rabelais (ˈræbəˌleɪ; *French* rablɛ) *n* **François** (frɑ̃swa). ?1494–1553, French writer. His written works, esp *Gargantua and Pantagruel* (1534), contain a lively mixture of earthy wit, common sense, and satire

Rabelaisian (ˌræbəˈleɪzɪən, -ʒən) *adj* **1** of, relating to, or resembling the work of François Rabelais, the French writer (?1494–1553), esp by broad, often bawdy humour and sharp satire ▷ *n* **2** a student or admirer of Rabelais ▷ **ˌRabeˈlaisianism** *n*

Rabi ('rɑːbɪ) *n* **Isidor Isaac**. 1898–1988, US physicist, born in Austria, who devised the atomic and molecular beam resonance method of observing atomic spectra. Nobel prize for physics 1944

Rabia *or* **Rabiah** ('rɑːbɪa) *n* full name *Rabia al-Adawiyyah*. c. 713–801 AD, Islamic saint, mystic, and religious leader; her teachings inspired the Sufi movement

rabid ('ræbɪd, 'reɪ-) *adj* **1** relating to or having rabies **2** zealous; fanatical; violent; raging [C17: from Latin *rabidus* frenzied, mad, from *rabere* to be mad] > **rabidity** (rə'bɪdɪtɪ) *or* **rabidness** *n* > **rabidly** *adv*

rabies ('reɪbiːz) *n pathol* an acute infectious viral disease of the nervous system transmitted by the saliva of infected animals, esp dogs. It is characterized by excessive salivation, aversion to water, convulsions, and paralysis [C17: from Latin: madness, from *rabere* to rave] > **rabic** ('ræbɪk) *or* **rabietic** (ˌreɪbɪ'etɪk) *adj*

Rabin (rə'biːn) *n* **Yitzhak**. 1922–95, Israeli statesman; prime minister of Israel (1974–77; 1992–95); assassinated

RAC *abbreviation* **1** Royal Automobile Club **2** Royal Armoured Corps

raccoon *or* **racoon** (rə'kuːn) *n, pl* **-coons** *or* **-coon 1** any omnivorous mammal of the genus *Procyon*, esp *P. lotor* (**North American raccoon**), inhabiting forests of North and Central America and the Caribbean: family *Procyonidae*, order *Carnivora* (carnivores). Raccoons have a pointed muzzle, long tail, and greyish-black fur with black bands around the tail and across the face **2** the fur of the North American raccoon [C17: from Algonquian *ärähkun*, from *ärähkunĕm* he scratches with his hands]

race¹ (reɪs) *n* **1** a contest of speed, as in running, swimming, driving, riding, etc **2** any competition or rivalry: *the race for the White House* **3** rapid or constant onward movement: *the race of time* **4** a rapid current of water, esp one through a narrow channel than has a tidal range greater at one end than the other **5** a channel of a stream, esp one for conducting water to or from a water wheel or other device for utilizing its energy: *a mill race* **6 a** a channel or groove that contains ball bearings or roller bearings or that restrains a sliding component **b** the inner or outer cylindrical ring in a ball bearing or roller bearing **7** *Austral & NZ* a narrow passage or enclosure in a sheep yard through which sheep pass individually, as to a sheep dip **8** *Austral* a wire tunnel through which footballers pass from the changing room onto a football field **9** *archaic* the span or course of life ▷ *vb* **10** to engage in a contest of speed with (another) **11** to engage (oneself or one's representative) in a race, esp as a profession or pastime: *to race pigeons* **12** to move or go as fast as possible **13** to run (an engine, shaft, propeller, etc) or (of an engine, shaft, propeller, etc) to run at high speed, esp after reduction of the load or resistance ▷ See also **races** [C13: from Old Norse *rās* running; related to Old English *rǣs* attack]

race² (reɪs) *n* **1** a group of people of common ancestry, distinguished from others by physical characteristics, such as hair type, colour of eyes and skin, stature, etc. Principal races are Caucasoid, Mongoloid, and Negroid **2 the human race** human beings collectively **3** a group of animals or plants having common characteristics that distinguish them from other members of the same species, usually forming a geographically isolated group; subspecies **4** a group of people sharing the same interests, characteristics, etc: *the race of authors* [C16: from French, from Italian *razza*, of uncertain origin]

Race (reɪs) *n* **Cape Race** a cape at the SE extremity of Newfoundland, Canada

racecard ('reɪsˌkɑːd) *n* a card or booklet at a race meeting with the times of the races, names of the runners, etc, printed on it

racecourse ('reɪsˌkɔːs) *n* a long broad track, usually of grass, enclosed between rails, and with starting and finishing points marked upon it, over which horses are raced. Also called (esp US and Canadian): **racetrack**

racehorse ('reɪsˌhɔːs) *n* a horse specially bred for racing

raceme (rə'siːm) *n* an inflorescence in which the flowers are borne along the main stem, with the oldest flowers at the base. It can be simple, as in the foxglove, or compound [C18: from Latin *racēmus* bunch of grapes]

> **racemose** ('ræsɪˌməʊs, -ˌməʊz) *adj* > **'race,mosely** *or* **'racemously** *adv*

race meeting *n* a prearranged fixture for racing horses (or sometimes greyhounds) over a set course at set times

racemic (rə'siːmɪk, -'sem-) *adj chem* of, concerned with, or being a mixture of equal amounts of enantiomers and consequently having no optical activity [C19: from RACEME (as in *racemic acid*) + -IC] > **racemism** ('ræsɪˌmɪzəm, rə'siːmɪzəm) *n*

racer ('reɪsə) *n* **1** a person, animal, or machine that races **2** a turntable used to traverse a heavy gun **3** any of several long slender nonvenomous North American snakes of the colubrid genus *Coluber* and related genera, such as *C. lateralis* (**striped racer**)

race relations *n* **1** (*functioning as plural*) the relations between members of two or more human races, esp within a single community **2** (*functioning as singular*) the branch of sociology concerned with such relations

race riot *n* a riot among members of different races in the same community

races ('reɪsɪz) *pl n* **the races** a series of contests of speed between horses (or sometimes greyhounds) over a set course at prearranged times; a race meeting

racetrack ('reɪsˌtræk) *n* **1** a circuit or course, esp an oval one, used for motor racing, speedway, etc **2** Also called: **racecourse** *chiefly US & Canadian* a long broad track, usually of grass, enclosed between rails, and with starting and finishing points marked upon it, over which horses are raced

raceway ('reɪsˌweɪ) *n* **1** another word for: **race¹** (sense 5) **2** a racetrack, esp one for banger racing

Rachel *n* **1** ('reɪtʃəl) *Old Testament* the second and best-loved wife of Jacob; mother of Joseph and Benjamin (Genesis 29–35) **2** (*French* raʃɛl) original name *Elisa Félix*. 1820–58, French tragic actress, famous for her roles in the plays of Racine and Corneille

rachis *or* **rhachis** ('reɪkɪs) *n, pl* **rachises, rhachises** *or* **rachides, rhachides** ('rækɪˌdiːz, 'reɪ-) **1** *botany* the main axis or stem of an inflorescence or compound leaf **2** *ornithol* the shaft of a feather, esp the part that carries the barbs **3** another name for **spinal column** [C17: via New Latin from Greek *rhakhis* ridge] > **rachial, rhachial** ('reɪkɪəl) *or* **rachidial, rhachidial** (rə'kɪdɪəl) *adj*

rachitis (rə'kaɪtɪs) *n pathol* another name for **rickets** [C18: New Latin, from Greek *rhakitis*; see RACHIS] > **rachitic** (rə'kɪtɪk) *adj*

Rachmaninoff *or* **Rachmaninov** (ræk'mænɪˌnɒf; *Russian* rax'maninəf) *n* **Sergei Vassilievich** (sɪr'gjej va'siljivitʃ). 1873–1943, Russian piano virtuoso and composer

Rachmanism ('rækməˌnɪzəm) *n* extortion or exploitation by a landlord of tenants of dilapidated or slum property, esp when involving intimidation or use of racial fears to drive out sitting tenants whose rent is fixed at a low rate [C20: after Perec *Rachman* (1920–62), British property-owner born in Poland]

racial ('reɪʃəl) *adj* **1** denoting or relating to the division of the human species into races on grounds of physical characteristics **2** characteristic of any such group > **'racially** *adv*

racial profiling *n* government activity directed at a suspect or group of suspects based solely on race

Racine (*French* rasin) *n* **Jean Baptiste** (ʒɑ̃ batist). 1639–99, French tragic poet and dramatist. His plays include *Andromaque* (1667), *Bérénice* (1670), and *Phèdre* (1677)

racism ('reɪsɪzəm) *or* **racialism** ('reɪʃəˌlɪzəm) *n* **1** the belief that races have distinctive cultural characteristics determined by hereditary factors and that this endows some races with an intrinsic superiority over others **2** abusive or aggressive behaviour towards members of another race on the basis of such a belief > **'racist** *or* **'racialist** *n, adj*

rack¹ (ræk) *n* **1** a framework for holding, carrying, or displaying a specific load or object **2** a toothed bar designed to engage a pinion to form a mechanism that will interconvert rotary and rectilinear motions **3** the rack an instrument of torture that stretched the body of the victim **4** a cause or state of mental or bodily stress, suffering, etc; anguish; torment (esp in the phrase **on the rack**) **5** *US & Canadian* (in pool, snooker, etc) **a** the triangular frame used to arrange the balls for the opening shot **b** the balls so grouped. Brit equivalent: frame ▷ *vb* (*tr*) **6** to torture on the rack **7** Also: **wrack** to cause great stress or suffering to: *guilt racked his conscience* **8** Also: **wrack** to strain or shake (something) violently, as by great physical force: *the storm racked the town* **9** to place or arrange in or on a rack **10** to move (parts of machinery or a mechanism) using a toothed rack **11** to raise (rents) exorbitantly; **rack-rent 12 rack one's brains** to strain in mental effort, esp to remember something or to find the solution to a problem [C14 *rekke*, probably from Middle Dutch *rec* framework; related to Old High German *recchen* to stretch, Old Norse *rekja* to spread out] ▷ '**racker** *n*

rack² (ræk) *n* destruction; wreck (obsolete except in the phrase **go to rack and ruin**) [C16: variant of WRACK¹]

rack³ (ræk) *n* another word for single-foot, a gait of the horse [C16: perhaps based on ROCK²]

rack⁴ (ræk) *n* **1** a group of broken clouds moving in the wind ▷ *vb* **2** (*intr*) (of clouds) to be blown along by the wind [Old English *wræc* what is driven; related to Gothic *wraks* persecutor, Swedish *vrak* wreckage]

rack⁵ (ræk) *vb* (*tr*) to clear (wine, beer, etc) as by siphoning it off from the dregs [C15: from Old Provençal *arraca*, from *raca* dregs of grapes after pressing]

rack-and-pinion *n* **1** a device for converting rotary into linear motion and vice versa, in which a gearwheel (the pinion) engages with a flat toothed bar (the rack) ▷ *adj* **2** (of a type of steering gear in motor vehicles) having a track rod with a rack along part of its length that engages with a pinion attached to the steering column

racket¹ ('rækɪt) *n* **1** a noisy disturbance or loud commotion; clamour; din **2** an illegal enterprise carried on for profit, such as extortion, fraud, prostitution, drug peddling, etc **3** *slang* a business or occupation: *what's your racket?* **4** *music* a medieval woodwind instrument of deep bass pitch ▷ *vb* **5** (*intr*; often foll by *about*) *now rare* to go about gaily or noisily, in search of pleasure, excitement, etc [C16: probably of imitative origin; compare RATTLE]

racket² or **racquet** ('rækɪt) *n* **1** a bat consisting of an open network of nylon or other strings stretched in an oval frame with a handle, used to strike the ball in tennis, badminton, etc **2** a snowshoe shaped like a tennis racket ▷ *vb* **3** (*tr*) to strike (a ball, shuttlecock, etc) with a racket ▷ See also **rackets** [C16: from French *raquette*, from Arabic *rāhat* palm of the hand] ▷ '**rackety** *adj*

racketeer (ˌrækɪ'tɪə) *n* **1** a person engaged in illegal enterprises for profit ▷ *vb* **2** (*intr*) to operate a racket ▷ ˌ**racke'teering** *n*

racket press *n* a device consisting of a frame closed by a spring mechanism, for keeping taut the strings of a tennis racket, squash racket, etc

rackets ('rækɪts) *n* (*functioning as singular*) **a** a game similar to squash played in a large four-walled court by two or four players using rackets and a small hard ball **b** (*as modifier*): *a rackets court; a rackets championship*

Rackham ('rækəm) *n* **Arthur**. 1867–1939, English artist, noted for his book illustrations, esp of fairy tales

rack off *vb* (*intr, adverb; usually imperative*) *Austral & NZ slang* to go away; depart

rack railway *n* a steep mountain railway having a middle rail fitted with a rack that engages a pinion on the locomotive to provide traction ▷ Also called: **cog railway**

rack-rent *n* **1** a high rent that annually equals or nearly equals the value of the property upon which it is charged **2** any extortionate rent ▷ *vb* **3** to charge an extortionate rent for (property, land, etc) [C17: from RACK¹ (sense 12) + RENT¹] ▷ '**rack-ˌrenter** *n*

rack saw *n* *building trades* a wide-toothed saw

raclette (ræ'klɛt) *n* a Swiss dish of melted cheese served on boiled potatoes [C20: from French, from *racler* to scrape, because the cheese is traditionally melted and scraped onto a plate]

racon ('reɪkɒn) *n* another name for **radar beacon** [C20: from *ra(dar)* + *(bea)con*]

raconteur (ˌrækɒn'tɜ:) *n* a person skilled in telling stories [C19: French, from *raconter* to tell]

racoon (rə'ku:n) *n, pl* **-coons** *or* **-coon** a variant spelling of **raccoon**

racquet ('rækɪt) *n* a variant spelling of **racket²**

racy ('reɪsɪ) *adj* **racier**, **raciest** **1** (of a person's manner, literary style, etc) having a distinctively lively and spirited quality; fresh **2** having a characteristic or distinctive flavour: *a racy wine* **3** suggestive; slightly indecent; risqué ▷ '**racily** *adv* ▷ '**raciness** *n*

rad¹ (ræd) *n* a former unit of absorbed ionizing radiation dose equivalent to an energy absorption per unit mass of 0.01 joule per kilogram of irradiated material. 1 rad is equivalent to 0.01 gray [C20: shortened from RADIATION]

rad² *symbol for* radian

rad. *abbreviation* **1** radical **2** radius

RADA ('rɑ:də) *n acronym for* (in Britain) Royal Academy of Dramatic Art

radar ('reɪdɑ:) *n* **1** a method for detecting the position and velocity of a distant object, such as an aircraft A narrow beam of extremely high-frequency radio pulses is transmitted and reflected by the object back to the transmitter, the signal being displayed on a radarscope. The direction of the reflected beam and the time between transmission and reception of a pulse determine the position of the object **2** the equipment used in such detection [C20 *ra(dio) d(etecting) a(nd) r(anging)*]

radar astronomy *n* the use of radar to map the surfaces of the planets, their satellites, and other bodies

radar beacon *n* a device for transmitting a coded radar signal in response to a signal from an aircraft or ship. The coded signal is then used by the navigator to determine his position ▷ Also called: **racon**

radarscope ('reɪdɑːˌskəʊp) *n* a cathode-ray oscilloscope on which radar signals can be viewed. In a **plan position indicator**, the target is represented by a blip on a radial line that rotates around a point, representing the antenna

radar trap *n* See **speed trap**

Radcliffe ('rædklɪf) *n* **1 Ann**. 1764–1823, British novelist, noted for her Gothic romances *The Mysteries of Udolpho* (1794) and *The Italian* (1797) **2 Paula** (**Jane**). born 1973, British athlete, winner of the London Marathon (2002, 2003, 2005), gold medallist in the marathon at the World Championships (2005), and European Record holder for the 10000m.

raddle ('ræd°l) *vb* **1** (*tr*) *chiefly Brit* to paint (the face) with rouge ▷ *n, vb* **2** another word for **ruddle** [C16: variant of RUDDLE]

raddled ('ræd°ld) *adj* (esp of a person) unkempt or run-down in appearance [C17: from RADDLE]

Radek (*Russian* rɑdjɪk) *n* **Karl** (**Bernhardovich**), original name *Karl Sobelsohn*. 1885–?1939, Soviet politician and journalist who was secretary of Comintern (1920–24). He was accused of treason (1937) and probably died in a labour camp

Radetzky (*German* ra'dɛtski) *n* Count **Joseph** ('jo:zɛf). 1766–1858, Austrian field marshal: served in the war against Sardinia (1848–9), winning brilliant victories at Custozza (1848) and Novara (1849): governor of Lombardy-Venetia in N Italy (1849-57)

radial ('reɪdɪəl) *adj* **1** (of lines, bars, beams of light, etc) emanating from a common central point; arranged like the radii of a circle **2** of, like, or relating to a radius or ray **3** *anatomy* of or relating to the radius or forearm **4** *astronomy* (of velocity) in a direction along the line of sight of a celestial object and measured by means of the red shift (or blue shift) of the spectral lines of the object ▷ *n* **5** a radial part or section [C16: from Medieval Latin *radiālis* from RADIUS] ▷ '**radially** *adv*

radial engine *n* an internal-combustion engine having a number of cylinders arranged about a central crankcase

radial-ply *adj* (of a motor tyre) having the fabric cords in the outer casing running radially to enable the sidewalls to be flexible

radial symmetry *n* a type of structure of an organism or part of an organism in which a vertical cut through the axis in any of two or more planes produces two halves that are mirror images of each other ▷ See bilateral symmetry

radian ('reɪdɪən) n an SI unit of plane angle; the angle between two radii of a circle that cut off on the circumference an arc equal in length to the radius. 1 radian is equivalent to 57.296 degrees and $\pi/2$ radians equals a right angle ▷ Symbol: rad [C19: from RADIUS]

radiance ('reɪdɪəns) or **radiancy** n, pl -ances or -ancies 1 the quality or state of being radiant 2 a measure of the amount of electromagnetic radiation leaving or arriving at a point on a surface. It is the radiant intensity in a given direction of a small element of surface area divided by the orthogonal projection of this area onto a plane at right angles to the direction

radiant ('reɪdɪənt) adj 1 sending out rays of light; bright; shining 2 characterized by health, intense joy, happiness, etc 3 emitted or propagated by or as radiation; radiated: radiant heat 4 sending out heat by radiation: a radiant heater 5 physics (of a physical quantity in photometry) evaluated by absolute energy measurements: radiant flux; radiant efficiency ▷ n 6 a point or object that emits radiation, esp the part of a heater that gives out heat 7 astronomy the point in space from which a meteor shower appears to emanate [C15: from Latin radiāre to shine, from radius ray of light, RADIUS] > 'radiantly adv

radiant energy n energy that is emitted or propagated in the form of particles or electromagnetic radiation. It is measured in joules

radiant heat n heat transferred in the form of electromagnetic radiation rather than by conduction or convection; infrared radiation

radiata pine (,reɪdɪ'ɑːtə) n a pine tree, Pinus radiata, native to the western USA. but grown in Australia, New Zealand, and elsewhere to produce building timber [from New Latin]

radiate vb ('reɪdɪ,eɪt) 1 Also called: eradiate to emit (heat, light, or some other form of radiation) or (of heat, light, etc) to be emitted as radiation 2 (intr) (of lines, beams, etc) to spread out from a centre or be arranged in a radial pattern 3 (tr) (of a person) to show (happiness, health, etc) to a great degree ▷ adj ('reɪdɪɪt, -,eɪt) 4 having rays; radiating 5 (of animals or their parts) showing radial symmetry [C17: from Latin radiāre to emit rays]

radiation (,reɪdɪ'eɪʃən) n 1 physics a the emission or transfer of radiant energy as particles, electromagnetic waves, sound, etc b the particles, etc, emitted, esp the particles and gamma rays emitted in nuclear decay 2 Also called: radiation therapy med treatment using a radioactive substance 3 the act, state, or process of radiating or being radiated > ,radi'ational adj

radiation sickness n pathol illness caused by overexposure of the body or a part of the body to ionizing radiations from radioactive material or X-rays. It is characterized by vomiting, diarrhoea, and in severe cases by sterility and cancer

radiative ('reɪdɪətɪv) or **radiatory** ('reɪdɪətərɪ, -trɪ) adj physics emitting or causing the emission of radiation: a radiative collision

radiator ('reɪdɪ,eɪtə) n 1 a device for heating a room, building, etc, consisting of a series of pipes through which hot water or steam passes 2 a device for cooling an internal-combustion engine, consisting of thin-walled tubes through which water passes. Heat is transferred from the water through the walls of the tubes to the airstream, which is created either by the motion of the vehicle or by a fan 3 electronics the part of an aerial or transmission line that radiates electromagnetic waves

radical ('rædɪkəl) adj 1 of, relating to, or characteristic of the basic or inherent constitution of a person or thing; fundamental: a radical fault 2 concerned with or tending to concentrate on fundamental aspects of a matter; searching or thoroughgoing: radical thought; a radical re-examination 3 favouring or tending to produce extreme or fundamental changes in political, economic, or social conditions, institutions, habits of mind, etc: a radical party 4 med (of treatment) aimed at removing the source of a disease: radical surgery 5 slang, chiefly US very good;

excellent 6 of, relating to, or arising from the root or the base of the stem of a plant: radical leaves 7 maths of, relating to, or containing roots of numbers or quantities 8 linguistics of or relating to the root of a word ▷ n 9 a person who favours extreme or fundamental change in existing institutions or in political, social, or economic conditions 10 maths a root of a number or quantity, such as $^3\sqrt{5}$, $\sqrt{x}$ 11 Also called: radicle chem a short for free radical b another name for group (sense 9) 12 linguistics another word for: root¹ (sense 8) [C14: from Late Latin rādīcālis having roots, from Latin rādix a root] > 'radicalness n

radicalism ('rædɪkə,lɪzəm) n 1 the principles, desires, or practices of political radicals 2 a radical movement, esp in politics > ,radical'istic adj > ,radical'istically adv

radicalize or **radicalise** ('rædɪkə,laɪz) vb (tr) to make (a person) more radical > ,radicali'zation or ,radicali'sation n

radically ('rædɪkəlɪ) adv thoroughly; completely; fundamentally: to alter radically

radical sign n the symbol $\sqrt{}$ placed before a number or quantity to indicate the extraction of a root, esp a square root. The value of a higher root is indicated by a raised digit in front of the symbol, as in $^3\sqrt{}$

radicand ('rædɪ,kænd, ,rædɪ'kænd) n a number or quantity from which a root is to be extracted, usually preceded by a radical sign: 3 is the radicand of $\sqrt{3}$ [C20: from Latin rādicandum, literally: that which is to be rooted, from rādicāre to take root, from rādix root]

radicchio (ræ'diːkɪəʊ) n, pl -chios an Italian variety of chicory, having purple leaves streaked with white that are eaten raw in salads

radices ('reɪdɪ,siːz) n a plural of radix

radicle ('rædɪkəl) n 1 botany a part of the embryo of seed-bearing plants that develops into the main root b a very small root or rootlike part 2 anatomy any bodily structure resembling a rootlet, esp one of the smallest branches of a vein or nerve 3 chem a variant spelling of radical (sense 11) [C18: from Latin rādicula a little root, from rādix root]

Radiguet (French radigɛ) n **Raymond** (rɛmɔ̃). 1903–23, French novelist; the author of The Devil in the Flesh (1923) and Count d'Orgel (1924)

radii ('reɪdɪ,aɪ) n a plural of radius

radio ('reɪdɪəʊ) n, pl -os 1 the use of electromagnetic waves, lying in the radio-frequency range, for broadcasting, two-way communications, etc 2 an electronic device designed to receive, demodulate, and amplify radio signals from sound broadcasting stations, etc 3 the broadcasting, content, etc, of sound radio programmes: he thinks radio is poor these days 4 a the occupation or profession concerned with any aspect of the broadcasting of sound radio programmes b (modifier) relating to, produced for, or transmitted by sound radio 5 short for radiotelegraph, radiotelegraphy, radiotelephone 6 (modifier) a of, relating to, employed in, or sent by radio signals: a radio station b of, concerned with, using, or operated by radio frequencies: radio spectrum 7 (modifier) (of a motor vehicle) equipped with a radio for communication ▷ vb -os, -oing, -oed 8 to transmit (a message) to (a person, radio station, etc) by means of radio waves ▷ Also called (esp Brit) wireless [C20: short for radiotelegraphy]

radio- combining form 1 denoting radio, broadcasting, or radio frequency: radiogram 2 indicating radioactivity or radiation [from French, from Latin radius ray; see RADIUS]

radioactive (,reɪdɪəʊ'æktɪv) adj exhibiting, using, or concerned with radioactivity > ,radio'actively adv

radioactive dating n another term for radiometric dating

radioactive decay n disintegration of a nucleus that occurs spontaneously or as a result of electron capture. One or more different nuclei are formed and usually particles and gamma rays are emitted. Also called: disintegration

radioactive series n physics a series of nuclides each of which undergoes radioactive decay into the next member of the series, ending with a stable element, usually lead

radioactive tracer n med See tracer (sense 3)

r

radioactive waste *n* any waste material containing radionuclides. Also called: **nuclear waste**

radioactivity (ˌreɪdɪəʊækˈtɪvɪtɪ) *n* the spontaneous emission of radiation from atomic nuclei. The radiation can consist of alpha, beta, and gamma radiation

radio astronomy *n* a branch of astronomy in which a radio telescope is used to detect and analyse radio signals received on earth from radio sources in space

radio beacon *n* a fixed radio transmitting station that broadcasts a characteristic signal by means of which a vessel or aircraft can determine its bearing or position

radiobiology (ˌreɪdɪəʊbaɪˈɒlədʒɪ) *n* the branch of biology concerned with the effects of radiation on living organisms and the study of biological processes using radioactive substances as tracers > **radiobiological** (ˌreɪdɪəʊˌbaɪəˈlɒdʒɪkᵊl) > ˌradioˌbioˈlogically *adv* > ˌradiobiˈologist *n*

radiocarbon (ˌreɪdɪəʊˈkɑːbᵊn) *n* a radioactive isotope of carbon, esp carbon-14. See **carbon** (sense 1)

radiocarbon dating *n* a technique for determining the age of organic materials, such as wood, based on their content of the radioisotope ^{14}C acquired from the atmosphere when they formed part of a living plant. The ^{14}C decays to the nitrogen isotope ^{14}N with a half-life of 5730 years. Measurement of the amount of radioactive carbon remaining in the material thus gives an estimate of its age. Also called: **carbon-14 dating**

radiochemistry (ˌreɪdɪəʊˈkemɪstrɪ) *n* the chemistry of radioactive elements and their compounds > ˌradioˈchemical *adj* > ˌradioˈchemist *n*

radio compass *n* any navigational device that gives a bearing by determining the direction of incoming radio waves transmitted from a particular radio station or beacon. See also **goniometer** (sense 2)

radio control *n* remote control by means of radio signals from a transmitter > **radio-controlled** *adj*

radioelement (ˌreɪdɪəʊˈelɪmənt) *n* an element that is naturally radioactive

radio frequency *n* **1 a** a frequency or band of frequencies that lie in the range 10 kilohertz to 300 000 megahertz and can be used for radio communications and broadcasting. Abbreviation: **RF b** (*as modifier*): *a radio-frequency amplifier* **2** the frequency transmitted by a particular radio station

radio galaxy *n* a galaxy that is a strong emitter of radio waves

radiogram (ˈreɪdɪəʊˌɡræm) *n* **1** *Brit* a unit comprising a radio and record player **2** a message transmitted by radiotelegraphy **3** another name for **radiograph**

radiograph (ˈreɪdɪəʊˌɡrɑːf, -ˌɡræf) *n* an image produced on a specially sensitized photographic film or plate by radiation, usually by X-rays or gamma rays

radiography (ˌreɪdɪˈɒɡrəfɪ) *n* the production of radiographs of opaque objects for use in medicine, surgery, industry, etc > ˌradiˈographer *n* > **radiographic** (ˌreɪdɪəʊˈɡræfɪk) *adj* > ˌradioˈgraphically *adv*

radioimmunoassay (ˈreɪdɪəʊˌɪmjʊnəʊˈæseɪ) *n* a sensitive immunological assay, making use of antibodies and radioactive labelling, for the detection and quantification of biologically important substances, such as hormone concentrations in the blood

radioisotope (ˌreɪdɪəʊˈaɪsətəʊp) *n* an isotope that is radioactive > **radioisotopic** (ˌreɪdɪəʊˌaɪsəˈtɒpɪk) *adj*

radiolarian (ˌreɪdɪəʊˈlɛərɪən) *n* any of various marine protozoans constituting the order *Radiolaria*, typically having a siliceous shell and stiff radiating cytoplasmic projections: phylum *Actinopoda* (actinopods) [C19: from New Latin *Radiolaria*, from Late Latin *radiolus* little sunbeam, from Latin *radius* ray, RADIUS]

radiology (ˌreɪdɪˈɒlədʒɪ) *n* the use of X-rays and radioactive substances in the diagnosis and treatment of disease > ˌradiˈologist *n*

radiometer (ˌreɪdɪˈɒmɪtə) *n* any instrument for the detection or measurement of radiant energy > **radiometric** (ˌreɪdɪəʊˈmetrɪk) *adj* > ˌradiˈometry *n*

radiometric dating *n* any method of dating material based on the decay of its constituent radioactive atoms, such as potassium-argon dating or rubidium-strontium dating. Also called: **radioactive dating**

radiopager (ˈreɪdɪəʊˌpeɪdʒə) *n* a small radio receiver fitted with a buzzer to alert a person to telephone their home, office, etc, to receive a message > ˈradioˌpaging *n*

radiopaque (ˌreɪdɪəʊˈpeɪk) or **radio-opaque** *adj* not permitting X-rays or other radiation to pass through > **radiopacity** (ˌreɪdɪəʊˈpæsɪtɪ) or **radio-oˈpacity** *n*

radio receiver *n* an apparatus that receives incoming modulated radio waves and converts them into sound

radioscopy (ˌreɪdɪˈɒskəpɪ) *n* another word for **fluoroscopy** > **radioscopic** (ˌreɪdɪəʊˈskɒpɪk) *adj* > ˌradioˈscopically *adv*

radiosonde (ˈreɪdɪəʊˌsɒnd) *n* an airborne instrument used to send meteorological information back to earth by radio [C20: RADIO- + French *sonde* sounding line]

radio source *n* a celestial object, such as a supernova remnant or quasar, that is a source of radio waves

radio spectrum *n* the range of electromagnetic frequencies used in radio transmission, lying between 10 kilohertz and 300 000 megahertz

radiotelegraphy (ˌreɪdɪəʊtɪˈlɛɡrəfɪ) *n* a type of telegraphy in which messages (usually in Morse code) are transmitted by radio waves; its use is no longer widespread as it has been superseded by satellite technology > **radiotelegraphic** (ˌreɪdɪəʊˌtelɪˈɡræfɪk) *adj* > **radiotelegraph** (ˌreɪdɪəʊˈtelɪˌɡrɑːf, -ˌɡræf) *vb, n*

radiotelephone (ˌreɪdɪəʊˈtelɪˌfəʊn) *n* **1** Also called: **radiophone, wireless telephone** a device for communication by means of radio waves rather than by transmitting along wires or cables ▷ *vb* **2** to telephone (a person) by radiotelephone ▷ Sometimes shortened to **radio** > **radiotelephonic** (ˌreɪdɪəʊˌtelɪˈfɒnɪk) *adj*

radio telescope *n* an instrument consisting of an antenna or system of antennas connected to one or more radio receivers, used in radio astronomy to detect and analyse radio waves from space

radioteletype (ˌreɪdɪəʊˈtelɪˌtaɪp) *n* **1** a teleprinter that transmits or receives information by means of radio waves rather than by cable or wire **2** a network of such devices widely used for communicating news, messages, information, etc

radiotherapy (ˌreɪdɪəʊˈθerəpɪ) *n* the treatment of disease, esp cancer, by means of alpha or beta particles emitted from an implanted or ingested radioisotope, or by means of a beam of high-energy radiation. See **chemotherapy** > **radiotherapeutic** (ˌreɪdɪəʊˌθerəˈpjuːtɪk) *adj* > ˌradioˈtherapist *n*

radio wave *n* an electromagnetic wave of radio frequency

radish (ˈrædɪʃ) *n* **1** any of various plants of the genus *Raphanus*, esp R. *sativus* of Europe and Asia, cultivated for its edible root: family *Brassicaceae* (crucifers) **2** the root of this plant, which has a pungent taste and is eaten raw in salads [Old English *rǣdīc*, from Latin *rādīx* root]

radium (ˈreɪdɪəm) *n* **a** a highly radioactive luminescent white element of the alkaline earth group of metals. It occurs in pitchblende, carnotite, and other uranium ores, and is used in radiotherapy and in luminous paints. Symbol: Ra; atomic no: 88; half-life of most stable isotope, ^{226}Ra: 1620 years; valency: 2; relative density: 5; melting pt: 700°C; boiling pt: 1140°C **b** (*as modifier*): *radium needle* [C20: from Latin *radius* ray]

radium therapy *n* treatment of disease, esp cancer, by exposing affected tissues to radiation from radium

radius (ˈreɪdɪəs) *n, pl* **-dii** (-dɪˌaɪ) *or* **-diuses 1** a straight line joining the centre of a circle or sphere to any point on the circumference or surface **2** the length of this line, usually denoted by the symbol r **3** *anatomy* the outer and slightly shorter of the two bones of the human forearm, extending from the elbow to the wrist **4** a corresponding bone in other vertebrates **5** any of the veins of an insect's wing **6** a group of ray florets, occurring in such plants as the daisy **7 a** any radial or radiating part, such as a spoke **b** (*as modifier*): *a radius arm* **8** a circular area of a size indicated by the length of its radius: *the police stopped every lorry within a radius of four miles* **9** the operational limit of a ship, aircraft, etc [C16: from Latin: rod, ray, spoke]

radix (ˈreɪdɪks) *n, pl* **-dices** (-dɪˌsiːz) *or* **-dixes 1** *maths* any number that is the base of a number system or of a system of logarithms: *10 is the radix of the decimal system* **2** *biology* the root or point of origin of a part or organ **3** *linguistics* a less common word for: **root**¹ (sense 8) [c16: from Latin *rādix* root; compare Greek *rhadix* small branch, *rhiza* root]

radix point *n* a point, such as the decimal point in the decimal system, separating the integral part of a number from the fractional part

Radnorshire (ˈrædnəˌʃɪə, -fə) *or* **Radnor** *n* (until 1974) a county of E Wales, now part of Powys

Radom (*Polish* ˈradɔm) *n* a city in E Poland: under Austria from 1795 to 1815 and Russia from 1815 to 1918. Pop: 232 000 (2005 est)

radome (ˈreɪdəʊm) *n* a protective housing for a radar antenna made from a material that is transparent to radio waves [c20: RA(DAR) + DOME]

radon (ˈreɪdɒn) *n* a colourless radioactive element of the rare gas group, the most stable isotope of which, radon-222, is a decay product of radium. It is used as an alpha particle source in radiotherapy. Symbol: Rn; atomic no: 86; half-life of ²²²Rn: 3.82 days; valency: o; density: 9.73 kg/m³; melting pt: −71°C; boiling pt: −61.7°C [c20: from RADIUM + -ON]

radula (ˈrædjʊlə) *n*, *pl* -lae (-ˌliː) a horny tooth-bearing strip on the tongue of molluscs that is used for rasping food [c19: from Late Latin: a scraping iron, from Latin *rādere* to scrape] > **ˈradular** *adj*

Raeburn (ˈreɪˌbɜːn) *n* Sir **Henry**. 1756–1823, Scottish portrait painter

RAF (*Not standard* ræf) *abbreviation* Royal Air Force

raff (ræf) *n archaic, or dialect* **1** rubbish; refuse **2** rabble or riffraff [c14: perhaps from Old French *rafle* a snatching up; compare RAFFLE, RIFFRAFF]

Rafferty (ˈræfətɪ) *or* **Rafferty's rules** *pl n Austral & NZ slang* no rules at all [c20: of uncertain origin]

raffia *or* **raphia** (ˈræfɪə) *n* **1** Also called: **raffia palm** a palm tree, *Raphia ruffia*, native to Madagascar, that has large plumelike leaves, the stalks of which yield a useful fibre **2** the fibre obtained from this plant, used for tying, weaving, etc **3** any of several related palms or the fibre obtained from them [c19: from Malagasy]

raffish (ˈræfɪʃ) *adj* **1** careless or unconventional in dress, manners, etc; rakish **2** tawdry; flashy; vulgar [c19: see RAFF] > **ˈraffishly** *adv* > **ˈraffishness** *n*

raffle (ˈræfᵊl) *n* **1** **a** a lottery in which the prizes are goods rather than money **b** (*as modifier*): *a raffle ticket* ▷ *vb* **2** (*tr*; often foll by *off*) to dispose of (goods) in a raffle [c14 (a dice game): from Old French, of obscure origin] > **ˈraffler** *n*

Raffles (ˈræfᵊlz) *n* Sir **Thomas Stamford**. 1781–1826, British colonial administrator: founded Singapore (1819) as a station for the British East India Company

rafflesia (ræˈfliːzɪə) *n* any of various tropical Asian parasitic leafless plants constituting the genus *Rafflesia*, esp *R. arnoldi*, the flowers of which grow up to 45 cm (18 inches) across, smell of putrid meat, and are pollinated by carrion flies: family *Rafflesiaceae* [c19: New Latin, named after Sir Stamford *Raffles* (1781–1826), British colonial administrator, who discovered it]

Rafsanjani (ˌræfsænˈdʒɑːnɪ) *n* **Hojatoleslam Hashemi Ali Akbar**. born 1934, Iranian politician: president of Iran (1989–97)

raft¹ (rɑːft) *n* **1** a buoyant platform of logs, planks, etc, used as a vessel or moored offshore **2** a thick slab of reinforced concrete laid over soft ground to provide a foundation for a building ▷ *vb* **3** to convey on or travel by raft, or make a raft from [c15: from Old Norse *raptr* RAFTER]

raft² (rɑːft) *n informal* a large collection or amount: *a raft of old notebooks discovered in a cupboard* [c19: from RAFF]

rafter (ˈrɑːftə) *n* any one of a set of sloping beams that form the framework of a roof [Old English *ræfter*; related to Old Saxon *rehter*, Old Norse *raptr*, Old High German *rāvo*; see RAFT¹]

RAFVR *abbreviation* Royal Air Force Volunteer Reserve

rag¹ (ræg) *n* **1** **a** a small piece of cloth, such as one torn from a discarded garment, or such pieces of cloth collectively **b** (*as modifier*): *a rag doll; a rag book; rag paper* **2** **a** fragmentary piece of any material; scrap; shred

3 *informal* a newspaper or other journal, esp one considered as worthless, sensational, etc **4** *informal* an item of clothing **5** *informal* a handkerchief **6** *Brit slang, esp naval* a flag or ensign [c14: probably back formation from RAGGED, from Old English *raggig*; related to Old Norse *rögg* tuft]

rag² (ræg) *vb* rags, ragging, ragged (*tr*) **1** to draw attention facetiously and persistently to the shortcomings or alleged shortcomings of (a person) **2** *Brit* to play rough practical jokes on ▷ *n* **3** *Brit* a boisterous practical joke, esp one on a fellow student **4** (in British universities) **a** a period, usually a week, in which various events are organized to raise money for charity, including a procession of decorated floats and tableaux **b** (*as modifier*): *rag day* [c18: of uncertain origin]

rag³ (ræg) *jazz* ▷ *n* **1** a piece of ragtime music ▷ *vb* rags, ragging, ragged **2** (*tr*) to compose or perform in ragtime [c20: shortened from RAGTIME]

raga (ˈrɑːgə) *n* (in Indian music) **1** any of several conventional patterns of melody and rhythm that form the basis for freely interpreted compositions. Each pattern is associated with different aspects of religious devotion **2** a composition based on one of these patterns [c18: from Sanskrit *rāga* tone, colour]

ragamuffin (ˈrægəˌmʌfɪn) *n* **1** a ragged unkempt person, esp a child **2** another name for **ragga** [c14 *Ragamoffyn*, name of a demon in the poem *Piers Plowman* (1393); probably based on RAG¹]

rag-and-bone man *n Brit* a man who buys and sells discarded clothing, furniture, etc

ragbag (ˈrægˌbæg) *n* **1** a bag for storing odd rags **2** a confused assortment; jumble [c19]

ragbolt (ˈrægˌbəʊlt) *n* a bolt that has angled projections on it to prevent it working loose once it has been driven home

rage (reɪdʒ) *n* **1** intense anger; fury **2** violent movement or action, esp of the sea, wind, etc **3** great intensity of hunger, sexual desire, or other feelings **4** aggressive behaviour associated with a specified environment or activity: *road rage; school rage* **5** a fashion or craze (esp in the phrase **all the rage**) **6** *Austral & NZ informal* a dance or party ▷ *vb* **7** to feel or exhibit intense anger **8** (esp of storms, fires, etc) to move or surge with great violence **9** (esp of a disease or epidemic) to spread rapidly and uncontrollably **10** *Austral & NZ informal* to have a good time [c13: via Old French from Latin *rabiēs* madness]

ragga (ˈrægə) *n* a dance-orientated style of reggae. Also called: **ragamuffin** [c20: shortened from RAGAMUFFIN]

ragged (ˈrægɪd) *adj* **1** (of clothes) worn to rags; tattered **2** (of a person) dressed in shabby tattered clothes **3** having a neglected or unkempt appearance: *ragged weeds* **4** having a loose, rough, or uneven surface or edge; jagged **5** uneven or irregular: *a ragged beat; a ragged shout* [c13: probably from *ragge* RAG¹] > **ˈraggedly** *adv* > **ˈraggedness** *n*

ragged robin *n* a caryophyllaceous plant, *Lychnis floscuculi*, native to Europe and Asia, that has pink or white flowers with ragged petals. See also **catchfly**

raggedy (ˈrægɪdɪ) *adj informal* somewhat ragged; tattered: *a raggedy doll*

raggle-taggle (ˈrægᵊl ˈtægᵊl) *adj* motley or unkempt: *a raggle-taggle band of volunteers and students* [augmented form of RAGTAG]

ragi, raggee *or* **raggy** (ˈrægɪ) *n* a cereal grass, *Eleusine coracana*, cultivated in Africa and Asia for its edible grain [c18: from Hindi]

raglan (ˈræglən) *n* **1** a coat with sleeves that continue to the collar instead of having armhole seams ▷ *adj* **2** cut in this design: *a raglan sleeve* [c19: named after Fitzroy James Henry Somerset, 1st Baron *Raglan* (1788–1855), British field marshal, diplomatist, and politician]

Raglan (ˈræglən) *n* **Fitzroy James Henry Somerset**, 1st Baron *Raglan*. 1788–1855, British field marshal, diplomatist, politician, and protégé of Wellington: commanded British troops (1854–55) in the Crimean War

Ragnarök *or* **Ragnarok** (ˈrɑːgnəˌrɒk) *n Norse myth* the ultimate destruction of the gods in a cataclysmic battle with evil, out of which a new order will arise. German equivalent: **Götterdämmerung** [Old Norse *ragnarökkr*, from *regin* the gods + *rökkr* twilight]

ragout (ræ'gu:) *n* **1** a richly seasoned stew of meat or poultry and vegetables ▷ *vb* -gouts (-'gu:z), -gouting (-'gu:ıŋ), -gouted (-'gu:d) **2** (*tr*) to make into a ragout [c17: from French, from *ragoûter* to stimulate the appetite again, from *ra-* RE- + *goûter* from Latin *gustāre* to taste]

rag-rolling *n* a decorating technique in which paint is applied with a roughly folded cloth in order to create a marbled effect

rags (rægz) *pl n* **1** torn, old, or shabby clothing **2** cotton or linen cloth waste used in the manufacture of rag paper **3** glad rags *informal* best clothes; finery **4** from rags to riches *informal* **a** from poverty to great wealth **b** (*as modifier*): *a rags-to-riches tale*

ragtag ('ræg,tæg) *n disparaging* the common people; rabble (esp in the phrase **ragtag and bobtail**) [c19]

ragtime ('ræg,taɪm) *n* a style of jazz piano music, developed by Scott Joplin around 1900, having a two-four rhythm base and a syncopated melody [c20: probably from RAGGED + TIME]

rag trade *n informal* the clothing business, esp the aspects concerned with the manufacture and sale of dresses

Ragusa (*Italian* ra'gu:za) *n* **1** an industrial town in SE Sicily. Pop: 68 956 (2001) **2** the Italian name (until 1918) for **Dubrovnik**

ragweed ('ræg,wi:d) *n* any plant of the chiefly North American genus *Ambrosia*, such as *A. artemisiifolia* (**common ragweed**): family *Asteraceae* (composites). Their green tassel-like flowers produce large amounts of pollen, which causes hay fever. Also called: ambrosia

ragworm ('ræg,wɜ:m) *n* any polychaete worm of the genus *Nereis*, living chiefly in burrows in sand or mud and having a flattened body with a row of fleshy parapodia along each side

ragwort ('ræg,wɜ:t) *n* any of several plants of the genus *Senecio*, esp *S. jacobaea* of Europe, that have yellow daisy-like flowers: family *Asteraceae* (composites). See also **groundsel** (sense 1)

rah (rɑ:) *interj informal, chiefly US* short for **hurrah**

rahui (,rɑ:'hu:ɪ) *n* NZ a Māori prohibition [Māori]

rai (raɪ) *n* a type of Algerian popular music based on traditional Algerian music influenced by modern Western pop [c20: Arabic, literally: opinion]

raid (reɪd) *n* **1** a sudden surprise attack **2** a surprise visit by police searching for criminals or illicit goods: *a fraud-squad raid* ▷ *vb* **3** to make a raid against (a person, thing, etc) **4** to sneak into (a place) in order to take something, steal, etc: *raiding the larder* ▷ See also (for senses 1, 2): **bear raid**, **dawn raid** [c15: Scottish dialect, from Old English *rād* military expedition; see ROAD] > 'raider *n*

rail¹ (reɪl) *n* **1** a horizontal bar of wood, metal, etc, supported by vertical posts, functioning as a fence, barrier, handrail, etc **2** a horizontal bar fixed to a wall on which to hang things: *a picture rail* **3** a horizontal framing member in a door or piece of panelling. See **stile**² **4** short for **railing 5** one of a pair of parallel bars laid on a prepared track, roadway, etc, that serve as a guide and running surface for the wheels of a railway train, tramcar, etc **6 a** short for **railway b** (*as modifier*): *rail transport* **7** *nautical* a trim for finishing the top of a bulwark **8** off the rails **a** into or in a state of dysfunction or disorder **b** eccentric or mad ▷ *vb* (*tr*) **9** to provide with a rail or railings **10** (*usually foll by* **in** or **off**) to fence (an area) with rails [c13: from Old French *raille* rod, from Latin *rēgula* ruler, straight piece of wood]

rail² (reɪl) *vb* (*intr*; *foll by* **at** or **against**) to complain bitterly or vehemently [c15: from Old French *railler* to mock, from Old Provençal *ralhar* to chatter, joke, from Late Latin *ragere* to yell, neigh] > 'railer *n*

rail³ (reɪl) *n* any of various small wading birds of the genus *Rallus* and related genera: family *Rallidae*, order *Gruiformes* (cranes, etc). They have short wings, long legs, and dark plumage [c15: from Old French *raale*, perhaps from Latin *rādere* to scrape]

railcar ('reɪl,kɑ:) *n* a passenger-carrying railway vehicle consisting of a single coach with its own power unit

railcard ('reɪl,kɑ:d) *n Brit* an identity card that young people or pensioners in Britain can buy, which allows

them to buy train tickets more cheaply

railhead ('reɪl,hɛd) *n* **1** a terminal of a railway **2** the farthest point reached by completed track on an unfinished railway

railing ('reɪlɪŋ) *n* **1** (*often plural*) a fence, balustrade, or barrier that consists of rails supported by posts **2** rails collectively or material for making rails

raillery ('reɪlərɪ) *n*, *pl* -leries **1** light-hearted satire or ridicule; banter **2** an example of this, esp a bantering remark [c17: from French, from *railler* to tease, banter; see RAIL²]

railroad ('reɪl,rəʊd) *n* **1** the usual US word for: **railway** ▷ *vb* **2** (*tr*) *informal* to force (a person) into (an action) with haste or by unfair means

railway ('reɪl,weɪ) *or US* **railroad** *n* **1** a permanent track composed of a line of parallel metal rails fixed to sleepers, for transport of passengers and goods in trains **2** any track on which the wheels of a vehicle may run: *a cable railway* **3** the entire equipment, rolling stock, buildings, property, and system of tracks used in such a transport system **4** the organization responsible for operating a railway network **5** (*modifier*) of, relating to, or used on a railway or railways: *a railway engine; a railway strike*

raiment ('reɪmənt) *n archaic or poetic* attire; clothing; garments [c15: shortened from *arrayment*, from Old French *areement*; see ARRAY]

rain (reɪn) *n* **1 a** precipitation from clouds in the form of drops of water, formed by the condensation of water vapour in the atmosphere **b** a fall of rain; shower **c** (*in combination*): *a raindrop* **2** a large quantity of anything falling rapidly or in quick succession: *a rain of abuse* **3** rain or shine *or* come rain or shine regardless of the weather **4** right as rain *Brit informal* perfectly all right; perfectly fit ▷ *vb* **5** (*intr*; *with* **it** *as subject*) to be the case that rain is falling **6** (*often with* **it** *as subject*) to fall or cause to fall like rain **7** (*tr*) to bestow in large measure: *to rain abuse on someone* **8** rained off cancelled or postponed on account of rain. US and Canadian term: rained out ▷ See also **rains** [Old English *regn*; related to Old Frisian *rein*, Old High German *regan*, Gothic *rign*] > 'rainless *adj*

rainbird ('reɪn,bɜ:d) *n* any of various birds, such as (in Britain) the green woodpecker, whose cry is supposed to portend rain

rainbow ('reɪn,bəʊ) *n* **1** a bow-shaped display in the sky of the colours of the spectrum, caused by the refraction and reflection of the sun's rays through rain or mist **2** (*as modifier*): *a rainbow pattern* **3** an illusory hope: *to chase rainbows* **4** (*modifier*) of or relating to a political grouping together by several minorities, esp of different races: *the rainbow coalition*

Rainbow Bridge *n* a natural stone bridge over a creek in SE Utah. Height: 94 m (309 ft). Span: 85 m (278 ft)

rainbow flag *n* a multi-coloured flag used as a symbol of peace; often used to represent gay and lesbian pride

rainbow lorikeet *n* a small Australasian parrot, *Trichoglossus haematodus*, with brightly-coloured plumage

rainbow nation *n South African* an epithet, alluding to its multiracial population, of **South Africa** [c20: coined by Nelson Mandela (born 1918), South African statesman, following the end of apartheid]

rainbow trout *n* a freshwater trout of North American origin, *Salmo gairdneri*, having a body marked with many black spots and two longitudinal red stripes

rain check *n* **1** *US & Canadian* a ticket stub for a baseball or other game that allows readmission on a future date if the event is cancelled because of rain **2** the deferral of acceptance of an offer, esp, a voucher issued to a customer wishing to purchase a sale item that is temporarily out of stock, enabling him to buy it at the special price when next the item is available **3** take a rain check *informal* to accept the postponement of an offer

raincoat ('reɪn,kəʊt) *n* a coat made of a waterproof material

rainfall ('reɪn,fɔ:l) *n* **1** precipitation in the form of raindrops **2** *meteorol* the amount of precipitation in a specified place and time

rainforest ('reɪn,fɒrɪst) *n* dense forest found in tropical areas of heavy rainfall. The trees are broad-leaved and evergreen, and the vegetation tends to grow in three layers (undergrowth, intermediate trees and shrubs, and very tall trees, which form a canopy)

rain gauge *n* an instrument for measuring rainfall or snowfall, consisting of a cylinder covered by a funnel-like lid

Rainier ('reɪnɪə, reɪ'nɪə, rə-) *n* Mount Rainier a mountain in W Washington State: the highest mountain in the state and in the Cascade Range. Height: 4392 m (14 410 ft)

Rainier III ('reɪnɪˌeɪ; *French* rɛnje) *n* full name *Rainier Louis Henri Maxence Bertrand de Grimaldi*. 1923–2005, ruling prince of Monaco from 1949. He married (1956) the US actress Grace Kelly (1929–82)

rainproof ('reɪnˌpruːf) *adj* 1 Also called: raintight (of garments, buildings, etc) impermeable to rainwater ▷ *vb* 2 (*tr*) to make rainproof

rains (reɪnz) *pl n* the rains the season of heavy rainfall, esp in the tropics

rain shadow *n* the relatively dry area on the leeward side of high ground in the path of rain-bearing winds

rainstorm ('reɪnˌstɔːm) *n* a storm with heavy rain

rainwater ('reɪnˌwɔːtə) *n* water from rain (as distinguished from spring water, tap water, etc)

rainy ('reɪnɪ) *adj* rainier, rainiest 1 characterized by a large rainfall: *a rainy climate* 2 wet or showery; bearing rain ▷ 'rainily *adv* ▷ 'raininess *n*

rainy day *n* a future time of need, esp financial

Rais (*French* res) *or* **Retz** *n* **Gilles de** (ʒil də). 1404–40, French nobleman who fought with Joan of Arc: marshal of France (1429–40). He was executed for the torture and murder of more than 140 children

raise (reɪz) *vb* (*mainly tr*) 1 to move, cause to move, or elevate to a higher position or level; lift 2 to set or place in an upright position 3 to construct, build, or erect: *to raise a barn* 4 to increase in amount, size, value, etc: *to raise prices* 5 to increase in degree, strength, intensity, etc: *to raise one's voice* 6 to advance in rank or status; promote 7 to arouse or awaken from or as if from sleep or death 8 to stir up or incite; activate: *to raise a mutiny* 9 raise Cain, raise the devil, raise hell *or* raise the roof to create a boisterous disturbance 10 to give rise to; cause or provoke: *to raise a smile* 11 to put forward for consideration: *to raise a question* 12 to cause to assemble or gather together; collect: *to raise an army* 13 to grow or cause to grow: *to raise a crop* 14 to bring up; rear: *to raise a family* 15 to cause to be heard or known; utter or express: *to raise a shout; to raise a protest* 16 to bring to an end; remove: *to raise a siege; raise a ban* 17 to cause (dough, bread, etc) to rise, as by the addition of yeast 18 *poker* to bet more than (the previous player) 19 *bridge* to bid (one's partner's suit) at a higher level 20 *nautical* to cause (something) to seem to rise above the horizon by approaching: *we raised land after 20 days* 21 to establish radio communications with: *we managed to raise Moscow last night* 22 to obtain (money, funds, capital, etc) 23 to bring (a surface, a design, etc) into relief; cause to project 24 to cause (a blister, welt, etc) to form on the skin 25 *maths* to multiply (a number) by itself a specified number of times: *8 is 2 raised to the power 3* 26 raise one's glass to to drink the health of; drink a toast to 27 raise one's hat *old-fashioned* to take one's hat briefly off one's head as a greeting or mark of respect ▷ *n* 28 the act or an instance of raising 29 *chiefly US & Canadian* an increase, esp in salary, wages, etc; rise [C12: from Old Norse *reisa*; related to Old English *rǣran* to REAR²] ▷ 'raisable, 'raiseable *adj*

raised beach *n* a wave-cut platform raised above the shoreline by a relative fall in the water level

raisin ('reɪz²n) *n* a dried grape [C13: from Old French: grape, ultimately from Latin *racēmus* cluster of grapes; compare Greek *rhax* berry, grape] ▷ 'raisiny *adj*

raison d'être *French* (rɛzɔ̃ dɛtrə) *n*, *pl* **raisons d'être** (rɛzɔ̃ dɛtrə) reason or justification for existence

raita ('reɪtə, raɪ'iːtə) *n* an Indian dish of finely chopped cucumber, peppers, mint, etc, in yoghurt, served with curries [C20: from Hindi]

raj (rɑːdʒ) *n* (in India) government; rule [C19: from

Hindi, from Sanskrit *rājya*, from *rājati* he rules]

Raj (rɑːdʒ) *n* the Raj the British government in India before 1947

rajah *or* **raja** ('rɑːdʒə) *n* 1 (in India, formerly) a ruler or landlord: sometimes used as a form of address or as a title preceding a name 2 a Malayan or Javanese prince or chieftain [C16: from Hindi *rājā*, from Sanskrit *rājan* king; see RAJ; compare Latin *rex* king]

Rajasthan (ˌrɑːdʒə'stɑːn) *n* a state of NW India, bordering on Pakistan: formed in 1958; contains the Thar Desert in the west; now the largest state in India. Capital: Jaipur. Pop: 56 473 122 (2001). Area: 342 239 sq km (132 111 sq miles)

Rajkot ('rɑːdʒkəʊt) *n* a city in W India, in S Gujarat. Pop: 966 642 (2001)

Rajput *or* **Rajpoot** ('rɑːdʒpʊt) *n* *Hinduism* one of a Hindu military caste claiming descent from the Kshatriya, the original warrior caste [C16: from Hindi, from Sanskrit *rājan* king; see RAJ]

Rajputana (ˌrɑːdʒpʊ'tɑːnə) *n* a former group of princely states in NW India: now mostly part of Rajasthan

Rakata (rə'kɑːtə) *n* another name for **Krakatoa**

rake¹ (reɪk) *n* 1 a hand implement consisting of a row of teeth set in a headpiece attached to a long shaft and used for gathering hay, straw, leaves, etc, or for smoothing loose earth 2 any of several mechanical farm implements equipped with rows of teeth or rotating wheels mounted with tines and used to gather hay, straw, etc 3 any of various implements similar in shape or function, such as a tool for drawing out ashes from a furnace 4 the act of raking ▷ *vb* 5 to scrape, gather, or remove (leaves, refuse, etc) with or as if with a rake 6 to level or prepare (a surface, such as a flower bed) with a rake or similar implement 7 (*tr*; sometimes foll by *out*) to clear (ashes, clinker, etc) from (a fire or furnace) 8 (*tr*; foll by *up* or *together*) to gather (items or people) with difficulty, as from a scattered area or limited supply 9 (*tr*; often foll by *through, over* etc) to search or examine carefully 10 (when *intr*, foll by *against, along* etc) to scrape or graze: *the ship raked the side of the quay* 11 (*tr*) to direct (gunfire) along the length of (a target): *machine-guns raked the column* 12 (*tr*) to sweep (one's eyes) along the length of (something); scan ▷ See also **rake in**, **rake-off**, etc [Old English *raca*; related to Old Norse *raka*, Old High German *rehho* a rake, Gothic *rikan* to heap up, Latin *rogus* funeral pile] ▷ 'raker *n*

rake² (reɪk) *n* a dissolute man, esp one in fashionable society; roué [C17: short for RAKEHELL]

rake³ (reɪk) *vb* (*mainly intr*) 1 to incline from the vertical by a perceptible degree, esp (of a ship's mast or funnel) towards the stern 2 (*tr*) to construct with a backward slope ▷ *n* 3 the degree to which an object, such as a ship's mast, inclines from the perpendicular, esp towards the stern 4 *theatre* the slope of a stage from the back towards the footlights 5 *aeronautics* the angle between the wings of an aircraft and the line of symmetry of the aircraft 6 the angle between the working face of a cutting tool and a plane perpendicular to the surface of the workpiece [C17: of uncertain origin; perhaps related to German *ragen* to project, Swedish *raka*]

rakehell ('reɪkˌhɛl) *archaic n* 1 a dissolute man; rake ▷ *adj* Also: rakehelly 2 profligate; dissolute [C16: from RAKE¹ + HELL; but compare Middle English *rakel* rash]

rake in *vb* (*tr, adverb*) *informal* to acquire (money) in large amounts

rake-off *slang* ▷ *n* 1 a share of profits, esp one that is illegal or given as a bribe ▷ *vb* rake off 2 (*tr, adverb*) to take or receive (such a share of profits)

rake up *vb* (*tr, adverb*) to revive, discover, or bring to light (something forgotten): *to rake up an old quarrel*

raki *or* **rakee** (rɑː'kiː, 'rækɪ) *n* a strong spirit distilled in Turkey, the former Yugoslavia, etc, from grain, usually flavoured with aniseed or other aromatics [C17: from Turkish *rāqī*]

raking ('reɪkɪŋ) *n* *rugby* the offence committed when a player deliberately scrapes an opponent's leg, arm, etc with the studs of his or her boots

rakish¹ ('reɪkɪʃ) *adj* dissolute; profligate [C18: from RAKE² + -ISH] ▷ 'rakishly *adv* ▷ 'rakishness *n*

r

rakish² ('reɪkɪʃ) *adj* **1** dashing; jaunty: *a hat set at a rakish angle* **2** *nautical* (of a ship or boat) having lines suggestive of speed [c19: probably from RAKE³ (sense 1), with reference to the sloping masts of pirate ships]

rale *or* **râle** (rɑːl) *n med* an abnormal coarse crackling sound heard on auscultation of the chest, usually caused by the accumulation of fluid in the lungs [c19: from French *râle*, from *râler* to breathe with a rattling sound]

Raleigh¹ ('rɔːlɪ, 'rɑː-) *n* a city in E central North Carolina, capital of the state. Pop: 316 802 (2003 est)

Raleigh² *or* **Ralegh** ('rɔːlɪ, 'rɑː-) *n* Sir **Walter**. ?1552–1618, English courtier, explorer, and writer; favourite of Elizabeth I. After unsuccessful attempts to colonize Virginia (1584–89), he led two expeditions to the Orinoco to search for gold (1595; 1616). He introduced tobacco and potatoes into England, and under imprisonment (1603–16) for conspiracy under James I. He was beheaded in 1618

rallentando (ˌrælɛn'tændəʊ) *adj, adv music* becoming slower. Also called: ritardando [c19: Italian, from *rallentare* to slow down]

rally¹ ('rælɪ) *vb* **-lies, -lying, -lied 1** to bring (a group, unit, etc) into order, as after dispersal, or (of such a group) to reform and come to order **2** (when *intr*, foll by *to*) to organize (supporters, etc) for a common cause or (of such people) to come together for a purpose **3** to summon up (one's strength, spirits, etc) or (of a person's health, strength, or spirits) to revive or recover **4** (*intr*) *stock exchange* to increase sharply after a decline **5** (*intr*) *tennis, squash, badminton* to engage in a rally ▷ *n, pl* **-lies 6** a large gathering of people for a common purpose, esp for some political cause **7** a marked recovery of strength or spirits, as during illness **8** a return to order after dispersal or rout, as of troops, etc **9** *stock exchange* a sharp increase in price or trading activity after a decline **10** *tennis, squash, badminton* an exchange of several shots before one player wins the point **11** a type of motoring competition over public and closed roads [c16: from Old French *rallier*, from RE- + *alier* to unite; see ALLY]
> 'rallier *n*

rally² ('rælɪ) *vb* **-lies, -lying, -lied** to mock or ridicule (someone) in a good-natured way; chaff; tease [c17: from Old French *railler* to tease; see RAIL²]

rallycross ('rælɪˌkrɒs) *n* a form of motor sport in which cars race over a one-mile circuit of rough grass with some hard-surfaced sections

rally round *vb* (*intr*) to come to the aid of (someone); offer moral or practical support

ram (ræm) *n* **1** an uncastrated adult sheep **2** a piston or moving plate, esp one driven hydraulically or pneumatically **3** the falling weight of a pile driver or similar device **4** short for **battering ram 5** Also called: rostrum, beak a pointed projection in the stem of an ancient warship for puncturing the hull of enemy ships **6** a warship equipped with a ram ▷ *vb* **rams, ramming, rammed 7** (*tr*; usually foll by *into*) to force or drive, as by heavy blows: *to ram a post into the ground* **8** (of a moving object) to crash with force (against another object) or (of two moving objects) to collide in this way **9** (*tr*; often foll by *in* or *down*) to stuff or cram (something into a hole, etc) **10** (*tr*; foll by *onto, against* etc) to thrust violently: *he rammed the books onto the desk* **11** (*tr*) to present (an idea, argument, etc) forcefully or aggressively (esp in the phrase **ram** (something) **down someone's throat**) **12** (*tr*) to drive (a charge) into a firearm [Old English *ramm*; related to Old High German *ram* ram, Old Norse *ramr* fierce, *rimma* to fight] > 'rammer *n*

Ram (ræm) *n* **the Ram** the constellation Aries, the first sign of the zodiac

RAM¹ (ræm) *n acronym computing* random access memory: semiconductor memory in which all storage locations can be rapidly accessed in the same amount of time. It forms the main memory of a computer, used by applications to perform tasks while the device is operating

RAM² *abbreviation* Royal Academy of Music

Ramadan, Rhamadhan (ˌræmə'dɑːn) *or* **Ramazan** (ˌræmə'zɑːn) *n* **1** the ninth month of the Muslim year, lasting 30 days, during which strict fasting is observed

from sunrise to sunset **2** the fast itself [c16: from Arabic, literally: the hot month, from *ramad* dryness]

Ramakrishna (ˌrɑːmə'krɪʃnə) *n* **Sri** (sriː). 1834–86, Hindu yogi and religious reformer. He preached the equal value of all religions as different paths to God

Ramallah (rə'mælə) *n* a town in the West Bank, serving as headquarters of the Palestinian National Authority. Pop: 51 000 (2005 est)

Raman effect ('rɑːmən) *n* a change in wavelength of light that is scattered by electrons within a material. The effect is used in **Raman spectroscopy** for studying molecules [c20: named after Sir Chandrasekhara *Raman* (1888–1970), Indian physicist]

Ramanuja (ˌræmə'nuːdʒə) *n* 11th century AD, Indian Hindu philosopher and theologian

Ramaphosa (ˌræmə'fɔːsə) *n* (**Matamela**) **Cyril**. born 1952, Black South African statesman and trade unionist

Ramat Gan (rɑː'mɑːt 'gɑːn) *n* a city in Israel, E of Tel Aviv. Pop: 126 500 (2003 est)

Rambert ('rɒmbeə) *n* Dame **Marie**. 1888–1982, British ballet dancer and teacher, born in Poland: founded the **Ballet Rambert** (1926)

ramble ('ræmbəl) *vb* (*intr*) **1** to stroll about freely, as for relaxation, with no particular direction **2** (of paths, streams, etc) to follow a winding course; meander **3** (of plants) to grow in a random fashion **4** (of speech, writing, etc) to lack organization ▷ *n* **5** a leisurely stroll, esp in the countryside [c17: probably related to Middle Dutch *rammelen* to ROAM (of animals); see RAM]

rambler ('ræmblə) *n* **1** a weak-stemmed plant, esp any of various cultivated hybrid roses that straggle over other vegetation **2** a person who rambles, esp one who takes country walks **3** a person who lacks organization in his speech or writing

rambling ('ræmblɪŋ) *adj* **1** straggling or sprawling haphazardly; unplanned: *a rambling old house* **2** (of speech or writing) lacking a coherent plan; diffuse and disconnected **3** (of a plant, esp a rose) profusely climbing and straggling **4** nomadic; wandering

Ramboesque (ˌræmbəʊ'esk) *adj* looking or behaving like, or characteristic of, Rambo, a fictional film character noted for his mindless brutality [c20: after *Rambo, First Blood II*, released in Britain 1985]
> 'Rambo,ism *n*

Rambouillet (French rɑbujɛ) *n* a town in N France, in the Yvelines department: site of the summer residence of French presidents. Pop: 24 758 (1999)

rambunctious (ræm'bʌŋkʃəs) *adj informal* boisterous; unruly [c19: probably from Icelandic *ram-* (intensifying prefix) + *-bunctious*, from BUMPTIOUS]
> ram'bunctiousness *n*

rambutan (ræm'buːtªn) *n* **1** a sapindaceous tree, *Nephelium lappaceum*, native to SE Asia, that has bright red edible fruit **2** the fruit of this tree [c18: from Malay, from *rambut* hair]

RAMC *abbreviation* Royal Army Medical Corps

Rameau (French ramo) *n* **Jean Philippe** (ʒɑ̃ filip). 1683–1764, French composer. His works include the opera *Castor et Pollux* (1737), chamber music, harpsichord pieces, church music, and cantatas. His *Traité de l'harmonie* (1722) was of fundamental importance in the development of modern harmony

ramekin *or* **ramequin** ('ræmɪkɪn) *n* **1** a savoury dish made from a cheese mixture baked in a fireproof container **2** the container itself [c18: French *ramequin*, of Germanic origin]

ramen ('rɑːmən) *n* **1** a Japanese dish consisting of a clear broth containing thin white noodles and sometimes vegetables, meat, etc ▷ *pl n* **2** thin white noodles served in such a broth [Japanese, from Chinese *la* to pull + *mian* noodles]

Rameses ('ræmɪˌsiːz) *n* same as **Ramses**

ramification (ˌræmɪfɪ'keɪʃən) *n* **1** the act or process of ramifying or branching out **2** an offshoot or subdivision **3** a structure of branching parts

ramify ('ræmɪˌfaɪ) *vb* **-fies, -fying, -fied 1** to divide into branches or branchlike parts **2** (*intr*) to develop complicating consequences; become complex [c16: from French *ramifier*, from Latin *rāmus* branch + *facere* to make]

Ramillies ('ræmɪliːz; *French* ramiji) *n* a village in central Belgium where the Duke of Marlborough defeated the French in 1706

ramjet *or* **ramjet engine** ('ræm,dʒɛt) *n* **a** a type of jet engine in which fuel is burned in a duct using air compressed by the forward speed of the aircraft **b** an aircraft powered by such an engine

ramose ('reɪməʊs, ræ'məʊs) *or* **ramous** ('reɪməs) *adj* having branches [c17: from Latin *rāmōsus*, from *rāmus* branch] > 'ramosely *or* 'ramously *adv* > ramosity (ræ'mɒsɪtɪ) *n*

ramp (ræmp) *n* **1** a sloping floor, path, etc, that joins two surfaces at different levels **2** a movable stairway by which passengers enter and leave an aircraft **3** the act of ramping **4** *Brit slang* a swindle, esp one involving exorbitant prices ▷ *vb* **5** (*intr*; often foll by *about* or *around*) (esp of animals) to rush around in a wild excited manner **6** to act in a violent or threatening manner, as when angry (esp in the phrase **ramp and rage**) **7** (*tr*) *finance* to buy (a security) in the market with the object of raising its price and enhancing the image of the company behind it for financial gain [c18 (n): from c13 *rampe*, from Old French *ramper* to crawl or rear, probably of Germanic origin; compare Middle Low German *ramp* cramp]

rampage *vb* (ræm'peɪdʒ) **1** (*intr*) to rush about in an angry, violent, or agitated fashion ▷ *n* ('ræmpeɪdʒ, ræm'peɪdʒ) **2** angry or destructive behaviour **3** on the rampage behaving violently or destructively [c18: from Scottish, of uncertain origin; perhaps based on RAMP] > ram'pageous *adj* > ram'pageously *adv* > ram'pager *n*

rampant ('ræmpənt) *adj* **1** unrestrained or violent in behaviour, desire, opinions, etc **2** growing or developing unchecked **3** (*postpositive*) *heraldry* (of a beast) standing on the hind legs, the right foreleg raised above the left **4** (of an arch) having one abutment higher than the other [c14: from Old French *ramper* to crawl, rear; see RAMP] > 'rampancy *n* > 'rampantly *adv*

rampart ('ræmpɑːt) *n* **1** the surrounding embankment of a fort, often including any walls, parapets, walks, etc, that are built on the bank **2** anything resembling a rampart in form or function, esp in being a defence or bulwark **3** *Canadian* a steep rock wall in a river gorge ▷ *vb* **4** (*tr*) to provide with a rampart; fortify [c16: from Old French, from *remparer*, from RE- + *emparer* to take possession of, from Old Provençal *antparar*, from Latin *ante* before + *parāre* to prepare]

Ramphal (,ræm'fɑːl) *n* Sir **Shridath Surendranath**, known as *Sunni*. born 1928, Guyanese diplomat and Commonwealth Secretary-General (1975–90)

Ramphele (ræm'fɛleɪ) *n* **Mamphela**. born 1947, Black South African political activist: partner of Steve Biko; a director of the World Bank from 2000

rampion ('ræmpɪən) *n* a campanulaceous plant, *Campanula rapunculus*, native to Europe and Asia, that has clusters of bluish flowers and an edible white tuberous root used in salads [c16: probably from Old French *raiponce*, from Old Italian *raponzo*, from *rapa* turnip, from Latin *rāpum* turnip; see RAPE²]

ramp up *vb* (*adverb*) **1** to increase or cause to increase **2** (*intr*) to increase the effort involved in a process

Rampur ('ræmpʊə) *n* a city in N India, in N Uttar Pradesh. Pop: 281 549 (2001)

ram raid *n informal* a raid in which a stolen car is driven through a shop window in order to steal goods from the shop > ram raider *n* > ram raiding *n*

ramrod ('ræm,rɒd) *n* a rod for cleaning the barrel of a rifle or other small firearms

Ramsay ('ræmzɪ) *n* **1 Allan**. ?1686–1758, Scottish poet, editor, and bookseller, noted particularly for his pastoral comedy *The Gentle Shepherd* (1725): first person to introduce the circulating library in Scotland **2** his son, **Allan** 1713–84, Scottish portrait painter **3** James Andrew Broun Ramsay See **Dalhousie** (sense 2) **4 Gordon**. born 1963, British chef and restaurateur; achieved a third Michelin star (2001) **5** Sir **William**. 1852–1916, Scottish chemist. He discovered argon (1894) with Rayleigh, isolated helium (1895), and identified neon, krypton, and xenon: Nobel prize for chemistry 1904

Ramses ('ræmsiːz) *or* **Rameses** *n* any of 12 kings of ancient Egypt, who ruled from ?1315 to ?1090 BC

Ramses II *or* **Rameses II** *n* died ?1225 BC, king of ancient Egypt (?1292–?25). His reign was marked by war with the Hittites and the construction of many colossal monuments, esp the rock temple at Abu Simbel

Ramses III *or* **Rameses III** *n* died ?1167 BC, king of ancient Egypt (?1198–?67). His reign was marked by wars in Libya and Syria

Ramsey ('ræmzɪ) *n* Sir **Alf(red) (Ernest)**. 1922–99, English footballer and football manager, who played for England 32 times and managed England when they won the World Cup (1966)

Ramsgate ('ræmz,geɪt) *n* a port and resort in SE England, in E Kent on the North Sea coast. Pop: 37 967 (2001)

ramshackle ('ræm,ʃækᵊl) *adj* (esp of buildings) badly constructed or maintained; rickety, shaky, or derelict [c17 *ramshackled*, from obsolete *ransackle* to RANSACK]

Ram Singh ('ræm 'sɪŋ) *n* 1816–85, Indian leader of a puritanical Sikh sect, the Kukas, who tried to remove the British from India through a policy of noncooperation

ramsons ('ræmzənz, -sənz) *pl n* (*usually functioning as singular*) **1** a broad-leaved garlic, *Allium ursinum*, native to Europe and Asia **2** the bulbous root of this plant, eaten as a relish [Old English *hramesa*; related to Middle Low German *ramese* Norwegian *rams*]

ran (ræn) *vb* the past tense of **run**

RAN *abbreviation* Royal Australian Navy

Rancagua (*Spanish* raŋ'kaɣwa) *n* a city in central Chile. Pop: 217 000 (2005 est)

ranch (rɑːntʃ) *n* **1** a large tract of land, esp one in North America, together with the necessary personnel, buildings, and equipment, for rearing livestock, esp cattle **2** a any large farm for the rearing of a particular kind of livestock or crop: *a mink ranch* **b** the buildings, land, etc, connected with it ▷ *vb* **3** (*intr*) to manage or run a ranch **4** (*tr*) to raise (animals) on or as if on a ranch [c19: from Mexican Spanish *rancho* small farm]

rancher ('rɑːntʃə) *n* a person who owns, manages, or works on a ranch

rancherie ('rɑːntʃərɪ) *n* (in British Columbia, Canada) a settlement of North American Indians, esp on a reserve [from Spanish *ranchería*]

Ranchi ('rɑːntʃɪ) *n* an industrial city in E India, between the coal and iron belts of the Chota Nagpur Plateau; the capital of Jharkhand from 2000. Pop: 846 454 (2001)

rancho ('rɑːntʃəʊ) *n, pl* **-chos** *Southwestern US* **1** a hut or group of huts for housing ranch workers **2** another word for **ranch** [c17: from Mexican Spanish: camp, from Old Spanish *ranchar* to be billeted, from Old French *ranger* to place]

rancid ('rænsɪd) *adj* **1** (of butter, bacon, etc) having an unpleasant stale taste or smell as the result of decomposition **2** (of a taste or smell) rank or sour; stale [c17: from Latin *rancidus* rank, from *rancēre* to stink] > rancidity (ræn'sɪdɪtɪ) *or* 'rancidness *n*

rancour *or US* **rancor** ('ræŋkə) *n* malicious resentfulness or hostility; spite [c14: from Old French, from Late Latin *rancor* rankness] > 'rancorous *adj* > 'rancorously *adv*

rand¹ (rænd, rɒnt) *n* the standard monetary unit of the Republic of South Africa, divided into 100 cents [c20: from Afrikaans, shortened from WITWATERSRAND, referring to the gold-mining there; related to RAND²]

rand² (rænd) *n* **1** *shoemaking* a leather strip put in the heel of a shoe before the lifts are put on **2** *dialect* **a** a strip or margin; border **b** a strip of cloth; selvage [Old English; related to Old High German *rant* border, rim of a shield, Old Norse *rönd* shield, rim]

Rand (rænd) *n* the Rand short for **Witwatersrand**

R & B *abbreviation* rhythm and blues

R & D *abbreviation* research and development

Randers (*Danish* 'ranərs) *n* a port and industrial centre in Denmark, in E Jutland on **Randers Fjord** (an inlet of the Kattegat). Pop: 55 739 (2004 est)

randlord ('rænd,lɔːd) *n South African* a mining magnate during the 19th-century gold boom in Johannesburg

Randolph ('rændɒlf, -dəlf) *n* **1** Edmund Jennings,

1753–1813, US politician. He was a member of the convention that framed the US constitution (1787), attorney general (1789–94), and secretary of state (1794–95) **2 John**, called *Randolph of Roanoke*. 1773–1833, US politician, noted for his eloquence: in 1820 he opposed the Missouri Compromise that outlawed slavery **3 Sir Thomas**; 1st Earl of Moray. Died 1332, Scottish soldier: regent after the death of Robert the Bruce (1329)

random ('rændəm) *adj* **1** lacking any definite plan or prearranged order; haphazard: *a random selection* **2** *statistics* **a** having a value which cannot be determined but only described probabilistically: *a random variable* **b** chosen without regard to any characteristics of the individual members of the population so that each has an equal chance of being selected: *random sampling* ▷ *n* **3 at random** in a purposeless fashion; not following any prearranged order [c14: from Old French *randon*, from *randir* to gallop, of Germanic origin; compare Old High German *rinnan* to run] > 'randomly *adv* > 'randomness *n*

random access *n* another name for **direct access**

randomize *or* **randomise** ('rændə,maɪz) *vb* (*tr*) to set up (a selection process, sample, etc) in a deliberately random way in order to enhance the statistical validity of any results obtained > ,randomi'zation *or* ,randomi'sation *n* > 'random,izer *or* 'random,iser *n*

random walk theory *n stock exchange* the theory that the future movement of share prices does not reflect past movements and therefore will not follow a discernible pattern

R and R *abbreviation US military* rest and recreation

randy ('rændɪ) *adj* **randier, randiest 1** *informal, chiefly Brit* sexually excited or aroused **2** *chiefly Scot* lacking any sense of propriety or restraint; reckless ▷ *n, pl* **randies 3** *chiefly Scot* a rude or reckless person [c17: probably from obsolete *rand* to RANT] > 'randily *adv* > 'randiness *n*

ranee ('rɑːnɪ) *n* a variant spelling of **rani**

rang (ræŋ) *vb* the past tense of **ring²**

◉ **USAGE** See at **ring²**

rangatira (,rʌŋɡə'tɪərə) *n NZ* a Māori chief of either sex [Māori]

rangatiratanga (,rʌŋɡətɪərə'tʌŋɡə) *n NZ* the condition of being a Māori chief; sovereignty [Māori]

range (reɪndʒ) *n* **1** the limits within which a person or thing can function effectively **2** the limits within which any fluctuation takes place: *a range of values* **3** the total products of a manufacturer, designer, or stockist: *the new autumn range* **4 a** the maximum effective distance of a projectile fired from a weapon **b** the distance between a target and a weapon **5** an area set aside for shooting practice or rocket testing **6** the total distance which a ship, aircraft, or land vehicle is capable of covering without taking on fresh fuel: *the range of this car is about 160 miles* **7** *maths, logic* (of a function) the set of values that the function takes for all possible arguments **8** *US & Canadian* **a** an extensive tract of open land on which livestock can graze **b** (*as modifier*): *range cattle* **9** the geographical region in which a species of plant or animal normally grows or lives **10** a rank, row, or series of items **11** a series or chain of mountains **12** a large stove with burners and one or more ovens, usually heated by solid fuel **13** the act or process of ranging ▷ *vb* **14** to establish or be situated in a line, row, or series **15** (*tr, often reflexive, foll by with*) to put into a specific category; classify: *she ranges herself with the angels* **16** (foll by *on*) to aim or point (a telescope, gun, etc) or (of a gun, telescope, etc) to be pointed or aimed **17** to establish the distance of (a target) from (a weapon) **18** (*intr*) (of a gun or missile) to have a specified range **19** (when *intr*, foll by *over*) to wander about (in) an area; roam (over) **20** (*intr*, foll by *over*) (of an animal or plant) to live or grow in its normal habitat **21** (*tr*) to put (cattle) to graze on a range **22** (*intr*) to fluctuate within specific limits **23** (*intr*) to extend or run in a specific direction **24** (*intr*) *nautical* (of a vessel) to swing back and forth while at anchor **25** (*tr*) to make (lines of printers' type) level or even at the margin [c13: from Old French: row, from *ranger* to position, from *renc* line]

rangefinder ('reɪndʒ,faɪndə) *n* an instrument for determining the distance of an object from the observer,

esp in order to sight a gun or focus a camera

ranger ('reɪndʒə) *n* **1** (*sometimes capital*) an official in charge of a forest, park, estate, nature reserve, etc **2** *chiefly US* a person employed to patrol a State or national park or forest. Brit equivalent: **warden 3** *US* one of a body of armed troops employed to police a State or district: *a Texas Ranger* **4** (in the US and certain other armies) a commando specially trained in making raids **5** a person who wanders about large areas of country; a rover

Ranger *or* **Ranger Guide** ('reɪndʒə) *n Brit* a member of the senior branch of the Guides

rangiora (,rʌŋɡɪ'ɔːrə, ,rʌŋɪ-) *n* an evergreen shrub or small tree, *Brachyglottis repanda*, of New Zealand, having large ovate leaves and small greenish-white flowers: family *Asteraceae* (composites) [Māori]

Rangoon (ræŋ'guːn) *n* the former official name (until 1989, but still widely used) of **Yangon**

rangy ('reɪndʒɪ) *adj* **rangier, rangiest 1** (of animals or people) having long slender limbs **2** adapted to wandering or roaming **3** allowing considerable freedom of movement; spacious; roomy [c19: from RANGE + -Y¹] > 'rangily *adv* > 'ranginess *n*

rani *or* **ranee** ('rɑːnɪ) *n* (in oriental countries, esp India) a queen or princess; the wife of a rajah [c17: from Hindi: queen, from Sanskrit *rājñī*, feminine of *rājan* RAJAH]

Ranjit Singh ('rʌndʒɪt 'sɪŋ) *n* called *the Lion of the Punjab*. 1780–1839, founder of the Sikh kingdom in the Punjab

rank¹ (ræŋk) *n* **1** a position, esp an official one, within a social organization, esp the armed forces: *the rank of captain* **2** high social or other standing; status **3** a line or row of people or things **4** the position of an item in any ordering or sequence **5** *Brit* a place where taxis wait to be hired **6** a line of soldiers drawn up abreast of each other. See **file¹**(sense 5) **7** any of the eight horizontal rows of squares on a chessboard **8 close ranks** to maintain discipline or solidarity, esp in anticipation of attack **9 pull rank** to get one's own way by virtue of one's superior position or rank ▷ *vb* **10** (*tr*) to arrange (people or things) in rows or lines; range **11** to accord or be accorded a specific position in an organization, society, or group **12** (*tr*) to array (a set of objects) as a sequence, esp in terms of the natural arithmetic ordering of some measure of the elements: *to rank students by their test scores* **13** (*intr*) to be important; rate: *money ranks low in her order of priorities* **14** *chiefly US* to take precedence or surpass in rank [c16: from Old French *ranc* row, rank, of Germanic origin; compare Old High German *hring* circle]

rank² (ræŋk) *adj* **1** showing vigorous and profuse growth: *rank weeds* **2** highly offensive or disagreeable, esp in smell or taste **3** (*prenominal*) complete or absolute; utter: *a rank outsider* **4** coarse or vulgar; gross: *his language was rank* [Old English *ranc* straight, noble; related to Old Norse *rakkr* upright, Dutch, Swedish *rank* tall and thin, weak] > 'rankly *adv* > 'rankness *n*

Rank *n* **1** (ræŋk) **J(oseph)** Arthur, 1st Baron. 1888–1972, British industrialist and film executive, whose companies dominated the British film industry in the 1940s and 1950s **2** (German raŋk) **Otto** ('ɔto). 1884–1939, Austrian psychoanalyst, noted for his theory that the trauma of birth may be reflected in certain forms of mental illness

rank and file *n* **1** the ordinary soldiers of an army, excluding the officers **2** the great mass or majority of any group or organization, as opposed to the leadership **3** (*modifier*) of, relating to, or characteristic of the rank and file: *rank-and-file opinion; rank-and-file support* > **rank and filer** *n*

ranker ('ræŋkə) *n* **1** a soldier in the ranks **2** a commissioned officer who entered service as a recruit, esp in the army

Rankin ('ræŋkɪn) *n* **Ian.** born 1960, Scottish novelist; best known for his series of novels featuring Edinburgh detective Inspector Rebus, beginning with *Knots and Crosses* (1987)

ranking ('ræŋkɪŋ) *adj* **1** *chiefly US & Canadian* prominent; high ranking **2** *Caribbean slang* possessed of style; fashionable; exciting ▷ *n* **3** a position on a scale; rating:

a ranking in a tennis tournament

rankism ('ræŋkˌɪzəm) *n* discriminination against people on the grounds of rank

rankle ('ræŋkəl) *vb* (*intr*) to cause severe and continuous irritation, anger, or bitterness; fester [c14 *ranclen*, from Old French *draoncler* to fester, from *draoncle* ulcer, from Latin *dracunculus* small serpent, from *dracō* serpent; see DRAGON]

ransack ('rænsæk) *vb* (*tr*) **1** to search through every part of (a house, box, etc); examine thoroughly **2** to plunder; pillage [c13: from Old Norse *rann* house + *saka* to search, SEEK] > 'ransacker *n*

ransom ('rænsəm) *n* **1** the release of captured prisoners, property, etc, on payment of a stipulated price **2** the price demanded or stipulated for such a release **3** hold to ransom **a** to keep (prisoners, property, etc) in confinement until payment for their release is made or received **b** to attempt to force (a person or persons) to comply with one's demands **4** a king's ransom a very large amount of money or valuables ▷ *vb* (*tr*) **5** to pay a stipulated price and so obtain the release of (prisoners, property, etc) **6** to set free (prisoners, property, etc) upon receiving the payment demanded **7** to redeem; rescue: *Christ ransomed men from sin* [c14: from Old French *ransoun*, from Latin *redemptiō* a buying back, REDEMPTION] > 'ransomer *n*

Ransom ('rænsəm) *n* **John Crowe**. 1888–1974, US poet and critic

Ransome ('rænsəm) *n* **Arthur**. 1884–1967, English writer, best known for his books for children, including *Swallows and Amazons* (1930) and *Great Northern?* (1947)

rant (rænt) *vb* **1** to utter (something) in loud, violent, or bombastic tones ▷ *n* **2** loud, declamatory, or extravagant speech; bombast [c16: from Dutch *ranten* to rave; related to German *ranzen* to gambol] > 'ranter *n* > 'rantingly *adv*

ranunculaceous (rəˌnʌŋkjʊ'leɪʃəs) *adj* of, relating to, or belonging to the *Ranunculaceae*, a N temperate family of flowering plants typically having flowers with five petals and numerous anthers and styles. The family includes the buttercup, clematis, hellebore, and columbine

ranunculus (rə'nʌŋkjʊləs) *n*, *pl* **-luses** *or* **-li** (-ˌlaɪ) any ranunculaceous plant of the genus *Ranunculus*, having finely divided leaves and typically yellow five-petalled flowers. The genus includes buttercup, crowfoot, spearwort, and lesser celandine [c16: from Latin: tadpole, from *rāna* a frog]

RAOC *abbreviation* Royal Army Ordnance Corps

rap¹ (ræp) *vb* **raps**, **rapping**, **rapped 1** to strike (a fist, stick, etc) against (something) with a sharp quick blow; knock **2** (*intr*) to make a sharp loud sound, esp by knocking **3** (*tr*) to rebuke or criticize sharply **4** (*tr*; foll by *out*) to put (forth) in sharp rapid speech; utter in an abrupt fashion: *to rap out orders* **5** (*intr*) slang to talk, esp volubly **6** (*intr*) to perform a rhythmic monologue with a musical backing **7** rap over the knuckles to reprimand ▷ *n* **8** a sharp quick blow or the sound produced by such a blow **9** a sharp rebuke or criticism **10** slang voluble talk; chatter **11 a** a fast, rhythmic monologue over a prerecorded instrumental track **b** (*as modifier*): *rap music* **12** beat the rap US & Canadian slang to escape punishment or be acquitted of a crime **13** take the rap slang to suffer the consequences of a mistake, misdeed, or crime, whether guilty or not [c14: probably from Scandinavian origin; compare Swedish *rappa* to beat]

rap² (ræp) *n* (*used with a negative*) the least amount (esp in the phrase **not to care a rap**) [c18: probably from *ropaire* counterfeit coin formerly current in Ireland]

rap³ (ræp) *vb*, *n* Austral informal a variant spelling of **wrap** (sense 8)

rapacious (rə'peɪʃəs) *adj* **1** practising pillage or rapine **2** greedy or grasping **3** (of animals, esp birds) subsisting by catching living prey [c17: from Latin *rapāx* grasping, from *rapere* to seize] > ra'paciously *adv* > rapacity (rə'pæsɪtɪ) *or* ra'paciousness *n*

Rapacki (Polish ra'patski) *n* **Adam** ('adam). 1909–70, Polish politician: foreign minister (1956–68): proposed (1957) the denuclearization of Poland, Czechoslovakia, East Germany, and West Germany (the **Rapacki Plan**):

rejected by the West because of Soviet predominance in conventional weapons

Rapallo (Italian ra'pallo) *n* a port and resort in NW Italy, in Liguria on the **Gulf of Rapallo** (an inlet of the Ligurian Sea): scene of the signing of two treaties after World War I. Pop: 29 159 (2001)

Rapa Nui ('rɑːpɑː 'nuːɪ) *n* the Polynesian name for **Easter Island**

rape¹ (reɪp) *n* **1** the offence of forcing a person, esp a woman, to submit to sexual intercourse against that person's will **2** the act of despoiling a country in warfare; rapine **3** any violation or abuse: *the rape of justice* **4** archaic abduction: *the rape of the Sabine women* ▷ *vb* (*mainly tr*) **5** to commit rape upon (a person) **6** archaic to carry off by force; abduct [c14: from Latin *rapere* to seize] > 'rapist *n*

rape² (reɪp) *n* a Eurasian plant, *Brassica napus*, that has bright yellow flowers and is cultivated for its seeds, which yield a useful oil, and as a fodder plant: family *Brassicaceae* (crucifers). Also called: colza, cole [c14: from Latin *rāpum* turnip]

rape³ (reɪp) *n* (*often plural*) the skins and stalks of grapes left after wine-making: used in making vinegar [c17: from French *râpe*, of Germanic origin; compare Old High German *raspōn* to scrape together]

Raphael¹ ('ræfeɪəl) *n* **1** Bible one of the archangels; the angel of healing and the guardian of Tobias (Tobit 3:17; 5–12). Feast day: Sept 29 **2** original name *Raffaello Santi* or *Sanzio*. 1483–1520, Italian painter and architect, regarded as one of the greatest artists of the High Renaissance. His many paintings include the *Sistine Madonna* (?1513) and the *Transfiguration* (unfinished, 1520) > ˌRaphael'esque *adj*

Raphael² ('ræfeɪəl) *n* Bible one of the archangels; the angel of healing and the guardian of Tobias (Tobit 3:17; 5–12). Feast day: Sept 29

raphia ('ræfɪə) *n* a variant spelling of **raffia**

raphide ('reɪfaɪd) *or* **raphis** ('reɪfɪs) *n*, *pl* **raphides** ('ræfɪˌdiːz) any of numerous needle-shaped crystals, usually of calcium oxalate, that occur in many plant cells as a metabolic product [c18: from French, from Greek *rhaphis* needle]

rapid¹ ('ræpɪd) *adj* **1** (of an action or movement) performed or occurring during a short interval of time; quick **2** acting or moving quickly; fast: *a rapid worker* ▷ See also **rapids** [c17: from Latin *rapidus* tearing away, from *rapere* to seize; see RAPE¹] > 'rapidly *adv* > rapidity (rə'pɪdɪtɪ) *or* 'rapidness *n*

rapid eye movement *n* movement of the eyeballs under closed eyelids during paradoxical sleep, which occurs while the sleeper is dreaming. Abbreviation: REM

rapid fire *n* **1** a fast rate of gunfire ▷ *adj* rapid-fire **2** firing shots rapidly **3** done, delivered, or occurring in rapid succession

rapids ('ræpɪdz) *pl n* part of a river where the current is very fast and turbulent

rapier ('reɪpɪə) *n* **1** a long narrow two-edged sword with a guarded hilt, used as a thrusting weapon, popular in the 16th and 17th centuries **2** a smaller single-edged 18th-century sword, used principally in France [c16: from Old French *espee rapiere*, literally: rasping sword; see RASP¹]

rapine ('ræpaɪn) *n* the seizure of property by force; pillage [c15: from Latin *rapīna* plundering, from *rapere* to snatch]

rap jumping *n* the sport of descending high buildings, attached to ropes and a pulley

rappee (ræ'piː) *n* a moist English snuff of the 18th and 19th centuries [c18: from French *tabac râpé*, literally: scraped tobacco, from *râper* to scrape; see RAPE³, RASP¹]

rappel (ræ'pɛl) *vb* **-pels**, **-pelling**, **-pelled 1** another word for **abseil** ▷ *n* **2** (formerly) a drumbeat to call soldiers to arms [c19: from French, from *rappeler* to call back, from Latin *appellāre* to summon]

rappé pie *or* **rappe** ('ræpeɪ) *n* Canadian an Acadian dish of grated potatoes and pork or chicken [from Acadian French *tarte râpée* grated pie]

rapport (ræ'pɔː) *n* (*often foll by* with) a sympathetic relationship or understanding. See also **en rapport** [c15:

r

from French, from *rapporter* to bring back, from RE- + *aporter*, from Latin *apportāre*, from *adto* + *portāre* to carry]

rapprochement *French* (raprɔʃmɑ̃) n a resumption of friendly relations, esp between two countries [C19: literally: bringing closer]

rapscallion (ræpˈskæljən) n a disreputable person; rascal or rogue [C17: from earlier *rascallion*; see RASCAL]

rap sheet n *chiefly US & Canadian informal* a police record of an individual's criminal history

rapt[1] (ræpt) adj 1 totally absorbed; engrossed; spellbound, esp through or as if through emotion: *rapt with wonder* 2 characterized by or proceeding from rapture: *a rapt smile* [C14: from Latin *raptus* carried away, from *rapere* to seize; see RAPE[1]] > **raptly** adv

rapt[2] (ræpt) adj Also: **wrapped** *Austral & NZ informal* very pleased: delighted

raptor (ˈræptə) n 1 another name for **bird of prey** 2 *informal* a carnivorous bipedal dinosaur of the late Cretaceous period [C17: from Latin: plunderer, from *rapere* to take by force]

raptorial (ræpˈtɔːrɪəl) adj *zoology* 1 (of the feet of birds) adapted for seizing prey 2 of or relating to birds of prey [C19: from Latin *raptor* a robber, from *rapere* to snatch]

rapture (ˈræptʃə) n 1 the state of mind resulting from feelings of high emotion; joyous ecstasy 2 (*often plural*) an expression of ecstatic joy 3 the act of transporting a person from one sphere of existence to another, esp from earth to heaven ▷ vb 4 (*tr*) *archaic or literary* to entrance; enrapture [C17: from Medieval Latin *raptūra*, from Latin *raptus* RAPT[1]] > **rapturous** adj > **rapturously** adv > **rapturousness** n

RAR *abbreviation* Royal Australian Regiment

rara avis (ˈrɛərə ˈeɪvɪs) n, pl **rarae aves** (ˈrɛəriː ˈeɪviːz) an unusual, uncommon, or exceptional person or thing [Latin: rare bird]

rare[1] (rɛə) adj 1 not widely known; not frequently used or experienced; uncommon or unusual: *a rare word* 2 not widely distributed; not generally occurring: *a rare herb* 3 (of a gas, esp at high altitudes) having a low density; thin; rarefied 4 uncommonly great; extreme: *kind to a rare degree* 5 exhibiting uncommon excellence; superlatively good or fine: *rare skill* [C14: from Latin *rārus* sparse] > **rareness** n

rare[2] (rɛə) adj (of meat, esp beef) very lightly cooked [Old English *hrēr*; perhaps related to *hreaw* RAW]

rarebit (ˈrɛəbɪt) n another name for **Welsh rabbit** [C18: by folk etymology from (WELSH) RABBIT; see RARE[2], BIT[1]]

rare earth n 1 any oxide of a lanthanide 2 Also called: **rare-earth element** another name for **lanthanide**

raree show (ˈrɛəriː) n 1 a street show or carnival 2 another name for **peepshow** [C17: *raree* from RARE[1]]

rarefaction (ˌrɛərɪˈfækʃən) or **rarefication** (ˌrɛərɪfɪˈkeɪʃən) n the act or process of making less dense or the state of being less dense > ˌrareˈfactional, ˌrarefiˈcational or ˌrareˈfactive adj

rarefied (ˈrɛərɪˌfaɪd) adj 1 exalted in nature or character; lofty: *a rarefied spiritual existence* 2 current within only a small group; esoteric or exclusive 3 (of a gas, esp the atmosphere at high altitudes) having a low density; thin

rarefy (ˈrɛərɪˌfaɪ) vb -**fies**, -**fying**, -**fied** to make or become rarer or less dense; thin out [C14: from Old French *raréfier*, from Latin *rārēfacere*, from *rārus* RARE[1] + *facere* to make] > ˈrareˌfiable adj > ˈrareˌfier n

rare gas n another name for **inert gas** (sense 1)

rarely (ˈrɛəlɪ) adv 1 hardly ever; seldom 2 to an unusual degree; exceptionally 3 *dialect* uncommonly well; excellently: *he did rarely at market yesterday*
 ● USAGE Since *rarely* means *hardly ever*, one should not say
 ● something *rarely ever* happens

raring (ˈrɛərɪŋ) adj ready; willing; enthusiastic (esp in the phrase **raring to go**) [C20: from *rare*, variant of REAR[2]]

rarity (ˈrɛərɪtɪ) n, pl -**ties** 1 a rare person or thing, esp something interesting or valued because it is uncommon 2 the state or quality of being rare

rark up vb (*tr, adverb*) *NZ informal* to give (someone) a severe reprimand

Rarotonga (ˌrɛərəˈtɒŋə) n an island in the S Pacific, in the SW Cook Islands: the chief island of the group. Chief

settlement: Avarua. Pop: 12 188 (2001). Area: 67 sq km (26 sq miles)

rasbora (ræzˈbɔːrə) n any of the small cyprinid fishes constituting the genus *Rasbora* of tropical Asia and East Africa. Many species are brightly coloured and are popular aquarium fishes [from New Latin, from an East Indian language]

rascal (ˈrɑːskəl) n 1 a disreputable person; villain 2 a mischievous or impish rogue 3 an affectionate or mildly reproving term for a child or old man: *you little rascal; the wicked old rascal kissed her* 4 *obsolete* a person of lowly birth ▷ adj 5 (*prenominal*) *obsolete* a belonging to the mob or rabble b dishonest; knavish [C14: from Old French *rascaille* rabble, perhaps from Old Norman French *rasque* mud, filth]

rascality (rɑːˈskælɪtɪ) n, pl -**ties** mischievous, disreputable, or dishonest character, behaviour, or action

rascally (ˈrɑːskəlɪ) adj 1 dishonest or mean; base ▷ adv 2 in a dishonest or mean fashion

rase (reɪz) vb a variant spelling of **raze**

rash[1] (ræʃ) adj 1 acting without due consideration or thought; impetuous 2 characterized by or resulting from excessive haste or impetuosity: *a rash word* [C14: from Old High German *rasc* hurried, clever; related to Old Norse *roskr* brave] > **rashly** adv > **rashness** n

rash[2] (ræʃ) n 1 *pathol* any skin eruption 2 a series of unpleasant and unexpected occurrences: *a rash of forest fires* [C18: from Old French *rasche*, from *raschier* to scratch, from Latin *rādere* to scrape]

rasher (ˈræʃə) n a thin slice of bacon or ham [C16: of unknown origin]

Rashid (ræˈʃiːd) n a town in N Egypt, on the Nile delta. Former name: Rosetta

Rasht (ræʃt) or **Resht** n a city in NW Iran, near the Caspian Sea: agricultural and commercial centre in a rice-growing area. Pop: 586 000 (2005 est)

Rask (*Danish* rasg) n **Rasmus Christian** (ˈrasmus ˈkresdjan). 1787–1832, Danish philologist. He pioneered comparative philology with his work on Old Norse (1818)

Rasmussen (*Danish* ˈrasmusən) n **Knud Johan Victor** (knuð joˈhan ˈviktɔr). 1879–1933, Danish arctic explorer and ethnologist. He led several expeditions through the Arctic in support of his theory that the North American Indians were originally migrants from Asia

rasp (rɑːsp) n 1 a harsh grating noise 2 a coarse file with rows of raised teeth ▷ vb 3 (*tr*) to scrape or rub (something) roughly, esp with a rasp; abrade 4 to utter with or make a harsh grating noise 5 to irritate (one's nerves or senses); grate (upon) [C16: from Old French *raspe*, of Germanic origin; compare Old High German *raspōn* to scrape] > **rasper** n > **rasping** or **raspy** adj

raspberry (ˈrɑːzbərɪ, -brɪ) n, pl -**ries** 1 any of the prickly shrubs of the rosaceous genus *Rubus*, such as R. *strigosus* of E North America and R. *idaeus* of Europe, that have pinkish-white flowers and typically red berry-like fruits (drupelets). See also **bramble** 2 a the fruit of any such plant b (*as modifier*): *raspberry jelly* 3 a a dark purplish-red colour b (*as adjective*): *a raspberry dress* 4 a spluttering noise made with the tongue and lips to express contempt (esp in the phrase **blow a raspberry**) [C17: from earlier *raspis* raspberry, of unknown origin + BERRY: C19 in sense 4, from rhyming slang *raspberry tart* fart]

Rasputin (ræˈspjuːtɪn; *Russian* rasˈputin) n **Grigori Efimovich** (griˈgɔrij jɪˈfiməvɪtʃ). ?1871–1916, Siberian peasant monk, notorious for his debauchery, who wielded great influence over Tsarina Alexandra. He was assassinated by a group of Russian noblemen

Rasta (ˈræstə) n, adj short for **Rastafarian**

Ras Tafari (ræs təˈfɑːrɪ) n See **Haile Selassie**

Rastafarian (ˌræstəˈfɛərɪən) n 1 a member of an originally Jamaican religion that regards **Ras Tafari** (the former emperor of Ethiopia, Haile Selassie (1892–1975)) as God ▷ adj 2 of, characteristic of, or relating to the Rastafarians

raster (ˈræstə) n a pattern of horizontal scanning lines traced by an electron beam, esp on a television screen [C20: via German from Latin: rake, from *rādere* to scrape]

rat (ræt) n 1 any of numerous long-tailed murine

rodents, esp of the genus *Rattus*, that are similar to but larger than mice and are now distributed all over the world **2** *informal* a person who deserts his friends or associates, esp in time of trouble **3** *informal* a worker who works during a strike; blackleg; scab **4** *informal* a despicable person **5** smell a rat to detect something suspicious ▷ *vb* rats, ratting, ratted **6** (*intr*; usually foll by *on*) *informal* **a** to divulge secret information (about); betray the trust (of) **b** to default (on); abandon **7** to hunt and kill rats [Old English *ræt*; related to Old Saxon *ratta*, Old High German *rato*]

rata ('rɑːtə) *n* either of two New Zealand myrtaceous forest trees, *Metrosideros robusta* or *M. lucida*, having crimson flowers and hard wood [c19: from Māori]

ratable *or* **rateable** ('reɪtəb°l) *adj* **1** able to be rated or evaluated **2** *Brit* (of property) liable to payment of rates > ,rata'bility *or* ,ratea'bility *n* > 'rateably *or* 'rateably *adv*

ratable value *or* **rateable value** *n Brit* (formerly) a fixed value assigned to a property by a local authority, on the basis of which variable annual rates are charged

ratafia (,rætə'fɪə) *or* **ratafee** (,rætə'fiː) *n* **1** any liqueur made from fruit or from brandy with added fruit **2** a flavouring essence made from almonds **3** Also called: ratafia biscuit *chiefly Brit* a small macaroon flavoured with almonds [c17: from West Indian Creole French]

ratan (ræ'tæn) *n* a variant spelling of **rattan**

Ratana ('rɑːtɑːnɑː) *adj* of or relating to the Ratana Church or the Māori Christian religious movement associated with it [from the Church's founder, TW *Ratana* (1873–1939)]

rat-arsed *adj Brit slang* drunk

rat-a-tat-tat ('rætə,tæt'tæt) *or* **rat-a-tat** ('rætə'tæt) *n* the sound of knocking on a door

ratatouille (,rætə'twiː) *n* a vegetable casserole made of tomatoes, aubergines, peppers, etc, fried in oil and stewed slowly [c19: from French, from *touiller* to stir, from Latin *tudiculāre*, from *tudes* hammer]

ratbag ('ræt,bæg) *n slang* a despicable person [c20: from RAT + BAG]

rat-catcher *n* a person whose job is to destroy or drive away vermin, esp rats

ratchet ('rætʃɪt) *n* **1** a device in which a toothed rack or wheel is engaged by a pawl to permit motion in one direction only **2** the toothed rack or wheel forming part of such a device ▷ *vb* **3** to operate using a ratchet [c17: from French *rochet*, from Old French *rocquet* blunt head of a lance, of Germanic origin: compare Old High German *rocko* distaff]

ratchet effect *n economics* an effect that occurs when a price or wage increases as a result of temporary pressure but fails to fall back when the pressure is removed

rate¹ (reɪt) *n* **1** a quantity or amount considered in relation to or measured against another quantity or amount: *a rate of 70 miles an hour* **2 a** a price or charge with reference to a standard or scale: *rate of interest; rate of discount* **b** (*as modifier*): *a rate card* **3** a charge made per unit for a commodity, service, etc **4** See **rates** **5** the relative speed of progress or change of something variable; pace: *he works at a great rate; the rate of production has doubled* **6 a** relative quality; class or grade **b** (*in combination*): *first-rate ideas* **7** at any rate in any case; at all events; anyway ▷ *vb* (*mainly tr*) **8** (*also intr*) to assign or receive a position on a scale of relative values; rank: *he is rated fifth in the world* **9** to estimate the value of; evaluate: *we rate your services highly* **10** to be worthy of; deserve: *this hotel does not rate four stars* **11** to consider; regard: *I rate him among my friends* **12** *Brit* to assess the value of (property) for the purpose of local taxation [c15: from Old French, from Medieval Latin *rata*, from Latin *prō ratā parte* according to a fixed proportion, from *ratus* fixed, from *rērī* to think, decide]

rate² (reɪt) *vb* (*tr*) to scold or criticize severely; rebuke harshly [c14: perhaps related to Swedish *rata* to chide]

rateable ('reɪtəb°l) *adj* a variant spelling of **ratable**

rate-cap ('reɪt,kæp) *vb* (*tr*) -caps, -capping, -capped (formerly in Britain) to impose on (a local authority) an upper limit on the level of the rate it may levy > 'rate-,capping *n*

ratel ('reɪt°l) *n* **1** Also called: honey badger a musteline mammal, *Mellivora capensis*, inhabiting wooded regions of Africa and S Asia. It has a massive body, strong claws, and a thick coat that is paler on the back and it feeds on honey and small animals **2** *South African* a six-wheeled armoured vehicle [c18: from Afrikaans]

rate of exchange *n* See **exchange rate**

rate of return *n finance* the ratio of the annual income from an investment to the original investment, often expressed as a percentage

ratepayer ('reɪt,peɪə) *n* a person who pays local rates, esp a householder

rates (reɪts) *pl n* (in some countries) a tax levied on property by a local authority

Rathenau (*German* 'raːtənau) *n* **Walther** ('valtər). 1867–1922, German industrialist and statesman: he organized the German war industries during World War I, became minister of reconstruction (1921) and of foreign affairs (1922), and was largely responsible for the treaty of Rapallo with Russia. His assassination by right-wing extremists caused a furore

rather *adv* ('rɑːðə) (*in senses 1-4, not used with a negative*) **1** relatively or fairly; somewhat: *it's rather dull* **2** to a significant or noticeable extent; quite: *she's rather pretty* **3** to a limited extent or degree: *I rather thought that was the case* **4** with better or more just cause: *this text is rather to be deleted than rewritten* **5** more readily or willingly; sooner: *I would rather not see you tomorrow* ▷ *sentence connector* **6** on the contrary: *it's not cold. Rather, it's very hot indeed* ▷ *sentence substitute* ('rɑː'ðɜː) **7** an expression of strong affirmation, often in answer to a question: *Is it worth seeing? Rather!* [Old English *hrathor* comparative of *hræth* READY, quick; related to Old Norse *hrathr*]

● USAGE Both *would* and *had* are used with *rather* in
● sentences such as I would rather (or had rather) go to the
● film than to the play. Had rather is less common and is
● now widely regarded as slightly old-fashioned

ratify ('rætɪ,faɪ) *vb* (*tr*) -fies, -fying, -fied to give formal approval or consent to [c14: via Old French from Latin *ratus* fixed (see RATE) + *facere* to make] > 'rati,fiable *adj* > ,ratifi'cation *n* > 'rati,fier *n*

rating¹ ('reɪtɪŋ) *n* **1** a classification according to order or grade; ranking **2** (in certain navies) a sailor who holds neither commissioned nor warrant rank; an ordinary seaman **3** *sailing* a handicap assigned to a racing boat based on its dimensions, sail area, weight, draught, etc **4** the estimated financial or credit standing of a business enterprise or individual **5** *radio, television* a figure based on statistical sampling indicating what proportion of the total listening and viewing audience tune in to a specific programme or network

rating² ('reɪtɪŋ) *n* a sharp scolding or rebuke

ratio ('reɪʃɪ,əʊ) *n, pl* -tios **1** a measure of the relative size of two classes expressible as a proportion: *the ratio of boys to girls is 2 to 1* **2** *maths* a quotient of two numbers or quantities. See also **proportion** (sense 5) [c17: from Latin: a reckoning, from *rērī* to think; see REASON]

ratiocinate (,rætɪ'ɒsɪ,neɪt) *vb* (*intr*) to reason or argue logically and methodically; reason [c17: from Latin *ratiōcinārī* to calculate, from *ratiō* REASON]
> ,ratioci'nation *n* > ,rati'ocinative *adj* > ,ratioci'nator *n*

ration ('ræʃən) *n* **1 a** a fixed allowance of food, provisions, etc, esp a statutory one for civilians in time of scarcity or soldiers in time of war **b** (*as modifier*): *a ration book* **2** a sufficient or adequate amount: *you've had your ration of television for today* ▷ *vb* (*tr*) **3** (often foll by *out*) to distribute (provisions), esp to an army **4** to restrict the distribution or consumption of (a commodity) by (people): *the government has rationed sugar; sugar is short, so I'll have to ration you* ▷ See also **rations** [c18: via French from Latin *ratiō* calculation; see REASON]

rational ('ræʃən°l) *adj* **1** using reason or logic in thinking out a problem **2** in accordance with the principles of logic or reason; reasonable **3** of sound mind; sane: *the patient seemed quite rational* **4** endowed with the capacity to reason; capable of logical thought: *man is a rational being* **5** *maths* expressible as a ratio of two integers or polynomials ▷ *n* **6** *maths* a rational number [c14: from Latin *ratiōnālis*, from *ratiō* REASON] > ,ratio'nality *n* > 'rationally *adv* > 'rationalness *n*

rationale (ˌræʃəˈnɑːl) *n* a reasoned exposition, esp one defining the fundamental reasons for a course of action, belief, etc [c17: from New Latin, from Latin *ratiōnālis*]

rationalism (ˈræʃənəˌlɪzəm) *n* 1 reliance on reason rather than intuition to justify one's beliefs or actions 2 *philosophy* the doctrine that knowledge about reality can be obtained by reason alone without recourse to experience 3 the belief that knowledge and truth are ascertained by rational thought and not by divine or supernatural revelation > ˈrationalist *n* > ˌrationalˈistic *adj* > ˌrationalˈistically *adv*

rationalize *or* **rationalise** (ˈræʃənəˌlaɪz) *vb* 1 to justify (one's actions, esp discreditable actions, or beliefs) with plausible reasons, esp after the event 2 to apply logic or reason to (something) 3 (*tr*) to eliminate unnecessary equipment, personnel, or processes from (a group of businesses, factory, etc), in order to make it more efficient 4 (*tr*) *maths* to eliminate one or more radicals without changing the value of (an expression) or the roots of (an equation) > ˌrationaliˈzation *or* ˌrationaliˈsation *n* > ˈrationalˌizer *or* ˈrationalˌiser *n*

rational number *n* any real number of the form *a/b*, where *a* and *b* are integers and *b* is not zero, as 7 or 7/3

rations (ˈræʃənz) *pl n* (*sometimes singular*) a fixed daily allowance of food, esp to military personnel or when supplies are limited

Ratisbon (ˈrætɪzˌbɒn) *n* the former English name for Regensburg

ratite (ˈrætaɪt) *adj* 1 (of flightless birds) having a breastbone that lacks a keel for the attachment of flight muscles 2 of or denoting the flightless birds, formerly classified as a group (the *Ratitae*), that have a flat breastbone, feathers lacking vanes, and reduced wings ▷ *n* 3 a bird, such as an ostrich, kiwi, or rhea, that belongs to this group; a flightless bird [c19: from Latin *ratis* raft]

rat kangaroo *n* any of several ratlike kangaroos of the genera *Bettongia, Potorous, Aepyprymnus*, etc, found on the Australian mainland and in Tasmania

ratline *or* **ratlin** (ˈrætlɪn) *n nautical* any of a series of light lines tied across the shrouds of a sailing vessel for climbing aloft [c15: of unknown origin]

ratoon *or* **rattoon** (ræˈtuːn) *n* 1 a new shoot that grows from near the root or crown of crop plants, esp the sugar cane, after the old growth has been cut back ▷ *vb* 2 to propagate or cause to propagate by such a growth [c18: from Spanish *retoño* young shoot, from RE- + *otoñar* to sprout in autumn, from *otoño* AUTUMN]

ratpack (ˈrætˌpæk) *n derogatory, slang* those members of the press who give wide, often intrusive, coverage of the private lives of celebrities: *the royal ratpack*

rat race *n* a continual routine of hectic competitive activity: *working in the City is a real rat race*

rat-running *n* the practice of driving through residential side streets to avoid congested main roads > ˈrat-ˌrun *n* > ˈrat-ˌrunner *n*

ratsbane (ˈrætsˌbeɪn) *n* rat poison, esp arsenic oxide

rat-tail *n* 1 a a horse's tail that has no hairs b a horse having such a tail 2 a style of spoon in which the line of the handle is prolonged in a tapering moulding along the back of the bowl

rattan *or* **ratan** (ræˈtæn) *n* 1 any of the climbing palms of the genus *Calamus* and related genera, having tough stems used for wickerwork and canes 2 the stems of such plants collectively 3 a stick made from one of these stems [c17: from Malay *rōtan*]

ratter (ˈrætə) *n* 1 a dog or cat that catches and kills rats 2 another word for **rat** (sense 2)

Rattigan (ˈrætɪgən) *n* Sir **Terence Mervyn**. 1911–77, English playwright. His plays include *The Winslow Boy* (1946), *Separate Tables* (1954), and *Ross* (1960)

rattle (ˈrætəl) *vb* 1 to make or cause to make a rapid succession of short sharp sounds, as of loose pellets colliding when shaken in a container 2 to send, move, drive, etc, with such a sound: *the car rattled along the country road* 3 (*intr*; foll by *on*) to chatter idly; talk, esp at length: *he rattled on about his work* 4 (*tr*; foll by *off, out* etc) to recite perfunctorily or rapidly 5 (*tr*) *informal* to disconcert; make frightened or anxious ▷ *n* 6 a rapid

succession of short sharp sounds 7 an object, esp a baby's toy, filled with small pellets that rattle when shaken 8 a series of loosely connected horny segments on the tail of a rattlesnake, vibrated to produce a rattling sound 9 any of various European scrophulariaceous plants having a capsule in which the seeds rattle, such as *Pedicularis palustris* (**red rattle**) and *Rhinanthus minor* (**yellow rattle**) 10 idle chatter 11 *med* another name for **rale** [c14: from Middle Dutch *ratelen*; related to Middle High German *razzen*, of imitative origin]

Rattle (ˈrætəl) *n* Sir **Simon**. born 1955, British conductor. Principal conductor (1980–91) and music director (1991–98) of the City of Birmingham Symphony Orchestra; chief conductor of the Berlin Philharmonic Orchestra from 2002

rattler (ˈrætlə) *n* 1 something that rattles 2 *chiefly US & Canadian* an informal name for **rattlesnake**

rattlesnake (ˈrætəlˌsneɪk) *n* any of the venomous New World snakes constituting the genera *Crotalus* and *Sistrurus*, such as *C. horridus* (**black** or **timber rattlesnake**): family *Crotalidae* (pit vipers). They have a series of loose horny segments on the tail that are vibrated to produce a buzzing or whirring sound

rattletrap (ˈrætəlˌtræp) *n informal* a broken-down old vehicle, esp an old car

rattling (ˈrætlɪŋ) *adv informal* (intensifier qualifying something good, fine, pleasant, etc): *a rattling good lunch*

ratty (ˈrætɪ) *adj* -tier, -tiest 1 *Brit & NZ informal* irritable; annoyed 2 *informal* (of the hair) unkempt or greasy 3 *US & Canadian slang* shabby; dilapidated 4 *Austral slang* a angry b mad 5 of, like, or full of rats > ˈrattily *adv* > ˈrattiness *n*

Ratushinskaya (ˌrætuːˈʃɪnskaɪjaː) *n* **Irina** (ɪˈriːnə). born 1954, Russian poet and writer: imprisoned (1983–86) in a Soviet labour camp on charges of subversion. Her publications include *Poems* (1984), *Grey is the Colour of Hope* (1988), and *The Odessans* (1992)

raucous (ˈrɔːkəs) *adj* (of voices, cries, etc) harshly or hoarsely loud [c18: from Latin *raucus* hoarse] > ˈraucously *adv* > ˈraucousness *or less commonly* raucity (ˈrɔːsɪtɪ) *n*

raunchy (ˈrɔːntʃɪ) *adj* -chier, -chiest *slang* 1 openly sexual; lusty; earthy 2 *chiefly US* slovenly or untidy [c20: of unknown origin] > ˈraunchiness *n*

raupatu (ˌraʊˈpɑːtuː) *n NZ* the confiscation or seizure of land [Māori]

raupo (rɑːuːpɒ) *n, pl* raupo a New Zealand bulrush, *Typha orientalis*, with sword-shaped leaves, traditionally used for construction and decoration [Māori]

Rauschenberg (ˈraʊʃənbɜːg) *n* **Robert**. born 1925, US artist; one of the foremost exponents of pop art

rauwolfia (rɔːˈwʊlfɪə, raʊ-) *n* 1 any tropical tree or shrub of the apocynaceous genus *Rauwolfia*, esp *R. serpentina* of SE Asia 2 the powdered root of *R. serpentina*: a source of various drugs, esp reserpine [c19: New Latin, named after Leonhard *Rauwolf* (died 1596), German botanist]

ravage (ˈrævɪdʒ) *vb* 1 to cause extensive damage to ▷ *n* 2 (*often plural*) destructive action: *the ravages of time* [c17: from French, from Old French *ravir* to snatch away, RAVISH] > ˈravagement *n* > ˈravager *n*

rave (reɪv) *vb* 1 to utter (something) in a wild or incoherent manner, as when mad or delirious 2 (*intr*) to speak in an angry uncontrolled manner 3 (*intr*) (of the sea, wind, etc) to rage or roar 4 (*intr*; foll by *over* or *about*) *informal* to write or speak (about) with great enthusiasm 5 (*intr*) *Brit slang* to enjoy oneself wildly or uninhibitedly ▷ *n* 6 *informal* a enthusiastic or extravagant praise b (*as modifier*): *a rave review* 7 *Brit slang* Also called: rave-up a party b a professionally organized party for young people, with electronic dance music, sometimes held in a field or disused building 8 a name given to various types of dance music, such as techno, that feature fast electronic rhythm [c14 *raven*, apparently from Old French *resver* to wander]

ravel (ˈrævəl) *vb* -els, -elling, -elled *or US* -els, -eling, -eled 1 to tangle (threads, fibres, etc) or (of threads, fibres, etc) to become entangled 2 (*often foll by out*) to tease or draw out (the fibres of a fabric or garment) or (of a garment or fabric) to fray out in loose ends; unravel 3 (*tr*; *usually* foll by *out*) to disentangle or resolve: *to ravel out a complicated story* ▷ *n* **4** a tangle or complication [c16: from Middle Dutch *ravelen*] > 'ravelly *adj*

Ravel (French ravɛl) *n* **Maurice** (**Joseph**) (mɔris). 1875–1937, French composer, noted for his use of unresolved dissonances and mastery of tone colour. His works include *Gaspard de la Nuit* (1908) and *Le Tombeau de Couperin* (1917) for piano, *Boléro* (1928) for orchestra, and the ballet *Daphnis et Chloé* (1912)

raven[1] ('reɪvᵊn) *n* **1** a large passerine bird, *Corvus corax*, having a large straight bill, long wedge-shaped tail, and black plumage: family *Corvidae* (crows). It has a hoarse croaking cry **2 a** a shiny black colour **b** (*as adjective*): *raven hair* [Old English *hræfn*; related to Old High German *hraban*, Old Norse *hrafn*]

raven[2] ('rævᵊn) *vb* **1** to seize or seek (plunder, prey, etc) **2** to eat (something) voraciously or greedily; be ravenous in eating [c15: from Old French *raviner* to attack impetuously; see RAVENOUS]

Raven ('reɪvᵊn) *n* a traditional trickster hero among the native peoples of the Canadian Pacific Northwest [from RAVEN[1]]

ravening ('rævənɪŋ) *adj* (esp of animals such as wolves) voracious; predatory > 'raveningly *adv*

Ravenna (rə'vɛnə; *Italian* ra'venna) *n* a city and port in NE Italy, in Emilia-Romagna: capital of the Western Roman Empire from 402 to 476, of the Ostrogoths from 493 to 526, and of the Byzantine exarchate from 584 to 751; famous for its ancient mosaics. Pop: 134 631 (2001)

ravenous ('rævᵊnəs) *adj* **1** famished; starving **2** rapacious; voracious [c16: from Old French *ravineux*, from Latin *rapīna* plunder, from *rapere* to seize] > 'ravenously *adv* > 'ravenousness *n*

raver ('reɪvə) *n* **1** *Brit slang* a person who leads a wild or uninhibited social life **2** *slang* a person who enjoys rave music, esp one who frequents raves

ravine (rə'viːn) *n* a deep narrow steep-sided valley, esp one formed by the action of running water [c15: from Old French: torrent, from Latin *rapīna* robbery, influenced by Latin *rapidus* RAPID, both from *rapere* to snatch]

raving ('reɪvɪŋ) *adj* **1 a** delirious; frenzied **b** (*as adv.*): *raving mad* **2** *informal* (intensifier): *a raving beauty* ▷ *n* **3** (*usually plural*) frenzied, irrational, or wildly extravagant talk or utterances > 'ravingly *adv*

ravioli (ˌrævɪ'əʊlɪ) *n* small squares of pasta containing a savoury mixture of meat, cheese, etc [c19: from Italian dialect, literally: little turnips, from Italian *rava* turnip, from Latin *rāpa*]

ravish ('rævɪʃ) *vb* (*tr*) **1** (*often passive*) to give great delight to; enrapture **2** to rape **3** *archaic* to carry off by force [c13: from Old French *ravir*, from Latin *rapere* to seize] > 'ravisher *n* > 'ravishment *n*

ravishing ('rævɪʃɪŋ) *adj* delightful; lovely; entrancing > 'ravishingly *adv*

raw (rɔː) *adj* **1** (of food) not cooked **2** (*prenominal*) in an unfinished, natural, or unrefined state; not treated by manufacturing or other processes: *raw materials for making steel; raw brick* **3** (of an edge of material) unhemmed; liabl to fray **4** (of the skin, a wound, etc) having the surface exposed or abraded, esp painfully **5** ignorant, inexperienced, or immature: *a raw recruit* **6** (*prenominal*) not selected or modified: *raw statistics* **7** frank or realistic: *a raw picture of the breakdown of a marriage* **8** (of spirits) undiluted **9** *chiefly US* coarse, vulgar, or obscene **10** (of the weather) harshly cold and damp **11** *informal* unfair; unjust (esp in the phrase **a raw deal**) ▷ *n* **12** the raw *Brit informal* a sensitive point: *his criticism touched me on the raw* **13** in the raw **a** *informal* without clothes; naked **b** in a natural or unmodified state [Old English *hreaw*; related to Old High German *hrao*, Old Norse *hrār* raw, Latin *cruor* thick blood, Greek *kreas* meat] > 'rawish *adj* > 'rawly *adv* > 'rawness *n*

Rawalpindi (rɔː'lpɪndɪ) *n* an ancient city in N Pakistan: interim capital of Pakistan (1959–67) during the building of Islamabad. Pop: 1 794 000 (2005 est)

rawboned ('rɔː'bəʊnd) *adj* having a lean bony physique

rawhide ('rɔːˌhaɪd) *n* **1** untanned hide **2** a whip or rope made of strips cut from such a hide

rawhide hammer *n* a hammer, used to avoid damaging a surface, having a head consisting of a metal tube from each end of which a tight roll of hide protrudes

rawinsonde ('reɪwɪnˌsɒnd) *n* a hydrogen balloon carrying meteorological instruments and a radar target, enabling the velocity of winds in the atmosphere to be measured [c20: blend of *radar* + *wind* + *radiosonde*]

Rawlplug ('rɔːlplʌg) *n trademark* a short fibre or plastic tube used to provide a fixing in a wall for a screw

raw material *n* **1** material on which a particular manufacturing process is carried out **2** a person or thing regarded as suitable for some particular purpose: *raw material for the army*

raw silk *n* **1** untreated silk fibres reeled from the cocoon **2** fabric woven from such fibres

Rawsthorne ('rɔːsˌθɔːn) *n* **Alan**. 1905–71, English composer, whose works include three symphonies, several concertos, and a set of *Symphonic Studies* (1939)

ray[1] (reɪ) *n* **1** a narrow beam of light; gleam **2** a slight indication, esp of something anticipated or hoped for: *a ray of solace* **3** *maths* a straight line extending from a point **4** a thin beam of electromagnetic radiation or particles **5** any of the bony or cartilaginous spines of the fin of a fish that form the support for the soft part of the fin **6** any of the arms or branches of a starfish or other radiate animal **7** *botany* any strand of tissue that runs radially through the vascular tissue of some higher plants ▷ *vb* **8** (of an object) to emit (light) in rays or (of light) to issue in the form of rays **9** (*intr*) (of lines, etc) to extend in rays or on radiating paths **10** (*tr*) to adorn (an ornament, etc) with rays or radiating lines [c14: from Old French *rai*, from Latin *radius* spoke, RADIUS]

ray[2] (reɪ) *n* any of various marine selachian fishes typically having a flattened body, greatly enlarged winglike pectoral fins, gills on the undersurface of the fins, and a long whiplike tail. They constitute the orders *Torpediniformes* (**electric rays**) and *Rajiformes* [c14: from Old French *raie*, from Latin *raia*]

ray[3] (reɪ) *n music* (in tonic sol-fa) the second degree of any major scale; supertonic [c14: see GAMUT]

Ray[1] (reɪ) *n* **Cape Ray** a promontory in SW Newfoundland, Canada

Ray[2] (reɪ) *n* **1 John**. 1627–1705, English naturalist. He originated natural botanical classification and the division of flowering plants into monocotyledons and dicotyledons **2 Man**, real name *Emmanuel Rudnitsky*. 1890–1976, US surrealist photographer **3 Satyajit** ('sætjədʒɪt). 1921–92, Indian film director, noted for his *Apu* trilogy (1955–59)

Raybans ('reɪˌbænz) *pl n trademark* a brand of sunglasses

ray floret *or* **ray flower** *n* any of the small strap-shaped flowers in the flower head of certain composite plants, such as the daisy

ray gun *n* (in science fiction) a gun that emits rays to paralyse, stun, or destroy

Rayleigh ('reɪlɪ) *n* **Lord**, title of *John William Strutt*, 1842–1919, British physicist. He discovered argon (1894) with Ramsay and made important contributions to the theory of sound, the theory of scattering of radiation, etc Nobel prize for physics 1904

rayless ('reɪlɪs) *adj* **1** dark; gloomy **2** lacking rays: *a rayless flower*

raylet ('reɪlɪt) *n* a small ray

rayon ('reɪɒn) *n* **1** any of a number of textile fibres made from wood pulp or other forms of cellulose **2** any fabric made from such a fibre **3** (*modifier*) consisting of or involving rayon: *a rayon shirt* [c20: from French, from Old French *rai* RAY[1]]

raze *or* **rase** (reɪz) *vb* (*tr*) **1** to demolish (a town, buildings, etc) completely; level (esp in the phrase **raze to the ground**) **2** to delete; erase **3** *archaic* to graze [c16: from Old French *raser* from Latin *rādere* to scrape] > 'razer *or* 'raser *n*

razoo (rə'zuː) *n Austral & NZ informal* an imaginary coin: *not a brass razoo; they took every last razoo* [c20: of uncertain origin]

razor ('reɪzə) *n* **1** a sharp implement used esp by men for shaving the face **2 on a razor's edge** *or* **on a razor-edge** in an acute dilemma ▷ *vb* **3** (*tr*) to cut or shave with a razor [C13: from Old French *raseor*, from *raser* to shave; see RAZE]

razorback ('reɪzə,bæk) *n* **1** Also called: **finback** the **common rorqual**. See **rorqual 2** a semiwild or wild pig of the southeastern US, having a narrow body, long legs, and a ridged back

razorbill ('reɪzə,bɪl) or **razor-billed auk** *n* a common auk, *Alca torda*, of the North Atlantic, having a thick laterally compressed bill with white markings

razor blade *n* a small rectangular piece of metal sharpened on one or both long edges for use in a razor for shaving

razor-shell *n* any of various sand-burrowing bivalve molluscs of the genera *Ensis* and *Solen*, which have a long tubular shell. US name: **razor clam**

razor wire *n* strong wire with pieces of sharp metal set across it at close intervals, used to make fences or barriers

razz (ræz) *US & Canadian slang* ▷ *vb* **1** (*tr*) to make fun of; deride ▷ *n* **2** short for **raspberry** (sense 4)

razzle ('ræzəl) *n* **on the razzle** or **on the razz** *Brit informal* out enjoying oneself or celebrating, esp while drinking freely [C20: from RAZZLE-DAZZLE]

razzle-dazzle ('ræzəl'dæzəl) or **razzmatazz** ('ræzmə'tæz) *n slang* noisy or showy fuss or activity [C19: rhyming compound based on DAZZLE]

Rb *the chemical symbol for* rubidium

RC *abbreviation* **1** Red Cross **2** Also: **R.C.** Roman Catholic

RCA *abbreviation* **1** (formerly) Radio Corporation of America **2** Royal College of Art

RCAF *abbreviation* Royal Canadian Air Force

RCM *abbreviation* Royal College of Music

RCMP *abbreviation* Royal Canadian Mounted Police

RCN *abbreviation* **1** Royal Canadian Navy **2** Royal College of Nursing

RCP *abbreviation* Royal College of Physicians

RCS *abbreviation* **1** Royal College of Science **2** Royal College of Surgeons

rd *abbreviation* **1** rod (unit of length) **2** road **3** round **4** *physics* rutherford

Rd *abbreviation* Road

RDA *abbreviation* **1** Recommended Daily or Dietary Amount or Allowance **2** (in England) Regional Development Agency

re¹ (reɪ, riː) *n music* a variant spelling of: **ray³**

re² (riː) *prep* with reference to [C18: from Latin *rē*, ablative case of *rēs* thing]
- USAGE *Re*, in contexts such as *re your letter, your remarks*
- *have been noted* or *he spoke to me re your complaint*, is
- common in business or official correspondence. In
- general English *with reference to* is preferable in the
- former case and *about* or *concerning* in the latter. Even
- in business correspondence, the use of *re* is often
- restricted to the letter heading

Re¹ (reɪ) *n* another name for **Ra²**

Re² *the chemical symbol for* rhenium

RE *abbreviation* **1** Reformed Episcopal **2** Royal Engineers

re- *prefix* **1** indicating return to a previous condition, restoration, withdrawal, etc: *rebuild; renew; retrace; reunite* **2** indicating repetition of an action: *recopy; remarry* [from Latin]
- USAGE Verbs beginning with *re-* indicate repetition or
- restoration. It is unnecessary to add an adverb such as
- *back* or *again*: *This must not occur again* (not *recur again*); *we*
- *recounted the votes* (not *recounted the votes again*, which
- implies that the votes were counted three times, not
- twice)

reach (riːtʃ) *vb* **1** (*tr*) to arrive at or get to (a place, person, etc) in the course of movement or action: *to reach the office* **2** to extend as far as (a point or place): *to reach the ceiling; can you reach?* **3** (*tr*) to come to (a certain condition, stage, or situation): *to reach the point of starvation* **4** (*intr*) to extend in influence or operation: *the Roman conquest reached throughout England* **5** (*tr*) *informal* to pass or give (something to a person) with the outstretched hand **6** (*intr*; foll by *out, for*, or *after*) to make a movement (towards), as if to grasp or touch **7** (*tr*) to make contact or communication with (someone): *we tried to reach him all day* **8** (*tr*) to strike, esp in fencing or boxing **9** (*tr*) to

amount to (a certain sum): *to reach the five million mark* **10** (*intr*) *nautical* to sail on a tack with the wind on or near abeam ▷ *n* **11** the act of reaching **12** the extent or distance of reaching: *within reach of safety; beyond her reach* **13** the range of influence, power, jurisdiction, etc **14** an open stretch of water, esp on a river **15** *nautical* the direction or distance sailed by a vessel on one tack **16** *marketing* the proportion of a market that an advertiser hopes to reach at least once in a campaign [Old English *rǣcan*; related to Old Frisian *rēka*, Old High German *reihhen*] > **'reachable** *adj* > **'reacher** *n*

reach-me-down *n informal* **1 a** (*often plural*) a garment that is cheaply ready-made or second-hand **b** (*as modifier*): *reach-me-down finery* **2** (*modifier*) not original; derivative; stale: *a stock of reach-me-down ideas*

react (rɪ'ækt) *vb* **1** (*intr*; foll by *to, upon* etc) (of a person or thing) to act in response to another person, a stimulus, etc or (of two people or things) to act together in a certain way **2** (*intr*; foll by *against*) to act in an opposing or contrary manner **3** (*intr*) *physics* to exert an equal force in the opposite direction to an acting force **4** *chem* to undergo or cause to undergo a chemical reaction [C17: from Late Latin *reagere*, from RE- + Latin *agere* to drive, do]

re-act (riː'ækt) *vb* (*tr*) to act or perform again

reactance (rɪ'æktəns) *n* the opposition to the flow of alternating current by the capacitance or inductance of an electrical circuit; the imaginary part of the impedance Z, $Z = R + iX$, where R is the resistance, $i = \sqrt{-1}$, and X is the reactance. It is expressed in ohms

reactant (rɪ'æktənt) *n* a substance that participates in a chemical reaction, esp a substance that is present at the start of the reaction

reaction (rɪ'ækʃən) *n* **1** a response to some foregoing action or stimulus **2** the reciprocal action of two things acting together **3** opposition to change, esp political change, or a desire to return to a former condition or system **4** a response indicating a person's feelings or emotional attitude **5** *med* **a** any effect produced by the action of a drug, esp an adverse effect **b** any effect produced by a substance (allergen) to which a person is allergic the simultaneous equal and opposite force that acts on a body whenever it exerts a force on another body **6** short for **chemical reaction, nuclear reaction** > **re'actional** *adj*
- USAGE *Reaction* is used to refer both to an instant
- response (*her reaction was one of amazement*) and to a
- considered response in the form of a statement (*the*
- *Minister gave his reaction to the court's decision*). Some
- people think this second use is incorrect

reactionary (rɪ'ækʃənərɪ, -ʃənrɪ) or **reactionist** *adj* **1** of, relating to, or characterized by reaction, esp against radical political or social change ▷ *n, pl* -**aries** or -**ists 2** a person opposed to radical change > **re'actionism** *n*

reaction engine or **reaction motor** *n* an engine, such as a jet or rocket engine, that ejects gas at high velocity and develops its thrust from the ensuing reaction

reaction turbine *n* a turbine in which the working fluid is accelerated by expansion in both the static nozzles and the rotor blades. Torque is produced by the momentum changes in the rotor and by reaction from fluid accelerating out of the rotor

reactivate (rɪ'æktɪ,veɪt) *vb* (*tr*) to make (something) active or functional again > **re,acti'vation** *n*

reactive (rɪ'æktɪv) *adj* **1** readily partaking in chemical reactions: *sodium is a reactive metal; free radicals are very reactive* **2** of, concerned with, or having a reactance **3** responsive to stimulus **4** (of mental illnesses) precipitated by an external cause > **reactivity** (,riːæk'tɪvɪtɪ) or **re'activeness** *n*

reactor (rɪ'æktə) *n* **1** *chem* a substance, such as a reagent, that undergoes a reaction **2** short for **nuclear reactor 3** a vessel, esp one in industrial use, in which a chemical reaction takes place **4** a coil of low resistance and high inductance that introduces reactance into a circuit **5** *med* a person sensitive to a particular drug or agent

read¹ (riːd) *vb* **reads, reading, read** (rɛd) **1** to comprehend the meaning of (something written or printed) by looking at and interpreting the written or printed characters **2** (when *tr*, often foll by *out*) to look at, interpret, and speak aloud (something written or printed) **3** (*tr*) to interpret the significance or meaning of through scrutiny and recognition: *he read the sky and predicted rain; to read a map* **4** (*tr*) to interpret or understand the meaning of (signs, characters, etc) other than by visual means: *to read Braille* **5** (*tr*) to have sufficient knowledge of (a language) to understand the written or printed word **6** (*tr*) to discover or make out the true nature or mood of: *to read someone's mind* **7** to interpret or understand (something read) in a specified way, or (of something read) to convey a particular meaning or impression: *I read this speech as satire; this book reads well* **8** (*tr*) to adopt as a reading in a particular passage: *for "boon" read "bone"* **9** (*intr*) to have or contain a certain form or wording: *the sentence reads as follows* **10** to undertake a course of study in (a subject): *to read history; read for the bar* **11** to gain knowledge by reading: *he read about the war* **12** (*tr*) to register, indicate, or show: *the meter reads 100* **13** (*tr*) to bring or put into a specified condition by reading: *to read a child to sleep* **14** (*tr*) to hear and understand, esp when using a two-way radio: *we are reading you loud and clear* **15** *computing* to obtain (data) from a storage device, such as magnetic tape **16 read a lesson** or **read a lecture** *informal* to censure or reprimand, esp in a long-winded manner ▷ *n* **17** matter suitable for reading: *this new book is a very good read* **18** the act of reading ▷ See also **read into, read out, read up** [Old English *rǣdan* to advise, explain; related to Old Frisian *rēda*, Old High German *rātan*, Gothic *garēdan*]

read² (red) *vb* **1** the past tense and past participle of **read¹** ▷ *adj* **2** having knowledge gained from books (esp in the phrases **widely read, well-read**) **3 take something as read** to take something for granted as a fact; understand or presume

readable ('riːdəb³l) *adj* **1** (of handwriting, etc) able to read or deciphered; legible **2** (of style of writing) interesting, easy, or pleasant to read ▷ ˌreada'bility or 'readableness *n* ▷ 'readably *adv*

read-across *n* a correlation or relationship between two separate things

Reade (riːd) *n* **Charles**. 1814–84, English novelist: author of *The Cloister and the Hearth* (1861), a historical romance

reader ('riːdə) *n* **1** a person who reads **2** a person who is fond of reading **3 a** *chiefly Brit* at a university, a member of staff having a position between that of a senior lecturer and a professor **b** *US* a teaching assistant in a faculty who grades papers, examinations, etc, on behalf of a professor **4 a** a book that is part of a planned series for those learning to read **b** a standard textbook, esp for foreign-language learning **5** a person who reads aloud in public **6** a person who reads and assesses the merit of manuscripts submitted to a publisher **7** a person employed to read proofs and indicate errors by comparison with the original copy; proofreader **8** short for **lay reader**

readership ('riːdəʃɪp) *n* all the readers collectively of a particular publication or author: *a readership of five million; Dickens's readership*

reading ('riːdɪŋ) *n* **1 a** the act of a person who reads **b** (as modifier): *a reading room; a reading lamp* **2 a** ability to read **b** (as modifier): *the reading public; a child of reading age* **3** any matter that can be read; written or printed text **4** a public recital or rendering of a literary work **5** the form of a particular word or passage in a given text, esp where more than one version exists **6** an interpretation, as of a piece of music, a situation, or something said or written **7** knowledge gained from books: *a person of little reading* **8** a measurement indicated by a gauge, dial, scientific instrument, etc **9** *parliamentary procedure* **a** the formal recital of the body or title of a bill in a legislative assembly in order to begin one of the stages of its passage **b** one of the three stages in the passage of a bill through a legislative assembly. See **first reading, second reading, third reading** **10** the formal recital of something written, esp a will

Reading ('rɛdɪŋ) *n* **1 a** a town in S England, in Reading unitary authority, Berkshire, on the River Thames: university (1892). Pop: 232 662 (2001) **2** a unitary

authority in S England, in Berkshire. Pop: 144 100 (2003 est). Area: 37 sq km (14 sq miles)

reading group *n* a group of people who meet regularly to discuss a book that they have all read

read into (riːd) *vb* (*tr*, *preposition*) to discern in or infer from a statement (meanings not intended by the speaker or writer)

read out (riːd) *vb* (*adverb*) **1** (*tr*) to read (something) aloud **2** to retrieve information from a computer memory or storage device **3** (*tr*) *US & Canadian* to expel (someone) from a political party or other society ▷ *n* **read-out 4 a** the act of retrieving information from a computer memory or storage device **b** the information retrieved

read up (riːd) *vb* (*adverb*; when *intr*, often foll by *on*) to acquire information about (a subject) by reading intensively

read-write head ('riːd'raɪt) *n* *computing* an electromagnet that can both read and write information on a magnetic medium such as magnetic tape or disk

ready ('rɛdɪ) *adj* **readier, readiest 1** in a state of completion or preparedness, as for use or action **2** willing or eager: *ready helpers* **3** prompt or rapid: *a ready response* **4** (*prenominal*) quick in perceiving; intelligent: *a ready mind* **5** (*postpositive*; foll by *to*) on the point (of) or liable (to): *ready to collapse* **6** (*postpositive*) conveniently near (esp in the phrase **ready to hand**) **7 make ready** or **get ready** to prepare oneself or something for use or action ▷ *n* **8** short for **ready money 9 at the ready a** poised for use or action: *with pen at the ready* **b** (of a rifle) in the position normally adopted immediately prior to aiming and firing ▷ *vb* **10** (*tr*) to put in a state of readiness; prepare [Old English (*ge*)*rǣde*; related to Old Frisian *rēde*, Old High German *reiti*, Old Norse *reithr* ready] ▷ 'readily *adv* ▷ 'readiness *n*

ready-made *adj* **1** made for purchase and immediate use by any customer **2** extremely convenient or ideally suited: *a ready-made solution* **3** unoriginal or conventional: *ready-made phrases* ▷ *n* **4** a ready-made article, esp a garment

ready-mix *n* **1** (*modifier*) consisting of ingredients blended in advance, esp of food that is ready to cook or eat after addition of milk or water: *a ready-mix cake* **2** concrete that is mixed before or during delivery to a building site

ready money or **ready cash** *n* funds for immediate use; cash. Also called: **the ready, the readies**

ready reckoner *n* a table of numbers used to facilitate simple calculations, esp one for applying rates of discount, interest, charging, etc to different sums

ready-to-wear *adj* (**ready to wear** when *postpositive*) **1** (of clothes) not tailored for the wearer; of a standard size ▷ *n* **2** an article or suit of such clothes

reafforest (ˌriːəˈfɒrɪst) or **reforest** *vb* (*tr*) to replant (an area that was formerly forested) ▷ ˌreafˌforest'ation or ˌreforest'ation *n*

Reagan ('reɪgən) *n* **Ronald**. 1911–2004, US film actor and Republican statesman: Governor of California (1966–74): 40th president of the US (1981–89)

reagent (riːˈeɪdʒənt) *n* a substance for use in a chemical reaction, esp for use in chemical synthesis and analysis

real¹ ('rɪəl) *adj* **1** existing or occurring in the physical world; not imaginary, fictitious, or theoretical; actual **2** (*prenominal*) true; actual; not false: *the real reason* **3** (*prenominal*) deserving the name; rightly so called: *a real friend; a real woman* **4** not artificial or simulated; genuine: *real sympathy; real fur* **5** (of food, etc) traditionally made and having a distinct flavour: *real ale; real cheese* **6** *philosophy* existent or relating to actual existence (as opposed to nonexistent, potential, contingent, or apparent) **7** (*prenominal*) *economics* (of prices, incomes, wages, etc) considered in terms of purchasing power rather than nominal currency value **8** (*prenominal*) denoting or relating to immovable property such as land and tenements **9** *maths* involving or containing real numbers alone; having no imaginary part **10** *informal* (intensifier): *a real fool; a real genius* **11 the real thing** the genuine article, not an inferior or mistaken substitute ▷ *n* **12 the real** that which exists in fact; reality **13 for real** *slang* not as a test or trial; in earnest [c15: from Old

French *réel*, from Late Latin *reālis*, from Latin *rēs* thing]
> 'realness *n*

real² (reɪˈɑːl; *Spanish* reˈal) *n, pl* reals or reales (*Spanish* reˈales) a former small Spanish or Spanish-American silver coin [C17: from Spanish, literally: royal, from Latin *rēgālis*; see REGAL]

real ale or **real beer** *n* any beer which is allowed to ferment in the cask and which when served is pumped up without using carbon dioxide

real estate *n* another term for **real property**

realgar (rɪˈælɡə) *n* a rare orange-red soft mineral consisting of arsenic sulphide in monoclinic crystalline form. It occurs in Utah and Romania and as a deposit from hot springs. It is an important ore of arsenic and is also used as a pigment. Formula: AsS [C14: via Medieval Latin from Arabic *rahj al-ghar* powder of the mine]

realism (ˈrɪəˌlɪzəm) *n* 1 awareness or acceptance of the physical universe, events, etc, as they are, as opposed to the abstract or ideal 2 a style of painting and sculpture that seeks to represent the familiar or typical in real life, rather than an idealized, formalized, or romantic interpretation of it 3 any similar school or style in other arts, esp literature 4 *philosophy* the thesis that general terms such as common nouns refer to entities that have a real existence separate from the individuals which fall under them 5 *philosophy* the theory that physical objects continue to exist whether they are perceived or not
> 'realist *n*

realistic (ˌrɪəˈlɪstɪk) *adj* 1 showing awareness and acceptance of reality 2 practical or pragmatic rather than ideal or moral 3 (of a book, film, etc) depicting or emphasizing what is real and actual rather than abstract or ideal 4 of or relating to philosophical realism > ˌreal'istically *adv*

reality (rɪˈælɪtɪ) *n, pl* -ties 1 the state of things as they are or appear to be, rather than as one might wish them to be 2 something that is real 3 the state of being real 4 *philosophy* **a** that which exists, independent of human awareness **b** the totality of facts as they are independent of human awareness of them 5 in reality actually; in fact

reality check *n* an occasion or opportunity to consider a matter realistically or honestly

reality principle *n psychoanal* control of behaviour by the ego to meet the conditions imposed by the external world

reality show *n* a television show in which members of the public or celebrities are filmed living their everyday lives or undertaking specific challenges

reality TV *n* television programmes focusing on members of the public living in conditions created especially by the programme makers

realize or **realise** (ˈrɪəˌlaɪz) *vb* 1 (when *tr, may take a clause as object*) to become conscious or aware of (something) 2 (*tr, often passive*) to bring (a plan, ambition, etc) to fruition; make actual or concrete 3 (*tr*) to give (something, such as a drama or film) the appearance of reality 4 (*tr*) (of goods, property, etc) to sell for or make (a certain sum): *this table realized £800* 5 (*tr*) to convert (property or goods) into cash 6 (*tr*) (of a musicologist or performer) to reconstruct (a composition) from an incomplete set of parts > 'real,izable or 'real,isable *adj* > 'real,izably or 'real,isably *adv* > ˌreali'zation or ˌreali'sation *n*

real life *n* actual human life, as lived by real people, esp contrasted with the lives of fictional or fantasy characters: *miracles don't happen in real life*

really (ˈrɪəlɪ) *adv* 1 in reality; in actuality; assuredly: *it's really quite harmless* 2 truly; genuinely: *really beautiful* ▷ *interj* 3 an exclamation of dismay, disapproval, doubt, surprise, etc 4 not really? an exclamation of surprise or polite doubt
● USAGE See at **very**

realm (rɛlm) *n* 1 a royal domain; kingdom (now chiefly in such phrases as **Peer of the Realm**) 2 a field of interest, study, etc: *the realm of the occult* [C13: from Old French *reialme*, from Latin *regimen* rule, influenced by Old French *reial* royal, from Latin *rēgālis* REGAL]

real number *n* a number expressible as a limit of rational numbers. See **number** (sense 1)

real presence *n* the doctrine that the body of Christ is actually present in the Eucharist

real property *n* immovable property, esp land and buildings, including proprietary rights over land, such as mineral rights. Compare **personal property**

real tennis *n* an ancient form of tennis played in a four-walled indoor court with various openings, a sloping-roofed corridor along three sides, and a buttress on the fourth side

real-time *adj* denoting or relating to a data-processing system in which a computer receives constantly changing data, such as information relating to air-traffic control, travel booking systems, etc, and processes it sufficiently rapidly to be able to control the source of the data

realtor (ˈrɪəltə, -ˌtɔː) *n US & Canadian* an estate agent, esp an accredited one [C20: from a trademark]

realty (ˈrɪəltɪ) *n* another term for **real property**

ream¹ (riːm) *n* 1 a number of sheets of paper, formerly 480 sheets (**short ream**), now 500 sheets (**long ream**) or 516 sheets (**printer's ream** or **perfect ream**). One ream is equal to 20 quires 2 (*often plural*) *informal* a large quantity, esp of written matter: *he wrote reams* [C14: from Old French *raime*, from Spanish *rezma*, from Arabic *rizmah* bale]

ream² (riːm) *vb* (*tr*) 1 to enlarge (a hole) by use of a reamer 2 *US* to extract (juice) from (a citrus fruit) using a reamer [C19: perhaps from C14 *remen* to open up, from Old English *rȳman* to widen]

reamer (ˈriːmə) *n* 1 a steel tool with a cylindrical or tapered shank around which longitudinal teeth are ground, used for smoothing the bores of holes accurately to size 2 *US* a utensil with a conical projection used for extracting juice from citrus fruits; lemon squeezer

reap (riːp) *vb* 1 to cut or harvest (a crop), esp corn, from (a field or tract of land) 2 (*tr*) to gain or get (something) as a reward for or result of some action or enterprise [Old English *riopan*; related to Norwegian *ripa* to scratch, Middle Low German *repen* to card, ripple (flax)]
> 'reapable *adj*

reaper (ˈriːpə) *n* 1 a person who reaps or a machine for reaping 2 the grim reaper death

rear¹ (rɪə) *n* 1 the back or hind part 2 the area or position that lies at the back: *a garden at the rear of the house* 3 the section of a military force or procession farthest from the front 4 the buttocks. See **buttock** 5 bring up the rear to be at the back in a procession, race, etc 6 in the rear at the back ▷ *adj* 7 (*modifier*) of or in the rear: *the rear legs; the rear side* [C17: probably abstracted from REARWARD or REARGUARD]

rear² (rɪə) *vb* 1 (*tr*) to care for and educate (children) until maturity; bring up; raise 2 (*tr*) to breed (animals) or grow (plants) 3 (*tr*) to place or lift (a ladder, etc) upright 4 (*tr*) to erect (a monument, building, etc); put up 5 (*intr; often foll by up*) (esp of horses) to lift the front legs in the air and stand nearly upright 6 (*intr; often foll by up or over*) (esp of tall buildings) to rise high; tower 7 (*intr*) to start with anger, resentment, etc [Old English *rǣran*; related to Old High German *rēren* to distribute, Old Norse *reisa* to RAISE] > 'rearer *n*

rear admiral *n* an officer holding flag rank in any of certain navies, junior to a vice admiral

Reardon (ˈrɪədən) *n* Ray. born 1932, Welsh snooker player: world champion 1970, 1973-76, 1978

rearguard (ˈrɪəˌɡɑːd) *n* 1 a detachment detailed to protect the rear of a military formation, esp in retreat 2 an entrenched or conservative element, as in a political party 3 rearguard action an action fought by a rearguard [C15: from Old French *rereguarde* (modern French *arrière-garde*), from *rer*, from Latin *retro* back + *guarde* GUARD; compare VANGUARD]

rear light or **rear lamp** *n* a red light, usually one of a pair, attached to the rear of a motor vehicle. Also called: tail-light, tail lamp

rearm (riːˈɑːm) *vb* 1 to arm again 2 (*tr*) to equip (an army, a nation, etc) with better weapons > re'armament *n*

rearmost (ˈrɪəˌməʊst) *adj* nearest the rear; coming last

rear-view mirror *n* a mirror on a motor vehicle enabling the driver to see traffic coming behind him or her

rearward ('rɪəwəd) *adj, adv* **1** towards or in the rear ▷ *n* **2** a position in the rear, esp the rear division of a military formation [c14 (as a noun: the part of an army positioned behind the main body of troops): from Anglo-French *rerewarde*, variant of *reregarde*; see REARGUARD]

Rea Silvia ('rɪə 'sɪlvɪə) *n* a variant spelling of **Rhea Silvia**

reason ('ri:z°n) *n* **1** the faculty of rational argument, deduction, judgment, etc **2** sound mind; sanity **3** a cause or motive, as for a belief, action, etc **4** an argument in favour of or a justification for something **5** *philosophy* the intellect regarded as a source of knowledge, as contrasted with experience **6** *logic* grounds for a belief; a premise of an argument supporting that belief **7 by reason of** because of **8 in reason** *or* **within reason** within moderate or justifiable bounds **9 it stands to reason** it is logical or obvious **10 listen to reason** to be persuaded peaceably **11 reasons of State** political justifications for an immoral act ▷ *vb* **12** (when *tr*, *takes a clause as object*) to think logically or draw (logical conclusions) from facts or premises **13** (*intr*; usually foll by *with*) to urge or seek to persuade by reasoning **14** (*tr*; often foll by *out*) to work out or resolve (a problem) by reasoning [c13: from Old French *reisun*, from Latin *ratiō* reckoning, from *rērī* to think] > 'reasoner *n*

● USAGE The expression *the reason is because...* should be
● avoided. Instead one should say either *this is because...*
● or *the reason is that...*

reasonable ('ri:zənəb°l) *adj* **1** showing reason or sound judgment **2** having the ability to reason **3** having modest or moderate expectations; not making unfair demands **4** moderate in price; not expensive **5** fair; average > 'reasonableness *n* > 'reasonably *adv*

reasoned ('ri:z°nd) *adj* well thought-out or well presented: *a reasoned explanation*

reasoning ('ri:zənɪŋ) *n* **1** the act or process of drawing conclusions from facts, evidence, etc **2** the arguments, proofs, etc, so adduced

reassortment (,ri:ə'sɔːtmənt) *n* the formation of a hybrid virus containing parts from the genomes of two distinct viruses in a mixed infection

reassure (,ri:ə'ʃʊə) *vb* (*tr*) **1** to relieve (someone) of anxieties; restore confidence to **2** another term for: **reinsure** > ,reas'surance *n* > ,reas'surer *n* > ,reas'suringly *adv*

Réaumur ('reɪə,mjʊə) *adj* indicating measurement on the Réaumur scale of temperature

Réaumur scale *n* a scale of temperature in which the freezing point of water is taken as 0° and the boiling point is 80° [c18: named after René Antoine Ferchault de Réaumur (1683–1757), French physicist, who introduced it]

reave (ri:v) *vb* **reaves, reaving, reaved** *or* **reft** (rɛft) *archaic* **1** to carry off (property, prisoners, etc) by force **2** (*tr*; foll by *of*) to deprive; strip. See also **reive** [Old English *rēafian*; related to Old High German *roubōn* to rob, Old Norse *raufa* to break open]

rebadge (ri:'bædʒ) *vb* (*tr*) to relaunch (a product) under a new name, brand, or logo

rebarbative (rɪ'bɑːbətɪv) *adj* fearsome; forbidding [c19: from French *rébarbatif*, from Old French *rebarber* to repel (an enemy), to withstand (him) face to face, from RE- + *barbe* beard, from Latin *barba*]

rebate¹ ('ri:beɪt) *n* **1** a refund of a fraction of the amount payable or paid, as for goods purchased in quantity; discount ▷ *vb* (rɪ'beɪt) (*tr*) **2** to deduct (a part) of a payment from (the total) **3** *archaic* to reduce or diminish (something or the effectiveness of something) [c15: from Old French *rabattre* to beat down, hence reduce, deduct, from RE- + *abatre* to put down; see ABATE] > 're'batable *or* re'bateable *adj* > 'rebater *n*

rebate² ('ri:beɪt, 'ræbɪt) *n, vb* another word for **rabbet**

rebec *or* **rebeck** ('ri:bɛk) *n* a medieval stringed instrument resembling the violin but having a lute-shaped body [c16: from Old French *rebebe*, from Arabic *rebāb*; perhaps also influenced by Old French *bec* beak]

Rebecca (rɪ'bɛkə) *n Old Testament* the sister of Laban, who became the wife of Isaac and the mother of Esau and Jacob (Genesis 24–27)

rebel *vb* (rɪ'bɛl) **-bels, -belling, -belled** (*intr*; often foll by *against*) **1** to resist or rise up against a government or other authority, esp by force of arms **2** to dissent from an accepted moral code or convention of behaviour, dress, etc **3** to show repugnance (towards) ▷ *n* ('rɛb°l) **4 a** a person who rebels **b** (*as modifier*): *a rebel soldier; a rebel leader* **5** a person who dissents from some accepted moral code or convention of behaviour, dress, etc [c13: from Old French *rebelle*, from Latin *rebellis* insurgent, from RE- + *bellum* war]

rebellion (rɪ'bɛljən) *n* **1** organized resistance or opposition to a government or other authority **2** dissent from an accepted moral code or convention of behaviour, dress, etc [c14: via Old French from Latin *rebelliō* revolt (of those conquered); see REBEL]

rebellious (rɪ'bɛljəs) *adj* **1** showing a tendency towards rebellion **2** (of a problem, etc) difficult to overcome; refractory > re'belliously *adv* > re'belliousness *n*

rebirth (ri:'bɜːθ) *n* **1** a revival or renaissance: *the rebirth of learning* **2** a second or new birth; reincarnation

reboot (ri:'buːt) *vb* to shut down and restart (a computer system) or (of a computer system) to shut down and restart

rebore *n* ('ri:,bɔː) **1** the process of boring out the cylinders of a worn reciprocating engine and fitting oversize pistons ▷ *vb* (ri:'bɔː) **2** (*tr*) to carry out this process

rebound *vb* (rɪ'baʊnd) (*tr*) **1** to spring back, as from a sudden impact **2** to misfire, esp so as to hurt the perpetrator ▷ *n* ('ri:,baʊnd) **3** the act or an instance of rebounding **4 on the rebound a** in the act of springing back **b** *informal* in a state of recovering from rejection, disappointment, etc: *he married her on the rebound from an unhappy love affair* [c14: from Old French *rebondir*, from RE- + *bondir* to BOUND²]

rebozo (rɪ'bəʊzəʊ; *Spanish* reˈβoθo) *n, pl* **-zos** (-zəʊz; *Spanish* -θos) a long wool or linen scarf covering the shoulders and head, worn by Latin American women [c19: from Spanish: shawl, from *rebozar* to muffle]

rebrand (ri:'brænd) *vb* (*tr*) to change or update the image of (an organization or product)

rebuff (rɪ'bʌf) *vb* (*tr*) **1** to snub, reject, or refuse (a person offering help or sympathy, an offer of help, etc) abruptly or out of hand **2** to beat back (an attack); repel ▷ *n* **3** a blunt refusal or rejection; snub [c16: from Old French *rebuffer*, from Italian *ribuffare*, from *ribuffo* a reprimand, from *ri-* RE- + *buffo* puff, gust, apparently of imitative origin]

rebuke (rɪ'bjuːk) *vb* **1** (*tr*) to scold or reprimand (someone) ▷ *n* **2** a reprimand or scolding [c14: from Old Norman French *rebuker*, from RE- + Old French *buchier* to hack down, from *busche* log, of Germanic origin] > re'bukable *adj* > re'buker *n*

rebus ('ri:bəs) *n, pl* **-buses 1** a puzzle consisting of pictures representing syllables and words; in such a puzzle the word *hear* might be represented by H followed by a picture of an ear **2** a heraldic emblem or device that is a pictorial representation of or pun on the name of the bearer [c17: from French *rébus*, from the Latin *rēbus* by things, from RES]

rebut (rɪ'bʌt) *vb* **-buts, -butting, -butted** (*tr*) to refute or disprove, esp by offering a contrary contention or argument [c13: from Old French *reboter*, from RE- + *boter* to thrust, BUTT³] > re'buttable *adj* > re'buttal *n*

rebutter (rɪ'bʌtə) *n* **1** *law* a defendant's pleading in reply to a claimant's surrejoinder **2** a person who rebuts

recalcitrant (rɪ'kælsɪtrənt) *adj* **1** not susceptible to control or authority; refractory ▷ *n* **2** a recalcitrant person [c19: via French from Latin *recalcitrāre*, from RE- + *calcitrāre* to kick, from *calx* heel] > re'calcitrance *n*

recalesce (,ri:kə'lɛs) ,reca'lesce *vb* (*intr*) to undergo recalescence

recalescence (,ri:kə'lɛsəns) *n* a sudden spontaneous increase in the temperature of cooling iron resulting from an exothermic change in crystal structure occurring at a particular temperature [c19: from Latin *recalēscere* to grow warm again, from RE- + *calēscere*, from *calēre* to be hot] > ˌreca'lescent *adj*

recall (rɪ'kɔ:l) *vb* (*tr*) 1 (*may take a clause as object*) to bring back to mind; recollect; remember 2 to order to return; call back permanently or temporarily 3 to revoke or take back 4 to cause (one's thoughts, attention, etc) to return from a reverie or digression ▷ *n* 5 the act of recalling or state of being recalled 6 revocation or cancellation 7 the ability to remember things; recollection 8 *military* (esp formerly) a signal to call back troops, etc, usually a bugle call 9 *US* the process by which elected officials may be deprived of office by popular vote > re'callable *adj*

recant (rɪ'kænt) *vb* to repudiate or withdraw (a former belief or statement), esp formally in public [c16: from Latin *recantāre* to sing again, from RE- + *cantāre* to sing; see CHANT] > recantation (ˌri:kæn'teɪʃən) *n* > re'canter *n*

recap *vb* ('ri:ˌkæp, ri:'kæp) -caps, -capping, -capped 1 *informal* short for **recapitulate** ▷ *n* ('ri:ˌkæp) 2 *informal* short for **recapitulation** > re'cappable *adj*

recapitulate (ˌri:kə'pɪtjʊˌleɪt) *vb* 1 to restate the main points of (an argument, speech, etc); summarize 2 (*tr*) (of an animal) to repeat (stages of its evolutionary development) during the embryonic stages of its life [c16: from Late Latin *recapitulāre*, literally: to put back under headings; see CAPITULATE] > ˌreca'pitulative *or* ˌreca'pitulatory *adj*

recapitulation (ˌri:kəˌpɪtjʊ'leɪʃən) *n* 1 the act of recapitulating, esp summing up, as at the end of a speech 2 *Also called:* palingenesis *biology* the apparent repetition in the embryonic development of an animal of the changes that occurred during its evolutionary history 3 *music* the repeating of earlier themes, esp when forming the final section of a movement in sonata form

recapture (ri:'kæptʃə) *vb* (*tr*) 1 to capture or take again 2 to recover, renew, or repeat (a lost or former ability, sensation, etc) ▷ *n* 3 the act of recapturing or fact of being recaptured

recce ('rɛkɪ) *n, vb* -ces, -ceing, -ced *or* -ceed a slang word for **reconnaissance, reconnoitre**

recd *or* **rec'd** *abbreviation* received

recede (rɪ'si:d) *vb* (*intr*) 1 to withdraw from a point or limit; go back: *the tide receded* 2 to become more distant: *hopes of rescue receded* 3 to slope backwards: *apes have receding foreheads* 4 a (of a man's hair) to cease to grow at the temples and above the forehead b (of a man) to start to go bald in this way 5 to decline in value or character 6 (*usually foll by from*) to draw back or retreat, as from a promise [c15: from Latin *recēdere* to go back, from RE- + *cēdere* to yield, CEDE]

re-cede (ri:'si:d) *vb* (*tr*) to restore to a former owner

receipt (rɪ'si:t) *n* 1 a written acknowledgment by a receiver of money, goods, etc, that payment or delivery has been made 2 the act of receiving or fact of being received 3 (*usually plural*) an amount or article received 4 *archaic* another word for **recipe** ▷ *vb* 5 (*tr*) to acknowledge payment of (a bill), as by marking it [c14: from Old Norman French *receite*, from Medieval Latin *recepta*, from Latin *recipere* to RECEIVE]

receivable (rɪ'si:vəb³l) *adj* 1 suitable for or capable of being received, esp as payment or legal tender 2 (of a bill, etc) awaiting payment: *accounts receivable* ▷ *n* 3 (*usually plural*) the part of the assets of a business represented by accounts due for payment

receive (rɪ'si:v) *vb* (*mainly tr*) 1 to take (something offered) into one's hand or possession 2 to have (an honour, blessing, etc) bestowed 3 to accept delivery or transmission of (a letter, telephone call, etc) 4 to be informed of (news or information) 5 to hear and consent to or acknowledge (an oath, confession, etc) 6 (of a vessel or container) to take or hold (a substance, commodity, or certain amount) 7 to support or sustain (the weight of something); bear 8 to apprehend or perceive (ideas, etc) 9 to experience, undergo, or meet with: *to receive a crack on the skull* 10 (*also intr*) to be at home to (visitors) 11 to greet or welcome (visitors or guests), esp in formal style 12 to admit (a person) to a place, society, condition, etc: *he was received into the priesthood* 13 to accept or acknowledge (a precept or principle) as

true or valid 14 to convert (incoming radio signals) into sounds, pictures, etc, by means of a receiver 15 (*also intr*) *tennis* to play at the other end from the server; be required to return (service) 16 (*also intr*) to partake of (the Christian Eucharist) 17 (*intr*) *chiefly Brit* to buy and sell stolen goods [c13: from Old French *receivre*, from Latin *recipere* to take back, from RE- + *capere* to take]

received (rɪ'si:vd) *adj* generally accepted or believed: *received wisdom*

Received Pronunciation *n* the accent of standard Southern British English. *Abbreviation:* RP

receiver (rɪ'si:və) *n* 1 a person who receives something; recipient 2 a person appointed by a court to manage property pending the outcome of litigation, during the infancy of the owner, or after the owner(s) has been declared bankrupt or of unsound mind 3 *chiefly Brit* a person who receives stolen goods knowing that they have been stolen 4 the equipment in a telephone, radio, or television that receives incoming electrical signals or modulated radio waves and converts them into the original audio or video signals 5 the part of a telephone containing the earpiece and mouthpiece that is held by the telephone user 6 *chem* a vessel in which the distillate is collected during distillation 7 *US sport* a player whose function is to receive the ball, esp a footballer who catches long passes

receivership (rɪ'si:vəʃɪp) *n law* 1 the office or function of a receiver 2 the condition of being administered by a receiver

receiving order *n Brit obsolete* a court order appointing a receiver to manage the property of a debtor or bankrupt

recension (rɪ'sɛnʃən) *n* 1 a critical revision of a literary work 2 a text revised in this way [c17: from Latin *recēnsiō*, from *recēnsēre* to survey, from RE- + *cēnsēre* to assess]

recent ('ri:s³nt) *adj* having appeared, happened, or been made not long ago; modern, fresh, or new [c16: from Latin *recens* fresh; related to Greek *kainos* new] > 'recently *adv* > 'recentness *or* 'recency *n*

Recent ('ri:s³nt) *adj, n geology* another word for **Holocene**

receptacle (rɪ'sɛptək³l) *n* 1 an object that holds something; container 2 *botany* a the enlarged or modified tip of the flower stalk that bears the parts of the flower b the part of lower plants that bears the reproductive organs or spores [c15: from Latin *receptāculum* a store-place, from *receptāre* to receive again, from *recipere* to RECEIVE]

reception (rɪ'sɛpʃən) *n* 1 the act of receiving or state of being received 2 the manner in which something, such as a guest or a new idea, is received: *a cold reception* 3 a formal party for guests, such as one after a wedding 4 an area in an office, hotel, etc, where visitors or guests are received and appointments or reservations dealt with 5 short for **reception room** 6 the quality or fidelity of a received radio or television broadcast: *the reception was poor* [c14: from Latin *receptiō* a receiving, from *recipere* to RECEIVE]

reception centre *n social welfare* (in Britain) a place to which distressed people, such as vagrants, addicts, victims of a disaster, refugees, etc, go pending more permanent arrangements

receptionist (rɪ'sɛpʃənɪst) *n* a person employed in an office, hotel, doctor's surgery, etc, to receive clients, guests, or patients, answer the telephone, and arrange appointments, etc

reception room *n* 1 a room in a private house suitable for entertaining guests, esp a lounge or dining room 2 a room in a hotel suitable for large parties, receptions, etc

receptive (rɪ'sɛptɪv) *adj* 1 able to apprehend quickly 2 tending to receive new ideas or suggestions favourably 3 able to hold or receive > re'ceptively *adv* > receptivity (ˌri:sɛp'tɪvɪtɪ) *or* re'ceptiveness *n*

receptor (rɪ'sɛptə) *n* 1 *physiol* a sensory nerve ending that changes specific stimuli into nerve impulses 2 any of various devices that receive information, signals, etc

recess *n* (rɪ'sɛs, 'ri:sɛs) 1 a space, such as a niche or alcove, set back or indented 2 (*often plural*) a secluded or secret place: *recesses of the mind* 3 a cessation of business, such as the closure of Parliament during a vacation 4 *anatomy* a small cavity or depression in a bodily organ, part, or structure **5** *US & Canadian* a break between classes at a school ▷ *vb* (rɪ'sɛs) **6** (*tr*) to place or set (something) in a recess **7** (*tr*) to build a recess or recesses in (a wall, building, etc) [C16: from Latin *recessus* a retreat, from *recēdere* to RECEDE]

recession[1] (rɪ'sɛʃən) *n* **1** a temporary depression in economic activity or prosperity **2** the withdrawal of the clergy and choir in procession from the chancel at the conclusion of a church service **3** the act of receding **4** a part of a building, wall, etc, that recedes [C17: from Latin *recessio*; see RECESS]

recession[2] (riː'sɛʃən) *n* the act of restoring possession to a former owner [C19: from RE- + CESSION]

recessional (rɪ'sɛʃənᵊl) *adj* **1** of or relating to recession ▷ *n* **2** a hymn sung as the clergy and choir withdraw from the chancel at the conclusion of a church service

recessive (rɪ'sɛsɪv) *adj* **1** tending to recede or go back; receding **2** *genetics* **a** (of a gene) capable of producing its characteristic phenotype in the organism only when its allele is identical **b** (of a character) controlled by such a gene. See **dominant** (sense 4) **3** *linguistics* (of stress) tending to be placed on or near the initial syllable of a polysyllabic word ▷ *n* **4** *genetics* a recessive gene or character ▷ re'cessively *adv* ▷ re'cessiveness *n*

recharge (riː'tʃɑːdʒ) *vb* (*tr*) **1** to cause (an accumulator, capacitor, etc) to take up and store electricity again **2** to revive or renew (one's energies) (esp in **recharge one's batteries**) ▷ re'chargeable *adj*

recherché (rə'ʃɛəʃeɪ; *French* rəʃɛrʃe) *adj* **1** known only to connoisseurs; choice or rare **2** studiedly refined or elegant [C18: from French: past participle of *rechercher* to make a thorough search for; see RESEARCH]

recidivism (rɪ'sɪdɪˌvɪzəm) *n* habitual relapse into crime [C19: from Latin *recidīvus* falling back, from RE- + *cadere* to fall] ▷ re'cidivist *n, adj* ▷ reˌcidi'vistic *or* reˌcidivous *adj*

Recife (rɛ'siːfə) *n* a port at the easternmost point of Brazil on the Atlantic: capital of Pernambuco state; built partly on an island, with many waterways and bridges. Pop: 3 527 000 (2005 est). Former name: **Pernambuco**

recipe ('rɛsɪpɪ) *n* **1** a list of ingredients and directions for making something, esp a food preparation **2** *med* (formerly) a medical prescription **3** a method for achieving some desired objective: *a recipe for success* [C14: from Latin, literally: take (it)! from *recipere* to take, RECEIVE]

recipient (rɪ'sɪpɪənt) *n* **1** a person who or thing that receives ▷ *adj* **2** a less common word for **receptive** [C16: via French from Latin *recipiēns*, from *recipere* to RECEIVE] ▷ re'cipience *n*

reciprocal (rɪ'sɪprəkᵊl) *adj* **1** of, relating to, or designating something given by each of two people, countries, etc, to the other; mutual: *reciprocal friendship; reciprocal trade* **2** given or done in return: *a reciprocal favour* **3** (of a pronoun) indicating that action is given and received by each subject; for example, *each other* in the sentence *they started to shout at each other* **4** *maths* of or relating to a number or quantity divided into one **5** *navigation* denoting a course or bearing that is 180° from the previous or assumed one ▷ *n* **6** something that is reciprocal **7** Also called: **inverse** *maths* a number or quantity that when multiplied by a given number or quantity gives a product of one: *the reciprocal of 2 is 0.5* [C16: from Latin *reciprocus* alternating] ▷ reˌcipro'cality *n* ▷ re'ciprocally *adv*

reciprocate (rɪ'sɪprəˌkeɪt) *vb* **1** to give or feel in return **2** to move or cause to move backwards and forwards **3** (*intr*) to be correspondent or equivalent [C17: from Latin *reciprocāre*, from *reciprocus* RECIPROCAL] ▷ reˌcipro'cation *n* ▷ re'ciprocative *or* re'ciproˌcatory *adj* ▷ re'ciproˌcator *n*

reciprocating engine *n* an engine in which one or more pistons move backwards and forwards inside a cylinder or cylinders

reciprocity (ˌrɛsɪ'prɒsɪtɪ) *n, pl* -ties **1** reciprocal action or relation **2** a mutual exchange of commercial or other privileges [C18: via French from Latin *reciprocus* RECIPROCAL]

recision (rɪ'sɪʒən) *n* the act of cancelling or rescinding; annulment: *the recision of a treaty* [C17: from Latin *recīsiō*, from *recīdere* to cut back]

recital (rɪ'saɪtᵊl) *n* **1** a musical performance by a soloist or soloists. See **concert** (sense 1) **2** the act of reciting or repeating something learned or prepared **3** an account, narration, or description **4** a detailed statement of facts, figures, etc ▷ re'citalist *n*

recitation (ˌrɛsɪ'teɪʃən) *n* **1** the act of reciting from memory, or a formal reading of verse before an audience **2** something recited

recitative[1] (ˌrɛsɪtə'tiːv) *n* a passage in a musical composition, esp the narrative parts in an oratorio, set for one voice with either continuo accompaniment only or full accompaniment, reflecting the natural rhythms of speech [C17: from Italian *recitativo*; see RECITE]

recitative[2] (rɪ'saɪtətɪv) *adj* of or relating to recital

recite (rɪ'saɪt) *vb* **1** to repeat (a poem, passage, etc) aloud from memory before an audience, teacher, etc **2** (*tr*) to give a detailed account of **3** (*tr*) to enumerate (examples, etc) [C15: from Latin *recitāre* to cite again, from RE- + *citāre* to summon; see CITE] ▷ re'citable *adj* ▷ re'citer *n*

reck (rɛk) *vb archaic* (*used mainly with a negative*) **1** to mind or care about (something): *to reck nought* **2** (*usually impersonal*) to concern or interest (someone) [Old English *reccan*; related to Old High German *ruohhen* to take care, Old Norse *rækja*, Gothic *rakjan*]

reckless ('rɛklɪs) *adj* having or showing no regard for danger or consequences; heedless; rash [Old English *recceleās* (see RECK, -LESS); related to Middle Dutch *roekeloos*, Old High German *ruahhalōs*] ▷ 'recklessly *adv* ▷ 'recklessness *n*

Recklinghausen (*German* rɛklɪŋ'hauzən) *n* an industrial city in NW Germany, in North Rhine-Westphalia on the N edge of the Ruhr. Pop: 123 144 (2003 est)

reckon ('rɛkən) *vb* **1** to calculate or ascertain by calculating; compute **2** (*tr*) to include; count as part of a set or class: *I reckon her with the angels* **3** (*usually passive*) to consider or regard: *he is reckoned clever* **4** (when *tr, takes a clause as object*) to think or suppose; be of the opinion: *I reckon you don't know where to go next* **5** (*intr*; foll by *with*) to settle accounts (with) **6** (*intr*; foll by *with* or *without*) to take into account or fail to take into account: *the bully reckoned without John's big brother* **7** (*intr*; foll by *on* or *upon*) to rely or depend: *I reckon on your support in this crisis* **8** (*tr*) *slang* to regard as good: *I don't reckon your chances of success* **9** (*tr*) *informal* to have a high opinion of: *she was sensitive to bad reviews, even from people she did not reckon* **10** to be reckoned with of considerable importance or influence [Old English (*ge*)*recenian* recount; related to Old Frisian *rekenia*, Old High German *rehhanón* to count]

reckoner ('rɛkənə) *n* any of various devices or tables used to facilitate reckoning, esp a ready reckoner

reckoning ('rɛkənɪŋ) *n* **1** the act of counting or calculating **2** settlement of an account or bill **3** a bill or account **4** retribution for one's actions (esp in the phrase **day of reckoning**) **5** *navigation* short for **dead reckoning**

reclaim (rɪ'kleɪm) *vb* (*tr*) **1** to claim back: *to reclaim baggage* **2** to convert (desert, marsh, waste ground, etc) into land suitable for growing crops **3** to recover (useful substances) from waste products **4** to convert (someone) from sin, folly, vice, etc **5** *falconry* to render (a hawk or falcon) tame ▷ *n* **6** the act of reclaiming or state of being reclaimed [C13: from Old French *réclamer*, from Latin *reclāmāre* to cry out, protest, from RE- + *clāmāre* to shout] ▷ re'claimable *adj* ▷ re'claimant *or* re'claimer *n*

reclamation (ˌrɛklə'meɪʃən) *n* **1** the conversion of desert, marsh, or other waste land into land suitable for cultivation **2** the recovery of useful substances from waste products **3** the act of reclaiming or state of being reclaimed

réclame *French* (reklam) *n* **1** public acclaim or attention; publicity **2** the capacity for attracting publicity

reclinate ('rɛklɪˌneɪt) *adj* (esp of a leaf or stem) naturally curved or bent backwards so that the upper part rests on the ground [C18: from Latin *reclīnātus* bent back]

recline (rɪ'klaɪn) *vb* to rest or cause to rest in a leaning position [C15: from Old French *recliner*, from Latin *reclīnāre* to lean back, from RE- + *clīnāre* to LEAN[1]] ▷ re'clinable *adj* ▷ reclination (ˌrɛklɪ'neɪʃən) *n*

recliner (rɪ'klaɪnə) *n* a type of armchair having a back that can be adjusted to slope at various angles and, usually, a leg rest

recluse (rɪˈkluːs) *n* **1** a person who lives in seclusion **2** a person who lives in solitude to devote himself to prayer and religious meditation; a hermit, anchorite, or anchoress ▷ *adj* **3** solitary; retiring [c13: from Old French *reclus*, from Late Latin *reclūdere* to shut away, from Latin RE- + *claudere* to close] > reclusion (rɪˈkluːʒən) *n* > reˈclusive *adj*

recognition (ˌrɛkəgˈnɪʃən) *n* **1** the act of recognizing or fact of being recognized **2** acceptance or acknowledgment of a claim, duty, fact, truth, etc **3** a token of thanks or acknowledgment **4** formal acknowledgment of a government or of the independence of a country [c15: from Latin *recognitiō*, from *recognoscere* to know again, from RE- + *cognoscere* to know, ascertain] > recognitive (rɪˈkɒgnɪtɪv) *or* reˈcognitory *adj*

recognizance *or* **recognisance** (rɪˈkɒgnɪzəns) *n* **1** *law* **a** a bond entered into before a court or magistrate by which a person binds himself to do a specified act, as to appear in court on a stated day, keep the peace, or pay a debt **b** a monetary sum pledged to the performance of such an act **2** an obsolete word for **recognition** [c14: from Old French *reconoissance*, from *reconoistre* to RECOGNIZE] > reˈcognizant *or* reˈcognisant *adj*

recognize *or* **recognise** (ˈrɛkəgˌnaɪz) *vb* (*tr*) **1** to perceive (a person, creature, or thing) to be the same as or belong to the same class as something previously seen or known; know again **2** to accept or be aware of (a fact, duty, problem, etc): *to recognize necessity* **3** to give formal acknowledgment of the status or legality of (a government, an accredited representative, etc) **4** *chiefly US & Canadian* to grant (a person) the right to speak in a deliberative body, debate, etc **5** to give a token of thanks for (a service rendered, etc) **6** to make formal acknowledgment of (a claim, etc) **7** to show approval or appreciation of (something good or pleasing) **8** to acknowledge or greet (a person), as when meeting by chance [c15: from Latin *recognoscere* to know again, from RE- + *cognoscere* to know, ascertain] > ˈrecogˌnizable *or* ˈrecogˌnisable *adj* > ˌrecogˌnizaˈbility *or* ˌrecogˌnisaˈbility *n* > ˈrecogˌnizably *or* ˈrecogˌnisably *adv* > ˈrecogˌnizer *or* ˈrecogˌniser *n*

recoil *vb* (rɪˈkɔɪl) (*intr*) **1** to jerk back, as from an impact or violent thrust **2** (*often foll by from*) to draw back in fear, horror, or disgust **3** (*foll by on or upon*) to go wrong, esp so as to hurt the perpetrator **4** (of a nucleus, atom, molecule, or elementary particle) to change momentum as a result of the emission of a photon or particle ▷ *n* (rɪˈkɔɪl, ˈriːkɔɪl) **5 a** the backward movement of a gun when fired **b** the distance moved **6** the motion acquired by a particle as a result of its emission of a photon or other particle **7** the act of recoiling [c13: from Old French *reculer*, from RE- + *cul* rump, from Latin *cūlus*] > reˈcoiler *n*

recollect (ˌrɛkəˈlɛkt) *vb* (when *tr*, *often takes a clause as object*) to recall from memory; remember [c16: from Latin *recolligere* to gather again, from RE- + *colligere* to COLLECT¹] > ˌrecolˈlection *n* > ˌrecolˈlective *adj* > ˌrecolˈlectively *adv*

recombinant (riːˈkɒmbɪnənt) *genetics* ▷ *adj* **1** produced by the combining of genetic material from more than one origin ▷ *n* **2** a chromosome, cell, organism, etc, the genetic makeup of which results from recombination

recombinant DNA *n* DNA molecules that are extracted from different sources and chemically joined together; for example DNA comprising an animal gene may be recombined with DNA from a bacterium

recombination (ˌriːkɒmbɪˈneɪʃən) *n genetics* any of several processes by which genetic material of different origins becomes combined. It most commonly occurs between two sets of parental chromosomes during production of germ cells

recommend (ˌrɛkəˈmɛnd) *vb* (*tr*) **1** (*may take a clause as object or an infinitive*) to advise as the best course or choice; counsel **2** to praise or commend: *to recommend a new book* **3** to make attractive or advisable: *the trip has little to recommend it* **4** *archaic* to entrust (a person or thing) to someone else's care; commend [c14: via Medieval Latin

from Latin RE- + *commendāre* to COMMEND] > ˌrecomˈmendable *adj* > recommendatory (ˌrɛkəˈmɛndətərɪ, -trɪ) *adj* > ˌrecomˈmender *n*

recommendation (ˌrɛkəmɛnˈdeɪʃən) *n* **1** the act of recommending **2** something that recommends, esp a letter presenting someone as suitable for a job, etc **3** something that is recommended, such as a course of action

recommit (ˌriːkəˈmɪt) *vb* -mits, -mitting, -mitted (*tr*) **1** to send (a bill) back to a committee for further consideration **2** to commit again > ˌrecomˈmitment *or* ˌrecomˈmittal *n*

recompense (ˈrɛkəmˌpɛns) *vb* **1** (*tr*) to pay or reward for service, work, etc **2** (*tr*) to compensate for loss, injury, etc ▷ *n* **3** compensation for loss, injury, etc **4** reward, remuneration, or repayment [c15: from Old French *recompenser*, from Latin RE- + *compensāre* to balance in weighing; see COMPENSATE] > ˈrecomˌpensable *adj* > ˈrecomˌpenser *n*

reconcile (ˈrɛkənˌsaɪl) *vb* (*tr*) **1** (*often passive; usually foll by to*) to make (oneself or another) no longer opposed; cause to acquiesce in something unpleasant: *she reconciled herself to poverty* **2** to become friendly with (someone) after estrangement or to re-establish friendly relations between (two or more people) **3** to settle (a quarrel or difference) **4** to make (two apparently conflicting things) compatible or consistent with each other **5** to reconsecrate (a desecrated church, etc) [c14: from Latin *reconciliāre* to bring together again, from RE- + *conciliāre* to make friendly, CONCILIATE] > ˈreconˌcilement *n* > ˈreconˌciler *n* > reconciliation (ˌrɛkənˌsɪlɪˈeɪʃən) *n* > reconciliatory (ˌrɛkənˈsɪlɪətərɪ, -trɪ) *adj*

recondite (rɪˈkɒndaɪt, ˈrɛkənˌdaɪt) *adj* **1** requiring special knowledge to be understood; abstruse **2** dealing with abstruse or profound subjects [c17: from Latin *reconditus* hidden away, from RE- + *condere* to conceal] > reˈconditely *adv* > reˈconditeness *n*

recondition (ˌriːkənˈdɪʃən) *vb* (*tr*) to restore to good condition or working order: *to recondition an engine* > reconˈditioned *adj*

reconfigure (ˌriːkənˈfɪgə) *vb* (*tr*) to rearrange the elements or settings of (a system, device, computer application, etc)

reconnaissance *or* **reconnoissance** (rɪˈkɒnɪsəns) *n* **1** the act of reconnoitring **2** the process of obtaining information about the position, activities, resources, etc, of an enemy or potential enemy **3** a preliminary inspection of an area of land before an engineering survey is made [c18: from French, from Old French *reconoistre* to explore, RECOGNIZE]

reconnoitre *or US* **reconnoiter** (ˌrɛkəˈnɔɪtə) *vb* **1** to survey or inspect (an enemy's position, region of land, etc); make a reconnaissance (of) ▷ *n* **2** the act or process of reconnoitring; a reconnaissance [c18: from obsolete French *reconnoître* to inspect, explore; see RECOGNIZE] > ˌreconˈnoitrer *or US* ˌreconˈnoiterer *n*

reconsider (ˌriːkənˈsɪdə) *vb* **1** to consider (something) again, with a view to changing one's policy or course of action **2** (in a legislative assembly or similar body) to consider again (a bill or other matter) that has already been voted upon > ˌreconˌsiderˈation *n*

reconstitute (riːˈkɒnstɪˌtjuːt) *vb* (*tr*) to restore (food, etc) to its former or natural state or a semblance of it, as by the addition of water to a concentrate > reconstituent (ˌriːkənˈstɪtjʊənt) *adj, n* > ˌreconstiˈtution *n*

reconstruct (ˌriːkənˈstrʌkt) *vb* (*tr*) to construct or form again; rebuild > ˌreconˈstructible *adj* > ˌreconˈstruction *n* > ˌreconˈstructive *or* ˌreconˈstructional *adj* > ˌreconˈstructor *n*

reconvert (ˌriːkənˈvɜːt) *vb* (*tr*) **1** to change (something) back to a previous state or form **2** to bring (someone) back to his or her former religion > reconversion (ˌriːkənˈvɜːʃən) *n*

record *n* (ˈrɛkɔːd) **1** an account in permanent form, esp in writing, preserving knowledge or information about facts or events **2** a written account of some transaction that serves as legal evidence of the transaction **3** a written official report of the proceedings of a court of justice or legislative body, including the judgments given or enactments made **4** anything serving as evidence or as a memorial: *the First World War is a record of human folly* **5** (*often plural*) information or data on a specific subject collected methodically over a long period: *weather records* **6 a** the best or most outstanding amount, rate, height, etc, ever attained, as in some field of sport: *an Olympic record; a world record; to break the record for the long jump* **b** (*as modifier*): *a record time* **7** the sum of one's recognized achievements, career, or performance: *the officer has an excellent record* **8** a list of crimes of which an accused person has previously been convicted, which are known to the police but may only be disclosed to a court in certain circumstances **9 have a record** to be a known criminal; have a previous conviction or convictions **10** *Also called:* **gramophone record, disc** a thin disc of a plastic material upon which sound has been recorded. Each side has a spiral groove, which undulates in accordance with the frequency and amplitude of the sound. Records were formerly made from a shellac-based compound but were later made from vinyl plastics **11** the markings made by a recording instrument such as a seismograph **12** *computing* a group of data or piece of information preserved as a unit in machine-readable form **13** (in some computer languages) a data structure designed to allow the handling of groups of related pieces of information as though the group was a single entity **14** **for the record** for the sake of a strict factual account **15 go on record** to state one's views publicly **16 on record a** stated in a public document **b** publicly known **17 put the record straight** *or* **set the record straight** to correct an error or misunderstanding ▷ *vb* (rɪˈkɔːd) (*mainly tr*) **18** to set down in some permanent form so as to preserve the true facts of: *to record the minutes of a meeting* **19** to contain or serve to relate (facts, information, etc) **20** to indicate, show, or register: *his face recorded his disappointment* **21** to remain as or afford evidence of: *these ruins record the life of the Romans in Britain* **22** (*also intr*) to make a recording of (music, speech, etc) for reproduction, or for later broadcasting **23** (*also intr*) (of an instrument) to register or indicate (information) on a scale: *the barometer recorded a low pressure* [C13: from Old French *recorder* to call to mind, from Latin *recordārī* to remember, from RE- + *cor* heart] > re'cordable *adj*

recorded delivery *n* a Post Office service by which an official record of posting and delivery is obtained for a letter or package. See **registered post**

recorder (rɪˈkɔːdə) *n* **1** a person who records, such as an official or historian **2** something that records, esp an apparatus that provides a permanent record of experiments, etc **3** short for **tape recorder 4** *music* a wind instrument of the flute family, blown through a fipple in the mouth end, having a reedlike quality of tone. There are four usual sizes: bass, tenor, treble, and descant **5** (in England) a barrister or solicitor of at least ten years' standing appointed to sit as a part-time judge in the crown court [sense 4 probably from *record* (*vb*) in the archaic sense "to sing"] > re'corder‚ship *n*

recording (rɪˈkɔːdɪŋ) *n* **1 a** the act or process of making a record, esp of sound on a gramophone record or magnetic tape **b** (*as modifier*): *recording studio; recording head* **2** the record or tape so produced **3** something that has been recorded, esp a radio or television programme

Recording Angel *n* an angel who supposedly keeps a record of every person's good and bad acts

record label *n* a company that produces and sells records, CDs, and recordings

record of achievement *n* *Brit* a statement of the personal and educational development of each pupil

record player *n* a device for reproducing the sounds stored on a record, consisting of a turntable, usually electrically driven, that rotates the record at a fixed speed of 33, 45, or (esp formerly) 78 revolutions a minute. A stylus vibrates in accordance with undulations in the groove in the record: these vibrations are converted into electric currents, which, after amplification, are recreated in the form of sound by one or more loudspeakers

recount (rɪˈkaʊnt) *vb* (*tr*) to tell the story or details of;

narrate [C15: from Old French *reconter*, from RE- + *conter* to tell, relate; see COUNT[1]] > re'countal *n*

re-count *vb* (riːˈkaʊnt) **1** to count (votes, etc) again ▷ *n* (ˈriːˌkaʊnt) **2** a second or further count, esp of votes in a closely contested election

recoup (rɪˈkuːp) *vb* **1** to regain or make good (a financial or other loss) **2** (*tr*) to reimburse or compensate (someone), as for a loss **3** *law* to keep back (something due), having rightful claim to do so; withhold; deduct [C15: from Old French *recouper* to cut back, from RE- + *couper* to cut, from *coper* to behead; see COUP[1]] > re'coupable *adj* > re'coupment *n*

recourse (rɪˈkɔːs) *n* **1** the act of resorting to a person, course of action, etc, in difficulty or danger (esp in the phrase **have recourse to**) **2** a person, organization, or course of action that is turned to for help, protection, etc **3** the right to demand payment, esp from the drawer or endorser of a bill of exchange or other negotiable instrument when the person accepting it fails to pay **4 without recourse** a qualified endorsement on such a negotiable instrument, by which the endorser protects himself from liability to subsequent holders [C14: from Old French *recours*, from Late Latin *recursus* a running back, from RE- + *currere* to run]

recover (rɪˈkʌvə) *vb* **1** (*tr*) to find again or obtain the return of (something lost) **2** to regain (loss of money, position, time, etc); recoup **3** (of a person) to regain (health, spirits, composure, etc), as after illness, a setback, or a shock, etc **4** to regain (a former and usually better condition): *industry recovered after the war* **5** *law* **a** (*tr*) to gain (something) by the judgment of a court of law: *to recover damages* **b** (*intr*) to succeed in a lawsuit **6** (*tr*) to obtain (useful substances) from waste **7** (*intr*) (in fencing, swimming, rowing, etc) to make a recovery [C14: from Old French *recoverer*, from Latin *recuperāre* RECUPERATE] > re‚covera'bility *n* > re'coverable *adj* > re'coverer *n*

re-cover (riːˈkʌvə) *vb* **1** to cover again **2** to provide (a piece of furniture, book, etc) with a new cover

recovery (rɪˈkʌvərɪ) *n, pl* -eries **1** the act or process of recovering, esp from sickness, a shock, or a setback; recuperation **2** restoration to a former or better condition **3** the regaining of something lost **4** the extraction of useful substances from waste **5** the recovery of a space capsule after a space flight **6** *law* **a** the obtaining of a right, etc, by the judgment of a court **b** (in the US) the final judgment or verdict in a case **7** *fencing* a return to the position of guard after making an attack **8** *swimming, rowing* the action of bringing the arm, oar, etc, forward for another stroke **9** *golf* a stroke played from the rough or a bunker to the fairway or green

recovery stock *n* *stock exchange* a security that has fallen in price but is believed to have the ability to recover

recreant (ˈrɛkrɪənt) *archaic* ▷ *adj* **1** cowardly; faint-hearted **2** disloyal ▷ *n* **3** a disloyal or cowardly person [C14: from Old French, from *recroire* to surrender, from RE- + Latin *crēdere* to believe; compare MISCREANT] > 'recreance *or* 'recreancy *n* > 'recreantly *adv*

recreate (ˈrɛkrɪ‚eɪt) *vb rare* to amuse (oneself or someone else) [C15: from Latin *recreāre* to invigorate, renew, from RE- + *creāre* to CREATE] > 'recreative *adj* > 'recreatively *adv* > 'recre‚ator *n*

re-create (‚riːkrɪˈeɪt) *vb* to create anew; reproduce > ‚re-cre'ator *n*

recreation (‚rɛkrɪˈeɪʃən) *n* **1** refreshment of health or spirits by relaxation and enjoyment **2** an activity or pastime that promotes this **3 a** an interval of free time between school lessons **b** (*as modifier*): *recreation period*

re-creation *n* **1** the state or instance of creating again or anew: *the re-creation of the Russian Empire* **2** a simulation or re-enactment of a scene, place, time, etc: *a re-creation of a vineyard kitchen*

recreational (‚rɛkrɪˈeɪʃənl) *adj* **1** of, relating to, or used for recreation: *recreational facilities* **2** (of a drug) taken for pleasure rather than for medical reasons or because of an addiction

recreational vehicle *n chiefly US* a large vanlike vehicle equipped to be lived in. Abbreviation: RV

r

recriminate (rɪˈkrɪmɪˌneɪt) *vb* (*intr*) to return an accusation against someone or engage in mutual accusations [C17: from Medieval Latin *recrīmināre*, from Latin *crīminārī* to accuse, from *crīmen* an accusation; see CRIME] > re'criminative *or* re'criminatory *adj* > re'crimiˌnator *n*

recrimination (rɪˌkrɪmɪˈneɪʃən) *n* the act or an instance of recriminating

recrudesce (ˌriːkruːˈdɛs) *vb* (*intr*) (of a disease, trouble, etc) to break out or appear again after a period of dormancy; recur [C19: from Latin *recrūdēscere* to become raw again, from RE- + *crūdēscere* to grow worse, from *crūdus* bloody, raw; see CRUDE] > ˌrecruˈdescence *n* > ˌrecruˈdescent *adj*

recruit (rɪˈkruːt) *vb* 1 to raise or strengthen (an army, navy, etc) by enlistment 2 (*tr*) to enrol or obtain (members, support, etc) 3 to furnish or be furnished with a fresh supply; renew 4 *archaic* to recover (health, strength, spirits, etc) ▷ *n* 5 a newly joined member of a military service 6 any new member or supporter [C17: from French *recrute* literally: new growth, from *recroître* to grow again, from Latin *recrēscere* from RE- + *crēscere* to grow] > re'cruitable *adj* > re'cruiter *n* > re'cruitment *n*

recta (ˈrɛktə) *n* a plural of **rectum**

rectal (ˈrɛktəl) *adj* of or relating to the rectum > 'rectally *adv*

rectangle (ˈrɛkˌtæŋɡəl) *n* a parallelogram having four right angles. See **rhombus** [C16: from Medieval Latin *rectangulum*, from Latin *rectus* straight + *angulus* angle]

rectangular (rɛkˈtæŋɡjʊlə) *adj* 1 shaped like a rectangle 2 having or relating to right angles 3 mutually perpendicular: *rectangular coordinates* 4 having a base or section shaped like a rectangle > recˌtanguˈlarity *n* > recˈtangularly *adv*

rectangular coordinates *pl n* the Cartesian coordinates in a system of mutually perpendicular axes

rectangular hyperbola *n* a hyperbola with perpendicular asymptotes

recti (ˈrɛktaɪ) *n* the plural of **rectus**

recti- *or before a vowel* **rect-** *combining form* straight or right: *rectilinear; rectangle* [from Latin *rectus*]

rectifier (ˈrɛktɪˌfaɪə) *n* 1 an electronic device, such as a semiconductor diode or valve, that converts an alternating current to a direct current by suppression or inversion of alternate half cycles 2 *chem* an apparatus for condensing a hot vapour to a liquid in distillation; condenser 3 a thing or person that rectifies

rectify (ˈrɛktɪˌfaɪ) *vb* **-fies, -fying, -fied** (*tr*) 1 to put right; correct; remedy 2 to separate (a substance) from a mixture or refine (a substance) by fractional distillation 3 to convert (alternating current) into direct current 4 *maths* to determine the length of (a curve) 5 to cause (an object) to assume a linear motion or characteristic [C14: via Old French from Medieval Latin *rectificāre* to adjust, from Latin *rectus* straight + *facere* to make] > 'rectiˌfiable *adj* > ˌrectifiˈcation *n*

rectilinear (ˌrɛktɪˈlɪnɪə) *or* **rectilineal** *adj* 1 in, moving in, or characterized by a straight line or lines 2 consisting of, bounded by, or formed by a straight line or lines > ˌrectiˈlinearly *or* ˌrectiˈlineally *adv*

rectitude (ˈrɛktɪˌtjuːd) *n* 1 moral or religious correctness 2 correctness of judgment [C15: from Late Latin *rectitūdō*, from Latin *rectus* right, straight, from *regere* to rule]

recto (ˈrɛktəʊ) *n*, *pl* **-tos** 1 the front of a sheet of printed paper 2 the right-hand pages of a book, bearing the odd numbers. See **verso** (sense 1b) [C19: from Latin *rectō* (*foliō*) on the right-hand page]

rectocele (ˈrɛktəʊˌsiːl) *n* *pathol* a protrusion or herniation of the rectum into the vagina [C19: New Latin, from RECTUM + -CELE]

rector (ˈrɛktə) *n* 1 *Church of England* a clergyman in charge of a parish in which, as its incumbent, he would formerly have been entitled to the whole of the tithes. See **vicar** 2 *RC Church* a cleric in charge of a college, religious house, or congregation 3 *Protestant Episcopal Church, Scottish Episcopal Church* a clergyman in charge of a parish 4 *chiefly Brit* the head of certain schools or colleges 5 (in Scotland) a high-ranking official in a university: now a public figure elected for three years by the students [C14: from Latin: director, ruler, from *regere* to rule] > 'rectorate *n* > rectorial (rɛkˈtɔːrɪəl) *adj* > 'rectorship *n*

rectory (ˈrɛktərɪ) *n*, *pl* **-ries** 1 the official house of a rector 2 *Church of England* the office and benefice of a rector

rectrix (ˈrɛktrɪks) *n*, *pl* **rectrices** (ˈrɛktrɪˌsiːz, rɛkˈtraɪsiːz) any of the large stiff feathers of a bird's tail, used in controlling the direction of flight [C17: from Late Latin, feminine of *rector* governor, RECTOR] > rectricial (rɛkˈtrɪʃəl) *adj*

rectum (ˈrɛktəm) *n*, *pl* **-tums** *or* **-ta** (-tə) the lower part of the alimentary canal, between the sigmoid flexure of the colon and the anus [C16: shortened from New Latin *rectum intestinum* the straight intestine]

rectus (ˈrɛktəs) *n*, *pl* **-ti** (-taɪ) *anatomy* a straight muscle, esp either of two muscles of the anterior abdominal wall (**rectus abdominis**) [C18: from New Latin *rectus musculus*]

recumbent (rɪˈkʌmbənt) *adj* 1 lying down; reclining 2 (of a part or organ) leaning or resting against another organ or the ground [C17: from Latin *recumbere* to lie back, from RE- + *cumbere* to lie] > re'cumbence *or* re'cumbency *n* > re'cumbently *adv*

recumbent bicycle *n* a type of bicycle that is ridden in a reclining position

recuperate (rɪˈkuːpəˌreɪt, -ˈkjuː-) *vb* 1 (*intr*) to recover from illness or exhaustion 2 to recover (losses of money, etc) [C16: from Latin *recuperāre* to recover, from RE- + *capere* to gain, take] > reˌcuperˈation *n* > re'cuperative *adj*

recur (rɪˈkɜː) *vb* **-curs, -curring, -curred** (*intr*) 1 to happen again, esp at regular intervals 2 (of a thought, idea, etc) to come back to the mind 3 (of a problem, etc) to come up again 4 *maths* (of a digit or group of digits) to be repeated an infinite number of times at the end of a decimal fraction [C15: from Latin *recurrere*, from RE- + *currere* to run] > re'curring *adj* > re'curringly *adv*

recurrent (rɪˈkʌrənt) *adj* 1 happening or tending to happen again or repeatedly 2 *anatomy* (of certain nerves, branches of vessels, etc) turning back, so as to run in the opposite direction > re'currence *n* > re'currently *adv*

recurrent fever *n* another name for **relapsing fever**

recurring decimal *n* a rational number that contains a pattern of digits repeated indefinitely after the decimal point

recursion (rɪˈkɜːʃən) *n* 1 the act or process of returning or running back 2 *logic, maths* the application of a function to its own values to generate an infinite sequence of values. The **recursion formula** or **clause** of a definition specifies the progression from one term to the next, as given the base clause $f(0) = 0$, $f(n + 1) = f(n) + 3$ specifies the successive terms of the sequence $f(n) = 3n$ [C17: from Latin *recursio*, from *recurrere* RECUR] > re'cursive *adj*

recurve (rɪˈkɜːv) *vb* to curve or bend (something) back or down or (of something) to be so curved or bent [C16: from Latin *recurvāre* from RE- + *curvāre* to CURVE]

recusant (ˈrɛkjʊzənt) *n* 1 (in 16th to 18th century England) a Roman Catholic who did not attend the services of the Church of England, as was required by law 2 any person who refuses to submit to authority ▷ *adj* 3 (formerly, of Catholics) refusing to attend services of the Church of England 4 refusing to submit to authority [C16: from Latin *recūsāns* refusing, from *recūsāre* from RE- + *causārī* to dispute, from *causa* a CAUSE] > 'recusance *or* 'recusancy *n*

recuse (rəˈkjuːz, rɪˈkjuːz) *vb* (*tr*) *US, Canadian & South African* (*reflexive*) to remove from participation in a court case due to potential prejudice or partiality [C19: see RECUSANT]

recycle (riːˈsaɪkᵊl) *vb* (*tr*) 1 to pass (a substance) through a system again for further treatment or use 2 to reclaim (packaging or products with a limited useful life) for further use 3 to institute a different cycle of processes or events in (a machine, system, etc) 4 to repeat (a series of operations) ▷ *n* 5 the repetition of a fixed sequence of events > re'cyclable *or* re'cycleable *adj*

red[1] (rɛd) *n* 1 any of a group of colours, such as that of a ripe tomato or fresh blood, that lie at one end of the visible spectrum, next to orange, and are perceived by the eye when light in the approximate wavelength

range 740–620 nanometres falls on the retina. Red is the complementary colour of cyan and forms a set of primary colours with blue and green **2** a pigment or dye of or producing these colours **3** red cloth or clothing: *dressed in red* **4** a red ball in snooker, billiards, etc **5** (in roulette and other gambling games) one of two colours on which players may place even bets, the other being black **6** Also called: inner *archery* a red ring on a target, between the blue and the gold, scoring seven points **7** in the red *informal* in debit; owing money **8** see red *informal* to become very angry ▷ *adj* redder, reddest **9** of the colour red **10** reddish in colour or having parts or marks that are reddish: *red hair; red deer* **11** having the face temporarily suffused with blood, being a sign of anger, shame, etc **12** (of the complexion) rosy; florid **13** (of the eyes) bloodshot **14** (of the hands) stained with blood, as after committing murder **15** bloody or violent: *red revolution* **16** (of wine) made from black grapes and coloured by their skins **17** denoting the highest degree of urgency in an emergency; used by the police and the army and informally (esp in the phrase **red alert**) ▷ *vb* reds, redding, redded **18** another word for **redden** [Old English *rēad*; compare Old High German *rōt*, Gothic *rauths*, Latin *ruber*, Greek *eruthros*, Sanskrit *rohita*]
> 'reddish *adj* > 'reddishly *adv* > 'reddishness *n*
> 'redness *n*

red² (rɛd) *vb* reds, redding, red *or* redded (*tr*) a variant spelling of **redd¹**

Red (rɛd) *informal* ▷ *adj* **1** Communist, Socialist, or Soviet **2** radical, leftist, or revolutionary ▷ *n* **3** a member or supporter of a Communist or Socialist Party or a national of a state having such a government, esp the former Soviet Union **4** a radical, leftist, or revolutionary [C19: from the colour chosen to symbolize revolutionary socialism]

redact (rɪˈdækt) *vb* (*tr*) **1** to compose or draft (an edict, proclamation, etc) **2** to put (a literary work, etc) into appropriate form for publication; edit [C15: from Latin *redigere* to bring back, from *red-* RE- + *agere* to drive]
> re'daction *n* > re'dactional *adj* > re'dactor *n*

red admiral *n* a nymphalid butterfly, *Vanessa atalanta*, of temperate Europe and Asia, having black wings with red and white markings. See also **white admiral**

red algae *pl n* the numerous algae that constitute the phylum *Rhodophyta*, which contain a red pigment in addition to chlorophyll. The group includes carrageen, dulse, and laver

Red Army Faction *n* another name for the **Baader-Meinhof Gang**

redback *or* **redback spider** *n* a small venomous Australian spider, *Latrodectus hasselti*, having long thin legs and, in the female, a red stripe on the back of its globular abdomen

red bark *n* a kind of cinchona containing a high proportion of alkaloids

red-bellied black snake *n* a highly venomous Australian black snake, *Pseudechis porphyriacus*, with a reddish underside

red biddy *n informal* cheap red wine fortified with methylated spirits

red blood cell *n* another name for **erythrocyte**

red-blooded *adj informal* vigorous; virile > ,red-'bloodedness *n*

red book *n* Brit(*sometimes capitals*) a government publication bound in red, esp the Treasury's annual forecast of revenue, expenditure, growth, and inflation

redbreast (ˈrɛd,brɛst) *n* any of various birds having a red breast, esp the Old World robin

redbrick (ˈrɛd,brɪk) *n* (*modifier*) denoting, relating to, or characteristic of a provincial British university of relatively recent foundation, esp as distinguished from Oxford and Cambridge

Redbridge (ˈrɛd,brɪdʒ) *n* a borough of NE Greater London: includes part of Epping Forest Pop: 245 100 (2003 est). Area: 56 sq km (22 sq miles)

redcap (ˈrɛd,kæp) *n* **1** Brit informal a military policeman **2** US & Canadian a porter at an airport or station

Redcar and Cleveland (ˈrɛdkɑː) *n* a unitary authority in NE England, in North Yorkshire: formerly (1975–96)

part of Cleveland county. Pop: 139 100 (2003 est). Area: 240 sq km (93 sq miles)

red card *sport* ▷ *n* **1** a card of a red colour displayed by a referee to indicate that a player has been sent off ▷ *vb* red-card **2** (*tr*) to send off (a player)

red carpet *n* **1** a strip of red carpeting laid for important dignitaries to walk on when arriving or departing **2** a deferential treatment accorded to a person of importance **b** (*as modifier*): *the returning hero had a red-carpet reception*

red cedar *n* **1** any of several North American coniferous trees, esp *Juniperus virginiana*, a juniper that has fragrant reddish wood used for making pencils, and *Thuja plicata*, an arbor vitae **2** the wood of any of these trees

red cent *n* (*used with a negative*) *informal, chiefly US* a cent considered as a trivial amount of money (esp in the phrases **not have a red cent**, **not worth a red cent**, etc)

Red China *n* an unofficial name for (the People's Republic of) **China**

redcoat (ˈrɛd,kəʊt) *n* (formerly) a British soldier [C16: from the colour of the uniform jacket]

red coral *n* any of several corals of the genus *Corallium*, the skeletons of which are pinkish red in colour and used to make ornaments, etc

red corpuscle *n* another name for **erythrocyte**

Red Crescent *n* a national branch of or the emblem of the Red Cross Society in a Muslim country

Red Cross *n* **1** an international humanitarian organization (**Red Cross Society**) formally established by the Geneva Convention of 1864. It was originally limited to providing medical care for war casualties, but its services now include liaison between prisoners of war and their families, relief to victims of natural disasters, etc **2** the emblem of this organization, consisting of a red cross on a white background

redcurrant (ˈrɛd,kʌrənt) *n* **1** a N temperate shrub, *Ribes rubrum*, having greenish flowers and small edible rounded red berries: family *Grossulariaceae* **2 a** the fruit of this shrub **b** (*as modifier*): *redcurrant jelly*

redd *or* **red** (rɛd) *Scot & northern English dialect* ▷ *vb* redds, redding, redd *or* redded **1** (*tr*; often foll by *up*) to bring order to; tidy (up) ▷ *n* **2** the act or an instance of redding [C15 *redden* to clear, perhaps a variant of RID] > 'redder *n*

red deer *n* a large deer, *Cervus elaphus*, formerly widely distributed in the woodlands of Europe and Asia. The coat is reddish brown in summer and the short tail is surrounded by a patch of light-coloured hair

Red Deer *n* **1** a town in S Alberta on the Red Deer River: trade centre for mixed farming, dairying region, and natural gas processing. Pop: 67 707 (2001) **2** a river in W Canada, in SW Alberta, flowing southeast into the South Saskatchewan River. Length: about 620 km (385 miles) **3** a river in W Canada, flowing east through **Red Deer Lake** into Lake Winnipegosis. Length: about 225 km (140 miles)

redden (ˈrɛdᵊn) *vb* **1** to make or become red **2** (*intr*) to flush with embarrassment, anger, etc; blush

Redding (ˈrɛdɪŋ) *n* **Otis.** 1941–67, US soul singer and songwriter. His recordings include "Respect" (1965), *Dictionary of Soul* (1966), and "(Sittin' on) The Dock of the Bay" (1968)

Redditch (ˈrɛdɪtʃ) *n* a town in W central England, in N Worcestershire: designated a new town in the mid-1960s; metal-working industries. Pop: 74 803 (2001)

reddle (ˈrɛdᵊl) *n*, *vb* a variant spelling of **ruddle**

red duster *n* Brit an informal name for the **Red Ensign**

red dwarf *n* one of a class of small cool main-sequence stars

rede (riːd) *archaic* ▷ *n* **1** advice or counsel **2** an explanation ▷ *vb* (*tr*) **3** to advise; counsel **4** to explain [Old English *rǣdan* to rule; see READ¹]

red earth *n* a clayey zonal soil of tropical savanna lands, formed by extensive chemical weathering, coloured by iron compounds, and less strongly leached than laterite

redeem (rɪˈdiːm) *vb* (*tr*) **1** to recover possession or ownership of by payment of a price or service; regain **2** to convert (bonds, shares, etc) into cash **3** to recover (something pledged, mortgaged, or pawned) **4** to convert (paper money) into bullion or specie **5** to fulfil (a promise, pledge, etc) **6** to exchange (trading stamps, coupons, etc) for goods **7** to reinstate in someone's estimation or good opinion; restore to favour: *he redeemed himself by his altruistic action* **8** to make amends for **9** *Christianity* (of Christ as Saviour) to free (mankind) from sin by his death on the Cross [C15: from Old French *redimer*, from Latin *redimere* to buy back, from *red-* RE- + *emere* to buy] ▷ re,deema'bility *n* ▷ redeemable (rɪ'diːməb^əl) *or* redemptible (rɪ'dɛmptəb^əl) *adj* (of bonds, shares, etc) ▷ re'deemably *adv* ▷ re'deemer *n*

Redeemer (rɪ'diːmə) *n* **The Redeemer** Jesus Christ as having brought redemption to mankind

redeeming (rɪ'diːmɪŋ) *adj* serving to compensate for faults or deficiencies in quality, etc: *one redeeming feature*

red emperor *n* *Austral* a brightly-coloured marine food fish, *Lutjanus sebae*, of the Great Barrier Reef

redemption (rɪ'dɛmpʃən) *n* **1** the act or process of redeeming **2** the state of being redeemed **3** *Christianity* **a** deliverance from sin through the incarnation, sufferings, and death of Christ **b** atonement for guilt [C14: via Old French from Latin *redemptiō* a buying back; see REDEEM] ▷ re'demptional, re'demptive *or* re'demptory *adj* ▷ re'demptively *adv*

redemption yield *n* *stock exchange* the yield produced by a redeemable gilt-edged security taking into account the annual interest it pays and an annualized amount to account for any profit or loss when it is redeemed

Red Ensign *n* the ensign of the British Merchant Navy, having the Union Jack on a red background at the upper corner of the vertical edge alongside the hoist

redeploy (,riːdɪ'plɔɪ) *vb* to assign new positions or tasks to (labour, troops, etc) ▷ ,rede'ployment *n*

redevelopment area *n* an urban area in which all or most of the buildings are demolished and rebuilt

redeye ('rɛd,aɪ) *n* **1** *US slang* inferior whiskey **2** *Canadian slang* a drink incorporating beer and tomato juice **3** another name for **rudd**

red-eye *n* *informal* **a** an aeroplane flight leaving late at night or arriving early in the morning **b** (*as modifier*): *a red-eye flight*

red-faced *adj* **1** flushed with embarrassment or anger **2** having a florid complexion ▷ red-facedly (,rɛd'feɪsɪdlɪ, -'feɪstlɪ) *adv*

redfin ('rɛd,fɪn) *n* any of various small cyprinid fishes of the genus *Notropis*, esp *N. cornutus*. They have reddish fins and are popular aquarium fishes

redfish ('rɛd,fɪʃ) *n*, *pl* **-fish** *or* **-fishes** a male salmon that has recently spawned. See **blackfish** (sense 2)

red flag *n* **1** a symbol of socialism, communism, or revolution **2** a warning of danger or a signal to stop

Redford ('rɛdfəd) *n* **Robert**. born 1937, US film actor and director. His films include (as actor) *Barefoot in the Park* (1966), *Butch Cassidy and the Sundance Kid* (1969), *The Sting* (1973), *All the President's Men* (1976), *Up Close and Personal* (1996) and (as director) *Ordinary People* (1980), *A River Runs Through It* (1992), and *The Horse Whisperer* (1998)

red fox *n* the common fox, *Vulpes vulpes*, which has a reddish-brown coat: family *Canidae*, order *Carnivora* (carnivores)

red giant *n* a giant star towards the end of its life, with a relatively low temperature of 2000–4000 K, that emits red light

Redgrave ('rɛd,greɪv) *n* **1 Lynn**. born 1944, British stage and film actress. Her films include *Georgy Girl* (1966), *The Happy Hooker* (1975), and *Gods and Monsters* (1999) **2** her father, Sir **Michael**. 1908–85, British stage and film actor. Among his films are *The Lady Vanishes* (1938), *The Dam Busters* (1955), *The Loneliness of the Long Distance Runner* (1963), and *The Go-Between* (1971) **3** Sir **Steve**. born 1962, British oarsman; won five gold medals in rowing events at consecutive Olympic Games (1984, 1988, 1992, 1996, 2000) **4** his elder daughter, **Vanessa**. born 1937, British stage and film actress, whose roles include performances in the films *Isadora* (1968), *Julia* (1977), *Howards End* (1992), *Mrs Dalloway* (1998), and *A Rumour of Angels* (2000): noted also for her active commitment to left-wing politics

red grouse *n* a reddish-brown grouse, *Lagopus scoticus*, of upland moors of Great Britain: an important game bird

Red Guard *n* a member of a Chinese youth movement that attempted to effect the Cultural Revolution (1965–71)

red-handed *adj* (*postpositive*) in the act of committing a crime or doing something wrong or shameful (esp in the phrase **catch red-handed**) [C19: earlier, C15 *red hand*)]

red hat *n* the broad-brimmed crimson hat given to cardinals as the symbol of their rank and office

redhead ('rɛd,hɛd) *n* **1** a person with red hair **2** a diving duck, *Aythya americana*, of North America, the male of which has a grey-and-black body and a reddish-brown head ▷ red-headed *adj*

red heat *n* **1** the temperature at which a substance is red-hot **2** the state or condition of being red-hot

red herring *n* **1** anything that diverts attention from a topic or line of inquiry **2** a herring cured by salting and smoking

red-hot *adj* **1** (esp of metal) heated to the temperature at which it glows red **2** extremely hot **3** keen, excited, or eager; enthusiastic **4** furious; violent: *red-hot anger* **5** very recent or topical: *red-hot information* **6** *Austral slang* extreme, unreasonable, or unfair: *the charges are red-hot*

red-hot poker *n* See **kniphofia**

Red Indian *n, adj* an old-fashioned name, now considered highly offensive, for **Native American** [see REDSKIN]

redingote ('rɛdɪŋ,gəʊt) *n* **1** a woman's coat with a close-fitting top and a full skirt **2** a man's or woman's full-skirted outer coat of the 18th and 19th centuries **3** a woman's light dress or coat of the 18th century, with an open-fronted skirt, revealing a decorative underskirt [C19: from French, from English *riding coat*]

redintegrate (rɛ'dɪntɪ,greɪt) *vb* (*tr*) to make whole or complete again; restore to a perfect state; renew [C15: from Latin *redintegrāre* to renew, from *red-* RE- + *integer* complete] ▷ re,dinte'gration *n* ▷ red'inte,grative *adj*

redistribution (,riːdɪstrɪ'bjuːʃən) *n* the act or instance of distributing or the state or manner of being distributed again

redivivus (,rɛdɪ'vaɪvəs) *adj* *rare* returned to life; revived [C17: from Late Latin, from Latin *red-* RE- + *vīvus* alive]

red lead (lɛd) *n* a bright-red poisonous insoluble oxide of lead usually obtained as a powder by heating litharge in air. It is used as a pigment in paints. Formula: Pb_3O_4

red-letter day *n* a memorably important or happy occasion [C18: from the red letters used in ecclesiastical calendars to indicate saints' days and feasts]

red light *n* **1** a signal to stop, esp a red traffic signal in a system of traffic lights **2** a danger signal **3 a** a red lamp in a window of or outside a house indicating that it is a brothel **b** (*as modifier*): *a red-light district*

redline ('rɛd,laɪn) *vb* (*tr*) (esp of a bank or group of banks) to refuse a loan to (a person or country) because of the presumed risks involved

red meat *n* any meat that is dark in colour, esp beef and lamb. See **white meat**

red mercury *n* a supposedly radioactive substance that could be used in a bomb made from nuclear waste, widely believed to be part of a confidence trick in which gangsters sold useless material to terrorists in the early 1990s

Redmond ('rɛdmənd) *n* **John Edward**. 1856–1918, Irish politician. He led the Parnellites from 1891 and helped to procure the Home Rule bill of 1912, but was considered too moderate by extreme nationalists

red mullet *n* any of the marine percoid fishes constituting the family *Mullidae*, esp *Mullus surmuletus*, a food fish of European waters. They have a pair of long barbels beneath the chin and a reddish coloration. US name: **goatfish**

redneck ('rɛd,nɛk) *n* *disparaging* **1** (in the southwestern US) a poor uneducated White farm worker **2** a person or institution that is extremely reactionary ▷ *adj* **3** reactionary and bigoted: *redneck laws*

redo (riː'duː) *vb* **-does, -doing, -did, -done** (*tr*) **1** to do over again **2** *informal* to redecorate, esp thoroughly: *we redid the house last summer*

red ochre *n* any of various natural red earths containing ferric oxide: used as pigments

redolent ('rɛdəʊlənt) *adj* **1** having a pleasant smell; fragrant **2** (*postpositive*; foll by *of* or *with*) having the odour or smell (of); scented (with): *a room redolent of country flowers* **3** (*postpositive*; foll by *of* or *with*) reminiscent or suggestive (of): *a picture redolent of the 18th century* [C14: from Latin *redolens* smelling (of), from *redolēre* to give off an odour, from *red-* RE + *olēre* to smell] ▷ '**redolence** or *less commonly* '**redolency** *n* ▷ '**redolently** *adv*

Redon (*French* rədɔ̃) *n* **Odilon** (ɔdilɔ̃). 1840–1916, French symbolist painter and etcher. He foreshadowed the surrealists in his paintings of fantastic dream images

redouble (rɪ'dʌbəl) *vb* **1** to make or become much greater in intensity, number, etc: *to redouble one's efforts* **2** to send back (sounds) or (of sounds) to be sent back; echo or re-echo **3** *bridge* to double (an opponent's double) ▷ *n* **4** the act of redoubling

redoubt (rɪ'daʊt) *n* **1** an outwork or detached fieldwork defending a pass, hilltop, etc **2** a temporary defence work built inside a fortification as a last defensive position [C17: via French from obsolete Italian *ridotta*, from Medieval Latin *reductus* shelter, from Latin *redūcere* to withdraw, from RE- + *dūcere* to lead]

redoubtable (rɪ'daʊtəbəl) *adj* **1** to be feared; formidable **2** worthy of respect [C14: from Old French, from *redouter* to dread, from RE- + *douter* to be afraid, DOUBT] ▷ re'**doubtableness** *n* ▷ re'**doubtably** *adv*

redound (rɪ'daʊnd) *vb* **1** (*intr*; foll by *to*) to have an advantageous or disadvantageous effect (on): *brave deeds redound to your credit* **2** (*intr*; foll by *on* or *upon*) to recoil or rebound **3** (*tr*) *archaic* to reflect; bring: *his actions redound dishonour upon him* [C14: from Old French *redonder*, from Latin *redundāre* to stream over, from *red-* RE + *undāre* to rise in waves, from *unda* a wave]

redox ('riːdɒks) *n* (*modifier*) another term for **oxidation-reduction** [C20: from RED(UCTION) + OX(IDATION)]

red pepper *n* **1** any of several varieties of the pepper plant *Capsicum frutescens*, cultivated for their hot pungent red podlike fruits **2** the fruit of any of these plants **3** the ripe red fruit of the sweet pepper **4** another name for **cayenne pepper**

red pine *n* a coniferous tree, *Dacrydium cupressinum*, of New Zealand, having narrow sharp pointed leaves: family *Podocarpaceae*. Also called: **rimu**

Red Planet *n* **the Red Planet** an informal name for **Mars²** (sense 1)

redpoll ('rɛd,pɒl) *n* either of two widely distributed finches, *Acanthis flammea* or *A. hornemanni* (**arctic** or **hoary redpoll**), having a greyish-brown plumage with a red crown and pink breast

red rag *n* a provocation; something that infuriates [so called because red objects supposedly infuriate bulls]

redress (rɪ'drɛs) *vb* (*tr*) **1** to put right (a wrong), esp by compensation; make reparation for **2** to correct or adjust (esp in the phrase **redress the balance**) **3** to make compensation to (a person) for a wrong ▷ *n* **4** the act or an instance of setting right a wrong; remedy or cure: *to seek redress of grievances* **5** compensation, amends, or reparation for a wrong, injury, etc [C14: from Old French *redrecier* to set up again, from RE- + *drecier* to straighten; see DRESS] ▷ re'**dressable** or re'**dressible** *adj* ▷ re'**dresser** or Also called: *less commonly* re'**dressor** *n*

re-dress (riː'drɛs) *vb* (*tr*) to dress (something) again

Red River *n* **1** Also called: **Red River of the South** a river in the S central US, flowing east from N Texas through Arkansas into the Mississippi in Louisiana. Length: 1639 km (1018 miles) **2** a river in the northern US, flowing north as the border between North Dakota and Minnesota and into Lake Winnipeg, Canada. Length: 515 km (320 miles) **3** a river in SE Asia, rising in SW China in Yunnan province and flowing southeast across N Vietnam to the Gulf of Tongkin: the chief river of N Vietnam, with an extensive delta. Length: 500 km (310 miles). Vietnamese name: **Song Koi**

red roman *n* *South African* a marine food fish, *Chrisoblephus laticeps*

red rose *n* *English history* the emblem of the House of Lancaster. See also **Wars of the Roses, white rose**

red salmon *n* any salmon having reddish flesh, esp the sockeye salmon

Red Sea *n* a long narrow sea between Arabia and NE Africa, linked with the Mediterranean in the north by the Suez Canal and with the Indian Ocean in the south: occasionally reddish in appearance through algae. Area: 438 000 sq km (169 000 sq miles)

redshank ('rɛd,ʃæŋk) *n* either of two large common European sandpipers, *Tringa totanus* or *T. erythropus* (**spotted redshank**), having red legs

redshift ('rɛd,ʃɪft) *n* a shift in the lines of the spectrum of an astronomical object towards a longer wavelength (the red end of an optical spectrum), relative to the wavelength of these lines in the terrestrial spectrum, usually as a result of the **Doppler effect** caused by the recession of the object

redskin ('rɛd,skɪn) *n* an old-fashioned informal name, now considered taboo, for a **Native American** [C17: so called because one particular tribe, the now extinct Beothuks of Newfoundland, painted themselves with red ochre]

red snapper *n* any of various marine percoid food fishes of the genus *Lutjanus*, esp *L. blackfordi*, having a reddish coloration, common in American coastal regions of the Atlantic: family *Lutjanidae* (snappers)

red spider *n* the red spider mite. See **spider mite**

Red Spot *n* See **Great Red Spot**

red squirrel *n* **1** a reddish-brown squirrel, *Sciurus vulgaris*, inhabiting woodlands of Europe and parts of Asia **2** American red squirrel Also called: **chickaree** either of two reddish-brown squirrels, *Tamiasciurus hudsonicus* or *T. douglasii*, inhabiting forests of North America

redstart ('rɛd,stɑːt) *n* **1** any European songbird of the genus *Phoenicurus*, esp *P. phoenicurus*, in which the male has a black throat, orange-brown tail and breast, and grey back: family *Muscicapidae* (thrushes, etc) **2** any North American warbler of the genus *Setophaga*, esp *S. ruticilla* [Old English *rēad* RED¹ + *steort* tail; compare German *Rotsterz*]

red tape *n* obstructive official routine or procedure; time-consuming bureaucracy [C18: from the red tape used to bind official government documents]

red-top *n* a tabloid newspaper characterized by sensationalism [C20: from the colour of the masthead on these publications]

reduce (rɪ'djuːs) *vb* (*mainly tr*) **1** (*also intr*) to make or become smaller in size, number, extent, degree, intensity, etc **2** to bring into a certain state, condition, etc: *to reduce a forest to ashes; to reduce someone to despair* **3** (*also intr*) to make or become slimmer; lose or cause to lose excess weight **4** to impoverish (esp in the phrase **in reduced circumstances**) **5** to bring into a state of submission to one's authority; subjugate: *the whole country was reduced after three months* **6** to bring down the price of (a commodity) **7** to lower the rank or status of; demote: *he was reduced from corporal to private; reduced to the ranks* **8** to set out systematically as an aid to understanding; simplify: *his theories have been reduced in a popular treatise* **9** *maths* to modify or simplify the form of (an expression or equation), esp by substitution of one term by another **10** *cookery* to make (a sauce, stock, etc) more concentrated by boiling away some of the water in it **11** to thin out (paint) by adding oil, turpentine, etc; dilute **12** (*also intr*) *chem* **a** to undergo or cause to undergo a chemical reaction with hydrogen or formation of a hydride **b** to lose or cause to lose oxygen atoms **c** to undergo or cause to undergo an increase in the number of electrons **13** *photog* to lessen the density of (a negative or print) by converting some of the blackened silver in the emulsion to soluble silver compounds by an oxidation process using a photographic reducer **14** *surgery* to manipulate or reposition (a broken or displaced bone, organ, or part) back to its normal site **15** (*also intr*) *biology* to undergo or cause to undergo meiosis [C14: from Latin *redūcere* to bring back, from RE- + *dūcere* to lead] ▷ re'**ducible** *adj* ▷ re,**duci'bility** *n* ▷ re'**ducibly** *adv*

reducer (rɪ'djuːsə) *n* **1** *photog* a chemical solution used to lessen the density of a negative or print by oxidizing some of the blackened silver to soluble silver compounds. See **intensifier** (sense 3) **2** a pipe fitting connecting two pipes of different diameters **3** a person or thing that reduces

reducing agent *n chem* a substance that reduces another substance in a chemical reaction, being itself oxidized in the process

reducing glass *n* a lens or curved mirror that produces an image smaller than the object observed

reductase (rɪˈdʌkteɪz) *n* any enzyme that catalyses a biochemical reduction reaction [C20: from REDUCTION + -ASE]

reductio ad absurdum (rɪˈdʌktɪəʊ æd æbˈsɜːdəm) *n* **1 a** method of disproving a proposition by showing that its inevitable consequences would be absurd **2** a method of indirectly proving a proposition by assuming its negation to be true and showing that this leads to an absurdity **3** application of a principle or proposed principle to an instance in which it is absurd [Latin, literally: reduction to the absurd]

reduction (rɪˈdʌkʃən) *n* **1** the act or process or an instance of reducing **2** the state or condition of being reduced **3** the amount by which something is reduced **4** a form of an original resulting from a reducing process, such as a copy on a smaller scale **5** a simplified form, such as an orchestral score arranged for piano **6** *maths* **a** the process of converting a fraction into its decimal form **b** the process of dividing out the common factors in the numerator and denominator of a fraction; cancellation ⊳ re'ductive *adj*

reduction formula *n maths* a formula, such as sin (90° ± A) = cos A, expressing the values of a trigonometric function of any angle greater than 90° in terms of a function of an acute angle

reductionism (rɪˈdʌkʃəˌnɪzəm) *n* **1** the analysis of complex things, data, etc, into less complex constituents **2** *often disparaging* any theory or method that holds that a complex idea, system, etc, can be completely understood in terms of its simpler parts or components ⊳ re'ductionist *n, adj* ⊳ re,duction'istic *adj*

redundancy (rɪˈdʌndənsɪ) *n, pl* -cies **1 a** the state or condition of being redundant or superfluous, esp superfluous in one's job **b** (*as modifier*): *a redundancy payment* **2** excessive proliferation or profusion, esp of superfluity

redundant (rɪˈdʌndənt) *adj* **1** surplus to requirements; unnecessary or superfluous **2** verbose or tautological **3** deprived of one's job because it is no longer necessary for efficient operation [C17: from Latin *redundans* overflowing, from *redundāre* to run back, stream over; see REDOUND] ⊳ re'dundantly *adv*

red underwing *n* a large noctuid moth, *Catocala nupta*, having dull forewings and hind wings coloured red and black

reduplicate *vb* (rɪˈdjuːplɪˌkeɪt) **1** to make or become double; repeat **2** to repeat (a sound or syllable) in a word or (of a sound or syllable) to be repeated, esp in forming inflections in certain languages ⊳ *adj* (rɪˈdjuːplɪkɪt) **3** doubled or repeated **4** (of petals or sepals) having the margins curving outwards ⊳ re,dupli'cation *n* ⊳ re'duplicative *adj*

red water *n* **1** a disease of cattle caused by the protozoan *Babesia* (or *Piroplasma*) *bovis*, which destroys the red blood cells, characterized by the passage of red or blackish urine. It is transmitted by tick bites **2** any of various other animal diseases characterized by haematuria

redwing (ˈrɛdˌwɪŋ) *n* a small European thrush, *Turdus iliacus*, having a speckled breast, reddish flanks, and brown back

redwood (ˈrɛdˌwʊd) *n* a giant coniferous tree, *Sequoia sempervirens*, of coastal regions of California, having reddish fibrous bark and durable timber: family *Taxodiaceae*. The largest specimen is over 120 metres (360 feet) tall

reebok (ˈriːbʌk, -bɒk) *n, pl* -boks *or* -bok a variant spelling of **rhebok**

re-echo (riːˈɛkəʊ) *vb* -oes, -oing, -oed to echo (a sound that is already an echo); resound **1** (*tr*) to repeat like an echo

reed (riːd) *n* **1** any of various widely distributed tall grasses of the genus *Phragmites*, esp *P. communis*, that grow in swamps and shallow water and have jointed hollow stalks **2** the stalk, or stalks collectively, of any of these plants, esp as used for thatching **3** *music* **a** a thin piece of cane or metal inserted into the tubes of certain wind instruments, which sets in vibration the air column inside the tube **b** a wind instrument or organ pipe that sounds by means of a reed **4** one of the several vertical parallel wires on a loom that may be moved upwards to separate the warp threads **5** a small semicircular architectural moulding **6** an archaic word for: **arrow 7 broken reed** a weak, unreliable, or ineffectual person ⊳ *vb* (*tr*) **8** to fashion into or supply with reeds or reeding **9** to thatch using reeds [Old English *hreod*; related to Old Saxon *hriod*, Old High German *hriot*]

Reed (riːd) *n* **1** Sir **Carol**. 1906–76, English film director. His films include *The Third Man* (1949), *An Outcast of the Islands* (1951), and *Oliver!* (1968), for which he won an Oscar **2 Lou**. born 1942, US rock singer, songwriter, and guitarist: member of the Velvet Underground (1965–70). His albums include *Transformer* (1972), *Berlin* (1973), *Street Hassle* (1978), *New York* (1989), *Set the Twilight Reeling* (1996), and *The Raven* (2003) **3 Walter**. 1851–1902, US physician, who proved that yellow fever is transmitted by mosquitoes (1900)

reedbuck (ˈriːdˌbʌk) *n, pl* -bucks *or* -buck any antelope of the genus *Redunca*, of Africa south of the Sahara, having a buff-coloured coat and inward-curving horns

reed bunting *n* a common European bunting, *Emberiza schoeniclus*, that occurs near reed beds and has a brown streaked plumage with, in the male, a black head

reed grass *n* a tall perennial grass, *Glyceria maxima*, of rivers and ponds of Europe, Asia, and Canada

reeding (ˈriːdɪŋ) *n* **1** a set of small semicircular architectural mouldings **2** the milling on the edges of a coin

reedling (ˈriːdlɪŋ) *n* a titlike Eurasian songbird, *Panurus biarmicus*, common in reed beds: family *Muscicapidae* (Old World flycatchers, etc). It has a tawny back and tail and, in the male, a grey-and-black head. Also called: **bearded tit**

reed mace *n* Also called: (*popularly*) **bulrush, false bulrush, cat's-tail** a tall reedlike marsh plant, *Typha latifolia*, with straplike leaves and flowers in long brown sausage-shaped spikes: family *Typhaceae*. See also **bulrush** (sense 2)

reed organ *n* **1** a wind instrument, such as the harmonium, accordion, or harmonica, in which the sound is produced by reeds, each reed producing one note only **2** a type of pipe organ, such as the regal, in which all the pipes are fitted with reeds

reed pipe *n* an organ pipe sounded by a vibrating reed

reed stop *n* an organ stop controlling a rank of reed pipes

reed warbler *n* any of various common Old World warblers of the genus *Acrocephalus*, esp *A. scirpaceus*, that inhabit marshy regions and have a brown plumage

reedy (ˈriːdɪ) *adj* reedier, reediest **1** (of a place, esp a marsh) abounding in reeds **2** of or like a reed **3** having a tone like a reed instrument; shrill or piping ⊳ 'reedily *adv* ⊳ 'reediness *n*

reef¹ (riːf) *n* **1** a ridge of rock, sand, coral, etc, the top of which lies close to the surface of the sea **2** a vein of ore, esp one of gold-bearing quartz [C16: from Middle Dutch *ref*, from Old Norse *rif* RIB¹, REEF²]

reef² (riːf) *nautical* ⊳ *n* **1** the part gathered in when sail area is reduced, as in a high wind ⊳ *vb* **2** to reduce the area (of sail) by taking in a reef **3** (*tr*) to shorten or bring inboard (a spar) [C14: from Middle Dutch *rif*; related to Old Norse *rif* reef, RIB¹, German *reffen* to reef; see REEF¹]

Reef (riːf) *n* **1** another name for the **Great Barrier Reef 2** another name for the **Witwatersrand**

reefer (ˈriːfə) *n* **1** *nautical* a person who reefs, such as a midshipman **2** another name for **reefing jacket 3** *slang* a hand-rolled cigarette, esp one containing cannabis [C19: from REEF²; applied to the cigarette because of its resemblance to the rolled reef of a sail]

reefing jacket *n* a man's short double-breasted jacket of sturdy wool

reef knot *n* a knot consisting of two overhand knots

turned opposite ways. Also called: square knot

reef point *n nautical* one of several short lengths of line stitched through a sail for tying a reef

reek (riːk) *vb* 1 (*intr*) to give off or emit a strong unpleasant odour; smell or stink 2 (*intr*; often foll by *of*) to be permeated (by); be redolent (of): *the letter reeks of subservience* 3 (*tr*) to treat with smoke; fumigate 4 (*tr*) *chiefly dialect* to give off or emit (smoke, fumes, vapour, etc) ▷ *n* 5 a strong offensive smell; stink 6 *chiefly dialect* smoke or steam; vapour [Old English *rēocan*; related to Old Frisian *riāka* to smoke, Old High German *rouhhan*, Old Norse *rjūka* to smoke, steam] > 'reeky *adj*

reel[1] (riːl, rɪəl) *n* 1 any of various cylindrical objects or frames that turn on an axis and onto which film, magnetic tape, paper tape, wire, thread, etc, may be wound. US equivalent: spool 2 *angling* a device for winding, casting, etc, consisting of a revolving spool with a handle, attached to a fishing rod ▷ *vb* (*tr*) 3 to wind (cotton, thread, etc) onto a reel 4 (foll by *in*, *out* etc) to wind or draw with a reel: *to reel in a fish* [Old English *hrēol*; related to Old Norse *hrǣll* weaver's rod, Greek *krekein* to weave] > 'reelable *adj* > 'reeler *n*

reel[2] (riːl, rɪəl) *vb* (*mainly intr*) 1 to sway, esp under the shock of a blow or through dizziness or drunkenness 2 to whirl about or have the feeling of whirling about: *his brain reeled* ▷ *n* 3 a staggering or swaying motion or sensation [c14 *relen*, probably from REEL[1]]

reel[3] (riːl, rɪəl) *n* 1 any of various lively Scottish dances, such as the **eightsome reel** and **foursome reel** for a fixed number of couples who combine in square and circular formations 2 a piece of music having eight quavers to the bar composed for or in the rhythm of this dance [c18: from REEL[2]]

reel-fed *adj printing* involving or printing on a web of paper: *a reel-fed press*

reel man *n Austral & NZ* (formerly) the member of a beach life-saving team who controlled the reel on which the line was wound

reel off *vb* (*tr, adverb*) to recite or write fluently and without apparent effort

reel-to-reel *adj* 1 (of magnetic tape) wound from one reel to another in use 2 (of a tape recorder) using magnetic tape wound from one reel to another, as opposed to cassettes

re-entrant (riːˈɛntrənt) *adj* 1 (of an angle, esp in fortifications) pointing inwards ▷ *n* 2 an angle or part that points inwards

re-entry (riːˈɛntrɪ) *n, pl* -tries 1 the act of retaking possession of land, etc, under a right reserved in an earlier transfer of the property, such as a lease 2 the return of a spacecraft into the earth's atmosphere

re-entry vehicle *n* the portion of a ballistic missile that carries a nuclear warhead and re-enters the earth's atmosphere

reeve[1] (riːv) *n* 1 *English history* the local representative of the king in a shire (under the ealdorman) until the early 11th century 2 in medieval England) a manorial steward who supervised the daily affairs of the manor: often a villein elected by his fellows 3 *Canadian government* (in certain provinces) the head of a local council, esp in a rural area 4 (formerly) a minor local official in any of several parts of England and the US [Old English *gerēva*; related to Old High German *ruova* number, array]

reeve[2] (riːv) *vb* reeves, reeving, reeved *or* rove (rəʊv) (*tr*) *nautical* 1 to pass (a rope or cable) through an eye or other narrow opening 2 to fasten by passing through or around something [c17: perhaps from Dutch *rēven* REEF[2]]

reeve[3] (riːv) *n* the female of the ruff (the bird) [c17: of uncertain origin]

re-export *vb* (ˌriːɪkˈspɔːt, riːˈɛkspɔːt) 1 to export (imported goods, esp after processing) ▷ *n* (riːˈɛkspɔːt) 2 the act of re-exporting 3 a re-exported commodity > ˌre-exporˈtation *n* > ˌre-exˈporter *n*

ref (rɛf) *n informal* short for **referee**

ref. *abbreviation* 1 referee 2 reference

refection (rɪˈfɛkʃən) *n* refreshment with food and drink [c14: from Latin *refectiō* a restoring, from *reficere* to remake, from RE- + *facere* to make]

refectory (rɪˈfɛktərɪ, -trɪ) *n, pl* -tories a communal dining hall in a religious, academic, or other institution [c15: from Late Latin *refectōrium*, from Latin *refectus* refreshed]

refectory table *n* a long narrow dining table supported by two trestles joined by a stretcher or set into a base

refer (rɪˈfɜː) *vb* -fers, -ferring, -ferred (often foll by *to*) 1 (*intr*) to make mention (of) 2 (*tr*) to direct the attention of (someone) for information, facts, etc: *the reader is referred to Chomsky, 1965* 3 (*intr*) to seek information (from): *I referred to Directory Enquiries; he referred to his notes* 4 (*intr*) to be relevant (to); pertain or relate (to) 5 (*tr*) to assign or attribute: *Cromwell referred his victories to God* 6 (*tr*) to hand over for consideration, reconsideration, or decision: *to refer a complaint to another department* 7 (*tr*) to hand back to the originator as unacceptable or unusable 8 (*tr*) *Brit* to fail (a student) in an examination 9 refer to drawer a request by a bank that the payee consult the drawer concerning a cheque payable by that bank (usually because the drawer has insufficient funds in his account), payment being suspended in the meantime 10 (*tr*) to direct (a patient) for treatment to another doctor, usually a specialist [c14: from Latin *referre* to carry back, from RE- + *ferre* to BEAR[1]] > referable (ˈrɛfərəb[ə]l) *or* referrable (rɪˈfɜːrəb[ə]l) *adj* > reˈferral *n* > reˈferrer *n*

⦿ **USAGE** The common practice of adding *back* to *refer* is
⦿ tautologous, since this meaning is already contained
⦿ in the re- of *refer*: *this refers to* (not *back to*) *what has already*
⦿ *been said.* However, when *refer* is used in the sense of
⦿ passing a document or question for further
⦿ consideration to the person from whom it was
⦿ received, it may be appropriate to say *he referred the*
⦿ *matter back*

referee (ˌrɛfəˈriː) *n* 1 a person to whom reference is made, esp for an opinion, information, or a decision 2 the umpire or judge in any of various sports, esp football and boxing, responsible for ensuring fair play according to the rules 3 a person who is willing to testify to the character or capabilities of someone 4 *law* See **Official Referee** ▷ *vb* -ees, -eeing, -eed 5 to act as a referee (in); preside (over)

reference (ˈrɛfərəns, ˈrɛfrəns) *n* 1 the act or an instance of referring 2 something referred, esp proceedings submitted to a referee in law 3 a direction of the attention to a passage elsewhere or to another book, document, etc 4 a book or passage referred to 5 a mention or allusion: *this book contains several references to the Civil War* 6 *philosophy* the relation between a word, phrase, or symbol and the object or idea to which it refers 7 a a source of information or facts b (*as modifier*): *a reference book; a reference library* 8 a written testimonial regarding one's character or capabilities 9 a person referred to for such a testimonial 10 a (foll by *to*) relation or delimitation, esp to or by membership of a specific class or group; respect or regard: *all people, without reference to sex or age* b (*as modifier*): *a reference group* 11 terms of reference the specific limits of responsibility that determine the activities of an investigating body, etc ▷ *vb* (*tr*) 12 to furnish or compile a list of references for (an academic thesis, publication, etc) 13 to make a reference to; refer to ▷ *prep* 14 *business* with reference to: *reference your letter of the 9th inst.* Abbreviation: re[1] > referential (ˌrɛfəˈrɛnʃəl) *adj*

referendum (ˌrɛfəˈrɛndəm) *n, pl* -dums *or* -da (-də) 1 submission of an issue of public importance to the direct vote of the electorate 2 a vote on such a measure ▷ See also (for senses 1, 2) **plebiscite** [c19: from Latin: something to be carried back, from *referre* to REFER]

referent (ˈrɛfərənt) *n* the object or idea to which a word or phrase refers [c19: from Latin *referens*, from *referre* to REFER]

referred pain *n psychol* pain felt in the body at some place other than its actual place of origin

refill *vb* (riːˈfɪl) 1 to fill (something) again ▷ *n* (ˈriːfɪl) 2 a replacement for a consumable substance in a permanent container 3 a second or subsequent filling > reˈfillable *adj*

refine (rɪˈfaɪn) *vb* 1 to make or become free from impurities, sediment, or other foreign matter; purify

2 (*tr*) to separate (a mixture) into pure constituents, as in an oil refinery **3** to make or become free from coarse characteristics; make or become elegant or polished **4** (*tr*; often foll by *out*) to remove (something impure or extraneous) **5** (*intr*; often foll by *on* or *upon*) to enlarge or improve (upon) by making subtle or fine distinctions **6** (*tr*) to make (language) more subtle or polished [c16: from RE- + FINE¹] ▷ re'finable *adj* ▷ re'finer *n*

refined (rɪ'faɪnd) *adj* **1** not coarse or vulgar; genteel, elegant, or polite **2** subtle; discriminating **3** freed from impurities; purified

refinement (rɪ'faɪnmənt) *n* **1** the act of refining or the state of being refined **2** a fine or delicate point, distinction, or expression; a subtlety **3** fineness or precision of thought, expression, manners, etc; polish or cultivation **4** a device, change, adaptation, etc, designed to improve performance or increase efficiency

refinery (rɪ'faɪnərɪ) *n*, *pl* **-eries** a factory for the purification of some crude material, such as ore, sugar, oil, etc

refit *vb* (ri:'fɪt) **-fits**, **-fitting**, **-fitted 1** to make or be made ready for use again by repairing, re-equipping, or resupplying ▷ *n* ('ri:,fɪt) **2** a repair or re-equipping, as of a ship, for further use ▷ re'fitment *n*

reflate (ri:'fleɪt) *vb* to inflate or be inflated again [c20: back formation from REFLATION]

reflation (ri:'fleɪʃən) *n* **1** an increase in economic activity **2** an increase in the supply of money and credit designed to cause such an increase ▷ Compare **inflation** (sense 2) [c20: from RE- + *-flation*, as in INFLATION or DEFLATION]

reflect (rɪ'flɛkt) *vb* **1** to undergo or cause to undergo a process in which light, other electromagnetic radiation, sound, particles, etc, are thrown back after impinging on a surface **2** (of a mirror, etc) to form an image of (something) by reflection **3** (*tr*) to show or express: *his tactics reflect his desire for power* **4** (*tr*) to bring as a consequence **5** (*intr*; foll by *on* or *upon*) to cause to be regarded in a specified way: *her behaviour reflects well on her* **6** (*intr*; foll by *on* or *upon*) to cast dishonour, discredit, etc (on) **7** (*intr*; usually foll by *on*) to think, meditate, or ponder [c15: from Latin *reflectere* to bend back, from RE- + *flectere* to bend; see FLEX]

reflectance (rɪ'flɛktəns) *or* reflection factor *n* a measure of the ability of a surface to reflect light or other electromagnetic radiation, equal to the ratio of the reflected flux to the incident flux

reflecting telescope *n* a type of telescope in which the initial image is formed by a concave mirror. Also called: **reflector** ▷ Compare **refracting telescope**

reflection *or less commonly* **reflexion** (rɪ'flɛkʃən) *n* **1** the act of reflecting or the state of being reflected **2** something reflected or the image so produced, as by a mirror **3** careful or long consideration or thought **4** implicit or explicit attribution of discredit or blame **5** *maths* a transformation in which the direction of one axis is reversed or which changes the sign of one of the variables **6** *anatomy* the bending back of a structure or part upon itself ▷ re'flectional *or* re'flexional *adj*

reflection density *n physics* a measure of the extent to which a surface reflects light or other electromagnetic radiation, equal to the logarithm to base ten of the reciprocal of the reflectance. Symbol: D

reflective (rɪ'flɛktɪv) *adj* **1** characterized by quiet thought or contemplation **2** capable of reflecting: *a reflective surface* **3** produced by reflection ▷ re'flectively *adv*

reflectivity (,ri:flɛk'tɪvɪtɪ) *n* **1** *physics* a measure of the ability of a surface to reflect radiation, equal to the reflectance of a layer of material sufficiently thick for the reflectance not to depend on the thickness **2** Also called: **reflectiveness** the quality or capability of being reflective

reflector (rɪ'flɛktə) *n* **1** a person or thing that reflects **2** a surface or object that reflects light, sound, heat, etc **3** another name for **reflecting telescope**

reflet (rə'fleɪ) *n* an iridescent glow or lustre, as on ceramic ware [c19: from French: a reflection, from Italian *riflesso*, from Latin *reflexus*, from *reflectere* to REFLECT]

reflex *n* ('ri:flɛks) **1 a** an immediate involuntary response, esp one that is innate, such as coughing or removal of the hand from a hot surface, evoked by a given stimulus **b** (*as modifier*): *a reflex action*. See also **reflex arc 2 a** a mechanical response to a particular situation, involving no conscious decision **b** (*as modifier*): *a reflex response* **3** a reflection; an image produced by or as if by reflection *adj* ('ri:flɛks) **4** *maths* (of an angle) between 180° and 360° **5** (*prenominal*) turned, reflected, or bent backwards ▷ *vb* (rɪ'flɛks) **6** (*tr*) to bend, turn, or reflect backwards [c16: from Latin *reflexus* bent back, from *reflectere* to reflect] ▷ re'flexible *adj* ▷ re,flexi'bility *n*

reflex arc *n physiol* the neural pathway over which impulses travel to produce a reflex action, consisting of at least one afferent (receptor) and one efferent (effector) neuron

reflex camera *n* a camera in which the image is composed and focused on a large ground-glass viewfinder screen. In a **single-lens reflex** the light enters through the camera lens and falls on the film when the viewfinder mirror is retracted. In a **twin-lens reflex** the light enters through a separate lens and is deflected onto the viewfinder screen

reflexion (rɪ'flɛkʃən) *n Brit* a less common spelling of: **reflection** ▷ re'flexional *adj*

reflexive (rɪ'flɛksɪv) *adj* **1** denoting a class of pronouns that refer back to the subject of a sentence or clause. Thus, in the sentence *that man thinks a great deal of himself*, the pronoun *himself* is reflexive **2** denoting a verb used transitively with the reflexive pronoun as its direct object, as the French *se lever* "to get up" (literally "to raise oneself") or English *to dress oneself* **3** *physiol* of or relating to a reflex ▷ *n* **4** a reflexive pronoun or verb ▷ re'flexively *adv* ▷ re'flexiveness *or* reflexivity (,ri:flɛk'sɪvɪtɪ) *n*

reflexology (,ri:flɛk'sɒlədʒɪ) *n* a form of therapy practised as a treatment in alternative medicine in which the soles of the feet are massaged: designed to stimulate the blood supply and nerves and thus relieve tension ▷ ,reflex'ologist *n*

reflux ('ri:flʌks) *vb* **1** *chem* to boil or be boiled in a vessel attached to a condenser, so that the vapour condenses and flows back into the vessel ▷ *n* **2** *chem* **a** an act of refluxing **b** (*as modifier*): *a reflux condenser* **3** the act or an instance of flowing back; ebb [c15: from Medieval Latin *refluxus*, from Latin *refluere* to flow back]

reflux oesophagitis (i:,sɒfə'dʒaɪtɪs) *n* inflammation of the gullet caused by regurgitation of stomach acids, producing heartburn: may be associated with a hiatus hernia

reform (rɪ'fɔ:m) *vb* **1** (*tr*) to improve (an existing institution, law, practice, etc) by alteration or correction of abuses **2** to give up or cause to give up a reprehensible habit or immoral way of life ▷ *n* **3** an improvement or change for the better, esp as a result of correction of legal or political abuses or malpractices **4** a principle, campaign, or measure aimed at achieving such change **5** improvement of morals or behaviour, esp by giving up some vice [c14: via Old French from Latin *reformāre* to form again] ▷ re'formable *adj* ▷ re'formative *adj* ▷ re'former *n*

re-form (ri:'fɔ:m) *vb* to form anew ▷ ,re-for'mation *n*

reformation (,rɛfə'meɪʃən) *n* the act or an instance of reforming or the state of being reformed ▷ ,refor'mational *adj*

Reformation (,rɛfə'meɪʃən) *n* a religious and political movement of 16th-century Europe that began as an attempt to reform the Roman Catholic Church and resulted in the establishment of the Protestant Churches

reformatory (rɪ'fɔ:mətərɪ, -trɪ) *n*, *pl* **-ries 1** Also called: **reform school** (formerly) a place of instruction where young offenders were sent for corrective training ▷ *adj* **2** having the purpose or function of reforming

Reformed (rɪ'fɔ:md) *adj* **1** of or designating a Protestant Church, esp the Calvinist as distinct from the Lutheran **2** of or designating Reform Judaism

reformism (rɪ'fɔ:mɪzəm) *n* a doctrine or movement advocating reform, esp political or religious reform, rather than abolition ▷ re'formist *n*, *adj*

Reform Judaism *n* a movement in Judaism originating in the 19th century, which does not require strict observance of the law, but adapts the historical forms of Judaism to the contemporary world

refract (rɪ'frækt) *vb* (*tr*) **1** to cause to undergo refraction **2** to measure the refractive capabilities of (the eye, a lens, etc) [c17: from Latin *refractus* broken up, from *refringere*, from RE- + *frangere* to break] > re'**fractable** *adj*

refracting telescope *n* a type of telescope in which the image is formed by a set of lenses. Also called: refractor Compare **reflecting telescope**

refraction (rɪ'frækʃən) *n* **1** *physics* the change in direction of a propagating wave, such as light or sound, in passing from one medium to another in which it has a different velocity **2** the amount by which a wave is refracted **3** the ability of the eye to refract light > re'**fractive** *adj* > re'**fractively** *adv* > re'**fractiveness** *or* refractivity (,riːfræk'tɪvɪtɪ) *n*

refractive index *n* *physics* a measure of the extent to which radiation is refracted on passing through the interface between two media. It is the ratio of the sine of the angle of incidence to the sine of the angle of refraction, which can be shown to be equal to the ratio of the phase speed in the first medium to that in the second. In the case of electromagnetic radiation, esp light, it is usual to give values of the **absolute refractive index** of a medium, that is for radiation entering the medium from free space

refractometer (,riːfræk'tɒmɪtə) *n* any instrument for determining the refractive index of a substance > refractometric (rɪ,fræktə'metrɪk) *adj* > ,refrac'tometry *n*

refractor (rɪ'fræktə) *n* **1** an object or material that refracts **2** another name for **refracting telescope**

refractory (rɪ'fræktərɪ) *adj* **1** unmanageable or obstinate **2** *med* not responding to treatment **3** (of a material) able to withstand high temperatures without fusion or decomposition ▷ *n*, *pl* -ries **4** a material, such as fireclay or alumina, that is able to withstand high temperatures: used to line furnaces, kilns, etc [c17: variant of obsolete *refractary*; see REFRACT] > re'**fractorily** *adv* > re'**fractoriness** *n*

refrain[1] (rɪ'freɪn) *vb* (*intr*; usually foll by *from*) to abstain (from action); forbear [c14: from Latin *refrēnāre* to check with a bridle, from RE- + *frēnum* a bridle] > re'**frainer** *n* > re'**frainment** *n*

refrain[2] (rɪ'freɪn) *n* **1** a regularly recurring melody, such as the chorus of a song **2** a much repeated saying or idea [c14: via Old French, ultimately from Latin *refringere* to break into pieces]

refrangible (rɪ'frændʒɪbᵊl) *adj* capable of being refracted [c17: from Latin *refringere* to break up, from RE- + *frangere* to break] > re,frangi'bility *or* re'frangibleness *n*

refresh (rɪ'freʃ) *vb* **1** (*usually tr or reflexive*) to make or become fresh or vigorous, as through rest, drink, or food; revive or reinvigorate **2** (*tr*) to enliven (something worn or faded), as by adding new decorations **3** (*tr*) to stimulate (the memory) **4** (*tr*) to replenish, as with new equipment or stores **5** *computing* to display the latest updated version (of a web page or document); reload [c14: from Old French *refreschir*; see RE-, FRESH] > re'**fresher** *n* > re'**freshing** *adj* > re'**freshingly** *adv*

refresher course *n* a short educational course for people to review their subject and developments in it

refreshment (rɪ'freʃmənt) *n* **1** the act of refreshing or the state of being refreshed **2** (*plural*) snacks and drinks served as a light meal

refresh rate *n* *computing* the frequency at which the image on a monitor is renewed

refrigerant (rɪ'frɪdʒərənt) *n* **1** a fluid capable of changes of phase at low temperatures: used as the working fluid of a refrigerator **2** a cooling substance, such as ice or solid carbon dioxide **3** *med* an agent that provides a sensation of coolness or reduces fever ▷ *adj* **4** causing cooling or freezing

refrigerate (rɪ'frɪdʒə,reɪt) *vb* to make or become frozen or cold, esp for preservative purposes; chill or freeze [c16: from Latin *refrīgerāre* to make cold, from RE- + *frīgus* cold] > re,friger'ation *n* > re'**frigerative** *adj* > re'**frigeratory** *adj*, *n*

refrigerator (rɪ'frɪdʒə,reɪtə) *n* a chamber in which food, drink, etc, are kept cool. Informal word: fridge

refringent (rɪ'frɪndʒənt) *adj* *physics* of, concerned with, or causing refraction; refractive [c18: from Latin *refringere* to break up; see REFRACT] > re'**fringency** *or* re'**fringence** *n*

reft (reft) *vb* a past tense and past participle of **reave**[1]

refuel (riː'fjuːəl) *vb* -els, -elling, -elled *or US* -els, -eling, -eled to supply or be supplied with fresh fuel

refuge ('refjuːdʒ) *n* **1** shelter or protection, as from the weather or danger **2** any place, person, action, or thing that offers or appears to offer protection, help, or relief [c14: via Old French from Latin *refugium*, from *refugere* to flee away, from RE- + *fugere* to escape]

refugee (,refjʊ'dʒiː) *n* **a** a person who has fled from some danger or problem, esp political persecution **b** (*as modifier*): *a refugee camp*; *a refugee problem* > ,refu'geeism *n*

refugee capital *n* *finance* money from abroad invested, esp for a short term, in the country offering the highest interest rate

refugium (rɪ'fjuːdʒɪəm) *n*, *pl* -gia (-dʒɪə) a geographical region that has remained unaltered by a climatic change affecting surrounding regions and that therefore forms a haven for relict fauna and flora [c20: Latin: refuge]

refulgent (rɪ'fʌldʒənt) *adj* *literary* shining, brilliant, or radiant [c16: from Latin *refulgēre* to shine brightly, from RE- + *fulgēre* to shine] > re'**fulgence** *or* *less commonly* re'**fulgency** *n* > re'**fulgently** *adv*

refund *vb* (rɪ'fʌnd) (*tr*) **1** to give back (money), as when an article purchased is unsatisfactory **2** to reimburse (a person) ▷ *n* ('riː,fʌnd) **3** return of money to a purchaser or the amount so returned [c14: from Latin *refundere* to pour back, from RE- + *fundere* to pour] > re'**fundable** *adj*

re-fund (riː'fʌnd) *vb* *finance* to discharge (an old or matured debt) by new borrowing, as by a new bond issue [c20: from RE- + FUND]

refurbish (riː'fɜːbɪʃ) *vb* (*tr*) to make neat, clean, or complete, as by renovating, re-equipping, or restoring > re'**furbishing** *or* re'**furbishment** *n*

refusal (rɪ'fjuːzᵊl) *n* **1** the act or an instance of refusing **2** the opportunity to reject or accept; option

refuse[1] (rɪ'fjuːz) *vb* **1** (*tr*) to decline to accept (something offered): *to refuse a present*; *to refuse promotion* **2** to decline to give or grant (something) to (a person, organization, etc) **3** (*when tr, takes an infinitive*) to express determination not (to do something); decline: *he refuses to talk about it* **4** (of a horse) to be unwilling to take (a jump), as by swerving or stopping [c14: from Old French *refuser*, from Latin *refundere* to pour back; see REFUND] > re'**fusable** *adj* > re'**fuser** *n*

refuse[2] ('refjuːs) *n* **a** anything thrown away; waste; rubbish **b** (*as modifier*): *a refuse collection* [c15: from Old French *refuser* to REFUSE[1]]

refusenik *or* **refusnik** (rɪ'fjuːznɪk) *n* **1** (formerly) a Jew in the Soviet Union who had been refused permission to emigrate **2** a person who refuses to cooperate with a system or comply with a law because of a moral conviction [c20: from REFUSE[1] + -NIK]

refute (rɪ'fjuːt) *vb* (*tr*) to prove (a statement, theory, charge, etc) of (a person) to be false or incorrect; disprove [c16: from Latin *refūtāre* to rebut] > refutable ('refjʊtəbᵊl, rɪ'fjuː-) *adj* > 'refutably *adv* > re'**futer** *n*

● **USAGE** The use of *refute* to mean *deny* is thought by many people to be incorrect

regain (rɪ'geɪn) *vb* (*tr*) **1** to take or get back; recover **2** to reach again > re'**gainer** *n*

regal ('riːgᵊl) *adj* of, relating to, or befitting a king or queen; royal [c14: from Latin *rēgālis* from *rēx* king] > 'regally *adv*

regale (rɪ'geɪl) *vb* (*tr*; usually foll by *with*) **1** to give delight or amusement to: *he regaled them with stories of his youth* **2** to provide with choice or abundant food or drink ▷ *n* **3** *archaic* **a** a feast **b** a delicacy of food or drink [c17: from French *régaler*, from *gale* pleasure; related to Middle Dutch *wale* riches; see also GALA] > re'**galement** *n*

regalia (rɪ'geɪlɪə) *pl n* (*sometimes functioning as singular*) **1** the ceremonial emblems or robes of royalty, high office, an order, etc **2** any splendid or special clothes; finery [c16: from Medieval Latin: royal privileges, from

Latin *rēgālis* REGAL]

regard (rɪˈgɑːd) *vb* **1** to look closely or attentively at (something or someone); observe steadily **2** (*tr*) to hold (a person or thing) in respect, admiration, or affection: *we regard your work very highly* **3** (*tr*) to look upon or consider in a specified way: *she regarded her brother as her responsibility* **4** (*tr*) to relate to; concern; have a bearing on **5** to take notice of or pay attention to (something); heed: *he has never regarded the conventions* **6** as regards (*preposition*) in respect of; concerning ▷ *n* **7** a gaze; look **8** attention; heed: *he spends without regard to his bank balance* **9** esteem, affection, or respect **10** reference, relation, or connection (esp in the phrases **with regard to** *or* **in regard to**) **11** (*plural*) good wishes or greetings (esp in the phrase **with kind regards**, used at the close of a letter) **12** in this regard on this point [c14: from Old French *regarder* to look at, care about, from RE- + *garder* to GUARD]

regardant (rɪˈgɑːdᵊnt) *adj* (*usually postpositive*) *heraldry* (of a beast) shown looking backwards over its shoulder [c15: from Old French; BC from Anglo-French]

regardful (rɪˈgɑːdfʊl) *adj* **1** (often foll by *of*) showing regard (for); heedful (of) **2** showing regard, respect, or consideration > reˈgardfully *adv*

regarding (rɪˈgɑːdɪŋ) *prep* in respect of; on the subject of

regardless (rɪˈgɑːdlɪs) *adj* **1** (usually foll by *of*) taking no regard or heed; heedless ▷ *adv* **2** in spite of everything; disregarding drawbacks > reˈgardlessly *adv* > reˈgardlessness *n*

regatta (rɪˈgætə) *n* an organized series of races of yachts, rowing boats, etc [c17: from obsolete Italian (Venetian dialect) *rigatta* contest, of obscure origin]

regd *abbreviation* registered

regelation (ˌriːdʒɪˈleɪʃən) *n* the rejoining together of two pieces of ice as a result of melting under pressure at the interface between them and subsequent refreezing [c19: from RE- + stem of participle of Latin *gelāre* to freeze] > ˈregeˌlate *vb*

regency (ˈriːdʒənsɪ) *n*, *pl* **-cies** **1** government by a regent or a body of regents **2** the office of a regent or body of regents **3** a territory under the jurisdiction of a regent or body of regents [c15: from Medieval Latin *regentia*, from Latin *regere* to rule]

Regency (ˈriːdʒənsɪ) **the Regency** *n* **1** (in the United Kingdom) the period (1811–20) during which the Prince of Wales (later George IV (1762–1830; king 1820–30)) acted as regent during his father's periods of insanity **2** (in France) the period of the regency of Philip, Duke of Orleans, during the minority (1715–23) of Louis XV (1710–74; king 1715–74) *adj* **3** characteristic of or relating to the Regency periods in France or the United Kingdom or to the styles of architecture, furniture, art, literature, etc, produced in them

regenerate *vb* (rɪˈdʒɛnəˌreɪt) **1** to undergo or cause to undergo moral, spiritual, or physical renewal or invigoration **2** to form or be formed again; come or bring into existence once again **3** to replace (lost or damaged tissues or organs) by new growth, or to cause (such tissues) to be replaced **4** (*tr*) *electronics* (in a digital system) to reshape (distorted incoming pulses) for onward transmission ▷ *adj* (rɪˈdʒɛnərɪt) **5** morally, spiritually, or physically renewed or reborn; restored or refreshed > reˈgeneracy *n* > reˌgeneˈration *n* > reˈgenerative *adj* > reˈgenerˌator *n*

Regensburg (German ˈreːɡənsbʊrk) *n* a city in SE Germany, in Bavaria on the River Danube: a free Imperial city from 1245 and the leading commercial city of S Germany in the 12th and 13th centuries; the Imperial Diet was held in the town hall from 1663 to 1806. Pop: 128 604 (2003 est). Former English name: Ratisbon

regent (ˈriːdʒənt) *n* **1** the ruler or administrator of a country during the minority, absence, or incapacity of its monarch **2** *US & Canadian* a member of the governing board of certain schools and colleges ▷ *adj* **3** (*usually postpositive*) acting or functioning as a regent: *a queen regent* [c14: from Latin *regēns* ruling, from *regere* to rule] > ˈregental *adj* > ˈregentship *n*

regent bowerbird *or* **regent bird** *n* an Australian bowerbird, *Sericulus chrysocephalus*, the male of which has

a showy yellow and velvety-black plumage [after the Prince Regent, the title of George IV (1762–1830) as regent of Great Britain and Ireland during the insanity of his father (1811–20)]

regent honeyeater *n* a large brightly-coloured Australian honeyeater, *Zanthomiza phrygia*

Reger (German ˈreːɡər) *n* **Max** (maks). 1873–1916, German composer, noted esp for his organ works

reggae (ˈrɛɡeɪ) *n* a type of West Indian popular music having four beats to the bar, the upbeat being strongly accented [c20: of West Indian origin]

reggaeton (ˌrɛɡeɪˈtɒn) *n* a type of Puerto Rican popular music that combines reggae rhythms with hip-hop influences and includes rapping in Spanish

Reggio di Calabria (Italian ˈreddʒo di kaˈlaːbrja) *n* a port in S Italy, in Calabria on the Strait of Messina: founded about 720 BC by Greek colonists. Pop: 180 353 (2001)

Reggio nell'Emilia (Italian ˈreddʒo nelleˈmiːlja) *n* a city in N central Italy, in Emilia-Romagna: founded in the 2nd century BC by Marcus Aemilius Lepidus; ruled by the Este family in the 15th–18th centuries. Pop: 141 877 (2001)

regicide (ˈrɛdʒɪˌsaɪd) *n* **1** the killing of a king **2** a person who kills a king [c16: from Latin *rēx* king + -CIDE] > ˌregiˈcidal *adj*

regime *or* **régime** (reɪˈʒiːm) *n* **1** a system of government or a particular administration: *a fascist regime; the regime of Fidel Castro* **2** a social system or order **3** *med* another word for **regimen** (sense 1) [c18: from French, from Latin *regimen* guidance, from *regere* to rule]

regime change *n* the transition from one political regime to another, esp through concerted political or military action

regimen (ˈrɛdʒɪˌmɛn) *n* **1** Also called: **regime** a systematic way of life or course of therapy, often including exercise and a recommended diet **2** administration or rule [c14: from Latin: guidance]

regiment *n* (ˈrɛdʒɪmənt) **1** a military formation varying in size from a battalion to a number of battalions **2** a large number in regular or organized groups ▷ *vb* (ˈrɛdʒɪˌmɛnt) (*tr*) **3** to force discipline or order on, esp in a domineering manner **4** to organize into a regiment or regiments **5** to form into organized groups [c14: via Old French from Late Latin *regimentum* government, from Latin *regere* to rule] > ˌregiˈmental *adj* > ˌregiˈmentally *adv* > ˌregimenˈtation *n*

regimentals (ˌrɛdʒɪˈmɛntᵊlz) *pl n* **1** the uniform and insignia of a regiment **2** military dress

Regin (ˈreɪɡɪn) *n* *Norse myth* a dwarf smith, tutor of Sigurd, whom he encouraged to kill Fafnir for the gold he guarded

Regina[1] (rɪˈdʒaɪnə) *n* queen: now used chiefly in documents, inscriptions, etc. Compare **Rex**

Regina[2] (rɪˈdʒaɪnə) *n* a city in W Canada, capital and largest city of Saskatchewan: founded in 1882 as Pile O'Bones. Pop: 178 225 (2001)

Regiomontanus (ˌriːdʒɪəʊmɒnˈteɪnəs, -ˈtɑː-, -ˈtæn-) *n* original name *Johann Müller*. 1436–76, German mathematician and astronomer, who furthered the development of trigonometry

region (ˈriːdʒən) *n* **1** any large, indefinite, and continuous part of a surface or space **2** an area considered as a unit for geographical, functional, social, or cultural reasons **3** an administrative division of a country **4** a realm or sphere of activity or interest **5** range, area, or scope: *in what region is the price likely to be?* **6** a division or part of the boday: *the lumbar region* [c14: from Latin *regiō*, from *regere* to govern]

regional (ˈriːdʒənᵊl) *adj* of, characteristic of, or limited to a region > ˈregionally *adv*

regionalism (ˈriːdʒənəˌlɪzəm) *n* **1** division of a country into administrative regions having partial autonomy **2** loyalty to one's home region; regional patriotism > ˈregionalist *n*, *adj*

régisseur French (reʒisœr) *n* an official in a dance company with varying duties, usually including directing productions [from *régir* to manage]

register (ˈrɛdʒɪstə) *n* **1** an official or formal list recording names, events, or transactions **2** the book in which such a list is written **3** an entry in such a list **4** a recording device that accumulates data, totals sums of money, etc: *a cash register* **5** a movable plate that controls the flow of air into a furnace, chimney, room, etc **6** *music* **a** the timbre characteristic of a certain manner of voice production **b** any of the stops on an organ as classified in respect of its tonal quality: *the flute register* **7** *printing* the exact correspondence of lines of type, columns, etc, on the two sides of a printed sheet of paper **8** a form of a language associated with a particular social situation or subject matter, such as obscene slang, legal language, or journalese **9** the act or an instance of registering ▷ *vb* **10** (*tr*) to enter or cause someone to enter (an event, person's name, ownership, etc) on a register; formally record **11** to show or be shown on a scale or other measuring instrument: *the current didn't register on the meter* **12** to show or be shown in a person's face, bearing, etc: *his face registered surprise* **13** (*intr*) to have an effect; make an impression: *the news of her uncle's death just did not register* **14** to send (a letter, package, etc) by registered post **15** (*tr*) *printing* to adjust (a printing press, forme, etc) to ensure that the printed matter is in register [C14: from Medieval Latin *registrum*, from Latin *regerere* to transcribe, from RE- + *gerere* to bear] ▷ 'registrable *adj*

Registered General Nurse *n* (in Britain) a nurse who has completed a three-year training course in all aspects of nursing care to enable the nurse to be registered with the United Kingdom Central Council for Nursing, Midwifery, and Health Visiting. Abbreviation: RGN

registered post *n* **1** a Post Office service by which compensation is paid for loss or damage to mail for which a registration fee has been paid **2** mail sent by this service

Registered Trademark *n* See **trademark** (sense 1)

register office *n* *Brit* a government office where civil marriages are performed and births, marriages, and deaths are recorded. Often called: registry office

register ton *n* the full name for: **ton**[1] (sense 6)

registrar (,redʒɪ'strɑː, 'redʒɪ,strɑː) *n* **1** a person who keeps official records **2** an administrative official responsible for student records, enrolment procedure, etc, in a school, college, or university **3** *Brit & NZ* a hospital doctor senior to a houseman but junior to a consultant, specializing in either medicine (**medical registrar**) or surgery (**surgical registrar**) **4** *chiefly US* a person employed by a company to maintain a register of its security issues ▷ 'registrarship *n*

registration (,redʒɪ'streɪʃən) *n* **1 a** the act of registering or state of being registered **b** (*as modifier*): *a registration number* **2** an entry in a register **3** a group of people, such as students, who register at a particular time **4** *Austral* **a** a tax payable by the owner of a motor vehicle **b** the period paid for

registration document *n* *Brit* a document giving identification details of a motor vehicle, including its manufacturer, date of registration, engine and chassis numbers, and owner's name

registration number *n* a sequence of letters and numbers assigned to a motor vehicle when it is registered, usually indicating the year and place of registration, displayed on numberplates at the front and rear of the vehicle, and by which the vehicle may be identified

registration plate *n* *Austral. & NZ* a plate mounted on the front and back of a motor vehicle bearing the registration number

registry ('redʒɪstrɪ) *n*, *pl* -tries **1** a place where registers are kept, such as the part of a church where the bride and groom sign a register after a wedding **2** the registration of a ship's country of origin: *a ship of Liberian registry* **3** another word for **registration**

registry office *n* *Brit* a name often used for a **register office**

Regius professor ('riːdʒɪəs) *n* *Brit* a person appointed by the Crown to a university chair founded by a royal patron [C17: *regius*, from Latin: royal, from *rex* king]

reglet ('reglɪt) *n* **1** a flat narrow architectural moulding **2** *printing* a strip of oiled wood used for spacing between lines of hot metal type [C16: from Old French, literally: a little rule, from *regle* rule, from Latin *rēgula*]

regmaker ('rex,mɑːkə) *n* *South African* a drink taken to relieve the symptoms of a hangover; a pick-me-up [Afrikaans]

regnal ('regnəl) *adj* **1** of a sovereign, reign, or kingdom **2** designating a year of a sovereign's reign calculated from the date of his or her accession [C17: from Medieval Latin *rēgnālis*, from Latin *rēgnum* sovereignty; see REIGN]

regnant ('regnənt) *adj* **1** (*postpositive*) reigning **2** prevalent; current [C17: from Latin *regnāre* to REIGN] ▷ 'regnancy *n*

regorge (rɪ'ɡɔːdʒ) *vb* **1** (*tr*) to vomit up; disgorge **2** (*intr*) (esp of water) to flow or run back [C17: from French *regorger*; see GORGE]

regress *vb* (rɪ'gres) **1** (*intr*) to return or revert, as to a former place, condition, or mode of behaviour **2** (*tr*) *statistics* to measure the extent to which (a dependent variable) is associated with one or more independent variables ▷ *n* ('riːgres) **3** movement in a backward direction; retrogression [C14: from Latin *regressus* a retreat, from *regredī* to go back, from RE- + *gradī* to go] ▷ re'gressive *adj* ▷ re'gressively *adv* ▷ re'gressiveness *n* ▷ re'gressor *n*

regression (rɪ'ɡreʃən) *n* **1** *psychol* the adoption by an adult or adolescent of behaviour more appropriate to a child, esp as a defence mechanism to avoid anxiety **2** *statistics* **a** the analysis or measure of the association between one variable (the dependent variable) and one or more other variables (the independent variables), usually formulated in an equation in which the independent variables have parametric coefficients, which may enable future values of the dependent variable to be predicted **b** (*as modifier*): *regression curve* **3** *geology* the retreat of the sea from the land **4** the act of regressing

regret (rɪ'ɡret) *vb* **-grets**, **-gretting**, **-gretted** (*tr*) **1** (*may take a clause as object or an infinitive*) to feel sorry, repentant, or upset about **2** to bemoan or grieve the death or loss of ▷ *n* **3** a sense of repentance, guilt, or sorrow, as over some wrong done or an unfulfilled ambition **4** a sense of loss or grief **5** (*plural*) a polite expression of sadness, esp in a formal refusal of an invitation [C14: from Old French *regrete*, of Scandinavian origin; compare Old Norse *grāta* to weep] ▷ re'gretful *adj* ▷ re'gretfully *adv* ▷ re'gretfulness *n* ▷ re'grettable *adj* ▷ re'grettably *adv*

● USAGE *Regretful* and *regretfully* are sometimes wrongly used where *regrettable* and *regrettably* are meant: *he gave a regretful smile; he smiled regretfully; this is a regrettable* (not *regretful*) *mistake; regrettably* (not *regretfully*), *I shall be unable to attend*

regroup (riː'ɡruːp) *vb* **1** to reorganize (military forces), esp after an attack or a defeat **2** (*tr*) to rearrange into a new grouping or groupings

Regt *abbreviation* **1** Regent **2** Regiment

regulable ('regjʊləbªl) *adj* able to be regulated

regular ('regjʊlə) *adj* **1** normal, customary, or usual **2** according to a uniform principle, arrangement, or order **3** occurring at fixed or prearranged intervals: *to make a regular call on a customer* **4** following a set rule or normal practice; methodical or orderly **5** symmetrical in appearance or form; even: *regular features* **6** (*prenominal*) organized, elected, conducted, etc, in a proper or officially prescribed manner **7** (*prenominal*) officially qualified or recognized: *he's not a regular doctor* **8** (*prenominal*) (*intensifier*): *a regular fool* **9** *US & Canadian informal* likable, dependable, or nice (esp in the phrase **a regular guy**) **10** denoting or relating to the personnel or units of the permanent military services: *a regular soldier; the regular army* **11** (of flowers) having any of their parts, esp petals, alike in size, shape, arrangement, etc; symmetrical **12** (of the formation, inflections, etc, of a word) following the usual pattern of formation in a language **13** *maths* **a** (of a polygon) equilateral and equiangular **b** (of a polyhedron) having identical regular polygons as faces that make identical angles with each other **c** (of a prism) having regular polygons as bases **d** (of a pyramid) having a regular polygon as a base and the altitude passing through the centre of the base **14** *botany* another word for **actinomorphic** **15** (*postpositive*) subject to the rule of an established religious order or community: *canons regular* ▷ *n* **16** a professional long-term serviceman in a military unit **17** *informal* a person who does something regularly, such as attending a theatre or patronizing a shop **18** a member of a religious order or congregation, as contrasted with a secular [C14: from Old French *reguler*, from Latin *rēgulāris* of a bar of wood or metal, from *rēgula* ruler, model] ▷ ˌregu'larity *n* ▷ regularize *or* regularise (ˈrɛɡjʊləˌraɪz) *vb* ▷ ˌregulari'zation *or* ˌregulari'sation *n* ▷ 'regularly *adv*

regulate (ˈrɛɡjʊˌleɪt) *vb* (*tr*) **1** to adjust (the amount of heat, sound, etc, of something) as required; control **2** to adjust (an instrument or appliance) so that it operates correctly **3** to bring into conformity with a rule, principle, or usage [C17: from Late Latin *rēgulāre* to control, from Latin *rēgula* a ruler] ▷ 'regulative *or* 'regulatory *adj* ▷ 'regulatively *adv*

regulation (ˌrɛɡjʊ'leɪʃən) *n* **1** the act or process of regulating **2** a rule, principle, or condition that governs procedure or behaviour **3** (*modifier*) as required by official rules or procedure: *regulation uniform* **4** (*modifier*) normal; usual; conforming to accepted standards: *a regulation haircut*

regulator (ˈrɛɡjʊˌleɪtə) *n* **1** a person or thing that regulates **2** the mechanism, including the hairspring and the balance wheel, by which the speed of a timepiece is regulated **3** any of various mechanisms or devices, such as a governor valve, for controlling fluid flow, pressure, temperature, voltage, etc

regulatory risk *n* a risk to which private companies are subject, arising from the possibility of legislation or regulations that will affect business being adopted by a government

regulo (ˈrɛɡjʊləʊ) *n* any of a number of temperatures to which a gas oven may be set: *cook at regulo 4 for 40 minutes* [C20: from *Regulo*, trademark for a type of thermostatic control on gas ovens]

regulus (ˈrɛɡjʊləs) *n, pl* -luses *or* -li (-ˌlaɪ) impure metal forming beneath the slag during the smelting of ores [C16: from Latin: a petty king, from *rēx* king; formerly used for antimony, because it combines readily with gold, thought of as the king of metals] ▷ 'reguline *adj*

Regulus¹ (ˈrɛɡjʊləs) *n* **Marcus Atilius** (ˈmɑːkəs əˈtɪlɪəs). died ?250 BC, Roman general; consul (267; 256). Captured by the Carthaginians in the First Punic War, he was sent to Rome on parole to deliver the enemy's peace terms, advised the Senate to refuse them, and was tortured to death on his return to Carthage

Regulus² (ˈrɛɡjʊləs) *n* the brightest star in the constellation Leo. Visual magnitude: 1.3; spectral type: B8; distance: 69 light years

regurgitate (rɪ'ɡɜːdʒɪˌteɪt) *vb* **1** to vomit forth (partially digested food) **2** (of some birds and certain other animals) to bring back to the mouth (undigested or partly digested food with which to feed the young) **3** (*intr*) to be cast up or out, esp from the mouth **4** (*intr*) *med* (of blood) to flow backwards, in a direction opposite to the normal one, esp through a defective heart valve [C17: from Medieval Latin *regurgitāre*, from RE- + *gurgitāre* to flood, from Latin *gurges* gulf, whirlpool] ▷ re'gurgitant *n, adj* ▷ reˌgurgi'tation *n*

rehabilitate (ˌriːə'bɪlɪˌteɪt) *vb* (*tr*) **1** to help (a person who has acquired a disability or addiction or who has just been released from prison) to readapt to society or a new job, as by vocational guidance, retraining, or therapy **2** to restore to a former position or rank **3** to restore the good reputation of [C16: from Medieval Latin *rehabilitāre* to restore, from RE- + Latin *habilitās* skill, ABILITY] ▷ reˌhabili'tation *n* ▷ ˌreha'bilitative *adj*

Rehabilitation Department *n NZ* a government department set up after World War II to assist ex-servicemen often shortened to: **rehab**

rehash *vb* (riː'hæʃ) **1** (*tr*) to rework, reuse, or make over (old or already used material) ▷ *n* (ˈriːˌhæʃ) **2** something consisting of old, reworked, or reused material [C19: from RE- + HASH¹ (to chop into pieces)]

rehearsal (rɪ'hɜːsəl) *n* **1** a session of practising a play, concert, speech etc, in preparation for public performance **2** the act of reciting **3** in rehearsal being

prepared for public performance

rehearse (rɪ'hɜːs) *vb* **1** to practise (a play, concert, etc), in preparation for public performance **2** (*tr*) to run through; recount; recite: *the official rehearsed the grievances of the committee* **3** (*tr*) to train or drill (a person or animal) for the public performance of a part in a play, show, etc [C16: from Anglo-Norman *rehearser*, from Old French *rehercier* to harrow a second time, from RE- + *herce* harrow] ▷ re'hearser *n*

reheat *vb* (riː'hiːt) **1** to heat or be heated again: *to reheat yesterday's soup* **2** (*tr*) to add fuel to (the exhaust gases of an aircraft jet engine) to produce additional heat and thrust ▷ *n* (ˈriːˌhiːt) Also called: **reheating 3** *aeronautics* another name (esp Brit) for **afterburning** (sense 1) ▷ re'heater *n*

rehoboam (ˌriːə'bəʊəm) *n* a wine bottle holding the equivalent of six normal bottles (approximately 156 ounces) [C19: named after *Rehoboam*, a son of King Solomon, from Hebrew, literally: the nation is enlarged]

Reich¹ (raɪk; German raiç) *n* **1** the Holy Roman Empire (**First Reich**) **2** the Hohenzollern empire from 1871 to 1919 (**Second Reich**) **3** the Nazi dictatorship from 1933 to 1945 (**Third Reich**) [German: kingdom]

Reich² (raɪk) *n* **1 Steve.** born 1936, US composer, whose works are characterized by the repetition and modification of small rhythmic motifs. His works include *Drumming* (1971), *The Desert Music* (1984), and *City Life* (1995) **2** (German raiç) **Wilhelm** (ˈvɪlhɛlm). 1897–1957, Austrian psychologist, lived in the US An ardent socialist and advocate of sexual freedom, he proclaimed a cosmic unity of all energy and built a machine (the orgone accumulator) to concentrate this energy on human beings. His books include *The Function of the Orgasm* (1927)

Reichenberg (ˈraiçənbɛrk) *n* the German name for **Liberec**

Reichsmark (ˈraiks,mɑːk; German ˈraiçsmark) *n, pl* -marks *or* -mark the standard monetary unit of Germany between 1924 and 1948, divided into 100 **Reichspfennigs**

Reichstag (ˈraiks,tɑːɡ; German ˈraiçstak) *n* **1** the legislative assembly representing the people in the North German Confederation (1867–71) and in the German empire (1871–1919) **2** the building in Berlin in which this assembly met and from 1999 in which the German government meets: its destruction by fire on Feb 27, 1933 (probably by agents of the Nazi government) marked the end of Weimar democracy. It was restored in the 1990s following German reunification

Reid (riːd) *n* **1 Sir George Houston.** 1845–1918, Australian statesman, born in Scotland: premier of New South Wales (1894–99); prime minister of Australia (1904–05) **2 Thomas.** 1710–96, Scottish philosopher and founder of what came to be known as the philosophy of common sense

reify (ˈriːɪˌfaɪ) *vb* -fies, -fying, -fied (*tr*) to consider or make (an abstract idea or concept) real or concrete [C19: from Latin *rēs* thing; compare DEIFY] ▷ ˌreifi'cation *n* ▷ ˌreifi'catory *adj* ▷ 're,fier *n*

Reigate (ˈraɪɡɪt, -ɡeɪt) *n* a town in S England, in Surrey at the foot of the North Downs. Pop (including Redhill): 50 436 (2001)

reign (reɪn) *n* **1** the period during which a monarch is the official ruler of a country **2** a period during which a person or thing is dominant, influential, or powerful: *the reign of violence is over* ▷ *vb* (*intr*) **3** to exercise the power and authority of a sovereign **4** to be accorded the rank and title of a sovereign without having ruling authority, as in a constitutional monarchy **5** to predominate; prevail: *a land where darkness reigns* **6** (*usually present participle*) to be the most recent winner of a competition, contest, etc: *the reigning heavyweight champion* [C13: from Old French *reigne*, from Latin *rēgnum* kingdom, from *rēx* king]
● USAGE *Reign* is sometimes wrongly written for *rein* in certain phrases: *he gave full rein* (not *reign*) *to his feelings; it will be necessary to rein in* (not *reign in*) *public spending*

reiki (ˈreɪkɪ) *n* a form of therapy in which the practitioner is believed to channel energy into the patient in order to encourage healing or restore wellbeing [Japanese, from *rei* universal + *ki* life force]

reimburse (ˌriːɪmˈbɜːs) *vb* (*tr*) to repay or compensate (someone) for (money already spent, losses, damages, etc) [c17: from RE- + *imburse*, from Medieval Latin *imbursāre* to put in a moneybag, from *bursa* PURSE] > ˌreimˈbursable *adj* > ˌreimˈbursement *n* > ˌreimˈburser *n*

reimport *vb* (ˌriːɪmˈpɔːt, riːˈɪmpɔːt) 1 (*tr*) to import (goods manufactured from exported raw materials) ▷ *n* (riːˈɪmpɔːt) 2 the act of reimporting 3 a reimported commodity > ˌreimporˈtation *n*

Reims *or* **Rheims** (riːmz; *French* rɛ̃s) *n* a city in NE France: scene of the coronation of most French monarchs. Pop: 187 206 (1999)

rein (reɪn) *n* 1 (*often plural*) one of a pair of long straps, usually connected together and made of leather, used to control a horse, running from the side of the bit or the headstall to the hand of the rider, driver, or trainer 2 a similar device used to control a very young child 3 any form or means of control: *to take up the reins of government* 4 the direction in which a rider turns (in phrases such as **on a left** (*or* **right**) **rein**, **change the rein**) 5 something that restrains, controls, or guides 6 **give free rein** *or* **give a free rein** to allow considerable freedom; remove restraints 7 **keep a tight rein on** to control carefully; limit: *we have to keep a tight rein on expenditure* ▷ *vb* 8 (*tr*) to check, restrain, hold back, or halt with or as if with reins 9 to control or guide (a horse) with a rein or reins: *they reined left* ▷ See also **rein in** [c13: from Old French *resne*, from Latin *retinēre* to hold back, from RE- + *tenēre* to hold; see RESTRAIN]
● USAGE See at **reign**

reincarnate *vb* (ˌriːɪnˈkɑːneɪt) (*tr; often passive*) 1 to cause to undergo reincarnation; be born again ▷ *adj* (ˌriːɪnˈkɑːnɪt) 2 born again in a new body

reincarnation (ˌriːɪnkɑːˈneɪʃən) *n* 1 the belief that on the death of the body the soul transmigrates to or is born again in another body 2 the incarnation or embodiment of a soul in a new body after it has left the old one at physical death 3 embodiment again in a new form, as of a principle or idea > ˌreincarˈnationist *n, adj*

reindeer (ˈreɪnˌdɪə) *n, pl* -**deer** *or* -**deers** a large deer, *Rangifer tarandus*, having large branched antlers in the male and female and inhabiting the arctic regions of Greenland, Europe, and Asia. It also occurs in North America, where it is known as a caribou [c14: from Old Norse *hreindȳri*, from *hreinn* reindeer + *dȳr* animal; related to Dutch *rendier*, German *Rentier*; see DEER]

Reindeer Lake *n* a lake in W Canada, in Saskatchewan and Manitoba: drains into the Churchill River via the **Reindeer River**. Area: 6390 sq km (2467 sq miles)

reindeer moss *n* any of various lichens of the genus *Cladonia*, esp *C. rangiferina*, which occur in arctic and subarctic regions, providing food for reindeer

reinforce (ˌriːɪnˈfɔːs) *vb* (*tr*) 1 to give added strength or support to 2 to give added emphasis to; stress, support, or increase: *his rudeness reinforced my determination* 3 to give added support to (a military force) by providing more men, supplies, etc [c17: from obsolete *renforce*, from French *renforcer*; see RE- + *inforce* ENFORCE] > ˌreinˈforcement *n*

reinforced concrete *n* concrete with steel bars, mesh, etc, embedded in it to enable it to withstand tensile and shear stresses

reinforced plastic *n* plastic with fibrous matter, such as carbon fibre, embedded in it to confer additional strength

Reinhardt (ˈraɪnˌhɑːt) *n* 1 **Django** (ˈdʒæŋɡəʊ), real name *Jean Baptiste Reinhardt*. 1910–53, French guitarist, whose work was greatly influenced by Gypsy music. With Stéphane Grappelli, he led the Quintet of the Hot Club of France between 1934 and 1939 2 **Max**, original name *Max Goldmann*. 1873–1943, Austrian theatre producer and director, in the US after 1933

rein in *vb* (*adverb*) to stop (a horse) by pulling on the reins

reins (reɪnz) *pl n archaic* the kidneys or loins [c14: from Old French, from Latin *rēnēs* the kidneys]

reinstate (ˌriːɪnˈsteɪt) *vb* (*tr*) to restore to a former rank or condition > ˌreinˈstatement *n* > ˌreinˈstator *n*

reinsure (ˌriːɪnˈʃʊə, -ˈʃɔː) *vb* (*tr*) 1 to insure again 2 (of an insurer) to obtain partial or complete insurance

coverage from another insurer for (a risk on which a policy has already been issued) > ˌreinˈsurance *n* > ˌreinˈsurer *n*

reinvent (ˌriːɪnˈvɛnt) *vb* (*tr*) 1 to replace (a product, etc) with an entirely new version 2 to duplicate (something that already exists) in what is therefore a wasted effort (esp in the phrase **reinvent the wheel**)

reissue (ˌriːˈɪʃjuː) *vb* (*tr*) 1 to issue (a recording, book, etc) again ▷ *n* 2 something, esp a recording or book, which has been issued again

reiterate (riːˈɪtəˌreɪt) *vb* (*tr; may take a clause as object*) to say or do again or repeatedly [c16: from Latin *reiterāre* to repeat, from RE- + *iterāre* to do again, from *iterum* again] > reˌiterˈation *n* > reˈiterative *adj* > reˈiteratively *adv*

Reith (riːθ) *n* **John** (**Charles Walsham**), 1st Baron. 1889–1971, British public servant: first general manager (1922–27) and first director general (1927–38) of the BBC > ˈReithian *or* ˈReithean *adj*

reive (riːv) *vb* (*intr*) *Scot & northern English dialect* to go on a plundering raid [variant of REAVE¹] > ˈreiver *n*

reject *vb* (rɪˈdʒɛkt) (*tr*) 1 to refuse to accept, acknowledge, use, believe, etc 2 to throw out as useless or worthless; discard 3 to rebuff (a person) 4 (of an organism) to fail to accept (a foreign tissue graft or organ transplant) because of immunological incompatibility ▷ *n* (ˈriːdʒɛkt) 5 something rejected as imperfect, unsatisfactory, or useless [c15: from Latin *rēicere* to throw back, from RE- + *jacere* to hurl] > reˈjecter *or* reˈjector *n* > reˈjection *n* > reˈjective *adj*

rejig (riːˈdʒɪɡ) *vb* -**jigs**, -**jigging**, -**jigged** (*tr*) 1 to re-equip (a factory or plant) 2 to rearrange, alter, or manipulate, sometimes in a slightly unscrupulous way ▷ *n* 3 the act or process of rejigging > reˈjigger *n*

rejoice (rɪˈdʒɔɪs) *vb* (when *tr, takes a clause as object or an infinitive*; when *intr*, often foll by *in*) to feel or express great joy or happiness [c14: from Old French *resjoir*, from RE- + *joir* to be glad, from Latin *gaudēre* to rejoice] > reˈjoicer *n*

rejoin¹ (riːˈdʒɔɪn) *vb* 1 to come again into company with (someone or something) 2 (*tr*) to put or join together again; reunite

rejoin² (rɪˈdʒɔɪn) *vb* (*tr*) 1 to say (something) in reply; answer, reply, or retort 2 *law* to answer (a claimant's reply) [c15: from Old French *rejoign-*, stem of *rejoindre*; see RE-, JOIN]

rejoinder (rɪˈdʒɔɪndə) *n* 1 a reply or response to a question or remark, esp a quick witty one; retort 2 *law* (in pleading) the answer made by a defendant to the claimant's reply [c15: from Old French *rejoindre* to REJOIN²]

rejuvenate (rɪˈdʒuːvɪˌneɪt) *vb* (*tr*) 1 to give new youth, restored vitality, or youthful appearance to 2 (*usually passive*) *geography* to cause (a river) to begin eroding more vigorously to a new lower base level, usually because of uplift of the land [c19: from RE- + Latin *juvenis* young] > reˌjuveˈnation *n* > reˈjuveˌnator *n*

rejuvenesce (rɪˌdʒuːvəˈnɛs) *vb* 1 to make or become youthful or restored to vitality 2 *biology* to convert (cells) or (of cells) to be converted into a more active form > reˌjuveˈnescence *n* > reˌjuveˈnescent *adj*

rel. *abbreviation* 1 relating 2 relative(ly)

relapse *vb* (rɪˈlæps) (*intr*) 1 to lapse back into a former state or condition, esp one involving bad habits 2 to become ill again after apparent recovery ▷ *n* (rɪˈlæps, ˈriːlæps) 3 the act or an instance of relapsing 4 the return of ill health after an apparent or partial recovery [c16: from Latin *relabī* to slip back, from RE- + *labī* to slip, slide] > reˈlapser *n*

relapsing fever *n* any of various infectious diseases characterized by recurring fever, caused by the bite of body lice or ticks infected with spirochaetes of the genus *Borrelia*. Also called: **recurrent fever**

relata (rɪˈleɪtə) *n* the plural of **relatum**

relate (rɪˈleɪt) *vb* 1 (*tr*) to tell or narrate (a story, information, etc) 2 (*often foll by* to) to establish association (between two or more things) or (of something) to have relation or reference (to something else) 3 (*intr; often foll by* to) to form a sympathetic or significant relationship (with other people, things, etc) [c16: from Latin *relātus* brought back, from *referre* to carry

back, from RE- + *ferre* to bear; see REFER] > re'latable *adj*
> re'later *n*

related (rɪ'leɪtɪd) *adj* **1** connected; associated
2 connected by kinship or marriage **3** (in diatonic music) denoting or relating to a key that has notes in common with another key or keys > re'latedness *n*

relation (rɪ'leɪʃən) *n* **1** the state or condition of being related or the manner in which things are related **2** connection by blood or marriage; kinship **3** a person who is connected by blood or marriage; relative; kinsman **4** reference or regard (esp in the phrase **in** or **with relation to**) **5** the position, association, connection, or status of one person or thing with regard to another or others **6** the act of relating or narrating **7** an account or narrative **8** *law* the principle by which an act done at one time is regarded in law as having been done antecedently **9** *logic, maths* **a** an association between ordered pairs of objects, numbers, etc, such as ... *is greater than* ... **b** the set of ordered pairs whose members have such an association ▷ See also **relations** [C14: from Latin *relātiō* a narration, a relation (between philosophical concepts)]

relational (rɪ'leɪʃənºl) *adj* **1** *grammar* indicating or expressing syntactic relation, as for example the case endings in Latin **2** having relation or being related **3** *computing* based on data stored in a tabular form

relations (rɪ'leɪʃənz) *pl n* **1** social, political, or other connections or dealings between or among individuals, groups, nations, etc **2** family or relatives **3** *euphemistic* sexual intercourse

relationship (rɪ'leɪʃənʃɪp) *n* **1** the state of being connected or related **2** association by blood or marriage; kinship **3** the mutual dealings, connections, or feelings that exist between two parties, countries, people, etc **4** an emotional or sexual affair or liaison

relative ('relətɪv) *adj* **1** having meaning or significance only in relation to something else; not absolute **2** (*prenominal*) (of a scientific quantity) being measured or stated relative to some other substance or measurement: *relative humidity; relative density* **3** (*prenominal*) comparative or respective: *the relative qualities of speed and accuracy* **4** (*postpositive*; foll by *to*) in proportion (to); corresponding (to): *earnings relative to production* **5** having reference (to); pertinent (to) **6** *grammar* denoting or belonging to a class of words that function as subordinating conjunctions in introducing relative clauses. In English, relative pronouns and determiners include *who*, *which*, and *that*. See **demonstrative** (sense 5) **7** *grammar* denoting or relating to a clause (**relative clause**) that modifies a noun or pronoun occurring earlier in the sentence **8** (of a musical key or scale) having the same key signature as another key or scale ▷ *n* **9** a person who is related by blood or marriage; relation **10** a relative pronoun, clause, or grammatical construction [C16: from Late Latin *relātīvus* referring] > 'relativeness *n*

relative aperture *n photog* the ratio of the equivalent focal length of a lens to the effective aperture of the lens; written as *f/n*, *f:n*, or *fn*, where *n* is the numerical value of this ratio and is equivalent to the f-number

relative atomic mass *n* the ratio of the average mass per atom of the naturally occurring form of an element to one-twelfth the mass of an atom of carbon-12. Symbol: A_r Former name: atomic weight

relative density *n* the ratio of the density of a substance to the density of a standard substance under specified conditions. For liquids and solids the standard is usually water at 4°C or some other specified temperature. For gases the standard is often air or hydrogen at the same temperature and pressure as the substance. Symbol: d^2 See also **specific gravity, vapour density**

relative frequency *n* the ratio of the actual number of favourable events to the total possible number of events; often taken as an estimate of probability

relative humidity *n* the mass of water vapour present in the air expressed as a percentage of the mass that would be present in an equal volume of saturated air at the same temperature

relatively ('relətɪvlɪ) *adv* in comparison or relation to something else; not absolutely

relative majority *n Brit* the excess of votes or seats won by the winner of an election over the runner-up when no candidate or party has more than 50 per cent. Compare **absolute majority**

relative molecular mass *n* the sum of all the relative atomic masses of the atoms in a molecule; the ratio of the average mass per molecule of a specified isotopic composition of a substance to one-twelfth the mass of an atom of carbon-12. Symbol: M_r Former name: molecular weight

relative permeability *n* the ratio of the permeability of a medium to that of free space

relative permittivity *n* the ratio of the permittivity of a substance to that of free space

relativism ('relətɪ,vɪzəm) *n* any theory holding that truth or moral or aesthetic value, etc, is not universal or absolute but may differ between individuals or cultures > 'relativist *n, adj* > relati'vistic *adj* > ,relativ'istically *adv*

relativity (,relə'tɪvɪtɪ) *n* **1** either of two theories developed by Albert Einstein, the **special theory of relativity**, which requires that the laws of physics shall be the same as seen by any two different observers in uniform relative motion, and the **general theory of relativity** which considers observers with relative acceleration and leads to a theory of gravitation **2** the state or quality of being relative

relator (rɪ'leɪtə) *n* **1** a person who relates a story; narrator **2** *English law* a person who gives information upon which the attorney general brings an action

relatum (rɪ'leɪtəm) *n, pl* -ta (-tə) *logic* one of the objects between which a relation is said to hold

relaunch *vb* (ri:'lɔ:ntʃ) (*tr*) **1** to launch again **2** to start, set in motion, or make available again ▷ *n* ('ri:,lɔ:ntʃ) **3** another launching, or something that is relaunched

relax (rɪ'læks) *vb* **1** to make (muscles, a grip, etc) less tense or rigid or (of muscles, a grip, etc) to become looser or less rigid **2** (*intr*) to take rest or recreation, as from work or effort **3** to lessen the force of (effort, concentration, etc) or (of effort) to become diminished **4** to make (rules or discipline) less rigid or strict or (of rules, etc) to diminish in severity **5** (*intr*) (of a person) to become less formal; unbend [C15: from Latin *relaxāre* to loosen, from RE- + *laxāre* to loosen, from *laxus* loose, LAX] > re'laxed *adj* > relaxedly (rɪ'læksɪdlɪ) *adv* > re'laxer *n*

relaxant (rɪ'læksºnt) *n* **1** *med* a drug or agent that relaxes, esp one that relaxes tense muscles ▷ *adj* **2** of, relating to, or tending to produce relaxation

relaxation (,ri:læk'seɪʃən) *n* **1** rest or refreshment, as after work or effort; recreation **2** a form of rest or recreation: *his relaxation is cricket* **3** a partial lessening of a punishment, duty, etc **4** the act of relaxing or state of being relaxed **5** *physics* the return of a system to equilibrium after a displacement from this state

relaxin (rɪ'læksɪn) *n* **1** a mammalian polypeptide hormone secreted by the corpus luteum during pregnancy, which relaxes the pelvic ligaments **2** a preparation of this hormone, used to facilitate childbirth [C20: from RELAX + -IN]

relay *n* ('ri:leɪ) **1** a person or team of people relieving others, as on a shift **2** a fresh team of horses, dogs, etc, posted at intervals along a route to relieve others **3** the act of relaying or process of being relayed **4** short for **relay race 5** an automatic device that controls the setting of a valve, switch, etc, by means of an electric motor, solenoid, or pneumatic mechanism **6** *electronics* an electrical device in which a small change in current or voltage controls the switching on or off of circuits or other devices **7** *radio* **a** a combination of a receiver and transmitter designed to receive radio signals and retransmit them, in order to extend their range **b** (*as modifier*): *a relay station* ▷ *vb* (rɪ'leɪ) (*tr*) **8** to carry or spread (something, such as news or information) by relays **9** to supply or replace with relays **10** to retransmit (a signal) by means of a relay **11** *Brit* to broadcast (a performance) by sending out signals through a transmitting station [C15 *relaien*, from Old French *relaier* to leave behind, from RE- + *laier* to leave, ultimately from Latin *laxāre* to loosen;

see RELAX]

relay race *n* a race between two or more teams of contestants in which each contestant covers a specified portion of the distance

release (rɪ'liːs) *vb* (*tr*) **1** to free (a person, animal, etc) from captivity or imprisonment **2** to free (someone) from obligation or duty **3** to free (something) from (one's grip); let go or fall **4** to issue (a record, film, book, etc) for sale or circulation **5** to make (news or information) known or allow (news, information, etc) to be made known **6** *law* to relinquish (a right, claim, title, etc) in favour of someone else ⊳ *n* **7** the act of freeing or state of being freed, as from captivity, imprisonment, duty, pain, life, etc **8** the act of issuing for sale or publication **9** something issued for sale or public showing, esp a film or a record: *a new release from Bob Dylan* **10** a news item, document, etc, made available for publication, broadcasting, etc **11** *law* the surrender of a claim, right, title, etc, in favour of someone else **12** a control mechanism for starting or stopping an engine **13** the control mechanism for the shutter in a camera [c13: from Old French *relesser*, from Latin *relaxāre* to slacken; see RELAX] > re'leaser *n*

relegate ('rɛlɪˌgeɪt) *vb* (*tr*) **1** to move to a position of less authority, importance, etc; demote **2** (*usually passive*) *chiefly Brit* to demote (a football team, etc) to a lower division **3** to assign or refer (a matter) to another or others, as for action or decision **4** (foll by *to*) to banish or exile **5** to assign (something) to a particular group or category [c16: from Latin *relēgāre* to send away, from RE- + *lēgāre* to send] > 'rele,gatable *adj* > ,rele'gation *n*

relent (rɪ'lɛnt) *vb* (*intr*) **1** to change one's mind about some decided course, esp a harsh one; become more mild or amenable **2** (of the pace or intensity of something) to slacken **3** (of the weather) to become more mild [c14: from RE- + Latin *lentāre* to bend, from *lentus* flexible, tenacious]

relentless (rɪ'lɛntlɪs) *adj* **1** (of an enemy, hostile attitude, etc) implacable; inflexible; inexorable **2** (of pace or intensity) sustained; unremitting > re'lentlessly *adv* > re'lentlessness *n*

Relenza (rɪ'lɛnzə) *n trademark* a preparation of an antiviral drug, zanamivir, used in the treatment of influenza to reduce the duration and severity of the illness

relevant ('rɛlɪvənt) *adj* having direct bearing on the matter in hand; pertinent [c16: from Medieval Latin *relevans*, from Latin *relevāre* to lighten, from RE- + *levāre* to raise, RELIEVE] > 'relevance *or* 'relevancy *n* > 'relevantly *adv*

reliable (rɪ'laɪəbᵊl) *adj* able to be trusted; predictable or dependable > re,lia'bility *or less commonly* re'liableness *n* > re'liably *adv*

reliance (rɪ'laɪəns) *n* **1** dependence, confidence, or trust **2** something or someone upon which one relies > re'liant *adj* > re'liantly *adv*

relic ('rɛlɪk) *n* **1** something that has survived from the past, such as an object or custom **2** something kept as a remembrance or treasured for its past associations; keepsake **3** (*usually plural*) a remaining part or fragment **4** *RC Church, Eastern Church* part of the body of a saint or something supposedly used by or associated with a saint, venerated as holy **5** *informal* an old or old-fashioned person or thing **6** (*plural*) *archaic* the remains of a dead person; corpse [c13: from Old French *relique*, from Latin *reliquiae* remains, from *relinquere* to leave behind, RELINQUISH]

relict ('rɛlɪkt) *n* **1** *ecology* **a** a group of animals or plants that exists as a remnant of a formerly widely distributed group in an environment different from that in which it originated **b** (*as modifier*): *a relict fauna* **2** *geology* a mountain, lake, glacier, etc, that is a remnant of a pre-existing formation after a destructive process has occurred **3** an archaic word for **widow** (sense 1) **4** an archaic word for **relic** (sense 6) [c16: from Latin *relictus* left behind, from *relinquere* to RELINQUISH]

relief (rɪ'liːf) *n* **1 a** a feeling of cheerfulness or optimism that follows the removal of anxiety, pain, or distress **2** deliverance from or alleviation of anxiety, pain,

distress, etc **3 a** help or assistance, as to the poor, needy, or distressed **b** (*as modifier*): *relief work* **4** short for **tax relief 5** something that affords a diversion from monotony **6** a person who replaces or relieves another at some task or duty **7** a bus, shuttle plane, etc, that carries additional passengers when a scheduled service is full **8** a road (**relief road**) carrying traffic round an urban area; bypass **9** a the act of freeing a beleaguered town, fortress, etc: *the relief of Mafeking* **b** (*as modifier*): *a relief column* **10** Also called: relievo, rilievo *sculpture, architect* **a** the projection of forms or figures from a flat ground, so that they are partly or wholly free of it **b** a piece of work of this kind **11** a printing process, such as engraving, letterpress, etc, that employs raised surfaces from which ink is transferred to the paper **12** any vivid effect resulting from contrast: *comic relief* **13** variation in altitude in an area; difference between highest and lowest level **14** *law* redress of a grievance or hardship: *to seek relief through the courts* **15** on relief *US & Canadian* (of people) in receipt of government aid because of personal need [c14: from Old French, from *relever* to raise up; see RELIEVE]

relief map *n* a map that shows the configuration and height of the land surface, usually by means of contours

relief pitcher *n baseball* a pitcher who replaces a side's main pitcher during a game. Also called: reliever

relieve (rɪ'liːv) *vb* (*tr*) **1** to bring alleviation of (pain, distress, etc) to (someone) **2** to bring aid or assistance to (someone in need, a disaster area, etc) **3** to take over the duties or watch of (someone) **4** to bring aid or a relieving force to (a besieged town, city, etc) **5** to free (someone) from an obligation **6** to make (something) less unpleasant, arduous, or monotonous **7** to bring into relief or prominence, as by contrast **8** (foll by *of*) *informal* to take from: *the thief relieved him of his watch* **9** relieve oneself to urinate or defecate [c14: from Old French *relever*, from Latin *relevāre* to lift up, relieve, from RE- + *levāre* to lighten] > re'lievable *adj* > re'liever *n*

relieved (rɪ'liːvd) *adj* (*postpositive*; often foll by *at, about,* etc) experiencing relief, esp from worry or anxiety

religieuse *French* (rəliʒjøz) *n* a nun [c18: feminine of RELIGIEUX]

religieux *French* (rəliʒjø) *n, pl -gieux* (-ʒjø) a member of a monastic order or clerical body [c17: from Latin *religiōsus* religious]

religion (rɪ'lɪdʒən) *n* **1** belief in, worship of, or obedience to a supernatural power or powers considered to be divine or to have control of human destiny **2** any formal or institutionalized expression of such belief: *the Christian religion* **3** the attitude and feeling of one who believes in a transcendent controlling power or powers **4** *chiefly RC Church* the way of life determined by the vows of poverty, chastity, and obedience entered upon by monks, friars, and nuns: *to enter religion* **5** something of overwhelming importance to a person: *football is his religion* [c12: via Old French from Latin *religiō* fear of the supernatural, piety, probably from *religāre* to tie up, from RE- + *ligāre* to bind]

religionism (rɪ'lɪdʒəˌnɪzəm) *n* extreme religious fervour > re'ligionist *n, adj*

religiose (rɪ'lɪdʒɪˌəʊs) *adj* affectedly or extremely pious; sanctimoniously religious > re'ligi,osely *adv* > religiosity (rɪˌlɪdʒɪ'ɒsɪtɪ) *n*

religious (rɪ'lɪdʒəs) *adj* **1** of, relating to, or concerned with religion **2 a** pious; devout; godly **b** (*as collective noun*; preceded by *the*): *the religious* **3** appropriate to or in accordance with the principles of a religion **4** scrupulous, exact, or conscientious **5** *Christianity* of or relating to a way of life dedicated to religion by the vows of poverty, chastity, and obedience, and defined by a monastic rule ⊳ *n* **6** *Christianity* a member of an order or congregation living by such a rule; a monk, friar, or nun > re'ligiously *adv* > re'ligiousness *n*

Religious Society of Friends *n* the official name for the Quakers

relinquish (rɪ'lɪŋkwɪʃ) *vb* (*tr*) to give up (a task, struggle, etc); abandon **1** to surrender or renounce (a claim, right, etc) **2** to release; let go [c15: from French *relinquir*, from Latin *relinquere* to leave behind, from RE- + *linquere* to leave] > re'linquisher *n* > re'linquishment *n*

r

reliquary ('rɛlɪkwərɪ) *n, pl* -quaries a receptacle or repository for relics, esp relics of saints [c17: from Old French *reliquaire*, from *relique* RELIC]

relique (rə'liːk, 'rɛlɪk) *n* an archaic spelling of **relic**

reliquiae (rɪ'lɪkwɪˌiː) *pl n archaic* fossil remains of animals or plants [c19: from Latin: remains]

relish ('rɛlɪʃ) *vb (tr)* 1 to savour or enjoy (an experience) to the full 2 to anticipate eagerly; look forward to 3 to enjoy the taste or flavour of (food, etc); savour ▷ *n* 4 liking or enjoyment, as of something eaten or experienced (esp in the phrase **with relish**) 5 pleasurable anticipation: *he didn't have much relish for the idea* 6 an appetizing or spicy food added to a main dish to enhance its flavour 7 an appetizing taste or flavour 8 a zestful trace or touch: *there was a certain relish in all his writing* [c16: from earlier *reles* aftertaste, from Old French: something remaining, from *relaisser* to leave behind; see RELEASE] > 'relishable *adj*

relive (riː'lɪv) *vb (tr)* to experience (a sensation, event, etc) again, esp in the imagination > re'livable *adj*

rellies ('rɛlɪz) *pl n Austral & NZ informal* relatives or relations

relocate (ˌriːləʊ'keɪt) *vb* to move or be moved to a new place, esp (of an employee, a business, etc) to a new area or place of employment > ˌrelo'cation *n*

reluct (rɪ'lʌkt) *vb (intr) archaic* 1 (often foll by *against*) to struggle or rebel 2 to object; show reluctance [c16: from Latin *reluctārī* to resist, from RE- + *luctārī* to struggle]

reluctance (rɪ'lʌktəns) *or less commonly* **reluctancy** *n* 1 lack of eagerness or willingness; disinclination 2 *physics* a measure of the resistance of a closed magnetic circuit to a magnetic flux, equal to the ratio of the magnetomotive force to the magnetic flux

reluctant (rɪ'lʌktənt) *adj* not eager; unwilling; disinclined [c17: from Latin *reluctārī* to resist; see RELUCT] > re'luctantly *adv*

reluctivity (ˌrɛlʌk'tɪvɪtɪ) *n, pl* -ties *physics* a specific or relative reluctance of a magnetic material [c19: RELUCT + -ivity from obs *reluct* to struggle]

rely (rɪ'laɪ) *vb* -lies, -lying, -lied *(intr;* foll by *on* or *upon)* 1 to be dependent (on): *he relies on his charm* 2 to have trust or confidence (in): *you can rely on us* [c14: from Old French *relier* to fasten together, repair, from Latin *religāre* to tie back, from RE- + *ligāre* to tie]

REM *abbreviation* rapid eye movement

remain (rɪ'meɪn) *vb (mainly intr)* 1 to stay behind or in the same place: *to remain at home; only Tom remained* 2 *(copula)* to continue to be: *to remain cheerful* 3 to be left, as after use, consumption, the passage of time, etc 4 to be left to be done, said, etc: *it remains to be pointed out* [c14: from Old French *remanoir*, from Latin *remanēre* to be left, from RE- + *manēre* to stay]

remainder (rɪ'meɪndə) *n* 1 a part or portion that is left, as after use, subtraction, expenditure, the passage of time, etc: *the remainder of the milk; the remainder of the day* 2 *maths* the amount left over when one quantity cannot be exactly divided by another: *for 10 ÷ 3, the remainder is 1* 3 *property law* a future interest in property; an interest in a particular estate that will pass to one at some future date, as on the death of the current possessor 4 a number of copies of a book left unsold when demand slows or ceases, which are sold at a reduced price by the publisher ▷ *vb* 5 *(tr)* to sell (copies of a book) as a remainder [c15: from Anglo-French, from Old French *remaindre* (infinitive used as noun), variant of *remanoir*; see REMAIN]

remains (rɪ'meɪnz) *pl n* 1 any pieces, scraps, fragments, etc, that are left unused or still extant, as after use, consumption, the passage of time, etc: *the remains of a meal; archaeological remains* 2 the body of a dead person; corpse 3 *Also called:* literary remains the unpublished writings of an author at the time of his death

remake *n* ('riːˌmeɪk) 1 something that is made again, esp a new version of an old film 2 the act of making again or anew ▷ *vb* (riː'meɪk) -makes, -making, -made 3 *(tr)* to make again or anew

remand (rɪ'mɑːnd) *vb (tr)* 1 *law* (of a court or magistrate) to send (a prisoner or accused person) back into custody or admit him to bail, esp on adjourning a case for further inquiries to be made 2 to send back ▷ *n* 3 the sending of a prisoner or accused person back into custody (or sometimes admitting him to bail) to await trial or continuation of his trial 4 the act of remanding or state of being remanded 5 **on remand** in custody or on bail awaiting trial or completion of one's trial [c15: from Medieval Latin *remandāre* to send back word, from Latin RE- + *mandāre* to command, confine; see MANDATE]

remand centre *n* (in Britain) an institution to which accused persons are sent for detention while awaiting appearance before a court. Until 1967 remand centres were for young people between 14 and 21 years of age

remanence ('rɛmənəns) *n physics* the ability of a material to retain magnetization, equal to the magnetic flux density of the material after the removal of the magnetizing field [c17: from Latin *remanēre* to stay behind, REMAIN]

remark (rɪ'mɑːk) *vb* 1 (when *intr,* often foll by *on* or *upon*; when *tr,* may take a clause as object) to pass a casual comment (about); reflect in informal speech or writing 2 *(tr;* may take a clause as object) to perceive; observe; notice ▷ *n* 3 a brief casually expressed thought or opinion; observation 4 notice, comment, or observation: *the event passed without remark* 5 *engraving* a variant spelling of **remarque** [c17: from Old French *remarquer* to observe, from RE- + *marquer* to note, MARK[1]] > re'marker *n*

remarkable (rɪ'mɑːkəbəl) *adj* 1 worthy of note or attention: *a remarkable achievement* 2 unusual, striking, or extraordinary: *a remarkable sight* > re'markableness, reˌmarka'bility *n* > re'markably *adv*

remarque *or* **remark** (rɪ'mɑːk) *n* a mark in the margin of an engraved plate to indicate the stage of production of the plate. It is removed before the plate is finished [c19: from French; see REMARK]

Remarque (rɪ'mɑːk) *n* **Erich Maria** ('eːrɪç ma'riːa). 1898–1970, US novelist, born in Germany, noted for his novel of World War I, *All Quiet on the Western Front* (1929)

remaster (riː'mɑːstə) *vb (tr)* to make a new master audio recording, now usually digital, from (an earlier recording), to produce compact discs or stereo records with improved sound reproduction

rematch *n* ('riːˌmætʃ) 1 *sport* a second or return match between contestants ▷ *vb* (riː'mætʃ) 2 *(tr)* to match (two contestants) again

Rembrandt ('rɛmbrænt) *n* full name *Rembrandt Harmensz* (or *Harmenszoon*) *van Rijn* (or *van Ryn*). 1606–69, Dutch painter, noted for his handling of shade and light, esp in his portraits > ˌRembrandt'esque *adj*

REME ('riːmiː) *n acronym for* Royal Electrical and Mechanical Engineers

remedial (rɪ'miːdɪəl) *adj* 1 affording a remedy; curative 2 denoting or relating to special teaching, teaching methods, or material for backward and slow learners: *remedial education* > re'medially *adv*

remediation (rɪˌmiːdɪ'eɪʃən) *n* the action of remedying something, esp the reversal or stopping of damage to the environment

remedy ('rɛmɪdɪ) *n, pl* -dies 1 (usually foll by *for* or *against*) any drug or agent that cures a disease or controls its symptoms 2 (usually foll by *for* or *against*) anything that serves to put a fault to rights, cure defects, improve conditions, etc: *a remedy for industrial disputes* 3 the legally permitted variation from the standard weight or quality of coins; tolerance ▷ *vb (tr)* 4 to relieve or cure (a disease, illness, etc) by or as if by a remedy 5 to put to rights (a fault, error, etc); correct [c13: from Anglo-Norman *remedie*, from Latin *remedium* a cure, from *remedērī* to heal again, from RE- + *medērī* to heal; see MEDICAL] > remediable (rɪ'miːdɪəbᵊl) *adj* > re'mediably *adv* > 'remediless *adj*

remember (rɪ'mɛmbə) *vb* 1 to become aware of (something forgotten) again; bring back to one's consciousness; recall 2 to retain (an idea, intention, etc) in one's conscious mind: *to remember Pythagoras' theorem; remember to do one's shopping* 3 *(tr)* to give money, etc, to (someone), as in a will or in tipping 4 *(tr;* foll by *to)* to mention (a person's name) to another person, as by way of greeting or friendship: *remember me to your mother* 5 *(tr)* to mention (a person) favourably, as in prayer 6 *(tr)* to commemorate (a person, event, etc): *to remember the dead of the wars* **7** *remember oneself* to recover one's good manners after a lapse; stop behaving badly [c14: from Old French *remembrer*, from Late Latin *rememorārī* to recall to mind, from Latin RE- + *memor* mindful; see MEMORY] > re'memberer *n*

remembrance (rɪ'mɛmbrəns) *n* **1** the act of remembering or state of being remembered **2** something that is remembered; reminiscence **3** a memento or keepsake **4** the extent in time of one's power of recollection **5** the act of honouring some past event, person, etc

remembrancer (rɪ'mɛmbrənsə) *n archaic* a reminder, memento, or keepsake

Remembrancer (rɪ'mɛmbrənsə) *n* (in Britain) **1** any of several officials of the Exchequer esp one (**Queen's** or **King's Remembrancer**) whose duties include collecting debts due to the Crown **2** an official (**City Remembrancer**) appointed by the Corporation of the City of London to represent its interests to Parliament and elsewhere

Remembrance Sunday *n Brit* the second Sunday in November, which is the Sunday closest to November 11, the anniversary of the armistice of 1918 that ended World War I, on which the dead of both World Wars are commemorated. Also called: **Remembrance Day**

remex ('riːmɛks) *n, pl* **remiges** ('rɛmɪˌdʒiːz) any of the large flight feathers of a bird's wing [c18: from Latin: a rower, from *rēmus* oar] > **remigial** (rɪ'mɪdʒɪəl) *adj*

remind (rɪ'maɪnd) *vb* (*tr*; usually foll by *of*; may take a clause as object or an infinitive) to cause (a person) to remember (something or to do something); make (someone) aware (of something he may have forgotten): *remind me to phone home; flowers remind me of holidays* > re'minder *n*

remindful (rɪ'maɪndfʊl) *adj* **1** serving to remind **2** (*postpositive*) bearing in mind; mindful

reminisce (ˌrɛmɪ'nɪs) *vb* (*intr*) to talk or write about old times, past experiences, etc

reminiscence (ˌrɛmɪ'nɪsəns) *n* **1** the act of recalling or narrating past experiences **2** (*often plural*) some past experience, event, etc, that is recalled or narrated; anecdote **3** an event, phenomenon, or experience that reminds one of something else **4** (in the philosophy of Plato) the doctrine that perception and recognition of particulars is possible because the mind has seen the universal forms of all things in a previous disembodied existence

reminiscent (ˌrɛmɪ'nɪsᵊnt) *adj* **1** (*postpositive*; foll by *of*) stimulating memories (of) or comparisons (with) **2** characterized by reminiscence **3** (of a person) given to reminiscing [c18: from Latin *reminisci* to call to mind, from RE- + *mēns* mind] > ˌremi'niscently *adv*

remise (rɪ'maɪz) *vb* **1** (*tr*) *law* to give up or relinquish (a right, claim, etc); surrender **2** *fencing* to make a renewed thrust on the same lunge after the first has missed ▷ *n* **3** *fencing* a second thrust made on the same lunge after the first has missed **4** *obsolete* a coach house [c17: from French *remettre* to put back, from Latin *remittere* to send back, from RE- + *mittere* to send]

remiss (rɪ'mɪs) *adj* (*postpositive*) **1** lacking in care or attention to duty; negligent **2** lacking in energy; dilatory [c15: from Latin *remissus* from *remittere* to release, from RE- + *mittere* to send] > re'missly *adv* > re'missness *n*

remissible (rɪ'mɪsəbᵊl) *adj* able to be remitted [c16: from Latin *remissibilis*; see REMIT] > reˌmissi'bility, re'missibleness *n*

remission (rɪ'mɪʃən) or less commonly **remittal** (rɪ'mɪtᵊl) *n* **1** the act of remitting or state of being remitted **2** a reduction of the term of a sentence of imprisonment, as for good conduct **3** forgiveness for sin **4** discharge or release from penalty, obligation, etc **5** lessening of intensity; abatement, as in the severity of symptoms of a disease > re'missive *adj* > re'missively *adv*

remit (rɪ'mɪt) -mits, -mitting, -mitted **1** (*also intr*) to send (money, payment, etc), as for goods or service, esp by post **2** *law* (esp of an appeal court) to send back (a case or proceeding) to an inferior court for further consideration or action **3** to cancel or refrain

from exacting (a penalty or punishment) **4** (*also intr*) to relax (pace, intensity, etc) or (of pace or the like) to slacken or abate **5** to postpone; defer **6** *archaic* to pardon or forgive (crime, sins, etc) ▷ *n* ('riːmɪt, rɪ'mɪt) **7** the area of authority or responsibility of an individual or a group **8** *law* the transfer of a case from one court or jurisdiction to another, esp from an appeal court to an inferior tribunal **9** the act of remitting [c14: from Latin *remittere* to send back, release, RE- + *mittere* to send] > re'mittable *adj* > re'mitter *n*

remittance (rɪ'mɪtəns) *n* **1** payment for goods or services received or as an allowance, esp when sent by post **2** the act of remitting

remittance man *n* a man living abroad on money sent from home, esp in the days of the British Empire

remittent (rɪ'mɪtᵊnt) *adj* (of a fever or the symptoms of a disease) characterized by periods of diminished severity > re'mittence *or* re'mittency *n* > re'mittently *adv*

remix *vb* (riː'mɪks) **1** to change the balance and separation of (a recording), usually to emphasize the rhythm section ▷ *n* ('riːˌmɪks) **2** a remixed version of a recording

remnant ('rɛmnənt) *n* **1** (*often plural*) a part left over after use, processing, etc **2** a surviving trace or vestige, as of a former era: *a remnant of imperialism* **3** a piece of material from the end of a roll, sold at a lower price ▷ *adj* **4** remaining; left over [c14: from Old French *remenant* remaining, from *remanoir* to remain]

remonetize *or* **remonetise** (riː'mʌnɪˌtaɪz) *vb* (*tr*) to reinstate as legal tender: *to remonetize silver* > reˌmoneti'zation *or* reˌmoneti'sation *n*

remonstrance (rɪ'mɒnstrəns) *n* **1** the act of remonstrating; protestation **2** a protest or reproof, esp a petition presented in protest against something

remonstrant (rɪ'mɒnstrənt) *n* **1** a person who remonstrates, esp one who signs a remonstrance ▷ *adj* **2** *rare* remonstrating or protesting

remonstrate ('rɛmənˌstreɪt) *vb* (*intr*)(usually foll by *with*, *against*, etc) to argue in protest or objection: *to remonstrate with the government* [c16: from Medieval Latin *remonstrāre* to point out (errors), from Latin RE- + *monstrāre* to show] > ˌremon'stration *n* > remonstrative (rɪ'mɒnstrətɪv) *adj* > 'remonˌstrator *n*

remontant (rɪ'mɒntənt) *adj* **1** (esp of cultivated roses) flowering more than once in a single season ▷ *n* **2** a rose having such a growth [c19: from French: coming up again, from *remonter*; see REMOUNT]

remora ('rɛmərə) *n* any of the marine spiny-finned fishes constituting the family *Echeneidae*. They have a flattened elongated body and attach themselves to larger fish, rocks, etc, by a sucking disc on the top of the head [c16: from Latin, from RE- + *mora* delay; an allusion to its alleged habit of delaying ships]

remorse (rɪ'mɔːs) *n* **1** a sense of deep regret and guilt for some misdeed **2** compunction; pity; compassion [c14: from Medieval Latin *remorsus* a gnawing, from Latin *remordēre* to bite again, from RE- + *mordēre* to bite] > re'morseful *adj* > re'morsefully *adv* > re'morsefulness *n* > re'morseless *adj*

remote (rɪ'məʊt) *adj* **1** located far away; distant **2** far from any centre of population, society, or civilization; out-of-the-way **3** distant in time **4** distantly related or connected: *a remote cousin* **5** slight or faint (esp in the phrases **not the remotest idea**, **a remote chance**) **6** (of a person's manner) aloof or abstracted [c15: from Latin *remōtus* far removed, from *removēre*, from RE- + *movēre* to move] > re'motely *adv* > re'moteness *n*

remote access *n computing* access to a computer from a physically separate terminal

remote control *n* control of a system or activity by a person at a different place, usually by means of radio or ultrasonic signals or by electrical signals transmitted by wire > re'mote-con'trolled *adj*

remote sensor *n* any instrument, such as a radar device or camera, that scans the earth or another planet from space in order to collect data about some aspect of it

rémoulade (ˌrɛmə'leɪd; *French* remulad) *n* a mayonnaise sauce flavoured with herbs, mustard, and capers, served with salads, cold meat, etc [c19: from French, from

Picard dialect *ramolas* horseradish, from Latin *armoracea*]

remould *vb* (riːˈməʊld) (*tr*) **1** to mould again **2** to bond a new tread onto the casing of (a worn pneumatic tyre) ▷ *n* (ˈriːˌməʊld) **3** a tyre made by this process

remount *vb* (riːˈmaʊnt) **1** to get on (a horse, bicycle, etc) again **2** (*tr*) to mount (a picture, jewel, exhibit, etc) again ▷ *n* (ˈriːˌmaʊnt) **3** a fresh horse, esp (formerly) to replace one killed or injured in battle

removal (rɪˈmuːvəl) *n* **1** the act of removing or state of being removed **2 a** a change of residence **b** (*as modifier*): *a removal company* **3** dismissal from office **4** *South African* the forced displacement of a community for political or social reasons

removalist (rɪˈmuːvəlɪst) *n* *Austral* a person or company that transports household effects to a new home

remove (rɪˈmuːv) *vb* (*mainly tr*) **1** to take away and place elsewhere **2** to displace (someone) from office; dismiss **3** to do away with (a grievance, cause of anxiety, etc); abolish **4** *euphemistic* to assassinate; kill **5** (*intr*) *formal* to change the location of one's home or place of business ▷ *n* **6** the act of removing, esp (formal) a removal of one's residence or place of work **7** the degree of difference separating one person, thing, or condition from another: *only one remove from madness* **8** *Brit* (in certain schools) a class or form, esp one for children of about 14 years, designed to introduce them to the greater responsibilities of a more senior position in the school [C14: from Old French *removoir*, from Latin *removēre*; see MOVE] ▷ re'**movable** *adj* ▷ re,**mova'bility** *or* re'**movableness** *n* ▷ re'**mover** *n*

removed (rɪˈmuːvd) *adj* **1** separated by distance or abstract distinction **2** (*postpositive*) separated by a degree of descent or kinship: *the child of a person's first cousin is his first cousin once removed*

Remscheid (*German* ˈrɛmʃait) *n* an industrial city in W Germany, in North Rhine-Westphalia. Pop: 117 717 (2003 est)

remunerate (rɪˈmjuːnəˌreɪt) *vb* (*tr*) to reward or pay for work, service, etc [C16: from Latin *remūnerārī* to reward, from RE- + *mūnerāre* to give, from *mūnus* a gift; see MUNIFICENT] ▷ re'**munerable** *adj* ▷ re'**munerative** *adj* ▷ re'**muneratively** *adv* ▷ re'**munerativeness** *n* ▷ re'**muner,ator** *n*

remuneration (rɪˌmjuːnəˈreɪʃən) *n* **1** the act of remunerating **2** pay; recompense

Remus (ˈriːməs) *n* *Roman myth* the brother of Romulus

renaissance (rəˈneɪsəns; *US* ˈrɛnəˌsɒns) *or* **renascence** *n* a revival or rebirth, esp of culture and learning [C19: from French, from Latin RE- + *nāscī* to be born]

Renaissance (rəˈneɪsəns; *US* ˈrɛnəˌsɒns) *n* **1** the Renaissance the period of European history marking the waning of the Middle Ages and the rise of the modern world: usually considered as beginning in Italy in the 14th century ▷ the spirit, culture, art, science, and thought of this period. Characteristics of the Renaissance are usually considered to include intensified classical scholarship, scientific and geographical discovery, a sense of individual human potentialities, and the assertion of the active and secular over the religious and contemplative life ▷ *adj* **3** of, characteristic of, or relating to the Renaissance, its culture, etc

renal (ˈriːnəl) *adj* of, relating to, resembling, or situated near the kidney [C17: from French, from Late Latin *rēnālis*, from Latin *rēnēs* kidneys, of obscure origin]

renal pelvis *n* a small funnel-shaped cavity of the kidney into which urine is discharged before passing into the ureter

Renan (*French* ranɑ̃) *n* (**Joseph**) **Ernest** (ernest). 1823–92, French philosopher, theologian, and historian; best known for his *Life of Jesus* (1863), which discounted the supernatural aspects of the Gospels

renascent (rɪˈnæsənt, -ˈneɪ-) *adj* becoming active or vigorous again; reviving: *renascent nationalism* [C18: from Latin *renascī* to be born again]

rencounter (rɛnˈkaʊntə) *archaic* Also: **rencontre** (rɛnˈkɒntə) ▷ *n* **1** an unexpected meeting **2** a hostile clash, as of two armies, adversaries, etc; skirmish ▷ *vb* **3** to meet (someone) unexpectedly [C16: from French

rencontre, from *rencontrer*; see ENCOUNTER]

rend (rɛnd) *vb* **rends**, **rending**, **rent 1** to tear with violent force or to be torn in this way; rip **2** (*tr*) to tear or pull (one's clothes, etc), esp as a manifestation of rage or grief **3** (*tr*) (of a noise or cry) to disturb (the air, silence, etc) with a shrill or piercing tone [Old English *rendan*; related to Old Frisian *renda*] ▷ '**rendible** *adj*

Rendell (ˈrɛndəl, rɛnˈdɛl) *n* **Ruth** (**Barbara**), Baroness. born 1930, British crime writer: author of detective novels, such as *Wolf to the Slaughter* (1967), and psychological thrillers, such as *The Lake of Darkness* (1980) and (under the name **Barbara Vine**) *A Fatal Inversion* (1987) and *The Chimney Sweeper's Boy* (1998)

render (ˈrɛndə) *vb* (*tr*) **1** to present or submit (accounts, etc) for payment, approval, or action **2** to give or provide (aid, charity, a service, etc) **3** to show (obedience), as due or expected **4** to give or exchange, as by way of return or requital: *to render blow for blow* **5** to cause to become: *grief had rendered him simple-minded* **6** to deliver (a verdict or opinion) formally **7** to portray or depict (something), as in painting, music, or acting **8** to translate (something) into another language or form **9** (sometimes foll by *up*) to yield or give: *the tomb rendered up its secret* **10** (often foll by *back*) to return (something); give back **11** to cover the surface of (brickwork, stone, etc) with a coat of plaster **12** (often foll by *down*) to extract (fat) from (meat) by melting ▷ *n* **13** a first thin coat of plaster applied to a surface [C14: from Old French *rendre*, from Latin *reddere* to give back (influenced by Latin *prendere* to grasp), from RE- + *dare* to give] ▷ '**renderable** *adj* ▷ '**renderer** *n*

rendezvous (ˈrɒndɪˌvuː) *n*, *pl* **-vous** (-ˌvuːz) **1** a meeting or appointment to meet at a specified time and place **2** a place where people meet ▷ *vb* **3** to meet or cause to meet at a specified time or place [C16: from French, from *rendez-vous!* present yourselves! from *se rendre* to present oneself; see RENDER]

rendition (rɛnˈdɪʃən) *n* **1** a performance of a musical composition, dramatic role, etc **2** a translation of a text **3** the act of rendering [C17: from obsolete French, from Late Latin *redditiō* see RENDER]

renegade (ˈrɛnɪˌgeɪd) *n* **a** a person who deserts his cause or faith for another; apostate; traitor **b** (*as modifier*): *a renegade priest* [C16: from Spanish *renegado*, from Medieval Latin *renegāre* to renounce, from Latin RE- + *negāre* to deny]

renege *or* **renegue** (rɪˈniːg, -ˈneɪg) *vb* **1** (*intr*; often foll by *on*) to go back (on one's promise, etc) ▷ *vb*, *n* **2** *cards* other words for **revoke** [C16 (in the sense: to deny, renounce): from Medieval Latin *renegāre* to renounce; see RENEGADE]

renew (rɪˈnjuː) *vb* (*mainly tr*) **1** to take up again (*also intr*) to begin (an activity) again; recommence **3** to restate or reaffirm (a promise, etc) **4** (*also intr*) to make (a lease, licence, or contract) valid or effective for a further period **5** to regain or recover (vigour, strength, activity, etc) **6** to restore to a new or fresh condition **7** to replace (an old or worn-out part or piece) **8** to replenish (a supply, etc) ▷ re'**newable** *adj* ▷ re'**newal** *n* ▷ re'**newer** *n*

renewable energy *n* another name for **alternative energy**

renewables *pl n* sources of alternative energy, such as wind and wave power

Renfrew (ˈrɛnfruː) *n* an industrial town in W central Scotland, in Renfrewshire, W of Glasgow. Pop: 20 251 (2001)

Renfrewshire (ˈrɛnfruːʃɪə, -ʃə) *n* **1** a council area of W central Scotland, on the River Clyde W of Glasgow: corresponds to part of the historical county of Renfrewshire; part of Strathclyde region from 1975 to 1996: agricultural and residential, with clothing and manufacturing industries in Paisley. Administrative centre: Paisley. Pop: 170 980 (2003 est). Area: 261 sq km (101 sq miles) **2** a former county of W central Scotland, on the Firth of Clyde: became part of Strathclyde region in 1975; now covered by the council areas of Renfrewshire, East Renfrewshire, and Inverclyde

Reni (*Italian* ˈrɛːni) *n* **Guido** (ˈgwiːdo). 1575–1642, Italian baroque painter and engraver

reni- *combining form* kidney or kidneys: *reniform* [from Latin *rēnēs*]

reniform ('rɛnɪˌfɔːm) *adj* having the shape or profile of a kidney: *a reniform leaf; a reniform mass of haematite*

renin ('riːnɪn) *n* a proteolytic enzyme secreted by the kidneys, which plays an important part in the maintenance of blood pressure [C20: from RENI- + -IN]

Rennes (*French* rɛn) *n* a city in NW France: the ancient capital of Brittany. Pop: 206 229 (1999)

rennet ('rɛnɪt) *n* **1 a** the membrane lining the fourth stomach (abomasum) of a young calf **b** the stomach of certain other young animals **2 a** substance, containing the enzyme rennin, prepared esp from the stomachs of calves and used for curdling milk in making cheese and junket [C15: related to Old English *gerinnan* to curdle, RUN]

Rennie ('rɛnɪ) *n* **John.** 1761–1821, British civil engineer who designed bridges, canals, docks, and harbours, including three London bridges and the London and East India docks

rennin ('rɛnɪn) *n* an enzyme that occurs in gastric juice and is a constituent of rennet. It coagulates milk by converting caseinogen to casein. Also called: chymosin [C20: from RENNET + -IN]

Reno ('riːnəʊ) *n* a city in W Nevada, at the foot of the Sierra Nevada: noted as a divorce, wedding, and gambling centre by reason of its liberal laws. Pop: 193 882 (2003 est)

Renoir ('rɛnwɑː; *French* rənwar) *n* **1 Jean** (ʒã). 1894–1979, French film director: his films include *La grande illusion* (1937), *La règle du jeu* (1939), and *Diary of a Chambermaid* (1945) **2** his father, **Pierre Auguste** (pjɛr ogyst). 1841–1919, French painter. One of the initiators of impressionism, he broke away from the movement with his later paintings, esp his many nude studies, which are more formal compositions

renounce (rɪ'naʊns) *vb* **1** (tr) to give up (a claim or right), esp by formal announcement: *to renounce a title* **2** (tr) to repudiate: *to renounce Christianity* **3** (tr) to give up (some habit, pursuit, etc) voluntarily: *to renounce smoking* **4** (intr) *cards* to fail to follow suit because one has no cards of the suit led ▷ *n* **5** *rare* a failure to follow suit in a card game [C14: from Old French *renoncer*, from Latin *renuntiāre* to disclaim, from RE- + *nuntiāre* to announce, from *nuntius* messenger] > re'nouncement *n* > re'nouncer *n*

renovate ('rɛnəˌveɪt) *vb* (tr) **1** to restore (something) to good condition **2** to revive or refresh (one's spirits, health, etc) [C16: from Latin *renovāre*, from RE- + *novāre* to make new, from *novus* NEW] > ˌreno'vation *n* > 'reno,vative *adj* > 'reno,vator *n*

renown (rɪ'naʊn) *n* widespread reputation, esp of a good kind; fame [C14: from Anglo-Norman *renoun*, from Old French *renom*, from *renomer* to celebrate, from RE- + *nomer* to name, from Latin *nōmināre*]

renowned (rɪ'naʊnd) *adj* having a widespread, esp good, reputation; famous

rent¹ (rɛnt) *n* **1 a** a payment made periodically by a tenant to a landlord or owner for the occupation or use of land, buildings, or by a user for the use of other property, such as a telephone **2** *economics* the return derived from the cultivation of land in excess of production costs **3 for rent** *chiefly US & Canadian* available for use and occupation subject to the payment of rent ▷ *vb* **4** (tr) to grant (a person) the right to use one's property in return for periodic payments **5** (tr) to occupy or use (property) in return for periodic payments **6** (intr; often foll by *at*) to be let or rented (for a specified rental) [C12: from Old French *rente* revenue, from Vulgar Latin *rendere* (unattested) to yield; see RENDER] > 'rentable *adj*

rent² (rɛnt) *n* **1 a** slit or opening made by tearing or rending; tear **2** a breach or division, as in relations ▷ *vb* **3** the past tense and past participle of **rend** > 'renter *n*

rent-a- *prefix* **1** denoting a rental service **2** *derogatory or facetious* denoting a person or group that performs a function as if hired from a rental service: *rent-a-mob*

rental ('rɛntᵊl) *n* **1 a** the amount paid by a tenant as rent **b** the amount paid by a user for the use of property **c** an income derived from rents received **2** property available for renting ▷ *adj* **3** of or relating to rent or renting

rent boy *n* a young male prostitute

rent control *n* regulation by law of the rent a landlord can charge for domestic accommodation and of his right to evict tenants

rent-free *adj, adv* without payment of rent

rentier *French* (rɑ̃tje) *n* a person whose income consists primarily of fixed unearned amounts, such as rent or bond interest [from *rente*; see RENT¹]

rent-roll *n* **1** a register of lands and buildings owned by a person, company, etc, showing the rent due and total amount received from each tenant **2** the total income arising from rented property

renunciation (rɪˌnʌnsɪ'eɪʃən) *n* **1** the act or an instance of renouncing **2** a formal declaration renouncing something **3** *stock exchange* the surrender to another of the rights to buy new shares in a rights issue [C14: from Latin *renunciātiō* a declaration, from *renuntiāre* to report, RENOUNCE] > re'nunciative *or* re'nunciatory *adj*

reo ('riːəʊ) *n* NZ a language [Māori]

reoffend ('riːəˌfɛnd) *vb* (intr) to commit another offence > 'reof,fender *n*

rep¹ *or* **repp** (rɛp) *n* a silk, wool, rayon, or cotton fabric with a transversely corded surface [C19: from French *reps*, perhaps from English *ribs*; see RIB¹] > repped *adj*

rep² (rɛp) *n* *theatre* short for **repertory company**

rep³ (rɛp) *n* short for **representative** (sense 2)

rep⁴ (rɛp) *n* *informal* short for **reputation**

Rep. *abbreviation* **1** US Representative **2** US Republican **3** Republic

repair¹ (rɪ'pɛə) *vb* (tr) **1** to restore (something damaged or broken) to good condition or working order **2** to heal (a breach or division) in (something): *to repair a broken marriage* **3** to make good or make amends for (a mistake, injury, etc) ▷ *n* **4** the act, task, or process of repairing **5** a part that has been repaired **6** state or condition: *in good repair* [C14: from Old French *reparer*, from Latin *reparāre*, from RE- + *parāre* to make ready] > re'pairable *adj* > re'pairer *n*

repair² (rɪ'pɛə) *vb* (intr) **1** (usually foll by *to*) to go (to a place) **2** (usually foll by *to*) to have recourse (to) for help, etc: *to repair to one's lawyer* ▷ *n* **3** *archaic* a haunt or resort [C14: from Old French *repairier*, from Late Latin *repatriāre* to return to one's native land, from Latin RE- + *patria* fatherland; compare REPATRIATE]

repairman (rɪ'pɛəˌmæn) *n, pl* -men a man whose job it is to repair machines, appliances, etc

repand (rɪ'pænd) *adj* *botany* having a wavy margin: *a repand leaf* [C18: from Latin *repandus* bent backwards, from RE- + *pandus* curved] > re'pandly *adv*

reparable ('rɛpərəbᵊl, 'rɛprə-) *adj* able to be repaired, recovered, or remedied: *a reparable loss* [C16: from Latin *reparābilis*, from *reparāre* to REPAIR¹] > 'reparably *adv*

reparation (ˌrɛpə'reɪʃən) *n* **1** the act or process of making amends **2** (*usually plural*) compensation exacted as an indemnity from a defeated nation by the victors: esp the compensation demanded by the Treaty of Versailles after World War I **3** the act or process of repairing or state of having been repaired [C14 *reparacioun*, ultimately from Latin *reparāre* to REPAIR¹] > reparative (rɪ'pærətɪv) *or* re'paratory *adj*

repartee (ˌrɛpɑː'tiː) *n* **1** a sharp, witty, or aphoristic remark made as a reply **2** skill in making sharp witty replies or conversation [C17: from French *repartie*, from *repartir* to retort, from RE- + *partir* to go away]

repast (rɪ'pɑːst) *n* a meal or the food provided at a meal: *a light repast* [C14: from Old French, from *repaistre* to feed, from Late Latin *repāscere* to nourish again, from Latin RE- + *pāscere* to feed, pasture (of animals)]

repatriate *vb* (riː'pætrɪˌeɪt) (tr) **1** to send back (a refugee, prisoner of war, etc) to the country of his birth or citizenship **2** to send back (a sum of money previously invested abroad) to its country of origin ▷ *n* (riː'pætrɪɪt) **3** a person who has been repatriated [C17: from Late Latin *repatriāre* from Latin RE- + *patria* fatherland; compare REPAIR²] > re,patri'ation *n*

repay (rɪ'peɪ) *vb* -pays, -paying, -paid **1** to pay back (money) to (a person); refund or reimburse **2** to make a return for (something) by way of compensation: *to repay kindness* > re'payable *adj* > re'payment *n*

repeal (rɪ'piːl) *vb* (tr) **1** to annul or rescind officially (something previously ordered); revoke: *these laws were* repealed ▷ n 2 an instance or the process of repealing; annulment [c14: from Old French *repeler*, from RE- + *apeler* to call, APPEAL] > re'**pealable** adj > re'**pealer** n

repeat (rɪ'piːt) vb 1 to do or experience (something) again once or several times 2 (*intr*) to occur more than once: *the last figure repeats* 3 (*tr; may take a clause as object*) to reproduce (the words, sounds, etc) uttered by someone else; echo 4 (*tr*) to utter (a poem, speech, etc) from memory; recite 5 (*intr*) **a** (of food) to be tasted again after ingestion as the result of belching or slight regurgitation **b** to belch 6 (*tr; may take a clause as object*) to tell to another person (the words, esp secrets, imparted to one by someone else) 7 (*intr*) (of a clock) to strike the hour or quarter-hour just past, when a spring is pressed 8 (*intr*) US to vote (illegally) more than once in a single election 9 **repeat oneself** to say or do the same thing more than once, esp so as to be tedious ▷ n 10 **a** the act or an instance of repeating **b** (*as modifier*): *a repeat performance* 11 a word, action, etc, that is repeated 12 an order made out for goods, provisions, etc, that duplicates a previous order 13 *radio, television* a further broadcast of a programme, film, etc, which has been broadcast before 14 *music* a passage that is an exact restatement of the passage preceding it [c14: from Old French *repeter*, from Latin *repetere* to seek again, from RE- + *petere* to seek] > re'**peatable** adj

● USAGE Since *again* is part of the meaning of *repeat*, one
● should not say something is *repeated again*

repeated (rɪ'piːtɪd) adj done, made, or said again and again; continual or incessant > re'**peatedly** adv

repeater (rɪ'piːtə) n 1 a person or thing that repeats 2 Also called: **repeating firearm** a firearm capable of discharging several shots without reloading 3 a timepiece having a mechanism enabling it to strike the hour or quarter-hour just past, when a spring is pressed 4 *electrical engineering* a device that amplifies or augments incoming electrical signals and retransmits them, thus compensating for transmission losses 5 Also called: **substitute** *nautical* one of three signal flags hoisted with others to indicate that one of the top three is to be repeated

repeating decimal n another name for **recurring decimal**

repechage (ˌrɛpɪ'ʃɑːʒ) n a heat of a competition, esp in rowing or fencing, in which eliminated contestants have another chance to qualify for the next round or the final [c19: from French *repêchage* literally: fishing out again, from RE- + *pêcher* to fish + -AGE]

repel (rɪ'pɛl) vb -**pels**, -**pelling**, -**pelled** (*mainly tr*) 1 to force or drive back (something or somebody, esp an attacker) 2 (*also intr*) to produce a feeling of aversion or distaste in (someone or something); be disgusting (to) 3 to be effective in keeping away, controlling, or resisting: *an aerosol spray that repels flies* 4 to have no affinity for; fail to mix with or absorb: *water and oil repel each other* 5 to disdain to accept (something); turn away from or spurn: *she repelled his advances* [c15: from Latin *repellere*, from RE- + *pellere* to push, drive] > re'**peller** n

● USAGE See at **repulse**

repellent (rɪ'pɛlənt) adj 1 giving rise to disgust or aversion; distasteful or repulsive 2 driving or forcing away or back; repelling ▷ n Also: **repellant** 3 something, esp a chemical substance, that repels: *insect repellent* 4 a substance with which fabrics are treated to increase their resistance to water > re'**pellence** or re'**pellency** n > re'**pellently** adv

repent¹ (rɪ'pɛnt) vb to feel remorse (for); be contrite (about); show penitence (for) [c13: from Old French *repentir* from RE- + *pentir* to be contrite, from Latin *paenitēre* to repent] > re'**penter** n

repent² ('riːpᵊnt) adj *botany* lying or creeping along the ground; reptant: *repent stems* [c17: from Latin *rēpere* to creep]

repentance (rɪ'pɛntəns) n 1 remorse or contrition for one's past actions or sins 2 an act or the process of being repentant; penitence > re'**pentant** adj > re'**pentantly** adv

repercussion (ˌriːpə'kʌʃən) n 1 (*often plural*) a result or consequence, esp one that is somewhat removed from the action or event which precipitated it: *the repercussions*

of the war are still keenly felt 2 a recoil after impact; a rebound 3 a reflection, esp of sound; echo or reverberation [c16: from Latin *repercussiō*, from *repercutere* to strike back; see PERCUSSION] > ˌreper'**cussive** adj

repertoire ('rɛpəˌtwɑː) n 1 all the plays, songs, operas, or other works collectively that a company, actor, singer, dancer, etc, has prepared and is competent to perform 2 the entire stock of things available in a field or of a kind 3 **in repertoire** denoting the performance of two or more plays, ballets, etc, by the same company in the same venue on different evenings over a period of time: *"Nutcracker" returns to Covent Garden over Christmas in repertoire with "Giselle"* [c19: from French, from Late Latin *repertōrium* inventory; see REPERTORY]

repertory ('rɛpətərɪ, -trɪ) n, pl -ries 1 the entire stock of things available in a field or of a kind; repertoire 2 a building or place where a stock of things is kept; repository 3 short for **repertory company** [c16: from Late Latin *repertōrium* storehouse, from Latin *reperīre* to obtain, from RE- + *parere* to bring forth] > ˌreper'**torial** adj

repertory company n a theatrical company that performs plays from a repertoire, esp at its own theatre

repetend ('rɛpɪˌtɛnd, ˌrɛpɪ'tɛnd) n 1 *maths* the digit or series of digits in a recurring decimal that repeats itself 2 anything repeated [c18: from Latin *repetendum* what is to be repeated, from *repetere* to REPEAT]

répétiteur *French* (repetitœr) n a member of an opera company who accompanies rehearsals on the piano and coaches the singers > **répétiteuse** (repetitøz) *fem* n

repetition (ˌrɛpɪ'tɪʃən) n 1 the act or an instance of repeating; reiteration 2 a thing, word, action, etc, that is repeated 3 a replica or copy

repetitious (ˌrɛpɪ'tɪʃəs) adj characterized by unnecessary repetition > ˌrepe'**titiously** adv > ˌrepe'**titiousness** n

repetitive (rɪ'pɛtɪtɪv) adj characterized by or given to unnecessary repetition; boring: *dull, repetitive work* > re'**petitively** adv > re'**petitiveness** n

repetitive strain injury or **repetitive stress injury** n a condition, characterized by arm or wrist pains, that can affect musicians, computer operators, etc, who habitually perform awkward hand movements. Abbreviation: RSI

repine (rɪ'paɪn) vb (*intr*) to be fretful or low-spirited through discontent [c16: from RE- + PINE²]

replace (rɪ'pleɪs) vb (*tr*) 1 to take the place of; supersede 2 to substitute a person or thing for (another which has ceased to fulfil its function); put in place of: *to replace an old pair of shoes* 3 to put back or return; restore to its rightful place > re'**placeable** adj > reˌplacea'**bility** n > re'**placer** n

replacement (rɪ'pleɪsmənt) n 1 the act or process of replacing 2 a person or thing that replaces another

replay n ('riːˌpleɪ) 1 Also called: **action replay** *television* a showing again of a sequence of action, esp of part of a sporting contest immediately after it happens either in slow motion (a **slow-motion replay**) or at normal speed 2 a rematch ▷ vb (riː'pleɪ) 3 to play again (a record, television sequence, sporting contest, etc)

replenish (rɪ'plɛnɪʃ) vb (*tr*) 1 to make full or complete again by supplying what has been used up or is lacking 2 to put fresh fuel on (a fire) [c14: from Old French *replenir*, from RE- + *plenir* to fill, from Latin *plēnus* full] > re'**plenisher** n > re'**plenishment** n

replete (rɪ'pliːt) adj (*usually postpositive*) 1 (*often foll by with*) copiously supplied (with); abounding (in) 2 having one's appetite completely or excessively satisfied by food and drink; stuffed; gorged; satiated [c14: from Latin *replētus*, from *replēre* to refill, from RE- + *plēre* to fill] > re'**pletely** adv > re'**pleteness** n > re'**pletion** n

replevin (rɪ'plɛvɪn) *law* ▷ n 1 the recovery of goods unlawfully taken, made subject to establishing the validity of the recovery in a legal action and returning the goods if the decision is adverse 2 (*formerly*) a writ of replevin ▷ vb 3 another word for **replevy** [c15: from Anglo-French *replevir*, from Old French *replevir* to give security for, from RE- + *plevir* to PLEDGE]

replevy (rɪ'plɛvɪ) *law* ▷ vb -**plevies**, -**plevying**, -**plevied** (*tr*) 1 to recover possession of (goods) by replevin ▷ n, pl -**plevies** 2 another word for **replevin** [c15: from Old

French *replevir*; see REPLEVIN] >re'pleviable *or*
re'plevisable *adj*

replica ('rɛplɪkə) *n* an exact copy or reproduction, esp on
a smaller scale [C19: from Italian, literally: a reply, from
replicare to repeat, from Latin: to bend back, repeat]

replicate ('rɛplɪˌkeɪt) *vb* (*mainly tr*) **1** (*also intr*) to make or
be a copy of; reproduce **2** to fold (something) over on
itself; bend back *adj* ('rɛplɪkɪt) **3** folded back on itself: *a
replicate leaf* [C19: from Latin *replicātus* bent back; see
REPLICA] >'repli·cation *n* >'replicative *adj*

reply (rɪ'plaɪ) *vb* -plies, -plying, -plied (*mainly intr*) **1** to
make answer (to) in words or writing or by an action;
respond **2** (*tr; takes a clause as object*) to say (something) in
answer: *he replied that he didn't want to come* **3** *law* to
answer a defendant's plea **4** to return (a sound); echo
▷ *n, pl* -plies **5** an answer made in words or writing or
through an action; response **6** the answer made by a
plaintiff or petitioner to a defendant's case [C14: from
Old French *replier* to fold again, reply, from Latin *replicāre*
to fold back, from RE- + *plicāre* to fold] >re'plier *n*

repo ('riːpəʊ) *n informal* short for **1** repurchase
agreement **2** a repossession of property **b** (*as modifier*): *a
repo car*

repoint (ˌriː'pɔɪnt) *vb* (*tr*) to repair the joints of
(brickwork, masonry, etc) with mortar or cement

report (rɪ'pɔːt) *n* **1** an account prepared for the benefit of
others, esp one that provides information obtained
through investigation and published in a newspaper or
broadcast **2** a statement made widely known; rumour:
according to report, he is not dead **3** an account of the
deliberations of a committee, body, etc: *a report of
parliamentary proceedings* **4** *Brit* a statement on the
progress, academic achievement, etc, of each child in a
school, written by teachers and sent to the parents or
guardian annually or each term **5** a written account of a
case decided at law, giving the main points of the
argument on each side, the court's findings, and the
decision reached **6** comment on a person's character or
actions; reputation: *he is of good report here* **7** a sharp loud
noise, esp one made by a gun ▷ *vb* (*when tr, may take a
clause as object; when intr, often foll by on*) **8** to give an
account (of); describe **9** to give an account of the results
of an investigation (into): *to report on housing conditions*
10 (of a committee, legislative body, etc) to make a
formal report on (a bill) **11** (*tr*) to complain about (a
person), esp to a superior **12** (*tr*) to reveal information
about (a fugitive, escaped prisoner, etc) esp concerning
his whereabouts **13** (*intr*) to present oneself or be present
at an appointed place or for a specific purpose: *report to
the manager's office* **14** (*intr*) to say or show that one is (in a
certain state): *to report fit* **15** (*intr; foll by to*) to be
responsible to and under the authority of **16** (*intr*) to act
as a reporter for a newspaper or for radio or television
17 *law* to take down in writing details of (the
proceedings of a court of law) as a record or for
publication [C14: from Old French, from *reporter* to carry
back, from Latin *reportāre*, from RE- + *portāre* to carry]
>re'portable *adj* >re'portedly *adv*

reportage (rɪ'pɔːtɪdʒ, ˌrəpɔː'tɑːʒ) *n* **1** the act or process of
reporting news or other events of general interest **2** a
journalist's style of reporting

reported speech *n* another term for **indirect speech**

reporter (rɪ'pɔːtə) *n* **1** a person who reports, esp one
employed to gather news for a newspaper, news agency,
or broadcasting organization **2** a person authorized to
report the proceedings of a legislature

reporter gene *n* a gene with an easily recognizable
phenotype, used in analysing the regulation of gene
structures

report stage *n* the stage preceding the third reading in
the passage of a bill through Parliament, at which the
bill, as amended in committee, is reported back to the
chamber considering it

repose¹ (rɪ'pəʊz) *n* **1** a state of quiet restfulness; peace or
tranquillity **2** dignified calmness of manner; composure
▷ *vb* **3** to place (oneself or one's body) in a state of quiet
relaxation; lie or lay down at rest **4** (*intr*) to lie when
dead, as in the grave **5** (*intr; foll by on, in, etc*) *formal* to
take support (from) or be based (on): *your plan reposes on a*

fallacy [C15: from Old French *reposer*, from Late Latin
repausāre from RE- + *pausāre* to stop; see PAUSE] >re'posal *n*
>re'poser *n* >re'poseful *adj* >re'posefully *adv*

repose² (rɪ'pəʊz) *vb* (*tr*) **1** to put (trust or confidence) in a
person or thing **2** to place or put (an object) somewhere
[C15: from Latin *repōnere* to store up, from RE- + *pōnere* to
put] >re'posal *n*

reposition (ˌriːpə'zɪʃən) *n* **1** the act or process of
depositing or storing ▷ *vb* (*tr*) **2** to place in a new
position **3** to target (a product or brand) at a new market
by changing its image

repository (rɪ'pɒzɪtərɪ, -trɪ) *n, pl* -ries **1** a place or
container in which things can be stored for safety **2** a
place where things are kept for exhibition; museum **3** a
place of burial; sepulchre **4** a person to whom a secret is
entrusted; confidant [C15: from Latin *repositōrium*, from
repōnere to place]

repossess (ˌriːpə'zɛs) *vb* (*tr*) to take back possession of
(property), esp for nonpayment of money due under a
hire-purchase agreement >repossession (ˌriːpə'zɛʃən) *n*
>ˌrepos'sessor *n*

repoussé (rə'puːseɪ) *adj* **1** raised in relief, as a design on
a thin piece of metal hammered through from the
underside ▷ *n* **2** a design or surface made in this way
[C19: from French, from *repousser* to push back, from RE- +
pousser to PUSH]

repp (rɛp) *n* a variant spelling of **rep¹**

reprehend (ˌrɛprɪ'hɛnd) *vb* (*tr*) to find fault with;
criticize [C14: from Latin *reprehendere* to hold fast, rebuke,
from RE- + *prendere* to grasp] >ˌrepre'hender *n*
>reprehension (ˌrɛprɪ'hɛnʃən) *n* >ˌrepre'hensive *or rarely*
ˌrepre'hensory *adj* >ˌrepre'hensively *adv*

reprehensible (ˌrɛprɪ'hɛnsəb³l) *adj* open to criticism or
rebuke; blameworthy [C14: from Late Latin *reprehensibilis*,
from Latin *reprehendere* to hold back, reprove; see
REPREHEND] >ˌrepre,hensi'bility *or* ˌrepre'hensibleness *n*
>ˌrepre'hensibly *adv*

represent (ˌrɛprɪ'zɛnt) *vb* (*tr*) **1** to stand as an equivalent
of; correspond to **2** to act as a substitute or proxy (for)
3 to act as or be the authorized delegate or agent for (a
person, country, etc): *an MP represents his constituency* **4** to
serve or use as a means of expressing: *letters represent the
sounds of speech* **5** to exhibit the characteristics of;
exemplify; typify: *romanticism in music is represented by
Beethoven* **6** to present an image of through the medium
of a picture or sculpture; portray **7** to bring clearly
before the mind **8** to set forth in words; state or explain
9 to describe as having a specified character or quality;
make out to be: *he represented her as a saint* **10** to act out the
part of on stage; portray [C14: from Latin *repraesentāre* to
exhibit, from RE- + *praesentāre* to PRESENT²]
>ˌrepre'sentable *adj* >ˌrepre,senta'bility *n*

re-present (ˌriːprɪ'zɛnt) *vb* (*tr*) to present again >re-
presentation (ˌriːprɛzən'teɪʃən) *n*

representation (ˌrɛprɪzɛn'teɪʃən) *n* **1** the act or an
instance of representing or the state of being
represented **2** anything that represents, such as a verbal
or pictorial portrait **3** anything that is represented, such
as an image brought clearly to mind **4** the principle by
which delegates act for a constituency **5** a body of
representatives **6** an instance of acting for another, on
his authority, in a particular capacity, such as executor
or administrator **7** a dramatic production or
performance **8** (*often plural*) a statement of facts, true or
alleged, esp one set forth by way of remonstrance or
expostulation

representational (ˌrɛprɪzɛn'teɪʃən³l) *adj* **1** *fine arts*
depicting or attempting to depict objects, scenes,
figures, etc, directly as seen; naturalistic **2** of or relating
to representation

representationalism (ˌrɛprɪzɛn'teɪʃənəˌlɪzəm) *or*
representationism *n* **1** *philosophy* the doctrine that in
perceptions of objects what is before the mind is not the
object but a representation of it. Compare
presentationism 2 *fine arts* the practice or advocacy of
attempting to depict objects, scenes, figures, etc,
directly as seen >ˌrepresen,tational'istic *adj*
>ˌrepresen'tationist *n, adj*

representative (ˌrɛprɪ'zɛntətɪv) *n* **1** a person or thing that represents another or others **2** a person who represents and tries to sell the products or services of a firm, esp a travelling salesman **3** a typical example **4** a person representing a constituency in a deliberative, legislative, or executive body, esp (*cap*) a member of the House of Representatives (the lower house of Congress). See also **House of Representatives** ▷ *adj* **5** serving to represent; symbolic **6 a** exemplifying a class or kind; typical **b** containing or including examples of all the interests, types, etc, in a group **7** acting as deputy or proxy for another or others **8** acting for or representing a constituency or the whole people in the process of government: *a representative council* **9** of, characterized by, or relating to the political principle of representation of the people: *representative government* **10** of or relating to a mental picture or representation > ,repre'sentatively *adv* > ,repre'sentativeness *n*

repress (rɪ'prɛs) *vb* (*tr*) **1** to keep (feelings, etc) under control; suppress or restrain **2** to put into a state of subjugation: *to repress a people* **3** *psychoanal* to banish (thoughts and impulses that conflict with conventional standards of conduct) from one's conscious mind [c14: from Latin *reprimere* to press back, from RE- + *premere* to PRESS¹] > re'pressed *adj* > re'presser *n* > re'pressible *adj* > re'pression *n*

repressive (rɪ'prɛsɪv) re'pressive *adj* **1** acting to control, suppress, or restrain **2** subjecting people, a society, etc to a state of subjugation > re'pressively *adv* > re'pressiveness *n*

reprieve (rɪ'priːv) *vb* (*tr*) **1** to postpone or remit the punishment of (a person, esp one condemned to death) **2** to give temporary relief to (a person or thing), esp from otherwise irrevocable harm ▷ *n* **3** a postponement or remission of punishment, esp of a person condemned to death **4** a warrant granting a postponement **5** a temporary relief from pain or harm; respite [c16: from Old French *repris* (something) taken back, from *reprendre* to take back, from Latin *reprehendere*; perhaps also influenced by obsolete English *repreve* to reprove] > re'prievable *adj* > re'priever *n*

reprimand ('rɛprɪ,mɑːnd) *n* **1** a reproof or formal admonition; rebuke ▷ *vb* **2** (*tr*) to admonish or rebuke, esp formally; reprove [c17: from French *réprimande*, from Latin *reprimenda* (things) to be repressed; see REPRESS]

reprint *n* ('riː,prɪnt) **1** a reproduction in print of any matter already published; offprint **2** a reissue of a printed work using the same type, plates, etc, as the original ▷ *vb* (riː'prɪnt) **3** (*tr*) to print again > re'printer *n*

reprisal (rɪ'praɪzᵊl) *n* **1** (*often plural*) retaliatory action against an enemy in wartime, such as the execution of prisoners of war, destruction of property, etc **2** the act or an instance of retaliation in any form **3** (formerly) the forcible seizure of the property or subjects of one nation by another [c15: from Old French *reprisaille*, from Old Italian *ripresaglia*, from *riprendere* to recapture, from Latin *reprehendere* to hold fast; see REPREHEND]

reprise (rɪ'priːz) *music* ▷ *n* **1** the repeating of an earlier theme ▷ *vb* **2** to repeat (an earlier theme) [c14: from Old French, from *reprendre* to take back, from Latin *reprehendere*; see REPREHEND]

repro (rɪ'prəʊ) *n*, *pl* -**pros** **1** short for **reproduction** (sense 2) *repro furniture* **2** short for **reproduction proof**

reproach (rɪ'prəʊtʃ) *vb* (*tr*) **1** to impute blame to (a person) for an action or fault; rebuke ▷ *n* **2** the act of reproaching **3** rebuke or censure; reproof **4** disgrace or shame: *to bring reproach upon one's family* **5** above reproach *or* beyond reproach perfect; beyond criticism [c15: from Old French *reprochier*, from Latin RE- + *prope* near] > re'proachable *adj* > re'proachableness *n* > re'proachably *adv* > re'proacher *n*

reproachful (rɪ'prəʊtʃfʊl) *adj* **1** full of or expressing reproach **2** *archaic* deserving of reproach; disgraceful > re'proachfully *adv* > re'proachfulness *n*

reprobate ('rɛprəʊ,beɪt) *adj* **1** morally unprincipled; depraved **2** *Christianity* destined or condemned to eternal punishment in hell ▷ *n* **3** an unprincipled, depraved, or damned person **4** a disreputable or roguish person: *the old reprobate* ▷ *vb* (*tr*) **5** to disapprove of; condemn **6** (of God) to destine, consign, or condemn to eternal

punishment in hell [c16: from Late Latin *reprobātus* held in disfavour, from Latin RE- + *probāre* to APPROVE¹] > reprobacy ('rɛprəbəsɪ) *n* > 'repro,bater *n*

reprocess (riː'prəʊsɛs) *vb* (*tr*) to treat or prepare (something) by a special method again > re'processing *adj*

reproduce (,riːprə'djuːs) *vb* (*mainly tr*) **1** to make a copy, representation, or imitation of; duplicate **2** (*also intr*) *biology* to undergo or cause to undergo a process of reproduction **3** to produce or exhibit again **4** to bring back into existence again; re-create **5** to bring before the mind again (a scene, event, etc) through memory or imagination **6** (*intr*) to come out (well, badly, etc), when copied **7** to replace (damaged parts or organs) by a process of natural growth; regenerate **8** to cause (a sound or television recording) to be heard or seen > ,repro'ducible *adj* > ,repro'ducibly *adv* > ,repro,duci'bility *n*

reproduction (,riːprə'dʌkʃən) *n* **1** *biology* any of various processes, either sexual or asexual, by which an animal or plant produces one or more individuals similar to itself **2 a** an imitation or facsimile of a work of art, esp of a picture made by photoengraving **b** (*as modifier*): *a reproduction portrait*. Sometimes shortened to **repro 3** the quality of sound from an audio system: *this amplifier gives excellent reproduction* **4** the act or process of reproducing **5** the state of being reproduced **6** a revival of an earlier production, as of a play

reproduction proof *n* *printing* a proof of very good quality used for photographic reproduction to make a printing plate. Sometimes shortened to **repro**

reproductive (,riːprə'dʌktɪv) *adj* of, relating to, characteristic of, or taking part in reproduction > ,repro'ductively *adv* > ,repro'ductiveness *n*

reprography (rɪ'prɒɡrəfɪ) *n* the art or process of copying, reprinting, or reproducing printed material > reprographic (,rɛprə'ɡræfɪk) *adj* > ,repro'graphically *adv*

reproof (rɪ'pruːf) *n* an act or expression of rebuke or censure. Also: **reproval** (rɪ'pruːvᵊl) [c14: *reproffe*, from Old French *reprove*, from Late Latin *reprobāre* to disapprove of; see REPROBATE]

re-proof (riː'pruːf) *vb* (*tr*) **1** to treat (a coat, jacket, etc) so as to renew its texture, waterproof qualities, etc **2** to provide a new proof of (a book, galley, etc)

reprove (rɪ'pruːv) *vb* (*tr*) to speak disapprovingly to (a person); rebuke or scold [c14: from Old French *reprover*, from Late Latin *reprobāre*, from Latin RE- + *probāre* to examine, APPROVE] > re'provable *adj* > re'prover *n* > re'proving *adj* > re'provingly *adv*

reptant ('rɛptənt) *adj* *biology* creeping, crawling, or lying along the ground. Also: **repent** [c17: from Latin *reptāre* to creep]

reptile ('rɛptaɪl) *n* **1** any of the cold-blooded vertebrates constituting the class *Reptilia*, characterized by lungs, an outer covering of horny scales or plates, and young produced in amniotic eggs. The class today includes the tortoises, turtles, snakes, lizards, and crocodiles; in Mesozoic times it was the dominant group, containing the dinosaurs and related forms **2** a grovelling insignificant person: *you miserable little reptile!* ▷ *adj* **3** creeping, crawling, or squirming **4** grovelling or insignificant; mean; contemptible [c14: from Late Latin *reptilis* creeping, from Latin *rēpere* to crawl] > rep'tilian *adj*, *n*

Repton ('rɛptᵊn) *n* **Humphry**. 1752–1818, English landscape gardener

republic (rɪ'pʌblɪk) *n* **1** a form of government in which the people or their elected representatives possess the supreme power **2** a political or national unit possessing such a form of government **3** a constitutional form in which the head of state is an elected or nominated president **4** any community or group that resembles a political republic in that its members or elements exhibit a general equality, shared interests, etc: *the republic of letters* [c17: from French *république*, from Latin *rēspublica* literally: the public thing: from *rēs* thing + *publica* PUBLIC]

republican (rɪ'pʌblɪkən) *adj* **1** of, resembling, or relating to a republic **2** supporting or advocating a republic ▷ *n*

3 a supporter or advocate of a republic

Republican (rɪˈpʌblɪkən) *adj* **1** of, belonging to, or relating to a Republican Party **2** of, belonging to, or relating to the Irish Republican Army ▷ *n* **3** a member or supporter of a Republican Party **4** a member or supporter of the Irish Republican Army

republicanism (rɪˈpʌblɪkəˌnɪzəm) *n* **1** the principles or theory of republican government **2** support for a republic **3** (*often capital*) support for a Republican Party or for the Irish Republican Army

Republican Party *n* **1** the more conservative of the two major political parties in the US: established around 1854 **2** any of a number of political parties in other countries, usually so named to indicate their opposition to monarchy

Republic of Ireland *n* See **Ireland¹** (sense 2)

repudiate (rɪˈpjuːdɪˌeɪt) *vb* (*tr*) **1** to reject the authority or validity of; refuse to accept or ratify: *Congress repudiated the treaty that the President had negotiated* **2** to refuse to acknowledge or pay (a debt) **3** to cast off or disown (a son, lover, etc) [c16: from Latin *repudiāre* to put away, from *repudium* a separation, divorce, from RE- + *pudēre* to be ashamed] > reˈpudiable *adj* > reˌpudiˈation *n* > reˈpudiative *adj* > reˈpudiˌator *n*

repugn (rɪˈpjuːn) *vb archaic* to oppose or conflict (with) [c14: from Old French *repugner*, from Latin *repugnāre* to fight against, from RE- + *pugnāre* to fight]

repugnant (rɪˈpʌɡnənt) *adj* **1** repellent to the senses; causing aversion **2** distasteful; offensive; disgusting **3** contradictory; inconsistent or incompatible [c14: from Latin *repugnāns* resisting; see REPUGN] > reˈpugnance or *now rarely* repugnancy *n* > reˈpugnantly *adv*

repulse (rɪˈpʌls) *vb* (*tr*) **1** to drive back or ward off (an attacking force); repel; rebuff **2** to reject with coldness or discourtesy: *she repulsed his advances* **3** to produce a feeling of aversion or distaste ▷ *n* **4** the act or an instance of driving back or warding off; rebuff **5** a cold discourteous rejection or refusal [c16: from Latin *repellere* to drive back, REPEL] > reˈpulser *n*

● **USAGE** Some people think that the use of *repulse* in
● sentences such as *he was repulsed by what he saw* is
● incorrect and that the correct word is *repel*

repulsion (rɪˈpʌlʃən) *n* **1** a feeling of disgust or aversion **2** *physics* a force tending to separate two objects, such as the force between two like electric charges or magnetic poles

repulsive (rɪˈpʌlsɪv) *adj* **1** causing or occasioning repugnance; loathsome; disgusting or distasteful: *a repulsive sight* **2** tending to repel, esp by coldness and discourtesy **3** *physics* concerned with, producing, or being a repulsion > reˈpulsively *adv* > reˈpulsiveness *n*

repurchase (riːˈpɜːtʃɪs) *vb* (*tr*) **1** to buy back or buy again goods, securities, assets, etc ▷ *n* **2** an act or instance of repurchasing

reputable (ˈrɛpjʊtəbᵊl) *adj* **1** having a good reputation; honoured, trustworthy, or respectable **2** (of words) acceptable as good usage; standard > ˌreputaˈbility *n* > ˈreputably *adv*

reputation (ˌrɛpjʊˈteɪʃən) *n* **1** the estimation in which a person or thing is generally held; opinion **2** a high opinion generally held about a person or thing; esteem **3** notoriety or fame, esp for some specified characteristic **4** have a reputation to be known or notorious, esp for promiscuity, excessive drinking, or the like [c14: from Latin *reputātiō* a reckoning, from *reputāre* to calculate, meditate; see REPUTE]

repute (rɪˈpjuːt) *vb* **1** (*tr; usually passive*) to consider (a person or thing) to be as specified: *he is reputed to be intelligent* ▷ *n* **2** public estimation; reputation: *a writer of little repute* [c15: from Old French *reputer*, from Latin *reputāre* to think over, from RE- + *putāre* to think]

reputed (rɪˈpjuːtɪd) *adj* (*prenominal*) generally reckoned or considered; supposed or alleged: *he is the reputed writer of a number of romantic poems* > reˈputedly *adv*

request (rɪˈkwɛst) *vb* (*tr*) **1** to express a desire for, ask politely; ask for or demand: *to request a bottle of wine* ▷ *n* **2** the act or an instance of requesting, esp in the form of a written statement; petition or solicitation: *a request for a song* **3** at the request of in accordance with the specific demand or wish of (someone) **4** by request in accordance with someone's desire **5** in request in demand; popular: *he is in request in concert halls all over the world* **6** on request on the occasion of a demand or request: *application forms are available on request* [c14: from Old French *requeste*, from Vulgar Latin *requaerere* (unattested) to seek after; see REQUIRE, QUEST] > reˈquester *n*

request stop *n* a point on a route at which a bus will stop only if signalled to do so. US equivalent: flag stop

Requiem (ˈrɛkwɪˌɛm) *n* **1** RC Church a Mass celebrated for the dead **2** a musical setting of this Mass **3** any piece of music composed or performed as a memorial to a dead person or persons [c14: from Latin *requiēs* rest, from the opening of the introit, *Requiem aeternam dona eis* Rest eternal grant unto them]

requiem shark *n* any shark of the family *Carcharhinidae*, occurring mostly in tropical seas and characterized by a nictitating membrane and a heterocercal tail. The family includes the tiger shark and the soupfin [c17: French *requiem* probably assimilated from a native name]

requiescat (ˌrɛkwɪˈɛskæt) *n* a prayer for the repose of the souls of the dead [Latin, from *requiescat in pace* may he rest in peace]

require (rɪˈkwaɪə) *vb* (*mainly tr; may take a clause as object or an infinitive*) **1** to have need of; depend upon; want **2** to impose as a necessity; make necessary: *this work requires precision* **3** (*also intr*) to make formal request (for); insist upon or demand, esp as an obligation **4** to call upon or oblige (a person) authoritatively; order or command: *to require someone to account for his actions* [c14: from Old French *requerre*, from Vulgar Latin *requaerere* (unattested) to seek after, from Latin *requīrere* to seek to know, but also influenced by *quaerere* to seek] > reˈquirer *n*

● **USAGE** The use of *require to* as in *I require to see the*
● *manager* or *you require to complete a special form* is thought
● by many people to be incorrect: *I need to see the manager;*
● *you are required to complete a special form*

requirement (rɪˈkwaɪəmənt) *n* **1** something demanded or imposed as an obligation **2** a thing desired or needed **3** the act or an instance of requiring

requisite (ˈrɛkwɪzɪt) *adj* **1** absolutely essential; indispensable ▷ *n* **2** something indispensable; necessity [c15: from Latin *requisītus* sought after, from *requīrere* to seek for, REQUIRE] > ˈrequisitely *adv*

requisition (ˌrɛkwɪˈzɪʃən) *n* **1** a request or demand, esp an authoritative or formal one **2** an official form on which such a demand is made **3** the act of taking something over, esp temporarily for military or public use in time of emergency ▷ *vb* (*tr*) **4** to demand and take for use or service, esp by military or public authority **5** (*may take an infinitive*) to require (someone) formally to do (something): *to requisition a soldier to drive a staff officer's car* > ˌrequiˈsitionary *adj*

requite (rɪˈkwaɪt) *vb* (*tr*) **1** to make return to (a person for a kindness or injury); repay with a similar action [c16: RE- + *obsolete quite* to discharge, repay; see QUIT] > reˈquitable *adj* > reˈquital *n* > reˈquitement *n* > reˈquiter *n*

reredos (ˈrɪədɒs) *n* **1** a screen or wall decoration at the back of an altar, in the form of a hanging, tapestry, painting, or piece of metalwork or sculpture **2** another word for **fireback** (sense 1) [c14: from Old French *areredos*, from *arere* behind + *dos* back, from Latin *dorsum*]

rerun *vb* (riːˈrʌn) -runs, -running, -ran (*tr*) **1** to broadcast or put on (a film, play, series, etc) again **2** to run (a race, etc) again ▷ *n* (ˈriːˌrʌn) **3** a film, play, series, etc, that is broadcast or put on again; repeat **4** a race that is run again **5** *computing* the repeat of a part of a computer program

res *Latin* (reɪs) *n, pl* res a thing, matter, or object

res. *abbreviation* **1** residence **2** resides **3** resigned **4** resolution

resale price maintenance *n* the practice by which a manufacturer establishes a fixed or minimum price for the resale of a brand product by retailers or other distributors. US equivalent: fair trade Abbreviation: rpm

reschedule (riːˈʃedjuːl; *esp US* -skɛdʒʊəl) *vb* (*tr*) **1** to change the time, date, or schedule of **2** to arrange a revised schedule for repayment of (a debt)

rescind (rɪˈsɪnd) *vb* (*tr*) to annul or repeal [c17: from Latin *rēscindere* to cut off, from *re-* (intensive) + *scindere* to cut] ▷ reˈscindable *adj* ▷ reˈscinder *n* ▷ reˈscindment *n*

rescission (rɪˈsɪʒən) *n* 1 the act of rescinding 2 *law* the right to have a contract set aside if it has been entered into mistakenly, as a result of misrepresentation, undue influence, etc

rescript (ˈriːˌskrɪpt) *n* 1 (in ancient Rome) an ordinance taking the form of a reply by the emperor to a question on a point of law 2 any official announcement or edict; a decree 3 something rewritten 4 the act or process of rewriting [c16: from Latin *rēscriptum* a reply, from *rēscribere* to write back]

rescue (ˈrɛskjuː) *vb* -cues, -cuing, -cued (*tr*) 1 to bring (someone or something) out of danger, attack, harm, etc; deliver or save 2 to free (a person) from legal custody by force 3 *law* to seize (goods or property) by force ▷ *n* 4 a the act or an instance of rescuing b (*as modifier*): *a rescue party* 5 the forcible removal of a person from legal custody 6 *law* the forcible seizure of goods or property [c14: *rescowen*, from Old French *rescourre*, from RE- + *escourre* to pull away, from Latin *excutere* to shake off, from *quatere* to shake] ▷ ˈrescuer *n*

research (rɪˈsɜːtʃ, ˈriːsɜːtʃ) *n* 1 systematic investigation to establish facts or principles or to collect information on a subject ▷ *vb* 2 to carry out investigations into (a subject, problem, etc) [c16: from Old French *recercher* to seek, search again, from RE- + *cercher* to SEARCH] ▷ reˈsearchable *adj* ▷ reˈsearcher *n*

research and development *n* the part of a commercial company's activity concerned with applying the results of scientific research to develop new products and improve existing ones. Abbreviation: R & D

research quantum *n Austral* the standard by which the contribution to a university of individual academics is measured and on the basis of which universities receive government funding and academics are promoted

reseat (riːˈsiːt) *vb* (*tr*) 1 to show (a person) to a new seat 2 to put a new seat on (a chair, etc) 3 to provide new seats for (a hall, theatre, etc) 4 to re-form the seating of (a valve)

resect (rɪˈsɛkt) *vb* (*tr*) *surgery* to cut out part of (a bone, an organ, or other structure or part) [c17: from Latin *resecāre* to cut away, from RE- + *secāre* to cut]

resection (rɪˈsɛkʃən) *n* 1 *surgery* excision of part of a bone, organ, or other part 2 *surveying* a method of fixing the position of a point by making angular observations to three fixed points ▷ reˈsectional *adj*

resemblance (rɪˈzɛmbləns) *n* 1 the state or quality of resembling; likeness or similarity in nature, appearance, etc 2 the degree or extent to which or the respect in which a likeness exists 3 something resembling something else; semblance; likeness ▷ reˈsemblant *adj*

resemble (rɪˈzɛmbəl) *vb* (*tr*) to possess some similarity to; be like [c14: from Old French *resembler*, from RE- + *sembler* to look like, from Latin *similis* like] ▷ reˈsembler *n*

resent (rɪˈzɛnt) *vb* (*tr*) to feel bitter, indignant, or aggrieved at [c17: from French *ressentir*, from RE- + *sentir* to feel, from Latin *sentīre* to perceive; see SENSE] ▷ reˈsentful *adj* ▷ reˈsentment *n*

reserpine (ˈrɛsəpɪn) *n* an insoluble alkaloid, extracted from the roots of the plant *Rauwolfia serpentina*, used medicinally to lower blood pressure and as a sedative and tranquillizer. Its main adverse effect is mental depression. Formula: $C_{33}H_{40}N_2O_9$ [c20: from German *Reserpin*, probably from the New Latin name of the plant]

reservation (ˌrɛzəˈveɪʃən) *n* 1 the act or an instance of reserving 2 something reserved, esp hotel accommodation, a seat on an aeroplane, in a theatre, etc 3 (*often plural*) a stated or unstated qualification of opinion that prevents one's wholehearted acceptance of a proposal, claim, statement, etc 4 an area of land set aside, esp (in the US) for American Indian peoples 5 *Brit* the strip of land between the two carriageways of a dual carriageway 6 the act or process of keeping back, esp for oneself; withholding 7 *law* a right or interest retained by the grantor in property granted, conveyed, leased,

etc, to another

reserve (rɪˈzɜːv) *vb* (*tr*) 1 to keep back or set aside, esp for future use or contingency; withhold 2 to keep for oneself; retain: *I reserve the right to question these men later* 3 to obtain or secure by advance arrangement: *I have reserved two tickets for tonight's show* 4 to delay delivery of (a judgment), esp in order to allow time for full consideration of the issues involved ▷ *n* 5 a something kept back or set aside, esp for future use or contingency b (*as modifier*): *a reserve stock* 6 the state or condition of being reserved: *I have plenty in reserve* 7 a tract of land set aside for the protection and conservation of wild animals, flowers, etc: *a nature reserve* 8 Also called: **reservation** *Canadian* an area of land set aside, esp (in the US and Canada) for American or Canadian Indian peoples 9 *Austral & NZ* an area of publicly owned land set aside for sport, recreation, etc 10 the act of reserving; reservation 11 a member of a team who only plays if a playing member drops out; a substitute 12 (*often plural*) a a part of an army or formation not committed to immediate action in a military engagement b that part of a nation's armed services not in active service 13 coolness or formality of manner; restraint, silence, or reticence 14 *finance* a a portion of capital not invested (a **capital reserve**) or a portion of profits not distributed (a **revenue** or **general reserve**) by a bank or business enterprise and held to meet legal requirements, future liabilities, or contingencies b (*often plural*) liquid assets held by an organization, government, etc, to meet expenses and liabilities 15 without reserve without reservations; fully; wholeheartedly [c14: from Old French *reserver*, from Latin *reservāre* to save up, from RE- + *servāre* to keep] ▷ reˈservable *adj* ▷ reˈserver *n*

re-serve (riːˈsɜːv) *vb* (*tr*) to serve again

reserve bank *n* one of the twelve banks forming part of the US Federal Reserve System

reserve currency *n* foreign currency that is acceptable as a medium of international payments and that is therefore held in reserve by many countries

reserved (rɪˈzɜːvd) *adj* 1 set aside for use by a particular person or people: *this table is reserved* 2 cool or formal in manner; restrained, silent, or reticent 3 destined; fated: *reserved for great things* 4 referring to matters that are the responsibility of the national parliament rather than a devolved regional assembly: *defence is a reserved issue* ▷ reˈservedly (rɪˈzɜːvɪdlɪ) *adv* ▷ reˈservedness *n*

reserved list *n Brit* a list of retired naval, army, or air-force officers available for recall to active service in an emergency

reserved occupation *n Brit* in time of war, an occupation from which one will not be called up for military service

reserve-grade *adj Austral* denoting a sporting team of the second rank in a club

reserve price *n* the minimum price acceptable to the owner of property being auctioned or sold. Also called (esp Scot and US): **upset price**

reserve tranche *n* the quota of 25 per cent to which a member of the IMF has unconditional access. Prior to 1978 it was paid in gold and known as the **gold tranche**

reservist (rɪˈzɜːvɪst) *n* one who serves in the reserve formations of a nation's armed forces

reservoir (ˈrɛzəˌvwɑː) *n* 1 a natural or artificial lake or large tank used for collecting and storing water, esp for community water supplies or irrigation 2 *biology* a vacuole or cavity in an organism, containing a secretion or some other fluid 3 a place where a great stock of anything is accumulated 4 a large supply of something; reserve: *a reservoir of talent* [c17: from French *réservoir*, from *réserver* to RESERVE]

reset¹ (riːˈsɛt) -sets, -setting, -set (*tr*) 1 to set again (a broken bone, matter in type, a gemstone, etc) 2 to restore (a gauge, dial, etc) to zero ▷ *n* (ˈriːˌsɛt) 3 the act or an instance of setting again 4 a thing that is set again ▷ reˈsetter *n*

reset² *Scot vb* (riːˈsɛt) -sets, -setting, -set 1 to receive or handle goods knowing they have been stolen ▷ *n* (ˈriːˌsɛt) 2 the receiving of stolen goods [c14: from Old French *receter*, from Latin *receptāre*, from *recipere* to receive]

> re'setter n

res gestae ('reɪs 'dʒɛstiː) pl n **1** things done or accomplished; achievements **2** law incidental facts and circumstances that are admissible in evidence because they introduce or explain the matter in issue [Latin]

Resht (rɛʃt) n a variant of **Rasht**

reside (rɪ'zaɪd) vb (intr) formal **1** to live permanently or for a considerable time (in a place); have one's home (in): he now resides in London **2** (of things, qualities, etc) to be inherently present (in); be vested (in): political power resides in military strength [c15: from Latin residēre to sit back, from RE- + sedēre to sit] > re'sider n

residence ('rɛzɪdəns) n **1** the place in which one resides; abode or home **2** a large imposing house; mansion **3** the fact of residing in a place or a period of residing **4** in residence **a** actually resident: the royal standard indicates that the Queen is in residence **b** designating a creative artist resident for a set period at a university, college, etc, whose role is to stimulate an active interest in the subject: composer in residence

residency ('rɛzɪdənsɪ) n, pl -cies **1** a variant of: **residence** **2** a regular series of concerts by a band or singer at one venue **3** US & Canadian the period, following internship, during which a physician undergoes further clinical training, usually in one medical speciality **4** (in India, formerly) the official house of the governor general at the court of a native prince

resident ('rɛzɪdənt) n **1** a person who resides in a place **2** (esp formerly) a representative of the British government in a British protectorate **3** (in India, formerly) a representative of the British governor general at the court of a native prince **4** a bird or other animal that does not migrate **5** US & Canadian a physician who lives in the hospital where he works while undergoing specialist training after completing his internship **6** Brit & NZ a junior doctor, esp a house officer, who lives in the hospital in which he works ▷ adj **7** living in a place; residing **8** living or staying at a place in order to discharge a duty, etc **9** (of qualities, characteristics, etc) existing or inherent (in) **10** (of birds and other animals) not in the habit of migrating > 'resident,ship n

residential (,rɛzɪ'dɛnʃəl) adj **1** suitable for or allocated for residence: a residential area **2** relating to or having residence > ,resi'dentially adv

residential school n (in Canada) a boarding school maintained by the Canadian government for Indian and Inuit children from sparsely populated settlements

residentiary (,rɛzɪ'dɛnʃərɪ) adj **1** residing in a place, esp officially; resident **2** subject to an obligation to reside in an official residence: a residentiary benefice ▷ n, pl -tiaries **3** a clergyman obliged to reside in the place of his official appointment

residual (rɪ'zɪdjʊəl) adj **1** of, relating to, or designating a residue or remainder; remaining; left over **2** of or relating to the payment of residuals ▷ n **3** something left over as a residue; remainder **4** statistics **a** the difference between the mean of a set of observations and one particular observation **b** the difference between the numerical value of one particular observation and the theoretical result **5** (often plural) payment made to an actor, actress, musician, etc, for subsequent use of film in which the person appears > re'sidually adv

residual unemployment n the unemployment that remains in periods of full employment, as a result of those mentally, physically, or emotionally unfit to work

residuary (rɪ'zɪdjʊərɪ) adj **1** of, relating to, or constituting a residue; residual **2** law entitled to the residue of an estate after payment of debts and distribution of specific gifts

residue ('rɛzɪ,djuː) n **1** matter remaining after something has been removed **2** law what is left of an estate after the discharge of debts and distribution of specific gifts [c14: from Old French residu, from Latin residuus remaining over, from residēre to stay behind, RESIDE]

residuum (rɪ'zɪdjʊəm) n, pl -ua (-jʊə) a more formal word for **residue**

resign (rɪ'zaɪn) vb **1** (when intr, often foll by from) to give

up tenure of (a job, office, etc) **2** (tr) to reconcile (oneself) to; yield: to resign oneself to death **3** (tr) to give up (a right, claim, etc); relinquish [c14: from Old French resigner, from Latin resignāre to unseal, invalidate, destroy, from RE- + signāre to seal; see SIGN] > re'signer n

re-sign (riː'saɪn) vb to sign (a document, etc) again

resignation (,rɛzɪg'neɪʃən) n **1** the act of resigning **2** a formal document stating one's intention to resign **3** a submissive unresisting attitude; passive acquiescence

resigned (rɪ'zaɪnd) adj characteristic of or proceeding from an attitude of resignation; acquiescent or submissive > resignedly (rɪ'zaɪnɪdlɪ) adv > re'signedness n

resile (rɪ'zaɪl) vb (intr) to spring or shrink back; recoil or resume original shape [c16: from Old French resilir, from Latin resilīre to jump back, from RE- + salīre to jump] > re'silement n

resilient (rɪ'zɪlɪənt) adj **1** (of an object or material) capable of regaining its original shape or position after bending, stretching, compression, or other deformation; elastic **2** (of a person) recovering easily and quickly from shock, illness, hardship, etc; irrepressible > re'silience n > re'siliently adv

resin ('rɛzɪn) n **1** any of a group of solid or semisolid amorphous compounds that are obtained directly from certain plants as exudations. They are used in medicine and in varnishes **2** any of a large number of synthetic, usually organic, materials that have a polymeric structure, esp such a substance in a raw state before it is moulded or treated with plasticizer, stabilizer, filler, etc ▷ vb **3** (tr) to treat or coat with resin [c14: from Old French resine, from Latin rēsīna, from Greek rhētīnē resin from a pine] > 'resinous adj > 'resinously adv > 'resinousness n

resinate ('rɛzɪ,neɪt) vb (tr) to impregnate with resin

resipiscence (,rɛsɪ'pɪsəns) n literary acknowledgment that one has been mistaken [c16: from Late Latin resipiscentia, from resipiscere to recover one's senses, from Latin sapere to know] > ,resi'piscent adj

resist (rɪ'zɪst) vb **1** to stand firm (against); not yield (to); fight (against) **2** (tr) to withstand the deleterious action of; be proof against: to resist corrosion **3** (tr) to oppose; refuse to accept or comply with: to resist arrest; to resist the introduction of new technology **4** (tr) to refrain from, esp in spite of temptation (esp in the phrases **cannot** or **could not resist (something)**) ▷ n **5** a substance used to protect something, esp a coating that prevents corrosion [c14: from Latin resistere to stand still, oppose, from RE- + sistere to stand firm] > re,sisti'bility n > re'sistible adj > re'sistibly adv > re'sistless adj > re'sistlessly adv

resistance (rɪ'zɪstəns) n **1** the act or an instance of resisting **2** the capacity to withstand something, esp the body's natural capacity to withstand disease **3 a** the opposition to a flow of electric current through a circuit component, medium, or substance. It is the magnitude of the real part of the impedance and is measured in ohms. Symbol: R **b** (as modifier): resistance coupling; a resistance thermometer **4** any force that tends to retard or oppose motion: air resistance; wind resistance **5** line of least resistance the easiest, but not necessarily the best or most honourable, course of action **6** See **passive resistance** > re'sistant adj, n

Resistance (rɪ'zɪstəns) n the Resistance an illegal organization fighting for national liberty in a country under enemy occupation, esp in France during World War II

resistance thermometer n an accurate type of thermometer in which temperature is calculated from the resistance of a coil of wire (usually of platinum) or of a semiconductor placed at the point at which the temperature is to be measured

Resistencia (Spanish resis'tenθja) n a city in NE Argentina, on the Paraná River. Pop: 423 000 (2005 est)

resistivity (,riːzɪs'tɪvɪtɪ) n **1** the electrical property of a material that determines the resistance of a piece of given dimensions. It is equal to RA/l, where R is the resistance, A the cross-sectional area, and l the length, and is the reciprocal of conductivity. It is measured in ohms **2** the power or capacity to resist; resistance

r

resistor (rɪˈzɪstə) *n* an electrical component designed to introduce a known value of resistance into a circuit

resit *vb* (riːˈsɪt) -sits, -sitting, -sat (*tr*) **1** to sit (an examination) again ▷ *n* (ˈriːsɪt) **2** an examination taken again by a person who has not been successful in a previous attempt

res judicata (ˈreɪs ˌdʒuːdɪˈkɑːtə) *or* **res adjudicata** *n law* a matter already adjudicated upon that cannot be raised again [Latin]

Resnais (*French* rɛnɛ) *n* **Alain** (alɛ̃). born 1922, French film director, whose films include *Hiroshima mon amour* (1959), *L'Année dernière à Marienbad* (1961), *La Vie est un roman* (1983), and *On Connaît la Chanson* (1998)

resoluble (rɪˈzɒljʊbᵊl, ˈrɛzəl-) *adj* another word for **resolvable**

re-soluble (riːˈsɒljʊbᵊl) *adj* capable of being dissolved again ▷ re-ˈsolubleness, re-ˌsoluˈbility *n* ▷ re-ˈsolubly *adv*

resolute (ˈrɛzəˌluːt) *adj* **1** firm in purpose or belief; steadfast **2** characterized by resolution; determined: *a resolute answer* [C16: from Latin *resolutus*, from *resolvere* to RESOLVE] ▷ ˈresoˌlutely *adv* ▷ ˈresoˌluteness *n*

resolution (ˌrɛzəˈluːʃən) *n* **1** the act or an instance of resolving **2** the condition or quality of being resolute; firmness or determination **3** something resolved or determined; decision **4** a formal expression of opinion by a meeting, esp one agreed by a vote **5** a judicial decision on some matter; verdict; judgment **6** the act or process of separating something into its constituent parts or elements **7** *med* subsidence of the symptoms of a disease, esp the disappearance of inflammation without the formation of pus **8** *music* the process in harmony whereby a dissonant note or chord is followed by a consonant one **9** the ability of a television or film image to reproduce fine detail **10** *physics* another word for **resolving power** ▷ ˌresoˈlutioner *or* ˌresoˈlutionist *n*

resolvable (rɪˈzɒlvəbᵊl) *or* **resoluble** *adj* able to be resolved or analysed ▷ reˌsolvaˈbility, reˌsoluˈbility, reˈsolvableness *or* reˈsolubleness *n*

resolve (rɪˈzɒlv) *vb* (*mainly tr*) **1** (*takes a clause as object or an infinitive*) to decide or determine firmly **2** to express (an opinion) formally, esp (of a public meeting) one agreed by a vote **3** (*also intr*; usually foll by *into*) to separate or cause to separate (into) (constituent parts or elements) **4** (*usually reflexive*) to change, alter, or appear to change or alter: *the ghost resolved itself into a tree* **5** to make up the mind of; cause to decide: *the tempest resolved him to stay at home* **6** to find the answer or solution to; solve **7** to explain away or dispel: *to resolve a doubt* **8** to bring to an end; conclude: *to resolve an argument* **9** *med* to cause (a swelling or inflammation) to subside, esp without the formation of pus **10** (*also intr*) to follow (a dissonant note or chord) or (of a dissonant note or chord) to be followed by one producing a consonance **11** *physics* to distinguish between (separate parts) of (an image) as in a microscope, telescope, or other optical instrument ▷ *n* **12** something determined or decided; resolution: *he had made a resolve to work all day* **13** firmness of purpose; determination: *nothing can break his resolve* [C14: from Latin *resolvere* to unfasten, reveal, from RE- + *solvere* to loosen; see SOLVE] ▷ reˈsolver *n*

resolved (rɪˈzɒlvd) *adj* fixed in purpose or intention; determined ▷ resolvedly (rɪˈzɒlvɪdlɪ) *adv* ▷ reˈsolvedness *n*

resolvent (rɪˈzɒlvənt) *adj* **1** serving to dissolve or separate something into its elements; resolving ▷ *n* **2** a drug or agent able to reduce swelling or inflammation

resolving power *n* **1** Also called: **resolution** *physics* the ability of a microscope, telescope, or other optical instrument to produce separate images of closely placed objects **2** *photog* the ability of an emulsion to show up fine detail in an image

resonance (ˈrɛzənəns) *n* **1** the condition or quality of being resonant **2** sound produced by a body vibrating in sympathy with a neighbouring source of sound **3** the condition of a body or system when it is subjected to a periodic disturbance of the same frequency as the natural frequency of the body or system. At this frequency the system displays an enhanced oscillation or vibration **4** amplification of speech sounds by sympathetic vibration in the bone structure of the head and chest, resounding in the cavities of the nose, mouth, and pharynx **5** *electronics* the condition of an electrical circuit when the frequency is such that the capacitive and inductive reactances are equal in magnitude. In a series circuit there is then maximum alternating current whilst in a parallel circuit there is minimum alternating current **6** *med* the sound heard when percussing a hollow bodily structure, esp the chest or abdomen. Change in the quality of the sound often indicates an underlying disease or disorder **7** *chem* the phenomenon in which the electronic structure of a molecule can be represented by two or more hypothetical structures involving single, double, and triple chemical bonds. The true structure is considered to be an average of these theoretical structures **8** *physics* the condition of a system in which there is a sharp maximum probability for the absorption of electromagnetic radiation or capture of particles [C16: from Latin *resonāre* to RESOUND]

resonant (ˈrɛzənənt) *adj* **1** (of sound) resounding or re-echoing **2** producing or enhancing resonance, as by sympathetic vibration **3** characterized by resonance ▷ ˈresonantly *adv*

resonate (ˈrɛzəˌneɪt) *vb* **1** to resound or cause to resound; reverberate **2** (of a mechanical system, electrical circuit, chemical compound, etc) to exhibit resonance or cause to exhibit resonance **3** (*intr*; often foll by *with*) to be understood or receive a sympathetic response: *themes which will resonate with voters* **4** (*intr*: foll by *with*) to be filled with: *simple words that seem to resonate with mystery and beauty* [C19: from Latin *resonāre*] ▷ ˌresoˈnation *n*

resonator (ˈrɛzəˌneɪtə) *n* any body or system that displays resonance, esp a tuned electrical circuit or a conducting cavity in which microwaves are generated by a resonant current

resorb (rɪˈsɔːb) *vb* (*tr*) to absorb again [C17: from Latin *resorbēre*, from RE- + *sorbēre* to suck in; see ABSORB] ▷ reˈsorbent *adj* ▷ reˈsorptive *adj*

resorcinol (rɪˈzɔːsɪˌnɒl) *n* a colourless crystalline phenol with a sweet taste, used in making dyes, drugs, resins, and adhesives. Formula: $C_6H_4(OH)_2$; relative density: 1.27; melting pt: 111°C; boiling pt at 1 atm.: 276°C [C19: New Latin, from RESIN + ORCINOL] ▷ reˈsorcinal *adj*

resorption (rɪˈsɔːpʃən) *n* **1** the process of resorbing or the state of being resorbed **2** *geology* the partial or complete remelting or dissolution of a mineral by magma, resulting from changes in temperature, pressure, or magma composition

resort (rɪˈzɔːt) *vb* (*intr*) **1** (usually foll by *to*) to have recourse (to) for help, use, etc: *to resort to violence* **2** to go, esp often or habitually; repair: *to resort to the beach* ▷ *n* **3** a place to which many people go for recreation, rest, etc: *a holiday resort* **4** the use of something as a means, help, or recourse **5** last resort the last possible course of action open to one [C14: from Old French *resortir* to come out again, from RE- + *sortir* to emerge] ▷ reˈsorter *n*

re-sort (riːˈsɔːt) *vb* (*tr*) to sort again

resound (rɪˈzaʊnd) *vb* (*intr*) **1** to ring or echo with sound; reverberate **2** to make a prolonged echoing noise: *the trumpet resounded* **3** (of sounds) to echo or ring **4** to be widely famous: *his achievements resounded throughout India* [C14: from Old French *resoner*, from Latin *resonāre* to sound again]

re-sound (riːˈsaʊnd) *vb* to sound or cause to sound again

resounding (rɪˈzaʊndɪŋ) *adj* **1** clear and emphatic; unmistakable: *a resounding vote of confidence* **2** full of or characterized by resonance; reverberating: *a resounding slap* ▷ reˈsoundingly *adv*

resource (rɪˈzɔːs, -ˈsɔːs) *n* **1** capability, ingenuity, and initiative; quick-wittedness: *a man of resource* **2** (*often plural*) a source of economic wealth, esp of a country (mineral, land, labour, etc) or business enterprise (capital, equipment, personnel, etc) **3** a supply or source of aid or support; something resorted to in time of need **4** a means of doing something; expedient [C17: from Old French *ressource* relief, from *resourdre* to rise again, from Latin *resurgere*, from RE- + *surgere* to rise] ▷ reˈsourceless *adj*

resourceful (rɪˈzɔːsfʊl, -ˈsɔːs-) *adj* ingenious, capable, and full of initiative, esp in dealing with difficult situations > re'sourcefully *adv* > re'sourcefulness *n*

respect (rɪˈspɛkt) *n* 1 an attitude of deference, admiration, or esteem; regard 2 the state of being honoured or esteemed 3 a detail, point, or characteristic; particular: *he differs in some respects from his son* 4 reference or relation (esp in the phrases **in respect of, with respect to**) 5 polite or kind regard; consideration: *respect for people's feelings* 6 (*often plural*) an expression of esteem or regard (esp in the phrase **pay one's respects**) ▷ *vb* (*tr*) 7 to have an attitude of esteem towards; show or have respect for: *to respect one's elders* 8 to pay proper attention to; not violate: *to respect Swiss neutrality* 9 *archaic* to concern or refer to [c14: from Latin *rēspicere* to look back, pay attention to, from RE- + *specere* to look] > re'specter *n*

respectable (rɪˈspɛktəbəl) *adj* 1 having or deserving the respect of other people; estimable; worthy 2 having good social standing or reputation 3 having socially or conventionally acceptable morals, standards, etc: *a respectable woman* 4 relatively or fairly good; considerable: *a respectable salary* 5 fit to be seen by other people; presentable > re,specta'bility *or less commonly* re'spectableness *n* > re'spectably *adv*

respectful (rɪˈspɛktfʊl) *adj* full of, showing, or giving respect > re'spectfully *adv* > re'spectfulness *n*

respecting (rɪˈspɛktɪŋ) *prep* concerning; regarding

respective (rɪˈspɛktɪv) *adj* belonging or relating separately to each of several people or things; several: *we took our respective ways home* > re'spectiveness *n*

respectively (rɪˈspɛktɪvlɪ) *adv* (in listing a number of items or attributes that refer to another list) separately in the order given: *he gave Janet and John a cake and a chocolate respectively*

Respighi (Italian resˈpiːgi) *n* **Ottorino** (ottoˈriːno). 1879–1936, Italian composer, noted esp for his suites *The Fountains of Rome* (1917) and *The Pines of Rome* (1924)

respirable (ˈrɛspɪrəbəl) *adj* 1 able to be breathed 2 suitable or fit for breathing > ,respira'bility *n*

respiration (ˌrɛspəˈreɪʃən) *n* 1 the process in living organisms of taking in oxygen from the surroundings and giving out carbon dioxide (**external respiration**). In terrestrial animals this is effected by breathing air 2 the chemical breakdown of complex organic substances, such as carbohydrates and fats, that takes place in the cells and tissues of animals and plants, during which energy is released and carbon dioxide produced (**internal respiration**)

respirator (ˈrɛspəˌreɪtə) *n* 1 an apparatus for providing long-term artificial respiration 2 Also called: **gas mask** a device worn over the mouth and nose to prevent inhalation of noxious fumes or to warm cold air before it is breathed

respiratory (ˈrɛspərətərɪ, -trɪ) *or rarely* **respirational** (ˌrɛspəˈreɪʃənəl) *adj* of, relating to, or affecting respiration or the organs used in respiration

respiratory failure *n* a condition in which the respiratory system is unable to provide an adequate supply of oxygen or to remove carbon dioxide efficiently

respiratory quotient *n biology* the ratio of the volume of carbon dioxide expired to the volume of oxygen consumed by an organism, tissue, or cell in a given time

respiratory syncytial virus *n* a myxovirus causing infections of the nose and throat, esp in young children. It is thought to be involved in some cot deaths. Abbreviation: **RSV**

respiratory system *n* the specialized organs, collectively, concerned with external respiration: in humans and other mammals it includes the trachea, bronchi, bronchioles, lungs, and diaphragm

respire (rɪˈspaɪə) *vb* 1 to inhale and exhale (air); breathe 2 (*intr*) to undergo the process of respiration [c14: from Latin *rēspīrāre* to exhale, from RE- + *spīrāre* to breathe; see SPIRIT[1]]

respite (ˈrɛspɪt, -paɪt) *n* 1 a pause from exertion; interval of rest 2 a temporary delay 3 a temporary stay of execution; reprieve ▷ *vb* 4 (*tr*) to grant a respite to; reprieve [c13: from Old French *respit*, from Latin *respectus*

a looking back; see RESPECT]

resplendent (rɪˈsplɛndənt) *adj* having a brilliant or splendid appearance [c15: from *rēsplendēre* to shine brightly, from RE- + *splendēre* to shine; see SPLENDOUR] > re'splendence *or* re'splendency *n* > re'splendently *adv*

respond (rɪˈspɒnd) *vb* 1 to state or utter (something) in reply 2 (*intr*) to act in reply; react: *to respond by issuing an invitation* 3 (*intr*; foll by *to*) to react favourably: *this patient will respond to treatment* 4 an archaic word for **correspond** ▷ *n* 5 *architect* a pilaster or an engaged column that supports an arch or a lintel 6 *Christianity* a choral anthem chanted in response to a lesson read at a church service [c14: from Old French *respondre*, from Latin *respondēre* to return like for like, from RE- + *spondēre* to pledge; see SPOUSE, SPONSOR] > re'spondence *or* re'spondency *n* > re'sponder *n*

respondent (rɪˈspɒndənt) *n* 1 *law* a person against whom a petition, esp in a divorce suit, or appeal is brought ▷ *adj* 2 a less common word for **responsive**

response (rɪˈspɒns) *n* 1 the act of responding; reply or reaction 2 *bridge* a bid replying to a partner's bid or double 3 (*usually plural*) *Christianity* a short sentence or phrase recited or sung by the choir or congregation in reply to the officiant at a church service 4 *electronics* the ratio of the output to the input level, at a particular frequency, of a transmission line or electrical device 5 any pattern of glandular, muscular, or electrical reactions that arises from stimulation of the nervous system [c14: from Latin *rēsponsum* answer, from *rēspondēre* to RESPOND] > re'sponseless *adj*

responser *or* **responsor** (rɪˈspɒnsə) *n* a radio or radar receiver used in conjunction with an interrogator to receive and display signals from a transponder

responsibility (rɪˌspɒnsəˈbɪlɪtɪ) *n*, *pl* -ties 1 the state or position of being responsible 2 a person or thing for which one is responsible

responsible (rɪˈspɒnsəbəl) *adj* 1 (*postpositive*; usually foll by *for*) having control or authority (over) 2 (*postpositive*; foll by *to*) being accountable for one's actions and decisions (to): *to be responsible to one's commanding officer* 3 (of a position, duty, etc) involving decision and accountability 4 (often foll by *for*) being the agent or cause (of some action): *to be responsible for a mistake* 5 able to take rational decisions without supervision; accountable for one's own actions 6 able to meet financial obligations; of sound credit [c16: from Latin *rēsponsus*, from *rēspondēre* to RESPOND] > re'sponsibleness *n* > re'sponsibly *adv*

responsive (rɪˈspɒnsɪv) *adj* 1 reacting or replying quickly or favourably, as to a suggestion, initiative, etc 2 (of an organism) reacting to a stimulus > re'sponsively *adv* > re'sponsiveness *n*

responsory (rɪˈspɒnsərɪ) *n*, *pl* -ries *Christianity* an anthem or chant consisting of versicles and responses and recited or sung after a lesson in a church service [c15: from Late Latin *rēsponsōrium*, from Latin *rēspondēre* to answer]

rest[1] (rest) *n* 1 a relaxation from exertion or labour b (*as modifier*): *a rest period* 2 repose; sleep 3 any relief or refreshment, as from worry or something troublesome 4 calm; tranquillity 5 death regarded as repose: *eternal rest* 6 cessation from motion 7 **at rest a** not moving; still b calm; tranquil c dead d asleep 8 a pause or interval 9 a mark in a musical score indicating a pause of specific duration 10 *prosody* a pause in or at the end of a line; caesura 11 a shelter or lodging: *a seaman's rest* 12 a thing or place on which to put something for support or to steady it; prop 13 *billiards, snooker* any of various special poles used as supports for the cue in shots that cannot be made using the hand as a support 14 **come to rest** to slow down and stop 15 **lay to rest** to bury (a dead person) 16 **set someone's mind at rest** to reassure someone or settle someone's mind ▷ *vb* 17 to take or give rest, as by sleeping, lying down, etc 18 to place or position (oneself, etc) for rest or relaxation 19 (*tr*) to place or position for support or steadying: *to rest one's elbows on the table* 20 (*intr*) to be at ease; be calm 21 to cease or cause to cease from motion or exertion; halt 22 (*intr*) to remain without further attention or action:

let the matter rest **23** to direct (one's eyes) or (of one's eyes) to be directed: *her eyes rested on the sleeping child* **24** to depend or cause to depend; base; rely: *the whole argument rests on one crucial fact* **25** to put pastry in a cool place to allow the gluten to contract **26** (*intr*; foll by *with*, *on*, *upon*, etc) to be a responsibility (of): *it rests with us to apportion blame* **27** *law* to finish the introduction of evidence in (a case) **28** *rest on one's oars* to stop doing anything for a time [Old English *ræst*, *reste*, of Germanic origin; related to Gothic *rasta* a mile, Old Norse *röst* mile] ▷ **'rester** *n*

rest² (rest) *the rest n* **1** something left or remaining; remainder **2** the others: *the rest of the world vb* **3** (*copula*) to continue to be (as specified); remain: *rest assured* [C15: from Old French *rester* to remain, from Latin *restāre*, from RE- + *stāre* to STAND]

rest area *n Austral & NZ* a motorists' stopping place, usually off a highway, equipped with tables, seats, etc

restaurant ('rɛstə,rɒŋ, 'rɛstrɒŋ, -rɒnt) *n* a commercial establishment where meals are prepared and served to customers [C19: from French, from RESTORE]

restaurant car *n Brit* a railway coach in which meals are served. Also called: dining car

restaurateur (,rɛstərə'tɜ:) *n* a person who owns or runs a restaurant [C18: via French from Late Latin *restaurātor* one who restores, from Latin *restaurāre* to RESTORE]
● USAGE Although the spelling *restauranteur* occurs
● frequently, it is a misspelling and should be avoided

rest-cure *n* **1** a rest taken as part of a course of medical treatment, as for stress, anxiety, etc **2** an easy undemanding time or assignment: usually used with a negative: *it's no rest-cure, I can assure you*

restful ('rɛstfʊl) *adj* **1** giving or conducive to rest **2** being at rest; tranquil; calm ▷ **'restfully** *adv* ▷ **'restfulness** *n*

restharrow ('rɛst,hærəʊ) *n* any of several Eurasian leguminous plants of the genus *Ononis*, such as *O. repens* and *O. spinosa*, with tough stems and roots [C16: from *rest* variant of ARREST (to hinder, stop) + HARROW]

resting ('rɛstɪŋ) *adj* **1** not moving or working; at rest **2** *euphemistic* (of an actor) out of work **3** (esp of plant spores) undergoing a period of dormancy before germination

restitution (,rɛstɪ'tju:ʃən) *n* **1** the act of giving back something that has been lost or stolen **2** *law* the act of compensating for loss or injury by reverting as far as possible to the position before such injury occurred **3** the return of an object or system to its original state, esp a restoration of shape after elastic deformation [C13: from Latin *restitūtiō*, from *restituere* to rebuild, from RE- + *statuere* to set up] ▷ **'resti,tutive** *or* **,resti'tutory** *adj*

restive ('rɛstɪv) *adj* **1** restless, nervous, or uneasy **2** impatient of control or authority [C16: from Old French *restif* balky, from *rester* to remain] ▷ **'restively** *adv* ▷ **'restiveness** *n*

restless ('rɛstlɪs) *adj* **1** unable to stay still or quiet **2** ceaselessly active or moving: *the restless wind* **3** worried; anxious; uneasy **4** not restful; without repose: *a restless night* ▷ **'restlessly** *adv* ▷ **'restlessness** *n*

rest mass *n* the mass of an object that is at rest relative to an observer. It is the mass used in Newtonian mechanics

restoration (,rɛstə'reɪʃən) *n* **1** the act of restoring or state of being restored, as to a former or original condition, place, etc **2** the replacement or giving back of something lost, stolen, etc **3** something restored, replaced, or reconstructed **4** a model or representation of an extinct animal, landscape of a former geological age, etc

Restoration (,rɛstə'reɪʃən) *n Brit history* **a** the re-establishment of the monarchy in 1660 or the reign of Charles II (1660–85) **b** (*as modifier*): *Restoration drama*

restorative (rɪ'stɒrətɪv) *adj* **1** tending to revive or renew health, spirits, etc ▷ *n* **2** anything that restores or revives, esp a drug or agent that promotes health or strength

restorative justice *n* a method of dealing with convicted criminals in which they are urged to accept responsibility for their offences through meeting victims, making amends to victims or the community, etc

restore (rɪ'stɔ:) *vb* (*tr*) **1** to return (something, esp a work of art or building) to an original or former condition **2** to bring back to health, good spirits, etc **3** to return (something lost, stolen, etc) to its owner **4** to reintroduce or re-enforce: *to restore discipline* **5** to reconstruct (an extinct animal, former landscape, etc) [C13: from Old French, from Latin *restaurāre* to rebuild, from RE- + *-staurāre*, as in *instaurāre* to renew] ▷ **re'storable** *adj* ▷ **re'storer** *n*

restrain (rɪ'streɪn) *vb* (*tr*) **1** to hold (someone) back from some action, esp by force **2** to deprive (someone) of liberty, as by imprisonment **3** to limit or restrict [C14 *restreyne*, from Old French *restreindre*, from Latin *restringere* to draw back tightly, from RE- + *stringere* to draw, bind; see STRAIN¹] ▷ **re'strainable** *adj* ▷ **re'strained** *adj* ▷ **restrainedly** (rɪ'streɪnɪdlɪ) *adv* ▷ **re'strainer** *n*

restraining order *n US law* an order issued by a civil court to a potential abuser to keep away from those named in the order

restraint (rɪ'streɪnt) *n* **1** the ability to control or moderate one's impulses, passions, etc **2** the act of restraining or the state of being restrained **3** something that restrains; restriction [C15: from Old French *restreinte*, from *restreindre* to RESTRAIN]

restraint of trade *n* action tending to interfere with the freedom to compete in business

restrict (rɪ'strɪkt) *vb* (often foll by *to*) to confine or keep within certain often specified limits or selected bounds [C16: from Latin *restrictus* bound up, from *restringere*; see RESTRAIN]

restricted (rɪ'strɪktɪd) *adj* **1** limited or confined **2** not accessible to the general public or (*esp US*) out of bounds to military personnel **3** *Brit* denoting or in a zone in which a speed limit or waiting restrictions for vehicles apply ▷ **re'strictedly** *adv* ▷ **re'strictedness** *n*

restriction (rɪ'strɪkʃən) *n* **1** something that restricts; a restrictive measure, law, etc **2** the act of restricting or the state of being restricted ▷ **re'strictionist** *n, adj*

restrictive (rɪ'strɪktɪv) *adj* **1** restricting or tending to restrict **2** *grammar* denoting a relative clause or phrase that restricts the number of possible referents of its antecedent. The relative clause in *Americans who live in New York* is restrictive; the relative clause in *Americans, who are generally extrovert*, is nonrestrictive ▷ **re'strictively** *adv* ▷ **re'strictiveness** *n*

restrictive practice *n Brit* **1** a trading agreement against the public interest **2** a practice of a union or other group tending to limit the freedom of other workers or employers

rest room *n* a room in a public building having lavatories, washing facilities, and sometimes couches

restructure (ri:'strʌktʃə) *vb* (*tr*) to organize (a system, business, society, etc) in a different way: *radical attempts to restructure the economy* ▷ **re'structuring** *n*

result (rɪ'zʌlt) *n* **1** something that ensues from an action, policy, course of events, etc; outcome; consequence **2** a number, quantity, or value obtained by solving a mathematical problem **3** *US* a decision of a legislative body **4** (*often plural*) the final score or outcome of a sporting contest **5** a favourable result, esp a victory or success ▷ *vb* (*intr*) **6** (often foll by *from*) to be the outcome or consequence (of) **7** (foll by *in*) to issue or terminate (in a specified way, state, etc); end: *to result in tragedy* [C15: from Latin *resultāre* to rebound, spring from, from RE- + *saltāre* to leap]

resultant (rɪ'zʌltənt) *adj* **1** that results; resulting ▷ *n* **2** *maths, physics* a single vector that is the vector sum of two or more other vectors

resume (rɪ'zju:m) *vb* **1** to begin again or go on with (something adjourned or interrupted) **2** (*tr*) to occupy again, take back, or recover: *to resume one's seat; to resume possession* **3** *archaic* to summarize; make a résumé of [C15: from Latin *resūmere* to take up again, from RE- + *sūmere* to take up] ▷ **re'sumable** *adj* ▷ **re'sumer** *n*

résumé ('rezjʊ,meɪ) *n* **1** a short descriptive summary, as of events **2** *US & Canadian* another name for **curriculum vitae** [C19: from French, from *résumer* to RESUME]

resumption (rɪ'zʌmpʃən) *n* the act of resuming or beginning again [C15: via Old French from Late Latin

resumptiō, from Latin *resūmere* to RESUME] > re'sumptive *adj* > re'sumptively *adv*

resupinate (rɪ'sju:pɪnɪt) *adj botany* (of plant parts, esp the flowers of many orchids) reversed or inverted in position, so as to appear to be upside down [c18: from Latin *resupīnātus* bent back, from *resupīnāre*, from RE- + *supīnāre* to place on the back; see SUPINE] > re͵supi'nation *n*

resurge (rɪ'sɜ:dʒ) *vb* (*intr*) *rare* to rise again from or as if from the dead [c16: from Latin *resurgere* to rise again, reappear, from RE- + *surgere* to lift, arise, SURGE]

resurgent (rɪ'sɜ:dʒənt) *adj* rising again, as to new life, vigour, etc: *resurgent nationalism* > re'surgence *n*

resurrect (͵rezə'rekt) *vb* **1** to rise or raise from the dead; bring or be brought back to life **2** (*tr*) to bring back into use or activity; revive **3** (*tr*) *facetious* (formerly) to exhume and steal (a body) from its grave, esp in order to sell it

resurrection (͵rezə'rekʃən) *n* **1** a supposed act or instance of a dead person coming back to life **2** belief in the possibility of this as part of a religious or mystical system **3** the condition of those who have risen from the dead: *we shall all live in the resurrection* **4** the revival of something: *a resurrection of an old story* [c13: via Old French from Late Latin *resurrectiō*, from Latin *resurgere* to rise again; see RESURGE] > ͵resur'rectional *or* ͵resur'rectionary *adj*

Resurrection (͵rezə'rekʃən) *n Christian theol* **1** the rising again of Christ from the tomb three days after his death **2** the rising again from the dead of all mankind at the Last Judgment

resurrectionism (͵rezə'rekʃə͵nɪzəm) *n* belief that men will rise again from the dead, esp the Christian doctrine of the Resurrection of Christ and of all mankind at the Last Judgment

resurrectionist (͵rezə'rekʃənɪst) *n* **1** *facetious* (formerly) a body snatcher **2** a person who believes in the Resurrection

resurrection plant *n* any of several unrelated desert plants that form a tight ball when dry and unfold and bloom when moistened. The best-known examples are the crucifer *Anastatica hierochuntica* (also called **rose of Jericho**), club mosses of the genus *Selaginella*, and the composite *Asteriscus pygmoeus*

resuscitate (rɪ'sʌsɪ͵teɪt) *vb* (*tr*) to restore to consciousness; revive [c16: from Latin *resuscitāre*, from RE- + *suscitāre* to raise, from *sub*- up from below + *citāre* to rouse, from *citus* quick] > re͵susci'tation *n* > re'suscitative *adj* > re'susci͵tator *n*

resveratrol (rɪ'sverə͵trɒl) *n* a compound found in red grapes, mulberries, peanuts, and certain plants, used medicinally as an antioxidant and anti-inflammatory [c20: from RES(ORCINOL) + VERATR(INE) + -OL[1]]

ret (ret) *vb* **rets**, **retting**, **retted** (*tr*) to moisten or soak (flax, hemp, jute, etc) to promote bacterial action in order to facilitate separation of the fibres from the woody tissue by beating [c15: of Germanic origin; related to Middle Dutch *reeten*, Swedish *röta*, German *rösten*; see ROT[1]]

retable (rɪ'teɪbəl) *n* an ornamental screenlike structure above and behind an altar, esp one used as a setting for a religious picture or carving [c19: from French, from Spanish *retablo*, from Latin *retrō* behind + *tabula* board; see REAR[1], TABLE]

retail ('ri:teɪl) *n* **1** the sale of goods individually or in small quantities to consumers. See **wholesale** (sense 1) ▷ *adj* **2** of, relating to, or engaged in such selling: *retail prices* ▷ *adv* **3** in small amounts or at a retail price ▷ *vb* **4** to sell or be sold in small quantities to consumers **5** (rɪ'teɪl) (*tr*) to relate (gossip, scandal, etc) in detail, esp persistently [c14: from Old French *retaillier* to cut off, from RE- + *taillier* to cut; see TAILOR] > 'retailer *n*

retail politics *n* (*functioning as plural*) *informal* the practice of a politician soliciting in person for votes from the public

retail price index *n* (in Britain) a list, based on government figures and usually published monthly, that shows the extent of change in the prices of a range of goods selected as being essential items in the budget

of a normal household. Abbreviation: RPI

retail therapy *n jocular* the action of shopping for clothes, etc in order to cheer oneself up

retain (rɪ'teɪn) *vb* (*tr*) **1** to keep in one's possession **2** to be able to hold or contain: *soil that retains water* **3** (of a person) to be able to remember (information, facts, etc) without difficulty **4** to hold in position **5** to keep for one's future use, as by paying a retainer or nominal charge **6** *law* to engage the services of (a barrister) by payment of a preliminary fee [c14: from Old French *retenir*, from Latin *retinēre* to hold back, from RE- + *tenēre* to hold] > re'tainable *adj* > re'tainment *n*

retained object *n grammar* a direct or indirect object of a passive verb The phrase *the drawings* in the sentence *Harry was given the drawings* is a retained object

retainer (rɪ'teɪnə) *n* **1** *history* a supporter or dependant of a person of rank, esp a soldier **2** a servant, esp one who has been with a family for a long time **3** a clip, frame, or similar device that prevents a part of a machine, engine, etc, from moving **4** a fee paid in advance to secure first option on the services of a barrister, jockey, etc **5** a reduced rent paid for a flat, room, etc, during absence to reserve it for future use

retaining wall *n* a wall constructed to hold back earth, loose rock, etc. Also called: revetment

retake *vb* (ri:'teɪk) **-takes**, **-taking**, **-took**, **-taken** (*tr*) **1** to take back or capture again: *to retake a fortress* **2** *films* to shoot again (a shot or scene) **3** to tape again (a recording) ▷ *n* ('ri:͵teɪk) **4** *films* a rephotographed shot or scene **5** a retaped recording > re'taker *n*

retaliate (rɪ'tælɪ͵eɪt) *vb* **1** (*intr*) to take retributory action, esp by returning some injury or wrong in kind **2** (*intr*) to cast (accustations) back upon a person [c17: from Late Latin *retāliāre*, from Latin RE- + *tālis* of such kind] > re͵tali'ation *n* > re'taliative *or* re'taliatory *adj*

retard *vb* (rɪ'tɑ:d) **1** (*tr*) to delay or slow down (the progress, speed, or development) of (something) ▷ *n* ('ri:tɑ:d) **2** *US offensive* a retarded person **3** *US offensive* a foolish person [c15: from Old French *retarder*, from Latin *retardāre*, from RE- + *tardāre* to make slow, from *tardus* sluggish; see TARDY]

retardant (rɪ'tɑ:dᵊnt) *n* **1** a substance that reduces the rate of a chemical reaction ▷ *adj* **2** having a slowing effect

retardation (͵ri:tɑ:'deɪʃən) *or less commonly* **retardment** (rɪ'tɑ:dmənt) *n* **1** the act of retarding or the state of being retarded **2** something that retards; hindrance > re'tardative *or* re'tardatory *adj*

retarded (rɪ'tɑ:dɪd) *adj* underdeveloped, esp mentally and esp having an IQ of 70 to 85

retarder (rɪ'tɑ:də) *n* **1** a person or thing that retards **2** a substance added to slow down the rate of a chemical change, such as one added to cement to delay its setting

retch (retʃ, ri:tʃ) *vb* **1** (*intr*) to undergo an involuntary spasm of ineffectual vomiting; heave ▷ *n* **2** an involuntary spasm of ineffectual vomiting [Old English *hrǣcan*; related to Old Norse *hrækja* to spit]

retd *abbreviation* **1** retired **2** retained **3** returned

rete ('ri:ti) *n, pl* **retia** ('ri:ʃɪə, -tɪə) *anatomy* any network of nerves or blood vessels; plexus [c14 (referring to a metal network used with an astrolabe): from Latin *rēte* net] > 'retial *adj*

retention (rɪ'tenʃən) *n* **1** the act of retaining or state of being retained **2** the capacity to hold or retain liquid **3** the capacity to remember **4** *pathol* the abnormal holding within the body of urine, faeces, etc, that are normally excreted **5** *commerce* a sum of money owed to a contractor but not paid for an agreed period as a safeguard against any faults found in the work carried out **6** (*plural*) *accounting* profits earned by a company but not distributed as dividends; retained earnings [c14: from Latin *retentiō*, from *retinēre* to RETAIN]

retentive (rɪ'tentɪv) *adj* having the capacity to retain or remember > re'tentively *adv* > re'tentiveness *n*

Réti ('reɪti) *n* **Richard**. 1889–1929, Hungarian chess player and theorist; influential in enunciating the theories of the hypermodern school

retiarius (͵ri:tɪ'eərɪəs, ͵ri:ʃɪ-) *n, pl* **-arii** (-'eərɪ͵aɪ) (in ancient Rome) a gladiator armed with a net and trident

[Latin, from *rēte* net]

reticent ('rɛtɪsənt) *adj* not open or communicative; not saying all that one knows; taciturn; reserved [c19: from Latin *reticēre* to keep silent, from RE- + *tacēre* to be silent] > 'reticence *n* > 'reticently *adv*

reticle ('rɛtɪkəl) *or less commonly* **reticule** *n* a network of fine lines, wires, etc, placed in the focal plane of an optical instrument to assist measurement of the size or position of objects under observation [c17: from Latin *rēticulum* a little net, from *rēte* net]

reticulate *adj* (rɪ'tɪkjʊlɪt) *Also:* reticular (rɪ'tɪkjʊlə) **1** in the form of a network or having a network of parts: *a reticulate leaf* ▷ *vb* (rɪ'tɪkjʊ,leɪt) **2** to form or be formed into a net [c17: from Late Latin *rēticulātus* made like a net] > re'ticulately *adv* > re,ticu'lation *n*

reticule ('rɛtɪ,kjuːl) *n* **1** (in the 18th and 19th centuries) a woman's small bag or purse, usually in the form of a pouch with a drawstring and made of net, beading, brocade, etc **2** a variant of **reticle** [c18: from French *réticule*, from Latin *rēticulum* RETICLE]

reticulum (rɪ'tɪkjʊləm) *n, pl* **-la** (-lə) **1** any fine network, esp one in the body composed of cells, fibres, etc **2** the second compartment of the stomach of ruminants, situated between the rumen and psalterium [c17: from Latin: little net, from *rēte* net]

retiform ('riːtɪ,fɔːm, 'rɛt-) *adj rare* netlike; reticulate [c17: from Latin *rēte* net + *forma* shape]

retina ('rɛtɪnə) *n, pl* **-nas, -nae** (-,niː) the light-sensitive membrane forming the inner lining of the posterior wall of the eyeball, composed largely of a specialized terminal expansion of the optic nerve. Images focused here by the lens of the eye are transmitted to the brain as nerve impulses [c14: from Medieval Latin, perhaps from Latin *rēte* net] > 'retinal *adj*

retinene ('rɛtɪ,niːn) *n* the aldehyde form of the polyene retinol (vitamin A) that associates with the protein opsin to form the visual purple pigment rhodopsin [c20: from RETINA + -ENE]

retinitis (,rɛtɪ'naɪtɪs) *n* inflammation of the retina [c20: from New Latin, from RETINA + -ITIS]

retinitis pigmentosa (,pɪgmən'təʊsə) *n* a degenerative hereditary disease of the human eye, characterized by pigmentary changes in the retina, night blindness, and eventual loss of vision [c19: *pigmentosa*, feminine of Latin *pigmentosus*]

retinopathy (,rɛtɪ'nɒpəθɪ) *n* any of various noninflammatory diseases of the retina which may have serious effects on vision

retinoscopy (,rɛtɪ'nɒskəpɪ) *n ophthalmol* a procedure for detecting errors of refraction in the eye by means of an instrument (**retinoscope**) that reflects a beam of light from a mirror into the eye. Diagnosis is made by observing the areas of shadow and the direction in which the light moves when the mirror is rotated > retinoscopic (,rɛtɪnə'skɒpɪk) *adj* >,retino'scopically *adv* >,reti'noscopist *n*

retinue ('rɛtɪ,njuː) *n* a body of aides and retainers attending an important person, royalty, etc [c14: from Old French *retenue*, from *retenir* to RETAIN]

retiral (rɪ'taɪərəl) *n Scot* the act of retiring from office, one's work, etc; retirement

retire (rɪ'taɪə) *vb* (*mainly intr*) **1** (*also tr*) to give up or to cause (a person) to give up his work, a post, etc, esp on reaching pensionable age (in Britain and Australia usually 65 for men, 60 for women) **2** to go away, as into seclusion, for recuperation, etc **3** to go to bed **4** to recede or disappear: *the sun retired behind the clouds* **5** to withdraw from a sporting contest, esp because of injury **6** (*also tr*) to pull back (troops, etc) from battle or an exposed position or (of troops, etc) to fall back **7** (*tr*) to remove (money) from circulation [c16: from French *retirer*, from Old French RE- + *tirer* to pull, draw] > re'tired *adj* > re'tirer *n*

retirement (rɪ'taɪəmənt) *n* **1 a** the act of retiring from one's work, office, etc **b** (*as modifier*): *retirement age* **2** the period of being retired from work: *she had many plans for her retirement* **3** seclusion from the world; privacy **4** the act of going away or retreating

retirement pension *n* a pension given to a person who has retired from regular employment, whether paid by the state, arising from the person's former employment, or the product of investment in a personal or stakeholder pension scheme

retiring (rɪ'taɪərɪŋ) *adj* shunning contact with others; shy; reserved > re'tiringly *adv*

retool (riː'tuːl) *vb* **1** to replace, re-equip, or rearrange the tools in (a factory, etc) **2** *chiefly US & Canadian* to revise or reorganize

retort¹ (rɪ'tɔːt) *vb* **1** (when *tr*, *takes a clause as object*) to utter (something) quickly, sharply, wittily, or angrily, in response **2** to use (an argument) against its originator; turn the tables by saying (something) ▷ *n* **3** a sharp, angry, or witty reply **4** an argument used against its originator [c16: from Latin *retorquēre* to twist back, from RE- + *torquēre* to twist, wrench] > re'torter *n*

retort² (rɪ'tɔːt) *n* **1** a glass vessel with a round bulb and long tapering neck that is bent down, used esp in a laboratory for distillation **2** a vessel in which large quantities of material may be heated, esp one used for heating ores in the production of metals or heating coal to produce gas ▷ *vb* **3** (*tr*) to heat in a retort [c17: from French *retorte*, from Medieval Latin *retorta*, from Latin *retorquēre* to twist back; see RETORT¹]

retouch (riː'tʌtʃ) *vb* (*tr*) **1** to restore, correct, or improve (a painting, make-up, etc) with new touches **2** *photog* to alter (a negative or print) by painting over blemishes or adding details ▷ *n* **3** the art or practice of retouching **4** a detail that is the result of retouching **5** a photograph, painting, etc, that has been retouched > re'toucher *n*

retrace (rɪ'treɪs) *vb* (*tr*) **1** to go back over (one's steps, a route, etc) again **2** to go over (a past event) in the mind; recall **3** to go over (a story, account, etc) from the beginning

re-trace (riː'treɪs) *vb* (*tr*) to trace (a map, drawing, etc) again

retract (rɪ'trækt) *vb* **1** (*tr*) to draw in (a part or appendage): *a snail can retract its horns; to retract the landing gear of an aircraft* **2** to withdraw (a statement, opinion, charge, etc) as invalid or unjustified **3** to go back on (a promise or agreement) [c16: from Latin *retractāre* to withdraw, from *tractāre* to pull, from *trahere* to drag] > retractation (,riː,træk'teɪʃən) *n* > re'tractable *or* re'tractible *adj* > re'traction *n* > re'tractive *adj*

retractile (rɪ'træktaɪl) *adj* capable of being drawn in: *the retractile claws of a cat* > retractility (,riː,træk'tɪlɪtɪ) *n*

retractor (rɪ'træktə) *n* **1** *anatomy* any of various muscles that retract an organ or part **2** *surgery* an instrument for holding back the edges of a surgical incision or organ or part **3** a person or thing that retracts

retral ('riːtrəl, 'rɛtrəl) *adj rare* at, near, or towards the back [c19: from Latin *retrō* backwards] > 'retrally *adv*

retread *vb* (riː'trɛd) **-treads, -treading, -treaded** **1** (*tr*) another word for **remould** (sense 2) ▷ *n* ('riː,trɛd) **2** another word for **remould** (sense 3) **3** *Austral & NZ informal* a pensioner who has resumed employment, esp in a former profession **4** a film, piece of music, etc which is a superficially altered version of an earlier original

re-tread (riː'trɛd) *vb* **-treads, -treading, -trod,** *or* **-trodden** (*tr*) to tread or walk over (one's steps) again

retreat (rɪ'triːt) *vb* (*mainly intr*) **1** *military* to withdraw or retire in the face of or from action with an enemy, either due to defeat or in order to adopt a more favourable position **2** to retire or withdraw, as to seclusion or shelter **3** (of a person's features) to slope back; recede **4** (*tr*) *chess* to move (a piece) back ▷ *n* **5** the act of retreating or withdrawing **6** *military* **a** a withdrawal or retirement in the face of the enemy **b** a bugle call signifying withdrawal or retirement, esp (formerly) to within a defended fortification **7** retirement or seclusion **8** a place, such as a sanatorium or monastery, to which one may retire for refuge, quiet, etc **9** a period of seclusion, esp for religious contemplation **10** an institution, esp a private one, for the care and treatment of the mentally ill, infirm, elderly, etc [c14: from Old French *retret*, from *retraire* to withdraw, from Latin *retrahere* to pull back; see RETRACT]

retrench (rɪ'trɛntʃ) *vb* **1** to reduce or curtail (costs);

economize **2** (*tr*) to shorten, delete, or abridge [C17: from Old French *retrenchier*, from RE- + *trenchier* to cut, from Latin *truncāre* to lop; see TRENCH] > re'trenchment *n*

retribution (ˌretrɪ'bjuːʃən) *n* **1** the act of punishing or taking vengeance for wrongdoing, sin, or injury **2** punishment or vengeance [C14: via Old French from Church Latin *retribūtiō*, from Latin *retribuere* to repay, from RE- + *tribuere* to pay; see TRIBUTE] > **retributive** (rɪ'trɪbjʊtɪv) *or less commonly* re'tributory *adj* > re'tributively *adv*

retrieval (rɪ'triːvᵊl) *n* **1** the act or process of retrieving **2** the possibility of recovery, restoration, or rectification (esp in the phrase **beyond retrieval**) **3** a computer filing operation that recalls records or other data from a file

retrieve (rɪ'triːv) *vb* (*mainly tr*) **1** to get or fetch back again; recover **2** to bring back to a more satisfactory state; revive **3** to extricate from trouble or danger; rescue or save **4** to recover or make newly available (stored information) from a computer system **5** (*also intr*) (of dogs) to find and fetch (shot game) **6** *tennis, squash, badminton* to return successfully (a shot difficult to reach) **7** to recall; remember ▷ *n* **8** the act of retrieving **9** the chance of being retrieved [C15: from Old French *retrover*, from RE- + *trouver* to find, perhaps from Vulgar Latin *tropāre* (unattested) to compose; see TROVER, TROUBADOUR] > re'trievable *adj*

retriever (rɪ'triːvə) *n* **1** one of a breed of large gun dogs that can be trained to retrieve game **2** any dog used to retrieve shot game **3** a person or thing that retrieves

retro ('retrəʊ) *n, pl* **-ros 1** short for **retrorocket** ▷ *adj* **2** denoting something associated with or revived from the past: *retro dressing; retro fashion*

retro- *prefix* **1** back or backwards: *retroactive* **2** located behind: *retrolental* [from Latin *retrō* behind, backwards]

retroact (ˌretrəʊ'ækt) *vb* (*intr*) **1** to act in opposition **2** to influence or have reference to past events > ˌretro'action *n*

retroactive (ˌretrəʊ'æktɪv) *adj* applying or referring to the past: *retroactive legislation* **2** effective or operative from a date or for a period in the past > ˌretro'actively *adv* > ˌretro'activeness *or* ˌretroac'tivity *n*

retrocede (ˌretrəʊ'siːd) *vb* **1** (*tr*) to give back; return **2** (*intr*) to go back or retire; recede > **retrocession** (ˌretrəʊ'seʃən) *or* ˌretro'cedence *n* > ˌretro'cessive *or* ˌretro'cedent *adj*

retrochoir ('retrəʊˌkwaɪə) *n* the space in a large church or cathedral behind the high altar

retrofire ('retrəʊˌfaɪə) *n* **1** the act of firing a retrorocket **2** the moment at which it is fired

retrofit ('retrəʊˌfɪt) *vb* **-fits, -fitting, -fitted** (*tr*) to equip (a vehicle, piece of equipment, etc) with new parts, safety devices, etc, after manufacture

retroflex ('retrəʊˌfleks) *or* **retroflexed** *adj* **1** bent or curved backwards **2** *phonetics* of, relating to, or involving retroflexion [C18: from Latin *retrōflexus*, from *retrōflectere*, from RETRO- + *flectere* to bend]

retroflexion *or* **retroflection** (ˌretrəʊ'flekʃən) *n* **1** the act or condition of bending or being bent backwards **2** *phonetics* the act of turning the tip of the tongue upwards and backwards towards the hard palate in the articulation of a vowel or a consonant

retrograde ('retrəʊˌgreɪd) *adj* **1** moving or bending backwards **2** (esp of order) reverse or inverse **3** tending towards an earlier worse condition; declining or deteriorating **4** *astronomy* **a** occurring or orbiting in a direction opposite to that of the earth's motion around the sun. See **direct** (sense 18) **b** occurring or orbiting in a direction around a planet opposite to the planet's rotational direction **c** appearing to move in a clockwise direction due to the rotational period exceeding the period of revolution around the sun: *Venus has retrograde rotation* ▷ *vb* (*intr*) **5** to move in a retrograde direction; retrogress [C14: from Latin *retrōgradī* to go backwards, from *gradī* to walk, go] > ˌretrogra'dation *n* > 'retroˌgradely *adv*

retrogress (ˌretrəʊ'gres) *vb* (*intr*) **1** to go back to an earlier, esp worse, condition; degenerate or deteriorate **2** to move backwards; recede [C19: from Latin *retrōgressus* having moved backwards, from *retrōgradī*; see

RETROGRADE] > ˌretro'gression *n* > ˌretro'gressive *adj* > ˌretro'gressively *adv*

retrorocket ('retrəʊˌrɒkɪt) *n* a small auxiliary rocket engine on a larger rocket, missile, or spacecraft, that produces thrust in the opposite direction to the direction of flight in order to decelerate the vehicle or make it move backwards. Often shortened to **retro**

retrorse (rɪ'trɔːs) *adj* (esp of plant parts) pointing backwards or in a direction opposite to normal [C19: from Latin *retrōrsus*, shortened form of *retrōversus* turned back, from RETRO- + *vertere* to turn] > re'trorsely *adv*

retrospect ('retrəʊˌspekt) *n* the act of surveying things past (often in the phrase **in retrospect**) [C17: from Latin *retrōspicere* to look back, from RETRO- + *specere* to look] > ˌretro'spection *n*

retrospective (ˌretrəʊ'spektɪv) *adj* **1** looking or directed backwards, esp in time; characterized by retrospection **2** applying to the past; retroactive ▷ *n* **3** an exhibition of an artist's life's work or a representative selection of it > ˌretro'spectively *adv*

retroussé (rə'truːseɪ; *French* rətruse) *adj* (of a nose) turned up [C19: from French *retrousser* to tuck up; see TRUSS]

retroversion (ˌretrəʊ'vɜːʃən) *n* **1** the act of turning or condition of being turned backwards **2** the condition of a part or organ, esp the uterus, that is turned or tilted backwards > 'retroˌverted *adj*

Retrovir ('retrəʊˌvɪə) *n trademark* a brand of the drug zidovudine

retrovirus ('retrəʊˌvaɪrəs) *n* any of several viruses whose genetic specification is encoded in RNA rather than DNA and that are able to reverse the normal flow of genetic information from DNA to RNA by transcribing RNA into DNA: many retroviruses are known to cause cancer in animals > 'retroˌviral *adj*

retsina (ret'siːnə, 'retsɪnə) *n* a Greek wine flavoured with resin [Modern Greek, from Italian *resina* RESIN]

retune (riː'tjuːn) *vb* **1** to tune (a musical instrument) differently or again **2** to tune (a radio, television, etc) to a different frequency

return (rɪ'tɜːn) *vb* **1** (*intr*) to come back to a former place or state **2** (*tr*) to give, take, or carry back; replace or restore **3** (*tr*) to repay or recompense, esp with something of equivalent value: *return the compliment* **4** (*tr*) to earn or yield (profit or interest) as an income from an investment or venture **5** (*intr*) to come back or revert in thought or speech: *I'll return to that later* **6** (*intr*) to recur or reappear: *the symptoms have returned* **7** to answer or reply **8** (*tr*) to vote into office; elect **9** *law* (of a jury) to deliver or render (a verdict) **10** (*tr*) to submit (a report, etc) about (someone or something) to someone in authority **11** (*tr*) *cards* to lead back (the suit led by one's partner) **12** (*tr*) *ball games* to hit, throw, or play (a ball) back **13 return thanks** (of Christians) to say grace before a meal ▷ *n* **14** the act or an instance of coming back **15** something that is given or sent back, esp unsatisfactory merchandise returned to the maker or supplier or a theatre ticket sent back by a purchaser for resale **16** the act or an instance of putting, sending, or carrying back; replacement or restoration **17** (*often plural*) the yield, revenue, or profit accruing from an investment, transaction, or venture **18** the act or an instance of reciprocation or repayment (esp in the phrase **in return for**) **19** a recurrence or reappearance **20** an official report, esp of the financial condition of a company **21 a** a form (a **tax return**) on which a statement concerning one's taxable income is made **b** the statement itself **22** (*often plural*) a statement of the votes counted at an election or poll **23** an answer or reply **24** *Brit* short for **return ticket** **25** *architect* a part of a building that forms an angle with the façade **26** *law* a report by a bailiff or other officer on the outcome of a formal document such as a claim, summons, etc, issued by a court **27** *cards* a lead of a card in the suit that one's partner has previously led **28** *ball games* the act of playing or throwing a ball back **29 by return** *or* **by return of post** *Brit* by the next post back to the sender **30 many happy returns** *or* **many happy returns of the day** a conventional greeting to someone on his or her birthday

▷ *adj* **31** of, relating to, or characterized by a return: *a return visit*; *a return performance* **32** denoting a second, reciprocated occasion: *a return match* [c14: from Old French *retorner*; see RE-, TURN] > re,turna'bility *n* > re'turnable *adj*

return crease *n cricket* one of two lines marked at right-angles to each bowling crease, from inside which a bowler must deliver the ball

returned soldier *n Austral & NZ* a soldier who has served abroad. Also called: (*Austral*) returned man

returner (rɪ'tɜ:nə) *n* **1** a person or thing that returns **2** a person who goes back to work after a break, esp a woman who has had children

returning officer *n* (in Britain, Canada, Australia, etc) an official in charge of conducting an election in a constituency or electoral district, who supervises the counting of votes and announces the results

return ticket *n Brit* a ticket entitling a passenger to travel to his destination and back again

retuse (rɪ'tju:s) *adj botany* having a rounded apex and a central depression [c18: from Latin *retundere* to make blunt, from RE- + *tundere* to pound]

Retz (French rets) *n* Gilles de Retz See **Rais**

Reuben ('ru:bɪn) *n Old Testament* **1** the eldest son of Jacob and Leah: one of the 12 patriarchs of Israel (Genesis 29:30) **2** the Israelite tribe descended from him **3** the territory of this tribe, lying to the northeast of the Dead Sea

Reuchlin (German 'rɔʏçli:n) *n* Johann (jo'han). 1455–1522, German humanist, who promoted the study of Greek and Hebrew

reunify (ri:'ju:nɪ,faɪ) *vb* -fies, -fying, -fied (*tr*) to bring together again (something, esp a country previously divided) > ,reunifi'cation *n*

reunion (ri:'ju:njən) *n* **1** the act or process of coming together again **2** the state or condition of having been brought together again **3** a gathering of relatives, friends, or former associates

Réunion (ri:'ju:njən; French reynjɔ̃) *n* an island in the Indian Ocean, in the Mascarene Islands: an overseas region of France, having been in French possession since 1642. A number of far-flung and uninhabited islands, some located on the opposite side of Madagascar, were also politically part of Réunion until 2007, when they were transferred to the French Southern and Antarctic Territories. Capital: Saint-Denis. Pop: 767 000 (2004 est). Area: 2510 sq km (970 sq miles)

reunite (,ri:ju:'naɪt) *vb* to bring or come together again > ,reu'nitable *adj*

Reus (Spanish rɛus) *n* a city in NE Spain, northwest of Tarragona: became commercially important after the establishment of an English colony (about 1750). Pop: 94 407 (2003 est)

Reuter ('rɔɪtə) *n* Baron Paul Julius von (paul 'ju:lius fɔn). original name *Israel Beer Josaphat*. 1816–99, German telegrapher, who founded a news agency in London (1851)

Reutlingen (German 'rɔʏtlɪŋən) *n* a city in SW Germany, in Baden-Württemberg: founded in the 11th century; an Imperial free city from 1240 until 1802; textile industry. Pop: 112 346 (2003 est)

rev (rɛv) *informal* ▷ *n* **1** revolution per minute ▷ *vb* revs, revving, revved **2** (often foll by *up*) to increase the speed of revolution of (an engine)

rev. *abbreviation* **1** revenue **2** reverse(d) **3** review **4** revise(d) **5** revision **6** revolution **7** revolving

Rev. *abbreviation* **1** *Bible* Revelation **2** Reverend

Reval ('re:val) *n* the German name for **Tallinn**

revalue (ri:'vælju:) *or US* **revaluate** *vb* **1** to adjust the exchange value of (a currency), esp upwards. See **devalue 2** (*tr*) to make a fresh valuation or appraisal of > re,valu'ation *n*

revamp (ri:'væmp) *vb* (*tr*) **1** to patch up or renovate; repair or restore ▷ *n* **2** something that has been renovated or revamped **3** the act or process of revamping [c19: from RE- + VAMP²]

revanchism (rɪ'væntʃɪzəm) *n* **1** a foreign policy aimed at revenge or the regaining of lost territories **2** desire or support for such a policy [c20: from French *revanche*

REVENGE] > re'vanchist *n*, *adj*

rev counter *n Brit* an informal name for **tachometer**

Revd *abbreviation* Reverend

reveal (rɪ'vi:l) *vb* (*tr*) **1** (may take a clause as object or an infinitive) to disclose (a secret); divulge **2** to expose to view or show (something concealed) **3** (of God) to disclose (divine truths) either directly or through the medium of prophets, etc ▷ *n* **4** *architect* the vertical side of an opening in a wall, esp the side of a window or door between the frame and the front of the wall [c14: from Old French *reveler*, from Latin *revēlāre* to unveil, from RE- + *vēlum* a VEIL] > re'vealable *adj* > re'vealer *n* > re'vealment *n*

revealed religion *n* **1** religion based on the revelation by God to man of ideas that he would not have arrived at by his natural reason alone **2** religion in which the existence of God depends on revelation

revealing (rɪ'vi:lɪŋ) *adj* **1** of significance or import: *a very revealing experience* **2** showing or designed to show more of the body than is usual or conventional: *a revealing costume* > re'vealingly *adv*

reveille (rɪ'vælɪ) *n* **1** a signal, given by a bugle, drum, etc, to awaken soldiers or sailors in the morning **2** the hour at which this takes place [c17: from French *réveillez!* awake! from RE- + Old French *esveillier* to be wakeful, ultimately from Latin *vigilāre* to keep watch; see VIGIL]

revel ('rɛvəl) *vb* -els, -elling, -elled *or US* -els, -eling, -eled (*intr*) **1** (foll by *in*) to take pleasure or wallow: *to revel in success* **2** to take part in noisy festivities; make merry ▷ *n* **3** (often plural) an occasion of noisy merrymaking [c14: from Old French *reveler* to be merry, noisy, from Latin *rebellāre* to revolt, REBEL] > 'reveller *n*

revelation (,rɛvə'leɪʃən) *n* **1** the act or process of disclosing something previously secret or obscure, esp something true **2** a fact disclosed or revealed, esp in a dramatic or surprising way **3** *Christianity* God's disclosure of his own nature and his purpose for mankind, esp through the words of human intermediaries [c14: from Church Latin *revēlātiō* from Latin *revēlāre* to REVEAL] > ,reve'lational *adj*

Revelation (,rɛvə'leɪʃən) *n* Also called: the Apocalypse, the Revelation of Saint John the Divine (popularly, often plural) the last book of the New Testament, containing visionary descriptions of heaven, of conflicts between good and evil, and of the end of the world

revelationist (,rɛvə'leɪʃənɪst) *n* a person who believes that God has revealed certain truths to man

revelry ('rɛvəlrɪ) *n*, *pl* -ries noisy or unrestrained merrymaking

revenant ('rɛvɪnənt) *n* something, esp a ghost, that returns [c19: from French: ghost, from *revenir* to come back, from Latin *revenīre*, from RE- + *venīre* to come]

revenge (rɪ'vɛndʒ) *n* **1** the act of retaliating for wrongs or injury received; vengeance **2** something done as a means of vengeance **3** the desire to take vengeance or retaliate **4** a return match, regarded as a loser's opportunity to even the score ▷ *vb* (*tr*) **5** to inflict equivalent injury or damage for (injury received); retaliate in return for **6** to take vengeance for (oneself or another); avenge [c14: from Old French *revenger*, from Late Latin *revindicāre*, from RE- + *vindicāre* to VINDICATE] > re'venger *n* > re'venging *adj* > re'vengingly *adv*

revengeful (rɪ'vɛndʒfʊl) *adj* full of or characterized by desire for vengeance; vindictive > re'vengefully *adv* > re'vengefulness *n*

revenue ('rɛvɪ,nju:) *n* **1** the income accruing from taxation to a government during a specified period of time, usually a year **2 a** a government department responsible for the collection of government revenue **b** (*as modifier*): *revenue men* **3** the gross income from a business enterprise, investment, property, etc **4** a particular item of income **5** something that yields a regular financial return; source of income [c16: from Old French, from *revenir* to return, from Latin *revenīre*; see REVENANT]

revenue cutter *n* a small lightly armed boat used to enforce customs regulations and catch smugglers

reverb ('ri:vɜ:b) *n* an electronic device that creates artificial acoustics

r

reverberate (rɪ'vɜːbəˌreɪt) *vb* **1** (*intr*) to resound or re-echo **2** to reflect or be reflected many times **3** (*intr*) to rebound or recoil **4** (*intr*) (of the flame or heat in a reverberatory furnace) to be deflected onto the metal or ore on the hearth **5** (*tr*) to heat, melt, or refine (a metal or ore) in a reverberatory furnace [c16: from Latin *reverberāre* to strike back, from RE- + *verberāre* to beat, from *verber* a lash] > re'verberantly *adv* > re'verber'ation *n* > re'verbeˌrator *n* > reverberatory (rɪ'vɜːbərətərɪ, -trɪ) *adj, n*

reverberation time *n* a measure of the acoustic properties of a room, equal to the time taken for a sound to fall in intensity by 60 decibels. It is usually measured in seconds

reverberatory furnace *n* a metallurgical furnace having a curved roof that deflects heat onto the charge so that the fuel is not in direct contact with the ore

revere (rɪ'vɪə) *vb* (*tr*) to be in awe of and respect deeply; venerate [c17: from Latin *reverērī*, from RE- + *verērī* to fear, be in awe of]

Revere (rɪ'vɪə) *n* **Paul**. 1735–1818, American patriot and silversmith, best known for his night ride on April 18, 1775, to warn the Massachusetts colonists of the coming of the British troops

reverence ('rɛvərəns) *n* **1** a feeling or attitude of profound respect, usually reserved for the sacred or divine; devoted veneration **2** an outward manifestation of this feeling, esp a bow or act of obeisance **3** the state of being revered or commanding profound respect ▷ *vb* **4** (*tr*) to revere or venerate

Reverence ('rɛvərəns) *n* (preceded by *Your* or *His*) a title sometimes used to address or refer to a Roman Catholic priest

reverend ('rɛvərənd) *adj* **1** worthy of reverence **2** relating to or designating a clergyman or the clergy ▷ *n* **3** *informal* a clergyman [c15: from Latin *reverendus* fit to be revered; see REVERE]

Reverend ('rɛvərənd) *adj* a title of respect for a clergyman. Abbrevs: **Rev, Revd**
● USAGE *Reverend* with a surname alone (*Reverend Smith*),
● as a term of address ("*Yes, Reverend*"), or in the
● salutation of a letter (*Dear Rev. Mr Smith*) are all
● generally considered to be wrong usage. Preferred are
● (*the*) *Reverend John Smith* or *Reverend Mr Smith* and *Dear Mr*
● *Smith*

reverent ('rɛvərənt, 'rɛvrənt) *adj* feeling, expressing, or characterized by reverence [c14: from Latin *reverēns* respectful] > 'reverently *adv*

reverential (ˌrɛvə'rɛnʃəl) *adj* resulting from or showing reverence > ˌrever'entially *adv*

reverie or **revery** ('rɛvərɪ) *n, pl* **-eries** **1** an act or state of absent-minded daydreaming: *to fall into a reverie* **2** a piece of instrumental music suggestive of a daydream **3** *archaic* a fanciful or visionary notion; daydream [c14: from Old French *resverie* wildness, from *resver* to behave wildly, of uncertain origin; see RAVE¹]

revers (rɪ'vɪə) *n, pl* **-vers** (-'vɪəz) (*usually plural*) the turned-back lining of part of a garment, esp a lapel or cuff [c19: from French, literally: REVERSE]

reversal (rɪ'vɜːsəl) *n* **1** the act or an instance of reversing **2** a change for the worse; reverse **3** the state of being reversed **4** the annulment of a judicial decision, esp by an appeal court on grounds of error or irregularity

reverse (rɪ'vɜːs) *vb* (*mainly tr*) **1** to turn or set in an opposite direction, order, or position **2** to change into something different or contrary; alter completely: *reverse one's policy* **3** (*also intr*) to move or cause to move backwards or in an opposite direction: *to reverse a car* **4** to run (machinery, etc) in the opposite direction to normal **5** to turn inside out **6** *law* to revoke or set aside (a judgment, decree, etc); annul **7 reverse the charge** or **reverse the charges** to make a telephone call at the recipient's expense ▷ *n* **8** the opposite or contrary of something **9** the back or rear side of something **10** a change to an opposite position, order, or direction **11** a change for the worse; setback or defeat **12 a** the mechanism or gears by which machinery, a vehicle, etc, can be made to reverse its direction **b** (*as modifier*): *reverse gear* **13** the side of a coin bearing a secondary design **14 a** printed matter in which normally black or coloured

areas, esp lettering, appear white, and vice versa **b** (*as modifier*): *reverse plates* **15 in reverse** in an opposite or backward direction **16 the reverse of** emphatically not; not at all: *he was the reverse of polite when I called* ▷ *adj* **17** opposite or contrary in direction, position, order, nature, etc; turned backwards **18** back to front; inverted **19** operating or moving in a manner contrary to that which is usual **20** denoting or relating to a mirror image [c14: from Old French, from Latin *reversus*, from *revertere* to turn back] > re'versely *adv* > re'verser *n*

reverse-charge *adj* (*prenominal*) (of a telephone call) made at the recipient's expense

reverse osmosis *n* a technique for purifying water, in which pressure is applied to force liquid through a semipermeable membrane in the opposite direction to that in normal osmosis

reverse swing *n cricket* a type of swing in which a ball that has been scuffed on one side will move in the opposite direction to that of a new ball

reverse takeover *n finance* the purchase of a larger company by a smaller company, esp a public company by a private company

reverse transcriptase (træn'skrɪpteɪz) *n* an enzyme present in retroviruses that copies RNA into DNA, thus reversing the usual flow of genetic information in which DNA is copied into RNA

reverse video *n computing* a highlighting feature achieved by reversing the colours of normal characters and background on a visual display unit

reversible (rɪ'vɜːsəbᵊl) *adj* **1** capable of being reversed: *a reversible decision* **2** capable of returning to an original condition **3** *chem, physics* capable of assuming or producing either of two possible states and changing from one to the other: *a reversible reaction* **4** (of a fabric or garment) woven, printed, or finished so that either side may be used as the outer side ▷ *n* **5** a reversible garment, esp a coat > reˌversi'bility *n* > re'versibly *adv*

reversing light *n* a light on the rear of a motor vehicle to warn others that the vehicle is being reversed

reversion (rɪ'vɜːʃən) *n* **1** a return to or towards an earlier condition, practice, or belief; act of reverting **2** *biology* the return of individuals, organs, etc, to a more primitive condition or type **3** *property law* **a** an interest in an estate that reverts to the grantor or his heirs at the end of a period, esp at the end of the life of a grantee **b** an estate so reverting **c** the right to succeed to such an estate **4** the benefit payable on the death of a life-insurance policyholder > re'versionary or re'versional *adj*

reversionary bonus *n insurance* a bonus added to the sum payable on death or at the maturity of a with-profits assurance policy

revert (rɪ'vɜːt) *vb* (*intr*; foll by *to*) **1** to go back to a former practice, condition, belief, etc: *she reverted to her old wicked ways* **2** to take up again or come back to a former topic **3** *biology* (of individuals, organs, etc) to return to a more primitive, earlier, or simpler condition or type **4** *property law* (of an estate or interest in land) to return to its former owner or his heirs when a grant, esp a grant for the lifetime of the grantee, comes to an end **5 revert to type** to resume characteristics that were thought to have disappeared [c13: from Latin *revertere* to return, from RE- + *vertere* to turn] > re'verter *n* > re'vertible *adj*
● USAGE Since *back* is part of the meaning of *revert*, one
● should not say that someone *reverts back* to a certain
● type of behaviour

revest (riː'vɛst) *vb* (often foll by *in*) to restore (former power, authority, status, etc, to a person) or (of power, authority, etc) to be restored [c16: from Old French *revestir* to clothe again, from Latin RE- + *vestīre* to clothe; see VEST]

revet (rɪ'vɛt) *vb* **-vets, -vetting, -vetted** to face (a wall or embankment) with stones [c19: from French *revêt*, from Old French *revestir* to reclothe; see REVEST]

revetment (rɪ'vɛtmənt) *n* **1** a facing of stones, sandbags, etc, to protect a wall, embankment, or earthworks **2** another name for **retaining wall** [c18: from French *revêtement* literally: a reclothing, from *revêtir*; see REVEST]

review (rɪ'vjuː) *vb* (*mainly tr*) **1** to look at or examine again: *to review a situation* **2** to look back upon (a period of

r

time, sequence of events, etc); remember: *he reviewed his achievements with pride* **3** to inspect, esp formally or officially: *the general reviewed his troops* **4** *law* to re-examine (a decision) judicially **5** to write a critical assessment of (a book, film, play, concert, etc), esp as a profession ▷ *n* **6** Also called: **reviewal** the act or an instance of reviewing **7** a general survey or report: *a review of the political situation* **8** a critical assessment of a book, film, play, concert, etc, esp one printed in a newspaper or periodical **9** a publication containing such articles **10** a second consideration; re-examination **11** a retrospective survey **12** a formal or official inspection **13** *US & Canadian* Also called (in Britain and certain other countries): **revision 14** *law* judicial re-examination of a case, esp by a superior court **15** a less common spelling of **revue** [c16: from French, from *revoir* to see again, from Latin *re-* RE- + *vidēre* to see] ▷ re'viewer *n*

revile (rɪˈvaɪl) *vb* to use abusive or scornful language against (someone or something) [c14: from Old French *reviler*, from RE- + *vil* VILE] ▷ re'vilement *n* ▷ re'viler *n*

revise (rɪˈvaɪz) *vb* **1** (*tr*) to change, alter, or amend: *to revise one's opinion* **2** *Brit* to reread (a subject or notes on it) so as to memorize it, esp in preparation for an examination **3** (*tr*) to prepare a new version or edition of (a previously printed work) ▷ *n* **4** the act, process, or result of revising; revision [c16: from Latin *revisere* to look back at, from RE- + *visere* to inspect, from *vidēre* to see; see REVIEW, VISIT] ▷ re'visal *n* ▷ re'viser *n*

Revised Standard Version *n* a revision by American scholars of the American Standard Version of the Bible. The New Testament was published in 1946 and the entire Bible in 1953

Revised Version *n* a revision of the Authorized Version of the Bible prepared by two committees of British scholars, the New Testament being published in 1881 and the Old in 1885

revision (rɪˈvɪʒən) *n* **1** the act or process of revising **2** *Brit* the process of rereading a subject or notes on it, esp in preparation for an examination **3** a corrected or new version of a book, article, etc ▷ re'visionary *adj*

revisionism (rɪˈvɪʒəˌnɪzəm) *n* **1** (*sometimes capital*) **a** a moderate, nonrevolutionary version of Marxism developed in Germany around 1900 **b** (in Marxist-Leninist ideology) any dangerous departure from the true interpretation of the teachings of Karl Marx, the German founder of modern Communism (1818–83) **2** the advocacy of revision of some political theory, religious doctrine, historical or critical interpretation, etc ▷ re'visionist *n, adj*

revisory (rɪˈvaɪzərɪ) *adj* of, relating to, or having the power to revise

revitalize *or* **revitalise** (riːˈvaɪtəˌlaɪz) *vb* (*tr*) to restore vitality or animation to

revival (rɪˈvaɪvəl) *n* **1** the act or an instance of reviving or the state of being revived **2** an instance of returning to life or consciousness; restoration of vigour or vitality **3** a renewed use, acceptance of, or interest in (past customs, styles, etc): *a revival of learning; the Gothic revival* **4** a new production of a play that has not been recently performed **5** a reawakening of faith or renewal of commitment to religion **6** an evangelistic meeting or service intended to effect such a reawakening in those present

revivalism (rɪˈvaɪvəˌlɪzəm) *n* **1** a movement, esp an evangelical Christian one, that seeks to reawaken faith **2** the tendency or desire to revive former customs, styles, etc ▷ re'vivalist *n, adj* ▷ re,vival'istic *adj*

revive (rɪˈvaɪv) *vb* **1** to bring or be brought back to life, consciousness, or strength; resuscitate or be resuscitated: *revived by a drop of whisky* **2** to give or assume new vitality; flourish again or cause to flourish again **3** to make or become operative or active again: *the youth movement was revived* **4** to bring or come back to mind **5** (*tr*) *theatre* to mount a new production of (an old play) [c15: from Old French *revivre* to live again, from Latin *revīvere*, from RE- + *vīvere* to live; see VIVID] ▷ re,viva'bility *n* ▷ re'viver *n* ▷ re'viving *adj*

revivify (rɪˈvɪvɪˌfaɪ) *vb* -fies, -fying, -fied (*tr*) to give new life or spirit to; revive ▷ re,vivifi'cation *n*

revocable (ˈrɛvəkəbəl) *or* **revokable** (rɪˈvəʊkəbəl) *adj* capable of being revoked; able to be cancelled ▷ ,revoca'bility *or* re,voka'bility *n* ▷ 'revocably *or* re'vokably *adv*

revocation (ˌrɛvəˈkeɪʃən) *n* **1** the act of revoking or state of being revoked; cancellation **2 a** the cancellation or annulment of a legal instrument, esp a will **b** the withdrawal of an offer, power of attorney, etc ▷ revocatory (ˈrɛvəkətərɪ, -trɪ) *adj*

revoice (riːˈvɔɪs) *vb* (*intr*) **1** to utter again; echo **2** to adjust the design of (an organ pipe or wind instrument) as after disuse or to conform with modern pitch

revoke (rɪˈvəʊk) *vb* **1** (*tr*) to take back or withdraw; cancel; rescind **2** (*intr*) *cards* to break a rule of play by failing to follow suit when able to do so; renege ▷ *n* **3** *cards* the act of revoking; a renege [c14: from Latin *revocāre* to call back, withdraw, from RE- + *vocāre* to call] ▷ re'voker *n*

revolt (rɪˈvəʊlt) *n* **1** a rebellion or uprising against authority **2** in revolt in the process or state of rebelling ▷ *vb* **3** (*intr*) to rise up in rebellion against authority **4** (*usually passive*) to feel or cause to feel revulsion, disgust, or abhorrence [c16: from French *révolter* to revolt, from Old Italian *rivoltare* to overturn, ultimately from Latin *revolvere* to roll back, REVOLVE]

revolting (rɪˈvəʊltɪŋ) *adj* **1** causing revulsion; nauseating, disgusting, or repulsive **2** *informal* unpleasant or nasty ▷ re'voltingly *adv*

revolute (ˈrɛvəˌluːt) *adj* (esp of the margins of a leaf) rolled backwards and downwards [c18: from Latin *revolūtus* rolled back; see REVOLVE]

revolution (ˌrɛvəˈluːʃən) *n* **1** the overthrow or repudiation of a regime or political system by the governed **2** (in Marxist theory) the violent and historically necessary transition from one system of production in a society to the next, as from feudalism to capitalism **3** a far-reaching and drastic change, esp in ideas, methods, etc **4 a** a movement in or as if in a circle **b** one complete turn in such a circle: *a turntable rotating at 33 revolutions per minute* **5 a** the orbital motion of one body, such as a planet or satellite, around another **b** one complete turn in such motion **6** a cycle of successive events or changes [c14: via Old French from Late Latin *revolūtiō*, from Latin *revolvere* to REVOLVE]

revolutionary (ˌrɛvəˈluːʃənərɪ) *n, pl* -aries **1** a person who advocates or engages in revolution ▷ *adj* **2** relating to or characteristic of a revolution **3** advocating or engaged in revolution **4** radically new or different: *a revolutionary method of making plastics*

Revolutionary (ˌrɛvəˈluːʃənərɪ) *adj* **1** *chiefly US* of or relating to the conflict or period of the War of American Independence (1775–83) **2** of or relating to any of various other Revolutions, esp the **Russian Revolution** (1917) or the **French Revolution** (1789)

Revolutionary calendar *n* the calendar adopted by the French First Republic in 1793 and abandoned in 1805. Dates were calculated from Sept 22, 1792. The months were called Vendémiaire, Brumaire, Frimaire, Nivôse, Pluviôse, Ventôse, Germinal, Floréal, Prairial, Messidor, Thermidor, and Fructidor

revolutionist (ˌrɛvəˈluːʃənɪst) *n* **1** a less common word for a: **revolutionary** ▷ *adj* **2** of, characteristic of, or relating to revolution or revolutionaries

revolutionize *or* **revolutionise** (ˌrɛvəˈluːʃəˌnaɪz) *vb* (*tr*) **1** to bring about a radical change in: *science has revolutionized civilization* **2** to inspire or infect with revolutionary ideas: *they revolutionized the common soldiers* **3** to cause a revolution in (a country, etc) ▷ ,revo'lution,izer *or* ,revo'lution,iser *n*

revolve (rɪˈvɒlv) *vb* **1** to move or cause to move around a centre or axis; rotate **2** (*intr*) to occur periodically or in cycles **3** to consider or be considered **4** (*intr*; foll by *around* or *about*) to be centred or focused (upon): *Juliet's thoughts revolved around Romeo* ▷ *n* **5** *theatre* a circular section of a stage that can be rotated by electric power to provide a scene change [c14: from Latin *revolvere*, from RE- + *volvere* to roll, wind] ▷ re'volvable *adj*

revolver (rɪˈvɒlvə) *n* a pistol having a revolving multichambered cylinder that allows several shots to be discharged without reloading

revolving (rɪ'vɒlvɪŋ) *adj* **1** moving around a central axis: *revolving door* **2** (of a fund) constantly added to from income from its investments to offset outgoing payments **3** (of a letter of credit, load, etc) available to be repeatedly drawn on by the beneficiary provided that a specified amount is never exceeded

revue *or less commonly* **review** (rɪ'vju:) *n* a form of light entertainment consisting of a series of topical sketches, songs, dancing, comic turns, etc [c20: from French; see REVIEW]

revulsion (rɪ'vʌlʃən) *n* **1** a sudden and unpleasant violent reaction in feeling, esp one of extreme loathing **2** the act or an instance of drawing back or recoiling from something **3** *obsolete* the diversion of disease or congestion from one part of the body to another by cupping, counterirritants, etc [c16: from Latin *revulsiō* a pulling away, from *revellere*, from RE- + *vellere* to pull, tear]

revulsive (rɪ'vʌlsɪv) *adj* **1** of or causing revulsion ▷ *n* **2** *med* a counterirritant ▷ re'vulsively *adv*

reward (rɪ'wɔːd) *n* **1** something given or received in return for a deed or service rendered **2** a sum of money offered, esp for help in finding a criminal or for the return of lost or stolen property **3** profit or return **4** something received in return for good or evil; deserts ▷ *vb* **5** (*tr*) to give (something) to (someone), esp in gratitude for a service rendered; recompense [c14: from Old Norman French *rewarder* to regard, from RE- + *warder* to care for, guard, of Germanic origin; see WARD] ▷ re'wardless *adj*

reward claim *n Austral history* a claim granted to a miner who discovered gold in a new area

rewarding (rɪ'wɔːdɪŋ) *adj* giving personal satisfaction; gratifying

rewa-rewa ('reɪwə'reɪwə) *n* a tall proteaceous tree of New Zealand, *Knightia excelsa*, yielding a beautiful reddish timber [c19: from Māori]

rewind *vb* (ri:'waɪnd) -winds, -winding, -wound **1** (*tr*) to wind back, esp a film or tape onto the original reel ▷ *n* ('ri:,waɪnd, ri:'waɪnd) **2** something rewound **3** the act of rewinding ▷ re'winder *n*

rewire (ri:'waɪə) *vb* (*tr*) to provide (a house, engine, etc) with new wiring ▷ re'wirable *adj*

reword (ri:'wɜːd) *vb* (*tr*) to alter the wording of; express differently

rework (ri:'wɜːk) *vb* (*tr*) **1** to use again in altered form **2** to rewrite or revise **3** to reprocess for use again

rewrite *vb* (ri:'raɪt) -writes, -writing, -wrote, -written (*tr*) **1** to write (written material) again, esp changing the words or form **2** *computing* to return (data) to a store when it has been erased during reading ▷ *n* ('ri:,raɪt) **3** something rewritten

Rex (rɛks) *n* king: part of the official title of a king, now used chiefly in documents, legal proceedings, inscriptions on coins, etc. Compare **Regina**[1] [Latin]

Rexine ('rɛksi:n) *n trademark* a form of artificial leather

Reye's syndrome (raɪz, reɪz) *n* a rare metabolic disease in children that can be fatal, involving damage to the brain, liver, and kidneys [c20: named after R. D. K. *Reye* (1912–78) Australian paediatrician]

Reykjavik ('reɪkjə,vi:k) *n* the capital and chief port of Iceland, situated in the southwest: its buildings are heated by natural hot water. Pop: 112 490 (2003 est)

Reynard ('rɛnəd, 'rɛnɑːd, 'reɪnəd, 'reɪnɑːd) *n* a name for a fox, used in medieval tales, fables, etc [from earlier *Renard, Renart*, hero of the French bestiary *Roman de Renart*: ultimately from the Old High German name *Reginhart*, literally: strong in counsel]

Reynaud (*French* rɛno) *n* **Paul** (pɔl). 1878–1966, French statesman: premier during the defeat of France by Germany (1940); later imprisoned by the Germans

Reynolds ('rɛnəldz) *n* **1** **Albert**. born 1935, Irish politician: leader of the Fianna Fáil party and prime minister of the Republic of Ireland (1994–96) **2** Sir **Joshua**. 1723–92, English portrait painter. He was the first president of the Royal Academy (1768): the annual lectures he gave there, published as *Discourses*, are important contributions to art theory and criticism

Reynosa (*Spanish* re'nosa) *n* a city in E Mexico, in

Tamaulipas state on the Rio Grande. Pop: 847 000 (2005 est)

RF *abbreviation* radio frequency

RFC *abbreviation* **1** Rugby Football Club **2** Royal Flying Corps

RFID *abbreviation* radio-frequency identity (*or* identification): a technology that uses tiny computer chips to track items such as consumer commodities at a distance

RGN *abbreviation* (in Britain) Registered General Nurse

RGS *abbreviation* Royal Geographical Society

rh *or* **RH** *abbreviation* right hand

Rh *the chemical symbol for* **1** rhodium ▷ *abbreviation* **2** rhesus (esp in **Rh factor**)

RHA *abbreviation* **1** Regional Health Authority **2** Royal Horse Artillery

rhabdomancy ('ræbdə,mænsɪ) *n* divination for water or mineral ore by means of a rod or wand; dowsing; divining [c17: via Late Latin from Late Greek *rhabdomanteia*, from *rhabdos* a rod + *manteia* divination] ▷ 'rhabdo,mantist *or* 'rhabdo,mancer *n*

rhachis ('reɪkɪs) *n*, *pl* rhachises *or* rhachides ('ræki,di:z, 'reɪ-) a variant spelling of **rachis**

Rhadamanthus *or* **Rhadamanthys** (,rædə'mænθəs) *n Greek myth* one of the judges of the dead in the underworld ▷ ,Rhada'manthine *adj*

Rhaetia ('ri:ʃɪə) *n* an Alpine province of ancient Rome including parts of present-day Tyrol and E Switzerland

Rhaetian Alps *pl n* a section of the central Alps along E Switzerland's borders with Austria and Italy. Highest peak: Piz Bernina, 4049 m (13 284 ft)

rhapsodic (ræp'sɒdɪk) *adj* **1** of or like a rhapsody **2** lyrical or romantic

rhapsodize *or* **rhapsodise** ('ræpsə,daɪz) *vb* **1** to speak or write (something) with extravagant enthusiasm **2** (*intr*) to recite or write rhapsodies

rhapsody ('ræpsədɪ) *n*, *pl* -dies **1** *music* a composition free in structure and highly emotional in character **2** an expression of ecstatic enthusiasm **3** (in ancient Greece) an epic poem or part of an epic recited by a rhapsodist **4** a literary work composed in an intense or exalted style **5** rapturous delight or ecstasy [c16: via Latin from Greek *rhapsōidia*, from *rhaptein* to sew together + *ōidē* song] ▷ 'rhapsodist *n* ▷ ,rhapso'distic *adj*

rhatany ('rætənɪ) *n*, *pl* -nies **1** either of two South American leguminous shrubs, *Krameria triandra* or *K. argentea*, that have thick fleshy roots **2** the dried roots of such shrubs used as an astringent ▷ Also called: krameria [c19: from New Latin *rhatānia*, ultimately from Quechua *ratánya*]

rhea ('rɪə) *n* either of two large fast-running flightless birds, *Rhea americana* or *Pterocnemia pennata*, inhabiting the open plains of S South America: order *Rheiformes*. They are similar to but smaller than the ostrich, having three-toed feet and a completely feathered body [c19: New Latin; arbitrarily named after RHEA]

Rhea ('rɪə) *n Greek myth* a Titaness, wife of Cronus and mother of several of the gods, including Zeus: a fertility goddess. Roman counterpart: **Ops**

Rhea Silvia *or* **Rea Silvia** ('sɪlvɪə) *n Roman myth* the mother of Romulus and Remus by Mars. See also **Ilia**

rhebok *or* **reebok** ('ri:bʌk, -bɒk) *n*, *pl* -boks *or* -bok an antelope, *Pelea capreolus*, of southern Africa, having woolly brownish-grey hair [c18: Afrikaans, from Dutch *reebok* ROEBUCK]

Rhee (ri:) *n* **Syngman** ('sɪŋmən). 1875–1965, Korean statesman, leader of the campaign for independence from Japan; first president of South Korea (1948–60). Popular unrest forced his resignation

Rheims (ri:mz; *French* rɛ̃s) *n* a variant spelling of **Reims**

Rhein (raɪn) *n* the German name for the **Rhine**

Rheinland ('raɪnlant) *n* the German name for the **Rhineland**

Rheinland-Pfalz ('raɪnlant'pfalts) *n* the German name for **Rhineland-Palatinate**

Rhenish ('rɛnɪʃ, 'ri:-) *adj* **1** of or relating to the River Rhine or the lands adjacent to it, esp the Rhineland-Palatinate ▷ *n* **2** another word for **hock**[2]

rhenium ('ri:nɪəm) *n* a dense silvery-white metallic

element that has a high melting point. It occurs principally in gadolinite and molybdenite and is used, alloyed with tungsten or molybdenum, in high-temperature thermocouples. Symbol: Re; atomic no: 75; atomic wt: 186.207; valency: –1 or 1–7; relative density: 21.02; melting pt: 3186°C; boiling pt: 5596°C (est) [c19: New Latin, from *Rhēnus* the Rhine]

rheo- *combining form* indicating stream, flow, or current [from Greek *rheos* stream, anything flowing, from *rhein* to flow]

rheology (rɪ'ɒlədʒɪ) *n* the branch of physics concerned with the flow and change of shape of matter
> rheological (,riːə'lɒdʒɪkᵊl) *adj* > rhe'ologist *n*

rheostat ('riːə,stæt) *n* a variable resistance, usually consisting of a coil of wire with a terminal at one end and a sliding contact that moves along the coil to tap off the current > ,rheo'static *adj*

Rhesus ('riːsəs) *n Greek myth* a king of Thrace, who arrived in the tenth year of the Trojan War to aid Troy. Odysseus and Diomedes stole his horses because an oracle had said that if these horses drank from the River Xanthus, Troy would not fall

rhesus baby ('riːsəs) *n* a baby suffering from haemolytic disease at birth as its red blood cells (which are Rh positive) have been attacked in the womb by antibodies from its Rh negative mother [c20: see Rh FACTOR]

rhesus factor *n* See Rh factor

rhesus monkey *n* a macaque monkey, *Macaca mulatta*, of S Asia: used extensively in medical research [c19: New Latin, arbitrarily from Greek *Rhesos* RHESUS]

rhetor ('riːtə) *n* 1 a teacher of rhetoric 2 (in ancient Greece) an orator [c14: via Latin from Greek *rhētōr*; related to *rhēma* word]

rhetoric ('rɛtərɪk) *n* 1 the study of the technique of using language effectively 2 the art of using speech to persuade, influence, or please; oratory 3 excessive use of ornamentation and contrivance in spoken or written discourse; bombast 4 speech or discourse that pretends to significance but lacks true meaning: *all the politician says is mere rhetoric* [c14: via Latin from Greek *rhētorikē (tekhnē)* (the art of) rhetoric, from *rhētōr* RHETOR]

rhetorical (rɪ'tɒrɪkᵊl) *adj* 1 concerned with effect or style rather than content or meaning; bombastic 2 of or relating to rhetoric or oratory > rhe'torically *adv*

rhetorical question *n* a question to which no answer is required: used esp for dramatic effect. An example is *Who knows?* (with the implication *Nobody knows*)

rhetorician (,rɛtə'rɪʃən) *n* 1 a teacher of the art of rhetoric 2 a stylish or eloquent writer or speaker 3 a person whose speech is pompous or extravagant

rheum (ruːm) *n* a watery discharge from the eyes or nose [c14: from Old French *reume*, ultimately from Greek *rheuma* bodily humour, stream, from *rhein* to flow]
> 'rheumy *adj*

rheumatic (ruː'mætɪk) *adj* 1 of, relating to, or afflicted with rheumatism ▷ *n* 2 a person afflicted with rheumatism [c14: ultimately from Greek *rheumatikos*, from *rheuma* a flow; see RHEUM] > rheu'matically *adv*

rheumatic fever *n* a disease characterized by sore throat, fever, inflammation, and pain in the joints

rheumatics (ruː'mætɪks) *n* (*functioning as singular*) *informal* rheumatism

rheumatism ('ruːmə,tɪzəm) *n* any painful disorder of joints, muscles, or connective tissue [c17: from Latin *rheumatismus* catarrh, from Greek *rheumatismos*; see RHEUM]

rheumatoid ('ruːmə,tɔɪd) *adj* (of the symptoms of a disease) resembling rheumatism

rheumatoid arthritis *n* a chronic disease of the musculoskeletal system, characterized by inflammation and swelling of joints (esp joints in the hands, wrists, knees, and feet), muscle weakness, and fatigue

rheumatology (,ruːmə'tɒlədʒɪ) *n* the branch of medicine concerned with the study of rheumatic diseases > rheumatological (,ruːmətə'lɒdʒɪkᵊl) *adj*

Rh factor *n* an agglutinogen commonly found in human blood: it may cause a haemolytic reaction, esp during pregnancy or following transfusion of blood that does not contain this agglutinogen. Full name: rhesus factor [c20: named after the rhesus monkey, in which it was first discovered]

rhinal ('raɪnᵊl) *adj* of or relating to the nose; nasal [c19: from Greek *rhis, rhin*]

Rhine (raɪn) *n* a river in central and W Europe, rising in SE Switzerland: flows through Lake Constance north through W Germany and west through the Netherlands to the North Sea. Length: about 1320 km (820 miles). Dutch name: Rijn. German name: Rhein

Rhineland ('raɪn,lænd, -lənd) *n* the region of Germany surrounding the Rhine. German name: Rheinland

Rhineland-Palatinate *n* a state of W Germany: formed in 1946 from the S part of the Prussian Rhine province, the Palatinate, and parts of Rhine-Hesse and Hesse-Nassau; part of West Germany until 1990: agriculture (with extensive vineyards) and tourism are important. Capital: Mainz. Pop: 4 059 000 (2003 est). Area: 19 832 sq km (7657 sq miles). German name: Rheinland-Pfalz

rhinestone ('raɪn,stəʊn) *n* an imitation gem made of paste [c19: translation of French *caillou du Rhin*, referring to Strasbourg, where such gems were made]

Rhine wine *n* any of several wines produced along the banks of the Rhine, characteristically a white table wine such as Riesling

rhinitis (raɪ'naɪtɪs) *n* inflammation of the mucous membrane that lines the nose > rhinitic (raɪ'nɪtɪk) *adj*

rhino¹ ('raɪnəʊ) *n, pl* -nos *or* -no short for rhinoceros

rhino² ('raɪnəʊ) *n Brit* a slang word for money [c17: of unknown origin]

rhino- *or before a vowel* **rhin-** *combining form* indicating the nose or nasal: *rhinology* [from Greek *rhis, rhin*]

rhinoceros (raɪ'nɒsərəs, -'nɒsrəs) *n, pl* -oses *or* -os any of several perissodactyl mammals constituting the family Rhinocerotidae of SE Asia and Africa and having either one horn on the nose, like the **Indian rhinoceros** (*Rhinoceros unicornis*), or two horns, like the African **white rhinoceros** (*Diceros simus*) They have a very thick skin, massive body, and three digits on each foot [c13: via Latin from Greek *rhinokerōs*, from *rhis* nose + *keras* horn] > rhinocerotic (,raɪnəʊsɪ'rɒtɪk) *adj*

rhinology (raɪ'nɒlədʒɪ) *n* the branch of medical science concerned with the nose and its diseases > rhinological (,raɪnᵊ'lɒdʒɪkᵊl) *adj* > rhi'nologist *n*

rhinoplasty ('raɪnəʊ,plæstɪ) *n* plastic surgery of the nose > ,rhino'plastic *adj*

rhinoscopy (raɪ'nɒskəpɪ) *n med* examination of the nasal passages, esp with a special instrument called a **rhinoscope** ('raɪnəʊ,skəʊp)

rhizo- *or before a vowel* **rhiz-** *combining form* root: *rhizomorphous* [from Greek *rhiza*]

rhizocarpous (,raɪzəʊ'kɑːpəs) *adj* 1 (of plants) producing subterranean flowers and fruit 2 (of perennial plants) having roots that persist throughout the year but stems and leaves that wither at the end of the growing season

rhizoid ('raɪzɔɪd) *n* any of various slender hairlike structures that function as roots in the gametophyte generation of mosses, ferns, and related plants > rhi'zoidal *adj*

rhizome ('raɪzəʊm) *n* a thick horizontal underground stem of plants such as the mint and iris whose buds develop new roots and shoots. Also called: rootstock, rootstalk [c19: from New Latin *rhizoma*, from Greek, from *rhiza* a root] > rhizomatous (raɪ'zɒmətəs, -'zəʊ-) *adj*

rhizopod ('raɪzəʊ,pɒd) *n* 1 any protozoan of the phylum Rhizopoda, characterized by naked protoplasmic processes (pseudopodia). The group includes the amoebas ▷ *adj* 2 of, relating to, or belonging to the Rhizopoda

rho (rəʊ) *n, pl* rhos the 17th letter in the Greek alphabet (Ρ, ρ), a consonant transliterated as *r* or *rh*

rhodamine ('rəʊdə,miːn, -mɪn) *n* any one of a group of synthetic red or pink basic dyestuffs used for wool and silk. They are made from phthalic anhydride and aminophenols [c20: from RHODO- + AMINE]

Rhode Island (rəʊd) *n* a state of the northeastern US, bordering on the Atlantic: the smallest state in the US; mainly low-lying and undulating, with an indented coastline in the east and uplands in the northwest Capital: Providence. Pop: 1 076 164 (2003 est). Area: 2717 sq km (1049 sq miles). Abbreviation: RI

Rhode Island Red *n* a breed of domestic fowl, originating in America, characterized by a dark reddish-brown plumage and the production of brown eggs

Rhodes¹ (rəʊdz) *n* **1** a Greek island in the SE Aegean Sea, about 16 km (10 miles) off the Turkish coast: the largest of the Dodecanese and the most easterly island in the Aegean. Capital: Rhodes. Pop (municipality): 55 086 (2001). Area: 1400 sq km (540 sq miles) **2** a port on this island, in the NE: founded in 408 BC; of great commercial and political importance in the 3rd century BC; suffered several earthquakes, notably in 225, when the Colossus was destroyed. Pop: 41 000 (latest est) Ancient Greek name: Rhodes. Modern Greek name: Ródhos

Rhodes² (rəʊdz) *n* **Cecil John**. 1853–1902, British colonial financier and statesman in South Africa. He made a fortune in diamond and gold mining and, as prime minister of the Cape Colony (1890–96), he helped to extend British territory. He established the annual Rhodes scholarships to Oxford ▷ See **Rhodes scholarship**

Rhodesia (rəʊˈdiːʃə, - zɪə) *n* a former name (1964–79) for **Zimbabwe** ▷ Rhoˈdesian *adj, n*

Rhodesian man *n* a type of early man, *Homo rhodesiensis* (or *H. sapiens rhodesiensis*), occurring in Africa in late Pleistocene times and resembling Neanderthal man in many features

Rhodes scholarship *n* one of 72 scholarships founded by Cecil Rhodes, awarded annually on merit to Commonwealth and US students to study for two or sometimes three years at Oxford University > Rhodes scholar *n*

Rhodian (ˈrəʊdɪən) *adj* **1** of or relating to the island of Rhodes ▷ *n* **2** a native or inhabitant of Rhodes

rhodium (ˈrəʊdɪəm) *n* a hard corrosion-resistant silvery-white element of the platinum metal group, occurring free with other platinum metals in alluvial deposits and in nickel ores. It is used as an alloying agent to harden platinum and palladium. Symbol: Rh; atomic no: 45; atomic wt: 102.90550; valency: 2–6; relative density: 12.41; melting pt: 1963±3°C; boiling pt: 3697±100°C [C19: New Latin, from Greek *rhodon* rose, from the pink colour of its compounds]

rhodo- *or before a vowel* **rhod-** *combining form* rose or rose-coloured: *rhododendron; rhodolite* [from Greek *rhodon* rose]

rhodochrosite (ˌrəʊdəʊˈkrəʊsaɪt) *n* a pink, red, grey, or brown mineral that consists of manganese carbonate in hexagonal crystalline form and occurs in ore veins. Formula: MnCO₃ [C19: from Greek *rhodokhrōs* of a rosy colour, from *rhodon* rose + *khrōs* colour]

rhododendron (ˌrəʊdəˈdɛndrən) *n* any ericaceous shrub of the genus *Rhododendron*, native to S Asia but widely cultivated in N temperate regions. They are mostly evergreen and have clusters of showy red, purple, pink, or white flowers [C17: from Latin: oleander, from Greek, from *rhodon* rose + *dendron* tree]

rhodolite (ˈrəʊdəˌlaɪt) *n* a pale violet or red variety of garnet, used as a gemstone

rhodonite (ˈrəʊdəˌnaɪt) *n* a brownish translucent mineral consisting of manganese silicate in triclinic crystalline form with calcium, iron, or magnesium sometimes replacing the manganese. It occurs in metamorphic rocks, esp in New Jersey and Russia, and is used as an ornamental stone, glaze, and pigment. Formula: MnSiO₃ [C19: from German *Rhodonit*, from Greek *rhodon* rose + -ITE]

Rhodope Mountains (ˈrɒdəpɪ, rɒˈdəʊ-) *pl n* a mountain range in SE Europe, in the Balkan Peninsula extending along the border between Bulgaria and Greece. Highest peak: Golyam Perelik (Bulgaria), 2191 m (7188 ft)

rhodopsin (rəʊˈdɒpsɪn) *n* a red pigment in the rods of the retina in vertebrates. It is dissociated by light into retinene, the light energy being converted into nerve signals, and is re-formed in the dark. Also called: visual purple See also **iodopsin** [C20: from RHODO- + -OPSIS + -IN]

Rhodos (ˈrɔðɔs) *n* the Ancient Greek name for **Rhodes¹**

rhomb (rɒm) *n* another name for **rhombus**

rhombencephalon (ˌrɒmbɛnˈsɛfəlɒn) *n* the part of the brain that develops from the posterior portion of the embryonic neural tube and comprises the cerebellum, pons, and the medulla oblongata [C20: from RHOMBUS + ENCEPHALON]

rhombic aerial *n* a directional travelling-wave aerial, usually horizontal, consisting of two conductors each forming a pair of adjacent sides of a rhombus

rhombohedral (ˌrɒmbəʊˈhiːdrəl) *adj* **1** of or relating to a rhombohedron **2** *crystallog* another term for **trigonal** (sense 2)

rhombohedron (ˌrɒmbəʊˈhiːdrən) *n* a six-sided prism whose sides are parallelograms [C19: from RHOMBUS + -HEDRON]

rhomboid (ˈrɒmbɔɪd) *n* **1** a parallelogram having adjacent sides of unequal length ▷ *adj* Also: rhomˈboidal **2** having such a shape [C16: from Late Latin *rhomboides*, from Greek *rhomboeidēs* shaped like a RHOMBUS]

rhombus (ˈrɒmbəs) *n, pl* -buses *or* -bi (-baɪ) an oblique-angled parallelogram having four equal sides. Also called: rhomb. See **square** (sense 1) [C16: from Greek *rhombos* something that spins; related to *rhembein* to whirl] > ˈrhombic *adj*

rhonchus (ˈrɒŋkəs) *n, pl* -chi (-kaɪ) a rattling or whistling respiratory sound resembling snoring, caused by secretions in the trachea or bronchi [C19: from Latin, from Greek *rhenkhos* snoring]

Rhondda (ˈrɒndə; *Welsh* ˈhrɔndə) *n* an urban area in S Wales, in Rhondda Cynon Taff county borough on two branches of the **Rhondda Valley**: the area developed into a major coal-mining centre after 1807: the last coal mine closed in 1990. Pop (Rhondda ward): 4690 (2001)

Rhondda Cynon Taff (ˈrɒndə ˈkʊnən ˈtæf) *n* a county borough in S Wales, created from part of Mid Glamorgan in 1996. Pop: 231 600 (2003 est). Area: 558 sq km (215 sq miles)

Rhône (rəʊn) *n* **1** a river in W Europe, rising in S Switzerland in the **Rhône glacier** and flowing to Lake Geneva, then into France through gorges between the Alps and Jura and south to its delta on the Gulf of Lions: important esp for hydroelectricity and for wine production along its valley. Length: 812 km (505 miles) **2** a department of E central France, in the Rhône-Alpes region. Capital: Lyon. Pop: 1 621 718 (2003 est). Area: 3233 sq km (1261 sq miles)

Rhône-Alpes (*French* rɔnalp) *n* a region of E France: mainly mountainous, rising to the edge of the Massif Central in the west and the French Alps in the east; drained by the Rivers Rhône, Saône, and Isère

RHS *abbreviation* **1** Royal Historical Society **2** Royal Horticultural Society **3** Royal Humane Society

rhubarb (ˈruːbɑːb) *n* **1** any of several temperate and subtropical plants of the polygonaceous genus *Rheum*, esp *R. rhaponticum* (**common garden rhubarb**), which has long green and red acid-tasting edible leafstalks, usually eaten sweetened and cooked **2** the leafstalks of this plant **3** a related plant, *Rheum officinale*, of central Asia, having a bitter-tasting underground stem that can be dried and used medicinally as a laxative or astringent **4** *US & Canadian slang* a heated discussion or quarrel ▷ *interj, n, vb* **5** the noise made by actors to simulate conversation, esp by repeating the word *rhubarb* at random [C14: from Old French *reubarbe*, from Medieval Latin *reubarbum*, probably a variant of *rha barbarum* barbarian rhubarb, from *rha* rhubarb (from Greek, perhaps from *Rha* ancient name of the Volga) + Latin *barbarus* barbarian]

rhumb (rʌm) *n* short for **rhumb line**

rhumba (ˈrʌmbə, ˈrʊm-) *n, pl* -bas a variant spelling of **rumba**

rhumb line *n* **1** an imaginary line on the surface of a sphere, such as the earth, that intersects all meridians at the same angle **2** the course navigated by a vessel or aircraft that maintains a uniform compass heading Often shortened to: **rhumb** [C16: from Old Spanish *rumbo*, apparently from Middle Dutch *ruum* space, ship's hold, but also influenced by Latin RHOMBUS]

rhyme *or archaic* **rime** (raɪm) *n* **1** identity of the terminal sounds in lines of verse or in words **2** a word that is identical to another in its terminal sound: *"while"* is a *rhyme for "mile"* **3** a verse or piece of poetry having corresponding sounds at the ends of the lines **4 rhyme or reason** sense, logic, or meaning ▷ *vb* **5** to use (a word) or (of a word) to be used so as to form a rhyme; be or make identical in sound **6** to render (a subject) into rhyme **7** to compose (verse) in a metrical pattern ▷ See also **eye rhyme** [C12: from Old French *rime*, from *rimer* to rhyme, from Old High German *rīm* a number; spelling influenced by RHYTHM]

rhymester, rimester ('raɪmstə) *or* **rhymer, rimer** *n* a poet, esp one considered to be mediocre or mechanical in diction; poetaster or versifier

rhyming slang *n* slang in which a word is replaced by another word or phrase that rhymes with it; for example, *apples and pears* meaning *stairs*

rhyolite ('raɪə,laɪt) *n* a fine-grained igneous rock consisting of quartz, feldspars, and mica or amphibole. It is the volcanic equivalent of granite [C19: *rhyo-* from Greek *rhuax* a stream of lava + LITE] > **rhyolitic** (,raɪə'lɪtɪk) *adj*

Rhys (riːs) *n* **Jean** (Ella Gwendolen Rees Williams). ?1890–1979, Welsh novelist and short-story writer, born in Dominica. Her novels include *Voyage in the Dark* (1934), *Good Morning, Midnight* (1939), and *Wide Sargasso Sea* (1966)

rhythm ('rɪðəm) *n* **1 a** the arrangement of the relative durations of and accents on the notes of a melody, usually laid out into regular groups (**bars**) of beats, the first beat of each bar carrying the stress **b** any specific arrangement of such groupings; time: *quadruple rhythm* **2** (in poetry) **a** the arrangement of words into a more or less regular sequence of stressed and unstressed or long and short syllables **b** any specific such arrangement; metre **3** (in painting, sculpture, architecture, etc) a harmonious sequence or pattern of masses alternating with voids, of light alternating with shade, of alternating colours, etc **4** any sequence of regularly recurring functions or events, such as the regular recurrence of certain physiological functions of the body, as the cardiac rhythm of the heartbeat [C16: from Latin *rhythmus*, from Greek *rhuthmos*; related to *rhein* to flow]

rhythm and blues *n* (*functioning as singular*) any of various kinds of popular music derived from or influenced by the blues. Abbreviation: **R & B**

rhythmic ('rɪðmɪk) *or* **rhythmical** ('rɪðmɪkəl) *adj* of, relating to, or characterized by rhythm, as in movement or sound; metrical, periodic, or regularly recurring > '**rhythmically** *adv* > **rhythmicity** (rɪð'mɪsɪtɪ) *n*

rhythm method *n* a method of controlling conception without the aid of a contraceptive device, by restricting sexual intercourse to those days in a woman's menstrual cycle on which conception is considered least likely to occur

rhythm section *n* those instruments in a band or group (usually piano, double bass, and drums) whose prime function is to supply the rhythm

RI *abbreviation* **1** Regina et Imperatrix [Latin: Queen and Empress] **2** Rex et Imperator [Latin: King and Emperor] **3** Rhode Island **4** Royal Institution **5** religious instruction

ria ('riːə) *n* a long narrow inlet of the seacoast, being a former valley that was submerged by a rise in the level of the sea. Rias are found esp on the coasts of SW Ireland and NW Spain [C19: from Spanish, from *rio* river]

Rialto (rɪ'æltəʊ) *n* an island in Venice, Italy, linked with San Marco Island by the **Rialto Bridge** (1590) over the Grand Canal: the business centre of medieval and renaissance Venice

rib[1] (rɪb) *n* **1** any of the 24 curved elastic arches of bone that together form the chest wall in man. All are attached behind to the thoracic part of the spinal column **2** the corresponding bone in other vertebrates **3** a cut of meat including one or more ribs **4** a part or element similar in function or appearance to a rib, esp a structural or supporting member or a raised strip or ridge **5** a structural member in a wing that extends from the leading edge to the trailing edge and maintains the shape of the wing surface **6** a projecting moulding or band on the underside of a vault or ceiling,

which may be structural or ornamental **7** one of a series of raised rows in knitted fabric **8** any of the transverse stiffening timbers or joists forming the frame of a ship's hull **9** any of the larger veins of a leaf **10** a projecting ridge of a mountain; spur ▷ *vb* **ribs, ribbing, ribbed** (*tr*) **11** to furnish or support with a rib or ribs **12** to mark with or form into ribs or ridges **13** to knit plain and purl stitches alternately in order to make raised rows in knitting [Old English *ribb*; related to Old High German *rippi*, Old Norse *rif* REEF[1]] > '**ribless** *adj*

rib[2] (rɪb) *informal vb* **ribs, ribbing, ribbed** (*tr*) to tease or ridicule [C20: short for *rib-tickle* (vb)]

riba ('riːbə) *n* (in Islam) interest or usury, as forbidden by the Koran [C21: from Arabic *al-Riba*, literally: to excess or increase]

RIBA *abbreviation* Royal Institute of British Architects

ribald ('rɪbəld) *adj* **1** coarse, obscene, or licentious, usually in a humorous or mocking way ▷ *n* **2** a ribald person [C13: from Old French *ribauld*, from *riber* to live licentiously, of Germanic origin]

ribaldry ('rɪbəldrɪ) *n* ribald language or behaviour

riband *or* **ribband** ('rɪbənd) *n* a ribbon, esp one awarded for some achievement [C14: variant of RIBBON]

Ribbentrop (German 'rɪbəntrɔp) *n* **Joachim von** ('joːaxɪm fɔn). 1893–1946, German Nazi politician: foreign minister under Hitler (1938–45). He was hanged after conviction as a war criminal at Nuremberg

ribbing ('rɪbɪŋ) *n* **1** a framework or structure of ribs **2** a raised pattern in woven or knitted material, made in knitting by doing purl and plain stitches alternately

Ribble ('rɪbəl) *n* a river in NW England, flowing south and west through Lancashire to the Irish Sea. Length: 121 km (75 miles)

ribbon ('rɪbən) *n* **1** a narrow strip of fine material, esp silk, used for trimming, tying, etc **2** something resembling a ribbon; a long strip **3** a long thin flexible band of metal used as a graduated measure, spring, etc **4** a long narrow strip of ink-impregnated cloth for making the impression of type characters on paper in a typewriter or similar device **5** (*plural*) ragged strips or shreds (esp in the phrase *torn to ribbons*) **6** a small strip of coloured cloth signifying membership of an order or award of military decoration, prize, or other distinction **7** a small, usually looped, strip of coloured cloth worn to signify support for a charity or cause: *a red AIDS ribbon* ▷ *vb* (*tr*) **8** to adorn with a ribbon or ribbons **9** to mark with narrow ribbon-like marks [C14 *ryban*, from Old French *riban*, apparently of Germanic origin; probably related to RING[1], BAND[2]]

ribbon development *n Brit* the building of houses in a continuous row along a main road: common in England between the two World Wars

ribbonfish ('rɪbən,fɪʃ) *n, pl* -**fish** *or* -**fishes** any of various soft-finned deep-sea teleost fishes, esp *Regalecus glesne* (see **oarfish**), that have an elongated compressed body. They are related to the opah and dealfishes

ribbonwood ('rɪbən,wʊd) *n* a small evergreen malvaceous tree, *Hoheria populnea*, of New Zealand. Its wood is used in furniture making and the tough bark for making cord. Also called: **lacebark**

ribcage ('rɪb,keɪdʒ) *n* the bony structure consisting of the ribs and their connective tissue that encloses and protects the lungs, heart, etc

Ribeirão Prêto (Portuguese riβəi'rəun 'pretu) *n* a city in SE Brazil, in São Paulo state. Pop: 550 000 (2005 est)

Ribera (Spanish ri'βera) *n* **José de** (xo'se de) also called *Jusepe da Ribera*, Italian nickname *Lo Spagnoletto* (The Little Spaniard). 1591–1652, Spanish artist, living in Italy. His religious pictures often dwell on horrible suffering, presented in realistic detail

riboflavin *or* **riboflavine** (,raɪbəʊ'fleɪvɪn) *n* a yellow water-soluble vitamin of the B complex that occurs in green vegetables, germinating seeds, and in milk, fish, egg yolk, liver, and kidney. It is essential for the carbohydrate metabolism of cells. It is used as a permitted food colour, yellow or orange-yellow (**E101**). Formula: $C_{17}H_{20}N_4O_6$ [C20: from RIBOSE + FLAVIN]

ribonuclease (,raɪbəʊ'njuːklɪ,eɪs, -,eɪz) *n* any of a group of enzymes that catalyse the hydrolysis of RNA [C20:

from RIBONUCLE(IC ACID) + -ASE]

ribonucleic acid (ˌraɪbəʊnjuːˈkliːɪk, -ˈkleɪ-) *n* the full name of RNA [C20: from RIBO(SE) + NUCLEIC ACID]

ribose (ˈraɪbəʊz, -bəʊs) *n biochem* a pentose sugar that is an isomeric form of arabinose and that occurs in RNA and riboflavin. Formula: CH₂OH(CHOH)₃CHO [C20: changed from ARABINOSE]

ribosomal RNA *n biochem* a type of RNA thought to be transcribed from DNA in the nucleoli of cell nuclei, subsequently forming the component of ribosomes on which the translation of messenger RNA into protein chains is accomplished. Sometimes shortened to: rRNA

ribosome (ˈraɪbəˌsəʊm) *n* any of numerous minute particles in the cytoplasm of cells, either free or attached to the endoplasmic reticulum, that contain RNA and protein and are the site of protein synthesis [C20: from RIBO(NUCLEIC ACID) + -SOME³] > ˌribo'somal *adj*

rib-tickler *n* a very amusing joke or story > rib-tickling *adj*

ribwort (ˈrɪbˌwɜːt) *n* a Eurasian plant, *Plantago lanceolata*, that has lancelike ribbed leaves, which form a rosette close to the ground, and a dense spike of small white flowers: family Plantaginaceae. Also called: ribgrass See also **plantain¹**

Ricardo (rɪˈkɑːdəʊ) *n* **David.** 1772–1823, British economist. His main work is *Principles of Political Economy and Taxation* (1817) > Ri'cardian *adj, n*

Ricci (Italian ˈrittʃi) *n* **Matteo** (maˈtɛo). 1552–1610, Italian Jesuit missionary and scholar, who introduced Christianity to China. He was later censured by the Church for allowing his converts to retain some of their ancient religious customs

Riccio (ˈrɪtsɪəʊ) *n* same as **Rizzio**

rice (raɪs) *n* **1** an erect grass, *Oryza sativa*, that grows in East Asia on wet ground and has drooping flower spikes and yellow oblong edible grains that become white when polished **2** the grain of this plant ▷ *vb* **3** (*tr*) *US & Canadian* to sieve (potatoes or other vegetables) to a coarse mashed consistency, esp with a ricer [C13 *rys*, via French, Italian, and Latin from Greek *orūza*, of Oriental origin]

Rice (raɪs) *n* **Elmer**, original name *Elmer Reizenstein*. 1892–1967, US dramatist. His plays include *The Adding Machine* (1923) and *Street Scene* (1929), which was made into a musical by Kurt Weill in 1947

rice bowl *n* **1** a small bowl for eating rice out of, esp a decorative one made of china or porcelain **2** a fertile rice-producing region

rice paper *n* **1** a thin semitransparent edible paper made from the straw of rice, on which macaroons and similar cakes are baked **2** a thin delicate Chinese paper made from an araliaceous plant, *Tetrapanax papyriferum* (**rice-paper plant**) of Taiwan, the pith of which is pared and flattened into sheets

ricercare (ˌriːtʃəˈkɑːreɪ) *or* **ricercar** (ˈriːtʃəˌkɑː) *n, pl* -cari (-ˈkɑːriː) *or* -cars (in music of the 16th and 17th centuries) **1** an elaborate polyphonic composition making extensive use of contrapuntal imitation and usually very slow in tempo **2** an instructive composition to illustrate instrumental technique; étude [Italian, literally: to seek again]

rich (rɪtʃ) *adj* **1 a** well supplied with wealth, property, etc; owning much **b** (*as collective noun; preceded by the*): *the rich* **2** (when *postpositive*, usually foll by *in*) having an abundance of natural resources, minerals, etc: *a land rich in metals* **3** producing abundantly; fertile: *rich soil* **4** (when *postpositive*, usually foll by *in* or *with*) well supplied (with desirable qualities); abundant (in): *a country rich with cultural interest* **5** of great worth or quality; valuable: *a rich collection of antiques* **6** luxuriant or prolific: *a rich growth of weeds* **7** expensively elegant, elaborate, or fine; costly: *a rich display* **8** (of food) having a large proportion of flavoursome or fatty ingredients, such as spices, butter, or cream **9** having a full-bodied flavour: *a rich ruby port* **10** (of a smell) pungent or fragrant **11** (of colour) intense or vivid; deep: *a rich red* **12** (of sound or a voice) full, mellow, or resonant **13** (of a fuel-air mixture) containing a relatively high proportion of fuel **14** very amusing, laughable, or ridiculous: *a rich joke; a rich*

situation ▷ *n* **15** See **riches** [Old English *rīce* (originally of persons: great, mighty), of Germanic origin, ultimately from Celtic (compare Old Irish *rī* king)] > 'rich,ness *n*

Rich (rɪtʃ) *n* **1 Adrienne.** born 1929, US poet and feminist writer; her volumes of poetry include *Snapshots of a Daughter-in-Law* (1963) and *Diving Into the Wreck* (1973) **2 Buddy**, real name *Bernard Rich*. 1917–87, US jazz drummer and band leader

Richard (ˈrɪtʃəd) *n* **1 Sir Cliff**, real name *Harry Rodger Webb*. born 1940, British pop singer. Film musicals include *The Young Ones* (1961) and *Summer Holiday* (1962) **2 Maurice**, known as *Rocket*. (1921–2000); Canadian ice hockey player

Richard I (ˈrɪtʃəd) *n* nicknamed *Coeur de Lion* or *the Lion-Heart*. 1157–99, king of England (1189–99); a leader of the third crusade (joining it in 1191). On his way home, he was captured in Austria (1192) and held to ransom. After a brief return to England, where he was crowned again (1194), he spent the rest of his life in France

Richard II *n* 1367–1400, king of England (1377–99), whose reign was troubled by popular discontent and baronial opposition. He was forced to abdicate in favour of Henry Bolingbroke, who became Henry IV

Richard III *n* 1452–85, king of England (1483–85), notorious as the suspected murderer of his two young nephews in the Tower of London. He proved an able administrator until his brief reign was ended by his death at the hands of Henry Tudor (later Henry VII) at the battle of Bosworth Field

Richards (ˈrɪtʃədz) *n* **1 I(vor) A(rmstrong)**. 1893–1979, British literary critic and linguist, who, with C. K. Ogden, wrote *The Meaning of Meaning* (1923) and devised Basic English **2 Sir Gordon**. 1904–86, British jockey **3 Sir Viv**, full name *Isaac Vivian Alexander Richards*. born 1952, West Indian cricketer; captained the West Indies (1985–91)

Richardson (ˈrɪtʃədsən) *n* **1 Dorothy M(iller)**. 1873–1957, British novelist, a pioneer of stream-of-consciousness writing: author of the novel sequence *Pilgrimage* (14 vols, 1915–67) **2 Henry Handel**. pen name of *Ethel Florence Lindesay Richardson*, 1870–1946, Australian novelist; author of the trilogy *The Fortunes of Richard Mahony* (1917–29) **3 Sir Owen Willans**. 1879–1959, British physicist; a pioneer in the study of atomic physics: Nobel prize for physics 1928 **4 Sir Ralph (David)**. 1902–83, British stage and screen actor **5 Samuel**. 1689–1761, British novelist whose psychological insight and use of the epistolary form exerted a great influence on the development of the novel. His chief novels are *Pamela* (1740) and *Clarissa* (1747)

Richelieu (ˈrɪʃəˌljɜː; *French* riʃəljø) *n* **Armand Jean du Plessis** (armɑ̃ ʒɑ̃ dy plɛsi). 1585–1642, French statesman and cardinal, principal minister to Louis XIII and virtual ruler of France (1624–42). He destroyed the power of the Huguenots and strengthened the crown in France and the role of France in Europe

Richelieu River (ˈrɪʃəˌljɜː; *French* riʃəljø) *n* a river in E Canada, in S Quebec, rising in Lake Champlain and flowing north to the St Lawrence River. Length: 338 km (210 miles)

riches (ˈrɪtʃɪz) *pl n* wealth; an abundance of money, valuable possessions, or property

Richler (ˈrɪʃlə) *n* **Mordecai**. 1931–2001, Canadian novelist. His novels include *St Urbain's Horseman* (1971), *Solomon Gursky Was Here* (1990), and *Barney's Version* (1997)

richly (ˈrɪtʃlɪ) *adv* **1** in a rich or elaborate manner: *a richly decorated carving* **2** fully and appropriately: *he was richly rewarded for his service*

Richmond (ˈrɪtʃmənd) *n* **1** a borough of Greater London, on the River Thames: formed in 1965 by the amalgamation of Barnes, Richmond, and Twickenham; site of Hampton Court Palace and the Royal Botanic Gardens at Kew. Pop: 179 200 (2003 est). Area: 55 sq km (21 sq miles) **2** a town in N England, in North Yorkshire: Norman castle. Pop: 8178 (2001) **3** a port in E Virginia, the state capital, at the falls of the James River: developed after the establishment of a trading post (1637); scene of the Virginia Conventions of 1774 and 1775; Confederate capital in the American Civil War. Pop: 194 729 (2003 est) **4** a county of SW New York City: coextensive with Staten Island borough; consists of

r

Staten Island and several smaller islands

Richter *n* 1 ('rɪktə) **Burton.** born 1931, US physicist: shared the 1976 Nobel prize for physics with Samuel Tring for discovering the subatomic particle known as the J/psi particle 2 (German 'rɪçtər) **Johann Friedrich** (jo'han 'fri:drɪç), wrote under the name *Jean Paul.* 1763–1825, German romantic novelist. His works include *Hesperus* (1795) and *Titan* (1800–03) 3 (Russian 'rixtır) **Sviatoslav** (svɪta'slaf). 1915–97, Ukrainian concert pianist

Richter scale ('rɪktə) *n* a scale for expressing the magnitude of an earthquake in terms of the logarithm of the amplitude of the ground wave; values range from 0 to over 9 [C20: named after Charles *Richter* (1900–85) US seismologist]

Richthofen (German 'rɪçtho:fən) *n* Baron **Manfred von** ('manfre:t fɔn), nickname *the Red Baron.* 1892–1918, German aviator; commander during World War I of the 11th Chasing Squadron (**Richthofen's Flying Circus**). He was credited with 80 air victories before he was shot down

rick¹ (rɪk) *n* 1 a large stack of hay, corn, peas, etc, built in the open in a regular-shaped pile, esp one with a thatched top ▷ *vb* 2 (tr) to stack or pile into ricks [Old English *hrēac*; related to Old Norse *hraukr*]

rick² (rɪk) *n* 1 a wrench or sprain, as of the back ▷ *vb* 2 (tr) to wrench or sprain (a joint, a limb, the back, etc) [C18: see WRICK]

rickets ('rɪkɪts) *n* (functioning as singular or plural) *pathol* a disease mainly of children, characterized by softening of developing bone, and hence bow legs, malnutrition, and enlargement of the liver and spleen, caused by a deficiency of vitamin D [C17: of unknown origin]

rickettsia (rɪ'kɛtsɪə) *n, pl* -siae (-sɪ,i:) *or* -sias any of a group of parasitic bacteria that live in the tissues of ticks, mites, and other arthropods, and cause disease when transmitted to man and other animals [C20: named after Howard T. *Ricketts* (1871–1910), US pathologist] > rick'ettsial *adj*

rickettsial disease *n* any of several acute infectious diseases caused by ticks, mites, or body lice infected with rickettsiae. The main types include typhus, spotted fever, Q fever, trench fever, and tsutsugamushi disease

rickety ('rɪkɪtɪ) *adj* 1 (of a structure, piece of furniture, etc) likely to collapse or break; shaky 2 feeble with age or illness; infirm 3 relating to, resembling, or afflicted with rickets [C17: from RICKETS] > 'ricketiness *n*

rickrack *or* **ricrac** ('rɪk,ræk) *n* a zigzag braid used for trimming [C20: dissimilated reduplication of RACK¹]

rickshaw ('rɪkʃɔ:) *or* **ricksha** ('rɪkʃə) *n* 1 Also called: jinrikisha a small two-wheeled passenger vehicle drawn by one or two men, used in parts of Asia 2 Also called: trishaw a similar vehicle with three wheels, propelled by a man pedalling as on a tricycle [C19: shortened from JINRIKISHA]

ricochet ('rɪkəʃeɪ, 'rɪkəʃɛt) *vb* -chets, -cheting (-,ʃeɪɪŋ), -cheted (-,ʃeɪd) *or* -chets, -chetting (-,ʃɛtɪŋ) , -chetted (-,ʃɛtɪd) 1 (intr) (esp of a bullet) to rebound from a surface or surfaces, usually with a characteristic whining or zipping sound ▷ *n* 2 the motion or sound of a rebounding object, esp a bullet ▷ an object, esp a bullet, that ricochets [C18: from French, of unknown origin]

Ricoeur (French rɪkœr) *n* **Paul** (pɔl) 1913–2005, French philosopher, noted for his work on theories of interpretation. His books include *Philosophy of the Will* (3 vols, 1950–60), *Freud and Philosophy* (1965), and *The Living Metaphor* (1975)

ricotta (rɪ'kɒtə) *n* a soft white unsalted cheese made from sheep's milk, used esp in making ravioli and gnocchi [C19: Italian, from Latin *recocta* recooked, from *recoquere*, from RE- + *coquere* to COOK]

RICS *abbreviation* Royal Institution of Chartered Surveyors

rictus ('rɪktəs) *n, pl* -tus *or* -tuses 1 the GAPE or cleft of an open mouth or beak 2 a fixed or unnatural grin or grimace, as in horror or death [C18: from Latin, from *ringī* to gape] > 'rictal *adj*

rid (rɪd) *vb* rids, ridding, rid *or* ridded (tr) 1 (foll by *of*) to relieve or deliver from something disagreeable or undesirable; make free (of) 2 get rid of to relieve or free

oneself of (something or someone unpleasant or undesirable) [C13 (meaning: to clear land): from Old Norse *rythja*; related to Old High German *riutan* to clear land]

riddance ('rɪdᵊns) *n* the act of getting rid of something undesirable or unpleasant; deliverance or removal (esp in the phrase **good riddance**)

ridden ('rɪdᵊn) *vb* 1 the past participle of: ride ▷ *adj* 2 (in combination) afflicted, affected, or dominated by something specified: *damp-ridden; disease-ridden*

riddle¹ ('rɪdᵊl) *n* 1 a question, puzzle, or verse so phrased that ingenuity is required for elucidation of the answer or meaning; conundrum 2 a person or thing that puzzles, perplexes, or confuses; enigma ▷ *vb* 3 to solve, explain, or interpret (a riddle or riddles) 4 (intr) to speak in riddles [Old English *rǣdelle, rǣdelse*, from *rǣd* counsel; related to Old Saxon *rādislo*, German *Rätsel*] > 'riddler *n*

riddle² ('rɪdᵊl) *vb* (tr) 1 (usually foll by *with*) to pierce or perforate with numerous holes: *riddled with bullets* 2 to put through a sieve; sift 3 to fill or pervade: *the report was riddled with errors* ▷ *n* 4 a sieve, esp a coarse one used for sand, grain, etc [Old English *hriddel* a sieve, variant of *hridder*; related to Latin *cribrum* sieve] > 'riddler *n*

ride (raɪd) *vb* rides, riding, rode, ridden 1 to sit on and control the movements of (a horse or other animal) 2 (tr) to sit on and propel (a bicycle or similar vehicle) 3 (intr; often foll by *on* or *in*) to be carried along or travel on or in a vehicle: *she rides to work on the bus* 4 (tr) to travel over or traverse: *they rode the countryside in search of shelter* 5 (tr) to take part in by riding: *to ride a race* 6 to travel through or be carried across (sea, sky, etc): *the small boat rode the waves; the moon was riding high* 7 (tr) US & Canadian to cause to be carried: *to ride someone out of town* 8 (intr) to be supported as if floating: *the candidate rode to victory on his new policies* 9 (intr) (of a vessel) to lie at anchor 10 (tr) (of a vessel) to be attached to (an anchor) 11 (tr) (of a male animal) to copulate with; mount 12 (tr) slang to have sexual intercourse with (someone) 13 (tr; usually passive) to tyrannize over or dominate: *ridden by fear* 14 (tr) informal to persecute, esp by constant or petty criticism: *don't ride me so hard over my failure* 15 (intr) informal to continue undisturbed: *I wanted to change something, but let it ride* 16 (tr) to endure successfully; ride out 17 (tr) to yield slightly to (a blow or punch) in order to lessen its impact 18 (intr; often foll by *on*) (of a bet) to remain placed: *let your winnings ride on the same number* 19 ride for a fall to act in such a way as to invite disaster 20 ride again informal to return to a former activity or scene of activity ▷ *n* 21 a journey or outing on horseback or in a vehicle 22 a path specially made for riding on horseback 23 transport in a vehicle, esp when given freely to a pedestrian; lift: *can you give me a ride to the station?* 24 a device or structure, such as a roller coaster at a fairground, in which people ride for pleasure or entertainment 25 slang an act of sexual intercourse 26 slang a partner in sexual intercourse 27 take for a ride informal **a** to cheat, swindle, or deceive **b** to take (someone) away in a car and murder him [Old English *rīdan*; related to Old High German *rītan*, Old Norse *rītha*] > 'ridable *or* 'rideable *adj*

Rideau Hall ('ri:dəʊ) *n* (in Canada) the official residence of the Governor General, in Ottawa

ride out *vb* (tr, adverb) to endure successfully; survive (esp in the phrase **ride out the storm**)

rider ('raɪdə) *n* 1 a person or thing that rides, esp a person who rides a horse, a bicycle, or a motorcycle 2 an additional clause, amendment, or stipulation added to a legal or other document, esp (in Britain) a legislative bill at its third reading 3 Brit a statement made by a jury in addition to its verdict, such as a recommendation for mercy 4 any of various objects or devices resting on, surmounting, or strengthening something else 5 geology a thin seam, esp of coal or mineral ore, overlying a thicker seam > 'riderless *adj*

ride up *vb* (intr, adverb) to move or work away from the proper place or position: *her new skirt rode up uncomfortably*

ridge (rɪdʒ) *n* 1 a long narrow raised land formation with sloping sides esp one formed by the meeting of two faces of a mountain or of a mountain buttress or spur 2 any long narrow raised strip or elevation, as on a fabric or in ploughed land **3** *anatomy* any elongated raised margin or border on a bone, tooth, tissue membrane, etc **4 a** the top of a roof at the junction of two sloping sides **b** (*as modifier*): *a ridge tile* **5** *meteorol* an elongated area of high pressure, esp an extension of an anticyclone ▷ Compare **trough** (sense 4) ▷ *vb* **6** to form into a ridge or ridges [Old English *hrycg*; related to Old High German *hrucki*, Old Norse *hryggr*] > 'ridge,like *adj* > 'ridgy *adj*

ridgepole ('rıdʒ,pəʊl) *n* **1** a timber laid along the ridge of a roof, to which the upper ends of the rafters are attached **2** the horizontal pole at the apex of a tent

ridgeway ('rıdʒ,weı) *n Brit* a road or track along a ridge, esp one of great antiquity

ridgy-didge ('rıdʒı,dıdʒ) *adj Austral & NZ informal* genuine; correct: *a ridgy-didge Aussie bloke*

ridicule ('rıdı,kjuːl) *n* **1** language or behaviour intended to humiliate or mock; derision ▷ *vb* **2** (*tr*) to make fun of, mock, or deride [c17: from French, from Latin *rīdiculus*, from *rīdēre* to laugh]

ridiculous (rı'dıkjʊləs) *adj* worthy of or exciting ridicule; absurd, preposterous, laughable, or contemptible [c16: from Latin *rīdiculōsus*, from *rīdēre* to laugh] > ri'diculousness *n*

riding¹ ('raıdıŋ) *n* **a** the art or practice of horsemanship **b** (*as modifier*): *riding school; riding techniques*

riding² ('raıdıŋ) *n* **1** (*capital when part of a name*) any of the three former administrative divisions of Yorkshire: **North Riding**, **East Riding** and **West Riding 2** (in Canada) a parliamentary constituency [from Old English *thriding*, from Old Norse *thrithjungr* a third. The *th*-was lost by assimilation to the -*t* or -*th* that preceded it, as in *west thriding*, etc]

riding crop *n* a short whip with a thong at one end and a handle for opening gates at the other

riding lamp *or* **riding light** *n* a light on a boat or ship showing that it is at anchor

Ridley ('rıdlı) *n* **Nicholas**. ?1500–55, English bishop, who helped to revise the liturgy under Edward VI. He was burnt at the stake for refusing to disavow his Protestant beliefs when Mary I assumed the throne

Rie (riː) *n* Dame **Lucie**, original name *Lucie Gomperz*. 1902–95, British potter, born in Austria

Riefenstahl (*German* 'riːfənʃtaːl) *n* **Leni** ('leːnı). 1902–2003, German photographer and film director, best known for her Nazi propaganda films, such as *Triumph of the Will* (1934)

Riel (riːˈɛl) *n* **Louis**. 1844–85, Canadian politician; hanged for treason after leading the Métis people in rebellion against the Canadian government

Riemann (*German* 'riːman) *n* **Georg Friedrich Bernhard** ('geːɔrk 'friːdrıç 'bɛrnhart). 1826–66, German mathematician whose non-Euclidean geometry was used by Einstein as a basis for his general theory of relativity > Rie'mannian *adj*

riempie ('rımpı) *n South African* a leather thong or lace used mainly to make chair seats [c19 (earlier *riem*): from Afrikaans, diminutive of *riem*, from Dutch: *rim*]

Rienzi (rı'ɛnzı; *Italian* 'rjɛntsı) *or* **Rienzo** (rı'ɛnzəʊ; *Italian* 'rjɛntso) *n* **Cola di** ('koːla di). 1313–54, Italian radical political reformer in Rome

Riesling ('riːzlıŋ, 'raız-) *n* **1** a white wine from the Rhine valley in Germany and from certain districts in other countries **2** the grape used to make this wine [c19: from German, from earlier *Rüssling*, of obscure origin]

rife (raıf) *adj* (*postpositive*) **1** of widespread occurrence; prevalent or current **2** very plentiful; abundant **3** (foll by *with*) abounding (in): *a land rife with poverty* [Old English *rīfe*; related to Old Norse *rīfr* generous, Middle Dutch *rive*] > 'rifely *adv* > 'rifeness *n*

riff (rıf) *music* ▷ *n* **1** (in jazz or rock music) a short series of chords ▷ *vb* **2** (*intr*) to play or perform riffs in jazz or rock music [c20: probably altered and shortened from REFRAIN²]

riffage ('rıfıdʒ) *n* (in jazz or rock music) the act or an instance of playing a short series of chords

riffle ('rıfəl) *vb* **1** (when *intr*, often foll by *through*) to flick rapidly through (the pages of a book, magazine, etc), esp in a desultory manner **2** to shuffle (playing cards) by halving the pack and flicking the adjacent corners

together ▷ *n* **3** *US & Canadian* **a** a rapid in a stream **b** a rocky shoal causing a rapid **c** a ripple on water **4** *mining* a contrivance on the bottom of a sluice, containing transverse grooves for trapping particles of gold **5** the act or an instance of riffling [c18: probably from RUFFLE¹, influenced by RIPPLE¹]

riffraff ('rıf,ræf) *n* (*sometimes functioning as plural*) **1** worthless people, esp collectively; rabble **2** *dialect* worthless rubbish [c15 *rif and raf*, from Old French *rif et raf*; related to *rifler* to plunder, and *rafle* a sweeping up; see RIFLE², RAFFLE]

rifle¹ ('raıfəl) *n* **1 a** a firearm having a long barrel with a spirally grooved interior, which imparts to the bullet spinning motion and thus greater accuracy over a longer range **b** (*as modifier*): *rifle fire* **2** (formerly) a large cannon with a rifled bore **3** one of the grooves in a rifled bore **4** (*plural*) **a** a unit of soldiers equipped with rifles **b** (*capital when part of a name*): *the Rifle Brigade* ▷ *vb* (*tr*) **5** to cut or mould spiral grooves inside the barrel of (a gun) [c18: from Old French *rifler* to scratch; related to Low German *rifeln* to groove, from *riefe* groove, furrow]

rifle² ('raıfəl) *vb* (*tr*) **1** to search (a house, safe, etc) and steal from it; ransack **2** to steal and carry off: *to rifle goods from a shop* [c14: from Old French *rifler* to plunder, scratch, of Germanic origin] > 'rifler *n*

riflebird ('raıfəl,bɜːd) *n* any of various birds of paradise of the genera *Ptiloris* and *Craspedophora*, such as *C. magnifica* (**magnificent riflebird**) [from its call, compared to a whistling bullet]

rifleman ('raıfəlmən) *n, pl* -**men 1** a person skilled in the use of a rifle, esp a soldier **2** Also called: titipounamu **a** wren, *Acanthisitta chloris*, of New Zealand: family *Xenicidae*

rifle range *n* an area used for target practice with rifles

rifling ('raıflıŋ) *n* **1** the cutting of spiral grooves on the inside of a firearm's barrel **2** the series of grooves so cut

rift (rıft) *n* **1** a gap or space made by cleaving or splitting; fissure **2** *geology* a long narrow zone of faulting resulting from tensional stress in the earth's crust **3** a gap between two cloud masses; break or chink **4** a break in friendly relations between people, nations, etc ▷ *vb* **5** to burst or cause to burst open; split [c13: from Old Norse; related to Danish *rift* cleft, Icelandic *ript* breach of contract]

rift valley *n* a long narrow valley resulting from the subsidence of land between two parallel faults, often associated with volcanism. The East African Rift Valley is an example

rig (rıg) *vb* **rigs, rigging, rigged** (*tr*) **1** *nautical* to equip (a vessel, mast, etc) with (sails, rigging, etc) **2** *nautical* to set up or prepare ready for use **3** to put the components of (an aircraft, etc) into their correct positions **4** to manipulate in a fraudulent manner, esp for profit: *to rig prices; to rig an election* ▷ *n* **5** *nautical* the distinctive arrangement of the sails, masts, and other spars of a vessel **6** the installation used in drilling for and exploiting natural oil and gas deposits: *an oil rig* **7** apparatus or equipment; gear **8** *chiefly US & Canadian* an articulated lorry ▷ See also **rig out**, **rig up**, etc [c15: from Scandinavian; related to Norwegian *rigga* to wrap]

Riga ('riːgə) *n* the capital of Latvia, on the Gulf of Riga at the mouth of the Western Dvina on the Baltic Sea: a port and major trading centre since Viking times. Pop: 739 232 (2002 est)

rigadoon (,rıgə'duːn) *or* **rigaudon** (*French* rigodɔ̃) *n* **1** an old Provençal couple dance, light and graceful, in lively duple time **2** a piece of music for or in the rhythm of this dance [c17: from French, allegedly from its inventor *Rigaud*, a dancing master at Marseille]

rigamarole ('rıgəmə,rəʊl) *n* a variant of **rigmarole**

-**rigged** *adj* (*in combination*) (of a sailing vessel) having a rig of a certain kind: *ketch-rigged; schooner-rigged*

rigger ('rıgə) *n* **1** a workman who rigs vessels, etc **2** *rowing* a bracket on a racing shell or other boat to support a projecting rowlock **3** a person skilled in the use of pulleys, lifting gear, cranes, etc

rigging ('rıgıŋ) *n* **1** the shrouds, stays, halyards, etc, of a vessel **2** the bracing wires, struts, and lines of a biplane, balloon, etc **3** any form of lifting gear, tackle, etc

right (raıt) *adj* **1** in accordance with accepted standards of moral or legal behaviour, justice, etc: *right conduct* **2** in accordance with fact, reason, or truth; correct or true: *the right answer* **3** appropriate, suitable, fitting, or proper: *the right man for the job* **4** most favourable or convenient; preferred: *the right time to act* **5** in a satisfactory condition; orderly: *things are right again now* **6** indicating or designating the correct time: *the clock is right* **7** correct in opinion or judgment **8** sound in mind or body; healthy or sane **9** (*usually prenominal*) of, designating, or located near the side of something or someone that faces east when the front is turned towards the north **10** (*usually prenominal*) worn on a right hand, foot, etc **11** (*sometimes capital*) of, designating, supporting, belonging to, or relating to the political or intellectual right (see sense 39) **12** (*sometimes capital*) conservative or reactionary: *the right wing of the party* **13** *geometry* **a** formed by or containing a line or plane perpendicular to another line or plane **b** having the axis perpendicular to the base: *a right circular cone* **c** straight: *a right line* **14** relating to or designating the side of cloth worn or facing outwards **15** *informal* (*intensifier*): *a right idiot* **16** in one's right mind sane **17** she'll be right *Austral & NZ informal* that's all right; not to worry **18** the right side of **a** in favour with: *you'd better stay on the right side of him* **b** younger than: *she's still on the right side of fifty* ▷ *adv* **19** too right *Austral & NZ informal* an exclamation of agreement **20** in accordance with correctness or truth; accurately: *to guess right* **21** in the appropriate manner; properly: *do it right next time!* **22** in a straight line; directly: *right to the top* **23** in the direction of the east from the point of view of a person or thing facing north **24** absolutely or completely; utterly: *he went right through the floor* **25** all the way: *the bus goes right to the city centre* **26** without delay; immediately or promptly: *I'll be right over* **27** exactly or precisely: *right here* **28** in a manner consistent with a legal or moral code; justly or righteously: *do right by me* **29** in accordance with propriety; fittingly or suitably: *it serves you right* **30** to good or favourable advantage; well: *it all came out right in the end* **31** (*esp in religious titles*) most or very: *right reverend* **32** *informal or dialect* (*intensifier*): *I'm right glad to see you* **33** right, left, and centre on all sides; from every direction **34** right off the bat *informal* as the first in a series; to begin with ▷ *n* **35** any claim, title, etc, that is morally just or legally granted as allowable or due to a person: *I know my rights* **36** anything that accords with the principles of legal or moral justice **37** the fact or state of being in accordance with reason, truth, or accepted standards (esp in the phrase in the right) **38** *Irish* an obligation or duty: *you had a right to lock the door* **39** the right side, direction, position, area, or part: *the right of the army; look to the right* **40** the right (*often capital*) the supporters or advocates of social, political, or economic conservatism or reaction, based generally on a belief that things are better left unchanged (opposed to *radical* or *left*) **41** *boxing* **a** a punch with the right hand **b** the right hand **42** *finance* **a** (*often plural*) the privilege of a company's shareholders to subscribe for new issues of the company's shares on advantageous terms **b** the negotiable certificate signifying this privilege **43** by right or by rights properly; justly: *by rights you should be in bed* **44** in one's own right having a claim or title oneself rather than through marriage or other connection: *a peeress in her own right* **45** to rights consistent with justice, correctness, or orderly arrangement: *he put the matter to rights* ▷ *vb* **46** (*also intr*) to restore to or attain a normal, esp an upright, position: *the raft righted in a few seconds* **47** to make (something) accord with truth or facts; correct **48** to restore to an orderly state or condition; put right **49** to make reparation for; compensate for or redress (esp in the phrase **right a wrong**) ▷ *interj* **50** an expression of agreement or compliance [Old English *riht, reoht*; related to Old High German *reht*, Gothic *raihts*, Latin *rēctus*] > **'righter** *n* > **'rightness** *n*

right about *n* **1 a** turn executed through 180° ▷ *adj, adv* **2** in the opposite direction

right angle *n* **1** the angle between two radii of a circle that cut off on the circumference an arc equal in length to one quarter of the circumference; an angle of 90° or $\pi/2$ radians **2** at right angles perpendicular or perpendicularly > **'right-,angled** *adj*

right-angled triangle *n* a triangle one angle of which is a right angle. US and Canadian name: right triangle

right ascension *n* *astronomy* the angular distance measured eastwards along the celestial equator from the vernal equinox to the point at which the celestial equator intersects a great circle passing through the celestial pole and the heavenly object in question

right away *adv* without delay; immediately or promptly

righteous ('raɪtʃəs) *adj* **1 a** characterized by, proceeding from, or in accordance with accepted standards of morality, justice, or uprightness; virtuous: *a righteous man* **b** (*as collective noun; preceded by the*): *the righteous* **2** morally justifiable or right, esp from one's own point of view: *righteous indignation* [Old English *rīhtwīs*, from RIGHT + WISE²] > **'righteously** *adv* > **'righteousness** *n*

rightful ('raɪtfʊl) *adj* **1** in accordance with what is right; proper or just **2** (*prenominal*) having a legally or morally just claim: *the rightful owner* **3** (*prenominal*) held by virtue of a legal or just claim: *my rightful property* > **'rightfully** *adv*

right-hand *adj* (*prenominal*) **1** of, relating to, located on, or moving towards the right: *a right-hand bend; this car has right-hand drive* **2** for use by the right hand; right-handed **3** right-hand man one's most valuable assistant or supporter

right-handed *adj* **1** using the right hand with greater skill or ease than the left **2** performed with the right hand **3** made for use by the right hand **4** turning from left to right; clockwise > **,right-'handedness** *n*

rightist ('raɪtɪst) *adj* **1** of, tending towards, or relating to the political right or its principles; conservative, traditionalist, or reactionary ▷ *n* **2** a person who supports or belongs to the political right > **'rightism** *n*

rightly ('raɪtlɪ) *adv* **1** in accordance with the facts; correctly **2** in accordance with principles of justice or morality **3** with good reason; justifiably: *he was rightly annoyed with her* **4** properly or suitably; appropriately **5** (*used with a negative*) *informal* with certainty; positively or precisely (usually in the phrases **I don't rightly know, I can't rightly say**)

right-minded *adj* holding opinions or principles that accord with what is right or with the opinions of the speaker

righto or **right oh** ('raɪt'əʊ) *sentence substitute Brit informal* an expression of agreement or compliance

right off *adv* immediately; right away

right of way *n, pl* rights of way **1** the right of one vehicle or vessel to take precedence over another, as laid down by law or custom **2 a** the legal right of someone to pass over another's land, acquired by grant or by long usage **b** the path or road used by this right **3** *US* the strip of land over which a power line, railway line, road, etc, extends

right on *adj* right-on *informal* modern, trendy, and socially aware or relevant: *right-on green politics*

Right Reverend *adj* (in Britain) a title of respect for an Anglican or Roman Catholic bishop

rights issue *n* *stock exchange* an issue of new shares offered by a company to its existing shareholders on favourable terms

rightsize ('raɪt,saɪz) *vb* to restructure (an organization) to cut costs and improve effectiveness without ruthlessly downsizing

right-thinking ('raɪt,θɪŋkɪŋ) *adj* possessing reasonable and generally acceptable opinions

rightward ('raɪtwəd) *adj* **1** situated on or directed towards the right ▷ *adv* **2** a variant of **rightwards**

rightwards ('raɪtwədz) or **rightward** *adv* towards or on the right

right whale *n* any large whalebone whale of the family *Balaenidae*. They are grey or black, have a large head, and, in most, no dorsal fin, and are hunted as a source of whalebone and oil. See also **bowhead** [c19: perhaps so named because it was *right* for hunting]

right wing *n* **1** (*often capitals*) the conservative faction of an assembly, party, etc **2** the part of an army or field of battle on the right from the point of view of one facing the enemy **3 a** the right-hand side of the field of play from the point of view of a team facing its opponent's goal **b** a player positioned in this area in any of various games ▷ *adj* right-wing **4** of, belonging to, or relating to the right wing > **'right-'winger** *n*

Rigi ('riːgɪ) *n* a mountain in the Alps of N central Switzerland, between Lakes Lucerne, Zug, and Lauerz

rigid ('rɪdʒɪd) *adj* **1** not bending; physically inflexible or stiff: *a rigid piece of plastic* **2** unbending; rigorously strict; severe: *rigid rules* [c16: from Latin *rigidus*, from *rigēre* to be stiff] > **'rigidly** *adv* or **ri'gidity** or **'rigidness** *n*

rigidify (rɪ'dʒɪdɪˌfaɪ) *vb* **-fies, -fying, -fied** to make or become rigid

rigmarole ('rɪɡməˌrəʊl) or **rigamarole** *n* **1** any long complicated procedure **2** a set of incoherent or pointless statements; garbled nonsense [c18: from earlier *ragman roll* a list, probably a roll used in a medieval game, wherein various characters were described in verse, beginning with *Ragemon le bon* Ragman the good]

rigor ('raɪɡɔː, 'rɪɡə) *n* **1** *med* a sudden feeling of chilliness, often accompanied by shivering: it sometimes precedes a fever **2** ('rɪɡə) *pathol* rigidity of a muscle; muscular cramp **3** a state of rigidity assumed by some animals in reaction to sudden shock [see RIGOUR]

rigor mortis ('rɪɡə 'mɔːtɪs) *n pathol* the stiffness of joints and muscular rigidity of a dead body, caused by depletion of ATP in the tissues. It begins two to four hours after death and lasts up to about four days, after which the muscles and joints relax [c19: Latin, literally: rigidity of death]

rigorous ('rɪɡərəs) *adj* **1** characterized by or proceeding from rigour; harsh, strict, or severe: *rigorous discipline* **2** severely accurate; scrupulous: *rigorous book-keeping* **3** (esp of weather) extreme or harsh **4** *maths, logic* (of a proof) making the validity of the successive steps completely explicit > **'rigorously** *adv*

rigour or US **rigor** ('rɪɡə) *n* **1** harsh but just treatment or action **2** a severe or cruel circumstance; hardship: *the rigours of famine* **3** strictness, harshness, or severity of character **4** strictness in judgment or conduct; rigorism [c14: from Latin *rigor*]

rig out *vb* **1** (*tr, adverb*; often foll by *with*) to equip or fit out (with): *his car is rigged out with gadgets* **2** to dress or be dressed: *rigged out smartly* ▷ *n* **rigout 3** *informal* a person's clothing or costume, esp a bizarre outfit

rig up *vb* (*tr, adverb*) to erect or construct, esp as a temporary measure: *cameras were rigged up to televise the event*

Rig-Veda (rɪɡ'veɪdə, -'viːdə) *n* a compilation of 1028 Hindu poems dating from 2000 BC or earlier [c18: from Sanskrit *rigveda*, from *ric* song of praise + VEDA]

Rijeka (rɪ'ɛkə; *Croatian* ri'jeka) *n* a port in Croatia: an ancient town, changing hands many times before passing to Yugoslavia in 1947 until Croatia became independent in 1991. Pop: 135 000 (2005 est). Italian name: **Fiume**

Rijksmuseum ('raɪksmjuːˌzɪəm) *n* a museum in Amsterdam housing the national art collection of the Netherlands

Rijn (rɛjn) *n* the Dutch name for the **Rhine**

Rijswijk ('raɪsvaɪk; *Dutch* 'rɛjswɛjk) *n* a town in the SW Netherlands, in South Holland province on the SE outskirts of The Hague: scene of the signing (1697) of the **Treaty of Rijswijk** ending the War of the Grand Alliance. Pop: 48 000 (2003 est). English name: **Ryswick**

rile (raɪl) *vb* (*tr*) **1** to annoy or anger; irritate **2** *US & Canadian* to stir up or agitate (water, etc); roil or make turbid [c19: variant of ROIL]

Riley ('raɪlɪ) *n* **1 Bridget** (**Louise**). born 1931, British painter, best known for her black-and-white op art paintings of the 1960s **2 Gina**. born 1961, Australian television actress and writer, best known for playing 'Kim' in the comedy series *Kath & Kim*

Rilke ('rɪlkə) *n* **Rainer Maria** ('raɪnər ma'riːa). 1875–1926, Austro-German poet, born in Prague. Author of intense visionary lyrics, notably in the *Duino Elegies* (1922) and *Sonnets to Orpheus* (1923)

rill (rɪl) *n* **1** a brook or stream; rivulet **2** a small channel or gulley, such as one formed during soil erosion **3** Also

called: **rille** one of many winding cracks on the moon [c15: from Low German *rille*; related to Dutch *ril*]

rim (rɪm) *n* **1** the raised edge of an object, esp of something more or less circular such as a cup or crater **2** the peripheral part of a wheel, to which the tyre is attached **3** *basketball* the hoop from which the net is suspended ▷ *vb* rims, rimming, rimmed (*tr*) **4** to put a rim on (a pot, cup, wheel, etc) **5** *slang* to lick, kiss, or suck the anus of (one's sexual partner) [Old English *rima*; related to Old Saxon *rimi*, Old Norse *rimi* ridge]

Rimbaud (*French* rɛ̃bo) *n* **Arthur** (artyr). 1854–91, French poet, whose work, culminating in the prose poetry of *Illuminations* (published 1884), greatly influenced the symbolists. *A Season in Hell* (1873) draws on his tempestuous homosexual affair with Verlaine, after which he abandoned writing (aged about 20) and spent the rest of his life travelling

rime¹ (raɪm) *n* **1** frost formed by the freezing of supercooled water droplets in fog onto solid objects ▷ *vb* **2** (*tr*) to cover with rime or something resembling rime [Old English *hrīm*; related to Dutch *rijm*, Middle High German *rīmeln* to coat with frost]

rime² (raɪm) *n, vb* an archaic spelling of **rhyme**

rim-fire *adj* **1** (of a cartridge) having the primer in the rim of the base **2** (of a firearm) adapted for such cartridges

Rimini ('rɪmɪnɪ) *n* a port and resort in NE Italy, in Emilia-Romagna on the N Adriatic coast. Pop: 128 656 (2001). Ancient name: Ariminum

rimose (raɪ'məʊs, -'məʊz) *adj* (esp of plant parts) having the surface marked by a network of intersecting cracks [c18: from Latin *rīmōsus*, from *rīma* a split, crack]

Rimsky-Korsakov ('rɪmskɪ'kɔːsəkɒf; *Russian* 'rimskij'kɔrsəkəf) *n* **Nikolai Andreyevich** (nika'laj an'drjejivitʃ). 1844–1908, Russian composer; noted for such works as the orchestral suite *Scheherazade* (1888) and the opera *Le Coq d'or* (first performed in 1910)

rimu ('riːmuː) *n* another name for **red pine** [from Māori]

rimy ('raɪmɪ) *adj* rimier, rimiest coated with rime

rind (raɪnd) *n* **1** a hard outer layer or skin on bacon, cheese, etc **2** the outer layer of a fruit or of the spore-producing body of certain fungi **3** the outer layer of the bark of a tree [Old English *rinde*; Old High German *rinta*, German *Rinde*]

rinderpest ('rɪndəˌpɛst) *n* an acute contagious viral disease of cattle, characterized by severe inflammation of the intestinal tract and diarrhoea [c19: German: cattle pest]

ring¹ (rɪŋ) *n* **1** a circular band usually of a precious metal, esp gold, often set with gems and worn upon the finger as an adornment or as a token of engagement or marriage **2** any object or mark that is circular in shape **3** a circular path or course: *to run around in a ring* **4** a group of people or things standing or arranged so as to form a circle: *a ring of spectators* **5** an enclosed space, usually circular in shape, where circus acts are performed **6** a square apron or raised platform, marked off by ropes, in which contestants box or wrestle **7** the ring the sport of boxing **8** throw one's hat in the ring to announce one's intention to be a candidate or contestant **9** a group of people usually operating illegally and covertly: *a drug ring; a paedophile ring; a ring of antique dealers* **10** (esp at country fairs) an enclosure, often circular, where horses, cattle, and other livestock are paraded and auctioned **11** an area reserved for betting at a racecourse **12** a circular strip of bark cut from a tree or branch, esp in order to kill it **13** a single turn in a spiral **14** *geometry* the area of space lying between two concentric circles **15** *maths* a set that is subject to two binary operations, addition and multiplication, such that the set is an Abelian group under addition and is closed under multiplication, this latter operation being associative **16** *botany* short for **annual ring 17** Also called: closed chain *chem* a closed loop of atoms in a molecule **18** *astronomy* any of the thin circular bands of small bodies orbiting a giant planet, esp Saturn **19** run rings around *informal* to be greatly superior to; outclass completely ▷ *vb* rings, ringing, ringed (*tr*) **20** to surround with or as if with or form a ring; encircle **21** to mark (a bird) with a ring or clip for subsequent identification **22** to fit a ring in the nose of (a bull, pig, etc) so that it can be led easily **23** Also called: **ringbark** to cut away a circular strip of bark from (a tree or branch) in order to kill it [Old English *hring*; related to Old Norse *hringr*] ▷ **ringed** *adj*

ring² (rɪŋ) *vb* **rings, ringing, rang, rung 1** to emit or cause to emit a sonorous or resonant sound, characteristic of certain metals when struck **2** to cause (a bell) to emit a ringing sound by striking it once or repeatedly or (of a bell) to emit such a sound **3 a** (*tr*) to cause (a large bell, esp a church bell) to emit a ringing sound by pulling on a rope that is attached to a wheel on which the bell swings back and forth, being sounded by a clapper inside it. See **chime¹** (sense 5) **b** (*intr*) (of a bell) to sound by being swung in this way **4** (*intr*) (of a building, place, etc) to be filled with sound; echo: *the church rang with singing* **5** (*intr*; foll by *for*) to call by means of a bell, buzzer, etc: *to ring for the butler* **6** Also called: **ring up** *chiefly Brit* to call (a person) by telephone **7** (*tr*) to strike or tap (a coin) in order to assess its genuineness by the sound produced **8** (*intr*) (of the ears) to have or give the sensation of humming or ringing **9** *slang* to change the identity of (a stolen vehicle) by using the licence plate, serial number, etc, of another, usually disused, vehicle **10 ring down the curtain a** to lower the curtain at the end of a theatrical performance **b** (foll by *on*) to put an end (to) **11 ring false** to give the impression of being false **12 ring true** to give the impression of being true ▷ *n* **13** the act of or a sound made by ringing **14** a sound produced by or suggestive of a bell **15** any resonant or metallic sound, esp one sustained or re-echoed: *the ring of trumpets* **16** *informal, chiefly Brit* a telephone call **17** the complete set of bells in a tower or belfry: *a ring of eight bells* **18** an inherent quality or characteristic: *his explanation has the ring of sincerity* ▷ See also **ring in, ring off**, etc [Old English *hringan*; related to Old High German *hringen* Old Norse *hringja*]

● **USAGE** *Rang* and *sang* are the correct forms of the past
● tenses of *ring* and *sing*, although *rung* and *sung* are still
● heard informally and dialectally: *he rung (rang) the bell*

ringbark (ˈrɪŋˌbɑːk) *vb* another term for **ring¹** (sense 23)

ring binder *n* a loose-leaf binder fitted with metal rings that can be opened to allow perforated paper to be inserted

ringbolt (ˈrɪŋˌbəʊlt) *n* a bolt with a ring fitted through an eye attached to the bolt head

ringdove (ˈrɪŋˌdʌv) *n* **1** another name for **wood pigeon 2** an Old World turtledove, *Streptopelia risoria*, having a greyish plumage with a black band around the neck

ringed plover *n* a European shorebird, *Charadrius hiaticula*, with a greyish-brown back, white underparts with a black throat band, and orange legs: family *Charadriidae* (plovers)

ringer (ˈrɪŋə) *n* **1** a person or thing that rings a bell **2** Also called: **dead ringer** *slang* a person or thing that is almost identical to another **3** a stolen vehicle the identity of which has been changed by the use of the licence plate, serial number, etc, of another, usually disused, vehicle **4** *US* a contestant, esp a horse, entered in a competition under false representations of identity, record, or ability **5** *Austral & NZ* the fastest shearer in a shed **6** *Austral informal* the fastest or best at anything **7** a quoit thrown so as to encircle a peg **8** such a throw

ring-fence *vb* **1** to assign (money, a grant, fund, etc) to one particular purpose, so as to restrict its use: *to ring-fence a financial allowance* **2** to oblige (a person or organization) to use money for a particular purpose: *to ring-fence a local authority* ▷ *n* **ring fence 3** an agreement, contract, etc, in which the use of money is restricted to a particular purpose

ring finger *n* the third finger, esp of the left hand, on which a wedding ring is traditionally worn

ring in *vb* (*adverb*) **1** (*intr*) *chiefly Brit* to report to someone by telephone **2** (*tr*) to accompany the arrival of with bells (esp in the phrase **ring in the new year**) ▷ *n* **ring-in 3** *Austral & NZ informal* a person or thing that is not normally a member of a particular group; outsider

ringing tone *n Brit* a sequence of pairs of tones heard by

the dialler on a telephone when the number dialled is ringing. Compare **engaged tone, dialling tone**

ringleader (ˈrɪŋˌliːdə) *n* a person who leads others in any kind of unlawful or mischievous activity

ringlet (ˈrɪŋlɪt) *n* **1** a lock of hair hanging down in a spiral curl **2** any of numerous butterflies of the genus *Erebia*, most of which occur in S Europe and have dark brown wings marked with small black-and-white eyespots: family *Satyridae* ▷ **ringleted** *adj*

ring main *n* a domestic electrical supply in which outlet sockets are connected to the mains supply through a ring circuit

ringmaster (ˈrɪŋˌmɑːstə) *n* the master of ceremonies in a circus

ring-necked *adj* (of animals, esp certain birds and snakes) having a band of distinctive colour around the neck

ring-necked pheasant *n* a common pheasant, *Phasianus colchicus*, originating in Asia. The male has a bright plumage with a band of white around the neck and the female is mottled brown

ring off *vb* (*intr, adverb*) *chiefly Brit* to terminate a telephone conversation by replacing the receiver; hang up

ring out *vb* (*adverb*) **1** (*tr*) to accompany the departure of with bells (esp in the phrase **ring out the old year**) **2** (*intr*) to send forth a loud resounding noise

ring ouzel *n* a European thrush, *Turdus torquatus*, common in rocky areas. The male has a blackish plumage with a white band around the neck and the female is brown

ring road *n* a main road that bypasses a town or town centre. US names: **belt, beltway**

ring rot *n* a virulent bacterial disease of potatoes occurring in the vascular ring of the potato tuber. Also called: **potato ring rot**

ringside (ˈrɪŋˌsaɪd) *n* **1** the area immediately surrounding an arena, esp the row of seats nearest a boxing or wrestling ring **2 a** any place affording a close uninterrupted view **b** (*as modifier*): *a ringside seat*

ringtail (ˈrɪŋˌteɪl) *n* Also called: **ringtail possum** *Austral* any of several possums having curling prehensile tails used to grasp branches while climbing

ringtone (ˈrɪŋˌtəʊn) *n* a musical tune played by a mobile phone when a call is received

ring up *vb* (*adverb*) **1** *chiefly Brit* to make a telephone call (to) **2** (*tr*) to record on a cash register **3 ring up the curtain a** to begin a theatrical performance **b** (often foll by *on*) to make a start (on)

ringworm (ˈrɪŋˌwɜːm) *n* any of various fungal infections of the skin (esp the scalp) or nails, often appearing as itching circular patches. Also called: **tinea**

rink (rɪŋk) *n* **1** an expanse of ice for skating on, esp one that is artificially prepared and under cover **2** an area for roller skating on **3** a building or enclosure for ice skating or roller skating **4** *bowls* a strip of the green, usually about 5–7 metres wide, on which a game is played **5** *curling* the strip of ice on which the game is played, usually 41 by 4 metres **6** (in bowls and curling) the players on one side in a game [C14 (Scots): from Old French *renc* row, RANK¹]

rinkhals (ˈrɪŋkˌhals) or **ringhals** (ˈrɪŋˌhals) *n, pl* **-hals** or **-halses** a venomous elapid snake, *Hemachatus hemachatus* of southern Africa, which spits venom at its enemies from a distance [Afrikaans, literally: ring neck]

rink rat *n Canadian informal* a young person who carries out chores at an ice-hockey rink in return for free skating time

rinse (rɪns) *vb* (*tr*) **1** to remove soap from (clothes, etc) by applying clean water in the final stage in washing **2** to wash lightly, esp without using soap **3** to give a light tint to (hair) ▷ *n* **4** the act or an instance of rinsing **5** *hairdressing* a liquid preparation put on the hair when wet to give a tint to it: *a blue rinse* [C14: from Old French *rincer*, from Latin *recens* fresh, new] ▷ **rinser** *n*

Rio Branco (*Portuguese* ˈriu ˈbrɐŋku) *n* **1** a city in W Brazil, capital of Acre state. Pop: 261 000 (2005 est) **2** a river in Brazil, flowing south to the Rio Negro. Length: 644 km (400 miles)

Río Bravo (*Spanish* 'rio 'βraβo) *n* the Mexican name for the **Rio Grande**

Rio de Janeiro ('ri:əʊ də dʒə'nɪərəʊ) *or* **Rio** *n* **1** a port in SE Brazil, on Guanabara Bay: the country's chief port and its capital from 1763 to 1960; backed by mountains, notably Sugar Loaf Mountain; founded by the French in 1555 and taken by the Portuguese in 1567. Pop: 11 469 000 (2005 est). Related noun: **Cariocan 2** a state of E Brazil. Capital: Rio de Janeiro. Pop: 14 724 475 (2002). Area: 42 911 sq km (16 568 sq miles)

Río de la Plata ('ri:əʊ də lɑ: 'plɑːtə) *n* See **Plata**

Río de Oro (*Spanish* 'rio ðe 'oro) *n* a former region of W Africa: comprised the S part of the Spanish Sahara (now Western Sahara)

Rio Grande *n* **1** ('ri:əʊ grænd, 'grændɪ) a river in North America, rising in SW Colorado and flowing southeast to the Gulf of Mexico, forming the border between the US and Mexico. Length: about 3030 km (1885 miles). Mexican name: **Río Bravo 2** (*Portuguese* 'riu 'grɒndi) a port in SE Brazil, in SE Rio Grande do Sul state: serves as the port for Porto Alegre. Pop: 188 000 (2005 est))

Rio Grande do Norte (*Portuguese* 'riu 'grɒndi du 'nɔrti) *n* a state of NE Brazil, on the Atlantic: much of it is semiarid plateau. Capital: Natal. Pop: 2 852 784 (2002). Area: 53 014 sq km (20 469 sq miles)

Rio Grande do Sul (*Portuguese* 'riu 'grɒndi du 'sul) *n* a state of S Brazil, on the Atlantic. Capital: Porto Alegre. Pop: 10 408 540 (2002). Area: 282 183 sq km (108 951 sq miles)

rioja (ri:'əʊxə) *n* a red or white wine, with a distinctive vanilla bouquet and flavour, produced around the Ebro river in central N Spain [c20: from *La Rioja*, the area where it is produced]

Río Negro ('ri:əʊ 'neɪgrəʊ, 'nɛg-; *Spanish* 'rio 'neɣro) *n* See **Negro²**

riot ('raɪət) *n* **1 a** a disturbance made by an unruly mob or (in law) three or more persons; tumult or uproar **b** (*as modifier*): *a riot gun; riot police; a riot shield* **2** boisterous activity; unrestrained revelry **3** an occasion of boisterous merriment **4** *slang* a person who occasions boisterous merriment **5** a dazzling or arresting display: *a riot of colour* **6** *hunting* the indiscriminate following of any scent by hounds **7** *archaic* wanton lasciviousness **8 run riot a** to behave wildly and without restraint **b** (of plants) to grow rankly or profusely ▷ *vb* **9** (*intr*) to take part in a riot **10** (*intr*) to indulge in unrestrained revelry or merriment **11** (*tr*; foll by *away*) to spend (time or money) in wanton or loose living [c13: from Old French *riote* dispute, from *ruihoter* to quarrel, probably from *ruir* to make a commotion, from Latin *rugīre* to roar] ▷ 'rioter *n*

Riot Act *n* **1** *criminal law* (formerly in England) a statute of 1715 by which persons committing a riot had to disperse within an hour of the reading of the act by a magistrate **2 read the riot act to someone** to warn or reprimand someone severely

riotous ('raɪətəs) *adj* **1** proceeding from or of the nature of riots or rioting **2** characterized by wanton or lascivious revelry: *riotous living* **3** characterized by boisterous or unrestrained merriment: *riotous laughter* ▷ 'riotously *adv* ▷ 'riotousness *n*

riot shield *n* a large oblong curved transparent shield used by police controlling crowds

rip¹ (rɪp) *vb* **rips, ripping, ripped 1** to tear or be torn violently or roughly; split or be rent **2** (*tr*; foll by *off* or *out*) to remove hastily, carelessly, or roughly **3** (*intr*) *informal* to move violently or precipitously; rush headlong **4** (*intr*; foll by *into*) *informal* to pour violent abuse (on); make a verbal attack (on) **5** (*tr*) to saw or split (wood) in the direction of the grain **6** (*tr*) *informal computing* to copy (music or software) without permission or making any payment **7 let rip** to act or speak without restraint ▷ *n* **8** the place where something is torn; a tear or split **9** short for **ripsaw** ▷ See also **rip off** [c15: perhaps from Flemish *rippen*; compare Middle Dutch *rippen* to pull]

rip² (rɪp) *n* short for **riptide** (sense 1) [c18: perhaps from **RIP¹**]

rip³ (rɪp) *n informal, archaic* **1** something or someone of

little or no value **2** an old worn-out horse [c18: perhaps altered from *rep*, shortened from **REPROBATE**]

RIP *abbreviation* requiescat *or* requiescant in pace [Latin: may he, she, *or* they rest in peace]

riparian (raɪ'pɛərɪən) *adj* **1** of, inhabiting, or situated on the bank of a river **2** denoting or relating to the legal rights of the owner of land on a river bank, such as fishing or irrigation ▷ *n* **3** *property law* a person who owns land on a river bank [c19: from Latin *rīpārius*, from *rīpa* a river bank]

ripcord ('rɪp,kɔːd) *n* **1** a cord that when pulled opens a parachute from its pack **2** a cord on the gas bag of a balloon that when pulled opens a panel, enabling gas to escape and the balloon to descend

ripe (raɪp) *adj* **1** (of fruit, grain, etc) mature and ready to be eaten or used; fully developed **2** mature enough to be eaten or used: *ripe cheese* **3** fully developed in mind or body **4** resembling ripe fruit, esp in redness or fullness: *a ripe complexion* **5** (*postpositive*; foll by *for*) ready or eager (to undertake or undergo an action) **6** (*postpositive*; foll by *for*) suitable; right or opportune: *the time is not yet ripe* **7** mature in judgment or knowledge **8** advanced but healthy (esp in the phrase **a ripe old age**) **9** *slang* **a** complete; thorough **b** excessive; exorbitant **10** *slang* slightly indecent; risqué [Old English *rīpe*; related to Old Saxon *rīpi*, Old High German *rīfi*, German *reif*] ▷ 'ripely *adv* ▷ 'ripeness *n*

ripen ('raɪpᵊn) *vb* to make or become ripe ▷ 'ripener *n*

ripieno (rɪ'pjɛːnəʊ; *Italian* ri'pjɛːno) *n, pl* -**ni** (-niː) *or* -**nos** (in baroque concertos and concerti grossi) the full orchestra, as opposed to the instrumental soloists [c18: from Italian: from *ri-* **RE-** + *pieno*, from Latin *plēnus* full]

Ripley ('rɪplɪ) *n* **George.** 1802–80, US social reformer and transcendentalist: founder of the Brook Farm experiment in communal living in Massachusetts (1841)

rip off *vb* **1** (*tr*) to tear violently or roughly (from) **2** (*adverb*) *slang* to steal from or cheat (someone) ▷ *n* **rip-off 3** *slang* an article or articles stolen **4** *slang* a grossly overpriced article **5** *slang* the act of stealing or cheating

Ripon ('rɪpᵊn) *n* a city in N England, in North Yorkshire: cathedral (12th–16th centuries). Pop: 16 468 (2001)

riposte *or* **ripost** (rɪ'pɒst, rɪ'pəʊst) *n* **1** a swift sharp reply in speech or action **2** *fencing* a counterattack made immediately after a successful parry ▷ *vb* **3** (*intr*) to make a riposte [c18: from French, from Italian *risposta*, from *rispondere* to reply, **RESPOND**]

ripper ('rɪpə) *n* **1** a person who rips **2** a murderer who dissects or mutilates his victims' bodies **3** *informal, chiefly Austral & NZ* a fine or excellent person or thing

ripping ('rɪpɪŋ) *adj archaic, Brit slang* excellent; splendid ▷ 'rippingly *adv*

ripple¹ ('rɪpᵊl) *n* **1** a slight wave or undulation on the surface of water **2** a small wave or undulation in fabric, hair, etc **3** a sound reminiscent of water flowing quietly in ripples: *a ripple of laughter* **4** *electronics* an oscillation of small amplitude superimposed on a steady value **5** *US & Canadian* another word for **riffle** (sense 3) ▷ *vb* **6** (*intr*) to form ripples or flow with a rippling or undulating motion **7** (*tr*) to stir up (water) so as to form ripples **8** (*tr*) to make ripple marks **9** (*intr*) (of sounds) to rise and fall gently [c17: perhaps from **RIP¹**] ▷ 'rippler *n* ▷ 'rippling *adj* ▷ 'ripply *adj*

ripple² ('rɪpᵊl) *n* **1** a special kind of comb designed to separate the seed from the stalks in flax, hemp, or broomcorn ▷ *vb* **2** (*tr*) to comb with this tool [c14: of Germanic origin; compare Middle Dutch *repelen*, Middle High German *reffen* to ripple] ▷ 'rippler *n*

ripple effect *n* the repercussions of an event or situation experienced far beyond its immediate location

ripple mark *n* one of a series of small wavy ridges of sand formed by waves on a beach, by a current in a sandy riverbed, or by wind on land: sometimes found fossilized on bedding planes of sedimentary rock

rip-roaring *adj informal* characterized by excitement, intensity, or boisterous behaviour

ripsaw ('rɪp,sɔː) *n* a handsaw for cutting along the grain of timber

ripsnorter ('rɪp,snɔːtə) *n slang* a person or thing noted for intensity or excellence [c19: from **RIP¹** + **SNORTER**]

r

riptide ('rɪp,taɪd) n **1** Also called: **rip, tide-rip** a stretch of turbulent water in the sea, caused by the meeting of currents or abrupt changes in depth **2** Also called: **rip current** a strong current, esp one flowing outwards from the shore, causing disturbance on the surface

RISC (rɪsk) n acronym for reduced instruction set computer: a computer in which the set of instructions which it can perform has been reduced to the minimum, resulting in very fast data processing

rise (raɪz) vb rises, rising, rose (rəʊz), risen ('rɪzᵊn) (mainly intr) **1** to get up from a lying, sitting, kneeling, or prone position **2** to get out of bed, esp to begin one's day: he always rises early **3** to move from a lower to a higher position or place; ascend **4** to ascend or appear above the horizon: the sun is rising **5** to increase in height or level: the water rose above the normal level **6** to attain higher rank, status, or reputation: he will rise in the world **7** to be built or erected: those blocks of flats are rising fast **8** to become apparent; appear: new troubles rose to afflict her **9** to increase in strength, degree, intensity, etc: her spirits rose; the wind is rising **10** to increase in amount or value: house prices are always rising **11** to swell up: dough rises **12** to become erect, stiff, or rigid: the hairs on his neck rose in fear **13** (of one's stomach or gorge) to manifest or feel nausea; retch **14** to become actively rebellious; revolt: the people rose against their oppressors **15** to slope upwards: the ground rises beyond the lake **16** to return from the dead; be resurrected **17** to originate; come into existence: that river rises in the mountains **18** (of a session of a court, legislative assembly, etc) to come to an end; adjourn **19** angling (of fish) to come to the surface of the water, as when taking flies **20** (often foll by to) informal to respond (to teasing, etc) or fall into a trap prepared for one ▷ n **21** the act or an instance of rising; ascent **22** an increase in height; elevation **23** an increase in rank, status, or position **24** an increase in amount, cost, or value **25** an increase in degree or intensity **26** Brit an increase in salary or wages. US and Canadian word: **raise** **27** the vertical height of a step or of a flight of stairs **28** the vertical height of a roof above the walls or columns **29** angling the act or instance of fish coming to the surface of the water to take flies, etc **30** the beginning, origin, or source; derivation [Old English rīsan; related to Old Saxon rīsan, Gothic reisan]

riser ('raɪzə) n **1** a person who rises, esp from bed: an early riser **2** the vertical part of a stair or step **3** a vertical pipe, esp one within a building

rise to vb (intr, preposition) to respond adequately to (the demands of something, esp a testing challenge)

risibility (,rɪzɪ'bɪlɪtɪ) n, pl -ties **1** a tendency to laugh **2** hilarity; laughter

risible ('rɪzɪbᵊl) adj **1** having a tendency to laugh **2** causing laughter; ridiculous [c16: from Late Latin rīsibilis, from Latin rīdēre to laugh] > 'risibly adv

rising ('raɪzɪŋ) n **1** an insurrection or rebellion; revolt **2** the yeast or leaven used to make dough rise in baking ▷ adj (prenominal) **3** increasing in rank, status, or reputation: a rising young politician **4** increasing in maturity; growing up to adulthood: the rising generation ▷ adv **5** informal approaching the age of; nearly: she's rising 40

rising damp n capillary movement of moisture from the ground into the walls of buildings. It results in structural damage up to a level of three feet

rising trot n a horse's trot in which the rider rises from the saddle every second beat

risk (rɪsk) n **1** the possibility of incurring misfortune or loss; hazard **2** insurance **a** a chance of a loss or other event on which a claim may be filed **b** the type of such an event, such as fire or theft **c** the amount of the claim should such an event occur **d** a person or thing considered with respect to the characteristics that may cause an insured event to occur **3 at risk** vulnerable; likely to be lost or damaged **4 take a risk** or **run a risk** to proceed in an action without regard to the possibility of danger involved in it ▷ vb (tr) **5** to expose to danger or loss; hazard **6** to act in spite of the possibility of (injury or loss): to risk a fall in climbing [c17: from French risque, from Italian risco, from rischiare to be in peril, from Greek

rhiza cliff (from the hazards of sailing along rocky coasts)]

risk capital n chiefly Brit capital invested in an issue of ordinary shares, esp of a speculative enterprise. Also called: **venture capital**

risk factor n med a factor, such as a habit or an environmental condition, that predisposes an individual to develop a particular disease

risky ('rɪskɪ) adj riskier, riskiest involving danger; perilous > 'riskily adv > 'riskiness n

risotto (rɪ'zɒtəʊ) n, pl -tos a dish of rice cooked in stock and served variously with tomatoes, cheese, chicken, etc [c19: from Italian, from riso RICE]

risqué ('rɪskeɪ) adj bordering on impropriety or indecency: a risqué joke [c19: from French risquer to hazard, RISK]

rissole ('rɪsəʊl) n a mixture of minced cooked meat coated in egg and breadcrumbs and fried [c18: from French, probably ultimately from Latin russus red; see RUSSET]

risus sardonicus ('riːsəs sɑː'dɒnɪkəs) n pathol fixed contraction of the facial muscles resulting in a peculiar distorted grin, caused esp by tetanus. Also called: **trismus cynicus** ('trɪzməs 'sɪnɪkəs) [c17: New Latin, literally: sardonic laugh]

rit. music abbreviation **1** ritardando **2** ritenuto

Ritalin ('rɪtəlɪn) n trademark a preparation of methylphenidate, a drug related to amphetamine, used to treat attention deficit disorder in children

ritardando (,rɪtɑː'dændəʊ) adj, adv another term for **rallentando** [c19: from Italian, from ritardare to slow down]

rite (raɪt) n **1** a formal act or procedure prescribed or customary in religious ceremonies: fertility rites; the rite of baptism **2** a particular body of such acts or procedures, esp of a particular Christian Church: the Latin rite **3** a Christian Church: the Greek rite [c14: from Latin rītus religious ceremony]

ritenuto (,rɪtə'nuːtəʊ) adj, adv music **1** held back momentarily **2** another term for **rallentando** [c19: from Italian, from past participle of ritenere, from Latin retinēre to hold back]

rite of passage or **rite de passage** (French rit də pasaʒ) n a ceremony performed in some cultures at times when an individual changes his status, as at puberty and marriage

ritornello (,rɪtə'nɛləʊ) n, pl -los or -li (-liː) music an orchestral passage between verses of an aria or song [c17: from Italian, literally: a little return, from ritorno a RETURN]

ritual ('rɪtjʊəl) n **1** the prescribed or established form of a religious or other ceremony **2** such prescribed forms in general or collectively **3** stereotyped activity or behaviour **4** any formal act, institution, or procedure that is followed consistently: the ritual of the law ▷ adj **5** of, relating to, or characteristic of religious, social, or other rituals [c16: from Latin rītuālis, from rītus RITE] > 'ritually adv

ritualism ('rɪtjʊə,lɪzəm) n **1** emphasis, esp exaggerated emphasis, on the importance of rites and ceremonies **2** the study of rites and ceremonies, esp magical or religious ones > 'ritualist n

ritualistic (,rɪtjʊə'lɪstɪk) adj of, relating to, or suggestive of ritualism > ,ritual'istically adv

ritualize or **ritualise** ('rɪtjʊə,laɪz) vb **1** (intr) to engage in ritualism or devise rituals **2** (tr) to make (something) into a ritual

ritzy ('rɪtsɪ) adj ritzier, ritziest slang luxurious or elegant > 'ritzily adv > 'ritziness n

rival ('raɪvᵊl) n **1 a** a person, organization, team, etc, that competes with another for the same object or in the same field **b** (as modifier): rival suitors; a rival company **2 a** person or thing that is considered the equal of another or others: she is without rival in the field of economics ▷ vb -vals, -valling, -valled or US -vals, -valing, -valed (tr) **3** to be the equal or near equal of: an empire that rivalled Rome **4** to try to equal or surpass; compete with in rivalry [c16: from Latin rīvalis, literally: one who shares the same brook, from rīvus a brook]

rivalry ('raɪvəlrɪ) *n*, *pl* -ries **1** the act of rivalling; competition **2** the state of being a rival or rivals

rive (raɪv) *vb* rives, riving, rived, *or* riven ('rɪvᵊn) (*usually passive*) **1** to split asunder: *a tree riven by lightning* **2** to tear apart: *riven to shreds* [C13: from Old Norse *rīfa*; related to Old Frisian *rīva*]

river ('rɪvə) *n* **1 a** a large natural stream of fresh water flowing along a definite course, usually into the sea, being fed by tributary streams **b** (*as modifier*): *river traffic; a river basin* **c** (*in combination*): *riverside; riverbed*. Related adjs: *fluvial, potamic* **2** any abundant stream or flow: *a river of blood* **3** *poker slang* the fifth and final community card to be dealt in a round of Texas holdem poker [C13: from Old French *riviere*, from Latin *rīpārius* of a river bank, from *rīpa* bank] > 'riverless *adj*

Rivera (*Spanish* ri'βera) *n* **Diego** ('djeɣo). 1886–1957, Mexican painter, noted for his monumental murals in public buildings, which are influenced by Aztec art and depict revolutionary themes

riverine ('rɪvə,raɪn) *adj* **1** of, like, relating to, or produced by a river **2** located or dwelling near a river; riparian

river red gum *n* a large Australian red gum tree, *Eucalyptus camaldulensis*, growing along river banks

Rivers ('rɪvəz) *n* a state of S Nigeria, in the Niger river delta on the Gulf of Guinea. Capital: Port Harcourt. Pop: 5 185 400 (2006). Area: 11 077 sq km (4277 sq miles)

Riverside ('rɪvə,saɪd) *n* a city in SW California. Pop: 281 514 (2003 est)

rivet ('rɪvɪt) *n* **1 a** a short metal pin for fastening two or more pieces together, having a head at one end, the other end being hammered flat after being passed through holes in the pieces ▷ *vb* -ets, -eting, -eted (*tr*) **2** to join by riveting **3** to hammer in order to form into a head **4** (*often passive*) to cause to be fixed or held firmly, as in fascinated attention, horror, etc: *to be riveted to the spot* [C14: from Old French, from *river* to fasten, fix, of unknown origin] > 'riveter *n* > 'riveting *adj*

riviera (,rɪvɪ'ɛərə) *n* a coastal region reminiscent of the Riviera

Riviera (,rɪvɪ'ɛərə) *n* the Mediterranean coastal region between Cannes, France, and La Spezia, Italy: contains some of Europe's most popular resorts [C18: from Italian literally: shore, ultimately from Latin *rīpa* bank, shore]

rivière (,rɪvɪ'ɛə) *n* a necklace the diamonds or other precious stones of which gradually increase in size up to a large centre stone [C19: from French: brook, river]

rivulet ('rɪvjʊlɪt) *n* a small stream [C16: from Italian *rivoletto*, from Latin *rīvulus*, from *rīvus* stream]

Riyadh (rɪ'jɑːd) *n* the joint capital (with Mecca) of Saudi Arabia, situated in a central oasis: the largest city in the country. Pop: 5 514 000 (2005 est)

riyal (rɪ'jɑːl) *n* the standard monetary unit of Qatar, divided into 100 dirhams; Saudi Arabia, divided into 100 halala; and Yemen, divided into 100 fils [from Arabic *riyāl*, from Spanish *real* REAL²]

Rizal¹ (*Spanish* ri'θal) *n* another name for **Pasay**

Rizal² (*Spanish* ri'θal) *n* **Jose** (xo'se). 1861–96, Philippine nationalist, executed by the Spanish during the Philippine revolution of 1896

Rizzio ('rɪtsɪəʊ) *or* **Riccio** *n* **David**. ?1533–66, Italian musician and courtier who became the secretary and favourite of Mary, Queen of Scots. He was murdered at the instigation of a group of nobles, including Mary's husband, Darnley

RL *abbreviation* Rugby League

rly *abbreviation* railway

rm *abbreviation* **1** ream **2** room

RM *abbreviation* **1** Royal Mail **2** Royal Marines **3** (in Canada) Rural Municipality

RMA *abbreviation* Royal Military Academy (Sandhurst)

RME *abbreviation* religious and moral education

rms *abbreviation* root mean square

Rn *the chemical symbol for* radon

RN *abbreviation* **1** (in Canada) Registered Nurse **2** Royal Navy

RNA *n biochem* ribonucleic acid; any of a group of nucleic acids, present in all living cells, that play an essential role in the synthesis of proteins. On hydrolysis they yield the pentose sugar ribose, the purine bases adenine

and guanine, the pyrimidine bases cytosine and uracil, and phosphoric acid

RNAS *abbreviation* **1** Royal Naval Air Service(s) **2** Royal Naval Air Station

RNIB *Brit abbreviation* Royal National Institute for the Blind

RNID *Brit abbreviation* Royal National Institute for Deaf People

RNLI *abbreviation* Royal National Lifeboat Institution

RNZAF *abbreviation* Royal New Zealand Air Force

RNZN *abbreviation* Royal New Zealand Navy

roach¹ (rəʊtʃ) *n*, *pl* roaches *or* roach a European freshwater cyprinid food fish, *Rutilus rutilus*, having a deep compressed body and reddish ventral and tail fins [C14: from Old French *roche*, of obscure origin]

roach² (rəʊtʃ) *n* **1** short for **cockroach 2** *slang* the butt of a cannabis cigarette

roach³ (rəʊtʃ) *n nautical* the curve at the foot of a square sail [C18: of unknown origin]

Roach (rəʊtʃ) *n* **Hal**, full name *Harald Eugene Roach*. 1892–1992, US film producer, whose company produced numerous comedy films in the 1920s and 1930s, including those featuring Harold Lloyd and Laurel and Hardy

roach clip *n slang* a small clip resembling tweezers, used to hold the butt of a cannabis cigarette, in order to prevent burning one's fingers

road (rəʊd) *n* **1 a** an open way, usually surfaced with asphalt or concrete, providing passage from one place to another **b** (*as modifier*): *road traffic; a road map; a road sign* **c** (*in combination*): *the roadside* **2 a** a street **b** (*capital when part of a name*): *London Road* **3 a** US short for **railroad b** *Brit* one of the tracks of a railway **4** a way, path, or course: *the road to fame* **5** Also called: roadstead (*often plural*) *nautical* a partly sheltered anchorage **6** a drift or tunnel in a mine, esp a level one **7** hit the road *slang* to start or resume travelling **8** on the road **a** travelling, esp as a salesman **b** leading a wandering life **9** take the road *or* take to the road to begin a journey or tour **10** one for the road *informal* a last alcoholic drink before leaving [Old English *rād*; related to *rīdan* to RIDE, and to Old Saxon *rēda*, Old Norse *reith*] > 'roadless *adj*

road allowance *n Canadian* land reserved by the government to be used for public roads

roadblock ('rəʊd,blɒk) *n* a barrier set up across a road by the police or military, in order to stop a fugitive, inspect traffic, etc

road-fund licence *n Brit* a licence showing that the tax payable in respect of a motor vehicle has been paid [C20: from the former *road fund* for the maintenance of public highways]

road hog *n informal* a selfish or aggressive driver

roadholding ('rəʊd,həʊldɪŋ) *n* the extent to which a motor vehicle is stable and does not skid, esp at high speeds, or on sharp bends or wet roads

roadhouse ('rəʊd,haʊs) *n* a pub, restaurant, etc, that is situated at the side of a road, esp a country road

road hump *n* the official name for **sleeping policeman**

roadie ('rəʊdɪ) *n informal* a person who transports and sets up equipment for a band or group [C20: shortened from *road manager*]

roadkill ('rəʊd,kɪl) *n chiefly US* the remains of an animal or animals killed on the road by motor vehicles

road map *n* **1** a map intended for drivers, showing roads, distances, etc in a country or area **2** a plan or guide for future actions

road metal *n* crushed rock, broken stone, etc, used to construct a road

road movie *n* a genre of film in which the chief character is on the run or travelling in search of, or to escape from, himself

road pricing *n* the practice of charging motorists for using certain stretches of road, in order to reduce congestion

road rage *n* aggressive behaviour by a motorist in response to the actions of another road user

road rash *n US & Canadian informal* grazing of the skin as a result of falling off a bicycle, skateboard, etc, onto a hard surface

r

roadroller ('rəʊd,rəʊlə) *n* a motor vehicle with heavy rollers for compressing road surfaces during road-making

road show *n* **1 a** a radio show broadcast live from one of a number of towns or venues being visited by a disc jockey who is touring an area **b** the touring disc jockey and the personnel and equipment needed to present such a show **2** a group of entertainers, esp pop musicians, on tour **3** any occasion when an organization attracts publicity while touring or visiting: *an antiques road show; a royal road show*

roadstead ('rəʊd,stɛd) *n nautical* another word for **road** (sense 5)

roadster ('rəʊdstə) *n* **1** an open car, esp one seating only two **2** a kind of bicycle

road tax *n* a tax paid, usually annually, on motor vehicles in use on the roads

road test *n* **1** a test to ensure that a vehicle is roadworthy, esp after repair or servicing, by driving it on roads **2** a test of something in actual use ▷ *vb* road-test (*tr*) **3** to test (a vehicle) in this way **4** to test (something) in a real and appropriate context

road train *n Austral* a line of linked trailers pulled by a truck, used for transporting stock, etc

roadway ('rəʊd,weɪ) *n* **1** the surface of a road **2** the part of a road that is used by vehicles

roadwork ('rəʊd,wɜːk) *n* sports training by running along roads

roadworks ('rəʊd,wɜːks) *pl n* repairs to a road or cable under a road, esp when forming a hazard or obstruction to traffic

roadworthy ('rəʊd,wɜːðɪ) *adj* (of a motor vehicle) mechanically sound; fit for use on the roads ▷ 'road,worthiness *n*

roam (rəʊm) *vb* **1** to travel or walk about with no fixed purpose or direction; wander ▷ *n* **2** the act of roaming [c13: origin unknown] ▷ 'roamer *n*

roan (rəʊn) *adj* **1** (of a horse) having a bay (**red roan**), chestnut (**strawberry roan**), or black (**blue roan**) coat sprinkled with white hairs ▷ *n* **2** a horse having such a coat **3** a soft unsplit sheepskin leather with a close tough grain, used in bookbinding, etc [c16: from Old French, from Spanish *roano*, probably from Gothic *rauths* red]

Roanoke Island ('rəʊə,nəʊk) *n* an island off the coast of North Carolina: site of the first attempted English settlement in America. Length: 19 km (12 miles). Average width: 5 km (3 miles)

roar (rɔː) *vb* (*mainly intr*) **1** (of lions and other animals) to utter characteristic loud growling cries **2** (*also tr*) (of people) to utter (something) with a loud deep cry, as in anger or triumph **3** to laugh in a loud hearty unrestrained manner **4** (of horses) to breathe with laboured rasping sounds **5** (of the wind, waves, etc) to blow or break loudly and violently, as during a storm **6** (of a fire) to burn fiercely with a roaring sound **7** (*tr*) to bring (oneself) into a certain condition by roaring: *to roar oneself hoarse* ▷ *n* **8** a loud deep cry, uttered by a person or crowd, esp in anger or triumph **9** a prolonged loud cry of certain animals, esp lions **10** any similar noise made by a fire, the wind, waves, artillery, an engine, etc **11** a loud unrestrained burst of laughter [Old English *rārian*; related to Old High German *rērēn*, Middle Dutch *reren*] ▷ 'roarer *n*

roaring ('rɔːrɪŋ) *adj* **1** *informal* very brisk and profitable (esp in the phrase **a roaring trade**) ▷ *adv* **2** noisily or boisterously (esp in the phrase **roaring drunk**) ▷ *n* **3** a loud prolonged cry

roast (rəʊst) *vb* (*mainly tr*) **1** to cook (meat or other food) by dry heat, usually with added fat and esp in an oven **2** to brown or dry (coffee, etc) by exposure to heat **3** *metallurgy* to heat (an ore) in order to produce a concentrate that is easier to smelt **4** to heat (oneself or something) to an extreme degree, as when sunbathing, sitting before the fire, etc **5** (*intr*) to be excessively and uncomfortably hot **6** *informal* to criticize severely ▷ *n* **7** something that has been roasted, esp meat [c13: from Old French *rostir*, of Germanic origin; compare Middle Dutch *roosten* to roast]

roasting ('rəʊstɪŋ) *informal* ▷ *adj* **1** extremely hot ▷ *n* **2** severe criticism

rob (rɒb) *vb* **robs, robbing, robbed 1** (*tr*) to take something from (someone) illegally, as by force or threat of violence **2** to plunder (a house, shop, etc) **3** (*tr*) to deprive unjustly: *to be robbed of an opportunity* [c13: from Old French *rober*, of Germanic origin; compare Old High German *roubōn* to rob] ▷ 'robber *n*

Robbe-Grillet (*French* rɔbgrijɛ) *n* **Alain** (alɛ̃). born 1922, French novelist and screenwriter. Author of *The Voyeur* (1955), *Jealousy* (1957), and *Djinn* (1981): he is one of the leading practitioners of the antinovel

Robben Island ('rɒbˀn) *n* a small island in South Africa, 11 km (7 miles) off the Cape Peninsula: formerly used by the South African government to house political prisoners

robbery ('rɒbərɪ) *n, pl* -beries **1** *criminal law* the stealing of property from a person by using or threatening to use force **2** the act or an instance of robbing

Robbia ('rɒbɪə; *Italian* 'rɔbbja) *n* **1 Andrea della** (anˈdrɛːa ˈdɛlla). 1435–1525, Florentine sculptor, best known for his polychrome reliefs and his statues of infants in swaddling clothes **2** his uncle, **Luca della** ('luːka ˈdɛlla). ?1400–82, Florentine sculptor, who perfected a technique of enamelling terra cotta for reliefs

Robbins ('rɒbɪnz) *n* **Jerome**. 1918–98, US ballet dancer and choreographer. He choreographed the musicals *The King and I* (1951) and *West Side Story* (1957)

robe (rəʊb) *n* **1** any loose flowing garment, esp the official vestment of a peer, judge, or academic **2** a dressing gown or bathrobe ▷ *vb* **3** to put a robe, etc, on (oneself or someone else); dress [c13: from Old French: of Germanic origin; compare Old French *rober* to ROB, Old High German *roub* booty]

Robert I ('rɒbət) *n* known as *Robert the Bruce*. 1274–1329, king of Scotland (1306–29): he defeated the English army of Edward II at Bannockburn (1314) and gained recognition of Scotland's independence (1328)

Robert II *n* 1316–90, king of Scotland (1371–90)

Robert III *n* ?1337–1406, king of Scotland (1390–1406), son of Robert II

Roberts ('rɒbəts) *n* **1 Frederick Sleigh**, 1st Earl. 1832–1914, British field marshal. He was awarded the Victoria Cross (1858) for his service during the Indian Mutiny and was commander in chief (1899–1900) in the second Boer War **2 Julia**. born 1967, US film actress; her films include *Pretty Woman* (1990), *Notting Hill* (1999), *Erin Brockovich* (2000), which earned her an Academy Award, and *Mona Lisa Smile* (2003)

Robertson *n* **George** (**Islay Macneill**), Baron. born 1946, Scottish Labour politician; secretary-general of NATO (1999–2003)

Robertson screw ('rɒbətsˀn) *n trademark* a screw having a square hole in the head into which a screwdriver with a square point (**Robertson screwdriver** (*Trademark*)) fits [c20: after its inventor P. L. Robertson (1896–1951), a Canadian industrialist]

Robeson ('rəʊbsən) *n* **Paul**. 1898–1976, US bass singer, actor, and leader in the Black civil rights movement

Robespierre ('rəʊbzpjɛə; *French* rɔbzpjɛr) *n* **Maximilien François Marie Isidore de**. (maksimiljɛ̃ frɑ̃swa mari izidɔr də). 1758–94, French revolutionary and Jacobin leader: established the Reign of Terror as a member of the Committee of Public Safety (1793–94): executed in the coup d'état of Thermidor (1794)

Robey ('rəʊbɪ) *n* **Sir George**, original name *George Edward Wade*, known as *the prime minister of mirth*. 1869–1954, British music-hall comedian, who also appeared in films

robin ('rɒbɪn) *n* **1** Also called: robin redbreast a small Old World songbird, *Erithacus rubecula*, related to the thrushes: family *Muscicapidae*. The male has a brown back, orange-red breast and face, and grey underparts **2** a North American thrush, *Turdus migratorius*, similar to but larger than the Old World robin [c16: arbitrary use of given name]

Robin Goodfellow ('rɒbɪn 'ɡʊd,fɛləʊ) *n* another name for **puck²**

Robin Hood *n* a legendary English outlaw of the reign

of Richard I, who according to tradition lived in Sherwood Forest and robbed the rich to give to the poor

robinia (rə'bɪnɪə) *n* any tree of the leguminous genus *Robinia*, esp the locust tree

Robinson ('rɒbɪnsən) *n* 1 **Edward G.**, real name *Emanuel Goldenberg*. 1893–1973, US film actor, born in Romania, famous esp for gangster roles. His films include *Little Caesar* (1930), *Brother Orchid* (1940), *Double Indemnity* (1944), and *All My Sons* (1948) 2 **Edward Arlington**. 1869–1935, US poet, author of narrative verse, often based on Arthurian legend. His works include *Collected Poems* (1922), *The Man Who Died Twice* (1924), and *Tristram* (1927) 3 (**William**) **Heath**. 1872–1944, British cartoonist and book illustrator, best known for his comic drawings of fantastic machines 4 **John** (**Arthur Thomas**)1919–83, British bishop and theologian, best known for his controversial *Honest to God* (1963), which popularized radical theological discussion. He was suffragan Bishop of Woolwich (1959–69) 5 **Mary**. born 1944, Irish barrister and politician: president of Ireland 1990–97; U.N. high commissioner for human rights (1997–2001) 6 **Smokey**, real name *William Robinson*. born 1940, US Motown singer, songwriter, and producer. His hits include "The Tears of a Clown" (1970) (with the Miracles) and "Being with you" (1981) 7 "**Sugar**" **Ray**, real name *Walker Smith*. 1921–89, US boxer, winner of the world middleweight championship on five separate occasions

roborant ('rəʊbərənt, 'rɒb-) *adj* 1 tending to fortify or increase strength ▷ *n* 2 a drug or agent that increases strength [c17: from Latin *roborāre* to strengthen, from *rōbur* an oak]

robot ('rəʊbɒt) *n* 1 any automated machine programmed to perform specific mechanical functions in the manner of a man 2 (*modifier*) not controlled by man; automatic: *a robot pilot* 3 a person who works or behaves like a machine; automaton 4 *South African* a set of traffic lights [c20: (used in R.U.R., a play by Karel Čapek) from Czech *robota* work; related to Old Slavonic *rabota* servitude, German *Arbeit* work] ▷ **ro'botic** *adj* ▷ **'robot-ˌlike** *adj*

robot bomb *n* another name for the **V-1**

robot dancing, robotics *or* **robotic dancing** *n* a dance of the 1980s characterized by jerky mechanical movements

robotics (rəʊ'bɒtɪks) *n* (*functioning as singular*) 1 the science or technology of designing, building, and using robots 2 another name for **robot dancing**

Rob Roy ('rɒb 'rɔɪ) *n* real name *Robert Macgregor*. 1671–1734, Scottish outlaw

Robson¹ ('rɒbsən) *n* **Mount Robson** a mountain in SW Canada, in E British Columbia: the highest peak in the Canadian Rockies. Height: 3954 m (12 972 ft)

Robson² ('rɒbsən) *n* 1 **Sir Bobby**, full name *Robert William*. born 1933, English footballer and manager of England (1982–90) 2 **Bryan**. born 1957, English footballer and manager: captain of England (1982–90) 3 **Dame Flora**. 1902–84, English stage and film actress

robust (rəʊ'bʌst, 'rəʊbʌst) *adj* 1 strong in constitution; hardy; vigorous 2 sturdily built: *a robust shelter* 3 requiring or suited to physical strength: *a robust sport* 4 (esp of wines) having a rich full-bodied flavour 5 rough or boisterous 6 (of thought, intellect, etc) straightforward and imbued with common sense [c16: from Latin *rōbustus*, from *rōbur* an oak, strength] ▷ **ro'bustly** *adv*

robusta (rəʊ'bʌstə) *n* 1 a species of coffee tree, *Coffea canephora* 2 coffee or coffee beans obtained from this plant [from Latin *rōbustus* strong]

robustious (rəʊ'bʌstʃəs) *adj archaic* 1 rough; boisterous 2 strong, robust, or stout ▷ **ro'bustiously** *adv* ▷ **ro'bustiousness** *n*

robustness (rəʊ'bʌstnɪs) *n* 1 the quality of being robust 2 *computing* the ability of a computer system to cope with errors during execution

roc (rɒk) *n* (in Arabian legend) a bird of enormous size and power [c16: from Arabic *rukhkh*, from Persian *rukh*]

ROC *abbreviation* Royal Observer Corps

Roca ('rəʊkə) *n* **Cape Roca** a cape in SW central Portugal, near Lisbon: the westernmost point of continental Europe

rocaille (rɒ'kaɪ) *n* decorative rock or shell work, esp as ornamentation in a rococo fountain, grotto, or interior [from French, from *roc* ROCK¹]

rocambole ('rɒkəm,bəʊl) *n* a variety of sand leek whose garlic-like bulb is used for seasoning [c17: from French, from German *Rockenbolle*, literally: distaff bulb (with reference to its shape)]

Rocard (*French* rɔka:r) *n* **Michel**. born 1930, French politician: prime minister of France (1988–91)

Rochdale ('rɒtʃ,deɪl) *n* 1 a town in NW England, in Rochdale unitary authority, Greater Manchester: former centre of the textile industry. Pop: 95 769 (2001) 2 a unitary authority in NW England, in Greater Manchester. Pop: 206 600 (2003 est). Area: 159 sq km (61 sq miles)

Rochelle salt *n* a white crystalline double salt, sodium potassium tartrate, used in Seidlitz powder. Formula: $KNaC_4H_4O_6.4H_2O$ [c18: after *La Rochelle*, French port]

roche moutonnée ('rəʊʃ ,mu:tɒ'neɪ) *n*, *pl* **roches moutonnées** ('rəʊʃ ,mu:tɒ'neɪz) a rounded mass of rock smoothed and striated by ice that has flowed over it [c19: French, literally: fleecy rock, from *mouton* sheep]

Rochester¹ ('rɒtʃɪstə) *n* 1 a city in SE England, in Medway unitary authority, Kent, on the River Medway. Pop: 27 123 (2001) 2 a city in NW New York State, on Lake Ontario. Pop: 215 093 (2003 est) 3 a city in the US, in Minnesota: site of the Mayo Clinic. Pop: 92 507 (2003 est)

Rochester² ('rɒtʃɪstə) *n* **2nd Earl of**, title of *John Wilmot*. 1647–80, English poet, wit, and libertine. His poems include satires, notably *A Satire against Mankind* (1675), love lyrics, and bawdy verse

rochet ('rɒtʃɪt) *n* a white surplice with tight sleeves, worn by bishops, abbots, and certain other Church dignitaries [c14: from Old French, from *roc* coat, outer garment, of Germanic origin; compare Old High German *roc* coat]

rock¹ (rɒk) *n* 1 *geology* any aggregate of minerals that makes up part of the earth's crust. It may be unconsolidated, such as a sand, clay, or mud, or consolidated, such as granite, limestone, or coal 2 any hard mass of consolidated mineral matter, such as a boulder 3 *chiefly US, Canadian & Austral* a stone 4 a person or thing suggesting a rock, esp in being dependable, unchanging, or providing firm foundation 5 *Brit* a hard sweet, typically a long brightly-coloured peppermint-flavoured stick, sold esp in holiday resorts 6 *slang* a jewel, esp a diamond 7 *slang* another name for **crack** (sense 29) 8 **on the rocks a** in a state of ruin or destitution **b** (of drinks, esp whisky) served with ice [c14: from Old French *roche*, of unknown origin]

rock² (rɒk) *vb* 1 to move or cause to move from side to side or backwards and forwards 2 to reel or sway or cause (someone) to reel or sway, as with a violent shock or emotion 3 (*tr*) to shake or move (something) violently 4 (*intr*) to dance in the rock-and-roll style ▷ *n* 5 a rocking motion 6 short for **rock and roll** 7 Also called: **rock music** any of various styles of pop music having a heavy beat, derived from rock and roll ▷ See also **rock up** [Old English *roccian*; related to Middle Dutch, Old High German *rocken*, German *rücken*]

Rock (rɒk) *n* the Rock 1 an informal name for **Gibraltar** 2 a Canadian informal name for **Newfoundland**

rockabilly ('rɒkə,bɪlɪ) *n* a fast, spare style of White rock music which originated in the mid-1950s in the US South [c20: from ROCK (AND ROLL) + (HILL)BILLY]

Rockall ('rɒkɔːl) *n* an uninhabited British island in the N Atlantic, 354 km (220 miles) W of the Outer Hebrides. Area: 0.07 ha (0.18 acres)

rock and roll *or* **rock'n'roll** *n* 1 a a type of pop music originating in the 1950s as a blend of rhythm and blues and country and western. It is generally based upon the twelve-bar blues, the first and third beats in each bar being heavily accented b (*as modifier*): *the rock-and-roll era* 2 dancing performed to such music, with exaggerated body movements stressing the beat ▷ *vb* 3 (*intr*) to perform this dance ▷ **rock and roller** *or* **rock'n'roller** *n*

rock bass (bæs) *n* a North American freshwater percoid fish, *Ambloplites rupestris*: an important food fish; family Centrarchidae (sunfishes, etc)

rock bottom n **a** the lowest possible level **b** (as modifier): rock-bottom prices

rock-bound adj hemmed in or encircled by rocks

rock cake n a small cake containing dried fruit and spice, with a rough surface supposed to resemble a rock

rock cod n Austral & NZ any of various marine fishes found in rocky habitats in Australian waters

rock crystal n a pure transparent colourless quartz, used in electronic and optical equipment. Formula: SiO_2

rock dove or **rock pigeon** n a common dove, Columba livia, from which domestic and feral pigeons are descended. It has a pale grey plumage with black-striped wings

Rockefeller ('rɒkə,felə) n **1** John D(avison). 1839–1937, US industrialist and philanthropist **2** his son, John D(avison). 1874–1960, US capitalist and philanthropist **3** his son, Nelson (Aldrich). 1908–79, US politician; governor of New York State (1958–74); vice president (1974–76)

rocker ('rɒkə) n **1** any of various devices that transmit or operate with a rocking motion. See also **rocker arm** **2** another word for **rocking chair** **3** either of two curved supports on the legs of a chair or other article of furniture on which it may rock **4 a** an ice skate with a curved blade **b** the curve itself **5** a rock-music performer, fan, or song **6** Brit an adherent of a youth movement rooted in the 1950s, characterized by motorcycle trappings. Compare **mod**[1] **7** off one's rocker slang crazy; demented

rocker arm n a lever that rocks about a pivot, esp a lever in an internal-combustion engine that transmits the motion of a pushrod or cam to a valve

rockery ('rɒkərı) n, pl -eries a garden constructed with rocks, esp one where alpine plants are grown. Also called: rock garden

rocket[1] ('rɒkɪt) n **1** a self-propelling device, esp a cylinder containing a mixture of solid explosives, used as a firework, distress signal, line carrier, etc **2 a** any vehicle propelled by a rocket engine, esp one used to carry a warhead, spacecraft, etc **b** (as modifier): rocket propulsion; rocket launcher **3** Brit & NZ informal a severe reprimand (esp in the phrase **get a rocket**) ▷ vb -ets, -eting, -eted **4** (tr) to propel (a missile, spacecraft, etc) by means of a rocket **5** (intr; foll by off, away, etc) to move off at high speed **6** (intr) to rise rapidly: he rocketed to the top [c17: from Old French roquette, from Italian rochetto a little distaff, from rocca distaff, of Germanic origin]

rocket[2] ('rɒkɪt) n **1** Also called: arugula a Mediterranean plant, Eruca sativa, having yellowish-white flowers and leaves used as a salad: family Brassicaceae (crucifers) **2** any of several plants of the related genus Sisymbrium, esp S. irio (**London rocket**), which grow on waste ground and have pale yellow flowers **3** yellow rocket any of several yellow-flowered plants of the related genus Barbarea, esp B. vulgaris ▷ See also **wall rocket** [c16: from French roquette, from Italian rochetta, from Latin ērūca a caterpillar, hairy plant]

rocket engine n a reaction engine in which a fuel and oxidizer are burnt in a combustion chamber, the products of combustion expanding through a nozzle and producing thrust

rocketry ('rɒkɪtrı) n the science and technology of the design, operation, maintenance, and launching of rockets

rocket science n informal an activity requiring considerable intelligence and ability (esp in the phrase **not exactly rocket science**) ▷ rocket scientist n

rockfish ('rɒk,fɪʃ) n, pl -fish or -fishes **1** any of various fishes that live among rocks, esp scorpaenid fishes of the genus Sebastodes and related genera, such as S. caurinus (**copper rockfish**) of North American Pacific coastal waters **2** Brit any of several coarse fishes when used as food, esp the dogfish or wolffish

Rockford ('rɒkfəd) n a city in N Illinois, on the Rock River. Pop: 151 725 (2003 est)

rock garden n a garden featuring rocks or rockeries

Rockhampton (rɒk'hæmptən, -'hæmtən) n a port in Australia, in E Queensland on the Fitzroy River. Pop: 59 475 (2001)

Rockies ('rɒkız) pl n another name for the **Rocky Mountains**

rocking chair n a chair set on curving supports so that the sitter may rock backwards and forwards

Rockingham ('rɒkıŋəm) n **Marquess of**, title of Charles Watson-Wentworth. 1730–82, British statesman and leader of the Whig opposition, whose members were known as the **Rockingham Whigs**; prime minister (1765–66; 1782). He opposed the war with the American colonists

rocking horse n a toy horse mounted on a pair of rockers on which a child can rock to and fro in a seesaw movement

rocking stone n a boulder so delicately poised that it can be rocked

rockling ('rɒklıŋ) n, pl -lings or -ling any small gadoid fish of the genera Gaidropsarus, Ciliata, etc (formerly all included in Motella), which have an elongated body with barbels around the mouth and occur mainly in the North Atlantic Ocean [c17: from ROCK[1] + -LING[1]]

rock lobster n another name for the **spiny lobster**

rock melon n US, Austral & NZ another name for **cantaloupe**

rock pigeon n another name for **rock dove**

rock plant n any plant that grows on rocks or in rocky ground

rock rabbit n South African another name for the **hyrax**

rockrose ('rɒk,rəʊz) n any of various cistaceous shrubs or herbaceous plants of the Eurasian genera Helianthemum, Tuberaria, and Cistus, cultivated for their yellow-white or reddish roselike flowers

rock salmon n Brit (formerly) any of several coarse fishes when used as food, esp the dogfish or wolffish: now called rockfish or catfish

rock salt n another name for **halite**

rock snake or **rock python** n any large Australasian python of the genus Liasis

rock tripe n Canadian any of various edible lichens, esp of the genus Umbilicaria, that grow on rocks and are used in the North as a survival food

rock steady n a type of slow Jamaican dance music

rock up vb (intr, adverb) informal to arrive late or unannounced

Rockwell ('rɒk,wel, -wəl) n **Norman**. 1894–1978, US illustrator, noted esp for magazine covers

rock wool n another name for **mineral wool**

rocky[1] ('rɒkı) adj rockier, rockiest **1** consisting of or abounding in rocks: a rocky shore **2** hard or unyielding: rocky determination **3** hard like rock: rocky muscles ▷ 'rockiness n

rocky[2] ('rɒkı) adj rockier, rockiest **1** weak, shaky, or unstable **2** informal (of a person) dizzy; sickly; nauseated ▷ 'rockily adv ▷ 'rockiness n

Rocky Mountains or **Rockies** pl n the chief mountain system of W North America, extending from British Columbia to New Mexico: forms the Continental Divide. Highest peak: Mount Elbert, 4399 m (14 431 ft). Mount McKinley (6194 m (20 320 ft)), in the Alaska Range, is not strictly part of the Rocky Mountains

Rocky Mountain spotted fever n an acute rickettsial disease characterized by high fever, chills, pain in muscles and joints, skin rash, etc It is caused by the bite of a tick infected with the microorganism Rickettsia rickettsii

rococo (rə'kəʊkəʊ) n (often capital) **1** a style of architecture and decoration that originated in France in the early 18th century, characterized by elaborate but graceful, light, ornamentation, often containing asymmetrical motifs **2** an 18th-century style of music characterized by petite prettiness, a decline in the use of counterpoint, and extreme use of ornamentation **3** any florid or excessively ornamental style ▷ adj **4** denoting, being in, or relating to the rococo **5** florid or excessively elaborate [c19: from French, from ROCAILLE, from roc ROCK[1]]

rod (rɒd) n **1** a slim cylinder of metal, wood, etc; stick or shaft **2** a switch or bundle of switches used to administer corporal punishment **3** any of various staffs of insignia or office **4** power, esp of a tyrannical kind: a dictator's iron rod **5** a straight slender shoot, stem, or cane of a woody plant **6** See **fishing rod** **7** Also called: pole, perch **a** a unit of length equal to 5½ yards **b** a unit of square measure equal to 301⅝4 square yards **8** *surveying* another name (esp US) for **staff¹** (sense 8) **9** Also called: retinal rod any of the elongated cylindrical cells in the retina of the eye, containing the visual purple (rhodopsin), which are sensitive to dim light but not to colour **10** any rod-shaped bacterium **11** *US slang* name for **pistol** (sense 1) **12** short for **hot rod** [Old English *rodd*; related to Old Norse *rudda* club, Norwegian *rudda*, *rydda* twig] > **'rod,like** *adj*

Rodchenko (rɒd'tʃɛŋkəʊ) *n* **Alexander** (Mikhailovich). 1891–1956, Soviet painter, sculptor, designer, and photographer, noted for his abstract geometrical style: a member of the constructivist movement

Roddick ('rɒdɪk) *n* **Anita**. 1942–2007, British entrepreneur, founder (1976) of the Body Shop chain, selling natural beauty and health products

rode (rəʊd) *vb* the past tense of **ride**

rodent ('rəʊdᵊnt) *n* **a** any of the relatively small placental mammals that constitute the order *Rodentia*, having constantly growing incisor teeth specialized for gnawing. The group includes porcupines, rats, mice, squirrels, marmots, etc **b** (*as modifier*): *rodent characteristics* [c19: from Latin *rōdere* to gnaw, corrode] > **'rodent-,like** *adj*

rodent ulcer *n* a slow-growing malignant tumour on the face, usually occurring at the edge of the eyelids, lips, or nostrils

rodeo ('rəʊdɪ,əʊ) *n*, *pl* -os *chiefly US & Canadian* **1** a display of the skills of cowboys, including bareback riding, steer wrangling, etc **2** the rounding up of cattle for branding, counting, inspection, etc **3** an enclosure for cattle that have been rounded up [c19: from Spanish, from *rodear* to go around, from *rueda* a wheel, from Latin *rota*]

Roderic ('rɒdərɪk) *n* See **Rory O'Connor**

Rodgers ('rɒdʒəz) *n* **Richard**. 1902–79, US composer of musical comedies. He collaborated with the librettist Lorenz Hart on such musicals as *A Connecticut Yankee* (1927), *On Your Toes* (1936), and *Pal Joey* (1940). After Hart's death his librettist was Oscar Hammerstein II. Two of their musicals, *Oklahoma!* (1943) and *South Pacific* (1949), received the Pulitzer Prize

Ródhos ('rɒðos) *n* transliteration of the Modern Greek name for **Rhodes¹**

Rodin (*French* rɔdɛ̃) *n* **Auguste** (ogyst). 1840–1917, French sculptor, noted for his portrayal of the human form. His works include *The Kiss* (1886), *The Burghers of Calais* (1896), and *The Thinker* (1905)

Rodney ('rɒdnɪ) *n* **George Brydges**, 1st Baron Rodney. 1719–92, English admiral: captured Martinique (1762): defeated the Spanish at Cape St Vincent (1780) and the French under Admiral de Grasse off Dominica (1782), restoring British superiority in the Caribbean

rodomontade (,rɒdəmɒn'teɪd, -'tɑːd) *literary* > *n* **1 a** boastful words or behaviour; bragging **b** (*as modifier*): *rodomontade behaviour* > *vb* **2** (*intr*) to boast, bluster, or rant [c17: from French, from Italian *rodomonte* a boaster, from *Rodomonte* the name of a braggart king of Algiers in epic poems by Boiardo and Ariosto]

Rodrigo (rɒ'driːgəʊ) *n* **Joaquín**. 1902–99, Spanish composer. His works include *Concierto de Aranjuez* (1940) for guitar and orchestra and *Concierto Pastorale* (1978)

roe¹ (rəʊ) *n* **1** Also called: hard roe the ovary of a female fish filled with mature eggs **2** Also called: soft roe the testis of a male fish filled with mature sperm [c15: from Middle Dutch *roge*, from Old High German *roga*; related to Old Norse *hrogn*]

roe² (rəʊ) *n*, *pl* roes *or* roe short for **roe deer** [Old English *rā(ha)*, related to Old High German *rēh(o)*, Old Norse *rā*]

Roe (rəʊ) *n* **Richard Roe** *law* (formerly) the defendant in a fictitious action, Doe versus Roe, to test a point of law. See also **Doe** (sense 1)

roebuck ('rəʊ,bʌk) *n*, *pl* -bucks *or* -buck the male of the roe deer

roe deer *n* a small graceful deer, *Capreolus capreolus*, of woodlands of Europe and Asia. The antlers are small and the summer coat is reddish-brown

Roeg ('rəʊəg) *n* **Nic(olas)**. born 1928, British film director and cinematographer. Films include *Walkabout* (1970),

Don't Look Now (1972), *Insignificance* (1984), and *The Witches* (1990)

roentgen *or* **röntgen** ('rɒntgən, -tjən, 'rɛnt-) *n* a unit of dose of electromagnetic radiation equal to the dose that will produce in air a charge of 0.258 × 10⁻³ coulomb on all ions of one sign, when all the electrons of both signs liberated in a volume of air of mass one kilogram are stopped completely [c20: named after German physicist W. K. *Roentgen* or *Röntgen* (1845–1923), who discovered X-rays]

Roentgen *or* **Röntgen** ('rɒntgən, -tjən, 'rɛnt-; *German* 'rœntgən) *n* **Wilhelm Konrad** ('vɪlhɛlm 'kɔnraːt). 1845–1923, German physicist, who in 1895 discovered X-rays: Nobel prize for physics 1901

roentgen ray *n* a former name for **X-ray**

Roeselare ('ruːsəlaːrə) *n* the Flemish name for **Roulers**

Roethke ('rɛtkə) *n* **Theodore**. 1908–63, US poet, whose books include *Words for the Wind* (1957) and *The Far Field* (1964)

rogation (rəʊ'geɪʃən) *n* (*usually plural*) Christianity a solemn supplication, esp in a form of ceremony prescribed by the Church [c14: from Latin *rogātiō*, from *rogāre* to ask, make supplication]

Rogation Days *pl n* April 25 (the **Major Rogation**) and the Monday, Tuesday, and Wednesday before Ascension Day, observed by Christians as days of solemn supplication for the harvest and marked by processions, special prayers, and blessing of the crops

roger ('rɒdʒə) *interj* **1** (used in signalling, telecommunications, etc) message received **2** an expression of agreement > *vb* **3** *slang* (of a man) to copulate (with) [c20: from the name *Roger*, representing R for *received*]

Roger II ('rɒdʒə) *n* 1095–1154, Norman king of Siciliy (1130–54). His court was an intellectual centre for Muslim and Christian scholars

Rogers ('rɒdʒəz) *n* **1 Ginger**, real name *Virginia McMath*. 1911–95, US dancer and film actress, who partnered Fred Astaire **2 Richard**, Baron Rogers of Riverside. born 1933, British architect. His works include the Pompidou Centre in Paris (1971–77; with Renzo Piano), the Lloyd's building in London (1986), and the Millennium Dome in Greenwich, London **3 William Penn Adair**, known as **Will**. 1879–1935, US actor, newspaper columnist, and humorist in the homespun tradition

Roget ('rɒʒeɪ) *n* **Peter Mark**. 1779–1869, English physician, who on retirement devised a *Thesaurus of English Words and Phrases* (1852), a classified list of synonyms

rogue (rəʊg) *n* **1** a dishonest or unprincipled person, esp a man; rascal; scoundrel **2** *often jocular* a mischievous or wayward person, often a child; scamp **3** a crop plant which is inferior, diseased, or of a different, unwanted variety **4 a** any inferior or defective specimen **b** (*as modifier*): *rogue heroin* **5** *archaic* a vagrant **6 a** an animal of vicious character that has separated from the main herd and leads a solitary life **b** (*as modifier*): *a rogue elephant* > *vb* **7** (*tr*) to rid (a field or crop) of plants that are inferior, diseased, or of an unwanted variety [c16: of unknown origin; perhaps related to Latin *rogāre* to beg]

rogue dialler *n* a dial-up connection placed on a computer without the user's knowledge which, when the user tries to connect to the internet, automatically connects to a premium-rate phone number

roguery ('rəʊgərɪ) *n*, *pl* -gueries **1** behaviour characteristic of a rogue **2** a roguish or mischievous act

rogues' gallery *n* **1** a collection of photographs of known criminals kept by the police for identification purposes **2** a group of undesirable people

rogue state *n* a state that conducts its policy in a dangerously unpredictable way, disregarding international law or diplomacy

rogue trader *n* a person who makes deals without due regard for normal business practices and controls

roguish ('rəʊgɪʃ) *adj* **1** dishonest or unprincipled **2** mischievous or arch > **'roguishly** *adv*

Röhm (*German* rœm) *n* **Ernst** (ɛrnst). 1887–1934, German soldier, who organized (1921–34) Hitler's storm troops: murdered on Hitler's orders

r

ROI *abbreviation* **1** Republic of Ireland **2** *finance* return on investment

roil (rɔɪl) *vb* **1** (*tr*) to make (a liquid) cloudy or turbid by stirring up dregs or sediment **2** (*intr*) (esp of a liquid) to be agitated or disturbed **3** (*intr*) *dialect* to be noisy or boisterous **4** (*tr*) another word (now rare) for **rile** (sense 1) [C16: of unknown origin; compare RILE]

roister ('rɔɪstə) *vb* (*intr*) **1** to engage in noisy merrymaking; revel **2** to brag, bluster, or swagger [C16: from Old French *rustre* lout, from *ruste* uncouth, from Latin *rusticus* rural; see RUSTIC] > 'roisterer *n* > 'roisterous *adj* > 'roisterously *adv*

Roland ('rəʊlənd) *n* the greatest of the legendary 12 peers (paladins, of whom Oliver was another) in attendance on Charlemagne; he died in battle at Roncesvalles (778 AD)

role *or* **rôle** (rəʊl) *n* **1** a part or character in a play, film, etc, to be played by an actor or actress **2** *psychol* the part played by a person in a particular social setting, influenced by his expectation of what is appropriate **3** usual or customary function: *what is his role in the organization?* [C17: from French *rôle* ROLL, an actor's script]

role model *n* a person regarded by others, esp younger people, as a good example to follow

role-playing *n* *psychol* activity in which a person imitates, consciously or unconsciously, a role uncharacteristic of himself. See also **psychodrama**

Rolf (rɒlf) *or* **Rolf the Ganger** *n* other names for **Rollo**

Rolfe (rɒlf) *n* Frederick William, also known as *Baron Corvo*. 1860–1913, British novelist. His best-known work is *Hadrian the Seventh* (1904)

roll (rəʊl) *vb* **1** to move or cause to move along by turning over and over **2** to move or cause to move along on wheels or rollers **3** to flow or cause to flow onwards in an undulating movement **4** (*intr*) (of animals, etc) to turn onto the back and kick: *the hills roll down to the sea* **5** (*intr*) to extend in undulations: *the hills roll down to the sea* **6** (*intr*; usually foll by *around*) to move or occur in cycles **7** (*intr*) (of a planet, the moon, etc) to revolve in an orbit **8** (*intr*; foll by *on*, *by*, etc) to pass or elapse: *the years roll by* **9** to rotate or cause to rotate wholly or partially: *to roll one's eyes* **10** to curl, cause to curl, or admit of being curled, so as to form a ball, tube, or cylinder; coil **11** to make or form by shaping into a ball, tube, or cylinder: *to roll a cigarette* **12** (often foll by *out*) to spread or cause to spread out flat or smooth under or as if under a roller: *to roll the lawn; to roll pastry* **13** to emit, produce, or utter with a deep prolonged reverberating sound: *the thunder rolled continuously* **14** to trill or cause to be trilled: *to roll one's r's* **15** (*intr*) (of a vessel, aircraft, rocket, etc) to turn from side to side around the longitudinal axis **16** to cause (an aircraft) to execute a roll or (of an aircraft) to execute a roll (sense 40) **17** (*intr*) to walk with a swaying gait, as when drunk; sway **18** to throw (dice) **19** (*intr*) to operate or begin to operate: *the presses rolled* **20** (*intr*) *informal* to make progress; move or go ahead: *let the good times roll* **21** (*tr*) *informal, chiefly US & NZ* to rob (a helpless person, such as someone drunk or asleep) ▷ *n* **22** the act or an instance of rolling **23** anything rolled up in a cylindrical form: *a roll of newspaper* **24** an official list or register, esp of names: *an electoral roll* **25** a rounded mass: *rolls of flesh* **26** a cylinder used to flatten something; roller **27** a small loaf of bread for one person: eaten plain, with butter, or as a light meal when filled with meat, cheese, etc **28** a flat pastry or cake rolled up with a meat (**sausage roll**), jam (**jam roll**), or other filling **29** a swell, ripple, or undulation on a surface: *the roll of the hills* **30** a swaying, rolling, or unsteady movement or gait **31** a deep prolonged reverberating sound: *the roll of thunder* **32** a trilling sound; trill **33** a very rapid beating of the sticks on a drum **34** a flight manoeuvre in which an aircraft makes one complete rotation about its longitudinal axis without loss of height or change in direction **35** *slang* an act of sexual intercourse or petting (esp in the phrase **a roll in the hay**) **36** *US slang* an amount of money, esp a wad of paper money **37** **on a roll** *slang* experiencing continued good luck or success **38** **strike off the roll** *or* **strike off the rolls a** to expel from membership **b** to debar (a solicitor) from practising, usually because of

dishonesty ▷ See also **roll in**, **roll on**, etc [C14 *rollen*, from Old French *roler*, from Latin *rotulus* a little wheel, from *rota* a wheel]

Rolland (French rɔlɑ̃) *n* **Romain** (rɔmɛ̃). 1866–1944, French novelist, dramatist, and essayist, known for his novels about a musical genius, *Jean-Christophe*, (1904–12): Nobel prize for literature 1915

rollbar ('rəʊl,bɑː) *n* a bar that reinforces the frame of a car, esp one used for racing, rallying, etc, to protect the driver if the car should turn over

roll call *n* the reading aloud of an official list of names, those present responding when their names are read out

rolled gold *n* a metal, such as brass, coated with a thin layer of gold, usually of above 9 carat purity. It is used in inexpensive jewellery

rolled-steel joist *n* a steel beam, esp one with a cross section in the form of a letter H or I

roller ('rəʊlə) *n* **1** a cylinder having an absorbent surface and a handle, used for spreading paint **2** Also called: **garden roller** a heavy cast-iron cylinder or pair of cylinders on an axle to which a handle is attached; used for flattening lawns **3** a long heavy wave of the sea, advancing towards the shore **4** a hardened cylinder of precision-ground steel that forms one of the rolling components of a roller bearing or of a linked driving chain **5** a cylinder fitted on pivots, used to enable heavy objects to be easily moved; castor **6** *printing* a cylinder, usually of hard rubber, used to ink a forme or plate before impression **7** any of various other cylindrical devices that rotate about a cylinder, used for any of various purposes **8** a small cylinder, esp one that is heated, onto which a woman's hair may be rolled to make it curl **9** *med* a bandage consisting of a long strip of muslin or cheesecloth rolled tightly into a cylindrical form before application **10** any of various Old World birds of the family *Coraciidae*, such as *Coracias garrulus* (**European roller**), that have a blue, green, and brown plumage, a slightly hooked bill, and an erratic flight: order *Coraciiformes* (kingfishers, etc) **11** (*often capital*) a variety of tumbler pigeon that performs characteristic backward somersaults in flight **12** a person or thing that rolls **13** short for **roadroller**

rollerball ('rəʊlə,bɔːl) *n* a pen having a small moving nylon, plastic, or metal ball as a writing point

roller bearing *n* a bearing in which a shaft runs on a number of hardened-steel rollers held within a cage

Rollerblade ('rəʊlə,bleɪd) *n* *trademark* a type of roller skate in which the wheels are set in a single straight line under the boot

roller chain *n* *engineering* a chain for transmitting power in which each link consists of two free-moving rollers held in position by pins connected to sideplates

roller coaster *n* another term for **big dipper**

roller derby *n* a race on roller skates, esp one involving aggressive tactics

roller skate *n* **1** a device having clamps and straps for fastening to a boot or shoe and four small wheels that enable the wearer to glide swiftly over a floor or other surface ▷ *vb* **roller-skate 2** (*intr*) to move on roller skates > roller skater *n*

roller towel *n* **1** a towel with the two ends sewn together, hung on a roller **2** a continuous towel wound inside a roller enabling a clean section to be pulled out when required

rollick ('rɒlɪk) *vb* **1** (*intr*) to behave in a carefree, frolicsome, or boisterous manner ▷ *n* **2** a boisterous or carefree escapade or event [C19: of Scottish dialect origin, probably from ROMP + FROLIC]

rollicking[1] ('rɒlɪkɪŋ) *adj* boisterously carefree and swaggering

rollicking[2] ('rɒlɪkɪŋ) *n* *Brit informal* a very severe telling-off; dressing-down [C20: from ROLLICK (vb) (in former sense: to be angry, make a fuss); perhaps influenced by BOLLOCKING]

roll in *vb* (*mainly intr*) **1** (*adverb*) to arrive in abundance or in large numbers **2** (*adverb*) *informal* to arrive at one's destination **3** (*preposition*) *informal* to abound or luxuriate in (wealth, money, etc)

rolling ('rəʊlɪŋ) *adj* **1** having gentle rising and falling slopes; undulating: *rolling country* **2** progressing or spreading by stages or by occurrences in different places in succession, with continued or increasing effectiveness: *three weeks of rolling strikes disrupted schools* **3** subject to regular review and updating: *a rolling plan for overseas development* **4** deeply resounding; reverberating: *rolling thunder* **5** *slang* extremely rich **6** that may be turned up or down: *a rolling hat brim* ▷ *adv* **7** *slang* swaying or staggering (in the phrase **rolling, drunk**)

rolling launch *n marketing* the process of introducing a new product into a market gradually. See **roll out** (sense 3)

rolling mill *n* **1** a mill or factory where ingots of heated metal are passed between rollers to produce sheets or bars of a required cross section and form **2** a machine having rollers that may be shaped to reduce ingots, etc, to a required cross section and form

rolling pin *n* a cylinder with handles at both ends, often of wood, used for rolling dough, pastry, etc, out flat

rolling stock *n* the wheeled vehicles collectively used on a railway, including the locomotives, passenger coaches, freight wagons, guard's vans, etc

rolling stone *n* a restless or wandering person

Rolling Stones *pl n* **the.** British rock group (formed 1962): comprising Mick Jagger, Keith Richards (born 1943; guitar, vocals), Brian Jones (1942–69; guitar), Charlie Watts (born 1941; drums), Bill Wyman (born 1936; bass guitar; now retired), and subsequently Mick Taylor (born 1948; guitar; with the group 1969–74) and Ron Wood (born 1947; guitar; with the group from 1975). See also **Jagger**

Rollins ('rɒlɪnz) *n* **Sonny**, original name *Theodore Walter Rollins*. born 1930, US jazz tenor saxophonist, noted for his improvization

rollmop ('rəʊlˌmɒp) *n* a herring fillet rolled, usually around onion slices, and pickled in spiced vinegar [c20: from German *Rollmops*, from *rollen* to ROLL + *Mops* pug dog]

rollneck ('rəʊlˌnɛk) *adj* **1** (of a garment) having a high neck that may be rolled over ▷ *n* **2** a rollneck sweater or other garment

Rollo ('rɒləʊ) *n* ?860–?930 AD, Norse war leader who received from Charles the Simple a fief that formed the basis of the duchy of Normandy. Also called: **Rolf, Rolf the Ganger**

roll of honour *n* a list of those who have died in war for their country, esp those from a particular locality or organization

roll on *vb* **1** *Brit* used to express the wish that an eagerly anticipated event or date will come quickly: *roll on Saturday* ▷ *adj* **roll-on 2** (of a deodorant, lip gloss, etc) dispensed by means of a revolving ball fitted into the neck of the container ▷ *n* **roll-on 3** a woman's foundation garment, made of elasticized material and having no fastenings

roll-on/roll-off *adj* denoting a cargo ship or ferry designed so that vehicles can be driven straight on and straight off

roll out *vb* (*tr, adverb*) **1** to cause (pastry) to become flatter and thinner by pressure with a rolling pin **2** to show (a new type of aircraft) to the public for the first time **3** to launch (a new film, product, etc) in a series of stages over an area, each stage involving an increased number of outlets ▷ *n* **roll-out 4** a presentation to the public of a new aircraft, product, etc; a launch

roll over *vb* (*adverb*) **1** (*intr*) to overturn **2** (*tr*) to allow (a loan, prize, etc) to continue in force for a further period ▷ *n* **rollover 3** an instance of such continuance of a loan, prize, etc

roll-top desk *n* a desk having a slatted wooden panel that can be pulled down over the writing surface when not in use

roll up *vb* (*adverb*) **1** to form or cause to form a cylindrical shape **2** (*tr*) to wrap (an object) round on itself or on an axis: *to roll up a map* **3** (*intr*) *informal* to arrive, esp in a vehicle **4** (*intr*) to proceed or develop **5** (*intr*) *Austral* to assemble; congregate ▷ *n* **roll-up 6** *Brit informal* a cigarette made by hand from loose tobacco and cigarette

paper **7** *Austral archaic* the attendance at any fixture

Rolodex ('rəʊləˌdɛks) *n trademark chiefly US* a small file for holding names, addresses, and telephone numbers, consisting of cards attached horizontally to a rotatable central cylinder

roly-poly ('rəʊlɪ'pəʊlɪ) *adj* **1** plump, buxom, or rotund ▷ *n, pl* -lies **2** *Brit* a strip of suet pastry spread with jam, fruit, or a savoury mixture, rolled up, and baked or steamed as a pudding [c17: apparently by reduplication from *roly*, from ROLL]

ROM (rɒm) *n acronym computing* read only memory: a storage device that holds data permanently and cannot in normal circumstances be altered by the programmer

rom. *printing abbreviation* roman (type)

Rom. *abbreviation* **1** Roman **2** Romance (languages) **3** *Bible* Romans **4** Romania(n)

Roma ('rɔːma) *n* the Italian name for **Rome**

Romagna (*Italian* rɔ'maɲɲa) *n* an area of N Italy: part of the Papal States up to 1860

Romaic (rəʊ'meɪɪk) *obsolete* ▷ *n* **1** the modern Greek vernacular, esp Demotic ▷ *adj* **2** of or relating to Greek, esp Demotic [c19: from Greek *Rhōmaikos* Roman, with reference to the Eastern Roman Empire]

Romains (*French* rɔmɛ̃) *n* **Jules** (ʒyl). pseudonym of *Louis Farigoule*. 1885–1972, French poet, dramatist, and novelist. His works include the novel *Men of Good Will* (1932–46)

roman ('rəʊmən) *adj* **1** of, relating to, or denoting a vertical style of printing type: the usual form of type for most printed matter. Compare **italic** ▷ *n* **2** roman type or print [c16: so called because the style of letters is that used in ancient Roman inscriptions]

Roman ('rəʊmən) *adj* **1** of or relating to Rome or its inhabitants in ancient or modern times **2** of or relating to Roman Catholicism or the Roman Catholic Church ▷ *n* **3** a citizen or inhabitant of ancient or modern Rome

roman à clef *French* (rɔmɑ̃ a kle) *n, pl romans à clef* (rɔmɑ̃ a kle) a novel in which real people are depicted under fictitious names [literally: novel with a key]

Roman alphabet *n* the alphabet evolved by the ancient Romans for the writing of Latin, based upon an Etruscan form derived from the Greeks and ultimately from the Phoenicians. The alphabet serves for writing most of the languages of W Europe and many other languages

Roman blind *n* a window blind consisting of a length of material which, when drawn up, gathers into horizontal folds from the bottom

Roman candle *n* a firework that produces a continuous shower of sparks punctuated by coloured balls of fire [c19: so called from its having been originated in Italy]

Roman Catholic *adj* **1** of or relating to the Roman Catholic Church ▷ *n* **2** a member of this Church Often shortened to: Catholic ▷ **Roman Catholicism** *n*

Roman Catholic Church *n* the Christian Church over which the pope presides, with administrative headquarters in the Vatican ▷ Also called: Catholic Church, Church of Rome

romance *n* (rə'mæns, 'rəʊmæns) **1** a love affair, esp an intense and happy but short-lived affair involving young people **2** love, esp romantic love idealized for its purity or beauty **3** a spirit of or inclination for adventure, excitement, or mystery **4** a mysterious, exciting, sentimental, or nostalgic quality, esp one associated with a place **5** a narrative in verse or prose, written in a vernacular language in the Middle Ages, dealing with strange and exciting adventures of chivalrous heroes **6** any similar narrative work dealing with events and characters remote from ordinary life **7** a story, novel, film, etc, dealing with love, usually in an idealized or sentimental way **8** an extravagant, absurd, or fantastic account or explanation **9** a lyrical song or short instrumental composition having a simple melody ▷ *vb* (rə'mæns) **10** (*intr*) to tell, invent, or write extravagant or romantic fictions **11** (*intr*) to tell extravagant or improbable lies **12** (*intr*) to have romantic thoughts **13** (*intr*) (of a couple) to indulge in romantic behaviour **14** (*tr*) to be romantically involved with [c13: *romauns*, from Old French *romans*, ultimately from Latin *Rōmānicus* Roman] ▷ ro'mancer *n*

r

Romance (rə'mæns, 'rəʊmæns) *adj* 1 denoting, relating to, or belonging to the languages derived from Latin, including Italian, Spanish, Portuguese, French, and Romanian 2 denoting a word borrowed from a Romance language ▷ *n* 3 this group of languages; the living languages that belong to the Italic branch of the Indo-European family

Roman Empire *n* 1 the territories ruled by ancient Rome. At its height under Trajan, the Roman Empire included W and S Europe, Africa north of the Sahara, and SW Asia. In 395 AD it was divided by Theodosius into the **Eastern Roman Empire** whose capital was Byzantium and which lasted until 1453, and the **Western Roman Empire** which lasted until the sack of Rome in 476 2 the government of Rome and its dominions by the emperors from 27 BC 3 the Byzantine Empire 4 the Holy Roman Empire

Romanesque (,rəʊmə'nɛsk) *adj* 1 denoting, relating to, or having the style of architecture used in W and S Europe from the 9th to the 12th century, characterized by the rounded arch, the groin vault, massive-masonry wall construction, and a restrained use of mouldings 2 denoting or relating to a corresponding style in painting, sculpture, etc [C18: see ROMAN, -ESQUE]

Roman holiday *n* entertainment or pleasure that depends on the suffering of others [C19: from Byron's poem *Childe Harold* (IV, 141)]

Romania (rəʊ'meɪnɪə), **Rumania** *or* **Roumania** *n* a republic in SE Europe, bordering on the Black Sea: united in 1861; became independent in 1878; Communist government set up in 1945; became a socialist republic in 1965; a more democratic regime was installed after a revolution in 1989; joined the EU in 2007. It consists chiefly of a great central arc of the Carpathian Mountains and Transylvanian Alps, with the plains of Walachia, Moldavia, and Dobriya on the south and east and the Pannonian Plain in the west Official language: Romanian. Religion: Romanian Orthodox (Christian) majority. Currency: leu. Capital: Bucharest Pop: 22 280 000 (2004 est). Area: 237 500 sq km (91 699 sq miles)

Romanian (rəʊ'meɪnɪən), **Rumanian** *or* **Roumanian** *n* 1 the official language of Romania, belonging to the Romance group of the Indo-European family 2 a native, citizen, or inhabitant of Romania ▷ *adj* 3 relating to, denoting, or characteristic of Romania, its people, or their language

Romanic (rəʊ'mænɪk) *adj* another word for **Roman**, **Romance**

Romanism ('rəʊmə,nɪzəm) *n* Roman Catholicism, esp when regarded as excessively or superstitiously ritualistic

Romanize *or* **Romanise** ('rəʊmə,naɪz) *vb* 1 (*tr*) to impart a Roman Catholic character to (a ceremony, practice, etc) 2 (*intr*) to be converted to Roman Catholicism 3 (*tr*) to transcribe or transliterate (a language) into the Roman alphabet

Roman law *n* the system of jurisprudence of ancient Rome, codified under Justinian and forming the basis of many modern legal systems

Roman nose *n* a nose having a high prominent bridge

Roman numerals *pl n* the letters used by the Romans for the representation of cardinal numbers, still used occasionally today. The integers are represented by the following letters: I (= 1), V (= 5), X (= 10), L (= 50), C (= 100), D (= 500), and M (= 1000). If a numeral is followed by another numeral of lower denomination, the two are added together; if it is preceded by one of lower denomination, the smaller numeral is subtracted from the greater. Thus VI = 6 (V + I), but IV = 4 (V − I). Other examples are XC (= 90), CL (= 150), XXV (= 25), XLIV (= 44). Multiples of a thousand are indicated by a superior bar: thus, $\bar{V}$ = 5000, $\bar{X}$ = 10 000, $\overline{XD}$ = 490 000, etc

Romano (*Italian* ro'ma:no) *n* See **Giulio Romano**

Romanov ('rəʊmənɒf; *Russian* ra'manəf) *n* any member of the Russian imperial dynasty that ruled from the crowning (1613) of Mikhail Fyodorovich to the abdication (1917) of Nicholas II during the February Revolution

Romansch *or* **Romansh** (rəʊ'mænʃ) *n* a group of Rhaetian dialects spoken in the Swiss canton of Graubünden; an official language of Switzerland since 1938 [C17: from Romansch, literally: Romance language, from Latin *Rōmānicus* ROMANIC]

romantic (rəʊ'mæntɪk) *adj* 1 of, relating to, imbued with, or characterized by romance 2 evoking or given to thoughts and feelings of love, esp idealized or sentimental love: *a romantic woman; a romantic setting* 3 impractical, visionary, or idealistic: *a romantic scheme* 4 *often euphemistic* imaginary or fictitious: *a romantic account of one's war service* 5 (*often capital*) of or relating to a movement in European art, music, and literature in the late 18th and early 19th centuries, characterized by an emphasis on feeling and content rather than order and form, on the sublime, supernatural, and exotic, and the free expression of the passions and individuality ▷ *n* 6 a person who is romantic, as in being idealistic, amorous, or soulful 7 a person whose tastes in art, literature, etc, lie mainly in romanticism; romanticist 8 (*often capital*) a poet, composer, etc, of the romantic period or whose main inspiration or interest is romanticism [C17: from French *romantique*, from obsolete *romant* story, romance, from Old French *romans* ROMANCE] ▷ ro'mantically *adv*

romanticism (rəʊ'mæntɪ,sɪzəm) *n* 1 (*often capital*) the theory, practice, and style of the romantic art, music, and literature of the late 18th and early 19th centuries, usually opposed to classicism 2 romantic attitudes, ideals, or qualities ▷ ro'manticist *n*

romanticize *or* **romanticise** (rəʊ'mæntɪ,saɪz) *vb* 1 (*intr*) to think or act in a romantic way 2 (*tr*) to interpret according to romantic precepts 3 to make or become romantic, as in style ▷ ro,mantici'zation *or* ro,mantici'sation *n*

Romany *or* **Romani** ('rɒmənɪ, 'rəʊ-) *n pl* -nies *or* -nis a another name for a: **Gypsy** b (*as modifier*): *Romany customs* 2 the language of the Gypsies, belonging to the Indic branch of the Indo-European family, but incorporating extensive borrowings from local European languages. Most of its 250 000 speakers are bilingual. It is extinct in Britain [C19: from Romany *romani* (adj) Gypsy, ultimately from Sanskrit *domba* man of a low caste of musicians, of Dravidian origin]

romanza (rə'mænzə) *n music* a short instrumental piece of song-like character [from Italian]

romaunt (rə'mɔːnt) *n archaic* a verse romance [C16: from Old French; see ROMANTIC]

Romberg ('rɒmbɜːg) *n* Sigmund. 1887–1951, US composer of operettas, born in Hungary. He wrote *The Student Prince* (1924) and *The Desert Song* (1926)

Rome (rəʊm) *n* 1 the capital of Italy, on the River Tiber: includes the independent state of the Vatican City; traditionally founded by Romulus on the Palatine Hill in 753 BC, later spreading to six other hills east of the Tiber; capital of the Roman Empire; a great cultural and artistic centre, esp during the Renaissance. Pop: 2 546 804 (2001). Italian name: Roma 2 the Roman Empire 3 the Roman Catholic Church or Roman Catholicism

Romeo ('rəʊmɪəʊ) *n pl* -os an ardent male lover [from the hero of Shakespeare's *Romeo and Juliet* (1594)]

Romish ('rəʊmɪʃ) *adj usually derogatory* of, relating to, or resembling Roman Catholic beliefs or practices

Rommel (*German* 'rɔməl) *n* Erwin ('ɛrviːn), nicknamed *the Desert Fox*. 1891–1944, German field marshal, noted for his brilliant generalship in N Africa in World War II. Later a commander in N France, he committed suicide after the officers' plot against Hitler

Romney ('rɒmnɪ, 'rʌm-) *n* George. 1734–1802, English painter, who painted more than 50 portraits of Lady Hamilton in various historical roles

Romney Marsh ('rɒmnɪ, 'rʌm-) *n* 1 a marshy area of SE England, on the Kent coast between New Romney and Rye: includes Dungeness 2 a type of hardy British sheep from this area, with long wool, bred for mutton

romp (rɒmp) *vb* (*intr*) 1 to play or run about wildly, boisterously, or joyfully 2 romp home *or* romp in to win a race easily ▷ *n* 3 a noisy or boisterous game or prank 4 an instance of sexual activity between two or more people that is entered into light-heartedly and without emotional judgment: *naked sex romps* **5** Also called: **romper** *archaic* a playful or boisterous child, esp a girl **6** an easy victory [c18: probably variant of RAMP, from Old French *ramper* to crawl, climb]

rompers ('rɒmpəz) *pl n* **1** a one-piece baby garment consisting of trousers and a bib with straps **2** NZ a type of costume worn by schoolgirls for games and gymnastics

Romulus ('rɒmjʊləs) *n Roman myth* the founder of Rome, suckled with his twin brother Remus by a she-wolf after they were abandoned in infancy. Their parents were Rhea Silvia and Mars. Romulus later killed Remus in an argument over the new city

Roncesvalles ('rɒnsə,vælz; *Spanish* rɔnθes'βaʎes) *n* a village in N Spain, in the Pyrenees: a nearby pass was the scene of the defeat of Charlemagne and death of Roland in 778

rondavel ('rɒndɑ:vəl) *n South African* a circular often thatched building with a conical roof [of uncertain origin]

rondeau ('rɒndəʊ) *n, pl* -deaux (-dəʊ, -dəʊz) a poem consisting of 13 or 10 lines with two rhymes and having the opening words of the first line used as an unrhymed refrain [c16: from Old French, from *rondel* a little round, from *rond* ROUND]

rondel ('rɒndəl) *n* a rondeau consisting of three stanzas of 13 or 14 lines with a two-line refrain appearing twice or three times [c14: from Old French, literally: a little circle, from *rond* ROUND]

rondo ('rɒndəʊ) *n, pl* -dos a piece of music in which a refrain is repeated between episodes: often constitutes the form of the last movement of a sonata or concerto [c18: from Italian, from French RONDEAU]

Rondônia (*Portuguese* rõ'donja) *n* a state of W Brazil: consists chiefly of tropical rainforest; a centre of the Amazon rubber boom until about 1912. Capital: Porto Velho. Pop: 1 431 777 (2002). Area: 243 043 sq km (93 839 sq miles). Former name (until 1956): Guaporé

rone (rəʊn; *Scot* rɒn) *or* **ronepipe** ('rəʊn,paɪp; *Scot* 'rɒn,pəɪp) *n Scot* a drainpipe or gutter for carrying rainwater from a roof [c19: origin unknown]

Ronsard (*French* rõsar) *n* Pierre de (pjɛr də). 1524–85, French poet, foremost of the *Pléiade*

röntgen ('rɒntgən, -tjən, 'rɛnt-) *n* a variant spelling of **roentgen**

Röntgen ('rɒntgən, -tjən, 'rɛnt-; *German* 'rœntgən) *n* a variant spelling of (Wilhelm Konrad) **Roentgen**

roo (ru:) *n Austral informal* a kangaroo

roo bars *pl n Austral* another name for **bull bars**

rood (ru:d) *n* **1** a a crucifix, esp one set on a beam or screen at the entrance to the chancel of a church **b** (*as modifier*): *rood beam; rood arch; rood screen* **2** the Cross on which Christ was crucified **3** a unit of area equal to one quarter of an acre or 0.10117 hectares **4** a unit of area equal to 40 square rods [Old English *rōd*; related to Old Saxon *rōda*, Old Norse *rōtha*]

Roodepoort ('ru:də,pʊət) *n* an industrial city in NE South Africa, in the Witwatersrand. Pop: 172 601 (2001)

roof (ru:f) *n, pl* roofs (ru:fs, ru:vz) **1** a a structure that covers or forms the top of a building **b** (*in combination*): *the rooftop* **c** (*as modifier*): *a roof garden* **2** the top covering of a vehicle, oven, or other structure: *the roof of a car* **3** *anatomy* any structure that covers an organ or part: *the roof of the mouth* **4** a highest or topmost point or part: *Mount Everest is the roof of the world* **5** a house or other shelter: *a poor man's roof* **6** hit the roof *or* go through the roof *informal* to get extremely angry; become furious ▷ *vb* **7** (*tr*) to provide or cover with a roof or rooflike part [Old English *hrōf*; related to Middle Dutch, Old Norse *hrōf*] ▷ 'roofer *n* ▷ 'roofless *adj*

roof garden *n* a garden on a flat roof of a building

roofing ('ru:fɪŋ) *n* **1** material used to construct a roof **2** the act of constructing a roof

roof rack *n* a rack attached to the roof of a motor vehicle for carrying luggage, skis, etc

rooftop ('ru:f,tɒp) *n* **1** the outside part of the roof of a building **2** shout from the rooftops to proclaim (something) publicly

rooftree ('ru:f,tri:) *n* another name for **ridgepole**

rooibos tea ('rɔɪbɒs) *n South African* tea prepared from any of several species of *Borbonia* or *Aspalanthus*, believed to have tonic properties [from Afrikaans *rooi* red + *bos* bush]

rooikat ('rɔɪ,kæt) *n* a South African lynx, *Felis caracal* [Afrikaans *rooi* red + *kat* cat]

rooinek ('rʊɪnɛk, 'rɔɪ-) *n South African* a contemptuous or jocular name for an English person or an English-speaking South African [c19: Afrikaans, literally: red neck]

rook¹ (rʊk) *n* **1** a large Eurasian passerine bird, *Corvus frugilegus*, with a black plumage and a whitish base to its bill: family *Corvidae* (crows) **2** *slang* a swindler or cheat, esp one who cheats at cards ▷ *vb* **3** (*tr*) *slang* to overcharge, swindle, or cheat [Old English *hrōc*; related to Old High German *hruoh*, Old Norse *hrōkr*]

rook² (rʊk) *n* a chesspiece that may move any number of unoccupied squares in a straight line, horizontally or vertically. Also called: **castle** [c14: from Old French *rok*, ultimately from Arabic *rukhkh*]

rookery ('rʊkərɪ) *n, pl* -eries **1** a group of nesting rooks **2** a clump of trees containing rooks' nests **3 a** a breeding ground or communal living area of certain other species of gregarious birds or mammals, esp penguins or seals **b** a colony of any such creatures **4** *archaic* an overcrowded slum tenement building or area of housing

rookie ('rʊkɪ) *n informal* an inexperienced person or newcomer, esp a raw recruit in the army [c20: changed from RECRUIT]

room (ru:m, rʊm) *n* **1** space or extent, esp unoccupied or unobstructed space for a particular purpose: *is there room to pass?* **2** an area within a building enclosed by a floor, a ceiling, and walls or partitions **3** (*functioning as singular or plural*) the people present in a room: *the whole room was laughing* **4** (*foll by for*) opportunity or scope: *room for manoeuvre* **5** (*plural*) a part of a house, hotel, etc that is rented out as separate accommodation; lodgings ▷ *vb* **6** (*intr*) *chiefly US* to occupy or share a room or lodging: *where does he room?* [Old English *rūm*; related to Gothic, Old High German *rūm*] ▷ 'roomer *n*

roomful ('ru:mfʊl, 'rʊm-) *n, pl* -fuls a number or quantity sufficient to fill a room: *a roomful of furniture*

rooming house *n US & Canadian* a house having self-contained furnished rooms or flats for renting

roommate ('ru:m,meɪt, 'rʊm-) *n* a person with whom one shares a room or lodging

room service *n* service in a hotel providing meals, drinks, etc, in guests' rooms

roomy ('ru:mɪ, 'rʊmɪ) *adj* roomier, roomiest having ample room; spacious ▷ 'roomily *adv* ▷ 'roominess *n*

Rooney ('ru:nɪ) *n* **Wayne.** born 1985, English footballer; he played for Everton (2002–2004) and plays for Manchester United (from 2004) and England (from 2003)

Roosevelt ('rəʊzə,vɛlt) *n* **1** (Anna) **Eleanor.** 1884–1962, US writer, diplomat, and advocate of liberal causes: delegate to the United Nations (1945–52) **2** her husband, **Franklin Delano** ('dɛlə,nəʊ), known as FDR. 1882–1945, 32nd president of the US (1933–45); elected four times. He instituted major reforms (the **New Deal**) to counter the economic crisis of the 1930s and was a forceful leader during World War II **3** Theodore. 1858–1919, 26th president of the US (1901–09). A proponent of extending military power, he won for the US the right to build the Panama Canal (1903). He won the Nobel peace prize (1906), for mediating in the Russo-Japanese war

roost (ru:st) *n* **1** a place, perch, branch, etc, where birds, esp domestic fowl, rest or sleep **2** a temporary place to rest or stay ▷ *vb* **3** (*intr*) to rest or sleep on a roost **4** (*intr*) to settle down or stay **5** come home to roost to have unfavourable repercussions [Old English *hrōst*; related to Old Saxon *hrost* loft, German *Rost* grid]

Roost (ru:st) *n* the Roost a powerful current caused by conflicting tides around the Shetland and Orkney Islands [c16: from Old Norse *rōst*]

rooster ('ru:stə) *n chiefly US & Canadian* the male of the domestic fowl; a cock

root¹ (ru:t) *n* **1** a the organ of a higher plant that anchors the rest of the plant in the ground, absorbs water and mineral salts from the soil, and does not bear leaves or buds **b** (loosely) any of the branches of such an organ **2** any plant part, such as a rhizome or tuber, that is similar to a root in structure, function, or appearance **3 a** the essential, fundamental, or primary part or nature of something: *your analysis strikes at the root of the problem* **b** (*as modifier*): *the root cause of the problem* **4** anatomy the embedded portion of a tooth, nail, hair, etc **5** origin or derivation, esp as a source of growth, vitality, or existence **6** (*plural*) a person's sense of belonging in a community, place, etc, esp the one in which he was born or brought up **7** Bible a descendant **8** the form of a word that remains after removal of all affixes; a morpheme with lexical meaning that is not further subdivisible into other morphemes with lexical meaning **9** maths a number or quantity that when multiplied by itself a certain number of times equals a given number or quantity: *3 is a cube root of 27* **10** Also called: solution maths a number that when substituted for the variable satisfies a given equation **11** music (in harmony) the note forming the foundation of a chord **12** Austral & NZ slang sexual intercourse **13** root and branch **a** (*adverb*) entirely; completely; utterly **b** (*adjective*) thorough; radical; complete. Related adjective: **radical** ▷ *vb* **14** Also: take root (*intr*) to put forth or establish a root and begin to grow **15** Also: take root (*intr*) to become established, embedded, or effective **16** (*tr*) to fix or embed with or as if with a root or roots **17** Austral & NZ slang to have sexual intercourse (with) ▷ See also **root out, roots,** etc [Old English *rōt*, from Old Norse; related to Old English *wyrt* WORT] ▷ 'rooter *n* ▷ 'root,like *adj* ▷ 'rooty *adj* ▷ 'rootiness *n*

root² (ruːt) *vb* (*intr*) **1** (of a pig) to burrow in or dig up the earth in search of food, using the snout **2** (foll by *about, around, in* etc) *informal* to search vigorously but unsystematically [c16: changed (through influence of ROOT¹) from earlier *wroot*, from Old English *wrōtan*; related to Old English *wrōt* snout, Middle Dutch *wrōte* mole] ▷ 'rooter *n*

root³ *vb* (*intr; usually foll by for*) *informal* to give support to (a contestant, team, etc), as by cheering [c19: perhaps a variant of Scottish *rout* to make a loud noise, from Old Norse *rauta* to roar]

root beer *n* US & Canadian an effervescent drink made from extracts of various roots and herbs

root canal *n* the passage in the root of a tooth through which its nerves and blood vessels enter the pulp cavity

root-canal therapy *n* another word for **root treatment**

root climber *n* any of various climbing plants, such as the ivy, that adhere to a supporting structure by means of small roots growing from the side of the stem

root crop *n* a crop, as of turnips or beets, cultivated for the food value of its roots

rooted ('ruːtɪd) *adj* **1** having roots **2** deeply felt: *rooted objections*

root ginger *n* the raw underground stem of the ginger plant used finely chopped or grated, esp in Chinese dishes

root hair *n* any of the hollow hairlike outgrowths of the outer cells of a root, just behind the tip, that absorb water and salts from the soil

rooting compound *n* horticulture a substance, usually a powder, containing auxins in which plant cuttings are dipped in order to promote root growth

rootkit ('ruːt,kɪt) *n* computers a set of programs used to gain unauthorized access to a computer's operating system, esp in order to destroy or alter files, attack other computers, etc

rootle ('ruːtªl) *vb* (*intr*) Brit another word for **root²**

rootless ('ruːtlɪs) *adj* having no roots, esp (of a person) having no ties with a particular place or community

rootlet ('ruːtlɪt) *n* a small root or branch of a root

root mean square *n* the square root of the average of the squares of a set of numbers or quantities: *the root mean square of 1, 2, and 4 is* $\sqrt{[(1^2 + 2^2 + 4^2)/3]} = \sqrt{7}$ Abbreviation: rms

root nodule *n* a swelling on the root of a leguminous plant, such as the pea or clover, that contains bacteria of the genus *Rhizobium*, capable of nitrogen fixation

root out *vb* (*tr, adverb*) to remove or eliminate completely: *we must root out inefficiency*

roots (ruːts) *adj* (of popular music) going back to the origins of a style, esp in being genuine and unpretentious: *roots rock* ▷ 'rootsy *adj*

rootserver ('ruːt,sɜːvə) *n* any of a small number of important large servers on the internet that match addresses at the top-domain level

roots music *n* **1** another name for **world music 2** reggae, esp when regarded as authentic and uncommercialized

rootstock ('ruːt,stɒk) *n* **1** another name for **rhizome 2** another name for **stock** (sense 7) **3** biology a basic structure from which offshoots have developed

root treatment *n* dentistry a procedure, used for treating an abscess at the tip of the root of a tooth, in which the pulp is removed and a filling (**root filling**) inserted in the root canal. Also called: root-canal therapy

ropable or **ropeable** ('rəʊpəbªl) *adj* **1** capable of being roped **2** Austral & NZ informal **a** angry **b** wild or intractable: *a ropable beast*

rope (rəʊp) *n* **1 a** a fairly thick cord made of twisted and intertwined hemp or other fibres or of wire or other strong material **b** (*as modifier*): *a rope bridge; a rope ladder* **2 a** row of objects fastened or united to form a line: *a rope of pearls; a rope of onions* **3** a quantity of material twisted or wound in the form of a cord **4** anything in the form of a filament or strand, esp something viscous or glutinous: *a rope of slime* **5** the rope **a** a rope, noose, or halter used for hanging **b** death by hanging, strangling, etc **6** give someone enough rope to hang himself to allow someone to accomplish his own downfall by his own foolish acts **7** know the ropes to have a thorough understanding of a particular sphere of activity **8** on the ropes **a** boxing driven against the ropes enclosing the ring by an opponent's attack **b** in a defenceless or hopeless position ▷ *vb* **9** (*tr*) to bind or fasten with or as if with a rope **10** (*tr; usually foll by off*) to enclose or divide by means of a rope **11** (when *intr*, foll by *up*) mountaineering to tie (climbers) together with a rope [Old English *rāp*; related to Old Saxon *rēp*, Old High German *reif*]

rope in *vb* (*tr, adverb*) **1** Brit to persuade to take part in some activity **2** US & Canadian to trick or entice into some activity

rope's end *n* a short piece of rope, esp as formerly used for flogging sailors

ropewalk ('rəʊp,wɔːk) *n* a long narrow usually covered path or shed where ropes are made

ropey or **ropy** ('rəʊpɪ) *adj* **ropier, ropiest 1** Brit informal **a** inferior or inadequate **b** slightly unwell; below par **2** (of a viscous or sticky substance) forming strands or filaments **3** resembling a rope ▷ 'ropily *adv* ▷ 'ropiness *n*

Roquefort ('rɒkfɔː) *n* a blue-veined cheese with a strong flavour, made from ewes' milk: matured in caves [c19: named after *Roquefort*, village in S France]

roquet ('rəʊkɪ) croquet ▷ *vb* **-quets** (-kɪz) , **-queting** (-kɪɪŋ), **-queted** (-kɪd) **1** to drive one's ball against (another person's ball) in order to be allowed to croquet ▷ *n* **2** the act of roqueting [c19: variant of CROQUET]

Roraima (Portuguese rɔ'raima) *n* a state of N Brazil: chiefly rainforest Capital: Boa Vista. Pop: 346 871 (2002). Area: 230 104 sq km (89 740 sq miles)

ro-ro ('rəʊrəʊ) *adj* acronym for **roll-on/roll-off**

rorqual ('rɔːkwəl) *n* any of several whalebone whales of the genus *Balaenoptera*, esp *B. physalus*: family *Balaenopteridae*. They have a dorsal fin and a series of grooves along the throat and chest. Also called: finback [c19: from French, from Norwegian *rörhval*, from Old Norse *reytharhvalr*, from *reythr* (from *rauthr* red) + *hvalr* whale]

Rorschach test ('rɔːʃɑːk; German 'rɔrʃax) *n* psychol a personality test consisting of a number of unstructured ink blots presented for interpretation [c20: named after Hermann *Rorschach* (1884–1922), Swiss psychiatrist]

rort (rɔːt) Austral informal ▷ *n* **1** a rowdy party or celebration **2** a dishonest scheme ▷ *vb* **3** to take unfair advantage of something [c20: back formation from *rorty* (in the sense: good, splendid)] ▷ 'rorty *adj*

rorter ('rɔːtə) *n Austral informal* a small-scale confidence trickster

Rory O'Connor (ˌrɔːrɪ əʊˈkɒnə) *n* Also called *Roderic*. ?1116–98, king of Connaught and last High King of Ireland

Rosa[1] ('rəʊzə; *Italian* 'rɔːza) Monte Rosa ('mɒntɪ; *Italian* 'monte) *n* a mountain between Italy and Switzerland: the highest in the Pennine Alps. Height: 4634 m (15 204 ft)

Rosa[2] (*Italian* 'rɔːza) *n* Salvator ('salvatɔr). 1615–73, Italian artist, noted esp for his romantic landscapes

rosace ('rəʊzeɪs) *n* 1 another name for **rose window** 2 another name for **rosette** [C19: from French, from Latin *rosāceus* ROSACEOUS]

rosacea (rəʊˈzeɪʃə) *n* a chronic inflammatory disease causing the skin of the face to become abnormally flushed and sometimes pustular. Also called: acne rosacea

rosaceous (rəʊˈzeɪʃəs) *adj* 1 of, relating to, or belonging to the *Rosaceae*, a family of flowering plants typically having white, yellow, pink, or red five-petalled flowers. The family includes the rose, strawberry, blackberry, and many fruit trees such as apple, cherry, and plum 2 of the colour rose; rose-coloured; rosy [C18: from Latin *rosāceus* composed of roses, from *rosa* ROSE[1]]

rosarian (rəʊˈzɛərɪən) *n* a person who cultivates roses, esp professionally

Rosario (rəʊˈsɑːrɪəʊ; *Spanish* rɔˈsarjo) *n* an inland port in E Argentina, on the Paraná River: the second largest city in the country; industrial centre. Pop: 1 312 000 (2005 est)

rosarium (rəʊˈzɛərɪəm) *n, pl* -sariums *or* -saria (-ˈzɛərɪə) a rose garden [C19: New Latin]

rosary ('rəʊzərɪ) *n, pl* -saries 1 *RC Church* a a series of prayers counted on a string of beads, usually consisting of five or 15 decades of Aves, each decade beginning with a Paternoster and ending with a Gloria b a string of 55 or 165 beads used to count these prayers as they are recited 2 (in other religions) a similar string of beads used in praying 3 an archaic word for **garland** (sense 1) [C14: from Latin *rosārium* rose garden, from *rosārius* of roses, from *rosa* ROSE[1]]

Roscius ('rɒskɪəs, -sɪəs) *n* 1 full name *Quintus Roscius Gallus*. died 62 BC, Roman actor 2 any actor > **Roscian** *adj*

Roscommon (rɒsˈkɒmən) *n* 1 an inland county of N central Republic of Ireland, in Connacht: economy based on cattle and sheep farming. County town: Roscommon. Pop: 53 774 (2002). Area: 2463 sq km (951 sq miles) 2 a former name for **Galway** (sense 3)

rose[1] (rəʊz) *n* 1 a any shrub or climbing plant of the rosaceous genus *Rosa*, typically having prickly stems, compound leaves, and fragrant flowers b (*in combination*): *rosebush; rosetree* 2 the flower of any of these plants 3 any of various similar plants, such as the rockrose and Christmas rose 4 a a moderate purplish-red colour; purplish pink b (*as adjective*): *rose paint* 5 a rose, or a representation of one, as the national emblem of England 6 *jewellery* a a cut for a diamond or other gemstone, having a hemispherical faceted crown and a flat base b a gem so cut 7 a perforated cap fitted to the spout of a watering can or the end of a hose, causing the water to issue in a spray 8 a design or decoration shaped like a rose; rosette 9 Also called: ceiling rose *electrical engineering* a circular boss attached to a ceiling through which the flexible lead of an electric-light fitting passes 10 *history* See **red rose**, **white rose** 11 bed of roses a situation of comfort or ease 12 under the rose in secret; privately; sub rosa ▷ *vb* 13 (*tr*) to make rose-coloured; cause to blush or redden [Old English, from Latin *rosa*, probably from Greek *rhodon* rose] > **'rose,like** *adj*

rose[2] (rəʊz) *vb* the past tense of **rise**

rosé ('rəʊzeɪ) *n* any pink wine, made either by removing the skins of red grapes after only a little colour has been extracted or by mixing red and white wines [C19: from French, literally: pink, from Latin *rosa* ROSE[1]]

roseate ('rəʊzɪˌeɪt) *adj* 1 of the colour rose or pink 2 excessively or idealistically optimistic

rosebay ('rəʊzˌbeɪ) *n* 1 *US* any of several rhododendrons, esp *Rhododendron maximum* of E North America 2 rosebay

willowherb a perennial onagraceous plant, *Chamerion* (formerly *Epilobium*) *angustifolium*, that has spikes of deep pink flowers and is widespread in open places throughout N temperate regions 3 another name for **oleander**

Rosebery ('rəʊzbərɪ, -brɪ) *n* Earl of, title of *Archibald Philip Primrose*. 1847–1929, British Liberal statesman; prime minister (1894–95)

rosebud ('rəʊz,bʌd) *n* 1 the bud of a rose 2 *literary* a pretty young woman

rose campion *n* a European caryophyllaceous plant, *Lychnis coronaria*, widely cultivated for its pink flowers. Its stems and leaves are covered with white woolly down. Also called: dusty miller

rose chafer *or* **rose beetle** *n* a British scarabaeid beetle, *Cetonia aurata*, that has a greenish-golden body with a metallic lustre and feeds on plants

rose-coloured *adj* 1 of the colour rose; rosy 2 see through rose-coloured glasses, see through rose-coloured spectacles, see through rose-tinted glasses *or* see through rose-tinted spectacles to view in an excessively optimistic light

rose-cut *adj* (of a gemstone) cut with a hemispherical faceted crown and a flat base

rosehip ('rəʊz,hɪp) *n* the berry-like fruit of a rose plant

rosella (rəʊˈzɛlə) *n* any of various Australian parrots of the genus *Platycercus*, such as *P. elegans* (**crimson rosella**), often kept as cage birds [C19: probably alteration of *Rose-hiller*, after *Rose Hill*, Parramatta, near Sydney]

rosemary ('rəʊzmərɪ) *n, pl* -maries an aromatic European shrub, *Rosmarinus officinalis*, widely cultivated for its grey-green evergreen leaves, which are used in cookery for flavouring and yield a fragrant oil used in the manufacture of perfumes: family *Lamiaceae* (labiates). It is the traditional flower of remembrance [C15: earlier *rosmarine*, from Latin *rōs* dew + *marīnus* marine; modern form influenced by folk etymology, as if ROSE[1] + MARY]

Rosenberg ('rəʊzənbɜːɡ) *n* 1 Alfred. 1893–1946, German Nazi politician and writer, who devised much of the racial ideology of Nazism: hanged for war crimes 2 Isaac. 1890–1918, British poet and painter, best known for his poems about life in the trenches during World War I: died in action 3 Julius. 1918–53, US spy, who, with his wife Ethel (1914–53), was executed for passing information about nuclear weapons to the Russians

rose of Sharon *n* Also called: Aaron's beard a creeping shrub, *Hypericum calycinum*, native to SE Europe but widely cultivated, having large yellow flowers: family *Hypericaceae*

roseola (rəʊˈziːələ) *n pathol* 1 a feverish condition of young children that lasts for some five days during the last two of which the patient has a rose-coloured rash. It is caused by the human herpes virus 2 any red skin eruption or rash [C19: from New Latin, diminutive of Latin *roseus* rosy] > **ro'seolar** *adj*

rosery ('rəʊzərɪ) *n, pl* -series a bed or garden of roses

Rosetta (rəʊˈzɛtə) *n* the former name of **Rashid**

Rosetta stone *n* a basalt slab discovered in 1799 at Rosetta, dating to the reign of Ptolemy V (196 BC) and carved with parallel inscriptions in Egyptian hieroglyphics, demotic characters, and Greek, which provided the key to the decipherment of ancient Egyptian texts

rosette (rəʊˈzɛt) *n* 1 a decoration or pattern resembling a rose, esp an arrangement of ribbons or strips formed into a rose-shaped design and worn as a badge or presented as a prize 2 another name for **rose window** 3 *botany* a circular cluster of leaves growing from the base of a stem [C18: from Old French: a little ROSE[1]]

Rosewall ('rəʊz,wɔːl) *n* Ken(neth). born 1934, Australian tennis player: Australian champion 1953, 1955, and 1971–72; US champion 1956 and 1970

rose-water *n* 1 scented water used as a perfume and in cooking, made by the distillation of rose petals or by impregnation with oil of roses 2 (*modifier*) elegant or delicate, esp excessively so

rose window *n* a circular window, esp one that has ornamental tracery radiating from the centre to form a symmetrical roselike pattern. Also called: wheel window, rosette

rosewood ('rəʊz,wʊd) *n* the hard dark wood of any of various tropical and subtropical leguminous trees, esp of the genus *Dalbergia*. It has a roselike scent and is used in cabinetwork

Rosh Hashanah or **Rosh Hashana** ('rɒʃ həˈʃɑːnə; *Hebrew* 'rɒʃ haʃaˈna) *n* the festival marking the Jewish New Year, celebrated on the first and second days of Tishri, and marked by penitential prayers and by the blowing of the shofar [from Hebrew *rōsh hasshānāh*, literally: beginning of the year, from *rōsh* head + *hash-shānāh* year]

Rosicrucian (,rəʊzɪˈkruːʃən) *n* 1 a member of a society professing esoteric religious doctrines, venerating the emblems of the rose and Cross as symbols of Christ's Resurrection and Redemption, and claiming various occult powers ▷ *adj* 2 of, relating to, or designating the Rosicrucians or Rosicrucianism [c17: from Latin *Rosae Crucis* Rose of the Cross, translation of the German name Christian *Rosenkreuz*, supposed founder of the society in the 15th century]

rosin ('rɒzɪn) *n* 1 Also called: colophony a translucent brittle amber substance produced in the distillation of crude turpentine oleoresin and used esp in making varnishes, printing inks, and sealing waxes and for treating the bows of stringed instruments 2 (not in technical usage) another name for **resin** (sense 1) ▷ *vb* 3 (*tr*) to treat or coat with rosin [c14: variant of RESIN] ▷ 'rosiny *adj*

Roskilde (*Danish* 'rɔskilə) *n* a city in Denmark, on NE Zealand west of Copenhagen: capital of Denmark from the 10th century to 1443; scene of the signing (1658) of the **Peace of Roskilde** between Denmark and Sweden. Pop: 44 205 (2004 est)

ROSPA ('rɒspə) *n acronym for* (in Britain) Royal Society for the Prevention of Accidents

Ross (rɒs) *n* 1 **Diana**. born 1944, US singer: lead vocalist (1961–69) with Motown group the Supremes, whose hits include *Baby Love* (1964). Her subsequent recordings include *Lady Sings the Blues* (film soundtrack, 1972), and *Chain Reaction* (1986) 2 **Sir James Clark**. 1800–62, British naval officer; explorer of the Arctic and Antarctic. He located the north magnetic pole (1831) and discovered the Ross Sea during an Antarctic voyage (1839–43) 3 his uncle, **Sir John**. 1777–1856, Scottish naval officer and Arctic explorer 4 **Sir Ronald**. 1857–1932, English bacteriologist, who discovered the transmission of malaria by mosquitoes: Nobel prize for physiology or medicine 1902

Ross and Cromarty (rɒs ənd 'krɒmətɪ) *n* (until 1975) a county of N Scotland, including the island of Lewis and many islets: now split between the Highland and Western Isles council areas

Ross Dependency *n* a section of Antarctica administered by New Zealand. (Claims are suspended under the Antarctic Treaty of 1959). Includes the coastal regions of Victoria Land and King Edward VII Land, the Ross Sea and islands, and the Ross Ice Shelf. Area: about 414 400 sq km (160 000 sq miles)

Rossellini (rɒsəˈliːnɪ) *n* **Roberto**. 1906–77, Italian film director. His films include *Rome, Open City* (1945), *Paisà* (1946), and *L'Amore* (1948)

Rossetti (rɒˈzɛtɪ) *n* 1 **Christina Georgina**. 1830–94, British poet 2 her brother, **Dante Gabriel**. 1828–82, British poet and painter: a leader of the Pre-Raphaelites

Rossini (rɒˈsiːnɪ) *n* **Gioacchino Antonio** (dʒoakˈkiːno anˈtɔːnjo). 1792–1868, Italian composer, esp of operas, such as *The Barber of Seville* (1816) and *William Tell* (1829)

Ross Island *n* an island in the W Ross Sea: contains the active volcano Mount Erebus

Rossiya (raˈsiːjə) *n* transliteration of the Russian name for **Russia**

Ross Sea *n* a large arm of the S Pacific in Antarctica, incorporating the Ross Ice Shelf and lying between Victoria Land and the Edward VII Peninsula

Rostand (*French* rɔstɑ̃) *n* **Edmond** (ɛdmɔ̃). 1868–1918, French playwright and poet in the romantic tradition; best known for his verse drama *Cyrano de Bergerac* (1897)

roster ('rɒstə) *n* 1 a list or register, esp one showing the order of people enrolled for duty ▷ *vb* 2 *marketing* the list of advertising agencies regularly used by a particular company 3 (*tr*) to place on a roster [c18: from Dutch *rooster* grating or list (the lined paper looking like a grid)]

Rostock ('rɒstɒk) *n* a port in NE Germany, in Mecklenburg-West Pomerania on the Warnow estuary 13 km (8 miles) from the Baltic and its outport, Warnemünde: the chief port of the former East Germany; university (1419). Pop: 198 303 (2003 est)

Rostov or **Rostov-on-Don** ('rɒstɒv) *n* a port in S Russia, on the River Don 48 km (30 miles) from the Sea of Azov: industrial centre. Pop: 1 081 000 (2005 est)

Rostropovich (,rɒstrəˈpəʊvɪtʃ) *n* **Mstislav Leopoldovich** ('mɪstɪslɑːv; *Russian* mstiˈslaf leaˈpɔldavitʃ). 1927–2007, Soviet cellist, composer, and conductor; became a US citizen in 1978 after losing Soviet citizenship (restored in 1990)

rostrum ('rɒstrəm) *n*, *pl* -**trums** or -**tra** (-trə) 1 any platform, stage, or dais on which public speakers stand to address an audience 2 a platform or dais in front of an orchestra on which the conductor stands 3 another word for **ram** (sense 5) 4 the prow or beak of an ancient Roman ship 5 *biology, zoology* a beak or beaklike part [c16: from Latin *rōstrum* beak, ship's prow, from *rōdere* to nibble, gnaw; in plural, *rōstra*, orator's platform, because this platform in the Roman forum was adorned with the prows of captured ships]

rosy ('rəʊzɪ) *adj* **rosier**, **rosiest** 1 of the colour rose or pink 2 having a healthy pink complexion: *rosy cheeks* 3 optimistic, esp excessively so: *a rosy view of social improvements* 4 resembling, consisting of, or abounding in roses ▷ 'rosily *adv* ▷ 'rosiness *n*

rot (rɒt) *vb* **rots**, **rotting**, **rotted** 1 to decay or cause to decay as a result of bacterial or fungal action 2 (*intr*; usually foll by *off* or *away*) to fall or crumble (off) or break (away), as from natural decay, corrosive action, or long use 3 (*intr*) to become weak, debilitated, or depressed through inertia, confinement, etc; languish: *rotting in prison* 4 to become or cause to become morally corrupt or degenerate ▷ *n* 5 the process of rotting or the state of being rotten 6 something decomposed, disintegrated, or degenerate. Related adj: **putrid** 7 short for **dry rot** 8 *pathol* any putrefactive decomposition of tissues 9 a condition in plants characterized by breakdown and decay of tissues, caused by bacteria, fungi, etc 10 *vet science* a contagious fungal disease of the feet of sheep characterized by inflammation, swelling, a foul-smelling discharge, and lameness 11 (*also interjection*) nonsense; rubbish [Old English *rotian* (vb); related to Old Norse *rotna*. c13 (noun), from Scandinavian]

rota ('rəʊtə) *n* *chiefly Brit* a register of names showing the order in which people take their turn to perform certain duties [c17: from Latin: a wheel]

Rota ('rəʊtə) *n* *RC Church* the supreme ecclesiastical tribunal for judging cases brought before the Holy See

rotachute ('rəʊtəˌʃuːt) *n* a device serving the same purpose as a parachute, in which the canopy is replaced by freely revolving rotor blades, used for the delivery of stores or recovery of missiles

rotaplane ('rəʊtəˌpleɪn) *n* an aircraft that derives its lift from freely revolving rotor blades

rotary ('rəʊtərɪ) *adj* 1 of, relating to, or operating by rotation 2 turning or able to turn; revolving ▷ *n*, *pl* -**ries** 3 a part of a machine that rotates about an axis 4 *US & Canadian* a roundabout (for traffic) [c18: from Medieval Latin *rotārius*, from Latin *rota* a wheel]

Rotary Club *n* any of the local clubs that form **Rotary International**, an international association of professional and businessmen founded in the US in 1905 to promote community service ▷ **Ro'tarian** *n*, *adj*

rotary engine *n* 1 an internal-combustion engine having radial cylinders that rotate about a fixed crankshaft 2 an engine, such as a turbine or wankel engine, in which power is transmitted directly to rotating components

rotary plough or **rotary tiller** *n* an implement with a series of blades mounted on a power-driven shaft, used to break up soil or weeds

rotary press *n* a machine for printing from a revolving cylinder, or a plate attached to one, usually onto a continuous strip of paper

rotate *vb* (rəʊˈteɪt) **1** to turn or cause to turn around an axis, line, or point; revolve or spin **2** to follow or cause to follow a set order or sequence **3** (of a position, presidency, etc) to pass in turn from one eligible party to each of the other eligible parties **4** (of staff) to replace or be replaced in turn ▷ *adj* (ˈrəʊteɪt) **5** *botany* designating a corolla the united petals of which radiate from a central point like the spokes of a wheel ▷ **roˈtatable** *adj*

rotating (rəʊˈteɪtɪŋ) *adj* **1** revolving around a central axis, line, or point: *the rotating blades of a helicopter* **2** passing in turn to each of two or more eligible parties: *the rotating presidency of the EU*

rotation (rəʊˈteɪʃən) *n* **1** the act of rotating; rotary motion **2** a regular cycle of events in a set order or sequence **3** a planned sequence of cropping according to which the crops grown in successive seasons on the same land are varied so as to make a balanced demand on its resources of fertility **4** *maths* **a** a circular motion of a configuration about a given point or line, without a change in shape **b** a transformation in which the coordinate axes are rotated by a fixed angle about the origin ▷ **roˈtational** *adj*

rotator (rəʊˈteɪtə) *n* **1** a person, device, or part that rotates or causes rotation **2** *anatomy* any of various muscles that revolve a part on its axis

rotator cuff *anatomy* the structure around the shoulder joint consisting of the capsule of the joint along with the tendons of the adjacent muscles

rotatory (ˈrəʊtətərɪ, -trɪ) *or less commonly* **rotative** (ˈrəʊtətɪv) *adj* of, relating to, possessing, or causing rotation

Rotavator *or* **Rotovator** (ˈrəʊtəˌveɪtə) *n* *trademark* a type of machine with rotating blades that will break up soil [c20: original form *Rotavator*, from *rota(ry) (culti)vator*]

Rotblat (ˈrɒtblæt) *n* See **Pugwash conferences**

rote (rəʊt) *n* a habitual or mechanical routine or procedure **1 by rote** by repetition; by heart (often in the phrase **learn by rote**) [c14: origin unknown]

rotenone (ˈrəʊtɪˌnəʊn) *n* a white odourless crystalline substance extracted from the roots of derris: a powerful insecticide. Formula: $C_{23}H_{22}O_6$; relative density: 1.27; melting pt: 163°C [c20: from Japanese *rōten* derris + -ONE]

ROTFL *text messaging abbreviation* rolling on the floor laughing

rotgut (ˈrɒtˌgʌt) *n* *facetious, slang* alcoholic drink, esp spirits, of inferior quality

Roth (rɒθ) *n* **Philip.** born 1933, US novelist. His works include *Goodbye, Columbus* (1959), *Portnoy's Complaint* (1969), *My Life as a Man* (1974), *Sabbath's Theater* (1995), *The Human Stain* (2000), and *The Plot Against America* (2004)

Rotherham (ˈrɒðərəm) *n* **1** an industrial town in N England, in Rotherham unitary authority, South Yorkshire. Pop: 117 262 (2001) **2** a unitary authority in N England, in South Yorkshire. Pop: 251 500 (2003 est). Area: 283 sq km (109 sq miles)

Rothermere (ˈrɒðəˌmɪə) *n* **Viscount.** title of *Harold Sidney Harmsworth*. 1868–1940, British newspaper magnate

Rothesay (ˈrɒθsɪ) *n* a town in SW Scotland, in Argyll and Bute, on the E coast of the Isle of Bute. Pop: 5017 (2001)

Rothko (ˈrɒθkəʊ) *n* **Mark.** 1903–70, US abstract expressionist painter, born in Russia

Rothschild (ˈrɒtʃaɪld, ˈrɒθs-) *n* a powerful family of European Jewish bankers, prominent members of which were **1 Lionel Nathan**, Baron de Rothschild. 1809–79, British banker and first Jewish member of Parliament **2** his grandfather **Meyer Amschel** (ˈmaɪər ˈamʃəl). 1743–1812, German financier and founder of the Rothschild banking firm **3** his son, **Nathan Meyer**, Baron de Rothschild. 1777–1836, British banker, born in Germany

rotifer (ˈrəʊtɪfə) *n* any minute aquatic multicellular invertebrate of the phylum *Rotifera*, having a ciliated wheel-like organ used in feeding and locomotion: common constituents of freshwater plankton. Also called: **wheel animalcule** [c18: from New Latin *Rotifera*, from Latin *rota* wheel + *ferre* to bear] ▷ **rotiferal**

(rəʊˈtɪfərəl) *or* **roˈtiferous** *adj*

rotisserie (rəʊˈtɪsərɪ) *n* **1** a rotating spit on which meat, poultry, etc, can be cooked **2** a shop or restaurant where meat is roasted to order [c19: from French, from Old French *rostir* to ROAST]

rotogravure (ˌrəʊtəʊɡrəˈvjʊə) *n* **1** a printing process using a cylinder etched with many small recesses, from which ink is transferred to a moving web of paper, plastic, etc, in a rotary press **2** printed material produced in this way, esp magazines [c20: from Latin *rota* wheel + GRAVURE]

rotor (ˈrəʊtə) *n* **1** the rotating member of a machine or device, esp the armature of a motor or generator or the rotating assembly of a turbine **2** a device having blades radiating from a central hub that is rotated to produce thrust to lift and propel a helicopter [c20: shortened form of ROTATOR]

Rotorua (ˌrəʊtəˈruːə) *n* a city in New Zealand, on N central North Island at the SW end of Lake Rotorua: centre of forestry; noted for volcanic activity. Pop: 67 800 (2004 est)

rotten (ˈrɒt³n) *adj* **1** affected with rot; decomposing, decaying, or putrid **2** breaking up, esp through age or hard use; disintegrating: *rotten ironwork* **3** morally despicable or corrupt **4** untrustworthy, disloyal, or treacherous **5** *informal* unpleasant, unfortunate, or nasty: *rotten luck; rotten weather* **6** *informal* unsatisfactory or poor: *rotten workmanship* **7** *informal* miserably unwell **8** *informal* distressed, uncomfortable, and embarrassed: *I felt rotten when I told him to go* ▷ *adv* *informal* **9** extremely; very much: *men fancy her rotten* [c13: from Old Norse *rottin*; related to Old English *rotian* to ROT¹] ▷ **ˈrottenly** *adv* ▷ **ˈrottenness** *n*

rotten borough *n* (before the Reform Act of 1832) any of certain English parliamentary constituencies with only a very few electors

rottenstone (ˈrɒt³nˌstəʊn) *n* a much-weathered limestone, rich in silica: used in powdered form for polishing metal

rotter (ˈrɒtə) *n* *slang, chiefly Brit* a worthless, unpleasant, or despicable person

Rotterdam (ˈrɒtəˌdæm) *n* a port in the SW Netherlands, in South Holland province: the second largest city of the Netherlands and one of the world's largest ports; oil refineries, shipbuilding yards, etc Pop: 600 000 (2003 est)

Rottweiler (ˈrɒtˌvaɪlə) *n* **1** a breed of large robustly built dog with a smooth coat of black with dark tan markings on the face, chest, and legs. It was previously a docked breed **2** (*often not capital*) an aggressive, ruthless, and unscrupulous person [German, named after *Rottweil*, German city where the dog was originally bred]

rotund (rəʊˈtʌnd) *adj* **1** rounded or spherical in shape **2** plump **3** sonorous or grandiloquent; full in tone, style of speaking, etc [c18: from Latin *rotundus* wheel-shaped, round, from *rota* wheel] ▷ **roˈtundity** *or* **roˈtundness** *n* ▷ **roˈtundly** *adv*

rotunda (rəʊˈtʌndə) *n* a building or room having a circular plan, esp one that has a dome [c17: from Italian *rotonda*, from Latin *rotundus* round, from *rota* a wheel]

Rouault (ruːˈəʊ; French rwo) *n* **Georges** (ʒɔrʒ). 1871–1958, French expressionist artist. His work is deeply religious; it includes much stained glass

Roubaix (French rubɛ) *n* a city in N France near the Belgian border: forms, with Tourcoing, a large industrial conurbation. Pop: 96 984 (1999)

Roubiliac *or* **Roubillac** (rubijak) *n* **Louis-François** (lwifrɑ̃swa). ?1695–1762, French sculptor: lived chiefly in England: his sculptures include the statue of Handel in Vauxhall Gardens (1737)

rouble *or* **ruble** (ˈruːb³l) *n* **1** the standard monetary unit of Belarus and Russia, divided into 100 kopecks **2** the former standard monetary unit of Tajikistan, divided into 100 tanga [c16: from Russian *rubl* silver bar, from Old Russian *rublĭ* bar, block of wood, from *rubiti* to cut up]

roué (ˈruːeɪ) *n* a debauched or lecherous man; rake [c19: from French, literally: one broken on the wheel, from *rouer*, from Latin *rotāre* to revolve, from *rota* a wheel; with reference to the fate deserved by a debauchee]

r

Rouen (*French* rwɑ̃) *n* a city in N France, on the River Seine: the chief river port of France; became capital of the duchy of Normandy in 912; scene of the burning of Joan of Arc (1431); university (1964). Pop: 106 592 (1999)

rouge (ruːʒ) *n* **1** a red powder, used as a cosmetic for adding redness to the cheeks **2** short for **jeweller's rouge** ▷ *vb* (*tr*) **3** to apply rouge to [c18: from French: red, from Latin *rubeus*]

rouge et noir ('ruːʒ eɪ 'nwɑː; *French* ruʒ e nwar) *n* a card game in which the players put their stakes on any of two red and two black diamond-shaped spots marked on the table [French, literally: red and black]

Rouget de Lisle (*French* ruʒɛ də lil) *n* **Claude Joseph** (klod ʒozɛf). 1760–1836, French army officer: composer of the *Marseillaise* (1792), the French national anthem

rough (rʌf) *adj* **1** (of a surface) not smooth; uneven or irregular **2** (of ground) covered with scrub, boulders, etc **3** denoting or taking place on uncultivated ground: *rough grazing; rough shooting* **4** shaggy or hairy **5** turbulent; agitated: *a rough sea* **6** (of the performance or motion of something) uneven; irregular: *a rough engine* **7** (of behaviour or character) rude, coarse, ill mannered, inconsiderate, or violent **8** harsh or sharp: *rough words* **9** informal severe or unpleasant: *a rough lesson* **10** (of work, a task, etc) requiring physical rather than mental effort **11** informal ill or physically upset: *he felt rough after an evening of heavy drinking* **12** unfair or unjust: *rough luck* **13** harsh or grating to the ear **14** without refinement, luxury, etc **15** not polished or perfected in any detail; rudimentary; not elaborate: *rough workmanship; rough justice* **16** not prepared or dressed: *rough gemstones* **17** (of a guess, estimate, etc) approximate **18** having the sound of *h*; aspirated **19** rough on informal, chiefly Brit **a** severe towards **b** unfortunate for (a person) **20** the rough side of one's tongue harsh words: *a reprimand, rebuke, or verbal attack* ▷ *n* **21** rough ground **22** a sketch or preliminary piece of artwork **23** an unfinished or crude state (esp in the phrase **in the rough**) **24** the rough *golf* the part of the course bordering the fairways where the grass is untrimmed **25** informal a rough or violent person; thug **26** the unpleasant side of something (esp in the phrase **take the rough with the smooth**) ▷ *adv* **27** in a rough manner; roughly **28** sleep rough to spend the night in the open; be without a home or without shelter ▷ *vb* **29** (*tr*) to make rough; roughen **30** (*tr*; foll by *out*, *in*, etc) to prepare (a sketch, report, piece of work, etc) in preliminary form **31** rough it informal to live without the usual comforts or conveniences of life ▷ See also **rough up** [Old English *rūh*; related to Old Norse *ruksa*, Middle Dutch *rūge, rūwe*, German *rauh*] ▷ **'roughly** *adv* ▷ **'roughness** *n*

roughage ('rʌfɪdʒ) *n* **1** the coarse indigestible constituents of food or fodder, which provide bulk to the diet and promote normal bowel function **2** any rough or coarse material

rough-and-ready *adj* **1** crude, unpolished, or hastily prepared, but sufficient for the purpose **2** (of a person) without formality or refinement; rudely vigorous

rough-and-tumble *n* **1** a fight or scuffle without rules ▷ *adj* **2** characterized by roughness, disorderliness, and disregard for rules or conventions

rough breathing *n* (in Greek) the sign (') placed over an initial letter, or a second letter if the word begins with a diphthong, indicating that (in ancient Greek) it was pronounced with an *h*

roughcast ('rʌf,kɑːst) *n* **1** a coarse plaster used to cover the surface of an external wall **2** any rough or preliminary form, model, etc ▷ *adj* **3** covered with or denoting roughcast ▷ *vb* -casts, -casting, -cast **4** to apply roughcast to (a wall, etc) **5** to prepare in rough ▷ **'rough,caster** *n*

rough-cut *n* a first edited version of a film with the scenes in sequence and the soundtrack synchronized

rough diamond *n* **1** an unpolished diamond **2** an intrinsically trustworthy or good person with uncouth manners or dress

rough-dry *adj* **1** (of clothes or linen) dried ready for pressing ▷ *vb* -dries, -drying, -dried **2** (*tr*) to dry (clothes or linen) without smoothing or pressing

roughen ('rʌfᵊn) *vb* to make or become rough

rough-hew *vb* -hews, -hewing, -hewed, -hewed *or* -hewn (*tr*) to cut or hew (timber, stone, etc) roughly without finishing the surface

roughhouse ('rʌf,haʊs) *n* slang rough, disorderly, or noisy behaviour

roughish ('rʌfɪʃ) *adj* somewhat rough

roughneck ('rʌf,nɛk) *n* slang **1** a rough or violent person; thug **2** a worker on an oil-drilling operation

rough puff pastry *n* a rich flaky pastry made with butter and used for pie-crusts, flans, etc

roughrider ('rʌf,raɪdə) *n* a rider of wild or unbroken horses

roughshod ('rʌf,ʃɒd) *adj* **1** (of a horse) shod with rough-bottomed shoes to prevent sliding ▷ *adv* **2** ride roughshod over to domineer over or act with complete disregard for

rough stuff *n* informal violence

rough trade *n* slang (in homosexual use) a tough or violent sexual partner, esp a lorry driver, construction worker, or docker, casually picked up

rough up *vb* (*tr, adverb*) **1** informal to treat violently; beat up **2** to cause (feathers, hair, etc) to stand up by rubbing against the grain

roulade (ruːˈlɑːd) *n* **1** a slice of meat rolled, esp around a stuffing, and cooked **2** an elaborate run in vocal music [c18: from French, literally: a rolling, from *rouler* to ROLL]

Roulers (ruːˈlɛəz; *French* rulɛrs) *n* a city in NW Belgium, in West Flanders province: electronics. Pop: 55 273 (2004 est). Flemish name: **Roeselare**

roulette (ruːˈlɛt) *n* **1** a gambling game in which a ball is dropped onto a spinning horizontal wheel divided into 37 or 38 coloured and numbered slots, with players betting on the slot into which the ball will fall **2** a toothed wheel for making a line of perforations **3** a curve generated by a point on one curve rolling on another ▷ *vb* (*tr*) **4** to use a roulette on (something), as in engraving, making stationery, etc [c18: from French, from *rouelle* a little wheel, from *roue* a wheel, from Latin *rota*]

Roumania (ruːˈmeɪnɪə) *n* a variant of **Romania** ▷ **Rou'manian** *n, adj*

round (raʊnd) *adj* **1** having a flat circular shape, as a disc or hoop **2** having the shape of a sphere or ball **3** curved; not angular **4** involving or using circular motion **5** (prenominal) complete; entire: *a round dozen* **6** maths **a** forming or expressed by an integer or whole number, with no fraction **b** expressed to the nearest ten, hundred, or thousand: *in round figures* **7** (of a sum of money) considerable; ample **8** fully depicted or developed, as a character in a book **9** full and plump: *round cheeks* **10** (of sound) full and sonorous **11** (of pace) brisk; lively **12** (prenominal) (of speech) candid; straightforward; unmodified: *a round assertion* **13** (of a vowel) pronounced with rounded lips ▷ *n* **14** a round shape or object **15** in the round **a** in full detail **b** theatre with the audience all round the stage **16** a session, as of a negotiation: *a round of talks* **17** a series, cycle, or sequence: *a giddy round of parties* **18** the daily round the usual activities of one's life: *he was eliminated in the first round* **20** (often plural) a series of calls, esp in a set order: *a doctor's rounds; a milkman's round* **21** a playing of all the holes on a golf course **22** a single turn of play by each player, as in a card game **23** one of a number of periods constituting a boxing, wrestling, or other match, each usually lasting three minutes **24** a single discharge by a number of guns or a single gun **25** a bullet, blank cartridge, or other charge of ammunition **26** a number of drinks bought at one time for a group of people **27** a single slice of bread or toast or two slices making a single serving of sandwiches **28** a general outburst of applause, cheering, etc **29** movement in a circle or around an axis **30** music a part song in which the voices follow each other at equal intervals at the same pitch **31** a sequence of bells rung in order of treble to tenor **32** a cut of beef from the thigh between the rump and the shank **33** go the rounds *or* make the rounds **a** to go from place to place, as in making deliveries or social calls **b** (of information,

rumour, etc) to be passed around, so as to be generally known ▷ *prep* **34** surrounding, encircling, or enclosing: *a band round her head* **35** on all or most sides of: *to look round one* **36** on or outside the circumference or perimeter of **37** from place to place in: *driving round Ireland* **38** reached by making a partial circuit about something: *the shop round the corner* **39** revolving round a centre or axis: *the earth's motion round its axis* ▷ *adv* **40** on all or most sides **41** on or outside the circumference or perimeter: *the racing track is two miles round* **42** to all members of a group: *pass the food round* **43** in rotation or revolution: *the wheels turn round* **44** by a circuitous route: *the road to the farm goes round by the pond* **45** to a specific place: *she came round to see me* **46** all year round throughout the year; in every month ▷ *vb* **47** to make or become round **48** (*tr*) to encircle; surround **49** to move or cause to move with circular motion: *to round a bend* **50** (*tr*) **a** to pronounce (a speech sound) with rounded lips **b** to purse (the lips) ▷ See also **round down, round off**, etc [c13: from Old French *ront*, from Latin *rotundus* round, from *rota* a wheel] > 'roundish *adj* > 'roundness *n*
⦿ USAGE See at **around**

roundabout ('raʊndə,baʊt) *n* **1** *Brit* a revolving circular platform provided with wooden animals, seats, etc, on which people ride for amusement; merry-go-round **2** a road junction in which traffic streams circulate around a central island ▷ *adj* **3** indirect or circuitous; devious ▷ *adv* round about *prep* **4** on all sides: *spectators standing round about* **5** approximately: *at round about 5 o'clock*

round dance *n* **1** a dance in which the dancers form a circle **2** a ballroom dance, such as the waltz, in which couples revolve

round down *vb* (*tr, adverb*) to lower (a number) to the nearest whole number or ten, hundred, or thousand below it

rounded ('raʊndɪd) *adj* **1** round or curved **2** full, mature, or complete **3** (of the lips) pursed, as in pronouncing the sound (u:) **4** (of a speech sound) articulated with rounded lips

roundel ('raʊndªl) *n* **1** a form of rondeau consisting of three stanzas each of three lines with a refrain after the first and the third **2** a circular identifying mark in national colours on military aircraft **3** a small ornamental circular window, panel, medallion, plate, disc, etc **4** a round plate of armour used to protect the armpit **5** another word for **roundelay** (sense 1) [c13: from Old French *rondel* a little circle; see RONDEL]

roundelay ('raʊndɪ,leɪ) *n* **1** Also called: **roundel** a slow medieval dance performed in a circle **2** a song in which a line or phrase is repeated as a refrain [c16: from Old French *rondelet* a little rondel, from *rondel*; also influenced by LAY⁴]

rounders ('raʊndəz) *n* (*functioning as singular*) *Brit* a ball game in which players run between posts after hitting the ball, scoring a 'rounder' if they run round all four before the ball is retrieved

round file *slang* ▷ *n* **1** a wastepaper basket ▷ *vb* round-file **2** (*tr*) to throw into a wastepaper basket; discard; reject

Roundhead ('raʊnd,hɛd) *n* *English history* a supporter of Parliament against Charles I during the Civil War [referring to their short-cut hair]

roundhouse ('raʊnd,haʊs) *n* **1** a circular building in which railway locomotives are serviced or housed, radial tracks being fed by a central turntable **2** *boxing slang* a swinging punch or style of punching **3** an obsolete word for **jail** **4** *obsolete* a cabin on the quarterdeck of a sailing ship

rounding ('raʊndɪŋ) *n* *computing* a process in which a number is approximated as the closest number that can be expressed using the number of bits or digits available

roundly ('raʊndlɪ) *adv* **1** frankly, bluntly, or thoroughly: *to be roundly criticized* **2** in a round manner or so as to be round

round off *vb* (*tr, adverb*) **1** (often foll by *with*) to bring to a satisfactory conclusion; complete, esp agreeably: *we rounded off the evening with a brandy* **2** to make round or less jagged

round on *vb* (*intr, preposition*) to attack or reply to (someone) with sudden irritation or anger

round robin *n* **1** a letter, esp a petition or protest, having the signatures in a circle in order to disguise the order of signing **2** *US & Canadian* a tournament, as in a competitive game or sport, in which each player plays against every other player

round-shouldered *adj* denoting a faulty posture characterized by drooping shoulders and a slight forward bending of the back

roundsman ('raʊndzmən) *n, pl* -men **1** *Brit* a person who makes rounds, as for inspection or to deliver goods **2** *Austral & NZ* a reporter covering a particular district or topic

round table *n* **a** a meeting of parties or people on equal terms for discussion **b** (*as modifier*): *a round-table conference*

Round Table the Round Table *n* **1** (in Arthurian legend) the table of King Arthur, shaped so that his knights could sit around it without any having precedence **2** Arthur and his knights collectively **3** one of an organization of clubs of young business and professional men who meet in order to further social and business activities and charitable work

round-the-clock *adj* (*or as adverb* **round the clock**) throughout the day and night

round tower *n* a freestanding circular stone belfry built in Ireland from the 10th century beside a monastery and used as a place of refuge

round trip *n* a trip to a place and back again, esp returning by a different route

roundtripping ('raʊnd,trɪpɪŋ) *n* *finance* a form of trading in which a company borrows a sum of money from one source and takes advantage of a short-term rise in interest rates to make a profit by lending it to another

round up *vb* (*tr, adverb*) **1** to gather (animals, suspects, etc) together: *to round ponies up* **2** to raise (a number) to the nearest whole number or ten, hundred, or thousand above it ▷ *n* roundup the act of gathering together livestock, esp cattle, so that they may be branded, counted, or sold **4** any similar act of collecting or bringing together: *a roundup of today's news*

roundworm ('raʊnd,wɜːm) *n* any nematode worm, esp *Ascaris lumbricoides*, a common intestinal parasite of man and pigs

roup (raʊp) *Scot & northern English dialect* ▷ *vb* (*tr*) **1** to sell by auction ▷ *n* **2** an auction [c16 (originally: to shout): of Scandinavian origin; compare Icelandic *raupa* to boast]

rouse (raʊz) *vb* **1** to bring (oneself or another person) out of sleep, unconsciousness, etc, or (of a person) to come to consciousness in this way **2** (*tr*) to provoke, stir, or excite: *to rouse someone's anger* **3** rouse oneself to become active or energetic **4** *hunting* to start or cause to start from cover: *to rouse game birds* **5** (*intr*) *falconry* (of hawks) to ruffle the feathers and cause them to stand briefly on end (a sign of contentment) **6** (raʊs) (*intr*; foll by *on*) *Austral* to speak scoldingly or rebukingly (to) [c15 (in sense 5): origin obscure] > 'rouser *n*

rouseabout ('raʊsə,baʊt) *n* *Austral & NZ* an unskilled labourer in a shearing shed. Also called: **roustabout**

rousing ('raʊzɪŋ) *adj* tending to rouse or excite; lively, brisk, or vigorous: *a rousing chorus* > 'rousingly *adv*

Rousseau (French ruso) *n* **1 Henri** (ãri), known as **le Douanier**. 1844–1910, French painter, who created bold dreamlike pictures, often of exotic landscapes in a naive style. Among his works are *Sleeping Gypsy* (1897) and *Jungle with a Lion* (1904–06). He also worked as a customs official **2 Jean Jacques** (ʒã ʒak). 1712–78, French philosopher and writer, born in Switzerland, who strongly influenced the theories of the French Revolution and the romantics. Many of his ideas spring from his belief in the natural goodness of man, whom he felt was warped by society. His works include *Du contrat social* (1762), *Émile* (1762), and his *Confessions* (1782) **3 Théodore** (teɔdɔr). 1812–67, French landscape painter: leader of the Barbizon school

Roussillon (French rusijõ) *n* a former province of S France: united with Aragon in 1172; passed to the French crown in 1659; now forms part of the region of Languedoc-Roussillon

roust (raʊst) *vb* (*tr*; often foll by *out*) to rout or stir, as out of bed [c17: perhaps an alteration of ROUSE]

roustabout (ˈraʊstəˌbaʊt) n 1 an unskilled labourer on an oil rig 2 Austral another word for **rouseabout**

rout¹ (raʊt) n 1 an overwhelming defeat 2 a disorderly retreat 3 a noisy rabble 4 law a group of three or more people proceeding to commit an illegal act 5 archaic a large party or social gathering ▷ vb 6 (tr) to defeat and cause to flee in confusion [C13: from Anglo-Norman rute, from Old French: disorderly band, from Latin ruptus broken, from rumpere to burst; see ROUTE]

rout² (raʊt) vb 1 to dig over or turn up (something), esp (of an animal) with the snout; root 2 (tr; usually foll by out or up) to get or find by searching 3 (tr; usually foll by out) to force or drive out: they routed him out of bed at midnight 4 (tr; often foll by out) to hollow or gouge out 5 (intr) to search, poke, or rummage [C16: variant of ROOT²]

route (ruːt) n 1 the choice of roads taken to get to a place 2 a regular journey travelled 3 (capital) US a main road between cities: Route 66 ▷ vb routes, routing or routeing, routed (tr) 4 to plan the route of; send by a particular route [C13: from Old French rute, from Vulgar Latin rupta via (unattested), literally: a broken (established) way, from Latin ruptus broken, from rumpere to break, burst]

● USAGE When forming the present participle or verbal
● noun from the verb to route it is preferable to retain
● the e in order to distinguish the word from routing, the
● present participle or verbal noun from rout¹, to defeat
● or rout², to dig, rummage: the routeing of buses from the city
● centre to the suburbs. The spelling routing in this sense is,
● however, sometimes encountered, esp in American
● English

routemarch (ˈruːtˌmɑːtʃ) n 1 military a long training march 2 informal any long exhausting walk

router (ˈraʊtə) n any of various tools or machines for hollowing out, cutting grooves, etc

routine (ruːˈtiːn) n 1 a usual or regular method of procedure, esp one that is unvarying 2 computing a program or part of a program performing a specific function: an input routine; an output routine 3 a set sequence of dance steps 4 informal a hackneyed or insincere speech ▷ adj 5 of, relating to, or characteristic of routine [C17: from Old French, from route a customary way, ROUTE] > rouˈtinely adv

roux (ruː) n, pl roux a mixture of equal amounts of fat and flour, heated, blended, and used as a basis for sauces [C19: from French: brownish, from Latin russus RUSSET]

ROV abbreviation remotely operated vehicle

rove¹ (rəʊv) vb 1 to wander about (a place) with no fixed direction; roam 2 (intr) (of the eyes) to look around; wander ▷ n 3 the act of roving [C15 roven (in archery) to shoot at a target chosen at random (C16: to wander, stray), from Scandinavian; compare Icelandic ráfa to wander]

rove² (rəʊv) vb 1 (tr) to pull out and twist (fibres of wool, cotton, etc) lightly, as before spinning or in carding ▷ n 2 wool, cotton, etc, thus prepared [C18: of obscure origin]

rove³ (rəʊv) vb a past tense and past participle of **reeve**²

rover¹ (ˈrəʊvə) n 1 a person who roves; wanderer 2 archery a mark selected at random for use as a target 3 Australian rules football one of the three players in the ruck, usually smaller than the other two, selected for his agility in play [C15: from ROVE¹]

rover² (ˈrəʊvə) n a pirate or pirate ship [C14: probably from Middle Dutch or Middle Low German, from roven to rob]

Rover or **Rover Scout** (ˈrəʊvə) n Brit the former name for **Venture Scout**

roving commission n authority or power given in a general area, without precisely defined terms of reference

row¹ (rəʊ) n 1 an arrangement of persons or things in a line: a row of chairs 2 chiefly Brit a street, esp a narrow one lined with identical houses 3 a line of seats, as in a cinema, theatre, etc 4 maths a horizontal linear arrangement of numbers, quantities, or terms, esp in a determinant or matrix 5 a horizontal rank of squares on a chessboard or draughtboard 6 in a row in succession; one after the other: he won two gold medals in a row 7 a hard

row to hoe a difficult task or assignment [Old English rāw, rǣw; related to Old High German rīga line, Lithuanian raiwe strip]

row² (rəʊ) vb 1 to propel (a boat) by using oars 2 (tr) to carry (people, goods, etc) in a rowing boat 3 to be propelled by means of (oars or oarsmen) 4 (intr) to take part in the racing of rowing boats as a sport, esp in eights, in which each member of the crew pulls one oar 5 (tr) to race against in a boat propelled by oars: Oxford row Cambridge every year ▷ n 6 an act, instance, period, or distance of rowing 7 an excursion in a rowing boat [Old English rōwan; related to Middle Dutch roien, Middle High German rüejen, Old Norse rōa, Latin rēmus oar] > ˈrower n

row³ (raʊ) n 1 a noisy quarrel or dispute 2 a noisy disturbance; commotion: we couldn't hear the music for the row next door 3 a reprimand ▷ vb 4 (intr; often foll by with) to quarrel noisily 5 (tr) archaic to reprimand [C18: origin unknown]

rowan (ˈrəʊən, ˈraʊ-) n another name for the (European) **mountain ash** [C16: from Scandinavian; compare Norwegian rogn, raun, Old Norse reynir]

rowdy (ˈraʊdɪ) adj -dier, -diest 1 tending to create noisy disturbances; rough, loud, or disorderly: a rowdy gang of football supporters ▷ n, pl -dies 2 a person who behaves in a rough disorderly fashion [C19: originally US slang, perhaps related to ROW³] > ˈrowdily adv > ˈrowdiness n > ˈrowdyism n

Rowe (rəʊ) n Nicholas. 1674–1718, English dramatist, who produced the first critical edition of Shakespeare; poet laureate (1715–18). His plays include Tamerlane (1702) and The Fair Penitent (1703)

rowel (ˈraʊəl) n 1 a small spiked wheel attached to a spur 2 vet science obsolete a piece of leather or other material inserted under the skin of a horse to allow drainage ▷ vb -els, -elling, -elled or US -els, -eling, -eled (tr) 3 to goad (a horse) using a rowel 4 vet science obsolete to insert a rowel in (the skin of a horse) to allow drainage [C14: from Old French roel a little wheel, from roe a wheel, from Latin rota]

rowing boat (ˈrəʊɪŋ) n chiefly Brit a small boat propelled by one or more pairs of oars

rowing machine n a device with oars and a sliding seat resembling a sculling boat, used to provide exercise

Rowlandson (ˈrəʊləndsən) n Thomas. 1756–1827, English caricaturist, noted for the vigour of his attack on sordid aspects of contemporary society and on statesmen such as Napoleon

Rowley (ˈrəʊlɪ, ˈraʊ-) n Thomas. ?1586–?1642, English dramatist, who collaborated with John Ford and Thomas Dekker on The Witch of Edmonton (1621) and with Thomas Middleton on The Changeling (1622)

Rowling (ˈrəʊlɪŋ) n J(oanne) K(athleen). born 1965, British novelist; author of the bestselling series of children's books featuring the boy wizard Harry Potter, which began with Harry Potter and the Philosopher's Stone (1995)

rowlock (ˈrɒlək) n a swivelling device attached to the gunwale of a boat that holds an oar in place and acts as a fulcrum during rowing. Usual US and Canadian word: oarlock

Roxas y Acuña (Spanish ˈroxas i aˈkuɲa) n Manuel (maˈnwel). 1892–1948, Philippine statesman; first president of the Republic of the Philippines (1946–48)

Roxburghshire (ˈrɒksbərəʃɪə, -ʃə) n (until 1975) a county of SE Scotland, now part of Scottish Borders council area

royal (ˈrɔɪəl) adj 1 of, relating to, or befitting a king, queen, or other monarch; regal 2 (prenominal; often capital) established, chartered by, under the patronage or in the service of royalty: the Royal Society of St George 3 being a member of a royal family 4 above the usual or normal in standing, size, quality, etc 5 informal unusually good or impressive; first-rate 6 nautical just above the topgallant (in the phrase **royal mast**) ▷ n 7 (sometimes capital) informal a member of a royal family 8 Also called: royal stag a stag with antlers having 12 or more branches 9 nautical a sail set next above the topgallant, on a royal mast 10 a size of printing paper, 20 by 25 inches [C14: from Old French roial, from Latin rēgālis, fit for a king, from *rēx* king; compare REGAL] ⊳ 'royally *adv*

Royal Academy *n* a society founded by George III in 1768 to foster a national school of painting, sculpture, and design in England. Full name: Royal Academy of Arts

Royal Air Force *n* the air force of the United Kingdom. Abbreviation: RAF

Royal and Ancient Club *n* the Royal and Ancient Club a golf club, headquarters of the sport's ruling body, based in St Andrews, Scotland

royal assent *n* (in Britain) the formal signing of an act of Parliament by the sovereign, by which it becomes law

royal blue *n* **a** a deep blue colour **b** (*as adjective*): *a royal-blue carpet*

Royal British Legion *n* Brit an organization founded in 1921 to provide services and assistance for former members of the armed forces

Royal Commission *n* (in Britain) a body set up by the monarch on the recommendation of the prime minister to gather information about the operation of existing laws or to investigate any social, educational, or other matter. The commission has prescribed terms of reference and reports to the government on how any change might be achieved

royal fern *n* a fern, *Osmunda regalis*, of damp regions, having large fronds up to 2 metres (7 feet) in height, some of which are modified for bearing spores: family *Osmundaceae*

royal flush *n* poker a hand made up of the five top honours of a suit

royalist ('rɔɪəlɪst) *n* **1** a supporter of a monarch or monarchy, esp a supporter of the Stuarts during the English Civil War **2** *informal* an extreme reactionary or conservative: *an economic royalist* ⊳ *adj* Also: royalistic **3** of, characteristic of, or relating to royalists ⊳ 'royalism *n*

royal jelly *n* a substance secreted by the pharyngeal glands of worker bees and fed to all larvae when very young or to larvae destined to become queens throughout their development

Royal Leamington Spa *n* the official name of **Leamington Spa**

Royal Marines *pl n* Brit a corps of soldiers specially trained in amphibious warfare. Abbreviation: RM

Royal Mint *n* a British organization having the sole right to manufacture coins since the 16th century. In 1968 it moved from London to Llantrisant in Wales

Royal National Theatre *n* a theatre complex in London, on the S bank of the Thames (opened 1976). The prefix Royal was added in 1988. It houses the Royal National Theatre Company

Royal Navy *n* the navy of the United Kingdom. Abbreviation: RN

royal palm *n* any of several palm trees of the genus *Roystonea*, esp *R. regia*, of tropical America, having a tall trunk with a tuft of feathery pinnate leaves

Royal Standard *n* a flag bearing the arms of the British sovereign, flown only when she (or he) is present

royal tennis *n* another name for **real tennis**

royalty ('rɔɪəltɪ) *n*, *pl* -ties **1** the rank, power, or position of a king or queen **2 a** royal persons collectively **b** one who belongs to the royal family **3** any quality characteristic of a monarch; kingliness or regal dignity **4** a percentage of the revenue from the sale of a book, performance of a theatrical work, use of a patented invention or of land, etc, paid to the author, inventor, or proprietor

royal warrant *n* an authorization to a tradesman to supply goods to a royal household

Royce (rɔɪs) *n* Josiah. 1855–1916, US philosopher of monistic idealism. In his ethical studies he emphasized the need for individual loyalty to the world community

rozzer ('rɒzə) *n* Cockney slang a policeman [C19: of unknown origin]

RPG *abbreviation* report program generator: a business-oriented computer programming language

RPI *abbreviation* (in Britain) retail price index

rpm *abbreviation* **1** revolutions per minute **2** resale price maintenance

RPV *abbreviation* remotely piloted vehicle

RR *abbreviation* **1** Right Reverend **2** (in the US and Canada) railroad **3** (in the US and Canada) rural route

-rrhagia *n combining form* (in pathology) an abnormal discharge or flow: *menorrhagia* [from Greek *-rrhagia* a bursting forth, from *rhēgnunai* to burst, break]

-rrhoea *or esp US* **-rrhea** *n combining form* (in pathology) a discharge or flow: *diarrhoea* [from New Latin, from Greek *-rrhoia*, from *rhoia* a flowing, from *rhein* to flow]

rRNA *abbreviation* ribosomal RNA

RRP *abbreviation* recommended retail price

RRSP *abbreviation* (in Canada) Registered Retirement Savings Plan

Rs *symbol for* rupees

RS *abbreviation* (in Britain) Royal Society

RSA *abbreviation* **1** Republic of South Africa **2** Royal Scottish Academy **3** Royal Scottish Academician **4** Royal Society of Arts **5** (in New Zealand) Returned Services Association

RSFSR *abbreviation* (formerly) Russian Soviet Federative Socialist Republic

RSI *abbreviation* repetitive strain (or stress) injury

RSL *abbreviation* (in Australia) Returned Services League

RSM *abbreviation* **1** regimental sergeant major **2** Royal School of Music **3** Royal Society of Medicine

RSNZ *abbreviation* Royal Society of New Zealand

RSPB *abbreviation* (in Britain) Royal Society for the Protection of Birds

RSPCA *abbreviation* (in Britain and Australia) Royal Society for the Prevention of Cruelty to Animals

RSS *abbreviation* **1 a** Rich Site Summary: a way of allowing web users to receive news headlines and updates on their browser from selected websites as soon as they are published **b** (*as modifier*): *an RSS newsfeed* **2** Really Simple Syndication: a way of allowing web users to receive syndicated newsletters and email alerts

RSV *abbreviation* Revised Standard Version (of the Bible)

RSVP *abbreviation* répondez s'il vous plaît [French: please reply]

rt *abbreviation* right

RTE *abbreviation* Radio Telefís Éireann [Irish Gaelic: Irish Radio and Television]

Rt Hon. *abbreviation* Right Honourable

RTS *abbreviation* real-time strategy: (of computer games, especially military) taking place in real time

Ru *the chemical symbol for* ruthenium

RU *abbreviation* Rugby Union

Ruanda-Urundi (ru'ændəʊ'rʊndɪ) *n* a former territory of central Africa: part of German East Africa from 1890; a League of Nations mandate under Belgian administration from 1919; a United Nations trusteeship from 1946; divided into the independent states of Rwanda and Burundi in 1962

rub (rʌb) *vb* rubs, rubbing, rubbed **1** to apply pressure and friction to (something) with a circular or backward and forward motion **2** to move (something) with pressure along, over, or against (a surface) **3** to chafe or fray **4** (*tr*) to bring into a certain condition by rubbing: *rub it clean* **5** (*tr*) to spread with pressure, esp in order to cause to be absorbed: *he rubbed ointment into his back* **6** (*tr*) to mix (fat) into flour with the fingertips, as in making pastry **7** (foll by *off, out, away*, etc) to remove or be removed by rubbing **8** bowls (of a bowl) to be slowed or deflected by an uneven patch on the green **9** (*tr*; often foll by *together*) to move against each other with pressure and friction (esp in the phrases **rub one's hands**, often a sign of glee, anticipation, or satisfaction, and **rub noses**, a greeting among the Inuit) **10** rub up the wrong way to arouse anger (in); annoy ⊳ *n* **11** the act of rubbing **12** the rub an obstacle or difficulty (esp in the phrase **there's the rub**) **13** something that hurts the feelings or annoys; rebuke **14** bowls an uneven patch in the green ⊳ See also **rub along, rub down,** etc [C15: perhaps from Low German *rubben*, of obscure origin]

Rub' al Khali ('rʊb æl 'kɑːlɪ) *n* a desert in S Arabia, mainly in Saudi Arabia, extending southeast from Nejd to Hadramaut and northeast from Yemen to the United Arab Emirates. Area: about 777 000 sq km (300 000 sq miles). English names: Great Sandy Desert, Empty Quarter Also called: Ar Rimal

r

rub along *vb* (*intr, adverb*) *Brit* **1** to continue in spite of difficulties **2** to maintain an amicable relationship; not quarrel

rubato (ruːˈbɑːtəʊ) *music* ▷ *n, pl* -tos **1** flexibility of tempo in performance ▷ *adj, adv* **2** to be played with a flexible tempo [C19: from the Italian phrase *tempo rubato*, literally: stolen time, from *rubare* to ROB]

rubber[1] (ˈrʌbə) *n* **1** Also called: India rubber, gum elastic, caoutchouc a cream to dark brown elastic material obtained by coagulating and drying the latex from certain plants, esp the tree *Hevea brasiliensis* **2** any of a large variety of elastomers produced by improving the properties of natural rubber or by synthetic means **3** *chiefly Brit* a piece of rubber or felt used for erasing something written, typed, etc; eraser **4** a cloth, pad, etc, used for polishing or buffing **5** a person who rubs something in order to smooth, polish, or massage **6** (*often plural*) *chiefly US & Canadian* a rubberized waterproof article, such as a mackintosh or overshoe **7** *slang* a male contraceptive; condom **8** (*modifier*) made of or producing rubber: *a rubber ball; a rubber factory* [C17: from RUB + -ER[1]; the tree was so named because its product was used for rubbing out writing] > **rubbery** *adj*

rubber[2] (ˈrʌbə) *n* **1** *bridge, whist* **a** a match of three games **b** the deal that wins such a match **2** a series of matches or games in any of various sports [C16: origin unknown]

rubber band *n* a continuous loop of thin rubber, used to hold papers, etc, together. Also called: elastic band

rubber cement *n* any of a number of adhesives made by dissolving rubber in a solvent such as benzene

rubberize *or* **rubberise** (ˈrʌbəˌraɪz) *vb* (*tr*) to coat or impregnate with rubber

rubberneck (ˈrʌbəˌnɛk) *slang* ▷ *n* **1** a person who stares or gapes inquisitively, esp in a naive or foolish manner **2** a sightseer or tourist ▷ *vb* **3** (*intr*) to stare in a naive or foolish manner

rubber plant *n* **1** a moraceous plant, *Ficus elastica*, with glossy leathery leaves: a tall tree in India and Malaya, it is cultivated as a house plant in Europe and America **2** any of several tropical trees, the sap of which yields rubber

rubber stamp *n* **1** a device used for imprinting dates or commonly used phrases on forms, invoices, etc **2** automatic authorization of a payment, proposal, etc, without challenge **3** a person who makes such automatic authorizations; a person or person of little account ▷ *vb* rubber-stamp (*tr*) **4** to imprint (forms, invoices, etc) with a rubber stamp **5** *informal* to approve automatically

rubber tree *n* a tropical American euphorbiaceous tree, *Hevea brasiliensis*, cultivated throughout the tropics, esp in Malaya, for the latex of its stem, which is the major source of commercial rubber

rubbing (ˈrʌbɪŋ) *n* an impression taken of an incised or raised surface, such as a brass plate on a tomb, by laying paper over it and rubbing with wax, graphite, etc

rubbing alcohol *n* a liquid usually consisting of 70 per cent denatured ethyl alcohol, used by external application as an antiseptic or rubefacient

rubbish (ˈrʌbɪʃ) *n* **1** worthless, useless, or unwanted matter **2** discarded or waste matter; refuse **3** foolish words or speech; nonsense ▷ *vb* **4** (*tr*) *informal* to criticize; attack verbally [C14 *robys*, of uncertain origin]

rubble (ˈrʌbᵊl) *n* **1** fragments of broken stones, bricks, etc **2** any fragmented solid material, esp the debris from ruined buildings **3** Also called: rubblework masonry constructed of broken pieces of rock, stone, etc [C14 *robyl*; perhaps related to Middle English *rubben* to rub, or to RUBBISH] > **rubbly** *adj*

Rubbra (ˈrʌbrə) *n* (**Charles**) **Edmund**. 1901–86, English composer of works in a traditional idiom

rubby (ˈrʌbɪ) *n, pl* -bies *Canadian slang* **1** rubbing alcohol, esp when mixed with cheap wine for drinking **2** a person who drinks such mixtures, esp a derelict alcoholic

rub down *vb* (*adverb*) **1** to dry or clean (a horse, athlete, oneself, etc) vigorously, esp after exercise **2** to make or become smooth by rubbing **3** (*tr*) to prepare (a surface) for painting by rubbing it with sandpaper ▷ *n* rubdown

4 the act of rubbing down

rube (ruːb) *n* *US & Canadian slang* an unsophisticated countryman [C20: probably from the name *Reuben*]

rubella (ruːˈbɛlə) *n* a mild contagious viral disease, somewhat similar to measles, characterized by cough, sore throat, skin rash, and occasionally vomiting. It can cause congenital defects if caught during the first three months of pregnancy. Also called: German measles [C19: from New Latin, from Latin *rubellus* reddish, from *rubeus* red]

rubellite (ˈruːbɪˌlaɪt, ruːˈbɛl-) *n* a red transparent variety of tourmaline, used as a gemstone [C18: from Latin *rubellus* reddish]

Rubens (ˈruːbɪnz) *n* Sir **Peter Paul**. 1577–1640, Flemish painter, regarded as the greatest exponent of the Baroque: appointed (1609) painter to Archduke Albert of Austria, who gave him many commissions, artistic and diplomatic. He was knighted by Charles I of England in 1629. His prolific output includes the triptych in Antwerp Cathedral, *Descent from the Cross* (1611–14), *The Rape of the Sabines* (1635), and his *Self-Portrait* (?1639)

rubeola (ruːˈbiːələ) *n* technical name for **measles** [C17: from New Latin, from Latin *rubeus* reddish, from *ruber* red]

Rubicon (ˈruːbɪkən) *n* **1** a stream in N Italy: in ancient times the boundary between Italy and Cisalpine Gaul. By leading his army across it and marching on Rome in 49 BC, Julius Caesar broke the law that a general might not lead an army out of the province to which he was posted and so committed himself to civil war with the senatorial party **2** (*sometimes not capital*) a point of no return **3** a penalty in piquet by which the score of a player who fails to reach 100 points in six hands is added to his opponent's **4** cross the Rubicon *or* pass the Rubicon to commit oneself irrevocably to some course of action

rubicund (ˈruːbɪkənd) *adj* of a reddish colour; ruddy; rosy [C16: from Latin *rubicundus*, from *rubēre* to be ruddy, from *ruber* red] > **rubicundity** (ˌruːbɪˈkʌndɪtɪ) *n*

rubidium (ruːˈbɪdɪəm) *n* a soft highly reactive radioactive element of the alkali metal group; the 16th most abundant element in the earth's crust (310 parts per million), occurring principally in pollucite, carnallite, and lepidolite. It is used in electronic valves, photocells, and special glass. Symbol: Rb; atomic no: 37; atomic wt: 85.4678; half-life of ^{87}Rb: 5 × 10^{11} years; valency: 1, 2, 3, or 4; relative density: 1.532 (solid), 1.475 (liquid); melting pt: 39.48°C; boiling pt: 688°C [C19: from New Latin, from Latin *rubidus* dark red, with reference to the two red lines in its spectrum] > **ru'bidic** *adj*

rubidium-strontium dating *n* a technique for determining the age of minerals based on the occurrence in natural rubidium of a fixed amount of the radioisotope ^{87}Rb which decays to the stable strontium isotope ^{87}Sr with a half-life of 4.7 × 10^{11} years. Measurement of the ratio of these isotopes thus gives the age of a mineral, for ages of up to about 4 × 10^9 years

rubiginous (ruːˈbɪdʒɪnəs) *adj* rust-coloured [C17: from Latin *rūbiginōsus*, from *rūbīgō* rust, from *ruber* red]

rub in *vb* (*tr, adverb*) **1** to spread with pressure, esp in order to cause to be absorbed **2** rub it in *informal* to harp on (something distasteful to a person, of which he or she does not wish to be reminded)

Rubinstein (ˈruːbɪnˌstaɪn) *n* **1** **Anton Grigorevich** (anˈtɔn griˈgɔrjivitʃ). 1829–94, Russian composer and pianist **2** **Artur** (ˈartur). 1886–1982, US pianist, born in Poland

ruble (ˈruːbᵊl) *n* a variant spelling of **rouble**

Rublyov (*Russian* ˈrubljɒv) *or* **Rublev** *n* **Andrey** (ˈandre). ?1370–1430, Russian icon painter. His masterpiece is *The Old Testament Trinity*

rub off *vb* **1** to remove or be removed by rubbing **2** (*intr*; often foll by *on* or *onto*) to have an effect through close association or contact, esp so as to make similar: *her crude manners have rubbed off on you*

rub out *vb* (*tr, adverb*) **1** to remove or be removed with a rubber **2** *US slang* to murder

rubric (ˈruːbrɪk) *n* **1** a title, heading, or initial letter in a book, manuscript, or section of a legal code, esp one printed or painted in red ink or in some similarly distinguishing manner **2** a set of rules of conduct or procedure **3** a set of directions for the conduct of Christian church services, often printed in red in a prayer book or missal [C15 *rubrike* red ochre, red lettering, from Latin *rubrīca* (*terra*) red (earth), ruddle, from *ruber* red] > '**rubrical** *adj* > '**rubrically** *adv*

ruby ('ru:bɪ) *n, pl* **-bies 1** a deep red transparent precious variety of corundum: occurs naturally in Myanmar and Sri Lanka but is also synthesized. It is used as a gemstone, in lasers, and for bearings and rollers in watchmaking. Formula: Al_2O_3 **2** the deep-red colour of a ruby **b** (*as adjective*): *ruby lips* **3** a something resembling, made of, or containing a ruby **b** (*as modifier*): *ruby necklace* **4** (*modifier*) denoting a fortieth anniversary: *our ruby wedding* [C14: from Old French *rubi*, from Latin *rubeus* reddish, from *ruber* red]

RUC *abbreviation* (the former) Royal Ulster Constabulary, now superseded by the Police Service of Northern Ireland

ruche *or* **rouche** (ru:ʃ) *n* a strip of pleated or frilled lawn, lace, etc, used to decorate blouses, dresses, etc, or worn around the neck like a small ruff as in the 16th century [C19: from French, literally: beehive, from Medieval Latin *rūsca* bark of a tree, of Celtic origin]

ruching ('ru:ʃɪŋ) *n* **1** material used for a ruche **2** a ruche or ruches collectively

ruck¹ (rʌk) *n* **1** a large number or quantity; mass, esp of ordinary or undistinguished people or things **2** (in a race) a group of competitors who are well behind the leaders at the finish **3** *rugby* a loose scrum that forms around the ball when it is on the ground **4** *Australian rules football* the three players, two ruckmen and a rover, that do not have fixed positions but follow the ball closely ▷ *vb* **5** (*intr*) *rugby* to try to win the ball by advancing over it when it is on the ground, driving opponents backward in the process [C13 (meaning "heap of firewood"): perhaps from Scandinavian; compare Old Norse *hraukr* RICK¹]

ruck² (rʌk) *n* **1** a wrinkle, crease, or fold ▷ *vb* **2** (usually foll by *up*) to become or make wrinkled, creased, or puckered [C18: from Scandinavian; related to Old Norse *hrukka*]

ruckman ('rʌk.mæn, -mən) *n, pl* **-men** *Australian rules football* a person who plays in the ruck

ruck-rover *n* *Australian rules football* a player playing a role midway between that of the rover and the ruckman

rucksack ('rʌk.sæk) *n* a large bag, usually having two straps and a supporting frame, carried on the back and often used by climbers, campers, etc. US and Canadian name: backpack [C19: from German, literally: back sack]

ruckus ('rʌkəs) *n, pl* **-uses** *informal* an uproar; ruction [C20: from RUCTION + RUMPUS]

ruction ('rʌkʃən) *n* *informal* **1** an uproar; noisy or quarrelsome disturbance **2** (*plural*) a violent and unpleasant row; trouble [C19: perhaps changed from INSURRECTION]

rudaceous (ru:'deɪʃəs) *adj* (of conglomerate, breccia, and similar rocks) composed of coarse-grained material. See arenaceous (sense 1) [C20: from Latin *rudis* coarse, rough + -ACEOUS]

Ruda Śląska ('ru:də 'ʃlɑnskə) *n* a town in SW Poland: coalmining. Pop: 144 914 (2007 est)

rudbeckia (rʌd'bɛkɪə) *n* any plant of the North American genus *Rudbeckia*, cultivated for their showy flowers, which have golden-yellow rays and green or black conical centres: family *Asteraceae* (composites). See also black-eyed Susan [C18: New Latin, named after Olaus *Rudbeck* (1630–1702), Swedish botanist]

rudd (rʌd) *n* a European freshwater cyprinid fish, *Scardinius erythrophthalmus*, having a compressed dark greenish body and reddish ventral and tail fins [C17: probably from dialect *rud* red colour, from Old English *rudu* redness]

Rudd (rʌd) *n* **1 Kevin.** born 1957, Australian politician: leader of the Australian Labor Party from 2005; prime minister from 2007 **2 Steele,** pen name of *Arthur Hoey Davis*, 1868–1935, Australian author. His works include *On Our Selection* (1899), *Our New Selection* (1902), *Back at Our Selection* (1906), and *Grandpa's Selection* (1916) which

featured the characters Dad and Dave

rudder ('rʌdə) *n* **1** *nautical* a pivoted vertical vane that projects into the water at the stern of a vessel and can be controlled by a tiller, wheel, or other apparatus to steer the vessel **2** a vertical control surface attached to the rear of the fin used to steer an aircraft, in conjunction with the ailerons **3** anything that guides or directs [Old English *rōther*; related to Old French *rōther*, Old High German *ruodar*, Old Norse *rōthr*. See ROW²] > '**rudderless** *adj*

rudderpost ('rʌdə.pəʊst) *n* *nautical* **1** Also called: rudderstock ('rʌdə.stɒk) a postlike member at the forward edge of a rudder **2** the part of the stern frame of a vessel to which a rudder is fitted

ruddle ('rʌdəl), **raddle** *or* **reddle** *n* **1** a red ochre, used esp to mark sheep ▷ *vb* **2** (*tr*) to mark (sheep) with ruddle [C16: diminutive formed from Old English *rudu* redness; see RUDD]

ruddy ('rʌdɪ) *adj* **-dier, -diest 1** (of the complexion) having a healthy reddish colour, usually resulting from an outdoor life **2** coloured red or pink: *a ruddy sky* ▷ *adv, adj informal, chiefly Brit* **3** (*intensifier*) bloody; damned: *a ruddy fool* [Old English *rudig*, from *rudu* redness (see RUDD); related to Old High German *rot* RED², Swedish *rod*, Old Norse *rythga* to make rusty] > '**ruddily** *adv* > '**ruddiness** *n*

rude (ru:d) *adj* **1** insulting or uncivil; discourteous; impolite **2** lacking refinement; coarse or uncouth **3** vulgar or obscene: *a rude joke* **4** unexpected and unpleasant: *a rude awakening to the facts of economic life* **5** roughly or crudely made: *we made a rude shelter on the island* **6** rough or harsh in sound, appearance, or behaviour **7** humble or lowly **8** (*prenominal*) robust or sturdy: *in rude health* **9** (*prenominal*) approximate or imprecise: *a rude estimate* [C14: via Old French from Latin *rudis* coarse, unformed] > '**rudely** *adv* > '**rudeness** *or informal* '**rudery** *n*

ruderal ('ru:dərəl) *n* **1** a plant that grows on waste ground ▷ *adj* **2** growing in waste places [C19: from New Latin *rūderālis*, from Latin *rūdus* rubble]

rudiment ('ru:dɪmənt) *n* **1** (*often plural*) the first principles or elementary stages of a subject **2** (*often plural*) a partially developed version of something **3** *biology* an organ or part in its earliest recognizable form, esp one in an embryonic or vestigial state [C16: from Latin *rudīmentum* a beginning, from *rudis* unformed; see RUDE]

rudimentary (.ru:dɪ'mɛntərɪ) *or less commonly* **rudimental** *adj* **1** basic; fundamental; not elaborated or perfected **2** incompletely developed; vestigial: *rudimentary leaves* > .rudi'mentarily *or less commonly* .rudi'mentally *adv*

rudish ('ru:dɪʃ) *adj* somewhat rude

Rudolf¹ ('ru:dɒlf) *n* Lake Rudolf the former name (until 1979) of (Lake) Turkana

Rudolf² *or* **Rudolph** ('ru:dɒlf) *n* 1858–89, archduke of Austria, son of emperor Franz Joseph: he and his mistress committed suicide at the royal hunting lodge in Mayerling

Rudolf I *or* **Rudolph I** ('ru:dɒlf) *n* 1218–91, king of Germany (1273–91): founder of the Hapsburg dynasty based on the duchies of Styria and Austria

rue¹ (ru:) *vb* **rues, ruing, rued 1** to feel sorrow, remorse, or regret for (one's own wrongdoing, past events with unpleasant consequences, etc) ▷ *n* **2** *archaic* sorrow, pity, or regret [Old English *hrēowan*; related to Old Saxon *hreuwan*, Old High German *hriuwan*] > '**ruer** *n*

rue² (ru:) *n* any rutaceous plant of the genus *Ruta*, esp *R. graveolens*, an aromatic Eurasian shrub with small yellow flowers and evergreen leaves which yield an acrid volatile oil, formerly used medicinally as a narcotic and stimulant [C14: from Old French, from Latin *rūta*, from Greek *rhutē*]

rueful ('ru:fʊl) *adj* **1** feeling or expressing sorrow or repentance: *a rueful face* **2** inspiring sorrow or pity > '**ruefully** *adv* > '**ruefulness** *n*

ruff¹ (rʌf) *n* **1** a circular pleated, gathered, or fluted collar of lawn, muslin, etc, often starched or wired, worn by both men and women in the 16th and 17th centuries **2** a natural growth of long or coloured hair or feathers around the necks of certain animals or birds **3 a** an Old World shore bird, *Philomachus pugnax*, the male of which has a large erectile ruff of feathers in the breeding season: family *Scolopacidae* (sandpipers, etc), order *Charadriiformes* **b** the male of this bird [c16: back formation from RUFFLE[1]] > 'ruff,like *adj*

ruff[2] (rʌf) *n cards* **1** (*also verb*) another word for **trump**[1] **2** an old card game similar to whist [c16: from Old French *roffle*; perhaps changed from Italian *trionfa* TRUMP[1]]

ruffe or **ruff** (rʌf) *n* a European freshwater teleost fish, *Acerina cernua*, having a single spiny dorsal fin: family *Percidae* (perches) [c15: perhaps an alteration of ROUGH (referring to its scales)]

ruffian ('rʌfɪən) *n* a violent or lawless person; hoodlum or villain [c16: from Old French *rufien*, from Italian *ruffiano*, perhaps related to Langobardic *hruf* scurf, scabbiness] > 'ruffianism *n* > 'ruffianly *adj*

ruffle[1] ('rʌfᵊl) *vb* **1** to make, be, or become irregular or rumpled: *to ruffle a child's hair; a breeze ruffling the water* **2** to annoy, irritate, or be annoyed or irritated **3** (*tr*) to make into a ruffle; pleat **4** (of a bird) to erect (its feathers) in anger, display, etc **5** (*tr*) to flick (cards, pages, etc) rapidly with the fingers ▷ *n* **6** an irregular or disturbed surface **7** a strip of pleated material used for decoration or as a trim **8** *zoology* another name for **ruff**[1] (sense 2) **9** annoyance or irritation [c13: of Germanic origin; compare Middle Low German *ruffelen* to crumple, Old Norse *hrufla* to scratch]

ruffle[2] ('rʌfᵊl) *n* **1** a low continuous drumbeat ▷ *vb* **2** (*tr*) to beat (a drum) with a low repetitive beat [c18: from earlier *ruff*, of imitative origin]

rufous ('ruːfəs) *adj* reddish-brown [c18: from Latin *rūfus*]

rug (rʌg) *n* **1** a floor covering, smaller than a carpet and made of thick wool or of other material, such as an animal skin **2** *chiefly Brit* a blanket, esp one used as a wrap or lap robe for travellers **3** *slang* a wig **4** pull the rug out from under to betray, expose, or leave defenceless [c16: from Scandinavian; compare Norwegian *rugga*, Swedish *rugg* coarse hair. See RAG[1]]

ruga ('ruːgə) *n*, *pl* **-gae** (-dʒiː) (*usually plural*) *anatomy* a fold, wrinkle, or crease [c18: Latin]

rugby or **rugby football** ('rʌgbɪ) *n* **1** Also called: **rugger** a form of football played with an oval ball in which the handling and carrying of the ball is permitted **2** *Canadian* another name for **Canadian football** ▷ See also **rugby league**, **rugby union** [c19: named after the public school at Rugby, where it was first played]

Rugby ('rʌgbɪ) *n* a town in central England, in E Warwickshire: famous public school, founded in 1567. Pop: 61 988 (2001)

rugby head *n NZ derogatory, slang* a male follower of rugby culture

rugby league *n* a form of rugby football played between teams of 13 players

rugby union *n* a form of rugby football played between teams of 15 players

rugged ('rʌgɪd) *adj* **1** having an uneven or jagged surface **2** rocky or steep: *rugged scenery* **3** (of the face) strong-featured or furrowed **4** rough, severe, or stern in character **5** without refinement or culture; rude: *rugged manners* **6** involving hardship; harsh: *he leads a rugged life in the mountains* **7** difficult or hard: *a rugged test* **8** (of equipment, machines, etc) designed to withstand rough treatment or use in rough conditions **9** *chiefly US & Canadian* sturdy or strong; robust [c14: from Scandinavian; compare Swedish *rugga* to make rough] > 'ruggedly *adv* > 'ruggedness *n*

rugger ('rʌgə) *n chiefly Brit* an informal name for **rugby**

rugose ('ruːgəʊs, -gəʊz), **rugous** or **rugate** ('ruːgeɪt, -gɪt) *adj* wrinkled: *rugose leaves* [c18: from Latin *rūgōsus*, from *rūga* a wrinkle] > 'rugosely *adv* > rugosity (ruː'gɒsɪtɪ) *n*

rug rat *n US & Canadian informal* a child not yet walking

Ruhr (rʊə; *German* ruːr) *n* the chief coalmining and industrial region of Germany: in North Rhine-Westphalia around the valley of the **River Ruhr** (a tributary of the Rhine 235 km (146 miles) long)

ruin ('ruːɪn) *n* **1** destroyed or decayed building or town **2** the state or condition of being destroyed or decayed

3 loss of wealth, position, etc, or something that causes such loss; downfall **4** something that is severely damaged: *his life was a ruin* **5** a person who has suffered a downfall, bankruptcy, etc **6** *archaic* loss of her virginity by a woman outside marriage ▷ *vb* **7** (*tr*) to bring to ruin; destroy **8** (*tr*) to injure or spoil: *the town has been ruined with tower blocks* **9** (*intr*) *archaic or poetic* to fall into ruins; collapse [c14: from Old French *ruine*, from Latin *ruīna* a falling down, from *ruere* to fall violently]

ruination (,ruːɪ'neɪʃən) *n* **1** the act of ruining or the state of being ruined **2** something that causes ruin

ruinous ('ruːɪnəs) *adj* causing, tending to cause, or characterized by ruin or destruction > 'ruinously *adv* > 'ruinousness *n*

Ruisdael or **Ruysdael** ('riːzdɑːl, -deɪl, 'raɪz-; *Dutch* 'rœɪzdaːl) *n* **Jacob van** ('jaːkɔp van). ?1628–82, Dutch landscape painter

rule (ruːl) *n* **1** an authoritative regulation or direction concerning method or procedure, as for a court of law, legislative body, game, or other human institution or activity: *judges' rules; play according to the rules* **2** the exercise of governmental authority or control: *the rule of Caesar* **3** the period of time in which a monarch or government has power: *his rule lasted 100 days* **4** a customary form or procedure; regular course of action: *he made a morning swim his rule* **5** the rule the common order of things; normal condition: *violence was the rule rather than the exception* **6** a prescribed method or procedure for solving a mathematical problem, or one constituting part of a computer program, usually expressed in an appropriate formalism **7** any of various devices with a straight edge for guiding or measuring; ruler: *a carpenter's rule* **8 a** a printed or drawn character in the form of a long thin line **b** another name for **dash**[1] (sense 12) *en rule*; *em rule* **c** a strip of brass or other metal used to print such a line **9** *Christianity* a systematic body of prescriptions defining the way of life to be followed by members of a religious order **10** *law* an order by a court or judge **11** as a rule normally or ordinarily ▷ *vb* **12** to exercise governing or controlling authority over (a people, political unit, individual, etc) **13** (when *tr*, often takes a clause as object) to decide authoritatively; decree: *the chairman ruled against the proposal* **14** (*tr*) to mark with straight parallel lines or make one straight line, as with a ruler **15** (*tr*) to restrain or control **16** (*intr*) to be customary or prevalent: *chaos rules in this school* **17** (*intr*) to be pre-eminent or superior: *football rules in the field of sport* **18** rule the roost or rule the roast to be pre-eminent; be in charge [c13: from Old French *riule*, from Latin *rēgula* a straight edge; see REGULATE] > 'rulable *adj*

rule of three *n* a mathematical rule asserting that the value of one unknown quantity in a proportion is found by multiplying the denominator of each ratio by the numerator of the other

rule of thumb *n* **a** a rough and practical approach, based on experience, rather than a scientific or precise one based on theory **b** (*as modifier*): *a rule-of-thumb decision*

rule out *vb* (*tr, adverb*) **1** to dismiss from consideration **2** to make impossible; preclude or prevent

ruler ('ruːlə) *n* **1** a person who rules or commands **2** Also called: **rule** a strip of wood, metal, or other material, having straight edges graduated usually in millimetres or inches, used for measuring and drawing straight lines

Rules (ruːlz) *pl n* **1** short for **Australian Rules** **2** the Rules *English history* the neighbourhood around certain prisons (esp the Fleet and King's Bench prison) in which trusted prisoners were allowed to live under specified restrictions

ruling ('ruːlɪŋ) *n* **1** a decision of someone in authority, such as a judge **2** one or more parallel ruled lines ▷ *adj* **3** controlling or exercising authority **4** prevalent or predominant

rum[1] (rʌm) *n* spirit made from sugar cane, either coloured brownish-red by the addition of caramel or by maturation in oak containers, or left white [c17: perhaps shortened from c16 *rumbullion*, of uncertain origin]

rum[2] (rʌm) *adj* **rummer**, **rummest** *Brit slang* strange; peculiar; odd [c19: perhaps from Romany *rom* man]

> 'rumly adv > 'rumness n

Rumania (ru:'meɪnɪə) n a variant of **Romania**
> Ru'manian adj, n

rumba or **rhumba** ('rʌmbə, 'rʊm-) n 1 a rhythmic and syncopated Cuban dance in duple time 2 a ballroom dance derived from this 3 a piece of music composed for or in the rhythm of this dance [c20: from Spanish: lavish display, of uncertain origin]

rumble ('rʌmbəl) vb 1 to make or cause to make a deep resonant sound: *thunder rumbled in the sky* 2 to move with such a sound: *the train rumbled along* 3 (tr) to utter with a rumbling sound: *he rumbled an order* 4 (tr) Brit informal to find out about (someone or something); discover (something): *the police rumbled their plans* 5 (intr) US slang to be involved in a gang fight ▷ n 6 a deep resonant sound 7 a widespread murmur of discontent 8 US, Canadian & NZ slang a gang fight [c14: perhaps from Middle Dutch *rummelen*; related to German *rummeln, rumpeln*] > 'rumbler n > 'rumbling adj

rumble seat n US & Canadian a folding outside seat at the rear of some early cars; dicky

rumbustious (rʌm'bʌstjəs) adj boisterous or unruly [c18: probably a variant of ROBUSTIOUS] > rum'bustiously adv > rum'bustiousness n

rumen ('ru:mɛn) n, pl -mens or -mina (-mɪnə) the first compartment of the stomach of ruminants, behind the reticulum, in which food is partly digested before being regurgitated as cud [c18: from Latin: throat, gullet]

Rumford ('rʌmfəd) n Count Rumford See **Thompson** (sense 1)

ruminant ('ru:mɪnənt) n 1 any artiodactyl mammal of the suborder *Ruminantia*, the members of which chew the cud and have a stomach of four compartments, one of which is the rumen. The group includes deer, antelopes, cattle, sheep, and goats 2 any other animal that chews the cud, such as a camel ▷ adj 3 of, relating to, or belonging to the suborder *Ruminantia* 4 (of members of this suborder and related animals, such as camels) chewing the cud; ruminating 5 meditating or contemplating in a slow quiet way

ruminate ('ru:mɪˌneɪt) vb 1 (of ruminants) to chew (the cud) 2 (when intr, often foll by upon, on, etc) to meditate or ponder (upon) [c16: from Latin *rūmināre* to chew the cud, from RUMEN] > ,rumi'nation n > 'ruminative adj > 'ruminatively adv > 'rumi,nator n

rummage ('rʌmɪdʒ) vb 1 (when intr, often foll by through) to search (through) while looking for something, often causing disorder or confusion ▷ n 2 an act of rummaging 3 a jumble of articles [c14 (in the sense: to pack a cargo): from Old French *arrumage*, from *arrumer* to stow in a ship's hold, probably of Germanic origin] > 'rummager n

rummage sale n 1 Also called (in Britain and certain other countries) **jumble sale** 2 US a sale of unclaimed property or unsold stock

rummer ('rʌmə) n a drinking glass, typically having an ovoid bowl on a short stem [c17: from Dutch *roemer* a glass for drinking toasts, from *roemen* to praise]

rummy ('rʌmɪ) or **rum** n a card game based on collecting sets and sequences [c20: perhaps from RUM²]

rumour or US **rumor** ('ru:mə) n 1 a information, often a mixture of truth and untruth, passed around verbally b (in combination): *a rumour-monger* 2 gossip or hearsay ▷ vb 3 (tr; usually passive) to pass around or circulate in the form of a rumour: *it is rumoured that the Queen is coming* [c14: via Old French *rumour*, from Latin *rūmor* common talk; related to Old Norse *rymja* to roar, Sanskrit *rāut* he cries]

rump (rʌmp) n 1 the hindquarters of a mammal, not including the legs 2 the rear part of a bird's back, nearest to the tail 3 a person's buttocks 4 Also called: **rump steak** a cut of beef from behind the loin and above the round 5 an inferior remnant [c15: from Scandinavian; compare Danish *rumpe*, Icelandic *rumpr*, German *Rumpf* trunk of the body] > 'rumpless adj

Rumpelstiltskin (ˌrʌmpəl'stɪltskɪn) n a dwarf in a German folktale who aids the king's bride on condition that she give him her first child or guess the dwarf's name. She guesses correctly and in his rage he destroys himself

rumple ('rʌmpəl) vb 1 to make or become wrinkled, crumpled, ruffled, or dishevelled ▷ n 2 a wrinkle, fold, or crease [c17: from Middle Dutch *rompelen*; related to Old English *gerumpen* creased, wrinkled] > 'rumply adj

rumpo ('rʌmpəʊ) n slang sexual intercourse

Rump Parliament or **the Rump** n English history the remainder of the Long Parliament after Pride's Purge. It sat from 1648–53

rumpus ('rʌmpəs) n, pl -puses a noisy, confused, or disruptive commotion [c18: of unknown origin]

rumpus room n US, Canadian & NZ a room used for noisy activities, such as parties or children's games

rumpy-pumpy ('rʌmpɪ'pʌmpɪ) n informal sexual intercourse

Rumsfeld ('rʌmsˌfɛlt, 'rʌmz-) n Donald H. born 1932, US Republican politician and businessman: US Secretary of Defense (2001–06)

run (rʌn) vb runs, running, ran, run 1 (intr) a (of a two-legged creature) to move on foot at a rapid pace so that both feet are off the ground together for part of each stride b (of a four-legged creature) to move at a rapid gait; gallop or canter 2 (tr) to pass over (a distance, route, etc) in running: *to run a mile; run a race* 3 (intr) to run in or finish a race as specified, esp in a particular position: *John is running third* 4 (tr) to perform or accomplish by or as if by running: *to run an errand* 5 (intr) to flee; run away 6 (tr) to bring into a specified state or condition by running: *to run oneself to a standstill* 7 (tr) to track down or hunt (an animal): *to run a fox to earth* 8 (tr) to set (animals) loose on (a field or tract of land) so as to graze freely 9 (intr; often foll by over, round or up) to make a short trip or brief informal visit: *I'll run over to your house this afternoon* 10 to move quickly and easily on wheels by rolling, or in any of certain other ways: *a ball running along the ground; a sledge running over snow* 11 to move or cause to move with a specified result or in a specified manner: *to run a ship aground; to run into a tree* 12 (often foll by over) to move or pass or cause to move or pass quickly: *to run a vacuum cleaner over the carpet; to run one's eyes over a page* 13 (tr; foll by into, out of, through, etc) to force, thrust, or drive: *she ran a needle into her finger* 14 (tr) to drive or maintain and operate (a vehicle) 15 (tr) to give a lift to (someone) in a vehicle; transport: *he ran her to the railway station* 16 to ply or cause to ply between places on a route: *the bus runs from Piccadilly to Golders Green* 17 to operate or be operated; function or cause to function: *the engine is running smoothly* 18 (tr) to perform or carry out: *to run tests* 19 to extend or continue or cause to extend or continue in a particular direction, for a particular duration or distance, etc: *the road runs north; the play ran for two years; the months ran into years* 20 (intr) law to have legal force or effect: *the lease runs for two more years* 21 (tr) to be subjected to, be affected by, or incur: *to run a risk; run a temperature* 22 (intr; often foll by to) to be characterized (by); tend or incline: *her taste runs to extravagant hats; to run to fat* 23 (intr) to recur persistently or be inherent: *red hair runs in my family* 24 to cause or allow (liquids) to flow or (of liquids) to flow, esp in a manner specified: *water ran from the broken pipe; the well has run dry* 25 (intr) to melt and flow: *the wax grew hot and began to run* 26 metallurgy a to melt or fuse b (tr) to mould or cast (molten metal): *to run lead into ingots* 27 (intr) (of waves, tides, rivers, etc) to rise high, surge, or be at a specified height: *a high sea was running that night* 28 (intr) to be diffused: *the colours in my dress ran when I washed it* 29 (intr) (of stitches) to unravel or come undone or (of a garment) to have stitches unravel or come undone 30 to sew (an article) with continuous stitches 31 (intr) (of growing vines, creepers, etc) to trail, spread, or climb: *ivy running over a cottage wall* 32 (intr) to spread or circulate quickly: *a rumour ran through the town* 33 (intr) to be stated or reported: *his story runs as follows* 34 to publish or print or be published or printed in a newspaper, magazine, etc: *they ran his story in the next issue* 35 (often foll by for) chiefly US & Canadian to be a candidate or present as a candidate for political or other office: *Anderson is running for president* 36 (tr) to get past or through; evade: *to run a blockade* 37 (tr) to deal in (arms, etc), esp by importing illegally: *he runs guns for the rebels* 38 nautical to sail (a vessel, esp a sailing vessel) or (of such a vessel) to be sailed with the wind coming from astern **39** (*intr*) (of fish) to migrate upstream from the sea, esp in order to spawn **40** (*tr*) *cricket* to score (a run or number of runs) by hitting the ball and running between the wickets **41** (*tr*) *billiards, snooker* to make (a number of successful shots) in sequence **42** (*tr*) *golf* to hit (the ball) so that it rolls along the ground **43** (*tr*) *bridge* to cash (all one's winning cards in a long suit) successively ▷ *n* **44** an act, instance, or period of running **45** a gait, pace, or motion faster than a walk: *she went off at a run* **46** a distance covered by running or a period of running: *a run of ten miles* **47** an act, instance, or period of travelling in a vehicle, esp for pleasure: *to go for a run in the car* **48** free and unrestricted access: *we had the run of the house and garden for the whole summer* **49 a** a period of time during which a machine, computer, etc, operates **b** the amount of work performed in such a period **50** a continuous or sustained period: *a run of good luck* **51** a continuous sequence of performances: *the play had a good run* **52** *cards* a sequence of winning cards in one suit, usually more than five: *a run of spades* **53** tendency or trend: *the run of the market* **54** type, class, or category: *the usual run of graduates* **55** (usually foll by *on*) a continuous and urgent demand: *a run on butter; a run on the dollar* **56** a series of unravelled stitches, esp in stockings or tights; ladder **57** the characteristic pattern or direction of something: *the run of the grain on a piece of wood* **58 a** a period during which water or other liquid flows **b** the amount of such a flow **59** a pipe, channel, etc, through which water or other liquid flows **60** *US* a small stream **61** a steeply inclined pathway or course, esp a snow-covered one used for skiing and bobsleigh racing **62** an enclosure for domestic fowls or other animals, in which they have free movement: *a chicken run* **63** (esp in Australia and New Zealand) a tract of land for grazing livestock **64** the migration of fish upstream in order to spawn **65** *military* a mission in a warplane **66** the movement of an aircraft along the ground during takeoff or landing **67** *music* a rapid scalelike passage of notes **68** *cricket* a score of one, normally achieved by both batsmen running from one end of the wicket to the other after one of them has hit the ball **69** *baseball* an instance of a batter touching all four bases safely, thereby scoring **70** *golf* the distance that a ball rolls after hitting the ground **71** a run for one's money **a** a strong challenge or close competition **b** pleasure derived from an activity **72** in the long run as the eventual outcome of a sequence of events, actions, etc; ultimately **73** in the short run as the immediate outcome of a series of events, etc **74** on the run **a** escaping from arrest; fugitive **b** in rapid flight; retreating: *the enemy is on the run* **c** hurrying from place to place: *she's always on the run* **75** the runs *slang* diarrhoea ▷ See also **runabout, run across**, etc [Old English *runnen*, past participle of (*ge*)*rinnan*; related to Old Frisian *runnen*, Old Norse *rinna*, Old Saxon, Gothic, Old High German *rinnan*]

runabout (ˈrʌnəˌbaʊt) *n* **1** a small car, esp one for use in a town ▷ *vb* run about **2** (*intr, adverb*) to move busily from place to place

run across *vb* (*intr, preposition*) to meet unexpectedly; encounter by chance

run along *vb* (*intr, adverb*) (often said patronizingly) to go away; leave

run around *vb* (*intr, adverb*) *informal* **1** (often foll by *with*) to associate habitually (with) **2** to behave in a fickle or promiscuous manner ▷ *n* run-around **3** *informal* deceitful or evasive treatment of a person (esp in the phrase *give* or *get the run-around*)

run away *vb* (*intr, adverb*) **1** to take flight; escape **2** to go away; depart **3** (of a horse) to gallop away uncontrollably **4** run away with **a** to abscond or elope with: *he ran away with his boss's daughter* **b** to make off with; steal **c** to escape from the control of: *his enthusiasm ran away with him* **d** to win easily or be assured of victory in (a competition): *he ran away with the race* ▷ *n* runaway **5 a** a person or animal that runs away **b** (*as modifier*): *a runaway horse* **6** the act or an instance of running away **7** (*modifier*) occurring as a result of the act of eloping: *a runaway wedding* **8** (*modifier*) (of a race, victory, etc) easily

won: *a runaway ten-shot victory*

runcible spoon (ˈrʌnsɪbəl) *n* a forklike utensil with two broad prongs and one sharp curved prong [*runcible* coined by Edward Lear in a nonsense poem (1871)]

Runcie (ˈrʌnsɪ) *n* **Robert** (**Alexander Kennedy**), Baron. 1921–2000, Archbishop of Canterbury (1980–91)

Runcorn (ˈrʌŋkɔːn) *n* a town in NW England, in Halton unitary authority, N Cheshire, on the Manchester Ship Canal: port and industrial centre; designated a new town in 1964. Pop: 60 072 (2001)

run down *vb* (*mainly adverb*) **1** to cause or allow (an engine, battery, etc) to lose power gradually and cease to function or (of an engine, battery, etc) to do this **2** to decline or reduce in number or size: *the firm ran down its sales force* **3** (*tr, usually passive*) to tire, sap the strength of, or exhaust: *he was thoroughly run down and needed a holiday* **4** (*tr*) to criticize adversely; denigrate; decry **5** (*tr*) to hit and knock to the ground with a moving vehicle **6** *nautical* (*tr*) to collide with and cause to sink **7** (*tr*) to pursue and find or capture: *to run down a fugitive* **8** (*tr*) to read swiftly or perfunctorily: *he ran down their list of complaints* ▷ *adj* run-down **9** tired; exhausted **10** worn-out, shabby, or dilapidated ▷ *n* rundown **11** a brief review, résumé, or summary **12** the process of a motor or mechanism coming gradually to a standstill after the source of power is removed **13** a reduction in number or size

Rundstedt (ˈrʊndstɛt; *German* ˈrʊntʃtɛt) *n* **Karl Rudolf Gerd von** (karl ˈruːdɔlf ɡɛrt fɔn). 1875–1953, German field marshal; directed the conquest of Poland and France in World War II; commander of the Western Front (1942–44); led the Ardennes counteroffensive (Dec 1944)

rune (ruːn) *n* **1** any of the characters of an ancient Germanic alphabet, derived from the Roman alphabet, in use, esp in Scandinavia, from the 3rd century AD to the end of the Middle Ages. Each character was believed to have a magical significance **2** any obscure piece of writing using mysterious symbols **3** a kind of Finnish poem or a stanza in such a poem [Old English *rūn*, from Old Norse *rūn* secret; related to Old Saxon, Old High German, Gothic *runa*] > ˈrunic *adj*

Runeberg (*Finnish* ˈruːnəˌbɜːɡ) (ˈrunəˌbærj) *n* **Johan Ludvig** 1804–77, Finnish poet, who wrote in Swedish. His works include the epic *King Fialar* (1844) and patriotic poems including the Finnish national anthem

rung[1] (rʌŋ) *n* **1** one of the bars or rods that form the steps of a ladder **2** a crosspiece between the legs of a chair, etc **3** *nautical* a spoke on a ship's wheel or a handle projecting from the periphery [Old English *hrung*; related to Old High German *runga*, Gothic *hrugga*] > ˈrungless *adj*

rung[2] (rʌŋ) *vb* the past participle of **ring**[2]

⊚ USAGE See at **ring**[2]

run in *vb* (*adverb*) **1** to run (an engine) gently, usually for a specified period when it is new, in order that the running surfaces may become polished **2** (*tr*) to insert or include **3** (*intr*) (of an aircraft) to approach a point or target **4** (*tr*) *informal* to take into custody; arrest ▷ *n* run-in **5** *informal* an argument or quarrel **6** an approach to the end of an event, etc: *the run-in to the championship* **7** *printing* matter inserted in an existing paragraph

run into *vb* (*preposition; mainly intr*) **1** (*also tr*) to collide with or cause to collide with: *her car ran into a tree* **2** to encounter unexpectedly **3** (*also tr*) to be beset by or cause to be beset by: *the project ran into financial difficulties* **4** to extend to; be of the order of: *debts running into thousands*

runnel (ˈrʌnəl) *n* *literary* a small stream [c16: from Old English *rynele*; related to **run**]

runner (ˈrʌnə) *n* **1** a person who runs, esp an athlete **2** a messenger for a bank or brokerage firm **3** a person engaged in the solicitation of business **4** a person on the run; fugitive **5 a** a person or vessel engaged in smuggling; smuggler **b** (*in combination*): *a rum-runner* **6** a person who operates, manages, or controls something **7 a** either of the strips of metal or wood on which a sledge runs **b** the blade of an ice skate **8** a roller or guide for a sliding component **9** *botany* **a** a slender stem with very long internodes, as of the strawberry, that arches down to the ground and propagates by producing roots and shoots at the nodes or tip **b** a plant that propagates in this way **10** a strip of lace, linen, etc, placed across a table, dressing table, etc for protection and decoration **11** another word for **rocker** (sense 3) **12** do a runner *slang* to run away in order to escape trouble or to avoid paying for something

runner bean *n* another name for **scarlet runner**

runner-up *n, pl* runners-up a contestant finishing a race or competition in second place

running ('rʌnɪŋ) *adj* **1** maintained continuously; incessant: *a running battle; running commentary* **2** (*postpositive*) without interruption; consecutive: *he lectured for two hours running* **3** denoting or relating to the scheduled operation of a public vehicle: *the running time of a train* **4** accomplished at a run: *a running jump* **5** (of a knot) sliding along the rope from which it is made, so as to form a noose which becomes smaller when the rope is pulled **6** (of a wound, sore, etc) discharging pus or a serous fluid **7** prevalent; current: *running prices* **8** repeated or continuous: *a running design* **9** (of certain plants, plant stems, etc) creeping along the ground **10** flowing: *running water* **11** (of handwriting) having the letters run together ▷ *n* **12** management or organization: *the running of a company* **13** operation or maintenance: *the running of a machine* **14** competition or a competitive situation (in the phrases **in the running**, **out of the running**) **15** make the running to set the pace in a competition or race **16** *rare* the power or ability to run

running board *n* a footboard along the side of a vehicle, esp an early motorcar

running head *or* **running title** *n* *printing* a heading printed at the top of every page or every other page of a book

running light *n* *nautical* one of several white, red, or green lights displayed by vessels operating at night

running mate *n* **1** *US* a candidate for the subordinate of two linked positions, esp a candidate for the vice-presidency **2** a horse that pairs another in a team

running repairs *pl n* repairs, as to a machine or vehicle, that are minor and can be made with little or no interruption in the use of the item

runny ('rʌnɪ) *adj* -nier, -niest **1** tending to flow; liquid **2** (of the nose or nasal passages) exuding mucus

Runnymede ('rʌnɪˌmiːd) *n* a meadow on the S bank of the Thames near Windsor, where King John met his rebellious barons in 1215 and acceded to Magna Carta

run off *vb* (*adverb*) **1** (*intr*) to depart in haste **2** (*tr*) to produce quickly, as copies on a duplicating machine **3** to drain (liquid) or (of liquid) to be drained **4** (*tr*) to decide (a race) by a runoff **5** run off with **a** to steal; purloin **b** to elope with ▷ *n* **runoff 6** an extra race to decide the winner after a tie **7** that portion of rainfall that runs into streams as surface water rather than being absorbed into ground water or evaporating **8** the overflow of a liquid from a container **9** *NZ* grazing land for store cattle

run-of-the-mill *adj* ordinary, average, or undistinguished in quality, character, or nature; not special or excellent

run on *vb* (*adverb*) **1** (*intr*) to continue without interruption **2** to write with linked-up characters **3** *printing* to compose text matter without indentation or paragraphing ▷ *n* **run-on** *printing* text matter composed without indenting **5 a** a word added at the end of a dictionary entry whose meaning can be easily inferred from the definition of the headword **b** (*as modifier*): *a run-on entry*

run out *vb* (*adverb*) **1** (*intr*; often foll by *of*) to exhaust (a supply of something) or (of a supply) to become exhausted **2** (*intr*) to expire; become no longer valid: *my passport has run out* **3** run out on *informal* to desert or abandon **4** (*tr*) *cricket* to dismiss (a running batsman) by breaking the wicket with the ball, or with the ball in the hand, while he is out of his ground ▷ *n* **run-out 5** *cricket* dismissal of a batsman by running him out

run over *vb* **1** (*tr, adverb*) to knock down (a person) with a moving vehicle **2** (*intr*) to overflow the capacity of (a container) **3** (*intr, preposition*) to examine hastily or make a rapid survey of **4** (*intr, preposition*) to exceed (a limit): *we've run over our time*

runt (rʌnt) *n* **1** the smallest and weakest young animal in a litter, esp the smallest piglet in a litter **2** *derogatory* an undersized or inferior person **3** a large pigeon, originally bred for eating [c16: origin unknown]
> 'runtish *adj* > 'runty *adj* > runtiness *n*

run through *vb* **1** (*tr, adverb*) to transfix with a sword or other weapon **2** (*intr, preposition*) to exhaust (money) by wasteful spending; squander **3** (*intr, preposition*) to practise or rehearse: *let's run through the plan* **4** (*intr, preposition*) to examine hastily ▷ *n* **run-through 5** a practice or rehearsal **6** a brief survey

run time *n* *computing* the time during which a computer program is executed

run to *vb* (*intr, preposition*) to be sufficient for: *my income doesn't run to luxuries*

run up *vb* (*tr, adverb*) **1** to amass or accumulate; incur: *to run up debts* **2** to make by sewing together quickly **3** to hoist: *to run up a flag* ▷ *n* **run-up 4** an approach run by an athlete for a long jump, pole vault, etc **5** a preliminary or preparatory period: *the run-up to the election*

runway ('rʌnˌweɪ) *n* **1** a hard level roadway or other surface from which aircraft take off and on which they land **2** *forestry* a chute for sliding logs down **3** a narrow ramp extending from the stage into the audience in a theatre, nightclub, etc, esp as used by models in a fashion show

Runyon ('rʌnjən) *n* (**Alfred**) **Damon**. 1884-1946, US short-story writer, best known for his humorous tales about racy Broadway characters. His story collections include *Guys and Dolls* (1932), which became the basis of a musical (1950)

RUOK *text messaging abbreviation* are you OK?

rupee (ruːˈpiː) *n* the standard monetary unit of India, Nepal, and Pakistan (divided into 100 paise), Sri Lanka, Mauritius, and the Seychelles (divided into 100 cents) [c17: from Hindi *rupaīyā*, from Sanskrit *rūpya* coined silver, from *rūpa* shape, beauty]

Rupert ('ruːpət) *n* **Prince**. 1619-82, German-born nephew of Charles I: Royalist general during the Civil War (until 1646) and commander of the Royalist fleet (1648-50). After the Restoration he was an admiral of the English fleet in wars against the Dutch

Rupert's Land *n* (formerly, in Canada) the territories granted by Charles II to the Hudson's Bay Company in 1670 and ceded to the Canadian Government in 1870, comprising all the land watered by rivers flowing into Hudson Bay

rupiah (ruːˈpiːə) *n, pl* -ah *or* -ahs the standard monetary unit of Indonesia, divided into 100 sen [from Hindi: RUPEE]

rupture ('rʌptʃə) *n* **1** the act of breaking or bursting or the state of being broken or burst **2** a breach of peaceful or friendly relations **3** *pathol* **a** the breaking or tearing of a bodily structure or part **b** another word for **hernia** ▷ *vb* **4** to break or burst or cause to break or burst **5** to affect or be affected with a rupture or hernia **6** to undergo or cause to undergo a breach in relations or friendship [c15: from Latin *ruptūra* a breaking, from *rumpere* to burst forth; see ERUPT] > 'rupturable *adj*

rural ('rʊərəl) *adj* **1** of, relating to, or characteristic of the country or country life **2** living in or accustomed to the country **3** of, relating to, or associated with farming ▷ See **urban** [c15: via Old French from Latin *rūrālis*, from *rūs* the country] > 'ruralism *n* > 'ruralist *n* > ru'rality *n* > 'rurally *adv*

rural dean *n* *chiefly Brit* a clergyman having authority over a group of parishes

rural district *n* (in England and Wales from 1888 to 1974 and Northern Ireland from 1898 to 1973) a rural division of a county

ruralize *or* **ruralise** ('rʊərəˌlaɪz) *vb* **1** (*tr*) to make rural in character, appearance, etc **2** (*intr*) to go into the country to live > ˌrurali'zation *or* ˌrurali'sation *n*

Rurik *or* **Ryurik** ('rʊərɪk) *n* died 879. Varangian (Scandinavian Viking) leader who founded the Russian monarchy. He gained control over Novgorod (?862) and his dynasty, the **Rurikids**, ruled until 1598

Ruritania (ˌrʊərɪˈteɪnɪə, -njə) *n* **1** an imaginary kingdom of central Europe: setting of several novels by Anthony

Hope, esp *The Prisoner of Zenda* (1894) **2** any setting of adventure, romance, and intrigue > ˌRuriˈtanian *adj, n*

ruse (ruːz) *n* an action intended to mislead, deceive, or trick; stratagem [c15: from Old French: trick, esp to evade capture, from *ruser* to retreat, from Latin *recūsāre* to refuse]

Ruse (ˈruːseɪ) *n* a city in NE Bulgaria, on the River Danube: the chief river port and one of the largest industrial centres in Bulgaria. Pop: 172 000 (2005 est)

rush¹ (rʌʃ) *vb* **1** to hurry or cause to hurry; hasten **2** to make a sudden attack upon (a fortress, position, person, etc) **3** (when *intr*, often foll by *at, in* or *into*) to proceed or approach in a reckless manner **4** rush one's fences to proceed with precipitate haste **5** (*intr*) to come, flow, swell, etc, quickly or suddenly: *tears rushed to her eyes* **6** *slang* to cheat, esp by grossly overcharging **7** (*tr*) *US & Canadian* to make a concerted effort to secure the agreement, participation, etc, of (a person) **8** (*intr*) *American football* to gain ground by running forwards with the ball ▷ *n* **9** the act or condition of rushing **10** a sudden surge towards someone or something: *a gold rush* **11** a sudden surge of sensation, esp produced by a drug **12** a sudden demand ▷ *adj* (*prenominal*) **13** requiring speed or urgency: *a rush job* **14** characterized by much movement, business, etc: *a rush period* [c14 *ruschen*, from Old French *ruser* to put to flight, from Latin *recūsāre* to refuse, reject] > ˈrusher *n*

rush² (rʌʃ) *n* **1** any annual or perennial plant of the genus *Juncus*, growing in wet places and typically having grasslike cylindrical leaves and small green or brown flowers: family *Juncaceae* Many species are used to make baskets **2** something valueless; a trifle; straw: *not worth a rush* **3** short for **rush light** [Old English *risce, rysce*; related to Middle Dutch *risch*, Norwegian *rusk*, Old Slavonic *rozga* twig, rod] > ˈrushˌlike *adj* > ˈrushy *adj*

Rushdie (ˈrʊʃdɪ) *n* Sir (**Ahmed**) **Salman** (sʌlˈmɑːn). born 1947, British writer, born in India, whose novels include *Midnight's Children* (1981), which won the Booker prize, *Shame* (1983), and *The Ground Beneath Her Feet* (1998). His novel *The Satanic Verses* (1988) was regarded as blasphemous by many Muslims and he was forced into hiding (1989) when the Ayatollah Khomeini called for his death; knighted in 2007

rushes (rʌʃɪz) *pl n* (*sometimes singular*) (in film-making) the initial prints of a scene or scenes before editing, usually prepared daily

rush hour *n* a period at the beginning and end of the working day when large numbers of people are travelling to or from work

rush light *or* **rush candle** *n* a narrow candle, formerly in use, made of the pith of various types of rush dipped in tallow

Rushmore (ˈrʌʃmɔː) *n* Mount Rushmore a mountain in W South Dakota, in the Black Hills: a national memorial, with the faces of Washington, Lincoln, Jefferson, and Roosevelt carved into its side by Gutzon Borglum between 1927 and 1941. Height: 1841 m (6040 ft)

rusk (rʌsk) *n* a light bread dough, plain or sweet, baked twice until it is brown, hard, and crisp: often given to babies [c16: from Spanish or Portuguese *rosca* screw, bread shaped in a twist, of unknown origin]

Rusk (rʌsk) *n* (**David**) **Dean**. 1909–94, US statesman: secretary of state (1961–69). He defended US military involvement in Vietnam and opposed recognition of communist China

Ruskin (ˈrʌskɪn) *n* **John**. 1819–1900, English art critic and social reformer. He was a champion of the Gothic Revival and the Pre-Raphaelites and saw a close connection between art and morality. From about 1860 he argued vigorously for social and economic planning. His works include *Modern Painters* (1843–60), *The Stones of Venice* (1851–53), *Unto this Last* (1862), *Time and Tide* (1867), and *Fors Clavigera* (1871–84)

Russ. *abbreviation* Russia(n)

Russell (ˈrʌsᵊl) *n* **1 Bertrand** (**Arthur William**), 3rd Earl. 1872–1970, British philosopher and mathematician. His books include *Principles of Mathematics* (1903), *Principia Mathematica* (1910–13) with A. N. Whitehead, *Introduction to Mathematical Philosophy* (1919), *The Problems of Philosophy*

(1912), *The Analysis of Mind* (1921), and *An Enquiry into Meaning and Truth* (1940): Nobel prize for literature 1950 **2 George William** pen name *æ*. 1867–1935, Irish poet and journalist **3 Henry Norris**. 1877–1957, US astronomer and astrophysicist, who originated one form of the Hertzsprung–Russell diagram **4 John**, 1st Earl. 1792–1878, British statesman; prime minister (1846–52; 1865–66). He led the campaign to carry the 1832 Reform Act **5 Ken**. born 1927, British film director. His films include *Women in Love* (1969), *The Music Lovers* (1970), *The Boy Friend* (1971), *Valentino* (1977), *Gothic* (1986), and *The Rainbow* (1989)

russet (ˈrʌsɪt) *n* **1** brown with a yellowish or reddish tinge **2** a rough homespun fabric, reddish-brown in colour, formerly in use for clothing **3** any of various apples with rough brownish-red skins ▷ *adj* **4** *archaic* simple; homely; rustic: *a russet life* **5** of the colour russet: *russet hair* [c13: from Anglo-Norman, from Old French *rosset*, from *rous*, from Latin *russus*; related to Latin *ruber* red] > ˈrussety *adj*

Russia (ˈrʌʃə) *n* (full name **Russian Federation**) **1** the largest country in the world, covering N Eurasia and bordering on the Pacific and Arctic Oceans and the Baltic, Black, and Caspian Seas: originating from the principality of Muscovy in the 17th century, it expanded to become the Russian Empire; the Tsar was overthrown in 1917 and the Communist Russian Soviet Federative Socialist Republic was created; this merged with neighbouring Soviet Republics in 1922 to form the Soviet Union; on the disintegration of the Soviet Union in 1991 the Russian Federation was established as an independent state. Official language: Russian. Religion: nonreligious and Russian orthodox Christian. Currency: rouble. Capital: Moscow. Pop: 142 397 000 (2004 est). Area: 17 074 984 sq km (6 592 658 sq miles) **2** another name for the **Russian Empire 3** another name for the former **Soviet Union 4** another name for the former **Russian Soviet Federative Socialist Republic** ▷ Russian name: Rossiya

Russia leather *n* a smooth dyed leather made from calfskin and scented with birch tar oil, originally produced in Russia

Russian (ˈrʌʃən) *n* **1** the official language of Russia: an Indo-European language belonging to the East Slavonic branch **2** a native or inhabitant of Russia ▷ *adj* **3** of, relating to, or characteristic of Russia, its people, or their language

Russian doll *n* any of a set of hollow wooden figures, each of which splits in half to contain the next smallest figure, down to the smallest. Also called: matryoshka, matrioshka

Russian Empire *n* the tsarist empire in Asia and E Europe, overthrown by the Russian Revolution of 1917

Russian Federation *n* See Russia

Russianize *or* **Russianise** (ˈrʌʃəˌnaɪz) *vb* to make or become Russian in style, character, etc > ˌRussianiˈzation *or* ˌRussianiˈsation *n*

Russian Orthodox Church *n* the national Church of Russia, constituting a branch of the Eastern Church presided over by the Patriarch of Moscow

Russian roulette *n* **1** a game of chance in which each player in turn spins the cylinder of a revolver loaded with only one cartridge and presses the trigger with the barrel against his own head **2** any act which, if repeated several times, is likely to have disastrous consequences

Russian salad *n* a salad of cold diced cooked vegetables mixed with Russian dressing

Russian Soviet Federative Socialist Republic *n* (formerly) the largest administrative division of the Soviet Union. Abbreviation: RSFSR

Russian Turkestan *n* See Turkestan

Russian Zone *n* another name for the **Soviet Zone**

Russo- (ˈrʌsəʊ-) *combining form* Russia or Russian: *Russo-Japanese*

rust (rʌst) *n* **1** a reddish-brown oxide coating formed on iron or steel by the action of oxygen and moisture **2** Also called: rust fungus *plant pathol* **a** any basidiomycetous fungus of the order *Uredinales*, parasitic on cereal plants, conifers, etc **b** any of various plant diseases characterized by reddish-brown discoloration of the leaves and stem, esp that caused by the rust fungi **3 a** a strong brown colour, sometimes with a reddish or yellowish tinge **b** (*as adjective*): *a rust carpet* **4** any corrosive or debilitating influence, esp lack of use ▷ *vb* **5** to become or cause to become coated with a layer of rust **6** to deteriorate or cause to deteriorate through some debilitating influence or lack of use: *he allowed his talent to rust over the years* [Old English *rūst*; related to Old Saxon, Old High German *rost*] > 'rustless *adj*

rust belt *n* an area where heavy industry is in decline, esp in the Midwest of the US

rustic ('rʌstɪk) *adj* **1** of, characteristic of, or living in the country; rural **2** having qualities ascribed to country life or people; simple; unsophisticated: *rustic pleasures* **3** crude, awkward, or uncouth **4** made of untrimmed branches: *a rustic seat* **5** (of masonry) having a rusticated finish ▷ *n* **6** a person who comes from or lives in the country **7** Also called: **rusticwork** brick or stone having a rough finish [c16: from Old French *rustique*, from Latin *rūsticus*, from *rūs* the country] > 'rustically *adv* > rusticity (rʌ'stɪsɪtɪ) *n*

rusticate ('rʌstɪˌkeɪt) *vb* **1** to banish or retire to the country **2** to make or become rustic in style, behaviour, etc **3** (*tr*) *architect* to finish (an exterior wall) with large blocks of masonry that are separated by deep joints and decorated with a bold, usually textured, design **4** (*tr*) *Brit* to send down from university for a specified time as a punishment [c17: from Latin *rūsticārī*, from *rūs* the country] > ˌrusti'cation *n* > 'rustiˌcator *n*

rustle¹ ('rʌsəl) *vb* **1** to make or cause to make a low crisp whispering or rubbing sound, as of dry leaves or paper **2** to move with such a sound ▷ *n* **3** such a sound or sounds [Old English *hrūxlian*; related to Gothic *hrukjan* to CROW², Old Norse *hraukr* raven, CROW¹]

rustle² ('rʌsəl) *vb* **1** *chiefly US & Canadian* to steal (cattle, horses, etc) **2** *US & Canadian informal* to move swiftly and energetically [c19: probably special use of RUSTLE¹ (in the sense: to move with quiet sound)] > 'rustler *n*

rustle up *vb* (*tr, adverb*) *informal* **1** to prepare (a meal, snack, etc) rapidly, esp at short notice **2** to forage for and obtain

rustproof ('rʌstˌpruːf) *adj* treated against rusting

rusty ('rʌstɪ) *adj* **rustier, rustiest 1** covered with, affected by, or consisting of rust: *a rusty machine; a rusty deposit* **2** of the colour rust **3** discoloured by age: *a rusty coat* **4** (of the voice) tending to croak **5** old-fashioned in appearance; seemingly antiquated: *a rusty old gentleman* **6** out of practice; impaired in skill or knowledge by inaction or neglect **7** (of plants) affected by the rust fungus > 'rustily *adv* > 'rustiness *n*

rut¹ (rʌt) *n* **1** a groove or furrow in a soft road, caused by wheels **2** a narrow or predictable way of life, set of attitudes, etc; dreary or undeviating routine (esp in the phrase **in a rut**) ▷ *vb* **ruts, rutting, rutted 3** (*tr*) to make a rut or ruts in [c16: probably from French *route* road]

rut² (rʌt) *n* **1** a recurrent period of sexual excitement and reproductive activity in certain male ruminants, such as the deer, that corresponds to the period of oestrus in females ▷ *vb* **ruts, rutting, rutted 2** (*intr*) (of male ruminants) to be in a period of sexual excitement and activity [c15: from Old French *rut* noise, roar, from Latin *rugītus*, from *rugīre* to roar]

rutabaga (ˌruːtəˈbeɪɡə) *n* Also called (in Britain and certain other countries): **swede 1** *US and Canadian* **a** Eurasian plant, *Brassica napus* (or *B. napobrassica*), cultivated for its bulbous edible root, which is used as a vegetable and as cattle fodder: family Brassicaceae (crucifors) **2** the root of this plant [c18: from Swedish dialect *rotabagge*, literally: root bag]

rutaceous (ruːˈteɪʃəs) *adj* of, relating to, or belonging to the *Rutaceae*, a family of tropical and temperate flowering plants many of which have aromatic leaves. The family includes rue and citrus trees [c19: from New Latin *Rutaceae*, from Latin *rūta* RUE²]

ruth (ruːθ) *n archaic* **1** pity; compassion **2** repentance; remorse [c12: from *rewen* to RUE¹]

Ruth¹ (ruːθ) *n* **1** *Old Testament* **a** a Moabite woman, who left her own people to remain with her mother-in-law Naomi, and became the wife of Boaz; an ancestress of David **b** the book in which these events are recounted **2** George Herman, nicknamed *Babe*. 1895–1948, US professional baseball player from 1914 to 1935

Ruth² (ruːθ) *n Old Testament* **a** a Moabite woman, who left her own people to remain with her mother-in-law Naomi, and became the wife of Boaz; an ancestress of David **b** the book in which these events are recounted

Ruthenia (ruːˈθiːnɪə) *n* a region of E Europe on the south side of the Carpathian Mountains: belonged to Hungary from the 14th century, to Czechoslovakia from 1918 to 1939, and was ceded to the former Soviet Union in 1945; in 1991 it became part of the newly independent Ukraine. Also called: **Carpatho-Ukraine**

ruthenium (ruːˈθiːnɪəm) *n* a hard brittle white element of the platinum metal group. It occurs free with other platinum metals in pentlandite and other ores and is used to harden platinum and palladium. Symbol: Ru; atomic no: 44; atomic wt: 101.07; valency: 0–8; relative density: 12.41; melting pt: 2334°C; boiling pt: 4150°C [c19: from Medieval Latin *Ruthenia* Russia, where it was first discovered]

rutherford ('rʌðəfəd) *n* a unit of activity equal to the quantity of a radioactive nuclide required to produce one million disintegrations per second [c20: named after Ernest Rutherford, 1st Baron *Rutherford* (1871–1937), New Zealand-born British physicist]

Rutherford ('rʌðəfəd) *n* **1 Ernest**, 1st Baron. 1871–1937, British physicist, born in New Zealand, who discovered the atomic nucleus (1909). Nobel prize for chemistry 1908 **2 Dame Margaret**. 1892–1972, British stage and screen actress. Her films include *Passport to Pimlico* (1949), *Murder She Said* (1962), and *The VIPs* (1963) **3 Mark**, original name *William Hale White*. 1831–1913, British novelist and writer, whose work deals with his religious uncertainties: best known for *The Autobiography of Mark Rutherford* (1881) and the novel *The Revolution in Tanner's Lane* (1887)

rutherfordium (ˌrʌðəˈfɔːdɪəm) *n* a transactinide element produced by bombarding californium-249 nuclei with carbon-12 nuclei. Symbol: Rf; atomic number.: 104; atomic wt: 261. Name in the former Soviet Union: **kurchatovium** [c20: named after Ernest Rutherford, 1st Baron *Rutherford* (1871–1937), New Zealand-born British physicist]

ruthful ('ruːθfʊl) *adj archaic* full of or causing sorrow or pity > 'ruthfully *adv* > 'ruthfulness *n*

ruthless ('ruːθlɪs) *adj* feeling or showing no mercy; hardhearted > 'ruthlessly *adv* > 'ruthlessness *n*

rutile ('ruːtaɪl) *n* a black, yellowish, or reddish-brown mineral, found in igneous rocks, metamorphosed limestones, and quartz veins. It is a source of titanium. Composition: titanium dioxide. Formula: TiO_2. Crystal structure: tetragonal [c19: via French from German *Rutil*, from Latin *rutilus* red, glowing]

Rutland ('rʌtlənd) *n* an inland county of central England: the smallest of the historical English counties, it became part of Leicestershire in 1974 but was reinstated as an independent unitary authority in 1997: mainly agricultural. Administrative centre: Oakham. Pop: 35 700 (2003 est). Area: 394 sq km (152 sq miles)

ruttish ('rʌtɪʃ) *adj* **1** (of an animal) in a condition of rut **2** lascivious or salacious > 'ruttishly *adv* > 'ruttishness *n*

rutty ('rʌtɪ) *adj* **-tier, -tiest** full of ruts or holes: *a rutty track* > 'ruttily *adv* > 'ruttiness *n*

Ruwenzori (ˌruːwɛnˈzɔːrɪ) *n* a mountain range in central Africa, on the border between Uganda and the Democratic Republic of Congo (formerly Zaïre) between Lakes Edward and Albert: generally thought to be Ptolemy's "Mountains of the Moon". Highest peak: Mount Stanley, 5109 m (16 763 ft)

Ruysdael ('riːzdɑːl, -deɪl, 'raɪz-; *Dutch* 'rœizdɑːl) *n* a variant spelling of **Ruisdael**

Ruyter ('raɪtə; *Dutch* 'rœitər) *n* **Michiel Adriaanszoon de** (miː'xiːl ˌɑːdriˈaːnsun də). 1607–76, Dutch admiral, noted for actions in the Anglo-Dutch wars in 1652–53, 1665–67, 1672, and 1673, when he prevented an Anglo-French invasion

RV *abbreviation* Revised Version (of the Bible)

Rwanda (rʊˈændə) *n* a republic in central Africa: part of

German East Africa from 1899 until 1917, when Belgium took over the administration; became a republic in 1961 after a Hutu revolt against the Tutsi (1959); fighting between the ethnic groups broke out repeatedly after independence, culminating in the genocide of Tutsis by Hutus in 1994. Official languages: Kinyarwanda, English, French, and Swahili. Religion: Roman Catholic, African Protestant, Muslim, and animist. Currency: Rwanda franc. Capital: Kigali. Pop: 8 481 000 (2004 est). Area: 26 338 sq km (10 169 sq miles) ▷ R'wandan *adj, n*

-ry *suffix forming nouns* a variant of **-ery:** *dentistry*

Ryazan (*Russian* rɪ'zanj) *n* a city in W central Russia: capital of a medieval principality; oil refineries and engineering industries. Pop: 523 000 (2005 est)

Rybinsk (*Russian* 'ribinsk) *n* a city in W central Russia, on the River Volga: an important river port, terminal of the Mariinsk Waterway (between Saint Petersburg and the Volga) at the SE end of the **Rybinsk Reservoir** (area: 4700 sq km (1800 sq miles)). Pop: 218 000 (2005 est). Former names: Shcherbakov, Andropov

Rydal ('raɪdᵊl) *n* a village in NW England, in Cumbria on **Rydal Water** (a small lake). **Rydal Mount**, home of Wordsworth from 1813 to 1850, is situated here

Ryder ('raɪdə) *n* **Susan**, Baroness Ryder of Warsaw. 1923–2000, British philanthropist; founder of the Sue Ryder Foundation for the Sick and Disabled, which is funded by a chain of charity shops: married to Leonard Cheshire

Ryder Cup (raɪdə) *n* the Ryder Cup the trophy awarded in a professional golfing competition between teams representing Europe and the US [c20: named after Samuel *Ryder* (1859–1936), British businessman and golf patron]

rye (raɪ) *n* **1** a tall hardy widely cultivated annual grass, *Secale cereale*, having soft bluish-green leaves, bristly flower spikes, and light brown grain **2** the grain of this grass, used in making flour and whiskey, and as a livestock food **3** Also called: **rye whiskey** whiskey distilled from rye. US whiskey must by law contain not less than 51 per cent rye **4** *US* short for **rye bread** [Old English *ryge*; related to Old Norse *rugr*, Old French *rogga*, Old Saxon *roggo*]

Rye (raɪ) *n* a resort in SE England, in East Sussex: one of the Cinque Ports. Pop: 4195 (2001)

rye bread *n* any of various breads made entirely or partly from rye flour, often with caraway seeds

rye-grass *n* any of various grasses of the genus *Lolium*, esp *L. perenne*, native to Europe, N Africa, and Asia and widely cultivated as forage crops. They have a flattened flower spike and hairless leaves

Ryle (raɪl) *n* **1 Gilbert**. 1900–76, British philosopher. His works include *The Concept of Mind* (1949) **2** Sir **Martin**. 1918–84, British astronomer, noted for his research on radio astronomy: Astronomer Royal 1972–82; shared the Nobel prize for physics in 1974

Ryswick ('rɪzwɪk) *n* the English name for **Rijswijk**

Ryukyu Islands (rɪ'uːkjuː) *pl n* a chain of 55 islands in the W Pacific, extending almost 650 km (400 miles) from S Japan to N Taiwan: an ancient kingdom, under Chinese rule from the late 14th century, invaded by Japan in the early 17th century, under full Japanese sovereignty from 1879 to 1945, and US control from 1945 to 1972; now part of Japan again. They are subject to frequent typhoons. Chief town: Naha (on Okinawa). Pop: 1 318 220 (2000). Area: 2196 sq km (849 sq miles)

Ryurik ('ruərɪk) *n* a variant spelling of **Rurik**

r

Ss

s¹ or **S** (ɛs) *n, pl* **s's, S's** or **Ss** **1** the 19th letter and 15th consonant of the modern English alphabet **2** a speech sound represented by this letter, usually an alveolar fricative, either voiceless, as in *sit*, or voiced, as in *dogs* **3 a** something shaped like an S **b** (*in combination*): *an S-bend in a road*

s² *symbol for* second (of time)

S *symbol for* **1** Society **2** small (size) **3** South **4** *chem* sulphur **5** *physics* **a** entropy **b** siemens **c** strangeness **6** *currency* (the former) schilling

s. *abbreviation* **1** shilling **2** singular **3** son **4** succeeded

S. *abbreviation* **1** *pl* **SS** Saint **2** school **3** Signor [Latin *socius*]

-s¹ or **-es** *suffix* forming the plural of most nouns: *boys; boxes* [from Old English *-as*, plural nominative and accusative ending of some masculine nouns]

-s² or **-es** *suffix* forming the third person singular present indicative tense of verbs: *he runs; she washes* [from Old English (northern dialect) *-es*, *-s*, originally the ending of the second person singular]

-'s *suffix* **1** forming the possessive singular of nouns and some pronouns: *man's; one's* **2** forming the possessive plural of nouns whose plurals do not end in *-s: children's* **3** forming the plural of numbers, letters, or symbols: *20's; p's and q's* **4** *informal* contraction of *is* or *has: he's here; John's coming; it's gone* **5** *informal* contraction of *us* with *let: let's* **6** *informal* contraction of *does* in some questions: *where's he live?; what's he do?* [senses 1, 2: assimilated contraction from Middle English *-es*, from Old English, masculine and neuter genitive singular; sense 3, equivalent to *-s¹*]

SA *abbreviation* **1** Salvation Army **2** [Spanish: limited company] **3** Société anonyme [French: limited company] **4** South Africa **5** South America **6** South Australia **7** *Sturmabteilung*: the Nazi terrorist militia, organized around 1924

Saadi (saː'diː) *n* a variant spelling of **Sadi**

Saar (saː; *German* zaːr) *n* **1** a river in W Europe, rising in the Vosges Mountains and flowing north to the Moselle River in Germany. Length: 246 km (153 miles). French name: **Sarre 2 the Saar** another name for **Saarland**

Saarbrücken (*German* zaːr'brykən) *n* an industrial city in W Germany, capital of Saarland state, on the Saar River. Pop: 181 860 (2003 est)

Saarinen ('saːrɪnən) *n* **Eero** ('eɪrəʊ). 1910–61, US architect, born in Finland. His works include the US Embassy, London (1960)

Saarland (*German* 'zaːrlant) *n* a state of W Germany: formed in 1919; under League of Nations administration until 1935; occupied by France (1945–57); part of West Germany (1957–90): contains rich coal deposits and is a major industrial region. Capital: Saarbrücken. Pop: 1 060 000 (2003 est). Area: 2567 sq km (991 sq miles)

Saba ('saːbə) *n* **1** an island in the NE Caribbean, in the Netherlands Antilles. Pop: 1491 (2007 est). Area: 13 sq km (5 sq miles) **2** another name for **Sheba¹** (sense 1)

Sabadell (*Spanish* saβa'ðel) *n* a town in NE Spain, near Barcelona: textile manufacturing. Pop: 191 057 (2003 est)

sabadilla (ˌsæbə'dɪlə) *n* **1** a tropical American liliaceous plant, *Schoenocaulon officinale* **2** the bitter brown seeds of this plant, which contain the alkaloids veratrine and veratridine and are used in insecticides [c19: from Spanish *cebadilla*, diminutive of *cebada* barley, from Latin *cibāre* to feed, from *cibus* food]

Sabaean or **Sabean** (sə'biːən) *n* **1** an inhabitant or native of ancient Saba **2** the ancient Semitic language of Saba ▷ *adj* **3** of or relating to ancient Saba, its inhabitants, or their language [c16: from Latin *Sabaeus*, from Greek *Sabaios* belonging to Saba (Sheba)]

Sabah ('saːbaː) *n* a state of Malaysia, occupying N Borneo and offshore islands in the South China and Sulu Seas: became a British protectorate in 1888; gained independence and joined Malaysia in 1963. Capital: Kota Kinabalu. Pop: 2 603 485 (2000). Area: 73 620 sq km (28 425 sq miles). Former name (until 1963): **North Borneo**

Sabatier (*French* sabatje) *n* **Paul** (pɔl). 1854–1941, French chemist, who discovered a process for the hydrogenation of organic compounds: shared the Nobel prize for chemistry (1912)

sabbat ('sæbæt, -ət) *n* another word for **Sabbath** (sense 4)

Sabbatarian (ˌsæbə'tɛərɪən) *n* **1** a person advocating the strict religious observance of Sunday **2** a person who observes Saturday as the Sabbath ▷ *adj* **3** of or relating to the Sabbath or its observance [c17: from Late Latin

S

sabbatārius a Sabbath-keeper] >,Sabba'tarianism *n*

Sabbath ('sæbəθ) *n* 1 the seventh day of the week, Saturday, devoted to worship and rest from work in Judaism and in certain Christian Churches 2 Sunday, observed by Christians as the day of worship and rest from work in commemoration of Christ's Resurrection 3 (*not capital*) a period of rest 4 Also called: sabbat, witches' Sabbath a midnight meeting or secret rendezvous for practitioners of witchcraft, sorcery, or devil worship [Old English *sabbat*, from Latin *sabbatum*, from Greek *sabbaton*, from Hebrew *shabbāth*, from *shābath* to rest]

sabbatical (sə'bætɪkᵊl) *adj* 1 denoting a period of leave granted to university staff, teachers, etc, esp approximately every seventh year: *a sabbatical year*; *sabbatical leave* 2 denoting a post that renders the holder eligible for such leave ▷ *n* 3 any sabbatical period [c16: from Greek *sabbatikos*; see SABBATH]

Sabbatical (sə'bætɪkᵊl) *adj* Also: Sabbatic of, relating to, or appropriate to the Sabbath as a day of rest and religious observance

SABC *abbreviation* South African Broadcasting Corporation

saber ('seɪbə) *n, vb* the US spelling of **sabre**

sabermetrics (,seɪbə'mɛtrɪks) *n* (*functioning as singular*) the statistical and mathematical analysis of baseball records [c20: from *saber* (from initials of *Society of American Baseball Research*) + -*metrics* as in ECONOMETRICS]

sabin ('sæbɪn, 'seɪ-) *n physics* a unit of acoustic absorption equal to the absorption resulting from one square foot of a perfectly absorbing surface [c20: introduced by Wallace C. *Sabine* (1868–1919), US physicist]

Sabin ('seɪbɪn) *n* **Albert Bruce**. 1906–93, US microbiologist, born in Poland. He developed the **Sabin vaccine** (1955), taken orally to immunize against poliomyelitis

Sabine ('sæbaɪn) *n* 1 a member of an ancient Oscan-speaking people who lived in central Italy northeast of Rome ▷ *adj* 2 of, characteristic of, or relating to this people or their language

sabkha ('sæbxə, -kə) *n* a flat coastal plain with a salt crust, common in Arabia [c19: from Arabic]

sable ('seɪbᵊl) *n, pl* -bles *or* -ble 1 a marten, *Martes zibellina*, of N Asian forests, with dark brown luxuriant fur 2 a the highly valued fur of this animal b (*as modifier*): *a sable coat* 3 American sable the brown, slightly less valuable fur of the American marten, *Martes americana* 4 the colour of sable fur: a dark brown to yellowish-brown colour ▷ *adj* 5 of the colour of sable fur 6 black; dark; gloomy 7 (*usually postpositive*) heraldry of the colour black [c15: from Old French, from Old High German *zobel*, of Slavic origin; related to Russian *sobol'*, Polish *sobol*]

Sable ('seɪbᵊl) Cape Sable *n* 1 a cape at the S tip of Florida: the southernmost point of continental US 2 the southernmost point of Nova Scotia, Canada

sable antelope *n* a large black E African antelope, *Hippotragus niger*, with long backward-curving horns

Sable Island pony *n* a variety of wild pony found on Sable Island, Nova Scotia

sabot ('sæbəʊ; *French* sabo) *n* 1 a shoe made from a single block of wood 2 a shoe with a wooden sole and a leather or cloth upper 3 *Austral* a small sailing boat with a shortened bow [c17: from French, probably from Old French *savate* an old shoe, also influenced by *bot* BOOT¹; related to Italian *ciabatta* old shoe, Old Provençal *sabata*]

sabotage ('sæbə,tɑ:ʒ) *n* 1 the deliberate destruction, disruption, or damage of equipment, a public service, etc, as by enemy agents, dissatisfied employees, etc 2 any similar action or behaviour ▷ *vb* 3 (*tr*) to destroy, damage, or disrupt, esp by secret means [c20: from French, from *saboter* to spoil through clumsiness (literally: to clatter in sabots)]

saboteur (,sæbə'tɜ:) *n* a person who commits sabotage [c20: from French; see SABOTAGE]

sabra ('sɑ:brə) *n* a native-born Israeli Jew [from Hebrew *Saber* prickly pear, common plant in the coastal areas of the country]

sabre *or US* **saber** ('seɪbə) *n* 1 a stout single-edged

cavalry sword, having a curved blade 2 a sword used in fencing, having a narrow V-shaped blade, a semicircular guard, and a slightly curved hand 3 a cavalry soldier ▷ *vb* 4 (*tr*) to injure or kill with a sabre [c17: via French from German (*dialect*) *Sabel*, from Middle High German *sebel*, perhaps from Magyar *szablya*; compare Russian *sablya* sabre]

sabre-rattling *n, adj informal* seeking to intimidate by an aggressive display of military power

sabre-toothed tiger *or* **sabre-toothed cat** *n* any of various extinct Tertiary felines of the genus *Smilodon* and related genera, with long curved upper canine teeth

sac (sæk) *n* a pouch, bag, or pouchlike part in an animal or plant [c18: from French, from Latin *saccus*; see SACK¹] >'sac,like *adj*

saccharide ('sækə,raɪd, -rɪd) *n* any sugar or other carbohydrate, esp a simple sugar

saccharimeter (,sækə'rɪmɪtə) *n* any instrument for measuring the strength of sugar solutions, esp a type of polarimeter for determining the concentration from the extent to which the solution rotates the plane of polarized light >,saccha'rimetry *n*

saccharin ('sækərɪn) *n* a very sweet white crystalline slightly soluble powder used as a nonfattening sweetener. Formula: $C_7H_5NO_3S$ [c19: from SACCHARO- + -IN]

saccharine ('sækə,raɪn, -,ri:n) *adj* 1 excessively sweet; sugary: *a saccharine smile* 2 of, relating to, of the nature of, or containing sugar or saccharin

saccharo- *or before a vowel* **sacchar-** *combining form* sugar: *saccharomycete* [via Latin from Greek *sakkharon*, ultimately from Sanskrit *śarkarā* sugar]

saccharose ('sækə,rəʊz, -,rəʊs) *n* a technical name for sugar (sense 1)

Sacco ('sækəʊ) *n* **Nicola** (ni'kɔ:la). 1891–1927, US radical agitator, born in Italy. With Bartolomeo Vanzetti, he was executed for murder (1927) despite suspicions that their political opinions influenced the verdict: the case caused international protests

saccule ('sækju:l) *or* **sacculus** ('sækjʊləs) *n, pl* -cules *or* -li (li:) 1 a small sac 2 the smaller of the two parts of the membranous labyrinth of the internal ear. See **utricle** (sense 1) [c19: from Latin *sacculus* diminutive of *saccus* SACK¹]

sacerdotal (,sæsə'dəʊtᵊl) *adj* of, relating to, or characteristic of priests [c14: from Latin *sacerdōtālis*, from *sacerdōs* priest, from *sacer* sacred] >,sacer'dotally *adv* >,sacer'dotalism *n*

sachem ('seɪtʃəm) *n* 1 *US* a leader of a political party or organization, esp of Tammany Hall 2 another name for **sagamore** [c17: from Narraganset *săchim* chief]

sachet ('sæʃeɪ) *n* 1 a small sealed envelope, usually made of plastic or paper, for containing sugar, salt, shampoo, etc 2 a a small soft bag containing perfumed powder, placed in drawers to scent clothing b the powder contained in such a bag [c19: from Old French: a little bag, from *sac* bag; see SACK¹]

Sachs (*German* zaks) *n* 1 **Hans** (hans). 1494–1576, German master shoemaker and Meistersinger, portrayed by Wagner in *Die Meistersinger von Nürnberg* 2 **Nelly** (**Leonie**). 1891–1970, German Jewish poet and dramatist, who escaped from Nazi Germany and settled in Sweden. Her works include *Eli: A Mystery Play of the Sufferings of Israel* (1951) and 'O the Chimneys', a poem about the Nazi extermination camps. Nobel prize for literature 1966 jointly with Shmuel Yosef Agnon

Sachsen ('zaksən) *n* the German name for **Saxony**

sack¹ (sæk) *n* 1 a large bag made of coarse cloth, thick paper, etc, used as a container 2 Also called: sackful the amount contained in a sack, sometimes used as a unit of measurement 3 a a woman's loose tube-shaped dress b Also called: sacque a woman's full loose hip-length jacket, worn in the 18th and mid-20th centuries 4 the sack *informal* dismissal from employment 5 a slang word for **bed** 6 hit the sack *slang* to go to bed ▷ *vb* (*tr*) 7 *informal* to dismiss from employment 8 to put into a sack or sacks [Old English *sacc*, from Latin *saccus* bag, from Greek *sakkos*; related to Hebrew *saq*] >'sack,like *adj*

sack² (sæk) *n* 1 the plundering of a place by an army or

mob, usually involving destruction, slaughter, etc
2 *American football* a tackle on a quarterback which brings
him down before he has passed the ball ▷ *vb* **3** (*tr*) to
plunder and partially destroy (a place) **4** *American football*
to tackle and bring down a quarterback before he has
passed the ball [c16: from French phrase *mettre à sac*,
literally: to put (loot) in a sack, from Latin *saccus* SACK¹]
> 'sacker *n*

sack³ (sæk) *n archaic or trademark* any dry white wine
formerly imported into Britain from SW Europe [C16
wyne seck, from French *vin sec* dry wine, from Latin *siccus*
dry]

sackable ('sækəb³l) *adj* of or denoting an offence,
infraction of rules, etc, that is sufficiently serious to
warrant dismissal from an employment

sackbut ('sæk,bʌt) *n* a medieval form of trombone [c16:
from French *saqueboute*, from Old French *saquer* to pull +
bouter to push; see BUTT³: used in the Bible (Daniel 3) as a
mistranslation of Aramaic *sabb'ka* stringed instrument]

sackcloth ('sæk,klɒθ) *n* **1** coarse cloth such as sacking
2 garments made of such cloth, worn formerly to
indicate mourning or penitence **3 sackcloth and ashes**
a public display of extreme grief, remorse, or repentance

sacking ('sækɪŋ) *n* coarse cloth used for making sacks,
woven from flax, hemp, jute, etc

sack race *n* a race in which the competitors' legs and
often bodies are enclosed in sacks

Sacks (sæks) *n* Sir **Jonathan** (**Henry**). born 1948, British
rabbi; Commonwealth chief rabbi from 1991; knighted
2005

Sackville ('sækvɪl) *n* **Thomas**, 1st Earl of Dorset.
1536–1608, English poet, dramatist, and statesman. He
collaborated with Thomas Norton on the early blank-
verse tragedy *Gorboduc* (1561)

Sackville-West (,sækvɪl 'wɛst) *n* **Victoria** (**Mary**), known
as *Vita*. 1892–1962, British writer and gardener, whose
works include the novel *The Edwardians* (1930) and the
poem *The Land* (1931). She is also noted for the gardens at
Sissinghurst Castle, Kent. Married to Harold Nicolson

sacral¹ ('seɪkrəl) *adj* of, relating to, or associated with
sacred rites [c19: from Latin *sacrum* sacred object]

sacral² ('seɪkrəl) *adj* of or relating to the sacrum [c18:
from New Latin *sacrālis* of the SACRUM]

sacrament ('sækrəmənt) *n* **1** an outward sign combined
with a prescribed form of words and regarded as
conferring some specific grace upon those who receive
it. The Protestant sacraments are baptism and the
Lord's Supper. In the Roman Catholic and Eastern
Churches they are baptism, penance, confirmation, the
Eucharist, holy orders, matrimony, and the anointing of
the sick (formerly extreme unction) **2** (*often capital*) the
Eucharist **3** the consecrated elements of the Eucharist,
esp the bread **4** something regarded as possessing a
sacred or mysterious significance **5** a symbol; pledge
[c12: from Church Latin *sacrāmentum* vow, from Latin
sacrāre to consecrate]

sacramental (,sækrə'mɛnt³l) *adj* **1** of, relating to, or
having the nature of a sacrament ▷ *n* **2** *RC Church* a
sacrament-like ritual action, such as the sign of the
cross or the use of holy water > **sacramentality**
(,sækrəmɛn'tælɪtɪ) *or* ,sacra'mentalness *n*

sacramentalism (,sækrə'mɛnt³,lɪzəm) *n* belief in or
special emphasis upon the efficacy of the sacraments
for conferring grace

Sacramento (,sækrə'mɛntəʊ) *n* **1** an inland port in N
central California, capital of the state at the confluence
of the American and Sacramento Rivers: became a boom
town in the gold rush of the 1850s. Pop: 445 335 (2003
est) **2** a river in N California, flowing generally south to
San Francisco Bay. Length: 615 km (382 miles)

sacrarium (sæ'krɛərɪəm) *n, pl* -**craria** (-'krɛərɪə) **1** the
sanctuary of a church **2** *RC Church* a place near the altar
of a church, similar in function to the piscina, where
materials used in the sacred rites are deposited or
poured away [c18: from Latin *sacrārium*, from *sacer*
SACRED]

sacred ('seɪkrɪd) *adj* **1** exclusively devoted to a deity or to
some religious ceremony or use; holy; consecrated
2 worthy of or regarded with reverence, awe, or respect

3 connected with or intended for religious use: *sacred
music* **4** dedicated to; in honour of [c14: from Latin *sacrāre*
to set apart as holy, from *sacer* holy] > 'sacredly *adv*
> 'sacredness *n*

sacred cow *n informal* a person, institution, custom, etc,
unreasonably held to be beyond criticism [alluding to
the Hindu belief that cattle are sacred]

sacred mushroom *n* **1** any of various hallucinogenic
mushrooms, esp species of *Psilocybe* and *Amanita*, that
have been eaten in rituals in various parts of the world
2 a mescal button, used in a similar way

sacred site *n Austral informal* a place of great significance

sacrifice ('sækrɪ,faɪs) *n* **1** a surrender of something of
value as a means of gaining something more desirable
or of preventing some evil **2** a ritual killing of a person
or animal with the intention of propitiating or pleasing
a deity **3** a symbolic offering of something to a deity
4 the person, animal, or object surrendered, destroyed,
killed, or offered **5** loss entailed by giving up or selling
something at less than its value **6** *chess* the act or an
instance of sacrificing a piece ▷ *vb* **7** to make a sacrifice
(of); give up, surrender, or destroy (a person, thing, etc)
8 *chess* to permit or force one's opponent to capture (a
piece) freely, as in playing a combination or gambit: *he
sacrificed his queen and checkmated his opponent on the next move*
[c13: via Old French from Latin *sacrificium*, from *sacer* holy
+ *facere* to make] > 'sacri,ficer *n*

sacrificial (,sækrɪ'fɪʃəl) *adj* used in or connected with a
sacrifice > ,sacri'ficially *adv*

sacrilege ('sækrɪlɪdʒ) *n* **1** the misuse or desecration of
anything regarded as sacred or as worthy of extreme
respect **2** the act or an instance of taking anything
sacred for secular use [c13: from Old French *sacrilège*,
from Latin *sacrilegium*, from *sacrilegus* temple-robber, from
sacra sacred things + *legere* to take] > sacrilegist
(,sækrɪ'li:dʒɪst) *n*

sacrilegious (,sækrɪ'lɪdʒəs) *adj* **1** of, relating to, or
involving sacrilege; impious **2** guilty of sacrilege
> ,sacri'legiously *adv*

sacring bell *n chiefly RC Church* a small bell rung at the
elevation of the Host and chalice during Mass

sacristan ('sækrɪstən) *or* **sacrist** ('sækrɪst, 'seɪ-) *n* **1** a
person who has charge of the contents of a church, esp
the sacred vessels, vestments, etc **2** a less common word
for **sexton** (sense 1) [c14: from Medieval Latin *sacristānus*,
from *sacrista*, from Latin *sacer* holy]

sacristy ('sækrɪstɪ) *n, pl* -**ties** a room attached to a
church or chapel where the sacred vessels, vestments,
etc, are kept and where priests attire themselves [c17:
from Medieval Latin *sacristia*; see SACRISTAN]

sacroiliac (,seɪkrəʊ'ɪlɪ,æk, ,sæk-) *anatomy* ▷ *adj* **1** of or
relating to the sacrum and ilium, their articulation, or
their associated ligaments ▷ *n* **2** the joint where these
bones meet

sacrosanct ('sækrəʊ,sæŋkt) *adj* very sacred or holy;
inviolable [c17: from Latin *sacrōsanctus* made holy by
sacred rite, from *sacrō* by sacred rite, from *sacer* holy +
sanctus from *sancīre* to hallow] > ,sacro'sanctity *n*

sacrum ('seɪkrəm, 'sækrəm) *n, pl* -**cra** (-krə) (*in man*)
the large wedge-shaped bone, consisting of five fused
vertebrae, in the lower part of the back [c18: from Latin
os sacrum holy bone, because it was used in sacrifices,
from *sacer* holy]

sad (sæd) *adj* **sadder**, **saddest 1** feeling sorrow; unhappy
2 causing, suggestive, or expressive of such feelings: *a
sad story* **3** unfortunate; unsatisfactory; shabby;
deplorable: *her clothes were of a sad state* **4** *Brit informal*
ludicrously contemptible; pathetic: *he's a sad, boring little
wimp* [Old English *sæd* weary; related to Old Norse *sathr*,
Gothic *saths*, Latin *satur*, *satis* enough] > 'sadly *adv*
> 'sadness *n*

SAD *abbreviation* seasonal affective disorder

Sadat (sə'dæt) *n* (**Mohammed**) **Anwar El** ('ænwɑː ɛl).
1918–81, Egyptian statesman: president of Egypt
(1970–81); assassinated; Nobel peace prize jointly with
Begin 1978

Saddam Hussein (sæ'dæm) *n* See **Hussein** (sense 2)

sadden ('sæd³n) *vb* to make or become sad

saddle ('sæd³l) *n* **1** a seat for a rider, usually made of leather, placed on a horse's back and secured with a girth under the belly **2** a similar seat on a bicycle, tractor, etc, made of leather or steel **3** a back pad forming part of the harness of a packhorse **4** anything that resembles a saddle in shape, position, or function **5** a cut of meat, esp mutton, consisting of part of the backbone and both loins **6** the part of a horse or similar animal on which a saddle is placed **7** the part of the back of a domestic chicken that is nearest to the tail **8** another name for **col** (sense 1) ▷ *vb* **9** (sometimes foll by *up*) to put a saddle on (a horse) **10** (*intr*) to mount into the saddle **11** (*tr*) to burden; charge: *I didn't ask to be saddled with this job* [Old English *sadol*, *sædel*; related to Old Norse *sothull*, Old High German *satul*] ▷ **'saddle-,like** *adj*

saddleback ('sæd³l,bæk) *n* a marking resembling a saddle on the backs of various animals

saddlebag ('sæd³l,bæg) *n* a pouch or small bag attached to the saddle of a horse, bicycle, etc

saddlebill ('sæd³l,bıl) *n* a large black-and-white stork, *Ephippiorhynchus senegalensis*, of tropical Africa, having a heavy red bill with a black band around the middle and a yellow patch at the base. Also called: **jabiru** [C19 (as *saddle-bill stork*): so called because of the appearance of its bill]

saddlebow ('sæd³l,bəʊ) *n* the pommel of a saddle

saddlecloth ('sæd³l,klɒθ) *n* a light cloth put under a horse's saddle, so as to prevent rubbing

saddle horse *n* a lightweight horse kept for riding only

saddler ('sædlə) *n* a person who makes, deals in, or repairs saddles and other leather equipment for horses

saddle roof *n* a roof that has a ridge and two gables

saddlery ('sædlərı) *n*, *pl* **-dleries 1** saddles, harness, and other leather equipment for horses collectively **2** the business, work, or place of work of a saddler

saddle soap *n* a soft soap containing neat's-foot oil used to preserve and clean leather

saddletree ('sæd³l,triː) *n* the frame of a saddle

saddo ('sædəʊ) *n*, *pl* **-dos** or **-does** *Brit slang* a socially inadequate or pathetic person [C20: from SAD (sense 4) + -o]

Sadducee ('sædjʊ,siː) *n Judaism* a member of an ancient Jewish sect that was opposed to the Pharisees, denying the resurrection of the dead, the existence of angels, and the validity of oral tradition [Old English *saddūcēas*, via Latin and Greek from Late Hebrew *sāddūqi*, probably from *Sadoq* Zadok, high priest and supposed founder of the sect] ▷ **,Saddu'cean** *adj*

Sade (sɑːd) *n* Comte **Donatien Alphonse François de** (dɔnasjɛ̃ alfɔ̃s frɑ̃swa də), known as the *Marquis de Sade*. 1740–1814, French soldier and writer, whose exposition of sexual perversion gave rise to the term sadism

sadhu or **saddhu** ('sɑːduː) *n* a Hindu wandering holy man [Sanskrit, from *sādhu* good]

Sadi or **Saadi** (sɑːˈdiː) *n* original name *Sheikh Muslih Addin*. ?1184–1292, Persian poet. His best-known works are *Gulistān* (Flower Garden) and *Būstān* (Tree Garden), long moralistic poems in prose and verse

sadiron ('sæd,aıən) *n* a heavy iron pointed at both ends, for pressing clothes [C19: from SAD (in the obsolete sense: heavy) + IRON]

sadism ('seıdızəm, 'sæ-) *n* the gaining of pleasure or sexual gratification from the infliction of pain and mental suffering on another person. See **masochism** [C19: from French, named after Comte Donatien Alphonse François de Sade, known as the *Marquis de Sade* (1740–1814), French soldier and writer of works describing sexual perversion] ▷ **'sadist** *n* ▷ **sadistic** (sə'dıstık) *adj* ▷ **sa'distically** *adv*

Sadler's Wells ('sædləz wɛlz) *n* (*functioning as singular*) a theatre in London. It was renovated in 1931 by Lilian Bayliss and became the home of the Sadler's Wells Opera Company and the Sadler's Wells Ballet (now the Royal Ballet) [named after the medicinal *wells* on the site and its owner Thomas *Sadler*, who founded the original theatre on the site]

sadomasochism (,seıdəʊ'mæsə,kızəm, ,sædəʊ-) *n* **1** the combination of sadistic and masochistic elements in one person, characterized by both aggressive and submissive periods in relationships with others

2 sexual practice in which one partner adopts a sadistic role and the other a masochistic one. Abbreviations: SM, S&M ▷ **,sadomaso'chistic** *adj*

Sadowa ('sɑːdəʊvə) *n* a village in the Czech Republic, in NE Bohemia: scene of the decisive battle of the Austro-Prussian war (1866) in which the Austrians were defeated by the Prussians. Czech name: **Sadová**

SADS (sædz) *n acronym for* sudden adult death syndrome: the sudden death of an apparently healthy adult, for which no cause can be found at postmortem [late C20: by analogy with SIDS (sudden infant death syndrome)]

s.a.e. *abbreviation* stamped addressed envelope

safari (sə'fɑːrı) *n*, *pl* **-ris 1** an overland journey or hunting expedition, esp in Africa **2** the people, animals, etc, that go on the expedition [C19: from Swahili: journey, from Arabic *safarīya*, from *safara* to travel]

safari park *n* an enclosed park in which lions and other wild animals are kept uncaged in the open and can be viewed by the public from cars, etc

safari suit *n* an outfit made of tough cotton, denim, etc, consisting of a bush jacket with matching trousers, shorts, or skirt

safe (seıf) *adj* **1** affording security or protection from harm: *a safe place* **2** (*postpositive*) free from danger: *you'll be safe here* **3** secure from risk; certain; sound: *a safe investment; a safe bet* **4** worthy of trust; prudent: *a safe companion* **5** tending to avoid controversy or risk: *a safe player* **6** unable to do harm; not dangerous: *a criminal safe behind bars; water safe to drink* **7** *Brit informal* excellent **8** **on the safe side** as a precaution ▷ *adv* **9** in a safe condition: *the children are safe in bed now* **10 play safe** to act in a way least likely to cause danger, controversy, or defeat ▷ *n* **11** a strong container, usually of metal and provided with a secure lock, for storing money or valuables **12** a small ventilated cupboard-like container for storing food [C13: from Old French *salf*, from Latin *salvus*; related to Latin *salus* safety] ▷ **'safely** *adv* ▷ **'safeness** *n*

safe-breaker *n* a person who breaks open and robs safes. Also called: **safe-cracker**

safe-conduct *n* **1** a document giving official permission to travel through a region, esp in time of war **2** the protection afforded by such a document

safe-deposit or **safety-deposit** *n* **a** a place or building with facilities for the safe storage of money or valuables **b** (*as modifier*): *a safe-deposit box*

safeguard ('seıf,gɑːd) *n* **1** a person or thing that ensures protection against danger, damage, injury, etc **2** a document authorizing safe-conduct ▷ *vb* **3** (*tr*) to defend or protect

safe house *n* a place used secretly by undercover agents, terrorists, etc, as a meeting place or refuge

safekeeping ('seıf'kiːpıŋ) *n* the act of keeping or state of being kept in safety

safe period *n informal* the period during the menstrual cycle when conception is considered least likely to occur

safe seat *n* a Parliamentary seat that at an election is sure to be held by the same party as held it before

safe sex or **safer sex** *n* sexual intercourse using physical protection, such as a condom, or nonpenetrative methods to prevent the spread of such diseases as AIDS

safety ('seıftı) *n*, *pl* **-ties 1** the quality of being safe **2** freedom from danger or risk of injury **3** a contrivance or device designed to prevent injury **4** *American football* Also called: **safetyman** either of two players who defend the area furthest back in the field

safety belt *n* **1** another name for **seat belt 2** a belt or strap worn by a person working at a great height and attached to a fixed object to prevent him from falling

safety curtain *n* a curtain made of fireproof material that can be lowered to separate the auditorium and stage in a theatre to prevent the spread of a fire

safety factor *n* another name for **factor of safety**

safety glass *n* glass made by sandwiching a layer of plastic or resin between two sheets of glass so that if broken the fragments will not shatter

Safety Islands *pl n* a group of three small French islands in the Atlantic, off the coast of French Guiana. French name: **Îles du Salut**

S

safety lamp *n* an oil-burning miner's lamp in which the flame is surrounded by a metal gauze to prevent it from igniting combustible gas

safety match *n* a match that will light only when struck against a specially prepared surface

safety net *n* **1** a net used in a circus to catch high-wire and trapeze artistes if they fall **2** any means of protection from hardship or loss, such as insurance

safety pin *n* a spring wire clasp with a covering catch, made so as to shield the point when closed and to prevent accidental unfastening

safety razor *n* a razor with a guard or guards fitted close to the cutting edge or edges so that deep cuts are prevented and the risk of accidental cuts reduced

safety touch *n Canadian football* a two-point play

safety valve *n* **1** a valve in a pressure vessel that allows fluid to escape when a predetermined level of pressure has been reached **2** a harmless outlet for emotion, energy, tension etc

saffian ('sæfɪən) *n* leather tanned with sumach and usually dyed a bright colour [c16: via Russian and Turkish from Persian *sakhtiyān* goatskin, from *sakht* hard]

safflower ('sæflaʊə) *n* **1** a thistle-like Eurasian annual plant, *Carthamus tinctorius*, having large heads of orange-yellow flowers and yielding a dye and an oil used in paints, medicines, etc: family *Asteraceae* (composites) **2** a red dye used for cotton and for colouring foods and cosmetics, or a drug obtained from the florets of this plant [c16: via Dutch *saffloer* or German *safflor* from Old French *saffleur*, from Early Italian *saffiore*, of uncertain origin. Influenced by SAFFRON, FLOWER]

saffron ('sæfrən) *n* **1** an Old World crocus, *Crocus sativus*, having purple or white flowers with orange stigmas **2** the dried stigmas of this plant, used to flavour or colour food **3** meadow saffron another name for **autumn crocus 4** false saffron another name for **safflower 5 a** an orange to orange-yellow colour **b** (*as adjective*): *a saffron dress* [c13: from Old French *safran*, from Medieval Latin *safranum*, from Arabic *za'farān*]

Safi (*French* safi) *n* a port in W Morocco, 170 km (105 miles) northwest of Marrakech, to which it is the nearest port. Pop: 470 000 (2003)

Safid Rud (sæ'fiːd 'ruːd) *n* a river in N Iran, flowing northeast to a delta on the Caspian Sea. Length: about 785 km (490 miles)

S.Afr. *abbreviation* South Africa(n)

safranine *or* **safranin** ('sæfrənɪn, -,niːn) *n* any of a class of azine dyes, used for textiles and biological stains [c19: from French *safran* SAFFRON + -INE²]

sag (sæg) *vb* **sags, sagging, sagged** (*mainly intr*) **1** (*also tr*) to sink or cause to sink in parts, as under weight or pressure: *the bed sags in the middle* **2** to fall in value: *prices sagged to a new low* **3** to hang unevenly; droop **4** (of courage, spirits, etc) to weaken; flag ▷ *n* **5** the act or an instance of sagging: *a sag in profits* **6** *nautical* the extent to which a vessel's keel sags at the centre [c15: from Scandinavian; compare Swedish *sacka*, Dutch *zakken*, Norwegian dialect *sakka* to subside, Danish *sakke* to lag behind]

saga ('sɑːgə) *n* **1** any of several medieval prose narratives written in Iceland and recounting the exploits of a hero or a family **2** any similar heroic narrative **3** Also called: **saga novel** a series of novels about several generations or members of a family **4** *informal* a series of events or a story stretching over a long period [c18: from Old Norse: a narrative; related to Old English *secgan* to SAY]

sagacious (sə'geɪʃəs) *adj* having or showing sagacity; wise [c17: from Latin *sagāx*, from *sāgīre* to be astute] > sa'**gaciously** *adv*

sagacity (sə'gæsɪtɪ) *n* foresight, discernment, or keen perception; ability to make good judgments

sagamore ('sægə,mɔː) *n* (among some North American Indians) a chief or eminent man. Also called: **sachem** [c17: from Abnaki *sāgimau*, literally: he overcomes]

Sagan (*French* sagã) *n* **1** Carl (Edward) 1934–96, US astronomer and writer on scientific subjects; presenter of the television series *Cosmos* (1980) **2** Françoise (frãswaːz), original name *Françoise Quoirez*. 1935–2004, French writer, best-known for the novels *Bonjour Tristesse*

(1954) and *Aimez-vous Brahms?* (1959)

Sagarmatha ('sɑːgɑːˌmɑːθə) *n* the Nepalese name for (Mount) **Everest**

sage¹ (seɪdʒ) *n* **1** a man revered for his profound wisdom ▷ *adj* **2** *obsolete* wise or prudent **3** *obsolete* solemn [c13: from Old French, from Latin *sapere* to be sensible; see SAPIENT] > '**sagely** *adv* > '**sageness** *n*

sage² (seɪdʒ) *n* **1** a perennial Mediterranean plant, *Salvia officinalis*, having grey-green leaves and purple, blue, or white flowers: family *Lamiaceae* (labiates) **2** the leaves of this plant, used in cooking for flavouring **3** short for **sagebrush** [c14: from Old French *saulge*, from Latin *salvia*, from *salvus* safe, in good health (from the curative properties attributed to the plant)]

sagebrush ('seɪdʒ,brʌʃ) *n* any of several aromatic plants of the genus *Artemisia*, esp *A. tridentata*, a shrub of W North America, having silver-green leaves and large clusters of small white flowers: family *Asteraceae* (composites)

saggar *or* **sagger** ('sægə) *n* a clay box in which fragile ceramic wares are placed for protection during firing [c17: perhaps alteration of SAFEGUARD]

Saghalien (sə'gɑːljən) *n* a variant of **Sakhalin**

sagittal suture *n* a serrated line on the top of the skull that marks the junction of the two parietal bones

Sagittarius (,sædʒɪ'tɛərɪəs) *n, Latin genitive* Sagittarii (,sædʒɪ'tɛərɪ,aɪ) **1** *astronomy* a large conspicuous zodiacal constellation in the S hemisphere lying between Scorpius and Capricornus on the ecliptic and crossed by the Milky Way and containing the galactic centre **2** Also called: the Archer *astrology* **a** the ninth sign of the zodiac, symbol ♐, having a mutable fire classification and ruled by the planet Jupiter. The sun is in this sign between Nov 22 and Dec 21 **b** a person born when the sun is in this sign [c14: from Latin: an archer, from *sagitta* an arrow]

sagittate ('sædʒɪ,teɪt) *or* **sagittiform** (sə'dʒɪtɪ,fɔːm, 'sædʒ-) *adj* (*esp of leaves*) shaped like the head of an arrow [c18: from New Latin *sagittātus*, from Latin *sagitta* arrow]

sago ('seɪgəʊ) *n* a starchy cereal obtained from the powdered pith of a sago palm, used for puddings and as a thickening agent [c16: from Malay *sāgū*]

saguaro (sə'gwɑːrəʊ, sə'wɑː-) *or* **sahuaro** (sə'wɑːrəʊ) *n*, *pl* -ros a giant cactus, *Carnegiea gigantea*, of desert regions of Arizona, S California, and Mexico, having white nocturnal flowers and edible red pulpy fruits [Mexican Spanish, variant of *sahuaro*, an Indian name]

Saguenay (,sægə'neɪ) *n* a river in SE Canada in S Quebec, rising as the Péribonca River on the central plateau and flowing south, then east to the St Lawrence. Length: 764 km (475 miles)

Sagunto (*Spanish* sa'ɣunto) *n* an industrial town in E Spain, near Valencia: allied to Rome and made a heroic resistance to the Carthaginian attack led by Hannibal (219–218 BC). Pop: 58 287 (2003 est)

Sahara (sə'hɑːrə) *n* a desert in N Africa, extending from the Atlantic to the Red Sea and from the Mediterranean to central Mali, Niger, Chad, and the Sudan: the largest desert in the world, occupying over a quarter of Africa; rises to over 3300 m (11 000 ft) in the central mountain system of the Ahaggar and Tibesti massifs; large reserves of iron ore, oil, and natural gas. Area: 9 100 000 sq km (3 500 000 sq miles). Average annual rainfall: less than 254 mm (10 in.). Highest recorded temperature: 58°C (136.4°F) > Sa'**haran** *n, adj*

sahib ('sɑːhɪb) *or* **saheb** ('sɑːhɛb) *n* (in India) a form of address or title placed after a man's name or designation, used as a mark of respect [c17: from Urdu, from Arabic *çāhib*, literally: friend]

said¹ (sɛd) *adj* **1** (*prenominal*) (in contracts, pleadings, etc) named or mentioned previously; aforesaid ▷ *vb* **2** the past tense and past participle of **say¹**

said² ('sɑːɪd) *n* a variant of **sayyid**

Saida ('sɑːɪdə) *n* a port in SW Lebanon, on the Mediterranean: on the site of ancient Sidon; terminal of the Trans-Arabian pipeline from Saudi Arabia. Pop: 150 000 (2005 est)

saiga ('saɪgə) *n* either of two antelopes, *Saiga tatarica* or *S.*

S

mongolica, of the plains of central Asia, having an enlarged slightly elongated nose [c19: from Russian]

Saigon (saɪˈɡɒn) *n* the former name (until 1976) of **Ho Chi Minh City**

Saigo Takamori (saɪˈiːɡəʊ ˌtækəˈmɔːrɪ) *n* 1828–77, Japanese samurai, who led (1868) the coup that restored imperial government. In 1877 he reluctantly led a samurai rebellion, committing suicide when it failed

sail (seɪl) *n* **1** an area of fabric, usually Terylene or nylon (formerly canvas), with fittings for holding it in any suitable position to catch the wind, used for propelling certain kinds of vessels, esp over water **2** a voyage on such a vessel: *a sail down the river* **3** a vessel with sails or such vessels collectively: *to travel by sail; we raised seven sail in the northeast* **4** a ship's sails collectively **5** something resembling a sail in shape, position, or function, such as the part of a windmill that is turned by the wind or the part of a Portuguese man-of-war that projects above the water **6** in sail having the sail set **7** make sail **a** to run up the sail or to run up more sail **b** to begin a voyage **8** set sail **a** to embark on a voyage by ship **b** to hoist sail **9** under sail **a** with sail hoisted **b** under way ▷ *vb* (mainly *intr*) **10** to travel in a boat or ship: *we sailed to Le Havre* **11** to begin a voyage; set sail: *we sail at 5 o'clock* **12** (of a vessel) to move over the water: *the liner is sailing to the Caribbean* **13** (*tr*) to manoeuvre or navigate a vessel: *he sailed the schooner up the channel* **14** (*tr*) to sail over: *she sailed the Atlantic single-handed* **15** (often foll by *over, through*, etc) to move fast or effortlessly: *we sailed through customs; the ball sailed over the fence* **16** to move along smoothly; glide **17** (often foll by *in* or *into*) *informal* **a** to begin (something) with vigour **b** to make an attack (on) violently with words or physical force [Old English *segl*; related to Old Frisian *seil*, Old Norse *segl*, German *Segel*] > **'sailable** *adj* > **'sailless** *adj*

sailboard (ˈseɪlˌbɔːd) *n* the craft used for windsurfing, consisting of a moulded board like a surfboard, to which a mast bearing a single sail is attached by a swivel joint

sailboarding (ˈseɪlˌbɔːdɪŋ) *n* another name for **windsurfing**

sailcloth (ˈseɪlˌklɒθ) *n* **1** any of various fabrics from which sails are made **2** a lighter cloth used for clothing, etc

sailer (ˈseɪlə) *n* a vessel, esp one equipped with sails, with specified sailing characteristics: *a good sailer*

sailfish (ˈseɪlˌfɪʃ) *n, pl* -fish or -fishes **1** any of several large scombroid game fishes of the genus *Istiophorus*, such as *I. albicans* (**Atlantic sailfish**), of warm and tropical seas: family Istiophoridae. They have an elongated upper jaw and a long sail-like dorsal fin **2** another name for **basking shark**

sailing ship *n* a large sailing vessel

sailor (ˈseɪlə) *n* **1** any member of a ship's crew, esp one below the rank of officer **2** a person who sails, esp with reference to the likelihood of his becoming seasick: *a good sailor*

sailplane (ˈseɪlˌpleɪn) *n* a high-performance glider

sainfoin (ˈsænfɔɪn) *n* a Eurasian perennial leguminous plant, *Onobrychis viciifolia*, widely grown as a forage crop, having pale pink flowers and curved pods [c17: from French, from Medieval Latin *sānum faenum* wholesome hay, referring to its former use as a medicine]

Sainsbury (ˈseɪnzbrɪ) *n* **David John**, Baron. born 1940, British businessman and politician, chief executive of the Sainsbury supermarket chain from 1992; science minister (1998–2006)

saint (seɪnt, *unstressed* sənt) *n* **1** a person who after death is formally recognized by a Christian Church, esp the Roman Catholic Church, as having attained, through holy deeds or behaviour, a specially exalted place in heaven and the right to veneration **2** a person of exceptional holiness or goodness **3** (*plural*) *Bible* the collective body of those who are righteous in God's sight ▷ *vb* **4** (*tr*) to canonize; recognize formally as a saint [c12: from Old French, from Latin *sanctus* holy, from *sancīre* to hallow] > **'saintlike** *adj* > **'sainthood** *n*

Saint Agnes's Eve *n* the night of Jan 20, when according to tradition a woman can discover the identity of her future husband in a dream by performing certain rites

Saint Albans (ˈɔːlbənz) *n* a city in SE England, in W Hertfordshire: founded in 948 AD around the Benedictine abbey first built in Saxon times on the site of the martyrdom (about 303 AD) of St Alban; present abbey built in 1077; Roman ruins. Pop: 82 429 (2001). Latin name: **Verulamium**

Saint Andrews *n* a city in E Scotland, in Fife on the North Sea: the oldest university in Scotland (1411); famous golf links. Pop: 14 209 (2001)

Saint Andrew's Cross *n* **1** a diagonal cross with equal arms **2** a white diagonal cross on a blue ground [c18: so called because Saint Andrew, one of the twelve apostles of Jesus, is reputed to have been crucified on a cross of this shape]

Saint Anthony's fire *n pathol* another name for **ergotism, erysipelas** [c16: so named because praying to St Anthony was believed to effect a cure]

Saint Augustine (ˈɔːɡəsˌtiːn) *n* a resort in NE Florida, on the Intracoastal Waterway: the oldest town in North America (1565); the northernmost outpost of the Spanish colonial empire for over 200 years. Pop: 11 915 (2003 est)

Saint Austell (ˈɔːstəl) *n* a town in SW England, in S Cornwall on **St Austell Bay** (an inlet of the English Channel): centre for the now-declining china clay industry; the Eden Project, a rainforest environment in the world's largest greenhouse, is nearby; administratively part of St Austell with Fowey 1968-74. Pop (with Fowey): 22 658 (2001)

Saint-Barthélemy (sɛbartɛɪleɪmɪ) *n* an island in the E Caribbean, in the Leeward Islands, belonging to France (as a dependency of Guadeloupe until 2007, then as a separate French Overseas Collectivity). Capital: Gustavia. Pop: 6852 (1999 census). Area: 21 sq km (8.1 sq miles)

Saint Bernard *n* a large breed of dog with a dense red-and-white coat, formerly used as a rescue dog in mountainous areas [c19: so called because they were kept by the monks of the hospice at the Great SAINT BERNARD PASS]

Saint Bernard Pass *n* either of two passes over the Alps: the **Great St Bernard Pass** 2472 m (8110 ft) high, east of Mont Blanc between Italy and Switzerland, or the **Little St Bernard Pass** 2157 m (7077 ft) high, south of Mont Blanc between Italy and France

Saint-Brieuc (French sēbriø) *n* a market town in NW France, near the N coast of Brittany. Pop: 46 087 (1999)

Saint Catharines *n* an industrial city in S central Canada, in S Ontario on the Welland Canal. Pop: 129 170 (2001)

Saint Christopher *n* another name for **Saint Kitts**

Saint Christopher-Nevis *n* the official name of **Saint Kitts-Nevis**

Saint Clair (klɛə) *n* **Lake Saint Clair** a lake between SE Michigan and Ontario: linked with Lake Huron by the **St Clair River** and with Lake Erie by the Detroit River. Area: 1191 sq km (460 sq miles)

Saint-Cloud (French sēklu) *n* a residential suburb of Paris: former royal palace; Sèvres porcelain factory. Pop: 28 157 (1999)

Saint Croix (krɔɪ) *n* an island in the Caribbean, the largest of the Virgin Islands of the US: purchased from Denmark by the US in 1917. Chief town: Christiansted. Pop: 53 234 (2000). Area: 207 sq km (80 sq miles). Also called: **Santa Cruz** (ˈsæntə ˈkruːz)

Saint Croix River *n* a river on the border between the northeast US and SE Canada, flowing from the Chiputneticook Lakes to Passamaquoddy Bay, forming the border between Maine, US, and New Brunswick, Canada. Length: 121 km (75 miles)

Saint David's *n* a town in SW Wales, in Pembrokeshire: its cathedral was a place of pilgrimage in medieval times. Pop: 1627 (2001)

Saint-Denis (French sēdni) *n* **1** a town in N France, on the Seine: 12th-century Gothic abbey church, containing the tombs of many French monarchs; an industrial suburb of Paris. Pop: 85 832 (1999) **2** the capital of the French overseas region of Réunion, a port on the N coast. Pop:

131 557 (1999)

Sainte-Beuve (French sɛ̃tbœv) n **Charles Augustin** (ʃarl ogystɛ̃). 1804–69, French critic, best known for his collections of essays *Port Royal* (1840–59) and *Les Causeries du Lundi* (1851–62)

sainted (ˈseɪntɪd) adj **1** canonized **2** like a saint in character or nature **3** hallowed or holy

Sainte Foy (seɪnt ˈfɔɪ, sənt) n a SW suburb of Quebec, on the St Lawrence River. Pop: 72 547 (2001)

Saint Elias Mountains pl n a mountain range between SE Alaska and the SW Yukon, Canada. Highest peak: Mount Logan, 5959 m (19 550 ft)

Saint Elmo's fire (ˈɛlməʊz) n (not in technical usage) a luminous region that sometimes appears around church spires, the masts of ships, etc. It is a corona discharge in the air caused by atmospheric electricity [c16: so called because it was associated with *Saint Elmo* (a corruption, via *Sant'Ermo*, of *Saint Erasmus*, died 303) the patron saint of Mediterranean sailors]

Saint-Étienne (French sɛ̃tetjɛn) n a town in E central France: a major producer of textiles and armaments. Pop: 180 210 (1999)

Saint-Exupéry (French sɛ̃tɛgzyperi) n **Antoine de** (ɑ̃twan də). 1900–44, French novelist and aviator. His novels of aviation include *Vol de nuit* (1931) and *Terre des hommes* (1939). He also wrote the fairy tale *Le petit prince* (1943)

Saint Gall (French sɛ̃ gal) n **1** a canton of NE Switzerland. Capital: St Gall. Pop: 455 200 (2002 est). Area: 2012 sq km (777 sq miles) **2** a town in NE Switzerland, capital of St Gall canton: an important educational centre in the Middle Ages. Pop: 72 626 (2000)

Saint George's n the capital of Grenada, a port in the southwest Pop: 3908 (2001)

Saint George's Channel n a strait between Wales and Ireland, linking the Irish Sea with the Atlantic. Length: about 160 km (100 miles). Width: up to 145 km (90 miles)

Saint Gotthard (ˈgɒtəd) n **1** a range of the Lepontine Alps in SE central Switzerland **2** a pass over the St Gotthard mountains, in S Switzerland. Height: 2114 m (6935 ft)

Saint Helena (ˌsɛntɪˈliːnə) n a volcanic island in the SE Atlantic, forming a UK Overseas Territory with its dependencies Tristan da Cunha and Ascension, and the uninhabited Gough, Inaccessible, and Nightingale Islands: discovered by the Portuguese in 1502 and annexed by England in 1651; scene of Napoleon's exile and death. Capital: Jamestown. Pop: 5644 (2003 est). Area: 122 sq km (47 sq miles)

Saint Helens n **1** a town in NW England, in St Helens unitary authority, Merseyside: glass industry. Pop: 102 629 (2001) **2** a unitary authority in NW England, in Merseyside. Pop: 176 700 (2003 est). Area: 130 sq km (50 sq miles) **3** a volcanic peak in S Washington state; it erupted in 1980 after lying dormant from 1857

Saint Helier (ˈhɛliə) n a market town and resort in the Channel Islands, the capital of Jersey, on the S coast. Pop: 28 310 (2001)

Saint James's Palace n a palace in Pall Mall, London: a residence of British monarchs from 1697 to 1837

Saint John n **1** a port in E Canada, at the mouth of the St John River: the largest city in New Brunswick; very often not abbreviated to 'St'. Pop: 90 762 (2001) **2** an island in the Caribbean, in the Virgin Islands of the US. Pop: 4197 (2000). Area: 49 sq km (19 sq miles) **3** Lake Saint John a lake in Canada, in S Quebec: drained by the Saguenay River. Area: 971 sq km (375 sq miles) **4** a river in E North America, rising in Maine, US, and flowing northeast to New Brunswick, Canada, then generally southeast to the Bay of Fundy. Length: 673 km (418 miles) Abbreviation: St John

St John (ˈsɪndʒən) n **Henry.** See (1st Viscount) **Bolingbroke**

Saint-John Perse (ˈsɪndʒən ˈpɜːs) n See **Perse**

Saint John's n **1** a port in Canada, capital of Newfoundland and Labrador, on the E coast of the Avalon Peninsula. Pop: 122 709 (2001) **2** the capital of Antigua and Barbuda: a port on the NW coast of the island of Antigua. Pop: 24 226 (2000 est)

Saint John's wort n **a** any of numerous shrubs or herbaceous plants of the temperate genus *Hypericum*, such as *H. perforatum*, having yellow flowers and glandular leaves: family Hypericaceae **b** a preparation of this plant often used to treat mild depression. See also **tutsan** [c15: so named because it was traditionally gathered on *Saint John's Eve* (June 23) as a protection against evil spirits]

Saint-Just (French sɛ̃ʒyst) n **Louis Antoine Léon de** (lwi ɑ̃twan leɔ̃ də). 1767–94, French Revolutionary leader and orator. A member of the Committee of Public Safety (1793–94), he was guillotined with Robespierre

Saint Kilda (ˈkɪldə) n **1** a group of volcanic islands in the Atlantic, in the Outer Hebrides: uninhabited since 1930; bird sanctuary **2** Also called: **Hirta** the main island of this group

Saint Kitts (kɪts) n an island in the E Caribbean, in the Leeward Islands: part of the state of St Kitts-Nevis. Capital: Basseterre. Pop: 34 703 (2001). Area: 168 sq km (65 sq miles). Also called: **Saint Christopher**

Saint Kitts-Nevis n an independent state in the E Caribbean; comprises the two islands of St Kitts and Nevis: with the island of Anguilla formed a colony (1882–1967) and a British associated state (1967–83); Anguilla formally separated from the group in 1983; gained full independence in 1983 as a member of the Commonwealth. Official language: English. Religion: Protestant majority. Currency: E Caribbean dollar. Capital: Basseterre. Pop: 42 000 (2003 est). Area: 262 sq km (101 sq miles)

Saint Laurent (French sɛ̃ lɔrɑ̃) n a W suburb of Montreal, Canada. Pop: 77 391 (2001)

Saint-Laurent (French sɛ̃lɔrɑ̃) n **1 Yves** (iv), full name *Yves-Mathieu.* born 1936, French couturier: popularized trousers for women for all occasions **2 Louis.** 1882–1973, Canadian politician; prime minister of Canada (1948–57)

Saint Lawrence n **1** a river in SE Canada, flowing northeast from Lake Ontario, forming part of the border between Canada and the US, to the Gulf of St Lawrence: commercially one of the most important rivers in the world as the easternmost link of the St Lawrence Seaway. Length: 1207 km (750 miles). Width at mouth: 145 km (90 miles) **2** Gulf of Saint Lawrence a deep arm of the Atlantic off the E coast of Canada between Newfoundland and the mainland coasts of Quebec, New Brunswick, and Nova Scotia

Saint Lawrence Seaway n an inland waterway of North America, passing through the Great Lakes, the St Lawrence River, and connecting canals and locks: one of the most important waterways in the world. Length: 3993 km (2480 miles)

Saint Leger (ˈlɛdʒə) n the Saint Leger an annual horse race run at Doncaster since 1776: one of the classics of the flat-racing season

Saint Leonard (ˈlɛnəd) n a N suburb of Montreal, Canada. Pop: 69 604 (2001)

Saint-Lô (French sɛ̃lo) n a market town in NW France: a Calvinist stronghold in the 16th century. Pop: 20 090 (1999)

Saint Louis (ˈlʊɪs) n a port in E Missouri, on the Mississippi River near its confluence with the Missouri: the largest city in the state; university; major industrial centre. Pop: 332 223 (2003 est)

Saint-Louis (French sɛ̃lwi) n a port in NW Senegal, on an island at the mouth of the Senegal River: the first French settlement in W Africa (1689); capital of Senegal until 1958. Pop: 183 000 (2005 est)

Saint Lucia (ˈluːʃə) n an island state in the Caribbean, in the Windward Islands group of the Lesser Antilles: a volcanic island; gained self-government in 1967 as a British Associated State; attained full independence within the Commonwealth in 1979. Official language: English. Religion: Roman Catholic majority. Currency: E Caribbean dollar. Capital: Castries. Pop: 150 000 (2004 est). Area: 616 sq km (238 sq miles)

saintly (ˈseɪntlɪ) adj -lier, -liest like, relating to, or suitable for a saint > **saintlily** adv > **saintliness** n

Saint Martin n an island in the E Caribbean, in the Leeward Islands: administratively divided since 1648, the north belonging to France (as a dependency of Guadeloupe until 2007, then as a separate French Overseas Collectivity) and the south belonging to the Netherlands (as part of the Netherlands Antilles); salt industry. Capital (French part): Marigot; (Dutch part) Philipsburg. Pop: (French) 33 102 (2004); (Dutch) 38 959 (2007 est). Areas: (French) 52 sq km (20 sq miles); (Dutch) 33 sq km (13 sq miles). Dutch name: **Sint Maarten**

Saint-Maur-des-Fossés (French sɛ̃mɔrdefose) n a town in N France, on the River Marne: a residential suburb of SE Paris. Pop: 73 069 (1999)

Saint-Mihiel (French sɛ̃mjɛl) n a village in NE France, on the River Meuse: site of a battle in World War I, in which the American army launched its first offensive in France

Saint Moritz (məˈrɪts) n a village in E Switzerland, in Graubünden canton in the Upper Engadine, at an altitude of 1856 m (6089 ft): sports and tourist centre. Pop: 5589 (2000)

Saint-Nazaire (French sɛ̃nazɛr) n a port in NW France, at the mouth of the River Loire: German submarine base in World War II; shipbuilding. Pop: 65 874 (1999)

Saint-Ouen (French sɛ̃twɛ̃) n a town in N France, on the Seine: an industrial suburb of Paris; famous flea market. Pop: 39 722 (1999)

Saint Paul n a port in SE Minnesota, capital of the state, at the head of navigation of the Mississippi: now contiguous with Minneapolis (the Twin Cities). Pop: 280 404 (2003 est)

saintpaulia (sənt'pɔːlɪə) n another name for **African violet** [c20: New Latin, named after Baron W. von *Saint Paul*, German soldier (died 1910), who discovered it]

Saint Paul's n a cathedral in central London, built between 1675 and 1710 to replace an earlier cathedral destroyed during the Great Fire (1666): regarded as Wren's masterpiece

Saint Peter Port n a port and resort in the Channel Islands: the capital of the Bailiwick of Guernsey, on the E coast of the island of Guernsey. Pop: 28 310 (2001)

Saint Peter's n the basilica of the Vatican City, built between 1506 and 1615 to replace an earlier church: the largest church in the world, 188 m (615 ft) long, and chief pilgrimage centre of Europe; designed by many architects, notably Bramante, Raphael, Sangallo, Michelangelo, and Bernini

Saint Petersburg ('piːtəz,bɜːg) n 1 a city and port in Russia, on the Gulf of Finland at the mouth of the Neva River: founded by Peter the Great in 1703 and built on low-lying marshes subject to frequent flooding; capital of Russia from 1712 to 1918; a cultural and educational centre, with a university (1819); a major industrial centre, with engineering, shipbuilding, chemical, textile, and printing industries. Pop: 5 315 000 (2005 est). Former names: Petrograd, Leningrad 2 a city and resort in W Florida, on Tampa Bay. Pop: 247 610 (2003 est)

Saint-Pierre[1] (French sɛ̃ pjɛr) n a town on the coast of the French island of Martinique, destroyed by the eruption of Mont Pelée in 1902 with the loss of about 30 000 lives; later partly rebuilt

Saint-Pierre[2] (French sɛ̃pjɛr) n Jacques Henri Bernardin de (ʒak ãri bɛrnardɛ̃ də). 1737–1814, French author; his work, which was greatly influenced by the writings of Rousseau, includes *Voyage à l'Île de France* (1773), *Études de la nature* (1784, 1788), and *La chaumière indienne* (1791)

Saint Pierre and Miquelon (,mɪkə'lɒn; French miklɔ̃) n an archipelago in the Atlantic, off the S coast of Newfoundland: an overseas department of France, the only remaining French possession in North America; consists of the islands of St Pierre, with most of the population, and Miquelon, about ten times as large; fishing industries. Capital: St Pierre. Pop: 6000 (2003 est). Area: 242 sq km (94 sq miles)

Saint Pölten ('pɜːltən) n See **Sankt Pölten**

Saint-Quentin (French sɛ̃kãtɛ̃) n a town in N France, on the River Somme: textile industry. Pop: 59 066 (1999)

Saint-Saëns (French sɛ̃sɑ̃s) n (**Charles**) **Camille** (kamij). 1835–1921, French composer, pianist, and organist. His works include the symphonic poem *Danse Macabre* (1874), the opera *Samson and Delilah* (1877), the humorous

orchestral suite *Carnival of Animals* (1886), five symphonies, and five piano concertos

Saintsbury ('seɪntsbəri, -brɪ) n **George Edward Bateman**. 1845–1933, British literary critic and historian; author of many works on English and French literature

saint's day n Christianity a day in the church calendar commemorating a saint

Saint-Simon (French sɛ̃simɔ̃) n 1 **Comte de** (kɔ̃t də), title of *Claude Henri de Rouvroy*. 1760–1825, French social philosopher, generally regarded as the founder of French socialism. He thought society should be reorganized along industrial lines and that scientists should be the new spiritual leaders. His most important work is *Nouveau Christianisme* (1825) 2 **Duc de** (dyk də), title of *Louis de Rouvroy*. 1675– 1755, French soldier, statesman, and writer: his *Mémoires* are an outstanding account of the period 1694–1723, during the reigns of Louis XIV and Louis XV

Saint Thomas n 1 an island in the E Caribbean, in the Virgin Islands of the US. Capital: Charlotte Amalie. Pop: 51 181 (2000). Area: 83 sq km (28 sq miles) 2 the former name (1921–37) of **Charlotte Amalie**

Saint Vincent n 1 **Cape Saint Vincent** a headland at the SW extremity of Portugal: scene of several important naval battles, notably in 1797, when the British defeated the French and Spanish 2 **Gulf Saint Vincent** a shallow inlet of SE South Australia, to the east of the Yorke Peninsula: salt industry

Saint Vincent and the Grenadines n an island state in the Caribbean, in the Windward Islands of the Lesser Antilles: comprises the island of St Vincent and the Northern Grenadines; formerly a British associated state (1969–79); gained full independence in 1979 as a member of the Commonwealth. Official language: English. Religion: Protestant majority. Currency: Caribbean dollar. Capital: Kingstown. Pop: 121 000 (2004 est). Area: 389 sq km (150 sq miles)

Saint Vitus's dance ('vaɪtəsɪz) n pathol a nontechnical name for: **Sydenham's chorea** [c17: so called because sufferers traditionally prayed to *Saint Vitus* (3rd-century child martyr) for relief and were said to be cured by a visit to his shrine]

Saipan (saɪ'pæn) n an island in the W Pacific, administrative centre of the US associated territory of the Northern Mariana Islands (on Capitol Hill); captured by the Americans and used as an air base until the end of World War II. Pop: 62 392 (2000). Area: 180 sq km (70 sq miles)

Saïs ('seɪɪs) n (in ancient Egypt) a city in the W Nile delta; the royal capital of the 24th dynasty (about 730–715 BC) and the 26th dynasty (about 664–525 BC)

saith (sɛθ) vb (used with he, she, or it) archaic a form of the present tense (indicative mood) of **say**[1]

saithe (seɪθ) n Brit another name for **coalfish** [c19: from Old Norse *seithr* coalfish; compare Gaelic *saigh*, *saighean* coalfish, Irish *saoidhean* young of fish]

Sakai (sɑːˈkaɪ) n a port in S Japan, on S Honshu on Osaka Bay: an industrial satellite of Osaka. Pop: 787 833 (2002 est)

sake[1] (seɪk) n 1 benefit or interest (esp in the phrase **for (someone's or one's own) sake**) 2 the purpose of obtaining or achieving (esp in the phrase **for the sake of (something)**) 3 used in various exclamations of impatience, urgency, etc: *for heaven's sake; for pete's sake* [c13 (in the phrase *for the sake of*, probably from legal usage): from Old English *sacu* lawsuit (hence, a cause); related to Old Norse *sok*, German *Sache* matter]

sake[2], **saké** or **saki** ('sækɪ) n a Japanese alcoholic drink made from fermented rice [c17: from Japanese]

saker ('seɪkə) n a large falcon, *Falco cherrug*, of E Europe and central Asia: used in falconry [c14 *sagre*, from Old French *sacre*, from Arabic *saqr*]

Sakhalin (Russian səxa'lin) or **Saghalien** n an island in the Sea of Okhotsk, off the SE coast of Russia north of Japan: fishing, forestry, and mineral resources (coal and petroleum). Capital: Yuzhno-Sakhalinsk. Pop: 546 500 (2002). Area: 76 000 sq km (29 300 sq miles). Japanese name (1905–24): **Karafuto**

Sakha Republic (Russian 'saxa) or **Yakutia** n an

administrative division in E Russia, in NE Siberia on the Arctic Ocean: the coldest inhabited region of the world; it has rich mineral resources. Capital: Yakutsk. Pop: 948 100 (2002). Area: 3 103 200 sq km (1 197 760 sq miles)

Sakharov (*Russian* za'xarəf) *n* **Andrei** (an'drjej). 1921–89, Soviet physicist and human-rights campaigner: Nobel peace prize 1975

saki ('saːkɪ) *n* **1** any of several small mostly arboreal New World monkeys of the genera *Pithecia* and *Chiropotes*, having long hair and a long bushy tail **2** another name for **sake²** [sense 1: C20: French, from Tupi *saqi*]

Saki ('saːkɪ) *n* pen name of (Hector Hugh) **Munro¹**

sal (sæl) *n* a pharmacological term for **salt** (sense 3) [Latin]

salaam (sə'laːm) *n* **1** a Muslim form of salutation consisting of a deep bow with the right palm on the forehead **2** a salutation signifying peace, used chiefly by Muslims ▷ *vb* **3** to make a salaam or salute (someone) with a salaam [C17: from Arabic *salām* peace, from the phrase *assalām 'alaikum* peace be to you]

salable ('seɪləbəl) *adj* the US spelling of **saleable**

salacious (sə'leɪʃəs) *adj* **1** having an excessive interest in sex **2** (of books, magazines, etc) erotic, bawdy, or lewd [C17: from Latin *salax* fond of leaping, from *salīre* to leap] ▷ **sa'laciously** *adv* ▷ **sa'laciousness** *or* **salacity** (sə'læsɪtɪ) *n*

salad ('sæləd) *n* **1** a dish of raw vegetables, such as lettuce, tomatoes, etc, served as a separate course with cold meat, eggs, etc, or as part of a main course **2** any dish of cold vegetables or fruit: *potato salad; fruit salad* **3** any green vegetable used in such a dish, esp lettuce [C15: from Old French *salade*, from Old Provençal *salada*, from *salar* to season with salt, from Latin *sal* salt]

salad days *pl n* a period of youth and inexperience [allusion to *Antony and Cleopatra* (1.v.73) by William Shakespeare: "my salad days When I was green in judgment, cold in blood"]

salad dressing *n* a sauce for salad, such as oil and vinegar or mayonnaise

salade niçoise (sæ'laːd niː'swaːz) *n* a cold dish consisting of hard-boiled eggs, anchovy fillets, olives, tomatoes, tuna fish, etc [C20: from French, literally salad of or from *Nice*, S France]

Saladin ('sælədɪn) *n* Arabic name *Salah-ed-Din Yusuf ibn-Ayyub*. ?1137–93, sultan of Egypt and Syria and opponent of the Crusaders. He defeated the Christians near Tiberias (1187) and captured Acre, Jerusalem, and Ashkelon. He fought against Richard I of England and Philip II of France during the Third Crusade (1189–92)

Salado (*Spanish* sa'laðo) *n* **1** a river in N Argentina, rising in the Andes as the Juramento and flowing southeast to the Paraná River. Length: 2012 km (1250 miles) **2** a river in W Argentina, rising near the Chilean border as the Desaguadero and flowing south to the Colorado River. Length: about 1365 km (850 miles)

Salamanca (*Spanish* sala'maŋka) *n* a city in W Spain: a leading cultural centre of Europe till the end of the 16th century; market town. Pop: 157 906 (2003 es

salamander ('sælə,mændə) *n* **1** any of various urodele amphibians, such as *Salamandra salamandra* (**European fire salamander**) of central and S Europe (family *Salamandridae*). They are typically terrestrial, have an elongated body, and only return to water to breed **2** *chiefly US & Canadian* any urodele amphibian **3** a mythical reptile supposed to live in fire **4** an elemental fire-inhabiting being [C14: from Old French *salamandre*, from Latin *salamandra*, from Greek]

Salambria (sə'læmbrɪə, ˌsaːlɑːm'brɪə) *n* a river in N Greece, in Thessaly, rising in the Pindus Mountains and flowing southeast and east to the Gulf of Salonika. Length: about 200 km (125 miles). Ancient name: Peneus. Modern Greek name: Piniós

salami (sə'laːmɪ) *n* a highly seasoned type of sausage, usually flavoured with garlic [C19: from Italian, plural of *salame*, from Vulgar Latin *salāre* (unattested) to salt, from Latin *sal* salt]

Salamis ('sæləmɪs) *n* an island in the Saronic Gulf, Greece: scene of the naval battle in 480 BC, in which the Greeks defeated the Persians. Pop (municipality): 28 423 (2001). Area: 95 sq km (37 sq miles)

sal ammoniac *n* another name for **ammonium chloride**

salaried ('sælərɪd) *adj* earning or yielding a salary: *a salaried worker; salaried employment*

salary ('sælərɪ) *n*, *pl* -ries **1** a fixed regular payment made by an employer, often monthly, for professional or office work as opposed to manual work. See **wage** (sense 1) ▷ *vb* -ries, -rying, -ried **2** (*tr*) to pay a salary to [C14: from Anglo-Norman *salarie*, from Latin *salārium* the sum given to Roman soldiers to buy salt, from *sal* salt]

Salazar (*Portuguese* sələ'zar) *n* **Antonio de Oliveira** (ən'tɔnju 'dɛ: oli'vəɪrə). 1889–1970, Portuguese statesman: dictator (1932–68)

salchow ('sɔːlkəʊ) *n* a figure-skating jump made from the inner backward edge of one foot with one, two, or three full turns in the air, returning to the outer backward edge of the opposite foot [C20: named after Ulrich *Salchow* (1877–1949), Swedish figure skater, who originated it]

Salduba (sæl'duːbə, 'sældəbə) *n* the pre-Roman (Celtiberian) name for **Zaragoza**

sale (seɪl) *n* **1** the exchange of goods, property, or services for an agreed sum of money or credit **2** the amount sold **3** the opportunity to sell; market: *there was no sale for luxuries* **4 a** an event at which goods are sold at reduced prices, usually to clear old stocks **b** (*as modifier*): *sale bargains* **5** an auction [Old English *sala*, from Old Norse *sala*. See also **SELL**]

Sale (seɪl) *n* **1** a town in NW England, in Trafford unitary authority, Greater Manchester: a residential suburb of Manchester. Pop: 55 234 (2001) **2** a city in SE Australia, in SE Victoria: centre of an agricultural region. Pop: 12 854 (2001)

Salé (*French* sale) *n* a port in NW Morocco, on the Atlantic adjoining Rabat. Pop: 880 000 (2003)

saleable *or US* **salable** ('seɪləbəl) *adj* fit for selling or capable of being sold ▷ ˌsalea'bility *or* ˌsaleableness *or US* ˌsala'bility *or* 'salableness *n*

Salem ('seɪləm) *n* **1** a city in S India, in Tamil Nadu: textile industries. Pop: 693 236 (2001) **2** a city in NE Massachusetts, on the Atlantic: scene of the execution of 19 people after the witch hunts of 1692. Pop: 42 067 (2003 est) **3** a city in the NW USA, the state capital of Oregon: food-processing. Pop: 142 914 (2003 est) **4** an Old Testament name for Jerusalem (Genesis 14:18; Psalms 76:2). See **Jerusalem**

sale of work *n Brit* a sale of goods and handicrafts made by the members of a club, church congregation, etc, to raise money

sale or return *or* **sale and return** *n* an arrangement by which a retailer pays only for goods sold, returning those that are unsold to the wholesaler or manufacturer

Salerno (*Italian* sa'lɛrno) *n* a port in SW Italy, in Campania on the **Gulf of Salerno**: first medical school of medieval Europe. Pop: 138 188 (2001)

saleroom ('seɪl,ruːm, -,rʊm) *n* *chiefly Brit* a room where objects are displayed for sale, esp by auction

salesclerk ('seɪlz,klaːrk) *n* *US & Canadian* a shop assistant. Sometimes shortened to **clerk**

salesman ('seɪlzmən) *n*, *pl* -men **1** Also called: (*fem*) saleswoman, (*fem*) salesgirl, (*fem*) saleslady, salesperson a person who sells merchandise or services either in a shop or by canvassing in a designated area **2** short for **travelling salesman**

salesmanship ('seɪlzmənʃɪp) *n* **1** the technique, skill, or ability of selling **2** the work of a salesman

sales pitch *or* **sales talk** *n* an argument or other persuasion used in selling

sales resistance *n* opposition of potential customers to selling, esp aggressive selling

sales tax *n* a tax levied on retail sales receipts and added to selling prices by retailers

sales trader *n* *stock exchange* a person employed by a market maker, or his firm, to find clients

Salford ('sɔːlfəd, 'sɒl-) *n* **1** a city in NW England in Salford unitary authority, Greater Manchester, on the Manchester Ship Canal: a major centre of the cotton industry in the 19th century; extensive dock area, now redeveloped, includes the Lowry arts centre; university (1967). Pop: 72 750 (2001) **2** a unitary authority in NW

England, in Greater Manchester. Pop: 216 500 (2003 est). Area: 97 sq km (37 sq miles)

Salian ('seɪlɪən) *adj* **1** denoting or relating to a group of Franks (the Salii) who settled in the Netherlands in the 4th century AD and later conquered large areas of Gaul, esp in the north ▷ *n* **2** a member of this group

salicin *or* **salicine** ('sælɪsɪn) *n* a colourless or white crystalline water-soluble glucoside obtained from the bark of poplar trees and used as a medical analgesic. Formula: $C_{13}H_{18}O_7$ [C19: from French *salicine*, from Latin *salix* willow]

Salic law *n history* **1** the code of laws of the Salic Franks and other Germanic tribes **2** a law excluding women from succession to the throne in certain countries, such as France and Spain

salicylate (sə'lɪsɪˌleɪt) *n* any salt or ester of salicylic acid

salicylic acid (ˌsælɪ'sɪlɪk) *n* a white crystalline slightly water-soluble substance with a sweet taste and bitter aftertaste, used in the manufacture of aspirin, dyes, and perfumes, and as a fungicide. Formula: $C_6H_4(OH)(COOH)$ [C19: from *salicyl* (via French from Latin *salix* a willow + -YL) + -IC]

salient ('seɪlɪənt) *adj* **1** prominent, conspicuous, or striking: *a salient feature* **2** (esp in fortifications) projecting outwards at an angle of less than 180° **3** *geometry* (of an angle) pointing outwards from a polygon and hence less than 180° **4** (esp of animals) leaping ▷ *n* **5** *military* a projection of the forward line into enemy-held territory **6** a salient angle [C16: from Latin *salīre* to leap] > 'salience *or* 'saliency *n* > 'saliently *adv*

saliantian (ˌseɪlɪ'enʃɪən) *n, adj* another word for **anuran** [C19: from New Latin *Salientia*, literally: leapers, from Latin *salīre* to leap]

Salieri (Italian ˌsal'jeri) *n* **Antonio** (an'tɔnjo). 1750–1825, Italian composer and conductor, who worked in Vienna (from 1766). The suggestion that he poisoned Mozart has no foundation

salina (sə'laɪnə) *n* a salt marsh, lake, or spring [C17: from Spanish, from Medieval Latin: salt pit, from Late Latin *salīnus* SALINE]

saline ('seɪlaɪn) *adj* **1** of, concerned with, consisting of, or containing common salt: *a saline taste* **2** *med* of or relating to a saline **3** of, concerned with, consisting of, or containing any chemical salt, esp a metallic salt resembling sodium chloride ▷ *n* **4** *med* an isotonic solution of sodium chloride in distilled water [C15: from Late Latin *salīnus*, from Latin *sal* salt]

Salinger ('sælɪndʒə) *n* **J**(erome) **D**(avid) born 1919, US writer, noted particularly for his novel of adolescence *The Catcher in the Rye* (1951). His first novel for 34 years, *Hapworth 16, 1924* was published in 1997

salinometer (ˌsælɪ'nɒmɪtə) *n* a hydrometer for determining the amount of salt in a solution, usually calibrated to measure concentration > ˌsali'nometry *n*

Salisbury¹ ('sɔːlzbəri, -brɪ) *n* **1** the former name (until 1982) of **Harare 2** a city in S Australia: an industrial suburb of N Adelaide. Pop: 118 422 (2006) **3** a city in S England, in SE Wiltshire: nearby Old Sarum was the site of an Early Iron Age hill fort; its cathedral (1220–58) has the highest spire in England. Pop: 43 355 (2001). Ancient name: Sarum

Salisbury² ('sɔːlzbəri, -brɪ) *n* **Robert Gascoyne Cecil** ('gæskɔɪn), 3rd Marquess of Salisbury. 1830–1903, British statesman; Conservative prime minister (1885–86; 1886–92; 1895–1902). His greatest interest was in foreign and imperial affairs

Salisbury Plain *n* an open chalk plateau in S England, in Wiltshire: site of Stonehenge; military training area. Average height: 120 m (400 ft)

saliva (sə'laɪvə) *n* the secretion of salivary glands, consisting of a clear usually slightly acid aqueous fluid of variable composition. It moistens the oral cavity, prepares food for swallowing, and initiates the process of digestion [C17: from Latin, of obscure origin] > salivary (sə'laɪvərɪ, 'sælɪvərɪ) *adj*

salivary gland *n* any of the glands in mammals that secrete saliva. In man the chief salivary glands are the **parotid, sublingual** and **submaxillary** glands

salivate ('sælɪˌveɪt) *vb* **1** (*intr*) to secrete saliva, esp an excessive amount **2** (*tr*) to cause (a laboratory animal, etc) to produce saliva, as by the administration of mercury > ˌsali'vation *n*

Salk (sɔːlk) *n* **Jonas Edward**. 1914–95, US virologist: developed an injected vaccine against poliomyelitis (1954)

sallee *or* **sally** ('sælɪ) *n Austral* **1** Also called: **snow gum** a SE Australian eucalyptus tree, *Eucalyptus pauciflora*, with a pale grey bark **2** any of various acacia trees [probably of native origin]

sallow¹ ('sæləʊ) *adj* **1** (esp of human skin) of an unhealthy pale or yellowish colour ▷ *vb* **2** (*tr*) to make sallow [Old English *salu*; related to Old Norse *sol* seaweed (Icelandic *sōlr* yellowish), Old High German *salo*, French *sale* dirty] > 'sallowish *adj* > 'sallowness *n*

sallow² ('sæləʊ) *n* **1** any of several small willow trees, esp the Eurasian *Salix cinerea* (**common sallow**), which has large catkins that appear before the leaves **2** a twig or the wood of any of these trees [Old English *sealh*; related to Old Norse *selja*, Old High German *salaha*, Middle Low German *salwīde*, Latin *salix*] > 'sallowy *adj*

Sallust ('sæləst) *n* full name *Gaius Sallustius Crispus*. 86–?34 BC, Roman historian and statesman, noted for his histories of the Catiline conspiracy and the Roman war against Jugurtha

sally ('sælɪ) *n, pl* -lies **1** a sudden violent excursion, esp by besieged forces to attack the besiegers; sortie **2** a sudden outburst or emergence into action, expression, or emotion **3** an excursion or jaunt **4** a jocular retort ▷ *vb* -lies, -lying, -lied (*intr*) **5** to make a sudden violent excursion **6** (often foll by *forth*) to go out on an expedition, etc **7** to come, go, or set out in an energetic manner **8** to rush out suddenly [C16: from Old French *saillie*, from *saillir* to dash forwards, from Latin *salīre* to leap] > 'sallier *n*

Sally Lunn (lʌn) *n* a flat round cake made from a sweet yeast dough, usually served hot [C19: said to be named after an 18th-century English baker who invented it]

salmagundi *or* **salmagundy** (ˌsælmə'gʌndɪ) *n* **1** a mixed salad dish of cooked meats, eggs, beetroot, etc, popular in 18th-century England **2** a miscellany; potpourri [C17: from French *salmigondis*, perhaps from Italian *salami conditi* pickled salami]

salmon ('sæmən) *n, pl* -ons *or* -on **1** any soft-finned fish of the family Salmonidae, esp *Salmo salar* of the Atlantic and *Oncorhynchus* species (sockeye, Chinook, etc) of the Pacific, which are important food fishes. They occur in cold and temperate waters and many species migrate to fresh water to spawn **2** *Austral* any of several unrelated fish, esp the Australian salmon [C13: from Old French *saumon*, from Latin *salmō*; related to Late Latin *salar* trout] > 'salmoˌnoid *adj, n*

Salmond ('sæmənd) *n* **Alex**(ander Elliot Anderson). born 1954, Scottish Nationalist politician; first minister of the Scottish Parliament from 2007

salmonella (ˌsælmə'nɛlə) *n, pl* -lae (-ˌliː) any Gram-negative rod-shaped aerobic bacterium of the genus *Salmonella*, including *S. typhosa*, which causes typhoid fever, and many species (notably *S. enteritidis*) that cause food poisoning (**salmonellosis**): family Enterobacteriaceae [C19: New Latin, named after Daniel E. *Salmon* (1850–1914), US veterinary surgeon]

salmon ladder *n* a series of steps in a river designed to enable salmon to bypass a dam and move upstream to their breeding grounds

Salome (sə'ləʊmɪ) *n New Testament* the daughter of Herodias, at whose instigation she beguiled Herod by her seductive dancing into giving her the head of John the Baptist

salon ('sælɒn) *n* **1** a room in a large house in which guests are received **2** an assembly of guests in a fashionable household, esp a gathering of major literary, artistic, and political figures from the 17th to the early 20th centuries **3** a commercial establishment in which hairdressers, beauticians, etc, carry on their businesses **4** a a hall for exhibiting works of art **b** such an exhibition, esp one showing the work of living artists [C18: from French, from Italian *salone*, augmented form of *sala* hall, of Germanic origin; compare Old English *sele* hall, Old High German *sal*, Old Norse *salr* hall]

Salonika *or* **Salonica** (səˈlɒnɪkə) *n* the English name for **Thessaloníki**

saloon (səˈluːn) *n* **1** Also called: **saloon bar** *Brit* another word for **lounge** (sense 5) **2** a large public room on a passenger ship **3** any large public room used for a specific purpose: *a dancing saloon* **4** *chiefly US & Canadian* a place where alcoholic drink is sold and consumed **5** a closed two-door or four-door car with four to six seats. US, Canadian, and NZ name: **sedan 6** an obsolete word for **salon** (sense 1) [c18: from French SALON]

Salop (ˈsæləp) *n* a former name (1974–80) of **Shropshire**

salopettes (ˌsæləˈpɛts) *pl n* a garment worn for skiing, consisting of quilted trousers reaching to the chest and held up by shoulder straps [c20: from French]

salpiglossis (ˌsælpɪˈɡlɒsɪs) *n* any solanaceous plant of the Chilean genus *Salpiglossis,* some species of which are cultivated for their bright funnel-shaped flowers [c19: New Latin, from Greek *salpinx* trumpet + *glōssa* tongue]

salpingitis (ˌsælpɪnˈdʒaɪtɪs) *n* inflammation of a Fallopian tube [c19: from SALPINX + -ITIS]

salpinx (ˈsælpɪŋks) *n, pl* **salpinges** (sælˈpɪndʒiːz) *anatomy* another name for **Fallopian tube, Eustachian tube** [c19: from Greek: trumpet] > **salpingectomy** (ˌsælpɪnˈdʒɛktəmɪ) *n* [c20: from SALPINX + -ECTOMY]

salsa (ˈsælsə) *n* **1** a type of Latin American big-band dance music **2** a dance performed to this kind of music **3** *Mexican cookery* a spicy tomato-based sauce [c20: from Spanish: sauce]

salsify (ˈsælsɪfɪ) *n, pl* **-fies 1** Also called: **oyster plant, vegetable oyster** a Mediterranean plant, *Tragopogon porrifolius,* having grasslike leaves, purple flower heads, and a long white edible taproot: family *Asteraceae* (composites) **2** the root of this plant, which tastes of oysters and is eaten as a vegetable [c17: from French *salsifis,* from Italian *sassefrica,* from Late Latin *saxifrica,* from Latin *saxum* rock + *fricāre* to rub]

sal soda *n* the crystalline decahydrate of sodium carbonate

salt (sɔːlt) *n* **1** a white powder or colourless crystalline solid, consisting mainly of sodium chloride and used for seasoning and preserving food **2** (*modifier*) preserved in, flooded with, containing, or growing in salt or salty water: *salt pork; salt marshes* **3** *chem* any of a class of usually crystalline solid compounds that are formed from, or can be regarded as formed from, an acid and a base by replacement of one or more hydrogen atoms in the acid molecules by positive ions from the base **4** liveliness or pungency: *his wit added salt to the discussion* **5** dry or laconic wit **6** a sailor, esp one who is old and experienced **7** short for **saltcellar 8** rub salt into someone's wounds to make someone's pain, shame, etc, even worse **9** salt of the earth a person or group of people regarded as the finest of their kind **10** with a grain of salt *or* with a pinch of salt with reservations; sceptically **11** worth one's salt efficient; worthy of one's pay ▷ *vb* (*tr*) **12** to season or preserve with salt **13** to scatter salt over (an icy road, path, etc) to melt the ice **14** to add zest to **15** (often foll by **down** *or* **away**) to preserve or cure with salt or saline solution **16** *chem* to treat with common salt or other chemical salt **17** to provide (cattle, etc) with salt **18** to give a false appearance of value to, esp to introduce valuable ore fraudulently into (a mine, sample, etc) ▷ *adj* **19** not sour, sweet, or bitter; salty ▷ See also **salt away, salts,** etc [Old English *sealt;* related to Old Norse, Gothic *salt,* German *Salz,* Lettish *sāls,* Latin *sāl,* Greek *hals*] > 'salt,like *adj* > 'saltness *n*

SALT (sɔːlt) *n acronym for* Strategic Arms Limitation Talks *or* Treaty

Salta (Spanish ˈsalta) *n* a city in NW Argentina: thermal springs. Pop: 504 000 (2005 est)

saltant (ˈsæltənt) *adj* (of an organism) differing from others of its species because of a saltation [c17: from Latin *saltāns* dancing, from *saltāre,* from *salīre* to spring]

saltation (sælˈteɪʃən) *n* **1** *biology* an abrupt variation in the appearance of an organism, species, etc, usually caused by genetic mutation **2** *geology* the leaping

movement of sand or soil particles carried in water or by the wind **3** a sudden abrupt movement or transition [c17: from Latin *saltātiō* a dance, from *saltāre* to leap about] > **saltatorial** (ˌsæltəˈtɔːrɪəl) *adj* [c17 *saltatory,* from Latin *saltātōrius* concerning dancing, from *saltātor* a dancer; see SALTANT]

salt away *or less commonly* **salt down** *vb* (*tr, adverb*) to hoard or save (money, valuables, etc)

saltbush (ˈsɔːltˌbʊʃ) *n* any of various chenopodiaceous shrubs of the genus *Atriplex* that grow in alkaline desert regions

salt cake *n* an impure form of sodium sulphate obtained as a by-product in several industrial processes: used in the manufacture of detergents, glass, and ceramic glazes

saltcellar (ˈsɔːltˌsɛlə) *n* **1** a small container for salt used at the table **2** *Brit informal* either of the two hollows formed above the collarbones of very slim people [changed (through influence of cellar) from C15 *salt saler; saler* from Old French *saliere* container for salt, from Latin *salārius* belonging to salt, from *sal* salt]

salt dome *or* **salt plug** *n* a domelike structure of stratified rocks containing a central core of salt: formed by the upward movement of a salt deposit

Salteaux *or* **Saulteaux** (ˈsəʊtəʊ) *n* a member of a Native Canadian people of Manitoba [from Ojibwa]

salted (ˈsɔːltɪd) *adj* seasoned, preserved, or treated with salt

salt flat *n* a flat expanse of salt left by the total evaporation of a body of water

saltie (ˈsɔːltɪ) *n Austral informal* a saltwater crocodile

saltigrade (ˈsæltɪˌɡreɪd) *adj* (of animals) adapted for moving in a series of jumps [c19: from New Latin *Saltigradae,* name formerly applied to jumping spiders, from Latin *saltus* a leap + *gradī* to move]

Saltillo (Spanish salˈtiʎo) *n* a city in N Mexico, capital of Coahuila state: resort and commercial centre of a mining region. Pop: 698 000 (2005 est)

salting (ˈsɔːltɪŋ) *n* (often plural) an area of low ground regularly inundated with salt water; often taken to include its halophyte vegetation; a salt marsh

saltire *or less commonly* **saltier** (ˈsɔːlˌtaɪə) *n heraldry* an ordinary consisting of a diagonal cross on a shield [c14 *sawtoure,* from Old French *sauteoure* cross-shaped barricade, from *saulter* to jump, from Latin *saltāre*]

Salt Lake City *n* a city in N central Utah, near the Great Salt Lake at an altitude of 1330 m (4300 ft): state capital; founded in 1847 by the Mormons as world capital of the Mormon Church; University of Utah (1850). Pop: 179 894 (2003 est)

salt lick *n* **1** a place where wild animals go to lick naturally occurring salt deposits **2** a block of salt or a salt preparation given to domestic or farm animals to lick

Salto (Spanish ˈsalto) *n* a port in NW Uruguay, on the Uruguay River. It is Uruguay's second largest city. Pop: 105 000 (2005 est)

saltpan (ˈsɔːltˌpæn) *n* a shallow basin, usually in a desert region, containing salt, gypsum, etc, that was deposited from an evaporated salt lake

saltpetre *or US* **saltpeter** (ˌsɔːltˈpiːtə) *n* **1** another name for **potassium nitrate 2** short for **Chile saltpetre** [c16: from Old French *salpetre,* from Latin *sal petrae* salt of rock]

salt pork *n* pork, esp the fat pork taken from the back, sides, and belly, that has been cured with salt

salts (sɔːlts) *pl n* **1** *med* any of various mineral salts, such as magnesium sulphate or sodium sulphate, for use as a cathartic **2** short for **smelling salts 3** like a dose of salts *informal* very fast

saltus (ˈsæltəs) *n, pl* **-tuses** a break in the continuity of a sequence, esp the omission of a necessary step in a logical argument [Latin: a leap]

saltwater (ˈsɔːltˌwɔːtə) *adj* of, relating to, or inhabiting salt water, esp the sea: *saltwater fishes*

saltworks (ˈsɔːltˌwɜːks) *n* (functioning as singular) a place, building, or factory where salt is produced

saltwort (ˈsɔːltˌwɜːt) *n* Also called: **glasswort, kali** any of several chenopodiaceous plants of the genus *Salsola,* esp *S. kali,* of beaches and salt marshes, which has prickly leaves, striped stems, and small green flowers

salty ('sɔ:ltɪ) *adj* **saltier, saltiest 1** of, tasting of, or containing salt **2** (*esp of humour*) sharp; piquant **3** relating to life at sea > **'saltiness**[n]

salubrious (sə'lu:brɪəs) *adj* conducive to or favourable to health; wholesome [c16: from Latin *salūbris*, from *salūs* health] > **sa'lubriously**[adv] > **sa'lubriousness**[or] **salubrity** (sə'lu:brɪtɪ) *n*

Saluki (sə'lu:kɪ) *n* a tall breed of hound with a smooth coat and long fringes on the ears and tail [c19: from Arabic *salūqiy* of Saluq, name of an ancient Arabian city]

salutary ('sæljʊtərɪ, -trɪ) *adj* **1** promoting or intended to promote an improvement or beneficial effect: *a salutary warning* **2** promoting or intended to promote health [c15: from Latin *salūtāris* wholesome, from *salūs* safety] > **'salutarily**[adv]

salutation (ˌsæljʊ'teɪʃən) *n* **1** an act, phrase, gesture, etc, that serves as a greeting **2** a form of words used as an opening to a speech or letter, such as *Dear Sir* or *Ladies and Gentlemen* [c14: from Latin *salūtātiō*, from *salūtāre* to greet; see SALUTE]

salutatory (sə'lu:tətərɪ, -trɪ) *adj* of, relating to, or resembling a salutation > **sa'lutatorily**[adv]

salute (sə'lu:t) *vb* **1** (*tr*) to address or welcome with friendly words or gestures of respect, such as bowing or lifting the hat; greet **2** (*tr*) to acknowledge with praise or honour: *we salute your gallantry* **3** *military* to pay or receive formal respect, as by presenting arms or raising the right arm ⊳ *n* **4** the act of saluting **5** a formal military gesture of respect [c14: from Latin *salūtāre* to greet, from *salūs* wellbeing] > **sa'luter**[n]

salvable ('sælvəb°l) *adj* capable of or suitable for being saved or salvaged [c17: from Late Latin *salvāre* to save, from Latin *salvus* safe]

Salvador ('sælvəˌdɔ:, *Portuguese* salva'dor) *n* a port in E Brazil, capital of Bahia state: founded in 1549 as capital of the Portuguese colony, which it remained until 1763; a major centre of the African slave trade in colonial times. Pop: 3 331 000 (2005 est). Former name: **Bahia**

salvage ('sælvɪdʒ) *n* **1** the act, process, or business of rescuing vessels or their cargoes from loss at sea **2 a** the act of saving any goods or property in danger of damage or destruction **b** (*as modifier*): *a salvage operation* **3** the goods or property so saved **4** compensation paid for the salvage of a vessel or its cargo **5** the proceeds from the sale of salvaged goods or property ⊳ *vb* (*tr*) **6** to save or rescue (goods or property) from fire, shipwreck, etc **7** to gain (something beneficial) from a failure [c17: from Old French, from Medieval Latin *salvāgium*, from *salvāre* to SAVE[1]] > **'salvageable**[adj] > **'salvager**[n]

salvation (sæl'veɪʃən) *n* **1** the act of preserving or the state of being preserved from harm **2** a person or thing that is the means of preserving from harm **3** *Christianity* deliverance by redemption from the power of sin and from the penalties ensuing from it [c13: from Old French *sauvacion*, from Late Latin *salvātiō*, from Latin *salvātus* saved, from *salvāre* to SAVE[1]]

Salvation Army *n* a Christian body founded in 1865 by William Booth and organized on quasi-military lines for evangelism and social work among the poor

salvationist (sæl'veɪʃənɪst) *n* **1** a member of an evangelical sect emphasizing the doctrine of salvation **2** (*often capital*) a member of the Salvation Army

salve (sælv, sɑ:v) *n* **1** an ointment for wounds, sores, etc **2** anything that heals or soothes ⊳ *vb* (*tr*) **3** to apply salve to (a wound, sore, etc) **4** to soothe, comfort, or appease [Old English *sealf*; related to Old High German *salba*, Greek *elpos* oil, Sanskrit *sarpis* lard]

salver ('sælvə) *n* a tray, esp one of silver, on which food, letters, visiting cards, etc, are presented [c17: from French *salve*, from Spanish *salva* tray from which the king's taster sampled food, from Latin *salvāre* to SAVE[1]]

salvia ('sælvɪə) *n* any herbaceous plant or small shrub of the genus *Salvia*, such as the sage, grown for their medicinal or culinary properties or for ornament: family *Lamiaceae* (labiates) [c19: from Latin: see SAGE[2]]

salvo ('sælvəʊ) *n, pl* **-vos**[or] **-voes 1** a discharge of fire from weapons in unison, esp on a ceremonial occasion **2** concentrated fire from many weapons, as in a naval battle **3** an outburst, as of applause [c17: from Italian *salva*, from Old French *salve*, from Latin *salvē!* greetings! from *salvēre* to be in good health, from *salvus* safe]

Salvo ('sælvəʊ) *n, pl* **-vos** *Austral slang* a member of the Salvation Army

sal volatile (vɒ'lætɪlɪ) *n* Also called: **spirits of ammonia,** (*archaic*) **hartshorn** a solution of ammonium carbonate in alcohol and aqueous ammonia, often containing aromatic oils, used as smelling salts [c17: from New Latin: volatile salt]

Salween ('sælwi:n) *n* a river in SW Asia, rising in the Tibetan Plateau and flowing east and south through SW China and Myanmar to the Gulf of Martaban. Length: 2400 km (1500 miles)

Salzburg ('sæltsbɜ:g; *German* 'zaltsburk) *n* **1** a city in W Austria, capital of Salzburg province: 7th-century Benedictine abbey; a centre of music since the Middle Ages and birthplace of Mozart; tourist centre. Pop: 142 662 (2001) **2** a state of W Austria. Pop: 521 238 (2003 est). Area: 7154 sq km (2762 sq miles)

Salzgitter (*German* zalts'gɪtər) *n* an industrial city in central Germany, in SE Lower Saxony. Pop: 109 855 (2003 est)

SAM (sæm) *n acronym for* surface-to-air missile

Sam. *abbreviation Bible* Samuel

S.Am. *abbreviation* South America(n)

Samar ('sɑ:mə) *n* an island in the E central Philippines, separated from S Luzon by the San Bernardino Strait: the third largest island in the republic. Capital: Catbalogan. Pop: 641 124 (2000). Area: 13 080 sq km (5050 sq miles)

samara (sə'mɑ:rə, 'sæmərə) *n* a dry indehiscent one-seeded fruit with a winglike extension to aid dispersal: occurs in the ash, maple, etc. Also called: **key fruit**[c16: from New Latin, from Latin: seed of an elm]

Samara (*Russian* sa'marə) *n* a port in SW Russia, on the River Volga: centre of an important industrial complex; oil refining. Pop: 1 140 000 (2005 est). Former name (1935–91): **Kuibyshev**

Samaria (sə'mɛərɪə) *n* **1** the region of ancient Palestine that extended from Judaea to Galilee and from the Mediterranean to the River Jordan; the N kingdom of Israel **2** the capital of this kingdom; constructed northwest of Shechem in the 9th century BC

Samaritan (sə'mærɪt°n) *n* **1** a native or inhabitant of Samaria **2** short for **Good Samaritan 3** a member of a voluntary organization (**the Samaritans**) which offers counselling to people in despair, esp by telephone

samarium (sə'mɛərɪəm) *n* a silvery metallic element of the lanthanide series occurring chiefly in monazite and bastnaesite and used in carbon-arc lighting, as a doping agent in laser crystals, and as a neutron-absorber. Symbol: Sm; atomic no: 62; atomic wt: 150.36; valency: 2 or 3; relative density: 7.520; melting pt: 1074°C; boiling pt: 1794°C [c19: New Latin, from SAMARSKITE + -IUM]

Samarkand ('sæməˌkænd; *Russian* səmar'kant) *n* a city in E Uzbekistan: under Tamerlane it became the chief economic and cultural centre of central Asia, on trade routes from China and India (the "silk road"). Pop: 289 000 (2005 est). Ancient name: **Maracanda**

samarskite (sə'mɑ:skaɪt) *n* a velvety black mineral of complex composition occurring in pegmatites: used as a source of uranium and certain rare earth elements [c19: named after Colonel von *Samarski*, 19th-century Russian inspector of mines]

samba ('sæmbə) *n, pl* **-bas 1** a lively modern ballroom dance from Brazil in bouncy duple time **2** a piece of music composed for or in the rhythm of this dance ⊳ *vb* **-bas, -baing, -baed 3** (*intr*) to perform such a dance [Portuguese, of African origin]

sambar[or] **sambur** ('sæmbə) *n, pl* **-bars, -bar**[or] **-burs,** **-bur**[a] a S Asian deer, *Cervus unicolor*, with three-tined antlers [c17: from Hindi, from Sanskrit *śambara*, of obscure origin]

Sambre (*French* sɑ̄brə) *n* a river in W Europe, rising in N France and flowing east into Belgium to join the Meuse at Namur. Length: 190 km (118 miles)

Sam Browne belt *n* a military officer's wide belt supported by a strap passing from the left side of the belt over the right shoulder [C20: named after Sir Samuel J. Browne (1824–1901), British general, who devised such a belt]

same (seɪm) *the same adj* **1** being the very one: *she is wearing the same hat she wore yesterday* **2 a** being the one previously referred to; aforesaid **b** (*as noun*): *a note received about same* **3 a** identical in kind, quantity, etc: *two girls of the same age* **b** (*as noun*): *we'd like the same, please* **4** unchanged in character or nature: *his attitude is the same as ever* **5** all the same **a** Also: just the same nevertheless; yet **b** immaterial: *it's all the same to me* ▷ *adv* **6** in an identical manner [C12: from Old Norse *samr*; related to Old English adverbial phrase *swā* same likewise, Gothic *sama*, Latin *similis*, Greek *homos* same] > ˈsamenessn
● USAGE The use of *same* exemplified in *if you send us your*
● *order for the materials, we will deliver same tomorrow* is
● common in business and official English. In general
● English, however, this use of the word is avoided: *may*
● *I borrow your book? I'll return it* (not *same*) *tomorrow*

samekh (ˈsɑːmək; *Hebrew* ˈsaməx) *n* the 15th letter in the Hebrew alphabet (ס) transliterated as *s* [Hebrew, literally: a support]

samfoo (ˈsæmfuː) *n* a style of casual dress worn by Chinese women, consisting of a waisted blouse and trousers [from Chinese (Cantonese) *sam* dress + *foo* trousers]

Sami (ˈsɑːmɪ) *n* **1** *pl* -mior -misa member of the indigenous people of Lapland **2** the language of this people, belonging to the Finno-Ugric family ▷ *adj* **3** of or relating to this people or their language
● USAGE The indigenous people of Lapland prefer to be
● called *Sami*, although *Lapp* is still in widespread use

Samian (ˈseɪmɪən) *adj* **1** of or relating to Samos or its inhabitants ▷ *n* **2** a native or inhabitant of Samos

Samian ware *n* a fine earthenware pottery, reddish-brown or black in colour, found in large quantities on Roman sites [C19: named after the island of SAMOS, source of a reddish-coloured earth resembling terra sigillata, similar to the earth from which the pottery was made]

samisen (ˈsæmɪˌsɛn) *n* a variant of **shamisen**

samite (ˈsæmaɪt, ˈseɪ-) *n* a heavy fabric of silk, often woven with gold or silver threads, used in the Middle Ages for clothing [C13: from Old French *samit*, from Medieval Latin *examitum*, from Greek *hexamiton*, from *hexamitos* having six threads, from *hex* six + *mitos* a thread]

samizdat (*Russian* səmizˈdat) *n* (in the former Soviet Union) **a** a system of clandestine printing and distribution of banned or dissident literature **b** (*as modifier*): *a samizdat publication* [C20: from Russian, literally: self-published]

Samnium (ˈsæmnɪəm) *n* an ancient country of central Italy inhabited by Oscan-speaking Samnites: corresponds to the present-day regions of Abruzzi, Molise, and part of Campania

Samoa (səˈməʊə) *n* **1** an independent state occupying four inhabited islands and five uninhabited islands in the S Pacific archipelago of the Samoa Islands: established as a League of Nations mandate under New Zealand administration in 1920 and a UN trusteeship in 1946; gained independence as Western Samoa in 1962 as the first fully independent Polynesian state; officially changed its name to Samoa in 1997; a member of the Commonwealth. Languages: Samoan and English. Religion: Christian. Currency: tala. Capital: Apia. Pop: 180 000 (2004 est). Area: 2841 sq km (1097 sq miles) **2** Also called: Samoa Islands a group of islands in the S Pacific, northeast of Fiji: an independent kingdom until the mid 19th century, when it was divided administratively into **American Samoa** (in the east) and **German Samoa** (in the west); the latter was mandated to New Zealand in 1919 and gained full independence in 1962 as Western Samoa, now called Samoa (as detailed in sense 1). Area: 3038 sq km (1173 sq miles) > Saˈmoan *adj, n*

Samos (ˈseɪmɒs) *n* a Greek island in the E Aegean Sea, off the SW coast of Turkey: a leading commercial centre of ancient Greece. Pop: 33 809 (2001). Area: 492 sq km

(190 sq miles)

samosa (səˈməʊsə) *n, pl* -sasor -sa(in Indian cookery) a small triangular pastry case containing spiced vegetables or meat and served fried [C20: from Hindi]

Samothrace (ˈsæməˌθreɪs) *n* a Greek island in the NE Aegean Sea: mountainous. Pop: 2723 (2001)

samovar (ˈsæməˌvɑː, ˌsæməˈvɑː) *n* (esp in Russia) a metal urn for making tea, in which the water is heated esp formerly by charcoal held in an inner container or nowadays more usually by electricity [C19: from Russian, from *samo-* self (related to SAME) + *varit'* to boil]

Samoyed (ˌsæməˈjed) *n* **1** *pl* -yedor -yedsa member of a group of peoples who migrated along the Russian Arctic coast and now live chiefly in the area of the N Urals: related to the Finns **2** the languages of these peoples, related to Finno-Ugric within the Uralic family **3** (səˈmɔɪed) a Siberian breed of dog of the spitz type, having a dense white or cream coat with a distinct ruff, and a tightly curled tail [C17: from Russian *Samoed*]

samp (sæmp) *n South African* crushed maize used for porridge [C17: from Narraganset *nasaump* softened by water]

sampan (ˈsæmpæn) *n* any small skiff, widely used in the Orient, that is propelled by oars or a scull [C17: from Chinese *san pan*, from *san* three + *pan* board]

samphire (ˈsæmˌfaɪə) *n* **1** Also called: rock samphire an umbelliferous plant, *Crithmum maritimum*, of Eurasian coasts, having fleshy divided leaves and clusters of small greenish-white flowers **2** golden samphire a Eurasian coastal plant, *Inula crithmoides*, with fleshy leaves and yellow flower heads: family *Asteraceae* (composites) **3** another name for **glasswort** (sense 1) **4** any of several other plants of coastal areas [C16 *sampiere*, from French *herbe de Saint Pierre* Saint Peter's herb; perhaps influenced by *camphire* CAMPHOR]

sample (ˈsɑːmpəl) *n* **1 a** a small part of anything, intended as representative of the whole; specimen **b** (*as modifier*): *a sample bottle* **2** Also called: sampling *statistics* a set of individuals or items selected from a population for analysis to yield estimates of, or to test hypotheses about, parameters of the whole population. A **biased sample** is one in which the items selected share some property which influences their distribution, while a **random sample** is devised to avoid any such interference so that its distribution is affected only by, and so can be held to represent, that of the whole population ▷ *vb* **3** (*tr*) to take a sample or samples of **4** *music* **a** to take a short extract from (one record) and mix it into a different backing track **b** to record (a sound) and feed it into a computerized synthesizer so that it can be reproduced at any pitch [C13: from Old French *essample*, from Latin *exemplum* EXAMPLE]

sampler (ˈsɑːmplə) *n* **1** a person who takes samples **2** a piece of embroidery executed as an example of the embroiderer's skill in using a variety of stitches: often incorporating numbers, letters, and the name and age of the embroiderer in a decorative panel **3** *music* a piece of electronic equipment used for sampling **4** a recording comprising a collection of tracks from other albums, intended to stimulate interest in the featured products

sampling (ˈsɑːmplɪŋ) *n* **1** the process of selecting a random sample **2** a variant of **sample** (sense 2) **3** the process of taking a short extract from (a record) and mixing it into a different backing track

sampling statistic *n* any function of observed data, esp one used to estimate the corresponding parameter of the underlying distribution, such as the sample mean, sample variance, etc. Compare **estimator** (sense 2)

Sampras (ˈsæmpˌræs) *n* **Pete**. born 1971, US tennis player: US singles champion (1990, 1993, 1995, 1996, 2002); Wimbledon singles champion (1993–95, 1997–2000)

Samson (ˈsæmsən) *n* **1** a judge of Israel, who performed herculean feats of strength against the Philistine oppressors until he was betrayed to them by his mistress Delilah (Judges 13–16) **2** any man of outstanding physical strength

Samsun (*Turkish* ˈsamsun) *n* a port in N Turkey, on the Black Sea. Pop: 395 000 (2005 est)

Samuel ('sæmjʊəl) n Old Testament **1** a Hebrew prophet, seer, and judge, who anointed the first two kings of the Israelites (I Samuel 1–3; 8–15) **2** either of the two books named after him, I and II Samuel

samurai ('sæmʊ,raɪ, 'sæmjʊ-) n, pl -rai **1** the Japanese warrior caste that provided the administrative and fighting aristocracy from the 11th to the 19th centuries **2** a member of this aristocracy [C19: from Japanese]

samurai bond n a bond issued in Japan and denominated in yen, available for purchase by nonresidents of Japan. See **shogun bond**

San¹ (sɑːn) n **1** an aboriginal people of southern Africa **2** a group of the Khoisan languages, spoken mostly by Bushmen

San² (sɑːn) n a river in E central Europe, rising in W Ukraine and flowing northwest across SE Poland to the Vistula River. Length: about 450 km (280 miles)

San'a or **Sanaa** (sɑːˈnɑː) n the administrative capital of Yemen, on the central plateau at an altitude of 2350 m (7700 ft): formerly the capital of North Yemen. Pop: 1 621 000 (2005 est)

San Antonio (sæn ænˈtəʊnɪˌəʊ) n a city in S Texas: site of the Alamo; the leading town in Texas until about 1930. Pop: 1 214 725 (2003 est)

sanative ('sænətɪv) adj a less common word for **curative** [C15: from Medieval Latin sānātīvus, from Latin sānāre to heal, from sānus healthy]

sanatorium (ˌsænəˈtɔːrɪəm) or US **sanitarium** n, pl -riums or -ria (-rɪə) **1** an institution for the medical care and recuperation of persons who are chronically ill **2** a health resort **3** Brit a room in a boarding school where sick pupils may be treated in isolation [C19: from New Latin, from Latin sānāre to heal]

San Bernardino (sæn ˌbɜːnəˈdiːnəʊ) n a city in SE California: founded in 1851 by Mormons from Salt Lake City. Pop: 195 357 (2003 est)

San Bernardino Pass n a pass over the Lepontine Alps in SE Switzerland. Highest point: 2062 m (6766 ft)

San Blas ('sɑːn 'blɑːs) n **1** Isthmus of San Blas the narrowest part of the Isthmus of Panama. Width: about 50 km (30 miles) **2** Gulf of San Blas an inlet of the Caribbean on the N coast of Panama

San Cristóbal (Spanish saŋ kriˈstoβal) n **1** an island in the Pacific, in the Galápagos Islands. Area: 505 sq km (195 sq miles). Former name: Chatham Island **2** a city in SW Venezuela: founded in 1561 by Spanish conquistadores. Pop: 395 000 (2005 est)

sanctified ('sæŋktɪˌfaɪd) adj **1** consecrated or made holy **2** a less common word for **sanctimonious**

sanctify ('sæŋktɪˌfaɪ) vb -fies, -fying, -fied (tr) **1** to make holy **2** to free from sin; purify **3** to sanction (an action or practice) as religiously binding: to sanctify a marriage **4** to declare or render (something) productive of or conducive to holiness, blessing, or grace **5** obsolete to authorize to be revered [C14: from Late Latin sanctificāre, from Latin sanctus holy + facere to make] > ˌsanctifiˈcation n > ˈsanctiˌfier n

sanctimonious (ˌsæŋktɪˈməʊnɪəs) adj affecting piety or making a display of holiness [C17: from Latin sanctimonia sanctity, from sanctus holy] > ˌsanctiˈmoniously adv > ˌsanctiˈmoniousness n > ˈsanctimony n

sanction ('sæŋkʃən) n **1** final permission; authorization **2** aid or encouragement **3** something, such as an ethical principle, that imparts binding force to a rule, oath, etc **4** the penalty laid down in a law for contravention of its provisions **5** (often plural) a coercive measure, esp one taken by one or more states against another guilty of violating international law ▷ vb (tr) **6** to give authority to; permit [C16: from Latin sanctiō the establishment of an inviolable decree, from sancīre to decree]

sanctitude ('sæŋktɪˌtjuːd) n saintliness; holiness

sanctity ('sæŋktɪtɪ) n, pl -ties **1** the condition of being sanctified; holiness **2** anything regarded as sanctified or holy **3** the condition of being inviolable; sacredness: the sanctity of marriage [C14: from Old French saincteté, from Latin sanctitās, from sanctus holy]

sanctuary ('sæŋktjʊərɪ) n, pl -aries **1** a holy place **2** a consecrated building or shrine **3** Old Testament **a** the Israelite temple at Jerusalem, esp the holy of holies

b the tabernacle in which the Ark was enshrined during the wanderings of the Israelites **4** the chancel, or that part of a sacred building surrounding the main altar **5** **a** a sacred building where fugitives were formerly entitled to immunity from arrest or execution **b** the immunity so afforded **6** a place of refuge; asylum **7** a place, protected by law, where animals, esp birds, can live and breed without interference [C14: from Old French sainctuarie, from Late Latin sanctuārium repository for holy things, from Latin sanctus holy]

sanctuary lamp n Christianity a lamp, usually red, placed in a prominent position in the sanctuary of a church, that when lit indicates the presence of the Blessed Sacrament

sanctum ('sæŋktəm) n, pl -tums, -ta (-tə) **1** a sacred or holy place **2** a room or place of total privacy or inviolability [C16: from Latin, from sanctus holy]

sanctum sanctorum (sæŋkˈtɔːrəm) n **1** Bible another term for the **holy of holies 2** often facetious an especially private place [C14: from Latin, literally: holy of holies, rendering Hebrew qōdesh haqqodāshīm]

Sanctus ('sæŋktəs) n **1** liturgy the hymn that occurs immediately after the preface in the celebration of the Eucharist **2** a musical setting of this, usually incorporated into the Ordinary of the Roman Catholic Mass [C14: from the first word of the hymn, Sanctus sanctus sanctus Holy, holy, holy, from Latin sancīre to consecrate]

Sanctus bell n chiefly RC Church a bell rung as the opening words of the Sanctus are pronounced and also at other important points during Mass

sand (sænd) n **1** loose material consisting of rock or mineral grains, esp rounded grains of quartz, between 0.05 and 2 mm in diameter **2** (often plural) a sandy area, esp on the seashore or in a desert **3 a** a greyish-yellow colour **b** (as adjective): sand upholstery **4** the grains of sandlike material in an hourglass ▷ vb **5** (tr) to smooth or polish the surface of with sandpaper or sand: to sand a floor **6** (tr) to sprinkle or cover with or as if with sand; add sand to [Old English; related to Old Norse sandr, Old High German sant, Greek hamathos] > ˈsandˌlike adj

Sand (French sɑ̃d) n George (ʒɔrʒ), pen name of Amandine Aurore Lucie Dupin. 1804–76, French novelist, best known for such pastoral novels as La Mare au diable (1846) and François le Champi (1847–48) and for her works for women's rights to independence

Sandage ('sændɪdʒ) n Allan Rex. born 1926, US astronomer, who discovered the first quasar (1961)

Sandakan (sɑːnˈdɑːkɑːn) n a port in Malaysia, on the NE coast of Sabah: capital (until 1947) of North Borneo. Pop: 347 334 (2000)

sandal ('sændᵊl) n **1** a light shoe consisting of a sole held on the foot by thongs, straps, etc **2** a strap passing over the instep or around the ankle to keep a low shoe on the foot [C14: from Latin sandalium, from Greek sandalion a small sandal, from sandalon sandal] > ˈsandalled adj

sandalwood ('sændᵊlˌwʊd) or **sandal** n **1** any of several evergreen hemiparasitic trees of the genus Santalum, esp S. album (white sandalwood), of S Asia and Australia, having hard light-coloured heartwood: family Santalaceae **2** the wood of any of these trees, which is used for carving, is burned as incense, and yields an aromatic oil used in perfumery **3** any of various similar trees or their wood, esp Pterocarpus santalinus (red sandalwood), a leguminous tree of SE Asia having dark red wood used as a dye [C14 sandal, from Medieval Latin sandalum, from Late Greek sandanon, from Sanskrit candana sandalwood]

Sandalwood Island n the former name for **Sumba**

sandarac or **sandarach** ('sændəˌræk) n **1** Also called: sandarac tree either of two coniferous trees, Tetraclinis articulata of N Africa or Callistris endlicheri of Australia, having hard fragrant dark wood: family Cupressaceae **2** a brittle pale yellow transparent resin obtained from the bark of this tree and used in making varnish and incense **3** Also called: citron wood the wood of this tree, used in building [C16 sandaracha, from Latin sandaraca red pigment, from Greek sandarakē]

sandbag ('sændˌbæg) n **1** a sack filled with sand used for protection against gunfire, floodwater, etc, or as ballast in a balloon, ship, etc **2** a bag filled with sand and used as a weapon ▷ *vb* **-bags, -bagging, -bagged** (*tr*) **3** to protect or strengthen with sandbags **4** to hit with or as if with a sandbag **5** *finance* to obstruct (an unwelcome takeover bid) by prolonging talks in the hope that an acceptable bidder will come forward > 'sand,bagger*n*

sandbank ('sænd,bæŋk) *n* a submerged bank of sand in a sea or river, that may be exposed at low tide

sand bar *n* a ridge of sand in a river or sea, built up by the action of tides, currents, etc, and often exposed at low tide

sandblast ('sænd,blɑːst) *n* **1** a jet of sand or grit blown from a nozzle under air, water, or steam pressure ▷ *vb* (*tr*) **2** to clean, grind, or decorate (a surface) with a sandblast > 'sand,blaster*n*

sand-blind *adj* not completely blind; partially able to see. See **stone-blind** [c15: changed (through influence of SAND) from Old English *samblind* (unattested), from *sam-* half, SEMI- + BLIND] > 'sand-blindness*n*

sandbox ('sænd,bɒks) *n* **1** a container on a railway locomotive from which sand is released onto the rails to assist the traction **2** a container of sand for small children to play in

sandboy ('sænd,bɔɪ) *n* **happy as a sandboy** *or* **jolly as a sandboy** very happy; high-spirited

Sandburg ('sændbɜːg, 'sænbɜːg) *n* **Carl.** 1878–1967, US writer, noted esp for his poetry, often written in free verse

sand castle *n* a mass of sand moulded into a castle-like shape, esp as made by a child on the seashore

sand eel *or* **sand lance** *n* any silvery eel-like marine spiny-finned fish of the family *Ammodytidae* found burrowing in sand or shingle

sander ('sændə) *n* **1** a power-driven tool for smoothing surfaces, esp wood, plastic, etc, by rubbing with an abrasive disc **2** a person who uses such a device

sanderling ('sændəlɪŋ) *n* a small sandpiper, *Crocethia alba*, that frequents sandy shores [c17: perhaps from SAND + Old English *erthling, eorthling* EARTHLING]

Sanderson ('sændəsən) *n* **Tessa.** born 1956, British javelin-thrower

sand flea *n* another name for the **chigoe** (sense 1) and **sand hopper**

sandfly ('sænd,flaɪ) *n, pl* **-flies 1** any of various small mothlike dipterous flies of the genus *Phlebotomus* and related genera: the bloodsucking females transmit diseases including leishmaniasis: family *Psychodidae* **2** any of various similar and related flies

sandgrouse ('sænd,graʊs) *n* any bird of the family *Pteroclididae*, of dry regions of the Old World, having very short feet, a short bill, and long pointed wings and tail: order *Columbiformes*

sand hopper *n* any of various small hopping amphipod crustaceans of the genus *Orchestia* and related genera, common in intertidal regions of seashores. Also called: **beach flea, sand flea**

Sandhurst ('sænd,hɜːst) *n* a village in S England, in Bracknell unitary authority, Berkshire: seat of the Royal Military Academy for the training of officer cadets in the British Army. Pop: 19 546 (2001)

Sandinista (,sændɪ'niːstə) *n* (in Nicaragua) **a** one of a left-wing group of revolutionaries who overthrew President Somoza in 1979 and formed a socialist coalition government. The Sandinistas were opposed militarily by the US-backed Contras during the 1980s and were defeated in a general election in 1990 **b** (*as modifier*): *the Sandinista revolution* [c20: from Spanish, named after Augusto César *Sandino* a Nicaraguan general and rebel leader, murdered in 1933]

San Diego (,sæn dɪ'eɪgəʊ) *n* a port in S California, on the Pacific: naval base; two universities. Pop: 1 266 753 (2003 est)

sandman ('sænd,mæn) *n, pl* **-men** (in folklore) a magical person supposed to put children to sleep by sprinkling sand in their eyes

sand martin *n* a small brown European songbird, *Riparia riparia*, with white underparts: it nests in tunnels bored in sand, river banks, etc: family *Hirundinidae* (swallows and martins)

sandpaper ('sænd,peɪpə) *n* **1** (formerly) a strong paper coated with sand for smoothing and polishing ▷ *vb* **2** (*tr*) to polish or grind (a surface) with or as if with sandpaper

sandpiper ('sænd,paɪpə) *n* **1** any of numerous N hemisphere shore birds of the genera *Tringa, Calidris*, etc, typically having a long slender bill and legs and cryptic plumage: family *Scolopacidae*, order *Charadriiformes* **2** any other bird of the family *Scolopacidae*, which includes snipes and woodcocks

sandpit ('sænd,pɪt) *n* **1** a shallow pit or container holding sand for children to play in **2** a pit from which sand is extracted

Sandringham ('sændrɪŋəm) *n* a village in E England, in Norfolk near the E shore of the Wash: site of **Sandringham House**, a residence of the royal family

Sandrocottus (,sændrəʊ'kɒtəs) *n* the Greek name of **Chandragupta**

sandshoe ('sænd,ʃuː) *n* *Brit & Austral* a light canvas shoe with a rubber sole; plimsoll

sandstone ('sænd,stəʊn) *n* any of a group of common sedimentary rocks consisting of sand grains consolidated with such materials as quartz, haematite, and clay minerals: used widely in building

sandstorm ('sænd,stɔːm) *n* a strong wind that whips up clouds of sand, esp in a desert

sand trap *n* another name (esp US) for **bunker** (sense 2)

sand viper *n* a S European viper, *Vipera ammodytes*, having a yellowish-brown coloration with a zigzag pattern along the back

Sandwell ('sændwɛl) *n* a unitary authority in central England, in West Midlands. Pop: 285 000 (2003 est). Area: 86 sq km (33 sq miles)

sandwich ('sænwɪdʒ, -wɪtʃ) *n* **1** two or more slices of bread, usually buttered, with a filling of meat, cheese, etc **2** anything that resembles a sandwich in arrangement ▷ *vb* (*tr*) **3** to insert tightly between two other things **4** to put into a sandwich **5** to place between two dissimilar things [c18: named after John Montagu, 4th Earl of *Sandwich* (1718–92), who ate sandwiches rather than leave the gambling table for meals]

sandwich board *n* one of two connected boards, usually bearing advertisements, that are hung over the shoulders in front of and behind a person

sandwich course *n* any of several courses consisting of alternate periods of study and industrial work

Sandwich Islands *pl n* the former name of **Hawaii**

sandwich man *n* a man who carries sandwich boards

sandwort ('sænd,wɜːt) *n* **1** any of numerous caryophyllaceous plants of the genus *Arenaria*, which grow in dense tufts on sandy soil and have white or pink solitary flowers **2** any of various related plants

sandy ('sændɪ) *adj* **sandier, sandiest 1** consisting of, containing, or covered with sand **2** (esp of hair) reddish-yellow **3** resembling sand in texture > 'sandiness*n*

sand yacht *n* a wheeled boat with sails, built to be propelled over sand, esp beaches, by the wind

sandy blight *n* *Austral* a nontechnical name for any of various eye inflammations

sane (seɪn) *adj* **1** sound in mind; free from mental disturbance **2** having or showing reason, good judgment, or sound sense [c17: from Latin *sānus* healthy] > 'sanely*adv* > 'saneness*n*

San Fernando (*Spanish* san fer'nando) *n* **1** a port in Trinidad and Tobago, on Trinidad on the Gulf of Paria: the second-largest town in the country. Pop: 55 190 (2000) **2** an inland port in W Venezuela, on the Apure River. Pop: 84 180 (latest est) **3** a port in SW Spain, on the Isla de León SE of Cádiz; site of an arsenal (founded 1790) and of the most southerly observatory in Europe. Pop: 88 490 (2003 est)

Sanforized *or* **Sanforised** ('sænfə,raɪzd) *adj* *trademark* (of a fabric) preshrunk using a patented process

San Francisco (,sæn fræn'sɪskəʊ) *n* a port in W California, situated around the Golden Gate: developed rapidly during the California gold rush; a major commercial centre and one of the world's finest

S

harbours. Pop: 751 682 (2003 est) >**San Fran'ciscan** *n, adj*

San Francisco Bay *n* an inlet of the Pacific in W California, linked with the open sea by the Golden Gate strait. Length: about 80 km (50 miles). Greatest width: 19 km (12 miles)

sang (sæŋ) *vb* the past tense of **sing**
● **USAGE** See at **ring²**

sangaree (ˌsæŋgəˈriː) *n* a spiced drink similar to sangria [c18: from Spanish *sangría* a bleeding, from *sangre* blood, from Latin *sanguis*; see **SANGUINE**]

sanger (ˈsæŋə) *n Austral slang* a sandwich. Also called: **sango**

Sanger (ˈsæŋə) *n* **1** Frederick. born 1918, English biochemist, who determined the molecular structure of insulin: awarded two Nobel prizes for chemistry (1958; 1980) **2** Margaret (**Higgins**). 1883–1966, US leader of the birth-control movement

sang-froid (*French* sɑ̃frwa) *n* composure; self-possession; calmness [c18: from French, literally: cold blood]

Sangiovese (ˌsændʒəʊˈveɪzɪ) *n* **1** a black grape grown in the Tuscany region of Italy, used for making Chianti and other wines **2** a red wine made from this grape

sangoma (sæŋˈgəʊmə, -ˈgɔːmə) *n South African* a witch doctor, healer, or herbalist [from Zulu *isangoma*]

Sangrail, Sangraal (sæŋˈgreɪl) *or* **Sangreal** (ˈsæŋgrɪəl) *n* another name for the **Holy Grail** [c15: from Old French *Saint Graal*. See **SAINT, HOLY GRAIL**]

Sangre de Cristo Mountains (ˈsæŋgrɪ də ˈkrɪstəʊ) *pl n* a mountain range in S Colorado and N New Mexico: part of the Rocky Mountains. Highest peak: Blanca Peak, 4364 m (14 317 ft)

sangria (sæŋˈgriːə) *n* a Spanish drink of red wine, sugar, spices, fruit, and soda water or lemonade, sometimes laced with rum or brandy [Spanish: a bleeding; see **SANGAREE**]

sanguinary (ˈsæŋgwɪnərɪ) *adj* **1** accompanied by much bloodshed **2** bloodthirsty **3** consisting of, flowing, or stained with blood [c17: from Latin *sanguinārius*] >ˈsanguinarily *adv* >ˈsanguinariness *n*

sanguine (ˈsæŋgwɪn) *adj* **1** cheerful and confident; optimistic **2** (esp of the complexion) ruddy in appearance **3** blood-red ▷ *n* **4** Also called: **red chalk** a red pencil containing ferric oxide, used in drawing [c14: from Latin *sanguineus* bloody, from *sanguis* blood] >ˈsanguinely *adv* >ˈsanguineness *or* sanˈguinity *n*

sanguineous (sæŋˈgwɪnɪəs) *adj* of, containing, relating to, or associated with blood >sanˈguineousness *n*

Sanhedrin (ˈsænɪdrɪn) *n Judaism* the supreme judicial, ecclesiastical, and administrative council of the Jews in New Testament times, having 71 members [c16: from Late Hebrew, from Greek *sunedrion* council, from *sun-* **SYN-** + *hedra* seat]

sanies (ˈseɪnɪˌiːz) *n pathol* a thin greenish foul-smelling discharge from a wound, ulcer, etc, containing pus and blood [c16: from Latin, of obscure origin]

San Ildefonso (*Spanish* san ildeˈfɔnso) *n* a town in central Spain, near Segovia: site of the 18th-century summer palace of the kings of Spain. Also called: La Granja

sanitarium (ˌsænɪˈtɛərɪəm) *n, pl* -riums *or* -ria (-rɪə) the US spelling of **sanatorium** [c19: from Latin *sānitās* health]

sanitary (ˈsænɪtərɪ, -trɪ) *adj* **1** of or relating to health and measures for the protection of health **2** conducive to or promoting health; free from dirt, germs, etc; hygienic [c19: from French *sanitaire*, from Latin *sānitās* health] >ˈsanitariness *n*

sanitary engineering *n* the branch of civil engineering associated with the supply of water, disposal of sewage, and other public health services >sanitary engineer *n*

sanitary towel *or esp US* **sanitary napkin** *n* an absorbent pad worn externally by women during menstruation to absorb the menstrual flow

sanitation (ˌsænɪˈteɪʃən) *n* the study and use of practical measures for the preservation of public health

sanitize *or* **sanitise** (ˈsænɪˌtaɪz) *vb* (tr) **1** to make sanitary or hygienic, as by sterilizing **2** to omit unpleasant details from (a news report, document, etc) to make it more palatable to the recipients >ˌsanitiˈzation *or* ˌsanitiˈsation *n*

sanity (ˈsænɪtɪ) *n* **1** the state of being sane **2** good sense or soundness of judgment [c15: from Latin *sānitās* health, from *sānus* healthy]

San Jose (ˌsæn həʊˈzeɪ) *n* a city in W central California: a leading world centre of the fruit drying and canning industry. Pop: 898 349 (2003 est)

San José (*Spanish* san xoˈse) *n* the capital of Costa Rica, on the central plateau: a major centre of coffee production in the mid-19th century; University of Costa Rica (1843). Pop: 1 145 000 (2005 est)

San Juan (*Spanish* san ˈxwan) *n* **1** the capital and chief port of Puerto Rico, on the NE coast; University of Puerto Rico; manufacturing centre. Pop: 433 733 (2003 est) **2** a city in W Argentina: almost completely destroyed by an earthquake in 1944. Pop: 455 000 (2005 est)

San Juan Bautista (*Spanish* san ˈxwan bauˈtista) *n* the former name of **Villahermosa**

San Juan Islands (ˌsæn ˈwɑːn, ˈhwɑːn) *pl n* a group of islands between NW Washington, US, and SE Vancouver Island, Canada: administratively part of Washington

San Juan Mountains *pl n* a mountain range in SW Colorado and N New Mexico: part of the Rocky Mountains. Highest peak: Uncompahgre Peak, 4363 m (14 314 ft)

sank (sæŋk) *vb* the past tense of **sink**

Sankara (ˈsænkɑːrə) *n* 8th century AD, Hindu philosopher, the leading exponent of the Vedantic school: noted for his commentaries on the great Hindu texts

Sankey (ˈsæŋkɪ) *n* **Ira David**. 1840–1908, US evangelist and hymnodist, noted for his revivalist campaigns in Britain and the US with D. L. Moody

Sankt Pölten (*German* zaŋkt ˈpœltən) *n* a city in NE Austria, the capital of Lower Austria state. Pop: 49 121 (2001)

San Luis Potosí (*Spanish* san ˈlwis potoˈsi) *n* **1** a state of central Mexico: mainly high plateau; economy based on mining (esp silver) and agriculture. Capital: San Luis Potosí. Pop: 927 000 (2005 est). Area: 62 849 sq km (24 266 sq miles) **2** an industrial city in central Mexico, capital of San Luis Potosí state, at an altitude of 1850 m (6000 ft). Pop: 628 134 (2000 est)

San Marino (ˌsæn məˈriːnəʊ) *n* a republic in S central Europe in the Apennines, forming an enclave in Italy: the smallest republic in Europe, according to tradition founded by St Marinus in the 4th century. Official language: Italian. Religion: Roman Catholic majority. Currency: euro. Capital: San Marino. Pop: 28 000 (2003 est). Area: 62 sq km (24 sq miles) >San Marinese (ˌsæn ˌmærɪˈniːz) *or* Sammarinese (sæˌmærɪˈniːz) *adj, n*

San Martín (*Spanish* san marˈtin) *n* José de (xoˈse de). 1778–1850, South American patriot, who played an important part in gaining independence for Argentina, Chile, and Peru. He was protector of Peru (1821–22)

Sanmicheli (*Italian* sanmiˈkeːli) *n* Michele (miˈkeːle). ?1484–1559, Italian mannerist architect

sannyasi, sanyasi (sʌnˈjɑːsɪ) *or* **sannyasin** (sʌnˈjɑːsɪn) *n* a Brahman who having attained the fourth and last stage of life as a beggar will not be reborn, but will instead be absorbed into the Universal Soul. Also called: **renunciate** [from Hindi: abandoning, from Sanskrit *samnyāsin*]

San Pedro Sula (*Spanish* san ˈpeðro ˈsula) *n* a city in NW Honduras: the country's chief industrial centre. Pop: 610 000 (2005 est)

San Remo (*Italian* san ˈrɛmo) *n* a port and resort in NW Italy, in Liguria on the slopes of the Maritime Alps; flower market. Pop: 50 608 (2001)

sans (sænz) *prep* an archaic word for **without** [c13: from Old French *sanz*, from Latin *sine* without, but probably also influenced by Latin *absentiā* in the absence of]

Sans. *or* **Sansk.** abbreviation Sanskrit

San Salvador (sæn ˈsælvəˌdɔː; *Spanish* san salˈβaˈðor) *n* the capital of El Salvador, situated in the SW central part: became capital in 1841; ruined by earthquakes in 1854 and 1873; university (1841). Pop: 1 472 000 (2005 est)

San Salvador Island *n* an island in the central Bahamas: the first land in the New World seen by Christopher Columbus (1492). Area: 156 sq km (60 sq miles). Also called: Watling Island

sans-culotte (ˌsænzkjʊˈlɒt; *French* sākylɔt) *n* **1** (during the French Revolution) **a** (originally) a revolutionary of the poorer class **b** (later) any revolutionary, esp one having extreme republican sympathies **2** any revolutionary extremist [C18: from French, literally: without knee breeches, because the revolutionaries wore pantaloons or trousers rather than knee breeches] > ˌsans-cuˈlottism *n* > ˌsans-cuˈlottist *n*

San Sebastián (ˌsæn səˈbæstjən; *Spanish* san seβasˈtjan) *n* a port and resort in N Spain on the Bay of Biscay: former summer residence of the Spanish court. Pop: 181 811 (2003 est)

sansevieria (ˌsænsɪˈvɪərɪə) *n* any herbaceous perennial plant of the liliaceous genus *Sansevieria*, of Old World tropical regions. Some are cultivated as house plants for their erect bayonet-like fleshy leaves of variegated green (mother-in-law's tongue); others yield useful fibre (bowstring hemp) [New Latin, named after Raimondo di Sangro (1710–71), Italian scholar and prince of *San Severo*]

Sanskrit (ˈsænskrɪt) *n* an ancient language of India, the language of the Vedas, of Hinduism, and of an extensive philosophical and scientific literature dating from the beginning of the first millennium BC. It is the oldest recorded member of the Indic branch of the Indo-European family of languages; recognition of the existence of the Indo-European family arose in the 18th century from a comparison of Sanskrit with Greek and Latin. Although it is used only for religious purposes, it is one of the official languages of India [C17: from Sanskrit *saṃskṛta* perfected, literally: put together]

sans serif *or* **sanserif** (sænˈsɛrɪf) *n* a style of printer's typeface in which the characters have no serifs

San Stefano (ˌsæn stɪˈfɑːnəʊ) *n* a village in NW Turkey, near Istanbul on the Sea of Marmara: scene of the signing (1878) of the treaty ending the Russo-Turkish War. Turkish name: Yeşilköy

San Suu Kyi *n* See Aung San Suu Kyi

Santa (ˈsæntə) *n informal* short for **Santa Claus**

Santa Ana *n* **1** (*Spanish* ˈsanta ˈana) a city in NW El Salvador: the second largest city in the country; coffee-processing industry. Pop: 172 000 (2005 est) **2** (ˈsæntə ˈænə) a city in SW California: commercial and processing centre of a rich agricultural region. Pop: 342 510 (2003 est)

Santa Catalina (ˈsæntə ˌkætᵊˈliːnə) *n* an island in the Pacific, off the coast of SW California: part of Los Angeles county: resort. Area: 181 sq km (70 sq miles). Also called: Catalina Island

Santa Catarina (*Portuguese* ˈsantə kətəˈrinə) *n* a state of S Brazil, on the Atlantic: consists chiefly of the Great Escarpment. Capital: Florianópolis. Pop: 5 527 707 (2002). Area: 95 985 sq km (37 060 sq miles)

Santa Clara (*Spanish* ˈsanta ˈklara) *n* a city in W central Cuba: sugar and tobacco industries. Pop: 216 000 (2005 est)

Santa Claus (ˈsæntə ˌklɔːz) *n* the legendary patron saint of children, commonly identified with Saint Nicholas, who brings presents to children on Christmas Eve or, in some European countries, on Saint Nicholas' Day. Often shortened to **Santa** Also called: Father Christmas

Santa Cruz[1] (ˈsæntə ˈkruːz; *Spanish* ˈsanta ˈkruθ) *n* **1** a province of S Argentina, on the Atlantic: consists of a large part of Patagonia, with the forested foothills of the Andes in the west Capital: Río Gallegos. Pop: 206 897 (2000 est). Area: 243 940 sq km (94 186 sq miles) **2** a city in E Bolivia: the second largest town in Bolivia. Pop: 1 352 000 (2005 est) **3** another name for **Saint Croix**

Santa Cruz[2] (*Spanish* ˈsanta ˈkruθ) *n* **Alvaro de Bazán.** 1526–88, Spanish naval commander, who proposed, assembled, and prepared the Spanish Armada but died shortly before it sailed for England

Santa Cruz de Tenerife (ˈsæntə ˈkruːz də ˌtɛnəˈriːf; *Spanish* ˈsanta ˈkruθ de teneˈrife) *n* a port and resort in the W Canary Islands, on NE Tenerife: oil refinery. Pop: 220 022 (2003 est)

Santa Fe *n* **1** (ˈsæntə ˈfeɪ) a city in N central New Mexico, capital of the state: one of the oldest European settlements in North America, founded in 1610 as the capital of the Kingdom of New Mexico; developed trade with the US by the Santa Fe Trail in the early 19th century. Pop: 66 476 (2003 est) **2** (*Spanish* ˈsanta ˈfe) an inland port in E Argentina, on the Salado River: University of the Littoral (1920). Pop: 492 000 (2005 est) > ˈSanta ˈFean *adj, n*

Santa Gertrudis (ˈsæntə gəˈtruːdɪs) *n* one of a breed of large red beef cattle developed in Texas

Santa Isabel (*Spanish* ˈsanta isaˈβɛl) *n* the former name (until 1973) of **Malabo**

Santa Maria *n* **1** (*Portuguese* ˈsantə maˈria) a city in S Brazil, in Rio Grande do Sul state. Pop: 252 000 (2005 est) **2** (*Spanish* ˈsanta maˈria) an active volcano in SW Guatemala. Height: 3768 m (12 362 ft)

Santa Marta (*Spanish* ˈsanta ˈmarta) *n* a port in NW Colombia, on the Caribbean: the oldest city in Colombia, founded in 1525; terminus of the Atlantic railway from Bogotá (opened 1961). Pop: 454 000 (2005 est)

Santa Maura (ˈsanta ˈmaura) *n* the Italian name for **Levkás**

Santander (*Spanish* santanˈdɛr) *n* a port and resort in N Spain, on an inlet of the Bay of Biscay: noted for its prehistoric collection from nearby caves; shipyards and an oil refinery. Pop: 184 778 (2003 est)

Santarém (*Portuguese* səntaˈrɐ̃j) *n* a port in N Brazil, in Pará state where the Tapajós River flows into the Amazon. Pop: 190 000 (2005 est)

Santa Rosa de Copán (*Spanish* ˈsanta ˈrɔsa de koˈpan) *n* a village in W Honduras: noted for the ruined Mayan city of Copán, which lies to the west

Santayana (ˌsæntɪˈænə) *n* **George.** 1863–1952, US philosopher, poet, and critic, born in Spain. His works include *The Life of Reason* (1905–06) and *The Realms of Being* (1927–40)

Santee (sænˈtiː) *n* a river in SE central South Carolina, formed by the union of the Congaree and Wateree Rivers: flows southeast to the Atlantic; part of the **Santee-Wateree-Catawba River System** an inland waterway 866 km (538 miles) long. Length: 230 km (143 miles)

Santer (ˈsæntə) *n* **Jacques.** born 1937, Luxembourg politician: prime minister of Luxembourg (1984–95); president of the European Commission (1994–99)

Santiago (ˌsæntɪˈɑːgəʊ; *Spanish* sanˈtjaɣo) *n* **1** the capital of Chile, at the foot of the Andes: commercial and industrial centre; two universities. Pop: 5 623 000 (2005 est) **2** a city in the N Dominican Republic. Pop: 479 000 (2005 est)

Santiago de Compostela (*Spanish* de kɔmpɔsˈtela) *n* a city in NW Spain: place of pilgrimage since the 9th century and the most visited (after Jerusalem and Rome) in the Middle Ages; cathedral built over the tomb of the apostle St James. Pop: 92 339 (2003 est)

Santiago de Cuba (*Spanish* de ˈkuβa) *n* a port in SE Cuba, on **Santiago Bay** (a large inlet of the Caribbean): capital of Cuba until 1589; university (1947); industrial centre. Pop: 456 000 (2005 est)

Santiago del Estero (*Spanish* del esˈtero) *n* a city in N Argentina: the oldest continuous settlement in Argentina, founded in 1553 by Spaniards from Peru. Pop: 385 000 (2005 est)

Santo Domingo (ˈsæntəʊ dəˈmɪŋgəʊ; *Spanish* ˈsanto ðoˈmiŋgo) *n* **1** the capital and chief port of the Dominican Republic, on the S coast: the oldest continuous European settlement in the Americas, founded in 1496; university (1538). Pop: 1 920 000 (2005 est). Former name (1936–61) Ciudad Trujillo **2** the former name (until 1844) of the **Dominican Republic 3** another name (esp in colonial times) for **Hispaniola**

santonica (sænˈtɒnɪkə) *n* **1** an oriental wormwood plant, *Artemisia cina* (or *maritima*) **2** the dried flower heads of this plant, formerly used as a vermifuge ▷ Also called: wormseed [C17: New Latin, from Late Latin *herba santonica* herb of the *Santones* (probably wormwood), from Latin *Santonī* a people of Aquitania]

santonin (ˈsæntənɪn) *n* a white crystalline soluble substance extracted from the dried flower heads of santonica and used in medicine as an anthelmintic. Formula: $C_{15}H_{18}O_3$ [C19: from SANTONICA + -IN]

S

Santos (Portuguese 'sɐntuʃ) n a port in S Brazil, in São Paulo state: the world's leading coffee port. Pop: 1 634 000 (2005 est)

Santos-Dumont (French sɑ̃tɔdymɔ̃) n **Alberto** (albɛrto). 1873–1932, Brazilian aeronaut, living in France. He constructed dirigibles and aircraft, including a monoplane (1909)

sanyasi (sʌn'jɑːsɪ) n a variant of **sannyasi**

São Francisco (Portuguese sɐu frɐ'sisku) n a river in E Brazil, rising in SW Minas Gerais state and flowing northeast, then southeast to the Atlantic northeast of Aracajú. Length: 3200 km (1990 miles)

São Luís (Portuguese sɐu 'lwis) or **São Luíz** ('lwiʃ) n a port in NE Brazil, capital of Maranhão state, on the W coast of São Luís Island: founded in 1612 by the French and taken by the Portuguese in 1615. Pop: 982 000 (2005 est)

São Miguel (Portuguese sɐu mi'ɣɛl) n an island in the E Azores: the largest of the group. Pop: 131 609 (2001). Area: 854 sq km (333 sq miles)

Saône (French son) n a river in E France, rising in Lorraine and flowing generally south to join the Rhône at Lyon, as its chief tributary: canalized for 375 km (233 miles) above Lyon; linked by canals with the Rhine, Marne, Seine, and Loire Rivers. Length: 480 km (298 miles)

Saône-et-Loire (French sonelwar) n a department of central France, in Burgundy region. Capital: Mâcon. Pop: 543 848 (2003 est). Area: 8627 sq km (3365 sq miles)

São Paulo (Portuguese sɐu 'paulu) n **1** a state of SE Brazil: consists chiefly of tableland draining west into the Paraná River. Capital: São Paulo. Pop: 38 177 742 (2002). Area: 247 239 sq km (95 459 sq miles) **2** a city in S Brazil, capital of São Paulo state: the largest city and industrial centre in Brazil, with one of the busiest airports in the world; three universities. Pop: 25 000 (1874); 2 017 025 (1950); Pop: 18 333 000 (2005 est)

Saorstat Eireann ('sɛəstɑːt 'ɛərən) n the Gaelic name for the **Irish Free State**

São Salvador (Portuguese sɐu salva'dor) n short for São Salvador da Bahia de Todos os Santos, the official name for Salvador. See **Salvador**

São Tomé and Príncipe or **São Tomé e Príncipe** (Portuguese sɐu tu'mɛ 'ɛ: 'prĩ:sipə) n a republic in the Gulf of Guinea, off the W coast of Africa, on the Equator: consists of the islands of Príncipe and São Tomé; colonized by the Portuguese in the late 15th century; became independent in 1975. Official language: Portuguese. Religion: Roman Catholic majority. Currency: dobra. Capital: São Tomé. Pop: 164 000 (2004 est). Area: 1001 sq km (386 sq miles)

sap¹ (sæp) n **1** a solution of mineral salts, sugars, etc, that circulates in a plant **2** any vital body fluid **3** energy; vigour **4** slang a gullible or foolish person **5** another name for **sapwood** ▷ vb saps, sapping, sapped (tr) **6** to drain of sap [Old English sæp; related to Old High German sapf, German Saft juice, Middle Low German sapp, Sanskrit sabar milk juice]

sap² (sæp) n **1** a deep and narrow trench used to approach or undermine an enemy position, esp in siege warfare ▷ vb saps, sapping, sapped **2** to undermine (a fortification, etc) by digging saps **3** (tr) to weaken [C16 zappe, from Italian zappa spade, of uncertain origin; perhaps from Old Italian (dialect) zappo a goat]

sapele (sə'piːlɪ) n **1** any of several W African meliaceous trees of the genus Entandrophragma, esp E. cylindricum, yielding a hard timber resembling mahogany **2** the timber obtained from such a tree, used to make furniture [C20: West African name]

sapid ('sæpɪd) adj **1** having a pleasant taste **2** agreeable or engaging [C17: from Latin sapidus, from sapere to taste] > sa'pidity (sə'pɪdɪtɪ) or 'sapidness n

sapient ('seɪpɪənt) adj often used ironically wise or sagacious [C15: from Latin sapere to taste] > 'sapience n > 'sapiently adv

sapiential (ˌseɪpɪ'ɛnʃəl, ˌsæpɪ-) adj showing, having, or providing wisdom

Sapir (sə'pɪə, 'seɪpɪə) n **Edward**. 1884–1939, US anthropologist and linguist, noted for his study of the ethnology and languages of North American Indians

sapling ('sæplɪŋ) n **1** a young tree **2** literary a youth

sapodilla (ˌsæpə'dɪlə) n **1** a large tropical American evergreen tree, Achras zapota, the latex of which yields chicle **2** Also called: **sapodilla plum** the edible brown rough-skinned fruit of this tree, which has a sweet yellowish pulp [C17: from Spanish zapotillo, diminutive of zapote sapodilla fruit, from Nahuatl tsapotl]

saponaceous (ˌsæpəʊ'neɪʃəs) adj resembling soap; soapy [C18: from New Latin sāpōnāceus, from Latin sāpō SOAP]

saponify (sə'pɒnɪˌfaɪ) vb -fies, -fying, -fied chem **1** to undergo or cause to undergo a process in which a fat is converted into a soap by treatment with alkali **2** to undergo or cause to undergo a reaction in which an ester is hydrolysed to an acid and an alcohol as a result of treatment with an alkali [C19: from French saponifier, from Latin sāpō SOAP] > sa'poni,fiable adj > sa'poni,fier n > sa,ponifi'cation n

saponin ('sæpənɪn) n any of a group of plant glycosides with a steroid structure that foam when shaken and are used in detergents [C19: from French saponine, from Latin sāpō SOAP]

sappanwood or **sapanwood** ('sæpənˌwʊd) n **1** a small leguminous tree, Caesalpinia sappan, of S Asia producing wood that yields a red dye **2** the wood of this tree [C16: sapan, via Dutch from Malay sapang]

sapper ('sæpə) n **1** a soldier who digs trenches **2** (in the British Army) a private of the Royal Engineers

Sapper ('sæpə) n real name Herman Cyril McNeile. 1888–1937, British novelist, author of the popular thriller Bull-dog Drummond (1920) and its sequels

Sapphic ('sæfɪk) adj **1** prosody denoting a metre associated with Sappho, the 6th century BC Greek lyric poetess of Lesbos, consisting generally of a trochaic pentameter line with a dactyl in the third foot **2** of or relating to Sappho or her poetry **3** lesbian ▷ n **4** prosody a verse, line, or stanza written in the Sapphic form

Sapphira (sæ'faɪrə) n New Testament the wife of Ananias, who together with her husband was struck dead for fraudulently concealing their wealth from the Church (Acts 5)

sapphire ('sæfaɪə) n **1 a** any precious corundum gemstone that is not red, esp the highly valued transparent blue variety. A synthetic form is used in electronics and precision apparatus. Formula: Al_2O_3 **b** (as modifier): a sapphire ring **2 a** the blue colour of sapphire **b** (as adjective): sapphire eyes [C13 safir, from Old French, from Latin sapphīrus, from Greek sappheiros, perhaps from Hebrew sappīr, ultimately perhaps from Sanskrit śanipriya, literally: beloved of the planet Saturn, from śani Saturn + priya beloved]

Sappho ('sæfəʊ) n 6th century BC, Greek lyric poetess of Lesbos

Sapporo ('sɑːpəʊˌrəʊ) n a city in N Japan, on W Hokkaido: commercial centre; university (1918). Pop: 1 822 992 (2002 est)

sappy ('sæpɪ) adj -pier, -piest **1** (of plants) full of sap **2** full of energy or vitality **3** slang silly or fatuous

sapro- or before a vowel **sapr-** combining form indicating dead or decaying matter: saprogenic; saprolite [from Greek sapros rotten]

saprogenic (ˌsæprəʊ'dʒɛnɪk) or **saprogenous** (sæ'prɒdʒɪnəs) adj **1** producing or resulting from decay **2** growing on decaying matter

saprophyte ('sæprəʊˌfaɪt) n any plant that lives and feeds on dead organic matter using mycorrhizal fungi associated with its roots; a saprotrophic plant > saprophytic (ˌsæprəʊ'fɪtɪk) adj

saprotroph ('sæprəʊˌtrɒf) n any organism, esp a fungus or bacterium, that lives and feeds on dead organic matter. Also called: saprobe, saprobiont > saprotrophic (ˌsæprəʊ'trɒfɪk) adj > ˌsapro'trophically adv

saprozoic (ˌsæprəʊ'zəʊɪk) adj **1** (of animals or plants) feeding on dead organic matter **2** of or relating to nutrition in which the nutrient substances are derived from dead organic matter

SAPS abbreviation South African Police Service

sapsucker ('sæpˌsʌkə) n either of two North American woodpeckers, Sphyrapicus varius or S. thyroideus, that have

S

white wing patches and feed on the sap from trees

sapwood ('sæpˌwʊd) *n* the soft wood, just beneath the bark in tree trunks, that consists of living tissue

sarabande *or* **saraband** ('særəˌbænd) *n* **1** a decorous 17th-century courtly dance **2** *music* a piece of music composed for or in the rhythm of this dance, in slow triple time, often incorporated into the classical suite [c17: from French, from Spanish *zarabanda*, of uncertain origin]

Saracen ('særəsən) *n* **1** *history* a member of one of the nomadic Arabic tribes, esp of the Syrian desert, that harassed the borders of the Roman Empire in that region **2** a Muslim, esp one who opposed the crusades **b** (in later use) any Arab ▷ *adj* **3** of or relating to Arabs of either of these periods, regions, or types [c13: from Old French *Sarrazin*, from Late Latin *Saracēnus*, from Late Greek *Sarakēnos*, perhaps from Arabic *sharq* sunrise, from *shāraqa* to rise] > **Saracenic** (ˌsærə'sɛnɪk) *or* ˌSara'cenical *adj*

Saragossa (ˌsærə'gɒsə) *n* the English name for **Zaragoza**

Sarah ('sɛərə) *n* *Old Testament* the wife of Abraham and mother of Isaac (Genesis 17:15–22)

Sarajevo (*Bosnian* 'sarajɛvɔ) *or* **Serajevo** *n* the capital of Bosnia-Herzegovina: developed as a Turkish town in the 15th century; capital of the Turkish and Austro-Hungarian administrations in 1850 and 1878 respectively; scene of the assassination of Archduke Franz Ferdinand in 1914, precipitating World War I; besieged by Bosnian Serbs (1992–95). Pop: 603 000 (2005 est)

Saramago (*Portuguese* ˌsara'magu) *or* **José**. born 1922, Portuguese novelist and writer; his works include the novel *O ano da morte de Ricardo Reis* (1984): Nobel prize for literature 1998

Sarandon ('særəndən) *n* **Susan Abigail**. born 1946, US film actress: her films include *Thelma and Louise* (1991), *Lorenzo's Oil* (1992), *The Client* (1994), *Dead Man Walking* (1996), and *Moonlight Mile* (2002)

Saransk (*Russian* sa'ransk) *n* a city in W central Russia, capital of the Mordovian Republic: university (1957). Pop: 304 000 (2005 est)

Saratov (*Russian* sa'ratəf) *n* an industrial city in W Russia, on the River Volga: university (1919). Pop: 868 000 (2005 est)

Sarawak (sə'rɑːwæk) *n* a state of Malaysia, on the NW coast of Borneo on the South China Sea: granted to Sir James Brooke by the Sultan of Brunei in 1841 as a reward for helping quell a revolt; mainly agricultural. Capital: Kuching. Pop: 2 071 506 (2000). Area: about 124 449 sq km (48 050 sq miles)

Sarazen ('særəzən) *n* **Gene**, original name *Eugenio Saraceni*. 1902–99, US golfer; won seven major tournaments between 1922 and 1935

sarcasm ('sɑːkæzəm) *n* **1** mocking, contemptuous, or ironic language intended to convey scorn or insult **2** the use or tone of such language [c16: from Late Latin *sarcasmus*, from Greek *sarkasmos*, from *sarkazein* to rend the flesh, from *sarx* flesh]

sarcastic (sɑː'kæstɪk) *adj* **1** characterized by sarcasm **2** given to the use of sarcasm > **sar'castically** *adv*

sarcenet *or* **sarsenet** ('sɑːsnɪt) *n* a fine soft silk fabric formerly from Italy and used for clothing, ribbons, etc [c15: from Old French *sarzinet*, from *Sarrazin* SARACEN]

sarco- *or before a vowel* **sarc-** *combining form* indicating flesh: *sarcoma* [from Greek *sark-*, *sarx* flesh]

sarcocarp ('sɑːkəʊˌkɑːp) *n* *botany* the fleshy mesocarp of such fruits as the peach or plum

sarcoma (sɑː'kəʊmə) *n*, *pl* **-mata** (-mətə) *or* **-mas** *pathol* a usually malignant tumour arising from connective tissue [c17: via New Latin from Greek *sarkōma* fleshy growth; see SARCO-, -OMA] > **sar'coma,toid**, sar'comatous *adj*

sarcomatosis (sɑːˌkəʊmə'təʊsɪs) *n* *pathol* a condition characterized by the development of several sarcomas at various bodily sites [c19: see SARCOMA, -OSIS]

sarcophagus (sɑː'kɒfəgəs) *n*, *pl* **-gi** (-ˌgaɪ) *or* **-guses** a stone or marble coffin or tomb, esp one bearing sculpture or inscriptions [c17: via Latin from Greek *sarkophagos* flesh-devouring; from the type of stone used,

which was believed to destroy the flesh of corpses]

sarcoplasm ('sɑːkəʊˌplæzəm) *n* the cytoplasm of a muscle fibre > ˌsarco'plasmic *adj*

sarcous ('sɑːkəs) *adj* (of tissue) muscular or fleshy [c19: from Greek *sarx* flesh]

sard (sɑːd) *or* **sardius** ('sɑːdɪəs) *n* an orange, red, or brown variety of chalcedony, used as a gemstone. Formula: SiO₂. Also called: sardine [c14: from Latin *sarda*, from Greek *sardios* stone from Sardis]

Sardanapalus (ˌsɑːdə'næpələs) *n* the Greek name of **Ashurbanipal**

sardar *or* **sirdar** (sə'dɑː) *n* (in India) **1** a title used before the name of Sikh men **2** a leader [Hindi, from Persian]

Sardegna (sar'deɲɲa) *n* the Italian name for **Sardinia**

sardine¹ (sɑː'diːn) *n*, *pl* **-dines**, **-dine** **1** any of various small marine food fishes of the herring family, esp a young pilchard **2** like sardines very closely crowded together [c15: via Old French from Latin *sardīna*, diminutive of *sarda* a fish suitable for pickling]

sardine² ('sɑːdiːn, -dən) *n* another name for **sard** [c14: from Late Latin *sardinus*, from Greek *sardinos lithos* Sardian stone, from *Sardeis* Sardis]

Sardinia (sɑː'dɪnɪə) *n* the second-largest island in the Mediterranean: forms, with offshore islands, an administrative region of Italy; ceded to Savoy by Austria in 1720 in exchange for Sicily and formed the Kingdom of Sardinia with Piedmont; became part of Italy in 1861. Capital: Cagliari. Pop: 1 637 639 (2003 est). Area: 24 089 sq km (9301 sq miles). Italian name: Sardegna

Sardinian (sɑː'dɪnɪən) *adj* **1** of or relating to Sardinia, its inhabitants, or their language ▷ *n* **2** a native or inhabitant of Sardinia **3** the spoken language of Sardinia, sometimes regarded as a dialect of Italian but containing many loan words from Spanish

Sardis ('sɑːdɪs) *or* **Sardes** ('sɑːdiːz) *n* an ancient city of W Asia Minor: capital of Lydia

sardonic (sɑː'dɒnɪk) *adj* characterized by irony, mockery, or derision [c17: from French *sardonique*, from Latin *sardonius*, from Greek *sardonios* derisive, literally: of Sardinia, alteration of Homeric *sardanios* scornful (laughter or smile)] > **sar'donically** *adv* > **sar'donicism** *n*

sardonyx ('sɑːdənɪks) *n* a variety of chalcedony with alternating reddish-brown and white parallel bands, used as a gemstone. Formula: SiO₂ [c14: via Latin from Greek *sardonux*, perhaps from *sardion* SARDINE² + *onux* nail]

Sardou (*French* sardu) *n* **Victorien** (viktɔrjɛ̃). 1831–1908, French dramatist. His plays include *Fédora* (1882) and *La Tosca* (1887), the source of Puccini's opera

SARFU *abbreviation* South African Rugby Football Union

sargasso *or* **sargasso weed** (sɑː'gæsəʊ) *n*, *pl* **-sos** another name for **gulfweed**, **sargassum** [c16: from Portuguese *sargaço*, of unknown origin]

Sargasso Sea *n* a calm area of the N Atlantic, between the Caribbean and the Azores, where there is an abundance of floating seaweed of the genus *Sargassum*

sargassum (sɑː'gæsəm) *or* **sargasso** (sɑː'gæsəʊ) *n* any floating brown seaweed of the genus *Sargassum*, such as gulfweed, of warm seas, having ribbon-like fronds containing air sacs [c18: from New Latin; see SARGASSO]

sarge (sɑːdʒ) *n* *informal* sergeant: used esp as a term of address

Sargent ('sɑːdʒənt) *n* **1** Sir (**Harold**) **Malcolm** (**Watts**). 1895–1967, English conductor **2** **John Singer**. 1856–1925, US painter, esp of society portraits; in London from 1885

Sargeson ('sɑːdʒəsən) *n* **Frank**. 1903–82, New Zealand short-story writer and novelist. His work includes the short-story collection *That Summer and Other Stories* (1946) and the novel *I Saw in my Dream* (1949)

Sargodha (sɑː'gəʊdə) *n* a city in NE Pakistan: grain market. Pop: 556 000 (2005 est)

Sargon II ('sɑːgɒn) *n* died 705 BC, king of Assyria (722–705). He developed a policy of transporting conquered peoples to distant parts of his empire

Sargon of Akkad ('sɑːgɒn, 'ækæd) *n* 24th to 23rd century BC, semilegendary Mesopotamian ruler whose empire extended from the Gulf to the Mediterranean

sari *or* **saree** ('sɑːrɪ) *n*, *pl* **-ris** *or* **-rees** the traditional dress of women of India, Pakistan, etc, consisting of a very long narrow piece of cloth elaborately swathed around the body [c18: from Hindi *sārī*, from Sanskrit *śātī*]

sark (saɛrk) *n Scot* a shirt or (formerly) chemise [Old English *serc*; related to Old Norse *serkr*]

Sark (saːk) *n* an island in the English Channel in the Channel Islands, consisting of **Great Sark** and **Little Sark**, connected by an isthmus: ruled by a hereditary Seigneur or Dame. Pop: 591 (2000). Area: 5 sq km (2 sq miles). French name: Sercq

Sarka ('zaːkə) *n* a variant spelling of **Zarqa**

sarking ('saːkɪŋ, 'særkɪŋ) *n Scot, northern English & NZ* a timber or felt cladding placed over the rafters of a roof before the tiles or slates are fixed in place [c15: from verbal use of SARK]

Sarkozy (saːˈkɔːzɪ) *n* **Nicolas** (niˈkɒˌlaː). born 1955, French centre-right politician, president of France from 2007

sarky ('saːkɪ) *adj* -kier, -kiest *Brit informal* sarcastic

Sarmatia (saːˈmeɪʃɪə) *n* the ancient name of a region between the Volga and Vistula Rivers now covering parts of Poland, Belarus, and SW Russia ⊳ Sar'matian *n, adj* ⊳ Sarmatic *adj*

sarmentose (saːˈmɛntəʊs), **sarmentous** (saːˈmɛntəs) or **sarmentaceous** (ˌsaːmənˈteɪʃəs) *adj* (of plants such as the strawberry) having stems in the form of runners [c18: from Latin *sarmentōsus* full of twigs, from *sarmentum* brushwood, from *sarpere* to prune]

sarmie ('saːmɪ) *n South African children's slang* a sandwich [c20: from Northern English SARNIE]

Sarnen (German 'zarnən) *n* a town in central Switzerland, capital of Obwalden demicanton: resort. Pop: 9145 (2000)

Sarnia ('saːnɪə) *n* an inland port in S central Canada, in SW Ontario at the S end of Lake Huron: oil refineries. Pop: 78 577 (2001)

sarnie ('saːnɪ) *n Brit informal* a sandwich [c20: probably from Northern or dialect pronunciation of first syllable of *sandwich*]

sarod (sæˈrəʊd) *n* an Indian stringed musical instrument that may be played with a bow or plucked [c19: from Hindi]

sarong (səˈrɒŋ) *n* **1** a draped skirtlike garment worn by men and women in the Malay Archipelago, Sri Lanka, the Pacific islands, etc **2** a fashionable Western adaptation of this garment [c19: from Malay, literally: sheath]

Saronic Gulf (səˈrɒnɪk) *n* an inlet of the Aegean on the SE coast of Greece. Length: about 80 km (50 miles). Width: about 48 km (30 miles). Also called: Aegina, Gulf of Aegina

saros ('sɛɪrɒs) *n* a cycle of about 18 years 11 days (6585.32 days) in which eclipses of the sun and moon occur in the same sequence and at the same intervals as in the previous such cycle [c19: from Greek, from Babylonian *šāru* 3600 (years); modern astronomical use apparently based on mistaken interpretation of *šāru* as a period of 18½ years]

Saros ('saːrɒs) *n* **Gulf of Saros** an inlet of the Aegean in NW Turkey, north of the Gallipoli Peninsula. Length: 59 km (37 miles). Width: 35 km (22 miles)

Sarpedon (saːˈpiːdɒn) *n Greek myth* a son of Zeus and Laodameia, or perhaps Europa, and king of Lycia. He was slain by Patroclus while fighting on behalf of the Trojans

Sarpi (Italian 'sarpi) *n* **Paolo** ('paolo), real name *Pietro Soave Polano*. 1552–1623, Italian scholar, theologian, and patriot, who championed the Venetian republic in its dispute with Pope Paul V, arguing against papal absolutism and for the separation of church and state

Sarraute (French sarot) *n* **Nathalie** (natali). 1900–99, French novelist, noted as an exponent of the antinovel. Her novels include *Portrait of a Man Unknown* (1948), *Martereau* (1953), and *Ici* (1995)

Sarre (sar) *n* the French name for the **Saar**

sarrusophone (səˈruːzəˌfəʊn) *n* a wind instrument resembling the oboe but made of brass [c19: named after *Sarrus*, French bandmaster, who invented it (1856)]

SARS (saːz) *n acronym for* severe acute respiratory syndrome; a severe viral infection of the lungs characterized by high fever, a dry cough, and breathing

difficulties. It is contagious, having an airborne mode of transmission

sarsaparilla (ˌsaːsəpəˈrɪlə, ˌsaːspə-) *n* **1** any of various prickly climbing plants of the tropical American genus *Smilax* having large aromatic roots and heart-shaped leaves: family *Smilacaceae* **2** the dried roots of any of these plants, formerly used as a medicine **3** a nonalcoholic drink prepared from these roots [c16: from Spanish *sarzaparrilla*, from *zarza* a bramble, (from Arabic *šaras*) + -*parrilla*, from Spanish *parra* a climbing plant]

sarsen ('saːsᵊn) *n* **1** *geology* a boulder of silicified sandstone, probably of Tertiary age, found in large numbers in S England **2** such a stone used in a megalithic monument ⊳ Also called: greywether [c17: probably a variant of SARACEN]

sarsenet ('saːsnɪt) *n* a variant spelling of **sarcenet**

Sarthe (French sart) *n* a department of NW France, in Pays de la Loire region. Capital: Le Mans. Pop: 536 857 (2003 est). Area: 6245 sq km (2436 sq miles)

Sarto (Italian 'sarto) *n* **Andrea del** (anˈdrɛːa del). 1486–1531, Florentine painter. His works include *The Nativity of the Virgin* (1514) in the church of Sant' Annunziata, Florence

sartor ('saːtə) *n* a humorous or literary word for **tailor** [c17: from Latin: a patcher, from *sarcīre* to patch]

sartorial (saːˈtɔːrɪəl) *adj* **1** of or relating to a tailor or to tailoring **2** *anatomy* of or relating to the sartorius [c19: from Late Latin *sartōrius* from SARTOR] ⊳ sar'torially *adv*

sartorius (saːˈtɔːrɪəs) *n, pl* -torii (-ˈtɔːrɪˌaɪ) *anatomy* a long ribbon-shaped muscle that aids in flexing the knee [c18: New Latin, from *sartorius musculus*, literally: tailor's muscle, because it is used when one sits in the cross-legged position in which tailors traditionally sat while sewing]

Sartre (French sartrə) *n* **Jean-Paul** (ʒ̃ãpɔl). 1905–80, French philosopher, novelist, and dramatist; chief French exponent of atheistic existentialism. His works include the philosophical essay *Being and Nothingness* (1943), the novels *Nausea* (1938) and *Les Chemins de la liberté* (1945–49), a trilogy, and the plays *Les Mouches* (1943), *Huis clos* (1944), and *Les Mains sales* (1948)

Sarum ('sɛərəm) *n* the ancient name of **Salisbury**[1] (sense 3)

Sarum use *n* the distinctive local rite or system of rites used at Salisbury cathedral in late medieval times

SAS *abbreviation* Special Air Service

Sasebo ('saːsəˌbəʊ) *n* a port in SW Japan, on NW Kyushu on Omura Bay: naval base. Pop: 242 474 (2002 est)

saser ('seizə) *n* a device for amplifying ultrasound, working on a similar principle to a laser [c20: s(ound) a(mplification by) s(timulated) e(mission) o(f) r(adiation)]

sash[1] (sæʃ) *n* a long piece of ribbon, silk, etc, worn around the waist like a belt or over one shoulder, as a symbol of rank [c16: from Arabic *shāsh* muslin]

sash[2] (sæʃ) *n* **1** a frame that contains the panes of a window or door ⊳ *vb* (*tr*) **2** to furnish with a sash, sashes, or sash windows [c17: originally plural *sashes*, variant of *shashes*, from CHASSIS]

sashay (sæˈʃeɪ) *vb* (*intr*) *informal* **1** to move, walk, or glide along casually **2** to move or walk in a showy way; parade [c19: from an alteration of *chassé*, a gliding dance step]

sash cord *n* a strong cord connecting a sash weight to a sliding sash

sashimi ('sæʃɪmɪ) *n* a Japanese dish of thin fillets of raw fish [c19: from Japanese *sashi* pierce + *mi* flesh]

sash saw *n* a small tenon saw used for cutting sashes

sash weight *n* a weight used to counterbalance the weight of a sliding sash in a sash window and thus hold it in position at any height

sash window *n* a window consisting of two sashes placed one above the other so that one or each can be slid over the other to open the window

Saskatchewan (sæsˈkætʃɪwən) *n* **1** a province of W Canada: consists of part of the Canadian Shield in the north and open prairie in the south; economy based chiefly on agriculture and mineral resources. Capital: Regina. Pop: 995 391 (2004 est). Area: 651 900 sq km (251 700 sq miles). Abbreviation: SK **2** a river in W

Canada, formed by the confluence of the North and South Saskatchewan Rivers: flows east to Lake Winnipeg. Length: 596 km (370 miles)
> Saskatchewanian (sæsˌkætʃəˈwɒnɪən) n, adj

Saskatchewan Party n (in Canada) a Saskatchewan political party formed by former members of the provincial Progressive Conservative and Liberal Parties

Saskatoon (ˌsæskəˈtuːn) n a city in W Canada, in S Saskatchewan on the South Saskatchewan River: oil refining; university (1907). Pop: 196 816 (2001)

sasquatch (ˈsæsˌkwætʃ) n (in Canadian folklore) in British Columbia, a hairy beast or manlike monster said to leave huge footprints [from Salish]

sass (sæs) US & Canadian informal ▷ n 1 insolent or impudent talk or behaviour ▷ vb (intr) 2 to talk or answer back in such a way [C20: back formation from SASSY]

sassaby (ˈsæsəbɪ) n, pl -bies an African antelope, Damaliscus lunatus, of grasslands and semideserts, having angular curved horns and an elongated muzzle: thought to be the swiftest hoofed mammal [C19: from Bantu tshêsêbê]

sassafras (ˈsæsəˌfræs) n 1 an aromatic deciduous lauraceous tree, Sassafras albidum, of North America, having three-lobed leaves and dark blue fruits 2 the aromatic dried root bark of this tree, used as a flavouring, and yielding sassafras oil 3 Austral any of several unrelated trees having a similar fragrant bark [C16: from Spanish sasafras, of uncertain origin]

Sassari (Italian ˈsassari) n a city in NW Sardinia, Italy: the second-largest city on the island; university (1565). Pop: 120 729 (2001)

Sassenach (ˈsæsəˌnæk; Scot, -næx) n Scot occasionally Irish an English person or a Lowland Scot [C18: from Scot Gaelic Sasunnach, Irish Sasanach, from Late Latin saxonēs Saxons]

Sassoon (sæˈsuːn) n 1 **Siegfried (Lorraine)**. 1886–1967, British poet and novelist, best known for his poems of the horrors of war collected in Counterattack (1918) and Satirical Poems (1926). He also wrote a semi-fictitious autobiographical trilogy The Memoirs of George Sherston (1928–36) 2 **Vidal**. born 1928, British hair stylist: founder and chairman of Vidal Sassoon Inc

sassy (ˈsæsɪ) adj -sier, -siest US informal insolent, impertinent [C19: variant of SAUCY] > **ˈsassily** adv > **ˈsassiness** n

sat (sæt) vb the past tense and past participle of **sit**

Sat. abbreviation 1 Saturday 2 Saturn

Satan (ˈseɪtᵊn) n the devil, adversary of God, and tempter of mankind: sometimes identified with Lucifer (Luke 4:5–8) [Old English, from Late Latin, from Greek, from Hebrew: plotter, from sātan to plot against]

satanic (səˈtænɪk) or now rarely **satanical** adj 1 of or relating to Satan 2 supremely evil or wicked; diabolic > **saˈtanically** adv

Satanism (ˈseɪtᵊˌnɪzəm) n 1 the worship of Satan 2 a form of such worship which includes blasphemous or obscene parodies of Christian prayers, etc 3 a satanic disposition or satanic practices > **ˈSatanist** n, adj

satay, satai or **saté** (ˈsæteɪ) n barbecued spiced meat cooked on skewers usually made from the stems of coconut leaves [from Malay]

SATB abbreviation soprano, alto, tenor, bass: a combination of voices in choral music

satchel (ˈsætʃəl) n a rectangular bag, usually made of leather or cloth and provided with a shoulder strap, used for carrying books, esp school books [C14: from Old French sachel a little bag, from Late Latin saccellus, from Latin saccus SACK¹] > **ˈsatchelled** adj

sate¹ (seɪt) vb (tr) 1 to satisfy (a desire or appetite) fully 2 to supply beyond capacity or desire [Old English sadian; related to Old High German satōn; see SAD, SATIATE]

sate² (sæt, seɪt) vb archaic a past tense and past participle of **sit**

sateen (sæˈtiːn) n a glossy linen or cotton fabric, woven in such a way that it resembles satin [C19: changed from SATIN, on the model of VELVETEEN]

satellite (ˈsætᵊˌlaɪt) n 1 a celestial body orbiting around a planet or star: the earth is a satellite of the sun 2 Also called: **artificial satellite** a man-made device orbiting around the earth, moon, or another planet transmitting to earth scientific information or used for communication. See also **communications satellite** 3 a person, esp one who is obsequious, who follows or serves another 4 a country or political unit under the domination of a foreign power 5 a subordinate area or community that is dependent upon a larger adjacent town or city 6 (modifier) subordinate to or dependent upon another: a satellite nation 7 (modifier) of, used in, or relating to the transmission of television signals from a satellite to the house: a satellite dish aerial ▷ vb 8 (tr) to transmit by communications satellite [C16: from Latin satelles an attendant, probably of Etruscan origin]

satellite navigation n navigation using data received from satellites

satellite navigation system n computing a computer-operated system of navigation that uses signals from orbiting satellites and mapping data to pinpoint the user's position and plot a subsequent course

satiable (ˈseɪʃɪəbᵊl, ˈseɪʃə-) adj capable of being satiated > **ˌsatiaˈbility** n > **ˈsatiably** adv

satiate (ˈseɪʃɪˌeɪt) vb (tr) 1 to fill or supply beyond capacity or desire, often arousing weariness 2 to supply to satisfaction or capacity [C16: from Latin satiāre to satisfy, from satis enough] > **ˌsatiˈation** n

Satie (French sati) n **Erik (Alfred Leslie)** (erik). 1866–1925, French composer, noted for his eccentricity, experimentalism, and his direct and economical style. His music, including numerous piano pieces and several ballets, exercised a profound influence upon other composers, such as Debussy and Ravel

satiety (səˈtaɪɪtɪ) n the state of being satiated [C16: from Latin satietās, from satis enough]

satin (ˈsætɪn) n 1 a fabric of silk, rayon, etc, closely woven to show much of the warp, giving a smooth glossy appearance 2 (modifier) of or like satin in texture: a satin finish [C14: via Old French from Arabic zaitūnī of Zaytūn, Arabic rendering of Chinese Tseutung (now Tsinkiang), port in southern China from which the cloth was probably first exported] > **ˈsatin-ˌlike** adj > **ˈsatiny** adj

satinet or **satinette** (ˌsætɪˈnɛt) n a thin or imitation satin [C18: from French: small satin]

satinflower (ˈsætɪnˌflaʊə) n the greater stitchwort. See **stitchwort**

satinwood (ˈsætɪnˌwʊd) n 1 a rutaceous tree, Chloroxylon swietenia, that occurs in the East Indies and has hard wood with a satiny texture 2 the wood of this tree, used in veneering, cabinetwork, marquetry, etc

satire (ˈsætaɪə) n 1 a novel, play, entertainment, etc, in which topical issues, folly, or evil are held up to scorn by means of ridicule and irony 2 the genre constituted by such works 3 the use of ridicule, irony, etc, to create such an effect [C16: from Latin satira a mixture, from satur sated, from satis enough]

satirical (səˈtɪrɪkᵊl) or **satiric** adj 1 of, relating to, or containing satire 2 given to the use of satire > **saˈtirically** adv

satirist (ˈsætərɪst) n 1 a person who writes satire 2 a person given to the use of satire

satirize or **satirise** (ˈsætəˌraɪz) vb to deride (a person or thing) by means of satire > **ˌsatiriˈzation** or **ˌsatiriˈsation** n > **ˈsatiˌrizer** or **ˈsatiˌriser** n

satisfaction (ˌsætɪsˈfækʃən) n 1 the act of satisfying or state of being satisfied 2 the fulfilment of a desire 3 the pleasure obtained from such fulfilment 4 a source of fulfilment 5 reparation or compensation for a wrong done or received 6 RC Church, Church of England the performance by a repentant sinner of a penance 7 Christianity the atonement for sin by the death of Christ [C15: via French from Latin satisfactionem, from satisfacere to SATISFY]

satisfactory (ˌsætɪsˈfæktərɪ, -trɪ) adj 1 adequate or suitable; acceptable 2 giving satisfaction 3 constituting or involving atonement, recompense, or expiation for sin > **ˌsatisˈfactorily** adv > **ˌsatisˈfactoriness** n

satisfice (ˈsætɪsˌfaɪs) vb 1 (intr) to act in such a way as to satisfy the minimum requirements for achieving a particular result 2 (tr) obsolete to satisfy [C16: altered from SATISFY] > 'satis,ficer n

satisficing behaviour ('sætɪs,faɪsɪŋ) n economics the form of behaviour demonstrated by firms who seek satisfactory profits and satisfactory growth rather than maximum profits

satisfy ('sætɪs,faɪ) vb -fies, -fying, -fied (mainly tr) 1 (also intr) to fulfil the desires or needs of (a person) 2 to provide amply for (a need or desire) 3 to relieve of doubt; convince 4 to dispel (a doubt) 5 to make reparation to or for 6 to discharge or pay off (a debt) to (a creditor) 7 to fulfil the requirements of; comply with: you must satisfy the terms of your lease 8 maths, logic to fulfil the conditions of (a theorem, assumption, etc); to yield a truth by substitution of the given value [c15: from Old French satisfier, from Latin satisfacere, from satis enough + facere to make, do] > 'satis,fiable adj > 'satis,fying adj > 'satis,fyingly adv

sat nav ('sæt næv) n informal a short for **satellite navigation** b short for **satellite navigation system**

Sato Eisaku ('saːtəʊ eɪsaku) n 1901–75, Japanese statesman: prime minister (1964–72). During his term of office Japan became a major economic power. He shared the Nobel peace prize (1974) for opposing the proliferation of nuclear weapons

satori (sə'tɔːrɪ) n Zen Buddhism the state of sudden indescribable intuitive enlightenment [from Japanese]

satrap ('sætrəp) n 1 (in ancient Persia) a provincial governor 2 a subordinate ruler, esp a despotic one [c14: from Latin satrapa, from Greek satrapēs, from Old Persian khshathrapāvan, literally: protector of the land]

satrapy ('sætrəpɪ) n, pl -trapies the province, office, or period of rule of a satrap

SATs (sæts) pl n acronym Brit education 1 standard assessment tasks 2 standard assessment tests

satsuma (sæt'suːmə) n 1 a small citrus tree, Citrus nobilis var. unshiu, cultivated, esp in Japan, for its edible fruit 2 the fruit of this tree, which has a loose rind and easily separable segments [c19: originally from the province of Satsuma, Japan]

Satsuma ('sætsʊ,maː) n a former province of SW Japan, on S Kyushu: famous for its porcelain

saturable ('sætʃərəbᵊl) adj chem capable of being saturated > ,satura'bility n

saturate vb ('sætʃə,reɪt) 1 to fill, soak, or imbue totally 2 to make (a chemical compound, vapour, solution, magnetic material, etc) saturated or (of a compound, vapour, etc) to become saturated 3 (tr) military to bomb or shell heavily ▷ adj ('sætʃərɪt, -,reɪt) 4 a less common word for **saturated** [c16: from Latin saturāre, from satur sated, from satis enough] > ,satu'rater or ,satu'rator n

saturated ('sætʃə,reɪtɪd) adj 1 (of a solution or solvent) containing the maximum amount of solute that can normally be dissolved at a given temperature and pressure. See also **supersaturated** 2 (of a chemical compound) **a** containing no multiple bonds and thus being incapable of undergoing additional reactions: a saturated hydrocarbon **b** containing no unpaired valence electrons 3 (of a fat, esp an animal fat) containing a high proportion of fatty acids having single bonds. See also **polyunsaturated, unsaturated** 4 (of a vapour) containing the equilibrium amount of gaseous material at a given temperature and pressure. See also **supersaturated** 5 (of a magnetic material) fully magnetized 6 extremely wet; soaked

saturation (,sætʃə'reɪʃən) n 1 the act of saturating or the state of being saturated 2 chem the state of a chemical compound, solution, or vapour when it is saturated 3 meteorol the state of the atmosphere when it can hold no more water vapour at its particular temperature and pressure, the relative humidity then being 100 per cent 4 the attribute of a colour that enables an observer to judge its proportion of pure chromatic colour. See also **colour** 5 physics the state of a ferromagnetic material in which it is fully magnetized. The magnetic domains are then all fully aligned 6 electronics the state of a valve or semiconductor device that is carrying the maximum current of which it is capable and is therefore unresponsive to further increases of input signal 7 the level beyond which demand for a product or service is

not expected to increase ▷ modifier 8 denoting the maximum possible intensity of coverage of an area: saturation bombing; a saturation release of a film

saturation point n the point at which no more (people, things, ideas, etc) can be absorbed, accommodated, used, etc

Saturday ('sætdɪ) n the seventh and last day of the week: the Jewish Sabbath [Old English sæternes dæg, translation of Latin Sāturnī diēs day of Saturn; compare Middle Dutch saterdach, Dutch zaterdag]

Saturn¹ ('sætɜːn) n the Roman god of agriculture and vegetation. Greek counterpart: **Cronus**

Saturn² ('sætɜːn) n 1 one of the **giant planets**, the sixth planet from the sun, around which revolve planar concentric rings (**Saturn's rings**) consisting of small frozen particles. The planet has at least 30 satellites. Mean distance from sun: 1425 million km; period of revolution around sun: 29.41 years; period of axial rotation: 10.23 hours; equatorial diameter and mass: 9.26 and 95.3 times that of the earth, respectively 2 the alchemical name for **lead²** > Saturnian (sæ'tɜːnɪən) adj, n

Saturnalia (,sætə'neɪlɪə) n, pl -lia or -lias 1 an ancient Roman festival celebrated in December: renowned for its general merrymaking 2 (sometimes not capital) a period or occasion of wild revelry [c14: from Latin Sāturnālis relating to SATURN¹] > ,Satur'nalian adj

saturnine ('sætə,naɪn) adj 1 having a gloomy temperament; taciturn 2 archaic a of or relating to lead **b** having or symptomatic of lead poisoning [c15: from French saturnin, from Medieval Latin sāturnīnus (unattested), from Latin Sāturnus Saturn, with reference to the gloomy influence attributed to the planet Saturn] > 'satur,ninely adv

satyagraha ('sɔːtjɑː,grɔːhɑː) n the policy of nonviolent resistance adopted by Mahatma Gandhi from about 1919 to oppose British rule in India [via Hindi from Sanskrit, literally: insistence on truth, from satya truth + agraha fervour]

satyr ('sætə) n 1 Greek myth one of a class of sylvan deities, represented as goatlike men who drank and danced in the train of Dionysus and chased the nymphs 2 a man who has strong sexual desires 3 any of various butterflies of the genus Satyrus and related genera, having dark wings often marked with eyespots: family Satyridae [c14: from Latin satyrus, from Greek saturos] > satyric (sə'tɪrɪk) or sa'tyrical adj

satyriasis (,sætɪ'raɪəsɪs) n a neurotic condition in men in which the symptoms are a compulsion to have sexual intercourse with as many women as possible and an inability to have lasting relationships with them [c17: via New Latin from Greek saturiasis; see SATYR, -IASIS]

sauce (sɔːs) n 1 any liquid or semiliquid preparation eaten with food to enhance its flavour 2 anything that adds piquancy 3 US & Canadian stewed fruit 4 informal impudent language or behaviour ▷ vb (tr) 5 to prepare (food) with sauce 6 to add zest to 7 informal to be saucy to [c14: from Old French from Latin salsus salted, from salīre to sprinkle with salt, from sal salt]

saucepan ('sɔːspən) n a metal or enamel pan with a long handle and often a lid, used for cooking food

saucer ('sɔːsə) n 1 a small round dish on which a cup is set 2 any similar dish [c14: from Old French saussier container for SAUCE] > 'saucerful n

saucy ('sɔːsɪ) adj saucier, sauciest 1 impertinent 2 pert; jaunty: a saucy hat > 'saucily adv > 'sauciness n

Saud (saʊd) n full name Saud ibn Abdul-Aziz. 1902–69, king of Saudi Arabia (1953–64); son of Ibn Saud. He was deposed by his brother Faisal

Saudi Arabia ('sɔːdɪ, 'saʊ-) n a kingdom in SW Asia, occupying most of the Arabian peninsula between the Persian Gulf and the Red Sea: founded in 1932 by Ibn Saud, who united Hejaz and Nejd; consists mostly of desert plateau; large reserves of petroleum and natural gas. Official language: Arabic. Official religion: (Sunni) Muslim. Currency: riyal. Capital: Riyadh (royal and administrative), Jiddah (diplomatic). Pop: 24 919 000 (2004 est.). Area: 2 260 353 sq km (872 722 sq miles) > 'Saudi or 'Saudi A'rabian adj, n

sauerkraut ('saʊə,kraʊt) n finely shredded and pickled

cabbage [German, from *sauer* SOUR + *Kraut* cabbage]

sauger ('sɔːɡə) *n* a small North American pikeperch, *Stizostedion canadense*, with a spotted dorsal fin: valued as a food and game fish [C19: of unknown origin]

Saul (sɔːl) *n* **1** *Old Testament* the first king of Israel (?1020–1000 BC). He led Israel successfully against the Philistines, but was in continual conflict with the high priest Samuel. He became afflicted with madness and died by his own hand; succeeded by David **2** *New Testament* the name borne by Paul prior to his conversion (Acts 9: 1–30)

sault (suː) *n Canad* a waterfall or rapids [C17: from Canad French, from French *saut* a leap]

Sault Sainte Marie ('suː seɪnt mə'riː) *n* **1** an inland port in central Canada, in Ontario on the St Mary's River, which links Lake Superior and Lake Huron, opposite Sault Ste Marie, Michigan: canal bypassing the rapids completed in 1895. Pop: 67 385 (2001) **2** an inland port in NE Michigan, opposite Sault Ste Marie, Ontario: canal around the rapids completed in 1855, enlarged and divided in 1896 and 1919 (popularly called **Soo Canals**). Pop: 14 184 (2003 est)

sauna ('sɔːnə) *n* **1** an invigorating bath originating in Finland in which the bather is subjected to hot steam, usually followed by a cold plunge or by being lightly beaten with birch twigs **2** the place in which such a bath is taken [C20: from Finnish]

Saunders ('sɔːndəz) *n* Dame **Cicely**. 1918–2005, British philanthropist: founded St Christopher's Hospice in 1967 for the care of the terminally ill, upon which the modern hospice movement is modelled. Her books include *Living with Dying* (1983)

saunter ('sɔːntə) *vb* (*intr*) **1** to walk in a casual manner; stroll ▷ *n* **2** a leisurely pace or stroll [C17: (meaning: to wander aimlessly), C15 (to muse): of obscure origin] > 'saunterer *n*

-saur or **-saurus** *n combining form* lizard: *dinosaur* [from New Latin *saurus*]

saurel ('sɔːrəl) *n* a US name for: **horse mackerel** (sense 1) [C19: via French from Late Latin *saurus*, from Greek *sauros*, of obscure origin]

saurian ('sɔːrɪən) *adj* **1** of, relating to, or resembling a lizard ▷ *n* **2** a former name for **lizard** [C15: from New Latin *Sauria*, from Greek *sauros*]

saury ('sɔːrɪ) *n*, *pl* **-ries** any teleost fish, such as the Atlantic *Scomberesox saurus* of the family *Scomberesocidae* of tropical and temperate seas, having an elongated body and long toothed jaws. Also called: skipper [C18: perhaps from Late Latin *saurus*; see SAUREL]

sausage ('sɒsɪdʒ) *n* **1** finely minced meat, esp pork or beef, mixed with fat, cereal or bread, and seasonings (**sausage meat**), and packed into a tube-shaped animal intestine or synthetic casing **2** an object shaped like a sausage **3** *aeronautics informal* a captive balloon shaped like a sausage **4** not a sausage nothing at all [C15: from Old Norman French *saussiche*, from Late Latin *salsīcia*, from Latin *salsus* salted; see SAUCE]

sausage dog *n* an informal name for **dachshund**

sausage roll *n Brit* a roll of sausage meat in pastry

Saussure (*French* sosyr) *n* **Ferdinand de** (fɛrdinɑ̃ də). 1857–1913, Swiss linguist. He pioneered structuralism in linguistics and the separation of scientific language description from historical philological studies > Saus'surean *adj*, *n*

sauté ('səʊteɪ) *vb* **-tés, -téing** or **-téeing, -téed 1** to fry (food) quickly in a little fat ▷ *n* **2** a dish of sautéed food, esp meat that is browned and then cooked in a sauce ▷ *adj* **3** sautéed until lightly brown: *sauté potatoes* [C19: from French: tossed, from *sauter* to jump, from Latin *saltāre* to dance, from *salīre* to spring]

Sauvignon Blanc ('səʊvɪnjɒn 'blɒŋk) *n* **1** a white grape grown in the Bordeaux and Loire regions of France, New Zealand, and elsewhere, used for making wine **2** any of various white wines made from this grape

Sava ('saːvə) or **Save** (saːv) *n* a river in SE Europe, rising in NW Slovenia and flowing east and south to the Danube at Belgrade. Length: 940 km (584 miles)

savage ('sævɪdʒ) *adj* **1** wild; untamed: *savage beasts of the jungle* **2** ferocious in temper; vicious: *a savage dog*

3 uncivilized; crude: *savage behaviour* **4** (of peoples) nonliterate or primitive: *a savage tribe* **5** (of terrain) rugged and uncultivated ▷ *n* **6** a member of a nonliterate society, esp one regarded as primitive **7** a fierce or vicious person or animal ▷ *vb* (*tr*) **8** to criticize violently **9** to attack ferociously and wound: *the dog savaged the child* [C13: from Old French *sauvage*, from Latin *silvāticus* belonging to a wood, from *silva* a wood] > 'savagedom *n* > 'savagely *adv* > 'savageness *n*

Savage ('sævɪdʒ) *n* **Michael Joseph**. 1872-1940, New Zealand statesman; prime minister of New Zealand (1935-40)

Savage Island *n* another name for **Niue**

savagery ('sævɪdʒrɪ) *n*, *pl* **-ries 1** an uncivilized condition **2** a savage act or nature **3** savages collectively

Savaii (saːˈvaiː) *n* the largest island in Samoa: mountainous and volcanic. Pop: 42 400 (2001). Area: 1174 sq km (662 sq miles)

savanna or **savannah** (səˈvænə) *n* open grasslands, usually with scattered bushes or trees, characteristic of much of tropical Africa [C16: from Spanish *zavana*, from Taino *zabana*]

Savannah (səˈvænə) *n* **1** a port in the US, in E Georgia, near the mouth of the Savannah River: port of departure of the *Savannah* for Liverpool (1819), the first steamship to cross the Atlantic. Pop: 127 573 (2003 est) **2** a river in the southeastern US, formed by the confluence of the Tugaloo and Seneca Rivers in NW South Carolina: flows southeast to the Atlantic. Length: 505 km (314 miles)

savant ('sævənt; *French* savɑ̃) *n* a man of great learning; sage [C18: from French, from *savoir* to know, from Latin *sapere* to be wise; see SAPIENT] > 'savante *fem n*

savate (səˈvæt) *n* a form of boxing in which blows may be delivered with the feet as well as the hands [C19: from French, literally: old worn-out shoe; related to SABOT]

save¹ (seɪv) *vb* **1** (*tr*) to rescue, preserve, or guard (a person or thing) from danger or harm **2** to avoid the spending, waste, or loss of (money, possessions, etc) **3** (*tr*) to deliver from sin; redeem **4** (often foll by *up*) to set aside or reserve (money, goods, etc) for future use **5** (*tr*) to treat with care so as to avoid or lessen wear or degeneration: *use a good light to save your eyes* **6** (*tr*) to prevent the necessity for; obviate the trouble of: *good work now will save future revision* **7** (*tr*) *sport* to prevent (a goal) by stopping (a struck ball or puck) ▷ *n* **8** *sport* the act of saving a goal **9** *computing* an instruction to write information from the memory onto a tape or disk [C13: from Old French *salver*, via Late Latin from Latin *salvus* safe] > 'savable or 'saveable *adj* > 'savableness or 'saveableness *n* > 'saver *n*

save² (seɪv) *archaic* or *literary* ▷ *prep* **1** Also called: saving (often foll by *for*) with the exception of ▷ *conj* **2** but; except [C13 *sauf*, from Old French, from Latin *salvō*, from *salvus* safe]

save as you earn *n* (in Britain) a savings scheme operated by the government, in which monthly contributions earn tax-free interest. Abbreviation: SAYE

saveloy ('sævɪˌlɔɪ) *n* a smoked sausage made from salted pork, well seasoned and coloured red with saltpetre [C19: probably via French from Italian *cervellato*, from *cervello* brain, from Latin *cerebellum*, diminutive of *cerebrum* brain]

Savery ('seɪvərɪ) *n* **Thomas**. ?1650–1715, English engineer, who built (1698) the first practical steam engine, used to pump water from mines

Savigny ('savɪɲɪ) *n* **Friedrich Karl von** ('friːdrɪç 'kɑːl fɒn). 1779–1861, German legal scholar, who pioneered the historical approach to jurisprudence, emphasizing custom and precedent

savin or **savine** ('sævɪn) *n* **1** a small spreading juniper bush, *Juniperus sabina*, of Europe, N Asia, and North America **2** the oil derived from the shoots and leaves of this plant, formerly used in medicine to treat rheumatism, etc **3** another name for **red cedar** (sense 1) [C14: from Old French *savine*, from Latin *herba Sabīna* the Sabine plant]

saving ('seɪvɪŋ) *adj* **1** tending to save or preserve **2** redeeming or compensating (esp in the phrase **saving grace**) **3** thrifty or economical **4** *law* denoting or relating to an exception or reservation: *a saving clause in an agreement* ▷ *n* **5** preservation or redemption, esp from loss or danger **6** economy or avoidance of waste **7** reduction in cost or expenditure **8** anything saved **9** (*plural*) money saved for future use ▷ *prep* **10** with the exception of ▷ *conj* **11** except ▷ '**savingly** *adv*

savings bank *n* a bank that accepts the savings of depositors and pays interest on them

savings ratio *n economics* the ratio of personal savings to disposable income, esp using the difference between national figures for disposable income and consumer spending as a measure of savings

saviour or US **savior** ('seɪvjə) *n* a person who rescues another person or a thing from danger or harm [C13 *saveour*, from Old French, from Church Latin *Salvātor* the Saviour; see SAVE]

Saviour or US **Savior** ('seɪvjə) *n Christianity* Jesus Christ regarded as the saviour of men from sin

Savitskaya (sæ'vɪtskaɪə) *n* **Svetlana** (svɛt'lɑːnə). born 1949, Soviet cosmonaut, the first woman to walk in space (1984). She was elected to the former Soviet parliament (1989)

Savoie (*French* savwa) *n* **1** a department of E France, in Rhône-Alpes region. Capital: Chambéry. Pop: 386 246 (2003 est). Area: 6188 sq km (2413 sq miles) **2** the French name for **Savoy**[1]

savoir-faire ('sævwɑːˈfɛə) *n* the ability to do the right thing in any situation [French, literally: a knowing how to do]

Savona (*Italian* sa'voːna) *n* a port in NW Italy, in Liguria on the Mediterranean: an important centre of the Italian iron and steel industry. Pop: 59 907 (2001)

Savonarola (*Italian* savona'roːla) *n* **Girolamo** (dʒi'roːlamo). 1452–98, Italian religious and political reformer. As a Dominican prior in Florence he preached against contemporary sinfulness and moral corruption. When the Medici were expelled from the city (1494) he instituted a severely puritanical republic but lost the citizens' support after being excommunicated (1497). He was hanged and burned as a heretic

savory ('seɪvərɪ) *n, pl* **-vories 1** any of numerous aromatic plants of the genus *Satureja*, esp *S. montana* (**winter savory**) and *S. hortensis* (**summer savory**), of the Mediterranean region, having narrow leaves and white, pink, or purple flowers: family *Lamiaceae* (labiates) **2** the leaves of any of these plants, used as a potherb [C14: probably from Old English *sætherie*, from Latin *satureia*, of obscure origin]

savour or US **savor** ('seɪvə) *n* **1** the quality in a substance that is perceived by the sense of taste or smell **2** a specific taste or smell: *the savour of lime* **3** a slight but distinctive quality or trace **4** the power to excite interest: *the savour of wit has been lost* ▷ *vb* **5** (*intr*; often foll by *of*) to possess the taste or smell (of) **6** (*intr*; often foll by *of*) to have a suggestion (of) **7** (*tr*) to give a taste to; season **8** (*tr*) to taste, smell, esp appreciatively **9** (*tr*) to relish or enjoy [C13: from Old French *savour*, from Latin *sapor* taste, from *sapere* to taste] ▷ '**savourless** or US '**savorless** *adj* ▷ '**savorous** *adj*

savoury or US **savory** ('seɪvərɪ) *adj* **1** attractive to the sense of taste or smell **2** salty or spicy; not sweet: *a savoury dish* **3** pleasant **4** respectable ▷ *n, pl* **-vouries 5** a savoury dish served as an hors d'oeuvre or dessert [C13 *savure*, from Old French *savouré*, from *savourer* to SAVOUR] ▷ '**savourily** or US '**savorily** *adv* ▷ '**savouriness** or US '**savoriness** *n*

savoy (sə'vɔɪ) *n* a cultivated variety of cabbage, *Brassica oleracea capitata*, having a compact head and wrinkled leaves [C16: named after the SAVOY region]

Savoy[1] (sə'vɔɪ) *n* an area of SE France, bordering on Italy, mainly in the Savoy Alps: a duchy in the late Middle Ages and part of the Kingdom of Sardinia from 1720 to 1860, when it became part of France. French name: **Savoie**

Savoy[2] (sə'vɔɪ) *n* a noble family of Italy that ruled over the duchy of Savoy and became the royal house of Italy (1861–1946): the oldest reigning dynasty in Europe before the dissolution of the Italian monarchy

Savoy Alps *pl n* a range of the Alps in SE France. Highest

peak: Mont Blanc, 4807 m (15 772 ft)

Savoyard (sə'vɔɪɑːd; *French* savwajar) *n* **1** a native of Savoy **2** the dialect of French spoken in Savoy ▷ *adj* **3** of or relating to Savoy, its inhabitants, or their dialect

savvy ('sævɪ) *slang* ▷ *vb* **-vies, -vying, -vied 1** to understand or get the sense of (an idea, etc) ▷ *n* **2** comprehension ▷ *adj* **-vier, -viest 3** *chiefly US* shrewd; well-informed [C18: corruption of Spanish *sabe(usted)* (you) know, from *saber* to know, from Latin *sapere* to be wise]

saw[1] (sɔː) *n* **1** any of various hand tools for cutting wood, metal, etc, having a blade with teeth along one edge **2** any of various machines or devices for cutting by use of a toothed blade, such as a power-driven circular toothed wheel or toothed band of metal ▷ *vb* **saws, sawing, sawed, sawed** or **sawn 3** to cut with a saw **4** to form by sawing **5** to cut as if wielding a saw: *to saw the air* **6** to move (an object) from side to side as if moving a saw [Old English *sagu*; related to Old Norse *sog*, Old High German *saga*, Latin *secāre* to cut, *secūris* axe] ▷ '**sawer** *n* ▷ '**saw,like** *adj*

saw[2] (sɔː) *vb* the past tense of **see**[1]

saw[3] (sɔː) *n* a wise saying, maxim, or proverb [Old English *sagu* a saying; related to SAGA]

sawbones ('sɔːˌbəʊnz) *n, pl* **-bones** or **-boneses** *slang* a surgeon or doctor

sawdust ('sɔːˌdʌst) *n* particles of wood formed by sawing

sawfish ('sɔːˌfɪʃ) *n, pl* **-fish** or **-fishes** any sharklike ray of the family *Pristidae* of subtropical coastal waters and estuaries, having a serrated bladelike mouth

sawfly ('sɔːˌflaɪ) *n, pl* **-flies** any of various hymenopterous insects of the family *Tenthredinidae* and related families, the females of which have a sawlike ovipositor

sawhorse ('sɔːˌhɔːs) *n* a stand for timber during sawing

sawmill ('sɔːˌmɪl) *n* an industrial establishment where timber is sawn into planks, etc

sawn (sɔːn) *vb* a past participle of **saw**[1]

sawn-off or esp US **sawed-off** *adj* (*prenominal*) (of a shotgun) having the barrel cut short, mainly to facilitate concealment of the weapon

saw-off *n Canadian* **1** a deadlock or stalemate **2** a compromise

saw set *n* a tool used for setting the teeth of a saw, consisting of a type of clamp used to bend each tooth in turn at a slight angle to the plane of the saw to improve cutting, alternate teeth being bent in the same direction

sawyer ('sɔːjə) *n* a person who saws timber for a living [C14 *sawier*, from SAW[1] + *-ier*, variant of *-ER*[1]]

sax (sæks) *n informal* short for **saxophone**

Saxe[1] (saks) *n* the French name for **Saxony**

Saxe[2] (*French* saks) *n* **Hermann Maurice** (ɛrman mɔris), comte de Saxe. 1696–1750, French marshal born in Saxony: he distinguished himself in the War of the Austrian Succession (1740–48)

saxe blue (sæks) *n* **a** a light greyish-blue colour **b** (*as adjective*): *a saxe-blue dress* [C19: from French *Saxe* Saxony, source of a dye of this colour]

Saxe-Coburg-Gotha (sæks'kəʊbɜːɡ'ɡəʊθə) *n* the ruling house of the former German duchy of Saxe-Coburg-Gotha (until 1918) and the name of the British royal family (1901–17) through Prince Albert

saxhorn ('sæksˌhɔːn) *n* a valved brass instrument used chiefly in brass and military bands, having a tube of conical bore and a brilliant tone colour. It resembles the tuba and constitutes a family of instruments related to the flugelhorn and cornet [C19: named after Adolphe *Sax* (see SAXOPHONE), who invented it (1845)]

saxicolous (sæk'sɪkələs) *adj* living on or among rocks: *saxicolous plants*. Also called: **saxicole, saxatile** ('sæksəˌtaɪl) [C19: from New Latin *saxicolus*, from Latin *saxum* rock + *colere* to dwell]

saxifrage ('sæksɪˌfreɪdʒ) *n* any saxifragaceous plant of the genus *Saxifraga*, characterized by smallish white, yellow, purple, or pink flowers [C15: from Late Latin *saxifraga*, literally: rock-breaker (probably alluding to its ability to dissolve kidney stones), from Latin *saxum* rock + *frangere* to break]

Saxo Grammaticus ('sæksəʊ grə'mætɪkəs) *n* ?1150–?1220, Danish chronicler, noted for his *Gesta Danorum*, a history of Denmark down to 1185, written in Latin, which is partly historical and partly mythological, and contains the Hamlet (Amleth) legend

Saxon ('sæksən) *n* 1 a member of a West Germanic people who in Roman times spread from Schleswig across NW Germany to the Rhine. Saxons raided and settled parts of S Britain in the fifth and sixth centuries AD. In Germany they established a duchy and other dominions, which changed and shifted through the centuries, usually retaining the name Saxony 2 a native or inhabitant of Saxony 3 a the Low German dialect of Saxony b any of the West Germanic dialects spoken by the ancient Saxons or their descendants ▷ *adj* 4 of, relating to, or characteristic of the ancient Saxons, the Anglo-Saxons, or their descendants 5 of, relating to, or characteristic of Saxony, its inhabitants, or their Low German dialect ▷ See also **Anglo-Saxon** [C13 (replacing Old English *Seaxe*): via Old French from Late Latin *Saxon-*, *Saxo*, from Greek; of Germanic origin and perhaps related to the name of a knife used by the Saxons]

Saxony ('sæksənɪ) *n* 1 a state in E Germany, formerly part of East Germany. Pop: 4 321 000 (2003 est) 2 a former duchy and electorate in SE and central Germany, whose territory changed greatly over the centuries 3 (in the early Middle Ages) any territory inhabited or ruled by Saxons ▷ See **Saxony-Anhalt, Lower Saxony**. German name: **Sachsen** French name: **Saxe**

Saxony-Anhalt ('sæksənɪ 'ɑːnhɑːlt) *n* a state of E Germany: created in 1947 from the state of Anhalt and those parts of Prussia formerly ruled by the duchy of Saxony: part of East Germany until 1990. Pop: 2 523 000 (2003 est)

saxophone ('sæksə,fəʊn) *n* a keyed wind instrument of mellow tone colour, used mainly in jazz and dance music. It is made in various sizes, has a conical bore, and a single reed. Often shortened to: **sax** [C19: named after Adolphe *Sax* (1814–94), Belgian musical-instrument maker, who invented it (1846)] ▷ **saxophonic** (,sæksə'fɒnɪk) *adj* ▷ **saxophonist** (sæk'sɒfənɪst) *n*

say (seɪ) *vb* **says** (sez), **saying, said** (mainly tr) 1 to speak, pronounce, or utter 2 (also intr) to express (an idea) in words; tell 3 (also intr; may take a clause as object) to state (an opinion, fact, etc) positively; declare; affirm 4 to recite: *to say grace* 5 (may take a clause as object) to report or allege: *they say we shall have rain today* 6 (may take a clause as object) to take as an assumption; suppose: *let us say that he is lying* 7 (may take a clause as object) to convey by means of artistic expression 8 to make a case for 9 **go without saying** to be so obvious as to need no explanation 10 **I say!** *chiefly Brit informal* an exclamation of surprise 11 **not to say** even; and indeed 12 **that is to say** in other words; more explicitly 13 **to say the least** without the slightest exaggeration; at the very least ▷ *adv* 14 approximately: *there were, say, 20 people present* 15 for example: *choose a number, fact, say, four* ▷ *n* 16 the right or chance to speak: *let him have his say* 17 authority, esp to influence a decision: *he has a lot of say in the company's policy* 18 a statement of opinion: *you've had your say, now let me have mine* ▷ *interj* 19 *US & Canadian informal* an exclamation to attract attention or express surprise, etc [Old English *secgan*; related to Old Norse *segja*, Old Saxon *seggian*, Old High German *sagēn*] ▷ **sayer** *n*

Sayan Mountains (sɑː'jæn) *pl n* a mountain range in S central Russia, in S Siberia. Highest peak: Munku-Sardyk, 3437 m (11 457 ft)

SAYE *abbreviation* save as you earn

Sayers ('seɪəz) *n* **Dorothy L(eigh)**. 1893–1957, English detective-story writer

saying ('seɪɪŋ) *n* a maxim, adage, or proverb

say-so *n informal* 1 an arbitrary assertion 2 an authoritative decision 3 the authority to make a final decision

sayyid, sayid ('saɪɪd) *or* **said** *n* 1 a Muslim claiming descent from Mohammed's grandson Husain 2 a Muslim honorary title [C17: from Arabic: lord]

Sb *the chemical symbol for* antimony [from New Latin *stibium*]

SBE *abbreviation* Southern British English

SBU *abbreviation* strategic business unit: a division within an organization responsible for marketing its own range of products

sc *abbreviation printing* small capitals

Sc *the chemical symbol for* scandium

SC *abbreviation* Signal Corps

sc. *abbreviation* 1 scene 2 scilicet

scab (skæb) *n* 1 the dried crusty surface of a healing skin wound or sore 2 a contagious disease of sheep, a form of mange, caused by a mite (*Psoroptes communis*) 3 a fungal disease of plants characterized by crusty spots on the fruits, leaves, etc 4 *derogatory* a Also called: **blackleg** a person who refuses to support a trade union's actions, esp one who replaces a worker who is on strike b (*as modifier*): *scab labour* 5 a despicable person ▷ *vb* **scabs, scabbing, scabbed** (*intr*) 6 to become covered with a scab 7 to replace a striking worker [Old English *sceabb*; related to Old Norse *skabb*, Latin *scabiēs*, Middle Low German *schabbe* scoundrel, German *schäbig* SHABBY]

scabbard ('skæbəd) *n* a holder for a bladed weapon such as a sword or bayonet; sheath [C13 *scauberc*, from Norman French *escaubers* (pl), of Germanic origin; related to Old High German *skār* blade and *bergan* to protect]

scabby ('skæbɪ) *adj* **-bier, -biest** 1 *pathol* having an area of the skin covered with scabs 2 *pathol obsolete* having scabies 3 *informal* despicable ▷ **scabbily** *adv* ▷ **scabbiness** *n*

scabby mouth *n Austral* another name for **orf**

scabies ('skeɪbiːz, -bɪˌiːz) *n* a contagious skin infection caused by the mite *Sarcoptes scabiei*, characterized by intense itching, inflammation, and the formation of vesicles and pustules [C15: from Latin: scurf, from *scabere* to scratch; see SHAVE]

scabious[1] ('skeɪbɪəs) *adj* 1 having or covered with scabs 2 of, relating to, or resembling scabies [C17: from Latin *scabiōsus*, from SCABIES]

scabious[2] ('skeɪbɪəs) *n* any plant of the genus *Scabiosa*, esp *S. atropurpurea*, of the Mediterranean region, having blue, red, or whitish dome-shaped flower heads: family Dipsacaceae [C14: from Medieval Latin *scabiōsa herba* the scabies plant, referring to its use in treating scabies]

scabrous ('skeɪbrəs) *adj* 1 roughened because of small projections; scaly 2 indelicate, indecent, or salacious: *scabrous humour* 3 difficult to deal with; knotty [C17: from Latin *scaber* rough; related to SCABIES] ▷ **scabrously** *adv* ▷ **scabrousness** *n*

scad (skæd) *n*, *pl* **scad** *or* **scads** any of various carangid fishes of the genus *Trachurus*, esp the horse mackerel [C17: of uncertain origin; compare Swedish *skädde* flounder]

scads (skædz) *pl n informal* a large amount or number [C19: of uncertain origin]

Scafell Pike (skɔː'fɛl) *n* a mountain in NW England, in Cumbria in the Lake District: the highest peak in England. Height: 977 m (3206 ft)

scaffold ('skæfəʊld, -fəʊld) *n* 1 a temporary metal or wooden framework that is used to support workmen and materials during the erection, repair, etc, of a building or other construction 2 a raised wooden platform on which plays are performed, tobacco, etc, is dried, or (esp formerly) criminals are executed ▷ *vb* (*tr*) 3 to provide with a scaffold 4 to support by means of a scaffold [C14: from Old French *eschaffaut*, from Vulgar Latin *catafalicum* (unattested); see CATAFALQUE] ▷ **scaffolder** *n*

scaffolding ('skæfəʊldɪŋ) *n* 1 a scaffold or system of scaffolds 2 the building materials used to make scaffolds

Scala ('skɑːlɑ) *n* See **La Scala**

scalability (,skeɪlə'bɪlɪtɪ) *n* the ability of something, esp a computer system, to adapt to increased demands

scalable ('skeɪləbᵊl) *adj* capable of being scaled or climbed ▷ **scalableness** *n* ▷ **scalably** *adv*

scalar ('skeɪlə) *n* 1 a quantity, such as time or temperature, that has magnitude but not direction 2 *maths* an element of a field associated with a vector space ▷ *adj* 3 having magnitude but not direction [C17 (meaning: resembling a ladder): from Latin *scālāris*, from *scāla* ladder]

S

scalar product *n* the product of two vectors to form a scalar, whose value is the product of the magnitudes of the vectors and the cosine of the angle between them. Written: *A•B* or *AB*. Also called: **dot product**

scalawag ('skælə,wæg) *n* a variant of **scallywag**

scald[1] (skɔːld) *vb* **1** to burn or be burnt with or as if with hot liquid or steam **2** (*tr*) to subject to the action of boiling water, esp so as to sterilize **3** (*tr*) to heat (a liquid) almost to boiling point **4** (*tr*) to plunge (tomatoes, peaches, etc) into boiling water briefly in order to skin them more easily ▷ *n* **5** the act or result of scalding **6** an abnormal condition in plants, characterized by discoloration and wrinkling of the skin of the fruits, caused by exposure to excessive sunlight, gases, etc [c13: via Old Norman French from Late Latin *excaldāre* to wash in warm water, from *calida (aqua)* warm (water), from *calēre* to be warm] ▷ 'scalder *n*

scald[2] (skɔːld) *n* a variant spelling of **skald**

scaldfish ('skɔːld,fɪʃ, 'skɑːld-) *n*, *pl* **-fish** or **-fishes** a small European flatfish, *Arnoglossus laterna*, covered with large fragile scales: family *Bothidae*

scale[1] (skeɪl) *n* **1** any of the numerous plates, made of various substances resembling enamel or dentine, covering the bodies of fishes **2 a** any of the horny or chitinous plates covering a part or the entire body of certain reptiles and mammals **b** any of the numerous minute structures covering the wings of lepidoptera **3 a** a thin flat piece or flake **4** a thin flake of dead epidermis shed from the skin: excessive shedding may be the result of a skin disease **5** a specialized leaf or bract, esp the protective covering of a bud or the dry membranous bract of a catkin **6** See **scale insect 7** any oxide formed on a metal during heat treatment **8** another word for **limescale** ▷ *vb* **9** (*tr*) to remove the scales or coating from **10** to peel off or cause to peel off in flakes or scales **11** (*intr*) to shed scales **12** to cover or become covered with scales, incrustation, etc **13** (*intr*) *Austral informal* to ride on public transport without paying a fare [c14: from Old French *escale*, of Germanic origin; compare Old English *scealu* SHELL]

scale[2] (skeɪl) *n* **1** (*often plural*) a machine or device for weighing **2** one of the pans of a balance **3 tip the scales a** to exercise a decisive influence **b** (foll by *at*) to amount in weight (to) ▷ *vb* (*tr*) **4** to weigh with or as if with scales [c13: from Old Norse *skāl* bowl, related to Old High German *scāla* cup, Old English *scealu* SHELL, SCALE[1]]

scale[3] (skeɪl) *n* **1** a sequence of marks either at regular intervals or else representing equal steps used as a reference in making measurements **2** a measuring instrument having such a scale **3** the ratio between the size of something real and that of a model or representation of it (*as modifier*): *a scale model* **4** a line, numerical ratio, etc, for showing this ratio **5** a progressive or graduated table of things, wages, etc, in order of size, value, etc: *a wage scale for carpenters* **6** an established measure or degree **7** a relative degree or extent: *he entertained on a grand scale* **8** *music* a group of notes taken in ascending or descending order, esp within the compass of one octave **9** *maths* the notation of a given number system: *the decimal scale* ▷ *vb* **10** to climb to the top of (a height) by or as if by a ladder **11** (*tr*) to make or draw (a model, plan, etc) according to a particular ratio of proportionate reduction **12** (*tr*; usually foll by *up* or *down*) to increase or reduce proportionately in size, etc [c15: via Italian from Latin *scāla* ladder; related to Old French *eschiele*, Spanish *escala*]

scaleboard ('skeɪl,bɔːd, 'skæbəd) *n* a very thin piece of board, used for backing a picture, as a veneer, etc

scale insect *n* any small homopterous insect of the family *Coccidae* and related families, which typically live and feed on plants and secrete a protective scale around themselves. Many species, such as the San Jose scale, are important pests

scalene ('skeɪliːn) *adj* **1** *maths* (of a triangle) having all sides of unequal length **2** *anatomy* of or relating to any of the scalenus muscles [c17: from Late Latin *scalēnus* with unequal sides, from Greek *skalēnos*]

scalenus (skə'liːnəs, skeɪ-) *n*, *pl* **-ni** (-naɪ) *anatomy* any one of the three muscles situated on each side of the

neck extending from the cervical vertebrae to the first or second pair of ribs [c18: from New Latin; see SCALENE]

Scaliger ('skælɪdʒə) *n* **1** Joseph Justus ('dʒʌstəs). 1540–1609, French scholar, who revolutionized the study of ancient chronology by his work *De Emendatione temporum* (1583) **2** his father, **Julius Caesar.** 1484–1558, Italian classical scholar, and writer on biology and medicine

scaling ladder *n* a ladder used to climb high walls, esp one used formerly to enter a besieged town, fortress, etc

scallion ('skæljən) *n* any of various onions or similar plants, such as the spring onion, that have a small bulb and long leaves and are eaten in salads [c14: from Anglo-French *scalun*, from Latin *Ascalōnia (caepa)* Ascalonian (onion), from *Ascalo* Ascalon, a Palestinian port]

scallop ('skɒləp, 'skæl-) *n* **1** any of various marine bivalves of the family *Pectinidae*, having a fluted fan-shaped shell: includes free-swimming species (genus *Pecten*) and species attached to a substratum (genus *Chlamys*) **2** the edible adductor muscle of certain of these molluscs **3** either of the shell valves of any of these molluscs **4** a scallop shell or similarly shaped dish, in which fish, esp shellfish, is cooked and served **5** one of a series of curves along an edge, esp an edge of cloth **6** the shape of a scallop shell used as the badge of a pilgrim, esp in the Middle Ages **7** *chiefly Austral* a potato cake fried in batter ▷ *vb* **8** (*tr*) to decorate (an edge) with scallops **9** to bake (food) in a scallop shell or similar dish [c14: from Old French *escalope* shell, of Germanic origin; see SCALP] ▷ 'scalloper *n* ▷ 'scalloping *n*

scally ('skælɪ) *n*, *pl* **-lies** *Northwest English dialect* a rascal; rogue [c20: from SCALLYWAG]

scallywag ('skælɪ,wæg) *n* *informal* a scamp; rascal. Also called: **scalawag, scallawag** [c19: (originally undersized animal) of uncertain origin]

scalp (skælp) *n* **1** *anatomy* the skin and subcutaneous tissue covering the top of the head **2** (among North American Indians) a part of this removed as a trophy from a slain enemy **3** a trophy or token signifying conquest **4** *Scot dialect* a projection of bare rock from vegetation ▷ *vb* (*tr*) **5** to cut the scalp from **6** *informal, chiefly US* to purchase and resell (securities) quickly so as to make several small profits **7** *informal* to buy (tickets) cheaply and resell at an inflated price [c13: probably from Scandinavian; compare Old Norse *skalpr* sheath, Middle Dutch *schelpe*, Danish *skalp* husk] ▷ 'scalper *n*

scalpel ('skælpᵊl) *n* a surgical knife with a short thin blade [c18: from Latin *scalpellum*, from *scalper* a knife, from *scalpere* to scrape]

scaly ('skeɪlɪ) *adj* **scalier, scaliest 1** resembling or covered in scales **2** peeling off in scales ▷ 'scaliness *n*

scaly anteater *n* another name for **pangolin**

scam (skæm) *slang* ▷ *n* **1** a stratagem for gain; a swindle ▷ *vb* **scams, scamming, scammed 2** (*tr*) to swindle (someone) by means of a trick

Scamander (skə'mændə) *n* the ancient name for the **Menderes** (sense 2)

scamp[1] (skæmp) *n* **1** an idle mischievous person; rascal **2** a mischievous child [c18: from *scamp* (vb) to be a highway robber, probably from Middle Dutch *schampen* to decamp, from Old French *escamper*, from *es-* EX-[1] + *-camper*, from Latin *campus* field] ▷ 'scampish *adj*

scamp[2] (skæmp) *vb* a less common word for **skimp** ▷ 'scamper *n*

scamper ('skæmpə) *vb* (*intr*) **1** to run about playfully **2** (often foll by *through*) to hurry quickly through (a place, task, book, etc) ▷ *n* **3** the act of scampering [c17: probably from *scamp* (vb); see SCAMP[1]]

scampi ('skæmpɪ) *n* (*usually functioning as singular*) large prawns, usually eaten fried in breadcrumbs [Italian: plural of *scampo* shrimp, of obscure origin]

scamto ('skæmtəʊ) *n* *South African* the argot of urban South African Black people [c20: of uncertain origin]

scan (skæn) *vb* **scans, scanning, scanned 1** (*tr*) to scrutinize minutely **2** (*tr*) to glance over quickly **3** (*tr*) *prosody* to read or analyse (verse) according to the rules of metre and versification **4** (*intr*) *prosody* to conform to the rules of metre and versification **5** (*tr*) *electronics* to move a beam of light, electrons, etc, in a predetermined pattern over (a surface or region) to obtain information, esp either to sense and transmit or to reproduce a television image **6** (tr) to examine data stored on (magnetic tape, etc), usually in order to retrieve information **7** to examine or search (a prescribed region) by systematically varying the direction of a radar or sonar beam **8** med to obtain an image of (a part of the body) by means of a scanner ▷ n **9** the act or an instance of scanning **10** med **a** the examination of a part of the body by means of a scanner: *a brain scan; ultrasound scan* **b** the image produced by a scanner [c14: from Late Latin *scandere* to scan (verse), from Latin: to climb] ▷ '**scannable** *adj*

scandal ('skænd³l) n **1** a disgraceful action or event: *his negligence was a scandal* **2** censure or outrage arising from an action or event **3** a person whose conduct causes reproach or disgrace **4** malicious talk, esp gossip about the private lives of other people **5** *law* a libellous action or statement [c16: from Late Latin *scandalum* stumbling block, from Greek *skandalon* a trap] ▷ '**scandalous** *adj* ▷ '**scandalously** *adv*

scandalize *or* **scandalise** ('skændə,laɪz) *vb* (tr) to shock, as by improper behaviour ▷ ,**scandali'zation** *or* ,**scandali'sation** *n*

scandalmonger ('skænd³l,mʌŋɡə) n a person who spreads or enjoys scandal, gossip, etc

Scanderbeg ('skændə,bɛɡ) n original name *George Castriota*; Turkish name *Iskender Bey*. ?1403–68, Albanian patriot. He was an army commander for the sultan of Turkey until 1443, when he changed sides and drove the Turks from Albania

Scandinavia (,skændɪ'neɪvɪə) n **1** Also called: the **Scandinavian Peninsula** the peninsula of N Europe occupied by Norway and Sweden **2** the countries of N Europe, esp considered as a cultural unit and including Norway, Sweden, Denmark, and often Finland, Iceland, and the Faeroes ▷ ,**Scandi'navian** *adj, n*

scandium ('skændɪəm) n a rare light silvery-white metallic element occurring in minute quantities in numerous minerals. Symbol: Sc; atomic no: 21; atomic wt: 44.955910; valency: 3; relative density: 2.989; melting pt: 1541°C; boiling pt: 2836°C [c19: from New Latin, from Latin *Scandia* Scandinavia, where it was discovered]

scanner ('skænə) n **1** a person or thing that scans **2** a device, usually electronic, used to measure or sample the distribution of some quantity or condition in a particular system, region, or area **3** an aerial or similar device designed to transmit or receive signals, esp radar signals, inside a given solid angle of space, thus allowing a particular region to be scanned **4** any of various devices used in medical diagnosis to obtain an image of an internal organ or part **5** short for **optical scanner 6** *printing* an electronic device which scans printed material and converts it to digital form

scanning electron microscope n a type of electron microscope that produces a three-dimensional image

scansion ('skænʃən) n the analysis of the metrical structure of verse [c17: from Latin: climbing up, from *scandere* to climb, SCAN]

scant (skænt) *adj* **1** scarcely sufficient; limited: *he paid her scant attention* **2** (prenominal) slightly short of the amount indicated; bare: *a scant ten inches* **3** (postpositive; foll by *of*) having a short supply (of) ▷ *vb* (tr) **4** to limit in size or quantity **5** to provide with a limited or inadequate supply of **6** to treat in a slighting or inadequate manner ▷ *adv* **7** scarcely; barely [c14: from Old Norse *skamt*, from *skammr*/short; related to Old High German *scam*] ▷ '**scantly** *adv*

scantling ('skæntlɪŋ) n **1** a piece of sawn timber, such as a rafter, that has a small cross section **2** the dimensions of a piece of building material or the structural parts of a ship, esp those in cross section **3** a building stone, esp one that is more than 6 feet in length **4** a small quantity or amount [c16: changed (through influence of SCANT and -LING¹) from earlier *scantillon*, a carpenter's gauge, from Old Norman French *escantillon*, ultimately from Latin *scandere* to climb; see SCAN]

scanty ('skæntɪ) *adj* scantier, scantiest **1** limited; barely enough; meagre **2** insufficient; inadequate **3** lacking fullness; small ▷ '**scantily** *adv* ▷ '**scantiness** *n*

Scapa Flow ('skæpə) n an extensive landlocked anchorage off the N coast of Scotland, in the Orkney Islands: major British naval base in both World Wars. Length: about 24 km (15 miles). Width: 13 km (8 miles)

scape *or* '**scape** (skeɪp) *vb, n* an archaic word for **escape**

-**scape** *suffix forming nouns* indicating a scene or view of something, esp a pictorial representation: *seascape* [abstracted from LANDSCAPE]

scapegoat ('skeɪp,ɡəʊt) n **1** a person made to bear the blame for others **2** *Old Testament* a goat used in the ritual of Yom Kippur (Leviticus 16); it was symbolically laden with the sins of the Israelites and sent into the wilderness to be destroyed ▷ *vb* **3** (tr) to make a scapegoat of [c16: from ESCAPE + GOAT, coined by William Tyndale to translate Biblical Hebrew *azāzēl* (probably) goat for Azazel, mistakenly thought to mean "goat that escapes"]

scapegrace ('skeɪp,ɡreɪs) n an idle mischievous person [c19: from SCAPE + GRACE, alluding to a person who lacks God's grace]

scaphocephalic (,skæfɪsɪ'fælɪk) *adj anatomy* having a head that is abnormally long and narrow as a result of the two parietal bones on the top of the skull closing prematurely. Compare **dolichocephalic, brachycephalic** ▷ '**scapho,cephaly** *or* '**scapho,cephalism** *n*

scaphoid ('skæfɔɪd) *adj anatomy* an obsolete word for **navicular** [c18: via New Latin from Greek *skaphoeidēs*, from *skaphē* boat]

scapula ('skæpjʊlə) n, pl -lae (-liː) *or* -las either of two large flat triangular bones, one on each side of the back part of the shoulder in man. Nontechnical name: **shoulder blade** [c16: from Late Latin: shoulder]

scapular ('skæpjʊlə) *adj* **1** *anatomy* of or relating to the scapula ▷ n **2** part of the monastic habit worn by members of many Christian, esp Roman Catholic, religious orders, consisting of a piece of woollen cloth worn over the shoulders, and hanging down in front and behind to the ankles **3** two small rectangular pieces of woollen cloth joined by tapes passing over the shoulders and worn under secular clothes in token of affiliation to a religious order **4** any of the small feathers that are attached to the humerus of a bird and lie along the shoulder

scar¹ (skɑː) n **1** any mark left on the skin or other tissue following the healing of a wound **2** a permanent change in a person's character resulting from emotional distress **3** the mark on a plant indicating the former point of attachment of a part, esp the attachment of a leaf to a stem **4** a mark of damage; blemish ▷ *vb* scars, scarring, scarred **5** to mark or become marked with a scar **6** (intr) to heal leaving a scar [c14: via Late Latin from Greek *eskhara* scab]

scar² (skɑː) n an irregular enlongated trench-like feature on a land surface that often exposes bedrock [c14: from Old Norse *sker* low reef, SKERRY]

scarab ('skærəb) n **1** any scarabaeid beetle, esp *Scarabaeus sacer* (**sacred scarab**), regarded by the ancient Egyptians as divine **2** the scarab as represented on amulets, etc, of ancient Egypt, or in hieroglyphics as a symbol of the solar deity [c16: from Latin *scarabaeus*; probably related to Greek *karabos* horned beetle]

scarabaeid (,skærə'biːɪd) *or* **scarabaean** (,skærə'biːən) n **1** any beetle of the family *Scarabaeidae*, including the sacred scarab and other dung beetles, the chafers, goliath beetles, and rhinoceros beetles ▷ *adj* **2** of, relating to, or belonging to the family *Scarabaeidae* [c19: from New Latin]

Scaramouch *or* **Scaramouche** ('skærə,maʊtʃ, -,muːtʃ) n a stock character who appears as a boastful coward in commedia dell'arte and farce [c17: via French from Italian *Scaramuccia*, from *scaramuccia* a SKIRMISH]

Scarborough ('skɑːbrə) n a fishing port and resort in NE England, in North Yorkshire on the North Sea: developed as a spa after 1660; ruined 12th-century castle. Pop: 38 364 (2001)

scarce (skeəs) *adj* **1** rarely encountered **2** insufficient to meet the demand **3** make oneself scarce *informal* to go away, esp suddenly ▷ *adv* **4** *archaic or literary* scarcely [c13:

from Old Norman French *scars*, from Vulgar Latin *excarpsus* (unattested) plucked out, from Latin *excerpere* to select; see EXCERPT] > 'scarceness *n*

scarcely ('skɛəslɪ) *adv* 1 hardly at all; only just 2 *often used ironically* probably not or definitely not: *that is scarcely justification for your actions*

● USAGE See at **hardly**

scarcity ('skɛəsɪtɪ) *n, pl* -ties 1 inadequate supply; dearth; paucity 2 rarity or infrequent occurrence

scare (skɛə) *vb* 1 to fill or be filled with fear or alarm 2 (*tr; often foll by away or off*) to drive (away) by frightening 3 (*tr) US & Canadian informal* (foll by *up*) **a** to produce (a meal) quickly from whatever is available **b** to manage to find (something) quickly or with difficulty: *brewers need to scare up more sales* ▷ *n* 4 a sudden attack of fear or alarm 5 a period of general fear or alarm ▷ *adj* 6 causing (needless) fear or alarm: *a scare story* [C12: from Old Norse *skirra*; related to Norwegian *skjerra*, Swedish dialect *skjarra*] > 'scarer *n*

scarecrow ('skɛə,krəʊ) *n* 1 an object, usually in the shape of a man, made out of sticks and old clothes to scare birds away from crops 2 a person or thing that appears frightening but is not actually harmful 3 *informal* an untidy-looking person

scaremonger ('skɛə,mʌŋgə) *n* a person who delights in spreading rumours of disaster > 'scare,mongering *n*

scarf[1] (skɑːf) *n, pl* **scarves** (skɑːvz) or **scarfs** a rectangular, triangular, or long narrow piece of cloth worn around the head, neck, or shoulders for warmth or decoration [C16: of uncertain origin; compare Old Norman French *escarpe*, Medieval Latin *scrippum* pilgrim's pack]

scarf[2] (skɑːf) *n, pl* **scarfs** 1 Also called: **scarf joint**, **scarfed joint** a lapped joint between two pieces of timber made by notching or grooving the ends and strapping, bolting, or gluing the two pieces together 2 the end of a piece of timber shaped to form such a joint 3 *whaling* an incision made along a whale's body before stripping off the blubber ▷ *vb* (*tr*) 4 to join (two pieces of timber) by means of a scarf 5 to make a scarf on (a piece of timber) 6 to cut a scarf in (a whale) [C14: probably from Scandinavian; compare Norwegian *skarv*, Swedish *skarf*, Low German, Dutch *scherf* SCARF[1]]

Scarfe (skɑːf) *n* **Gerald.** born 1936, British cartoonist, famous for his scathing caricatures of politicians and celebrities

scarfskin ('skɑːf,skɪn) *n* the outermost layer of the skin; epidermis or cuticle [C17: from SCARF[1] (in the sense: an outer covering)]

Scargill ('skɑːgɪl) *n* **Arthur.** born 1941, British trades union leader; president of the National Union of Mineworkers (1982–2002). He led the miners in a long and bitter strike (1984–85), but failed to prevent pit closures

scarify ('skɛərɪ,faɪ, 'skɑːrɪ-) *vb* -fies, -fying, -fied (*tr*) 1 *surgery* to make tiny punctures or superficial incisions in (the skin or other tissue), as for inoculating 2 *agriculture* to break up and loosen (soil) to a shallow depth 3 to wound with harsh criticism [C15: via Old French from Latin *scarīfāre* to scratch open, from Greek *skariphasthai* to draw, from *skariphos* a pencil] > ,scarifi'cation *n* > 'scari,fier *n*

scarlatina (,skɑːlə'tiːnə) *n* the technical name for **scarlet fever** [C19: from New Latin, from Italian *scarlattina*, diminutive of *scarlatto* SCARLET]

Scarlatti (skɑː'lætɪ) *n* 1 **Alessandro** (ales'sandro). ?1659–1725, Italian composer; regarded as the founder of modern opera 2 his son, (**Giuseppe**) **Domenico** (do'me:niko). 1685–1757, Italian composer and harpsichordist, in Portugal and Spain from 1720. He wrote over 550 single-movement sonatas for harpsichord, many of them exercises in virtuoso technique

scarlet ('skɑːlɪt) *n* 1 a vivid red colour, sometimes with an orange tinge 2 cloth or clothing of this colour ▷ *adj* 3 of the colour scarlet 4 sinful or immoral, esp unchaste [C13: from Old French *escarlate* fine cloth, of unknown origin]

scarlet fever *n* an acute communicable disease

characterized by fever, strawberry-coloured tongue, and a typical rash starting on the neck and chest and spreading to the abdomen and limbs, caused by all group A haemolytic *Streptococcus* bacteria. Technical name: **scarlatina**

scarlet letter *n* (esp among US Puritans) a scarlet letter *A* formerly worn by a person convicted of adultery

scarlet pimpernel *n* a weedy primulaceous plant, *Anagallis arvensis*, of temperate regions, having small red, purple, or white star-shaped flowers that close in bad weather. Also called: **poor man's weatherglass**, **shepherd's weatherglass**

scarlet runner *n* a climbing perennial bean plant, *Phaseolus multiflorus* (or *P. coccineus*), of tropical America, having scarlet flowers: widely cultivated for its long green edible pods containing edible seeds. Also called: **runner bean**

scarlet woman *n* 1 *New Testament* a sinful woman described in Revelation 17, interpreted as a figure either of pagan Rome or of the Roman Catholic Church regarded as typifying vice overlaid with gaudy pageantry 2 any sexually promiscuous woman, esp a prostitute

scarp (skɑːp) *n* 1 a steep slope, esp one formed by erosion or faulting; escarpment 2 *fortifications* the side of a ditch cut nearest to and immediately below a rampart ▷ *vb* 3 (*tr; often passive*) to wear or cut so as to form a steep slope [C16: from Italian *scarpa*]

scarper ('skɑːpə) *Brit slang* ▷ *vb* (*intr*) 1 to depart in haste ▷ *n* 2 a hasty departure [C19: probably an adaptation of Italian *scappare* to escape; perhaps influenced by folk etymology *Scapa Flow* Cockney rhyming slang for *go*]

Scarron (*French* skarɔ̃) *n* **Paul** (pɔl). 1610–60, French comic dramatist and novelist, noted particularly for his picaresque novel *Le Roman comique* (1651–57)

Scart or **SCART** (skɑːt) *n electronics* **a** a 21-pin plug-and-socket system which carries picture, sound, and other signals, used especially in home entertainment systems **b** (*as modifier*): *a Scart cable* [C20: abbrev *Syndicat des Constructeurs des Appareils Radiorécepteurs et Téléviseurs*, the company that designed it]

scarves (skɑːvz) *n* a plural of **scarf**[1]

scary ('skɛərɪ) *adj* **scarier, scariest** *informal* causing fear or alarm; frightening

scat[1] (skæt) *vb* **scats, scatting, scatted** (*intr; usually imperative*) *informal* to go away in haste [C19: perhaps from a hiss + the word *cat*, used to frighten away cats]

scat[2] (skæt) *n* 1 a type of jazz singing characterized by improvised vocal sounds instead of words ▷ *vb* **scats, scatting, scatted** 2 (*intr*) to sing jazz in this way [C20: perhaps imitative]

scathe (skeɪð) *vb* (*tr*) 1 *rare* to attack with severe criticism 2 *archaic or dialect* to injure ▷ *n* 3 *archaic, or dialect* harm [Old English *sceatha*; related to Old Norse *skathi*, Old Saxon *scatho*]

scathing ('skeɪðɪŋ) *adj* 1 harshly critical; scornful 2 damaging; painful > 'scathingly *adv*

scatology (skæ'tɒlədʒɪ) *n* 1 the scientific study of excrement, esp in medicine for diagnostic purposes, and in palaeontology of fossilized excrement 2 obscenity or preoccupation with obscenity, esp in the form of references to excrement > scatological (,skætə'lɒdʒɪkᵊl) or (*less commonly*) scatologic (,skætə'lɒdʒɪk) *adj*

scatter ('skætə) *vb* 1 (*tr*) to throw about in various directions; strew 2 to separate and move or cause to separate and move in various directions; disperse 3 to deviate or cause to deviate in many directions, as in the diffuse reflection or refraction of light ▷ *n* 4 the act of scattering 5 a substance or a number of objects scattered about [C13: probably a variant of SHATTER] > 'scatterer *n*

scatterbrain ('skætə,breɪn) *n* a person who is incapable of serious thought or concentration > 'scatter,brained *adj*

scatter diagram *n statistics* a graph that plots along two axes at right angles to each other the relationship between two variable quantities, such as height and weight

scattering ('skætərɪŋ) *n* 1 a small amount 2 *physics* the process in which particles, atoms, etc, are deflected as a result of collision

scattershot ('skætə,ʃɒt) *adj* random; haphazard: *their approach to conservation is scattershot and unscientific*

scatty ('skætɪ) *adj* -tier, -tiest *Brit informal* **1** empty-headed, frivolous, or thoughtless **2** distracted (esp in **drive someone scatty**) [C20: from SCATTERBRAINED] > **'scattily** *adv* > **'scattiness** *n*

scaup *or* **scaup duck** (skɔːp) *n* either of two diving ducks, *Aythya marila* (**greater scaup**) or *A. affinis* (**lesser scaup**), of Europe and America, having a black-and-white plumage in the male [C16: Scottish variant of SCALP]

scavenge ('skævɪndʒ) *vb* **1** to search for (anything usable) among discarded material **2** (*tr*) to purify (a molten metal) by bubbling a suitable gas through it. The gas may be inert or may react with the impurities **3** to clean up filth from (streets, etc)

scavenger ('skævɪndʒə) *n* **1** a person who collects things discarded by others **2** any animal that feeds on decaying organic matter, esp on refuse **3** a person employed to clean the streets [C16: from Anglo-Norman *scawager*, from Old Norman French *escauwage* examination, from *escauwer* to scrutinize, of Germanic origin; related to Flemish *scauwen*] > **'scavengery** *n*

ScD *abbreviation* Doctor of Science [Latin *scientiae doctor* doctor of the sciences]

SCE *abbreviation* (in Scotland) Scottish Certificate of Education: either of two public examinations in specific subjects taken as school-leaving qualifications or as qualifying examinations for entry into a university, college, etc

scena ('ʃeɪnə) *n, pl* -ne (-,neɪ) a dramatic vocal piece written in operatic style

scenario (sɪ'nɑːrɪ,əʊ) *n, pl* -narios **1** a summary of the plot of a play, etc, including information about its characters, scenes, etc **2** a predicted sequence of events [C19: via Italian from Latin *scēnārium*, from *scēna*; see SCENE]

scene (siːn) *n* **1** the place where an action or event, real or imaginary, occurs **2** the setting for the action of a play, novel, etc **3** an incident or situation, real or imaginary, esp as described or represented **4 a** a subdivision of an act of a play, in which the time is continuous and the setting fixed **b** a single event, esp a significant one, in a play **5** *films* a shot or series of shots that constitutes a unit of the action **6** the backcloths, stage setting, etc, for a play or film set; scenery **7** the prospect of a place, landscape, etc **8** a display of emotion, esp an embarrassing one to the onlookers **9** *informal* the environment for a specific activity: *the fashion scene* **10** *informal* interest or chosen occupation: *classical music is not my scene* **11** *rare* the stage, esp of a theatre in ancient Greece or Rome **12** **behind the scenes** out of public view; privately [C16: from Latin *scēna* theatrical stage, from Greek *skēnē* tent, stage]

scene dock *or* **scene bay** *n* a place in a theatre where scenery is stored, usually near the stage

scenery ('siːnərɪ) *n, pl* -eries **1** the natural features of a landscape **2** *theatre* the painted backcloths, stage structures, etc, used to represent a location in a theatre or studio [C18: from Italian SCENARIO]

scenic ('siːnɪk, 'sɛn-) *adj* **1** of or relating to natural scenery **2** having beautiful natural scenery: *a scenic drive* **3** of or relating to the stage or stage scenery **4** (in painting) representing a scene, such as a scene of action or a historical event > **'scenically** *adv*

scenic railway *n* a miniature railway used for amusement in a park, zoo, etc

scenic reserve *n* NZ an area of natural beauty, set aside for public recreation

scent (sɛnt) *n* **1** a distinctive smell, esp a pleasant one **2** a smell left in passing, by which a person or animal may be traced **3** a trail, clue, or guide **4** an instinctive ability for finding out or detecting **5** another word (esp Brit) for **perfume** ▷ *vb* **6** (*tr*) to recognize or be aware of by or as if by the smell **7** (*tr*) to have a suspicion of; detect: *I scent foul play* **8** (*tr*) to fill with odour or fragrance **9** (*intr*) (of hounds, etc) to hunt by the sense of smell

10 to smell (at): *the dog scented the air* [C14: from Old French *sentir* to sense, from Latin *sentīre* to feel; see SENSE] > **'scented** *adj*

sceptic *or archaic and US* **skeptic** ('skɛptɪk) *n* **1** a person who habitually doubts the authenticity of accepted beliefs **2** a person who mistrusts people, ideas, etc, in general **3** a person who doubts the truth of religion, esp Christianity ▷ *adj* **4** of or relating to sceptics; sceptical [C16: from Latin *scepticus*, from Greek *skeptikos* one who reflects upon, from *skeptesthai* to consider] > **'scepticism** *or archaic and US* **'skepticism** *n* **'sceptical** *or archaic and US* **'skeptical** *adj* > **'sceptically,** *or archaic and US* **'skeptically** *adv*

Sceptic *or archaic and US* **Skeptic** ('skɛptɪk) *n* **1** a member of one of the ancient Greek schools of philosophy, esp that of Pyrrho (?365–?275 BC), who believed that real knowledge of things is impossible ▷ *adj* **2** of or relating to the Sceptics > **'Scepticism** *or* Skepticism *archaic and US* **'Skepticism** *n*

sceptre *or US* **scepter** ('sɛptə) *n* a ceremonial staff held by a monarch as the symbol of authority **2** imperial authority; sovereignty [C13: from Old French *sceptre*, from Latin *scēptrum*, from Greek *skeptron* staff] > **'sceptred** *or US* **'sceptered** *adj*

Schaerbeek (Flemish 'sxaːrbeːk) *n* a city in central Belgium: an industrial suburb of Brussels. Pop: 110 253 (2004 est)

Schaffhausen (German ʃaːfˈhauzən) *n* **1** a small canton of N Switzerland. Pop: 73 900 (2002 est). Area: 298 sq km (115 sq miles) **2** a town in N Switzerland, capital of Schaffhausen canton, on the Rhine. Pop: 33 628 (2000)

Schama ('ʃɑːmə) *n* **Simon** (**Michael**). born 1945, British historian, art critic, and broadcaster, based in the US; his work includes *The Embarrassment of Riches* (1987), *Landscape and Memory* (1995), and the BBC television series *A History of Britain* (2000–02)

Schaumburg-Lippe (German 'ʃaumbʊrk'lɪpə) *n* a former state of NW Germany, between Westphalia and Hanover: part of Lower Saxony since 1946

schedule ('ʃɛdjuːl; *esp US* 'skɛdʒʊəl) *n* **1** a plan of procedure for a project, allotting the work to be done and the time for it **2** a list of items: *a schedule of fixed prices* **3** a list of times, esp of arrivals and departures; timetable **4** a list of tasks to be performed, esp within a set period **5** *law* a list or inventory, usually supplementary to a contract, will, etc ▷ *vb* **6** to make a schedule of or place in a schedule **7** to plan to occur at a certain time [C14: earlier *cedule, sedule* via Old French from Late Latin *schedula* small piece of paper, from Latin *scheda* sheet of paper]

scheduled castes *pl n* certain classes in Indian society officially granted special concessions. See **Harijan**

scheduled territories *pl n* the scheduled territories another name for **sterling area**

scheduler ('ʃɛdjuːlə; US 'skɛdʒʊələ) *n* **1** a person whose job is to allot times for television or radio programmes to be broadcast **2** *computing* a computer program designed to aid in scheduling tasks

Scheele (Swedish 'ʃeːlə) *n* **Karl Wilhelm** (kɑːrl 'vɪlhɛlm). 1742–86, Swedish chemist. He discovered oxygen, independently of Priestley, and many other substances

scheelite ('ʃiːlaɪt) *n* a white, brownish, or greenish mineral, usually fluorescent, consisting of calcium tungstate in tetragonal crystalline form with some tungsten often replaced by molybdenum: occurs principally in contact metamorphic rocks and quartz veins, and is an important source of tungsten and purified calcium tungstate. Formula: CaWO$_4$ [C19: from German *Scheelit*, named after Karl Wilhelm Scheele (1742–86), Swedish chemist]

Scheldt (ʃɛlt, skɛlt) *n* a river in W Europe, rising in NE France and flowing north and northeast through W Belgium to Antwerp, then northwest to the North Sea in the SW Netherlands. Length: 435 km (270 miles). French name: **Escaut**

Schelling (German 'ʃɛlɪŋ) *n* **Friedrich Wilhelm Joseph von** ('friːdrɪç 'vɪlhɛlm 'joːzɛf fɔn). 1775–1854, German philosopher. He expanded Fichte's idea that there is one reality, the infinite and absolute Ego, by regarding nature as an absolute being working towards self-consciousness. His works include *Ideas towards a Philosophy of Nature* (1797) and *System of Transcendental Idealism* (1800) > **Schellingian** (ʃɛˈlɪŋɪən) *adj*

schema (ˈskiːmə) *n*, *pl* **-mata** (-mətə) **1** a plan, diagram, or scheme **2** (in the philosophy of Kant) a rule or principle that enables the understanding to apply its categories and unify experience [c19: from Greek: form]

schematic (skɪˈmætɪk, skiː-) *adj* **1** of or relating to the nature of a diagram, plan, or schema ▷ *n* **2** a schematic diagram, esp of an electrical circuit > **scheˈmatically** *adv*

schematism (ˈskiːməˌtɪzəm) *n* the general form, arrangement, or classification of something

schematize or **schematise** (ˈskiːməˌtaɪz) *vb* (*tr*) to form into or arrange in a scheme > ˌschematiˈzation or ˌschematiˈsation *n*

scheme (skiːm) *n* **1** a systematic plan for a course of action **2** a systematic arrangement of correlated parts; system **3** a secret plot **4** a visionary or unrealizable project **5** a chart, diagram, or outline **6** an astrological diagram giving the aspects of celestial bodies at a particular time **7** *chiefly Brit* a plan formally adopted by a commercial enterprise or governmental body, as for pensions, etc **8** *chiefly Scot* an area of housing that is laid out esp by a local authority; estate ▷ *vb* **9** (*tr*) to devise a system for **10** to form intrigues (for) in an underhand manner [c16: from Latin *schema*, from Greek *skhēma* form] > ˈschemer *n*

scheming (ˈskiːmɪŋ) *adj* **1** given to making plots; cunning ▷ *n* **2** intrigues

Schengen Convention or **Schengen Agreement** (ˈʃɛŋən) *n* an agreement, signed in 1985, but not implemented until 1995, to abolish border controls within Europe: ten countries had acceded by 1995; the UK is not a signatory

Schepisi (ʃəˈpiːzɪ) *n* **Fred**, full name *Frederick Alan Schepisi*. born 1939, Australian film director. His films include *The Chant of Jimmie Blacksmith* (1978), *A Cry in the Dark* (1988) and *Last Orders* (2001)

scherzando (skɛəˈtsændəʊ) *music* ▷ *adj*, *adv* **1** to be performed in a light-hearted manner ▷ *n*, *pl* **-di** (-diː) or **-dos 2** a movement, passage, etc, directed to be performed in this way [Italian, literally: joking. See SCHERZO]

scherzo (ˈskɛətsəʊ) *n*, *pl* **-zos** or **-zi** (-tsiː) a brisk lively movement, developed from the minuet, with a contrastive middle section (a trio) [Italian: joke, of Germanic origin; compare Middle High German *scherzen* to jest]

Schiaparelli (Italian skjapaˈrɛlli) *n* **1 Elsa** (ˈelsa). 1896–1973, Italian couturière, noted esp for the dramatic colours of her designs **2 Giovanni Virginio** (dʒoˈvanni virˈdʒiːnjo). 1835–1910, Italian astronomer, who discovered the asteroid Hesperia (1861) and the so-called canals of Mars (1877)

Schick test (ʃɪk) *n med* a skin test to determine immunity to diphtheria: a dilute diphtheria toxin is injected into the skin; within two or three days a red inflamed area will develop if no antibodies are present [c20: named after Bela *Schick* (1877–1967), US paediatrician]

Schiedam (Dutch sxiˈdɑm) *n* a port in the SW Netherlands, in South Holland province west of Rotterdam: gin distilleries. Pop: 76 000 (2003 est)

Schiele (German ˈʃiːlə) *n* **Egon** (ˈeːɡɔn). 1890–1918, Austrian painter and draughtsman: a leading exponent of Austrian expressionism

Schiff (ʃɪf) *n* **Andras** (ˈɑndrəs). born 1953, Hungarian concert pianist; became British citizen in 2001

schiller (ˈʃɪlə) *n* an unusual iridescent or metallic lustre in some minerals caused by internal reflection from certain inclusions such as gas cavities or mineral intergrowths. Formula: $NaFe_3B_3Al_3(Al_3Si_6O_{27})(OH)_4$ [c19: from German *Schiller* iridescence, from Old High German *scilihen* to blink]

Schiller (German ˈʃɪlər) *n* **Johann Christoph Friedrich von** (joˈhan ˈkrɪstɔf ˈfriːdrɪç fɔn). 1759–1805, German poet, dramatist, historian, and critic. His concern with the ideal freedom of the human spirit to rise above the

constraints placed upon it is reflected in his great trilogy *Wallenstein* (1800) and in *Maria Stuart* (1800)

schilling (ˈʃɪlɪŋ) *n* the former standard monetary unit of Austria, divided into 100 groschen; replaced by the euro in 2002 [c18: from German: SHILLING]

schism (ˈskɪzəm, ˈsɪz-) *n* **1** the division of a group into opposing factions **2** the factions so formed **3** division within or separation from an established Church, esp the Roman Catholic Church, not necessarily involving differences in doctrine [c14: from Church Latin *schisma*, from Greek *skhisma* a cleft, from *skhizein* to split]

schismatic (skɪzˈmætɪk, sɪz-) or **schismatical** *adj* **1** of, relating to, or promoting schism ▷ *n* **2** a person who causes schism or belongs to a schismatic faction > **schisˈmatically** *adv*

schist (ʃɪst) *n* any metamorphic rock that can be split into thin layers because its micaceous minerals have become aligned in thin parallel bands [c18: from French *schiste*, from Latin *lapis schistos* stone that may be split, from Greek *skhizein* to split] > ˈschistose *adj*

schistosome (ˈʃɪstəˌsəʊm) *n* any of various blood flukes of the chiefly tropical genus *Schistosoma*, which cause disease in man and domestic animals. Also called: bilharzia [c19: from New Latin *Schistosoma*; see SCHIST, -SOME³]

schistosomiasis (ˌʃɪstəsəʊˈmaɪəsɪs) *n* a disease caused by infestation of the body with blood flukes of the genus *Schistosoma*. Also called: bilharziasis

schizanthus (skɪtˈsænθəs) *n* any plant of the Chilean annual genus *Schizanthus*, some species of which are grown as pot or garden plants for their showy red, white, or yellow orchid-like flowers: family Solanaceae [New Latin, from Greek *schizein* to cut + *anthos* flower (from the deeply divided corolla)]

schizo (ˈskɪtsəʊ) *highly offensive* ▷ *adj* **1** schizophrenic ▷ *n*, *pl* **-os 2** a schizophrenic person

schizo- or before a vowel **schiz-** *combining form* indicating a cleavage, split, or division: *schizocarp*; *schizophrenia* [from Greek *skhizein* to split]

schizocarp (ˈskɪzəˌkɑːp) *n botany* a dry fruit that splits into two or more one-seeded portions at maturity > ˌschizoˈcarpous or ˌschizoˈcarpic *adj*

schizoid (ˈskɪtsɔɪd) *adj* **1** *psychol* denoting a personality disorder characterized by lack of close relationships with other people and more than usual self-absorption **2** *informal*, *offensive* characterized by or showing conflicting or contradictory attitudes, ideas, etc ▷ *n* **3** a person who has a schizoid personality

schizomycete (ˌskɪtsəʊmaɪˈsiːt) *n* (formerly) any microscopic organism of the now obsolete class *Schizomycetes*, which included the bacteria

schizophrenia (ˌskɪtsəʊˈfriːnɪə) *n* **1** any of a group of psychotic disorders characterized by progressive deterioration of the personality, withdrawal from reality, hallucinations, delusions, social apathy, emotional instability, etc **2** *informal* behaviour that appears to be motivated by contradictory or conflicting principles [c20: from SCHIZO- + Greek *phrēn* mind + -IA] > ˌschizoˈphrenic *adj*, *n*

● USAGE It is preferable to refer to a person as *someone* ● *with a diagnosis of schizophrenia* rather than as *a* ● *schizophrenic*. The general use of the word to mean ● 'contradictory' is also best avoided. Suitable ● alternatives are *contradictory*, *inconsistent*, *incoherent*

schizothymia (ˌskɪtsəʊˈθaɪmɪə) *n psychiatry* the condition of being schizoid or introverted. It encompasses elements of schizophrenia but does not involve the same depth of psychological disturbance [c20: New Latin, from SCHIZO- + -thymia, from Greek *thumos* spirit] > ˌschizoˈthymic *adj*

Schlegel (German ˈʃleːɡəl) *n* **1 August Wilhelm von** (ˈaʊɡʊst ˈvɪlhɛlm fɔn). 1767–1845, German romantic critic and scholar, noted particularly for his translations of Shakespeare **2** his brother, **Friedrich von** (ˈfriːdrɪç fɔn). 1772–1829, German philosopher and critic; a founder of the romantic movement in Germany

Schleiermacher (German ˈʃlaɪərˌmaxər) *n* **Friedrich Ernst Daniel** (ˈfriːdrɪç ɛrnst ˈdaːnjeːl). 1768–1834, German Protestant theologian and philosopher. His works include *The Christian Faith* (1821–22)

Schlesien ('ʃleːziən) *n* the German name for **Silesia**

Schlesinger ('ʃlɛzɪŋə) *n* **John** (**Richard**). 1926–2003, British film and theatre director. Films include *Billy Liar* (1963), *Midnight Cowboy* (1969), *Sunday Bloody Sunday* (1971), and *Eye for an Eye* (1995)

Schleswig (German 'ʃleːsvɪç) *n* **1** a fishing port in N Germany, in Schleswig-Holstein state: on an inlet of the Baltic. Pop: 24 288 (2003 est) **2** a former duchy, in the S Jutland Peninsula: annexed by Prussia in 1864; N part returned to Denmark after a plebiscite in 1920; S part forms part of the German state of Schleswig-Holstein. Danish name: **Slesvig**

Schleswig-Holstein (German 'ʃleːsvɪç'hɔlʃtaɪn) *n* a state of N Germany: drained chiefly by the River Elbe; mainly agricultural. Capital: Kiel. Pop: 2 823 000 (2003 est). Area: 15 658 sq km (6045 sq miles)

Schlick (ʃlɪk) *n* **Moritz**. 1882–1936, German philosopher, working in Austria, who founded (1924) the Vienna Circle to develop the doctrine of logical positivism. His works include the *General Theory of Knowledge* (1918) and *Problems of Ethics* (1930)

Schlieffen (German 'ʃliːfən) *n* **Alfred** ('alfreːt), Count von Schlieffen. 1833–1913, German field marshal, who devised the **Schlieffen Plan** (1905): it was intended to ensure German victory over a Franco-Russian alliance by holding off Russia with minimal strength and swiftly defeating France by a massive flanking movement through the Low Countries. In a modified form, it was unsuccessfully employed in World War I (1914)

Schliemann (German 'ʃliːman) *n* **Heinrich** ('haɪnrɪç). 1822–90, German archaeologist, who discovered nine superimposed city sites of Troy (1871–90). He also excavated the site of Mycenae (1876)

schlieren ('ʃliːrən) *n* **1** *physics* visible streaks produced in a transparent medium as a result of variations in the medium's density leading to variations in refractive index. They can be recorded by flash photography (**schlieren photography**) **2** streaks or platelike masses of mineral in a rock mass, that differ in texture or composition from the main mass [German, plural of *Schliere* streak]

schmaltz *or* **schmalz** (ʃmælts, ʃmɔːlts) *n* excessive sentimentality, esp in music [C20: from German (*Schmalz*) and Yiddish: melted fat, from Old High German *smalz*]

schmaltzy (ʃmæltsɪ, ʃmɔːltsɪ) *adj* **-ier, -iest** excessively sentimental

schmick (ʃmɪk) *adj Austral informal* excellent, elegant, or stylish [C20: of unknown origin]

Schmidt (ʃmɪt) *n* **Helmut** (**Heinrich Waldemar**) ('hɛlmuːt). born 1918, German Social Democrat statesman; chancellor of West Germany (1974–82)

Schmidt telescope *or* **Schmidt camera** *n* a catadioptric telescope designed to produce a very sharp image of a large area of sky in one photographic exposure. It incorporates a thin specially shaped glass plate at the centre of curvature of a short-focus spherical primary mirror so that the resulting image, which is focused on a photographic plate, is free from spherical aberration, coma, and astigmatism [C20: named after B. V. *Schmidt* (1879–1935), Estonian-born German inventor]

Schnabel ('ʃnaːbʰl) *n* **Artur** ('artʊr). 1882–1951, US pianist and composer, born in Austria

schnapper ('ʃnæpə) *n* a variant of **snapper** (senses 1, 2)

schnapps *or* **schnaps** (ʃnæps) *n* **1** a Dutch spirit distilled from potatoes **2** (in Germany) any strong spirit [C19: from German *Schnaps*, from *schnappen* to SNAP]

schnauzer ('ʃnaʊtsə) *n* a wire-haired breed of dog of the terrier type, originally from Germany, having a greyish coat and distinctive beard, moustache, and eyebrows [C19: from German *Schnauze* SNOUT]

Schnittke ('ʃnɪtkə) *n* **Alfred**. 1934–98, Russian composer: his works include four symphonies, four violin concertos, choral, chamber, and film music

schnitzel ('ʃnɪtsəl) *n* a thin slice of meat, esp veal. See also **Wiener schnitzel** [German: cutlet, from *schnitzen* to carve, *schnitzeln* to whittle]

Schnitzler (German 'ʃnɪtslər) *n* **Arthur** ('artʊr). 1862–1931, Austrian dramatist and novelist. His best-known works are *Anatol* (1893) a series of one-act plays, and *Reigen* (1900), both of which reveal his psychological insight and preoccupation with sexuality

schnorkel ('ʃnɔːkʰl) *n, vb* a less common variant of **snorkel**

schnozzle ('ʃnɒzʰl) *n* *chiefly US* a slang word for **nose** (sense 1) [alteration of Yiddish *shnoitsl*, diminutive of *shnoits*, from German *Schnauze* SNOUT]

Schoenberg *or* **Schönberg** ('ʃɜːnbɜːg; German 'ʃøːnbɛrk) *n* **Arnold** ('arnɔlt). 1874–1951, Austrian composer and musical theorist, in the US after 1933. The harmonic idiom of such early works as the string sextet *Verklärte Nacht* (1899) gave way to his development of atonality, as in the song cycle *Pierrot Lunaire* (1912), and later of the twelve-tone technique. He wrote many choral, orchestral, and chamber works and the unfinished opera *Moses and Aaron*

scholar ('skɒlə) *n* **1** a learned person, esp in the humanities **2** a person, esp a child, who studies; pupil **3** a student of merit at an educational establishment who receives financial aid, esp from an endowment given for such a purpose **4** *South African* a school pupil [C14: from Old French *escoler*, via Late Latin from Latin *schola* SCHOOL¹] > **'scholarly** *adj* > **'scholarliness** *n*

scholarship ('skɒləʃɪp) *n* **1** academic achievement; erudition; learning **2 a** financial aid provided for a scholar because of academic merit **b** the position of a student who gains this financial aid **c** (*as modifier*): *a scholarship student* **3** the qualities of a scholar

scholastic (skə'læstɪk) *adj* **1** of, relating to, or befitting schools, scholars, or education **2** pedantic or precise **3** (*often capital*) characteristic of or relating to the medieval Schoolmen ▷ *n* **4** a student or pupil **5** a person who is given to quibbling or logical subtleties; pedant **6** (*often capital*) a disciple or adherent of scholasticism; Schoolman **7** a Jesuit student who is undergoing a period of probation prior to commencing his theological studies [C16: via Latin from Greek *skholastikos* devoted to learning, ultimately from *skholē* SCHOOL¹] > **scho'lastically** *adv*

scholasticism (skə'læstɪˌsɪzəm) *n* (*sometimes capital*) the system of philosophy, theology, and teaching that dominated medieval western Europe and was based on the writings of the Church Fathers and (from the 12th century) Aristotle, the Greek philosopher (384–322 BC)

scholiast ('skəʊlɪˌæst) *n* a medieval annotator, esp of classical texts [C16: from Late Greek *skholiastēs*, from *skholiazein* to write a SCHOLIUM] > **ˌscholi'astic** *adj*

scholium ('skəʊlɪəm) *n, pl* **-lia** (-lɪə) a commentary or annotation, esp on a classical text [C16: from New Latin, from Greek *skholion* exposition, from *skholē* SCHOOL¹]

Schönberg ('ʃɜːnbɜːg; German 'ʃøːnbɛrk) *n* See **Schoenberg**

Schongauer (German 'ʃɔːngaʊər) *n* **Martin** ('martiːn). ?1445–91, German painter and engraver

school¹ (skuːl) *n* **1 a** an institution or building at which children and young people usually under 19 receive education **b** (*as modifier*): *school bus; school day* **c** (*in combination*): *schoolroom; schoolwork* **2** a faculty, institution, or department specializing in a particular subject **3** the staff and pupils of a school **4** the period of instruction in a school or one session of this: *he stayed after school to do extra work* **5** a place or sphere of activity that instructs: *the school of hard knocks* **6** a body of people or pupils adhering to a certain set of principles, doctrines, or methods **7** a group of artists, writers, etc, linked by the same style, teachers, or aims **8** a style of life: *a gentleman of the old school* **9** *informal* a group assembled for a common purpose, esp gambling or drinking ▷ *vb* (*tr*) **10** to train or educate in or as in a school **11** to discipline or control [Old English *scōl*, from Latin *schola* school, from Greek *skholē* leisure spent in the pursuit of knowledge]

school² (skuːl) *n* **1** a group of porpoises or similar aquatic animals that swim together ▷ *vb* **2** (*intr*) to form such a group [Old English *scolu* SHOAL²]

school board *n* **1** (formerly in Britain) an elected board of ratepayers who provided local elementary schools between 1870 and 1902 **2** (in the US and Canada) a local board of education

schoolboy ('sku:l,bɔɪ) *or feminine* **schoolgirl** *n* a child attending school

schoolhouse ('sku:l,haʊs) *n* **1** a building used as a school, esp a rural school **2** a house attached to a school

schoolie ('sku:lɪ) *n Austral slang* **1** a schoolteacher **2** a high-school student **3** a holiday away from home in which large numbers of school leavers join together

Schoolies Week ('sku:li:z) *n* (in Australia) a week when large numbers of school leavers gather together for a holiday away from home after the end of their final exams

schooling ('sku:lɪŋ) *n* **1** education, esp when received at school **2** the process of teaching or being taught in a school **3** the training of an animal, esp of a horse for dressage

schoolman ('sku:lmən) *n, pl* -men (*sometimes capital*) a scholar versed in the learning of the Schoolmen

Schoolman ('sku:lmən) *n, pl* men a master in one of the schools or universities of the Middle Ages who was versed in scholasticism

schoolmarm ('sku:l,mɑ:m) *n informal* **1** a woman schoolteacher, esp when considered to be prim, prudish, or old-fashioned **2** *Brit* any woman considered to be prim, prudish, or old-fashioned [C19: from SCHOOL¹ + *marm*, variant of MA'AM. See MADAM]
> 'school,marmish *adj*

schoolmaster ('sku:l,mɑ:stə) *n* **1** a man who teaches in or runs a school **2** a person or thing that acts as an instructor

schoolmate ('sku:l,meɪt) *or* **schoolfellow** *n* a companion at school; fellow pupil

schoolmistress ('sku:l,mɪstrɪs) *n* a woman who teaches in or runs a school > 'school,mistressy *adj*

school of arts *n Austral* a public building in a small town, originally one used for adult education

school prawn *n Austral* a common olive-green prawn, *Metapenaeus macleayi*

Schools (sku:lz) *pl n* **1** the Schools the medieval Schoolmen collectively **2** (at Oxford University) **a** the Examination Schools, the University building in which examinations are held **b** *informal* the Second Public Examination for the degree of Bachelor of Arts; finals

school shark *n Austral* an Australian shark resembling the tope, *Notogaleus australis*

schoolteacher ('sku:l,ti:tʃə) *n* a person who teaches in a school > 'school,teaching *n*

school year *n* **1** a twelve-month period, (in Britain) usually starting in late summer and continuing for three terms until the following summer, during which pupils remain in the same class **2** the time during this period when the school is open

schooner ('sku:nə) *n* **1** a sailing vessel with at least two masts, with all lower sails rigged fore-and-aft, and with the main mast stepped aft **2** *Brit* a large glass for sherry **3** *US, Canadian, Austral & NZ* a large glass for beer [C18: origin uncertain]

Schopenhauer (*German* 'ʃoːpənhaʊər) *n* **Arthur** ('ɑrtʊr). 1788–1860, German pessimist philosopher. In his chief work, *The World as Will and Idea* (1819), he expounded the view that will is the creative primary factor and idea the secondary receptive factor > Schopenhauerian (ˌʃəʊpən'haʊərɪən) *adj* > 'Schopen,hauer,ism *n*

schottische (ʃɒ'tiːʃ) *n* **1** a 19th-century German dance resembling a slow polka **2** a piece of music composed for or in the manner of this dance [C19: from German *der schottische Tanz* the Scottish dance]

Schottky effect *n physics* a reduction in the energy required to remove an electron from a solid surface in a vacuum when an electric field is applied to the surface [C20: named after Walter *Schottky* (1886–1976), German physicist]

Schouten Islands ('ʃaʊtⁿn) *pl n* a group of islands in the Pacific, off the N coast of Papua New Guinea. Area: 3185 sq km (1230 sq miles)

Schreiner ('ʃraɪnə) *n* **Olive** (**Emilie Albertina**). 1855–1920, South African novelist and feminist writer, whose works include the autobiographical *The Story of an African Farm* (1883) and *Women and Labour* (1911)

Schröder (*German* 'ʃrøːdɜːr) *n* **Gerhard** ('gerhat). born 1944, German Social Democrat politician; chancellor of Germany from 1998–2005

Schrödinger (*German* 'ʃrøːdɪŋər) *n* **Erwin** ('ɛrviːn). 1887–1961, Austrian physicist, who discovered the wave equation: shared the Nobel prize for physics 1933

Schubert ('ʃuːbət) *n* **Franz** (**Peter**) (frants). 1797–1828, Austrian composer; the originator and supreme exponent of the modern German lied. His many songs include the cycles *Die Schöne Müllerin* (1823) and *Die Winterreise* (1827). His other works include symphonies and much piano and chamber music including string quartets and the *Trout* piano quintet (1819)

Schumacher (*German* 'ʃuːmaxər) *n* **1** **Ernst Friedrich** (ɛrnst 'friːdrɪç). 1911–77, British economist, born in Germany. He is best known for his book *Small is Beautiful* (1973) **2** **Michael**. born 1969, German motor racing driver, who has won more Grand Prix races than any other; Formula One world champion (1994–1995, 2000–2004)

Schuman (*French* ʃuman) *n* **Robert** (rɔbɛr). 1886–1963, French statesman; prime minister (1947–48). He proposed (1950) pooling the coal and steel resources of W Europe (ˈʃuːmən) **William** (**Howard**). 1910–91, US composer

Schumann ('ʃuːmən) *n* **1** **Elisabeth**. (e'liːzabɛt). 1885–1952, German soprano, noted esp for her interpretations of lieder **2** **Robert Alexander**. ('roːbɛrt alɛ'ksandər). 1810–56, German romantic composer, noted esp for his piano music, such as *Carneval* (1835) and *Kreisleriana* (1838), his songs, and four symphonies

schuss (ʃʊs) *skiing* ⊳ *n* **1** a straight high-speed downhill run ⊳ *vb* **2** (*intr*) to perform a schuss [German: SHOT¹]

Schuster ('ʃuːstə) *n* **Leon**. born 1952, South African comedian and film maker. His films include *You Must Be Joking* (1986) and *Mr Bones* (2001)

Schütz (*German* ʃyts) *n* **Heinrich** ('haɪnrɪç). 1585–1672, German composer, esp of church music and madrigals

schwa *or* **shwa** (ʃwɑ:) *n* **1** a central vowel represented in the International Phonetic Alphabet by (ə). The sound occurs in unstressed syllables in English, as in *around, mother*, and *sofa* **2** the symbol (ə) used to represent this sound [C19: via German from Hebrew *shewā*, a diacritic indicating lack of a vowel sound]

Schwaben ('ʃvaːbən) *n* the German name for **Swabia**

Schwann (*German* ʃvan) *n* **Theodor** ('teːodoːr). 1810–82, German physiologist, who founded the theory that all animals consist of cells or cell products

Schwarzkopf (*German* 'ʃvartskɔpf) *n* **1** **Elisabeth** (e'liːzabɛt). 1915–2006, Austro-British operatic soprano, born in Germany **2** (ˈʃwɔːts,kɒpf) **Norman**, nicknamed *Stormin' Norman*. born 1934, US general. As head of Central Command, the US military district covering the Middle East, he became the victorious commander-in-chief of the US-led forces in the Gulf War (1991)

Schwarzwald ('ʃvartsvalt) *n* the German name for the **Black Forest**

Schweinfurt (*German* 'ʃvainfʊrt) *n* a city in central Germany, in N Bavaria on the River Main. Pop: 54 601 (2003 est)

Schweitzer ('ʃwaɪtsə, 'ʃvaɪt-) *n* **Albert**. 1875–1965, Franco-German medical missionary, philosopher, theologian, and organist, born in Alsace. He took up medicine in 1905 and devoted most of his life after 1913 to a medical mission at Lambaréné, Gabon: Nobel peace prize 1952

Schweiz (ʃvaits) *n* the German name for **Switzerland**

Schwerin (*German* ʃve'riːn) *n* a city in N Germany, in Mecklenburg-West Pomerania on **Lake Schwerin**. Pop: 97 694 (2003 est)

Schwitters (*German* 'ʃvɪtərs) *n* **Kurt** (kʊrt). 1887–1948, German dadaist painter and poet, noted for his collages composed of discarded materials

Schwyz (*German* ʃviːts) *n* **1** a canton of central Switzerland: played an important part in the formation of the Swiss confederation, to which it gave its name. Capital: Schwyz. Pop: 133 300 (2002 est). Area: 908 sq km (351 sq miles) **2** a town in E central Switzerland, capital of Schwyz canton: tourism. Pop: 13 802 (2000)

sci. *abbreviation* **1** science **2** scientific

sciatic (saɪˈætɪk) *adj* **1** *anatomy* of or relating to the hip or the hipbone **2** of, relating to, or afflicted with sciatica [c16: from French *sciatique*, from Late Latin *sciaticus*, from Latin *ischiadicus* relating to pain in the hip, from Greek *iskhiadikos*, from *iskhia* hip joint]

sciatica (saɪˈætɪkə) *n* a form of neuralgia characterized by intense pain and tenderness along the course of the body's longest nerve (**sciatic nerve**), extending from the back of the thigh down to the calf of the leg [c15: from Late Latin *sciatica*; see SCIATIC]

science (ˈsaɪəns) *n* **1** the systematic study of the nature and behaviour of the material and physical universe, based on observation, experiment, and measurement, and the formulation of laws to describe these facts in general terms **2** the knowledge so obtained or the practice of obtaining it **3** any particular branch of this knowledge: *the pure and applied sciences* **4** any body of knowledge organized in a systematic manner **5** skill or technique **6** *archaic* knowledge [c14: via Old French from Latin *scientia* knowledge, from *scīre* to know]

science fiction *n* **a** a literary genre that makes imaginative use of scientific knowledge or conjecture **b** (*as modifier*): *a science fiction writer*

Science Museum *n* a museum in London, originating from 1852 and given its present name and site in 1899: contains collections relating to the history of science, technology, and industry

science park *n* an area usually linked with a university where scientific research and commercial development are carried on in cooperation

scienter (saɪˈɛntə) *adv law* knowingly; wilfully [from Latin]

sciential (saɪˈɛnʃəl) *adj* **1** of or relating to science **2** skilful or knowledgeable

scientific (ˌsaɪənˈtɪfɪk) *adj* **1** (*prenominal*) of, relating to, derived from, or used in science: *scientific equipment* **2** (*prenominal*) occupied in science: *scientific manpower* **3** conforming with the principles or methods used in science > **ˌscienˈtifically** *adv*

scientism (ˈsaɪənˌtɪzəm) *n* **1** the application of, or belief in, the scientific method **2** the uncritical application of scientific or quasi-scientific methods to inappropriate fields of study or investigation > **ˌscienˈtistic** *adj*

scientist (ˈsaɪəntɪst) *n* a person who studies or practises any of the sciences or who uses scientific methods

Scientology (ˌsaɪənˈtɒlədʒɪ) *n trademark* the philosophy of the Church of Scientology, a nondenominational movement founded in the US in the 1950s, which emphasizes self-knowledge as a means of realizing full spiritual potential [c20: from Latin *scient(ia)* SCIENCE + -LOGY] > **ˌScienˈtologist** *n*

sci-fi (ˈsaɪˌfaɪ) *n* short for **science fiction**

scilicet (ˈsɪlɪˌsɛt) *adv* namely; that is: used esp in explaining an obscure text or an ambiguity, or supplying a missing word [Latin: shortened from *scīre licet* it is permitted to know]

scilla (ˈsɪlə) *n* any liliaceous plant of the genus *Scilla*, of Old World temperate regions, having small bell-shaped flowers. See also **squill** (sense 3) [c19: via Latin from Greek *skilla*; compare SQUILL]

Scilly Isles, Scilly Islands (ˈsɪlɪ) or **Scillies** (ˈsɪlɪz) *pl n* a group of about 140 small islands (only five inhabited) off the extreme SW coast of England: tourist centre. Capital: Hugh Town. Pop: 2100 (2003 est). Area: 16 sq km (6 sq miles)

scimitar or rarely **simitar** (ˈsɪmɪtə) *n* an oriental sword with a curved blade broadening towards the point [c16: from Old Italian *scimitarra*, probably from Persian *shimshīr*, of obscure origin]

scintigraphy (ˌsɪnˈtɪɡrəfɪ) *n med* a diagnostic technique using a radioactive tracer and scintillation counter for producing pictures (**scintigrams**) of internal parts of the body [c20: from SCINTI(LLATION) + -GRAPHY]

scintilla (sɪnˈtɪlə) *n* a minute amount; hint, trace, or particle [c17: from Latin: a spark]

scintillate (ˈsɪntɪˌleɪt) *vb* (*mainly intr*) **1** (*also tr*) to give off (sparks); sparkle; twinkle **2** to be animated or brilliant **3** *physics* to give off flashes of light as a result of the impact of particles or photons [c17: from Latin *scintillāre*,

from *scintilla* a spark] > **ˈscintillant** *adj*

scintillating (ˈsɪntɪˌleɪtɪŋ) *adj* **1** sparkling; twinkling **2** animated or brilliant

scintillation (ˌsɪntɪˈleɪʃən) *n* **1** the act of scintillating **2** a spark or flash **3** the twinkling of stars or radio sources, caused by rapid changes in the density of the earth's atmosphere, the interplanetary medium, or the interstellar medium producing uneven refraction of starlight **4** *physics* a flash of light produced when a material scintillates

scintillation counter *n* an instrument for detecting and measuring the intensity of high-energy radiation. It consists of a phosphor with which particles collide producing flashes of light that are detected by a photomultiplier and converted into pulses of electric current that are counted by electronic equipment

sciolism (ˈsaɪəˌlɪzəm) *n rare* the practice of opinionating on subjects of which one has only superficial knowledge [c19: from Late Latin *sciolus* someone with a smattering of knowledge, from Latin *scīre* to know] > **ˈsciolist** *n* > **ˌscioˈlistic** *adj*

scion (ˈsaɪən) *n* **1** a descendant, heir, or young member of a family **2** a shoot or twig of a plant used to form a graft [c14: from Old French *cion*, of Germanic origin; compare Old High German *chīnan* to sprout]

Scipio (ˈskɪpɪˌəʊ, ˈsɪpɪˌəʊ) *n* **1** full name *Publius Cornelius Scipio Africanus Major*. 237–183 BC, Roman general. He commanded the Roman invasion of Carthage in the Second Punic War, defeating Hannibal at Zama (202) **2** full name *Publius Cornelius Scipio Aemilianus Africanus Minor*. ?185–129 BC, Roman statesman and general; the grandson by adoption of Scipio Africanus Major. He commanded an army against Carthage in the last Punic War and razed the city to the ground (146). He became the leader (132) of the opposition in Rome to popular reforms

scirrhus (ˈsɪrəs) *n*, *pl* -**rhi** (-raɪ) or -**rhuses** *pathol* a hard cancerous growth composed of fibrous tissues. Also called: **scirrhous carcinoma** [c17: from New Latin, from Latin *scirros*, from Greek *skirros*, from *skiros* hard] > **scirrhoid** (ˈsɪrɔɪd) *adj*

scission (ˈsɪʃən) *n* the act or an instance of cutting, splitting, or dividing [c15: from Late Latin *scissiō*, from *scindere* to split]

scissor (ˈsɪzə) *n* (*modifier*) of or relating to scissors

scissors (ˈsɪzəz) *pl n* **1** Also called: **pair of scissors** a cutting instrument used for cloth, hair, etc, having two crossed pivoted blades that cut by a shearing action, with ring-shaped handles at one end **2** a wrestling hold in which a wrestler wraps his legs round his opponent's body or head, locks his feet together, and squeezes **3** any gymnastic or athletic feat in which the legs cross and uncross in a scissor-like movement [c14 *sisoures*, from Old French *cisoires*, from Vulgar Latin *cīsōria* (unattested), ultimately from Latin *caedere* to cut; see CHISEL]

scissors kick *n* a type of swimming kick used esp in the sidestroke, in which one leg is moved forward and the other bent back and they are then brought together again in a scissor-like action

sciurine (ˈsaɪjʊrɪn, -ˌraɪn) *adj* of, relating to, or belonging to the *Sciuridae*, a family of rodents inhabiting most parts of the world except Australia and southern South America: includes squirrels, marmots, and chipmunks [c19: from Latin *sciūrus*, from Greek *skiouros* squirrel, from *skia* a shadow + *oura* a tail]

sclera (ˈsklɪərə) *n* the firm white fibrous membrane that forms the outer covering of the eyeball [c19: from New Latin, from Greek *sklēros* hard] > **scleritis** (sklɪəˈraɪtɪs) or **sclerotitis** (ˌsklɪərəʊˈtaɪtɪs) *n*

sclerenchyma (sklɪəˈrɛŋkɪmə) *n* a supporting tissue in plants consisting of dead cells with very thick lignified walls [c19: from SCLERO- + PARENCHYMA]

sclero- or before a vowel **scler-** *combining form* **1** indicating hardness: *sclerosis* **2** of or relating to the sclera: *sclerotomy* [from Greek *sklēros* hard]

scleroderma (ˌsklɪərəʊˈdɜːmə), **sclerodermia** (ˌsklɪərəʊˈdɜːmɪə) or **scleriasis** (sklɪˈraɪəsɪs) *n* a chronic progressive disease most common among women, characterized by a local or diffuse thickening and hardening of the skin [C19: from New Latin *sclerōdermus*, from Greek, from *sklēros* hard + *derma* skin]

scleroma (sklɪəˈrəʊmə) *n*, *pl* **-mata** (-ˈmətə) *or* **-mas** *pathol* any small area of abnormally hard tissue, esp in a mucous membrane [C17: from New Latin, from Greek, from *sklēroun* to harden, from *sklēros* hard]

scleroprotein (ˌsklɪərəʊˈprəʊtiːn) *n* any of a group of insoluble stable proteins such as keratin, elastin, and collagen that occur in skeletal and connective tissues. Also called: **albuminoid**

sclerosis (sklɪəˈrəʊsɪs) *n*, *pl* **-ses** (-siːz) **1** *pathol* a hardening or thickening of organs, tissues, or vessels from chronic inflammation, abnormal growth of fibrous tissue, or degeneration of the myelin sheath of nerve fibres, or (esp on the inner walls of arteries) deposition of fatty plaques **2** the hardening of a plant cell wall or tissue by the deposition of lignin [C14: via Medieval Latin from Greek *sklērōsis* a hardening]

sclerotic (sklɪəˈrɒtɪk) *adj* **1** of or relating to the sclera **2** of, relating to, or having sclerosis [C16: from Medieval Latin *sclerōticus*, from Greek; see SCLEROMA]

sclerous (ˈsklɪərəs) *adj* *anatomy*, *pathol* hard; bony; indurated [C19: from Greek *sklēros* hard]

SCM *abbreviation* (in Britain) **1** State Certified Midwife **2** Student Christian Movement

scody (ˈskəʊdɪ) *adj* *NZ informal* unkempt; dirty: *they lived in a scody student flat*

scoff[1] (skɒf) *vb* **1** (*intr*; often foll by *at*) to speak contemptuously (about); express derision (for); mock **2** (*tr*) *obsolete* to regard with derision ▷ *n* **3** an expression of derision **4** an object of derision [C14: probably from Scandinavian; compare Old Frisian *skof* mockery, Danish *skof*, *skuf* jest] > **ˈscoffer** *n* > **ˈscoffing** *adj*

scoff[2] (skɒf) *informal*, *chiefly Brit* ▷ *vb* **1** to eat (food) fast and greedily; devour ▷ *n* **2** food or rations [C19: variant of *scaff* food; related to Afrikaans, Dutch *schoft* quarter of the day, one of the four daily meals]

Scofield (ˈskəʊfiːld) *n* (**David**) **Paul**. (1922–2008), English stage and film actor

scold (skəʊld) *vb* **1** to find fault with or reprimand (a person) harshly; chide **2** (*intr*) to use harsh or abusive language ▷ *n* **3** a person, esp a woman, who constantly finds fault [C13: from Old Norse SKALD] > **ˈscolder** *n* > **ˈscolding** *n*

scoliosis (ˌskɒlɪˈəʊsɪs) *n* *pathol* an abnormal lateral curvature of the spine, of congenital origin or caused by trauma or disease of the vertebrae or hipbones [C18: from New Latin, from Greek: a curving, from *skolios* bent] > **scoliotic** (ˌskɒlɪˈɒtɪk) *adj*

scollop (ˈskɒləp) *n*, *vb* a variant of **scallop**

scombroid (ˈskɒmbrɔɪd) *adj* **1** of, relating to, or belonging to the *Scombroidea*, a suborder of marine spiny-finned fishes having a spindle-shaped body and a forked powerful tail: includes the mackerels, tunnies, bonitos, swordfish, and sailfish ▷ *n* **2** any fish belonging to the suborder *Scombroidea* [C19: from Greek *skombros* a mackerel; see -OID]

sconce[1] (skɒns) *n* **1** a bracket fixed to a wall for holding candles or lights **2** a flat candlestick with a handle [C14: from Old French *esconse* hiding place, lantern, or from Late Latin *sconsa*, from *absconsa* dark lantern]

sconce[2] (skɒns) *n* a small protective fortification, such as an earthwork [C16: from Dutch *schans*, from Middle High German *schanze* bundle of brushwood]

scone *n* (skɒn, skəʊn) a light plain doughy cake made from flour with very little fat, cooked in an oven or (esp originally) on a griddle, usually split open and buttered [C16: Scottish, perhaps from Middle Low German *schonbrot*, Middle Dutch *schoonbrot* fine bread]

Scone (skuːn) *n* a parish in Perth and Kinross, E Scotland, consisting of the two villages of New Scone and Old Scone, formerly the site of the Pictish capital and the stone upon which medieval Scottish kings were crowned. The stone was removed to Westminster Abbey by Edward I in 1296; it was returned to Scotland in 1996 and placed in Edinburgh Castle. Scone Palace was rebuilt in the Neo-Gothic style in the 19th century

scooby doo (ˌskuːbɪ ˈduː) *n* *rhyming slang* a clue: *I don't have a scooby doo what you're talking about* [C20: from *Scooby*

Doo, a cartoon character on children's television]

scoop (skuːp) *n* **1** a utensil used as a shovel or ladle, esp a small shovel with deep sides and a short handle, used for taking up flour, corn, etc **2** a utensil with a long handle and round bowl used for dispensing liquids **3** a utensil with a round bowl and short handle, sometimes with a mechanical device to empty the bowl, for serving ice cream or mashed potato **4** anything that resembles a scoop in action, such as the bucket on a dredge **5** a spoonlike surgical instrument for scraping or extracting foreign matter, etc, from the body **6** the quantity taken up by a scoop **7** the act of scooping, dredging, etc **8** a hollow cavity **9** *slang* a large quick gain, as of money **10** a news story reported in one newspaper before all the others; an exclusive ▷ *vb* (*mainly tr*) **11** (often foll by *up*) to take up and remove (an object or substance) with or as if with a scoop **12** (often foll by *out*) to hollow out with or as if with a scoop **13** to win (a prize, award, or large amount of money) **14** to beat (rival newspapers) in uncovering a news item [C14: via Middle Dutch *schōpe* from Germanic; compare Old High German *scephan* to ladle, German *schöpfen*, *Schaufel* SHOVEL, Dutch *schoep* vessel for baling] > **ˈscooper** *n* > **ˈscoopˌful** *n*

scoot (skuːt) *vb* **1** to go or cause to go quickly or hastily; dart or cause to dart off or away ▷ *n* **2** the act of scooting [C19 probably of Scandinavian origin; compare SHOOT]

scooter (ˈskuːtə) *n* **1** a child's vehicle consisting of a low footboard on wheels, steered by handlebars. It is propelled by pushing one foot against the ground **2** See **motor scooter**

Scopas (ˈskəʊpəs) *n* 4th century BC, Greek sculptor and architect

scope (skəʊp) *n* **1** opportunity for exercising the faculties or abilities; capacity for action: *plenty of scope for improvement* **2** range of view, perception, or grasp; outlook **3** the area covered by an activity, topic, etc; range: *the scope of his thesis was vast* **4** *nautical* slack left in an anchor cable **5** *logic, linguistics* that part of an expression that is governed by a given operator: the scope of the negation in $PV-(q \wedge r)$ is $-(q \wedge r)$ **6** *informal* short for **telescope, microscope, oscilloscope** **7** *archaic* purpose or aim [C16: from Italian *scopo* goal, from Latin *scopus*, from Greek *skopos* target; related to Greek *skopein* to watch]

-scope *n combining form* indicating an instrument for observing, viewing, or detecting: *microscope; stethoscope* [from New Latin *-scopium*, from Greek *-skopion*, from *skopein* to look at] > **-scopic** *adj combining form*

scoping study *n* a preliminary study to define the scope of a project

scopolamine (skəˈpɒləˌmiːn, -mɪn, ˌskəʊpəˈlæmɪn) *n* a colourless viscous liquid alkaloid extracted from certain plants, such as henbane: used in preventing travel sickness and as an anticholinergic, sedative, and truth serum. Formula: $C_{17}H_{21}NO_4$. Also called: hyoscine See also **atropine** [C20 *scopol-* from New Latin *scopolia Japonica* Japanese belladonna (from which the alkaloid is extracted), named after G. A. *Scopoli* (1723–88), Italian naturalist, + AMINE]

Scopus (ˈskəʊpəs) *n* Mount Scopus a mountain in central Israel, east of Jerusalem: a N extension of the Mount of Olives; site of the Hebrew University (1925). Height: 834 m (2736 ft)

-scopy *n combining form* indicating a viewing or observation: *microscopy* [from Greek *-skopia*, from *skopein* to look at]

scorbutic (skɔːˈbjuːtɪk) *adj* of, relating to, or having scurvy [C17: from New Latin *scorbūticus*, from Medieval Latin *scorbūtus*, probably of Germanic origin; compare Old English *sceorf* scurf, Middle Low German *scorbuk* scurvy] > **scorˈbutically** *adv*

scorch (skɔːtʃ) *vb* **1** to burn or become burnt, so as to affect the colour, taste, etc, or to cause or feel pain **2** to wither or parch or cause to wither from exposure to heat **3** (*intr*) *informal* to be very hot: *it is scorching outside* **4** (*tr*) *informal* to criticize harshly ▷ *n* **5** a slight burn **6** a mark caused by the application of too great heat **7** *horticulture* a mark or series of marks on fruit, vegetables, etc, caused by pests or insecticides [C15: probably from Old

Norse *skorpna* to shrivel up] > '**scorching** *adj*

scorched earth policy *n* **1** the policy in warfare of removing or destroying everything that might be useful to an invading enemy, esp by fire **2** *business* a manoeuvre by a company expecting an unwelcome takeover bid in which apparent profitability is greatly reduced by a reversible operation, such as borrowing at an exorbitant interest rate

scorcher ('skɔːtʃə) *n* **1** a person or thing that scorches **2** something severe or caustic **3** *Brit informal* something remarkable

score (skɔː) *n* **1** an evaluative usually numerical record of a competitive game or match **2** the total number of points made by a side or individual in a game or match **3** the act of scoring, esp a point or points **4** **the score** *informal* the actual situation; the true facts: *to know the score* **5** a group or set of twenty: *three score years and ten* **6** (*usually plural*; foll by *of*) a great number; lots: *I have scores of things to do* **7** *music* **a** the written or printed form of a composition in which the instrumental or vocal parts appear on separate staves vertically arranged on large pages (**full score**) or in a condensed version, usually for piano (**short score**) or voices and piano (**vocal score**) **b** the incidental music for a film or play **c** the songs, music, etc, for a stage or film musical **8** a mark or notch, esp one made in keeping a tally **9** an account of amounts due **10** an amount recorded as due **11** a reason or account: *the book was rejected on the score of length* **12** a grievance **13 a** a line marking a division or boundary **b** (*as modifier*): *score line* **14** **over the score** *informal* excessive; unfair **15** **settle a score** *or* **pay off a score** **a** to avenge a wrong **b** to repay a debt ▷ *vb* **16** to gain (a point or points) in a game or contest **17** (*tr*) to make a total score of **18** to keep a record of the score (of) **19** (*tr*) to be worth (a certain amount) in a game **20** (*tr*) to record by making notches in **21** to make (cuts, lines, etc) in or on **22** (*intr*) *slang* to obtain something desired, esp to purchase an illegal drug **23** (*intr*) *slang* (of a man) to be successful in seducing a person **24** (*tr*) **a** to set or arrange (a piece of music) for specific instruments or voices **b** to write the music for (a film, play, etc) **25** to achieve (success or an advantage): *your idea really scored with the boss* [Old English *scora*; related to Old Norse *skor* notch, tally, twenty] > '**scorer** *n*

scoreboard ('skɔːˌbɔːd) *n* *sport* a board for displaying the score of a game or match

scorecard ('skɔːˌkɑːd) *n* **1** a card on which scores are recorded in various games, esp golf **2** a card identifying the players in a sports match, esp cricket or baseball

score off *vb* (*intr, preposition*) to gain an advantage at someone else's expense

scoria ('skɔːrɪə) *n, pl* **-riae** (-rɪˌiː) **1** a rough cindery crust on top of solidified lava flows containing numerous vesicles **2** refuse obtained from smelted ore; slag [c17: from Latin: dross, from Greek *skōria*, from *skōr* excrement]

scorify ('skɔːrɪˌfaɪ) *vb* **-fies, -fying, -fied** to remove (impurities) from metals by forming scoria > ˌscorifi'cation *n* > 'scoriˌfier *n*

scoring ('skɔːrɪŋ) *n* orchestration. See **orchestrate**

scorn (skɔːn) *n* **1** open contempt or disdain for a person or thing; derision **2** an object of contempt or derision ▷ *vb* **3** to treat with contempt or derision **4** (*tr*) to reject with contempt [c12 *schornen*, from Old French *escharnir*, of Germanic origin; compare Old High German *scerōn* to behave rowdily, obsolete Dutch *schern* mockery] > 'scorner *n* > 'scornful *adj* > 'scornfully *adv*

Scorpio ('skɔːpɪˌəʊ) *n* Also called: **the Scorpion** *astrology* the eighth sign of the zodiac, symbol ♏, having a fixed water classification and ruled by the planet Mars and the dwarf planet Pluto. The sun is in this sign between about Oct 23 and Nov 21 [Latin: SCORPION]

scorpion ('skɔːpɪən) *n* **1** any arachnid of the order *Scorpionida*, of warm dry regions, having a segmented body with a long tail terminating in a venomous sting **2** false scorpion any small nonvenomous arachnid of the order *Pseudoscorpionida* (or *Chelonethida*), which superficially resemble scorpions but lack the long tail **3** *Old Testament* a barbed scourge (I Kings 12:11) [c13: via

Old French from Latin *scorpiō*, from Greek *skorpios*, of obscure origin]

Scorpion ('skɔːpɪən) *n* **the Scorpion** the constellation Scorpio, the eighth sign of the zodiac

scorpion fish *n* any of various scorpaenid fishes of the genus *Scorpaena* and related genera, of temperate and tropical seas, having venomous spines on the dorsal and anal fins

Scorsese (skɔːˈseɪzɪ) *n* **Martin.** born 1942, US film director, whose films include *Taxi Driver* (1976), *Raging Bull* (1980), the controversial *The Last Temptation of Christ* (1988), *Casino* (1995), and *Gangs of New York* (2002), and *The Aviator* (2004)

Scot (skɒt) *n* **1** a native or inhabitant of Scotland **2** a member of a tribe of Celtic raiders from the north of Ireland who carried out periodic attacks against the British mainland coast from the 3rd century AD, eventually settling in N Britain during the 5th and 6th centuries

Scot. *abbreviation* **1** Scotch (whisky) **2** Scotland **3** Scottish

scot and lot *n* *Brit history* a municipal tax paid by burgesses and others that came to be regarded as a qualification for the borough franchise in parliamentary elections (until the Reform Act of 1832) [C13 *scot* tax, from Germanic; compare Old Norse *skot*; related to Old French *escot* (French *écot*) + LOT (in the obsolete sense: tax)]

scotch¹ (skɒtʃ) *vb* (*tr*) **1** to put an end to; crush: *bad weather scotched our plans* **2** obsolete to cut or score ▷ *n* **3** archaic a gash; scratch **4** a line marked down, as for hopscotch [c15: of obscure origin]

scotch² (skɒtʃ) *vb* **1** (*tr*) to block, prop, or prevent from moving with or as if with a wedge ▷ *n* **2** a block or wedge to prevent motion [c17: of obscure origin]

Scotch¹ (skɒtʃ) *adj* **1** another word for **Scottish** ▷ *n* **2** the Scots or their language

● USAGE In the north of England and in Scotland, *Scotch*
● is not used outside fixed expressions such as *Scotch*
● *whisky*. The use of *Scotch* for *Scots* or *Scottish* is otherwise
● felt to be incorrect, esp when applied to people

Scotch² (skɒtʃ) *n* Also called: **Scotch whisky** whisky distilled esp from fermented malted barley and made in Scotland

Scotch broth *n* *Brit* a thick soup made from mutton, lamb, or beef stock, vegetables, and pearl barley

Scotch egg *n* *Brit* a hard-boiled egg enclosed in a layer of sausage meat, covered in egg and crumbs, and fried

Scotchman ('skɒtʃmən) *n, pl* **-men** (*regarded as bad usage by the Scots*) another word for **Scotsman**

Scotch mist *n* **1** a heavy wet mist **2** drizzle [c16: so called because it is common on Scottish hills]

Scotch snap *n* *music* a rhythmic pattern consisting of a short note followed by a long one. Also called: **Scotch catch** [c19: so named because it is characteristic of, though not exclusive to, Scottish dance music, esp that for strathspeys]

Scotch terrier *n* another name for **Scottish terrier**

scoter ('skəʊtə) *n, pl* **-ters** *or* **-ter** any sea duck of the genus *Melanitta*, such as *M. nigra* (**common scoter**), of northern regions. The male plumage is black with white patches around the head and eyes [c17: origin unknown]

scot-free *adv, adj* (*predicative*) without harm, loss, or penalty [c16: see SCOT AND LOT]

Scotland ('skɒtlənd) *n* a country that is part of the United Kingdom, occupying the north of Great Britain: the English and Scottish thrones were united under one monarch in 1603 and the parliaments in 1707: a separate Scottish parliament was established in 1999. Scotland consists of the Highlands in the north, the central Lowlands, and hilly uplands in the south; has a deeply indented coastline, about 800 offshore islands (mostly in the west), and many lochs. Capital: Edinburgh. Pop: 5 057 400 (2003 est). Area: 78 768 sq km (30 412 sq miles) Related adjs: **Scots, Caledonian, Scottish**

Scotland Yard *n* the headquarters of the police force of metropolitan London, controlled directly by the British Home Office and hence having certain national responsibilities. Official Name: **New Scotland Yard**

S

scotoma (skɒˈtəʊmə) *n*, *pl* **-mas** or **-mata** (-mətə) **1** *pathol* a blind spot; a permanent or temporary area of depressed or absent vision caused by lesions of the visual system, viewing the sun directly (**eclipse scotoma**), squinting, etc **2** *psychol* a mental blind spot; inability to understand or perceive certain matters [c16: via Medieval Latin from Greek *skotōma* giddiness, from *skotoun* to make dark, from *skotos* darkness]

Scots (skɒts) *adj* **1** of, relating to, or characteristic of Scotland, its people, their English dialects, or their Gaelic language ▷ *n* **2** any of the English dialects spoken or written in Scotland

Scotsman (ˈskɒtsmən) *n*, *pl* **-men** a native or inhabitant of Scotland

Scots pine or **Scotch pine** *n* **1** a coniferous tree, *Pinus sylvestris*, of Europe and W and N Asia, having blue-green needle-like leaves and brown cones with a small prickle on each scale: a valuable timber tree **2** the wood of this tree

Scott (skɒt) *n* **1** Sir George Gilbert. 1811–78, British architect, prominent in the Gothic revival. He restored many churches and cathedrals and designed the Albert Memorial (1863) and St Pancras Station (1865) **2** his grandson, **Sir Giles Gilbert**. 1880–1960, British architect, whose designs include the Anglican cathedral in Liverpool (1904–78) and the new Waterloo Bridge (1939–45) **3** Paul (**Mark**). 1920–78, British novelist, who is best known for the series of novels known as the "Raj Quartet": *The Jewel in the Crown* (1966), *The Day of the Scorpion* (1968), *The Towers of Silence* (1972), and *A Division of the Spoils* (1975). *Staying On* (1977) won the Booker Prize **4** Sir Peter (**Markham**). 1909–89, British naturalist, wildlife artist, and conservationist, noted esp for his paintings of birds. He founded (1946) the Slimbridge refuge for waterfowl in Gloucestershire **5** his father, **Robert Falcon**. 1868–1912, British naval officer and explorer of the Antarctic. He commanded two Antarctic expeditions (1901–04; 1910–12) and reached the South Pole on Jan 18, 1912, shortly after Amundsen; he and the rest of his party died on the return journey **6** Sir Walter. 1771–1832, Scottish romantic novelist and poet. He is remembered chiefly for the "Waverley" historical novels, including *Waverley* (1814), *Rob Roy* (1817), *The Heart of Midlothian* (1818), inspired by Scottish folklore and history, and *Ivanhoe* (1819), *Kenilworth* (1821), *Quentin Durward* (1823), and *Redgauntlet* (1824). His narrative poems include *The Lay of the Last Minstrel* (1805), *Marmion* (1808), and *The Lady of the Lake* (1810)

Scotticism (ˈskɒtɪˌsɪzəm) *n* a Scottish idiom, word, etc

Scottie or **Scotty** (ˈskɒtɪ) *n*, *pl* **-ties 1** See **Scottish terrier 2** *informal* a Scotsman

Scottish (ˈskɒtɪʃ) *adj* of, relating to, or characteristic of Scotland, its people, their Gaelic language, or their English dialect

Scottish Borders *n* a council area in SE Scotland, on the English border: created in 1996, it has the same boundaries as the former Borders Region: it is mainly hilly, with agriculture (esp sheep farming) the chief economic activity. Administrative centre: Newtown St Boswells. Pop: 108 280 (2003 est). Area: 4734 sq km (1827 sq miles)

Scottish Certificate of Education *n* See SCE

Scottish Gaelic *n* the Goidelic language of the Celts of Scotland, spoken in the Highlands and Western Isles

Scottish National Party *n* a political party advocating the independence of Scotland, founded in 1934. Abbreviation: SNP

Scottish terrier *n* a small but sturdy breed of terrier, having short legs and erect ears and tail and a longish, wiry, usually black coat

Scotus (ˈskəʊtəs) *n* See **Duns Scotus**

scoundrel (ˈskaʊndrəl) *n* a worthless or villainous person [c16: of unknown origin]

scour¹ (skaʊə) *vb* **1** to clean or polish (a surface) by washing and rubbing, as with an abrasive cloth **2** to remove dirt from or have the dirt removed from **3** (tr) to clear (a channel) by the force of water; flush **4** (tr) to remove by or as if by rubbing **5** (tr) to cause (livestock) to purge their bowels ▷ *n* **6** the act of scouring **7** the place

scoured, esp by running water **8** something that scours, such as a cleansing agent **9** (*often plural*) prolonged diarrhoea in livestock, esp cattle [c13: via Middle Low German *schüren*, from Old French *escurer*, from Late Latin *excūrāre* to cleanse, from *cūrāre*; see CURE] > ˈscourer *n*

scour² (skaʊə) *vb* **1** to range over (territory), as in making a search **2** to move swiftly or energetically over (territory) [c14: from Old Norse *skūr*]

scourge (skɜːdʒ) *n* **1** a person who harasses, punishes, or causes destruction **2** a means of inflicting punishment or suffering **3** a whip used for inflicting punishment or torture ▷ *vb* (tr) **4** to whip; flog **5** to punish severely [c13: from Anglo-French *escorge*, from Old French *escorgier* (unattested) to lash, from *es-* EX-¹ + Latin *corrigia* whip] > ˈscourger *n*

scourings (ˈskaʊərɪŋz) *pl n* **1** the residue left after cleaning grain **2** residue that remains after scouring

scouse (skaʊs) *n Liverpool dialect* a stew made from left-over meat [c19: shortened from LOBSCOUSE]

Scouse (skaʊs) *Brit informal* ▷ *n* **1** Also called: **Scouser** a person who lives in or comes from Liverpool **2** the dialect spoken by such a person ▷ *adj* **3** of or from Liverpool; Liverpudlian [c20: from SCOUSE]

scout¹ (skaʊt) *n* **1** a person, ship, or aircraft sent out to gain information **2** *military* a person or unit despatched to reconnoitre the position of the enemy **3** the act or an instance of scouting **4** (esp at Oxford University) a college servant **5** *informal* a fellow or companion ▷ *vb* **6** to examine or observe (anything) in order to obtain information **7** (tr; sometimes foll by *out* or *up*) to seek **8** (intr; foll by *about* or *around*) to go in search (for) [c14: from Old French *ascouter* to listen to, from Latin *auscultāre* to AUSCULTATE] > ˈscouter *n*

scout² (skaʊt) *vb archaic* to reject (a person or thing) with contempt [c17: from Old Norse *skūta* derision]

Scout (skaʊt) *n* (*sometimes not capital*) a boy or (in some countries) a girl who is a member of a worldwide movement (the **Scout Association**) founded as the Boy Scouts in England in 1908 by Lord Baden-Powell with the aim of developing character and responsibility > ˈScouting *n*

scow (skaʊ) *n* an unpowered barge used for freight; lighter [c18: via Dutch *schouw* from Low German *schalde*, related to Old Saxon *skaldan* to push (a boat) into the sea]

scowl (skaʊl) *vb* **1** (intr) to contract the brows in a threatening or angry manner ▷ *n* **2** a gloomy or threatening expression [c14: probably from Scandinavian; compare Danish *skule* to look down, Old English *scūlēgede* squint-eyed]

scrabble (ˈskræb³l) *vb* **1** (intr; often foll by *about* or *at*) to scrape (at) or grope (for), as with hands or claws **2** to struggle (with) **3** (intr; often foll by *for*) to struggle to gain possession, esp in a disorderly manner **4** to scribble ▷ *n* **5** the act or an instance of scrabbling **6** a scribble **7** a disorderly struggle [c16: from Middle Dutch *shrabbelen*, frequentative of *shrabben* to scrape]

Scrabble (ˈskræb³l) *n trademark* a board game in which words are formed by placing lettered tiles in a pattern similar to a crossword puzzle

scrag (skræg) *n* **1** a thin or scrawny person or animal **2** the lean end of a neck of veal or mutton **3** *informal* the neck of a human being ▷ *vb* **scrags, scragging, scragged** (tr) **4** *informal* to wring the neck of; throttle [c16: perhaps variant of CRAG; related to Norwegian *skragg*, German *Kragen* collar]

scraggly (ˈskræglɪ) *adj* **-glier, -gliest** untidy or irregular

scraggy (ˈskrægɪ) *adj* **-gier, -giest 1** lean or scrawny **2** rough; unkempt > ˈscraggily *adv* > ˈscragginess *n*

scram¹ (skræm) *vb* **scrams, scramming, scrammed** (intr; often imperative) *informal* to go away hastily; get out [c20: shortened from SCRAMBLE]

scram² (skræm) *n* **1** an emergency shutdown of a nuclear reactor ▷ *vb* **2** (of a nuclear reactor) to shut down or be shut down in an emergency [c20: perhaps from SCRAM¹]

scramble (ˈskræmb³l) *vb* **1** (intr) to climb or crawl, esp by using the hands to aid movement **2** (intr) to proceed hurriedly or in a disorderly fashion **3** (intr; often foll by *for*) to compete with others, esp in a disordered manner

4 (*intr; foll by through*) to deal with hurriedly and unsystematically **5** (*tr*) to throw together in a haphazard manner; jumble **6** (*tr*) to collect in a hurried or disorganized manner **7** (*tr*) to cook (eggs that have been whisked up with milk and seasoning) in a pan containing a little melted butter **8** *military* to order (a crew or aircraft) to take off immediately or (of a crew or aircraft) to take off immediately **9** (*tr*) to render (speech) unintelligible during transmission by means of an electronic scrambler ▷ *n* **10** the act of scrambling **11** a climb over rocks that involves the use of the hands but not ropes, etc **12** a disorderly struggle, esp to gain possession **13** *military* an immediate preparation for action, as of crew, aircraft, etc **14** *Brit* a motorcycle rally in which competitors race across rough open ground [C16: blend of SCRABBLE and RAMP]

scrambler ('skræmblə) *n* an electronic device that renders speech unintelligible during transmission, normal speech being restored at the receiving system

scramjet ('skræm,dʒɛt) *n* **a** a type of ramjet in which the forward motion of the craft forces oxygen to mix with fuel (usually hydrogen) at supersonic speeds within a duct in the engine **b** an aircraft powered by such an engine [C20: from s(*upersonic*) + c(*ombustion*) + RAMJET]

scrannel ('skræn⁰l) *adj archaic* **1** thin **2** harsh [C17: probably from Norwegian *skran* lean. Compare SCRAWNY]

Scranton ('skræntən) *n* an industrial city in NE Pennsylvania: university (1888). Pop: 74 320 (2003 est)

scrap¹ (skræp) *n* **1** a small piece of something larger; fragment **2** an extract from something written **3** a waste material or used articles, esp metal, often collected and reprocessed **b** (*as modifier*): *scrap iron* **4** (*plural*) pieces of discarded food ▷ *vb* **scraps, scrapping, scrapped** (*tr*) **5** to discard as useless [C14: from Old Norse *skrap*; see SCRAPE]

scrap² (skræp) *informal n* **1** a fight or argument ▷ *vb* **scraps, scrapping, scrapped 2** (*intr*) to quarrel or fight [C17: perhaps from SCRAPE]

scrapbook ('skræp,bʊk) *n* a book or album of blank pages in which to mount newspaper cuttings, pictures, etc

scrape (skreɪp) *vb* **1** to move (a rough or sharp object) across (a surface), esp to smooth or clean **2** (*tr; often foll by away or off*) to remove (a layer) by rubbing **3** to produce a harsh or grating sound by rubbing against (an instrument, surface, etc) **4** (*tr*) to injure or damage by rough contact: *to scrape one's knee* **5** (*intr*) to be very economical or sparing in the use (of) (esp in the phrase **scrimp and scrape**) **6** (*intr*) to draw the foot backwards in making a bow ▷ *n* **7** the act of scraping **8** a scraped place **9** a harsh or grating sound **10** *informal* an awkward or embarrassing predicament **11** *informal* a conflict or struggle [Old English *scrapian*; related to Old Norse *skrapa*, Middle Dutch *schrapen*, Middle High German *schraffen*] > 'scraper_n

scraperboard ('skreɪpə,bɔːd) *n* thin card covered with a layer of white china clay and a black top layer of Indian ink, which can be scraped away with a special tool to leave a white line

scrape through (*adverb*) **1** (*intr*) to manage or survive with difficulty **2** to succeed in with difficulty or by a narrow margin

scrape together or **scrape up** *vb* (*tr, adverb*) to collect with difficulty: *to scrape together money for a new car*

scrapheap ('skræp,hiːp) *n* **1** a pile of discarded material **2** on the scrapheap (of people or things) having outlived their usefulness

scrappy ('skræpɪ) *adj* **-pier, -piest** fragmentary; disjointed > 'scrappily_{adv}

scratch (skrætʃ) *vb* **1** to mark or cut (the surface of something) with a rough or sharp instrument **2** (often foll by *at, out, off*, etc) to scrape (the surface of something), as with claws, nails, etc **3** to scrape (the surface of the skin) with the nails, as to relieve itching **4** to chafe or irritate (a surface, esp the skin) **5** to make or cause to make a grating sound; scrape **6** (*tr; sometimes foll by out*) to erase by or as if by scraping **7** (*tr*) to write or draw awkwardly **8** (*intr; sometimes foll*

by *along*) to earn a living, manage, etc, with difficulty **9** to withdraw (an entry) from a race, match, etc ▷ *n* **10** the act of scratching **11** a slight injury **12** a mark made by scratching **13** a slight grating sound **14** (in a handicap sport) a competitor or the status of a competitor who has no allowance or receives a penalty **15 a** the line from which competitors start in a race **b** (*formerly*) a line drawn on the floor of a prize ring at which the contestants stood to begin or continue fighting **16** *billiards, snooker* a lucky shot **17** up to scratch (*usually used with a negative*) *informal* up to standard ▷ *adj* **18** *sport* (of a team) assembled hastily **19** (in a handicap sport) with no allowance or penalty **20** *informal* rough or haphazard [C15: via Old French *escrater* from Germanic; compare Old High German *krazzōn* (German *kratzen*); related to Old French *gratter* to GRATE¹] > 'scratchy_{adj} > 'scratcher_n

scratchcard ('skrætʃ,kɑːd) *n* a ticket that reveals whether or not the holder is eligible for a prize when the surface is removed by scratching

scratch file *n computing* a temporary store for use during the execution of a program

scratching ('skrætʃɪŋ) *n* a percussive effect obtained by rotating a gramophone record manually: a disc-jockey and dub technique

scratch pad *n* **1** *chiefly US & Canadian* a notebook, esp one with detachable leaves **2** *computing* a small semiconductor memory for temporary storage

scratch video *n* the technique or practice of recycling images from films or television to make collages

scrawl (skrɔːl) *vb* **1** to write or draw (signs, words, etc) carelessly or hastily; scribble ▷ *n* **2** careless or scribbled writing, drawing, or marks [C17: perhaps a blend of SPRAWL and CRAWL¹] > 'scrawly_{adj}

scrawny ('skrɔːnɪ) *adj* **scrawnier, scrawniest 1** very thin and bony; scraggy **2** meagre or stunted [C19: variant of dialect *scranny*; see SCRANNEL] > 'scrawnily_{adv} > 'scrawniness_n

scream (skriːm) *vb* **1** to utter or emit (a sharp piercing cry or similar sound or sounds), esp as of fear, pain, etc **2** (*intr*) to laugh wildly **3** (*intr*) to speak, shout, or behave in a wild or impassioned manner **4** (*tr*) to bring (oneself) into a specified state by screaming: *she screamed herself hoarse* **5** (*intr*) to be extremely conspicuous: *these orange curtains scream, you need more restful colours in a bedroom* ▷ *n* **6** a sharp piercing cry or sound, esp one denoting fear or pain **7** *informal* a person or thing that causes great amusement [C13: from Germanic; compare Middle Dutch *schreem*, West Frisian *skrieme* to weep]

screamer ('skriːmə) *n* **1** a person or thing that screams **2** any goose-like aquatic bird, such as *Chauna torquata* (**crested screamer**), of the family *Anhimidae* of tropical and subtropical South America: order *Anseriformes* (ducks, geese, etc) **3** someone or something that raises screams of laughter or astonishment **4** *US & Canadian slang* a sensational headline **5** *Austral slang* a person or thing that is excellent of its kind

scree (skriː) *n* an accumulation of weathered rock fragments at the foot of a cliff or hillside, often forming a sloping heap [Old English *scrithan* to slip; related to Old Norse *skritha* to slide, German *schreiten* to walk]

screech¹ (skriːtʃ) *n* **1** a shrill, harsh, or high-pitched sound or cry ▷ *vb* **2** to utter with or produce a screech [C16: variant of earlier *scritch*, of imitative origin] > 'screecher_n > 'screechy_{adj}

screech² (skriːtʃ) *n Canadian* (esp in Newfoundland) a dark rum [perhaps special use of SCREECH¹]

screech owl *n* a small North American owl, *Otus asio*, having ear tufts and a reddish-brown or grey plumage

screed (skriːd) *n* **1** a long or prolonged speech or piece of writing **2** a strip of wood, plaster, or metal placed on a surface to act as a guide to the thickness of the cement or plaster coat to be applied **3** a mixture of cement, sand, and water applied to a concrete slab, etc, to give a smooth surface finish [C14: probably variant of Old English *scrēade* SHRED]

screen (skriːn) *n* **1** a light movable frame, panel, or partition serving to shelter, divide, hide, etc **2** anything that serves to shelter, protect, or conceal **3** a frame

S

containing a mesh that is placed over a window or opening to keep out insects **4** a decorated partition, esp in a church around the choir **5** a sieve **6** the wide end of a cathode-ray tube, esp in a television set, on which a visible image is formed **7** a white or silvered surface, usually fabric, placed in front of a projector to receive the enlarged image of a film or of slides **8** the screen the film industry or films collectively **9** *photog* a plate of ground glass in some types of camera on which the image of a subject is focused before being photographed **10** men or ships deployed around and ahead of a larger military formation to warn of attack or protect from a specific threat **11** *electronics* See **screen grid** ▷ *vb* (*tr*) **12** (sometimes foll by *off*) to shelter, protect, or conceal **13** to sieve or sort **14** to test or check (an individual or group) so as to determine suitability for a task, etc **15** to examine for the presence of a disease, weapons, etc **16** to provide with a screen or screens **17** to project (a film) onto a screen, esp for public viewing [C15: from Old French *escren* (French *écran*); related to Old High German *skrank*, German *Schrank* cupboard] ▷ **'screenable** *adj* ▷ **'screener** *n* ▷ **'screen₁ful** *n*

screenager ('skriːnˌeɪdʒə) *n informal* a teenager who is dully conversant with and skilled in the use of computers and other electronic devices

screen grid *n electronics* an electrode placed between the control grid and anode of a valve and having a fixed positive potential relative to the grid. It acts as an electrostatic shield preventing capacitive coupling between grid and anode, thus increasing the stability of the device. Sometimes shortened to **screen**

screenings ('skriːnɪŋz) *pl n* refuse separated by sifting

screening test *n* a simple test performed on a large number of people to identify those who have or are likely to develop a specified disease

screenplay ('skriːnˌpleɪ) *n* the script for a film, including instructions for sets and camera work

screen process *n* a method of printing using a fine mesh of silk, nylon, etc, treated with an impermeable coating except in the areas through which ink is subsequently forced onto the paper behind. Also called: **silk-screen printing**

screensaver ('skriːnˌseɪvə) *n* a computer program that reduces screen damage resulting from an unchanging display when a computer is switched on but not in use by blanking the screen or generating moving patterns, etc

screenshot ('skriːnˌʃɒt) *n* an image created by copying part or all of the display on a computer screen at a particular moment, for example in order to demonstrate the use of a piece of software

screenwriter ('skriːnˌraɪtə) *n* a person who writes screenplays

screw (skruː) *n* **1** a device used for fastening materials together, consisting of a threaded and usually tapered shank that has a slotted head by which it may be rotated so as to cut its own thread as it bores through the material **2** Also called: **screw-bolt** a threaded cylindrical rod that engages with a similarly threaded cylindrical hole; bolt **3** a thread in a cylindrical hole corresponding with that on the bolt or screw with which it is designed to engage **4** anything resembling a screw in shape or spiral form **5** a twisting movement of or resembling that of a screw **6** Also called: **screw-back** *billiards, snooker* a stroke in which the cue ball recoils or moves backward after striking the object ball, made by striking the cue ball below its centre **7** another name for **propeller** (sense 1) **8** *slang* a prison guard **9** *Brit slang* salary, wages, or earnings **10** *Brit* a small amount of salt, tobacco, etc, in a twist of paper **11** *slang* a person who is mean with money **12** *slang* an old, unsound, or worthless horse **13** (*often plural*) *slang* force or compulsion (esp in the phrase **put the screws on**) **14** *slang* sexual intercourse **15** **have a screw loose** *informal* to be insane ▷ *vb* **16** (*tr*) to rotate (a screw or bolt) so as to drive it into or draw it out of a material **17** (*tr*) to cut a screw thread in (a rod or hole) with a tap or die or on a lathe **18** to screw or turn to turn in the manner of a screw **19** (*tr*) to attach or fasten with a screw or screws **20** (*tr*) *informal* to

take advantage of; cheat **21** (*tr*; often foll by *up*) to distort or contort: *he screwed his face into a scowl* **22** (*tr*, often foll by *from* or *out of*) to coerce or force out of; extort **23** *slang* to have sexual intercourse (with) **24** (*tr*) *slang* to burgle **25** **have one's head screwed on** *or* **have one's head screwed on the right way** *informal* to be wise or sensible ▷ See also **screw up** [C15: from French *escroe*, from Medieval Latin *scrōfa* screw, from Latin: sow, presumably because the thread of the screw is like the spiral of the sow's tail] ▷ **'screwer** *n*

screwball ('skruːˌbɔːl) *slang, chiefly US & Canadian* ▷ *n* **1** an odd or eccentric person ▷ *adj* **2** odd; zany; eccentric

screwdriver ('skruːˌdraɪvə) *n* **1** a tool used for turning screws, usually having a handle of wood, plastic, etc, and a steel shank with a flattened square-cut tip that fits into a slot in the head of the screw **2** an alcoholic beverage consisting of orange juice and vodka

screwed (skruːd) *adj* **1** fastened by a screw or screws **2** having spiral grooves like a screw; threaded **3** twisted or distorted **4** *Brit* a slang word for **drunk**

screw eye *n* a wood screw with its shank bent into a ring

screw pine *n* any of various pandanaceous plants of the Old World tropical genus *Pandanus*, having a spiral mass of pineapple-like leaves and heavy conelike fruits

screw propeller *n* an early form of ship's propeller in which an Archimedes' screw is used to produce thrust by accelerating a flow of water

screw top *n* **1** a lid with a threaded rim that is turned on the corresponding thread on the neck of a bottle or container to close it securely **2** a bottle or container having such a lid ▷ **'screw-ˌtop** *or* **'screw-ˌtopped** *adj*

screw up *vb* (*tr, adverb*) **1** to twist out of shape or distort **2** to summon up or call upon: *to screw up one's courage* **3** (*also intr*) *informal* to mishandle or make a mess (of)

screwy ('skruːɪ) *adj* **screwier, screwiest** *informal* odd, crazy, or eccentric

Scriabin *or* **Skryabin** ('skrɪəbɪn; *Russian* 'skrjabin) *n* **Aleksandr Nikolayevich** (alɪk'sandr nika'lajɪvitʃ). 1872–1915, Russian composer, whose works came increasingly to express his theosophic beliefs. He wrote many piano works; his orchestral compositions include *Prometheus* (1911)

scribble ('skrɪbəl) *vb* **1** to write or draw in a hasty or illegible manner **2** to make meaningless or illegible marks (on) **3** *derogatory or facetious* to write poetry, novels, etc ▷ *n* **4** hasty careless writing or drawing **5** meaningless or illegible marks [C15: from Medieval Latin *scrībillāre* to write hastily, from Latin *scrībere* to write] ▷ **'scribbly** *adj* ▷ **'scribbler** *n*

scribe (skraɪb) *n* **1** a person who copies documents, esp a person who made handwritten copies before the invention of printing **2** a clerk or public copyist **3** *Old Testament* a recognized scholar and teacher of the Jewish Law ▷ *vb* **4** to score a line on (a surface) with a pointed instrument, as in metalworking [(in the senses: writer, etc) C14: from Latin *scrība* clerk, from *scrībere* to write; C17 (vb): perhaps from INSCRIBE] ▷ **'scribal** *adj*

Scribe (French skrib) *n* **Augustin Eugène** (ogystɛ øʒɛn). 1791–1861, French author or coauthor of over 350 vaudevilles, comedies, and libretti for light opera

scriber ('skraɪbə) *n* a pointed steel tool used to score materials as a guide to cutting, etc. Also called: **scribe**

scrim (skrɪm) *n* an open-weave muslin or hessian fabric, used in upholstery, lining, building, and in the theatre to create the illusion of a solid wall or to suggest haziness, etc, according to the lighting [C18: origin unknown]

scrimmage ('skrɪmɪdʒ) *n* **1** a rough or disorderly struggle **2** *American football* the clash of opposing linemen at every down ▷ *vb* **3** (*intr*) to engage in a scrimmage **4** (*tr*) to put (the ball) into a scrimmage [C15: from earlier *scrimish*, variant of SKIRMISH] ▷ **'scrimmager** *n*

scrimp (skrɪmp) *vb* **1** (when *intr*, sometimes foll by *on*) to be very economical or sparing in the use (of) (esp in the phrase **scrimp and save**) **2** (*tr*) to treat meanly: *he is scrimping his children* [C18: Scottish, origin unknown] ▷ **'scrimpy** *adj* ▷ **'scrimpiness** *n*

scrimshank ('skrɪmˌʃæŋk) vb (intr) Brit military slang to shirk work [c19: of unknown origin]

scrimshaw ('skrɪmˌʃɔ:) n 1 the art of decorating or carving shells, ivory, etc, done by sailors as a leisure activity 2 an article made in this manner [c19: origin uncertain, perhaps after a surname]

scrip¹ (skrɪp) n 1 a written certificate, list, etc 2 a small scrap, esp of paper with writing on it 3 finance a a certificate representing a claim to part of a share of stock b the shares allocated in a bonus issue [c18: in some senses, probably from SCRIPT; otherwise, short for subscription receipt]

scrip² (skrɪp) or **script** n informal a medical prescription [c20: short for PRESCRIPTION]

script (skrɪpt) n 1 handwriting as distinguished from print, esp cursive writing 2 the letters, characters, or figures used in writing by hand 3 any system or style of writing 4 written copy for the use of performers in films and plays 5 law an original or principal document 6 any of various typefaces that imitate handwriting 7 computing a series of instructions that is executed by a computer program 8 an answer paper in an examination ▷ vb 9 (tr) to write a script for [c14: from Latin scriptum something written, from scrībere to write]

script kiddie n slang a child or teenager who gains illegal access to computer systems, often by using hacking programs downloaded from the internet

scriptorium (skrɪp'tɔ:rɪəm) n, pl -riums or -ria (-rɪə) a room, esp in a monastery, set apart for the writing or copying of manuscripts [from Medieval Latin]

scripture ('skrɪptʃə) n a sacred, solemn, or authoritative book or piece of writing [c13: from Latin scriptūra written material, from scrībere to write] > 'scriptural adj > 'scripturally adv

Scripture ('skrɪptʃə) n 1 Also called: Holy Scripture, Holy Writ, the Scriptures Christianity the Old and New Testaments 2 any book or body of writings, esp when regarded as sacred by a particular religious group

scriptwriter ('skrɪptˌraɪtə) n a person who prepares scripts, esp for a film > 'script,writing n

scrivener ('skrɪvnə) n archaic 1 a person who writes out deeds, letters, etc; copyist 2 a notary [c14: from scrivein clerk, from Old French escrivain, ultimately from Latin scrība SCRIBE]

scrod (skrɒd) n US a young cod or haddock, esp one split and prepared for cooking [c19: perhaps from obsolete Dutch schrood, from Middle Dutch schrode SHRED (n); the name perhaps refers to the method of preparing the fish for cooking]

scrofula ('skrɒfjʊlə) n pathol (no longer in technical use) tuberculosis of the lymphatic glands. Also called (formerly): the king's evil [c14: from Medieval Latin, from Late Latin scrōfulae swollen glands in the neck, literally: little sows (sows were thought to be particularly prone to the disease), from Latin scrōfa sow] > 'scrofulous adj > 'scrofulously adv > 'scrofulousness n

scroggin ('skrɒgɪn) n NZ informal a tramper's home-made high-calorie sweetmeat

scroll (skrəʊl) n 1 a roll of parchment, paper, etc, usually inscribed with writing 2 an ancient book in the form of a roll of parchment, papyrus, etc 3 a decorative carving or moulding resembling a scroll ▷ vb 4 (tr) to saw into scrolls 5 to roll up like a scroll 6 computing to move (text) from right to left or up and down on a screen in order to view text that cannot be contained within a single display image [c15 scrowle, from scrowe, from Old French escroe scrap of parchment, but also influenced by ROLL]

scroll saw n a saw with a narrow blade for cutting intricate ornamental curves in wood

scrollwork ('skrəʊl,wɜːk) n ornamental work in scroll-like patterns, esp when done with a scroll saw

Scrooge (skru:dʒ) n a mean or miserly person [c19: after a character in Dickens' story A Christmas Carol (1843)]

scrophulariaceous (ˌskrɒfjʊ,lɛərɪ'eɪʃəs) adj of, relating to, or belonging to the Scrophulariaceae, a family of plants including figwort, snapdragon, foxglove, toadflax, speedwell, and mullein [c19: from New Latin (herba) scrophularia scrofula (plant), from the use of such plants in treating scrofula]

scrotum ('skrəʊtəm) n, pl -ta (-tə) or -tums the pouch of skin containing the testes in most mammals [c16: from Latin] > 'scrotal adj

scrounge (skraʊndʒ) vb informal 1 (when intr, sometimes foll by around) to search in order to acquire (something) without cost 2 to obtain or seek to obtain (something) by cadging or begging [c20: variant of dialect scrunge to steal, of obscure origin] > 'scrounger n

scrub¹ (skrʌb) vb scrubs, scrubbing, scrubbed 1 to rub (a surface) hard, with or as if with a brush, soap, and water, in order to clean it 2 to remove (dirt), esp by rubbing with a brush and water 3 (intr; foll by up) (of a surgeon) to wash the hands and arms thoroughly before operating 4 (tr) to purify (a vapour or gas) by removing impurities 5 (tr) informal to delete or cancel ▷ n 6 the act of or an instance of scrubbing [c14: from Middle Low German schrubben, or Middle Dutch schrobben]

scrub² (skrʌb) n 1 a vegetation consisting of stunted trees, bushes, and other plants growing in an arid area b (as modifier): scrub vegetation 2 an area of arid land covered with such vegetation 3 a an animal of inferior breeding or condition b (as modifier): a scrub bull 4 a small or insignificant person 5 anything stunted or inferior 6 sport, US & Canadian a player not in the first team 7 the scrub Austral informal a remote place, esp one where contact with people can be avoided ▷ adj prenominal 8 small, stunted, or inferior 9 sport, US & Canadian a (of a player) not in the first team b (of a team) composed of such players [c16: variation of SHRUB]

scrubber ('skrʌbə) n 1 a person or thing that scrubs 2 an apparatus for purifying a gas 3 Brit & Austral derogatory, slang a promiscuous woman

scrubby ('skrʌbɪ) adj -bier, -biest 1 covered with or consisting of scrub 2 (of trees or vegetation) stunted in growth 3 Brit informal messy

scrubland ('skrʌb,lænd) n an area of scrub vegetation

scrubs (skrʌbs) pl n the hygienic clothing worn by surgeons and other operating theatre staff during an operation

scrub turkey n another name for **megapode**

scrub typhus n an acute febrile disease characterized by severe headache, skin rash, chills, and swelling of the lymph nodes, caused by the bite of mites infected with the microorganism Rickettsia tsutsugamushi: occurs mainly in Asia, Australia, and the islands of the western Pacific

scruff¹ (skrʌf) n the nape of the neck (esp in the phrase **by the scruff of the neck**) [c18: variant of scuft, perhaps from Old Norse skoft hair; related to Old High German scuft]

scruff² (skrʌf) n informal 1 an untidy scruffy person 2 a disreputable person, ruffian

scruffy ('skrʌfɪ) adj scruffier, scruffiest unkempt or shabby

scrum (skrʌm) n 1 rugby the act or method of restarting play after an infringement when the two opposing packs of forwards group together with heads down and arms interlocked and push to gain ground while the scrum half throws the ball in and the hookers attempt to scoop it out to their own team. A scrum is usually called by the referee (**set scrum**) but may be formed spontaneously (**loose scrum**) 2 informal a disorderly struggle ▷ vb scrums, scrumming, scrummed 3 (intr; usually foll by down) rugby to form a scrum [c19: shortened from SCRUMMAGE]

scrum half n rugby 1 a player who puts in the ball at scrums and tries to get it away to his three-quarter backs 2 this position in a team

scrummage ('skrʌmɪdʒ) n, vb 1 rugby another word for **scrum** 2 a variant of **scrimmage** [c19: variant of SCRIMMAGE]

scrump (skrʌmp) vb dialect to steal (apples) from an orchard or garden [dialect variant of SCRIMP]

scrumptious ('skrʌmpʃəs) adj informal very pleasing; delicious [c19: probably changed from SUMPTUOUS] > 'scrumptiously adv

scrumpy ('skrʌmpɪ) n a rough dry cider, brewed esp in the West Country [from scrump, variant of SCRIMP (in obsolete sense: withered), referring to the apples used]

scrunch (skrʌntʃ) vb 1 to crumple, crush, or crunch or to be crumpled, crushed, or crunched ▷ *n* **2** the act or sound of scrunching [C19: variant of CRUNCH]

scruncheon *or* **scrunchion** ('skrʌntʃən) *n Canadian* (in Newfoundland) a small crisp piece of fried pork fat [origin unknown]

scrunchie ('skrʌntʃɪ) *n* a loop of elastic covered loosely with fabric, used to hold the hair in a ponytail, etc

scruple ('skruːpəl) *n* **1** (*often plural*) a doubt or hesitation as to what is morally right in a certain situation **2** *archaic* a very small amount **3** a unit of weight equal to 20 grains (1.296 grams) ▷ *vb* **4** (*obsolete when tr*) to have doubts (about), esp for a moral reason [C16: from Latin *scrūpulus* a small weight, from *scrūpus* rough stone]

scrupulous ('skruːpjʊləs) *adj* **1** characterized by careful observation of what is morally right **2** very careful or precise [C15: from Latin *scrūpulōsus* punctilious] > **'scrupulously** *adv* > **'scrupulousness** *n*

scrutineer (ˌskruːtɪ'nɪə) *n* a person who examines, esp one who scrutinizes the conduct of an election poll

scrutinize *or* **scrutinise** ('skruːtɪˌnaɪz) *vb* (*tr*) to examine carefully or in minute detail > **'scruti,nizer** *or* **'scruti,niser** *n*

scrutiny ('skruːtɪnɪ) *n*, *pl* **-nies** **1** close or minute examination **2** a searching look **3** (in the early Christian Church) a formal testing that catechumens had to undergo before being baptized [C15: from Late Latin *scrūtinium* an investigation, from *scrūtārī* to search (originally referring to rag-and-bone men), from *scrūta* rubbish]

scry (skraɪ) *vb* **scries**, **scrying**, **scried** (*intr*) to divine, esp by crystal gazing [C16: from DESCRY]

scuba ('skjuːbə) *n* an apparatus used in skindiving, consisting of a cylinder or cylinders containing compressed air attached to a breathing apparatus [C20: from the initials of *self-contained underwater breathing apparatus*]

scud (skʌd) *vb* **scuds**, **scudding**, **scudded** **1** (*intr*) (esp of clouds) to move along swiftly and smoothly **2** (*intr*) *nautical* to run before a gale ▷ *n* **3** the act of scudding **4** *meteorol* a formation of low fractostratus clouds driven by a strong wind beneath rain-bearing clouds **b** a sudden shower or gust of wind [C16: probably of Scandinavian origin; related to Norwegian *skudda* to thrust, Swedish *skudda* to shake]

scuff (skʌf) *vb* **1** to scrape or drag (the feet) while walking **2** to rub or scratch (a surface) or (of a surface) to become rubbed or scratched **3** (*tr*) *US* to poke at (something) with the foot ▷ *n* **4** the act or sound of scuffing **5** a rubbed place caused by scuffing **6** a backless slipper [C19: probably of imitative origin]

scuffle ('skʌfəl) *vb* (*intr*) **1** to fight in a disorderly manner **2** to move by shuffling ▷ *n* **3** a disorderly struggle **4** the sound made by scuffling or shuffling [C16: from Scandinavian; compare Swedish *skuff, skuffa* to push]

scull (skʌl) *n* **1** a single oar moved from side to side over the stern of a boat to propel it **2** one of a pair of short-handled oars, both of which are pulled by one oarsman, esp in a racing skiff **3** a racing shell propelled by an oarsman or oarsmen pulling two oars **4** an act, instance, period, or distance of sculling ▷ *vb* **5** to propel (a boat) with a scull [C14: of unknown origin] > **'sculler** *n*

scullery ('skʌlərɪ) *n*, *pl* **-leries** *chiefly Brit* a small room or part of a kitchen where washing up, vegetable preparation, etc is done [C15: from Anglo-Norman *squillerie*, from Old French *escuelerie*, from *escuele* a bowl, from Latin *scutella*, from *scutra* a flat tray]

Scullin ('skʌlɪn) *n* James Henry. 1876–1953, Australian statesman; prime minister of Australia (1929–31)

scullion ('skʌljən) *n* **1** a mean or despicable person **2** *archaic* a servant employed to do rough household work in a kitchen [C15: from Old French *escouillon* cleaning cloth, from *escouve* a broom, from Latin *scōpa* a broom]

sculpt (skʌlpt) *vb* (*intr*) to practise sculpture. Also called: sculp [C19: from French *sculpter*, from Latin *sculpere* to carve]

sculptor ('skʌlptə) *or feminine* **sculptress** *n* a person who practises sculpture

sculpture ('skʌlptʃə) *n* **1** the art of making figures or

designs in relief or the round by carving wood, moulding plaster, etc, or casting metals, etc **2** works or a work made in this way **3** ridges or indentations as on a shell, formed by natural processes ▷ *vb* (*mainly tr*) **4** (*also intr*) to carve, cast, or fashion (stone, bronze, etc) three dimensionally **5** to portray (a person, etc) by means of sculpture **6** to form in the manner of sculpture, esp to shape (landscape) by erosion **7** to decorate with sculpture [C14: from Latin *sculptūra* a carving; see SCULPT] > **'sculptural** *adj*

sculpturesque (ˌskʌlptʃə'rɛsk) *adj* resembling sculpture > ˌsculptur'esquely *adv*

scum (skʌm) *n* **1** a layer of impure matter that forms on the surface of a liquid, often as the result of boiling or fermentation **2** the greenish film of algae and similar vegetation surface of a stagnant pond **3** Also called: dross, scruff the skin of oxides or impurities on the surface of a molten metal **4** waste matter **5** a worthless person or group of people ▷ *vb* **scums**, **scumming**, **scummed** **6** (*tr*) to remove scum from **7** (*intr*) *rare* to form a layer of or become covered with scum [C13: of Germanic origin; related to Old High German *scūm*, Middle Dutch *schūm*, Old French *escume*; see SKIM] > **'scummy** *adj*

scumbag ('skʌmˌbæg) *n slang* an offensive or despicable person [C20: perhaps from earlier US sense: condom, from US slang *scum* semen + *bag*]

scumble ('skʌmbəl) *vb* **1** (in painting and drawing) to soften or blend (an outline or colour) with an upper coat of opaque colour, applied very thinly ▷ *n* **2** the upper layer of colour applied in this way [C18: probably from SCUM]

scuncheon ('skʌntʃən) *n* the inner part of a door jamb or window frame [C15: from Old French *escoinson*, from *coin* angle]

scungy ('skʌndʒɪ) *adj* **-gier**, **-giest** *Austral & NZ informal* miserable; sordid; dirty [C20: of uncertain origin]

scunner ('skʌnə; *Scot* 'skʌnər) *dialect, chiefly Scot* ▷ *vb* **1** (*intr*) to feel aversion **2** (*tr*) to produce a feeling of aversion in ▷ *n* **3** a strong aversion (often in the phrase **take a scunner to**) **4** an object of dislike; nuisance [C14: from Scottish *skunner*, of unknown origin]

Scunthorpe ('skʌnˌθɔːp) *n* a town in E England, in North Lincolnshire unitary authority, Lincolnshire: developed rapidly after the discovery of local iron ore in the late 19th century; iron and steel industries have declined. Pop: 72 660 (2001)

scup (skʌp) *n* a common sparid fish, *Stenotomus chrysops*, of American coastal regions of the Atlantic. Also called: northern porgy [C19: from Narraganset *mishcup*, from *mishe* big + *kuppe* close together; from the form of the scales]

scupper[1] ('skʌpə) *n nautical* a drain or spout allowing water on the deck of a vessel to flow overboard [C15 *skopper*, of uncertain origin; perhaps related to SCOOP]

scupper[2] ('skʌpə) *vb* (*tr*) *Brit* **1** *slang* to overwhelm, ruin, or disable **2** to sink (one's ship) deliberately [C19: of unknown origin]

scurf (skɜːf) *n* **1** another name for **dandruff** **2** flaky or scaly matter adhering to or peeling off a surface [Old English *scurf*; related to Old Norse *skurfõttr* scurfy, Old High German *scorf*, Danish *skurv*] > **'scurfy** *adj*

scurrilous ('skʌrɪləs) *adj* **1** grossly or obscenely abusive or defamatory **2** characterized by gross or obscene humour [C16: from Latin *scurrīlis* derisive, from *scurra* buffoon] > **scurrility** (skə'rɪlɪtɪ) *or* **'scurrilousness** *n* > **'scurrilously** *adv*

scurry ('skʌrɪ) *vb* **-ries**, **-rying**, **-ried** **1** to move about or proceed hurriedly **2** (*intr*) to whirl about ▷ *n*, *pl* **-ries** **3** the act or sound of scurrying **4** a brisk light whirling movement, as of snow [C19: probably shortened from *hurry-scurry*]

scurvy ('skɜːvɪ) *n* **1** a disease caused by a lack of vitamin C, characterized by anaemia, spongy gums, bleeding beneath the skin, and (in infants) malformation of bones and teeth ▷ *adj* **-vier**, **-viest** **2** mean or despicable [C16: see SCURF] > **'scurvily** *adv* > **'scurviness** *n*

scurvy grass *n* any of various plants of the genus

Cochlearia, esp *C. officinalis*, of Europe and North America, formerly used to treat scurvy: family *Brassicaceae* (crucifers)

scut (skʌt) *n* the short tail of animals such as the deer and rabbit [c15: probably of Scandinavian origin; compare Old Norse *skutr* end of a vessel, Icelandic *skott* tail]

Scutari *n* 1 ('sku:tərɪ, sku:'ta:rɪ) the former name of **Üsküdar** 2 (sku'tari) the Italian name for **Shkodër**

scutate ('skju:teɪt) *adj* 1 (of animals) having or covered with large bony or horny plates 2 *botany* shaped like a round shield or buckler [c19: from Latin *scūtātus* armed with a shield, from *scūtum* a shield]

scutcheon ('skʌtʃən) *n* 1 a variant of **escutcheon** 2 any rounded or shield-shaped structure, esp a scute

scutch grass *n* another name for **couch grass** [variant of COUCH GRASS]

scute (skju:t) *n* *zoology* a horny or chitinous plate that makes up part of the exoskeleton in armadillos, turtles, fishes, etc [c14 (the name of a French coin; c19 in zoological sense): from Latin *scūtum* shield]

scutellum (skju:'teləm) *n, pl* **-la** (-lə) *biology* 1 the last of three plates into which the notum of an insect's thorax is divided 2 one of the scales on the tarsus of a bird's leg 3 an outgrowth from a germinating grass seed that probably represents the cotyledon [c18: from New Latin: a little shield, from Latin *scūtum* a shield] > **scutellate** ('skju:tɪˌleɪt, -lɪt) *adj*

scutter ('skʌtə) *vb, n* *Brit* an informal word for **scurry** [c18: probably from SCUTTLE², with -ER¹ as in SCATTER]

scuttle¹ ('skʌt°l) *n* 1 See **coal scuttle** 2 *dialect, chiefly Brit* a shallow basket, esp for carrying vegetables 3 the part of a motor-car body lying immediately behind the bonnet [Old English *scutel* trencher, from Latin *scutella* bowl, diminutive of *scutra* platter; related to Old Norse *skutill*, Old High German *scuzzila*, perhaps to Latin *scūtum* shield]

scuttle² ('skʌt°l) *vb* 1 (*intr*) to run or move about with short hasty steps ▷ *n* 2 a hurried pace or run [c15: perhaps from SCUD, influenced by SHUTTLE]

scuttle³ ('skʌt°l) *vb* 1 (*tr*) *nautical* to cause (a vessel) to sink by opening the seacocks or making holes in the bottom 2 (*tr*) to give up (hopes, plans, etc) ▷ *n* 3 a small hatch or its cover [c15 (n): via Old French from Spanish *escotilla* a small opening, from *escote* opening in a piece of cloth, from *escotar* to cut out]

scuttlebutt ('skʌt°lˌbʌt) *n* *nautical* 1 a drinking fountain 2 (formerly) a cask of drinking water aboard a ship 3 *chiefly US slang* rumour or gossip [c19: from SCUTTLE³ + BUTT⁴]

scutum ('skju:təm) *n, pl* **-ta** (-tə) 1 the middle of three plates into which the notum of an insect's thorax is divided 2 another word for **scute** [Latin: shield]

scuzzy ('skʌzɪ) *adj* **-zier, -ziest** *slang, chiefly US* unkempt, dirty, or squalid [c20: perhaps from *disgusting* or perhaps from a blend of *scum* and *fuzz*]

Scylla ('sɪlə) *n* 1 *Greek myth* a sea nymph transformed into a sea monster believed to drown sailors navigating the Strait of Messina. She was identified with a rock off the Italian coast. See **Charybdis** 2 **between Scylla and Charybdis** in a predicament in which avoidance of either of two dangers means exposure to the other

scythe (saɪð) *n* 1 a manual implement for cutting grass, etc, having a long handle held with both hands and a curved sharpened blade that moves in a plane parallel to the ground ▷ *vb* 2 (*tr*) to cut (grass, etc) with a scythe [Old English *sigthe*; related to Old Norse *sigthr*, Old High German *segansa*]

Scythia ('sɪðɪə) *n* an ancient region of SE Europe and Asia, north of the Black Sea: now part of Ukraine > **'Scythian** *adj, n*

SD *abbreviation* 1 South Dakota 2 Also called: **sd** *statistics* standard deviation

S. Dak. *abbreviation* South Dakota

SDI *abbreviation* Strategic Defense Initiative. See **Star Wars**

SDK *abbreviation* *computing* software development kit

SDLP *abbreviation* (in Northern Ireland) Social Democratic and Labour Party

SDP *abbreviation* Social Democratic Party

SDRs *abbreviation* special drawing rights

SDSL *abbreviation* symmetric digital subscriber line: a telephone line that carries data in the form of digital pulses, but not at the same time as voice messages are being sent

Se *the chemical symbol for* selenium

SE *symbol for* southeast(ern)

sea (si:) *n* 1 a **the sea** the mass of salt water on the earth's surface as differentiated from the land b (*as modifier*): *sea air* 2 (*capital when part of place name*) a one of the smaller areas of ocean: *the Irish Sea* b a large inland area of water: *the Caspian Sea* 3 turbulence or swell, esp of considerable size: *heavy seas* 4 (*capital when part of a name*) *astronomy* any of many huge dry plains on the surface of the moon. See also **mare²** 5 anything resembling the sea in size or apparent limitlessness 6 **at sea** a on the ocean b in a state of confusion 7 **go to sea** to become a sailor 8 **put to sea** *or* **put out to sea** to embark on a sea voyage [Old English *sǣ*; related to Old Norse *sǣr*, Old Frisian *sē*, Gothic *saiws*, Old High German *sēo*]

sea anchor *n* *nautical* any device, such as a bucket or canvas funnel, dragged in the water to keep a vessel heading into the wind or reduce drifting

sea anemone *n* any of various anthozoan coelenterates, esp of the order *Actiniaria*, having a polypoid body with oral rings of tentacles

sea bag *n* a canvas bag, closed by a line threaded through grommets at the top, used by a seaman for his belongings

sea bass (bæs) *n* any of various American coastal percoid fishes of the genus *Centropristes* and related genera, such as *C. striatus* (**black sea bass**), having an elongated body with a long spiny dorsal fin almost divided into two: family *Serranidae*

sea bird *n* a bird such as a gull, that lives on the sea

seaboard ('si:ˌbɔ:d) *n* land bordering on the sea; the seashore

Seaborg ('si:bɔ:g) *n* **Glenn Theodore**. 1912–99, US chemist and nuclear physicist. With E.M. McMillan, he discovered several transuranic elements, including plutonium (1940), curium, and americium (1944), and shared a Nobel prize for chemistry 1951

seaborgium ('si:bɔ:gɪəm) *n* a synthetic transuranic element, synthesized and identified in 1974. Symbol: Sg; atomic no: 106 [c20: named after Glenn *Seaborg* (1912–99), US chemist and nuclear physicist]

seaborne ('si:ˌbɔ:n) *adj* 1 carried on or by the sea 2 transported by ship

sea bream *n* any sparid fish, esp *Pagellus centrodontus*, of European seas, valued as a food fish

sea breeze *n* a wind blowing from the sea to the land, esp during the day when the land surface is warmer

sea change *n* a seemingly magical change, as brought about by the action of the sea [coined by Shakespeare, in Ariel's song "Full Fathom Five" in *The Tempest* (1611)]

seacoast ('si:ˌkəʊst) *n* land bordering on the sea; a coast

seacock ('si:ˌkɒk) *n* *nautical* a valve in the hull of a vessel below the water line for admitting sea water or for pumping out bilge water

sea cow *n* 1 any sirenian mammal, such as a dugong or manatee 2 an archaic name for **walrus**

sea cucumber *n* any echinoderm of the class *Holothuroidea*, having an elongated body covered with a leathery skin and bearing a cluster of tentacles at the oral end. They usually creep on the sea bed or burrow in sand [c17: so named because of its cucumber-like shape]

sea dog *n* an experienced or old sailor

Sea-Doo ('si:ˌdu:) *n* *trademark Canadian* a small self-propelled watercraft for one person

sea eagle *n* any of various fish-eating eagles that live near the sea, esp *Haliaetus albicilla* (**European sea eagle** or **white-tailed eagle**) having a brown plumage and white tail

seafarer ('si:ˌfɛərə) *n* 1 a traveller who goes by sea 2 a less common word for **sailor**

seafaring ('si:ˌfɛərɪŋ) *adj* (*prenominal*) 1 travelling by sea 2 working as a sailor ▷ *n* 3 the act of travelling by sea 4 the career or work of a sailor

seafood ('si:ˌfu:d) *n* edible saltwater fish or shellfish

seafront ('si:ˌfrʌnt) n a built-up area facing the sea

sea-girt adj literary surrounded by the sea

seagoing ('si:ˌgəʊɪŋ) adj intended for or used at sea

sea green n **a** a moderate green colour, sometimes with a bluish or yellowish tinge **b** (as adjective): a sea-green carpet

seagull ('si:ˌgʌl) n **1** a popular name for **gull¹** **2** NZ a casual wharf labourer who is not a trade-union member

Seahenge (ˌsɪːˈhɛndʒ) n a Bronze Age timber circle discovered off the coast of Norfolk in E England. Dating from 2050 BC, it is thought to have been used as a ceremonial site

sea holly n a European umbelliferous plant, Eryngium maritimum, of sandy shores, having spiny bluish-green stems and blue flowers

sea horse n **1** any marine teleost fish of the temperate and tropical genus Hippocampus, having a bony-plated body, a prehensile tail, and a horselike head and swimming in an upright position: family Syngnathidae (pipefishes) **2** an archaic name for the **walrus** **3** a fabled sea creature with the tail of a fish and the front parts of a horse

sea-island cotton n **1** a cotton plant, Gossypium barbadense, of the Sea Islands, widely cultivated for its fine long fibres **2** the fibre of this plant or the material woven from it

Sea Islands pl n a chain of islands in the Atlantic off the coasts of South Carolina, Georgia, and Florida

sea kale n a European coastal plant, Crambe maritima, with broad fleshy leaves and white flowers, cultivated for its edible asparagus-like shoots: family Brassicaceae (crucifers). See **kale¹**

seal¹ (si:l) n **1** a device impressed on a piece of wax, moist clay, etc, fixed to a letter, document, etc, as a mark of authentication **2** a stamp, ring, etc, engraved with a device to form such an impression **3** a substance, esp wax, so placed over an envelope, document, etc, that it must be broken before the object can be opened or used **4** any substance or device used to close or fasten tightly **5** a small amount of water contained in the trap of a drain to prevent the passage of foul smells **6** anything that gives a pledge or confirmation **7** a decorative stamp often sold in aid of charity **8** Also called: seal of confession RC Church the obligation never to reveal anything said by a penitent in confession **9** set one's seal on or set one's seal to **a** to mark with one's sign or seal **b** to endorse ▷ vb (tr) **10** to affix a seal to, as proof of authenticity **11** to stamp with or as if with a seal **12** to approve or authorize **13** (sometimes foll by up) to close or secure with or as if with a seal: to seal one's lips; seal up a letter **14** (foll by off) to enclose (a place) with a fence, wall, etc **15** to decide irrevocably **16** to subject (the outside of meat, etc) to fierce heat so as to retain the juices during cooking **17** to close tightly so as to render airtight or watertight **18** to paint (a porous material) with a nonporous coating **19** Austral & NZ to consolidate (a road surface) with bitumen, tar, etc [C13 seel, from Old French, from Latin sigillum little figure, from signum a sign] ▷ 'sealable adj

seal² (si:l) n **1** any pinniped mammal of the families Otariidae (eared seals) and Phocidae (earless seals) that are aquatic but come on shore to breed **2** sealskin ▷ vb **3** (intr) to hunt for seals [Old English seolh; related to Old Norse selr, Old High German selah, Old Irish selige tortoise] ▷ 'seal-ˌlike adj

sea lane n an established route for ships

sealant ('si:lənt) n **1** any substance, such as wax, used for sealing documents, bottles, etc **2** any of a number of substances used for stopping leaks, waterproofing wood, etc

sea lavender n any of numerous perennial plants of the plumbaginaceous genus Limonium, of temperate salt marshes, having spikes of white, pink, or mauve flowers, several species of which are grown as garden plants

sealed-beam adj (esp of a car headlight) having a lens and prefocused reflector sealed in the lamp vacuum

sealed road n Austral & NZ a road surfaced with bitumen or some other hard material

sea legs pl n informal **1** the ability to maintain one's balance on board ship, esp in rough weather **2** the ability to resist seasickness, esp in rough weather

sealer ('si:lə) n **1** a person or thing that seals **2** (formerly in Britain and currently in the US) an official who examines the accuracy of weights and measures **3** a coating of paint, varnish, etc, applied to a surface to prevent the absorption of subsequent coats

sea level n the level of the surface of the sea with respect to the land, taken to be the mean level between high and low tide, and used as a standard base for measuring heights and depths

sea lily n any of various sessile echinoderms, esp of the genus Ptilocrinus, in which the body consists of a long stalk attached to a hard surface and bearing a central disc with delicate radiating arms: class Crinoidea (crinoids)

sealing wax n a hard material made of shellac, turpentine, and pigment that softens when heated. It is used for sealing documents, parcels, letters, etc

sea lion n any of various large eared seals, such as Zalophus californianus (**Californian sea lion**), of the N Pacific, often used as a performing animal

Sea Lord n (in Britain) either of the two serving naval officers (**First** and **Second Sea Lords**) who sit on the admiralty board of the Ministry of Defence

seal ring n another term for **signet ring**

sealskin ('si:lˌskɪn) n **a** the skin or pelt of a fur seal, esp when dressed with the outer hair removed and the underfur dyed dark brown **b** (as modifier): a sealskin coat

Sealyham terrier ('si:lɪəm) n a short-legged wire-haired breed of terrier with a medium-length white coat [named after Sealyham, village in S Wales, where it was bred in the 19th century]

seam (si:m) n **1** the line along which pieces of fabric are joined, esp by stitching **2** a ridge or line made by joining two edges **3** a stratum of coal, ore, etc **4** a linear indentation, such as a wrinkle or scar **5** (modifier) cricket of or relating to a style of bowling in which the bowler utilizes the stitched seam round the ball in order to make it swing in flight and after touching the ground: a seam bowler **6** bursting at the seams full to overflowing ▷ vb **7** (tr) to join or sew together by or as if by a seam **8** to mark or become marked with or as if with a seam or wrinkle [Old English; related to Old Norse saumr, Old High German soum]

seaman ('si:mən) n, pl -men **1** a rating trained in seamanship as opposed to electrical engineering, etc **2** a man who serves as a sailor **3** a person skilled in seamanship ▷'seaman-ˌlike adj ▷'seamanly adj, adv

seamanship ('si:mənʃɪp) n skill in and knowledge of the work of navigating, maintaining, and operating a vessel

Seami (si:ˈɑːmɪ) n a variant spelling of **Zeami**

sea mile n a unit of distance used in navigation, defined as the length of one minute of arc, measured along the meridian, in the latitude of the position. Its actual length varies slightly with latitude but is about 1853 metres (6080 feet). Symbol: M See also **nautical mile**

seamless ('si:mlɪs) adj **1** (of a garment) having no seams **2** continuous or flowing: seamless output; a seamless performance

sea mouse n any of several large polychaete worms of the genus Aphrodite and related genera, having a broad flattened body covered dorsally with a dense mat of iridescent hairlike chaetae [c16: so called because of its appearance]

seamstress ('sɛmstrɪs) or rarely **sempstress** ('sɛmpstrɪs) n a woman who sews and makes clothes, esp professionally

seamy ('si:mɪ) adj seamier, seamiest showing the least pleasant aspect; sordid ▷'seaminess n

Seanad Éireann ('ʃænəð 'eːrən) n (in the Republic of Ireland) the upper chamber of parliament; the Senate [from Irish, literally: senate of Ireland]

seance or **séance** ('seɪɑ̃ns, -ɑːns) n a meeting at which spiritualists attempt to receive messages from the spirits of the dead [c19: from French, literally: a sitting, from Old French seoir to sit, from Latin sedēre]

sea otter n a large marine otter, Enhydra lutris, of N

Pacific coasts, formerly hunted for its thick dark brown fur

sea pink *n* another name for **thrift** (sense 2)

seaplane ('si:ˌpleɪn) *n* any aircraft that lands on and takes off from water

seaport ('si:ˌpɔːt) *n* **1** a port or harbour accessible to seagoing vessels **2** a town or city located at such a place

SEAQ ('si:ˌæk) *n acronym for* (in Britain) Stock Exchange Automated Quotation: a computerized system that collects and displays the prices and transactions in securities

sear (sɪə) *vb* (*tr*) **1** to scorch or burn the surface of **2** to brand with a hot iron **3** to cause to wither or dry up **4** *rare* to make callous or unfeeling ▷ *adj* **5** *poetic* dried up [Old English *sēarian* to become withered, from *sēar* withered; related to Old High German *sōrēn*, Greek *hauos* dry, Sanskrit *sōsa* drought]

search (sɜːtʃ) *vb* **1** to look through (a place, records, etc) thoroughly in order to find someone or something **2** (*tr*) to examine (a person) for concealed objects by running one's hands over the clothing **3** to look at or examine (something) closely: *to search one's conscience* **4** (*tr*; foll by *out*) to discover by investigation **5** *surgery* to probe (a wound) **6** *computing* to review (a file) to locate specific information **7** *archaic* to penetrate **8 search me** *informal* I don't know ▷ *n* **9** the act or an instance of searching **10** the examination of a vessel by the right of search **11 right of search** *international law* the right possessed by the warships of a belligerent state in time of war to board and search merchant vessels to ascertain whether ship or cargo is liable to seizure [C14: from Old French *cerchier*, from Late Latin *circāre* to go around, from Latin *circus* CIRCLE] ▷ 'searchable *adj* ▷ 'searcher *n*

search engine *n computing* a service provided on the internet enabling users to search for items of interest

search-engine optimization *n* the process of adjusting the content, structure, etc of a website so that it will be displayed prominently by a search engine

searching ('sɜːtʃɪŋ) *adj* keenly penetrating: *a searching look* ▷ 'searchingly *adv*

searchlight ('sɜːtʃˌlaɪt) *n* **1** a device, consisting of a light source and a reflecting surface behind it, that projects a powerful beam of light in a particular direction **2** the beam of light produced by such a device

search party *n* a group of people taking part in an organized search, as for a lost, missing, or wanted person

search warrant *n* a written order issued by a justice of the peace authorizing a constable or other officer to enter and search premises for stolen goods, drugs, etc

Searle (sɜːl) *n* **Ronald (William Fordham)**. born 1920, British cartoonist, best known as the creator of the schoolgirls of St Trinian's

seascape ('si:ˌskeɪp) *n* a sketch, picture, etc, of the sea

sea scorpion *n* any of various northern marine scorpaenoid fishes of the family *Cottidae*, esp *Taurulus bubalis* (**long-spined sea scorpion**). They have a tapering body and a large head covered with bony plates and spines

Sea Scout *n* a Scout belonging to any of a number of Scout troops whose main activities are canoeing, sailing, etc, and who wear sailors' caps as part of their uniform

sea serpent *n* a huge legendary creature of the sea resembling a snake or dragon

sea shanty *n* same as **shanty²**

seashell ('si:ˌʃɛl) *n* the empty shell of a marine mollusc

seashore ('si:ˌʃɔː) *n* **1** land bordering on the sea **2** the land between the marks of high and low water

seasick ('si:ˌsɪk) *adj* suffering from nausea and dizziness caused by the motion of a ship at sea ▷ 'sea,sickness *n*

seaside ('si:ˌsaɪd) *n* **a** any area bordering on the sea, esp one regarded as a resort **b** (*as modifier*): *a seaside hotel*

sea snail *n* any small spiny-finned fish of the family *Liparidae*, esp *Liparis liparis*, of cold seas, having a soft scaleless tadpole-shaped body with the pelvic fins fused into a sucker

sea snake *n* any venomous snake of the family *Hydrophiidae*, of tropical seas, that swims by means of a

laterally compressed oarlike tail

season ('si:zən) *n* **1** one of the four equal periods into which the year is divided by the equinoxes and solstices, resulting from the apparent movement of the sun north and south of the equator during the course of the earth's orbit around it. These periods (spring, summer, autumn, and winter) have their characteristic weather conditions in different regions, and occur at opposite times of the year in the N and S hemispheres **2** a period of the year characterized by particular conditions or activities: *the rainy season* **3** the period during which any particular species of animal, bird, or fish is legally permitted to be caught or killed: *open season on red deer* **4** a period during which a particular entertainment, sport, etc, takes place: *a season at the National Theatre; the football season; the tourist season* **5** any definite or indefinite period **6** any of the major periods into which the ecclesiastical calendar is divided, such as Lent, Advent, or Easter **7 in good season** early enough **8 in season a** (of game) permitted to be caught or killed **b** (of fresh food) readily available **c** Also called: **in heat, on heat** (of some female mammals) sexually receptive **d** appropriate ▷ *vb* **9** (*tr*) to add herbs, salt, pepper, or spice to (food) **10** (*tr*) to add zest to **11** (in the preparation of timber) to undergo or cause to undergo drying **12** (*tr; usually passive*) to make or become mature or experienced: *seasoned troops* **13** (*tr*) to mitigate or temper [C13: from Old French *seson*, from Latin *satiō* a sowing, from *serere* to sow] ▷ **seasoned** *adj* ▷ 'seasoner *n*

seasonable ('si:zənəbəl) *adj* **1** suitable for the season **2** taking place at the appropriate time ▷ 'seasonableness *n* ▷ 'seasonably *adv*

seasonal ('si:zənəl) *adj* of, relating to, or occurring at a certain season or certain seasons of the year: *seasonal labour* ▷ 'seasonally *adv*

seasonal affective disorder *n* a state of depression sometimes experienced by people in winter, thought to be related to lack of sunlight. Abbreviation: **SAD**

seasoning ('si:zənɪŋ) *n* **1** something that enhances the flavour of food, such as salt or herbs **2** another term (not now in technical usage) for **drying** (sense 1)

season ticket *n* a ticket for a series of events, number of journeys, etc, within a limited time, usually obtained at a reduced rate

sea squirt *n* any minute primitive marine animal of the class *Ascidiacea*, most of which are sedentary, having a saclike body with openings through which water enters and leaves

sea swallow *n* a popular name for **tern¹**

seat (si:t) *n* **1** a piece of furniture designed for sitting on, such as a chair or sofa **2** the part of a chair, bench, etc, on which one sits **3** a place to sit, esp one that requires a ticket: *I have two seats for the film tonight* **4** the buttocks **5** the part of a garment covering the buttocks **6** the part or area serving as the base of an object **7** the part or surface on which the base of an object rests **8** the place or centre in which something is located: *a seat of government* **9** a place of abode, esp a country mansion that is or was originally the chief residence of a family **10** a membership or the right to membership in a legislative or similar body **11** *chiefly Brit* a parliamentary constituency **12** the manner in which a rider sits on a horse ▷ *vb* **13** (*tr*) to bring to or place on a seat; cause to sit down **14** (*tr*) to provide with seats **15** (*tr; often passive*) to place or centre: *the ministry is seated in the capital* **16** (*tr*) to set firmly in place **17** (*tr*) to fix or install in a position of power **18** (*intr*) (of garments) to sag in the area covering the buttocks: *your thin skirt has seated badly* [Old English *gesete*; related to Old Norse *sæti*, Old High German *gasāzi*, Middle Dutch *gesaete*]

seat belt *n* **1** Also called: **safety belt** a belt or strap worn in a vehicle to restrain forward motion in the event of a collision **2** a similar belt or strap worn in an aircraft at takeoff and landing and in rough weather

seating ('si:tɪŋ) *n* **1** the act of providing with a seat or seats **2** the provision of seats, as in a theatre, cinema, etc **b** (*as modifier*): *seating arrangements* **3** material used for covering or making seats

Seaton Valley ('si:tən) *n* a region in NE England, in SE

Northumberland: consists of a group of former coal-mining villages

sea trout *n* a silvery marine variety of the brown trout that migrates to fresh water to spawn

Seattle (sɪˈætˤl) *n* a port in W Washington, on the isthmus between Lake Washington and Puget Sound: the largest city in the state and chief commercial centre of the Northwest; two universities. Pop: 569 101 (2003 est)

sea urchin *n* any echinoderm of the class *Echinoidea*, such as *Echinus esculentus* (**edible sea urchin**), typically having a globular body enclosed in a rigid spiny test and occurring in shallow marine waters

sea vegetable *n* an edible seaweed

sea wall *n* a wall or embankment built to prevent encroachment or erosion by the sea or to serve as a breakwater

seaward (ˈsiːwəd) *adv* ▷ *adj* **1** directed or moving towards the sea **2** (esp of a wind) coming from the sea

seaway (ˈsiːˌweɪ) *n* **1** a waterway giving access to an inland port, navigable by ocean-going ships **2** a vessel's progress **3** a rough or heavy sea

seaweed (ˈsiːˌwiːd) *n* any of numerous multicellular marine algae that grow on the seashore, in salt marshes, in brackish water, or submerged in the ocean

seaworthy (ˈsiːˌwɜːðɪ) *adj* in a fit condition or ready for a sea voyage ▷ ˈseaˌworthiness *n*

sebaceous (sɪˈbeɪʃəs) *adj* **1** of or resembling sebum, fat, or tallow; fatty **2** secreting fat or a greasy lubricating substance [c18: from Late Latin *sēbāceus*, from SEBUM]

sebaceous glands *pl n* the small glands in the skin that secrete sebum into hair follicles and onto most of the body surface except the soles of the feet and the palms of the hands

Sebastian (sɪˈbæstjən) *n* **Saint.** died ?288 AD, Christian martyr. According to tradition, he was first shot with arrows and then beaten to death. Feast day: Jan 20

Sebastopol (sɪˈbæstəpəl) *n* the English name for Sevastopol

seborrhoea *or esp US* **seborrhea** (ˌsɛbəˈrɪə) *n* any disease of the skin characterized by excessive secretion of sebum by the sebaceous glands and its accumulation on the skin surface

sebum (ˈsiːbəm) *n* the oily secretion of the sebaceous glands that acts as a lubricant for the hair and skin and provides some protection against bacteria [c19: from New Latin, from Latin: tallow]

sec¹ (sɛk) *adj* **1** (of wines) dry **2** (of champagne) of medium sweetness [c19: from French, from Latin *siccus*]

sec² (sɛk) *n informal* short for **second²**: *wait a sec*

sec³ (sɛk) *abbreviation* secant

SEC *abbreviation* Securities and Exchange Commission

sec. *abbreviation* **1** second (of time) **2** secondary **3** secretary **4** section **5** sector

secant (ˈsiːkənt) *n* **1** (of an angle) a trigonometric function that in a right-angled triangle is the ratio of the length of the hypotenuse to that of the adjacent side; the reciprocal of cosine. Abbreviation: sec **2** a line that intersects a curve [c16: from Latin *secāre* to cut]

secateurs (ˈsɛkətəz, ˌsɛkəˈtɜːz) *pl n chiefly Brit* a small pair of shears for pruning, having a pair of pivoted handles, sprung so that they are normally open, and usually a single cutting blade that closes against a flat surface [c19: plural of French *sécateur*, from Latin *secāre* to cut]

secede (sɪˈsiːd) *vb* (*intr*; often foll by *from*) (of a person, section, etc) to make a formal withdrawal of membership, as from a political alliance, church, organization, etc [c18: from Latin *sēcēdere* to withdraw, from *sē-* apart + *cēdere* to go] ▷ seˈceder *n*

secern (sɪˈsɜːn) *vb* (*tr*) *rare* **1** (of a gland or follicle) to secrete **2** to distinguish or discriminate [c17: from Latin *sēcernere* to separate, from *sē-* apart + *cernere* to distinguish] ▷ seˈcernment *n*

secession (sɪˈsɛʃən) *n* **1** the act of seceding **2** (*often capital*) *chiefly US* the withdrawal in 1860–61 of 11 Southern states from the Union to form the Confederacy, precipitating the American Civil War [c17: from Latin *sēcessiō* a withdrawing, from *sēcēdere* to SECEDE] ▷ seˈcessionist *n, adj*

sech (ʃɛk, sɛtʃ, ˈsɛkˈeɪtʃ) *n* hyperbolic secant; a hyperbolic function that is the reciprocal of cosh

seclude (sɪˈkluːd) *vb* (*tr*) **1** to remove from contact with others **2** to shut off or screen from view [c15: from Latin *sēclūdere* to shut off, from *sē-* + *claudere* to imprison]

secluded (sɪˈkluːdɪd) *adj* **1** kept apart from the company of others: *a secluded life* **2** sheltered; private ▷ seˈcludedly *adv* ▷ seˈcludedness *n*

seclusion (sɪˈkluːʒən) *n* **1** the act of secluding or the state of being secluded **2** a secluded place [c17: from Medieval Latin *sēclūsiō*; see SECLUDE]

second¹ (ˈsɛkənd) *adj* (*usually prenominal*) **1 a** coming directly after the first in numbering or counting order, position, time, etc; being the ordinal number of *two*: often written 2nd **b** (*as noun*): *the second in line* **2** rated, graded, or ranked between the first and third levels **3** alternate: *every second Thursday* **4** additional; extra: *a second opportunity* **5** resembling a person or event from an earlier period of history; unoriginal: *a second Wagner* **6** of lower quality; inferior **7** denoting the lowest but one forward ratio of a gearbox in a motor vehicle **8** *music* relating to or denoting a musical part, voice, or instrument lower in pitch than another part, voice, or instrument (the first): *the second tenors* **9** at second hand by hearsay ▷ *n* **10** *Brit education* an honours degree of the second class, usually further divided into an upper and lower designation. Full term: **second-class honours degree** **11** the lowest but one forward ratio of a gearbox in a motor vehicle **12** (in boxing, duelling, etc) an attendant who looks after a competitor **13** a speech seconding a motion or the person making it **14** *music* the interval between one note and another lying next above or below it in the diatonic scale **15** (*plural*) goods of inferior quality **16** (*plural*) *informal* a second helping of food **17** (*plural*) the second course of a meal ▷ *vb* (*tr*) **18** to give aid or backing to **19** (in boxing, etc) to act as second to (a competitor) **20** to make a speech or otherwise express formal support for (a motion already proposed) ▷ *adv* **21** Also called: **secondly** in the second place ▷ *sentence connector* **22** Also called: **secondly** as the second point: linking what follows with the previous statement [c13: via Old French from Latin *secundus* coming next in order, from *sequī* to follow] ▷ ˈseconder *n*

second² (ˈsɛkənd) *n* **1 a** 1/60 of a minute of time **b** the basic SI unit of time: the duration of 9 192 631 770 periods of radiation corresponding to the transition between two hyperfine levels of the ground state of caesium-133. Symbol: s **2** 1/60 of a minute of angle. Symbol: ″ **3** a very short period of time; moment [c14: from Old French, from Medieval Latin *pars minūta secunda* the second small part (a minute being the first small part of an hour); see SECOND¹]

second³ (sɪˈkɒnd) *vb* (*tr*) *Brit* **1** to transfer (an employee) temporarily to another branch, etc **2** *military* to transfer (an officer) to another post, often retiring him to a staff or nonregimental position [c19: from French *en second* in second rank (or position)] ▷ seˈcondment *n* [c19: from French *en second* in second rank (or position)]

secondary (ˈsɛkəndərɪ, -drɪ) *adj* **1** one grade or step after the first; not primary **2** derived from or depending on what is primary, original, or first: *a secondary source* **3** below the first in rank, importance, etc; not of major importance **4** (*prenominal*) of or relating to the education of young people between the ages of 11 and 18: *secondary education* **5** (of the flight feathers of a bird's wing) growing from the ulna **6 a** being the part of an electric circuit, such as a transformer or induction coil, in which a current is induced by a changing current in a neighbouring coil: *a secondary coil* **b** (of a current) flowing in such a circuit **7** *chem* **a** (of an amine) having only two organic groups attached to a nitrogen atom; containing the group NH **b** (of a salt) derived from a tribasic acid by replacement of two acidic hydrogen atoms with metal atoms or electropositive groups ▷ *n, pl* **-aries 8** a person or thing that is secondary **9** a subordinate, deputy, or inferior **10** a secondary coil, winding, inductance, or current in an electric circuit **11** *ornithol* any of the flight feathers that grow from the ulna of a bird's wing. See **primary** (sense 6) **12** *astronomy* a celestial body that orbits

S

around a specified primary body: *the moon is the secondary of the earth* **13** *American football* **a** the secondary cornerbacks and safeties collectively **b** their area in the field **14** short for **secondary colour** ▷ˈsecondarily *adv* ▷ˈsecondariness *n*

secondary cell *n* an electric cell that can be recharged and can therefore be used to store electrical energy in the form of chemical energy

secondary colour *n* a colour formed by mixing two primary colours

secondary emission *n physics* the emission of electrons (**secondary electrons**) from a solid as a result of bombardment with a beam of electrons, ions, or metastable atoms: used in electron multipliers

secondary picketing *n* the picketing by strikers of a place of work that supplies goods to or distributes goods from their employer

secondary sexual characteristic *n* any of various features distinguishing individuals of different sex but not directly concerned in reproduction. Examples are the antlers of a stag and the beard of a man

second ballot *n* an electoral procedure in which if no candidate emerges as a clear winner in a first ballot, candidates at the bottom of the poll are eliminated and another ballot is held among the remaining candidates

second-best *adj* **1** next to the best **2** come off second best *informal* to be defeated in competition ▷ *n* second best **3** an inferior alternative

second chamber *n* the upper house of a bicameral legislative assembly

second childhood *n* dotage; senility (esp in the phrases **in his, her, etc, second childhood**)

second class *n* **1** the class or grade next in value, quality, etc, to the first ▷ *adj* **second-class** when prenominal **2** of the class or grade next to the best in quality, etc **3** shoddy or inferior **4** of or denoting the class of accommodation in a hotel or on a train, etc, lower in quality and price than first class **5** (in Britain) of or relating to mail that is processed more slowly than first-class mail **6** *education* See **second**¹ (sense 10) ▷ *adv* **7** by second-class mail, transport, etc

second-class citizen *n* a person whose rights and opportunities are treated as less important than those of other people in the same society

Second Coming *or less commonly* **Second Advent** *n* the prophesied return of Christ to earth at the Last Judgment

second cousin *n* the child of a first cousin of either of one's parents

second-degree burn *n pathol* See **burn**¹ (sense 15)

seconde (sɪˈkɒnd; *French* səɡɔ̃d) *n* the second of eight positions from which a parry or attack can be made in fencing [C18: from French *seconde parade* the second parry]

Second Empire *n* **1** the period during which this government functioned (1852–70) **2** the style of furniture and decoration of the Second Empire, reviving the Empire style, but with fussier ornamentation

second fiddle *n informal* **1 a** the second violin in a string quartet or one of the second violins in an orchestra **b** the musical part assigned to such an instrument **2 a** person who has a secondary status

second floor *n Brit* the storey of a building immediately above the first and two floors up from the ground

second generation *n* **1** offspring of parents born in a given country ▷ *modifier* **2** of an improved or refined stage of development in manufacture: *a second-generation robot*

second growth *or* **secondary growth** *n* natural regrowth of a forest after fire, cutting, or some other disturbance

second hand *n* a pointer on the face of a timepiece that indicates the seconds

second-hand *adj* **1** previously owned or used **2** not from an original source or experience (a parry or attack) **3** dealing in or selling goods that are not new: *a second-hand car dealer* ▷ *adv* **4** from a source of previously owned or used goods: *he prefers to buy second-hand* **5** not directly: *he got the news second-hand*

second language *n* **1** a language other than the mother

tongue that a person or community uses for public communication, esp in trade, higher education, and administration **2** a non-native language officially recognized and adopted in a multilingual country as a means of public communication

second lieutenant *n* an officer holding the lowest commissioned rank in the armed forces of certain nations

secondly (ˈsɛkəndlɪ) *adv* another word for second, usually used to precede the second item in a list of topics

second nature *n* a habit, characteristic, etc, not innate but so long practised or acquired as to seem so

second person *n* a grammatical category of pronouns and verbs used when referring to or describing the individual or individuals being addressed

second-rate *adj* **1** not of the highest quality; mediocre **2** second in importance, etc

second reading *n* the second presentation of a bill in a legislative assembly, as to approve its general principles (in Britain), or to discuss a committee's report on it (in the US)

second row *n* (*functioning as singular or plural*) *rugby union* **a** the forwards in the second row of a scrum **b** (*as modifier*): *a second-row forward*

second sight *n* the alleged ability to foresee the future, see actions taking place elsewhere, etc; clairvoyance ▷ˈsecond-ˈsighted *adj*

second string *n* **1** *chiefly Brit* an alternative course of action, etc, intended to come into use should the first fail (esp in the phrase **a second string to one's bow**) ▷ *adj* second-string *chiefly US & Canadian* **2** *sport* being a substitute player

second thought *n* (*usually plural*) a revised opinion or idea on a matter already considered

second wind (wɪnd) *n* **1** the return of the ability to breathe at a comfortable rate, esp following a period of exertion **2** renewed ability to continue in an effort

secrecy (ˈsiːkrɪsɪ) *n, pl* -cies **1** the state or quality of being secret **2** the state of keeping something secret **3** the ability or tendency to keep things secret

secret (ˈsiːkrɪt) *adj* **1** kept hidden or separate from the knowledge of others. Related adj: **cryptic** **2** known only to initiates: *a secret password* **3** hidden from general view or use: *a secret garden* **4** able or tending to keep things private or to oneself **5** operating without the knowledge of outsiders: *a secret society* ▷ *n* **6** something kept or to be kept hidden **7** something unrevealed; mystery **8** an underlying explanation, reason, etc, that is not apparent: *the secret of success* **9** a method, plan, etc, known only to initiates **10** *liturgy* a variable prayer, part of the Mass, said by the celebrant after the offertory and before the preface [C14: via Old French from Latin *sēcrētus* concealed, from *sēcernere* to sift; see SECERN] ▷ˈsecretly *adv*

secret agent *n* a person employed in espionage

secretaire (ˌsɛkrɪˈtɛə) *n* an enclosed writing desk, usually having an upper cabinet section [C19: from French *secrétaire*; see SECRETARY]

secretariat (ˌsɛkrɪˈtɛərɪət) *n* **1 a** an office responsible for the secretarial, clerical, and administrative affairs of a legislative body, executive council, or international organization **b** the staff of such an office **2 a** body of secretaries **3** a secretary's place of work; office **4** the position of a secretary [C19: via French from Medieval Latin *sēcrētāriātus*, from *sēcrētārius* SECRETARY]

secretary (ˈsɛkrətrɪ) *n, pl* -taries **1** a person who handles correspondence, keeps records, and does general clerical work for an individual, organization, etc **2** the official manager of the day-to-day business of a society or board **3** (in Britain) a senior civil servant who assists a government minister **4** (in the US and New Zealand) the head of a government administrative department **5** (in Britain) See **secretary of state** **6** another name for **secretaire** [C14: from Medieval Latin *sēcrētārius*, from Latin *sēcrētum* something hidden; see SECRET] ▷secretarial (ˌsɛkrɪˈtɛərɪəl) *adj* ▷ˈsecretaryship *n*

secretary bird *n* a large African long-legged diurnal bird of prey, *Sagittarius serpentarius*, having a crest and tail of long feathers and feeding chiefly on snakes: family *Sagittariidae*, order *Falconiformes* (hawks, falcons, etc) [C18: so called because its crest resembles a group of quill pens stuck behind the ear]

secretary-general *n*, *pl* secretaries-general a chief administrative official, as of the United Nations

secretary of state *n* **1** (in Britain) the head of any of several government departments **2** (in the US) the head of the government department in charge of foreign affairs (**State Department**)

secrete¹ (sɪˈkriːt) *vb* (of a cell, organ, etc) to synthesize and release (a secretion) [C18: back formation from SECRETION] > seˈcretor *n* > seˈcretory *adj*

secrete² (sɪˈkriːt) *vb* (tr) to put in a hiding place [C18: variant of obsolete *secret* to hide away; see SECRET (*n*)]

secretion (sɪˈkriːʃən) *n* **1** a substance that is released from a cell, esp a glandular cell, and is synthesized in the cell **2** the process involved in producing and releasing such a substance from the cell [C17: from Medieval Latin *sēcrētiō*, from Latin: a separation; see SECERN]

secretive (ˈsiːkrɪtɪv, sɪˈkriːtɪv) *adj* inclined to secrecy; reticent > 'secretively *adv* > 'secretiveness *n*

secret police *n* a police force that operates relatively secretly to check subversion or political dissent

secret Santa *n* **a** a system whereby each member of a group chooses at random another member of the group for whom to buy a Christmas present at an agreed cost, so that each member buys one present and receives one present **b** a person chosen in this way to buy another person's Christmas present

secret service *n* a government agency or department that conducts intelligence or counterintelligence operations

sect (sɛkt) *n* **1** a subdivision of a larger religious group (esp the Christian Church as a whole) the members of which have to some extent diverged from the rest by developing deviating beliefs, practices, etc **2** *often disparaging* **a** a schismatic religious body characterized by an attitude of exclusivity in contrast to the more inclusive religious groups called denominations or Churches **b** a religious group regarded as extreme or heretical **3** a group of people with a common interest, doctrine, etc; faction [C14: from Latin *secta* faction, following, from the stem of *sequī* to follow]

-sect *vb combining form* to cut or divide, esp into a specified number of parts: *trisect* [from Latin *sectus* cut, from *secāre* to cut; see SAW¹]

sectarian (sɛkˈtɛərɪən) *adj* **1** of, belonging or relating to, or characteristic of sects or sectaries **2** adhering to a particular sect, faction, or doctrine **3** narrow-minded, esp as a result of rigid adherence to a particular sect ⊳ *n* **4** a member of a sect or faction, esp one who is bigoted in his adherence to its doctrines or in his intolerance towards other sects, etc > secˈtarianˌism *n*

sectary (ˈsɛktərɪ) *n*, *pl* -taries **1** a member of a sect, esp a person who belongs to a religious sect that is regarded as heretical or schismatic **2** a member of a Nonconformist denomination, esp one that is small [C16: from Medieval Latin *sectārius*, from Latin *secta* SECT]

section (ˈsɛkʃən) *n* **1** a part cut off or separated from the main body of something **2** a part or subdivision of a piece of writing, book, etc: *the sports section of the newspaper* **3** one of several component parts **4** a distinct part or subdivision of a country, community, etc **5** *US & Canadian* an area one mile square (640 acres) in a public survey, esp in the western parts of the US and Canada **6** *NZ* a plot of land for building on, esp in a suburban area **7** the section of a railway track that is maintained by a single crew or is controlled by a particular signal box **8** the act or process of cutting or separating by cutting **9** a representation of a portion of a building or object exposed when cut by an imaginary vertical plane so as to show its construction and interior **10** *geometry* a plane surface formed by cutting through a solid **11** a thin slice of biological tissue, mineral, etc, prepared for examination by a microscope **12** a segment of an orange or other citrus fruit **13** a small military formation, typically comprising two or more squads or aircraft

14 *Austral & NZ* a fare stage on a bus, tram, etc **15** *music* **a** an extended division of a composition or movement that forms a coherent part of the structure: *the development section* **b** a division in an orchestra, band, etc, containing instruments belonging to the same class: *the brass section* **16** Also called: **signature, gathering, gather, quire** a folded printing sheet or sheets ready for gathering and binding ⊳ *vb* (tr) **17** to cut or divide into sections **18** to cut through so as to reveal a section **19** (in drawing, esp mechanical drawing) to shade so as to indicate sections **20** *Brit social welfare* to have (a mentally disturbed person) confined in a mental hospital under an appropriate section of the mental health legislation [C16: from Latin *sectiō*, from *secāre* to cut]

sectional (ˈsɛkʃənᵊl) *adj* **1** composed of several sections **2** of or relating to a section > 'sectionally *adv* > sectionalize or sectionalise (ˈsɛkʃənəˌlaɪz) *vb* (tr)

sectionalism (ˈsɛkʃənəˌlɪzəm) *n* excessive or narrow-minded concern for local or regional interests as opposed to the interests of the whole > 'sectionalist *n*, *adj*

sector (ˈsɛktə) *n* **1** a part or subdivision, esp of a society or an economy: *the private sector* **2** *geometry* either portion of a circle included between two radii and an arc. Area: $\frac{1}{2}r^2\theta$, where *r* is the radius and θ is the central angle subtended by the arc (in radians) **3** a measuring instrument consisting of two graduated arms hinged at one end **4** a part or subdivision of an area of military operations **5** *computing* the smallest addressable portion of the track on a magnetic tape, disk, or drum store [C16: from Late Latin: sector, from Latin: a cutter, from *secāre* to cut] > 'sectoral *adj*

sectorial (sɛkˈtɔːrɪəl) *adj* **1** of or relating to a sector **2** *zoology* adapted for cutting: *the sectorial teeth of carnivores*

secular (ˈsɛkjʊlə) *adj* **1** of or relating to worldly as opposed to sacred things; temporal **2** not concerned with or related to religion **3** not within the control of the Church **4** (of an education, etc) having no particular religious affinities **5** (of clerics) not bound by religious vows to a monastic or other order **6** occurring or appearing once in an age or century **7** lasting for a long time **8** *astronomy* occurring slowly over a long period of time ⊳ *n* **9** a member of the secular clergy [C13: from Old French *seculer*, from Late Latin *saeculāris* temporal, from Latin: concerning an age, from *saeculum* an age] > 'secularly *adv* > ˌsecu'larity *n*

secularism (ˈsɛkjʊləˌrɪzəm) *n* **1** *philosophy* a doctrine that rejects religion, esp in ethics **2** the attitude that religion should have no place in civil affairs > 'secularist *n*, *adj*

secularize or **secularise** (ˈsɛkjʊləˌraɪz) *vb* (tr) **1** to change from religious or sacred to secular functions, etc **2** to dispense from allegiance to a religious order **3** *law* to transfer (property) from ecclesiastical to civil possession or use > ˌsecular'zation or ˌseculari'sation *n*

secund (sɪˈkʌnd) *adj botany* having or designating parts arranged on or turned to one side of the axis [C18: from Latin *secundus* following, from *sequī* to follow; see SECOND¹]

Secunderabad (səˈkʌndərəˌbæd, -ˌbɑːd) *n* a former town in S central India, in N Andra Pradesh: one of the largest British military stations in India: now part of Hyderabad city

secure (sɪˈkjʊə) *adj* **1** free from danger, damage, etc **2** free from fear, care, etc **3** in safe custody **4** not likely to fail, become loose, etc **5** able to be relied on; certain **6** *archaic* careless or overconfident ⊳ *vb* (tr) **7** to obtain or get possession of: *I will secure some good seats* **8** (when *intr*, often foll by *against*) to make or become free from danger, fear, etc **9** (tr) to make fast or firm; fasten **10** (when *intr*, often foll by *against*) to make or become certain; guarantee: *this plan will secure your happiness* **11** (tr) to assure (a creditor) of payment, as by giving security **12** (tr) to make (a military position) safe from attack **13** *nautical* to make (a vessel or its contents) safe or ready by battening down hatches, stowing gear, etc [C16: from Latin *sēcūrus* free from care, from *sē-* without + *cūra* care] > se'curable *adj* > se'curely *adv* > se'curement *n* > se'curer *n*

secure unit *n* an establishment providing secure

accommodation, education and training, psychiatric help, etc for offenders and people who are mentally ill

Securities and Investments Board n (from 1986 to 1997) a British regulatory body that oversaw London's financial markets, each of which has its own self-regulatory organization: replaced by the Financial Services Authority. Abbreviation: SIB

securitization or **securitisation** (sɪˌkjʊərɪtaɪˈzeɪʃən) n finance the use of such securities as eurobonds to enable investors to lend directly to borrowers with a minimum of risk but without using banks as intermediaries

security (sɪˈkjʊərɪtɪ) n, pl -ties 1 the state of being secure 2 assured freedom from poverty or want: he needs the security of a permanent job 3 a person or thing that secures, guarantees, etc 4 precautions taken to ensure against theft, espionage, etc 5 (often plural) a a certificate of creditorship or property carrying the right to receive interest or dividend, such as shares or bonds b the financial asset represented by such a certificate 6 the specific asset that a creditor can claim title to in the event of default on an obligation 7 something given or pledged to secure the fulfilment of a promise or obligation 8 the protection of data to ensure that only authorized personnel have access to computer files

security blanket n 1 a policy of temporary secrecy by police or those in charge of security, in order to protect a person, place, etc, threatened with danger, from further risk 2 a baby's blanket, soft toy, etc, to which a baby or young child becomes very attached, using it as a comforter 3 informal anything used or thought of as providing reassurance

Security Council n a permanent organ of the United Nations established to maintain world peace. It consists of five permanent members (China, France, Russia, the UK, and the US) and ten nonpermanent members

security guard n a person employed to protect buildings, people, etc, and to collect and deliver large sums of money

security risk n a person deemed to be a threat to state security in that he could be open to pressure, have subversive political beliefs, etc

secy or **sec'y** abbreviation secretary

sedan (sɪˈdæn) n 1 US, Canadian & NZ a closed two-door or four-door car with four to six seats 2 short for **sedan chair** [C17: of uncertain origin; compare Latin sēdēs seat]

Sedan (French sədã; English sɪˈdæn) n a town in NE France, on the River Meuse: passed to France in 1642; a Protestant stronghold (16th–17th centuries); scene of a French defeat (1870) during the Franco-Prussian War and of a battle (1940) in World War II, which began the German invasion of France. Pop: 20 548 (1999)

sedan chair n a closed chair for one passenger, carried on poles by two bearers. It was commonly used in the 17th and 18th centuries

sedate[1] (sɪˈdeɪt) adj 1 habitually calm and composed in manner; serene 2 staid, sober, or decorous [C17: from Latin sēdāre to soothe; related to sedēre to sit] > se'dately adv > se'dateness n

sedate[2] (sɪˈdeɪt) vb (tr) to administer a sedative to [C20: back formation from SEDATIVE]

sedation (sɪˈdeɪʃən) n 1 a state of calm or reduced nervous activity 2 the administration of a sedative

sedative (ˈsɛdətɪv) adj 1 having a soothing or calming effect 2 of or relating to sedation ▷ n 3 med a sedative drug or agent [C15: from Medieval Latin sēdātīvus, from Latin sēdātus assuaged; see SEDATE[1]]

Seddon (ˈsɛdən) n **Richard John**, known as *King Dick*. 1845–1906, New Zealand statesman, born in England; prime minister of New Zealand (1893–1906)

sedentary (ˈsɛdəntərɪ, -trɪ) adj 1 characterized by or requiring a sitting position: sedentary work 2 tending to sit about without taking much exercise 3 (of animals) moving about very little, usually because of attachment to a rock or other surface 4 (of animals) not migratory [C16: from Latin sedentārius, from sedēre to sit] > 'sedentarily adv > 'sedentariness n

Seder (ˈseɪdə) n Judaism a ceremonial meal with prescribed ritual reading of the Haggadah observed in Jewish homes on the first night or first two nights of Passover [from Hebrew sēdher order]

sedge (sɛdʒ) n any grasslike cyperaceous plant of the genus *Carex*, typically growing on wet ground and having rhizomes, triangular stems, and minute flowers in spikelets [Old English secg; related to Middle High German segge sedge, Old English sagu SAW[1]] > 'sedgy adj

Sedgemoor (ˈsɛdʒˌmʊə) n a low-lying plain in SW England, in central Somerset: scene of the defeat (1685) of the Duke of Monmouth

sedge warbler n a European songbird, *Acrocephalus schoenobaenus*, of reed beds and swampy areas, having a streaked brownish plumage with white eye stripes: family *Muscicapidae* (Old World flycatchers, etc)

Sedgwick (ˈsɛdʒwɪk) n **Adam**. 1785–1873, English geologist; played a major role in establishing parts of the geological time scale, esp the Cambrian and Devonian periods

sedilia (sɛˈdaɪlɪə) n (functioning as singular) the group of three seats, each called a sedile (sɛˈdaɪlɪ), often recessed, on the south side of a sanctuary where the celebrant and ministers sit at certain points during High Mass [C18: from Latin, from sedīle a chair, from sedēre to sit]

sediment (ˈsɛdɪmənt) n 1 matter that settles to the bottom of a liquid 2 material that has been deposited from water, ice, or wind [C16: from Latin sedimentum a settling, from sedēre to sit] > sedimentous (ˌsɛdɪˈmɛntəs) adj > ˌsedimen'tation n

sedimentary (ˌsɛdɪˈmɛntərɪ) adj 1 characteristic of, resembling, or containing sediment 2 (of rocks) formed by the accumulation and consolidation of mineral and organic fragments that have been deposited by water, ice, or wind > ˌsedi'mentarily adv

sedimentation tank n a tank into which sewage is passed to allow suspended solid matter to separate out

sedition (sɪˈdɪʃən) n 1 speech or behaviour directed against the peace of a state 2 an offence that tends to undermine the authority of a state 3 an incitement to public disorder [C14: from Latin sēditiō discord, from sēd-apart + itiō a going, from īre to go] > se'ditionary n, adj

seditious (sɪˈdɪʃəs) adj 1 of, like, or causing sedition 2 inclined to or taking part in sedition

Sedna (ˈsɛdnə) n a large planet-like object discovered in 2003, orbiting the sun but considerably beyond Pluto [C21: after the Inuit goddess of the ocean]

seduce (sɪˈdjuːs) vb (tr) 1 to persuade to engage in sexual intercourse 2 to lead astray, as from the right action 3 to win over, attract, or lure [C15: from Latin sēdūcere to lead apart, from sē- apart + dūcere to lead] > se'ducible or se'duceable adj

seducer (sɪˈdjuːsə) or feminine **seductress** (sɪˈdʌktrɪs) n a person who entices, allures, or seduces, esp one who entices another to engage in sexual intercourse

seduction (sɪˈdʌkʃən) n 1 the act of seducing or the state of being seduced 2 a means of seduction

seductive (sɪˈdʌktɪv) adj tending to seduce or capable of seducing; enticing; alluring > se'ductively adv > se'ductiveness n

sedulous (ˈsɛdjʊləs) adj constant or persistent in use or attention; assiduous; diligent [C16: from Latin sēdulus, of uncertain origin] > sedulity (sɪˈdjuːlɪtɪ) or 'sedulousness n > 'sedulously adv

sedum (ˈsiːdəm) n any crassulaceous rock plant of the genus *Sedum*, having thick fleshy leaves and clusters of white, yellow, or pink flowers [C15: from Latin: houseleek]

see[1] (siː) vb sees, seeing, saw, seen 1 to perceive with the eyes 2 (when tr, may take a clause as object) to perceive (an idea) mentally; understand: I explained the problem but he could not see it 3 (tr) to perceive with any or all of the senses: I hate to see you so unhappy 4 (tr; may take a clause as object) to be aware of in advance; foresee: I can see what will happen if you don't help 5 (when tr, may take a clause as object) to ascertain or find out (a fact); learn: see who is at the door 6 (when tr, takes a clause as object; when intr, foll by to) to make sure (of something) or take care (of something): see that he gets to bed early 7 (when tr, may take a clause as object) to consider, deliberate, or decide: see if you can come next week 8 (tr) to have experience of; undergo: he had seen much unhappiness in his life 9 (tr) to allow to be in a specified condition: *I cannot stand by and see a child in pain* **10** (*tr*) to be characterized by: *this period of history has seen much unrest* **11** (*tr*) to meet or pay a visit to: *to see one's solicitor* **12** (*tr*) to receive, esp as a guest or visitor: *the Prime Minister will see the deputation now* **13** (*tr*) to frequent the company of: *she is seeing a married man* **14** (*tr*) to accompany or escort: *I saw her to the door* **15** (*tr*) to refer to or look up: *for further information see the appendix* **16** (in gambling, esp in poker) to match (another player's bet) or match the bet of (another player) by staking an equal sum **17 as far as I can see** to the best of my judgment or understanding **18 see fit** (*takes an infinitive*) to consider proper, desirable, etc: *I don't see fit to allow her to come here* **19 see someone hanged first** *or* **see someone damned first** *informal* to refuse absolutely to do what one has been asked **20 see you, see you later** *or* **be seeing you** an expression of farewell ▷ See also **see about, see into**, etc [Old English *sēon*; related to Old Norse *sjā*, Gothic *saihwan*, Old Saxon *sehan*]

see² (siː) *n* the diocese of a bishop, or the place within it where his cathedral or procathedral is situated [C13: from Old French *sed*, from Latin *sēdēs* a seat; related to *sedēre* to sit]

see about *vb* (*intr, preposition*) **1** to take care of; look after: *he couldn't see about the matter because he was ill* **2** to investigate; enquire into: *to see about a new car*

Seebeck effect (ˈsiːbɛk; *German* ˈzeːbɛk) *n* the phenomenon in which a current is produced in a circuit containing two or more different metals when the junctions between the metals are maintained at different temperatures. Also called: **thermoelectric effect** [C19: named after Thomas *Seebeck* (1770–1831), German physicist]

seed (siːd) *n* **1** *botany* a mature fertilized plant ovule, consisting of an embryo and its food store surrounded by a protective seed coat (testa). Related adj: **seminal 2** the small hard seedlike fruit of plants such as wheat **3** (loosely) any propagative part of a plant, such as a tuber, spore, or bulb **4** the source, beginning, or germ of anything: *the seeds of revolt* **5** *chiefly Bible* offspring or descendants: *the seed of Abraham* **6** an archaic or dialect term for **sperm¹, semen 7** *sport* a seeded player **8** *chem* a small crystal added to a supersaturated solution or supercooled liquid to induce crystallization **9 go to seed** *or* **run to seed a** (of plants) to produce and shed seeds **b** to lose vigour, usefulness, etc ▷ *vb* **10** to plant (seeds, grain, etc) in (soil): *we seeded this field with oats* **11** (*intr*) (of plants) to form or shed seeds **12** (*tr*) to remove the seeds from (fruit, etc) **13** (*tr*) *chem* to add a small crystal to (a supersaturated solution or supercooled liquid) in order to cause crystallization **14** (*tr*) to scatter certain substances, such as silver iodide, in (clouds) in order to cause rain **15** (*tr*) to arrange (the draw of a tournament) so that outstanding teams or players will not meet in the early rounds [Old English *sǣd*; related to Old Norse *sāth*, Gothic *sēths*, Old High German *sāt*] ▷ '**seedless** *adj* ▷ '**seeder** *n*

seedbed (ˈsiːdˌbɛd) *n* **1** a plot of land in which seeds or seedlings are grown before being transplanted **2** the place where something develops

seedcake (ˈsiːdˌkeɪk) *n* a sweet cake flavoured with caraway seeds and lemon rind or essence

seed capital *n* *finance* a small amount of capital required to finance the research necessary to produce a business plan for a new company

seed coral *n* small pieces of coral used in jewellery, etc

seed corn *n* **1** the good quality ears or kernels of corn that are used as seed **2** assets or investments that are expected to provide profits in the future

seed leaf *n* the nontechnical name for **cotyledon**

seedling (ˈsiːdlɪŋ) *n* a very young plant produced from a seed

seed money *n* money used for the establishment of an enterprise

seed oyster *n* a young oyster, esp a cultivated oyster, ready for transplantation

seed pearl *n* a tiny pearl weighing less than a quarter of a grain

seed pod *n* a carpel or pistil enclosing the seeds of a plant, esp a flowering plant

seed potato *n* a potato tuber used for planting

seed vessel *n* *botany* a dry fruit, such as a capsule

seedy (ˈsiːdɪ) *adj* **seedier, seediest 1** shabby or unseemly in appearance: *seedy clothes* **2** (of a plant) at the stage of producing seeds **3** *informal* not physically fit; sickly ▷ '**seedily** *adv* ▷ '**seediness** *n*

Seeger (ˈsiːgə) *n* **Pete.** born 1919. US folk singer and songwriter, noted for his protest songs, which include "We shall Overcome" (1960), "Where have all the Flowers gone?" (1961), "If I had a Hammer" (1962), and "Little Boxes" (1962)

seeing (ˈsiːɪŋ) *n* **1** the sense or faculty of sight; vision **2** *astronomy* the quality of the observing conditions (especially the turbulence of the atmosphere) during an astronomical observation ▷ *conj* **3** (*subordinating; often foll by that*) in light of the fact (that); inasmuch as; since
● USAGE The use of *seeing as how* as in *seeing as (how) the bus is always late, I don't need any reason to hurry* is generally thought to be incorrect or non-standard

seeing-eye dog *n* the US name for **guide dog**

see into *vb* (*intr, preposition*) to discover the true nature of: *I can't see into your thoughts*

seek (siːk) *vb* **seeks, seeking, sought** (*mainly tr*) **1** (when *intr*, often foll by *for* or *after*) to try to find by searching; look for: *to seek a solution* **2** (*also intr*) to try to obtain or acquire: *to seek happiness* **3** to attempt (to do something); try: *I'm only seeking to help* **4** (*also intr*) to enquire about or request (something): *to seek help* **5** to go or resort to: *to seek the garden for peace* [Old English *sēcan*; related to Old Norse *sōkja*, Gothic *sōkjan*, Old High German *suohhen*, Latin *sāgīre* to perceive by scent; see BESEECH] ▷ '**seeker** *n*

seek out *vb* (*tr, adverb*) to search hard for a specific person or thing and find: *she sought out her friend from amongst the crowd*

Seeland (ˈzeːlant) *n* the German name for **Zealand**

seem (siːm) *vb* (*may take an infinitive*) **1** (*copula*) to appear to the mind or eye; look: *this seems nice; the car seems to be running well* **2** to give the impression of existing; appear to be: *there seems no need for all this nonsense* **3** used to diminish the force of a following infinitive to be polite, more noncommittal, etc: *I can't seem to get through to you* [C12: perhaps from Old Norse *soma* to beseem, from *sæmr* befitting; related to Old English *sēman* to reconcile; see SAME]
● USAGE See at **like¹**

seeming (ˈsiːmɪŋ) *adj* **1** (*prenominal*) apparent but not actual or genuine ▷ *n* **2** outward or false appearance ▷ '**seemingly** *adv*

seemly (ˈsiːmlɪ) *adj* **-lier, -liest 1** proper or fitting **2** *obsolete* pleasing or handsome in appearance ▷ *adv* **3** *archaic* properly or decorously [C13: from Old Norse *sœmiligr*, from *sæmr* befitting]

seen (siːn) *vb* the past participle of **see¹**

see off *vb* (*tr, adverb*) **1** to be present at the departure of (a person making a journey) **2** *informal* to cause to leave or depart, esp by force

seep (siːp) *vb* **1** (*intr*) to pass gradually or leak through or as if through small openings; ooze ▷ *n* **2** a small spring or place where water, oil, etc, has oozed through the ground [Old English *sīpian*; related to Middle High German *sīfen*, Swedish dialect *sipa*] ▷ '**seepage** *n*

seer¹ (sɪə) *n* **1** a person who can supposedly see into the future; prophet **2** a person who professes supernatural powers **3** a person who sees

seer² (sɪə) *n* a variant spelling of **ser**

seersucker (ˈsɪəˌsʌkə) *n* a light cotton, linen, or other fabric with a crinkled surface and often striped [C18: from Hindi *śīrśakar*, from Persian *shīr o shakkar*, literally: milk and sugar]

seesaw (ˈsiːˌsɔː) *n* **1** a plank balanced in the middle so that two people seated on the ends can ride up and down by pushing on the ground with their feet **2** the pastime of riding up and down on a seesaw **3** an up-and-down or back-and-forth movement ▷ *vb* **4** (*intr*) to move up and down or back and forth in such a manner; oscillate [C17: reduplication of SAW¹, alluding to the movement from side to side, as in sawing]

seethe (siːð) *vb* **1** (*intr*) to boil or to foam as if boiling

2 (*intr*) to be in a state of extreme agitation, esp through anger **3** (*tr*) to soak in liquid **4** (*tr*) *archaic* to cook or extract the essence of (a food) by boiling [Old English *sēothan*; related to Old Norse *sjōtha*, Old High German *siodan* to seethe]

seething ('si:ðɪŋ) *adj* **1** boiling or foaming as if boiling **2** crowded and full of restless activity **3** in a state of extreme agitation, esp through anger

see through *vb* **1** (*tr*) to help out in time of need or trouble **2** (*tr, adverb*) to remain with until the end or completion: *let's see the job through* **3** (*intr, preposition*) to perceive the true nature of: *I can see through your evasion* ▷ *adj* **see-through 4** partly or wholly transparent or translucent, esp (of clothes) in a titillating way

Seferis (sə'fɛərɪs) *n* **George**. pen name of *Georgios Seferiades*. 1900–71, Greek poet and diplomat: Nobel prize for literature 1963

Sefton ('sɛftən) *n* a unitary authority in NW England, in Merseyside. Pop: 281 600 (2003 est). Area: 150 sq km (58 sq miles)

segment *n* ('sɛgmənt) **1** *maths* **a** a part of a line or curve between two points **b** a part of a plane or solid figure cut off by an intersecting line, plane, or planes, esp one between a chord and an arc of a circle **2** one of several parts or sections into which an object is divided; portion **3** *zoology* any of the parts into which the body or appendages of an annelid or arthropod are divided **4** *linguistics* a speech sound considered in isolation ▷ *vb* (sɛg'mɛnt) **5** to cut or divide (a whole object) into segments [c16: from Latin *segmentum*, from *secāre* to cut] > **segmentary** ('sɛgməntərɪ, -trɪ) *adj* > **seg'mental** *adj* > **seg'mentally** *adv*

segmentation (ˌsɛgmɛn'teɪʃən) *n* **1** the act or an instance of dividing into segments **2** *embryol* another name for **cleavage** (sense 4)

Segovia¹ (sɪ'gəʊvɪə; *Spanish* se'ɣoβja) *n* a town in central Spain: site of a Roman aqueduct, still in use, and the fortified palace of the kings of Castile (the Alcázar). Pop: 55 640 (2003 est)

Segovia² (sɪ'gəʊvɪə; *Spanish* se'ɣoβja) *n* **Andrés** (an'dres), Marquis of Salobreña. 1893–1987, Spanish classical guitarist

Segrè (sə'greɪ) *n* **Emilio** (ɛm'i:lɪəʊ). 1905–89, US physicist, born in Italy, who was the first to produce an artificial element. He shared the Nobel prize for physics (1959) with Owen Chamberlain for their discovery (1955) of the antiproton

segregate ('sɛgrɪˌgeɪt) *vb* **1** to set or be set apart from others or from the main group **2** (*tr*) to impose segregation on (a racial or minority group) **3** *genetics, metallurgy* to undergo or cause to undergo segregation [c16: from Latin *sēgregāre*, from *sē-* apart + *grex* a flock] > **'segreˌgative** *adj* > **'segreˌgator** *n*

segregation (ˌsɛgrɪ'geɪʃən) *n* **1** the act of segregating or state of being segregated **2** *sociol* the practice or policy of creating separate facilities within the same society for the use of a minority group **3** *genetics* the separation at meiosis of the two members of any pair of alleles into separate gametes > ˌsegre'gational *adj* > ˌsegre'gationist *n*

segue ('sɛgweɪ) *vb* **segues, segueing, segued** (*intr*) **1** (often foll by *into*) to proceed from one section or piece of music to another without a break ▷ *n* **2** the practice or an instance of playing music in this way [from Italian: follows, from *seguire* to follow, from Latin *sequī*]

seguidilla (ˌsɛgɪ'di:ljə) *n* **1** a Spanish dance in a fast triple rhythm **2** a piece of music composed for or in the rhythm of this dance [Spanish: a little dance, from *seguida* a dance, from *seguir* to follow, from Latin *sequī*]

seiche (seɪʃ) *n* a periodic oscillation of the surface of an enclosed or semienclosed body of water (lake, inland sea, bay, etc) caused by such phenomena as atmospheric pressure changes, winds, tidal currents, and earthquakes [c19: from Swiss French, first used to describe rise and fall of water in Lake Geneva; of obscure origin]

Seidlitz powder or **Seidlitz powders** ('sɛdlɪts) *n* a laxative consisting of two powders, tartaric acid and a mixture of sodium bicarbonate and Rochelle salt

(sodium potassium tartrate) [c19: named after *Seidlitz*, a village in Bohemia with mineral springs having similar laxative effects]

seif dune (seɪf) *n* (in deserts, esp the Sahara) a long ridge of blown sand, often several miles long [*seif*, from Arabic: sword, from the shape of the dune]

Seifert ('si:fət) *n* **Jaroslav** ('jærəslæf). 1901–86, Czech poet and journalist, noted esp for poems dealing with the German occupation of Prague during World War II. Nobel prize for literature 1984

seigneur (se'njɜː, *French* sɛɲœr) *n* a feudal lord, esp in France [c16: from Old French, from Vulgar Latin *senior*, from Latin: an elderly man; see SENIOR] > **sei'gneurial** *adj*

seigneury ('seɪnjərɪ) *n, pl* **-gneuries** the estate of a seigneur

seignior ('seɪnjə) *n* **1** a less common name for a **seigneur 2** (in England) the lord of a seigniory [c14: from Anglo-French *segnour*; see SEIGNEUR] > **seigniorial** (seɪ'njɔːrɪəl) *adj*

seigniory ('seɪnjərɪ) or **signory** ('si:njərɪ) *n, pl* **-gniories** or **-gnories 1** less common names for a **seigneury 2** (in England) the fee or manor of a seignior; a feudal domain **3** the authority of a seignior or the relationship between him and his tenants

seine (seɪn) *n* **1** a large fishing net that hangs vertically in the water by means of floats at the top and weights at the bottom ▷ *vb* **2** to catch (fish) using this net [Old English *segne*, from Latin *sagēna*, from Greek *sagēnē*; related to Old High German *segina*, Old French *saïne*]

Seine (seɪn; *French* sɛn) *n* a river in N France, rising on the Plateau de Langres and flowing northwest through Paris to the English Channel: the second longest river in France, linked by canal with the Rivers Somme, Scheldt, Meuse, Rhine, Saône, and Loire. Length: 776 km (482 miles)

Seine-et-Marne (*French* sɛnemarn) *n* a department of N central France, in Île-de-France region. Capital: Melun. Pop: 1 232 467 (2003 est). Area: 5931 sq km (2313 sq miles)

Seine-Maritime (*French* sɛnmaritim) *n* a department of N France, in Haute-Normandie region. Capital: Rouen. Pop: 1 237 263 (2003 est). Area: 6342 sq km (2473 sq miles)

Seine-Saint-Denis (*French* sɛnsɛdni) *n* a department of N central France, in Île-de-France region. Capital: Bobigny. Pop: 1 396 122 (2003 est). Area: 236 sq km (92 sq miles)

seise or *US* **seize** (si:z) *vb* to put into legal possession of (property, etc) [variant of SEIZE] > **seiser** *n*

seisin or *US* **seizin** ('si:zɪn) *n* property law feudal possession of an estate in land [c13: from Old French *seisine*, from *seisir* to SEIZE]

seismic ('saɪzmɪk) *adj* relating to or caused by earthquakes or artificially produced earth tremors

seismo- or before a vowel **seism-** *combining form* earthquake: *seismology* [from Greek *seismos*]

seismograph ('saɪzməˌgrɑːf, -ˌgræf) *n* an instrument that registers and records the features of earthquakes. A **seismogram** ('saɪzməˌgræm) is the record from such an instrument. Also called: **seismometer** > **seismographic** (ˌsaɪzmə'græfɪk) *adj* > **seismographer** (saɪz'mɒgrəfə) *n* > **seis'mography** *n*

seismology (saɪz'mɒlədʒɪ) *n* the branch of geology concerned with the study of earthquakes and seismic waves > **seismologic** (ˌsaɪzmə'lɒdʒɪk) or ˌseismo'logical *adj* > ˌseismo'logically *adv* > **seis'mologist** *n*

seize (si:z) *vb* (*mainly tr*) **1** (*also intr*, foll by *on*) to take hold of quickly; grab **2** (sometimes foll by *on* or *upon*) to grasp mentally, esp rapidly: *she immediately seized his idea* **3** to take mental possession of: *alarm seized the crowd* **4** to take possession of rapidly and forcibly: *the thief seized the woman's purse* **5** to take legal possession of; take into custody **6** to take by force or capture: *the army seized the undefended town* **7** to take immediate advantage of: *to seize an opportunity* **8** *nautical* to bind (two ropes together or a piece of gear to a rope) **9** (*intr*, often foll by *up*) (of mechanical parts) to become jammed, esp because of excessive heat **10** the usual US spelling of **seise** [c13 *saisen*, from Old French *saisir*, from Medieval Latin *sacīre* to position, of Germanic origin; related to Gothic *satjan* to

SET¹ > 'seizable adj

seizure ('siːʒə) n **1** the act or an instance of seizing or the state of being seized **2** pathol a sudden manifestation or recurrence of a disease, such as an epileptic convulsion

Sekondi (ˌsɛkən'diː) n a port in SW Ghana, 8 km (5 miles) northeast of Takoradi: linked administratively with Takoradi in 1946. Pop (with Takoradi): 335 000 (2005 est)

selachian (sɪ'leɪkɪən) adj of, relating to, or belonging to the Selachii (or Elasmobranchii), a large subclass of cartilaginous fishes including the sharks, rays, dogfish, and skates [c19: from New Latin Selachii, from Greek selakhē a shark; related to Greek selas brightness]

Selangor (sə'læŋə) n a state of Peninsular Malaysia, on the Strait of Malacca: established as a British protectorate in 1874, became a Federated Malay State in 1896 and part of Malaysia in 1946; tin producer. Capital: Shah Alam. Pop: 4 188 876 (2000). Area: 7955 sq km (3071 sq miles)

Selby ('sɛlbɪ) n an inland port in N England, in North Yorkshire, on the River Ouse: centre for a coalfield since 1983: agricultural products. Pop: 15 807 (2001)

Selden ('sɛldən) n John. 1584–1654, English antiquary and politician. As a member of Parliament, he was twice imprisoned for opposing the king

seldom ('sɛldəm) adv not often; rarely [Old English seldon; related to Old Norse sjáldan, Old High German seltan]

select (sɪ'lɛkt) vb **1** to choose (someone or something) in preference to another or others ▷ adj Also: selected **2** chosen in preference to another or others **3** of particular quality or excellence **4** limited as to membership or entry: a select gathering [c16: from Latin sēligere to sort, from sē- apart + legere to choose] > se'lectness n > se'lector n

select committee n (in Britain) a small committee composed of members of parliament, set up by either House of Parliament to investigate and report back on a specified matter of interest

selection (sɪ'lɛkʃən) n **1** the act or an instance of selecting or the state of being selected **2** a thing or number of things that have been selected **3** a range from which something may be selected: this shop has a good selection of clothes **4** biology the natural or artificial process by which certain organisms or characters are reproduced and perpetuated in the species in preference to others

selective (sɪ'lɛktɪv) adj **1** of or characterized by selection **2** tending to choose carefully or characterized by careful choice **3** electronics occurring at, operating at, or capable of separating out a particular frequency or band of frequencies > se'lectively adv

selectivity (sɪˌlɛk'tɪvɪtɪ) n **1** the state or quality of being selective **2** the degree to which a radio receiver or other circuit can respond to and separate the frequency of a desired signal from other frequencies by tuning

Selene (sɪ'liːnɪ) n the Greek goddess of the moon. Roman counterpart: Luna

selenite ('sɛlɪˌnaɪt) n a colourless glassy variety of gypsum [c17: via Latin from Greek selēnitēs lithos moonstone, from selēnē moon; so called because it was believed to wax and wane with the moon]

selenium (sɪ'liːnɪəm) n a nonmetallic element that exists in several allotropic forms. It occurs free in volcanic areas and in sulphide ores, esp pyrite. The common form is a grey crystalline solid that is photoconductive, photovoltaic, and semiconducting: used in photocells, solar cells, and in xerography. Symbol: Se; atomic no: 34; atomic wt: 78.96; valency: –2, 4, or 6; relative density: 4.79 (grey); melting pt: 221°C (grey); boiling pt: 685°C (grey) [c19: from New Latin, from Greek selēnē moon; named by analogy to TELLURIUM (from Latin tellus earth)]

seleno- or before a vowel **selen-** combining form denoting the moon: selenology [from Greek selēnē moon]

selenography (ˌsiːlɪ'nɒɡrəfɪ) n the branch of astronomy concerned with the description and mapping of the surface features of the moon > sele'nographer or ˌsele'nographist n > selenographic (sɪˌliːnəʊ'ɡræfɪk) adj

Seles ('sɛlɛz, -lɛʃ) n **Monica.** born 1973, US tennis player, born in Yugoslavia: winner of the US Open (1991, 1992); stabbed while on court in an unprovoked attack

Seleucia (sɪ'luːʃɪə) n **1** an ancient city in Mesopotamia, on the River Tigris: founded by Seleucus Nicator in 312 BC; became the chief city of the Seleucid empire; sacked by the Romans around 162 AD **2** an ancient city in SE Asia Minor, on the River Calycadnus (modern Goksu Nehri): captured by the Turks in the 13th century; site of present-day Silifke (Turkey) **3** an ancient port in Syria, on the River Orontes: the port of Antioch, of military importance during the wars between the Ptolemies and Seleucids; largely destroyed by earthquake in 526; site of present-day Samandağ (Turkey)

Seleucid (sɪ'luːsɪd) n, pl -cids, -cidae (-sɪˌdiː) **1** a member of a royal dynasty (312–64 BC) that at the zenith of its power ruled over an area extending from Thrace to India ▷ adj **2** of, relating to, or supporting the Seleucids or their dynasty > Seleucidan (sɪ'luːsɪdᵊn) adj

Seleucus I (sɪ'luːkəs) n surname Nicator. ?358–280 BC, Macedonian general under Alexander the Great, who founded the Seleucid kingdom

self (sɛlf) n, pl selves (sɛlvz) **1** the distinct individuality or identity of a person or thing **2** a person's usual or typical bodily make-up or personal characteristics: she looked her old self again **3** one's own welfare or interests: he only thinks of self **4** an individual's consciousness of his own identity or being **5** a bird, animal, etc, that is a single colour throughout, esp a self-coloured pigeon ▷ pron **6** not standard myself, yourself, etc: seats for self and wife ▷ adj **7** of the same colour or material **8** obsolete the same [Old English seolf; related to Old Norse sjálfr, Gothic silba, Old High German selb]

self- combining form **1** of oneself or itself: self-defence; self-rule **2** by, to, in, due to, for, or from the self: self-employed; self-inflicted; self-respect **3** automatic or automatically: self-propelled

self-abnegation n the denial of one's own interests in favour of the interests of others

self-absorption n **1** preoccupation with oneself to the exclusion of others or the outside world **2** physics the process in which some of the radiation emitted by a material is absorbed by the material itself

self-abuse n disparagement or misuse of one's own abilities, etc

self-acting adj not requiring an external influence or control to function; automatic

self-addressed adj **1** addressed for return to the sender **2** directed to oneself: a self-addressed remark

self-aggrandizement n the act of increasing one's own power, importance, etc, esp in an aggressive or ruthless manner > ˌself-ag'granˌdizing adj

self-appointed adj having assumed authority without the agreement of others: a self-appointed critic

self-assertion n the act or an instance of putting forward one's own opinions, etc, esp in an aggressive or conceited manner > ˌself-as'serting adj > ˌself-as'sertive adj

self-assurance n confidence in the validity, value, etc, of one's own ideas, opinions, etc > self-assured adj > ˌself-as'suredly adv > ˌself-as'suredness n

self-centred adj totally preoccupied with one's own concerns > ˌself-'centredness n

self-certification n (in Britain) a formal assertion by a worker to his employer that absence from work for up to seven days was due to sickness. From 1982 this replaced a doctor's certificate for the purposes of paying sickness benefit

self-coloured adj **1** having only a single and uniform colour: self-coloured flowers; a self-coloured dress **2** (of cloth, material, etc) having the natural or original colour

self-command n another term for self-control

self-confessed adj according to one's own testimony or admission: a self-confessed liar

self-confidence n confidence in one's own powers, judgment, etc > ˌself-'confident adj > ˌself-'confidently adv

self-conscious adj **1** unduly aware of oneself as the object of the attention of others; embarrassed

S

2 conscious of one's existence > ˌself-ˈconsciously *adv* > ˌself-ˈconsciousness *n*

self-contained *adj* **1** containing within itself all parts necessary for completeness **2** (of a flat) having its own kitchen, bathroom, and lavatory not shared by others and usually having its own entrance **3** able or tending to keep one's feelings, thoughts, etc, to oneself; reserved > ˌself-conˈtainedness *n*

self-control *n* the ability to exercise restraint or control over one's feelings, emotions, reactions, etc > ˌself-conˈtrolled *adj*

self-deception *or* **self-deceit** *n* the act or an instance of deceiving oneself, esp as to the true nature of one's feelings or motives > ˌself-deˈceptive *adj*

self-defence *n* **1** the act of defending oneself, one's actions, ideas, etc **2** boxing as a means of defending the person (esp in the phrase **noble art of self-defence**) **3** *law* the right to defend one's person, family, or property against attack or threat of attack by the use of no more force than is reasonable > ˌself-deˈfensive *adj*

self-denial *n* the denial or sacrifice of one's own desires > ˌself-deˈnying *adj*

self-deprecating *or* **self-depreciating** *adj* having a tendency to disparage oneself

self-determination *n* **1** the power or ability to make a decision for oneself without influence from outside **2** the right of a nation or people to determine its own form of government without influence from outside > ˌself-deˈtermined *adj* > ˌself-deˈtermining *adj*

self-discipline *n* the act of disciplining or power to discipline one's own feelings, desires, etc, esp with the intention of improving oneself > ˌself-ˈdisciplined *adj*

self-drive *adj* denoting or relating to a hired car that is driven by the hirer

self-educated *adj* **1** educated through one's own efforts without formal instruction **2** educated at one's own expense, without financial aid > ˌself-eduˈcation *n*

self-effacement *n* the act of making oneself, one's actions, etc, inconspicuous, esp because of humility or timidity > self-effacing *adj* > ˌself-efˈfacingly *adv*

self-employed *adj* earning one's living in one's own business or through freelance work, rather than as the employee of another > ˌself-emˈployment *n*

self-esteem *n* **1** respect for or a favourable opinion of oneself **2** an unduly high opinion of oneself; vanity

self-evident *adj* containing its own evidence or proof without need of further demonstration > ˌself-ˈevidence *n* > ˌself-ˈevidently *adv*

self-existent *adj* *philosophy* existing independently of any other being or cause

self-explanatory *or less commonly* **self-explaining** *adj* understandable without explanation; self-evident

self-expression *n* the expression of one's own personality, feelings, etc, as in painting, poetry, or other creative activity > ˌself-exˈpressive *adj*

self-government *n* **1** the government of a country, nation, etc, by its own people **2** the state of being self-controlled > ˌself-ˈgoverned *adj* > ˌself-ˈgoverning *adj*

self-harm *n* the practice of cutting or otherwise wounding oneself, usually considered as indicating psychological disturbance > ˌself-ˈharming *n*

selfheal (ˈsɛlfˌhiːl) *n* **1 a** low-growing European herbaceous plant, *Prunella vulgaris*, with tightly clustered violet-blue flowers and reputedly having healing powers: family *Lamiaceae* (labiates) **2** any of several other plants thought to have healing powers

self-help *n* **1** the act or state of providing the means to help oneself without relying on the assistance of others **2 a** the practice of solving one's problems by joining or forming a group designed to help those suffering from a particular problem **b** (*as modifier*): *a self-help group*

self-image *n* one's own idea of oneself or sense of one's worth

self-important *adj* having or showing an unduly high opinion of one's own abilities, importance, etc > ˌself-imˈportantly *adv* > ˌself-imˈportance *n*

self-improvement *n* the improvement of one's status, position, education, etc, by one's own efforts

self-induced *adj* **1** induced or brought on by oneself or

itself **2** *electronics* produced by self-induction

self-induction *n* the production of an electromotive force in a circuit when the magnetic flux linked with the circuit changes as a result of a change in current in the same circuit

self-indulgent *adj* tending to indulge one's own desires, etc > ˌself-inˈdulgence *n*

self-interest *n* **1** one's personal interest or advantage **2** the act or an instance of pursuing one's own interest > ˌself-ˈinterested *adj*

selfish (ˈsɛlfɪʃ) *adj* **1** chiefly concerned with one's own interest, advantage, etc, esp to the total exclusion of the interests of others **2** relating to or characterized by self-interest > ˈselfishly *adv* > ˈselfishness *n*

self-justification *n* the act or an instance of justifying or providing excuses for one's own behaviour, etc

selfless (ˈsɛlflɪs) *adj* having little concern for one's own interests > ˈselflessly *adv* > ˈselflessness *n*

self-loading *adj* (of a firearm) utilizing some of the force of the explosion to eject the empty shell and replace it with a new one > ˌself-ˈloader *n*

self-love *n* the instinct or tendency to seek one's own well-being or to further one's own interest

self-made *adj* **1** having achieved wealth, status, etc, by one's own efforts **2** made by oneself

self-opinionated *or less commonly* **self-opinioned** *adj* **1** having an unduly high regard for oneself or one's own opinions **2** clinging stubbornly to one's own opinions

self-pity *n* the act or state of pitying oneself, esp in an exaggerated or self-indulgent manner > ˌself-ˈpitying *adj* > ˌself-ˈpityingly *adv*

self-pollination *n* the transfer of pollen from the anthers to the stigma of the same flower or of another flower on the same plant > ˌself-ˈpolliˌnated *adj*

self-possessed *adj* having control of one's emotions, etc > ˌself-posˈsession *n*

self-preservation *n* the preservation of oneself from danger or injury, esp as a basic instinct

self-pronouncing *adj* (in a phonetic transcription) of, relating to, or denoting a word that, except for additional diacritic marks of stress, may keep the letters of its ordinary orthography to represent its pronunciation

self-propelled *adj* (of a vehicle) provided with its own source of tractive power rather than requiring an external means of propulsion > ˌself-proˈpelling *adj*

self-raising *adj* (of flour) having a raising agent, such as baking powder, already added

self-realization *n* the realization or fulfilment of one's own potential or abilities

self-regard *n* **1** concern for one's own interest **2** proper esteem for oneself

self-regulating organization *n* one of several British organizations set up in 1986 under the auspices of the Securities and Investment Board to regulate the activities of London investment markets. Abbreviation: **SRO**

self-reliance *n* reliance on one's own abilities, decisions, etc > ˌself-reˈliant *adj*

self-reproach *n* the act of finding fault with or blaming oneself > ˌself-reˈproachful *adj*

self-respect *n* a proper sense of one's own dignity and integrity > ˌself-reˈspectful *or* ˌself-reˈspecting *adj*

self-restraint *n* restraint imposed by oneself on one's own feelings, desires, etc

self-righteous *adj* having or showing an exaggerated awareness of one's own virtuousness or rights > ˌself-ˈrighteously *adv* > ˌself-ˈrighteousness *n*

self-rule *n* another term for **self-government** (sense 1)

self-sacrifice *n* the sacrifice of one's own desires, interest, etc, for the sake of duty or for the well-being of others > ˌself-ˈsacriˌficing *adj*

selfsame (ˈsɛlfˌseɪm) *adj* (*prenominal*) the very same

self-satisfied *adj* having or showing a complacent satisfaction with oneself, one's own actions, behaviour, etc > ˌself-ˌsatisˈfaction *n*

self-sealing *adj* (esp of an envelope) designed to become sealed with the application of pressure only

self-seeking *n* **1** the act or an instance of seeking one's own profit or interest, esp exclusively ▷ *adj* **2** having or showing an exclusive preoccupation with one's own profit or interest: *a self-seeking attitude* > ˌself-'seeker *n*

self-service *adj* **1** of or denoting a shop, restaurant, petrol station, etc, where the customer serves himself ▷ *n* **2** the practice of serving oneself, as in a shop, etc

self-serving *adj* habitually seeking one's own advantage, esp at the expense of others

self-sown *adj* (of plants) growing from seed dispersed by any means other than by the agency of man or animals. Also called: **self-seeded**

self-starter *n* a person who is strongly motivated and shows initiative, esp at work

self-styled *adj* (*prenominal*) claiming to be of a specified nature, quality, profession, etc: *a self-styled expert*

self-sufficient *or* **self-sufficing** *adj* able to provide for or support oneself without the help of others > ˌself-sufficiency *n* > ˌself-sufficiently *adv*

self-supporting *adj* **1** able to support or maintain oneself without the help of others **2** able to stand up or hold firm without support, props, attachments, etc

self-talk *n* the act or practice of talking to oneself, either aloud or silently and mentally: *positive self-talk*

self-tender *n* an offer by a company to buy back some or all of its shares from its shareholders, esp as a protection against an unwelcome takeover bid

self-will *n* stubborn adherence to one's own will, desires, etc, esp at the expense of others > ˌself-'willed *adj*

self-winding *adj* (of a wrist watch) having a mechanism, activated by the movements of the wearer, in which a rotating or oscillating weight rewinds the mainspring

Seljuk (sɛl'dʒuːk) *or* **Seljukian** (sɛl'dʒuːkɪən) *n* **1** a member of any of the pre-Ottoman Turkish dynasties ruling over large parts of Asia in the 11th, 12th, and 13th centuries AD ▷ *adj* **2** of or relating to these dynasties or to their subjects [c19: from Turkish]

Selkirk ('sɛlˌkɜːk) *n* **Alexander**. original name *Alexander Selcraig*. 1676–1721, Scottish sailor, who was marooned on one of the islets of Juan Fernández and is regarded as the prototype of Defoe's *Robinson Crusoe*

Selkirk Mountains *pl n* a mountain range in SW Canada, in SE British Columbia. Highest peak: Mount Sir Sandford, 3533 m (11 590 ft)

Selkirkshire ('sɛlkɜːkˌʃɪə, -ʃə) *n* (until 1975) a county of SE Scotland, now part of Scottish Borders

sell (sɛl) *vb* **sells, selling, sold 1** to dispose of or transfer or be disposed of or transferred to a purchaser in exchange for money or other consideration; put or be on sale **2** to deal in (objects, property, etc): *he sells used cars for a living* **3** (*tr*) to give up or surrender for a price or reward: *to sell one's honour* **4** to promote or facilitate the sale of (objects, property, etc): *publicity sells many products* **5** to induce or gain acceptance of: *to sell an idea* **6** (*intr*) to be in demand on the market: *these dresses sell well in the spring* **7** (*tr*) *informal* to deceive or cheat **8** **sell down the river** *informal* to betray **9** **sell oneself a** to convince someone else of one's potential or worth **b** to give up one's moral or spiritual standards, etc **10** **sell short a** *informal* to disparage or belittle **b** *finance* to sell securities or goods without owning them in anticipation of buying them before delivery at a lower price ▷ *n* **11** the act or an instance of selling **12** *informal* a trick, hoax, or deception ▷ See also **sell in, sell off**, etc [Old English *sellan* to lend, deliver; related to Old Norse *selja* to sell, Gothic *saljan* to offer sacrifice, Old High German *sellen* to sell, Latin *cōnsilium* advice] > 'sellable *adj* > 'seller *n*

Sella (French sela) *n* **Phillipe** (filip). French Rugby Union football player; played 111 internationals for France (1982–95)

Sellafield ('sɛləˌfiːld) *n* the site of an atomic power station and nuclear reprocessing plant in NW England, in W Cumbria. Former name: **Windscale**

sell-by date *n* **1** a date printed on the packaging of perishable goods, indicating the date after which the goods should not be offered for sale **2** past one's sell-by date *informal* beyond one's prime

Sellers ('sɛləz) *n* **Peter**. 1925–80, English radio, stage, and film actor and comedian: noted for his gift of precise

vocal mimicry, esp in *The Goon Show* (with Spike Milligan and Harry Secombe; BBC Radio, 1952–60). His films include *I'm All Right, Jack* (1959), *The Millionairess* (1961), *The Pink Panther* (1963), *Dr Strangelove* (1964), and *Being There* (1979)

sell in *vb* (*adverb*) **1** (*tr*) to sell (new products) to a retail outlet to be sold to the public **2** (*intr*) to use the established system to one's advantage, rather than attempting to fight against it

selling race *or* **selling plate** *n* a horse race in which the winner must be offered for sale at auction

sell off *vb* (*tr, adverb*) to sell (remaining or unprofitable items), esp at low prices

Sellotape ('sɛləˌteɪp) *n* **1** *trademark* a type of transparent adhesive tape made of cellulose or a similar substance ▷ *vb* **2** (*tr*) to seal or stick using adhesive tape

sell out *vb* (*adverb*) **1** to dispose of (supplies of something) completely by selling. Also (chiefly *Brit*): **sell up 2** (*tr*) *informal* to betray, esp through a secret agreement **3** (*intr*) *informal* to abandon one's principles, standards, etc ▷ *n* **sellout 4** *informal* a performance for which all tickets are sold **5** a commercial success **6** *informal* a betrayal

sell-through *n* the sale of prerecorded video cassettes or DVDs, as opposed to their being available for hire only

sell up *vb* (*adverb*) chiefly *Brit* **1** (*tr*) to sell all (the possessions or assets) of (a bankrupt debtor) in order to discharge his debts as far as possible **2** (*intr*) to sell a business

selsyn ('sɛlsɪn) *n* another name for **synchro** [from SEL(F-) + SYN(CHRONOUS)]

Seltzer ('sɛltsə) *n* **1** a natural effervescent water with a high content of minerals **2** a similar synthetic water, used as a beverage [c18: changed from German *Selterser Wasser* water from (*Nieder*) *Selters*, district where mineral springs are located, near Wiesbaden, Germany]

selva ('sɛlvə) *n* **1** dense equatorial forest, esp in the Amazon basin, characterized by tall broad-leaved evergreen trees, epiphytes, lianas, etc **2** a tract of such forest [c19: from Spanish and Portuguese, from Latin *silva* forest]

selvage *or* **selvedge** ('sɛlvɪdʒ) *n* **1** the finished nonfraying edge of a length of woven fabric **2** a similar strip of material allowed in fabricating a metal or plastic article, used esp for handling components during manufacture [c15: from SELF + EDGE; related to Dutch *selfegghe*, German *Selbende*] > 'selvaged *adj*

selves (sɛlvz) *n* **a** the plural of **self b** (*in combination*): *ourselves; yourselves; themselves*

Selznick ('sɛlznɪk) *n* **David O**(liver). 1902–62, US film producer, who produced such films as *A Star is Born* (1937), *Gone with the Wind* (1939), and *A Farewell to Arms* (1957)

semantic (sɪ'mæntɪk) *adj* **1** of or relating to meaning or arising from distinctions between the meanings of different words or symbols **2** of or relating to semantics [c19: from Greek *sēmantikos* having significance, from *sēmainein* to signify, from *sēma* a sign] > se'mantically *adv*

semantics (sɪ'mæntɪks) *n* (*functioning as singular*) **1** the branch of linguistics that deals with the study of meaning, changes in meaning, and the principles that govern the relationship between sentences or words and their meanings **2** the study of the relationships between signs and symbols and what they represent **3** *logic* (of a formal theory) the principles that determine the truth or falsehood of sentences within the theory, and the references of its terms > se'manticist *n*

semaphore ('sɛməˌfɔː) *n* **1** an apparatus for conveying information by means of visual signals, as with movable arms or railway signals, flags, etc **2** a system of signalling by holding a flag in each hand and moving the arms to designated positions to denote each letter of the alphabet ▷ *vb* **3** to signal (information) by means of semaphore [c19: via French, from Greek *sēma* a signal + -PHORE] > semaphoric (ˌsɛmə'fɒrɪk) *or* ˌsema'phorical *adj*

Semarang *or* **Samarang** (səˈmɑːrɑːŋ) *n* a port in S Indonesia, in N Java. Pop: 1 348 803 (2000)

semasiology (sɪˌmeɪsɪ'ɒlədʒɪ) *n* another name for **semantics** [c19: from Greek *sēmasia* meaning, from *sēmainein* to signify + -LOGY]

S

sematic (sɪ'mætɪk) *adj* (of the conspicuous coloration of certain animals) acting as a warning, esp to potential predators [C19: from Greek *sēma* a sign]

semblance ('sɛmbləns) *n* **1** outward appearance, esp without any inner substance or reality **2** a resemblance or copy [C13: from Old French, from *sembler* to seem, from Latin *simulāre* to imitate, from *similis* like]

Semele ('sɛmɪlɪ) *n Greek myth* mother of Dionysus by Zeus

semelparous ('sɛməl,pærəs) *adj* **1** Also called: **hapaxanthic, monocarpic** (of a plant) producing flowers and fruit only once before dying **2** (of an animal) producing offspring only once during its lifetime > **'semel,parity** *n*

sememe ('si:mi:m) *n linguistics* the meaning of a morpheme [C20 (coined in 1933 by Leonard Bloomfield (1887–1949), US linguist): from Greek *sēma* a sign + -EME]

semen ('si:mɛn) *n* **1** the thick whitish fluid containing spermatozoa that is ejaculated from the male genital tract **2** another name for **sperm**[1] [C14: from Latin: seed]

Semeru *or* **Semeroe** (sə'mɛru:) *n* a volcano in Indonesia: the highest peak in Java. Height: 3676 m (12 060 ft)

semester (sɪ'mɛstə) *n* **1** (in some universities) either of two divisions of the academic year, ranging from 15 to 18 weeks **2** (in German universities) a session of six months [C19: via German from Latin *sēmestris* half-yearly, from *sex* six + *mensis* a month]

semi ('sɛmɪ) *n, pl* **semis 1** *Brit* a semidetached house **2** short for **semifinal**

semi- *prefix* **1** half: *semicircle* **2** partially, partly, not completely, or almost: *semiprofessional; semifinal* **3** occurring twice in a specified period of time: *semiannual; semiweekly* [from Latin; compare Old English *sōm-, sām-* half, Greek *hēmi-*]

semiannual (,sɛmɪ'ænjʊəl) *adj* **1** occurring every half-year **2** lasting for half a year > **,semi'annually** *adv*

semiarid (,sɛmɪ'ærɪd) *adj* characterized by scanty rainfall and scrubby vegetation, often occurring in continental interiors

semiautomatic (,sɛmɪ,ɔːtə'mætɪk) *adj* **1** partly automatic **2** (of a firearm) self-loading but firing only one shot at each pull of the trigger ▷ *n* **3** a semiautomatic firearm > **,semi,auto'matically** *adv*

semibreve ('sɛmɪ,bri:v) *n music* a note, now the longest in common use, having a time value that may be divided by any power of 2 to give all other notes. Usual US and Canadian name: **whole note**

semicircle ('sɛmɪ,sɜːk³l) *n* **1 a** one half of a circle **b** half the circumference of a circle **2** anything having the shape or form of half a circle > **semicircular** (,sɛmɪ'sɜːkjʊlə) *adj*

semicircular canal *n anatomy* any of the three looped fluid-filled membranous tubes, at right angles to one another, that comprise the labyrinth of the ear: concerned with the sense of orientation and equilibrium

semicolon (,sɛmɪ'kəʊlən) *n* the punctuation mark (;) used to indicate a pause intermediate in value or length between that of a comma and that of a full stop

semiconductor (,sɛmɪkən'dʌktə) *n* **1** a substance, such as germanium or silicon, that has an electrical conductivity that increases with temperature and is intermediate between that of a metal and an insulator **2 a** a device, such as a transistor or integrated circuit, that depends on the properties of such a substance **b** (*as modifier*): *a semiconductor diode*

semiconscious (,sɛmɪ'kɒnʃəs) *adj* not fully conscious > **,semi'consciously** *adv* > **,semi'consciousness** *n*

semidetached (,sɛmɪdɪ'tætʃt) *adj* **a** (of a building) joined to another on one side by a common wall **b** (*as noun*): *they live in a suburban semidetached*

semifinal (,sɛmɪ'faɪn³l) *n* **a** the round before the final in a competition **b** (*as modifier*): *the semifinal draw* > **,semi'finalist** *n*

semifluid (,sɛmɪ'flu:ɪd) *or* **semifluidic** (,sɛmɪflu:'ɪdɪk) *adj* **1** having properties between those of a liquid and those of a solid **2** a substance that has such properties because of high viscosity: *tar is a semifluid* ▷ Also called: **semiliquid**

semiliterate (,sɛmɪ'lɪtərɪt) *adj* **1** hardly able to read or write **2** able to read but not to write

semilunar (,sɛmɪ'lu:nə) *adj* shaped like a crescent or half-moon

semilunar valve *n anatomy* either of two crescent-shaped valves, one in the aorta and one in the pulmonary artery, that prevent regurgitation of blood into the heart

seminal ('sɛmɪn³l) *adj* **1** potentially capable of development **2** highly original, influential and important **3** rudimentary or unformed **4** of or relating to semen: *seminal fluid* **5** *biology* of or relating to seed [C14: from Late Latin *sēminālis* belonging to seed, from Latin *sēmen* seed] > **'seminally** *adv*

seminar ('sɛmɪ,nɑ:) *n* **1** a small group of students meeting regularly under the guidance of a tutor, professor, etc, to exchange information, discuss theories, etc **2** one such meeting or the place in which it is held **3** a higher course for postgraduates **4** any group or meeting for holding discussions or exchanging information [C19: via German from Latin *sēminārium* SEMINARY]

seminary ('sɛmɪnərɪ) *n, pl* **-naries** an academy for the training of priests, rabbis, etc [C15: from Latin *sēminārium* a nursery garden, from *sēmen* seed] > **,semi'narial** *adj* > **,semi'narian** *n*

seminiferous (,sɛmɪ'nɪfərəs) *adj* **1** containing, conveying, or producing semen: *the seminiferous tubules of the testes* **2** (of plants) bearing or producing seeds [C17: from Latin *sēmin-, sēmen* seed + connecting vowel + -FEROUS]

seminoma (,sɛmɪ'nəʊmə) *n, pl* **-mas** *or* **-mata** (-mətə) *pathol* a malignant tumour of the testicle [C20: from French *seminome*, from Latin *sēmen* semen + -OMA]

semiotics *or* **semeiotics** (,sɛmɪ'ɒtɪks, ,si:mɪ-) *n* (*functioning as singular*) **1** the study of signs and symbols, esp the relations between written or spoken signs and their referents in the physical world or the world of ideas **2** the scientific study of the symptoms of disease; symptomatology ▷ Also called: **semiology, semeiology** > **semiotic** *or* **semeiotic** (,sɛmɪ'ɒtɪk, ,si:mɪ-) *adj* [C17: from Greek *sēmeiōtikos* taking note of signs, from *sēmeion* a sign]

Semipalatinsk (*Russian* sɪmɪpa'latinsk) *n* a city in NE Kazakhstan on the Irtysh River; an important communications centre. Pop: 282 000 (2005 est)

semipermeable (,sɛmɪ'pɜːmɪəb³l) *adj* (esp of a cell membrane) selectively permeable > **,semi,permea'bility** *n*

semiprecious (,sɛmɪ'prɛʃəs) *adj* (of certain stones) having commercial value, but less than a precious stone

semiprofessional (,sɛmɪprə'fɛʃən³l) *adj* **1** (of a person) engaged in an activity or sport part-time but for pay **2** (of an activity or sport) engaged in by semiprofessional people **3** of or relating to a person whose activities are professional in some respects ▷ *n* **4** a semiprofessional person > **,semipro'fessionally** *adv*

semiquaver ('sɛmɪ,kweɪvə) *n music* a note having the time value of one-sixteenth of a semibreve. Usual US and Canadian name: **sixteenth note**

Semiramis (sɛ'mɪrəmɪs) *n* the legendary founder of Babylon and wife of Ninus, king of Assyria, which she ruled with great skill after his death

semirigid (,sɛmɪ'rɪdʒɪd) *adj* **1** partly but not wholly rigid **2** (of an airship) maintaining shape by means of a main supporting keel and internal gas pressure

semiskilled (,sɛmɪ'skɪld) *adj* partly skilled or trained but not sufficiently so to perform specialized work

semisolid (,sɛmɪ'sɒlɪd) *adj* having a viscosity and rigidity intermediate between that of a solid and a liquid

semisolus (,sɛmɪ'səʊləs) *n* an advertisement that appears on the same page as another advertisement but not adjacent to it

Semite ('si:maɪt) *or less commonly* **Shemite** *n* a member of the group of Caucasoid peoples who speak a Semitic language, including the Jews and Arabs as well as the ancient Babylonians, Assyrians, and Phoenicians [C19:

from New Latin *sēmīta* descendant of Shem, via Greek *Sēm*, from Hebrew SHEM]

Semitic (sɪ'mɪtɪk) *or less commonly* **Shemitic** *n* **1** a branch or subfamily of the Afro-Asiatic family of languages that includes Arabic, Hebrew, Aramaic, Amharic, and such ancient languages as Akkadian and Phoenician ▷ *adj* **2** denoting, relating to, or belonging to this group of languages **3** denoting, belonging to, or characteristic of any of the peoples speaking a Semitic language, esp the Jews or the Arabs **4** another word for **Jewish**

semitone ('sɛmɪˌtəʊn) *n* an interval corresponding to a frequency difference of 100 cents as measured in the system of equal temperament, and denoting the pitch difference between certain adjacent degrees of the diatonic scale (**diatonic semitone**) or between one note and its sharpened or flattened equivalent (**chromatic semitone**); minor second. Also called (US and Canadian) half step. See **whole tone** > semitonic (ˌsɛmɪ'tɒnɪk) *adj*

semitrailer (ˌsɛmɪ'treɪlə) *n* a type of trailer or articulated lorry that has wheels only at the rear, the front end being supported by the towing vehicle

semitropical (ˌsɛmɪ'trɒpɪkᵊl) *adj* partly tropical > ˌsemi'tropics *pl n*

semivowel ('sɛmɪˌvaʊəl) *n* phonetics a vowel-like sound that acts like a consonant, in that it serves the same function in a syllable carrying the same amount of prominence as a consonant relative to a true vowel, the nucleus of the syllable. Also called: glide

semiyearly (ˌsɛmɪ'jɪəlɪ) *adj* another word for **semiannual**

Semmelweis ('sɛmᵊlˌvaɪs) *n* **Ignaz Philipp.** 1818–65, Hungarian obstetrician, who discovered the cause of puerperal infection and pioneered the use of antiseptics

semolina (ˌsɛmə'liːnə) *n* the large hard grains of wheat left after flour has been bolted, used for puddings, soups, etc [c18: from Italian *semolino*, diminutive of *semola* bran, from Latin *simila* very fine wheat flour]

Sempach (German 'zɛmpax) *n* a village in central Switzerland, in Lucerne canton on **Lake Sempach**: scene of the victory (1386) of the Swiss over the Hapsburgs

sempervivum (ˌsɛmpə'vaɪvəm) *n* See **houseleek** [New Latin, from Latin *sempervivus* ever-living, from *semper* always + *vivere* to live]

sempiternal (ˌsɛmpɪ't3:nᵊl) *adj* literary everlasting; eternal [c15: from Old French *sempiternel*, from Late Latin *sempiternālis*, from Latin *sempiternus*, from *semper* always + *aeternus* ETERNAL] > ˌsempi'ternally *adv*

semplice ('sɛmplɪtʃɪ) *adj, adv* music to be performed in a simple manner [Italian: simple, from Latin *simplex*]

sempre ('sɛmprɪ) *adv* music (preceding a tempo or dynamic marking) always; consistently. It is used to indicate that a specified volume, tempo, etc, is to be sustained throughout a piece or passage [Italian: always, from Latin *semper*]

sempstress ('sɛmpstrɪs) *n* a rare word for **seamstress**

Semtex ('sɛmtɛks) *n* a pliable plastic explosive originally produced in the Czech Republic [c20: originally a trade name]

Sen. *or* **sen.** abbreviation **1** senator **2** senior

senate ('sɛnɪt) *n* **1** any legislative or governing body considered to resemble a Senate **2** the main governing body at some colleges and universities [c13: from Latin *senātus* council of the elders, from *senex* an old man]

Senate ('sɛnɪt) *n* (*sometimes not capital*) **1** the upper chamber of the legislatures of the US, Canada, Australia, and many other countries **2** the legislative council of ancient Rome. Originally the council of the kings, the Senate became the highest legislative, judicial, and religious authority in republican Rome

senator ('sɛnətə) *n* **1** (*often capital*) a member of a Senate or senate **2** any legislator or statesman > ˌsena'torial *adj* > ˌsena'torially *adv*

send (sɛnd) *vb* **sends, sending, sent 1** (*tr*) to cause or order (a person or thing) to be taken, directed, or transmitted to another place: *he sent the salesman away* **2** (when *intr*, foll by *for*; when *tr*, *takes an infinitive*) to dispatch a request or command (for something or to do something): *he sent for a bottle of wine; he sent his son to come home* **3** (*tr*) to direct or cause to go to a place or point: *his blow sent the champion to the floor*

4 (*tr*) to bring to a state or condition: *this noise will send me mad* **5** (*tr*; often foll by *forth, out*, etc) to cause to issue; emit: *his cooking sent forth a lovely smell from the kitchen* **6** (*tr*) to cause to happen or come: *misery sent by fate* **7** to transmit (a message) by radio, esp in the form of pulses **8** (*tr*) slang to move to excitement or rapture: *this music really sends me* ▷ *n* **9** another word for **swash** (sense 4) [Old English *sendan*; related to Old Norse *senda*, Gothic *sandjan*, Old High German *senten*] > **sendable** *adj* > **sender** *n*

Sendai (sɛn'daɪ) *n* a city in central Japan, on NE Honshu: university (1907). Pop: 986 713 (2002 est)

Sendak ('sɛndæk) *n* **Maurice (Bernard).** born 1928, US artist, writer, and set designer, best known as an illustrator of children's books, including *Where the Wild Things Are* (1963), which he also wrote, *In the Night Kitchen* (1971), and *Nutcracker* (1984)

send down *vb* (*tr, adverb*) *Brit* **1** to expel from a university, esp permanently **2** *informal* to send to prison

sendoff ('sɛndˌɒf) *n* informal **1** a demonstration of good wishes to a person about to set off on a journey, new career, etc ▷ *vb* **send off** (*tr, adverb*) **2** to cause to depart; despatch **3** *sport* (of the referee) to dismiss (a player) from the field of play for some offence **4** *informal* to give a sendoff

send up *vb* (*tr, adverb*) **1** *slang* to send to prison **2** *Brit informal* to make fun of, esp by doing an imitation or parody of ▷ *n* **send-up 3** *Brit informal* a parody or imitation

Seneca ('sɛnɪkə) *n* **1 Lucius Annaeus** (ə'niːəs), called *the Younger.* ?4 BC–65 AD, Roman philosopher, statesman, and dramatist; tutor and adviser to Nero. He was implicated in a plot to murder Nero and committed suicide. His works include Stoical essays on ethical subjects and tragedies that had a considerable influence on Elizabethan drama **2** his father, **Marcus** ('mɑːkəs) or **Lucius Annaeus,** called *the Elder* or *the Rhetorician.* ?55 BC–?39 AD, Roman writer on oratory and history

Senefelder ('zenəˌfɛldə) *n* (**Johan Nepomuk Franz**) **Aloys** ('aloɪs). 1771–1834, German dramatist and engraver, born in Czechoslovakia, who invented (1796) lithography

Senegal (ˌsɛnɪ'ɡɔːl) *n* a republic in West Africa, on the Atlantic: made part of French West Africa in 1895; became fully independent in 1960; joined with The Gambia to form the Confederation of Senegambia (1982–89); mostly low-lying, with semidesert in the north and tropical forest in the southwest Official language: French. Religion: Muslim majority. Currency: franc. Capital: Dakar. Pop: 10 339 000 (2004 est). Area: 197 160 sq km (76 124 sq miles) > ˌSenega'lese *adj, n*

Senegambia (ˌsɛnə'ɡæmbɪə) *n* a region of W Africa, between the Senegal and Gambia Rivers: now mostly in Senegal

Senegambia Confederation *n* an economic and political union (1982–89) between Senegal and The Gambia

senescent (sɪ'nɛsᵊnt) *adj* **1** growing old **2** characteristic of old age [c17: from Latin *senēscere* to grow old, from *senex* old] > se'nescence *n*

seneschal ('sɛnɪʃəl) *n* **1** a steward of the household of a medieval prince or nobleman who took charge of domestic arrangements, etc **2** *Brit* a cathedral official [c14: from Old French, from Medieval Latin *siniscalus*, of Germanic origin; related to Old High German *seneschalh* oldest servant, from *sene-* old + *scalh* a servant]

Senghor (French sɑ̃ɡɔr) *n* **Léopold Sédar** (leɔpɔl sedar). 1906–2001, Senegalese statesman and writer; president of Senegal (1960–80)

senile ('siːnaɪl) *adj* **1** of, relating to, or characteristic of old age **2** mentally or physically weak or infirm on account of old age [c17: from Latin *senīlis*, from *senex* an old man] > senility (sɪ'nɪlɪtɪ) *n*

senile dementia *n* dementia starting in old age with no precipitating physical cause

senior ('siːnjə) *adj* **1** higher in rank or length of service **2** older in years: *senior citizens* **3** of or relating to adulthood, maturity, or old age: *senior privileges* **4** education **a** of, relating to, or designating more advanced or older pupils **b** of or relating to a secondary school **5** *US* of, relating to, or designating students in the fourth and final year at college [c14: from Latin: older, from *senex* old]

Senior ('si:njə) *adj chiefly US* being the older: used to distinguish the father from the son with the same first name or names: *Charles Parker, Senior* Abbreviation: **Sr**

senior aircraftman *n* a rank in the Royal Air Force comparable to that of a private in the army, though not the lowest rank in the Royal Air Force

senior citizen *n* an old age pensioner

senior common room *n* (in British universities, colleges, etc) a common room for the use of academic staff

seniority (,si:nɪ'ɒrɪtɪ) *n, pl* **-ties** 1 the state of being senior 2 precedence in rank, etc, due to senior status

senior moment *n jocular* a lapse of memory common in elderly people

senior service *n Brit* the Royal Navy

Senlac ('sɛnlæk) *n* a hill in Sussex: site of the Battle of Hastings in 1066

senna ('sɛnə) *n* 1 any of various tropical plants of the leguminous genus *Cassia*, esp *C. angustifolia* (**Arabian senna**) and *C. acutifolia* (**Alexandrian senna**), having typically yellow flowers and long pods 2 **senna leaf** the dried leaflets of any of these plants, used as a cathartic and laxative 3 **senna pods** the dried fruits of any of these plants, used as a cathartic and laxative [c16: via New Latin from Arabic *sanā*]

Senna ('sɛnə) *n* **Ayrton** ('ɛətən). 1960–94, Brazilian racing driver: world champion (1988, 1990, 1991)

Sennacherib (sɛ'nækərɪb) *n* died 681 BC, king of Assyria (705–681); son of Sargon II. He invaded Judah twice, defeated Babylon, and rebuilt Nineveh

Sennar ('sɛnɑ:, sɛ'nɑ:) *n* 1 a region of the E Sudan, between the White Nile and the Blue Nile: a kingdom from the 16th to 19th centuries 2 a town in this region, on the Blue Nile: the nearby **Sennar Dam** (1925) supplies irrigation water to Gezira. Pop: 135 000 (2005 est)

Sennett ('sɛnət) *n* **Mack**, original name *Michael Sinott*. 1884–1960, US film producer and director, born in Canada, who produced many silent comedy films featuring the Keystone Kops, Charlie Chaplin, and Harold Lloyd, for the Keystone Company

sennight *or* **se'nnight** ('sɛnaɪt) *n* an archaic word for **week** [Old English *seofan nihte*; see SEVEN, NIGHT]

señor (sɛ'njɔ:; *Spanish* se'ɲɔr) *n, pl* **-ñors** *or* **-ñores** (*Spanish* -'ɲores) a Spaniard or Spanish-speaking man: a title of address equivalent to *Mr* when placed before a name or *sir* when used alone [Spanish, from Latin *senior* an older man, SENIOR]

señora (sɛ'njɔ:rə; *Spanish* se'ɲora) *n, pl* **-ras** (-rəz; *Spanish* -ras) a married Spanish or Spanish-speaking woman: a title of address equivalent to *Mrs* when placed before a name or *madam* when used alone

señorita (,sɛnjɔ:'ri:tə; *Spanish* seɲo'rita) *n, pl* **-tas** (-təz; *Spanish* -tas) an unmarried Spanish or Spanish-speaking woman: a title of address equivalent to *Miss* when placed before a name or *madam* or *miss* when used alone

sensate ('sɛnseɪt) *adj* 1 perceived by the senses 2 *obsolete* having the power of sensation [c16: from Late Latin *sensātus* endowed with sense, from Latin *sensus* SENSE] > 'sensately *adv*

sensation (sɛn'seɪʃən) *n* 1 the power of perceiving through the senses 2 a physical condition or experience resulting from the stimulation of one of the sense organs 3 a state of widespread public excitement: *his announcement caused a sensation* 4 anything that causes such a state: *your speech was a sensation* [c17: from Medieval Latin *sensātiō*, from Late Latin *sensātus* SENSATE]

sensational (sɛn'seɪʃənəl) *adj* 1 causing or intended to cause intense feelings, esp of curiosity, horror, etc: *sensational disclosures in the press* 2 *informal* extremely good: *a sensational skater* 3 of or relating to the faculty of sensation > sen'sationally *adv*

sensationalism (sɛn'seɪʃənə,lɪzəm) *n* 1 the use of sensational language, etc, to arouse an intense emotional response 2 such sensational matter itself 3 *philosophy* the doctrine that knowledge cannot go beyond the analysis of experience. Also called: sensualism > sen'sationalist *n, adj* > sen,sational'istic *adj*

sensationalize *or* **sensationalise** (sɛn'seɪʃənə,laɪz) *vb* (*tr*) to cause (events, esp in newspaper reports) to seem more vivid, shocking, etc, than they really are

sense (sɛns) *n* 1 any of the faculties by which the mind receives information about the external world or about the state of the body. In addition to the five traditional faculties of sight, hearing, touch, taste, and smell, the term includes the means by which bodily position, temperature, pain, balance, etc, are perceived 2 such faculties collectively; the ability to perceive 3 a feeling perceived through one of the senses: *a sense of warmth* 4 a mental perception or awareness: *a sense of happiness* 5 moral discernment; understanding: *a sense of right and wrong* 6 (*sometimes plural*) sound practical judgment or intelligence 7 reason or purpose: *what is the sense of going out in the rain?* 8 substance or gist; meaning: *what is the sense of this proverb?* 9 specific meaning; definition: *in what sense are you using the word?* 10 an opinion or consensus 11 *maths* one of two opposite directions measured on a directed line; the sign as contrasted with the magnitude of a vector 12 **make sense** to be reasonable or understandable 13 **take leave of one's senses** ▷ *vb* (*tr*) 14 to perceive through one or more of the senses 15 to apprehend or detect without or in advance of the evidence of the senses 16 to understand 17 *computing* a to test or locate the position of (a part of computer hardware) b to read (data) [c14: from Latin *sēnsus*, from *sentīre* to feel]

sense datum *n philosophy* a sensation detached both from any information it may convey and from its putative source in the external world, such as the bare awareness of a red visual field. Sense data are held by some philosophers to be the immediate objects of experience providing certain knowledge from which knowledge of material objects is inferred

senseless ('sɛnslɪs) *adj* 1 lacking in sense; foolish: *a senseless plan* 2 lacking in feeling; unconscious 3 lacking in perception; stupid > 'senselessly *adv* > 'senselessness *n*

sense organ *n* a structure in animals that is specialized for receiving external or internal stimuli and transmitting them in the form of nervous impulses to the brain

sensibility (,sɛnsɪ'bɪlɪtɪ) *n, pl* **-ties** 1 the ability to perceive or feel 2 (*often plural*) the capacity for responding to emotion, impression, etc 3 (*often plural*) the capacity for responding to aesthetic stimuli 4 mental responsiveness; discernment; awareness 5 (*usually plural*) emotional or moral feelings: *cruelty offends most people's sensibilities*

sensible ('sɛnsɪbəl) *adj* 1 having or showing good sense or judgment 2 (of clothing) serviceable; practical 3 having the capacity for sensation; sensitive 4 capable of being apprehended by the senses 5 perceptible to the mind 6 (sometimes foll by *of*) having perception; aware: *sensible of your kindness* 7 readily perceived; considerable: *a sensible difference* [c14: from Old French, from Late Latin *sēnsibilis*, from Latin *sentīre* to sense] > 'sensibleness *n* > 'sensibly *adv*

sensitive ('sɛnsɪtɪv) *adj* 1 having the power of sensation 2 responsive to or aware of feelings, moods, reactions, etc 3 easily irritated; delicate 4 affected by external conditions or stimuli 5 easily offended 6 of or relating to the senses or the power of sensation 7 capable of registering small differences or changes in amounts, quality, etc: *a sensitive instrument* 8 *photog* having a high sensitivity: *a sensitive emulsion* 9 connected with matters affecting national security, esp through access to classified information 10 (of a stock market or prices) quickly responsive to external influences and thus fluctuating or tending to fluctuate [c14: from Medieval Latin *sēnsitīvus*, from Latin *sentīre* to feel] > 'sensitively *adv* > sensitivity (,sɛnsɪ'tɪvɪtɪ) *n*

sensitive plant *n* a tropical American mimosa plant, *Mimosa pudica*, the leaflets and stems of which fold if touched

sensitize *or* **sensitise** ('sɛnsɪ,taɪz) *vb* 1 to make or become sensitive 2 (*tr*) to render (an individual) sensitive to a drug, allergen, etc 3 (*tr*) *photog* to make (a

S

material) sensitive to light or to other actinic radiation, esp to light of a particular colour, by coating it with a photographic emulsion often containing special chemicals, such as dyes > ˌsensiti'zation or ˌsensiti'sation n > 'sensiˌtizer or 'sensiˌtiser n

sensitometer (ˌsensɪ'tɒmɪtə) n an instrument for measuring the sensitivity to light of a photographic material over a range of exposures

sensor ('sensə) n anything, such as a photoelectric cell, that receives a signal or stimulus and responds to it [C19: from Latin *sēnsus* perceived, from *sentīre* to observe]

sensorimotor (ˌsensərɪ'məutə) or **sensomotor** (ˌsensə'məutə) adj of or relating to both the sensory and motor functions of an organism or to the nerves controlling them

sensorium (sen'sɔːrɪəm) n, pl -riums or -ria (-rɪə) 1 the area of the brain considered responsible for receiving and integrating sensations from the outside world 2 physiol the entire sensory and intellectual apparatus of the body [C17: from Late Latin, from Latin *sēnsus* felt, from *sentīre* to perceive]

sensor network or **wireless sensor network** n computing a network of tiny autonomous devices embedded in everyday objects or sprinkled on the ground, able to communicate using wireless links

sensory ('sensərɪ) or less commonly **sensorial** (sen'sɔːrɪəl) adj of or relating to the senses or the power of sensation [C18: from Latin *sensōrius*, from *sentīre* to feel]

sensual ('sensjʊəl) adj 1 of or relating to any of the senses or sense organs; bodily 2 strongly or unduly inclined to gratification of the senses 3 tending to arouse the bodily appetites, esp the sexual appetite [C15: from Late Latin *sensuālis*, from Latin *sēnsus* SENSE. Compare French *sensuel*, Italian *sensuale*] > 'sensually adv

sensualism ('sensjʊəˌlɪzəm) n the quality or state of being sensual

sensuality (ˌsensjʊ'ælɪtɪ) n, pl -ties 1 the quality or state of being sensual 2 excessive indulgence in sensual pleasures > sensualist ('sensjʊəlɪst) n

sensuous ('sensjʊəs) adj 1 aesthetically pleasing to the senses 2 appreciative of or moved by qualities perceived by the senses 3 of, relating to, or derived from the senses [C17: apparently coined by Milton to avoid the unwanted overtones of SENSUAL; not in common use until C19: from Latin *sēnsus* SENSE + -OUS] > 'sensuously adv > 'sensuousness n

sent (sent) vb the past tense and past participle of **send**

sentence ('sentəns) n 1 a sequence of words capable of standing alone to make an assertion, ask a question, or give a command, usually consisting of a subject and a predicate containing a finite verb 2 the judgment formally pronounced upon a person convicted in criminal proceedings, esp the decision as to what punishment is to be imposed 3 music a passage or division of a piece of music, usually consisting of two or more contrasting musical phrases and ending in a cadence 4 archaic a proverb, maxim, or aphorism ▷ vb 5 (tr) to pronounce sentence on (a convicted person) in a court of law [C13: via Old French from Latin *sententia* a way of thinking, from *sentīre* to feel] > sentential (sen'tenʃəl) adj

sentence connector n a word or phrase that introduces a clause or sentence and serves as a transition between it and a previous clause or sentence, as for example *also* in *I'm buying eggs and also I'm looking for a dessert for tonight.* It may be preceded by a coordinating conjunction such as *and* in the above example

sentence substitute n a word or phrase, esp one traditionally classified as an adverb, that is used in place of a finite sentence, such as *yes, no, certainly,* and *never*

sentencing circle n a method of dispensing justice amongst native Canadian peoples involving discussion between offenders, victims, and members of the community

sententious (sen'tenʃəs) adj 1 characterized by or full of aphorisms, terse pithy sayings, or axioms 2 constantly using aphorisms, etc 3 tending to indulge in pompous moralizing [C15: from Latin *sententiōsus* full of meaning, from *sententia*; see SENTENCE] > sen'tentiously adv

> sen'tentiousness n

sentient ('sentiənt) adj 1 having the power of sense perception or sensation; conscious ▷ n 2 rare a sentient person or thing [C17: from Latin *sentiēns* feeling, from *sentīre* to perceive] > 'sentiently adv > sentience ('senʃəns)

sentiment ('sentimənt) n 1 susceptibility to tender, delicate, or romantic emotion: *she has too much sentiment to be successful* 2 (often plural) a thought, opinion, or attitude 3 exaggerated, overindulged, or mawkish feeling or emotion 4 an expression of response to deep feeling, esp in art or literature 5 a feeling, emotion, or awareness: *a sentiment of pity* 6 a mental attitude modified or determined by feeling: *there is a strong revolutionary sentiment in his country* 7 a feeling conveyed, or intended to be conveyed, in words [C17: from Medieval Latin *sentīmentum*, from Latin *sentīre* to feel]

sentimental (ˌsentɪ'mentəl) adj 1 tending to indulge the emotions excessively 2 making a direct appeal to the emotions, esp to romantic feelings 3 relating to or characterized by sentiment > ˌsenti'mentally adv > ˌsenti'mentalism n > ˌsenti'mentalist n

sentimentality (ˌsentɪmen'tælɪtɪ) n, pl -ties 1 the state, quality, or an instance of being sentimental 2 an act, statement, etc, that is sentimental

sentimentalize or **sentimentalise** (ˌsentɪ'mentəˌlaɪz) vb to make sentimental or behave sentimentally > ˌsentiˌmentali'zation or ˌsentiˌmentali'sation n

sentimental value n the value of an article in terms of its sentimental associations for a particular person

sentinel ('sentɪnəl) n 1 a person, such as a sentry, assigned to keep guard ▷ vb -nels, -nelling, -nelled (tr) 2 to guard as a sentinel 3 to post as a sentinel [C16: from Old French *sentinelle*, from Old Italian *sentinella*, from *sentina* watchfulness, from *sentire* to notice, from Latin]

sentry ('sentrɪ) n, pl -tries a soldier who guards or prevents unauthorized access to a place, keeps watch for danger, etc [C17: perhaps shortened from obsolete *centrinel*, C16 variant of SENTINEL]

sentry box n a small shelter with an open front in which a sentry may stand to be sheltered from the weather

senza ('sentsaː) prep music without; omitting [Italian]

SEO abbreviation search-engine optimization

Seoul (səul) n the capital of South Korea, in the west on the Han River: capital of Korea from 1392 to 1910, then seat of the Japanese administration until 1945; became capital of South Korea in 1948; cultural and educational centre. Pop: 9 592 000 (2005 est)

sepal ('sepəl) n any of the separate parts of the calyx of a flower [C19: from New Latin *sepalum*: sep-, from Greek *skepē* a covering + -alum, from New Latin *petalum* PETAL]

-sepalous adj combining form having sepals of a specified type or number: *polysepalous* > -sepaly n combining form

separable ('sepərəbəl, 'seprəbəl) adj able to be separated, divided, or parted > ˌsepara'bility or 'separableness n > 'separably adv

separate vb ('sepəˌreit) 1 (tr) to act as a barrier between: *a range of mountains separates the two countries* 2 to part or be parted from a mass or group 3 (tr) to distinguish between: *to separate the men from the boys* 4 to divide or be divided into component parts; sort or be sorted 5 to sever or be severed 6 (intr) (of a married couple) to cease living together by mutual agreement or after obtaining a decree of judicial separation ▷ adj ('seprit, 'separit) 7 existing or considered independently: *a separate problem* 8 disunited or apart 9 set apart from the main body or mass 10 distinct, individual, or particular 11 solitary or withdrawn [C15: from Latin *sēparāre*, from *sē-* apart + *parāre* to obtain] > 'separately adv > 'separateness n > separative ('sepərətɪv, 'seprə-) adj > 'separatively adv > 'separativeness n > 'sepaˌrator n > 'separatory adj

separates ('seprits, 'sepərits) pl n women's outer garments that only cover part of the body and so are worn in combination with others, usually unmatching; skirts, blouses, jackets, trousers, etc

separate school n (in Canada) a school for a large religious minority financed by its rates and administered by its own school board but under the

separation (ˌsɛpəˈreɪʃən) *n* **1** the act of separating or state of being separated **2** the place or line where a separation is made **3** a gap that separates **4** *family law* the cessation of cohabitation between a man and wife, either by mutual agreement or under a decree of a court

separation anxiety *n psychoanal* a state of distress felt at the prospect of being separated from a familiar or beloved person

separatist (ˈsɛpərətɪst, ˈsɛprə-) *or* **separationist** *n* **a** a person who advocates or practises secession from an organization or group **b** (*as modifier*): *a separatist movement* > **ˈsepara,tism** *n*

Separatist (ˈsɛpərətɪst, ˈsɛprə-) *n* (*sometimes not capital*) a person who advocates the secession of a province, esp Quebec, from Canada > **ˈSepara,tism** *n*

Sephardi (sɪˈfɑːdɪ) *n, pl* **-dim** (-dɪm) *Judaism* **1** a Jew of Spanish, Portuguese, or North African descent **2** the pronunciation of Hebrew used by these Jews, and of Modern Hebrew as spoken in Israel ▷ See **Ashkenazi** [C19: from Late Hebrew, from Hebrew *sepharad* a region mentioned in Obadiah 20, thought to have been Spain] > **Seˈphardic** *adj*

sepia (ˈsiːpɪə) *n* **1** a dark reddish-brown pigment obtained from the inky secretion of the cuttlefish **2** a brownish tone imparted to a photograph, esp an early one such as a calotype. It can be produced by first bleaching a print (after fixing) and then immersing it for a short time in a solution of sodium sulphide or of alkaline thiourea **3** a brownish-grey to dark yellowish-brown colour **4** a drawing or photograph in sepia ▷ *adj* **5** of the colour sepia or done in sepia: *a sepia print* [C16: from Latin: a cuttlefish, from Greek; related to Greek *sēpein* to make rotten]

sepoy (ˈsiːpɔɪ) *n* (formerly) an Indian soldier in the service of the British [C18: from Portuguese *sipaio*, from Urdu *sipāhī*, from Persian: horseman, from *sipāh* army]

Seppo (ˈsɛpəʊ) *n Austral slang* an American [C20: from *Septic Tank*, rhyming slang for YANK; see YANKEE]

seppuku (sɛˈpuːkuː) *n* another word for **hara-kiri** [from Japanese, from Chinese *ch'ieh* to cut + *fu* bowels]

sepsis (ˈsɛpsɪs) *n* the presence of pus-forming bacteria in the body [C19: via New Latin from Greek *sēpsis* a rotting; related to Greek *sēpein* to cause to decay]

sept (sɛpt) *n* **1** *anthropol* a clan or group that believes itself to be descended from a common ancestor **2** a branch of a tribe or nation, esp in medieval Ireland or Scotland [C16: perhaps variant of SECT]

Sept *abbreviation* **1** September **2** Septuagint

septa (ˈsɛptə) *n* the plural of **septum**

septal (ˈsɛptəl) *adj* of or relating to a septum

September (sɛpˈtɛmbə) *n* the ninth month of the year, consisting of 30 days [Old English, from Latin: the seventh (month) according to the original calendar of ancient Rome, from *septem* seven]

septenary (ˈsɛptɪnərɪ) *adj* **1** of or relating to the number seven **2** forming a group of seven ▷ *n, pl* **-naries** **3** the number seven **4** a group of seven things **5** a period of seven years [C16: from Latin *septēnārius*, from *septēnī* seven each, from *septem* seven]

septennial (sɛpˈtɛnɪəl) *adj* **1** occurring every seven years **2** relating to or lasting seven years [C17: from Latin *septennis*, from *septem* seven + *annus* a year]

septet *or* **septette** (sɛpˈtɛt) *n* **1** *music* a group of seven singers or instrumentalists or a piece of music composed for such a group **2** a group of seven people or things [C19: from German, from Latin *septem* seven]

septic (ˈsɛptɪk) *adj* **1** of, relating to, or caused by sepsis **2** of, relating to, or caused by putrefaction ▷ *n* **3** *Austral & NZ informal* short for **septic tank** [C17: from Latin *sēpticus*, from Greek *sēptikos*, from *sēptos* decayed, from *sēpein* to make rotten] > **ˈseptically** *adv* > **septicity** (sɛpˈtɪsɪtɪ) *n*

septicaemia *or US* **septicemia** (ˌsɛptɪˈsiːmɪə) *n* a condition caused by pus-forming microorganisms in the blood. Nontechnical name: **blood poisoning** [C19: from New Latin, from Greek *sēptik(os)* SEPTIC + -AEMIA] > **ˌseptiˈcaemic** *or US* **ˌseptiˈcemic** *adj*

septic tank *n* a tank, usually below ground, for containing sewage to be decomposed by the action of anaerobic bacteria

septillion (sɛpˈtɪljən) *n, pl* **-lions** *or* **-lion** **1** (in Britain, France, and Germany) the number represented as one followed by 42 zeros (10^{42}) **2** (in the US and Canada) the number represented as one followed by 24 zeros (10^{24}). Brit word: **quadrillion** [C17: from French, from *sept* seven + *-illion*, on the model of *million*] > **sepˈtillionth** *adj, n*

septime (ˈsɛptiːm) *n* the seventh of eight basic positions from which a parry or attack can be made in fencing [C19: from Latin *septimus* seventh, from *septem* seven]

septuagenarian (ˌsɛptjʊədʒɪˈnɛərɪən) *n* **1** a person who is from 70 to 79 years old ▷ *adj* **2** being between 70 and 79 years old **3** of or relating to a septuagenarian [C18: from Latin *septuāgēnārius*, from *septuāgēnī* seventy each, from *septuāgintā* seventy]

Septuagesima (ˌsɛptjʊəˈdʒɛsɪmə) *n* the third Sunday before Lent [C14: from Church Latin *septuāgēsima* (*diēs*) the seventieth (day); compare QUINQUAGESIMA]

Septuagint (ˈsɛptjʊəˌdʒɪnt) *n* the principal Greek version of the Old Testament, including the Apocrypha, believed to have been translated by 70 or 72 scholars [C16: from Latin *septuāgintā* seventy]

septum (ˈsɛptəm) *n, pl* **-ta** (-tə) *biology, anatomy* a dividing partition between two tissues or cavities [C18: from Latin *saeptum* wall, from *saepīre* to enclose; related to Latin *saepēs* a fence]

septuple (ˈsɛptjʊp⁹l) *adj* **1** seven times as much or many; sevenfold **2** consisting of seven parts or members ▷ *vb* **3** (*tr*) to multiply by seven [C17: from Late Latin *septuplus*, from *septem* seven; compare QUADRUPLE] > **sepˈtuplicate** *n, adj*

sepulchral (sɪˈpʌlkrəl) *adj* **1** suggestive of a tomb; gloomy **2** of or relating to a sepulchre > **seˈpulchrally** *adv*

sepulchre *or US* **sepulcher** (ˈsɛpəlkə) *n* **1** a burial vault, tomb, or grave **2** Also called: **Easter sepulchre** a separate alcove in some medieval churches in which the Eucharistic elements were kept from Good Friday until the Easter ceremonies ▷ *vb* **3** (*tr*) to bury in a sepulchre [C12: from Old French *sépulcre*, from Latin *sepulcrum*, from *sepelīre* to bury]

sepulture (ˈsɛpəltʃə) *n* the act of placing in a sepulchre [C13: via Old French from Latin *sepultūra*, from *sepultus* buried, from *sepelīre* to bury]

seq. *abbreviation* **1** sequel **2** sequens [Latin: the following (one)]

sequel (ˈsiːkwəl) *n* **1** anything that follows from something else; development **2** a consequence or result **3** a novel, play, etc, that continues a previously related story [C15: from Late Latin *sequēla*, from Latin *sequī* to follow]

sequela (sɪˈkwiːlə) *n, pl* **-lae** (-liː) (*often plural*) *med* **1** any abnormal bodily condition or disease related to or arising from a pre-existing disease **2** any complication of a disease [C18: from Latin: SEQUEL]

sequence (ˈsiːkwəns) *n* **1** an arrangement of two or more things in a successive order **2** the successive order of two or more things: *chronological sequence* **3** an action or event that follows another or others **4 a** *cards* a set of three or more consecutive cards, usually all of the same suit **b** *bridge* a set of two or more consecutive cards **5** *music* an arrangement of notes or chords repeated several times at different pitches **6** *maths* an ordered set of numbers or other mathematical entities in one-to-one correspondence with the integers 1 to *n* **7** a section of a film constituting a single continuous uninterrupted episode **8** *biochem* the unique order of amino acids in the polypeptide chain of a protein or of nucleotides in the polynucleotide chain of DNA or RNA ▷ *vb* (*tr*) **9** to arrange in a sequence [C14: from Medieval Latin *sequentia* that which follows, from Latin *sequī* to follow]

sequence of tenses *n grammar* the sequence according to which the tense of a subordinate verb in a sentence is determined by the tense of the principal verb, as in I *believe he is lying, I believed he was lying*, etc

sequencing (ˈsiːkwənsɪŋ) *n biochem* the procedure of determining the order of amino acids in the polypeptide chain of a protein (**protein sequencing**) or of nucleotides in a DNA section comprising a gene (**gene sequencing**)

S

sequent ('si:kwənt) *adj* 1 following in order or succession 2 following as a result; consequent ▷ *n* 3 something that follows; consequence [c16: from Latin *sequēns*, from *sequī* to follow] > 'sequently *adv*

sequential (sɪ'kwɛnʃəl) *adj* 1 characterized by or having a regular sequence 2 another word for **sequent** > sequentiality (sɪ,kwɛnʃɪ'ælɪtɪ) *n* > se'quentially *adv*

sequential access *n* a method of reaching and reading data from a computer file by reading through the file from the beginning

sequester (sɪ'kwɛstə) *vb* (*tr*) 1 to remove or separate 2 (*usually passive*) to retire into seclusion 3 *law* to take (property) temporarily out of the possession of its owner, esp until the claims of creditors are satisfied or a court order is complied with 4 *international law* to requisition or appropriate (enemy property) [c14: from Late Latin *sequestrāre* to surrender for safekeeping, from Latin *sequester* a trustee]

sequestrate (sɪ'kwɛstreɪt) *vb* (*tr*) *law* a variant of **sequester** (sense 3) [c16: from Late Latin *sequestrāre* to SEQUESTER] > sequestrator ('si:kwɛs,treɪtə, sɪ'kwɛs,treɪtə) *n*

sequestration (,si:kwɛ'streɪʃən) *n* 1 the act of sequestering or state of being sequestered 2 *law* the sequestering of property 3 *chem* the effective removal of ions from a solution by coordination with another type of ion or molecule to form complexes that do not have the same chemical behaviour as the original ions

sequestrum (sɪ'kwɛstrəm) *n*, *pl* -tra (-trə) *pathol* a detached piece of necrotic bone that often migrates to a wound, abscess, etc [c19: from New Latin, from Latin: something deposited;] > se'questral *adj*

sequin ('si:kwɪn) *n* 1 a small piece of shiny often coloured metal foil or plastic, usually round, used to decorate garments, etc 2 Also called: **zecchino** any of various gold coins that were formerly minted in Italy, Turkey, and Malta [c17: via French from Italian *zecchino*, from *zecca* mint, from Arabic *sikkah* die for striking coins] > 'sequined *adj*

sequoia (sɪ'kwɔɪə) *n* either of two giant Californian coniferous trees, *Sequoia sempervirens* (**redwood**) or *Sequoiadendron giganteum* (formerly *Sequoia gigantea*) (**big tree** or **giant sequoia**): family *Taxodiaceae* [c19: New Latin, named after *Sequoya*, known also as George Guess, (?1770–1843), American Indian scholar and leader]

Sequoia National Park *n* a national park in central California, in the Sierra Nevada Mountains: established in 1890 to protect groves of giant sequoias, some of which are about 4000 years old. Area: 1556 sq km (601 sq miles)

ser *or* **seer** (sɪə) *n* a unit of weight used in India, usually taken as one fortieth of a maund [from Hindi]

sérac ('sɛræk) *n* a pinnacle of ice among crevasses on a glacier, usually on a steep slope [c19: from Swiss French: a variety of white cheese (hence the ice that it resembles) from Medieval Latin *serācium*, from Latin *serum* whey]

seraglio (sɛ'rɑːlɪ,əʊ) *or* **serail** (sə'raɪl, -'raɪl, -'reɪl) *n*, *pl* -raglios *or* -rails 1 the harem of a Muslim house or palace 2 a sultan's palace, esp in the former Turkish empire [c16: from Italian *serraglio* animal cage, from Medieval Latin *serrāculum* bolt, from Latin *sera* a door bar; associated also with Turkish *seray* palace]

Serajevo (*Bosnian* 'serajevɔ) *n* a variant of **Sarajevo**

Seram *or* **Ceram** (sɪ'ræm) *n* an island in Indonesia, in the Moluccas, separated from New Guinea by the **Ceram Sea**: mountainous and densely forested. Area: 17 150 sq km (6622 sq miles). Also called: Serang (sə'ræŋ)

serape (sə'rɑːpɪ) *n* 1 a blanket-like shawl often of brightly-coloured wool worn by men in Latin America 2 a large shawl worn around the shoulders by women as a fashion garment [C19 Mexican Spanish]

seraph ('sɛrəf) *n*, *pl* -aphs *or* -aphim (-əfɪm) *theol* a member of the highest order of angels in the celestial hierarchies, often depicted as the winged head of a child [c17: back formation from plural *seraphim*, via Late Latin from Hebrew] > se'raphic *or* se'raphical *adj* > se'raphically *adv*

Serapis ('sɛrəpɪs) *n* a Graeco-Egyptian god combining attributes of Apis and Osiris

Serb (sɜːb) *n, adj* another word for **Serbian** [c19: from Serbian *Srb*]

Serbia ('sɜːbɪə) *n* a republic in SE Europe: declared a kingdom in 1882; precipitated World War I by the conflict with Austria; became part of the Kingdom of the Serbs, Croats, and Slovenes (later called Yugoslavia) in 1918; with Montenegro formed the Federal Republic of Yugoslavia when the other constituent republics became independent in 1991–92; a Union of Serbia and Montenegro formed in 2003 and dissolved in 2006. The autonomous region of Kosovo (administered by the U.N. following the conflict of 1999) unilaterally declared its independence from Serbia in 2008. Mountainous in the S, with the Danube plains in the N. Religion: Serbian Orthodox majority, with Roman Catholic and Muslim minorities. Currencies: new dinar and euro (in Kosovo). Capital: Belgrade. Pop: 7 479 437 (2002). Area: 88 361 sq km (34 109 sq miles). Former name: **Servia**. Serbian name: Srbija

Serbian ('sɜːbɪən) *or* **Serb** *adj* 1 of, relating to, or characteristic of Serbia, its people, or their language (formerly regarded as a dialect of Serbo-Croat) ▷ *n* 2 the language spoken in Serbia 3 a native or inhabitant of Serbia

Serbo-Croat *or* **Serbo-Croatian** *n* 1 Also called: Croato-Serb a name for the Serbian and Croatian languages considered together as branches of the same language, belonging to the South Slavonic branch of the Indo-European family. The Serbian dialect is usually written in the Cyrillic alphabet, the Croatian in Roman ▷ *adj* 2 of or relating to this language

Sercq (sɛrk) *n* the French name for **Sark**

sere[1] *or* **sear** (sɪə) *adj* 1 *archaic* dried up or withered ▷ *vb, n* 2 a rare spelling of **sear**[1] (sense 1) [Old English *sēar*; see SEAR]

sere[2] (sɪə) *n* the series of changes occurring in the ecological succession of a particular community [c20: from SERIES]

Seremban (sə'rɛmbən) *n* a town in Peninsular Malaysia, capital of Negri Sembilan state. Pop: 332 000 (2005 est)

serenade (,sɛrɪ'neɪd) *n* 1 a piece of music appropriate to the evening, characteristically played outside the house of a woman 2 a piece of music indicative or suggestive of this 3 an extended composition in several movements similar to the modern suite or divertimento ▷ *vb* 4 (*tr*) to play a serenade for (someone) 5 (*intr*) to play a serenade [c17: from French *sérénade*, from Italian *serenata*, from *sereno* peaceful, from Latin *serēnus* calm; also influenced in meaning by Italian *sera* evening, from Latin *sērus* late] > ,sere'nader *n*

serendipity (,sɛrən'dɪpɪtɪ) *n* the faculty of making fortunate discoveries by accident [c18: coined by Horace Walpole, from the Persian fairytale *The Three Princes of Serendip*, in which the heroes possess this gift] > ,seren'dipitous *adj*

serene (sɪ'riːn) *adj* 1 peaceful or tranquil; calm 2 clear or bright: *a serene sky* 3 (*often capital*) honoured: used as part of certain royal titles: *His Serene Highness* [c16: from Latin *serēnus*] > se'renely *adv* > se'renity *n*

serf (sɜːf) *n* (esp in medieval Europe) an unfree person, esp one bound to the land. If his lord sold the land, the serf was passed on to the new landlord [c15: from Old French, from Latin *servus* a slave; see SERVE] > 'serfdom *or* 'serfhood *n*

serge (sɜːdʒ) *n* 1 a twill-weave woollen or worsted fabric used for clothing 2 a similar twilled cotton, silk, or rayon fabric [c14: from Old French *sarge*, from Vulgar Latin *sārica* (unattested), from Latin *sēricum*, from Greek *sērikon* silk, from *sērikos* silken, from *sēr* silkworm]

sergeant ('sɑːdʒənt) *n* 1 a noncommissioned officer in certain armed forces, usually ranking above a corporal 2 a (in Britain) a police officer ranking between constable and inspector b (in the US) a police officer ranking below a captain 3 a court or municipal officer who has ceremonial duties ▷ Also: serjeant [c12: from Old French *sergent*, from Latin *serviēns*, literally: serving, from *servīre* to SERVE]

sergeant at arms *n* an officer of a legislative or fraternal body responsible for maintaining internal order. Also called: **sergeant**, **serjeant at arms**, **serjeant**

sergeant baker *n* a large brightly-coloured fish of the genus *Latropiscis*, found in temperate reef waters of Australasia [named after *Sergeant* (*William*) *Baker*, a Norfolk Island colonist]

sergeant major *n* a noncommissioned officer of the highest rank or having specific administrative tasks in branches of the armed forces of various countries

Sergipe (*Portuguese* ser'ʒipi) *n* a state of NE Brazil: the smallest Brazilian state; a centre of resistance to Dutch conquest (17th century). Capital: Aracajú. Pop: 1 846 039 (2002). Area: 13 672 sq km (8492 sq miles)

Sergt *abbreviation* Sergeant

serial ('sɪərɪəl) *n* **1** a novel, play, etc, presented in separate instalments at regular intervals **2** a publication, usually regularly issued and consecutively numbered ▷ *adj* **3** of, relating to, or resembling a series **4** published or presented as a serial **5** of or relating to such publication or presentation **6** *computing* of or operating on items of information, instructions, etc, in the order in which they occur **7** of, relating to, or using the techniques of serialism [c19: from New Latin *seriālis*, from Latin *seriēs* SERIES] ▷ **'serially** *adv*

serialism ('sɪərɪə,lɪzəm) *n* (in 20th-century music) the use of a sequence of notes in a definite order as a thematic basis for a composition and a source from which the musical material is derived. See also **twelve-tone**

serialize *or* **serialise** ('sɪərɪə,laɪz) *vb* (*tr*) to publish or present in the form of a serial ▷ **,seriali'zation** *or* **,seriali'sation** *n*

serial killer *n* a person who carries out a series of murders

serial monogamy *n* the practice of having a number of long-term romantic or sexual partners in succession

serial number *n* any of the consecutive numbers assigned to machines, tools, books, etc

serial port *n* *computing* (on a computer) a socket that can be used for connecting devices that send data one bit at a time; often used for connecting the mouse or a modem

seriate ('sɪərɪɪt) *adj* forming a series

seriatim (,sɪərɪ'ætɪm, ,sɛr-) *adv* in a series; one after another in regular order [c17: from Medieval Latin, from Latin *seriēs* SERIES]

sericeous (sɪ'rɪʃəs) *adj* *botany* **1** covered with a layer of small silky hairs: *a sericeous leaf* **2** silky [c18: from Late Latin *sēriceus* silken, from Latin *sēricus*; see SERGE]

sericulture ('sɛrɪ,kʌltʃə) *n* the rearing of silkworms for the production of raw silk [c19: via French; *seri*- from Latin *sēricum* silk, from Greek *sērikos* silken, from *sēr* a silkworm] ▷ **,seri'cultural** *adj* ▷ **,seri'culturist** *n*

series ('sɪəriːz, -rɪz) *n, pl* **-ries 1** a group or connected succession of similar or related things, usually arranged in order **2** a set of radio or television programmes having the same characters and setting but different stories **3** a set of books having the same format, related content, etc, published by one firm **4** a set of stamps, coins, etc, issued at a particular time **5** *maths* the sum of a finite or infinite sequence of numbers or quantities **6** *electronics* **a** a configuration of two or more components connected in a circuit so that the same current flows in turn through each of them (esp in the phrase **in series**) **b** (*as modifier*): *a series circuit.* See **parallel** (sense 10) **7** *geology* a stratigraphical unit that is a subdivision of a system and represents the rocks formed during an epoch [c17: from Latin: a row, from *serere* to link]

series-wound ('sɪəriːz,waʊnd, -rɪz-) *adj* (of a motor or generator) having the field and armature circuits connected in series

serif *or rarely* **seriph** ('sɛrɪf) *n* *printing* a small line at the extremities of a main stroke in a type character [c19: perhaps from Dutch *schreef* dash, probably of Germanic origin, compare Old High German *screvōn* to engrave]

serigraph ('sɛrɪ,græf, -,grɑːf) *n* a colour print made by an adaptation of the silk-screen process [c19: from *seri*-,

from Latin *sēricum* silk + -GRAPH] ▷ **serigraphy** (sə'rɪgrəfɪ) *n*

serin ('sɛrɪn) *n* any of various small yellow-and-brown finches of the genus *Serinus*, esp *S. serinus*, of parts of Europe and North Africa [c16: from French, perhaps from Old Provençal *sirena* a bee-eater, from Latin *sīren*, a kind of bird, from SIREN]

seringa (sə'rɪŋgə) *n* **1** any of several euphorbiaceous trees of the Brazilian genus *Hevea*, that yield rubber **2** a deciduous simaroubaceous tree, *Kirkia acuminata*, of southern Africa with a graceful shape [c18: from Portuguese, variant of SYRINGA]

Seringapatam (sə,rɪŋgəpə'tæm) *n* a small town in S India, in Karnataka on **Seringapatam Island** in the Cauvery River: capital of Mysore from 1610 to 1799, when it was besieged and captured by the British. Pop: 23 448 (2001)

seriocomic (,sɪərɪəʊ'kɒmɪk) *or less commonly* **seriocomical** *adj* mixing serious and comic elements ▷ **,serio'comically** *adv*

serious ('sɪərɪəs) *adj* **1** grave in nature or disposition; thoughtful: *a serious person* **2** marked by deep feeling; in earnest; sincere: *is he serious or joking?* **3** concerned with important matters: *a serious conversation* **4** requiring effort or concentration: *a serious book* **5** giving rise to fear or anxiety; critical: *a serious illness* **6** *informal* worthy of regard because of substantial quantity or quality: *serious money; serious wine* **7** *informal* extreme or remarkable: *a serious haircut* [c15: from Late Latin *sēriōsus*, from Latin *sērius*; probably related to Old English *swǣr* gloomy, Gothic *swers* esteemed] ▷ **'seriousness** *n*

seriously ('sɪərɪəslɪ) *adv* **1** in a serious manner or to a serious degree **2** *informal* extremely or remarkably: *seriously tall*

serjeant ('sɑːdʒənt) *n* a variant spelling of **sergeant**

serjeant at law *n* (formerly in England) a barrister of a special rank, to which he was raised by a writ under the Great Seal. Also called: **serjeant**, **sergeant at law**, **sergeant**

Serlio (*Italian* 'sɛrʎo) *n* **Sebastiano** 1475–1554, Italian architect and painter, best known for his treatise *Complete Works on Architecture and Perspective* (1537–75), the first to set out the principles of classical architecture and to give rules for their application

sermon ('sɜːmən) *n* **1 a** an address of religious instruction or exhortation, often based on a passage from the Bible, esp one delivered during a church service **b** a written version of such an address **2 a** serious speech, esp one administering reproof [c12: via Old French from Latin *sermō* discourse, probably from *serere* to join together]

sermonize *or* **sermonise** ('sɜːmə,naɪz) *vb* to talk to or address (a person or audience) as if delivering a sermon ▷ **'sermon,izer** *or* **'sermon,iser** *n*

Sermon on the Mount *n* *New Testament* a major discourse delivered by Christ, including the Beatitudes and the Lord's Prayer (Matthew 5–7)

sero- *combining form* indicating a serum

seroconvert (,sɪərəʊkən'vɜːt) *vb* (*intr*) (of an individual) to produce antibodies specific to, and in response to the presence in the blood of, a particular antigen, such as a virus or vaccine ▷ **,serocon'version** *n*

serology (sɪ'rɒlədʒɪ) *n* the science concerned with serums ▷ **serologic** (,sɪərə'lɒdʒɪk) *or* **,sero'logical** *adj*

seropositive (,sɪərəʊ'pɒzɪtɪv) *adj* (of a person whose blood has been tested for a specific disease, such as AIDS) showing a serological reaction indicating the presence of the disease

serotine ('sɛrə,taɪn) *adj* **1** Also called: **serotinal** (sɪ'rɒtɪnəl), **serotinous** *biology* produced, flowering, or developing late in the season ▷ *n* **2** either of two insectivorous bats, *Eptesicus serotinus* or *Vespertilio serotinus*: family *Vespertilionidae* [c16: from Latin *sērōtinus* late, from *sērus* late; applied to the bats because they fly late in the evening]

serotonin (,sɛrə'təʊnɪn) *n* a compound that occurs in the brain, intestines, and blood platelets and acts as a neurotransmitter, as well as inducing vasoconstriction and contraction of smooth muscle;

S

5-hydroxytryptamine (5HT) [from SERO- + TON(IC) + -IN]

serotype ('sɪərəʊˌtaɪp) n medicine a category into which material, usually a bacterium, is placed based on its serological activity, esp in terms of the antigens it contains or the antibodies produced against it

serous ('sɪərəs) adj of, resembling, producing, or containing serum [c16: from Latin serōsus, from SERUM] > serosity (sɪ'rɒsɪtɪ) n

serous fluid n a thin watery fluid found in many body cavities, esp those lined with serous membrane

serous membrane n any of the smooth moist delicate membranes, such as the pleura or peritoneum, that line the closed cavities of the body and secrete a watery exudate

serow ('sɛrəʊ) n either of two antelopes, Capricornis sumatraensis and C. crispus, of mountainous regions of S and SE Asia, having a dark coat and conical backward-pointing horns [c19: from Lepcha să-ro Tibetan goat]

Seroxat ('sɛˌrɒksæt) n trademark a drug that prolongs the action of serotonin in the brain; used to treat depression and social anxiety

serpent ('sɜːpənt) n 1 a literary or dialect word for **snake** 2 Old Testament a manifestation of Satan as a guileful tempter (Genesis 3:1–5) 3 a sly, deceitful, or unscrupulous person 4 an obsolete wind instrument resembling a snake in shape, the bass form of the cornett [c14: via Old French from Latin serpēns a creeping thing, from serpere to creep; related to Greek herpein to crawl]

serpentine[1] ('sɜːpənˌtaɪn) adj 1 of, relating to, or resembling a serpent 2 twisting; winding [c14: from Late Latin serpentīnus, from serpēns SERPENT]

serpentine[2] ('sɜːpənˌtaɪn) n a dark green or brown mineral with a greasy or silky lustre, found in igneous and metamorphic rocks. It is used as an ornamental stone; and one variety (chrysotile) is known as asbestos. Composition: hydrated magnesium silicate. Formula: $Mg_3Si_2O_5(OH)_4$. Crystal structure: monoclinic [c15 serpentyn, from Medieval Latin serpentīnum SERPENTINE[1]; referring to the snakelike patterns of these minerals]

serpigo (sɜː'paɪɡəʊ) n pathol any progressive skin eruption, such as ringworm or herpes [c14: from Medieval Latin, from Latin serpere to creep]

SERPS or **Serps** (sɜːps) n acronym for (in Britain) state earnings-related pension scheme

Serrano ham (sə'rɑːnəʊ) n cured ham from Spain

serrate adj ('sɛrɪt, -eɪt) 1 (of leaves) having a margin of forward pointing teeth 2 having a notched or sawlike edge ▷ vb ('sɛreɪt) 3 (tr) to make serrate [c17: from Latin serrātus saw-shaped, from serra a saw]

serrated (sə'reɪtɪd) adj having a notched or sawlike edge

serration (sə'reɪʃən) or less commonly **serrature** ('sɛrətʃə) n 1 the state or condition of being serrated 2 a row of notches or toothlike projections on an edge

serried ('sɛrɪd) adj in close or compact formation: serried ranks of troops [c17: from Old French serré close-packed, from serrer to shut up]

serriform ('sɛrɪˌfɔːm) adj biology resembling a notched or sawlike edge [serri-, from Latin serra saw]

serrulate ('sɛrʊˌleɪt, -lɪt) or **serrulated** adj (esp of leaves) minutely serrate [c18: from New Latin serrulātus, from Latin serrula diminutive of serra a saw] > ˌserruˈlation n

Sertorius (sɜː'tɔːrɪəs) n **Quintus** ('kwɪntəs). ?123–72 BC, Roman soldier who fought with Marius in Gaul (102) and led an insurrection in Spain against Sulla until he was assassinated

serum ('sɪərəm) n, pl -rums or -ra (-rə) 1 antitoxin obtained from the blood serum of immunized animals 2 physiol, zoology clear watery fluid, esp that exuded by serous membranes 3 a less common word for **whey** [c17: from Latin: whey]

serum albumin n a form of albumin that is the most abundant protein constituent of blood plasma

serum hepatitis n a former name for **hepatitis B**

serum sickness n an allergic reaction, such as vomiting, skin rash, etc, that sometimes follows 2-3 weeks after an injection of a foreign serum

serval ('sɜːvəl) n, pl -vals or -val a slender feline mammal, Felis serval, of the African bush, having an orange-brown coat with black spots, large ears, and long legs [c18: via French from Late Latin cervālis staglike, from Latin cervus a stag]

servant ('sɜːvᵊnt) n 1 a person employed to work for another, esp one who performs household duties 2 See **public servant** [c13: via Old French, from servant serving, from servir to SERVE]

serve (sɜːv) vb 1 to be in the service of (a person) 2 to render or be of service to (a person, cause, etc); help 3 (in a shop) to give (customers) information about articles for sale and to hand over articles purchased 4 (tr) to provide (guests, customers, etc) with food, drink, etc: she served her guests with cocktails 5 to distribute or provide (food, drink, etc) for guests, customers, etc: do you serve coffee? 6 (tr; sometimes foll by up) to present (food, drink, etc) in a specified manner: cauliflower served with cheese sauce 7 (tr) to provide with a regular supply of 8 (tr) to work actively for: to serve the government 9 (tr) to pay homage to: to serve God 10 to answer the requirements of; suit: this will serve my purpose 11 (intr; may take an infinitive) to have a use; function: this wood will serve to build a fire 12 to go through (a period of service, enlistment, imprisonment, etc) 13 (intr) (of weather, conditions, etc) to be favourable or suitable 14 Also called: **service** (tr) (of a male animal) to copulate with (a female animal) 15 sport to put (the ball) into play 16 (tr) to deliver (a legal document, esp a writ or summons) to (a person) 17 (tr) nautical to bind (a rope, spar, etc) with wire or fine cord to protect it from chafing, etc 18 **serve a person right** informal to pay a person back, esp for wrongful or foolish treatment or behaviour ▷ n 19 sport short for **service**[1] (sense 15) 20 Austral a portion or helping of food or drink [c13: from Old French servir, from Latin servīre, from servus a slave] > 'servable or 'serveable adj

server ('sɜːvə) n 1 a person who serves 2 chiefly RC Church a person who acts as acolyte or assists the priest at Mass 3 something that is used in serving food and drink 4 the player who serves in racket games 5 computing a computer or program that supplies data or resources to other machines on a network

Servetus (sɜː'viːtəs) n **Michael,** Spanish name Miguel Serveto. 1511–53, Spanish theologian and physician. He was burnt at the stake by order of Calvin for denying the doctrine of the Trinity and the divinity of Christ

Servia ('sɜːvɪə) n the former name of **Serbia**

service ('sɜːvɪs) n 1 an act of help or assistance 2 an organized system of labour and material aids used to supply the needs of the public: telephone service; bus service 3 the supply, installation, or maintenance of goods carried out by a dealer 4 the state of availability for use by the public (esp in the phrases **into** or **out of service**) 5 a periodic overhaul made on a car, machine, etc 6 the act or manner of serving guests, customers, etc, in a shop, hotel, restaurant, etc 7 a department of public employment and its employees: civil service 8 employment in or performance of work for another: he has been in the service of our firm for ten years 9 a one of the branches of the armed forces b (as modifier): service life 10 the state, position, or duties of a domestic servant (esp in the phrase **in service**) 11 the act or manner of serving food 12 a complete set of dishes, cups, etc, for use at table 13 public worship carried out according to certain prescribed forms: divine service 14 the prescribed form according to which a specific kind of religious ceremony is to be carried out: the burial service 15 sport a the act, manner, or right of serving a ball b the game in which a particular player serves: he has lost his service 16 the serving of a writ, summons, etc, upon a person 17 (of male animals) the act of mating 18 (modifier) of, relating to, or for the use of servants or employees 19 (modifier) serving the public rather than producing goods ▷ vb (tr) 20 to provide service or services 21 to make fit for use 22 to supply with assistance 23 to overhaul (a car, machine, etc) 24 (of a male animal) to mate with (a female) 25 Brit to meet interest and capital payments on (debt) ▷ See also **services** [c12 servise, from Old French, from Latin servitium condition of a slave, from servus a slave]

Service ('sɜːvɪs) n **Robert (William)**. 1874–1958, Canadian poet, born in England; noted for his ballad-like poems of gold-rush era Yukon, such as 'The Shooting of Dan McGrew'; his books include *Songs of a Sourdough* (1907)

serviceable ('sɜːvɪsəbᵊl) *adj* **1** capable of or ready for service; usable **2** capable of giving good service; durable > ˌservicea'bility *or* 'serviceableness *n* > 'serviceably *adv*

service area *n* a place on a motorway providing garage services, restaurants, toilet facilities, etc

service charge *n* a percentage of a bill, as at a restaurant or hotel, added to the total to pay for service

service contract *n* a contract between an employer and a senior employee, esp a director, executive, etc

service flat *n Brit* a flat in which domestic services are provided by the management

serviceman ('sɜːvɪsˌmæn, -mən) *n, pl* -men **1** Also called (feminine): **servicewoman** a person who serves in the armed services of a country **2** a man employed to service and maintain equipment

service road *n Brit* a relatively narrow road running parallel to a main road and providing access to houses, shops, offices, factories, etc, situated along its length

services ('sɜːvɪsɪz) *pl n* **1** work performed for remuneration **2** the services the armed forces **3** (*sometimes singular*) *economics* commodities, such as banking, that are mainly intangible and usually consumed concurrently with their production **4** a system of providing the public with gas, water, etc

service station *n* a place that supplies fuel, oil, etc, for motor vehicles and often carries out repairs, servicing, etc

service tree *n* **1** Also called: **sorb** a Eurasian rosaceous tree, *Sorbus domestica*, cultivated for its white flowers and brown edible apple-like fruits **2** wild service tree a similar and related Eurasian tree, *Sorbus torminalis* [*service*, from Old English *syrfe*, from Vulgar Latin *sorbea* (unattested), from Latin *sorbus* SORB]

serviette (ˌsɜːvɪ'ɛt) *n chiefly Brit* a small square of cloth or paper used while eating to protect the clothes, wipe the mouth and hands, etc [c15: from Old French, from *servir* to SERVE; formed on the model of OUBLIETTE]

servile ('sɜːvaɪl) *adj* **1** obsequious or fawning in attitude or behaviour; submissive **2** of or suitable for a slave **3** existing in or relating to a state of slavery **4** (when *postpositive*, foll by *to*) submitting or obedient [c14: from Latin *servīlis*, from *servus* slave] > **servility** (sɜː'vɪlɪtɪ) *n*

serving ('sɜːvɪŋ) *n* a portion or helping of food or drink

servitor ('sɜːvɪtə) *n archaic* a person who serves another [c14: from Old French *servitour*, from Late Latin *servītor*, from Latin *servīre* to SERVE]

servitude ('sɜːvɪˌtjuːd) *n* **1** the state or condition of a slave; bondage **2** the state or condition of being subjected to or dominated by a person or thing **3** *law* a burden attaching to an estate for the benefit of an adjoining estate or of some definite person. See also **easement** [c15: via Old French from Latin *servitūdō*, from *servus* a slave]

servlet ('sɜːvlɪt) *n computing* a small program that runs on a web server often accessing databases in response to client input

servo ('sɜːvəʊ) *adj* **1** (*prenominal*) of, relating to, forming part of, or activated by a servomechanism: *servo brakes* ▷ *n, pl* -vos **2** *informal* short for **servomechanism** [see SERVOMOTOR]

servomechanism ('sɜːvəʊˌmɛkəˌnɪzəm, ˌsɜːvəʊ'mɛk-) *n* a mechanical or electromechanical system for control of the position or speed of an output transducer. Negative feedback is incorporated to minimize discrepancies between the output state and the input control setting

servomotor ('sɜːvəʊˌməʊtə) *n* any motor that supplies power to a servomechanism [c19: from French *servo-moteur*, from Latin *servus* slave + French *moteur* MOTOR]

servqual ('sɜːvˌkwɒl) *n marketing* the provision of high-quality products by an organization backed by a high level of service for consumers [c20: from SERV(ICE)¹ + QUAL(ITY)]

sesame ('sɛsəmɪ) *n* **1** a tropical herbaceous plant, *Sesamum indicum*, of the East Indies, cultivated, esp in India, for its small oval seeds: family *Pedaliaceae* **2** the seeds of this plant, used in flavouring bread and

yielding an edible oil (**benne oil** *or* **gingili**) [c15: from Latin, from Greek *sēsamon*, *sēsamē*, of Semitic origin; related to Arabic *simsim*]

sesamoid ('sɛsəˌmɔɪd) *adj anatomy* **1** of or relating to various small bones formed in tendons, such as the patella **2** of or relating to any of various small cartilages, esp those of the nose [c17: from Latin *sēsamoīdēs* like sesame (seed), from Greek]

sesh (sɛʃ) *n slang* short for **session**

Sesostris I (sɛ'sɒstrɪs) *n* 20th century BC, king of Egypt of the 12th dynasty. He conquered Nubia and brought ancient Egypt to the height of its prosperity. The funerary complex at Lisht was built during his reign

sesqui- *prefix* **1** indicating one and a half: *sesquicentennial* **2** (in a chemical compound) indicating a ratio of two to three [from Latin, contraction of SEMI- + *as* AS² + -*que* and]

sesquicentennial (ˌsɛskwɪsɛn'tɛnɪəl) *adj* **1** of or relating to a period of 150 years ▷ *n* **2** a period or cycle of 150 years **3** a 150th anniversary or its celebration > ˌsesquicen'tennially *adv*

Sesshu ('sɛʃuː) *n* original family name *Oda*, also called *Toyo*. 1420–1506, Japanese landscape painter, who introduced the Chinese technique of ink painting on long scrolls to Japan

sessile ('sɛsaɪl) *adj* **1** (of flowers or leaves) having no stalk; growing directly from the stem **2** (of animals such as the barnacle) permanently attached to a substratum [c18: from Latin *sēssilis* concerning sitting, from *sedēre* to sit] > **sessility** (sɛ'sɪlɪtɪ) *n*

sessile oak *n* another name for the **durmast** (sense 1)

session ('sɛʃən) *n* **1** the meeting of a court, legislature, judicial body, etc, for the execution of its function or the transaction of business **2** a single continuous meeting of such a body **3** a series or period of such meetings **4** *education* **a** the time during which classes are held **b** a school or university term or year **5** *Presbyterian Church* the judicial and administrative body presiding over a local congregation and consisting of the minister and elders **6** a meeting of a group of musicians to record in a studio **7** any period devoted to an activity [c14: from Latin *sessiō* a sitting, from *sedēre* to sit] > 'sessional *adj*

Sessions ('sɛʃənz) *n* **Roger (Huntington)**. 1896–1985, US composer

sesterce ('sɛstɜːs) *or* **sestertius** (sɛ'stɜːtɪəs) *n* a silver or, later, bronze coin of ancient Rome worth a quarter of a denarius [c16: from Latin *sēstertius* a coin worth two and a half asses, from *sēmis* half + *tertius* a third]

sestet (sɛ'stɛt) *n* **1** *prosody* the last six lines of a Petrarchan sonnet **2** another word for **sextet** (sense 1) [c19: from Italian *sestetto*, from *sesto* sixth, from Latin *sextus*, from *sex* six]

sestina (sɛ'stiːnə) *n* an elaborate verse form of Italian origin, normally unrhymed, consisting of six stanzas of six lines each and a concluding tercet. The six final words of the lines in the first stanza are repeated in a different order in each of the remaining five stanzas and also in the concluding tercet [c19: from Italian, from *sesto* sixth, from Latin *sextus*]

Sestos ('sɛstɒs) *n* a ruined town in NW Turkey, at the narrowest point of the Dardanelles: N terminus of the bridge of boats built by Xerxes in 481 BC for the crossing of his armies of invasion

set¹ (sɛt) *vb* **sets, setting, set** (*mainly tr*) **1** to put or place in position or into a specified state or condition: *to set a book on the table; to set someone free* **2** (*also intr*; foll by *to* or *on*) to put or be put (to); apply or be applied: *he set fire to the house; they set the dogs on the scent* **3** to put into order or readiness for use; prepare: *to set a trap; to set the table for dinner* **4** (*also intr*) to put, form, or be formed into a jelled, firm, fixed, or rigid state: *the jelly set in three hours* **5** (*also intr*) to put or be put into a position that will restore a normal state: *to set a broken bone* **6** to adjust (a clock or other instrument) to a position **7** to determine or fix or establish: *we have set the date for our wedding* **8** to prescribe or allot (an undertaking, course of study, etc): *the examiners have set "Paradise Lost"* **9** to arrange in a particular fashion, esp an attractive one: *she set her hair; the jeweller set the diamonds in silver* **10** Also called: **set to**

music to provide music for (a poem or other text to be sung) **11** Also called: **set up** *printing* to arrange or produce (type, film, etc) from (text or copy); compose **12** to arrange (a stage, television studio, etc) with scenery and props **13** to describe or present (a scene or the background to a literary work, story, etc) in words: *his novel is set in Russia* **14** to present as a model of good or bad behaviour (esp in the phrases **set an example, set a good example, set a bad example**) **15** (foll by *on* or *by*) to value (something) at a specified price or estimation of worth: *he set a high price on his services* **16** (*also intr*) to give or be given a particular direction: *his course was set to the East* **17** (*also intr*) to rig (a sail) or (of a sail) to be rigged so as to catch the wind **18** (*intr*) (of the sun, moon, etc) to disappear beneath the horizon **19** to leave (dough, etc) in one place so that it may prove **20** to sink (the head of a nail) below the surface surrounding it by using a nail set **21** *computing* to give (a binary circuit) the value 1 **22** (of plants) to produce (fruits, seeds, etc) after pollination or (of fruits or seeds) to develop after pollination **23** to plant (seeds, seedlings, etc) **24** to place (a hen) on (eggs) for the purpose of incubation **25** (*intr*) (of a gun dog) to turn in the direction of game, indicating its presence **26** *bridge* to defeat (one's opponents) in their attempt to make a contract **27** a dialect word for **sit** ▷ *n* **28** the act of setting or the state of being set **29** a condition of firmness or hardness **30** bearing, carriage, or posture: *the set of a gun dog when pointing* **31** the scenery and other props used in and identifying the location of a stage or television production, film, etc **32** Also called: **set width** *printing* **a** the width of the body of a piece of type **b** the width of the lines of type in a page or column **33** *psychol* a temporary bias disposing an organism to react to a stimulus in one way rather than in others **34** a seedling, cutting, or similar part that is ready for planting: *onion sets* **35** a variant spelling of **sett** ▷ *adj* **36** fixed or established by authority or agreement: *set hours of work* **37** (*usually postpositive*) rigid or inflexible: *she is set in her ways* **38** unmoving; fixed: *a set expression on his face* **39** conventional, artificial, or stereotyped, rather than spontaneous: *she made her apology in set phrases* **40** (*postpositive*; foll by *on* or *upon*) resolute in intention: *he is set upon marrying* **41** (of a book, etc) prescribed for students' preparation for an examination ▷ See also **set about, set against**, etc [Old English *settan*, causative of *sittan* to SIT; related to Old Frisian *setta*, Old High German *sezzan*]

set² (sɛt) *n* **1** a number of objects or people grouped or belonging together, often forming a unit or having certain features or characteristics in common: *a set of coins; John is in the top set for maths* **2** a group of people who associate together, esp a clique: *he's part of the jet set* **3** *maths, logic* Also called: **class** a collection of numbers, objects, etc, that is treated as an entity: *3, the moon is the set the two members of which are the number 3 and the moon* **4** any apparatus that receives or transmits television or radio signals **5** *tennis, squash, badminton* one of the units of a match, in tennis one in which one player or pair of players must win at least six games: *Graf lost the first set* **6 a** the number of couples required for a formation dance **b** a series of figures that make up a formation dance **7 a** a band's or performer's concert repertoire on a given occasion: *the set included no new numbers* **b** a continuous performance: *the Who played two sets* ▷ *vb* **sets, setting, set 8** (*intr*) (in square dancing and country dancing) to perform a sequence of steps while facing towards another dancer **9** (*usually tr*) to divide into sets: *in this school we set our older pupils for English* [C14 (in the obsolete sense: a religious sect): from Old French *sette*, from Latin *secta* SECT; later sense development influenced by the verb SET¹]

seta ('siːtə) *n, pl* **-tae** (-tiː) (in invertebrates and some plants) any bristle or bristle-like appendage [C18: from Latin] > **setaceous** (sɪ'teɪʃəs) *adj*

set about *vb* (*intr, preposition*) **1** to start or begin to **2** to attack physically or verbally

set against *vb* (*tr, preposition*) **1** to balance or compare **2** to cause to be hostile or unfriendly to

set aside *vb* (*tr, adverb*) **1** to reserve for a special purpose; put to one side **2** to discard, dismiss, or quash ▷ *n* **set-aside 3 a** (in the European Union) a scheme in which a proportion of farmland is taken out of production in order to reduce surpluses or maintain or increase prices of a specific crop **b** (*as modifier*): *set-aside land*

set back *vb* (*tr, adverb*) **1** to hinder; impede **2** *informal* to cost (a person) a specified amount ▷ *n* **setback 3** anything that serves to hinder or impede **4** a recession in the upper part of a high building, esp one that increases the daylight at lower levels **5** Also called: **offset, setoff** a steplike shelf where a wall is reduced in thickness

set down *vb* (*tr, adverb*) **1** to write down or record **2** to judge, consider, or regard: *he set him down as an idiot* **3** (foll by *to*) to ascribe; attribute: *his attitude was set down to his illness* **4** to reprove; rebuke **5** to snub; dismiss **6** *Brit* to allow (passengers) to alight from a bus, taxi, etc

set forth *vb* (*adverb*) *formal or archaic* **1** (*tr*) to state, express, or utter **2** (*intr*) to start out on a journey

Seth (sɛθ) *n Old Testament* Adam's third son, given by God in place of the murdered Abel (Genesis 4:25)

SETI ('sɛtɪ) *n acronym for* Search for Extraterrestrial Intelligence; the attempt to detect signals, esp radiowaves or light, from an intelligent extraterrestrial source

setiferous (sɪ'tɪfərəs) *or* **setigerous** (sɪ'tɪdʒərəs) *adj biology* bearing bristles [C19: see SETA, -FEROUS, -GEROUS]

set in *vb* (*intr, adverb*) **1** to become established: *the winter has set in* **2** (of wind) to blow or (of current) to move towards shore ▷ *adj* **set-in 3** (of a part) made separately and then added to a larger whole: *a set-in sleeve*

setline ('sɛt,laɪn) *n* any of various types of fishing line that consist of a long line suspended across a stream, between buoys, etc, and having shorter hooked and baited lines attached

set off *vb* (*adverb*) **1** (*intr*) to embark on a journey **2** (*tr*) to cause (a person) to act or do something, such as laugh or tell stories **3** (*tr*) to cause to explode **4** (*tr*) to act as a foil or contrast to, esp so as to improve: *that brooch sets your dress off well* **5** (*tr*) *accounting* to cancel a credit on (one account) against a debit on another, both of which are in the name of the same person, enterprise, etc ▷ *n* **setoff 6** anything that serves to contrast with or enhance something else; foil **7** a cross claim brought by a debtor that partly offsets the creditor's claim

set-off *n printing* a fault in which ink is transferred from a heavily inked or undried printed sheet to the sheet next to it in a pile

set on *vb* (*tr*) **1** (*preposition*) to cause to attack: *they set the dogs on him* **2** (*adverb*) to instigate or incite; urge

Seton ('siːt∘n) *n* **Ernest Thompson**. 1860–1946, US author and illustrator of animal books, born in England

Seto Naikai ('sɛtəʊ 'naɪkaɪ) *n* transliteration of the Japanese name for the **Inland Sea**

setose ('siːtəʊs) *adj biology* covered with setae; bristly [C17: from Latin *saetōsus*, from *saeta* a bristle]

set out *vb* (*adverb, mainly tr*) **1** to present, arrange, or display **2** to give a full account of; explain exactly: *he set out the matter in full* **3** to plan or lay out (a garden, etc) **4** (*intr*) to begin or embark on an undertaking, esp a journey

set piece *n* **1** a work of literature, music, etc, often having a conventional or prescribed theme, intended to create an impressive effect **2** a display of fireworks **3** *sport* a rehearsed team manoeuvre, usually attempted in continuous games at a restart of play, esp when the other side has been penalized for improper play

setscrew ('sɛt,skruː) *n* a screw that fits into the boss or hub of a wheel, coupling, cam, etc, and prevents motion of the part relative to the shaft on which it is mounted

set square *n* a thin flat piece of plastic, metal, etc, in the shape of a right-angled triangle, used in technical drawing

sett *or* **set** (sɛt) *n* **1** a small rectangular paving block made of stone, such as granite, used to provide a durable road surface **2** the burrow of a badger **3 a** a square in a pattern of tartan **b** the pattern itself [C19: variant of SET¹ (n)]

settee (sɛˈtiː) n a seat, for two or more people, with a back and usually with arms [c18: changed from SETTLE²]

setter (ˈsɛtə) n any of various breeds of large gun dog, having silky coats and plumed tails [c16: so called because they can be used to indicate where game is: see SET¹]

set theory n maths the branch of mathematics concerned with the properties and interrelationships of sets

setting (ˈsɛtɪŋ) n 1 the surroundings in which something is set; scene 2 the scenery, properties, or background, used to create the location for a stage play, film, etc 3 music a composition consisting of a certain text and music provided or arranged for it 4 the metal mounting and surround of a gem 5 the tableware, cutlery, etc, for a single place at table 6 any of a series of points on a scale or dial that can be selected to control the level as of temperature, speed, etc, at which a machine functions

settle¹ (ˈsɛtəl) vb 1 (tr) to put in order; arrange in a desired state or condition: he settled his affairs before he died 2 to arrange or be arranged in a fixed or comfortable position: he settled himself by the fire 3 (intr) to come to rest or a halt: a bird settled on the hedge 4 to take up or cause to take up residence: the family settled in the country 5 to establish or become established in a way of life, job, residence, etc 6 (tr) to migrate to and form a community; colonize 7 to make or become quiet, calm, or stable 8 to cause (sediment) to sink to the bottom, as in a liquid, or (of sediment) to sink thus 9 to subside or cause to subside and become firm or compact: the dust settled 10 (sometimes foll by up) to pay off or account for (a bill, debt, etc) 11 (tr) to decide, conclude, or dispose of: to settle an argument 12 (intr; often foll by on or upon) to agree or fix: to settle upon a plan 13 (tr; usually foll by on or upon) to secure (title, property, etc) to a person, as by making a deed of settlement, will, etc: he settled his property on his wife 14 to determine (a legal dispute, etc) by agreement of the parties without resort to court action (esp in the phrase **settle out of court**) [Old English setlan; related to Dutch zetelen; see SETTLE²] ▷ **settleable** adj

settle² (ˈsɛtəl) n a seat, for two or more people, usually made of wood with a high back and arms, and sometimes having a storage space in the boxlike seat [Old English setl; related to Old Saxon, Old High German sezzal]

settle down vb (adverb, mainly intr) 1 (also tr) to make or become quiet and orderly 2 (often foll by to) to apply oneself diligently: please settle down to work 3 to adopt an orderly and routine way of life, take up a permanent post, etc, esp after marriage

settle for vb (intr, preposition) to accept or agree to in spite of dispute or dissatisfaction

settlement (ˈsɛtəlmənt) n 1 the act or state of settling or being settled 2 the establishment of a new region; colonization 3 a place newly settled; colony 4 a community formed by members of a group, esp of a religious sect 5 a public building used to provide educational and general welfare facilities for persons living in deprived areas 6 a subsidence of all or part of a structure 7 a the payment of an outstanding account, invoice, charge, etc b (as modifier): settlement day 8 an adjustment or agreement reached in matters of finance, business, etc 9 law a a conveyance, usually to trustees, of property to be enjoyed by several persons in succession b the deed or other instrument conveying such property

settler (ˈsɛtlə) n a person who settles in a new country or a colony

settlings (ˈsɛtlɪŋz) pl n any matter or substance that has settled at the bottom of a liquid; sediment; dregs

set to vb (intr, adverb) 1 to begin working 2 to start fighting ▷ n **set-to** 3 informal a brief disagreement or fight

set-top box n a device which converts the signals from a digital television broadcast into a form which can be viewed on a standard television set

Setúbal (Portuguese səˈtuβal) n a port in SW Portugal, on **Setúbal Bay** south of Lisbon: an earthquake in 1755

destroyed most of the old town. Pop: 113 937 (2001)

set up vb (adverb, mainly tr) 1 (also intr) to put into a position of power, etc 2 (also intr) to begin or enable (someone) to begin (a new venture), as by acquiring or providing means, equipment, etc 3 to build or construct: to set up a shed 4 to raise, cause, or produce: to set up a wail 5 to advance or propose: to set up a theory 6 to restore the health of: the sea air will set you up again 7 to establish (a record) 8 informal to cause (a person) to be blamed, accused, etc ▷ n **setup** 9 informal the way in which anything is organized or arranged 10 slang an event the result of which is prearranged: it's a setup 11 a prepared arrangement of materials, machines, etc, for a job or undertaking ▷ adj **set-up** 12 physically well-built

Seurat (French sœra) n **Georges** (ʒɔrʒ). 1859–91, French neoimpressionist painter. He developed the pointillist technique of painting, characterized by brilliant luminosity, as in Dimanche à la Grande-Jatte (1886)

Sevan (sɛˈvɑːn) n Lake Sevan a lake in Armenia at an altitude of 1914 m (6279 ft). Area: 1417 sq km (547 sq miles)

Sevastopol (Russian sivasˈtopəlj) n a port, resort, and naval base in S Ukraine, in the Crimea, on the Black Sea: captured and destroyed by British, French, and Turkish forces after a siege of 11 months (1854–55) during the Crimean War; taken by the Germans after a siege of 8 months (1942) during World War II. Pop: 338 000 (2005 est). English name: Sebastopol

seven (ˈsɛvən) n 1 the cardinal number that is the sum of six and one and is a prime number 2 a numeral, 7, VII, etc, representing this number 3 the amount or quantity that is one greater than six 4 anything representing, represented by, or consisting of seven units, such as a playing card with seven symbols on it 5 Also called: **seven o'clock** seven hours after noon or midnight ▷ determiner 6 a amounting to seven: seven swans a-swimming b (as pronoun): you've eaten seven already ▷ See also **sevens** [Old English seofon; related to Gothic sibun, German sieben, Old Norse sjau, Latin septem, Greek hepta, Sanskrit saptá]

Seven against Thebes pl n Greek myth the seven members of an expedition undertaken to regain for Polynices, a son of Oedipus, his share in the throne of Thebes from his usurping brother Eteocles. The seven are usually listed as Polynices, Adrastus, Amphiaraus, Capaneus, Hippomedon, Tydeus, and Parthenopaeus. The campaign failed and the warring brothers killed each other in single combat before the Theban walls. See also **Adrastus**

seven deadly sins pl n a fuller name for the **deadly sins**

sevenfold (ˈsɛvənˌfəʊld) adj 1 equal to or having seven times as many or as much 2 composed of seven parts ▷ adv 3 by or up to seven times as many or as much

Seven Hills of Rome pl n the hills on which the ancient city of Rome was built: the Palatine, Capitoline, Quirinal, Caelian, Aventine, Esquiline, and Viminal

sevens (ˈsɛvənz) n (functioning as singular) a Rugby Union match or series of matches played with seven players on each side

seven seas pl n the oceans of the world considered as the N and S Pacific, the N and S Atlantic, and the Arctic, Antarctic, and Indian Oceans

seven-segment display n an arrangement of seven bars forming a square figure of eight, used in electronic displays of alphanumeric characters: any letter or figure can be represented by illuminating selected bars

seven-seven, 7-7 or **7/7** n the 7th of July 2005, the day on which a series of suicide bombings were carried out on the London public transport system by Islamic fundamentalists [c21: by analogy with NINE-ELEVEN]

Seven Sleepers pl n seven Christian youths from Ephesus who were walled up in a cave by the Emperor Decius in 250 AD and, according to legend, slept for 187 years

seventeen (ˈsɛvənˈtiːn) n 1 the cardinal number that is the sum of ten and seven and is a prime number 2 a numeral, 17, XVII, etc, representing this number 3 the amount or quantity that is seven more than ten 4 something represented by, representing, or consisting

S

of 17 units ▷ *determiner* **5 a** amounting to seventeen: *seventeen attempts* **b** (*as pronoun*): *seventeen were sold* [Old English *seofontīene*] > **'seventeen'th** *adj, n*

seventh ('sɛv°nθ) *adj* **1** (*usually prenominal*) **a** coming after the sixth and before the eighth in numbering or counting order, position, time, etc; being the ordinal number of *seven*: often written 7th **b** (*as noun*): *she left on the seventh; he was the seventh to arrive* ▷ *n* **2 a** one of seven equal or nearly equal parts of an object, quantity, measurement, etc **b** (*as modifier*): *a seventh part* **3** the fraction equal to one divided by seven (1/7) **4** *music* **a** the interval between one note and another seven notes away from it counting inclusively along the diatonic scale **b** one of two notes constituting such an interval in relation to the other ▷ *adv* **5** Also called: **seventhly** after the sixth person, position, event, etc

Seventh-Day Adventist *n* Protestant theol a member of that branch of the Adventists which constituted itself as a separate body after the expected Second Coming of Christ failed to be realized in 1844. They are strongly Protestant, believe that Christ's coming is imminent, and observe Saturday instead of Sunday as their Sabbath

seventh heaven *n* the final state of eternal bliss, esp according to Talmudic and Muslim eschatology [c19: so named from the belief that there are seven levels of heaven, the seventh and most exalted being the abode of God and the angels]

seventieth ('sɛv°ntɪɪθ) *adj* **1** (*usually prenominal*) **a** being the ordinal number of *seventy* in numbering or counting order, position, time, etc: often written 70th **b** (*as noun*): *the seventieth in line* ▷ *n* **2 a** one of 70 approximately equal parts of something **b** (*as modifier*): *a seventieth part* **3** the fraction equal to one divided by 70 (1/70)

seventy ('sɛv°ntɪ) *n, pl* **-ties 1** the cardinal number that is the product of ten and seven **2** a numeral, 70, LXX, etc, representing this number **3** (*plural*) the numbers 70–79, esp the 70th to the 79th year of a person's life or of a particular century **4** the amount or quantity that is seven times as big as ten **5** something represented by, representing, or consisting of 70 units ▷ *determiner* **6 a** amounting to seventy: *the seventy varieties of fabric* **b** (*as pronoun*): *to invite seventy to the wedding* [Old English *seofentig*]

Seven Wonders of the World *pl n* the seven structures considered by ancient and medieval scholars to be the most wondrous of the ancient world. The list varies, but generally consists of the Pyramids of Egypt, the Hanging Gardens of Babylon, Phidias' statue of Zeus at Olympia, the temple of Artemis at Ephesus, the mausoleum of Halicarnassus, the Colossus of Rhodes, and the Pharos (or lighthouse) of Alexandria

Seven Years' War *n* the war (1756–63) of Britain and Prussia, who emerged in the ascendant, against France and Austria, resulting from commercial and colonial rivalry between Britain and France and from the conflict in Germany between Prussia and Austria

sever ('sɛvə) *vb* **1** to put or be put apart; separate **2** to divide or be divided into parts **3** (*tr*) to break off or dissolve (a tie, relationship, etc) [c14 *severen*, from Old French *severer*, from Latin *sēparāre* to SEPARATE] > **'severable** *adj*

several ('sɛvrəl) *determiner* **1 a** more than a few; an indefinite small number: *several people objected* (*as pronoun; functioning as plural*): *several of them know* ▷ *adj* **2** (*prenominal*) various; separate: *the members with their several occupations* **3** (*prenominal*) different; three: *three several times* **4** *law* capable of being dealt with separately; not shared [c15: via Anglo-French from Medieval Latin *sēparālis*, from Latin *sēpar*, from *sēparāre* to SEPARATE]

severally ('sɛvrəlɪ) *adv* **1** separately, individually, or distinctly **2** each in turn; respectively

severalty ('sɛvrəltɪ) *n, pl* **-ties 1** the state of being several or separate **2** (*usually preceded by in*) *property law* the tenure of property, esp land, in a person's own right and not jointly with another or others

severance ('sɛvərəns) *n* **1** the act of severing or state of being severed **2** a separation **3** *law* the division into separate parts of a joint estate, contract, etc

severance pay *n* compensation paid by an organization to an employee who leaves because, through no fault of his own, the job to which he was appointed ceases to exist, as during rationalization, and no comparable job is available to him

severe (sɪ'vɪə) *adj* **1** rigorous or harsh in the treatment of others; strict: *a severe parent* **2** serious in appearance or manner; stern **3** critical or dangerous: *a severe illness* **4** causing misery or discomfort by its harshness: *severe weather* **5** strictly restrained in appearance; austere: *a severe way of dressing* **6** hard to endure, perform, or accomplish: *a severe test* [c16: from Latin *sevērus*] > **se'verely** *adv* > **se'vereness** or **severity** (sɪ'vɛrɪtɪ) *n*

Severn ('sɛv°n) *n* **1 a** river in E Wales and W England, rising in Powys and flowing northeast and east into England, then south to the Bristol Channel. Length: about 354 km (220 miles) **2** a river in SE central Canada, in Ontario, flowing northeast to Hudson Bay. Length: about 676 km (420 miles)

Severnaya Zemlya (*Russian* 'sjevɪrnəjə zɪm'lja) *n* an archipelago in the Arctic Ocean off the coast of N central Russia

Severus (sɪ'vɪərəs) *n* **Lucius Septimius** (sɛp'tɪmɪəs). 146–211 AD, Roman soldier and emperor (193–211). He waged war successfully against the Parthians (197–202) and spent his last years in Britain (208–11)

Seveso (sɛ'veɪsəu) *n* a town in N Italy, near Milan: evacuated in 1976 after contamination with a poisonous cloud of dioxin gas released from a factory

Sévigné (*French* seviɲe) *n* **Marquise de**, title of *Marie de Rabutin-Chantal*. 1626–96, French letter writer. Her correspondence with her daughter and others provides a vivid account of society during the reign of Louis XIV

Seville (sə'vɪl) *n* a port in SW Spain, on the Guadalquivir River: chief town of S Spain under the Vandals and Visigoths (5th–8th centuries); centre of Spanish colonial trade (16th–17th centuries); tourist centre. Pop: 709 975 (2003 est)

Seville orange *n* **1** an orange tree, *Citrus aurantium*, of tropical and semitropical regions: grown for its bitter fruit, which is used to make marmalade **2** the fruit of this tree

Sèvres (*French* sɛvrə) *n* porcelain ware manufactured at Sèvres, near Paris, from 1756, characterized by the use of clear colours and elaborate decorative detail

sew (səu) *vb* **sews, sewing, sewed, sewn** or **sewed 1** to join or decorate (pieces of fabric, etc) by means of a thread repeatedly passed through with a needle or similar implement **2** (*tr, often foll by on or up*) to attach, fasten, or close by sewing **3** (*tr*) to make (a garment, etc) by sewing ▷ See also **sew up** [Old English *sēowan*; related to Old Norse *sȳja*, Gothic *siujan*, Old High German *siuwen*, Latin *suere* to sew, Sanskrit *sīvjati* he sews]

sewage ('su:ɪdʒ) *n* waste matter from domestic or industrial establishments that is carried away in sewers or drains for dumping or conversion into a form that is not toxic [c19: back formation from SEWER¹]

sewage farm *n* a place where sewage is treated, esp for use as manure

Seward ('sju:əd) *n* **William Henry**. 1801–72, US statesman; secretary of state (1861–69). He was a leading opponent of slavery and was responsible for the purchase of Alaska (1867)

Seward Peninsula ('sju:əd) *n* a peninsula of W Alaska, on the Bering Strait. Length: about 290 km (180 miles)

Sewell ('su:əl) *n* **Henry**. 1807–79, New Zealand statesman, born in England: first prime minister of New Zealand (1856)

sewer¹ ('su:ə) *n* **1 a** drain or pipe, esp one that is underground, used to carry away surface water or sewage ▷ *vb* **2** (*tr*) to provide with sewers [c15: from Old French *esseveur*, from *essever* to drain, from Vulgar Latin *exaquāre* (unattested), from Latin EX-¹ + *aqua* water]

sewer² ('səuə) *n* a person or thing that sews

sewerage ('su:ərɪdʒ) *n* **1** an arrangement of sewers **2** the removal of surface water or sewage by means of sewers **3** another word for **sewage**

sewing ('səuɪŋ) *n* **a** a piece of cloth, etc, that is sewn or to be sewn **b** (*as modifier*): *sewing basket*

sewing machine *n* any machine designed to sew

material. It is now usually driven by electric motor but is sometimes operated by a foot treadle or by hand

sewn (səʊn) *vb* a past participle of **sew**

sew up *vb* (*tr, adverb*) **1** to fasten or mend completely by sewing **2** *US* to acquire sole use or control of **3** *informal* to complete or negotiate successfully: *to sew up a deal*

sex (sɛks) *n* **1** the sum of the characteristics that distinguish organisms on the basis of their reproductive function **2** either of the two categories, male or female, into which organisms are placed on this basis **3** short for **sexual intercourse 4** feelings or behaviour resulting from the urge to gratify the sexual instinct **5** sexual matters in general ▷ *modifier* **6** of or concerning sexual matters: *sex education; sex hygiene* **7** based on or arising from the difference between the sexes: *sex discrimination* ▷ *vb* **8** (*tr*) to ascertain the sex of [c14: from Latin *sexus*; compare *secāre* to divide]

sex- *combining form* six: *sexcentennial* [from Latin]

sexagenarian (ˌsɛksədʒɪˈnɛərɪən) *n* **1** a person from 60 to 69 years old ▷ *adj* **2** being from 60 to 69 years old **3** of or relating to a sexagenarian [c18: from Latin *sexāgēnārius*, from *sexāgēnī* sixty each, from *sexāgintā* sixty]

Sexagesima (ˌsɛksəˈdʒɛsɪmə) *n* the second Sunday before Lent [c16: from Latin: sixtieth, from *sexāgintā* sixty]

sexagesimal (ˌsɛksəˈdʒɛsɪməl) *adj* **1** relating to or based on the number 60: *sexagesimal measurement of angles* ▷ *n* **2** a fraction in which the denominator is some power of 60; a sixtieth

sexaholic (ˌsɛksəˈhɒlɪk) *n* a person who is addicted to sex

sex-and-shopping *adj* (*prenominal*) (of a novel) belonging to a genre of novel in which the central character, a woman, has a number of sexual encounters, and the author mentions the name of many up-market products

sex appeal *n* the quality or power of attracting the opposite sex

sexcentenary (ˌsɛksɛnˈtiːnərɪ) *adj* **1** of or relating to 600 or a period of 600 years **2** of, relating to, or celebrating a 600th anniversary ▷ *n, pl* **-naries 3** a 600th anniversary or its celebration [c18: from Latin *sexcentēnī* six hundred each]

sex chromosome *n* either of the chromosomes determining the sex of animals

sexed (sɛkst) *adj* **1** (*in combination*) having a specified degree of sexuality: *undersexed* **2** of, relating to, or having sexual differentiation

sex hormone *n* an animal hormone affecting development and growth of reproductive organs and related parts

sexism (ˈsɛksɪzəm) *n* discrimination on the basis of sex, esp the oppression of women by men [c20: from SEX + -ISM, on the model of RACISM] > **'sexist** *n, adj*

sexless (ˈsɛkslɪs) *adj* **1** having or showing no sexual differentiation **2** having no sexual desires **3** sexually unattractive

sex linkage *n genetics* the condition in which a particular gene is located on a sex chromosome, esp on the X-chromosome, so that the character controlled by the gene is associated with either of the sexes > **'sex,linked** *adj*

sex object *n* a person viewed or treated as a means of obtaining sexual gratification

sexology (sɛkˈsɒlədʒɪ) *n* the study of sexual behaviour in human beings > **sex'ologist** *n* > **sexological** (ˌsɛksəˈlɒdʒɪkᵊl) *adj*

sexpartite (sɛksˈpɑːtaɪt) *adj* **1** (esp of vaults, arches, etc) divided into or composed of six parts **2** maintained by or involving six participants or groups of participants

sex shop *n* a shop selling aids purporting to increase the pleasurableness of sexual activity

sext (sɛkst) *n chiefly RC Church* the fourth of the seven canonical hours of the divine office or the prayers prescribed for it: originally the sixth hour of the day (noon) [c15: from Church Latin *sexta hōra* the sixth hour]

sextan (ˈsɛkstən) *adj* (of a fever) marked by paroxysms that recur after an interval of five days [c17: from Medieval Latin *sextana* (*febris*) (fever) of the sixth (day)]

sextant (ˈsɛkstənt) *n* **1** an optical instrument used in

navigation and consisting of a telescope through which a sighting of a heavenly body is taken, with protractors for determining its angular distance above the horizon or from another heavenly body **2** a sixth part of a circle having an arc which subtends an angle of 60° [c17: from Latin *sextāns* one sixth of a unit]

sextet *or* **sextette** (sɛksˈtɛt) *n* **1** *music* a group of six singers or instrumentalists or a piece of music composed for such a group **2** a group of six people or things [c19: variant of SESTET, with Latinization of *ses-*]

sex-text *vb* (*tr*) to send a text message of a sexual nature to (someone)

sextillion (sɛksˈtɪljən) *n, pl* **-lions** *or* **-lion 1** (in Britain, France, and Germany) the number represented as one followed by 36 zeros (10^{36}) **2** (in the US and Canada) the number represented as one followed by 21 zeros (10^{21}) [c17: from French, from SEX- + -*illion*, on the model of SEPTILLION]

sexto (ˈsɛkstəʊ) *n, pl* **-tos** another word for **sixmo** [c19: from Latin *sextus* sixth]

sexton (ˈsɛkstən) *n* a person employed to act as caretaker of a church and its contents and graveyard, and often also as bell-ringer, gravedigger, etc [c14: from Old French *secrestein*, from Medieval Latin *sacristānus* SACRISTAN]

sextuple (ˈsɛkstjʊpᵊl) *n* **1** a quantity or number six times as great as another ▷ *adj* **2** six times as much or many; sixfold **3** consisting of six parts or members [c17: Latin *sextus* sixth + -*uple*, as in QUADRUPLE]

sextuplet (ˈsɛkstjʊplɪt) *n* **1** one of six offspring born at one birth **2** a group of six things **3** *music* a group of six notes played in a time value of four

sexual (ˈsɛksjʊəl) *adj* **1** of, relating to, or characterized by sex or sexuality **2** (of reproduction) characterized by the union of male and female gametes. See **asexual** (sense 2) [c17: from Late Latin *sexuālis*; see SEX] > **'sexually** *adv* > **,sexu'ality** *n*

sexual harassment *n* the persistent unwelcome directing of sexual remarks and looks, and unnecessary physical contact at a person, usually a woman, esp in the workplace

sexual intercourse *n* the act carried out for procreation or for pleasure in which, typically, the insertion of the male's erect penis into the female's vagina is followed by rhythmic thrusting usually culminating in orgasm; copulation; coitus

sexual reproduction *n* reproduction involving the fusion of a male and female haploid gamete

sexual selection *n* an evolutionary process in animals, in which selection by females of males with certain characters, such as large antlers or bright plumage, results in the preservation of these characters in the species

sex up *vb* (*tr, adverb*) *informal* to make (something) more interesting or exciting: *the BBC decided to sex up the book's title*

Sexwale (sɛksˈwɑleɪ) *n* **Tokyo**. full name *Mosima Gabriel Sexwale*. born 1953; South African political activist and businessman

sex worker *n* a prostitute

sexy (ˈsɛksɪ) *adj* **sexier, sexiest** *informal* **1** provoking or intended to provoke sexual interest: *a sexy dress; a sexy book* **2** feeling sexual interest; aroused **3** interesting, exciting, or trendy: *a sexy project; a sexy new car* > **'sexily** *adv* > **'sexiness** *n*

Seychelles (seɪˈʃɛl, -ˈʃɛlz) *pl n* a group of volcanic islands in the W Indian Ocean: taken by the British from the French in 1744: became an independent republic within the Commonwealth in 1976, incorporating the British Indian Ocean Territory islands of Aldabra, Farquhar and Desroches. Languages: Creole, English, and French. Religion: Roman Catholic majority. Currency: rupee. Capital: Victoria. Pop: 81 000 (2003 est). Area: 455 sq km (176 sq miles)

Seyhan (seɪˈhɑːn) *n* another name for **Adana**

Seymour (ˈsiːmɔː) *n* **Jane**. ?1509–37, third wife of Henry VIII of England; mother of Edward VI

sf, sf., sfz *or* **sfz.** *abbreviation music* sforzando

SF *or* **sf** *abbreviation* science fiction

SFA *abbreviation* **1** Scottish Football Association **2** Sweet Fanny Adams. See **fanny adams**

Sfax (sfæks) *n* a port in E Tunisia, on the Gulf of Gabès: the second largest town in Tunisia; commercial centre of a phosphate region. Pop: 570 000 (2005 est)

SFO *abbreviation* Serious Fraud Office: the department of the British government which investigates cases of serious financial fraud

Sforza (Italian 'sfɔrtsa) *n* **1** Count **Carlo** ('karlo). 1873–1952, Italian statesman; leader of the anti-Fascist opposition **2 Francesco** (fran'tʃesko). 1401–66, duke of Milan (1450–66) **3** his father **Giacomuzzo** (dʒako'muttso) or **Muzio** ('muttsjo), original name *Attendolo*. 1369–1424, Italian condottiere and founder of the dynasty that ruled Milan (1450–1535) **4 Lodovico** (lodo'vi:ko), called *the Moor*. 1451–1508, duke of Milan (1494–1500), but effective ruler from 1480; patron of Leonardo da Vinci

sforzando (sfɔ:'tsa:ndəʊ) or **sforzato** (sfɔ:'tsa:təʊ) *music* ▷ *adj, adv* **1** to be played with strong initial attack. Abbreviation: **sf** ▷ *n* **2** a symbol, mark, etc, such as >, written above a note, indicating this [C19: from Italian, from *sforzare* to force, from EX-¹ + *forzare*, from Vulgar Latin *fortiāre* (unattested) to FORCE¹]

SFW *abbreviation* (in South Africa) Stellenbosch Farmers' Winery, South Africa's leading wine producer

SG *abbreviation* solicitor general

sgd *abbreviation* signed

sgian-dhu ('ski:ən'du:, 'ski:n-) *n Scot* a dirk carried in the stocking by Highlanders

SGML *abbreviation* standard generalized mark-up language: an international standard used in publishing for defining the structure and formatting of documents

sgraffito (sgræ'fi:təʊ) *n, pl* -ti (-tɪ) **1** a technique in mural or ceramic decoration in which the top layer of glaze, plaster, etc, is incised with a design to reveal parts of the ground **2** such a decoration [C18: from Italian, from *sgraffire* to scratch; see GRAFFITI]

's Gravenhage (sxra:vən'ha:xə) *n* a Dutch name for (The) **Hague**¹

Sgt *abbreviation* Sergeant

sh (*spelling pron* ʃʃʃ) *interj* an exclamation to request silence or quiet

Shaanxi ('ʃæn'ʃi:) or **Shensi** *n* a province of NW China: one of the earliest centres of Chinese civilization; largely mountainous. Capital: Xi'an. Pop: 36 900 000 (2003 est). Area: 195 800 sq km (75 598 sq miles)

Shaba ('ʃɑ:bə) *n* the former name (1972–97) of **Katanga**

shabby ('ʃæbɪ) *adj* -bier, -biest **1** threadbare or dilapidated in appearance **2** wearing worn and dirty clothes; seedy **3** mean, despicable, or unworthy: *shabby treatment* **4** dirty or squalid [C17: from Old English *sceabb* SCAB + -Y¹] > 'shabbily *adv* > 'shabbiness *n*

Shache ('ʃæ'tʃeɪ, **Soche** or **So-ch'e** *n* a town in W China, in the W Xinjiang: a centre of the caravan trade between China, India, and Transcaspian areas. Also called: Yarkand

shack (ʃæk) *n* **1** a roughly built hut ▷ *vb* **2** See **shack up** [C19: perhaps from dialect *shackly* ramshackle, from dialect *shack* to shake]

shackle ('ʃækᵊl) *n* **1** (*often plural*) a metal ring or fastening, usually part of a pair used to secure a person's wrists or ankles; fetter **2** (*often plural*) anything that confines or restricts freedom **3** a U-shaped bracket, the open end of which is closed by a bolt (**shackle pin**), used for securing ropes, chains, etc ▷ *vb* (*tr*) **4** to confine with or as if with shackles **5** to fasten or connect with a shackle [Old English *sceacel*; related to Dutch *schakel*, Old Norse *skokull* wagon pole, Latin *cingere* to surround] > 'shackler *n*

Shackleton ('ʃækəltən) *n* Sir **Ernest Henry**. 1874–1922, British explorer. He commanded three expeditions to the Antarctic (1907–09; 1914–17; 1921–22), during which the south magnetic pole was located (1909)

shack up *vb* (*intr, adverb*; usually foll by *with*) *slang* to live or take up residence, esp with a mistress or lover

shad (ʃæd) *n, pl* **shad** or **shads** any of various herring-like food fishes of the genus *Alosa* and related genera, such as *A. alosa* (**allis shad**) of Europe, that migrate from the sea to freshwater to spawn: family *Clupeidae* (herrings) [Old English *sceadd*; related to Norwegian *skadd*, German

Schade shad, Old Irish *scatān* herring, Latin *scatēre* to well up]

Shadbolt ('ʃæd,bəʊlt) *n* **Maurice**. 1932–2004, New Zealand novelist

shaddock ('ʃædək) *n* another name for **pomelo** [C17: named after Captain *Shaddock*, who brought its seed from the East Indies to Jamaica in 1696]

shade (ʃeɪd) *n* **1** relative darkness produced by the blocking out of light **2** a place made relatively darker or cooler than other areas by the blocking of light, esp sunlight **3** a position of relative obscurity **4** something used to provide a shield or protection from a direct source of light, such as a lampshade **5** a darker area indicated in a painting, drawing, etc, by shading **6** a colour that varies slightly from a standard colour due to a difference in hue, saturation, or luminosity: *a darker shade of green* **7** a slight amount: *a shade of difference* **8** literary a ghost ▷ *vb* (*mainly tr*) **9** to screen or protect from heat, light, view, etc **10** to make darker or dimmer **11** to represent (a darker area) in (a painting, drawing, etc), by means of hatching, using a darker colour, etc **12** (*also intr*) to change or cause to change slightly **13** to lower (a price) slightly [Old English *sceadu*; related to Gothic *skadus*, Old High German *skato*, Old Irish *scáth* shadow, Greek *skotos* darkness, Swedish *skäddä* fog] > 'shadeless *adj*

shades (ʃeɪdz) *pl n* **1** gathering darkness at nightfall **2** a slang word for **sunglasses 3 the shades** (*often capital*) a literary term for **Hades 4** (foll by *of*) undertones or suggestions: *shades of my father!*

shading ('ʃeɪdɪŋ) *n* the graded areas of tone, lines, dots, etc, indicating light and dark in a painting or drawing

shadoof or **shaduf** (ʃə'du:f) *n* a mechanism for raising water, consisting of a pivoted pole with a bucket at one end and a counterweight at the other, esp as used in Egypt and the Near East [C19: from Egyptian Arabic]

shadow ('ʃædəʊ) *n* **1** a dark image or shape cast on a surface by the interception of light rays by an opaque body **2** an area of relative darkness **3** the dark portions of a picture **4** a hint, image, or faint semblance: *beyond a shadow of a doubt* **5** a remnant or vestige: *a shadow of one's past self* **6** a reflection **7** a threatening influence; blight: *a shadow over one's happiness* **8** a spectre **9** an inseparable companion **10** a person who trails another in secret, such as a detective **11** *med* a dark area on an X-ray film representing an opaque structure or part **12** (in Jungian psychology) the archetype that represents man's animal ancestors **13** *archaic or rare* protection or shelter **14** (*modifier*) *Brit* designating a member or members of the main opposition party in Parliament who would hold ministerial office if their party were in power: *shadow Chancellor; shadow cabinet* ▷ *vb* (*tr*) **15** to cast a shadow over **16** to make dark or gloomy; blight **17** to shade from light **18** to follow or trail secretly **19** (*often* foll by *forth*) to represent vaguely [Old English *sceadwe*, oblique case of *sceadu* SHADE; related to Dutch *schaduw*] > 'shadower *n*

shadow-box *vb* (*intr*) *boxing* to practise blows and footwork against an imaginary opponent > 'shadow-boxing *n*

shadowgraph ('ʃædəʊ,grɑ:f, -,græf) *n* **1** a silhouette made by casting a shadow, usually of the hands, on a lighted surface **2** another name for **radiograph**

shadow play *n* a theatrical entertainment using shadows thrown by puppets or actors onto a lighted screen

shadow price *n economics* the calculated price of a good or service for which no market price exists

shadowy ('ʃædəʊɪ) *adj* **1** full of shadows; dark; shady **2** resembling a shadow in faintness; vague **3** illusory or imaginary **4** mysterious or secretive: *a shadowy underworld figure* > 'shadowiness *n*

Shadrach ('ʃædræk, 'ʃeɪ-) *n Old Testament* one of Daniel's three companions, who, together with Meshach and Abednego, was miraculously saved from destruction in Nebuchadnezzar's fiery furnace (Daniel 3:12–30)

Shadwell ('ʃædwəl) *n* **Thomas**. ?1642–92, English dramatist; poet laureate (1688–92). He was satirized by Dryden

shady ('ʃeɪdɪ) *adj* **shadier, shadiest** **1** full of shade; shaded **2** affording or casting a shade **3** dim, quiet, or concealed **4** *informal* dubious or questionable as to honesty or legality > 'shadily *adv* > 'shadiness *n*

SHAEF (ʃeɪf) *n, acronym for* (in World War II) Supreme Headquarters Allied Expeditionary Forces

Shaffer ('ʃæfə) *n* Sir **Peter.** born 1926, British dramatist. His plays include *The Royal Hunt of the Sun* (1964), *Equus* (1973), *Amadeus* (1979), and *The Gift of the Gorgon* (1992)

shaft (ʃɑːft) *n* **1** the long narrow pole that forms the body of a spear, arrow, etc **2** something directed at a person in the manner of a missile **3** a ray, beam, or streak, esp of light **4** a rod or pole forming the handle of a hammer, axe, golf club, etc **5** a revolving rod that transmits motion or power: usually used of axial rotation **6** one of the two wooden poles by which an animal is harnessed to a vehicle **7** *anatomy* the middle part (diaphysis) of a long bone **8** the middle part of a column or pier, between the base and the capital **9** *architect* a column that supports a vaulting rib, sometimes one of a set **10** a vertical passageway through a building, as for a lift **11** a vertical passageway into a mine **12** *ornithol* the central rib of a feather **13** an archaic or literary word for **arrow** ▷ *vb* **14** *slang* to trick or cheat [Old English *sceaft*; related to Old Norse *skapt*, German *Schaft*, Latin *scāpus* shaft, Greek *skeptron* SCEPTRE, Lettish *skeps* javelin]

Shaftesbury ('ʃɑːftsbərɪ, -brɪ) *n* **1 1st Earl of**, title of *Anthony Ashley Cooper*. 1621–83, English statesman, a major figure in the Whig opposition to Charles II **2 7th Earl of**, title of *Anthony Ashley Cooper*. 1801–85, English evangelical churchman and social reformer. He promoted measures to improve conditions in mines (1842), factories (1833; 1847; 1850), and schools

shag¹ (ʃæg) *n* **1** a matted tangle, esp of hair, wool, etc **2** a napped fabric, usually a rough wool **3** shredded coarse tobacco [Old English *sceacga*; related to *sceaga* SHAW¹, Old Norse *skegg* beard, *skagi* tip, *skōgr* forest]

shag² (ʃæg) *n* **1** another name for the **green cormorant** (*Phalacrocorax aristotelis*) **2** like a shag on a rock *Austral, slang* abandoned and alone [C16: special use of SHAG¹, with reference to its crest]

shag³ (ʃæg) *Brit slang* ▷ *vb* **shags, shagging, shagged 1** to have sexual intercourse with (a person) **2** (*tr; often foll by out; usually passive*) to exhaust; tire ▷ *n* **3** an act of sexual intercourse [C20: of unknown origin]

shaggable ('ʃægəbˀl) *adj* *Brit slang* sexually attractive

shaggy ('ʃægɪ) *adj* **-gier, -giest 1** having or covered with rough unkempt fur, hair, wool, etc: *a shaggy dog* **2** rough or unkempt > 'shaggily *adv* > 'shagginess *n*

shaggy dog story *n* *informal* a long rambling joke ending in a deliberate anticlimax, such as a pointless punch line

shagreen (ʃæ'griːn) *n* **1** the rough skin of certain sharks and rays, used as an abrasive **2** a rough grainy leather made from certain animal hides [C17: from French *chagrin*, from Turkish *çagri* rump; also associated through folk etymology with SHAG¹, GREEN]

shagtastic (ʃæg'tæstɪk) *adj* *Brit slang* **1** sexually attractive; sexy **2** excellent; wonderful [C20: from SHAG³ + (FAN)TASTIC]

shah (ʃɑː) *n* a ruler of certain Middle Eastern countries, esp (formerly) Iran [C16: from Persian: king] > 'shahdom *n*

Shah Jahan (dʒə'hɑːn) *n* 1592–1666, Mogul emperor (1628–58). During his reign the finest monuments of Mogul architecture in India were built, including the Taj Mahal and the Pearl Mosque at Agra

Shahjahanpur (ʃɑːdʒə,hɑːn'pʊə) *n* a city in N India, in central Uttar Pradesh: founded in 1647 in the reign of Shah Jahan. Pop: 297 932 (2001)

Shahn (ʃɑːn) *n* **Ben.** 1898–1969, US artist, born in Lithuania, best known as an exponent of social realism, especially in the series (1931–32) inspired by the executions of Sacco and Vanzetti

Shah of Iran (ʃɑː) *n* See **Pahlavi**

shahtoosh (ʃɑː'tuːʃ) *n* a soft wool that comes from the protected Tibetan antelope

Shaka *or* **Chaka** ('ʃaka) *n* died 1828, Zulu military leader, who founded the Zulu Empire in southern Africa

shake (ʃeɪk) *vb* **shakes, shaking, shook, shaken** ('ʃeɪkˀn) **1** to move or cause to move up and down or back and forth with short quick movements; vibrate **2** to sway or totter or cause to sway or totter **3** to clasp or grasp (the hand) of (a person) in greeting, agreement, etc: *he shook John by the hand; he shook John's hand; they shook and were friends* **4** shake hands to clasp hands in greeting, agreement, etc **5** shake on it *informal* to shake hands in agreement, reconciliation, etc **6** to bring or come to a specified condition by or as if by shaking: *he shook free and ran* **7** (*tr*) to wave or brandish: *he shook his sword* **8** (*tr; often foll by up*) to rouse, stir, or agitate **9** (*tr*) to shock, disturb, or upset: *he was shaken by the news of her death* **10** (*tr*) to undermine or weaken: *the crisis shook his faith* **11** to mix (dice) by rattling in a cup or the hand before throwing **12** (*tr*) *Austral archaic, slang* to steal **13** (*tr*) *US & Canadian informal* to escape from **14** *music* to perform a trill on (a note) **15** shake in one's shoes to tremble with fear or apprehension **16** shake one's head to indicate disagreement or disapproval by moving the head from side to side ▷ *n* **17** the act or an instance of shaking **18** a tremor or vibration **19** the shakes *informal* a state of uncontrollable trembling or a condition that causes it, such as a fever **20** *informal* a very short period of time; jiffy: *in half a shake* **21** a fissure or crack in timber or rock **22** an instance of shaking dice before casting **23** *music* another word for **trill¹** (sense 1) **24** an informal name for **earthquake 25** short for **milk shake 26** no great shakes *informal* of no great merit or value; ordinary ▷ See also **shake down, shake off**, etc [Old English *sceacan*; related to Old Norse *skaka* to shake, Old High German *untscachōn* to be driven] > 'shakable *or* 'shakeable *adj*

shake down *vb* (*adverb*) **1** to fall or settle or cause to fall or settle by shaking **2** (*tr*) *US slang* to extort money from, esp by blackmail or threats of violence **3** (*tr*) *informal, chiefly US* to submit (a vessel, etc) to a shakedown test **4** (*intr*) to go to bed, esp to a makeshift bed ▷ *n* **shakedown 5** *US slang* a swindle or act of extortion **6** a makeshift bed, esp of straw, blankets, etc **7** *informal, chiefly US* **a** a voyage to test the performance of a ship or aircraft or to familiarize the crew with their duties **b** (*as modifier*): *a shakedown run*

shaken baby syndrome *n* a combination of physical injuries and conditions such as brain damage and broken bones, sometimes leading to death, caused by the vigorous shaking of an infant or young child

shake off *vb* (*adverb*) **1** to remove or be removed with or as if with a quick movement: *she shook off her depression* **2** (*tr*) to escape from; elude: *they shook off the police*

shaker ('ʃeɪkə) *n* **1** a person or thing that shakes **2** a container, often having a perforated top, from which something, such as a condiment, is shaken **3** a container in which the ingredients of alcoholic drinks are shaken together

Shakers ('ʃeɪkəz) *pl n* the Shakers an American millenarian sect, founded in 1747 as an offshoot of the Quakers, given to ecstatic shaking, advocating celibacy for its members, and practising common ownership of property

Shakespeare ('ʃeɪkspɪə) *n* **William.** 1564–1616, English dramatist and poet. He was born and died at Stratford-upon-Avon but spent most of his life as an actor and playwright in London. His plays with approximate dates of composition are: *Henry VI, Parts I–III* (1590); *Richard III* (1592); *The Comedy of Errors* (1592); *Titus Andronicus* (1593); *The Taming of the Shrew* (1593); *The Two Gentlemen of Verona* (1594); *Love's Labour's Lost* (1594); *Romeo and Juliet* (1594); *Richard II* (1595); *A Midsummer Night's Dream* (1595); *King John* (1596); *The Merchant of Venice* (1596); *Henry IV, Parts I–II* (1597); *Much Ado about Nothing* (1598); *Henry V* (1598); *Julius Caesar* (1599); *As You Like It* (1599); *Twelfth Night* (1599); *Hamlet* (1600); *The Merry Wives of Windsor* (1600); *Troilus and Cressida* (1601); *All's Well that Ends Well* (1602); *Measure for Measure* (1604); *Othello* (1604); *King Lear* (1605); *Macbeth* (1605); *Antony and Cleopatra* (1606); *Coriolanus* (1607); *Timon of Athens* (1607); *Pericles* (1608); *Cymbeline* (1609); *The Winter's Tale* (1610); *The Tempest* (1611); and, possibly in collaboration with John Fletcher, *Two Noble Kinsmen* (1612) and *Henry VIII* (1612). His *Sonnets*, variously addressed to a fair young man and a dark lady,

S

were published in 1609

Shakespearean or **Shakespearian** (ʃeɪkˈspɪərɪən) adj
1 of, relating to, or characteristic of William
Shakespeare, the English dramatist and poet
(1564–1616), or his works ▷ n **2** a student of or specialist
in Shakespeare's works

Shakespearean sonnet n a sonnet form developed in
16th-century England and employed by Shakespeare,
having the rhyme scheme a b a b c d c d e f e f g g

shake up vb (tr, adverb) **1** to shake or agitate in order to
mix **2** to reorganize drastically **3** to stir or rouse **4** to
restore the shape of (a pillow, cushion, etc) **5** informal to
disturb or shock mentally or physically ▷ n shake-up
6 informal a radical or drastic reorganization

Shakhty (Russian ˈʃaxtɪ) n an industrial city in W Russia:
the chief town of the E Donets Basin; a major coal-
mining centre. Pop: 219 000 (2005 est)

shako or **shacko** (ˈʃækəʊ) n, pl shakos, shakoes or
shackos, shackoes a tall usually cylindrical military
headdress, having a plume and often a peak, popular
esp in the 19th century [C19: via French from Hungarian
csákó, from Middle High German zacke a sharp point]

shaky (ˈʃeɪkɪ) adj shakier, shakiest **1** tending to shake or
tremble **2** liable to prove defective; unreliable
3 uncertain or questionable: your arguments are very shaky
> ˈshakily adv > ˈshakiness n

shale (ʃeɪl) n a dark fine-grained laminated
sedimentary rock formed by compression of successive
layers of clay-rich sediment [Old English scealu SHELL;
compare German Schalstein laminated limestone; see
SCALE¹, SCALE²] > ˈshaly adj

shale oil n an oil distilled from shales and used as fuel

shall (ʃæl; unstressed ʃəl) vb, past should (takes an
infinitive without to or an implied infinitive) **1** (esp
with I or we as subject) used as an auxiliary to make the
future tense: we shall see you tomorrow. See will¹ (sense 1)
2 (with you, he, she, it, they, or a noun as subject) **a** used as
an auxiliary to indicate determination on the part of the
speaker, as in issuing a threat: you shall pay for this! **b** used
as an auxiliary to indicate compulsion, now esp in
official documents **c** used as an auxiliary to indicate
certainty or inevitability: our day shall come **3** (with any
noun or pronoun as subject, esp in conditional clauses or clauses
expressing doubt) used as an auxiliary to indicate
nonspecific futurity: I don't think I shall ever see her again; he
doubts whether he shall be in tomorrow [Old English sceal;
related to Old Norse skal, Old High German scal, Dutch
zal]

● USAGE The usual rule given for the use of shall and will
● is that where the meaning is one of simple futurity,
● shall is used for the first person of the verb and will for
● the second and third: I shall go tomorrow; they will be there
● now. Where the meaning involves command,
● obligation, or determination, the positions are
● reversed: it shall be done; I will definitely go. However, shall
● has come to be largely neglected in favour of will,
● which has become the commonest form of the future
● in all three persons

shallop (ˈʃæləp) n a light boat used for rowing in
shallow water [C16: from French chaloupe, from Dutch
sloep SLOOP]

shallot (ʃəˈlɒt) n **1** Also called: scallion an alliaceous
plant, Allium ascalonicum, cultivated for its edible bulb
2 the bulb of this plant, which divides into small
sections and is used in cooking for flavouring and as a
vegetable [C17: from Old French eschalotte, from Old
French eschalogne, from Latin Ascalōnia caepa Ascalonian
onion, from Ascalon, a Palestinian town]

shallow (ˈʃæləʊ) adj **1** having little depth **2** lacking
intellectual or mental depth or subtlety; superficial ▷ n
3 (often plural) a shallow place in a body of water; shoal
▷ vb **4** to make or become shallow [C15: related to Old
English sceald shallow; see SHOAL¹] > ˈshallowly adv
> ˈshallowness n

shalom aleichem Hebrew (ʃaˈlɔm aˈlexɛm; English ʃəˈlɒm
əˈleɪxəm) interj peace be to you: used by Jews as a
greeting or farewell. Often shortened to: shalom

shalt (ʃælt) vb archaic or dialect (used with the pronoun
thou or its relative equivalent) a singular form of the

present tense (indicative mood) of shall

shalwar (ˈʃælwɑː) n a pair of loose-fitting trousers
tapering to a narrow fit around the ankles, worn in the
Indian subcontinent, often with a kameez [from Urdu
and Persian shalwār]

sham (ʃæm) n **1** anything that is not what it purports or
appears to be **2** something false, fake, or fictitious that
purports to be genuine **3** a person who pretends to be
something other than he is ▷ adj **4** counterfeit or false;
simulated ▷ vb shams, shamming, shammed **5** to falsely
assume the appearance of (something); counterfeit: to
sham illness [C17: perhaps a Northern English dialect
variant of SHAME]

shaman (ˈʃæmən) n **1** a priest of shamanism **2** a
medicine man of a similar religion, esp among certain
tribes of North American Indians [C17: from Russian
shaman, from Tungusian šaman, from Pali samana
Buddhist monk, ultimately from Sanskrit śrama
religious exercise]

shamanism (ˈʃæməˌnɪzəm) n **1** the religion of certain
peoples of northern Asia, based on the belief that the
world is pervaded by good and evil spirits who can be
influenced or controlled only by the shamans **2** any
similar religion involving forms of spiritualism
> ˈshamanist n, adj

Shamash (ˈʃɑːmæʃ) n the sun god of Assyria and
Babylonia [from Akkadian: sun]

shamateur (ˈʃæməˌtɜː, -ˌtjʊə, -tə, -tʃə) n a sportsperson
who is officially an amateur but accepts payment [C20:
from a blend of SHAM + AMATEUR]

shamble (ˈʃæmbᵊl) vb **1** (intr) to walk or move along in an
awkward or unsteady way ▷ n **2** an awkward or
unsteady walk [C17: from shamble (adj) ungainly, perhaps
from the phrase shamble legs legs resembling those of a
meat vendor's table; see SHAMBLES] > ˈshambling adj, n

shambles (ˈʃæmbᵊlz) n (functioning as singular or plural) **1** a
place of great disorder: the room was a shambles after the
party **2** a place where animals are brought to be
slaughtered **3** any place of slaughter or carnage [C14
shamble table used by meat vendors, from Old English
sceamel stool, from Late Latin scamellum a small bench,
from Latin scamnum stool]

shambolic (ʃæmˈbɒlɪk) adj informal completely
disorganized; chaotic [C20: irregularly formed from
SHAMBLES]

shame (ʃeɪm) n **1** a painful emotion resulting from an
awareness of having done something dishonourable,
unworthy, degrading, etc **2** capacity to feel such an
emotion **3** ignominy or disgrace **4** a person or thing
that causes this **5** an occasion for regret,
disappointment, etc: it's a shame you can't come with us
6 put to shame **a** to disgrace **b** to surpass totally ▷ vb
(tr) **7** to cause to feel shame **8** to bring shame on;
disgrace **9** (often foll by into) to compel through a sense
of shame **10** name and shame See name (sense 15) [Old
English scamu; related to Old Norse skömm, Old High
German skama] > ˈshamable or ˈshameable adj

shamefaced (ˈʃeɪmˌfeɪst) adj **1** bashful or modest
2 showing a sense of shame [C16: alteration of earlier
shamefast, from Old English sceamfaest; see SHAME, FAST¹]
> shamefacedly (ʃeɪmˈfeɪsɪdlɪ, ˈʃeɪmˌfeɪstlɪ) adv

shameful (ˈʃeɪmfʊl) adj causing or deserving shame;
scandalous > ˈshamefully adv > ˈshamefulness n

shameless (ˈʃeɪmlɪs) adj **1** having no sense of shame;
brazen **2** done without shame; without decency or
modesty > ˈshamelessly adv > ˈshamelessness n

Shamir (ʃæˈmɪə) n **Yitzhak** (ˈjɪtzæk). born 1915, Israeli
statesman, born in Poland: prime minister (1983–84;
1986–92): foreign minister (1980–83; 1984–86)

shamisen (ˈʃæmɪˌsɛn) or **samisen** (ˈsæmɪˌsɛn) n a
Japanese plucked stringed instrument with a long neck,
an unfretted fingerboard, and a rectangular soundbox
[Japanese, from Chinese san-hsien, from san three + hsien
string]

shammes or **shammash** (ˈʃɑːməs; Hebrew ʃaˈmaʃ) n, pl
shammosim or shammashim (Hebrew ʃaˈmɔsɪm) Judaism
1 an official acting as the beadle, sexton, and caretaker
of a synagogue **2** the extra candle used on the Feast of
Hanukkah to kindle the lamps or candles of the

menorah [from Hebrew *shāmmāsh*, from Aramaic *shēmash* to serve]

shammy ('ʃæmɪ) *n, pl* -mies *informal* another word for **chamois** (sense 3). Also called: **shammy leather** [c18: variant, influenced by the pronunciation, of CHAMOIS]

Shamo ('ʃɑːˈməʊ) *n* transliteration of the Chinese name for the **Gobi**

shampoo (ʃæmˈpuː) *n* 1 a liquid or cream preparation of soap or detergent to wash the hair 2 a similar preparation for washing carpets, etc ▷ *vb* -poos, -pooing, -pooed 3 (*tr*) to wash (the hair, etc) with such a preparation [c18: from Hindi *chāmpo*, from *chāmpnā* to knead]

shamrock ('ʃæm,rɒk) *n* a plant having leaves divided into three leaflets, variously identified as the wood sorrel, red clover, white clover, and black medick: the national emblem of Ireland [c16: from Irish Gaelic *seamrōg*, diminutive of *seamar* clover]

shamus ('ʃɑːməs, 'ʃeɪ-) *n, pl* -muses *US slang* a police or private detective [probably from SHAMMES, influenced by Irish *Séamas* James]

Shandong ('ʃænˈdʌŋ) *or* **Shantung** *n* a province of NE China, on the Yellow Sea and the Gulf of Chihli: part of the earliest organized state of China (1520–1030 BC); consists chiefly of the fertile plain of the lower Yellow River, with mountains over 1500 m (5000 ft) high in the centre. Capital: Jinan. Pop: 91 250 000 (2003 est). Area: 153 300 sq km (59 189 sq miles)

shandy ('ʃændɪ) *n, pl* -dies an alcoholic drink made of beer and ginger beer or lemonade [c19: of unknown origin]

Shang (ʃæŋ) *n* 1 the dynasty ruling in China from about the 18th to the 12th centuries BC ▷ *adj* 2 of or relating to the pottery produced during the Shang dynasty

shanghai ('ʃæŋhaɪ, ʃæŋˈhaɪ) *slang* ▷ *vb* -hais, -haiing, -haied (*tr*) 1 to kidnap (a man or seaman) for enforced service at sea, esp on a merchant ship 2 to force or trick (someone) into doing something, going somewhere, etc 3 *Austral & NZ* to shoot with a catapult ▷ *n* 4 *Austral & NZ* a catapult [c19: from the city of SHANGHAI; from the forceful methods formerly used to collect crews for voyages to the Orient]

Shanghai ('ʃæŋˈhaɪ) *n* a port in E China, capital of Shanghai municipality (traditionally in SE Jiangsu) near the estuary of the Yangtze: the largest city in China and one of the largest ports in the world; a major cultural and industrial centre, with many universities. Pop: 12 665 000 (2005 est)

Shangri-la ('ʃæŋɡrɪ'lɑː) *n* a remote or imaginary utopia [c20: from the name of an imaginary valley in the Himalayas, from *Lost Horizon* (1933), a novel by James Hilton]

shank (ʃæŋk) *n* 1 *anatomy* the shin 2 the corresponding part of the leg in vertebrates other than man 3 a cut of meat from the top part of an animal's shank 4 the main part of a tool, between the working part and the handle 5 the ring or stem on the back of some buttons 6 the stem or long narrow part of a key, anchor, hook, spoon handle, nail, pin, etc 7 the band of a ring as distinguished from the setting 8 the part of a shoe connecting the wide part of the sole with the heel 9 *printing* the body of a piece of type, between the shoulder and the foot ▷ *vb* 10 (*intr*) (of fruits, roots, etc) to show disease symptoms, esp discoloration 11 (*tr*) *golf* to mishit (the ball) with the foot of the shaft rather than the face of the club [Old English *scanca*; related to Old Frisian *schanke*, Middle Low German *schenke*, Danish, Swedish *skank* leg]

Shankar ('ʃæŋkɑː) *n* **Ravi** ('rɑːviː). born 1920, Indian sitarist

Shankaracharya ('ʃʌŋkərɑːˈtʃɑːrjə) *or* **Shankara** ('ʃʌŋkərə) *n* 9th century AD, Hindu philosopher and teacher; chief exponent of Vedanta philosophy

Shankly ('ʃæŋklɪ) *n* **Bill**. 1913–81, Scottish footballer and manager of Liverpool FC (1959–74)

shanks's pony *or US and Canadian* **shanks's mare** ('ʃæŋksɪz) *n informal* one's legs as a means of transportation [c18: from SHANK (in the sense: lower leg); probably with a pun on the surname *Shanks*]

Shannon[1] ('ʃænən) *n* a river in the Republic of Ireland, rising in NW Co Cavan and flowing south to the Atlantic by an estuary 113 km (70 miles) long: the longest river in the Republic of Ireland. Length: 260 km (161 miles)

Shannon[2] ('ʃænən) *n* **Claude** (**Elwood**). 1916–2000, US mathematician, who first developed information theory

shanny ('ʃænɪ) *n, pl* -nies a European blenny, *Blennius pholis*, of rocky coastal waters [c19: of obscure origin]

Shansi ('ʃænˈsiː) *n* a variant transliteration of the Chinese name for **Shanxi**

Shan State ('ʃɑːn, ʃæn) *n* an administrative division of E Myanmar: formed in 1947 from the joining of the Federation of Shan States with the Wa States; consists of the **Shan plateau** crossed by forested mountain ranges reaching over 2100 m (7000 ft). Pop: 4 416 000 (1994 est). Area: 149 743 sq km (57 816 sq miles)

shan't (ʃɑːnt) *contraction of* shall not

Shantou *or* **Shantow** ('ʃænˈtaʊ) *n* a port in SE China, in E Guangdong near the mouth of the Han River: became a treaty port in 1869. Pop: 1 356 000 (2005 est). Also called: **Swatow**

shantung (ʃænˈtʌŋ) *n* 1 a heavy silk fabric with a knobbly surface 2 a cotton or rayon imitation of this [c19: so called because it was first imported to Britain from SHANTUNG in China]

Shantung ('ʃænˈtʌŋ) *n* a variant transliteration of the Chinese name for **Shandong**

shanty[1] ('ʃæntɪ) *n, pl* -ties 1 a ramshackle hut; crude dwelling 2 *Austral & NZ* a public house, esp an unlicensed one [c19: from Canadian French *chantier* cabin built in a lumber camp, from Old French *gantier* GANTRY]

shanty[2], **shantey** ('ʃæntɪ) *or* **chanty**, *US* **chantey** ('ʃæntɪ, 'tʃæn-) *n, pl* -ties *or* -teys a song originally sung by sailors, esp a rhythmic one forming an accompaniment to work [c19: from French *chanter* to sing; see CHANT]

shantytown ('ʃæntɪˌtaʊn) *n* a town or section of a town or city inhabited by very poor people living in shanties, esp in a developing country

Shanxi ('ʃænˈʃiː) *or* **Shansi** *n* a province of N China: China's richest coal reserves and much heavy industry. Capital: Taiyuan. Pop: 33 140 000 (2003 est). Area: 157 099 sq km (60 656 sq miles)

shape (ʃeɪp) *n* 1 the outward form of an object defined by outline 2 the figure or outline of the body of a person 3 a phantom 4 organized or definite form: *my plans are taking shape* 5 the form that anything assumes; guise 6 something used to provide or define form; pattern; mould 7 condition or state of efficiency: *to be in good shape* 8 out of shape a in bad physical condition b bent, twisted, or deformed 9 take shape to assume a definite form ▷ *vb* 10 (when *intr*, often foll by *into* or *up*) to receive or cause to receive shape or form 11 (*tr*) to mould into a particular pattern or form; modify 12 (*tr*) to plan, devise, or prepare: *to shape a plan of action* [Old English *gesceap*, literally: that which is created, from *scieppan* to create; related to *sceap* sexual organs, Old Norse *skap* destiny, Old High German *scaf* form] > 'shapable *or* 'shapeable *adj* > 'shaper *n*

SHAPE (ʃeɪp) *n acronym for* Supreme Headquarters Allied Powers Europe

-shaped (ʃeɪpt) *adj combining form* having the shape of: *an L-shaped room; a pear-shaped figure*

shapeless ('ʃeɪplɪs) *adj* 1 having no definite shape or form: *a shapeless mass; a shapeless argument* 2 lacking a symmetrical or aesthetically pleasing shape: *a shapeless figure* > 'shapelessness *n*

shapely ('ʃeɪplɪ) *adj* -lier, -liest (esp of a woman's body or legs) pleasing or attractive in shape > 'shapeliness *n*

shape up *vb* (*intr, adverb*) 1 *informal* to proceed or develop satisfactorily 2 *informal* to develop a definite or proper form

Shapiro (ʃəˈpiːrəʊ) *n* **Jonathan**. publishing as *Zapiro*. born 1958, South African political cartoonist

Shapley ('ʃæplɪ) *n* **Harlow**. 1885–1972, US astronomer, director of the Harvard College Observatory (1922–56): noted for his work on the size and structure of the galaxy

S

shard (ʃɑːd) *or* **sherd** *n* **1** a broken piece or fragment of a brittle substance, esp of pottery **2** *zoology* a tough sheath, scale, or shell, esp the elytra of a beetle [Old English *sceard*; related to Old Norse *skarth* notch, Middle High German *scharte* notch]

share¹ (ʃɛə) *n* **1** a part or portion of something owned, allotted to, or contributed by a person or group **2** (*often plural*) any of the equal parts, usually of low par value, into which the capital stock of a company is divided: ownership of shares carries the right to receive a proportion of the company's profits **3** go shares *informal* to share (something) with another or others ▷ *vb* **4** (*tr*; *often foll by* out) to divide or apportion, esp equally **5** (*when* intr, *often foll by* in) to receive or contribute a portion of: *we can share the cost of the petrol; six people shared in the inheritance* **6** to join with another or others in the use of (something): *can I share your umbrella?* [Old English *scearu*; related to Old Norse *skor* amount, Old High German *scara* crowd; see SHEAR] ▷ **'sharable** *or* **'shareable** *adj* ▷ **'sharer** *n*

share² (ʃɛə) *n* short for **ploughshare** [Old English *scear*; related to Old Norse *skeri*, Old High German *scaro*]

sharecrop (ˈʃɛəˌkrɒp) *vb* **-crops, -cropping, -cropped** *chiefly US* to cultivate (farmland) as a sharecropper

sharecropper (ˈʃɛəˌkrɒpə) *n chiefly US* a farmer, esp a tenant farmer, who pays over a proportion of a crop or crops as rent

shared ownership *n* (in Britain) a form of house purchase whereby the purchaser buys a proportion of the dwelling, usually from a local authority or housing association, and rents the rest

sharefarmer (ˈʃɛəˌfɑːmə) *n chiefly Austral* a farmer who pays a fee to another in return for use of land to raise crops, etc

shareholder (ˈʃɛəˌhəʊldə) *n* the owner of one or more shares in a company

share index *n* an index showing the movement of share prices

share market *n Austral & NZ* a highly organized market facilitating the purchase and sale of securities and operated by professional stockbrokers and market makers according to fixed rules

share-milker *n* (in New Zealand) a person who lives on a dairy farm milking the owner's herd for an agreed share of the profits and, usually, building his own herd simultaneously

share option *n* a scheme giving employees an option to buy shares in the company for which they work at a favourable price or discount

share premium *n Brit* the excess of the amount actually subscribed for an issue of corporate capital over its par value

Sharesave (ˈʃɛəˌseɪv) *n* (in Britain) a system by which employees can invest, risk-free, in their company's shares

share shop *n* a stockbroker, bank, or other financial intermediary that handles the buying and selling of shares for members of the public, esp during a privatization issue

shareware (ˈʃɛəˌwɛə) *n computing* software available to all users without the need for a licence and for which a token fee is requested

sharia *or* **sheria** (ʃəˈriːə) *n* the body of canonical law based on the Koran that lays down certain duties and penalties for Muslims [Arabic]

sharif (ʃæˈriːf) *n* a variant transliteration of **sherif**

shark¹ (ʃɑːk) *n* any of various usually ferocious selachian fishes, typically marine with a long body, two dorsal fins, rows of sharp teeth, and between five and seven gill slits on each side of the head [c16: of uncertain origin] ▷ **'shark,like** *adj*

shark² (ʃɑːk) *n* a person who preys on or victimizes others, esp by swindling or extortion [c18: probably from German *Schurke* rogue; perhaps also influenced by SHARK¹]

sharkskin (ˈʃɑːkˌskɪn) *n* a smooth glossy fabric of acetate rayon, used for sportswear, etc

shark watcher *n informal* a business consultant who assists companies in identifying and preventing unwelcome takeover bids

Sharon¹ (ˈʃærən) *n* **Plain of Sharon** a plain in W Israel, between the Mediterranean and the hills of Samaria, extending from Haifa to Tel Aviv

Sharon² (ʃəˈrɒn) *n* **Ariel** (ˈɑːrɪəl). born 1928, Israeli soldier and politician; Likud prime minister (2001–06)

sharon fruit (ˈʃærən) *n* another name for **persimmon** (sense 2)

sharp (ʃɑːp) *adj* **1** having a keen edge suitable for cutting **2** having an edge or point; not rounded or blunt **3** involving a sudden change, esp in direction: *a sharp bend* **4** moving, acting, or reacting quickly, efficiently, etc: *sharp reflexes* **5** clearly defined **6** mentally acute; clever; astute **7** sly or artful; clever in an underhand way: *sharp practice* **8** bitter or harsh: *sharp words* **9** shrill or penetrating: *a sharp cry* **10** having an acrid taste **11** keen; biting: *a sharp wind; sharp pain* **12** *music* **a** (*immediately postpositive*) denoting a note that has been raised in pitch by one chromatic semitone: *B sharp* **b** (of an instrument, voice, etc) out of tune by being or tending to be too high in pitch. See **flat¹** (sense 22) **13** *informal* **a** stylish **b** too smart **14** at the sharp end involved in the area of any activity where there is most difficulty, competition, danger, etc ▷ *adv* **15** in a sharp manner **16** exactly: *six o'clock sharp* **17** *music* **a** higher than a standard pitch **b** out of tune by being or tending to be too high in pitch: *she sings sharp*. See **flat¹** (sense 27) ▷ *n* **18** *music* **a** an accidental that raises the pitch of the following note by one chromatic semitone. usual symbol: ♯ **b** a note affected by this accidental. See **flat¹** (sense 33) **19** a thin needle with a sharp point **20** *informal* a sharper ▷ *vb* **21** (*tr*) *music, US & Canadian* to raise the pitch of (a note), esp by one chromatic semitone. Usual equivalent in Britain and certain other countries: **sharpen** [Old English *scearp*; related to Old Norse *skarpr*, Old High German *scarpf*, Old Irish *cerb*, Lettish *skarbs*] ▷ **'sharply** *adv* ▷ **'sharpness** *n*

Sharp (ʃɑːp) *n* **Cecil** (**James**). 1859–1924, British musician, best known for collecting, editing, and publishing English folk songs

sharpbender (ˈʃɑːpˌbɛndə) *n informal* an organization that has been underperforming its competitors but suddenly becomes more successful, often as a result of new management or changes in its business strategy [c20: from the sharp upward bend in its sales or profits]

sharpen (ˈʃɑːpən) *vb* **1** to make or become sharp or sharper **2** *music* to raise the pitch of (a note), esp by one chromatic semitone ▷ **'sharpener** *n*

sharper (ˈʃɑːpə) *n* a person who cheats or swindles; fraud

Sharpeville (ˈʃɑːpvɪl) *n* a town in E South Africa: scene of riots in 1960 (when 69 demonstrators died), 1984, and 1985 (when 19 died)

sharpish (ˈʃɑːpɪʃ) *adj* **1** fairly sharp ▷ *adv* **2** *informal* promptly; quickly

sharp-set *adj* **1** set to give an acute cutting angle **2** keenly hungry **3** keen or eager

sharpshooter (ˈʃɑːpˌʃuːtə) *n* an expert marksman, esp with a rifle ▷ **'sharp,shooting** *n*

sharp-tongued *adj* bitter or critical in speech; sarcastic

sharp-witted *adj* having or showing a keen intelligence; perceptive ▷ **,sharp-'wittedly** *adv* ▷ **,sharp-'wittedness** *n*

Shasta daisy (ˈʃæstə) *n* a Pyrenean plant, *Chrysanthemum maximum*, widely cultivated for its large white daisy-like flowers: family *Asteraceae* (composites) [named after Mount Shasta in California]

shastra (ˈʃɑːstrə), **shaster** (ˈʃɑːstə) *or* **sastra** *n* any of the sacred writings of Hinduism [c17: from Sanskrit *śāstra*, from *śās* to teach]

shat (ʃæt) *vb taboo* a past tense and past participle of **shit**

Shatt-al-Arab (ˌʃætælˈærəb) *n* a river in SE Iraq, formed by the confluence of the Tigris and Euphrates Rivers: flows southeast as part of the border between Iraq and Iran to the Persian Gulf. Length: 193 km (120 miles)

shatter (ˈʃætə) *vb* **1** to break or be broken into many small pieces **2** (*tr*) to impair or destroy: *his nerves were shattered by the torture* **3** (*tr*) to dumbfound or thoroughly upset: *she was shattered by the news* **4** (*tr*) *informal* to cause to be tired out or exhausted [c12: perhaps obscurely related to SCATTER] ⊳ '**shattering** *adj* ⊳ '**shatteringly** *adv* ⊳ '**shattered** *adj*

shatterproof ('ʃætə,pruːf) *adj* designed to resist shattering

shave (ʃeɪv) *vb* shaves, shaving, shaved, shaved *or* shaven (*mainly tr*) **1** (*also intr*) to remove (the beard, hair, etc) from (the face, head, or body) by scraping the skin with a razor **2** to cut or trim very closely **3** to reduce to shavings **4** to remove thin slices from (wood, etc) with a sharp cutting tool; plane or pare **5** to touch or graze in passing **6** *informal* to reduce (a price) by a slight amount ⊳ *n* **7** the act or an instance of shaving **8** any tool for scraping **9** a thin slice or shaving [Old English *sceafan*; related to Old Norse *skafa*, Gothic *skaban* to shave, Latin *scabere* to scrape] ⊳ '**shavable** *or* '**shaveable** *adj*

shaveling ('ʃeɪvlɪŋ) *n archaic* **1** *derogatory* a priest or clergyman with a shaven head **2** a young fellow; youth

shaven ('ʃeɪvᵊn) *adj* **a** closely shaved or tonsured **b** (*in combination*): *clean-shaven*

shaver ('ʃeɪvə) *n* **1** a person or thing that shaves **2** Also called: **electric razor, electric shaver** an electrically powered implement for shaving, having reciprocating or rotating blades behind a fine metal comb or pierced foil **3** *informal* a youngster, esp a young boy

Shavian ('ʃeɪvɪən) *adj* **1** of, relating to, or like George Bernard Shaw (1856–1950), the Irish dramatist and critic, his works, ideas, etc ⊳ *n* **2** an admirer of Shaw or his works

shaving ('ʃeɪvɪŋ) *n* **1** a thin paring or slice, esp of wood, that has been shaved from something ⊳ *modifier* **2** used when shaving the face, etc: *shaving cream*

Shavuot *or* **Shabuoth** (ʃəˈvuːəs, -ɒs; *Hebrew* ʃavuˈʔɔt) *n* the Hebrew name for **Pentecost** (sense 2) [from Hebrew *shābhū'ōth*, plural of *shābhūā'* week]

shaw¹ (ʃɔː) *n archaic, or dialect* a small wood; thicket; copse [Old English *sceaga*; related to Old Norse *skagi* tip, *skaga* to jut out, *skōgr* forest, *skegg* beard]

shaw² (ʃɔː) *Scot vb* **1** to show ⊳ *n* **2** a show **3** the part of a potato plant that is above ground

Shaw (ʃɔː) *n* **1 Artie**, original name *Arthur Arshawsky*. 1910–2004, US jazz clarinetist, band leader, and composer **2 George Bernard**, often known as *GBS*. 1856–1950, Irish dramatist and critic, in England from 1876. He was an active socialist and became a member of the Fabian Society but his major works are effective as satiric attacks rather than political tracts. These include *Arms and the Man* (1894), *Candida* (1894), *Man and Superman* (1903), *Major Barbara* (1905), *Pygmalion* (1913), *Back to Methuselah* (1921), and *St Joan* (1923): Nobel prize for literature 1925 **3 Richard Norman**. 1831–1912, English architect **4 Thomas Edward**. the name assumed by (T. E.) **Lawrence** after 1927

shawl (ʃɔːl) *n* a piece of fabric or knitted or crocheted material worn around the shoulders by women or wrapped around a baby [c17: from Persian *shāl*]

shawm (ʃɔːm) *n music* a medieval form of the oboe with a conical bore and flaring bell, blown through a double reed [c14 *shalmye*, from Old French *chalemie*, ultimately from Latin *calamus* a reed, from Greek *kalamos*]

shay (ʃeɪ) *n* a dialect word for **chaise** [c18: back formation from CHAISE, mistakenly thought to be plural]

Shays (ʃeɪz) *n* **Daniel**. ?1747–1825, American soldier and revolutionary leader of a rebellion of Massachusetts farmers against the US government (1786–87)

Shcheglovsk (*Russian* ʃtʃɪgˈlɔfsk) *n* the former name (until 1932) of **Kemerovo**

Shcherbakov (*Russian* ʃtʃɪrbaˈkɔf) *n* a former name (from the Revolution until 1957) of **Rybinsk**

she (ʃiː) *pron* (*subjective*) **1** refers to a female person or animal: *she is a doctor; she's a fine mare* **2** refers to things personified as feminine, such as cars, ships, and nations **3** *Austral & NZ* an informal word for **it**¹ (sense 3) *she's apples; she'll be right* ⊳ *n* **4 a** a female person or animal **b** (*in combination*): *she-cat* [Old English *sīe*, accusative of *sēo*, feminine demonstrative pronoun]

shea ('ʃɪə) *n* **1** a tropical African sapotaceous tree,

Butyrospermum parkii, with oily seeds **2** shea butter the white butter-like fat obtained from the seeds of this plant and used as food, to make soaps, etc [c18: from Bambara *si*]

sheading ('ʃiːdɪŋ) *n* any of the six subdivisions of the Isle of Man [variant of *shedding*; see SHED²]

sheaf (ʃiːf) *n, pl* sheaves (ʃiːvz) **1** a bundle of reaped but unthreshed corn tied with one or two bonds **2** a bundle of objects tied together **3** the arrows contained in a quiver ⊳ *vb* **4** (*tr*) to bind or tie into a sheaf [Old English *sceaf*, related to Old High German *skoub* sheaf, Old Norse *skauf* tail, Gothic *skuft* tuft of hair]

shear (ʃɪə) *vb* shears, shearing, sheared *or Austral. and NZ* shore, sheared *or* shorn **1** (*tr*) to remove (the fleece or hair) of (sheep, etc) by cutting or clipping **2** to cut or cut through (something) with shears or a sharp instrument **3** *engineering* to cause (a part, member, shaft, etc) to deform or fracture or (of a part, etc) to deform or fracture as a result of excess torsion or transverse load **4** (*tr*; often foll by *of*) to strip or divest: *to shear someone of his power* **5** (when *intr*, foll by *through*) to move through (something) by or as if by cutting ⊳ *n* **6** the act, process, or an instance of shearing **7** a shearing of a sheep or flock of sheep, esp when referred to as an indication of age: *a sheep of two shears* **8** a form of deformation or fracture in which parallel planes in a body or assembly slide over one another **9** *physics* the deformation of a body, part, etc, expressed as the lateral displacement between two points in parallel planes divided by the distance between the planes **10** either one of the blades of a pair of shears, scissors, etc See also **shears, shore** [Old English *sceran*; related to Old Norse *skera* to cut, Old Saxon, Old High German *skeran* to shear; see SHARE²] ⊳ '**shearer** *n*

shearling ('ʃɪəlɪŋ) *n* **1** a young sheep after its first shearing **2** the skin of such an animal

shear pin *n* an easily replaceable pin inserted in a machine at a critical point and designed to shear and stop the machine if the load becomes too great

shears (ʃɪəz) *pl n* **1 a** large scissors, as for cutting cloth, jointing poultry, etc **b** a large scissor-like and usually hand-held cutting tool with flat blades, as for cutting hedges **2** any of various analogous cutting or clipping implements or machines

shearwater ('ʃɪə,wɔːtə) *n* any of several oceanic birds of the genera *Puffinus*, such as *P. puffinus* (**Manx shearwater**), *Procellaria*, etc, specialized for an aerial or aquatic existence: family Procellariidae, order Procellariiformes (petrels) [c17: so named because their wings seem to clip the waves when they are flying low]

sheatfish ('ʃiːt,fɪʃ) *n, pl* **-fish** *or* **-fishes** the European catfish. See **silurid** (sense 1) [c16: variant of *sheathfish*; perhaps influenced by German *Schaid* sheatfish; see SHEATH, FISH]

sheath (ʃiːθ) *n, pl* sheaths (ʃiːðz) **1** a case or covering for the blade of a knife, sword, etc **2** any similar close-fitting case **3** *biology* an enclosing or protective structure, such as a leaf base encasing the stem of a plant **4** the protective covering on an electric cable **5** a figure-hugging dress with a narrow tapering skirt **6** another name for **condom** [Old English *scēath*; related to Old Norse *skeithir*, Old High German *sceida* a dividing; compare Old English *scādan* to divide]

sheathe (ʃiːð) *vb* (*tr*) **1** to insert (a knife, sword, etc) into a sheath **2** (esp of cats) to retract (the claws) **3** to surface with or encase in a sheath or sheathing

sheathing ('ʃiːðɪŋ) *n* **1** any material used as an outer layer, as on a ship's hull **2** boarding, etc, used to cover the wall studding or roof joists of a timber frame

sheath knife *n* a knife carried in or protected by a sheath

sheave¹ (ʃiːv) *vb* (*tr*) to gather or bind into sheaves

sheave² (ʃiːv) *n* a wheel with a grooved rim, esp one used as a pulley [c14: of Germanic origin; compare Old High German *sciba* disc]

sheaves (ʃiːvz) *n* the plural of **sheaf**

Sheba¹ ('ʃiːbə) *n* **1** Also called: **Saba** the ancient kingdom of the Sabeans: a rich trading nation dealing in gold, spices, and precious stones (I Kings 10) **2** the region inhabited by this nation, located in the SW corner of the Arabian peninsula: modern Yemen

Sheba² (ˈʃiːbə) n Queen of Sheba Old Testament a queen of the Sabeans, who visited Solomon (I Kings 10:1–13)

shebang (ʃɪˈbæŋ) n slang a situation, matter, or affair (esp in the phrase **the whole shebang**) [c19: of uncertain origin]

shebeen or **shebean** (ʃɪˈbiːn) n 1 Irish, Scot & South African a place where alcoholic drink is sold illegally 2 (in Ireland) alcohol, esp home-distilled whiskey, sold without a licence 3 (in South Africa) a place where Black African men engage in social drinking [c18: from Irish Gaelic síbín beer of poor quality]

Shechem (ˈʃɛkəm, -ɛm) n the ancient name of **Nablus**

shed¹ (ʃɛd) n 1 a small building or lean-to of light construction, used for storage, shelter, etc 2 a large roofed structure, esp one with open sides, used for storage, repairing locomotives, sheepshearing, etc [Old English sced; probably variant of scead shelter, SHADE]

shed² (ʃɛd) vb sheds, shedding, shed (mainly tr) 1 to pour forth or cause to pour forth: to shed tears; shed blood 2 shed light on, shed light upon, throw light on or throw light upon to clarify or supply additional information about 3 to cast off or lose: the snake shed its skin; trees shed their leaves 4 (of a lorry) to drop (its load) on the road by accident 5 to abolish or get rid of (jobs, workers, etc) 6 to repel: this coat sheds water 7 (tr) dialect to make a parting in (the hair) ▷ n 8 short for **watershed** [Old English sceadan; related to Gothic skaidan, Old High German skeidan to separate; see SHEATH] > 'shedable or 'sheddable adj

shed³ (ʃɛd) vb sheds, shedding, shed 1 (tr) to separate or divide off (some farm animals) from the remainder of a group: a good dog can shed his sheep in a matter of minutes ▷ n 2 (of a dog) the action of separating farm animals [from SHED²] > 'shedding n

she'd (ʃiːd) contraction of she had or she would

shedder (ˈʃɛdə) n 1 a person or thing that sheds 2 an animal, such as a llama, snake, or lobster, that moults

shedful (ˈʃɛdfʊl) n 1 the quantity or amount contained in a shed 2 informal a lot: a shedful of helpful hints

shed hand n chiefly Austral & NZ a worker in a sheepshearing shed

shedload (ˈʃɛdˌləʊd) n slang a very large amount or number

shed out vb (tr, adverb) NZ to separate off (sheep that have lambed) and move them to better pasture

sheen (ʃiːn) n 1 a gleaming or glistening brightness; lustre 2 poetic splendid clothing ▷ adj 3 rare shining and beautiful; radiant [Old English sciene; related to Old Norse skjóni white horse, Gothic skauns beautiful, Old High German scōni bright] > 'sheeny adj

Sheene (ʃiːn) n Barry (Stephen Frank). 1950–2003, British racing motorcyclist: 500 cc. world champion (1976, 1977)

sheep (ʃiːp) n, pl sheep 1 any of various bovid mammals of the genus Ovis and related genera, esp O. aries (**domestic sheep**), having transversely ribbed horns and a narrow face. There are many breeds of domestic sheep, raised for their wool and for meat 2 Barbary sheep another name for **aoudad** 3 a meek or timid person, esp one without initiative 4 separate the sheep from the goats to pick out the members of any group who are superior in some respects [Old English sceap; related to Old Frisian skēp, Old Saxon scāp, Old High German scāf] > 'sheep,like adj

sheepcote (ˈʃiːpˌkəʊt) n chiefly Brit another word for **sheepfold**

sheep-dip n 1 any of several liquid disinfectants and insecticides in which sheep are immersed to kill vermin and germs in their fleece 2 a deep trough containing such a liquid

sheepdog (ˈʃiːpˌdɒg) n 1 Also called: **shepherd dog** a dog used for herding sheep 2 any of various breeds of dog reared originally for herding sheep. See **Old English sheepdog, Shetland sheepdog**

sheepdog trial n (often plural) a competition in which sheepdogs are tested in their tasks

sheepfold (ˈʃiːpˌfəʊld) n a pen or enclosure for sheep

sheepish (ˈʃiːpɪʃ) adj 1 abashed or embarrassed, esp through looking foolish or being in the wrong 2 resembling a sheep in timidity or lack of initiative > 'sheepishly adv > 'sheepishness n

sheepo (ˈʃiːpəʊ) n, pl sheepos NZ a person employed to bring sheep to the catching pen in a shearing shed

sheep's eyes pl n old-fashioned amorous or inviting glances

sheepshank (ˈʃiːpˌʃæŋk) n a knot consisting of two hitches at the ends of a bight made in a rope to shorten it temporarily

sheepskin (ˈʃiːpˌskɪn) n a the skin of a sheep, esp when used for clothing, etc, or with the fleece removed and used for parchment b (as modifier): a sheepskin coat

sheepwalk (ˈʃiːpˌwɔːk) n chiefly Brit a tract of land for grazing sheep

sheer¹ (ʃɪə) adj 1 perpendicular; very steep: a sheer cliff 2 (of textiles) so fine as to be transparent 3 (prenominal) absolute; unmitigated: sheer folly 4 obsolete bright or shining ▷ adv 5 steeply or perpendicularly 6 completely or absolutely [Old English scīr; related to Old Norse skírr bright, Gothic skeirs clear, Middle High German schīr] > 'sheerly adv > 'sheerness n

sheer² (ʃɪə) vb (foll by off or away (from)) 1 to deviate or cause to deviate from a course 2 (intr) to avoid an unpleasant person, thing, topic, etc ▷ n 3 nautical the position of a vessel relative to its mooring [c17: perhaps variant of SHEAR]

sheerlegs or **shearlegs** (ˈʃɪəˌlɛgz) n (functioning as singular) a device for lifting heavy weights consisting of two or more spars lashed together at the upper ends from which a lifting tackle is suspended. Also called: shears [c19: variant of shear legs]

Sheerness (ʃɪəˈnɛs) n a port and resort in SE England, in N Kent at the junction of the Medway estuary and the Thames: administratively part of Queenborough in Sheppey since 1968

sheet¹ (ʃiːt) n 1 a large rectangular piece of cotton, linen, etc, generally one of a pair used as inner bedclothes 2 a a thin piece of a substance such as paper, glass, or metal, usually rectangular in form b (as modifier): sheet iron 3 a broad continuous surface; expanse or stretch: a sheet of rain 4 a newspaper, esp a tabloid 5 a piece of printed paper to be folded into a section for a book ▷ vb 6 (tr) to provide with, cover, or wrap in a sheet [Old English sciete; related to sceat corner, lap, Old Norse skaut, Old High German scōz lap]

sheet² (ʃiːt) n nautical a line or rope for controlling the position of a sail relative to the wind [Old English scēata corner of a sail; related to Middle Low German schōte rope attached to a sail; see SHEET¹]

sheet anchor n 1 nautical a large strong anchor for use in emergency 2 a person or thing to be relied upon in an emergency [c17: from earlier shute anker, from shoot (obsolete) the sheet of a sail]

sheet bend n a knot used esp for joining ropes of different sizes

sheeting (ˈʃiːtɪŋ) n fabric from which sheets are made

sheet lightning n lightning that appears as a broad sheet, caused by the reflection of more distant lightning

sheet metal n metal in the form of a sheet, the thickness being intermediate between that of plate and that of foil

sheet music n 1 the printed or written copy of a short composition or piece, esp in the form of unbound leaves 2 music in its written or printed form

Sheffield (ˈʃɛfiːld) n 1 a city in N England, in Sheffield unitary authority, South Yorkshire on the River Don: important centre of steel manufacture and of the cutlery industry; Sheffield university (1905) and Sheffield Hallam University (1992). Pop: 439 866 (2001) 2 a unitary authority in N England, in South Yorkshire. Pop: 512 500 (2003 est). Area: 368 sq km (142 sq miles)

Sheffield Shield n (in Australia) the former name for the trophy of the annual interstate cricket competition

sheikh or **sheik** (ʃeɪk) n (in Muslim countries) a the head of an Arab tribe, village, etc b a high priest or religious leader, esp a Sufi master [c16: from Arabic shaykh old man]

sheila ('ʃiːlə) *n Austral & NZ old-fashioned* an informal word for **girl, woman** [C19: from the girl's name *Sheila*]

shekel *or* **sheqel** ('ʃekəl) *n* 1 the standard monetary unit of modern Israel, divided into 100 agorot 2 any of several former coins and units of weight of the Near East 3 *(often plural) informal* any coin or money [C16: from Hebrew *sheqel*]

Shelburne ('ʃelbɜːn) *n* **2nd Earl of**, title of *William Petty Fitzmaurice*, also called *(from 1784)* 1st Marquess of Lansdowne. 1737–1805, British statesman; prime minister (1782–83)

shelduck ('ʃel,dʌk) *or masculine* **sheldrake** ('ʃel,dreɪk) *n, pl* -ducks, -duck *or* -drakes, -drake any of various large usually brightly coloured gooselike ducks, such as *Tadorna tadorna* (**common shelduck**), of the Old World [C14 *shel*, probably from dialect *sheld* pied; related to Middle Dutch *schillede* variegated]

shelf (ʃelf) *n, pl* **shelves** (ʃelvz) 1 a thin flat plank of wood, metal, etc, fixed horizontally against a wall, etc, for the purpose of supporting objects 2 something resembling this in shape or function 3 the objects placed on a shelf, regarded collectively: *a shelf of books* 4 a projecting layer of ice, rock, etc, on land or in the sea 5 See **off the shelf** 6 **on the shelf** put aside or abandoned: used esp of unmarried women considered to be past the age of marriage ▷ *vb* 7 *(tr) Austral slang* to inform upon [Old English *scylfe* ship's deck; related to Middle Low German *schelf* shelf, Old English *scylf* crag] > 'shelf,like *adj*

shelf life *n* the length of time a packaged food, chemical, etc, will last without deteriorating

shell (ʃel) *n* 1 the protective calcareous or membranous outer layer of an egg, esp a bird's egg 2 the hard outer covering of many molluscs that is secreted by the mantle 3 any other hard outer layer, such as the exoskeleton of many arthropods 4 the hard outer layer of some fruits, esp of nuts 5 any hard outer case 6 a hollow artillery projectile filled with explosive primed to explode either during flight, on impact, or after penetration 7 a small-arms cartridge comprising a hollow casing inside which is the primer, charge, and bullet 8 *rowing* a very light narrow racing boat 9 the external structure of a building, esp one that is unfinished or one that has been gutted by fire 10 *physics* **a** a class of electron orbits in an atom in which the electrons have the same principal quantum number and orbital angular momentum quantum number and differences in their energy are small compared with differences in energy between shells **b** an analogous energy state of nucleons in certain theories (**shell models**) of the structure of the atomic nucleus 11 **come out of one's shell** to become less shy and reserved ▷ *vb* 12 to divest or be divested of a shell, husk, pod, etc 13 to separate or be separated from an ear, husk, cob, etc 14 *(tr)* to bombard with artillery shells ▷ See also **shell out** [Old English *sciell*; related to Old Norse *skel* shell, Gothic *skalja* tile, Middle Low German *schelle* shell; see SCALE¹, SHALE] > 'shell-less *adj* > 'shell-,like *adj* > 'shelly *adj*

she'll (ʃiːl; *unstressed* ʃɪl) *contraction of* she will *or* she shall

shellac (ʃə'læk, 'ʃelæk) *n* 1 a yellowish resin secreted by the lac insect, esp a commercial preparation of this used in varnishes, polishes, and leather dressings 2 Also called: **shellac varnish** a varnish made by dissolving shellac in ethanol or a similar solvent ▷ *vb* -lacs, -lacking, -lacked *(tr)* 3 to coat or treat (an article) with a shellac varnish [C18: SHELL + LAC¹, translation of French *laque en écailles*, literally: lac in scales, that is, in thin plates]

shellback ('ʃel,bæk) *n informal* a sailor who has crossed the equator

shell company *n business* 1 a near-defunct company, esp one with a stock-exchange listing, used as a vehicle for a thriving company 2 a company that has ceased to trade but retains its registration and is sold for a small sum to enable its new owners to avoid the cost and trouble of registering a new company

Shelley ('ʃelɪ) *n* 1 **Mary (Wollstonecraft)** ('wʊlstən,krɑːft). 1797–1851, British writer; author of *Frankenstein* (1818); the

daughter of William Godwin and Mary Wollstonecraft, she eloped with Percy Bysshe Shelley 2 **Percy Bysshe** (bɪʃ). 1792–1822, British romantic poet. His works include *Queen Mab* (1813), *Prometheus Unbound* (1820), and *The Triumph of Life* (1824). He wrote an elegy on the death of Keats, *Adonais* (1821), and shorter lyrics, including the odes 'To the West Wind' and 'To a Skylark' (both 1820). He was drowned in the Ligurian Sea while sailing from Leghorn to La Spezia

shellfire ('ʃel,faɪə) *n* the firing of artillery shells

shellfish ('ʃel,fɪʃ) *n, pl* -fish *or* -fishes any aquatic invertebrate having a shell or shell-like carapace, esp such an animal used as human food. Examples are crustaceans such as crabs and lobsters and molluscs such as oysters

shell out *vb (adverb) informal* to pay out or hand over (money) [C19: from SHELL (in the sense: to remove from a pod or (figuratively) a purse]

shell program *n computing* a basic low-cost computer program that provides a framework within which the user can develop the program to suit his personal requirements

shellproof ('ʃel,pruːf) *adj* designed, intended, or able to resist shellfire

shell shock *n* loss of sight, memory, etc, resulting from psychological strain during prolonged engagement in warfare. Also called: **combat neurosis**

shell suit *n* a lightweight tracksuit consisting of an inner cotton layer covered by a waterproof nylon layer

Shelta ('ʃeltə) *n* a secret language used by some itinerant tinkers in Ireland and parts of Britain, based on systematically altered Gaelic [C19: from earlier *sheldrū*, perhaps an arbitrary alteration of Old Irish *bēlre* speech]

shelter ('ʃeltə) *n* 1 something that provides cover or protection, as from weather or danger; place of refuge 2 the protection afforded by such a cover; refuge 3 the state of being sheltered ▷ *vb* 4 *(tr)* to provide with or protect by a shelter 5 *(intr)* to take cover, as from rain; find refuge 6 *(tr)* to act as a shelter for; take under one's protection [C16: of uncertain origin] > 'shelterer *n*

sheltered ('ʃeltəd) *adj* 1 protected from wind or weather 2 protected from outside influences: *a sheltered upbringing* 3 (of buildings) specially designed to provide a safe environment for the elderly, handicapped, or disabled

sheltie *or* **shelty** ('ʃeltɪ) *n, pl* -ties another name for **Shetland pony, Shetland sheepdog** [C17: probably from Orkney dialect *sjalti*, from Old Norse *Hjalti* Shetlander, from *Hjaltland* Shetland]

shelve¹ (ʃelv) *vb (tr)* 1 to place on a shelf 2 to provide with shelves 3 to put aside or postpone from consideration 4 to dismiss or cause to retire [C16: from *shelves*, plural of SHELF] > 'shelver *n*

shelve² (ʃelv) *vb (intr)* to slope away gradually; incline [C16: origin uncertain]

shelves (ʃelvz) *n* the plural of **shelf**

shelving ('ʃelvɪŋ) *n* 1 material for making shelves 2 a set of shelves; shelves collectively

Shem (ʃem) *n Old Testament* the eldest of Noah's three sons (Genesis 10:21)

she-male *n informal* a male-to-female transsexual

shemozzle (ʃɪ'mɒzəl) *n informal* a noisy confusion or dispute; uproar [C19: perhaps from Yiddish *shlimazl* misfortune]

shenanigan (ʃɪ'nænɪɡən) *n informal* 1 *(usually plural)* roguishness; mischief 2 an act of treachery; deception [C19: of unknown origin]

Shensi ('ʃen'siː) *n* a variant transliteration of the Chinese name for **Shaanxi**

Shenyang ('ʃen'jæŋ) *n* a walled city in NE China in S Manchuria, capital of Liaoning province: capital of the Manchu dynasty from 1644–1912; seized by the Japanese in 1931. Pop: 4 916 000 (2005 est). Former name: **Mukden**

Shenzhou ('ʃen'dʒəʊ) *n* any of a series of manned Chinese spacecraft [C20: Chinese: divine craft or divine mechanism]

she-oak *n* any of various Australian trees of the genus *Casuarina*. See **casuarina** [C18 *she* (in the sense: inferior) + OAK]

Sheol ('ʃiːəʊl, -ɒl) *n Old Testament* 1 the abode of the dead

S

2 (*often not capital*) hell [C16: from Hebrew *shĕ'ōl*]

Shepard ('ʃepəd) *n* **1 Alan Bartlett, Jr.** 1923–98, US naval officer; first US astronaut in space (1961) **2 Sam**, original name *Samuel Shepard Rogers*. born 1943, US dramatist, film actor, and director. His plays include *Chicago* (1966), *The Tooth of Crime* (1972), and *Buried Child* (1978): films as actor include *Days of Heaven* (1978) and *The Right Stuff* (1983); films as director include *Far North* (1989) and *Silent Tongue* (1994)

shepherd ('ʃepəd) *n* **1** a person employed to tend sheep. Female equivalent: **shepherdess 2** a person, such as a clergyman, who watches over or guides a group of people ▷ *vb* (*tr*) **3** to guide or watch over in the manner of a shepherd **4** *Australian rules football* to prevent opponents from tackling (a member of one's own team) by blocking their path [from Old English *sceaphirde*. See SHEEP, HERD²]

shepherd dog *n* another term for **sheepdog** (sense 1)

shepherd's pie *n chiefly Brit* a baked dish of minced meat covered with mashed potato. Also called: cottage pie

shepherd's-purse *n* a plant, *Capsella bursa-pastoris*, having small white flowers and flattened triangular seed pods: family Brassicaceae (crucifers) [C15: compare Latin *bursa pastoris*, French *bourse-de-berger*, German *Hirtentasche*, Dutch *herdentasch*]

shepherd's weatherglass *n Brit* another name for the **scarlet pimpernel**

Sheppard ('ʃepəd) *n* **Jack.** 1702–24, English criminal, whose daring escapes from prison were celebrated in many contemporary ballads and plays

Sheppey ('ʃepɪ) *n* **Isle of Sheppey** an island in SE England, off the N coast of Kent in the Thames estuary: separated from the mainland by **The Swale**, a narrow channel. Chief towns: Sheerness, Minster. Pop: 37 852 (2001 est). Area: 80 sq km (30 sq miles)

Sher (ʃɜː) *n* **Sir Antony.** born 1953, British actor and writer, born in South Africa

sherang (ʃəˈræŋ) *n* head sherang *Austral & NZ* the boss; person in authority: *who is the head sherang around here?* [C20 from Anglo-Indian *şerang* boatswain]

Sheraton¹ ('ʃerətən) *n* **Thomas.** 1751–1806, English furniture maker, author of the influential *Cabinet-Maker and Upholsterer's Drawing Book* (1791)

Sheraton² ('ʃerətən) *adj* denoting furniture made by or in the style of Thomas Sheraton, the English furniture maker (1751–1806), characterized by lightness, elegance, and the extensive use of inlay

sherbet ('ʃɜːbət) *n* **1** a fruit-flavoured slightly effervescent powder, eaten as a sweet or used to make a drink **2** *US & Canadian* another word for: **sorbet** (sense 1) **3** *Austral slang* beer **4** a cooling Oriental drink of sweetened fruit juice [C17: from Turkish *şerbet*, from Persian *sharbat*, from Arabic *sharbah* drink, from *shariba* to drink]

Sherborne ('ʃɛːbɔːn) *n* a town in S England in Dorset: noted for its medieval abbey, ruined medieval castle, and Sherborne Castle, a mansion built by Sir Walter Raleigh in 1594. Pop: 9350 (2001)

Sherbrooke ('ʃɜːbrʊk) *n* a city in E Canada, in S Quebec: university. It is an industrial and commercial centre. Pop: 127 354 (2001)

sherd (ʃɜːd) *n* a variant of **shard**

Sheridan ('ʃerɪdən) *n* **1 Philip Henry.** 1831–88, American Union cavalry commander in the Civil War. He forced Lee's surrender to Grant (1865) **2 Richard Brinsley** ('brɪnzlɪ). 1751–1816, Irish dramatist, politician, and orator, noted for his comedies of manners *The Rivals* (1775), *School for Scandal* (1777), and *The Critic* (1779)

sherif, shereef (ʃɛˈriːf) *or* **sharif** *n, pl* ashraf *Islam* **1 a** a descendant of Mohammed through his daughter Fatima **2** an honorific title accorded to any Muslim ruler [C16: from Arabic *sharīf* noble]

sheriff ('ʃerɪf) *n* **1** (in the US) the chief law-enforcement officer in a county: popularly elected, except in Rhode Island **2** (in England and Wales) the chief executive officer of the Crown in a county, having chiefly ceremonial duties **3** (in Scotland) a judge in any of the sheriff courts **4** (in New Zealand) an officer of the High Court [Old English *scīrgerēfa*, from *scīr* SHIRE¹ + *gerēfa* REEVE¹] ▷ 'sheriffdom *n*

sheriff court *n* (in Scotland) a court having jurisdiction to try summarily or on indictment all but the most serious crimes and to deal with most civil actions

Sherman ('ʃɜːmən) *n* **William Tecumseh** (tɪˈkʌmsə). 1820–91, American Union commander during the Civil War. He led the victorious march through Georgia (1864), becoming commander of the army in 1869

Sherpa ('ʃɜːpə) *n, pl* **-pas** *or* **-pa** a member of a people of Mongolian origin living on the southern slopes of the Himalayas in Nepal, noted as mountaineers

Sherriff ('ʃerɪf) *n* **R(obert) C(edric).** 1896–1975, British dramatist and film writer, best known for his play of World War I *Journey's End* (1928). His film scripts include *Goodbye Mr. Chips* (1936) and *The Dam Busters* (1955)

Sherrington ('ʃerɪŋtən) *n* **Sir Charles Scott.** 1857–1952, English physiologist, noted for his work on reflex action, published in *The Integrative Action of the Nervous System* (1906): shared the Nobel prize for physiology or medicine with Adrian (1932)

sherry ('ʃerɪ) *n, pl* **-ries** a fortified wine, originally from the Jerez region in S Spain, usually drunk as an apéritif [C16: from earlier *sherris* (assumed to be plural), from Spanish *Xeres*, now *Jerez*]

's Hertogenbosch (Dutch shɛrtoːxənˈbɔs) *n* a city in the S Netherlands, capital of North Brabant province: birthplace of Hieronymus Bosch. Pop: 133 000 (2003 est). Also called: **Den Bosch** French name: **Bois-le-Duc**

sherwani (ʃɛəˈwɑːnɪ) *n, pl* **-nis** a long coat closed up to the neck, worn by men in India [Hindi]

Sherwood ('ʃɜːwʊd) *n* **Robert Emmet.** 1896–1955, US dramatist. His plays include *The Petrified Forest* (1935), *Idiot's Delight* (1936), and *There shall be no Night* (1940)

Sherwood Forest ('ʃɜːwʊd) *n* an ancient forest in central England, in Nottinghamshire: formerly a royal hunting ground and much more extensive; famous as the home of Robin Hood

she's (ʃiːz) *contraction of* she is *or* she has

Shetland ('ʃetlənd) *n* Also called: **Shetland Islands** a group of about 100 islands (fewer than 20 inhabited), off the N coast of Scotland, which constitute an island authority of Scotland: a Norse dependency from the 8th century until 1472; noted for the breeding of Shetland ponies, knitwear manufacturing, and fishing; oil-related industries. Administrative centre: Lerwick. Pop: 21 870 (2003 est). Area: 1426 sq km (550 sq miles). Official name (until 1974): **Zetland**

Shetland pony *n* a very small sturdy breed of pony with a long shaggy mane and tail. Also called: **sheltie**

Shetland sheepdog *n* a small dog similar in appearance to a rough collie. Also called: **sheltie**

Shevardnadze (ʃevədˈnɑːdze) *n* **Eduard (Amvrosiyevich).** born 1928, Georgian statesman; president of Georgia (1992–2003); Soviet minister of foreign affairs (1985–91), who played an important part in arms negotiations with the US

shew (ʃəʊ) *vb* shews, shewing, shewed, shewn (ʃəʊn) *or* shewed an archaic spelling of **show** ▷ 'shewer *n*

shewbread *or* **showbread** ('ʃəʊ,bred) *n Old Testament* the loaves of bread placed every Sabbath on the table beside the altar of incense in the tabernacle or temple of ancient Israel (Exodus 25:30; Leviticus 24:5–9) [on the model of German *Schaubrot*, a translation of the Greek *artoi enōpioi*, a translation of the Hebrew *lechem pānīm*, literally: bread of the presence]

SHF *or* **shf** *radio abbreviation* superhigh frequency

Shiah *or* **Shia** ('ʃiːə) *n* **1** one of the two main branches of Islam (the other being the Sunni), making up a tenth or more of the entire Muslim population, and forming the majority in Iran and Iraq, and which regards Mohammed's cousin Ali and his successors as the true imams ▷ *adj* **2** designating or characteristic of this sect or its beliefs and practices [C17: from Arabic *shī'ah* sect, from *shā'a* to follow]

shiatsu (ʃiːˈætsuː) *n* massage in which pressure is applied to the same points of the body as in acupuncture. Also called: **acupressure** [Japanese, from Chinese *chī* finger + *yā* pressure]

shibboleth ('ʃɪbə,lεθ) *n* **1** a belief, principle, or practice which is commonly adhered to but which is thought by some people to be inappropriate or out of date **2** a custom, phrase, or use of language that acts as a test of belonging to, or as a stumbling block to becoming a member of, a particular social class, profession, etc [c14: from Hebrew, literally: ear of grain; the word is used in the Old Testament by the Gileadites as a test word for the Ephraimites, who could not pronounce the sound *sh*]

shickered ('ʃɪkəd) *adj Austral & NZ slang* drunk; intoxicated [via Yiddish from Heb.]

shied (ʃaɪd) *vb* the past tense and past participle of **shy**[1,2]

shield (ʃiːld) *n* **1** any protection used to intercept blows, missiles, etc, such as a tough piece of armour carried on the arm **2** any similar protective device **3** Also called: **scutcheon, escutcheon** *heraldry* a pointed stylized shield used for displaying armorial bearings **4** anything that resembles a shield in shape, such as a prize in a sports competition **5** *physics* a structure of concrete, lead, etc, placed around a nuclear reactor or other source of radiation in order to prevent the escape of radiation **6** a broad stable plateau of ancient Precambrian rocks forming the rigid nucleus of a particular continent **7 the shield** *informal* **a** *Austral* short for the **Sheffield Shield b** NZ short for the **Ranfurly Shield,** a trophy competed for by provincial rugby teams ▷ *vb* **8** (*tr*) to protect, hide, or conceal (something) from danger or harm [Old English *scield*; related to Old Norse *skjöldr*, Gothic *skildus*, Old High German *scilt* shield, Old English *sciell* SHELL] > '**shield,like** *adj*

shield match *n* **a** *Austral* a cricket match for the Sheffield Shield **b** NZ a rugby match for the Ranfurly Shield

Shields (ʃiːldz) *n* Carol (Ann). 1935–2003, Canadian novelist and writer, born in the US; her novels include *Happenstance* (1980), *The Stone Diaries* (1995), and *Unless* (2002)

shield volcano *n* a broad volcano built up from the repeated nonexplosive eruption of basalt to form a low dome or shield, usually having a large caldera at the summit

shieling ('ʃiːlɪŋ) *or* **shiel** (ʃiːl) *n chiefly Scot* **1** a rough, sometimes temporary, hut or shelter used by people tending cattle on high or remote ground **2** pasture land for the grazing of cattle in summer [c16: from Middle English *shale* hut, of unknown origin]

shier ('ʃaɪə) *adj* a comparative of **shy**[1]

shiest ('ʃaɪɪst) *adj* a superlative of **shy**[1]

shift (ʃɪft) *vb* **1** to move or cause to move from one place or position to another **2** (*tr*) to change for another or others **3** to change (gear) in a motor vehicle **4** (*intr*) (of a sound or set of sounds) to alter in a systematic way **5** (*intr*) to provide for one's needs (esp in the phrase **shift for oneself**) **6** to remove or be removed, esp with difficulty: *no detergent can shift these stains* **7** (*intr*) *slang* to move quickly **8** (*tr*) *computing* to move (bits held in a store location) to the left or right ▷ *n* **9** the act or an instance of shifting **10** a group of workers who work for a specific period **11** the period of time worked by such a group **12** an expedient, contrivance, or artifice **13** an underskirt or dress with little shaping [Old English *sciftan*; related to Old Norse *skipta* to divide, Middle Low German *schiften,* to separate] > '**shifter** *n*

shiftless ('ʃɪftlɪs) *adj* lacking in ambition or initiative > '**shiftlessness** *n*

shifty ('ʃɪftɪ) *adj* shiftier, shiftiest **1** given to evasions; artful **2** furtive in character or appearance > '**shiftily** *adv* > '**shiftiness** *n*

shigella (ʃɪ'gεlə) *n* any rod-shaped Gram-negative bacterium of the genus *Shigella*; some species cause dysentery [c20: named after K. *Shiga* (1870–1957), Japanese bacteriologist, who discovered it]

shiitake (ʃɪɪ'taːkeɪ) *or* **shitake** *n, pl* **-take** a kind of mushroom widely used in Oriental cookery [c20: from Japanese *shii* tree + *take* mushroom]

Shiite ('ʃiːaɪt) *or* **Shiah** *Islam n* **1** an adherent of Shiah ▷ *adj* **2** of or relating to Shiah > **Shiitic** (ʃiː'ɪtɪk) *adj* > **Shiism** ('ʃiːɪzəm) *n*

Shijiazhuang ('ʃiːdʒaː'dʒwæn), **Shihchiachuang** *or* **Shihkiachwang** (ʃiːtʃjaː'tʃwæn) *n* a city in NE China, capital of Hebei province: textile manufacturing. Pop: 1 733 000 (2005 est)

Shikoku ('ʃiːkəʊ,kuː) *n* the smallest of the four main islands of Japan, separated from Honshu by the Inland Sea: forested and mountainous. Pop: 4 137 000 (2002 est). Area: 17 759 sq km (6857 sq miles)

shillelagh *or* **shillala** (ʃə'leɪlə, -lɪ; *Irish* ʃɪ'leːlə) *n* (in Ireland) a stout club or cudgel, esp one made of oak or blackthorn [c18: from Irish Gaelic *sail* cudgel + *éille* leash, thong]

shilling ('ʃɪlɪŋ) *n* **1** a former British and Australian silver or cupronickel coin worth one twentieth of a pound: not minted in Britain since 1970. Abbreviation: **s.** **2** the standard monetary unit of Kenya, Somalia, Tanzania, and Uganda: divided into 100 cents [Old English *scilling*; related to Old Norse *skillingr*, Gothic *skilliggs*, Old High German *skilling*]

Shillong (ʃɪ'lɒŋ) *n* a city in NE India, capital of Meghalaya: situated on the Shillong Plateau at an altitude of 1520 m (4987 ft); destroyed by earthquake in 1897 and rebuilt. Pop: 132 876 (2001)

shillyshally ('ʃɪlɪ,ʃælɪ) *informal* ▷ *vb* **-lies, -lying, -lied 1** (*intr*) to be indecisive, esp over unimportant matters; hesitate ▷ *adv* **2** in an indecisive manner ▷ *adj* **3** indecisive or hesitant ▷ *n, pl* **-lies 4** indecision or hesitation; vacillation [c18: from *shall I shall I*, by reduplication of *shall* I] > '**shilly,shallier** *n*

Shiloh ('ʃaɪləʊ) *n* a town in central ancient Palestine, in Canaan on the E slope of Mount Ephraim: keeping place of the tabernacle and the ark; destroyed by the Philistines

shily ('ʃaɪlɪ) *adv* a less common spelling of **shyly**

shim (ʃɪm) *n* **1** a thin packing strip or washer often used with a number of similar washers or strips to adjust a clearance for gears, etc ▷ *vb* **shims, shimming, shimmed 2** (*tr*) to modify a load, clearance, or magnetic field by the use of shims [c18 from ?]

shimmer ('ʃɪmə) *vb* **1** (*intr*) to shine with a glistening or tremulous light ▷ *n* **2** a faint, glistening, or tremulous light [Old English *scimerian*; related to Middle Low German *schēmeren* to grow dark, Old Norse *skimi* brightness] > '**shimmering** *adj*

shimmy ('ʃɪmɪ) *n, pl* **-mies 1** an American ragtime dance with much shaking of the hips and shoulders **2** abnormal wobbling motion in a motor vehicle, esp in the front wheels or steering ▷ *vb* **-mies, -mying, -mied** (*intr*) **3** to dance the shimmy **4** to vibrate or wobble [c19: changed from CHEMISE, mistakenly assumed to be plural]

Shimonoseki (ʃɪmənəʊ'sεkɪ) *n* a port in SW Japan, on SW Honshu: scene of the peace treaty (1895) ending the Sino-Japanese War; a heavy industrial centre. Pop: 246 924 (2002 est)

shin (ʃɪn) *n* **1** the front part of the lower leg **2** the front edge of the tibia **3** *chiefly Brit* a cut of beef, the lower foreleg ▷ *vb* **shins, shinning, shinned 4** (when *intr*, often foll by *up*) to climb (a pole, tree, etc) by gripping with the hands or arms and the legs and hauling oneself up **5** (*tr*) to kick (a person) in the shins [Old English *scinu*; related to Old High German *scina* needle, Norwegian dialect *skina* small disc]

Shinar ('ʃaɪnə) *n Old Testament* the southern part of the valley of the Tigris and Euphrates, often identified with Sumer; Babylonia

shinbone ('ʃɪn,bəʊn) *n* the nontechnical name for **tibia** (sense 1)

shindig ('ʃɪn,dɪɡ) *n informal* a noisy party, dance, etc [c19: variant of SHINDY]

shindy ('ʃɪndɪ) *n, pl* **-dies** *informal* **1** a quarrel or commotion (esp in the phrase **kick up a shindy**) **2** another word for **shindig** [c19: variant of SHINTY]

shine (ʃaɪn) *vb* **shines, shining, shone 1** (*intr*) to emit light **2** (*intr*) to glow or be bright with reflected light **3** (*tr*) to direct the light of (a lamp, etc): *he shone the torch in my eyes* **4** (*tr; past tense and past participle* **shined**) to cause to gleam by polishing: *to shine shoes* **5** (*intr*) to be conspicuously competent; excel: *she shines at tennis* **6** (*intr*) to appear clearly; be conspicuous ▷ *n* **7** the state or quality of shining; sheen; lustre **8** *informal* a liking or fancy (esp in the phrase **take a shine to**) [Old English *scīnan*; related to Old Norse *skīna*, Gothic *skeinan*, Old High German *scīnan* to shine, Greek *skia* shadow]

shiner ('ʃaɪnə) *n* **1** something that shines, such as a polishing device **2** any of numerous small North American freshwater cyprinid fishes of the genus *Notropis* and related genera, such as *N. cornutus* (**common shiner**) and *Notemigonus crysoleucas* (**golden shiner**) **3** *informal* a black eye **4** *NZ old-fashioned, informal* a vagrant or tramp

shingle[1] ('ʃɪŋɡ³l) *n* **1** a thin rectangular tile, esp one made of wood, that is laid with others in overlapping rows to cover a roof or a wall **2** a woman's short-cropped hairstyle **3** *US & Canadian* a small signboard or nameplate fixed outside the office of a doctor, lawyer, etc ▷ *vb* (*tr*) **4** to cover (a roof or a wall) with shingles **5** to cut (the hair) in a short-cropped style [C12 *scingle*, from Late Latin *scindula* a split piece of wood, from Latin *scindere* to split] > 'shingler *n*

shingle[2] ('ʃɪŋɡ³l) *n* **1** coarse gravel, esp the pebbles found on beaches **2** a place or area strewn with shingle [C16: of Scandinavian origin; compare Norwegian *singl* pebbles, Frisian *singel* gravel] > 'shingly *adj*

shingles ('ʃɪŋɡ³lz) *n* (*functioning as singular*) an acute viral disease affecting the ganglia of certain nerves, characterized by inflammation, pain, and skin eruptions along the course of the affected nerve. Technical names: **herpes zoster, zoster** [C14: from Medieval Latin *cingulum* girdle, rendering Greek *zōnē* ZONE]

Shinto ('ʃɪntəʊ) *n* the indigenous religion of Japan, polytheistic in character and incorporating the worship of a number of ethnic divinities, from the chief of which the emperor is believed to be descended [c18: from Japanese: the way of the gods, from Chinese *shên* gods + *tao* way] > 'Shintoism *n* > 'Shintoist *n, adj*

shinty ('ʃɪntɪ) *or US and Canadian* **shinny** ('ʃɪnɪ) *n, pl* -**ties** *or* -**nies 1** a simple form of hockey of Scottish origin played with a ball and sticks curved at the lower end **2** the stick used in this game ▷ *vb* -**ties, -tying, -tied** *or US and Canadian* -**nies, -nying, -nied** (*intr*) **3** to play shinty [C17: possibly from Scottish Gaelic *sinteag* a pace, bound]

shiny ('ʃaɪnɪ) *adj* **shinier, shiniest 1** glossy or polished; bright **2** (of clothes or material) worn to a smooth and glossy state, as by continual rubbing > 'shininess *n*

ship (ʃɪp) *n* **1 a** a vessel propelled by engines or sails for navigating on the water, esp a large vessel that cannot be carried aboard another, as distinguished from a boat **2** *nautical* a large sailing vessel with three or more square-rigged masts **3** the crew of a ship **4** short for **airship, spaceship 5 when one's ship comes in** when one has become successful or wealthy ▷ *vb* **ships, shipping, shipped 6** to place, transport, or travel on any conveyance, esp aboard a ship **7** (*tr*) *nautical* to take (water) over the side **8** to bring or go aboard a vessel: *to ship oars* **9** (*tr*; often foll by *off*) *informal* to send away, often in order to be rid of: *they shipped the children off to boarding school* **10** (*intr*) to engage to serve aboard a ship: *I shipped aboard a Liverpool liner* [Old English *scip*; related to Old Norse *skip*, Old High German *skif* ship, *scipfi* cup] > 'shippable *adj*

-ship *suffix forming nouns* **1** indicating state or condition: *fellowship* **2** indicating rank, office, or position: *lordship* **3** indicating craft or skill: *horsemanship; workmanship; scholarship* [Old English *-scipe*; compare SHAPE]

shipboard ('ʃɪp,bɔːd) *n* (*modifier*) taking place, used, or intended for use aboard a ship: *a shipboard encounter*

shipbuilder ('ʃɪp,bɪldə) *n* a person or business engaged in the building of ships > 'ship,building *n*

ship chandler *n* a person or business dealing in supplies for ships > **ship chandlery** *n*

Shipka Pass ('ʃɪpkə) *n* a pass over the Balkan Mountains in central Bulgaria: scene of a bloody Turkish defeat in the Russo-Turkish War (1877–78). Height: 1334 m (4376 ft)

shipload ('ʃɪp,ləʊd) *n* the quantity carried by a ship

shipmate ('ʃɪp,meɪt) *n* a sailor who serves on the same ship as another

shipment ('ʃɪpmənt) *n* **1 a** goods shipped together as part of the same lot: *a shipment of grain* **b** (*as modifier*): *a shipment schedule* **2** the act of shipping cargo

ship money *n English history* a tax levied to finance the fitting out of warships: abolished 1640

ship of the line *n nautical* (formerly) a warship large enough to fight in the first line of battle

shipowner ('ʃɪp,əʊnə) *n* a person who owns or has shares in a ship or ships

shipper ('ʃɪpə) *n* a person or company in the business of shipping freight

shipping ('ʃɪpɪŋ) *n* **1 a** the business of transporting freight, esp by ship **b** (*as modifier*): *a shipping magnate; shipping line* **2** ships collectively: *there is a lot of shipping in the Channel*

ship's biscuit *n* another name for **hardtack**

shipshape ('ʃɪp,ʃeɪp) *adj* **1** neat; orderly ▷ *adv* **2** in a neat and orderly manner

shipworm ('ʃɪp,wɜːm) *n* any wormlike marine bivalve mollusc of the genus *Teredo* and related genera and family *Teredinidae*. They bore into wooden piers, ships, etc, by means of drill-like shell valves

shipwreck ('ʃɪp,rɛk) *n* **1** the partial or total destruction of a ship at sea **2** a wrecked ship or part of such a ship **3** ruin or destruction: *the shipwreck of all my hopes* ▷ *vb* (*tr*) **4** to wreck or destroy (a ship) **5** to bring to ruin or destruction [Old English *scipwræc*, from SHIP + *wræc* something driven by the sea; see WRACK[2]]

shipwright ('ʃɪp,raɪt) *n* an artisan skilled in one or more of the tasks required to build vessels

shipyard ('ʃɪp,jɑːd) *n* a place or facility for the building, maintenance, and repair of ships

shiralee (,ʃɪrə'liː) *n Austral history informal* a swag; swagman's bundle [c19: of unknown origin]

Shiraz[1] (ʃɪə'rɑːz) *n* a city in SW Iran, at an altitude of 1585 m (5200 ft): an important Muslim cultural centre in the 14th century; university (1948); noted for fine carpets. Pop: 1 230 000 (2005 est)

Shiraz[2] (ʃɪə'rɑːz) *n* the name used in Australia for the Syrah grape and wines [from SHIRAZ[1], where the wine supposedly originated]

shire (ʃaɪə) *n* **1 a** one of the British counties **b** (*in combination*): *Yorkshire* **2** (in Australia) a rural district having its own local council **3** See **shire horse 4** the Midland counties of England, esp Northamptonshire and Leicestershire, famous for hunting, etc [Old English *scīr* office; related to Old High German *scīra* business]

Shire ('ʃɪəreɪ) *or* **Shiré** *n* a river in E central Africa, flowing from Lake Malawi through Malawi and Mozambique to the Zambezi. Length: 596 km (370 miles)

Shire Highlands *or* **Shiré Highlands** *pl n* an upland area of S Malawi. Average height: 900 m (3000 ft)

shire horse *n* a large heavy breed of carthorse with long hair on the fetlocks [c19: so called because the breed was originally reared in *the Shires*. See SHIRE[1]]

shirk (ʃɜːk) *vb* **1** to avoid discharging (work, a duty, etc); evade ▷ *n* Also: **shirker** **2** a person who shirks [c17: probably from German *Schurke* rogue; see SHARK[2]]

shirr (ʃɜː) *vb* **1** to gather (fabric) into two or more parallel rows to decorate a dress, blouse, etc, often using elastic thread **2** (*tr*) to bake (eggs) out of their shells ▷ *n* Also: **shirring 3** a series of gathered rows decorating a dress, blouse, etc [c19: of unknown origin]

shirt (ʃɜːt) *n* **1 a** garment worn on the upper part of the body, esp by men, usually of light material and typically having a collar and sleeves and buttoning up the front **2** short for **nightshirt, undershirt 3 keep your shirt on** *informal* refrain from losing your temper (often used as an exhortation to another) **4 put one's shirt on** *informal* to bet all one has on (a horse, etc) [Old English *scyrte*; related to Old English *sceort* SHORT, Old Norse *skyrta* skirt, Middle High German *schurz* apron]

shirting ('ʃɜːtɪŋ) *n* fabric used in making men's shirts

shirt-lifter *n derogatory, slang* a homosexual

shirtsleeve ('ʃɜːt,sliːv) *n* **1** the sleeve of a shirt **2 in one's shirtsleeves** not wearing a jacket

shirt-tail *n* the part of a shirt that extends below the waist

shirtwaister ('ʃɜːt,weɪstə) *or US and Canadian* **shirtwaist**

n a woman's dress with a tailored bodice resembling a shirt

shirty ('ʃɜːtɪ) *adj* **shirtier, shirtiest** *slang, chiefly Brit* bad-tempered or annoyed [C19: perhaps based on such phrases as *to get someone's shirt out* to annoy someone] > **'shirtily** *adv*

shisha ('ʃiːʃə) *n* another name for **hookah** [C21: from Persian *shishe* a bottle]

shish kebab ('ʃiːʃ kə'bæb) *n* a dish consisting of small pieces of meat and vegetables threaded onto skewers and grilled [from Turkish şiş *kebab*, from şiş skewer; see KEBAB]

shiso ('ʃiːsəʊ) *n* another name for **beefsteak plant** [Japanese]

shit (ʃɪt) *taboo vb* **shits, shitting, shitted, shit** *or* **shat** to defecate **1** (usually foll by *on*) *slang* to give the worst possible treatment (to) ▷ *n* **2** faeces; excrement **3** an act of defacation **4** rubbish; nonsense **5** an obnoxious or worthless person ▷ *interj* **6** an exclamation expressing anger, disgust, etc [Old English *scite* (unattested) dung, *scitan* to defecate, of Germanic origin; related to Old English *scēadan* to separate, Old Norse *skíta* to defecate, Middle Dutch *schitte* excrement] > **'shitty** *adj*

shitake (ʃɪ'tɑːkeɪ) *n* a variant of **shiitake**

shitload ('ʃɪt,ləʊd) *n taboo, slang* a lot; large amount: *a shitload of money*

shit-stir *vb* (intr) *slang* to make trouble > **'shit-,stirrer** *n*

Shittim ('ʃɪtɪm) *n Old Testament* the site to the east of the Jordan and northeast of the Dead Sea where the Israelites encamped before crossing the Jordan (Numbers 25:1–9)

shiv (ʃɪv) *n* a variant spelling of **chiv**

Shiva ('ʃiːvə, 'ʃɪvə) *n* a variant spelling of **Siva**

shivaree (ʃɪvə'riː) *n US & Canadian* **1** a discordant mock serenade to newlyweds, made with pans, kettles, etc **2** a confused noise; din ▷ Also called: **charivari**

shiver¹ ('ʃɪvə) *vb* (intr) **1** to shake or tremble, as from cold or fear ▷ *n* **2** the act of shivering; a tremulous motion **3** the shivers an attack of shivering, esp through fear or illness [C13 *chiveren*, perhaps variant of *chevelen* to chatter (used of teeth), from Old English *ceafl* JOWL¹] > **'shiverer** *n* > **'shivering** *adj*

shiver² ('ʃɪvə) *vb* **1** to break or cause to break into fragments ▷ *n* **2** a splintered piece [C13: of Germanic origin; compare Old High German *scivaro*, Middle Dutch *scheveren* to splinter, Old Norse *skífa* to split]

Shizuoka (ʃiːzuː'əʊkə) *n* a city in central Japan, on S Honshu: a centre for green tea; university (1949). Pop: 468 775 (2002 est)

Shkodër (Albanian 'ʃkɔdər) *n* a market town in NW Albania, on **Lake Shkodër**: an Illyrian capital in the first millennium BC. Pop: about 90 000 (2003 est). Italian name: **Scutari**

shoal¹ (ʃəʊl) *n* **1** a stretch of shallow water **2** a sandbank or rocky area in a stretch of water, esp one that is visible at low water ▷ *vb* **3** to make or become shallow **4** (intr) *nautical* to sail into shallower water ▷ *adj* Also: **shoaly** **5** a less common word for **shallow** [Old English *sceald* SHALLOW]

shoal² (ʃəʊl) *n* **1** a large group of certain aquatic animals, esp fish **2** a large group of people or things ▷ *vb* **3** (intr) to collect together in such a group [Old English *scolu*; related to Middle Low German, Middle Dutch *schōle* SCHOOL²]

shock¹ (ʃɒk) *vb* **1** to experience or cause to experience extreme horror, disgust, surprise, etc: *the atrocities shocked us; she shocks easily* **2** to cause a state of shock in (a person) **3** to come or cause to come into violent contact; jar ▷ *n* **4** a sudden and violent jarring blow or impact **5** something that causes a sudden and violent disturbance in the emotions **6** *pathol* a state of bodily collapse or near collapse caused by circulatory failure or sudden lowering of the blood pressure, as from severe bleeding, burns, fright, etc Also called: **electric shock 7** *pathol* pain and muscular spasm as the physical reaction to an electric current passing through the body [C16: from Old French *choc*, from *choquier* to make violent contact with, of Germanic origin; related to Middle High German *schoc*] > **'shockable** *adj* > **,shocka'bility** *n*

shock² (ʃɒk) *n* **1** a number of sheaves set on end in a field to dry **2** a pile or stack of unthreshed corn ▷ *vb* **3** (tr) to set up (sheaves) in shocks [C14: probably of Germanic origin; compare Middle Low German, Middle Dutch *schok* shock of corn, group of sixty]

shock³ (ʃɒk) *n* a thick bushy mass, esp of hair [C19: perhaps from SHOCK²]

shock absorber *n* any device designed to absorb mechanical shock, esp one fitted to a motor vehicle to damp the recoil of the suspension springs

shocker ('ʃɒkə) *n informal* **1** a person or thing that shocks or horrifies **2** a sensational novel, film, or play

shockheaded ('ʃɒk,hɛdɪd) *adj* having a head of bushy or tousled hair

shock-horror *adj facetious* (esp of newspaper headlines) sensationalistic: *shock-horror stories about the British diet* [C20: SHOCK² + HORROR]

shocking ('ʃɒkɪŋ) *adj* **1** causing shock, horror, or disgust **2 shocking pink** a vivid or garish shade of pink **3** *informal* very bad or terrible: *shocking weather* > **'shockingly** *adv*

Shockley ('ʃɒklɪ) *n* **William Bradfield**. 1910–89, US physicist, born in Britain, who shared the Nobel prize for physics (1956) with John Bardeen and Walter Brattain for developing the transistor. He also held controversial views on the connection between race and intelligence

shockproof ('ʃɒk,pruːf) *adj* capable of absorbing shock without damage

shock therapy or **shock treatment** *n* the treatment of certain psychotic conditions by injecting drugs or by passing an electric current through the brain (**electroconvulsive therapy**) to produce convulsions or coma

shock troops *pl n* soldiers specially trained and equipped to carry out an assault

shock wave *n* a region across which there is a rapid pressure, temperature, and density rise, usually caused by a body moving supersonically in a gas or by a detonation. See also **sonic boom**

shod (ʃɒd) *vb* the past participle of **shoe**

shoddy ('ʃɒdɪ) *adj* **-dier, -diest 1** imitating something of better quality **2** of poor quality; trashy ▷ *n, pl* **-dies 3** a yarn or fabric made from wool waste or clippings **4** anything of inferior quality that is designed to simulate superior quality [C19: of unknown origin] > **'shoddily** *adv* > **'shoddiness** *n*

shoe (ʃuː) *n* **1 a** one of a matching pair of coverings shaped to fit the foot, esp one ending below the ankle, having an upper of leather, plastic, etc, on a sole and heel of heavier leather, rubber, or synthetic material **b** (as modifier): *shoe cleaner* **2** anything resembling a shoe in shape, function, position, etc, such as a horseshoe **3** a band of metal or wood on the bottom of the runner of a sledge **4** *engineering* a lining to protect from and withstand wear. See **brake shoe 5 be in a person's shoes** *informal* to be in another person's situation ▷ *vb* **shoes, shoeing, shod** (tr) **6** to furnish with shoes **7** to fit (a horse) with horseshoes **8** to furnish with a hard cover, such as a metal plate, for protection against friction or bruising [Old English *scōh*; related to Old Norse *skōr*, Gothic *skōhs*, Old High German *scuoh*]

shoeblack ('ʃuː,blæk) *n* (esp formerly) a person who shines boots and shoes

shoehorn ('ʃuː,hɔːn) *n* **1** a smooth curved implement of horn, metal, plastic, etc, inserted at the heel of a shoe to ease the foot into it ▷ *vb* **2** (tr) to cram (people or things) into a very small space

shoelace ('ʃuː,leɪs) *n* a cord or lace for fastening shoes

shoe leather *n* **1** leather used to make shoes **2 save shoe leather** to avoid wearing out shoes, as by taking a bus rather than walking

shoemaker ('ʃuː,meɪkə) *n* a person who makes or repairs shoes or boots > **'shoe,making** *n*

shoer ('ʃuːə) *n rare* a person who shoes horses; farrier

shoeshine ('ʃuː,ʃaɪn) *n* the act or an instance of polishing a pair of shoes

shoestring ('ʃuː,strɪŋ) *n* **1** another word for **shoelace 2** *informal* a very small or petty amount of money (esp in the phrase **on a shoestring**)

S

shoetree ('ʃuːˌtriː) n a wooden or metal form inserted into a shoe or boot to stretch it or preserve its shape

shofar or **shophar** ('ʃəʊfɑː; Hebrew ʃɔ'far) n, pl -fars, -phars or -froth, -phroth (Hebrew -'frɔt) Judaism a ram's horn sounded in the synagogue daily during the month of Elul and repeatedly on Rosh Hashanah, and by the ancient Israelites as a warning, summons, etc [from Hebrew shōphār ram's horn]

shogun ('ʃəʊˌguːn) n Japanese history (from about 1192 to 1867) any of a line of hereditary military dictators who relegated the emperors to a position of purely theoretical supremacy [C17: from Japanese, from Chinese chiang chün general, from chiang to lead + chün army] > **shogunate** ('ʃəʊgʊnɪt, -ˌneɪt)

shogun bond n a bond sold on the Japanese market by a foreign institution and denominated in a foreign currency. See **samurai bond**

Sholapur ('ʃəʊləˌpʊə) n a city in SW India, in S Maharashtra: major textile centre. Pop: 873 037 (2001)

Sholem Aleichem n See **Aleichem**

Sholes (ʃəʊlz) n Christopher Latham. 1819–90, US inventor, who invented (1868) the typewriter and sold the patent to the Remington company (1873)

Sholokhov (Russian 'ʃɔləxəf) n Mikhail Aleksandrovich (mɪxaˈil alɪkˈsandrəvitʃ). 1905–84, Soviet author, noted particularly for And Quiet flows the Don (1934) and The Don flows Home to the Sea (1940), describing the effect of the Revolution and civil war on the life of the Cossacks: Nobel prize for literature 1965

shone (ʃɒn; US ʃəʊn) vb the past tense and past participle of **shine**

shonky ('ʃɒŋkɪ) adj -kier, -kiest Austral & NZ informal 1 of dubious integrity or legality 2 unreliable; unsound [C19: perhaps from Yiddish shonniker or from SH(ODDY) + (W)ONKY]

shoo (ʃuː) interj 1 go away!: used to drive away unwanted or annoying people, animals, etc ▷ vb **shoos**, **shooing**, **shooed** 2 (tr) to drive away by or as if by crying "shoo." 3 (intr) to cry "shoo." [C15: imitative; related to Middle High German schū, French shou, Italian scio]

shoo-in n 1 a person or thing that is certain to win or succeed 2 a match or contest that is easy to win

shook[1] (ʃʊk) n 1 (in timber working) a set of parts ready for assembly, esp of a barrel 2 a group of sheaves piled together on end; shock [C18: of unknown origin]

shook[2] (ʃʊk) vb the past tense of **shake**

shoon (ʃuːn) n dialect, chiefly Scot a plural of **shoe**

shoot (ʃuːt) vb **shoots**, **shooting**, **shot** 1 (tr) to hit, wound, damage, or kill with a missile discharged from a weapon 2 to discharge (a missile or missiles) from a weapon 3 to fire (a weapon) or (of a weapon) to be fired 4 to send out or be sent out as if from a weapon: he shot questions at her 5 (intr) to move very rapidly; dart 6 (tr) to slide or push into or out of a fastening: to shoot a bolt 7 to emit (a ray of light) or (of a ray of light) to be emitted 8 (tr) to go or pass quickly over or through: to shoot rapids 9 (intr) to hunt game with a gun for sport 10 (tr) to pass over (an area) in hunting game 11 (intr) (of a plant) to produce (buds, branches, etc) 12 to photograph or record (a sequence, subject, etc) 13 (tr; usually passive) to variegate or streak, as with colour 14 sport to hit or propel (the ball, etc) towards the goal 15 (tr) sport chiefly US & Canadian to score (points, strokes, etc): he shot 72 on the first round 16 (tr) to measure the altitude of (a celestial body) 17 (often foll by up) slang to inject (someone, esp oneself) with (a drug, esp heroin) 18 **shoot oneself in the foot** informal to damage one's own cause inadvertently ▷ n 19 the act of shooting 20 the action or motion of something that is shot 21 the first aerial part of a plant to develop from a germinating seed 22 any new growth of a plant, such as a bud, young branch, etc 23 chiefly Brit a meeting or party organized for hunting game with guns 24 an area or series of coverts and woods where game can be hunted with guns 25 a steep descent in a stream; rapid 26 informal a photographic assignment 27 the whole shoot slang everything ▷ interj 28 US & Canadian an exclamation expressing disbelief, scepticism, disgust, disappointment, etc ▷ See also **shoot down**, **shoot through**, etc [Old English scēotan;

related to Old Norse skjōta, Old High German skiozan to shoot, Old Slavonic iskydati to throw out]

shootaround ('ʃuːtəˌraʊnd) n basketball an informal match or practice session

shoot down vb (tr, adverb) 1 to shoot callously 2 to defeat or disprove: he shot down her argument

shoot-'em-up or **shoot-em-up** n informal 1 a type of computer game, the object of which is to shoot as many enemies, targets, etc, as possible 2 a fast-moving film involving many gunfights, battles, etc

shooter ('ʃuːtə) n 1 a person or thing that shoots 2 slang a gun

shooting box n a small country house providing accommodation for a shooting party during the shooting season. Also called: **shooting lodge**

shooting brake n Brit a former name for **estate car**

shooting star n an informal name for **meteor**

shooting stick n a device that resembles a walking stick, having a spike at one end and a folding seat at the other

shoot through vb (intr, adverb) informal, chiefly Austral to leave; depart

shop (ʃɒp) n 1 a place, esp a small building, for the retail sale of goods and services 2 an act or instance of shopping, esp household shopping 3 a place for the performance of a specified type of work; workshop 4 **all over the shop** informal a in disarray: his papers were all over the shop b in every direction: I've searched for it all over the shop 5 **shut up shop** a to close business at the end of the day or permanently b to become defensive or inactive 6 **talk shop** to speak about one's work, esp when meeting socially, sometimes with the effect of excluding those not similarly employed ▷ vb **shops**, **shopping**, **shopped** 7 (intr; often foll by for) to visit a shop or shops in search of (goods) with the intention of buying them 8 (tr) slang, chiefly Brit to inform on or betray, esp to the police [Old English sceoppa stall, booth; related to Old High German scopf shed, Middle Dutch schoppe stall]

shop around vb (intr, adverb) informal 1 to visit a number of shops or stores to compare goods and prices 2 to consider a number of possibilities before making a choice

shop assistant n a person who serves in a shop

shop floor n 1 the part of a factory housing the machines and men directly involved in production 2 workers, esp factory workers organized in a union

shopkeeper ('ʃɒpˌkiːpə) n a person who owns or manages a shop or small store > '**shop**ˌ**keeping** n

shoplifter ('ʃɒpˌlɪftə) n a person who steals goods from a shop during shopping hours > '**shop**ˌ**lifting** n

shopper ('ʃɒpə) n a person who buys goods in a shop

shopping ('ʃɒpɪŋ) n 1 a number or collection of articles purchased 2 the act or an instance of making purchases

shopping basket n 1 a metal or plastic container with one or two handles, used to carry shopping in a shop 2 the list of items an internet shopper chooses to buy at one time from a website

shopping cart n the usual US and Canadian word for **shopping basket**

shopping centre n 1 a purpose-built complex of shops, restaurants, etc, for the use of pedestrians 2 the area of a town where most of the shops are situated

shopping mall n a large enclosed shopping centre

shopsoiled ('ʃɒpˌsɔɪld) adj worn, faded, tarnished, etc, from being displayed in a shop or store

shop steward n a coworker elected by trade union members to represent them in discussions and negotiations with the management

shoptalk ('ʃɒpˌtɔːk) n conversation concerning one's work, esp when carried on outside business hours

shopwalker ('ʃɒpˌwɔːkə) n Brit a person employed by a departmental store to supervise sales personnel, assist customers, etc

shoran ('ʃɔːræn) n a short-range radar system by which an aircraft, ship, etc, can accurately determine its position by the time taken for a signal to be sent to two radar beacons at known locations and be returned [C20: sho(rt) ra(nge) n(avigation)]

shore¹ (ʃɔː) n **1** the land along the edge of a sea, lake, or wide river. Related adj: **littoral 2 a** land, as opposed to water (esp in the phrase **on shore**) **b** (as modifier): shore duty **3** law the tract of coastland lying between the ordinary marks of high and low water **4** (often plural) a country: his native shores [c14: probably from Middle Low German, Middle Dutch schōre; compare Old High German scorra cliff; see SHEAR]

shore² (ʃɔː) n **1 a** prop, post, or beam used to support a wall, building, ship in dry dock, etc ▷ vb **2** (tr; often foll by up) to prop or make safe with or as if with a shore [c15: from Middle Dutch schōre; related to Old Norse skortha prop] > 'shoring n

shore³ (ʃɔː) vb Austral & NZ a past tense of shear

shore bird n any of various birds that live close to water, esp any bird of the families Charadriidae or Scolopacidae (plovers, sandpipers, etc). Also called (Brit): wader

shore leave n naval **1** permission to go ashore **2** time spent ashore during leave

shoreless ('ʃɔːlɪs) adj **1** without a shore suitable for landing **2** poetic boundless; vast

shoreline ('ʃɔːˌlaɪn) n the edge of a body of water

shoreward ('ʃɔːwəd) adj **1** near or facing the shore ▷ adv Also: **shorewards 2** towards the shore

shorn (ʃɔːn) vb a past participle of shear

short (ʃɔːt) adj **1** of little length; not long **2** of little height; not tall **3** of limited duration **4** not meeting a requirement; deficient: the number of places laid at the table was short by four **5** (postpositive; often foll by of or on) lacking (in) or needful (of): I'm always short of money **6** concise; succinct **7** lacking in the power of retentiveness: a short memory **8** abrupt to the point of rudeness: the salesgirl was very short with him **9** finance **a** not possessing the securities or commodities that have been sold under contract and therefore obliged to make a purchase before the delivery date **b** of or relating to such sales, which depend on falling prices for profit **10** phonetics **a** denoting a vowel of relatively brief temporal duration **b** (in popular usage) denoting the qualities of the five English vowels represented orthographically in the words pat, pet, pit, pot, put, and putt **11** prosody **a** denoting a vowel that is phonetically short or a syllable containing such a vowel. In classical verse short vowels are followed by one consonant only or sometimes one consonant plus a following l or r **b** (of a vowel or syllable in verse that is not quantitative) not carrying emphasis or accent; unstressed **12** (of pastry) crumbly in texture **13** (of a drink of spirits) undiluted; neat **14** (of betting odds) almost even **15 in short supply** scarce **16 short and sweet** unexpectedly brief **17 short for** an abbreviation for ▷ adv **18** abruptly: to stop short **19** briefly or concisely **20** rudely or curtly **21** finance without possessing the securities or commodities at the time of their contractual sale: to sell short **22 caught short** or **taken short** having a sudden need to urinate or defecate **23 go short** not to have a sufficient amount, etc **24 short of** except: nothing short of a miracle can save him now ▷ n **25** anything that is short **26** a drink of spirits as opposed to a long drink such as beer **27** phonetics, prosody a short vowel or syllable **28** finance **a** a short contract or sale **b** a short seller **29** a short film, usually of a factual nature **30** See **short circuit** (sense 1) **31 for short** informal as an abbreviation: he is called Jim for short **32 in short a** as a summary **b** in a few words ▷ vb **33** See **short circuit** (sense 2) ▷ See also **shorts** [Old English scort; related to Old Norse skortr a lack, skera to cut, Old High German scurz short] > 'shortness n

short-acting adj (of a drug) quickly effective, but requiring regularly repeated doses for long-term treatment, being rapidly absorbed, distributed in the body, and excreted. See **intermediate-acting, long-acting**

shortage ('ʃɔːtɪdʒ) n a deficiency or lack in the amount needed, expected, or due; deficit

shortboard ('ʃɔːtˌbɔːd) n a type of surfboard that is shorter than standard

shortbread ('ʃɔːtˌbrɛd) n a rich crumbly biscuit made from dough with a large proportion of butter [c19: from SHORT (in the sense: crumbly)]

shortcake ('ʃɔːtˌkeɪk) n **1** a kind of shortbread made from a rich biscuit dough **2** a dessert made of layers of shortcake filled with fruit and cream [c16: from SHORT (in the sense: crumbly)]

short-change vb (tr) **1** to give less than correct change to **2** slang to treat unfairly or dishonestly, esp by giving less than is deserved or expected

short circuit n **1** a faulty or accidental connection between two points of different potential in an electric circuit, bypassing the load and establishing a path of low resistance through which an excessive current can flow. It can cause damage to the components if the circuit is not protected by a fuse ▷ vb **short-circuit 2** to develop or cause to develop a short circuit **3** (tr) to bypass (a procedure, regulation, etc) **4** (tr) to hinder or frustrate (plans, etc) ▷ Sometimes (for senses 1, 2) shortened to: **short**

shortcoming ('ʃɔːtˌkʌmɪŋ) n a failing, defect, or deficiency

short corner n hockey another name for **penalty corner**

short covering n the purchase of securities or commodities by a short seller to meet delivery requirements

shortcrust pastry ('ʃɔːtˌkrʌst) n a basic type of pastry that is made with half the quantity of fat to flour, and has a crisp but crumbly texture. Also called: **short pastry**

short cut n **1** a route that is shorter than the usual one **2** a means of saving time or effort ▷ vb **short-cut -cuts, -cutting, -cut 3** (intr) to use a short cut [c16: from CUT (in the sense: a direct route)]

short-dated adj (of a gilt-edged security) having less than five years to run before redemption. See **medium-dated, long-dated**

short-day adj (of plants) able to flower only if exposed to short periods of daylight (less than 12 hours), each followed by a long dark period. See **long-day**

shorten ('ʃɔːtən) vb **1** to make or become short or shorter **2** (tr) nautical to reduce the area of (sail) **3** (tr) to make (pastry, bread, etc) short, by adding butter or another fat **4** gambling to cause (the odds) to lessen or (of odds) to become less

shortening ('ʃɔːtənɪŋ) n butter, lard, or other fat, used in a dough, cake mixture, etc, to make the mixture short

Shorter Catechism n chiefly Presbyterian Church the more widely used and influential of two catechisms on religious instruction drawn up in 1647

shortfall ('ʃɔːtˌfɔːl) n **1** failure to meet a goal or a requirement **2** the amount of such a failure; deficiency

shorthand ('ʃɔːtˌhænd) n **a** a system of rapid handwriting employing simple strokes and other symbols to represent words or phrases **b** (as modifier): a shorthand typist

short-handed adj **1** lacking the usual or necessary number of assistants, workers, etc **2** sport, US & Canadian with less than the full complement of players

shorthand typist n Brit a person skilled in the use of shorthand and in typing. US and Canadian name: **stenographer**

short head n horse racing a distance shorter than the length of a horse's head

shorthorn ('ʃɔːtˌhɔːn) n a short-horned breed of cattle with several regional varieties. Also called: **Durham**

shortie or **shorty** ('ʃɔːtɪ) n pl **shorties a** person or thing that is extremely short **b** (as modifier): a shortie nightdress

short list chiefly Brit ▷ n **1** a list of suitable applicants for a job, post, etc, from which the successful candidate will be selected ▷ vb **short-list** (tr) **2** to put (someone) on a short list

short-lived adj living or lasting only for a short time

shortly ('ʃɔːtlɪ) adv **1** in a short time; soon **2** in a few words; briefly **3** in a curt or rude manner

short order n chiefly US & Canadian food that is easily and quickly prepared

short-range adj of small or limited extent in time or distance: a short-range forecast; a short-range gun

shorts (ʃɔːts) pl n **1** trousers reaching the top of the thigh or partway to the knee, worn by both sexes for sport, relaxing in summer, etc **2** chiefly US & Canadian men's underpants that usually reach mid-thigh **3** short-dated

S

gilt-edged securities **4** short-term bonds **5** securities or commodities that have been sold short **6** a livestock feed containing a large proportion of bran and wheat germ

short selling n *finance* the practice of selling commodities, securities, currencies, etc that one does not have in the expectation that falling prices will enable one to buy them in at a profit before they have to be delivered

short shrift n **1** brief and unsympathetic treatment **2** (formerly) a brief period allowed to a condemned prisoner to make confession **3** make short shrift of to dispose of quickly and unsympathetically

short-sighted adj **1** relating to or suffering from myopia **2** lacking foresight: *a short-sighted plan* > ,short-'sightedly adv > ,short-'sightedness n

short-spoken adj tending to be abrupt in speech

short story n a prose narrative of shorter length than the novel, esp one that concentrates on a single theme

short straw n draw the short straw be the person (as in drawing lots) to whom an unwelcome task or fate falls

short-tempered adj easily moved to anger; irascible

short-term adj **1** of, for, or extending over a limited period **2** *finance* extending over, maturing within, or required within a short period of time, usually twelve months: *short-term credit; short-term capital*

short-termism n the tendency to focus attention on short-term gains, often at the expense of long-term success or stability

short time or **short-time working** n a system of working, usually for a temporary period, when employees are required to work and be paid for fewer than their normal hours per week due to a shortage of work

short ton n the full name for **ton**¹ (sense 2)

short-waisted adj unusually short from the shoulders to the waist

short wave n **a** a radio wave with a wavelength in the range 10–100 metres **b** (*as modifier*): *a short-wave broadcast*

short-winded adj **1** tending to run out of breath, esp after exertion **2** (of speech or writing) terse or abrupt

Shostakovich (ˌʃɒstəˈkəʊvɪtʃ; *Russian* ʃɒstaˈkɔvitʃ) n **Dmitri Dmitriyevich** (ˈdmitrij ˈdmitrijɪvitʃ). 1906–75, Soviet composer, noted esp for his 15 symphonies and his chamber music

shot¹ (ʃɒt) n **1** the act or an instance of discharging a projectile **2** pl shot a solid missile, such as an iron ball or a lead pellet, discharged from a firearm **3** a small round pellets of lead collectively, as used in cartridges **b** metal in the form of coarse powder or small pellets **4** the distance that a discharged projectile travels or is capable of travelling **5** a person who shoots, esp with regard to his ability: *he is a good shot* **6** *informal* an attempt; effort **7** *informal* a guess or conjecture **8** any act of throwing or hitting something, as in certain sports **9** the launching of a rocket, missile, etc, esp to a specified destination: *a moon shot* **10 a** a single photograph **b** a length of film taken by a single camera without breaks, used with others to build up a full motion picture or television film **11** *informal* an injection, as of a vaccine or narcotic drug **12** *informal* a glass of alcoholic drink, esp spirits **13** *sport* a heavy metal ball used in the shot put **14 call the shots** *slang* to have control over an organization, course of action, etc **15 have a shot at** *informal* to attempt **16 like a shot** very quickly, esp willingly **17 shot in the arm** *informal* anything that regenerates, increases confidence or efficiency, etc **18 shot in the dark** a wild guess [Old English *scot*; related to Old Norse *skot*, Old High German *scoz* missile; see SHOOT]

shot² (ʃɒt) vb **1** the past tense and past participle of **shoot** > adj **2** (of textiles) woven to give a changing colour effect: *shot silk* **3** streaked with colour

shotgun (ˈʃɒtˌɡʌn) n **1** a shoulder firearm with unrifled bore designed for the discharge of small shot at short range and used mainly for hunting small game **2** *American football* an offensive formation in which the quarterback lines up for a snap unusually far behind the line of scrimmage > adj **3** *chiefly US* involving coercion or duress: *a shotgun merger*

shotgun wedding n *informal* a wedding into which one or both partners are coerced, usually because the woman is pregnant

shot put n an athletic event in which contestants hurl or put a heavy metal ball or shot as far as possible > 'shot-ˌputter n

shotten (ˈʃɒtᵊn) adj **1** (of fish, esp herring) having recently spawned **2** *archaic* worthless or undesirable [C15: from obsolete past participle of SHOOT]

shot tower n a building formerly used in the production of shot, in which molten lead was graded and dropped from a great height into water, thus cooling it and forming the shot

should (ʃʊd) vb the past tense of **shall**: used as an auxiliary verb to indicate that an action is considered by the speaker to be obligatory (*you should go*) or to form the subjunctive mood with I or *we* (*I should like to see you; if I should be late, go without me*). See also **shall** [Old English *sceold*; see SHALL]

● USAGE *Should* has, as its most common meaning in
● modern English, the sense *ought* as in *I should go to the*
● *graduation, but I don't see how I can*. However, the older
● sense of the subjunctive of *shall* is often used with I or
● *we* to indicate a more polite form than *would*: *I should*
● *like to go, but I can't*. In much speech and writing, *should*
● has been replaced by *would* in contexts of this kind,
● but it remains in formal English when a conditional
● subjunctive is used: *should he choose to remain, he would be*
● *granted asylum*

shoulder (ˈʃəʊldə) n **1** the part of the vertebrate body where the arm or a corresponding forelimb joins the trunk: the pectoral girdle and associated structures **2** the joint at the junction of the forelimb with the pectoral girdle **3** a cut of meat including the upper part of the foreleg **4** *printing* the flat surface of a piece of type from which the face rises **5** the part of a garment that covers the shoulder **6** anything that resembles a shoulder in shape or position **7** the strip of unpaved land that borders a road **8 a shoulder to cry on** a person one turns to for sympathy with one's troubles **9 give someone the cold shoulder** *informal* **a** to treat someone in a cold manner; snub **b** to ignore or shun someone **10 put one's shoulder to the wheel** *informal* to work very hard **11 rub shoulders with** See rub (sense 10) **12 shoulder to shoulder a** side by side or close together **b** in a corporate effort > vb **13** (tr) to bear or carry (a burden, responsibility, etc) as if on one's shoulders **14** to push (something) with or as if with the shoulder **15** (tr) to lift or carry on the shoulders **16 shoulder arms** *military* to bring the rifle vertically close to the right side with the muzzle uppermost and held at the trigger guard [Old English *sculdor*; related to Old High German *scultera*]

shoulder blade n the nontechnical name for **scapula**

shoulder strap n a strap over one or both of the shoulders, as to hold up a garment or to support a bag, etc

shouldn't (ˈʃʊdᵊnt) vb contraction of should not

shouldst (ʃʊdst) or **shouldest** (ˈʃʊdɪst) vb *archaic or dialect* (used with the pronoun *thou* or its relative equivalent) a form of the past tense of **shall**

shout (ʃaʊt) n **1** a loud cry, esp to convey emotion or a command **2** *informal, Brit, Austral & NZ* **a** a round, esp of drinks **b** one's turn to buy a round of drinks **3** *informal* a greeting (to family, friends, etc) sent to a radio station for broadcasting > vb **4** to utter (something) in a loud cry; yell **5** (intr) to make a loud noise **6** (tr) *Austral & NZ informal* to treat (someone) to (something), esp a drink [C14: probably from Old Norse *skúta* taunt; related to Old Norse *skjōta* to shout] > 'shouter n

shout down vb (tr, adverb) to drown, overwhelm, or silence by shouting or talking loudly

shove (ʃʌv) vb **1** to give a thrust or push to (a person or thing) **2** (tr) to give a violent push to; jostle **3** (intr) to push one's way roughly **4** (tr) *informal* to put (something) somewhere, esp hurriedly or carelessly: *shove it in the bin* > n **5** the act or an instance of shoving > See also **shove off** [Old English *scūfan*; related to Old Norse *skúfa* to push, Gothic *afskiuban* to push away, Old High German *skioban* to shove] > 'shover n

shove-halfpenny n Brit a game in which players try to propel old halfpennies or polished discs with the hand into lined sections of a wooden or slate board

shovel ('ʃʌvᵊl) n 1 an instrument for lifting or scooping loose material, such as earth, coal, etc, consisting of a curved blade or scoop attached to a handle 2 any machine or part resembling a shovel in action 3 Also called: **shovelful** the amount that can be contained in a shovel ▷ vb -els, -elling, -elled or US -els, -eling, -eled 4 to lift (earth, etc) with a shovel 5 (tr) to clear or dig (a path) with or as if with a shovel 6 (tr) to gather, load, or unload in a hurried or careless way [Old English scofl; related to Old High German scūfla shovel, Dutch schoffel hoe; see SHOVE] > 'shoveller or US 'shoveler n

shoveler ('ʃʌvələ) n a duck, Anas (or Spatula) clypeata, of ponds and marshes, having a spoon-shaped bill, a blue patch on each wing, and in the male a green head, white breast, and reddish-brown body

shovelhead ('ʃʌvᵊl,hɛd) n a common shark, Sphyrna tiburo, of the Atlantic and Pacific Oceans, having a shovel-shaped head: family Sphyrnidae (hammerheads)

shove off vb (intr, adverb; often imperative) 1 to move from the shore in a boat 2 informal to go away; depart

show (ʃəʊ) vb shows, showing, showed, shown or showed 1 to make, be, or become visible or noticeable: to show one's dislike 2 (tr) to present to view; exhibit: he showed me a picture 3 (tr) to indicate or explain; prove: to show that the earth moves round the sun 4 (tr) to exhibit or present (oneself or itself) in a specific character: to show oneself to be trustworthy 5 (tr; foll by how and an infinitive) to instruct by demonstration: show me how to swim 6 (tr) to indicate or register: a barometer shows changes in the weather 7 (tr) to grant or bestow: to show favour to someone 8 (intr) to appear: to show to advantage 9 to exhibit, display, or offer (goods, etc) for sale: three artists were showing at the gallery 10 (tr) to allege, as in a legal document: to show cause 11 to present (a play, film, etc) or (of a play, etc) to be presented, as at a theatre or cinema 12 (tr) to guide or escort: please show me to my room 13 show in to conduct a person into a room or building by opening the door for him 14 show out to conduct a person out of a room or building by opening the door for him 15 a display or exhibition 16 a public spectacle 17 an ostentatious or pretentious display 18 a theatrical or other entertainment 19 a trace or indication 20 obstetrics a discharge of blood at the onset of labour 21 US, Austral & NZ informal a chance; opportunity (esp in the phrases give someone a show, he's got no show of winning, etc) 22 for show in order to attract attention 23 run the show informal to take charge of or manage an affair, business, etc 24 steal the show to draw the most attention or admiration, esp unexpectedly 25 stop the show to be received with great enthusiasm ▷ See also **show off**, **show up**, etc [Old English scēawian; related to Old High German scouwōn to look, Old Norse örskār careful, Greek thuoskoos seer]

show bag n a bag containing samples, promotional material, etc, given out at trade fairs and other such events

showboat ('ʃəʊ,bəʊt) n 1 a paddle-wheel river steamer with a theatre and a repertory company ▷ vb 2 (intr) to perform or behave in a showy and flamboyant way

showbread ('ʃəʊ,brɛd) n a variant spelling of **shewbread**

show business n the entertainment industry, including theatre, films, television, and radio. Informal term: **show biz**

show card n commerce a tradesman's advertisement mounted on card as a poster

showcase ('ʃəʊ,keɪs) n 1 a glass case used to display objects in a museum or shop 2 a setting in which anything may be displayed to best advantage ▷ vb 3 (tr) to exhibit or display

show day n (in Australia) a public holiday in a state on the date of its annual agricultural and industrial show

showdown ('ʃəʊ,daʊn) n 1 informal an action that brings matters to a head or acts as a conclusion or point of decision 2 poker the exposing of the cards in the players' hands on the table at the end of the game

shower¹ ('ʃaʊə) n 1 a brief period of rain, hail, sleet, or snow 2 a sudden abundant fall or downpour, as of tears, sparks, or light 3 a rush; outpouring: a shower of praise 4 a a kind of bath in which a person stands upright and is sprayed with water from a nozzle b the room, booth, etc, containing such a bath 5 Brit slang a derogatory term applied to a person or group, esp to a group considered as being slack, untidy, etc 6 US, Canadian, Austral & NZ a party held to honour and present gifts to a person, as to a prospective bride 7 a large number of particles formed by the collision of a cosmic-ray particle with a particle in the atmosphere 8 NZ a light fabric cover thrown over a tea table to protect the food from flies, dust, etc ▷ vb 9 (tr) to sprinkle or spray with or as if with a shower 10 (often with it as subject) to fall or cause to fall in the form of a shower 11 (tr) to give (gifts, etc) in abundance or present (a person) with (gifts, etc): they showered gifts on him 12 (intr) to take a shower [Old English scūr; related to Old Norse skūr, Old High German skūr shower, Latin caurus northwest wind] > 'showery adj

shower² ('ʃəʊə) n a person or thing that shows

showgirl ('ʃəʊ,gɜːl) n a girl who appears in variety shows, nightclub acts, etc, esp as a singer or dancer

show house n a house on a new estate that is decorated and furnished for prospective buyers to view

showing ('ʃəʊɪŋ) n 1 a presentation, exhibition, or display 2 manner of presentation; performance

showjumping ('ʃəʊ,dʒʌmpɪŋ) n the riding of horses in competitions to demonstrate skill in jumping over or between various obstacles > 'show-jumper n

showman ('ʃəʊmən) n, pl -men 1 a person who presents or produces a theatrical show, etc 2 a person skilled at presenting anything in an effective manner > 'showmanship n

shown (ʃəʊn) vb a past participle of **show**

show off vb (adverb) 1 (tr) to exhibit or display so as to invite admiration 2 (intr) informal to behave in such a manner as to make an impression ▷ n **show-off** 3 informal a person who makes a vain display of himself

showplace ('ʃəʊ,pleɪs) n a place exhibited or visited for its beauty, historic interest, etc

showroom ('ʃəʊ,ruːm, -,rʊm) n a room in which goods, such as cars, are on display

show up vb (adverb) 1 to reveal or be revealed clearly 2 (tr) to expose or reveal the faults or defects of by comparison 3 (tr) informal to put to shame; embarrass 4 (intr) informal to appear or arrive

showy ('ʃəʊɪ) adj showier, showiest 1 gaudy, flashy, or ostentatious 2 making a brilliant or imposing display > 'showily adv > 'showiness n

shrank (ʃræŋk) vb a past tense of **shrink**

shrapnel ('ʃræpnᵊl) n 1 a projectile containing a number of small pellets or bullets exploded before impact 2 fragments from this or any other type of shell [C19: named after H. Shrapnel (1761–1842), English army officer, who invented it]

shred (ʃrɛd) n 1 a long narrow strip or fragment torn or cut off 2 a very small piece or amount; scrap ▷ vb shreds, shredding, shredded or shred 3 (tr) to tear or cut into shreds [Old English scread; related to Old Norse skrjōthr torn-up book, Old High German scrōt cut-off piece; see SCROLL, SHROUD, SCREED] > 'shredder n

Shreveport ('ʃriːv,pɔːt) n a city in NW Louisiana, on the Red River: centre of an oil and natural-gas region. Pop: 198 364 (2003 est)

shrew (ʃruː) n Also called: **shrewmouse** any small mouse-like long-snouted mammal, such as Sorex araneus (**common shrew**), of the family Soricidae: order Insectivora (insectivores) [Old English scrēawa; related to Old High German scrawaz dwarf, Icelandic skröggr old man, Norwegian skrugg dwarf]

shrewd (ʃruːd) adj 1 astute and penetrating, often with regard to business 2 artful and crafty: a shrewd politician 3 obsolete piercing: a shrewd wind [C14: from shrew (obsolete vb) to curse, from SHREW] > 'shrewdly adv > 'shrewdness n

shrewish ('ʃruːɪʃ) adj (esp of a woman) bad-tempered and nagging

Shrewsbury ('ʃrəʊzbərɪ, -brɪ, 'ʃruːz-) n a town in W central England, administrative centre of Shropshire, on the River Severn: strategically situated near the Welsh border; market town. Pop: 67 126 (2001)

shriek (ʃriːk) *n* **1** a shrill and piercing cry ▷ *vb* **2** to produce or utter (words, sounds, etc) in a shrill piercing tone [c16: probably from Old Norse *skrækja* to SCREECH¹] > **'shrieker** *n*

shrieval (ʃriːvəl) *adj* of or relating to a sheriff

shrievalty (ʃriːvəltɪ) *n, pl* **-ties** **1** the office or term of office of a sheriff **2** the jurisdiction of a sheriff [c16: from SHRIEVE, on the model of *mayoralty*]

shrieve (ʃriːv) *n* an archaic word for **sheriff**

shrift (ʃrɪft) *n* archaic the act or an instance of shriving or being shriven. See also **short shrift** [Old English *scrift*, from Latin *scriptum* SCRIPT]

shrike (ʃraɪk) *n* Also called: **butcherbird** any songbird of the chiefly Old World family *Laniidae*, having a heavy hooked bill and feeding on smaller animals which they sometimes impale on thorns, barbed wire, etc [Old English *scríc* thrush; related to Middle Dutch *schrīk* corncrake; see SCREECH¹, SHRIEK]

shrill (ʃrɪl) *adj* **1** sharp and high-pitched in quality **2** emitting a sharp high-pitched sound ▷ *vb* **3** to utter (words, sounds, etc) in a shrill tone [c14: probably from Old English *scralletan*; related to German *schrill* shrill, Dutch *schrallen* to shriek] > **'shrillness** *n* > **'shrilly** *adv*

shrimp (ʃrɪmp) *n* **1** any of various chiefly marine decapod crustaceans of the genus *Crangon* and related genera, having a slender flattened body with a long tail and a single pair of pincers **2** *informal* a diminutive person, esp a child ▷ *vb* **3** (*intr*) to fish for shrimps [c14: probably of Germanic origin; compare Middle Low German *schrempen* to shrink; see SCRIMP, CRIMP] > **'shrimper** *n*

shrine (ʃraɪn) *n* **1** a place of worship hallowed by association with a sacred person or object **2** a container for sacred relics **3** the tomb of a saint or other holy person **4** a place or site venerated for its association with a famous person or event **5** *RC Church* a building, alcove, or shelf arranged as a setting for a statue, picture, or other representation of Christ, the Virgin Mary, or a saint ▷ *vb* **6** short for **enshrine** [Old English *scrín*, from Latin *scrínium* bookcase; related to Old Norse *skrín*, Old High German *skríni*] > **'shrine,like** *adj*

shrink (ʃrɪŋk) *vb* shrinks, shrinking, shrank *or* shrunk, shrunk *or* shrunken **1** to contract or cause to contract as from wetness, heat, cold, etc **2** to become or cause to become smaller in size **3** (*intr*; often foll by *from*) **a** to recoil or withdraw: *to shrink from the sight of blood* **b** to feel great reluctance (at) ▷ *n* **4** the act or an instance of shrinking [Old English *scrincan*; related to Old Norse *skrokkr* torso, Old Swedish *skrunkin* wrinkled, Old Norse *hrukka* a crease, Icelandic *skrukka* wrinkled woman] > **'shrinkable** *adj* > **'shrinker** *n* > **'shrinking** *adj*

shrinkage (ʃrɪŋkɪdʒ) *n* **1** the act or fact of shrinking **2** the amount by which anything decreases in size, value, weight, etc **3** the loss of merchandise in a retail store through theft or damage

shrinking violet *n* informal a shy person

shrink-wrap *vb* **-wraps, -wrapping, -wrapped** (*tr*) to package (a product) in a flexible plastic wrapping designed to shrink about its contours to protect and seal it

shrive (ʃraɪv) *vb* shrives, shriving, shrove *or* shrived, shriven (ʃrɪvən) *or* shrived chiefly *RC Church* **1** to hear the confession of (a penitent) **2** (*tr*) to impose a penance upon (a penitent) and grant him sacramental absolution **3** (*intr*) to confess one's sins to a priest in order to obtain sacramental forgiveness [Old English *scrífan*, from Latin *scríbere* to write] > **'shriver** *n*

shrivel (ʃrɪvəl) *vb* **-els, -elling, -elled** *or US* **-els, -eling, -eled** **1** to make or become shrunken and withered **2** to lose or cause to lose vitality [c16: probably of Scandinavian origin; compare Swedish dialect *skryvla* wrinkle]

Shropshire (ʃrɒpʃɪə, -ʃə) *n* **1** a county of W central England: Telford and Wrekin became an independent unitary authority in 1998; mainly agricultural. Administrative centre: Shrewsbury. Pop (excluding Telford and Wrekin): 286 700 (2003 est). Area (excluding

Telford and Wrekin): 3201 sq km (1236 sq miles) **2** a breed of medium-sized sheep having a dense fleece, originating from Shropshire and Staffordshire, England

shroud (ʃraʊd) *n* **1** a garment or piece of cloth used to wrap a dead body **2** anything that envelops like a garment: *a shroud of mist* **3** a protective covering for a piece of equipment **4** *astronautics* a streamlined protective covering used to protect the payload during a rocket-powered launch **5** *nautical* one of a pattern of ropes or cables used to stay a mast ▷ *vb* **6** (*tr*) to wrap in a shroud **7** (*tr*) to cover, envelop, or hide [Old English *scrúd* garment; related to Old Norse *skrúth* gear] > **'shroudless** *adj*

shrove (ʃraʊv) *vb* a past tense of **shrive**

Shrovetide (ʃraʊv,taɪd) *n* the Sunday, Monday, and Tuesday before Ash Wednesday, formerly a time when confessions were made in preparation for Lent

Shrove Tuesday *n* the last day of Shrovetide; Pancake Day

shrub¹ (ʃrʌb) *n* a woody perennial plant, smaller than a tree, with several major stems arising from near the base of the main stem [Old English *scrybb*; related to Middle Low German *schrubben* coarse, uneven, Old Swedish *skrubba* to SCRUB¹] > **'shrub,like** *adj*

shrub² (ʃrʌb) *n* a mixed drink of rum, fruit juice, sugar, and spice [c18: from Arabic *sharāb*, variant of *shurb* drink; see SHERBET]

shrubbery (ʃrʌbərɪ) *n, pl* **-beries** **1** a place where a number of shrubs are planted **2** shrubs collectively

shrubby (ʃrʌbɪ) *adj* **-bier, -biest** **1** consisting of, planted with, or abounding in shrubs **2** resembling a shrub > **'shrubbiness** *n*

shrug (ʃrʌg) *vb* shrugs, shrugging, shrugged **1** to draw up and drop (the shoulders) abruptly in a gesture expressing indifference, contempt, ignorance, etc ▷ *n* **2** the gesture so made [c14: of uncertain origin]

shrug off *vb* (*tr, adverb*) **1** to minimize the importance of; dismiss **2** to get rid of

shrunk (ʃrʌŋk) *vb* a past participle and past tense of **shrink**

shrunken (ʃrʌŋkən) *vb* **1** a past participle of **shrink** ▷ *adj* **2** (*usually prenominal*) reduced in size

shtoom (ʃtʊm) *adj* slang silent; dumb (esp in the phrase **keep shtoom**) [from Yiddish, from German *stumm* silent]

shuck (ʃʌk) *n* **1** the outer covering of something, such as the husk of a grain of maize, a pea pod, or an oyster shell ▷ *vb* **2** to remove the shucks from [c17: American dialect, of unknown origin] > **'shucker** *n*

shucks (ʃʌks) *US & Canadian informal interj* an exclamation of disappointment, annoyance, etc

shudder (ʃʌdə) *vb* **1** (*intr*) to shake or tremble suddenly and violently, as from horror, fear, aversion, etc ▷ *n* **2** the act of shuddering; convulsive shiver [c18: from Middle Low German *schoderen*; related to Old Frisian *skedda* to shake, Old High German *skutten* to shake] > **'shuddering** *adj* > **'shudderingly** *adv* > **'shuddery** *adj*

shuffle (ʃʌfəl) *vb* **1** to walk or move (the feet) with a slow dragging motion **2** to change the position of (something), esp quickly or in order to deceive others **3** (*tr*) to mix together in a careless manner: *he shuffled the papers nervously* **4** to mix up (cards in a pack) to change their order **5** (*intr*) to behave in an awkward, evasive, or underhand manner; equivocate **6** (when *intr*, often foll by *into* or *out of*) to move or cause to move clumsily: *he shuffled out of the door* ▷ *n* **7** the act or an instance of shuffling **8** a dance or dance step with short dragging movements of the feet [c16: probably from Low German *schüffeln*; see SHOVE] > **'shuffler** *n*

shuffleboard (ʃʌfəl,bɔːd) *n* **1** a game in which players push wooden or plastic discs with a long cue towards numbered scoring sections marked on a floor, esp a ship's deck **2** the marked area on which this game is played

shuffle off *vb* (*tr, adverb*) to thrust off or put aside: *shuffle off responsibility*

shuffle play *n* a facility on a compact disc player that randomly selects a track from one of a number of compact discs

shufty *or* **shufti** (ʃʊftɪ, ʃʌftɪ) *n, pl* **-ties** *Brit slang* a look;

peep [c20: from Arabic]

shun (ʃʌn) vb shuns, shunning, shunned (tr) to avoid deliberately; keep away from [Old English *scunian*, of obscure origin]

shunt (ʃʌnt) vb **1** to turn or cause to turn to one side; move or be moved aside **2** *railways* to transfer (rolling stock) from track to track **3** *electronics* to divert or be diverted through a shunt **4** (tr) to evade by putting off onto someone else ▷ n **5** the act or an instance of shunting **6** a railway point **7** *electronics* a low-resistance conductor connected in parallel across a device, circuit, or part of a circuit to provide an alternative path for a known fraction of the current **8** *med* a channel that bypasses the normal circulation of the blood: a congenital abnormality or surgically induced **9** *Brit informal* a collision which occurs when a vehicle runs into the back of the vehicle in front [c13: perhaps from *shunen* to SHUN]

shunt-wound (ˈʃʌntˌwaʊnd) adj *electrical engineering* (of a motor or generator) having the field and armature circuits connected in parallel

shush (ʃʊʃ) interj **1** be quiet! hush! ▷ vb **2** to silence or calm (someone) by or as if by saying "shush" [c20: reduplication of SH, influenced by HUSH[1]]

Shushan (ˈʃuːʃæn) n the Biblical name for **Susa**

shut (ʃʌt) vb shuts, shutting, shut **1** to move (something) so as to cover an aperture; close: *to shut a door* **2** to close (something) by bringing together the parts: *to shut a book* **3** (tr; often foll by *up*) to close or lock the doors of: *to shut up a house* **4** (tr; foll by *in*, *out*, etc) to confine, enclose, or exclude **5** (tr) to prevent (a business, etc) from operating **6** shut the door on **a** to refuse to think about **b** to render impossible ▷ adj **7** closed or fastened ▷ n **8** the act or time of shutting ▷ See also **shutdown, shut-off**, etc [Old English *scyttan*; related to Old Frisian *sketta* to shut in, Middle Dutch *schutten* to obstruct]

shutdown (ˈʃʌtˌdaʊn) n **1 a** the closing of a factory, shop, etc **b** (as modifier): *shutdown costs* ▷ vb **shut down** (adverb) **2** to cease or cause to cease operation **3** (tr) to close by lowering

Shute (ʃuːt) n **Nevil**, real name *Nevil Shute Norway*. 1899–1960, English novelist, in Australia after World War II: noted for his novels set in Australia, esp *A Town like Alice* (1950) and *On the Beach* (1957)

shuteye (ˈʃʌtˌaɪ) n an informal term for **sleep**

shut-in n *chiefly US & Canadian* **a** a person confined indoors by illness **b** (as modifier): *a shut-in patient*

shut-off n **1** a device that shuts something off, esp a machine control **2** a stoppage or cessation ▷ vb **shut off** (tr, adverb) **3** to stem the flow of **4** to block off the passage through **5** to isolate or separate

shutout (ˈʃʌtˌaʊt) n **1** *sport* a game in which the opposing team does not score ▷ vb **shut out** (tr, adverb) **2** to keep out or exclude **3** to conceal from sight: *we planted trees to shut out the view of the road*

shutter (ˈʃʌtə) n **1** a hinged doorlike cover, often louvred and usually one of a pair, for closing off a window **2** put up the shutters to close business at the end of the day or permanently **3** *photog* an opaque shield in a camera that, when tripped, admits light to expose the film or plate for a predetermined period, usually a fraction of a second. It is either built into the lens system or lies in the focal plane of the lens (**focal-plane shutter**) **4** *music* one of the louvred covers over the mouths of organ pipes, operated by the swell pedal **5** a person or thing that shuts ▷ vb (tr) **6** to close with or as if with a shutter or shutters **7** to equip with a shutter or shutters

shuttering (ˈʃʌtərɪŋ) n another word (esp Brit) for **formwork**

shuttle (ˈʃʌtəl) n **1** a bobbin-like device used in weaving for passing the weft thread between the warp threads **2** a small bobbin-like device used to hold the thread in a sewing machine or in tatting, knitting, etc **3 a** a bus, train, aircraft, etc, that plies between two points, esp one that offers a frequent service over a short route **b** short for **space shuttle 4 a** the movement between various countries of a diplomat in order to negotiate with rulers who refuse to meet each other **b** (as modifier):

shuttle diplomacy 5 *badminton* short for **shuttlecock** ▷ vb **6** to move or cause to move by or as if by a shuttle [Old English *scytel* bolt; related to Middle High German *schüzzel*, Swedish *skyttel*. See SHOOT, SHOT]

shuttlecock (ˈʃʌtəlˌkɒk) n **1** a light cone consisting of a cork stub with feathered flights, struck to and fro in badminton and battledore **2** anything moved to and fro, as in an argument [c16: from SHUTTLE + COCK[1]]

shut up vb **1** (tr) to prevent all access to **2** (tr) to confine or imprison **3** *informal* to cease to talk or make a noise or cause to cease to talk or make a noise: often used in commands

shwa (ʃwɑː) n a variant spelling of **schwa**

shy[1] (ʃaɪ) adj shyer, shyest or shier, shiest **1** not at ease in the company of others **2** easily frightened; timid **3** (often foll by *of*) watchful or wary **4** (foll by *of*) *informal, chiefly US & Canadian* short (of) **5** (in combination) showing reluctance or disinclination: *workshy* ▷ vb shies, shying, shied (intr) **6** to move suddenly, as from fear: *the horse shied at the snake in the road* **7** (usually foll by *off* or *away*) to draw back; recoil ▷ n, pl shies **8** a sudden movement, as from fear [Old English *sceoh*; related to Old High German *sciuhen* to frighten away, Dutch *schuw* shy, Swedish *skygg*] > ˈshyer n > ˈshyly adv > ˈshyness n

shy[2] (ʃaɪ) vb shies, shying, shied **1** to throw (something) with a sideways motion ▷ n, pl shies **2** a quick throw **3** *informal* a gibe **4** *informal* an attempt; experiment [c18: of Germanic origin; compare Old High German *sciuhen* to make timid, Middle Dutch *schüchteren* to chase away] > ˈshyer n

Shylock (ˈʃaɪˌlɒk) n a heartless or demanding creditor [c19: after *Shylock*, the name of the heartless usurer in Shakespeare's *The Merchant of Venice* (1596)]

Shymkent (ʃɪmˈkɛnt) n a city in S Kazakhstan; a major railway junction. Pop: 469 000 (2005 est). Russian name: **Chimkent**

shyster (ˈʃaɪstə) n *informal, chiefly US* a person, esp a lawyer or politician, who uses discreditable or unethical methods [c19: probably based on *Scheuster*, name of a disreputable 19th-century New York lawyer]

si (siː) n *music* a variant of **te**

Si[1] (siː) or **Si Kiang** n a variant transliteration of the Chinese name for the **Xi**

Si[2] the chemical symbol for silicon

SI symbol for **1** Système International (d'Unités). See SI unit ▷ abbreviation **2** *NZ* South Island

sial (ˈsaɪəl) n the silicon-rich and aluminium-rich rocks of the earth's continental upper crust, the most abundant individual rock being granite [c20: si(licon) + al(uminium)] > ˈsialic (saɪˈælɪk) adj

Sialkot (sɪˈælkɒt) n a city in NE Pakistan: shrine of Guru Nanak. Pop: 487 000 (2005 est)

Siam (saɪˈæm, ˈsaɪæm) n **1** the former name (until 1939 and 1945–49) of **Thailand 2 Gulf of Siam** an arm of the South China Sea between the Malay Peninsula and Indochina

siamang (ˈsaɪəˌmæŋ) n a large black gibbon, *Hylobates* (or *Symphalangus*) *syndactylus*, of Sumatra and the Malay Peninsula, having a large reddish-brown vocal sac beneath the chin and the second and third toes united [c19: from Malay]

Siamese (ˌsaɪəˈmiːz) n, pl -mese **1** See **Siamese cat** ▷ adj **2** characteristic of, relating to, or being a Siamese twin ▷ adj, n **3** another word for **Thai**

Siamese cat n a short-haired breed of cat with a tapering tail, blue eyes, and dark ears, mask, tail, and paws [so called because the breed is believed to have originated in SIAM]

Siamese fighting fish n a brightly coloured labyrinth fish, *Betta splendens*, of Thailand and Malaysia, having large sail-like fins: the males are very pugnacious

Siamese twins pl n non-technical name for **conjoined twins** [c19: named after a famous pair of conjoined twins, Chang and Eng (1811–74), who were born in SIAM]

Sian (ʃjɑːn) n a variant transliteration of the Chinese name for **Xi'an**

Siang (ʃjɑːŋ) n a variant transliteration of the Chinese name for the **Xiang**

Siangtan (ˈʃjɑːŋˈtɑːn) n a variant transliteration of the

Chinese name for **Xiangtan**

sib (sɪb) *n* **1** a blood relative **2** a brother or sister; sibling **3** kinsmen collectively; kindred [Old English *sibb*; related to Old Norse *sifjar* relatives, Old High German *sippa* kinship, Latin *suus* one's own; see GOSSIP]

SIB *abbreviation* (in Britain) (the former) Securities and Investments Board

Sibelius (sɪˈbeɪlɪəs) *n* **Jean** (ʒɑn). 1865–1957, Finnish composer, noted for his seven symphonies, his symphonic poems, such as *Finlandia* (1900) and *Tapiola* (1925), and his violin concerto (1905)

Siberia (saɪˈbɪərɪə) *n* a vast region of Russia and N Kazakhstan: extends from the Ural Mountains to the Pacific and from the Arctic Ocean to the borders with China and Mongolia; colonized after the building of the Trans-Siberian Railway. Area: 13 807 037 sq km (5 330 896 sq miles) ⊳ Si'berian *adj, n*

sibilant ('sɪbɪlənt) *adj* **1** *phonetics* relating to or denoting the consonants (s, z, ʃ, ʒ), all pronounced with a characteristic hissing sound **2** having a hissing sound ⊳ *n* **3** a sibilant consonant [C17: from Latin *sībilāre* to hiss, of imitative origin; compare Greek *sizein* to hiss] ⊳ 'sibilance *or* 'sibilancy *n* ⊳ 'sibilantly *adv*

sibilate ('sɪbɪˌleɪt) *vb* to pronounce or utter (words or speech) with a hissing sound ⊳ ˌsibi'lation *n*

Sibiu (*Romanian* siˈbiu) *n* an industrial town in W central Romania: originally a Roman city, refounded by German colonists in the 12th century. Pop: 133 000 (2005 est). German name: Hermannstadt. Hungarian name: Nagyszeben

sibling ('sɪblɪŋ) *n* **1 a** a person's brother or sister **b** (*as modifier*): *sibling rivalry* **2** any fellow member of a sib [C19: specialized modern use of Old English *sibling* relative, from SIB; see -LING¹]

sibyl ('sɪbɪl) *n* **1** (in ancient Greece and Rome) any of a number of women believed to be oracles or prophetesses, one of the most famous being the sibyl of Cumae, who guided Aeneas through the underworld **2** a witch, fortune-teller, or sorceress [C13: ultimately from Greek *Sibulla*, of obscure origin] ⊳ sibylline ('sɪbɪˌlaɪn, sɪˈbɪlaɪn) *adj*

sic¹ (sɪk) *adv* so or thus: inserted in brackets in a written or printed text to indicate that an odd or questionable reading is what was actually written or printed [Latin]

sic² (sɪk) *vb* **sics, sicking, sicked** (*tr*) **1** to turn on or attack: used only in commands, as to a dog **2** to urge (a dog) to attack [C19: dialect variant of SEEK]

Sica (*Italian* 'siːka) *n* See **de Sica**

siccative ('sɪkətɪv) *n* a substance added to a liquid to promote drying: used in paints and some medicines [C16: from Late Latin *siccātīvus*, from Latin *siccāre* to dry up, from *siccus* dry]

Sichuan, Szechuan *or* **Szechwan** *n* a province of SW China: the most populous administrative division in the country, esp in the central Red Basin, where it is crossed by three main tributaries of the Yangtze. Capital: Chengdu. Pop: 81 000 000 (2003 est). Area: about 569 800 sq km (220 000 sq miles)

Sicilia (siˈtʃiːlja) *n* the Latin and Italian name for **Sicily**

siciliano (sɪˌsɪlɪˈɑːnəʊ, ˌsiːtʃɪˈljɑːnəʊ) *n, pl* **-ianos 1** an old dance in six-beat or twelve-beat time **2** music composed for or in the rhythm of this dance [Italian: Sicilian]

Sicily ('sɪsɪlɪ) *n* the largest island in the Mediterranean, separated from the tip of SW Italy by the Strait of Messina: administratively an autonomous region of Italy; settled by Phoenicians, Greeks, and Carthaginians before the Roman conquest of 241 BC; under Normans (12th–13th centuries); formed the **Kingdom of the Two Sicilies** with Naples in 1815; mountainous and volcanic. Capital: Palermo. Pop: 4 972 124 (2003 est). Area: 25 460 sq km (9830 sq miles) Latin names: Sicilia, Trinacria Italian name: Sicilia ⊳ Si'cilian *adj, n*

sick¹ (sɪk) *adj* **1** inclined or likely to vomit **2 a** suffering from ill health **b** (*as collective noun; preceded by the*): *the sick* **3 a** of, relating to, or used by people who are unwell: *sick benefits* **b** (*in combination*): *a sickroom* **4** deeply affected with a mental or spiritual feeling akin to physical sickness: *sick at heart* **5** mentally,

psychologically, or spiritually disturbed **6** *informal* delighting in or catering for the macabre or sadistic; morbid: *sick humour* **7** Also: **sick and tired** (often foll by *of*) *informal* disgusted or weary, esp because satiated: *I am sick of his everlasting laughter* **8** (often foll by *for*) weary with longing; pining: *I am sick for my own country* **9** pallid or sickly **10** not in working order ⊳ *n, vb* **11** an informal word for **vomit** [Old English *sēoc*; related to Old Norse *skjūkr*, Gothic *siuks*, Old High German *sioh*] ⊳ 'sickish *adj*

sick² (sɪk) *vb* a variant spelling of **sic²**

sickbay ('sɪkˌbeɪ) *n* a room or area for the treatment of the sick or injured, as on board a ship or at a boarding school

sick building syndrome *n* a group of symptoms, such as headaches, eye irritation, and lethargy, that may be experienced by workers in offices with limited ventilation

sicken ('sɪkən) *vb* **1** to make or become sick, nauseated, or disgusted **2** (*intr*; often foll by *for*) to show symptoms (of an illness) ⊳ 'sickener *n*

sickening ('sɪkənɪŋ) *adj* **1** causing sickness or revulsion **2** *informal* extremely annoying ⊳ 'sickeningly *adv*

Sickert ('sɪkət) *n* **Walter Richard.** 1860–1942, British impressionist painter, esp of scenes of London music halls

sick headache *n* **1** a headache accompanied by nausea **2** a nontechnical name for **migraine**

sickie ('sɪkɪ) *n informal* a day of sick leave from work, whether for genuine sickness or not [C20: from SICK¹ + -IE]

sickle ('sɪkᵊl) *n* an implement for cutting grass, corn, etc, having a curved blade and a short handle [Old English *sicol*, from Latin *sēcula*; related to *secāre* to cut]

sick leave *n* leave of absence from work through illness

sicklebill ('sɪkᵊlˌbɪl) *n* any of various birds having a markedly curved bill, such as *Falculea palliata*, a Madagascan bird of the family *Vangidae*, *Hemignathus procerus*, a Hawaiian honey creeper, and certain hummingbirds and birds of paradise

sickle-cell anaemia *n* a hereditary haemolytic anaemia, occurring in Black populations, and caused by mutant haemoglobin. The red blood cells become sickle-shaped. It is characterized by fever, abdominal pain, jaundice, leg ulcers, etc

sick list *n* a list of the sick, esp in the army or navy

sickly ('sɪklɪ) *adj* **-lier, -liest 1** disposed to frequent ailments; not healthy; weak **2** of, relating to, or caused by sickness **3** (of a smell, taste, etc) causing revulsion or nausea **4** mawkish; insipid ⊳ *adv* **5** in a sick or sickly manner ⊳ 'sickliness *n*

sickness ('sɪknɪs) *n* **1** an illness or disease **2** nausea or queasiness **3** the state or an instance of being sick

sick pay *n* wages paid to an employee while he is on sick leave

sic transit gloria mundi *Latin* (sɪk ˈtrænsɪt ˈɡlɔːrɪˌɑː ˈmʊndiː) thus passes the glory of the world

Sicyon (ˈsɪsɪˌɒn, ˈsɪsɪən) *n* an ancient city in S Greece, in the NE Peloponnese near Corinth: declined after 146 BC

sidalcea (sɪˈdælsɪə) *n* any plant of the mostly perennial N American genus *Sidalcea*, related to and resembling mallow, esp *S. malvaeflora*, grown for its spikes of lilac, pink, or red flowers: family *Malvaceae*. Also called: Greek mallow [New Latin, from Greek *sidē* a plant name + *alkea* a kind of mallow]

Siddhartha (sɪˈdɑːtə) *n* the personal name of the **Buddha**

Siddons ('sɪdᵊnz) *n* **Sarah.** 1755–1831, English tragedienne

side (saɪd) *n* **1** a line or surface that borders anything **2** *geometry* **a** any line segment forming part of the perimeter of a plane geometric figure **b** another name for **face** (sense 13) **3** either of two parts into which an object, surface, area, etc, can be divided, esp by a line, median, space, etc: *the right side and the left side* **4** a surface or part of an object that extends vertically: *the side of a cliff* **5** either half of a human or animal body, esp the area around the waist, as divided by the median plane: *I have a pain in my side* **6** the area immediately next to a person or thing: *he stood at her side* **7** a district, point, or direction within an area identified by reference to a central point: *the south side of the city* **8** the area at the edge of a room, road, etc, as distinguished from the middle **9** aspect or part: *look on the bright side; his cruel side* **10** one of two or more contesting factions, teams, etc **11** a page in an essay, book, etc **12** a position, opinion, etc, held in opposition to another in a dispute **13** line of descent: *he gets his brains from his mother's side* **14** *informal* a television channel **15** *billiards, snooker* spin imparted to a ball by striking it off-centre with the cue. US and Canadian equivalent: **English 16** *Brit slang* insolence, arrogance, or pretentiousness: *to put on side* **17** on one side set apart from the rest, as provision for emergencies, etc, or to avoid muddling **18** on the side **a** apart from or in addition to the main object **b** as a sideline **c** *US* as a side dish **19** take sides to support one group, opinion, etc, as against another ▷ *adj* **20** being on one side; lateral **21** from or viewed as if from one side **22** not main; subordinate or incidental: *side door; side road* ▷ *vb* **23** (*intr*; usually foll by *with*) to support or associate oneself with a faction, interest, etc [Old English *side*; related to *sīd* wide, Old Norse *sītha* side, Old High German *sīta*]

side arms *pl n* weapons carried on the person, by sling, belt, or holster, such as a sword, pistol, etc

sideband ('saɪd,bænd) *n* the frequency band either above (**upper sideband**) or below (**lower sideband**) the carrier frequency, within which fall the spectral components produced by modulation of a carrier wave

sideboard ('saɪd,bɔːd) *n* a piece of furniture intended to stand at the side of a dining room, with drawers, cupboards, and shelves to hold silver, china, linen, etc

sideboards ('saɪd,bɔːdz) *pl n* another term for **sideburns**

sideburns ('saɪd,bɜːnz) *pl n* a man's whiskers grown down either side of the face in front of the ears. Also called: **sideboards**, **side whiskers**, (*Austral.*) **sidelevers** [C19: variant of BURNSIDES]

sidecar ('saɪd,kɑː) *n* a small car attached on one side to a motorcycle, usually for one passenger, the other side being supported by a single wheel

side chain *n chem* a group of atoms bound to an atom, usually a carbon, that forms part of a larger chain or ring in a molecule

-sided *adj* (*in combination*) having a side or sides as specified: *three-sided; many-sided*

side deal *n* a transaction between two people for their private benefit, which is subsidiary to a contract negotiated by them on behalf of the organizations they represent

side dish *n* a portion of food served in addition to the main dish

side drum *n* a small double-headed drum carried at the side with snares that produce a rattling effect

side effect *n* **1** any unwanted nontherapeutic effect caused by a drug **2** any secondary effect, esp an undesirable one

side-foot *soccer* ▷ *n* **1** a shot or pass played with the side of the foot ▷ *vb* **2** (*tr*) to strike (a ball) with the side of the foot

sidekick ('saɪd,kɪk) *n informal* a close friend or follower who accompanies another on adventures, etc

sidelight ('saɪd,laɪt) *n* **1** light coming from the side **2** a side window **3** either of the two navigational running lights used by vessels at night, a red light on the port and a green on the starboard **4** *Brit* either of two small lights on the front of a motor vehicle, used to indicate the presence of the vehicle at night rather than to assist the driver **5** additional or incidental information

sideline ('saɪd,laɪn) *n* **1** *sport* a line that marks the side boundary of a playing area **2** a subsidiary interest or source of income **3** an auxiliary business activity or line of merchandise ▷ *vb* (*tr*) **4** to prevent (a player) from taking part in a game

sidelines ('saɪd,laɪnz) *pl n* **1** *sport* the area immediately outside the playing area, where substitute players sit **2** the peripheral areas of any region, organization, etc

sidelong ('saɪd,lɒŋ) *adj* (*prenominal*) **1** directed or inclining to one side **2** indirect or oblique ▷ *adv* **3** from the side; obliquely

sidereal (saɪ'dɪərɪəl) *adj* **1** of, relating to, or involving the stars **2** determined with reference to one or more stars: *the sidereal day* [C17: from Latin *sīdereus*, from *sīdus* a star, a constellation] > si'dereally *adv*

sidereal day *n* See **day** (sense 5)

sidereal period *n astronomy* the period of revolution of a body about another with respect to one or more distant stars

sidereal time *n* time based upon the rotation of the earth with respect to the distant stars, the sidereal day being the unit of measurement. See also **sidereal day**

sidereal year *n* See **year** (sense 5)

siderite ('saɪdə,raɪt) *n* Also called: **chalybite** a pale yellow to brownish-black mineral consisting chiefly of iron carbonate in hexagonal crystalline form. It occurs mainly in ore veins and sedimentary rocks and is an important source of iron. Formula: $FeCO_3$

sidero- or before a vowel **sider-** *combining form* indicating iron: *siderolite* [from Greek *sidēros*]

siderolite ('saɪdərə,laɪt) *n* a meteorite consisting of a mixture of iron, nickel, and such ferromagnesian minerals as olivine and pyroxene

siderosis (,saɪdə'rəʊsɪs) *n* a lung disease caused by breathing in fine particles of iron or other metallic dust

siderostat ('saɪdərəʊ,stæt) *n* an astronomical instrument consisting essentially of a plane mirror driven about two axes so that light from a celestial body, esp the sun, is reflected along a constant direction for a long period of time [C19: from *sidero-*, from Latin *sidus* a star + -STAT, on the model of HELIOSTAT]

side-saddle *n* **1** a riding saddle originally designed for women riders in skirts who sit with both legs on the near side of the horse ▷ *adv* **2** on or as if on a side-saddle

sideshow ('saɪd,ʃəʊ) *n* **1** a small show or entertainment offered in conjunction with a larger attraction, as at a circus or fair **2** a subordinate event or incident

sideslip ('saɪd,slɪp) *n* **1** a sideways skid, as of a motor vehicle ▷ *vb* **2** -slips, -slipping, -slipped **3** another name for slip¹ (sense 11)

sidesman ('saɪdzmən) *n, pl* -men *Church of England* a man elected to help the parish church warden

side-splitting *adj* **1** producing great mirth **2** (of laughter) uproarious or very hearty

sidestep ('saɪd,stɛp) *vb* -steps, -stepping, -stepped **1** to step aside from or out of the way of (something) **2** (*tr*) to dodge or circumvent ▷ *n* side step **3** a movement to one side, as in dancing, boxing, etc > 'side,stepper *n*

sidestream smoke *n* cigarette smoke that passes into the air without first being inhaled by the smoker

sidestroke ('saɪd,strəʊk) *n* a type of swimming stroke in which the swimmer lies sideways in the water paddling with his arms and making a scissors kick with his legs

sideswipe ('saɪd,swaɪp) *n* **1** a glancing blow or hit along or from the side **2** an unexpected criticism of someone or something while discussing another subject ▷ *vb* **3** to strike (someone) with such a blow > 'side,swiper *n*

side tone *n* sound diverted from a telephone microphone to the earpiece so that a speaker hears his own voice at the same level and position as that of the respondent

sidetrack ('saɪd,træk) *vb* **1** to distract or be distracted from a main subject or topic ▷ *n* **2** *US & Canadian* a railway siding **3** the act or an instance of sidetracking; digression

side-valve engine *n* a type of internal-combustion engine in which the inlet and exhaust valves are in the cylinder block at the side of the pistons

sidewalk ('saɪd,wɔːk) *n US & Canadian* a hard-surfaced path for pedestrians alongside and a little higher than a road. Also called (in Britain and certain other countries): pavement

sidewall ('saɪd,wɔːl) *n* either of the sides of a pneumatic tyre between the tread and the rim

sideward ('saɪdwəd) *adj* **1** directed or moving towards one side ▷ *adv* Also: **sidewards 2** towards one side

sideways ('saɪd,weɪz) *adv* **1** moving, facing, or inclining towards one side **2** from one side; obliquely **3** with one side forward ▷ *adj* (*prenominal*) **4** moving or directed to or from one side **5** towards or from one side

S

side whiskers *pl n* another name for **sideburns**

sidewinder ('saɪdˌwaɪndə) *n* **1** a North American rattlesnake, *Crotalus cerastes*, that moves forwards by a sideways looping motion **2** *boxing*, *US* a heavy swinging blow from the side

Sidi-bel-Abbès (*French* sidibɛlabɛs) *n* a city in NW Algeria: headquarters of the Foreign Legion until Algerian independence (1962). Pop: 201 000 (2005 est)

siding ('saɪdɪŋ) *n* **1** a short stretch of railway track connected to a main line, used for storing rolling stock or to enable trains on the same line to pass **2** a short railway line giving access to the main line for freight from a factory, mine, quarry, etc **3** *US & Canadian* material attached to the outside of a building to make it weatherproof

sidle ('saɪdᵊl) *vb* (*intr*) **1** to move in a furtive or stealthy manner; edge along **2** to move along sideways [C17: back formation from obsolete *sideling* sideways]

Sidmouth ('sɪdmʊθ) *n* **1st Viscount.** See (Henry) Addington

Sidney *or* **Sydney** ('sɪdnɪ) *n* **1** Algernon. 1622–83, English Whig politician, beheaded for his supposed part in the Rye House Plot to assassinate Charles II and the future James II: author of *Discourses Concerning Government* (1689) **2** Sir **Philip.** 1554–86, English poet, courtier, and soldier. His works include the pastoral romance *Arcadia* (1590), the sonnet sequence *Astrophel and Stella* (1591), and *The Defence of Poesie* (1595), one of the earliest works of literary criticism in English

Sidon ('saɪdᵊn) *n* the chief city of ancient Phoenicia: founded in the third millennium BC; wealthy through trade and the making of glass and purple dyes; now the Lebanese city of Saïda > Si'donian *adj, n*

Sidra ('sɪdrə) *n* Gulf of Sidra a wide inlet of the Mediterranean on the N coast of Libya

SIDS *abbreviation* sudden infant death syndrome. See **cot death**

siècle *French* (sjɛklə) *n* a century, period, or era

Siegbahn ('siːgbɑːn) *n* **1** Kai (kaɪ). 1918–2007, Swedish physicist who worked on electron spectroscopy: Nobel prize for physics 1981 **2** his father, **Karl Manne Georg** (kɑːrl 'manə 'jeːɔrj). 1886–1978, Swedish physicist, who discovered the M series in X-ray spectroscopy: Nobel prize for physics 1924

siege (siːdʒ) *n* **1 a** the offensive operations carried out to capture a fortified place by surrounding it, severing its communications and supply lines, and deploying weapons against it **b** (*as modifier*): *siege warfare* **2** a persistent attempt to gain something **3** *obsolete* a seat or throne **4** **lay siege to** to besiege [C13: from Old French *sege* a seat, from Vulgar Latin *sēdicāre* (unattested) to sit down, from Latin *sedēre*]

siege mentality *n* a state of mind in which a person believes that he or she is being constantly oppressed or attacked

Siegen ('siːgən) *n* a city in NW Germany, in North Rhine-Westphalia: manufacturing centre; birthplace of Rubens. Pop: 107 768 (2003 est)

Siegfried ('siːgfriːd; *German* 'ziːkfriːt) *n* German myth a German prince, the son of Sigmund and husband of Kriemhild, who, in the *Nibelungenlied*, assumes possession of the treasure of the Nibelungs by slaying the dragon that guards it, wins Brunhild for King Gunther, and is eventually killed by Hagen. Norse equivalent: **Sigurd**

siemens ('siːmənz) *n, pl* **siemens** the derived SI unit of electrical conductance equal to 1 reciprocal ohm. Symbol: S Formerly called: **mho**

Siemens ('siːmənz) *n* **1** Ernst Werner von (ɛrnst 'vɛrnər fɔn). 1816–92, German engineer, inventor, and pioneer in telegraphy. Among his inventions are the self-excited dynamo and an electrolytic refining process **2** his brother, Sir **William**, original name *Karl Wilhelm Siemens*. 1823–83, British engineer, born in Germany, who invented the open-hearth process for making steel

Siena (sɪ'ɛnə; *Italian* 'sjɛːna) *n* a walled city in central Italy, in Tuscany: founded by the Etruscans; important artistic centre (13th–14th centuries); university (13th century). Pop: 52 625 (2001)

Sienkiewicz (*Polish* ʃɛŋ'kjɛvitʃ) *n* Henryk ('xɛnrik). 1846–1916, Polish novelist. His best-known works are *Quo Vadis?* (1896), set in Nero's Rome, and the war trilogy *With Fire and Sword* (1884), *The Deluge* (1886), and *Pan Michael* (1888), set in 17th-century Poland: Nobel prize for literature 1905

sienna (sɪ'ɛnə) *n* **1** a natural earth containing ferric oxide used as a yellowish-brown pigment when untreated (**raw sienna**) or a reddish-brown pigment when roasted (**burnt sienna**) **2** the colour of this pigment. See also **burnt sienna** [C18: from Italian *terra di Siena* earth of SIENA]

sierra (sɪ'ɛərə) *n* a range of mountains with jagged peaks, esp in Spain or America [C17: from Spanish, literally: saw, from Latin *serra*; see SERRATE] > si'erran *adj*

Sierra Leone (sɪ'ɛərə lɪ'əʊnɪ, lɪ'əʊn) *n* a republic in W Africa, on the Atlantic: became a British colony in 1808 and gained independence (within the Commonwealth) in 1961; declared a republic in 1971; became a one-party state in 1978; multiparty democracy restored in 1991 but military rule was imposed following a coup in 1992, which led to civil unrest; consists of coastal swamps rising to a plateau in the east. Official language: English. Religion: Muslim majority and animist. Currency: leone. Capital: Freetown. Pop: 5 169 000 (2004 est). Area: 71 740 sq km (27 699 sq miles)

Sierra Madre (*Spanish* 'sjɛrra 'maðre) *n* (*functioning as singular*) the main mountain system of Mexico, extending for 2500 km (1500 miles) southeast from the N border: consists of the **Sierra Madre Oriental** in the east, the **Sierra Madre Occidental** in the west, and the **Sierra Madre del Sur** in the south. Highest peak: Citlaltépetl, 5636 m (18 492 ft) (disputed)

Sierra Morena (*Spanish* 'sjɛrra mo'rena) *n* (*functioning as singular*) a mountain range in SW Spain, between the Guadiana and Guadalquivir Rivers. Highest peak: Estrella, 1299 m (4262 ft)

Sierra Nevada *n* (*functioning as singular*) **1** (sɪ'ɛərə nɪ'vɑːdə) a mountain range in E California, parallel to the Coast Ranges. Highest peak: Mount Whitney, 4418 m (14 495 ft) **2** (*Spanish* 'sjɛrra ne'βaða) a mountain range in SE Spain, mostly in Granada and Almería provinces. Highest peak: Cerro de Mulhacén, 3478 m (11 411 ft)

siesta (sɪ'ɛstə) *n* a rest or nap, usually taken in the early afternoon, as in hot countries [C17: from Spanish, from Latin *sexta hōra* the sixth hour, that is, noon]

sieve (sɪv) *n* **1** a device for separating lumps from powdered material, straining liquids, grading particles, etc, consisting of a container with a mesh or perforated bottom through which the material is shaken or poured ▷ *vb* **2** to pass or cause to pass through a sieve **3** (*tr*; often foll by *out*) to separate or remove (lumps, materials, etc) by use of a sieve [Old English *sife*; related to Old Norse *sef* reed with hollow stalk, Old High German *sib* sieve, Dutch *zeef*] > 'sieve͵like *adj*

Sieyès (*French* sjɛjɛs) *n* Emmanuel Joseph (ɛmanɥɛl ʒozɛf), called *Abbé Sieyès*. 1748–1836, French statesman, political theorist, and churchman, who became prominent during the Revolution following the publication of his pamphlet *Qu'est-ce que le tiers état?* (1789). He was instrumental in bringing Napoleon I to power (1799)

sift (sɪft) *vb* **1** (*tr*) to sieve (sand, flour, etc) in order to remove the coarser particles **2** to scatter (something) over a surface through a sieve **3** (*tr*) to separate with or as if with a sieve; distinguish between **4** (*tr*) to examine minutely: *to sift evidence* **5** (*intr*) to move as if through a sieve [Old English *siftan*; related to Middle Low German *siften* to sift, Dutch *ziften*; see SIEVE] > 'sifter *n*

siftings ('sɪftɪŋz) *pl n* material or particles separated out by or as if by a sieve

sigh (saɪ) *vb* **1** (*intr*) to draw in and exhale audibly a deep breath as an expression of weariness, despair, relief, etc **2** (*intr*) to make a sound resembling this **3** (*intr*; often foll by *for*) to yearn, long, or pine **4** (*tr*) to utter or express with sighing ▷ *n* **5** the act or sound of sighing [Old English *sīcan*, of obscure origin] > 'sigher *n*

sight (saɪt) *n* **1** the power or faculty of seeing; perception by the eyes; vision. Related adjs: **visual 2** the act or an instance of seeing **3** the range of vision: *within sight of land* **4** range of mental vision; point of view; judgment: *in his sight she could do nothing wrong* **5** a glimpse or view (esp in the phrases **catch sight of, lose sight of**) **6** anything that is seen **7** (*often plural*) anything worth seeing; spectacle: *the sights of London* **8** *informal* anything unpleasant or undesirable to see: *his room was a sight!* **9** any of various devices or instruments used to assist the eye in making alignments or directional observations, esp such a device used in aiming a gun **10** an observation or alignment made with such a device **11** **a sight** *informal* a great deal: *she's a sight too good for him* **12** **a sight for sore eyes** a person or thing that one is pleased or relieved to see **13** **at sight** or **on sight** **a** as soon as seen **b** on presentation: *a bill payable at sight* **14** **know by sight** to be familiar with the appearance of without having personal acquaintance **15** **out by a long sight** *informal* on no account; not at all **16** **set one's sights on** to have (a specified goal) in mind; aim for **17** **sight unseen** without having seen the object at issue: *to buy a car sight unseen* ▷ *vb* **18** (*tr*) to see, view, or glimpse **19** (*tr*) **a** to furnish with a sight or sights **b** to adjust the sight of **20** to aim (a firearm) using the sight [Old English *sihth*; related to Old High German *siht*; see SEE[1]] ▷ '**sightable** *adj*

sighted ('saɪtɪd) *adj* (*in combination*) having sight of a specified kind: *short-sighted*

sighting ('saɪtɪŋ) *n* **1** an occasion on which something is seen **2** Another name for **sight** (sense 10)

sightless ('saɪtlɪs) *adj* **1** blind **2** invisible ▷ '**sightlessly** *adv* ▷ '**sightlessness** *n*

sightly ('saɪtlɪ) *adj* **-lier, -liest** pleasing or attractive to see ▷ '**sightliness** *n*

sight-read ('saɪt,riːd) *vb* **-reads, -reading, -read** (-,rɛd) to sing or play (music in a printed or written form) without previous preparation ▷ '**sight-,reader** *n* ▷ '**sight-,reading** *n*

sightscreen ('saɪt,skriːn) *n* *cricket* a large white screen placed near the boundary behind the bowler to help the batsman see the ball

sightsee ('saɪt,siː) *vb* **-sees, -seeing, -saw, -seen** *informal* to visit the famous or interesting sights of (a place) ▷ '**sight,seer** *n*

sightseeing ('saɪt,siːɪŋ) *n* *informal* **a** the activity of visiting the famous or interesting sights of a place **b** (*as modifier*): *sightseeing trip*

Sigismund ('sɪɡɪsmənd) *n* 1368–1437, king of Hungary (1387–1437) and of Bohemia (1419–37); Holy Roman Emperor (1411–37). He helped to end the Great Schism in the Church; implicated in the death of Huss

Sigismund II *n* called *Sigismund Augustus*. 1520–72, king of Poland (1548–72), who united Poland, Lithuania, and their dependencies by the Union of Lublin (1569)

sigla ('sɪɡlə) *n* the list of symbols used in a book, usually collected together as part of the preliminaries [Latin: plural of *siglum*, diminutive of *signum* sign]

sigma ('sɪɡmə) *n* **1** the 18th letter in the Greek alphabet (Σ, σ or, when final, ς), a consonant, transliterated as *S* **2** *maths* the symbol Σ, indicating summation of the numbers or quantities indicated [Greek, of Semitic origin; related to Hebrew SAMEKH]

sigmoid ('sɪɡmɔɪd) or **sigmoidal** *adj* **1** shaped like the letter S **2** of or relating to the sigmoid colon of the large intestine [c17: from Greek *sigmoeidēs* sigma-shaped]

sigmoid flexure *n* *zoology* an S-shaped curve, as in the necks of certain birds

Sigmund ('sɪɡmənd, 'siːɡmʊnd; German 'ziːkmʊnt) *n* **1** *Norse myth* the father of the hero Sigurd **2** Also called: Siegmund (German 'ziːkmʊnt) *German myth* king of the Netherlands, father of Siegfried

sign (saɪn) *n* **1** something that indicates or acts as a token of a fact, condition, etc, that is not immediately or outwardly observable **2** an action or gesture intended to convey information, a command, etc **3 a** a board, placard, etc, displayed in public and inscribed with words or designs intended to inform, warn, etc **b** (*as modifier*): *a sign painter* **4** an arbitrary or conventional mark or device that stands for a word, phrase, etc **5** *maths, logic* **a** any symbol indicating an operation: *a plus*

sign; an implication sign **b** the positivity or negativity of a number, quantity, or expression **6** an indication or vestige: *the house showed no signs of being occupied* **7** a portentous or significant event **8** an indication, such as a scent or spoor, of the presence of an animal **9** *med* any objective evidence of the presence of a disease or disorder **10** *astrology* See **sign of the zodiac** ▷ *vb* **11** to write (one's name) as a signature to (a document, etc) in attestation, confirmation, ratification, etc **12** (*intr*; often foll by *to*) to make a sign; signal **13** to engage or be engaged by written agreement, as a player for a team, etc **14** (*tr*) to outline in gestures a sign over, esp the sign of the cross **15** (*tr*) to indicate by or as if by a sign; betoken ▷ See also **sign away, sign in**, etc [c13: from Old French *signe*, from Latin *signum* a sign] ▷ '**signable** *adj* ▷ '**signer** *n*

Signac (French siɲak) *n* **Paul** (pɔl). 1863–1935, French neoimpressionist painter, influenced by Seurat

signal ('sɪɡn³l) *n* **1** any sign, gesture, token, etc, that serves to communicate information **2** anything that acts as an incitement to action: *the rise in prices was a signal for rebellion* **3 a** a variable parameter, such as a current or electromagnetic wave, by which information is conveyed through an electronic circuit, communications system, etc **b** the information so conveyed **c** (*as modifier*): *signal strength; a signal generator* ▷ *adj* **4** distinguished or conspicuous **5** used to give or act as a signal ▷ *vb* **-nals, -nalling, -nalled** or *US* **-nals, -naling, -naled** **6** to communicate (a message, etc) to (a person) [c16: from Old French *seignal*, from Medieval Latin *signāle*, from Latin *signum* SIGN] ▷ '**signaller** or *US* '**signaler** *n*

signal box *n* a control point for a large area of a railway system, operated electrically and semiautomatically

signalize or **signalise** ('sɪɡnə,laɪz) *vb* (*tr*) **1** to make noteworthy or conspicuous **2** to point out carefully

signally ('sɪɡnəlɪ) *adv* conspicuously or especially

signalman ('sɪɡn³lmən) *n, pl* **-men** a railway employee in charge of the signals and points within a section

signal-to-noise ratio *n* the ratio of one parameter, such as power of a wanted signal to the same parameter of the noise at a specified point in an electronic circuit, etc

signatory ('sɪɡnətərɪ, -trɪ) *n, pl* **-ries** **1** a person who has signed a document such as a treaty or contract or an organization, state, etc, on whose behalf such a document has been signed ▷ *adj* **2** having signed a document, treaty, etc [c17: from Latin *signātōrius* concerning sealing, from *signāre* to seal, from *signum* a mark]

signature ('sɪɡnɪtʃə) *n* **1** the name of a person or a mark or sign representing his name, marked by himself or by an authorized deputy **2** the act of signing one's name **3 a** a distinctive mark, characteristic, etc, that identifies a person or thing **b** (*as modifier*): *a signature fragrance* **4** *music* See **key signature, time signature** **5** *printing* **a** a sheet of paper printed with several pages that upon folding will become a section or sections of a book **b** such a sheet so folded **c** a mark, esp a letter, printed on the first page of a signature [c16: from Old French, from Medieval Latin *signātura*, from Latin *signāre* to sign]

signature tune *n* *Brit* a melody used to introduce or identify a television or radio programme, a dance band, a performer, etc

sign away *vb* (*tr, adverb*) to dispose of or lose by or as if by signing a document

signboard ('saɪn,bɔːd) *n* a board carrying a sign or notice, esp one used to advertise a product, event, etc

signet ('sɪɡnɪt) *n* **1** a small seal, esp one as part of a finger ring **2** a seal used to stamp or authenticate documents **3** the impression made by such a seal [c14: from Medieval Latin *signētum* a little seal, from Latin *signum* a SIGN]

signet ring *n* a finger ring bearing a signet

significance (sɪɡ'nɪfɪkəns) *n* **1** consequence or importance **2** something signified, expressed, or intended **3** the state or quality of being significant **4** *statistics* a measure of the confidence that can be placed in a result, esp a substantive causal hypothesis, as not being merely a matter of chance

S

significant (sɪgˈnɪfɪkənt) *adj* **1** having or expressing a meaning; indicative **2** having a covert or implied meaning; suggestive **3** important, notable, or momentous **4** *statistics* of or relating to a difference between a result derived from a hypothesis and its observed value that is too large to be attributed to chance and that therefore tends to refute the hypothesis [c16: from Latin *significāre* to SIGNIFY] ▷ sig'nificantly *adv*

significant figures *or esp US* **significant digits** *pl n* **1** the figures of a number that express a magnitude to a specified degree of accuracy, rounding up or down the final figure: *3.141 59 to four significant figures is 3.142* **2** the number of such figures: *3.142 has four significant figures*

significant other *n US informal* a spouse or lover

signification (ˌsɪgnɪfɪˈkeɪʃən) *n* **1** something that is signified; meaning or sense **2** the act of signifying

signify (ˈsɪgnɪˌfaɪ) *vb* -**fies**, -**fying**, -**fied** (when *tr, may take a clause as object*) **1** (*tr*) to indicate, show, or suggest **2** (*tr*) to imply or portend: *the clouds signified the coming storm* **3** (*tr*) to stand as a symbol, sign, etc (for) **4** (*intr*) *informal* to be significant or important [c13: from Old French *signifier*, from Latin *significāre*, from *signum* a sign, mark + *facere* to make] ▷ ˈsigniˌfier *n* ▷ **significative** (sɪgˈnɪfɪkətɪv, sɪgˈnɪfɪkeɪ-) *adj*

sign in *vb* (*adverb*) **1** to sign or cause to sign a register, as at a hotel, club, etc **2** to make or become a member, as of a club

signing (ˈsaɪnɪŋ) *n* a specific set of manual signs used to communicate with deaf people

sign language *n* any system of communication by manual signs or gestures

sign off *vb* (*adverb*) **1** (*intr*) to announce the end of a radio or television programme, esp at the end of a day **2** (*tr*) (of a doctor) to declare (someone) unfit for work, because of illness **3** (*intr*) *Brit* to terminate one's claim to unemployment benefit

sign of the zodiac *n* any of the 12 equal areas, 30° wide, into which the zodiac can be divided, named after the 12 zodiacal constellations. In astrology, it is thought that a person's psychological type and attitudes to life can be correlated with the sign in which the sun lay at the moment of his birth, with the ascendant sign, and to a lesser extent with the signs in which other planets lay at this time. Also called: **sign, star sign, sun sign**

sign on *vb* (*adverb*) **1** (*tr*) to hire or employ **2** (*intr*) to commit oneself to a job, activity, etc **3** (*intr*) *Brit* to register as unemployed with the Department of Social Security

signor *or* **signior** (ˈsiːnjɔː; *Italian* sinˈɲor) *n, pl* -**gnors** *or* -**gnori** (*Italian* -ˈɲori) an Italian man: usually used before a name as a title equivalent to *Mr*

signora (siːnˈjɔːrə; *Italian* sinˈɲora) *n, pl* -**ras** *or* -**re** (*Italian* -re) a married Italian woman: a title of address equivalent to *Mrs* when placed before a name or *madam* when used alone [Italian, feminine of SIGNORE]

signore (siːnˈjɔːriː; *Italian* sinˈɲore) *n, pl* -**ri** (-rɪ; *Italian* -ri) an Italian man: a title of respect equivalent to *sir* [Italian, ultimately from Latin *senior* an elder, from *senex* an old man]

Signorelli (*Italian* siɲɲoˈrɛlli) *n* **Luca** (ˈluːka). ?1441–1523, Italian painter, noted for his frescoes

Signoret (*French* siɲore) *n* **Simone** (simɔ̃), original name *Simone Kaminker*. 1921–85, French stage and film actress, whose films include *La Ronde* (1950), *Casque d'Or* (1952), *Room at the Top* (1958), and *Ship of Fools* (1965): married the actor and singer Yves Montand (1921–91)

signorina (ˌsiːnjɔːˈriːnə; *Italian* siɲɲoˈrina) *n, pl* -**nas** *or* -**ne** (*Italian* -ne) an unmarried Italian woman: a title of address equivalent to *Miss* when placed before a name or *madam* or *miss* when used alone [Italian, diminutive of SIGNORA]

signory (ˈsiːnjərɪ) *n, pl* -**gnories** a variant spelling of **seigniory**

sign out *vb* (*adverb*) to sign (one's name) to indicate that one is leaving a place: *he signed out for the evening*

signpost (ˈsaɪnˌpəʊst) *n* **1** a post bearing a sign that shows the way, as at a roadside **2** something that serves as a clue or indication; sign ▷ *vb* (*tr; usually passive*) **3** to mark with signposts **4** to indicate direction towards

sign up *vb* (*adverb*) to enlist or cause to enlist, as for military service

Sigurd (ˈsɪgʊəd; *German* ˈziːɡʊrt) *n Norse myth* a hero who killed the dragon Fafnir to gain the treasure of Andvari, won Brynhild for Gunnar by deception, and then was killed by her when she discovered the fraud. His wife was Gudrun. German counterpart: **Siegfried**

Sihanouk (ˈsɪənʊk) *n* **King Norodom** (ˌnɒrəˈdɒm). born 1922, Cambodian statesman; king of Cambodia (1941–55 and from 1993); prime minister (1955–60), after which he became head of state. He was deposed in 1970 but reinstated (1975–76) following the victory of the Khmer Rouge in the civil war. He was head of state in exile from 1982; returned in 1991 and became monarch in 1993 under a new constitution; abdicated 2004

sika (ˈsiːkə) *n* a Japanese forest-dwelling deer, *Cervus nippon*, having a brown coat, spotted with white in summer, and a large white patch on the rump [from Japanese *shika*]

Sikang (ˈʃiːˈkæŋ) *n* a former province of W China: established in 1928 from part of W Sichuan and E Tibet; dissolved in 1955

Sikh (siːk) *n* **1** a member of an Indian religion that separated from Hinduism and was founded in the 16th century, that teaches monotheism and that has the Granth as its chief religious document, rejecting the authority of the Vedas ▷ *adj* **2** of or relating to the Sikhs or their religious beliefs and customs [c18: from Hindi, literally: disciple, from Sanskrit *śikṣati* he studies] ▷ ˈSikhˌism *n*

Si Kiang (ˈʃiː ˈkjæŋ, kaɪˈæŋ) *n* See **Xi**

Siking (ˈsiːˈkɪŋ) *n* a former name for **Xi'an**

Sikkim (ˈsɪkɪm) *n* a state of NE India. formerly an independent state: under British control (1861–1947); became an Indian protectorate in 1950 and an administrative division of India in 1975; lies in the Himalayas, rising to 8600 m (28 216 ft) at Kanchenjunga in the north. Capital: Gangtok. Pop: 540 493 (2001). Area: 7096 sq km (2740 sq miles) ▷ ˌSikkiˈmese *adj, n*

Sikorski (sɪˈkɔːskiː) *n* **Władysław** (ˈvlædɪslæf). 1881–1943, Polish general and statesman: prime minister (1922–23) and prime minister of the Polish government in exile during World War II: died in an air crash

Sikorsky (sɪˈkɔːskɪ) *n* **Igor**. 1889–1972, US aeronautical engineer, born in Russia. He designed and flew the first four-engined aircraft (1913) and designed the first successful helicopter (1939)

silage (ˈsaɪlɪdʒ) *n* any crop harvested while green for fodder and kept succulent by partial fermentation in a silo. Also called: **ensilage** [c19: alteration (influenced by SILO) of ENSILAGE]

sild (sɪld) *n* any of various small young herrings, esp when prepared and canned in Norway [Norwegian]

silence (ˈsaɪləns) *n* **1** the state or quality of being silent **2** the absence of sound or noise; stillness **3** refusal or failure to speak, communicate, etc, when expected: *his silence on the subject of their promotion was alarming* **4** a period of time without noise **5** oblivion or obscurity ▷ *vb* (*tr*) **6** to bring to silence **7** to put a stop to; extinguish: *to silence all complaint* [c13: via Old French from Latin *silentium*, from *silēre* to be quiet. See SILENT]

silencer (ˈsaɪlənsə) *n* **1** any device designed to reduce noise, esp the tubular device containing baffle plates in the exhaust system of a motor vehicle. US and Canadian name: **muffler 2** a tubular device fitted to the muzzle of a firearm to deaden the report **3** a person or thing that silences

silene (saɪˈliːnɪ) *n* any plant of the large perennial genus *Silene*, with mostly red or pink flowers; many, esp *S.* or *Agrostemma coeli-rosa*, are grown as garden plants: family *Carophyllaceae* [New Latin from Latin *silenus* viscaria]

silent (ˈsaɪlənt) *adj* **1** characterized by an absence or near absence of noise or sound: *a silent house* **2** tending to speak very little or not at all **3** unable to speak **4** failing to speak, communicate, etc, when expected: *the witness chose to remain silent* **5** not spoken or expressed **6** (of a letter) used in the conventional orthography of a word but no longer pronounced in that word: *the "k" in "know" is silent* **7** denoting a film that has no accompanying soundtrack, esp one made before 1927, when such soundtracks were developed [c16: from Latin *silēns*, from *silēre* to be quiet] > **'silently** *adv* > **'silentness** *n*

silent cop *n Austral informal* a small hemispherical traffic marker at an intersection

silent majority *n* a presumed moderate majority of the citizens who are too passive to make their views known

Silenus (saɪˈliːnəs) *n Greek myth* **1** chief of the satyrs and foster father to Dionysus: often depicted riding drunkenly on a donkey **2** *pl* **Sileni** (saɪˈliːnaɪ) *(often not capital)* one of a class of woodland deities, closely similar to the satyrs

Silesia (saɪˈliːʃɪə) *n* a region of central Europe around the upper and middle Oder valley: mostly annexed by Prussia in 1742 but became almost wholly Polish in 1945; rich coal and iron-ore deposits. Polish name: **Śląsk**. Czech name: **Slezsko**. German name: **Schlesien** > **Si'lesian** *adj, n*

silex (ˈsaɪlɛks) *n* a type of heat-resistant glass made from fused quartz [c16: from Latin: hard stone, flint]

silhouette (ˌsɪluːˈɛt) *n* **1** the outline of a solid figure as cast by its shadow **2** an outline drawing filled in with black, often a profile portrait cut out of black paper and mounted on a light ground ▷ *vb* **3** *(tr)* to cause to appear in silhouette [c18: named after Étienne de *Silhouette* (1709–67), French politician, perhaps referring to silhouettes as partial portraits, with a satirical allusion to Silhouette's brief career as controller general (1759)]

silica (ˈsɪlɪkə) *n* the dioxide of silicon, occurring naturally as quartz, cristobalite, and tridymite. It is a refractory insoluble material used in the manufacture of glass, ceramics, and abrasives [c19: New Latin, from Latin: SILEX]

silica gel *n* an amorphous form of silica capable of absorbing large quantities of water: used in drying gases and oils, as a carrier for catalysts and an anticaking agent for cosmetics

silicate (ˈsɪlɪkɪt, -ˌkeɪt) *n* a salt or ester of silicic acid, esp one of a large number of usually insoluble salts with polymeric negative ions having a structure formed of tetrahedrons of SiO_4 groups linked in rings, chains, sheets, or three dimensional frameworks. Silicates constitute a large proportion of the earth's minerals and are present in cement and glass

siliceous *or* **silicious** (sɪˈlɪʃəs) *adj* **1** of, relating to, or containing abundant silica: *siliceous deposits; a siliceous clay* **2** (of plants) growing in or needing soil rich in silica

silicic (sɪˈlɪsɪk) *adj* of, concerned with, or containing silicon or an acid obtained from silicon

silicic acid *n* a white gelatinous substance obtained by adding an acid to a solution of sodium silicate. It has an ill-defined composition and is best regarded as hydrated silica, $SiO_2.nH_2O$

silicify (sɪˈlɪsɪˌfaɪ) *vb* **-fies, -fying, -fied** to convert or be converted into silica: *silicified wood* > **si,licifi'cation** *n*

silicon (ˈsɪlɪkən) *n* **a** a brittle metalloid element that exists in two allotropic forms; occurs principally in sand, quartz, granite, feldspar, and clay. It is usually a grey crystalline solid but is also found as a brown amorphous powder. It is used in transistors, rectifiers, solar cells, and alloys. Its compounds are widely used in glass manufacture, the building industry, and in the form of silicones. Symbol: Si; atomic no: 14; atomic wt: 28.0855; valency: 4; relative density: 2.33; melting pt: 1414°C; boiling pt: 3267°C **b** *(modifier; sometimes capital)* denoting an area of a country that contains a density of high-technology industry [c19: from SILICA, on the model of *boron, carbon*]

Silicon Alley *n* an area of New York City in which industries associated with information technology are concentrated

silicon carbide *n* an extremely hard bluish-black insoluble crystalline substance produced by heating carbon with sand at a high temperature and used as an abrasive and refractory material. Silicon carbide whiskers have a high tensile strength and are used in composites; very pure crystals are used as semiconductors. Formula: SiC

silicon chip *n* another term for **chip** (sense 6)

silicon-controlled rectifier *n* a semiconductor rectifier whose forward current between two electrodes, the anode and cathode, is initiated by means of a signal applied to a third electrode, the gate. The current subsequently becomes independent of the signal. It is a type of thyristor

silicone (ˈsɪlɪˌkəʊn) *n chem* **a** any of a large class of polymeric synthetic materials that usually have resistance to temperature, water, and chemicals, and good insulating and lubricating properties, making them suitable for wide use as oils, water-repellents, resins, etc Chemically they have alternate silicon and oxygen atoms with the silicon atoms bound to organic groups **b** *(as modifier): silicone rubber*

Silicon Fen *n* an area of Cambridgeshire, esp around the city of Cambridge, in which industries associated with information technology are concentrated

Silicon Glen *n* a collective term for the industries in Scotland associated with information technology, esp those concentrated in the central conurbation between Glasgow and Edinburgh

Silicon Valley *n* an industrial strip in W California, extending S of San Francisco, in which the US information technology industry is concentrated

silicosis (ˌsɪlɪˈkəʊsɪs) *n pathol* a form of pneumoconiosis caused by breathing in tiny particles of silica, quartz, or slate, and characterized by shortness of breath and fibrotic changes in the tissues of the lungs

siliqua (sɪˈliːkwə, ˈsɪlɪkwə) *or* **silique** (sɪˈliːk, ˈsɪlɪk) *n, pl* **-liquae** (-ˈliːkwiː), **-liquas** *or* **-liques** the long dry dehiscent fruit of cruciferous plants, such as the wallflower, consisting of two compartments separated by a central septum to which the seeds are attached [c18: via French from Latin *siliqua* a pod] > **siliquose** (ˈsɪlɪˌkwəʊs) *or* **siliquous** (ˈsɪlɪkwəs) *adj*

silk (sɪlk) *n* **1** the very fine soft lustrous fibre produced by a silkworm to make its cocoon **2 a** a thread or fabric made from this fibre **b** *(as modifier): a silk dress* **3** a garment made of this **4** a very fine fibre produced by a spider to build its web, nest, or cocoon **5** the tuft of long fine styles on an ear of maize **6** *Brit* **a** the gown worn by a Queen's (or King's) Counsel **b** *informal* a Queen's (or King's) Counsel **c take silk** to become a Queen's (or King's) Counsel [Old English *sioluc*; compare Old Norse *silki*, Greek *sērikon*, Korean *sir*; all ultimately from Chinese *ssŭ* silk] > **'silk,like** *adj*

silk cotton *n* another name for **kapok**

silk-cotton tree *n* any of several tropical bombacaceous trees of the genus *Ceiba*, esp *Ceiba pentandra*, having seeds covered with silky hairs from which kapok is obtained. Also called: **kapok tree**

silken (ˈsɪlkən) *adj* **1** made of silk **2** resembling silk in smoothness or gloss **3** dressed in silk **4** soft and delicate

silk hat *n* a man's top hat covered with silk

silkworm (ˈsɪlk,wɜːm) *n* **1** the larva of the Chinese moth *Bombyx mori*, that feeds on the leaves of the mulberry tree: widely cultivated as a source of silk **2** any of various similar or related larvae

silky (ˈsɪlkɪ) *adj* **silkier, silkiest 1** resembling silk in texture; glossy **2** made of silk **3** (of a voice, manner, etc) suave; smooth **4** *botany* covered with long fine soft hairs: *silky leaves* > **'silkily** *adv* > **'silkiness** *n*

silky oak *n* any of several trees of the Australian genus *Grevillea*, esp *G. robusta*, having divided leaves, smooth glossy wood, and showy clusters of orange, red, or white flowers: cultivated in the tropics as shade trees: family *Proteaceae*

sill (sɪl) *n* **1** a shelf at the bottom of a window inside a room **2** a horizontal piece along the outside lower member of a window, that throws water clear of the wall below **3** the lower horizontal member of a window or door frame **4** a continuous horizontal member placed on top of a foundation wall in order to carry a timber framework **5** a flat usually horizontal mass of igneous rock, situated between two layers of older sedimentary rock, that was formed by an intrusion of magma [Old English *syll*; related to Old Norse *svill* sill, Icelandic *svoli* tree trunk, Old High German *swella* sill, Latin *solum* ground]

S

sillabub ('sɪləˌbʌb) n a variant spelling of **syllabub**

Sillanpää (Finnish 'sillɑmpæː) n **Frans Eemil** (frans 'eːmil). 1888–1964, Finnish writer, noted for his novels *Meek Heritage* (1919) and *The Maid Silja* (1931): Nobel prize for literature 1939

Sillitoe ('sɪlɪtəʊ) n **Alan**. born 1928, British novelist. His best-known works include *Saturday Night and Sunday Morning* (1958) and *The Loneliness of the Long Distance Runner* (1959)

Sills (sɪlz) n **Beverley**, original name *Belle Silverman*. 1929–2007, US soprano: director of the New York City Opera (1979–89)

silly ('sɪlɪ) adj -lier, -liest **1** lacking in good sense; absurd **2** frivolous, trivial, or superficial **3** feeble-minded **4** dazed, as from a blow ▷ n **5** (modifier) cricket (of a fielding position) near the batsman's wicket: *silly mid-on* **6** pl -lies Also called: **silly-billy** informal a foolish person [c15 (in the sense: pitiable, hence the later senses: foolish): from Old English *sǣlig* (unattested) happy, from *sǣl* happiness; related to Gothic *sēls* good] > **'silliness** n

silly season n Brit a period, usually during the hot summer months, when journalists fill space reporting on frivolous events and activities

silo ('saɪləʊ) n, pl -los **1** a pit, trench, horizontal container, or tower, often cylindrical in shape, in which silage is made and stored **2** a strengthened underground position in which missile systems are sited for protection against attack [c19: from Spanish, perhaps from Celtic]

Siloam (saɪ'ləʊəm, sɪ-) n Bible a pool in Jerusalem where Jesus cured a man of his blindness (John 9)

Silone (Italian si'loːne) n **Ignazio** (iɲ'nattsjo). 1900–78, Italian writer, noted for his humanitarian socialistic novels, *Fontamara* (1933) and *Bread and Wine* (1937)

silt (sɪlt) n **1** a fine deposit of mud, clay, etc, esp one in a river or lake ▷ vb **2** (usually foll by up) to fill or become filled with silt; choke [c15: of Scandinavian origin; compare Norwegian, Danish *sylt* salt marsh; related to Old High German *sulza* salt marsh; see **SALT**] > **sil'tation** n > **'silty** adj

Silurian (saɪ'lʊərɪən) adj **1** of, denoting, or formed in the third period of the Palaeozoic era, between the Ordovician and Devonian periods, which lasted for 25 million years, during which fishes first appeared ▷ n **2 the Silurian** the Silurian period or rock system

silurid (saɪ'lʊərɪd) n **1** any freshwater teleost fish of the Eurasian family *Siluridae*, including catfish, such as *Silurus glanis* (**European catfish**), that have an elongated body, naked skin, and a long anal fin ▷ adj **2** of, relating to, or belonging to the family *Siluridae* [c19: from Latin *silūrus*, from Greek *silouros* a river fish]

silva ('sɪlvə) n a variant spelling of **sylva**

silvan ('sɪlvən) adj a variant spelling of **sylvan**

Silvanus or **Sylvanus** (sɪl'veɪnəs) n Roman myth the Roman god of woodlands, fields, and flocks. Greek counterpart: **Pan** [Latin: from *silva* woodland]

silver ('sɪlvə) n **1 a** a very ductile malleable brilliant greyish-white element having the highest electrical and thermal conductivity of any metal. It occurs free and in argentite and other ores: used in jewellery, tableware, coinage, electrical contacts, and in electroplating. Its compounds are used in photography. Symbol: Ag; atomic no: 47; atomic wt: 107.8682; valency: 1 or 2; relative density: 10.50; melting pt: 961.93°C; boiling pt: 2163°C **b** (as modifier): *a silver coin*. Related adj: **argent** **2** coin made of, or having the appearance of, this metal **3** cutlery, whether made of silver or not **4** any household articles made of silver **5 a** a brilliant or light greyish-white colour **b** (as adjective): *silver hair* **6** short for **silver medal** ▷ adj **7** well-articulated: *silver speech* **8** (prenominal) denoting the 25th in a series, esp an annual series: *a silver wedding anniversary* ▷ vb **9** (tr) to coat with silver or a silvery substance: *to silver a spoon* **10** to become or cause to become silvery in colour [Old English *siolfor*; related to Old Norse *silfr*, Gothic *silubr*, Old High German *silabar*, Old Slavonic *sĭrebro*] > **'silvering** n

silver age n **1** (in Greek and Roman mythology) the second of the world's major epochs, inferior to the preceding golden age and characterized by opulence and irreligion **2** the postclassical period of Latin literature, occupying the early part of the Roman imperial era, characterized by an overindulgence in elegance for its own sake and empty scholarly rhetoric

silver beet n a variety of beet, *Beta vulgaris cicla*, having large firm green leaves: staple cooked green vegetable in Australia and New Zealand

silver bell n any of various deciduous trees of the styracaceous genus *Halesia*, esp *H. carolina*, of North America and China, having white bell-shaped flowers. Also called: **snowdrop tree**

silver birch n a betulaceous tree, *Betula pendula*, of N temperate regions of the Old World, having silvery-white peeling bark

silver bromide n a yellowish insoluble powder that darkens when exposed to light: used in making photographic emulsions. Formula: AgBr

Silverchair ('sɪlvəˌtʃɛə) pl n Australian rock group (formed 1994): comprising Daniel Johns (born 1979; vocals, guitar), Ben Gillies (born 1979, drums) and Chris Joannou (born 1979, bass guitar); their albums include *Frogstomp* (1995) and *Young Modern* (2007)

silver chloride n a white insoluble powder that darkens on exposure to light because of the production of metallic silver: used in making photographic emulsions and papers. Formula: AgCl

silver disc n (in Britain) an album certified to have sold 60 000 copies or a single certified to have sold 200 000 copies

silver-eye n Austral & NZ another name for **white-eye**

silver fern n NZ **1** another name for **ponga** **2** a formalized spray of fern leaf, silver on a black background: the symbol of New Zealand sporting teams, esp the All Blacks

Silver Ferns pl n **the Silver Ferns** the women's international netball team of New Zealand

silver fir n any of various fir trees the leaves of which have a silvery undersurface, esp *Abies alba*, an important timber tree of central and S Europe

silverfish ('sɪlvəˌfɪʃ) n, pl -fish or -fishes **1** a silver variety of the goldfish *Carassius auratus* **2** any of various other silvery fishes, such as the moonfish *Monodactylus argenteus* **3** any of various small primitive wingless insects of the genus *Lepisma*, esp *L. saccharina*, that have long antennae and tail appendages and occur in buildings, feeding on food scraps, bookbindings, etc: order *Thysanura* (bristletails)

silver fox n **1** an American red fox in a colour phase in which the fur is black with long silver-tipped hairs **2** the valuable fur or pelt of this animal

silver-gilt n silver covered with a thin film of gold

silver goal n soccer (in certain competitions) a goal scored in a full half of extra time that is played if a match is drawn. This goal counts as the winner if it is the only goal scored in the full half or full period of extra time

silver iodide n a yellow insoluble powder that darkens on exposure to light: used in photography and artificial rainmaking. Formula: AgI

silver lining n a comforting or hopeful aspect of an otherwise desperate or unhappy situation (esp in the phrase **every cloud has a silver lining**)

silver medal n a medal of silver awarded to a competitor who comes second in a contest or race

silver nitrate n a white crystalline soluble poisonous substance used in making photographic emulsions, other silver salts, and as a medical antiseptic and astringent. Formula: $AgNO_3$

silver plate n **1** a thin layer of silver deposited on a base metal **2** articles, esp tableware, made of silver plate ▷ vb **silver-plate 3** (tr) to coat (a metal, object, etc) with silver, as by electroplating

silver screen the silver screen n informal **1** films collectively or the film industry **2** the screen onto which films are projected

silver service n (in restaurants) a style of serving food using a spoon and fork in one hand like a pair of tongs

silverside ('sɪlvəˌsaɪd) n **1** Brit & NZ a coarse cut of beef below the aitchbone and above the leg **2** Also called:

silversides any small marine or freshwater teleost fish of the family *Atherinidae*, related to the grey mullets: includes the jacksmelt

silversmith ('sɪlvəˌsmɪθ) *n* a craftsman who makes or repairs articles of silver ▷ 'silverˌsmithing *n*

silver surfer *n informal* an older, esp retired, person who uses the internet

silver thaw *n Canadian* 1 a freezing rainstorm 2 another name for **glitter** (sense 7)

silverware ('sɪlvəˌwɛə) *n* articles, esp tableware, made of or plated with silver

silverweed ('sɪlvəˌwiːd) *n* 1 a rosaceous perennial creeping plant, *Potentilla anserina*, with silvery pinnate leaves and yellow flowers 2 any of various convolvulaceous shrubs of the genus *Argyreia*, of SE Asia and Australia, having silvery leaves and purple flowers

silvery ('sɪlvərɪ) *adj* 1 of or having the appearance of silver: *the silvery moon* 2 containing or covered with silver 3 having a clear ringing sound ▷ 'silveriness *n*

silviculture ('sɪlvɪˌkʌltʃə) *n* the branch of forestry that is concerned with the cultivation of trees [C20: *silvi-*, from Latin *silva* woodland + CULTURE] ▷ ˌsilvi'cultural *adj* ▷ ˌsilvi'culturist *n*

silymarin (sə'laɪmərɪn) *n* an antioxidant flavonoid found in milk thistle [C20: from the genus name *Silybum*]

sim (sɪm) *n* a computer game which simulates an activity such as playing a sport or flying an aircraft

sima ('saɪmə) *n* 1 the silicon-rich and magnesium-rich rocks of the earth's oceanic crust, the most abundant individual rock being basalt 2 the earth's continental lower crust, probably comprised of gabbro rather than basalt [C20: from SI(LICA) + MA(GNESIA)]

Si-ma Qian ('siːmɑː 'tʃɪən) *or* **Ssu-ma Ch'ien** *n* ?145–?85 BC, Chinese historian, author of the *Shih-chi*, a history of China from earliest times to the 2nd century BC, usually considered the greatest historical work in Chinese

Simbirsk (*Russian* sim'birsk) *n* the former name (1924–91) of Ulyanovsk

Simenon ('siːmənɒn; *French* simnɔ̃) *n* **Georges** (ʒɔrʒ). 1903–89, Belgian novelist. He wrote over two hundred novels, including the detective series featuring Maigret

Simeon ('sɪmɪən) *n* 1 a *Old Testament* the second son of Jacob and Leah b the tribe descended from him c the territory once occupied by this tribe in the extreme south of the land of Canaan 2 *New Testament* a devout Jew, who recognized the infant Jesus as the Messiah and uttered the canticle *Nunc Dimittis* over him in the Temple (Luke 2:25–35)

Simeon Stylites (staɪ'laɪtiːz) *n* **Saint**. ?390–459 AD, Syrian monk, first of the ascetics who lived on pillars. Feast day: Jan 5 or Sept 1

Simferopol (*Russian* simfɪ'rɔpəlj) *n* a city in S Ukraine on the S Crimean Peninsula: a Scythian town in the 1st century BC; seized by the Russians in 1736. Pop: 344 000 (2005 est)

simian ('sɪmɪən) *adj* 1 of, relating to, or resembling a monkey or ape ▷ *n* 2 a monkey or ape [C17: from Latin *sīmia* an ape, probably from *sīmus* flat-nosed, from Greek *sīmos*]

similar ('sɪmɪlə) *adj* 1 showing resemblance in qualities, characteristics, or appearance; alike but not identical 2 *geometry* (of two or more figures) having corresponding angles equal and all corresponding sides in the same ratio [C17: from Old French *similaire*, from Latin *similis*] ▷ **similarity** (ˌsɪmɪ'lærɪtɪ) *n* ▷ 'similarly *adv*
● USAGE *As* should not be used after *similar: Wilson held a*
  ● *similar position to Jones* (not *a similar position as Jones*); *the*
  ● *system is similar to the one in France* (not *similar as in France*)

simile ('sɪmɪlɪ) *n* a figure of speech that expresses the resemblance of one thing to another of a different category, usually introduced by *as* or *like*. See **metaphor** [C14: from Latin *simile* something similar, from *similis* like]

similitude (sɪ'mɪlɪˌtjuːd) *n* 1 likeness; similarity 2 a thing or sometimes a person that is like or the counterpart of another 3 *archaic* a simile, allegory, or parable [C14: from Latin *similitūdō*, from *similis* like]

Simla ('sɪmlə) *n* a city in N India, capital of Himachal Pradesh state: summer capital of India (1865–1939); hill resort and health centre. Pop: 142 161 (2001)

simmer ('sɪmə) *vb* 1 to cook (food) gently at or just below the boiling point 2 (*intr*) to be about to break out in rage or excitement ▷ *n* 3 the act, sound, or state of simmering [C17: perhaps of imitative origin; compare German *summen* to hum]

simmer down *vb* (*adverb*) 1 (*intr*) *informal* to grow calmer or quieter, as after intense rage or excitement 2 (*tr*) to reduce the volume of (a liquid) by boiling slowly

simnel cake ('sɪmn²l) *n Brit* a fruit cake containing a layer of marzipan, often coloured with saffron and topped with marzipan, traditionally eaten at Lent or Easter [C13: *simenel*, from Old French, from Latin *simila* fine flour, probably of Semitic origin; related to Greek *semidalis* fine flour]

Simon ('saɪmən) *n* 1 the original name of (Saint) **Peter²** 2 *New Testament* a See **Simon Zelotes** b a relative of Jesus, who may have been identical with Simon Zelotes (Matthew 13:55) c Also called: **Simon the Tanner** a Christian of Joppa with whom Peter stayed (Acts of the Apostles 9:43) 3 **John** (**Allsebrook**), 1st Viscount Simon. 1873–1954, British statesman and lawyer. He was Liberal home secretary (1915–16) and, as a leader of the National Liberals, foreign secretary (1931–35), home secretary (1935–37), Chancellor of the Exchequer (1937–40), Lord Chancellor (1940–45) 4 (**Marvin**) **Neil**. born 1927, US dramatist and librettist, whose plays include *Barefoot in the Park* (1963), *California Suite* (1976), *Biloxi Blues* (1985), *Lost in Yonkers* (1990), and *London Suite* (1995): many have been made into films 5 **Paul**. born 1942, US pop singer and songwriter. His albums include: with Art Garfunkel (born 1941), *The Sounds of Silence* (1966), and *Bridge over Troubled Water* (1970); and, solo, *Graceland* (1986), *The Rhythm of the Saints* (1990), and *You're The One* (2000)

Simonides (saɪ'mɒnɪˌdiːz) *n* ?556–?468 BC, Greek lyric poet and epigrammatist, noted for his odes to victory

Simon Magus *n New Testament* a Samaritan sorcerer, probably from Gitta, of the 1st century AD After being converted to Christianity, he tried to buy miraculous powers from the apostles (Acts of the Apostles 8:9–24). He is also identified as the founder of a Gnostic sect

Simon Peter *n New Testament* the full name of the apostle Peter, a combination of his original name and the name given him by Christ (Matthew 16:17–18)

simon-pure *adj* real; genuine; authentic [C19: from the phrase *the real Simon Pure*, name of a character in the play *A Bold Stroke for a Wife* (1717) by Susannah Centlivre (1669–1723) who is impersonated by another character in some scenes]

simony ('saɪmənɪ) *n Christianity* the practice, now usually regarded as a sin, of buying or selling spiritual or Church benefits such as pardons, relics, etc, or preferments [C13: from Old French *simonie*, from Late Latin *sīmōnia*, from the name of *Simon Magus*, a Samaritan sorceror of the 1st century AD] ▷ 'simonist *n*

Simon Zelotes (zɪ'ləʊtiːz) *n* Saint **Simon Zelotes** one of the 12 apostles, who had probably belonged to the Zealot party before becoming a Christian (Luke 6:15). Owing to a misinterpretation of two similar Aramaic words he is also, but mistakenly, called the Canaanite (Matthew 10:4). Feast day: Oct 28 or May 10

simoom (sɪ'muːm) *or* **simoon** (sɪ'muːn) *n* a strong suffocating sand-laden wind of the deserts of Arabia and North Africa. Also called: **samiel** [from Arabic *samūm* poisonous, from *sam* poison, from Aramaic *sammā* poison]

simpatico (sɪm'pɑːtɪˌkəʊ, -'pæt-) *adj informal* 1 pleasant or congenial 2 of similar mind or temperament; compatible [Italian: from *simpatia* SYMPATHY]

simper ('sɪmpə) *vb* 1 (*intr*) to smile coyly, affectedly, or in a silly self-conscious way 2 (*tr*) to utter (something) in a simpering manner ▷ *n* 3 a simpering smile; smirk [C16: probably from Dutch *simper* affected] ▷ 'simperer *n* ▷ 'simpering *adj, n* ▷ 'simperingly *adv*

simple ('sɪmp²l) *adj* 1 not involved or complicated; easy to understand or do: *a simple problem* 2 plain; unadorned: *a simple dress* 3 consisting of one element or part only; not combined or complex: *a simple mechanism* 4 unaffected or unpretentious: *although he became famous,* he remained a simple and well-liked man **5** not guileful; sincere; frank: *her simple explanation was readily accepted* **6** of humble condition or rank: *the peasant was of simple birth* **7** weak in intelligence; feeble-minded **8** (*prenominal*) without additions or modifications; mere: *the witness told the simple truth* **9** (*prenominal*) ordinary or straightforward: *a simple case of mumps* **10** *chem* (of a substance or material) consisting of only one chemical compound rather than a mixture of compounds **11** *maths* **a** (of a fraction) containing only integers **b** (of an equation) containing variables to the first power only; linear **12** *biology* **a** not divided into parts: *a simple leaf; a simple eye* **b** formed from only one ovary: *simple fruit* **13** *music* relating to or denoting a time where the number of beats per bar may be two, three, or four ▷ *n archaic* **14** a simpleton; fool **15** a plant, esp a herbaceous plant, having medicinal properties [c13: via Old French from Latin *simplex* plain] > 'simpleness *n* > simplicity (sɪm'plɪsɪtɪ) *n*

simple fraction *n* a fraction in which the numerator and denominator are both integers expressed as a ratio rather than a decimal. Also called: **common fraction**, **vulgar fraction**

simple fracture *n* a fracture in which the broken bone does not pierce the skin

simple harmonic motion *n* a form of periodic motion of a particle, etc, in which the acceleration is always directed towards some equilibrium point and is proportional to the displacement from this point. Abbreviation: **SMH**

simple-hearted *adj* free from deceit; open; frank; sincere

simple interest *n* interest calculated or paid on the principal alone. See **compound interest**

simple machine *n* a simple device for altering the magnitude or direction of a force. The six basic types are the lever, wheel and axle, pulley, screw, wedge, and inclined plane

simple-minded *adj* **1** stupid; foolish; feeble-minded **2** unsophisticated; artless > ,simple-'mindedly *adv* > ,simple-'mindedness *n*

simple sentence *n* a sentence consisting of a single main clause

simpleton ('sɪmpᵊltən) *n* a foolish or ignorant person

simplify ('sɪmplɪˌfaɪ) *vb* **-fies, -fying, -fied** (*tr*) **1** to make less complicated, clearer, or easier **2** *maths* to reduce (an equation, fraction, etc) to a simpler form by cancellation of common factors, regrouping of terms in the same variable, etc [c17: via French from Medieval Latin *simplificāre*, from Latin *simplus* simple + *facere* to make] > ,simplifi'cation *n*

simplistic (sɪm'plɪstɪk) *adj* **1** characterized by extreme simplicity; naive **2** oversimplifying complex problems; making unrealistically simple judgments or analyses > 'simplism *n* > sim'plistically *adv*

● USAGE Since *simplistic* already has *too* as part of its
● meaning, it is tautologous to talk about something
● being *too simplistic* or *over-simplistic*

Simplon Pass ('sɪmplɒn) *n* a pass over the Lepontine Alps in S Switzerland, between Brig (Switzerland) and Iselle (Italy). Height: 2009 m (6590 ft)

simply ('sɪmplɪ) *adv* **1** in a simple manner **2** merely; only **3** absolutely; altogether; really: *a simply wonderful holiday* **4** (*sentence modifier*) frankly; candidly

Simpson ('sɪmpsᵊn, 'sɪmsᵊn) *n* **1** Sir **James Young**. 1811–70, Scottish obstetrician, who pioneered the use of chloroform as an anaesthetic **2 Wallis** (**Warfield**) ('wɒlɪs). See **Edward VIII**

Simpson Desert ('sɪmpsən) *n* an uninhabited arid region in central Australia, mainly in the Northern Territory. Area: about 145 000 sq km (56 000 sq miles)

simulacrum (ˌsɪmjʊ'leɪkrəm) *n, pl* **-cra** (-krə) *archaic* **1** any image or representation of something **2** a slight, unreal, or vague semblance of something; superficial likeness [c16: from Latin: likeness, from *simulāre* to imitate, from *similis* like]

simulate *vb* ('sɪmjʊˌleɪt) (*tr*) **1** to make a pretence of; feign: *to simulate anxiety* **2** to reproduce the conditions of (a situation, etc), as in carrying out an experiment: *to simulate weightlessness* **3** to assume or have the appearance

of; imitate ▷ *adj* ('sɪmjʊlɪt, -ˌleɪt) **4** *archaic* assumed or simulated [c17: from Latin *simulāre* to copy, from *similis* like] > 'simulative *adj* > ˌsimu'lation *n*

simulated ('sɪmjʊˌleɪtɪd) *adj* **1** (of fur, leather, pearls, etc) being an imitation of the genuine article, usually made from cheaper material **2** (of actions, qualities, emotions, etc) imitated; feigned

simulator ('sɪmjʊˌleɪtə) *n* **1** any device or system that simulates specific conditions or the characteristics of a real process or machine for the purposes of research or operator training: *space simulator* **2** a person who simulates

simulcast ('sɪmᵊlˌkɑːst) *vb* **1** (*tr*) to broadcast (a programme, etc) simultaneously on radio and television ▷ *n* **2** a programme, etc, so broadcast [c20: from SIMUL(TANEOUS) + (BROAD)CAST]

simultaneous (ˌsɪmᵊl'teɪnɪəs; US ˌsaɪmᵊl'teɪnɪəs) *adj* occurring, existing, or operating at the same time; concurrent [c17: formed on the model of INSTANTANEOUS from Latin *simul* at the same time, together] > ˌsimul'taneously *adv* > ˌsimul'taneousness *or* simultaneity (ˌsɪmᵊltə'niːɪtɪ; US ˌsaɪmᵊltə'niːɪtɪ) *n*

simultaneous equations *pl n* a set of equations that are all satisfied by the same values of the variables

sin¹ (sɪn) *n* **1** *theol* **a** a transgression of God's known will or any principle or law regarded as embodying this **b** the condition of estrangement from God arising from such transgression **2** any serious offence, as against a religious or moral principle **3** any offence against a principle or standard **4 live in sin** *informal* (of an unmarried couple) to live together ▷ *vb* **sins, sinning, sinned** (*intr*) **5** *theol* to commit a sin **6** (usually foll by *against*) to commit an offence (against a person, principle, etc) [Old English *synn*; related to Old Norse *synth*, Old High German *suntea* sin, Latin *sons* guilty] > 'sinner *n*

sin² (saɪn) *abbreviation maths* sine

SIN *or* **S.I.N.** *abbreviation* (in Canada) social insurance number

Sinai ('saɪnaɪ, 'saɪnɪˌaɪ) *n* **1** a mountainous peninsula of NE Egypt at the N end of the Red Sea, between the Gulf of Suez and the Gulf of Aqaba: occupied by Israel in 1967; fully restored by 1982 **2 Mount Sinai** the mountain where Moses received the Law from God (Exodus 19–20): often identified as Jebel Musa, sometimes as Jebel Serbal, both on the S Sinai Peninsula > Sinaitic (ˌsaɪnɪ'ɪtɪk) *or* Sinaic (sɪ'neɪɪk) *adj*

Sinaloa (ˌsiːnə'ləʊə, ˌsɪn-; *Spanish* sina'loa) *n* a state of W Mexico. Capital: Culiacán. Pop: 2 534 835 (2000). Area: 58 092 sq km (22 425 sq miles)

sinanthropus (sɪn'ænθrəpəs) *n* a primitive apelike man of the genus *Sinanthropus*, now considered a subspecies of *Homo erectus* [c20: from New Latin, from Late Latin *Sīnae* the Chinese + *-anthropus*, from Greek *anthrōpos* man]

Sinatra (sɪ'nɑːtrə) *n* **Francis Albert**, known as **Frank**. 1915–98, US popular singer and film actor. His recordings include "One for My Baby (and One More for the Road)" (1955) and "My Way" (1969)

sin bin *n* **1** *slang* (in ice hockey, rugby, etc) an area off the field of play where a player who has committed a foul can be sent to sit for a specified period **2** *Brit informal* a special unit on a separate site from a school that disruptive schoolchildren attend until they can be reintegrated into their normal classes

since (sɪns) *prep* **1** during or throughout the period of time after: *since May it has only rained once* ▷ *conj* (*subordinating*) **2** (sometimes preceded by *ever*) continuously from or starting from the time when **3** seeing that; because ▷ *adv* **4** since that time: *he left yesterday and I haven't seen him since* [Old English *sīththan*, literally: after that; related to Old High German *sīd* since, Latin *sērus* late]

● USAGE See at **ago**

sincere (sɪn'sɪə) *adj* **1** not hypocritical or deceitful; open; genuine: *a sincere person; sincere regret* **2** *archaic* pure; unadulterated; unmixed [c16: from Latin *sincērus*] > sin'cerely *adv* > sincerity (sɪn'sɛrɪtɪ) *or* sin'cereness *n*

sinciput ('sɪnsɪˌpʌt) *n, pl* **sinciputs** *or* **sincipita** (sɪn'sɪpɪtə) *anatomy* the forward upper part of the skull [c16: from

Latin: half a head, from SEMI- + *caput* head]
> sin'cipital *adj*

Sinclair (sɪŋ'kleə, 'sɪŋkleə) *n* 1 Sir **Clive** (**Marles**). born 1940, British electronics engineer, inventor, and entrepreneur, who produced such electronic goods as pocket calculators and some of the first home computers; however, the Sinclair C5, a small light electric vehicle for one person, proved a commercial failure 2 **Upton** (**Beall**). 1878–1968, US novelist, whose *The Jungle* (1906) exposed the working and sanitary conditions of the Chicago meat-packing industry and prompted the passage of food inspection laws

Sind (sɪnd) *n* a province of SE Pakistan, mainly in the lower Indus valley: formerly a province of British India; became a province of Pakistan in 1947; divided in 1955 between Hyderabad and Khairpur; reunited as a province in 1970. Capital: Karachi. Pop: 34 240 000 (2003 est). Area: 140 914 sq km (54 407 sq miles)

sine¹ (saɪn) *n* (of an angle) a trigonometric function that in a right-angled triangle is the ratio of the length of the opposite side to that of the hypotenuse [C16: from Latin *sinus* a bend; in New Latin, *sinus* was mistaken as a translation of Arabic *jība* sine (from Sanskrit *jīva*, literally: bowstring) because of confusion with Arabic *jaib* curve]

sine² ('saɪnɪ) *prep* (esp in Latin phrases or legal terms) lacking; without

sinecure ('saɪnɪ,kjʊə) *n* 1 a paid office or post involving minimal duties 2 a Church benefice to which no spiritual or pastoral charge is attached [C17: from Medieval Latin phrase (*beneficium*) *sine cūrā* (benefice) without cure (of souls), from Latin *sine* without + *cūra* cure, care] > 'sine,curism *n* > 'sine,curist *n*

sine curve *n* a curve of the equation *y* = sin *x*. Also called: sinusoid

sine die Latin ('saɪnɪ 'daɪɪ) *adv, adj* without a day fixed [literally: without a day]

sine qua non Latin ('saɪnɪ kweɪ 'nɒn) *n* an essential condition or requirement [literally: without which not]

sinew ('sɪnjuː) *n* 1 *anatomy* another name for **tendon** 2 (*often plural*) a source of strength or power **b** a literary word for **muscle** [Old English *sionu*; related to Old Norse *sin*, Old Saxon *sinewa*, Old High German *senawa* sinew, Lettish *pasainis* string] > 'sinewless *adj*

sine wave *n* any oscillation, such as a sound wave or alternating current, whose waveform is that of a sine curve

sinewy ('sɪnjuɪ) *adj* 1 consisting of or resembling a tendon or tendons 2 muscular; brawny 3 (esp of language, style, etc) vigorous; forceful 4 (of meat, etc) tough; stringy > 'sinewiness *n*

sinfonia (,sɪnfə'nɪə) *n, pl* -nie (-'niːeɪ) 1 another word for **symphony** (sense 2) 2 (*capital when part of a name*) a symphony orchestra [Italian]

sinfonietta (,sɪnfən'jetə, -fəʊn-) *n* 1 a short or light symphony 2 (*capital when part of name*) a small symphony orchestra [Italian: a little symphony, from SINFONIA]

sinful ('sɪnfʊl) *adj* 1 having committed or tending to commit sin: *a sinful person* 2 characterized by or being a sin: *a sinful act* > 'sinfully *adv* > 'sinfulness *n*

sing (sɪŋ) *vb* sings, singing, sang, sung 1 to produce or articulate (sounds, words, a song, etc) with definite and usually specific musical intonation 2 (when *intr*, often foll by *to*) to perform (a song) to the accompaniment (of): *to sing to a guitar* 3 (*intr*; foll by *of*) to tell a story or tale in song (about): *I sing of a maiden* 4 (*intr*) to perform songs for a living, as a professional singer 5 (*intr*) (esp of certain birds and insects) to utter calls or sounds reminiscent of music 6 (when *intr*, usually foll by *of*) to tell (something) or give praise (to someone), esp in verse: *the poet who sings of the Trojan dead* 7 (*intr*) to make a whining, ringing, or whistling sound: *the kettle is singing; the arrow sang past his ear* 8 (*intr*) (of the ears) to experience a continuous ringing or humming sound 9 (*tr*) to bring to a given state by singing: *to sing a child to sleep* 10 (*intr*) *slang, chiefly US* to confess or act as an informer ▷ *n* 11 *informal* an act or performance of singing ▷ See also **sing out** [Old English *singan*; related to Old Norse *syngja* to sing, Gothic *siggwan*, Old High German *singan*] > 'singable

adj > 'singing *adj, n*
● USAGE See at **ring²**

sing. *abbreviation* singular

Singapore (,sɪŋə'pɔː, ,sɪŋgə-) *n* 1 a republic in SE Asia, occupying one main island and over 50 small islands at the S end of the Malay Peninsula: established as a British trading post in 1819 and became part of the Straits Settlements in 1826; occupied by the Japanese (1942–45); a British colony from 1946, becoming self-governing in 1959; part of the Federation of Malaysia from 1963 to 1965, when it became an independent republic (within the Commonwealth). Official languages: Chinese, Malay, English, and Tamil. Religion: Buddhist, Taoist, traditional beliefs, and Muslim. Currency: Singapore dollar. Capital: Singapore. Pop: 4 315 000 (2004 est). Area: now over 700 sq km (270 sq miles), increased in recent years as a result of land reclamation schemes 2 the capital of the republic of Singapore: a major international port; administratively not treated as a city > ,Singa'porean *adj, n*

singe (sɪndʒ) *vb* singes, singeing, singed 1 to burn or be burnt superficially; scorch: *to singe one's clothes* 2 (*tr*) to burn the ends of (hair, etc) 3 (*tr*) to expose (a carcass) to flame to remove bristles or hair ▷ *n* 4 a superficial burn [Old English *sengan*; related to Middle High German *sengen* to singe, Dutch *sengel* spark, Norwegian *sengla* to smell of burning, Swedish *sjängla* to singe, Icelandic *sāngr*]

singer ('sɪŋə) *n* 1 a person who sings, esp one who earns a living by singing 2 a singing bird

Singer ('sɪŋə) *n* 1 **Isaac Bashevis**. 1904–91, US writer of Yiddish novels and short stories; born in Poland. His works include *Satan in Goray* (1935), *The Family Moscat* (1950), the autobiographical *In my Father's Court* (1966), and *The King of the Fields* (1989): Nobel prize for literature 1978 2 **Isaac Merrit**. 1811–75, US inventor, who originated and developed an improved chain-stitch sewing machine (1852)

Singh (sɪŋ) *n* a title assumed by a Sikh when he becomes a full member of the community [from Hindi, from Sanskrit *sinhá* a lion]

Singhalese (,sɪŋgə'liːz) *n, pl* -leses or -lese 1 a variant spelling of **Sinhalese** ▷ *adj* 2 a variant spelling of **Sinhalese**

singing telegram *n* a greetings service in which a person is employed to present greetings by singing to the person celebrating

single ('sɪŋgªl) *adj* (*usually prenominal*) 1 existing alone; solitary: *upon the hill stood a single tower* 2 distinct from other things; unique or individual 3 composed of one part 4 designed for one user: *a single room; a single bed* 5 (*also postpositive*) unmarried 6 connected with the condition of being unmarried: *he led a single life* 7 (esp of combat) involving two individuals; one against one 8 even one: *there wasn't a single person on the beach* 9 (of a flower) having only one set or whorl of petals 10 determined; single-minded: *a single devotion to duty* 11 *rare* honest or sincere; genuine ▷ *n* 12 something forming one individual unit 13 an unmarried person 14 a gramophone record, CD, or cassette with a short recording, usually of pop music, on it 15 *cricket* a hit from which one run is scored 16 **a** *Brit* a pound note **b** *US & Canadian* a dollar note 17 See **single ticket** ▷ *vb* 18 (*tr*; usually foll by *out*) to select from a group of people or things; distinguish by separation: *he singled him out for special mention* ▷ See also **singles** [C14: from Old French *sengle*, from Latin *singulus* individual] > 'singleness *n*

single-acting *adj* (of a reciprocating engine or pump) having a piston or pistons that are pressurized on one side only

single-breasted *adj* (of a garment) having the fronts overlapping only slightly and with one row of fastenings

single cream *n* cream having a low fat content that does not thicken with beating

single-decker *n* *Brit informal* a bus with only one passenger deck

single-end *n* *Scot dialect* accommodation consisting of a single room

single entry n **a** a simple book-keeping system in which transactions are entered in one account only **b** (as modifier): a single-entry account

single file n a line of persons, animals, or things ranged one behind the other, either stationary or moving

single-foot n **1** a rapid showy gait of a horse in which each foot strikes the ground separately, as in a walk ▷ vb **2** to move or cause to move at this gait

single-handed adj, adv **1** unaided or working alone: a single-handed crossing of the Atlantic **2** having or operated by one hand or one person only > ,single-'handedly adv > ,single-'handedness n

single-lens reflex n See **reflex camera**

single-minded adj having but one aim or purpose; dedicated > ,single-'mindedly adv > ,single-'mindedness n

single parent n **a** a person who has a dependent child or dependent children and who is widowed, divorced, or unmarried **b** (as modifier): a single-parent family Also called (NZ): solo parent

singles ('sɪŋɡ³lz) pl n tennis, badminton a match played with one person on each side

singles bar n a bar or club that is a social meeting place for single people

single-sex adj (of schools, etc) admitting members of one sex only; not coeducational

single sideband transmission n a method of transmitting radio waves in which either the upper or the lower sideband is transmitted, the carrier being either wholly or partially suppressed. This reduces the required bandwidth and improves the signal-to-noise ratio

singlestick ('sɪŋɡ³l,stɪk) n **1** a wooden stick used instead of a sword for fencing **2** fencing with such a stick **3** any short heavy stick

singlet ('sɪŋɡlɪt) n **1** Austral a similar sleeveless garment worn as outerwear **2** chiefly Brit a garment worn with shorts by athletes, boxers, etc [c18: from SINGLE, on the model of doublet]

single ticket n Brit a ticket entitling a passenger to travel only to his destination, without returning

singleton ('sɪŋɡ³ltən) n **1** bridge an original holding of one card only in a suit **2** a single object, individual, etc, separated or distinguished from a pair or group **3** maths a set containing only one member **4** a person who is neither married nor in a relationship [c19: from SINGLE, on the model of SIMPLETON]

singletrack ('sɪŋɡ³l,træk) n an off-road trail used by cyclists, wide enough for only one bicycle at a time

single-track adj **1** (of a railway) having only a single pair of lines, so that trains can travel in only one direction at a time **2** (of a road) only wide enough for one vehicle

Single Transferable Vote n (modifier) of or relating to a system of voting in which voters list the candidates in order of preference. Any candidate achieving a predetermined proportion of the votes in a constituency is elected. Votes exceeding this amount and those cast for the bottom candidate are redistributed according to the stated preferences. Redistribution continues until all the seats are filled. Abbreviation: STV See **proportional representation**

singletree ('sɪŋɡ³l,tri:) n a variant, esp US and Austral., of **swingletree**

singly ('sɪŋlɪ) adv **1** one at a time; one by one **2** apart from others; separately; alone

sing out vb (tr, adverb) to call out in a loud voice; shout

singsong ('sɪŋ,sɒŋ) n **1** an accent, metre, or intonation that is characterized by an alternately rising and falling rhythm, as in a person's voice, piece of verse, etc **2** Brit an informal session of singing, esp of popular or traditional songs ▷ adj **3** having a regular or monotonous rising and falling rhythm: a singsong accent

singular ('sɪŋɡjʊlə) adj **1** remarkable; exceptional; extraordinary: a singular feat **2** unusual; odd: a singular character **3** unique **4** denoting a word or an inflected form of a word indicating that not more than one referent is being referred to or described **5** logic of or referring to a specific thing or person as opposed to something general ▷ n **6** grammar **a** the singular number **b** a singular form of a word [c14: from Latin singulāris

SINGLE] > 'singularly adv

singularity (,sɪŋɡjʊ'lærɪtɪ) n, pl -ties **1** the state, fact, or quality of being singular **2** something distinguishing a person or thing from others **3** something remarkable or unusual **4** maths a point at which a function is not differentiable although it is differentiable in a neighbourhood of that point **5** astronomy a hypothetical point in space-time at which matter is infinitely compressed to infinitesimal volume

singularize or **singularise** ('sɪŋɡjʊlə,raɪz) vb (tr) **1** to make (a word, etc) singular **2** to make conspicuous > ,singulari'zation or ,singulari'sation n

singultus (sɪŋ'ɡʌltəs) n a technical name for **hiccup** [c18: from Latin, literally: a sob]

sinh (ʃaɪn, sɪnʃ) n hyperbolic sine; a hyperbolic function, sinh $z = \frac{1}{2}(e^z - e^{-z})$, related to sine by the expression sinh iz = i sin z, where i = √–1 [c20: from SIN(E)^1 + H(YPERBOLIC)]

Sinhailien ('ʃɪn'haɪ'ljɛn) n a variant transliteration of the alternative name for **Lianyungang**

Sinhalese (,sɪnhə'li:z) or **Singhalese** n **1** pl -leses or -lese a member of a people living chiefly in Sri Lanka, where they constitute the majority of the population **2** the language of this people, belonging to the Indic branch of the Indo-European family: the official language of Sri Lanka. It is written in a script of Indian origin ▷ adj **3** of or relating to this people or their language

Sining ('ʃiː'nɪŋ) n variant transliteration of the Chinese name for **Xining**

sinister ('sɪnɪstə) adj **1** threatening or suggesting evil or harm; ominous: a sinister glance **2** evil or treacherous, esp in a mysterious way **3** (usually postpositive) heraldry of, on, or starting from the left side from the bearer's point of view and therefore on the spectator's right **4** archaic located on the left side [c15: from Latin sinister on the left-hand side, considered by Roman augurs to be the unlucky one] > 'sinisterly adv > 'sinisterness n

sinistral ('sɪnɪstrəl) adj **1** of, relating to, or located on the left side, esp the left side of the body **2** a technical term for **left-handed** **3** (of the shells of certain gastropod molluscs) coiling in a clockwise direction from the apex [c15 (in the obsolete sense: adverse, evil); c19 (in current senses): from Medieval Latin sinistrālis. See SINISTER] > 'sinistrally adv

sinistrorse (,sɪnɪ'strɔ:s, ,sɪnɪ'strɔ:s) adj (of some climbing plants) growing upwards in a spiral from right to left, or clockwise [c19: from Latin sinistrōrsus turned towards the left, from sinister on the left + vertere to turn] > ,sinis'trorsal adj

Sinitic (sɪ'nɪtɪk) n **1** a branch of the Sino-Tibetan family of languages, consisting of the various languages or dialects of Chinese ▷ adj **2** belonging or relating to this group of languages

sink (sɪŋk) vb sinks, sinking, sank, sunk or sunken **1** to descend or cause to descend, esp beneath the surface of a liquid or soft substance **2** (intr) to appear to move down towards or descend below the horizon **3** (intr) to slope downwards; dip **4** (intr; often foll by in or into) to pass into or gradually enter a specified lower state or condition: to sink into apathy **5** to make or become lower in volume, pitch, etc **6** (intr) to become weaker in health, strength, etc **7** (intr) to seep or penetrate **8** (tr) to dig, cut, drill, bore, or excavate (a hole, shaft, etc) **9** (tr) to drive into the ground: to sink a stake **10** (tr; usually foll by in or into) **a** to invest (money) **b** to lose (money) in an unwise or unfortunate investment **11** (tr) to pay (a debt) **12** (intr) to become hollow; cave in: his cheeks had sunk during his illness **13** (tr) to hit, throw, or propel (a ball) into a hole, basket, pocket, etc: he sank a 15-foot putt **14** (tr) Brit informal to drink up quickly: he sank three pints in half an hour **15** sink or swim to take risks where the alternatives are loss and failure or security and success ▷ n **16** a fixed basin, esp in a kitchen, made of stone, earthenware, metal, etc, used for washing **17** a place of vice or corruption **18** an area of ground below that of the surrounding land, where water collects **19** physics a device or part of a system at which energy is removed from the system: a heat sink ▷ adj **20** informal (of a housing estate or school) deprived or having low standards of achievement [Old English *sincan*; related to Old Norse *sökkva* to sink, Gothic *siggan*, Old High German *sincan*, Swedish *sjunka*] > 'sinkable *adj*

sinker ('sɪŋkə) *n* 1 a weight attached to a fishing line, net, etc, to cause it to sink in water 2 a person who sinks shafts, etc

sinkhole ('sɪŋk,həʊl) *n* 1 a depression in the ground surface, esp in limestone, where a surface stream disappears underground. Also called (esp Brit): **swallow hole** 2 a place into which foul matter runs

Sinkiang-Uighur Autonomous Region ('sɪn'kjæŋ 'wiːɡʊə) *n* a variant transliteration of the Chinese name for the **Xinjiang Uygur Autonomous Region**

sink in *vb* (*intr, adverb*) to enter or penetrate the mind: *eventually the news sank in*

sinking ('sɪŋkɪŋ) *n* **a** a feeling in the stomach caused by hunger or uneasiness **b** (*as modifier*): *a sinking feeling*

sinking fund *n* a fund accumulated out of a business enterprise's earnings or a government's revenue and invested to repay a long-term debt or meet a depreciation charge

sinless ('sɪnlɪs) *adj* free from sin or guilt; innocent; pure > 'sinlessly *adv* > 'sinlessness *n*

Sinn Féin ('ʃɪn 'feːn) *n* an Irish republican political movement founded about 1905 and linked to the revolutionary Irish Republican Army: divided into a Provisional and an Official movement since a similar split in the IRA in late 1969 [c20: from Irish: we ourselves] > Sinn Féiner *n* > Sinn Féinism *n*

Sino- combining form Chinese: *Sino-Tibetan*; *Sinology* [from French, from Late Latin *Sīnae* the Chinese, from Late Greek *Sinai*, from Arabic *Sīn* China, probably from Chinese *Ch'in*]

Sinology (saɪˈnɒlədʒɪ, sɪ-) *n* the study of Chinese history, language, culture, etc > **Sinological** (,saɪnəˈlɒdʒɪkᵊl, ,sɪn-) *adj* > 'Sinologist *n* > Sinologue ('saɪnə,lɒɡ) *n*

Sino-Tibetan ('saɪnəʊ-) *n* 1 a family of languages that includes most of the languages of China, as well as Tibetan, Burmese, and possibly Thai. Their most noticeable phonological characteristic is the phonemic use of tones ▷ *adj* 2 belonging or relating to this family of languages

sinsemilla (,sɪnsəˈmiːljə) *n* 1 a type of marijuana with a very high narcotic content 2 the plant from which it is obtained [c20: from American Spanish, literally: without seed]

sinter ('sɪntə) *n* 1 a whitish porous incrustation, usually consisting of silica, that is deposited from hot springs 2 the product of a sintering process ▷ *vb* 3 (*tr*) to form large particles, lumps, or masses from (metal powders or powdery ores) by heating or pressure or both [c18: German: CINDER]

Sint Maarten (sɪnt ˈmaːrtən) *n* the Dutch name for **Saint Martin**

Sintra ('sɪntrə) *n* a town in central Portugal, near Lisbon, in the Sintra mountains: noted for its castles and palaces and the beauty of its setting: tourism. Former name: Cintra

sinuate ('sɪnjʊɪt, -,eɪt) *adj* 1 Also called: **sinuous** (of leaves) having a strongly waved margin 2 another word for **sinuous** [c17: from Latin *sinuātus* curved; see SINUS, -ATE¹] > 'sinuately *adv*

Sinŭiju (sɪ,nuːɪˈdʒuː) *n* a port in North Korea, on the Yalu River opposite Dandong, China: developed by the Japanese during their occupation (1910–45); industrial centre. Pop: 349 000 (2005 est)

sinuous ('sɪnjʊəs) *adj* 1 full of turns or curves; intricate 2 devious; not straightforward 3 supple; lithe [c16: from Latin *sinuōsus* winding, from *sinus* a curve] > 'sinuously *adv* > sinuosity (,sɪnjʊˈɒsɪtɪ) *or* (*less commonly*) sinuation *n*,

sinus ('saɪnəs) *n, pl* -nuses 1 anatomy **a** any bodily cavity or hollow space **b** a large channel for venous blood, esp between the brain and the skull **c** any of the air cavities in the cranial bones 2 pathol a passage leading to a cavity containing pus [c16: from Latin: a curve, bay]

sinusitis (,saɪnəˈsaɪtɪs) *n* inflammation of the membrane lining a sinus, esp a nasal sinus

sinusoid ('saɪnə,sɔɪd) *n* 1 any of the irregular terminal blood vessels that replace capillaries in certain organs,

such as the liver, heart, spleen, and pancreas 2 another name for **sine curve** ▷ *adj* 3 resembling a sinus [c19: from French *sinusoïde*. See SINUS, -OID]

sinusoidal projection *n* an equal-area map projection on which all parallels are straight lines and all except the prime meridian are sine curves, often used to show tropical latitudes

Sion *n* 1 (*French* sjɔ̃) a town in SW Switzerland, capital of Valais canton, on the River Rhône. Pop: 27 171 (2000) 2 ('saɪən) a variant of **Zion**

Siouan ('suːən) *n* a family of North American Indian languages including Sioux, probably related to Iroquoian

Sioux (suː) *n* 1 *pl* Sioux (suː, suːz) a member of a group of North American Indian peoples formerly ranging over a wide area of the Plains from Lake Michigan to the Rocky Mountains 2 any of the Siouan languages [from French, shortened from *Nadowessioux*, from Chippewa *Nadoweisiw*]

sip (sɪp) *vb* sips, sipping, sipped 1 to drink (a liquid) by taking small mouthfuls; drink gingerly or delicately ▷ *n* 2 a small quantity of a liquid taken into the mouth and swallowed 3 an act of sipping [c14: probably from Low German *sippen*] > 'sipper *n*

siphon *or* **syphon** ('saɪfᵊn) *n* 1 a tube placed with one end at a certain level in a vessel of liquid and the other end outside the vessel below this level, so that atmospheric pressure forces the liquid through the tube and out of the vessel 2 See **soda siphon** 3 zoology any of various tubular organs in different aquatic animals, such as molluscs and elasmobranch fishes, through which a fluid, esp water, passes ▷ *vb* 4 (*often foll by off*) to pass or draw off through or as if through a siphon [c17: from Latin *siphō*, from Greek *siphōn* siphon] > 'siphonal, *or* siphonic (saɪˈfɒnɪk) *adj*

siphon bottle *n* another name (esp US) for **soda siphon**

siphonophore ('saɪfənə,fɔː, saɪˈfɒnə-) *n* any marine colonial hydrozoan of the order *Siphonophora*, including the Portuguese man-of-war [c19: from New Latin *siphonophora*, from Greek *siphōnophoros* tube-bearing]

Siple ('saɪpᵊl) *n* **Mount Siple** a mountain in Antarctica, on the coast of Byrd Land. Height: 3100 m (10 171 ft)

sippet ('sɪpɪt) *n* a small piece of something, esp a piece of toast or fried bread eaten with soup or gravy [c16: used as diminutive of SOP; see -ET]

sippy cup *n* US & Canadian a plastic cup for young children which has a tight-fitting lid with a perforated spout

Siqueiros (*Spanish* siˈkeɪrɒs) *n* **David Alfaro** (daˈβið alˈfaro). 1896–1974, Mexican painter, noted for his murals expressing a revolutionary message

sir (sɜː) *n* 1 a formal or polite term of address for a man 2 archaic a gentleman of high social status [c13: variant of SIRE]

Sir (sɜː) *n* 1 a title of honour placed before the name of a knight or baronet: *Sir Walter Raleigh* 2 archaic a title placed before the name of a figure from ancient history

Siracusa (sira'kuːza) *n* the Italian name for **Syracuse**

Siraj-ud-daula (sɪˈrɑːdʒʊdˈdaʊlə) *n* ?1728–57, Indian leader who became the Great Mogul's deputy in Bengal (1756); opponent of English colonization. He captured Calcutta (1756) from the English and many of his prisoners suffocated in a crowded room that became known as the Black Hole of Calcutta. He was defeated (1757) by a group of Indian nobles in alliance with Robert Clive

sirdar ('sɜːdɑː) *n* 1 a general or military leader in Pakistan and India 2 (formerly) the title of the British commander in chief of the Egyptian Army 3 a variant spelling of **sardar** [from Hindi *sardār*, from Persian, from *sar* head + *dār* possession]

sire (saɪə) *n* 1 a male parent, esp of a horse or other domestic animal 2 a respectful term of address, now used only in addressing a male monarch ▷ *vb* 3 (*tr*) (esp of a domestic animal) to father; beget [c13: from Old French, from Latin *senior* an elder, from *senex* an old man]

siren ('saɪərən) *n* 1 a device for emitting a loud wailing sound, esp as a warning or signal, typically consisting of a rotating perforated metal drum through which air or steam is passed under pressure **2** (*sometimes capital*) *Greek myth* one of several sea nymphs whose seductive singing was believed to lure sailors to destruction on the rocks the nymphs inhabited **3** a woman considered to be dangerously alluring or seductive **4** any aquatic eel-like salamander of the North American family *Sirenidae*, having external gills, no hind limbs, and reduced forelimbs [C14: from Old French *sereine*, from Latin *sīrēn*, from Greek *seirēn*]

sirenian (saɪˈriːnɪən) *adj* **1** of, relating to, or belonging to the *Sirenia*, an order of aquatic herbivorous placental mammals having forelimbs modified as paddles, no hind limbs, and a horizontally flattened tail: contains only the dugong and manatees ▷ *n* **2** any animal belonging to the order *Sirenia*; a sea cow

Siret (sɪˈrɛt) *n* a river in SE Europe, rising in Ukraine and flowing southeast through E Romania to the Danube. Length: about 450 km (280 miles)

Sirius (ˈsɪrɪəs) *n* the brightest star in the sky after the sun, lying in the constellation Canis Major. It is a binary star whose companion, **Sirius B**, is a very faint white dwarf. Distance: 8.6 light years. Also called: **the Dog Star** [C14: via Latin from Greek *Seirios*, of obscure origin]

sirloin (ˈsɜːˌlɔɪn) *n* a prime cut of beef from the loin, esp the upper part [C16 *surloyn*, from Old French *surlonge*, from *sur* above + *longe*, from *loigne* LOIN]

sirocco (sɪˈrɒkəʊ) *n*, *pl* **-cos** a hot oppressive and often dusty wind usually occurring in spring, beginning in N Africa and reaching S Europe [C17: from Italian, from Arabic *sharq* east wind]

sironize *or* **sironise** (ˈsaɪrəˌnaɪz) *vb* (*tr*) *Austral* to treat (a woollen fabric) chemically to prevent it wrinkling after being washed [C20: from (C)SIRO + *-n-* + *-IZE*]

siroset (ˈsaɪrəʊˌsɛt) *adj Austral* of or relating to the chemical treatment of woollen fabrics to give a permanent-press effect, or a garment so treated

sirrah (ˈsɪrə) *n archaic* a contemptuous term used in addressing a man or boy [C16: probably variant of SIRE]

sirree (səˈriː) *interj* (*sometimes capital*) *US informal* an emphatic exclamation used with *yes* or *no*

sirup (ˈsɪrəp) *n US* a less common spelling of **syrup**

sis[1] (sɪs) *n informal* short for **sister**

sis[2] *or* **sies** (sɪs, siːs) *interj South African informal* an exclamation of disgust [Afrikaans, possibly from Khoi]

SIS *abbreviation* Also called: **MI6** (in Britain) Secret Intelligence Service

sisal (ˈsaɪs[ə]l) *n* **1** a Mexican agave plant, *Agave sisalana*, cultivated for its large fleshy leaves, which yield a stiff fibre used for making rope **2** the fibre of this plant ▷ Also called: **sisal hemp** [C19: from Mexican Spanish, named after *Sisal*, a port in Yucatán, Mexico]

Sisera (ˈsɪsərə) *n* a defeated leader of the Canaanites, who was assassinated by Jael (Judges 4:17–21)

siskin (ˈsɪskɪn) *n* **1** a yellow-and-black Eurasian finch, *Carduelis spinus* **2** pine siskin a North American finch, *Spinus pinus*, having a streaked yellowish-brown plumage [C16: from Middle Dutch *sīseken*, from Middle Low German *sīsek*; related to Czech *čížek*, Russian *chizh*]

Sisley (ˈsɪslɪ; *French* sislɛ) *n* **Alfred** (alfrɛd). 1839–99, French painter, esp of landscapes; one of the originators of impressionism

Sismondi (sɪsˈmɒndɪ; *French* sismɔ̃di) *n* **Jean Charles Léonard Simonde de** (ʒɑ̃ ʃarl leɔnar simɔ̃d də). 1773–1842, Swiss historian and economist. His *Histoire des républiques italiennes du moyen âge* (1807–18) contributed to the movement for Italian unification

sissy *or* **cissy** (ˈsɪsɪ) *n*, *pl* **-sies 1** an effeminate, weak, or cowardly boy or man ▷ *adj* **2** effeminate, weak, or cowardly

sister (ˈsɪstə) *n* **1** a female person having the same parents as another person **2** a female person who belongs to the same group, trade union, etc, as another or others **3** a senior nurse **4** *chiefly RC Church* a nun or a title given to a nun **5** a woman fellow member of a Church or religious body **6** (*modifier*) belonging to the same class, fleet, etc, as another or others: *a sister ship* **7** (*modifier*) *biology* denoting any of the cells or cell components formed by division of a parent cell or cell component: *sister nuclei* [Old English *sweostor*; related to

Old Norse *systir*, Old High German *swester*, Gothic *swistar*]

sisterhood (ˈsɪstəˌhʊd) *n* **1** the state of being related as a sister or sisters **2** a religious body or society of sisters, esp a community, order, or congregation of nuns

sister-in-law *n*, *pl* **sisters-in-law 1** the sister of one's husband or wife **2** the wife of one's brother

sisterly (ˈsɪstəlɪ) *adj* of, resembling, or suitable to a sister, esp in showing kindness and affection ▷ **sisterliness** *n*

Sistine Chapel (ˈsɪstaɪn, -tiːn) *n* the chapel of the pope in the Vatican at Rome, built for Sixtus IV and decorated with frescoes by Michelangelo and others [Sistine, from Italian *Sistino* relating to *Sisto* Sixtus (Pope Sixtus IV)]

sistrum (ˈsɪstrəm) *n*, *pl* **-tra** (-trə) a musical instrument of ancient Egypt consisting of a metal rattle [C14: via Latin from Greek *seistron*, from *seiein* to shake]

Sisyphean (ˌsɪsɪˈfiːən) *adj* **1** relating to Sisyphus **2** actually or seemingly endless and futile

Sisyphus (ˈsɪsɪfəs) *n Greek myth* a king of Corinth, punished in Hades for his misdeeds by eternally having to roll a heavy stone up a hill: every time he approached the top, the stone escaped his grasp and rolled to the bottom

sit (sɪt) *vb* **sits**, **sitting**, **sat** (*mainly intr*) **1** (*also tr*; when intr, often foll by *down*, *in*, or *on*) to adopt or rest in a posture in which the body is supported on the buttocks and thighs and the torso is more or less upright: *to sit on a chair*; *sit a horse* **2** (*tr*) to cause to adopt such a posture **3** (of an animal) to adopt or rest in a posture with the hindquarters lowered to the ground **4** (of a bird) to perch or roost **5** (of a hen or other bird) to cover eggs to hatch them; brood **6** to be situated or located **7** (of the wind) to blow from the direction specified **8** to adopt and maintain a posture for one's portrait to be painted, etc **9** to occupy or be entitled to a seat in some official capacity, as a judge, elected representative, etc **10** (of a deliberative body) to be convened or in session **11** to remain inactive or unused: *his car sat in the garage for a year* **12** (of a garment) to fit or hang as specified: *that dress sits well on you* **13** to weigh, rest, or lie as specified: *greatness sits easily on him* **14** (*tr*) *chiefly Brit* to take (an examination): *he's sitting his bar finals* **15** (usually foll by *for*) *chiefly Brit* to be a candidate (for a qualification): *he's sitting for a BA* **16** (*intr*; in combination) to look after a specified person or thing for someone else: *granny-sit* **17** (*tr*) to have seating capacity for **18 sit tight a** to wait patiently; bide one's time **b** to maintain one's position, stand, or opinion firmly ▷ See also **sit back**, **sit down**, etc [Old English *sittan*; related to Old Norse *sitja*, Gothic *sitan*, Old High German *sizzen*, Latin *sedēre* to sit, Sanskrit *sīdati* he sits]

SIT *abbreviation text messaging* stay in touch

sitar (sɪˈtɑː, ˈsɪtɑː) *n* a stringed musical instrument, esp of India, having a long neck, a rounded body, and movable frets. The main strings, three to seven in number, overlie other sympathetic strings, the tuning depending on the raga being performed [from Hindi *sitār*, literally: three-stringed] ▷ **si'tarist** *n*

sit back *vb* (*intr*, *adverb*) to relax, as when action should be taken: *many people just sit back and ignore the problems of today*

sitcom (ˈsɪtˌkɒm) *n* an informal term for **situation comedy**

sit down *vb* (*adverb*) **1** to adopt or cause (oneself or another) to adopt a sitting posture **2** (*intr*; foll by *under*) to suffer (insults, etc) without protests or resistance ▷ *n* **sit-down 3** a form of civil disobedience in which demonstrators sit down in a public place as a protest or to draw attention to a cause **4** See **sit-down strike** ▷ *adj* **sit-down 5** (of a meal, etc) eaten while sitting down at a table

sit-down strike *n* a strike in which workers refuse to leave their place of employment until a settlement is reached

site (saɪt) *n* **1 a** the piece of land where something was, is, or is intended to be located: *a building site*; *archaeological site* **b** (*as modifier*): *site office* **2** an internet location where information relating to a specific subject or group of subjects can be accessed ▷ *vb* **3** (*tr*) to locate, place, or install (something) in a specific place [c14: from Latin *situs* situation, from *sinere* to be placed]

site map *n computing* a plan of a website showing its contents and where it can be viewed

sith (sɪθ) *adv, conj, prep* an archaic word for **since** [Old English *siththa*, short for *siththan* SINCE]

sit-in *n* **1** a form of civil disobedience in which demonstrators occupy seats in a public place and refuse to move as a protest **2** another term for **sit-down strike** ▷ *vb* **sit in** (*intr, adverb*) **3** (often foll by *for*) to deputize (for) **4** (foll by *on*) to take part (in) as a visitor or guest **5** to organize or take part in a sit-in

Sitka (ˈsɪtkə) *n* a town in SE Alaska, in the Alexander Archipelago on W Baranof Island: capital of Russian America (1804–67) and of Alaska (1867–1906). Pop: 8876 (2003 est)

sitkamer (ˈsɪtˌkɑːmə) *n South African* a sitting room; lounge [from Afrikaans *sit* sitting + *kamer* room]

sitka spruce (ˈsɪtkə) *n* a tall North American spruce tree, *Picea sitchensis*, having yellowish-green needle-like leaves: yields valuable timber [c19: from SITKA]

sit on *vb* (*intr, preposition*) **1** to be a member of (a committee, etc) **2** *informal* to suppress **3** *informal* to check or rebuke

sit out *vb* (*adverb*) **1** (*tr*) to endure to the end: *I sat out the play although it was terrible* **2** (*tr*) to remain seated throughout (a dance, etc)

Sitsang (ˈsiːˈtsæŋ) *n* a Chinese name for **Tibet**

sitter (ˈsɪtə) *n* **1** a person or animal that sits **2** a person who is posing for his or her portrait to be painted, carved, etc **3** a broody hen or other bird that is sitting on its eggs to hatch them **4** (*in combination*) a person who looks after a specified person or thing for someone else: *flat-sitter* **5** short for **baby-sitter** **6** anyone, other than the medium, taking part in a seance **7** anything that is extremely easy, such as an easy catch in cricket

Sitter (ˈsɪtə) *n* **Willem de** (ˈwɪləm də). 1872–1934, Dutch astronomer, who calculated the size of the universe and conceived of it as expanding

sitting (ˈsɪtɪŋ) *n* **1** a continuous period of being seated: *I read his novel at one sitting* **2** such a period in a restaurant, canteen, etc, where space and other facilities are limited: *dinner will be served in two sittings* **3** the act or period of posing for one's portrait to be painted, carved, etc **4** a meeting, esp of an official body, to conduct business **5** the incubation period of a bird's eggs during which the mother sits on them to keep them warm ▷ *adj* **6** in office: *a sitting Member of Parliament* **7** seated: *in a sitting position*

Sitting Bull *n* Indian name *Tatanka Yotanka*. ?1831–90, American Indian chief of the Teton Dakota Sioux. Resisting White encroachment on his people's hunting grounds, he led the Sioux tribes against the US Army in the Sioux War (1876–77) in which Custer was killed. The hunger of the Sioux, whose food came from the diminishing buffalo, forced his surrender (1881). He was killed during renewed strife

sitting room *n* a room in a private house or flat used for relaxation and entertainment of guests

sitting target *n* a person or thing in a defenceless or vulnerable position. Also called: **sitting duck**

sitting tenant *n* a tenant occupying a house, flat, etc

situate (ˈsɪtjʊˌeɪt) *vb* **1** (*tr; often passive*) to allot a site to; place; locate ▷ *adj* **2** (now used esp in legal contexts) situated [c16: from Late Latin *situāre* to position, from Latin *situs* a SITE]

situation (ˌsɪtjʊˈeɪʃən) *n* **1** physical placement, esp with regard to the surroundings **2 a** state of affairs; combination of circumstances **b** a complex or critical state of affairs in a novel, play, etc **3** social or financial status, position, or circumstances **4** a position of employment; post > ˌsitu'ational *adj*

● USAGE *Situation* is often used in contexts in which it is
● redundant or imprecise. Typical examples are: *the*
● *company is in a crisis situation* or *people in a job situation*. In
● the first example, *situation* does not add to the
● meaning and should be omitted. In the second
● example, it would be clearer and more concise to
● substitute a phrase such as *people at work*

situation comedy *n* (on television or radio) a comedy series involving the same characters in various day-to-day situations which are developed as separate stories for each episode. Also called: **sitcom**

sit up *vb* (*adverb*) **1** to raise (oneself or another) from a recumbent to an upright or alert sitting posture **2** (*intr*) to remain out of bed and awake, esp until a late hour **3** (*intr*) *informal* to become suddenly interested or alert: *devaluation of the dollar made the money market sit up* ▷ *n* **sit-up** **4** a physical exercise in which the body is brought into a sitting position from one lying on the back. Also: **trunk curl**

Sitwell (ˈsɪtwəl) *n* **1** Dame **Edith**. 1887–1964, English poet and critic, noted esp for her collection *Façade* (1922) **2** her brother, Sir **Osbert**. 1892–1969, English writer, best known for his five autobiographical books (1944–50) **3** his brother, Sir **Sacheverell** (səˈʃɛvərəl). 1897–1988, English poet and writer of books on art, architecture, music, and travel

sitz bath (sɪts, zɪts) *n* a bath in which the buttocks and hips are immersed in hot water, esp for therapeutic effects, as after perineal or pelvic surgery [half translation of German *Sitzbad*, from *Sitz* SEAT + *Bad* BATH¹]

SI unit *n* any of the units adopted for international use under the Système International d'Unités, now employed for all scientific and most technical purposes. There are seven fundamental units: the metre, kilogram, second, ampere, kelvin, candela, and mole; and two supplementary units: the radian and the steradian. All other units are derived by multiplication or division of these units without the use of numerical factors

Siva (ˈsiːvə, ˈsɪvə) *n Hinduism* the destroyer, one of the three chief divinities of the later Hindu pantheon, the other two being Brahma and Vishnu. Siva is also the god presiding over personal destinies [from Sanskrit *Śiva*, literally: the auspicious (one)] > ˈSiva,ism *n*

Sivaji (sɪˈvɑːʒi) *n* 1627–80, Indian king (1674–80), who led an uprising of Hindus against Muslim rule and founded the Masatha kingdom

Sivas (Turkish ˈsivas) *n* a city in central Turkey, at an altitude of 1347 m (4420 ft): one of the chief cities in Asia Minor in ancient times; scene of the national congress (1919) leading to the revolution that established modern Turkey. Pop: 266 000 (2005 est)

six (sɪks) *n* **1** the cardinal number that is the sum of five and one **2** a numeral, 6, VI, etc, representing this number **3** something representing, represented by, or consisting of six units, such as a playing card with six symbols on it **4** Also called: **six o'clock** six hours after noon or midnight **5** Also called: **sixer** *cricket* **a** a stroke in which the ball crosses the boundary without bouncing **b** the six runs scored for such a stroke **6** a division of a Brownie Guide or Cub Scout pack **7 at sixes and sevens a** in disagreement **b** in a state of confusion **8 knock someone for six** *informal* to upset or overwhelm someone completely; stun **9 six of one and half a dozen of the other** Also called: **six and two threes** a situation in which the alternatives are considered equivalent ▷ *determiner* **10 a** amounting to six: *six nations* **b** (as pronoun): *set the table for six* [Old English *siex*; related to Old Norse *sex*, Gothic *saihs*, Old High German *sehs*, Latin *sex*, Greek *hex*, Sanskrit *sastha*]

Six (French sis) *n* **Les Six** (le) a group of six young composers in France, who from about 1916 formed a temporary association as a result of interest in neoclassicism and in the music of Satie and the poetry of Cocteau. Its members were Darius Milhaud, Arthur Honegger, Francis Poulenc, Georges Auric, Louis Durey, and Germaine Tailleferre

Six Counties *pl n* the historic counties of Northern Ireland, which no longer have a local government function

sixer (ˈsɪksə) *n* a leader of a Brownie Guide or Cub Scout six

sixfold (ˈsɪksˌfəʊld) *adj* **1** equal to or having six times as many or as much **2** composed of six parts ▷ *adv* **3** by or up to six times as many or as much

sixmo (ˈsɪksməʊ) *n, pl* **-mos 1** Also called: **sexto** a book size resulting from folding a sheet of paper into six leaves or twelve pages, each one sixth the size of the sheet. Often written: 6mo, 6° **2** a book of this size

Six Nations *pl n* (in North America) the Indian confederacy of the Cayugas, Mohawks, Oneidas, Onondagas, Senecas, and Tuscaroras. Also called: **Iroquois** See also **Five Nations**

Six Nations Championship *n rugby union* the annual competition involving national sides representing England, France, Ireland, Italy, Scotland, and Wales. Until the admission of Italy in 2000, it was known as the Five Nations Championship

six-pack *n* **1** *informal* a package containing six units, esp six cans of beer **2** a set of highly developed abdominal muscles in a man

sixpence ('sɪkspəns) *n* a small British cupronickel coin with a face value of six pennies, worth 2½ (new) pence, not minted since 1970

six-pointer *n Informal* a football match between two teams in similar positions in the league table, considered as being worth six points as it not only gains the winning team three points but denies three points to the losing team

six-shooter *n US informal* a revolver with six chambers. Also called: **six-gun**

sixte (sɪkst) *n* the sixth of eight basic positions from which a parry or attack can be made in fencing [from French: (the) sixth (parrying position), from Latin *sextus* sixth]

sixteen ('sɪks'tiːn) *n* **1** the cardinal number that is the sum of ten and six **2** a numeral, 16, XVI, etc, representing this number **3** something represented by, representing, or consisting of 16 units ▷ *determiner* **4 a** amounting to sixteen: *sixteen tons* **b** (*as pronoun*): *sixteen are known to the police* [Old English *sextyne*] ▷ 'six'teenth *adj, n*

sixteenmo ('sɪks'tiːnməʊ) *n, pl* -mos a book size resulting from folding a sheet of paper into 16 leaves or 32 pages, each one sixteenth the size of the sheet Also called: **sextodecimo**. Often written: 16mo, 16°

sixteenth note *n US & Canadian music* a note having the time value of one-sixteenth of a semibreve. Also called (in certain other countries): **semiquaver**

sixth (sɪksθ) *adj* **1** (*usually prenominal*) a coming after the fifth and before the seventh in numbering or counting order, position, time, etc; being the ordinal number of *six*: often written 6th **b** (*as noun*): *the sixth to go* ▷ *n* **2 a** one of six equal or nearly equal parts of an object, quantity, measurement, etc **b** (*as modifier*): *a sixth part* **3** the fraction equal to one divided by six (1/6) **4** *music* **a** the interval between one note and another note six notes away from it counting inclusively along the diatonic scale **b** one of two notes constituting such an interval in relation to the other ▷ *adv* **5** Also called: **sixthly** after the fifth person, position, etc ▷ *sentence connector* **6** Also called: **sixthly** as the sixth point: linking what follows to the previous statements

sixth form *n* (in England and Wales) the most senior class in a secondary school to which pupils, usually above the legal leaving age, may proceed to take A levels, retake GCSEs, etc ▷ 'sixth-ˌformer *n*

sixth sense *n* any supposed sense or means of perception, such as intuition or clairvoyance, other than the five senses of sight, hearing, touch, taste, and smell

Sixtus IV ('sɪkstəs) *n* original name *Francesco della Rovere.* 1414–84, Italian ecclesiastic; pope (1471–84). Notorious for his nepotism and political intrigue, he was also a patron of the arts and commissioned the building (1473–81) of the Sistine Chapel

Sixtus V *n* original name *Felice Peretti.* 1520–90, Italian ecclesiastic; pope (1585–90). He is noted for vigorous administrative reforms that contributed to the Counter-Reformation

sixty ('sɪkstɪ) *n, pl* -ties **1** the cardinal number that is the product of ten and six **2** a numeral, 60, LX, etc, representing sixty **3** something represented by, representing, or consisting of 60 units ▷ *determiner* **4 a** amounting to sixty: *sixty soldiers* **b** (*as pronoun*): *sixty are dead* [Old English *sixtig*] ▷ 'sixtieth *adj, n*

sixty-fourmo (ˌsɪkstɪ'fɔːməʊ) *n, pl* -mos a book size resulting from folding a sheet of paper into 64 leaves or 128 pages, each one sixty-fourth the size of the sheet. Often written: 64mo, 64°

sixty-fourth note *n music, US & Canadian* a note having the time value of one sixty-fourth of a semibreve. Also called (in Britain and certain other countries): **hemidemisemiquaver**

sixty-nine *n* another term for **soixante-neuf**

sizable *or* **sizeable** ('saɪzəb³l) *adj* quite large ▷ 'sizably *or* 'sizeably *adv*

size¹ (saɪz) *n* **1** the dimensions, proportions, amount, or extent of something **2** large or great dimensions, etc **3** one of a series of graduated measurements, as of clothing: *she takes size 4 shoes* **4** state of affairs as summarized: *he's bankrupt, that's the size of it* ▷ *vb* **5** to sort according to size **6** (*tr*) to make or cut to a particular size or sizes [c13: from Old French *sise*, shortened from *assise* ASSIZE] ▷ 'sizer *n*

size² (saɪz) *n* **1** Also called: **sizing** a thin gelatinous mixture, made from glue, clay, or wax, that is used as a sealer or filler on paper, cloth, or plaster surfaces ▷ *vb* **2** (*tr*) to treat or coat (a surface) with size [c15: perhaps from Old French *sise*; see SIZE¹]

sized (saɪzd) *adj* of a specified size: *medium-sized*

sizeism ('saɪzɪzəm) *n* discrimination on the basis of a person's size, esp against people considered to be overweight [c20: from SIZE¹ + -ISM, on the model of RACISM]

size up *vb* (*adverb*) **1** (*tr*) to make an assessment of (a person, problem, etc) **2** to conform to or make so as to conform to certain specifications of dimension

size zero *n* a very small size in women's clothes, originating in the US, equivalent to a UK size 4

sizzle ('sɪz³l) *vb* (*intr*) **1** to make the hissing sound characteristic of frying fat **2** *informal* to be very hot **3** *informal* to be very angry ▷ *n* **4** a hissing sound [c17: of imitative origin. Compare *siss* (now dialect) to hiss, West Frisian *size, sizje*. See also FIZZ and FIZZLE] ▷ 'sizzler *n*

sizzling ('sɪzlɪŋ) *adj* **1** extremely hot **2** very passionate or erotic: *a sizzling sex scene*

SJ *abbreviation* Society of Jesus

SJA *abbreviation* Saint John's Ambulance (Brigade or Association)

Sjælland (*Danish* 'sjɛlan) *n* the Danish name for **Zealand**

sjambok ('ʃæmbʌk, -bɒk) (in South Africa) *n* a heavy whip of rhinoceros or hippopotamus hide [c19: from Afrikaans, from Malay *samboq, chamboq*, from Urdu *chābuk*]

SK *abbreviation* (esp in postal addresses) Saskatchewan

ska (skɑː) *n* a type of West Indian pop music of the 1960s, accented on the second and fourth beats of a four-beat bar [c20: origin unknown]

Skagen ('skɑːɡən) *n* Cape Skagen another name for the **Skaw**

Skagerrak ('skæɡəˌræk) *n* an arm of the North Sea between Denmark and Norway, merging with the Kattegat in the southeast

skald *or* **scald** (skɔːld) *n* (in ancient Scandinavia) a bard or minstrel [from Old Norse, of unknown origin] ▷ 'skaldic *or* 'scaldic *adj*

skanky ('skæŋkɪ) *adj* -kier, -kiest *slang* **1** dirty, foul-smelling, or unattractive **2** promiscuous ▷ 'skankiness *n*

Skara Brae ('skærə) *n* a Neolithic village in NE Scotland, in the Orkney Islands: one of Europe's most perfectly preserved Stone Age villages, buried by a sand dune until uncovered by a storm in 1850

Skase ('skeɪs) *n* **do a Skase** *Austral informal* to skip the country while owing a large amount of money [c20: after the Australian businessman Christopher *Skase* (1948–2001), who fled Australia after the collapse of his business empire, owing millions of dollars]

skat (skæt) *n* a three-handed card game using 32 cards, popular in German-speaking communities [c19: from German, from Italian *scarto* played cards, from *scartare* to discard, from *s-* EX-¹ + *carta*, from Latin *charta* CARD¹]

skate¹ (skeɪt) *n* **1** See **roller skate, ice skate 2** the steel blade or runner of an ice skate **3** such a blade fitted with straps for fastening to a shoe **4** get one's skates on to hurry ▷ *vb* (*intr*) **5** to glide swiftly on skates **6** to slide smoothly over a surface **7** skate on thin ice to place oneself in a dangerous or delicate situation [C17: via Dutch from Old French *éschasse* stilt, probably of Germanic origin] > 'skater *n*

skate² (skeɪt) *n*, *pl* skate *or* skates any large ray of the family *Rajidae*, of temperate and tropical seas, having flat pectoral fins continuous with the head, two dorsal fins, a short spineless tail, and a long snout [C14: from Old Norse *skata*]

skateboard ('skeɪt,bɔːd) *n* **1** a narrow board mounted on roller-skate wheels, usually ridden while standing up ▷ *vb* **2** (*intr*) to ride on a skateboard > 'skate,boarder *n* > 'skate,boarding *n*

skate over *vb* (*intr*, *preposition*) **1** to cross on or as if on skates **2** to avoid dealing with (a matter) fully

Skaw (skɔː) *n* the Skaw a cape at the N tip of Denmark. Also known as: Skagen

skean-dhu ('skiːən'duː, 'skiːn-) *n Scot* a variant of **sgian-dhu**

skedaddle (skɪ'dædᵊl) *informal* ▷ *vb* **1** (*intr*) to run off hastily ▷ *n* **2** a hasty retreat [C19: of unknown origin]

skeet (skiːt) *n* a form of clay-pigeon shooting in which targets are hurled from two traps at varying speeds and angles [C20: changed from Old Norse *skeyti* a thrown object, from *skjóta* to shoot]

skein (skeɪn) *n* **1** a length of yarn, etc, wound in a long coil **2** something resembling this, such as a lock of hair **3** a flock of geese flying [C15: from Old French *escaigne*, of unknown origin]

skeleton ('skɛlɪtən) *n* **1** a hard framework consisting of inorganic material that supports and protects the soft parts of an animal's body and provides attachment for muscles: may be internal (an endoskeleton), as in vertebrates, or external(an exoskeleton), as in arthropods **2** *informal* a very thin emaciated person or animal **3** the essential framework of any structure, such as a building or leaf, that supports or determines the shape of the rest of the structure **4** an outline consisting of bare essentials: *the skeleton of a novel* **5** (*modifier*) *US & Canadian* reduced to a minimum: *a skeleton staff* **6** skeleton in the cupboard *or US & Canadian* skeleton in the closet a scandalous fact or event in the past that is kept secret [C16: via New Latin from Greek: something desiccated, from *skellein* to dry up] > 'skeletal *adj* > 'skeleton-,like *adj*

skeletonize *or* **skeletonise** ('skɛlɪtə,naɪz) *vb* (*tr*) **1** to reduce to a minimum framework, number, or outline **2** to create the essential framework of

skeleton key *n* a key with the serrated edge filed down so that it can open numerous locks. Also called: passkey [C19: so called because it has been reduced to its essential parts]

skelm ('skɛlᵊm) *n South African informal* a villain or crook [Afrikaans]

Skelmersdale ('skɛlməz,deɪl) *n* a town in NW England, in Lancashire: designated a new town in 1962. Pop: 39 279 (2001)

Skelton ('skɛltən) *n* John. ?1460–1529, English poet celebrated for his short rhyming lines using the rhythms of colloquial speech > Skel'tonic *adj*

skep (skɛp) *n* **1** a beehive, esp one constructed of straw **2** *now chiefly dialect* a large basket of wickerwork or straw [Old English *sceppe*, from Old Norse *skeppa* bushel; related to Old High German *sceffil* bushel]

skeptic ('skɛptɪk) *n*, *adj* an archaic, and the usual US, spelling of **sceptic**

skerrick ('skɛrɪk) *n US, Austral & NZ* a small fragment or amount (esp in the phrase **not a skerrick**) [C20: northern English dialect, probably of Scandinavian origin]

skerry ('skɛrɪ) *n*, *pl* -ries *chiefly Scot* **1** a small rocky island **2** a reef [C17: Orkney dialect, from Old Norse *sker* SCAR²]

sketch (skɛtʃ) *n* **1** a rapid drawing or painting, often a study for subsequent elaboration **2** a brief usually descriptive and informal essay or other literary composition **3** a short play, often comic, forming part of a revue **4** a short evocative piece of instrumental music, esp for piano **5** any brief outline ▷ *vb* **6** to make a rough drawing (of) **7** (*tr*; often foll by *out*) to make a brief

description of [C17: from Dutch *schets*, via Italian from Latin *schedius* hastily made, from Greek *skhedios* unprepared] > 'sketcher *n*

sketchbook ('skɛtʃ,bʊk) *n* **1** a book of plain paper containing sketches or for making sketches in **2** a book of literary sketches

sketchy ('skɛtʃɪ) *adj* sketchier, sketchiest **1** characteristic of a sketch; existing only in outline **2** superficial or slight > 'sketchily *adv* > 'sketchiness *n*

skew (skjuː) *adj* **1** placed in or turning into an oblique position or course **2** *machinery* having a component that is at an angle to the main axis of an assembly or is in some other way asymmetrical: *a skew bevel gear* **3** *maths* composed of or being elements that are neither parallel nor intersecting as, for example, two lines not lying in the same plane in a three-dimensional space **4** (of a statistical distribution) not having equal probabilities above and below the mean; non-normal **5** distorted or biased ▷ *n* **6** an oblique, slanting, or indirect course or position ▷ *vb* **7** to take or cause to take an oblique course or direction **8** (*intr*) to look sideways; squint **9** (*tr*) to distort or bias [C14: from Old Norman French *escuer* to shun, of Germanic origin; compare Middle Dutch *schuwen* to avoid] > 'skewness *n*

skewback ('skjuː,bæk) *n* the sloping surface on both sides of a segmental arch that takes the thrust

skewbald ('skjuː,bɔːld) *adj* **1** marked or spotted in white and any colour except black ▷ *n* **2** a horse with this marking [C17: see SKEW, PIEBALD]

skewer ('skjʊə) *n* **1** a long pin for holding meat in position while being cooked, etc **2** a similar pin having some other function ▷ *vb* **3** (*tr*) to drive a skewer through or fasten with a skewer [C17: probably from dialect *skiver*]

skewwhiff ('skjuː'wɪf) *adj* (*postpositive*) *Brit informal* not straight; askew [C18: probably influenced by ASKEW]

ski (skiː) *n*, *pl* ski *or* skis **1** a one of a pair of wood, metal, or plastic runners that are used for gliding over snow. Skis are commonly attached to shoes for sport, but may also be used as landing gear for aircraft, etc **b** (*as modifier*): *a ski boot* **2** a water-ski ▷ *vb* skis, skiing, skied *or* ski'd **3** (*intr*) to travel on skis [C19: from Norwegian, from Old Norse *skith* snowshoes; related to Old English *scíd* piece of split wood] > 'skier *n* > 'skiing *n*

skibob ('skiː,bɒb) *n* a vehicle made of two short skis, the forward one having a steering handle and the rear one supporting a low seat, for gliding down snow slopes [C20: from SKI + BOB². See BOBSLEIGH] > 'skibobber *n*

skid (skɪd) *vb* skids, skidding, skidded **1** to cause (a vehicle) to slide sideways or (of a vehicle) to slide sideways while in motion, esp out of control **2** (*intr*) to slide without revolving, as the wheel of a moving vehicle after sudden braking ▷ *n* **3** an instance of sliding, esp sideways **4** a support on which heavy objects may be stored and moved short distances by sliding **5** a shoe or drag used to apply pressure to the metal rim of a wheel to act as a brake [C17: perhaps of Scandinavian origin; compare SKI]

Skidoo (skɪ'duː) *n trademark Canadian* another name for **snowmobile**

skid row (rəʊ) *or* **skid road** *n slang, chiefly US & Canadian* a dilapidated section of a city inhabited by vagrants, etc

skied¹ (skaɪd) *vb* the past tense and past participle of **sky**

skied² (skiːd) *vb* a past tense and past participle of **ski**

Skien (Norwegian *ʃeːən*) *n* a port in S Norway, on the **Skien River**: one of the oldest towns in Norway; timber industry. Pop: 50 507 (2004 est)

skiff (skɪf) *n* any of various small boats propelled by oars, sail, or motor [C18: from French *esquif*, from Old Italian *schifo* a boat, of Germanic origin; related to Old High German *schif* SHIP]

skiffle ('skɪfᵊl) *n* a style of popular music of the 1950s, played chiefly on guitars and improvised percussion instruments [C20: of unknown origin]

skijoring (skiː'dʒɔːrɪŋ) *n* a sport in which a skier is pulled over snow or ice, usually by a horse [Norwegian *skikjöring*, literally: ski-driving] > ski'jorer *n*

ski jump *n* **1** a high ramp overhanging a slope from which skiers compete to make the longest jump ▷ *vb* ski-jump **2** (*intr*) to perform a ski jump > ski jumper *n*

S

Skikda ('skɪkdɑː) n a port in NE Algeria, on an inlet of the Mediterranean: founded by the French in 1838 on the site of a Roman city. Pop: 170 000 (2005 est). Former name: **Philippeville**

skilful or US **skillful** ('skɪlfʊl) adj 1 possessing or displaying accomplishment or skill 2 involving or requiring accomplishment or skill > **'skilfully** or US **'skillfully** adv

ski lift n any of various devices for carrying skiers up a slope, such as a chairlift

skill (skɪl) n 1 special ability in a task, sport, etc, esp ability acquired by training 2 something, esp a trade or technique, requiring special training or manual proficiency [c12: from Old Norse skil distinction; related to Middle Low German schēle, Middle Dutch geschil difference] > **'skill-less** or **'skilless** adj

skilled (skɪld) adj 1 possessing or demonstrating accomplishment, skill, or special training 2 (prenominal) involving skill or special training: a skilled job

skillet ('skɪlɪt) n 1 a small frying pan 2 chiefly Brit a saucepan [c15: probably from skele bucket, of Scandinavian origin; related to Old Norse skjōla bucket]

skilly ('skɪlɪ) n chiefly Brit a thin soup or gruel [c19: shortened from skilligallee, probably a fanciful formation]

skim (skɪm) vb skims, skimming, skimmed 1 (tr) to remove floating material from the surface of (a liquid), as with a spoon: to skim milk 2 to glide smoothly or lightly over (a surface) 3 (tr) to throw (something) in a path over a surface, so as to bounce or ricochet: to skim stones over water 4 (when intr, usually foll by through) to read (a book) in a superficial or cursory manner ▷ n 5 the act or process of skimming 6 material skimmed off a liquid, esp off milk 7 any thin layer covering a surface [c15 skimmen, probably from scumen to skim; see SCUM]

skimmed milk n milk from which the cream has been removed. Also called: **skim milk**

skimmer ('skɪmə) n 1 a person or thing that skims 2 any of several mainly tropical coastal aquatic birds of the genus Rhynchops, having long narrow wings and a bill with an elongated lower mandible for skimming food from the surface of the water: family Rynchopidae, order Charadriiformes 3 a flat perforated spoon used for skimming fat from liquids

skimmia ('skɪmɪə) n any rutaceous shrub of the S and SE Asian genus Skimmia, grown for their ornamental red berries and evergreen foliage [c18: New Latin from Japanese (mijama-)shikimi, a native name of the plant]

skimp (skɪmp) vb 1 to be extremely sparing or supply (someone) sparingly; stint 2 to perform (work, etc) carelessly, hastily, or with inadequate materials [c17: perhaps a combination of SCANT and SCRIMP]

skimpy ('skɪmpɪ) adj skimpier, skimpiest 1 (of clothes, etc) made of too little material; scanty 2 excessively thrifty; mean; stingy > **'skimpily** adv > **'skimpiness** n

skin (skɪn) n 1 the tissue forming the outer covering of the vertebrate body: it consists of two layers (the dermis and epidermis), the outermost of which may be covered with hair, scales, feathers, etc It is mainly protective and sensory in function 2 a person's complexion: a fair skin 3 any similar covering in a plant or lower animal 4 any coating or film, such as one that forms on the surface of a liquid 5 the outer covering of a fur-bearing animal, dressed and finished with the hair on 6 a container made from animal skin 7 the outer covering surface of a vessel, rocket, etc 8 a person's skin regarded as his life: to save one's skin 9 (often plural) informal (in jazz or pop use) a drum 10 informal short for **skinhead** 11 by the skin of one's teeth by a narrow margin; only just 12 get under one's skin informal to irritate one 13 no skin off one's nose informal not a matter that affects one adversely 14 skin and bone extremely thin 15 thick skin an insensitive nature 16 thin skin a sensitive nature ▷ vb skins, skinning, skinned 17 (tr) to remove the outer covering from (fruit, etc) 18 (tr) to scrape a small piece of skin from (a part of oneself) in falling, etc: he skinned his knee 19 (often foll by over) to cover (something) with skin or a skinlike substance or (of something) to become covered in this way 20 (tr) slang to strip of money;

swindle ▷ adj 21 relating to or for the skin: skin cream [Old English scinn, from Old Norse skinn] > **'skinless** adj > **'skin,like** adj

skin-deep adj 1 superficial; shallow ▷ adv 2 superficially

skin diving n the sport or activity of diving and underwater swimming without wearing a diver's costume > **'skin-,diver** n

skin flick n slang a film containing much nudity and explicit sex for sensational purposes

skinflint ('skɪn,flɪnt) n an ungenerous or niggardly person; miser [c18: referring to a person so avaricious that he would skin (swindle) a flint]

skinful ('skɪn,fʊl) n, pl -fuls slang sufficient alcoholic drink to make one drunk (esp in the phrase **have a skinful**)

skin graft n a piece of skin removed from one part of the body and surgically grafted at the site of a severe burn or similar injury

skinhead ('skɪn,hɛd) n 1 a member of a group of White youths, noted for their closely cropped hair, aggressive behaviour, and overt racism 2 a closely cropped hairstyle

skink (skɪŋk) n any lizard of the family Scincidae, commonest in tropical Africa and Asia, having reduced limbs and an elongated body covered with smooth scales [c16: from Latin scincus a lizard, from Greek skinkos]

skinned (skɪnd) adj 1 stripped of the skin 2 a having a skin as specified b (in combination): thick-skinned

Skinner ('skɪnə) n B(urrhus) F(rederic). 1904–90, US behavioural psychologist. His "laws of learning", derived from experiments with animals, have been widely applied to education and behaviour therapy

skinny ('skɪnɪ) adj -nier, -niest 1 lacking in flesh; thin 2 consisting of or resembling skin

skint (skɪnt) adj (usually postpositive) Brit slang without money [variant of skinned, past participle of SKIN]

skin test n med any test to determine immunity to a disease or hypersensitivity by introducing a small amount of the test substance beneath the skin or rubbing it into a fresh scratch

skintight ('skɪn'taɪt) adj (of garments) fitting tightly over the body; clinging

skip¹ (skɪp) vb skips, skipping, skipped 1 (when intr, often foll by over, along, into, etc) to spring or move lightly, esp to move by hopping from one foot to the other 2 (intr) to jump over a skipping-rope 3 (tr) to cause (a stone, etc) to bounce or skim over a surface or (of a stone) to move in this way 4 to omit (intervening matter), as in passing from one part or subject to another: he skipped a chapter of the book 5 (intr; foll by through) to read or deal with quickly or superficially 6 skip it! informal it doesn't matter! 7 (tr) informal to miss deliberately: to skip school 8 (tr) informal, chiefly US & Canadian to leave (a place) in haste or secrecy: to skip town ▷ n 9 a skipping movement or gait 10 the act of passing over or omitting [c13: probably of Scandinavian origin; related to Old Norse skopa to run, obsolete Swedish skuppa to skip]

skip² (skɪp) n, vb skips, skipping, skipped informal short for **skipper¹**

skip³ (skɪp) n 1 a large open container for transporting building materials, etc 2 a cage used as a lift in mines, etc [c19: variant of SKEP]

ski pants pl n trousers usually of stretch material and kept taut by a strap under the foot, worn for skiing or as a fashion garment

skip distance n the shortest distance between a transmitter and a receiver that will permit reception of radio waves of a specified frequency by one reflection from the ionosphere

skipjack ('skɪp,dʒæk) n, pl -jack or -jacks 1 Also called: skipjack tuna an important food fish, Katsuwonus pelamis, that has a striped abdomen and occurs in all tropical seas: family Scombridae (mackerels and tunas) 2 black skipjack a small spotted tuna, Euthynnus yaito, of Indo-Pacific seas [c18: from SKIP¹ + JACK¹]

skiplane ('skiː,pleɪn) n an aircraft fitted with skis to enable it to land on and take off from snow

skipper¹ ('skɪpə) n 1 the captain of any vessel 2 the captain of an aircraft 3 a manager or leader, as of a sporting team ▷ *vb* **4** to act as skipper (of) [C14: from Middle Low German, Middle Dutch *schipper* shipper]

skipper² ('skɪpə) *n* **1** a person or thing that skips **2** any small butterfly of the family *Hesperiidae*, having a hairy mothlike body and erratic darting flight

skipping ('skɪpɪŋ) *n* the act of jumping over a rope that is held and swung either by the person jumping or by two other people, as a game or for exercise

skipping-rope *n Brit* a cord, usually having handles at each end, that is held in the hands and swung round and down so that the holder or others can jump over it

Skipton ('skɪptən) *n* a market town in N England, in North Yorkshire: 11th-century castle. Pop: 14 313 (2001)

skip-tooth saw *n* a saw with alternate teeth absent

skip zone *n* a region surrounding a broadcasting station that cannot receive transmissions either directly or by reflection of the ionosphere

skirl (skɜːl; *Scot* skɪrl) *vb* (*intr*) **1** *Scot & northern English dialect* (esp of bagpipes) to emit a shrill sound ▷ *n* **2** the sound of bagpipes [C14: probably of Scandinavian origin; see SHRILL]

skirmish ('skɜːmɪʃ) *n* **1** a minor short-lived military engagement **2** any brisk clash or encounter, usually of a minor nature ▷ *vb* **3** (*intr*; often foll by *with*) to engage in a skirmish [C14: from Old French *eskirmir*, of Germanic origin; related to Old High German *skirmen* to defend] > 'skirmisher *n*

Skíros ('skirɒs) *n* transliteration of the Modern Greek name for **Skyros**

skirt (skɜːt) *n* **1** a garment hanging from the waist, worn chiefly by women and girls **2** the part of a dress below the waist **3** Also called: **apron** a frieze or circular flap, as round the base of a hovercraft **4** the flaps on a saddle that protect a rider's legs **5** *Brit* a cut of beef from the flank **6** (*often plural*) a margin or outlying area **7** bit of skirt *slang* a girl or woman ▷ *vb* **8** (*tr*) to form the edge of **9** (*tr*) to provide with a border **10** (when *intr*, foll by *around, along*, etc) to pass (by) or be situated (near) the outer edge of (an area, etc) **11** (*tr*) to avoid (a difficulty, etc): *he skirted the issue* **12** *chiefly Austral & NZ* to remove the trimmings or inferior wool from (a fleece) [C13: from Old Norse *skyrta* SHIRT] > 'skirted *adj*

skirting ('skɜːtɪŋ) *n* **1** a border, esp of wood or tiles, fixed round the base of an interior wall to protect it from kicks, dirt, etc **2** material used or suitable for skirts

skirting board *n* a skirting made of wood

skirtings ('skɜːtɪŋz) *pl n* ragged edges trimmed from the fleece of a sheep

ski stick *or* **ski pole** *n* a stick, usually with a metal point and a disc to prevent it from sinking into the snow, used by skiers to gain momentum and maintain balance

skit (skɪt) *n* **1** a brief satirical theatrical sketch **2** a short satirical piece of writing [C18: related to earlier verb *skit* to move rapidly, hence to score a satirical hit, probably of Scandinavian origin; related to Old Norse *skjóta* to shoot]

skite¹ (skaɪt) *Scot* ▷ *vb* **1** (*intr*) to slide or slip, as on ice **2** (*tr*) to strike with a sharp or glancing blow ▷ *n* **3** an instance of sliding or slipping **4** a sharp or glancing blow [C18: of uncertain origin]

skite² (skaɪt) *Austral & NZ informal* ▷ *vb* (*intr*) **1** to boast ▷ *n* **2** boastful talk **3** a person who boasts [C19: from Scottish and northern English dialect]

ski tow *n* a device for pulling skiers uphill, usually a motor-driven rope grasped by the skier while riding on his skis

skitter ('skɪtə) *vb* **1** (*intr*; often foll by *off*) to move or run rapidly or lightly; scamper **2** to skim or cause to skim lightly and rapidly, as across the surface of water **3** (*intr*) *angling* to draw a bait lightly over the surface of water [C19: probably from dialect *skite* to dash about; related to Old Norse *skjóta* to SHOOT]

skittish ('skɪtɪʃ) *adj* **1** playful, lively, or frivolous **2** difficult to handle or predict [C15: probably of Scandinavian origin; compare Old Norse *skjóta* to SHOOT; see -ISH] > 'skittishly *adv* > 'skittishness *n*

skittle ('skɪtᵊl) *n* **1** a wooden or plastic pin, typically widest just above the base **2** (*plural; functioning as singular*) a bowling game in which players knock over as many

skittles as possible by rolling a wooden ball at them. Also called (esp US): **ninepins** [C17: of obscure origin; perhaps related to Swedish *skyttel* shuttle]

skive¹ (skaɪv) *vb* (*tr*) to shave or remove the surface of (leather) [C19: from Old Norse *skifa*; related to English dialect *shive* a slice of bread] > 'skiver *n*

skive² (skaɪv) *vb* (when *intr*, often foll by *off*) *Brit informal* to evade (work or responsibility) [C20: of unknown origin] > 'skiver *n*

skivvy¹ ('skɪvɪ) *n, pl* **-vies** *chiefly Brit, often contemptuous* a servant, esp a female, who does menial work of all kinds; drudge ▷ *vb* **-vies, -vying, -vied** **2** (*intr*) *Brit* to work as a skivvy [C20: of unknown origin]

skivvy² ('skɪvɪ) *n, pl* **-vies** *Austral & NZ* a garment resembling a sweater with long sleeves and a polo neck, usually made of stretch cotton or cotton and polyester and worn by either sex [of unknown origin]

skol (skɒl) *or* **skoal** (skəʊl) *sentence substitute* good health! (a drinking toast) [C16: from Danish *skaal* bowl, from Old Norse *skal*; see SCALE²]

skookum ('skuːkəm) *adj Canadian* strong or brave [C19: from Chinook Jargon]

Skopje ('skɔːpjɛ) *n* the capital of (the Former Yugoslav Republic of) Macedonia, on the Vardar River: became capital of Serbia in 1346 and of Macedonia in 1945; suffered a severe earthquake in 1963; university (1949). Pop: 449 000 (2005 est.). Turkish name (1392–1913): Üsküb

Skryabin *n* a variant spelling of **Scriabin**

Skt *or* **Skr.** *abbreviation* Sanskrit

skua ('skjuːə) *n* any predatory gull-like bird of the family *Stercorariidae*, such as the **great skua** or **bonxie** (*Stercorarius skua*) or **arctic skua** (*S. parasiticus*) both of which harass terns or gulls into dropping or disgorging fish they have caught [C17: from New Latin, from Faeroese *skúgvur*, from Old Norse *skúfr*]

skulduggery *or US* **skullduggery** (skʌl'dʌgərɪ) *n informal* underhand dealing; trickery [C19: altered from earlier Scot *sculduddery*; of obscure origin]

skulk (skʌlk) *vb* (*intr*) **1** to move stealthily so as to avoid notice **2** to lie in hiding; lurk **3** to shirk duty or evade responsibilities; malinger ▷ *n* **4** a person who skulks **5** *obsolete* a pack of foxes or other animals that creep about stealthily [C13: of Scandinavian origin; compare Norwegian *skulka* to lurk, Swedish *skolka*, Danish *skulke* to shirk] > 'skulker *n*

skull (skʌl) *n* **1** the bony skeleton of the head of vertebrates **2** *often derogatory* the head regarded as the mind or intelligence: *to have a dense skull* **3** a picture of a skull used to represent death or danger [C13: of Scandinavian origin; compare Old Norse *skoltr*, Norwegian *skult*, Swedish dialect *skulle*]

skull and crossbones *n* a picture of the human skull above two crossed thighbones, formerly on the pirate flag, now used as a warning of danger or death

skullcap ('skʌl,kæp) *n* **1** a rounded brimless hat fitting the crown of the head **2** the nontechnical name for **calvaria** **3** any of various perennial plants of the genus *Scutellaria*, esp *S. galericulata*, that typically have helmet-shaped flowers: family *Lamiaceae* (labiates)

skunk (skʌŋk) *n, pl* **skunks** *or* **skunk** **1** any of various American musteline mammals of the subfamily *Mephitinae*, esp *Mephitis mephitis* (**striped skunk**), typically having a black and white coat and bushy tail: they eject an unpleasant-smelling fluid from the anal gland when attacked **2** *informal* a despicable person [C17: from Algonquian; compare Abnaki *segâkw* skunk]

skunk cabbage *n* a low-growing fetid aroid swamp plant, *Symplocarpus foetidus* of E North America, having broad leaves and minute flowers enclosed in a mottled greenish or purple spathe

sky (skaɪ) *n, pl* **skies** **1** (*sometimes plural*) the apparently dome-shaped expanse extending upwards from the horizon that is characteristically blue or grey during the day, red in the evening, and black at night **2** outer space, as seen from the earth **3** (*often plural*) weather, as described by the appearance of the upper air: *sunny skies* **4** the source of divine power; heaven **5** *informal* the highest level of attainment: *the sky's the limit* **6** **to the skies** highly; extravagantly ▷ *vb* **skies, skying, skied**

7 *rowing* to lift (the blade of an oar) too high before a stroke **8** (*tr*) *informal* to hit (a ball) high in the air [c13: from Old Norse *skȳ*; related to Old English *scio* cloud, Old Saxon *skio*, Old Norse *skjār* transparent skin]

sky blue *n* **a** a light or pale blue colour **b** (*as adjective*): *a sky-blue jumper*

skydiving ('skaɪˌdaɪvɪŋ) *n* the sport of parachute jumping, in which participants perform manoeuvres before opening the parachute and attempt to land accurately ▷ **'sky,dive** *vb* ▷ **'sky,diver** *n*

Skye (skaɪ) *n* a mountainous island off the NW coast of Scotland, the largest island of the Inner Hebrides: tourist centre. Chief town: Portree. Pop: 9232 (2001). Area: 1735 sq km (670 sq miles)

Skye terrier *n* a short-legged long-bodied breed of terrier with long wiry hair and erect ears

sky-high *adj, adv* **1** at or to an unprecedented or excessive level: *prices rocketed sky-high* ▷ *adv* **2** high into the air **3 blow sky-high** to destroy completely

skyjack ('skaɪˌdʒæk) *vb* (*tr*) to commandeer (an aircraft), usually at gunpoint during flight, forcing the pilot to fly somewhere other than to the scheduled destination [c20: from SKY + HIJACK]

skylark ('skaɪˌlɑːk) *n* **1** an Old World lark, *Alauda arvensis*, noted for singing while hovering at a great height ▷ *vb* **2** (*intr*) *informal* to romp or play jokes

skylight ('skaɪˌlaɪt) *n* a window placed in a roof or ceiling to admit daylight. Also called: **fanlight**

skyline ('skaɪˌlaɪn) *n* **1** the line at which the earth and sky appear to meet; horizon **2** the outline of buildings, mountains, trees, etc, seen against the sky

sky marshal *n* an armed security guard on a commercial aircraft

Skype (skaɪp) *n trademark* a system for making telephone calls over the internet

sky pilot *n slang* a chaplain in one of the military services

skyrocket ('skaɪˌrɒkɪt) *n* **1** another word for **rocket¹** (sense 1) ▷ *vb* **2** (*intr*) *informal* to rise rapidly, as in price

Skyros or **Scyros** ('skiːrɒs) *n* a Greek island in the Aegean, the largest island in the N Sporades. Pop: 2602 (2001). Area: 199 sq km (77 sq miles). Modern Greek name: **Skíros**

skysail ('skaɪˌseɪl) *n nautical* a square sail set above the royal on a square-rigger

skyscraper ('skaɪˌskreɪpə) *n* a very tall multistorey building

sky show *n Austral* a fireworks display

skyward ('skaɪwəd) *adj* **1** directed or moving towards the sky ▷ *adv* **2** Also called: **skywards** towards the sky

skywriting ('skaɪˌraɪtɪŋ) *n* **1** the forming of words in the sky by the release of smoke or vapour from an aircraft **2** the words so formed ▷ **'sky,writer** *n*

slab (slæb) *n* **1** a broad flat thick piece of wood, stone, or other material **2** a thick slice of cake, etc **3** any of the outside parts of a log that are sawn off while the log is being made into planks **4** (*modifier*) *Austral & NZ* made or constructed of coarse wooden planks: *a slab hut* **5** *informal, chiefly Brit* an operating or mortuary table **6** *chiefly Brit & Austral informal* a package containing 24 cans of beer ▷ *vb* **slabs, slabbing, slabbed** (*tr*) **7** to make or cut into a slab or slabs **8** to saw slabs from (a log) [c13: of unknown origin]

slack¹ (slæk) *adj* **1** not tight, tense, or taut **2** negligent or careless **3** (esp of water, etc) moving slowly **4** (of trade, etc) not busy **5** *phonetics* another term for **lax** (sense 4) ▷ *adv* **6** in a slack manner ▷ *n* **7** a part of a rope, etc, that is slack: *take in the slack* **8** a period of decreased activity ▷ *vb* **9** to neglect (one's duty, etc) **10** (often foll by *off*) to loosen; to make slack **11** *chem* a less common word for **slake** (sense 3) ▷ See also **slacks** [Old English *slæc, sleac*; related to Old High German *slah, Old Norse *slākr* bad, Latin *laxus* LAX] ▷ **'slackly** *adv* ▷ **'slackness** *n*

slack² (slæk) *n* small pieces of coal with a high ash content [c15: probably from Middle Low German *slecke*; related to Dutch *slak*, German *Schlacke* dross]

slacken ('slækən) *vb* (often foll by *off*) **1** to make or become looser **2** to make or become slower, less intense, etc

slacker ('slækə) *n* a person who evades work or duty; shirker

slacks (slæks) *pl n informal* trousers worn by both sexes

slack water *n* the period of still water around the turn of the tide, esp at low tide

slag (slæg) *n* **1** Also called: **cinder** the fused material formed during the smelting or refining of metals by combining the flux with gangue, impurities in the metal, etc It usually consists of a mixture of silicates with calcium, phosphorus, sulphur, etc **2** a mass of rough fragments of pyroclastic rock and cinders derived from a volcanic eruption; scoria **3** a mixture of shale, clay, coal dust, and other mineral waste produced during coal mining **4** *Brit slang* a coarse or dissipated girl or woman ▷ *vb* **slags, slagging, slagged 5** (*tr*) *Brit slang* to abuse (someone) verbally [c16: from Middle Low German *slagge*, perhaps from *slagen* to SLAY] ▷ **'slagging** *n* ▷ **'slaggy** *adj*

slag heap *n* a hillock of waste matter from coal mining, etc

slain (sleɪn) *vb* the past participle of **slay**

slake (sleɪk) *vb* **1** (*tr*) *literary* to satisfy (thirst, desire, etc) **2** (*tr*) *poetic* to cool or refresh **3** Also called: **slack** to undergo or cause to undergo the process in which lime reacts with water or moist air to produce calcium hydroxide [Old English *slacian*, from *slæc* SLACK¹; related to Dutch *slaken* to diminish, Icelandic *slaka*] ▷ **'slakable** or **'slakeable** *adj*

slaked lime *n* another name for calcium hydroxide, esp when made by adding water to calcium oxide

slalom ('slɑːləm) *n skiing* a race, esp one downhill, over a winding course marked by artificial obstacles [Norwegian, from *slad* sloping + *lom* path]

slam¹ (slæm) *vb* **slams, slamming, slammed 1** to cause (a door or window) to close noisily and with force or (of a door, etc) to close in this way **2** (*tr*) to throw (something) down noisily and violently **3** (*tr*) *slang* to criticize harshly **4** (*intr*; usually foll by *into* or *out of*) *informal* to go (into or out of a room, etc) in violent haste or anger **5** (*tr*) to strike with violent force **6** (*tr*) *informal* to defeat easily ▷ *n* **7** the act or noise of slamming [c17: of Scandinavian origin; compare Old Norse *slamra*, Norwegian *slemma*, Swedish dialect *slämma*]

slam² (slæm) *n* **a** the winning of all (grand slam) or all but one (little slam or small slam) of the 13 tricks at bridge or whist **b** the bid to do so in bridge ▷ See **grand slam, little slam** [c17: of uncertain origin]

slam³ (slæm) *n* a poetry contest in which entrants compete with each other by reciting their work and are awarded points by the audience [c20: origin unknown]

slam dance *vb* to hurl oneself repeatedly into or through a crowd at a rock-music concert

slam dunk *basketball* ▷ *n* **1** a scoring shot in which a player jumps up and forces the ball down through the basket **2** *informal* a task so easy that success in it is deemed a certainty ▷ *vb* **slam-dunk 3** to jump up and force (a ball) through a basket

slammer ('slæmə) *n* **the slammer** *slang* prison

slander ('slɑːndə) *n* **1** *law* **a** defamation in some transient form, as by spoken words, gestures, etc **b** a slanderous statement, etc **2** any false or defamatory words spoken about a person; calumny ▷ *vb* **3** to utter or circulate slander (about) [c13: via Anglo-French from Old French *escandle*, from Late Latin *scandalum* a cause of offence; see SCANDAL] ▷ **'slanderer** *n* ▷ **'slanderous** *adj*

slang (slæŋ) *n* **1 a** vocabulary, idiom, etc, that is not appropriate to the standard form of a language or to formal contexts, may be restricted as to social status or distribution, and is characteristically more metaphorical and transitory than standard language **b** (*as modifier*): *a slang word* ▷ *vb* **2** to abuse (someone) with vituperative language; insult [c18: of unknown origin] ▷ **'slangy** *adj* ▷ **'slangily** *adv* ▷ **'slanginess** *n*

slant (slɑːnt) *vb* **1** to incline or be inclined at an oblique or sloping angle **2** (*tr*) to write or present (news, etc) with a bias **3** (*intr*; foll by *towards*) (of a person's opinions) to be biased ▷ *n* **4** an inclined or oblique line or direction; slope **5** a way of looking at something **6** a bias or opinion, as in an article **7 on a slant** *or* **on the**

slant sloping ▷ *adj* **8** oblique, sloping [c17: short for ASLANT, probably of Scandinavian origin] > **'slanting** *adj*

slantwise ('slɑːntˌwaɪz) *or* **slantways** ('slɑːntˌweɪz) *adv, adj* (prenominal) in a slanting or oblique direction

slap (slæp) *n* **1** a sharp blow or smack, as with the open hand, something flat, etc **2** the sound made by or as if by such a blow **3** a bit of slap and tickle *or* slap and tickle *Brit informal* sexual play **4** a slap in the face an insult or rebuff **5** a slap on the back congratulation ▷ *vb* slaps, slapping, slapped **6** (*tr*) to strike (a person or thing) sharply, as with the open hand or something flat **7** (*tr*) to bring down (the hand, something flat, etc) sharply **8** (when *intr*, usually foll by *against*) to strike (something) with or as if with a slap **9** (*tr*) *informal, chiefly Brit* to apply in large quantities, haphazardly, etc: *she slapped butter on the bread* **10** slap on the back to congratulate ▷ *adv informal* **11** exactly; directly: *slap on time* **12** forcibly or abruptly: *to fall slap on the floor* [c17: from Low German *slapp*, German *Schlappe*, of imitative origin]

slap bass *n* a rock or jazz style of playing the electric or double bass in which the strings are plucked and released so as to vibrate sharply against the fretboard or fingerboard

slapdash ('slæpˌdæʃ) *adv* **1** in a careless, hasty, or haphazard manner ▷ *adj* **2** careless, hasty, or haphazard ▷ *n* **3** slapdash activity or work [c17: from SLAP + DASH[1]]

slap-happy *adj* **-happier, -happiest** *informal* **1** cheerfully irresponsible or careless **2** dazed or giddy from or as if from repeated blows; punch-drunk

slaphead ('slæpˌhɛd) *n* *derogatory, slang* a bald person [c20: from SLAP + HEAD]

slapstick ('slæpˌstɪk) *n* **1** a comedy characterized by horseplay and physical action **b** (*as modifier*): *slapstick humour* **2** a flexible pair of paddles bound together at one end, formerly used in pantomime to strike a blow to a person with a loud clapping sound but without injury

slap-up *adj* (prenominal) *Brit informal* (esp of meals) lavish; excellent; first-class

slash (slæʃ) *vb* (*tr*) **1** to cut or lay about (a person or thing) with sharp sweeping strokes, as with a sword, knife, etc **2** to lash with a whip **3** to make large gashes in: *to slash tyres* **4** to reduce (prices, etc) drastically **5** *chiefly US* to criticize harshly **6** to slit (the outer fabric of a garment) so that the lining material is revealed **7** to clear (scrub or undergrowth) by cutting ▷ *n* **8** a sharp, sweeping stroke, as with a sword or whip **9** a cut or rent made by such a stroke **10** a decorative slit in a garment revealing the lining material **11** *US & Canadian* littered wood chips and broken branches that remain after trees have been cut down **12** Also called: **diagonal, forward slash, separatrix, shilling mark, solidus, stroke, virgule** a short oblique stroke used in text to separate items of information, such as days, months, and years in dates (18/7/80), alternative words (*and/or*), numerator from denominator in fractions (55/103), etc **13** *Brit slang* the act of urinating (esp in the phrase **have a slash**) [C14 *slaschen*, perhaps from Old French *esclachier* to break]

Slashdot effect ('slæʃˌdɒt) *n* *computing* a temporary surge in the numbers visiting a website and consequent service slowdown or even server crash that sometimes arises as a result of a new link being set up from a more popular website [c21: from the symbols SLASH + DOT, which are conventions of website addresses]

slasher ('slæʃə) *n* **1** a person or thing that slashes **2** *Austral & NZ* a wooden-handled cutting tool or tractor-drawn machine used for cutting scrub or undergrowth in the bush

slasher movie *n* *slang* a film in which victims, usually women, are slashed with knives, razors, etc

slashing ('slæʃɪŋ) *adj* aggressively or harshly critical (esp in the phrase **slashing attack**)

Śląsk (ʃlõsk) *n* the Polish name for **Silesia**

slat (slæt) *n* **1** a narrow thin strip of wood or metal, as used in a Venetian blind, etc **2** a movable or fixed auxiliary aerofoil attached to the leading edge of an aircraft wing to increase lift, esp during landing and takeoff [c14: from Old French *esclat* splinter, from *esclater* to shatter]

slate[1] (sleɪt) *n* **1 a** a compact fine-grained metamorphic rock formed by the effects of heat and pressure on shale. It can be split into thin layers along natural cleavage planes and is used as a roofing and paving material **b** (*as modifier*): *a slate tile* **2** a roofing tile of slate **3** (formerly) a writing tablet of slate **4** a dark grey colour, often with a purplish or bluish tinge **5** *chiefly US & Canadian* a list of candidates in an election **6** clean slate a record without dishonour **7** have a slate loose *Brit & Irish informal* to be eccentric or crazy **8** on the slate *Brit informal* on credit ▷ *vb* (*tr*) **9** to cover (a roof) with slates **10** *chiefly US* to enter (a person's name) on a list, esp on a political slate ▷ *adj* **11** of the colour slate [c14: from Old French *esclate*, from *esclat* a fragment; see SLAT[1]] > **'slaty** *adj*

slate[2] (sleɪt) *vb* (*tr*) *informal, chiefly Brit* to criticize harshly; censure [c19: probably from SLATE[1]] > **'slating** *n*

slater ('sleɪtə) *n* **1** a person trained in laying roof slates **2** *dialect, Austral & NZ* a woodlouse

slather ('slæðə) *n* **1** (usually plural) *informal* a large quantity **2** open slather *Austral & NZ slang* a situation in which there are no restrictions; free-for-all [c19: of unknown origin]

Slatkin ('slætkɪn) *n* **Leonard.** born 1944, US conductor; musical director of the St Louis Symphony Orchestra (1979–96) and of the National Symphony Orchestra from 1996

slattern ('slætən) *n* a slovenly woman or girl; slut [c17: probably from *slattering*, from dialect *slatter* to slop; perhaps from Scandinavian; compare Old Norse *sletta* to slap] > **'slatternly** *adj* > **'slatterliness** *n*

slaughter ('slɔːtə) *n* **1** the killing of animals, esp for food **2** the savage killing of a person **3** the indiscriminate or brutal killing of large numbers of people, as in war; massacre ▷ *vb* (*tr*) **4** to kill (animals), esp for food **5** to kill in a brutal manner **6** to kill indiscriminately or in large numbers **7** *informal* to defeat resoundingly [Old English *sleaht*; related to Old Norse *slāttar* hammering, *slātr* butchered meat, Old High German *slahta*, Gothic *slauhts*, German *Schlacht* battle] > **'slaughterer** *n* > **'slaughterous** *adj*

slaughterhouse ('slɔːtəˌhaʊs) *n* a place where animals are butchered for food; abattoir

Slav (slɑːv) *n* a member of any of the peoples of E Europe or NW Asia who speak a Slavonic language [c14: from Medieval Latin *Sclāvus* a captive Slav; see SLAVE]

slave (sleɪv) *n* **1** a person legally owned by another and having no freedom of action or right to property **2** a person who is forced to work for another against his will **3** a person under the domination of another person or some habit or influence **4** a person who works in harsh conditions for low pay **5** a device that is controlled by or that duplicates the action of another similar device (the master device) ▷ *vb* **6** (*intr*; often foll by *away*) to work like a slave [c13: via Old French from Medieval Latin *Sclāvus* a Slav, one held in bondage (from the fact that the Slavonic races were frequently conquered in the Middle Ages), from Late Greek *Sklabos* a Slav]

Slave Coast *n* the coast of W Africa between the Volta River and Mount Cameroon, chiefly along the Bight of Benin: the main source of African slaves (16th–19th centuries)

slave cylinder *n* a small cylinder containing a piston that operates the brake shoes or pads in hydraulic brakes or the working part in any other hydraulically operated system

slave-driver *n* **1** (esp formerly) a person forcing slaves to work **2** an employer who demands excessively hard work from his employees

slaveholder ('sleɪvˌhəʊldə) *n* a person who owns slaves > **'slaveˌholding** *n*

slaver[1] ('sleɪvə) *n* **1** an owner of or dealer in slaves **2** another name for **slave ship**

slaver[2] ('slævə) *vb* (*intr*) **1** to dribble saliva **2** (often foll by *over*) **a** to fawn or drool (over someone) **b** to show great desire (for); lust (after) ▷ *n* **3** saliva dribbling from the mouth **4** *informal* drivel [c14: probably of Low Dutch origin; related to SLOBBER] > **'slaverer** *n*

Slave River *n* a river in W Canada, in the Northwest Territories and NE Alberta, flowing from Lake Athabaska northwest to Great Slave Lake. Length: about

420 km (260 miles). Also called: **Great Slave River**

slavery ('sleɪvərɪ) n **1** the state or condition of being a slave; a civil relationship whereby one person has absolute power over another and controls his life, liberty, and fortune **2** the subjection of a person to another person, esp in being forced into work **3** the condition of being subject to some influence or habit **4** work done in harsh conditions for low pay

slave ship n a ship used to transport slaves, esp formerly from Africa to the New World

Slave State n US history any of the 15 Southern states in which slavery was legal until the Civil War

slave trade n the business of trading in slaves, esp the transportation of Black Africans to America from the 16th to 19th centuries > **slave-,trader** n > **slave-,trading** n

slavey ('sleɪvɪ) n Brit informal a female general servant [C19: from SLAVE + -Y²]

Slavey ('sleɪvɪ) n a member of a Dene Native Canadian people of northern Canada [from Athapascan]

Slavic ('slɑːvɪk) n, adj another word (esp US) for **Slavonic**

slavish ('sleɪvɪʃ) adj **1** of or befitting a slave **2** being or resembling a slave; servile **3** unoriginal; imitative > **'slavishly** adv

Slavkov ('slafkɔf) n the Czech name for **Austerlitz**

Slavonia (slə'vəʊnɪə) n a region in Croatia, mainly between the Drava and Sava Rivers > **Sla'vonian** adj, n

Slavonic (slə'vɒnɪk) or esp US **Slavic** n **1** a branch of the Indo-European family of languages, usually divided into three subbranches: **South Slavonic** (including Old Church Slavonic, Serbian, Croatian, Bulgarian, etc), **East Slavonic** (including Ukrainian, Russian, etc), and **West Slavonic** (including Polish, Czech, Slovak, etc) ▷ adj **2** of, denoting, or relating to this group of languages **3** of, denoting, or relating to the people who speak these languages [C17: from Medieval Latin Slavonicus, Sclavonicus, from SLAVONIA]

slaw (slɔː) n chiefly US & Canadian short for **coleslaw** [C19: from Dutch sla, short for salade SALAD]

slay (sleɪ) vb slays, slaying, slew, slain (tr) **1** archaic or literary to kill, esp violently **2** slang to impress (someone of the opposite sex) [Old English slēan; related to Old Norse slā, Gothic, Old High German slahan to strike, Old Irish slacaim I beat] > **'slayer** n

SLCM abbreviation sea-launched cruise missile: a type of cruise missile that can be launched from either a submarine or a surface ship

sleaze (sliːz) n informal **1** sleaziness **2** dishonest, disreputable, or immoral behaviour, especially of public officials or employees: political sleaze

sleazy ('sliːzɪ) adj -zier, -ziest **1** sordid; disreputable: a sleazy nightclub **2** thin or flimsy, as cloth [C17: origin uncertain] > **'sleazily** adv > **'sleaziness** n

sledge¹ (slɛdʒ) or esp US and Canadian **sled** (slɛd) n **1** Also called: **sleigh** a vehicle mounted on runners, drawn by horses or dogs, for transporting people or goods, esp over snow **2** a light wooden frame used, esp by children, for sliding over snow; toboggan ▷ vb **3** to convey, travel, or go by sledge [C17: from Middle Dutch sleedse; C14 sled, from Middle Low German, from Old Norse slethi, related to SLIDE] > **'sledger** n

sledge² (slɛdʒ) n short for **sledgehammer**

sledge³ (slɛdʒ) vb (tr) to bait (an opponent, esp a batsman in cricket) in order to upset his concentration [of uncertain origin; perhaps from SLEDGEHAMMER]

sledgehammer ('slɛdʒ,hæmə) n **1** a large heavy hammer with a long handle used with both hands for heavy work such as forging iron, breaking rocks, etc **2** (modifier) resembling the action of a sledgehammer in power, ruthlessness, etc: a sledgehammer blow [C15 sledge, from Old English slecg a large hammer; related to Old Norse sleggja, Middle Dutch slegge]

sleek (sliːk) adj **1** smooth and shiny; polished **2** polished in speech or behaviour; unctuous **3** (of an animal or bird) having a shiny healthy coat or feathers **4** (of a person) having a prosperous appearance ▷ vb (tr) **5** to make smooth and glossy, as by grooming, etc **6** (usually foll by over) to cover (up), as by making more agreeable; gloss (over) [C16: variant of SLICK] > **'sleekly** adv

> **'sleekness** n > **'sleeky** adj

sleep (sliːp) n **1** a periodic state of physiological rest during which consciousness is suspended and metabolic rate is decreased **2** botany the nontechnical name for **nyctitropism 3** a period spent sleeping **4** a state of quiescence or dormancy **5** a poetic or euphemistic word for **death** ▷ vb sleeps, sleeping, slept **6** (intr) to be in or as in the state of sleep **7** (intr) (of plants) to show nyctitropism **8** (intr) to be inactive or quiescent **9** (tr) to have sleeping accommodation for (a certain number): the boat could sleep six **10** (tr; foll by away) to pass (time) sleeping **11** (intr) poetic or euphemistic to be dead **12** sleep on it to give (something) extended consideration, esp overnight ▷ See also **sleep around, sleep in**, etc [Old English slǣpan; related to Old Frisian slēpa, Old Saxon slāpan, Old High German slāfan, German schlaff limp]

sleep around vb (intr, adverb) informal to be sexually promiscuous

sleeper ('sliːpə) n **1** a person, animal, or thing that sleeps **2** a railway sleeping car or compartment **3** Brit one of the blocks supporting the rails on a railway track **4** a heavy timber beam, esp one that is laid horizontally on the ground **5** chiefly Brit a small plain gold circle worn in a pierced ear lobe to prevent the hole from closing up **6** informal a person or thing that achieves unexpected success after an initial period of obscurity **7** a spy planted in advance for future use, but not currently active

sleep in vb (intr, adverb) **1** Brit to sleep longer than usual **2** to sleep at the place of one's employment

sleeping bag n a large well-padded bag designed for sleeping in, esp outdoors

sleeping car n a railway car fitted with compartments containing bunks for people to sleep in

sleeping partner n a partner in a business who does not play an active role, esp one who supplies capital. Also called: **silent partner**

sleeping pill n a pill or tablet containing a sedative drug, such as a barbiturate, used to induce sleep

sleeping policeman n a bump built across roads, esp in housing estates, to deter motorists from speeding. Also called: **road hump**

sleeping sickness n **1** Also called: **African sleeping sickness** an African disease caused by infection with protozoans of the genus Trypanosoma, characterized by fever, wasting, and sluggishness **2** an epidemic viral form of encephalitis characterized by extreme drowsiness. Technical name: encephalitis lethargica

sleepless ('sliːplɪs) adj **1** without sleep or rest: a sleepless journey **2** unable to sleep **3** always watchful or alert **4** chiefly poetic always active or moving > **'sleeplessly** adv > **'sleeplessness** n

sleep off vb (tr, adverb) informal to lose by sleeping: to sleep off a hangover

sleep out vb (intr, adverb) **1** (esp of a tramp) to sleep in the open air **2** to sleep away from the place of work ▷ n sleep-out **3** Austral & NZ an area of a veranda that has been glassed in or partitioned off so that it may be used as a bedroom

sleepover ('sliːp,əʊvə) n informal, chiefly US an instance of spending the night at someone else's home

sleepwalk ('sliːp,wɔːk) vb (intr) to walk while asleep > **'sleep,walker** n > **'sleep,walking** n, adj

sleep with vb (intr, preposition) to have sexual intercourse and (usually) spend the night with. Also called: **sleep together**

sleepy ('sliːpɪ) adj sleepier, sleepiest **1** inclined to or needing sleep; drowsy **2** characterized by or exhibiting drowsiness, sluggishness, etc **3** conducive to sleep; soporific **4** without activity or bustle: a sleepy town > **'sleepily** adv > **'sleepiness** n

sleet (sliːt) n **1** partly melted falling snow or hail or (esp US) partly frozen rain **2** chiefly US the thin coat of ice that forms when sleet or rain freezes on cold surfaces ▷ vb **3** (intr) to fall as sleet [C13: from Germanic; compare Middle Low German slöten hail, Middle High German slōze, German Schlossen hailstones] > **'sleety** adj

sleeve (sliːv) n **1** the part of a garment covering the arm

2 a tubular piece that is forced or shrunk into a cylindrical bore to reduce the diameter of the bore or to line it with a different material; liner **3** a tube fitted externally over two cylindrical parts in order to join them; bush **4** a flat cardboard or plastic container to protect a gramophone record. US name: jacket **5 up one's sleeve** secretly ready **6 roll up one's sleeves** to prepare oneself for work, a fight, etc ▷ *vb* **7** (*tr*) to provide with a sleeve or sleeves [Old English *slīf, slēf*; related to Dutch *sloof* apron] > 'sleeveless *adj* > 'sleeve,like *adj*

sleeve board *n* a small ironing board for pressing sleeves, fitted onto an ironing board or table

sleeving ('sliːvɪŋ) *n electronics chiefly Brit* tubular flexible insulation into which bare wire can be inserted

sleigh (sleɪ) *n* **1** another name for **sledge¹** (sense 1) ▷ *vb* **2** (*intr*) to travel by sleigh [c18: from Dutch *slee*, variant of *slede* SLEDGE¹]

sleight (slaɪt) *n archaic* **1** skill; dexterity **2** a trick or stratagem **3** cunning; trickery [c14: from Old Norse *slægth*, from *slægr* SLY]

sleight of hand *n* **1** manual dexterity used in performing conjuring tricks **2** the performance of such tricks

slender ('slɛndə) *adj* **1** of small width relative to length or height **2** (esp of a person's figure) slim and well-formed **3** small or inadequate in amount, size, etc: *slender resources* **4** (of hopes, etc) having little foundation; feeble **5** very small: *a slender margin* [c14 *slendre*, of unknown origin] > 'slenderly *adv* > 'slenderness *n*

slenderize or **slenderise** ('slɛndə,raɪz) *vb chiefly US & Canadian* to make or become slender

slept (slɛpt) *vb* the past tense and past participle of **sleep**

Slesvig ('slesviː) *n* the Danish name for **Schleswig**

sleuth (sluːθ) *n* **1** an informal word for **detective 2** short for **sleuthhound** (sense 1) ▷ *vb* **3** (*tr*) to track or follow [c19: short for *sleuthhound*, from c12 *sleuth* trail, from Old Norse *sloth*; see SLOT²]

sleuthhound ('sluːθ,haʊnd) *n* **1** a dog trained to track people, esp a bloodhound **2** an informal word for **detective**

S level *n Brit* a public examination in a subject taken for the General Certificate of Education: usually taken at the same time as A2 levels as an additional qualification

slew¹ (sluː) *vb* the past tense of **slay**

slew² or esp US **slue** (sluː) *vb* **1** to twist or be twisted sideways, esp awkwardly **2** *nautical* to cause (a mast) to rotate in its step or (of a mast) to rotate in its step ▷ *n* **3** the act of slewing [c18: of unknown origin]

slew³ (sluː) *n* a variant spelling (esp US) of **slough¹** (sense 2)

slew⁴ or **slue** (sluː) *n informal, chiefly US & Canadian* a great number or amount; a lot [c20: from Irish Gaelic *sluagh*; related to Old Irish *slōg* army]

Slezsko ('slɛsko) *n* the Czech name for **Silesia**

slice (slaɪs) *n* **1** a thin flat piece cut from something having bulk: *a slice of pork* **2** a share or portion: *a slice of the company's revenue* **3** any of various utensils having a broad flat blade and resembling a spatula **4** (in golf, tennis, etc) **a** the flight of a ball that travels obliquely because it has been struck off centre **b** the action of hitting such a shot **c** the shot so hit ▷ *vb* **5** to divide or cut (something) into parts or slices **6** (when *intr*, usually foll by *through*) to cut in a clean and effortless manner **7** (when *intr*, foll by *through*) to move or go (through something) like a knife: *the ship sliced through the water* **8** (usually foll by *off, from, away*, etc) to cut or be cut (from) a larger piece **9** (*tr*) to remove by use of a slicing implement **10** to hit (a ball) with a slice [c14: from Old French *esclice* a piece split off, from *esclicier* to splinter] > 'sliceable *adj* > 'slicer *n*

slick (slɪk) *adj* **1** flattering and glib: *a slick salesman* **2** adroitly devised or executed: *a slick show* **3** *informal, chiefly US & Canadian* shrewd; sly **4** *informal* superficially attractive: *a slick publication* **5** *chiefly US & Canadian* smooth and glossy; slippery ▷ *n* **6** a slippery area, esp a patch of oil floating on water ▷ *vb* (*tr*) **7** *chiefly US & Canadian* to make smooth or sleek **8** (often foll by *up*) to make smooth or glossy [c14: probably of Scandinavian origin; compare Icelandic, Norwegian *slikja* to be or make

smooth] > 'slickly *adv* > 'slickness *n*

slicker ('slɪkə) *n* **1** *informal* a sly or untrustworthy person (esp in the phrase **city slicker**) **2** *US & Canadian* a shiny raincoat, esp an oilskin

slide (slaɪd) *vb* **slides, sliding, slid** (slɪd), **slid** or **slidden** ('slɪdᵊn) **1** to move or cause to move smoothly along a surface in continual contact with it: *doors that slide open; children sliding on the ice* **2** (*intr*) to lose grip or balance: *he slid on his back* **3** (*intr*; usually foll by *into, out of, away from*, etc) to pass or move gradually and unobtrusively: *she slid into the room* **4** (*intr*; usually foll by *into*) to go (into a specified condition) by degrees, imperceptibly, etc: *he slid into loose living* **5** (foll by *in, into*, etc) to move (an object) unobtrusively or (of an object) to move in this way: *he slid the gun into his pocket* **6** (*intr*) *music* to execute a portamento **7 let slide** to allow to follow a natural course, esp one leading to deterioration: *to let things slide* ▷ *n* **8** the act or an instance of sliding **9** a smooth surface, as of ice or mud, for sliding on **10** a construction incorporating an inclined smooth slope for sliding down in playgrounds, etc **11** a thin glass plate on which specimens are mounted for microscopic study **12** Also called: **transparency** a positive photograph on a transparent base, mounted in a cardboard or plastic frame or between glass plates, that can be viewed by means of a slide projector **13** Also called: **hair slide** *chiefly Brit* an ornamental clip to hold hair in place. US and Canadian name: **barrette 14** *machinery* a sliding part or member **15** *music* **a** the sliding curved tube of a trombone that is moved in or out to allow the production of different harmonic series and a wider range of notes **b** a portamento **16** *music* **a** a metal or glass tube placed over a finger held against the frets of a guitar to produce a portamento **b** the style of guitar playing using a slide **17** *geology* **a** the rapid downward movement of a large mass of earth, rocks, etc, caused by erosion, faulting, etc **b** the mass of material involved in this descent. See also **landslide** [Old English *slīdan*; related to *slidor* slippery, *sliderian* to SLITHER, Middle High German *slīten*] > 'slidable *adj* > 'slider *n*

slide over *vb* (*intr, preposition*) **1** to cross by or as if by sliding **2** to avoid dealing with (a matter) fully

slide rule *n obsolete* a mechanical calculating device consisting of two strips, one sliding along a central groove in the other, each strip graduated in two or more logarithmic scales of numbers, trigonometric functions, etc It employs the same principles as logarithm tables

slide show *n* **1** a display of photographic transparencies using a slide projector **2** any display in the form of a series of static images, such as on a computer screen ▷ *adj* **3** (*prenominal*) presented as a series of static images: *slide-show presentation*

sliding scale *n* a variable scale according to which specified wages, tariffs, prices, etc, fluctuate in response to changes in some other factor, standard, or conditions

slier ('slaɪə) *adj* a comparative of **sly**

sliest ('slaɪɪst) *adj* a superlative of **sly**

slight (slaɪt) *adj* **1** small in quantity or extent **2** of small importance; trifling **3** slim and delicate **4** lacking in strength or substance ▷ *vb* (*tr*) **5** to show indifference or disregard for (someone); snub **6** to treat as unimportant or trifling **7** *US* to devote inadequate attention to (work, duties, etc) ▷ *n* **8** an act or omission indicating superscilious neglect or indifference [c13: from Old Norse *slēttr* smooth; related to Old High German *slehtr*, Gothic *slaihts*, Middle Dutch *slecht* simple] > 'slightness *n*

slightly ('slaɪtlɪ) *adv* in small measure or degree

Sligo ('slaɪgəʊ) *n* **1** a county of NW Republic of Ireland, on the Atlantic: has a deeply indented low-lying coast; livestock and dairy farming. County town: Sligo. Pop: 58 200 (2002). Area: 1795 sq km (693 sq miles) **2** a port in NW Republic of Ireland, county town of Co Sligo on **Sligo Bay**. Pop: 19 735 (2002)

slily ('slaɪlɪ) *adv* a variant spelling of **slyly**

slim (slɪm) *adj* **slimmer, slimmest** small in width relative to height or length **1** small in amount or quality: *slim chances of success* ▷ *vb* **slims, slimming, slimmed 2** to make or become slim, esp by diets and exercise **3** to reduce or decrease or cause to be reduced or decreased [c17: from Dutch: crafty, from Middle Dutch *slimp* slanting; compare Old High German *slimbi* obliquity] ▷ **'slimmer** *n* ▷ **'slimness** *n*

Slim[1] (slɪm) *n* the E African name for **AIDS** [from its wasting effects]

Slim[2] (slɪm) *n* **William Joseph**, 1st Viscount. 1891–1970, British field marshal, who commanded (1943–45) the 14th Army in the reconquest of Burma (now called Myanmar) from the Japanese; governor general of Australia (1953–60)

slim down *vb* (*adverb*) **1** to make or become slim, esp intentionally **2** to make (an organization) more efficient or (of an organization) to become more efficient, esp by cutting staff ▷ *n* slimdown **3** an instance of an organization slimming down

slime (slaɪm) *n* **1** soft thin runny mud or filth **2** any moist viscous fluid, esp when noxious or unpleasant **3** a mucous substance produced by various organisms, such as fish, slugs, and fungi ▷ *vb* (*tr*) **4** to cover with slime [Old English *slīm*; related to Old Norse *slīm*, Old High German *slīmen* to smooth, Russian *slimák* snail, Latin *līmax* snail]

slimline ('slɪm,laɪn) *adj* slim; giving the appearance of or conducive to slimness

slimy ('slaɪmɪ) *adj* **slimier**, **slimiest 1** characterized by, covered with, containing, secreting, or resembling slime **2** offensive or repulsive **3** chiefly *Brit* characterized by servility

sling[1] (slɪŋ) *n* **1** a simple weapon consisting of a loop of leather, etc, in which a stone is whirled and then let fly **2** a rope or strap by which something may be secured or lifted **3** *med* a wide piece of cloth suspended from the neck for supporting an injured hand or arm across the front of the body **4** a loop or band attached to an object for carrying **5** *mountaineering* a loop of rope or tape used for support in belays, abseils, etc **6** the act of slinging ▷ *vb* **slings, slinging, slung 7** (*tr*) to hurl with or as if with a sling **8** to attach a sling or slings to (a load, etc) **9** (*tr*) to carry or hang loosely from or as if from a sling: *to sling washing from the line* **10** *informal* to throw [c13: perhaps of Scandinavian origin; compare Old Norse *slyngva* to hurl, Old High German *slingan*]

sling[2] (slɪŋ) *n* a mixed drink with a spirit base, usually sweetened [c19: of uncertain origin]

slingback ('slɪŋ,bæk) *n* a shoe with a strap instead of a full covering for the heel

sling off *vb* (*intr, adverb*; often foll by *at*) *Austral & NZ informal* to laugh or jeer (at)

slingshot ('slɪŋ,ʃɒt) *n* **1** *US & Canadian* a catapult **2** another name for **sling**[1] (sense 1)

slink (slɪŋk) *vb* **slinks, slinking, slunk 1** (*intr*) to move or act in a furtive or cringing manner from or as if from fear, guilt, etc **2** (*intr*) to move in a sinuous alluring manner **3** (*tr*) (of animals, esp cows) to give birth to prematurely ▷ *n* **4** an animal, esp a calf, born prematurely [Old English *slincan*; related to Middle Low German *slinken* to shrink, Old Swedish *slinka* to creep, Danish *slunken* limp]

slinky ('slɪŋkɪ) *adj* **slinkier, slinkiest** *informal* **1** moving in a sinuously graceful or provocative way **2** (of clothes) figure-hugging; clinging ▷ **'slinkily** *adv* ▷ **'slinkiness** *n*

slip[1] (slɪp) *vb* **slips, slipping, slipped 1** to move or cause to move smoothly and easily **2** (*tr*) to place, insert, or convey quickly or stealthily **3** (*tr*) to put on or take off easily or quickly: *to slip on a sweater* **4** (*intr*) to lose balance and slide unexpectedly: *he slipped on the ice* **5** to let loose or be let loose **6** to be released from (something); escape **7** (*tr*) to let go (mooring or anchor lines) over the side **8** (when *intr*, often foll by *from* or *out of*) to pass out of (the mind or memory) **9** (*intr*) to move or pass swiftly or unperceived: *to slip quietly out of the room* **10** (*intr*; sometimes foll by *up*) to make a mistake **11** Also called: **sideslip** to cause (an aircraft) to slide sideways or (of an aircraft) to slide sideways **12** (*intr*) to decline in health, mental ability, etc **13** (*intr*) (of an intervertebral disc) to become displaced from the normal position **14** (*tr*) to dislocate (a bone) **15** (of animals) to give birth to (offspring) prematurely **16** (*tr*) to pass (a stitch) from one needle to another without knitting or purling **17 a** (*tr*) to operate

(the clutch of a motor vehicle) so that it partially disengages **b** (*intr*) (of the clutch of a motor vehicle) to fail to engage, esp as a result of wear **18 let slip a** to allow to escape **b** to say unintentionally ▷ *n* **19** the act or an instance of slipping **20** a mistake or oversight: *a slip of the pen* **21** a moral lapse or failing **22** a woman's sleeveless undergarment, worn as a lining for and to give support to a dress **23** See **slipway 24** *cricket* **a** the position of the fielder who stands a little way behind and to the offside of the wicketkeeper **b** the fielder himself **25** the relative movement of rocks along a fault plane **26** a landslide, esp one blocking a road or railway line **27** *metallurgy, crystallog* the deformation of a metallic crystal caused when one part glides over another part along a plane **28** the deviation of a propeller from its helical path through a fluid, expressed as the difference between its actual forward motion and its theoretical forward motion in one revolution **29** another name for **sideslip** (sense 1) **30** give someone the slip to elude or escape from someone ▷ See also **slip up** [c13: from Middle Low German or Dutch *slippen*] ▷ **'slipless** *adj*

slip[2] (slɪp) *n* **1** a narrow piece; strip **2** a small piece of paper: *a receipt slip* **3** a part of a plant that, when detached from the parent, will grow into a new plant; cutting; scion **4** a young slender person: *a slip of a child* **5** *printing* **a** a long galley **b** a less common name for a **galley proof 6** chiefly *US* a pew or similar long narrow seat ▷ *vb* **slips, slipping, slipped 7** (*tr*) to detach (portions of stem, etc) from (a plant) for propagation [c15: probably from Middle Low German, Middle Dutch *slippe* to cut, strip]

slip[3] (slɪp) *n* clay mixed with water to a creamy consistency, used for decorating or patching a ceramic piece [Old English *slyppe* slime; related to Norwegian *slipa* slime on fish; see **SLOP**[1]]

slipcase ('slɪp,keɪs) *n* a protective case for a book or set of books that is open at one end so that only the spines of the books are visible

slipcover ('slɪp,kʌvə) *n* **1** *US & Canadian* a fitted but easily removable cloth cover for a chair, sofa, etc. Also called (in Britain and certain other countries): **loose cover 2** *US & Canadian* a book jacket; dust cover

slipe (slaɪp) *n* *NZ* a wool removed from the pelt of a slaughtered sheep by immersion in a chemical bath **b** (*as modifier*): *slipe wool* [from English dialect]

slipknot ('slɪp,nɒt) *n* **1** Also called: **running knot** a nooselike knot tied so that it will slip along the rope round which it is made **2** a knot that can be easily untied by pulling one free end

slip-on *adj* **1** (of a garment or shoe) made so as to be easily and quickly put on or off ▷ *n* **2** a slip-on garment or shoe

slipover ('slɪp,əʊvə) *adj* **1** of or denoting a garment that can be put on easily over the head ▷ *n* **2** such a garment, esp a sleeveless pullover

slippage ('slɪpɪdʒ) *n* **1** the act or an instance of slipping **2** the amount of slipping or the extent to which slipping occurs **3 a** an instance of not reaching a norm, target, etc **b** the extent of this

slipped disc *n* *pathol* a herniated intervertebral disc, often resulting in pain because of pressure on the spinal nerves

slipper ('slɪpə) *n* **1** a light shoe of some soft material, for wearing around the house **2** a woman's evening or dancing shoe ▷ *vb* **3** (*tr*) *informal* to hit or beat with a slipper ▷ **'slippered** *adj*

slipper bath *n* a bath in the shape of a slipper, with a covered end

slipperwort ('slɪpə,wɜːt) *n* another name for: **calceolaria** [c19: so called because of the slipper-like shape of the flower]

slippery ('slɪpərɪ, -prɪ) *adj* **1** causing or tending to cause objects to slip: *a slippery road* **2** liable to slip from the grasp, a position, etc **3** not to be relied upon; cunning and untrustworthy: *a slippery character* **4** (esp of a situation) liable to change; unstable [c16: probably coined by Coverdale to translate German *schlipfferig* in Luther's Bible (Psalm 35:6); related to Old English *slipor* slippery] ▷ **'slipperiness** *n*

slippery elm *n* **1** a tree, *Ulmus fulva*, of E North America, having oblong serrated leaves, notched winged fruits, and a mucilaginous inner bark **2** the bark of this tree, used medicinally as a demulcent ▷ Also called: **red elm**

slippy ('slɪpɪ) *adj* **-pier, -piest** **1** *informal or dialect* another word for **slippery** (senses 1, 2) **2** *Brit informal* alert; quick ▷ 'slippiness *n*

slip rail *n Austral & NZ* a rail in a fence that can be slipped out of place to make an opening

slip road *n Brit* a short road connecting a motorway, etc, to another road

slipshod ('slɪp,ʃɒd) *adj* **1** (of an action) negligent; careless **2** (of a person's appearance) slovenly; down-at-heel [c16: from SLIP¹ + SHOD]

slipstream ('slɪp,striːm) *n* **1** Also called: **airstream, race a** the stream of air forced backwards by an aircraft propeller **b** a stream of air behind any moving object ▷ *vb* **2** *motor racing* to follow (another car, etc) closely in order to take advantage of the decreased wind resistance immediately behind it

slip up *vb* (*intr, adverb*) **1** *informal* to make a blunder or mistake; err ▷ *n* **slip-up** **2** *informal* a mistake, blunder, or mishap

slipware ('slɪp,wɛə) *n* pottery that has been decorated with slip

slipway ('slɪp,weɪ) *n* **1** the sloping area in a shipyard, containing the ways **2** Also called: **marine railway** the ways on which a vessel is launched

slit (slɪt) *vb* **slits, slitting, slit** (*tr*) **1** to make a straight long incision in; split open **2** to cut into strips lengthwise ▷ *n* **3** a long narrow cut **4** a long narrow opening [Old English *slītan* to slice; related to Old Norse *slita*, Old High German *slīzen*] ▷ 'slitter *n*

slither ('slɪðə) *vb* **1** to move or slide or cause to move or slide unsteadily, as on a slippery surface **2** (*intr*) to travel with a sliding motion ▷ *n* **3** a slithering motion [Old English *slidrian*, from *slīdan* to SLIDE]

slit trench *n military* a narrow trench dug for the protection of a small number of people

sliver ('slɪvə) *n* **1 a** a thin piece that is cut or broken off lengthwise; splinter **2** a loose strand or fibre obtained by carding ▷ *vb* **3** to divide or be divided into splinters; split **4** (*tr*) to form (wool, etc) into slivers [c14: from *sliven* to split]

Sloan (sləʊn) *n* **John.** 1871–1951, US painter and etcher, a leading member of the group of realistic painters known as the Ash Can School. His pictures of city scenes include *McSorley's Bar* (1912) and *Backyards, Greenwich Village* (1914)

Sloane Ranger (sləʊn) *n* (in Britain) *informal* a young upper-class or upper-middle-class person, esp a woman, having a home in London and in the country, characterized typically as wearing expensive informal country clothes. Also called: **Sloane** [c20: coined by Peter York, punning on *Sloane* Square, London SW1, and *Lone Ranger*, television cowboy character]

slob (slɒb) *n* **1** *informal* a slovenly, unattractive, and lazy person **2** *Irish* mire [c19: from Irish *slab* mud; compare SLAB] ▷ 'slobbish *adj*

slobber ('slɒbə) *or* **slabber** *vb* **1** to dribble (saliva, food, etc) from the mouth **2** (*intr*) to speak or write mawkishly **3** (*tr*) to smear with matter dribbling from the mouth ▷ *n* **4** liquid or saliva spilt from the mouth **5** maudlin language or behaviour [c15: from Middle Low German, Middle Dutch *slubberen*; see SLAVER²] ▷ 'slobberer *or* 'slabberer *n* ▷ 'slobbery *or* 'slabbery *adj*

sloe (sləʊ) *n* **1** the small sour blue-black fruit of the blackthorn **2** another name for **blackthorn** [Old English *slāh*; related to Old High German *slēha*, Middle Dutch *sleuuwe*]

sloe-eyed *adj* having dark slanted or almond-shaped eyes

sloe gin *n* gin flavoured with sloe juice

slog (slɒg) *vb* **slogs, slogging, slogged** **1** to hit with heavy blows, as in boxing **2** (*intr*) to work hard; toil **3** (*intr*; foll by *down, up, along*, etc) to move with difficulty; plod **4** *cricket* to score freely by taking large swipes at the ball ▷ *n* **5** a tiring hike or walk **6** long exhausting work **7** a heavy blow or swipe [c19: of unknown origin]

▷ 'slogger *n*

slogan ('sləʊgən) *n* **1** a distinctive or topical phrase used in politics, advertising, etc **2** *Scot history* a Highland battle cry [c16: from Gaelic *sluagh-ghairm* war cry, from *sluagh* army + *gairm* cry]

slommock ('slɒmək) *vb* (*intr*) *Midland English dialect* to walk assertively with a hip-rolling gait

sloop (sluːp) *n* a single-masted sailing vessel, rigged fore-and-aft, with the mast stepped about one third of the overall length aft of the bow [c17: from Dutch *sloep*; related to French *chaloupe* launch, Old English *slūpan* to glide]

sloot (sluːt) *n South African* a ditch for irrigation or drainage [from Afrikaans, from Dutch *sluit, sluis* SLUICE]

slop¹ (slɒp) *vb* **slops, slopping, slopped** **1** (when *intr*, often foll by *about*) to cause (liquid) to splash or spill or (of liquid) to splash or spill **2** (*intr*; foll by *along, through*, etc) to tramp (through) mud or slush **3** (*tr*) to feed slop or swill to: *to slop the pigs* **4** (*tr*) to ladle or serve, esp clumsily **5** (*intr*; foll by *over*) *informal, chiefly US & Canadian* to be unpleasantly effusive ▷ *n* **6** a puddle of spilt liquid **7** (*plural*) wet feed, esp for pigs, made from kitchen waste, etc **8** (*plural*) waste food or liquid refuse **9** (often *plural*) *informal* liquid or semiliquid food of low quality **10** soft mud, snow, etc [c14: probably from Old English *-sloppe* in *cūsloppe* COWSLIP; see SLIP³]

slop² (slɒp) *n* **1** (*plural*) sailors' clothing and bedding issued from a ship's stores **2** any loose article of clothing, esp a smock **3** (*plural*) shoddy manufactured clothing [Old English *oferslop* surplice; related to Old Norse *slopps* gown, Middle Dutch *slop*]

slop basin *n* a bowl or basin into which the dregs from teacups are emptied at the table

slope (sləʊp) *vb* **1** to lie or cause to lie at a slanting or oblique angle **2** (*intr*) (esp of natural features) to follow an inclined course: *many paths sloped down the hillside* **3** (*intr*; foll by *off, away*, etc) to go furtively **4** (*tr*) *military* (formerly) to hold (a rifle) in the slope position (esp in the command **slope arms**) ▷ *n* **5** an inclined portion of ground **6** (*plural*) hills or foothills **7** any inclined surface or line **8** the degree or amount of such inclination **9** *maths* (of a line) the tangent of the angle between the line and another line parallel to the *x*-axis **10** (formerly) the position adopted for British military drill when the rifle is rested on the shoulder [c15: short for *aslope*, perhaps from the past participle of Old English *āslūpan* to slip away, from *slūpan* to slip] ▷ 'sloper *n* ▷ 'sloping *adj*

slop out *vb* (*intr, adverb*) (of prisoners) to empty chamber pots and collect water for washing

sloppy ('slɒpɪ) *adj* **-pier, -piest** **1** (esp of ground conditions, etc) wet; slushy **2** *informal* careless; untidy **3** *informal* mawkishly sentimental **4** (of food or drink) watery and unappetizing **5** splashed with slops **6** (of clothes) loose; baggy ▷ 'sloppily *adv* ▷ 'sloppiness *n*

slosh (slɒʃ) *n* **1** watery mud, snow, etc **2** *Brit slang* a heavy blow **3** the sound of splashing liquid ▷ *vb* **4** (*tr*; foll by *around, on, in*, etc) *informal* to throw or pour (liquid) **5** (when *intr*, often foll by *about* or *around*) *informal* **a** to shake or stir (something) in a liquid **b** (of a person) to splash (around) in water, etc **6** *Brit slang* to deal a heavy blow to **7** (usually foll by *about* or *around*) *informal* to shake (a container of liquid) or (of liquid within a container) to be shaken [c19: variant of SLUSH, influenced by SLOP¹] ▷ 'sloshy *adj*

sloshed (slɒʃt) *adj chiefly Brit* a slang word for **drunk**

slot¹ (slɒt) *n* **1** an elongated aperture or groove, such as one in a vending machine for inserting a coin **2** *informal* a place in a series or scheme ▷ *vb* **slots, slotting, slotted** **3** (*tr*) to furnish with a slot or slots **4** (usually foll by *in* or *into*) to fit or adjust in a slot **5** *informal* to situate or be situated in a series or scheme [c13: from Old French *esclot* the depression of the breastbone, of unknown origin] ▷ 'slotter *n*

slot² (slɒt) *n* the trail of an animal, esp a deer [c16: from Old French *esclot* horse's hoof-print, probably of Scandinavian origin; compare Old Norse *sloth* track; see SLEUTH]

sloth (sləʊθ) *n* **1** any of several shaggy-coated arboreal edentate mammals of the family *Bradypodidae*, esp

Bradypus tridactylus (**three-toed sloth** or **ai**) or *Choloepus didactylus* (**two-toed sloth** or **unau**), of Central and South America. They are slow-moving, hanging upside down by their long arms and feeding on vegetation **2** reluctance to work or exert oneself [Old English *slǣwth*; from *slǣw*, variant of *slǎw* SLOW]

sloth bear *n* a bear, *Melursus ursinus*, of forests of S India and Sri Lanka, having a shaggy coat and an elongated snout specialized for feeding on termites

slothful ('sləʊθfʊl) *adj* indolent ⊳ 'slothfully *adv* ⊳ 'slothfulness *n*

slot machine *n* a machine, esp one for selling small articles or for gambling, activated by placing a coin or metal disc in a slot

slouch (slaʊtʃ) *vb* **1** (*intr*) to sit or stand with a drooping bearing **2** (*intr*) to walk or move with an awkward slovenly gait **3** (*tr*) to cause (the shoulders) to droop ⊳ *n* **4** a drooping carriage **5** (*usually used in negative constructions*) *informal* an incompetent or slovenly person: *he's no slouch at football* [c16: of unknown origin] ⊳ 'slouching *adj*

slouch hat *n* any soft hat with a brim that can be pulled down over the ears, esp an Australian army hat with the left side of the brim turned up

slough¹ (slaʊ) *n* **1** a hollow filled with mud; bog **2** (slu:) *US & Canadian* **a** (in the prairies) a large hole where water collects or the water in such a hole **b** (on the Pacific coast) a marshy saltwater inlet **3** despair or degradation [Old English *slōh*; related to Middle High German *sluoche* ditch, Swedish *slaga* swamp] ⊳ 'sloughy *adj*

slough² (slʌf) *n* **1** any outer covering that is shed, such as the dead outer layer of the skin of a snake, the cellular debris in a wound, etc ⊳ *vb* **2** (often foll by *off*) to shed (a skin, etc) or (of a skin, etc) to be shed [c13: of Germanic origin; compare Middle Low German *slū* husk, German *Schlauch* hose, Norwegian *slō* fleshy part of a horn] ⊳ 'sloughy *adj*

Slough (slaʊ) *n* **1** an industrial town in SE central England, in Slough unitary authority, Berkshire; food products, high-tech industries. Pop: 126 276 (2001) **2** a unitary authority in SE central England, in Berkshire. Pop: 118 800 (2003 est). Area: 28 sq km (11 sq miles)

slough off (slʌf) *vb* (*tr, adverb*) to cast off (cares, etc)

Slovak ('sləʊvæk) *adj* **1** of, relating to, or characteristic of Slovakia, its people, or their language ⊳ *n* **2** the official language of Slovakia, belonging to the West Slavonic branch of the Indo-European family. Slovak is closely related to Czech, they are mutually intelligible **3** a native or inhabitant of Slovakia

Slovakia (sləʊ'vækɪə) *n* a country in central Europe: part of Hungary from the 11th century until 1918, when it united with Bohemia and Moravia to form Czechoslovakia; it became independent in 1993 and joined the EU in 2004. Official language: Slovak. Religion: Roman Catholic majority. Currency: koruna. Capital: Bratislava. Pop: 5 407 000 (2004 est). Area: 49 036 sq km (18 940 sq miles) ⊳ Slo'vakian *adj, n*

sloven ('slʌvᵊn) *n* a person who is habitually negligent in appearance, hygiene, or work [c15: probably related to Flemish *sloef* dirty, Dutch *slof* negligent]

Slovene (sləʊ'vi:n) *adj* **1** Also called: **Slovenian** of, relating to, or characteristic of Slovenia, its people, or their language ⊳ *n* **2** Also called: **Slovenian** a South Slavonic language spoken in Slovenia, closely related to Croatian **3** a native or inhabitant of Slovenia

Slovenia (sləʊ'vi:nɪə) *n* a republic in S central Europe: settled by the Slovenes in the 6th century; joined Yugoslavia in 1918 and became an autonomous republic in 1946; became fully independent in 1992 and joined the EU in 2004; rises over 2800 m (9000 ft) in the Julian Alps. Official language: Slovene. Religion: Roman Catholic majority. Currency: euro (replacing the tolar in 2007). Capital: Ljubljana. Pop: 1 982 000 (2004 est). Area: 20 251 sq km (7819 sq miles)

slovenly ('slʌvᵊnlɪ) *adj* **1** frequently or habitually unclean or untidy **2** negligent and careless; slipshod: *slovenly manners* ⊳ *adv* **3** in a negligent or slovenly manner ⊳ 'slovenliness *n*

slow (sləʊ) *adj* **1** performed or occurring during a comparatively long interval of time **2** lasting a comparatively long time: *a slow journey* **3** characterized by lack of speed: *a slow walker* **4** (*prenominal*) adapted to or productive of slow movement: *the slow lane of a motorway* **5** (of a clock, etc) indicating a time earlier than the correct time **6** not readily responsive to stimulation; intellectually unreceptive: *a slow mind* **7** dull or uninteresting: *the play was very slow* **8** not easily aroused: *a slow temperament* **9** lacking promptness or immediacy: *a slow answer* **10** unwilling to perform an action or enter into a state: *slow to anger* **11** behind the times **12** (of trade, etc) unproductive; slack **13** (of a fire) burning weakly **14** (of an oven) cool **15** *photog* requiring a relatively long time of exposure to produce a given density: *a slow lens* **16** *sport* (of a track, etc) tending to reduce the speed of the ball or the competitors **17** *cricket* (of a bowler, etc) delivering the ball slowly, usually with spin ⊳ *adv* **18** in a manner characterized by lack of speed; slowly ⊳ *vb* **19** (often foll by *up* or *down*) to decrease or cause to decrease in speed, efficiency, etc [Old English *slāw* sluggish; related to Old High German *slēo* dull, Old Norse *slēr*, Dutch *sleeuw* slow] ⊳ 'slowly *adv* ⊳ 'slowness *n*

slowcoach ('sləʊ,kəʊtʃ) *n* *Brit informal* a person who moves, acts, or works slowly. US and Canadian name: **slowpoke**

slow handclap *n* *Brit* slow rhythmic clapping, esp used by an audience to indicate dissatisfaction or impatience

slow march *n* *military* a march in slow time

slow match *n* a match or fuse that burns slowly without flame, esp a wick impregnated with potassium nitrate

slow-mo or **slo-mo** ('sləʊ,məʊ) *n, adj informal* short for **slow motion**

slow motion *n* **1** *films, television* action that is made to appear slower than normal by passing the film through the taking camera at a faster rate than normal or by replaying a video tape recording more slowly ⊳ *adj* **slow-motion 2** *films, television* of or relating to such action **3** moving or functioning at less than usual speed

slow virus *n* any of a class of virus-like disease-causing agents known as prions that are present in the body for a long time before becoming active or infectious and are very resistant to radiation and similar factors: believed to be the cause of BSE and scrapie

slowworm ('sləʊ,wɜ:m) *n* a Eurasian legless lizard, *Anguis fragilis*, with a brownish-grey snakelike body: family Anguidae. Also called: **blindworm**

SLR *abbreviation* single-lens reflex. See **reflex camera**

SLSC *abbreviation* (in Australia) Surf Life Saving Club

slub (slʌb) *n* **1** a lump in yarn or fabric, often made intentionally to give a knobbly effect **2** a loosely twisted roll of fibre prepared for spinning ⊳ *vb* **slubs, slubbing, slubbed 3** (*tr*) to draw out and twist (a sliver of fibre) preparatory to spinning ⊳ *adj* **4** (of material) having an irregular appearance [c18: of unknown origin]

sludge (slʌdʒ) *n* **1** soft mud, snow, etc **2** any deposit or sediment **3** a surface layer of ice that has a slushy appearance **4** (in sewage disposal) the solid constituents of sewage that precipitate during treatment and are removed for subsequent purification [c17: probably related to SLUSH] ⊳ 'sludgy *adj*

slue¹ (slu:) *n, vb* a variant spelling (esp US) of **slew²**

slue² (slu:) *n* a variant spelling of **slough¹** (sense 2)

slug¹ (slʌg) *n* **1** any of various terrestrial gastropod molluscs of the genera *Limax, Arion*, etc, in which the body is elongated and the shell is absent or very much reduced **2** any of various other invertebrates having a soft slimy body, esp the larvae of certain sawflies [c15 (in the sense: a slow person or animal): probably of Scandinavian origin; compare Norwegian (dialect) *sluggje*]

slug² (slʌg) *n* **1** an fps unit of mass; the mass that will acquire an acceleration of 1 foot per second per second when acted upon by a force of 1 pound. 1 slug is approximately equal to 32.17 pounds **2** *metallurgy* a metal blank from which small forgings are worked **3** a bullet or pellet larger than a pellet of buckshot **4** *chiefly US & Canadian* a metal token for use in slot machines, etc **5** *printing* **a** a thick strip of type metal that is less than type-high and is used for spacing **b** a metal strip

S

containing a line of characters as produced by a
linecaster [C17 (bullet), C19 (printing): perhaps from sʟᴜɢ¹, with
allusion to the shape of the animal]

slug³ (slʌɡ) vb **slugs, slugging, slugged 1** to hit very hard
and solidly, as in boxing **2** (tr) Austral & NZ informal to
charge (someone) an exorbitant price ▷ n **3** an act of
slugging; heavy blow **4** Austral & NZ informal an
exorbitant charge or price [c19: perhaps from sʟᴜɢ²
(bullet)]

sluggard ('slʌɡəd) n **1** a person who is habitually
indolent ▷ adj **2** lazy [C14 slogarde; related to sʟᴜɢ¹]
> 'sluggardly adj

sluggish ('slʌɡɪʃ) adj **1** lacking energy; inactive; slow-
moving **2** functioning at below normal rate or level
3 exhibiting poor response to stimulation
> 'sluggishly adv

sluice (sluːs) n **1** Also called: sluiceway a channel that
carries a rapid current of water, esp one that has a
sluicegate to control the flow **2** the body of water
controlled by a sluicegate **3** See sluicegate **4** mining an
inclined trough for washing ore, esp one having riffles
on the bottom to trap particles **5** an artificial channel
through which logs can be floated ▷ vb **6** (tr) to draw out
or drain (water, etc) from (a pond, etc) by means of a
sluice **7** (tr) to wash or irrigate with a stream of water
8 (tr) mining to wash in a sluice **9** (tr) to send (logs, etc)
down a sluice **10** (intr; often foll by away or out) (of water,
etc) to run or flow from or as if from a sluice **11** (tr) to
provide with a sluice [c14: from Old French escluse, from
Late Latin exclūsa aqua water shut out, from Latin exclūdere
to shut out, ᴇxᴄʟᴜᴅᴇ] > 'sluice,like adj

sluicegate ('sluːs,ɡeɪt) n a valve or gate fitted to a sluice
to control the rate of flow of water. See also floodgate
(sense 1)

slum (slʌm) n **1** a squalid overcrowded house, etc **2** (often
plural) a squalid section of a city, characterized by
inferior living conditions and usually by overcrowding
3 (modifier) of, relating to, or characteristic of slums: slum
conditions ▷ vb **slums, slumming, slummed** (intr) **4** to visit
slums, esp for curiosity **5** Also called: slum it to suffer
conditions below those to which one is accustomed [c19:
originally slang, of obscure origin] > 'slummy adj

slumber ('slʌmbə) vb **1** (intr) to sleep, esp peacefully
2 (intr) to be quiescent or dormant **3** (tr; foll by away) to
spend (time) sleeping ▷ n **4** (sometimes plural) sleep **5** a
dormant or quiescent state [Old English slūma sleep (n);
related to Middle High German slummeren, Dutch
sluimeren] > 'slumberer n

slumberous ('slʌmbərəs, -brəs) adj chiefly poetic **1** sleepy;
drowsy **2** inducing sleep > 'slumberously adv
> 'slumberousness n

slump (slʌmp) vb (intr) **1** to sink or fall heavily and
suddenly **2** to relax ungracefully **3** (of business activity,
etc) to decline suddenly; collapse **4** (of health, interest,
etc) to deteriorate or decline suddenly or markedly ▷ n
5 a sudden or marked decline or failure, as in progress or
achievement; collapse **6** a decline in commercial
activity, prices, etc **7** economics another word for
depression **8** the act of slumping [c17: probably of
Scandinavian origin; compare Low German slump bog,
Norwegian slumpa to fall]

slung (slʌŋ) adj the past tense and past participle of
sling¹

slunk (slʌŋk) vb the past tense and past participle of
slink

slur (slɜː) vb **slurs, slurring, slurred** (mainly tr) **1** (often foll
by over) to treat superficially, hastily, or without due
deliberation; gloss **2** (also intr) to pronounce or utter
(words, etc) indistinctly **3** to speak disparagingly of or
cast aspersions on **4** music to execute (a melodic interval
of two or more notes) smoothly, as in legato
performance ▷ n **5** an indistinct sound or utterance **6** a
slighting remark; aspersion **7** a stain or disgrace, as
upon one's reputation; stigma **8** music **a** a performance
or execution of a melodic interval of two or more notes
in a part **b** the curved line (⌢ or ⌣) indicating this [c15:
probably from Middle Low German; compare Middle
Low German slūren to drag, trail, Middle Dutch sloren,

Dutch sleuren]

slurp (slɜːp) informal ▷ vb **1** to eat or drink (something)
noisily ▷ n **2** a sound produced in this way [c17: from
Middle Dutch slorpen to sip; related to German schlürfen]

slurry ('slʌrɪ) n, pl -ries a suspension of solid particles in
a liquid, as in a mixture of cement, clay, coal dust,
manure, meat, etc with water [C15 slory; see sʟᴜʀ]

slush (slʌʃ) n **1** any watery muddy substance, esp
melting snow **2** informal sloppily sentimental language
▷ vb **3** (intr; foll by along) to make one's way
through or as if through slush [c17: related to Danish
slus sleet, Norwegian slusk slops; see sʟᴜᴅɢᴇ, sʟᴏsʜ]
> 'slushy adj > 'slushiness n

slush fund n a fund for financing political or
commercial corruption

slut (slʌt) n derogatory **1** a dirty slatternly woman **2** an
immoral woman [c14: of unknown origin] > 'sluttish adj
> 'sluttishness n

Sluter (Dutch 'slyːtər) n Claus (klaʊs). ?1345–1406, Dutch
sculptor, working in Burgundy, whose realism
influenced many sculptors and painters in 15th-century
Europe. He is best known for the portal sculptures and
the Well of Moses in the Carthusian monastery at
Champnol

sly (slaɪ) adj **slyer, slyest** or **slier, sliest 1** crafty; artful: a
sly dodge **2** insidious; furtive: a sly manner **3** playfully
mischievous; roguish: sly humour ▷ n **4** on the sly in a
secretive manner [c12: from Old Norse slǣgr clever,
literally: able to strike, from slā to sʟᴀʏ] > 'slyly or 'slily
adv > 'slyness n

slype (slaɪp) n a covered passageway in a cathedral or
church that connects the transept to the chapterhouse
[c19: probably from Middle Flemish slijpen to slip]

Sm the chemical symbol for samarium

SM abbreviation **1** sergeant major **2** sadomasochism

smack¹ (smæk) n **1** a smell or flavour that is distinctive
though faint **2** a distinctive trace or touch: the smack of
corruption **3** a small quantity, esp a mouthful or taste ▷ vb
(intr; foll by of) **4** to have the characteristic smell or
flavour (of something): to smack of the sea **5** to have an
element suggestive (of something): his speeches smacked of
bigotry [Old English smæc; related to Old High German
smoc, Icelandic smekkr a taste, Dutch smaak]

smack² (smæk) vb **1** (tr) to strike or slap smartly, with or
as if with the open hand **2** to strike or send forcibly or
loudly or to be struck or sent forcibly or loudly **3** to open
and close (the lips) loudly, esp to show pleasure ▷ n **4** a
sharp resounding slap or blow with something flat, or
the sound of such a blow **5** a loud kiss **6** a sharp sound
made by the lips, as in enjoyment **7** have a smack at
informal, chiefly Brit to attempt **8** smack in the eye
informal, chiefly Brit a snub or setback ▷ adv informal
9 directly; squarely **10** with a smack; sharply and
unexpectedly [c16: from Middle Low German or Middle
Dutch smacken, probably of imitative origin]

smack³ (smæk) n a slang word for heroin [c20: perhaps
from Yiddish schmeck]

smack⁴ (smæk) n a sailing vessel, usually sloop-rigged,
used in coasting and fishing along the British coast [c17:
from Low German smack or Dutch smak, of unknown
origin]

smacker ('smækə) n slang **1** a loud kiss; smack **2** a pound
note or dollar bill

smackhead ('smæk,hɛd) n Brit slang a person who is
addicted to heroin

small (smɔːl) adj **1** comparatively little; limited in size,
number, importance, etc **2** of little importance or on a
minor scale: a small business **3** lacking in moral or mental
breadth or depth: a small mind **4** modest or humble: small
beginnings **5** of low or inferior status, esp socially **6** (of a
child or animal) young; not mature **7** unimportant,
trivial: a small matter **8** of, relating to, or designating the
ordinary modern minuscule letter used in printing and
cursive writing **9** lacking great strength or force: a small
effort **10** in fine particles: small gravel ▷ adv **11** into small
pieces: you have to cut it small **12** in a small or soft manner
▷ n **13** the small an object, person, or group considered
to be small: do you want the small or the large? **14** a small
slender part, esp of the back **15** (plural) informal, chiefly Brit

items of personal laundry, such as underwear [Old English *smæl*; related to Old High German *smal*, Old Norse *smali* small cattle] > 'smallish *adj* > 'smallness *n*

small arms *pl n* portable firearms of relatively small calibre

small beer *n* *informal, chiefly Brit* people or things of no importance

small change *n* **1** coins, esp those of low value **2** a person or thing that is not outstanding or important

small circle *n* a circular section of a sphere that does not contain the centre of the sphere

small claims court *n* *Brit & Canadian* a local court with jurisdiction to try civil actions involving small claims

small fry *pl n* **1** people or things regarded as unimportant **2** young children **3** young or small fishes

small goods *pl n* *Austral & NZ* meats bought from a delicatessen, such as sausages

smallholding ('smɔːlˌhəʊldɪŋ) *n* a holding of agricultural land smaller than a small farm > 'smallˌholder *n*

small hours *pl n* the small hours the early hours of the morning, after midnight and before dawn

small intestine *n* the longest part of the alimentary canal, consisting of the duodenum, jejunum, and ileum, in which digestion is completed. See **large intestine**

small-minded *adj* narrow-minded; petty; intolerant; mean > ˌsmall-'mindedly *adv* > ˌsmall-'mindedness *n*

smallpox ('smɔːlˌpɒks) *n* an acute highly contagious viral disease characterized by high fever, severe prostration, and a pinkish rash changing in form from papules to pustules, which dry up and form scabs that are cast off, leaving pitted depressions. Technical name: variola [c16: from SMALL + POX. So called to distinguish it from *the Great Pox*, an archaic name for syphilis]

small print *n* matter in a contract, etc, printed in small type, esp when considered to be a trap for the unwary

small-scale *adj* **1** of limited size or scope **2** (of a map, model, etc) giving a relatively small representation of something, usually missing out details

small screen *n* an informal name for **television**

small slam *n* *bridge* another name for **little slam**

small talk *n* light conversation for social occasions

small-time *adj informal* insignificant; minor: *a small-time criminal* > 'small-'timer *n*

smalt (smɔːlt) *n* **1** a type of silica glass coloured deep blue with cobalt oxide **2** a pigment made by crushing this glass, used in colouring enamels [c16: via French from Italian SMALTO, of Germanic origin; related to SMELT¹]

smalto ('smɑːltəʊ) *n*, *pl* -tos *or* -ti (-tiː) coloured glass, etc, used in mosaics [c18: from Italian; see SMALT]

smarm (smɑːm) *Brit informal* *vb* **1** (*tr*; often foll by *down*) to flatten (the hair, etc) with cream or grease **2** (when *intr*, foll by *up to*) to ingratiate oneself (with) [c19: of unknown origin]

smarmy ('smɑːmɪ) *adj* smarmier, smarmiest *Brit informal* obsequiously flattering or unpleasantly suave > 'smarmily *adv* > 'smarminess *n*

smart (smɑːt) *adj* **1** astute, as in business; clever or bright **2** quick, witty, and often impertinent in speech: *a smart talker* **3** fashionable; chic: *a smart hotel* **4** well-kept; neat **5** causing a sharp stinging pain **6** vigorous or brisk **7** (of systems) operating as if by human intelligence by using automatic computer control **8** (of a projectile or bomb) containing a device that allows it to be guided to its target ▷ *vb* (*mainly intr*) **9** to feel, cause, or be the source of a sharp stinging physical pain or keen mental distress: *a nettle sting smarts; he smarted under their abuse* **10** (often foll by *for*) to suffer a harsh penalty ▷ *n* **11** a stinging pain or feeling ▷ *adv* **12** in a smart manner [Old English *smeortan*; related to Old High German *smerzan*, Latin *mordēre* to bite, Greek *smerdnos* terrible] > 'smartly *adv* > 'smartness *n*

Smart (smɑːt) *n* **Christopher.** 1722–71, British poet, author of *A Song to David* (1763) and *Jubilate Agno* (written 1758–63, published 1939). He was confined (1756–63) for religious mania and died in a debtors' prison

smart aleck ('ælɪk) *n*, *pl* smart alecks *informal* an irritatingly oversmart person [c19: from *Aleck, Alec,* short for *Alexander*] > 'smart-ˌaleck *or* 'smart-ˌalecky *adj*

smart card *n* a plastic card with integrated circuits used for storing and processing computer data. Also called: laser card, intelligent card

smart dust *n* *computing slang* same as **sensor network**

smarten ('smɑːtᵊn) *vb* (usually foll by *up*) **1** (*intr*) to make oneself neater **2** (*tr*) to make quicker or livelier

smart money *n* **1 a** money bet or invested by experienced gamblers or investors, esp with inside information **b** the gamblers or investors themselves **2** money paid in order to extricate oneself from an unpleasant situation or agreement, esp from military service **3** *US law* damages awarded to a plaintiff where the wrong was aggravated by fraud, malice, etc

smartphone ('smɑːtˌfəʊn) *n* *computing* a mobile telephone with computer features that may enable it to interact with computerized systems, send e-mails, and access the web

smarts (smɑːts) *pl n* *slang, chiefly US* know-how, intelligence, or wits: *street smarts*

smart set *n* (*functioning as singular or plural*) fashionable sophisticated people considered as a group

smash (smæʃ) *vb* **1** to break into pieces violently and usually noisily **2** (when *intr*, foll by *against, through, into,* etc) to throw or crash (against) vigorously, causing shattering: *he smashed the equipment; it smashed against the wall* **3** (*tr*) to hit forcefully and suddenly **4** (*tr*) *tennis, squash, badminton* to hit (the ball) fast and powerfully, esp with an overhead stroke **5** (*tr*) to defeat or wreck (persons, theories, etc) **6** (*tr*) to make bankrupt **7** (*intr*) to collide violently; crash ▷ *n* **8** an act, instance, or sound of smashing or the state of being smashed **9** a violent collision, esp of vehicles **10** a total failure or collapse, as of a business **11** *tennis, squash, badminton* a fast and powerful overhead stroke **12** *informal* **a** something having popular success **b** (*in combination*): *smash-hit* ▷ *adv* **13** with a smash [c18: probably from SM(ACK² + M)ASH] > 'smashable *adj*

smash-and-grab *adj informal* of or relating to a robbery in which a shop window is broken and the contents removed

smashed (smæʃt) *adj slang* noticeably under the influence of a drug

smasher ('smæʃə) *n informal, chiefly Brit* a person or thing that is very attractive or outstanding

smashing ('smæʃɪŋ) *adj informal, chiefly Brit* excellent or first-rate; wonderful: *we had a smashing time*

smash-up *informal* ▷ *n* **1** a bad collision, esp of cars ▷ *vb* smash up **2** (*tr, adverb*) to damage to the point of complete destruction: *they smashed the place up*

smatter ('smætə) *n* **1** a smattering ▷ *vb* **2** (*intr*) *rare* to prattle **3** (*tr*) *archaic* to dabble in [c14 (in the sense: to prattle): of uncertain origin; compare Middle High German *smetern* to gossip] > 'smatterer *n*

smattering ('smætərɪŋ) *n* **1** a slight or superficial knowledge **2** a small amount

smear (smɪə) *vb* (*mainly tr*) **1** to bedaub or cover with oil, grease, etc **2** to rub over or apply thickly **3** to rub so as to produce a smudge **4** to slander **5** *US slang* to defeat completely **6** (*intr*) to be or become smeared or dirtied ▷ *n* **7** a dirty mark or smudge **8 a** a slanderous attack **b** (*as modifier*): *smear tactics* **9** a preparation of blood, secretions, etc, smeared onto a glass slide for examination under a microscope [Old English *smeoru* (n); related to Old Norse *smjör* fat, Old High German *smero*, Greek *muron* ointment] > 'smeary *adj* > 'smearily *adv* > 'smeariness *n*

smear test *n med* another name for **Pap test**

smectic ('smɛktɪk) *adj chem* (of a substance) existing in or having a mesomorphic state in which the molecules are oriented in layers [c17: via Latin from Greek *smēktikos*, from *smēkhein* to wash; from the soaplike consistency of a smectic substance]

smegma ('smɛgmə) *n physiol* a whitish sebaceous secretion that accumulates beneath the prepuce [c19: via Latin from Greek *smēgma* detergent, from *smekhein* to wash]

smell (smɛl) *vb* smells, smelling, smelt *or* smelled **1** (*tr*) to perceive the scent or odour of (a substance) by means of the olfactory nerves **2** (*copula*) to have a specified smell; appear to the sense of smell to be: *the beaches smell of seaweed; some tobacco smells very sweet* **3** (*intr; often foll by of*) to emit an odour (of): *the park smells of flowers* **4** (*intr*) to emit an unpleasant odour; stink **5** (*tr; often foll by out*) to detect through shrewdness or instinct **6** (*intr*) to have or use the sense of smell; sniff **7** (*intr; foll by of*) to give indications (of): *he smells of money* **8** (*intr; foll by around, about,* etc) to search, investigate, or pry **9** (*copula*) to be or seem to be untrustworthy or corrupt ▷ *n* **10** that sense (olfaction) by which scents or odours are perceived. Related adj: **olfactory 11** anything detected by the sense of smell; odour; scent **12** a trace or indication **13** the act or an instance of smelling [c12: of uncertain origin; compare Middle Dutch *smölen* to scorch] > 'smeller *n*

smelling salts *pl n* a pungent preparation containing crystals of ammonium carbonate that has a stimulant action when sniffed in cases of faintness, headache, etc

smelly ('smɛlɪ) *adj* smellier, smelliest having a strong or nasty smell > 'smelliness *n*

smelt¹ (smɛlt) *vb* (*tr*) to extract (a metal) from (an ore) by heating [c15: from Middle Low German, Middle Dutch *smelten*; related to Old High German *smelzan* to melt]

smelt² (smɛlt) *n, pl* smelt *or* smelts any marine or freshwater salmonoid food fish of the family *Osmeridae*, such as *Osmerus eperlanus* of Europe, having a long silvery body and occurring in temperate and cold northern waters [Old English *smylt*; related to Dutch, Danish *smelt*, Norwegian *smelta*, German *Schmelz*]

smelt³ (smɛlt) *vb* a past tense and past participle of **smell**

smelter ('smɛltə) *n* **1** a person engaged in smelting **2** Also called: **smeltery** ('smɛltərɪ) an industrial plant in which smelting is carried out

Smetana (*Czech* 'smɛtana) *n* **Bedřich** ('bɛdrȝix). 1824–84, Czech composer, founder of his country's national school of music. His works include *My Fatherland* (1874–79), a cycle of six symphonic poems, and the opera *The Bartered Bride* (1866)

smew (smju:) *n* a merganser, *Mergus albellus*, of N Europe and Asia, having a male plumage of white with black markings [c17: of uncertain origin]

smidgen *or* **smidgin** ('smɪdȝən) *n informal* a very small amount or part [c20: of obscure origin]

smilax ('smaɪlæks) *n* **1** any typically climbing shrub of the smilacaceous genus *Smilax*, of warm and tropical regions, having slightly lobed leaves, small greenish or yellow flowers, and berry-like fruits: includes the sarsaparilla plant and greenbrier **2** a fragile, much branched liliaceous vine, *Asparagus asparagoides*, of southern Africa: cultivated by florists for its glossy bright green foliage [c17: via Latin from Greek: bindweed]

smile (smaɪl) *n* **1** a facial expression characterized by an upturning of the corners of the mouth, usually showing amusement, friendliness, etc, but sometimes scorn, etc **2** favour or blessing: *the smile of fortune* ▷ *vb* **3** (*intr*) to wear or assume a smile **4** (*intr; foll by at*) **a** to look (at) with a kindly or amused expression **b** to look derisively (at) instead of being annoyed **c** to bear (troubles, etc) patiently **5** (*intr; foll by on or upon*) to show approval; bestow a blessing **6** (*tr*) to express by means of a smile: *she smiled a welcome* **7** (*tr; often foll by away*) to drive away or change by smiling: *smile away one's tears* **8** come up smiling to recover cheerfully from misfortune [c13: probably of Scandinavian origin; compare Swedish *smila*, Danish *smile*; related to Middle High German *smielen*] > 'smiler *n* > 'smiling *adj* > 'smilingly *adv*

Smiles (smaɪlz) *n* **Samuel**. 1812–1904, British writer: author of the didactic work *Self-Help* (1859)

smiley ('smaɪlɪ) *adj* **1** given to smiling; cheerful **2** depicting a smile: *a smiley badge* ▷ *n* **3** any of a group of symbols depicting a smile, or other facial expression, used in electronic mail

smirch (smɜ:tʃ) *vb* (*tr*) **1** to dirty; soil ▷ *n* **2** the act of smirching or state of being smirched **3** a smear or stain [c15 *smorchen*; of unknown origin]

smirk (smɜ:k) *n* **1** a smile expressing scorn, smugness, etc, rather than pleasure ▷ *vb* **2** (*intr*) to give such a smile

3 (*tr*) to express with such a smile [Old English *smearcian*; related to *smer* derision, Old High German *bismer* contempt, *bismerōn* to scorn] > 'smirker *n* > 'smirking *adj* > 'smirkingly *adv*

smite (smaɪt) *vb* smites, smiting, smote, smitten *or* smit (*mainly tr*) *in most senses archaic* **1** to strike with a heavy blow or blows **2** to damage with or as if with blows **3** to afflict or affect severely: *smitten with flu* **4** to afflict in order to punish **5** (*intr; foll by on*) to strike forcibly or abruptly: *the sun smote down on him* [Old English *smītan*; related to Old High German *smīzan* to smear, Gothic *bismeitan*, Old Swedish *smēta* to daub] > 'smiter *n*

smith (smɪθ) *n* **1 a** a person who works in metal, esp one who shapes metal by hammering **b** (*in combination*): *a silversmith* **2** See **blacksmith** [Old English; related to Old Norse *smithr*, Old High German *smid*, Middle Low German *smīde* jewellery, Greek *smilē* carving knife]

Smith (smɪθ) *n* **1 Adam**. 1723–90, Scottish economist and philosopher, whose influential book *The Wealth of Nations* (1776) advocated free trade and private enterprise and opposed state interference **2 Alexander McCall**. born 1948, Scottish writer and academic, born in Zimbabwe. His novels include *The No. 1 Ladies' Detective Agency* (1998), *The Sunday Philosophy Club* (2004) and *44 Scotland Street* (2005) **3 Bessie**, known as *Empress of the Blues*. 1894–1937, US blues singer and songwriter **4 Delia**. born 1941, British cookery writer and broadcaster: her publications include *The Complete Cookery Course* (1982) **5 F.E.** See (1st Earl of) **Birkenhead¹ 6 Harvey**. born 1938, British showjumper **7 Ian** (**Douglas**). 1919–2007, Zimbabwean statesman; prime minister of Rhodesia (1964–79). He declared independence from Britain unilaterally (1965) **8 John**. ?1580–1631, English explorer and writer, who helped found the North American colony of Jamestown, Virginia. He was reputedly saved by the Indian chief's daughter Pocahontas from execution by her tribe. Among his works is a *Description of New England* (1616) **9 John**. 1938–94, British Labour politician; leader of the Labour Party 1992–94 **10 Joseph**. 1805–44, US religious leader; founder of the Mormon Church **11 Dame Maggie**. born 1934, British actress. Her films include *The Prime of Miss Jean Brodie* (1969), *California Suite* (1978), *The Lonely Passion of Judith Hearne* (1988), *The Secret Garden* (1993), and *Gosford Park* (2001) **12 Stevie**, real name *Florence Margaret Smith*. 1902–71, British poet. Her works include *Novel on Yellow Paper* (1936), and the poems 'A Good Time was had by All' (1937) and 'Not Waving but Drowning' (1957) **13 Sydney**. 1771–1845, British clergyman and writer, noted for *The Letters of Peter Plymley* (1807–08), in which he advocated Catholic emancipation **14 Will(ard Christopher)**. born 1968, US film actor and rap singer; star of the television series *The Fresh Prince of Bel Air* (1990–96) and the films *Men In Black* (1997), *Wild Wild West* (1999), and *Ali* (2001) **15 Wilbur**. born 1933, British novelist, born in Zambia. His novels include *Where the Lion Feeds* (1964), *Monsoon* (1999) and *The Quest* (2007) **16 William**. 1769–1839, English geologist, who founded the science of stratigraphy by proving that rock strata could be dated by the fossils they contained

smithereens (ˌsmɪðə'ri:nz) *pl n* little shattered pieces or fragments [c19: from Irish Gaelic *smidirín*, from *smiodar*]

smithery ('smɪθərɪ) *n, pl* -eries **1** the trade or craft of a blacksmith **2** a rare word for **smithy**

Smithson ('smɪθsən) *n* **James**. original name *James Lewes Macie*. 1765–1829, English chemist and mineralogist, who left a bequest to found the Smithsonian Institution

smithy ('smɪðɪ) *n, pl* smithies a place in which metal, usually iron or steel, is worked by heating and hammering; forge [Old English *smiththe*; related to Old Norse *smithja*, Old High German *smidda*, Middle Dutch *smisse*]

smitten ('smɪtᵊn) *vb* **1** a past participle of **smite** ▷ *adj* **2** (*postpositive*) affected by love (for)

smock (smɒk) *n* **1** any loose protective garment, worn by artists, laboratory technicians, etc **2** a woman's loose blouse-like garment, reaching to below the waist, worn over slacks, etc **3** Also called: **smock frock** a loose protective overgarment decorated with smocking, worn formerly esp by farm workers **4** *archaic* a woman's loose undergarment, worn from the 16th to the 18th centuries ▷ *vb* **5** to ornament (a garment) with smocking [Old English *smocc*; related to Old High German *smocco*, Old Norse *smokkr* blouse, Middle High German *gesmuc* decoration] > 'smock,like *adj*

smocking ('smɒkɪŋ) *n* ornamental needlework used to gather and stitch material in a honeycomb pattern so that the part below the gathers hangs in even folds

smog (smɒg) *n* a mixture of smoke, fog, and chemical fumes [C20: from SM(OKE + F)OG[1]] > '**smoggy** *adj*

smoke (sməʊk) *n* **1** the product of combustion, consisting of fine particles of carbon carried by hot gases and air **2** any cloud of fine particles suspended in a gas **3 a** the act of smoking tobacco or other substances, esp in a pipe or as a cigarette or cigar **b** the duration of smoking such substances **4** *informal* **a** a cigarette or cigar **b** a substance for smoking, such as pipe tobacco or marijuana **5** something with no concrete or lasting substance: *everything turned to smoke* **6** a thing or condition that obscures **7 go up in smoke** *or* **end up in smoke a** to come to nothing **b** to burn up vigorously **c** to flare up in anger ▷ *vb* **8** (*intr*) to emit smoke or the like, sometimes excessively or in the wrong place **9** to draw in on (a burning cigarette, etc) and exhale the smoke **10** (*tr*) to bring (oneself) into a specified state by smoking **11** (*tr*) to subject or expose to smoke **12** (*tr*) to cure (meat, fish, cheese, etc) by treating with smoke **13** (*tr*) to fumigate or purify the air of (rooms, etc) **14** (*tr*) to darken (glass, etc) by exposure to smoke ▷ See also **smoke out** [Old English *smoca* (n); related to Middle Dutch *smieken* to emit smoke] > '**smokable** *or* '**smokeable** *adj*

Smoke (sməʊk) *n* **the Smoke** short for **Big Smoke**

smoke and mirrors *n* irrelevant or misleading information serving to obscure the truth of a situation [C20: reference to the use of smoke and mirrors in conjuring illusions]

smoke-dried *adj* (of fish, meat, etc) cured in smoke

smoked rubber *n* a type of crude natural rubber in the form of brown sheets obtained by coagulating latex with an acid, rolling it into sheets, and drying over open wood fires. It is the main raw material for natural rubber products

smokeho ('sməʊkəʊ) *n* a variant spelling of **smoko**

smokehouse ('sməʊk,haʊs) *n* a building or special construction for curing meat, fish, etc, by smoking

smokeless ('sməʊklɪs) *adj* having or producing little or no smoke: *smokeless fuel*

smokeless zone *n* an area designated by the local authority where only smokeless fuels are permitted

smoke out *vb* (*tr, adverb*) **1** to subject to smoke in order to drive out of hiding **2** to bring into the open; expose to the public: *they smoked out the plot*

smoker ('sməʊkə) *n* **1** a person who habitually smokes tobacco **2** Also called: **smoking compartment** a compartment in a train where smoking is permitted **3** an informal social gathering, as at a club

smoke screen *n* **1** *military* a cloud of smoke produced by artificial means to obscure movements or positions **2** something said or done to hide the truth

smokestack ('sməʊk,stæk) *n* a tall chimney that conveys smoke into the air

smokestack industry *n* *informal* any of the traditional British industries, esp heavy engineering or manufacturing, as opposed to such modern industries as electronics

smoking jacket *n* a man's comfortable jacket of velvet, etc, closed by a tie belt or fastenings, worn at home [so called because it was formerly worn for smoking]

smoko *or* **smokeho** ('sməʊkəʊ) *n, pl* -kos *or* -hos *Austral & NZ informal* **1** a short break from work for tea, a cigarette, etc **2** a refreshment taken during this break [C19: from SMOKE + -O]

smoky ('sməʊkɪ) *adj* smokier, smokiest **1** emitting, containing, or resembling smoke **2** emitting smoke excessively or in the wrong place: *a smoky fireplace* **3** having the flavour of having been cured by smoking **4** made dark, dirty, or hazy by smoke > '**smokily** *adv* > '**smokiness** *n*

Smoky Mountains *pl n* See **Great Smoky Mountains**

smolder ('sməʊldə) *vb, n* the US spelling of **smoulder**

Smolensk (*Russian* sma'ljɛnsk; *English* 'smɒlɛnsk) *n* a city in W Russia, on the Dnieper River: a major commercial centre in medieval times; scene of severe fighting (1941 and 1943) in World War II. Pop: 323 000 (2005 est)

Smollett ('smɒlɪt) *n* **Tobias George.** 1721–71, Scottish novelist, whose picaresque satires include *Roderick Random* (1748), *Peregrine Pickle* (1751), and *Humphry Clinker* (1771)

smolt (sməʊlt) *n* a young salmon at the stage when it migrates from fresh water to the sea [C14: Scottish, of uncertain origin; perhaps related to SMELT[2]]

smooch (smuːtʃ) *informal* ▷ *vb* (*intr*) **1** (of two people) to kiss and cuddle. Also (Austral. and NZ): **smoodge**, **smooge 2** *Brit* to dance very slowly and amorously with one's arms around another person, or (of two people) to dance together in such a way ▷ *n* **3** the act of smooching [C20: variant of dialect *smouch*, of imitative origin]

smoodge *or* **smooge** (smuːdʒ) *vb Austral & NZ* variants of **smooch** (sense 1)

smooth (smuːð) *adj* **1** resting in the same plane; without bends or irregularities **2** silky to the touch: *smooth velvet* **3** lacking roughness of surface; flat **4** tranquil or unruffled: *smooth temper* **5** lacking obstructions or difficulties **6 a** suave or persuasive, esp as suggestive of insincerity **b** (*in combination*): *smooth-tongued* **7** (of the skin) free from hair **8** of uniform consistency: *smooth batter* **9** not erratic; free from jolts: *smooth driving* **10** not harsh or astringent: *a smooth wine* **11** having all projections worn away: *smooth tyres* **12** *phonetics* without preliminary or simultaneous aspiration **13** *physics* (of a plane, surface, etc) regarded as being frictionless ▷ *adv* **14** in a calm or even manner; smoothly ▷ *vb* (*mainly tr*) **15** (*also intr*; often foll by *down*) to make or become flattened or without roughness or obstructions **16** (often foll by *out* or *away*) to take or rub (away) in order to make smooth: *she smoothed out the creases in her dress* **17** to make calm; soothe **18** to make easier: *smooth his path* ▷ *n* **19** the smooth part of something **20** the act of smoothing **21** *tennis, squash, badminton* the side of a racket on which the binding strings form a continuous line ▷ See also **smooth over** [Old English *smōth*; related to Old Saxon *māthmundi* gentle-minded, *smōthi* smooth] > '**smoother** *n* > '**smoothly** *adv* > '**smoothness** *n*

smoothbore ('smuːð,bɔː) *n* (*modifier*) (of a firearm) having an unrifled bore: *a smoothbore musket* > '**smooth,bored** *adj*

smooth breathing *n* (in Greek) the sign (ʼ) placed over an initial vowel, indicating that (in ancient Greek) it was not pronounced with an *h*

smoothen ('smuːðən) *vb* to make or become smooth

smooth hound *n* any of several small sharks of the genus *Mustelus*, esp *M. mustelus*, a species of North Atlantic coastal regions: family Triakidae [C17: from HOUND(FISH); so called because it has no dorsal spines]

smoothie *or* **smoothy** ('smuːðɪ) *n, pl* smoothies **1** *slang, usually derogatory* a person, esp a man, who is suave or slick, esp in speech, dress, or manner **2** a smooth, thick drink made with puréed fresh fruit and yogurt, ice cream, or milk

smoothing iron *n* a former name for **iron** (sense 3)

smooth muscle *n* muscle that is capable of slow rhythmic involuntary contractions: occurs in the walls of the blood vessels, alimentary canal, etc [so called because there is no cross-banding on the muscle]

smooth over *vb* (*tr*) to ease or gloss over: *to smooth over a situation*

smooth snake *n* any of several slender nonvenomous colubrid snakes of the European genus *Coronella*, esp *C. austriaca*, having very smooth scales and a reddish-brown coloration

smooth-spoken *adj* speaking or spoken in a gently persuasive or competent manner

smooth-tongued *adj* suave or persuasive in speech

smorgasbord ('smɔːgəs,bɔːd, 'smɑː-) *n* a variety of cold or hot savoury dishes, such as pâté, smoked salmon, etc, served in Scandinavia as hors d'oeuvres or as a buffet meal [Swedish, from *smörgås* sandwich + *bord* table]

S

smote (sməʊt) *vb* the past tense of **smite**

smother ('smʌðə) *vb* **1** to suffocate or stifle by cutting off or being cut off from the air **2** (*tr*) to surround (with) or envelop (in): *he smothered her with love* **3** (*tr*) to extinguish (a fire) by covering so as to cut it off from the air **4** to be or cause to be suppressed or stifled: *smother a giggle* **5** (*tr*) to cook or serve (food) thickly covered with sauce, etc ▷ *n* **6** anything, such as a cloud of smoke, that stifles **7** a profusion or turmoil [Old English *smorian* to suffocate; related to Middle Low German *smōren*] > 'smothery *adj*

smothered mate *n chess* checkmate given by a knight when the king is prevented from moving by surrounding men

smoulder *or US* **smolder** ('sməʊldə) *vb* (*intr*) **1** to burn slowly without flame, usually emitting smoke **2** (esp of anger, etc) to exist in a suppressed or half-suppressed state **3** to have strong repressed or half repressed feelings, esp anger ▷ *n* **4** dense smoke, as from a smouldering fire [c14: from *smolder* (n), of obscure origin]

SMP *abbreviation* statutory maternity pay

SMTP *abbreviation* simple mail transfer protocol: a protocol that enables e-mails to be sent between different servers

smudge (smʌdʒ) *vb* **1** to smear, blur, or soil or cause to do so **2** (*tr*) *chiefly US & Canadian* to fill (an area) with smoke in order to drive insects away or guard against frost ▷ *n* **3** a smear or dirty mark **4** a blurred form or area: *that smudge in the distance is a quarry* **5** *chiefly US & Canadian* a smoky fire for driving insects away or protecting fruit trees or plants from frost [c15: of uncertain origin] > 'smudgily *or* 'smudgedly *adv*

smug (smʌg) *adj* **smugger, smuggest** excessively self-satisfied or complacent [c16: of Germanic origin; compare Low German *smuck* neat] > 'smugly *adv* > 'smugness *n*

smuggle ('smʌgəl) *vb* **1** to import or export (prohibited or dutiable goods) secretly **2** (*tr*; often foll by *into* or *out of*) to bring or take secretly, as against the law or rules [c17: from Low German *smukkelen* and Dutch *smokkelen*, perhaps from Old English *smūgen* to creep; related to Old Norse *smjūga*] > 'smuggler *n* > 'smuggling *n*

smut (smʌt) *n* **1** a small dark smudge or stain, esp one caused by soot **2** a speck of soot or dirt **3** something obscene or indecent **4 a** any of various fungal diseases of flowering plants, esp cereals, in which black sooty masses of spores cover the affected parts **b** any parasitic basidiomycetous fungus of the order *Ustilaginales* that causes such a disease ▷ *vb* **smuts, smutting, smutted** **5** to mark or become marked or smudged, as with soot **6** to affect (grain) or (of grain) to be affected with smut [Old English *smitte*; related to Middle High German *smitze*; associated with SMUDGE, SMUTCH] > 'smutty *adj* > 'smuttily *adv* > 'smuttiness *n*

smutch (smʌtʃ) *vb* **1** (*tr*) to smudge; mark ▷ *n* **2** a mark; smudge **3** soot; dirt [c16: probably from Middle High German *smutzen* to soil; see SMUT] > 'smutchy *adj*

Smuts (smʌts) *n* **Jan Christiaan** (jan 'kristi,an). 1870–1950, South African statesman; prime minister (1919–24; 1939–48). He fought for the Boers during the Boer War, then worked for Anglo-Boer reconciliation and served the Allies during World Wars I and II

Smyrna ('smɜːnə) *n* an ancient city on the W coast of Asia Minor: a major trading centre in the ancient world; a centre of early Christianity. Modern name: Izmir

Smyth (smaɪð) *n* Dame **Ethel (Mary)**. 1858–1944, British composer, best known for her operas, such as *The Wreckers* (1906). She was imprisoned for supporting the suffragette movement

Sn *the chemical symbol for* tin [from New Latin *stannum*]

snack (snæk) *n* **1 a** light quick meal eaten between or in place of main meals **2** a sip or bite ▷ *vb* **3** (*intr*) to eat a snack [c15: probably from Middle Dutch *snacken*, variant of *snappen* to SNAP]

snack bar *n* a place where light meals or snacks can be obtained, often with a self-service system

snaffle ('snæfəl) *n* **1** Also called: **snaffle bit** a simple jointed bit for a horse ▷ *vb* (*tr*) **2** *Brit informal* to steal or take for oneself **3** to equip or control with a snaffle [c16: of uncertain origin; compare Old Frisian *snavel* mouth,

Old High German *snabul* beak]

snafu (snæ'fuː) *slang, chiefly military* ▷ *n* **1** confusion or chaos regarded as the normal state ▷ *adj* **2** (*postpositive*) confused or muddled up, as usual ▷ *vb* **-fus, -fuing, -fued** **3** (*tr*) *US & Canadian* to throw into chaos [c20: from *s*(ituation) *n*(ormal): *a*(ll) *f*(ucked or ouled) *u*(p)]

snag (snæg) *n* **1 a** difficulty or disadvantage: *the snag is that I have nothing suitable to wear* **2** a sharp protuberance, such as a tree stump **3** a small loop or hole in a fabric caused by a sharp object **4** *chiefly US & Canadian* a tree stump in a riverbed that is dangerous to navigation **5** *US & Canadian* a standing dead tree, esp one used as a perch by an eagle ▷ *vb* **snags, snagging, snagged** **6** (*tr*) to hinder or impede **7** (*tr*) to tear or catch (fabric) **8** (*intr*) to develop a snag **9** (*intr*) *chiefly US & Canadian* (of a boat) to strike or be damaged by a snag **10** (*tr*) *chiefly US & Canadian* to clear (a stretch of water) of snags **11** (*tr*) *US* to seize (an opportunity, benefit, etc) [c16: of Scandinavian origin; compare Old Norse *snaghyrndr* sharp-pointed, Norwegian *snage* spike, Icelandic *snagi* peg]

snaggletooth ('snægəl,tuːθ) *n, pl* **-teeth** a tooth that is broken or projecting

snail (sneɪl) *n* **1** any of numerous terrestrial or freshwater gastropod molluscs with a spirally coiled shell, esp any of the family *Helicidae*, such as *Helix aspersa* (**garden snail**) **2** any other gastropod with a spirally coiled shell, such as a whelk **3** a slow-moving or lazy person or animal [Old English *snægl*; related to Old Norse *snigill*, Old High German *snecko*] > 'snail-,like *adj*

snail mail *informal* ▷ *n* **1** the conventional postal system, as opposed to electronic mail ▷ *vb* **snail-mail 2** (*tr*) to send by the conventional postal system, rather than by electronic mail [c20: so named because of the relative slowness of the conventional postal system]

snail's pace *n* a very slow or sluggish speed or rate

snake (sneɪk) *n* **1** any reptile of the suborder *Ophidia* (or *Serpentes*), typically having a scaly cylindrical limbless body, fused eyelids, and a jaw modified for swallowing large prey: includes venomous forms such as cobras and rattlesnakes, large nonvenomous constrictors (boas and pythons), and small harmless types such as the grass snake **2** Also called: **snake in the grass** a deceitful or treacherous person **3** anything resembling a snake in appearance or action **4** (in the European Union) a former system of managing a group of currencies by allowing the exchange rate of each of them only to fluctuate within narrow limits **5** a tool in the form of a long flexible wire for unblocking drains ▷ *vb* **6** (*intr*) to glide or move like a snake **7** (*tr*) to move in or follow (a sinuous course) [Old English *snaca*; related to Old Norse *snākr* snake, Old High German *snahhan* to crawl, Norwegian *snōk* snail] > 'snake,like *adj*

snakebird ('sneɪk,bɜːd) *n* another name for **darter**

snakebite ('sneɪk,baɪt) *n* **1** a bite inflicted by a snake, esp a venomous one **2** a drink of cider and lager

snake charmer *n* an entertainer, esp in Asia, who charms or appears to charm snakes by playing music and by rhythmic body movements

Snake River *n* a river in the northwestern US, rising in NW Wyoming and flowing west through Idaho, turning north as part of the border between Idaho and Oregon, and flowing west to the Columbia River near Pasco, Washington. Length: 1670 km (1038 miles)

snakeroot ('sneɪk,ruːt) *n* **1** any of various North American plants, such as *Aristolochia serpentaria* (**Virginia snakeroot**) and *Eupatorium urticaefolium* (**white snakeroot**), the roots or rhizomes of which have been used as a remedy for snakebite **2** the rhizome or root of any such plant

snakes and ladders *n* (*functioning as singular*) a board game in which players move counters along a series of squares according to throws of a dice. A ladder provides a short cut to a square nearer the finish and a snake obliges a player to return to a square nearer the start

snake's head *n* a European fritillary plant, *Fritillaria meleagris*, of damp meadows, having purple-and-white chequered flowers [c19: so called because its buds are claimed to resemble a snake's head]

snakeskin ('sneɪk,skɪn) *n* the skin of a snake, esp when

S

made into a leather valued for handbags, shoes, etc

snaky ('sneɪkɪ) *adj* snakier, snakiest 1 of or like a snake; sinuous 2 treacherous or insidious 3 infested with snakes 4 *Austral & NZ informal* angry or bad-tempered > 'snakily *adv* > 'snakiness *n*

snap (snæp) *vb* snaps, snapping, snapped 1 to break or cause to break suddenly, esp with a sharp sound 2 to make or cause to make a sudden sharp cracking sound 3 (*intr*) to give way or collapse suddenly, esp from strain 4 to move, close, etc, or cause to move, close, etc, with a sudden sharp sound 5 to move or cause to move in a sudden or abrupt way 6 (*intr*; often foll by *at* or *up*) to seize something suddenly or quickly 7 (when *intr*, often foll by *at*) to bite at (something) bringing the jaws rapidly together 8 to speak (words) sharply or abruptly 9 to take a snapshot of (something) 10 (*tr*) *American football* to put (the ball) into play by sending it back from the line of scrimmage to a teammate 11 **snap one's fingers at** *informal* **a** to dismiss with contempt **b** to defy 12 **snap out of it** *informal* to recover quickly, esp from depression, anger, or illness ▷ *n* 13 the act of breaking suddenly or the sound produced by a sudden breakage 14 a sudden sharp sound, esp of bursting, popping, or cracking 15 a catch, clasp, or fastener that operates with a snapping sound 16 a sudden grab or bite 17 a thin crisp biscuit: *ginger snaps* 18 *informal* See **snapshot** 19 *informal* vigour, liveliness, or energy 20 *informal* a task or job that is easy or profitable to do 21 a short spell or period, esp of cold weather 22 *Brit* a card game in which the word *snap* is called when two cards of equal value are turned up on the separate piles dealt by each player 23 *American football* the start of each play when the centre passes the ball back from the line of scrimmage to a teammate 24 (*modifier*) done on the spur of the moment, without consideration or warning: *a snap decision* 25 (*modifier*) closed or fastened with a snap ▷ *adv* 26 with a snap ▷ *interj* 27 **a** *cards* the word called while playing snap **b** an exclamation used to draw attention to the similarity of two things ▷ See also **snap up** [c15: from Middle Low German or Middle Dutch *snappen* to seize; related to Old Norse *snapa* to snuffle] > 'snapless *adj*

snapdragon ('snæp,drægən) *n* any of several scrophulariaceous chiefly Old World plants of the genus *Antirrhinum*, esp *A. majus*, of the Mediterranean region, having spikes of showy white, yellow, pink, red, or purplish flowers. Also called: antirrhinum [c16: so named because the flowers, which are claimed to look like a dragon's head, have a "mouth" which snaps shut if squeezed open and then released]

snap fastener *n* another name for **press stud**

snapper ('snæpə) *n, pl* -per *or* -pers 1 any large sharp-toothed percoid food fish of the family *Lutjanidae* of warm and tropical coastal regions. See also **red snapper** 2 a sparid food fish, *Chrysophrys auratus*, of Australia and New Zealand, that has a pinkish body covered with blue spots 3 another name for **snapping turtle** 4 a person or thing that snaps ▷ Also called (for senses 1, 2): schnapper

snapping turtle *n* any large aggressive North American river turtle of the family *Chelydridae*, esp *Chelydra serpentina* (**common snapping turtle**), having powerful hooked jaws and a rough shell. Also called: snapper

snappy ('snæpɪ) *adj* -pier, -piest 1 Also called: snappish apt to speak sharply or irritably 2 Also called: snappish apt to snap or bite 3 crackling in sound: *a snappy fire* 4 brisk, sharp, or chilly: *a snappy pace; snappy weather* 5 smart and fashionable: *a snappy dresser* 6 **make it snappy** *slang* be quick! hurry up! > 'snappily *adv* > 'snappiness *n*

snap ring *n* *mountaineering* another name for **karabiner**

snapshot ('snæp,ʃɒt) *n* an informal photograph taken with a simple camera. Often shortened to **snap**

snap shot *n* *sport* a sudden, fast shot at goal

snap up *vb* (*tr, adverb*) 1 to avail oneself of eagerly and quickly: *she snapped up the bargains* 2 to interrupt abruptly

snare¹ (snɛə) *n* 1 a device for trapping birds or small animals, esp a flexible loop that is drawn tight around the prey 2 a surgical instrument for removing certain tumours, consisting of a wire loop that may be drawn tight around their base to sever or uproot them

3 anything that traps or entangles someone or something unawares ▷ *vb* (*tr*) 4 to catch (birds or small animals) with a snare 5 to catch or trap in or as if in a snare; capture by trickery [Old English *sneare*, from Old Norse *snara*; related to Old High German *snaraha*] > 'snarer *n*

snare² (snɛə) *n* *music* a set of gut strings wound with wire fitted against the lower drumhead of a snare drum. They produce a rattling sound when the drum is beaten [c17: from Middle Dutch *snaer* or Middle Low German *snare* string; related to Gothic *snōrjō* basket]

snare drum *n* *music* a cylindrical drum with two drumheads, the upper of which is struck and the lower fitted with a snare. See **snare²**

snarf (snɑːf) *vb* *informal* to eat or drink greedily

snarky ('snɑːkɪ) *adj* snarkier, snarkiest *informal* unpleasant and scornful [c20: from SARCASTIC + NASTY]

snarl¹ (snɑːl) *vb* 1 (*intr*) (of an animal) to growl viciously, baring the teeth 2 to speak or express (something) viciously or angrily ▷ *n* 3 a vicious growl, utterance, or facial expression 4 the act of snarling [c16: of Germanic origin; compare Middle Low German *snarren*, Middle Dutch *snerren* to drone] > 'snarling *adj* > 'snarly *adj* > 'snarler *n*

snarl² (snɑːl) *n* 1 a tangled mass of thread, hair, etc 2 a complicated or confused state or situation 3 a knot in wood ▷ *vb* 4 (often foll by *up*) to be, become, or make tangled or complicated 5 (*tr*; often foll by *up*) to confuse mentally 6 (*tr*) to flute or emboss (metal) by hammering on a tool held against the under surface [c14: of Scandinavian origin; compare Old Swedish *snarel* noose, Old Norse *snara* SNARE¹] > 'snarly *adj*

snarl-up *n* *informal, chiefly Brit* a confusion, obstruction, or tangle, esp a traffic jam

snatch (snætʃ) *vb* 1 (*tr*) to seize or grasp (something) suddenly or peremptorily: *he snatched the chocolate out of my hand* 2 (*intr*; usually foll by *at*) to seize or attempt to seize suddenly 3 (*tr*) to take hurriedly: *to snatch some sleep* 4 (*tr*) to remove suddenly: *she snatched her hand away* 5 (*tr*) to gain, win, or rescue, esp narrowly: *they snatched victory in the closing seconds* ▷ *n* 6 an act of snatching 7 a fragment or small incomplete part: *snatches of conversation* 8 a brief spell: *snatches of time off* 9 *weightlifting* a lift in which the weight is raised in one quick motion from the floor to an overhead position 10 *slang, chiefly US* an act of kidnapping 11 *Brit slang* a robbery: *a diamond snatch* [c13 *snacchen*; related to Middle Dutch *snakken* to gasp, Old Norse *snaka* to sniff around] > 'snatcher *n*

snatchy ('snætʃɪ) *adj* snatchier, snatchiest disconnected or spasmodic > 'snatchily *adv*

snazzy ('snæzɪ) *adj* -zier, -ziest *informal* (esp of clothes) stylishly and often flashily attractive [c20: perhaps from SN(APPY + J)AZZY] > 'snazzily *adv* > 'snazziness *n*

Snead (sniːd) *n* Sam(uel Jackson). 1912–2002, US golfer; winner of seven major tournaments between 1938 and 1951

sneak (sniːk) *vb* 1 (*intr*; often foll by *along, off, in*, etc) to move furtively 2 (*intr*) to behave in a cowardly or underhand manner 3 (*tr*) to bring, take, or put stealthily 4 (*intr*) *informal, chiefly Brit* to tell tales (esp in schools) 5 (*tr*) *informal* to steal 6 (*intr*; foll by *off, out, away*, etc) *informal* to leave unobtrusively ▷ *n* 7 a person who acts in an underhand or cowardly manner, esp as an informer 8 **a** a stealthy act or movement **b** (*as modifier*): *a sneak attack* [Old English *snīcan* to creep; from Old Norse *snīkja* to hanker after] > 'sneaky *adj* > 'sneakily *adv* > 'sneakiness *n*

sneakers ('sniːkəz) *pl n* *chiefly US & Canadian* canvas shoes with rubber soles worn for sports or informally

sneaking ('sniːkɪŋ) *adj* 1 acting in a furtive or cowardly way 2 secret: *a sneaking desire to marry a millionaire* 3 slight but nagging (esp in the phrase **a sneaking suspicion**) > 'sneakingly *adv*

sneak thief *n* a person who steals paltry articles from premises, which he enters through open doors, windows, etc

sneer (snɪə) *n* 1 a facial expression of scorn or contempt, typically with the upper lip curled 2 a scornful or contemptuous remark or utterance ▷ *vb* 3 (*intr*) to assume a facial expression of scorn or contempt **4** to say or utter (something) in a scornful or contemptuous manner [c16: perhaps from Low Dutch; compare North Frisian *sneere* contempt] > 'sneerer *n* > 'sneering *adj, n*

sneeze (sni:z) *vb* **1** (*intr*) to expel air and nasal secretions from the nose involuntarily, esp as the result of irritation of the nasal mucous membrane ▷ *n* **2** the act or sound of sneezing [Old English *fnēosan* (unattested); related to Old Norse *fnȳsa*, Middle High German *fnūsen*, Greek *pneuma* breath] > 'sneezer *n* > 'sneezy *adj*

sneeze at *vb* (*intr, prep.*; usually with a negative) *informal* to dismiss lightly: *his offer is not to be sneezed at*

sneezewood ('sni:z,wʊd) *n* **1** a tree, *Ptaeroxylon utile*, native to southern Africa: family *Ptaeroxylaceae* **2** the tough wood of this tree, which has a peppery smell and is used for bridges, piers, fencing posts, etc

sneezewort ('sni:z,wɜ:t) *n* a Eurasian plant, *Achillea ptarmica*, having daisy-like flowers and long grey-green leaves, which cause sneezing when powdered: family *Asteraceae* (composites)

Snell (snɛl) *n* Peter (George). born 1938, New Zealand athlete; winner of three Olympic gold medals: for the 800 metres in 1960, and again in 1964, when he also won gold for the 1500 metres

snick (snɪk) *n* **1** a small cut; notch **2** *cricket* **a** a glancing blow off the edge of the bat **b** the ball so hit ▷ *vb* (*tr*) **3** to cut a small corner or notch in (material, etc) **4** *cricket* to hit (the ball) with a snick [c18: probably of Scandinavian origin; compare Old Norse *snikka* to whittle, Swedish *snicka*]

snicker ('snɪkə) *n* **1** *chiefly US & Canadian* a sly or disrespectful laugh, esp one partly stifled ▷ *vb* **2** to utter such a laugh. Equivalent term (in Britain and certain other countries): **snigger** **3** (of a horse) to whinny [c17: probably of imitative origin]

Snickometer (snɪ'kɒmɪtə) *n* *trademark cricket* a device, which uses sound waves recorded by the stump microphone, employed by TV commentators to determine whether or not a batsman has made contact with the ball [c20: from SNICK (sense 5) + -METER]

snide (snaɪd) *adj* **1** Also called: **snidey** ('snaɪdɪ) (of a remark, etc) maliciously derogatory; supercilious **2** counterfeit; sham ▷ *n* **3** *slang* sham jewellery [c19: of unknown origin] > 'snidely *adv* > 'snideness *n*

sniff (snɪf) *vb* **1** to inhale through the nose, usually in short rapid audible inspirations, as for the purpose of identifying a scent, for clearing a congested nasal passage, or for taking a drug or intoxicating fumes **2** (when *intr*, often foll by *at*) to perceive or attempt to perceive (a smell) by inhaling through the nose ▷ *n* **3** the act or sound of sniffing **4** a smell perceived by sniffing, esp a faint scent [c14: probably related to *sniveln* to SNIVEL] > 'sniffing *n, adj* > 'sniffer *n*

sniff at *vb* (*intr, preposition*) to express contempt or dislike for

sniffer dog *n* a police dog trained to detect drugs or explosives by smell

sniffle ('snɪfᵊl) *vb* **1** (*intr*) to breathe audibly through the nose, as when the nasal passages are congested ▷ *n* **2** the act, sound, or an instance of sniffling > 'sniffler *n* > 'sniffly *adj*

sniffles ('snɪfᵊlz) or **snuffles** *pl n* *informal* the sniffles a cold in the head

sniff out *vb* (*tr, adverb*) to detect through shrewdness or instinct

sniffy ('snɪfɪ) *adj* -fier, -fiest *informal* contemptuous or disdainful > 'sniffily *adv* > 'sniffiness *n*

snifter ('snɪftə) *n* **1** a pear-shaped glass with a short stem and a bowl that narrows towards the top so that the aroma of brandy or a liqueur is retained **2** *informal* a small quantity of alcoholic drink [c19: perhaps from dialect *snifter* to sniff, perhaps of Scandinavian origin; compare Danish *snifta* (obsolete) to sniff]

snig (snɪg) *vb* **snigs, snigging, snigged** (*tr*) *Austral & NZ* to drag (a log) along the ground by a chain fastened at one end [from English dialect]

snigger ('snɪgə) *n* **1** a sly or disrespectful laugh, esp one partly stifled ▷ *vb* (*intr*) **2** to utter such a laugh [c18: variant of SNICKER]

snigging chain *n* *Austral & NZ* a chain attached to a log when being hauled out of the bush

snip (snɪp) *vb* **snips, snipping, snipped** **1** to cut or clip with a small quick stroke or a succession of small quick strokes, esp with scissors or shears ▷ *n* **2** the act of snipping **3** the sound of scissors or shears closing **4** Also called: **snipping** a small piece of anything, esp one that has been snipped off **5** a small cut made by snipping **6** *chiefly Brit* an informal word for **bargain** **7** *informal* something easily done; cinch ▷ See also **snips** [c16: from Low German, Dutch *snippen*; related to Middle High German *snipfen* to snap the fingers]

snipe (snaɪp) *n, pl* **snipe** or **snipes** **1** any of various birds of the genus *Gallinago* (or *Capella*) and related genera, such as *G. gallinago* (**common** or **Wilson's snipe**), of marshes and river banks, having a long straight bill: family *Scolopacidae* (sandpipers, etc), order *Charadriiformes* **2** a shot, esp a gunshot, fired from a place of concealment ▷ *vb* **3** (when *intr*, often foll by *at*) to attack (a person or persons) with a rifle from a place of concealment **4** (*intr*; often foll by *at*) to criticize adversely a person or persons from a position of security **5** (*intr*) to hunt or shoot snipe [c14: from Old Norse *snīpa*; related to Old High German *snepfa* Middle Dutch *snippe*] > 'sniper *n*

snipefish ('snaɪp,fɪʃ) *n, pl* -fish or -fishes any teleost fish of the family *Macrorhamphosidae*, of tropical and temperate seas, having a deep body, long snout, and a single long dorsal fin: order *Solenichthyes* (sea horses, etc). Also called: **bellows fish** [c17: so called because of the resemblance between its snout and a snipe's bill]

snippet ('snɪpɪt) *n* a small scrap or fragment [c17: from SNIP + -ET] > 'snippetiness *n* > 'snippety *adj*

snips (snɪps) *pl n* a small pair of shears used for cutting sheet metal

snitch (snɪtʃ) *slang* ▷ *vb* **1** (*tr*) to steal; take, esp in an underhand way **2** (*intr*) to act as an informer ▷ *n* **3** an informer; telltale **4** the nose [c17: of unknown origin]

snitch line *n* *Canadian* a direct telephone or other communications link set up to allow people to report neighbours, colleagues, etc suspected of wrongdoing

snitchy ('snɪtʃɪ) *adj* snitchier, snitchiest *NZ informal* bad-tempered or irritable

snivel ('snɪvᵊl) *vb* -els, -elling, -elled or US -els, -eling, -eled **1** (*intr*) to sniffle as a sign of distress, esp contemptibly **2** to utter (something) tearfully; whine **3** (*intr*) to have a runny nose ▷ *n* **4** an instance of snivelling [c14 *snivelen*; related to Old English *snyflung* mucus, Dutch *snuffelen* to smell out, Old Norse *snoppa* snout] > 'sniveller *n* > 'snivelling *adj, n*

snob (snɒb) *n* **1 a** a person who strives to associate with those of higher social status and who behaves condescendingly to others **b** (*as modifier*): snob appeal **2** a person having similar pretensions with regard to his tastes, etc: *an intellectual snob* [c18 (in the sense: shoemaker; hence, c19: a person who flatters those of higher station, etc): of unknown origin] > 'snobbery *n* > 'snobbish *adj* > 'snobbishly *adv*

SNOBOL ('snəʊbɒl) *n* String Oriented Symbolic Language: a computer-programming language for handling strings of symbols

Sno-Cat ('snəʊ,kæt) *n* *trademark* a type of snowmobile

snoek (snʊk) *n* a South African edible marine fish, *Thyrsites atun* [Afrikaans, from Dutch *snoek* pike]

snoep (snʊp) *adj* *South African informal* mean or tight-fisted [Afrikaans *snoep* greedy]

snog (snɒg) *Brit slang* ▷ *vb* **snogs, snogging, snogged** **1** to kiss and cuddle (someone) ▷ *n* **2** the act of kissing and cuddling [of obscure origin]

snood (snu:d) *n* **1** a pouchlike hat, often of net, loosely holding a woman's hair at the back **2** a headband, esp one formerly worn by young unmarried women in Scotland [Old English *snōd*; of obscure origin]

snook¹ (snu:k) *n, pl* snook or snooks **1** any of several large game fishes of the genus *Centropomus*, esp *C. undecimalis* of tropical American marine and fresh waters: family *Centropomidae* (robalos) **2** *Austral* the sea pike *Australuzza novaehollandiae* [c17: from Dutch *snoek* pike]

snook² (snu:k) *n* **cock a snook** *Brit* to make a rude gesture by putting one thumb to the nose with the fingers of the hand outstretched [C19: of obscure origin]

snooker ('snu:kə) *n* **1** a game played on a billiard table with 15 red balls, six balls of other colours, and a white cue ball. The object is to pot the balls in a certain order **2** a shot in which the cue ball is left in a position such that another ball blocks the object ball. The opponent is then usually forced to play the cue ball off a cushion ▷ *vb* (*tr*) **3** to leave (an opponent) in an unfavourable position by playing a snooker **4** to place (someone) in a difficult situation **5** (*often passive*) to thwart; defeat [C19: of unknown origin]

snoop (snu:p) *informal* ▷ *vb* **1** (*intr*; often foll by *about* or *around*) to pry into the private business of others ▷ *n* **2** a person who pries into the business of others **3** an act or instance of snooping [C19: from Dutch *snoepen* to eat furtively] > 'snoopy *adj* > 'snooper *n*

snooperscope ('snu:pə,skəʊp) *n military US* an instrument that enables the user to see objects in the dark by illuminating the object with infrared radiation and converting the reflected radiation to a visual image

snoot (snu:t) *n slang* the nose [C20: variant of SNOUT]

snooty ('snu:tı) *adj* **snootier, snootiest** *informal* **1** aloof or supercilious **2** snobbish or exclusive: *a snooty restaurant* > 'snootily *adv* > 'snootiness *n*

snooze (snu:z) *informal* ▷ *vb* **1** (*intr*) to take a brief light sleep ▷ *n* **2** a nap [C18: of unknown origin] > 'snoozer *n* > 'snoozy *adj*

snore (snɔ:) *vb* **1** (*intr*) to breathe through the mouth and nose while asleep with snorting sounds caused by vibrations of the soft palate ▷ *n* **2** the act or sound of snoring [C14: of imitative origin; related to Middle Low German, Middle Dutch *snorken*; see SNORT] > 'snorer *n*

snorkel ('snɔ:kᵊl) *n* **1** a device allowing a swimmer to breathe while face down on the surface of the water, consisting of a bent tube fitting into the mouth and projecting above the surface **2** (on a submarine) a retractable vertical device containing air-intake and exhaust pipes for the engines and general ventilation: its use permits extended periods of submergence at periscope depth ▷ *vb* **-kels, -kelling, -kelled** or *US* **-kels, -keling, -keled 3** (*intr*) to swim with a snorkel [C20: from German *Schnorchel*; related to German *schnarchen* to SNORE]

Snorri Sturluson ('snɔ:rı 'stɜ:ləsᵊn) *n* 1179–1241, Icelandic historian and poet; author of *Younger* or *Prose Edda* (?1222), containing a collection of Norse myths and a treatise on poetry, and the *Heimskringla* sagas of the Norwegian kings from their mythological origins to the 12th century

snort (snɔ:t) *vb* **1** (*intr*) to exhale forcibly through the nostrils, making a characteristic noise **2** (*intr*) (of a person) to express contempt or annoyance by such an exhalation **3** (*tr*) to utter in a contemptuous or annoyed manner **4** *slang* to inhale (a powdered drug) through the nostrils ▷ *n* **5** a forcible exhalation of air through the nostrils, esp (of persons) as a noise of contempt or annoyance **6** *slang* an instance of snorting a drug [C14 *snorten*; probably related to *snoren* to SNORE] > 'snorting *n*, *adj* > 'snortingly *adv*

snorter ('snɔ:tə) *n* **1** a person or animal that snorts **2** *Brit slang* something outstandingly impressive or difficult

snot (snɒt) *n* (*usually considered vulgar*) **1** nasal mucus or discharge **2** *slang* a contemptible person [Old English *gesnot*; related to Old High German *snuzza*, Norwegian, Danish *snot*, German *schneuzen* to blow one's nose]

snotty ('snɒtı) (*considered vulgar*) *adj* **-tier, -tiest 1** dirty with nasal discharge **2** *slang* contemptible; nasty **3** snobbish; conceited > 'snottily *adv* > 'snottiness *n*

snout (snaʊt) *n* **1** the part of the head of a vertebrate, esp a mammal, consisting of the nose, jaws, and surrounding region, esp when elongated **2** the corresponding part of the head of such insects as weevils **3** anything projecting like a snout, such as a nozzle or the lower end of a glacier **4** *slang* a person's nose **5** *Brit slang* a cigarette or tobacco **6** *slang* an informer [C13: of Germanic origin; compare Old Norse *snyta*, Middle Low German, Middle Dutch *snūte*] > 'snouted *adj* > 'snoutless *adj* > 'snout,like *adj*

snout beetle *n* another name for **weevil** (sense 1) [C19:

so named because of its long proboscis]

snow (snəʊ) *n* **1** precipitation from clouds in the form of flakes of ice crystals formed in the upper atmosphere **2** a layer of snowflakes on the ground **3** a fall of such precipitation **4** anything resembling snow in whiteness, softness, etc **5** the random pattern of white spots on a television or radar screen, produced by noise in the receiver and occurring when the signal is weak or absent **6** *slang* cocaine ▷ *vb* **7** (*intr*; with *it* as subject) to be the case that snow is falling **8** (*tr*; usually passive, foll by *over, under, in,* or *up*) to cover or confine with a heavy fall of snow **9** (often with *it* as subject) to fall or cause to fall as or like snow **10** (*tr*) *US & Canadian slang* to deceive or overwhelm with elaborate often insincere talk **11 be snowed under** to be overwhelmed, esp with paperwork [Old English *snāw*; related to Old Norse *snjōr*, Gothic *snaiws*, Old High German *snēo*, Greek *nipha*] > 'snowless *adj* > 'snow,like *adj*

Snow (snəʊ) *n* **C**(harles) **P**(ercy), Baron. 1905–80, British novelist and physicist. His novels include the series *Strangers and Brothers* (1949–70)

snow apple *n* a Canadian variety of eating apple

snowball ('snəʊ,bɔ:l) *n* **1** snow pressed into a ball for throwing, as in play **2** a drink made of advocaat and lemonade ▷ *vb* **3** (*intr*) to increase rapidly in size, importance, etc **4** (*tr*) to throw snowballs at

snowball tree *n* any of several caprifoliaceous shrubs of the genus *Viburnum*, esp *V. opulus* var. *roseum*, a sterile cultivated variety with spherical clusters of white or pinkish flowers

snowberry ('snəʊbərı, -brı) *n*, *pl* **-ries 1** any of several caprifoliaceous shrubs of the genus *Symphoricarpos*, esp *S. albus*, cultivated for their small pink flowers and white berries **2** Also called: **waxberry** any of the berries of such a plant

snow-blind *adj* temporarily unable to see or having impaired vision because of the intense reflection of sunlight from snow > **snow blindness** *n*

snowblower ('snəʊ,bləʊə) *n* a snow-clearing machine that sucks in snow and blows it away to one side

snowboard ('snəʊ,bɔ:d) *n* a shaped board, resembling a skateboard without wheels, on which a person can stand to slide across snow [C20: on the model of SURFBOARD] > 'snow,boarder *n* > 'snow,boarding *n*

snowbound ('snəʊ,baʊnd) *adj* confined to one place by heavy falls or drifts of snow; snowed-in

snow bunting *n* a bunting, *Plectrophenax nivalis*, of northern and arctic regions, having a white plumage with dark markings on the wings, back, and tail

snowcap ('snəʊ,kæp) *n* a cap of snow, as on the top of a mountain

snowcapped ('snəʊ,kæpt) *adj* (of a mountain, hill, etc) having a cap of snow on the top

snow crab *n Canadian* an edible crab with long thin legs found off the coasts of Eastern Canada

Snowdon¹ ('snəʊdən) *n* a mountain in NW Wales, in Gwynedd: the highest peak in Wales. Height: 1085 m (3560 ft)

Snowdon² ('snəʊdən) *n* **1st Earl of,** title of *Antony Armstrong-Jones*. born 1930, British photographer, whose work includes television documentaries, photographic books, and the design of the Snowdon Aviary, London Zoo (1965). His marriage (1960–78) to Princess Margaret ended in divorce

Snowdonia (snəʊ'dəʊnıə) *n* **1** a massif in NW Wales, in Gwynedd, the highest peak being Snowdon **2** a national park in NW Wales, in Gwynedd and Conwy: includes the Snowdonia massif in the north. Area: 2189 sq km (845 sq miles)

snowdrift ('snəʊ,drıft) *n* a bank of deep snow driven together by the wind

snowdrop ('snəʊ,drɒp) *n* any of several amaryllidaceous plants of the Eurasian genus *Galanthus*, esp *G. nivalis*, having drooping white bell-shaped flowers that bloom in early spring

snowfall ('snəʊ,fɔ:l) *n* **1** a fall of snow **2** *meteorol* the amount of snow received in a specified place and time

snow fence *n* a portable wire-and-paling fence erected to prevent snow from drifting across a road, drive, ski

S

run, or other space

snowfield ('snəʊˌfiːld) *n* a large area of permanent snow

snowflake ('snəʊˌfleɪk) *n* **1** one of the mass of small thin delicate arrangements of ice crystals that fall as snow **2** any of various European amaryllidaceous plants of the genus *Leucojum*, such as *L. vernum* (**spring snowflake**), that have white nodding bell-shaped flowers

snow goose *n* a North American goose, *Anser hyperboreus* (or *Chen hyperborea* or *A. caerulescens*), having a white plumage with black wing tips

snow gum *n* any of various eucalyptus trees that grow at high altitude, esp *Eucalyptus pauciflora* [so called because it grows at high altitude]

snow-in-summer *n* another name for **dusty miller** (sense 1) [c19: so called from the appearance of its flowers]

snow leopard *n* a large feline mammal, *Panthera uncia*, of mountainous regions of central Asia, closely related to the leopard but having a long pale brown coat marked with black rosettes

snow line *n* the altitudinal or latitudinal limit of permanent snow

snowman ('snəʊˌmæn) *n*, *pl* -men a figure resembling a man, made of packed snow

snowmobile ('snəʊməˌbiːl) *n* a small open motor vehicle for travelling on snow, steered by two skis at the front and driven by a caterpillar track underneath

snowplough ('snəʊˌplaʊ) *n* an implement or vehicle for clearing away snow

snowshoe ('snəʊˌʃuː) *n* **1** a device to facilitate walking on snow, esp a racket-shaped frame with a network of thongs stretched across it ▷ *vb* -shoes, -shoeing, -shoed **2** (*intr*) to walk or go using snowshoes > 'snow,shoer *n*

snowstorm ('snəʊˌstɔːm) *n* a storm with heavy snow

snow tyre *n* a motor vehicle tyre with deep treads and ridges to give improved grip on snow and ice

snow-white *adj* **1** white as snow **2** pure as white snow

snowy ('snəʊɪ) *adj* snowier, snowiest **1** covered with or abounding in snow: *snowy hills* **2** characterized by snow: *snowy weather* **3** resembling snow in whiteness, purity, etc > 'snowily *adv* > 'snowiness *n*

Snowy Mountains *pl n* a mountain range in SE Australia, part of the Australian Alps: famous hydroelectric scheme > Snowy Mountain *adj*

snowy owl *n* a large owl, *Nyctea scandiaca*, of tundra regions, having a white plumage flecked with brown

Snowy River *n* a river in SE Australia, rising in SE New South Wales: waters diverted through a system of dams and tunnels across the watershed into the Murray and Murrumbidgee Rivers for hydroelectric power and to provide water for irrigation. Length: 426 km (265 miles)

SNP *abbreviation* Scottish National Party

Snr *or* **snr** *abbreviation* senior

snub (snʌb) *vb* snubs, snubbing, snubbed (*tr*) **1** to insult (someone) deliberately **2** to stop or check the motion of (a boat, horse, etc) by taking turns of a rope or cable around a post or other fixed object ▷ *n* **3** a deliberately insulting act or remark **4** *nautical* an elastic shock absorber attached to a mooring line ▷ *adj* **5** short and blunt. See also **snub-nosed** [c14: from Old Norse *snubba* to scold; related to Norwegian, Swedish dialect *snubba* to cut short, Danish *snubbe*] > 'snubber *n* > 'snubby *adj*

snub-nosed *adj* **1** having a short turned-up nose **2** (of a pistol) having an extremely short barrel

snuff¹ (snʌf) *vb* **1** (*tr*) to inhale through the nose **2** (when *intr*, often foll by *at*) (esp of an animal) to examine by sniffing ▷ *n* **3** an act or the sound of snuffing [c16: probably from Middle Dutch *snuffen* to snuffle, ultimately of imitative origin] > 'snuffer *n*

snuff² (snʌf) *n* **1** finely powdered tobacco for sniffing up the nostrils or less commonly for chewing **2** a small amount of this **3** up to snuff *informal* **a** in good health or in good condition **b** chiefly Brit not easily deceived ▷ *vb* **4** (*intr*) to use or inhale snuff [c17: from Dutch *snuf*, shortened from *snuftabale*, literally: tobacco for snuffing; see SNUFF¹]

snuff³ (snʌf) *vb* (*tr*) **1** (often foll by *out*) to extinguish (a

light from a naked flame, esp a candle) **2** to cut off the charred part of (the wick of a candle, etc) **3** (usually foll by *out*) *informal* to suppress; put an end to **4** snuff it *Brit informal* to die ▷ *n* **5** the burned portion of the wick of a candle [c14 *snoffe*, of obscure origin]

snuffbox ('snʌfˌbɒks) *n* a container, often of elaborate ornamental design, for holding small quantities of snuff

snuff-dipping *n* the practice of absorbing nicotine by holding in one's mouth, between the cheek and the gum, a small amount of tobacco, either loose or enclosed in a sachet

snuffer ('snʌfə) *n* **1** a cone-shaped implement for extinguishing candles **2** (*plural*) an instrument resembling a pair of scissors for trimming the wick or extinguishing the flame of a candle

snuffle ('snʌfəl) *vb* **1** (*intr*) to breathe noisily or with difficulty **2** to say or speak in a nasal tone **3** (*intr*) to snivel ▷ *n* **4** an act or the sound of snuffling **5** a nasal tone or voice **6** the snuffles a condition characterized by snuffling [c16: from Low German or Dutch *snuffelen*; see SNUFF¹, SNIVEL] > 'snuffly *adj*

snuff movie *or* **snuff film** *n* *slang* a pornographic film in which an unsuspecting actress or actor is murdered as the climax of the film

snuffy ('snʌfɪ) *adj* snuffier, snuffiest **1** of, relating to, or resembling snuff **2** covered with or smelling of snuff **3** unpleasant; disagreeable > 'snuffiness *n*

snug (snʌg) *adj* snugger, snuggest **1** comfortably warm and well-protected; cosy: *the children were snug in bed during the blizzard* **2** small but comfortable: *a snug cottage* **3** well-ordered; compact: *a snug boat* **4** sheltered and secure: *a snug anchorage* **5** fitting closely and comfortably **6** offering safe concealment ▷ *n* **7** (in Britain and Ireland) one of the bars in certain pubs, offering intimate seating for only a few persons ▷ *vb* snugs, snugging, snugged **8** to make or become comfortable and warm [c16 (in the sense: prepared for storms (used of a ship)): related to Old Icelandic *snöggr* short-haired, Swedish *snygg* tidy, Low German *snögger* smart] > 'snugly *adv* > 'snugness *n*

snuggery ('snʌgərɪ) *n*, *pl* -geries **1** a cosy and comfortable place or room **2** another name for **snug** (sense 7)

snuggle ('snʌgəl) *vb* **1** (usually *intr*; usually foll by *down*, *up*, or *together*) to nestle into or draw close to (somebody or something) for warmth or from affection ▷ *n* **2** the act of snuggling [c17: frequentative SNUG (vb)]

so¹ (səʊ) *adv* **1** (foll by an adjective or adverb and a correlative clause often introduced by *that*) to such an extent: *the river is so dirty that it smells* **2** (used with a negative; it replaces the first *as* in an equative comparison) to the same extent as: *she is not so old as you* **3** (intensifier): *it's so lovely; I love you so* **4** in the state or manner expressed or implied: *they're happy and will remain so* **5** (not used with a negative; foll by an auxiliary verb or *do*, *have*, or *be* used as main verbs) also; likewise: *I can speak Spanish and so can you* **6** *informal* indeed: used to contradict a negative statement: *You didn't tell the truth. I did so!* **7** *archaic* provided that **8** and so on *or* and so forth and continuing similarly **9** or so approximately: *fifty or so people came to see me* **10** so be it used to express agreement or resignation **11** so much **a** a certain degree or amount (of): *it's just so much nonsense* **12** so much for **a** no more can or need be said about **b** used to express contempt for something that has failed ▷ *conj* (subordinating; often foll by *that*) **13** in order (that): *to die so that you might live* **14** with the consequence (that): *he was late home, so that there was trouble* **15** so as (takes an infinitive) in order (to): *to slim so as to lose weight* ▷ *sentence connector* **16** in consequence; hence: *she wasn't needed, so she left* **17** thereupon; and then: *and so we ended up in France* **18** so what! *informal* what importance does that have? ▷ *pron* **19** used to substitute for a clause or sentence, which may be understood: *you'll stop because I said so* **20** (used with *is*, *was*, etc) factual; true: *it can't be so* ▷ *interj* **21** an exclamation of agreement, surprise, etc [Old English *swā*; related to Old Norse *svā*, Old High German *sō*, Dutch *zoo*]

● USAGE In formal English, *so* is not used as a
● conjunction, to indicate either purpose (*he left by a back*
● *door so he could avoid photographers*) or result (*the project was*
● *abandoned so his services were no longer needed*). In the
● former case *to* or *in order to* should be used instead, and
● in the latter case *and so* or *and therefore* would be more
● acceptable. The expression *so therefore* should not be
● used

so² ('səʊ) *n music* a variant spelling of **soh**

soak (səʊk) *vb* **1** to make, become, or be thoroughly wet
or saturated, esp by immersion in a liquid **2** (when *intr*,
usually foll by *in* or *into*) (of a liquid) to penetrate or
permeate **3** (*tr*; usually foll by *in* or *up*) (of a permeable
solid) to take in (a liquid) by absorption: *the earth soaks up*
rainwater **4** (*tr*; foll by *out* or *out of*) to remove by
immersion in a liquid: *she soaked the stains out of the dress*
5 *informal* to drink excessively or make someone drunk
6 (*tr*) *US & Canadian slang* to overcharge ▷ *n* **7** the act of
immersing in a liquid or the period of immersion **8** the
liquid in which something may be soaked, esp a
solution containing detergent **9** *slang* a person who
drinks to excess [Old English *sōcian* to cook; see **suck**]
▷ '**soaker** *n* ▷ '**soaking** *n, adj*

soakaway ('səʊkə,weɪ) *n* a pit filled with rubble, etc,
into which rain or waste water drains

so-and-so *n, pl* **so-and-sos** *informal* **1** a person whose
name is forgotten or ignored **2** *euphemistic* a person or
thing regarded as unpleasant or difficult: *which so-and-so*
broke my razor?

Soane (səʊn) *n* Sir **John**. 1753–1837, British architect. His
work includes Dulwich College Art Gallery (1811–14) and
his own house in Lincoln's Inn Fields, London (1812–13),
which is now the Sir John Soane's Museum

soap (səʊp) *n* **1** a cleaning or emulsifying agent made by
reacting animal or vegetable fats or oils with potassium
or sodium hydroxide. Soaps often contain colouring
matter and perfume and act by emulsifying grease and
lowering the surface tension of water, so that it more
readily penetrates open materials such as textiles **2** any
metallic salt of a fatty acid, such as palmitic or stearic
acid **3** *slang* flattery or persuasive talk (esp in the phrase
soft soap) **4** *informal* short for **soap opera 5** no soap *US &*
Canadian slang not possible or successful ▷ *vb* **6** (*tr*) to
apply soap to **7** (*tr*; often foll by *up*) *slang* to flatter or talk
persuasively to [Old English *sāpe*; related to Old High
German *seipfa*, Old French *savon*, Latin *sāpō*] ▷ '**soapless**
adj ▷ '**soap,like** *adj*

soapberry ('səʊp,bɛrɪ) *n, pl* **-ries 1** any of various chiefly
tropical American sapindaceous trees of the genus
Sapindus, esp *S. saponaria* (or *S. marginatus*), having pulpy
fruit containing saponin **2** the fruit of any of these trees

soapbox ('səʊp,bɒks) *n* **1** a box or crate for packing soap
2 a crate used as a platform for speech-making **3** a
child's homemade racing cart consisting of a wooden
box set on a wooden frame with wheels and a steerable
front axle

soapie *or* **soapy** ('səʊpɪ) *n Austral* an informal word for
soap opera

soap opera *n* a serialized drama, usually dealing with
domestic themes and characterized by sentimentality,
broadcast on radio or television [c20: so called because
manufacturers of soap were typical sponsors]

soapstone ('səʊp,stəʊn) *n* a massive compact soft
variety of talc, used for making tabletops, hearths,
ornaments, etc. Also called: **steatite** [c17: so called
because it has a greasy feel and was sometimes used as
soap]

soapsuds ('səʊp,sʌdz) *pl n* foam or lather made from
soap ▷ '**soap,sudsy** *adj*

soapwort ('səʊp,wɜːt) *n* a Eurasian caryophyllaceous
plant, *Saponaria officinalis*, having rounded clusters of
fragrant pink or white flowers and leaves that were
formerly used as a soap substitute. Also called:
bouncing Bet

soapy ('səʊpɪ) *adj* **soapier, soapiest 1** containing or
covered with soap: *soapy water* **2** resembling or
characteristic of soap **3** *slang* flattering or persuasive
▷ '**soapily** *adv* ▷ '**soapiness** *n*

soar (sɔː) *vb* (*intr*) **1** to rise or fly upwards into the air

2 (of a bird, aircraft, etc) to glide while maintaining
altitude by the use of ascending air currents **3** to rise or
increase in volume, size, etc: *soaring prices* [c14: from Old
French *essorer*, from Vulgar Latin *exaurāre* (unattested) to
expose to the breezes, from Latin **EX-**¹ + *aura* a breeze]
▷ '**soarer** *n* ▷ '**soaring** *n, adj*

Soares (Portuguese 'swarɪʃ) *n* **Mário** ('marju). born 1924,
Portuguese statesman; prime minister of Portugal
(1976–77; 1978–80; 1983–86); president of Portugal
(1986–96)

sob (sɒb) *vb* **sobs, sobbing, sobbed 1** (*intr*) to weep with
convulsive gasps **2** (*tr*) to utter with sobs **3** to cause
oneself to be in a specified state by sobbing: *to sob*
oneself to sleep ▷ *n* **4** a convulsive gasp made in weeping
[c12: probably from Low German; compare Dutch *sabben*
to suck] ▷ '**sobbing** *n, adj*

soba ('səʊbə) *n* (in Japanese cookery) noodles made from
buckwheat flour [Japanese]

sober ('səʊbə) *adj* **1** not drunk **2** not given to excessive
indulgence in drink or any other activity **3** sedate and
rational: *a sober attitude to a problem* **4** (of colours) plain
and dull or subdued **5** free from exaggeration or
speculation: *he told us the sober truth* ▷ *vb* **6** (usually foll by
up) to make or become less intoxicated, reckless, etc [c14:
sobre, from Old French, from Latin *sōbrius*] ▷ '**sobering** *adj*
▷ '**soberly** *adv*

Sobers ('səʊbəz) *n* Sir **Garfield St Auburn**, known as
Garry. born 1936, West Indian (Barbadian) cricketer; one
of the finest all-rounders of all time

sobriety (sə'braɪətɪ) *n* **1** the state or quality of being
sober **2** the quality of refraining from excess **3** the
quality of being serious or sedate

sobriquet *or* **soubriquet** ('səʊbrɪ,keɪ) *n* a humorous
epithet, assumed name, or nickname [c17: from French
soubriquet, of uncertain origin]

sob story *n* a tale of personal distress intended to
arouse sympathy, esp one offered as an excuse or
apology

Soc. *or* **soc.** *abbreviation* **1** socialist **2** society

soca ('səʊkə) *n* a mixture of soul and calypso music
typical of the E Caribbean [c20: a blend of *soul* and
calypso]

SOCA ('səʊkə) *n* acronym for Serious Organized Crime
Agency: a British government organization set up in
2004 specifically to combat organized crime

socage ('sɒkɪdʒ) *n English legal history* the tenure of land
by certain services, esp of an agricultural nature [c14:
from Anglo-French, from *soc* **SOKE**]

so-called *adj* **a** (*prenominal*) designated or styled by the
name or word mentioned, esp (in the speaker's opinion)
incorrectly: *a so-called genius* **b** (*also used parenthetically after*
a noun): *these experts, so-called, are no help*

soccer ('sɒkə) *n* **a** a game in which two teams of eleven
players try to kick or head a ball into their opponent's
goal, only the goalkeeper on either side being allowed to
touch the ball with his hands and arms except in the
case of throw-ins **b** (*as modifier*): *a soccer player* ▷ Also
called: **Association Football** [c19: from (*as*)*soc.* + -*er*]

Socceroos (,sɒkə'ruːz) *pl n* the Australian men's
national soccer team [from **SOCCER** + (**KANGAR**)**OO**]

Soche *or* **So-ch'e** ('səʊ'tʃɛ) *n* a variant transliteration of
the Chinese name for **Shache**

Sochi (Russian 'sɒtʃɪ) *n* a city and resort in SW Russia, in
the Krasnodar Territory on the Black Sea: hot mineral
springs. Pop: 328 000 (2005 est)

sociable ('səʊʃəbəl) *adj* **1** friendly or companionable **2** (of
an occasion) providing the opportunity for friendliness
and conviviality ▷ *n* **3** *chiefly US* another name for **social**
(sense 9) **4** a type of open carriage with two seats facing
each other [c16: via French from Latin *sociābilis*, from
sociāre to unite, from *socius* an associate] ▷ ,**socia'bility** *or*
'**sociableness** *n* ▷ '**sociably** *adv*

social ('səʊʃəl) *adj* **1** living or preferring to live in a
community rather than alone **2** denoting or relating to
human society or any of its subdivisions **3** of, relating
to, or characteristic of the experience, behaviour, and
interaction of persons forming groups **4** relating to or
having the purpose of promoting companionship,
communal activities, etc: *a social club* **5** relating to or

engaged in social services: *a social worker* **6** relating to or considered appropriate to a certain class of society, esp one thought superior **7** (esp of certain species of insects) living together in organized colonies: *social bees* **8** (of plant species) growing in clumps, usually over a wide area ▷ *n* **9** an informal gathering, esp of an organized group, to promote companionship, communal activity, etc [c16: from Latin *sociālis* companionable, from *socius* a comrade] > 'socially *adv*

Social and Liberal Democratic Party *n* (in Britain) a centrist political party formed in 1988 by the merging of the Liberal Party and part of the Social Democratic Party. In 1989 it changed its name to the Liberal Democrats

social anthropology *n* the branch of anthropology that deals with cultural and social phenomena such as kinship systems or beliefs, esp of nonliterate peoples

social capital *n* the network of social connections that exist between people, and their shared values and norms of behaviour, which enable and encourage mutually advantageous social cooperation

Social Chapter *n* the section of the **Maastricht Treaty** concerning working conditions, consultation of workers, employment rights, and social security. The UK government negotiated an opt-out clause from this section of the treaty in 1993 but adopted it in 1997

Social Charter *n* a declaration of the rights, minimum wages, maximum hours, etc, of workers in the European Union, later adopted in the Social Chapter

social climber *n* a person who seeks advancement to a higher social class, esp by obsequious behaviour > **social climbing** *n*

social contract *or* **social compact** *n* (in the theories of Locke, Hobbes, Rousseau, and others) an agreement, entered into by individuals, that results in the formation of the state or of organized society, the prime motive being the desire for protection, which entails the surrender of some or all personal liberties

Social Credit *n* (esp in Canada) a right-wing Populist political party, movement, or doctrine based on the socioeconomic theories of Major C. H. Douglas

social democrat *n* **1** any socialist who believes in the gradual transformation of capitalism into democratic socialism **2** (*usually capital*) a member of a Social Democratic Party > **social democracy** *n*

Social Democratic and Labour Party *n* a Northern Irish political party, which advocates peaceful union with the Republic of Ireland

Social Democratic Party *n* **1** (in Britain 1981–90) a centre political party founded by ex-members of the Labour Party. It formed an alliance with the Liberal Party and continued in a reduced form after many members left to join the Social and Liberal Democratic Party in 1988 **2** one of the two major political parties in Germany (formerly in West Germany), favouring gradual reform **3** any of the parties in many other countries similar to that of Germany

social dumping *n* the practice of allowing employers to lower wages and reduce employees' benefits in order to attract and retain employment and investment

social engineering *n* the manipulation of the social position and function of individuals in order to manage change in a society

social exclusion *n sociol* the failure of society to provide certain individuals and groups with those rights and benefits normally available to its members, such as employment, adequate housing, health care, education and training, etc

social fund *n* (in Britain) a social security fund from which loans or payments may be made to people in cases of extreme need

social inclusion *n sociol* the provision of certain rights to all individuals and groups in society, such as employment, adequate housing, health care, education and training, etc

social insurance *n* government insurance providing coverage for the unemployed, the injured, the old, etc: usually financed by contributions from employers and employees, as well as general government revenue

Social Insurance Number *n Canadian* a nine-digit number used by the federal government to identify a citizen

socialism ('səʊʃə,lɪzəm) *n* **1** an economic theory or system in which the means of production, distribution, and exchange are owned by the community collectively, usually through the state. It is characterized by production for use rather than profit, by equality of individual wealth, by the absence of competitive economic activity, and, usually, by government determination of investment, prices, and production levels. See **capitalism 2** any of various social or political theories or movements in which the common welfare is to be achieved through the establishment of a socialist economic system **3** (in Leninist theory) a transitional stage after the proletarian revolution in the development of a society from capitalism to communism: characterized by the distribution of income according to work rather than need

socialist ('səʊʃəlɪst) *n* **1** a supporter or advocate of socialism or any party promoting socialism (**socialist party**) ▷ *adj* **2** of, characteristic of, implementing, or relating to socialism **3** (*sometimes capital*) of, characteristic of, or relating to socialists or a socialist party > ,soci'listic *adj*

Socialist International *n* an international association of largely anti-Communist Social Democratic Parties founded in Frankfurt in 1951

socialist realism *n* (in Communist countries, esp formerly) the doctrine that art, literature, etc should present an idealized portrayal of reality, which glorifies the achievements of the Communist Party

socialite ('səʊʃə,laɪt) *n* a person who is or seeks to be prominent in fashionable society

sociality (,səʊʃɪ'ælɪtɪ) *n, pl* **-ties 1** the tendency of groups and persons to develop social links and live in communities **2** the quality or state of being social

socialize *or* **socialise** ('səʊʃə,laɪz) *vb* **1** (*intr*) to behave in a friendly or sociable manner **2** (*tr*) to prepare for life in society **3** (*tr*) *chiefly US* to alter or create so as to be in accordance with socialist principles, as by nationalization

social market *n* **a** an economic system in which industry and commerce are run by private enterprise within limits set by the government to ensure equality of opportunity and social and environmental responsibility **b** (*as modifier*): *a social-market economy*

social realism *n* **1** the use of realist art, literature, etc as a medium for social or political comment **2** another name for **socialist realism**

social science *n* **1** the study of society and of the relationship of individual members within society, including economics, history, political science, psychology, anthropology, and sociology **2** any of these subjects studied individually > **social scientist** *n*

social secretary *n* **1** a member of an organization who arranges its social events **2** a personal secretary who deals with private correspondence, etc

social security *n* **1** public provision for the economic, and sometimes social, welfare of the aged, unemployed, etc, esp through pensions and other monetary assistance **2** (*often capitals*) a government programme designed to provide such assistance

social services *pl n* welfare activities organized by the state or a local authority and carried out by trained personnel

social studies *n* (*functioning as singular*) the study of how people live and organize themselves in society, embracing geography, history, economics, and other subjects

social welfare *n* **1** the various social services provided by a state for the benefit of its citizens **2** (*capitals*) (in New Zealand) a government department concerned with pensions and benefits for the elderly, the sick, etc

social work *n* any of various social services designed to alleviate the conditions of the poor and aged and to increase the welfare of children > **social worker** *n*

societal (sə'saɪətˀl) *adj* of or relating to society, esp human society or social relations > so'cietally *adv*

societal marketing *n* **1** marketing that takes into

account society's long-term welfare **2** the marketing of a social or charitable cause, such as an environmental campaign

society (sə'saɪətɪ) *n, pl* **-ties 1** the totality of social relationships among organized groups of human beings or animals **2** a system of human organizations generating distinctive cultural patterns and institutions and usually providing protection, safety, continuity, and a national identity for its members **3** such a system with reference to its mode of social and economic organization or its dominant class: *middle-class society* **4** those with whom one has companionship **5** an organized group of people associated for some specific purpose or on account of some common interest: *a learned society* **6 a** the privileged class of people in a community, esp as considered superior or fashionable **b** (*as modifier*): *a society woman* **7** the social life and intercourse of such people: *to enter society as a debutante* **8** companionship; the fact or state of being together with someone else: *I enjoy her society* **9** *ecology* a small community of plants within a larger association [c16: via Old French *societé* from Latin *societās*, from *socius* a comrade]

Society Islands *pl n* a group of islands in the S Pacific: administratively part of French Polynesia; consists of the Windward Islands and the Leeward Islands; became a French protectorate in 1843 and a colony in 1880. Pop: 214 445 (2002). Area: 1595 sq km (616 sq miles)

Society of Jesus *n* the religious order of the Jesuits, founded by Ignatius Loyola

Socinus (səʊ'saɪnəs) *n* **Faustus** ('fɔːstəs), Italian name *Fausto Sozzini*, 1539–1604, and his uncle, **Laelius** ('liːlɪəs), Italian name *Lelio Sozzini*, 1525–62, Italian Protestant theologians and reformers

socio- *combining form* denoting social or society: *socioeconomic; sociopolitical; sociology*

sociobiology (ˌsəʊsɪəʊbaɪ'ɒlədʒɪ) *n* the study of social behaviour in animals and humans, esp in relation to its survival value and evolutionary origins > ˌsociobi'ologist *n*

socioeconomic (ˌsəʊsɪəʊˌiːkə'nɒmɪk, -ˌɛkə-) *adj* of, relating to, or involving both economic and social factors > ˌsocio,eco'nomically *adv*

sociolinguistics (ˌsəʊsɪəʊlɪŋ'gwɪstɪks) *n* (*functioning as singular*) the study of language in relation to its social context > ˌsocio'linguist *n*

sociology (ˌsəʊsɪ'ɒlədʒɪ) *n* the study of the development, organization, functioning, and classification of human societies > sociological (ˌsəʊsɪə'lɒdʒɪkªl) *adj* > ˌsoci'ologist *n*

sociometry (ˌsəʊsɪ'ɒmɪtrɪ) *n* the study of sociological relationships, esp of preferences, within social groups > sociometric (ˌsəʊsɪə'mɛtrɪk) *adj* > ˌsoci'ometrist *n*

sociopath ('səʊsɪəˌpæθ) *n psychiatry* another name for **psychopath** > ˌsocio'pathic *adj* > sociopathy (ˌsəʊsɪ'ɒpəθɪ) *n*

sociopolitical (ˌsəʊsɪəʊpə'lɪtɪkªl) *adj* of, relating to, or involving both political and social factors

sock¹ (sɒk) *n* **1** a cloth covering for the foot, reaching to between the ankle and knee and worn inside a shoe **2** an insole put in a shoe, as to make it fit better **3** a light shoe worn by actors in ancient Greek and Roman comedy, sometimes taken to allude to comic drama in general (as in the phrase **sock and buskin**) **4** **pull one's socks up** *Brit informal* to make a determined effort, esp in order to regain control of a situation **5** **put a sock in it** *Brit slang* to be quiet! [Old English *socc* a light shoe, from Latin *soccus*, from Greek *sukkhos*]

sock² (sɒk) *slang* > *vb* **1** (*usually tr*) to hit with force **2** **sock it to** to make a forceful impression on > *n* **3** a forceful blow [c17: of obscure origin]

socket ('sɒkɪt) *n* **1** a device into which an electric plug can be inserted in order to make a connection in a circuit **2** *chiefly Brit* such a device mounted on a wall and connected to the electricity supply **3** a part with an opening or hollow into which some other part, such as a pipe, probe, etc, can be fitted **4** *anatomy* **a** a bony hollow into which a part or structure fits: *a tooth socket; an eye socket* **b** the receptacle of a ball-and-socket joint > *vb*

5 (*tr*) to furnish with or place into a socket [c13: from Anglo-Norman *soket* a little ploughshare, from *soc*, of Celtic origin; compare Cornish *soch* ploughshare]

sockeye ('sɒkˌaɪ) *n* a Pacific salmon, *Oncorhynchus nerka*, having red flesh and valued as a food fish. Also called: **red salmon** [by folk etymology from Salishan *sukkegh*]

socle ('səʊkªl) *n* another name for **plinth** (sense 1) [c18: via French from Italian *zoccolo*, from Latin *socculus* a little shoe, from *soccus* a SOCK¹]

Socotra, Sokotra *or* **Suqutra** (sə'kəʊtrə) *n* an island in the Indian Ocean, about 240 km (150 miles) off Cape Guardafui, Somalia: administratively part of Yemen. Capital: Hadiboh (Tamrida). Area: 3100 sq km (1200 sq miles)

Socrates ('sɒkrəˌtiːz) *n* ?470–399 BC, Athenian philosopher, whose beliefs are known only through the writings of his pupils Plato and Xenophon. He taught that virtue was based on knowledge, which was attained by a dialectical process that took into account many aspects of a stated hypothesis. He was indicted for impiety and corruption of youth (399) and was condemned to death. He refused to flee and died by drinking hemlock

Socratic (sɒ'krætɪk) *adj* **1** of or relating to Socrates, the Athenian philosopher (?470–399 BC), his methods, etc > *n* **2** a person who follows the teachings of Socrates > So'cratically *adv* > So'crati,cism *n* > Socratist ('sɒkrətɪst) *n*

Socratic irony *n philosophy* a means by which the pretended ignorance of a skilful questioner leads the person answering to expose his own ignorance

Socratic method *n philosophy* the method of instruction by question and answer used by Socrates in order to elicit from his pupils truths he considered to be implicitly known by all rational beings

sod¹ (sɒd) *n* **1** a piece of grass-covered surface soil held together by the roots of the grass; turf **2** *poetic* the ground > *vb* **sods, sodding, sodded 3** (*tr*) to cover with sods [c15: from Low German; compare Middle Low German, Middle Dutch *sode*; related to Old Frisian *satha*]

sod² (sɒd) *slang, chiefly Brit* > *n* **1** a person considered to be obnoxious **2** a jocular word for a person **3 sod all** *slang* nothing > *interj* **4 sod it** a strong exclamation of annoyance > *See also* **sod off** [c19: shortened from SODOMITE] > 'sodding *adj*

soda ('səʊdə) *n* **1** any of a number of simple inorganic compounds of sodium, such as sodium carbonate (**washing soda**), sodium bicarbonate (**baking soda**), and sodium hydroxide (**caustic soda**) **2** See **soda water 3** *US & Canadian* a fizzy drink [c16: from Medieval Latin, from *sodanum* barilla, a plant that was burned to obtain a type of sodium carbonate, perhaps of Arabic origin]

soda ash *n* the anhydrous commercial form of sodium carbonate

soda bread *n* a type of bread leavened with sodium bicarbonate combined with milk and cream of tartar

soda fountain *n US & Canadian* **1** a counter that serves drinks, snacks, etc **2** an apparatus dispensing soda water

sodality (səʊ'dælɪtɪ) *n, pl* **-ties 1** *RC Church* a religious or charitable society **2** fraternity; fellowship [c16: from Latin *sodālitās* fellowship, from *sodālis* a comrade]

sodamide ('səʊdəˌmaɪd) *n* a white crystalline compound used as a dehydrating agent, as a chemical reagent, and in making sodium cyanide. Formula: $NaNH_2$ [c19: from SOD(IUM) + AMIDE]

soda siphon *n* a sealed bottle containing and dispensing soda water. The water is forced up a tube reaching to the bottom of the bottle by the pressure of gas above the water

soda water *n* an effervescent beverage made by charging water with carbon dioxide under pressure. Sometimes shortened to **soda**

sodden ('sɒdªn) *adj* **1** completely saturated **2 a** dulled, esp by excessive drinking **b** (*in combination*): *a drink-sodden mind* **3** heavy or doughy, as bread is when improperly cooked > *vb* **4** to make or become sodden [c13 *soden*, past participle of SEETHE] > 'soddenness *n*

Soddy ('sɒdɪ) *n* **Frederick.** 1877–1956, English chemist, whose work on radioactive disintegration led to the discovery of isotopes: Nobel prize for chemistry 1921

sodium ('səʊdɪəm) n **a** a very reactive soft silvery-white element of the alkali metal group occurring principally in common salt, Chile saltpetre, and cryolite. Sodium and potassium ions maintain the essential electrolytic balance in living cells. It is used in the production of chemicals, in metallurgy, and, alloyed with potassium, as a cooling medium in nuclear reactors. Symbol: Na; atomic no: 11; atomic wt: 22.989768; valency: 1; relative density: 0.971; melting pt: 97.81±0.03°C; boiling pt: 892.9°C **b** (as modifier): sodium light [C19: New Latin, from SODA + -IUM]

sodium amytal n another name for **Amytal**

sodium benzoate n a white crystalline soluble compound used as an antibacterial and antifungal agent in preserving food (**E211**), as an antiseptic, and in making dyes and pharmaceuticals. Formula: (C_6H_5COO)Na

sodium bicarbonate n a white crystalline soluble compound usually obtained by the Solvay process and used in effervescent drinks, baking powders, fire extinguishers, and in medicine as an antacid; sodium hydrogen carbonate. Formula: $NaHCO_3$. Also called: **bicarbonate of soda, baking soda**

sodium carbonate n a colourless or white odourless soluble crystalline compound existing in several hydrated forms and used in the manufacture of glass, ceramics, soap, and paper and as an industrial and domestic cleansing agent. It is made by the Solvay process and commonly obtained as the decahydrate (washing soda or sal soda) or a white anhydrous powder (soda ash). Formula: Na_2CO_3

sodium chlorate n a colourless crystalline soluble compound used as a bleaching agent, weak antiseptic, and weedkiller. Formula: $NaClO_3$

sodium chloride n common table salt; a soluble colourless crystalline compound occurring naturally as halite and in sea water: widely used as a seasoning and preservative for food and in the manufacture of chemicals, glass, and soap. Formula: NaCl. Also called: **salt**

sodium cyanide n a white odourless crystalline soluble poisonous compound with an odour of hydrogen cyanide when damp. It is used for extracting gold and silver from their ores and for case-hardening steel. Formula: NaCN

sodium glutamate ('glu:tə,meɪt) n another name for **monosodium glutamate**

sodium hydroxide n a white deliquescent strongly alkaline solid used in the manufacture of rayon, paper, aluminium, soap, and sodium compounds. Formula: NaOH. Also called: **caustic soda**

sodium hyposulphite n another name (not in technical usage) for **sodium thiosulphate**

sodium lamp n another name for **sodium-vapour lamp**

sodium nitrate n a white crystalline soluble solid compound occurring naturally as Chile saltpetre and caliche and used in matches, explosives, and rocket propellants, as a fertilizer, and as a curing salt for preserving food such as bacon, ham, and cheese (**E251**). Formula: $NaNO_3$

Sodium Pentothal n trademark another name for **thiopental sodium**

sodium silicate n any sodium salt of orthosilicic acid or metasilicic acid

sodium sulphate n a solid white substance that occurs naturally as thenardite and is usually used as the white anhydrous compound (**salt cake**) or the white crystalline decahydrate (**Glauber's salt**) in making glass, detergents, and pulp. Formula: Na_2SO_4

sodium thiosulphate n a white soluble substance used, in the pentahydrate form, in photography as a fixer to dissolve unchanged silver halides and also to remove excess chlorine from chlorinated water. Formula: $Na_2S_2O_3$. Also called (not in technical usage): **sodium, hyposulphitehypo**

sodium-vapour lamp n a type of electric lamp consisting of a glass tube containing neon and sodium vapour at low pressure through which an electric current is passed to give an orange light. They are used in street lighting

sod off vb (intr, adverb; usually imperative) slang, chiefly Brit to go away; depart

● **USAGE** This phrase was formerly considered to be
● taboo, and it was labelled as such in previous editions
● of Collins English Dictionary. However, it has now become
● acceptable in speech, although some older or more
● conservative people may object to its use

Sodom ('sɒdəm) n **1** Old Testament a city destroyed by God for its wickedness that, with Gomorrah, traditionally typifies depravity (Genesis 19:24) **2** this city as representing homosexuality **3** any place notorious for depravity

sodomite ('sɒdə,maɪt) n a person who practises sodomy

sodomize or **sodomise** ('sɒdə,maɪz) vb (tr) to be the active partner in anal intercourse

sodomy ('sɒdəmɪ) n anal intercourse committed by a man with another man or a woman [C13: via Old French sodomie from Latin (Vulgate) Sodoma Sodom]

Sod's law (sɒdz) n informal a humorous or facetious precept stating that if something can go wrong or turn out inconveniently it will

Soekarno (su:'kɑ:nəʊ) n a variant spelling of (Achmed) **Sukarno**

Soembawa (su:m'bɑ:wə) n the former spelling of **Sumbawa**

soever (səʊ'ɛvə) adv in any way at all: used to emphasize or make less precise a word or phrase, usually in combination with what, where, when, how, etc, or else separated by intervening words. See **whatsoever**

sofa ('səʊfə) n an upholstered seat with back and arms for two or more people [C17 (in the sense: dais upholstered as a seat): from Arabic suffah]

soffit ('sɒfɪt) n the underside of a part of a building or a structural component, such as an arch, beam, stair, etc [C17: via French from Italian soffitto, from Latin suffixus something fixed underneath, from suffigere, from sub- under + figere to fasten]

Sofia ('səʊfɪə) n the capital of Bulgaria, in the west: colonized by the Romans in 29 AD; became capital of Bulgaria in 1879; university (1880). Pop: 1 045 000 (2005 est)

S. of Sol. abbreviation Bible Song of Solomon

soft (sɒft) adj **1** easy to dent, work, or cut without shattering; malleable **2** not hard; giving little or no resistance to pressure or weight **3** fine, light, smooth, or fluffy to the touch **4** gentle; tranquil **5** (of music, sounds, etc) low and pleasing **6** (of light, colour, etc) not excessively bright or harsh **7** (of a breeze, climate, etc) temperate, mild, or pleasant **8** slightly blurred; not sharply outlined: soft focus **9** (of a diet) consisting of easily digestible foods **10** kind or lenient, often excessively so **11** easy to influence or impose upon **12** prepared to compromise; not doctrinaire: the soft left **13** informal feeble or silly; simple (often in the phrase **soft in the head**) **14** unable to endure hardship, esp through too much pampering **15** physically out of condition; flabby: soft muscles **16** loving; tender: soft words **17** informal requiring little exertion; easy: a soft job **18** chem (of water) relatively free of mineral salts and therefore easily able to make soap lather **19** (of a drug such as cannabis) nonaddictive or only mildly addictive **20** phonetics (not in technical usage) denoting the consonants c and g in English when they are pronounced as palatal or alveolar fricatives or affricates (s, dʒ, ʃ, ð, tʃ) before e and i, rather than as velar stops (k, g) **21** finance chiefly US (of prices, a market, etc) unstable and tending to decline **22** (of a currency) in relatively little demand, esp because of a weak balance of payments situation **23** (of radiation, such as X-rays and ultraviolet radiation) having low energy and not capable of deep penetration of materials **24** related to the performance of non-specific, undefinable tasks: soft skills such as customer services and office support **25 soft on** or **soft about a** gentle, sympathetic, or lenient towards **b** feeling affection or infatuation for ▷ adv **26** in a soft manner: to speak soft ▷ n **27** a soft object, part, or piece

S

28 *informal* See **softie** ▷ *interj archaic* **29** quiet! **30** wait! [Old English *sōfte*; related to Old Saxon *sāfti*, Old High German *semfti* gentle] > 'softly *adv* > 'softness *n*

softa ('sɒftə) *n* a Muslim student of divinity and jurisprudence, esp in Turkey [c17: from Turkish, from Persian *sōkhtah* aflame (with love of learning)]

softball ('sɒft,bɔːl) *n* **1** a variation of baseball using a larger softer ball, pitched underhand **2** the ball used **3** *cookery* the stage in the boiling of a sugar syrup at which it may be rubbed into balls after dipping in cold water

soft-boiled *adj* (of an egg) boiled for a short time so that the yolk is still soft

soft coal *n* another name for **bituminous coal**

soft commodities *pl n* nonmetal commodities such as cocoa, sugar, and grains, bought and sold on a futures market. Also called: **softs**

soft-core *adj* (of pornography) suggestive and titillating through not being totally explicit or detailed

soft-cover *adj* a less common word for **paperback**

soft drink *n* a nonalcoholic drink, usually cold

soften ('sɒfⁿn) *vb* **1** to make or become soft or softer **2** to make or become gentler > 'softener *n*

softening of the brain *n* an abnormal softening of the tissues of the cerebrum characterized by various degrees of mental impairment

soft-focus lens *n photog* a lens designed to produce an image that is uniformly very slightly out of focus: typically used for portrait work

soft furnishings *pl n Brit* curtains, hangings, rugs, etc

soft goods *pl n* textile fabrics and related merchandise

soft-headed *adj informal* feeble-minded; stupid; simple > ,soft-'headedness *n*

softhearted (,sɒft'hɑːtɪd) *adj* easily moved to pity > ,soft'heartedly *adv* > ,soft'heartedness *n*

softie *or* **softy** ('sɒftɪ) *n, pl* **softies** *informal* a person who is sentimental, weakly foolish, or lacking in physical endurance

soft landing *n* **1** a landing by a spacecraft on the moon or a planet at a sufficiently low velocity for the equipment or occupants to remain unharmed **2** a decrease in demand that does not result in a country's economy falling into recession ▷ Compare **hard landing**

soft launch *n* **1** the launch of a website in stages, with regular updating ▷ *vb* **soft-launch 2** (*tr*) to implement the soft launch of (a website)

soft option *n* in a number of choices, the one considered to be easy or the easiest to do, involving the least difficulty or exertion

soft palate *n* the posterior fleshy portion of the roof of the mouth. It forms a movable muscular flap that seals off the nasopharynx during swallowing and speech

soft paste *n* **a** artificial porcelain made from clay, bone ash, etc **b** (*as modifier*): *softpaste porcelain* [c19: from PASTE¹ (in the sense: the mixture from which porcelain is made); so called because of its consistency]

soft-pedal *vb* **-als, -alling, -alled** *or US* **-als, -aling, -aled** (*tr*) **1** to mute the tone of (a piano) by depressing the soft pedal **2** *informal* to make (something, esp something unpleasant) less obvious by deliberately failing to emphasize or allude to it ▷ *n* **soft pedal 3** a foot-operated lever on a piano, the left one of two, that either moves the whole action closer to the strings so that the hammers strike with less force or causes fewer of the strings to sound

soft porn *n informal* soft-core pornography

softs (sɒfts) *pl n* another name for **soft commodities**

soft science *n* a science, such as sociology or anthropology, that deals with humans as its principle subject matter, and is therefore not generally considered to be based on rigorous experimentation

soft sell *n* a method of selling based on indirect suggestion or inducement

soft shoulder *or* **soft verge** *n* a soft edge along the side of a road that is unsuitable for vehicles to drive on

soft skills *pl n* desirable qualities for certain forms of employment that do not depend on acquired knowledge: they include common sense, the ability to deal with people, and a positive flexible attitude

soft soap *n* **1** *med* another name for **green soap 2** *informal* flattering, persuasive, or cajoling talk ▷ *vb* **soft-soap 3** *informal* to use such talk on (a person)

soft-spoken *adj* **1** speaking or said with a soft gentle voice **2** able to persuade or impress by glibness of tongue

soft spot *n* a sentimental fondness (esp in the phrase **have a soft spot for**)

soft touch *n informal* a person easily persuaded or imposed on, esp to lend money

software ('sɒft,wɛə) *n computing* the programs that can be used with a particular computer system. See **hardware** (sense 2)

softwood ('sɒft,wʊd) *n* **1** the open-grained wood of any of numerous coniferous trees, such as pine and cedar, as distinguished from that of a dicotyledonous tree **2** any tree yielding this wood

Sogdiana (,sɒgdɪ'ɑːnə) *n* a region of ancient central Asia. Its chief city was Samarkand > 'Sogdian *n, adj*

soggy ('sɒgɪ) *adj* **-gier, -giest 1** soaked with liquid **2** (of bread, pastry, etc) moist and heavy **3** *informal* lacking in spirit or positiveness [c18: probably from dialect *sog* marsh, of obscure origin] > 'soggily *adv* > 'sogginess *n*

soh *or* **so** (səʊ) *n music* (in tonic sol-fa) the name used for the fifth note or dominant of any scale [c13: see GAMUT]

Soho ('səʊhəʊ) *n* a district of central London, in the City of Westminster: a foreign quarter since the late 17th century, now chiefly known for restaurants, nightclubs, striptease clubs, etc

soi-disant *French* (swadizɑ̃) *adj* so-called; self-styled [literally: calling oneself]

soigné *or feminine* **soignée** ('swɑːnjeɪ; *French* swaɲe) *adj* well-groomed; elegant [French, from *soigner* to take good care of, of Germanic origin; compare Old Saxon *sunnea* care]

soil¹ (sɔɪl) *n* **1** the top layer of the land surface of the earth that is composed of disintegrated rock particles, humus, water, and air **2** a type of this material having specific characteristics: *loamy soil* **3** land, country, or region: *one's native soil* **4** the soil life and work on a farm; land: *he belonged to the soil, as his forefathers had* **5** any place or thing encouraging growth or development [c14: from Anglo-Norman, from Latin *solium* a seat, but confused with Latin *solum* the ground]

soil² (sɔɪl) *vb* **1** to make or become dirty or stained **2** (*tr*) to pollute with sin or disgrace; sully; defile ▷ *n* **3** the state or result of soiling **4** refuse, manure, or excrement [c13: from Old French *soillier* to defile, from *soil* pigsty, probably from Latin *sūs* a swine]

soil³ (sɔɪl) *vb* (*tr*) to feed (livestock) freshly cut green fodder either to fatten or purge them [c17: perhaps from obsolete *sull* (c16) *soil* to manure, from SOIL² (n)]

soil pipe *n* a pipe that conveys sewage or waste water from a toilet, etc, to a soil drain or sewer

soiree ('swɑːreɪ) *n* an evening party or other gathering given usually at a private house, esp where guests are invited to listen to, play, or dance to music [c19: from French, from Old French *soir* evening, from Latin *sērum* a late time, from *sērus* late]

Soissons (*French* swasɔ̃) *n* a city in N France, on the Aisne River: has Roman remains and an 11th-century abbey. Pop: 29 453 (1999)

soixante-neuf *French* (swasɑ̃tnœf) *n* a sexual activity in which two people simultaneously stimulate each other's genitalia with their mouths. Also called: **sixty-nine** [literally: sixty-nine, from the position adopted by the participants]

sojourn ('sɒdʒɜːn, 'sʌdʒ-) *n* **1** a temporary stay ▷ *vb* **2** (*intr*) to stay or reside temporarily [c13: from Old French *sojorner*, from Vulgar Latin *subdiurnāre* (unattested) to spend a day, from Latin *sub-* during + Late Latin *diurnum* day] > 'sojourner *n*

soke (səʊk) *n English legal history* **1** the right to hold a local court **2** the territory under the jurisdiction of a particular court [c14: from Medieval Latin *sōca*, from Old English *sōcn* a seeking; see SEEK]

Sokoto ('səʊkə,təʊ) *n* **1** a state of NW Nigeria. Capital: Sokoto. Pop: 3 696 999 (2006). Area: 25 973 sq km (10 028 sq miles) **2** a town in NW Nigeria, capital of Sokoto state: capital of the Fulah Empire in the 19th century; Muslim place of pilgrimage. Pop: 444 000 (2005 est)

sol¹ (sɒl) *n music* another name for **soh** [c14: see GAMUT]

sol² (sɒl) *n* a colloid that has a continuous liquid phase, esp one in which a solid is suspended in a liquid [c20: shortened from HYDROSOL]

Sol (sɒl) *n* **1** the Roman god personifying the sun **2** a poetic word for the **sun**

Sol. *abbreviation* **1** Also called: **Solr** solicitor **2** *Bible* Solomon

sola *Latin* ('səʊlə) *adj* the feminine form of **solus**

solace ('sɒlɪs) *n* **1** comfort in misery, disappointment, etc **2** something that gives comfort or consolation ▷ *vb* (*tr*) **3** to give comfort or cheer to (a person) in time of sorrow, distress, etc **4** to alleviate (sorrow, misery, etc) [c13: from Old French *solas*, from Latin *sōlātium* comfort, from *sōlārī* to console] ▷ '**solacer** *n*

solan *or* **solan goose** ('səʊlən) *n* an archaic name for the **gannet** [c15 *soland*, of Scandinavian origin; compare Old Norse *sūla* gannet, *ōnd* duck]

Solana (səʊ'lɑːnə) *or* **Solana Madariaga** (səʊ'lɑːnə ˌmædərɪ'ɑːgə) *n* **Javier** ('hævɪeɪ). born 1942, Spanish socialist politician; minister for foreign affairs (1992–95), secretary-general of NATO (1995–99), and EU high representative for foreign policy from 1999

solanaceous (ˌsɒlə'neɪʃəs) *adj* of, relating to, or belonging to the *Solanaceae*, a family of plants having typically tubular flowers with reflexed petals, protruding anthers, and often poisonous or narcotic properties: includes the potato, tobacco, henbane, mandrake, and several nightshades [c19: from New Latin *Sōlānāceae*, from Latin *sōlānum* nightshade]

solanum (səʊ'leɪnəm) *n* any tree, shrub, or herbaceous plant of the mainly tropical solanaceous genus *Solanum*: includes the potato, aubergine, and certain nightshades [c16: from Latin: nightshade]

solar ('səʊlə) *adj* **1** of or relating to the sun **2** operating by or utilizing the energy of the sun: *solar cell* **3** *astronomy* determined from the motion of the earth relative to the sun: *solar year* **4** *astrology* subject to the influence of the sun [c15: from Latin *sōlāris*, from *sōl* the sun]

solar cell *n* a photovoltaic cell that produces electricity from the sun's rays, used esp in spacecraft

solar constant *n* the rate at which the sun's energy is received per unit area at the top of the earth's atmosphere when the sun is at its mean distance from the earth and atmospheric absorption has been corrected for. Its value is 1367 watts per square metre

solar day *n* the period of time during which the earth makes one complete revolution on its axis relative to the sun

solar energy *n* energy obtained from solar power

solar flare *n* a brief powerful eruption of particles and intense electromagnetic radiation from the sun's surface, associated with sunspots and causing disturbances to radio communication on earth

solarium (səʊ'lɛərɪəm) *n, pl* -**lariums** *or* -**laria** (-'lɛərɪə) **1** a room built largely of glass to afford exposure to the sun **2** a bed equipped with ultraviolet lights used for acquiring an artificial suntan **3** an establishment offering such facilities [c19: from Latin: a terrace, from *sōl* sun]

solar month *n* See **month** (sense 4)

solar plexus *n* **1** Also called: **coeliac plexus** *anatomy* the network of sympathetic nerves situated behind the stomach that supply the abdominal organs **2** (*not in technical usage*) the part of the stomach beneath the diaphragm; pit of the stomach [c18: referring to resemblance between the radial network of nerves and ganglia and the rays of the sun]

solar power *n* heat radiation from the sun converted into electrical power

solar sail *n* a device that reflects light particles from the Sun, gaining momentum in the opposite direction to propel spacecraft forwards

solar system *n* the system containing the sun and the bodies held in its gravitational field, including the planets (Mercury, Venus, Earth, Mars, Jupiter, Saturn, Uranus, and Neptune), the dwarf planets (Eris, Pluto,

and Ceres), the asteroids, and comets

solar wind (wɪnd) *n* the constant stream of charged particles, esp protons and electrons, emitted by the sun at high velocities, its density and speed varying during periods of solar activity. It interacts with the earth's magnetic field, some of the particles being trapped by the magnetic lines of force, and causes auroral displays

solar year *n* See **year** (sense 4)

solatium (səʊ'leɪʃɪəm) *n, pl* -**tia** (-ʃɪə) *law chiefly US & Scot* compensation awarded to a party for injury to the feelings as distinct from physical suffering and pecuniary loss [c19: from Latin: see SOLACE]

sold (səʊld) *vb* **1** the past tense and past participle of **sell** ▷ *adj* **2 sold on** *slang* uncritically attached to or enthusiastic about

solder ('səʊldə; *US* 'sɒdər) *n* **1** an alloy for joining two metal surfaces by melting the alloy so that it forms a thin layer between the surfaces. **Soft solders** are alloys of lead and tin; **brazing solders** are alloys of copper and zinc **2** something that joins things together firmly; a bond ▷ *vb* **3** to join or mend or be joined or mended with or as if with solder [c14: via Old French from Latin *solidāre* to strengthen, from *solidus* SOLID] ▷ '**solderable** *adj* ▷ '**solderer** *n*

soldering iron *n* a hand tool consisting of a handle fixed to a copper tip that is heated, electrically or in a flame, and used to melt and apply solder

soldier ('səʊldʒə) *n* **1 a** a person who serves or has served in an army **b** Also called: **common soldier** a noncommissioned member of an army as opposed to a commissioned officer **2** a person who works diligently for a cause **3** *zoology* an individual in a colony of social insects, esp ants, that has powerful jaws adapted for defending the colony, crushing large food particles, etc ▷ *vb* (*intr*) **4** to serve as a soldier [c13: from Old French *soudier*, from *soude* (army) pay, from Late Latin *solidus* a gold coin, from *solidus* firm] ▷ '**soldierly** *adj*

soldier of fortune *n* a man who seeks money or adventure as a soldier; mercenary

soldier on *vb* (*intr, adverb*) to persist in one's efforts in spite of difficulties, pressure, etc

soldiery ('səʊldʒərɪ) *n, pl* -**dieries 1** soldiers collectively **2** a group of soldiers **3** the profession of being a soldier

sole¹ (səʊl) *adj* **1** (*prenominal*) being the only one; only **2** (*prenominal*) of or relating to one individual or group and no other: *sole rights on a patent* **3** *law* having no wife or husband **4** an archaic word for **solitary** [c14: from Old French *soule*, from Latin *sōlus* alone] ▷ '**soleness** *n*

sole² (səʊl) *n* **1** the underside of the foot **2** the underside of a shoe **3 a** the bottom of a furrow **b** the bottom of a plough **4** the underside of a golf-club head ▷ *vb* (*tr*) **5** to provide (a shoe) with a sole [c14: via Old French from Latin *solea* sandal; probably related to *solum* the ground]

sole³ (səʊl) *n, pl* **sole** *or* **soles** any tongue-shaped flatfish of the family *Soleidae*, esp *Solea solea* (**European sole**): most common in warm seas and highly valued as food fishes [c14: via Old French from Vulgar Latin *sola* (unattested), from Latin *solea* a sandal (from the fish's shape)]

sole-charge school *n* NZ a rural school with only one teacher

solecism ('sɒlɪˌsɪzəm) *n* **1 a** the nonstandard use of a grammatical construction **b** any mistake, incongruity, or absurdity **2** a violation of good manners [c16: from Latin *soloecismus*, from Greek *soloikismos*, from *soloikos* speaking incorrectly, from *Soloi* an Athenian colony of Cilicia where the inhabitants spoke a corrupt form of Greek] ▷ '**solecist** *n* ▷ ˌsole'**cistic** *or* ˌsole'**cistical** *adj* ▷ ˌsole'**cistically** *adv*

solely ('səʊllɪ) *adv* **1** only; completely; entirely **2** without another or others; singly; alone **3** for one thing only

solemn ('sɒləm) *adj* **1** characterized or marked by seriousness or sincerity: *a solemn vow* **2** characterized by pomp, ceremony, or formality **3** serious, glum, or pompous **4** inspiring awe: *a solemn occasion* **5** performed with religious ceremony **6** gloomy or sombre: *solemn colours* [c14: from Old French *solempne*, from Latin *sōllemnis* appointed, perhaps from *sollus* whole] ▷ '**solemnly** *adv* ▷ '**solemnness** *or* '**solemness** *n*

solemnify (səˈlɛmnɪˌfaɪ) *vb* **-fies, -fying, -fied** (*tr*) to make serious or grave > so,lemnifiˈcation *n*

solemnity (səˈlɛmnɪtɪ) *n*, *pl* **-ties** **1** the state or quality of being solemn **2** (*often plural*) solemn ceremony, observance, celebration, etc **3** *law* a formality necessary to validate a deed, act, contract, etc

solemnize *or* **solemnise** (ˈsɒləmˌnaɪz) *vb* (*tr*) **1** to celebrate or observe with rites or formal ceremonies, as a religious occasion **2** to celebrate or perform the ceremony of (marriage) **3** to make solemn or serious **4** to perform or hold (ceremonies, etc) in due manner > ,solemniˈzation *or* ,solemniˈsation *n* > ˈsolem,nizer *or* ˈsolem,niser *n*

solenodon (səˈlɛnədən) *n* either of two rare shrewlike nocturnal mammals of the Caribbean, *Atopogale cubana* (**Cuban solenodon**) or *Solenodon paradoxus* (**Haitian solenodon**), having a long hairless tail and an elongated snout: family *Solenodontidae*, order *Insectivora* (insectivores) [C19: from New Latin, from Latin *sōlēn* sea mussel, razor-shell (from Greek: pipe) + Greek *odōn* tooth]

solenoid (ˈsəʊlɪˌnɔɪd) *n* **1** a coil of wire, usually cylindrical, in which a magnetic field is set up by passing a current through it **2** a coil of wire, partially surrounding an iron core, that is made to move inside the coil by the magnetic field set up by a current: used to convert electrical to mechanical energy, as in the operation of a switch [C19: from French *solénoïde*, from Greek *sōlēn* a pipe, tube] > ,soleˈnoidal *adj*

Solent (ˈsəʊlənt) *n* **the Solent** a strait of the English Channel between the coast of Hampshire, on the English mainland, and the Isle of Wight. Width: up to 6 km (4 miles)

Soleure (sɔlœr) *n* the French name for **Solothurn**

sol-fa (ˈsɒlˈfɑː) *n* **1** short for **tonic sol-fa** ▷ *vb* **-fas, -faing, -faed 2** *US* to use tonic sol-fa syllables in singing (a tune) [C16: see GAMUT]

solfatara (ˌsɒlfəˈtɑːrə) *n* a volcanic vent emitting only sulphurous gases and water vapour or sometimes hot mud [C18: from Italian: a sulphurous volcano near Naples, from *solfo* SULPHUR]

solfeggio (sɒlˈfɛdʒɪəʊ) *or* **solfège** (sɒlˈfɛʒ) *n*, *pl* **-feggi** (-ˈfɛdʒiː), **-feggios** *or* **-fèges** *music* **1** a voice exercise in which runs, scales, etc, are sung to the same syllable or syllables **2** solmization, esp the French or Italian system, in which the names correspond to the notes of the scale of C major [C18: from Italian *solfeggiare* to use the syllables sol-fa; see GAMUT]

soli (ˈsəʊlɪ) *adj, adv music* (of a piece or passage) to be performed by or with soloists [plural of SOLO]

solicit (səˈlɪsɪt) *vb* **-its, -iting, -ited 1** (when *intr,* foll by *for*) to make a request, application, or entreaty to (a person for business, support, etc) **2** to accost (a person) with an offer of sexual relations in return for money **3** to provoke or incite (a person) to do something wrong or illegal [C15: from Old French *solliciter* to disturb, from Latin *sollicitāre* to harass, from *sollicitus* agitated, from *sollus* whole + *citus* to excite] > so,liciˈtation *n*

solicitor (səˈlɪsɪtə) *n* **1** (in Britain) a lawyer who advises clients on matters of law, draws up legal documents, prepares cases for barristers, etc, and who may represent clients in certain courts **2** (in the US) an officer responsible for the legal affairs of a town, city, etc **3** a person who solicits > soˈlicitorship *n*

Solicitor General *n*, *pl* **Solicitors General 1** (in Britain) the law officer of the Crown ranking next to the Attorney General (in Scotland to the Lord Advocate) and acting as his assistant **2** (in New Zealand) the government's chief lawyer: head of the Crown Law Office and prosecutor for the Crown

solicitous (səˈlɪsɪtəs) *adj* **1** showing consideration, concern, attention, etc **2** keenly anxious or willing; eager [C16: from Latin *sollicitus* anxious; see SOLICIT] > soˈlicitousness *n*

solicitude (səˈlɪsɪˌtjuːd) *n* **1** the state or quality of being solicitous **2** (*often plural*) something that causes anxiety or concern **3** anxiety or concern

solid (ˈsɒlɪd) *adj* **1** of, concerned with, or being a substance in a physical state in which it resists changes in size and shape. See **liquid** (sense 1), **gas** (sense 1)

2 consisting of matter all through **3** of the same substance all through: *solid rock* **4** sound; proved or provable: *solid facts* **5** reliable or sensible; upstanding: *a solid citizen* **6** firm, strong, compact, or substantial: *a solid table; solid ground* **7** (of a meal or food) substantial **8** (*often postpositive*) without interruption or respite; continuous: *solid bombardment* **9** financially sound or solvent: *a solid institution* **10** strongly linked or consolidated: *a solid relationship* **11** *geometry* having or relating to three dimensions **12** (of a word composed of two or more other words or elements) written or printed as a single word without a hyphen **13** *printing* with no space or leads between lines of type **14** solid for unanimously in favour of **15** (of a writer, work, performance, etc) adequate; sensible **16** of or having a single uniform colour or tone **17** *NZ informal* excessive; unreasonably strict ▷ *n* **18** *geometry* **a** a closed surface in three-dimensional space **b** such a surface together with the volume enclosed by it **19** a solid substance, such as wood, iron, or diamond **20** (*plural*) solid food, as opposed to liquid [C14: from Old French *solide*, from Latin *solidus* firm; related to Latin *sollus* whole] > **solidity** (səˈlɪdɪtɪ) *n* > ˈsolidly *adv* > ˈsolidness *n*

solidago (ˌsɒlɪˈdeɪɡəʊ) *n*, *pl* **-gos** any plant of the chiefly American genus *Solidago*, which includes the goldenrods: family *Asteraceae* (composites) [C18: via New Latin from Medieval Latin *soldago* a plant reputed to have healing properties, from *soldāre* to strengthen, from Latin *solidāre*, from *solidus* SOLID]

solid angle *n* a geometric surface consisting of lines originating from a common point (the vertex) and passing through a closed curve or polygon: measured in steradians

solidarity (ˌsɒlɪˈdærɪtɪ) *n*, *pl* **-ties** unity of interests, sympathies, etc, as among members of the same class

solid fuel *n* **1** a domestic or industrial fuel, such as coal or coke, that is a solid rather than an oil or gas **2** Also called: **solid propellant** a rocket fuel that is a solid rather than a liquid or a gas

solid geometry *n* the branch of geometry concerned with the properties of three-dimensional geometric figures

solidify (səˈlɪdɪˌfaɪ) *vb* **-fies, -fying, -fied 1** to make or become solid or hard **2** to make or become strong, united, determined, etc > so,lidifiˈcation *n* > soˈlidi,fier *n*

solid-state *n* **1** (*modifier*) (of an electronic device) activated by a semiconductor component in which current flow is through solid material rather than in a vacuum **2** (*modifier*) of, concerned with, characteristic of, or consisting of solid matter

solid-state physics *n* (*functioning as singular*) the branch of physics concerned with experimental and theoretical investigations of the properties of solids, such as superconductivity, photoconductivity, and ferromagnetism

solidus (ˈsɒlɪdəs) *n*, *pl* **-di** (-ˌdaɪ) **1** a technical name for **slash** (sense 12) **2** a gold coin of the Byzantine empire [C14: from Late Latin *solidus* (*nummus*) a gold coin (from *solidus* solid); in Medieval Latin, *solidus* referred to a shilling and was indicated by a long *s*, which ultimately became the virgule]

solifluction *or* **solifluxion** (ˌsɒlɪˈflʌkʃən, ˌsəʊlɪ-) *n* slow downhill movement of soil, saturated with meltwater, over a permanently frozen subsoil in tundra regions [C20: from Latin *solum* soil + *fluctio* act of flowing]

Solihull (ˌsəʊlɪˈhʌl) *n* **1** a town in central England, in Solihull unitary authority in the S West Midlands near Birmingham: mainly residential. Pop: 94 753 (2001) **2** a unitary authority in central England, in the West Midlands. Pop: 200 300 (2003 est). Area: 180 sq km (70 sq miles)

soliloquize *or* **soliloquise** (səˈlɪləˌkwaɪz) *vb* (*intr*) to utter a soliloquy > **soliloquist** (səˈlɪləkwɪst) *or* soˈlilo,quizer *or* soˈlilo,quiser *n*

soliloquy (səˈlɪləkwɪ) *n*, *pl* **-quies 1** the act of speaking alone or to oneself, esp as a theatrical device **2** a speech in a play that is spoken in soliloquy [C17: via Late Latin *sōliloquium*, from Latin *sōlus* sole + *loquī* to speak]

● USAGE *Soliloquy* is sometimes wrongly used where
● *monologue* is meant. Both words refer to a long speech
● by one person, but a *monologue* can be addressed to
● other people, whereas in a *soliloquy* the speaker is
● always talking to himself or herself

Soliman ('sɒlɪmən) *n* a variant spelling of **Suleiman I**

Solimões (suli'mõəʃ) *n* the Solimões the Brazilian name
for the Amazon from the Peruvian border to the Rio
Negro

Solingen (*German* 'zoːlɪŋən) *n* a city in W Germany, in
North Rhine-Westphalia: a major European centre of
the cutlery industry. Pop: 164 543 (2003 est)

solipsism ('sɒlɪpˌsɪzəm) *n philosophy* the extreme form of
scepticism which denies the possibility of any
knowledge other than of one's own existence [c19: from
Latin *sōlus* alone + *ipse* self] > **solipsist** *n, adj*
> ˌsolip'sistic *adj*

solitaire ('sɒlɪˌtɛə, ˌsɒlɪ'tɛə) *n* **1** Also called: **pegboard** a
game played by one person, esp one involving moving
and taking pegs in a pegboard or marbles on an
indented circular board with the object of being left
with only one **2** the US name for **patience** (sense 3) **3** a
gem, esp a diamond, set alone in a ring **4** any of several
extinct birds of the genus *Pezophaps*, related to the dodo
5 any of several dull grey North American songbirds
of the genus *Myadestes*: subfamily *Turdinae* (thrushes) [c18:
from Old French: SOLITARY]

solitary ('sɒlɪtərɪ, -trɪ) *adj* **1** following or enjoying a life
of solitude: *a solitary disposition* **2** experienced or
performed alone: *a solitary walk* **3** (of a place)
unfrequented **4** (*prenominal*) single; sole: *a solitary speck in
the sky* **5** having few companions; lonely **6** (of animals)
not living in organized colonies or large groups: *solitary
bees; a solitary elephant* **7** (of flowers) growing singly ▷ *n, pl*
-taries 8 a person who lives in seclusion; hermit; recluse
9 *informal* short for **solitary confinement** [c14: from
Latin *sōlitārius*, from *sōlus* SOLE[1]] > **solitarily** *adv*
> **solitariness** *n*

solitary confinement *n* isolation imposed on a
prisoner, as by confinement in a special cell

solitude ('sɒlɪˌtjuːd) *n* **1** the state of being solitary or
secluded **2** *poetic* a solitary place [c14: from Latin *sōlitūdō*,
from *sōlus* alone, SOLE[1]] > ˌsoli'tudinous *adj*

solmization *or* **solmisation** (ˌsɒlmɪ'zeɪʃən) *n music* a
system of naming the notes of a scale by syllables
instead of letters derived from the 11th-century
hexachord system of Guido d'Arezzo, which assigns the
names *ut* (or *do*), *re, mi, fa, sol, la, si* (or *ti*) to the degrees of
the major scale of C (**fixed system**) or (excluding the
syllables *ut* and *si*) to the major scale in any key
(**movable system**). See also **tonic sol-fa** [c18: from French
solmisation, from *solmiser* to use the sol-fa syllables, from
SOL[1] + MI]

solo ('səʊləʊ) *n, pl* **-los 1** *pl* **-los** *or* **-li** (-liː) a musical
composition for one performer with or without
accompaniment **2** any of various card games in which
each person plays on his own instead of in partnership
with another, such as solo whist **3** a flight in which an
aircraft pilot is unaccompanied **4 a** any performance,
mountain climb, or other undertaking carried out by an
individual without assistance from others **b** (*as modifier*):
a solo attempt ▷ *adj* **5** *music* unaccompanied: *a sonata for
cello solo* ▷ *adv* **6** by oneself; alone: *to fly solo* ▷ *vb* **7** (*intr*) to
undertake a venture alone, esp to operate an aircraft
alone or climb alone [c17: via Italian from Latin *sōlus*
alone, SOLE[1]] > **soloist** ('səʊləʊɪst) *n*

Solomon ('sɒləmən) *n* 10th century BC, king of Israel,
son of David and Bathsheba, credited with great wisdom
> **Solomonic** (ˌsɒlə'mɒnɪk) *or* **Solomonian**
(ˌsɒlə'məʊnɪən) *adj*

Solomon Gundy ('sɒləmən 'gʌndɪ) *n Canadian* a dish of
salted marinated herring in vinegar and spices [from
SALMAGUNDI]

Solomon Islands *pl n* an independent state in the SW
Pacific comprising an archipelago extending for almost
1450 km (900 miles) in a northwest–southeast direction:
the northernmost islands of the archipelago (Buka and
Bougainville) form part of Papua New Guinea; the main
islands are Guadalcanal, Malaita, San Cristobal, New

Georgia, Santa Isabel, and Choiseul: a member of the
Commonwealth. Official language: English. Religion:
Christian majority. Currency: Solomon Islands dollar.
Capital: Honiara. Pop: 491 000 (2004 est). Area: 29 785 sq
km (11 500 sq miles)

Solomon's seal *n* **1** another name for **Star of David**
2 any of several liliaceous plants of the genus
Polygonatum of N temperate regions, having greenish or
yellow paired flowers, long narrow waxy leaves, and a
thick underground stem with prominent leaf scars [c16:
translation of Medieval Latin *sigillum Solomonis*, perhaps
referring to the resemblance of the leaf scars to seals]

Solon ('səʊlən) *n* ?638–?559 BC, Athenian statesman,
who introduced economic, political, and legal reforms
> **Solonian** (səʊ'ləʊnɪən) *or* **Solonic** (səʊ'lɒnɪk) *adj*

so long *sentence substitute* **1** *informal* farewell; goodbye
▷ *adv* **2** *South African slang* for the time being; meanwhile

solo parent *n NZ* the usual name for **single parent**

Solothurn (*German* 'zoːlotʊrn) *n* **1** a canton of NW
Switzerland. Capital: Solothurn. Pop: 246 500 (2002 est).
Area: 793 sq km (306 sq miles) **2** a town in NW
Switzerland, capital of Solothurn canton, on the Aare
River. Pop: 15 489 (2000) ▷ French name: **Soleure**

solo whist *n* a version of whist for four players acting
independently, each of whom may bid to win or lose a
fixed number of tricks before play starts, trumps having
usually been decided by cutting

solstice ('sɒlstɪs) *n* **1** either the shortest day of the year
(**winter solstice**) or the longest day of the year (**summer
solstice**) **2** either of the two points on the ecliptic at
which the sun is overhead at the tropic of Cancer or
Capricorn at the summer and winter solstices [c13: via
Old French from Latin *sōlstitium*, literally: the (apparent)
standing still of the sun, from *sōl* sun + *sistere* to stand
still] > **solstitial** (sɒl'stɪʃəl) *adj*

Solti ('ʃɒltɪ) *n* Sir **Georg** ('geːɔrk). 1912–97, British
conductor, born in Hungary

soluble ('sɒljʊbʰl) *adj* **1** (of a substance) capable of being
dissolved, esp easily dissolved in some solvent, usually
water **2** capable of being solved or answered [c14: from
Late Latin *solūbilis*, from Latin *solvere* to dissolve]
> **solubly** *adv* > ˌsolu'bility *n*

solus ('səʊləs) *adj* **1** alone; separate **2** of or denoting the
position of an advertising poster or press advertisement
that is separated from competing advertisements: *a solus
position* **3** of or denoting a retail outlet, such as a petrol
station, that sells the products of one company
exclusively: *a solus site* **4** *fem* **sola** alone; by oneself
(formerly used in stage directions) [c17: from Latin *sōlus*
alone]

solute (sɒ'ljuːt) *n* **1** the component of a solution that
changes its state in forming the solution or the
component that is not present in excess; the substance
that is dissolved in another substance ▷ *adj* **2** *botany now
rare* loose or unattached; free [c16: from Latin *solūtus*
free, unfettered, from *solvere* to release]

solution (sə'luːʃən) *n* **1** a homogeneous mixture of two or
more substances in which the molecules or atoms of the
substances are completely dispersed. The constituents
can be solids, liquids, or gases **2** the act or process of
forming a solution **3** the state of being dissolved (esp in
the phrase **in solution**) **4** a mixture of two or more
substances in which one or more components are
present as small particles with colloidal dimension;
colloid: *a colloidal solution* **5** a specific answer to or way of
answering a problem **6** the act or process of solving a
problem **7** *maths* **a** the unique set of values that yield a
true statement when substituted for the variables in an
equation **b** a member of a set of assignments of values
to variables under which a given statement is satisfied;
a member of a solution set [c14: from Latin *solūtiō* an
unloosing, from *solūtus*; see SOLUTE]

solution set *n* another name for **truth set**

Solutrean (sə'luːtrɪən) *adj* of or relating to an Upper
Palaeolithic culture of Europe that was characterized by
leaf-shaped flint blades [c19: named after *Solutré*, village
in central France where traces of this culture were
originally found]

solvation (sɒl'veɪʃən) *n* the process in which there is some chemical association between the molecules of a solute and those of the solvent. An example is an aqueous solution of copper sulphate which contains complex ions of the type $[Cu(H_2O)_4]^{2+}$

Solvay process ('sɒlveɪ) *n* an industrial process for manufacturing sodium carbonate. Carbon dioxide is passed into a solution of sodium chloride saturated with ammonia. Sodium bicarbonate is precipitated and heated to form the carbonate [C19: named after Ernest *Solvay* (1838–1922), Belgian chemist who invented a process using salt, limestone, and ammonia]

solve (sɒlv) *vb* (*tr*) **1** to find the explanation for or solution to (a mystery, problem, etc) **2** *maths* **a** to work out the answer to (a problem) **b** to obtain the roots of (an equation) [C15: from Latin *solvere* to loosen, release, free from debt] > 'solvable *adj*

solvent ('sɒlvənt) *adj* **1** capable of meeting financial obligations **2** (of a substance, esp a liquid) capable of dissolving another substance ▷ *n* **3** a liquid capable of dissolving another substance **4** something that solves [C17: from Latin *solvēns* releasing, from *solvere* to free, SOLVE] > 'solvency *n*

solvent abuse *n* the deliberate inhaling of intoxicating fumes given off by certain solvents such as toluene

Solway Firth ('sɒlweɪ) *n* an inlet of the Irish Sea between SW Scotland and NW England. Length: about 56 km (35 miles)

Solyman ('sɒlɪmən) *n* a variant spelling of **Suleiman I**

Solyom ('sɒljəm) *n* **Laszlo**, born 1942, Hungarian politician, president of Hungary from 2005

Solzhenitsyn (ˌsɒlʒə'nɪtsɪn; *Russian* səlʒə'nitsin) *n* **Alexander Isayevich** (alɪk'sandr iˈsajɪvitʃ). born 1918, Russian novelist. His books include *One Day in the Life of Ivan Denisovich* (1962), *The First Circle* (1968), *Cancer Ward* (1968), *August 1914* (1971), *The Gulag Archipelago* (1974), and *October 1916* (1985). His works criticize the Soviet regime and he was imprisoned (1945–53) and exiled to Siberia (1953–56). He was deported to the West from the Soviet Union in 1974; all charges against him were dropped in 1991 and he returned to Russia in 1994. Nobel prize for literature 1970

Som. *abbreviation* Somerset

soma[1] ('səʊmə) *n*, *pl* **-mata** (-mətə) *or* **-mas** the body of an organism, esp an animal, as distinct from the germ cells [C19: via New Latin from Greek *sōma* the body]

soma[2] ('səʊmə) *n* an intoxicating plant juice drink used in Vedic rituals [from Sanskrit]

Somali (səʊ'mɑːlɪ) *n* **1** *pl* **-lis** *or* **-li** a member of a tall dark-skinned people inhabiting Somalia **2** the language of this people, belonging to the Cushitic subfamily of the Afro-Asiatic family of languages ▷ *adj* **3** of, relating to, or characteristic of Somalia, the Somalis, or their language

Somalia (səʊ'mɑːlɪə) *n* a republic in NE Africa, on the Indian Ocean and the Gulf of Aden: the north became a British protectorate in 1884; the east and south were established as an Italian protectorate in 1889; gained independence and united as Somalia (or the Somali Republic) in 1960. In 1991 the former British Somaliland region in the north unilaterally declared itself independent as the Republic of Somaliland, and Puntland and other areas are also operating effectively as separate states, but this has not been recognized officially. Official languages: Arabic and Somali. Official religion: (Sunni) Muslim. Currency: Somali shilling. Capital: Mogadishu. Pop: 10 312 000 (2004 est). Area: 637 541 sq km (246 154 sq miles) > So'malian *adj, n*

Somaliland (səʊ'mɑːlɪˌlænd) *n* a former region of E Africa, between the equator and the Gulf of Aden: includes Somalia, Djibouti, and SE Ethiopia

somatic (səʊ'mætɪk) *adj* **1** of or relating to the soma: *somatic cells* **2** of or relating to an animal body or body wall as distinct from the viscera, limbs, and head **3** of or relating to the human body as distinct from the mind: *a somatic disease* [C18: from Greek *sōmatikos* concerning the body, from *sōma* the body] > so'matically *adv*

somatic cell nuclear transfer *n* another name for **therapeutic cloning**

somato- *or before a vowel* **somat-** *combining form* body: *somatoplasm* [from Greek *sōma, sōmat-* body]

somatogenic (səˌmætəʊ'dʒɛnɪk) *adj med* originating in the cells of the body: of organic, rather than mental, origin: *a somatogenic disorder*

somatotype ('səʊmətəˌtaɪp) *n* a type or classification of physique or body build. See **endomorph, mesomorph, ectomorph**

sombre *or US* **somber** ('sɒmbə) *adj* **1** dismal; melancholy: *a sombre mood* **2** dim, gloomy, or shadowy **3** (of colour, clothes, etc) sober, dull, or dark [C18: from French, from Vulgar Latin *subumbrāre* (unattested) to shade, from Latin *sub* beneath + *umbra* shade] > 'sombrely *or US* 'somberly *adv* > 'sombreness *or US* 'somberness *n* > sombrous ('sɒmbrəs) *adj*

sombrero (sɒm'brɛərəʊ) *n, pl* **-ros** a felt or straw hat with a wide brim, as worn by men in Mexico [C16: from Spanish, from *sombrero de sol* shade from the sun]

some (sʌm; *unstressed* səm) *determiner* **1 a** (a) certain unknown or unspecified: *some lunatic drove into my car; some people never learn* **b** (as pronoun; functioning as sing or plural): *some can teach and others can't* **2 a** an unknown or unspecified quantity or amount of: *there's some rice on the table; he owns some horses* **b** (as pronoun; functioning as sing or plural): *we'll buy some* **3 a** a considerable number or amount of: *he lived some years afterwards* **b** a little: *show him some respect* **4** (usually stressed) *informal* an impressive or remarkable: *that was some game!* **5** a certain amount (more) (in the phrases **some more** and (informal) **and then some**) **6** about; approximately: *he owes me some thirty pounds* ▷ *adv* **7** *US not standard* to a certain degree or extent: *I guess I like him some* [Old English *sum*; related to Old Norse *sumr*, Gothic *sums*, Old High German *sum* some, Sanskrit *samá* any, Greek *hamē* somehow]

-some[1] *suffix forming adjectives* characterized by; tending to: *awesome; tiresome* [Old English *-sum*; related to Gothic *-sama*, German *-sam*]

-some[2] *suffix forming nouns* indicating a group of a specified number of members: *threesome* [Old English *sum*, special use of SOME (determiner)]

-some[3] (-səʊm) *n combining form* a body: *chromosome* [from Greek *sōma* body]

somebody ('sʌmbədɪ) *pron* **1** some person; someone ▷ *n, pl* **-bodies 2** a person of greater importance than others: *he seems to be somebody in this town*
 ⊙ USAGE See at **everyone**

someday ('sʌmˌdeɪ) *adv* at some unspecified time in the (distant) future

somehow ('sʌmˌhaʊ) *adv* **1** in some unspecified way **2** Also called: **somehow or other** by any means that are necessary

someone ('sʌmˌwʌn, -wən) *pron* some person; somebody
 ⊙ USAGE See at **everyone**

someplace ('sʌmˌpleɪs) *adv US & Canadian informal* in, at, or to some unspecified place or region

somersault *or* **summersault** ('sʌməˌsɔːlt) *n* **1 a** a forward roll in which the head is placed on the ground and the trunk and legs are turned over it **b** a similar roll in a backward direction **2** an acrobatic feat in which either of these rolls are performed in midair, as in diving or gymnastics **3** a complete reversal of opinion, policy, etc ▷ *vb* **4** (*intr*) to perform a somersault [C16: from Old French *soubresault*, probably from Old Provençal *sobresaut*, from *sobre* over (from Latin *super*) + *saut* a jump, leap (from Latin *saltus*)]

Somerset[1] ('sʌməsɪt, -ˌsɛt) *n* a county of SW England, on the Bristol Channel: the Mendip Hills lie in the north and Exmoor in the west: the geographical and ceremonial county includes the unitary authorities of North Somerset and Bath and North East Somerset (both part of Avon county from 1975 until 1996): mainly agricultural (esp dairying and fruit). Administrative centre: Taunton. Pop (excluding unitary authorities): 507 500 (2003 est). Area (excluding unitary authorities): 3452 sq km (1332 sq miles)

Somerset[2] ('sʌməsɪt) *n* **1st Duke of,** title of *Edward Seymour*. ?1500–52, English statesman, protector of England (1547–49) during Edward VI's minority. He defeated the Scots (1547) and furthered the Protestant Reformation: executed

Somerville ('sʌməvɪl) *n* **Mary,** original name *Mary*

Fairfax. 1780–1872, British scientific writer, author of *Physical Geography* (1848) and other textbooks. Somerville College, Oxford, was named after her

something ('sʌmθɪŋ) *pron* **1** an unspecified or unknown thing; some thing: *he knows something you don't; take something warm with you* **2** an unspecified or unknown amount; bit: *something less than a hundred* **3** an impressive or important person, thing, or event: *isn't that something?* **4** something else a remarkable person or thing **5** something or other one unspecified thing or an alternative thing ▷ *adv* **6** to some degree; a little; somewhat: *to look something like me* **7** (foll by an adjective) *informal* (intensifier): *it hurts something awful*

-something *n combining form* **a** a person whose age can be approximately expressed by a specified decade **b** (as modifier): *the thirtysomething market* [C20: from the US television series *thirtysomething*]

sometime ('sʌmˌtaɪm) *adv* **1** at some unspecified point of time ▷ *adj* **2** (prenominal) having been at one time; former: *the sometime President*
• USAGE The form *sometime* should not be used to refer
• to a fairly long period of time: *he has been away for some*
• *time* (not for *sometime*)

sometimes ('sʌmˌtaɪmz) *adv* **1** now and then; from time to time; occasionally **2** *obsolete* formerly; sometime

someway ('sʌmˌweɪ) *adv* in some unspecified manner

somewhat ('sʌmˌwɒt) *adv* (not used with a negative) rather; a bit: *she found it somewhat less easy than he*

somewhere ('sʌmˌwɛə) *adv* **1** in, to, or at some unknown or unspecified place or point: *somewhere in England; somewhere between 3 and 4 o'clock* **2** get somewhere *informal* to make progress

Somme (French sɒm) *n* **1** a department of N France, in Picardy region. Capital: Amiens. Pop: 557 061 (2003 est). Area: 6277 sq km (2448 sq miles) **2** a river in N France, rising in Aisne department and flowing west to Amiens, then northwest to the English Channel: scene of heavy fighting in World War I. Length: 245 km (152 miles)

sommelier ('sʌməlˌjeɪ) *n* a wine steward in a restaurant or hotel [French: butler, via Old French from Old Provençal *saumalier* pack-animal driver, from Late Latin *sagma* a packsaddle, from Greek]

somnambulate (sɒmˈnæmbjʊˌleɪt) *vb* (intr) to walk while asleep [C19: from Latin *somnus* sleep + *ambulāre* to walk] > som'nambulance *n* > som'nambulant *adj, n* > som,nambu'lation *n* > som'nambu,lator *n*

somnambulism (sɒmˈnæmbjʊˌlɪzəm) *n* a condition that is characterized by walking while asleep or in a hypnotic trance. Also called: noctambulism > som'nambulist *n*

somniferous (sɒmˈnɪfərəs) *or* **somnific** *adj rare* tending to induce sleep [C17: from Latin *somnifer* (from *somnus* sleep + *ferre* to do) + -OUS]

somnolent ('sɒmnələnt) *adj* **1** drowsy; sleepy **2** causing drowsiness [C15: from Latin *somnus* sleep] > 'somnolence *or* 'somnolency *n* > 'somnolently *adv*

Somnus ('sɒmnəs) *n* the Roman god of sleep. Greek counterpart: Hypnos

son (sʌn) *n* **1** a male offspring; a boy or man in relation to his parents **2** a male descendant **3** (often capital) a familiar term of address for a boy or man **4** a male from a certain country, place, etc, or one closely connected with a certain environment: *a son of the circus; a son of the manse* Related adjective: **filial** [Old English *sunu*; related to Old Norse *sunr*, Gothic *sunus*, Old High German *sunu*, Lithuanian *sūnus*, Sanskrit *sūnu*] > 'sonless *adj*

Son (sʌn) *n Christianity* the second person of the Trinity, Jesus Christ

sonant ('səʊnənt) *adj* **1** *phonetics* denoting a voiced sound capable of forming a syllable or syllable nucleus **2** inherently possessing, exhibiting, or producing a sound ▷ *n* **3** *phonetics* a voiced sound belonging to the class of frictionless continuants or nasals (l, r, m, n, ŋ) considered from the point of view of being a vowel and, in this capacity, able to form a syllable or syllable nucleus [C19: from Latin *sonāns* sounding, from *sonāre* to make a noise, resound] > 'sonance *n*

sonar ('səʊnɑː) *n* a communication and position-finding device used in underwater navigation and

target detection using echolocation [C20: from *so(und) na(vigation and) r(anging)*]

sonata (səˈnɑːtə) *n* **1** an instrumental composition, usually in three or more movements, for piano alone (**piano sonata**) or for any other instrument with or without piano accompaniment (**violin sonata, cello sonata**, etc). See also **sonata form** **2** a one-movement keyboard composition of the baroque period [C17: from Italian, from *sonare* to sound, from Latin]

sonata form *n* a musical structure consisting of an expanded ternary form whose three sections (exposition, development, and recapitulation), followed by a coda, are characteristic of the first movement in a sonata, symphony, string quartet, concerto, etc

sondage (sɒnˈdɑːʒ) *n, pl* **-dages** (-ˈdɑːʒɪz, -ˈdɑːʒ) *archaeol* a deep trial trench for inspecting stratigraphy [C20: from French: a sounding, from *sonder* to sound]

sonde (sɒnd) *n* a rocket, balloon, or probe used for observing in the upper atmosphere [C20: from French: plummet, plumb line; see SOUND³]

Sondheim ('sɒndhaɪm) *n* **Stephen** (**Joshua**). born 1930, US songwriter. He wrote the lyrics for *West Side Story* (1957), the score for *Company* (1971), and both for *A Little Night Music* (1973), *Into the Woods* (1987), and *Passion* (1994)

sone (səʊn) *n* a subjective unit of loudness equal to that experienced by a normal person hearing a 1 kHz tone at 40 dB [C20: from Latin *sonus* a sound]

son et lumière ('sɒn eɪ 'luːmɪˌɛə; French sɔ̃ e lymjɛr) *n* an entertainment staged at night at a famous building, historical site, etc, whereby the history of the location is presented by means of lighting effects, sound effects, and narration [French, literally: sound and light]

song (sɒŋ) *n* **1 a** a piece of music, usually employing a verbal text, composed for the voice, esp one intended for performance by a soloist **b** the whole repertory of such pieces **c** (as modifier): *a song book* **2** poetical composition; poetry **3** the characteristic tuneful call or sound made by certain birds or insects **4** the act or process of singing: *they raised their voices in song* **5** for a song at a bargain price **6** on song *Brit informal* performing at peak efficiency or ability [Old English *sang*; related to Gothic *saggws*, Old High German *sang*; see SING]

Song (sʊŋ) *n* the Pinyin transliteration of the Chinese name for **Sung**

song and dance *n informal* **1** *Brit* a fuss, esp one that is unnecessary **2** *US & Canadian* a long or elaborate story or explanation, esp one that is evasive

songbird ('sɒŋˌbɜːd) *n* **1** any passerine bird of the suborder *Oscines*, having highly developed vocal organs and, in most, a musical call **2** any bird having a musical call

song cycle *n* any of several groups of songs written by composers during and after the Romantic period, each series employing texts, usually by one poet, relating a story or grouped around a central motif

Songhua (ˈsʌŋˈwɑː) *n* a river in NE China, rising in SE Jilin province and flowing north and northeast to the Amur River near Tongjiang: the chief river of Manchuria and largest tributary of the Amur; frozen from November to April. Length: over 1300 km (800 miles). Also called: Sungari

Song Koi *or* **Song Coi** ('sɒŋ 'kɔɪ) *n* transliteration of the Vietnamese name for the **Red River** (sense 3)

songololo (ˌsɒŋɡəˈləʊləʊ) *n, pl* **-los** *South African* a millipede, *Jurus terrestris*, having a hard shiny dark brown segmented exoskeleton [from Nguni *ukusonga* to roll up]

songster ('sɒŋstə) *n* **1** a singer or poet **2** a singing bird; songbird > 'songstress *fem n*

song thrush *n* a common Old World thrush, *Turdus philomelos*, that has a brown back and spotted breast and is noted for its song

songwriter ('sɒŋˌraɪtə) *n* a person who composes the words or music for songs in a popular idiom

sonic ('sɒnɪk) *adj* **1** of, involving, or producing sound **2** having a speed about equal to that of sound in air: 331 metres per second (741 miles per hour) at 0°C [C20: from Latin *sonus* sound]

sonic barrier *n* another name for **sound barrier**

sonic boom *n* a loud explosive sound caused by the

shock wave of an aircraft, etc, travelling at supersonic speed

sonic depth finder *n* an instrument for detecting the depth of water or of a submerged object by means of sound waves; Fathometer

sonics ('sɒnɪks) *n* (*functioning as singular*) *physics* the study of mechanical vibrations in matter

son-in-law *n*, *pl* **sons-in-law** the husband of one's daughter

sonnet ('sɒnɪt) *prosody* ▷ *n* **1** a verse form of Italian origin consisting of 14 lines in iambic pentameter with rhymes arranged according to a fixed scheme, usually divided either into octave and sestet or, in the English form, into three quatrains and a couplet ▷ *vb* **2** (*intr*) to compose sonnets **3** (*tr*) to celebrate in a sonnet [c16: via Italian from Old Provençal *sonet* a little poem, from *son* song, from Latin *sonus* a sound]

sonneteer (ˌsɒnɪ'tɪə) *n* a writer of sonnets

sonny ('sʌnɪ) *n*, *pl* -**nies** a familiar or patronizing term of address to a boy or man [c19: from SON + -Y²]

sonobuoy ('səʊnəˌbɔɪ) *n* a buoy equipped to detect underwater noises and transmit them by radio [from SONIC + BUOY]

Son of Man *n Bible* a title of Jesus Christ

sonoluminescence (ˌsəʊnəʊˌluːmɪ'nɛsəns) *n* luminescence produced by ultrasound

Sonora (*Spanish* so'nora) *n* a state of NW Mexico, on the Gulf of California: consists of a narrow coastal plain rising inland to the Sierra Madre Occidental; an important mining area in colonial times. Capital: Hermosillo. Pop: 2 213 370 (2000). Area: 184 934 sq km (71 403 sq miles)

sonorant ('sɒnərənt) *n phonetics* **1** one of the frictionless continuants or nasals (l, r, m, n, ŋ) having consonantal or vocalic functions depending on its situation within the syllable **2** either of the two consonants represented in English orthography by *w* or *y* and regarded as either consonantal or vocalic articulations of the vowels (i:) and (u:) [from Latin *sonor* a noise + -ANT]

sonorous (sə'nɔːrəs, 'sɒnərəs) *adj* **1** producing or capable of producing sound **2** (of language, sound, etc) deep or resonant **3** (esp of speech) high-flown; grandiloquent [c17: from Latin *sonōrus* loud, from *sonor* a noise] > **sonority** (sə'nɒrɪtɪ) *n* > **so'norously** *adv* > **so'norousness** *n*

sonsy or **sonsie** ('sɒnsɪ) *adj* -**sier**, -**siest** *Scot, Irish & English dialect* **1** plump; buxom; comely **2** cheerful; good-natured **3** lucky [c16: from Gaelic *sonas* good fortune]

Sontag ('sɒntæg) *n* **Susan.** 1933–2004, US intellectual and essayist, noted esp for her writings on modern culture. Her works include 'Notes on Camp' (1964), 'Against Interpretation' (1968), *On Photography* (1977), *Illness as Metaphor* (1978), and the novel *The Volcano Lover* (1992)

Soo Canals (suː) *pl n* the **Soo Canals** the two ship canals linking Lakes Superior and Huron. There is a canal on the Canadian and on the US side of the rapids of the St Mary's River. See also **Sault Sainte Marie**

Soochow ('suː'tʃaʊ) *n* a variant transliteration of the Chinese name for **Suzhou**

sook (sʊk) *n* **1** *Southwest English dialect* a baby **2** *derogatory* a coward [perhaps from Old English *sūcan* to suck, influenced by Welsh *swci swead* tame]

sool (suːl) *vb* (*tr*) **1** to incite (a dog) to attack **2** to attack [c17: from English dialect *sowl* (esp of a dog) to pull or seize roughly] > **'sooler** *n*

soon (suːn) *adv* **1** in or after a short time; in a little while; before long **2** as soon as at the very moment that: *she burst into tears as soon as she saw him* **3** as soon...as used to indicate that the second alternative mentioned is not preferable to the first: *I'd just as soon go by train as drive* [Old English *sōna*; related to Old High German *sāno*, Gothic *suns*]

sooner ('suːnə) *adv* **1** the comparative of **soon**: *he came sooner than I thought* **2** rather; in preference: *I'd sooner die than give up* **3** no sooner...than immediately after or when: *no sooner had he got home than the rain stopped*; *no sooner said than done* **4** sooner or later eventually; inevitably

● USAGE *When* is sometimes used instead of *than* after *no sooner*, but this use is generally regarded as incorrect: *no sooner had he arrived than* (not *when*) *the telephone rang*

Soong or **Song** (sʊŋ) *n* an influential Chinese family, notably **Soong Ch'ing-ling** (1890–1981), who married **Sun Yat-sen** and became a vice-chairman of the People's Republic of China (1959); and **Soong Mei-ling** (1898-2003), who married **Chiang Kai-shek**

soot (sʊt) *n* **1** finely divided carbon deposited from flames during the incomplete combustion of organic substances such as coal ▷ *vb* **2** (*tr*) to cover with soot [Old English *sōt*; related to Old Norse, Middle Low German *sōt*, Lithuanian *sódis*, Old Slavonic *sažda*, Old Irish *súide*]

sooth (suːθ) *archaic* or *poetic* ▷ *n* **1** truth or reality (esp in the phrase **in sooth**) ▷ *adj* **2** true or real [Old English *sōth*; related to Old Norse *sathr* true, Old Norse *sand*, Gothic *sunja* truth, Latin *sōns* guilty, *sonticus* critical]

soothe (suːð) *vb* **1** (*tr*) to make calm or tranquil **2** (*tr*) to relieve or assuage (pain, longing, etc) **3** (*intr*) to bring tranquillity or relief [C16 (in the sense: to mollify): from Old English *sōthian* to prove; related to Old Norse *sanna* to assert; see SOOTH] > **'soother** *n* > **'soothing** *adj* > **'soothingly** *adv* > **'soothingness** *n*

soothsayer ('suːθˌseɪə) *n* a seer or prophet

sooty ('sʊtɪ) *adj* **sootier**, **sootiest** **1** covered with soot **2** resembling or consisting of soot > **'sootily** *adv* > **'sootiness** *n*

sop (sɒp) *n* **1** (*often plural*) food soaked in a liquid before being eaten **2** a concession, bribe, etc, given to placate or mollify: *a sop to one's feelings* **3** *informal* a stupid or weak person ▷ *vb* **sops**, **sopping**, **sopped** **4** (*tr*) to dip or soak (food) in liquid **5** (when *intr*, often foll by *in*) to soak or be soaked ▷ See also **sop up** [Old English *sopp*; related to Old Norse *soppa* soup, Old High German *sopfa* milk with bread; see SUP²]

SOP *abbreviation* standard operating procedure

sop. *abbreviation* soprano

Soper ('səʊpə) *n* **Donald** (**Oliver**), **Baron.** 1903–98, British Methodist minister and publicist, noted esp for his pacifist convictions. His books include *All His Grace* (1953) and *Calling for Action* (1984)

Sophia (səʊ'faɪə) *n* 1630–1714, electress of Hanover (1658–1714), in whom the Act of Settlement (1701) vested the English Crown. She was a granddaughter of James I of England and her son became George I of Great Britain and Ireland

sophism ('sɒfɪzəm) *n* an instance of sophistry. See **paralogism** [c14: from Latin *sophisma*, from Greek: ingenious trick, from *sophizesthai* to use clever deceit, from *sophos* wise, clever]

sophist ('sɒfɪst) *n* **1** (*often capital*) one of the pre-Socratic philosophers who were itinerant professional teachers of oratory and argument and who were prepared to enter into debate on any matter however specious **2** a person who uses clever or quibbling arguments that are fundamentally unsound [c16: from Latin *sophista*, from Greek *sophistēs* a wise man, from *sophizesthai* to act craftily]

sophistic (sə'fɪstɪk) or **sophistical** *adj* **1** of or relating to sophists or sophistry **2** consisting of sophisms or sophistry; specious > **so'phistically** *adv*

sophisticate *vb* (sə'fɪstɪˌkeɪt) **1** (*tr*) to make (someone) less natural or innocent, as by education **2** to pervert or corrupt (an argument, etc) by sophistry **3** (*tr*) to make more complex or refined **4** *rare* to falsify (a text, etc) by alterations ▷ *n* (sə'fɪstɪˌkeɪt, -kɪt) **5** a sophisticated person [c14: from Medieval Latin *sophisticāre*, from Latin *sophisticus* sophistic] > **so,phisti'cation** *n* > **so'phisti,cator** *n*

sophisticated (sə'fɪstɪˌkeɪtɪd) *adj* **1** having refined or cultured tastes and habits **2** appealing to sophisticates: *a sophisticated restaurant* **3** unduly refined or cultured **4** pretentiously or superficially wise **5** (of machines, methods, etc) complex and refined

sophistry ('sɒfɪstrɪ) *n*, *pl* -**ries** **1 a** a method of argument that is seemingly plausible though actually invalid and misleading **b** the art of using such arguments **2** subtle but unsound or fallacious reasoning **3** an instance of this; sophism

Sophocles ('sɒfəˌkliːz) n ?496–406 BC, Greek dramatist; author of seven extant tragedies: *Ajax, Antigone, Oedipus Rex, Trachiniae, Electra, Philoctetes,* and *Oedipus at Colonus* > Sophoclean (ˌsɒfə'kliːən) *adj*

sophomore ('sɒfəˌmɔː) n 1 *chiefly US & Canadian* a second-year student at a secondary (high) school or college ▷ *adj* 2 (of a book, recording, etc by an artist) second: *her sophomore album* [C17: perhaps from earlier *sophumer*, from *sophum*, variant of SOPHISM + -ER¹]

Sophy or **Sophi** ('səʊfɪ) n, pl **-phies** (formerly) a title of the Persian monarchs [C16: from Latin *sophī* wise men, from Greek *sophos* wise]

-sophy n *combining form* indicating knowledge or an intellectual system: *philosophy; theosophy* [from Greek *-sophia,* from *sophia* wisdom, from *sophos* wise] > -sophic or -sophical *adj combining form*

soporific (ˌsɒpə'rɪfɪk) *adj* Also called: (*archaic*) soporiferous 1 inducing sleep 2 drowsy; sleepy ▷ *n* 3 a drug or other agent that induces sleep

sopping ('sɒpɪŋ) *adj* completely soaked; wet through. Also called: **sopping wet**

soppy ('sɒpɪ) *adj* **-pier, -piest** 1 wet or soggy 2 *Brit informal* silly or sentimental > **soppily** *adv* > **soppiness** *n*

sopranino (ˌsɒprə'niːnəʊ) n, pl **-nos** a the instrument with the highest possible pitch in a family of instruments b (*as modifier*): *a sopranino recorder* [Italian, diminutive of SOPRANO]

soprano (sə'prɑːnəʊ) n, pl **-pranos** or **-prani** (-'prɑːniː) 1 the highest adult female voice, having a range approximately from middle C to the A a thirteenth above it 2 the voice of a young boy before puberty 3 a singer with such a voice 4 the highest part of a piece of harmony 5 a the highest or second highest instrument in a family of instruments b (*as modifier*): *a soprano saxophone* ▷ See also **treble** [C18: from Italian, from *sopra* above, from Latin *suprā*]

soprano clef n the clef that establishes middle C as being on the bottom line of the staff

sop up *vb* (*tr, adverb*) to mop or take up (spilt water, etc) with or as if with a sponge

Sopwith ('sɒpwɪθ) n Sir **Thomas Octave Murdoch.** 1888–1989, British aircraft designer, who built the Sopwith Camel biplane used during World War I. He was chairman (1935–63) of the Hawker Siddeley Group, which developed the Hurricane fighter

Sorata (*Spanish* so'rata) n Mount Sorata a mountain in W Bolivia, in the Andes: the highest mountain in the Cordillera Real, with two peaks, Ancohama, 6550 m (21 490 ft), and Illampu, 6485 m (21 276 ft)

sorb (sɔːb) n 1 another name for **service tree** (sense 1) 2 any of various related trees, esp the mountain ash 3 Also called: **sorb apple** the fruit of any of these trees [C16: from Latin *sorbus* the sorb, service tree]

sorbefacient (ˌsɔːbɪ'feɪʃənt) *adj* 1 inducing absorption ▷ *n* 2 a sorbefacient drug [C19: from Latin *sorbē(re)* to absorb + -FACIENT]

sorbet ('sɔːbeɪ, -bɪt) n 1 a water ice made from fruit juice, egg whites, milk, etc 2 a US word for **sherbet** (sense 2) [C16: from French, from Old Italian *sorbetto,* from Turkish *şerbet,* from Arabic *sharbah* a drink]

sorbic acid ('sɔːbɪk) n a white crystalline unsaturated carboxylic acid found in berries of the mountain ash and used to inhibit the growth of moulds and as an additive for certain synthetic coatings, as of cheese (E200); 2,4-hexadienoic acid. It exists as *cis-* and *trans-* isomers, the latter being the one usually obtained. Formula: $CH_3CH:CHCH:CHCOOH$ [C19: from SORB (the tree), from its discovery in the berries of the mountain ash]

sorbitol ('sɔːbɪˌtɒl) n a white water-soluble crystalline alcohol with a sweet taste, found in certain fruits and berries and manufactured by the catalytic hydrogenation of sucrose: used as a sweetener (E420) and in the manufacture of ascorbic acid and synthetic resins. Formula: $C_6H_8(OH)_6$ [C19: from SORB + -ITOL]

Sorbonne (*French* sɔrbɔn) n the Sorbonne a part of the University of Paris containing the faculties of science and literature: founded in 1253 by Robert de Sorbon as a theological college; given to the university in 1808

sorbo rubber ('sɔːbəʊ) n *Brit* a spongy form of rubber [C20: from ABSORB]

sorcerer ('sɔːsərə) or feminine **sorceress** ('sɔːsərɪs) n a person who seeks to control and use magic powers; a wizard or magician [C16: from Old French *sorcier,* from Vulgar Latin *sortiārius* (unattested) caster of lots, from Latin *sors* lot]

sorcery ('sɔːsərɪ) n, pl **-ceries** the art, practices, or spells of magic, esp black magic, by which it is sought to harness occult forces or evil spirits in order to produce preternatural effects in the world [C13: from Old French *sorcerie,* from *sorcier* SORCERER]

Sordello (*Italian* sor'dɛllo) n born ?1200, Italian troubadour

sordid ('sɔːdɪd) *adj* 1 dirty, foul, or squalid 2 degraded; vile; base 3 selfish and grasping: *sordid avarice* [C16: from Latin *sordidus,* from *sordēre* to be dirty] > **sordidly** *adv* > **sordidness** *n*

sordino (sɔː'diːnəʊ) n, pl **-ni** (-niː) 1 a mute for a stringed or brass musical instrument 2 any of the dampers that arrest the vibrations of piano strings 3 **con sordino** or **con sordini** a musical direction to play with a mute 4 **senza sordino** or **senza sordini** a musical direction to remove or play without the mute or (on the piano) with the sustaining pedal pressed down [Italian: from *sordo* deaf, from Latin *surdus*]

sore (sɔː) *adj* 1 (esp of a wound, injury, etc) painfully sensitive; tender 2 causing annoyance: *a sore point* 3 resentful; irked 4 urgent; pressing: *in sore need* 5 (*postpositive*) grieved; distressed 6 causing grief or sorrow ▷ *n* 7 a painful or sensitive wound, injury, etc 8 any cause of distress or vexation ▷ *adv* 9 *archaic* direly; sorely (now only in such phrases as **sore pressed, sore afraid**) [Old English *sār;* related to Old Norse *sārr,* Old High German *sēr,* Gothic *sair* sore, Latin *saevus* angry] > **soreness** *n*

sorehead ('sɔːˌhɛd) n *informal, chiefly US & Canadian* a peevish or disgruntled person

Sorel (*French* sɔrɛl) n **Georges** (**Eugène**) (ʒɔrʒ). 1847–1922, French social philosopher, who advocated revolutionary syndicalism and preached the creative role of violence and myth

sorely ('sɔːlɪ) *adv* 1 painfully or grievously: *sorely wounded* 2 pressingly or greatly: *sorely taxed; sorely missed*

Sorenstam ('sɔːrənstəm) n **Annika** ('ænɪka). born 1970, Swedish golfer; winner of the US Women's Open (1995, 1996, 2006), the LPGA Championship (2003, 2004, 2005), and the British Women's Open (2003)

sorghum ('sɔːgəm) n any grass of the Old World genus *Sorghum,* having solid stems, large flower heads, and glossy seeds: cultivated for grain, hay, and as a source of syrup [C16: from New Latin, from Italian *sorgo,* probably from Vulgar Latin *Syricum grānum* (unattested) Syrian grain]

Sorocaba (*Portuguese* soro'kaba) n a city in S Brazil, in São Paulo state: industrial centre. Pop: 671 000 (2005 est)

Soroptimist (sə'rɒptɪmɪst) n a member of an organization of clubs (**Soroptimist International**) for professional and executive businesswomen [C20: from Latin *soror* sister + OPTIMIST]

sororal (sə'rɔːrəl) *adj* of or relating to a sister or sisters [C17: from Latin *soror* a sister]

sorority (sə'rɒrɪtɪ) n, pl **-ties** *chiefly US* a social club or society for university women [C16: from Medieval Latin *sorōritās,* from Latin *soror* sister]

sorption ('sɔːpʃən) n the process in which one substance takes up or holds another; adsorption or absorption [C20: back formation from ABSORPTION, ADSORPTION]

sorrel¹ ('sɒrəl) n 1 a a light brown to brownish-orange colour b (*as adjective*): *a sorrel carpet* 2 a horse of this colour [C15: from Old French *sorel,* from *sor* a reddish brown, of Germanic origin; related to Middle Dutch *soor* desiccated]

sorrel² ('sɒrəl) n 1 any of several polygonaceous plants of the genus *Rumex,* esp *R. acetosa,* of Eurasia and North America, having acid-tasting leaves used in salads and sauces 2 short for **wood sorrel** [C14: from Old French *surele,* from *sur* sour, of Germanic origin; related to Old High German *sūr* SOUR]

S

Sorrento (səˈrɛntəʊ; *Italian* sorˈrɛnto) *n* a port in SW Italy, in Campania on a mountainous peninsula between the Bay of Naples and the Gulf of Salerno: a resort since Roman times. Pop: 16 536 (2001)

sorrow (ˈsɒrəʊ) *n* **1** the characteristic feeling of sadness, grief, or regret associated with loss, bereavement, sympathy for another's suffering, for an injury done, etc **2** a particular cause or source of regret, grief, etc **3** Also called: **sorrowing** the outward expression of grief or sadness ▷ *vb* **4** (*intr*) to mourn or grieve [Old English *sorg*; related to Old Norse *sorg*, Gothic *saurga*, Old High German *sworga*] > ˈsorrowful *adj* > ˈsorrowfully *adv* > ˈsorrowfulness *n*

sorry (ˈsɒrɪ) *adj* **-rier, -riest** **1** (*usually postpositive*; often foll by *for*) feeling or expressing pity, sympathy, remorse, grief, or regret: *I feel sorry for him* **2** pitiful, wretched, or deplorable: *a sorry sight* **3** poor; paltry: *a sorry excuse* **4** affected by sorrow; sad **5** causing sorrow or sadness ▷ *interj* **6** an exclamation expressing apology, used esp at the time of the misdemeanour, offence, etc [Old English *sārig*; related to Old High German *sērag*; see SORE] > ˈsorrily *adv* > ˈsorriness *n*

sort (sɔːt) *n* **1** a class, group, kind, etc, as distinguished by some common quality or characteristic **2** *informal* type of character, nature, etc: *he's a good sort* **3** a more or less definable or adequate example: *it's a sort of review* **4** (*often plural*) *printing* any of the individual characters making up a fount of type **5** *archaic* manner; way: *in this sort we struggled home* **6** **after a sort** to some extent **7** **of sorts** *or* **of a sort** **a** of an inferior kind **b** of an indefinite kind **8** **out of sorts** not in normal good health, temper, etc **9** **sort of** in some way or other; as it were; rather ▷ *vb* **10** (*tr*) to arrange according to class, type, etc **11** (*tr*) to put (something) into working order **12** (*tr*) to arrange (computer information) by machine in an order convenient to the computer user **13** (*intr*) *archaic* to agree; accord [c14: from Old French, from Medieval Latin *sors* kind, from Latin: fate] > ˈsortable *adj* > ˈsorter *n*
● USAGE See at kind²

sort code *n* a sequence of numbers printed on a cheque or embossed on a bank or building-society card that identifies the branch holding the account

sortie (ˈsɔːtɪ) *n* **1 a** (of troops, etc) the act of emerging from a contained or besieged position **b** the troops doing this **2** an operational flight made by one aircraft **3** a short or relatively short return trip ▷ *vb* **-ties, -tieing, -tied** **4** (*intr*) to make a sortie [c17: from French: a going out, from *sortir* to go out]

sortilege (ˈsɔːtɪlɪdʒ) *n* the act or practice of divination by drawing lots [c14: via Old French from Medieval Latin *sortilegium*, from Latin *sortilegus* a soothsayer, from *sors* fate + *legere* to select]

sort out *vb* (*tr, adverb*) **1** to find a solution to (a problem, etc), esp to make clear or tidy: *it took a long time to sort out the mess* **2** to take or separate, as from a larger group: *he sorted out the most likely ones* **3** to organize into an orderly and disciplined group **4** *informal* to beat or punish

SOS *n* **1** an internationally recognized distress signal in which the letters SOS are repeatedly spelt out, as by radio-telegraphy: used esp by ships and aircraft **2** a message broadcast in an emergency for people otherwise unobtainable **3** *informal* a call for help [c20: letters chosen as the simplest to transmit and receive in Morse code; by folk etymology taken to be abbrev. for *save our souls*]

sosatie (səˈsɑːtɪ) *n* *South African* a skewer of curried meat pieces [Afrikaans]

Sosnowiec (*Polish* sɔsˈnɔvjɛts) *n* an industrial town in S Poland. Pop: 223 284 (2007 est)

so-so *informal* ▷ *adj* **1** (*postpositive*) neither good nor bad ▷ *adv* **2** in an average or indifferent manner

sostenuto (ˌsɒstəˈnuːtəʊ) *adj, adv* *music* (preceded by a tempo marking) to be performed in a smooth sustained manner [c18: from Italian, from *sostenere* to sustain, from Latin *sustinēre* to uphold]

sot (sɒt) *n* **1 a** a habitual or chronic drunkard **2** a person stupefied by or as if by drink [Old English, from Medieval Latin *sottus*; compare French *sot* a fool] > ˈsottish *adj*

soteriology (sɒˌtɪərɪˈɒlədʒɪ) *n* *theol* the doctrine of salvation [c19: from Greek *sōtēria* deliverance (from *sōtēr* a saviour) + -LOGY]

Soto *n* See **De Soto**

sotto voce (ˈsɒtəʊ ˈvəʊtʃɪ) *adv* in an undertone [c18: from Italian: under (one's) voice]

sou (suː) *n* **1** a former French coin of low denomination **2** a very small amount of money: *I haven't a sou to my name* [c19: from French, from Old French *sol*, from Latin: SOLIDUS]

soubrette (suːˈbrɛt) *n* **1** a minor female role in comedy, often that of a pert lady's maid **2** any pert or flirtatious girl [c18: from French: maidservant, from Provençal *soubreto*, from *soubret* conceited, from *soubra* to exceed, from Latin *superāre* to surmount, from *super* above]

soubriquet (ˈsəʊbrɪˌkeɪ) *n* a variant spelling of **sobriquet**

Soudan (sudɑ̃) *n* the French name for the **Sudan**

soufflé (ˈsuːfleɪ) *n* **1** a very light fluffy dish made with egg yolks and stiffly beaten egg whites combined with cheese, fish, etc **2** a similar sweet or savoury cold dish, set with gelatine ▷ *adj* Also: **souffléed** **3** made light and puffy, as by beating and cooking [c19: from French, from *souffler* to blow, from Latin *sufflāre*]

Soufrière (*French* sufrjɛr) *n* **1** a volcano in the Caribbean, on N St Vincent: erupted in 1902, killing about 2000 people. Height: 1234 m (4048 ft) **2** a volcano in the Caribbean, on S Montserrat: the highest point on the island; erupted 1997, causing the effective destruction of the capital, Plymouth, and requiring the partial evacuation of the island. Height: 915 m (3002 ft) **3** a volcano in the Caribbean, on Guadeloupe. Height: 1484 m (4869 ft)

sough (saʊ) *vb* **1** (*intr*) (esp of the wind) to make a characteristic sighing sound ▷ *n* **2** a soft continuous murmuring sound [Old English *swōgan* to resound; related to Gothic *gaswogjan* to groan, Lithuanian *svageti* to sound, Latin *vāgīre* to lament]

sought (sɔːt) *vb* the past tense and past participle of **seek**

souk *or* **suq** (suːk) *n* (in Muslim countries, esp North Africa and the Middle East) an open-air marketplace [c20: from Arabic *sūq*]

soukous (ˈsuːkʊs) *n* a style of African popular music that originated in Zaïre (now the Democratic Republic of Congo), characterized by syncopated rhythms and intricate contrasting guitar melodies [c20: perhaps from French *secouer* to shake]

soul (səʊl) *n* **1** the spirit or immaterial part of man, the seat of human personality, intellect, will, and emotions, regarded as an entity that survives the body after death **2** *Christianity* the spiritual part of a person, capable of redemption from the power of sin through divine grace **3** the essential part or fundamental nature of anything **4** a person's feelings or moral nature as distinct from other faculties **5 a** Also called: **soul music** a type of Black music resulting from the addition of jazz, gospel, and pop elements to the urban blues style **b** (*as modifier*): *a soul singer* **6** (*modifier*) of or relating to Black Americans and their culture: *soul brother*; *soul food* **7** nobility of spirit or temperament: *a man of great soul and courage* **8** an inspiring spirit or leading figure, as of a cause or movement **9** a person regarded as typifying some characteristic or quality: *the soul of discretion* **10** a person; individual: *an honest soul* **11** **upon my soul!** an exclamation of surprise [Old English *sāwol*; related to Old Frisian *sēle*, Old Saxon *sēola*, Old High German *sēula* soul]

soul-destroying *adj* (of an occupation, situation, etc) unremittingly monotonous

soul food *n* *informal* food, such as chitterlings or yams, traditionally eaten by Black people in the southern US

soulful (ˈsəʊlfʊl) *adj* *sometimes ironic* expressing profound thoughts or feelings > ˈsoulfully *adv* > ˈsoulfulness *n*

soulless (ˈsəʊllɪs) *adj* **1** lacking any humanizing qualities or influences; dead; mechanical: *soulless work* **2** (of a person) lacking in sensitivity or nobility > ˈsoullessness *n*

soul mate *n* a person for whom one has a deep affinity, esp a lover, wife, husband, etc

soul-searching *n* **1** deep or critical examination of one's motives, actions, beliefs, etc ▷ *adj* **2** displaying the characteristics of deep or painful self-analysis

Soult (*French* sult) *n* **Nicolas Jean de Dieu** (nikɔla ʒɑ̃ də dyø). 1769–1851, French marshal under Napoleon I. Under Louis-Philippe he was minister of war (1830–34; 1840–44)

sound¹ (saʊnd) *n* **1 a** a periodic disturbance in the pressure or density of a fluid or in the elastic strain of a solid, produced by a vibrating object. It has a velocity in air at sea level at 0°C of 331 metres per second (741 miles per hour) and travels as longitudinal waves **b** (*as modifier*): *a sound wave* **2** the sensation produced by such a periodic disturbance in the organs of hearing **3** anything that can be heard **4** a particular instance, quality, or type of sound: *the sound of running water* **5** volume or quality of sound: *a radio with poor sound* **6** the area or distance over which something can be heard: *to be born within the sound of Big Ben* **7** the impression or implication of something: *I don't like the sound of that* **8** (*often plural*) *slang* music, esp rock, jazz, or pop ▷ *vb* **9** to cause (something, such as an instrument) to make a sound or (of an instrument, etc) to emit a sound **10** to announce or be announced by a sound: *to sound the alarm* **11** (*intr*) (of a sound) to be heard **12** (*intr*) to resonate with a certain quality or intensity: *to sound loud* **13** (*copula*) to give the impression of being as specified when read, heard, etc: *to sound reasonable* **14** (*tr*) to pronounce distinctly or audibly: *to sound one's consonants* [C13: from Old French *soner* to make a sound, from Latin *sonāre*, from *sonus* a sound] > 'soundable *adj*

sound² (saʊnd) *adj* **1** free from damage, injury, decay, etc **2** firm; solid; substantial: *a sound basis* **3** financially safe or stable: *a sound investment* **4** showing good judgment or reasoning; sensible; wise: *sound advice* **5** valid, logical, or justifiable: *a sound argument* **6** holding approved beliefs; ethically correct; upright; honest **7** (of sleep) deep; peaceful; unbroken **8** thorough; complete: *a sound examination* ▷ *adv* **9** soundly; deeply: now archaic except when applied to sleep [Old English *sund*; related to Old Saxon *gisund*, Old High German *gisunt*] > 'soundly *adv* > 'soundness *n*

sound³ (saʊnd) *vb* **1** to measure the depth of (a well, the sea, etc) by lowering a plumb line, by sonar, etc **2** to seek to discover (someone's views, etc), as by questioning **3** (*intr*) (of a whale, etc) to dive downwards swiftly and deeply **4** *med* **a** to probe or explore (a bodily cavity or passage) by means of a sound **b** to examine (a patient) by means of percussion and auscultation ▷ *n* **5** *med* an instrument for insertion into a bodily cavity or passage to dilate strictures, dislodge foreign material, etc ▷ See also **sound out** [C14: from Old French *sonder*, from *sonde* sounding line, probably of Germanic origin; related to Old English *sundgyrd* sounding pole, Old Norse *sund* strait, SOUND⁴; see SWIM]

sound⁴ (saʊnd) *n* **1 a** a relatively narrow channel between two larger areas of sea or between an island and the mainland **2** an inlet or deep bay of the sea **3** the air bladder of a fish [Old English *sund* swimming, narrow sea; related to Middle Low German *sunt* strait; see SOUND³]

Sound (saʊnd) *n* **the Sound** a strait between SW Sweden and Zealand (Denmark), linking the Kattegat with the Baltic: busy shipping lane; spanned by a bridge in 2000. Length of the strait: 113 km (70 miles). Narrowest point: 5 km (3 miles). Danish name: **Øresund** Swedish name: **Öresund**

soundalike ('saʊndə,laɪk) *n* **a** a person or thing that sounds like another, often well known, person or thing **b** (*as modifier*): *a soundalike band*

sound barrier *n* (*not in technical usage*) a hypothetical barrier to flight at or above the speed of sound, when a sudden large increase in drag occurs. Also called: **sonic barrier**

sound bite *n* a short pithy sentence or phrase coined with the aim of being repeated when a longer speech is reported on radio or television

soundbox ('saʊnd,bɒks) *n* the resonating chamber of the hollow body of a violin, guitar, etc

soundcard ('saʊnd,kɑːd) *n* a printed circuit board inserted into a computer, enabling the output and manipulation of sound

sound effect *n* any sound artificially produced, reproduced from a recording, etc, to create a theatrical effect, such as the bringing together of two halves of a hollow coconut shell to simulate a horse's gallop; used in plays, films, etc

sounding¹ ('saʊndɪŋ) *adj* **1** resounding; resonant **2** having an imposing sound and little content; pompous: *sounding phrases*

sounding² ('saʊndɪŋ) *n* **1** (*sometimes plural*) the act or process of measuring depth of water or examining the bottom of a river, lake, etc, as with a sounding line **2** an observation or measurement of atmospheric conditions, as made using a radiosonde or rocketsonde **3** (*often plural*) measurements taken by sounding **4** (*plural*) a place where a sounding line will reach the bottom, esp less than 100 fathoms in depth

sounding board *n* **1** Also called: **soundboard** a thin wooden board in a piano or comprising the upper surface of a resonating chamber in a violin, cello, etc, serving to amplify the vibrations produced by the strings passing across it **2** Also called: **soundboard** a thin screen suspended over a pulpit, stage, etc, to reflect sound towards an audience **3** a person, group, experiment, etc, used to test a new idea, policy, etc, for acceptance or applicability

sounding line *n* a line marked off to indicate its length and having a sounding lead at one end. It is dropped over the side of a vessel to determine the depth of the water

soundless ('saʊndlɪs) *adj* extremely still or silent > 'soundlessness *n*

sound out *vb* (*tr, adverb*) to question (someone) in order to discover (opinions, facts, etc)

soundpost ('saʊnd,pəʊst) *n music* a small post, usually of pine, on guitars, violins, etc, that joins the front surface to the back, helps to support the bridge, and allows the whole body of the instrument to vibrate

soundproof ('saʊnd,pruːf) *adj* **1** not penetrable by sound ▷ *vb* **2** (*tr*) to render soundproof

sound spectrograph *n* an electronic instrument that produces a record (**sound spectrogram**) of the way in which the frequencies and intensities of the components of a sound, such as a spoken word, vary with time

sound system *n* **1** any system of sounds, as in the speech of a language **2** integrated equipment for producing amplified sound, as in a hi-fi or a mobile disco, or as a public-address system on stage

soundtrack ('saʊnd,træk) *n* **1** the recorded sound accompaniment to a film **2** a narrow strip along the side of a spool of film, which carries the sound accompaniment

sound wave *n* a wave that propagates sound

Souness ('suːnɪs) *n* **Graeme**. born 1953, Scottish footballer and manager

soup (suːp) *n* **1** a liquid food made by boiling or simmering meat, fish, vegetables, etc, usually served hot at the beginning of a meal **2** *informal* a photographic developer **3** *informal* anything resembling soup in appearance or consistency, esp thick fog **4** a slang name for **nitroglycerine** **5** **in the soup** *informal* in trouble or difficulties [C17: from Old French *soupe*, from Late Latin *suppa*, of Germanic origin; compare Middle High German *suppe*, Old Norse *soppa* soup]

soupçon *French* (supsɔ̃) *n* a slight amount; dash [C18: from French, ultimately from Latin *suspicio* SUSPICION]

Souphanouvong (,suːfænuːˈvɒŋ) *n* **Prince**. 1902–95, Laotian statesman; president of Laos (1975–86)

soup kitchen *n* **1** a place or mobile stall where food and drink, esp soup, is served to destitute people **2** *military* a mobile kitchen

soup plate *n* a deep plate with a wide rim, used esp for drinking soup

soup up *informal* ▷ *vb* (*tr, adverb*) **1** to modify (a vehicle or vehicle engine) in order to increase its power **2** Also called: **hot up**, (*esp US and Canadian*) **hop up** to make (something) more exciting or interesting

sour ('saʊə) *adj* **1** having or denoting a sharp biting taste like that of lemon juice or vinegar **2** made acid or bad, as in the case of milk or alcohol, by the action of microorganisms **3** having a rancid or unwholesome smell **4** (of a person's temperament) sullen, morose, or disagreeable **5** (esp of the weather or climate) harsh and unpleasant **6** disagreeable; distasteful: *a sour experience* **7** (of land, etc) lacking in fertility, esp due to excessive acidity **8** (of oil, gas, or petrol) containing a relatively large amount of sulphur compounds **9 go sour** *or* **turn sour** to become unfavourable or inharmonious: *his marriage went sour* ▷ *n* **10** something sour **11** *chiefly US* any of several iced drinks usually made with spirits, lemon juice, and ice: *a whiskey sour* **12** an acid used in laundering and bleaching clothes or in curing animal skins ▷ *vb* **13** to make or become sour [Old English *sūr*; related to Old Norse *sūrr*, Lithuanian *suras* salty, Old Slavonic *syrŭ* wet, raw, *surovu* green, raw, Sanskrit *surā* brandy] > 'sourish *adj* > 'sourly *adv* > 'sourness *n*

source (sɔːs) *n* **1** the point or place from which something originates **2 a** a spring that forms the starting point of a stream; headspring **b** the area where the headwaters of a river rise **3** a person, group, etc, that creates, issues, or originates something: *the source of a complaint* **4 a** any person, book, organization, etc, from which information, evidence, etc, is obtained **b** (*as modifier*): *source material* **5** anything, such as a story or work of art, that provides a model or inspiration for a later work **6 at source** at the point of origin ▷ *vb* **7** to determine the source of a news report or stor **8** (*tr; foll by from*) to originate from **9** (*tr*) to establish an originator or source of (a product, piece of information, etc) [c14: from Old French *sors*, from *sourdre* to spring forth, from Latin *surgere* to rise]

source code *n* *computing* the original form of a computer program before it is converted into a machine-readable code

source program *n* an original computer program written by a programmer that is converted into the equivalent object program, written in machine language, by the compiler or assembler

sour cherry *n* **1** a Eurasian rosaceous tree, *Prunus cerasus*, with white flowers: cultivated for its tart red fruits **2** the fruit of this tree

sour cream *n* cream soured by lactic acid bacteria, used in making salads, dips, etc

sourdough ('saʊə,dəʊ) *adj* **1** *dialect* (of bread) made with fermented dough used as a leaven ▷ *n* **2** (in Western US, Canada, and Alaska) an old-time prospector or pioneer

sour gourd *n* **1** a large bombacaceous tree, *Adansonia gregorii*, of N Australia, having gourdlike fruit **2** the acid-tasting fruit of this tree, which has a woody rind and large seeds **3** the fruit of the baobab tree

sour grapes *n* (*functioning as singular*) the attitude of affecting to despise something because one cannot or does not have it oneself [from a fable by Aesop]

sourpuss ('saʊə,pʊs) *n* *informal* a person whose facial expression or nature is habitually gloomy or sullen

sourveld ('saʊə,fɛlt) *n* (in South Africa) a type of grazing characterized by long coarse grass [from Afrikaans *suur* sour + VELD grassland]

Sousa ('suːzə) *n* **John Philip.** 1854–1932, US bandmaster and composer of military marches, such as *The Stars and Stripes Forever* (1897) and *The Liberty Bell* (1893)

sousaphone ('suːzə,fəʊn) *n* *music* a large tuba that encircles the player's body and has a bell facing forwards [c20: named after John Philip *Sousa* (1854–1932), US bandmaster and composer of military marches] > 'sousa,phonist *n*

souse (saʊs) *vb* **1** to plunge (something, oneself, etc) into water or other liquid **2** to drench or be drenched **3** (*tr*) to pour or dash (liquid) over (a person or thing) **4** to steep or cook (food) in a marinade **5** (*tr; usually passive*) *slang* to make drunk ▷ *n* **6** the liquid or brine used in pickling **7** the act or process of sousing **8** *slang* a habitual drunkard [c14: from Old French *sous*, of Germanic origin; related to Old High German *sulza* brine]

Sousse (suːs), **Susa** *or* **Susah** *n* a port in E Tunisia, on the Mediterranean: founded by the Phoenicians in the 9th century BC. Pop: 191 000 (2005 est)

soutane (suːˈtæn) *n* *RC Church* a priest's cassock [c19: from French, from Old Italian *sottana*, from Medieval Latin *subtanus* (adj) (worn) beneath, from Latin *subtus* below]

souterrain ('suːtə,reɪn) *n* *archaeol* an underground chamber or passage [c18: from French]

south (saʊθ) *n* **1** one of the four cardinal points of the compass, at 180° from north and 90° clockwise from east and anticlockwise from west **2** the direction along a meridian towards the South Pole **3** the south (*often capital*) any area lying in or towards the south **4** (*usually capital*) cards the player or position at the table corresponding to south on the compass ▷ *adj* **5** situated in, moving towards, or facing the south **6** (esp of the wind) from the south ▷ *adv* **7** in, to, or towards the south [Old English *sūth*; related to Old Norse *suthr* southward, Old High German *sundan* from the south]

South (saʊθ) **the South** *n* **1** the southern part of England, generally regarded as lying to the south of an imaginary line between the Wash and the Severn **2** (in the US) **a** the area approximately south of Pennsylvania and the Ohio River, esp those states south of the Mason-Dixon line that formed the Confederacy during the Civil War **b** the Confederacy itself **3** the countries of the world that are not economically and technically advanced *adj* **4** of or denoting the southern part of a specified country, area, etc

South Africa *n* Republic of South Africa a republic occupying the southernmost part of the African continent: the Dutch Cape Colony (1652) was acquired by Britain in 1806 and British victory in the Boer War resulted in the formation of the Union of South Africa in 1910, which became a republic in 1961; implementation of the apartheid system began in 1948 and was abolished, following an intense civil rights campaign, in 1993, with multiracial elections held in 1994; a member of the Commonwealth, it withdrew in 1961 but was re-admitted in 1994. Mainly plateau with mountains in the south and east. Mineral production includes gold, diamonds, coal, and copper. Official languages: Afrikaans; English; Ndebele; Pedi; South Sotho; Swazi; Tsonga; Tswana; Venda; Xhosa; Zulu. Religion: Christian majority. Currency: rand. Capitals: Cape Town (legislative), Pretoria (administrative), Bloemfontein (judicial). Pop: 45 214 000 (2004 est). Area: 1 221 044 sq km (471 445 sq miles). Former name (1910–61): Union of South Africa > South African *adj, n*

South America *n* the fourth largest of the continents, bordering on the Caribbean in the north, the Pacific in the west, and the Atlantic in the east and joined to Central America by the Isthmus of Panama. It is dominated by the Andes Mountains, which extend over 7250 km (4500 miles) and include many volcanoes; ranges from dense tropical jungle, desert, and temperate plains to the cold wet windswept region of Tierra del Fuego. Pop (Latin America and the Caribbean): Pop: 558 281 000 (2005 est). Area: 17 816 600 sq km (6 879 000 sq miles) > South American *adj, n*

Southampton[1] (saʊθˈæmptən, -ˈhæmp-) *n* **1** a port in S England, in Southampton unitary authority, Hampshire on **Southampton Water** (an inlet of the English Channel): chief English passenger port; university (1952); shipyards and oil refinery. Pop: 234 224 (2001) **2** a unitary authority in S England, in Hampshire. Pop: 221 100 (2003 est). Area: 49 sq km (19 sq miles)

Southampton[2] (saʊθˈæmptən, -ˈhæmp-) *n* **3rd Earl of,** title of *Henry Wriothesley.* 1573–1624, English courtier and patron of Shakespeare, who dedicated *Venus and Adonis* (1593) and *The Rape of Lucrece* (1594) to him: sentenced to death (1601) for his part in the Essex rebellion but reprieved

Southampton Island *n* an island in N Canada, in Nunavut at the entrance to Hudson Bay: inhabited chiefly by Inuit. Area: 49 470 sq km (19 100 sq miles)

South Arabia *n* Federation of South Arabia the former name (1963–67) of South Yemen (excluding Aden). See also **South Yemen** > South Arabian *adj, n*

S

South Australia *n* a state of S central Australia, on the Great Australian Bight: generally arid, with the Great Victoria Desert in the west central part, the Lake Eyre basin in the northeast, and the Flinders Ranges, Murray River basin, and salt lakes in the southeast. Capital: Adelaide. Pop: 1 531 375 (2003 est). Area: 984 395 sq km 380 070 sq miles) > **South Australian** *adj, n*

South Ayrshire ('ɛəʃɪə, -ʃə) *n* a council area of SW Scotland, on the Firth of Clyde: comprises the S part of the historical county of Ayrshire; formerly part of Strathclyde Region (1975–96): chiefly agricultural, with fishing and tourism. Administrative centre: Ayr. Pop: 111 580 (2003 est). Area: 1202 sq km (464 sq miles)

South Bend *n* a city in the US, in N Indiana: university (1842). Pop: 105 540 (2003 est)

southbound ('saʊθ,baʊnd) *adj* going or leading towards the south

south by east *n* **1** one point on the compass east of south; 168° 45′ clockwise from north ▷ *adj, adv* **2** in, from, or towards this direction

south by west *n* **1** one point on the compass west of south; 191° 15′ clockwise from north ▷ *adj, adv* **2** in, from, or towards this direction

South Carolina *n* a state of the southeastern US, on the Atlantic: the first state to secede from the Union in 1860; consists largely of low-lying coastal plains, rising in the northwest to the Blue Ridge Mountains; the largest US textile producer. Capital: Columbia. Pop: 4 147 152 (2003 est). Area: 78 282 sq km (30 225 sq miles). Abbreviation and zip code: SC > **South ˌCaroˈlinian** *adj, n*

South China Sea *n* part of the Pacific surrounded by SE China, Vietnam, the Malay Peninsula, Borneo, and the Philippines

Southcott ('saʊθkɒt) *n* **Joanna**. 1750–1814, British religious fanatic, who claimed that she would give birth to the second Messiah

South Dakota *n* a state of the western US: lies mostly in the Great Plains; the chief US producer of gold and beryl. Capital: Pierre. Pop: 764 309 (2003 est). Area: 196 723 sq km (75 955 sq miles) Abbreviations: S. Dak., (with zip code) SD > **South Dakotan** *adj, n*

Southdown ('saʊθ,daʊn) *n* an English breed of sheep with short wool and a greyish-brown face and legs [C18: so called because it was originally bred on the SOUTH DOWNS]

South Downs *pl n* a range of low hills in S England, extending from E Hampshire to East Sussex: proposed (since 1999) as a national park

southeast (ˌsaʊθˈiːst; *Nautical* ˌsaʊˈiːst) *n* **1** the point of the compass or the direction midway between south and east, 135° clockwise from north **2** (*often cap*; *usually preceded by the*) any area lying in or towards this direction ▷ *adj* Also: **southeastern** (*sometimes capital*) of or denoting the southeastern part of a specified country, area, etc **4** situated in, proceeding towards, or facing the southeast **5** (esp of the wind) from the southeast ▷ *adv* **6** in, to, towards, or (esp of the wind) from the southeast > ˌsouthˈeasternmost *adj*

Southeast (ˌsaʊθˈiːst) *n* **the Southeast** the southeastern part of Britain, esp the London area

Southeast Asia *n* a region including Brunei, Cambodia, Indonesia, Laos, Malaysia, Myanmar, the Philippines, Thailand, and Vietnam > **Southeast Asian** *adj, n*

southeast by east *n* **1** one point on the compass north of southeast; 123° 45′ clockwise from north ▷ *adj, adv* **2** in, from, or towards this direction

southeast by south *n* **1** one point on the compass south of southeast; 146° 15′ clockwise from north ▷ *adj, adv* **2** in, from, or towards this direction

southeaster (ˌsaʊθˈiːstə; *Nautical* ˌsaʊˈiːstə) *n* a strong wind or storm from the southeast

southeasterly (ˌsaʊθˈiːstəlɪ; *Nautical* ˌsaʊˈiːstəlɪ) *adj, adv* **1** in, towards, or (esp of a wind) from the southeast ▷ *n, pl* **-lies 2** a strong wind or storm from the southeast

southeastward (ˌsaʊθˈiːstwəd; *Nautical* ˌsaʊˈiːstwəd) *adj* **1** towards or (esp of a wind) from the southeast ▷ *n* **2** a direction towards or area in the southeast ▷ *adv*

Southend-on-Sea (ˌsaʊθˈend-) *n* **1 a** a town in SE England, in SE Essex on the Thames estuary: one of England's

largest resorts, extending for about 11 km (7 miles) along the coast. Pop: 160 257 (2001) **2 a** unitary authority in SE England, in Essex. Pop: 160 300 (2003 est). Area: 42 sq km (16 sq miles)

souther ('saʊðə) *n* a strong wind or storm from the south

southerly ('sʌðəlɪ) *adj* **1** of, relating to, or situated in the south ▷ *adv, adj* **2** towards or in the direction of the south **3** from the south ▷ *n, pl* **-lies 4** a wind from the south > ˈsoutherliness *n*

southern ('sʌðən) *adj* **1** situated in or towards the south **2** (of a wind, etc) coming from the south **3** native to, inhabiting, or growing in the south > ˈsouthernˌmost *adj*

Southern ('sʌðən) *adj* of, relating to, or characteristic of the south of a particular region or country

Southern Alps *pl n* a mountain range in New Zealand, on South Island: the highest range in Australasia. Highest peak: Mount Cook (also known as Aoraki or Aorangi), 3754 m (12 316 ft)

Southern Cross *n* a small conspicuous constellation in the S hemisphere lying in the Milky Way near Centaurus. The four brightest stars form a cross the longer arm of which points to the south celestial pole

Southerner ('sʌðənə) *n* (*sometimes not capital*) a native or inhabitant of the south of any specified region, esp the South of England or the Southern states of the US

southern hemisphere *n* (*often capitals*) that half of the earth lying south of the equator

Southern Ireland *n* See **Ireland¹** (sense 2)

southern lights *pl n* another name for **aurora australis**

Southern Ocean *n* another name for the **Antarctic Ocean**

Southern Rhodesia *n* the former name (until 1964) of **Zimbabwe** > **Southern Rhodesian** *adj, n*

Southern Stars *pl n* the Australian women's national cricket team

Southern Uplands *pl n* a hilly region extending across S Scotland: includes the Lowther, Moorfoot, and Lammermuir hills

Southey ('saʊðɪ, 'sʌðɪ) *n* **Robert**. 1774–1843, English poet, a friend of Wordsworth and Coleridge, attacked by Byron; poet laureate (1813–43)

South Georgia *n* an island in the S Atlantic, about 1300 km (800 miles) southeast of the Falkland Islands, part of the UK Overseas Territory of **South Georgia and the South Sandwich Islands**; no permanent population. Area: 3755 sq km (1450 sq miles) > **South Georgian** *adj, n*

South Glamorgan *n* a former county of S Wales, formed in 1974 from parts of Glamorgan and Monmouthshire plus the county borough of Cardiff: replaced in 1996 by the county boroughs of Cardiff and Vale of Glamorgan

South Gloucestershire *n* a unitary authority of SW England, in Gloucestershire: formerly (1975–96) part of the county of Avon. Pop: 246 800 (2003 est). Area: 510 sq km (197 sq miles)

South Holland *n* a province of the SW Netherlands, on the North Sea: lying mostly below sea level, it has a coastal strip of dunes and is drained chiefly by distributaries of the Rhine, with large areas of reclaimed land; the most densely populated province in the country, intensively cultivated and industrialized. Capital: The Hague. Pop: 3 440 000 (2003 est). Area: 3196 sq km (1234 sq miles). Dutch name: **Zuidholland**

southing ('saʊðɪŋ) *n* **1** *navigation* movement, deviation, or distance covered in a southerly direction **2** *astronomy* a south or negative declination

South Island *n* **the South Island** the largest island of New Zealand, separated from the North Island by the Cook Strait. Pop: 973 000 (2004 est). Area: 153 947 sq km (59 439 sq miles)

South Korea *n* a republic in NE Asia: established as a republic in 1948; invaded by North Korea and Chinese Communists in 1950 but division remained unchanged at the end of the war (1953); includes over 3000 islands; rapid industrialization. Language: Korean. Religions: Buddhist, Confucianist, Shamanist, and Chondokyo. Currency: won. Capital: Seoul. Pop: 47 950 000 (2004 est). Area: 98 477 sq km (38 022 sq miles). Korean name:

S

Hanguk > **South Korean** *adj, n*

South Lanarkshire ('lænək,ʃɪə, -ʃə) *n* a council area of S Scotland, comprising the S part of the historical county of Lanarkshire: included within Strathclyde Region from 1975 to 1996: has uplands in the S and part of the Glasgow conurbation in the N: mainly agricultural. Administrative centre: Hamilton. Pop: 303 010 (2003 est). Area: 1771 sq km (684 sq miles)

South Orkney Islands *pl n* an uninhabited group of islands in the S Atlantic, southeast of Cape Horn: formerly a dependency of the Falkland Islands; part of the British Antarctic Territory since 1962 (claims are suspended under the Antarctic Treaty). Area: 621 sq km (240 sq miles)

South Ossetia (ə'siːʃə) *n* a region in Georgia on the S slopes of the Caucasus Mountains, in 1990 it voted to join Russia, leading to armed conflict with Georgian forces; it became an autonomous region in 1997 but later lost this status under a nationwide reorganization of local government. Capital: Tskhinvali. Pop: about 70 000 (2000 est). Area: 3900 sq km (1500 sq miles). Also called: South Ossetian Autonomous Region

southpaw ('saʊθ,pɔː) *informal* ▷ *n* **1** a boxer who leads with his right hand and off his right foot as opposed to the orthodox style of leading with the left **2** any left-handed person ▷ *adj* **3** of or relating to a southpaw [c20: from PAW (in the sense: hand): originally a term applied to a left-handed baseball player: perhaps so called because baseball pitchers traditionally face west, so that a left-handed pitcher would throw with the hand on the south side of his body]

South Pole *n* **1** the southernmost point on the earth's axis, at the latitude of 90°S **2** *astronomy* the point of intersection, in the constellation Octans, of the earth's extended axis and the southern half of the celestial sphere **3** (*usually not capitals*) the south-seeking pole of a freely suspended magnet

Southport ('saʊθ,pɔːt) *n* a town and resort in NW England, in Sefton unitary authority, Merseyside on the Irish Sea. Pop: 91 404 (2001)

South Saskatchewan *n* a river in S central Canada, rising in S Alberta and flowing east and northeast to join the North Saskatchewan River, forming the Saskatchewan River. Length: 1392 km (865 miles)

South Sea Bubble *n* *Brit history* the financial crash that occurred in 1720 after the **South Sea Company** had taken over the national debt in return for a monopoly of trade with the South Seas, causing feverish speculation in their stocks [so named because the rapid expansion and sudden collapse of investment resembled the blowing up and bursting of a bubble]

South Sea Islands *pl n* the islands in the S Pacific that constitute Oceania

South Seas *pl n* the seas south of the equator

South Shetland Islands *pl n* a group of uninhabited islands in the S Atlantic, north of the Antarctic Peninsula: formerly a dependency of the Falkland Islands; part of British Antarctic Territory since 1962. (Claims are suspended under the Antarctic Treaty). Area: 4662 sq km (1800 sq miles)

South Shields *n* a port in NE England, in South Tyneside unitary authority, Tyne and Wear on the Tyne estuary opposite North Shields. Pop: 82 854 (2001)

south-southeast *n* **1** the point on the compass or the direction midway between southeast and south; 157° 30′ clockwise from north ▷ *adj, adv* **2** in, from, or towards this direction

south-southwest *n* **1** the point on the compass or the direction midway between south and southwest; 202° 30′ clockwise from north ▷ *adj, adv* **2** in, from, or towards this direction

South Tyneside ('taɪn,saɪd) *n* a unitary authority of NE England, in Tyne and Wear. Pop: 151 700 (2003 est). Area: 64 sq km (25 sq miles)

South Tyrol or **South Tirol** *n* a former part of the Austrian state of Tyrol: ceded to Italy in 1919, becoming the Bolzano and Trento provinces of the Trentino-Alto Adige Autonomous Region. Area: 14 037 sq km (5420 sq miles)

South Vietnam *n* a former republic (1955–76) occupying the S of present-day Vietnam on the South China Sea and the Gulf of Thailand > **South Vietnamese** *adj, n*

southward ('saʊθwəd; *Nautical* 'sʌðəd) *adj* **1** situated, directed, or moving towards the south ▷ *n* **2** the southward part, direction, etc; the south ▷ *adv* a variant of **southwards**

southwards ('saʊθwədz; *Nautical* 'sʌðədz) or **southward** *adv* towards the south

Southwark ('sʌðək) *n* a borough of S central Greater London, on the River Thames: site of the Globe Theatre, now reconstructed; the former docks and warehouses have been redeveloped. Pop: 253 800 (2003 est). Area: 29 sq km (11 sq miles)

Southwell ('saʊθwel) *n* **Saint Robert**. ?1561–95, English poet and Roman Catholic martyr, who was imprisoned, tortured, and executed for his Jesuit activities. His best known poem is 'The Burning Babe'

southwest (,saʊθ'west; *Nautical* ,saʊ'west) *n* **1** the point of the compass or the direction midway between west and south, 225° clockwise from north **2** (*often cap; usually preceded by the*) any area lying in or towards this direction ▷ *adj* Also: **southwestern 3** (*sometimes capital*) of or denoting the southwestern part of a specified country, area, etc: *southwest Italy* **4** situated in or towards the southwest **5** (*esp of the wind*) from the southwest ▷ *adv* **6** in, to, towards, or (*esp of the wind*) from the southwest > ,**south'westernmost** *adj*

Southwest (,saʊθ'west) *n* **the Southwest** the southwestern part of Britain, esp Cornwall, Devon, and Somerset

South West Africa *n* another name for **Namibia**

southwest by south *n* **1** one point on the compass south of southwest; 213° 45′ clockwise from north ▷ *adj, adv* **2** in, from, or towards this direction

southwest by west *n* **1** one point on the compass north of southwest, 236° 15′ clockwise from north ▷ *adj, adv* **2** in, from, or towards this direction

southwester (,saʊθ'westə; *Nautical* ,saʊ'westə) *n* a strong wind or storm from the southwest

southwesterly (,saʊθ'westəlɪ; *Nautical* ,saʊ'westəlɪ) *adj, adv* **1** in, towards, or (*esp of a wind*) from the southwest ▷ *n, pl* **-lies 2** a wind or storm from the southwest

southwestward (,saʊθ'westwəd; *Nautical* ,saʊ'westwəd) *adj* **1** from or towards the southwest ▷ *adv* ▷ *n* **2** a direction towards or area in the southwest

South Yemen *n* a former republic in SW Arabia, on the Gulf of Aden; now a part of Yemen: became a republic in 1967; merged with North Yemen in 1990. Name from 1963 to 1967 (excluding Aden): South Arabia See also **Yemen, North Yemen**

South Yorkshire *n* a metropolitan county of N England, administered since 1986 by the unitary authorities of Barnsley, Doncaster, Sheffield, and Rotherham. Area: 1560 sq km (602 sq miles)

Soutine (French sutin) *n* **Chaim** (xaɪɪm). 1893–1943, French expressionist painter, born in Russia; noted for his portraits and still lifes, esp of animal carcasses

souvenir (,suːvə'nɪə, 'suːvə,nɪə) *n* **1** an object that recalls a certain place, occasion, or person; memento ▷ *vb* (*tr*) **2** *Austral & NZ euphemistic, slang* to steal or keep (something, esp a small article) for one's own use; purloin [c18: from French, from (*se*) *souvenir* to remember, from Latin *subvenīre* to come to mind, from *sub-* up to + *venīre* to come]

sou'wester (saʊ'westə) *n* a waterproof hat having a very broad rim behind, worn esp by seamen [c19: a contraction of SOUTHWESTER]

sovereign ('sɒvrɪn) *n* **1** a person exercising supreme authority, esp a monarch **2** a former British gold coin worth one pound sterling ▷ *adj* **3** supreme in rank or authority: *a sovereign lord* **4** excellent or outstanding: *a sovereign remedy* **5** of, relating to, or characteristic of a sovereign **6** independent of outside authority: *a sovereign state* [c13: from Old French *soverain*, from Vulgar Latin *superānus* (unattested), from Latin *super* above; also influenced by REIGN] > '**sovereignly** *adv*

sovereigntist ('sɒvrəntɪst) *n* (in Canada) **1** a supporter of sovereignty association ▷ *adj* **2** supporting sovereignty association

sovereignty ('sɒvrəntı) *n, pl* -ties 1 supreme and unrestricted power, as of a state 2 the position, dominion, or authority of a sovereign 3 an independent state

sovereignty association *n* (in Canada) a proposed arrangement by which Quebec would become independent but would maintain a formal association with Canada

Sovetsk (*Russian* sa'vjɛtsk) *n* a town in W Russia, in the Kaliningrad Region on the Neman River: scene of the signing of the treaty (1807) between Napoleon I and Tsar Alexander I; passed from East Prussia to the Soviet Union in 1945. Former name (until 1945): **Tilsit**

soviet ('səuvɪət, 'sɒv-) *n* 1 (in the former Soviet Union) an elected government council at the local, regional, and national levels, which culminated in the Supreme Soviet ▷ *adj* 2 of or relating to a soviet [c20: from Russian *sovyet* council, from Old Russian *sŭvĕtŭ*] > 'sovie,tism *n* (*sometimes capital*)

Soviet ('səuvɪət, 'sɒv-) *adj* of, characteristic of, or relating to the former Soviet Union, its people, or its government

Soviet Central Asia *n* the region of the former Soviet Union now occupied by Kazakhstan, Kyrgyzstan, Tajikistan, Turkmenistan, and Uzbekistan. Also called: **Russian Turkestan, West Turkestan**

sovietize *or* **sovietise** ('səuvɪɪ,taɪz, 'sɒv-) *vb* (*tr; often capital*) 1 to bring (a country, person, etc) under Soviet control or influence 2 to cause (a country) to conform to the Soviet model in its social, political, and economic structure > ,sovieti'zation *or* ,sovieti'sation *n*

Soviet Russia *n* (formerly) another name for **Russian Soviet Federative Socialist Republic, Soviet Union**

Soviets ('səuvɪəts, 'sɒv-) *n* the people or government of the former Soviet Union

Soviet Union *n* a former federal republic in E Europe and central and N Asia: the revolution of 1917 achieved the overthrow of the Russian monarchy and the Soviet Union (the USSR) was established in 1922 as a Communist state. It was the largest country in the world, occupying a seventh of the total land surface. The collapse of Communist rule in 1991 was followed by declarations of independence by the constituent republics and the consequent break-up of the Soviet Union. Official name: **Union of Soviet Socialist Republics** Also called: **Russia, Soviet Russia** Abbreviation: **USSR**

Soviet Zone *n* that part of Germany occupied by Soviet forces in 1945–49: transformed into the German Democratic Republic in 1949–50. Also called: **Russian Zone**

sow[1] (səu) *vb* sows, sowing, sowed, sown *or* sowed 1 to scatter or place (seed, a crop, etc) in or on (a piece of ground, field, etc) so that it may grow: *to sow wheat; to sow a strip of land* 2 (*tr*) to implant or introduce: *to sow a doubt in someone's mind* [Old English *sāwan*; related to Old Norse *sā*, Old High German *sāen*, Old Slavonic *seja*, Latin *serere* to sow] > 'sower *n*

sow[2] (sau) *n* 1 a female adult pig 2 the female of certain other animals, such as the mink 3 *metallurgy* a the channels for leading molten metal to the moulds in casting pig iron b iron that has solidified in these channels [Old English *sugu*; related to Old Norse *sȳr*, Old High German *sū*, Latin *sūs*, Norwegian *sugga*, Dutch *zeug*: see SWINE]

Soweto (sə'wɛtəu, -'weɪtəu) *n* a contiguous group of Black African townships southwest of Johannesburg, South Africa: the largest purely Black African urban settlement in southern Africa: scene of riots (1976) following protests against the use of Afrikaans in schools for Black African children. Area: 62 sq km (24 sq miles). Pop: 858 649 (2001) [c20: from *So(uth) we(st) to(wnship)*]

sown (səun) *vb* a past participle of **sow**[1]

sow thistle (sau) *n* any of various plants of the Old World genus *Sonchus*, esp *S. oleraceus*, having milky juice, prickly leaves, and heads of yellow flowers: family *Asteraceae* (composites) [c13: from *sugethistel*, perhaps

variant of Old English *thugethistel, thuthistel* thowthistle, a dialect name of the sow thistle. See sow[2], THISTLE]

soya bean ('sɔɪə) *or US and Canadian* **soybean** ('sɔɪ,biːn) *n* 1 an Asian bean plant, *Glycine max* (or *G. soja*), cultivated for its nutritious seeds, for forage, and to improve the soil 2 the seed of this plant, used as food, forage, and as the source of an oil [c17 *soya*, via Dutch *soya* from Japanese *shōyu*, from Chinese *chiang yu*, from *chiang* paste + *yu* sauce]

Soyinka (sɔ'jɪŋkə) *n* **Wole** ('wɔːle). born 1934, Nigerian dramatist, novelist, poet, and literary critic. His works include the plays *The Strong Breed* (1963), *The Road* (1965), and *Kongi's Harvest* (1966), the novel *The Interpreters* (1965), and the political essays *The Burden of Memory, the Muse of Forgiveness* (1999); forced into exile by the military regime (1993–98). Nobel prize for literature 1986

soy sauce (sɔɪ) *n* a salty dark brown sauce made from fermented soya beans, used esp in Japanese and Chinese cookery. Also called: **soya sauce**

sozzled ('sɒzəld) *adj* an informal word for **drunk** [c19: perhaps from obsolete *sozzle* stupor; related to SOUSE[1]]

SP *abbreviation* starting price

sp. *abbreviation* 1 special 2 *pl* spp species 3 specific

Sp. *abbreviation* 1 Spain 2 Spaniard 3 Spanish

spa (spɑː) *n* a mineral spring or a place or resort where such a spring is found [c17: named after Spa, Belgium]

Spa (spɑː) *n* a town in E Belgium, in Liège province: a resort with medicinal mineral springs (discovered in the 14th century). Pop: 10 491 (2004 est)

Spaak (spɑːk) *n* **Paul Henri** (pɔl ɑ̃ri). 1899–1972, Belgian statesman, first socialist premier of Belgium (1937–38); a leading advocate of European unity, he was president of the consultative assembly of the Council of Europe (1949–51) and secretary-general of NATO (1957–61)

space (speɪs) *n* 1 the unlimited three-dimensional expanse in which all material objects are located. Related adj: **spatial** 2 an interval of distance or time between two points, objects, or events 3 a blank portion or area 4 a unoccupied area or room: *there is no space for a table* b (*in combination*): *space-saving*. Related adj: **spacious** 5 a the region beyond the earth's atmosphere containing the other planets of the solar system, stars, galaxies, etc; universe b (*as modifier*): *a space probe; space navigation* 6 a seat or place, as on a train, aircraft, etc 7 *printing* a piece of metal, less than type-high, used to separate letters or words in hot-metal printing 8 *music* any of the gaps between the lines that make up the staff 9 Also called: **spacing** *telegraphy* the period of time that separates complete letters, digits, and other characters in Morse code ▷ *vb* (*tr*) 10 to place or arrange at intervals or with spaces between 11 to divide into or by spaces: *to space one's time evenly* 12 *printing* to separate (letters, words, or lines) by the insertion of spaces [c13: from Old French *espace*, from Latin *spatium*] > 'spacer *n*

space age *n* 1 the period in which the exploration of space has become possible ▷ *adj* space-age 2 (*usually prenominal*) futuristic or ultramodern, esp when suggestive of space technology

space-bar *n* a horizontal bar on a typewriter that is depressed in order to leave a space between words, letters, etc

space capsule *n* a vehicle, sometimes carrying people or animals, designed to obtain scientific information from space, planets, etc, and be recovered on returning to earth

spacecraft ('speɪs,krɑːft) *n* a manned or unmanned vehicle designed to orbit the earth or travel to celestial objects for the purpose of research, exploration, etc

spaced out *adj slang* intoxicated through or as if through taking a drug

space heater *n* a heater used to warm the air in an enclosed area, such as a room or office

Space Invaders *n* (*functioning as singular*) *trademark* a video or computer game, the object of which is to destroy attacking alien spacecraft

spaceman ('speɪs,mæn) *or feminine* **spacewoman** *n, pl* -men *or feminine* -women a person who travels in outer space, esp one trained to participate in a space flight

space platform *n* another name for **space station**

S

spaceport ('speɪsˌpɔːt) *n* a base equipped to launch, maintain, and test spacecraft

space probe *n* a vehicle, such as a satellite, equipped to obtain scientific information, normally transmitted back to earth by radio, about the atmosphere, surface, and temperature of a planet, conditions in space, etc

spaceship ('speɪsˌʃɪp) *n* a manned spacecraft

space shuttle *n* any of a series of reusable US space vehicles (*Columbia* (exploded 2003), *Challenger* (exploded 1986), *Discovery, Atlantis, Endeavour*) that can be launched into earth orbit transporting astronauts and equipment for a period of observation, research, etc, before re-entry and an unpowered landing on a runway; the first operational flight occurred in 1982

space station *n* any large manned artificial satellite designed to orbit the earth during a long period of time thus providing a base for scientific and medical research in space and a construction site, launch pad, and docking arrangements for spacecraft

spacesuit ('speɪsˌsuːt, -ˌsjuːt) *n* any of various types of sealed and pressurized suits worn by astronauts or cosmonauts that provide an artificial atmosphere, acceptable temperature, radiocommunication link, and protection from radiation for work outside a spacecraft

space-time *or* **space-time continuum** *n physics* the four-dimensional continuum having three spatial coordinates and one time coordinate that together completely specify the location of a particle or an event

spacewalk ('speɪsˌwɔːk) *n* **1** the act or an instance of floating and manoeuvring in space, outside but attached by a lifeline to a spacecraft ▷ *vb* **2** (*intr*) to float and manoeuvre in space while outside but attached to a spacecraft

spacey ('speɪsɪ) *adj* spacier, spaciest *slang* vague and dreamy, as if under the influence of drugs [C20: SPACE + -EY]

Spacey ('speɪsɪ) *n* **Kevin**, original name *Kevin Spacey Fowler*. born 1959, US actor; films include *Glengarry Glen Ross* (1992), *The Usual Suspects* (1995), *American Beauty* (1999), which earned him an Academy Award, *The Shipping News* (2001), and *Beyond the Sea* (2004); artistic director of Old Vic Theatre Company, London, from 2003

spacial ('speɪʃəl) *adj* a variant spelling of **spatial**

spacing ('speɪsɪŋ) *n* **1** the arrangement of letters, words, etc, on a page in order to achieve legibility or aesthetic appeal **2** the arrangement of objects in a space

spacious ('speɪʃəs) *adj* having a large capacity or area [C14: from Latin *spātiosus*, from *spatium* SPACE]
> **'spaciously** *adv* > **'spaciousness** *n*

SPAD (spæd) *n acronym for* signal passed at danger: an incident in which a train goes through a red light

spade¹ (speɪd) *n* **1** a tool for digging, typically consisting of a flat rectangular steel blade attached to a long wooden handle **2** an object or part resembling a spade in shape **3** a cutting tool for stripping the blubber from a whale or skin from a carcass **4** call a spade a spade to speak plainly and frankly ▷ *vb* **5** (*tr*) to use a spade on [Old English *spadu*; related to Old Norse *spathi*, Old High German *spato*, Greek *spathē* blade] > **'spader** *n*

spade² (speɪd) *n* **1** **a** the black symbol on a playing card resembling a heart-shaped leaf with a stem **b** a card with one or more of these symbols or (*when pl.*) the suit of cards so marked, usually the highest ranking of the four **2** a derogatory word for **Black¹** **3** in spades *informal* in an extreme or emphatic way [C16: from Italian *spada* sword, used as an emblem on playing cards, from Latin *spatha*, from Greek *spathē* blade, broadsword]

spadework ('speɪdˌwɜːk) *n* dull or routine preparatory work

spadix ('speɪdɪks) *n, pl* spadices (speɪˈdaɪsɪːz) a racemose inflorescence having many small sessile flowers borne on a fleshy stem, the whole usually being surrounded by a spathe: typical of aroid plants [C18: from Latin: pulled-off branch of a palm, with its fruit, from Greek: torn-off frond; related to Greek *span* to pull off]

spaghetti (spəˈɡetɪ) *n* pasta in the form of long strings [C19: from Italian: little cords, from *spago* a cord]

spaghetti junction *n* an interchange, usually between motorways, in which there are a large number of underpasses and overpasses and intersecting roads used by a large volume of high-speed traffic [C20: from the nickname of the Gravelly Hill Interchange, Birmingham, where the M6, A38M, A38, and A5127 intersect]

spaghetti western *n* a cowboy film about the American West made, esp by an Italian director, in Europe

spahi *or* **spahee** ('spaːhiː, 'spaːiː) *n, pl* -his *or* -hees **1** (formerly) an irregular cavalryman in the Turkish armed forces **2** a member of a body of native Algerian cavalrymen in the French armed forces: disbanded after Algerian independence [C16: from Old French, from Turkish *sipahi*, from Persian *sipāhī* soldier; see SEPOY]

Spain (speɪn) *n* a kingdom of SW Europe, occupying the Iberian peninsula between the Mediterranean and the Atlantic: a leading European power in the 16th century, with many overseas possessions, esp in the New World; became a republic in 1931; under the fascist dictatorship of Franco following the Civil War (1936–39) until his death in 1975; a member of the European Union. It consists chiefly of a central plateau (the Meseta), with the Pyrenees and the Cantabrian Mountains in the north and the Sierra Nevada in the south. Official language: Castilian Spanish, with Catalan, Galician, and Basque official regional languages. Religion: Roman Catholic majority. Currency: euro. Capital: Madrid. Pop: 41 128 000 (2004 est). Area: 504 748 sq km (194 883 sq miles). Spanish name: **España**

spake (speɪk) *vb archaic or dialect* a past tense of **speak**

Spalato (spaːˈlato) *n* the Italian name for **Split**

Spalding ('spɔːldɪŋ) *n* a town in E England, in S Lincolnshire: noted for its bulbfields. Pop: 22 081 (2001)

Spallanzani (ˌspælənt'saːnɪ) *n* **Lazzaro**. 1729–99, Italian physiologist, noted esp for his experimental studies of microorganisms and his work on animal reproduction and digestion

spam (spæm) *computing slang* ▷ *vb* spams, spamming, spammed **1** to send unsolicited electronic mail simultaneously to a number of newsgroups on the internet ▷ *n* **2** unsolicited electronic mail or text messages sent in this way [C20: from the repeated use of the word *Spam* in a popular sketch from the British television show *Monty Python's Flying Circus*, first broadcast in 1969] > **'spammer** *n* > **'spamming** *n*

Spam (spæm) *n trademark* a kind of tinned luncheon meat, made largely from pork

spammie ('spæmɪ) *n Northern English dialect* a love bite

span¹ (spæn) *n* **1** the interval, space, or distance between two points, such as the ends of a bridge or arch **2** the complete duration or extent: *the span of his life* **3** *psychol* the amount of material that can be processed in a single mental act: *apprehension span; span of attention* **4** short for **wingspan** **5** a unit of length based on the width of an expanded hand, usually taken as nine inches ▷ *vb* spans, spanning, spanned (*tr*) **6** to stretch or extend across, over, or around **7** to provide with something that extends across or around: *to span a river with a bridge* **8** to measure or cover, esp with the extended hand [Old English *spann*; related to Old Norse *sponn*, Old High German *spanna*]

span² (spæn) *n* a team of horses or oxen, esp two matched animals [C16 (in the sense: yoke): from Middle Dutch: something stretched, from *spannen* to stretch; see SPAN¹]

span³ (spæn) *vb archaic or dialect* a past tense of **spin**

Span. *abbreviation* Spanish

spandrel *or* **spandril** ('spændrəl) *n architect* **1** an approximately triangular surface bounded by the outer curve of an arch and the adjacent wall **2** the surface area between two adjacent arches and the horizontal cornice above them [C15 *spaundrell*, from Anglo-French *spaundre* spandrel, from Old French *spandre* to spread, EXPAND]

spangle ('spæŋɡəl) *n* **1** a small thin piece of metal or other shiny material used as a decoration, esp on clothes; sequin **2** any glittering or shiny spot or object ▷ *vb* **3** (*intr*) to glitter or shine with or like spangles **4** (*tr*) to decorate or cover with spangles [C15: diminutive of *spange*, perhaps from Middle Dutch: clasp; compare Old

Norse *spöng*] >'spangly *adj*

Spaniard ('spænjəd) *n* a native or inhabitant of Spain

spaniel ('spænjəl) *n* 1 any of several breeds of gundog with long drooping ears, a silky coat, and formerly a docked tail 2 an obsequiously devoted person [C14: from Old French *espaigneul* Spanish (dog), from Old Provençal *espanhol*, ultimately from Latin *Hispāniolus* Spanish]

Spanish ('spænɪʃ) *n* 1 the official language of Spain, Mexico, and most countries of South and Central America except Brazil: also spoken in Africa, the Far East, and elsewhere. It is the native language of approximately 200 million people throughout the world. Spanish is an Indo-European language belonging to the Romance group 2 **the Spanish** (*functioning as plural*) Spaniards collectively ▷ *adj* 3 of or relating to the Spanish language or its speakers 4 of or relating to Spain or Spaniards

Spanish Armada *n* the great fleet sent by Philip II of Spain against England in 1588: defeated in the Channel by the English fleets and almost completely destroyed by storms off the Hebrides. Also called: **the Armada**

Spanish America *n* the parts of America colonized by Spaniards from the 16th century onwards and now chiefly Spanish-speaking: includes all of South America (except Brazil, Guyana, French Guiana, and Surinam), Central America (except Belize), Mexico, Cuba, Puerto Rico, the Dominican Republic, and a number of small Caribbean islands

Spanish-American *adj* 1 of or relating to any of the Spanish-speaking countries or peoples of the Americas ▷ *n* 2 a native or inhabitant of Spanish America 3 a Spanish-speaking person in the US

Spanish customs *or* **Spanish practices** *pl n informal* irregular practices among a group of workers to gain increased financial allowances, reduced working hours, etc

Spanish fly *n* 1 a European blister beetle, *Lytta vesicatoria* (family *Meloidae*), the dried bodies of which yield the pharmaceutical product cantharides 2 another name for **cantharides**

Spanish Guinea *n* the former name (until 1964) of **Equatorial Guinea**

Spanish guitar *n* the classic form of the guitar; a six-stringed guitar with a waisted body and a central sound hole

Spanish Main *n* 1 the mainland of Spanish America, esp the N coast of South America from the Isthmus of Panama to the mouth of the Orinoco River, Venezuela 2 the Caribbean Sea, the S part of which in colonial times was the route of Spanish treasure galleons and the haunt of pirates

Spanish Morocco *n* a former Spanish colony on the N coast of Morocco: part of the kingdom of Morocco since 1956 >**Spanish Moroccan** *adj*, *n*

Spanish moss *n* 1 an epiphytic bromeliaceous plant, *Tillandsia usneoides*, growing in tropical and subtropical regions as long bluish-grey strands suspended from the branches of trees 2 a tropical lichen, *Usnea longissima*, growing as long trailing green threads from the branches of trees

Spanish omelette *n* an omelette made by adding green peppers, onions, tomato, etc, to the eggs

Spanish rice *n* rice cooked with tomatoes, onions, green peppers, etc, and often flavoured with saffron

Spanish Sahara *n* the former name (until 1975) of **Western Sahara**

Spanish West Africa *n* a former overseas territory of Spain in NW Africa: divided in 1958 into the overseas provinces of Ifni and Spanish Sahara >**Spanish West African** *adj*, *n*

spank¹ (spæŋk) *vb* 1 (*tr*) to slap or smack with the open hand, esp on the buttocks ▷ *n* 2 a slap or series of slaps with the flat of the hand [C18: probably of imitative origin]

spank² (spæŋk) *vb* (*intr*) to go at a quick and lively pace [C19: back formation from SPANKING²]

spanker ('spæŋkə) *n* 1 *nautical* a fore-and-aft sail or a mast that is aftermost in a sailing vessel 2 *informal* something outstandingly fine or large

spanking¹ ('spæŋkɪŋ) *n* a series of spanks, esp on the buttocks, usually as a punishment for children

spanking² ('spæŋkɪŋ) *adj* (*prenominal*) 1 *informal* outstandingly fine, smart, large, etc 2 quick and energetic; lively 3 (esp of a breeze) fresh and brisk [C17: of uncertain origin. Compare Danish *spanke* to strut]

spanner ('spænə) *n* 1 a steel hand tool with a handle carrying jaws or a hole of particular shape designed to grip a nut or bolt head 2 *Brit informal* a source of impediment or annoyance (esp in the phrase **throw a spanner in the works**) [C17: from German, from *spannen* to stretch, SPAN¹]

span-new *adj archaic or dialect* absolutely new [C14: from Old Norse *spānnȳr*, from *spānn* chip + *nȳr* NEW]

span roof *n* a roof consisting of two equal sloping sides

spanspek ('spɑn,spek) *n South African* a sweet rough-skinned melon; a cantaloupe: family *Cucurbitaceae* [C19: possibly from Afrikaans: literally, Spanish bacon]

spar¹ (spɑː) *n* 1 any piece of nautical gear resembling a pole and used as a mast, boom, gaff, etc 2 a principal supporting structural member of an aerofoil that runs from tip to tip or root to tip [C13: from Old Norse *sperra* beam; related to Old High German *sparro*, Old French *esparre*]

spar² (spɑː) *vb* spars, sparring, sparred (*intr*) 1 *boxing*, *martial arts* to fight using light blows, as in training 2 to dispute or argue 3 (of gamecocks) to fight with the feet or spurs ▷ *n* 4 an unaggressive fight 5 an argument or wrangle [Old English, perhaps from SPUR]

spar³ (spɑː) *n* any of various minerals, such as feldspar or calcite, that are light-coloured, microcrystalline, transparent to translucent, and easily cleavable [C16: from Middle Low German *spar*; related to Old English *spærstān*; see FELDSPAR]

sparaxis (spə'ræksɪs) *n* any plant of the cormous S African genus *Sparaxis*, esp *S. grandiflora* and *S. tricolor*, grown for their dainty spikes of star-shaped purple, red, or orange flowers: family *Iridaceae* [New Latin, from Greek *sparassein* to tear (from the appearance of the spathes)]

spare (spɛə) *vb* 1 (*tr*) to refrain from killing, punishing, harming, or injuring 2 (*tr*) to release or relieve, as from pain, suffering, etc 3 (*tr*) to refrain from using: *spare the rod, spoil the child* 4 (*tr*) to be able to afford or give: *I can't spare the time* 5 (*usually passive*) (esp of Providence) to allow to survive: *I'll see you again next year if we are spared* 6 (*intr*) *now rare* to act or live frugally 7 **not spare oneself** to exert oneself to the full 8 **to spare** more than is required: *two minutes to spare* ▷ *adj* 9 (often immediately *postpositive*) in excess of what is needed; additional 10 able to be used when needed: *a spare part* 11 (of a person) thin and lean 12 scanty or meagre 13 (*postpositive*) *Brit slang* upset, angry, or distracted (esp in the phrase **go spare**) ▷ *n* 14 a duplicate kept as a replacement in case of damage or loss 15 a spare tyre 16 *tenpin bowling* **a** the act of knocking down all the pins with the two bowls of a single frame **b** the score thus made [Old English *sparian* to refrain from injuring; related to Old Norse *spara*, Old High German *sparōn*] >'sparely *adv* >'spareness *n* >'sparer *n*

spare-part surgery *n* surgical replacement of defective or damaged organs by transplant or insertion of artificial devices

sparerib (,spɛə'rɪb) *n* a cut of pork ribs with most of the meat trimmed off

spare tyre *n* 1 an additional tyre, usually mounted on a wheel, carried by a motor vehicle in case of puncture 2 *Brit slang, jocular* a deposit of fat just above the waist

sparing ('spɛərɪŋ) *adj* 1 (sometimes foll by *with* or *of*) economical or frugal (with) 2 scanty; meagre 3 merciful or lenient ▷ *adv* >'sparingly *adv* >'sparingness *n*

spark¹ (spɑːk) *n* 1 a a fiery particle thrown out or left by burning material or caused by the friction of two hard surfaces 2 a a momentary flash of light accompanied by a sharp crackling noise, produced by a sudden electrical discharge through the air or some other insulating medium between two points **b** the electrical discharge itself **c** (*as modifier*): *a spark gap* 3 anything that serves to animate, kindle, or excite 4 a trace or hint: *she doesn't* show a spark of interest **5** vivacity, enthusiasm, or humour **6** a small piece of diamond, as used in the cutting of glass ▷ *vb* **7** (*intr*) to give off sparks **8** (*intr*) (of the sparking plug or ignition system of an internal-combustion engine) to produce a spark **9** (*tr; often foll by off*) to kindle, excite, or animate ▷ See also **sparks** [Old English *spearca*; related to Middle Low German *sparke*, Middle Dutch *spranke*, Lettish *spirgsti* cinders, Latin *spargere* to strew]

spark² (spɑːk) *n rare* **1** a fashionable or gallant young man **2** bright spark *Brit usually ironic* a person who appears clever or witty ▷ *vb* **3** *rare* to woo (a person) [C16 (in the sense: beautiful or witty woman): perhaps of Scandinavian origin; compare Old Norse *sparkr* vivacious] > **'sparkish** *adj*

Spark (spɑːk) *n* Dame Muriel (Sarah). 1918–2006, British novelist and writer; her novels include *Memento Mori* (1959), *The Prime of Miss Jean Brodie* (1961), *The Takeover* (1976), *A Far Cry from Kensington* (1988), *Symposium* (1990), and *The Finishing School* (2004)

spark gap *n* the space between two electrodes across which a spark can jump

sparkie ('spɑːkɪ) *n* an informal name for **electrician**

sparking plug *n* a device screwed into the cylinder head of an internal-combustion engine to ignite the explosive mixture by means of an electric spark which jumps across a gap between a point earthed to the body of the plug and the tip of a central insulated rod. Also called: **spark plug**

sparkle ('spɑːkᵊl) *vb* **1** to issue or reflect or cause to issue or reflect bright points of light **2** (*intr*) (of wine, mineral water, etc) to effervesce **3** (*intr*) to be vivacious or witty ▷ *n* **4** a point of light, spark, or gleam **5** vivacity or wit [C12 *sparklen*, frequentative of *sparken* to SPARK¹]

sparkler ('spɑːklə) *n* **1** a type of firework that throws out showers of sparks **2** *informal* a sparkling gem

sparkling wine *n* a wine made effervescent by carbon dioxide gas, introduced artificially or produced naturally by secondary fermentation

spark plug *n* another name for **sparking plug**

sparks (spɑːks) *n* (*functioning as singular*) *informal* **1** an electrician **2** a radio officer, esp on a ship

sparky ('spɑːkɪ) *adj* sparkier, sparkiest lively; vivacious; spirited

sparring partner ('spɑːrɪŋ) *n* **1** a person who practises with a boxer during training **2** a person with whom one has friendly arguments

sparrow ('spærəʊ) *n* **1** any weaverbird of the genus *Passer* and related genera, esp the house sparrow, having a brown or grey plumage and feeding on seeds or insects **2** *US & Canadian* any of various North American finches, such as the chipping sparrow (*Spizella passerina*), that have a dullish streaked plumage ▷ See also **hedge sparrow, tree sparrow**, etc [Old English *spearwa*; related to Old Norse *spörr*, Old High German *sparo*]

sparrowgrass ('spærəʊˌgrɑːs) *n* a dialect or popular name for **asparagus** [C17: variant of ASPARAGUS, associated by folk etymology with SPARROW and GRASS]

sparrowhawk ('spærəʊˌhɔːk) *n* any of several small hawks, esp *Accipiter nisus*, of Eurasia and N Africa that prey on smaller birds

sparrow hawk *n* a very small North American falcon, *Falco sparverius*, that is closely related to the kestrels

sparse (spɑːs) *adj* scattered or scanty; not dense [C18: from Latin *sparsus*, from *spargere* to scatter] > **'sparsely** *adv* > **'sparseness** or **'sparsity** *n*

Sparta ('spɑːtə) *n* an ancient Greek city in the S Peloponnese, famous for the discipline and military prowess of its citizens and for their austere way of life

Spartacus ('spɑːtəkəs) *n* died 71 BC, Thracian slave, who led an ultimately unsuccessful revolt of gladiators against Rome (73–71 BC)

Spartan ('spɑːtᵊn) *adj* **1** of or relating to Sparta or its citizens **2** (*sometimes not capital*) very strict or austere: *a Spartan upbringing* **3** (*sometimes not capital*) possessing courage and resolve ▷ *n* **4** a citizen of Sparta (*sometimes not capital*) **5** (*sometimes not capital*) a disciplined or brave person

spasm ('spæzəm) *n* **1** an involuntary muscular contraction, esp one resulting in cramp or convulsion

2 a sudden burst of activity, emotion, etc [C14: from Latin *spasmus*, from Greek *spasmos* a cramp, from *span* to tear]

spasmodic (spæz'mɒdɪk) *or rarely* **spasmodical** *adj* **1** taking place in sudden brief spells **2** of or characterized by spasms [C17: New Latin, from Greek *spasmos* SPASM] > **spas'modically** *adv*

Spassky ('spæskɪ; *Russian* 'spaskij) *n* **Boris** (ba'ris). born 1937, Russian chess player; world champion (1969–72)

spastic ('spæstɪk) *n* **1** an old-fashioned and now offensive name for a person who has cerebral palsy **2** *taboo, slang* a clumsy, incapable, or incompetent person ▷ *adj* **3** affected by or resembling spasms **4** *taboo, slang* clumsy, incapable or incompetent [C18: from Latin *spasticus*, from Greek *spastikos*, from *spasmos* SPASM] > **'spastically** *adv* > **spasticity** (spæs'tɪsɪtɪ) *n*

spat¹ (spæt) *n* **1** *now rare* a slap or smack **2** a slight quarrel ▷ *vb* spats, spatting, spatted **3** *now rare* to slap (someone) **4** (*intr*) *US, Canadian & NZ* to have a slight quarrel [C19: probably imitative of the sound of quarrelling]

spat² (spæt) *vb* a past tense and past participle of **spit¹**

spat³ (spæt) *n* another name for **gaiter** (sense 2) [C19: short for SPATTERDASH]

spat⁴ (spæt) *n* **1** a larval oyster or similar bivalve mollusc, esp when it settles to the sea bottom and starts to develop a shell **2** such oysters or other molluscs collectively [C17: from Anglo-Norman *spat*; perhaps related to SPIT¹]

spatchcock ('spætʃˌkɒk) *n* **1** a chicken or game bird split down the back and grilled ▷ *vb* (*tr*) **2** to interpolate (words, a story, etc) into a sentence, narrative, etc, esp inappropriately [C18: perhaps variant of *spitchcock* eel when prepared and cooked]

spate (speɪt) *n* **1** a fast flow, rush, or outpouring: *a spate of words* **2** *chiefly Brit* a sudden flood: *the rivers were in spate* **3** *chiefly Brit* a sudden heavy downpour [C15 (Northern and Scottish): of unknown origin]

spathe (speɪð) *n* a large bract, often coloured, that surrounds the inflorescence of aroid plants and palms [C18: from Latin *spatha*, from Greek *spathē* a blade] > **spathaceous** (spə'θeɪʃəs) *adj*

spathic ('spæθɪk) *or* **spathose** ('spæθəʊs) *adj* (of minerals) resembling spar, esp in having good cleavage [C18: from German *Spat*, *Spath* SPAR³; related to Old High German *spān* chip; see SPOON]

spatial *or* **spacial** ('speɪʃəl) *adj* **1** of or relating to space **2** existing or happening in space > **spatiality** (ˌspeɪʃɪ'ælɪtɪ) *n* > **'spatially** *adv*

spatiotemporal (ˌspeɪʃɪəʊ'tempərəl, -'temprəl) *adj* **1** of or existing in both space and time **2** of or concerned with space-time [C20: from Latin *spatium* space + *temporālis*, from *tempus* time] > **ˌspatio'temporally** *adv*

spatter ('spætə) *vb* **1** to scatter or splash (a substance, esp a liquid) or (of a substance) to splash (something) in scattered drops: *to spatter mud on the car; mud spattered in her face* **2** (*tr*) to sprinkle, cover, or spot (with a liquid) **3** (*tr*) to slander or defame **4** (*intr*) to shower or rain down: *bullets spattered around them* ▷ *n* **5** the sound of something spattering **6** something spattered, such as a spot or splash **7** the act or an instance of spattering [C16: of imitative origin; related to Low German, Dutch *spatten* to spout, Frisian *spatteren* to splash]

spatterdash ('spætəˌdæʃ) *n* **1** *US* another name for **roughcast** **2** (*plural*) long leather leggings worn in the 18th century, as to protect from mud when riding [C17: see SPATTER, DASH¹]

spatula ('spætjʊlə) *n* a utensil with a broad flat, often flexible blade, used for lifting, spreading, or stirring foods, etc [C16: from Latin: a broad piece, from *spatha* a flat wooden implement; see SPATHE] > **'spatular** *adj*

spatulate ('spætjʊlɪt) *adj* **1** shaped like a spatula **2** Also called: **spathulate** *botany* having a narrow base and a broad rounded apex

spavin ('spævɪn) *n vet science* enlargement of the hock of a horse by a bony growth (**bony spavin**) or fluid accumulation in the joint (**bog spavin**), usually caused by inflammation or injury, and often resulting in lameness [C15: from Old French *espavin*, of unknown origin] > **'spavined** *adj*

S

spawn (spɔːn) n 1 the mass of eggs deposited by fish, amphibians, or molluscs 2 *often derogatory* offspring, product, or yield 3 *botany* the nontechnical name for **mycelium** ▷ vb 4 (of fish, amphibians, etc) to produce or deposit (eggs) 5 *often derogatory* (of people) to produce (offspring) 6 (tr) to produce or engender [c14: from Anglo-Norman *espaundre*, from Old French *spandre* to spread out, EXPAND] >'spawner n

spay (speɪ) vb (tr) to remove the ovaries, and usually the uterus, from (a female animal) [c15: from Old French *espeer* to cut with the sword, from *espee* sword, from Latin *spatha*]

spaza shop ('spɑːzə) n *South African slang* a small informal shop in a township, often run from a private house [from township slang: dummy, camouflaged]

SPCK *abbreviation* (in Britain) Society for Promoting Christian Knowledge

speak (spiːk) vb speaks, speaking, spoke, spoken 1 to make (verbal utterances); utter (words) 2 to communicate or express (something) in or as if in words 3 (intr) to deliver a speech, discourse, etc 4 (tr) to know how to talk in (a language or dialect): *he does not speak German* 5 (intr) to make a characteristic sound: *the clock spoke* 6 (intr) (of dogs, esp hounds used in hunting) to give tongue; bark 7 (tr) *nautical* to hail and converse or communicate with (another vessel) at sea 8 (intr) (of a musical instrument) to produce a sound 9 on speaking terms on good terms; friendly 10 so to speak in a manner of speaking; as it were 11 speak one's mind to express one's opinions frankly and plainly 12 to speak of of a significant or worthwhile nature: *we have had no support to speak of* ▷ See also **speak for, speak out**, etc [Old English *specan*; related to Old High German *spehhan*, Middle High German *spechten* to gossip, Middle Dutch *speken*; see SPEECH] >'speakable adj

speakeasy ('spiːkˌiːzɪ) n, pl-easies US a place where alcoholic drink was sold illicitly during Prohibition [c19: from SPEAK + EASY (in the sense: gently, quietly)]

speaker ('spiːkə) n 1 a person who speaks, esp at a formal occasion 2 See **loudspeaker** >'speakership n

Speaker ('spiːkə) n the presiding officer in any of numerous legislative bodies, including the House of Commons in Britain and Canada and the House of Representatives in the US, Australia, and New Zealand

speakerphone ('spiːkəˌfəʊn) n a telephone incorporating an external microphone and loudspeaker, allowing several people to participate in a call at the same time

speak for vb (intr, preposition) 1 to speak as a representative of (other people) 2 speak for itself to be so evident that no further comment is necessary 3 speak for yourself *informal* (used as an imperative) do not presume that other people agree with you

speaking ('spiːkɪŋ) adj 1 (prenominal) eloquent, impressive, or striking 2 a able to speak b (in combination) able to speak a particular language: *French-speaking*

speaking clock n Brit a telephone service that gives a precise verbal statement of the correct time

speaking in tongues n another term for **gift of tongues**

speaking tube n a tube or pipe for conveying a person's voice from one room, area, or building to another

speak out vb (intr, adverb) 1 to state one's beliefs, objections, etc, bravely and firmly 2 to speak more loudly and clearly

speak to vb (intr, preposition) 1 to address (a person) 2 to reprimand 3 *formal* to give evidence of or comments on (a subject)

speak up vb (intr, adverb) 1 to speak more loudly 2 to state one's beliefs, objections, etc, bravely and firmly

spear¹ (spɪə) n 1 a weapon consisting of a long shaft with a sharp pointed end of metal, stone, or wood that may be thrown or thrust 2 a similar implement used to catch fish 3 another name for **spearman** ▷ vb 4 to pierce (something) with or as if with a spear [Old English *spere*; related to Old Norse *spjör* spears, Greek *sparos* gilthead]

spear² (spɪə) n a shoot, slender stalk or blade, as of grass, asparagus, or broccoli [c16: probably variant of SPIRE¹, influenced by SPEAR¹]

spear grass n NZ any of various grasses with sharp stiff blades or seeds

spear gun n a device for shooting spears underwater

spearhead ('spɪəˌhɛd) n 1 the pointed head of a spear 2 the leading force in a military attack 3 any person or thing that leads or initiates an attack, a campaign, etc ▷ vb 4 (tr) to lead or initiate (an attack, a campaign, etc)

spearman ('spɪəmən) n, pl-men a soldier armed with a spear

spearmint ('spɪəmɪnt) n a purple-flowered mint plant, *Mentha spicata*, of S and central Europe, cultivated for its leaves, which yield an oil used for flavouring [c16: so called because of its long narrow leaves]

Spears (spɪəz) n **Britney** ('brɪtnɪ). born 1981, US pop singer; records include the single "Baby One More Time" (1998) and the album *Britney* (2001)

spec (spɛk) *informal* ▷ n 1 on spec as a speculation or gamble: *all the tickets were sold so I went to the theatre on spec* ▷ adj 2 (prenominal) Austral & NZ speculative: *a spec developer* [c19: short for SPECULATION or SPECULATIVE]

spec. *abbreviation* 1 specification 2 speculation

speccy ('spɛkɪ) adj speccier, specciest *slang* wearing spectacles

special ('spɛʃəl) adj 1 distinguished, set apart from, or excelling others of its kind 2 (prenominal) designed or reserved for a particular purpose 3 not usual or commonplace 4 (prenominal) particular or primary: *his special interest was music* ▷ n 5 a special person or thing, such as an extra edition of a newspaper or a train reserved for a particular purpose 6 a dish or meal given prominence, esp at a low price, in a café, etc 7 short for **special constable** 8 Austral, NZ, US & Canadian informal an item in a store that is advertised at a reduced price; a loss leader ▷ vb -cials, -cialling, -cialled (tr) 9 NZ informal to advertise and sell (an item) at a reduced price [c13: from Old French *especial*, from Latin *speciālis* individual, special, from *speciēs* appearance, SPECIES] >'specially adv >'specialness n

Special Branch n (in Britain) the department of the police force that is concerned with political security

special clearing n banking (in Britain) the clearing of a cheque through a bank in less than the usual three days, for an additional charge

special constable n a person recruited for temporary or occasional police duties, esp in time of emergency

special delivery n the delivery of a piece of mail outside the time of a scheduled delivery

special drawing rights pl n (sometimes capitals) the reserve assets of the International Monetary Fund on which member nations may draw in proportion to their contribution to the Fund

special effects pl n *films* techniques used in the production of scenes that cannot be achieved by normal techniques

special forces pl n élite, highly trained military forces, specially selected to work on difficult missions

specialist ('spɛʃəlɪst) n a person who specializes in or devotes himself to a particular area of activity, field of research, etc >ˌspecial'istic adj >'specialˌism n

specialist registrar n a hospital doctor senior to a house officer but junior to a consultant, specializing in medicine (**medical specialist registrar**), surgery (**surgical specialist registrar**), or some subspeciality of either

speciality (ˌspɛʃɪ'ælɪtɪ) or chiefly US and Canadian **specialty** n, pl-ties 1 a special interest or skill 2 a service or product specialized in, as at a restaurant b (as modifier): *a speciality dish* 3 a special or distinguishing feature or characteristic

specialize or **specialise** ('spɛʃəˌlaɪz) vb 1 (intr) to train in or devote oneself to a particular area of study, occupation, or activity 2 (usually passive) to cause (organisms or their parts) to develop in a way most suited to a particular environment or way of life or (of organisms, etc) to develop in this way 3 (tr) to modify or make suitable for a special use or purpose >ˌspecialiˈzation or ˌspecialiˈsation n

special licence n Brit a licence permitting a marriage to take place by dispensing with the usual legal conditions

special needs or **special educational needs** pl n a the educational requirements of pupils or students suffering from any of a wide range of physical disabilities, medical conditions, intellectual difficulties, or emotional problems, including deafness, blindness, dyslexia, learning difficulties, and behavioural problems **b** (*as modifier*): *special-needs teachers*

special pleading *n law* **1** a pleading that alleges new facts that offset those put forward by the other side rather than directly admitting or denying those facts **2** a pleading that emphasizes the favourable aspects of a case while omitting the unfavourable

special school *n Brit* a school for children who are unable to benefit from ordinary schooling because they have learning difficulties, physical or mental handicaps, etc

special team *n American football* any of several predetermined permutations of the players within a team that play in situations, such as kickoffs and attempts at field goals, where the standard offensive and defensive formations are not appropriate

specialty ('spɛʃəltɪ) *n*, *pl* **-ties 1** *law* a formal contract or obligation expressed in a deed. **2** another for for **speciality**

speciation (ˌspiːʃɪˈeɪʃən) *n* the evolutionary development of a biological species, as by geographical isolation of a group of individuals from the main stock [C20: from SPECIES + -ATION]

specie ('spiːʃiː) *n* **1** coin money, as distinguished from bullion or paper money **2** in specie **a** (of money) in coin **b** in kind [C16: from the Latin phrase *in speciē* in kind]

species ('spiːʃiːz; *Latin* 'spiːʃɪˌiːz) *n*, *pl* **-cies 1** *biology* **a** any of the taxonomic groups into which a genus is divided, the members of which are capable of interbreeding: often containing subspecies, varieties, or races. A species is designated in italics by the genus name followed by the specific name, for example *Felis domesticus* (the domestic cat) **b** the animals of such a group **c** any group of related animals or plants not necessarily of this taxonomic rank **2** (*modifier*) denoting a plant that is a natural member of a species rather than a hybrid or cultivar: *a species clematis* **3** *logic* a group of objects or individuals, all sharing at least one common attribute, that forms a subdivision of a genus **4** a kind, sort, or variety: *a species of treachery* **5** *chiefly RC Church* the outward form of the bread and wine in the Eucharist **6** *obsolete* an outward appearance or form [C16: from Latin: appearance, from *specere* to look]

specific (spɪˈsɪfɪk) *adj* **1** explicit, particular, or definite **2** relating to a specified or particular thing: *a specific treatment for arthritis* **3** of or relating to a biological species **4** (of a disease) caused by a particular pathogenic agent **5** *physics* **a** characteristic of a property of a particular substance, esp in relation to the same property of a standard reference substance: *specific gravity* **b** characteristic of a property of a particular substance per unit mass, length, area, volume, etc: *specific heat* **c** (of an extensive physical quantity) divided by mass: *specific heat capacity; specific volume* **6** *international trade* denoting a tariff levied at a fixed sum per unit of weight, quantity, volume, etc, irrespective of value ▷ *n* **7** (*sometimes plural*) a designated quality, thing, etc **8** *med* any drug used to treat a particular disease [C17: from Medieval Latin *specificus*, from Latin SPECIES] > spe'cifically *adv* > specificity (ˌspɛsɪˈfɪsɪtɪ) *n*

specification (ˌspɛsɪfɪˈkeɪʃən) *n* **1** the act or an instance of specifying **2** (in patent law) a written statement accompanying an application for a patent that describes the nature of an invention **3** a detailed description of the criteria for the constituents, construction, appearance, performance, etc, of a material, apparatus, etc, or of the standard of workmanship required in its manufacture **4** an item, detail, etc, specified

specific charge *n physics* the charge-to-mass ratio of an elementary particle

specific gravity *n* the ratio of the density of a substance to that of water

specific heat capacity *n* the heat required to raise unit mass of a substance by unit temperature interval under specified conditions, such as constant pressure: usually measured in joules per kelvin per kilogram. Also called:

specific heat

specific humidity *n* the mass of water vapour in a sample of moist air divided by the mass of the sample

specific volume *n physics* the volume of matter per unit mass; the reciprocal of the density

specify ('spɛsɪˌfaɪ) *vb* **-fies**, **-fying**, **-fied** (*tr; may take a clause as object*) **1** to refer to or state specifically **2** to state as a condition **3** to state or include in the specification of [C13: from Medieval Latin *specificāre* to describe] > specificative (ˈspɛsɪfɪˌkeɪtɪv) *adj* > 'speci,fiable *adj*

specimen ('spɛsɪmɪn) *n* **1 a** an individual, object, or part regarded as typical of the group or class to which it belongs **b** (*as modifier*): *a specimen signature; a specimen page* **2** *med* a sample of tissue, blood, urine, etc, taken for diagnostic examination or evaluation **3** the whole or a part of an organism, plant, rock, etc, collected and preserved as an example of its class, species, etc **4** *informal, often derogatory* a person [C17: from Latin: mark, evidence, proof, from *specere* to look at]

specious ('spiːʃəs) *adj* **1** apparently correct or true, but actually wrong or false **2** deceptively attractive in appearance [C14 (originally: fair): from Latin *speciōsus* plausible, from *speciēs* outward appearance, from *specere* to look at] > 'speciously *adv* > 'speciousness *n* > speciosity (ˌspiːʃɪˈɒsɪtɪ) *n*

speck (spɛk) *n* **1 a** a very small mark or spot **2** a small or tiny piece of something ▷ *vb* **3** (*tr*) to mark with specks or spots [Old English *specca*; related to Middle Dutch *spekelen* to sprinkle]

speckle ('spɛkəl) *n* **1** a small or slight mark usually of a contrasting colour, as on the skin, a bird's plumage, or eggs ▷ *vb* **2** (*tr*) to mark with or as if with speckles [C15: from Middle Dutch *spekkel*; see SPECK] > 'speckled *adj*

specs (spɛks) *pl n informal* short for **spectacles**

spectacle ('spɛktəkəl) *n* **1** a public display or performance, esp a showy or ceremonial one **2** a thing or person seen, esp an unusual or ridiculous one: *he makes a spectacle of himself* **3** a strange or interesting object or phenomenon [C14: via Old French from Latin *spectaculum* a show, from *spectāre* to watch, from *specere* to look at]

spectacles ('spɛktəkəlz) *pl n* a pair of glasses for correcting defective vision. Often (*informal*) shortened to **specs** > 'spectacled *adj*

spectacular (spɛkˈtækjʊlə) *adj* **1** of or resembling a spectacle; impressive, grand, or dramatic **2** unusually marked or great: *a spectacular increase in spending* ▷ *n* **3** a lavishly produced performance > spec'tacularly *adv*

spectate (spɛkˈteɪt) *vb* (*intr*) to be a spectator, esp at a sporting event; watch [C20: back formation from SPECTATOR]

spectator (spɛkˈteɪtə) *n* a person viewing anything; onlooker; observer [C16: from Latin, from *spectāre* to watch; see SPECTACLE]

spectator sport *n* a sport that attracts more people as spectators than as participants

Spector ('spɛktə) *n* **Phil.** born 1940, US record producer and songwriter, noted for the densely orchestrated "Wall of Sound" in his work with groups such as the Ronettes and the Crystals; arrested on a murder charge in 2003

spectra ('spɛktrə) *n* the plural of **spectrum**

spectral ('spɛktrəl) *adj* **1** of or like a spectre **2** of or relating to a spectrum > spectrality (spɛkˈtrælɪtɪ) *n* > 'spectrally *adv*

spectral type *or* **spectral class** *n* any of various groups into which stars are classified according to characteristic spectral lines and bands. The most important classification (**Harvard classification**) has a series of classes O, B, A, F, G, K, M, the series also being a scale of diminishing surface temperature

spectre *or US* **specter** ('spɛktə) *n* **1** a ghost; phantom; apparition **2** a mental image of something unpleasant or menacing: *the spectre of redundancy* [C17: from Latin *spectrum*, from *specere* to look at]

spectro- *combining form* indicating a spectrum: *spectrogram*

spectrograph ('spɛktrəʊˌɡrɑːf, -ˌɡræf) *n* a spectroscope or spectrometer that produces a photographic record (**spectrogram**) of a spectrum. See also **sound**

spectrograph > ˌspectro'graphic *adj*
> ˌspectro'graphically *adv* > spec'trography *n*
spectroheliograph (ˌspɛktrəʊ'hiːlɪəˌɡrɑːf, -ˌɡræf) *n* an instrument used to obtain an image of the sun in light of a particular wavelength, such as calcium or hydrogen, to show the distribution of the element over the surface and in the solar atmosphere. The image obtained is a **spectroheliogram** [C19: from SPECTRO- + HELIO- + -GRAPH] > ˌspectroˌhelio'graphic *adj*
spectrometer (spɛk'trɒmɪtə) *n* any instrument for producing a spectrum, esp one in which wavelength, energy, intensity, etc, can be measured. See also **mass spectrometer** > spectrometric (ˌspɛktrəʊ'mɛtrɪk) *adj* > spec'trometry *n*
spectrophotometer (ˌspɛktrəʊfəʊ'tɒmɪtə) *n* an instrument for producing or recording a spectrum and measuring the photometric intensity of each wavelength present, esp such an instrument used for infrared, visible, and ultraviolet radiation [C19: from SPECTRO- + PHOTO- + -METER] > spectrophotometric (ˌspɛktrəʊˌfəʊtə'mɛtrɪk) *adj* > ˌspectropho'tometry *n*
spectroscope ('spɛktrəˌskəʊp) *n* any of a number of instruments for dispersing electromagnetic radiation and thus forming or recording a spectrum [C19: from SPECTRO- + -SCOPE; from French, or on the model of German *Spektroskop*] > spectroscopic (ˌspɛktrə'skɒpɪk) or ˌspectro'scopical *adj*
spectroscopy (spɛk'trɒskəpɪ) *n* the science and practice of using spectrometers and spectroscopes and of analysing spectra, the methods employed depending on the radiation being examined. The techniques are widely used in chemical analysis and in studies of the properties of atoms, molecules, ions, etc
> spec'troscopist *n*
spectrum ('spɛktrəm) *n*, *pl* -tra (-trə) 1 the distribution of colours produced when white light is dispersed by a prism or diffraction grating. There is a continuous change in wavelength from red, the longest wavelength, to violet, the shortest Seven colours are usually distinguished: violet, indigo, blue, green, yellow, orange, and red 2 the whole range of electromagnetic radiation with respect to its wavelength or frequency 3 any particular distribution of electromagnetic radiation often showing lines or bands characteristic of the substance emitting the radiation or absorbing it 4 any similar distribution or record of the energies, velocities, masses, etc, of atoms, ions, electrons, etc: *a mass spectrum* 5 any range or scale, as of capabilities, emotions, or moods 6 another name for an **afterimage** [C17: from Latin: appearance, image, from *spectāre* to observe, from *specere* to look at]
spectrum analysis *n* the analysis of a spectrum to determine the properties of its source, such as the analysis of the emission spectrum of a substance to determine the electron distribution in its molecules
specular ('spɛkjʊlə) *adj* 1 of, relating to, or having the properties of a mirror 2 of or relating to a speculum [C16: from Latin *speculāris*, from *speculum* a mirror, from *specere* to look at]
speculate ('spɛkjʊˌleɪt) *vb* 1 (when *tr, takes a clause as object*) to conjecture without knowing the complete facts 2 (*intr*) to buy or sell securities, property, etc, in the hope of deriving capital gains 3 (*intr*) to risk loss for the possibility of considerable gain 4 (*intr*) NZ *rugby* to make an emergency forward kick of the ball without taking any particular aim [C16: from Latin *speculārī* to spy out, from *specula* a watchtower, from *specere* to look at]
speculation (ˌspɛkjʊ'leɪʃən) *n* 1 the act or an instance of speculating 2 a supposition, theory, or opinion arrived at through speculating 3 investment involving high risk but also the possibility of high profits
> 'speculative *adj*
speculative fiction *n* a broad literary genre encompassing any fiction with supernatural, fantastical or futuristic elements [C20]
speculator ('spɛkjʊˌleɪtə) *n* 1 a person who speculates 2 NZ *rugby* an undirected kick of the ball
speculum ('spɛkjʊləm) *n*, *pl* -la (-lə) or -lums 1 a mirror, esp one made of polished metal for use in a telescope,

etc 2 *med* an instrument for dilating a bodily cavity or passage to permit examination of its interior 3 a patch of distinctive colour on the wing of a bird, esp in certain ducks [C16: from Latin: mirror, from *specere* to look at]
sped (spɛd) *vb* a past tense and past participle of **speed**
speech (spiːtʃ) *n* 1 a the act or faculty of speaking, esp as possessed by persons b (*as modifier*): *speech therapy* 2 that which is spoken; utterance 3 a talk or address delivered to an audience 4 a person's characteristic manner of speaking 5 a national or regional language or dialect 6 *linguistics* another word for **parole** (sense 3) [Old English *spēc*; related to *specan* to SPEAK]
speech day *n* *Brit* (in schools) an annual day on which prizes are presented, speeches are made by guest speakers, etc
speechify ('spiːtʃɪˌfaɪ) *vb* -fies, -fying, -fied (*intr*) 1 to make a speech or speeches 2 to talk pompously and boringly > 'speechiˌfier *n*
speechless ('spiːtʃlɪs) *adj* 1 not able to speak 2 temporarily deprived of speech 3 not expressed or able to be expressed in words: *speechless fear* > 'speechlessly *adv* > 'speechlessness *n*
speed (spiːd) *n* 1 the act or quality of acting or moving fast; rapidity 2 the rate at which something moves, is done, or acts 3 *physics* a scalar measure of the rate of movement of a body expressed either as the distance travelled divided by the time taken (**average speed**) or the rate of change of position with respect to time at a particular point (**instantaneous speed**). It is measured in metres per second, miles per hour, etc 4 a rate of rotation, usually expressed in revolutions per unit time 5 a a gear ratio in a motor vehicle, bicycle, etc b (*in combination*): *a three-speed gear* 6 *photog* a numerical expression of the sensitivity to light of a particular type of film, paper, or plate. See also **ISO rating** 7 *photog* a measure of the ability of a lens to pass light from an object to the image position, determined by the aperture and also the transmitting power of the lens. It increases as the f-number is decreased and vice versa 8 a slang word for **amphetamine** 9 *archaic* prosperity or success 10 at speed quickly 11 up to speed a operating at an acceptable or competitive level b in possession of all the relevant or necessary information ▷ *vb* speeds, speeding, sped *or* speeded 12 to move or go or cause to move or go quickly 13 (*intr*) to drive (a motor vehicle) at a high speed, esp above legal limits 14 (*tr*) to help further the success or completion of 15 (*intr*) *slang* to take or be under the influence of amphetamines 16 (*intr*) to operate or run at a high speed 17 *archaic* a (*intr*) to prosper or succeed b (*tr*) to wish success to ▷ See also **speed up** [Old English *spēd* (originally in the sense: success); related to *spōwan* to succeed, Latin *spēs* hope, Old Slavonic *spěti* to be lucky] > 'speeder *n*
speedball ('spiːdˌbɔːl) *n* *slang* a mixture of heroin with amphetamine or cocaine
speedboat ('spiːdˌbəʊt) *n* a high-speed motorboat having either an inboard or outboard motor
speed camera *n* a fixed camera that photographs vehicles breaking the speed limit on a certain stretch of road
speed chess *n* a form of chess in which each player's game is limited to a total stipulated time, usually half an hour; the first player to exceed the time limit loses
speed dating *n* a method of meeting potential partners in which each participant has only a few minutes to talk to each of his or her dates before being moved on to the next one. At the end of the event, paticipants decide which dates they would like to see again
speed limit *n* the maximum permitted speed at which a vehicle may travel on certain roads
speedo ('spiːdəʊ) *n*, *pl* speedos an informal name for **speedometer, odometer**
speedometer (spɪ'dɒmɪtə) *n* a device fitted to a vehicle to measure and display the speed of travel. See also **mileometer**
speed ramp *n* *Brit* a raised band across a road, designed to make motorists reduce their speed, esp in built-up areas
speed trap *n* a section of road on which the police check

the speed of vehicles, often using radar

speed up *vb* (*adverb*) **1** to increase or cause to increase in speed or rate; accelerate ▷ *n* **speed-up 2** an instance of this; acceleration

● USAGE The past tense and past participle of *speed up* is
● *speeded up*, not *sped up*

speedway ('spiːdˌweɪ) *n* **1** the sport of racing on light powerful motorcycles round cinder tracks **2** the track or stadium where such races are held **3** *US & Canadian* **a** a racetrack for cars **b** a road on which fast driving is allowed

speedwell ('spiːdˌwɛl) *n* any of various temperate scrophulariaceous plants of the genus *Veronica*, such as *V. officinalis* (**heath speedwell**) and *V. chamaedrys* (**germander speedwell**), having small blue or pinkish white flowers [c16: from SPEED + WELL[1]]

speedy ('spiːdɪ) *adj* **speedier, speediest 1** characterized by speed of motion **2** done or decided without delay; quick >'**speedily** *adv* >'**speediness** *n*

spek (spek) *n* *South African* bacon, fat, or fatty pork used for larding venison or other game [Afrikaans]

speleology or**spelaeology** (ˌspiːlɪ'ɒlədʒɪ) *n* **1** the scientific study of caves, esp in respect of their geological formation, flora and fauna, etc **2** the sport or pastime of exploring caves [c19: from Latin *spēlaeum* cave] >**speleological** or**spelaeological** (ˌspiːlɪə'lɒdʒɪk²l) *adj* >ˌspele'ologist or ˌspelae'ologist *n*

spell[1] (spɛl) *vb* **spells, spelling, spelt** or**spelled 1** to write or name in correct order the letters that comprise the conventionally accepted form of (a word or part of a word) **2** (*tr*) (of letters) to go to make up the conventionally established form of (a word) when arranged correctly: *d-o-g spells dog* **3** (*tr*) to indicate or signify: *such actions spell disaster for our cause* ▷ See also **spell out** [c13: from Old French *espeller*, of Germanic origin; related to Old Norse *spialla* to talk, Middle High German *spellen*] >'**spellable** *adj*

spell[2] (spɛl) *n* **1 a** a verbal formula considered as having magical force **2** any influence that can control the mind or character; fascination **3** a state induced by or as if by the pronouncing of a spell; trance: *to break the spell* **4** under a spell **held** in or as if in a spell ▷ *vb* **5** (*tr*) *rare* to place under a spell [Old English *spell* speech; related to Old Norse *spjall* tale, Gothic *spill*, Old High German *spel*]

spell[3] (spɛl) *n* **1** an indeterminate, usually short, period of time: *a spell of cold weather* **2** a period or tour of duty after which one person or group relieves another **3** *Scot, Austral & NZ* a period or interval of rest ▷ *vb* **4** (*tr*) to take over from (a person) for an interval of time; relieve temporarily [Old English *spelian* to take the place of, of obscure origin]

spellbind ('spɛlˌbaɪnd) *vb* **-binds, -binding, -bound** (*tr*) to cause to be spellbound; entrance or enthral

spellbound ('spɛlˌbaʊnd) *adj* having one's attention held as though one is bound by a spell

spellchecker ('spɛlˌtʃɛkə) *n* *computing* a program that highlights any word in a word-processed document that is not recognized as being correctly spelt

speller ('spɛlə) *n* **1** a person who spells words in the manner specified: *a bad speller* **2** a book designed to teach or improve spelling

spelling ('spɛlɪŋ) *n* **1** the act or process of writing words by using the letters conventionally accepted for their formation; orthography **2** the art or study of orthography **3** the actual way in which a word is spelt **4** the ability of a person to spell

spelling bee *n* a contest in which players are required to spell words according to orthographic conventions [c19: from BEE[2]]

spell out *vb* (*tr, adverb*) **1** to make clear, distinct, or explicit; clarify in detail: *let me spell out the implications* **2** to read laboriously or with difficulty, working out each word letter by letter **3** to discern by study; puzzle out

spelt[1] (spɛlt) *vb* a past tense and past participle of **spell**[1]

spelt[2] (spɛlt) *n* a species of wheat, *Triticum spelta*, that was formerly much cultivated and was used to develop present-day cultivated wheats [Old English; related to Old Saxon *spelta*, Old High German *spelza*]

spelter ('spɛltə) *n* impure zinc, usually containing

about 3 per cent of lead and other impurities [c17: probably from Middle Dutch *speauter*, of obscure origin; compare Old French *peautre* pewter, Italian *peltro* PEWTER]

spelunker (spɪ'lʌŋkə) *n* a person whose hobby is the exploration and study of caves [c20: from Latin *spēlunca*, from Greek *spēlunx* a cave] >spe'lunking *n*

Spence (spɛns) *n* Sir **Basil** (**Unwin**). 1907-76, Scottish architect, born in India; designed Coventry Cathedral (1951)

spencer[1] ('spɛnsə) *n* **1** a short fitted coat or jacket **2** a woman's knitted vest [c18: named after Earl *Spencer* (1758-1834)]

spencer[2] ('spɛnsə) *n* *nautical* a large loose-footed gaffsail on a square-rigger or barque [c19: perhaps after the surname *Spencer*]

Spencer ('spɛnsə) *n* **1 Herbert**. 1820-1903, English philosopher, who applied evolutionary theory to the study of society, favouring laissez-faire doctrines **2** Sir **Stanley**. 1891-1959, English painter, noted esp for his paintings of Christ in a contemporary English setting

Spencer Gulf *n* an inlet of the Indian Ocean in S Australia, between the Eyre and Yorke Peninsulas. Length: about 320 km (200 miles). Greatest width: about 145 km (90 miles)

spend (spɛnd) *vb* **spends, spending, spent 1** to pay out (money, wealth, etc) **2** (*tr*) to concentrate (time, effort, thought, etc) upon an object, activity, etc **3** (*tr*) to pass (time) in a specific way, activity, place, etc **4** (*tr*) to use up completely: *the hurricane spent its force* **5** (*tr*) to give up (one's blood, life, etc) in a cause [Old English *spendan*, from Latin *expendere*; influenced also by Old French *despendre* to spend, from Latin *dispendere*; see EXPEND, DISPENSE] >'**spendable** *adj*

Spender ('spɛndə) *n* Sir **Stephen**. 1909-95, English poet and critic, who played an important part in the left-wing literary movement of the 1930s. His works include *Journals 1939-83* (1985) and *Collected Poems* (1985)

spendthrift ('spɛnd,θrɪft) *n* **1** a person who spends money in an extravagant manner ▷ *adj* **2** (*usually prenominal*) of or like a spendthrift [c17: from SPEND + THRIFT]

Spengler ('spɛŋlə; German 'ʃpɛŋlər) *n* **Oswald** ('ɔsvalt). 1880-1936, German philosopher of history, noted for *The Decline of the West* (1918-22), which argues that civilizations go through natural cycles of growth and decay

Spenser ('spɛnsə) *n* **Edmund**. ?1552-99, English poet celebrated for *The Faerie Queene* (1590; 1596), an allegorical romance. His other verse includes the collection of eclogues *The Shepheardes Calendar* (1579) and the marriage poem *Epithalamion* (1594)

Spenserian (spɛn'sɪərɪən) *adj* **1** relating to, in the style of, or characteristic of Edmund Spenser, the English poet (??1552-99), or his poetry ▷ *n* **2** a student or imitator of Edmund Spenser

Spenserian stanza *n* *prosody* the stanza form used by the poet Spenser in his poem *The Faerie Queene*, consisting of eight lines in iambic pentameter and a concluding Alexandrine, rhyming a b a b b c b c c

spent (spɛnt) *vb* **1** the past tense and past participle of **spend** ▷ *adj* **2** used up or exhausted; consumed **3** (of a fish) exhausted by spawning

Speranski (spe'ranskɪ) *n* **Mikhail Mikhailovich** (mixa'il). 1772-1839, Russian statesman, chief adviser (1807-12) to Alexander I. His greatest achievement was the codification of Russian law (begun 1826)

sperm[1] (spɜːm) *n*, *pl* **sperms** or**sperm 1** another name for **semen 2** a male reproductive cell; male gamete [c14: from Late Latin *sperma*, from Greek; related to Greek *speirein* to sow]

sperm[2] (spɜːm) *n* short for **sperm whale, spermaceti, sperm oil**

-sperm *n combining form* (in botany) a seed: *gymnosperm* >-**spermous** or-**spermal** *adj combining form*

spermaceti (ˌspɜːmə'sɛtɪ, -'siːtɪ) *n* a white waxy substance obtained from oil from the head of the sperm whale: used in cosmetics, candles, ointments, etc [c15: from Medieval Latin *sperma cētī* whale's sperm, from *sperma* SPERM[1] + Latin *cētus* whale, from Greek *kētos*]

spermatic (spɜ:ˈmætɪk), **spermic** (ˈspɜ:mɪk) or **spermous** (ˈspɜ:məs) *adj* **1** of or relating to spermatozoa: *spermatic fluid* **2** of or relating to the testis: *the spermatic artery* [c16: from Late Latin *spermaticus*, from Greek *spermatikos* concerning seed, from *sperma* seed, SPERM[1]] > sperˈmatically *adv*

spermatid (ˈspɜ:mətɪd) *n zoology* any of four immature male gametes that are formed from a spermatocyte, each of which develops into a spermatozoon

spermato-, spermo-, *before a vowel* **spermat-** *or before a vowel* **sperm-** *combining form* **1** indicating sperm **2** indicating seed: *spermatophyte* [from Greek *sperma*, *spermat-*, seed; see SPERM[1]]

spermatocyte (ˈspɜ:mətəʊˌsaɪt) *n zoology* an immature male germ cell, developed from a spermatogonium, that gives rise, by meiosis, to four spermatids

spermatogenesis (ˌspɜ:mətəʊˈdʒɛnɪsɪs) *n* the formation and maturation of spermatozoa in the testis > spermatogenetic (ˌspɜ:mətəʊdʒəˈnɛtɪk) *adj*

spermatogonium (ˌspɜ:mətəˈɡəʊnɪəm) *n*, *pl* **-nia** (-nɪə) *zoology* an immature male germ cell that divides to form many spermatocytes [c19: from SPERMATO- + -GONIUM]

spermatophyte (ˈspɜ:mətəʊˌfaɪt) or **spermophyte** *n* (in traditional classifications) any plant of the major division *Spermatophyta*, which includes all seed-bearing plants: an angiosperm or a gymnosperm. Former name: phanerogam > spermatophytic (ˌspɜ:mətəʊˈfɪtɪk) *adj*

spermatozoon (ˌspɜ:mətəʊˈzəʊɒn) *n*, *pl* **-zoa** (-ˈzəʊə) any of the male reproductive cells released in the semen during ejaculation, consisting of a flattened egg-shaped head, a long neck, and a whiplike tail by which it moves to fertilize the female ovum. Also called: **sperm**, **zoosperm** > ˌspermatoˈzoal, ˌspermatoˈzoan or ˌspermatoˈzoic *adj*

spermicide (ˈspɜ:mɪˌsaɪd) *n* any drug or other agent that kills spermatozoa > ˌspermiˈcidal *adj*

sperm oil *n* an oil obtained from the head of the sperm whale, used as a lubricant

spermous (ˈspɜ:məs) *adj* **1** of or relating to the sperm whale or its products **2** another word for **spermatic**

sperm whale *n* a large toothed whale, *Physeter catodon*, having a square-shaped head and hunted for sperm oil, spermaceti, and ambergris: family *Physeteridae* [c19: short for SPERMACETI *whale*]

spew (spju:) *vb* **1** to eject (the contents of the stomach) involuntarily through the mouth; vomit **2** to spit (spittle, phlegm, etc) out of the mouth **3** (usually foll by *out*) to send or be sent out in a stream: *flames spewed out* ▷ *n* **4** something ejected from the mouth ▷ Also (archaic): **spue** [Old English *spīwan*; related to Old Norse *spȳja*, Gothic *speiwan*, Old High German *spīwan*, Latin *spuere*, Lithuanian *spiauti*] > ˈspewer *n*

Spey (speɪ) *n* a river in E Scotland, flowing generally northeast through the Grampian Mountains to the Moray Firth: salmon fishing; parts of the surrounding area (**Speyside**) are famous for whisky distilleries. Length: 172 km (107 miles)

Speyer (*German* ˈʃpaɪər) *n* a port in SW Germany, in Rhineland-Palatinate on the Rhine: the scene of 50 imperial diets. Pop: 50 247 (2003 est). English name: **Spires**

SPF *abbreviation* **1** sender policy framework: a mechanism designed to prevent an e-mail address being duplicated and used as a false address from which to send unsolicited e-mails **2** sun protection factor: an indicator of how effectively a sun cream, lotion, cosmetic, etc, protects the skin from the harmful rays of the sun: *SPF 25*

sp. gr. *abbreviation* specific gravity

sphagnum (ˈsfæɡnəm) *n* any moss of the genus *Sphagnum*, of temperate bogs, having leaves capable of holding much water: layers of these mosses decay to form peat. Also called: **peat moss**, **bog moss** [c18: from New Latin, from Greek *sphagnos* a variety of moss] > ˈsphagnous *adj*

sphairee (sfaɪˈri:) *n Austral* a game resembling tennis played with wooden bats and a perforated plastic ball, devised by F. A. Beck in 1961 [from Greek *sphaira* a ball]

sphalerite (ˈsfæləˌraɪt, ˈsfeɪlə-) *n* a yellow to brownish-black mineral consisting of zinc sulphide in cubic crystalline form with varying amounts of iron, manganese, cadmium, gallium, and indium: the chief source of zinc. Formula: ZnS. Also called: **zinc blende** [c19: from Greek *sphaleros* deceitful, from *sphallein* to cause to stumble]

sphene (sfi:n) *n* a brown, yellow, green, or grey lustrous mineral consisting of calcium titanium silicate in monoclinic crystalline form. It occurs in metamorphic and acid igneous rocks and is used as a gemstone. Formula: $CaTiSiO_5$. Also called: **titanite** [c19: from French *sphène*, from Greek *sphēn* a wedge, alluding to its crystals]

sphenoid (ˈsfi:nɔɪd) *adj* Also: **sphenoidal** **1** wedge-shaped **2** of or relating to the sphenoid bone ▷ *n* **3** See **sphenoid bone**

sphenoid bone *n* the large butterfly-shaped compound bone at the base of the skull, containing a protective depression for the pituitary gland

sphere (sfɪə) *n* **1** *maths* **a** a three-dimensional closed surface such that every point on the surface is equidistant from a given point, the centre **b** the solid figure bounded by this surface or the space enclosed by it. Equation: $(x-a)^2 + (y-b)^2 + (z-c)^2 = r^2$, where *r* is the radius and (*a, b, c*) are the coordinates of the centre; surface area: $4\pi r^2$; volume: $4\pi r^3/3$ **2** any object having approximately this shape; globe **3** the night sky considered as a vaulted roof; firmament **4** any heavenly object such as a planet, natural satellite, or star **5** (in the Ptolemaic or Copernican systems of astronomy) one of a series of revolving hollow globes, arranged concentrically, on whose transparent surfaces the sun (or in the Copernican system the earth), the moon, the planets, and fixed stars were thought to be set, revolving around the earth (or in the Copernican system the sun) **6** a social class or stratum of society ▷ *vb* (*tr*) *chiefly poetic* **7** to surround or encircle **8** to place aloft or in the heavens [c14: from Late Latin *sphēra*, from Latin *sphaera* globe, from Greek *sphaira*]

-sphere *n combining form* **1** having the shape or form of a sphere: *bathysphere* **2** indicating a spherelike enveloping mass: *atmosphere* > **-spheric** *adj combining form*

spherical (ˈsfɛrɪkᵊl) or **spheric** *adj* **1** shaped like a sphere **2** of or relating to a sphere: *spherical geometry* **3** *geometry* formed on the surface of or inside a sphere: *a spherical triangle* **4** **a** of or relating to heavenly bodies **b** of or relating to the spheres of the Ptolemaic or the Copernican system > ˈspherically *adv* > ˈsphericalness *n*

spherical aberration *n physics* a defect of optical systems that arises when light striking a mirror or lens near its edge is focused at different points on the axis to the light striking near the centre. The effect occurs when the mirror or lens has spherical surfaces

spherical angle *n* an angle formed at the intersection of two great circles of a sphere

spherical coordinates *pl n* three coordinates that define the location of a point in three-dimensional space in terms of the length *r* of its radius vector, the angle, θ, which this vector makes with one axis, and the angle, φ, made by a second axis, perpendicular to the first, with the plane containing the first axis and the point. Usually written (*r*, θ, φ)

spherical trigonometry *n* the branch of trigonometry concerned with the measurement of the angles and sides of spherical triangles

spheroid (ˈsfɪərɔɪd) *n* **1** *maths* another name for **ellipsoid of revolution** ▷ *adj* **2** shaped like but not exactly a sphere > spheˈroidal *adj* > ˌspheroidˈicity *n*

spherometer (sfɪəˈrɒmɪtə) *n* an instrument for measuring the curvature of a surface

spherule (ˈsfɛruːl) *n* a very small sphere or globule [c17: from Late Latin *sphaerula* a little SPHERE] > ˈspherular *adj*

spherulite (ˈsfɛruˌlaɪt) *n* any of several spherical masses of radiating needle-like crystals of one or more minerals occurring in rocks such as obsidian > spherulitic (ˌsfɛruˈlɪtɪk) *adj*

sphincter (ˈsfɪŋktə) *n anatomy* a ring of muscle surrounding the opening of a hollow organ or body and contracting to close it [c16: from Late Latin, from Greek *sphinkter*, from *sphingein* to grip tightly] >'**sphincteral** *adj*

sphinx (sfɪŋks) *n*, *pl* **sphinxes** *or* **sphinges** ('sfɪndʒi:z) **1** any of a number of huge stone statues built by the ancient Egyptians, having the body of a lion and the head of a man **2** an inscrutable person

Sphinx (sfɪŋks) the Sphinx *n* **1** *Greek myth* a monster with a woman's head and a lion's body. She lay outside Thebes, asking travellers a riddle and killing them when they failed to answer it. Oedipus answered the riddle and the Sphinx then killed herself **2** the huge statue of a sphinx near the pyramids at El Gîza in Egypt, of which the head is a carved portrait of the fourth-dynasty Pharaoh, Chephrēn [c16: via Latin from Greek, apparently from *sphingein* to hold fast]

sphragistics (sfrəˈdʒɪstɪks) *n* (*functioning as singular*) the study of seals and signet rings [c19: from Greek *sphragistikos*, from *sphragizein* to seal, from *sphragis* a seal] >**sphra'gistic** *adj*

sphygmo- *or before a vowel* **sphygm-** *combining form* indicating the pulse [from Greek *sphugmos* pulsation, from *sphuzein* to throb]

sphygmograph ('sfɪɡməʊˌɡrɑːf, -ˌɡræf) *n med* an instrument for making a recording (**sphygmogram**) of variations in blood pressure and pulse >**sphygmographic** (ˌsfɪɡməʊˈɡræfɪk) *adj* >**sphygmography** (sfɪɡˈmɒɡrəfɪ) *n*

sphygmomanometer (ˌsfɪɡməʊməˈnɒmɪtə) *n med* an instrument for measuring arterial blood pressure [c19: from SPHYGMO- + MANOMETER, on the model of French *sphygmomanomètre*]

spica ('spaɪkə) *n*, *pl* **-cae** (-siː) *or* **-cas** **1** *med* a spiral bandage formed by a series of overlapping figure-of-eight turns **2** *botany* another word for: **spike**² (sense 1) [c15: from Latin: ear of corn]

spicate ('spaɪkeɪt) *adj botany* having, arranged in, or relating to spikes: *a spicate inflorescence* [c17: from Latin *spīcātus* having spikes, from *spīca* a point]

spiccato (spɪˈkɑːtəʊ) *music* ▷ *n* **1** a style of playing a bowed stringed instrument in which the bow bounces lightly off the strings ▷ *adj, adv* **2** to be played in this manner [Italian: detached, from *spiccare* to make distinct]

spice (spaɪs) *n* **1a** any of a variety of aromatic vegetable substances, such as ginger, cinnamon, nutmeg, used as flavourings **b** these substances collectively **2** something that represents or introduces zest, charm, or gusto **3** *rare* a small amount ▷ *vb* (*tr*) **4** to prepare or flavour (food) with spices **5** to introduce charm or zest into [c13: from Old French *espice*, from Late Latin *speciēs* (pl) spices, from Latin *speciēs* (sing.) kind; also associated with Late Latin *spīcea* (unattested) fragrant herb, from Latin *spīceus* having spikes of foliage; see SPICA]

spicebush ('spaɪsˌbʊʃ) *n* a North American lauraceous shrub, *Lindera benzoin*, having yellow flowers and aromatic leaves and bark

Spice Islands *pl n* the former name of the **Moluccas**

spick-and-span *or* **spic-and-span** ('spɪkənˈspæn) *adj* **1** extremely neat and clean **2** new and fresh [c17: shortened from *spick-and-span-new*, from obsolete *spick* spike, nail + SPAN-NEW]

spicule ('spɪkjuːl) *n* **1** Also called: **spiculum** a small slender pointed structure or crystal, esp any of the calcareous or siliceous elements of the skeleton of sponges, corals, etc **2** *astronomy* a spiked ejection of hot gas occurring over 5000 kilometres above the sun's surface (in its atmosphere) and having a diameter of about 1000 kilometres [c18: from Latin: SPICULUM] >**spiculate** ('spɪkjʊˌleɪt, -lɪt) *adj*

spiculum ('spɪkjʊləm) *n*, *pl* **-la** (-lə) another word for: **spicule** (sense 1) [c18: from Latin: small sharp point, from SPICA]

spicy ('spaɪsɪ) *adj* **spicier, spiciest** **1** seasoned with or containing spice **2** highly flavoured; pungent **3** *informal* suggestive of scandal or sensation **4** producing or yielding spices >**spicily** *adv* >**spiciness** *n*

spider ('spaɪdə) *n* **1** any predatory silk-producing arachnid of the order *Araneae*, having four pairs of legs and a rounded unsegmented body consisting of abdomen and cephalothorax **2** any of various similar or related arachnids **3** any implement or tool having the shape of a spider **4** any part of a machine having a number of radiating spokes, tines, or arms **5** Also called: **octopus** *Brit* a cluster of elastic straps fastened at a central point and used to hold a load on a car rack, motorcycle, etc **6** *billiards, snooker* a rest having long legs, used to raise the cue above the level of the height of the ball **7** *computing* a computer program that is capable of performing sophisticated recursive searches on the internet [Old English *spīthra*; related to Danish *spinder*, German *Spinne*; see SPIN] >**spidery** *adj*

spider crab *n* any of various crabs of the genera *Macropodia, Libinia*, etc, having a small triangular body and very long legs

spiderman ('spaɪdəˌmæn) *n*, *pl* **-men** *informal chiefly Brit* a person who erects the steel structure of a building

spider mite *n* any of various plant-feeding mites of the family *Tetranychidae*, esp *Panonychus ulmi* (**red spider mite**), which is a serious orchard pest

spider monkey *n* **1** any of several arboreal New World monkeys of the genus *Ateles*, of Central and South America, having very long legs, a long prehensile tail, and a small head **2** **woolly spider monkey** a rare related monkey, *Brachyteles arachnoides*, of SE Brazil [c18: so called because its long limbs resemble the legs of a spider]

spider plant *n* any of various house plants, esp *Chlorophytum elatum*

spiderwort ('spaɪdəˌwɜːt) *n* **1** any of various plants of the American genus *Tradescantia*, esp *T. virginiana*, having blue, purplish, or pink flowers and widely grown as house plants: family *Commelinaceae*. See also **tradescantia** **2** any of various similar or related plants [c17: so called because of the spidery shape of its stamens]

spiel (ʃpiːl) *n* **1** a glib plausible style of talk, associated esp with salesmen ▷ *vb* **2** (*intr*) to deliver a prepared spiel **3** (*tr*; usually foll by *off*) to recite (a prepared oration) [c19: from German *Spiel* play] >**spieler** *n*

Spielberg ('spiːlbɜːɡ) *n* Steven. born 1947, US film director, noted esp for the commercial success of such films as *Jaws* (1975), *Close Encounters of the Third Kind* (1977), *Raiders of the Lost Ark* (1981) and its sequels, *E.T.* (1982), and *Jurassic Park* (1993). Other films include *The Color Purple* (1986), *Schindler's List* (1993), *Saving Private Ryan* (1998), and *The Terminal* (2004)

spiffing ('spɪfɪŋ) *adj Brit slang, old-fashioned* excellent; splendid [c19: probably from dialect *spiff* spruce, smartly dressed]

spiffy ('spɪfɪ) *adj* **-fier, -fiest** *US & Canadian slang* smart; stylish [c19: from dialect *spiff*] >**spiffily** *adv*

spigot ('spɪɡət) *n* **1** a stopper for the vent hole of a cask **2** a tap, usually of wood, fitted to a cask **3** a US name for **tap**² (sense 1) **4** a short cylindrical projection on one component designed to fit into a hole on another, esp the male part of a joint (**spigot and socket joint**) between two pipes [c14: probably from Old Provençal *espiga* a head of grain, from Latin *spīca* a point]

spike¹ (spaɪk) *n* **1** a sharp point **2** any sharp-pointed object, esp one made of metal **3** a long metal nail **4** (*plural*) shoes with metal projections on the sole and heel for greater traction, as used by athletes **5** *Brit slang* another word for **dosshouse** ▷ *vb* (*tr*) **6** to secure or supply with or as with spikes **7** to render ineffective or block the intentions of; thwart **8** to impale on a spike **9** to add alcohol to (a drink) **10** *volleyball* to hit (a ball) sharply downwards with an overarm motion from the front of one's own court into the opposing court **11** (formerly) to render (a cannon) ineffective by blocking its vent with a spike **12** **spike someone's guns** to thwart someone's purpose [c13 *spyk*; related to Old English *spīcing* nail, Old Norse *spīk* splinter, Middle Low German *spīker* spike, Norwegian *spīk* SPOKE², Latin *spīca* sharp point; see SPIKE²] >**spiky** *adj*

spike² (spaɪk) *n botany* **1** an inflorescence consisting of a raceme of sessile flowers, as in the gladiolus and sedges **2** an ear of wheat, barley, or any other grass that has sessile spikelets [c14: from Latin *spīca* ear of corn]

spikelet ('spaɪklɪt) *n* the small inflorescence of plants of other families, esp the sedges

spikenard ('spaɪknɑːd, 'spaɪkəˌnɑːd) *n* **1** an aromatic

Indian valerianaceous plant, *Nardostachys jatamans*, having rose-purple flowers **2** an aromatic ointment obtained from this plant **3** any of various similar or related plants **4** a North American araliaceous plant, *Aralia racemosa*, having small green flowers and an aromatic root ▷ Also called (for senses 1, 2): nard [c14: from Medieval Latin *spīca nardī*; see SPIKE², NARD]

spile (spaɪl) *n* **1** a heavy timber stake or pile **2** *US & Canadian* a spout for tapping sap from the sugar maple tree **3** a plug or spigot ▷ *vb* (*tr*) **4** to provide or support with a spile **5** *US* to tap (a tree) with a spile [c16: probably from Middle Dutch *spile* peg; related to Icelandic *spila* skewer, Latin *spīna* thorn]

spill¹ (spɪl) *vb* **spills, spilling, spilt** *or* **spilled** (*mainly tr*) **1** (when *intr*, usually foll by *from, out of*, etc) to fall or cause to fall from or as from a container, esp unintentionally **2** to disgorge (contents, occupants, etc) or (of contents, occupants, etc) to be disgorged: *the car spilt its passengers onto the road; the crowd spilt out of the theatre* **3** to shed (blood) **4** Also called: **spill the beans** *informal* to disclose something confidential **5** *nautical* to let (wind) escape from a sail or (of the wind) to escape from a sail ▷ *n* **6** *informal* a fall or tumble **7** short for **spillway 8** a spilling of liquid, etc, or the amount spilt **9** *Austral* the declaring of several political jobs vacant when one higher up becomes so [Old English *spillan* to destroy; related to *spildan*, Old High German *spaltan* to split; see SPOIL] ▷ **spiller** *n* ▷ **spillage** *n*

spill² (spɪl) *n* a splinter of wood or strip of twisted paper with which pipes, fires, etc, are lit [c13: of Germanic origin; compare Old High German *spilla*, Middle Dutch *spile* stake]

Spillane (spɪ'leɪn) *n* **Mickey**, original name *Frank Morrison Spillane*. 1918–2006, US detective-story writer, best known for his books featuring the detective Mike Hammer, for example *I, the Jury* (1947) and *The Twisted Thing* (1966)

spillikin, spilikin ('spɪlɪkɪn) *or* **spellican** ('spɛlɪkən) *n* a thin strip of wood, cardboard, or plastic, esp one used in spillikins

spillikins ('spɪlɪkɪnz) *n* (*functioning as singular*) *Brit* a game in which players try to pick each spillikin from a heap without moving any of the others. Also called: **jackstraws** [c18: from SPILL² + diminutive ending. See -KIN]

spill over *vb* **1** (*intr, adverb*) to overflow or be forced out of an area, container, etc ▷ *n* **spillover 2** *chiefly US & Canadian* the act of spilling over **3** *chiefly US & Canadian* the excess part of something

spillway ('spɪl,weɪ) *n* a channel that carries away surplus water, as from a dam

spilt (spɪlt) *vb* a past tense and past participle of **spill¹**

spim (spɪm) *n* unsolicited commercial communications received on a computer via an instant-messaging system [from *sp(am)* + *i(nstant)* *m(essaging)*]

spin (spɪn) *vb* **spins, spinning, spun 1** to rotate or cause to rotate rapidly, as on an axis **2 a** to draw out and twist (natural fibres, as of silk or cotton) into a long continuous thread **b** to make such a thread or filament from (synthetic resins, etc), usually by forcing through a nozzle **3** (of spiders, silkworms, etc) to form (webs, cocoons, etc) from a silky fibre exuded from the body **4** (*tr*) to shape (metal) into a rounded form on a lathe **5** (*tr*) *informal* to tell (a tale, story, etc) by drawing it out at great length (esp in the phrase **spin a yarn**) **6** to bowl, pitch, hit, or kick (a ball) so that it rotates in the air and changes direction or speed on bouncing, or (of a ball) to be projected in this way **7** (*intr*) (of wheels) to revolve rapidly without causing propulsion **8** to cause (an aircraft) to dive in a spiral descent or (of an aircraft) to dive in a spiral descent **9** (*intr*; foll by *along*) to drive or travel swiftly **10** Also called: **spin-dry** (*tr*) to rotate (clothes) in a washing machine in order to extract surplus water **11** (*intr*) to reel or grow dizzy, as from turning around: *my head is spinning* **12** (*intr*) to fish by drawing a revolving lure through the water **13** (*intr*) *informal* to present news or information in a way that creates a favourable impression ▷ *n* **14** a swift rotating motion; instance of spinning **15** *physics* **a** the intrinsic angular momentum of an elementary particle or atomic

nucleus, as distinguished from any angular momentum resulting from its motion **b** a quantum number determining values of this angular momentum in units of the Dirac constant, having integral or half-integral values **16** a condition of loss of control of an aircraft or an intentional flight manoeuvre in which the aircraft performs a continuous spiral descent because the angle of maximum lift is less than the angle of incidence **17** a spinning motion imparted to a ball, etc **18** flat spin *informal, chiefly Brit* a state of agitation or confusion **19** on the spin *informal* one after another: *they have lost two finals on the spin* ▷ See also **spin off, spin out**, etc [Old English *spinnan*; related to Old Norse *spinna*, Old High German *spinnan* to spin, Lithuanian *pinu* to braid]

spina bifida ('spaɪnə 'bɪfɪdə) *n* a congenital condition in which the meninges of the spinal cord protrude through a gap in the backbone, sometimes causing enlargement of the skull (due to accumulation of cerebrospinal fluid) and paralysis [New Latin; see SPINE, BIFID]

spinach ('spɪnɪdʒ, -ɪtʃ) *n* **1** a chenopodiaceous annual plant, *Spinacia oleracea*, cultivated for its dark green edible leaves **2** the leaves of this plant, eaten as a vegetable [c16: from Old French *espinache*, from Old Spanish *espinaca*, from Arabic *isfānākh*, from Persian]

spinal ('spaɪnˀl) *adj* **1** of or relating to the spine or the spinal cord ▷ *n* **2** short for **spinal anaesthesia** ▷ **spinally** *adv*

spinal anaesthesia *n* **1** *surgery* anaesthesia of the lower half of the body produced by injecting an anaesthetic beneath the arachnoid membrane surrounding the spinal cord. See also **epidural** (sense 2) **2** *pathol* loss of sensation in some part of the body as the result of injury of the spinal cord

spinal canal *n* the natural passage through the centre of the spinal column that contains the spinal cord

spinal column *n* a series of contiguous or interconnecting bony or cartilaginous segments that surround and protect the spinal cord

spinal cord *n* the thick cord of nerve tissue within the spinal canal, which in man gives rise to 31 pairs of spinal nerves, and together with the brain forms the central nervous system

spin bowler *n* *cricket* a bowler who specializes in bowling balls with a spinning motion

spindle ('spɪndˀl) *n* **1** a rod or stick that has a notch in the top, used to draw out natural fibres for spinning into thread, and a long narrow body around which the thread is wound when spun **2** one of the thin rods or pins bearing bobbins upon which spun thread is wound in a spinning wheel or machine **3** any of various parts in the form of a rod, esp a rotating rod that acts as an axle, mandrel, or arbor **4** a piece of wood that has been turned, such as a baluster or table leg **5** a small square metal shaft that passes through the lock of a door and to which the door knobs or handles are fixed **6** *biology* a spindle-shaped structure formed by microtubules during mitosis or meiosis which draws the duplicated chromosomes apart as the cell divides **7** a device consisting of a sharp upright spike on a pedestal on which bills, order forms, etc, are impaled **8** short for **spindle tree** ▷ *vb* **9** (*tr*) to form into a spindle or equip with spindles **10** (*intr*) *rare* (of a plant, stem, shoot, etc) to grow rapidly and become elongated and thin [Old English *spinel*; related to *spinnan* to SPIN, Old Saxon *spinnila* spindle, Old High German *spinnala*]

spindlelegs ('spɪndˀl,lɛgz) *or* **spindleshanks** *pl n* **1** long thin legs **2** (*functioning as singular*) a person who has long thin legs

spindle tree *n* any of various shrubs or trees of the genus *Euonymus*, esp *E. europaeus*, of Europe and W Asia, typically having red fruits and yielding a hard wood formerly used in making spindles: family *Celastraceae*

spindly ('spɪndlɪ) *adj* **-dlier, -dliest** tall, slender, and frail; attenuated

spin doctor *n* *informal* a person who provides a favourable slant to an item of news, potentially unpopular policy, etc, esp on behalf of a political personality or party [c20: from the spin given to a ball in various sports to make it go in the desired direction]

spindrift ('spɪn,drɪft) n spray blown up from the surface of the sea. Also called: spoondrift [C17: of Scottish origin, possibly from a variant of obsolete *spoon* to scud + DRIFT]

spin-dry vb -dries, -drying, -dried (tr) to dry (clothes, linen, etc) in a spin-dryer

spin-dryer n a device that extracts water from clothes, linen, etc, by spinning them in a perforated drum

spine (spaɪn) n 1 the spinal column 2 the sharply pointed tip or outgrowth of a leaf, stem, etc 3 zoology a hard pointed process or structure, such as the ray of a fin, the quill of a porcupine, or the ridge on a bone 4 the back of a book, record sleeve, etc 5 a ridge, esp of a hill 6 strength of endurance, will, etc 7 anything resembling the spinal column in function or importance; main support or feature [C14: from Old French *espine* spine, from Latin *spīna* thorn, backbone] > spined adj

spine-chiller n a book, film, etc, that arouses terror

spinel (spɪ'nɛl) n any of a group of hard glassy minerals of variable colour consisting of oxides of aluminium, magnesium, chromium, iron, zinc, or manganese and occurring in the form of octahedral crystals: used as gemstones [C16: from French *spinelle*, from Italian *spinella*, diminutive of *spina* a thorn, from Latin; so called from the shape of the crystals]

spineless ('spaɪnlɪs) adj 1 lacking a backbone; invertebrate 2 having no spiny processes: *spineless stems* 3 lacking strength of character, resolution, or courage > 'spinelessly adv > 'spinelessness n

spinet (spɪ'nɛt, 'spɪnɪt) n a small type of harpsichord having one manual [C17: from Italian *spinetta*, perhaps from Giovanni Spinetti, 16th-century Italian maker of musical instruments and its supposed inventor]

spinifex ('spɪnɪ,fɛks) n 1 Also called: porcupine grass *Austral* any of various coarse spiny-leaved inland grasses of the genus *Triodia* 2 any grass of the SE Asian genus *Spinifex*, having pointed leaves and spiny seed heads: often planted to bind loose sand [C19: from New Latin, from Latin *spīna* a thorn + *-fex* maker, from *facere* to make]

spinmeister ('spɪn,maɪstə) n another name for spin doctor [C20: from SPIN (sense 23) + -MEISTER]

spinnaker ('spɪnəkə; Nautical 'spæŋkə) n a large light triangular racing sail set from the foremast of a yacht when running or on a broad reach [C19: probably from SPIN + (MO)NIKER, but traditionally derived from Sphinx, the yacht that first adopted this type of sail]

spinner ('spɪnə) n 1 a person or thing that spins 2 cricket a a ball that is bowled with a spinning motion b a bowler who specializes in bowling such balls 3 a streamlined fairing that fits over and revolves with the hub of an aircraft propeller 4 a fishing lure with a fin or wing that revolves when drawn through the water

spinneret ('spɪnə,rɛt) n 1 any of several organs in spiders and certain insects through which silk threads are exuded 2 a finely perforated dispenser through which a viscous liquid is extruded in the production of synthetic fibres [C18: from SPINNER + -ET]

spinney ('spɪnɪ) n chiefly Brit a small wood or copse [C16: from Old French *espinei*, from *espine* thorn, from Latin *spīna*]

spinning ('spɪnɪŋ) n 1 the act or process of spinning 2 the act or technique of casting and drawing a revolving lure through the water so as to imitate the movement of a live fish, etc

spinning jenny n an early type of spinning frame with several spindles, invented by James Hargreaves in 1764 [C18: see JENNY; the reason for the adoption of the woman's name is unclear]

spinning wheel n a wheel-like machine for spinning at home, having one hand- or foot-operated spindle

spin off vb 1 (tr, preposition) to turn (a part of a business enterprise) into a separate company ▷ n spin-off 2 any product or development derived incidentally from the application of existing knowledge or enterprise 3 a book, film, or television series derived from a similar successful book, film, or television series

spin out vb (tr, adverb) 1 to extend or protract (a story, etc)

by including superfluous detail; prolong 2 to spend or pass (time) 3 to contrive to cause (money, etc) to last as long as possible

Spinoza (spɪ'nəʊzə) n **Baruch** (bə'ru:k). 1632–77, Dutch philosopher who constructed a holistic metaphysical system derived from a series of hypotheses that he judged self-evident. His chief work is *Ethics* (1677)

spinster ('spɪnstə) n 1 an unmarried woman regarded as being beyond the age of marriage 2 law (in legal documents) a woman who has never married 3 (formerly) a woman who spins thread for her living [C14 (in the sense: a person, esp a woman, whose occupation is spinning; C17: a woman still unmarried): from SPIN + -STER] > 'spinster,hood n > 'spinsterish adj

spiny ('spaɪnɪ) adj spinier, spiniest 1 (of animals) having or covered with quills or spines 2 (of plants) covered with spines; thorny 3 troublesome to handle; puzzling > 'spininess n

spiny anteater n another name for echidna

spiny-finned adj (of certain fishes) having fins that are supported by stiff bony spines

spiny lobster n any of various large edible marine decapod crustaceans of the genus *Palinurus* and related genera, having a very tough spiny carapace. Also called: rock lobster, crawfish, langouste

spiracle ('spaɪərək³l, 'spaɪrə-) n 1 any of several paired apertures in the cuticle of an insect, by which air enters and leaves the trachea 2 a small paired rudimentary gill slit just behind the head in skates, rays, and related fishes 3 any similar respiratory aperture, such as the blowhole in whales [C14 (originally: breath): from Latin *spīrāculum* vent, from *spīrāre* to breathe] > spiracular (spɪ'rækjʊlə) adj > spi'raculate adj

spiraea or esp US **spirea** (spaɪ'rɪə) n any rosaceous plant of the genus *Spiraea*, having sprays of small white or pink flowers. See also meadowsweet (sense 2) [C17: via Latin from Greek *speiraia*, from *speira* SPIRE²]

spiral ('spaɪərəl) n 1 geometry one of several plane curves formed by a point winding about a fixed point at an ever-increasing distance from it. Polar equation of Archimedes spiral: $r = a\theta$; of logarithmic spiral: $\log r = a\theta$; of hyperbolic spiral: $r\theta = a$, (where a is a constant) 2 another name for helix (sense 1) 3 something that pursues a winding, usually upward, course or that displays a twisting form or shape 4 a flight manoeuvre in which an aircraft descends describing a helix of comparatively large radius with the angle of attack within the normal flight range. See spin (sense 16) 5 economics a continuous upward or downward movement in economic activity or prices, caused by interaction between prices, wages, demand, and production ▷ adj 6 having the shape of a spiral ▷ vb -rals, -ralling, -ralled or US -rals, -raling, -raled 7 to assume or cause to assume a spiral course or shape 8 (intr) to increase or decrease with steady acceleration: *wages and prices continue to spiral* [C16: via French from Medieval Latin *spīrālis*, from Latin *spīra* a coil; see SPIRE²] > 'spirally adv

spiral galaxy n a galaxy consisting of an ellipsoidal nucleus of old stars from opposite sides of which arms, containing younger stars, spiral outwards around the nucleus. In a barred spiral the arms originate at the ends of a bar-shaped nucleus

spirant ('spaɪərənt) adj 1 phonetics another word for fricative ▷ n 2 a fricative consonant [C19: from Latin *spīrāns* breathing, from *spīrāre* to breathe]

spire¹ (spaɪə) n 1 Also called: steeple a tall structure that tapers upwards to a point, esp one on a tower or roof or one that forms the upper part of a steeple 2 a slender tapering shoot or stem, such as a blade of grass 3 the apical part of any tapering formation; summit ▷ vb 4 (intr) to assume the shape of a spire; point up 5 (tr) to furnish with a spire or spires [Old English *spīr* blade; related to Old Norse *spīra* stalk, Middle Low German *spīr* shoot, Latin *spīna* thorn] > 'spiry adj

spire² (spaɪə) n 1 any of the coils or turns in a spiral structure 2 the apical part of a spiral shell [C16: from Latin *spīra* a coil, from Greek *speira*]

Spires (spaɪəz) n the English name for Speyer

spirillum (spaɪˈrɪləm) *n*, *pl* **-la** (-lə) **1** any bacterium having a curved or spirally twisted rodlike body **2** any bacterium of the genus *Spirillum*, such as *S. minus*, which causes ratbite fever [C19: from New Latin, literally: a little coil, from *spīra* a coil]

spirit¹ (ˈspɪrɪt) *n* **1** the force or principle of life that animates the body of living things **2** temperament or disposition: *truculent in spirit* **3** liveliness; mettle: *they set to it with spirit* **4** the fundamental, emotional, and activating principle of a person; will: *the experience broke his spirit* **5** a sense of loyalty or dedication: *team spirit* **6** the prevailing element; feeling: *a spirit of joy pervaded the atmosphere* **7** state of mind or mood; attitude: *he did it in the wrong spirit* **8** (*plural*) an emotional state, esp with regard to exaltation or dejection: *in high spirits* **9** a person characterized by some activity, quality, or disposition: *a leading spirit of the movement* **10** the deeper more significant meaning as opposed to a pedantic interpretation: *the spirit of the law* **11** that which constitutes a person's intangible being as contrasted with his physical presence: *I shall be with you in spirit* **12 a** an incorporeal being, esp the soul of a dead person **b** (*as modifier*): *spirit world* ▷ *vb* (*tr*) **13** (usually foll by *away* or *off*) to carry off mysteriously or secretly **14** (often foll by *up*) to impart animation or determination to [C13: from Old French *esperit*, from Latin *spīritus* breath, spirit; related to *spīrāre* to breathe] > **ˈspiritless** *adj*

spirit² (ˈspɪrɪt) *n* **1** (*often plural*) any distilled alcoholic liquor such as brandy, rum, whisky, or gin **2** *chem* **a** an aqueous solution of ethanol, esp one obtained by distillation **b** the active principle or essence of a substance, extracted as a liquid, esp by distillation **3** *pharmacol* a solution of a volatile substance, esp a volatile oil, in alcohol **4** *alchemy* any of the four substances sulphur, mercury, sal ammoniac, or arsenic [C14: special use of SPIRIT¹, name applied to alchemical substances (as in sense 4), hence extended to distilled liquids]

Spirit (ˈspɪrɪt) **the Spirit** *n* God, esp when regarded as transcending material limitations

spirited (ˈspɪrɪtɪd) *adj* **1** displaying animation, vigour, or liveliness **2** (*in combination*) characterized by mood, temper, or disposition as specified: *high-spirited; public-spirited* > **ˈspiritedly** *adv* > **ˈspiritedness** *n*

spirit gum *n* a glue made from gum dissolved in ether used to stick a false beard, etc, onto the face

spiritism (ˈspɪrɪˌtɪzəm) *n* a less common word for **spiritualism** > **ˈspiritist** *n* > **ˌspiritˈistic** *adj*

spirit lamp *n* a lamp that burns methylated or other spirits instead of oil

spirit level *n* a device for setting horizontal surfaces, consisting of an accurate block of material in which a sealed slightly curved tube partially filled with liquid is set so that the air bubble rests between two marks on the tube when the block is horizontal

spiritous (ˈspɪrɪtəs) *adj* a variant spelling of **spirituous**

spirits of ammonia *n* (*functioning as singular or plural*) another name for **sal volatile** (sense 2)

spirits of hartshorn *n* (*functioning as singular or plural*) See **ammonium hydroxide**

spirits of salt *n* (*functioning as singular or plural*) a solution of hydrochloric acid in water

spiritual (ˈspɪrɪtjʊəl) *adj* **1** relating to the spirit or soul and not to physical nature or matter; intangible **2** of, relating to, or characteristic of sacred things, the Church, religion, etc **3** standing in a relationship based on communication between the souls or minds of the persons involved: *a spiritual father* **4** having a mind or emotions of a high and delicately refined quality ▷ *n* **5** (*often plural*) the sphere of religious, spiritual, or ecclesiastical matters, or such matters in themselves > **ˈspiritually** *adv* > **ˌspirituˈality** *n*

spiritualism (ˈspɪrɪtjʊəˌlɪzəm) *n* **1** the belief that the disembodied spirits of the dead, surviving in another world, can communicate with the living in this world, esp through mediums **2** the doctrines and practices associated with this belief **3** *philosophy* the belief that because reality is to some extent immaterial it is therefore spiritual **4** any doctrine (in philosophy, religion, etc) that prefers the spiritual to the material > **ˈspiritualist** *n*

spiritualize or **spiritualise** (ˈspɪrɪtjʊəˌlaɪz) *vb* (*tr*) to make spiritual or infuse with spiritual content > **ˌspiritualiˈzation** or **ˌspiritualiˈsation** *n* > **ˈspiritualˌizer** or **ˈspiritualˌiser** *n*

spirituel (ˌspɪrɪtjʊˈɛl) *adj* having a refined and lively mind or wit. Also (feminine): **spirituelle** [C17: from French]

spirituous (ˈspɪrɪtjʊəs) *adj* **1** characterized by or containing alcohol **2** (of a drink) being a spirit > **spirituosity** (ˌspɪrɪtjʊˈɒsɪtɪ) or **ˈspirituousness** *n*

spiro-¹ *combining form* indicating breath or respiration: *spirograph* [from Latin *spīrāre* to breathe]

spiro-² *combining form* spiral; coil: *spirochaete* [from Latin *spīra*, from Greek *speira* a coil]

spirochaete or US **spirochete** (ˈspaɪrəʊˌkiːt) *n* any of a group of spirally coiled rodlike bacteria that includes the causative agent of syphilis [C19: from New Latin *spīrochaeta*; see SPIRO-², CHAETA]

spirograph (ˈspaɪrəˌɡrɑːf, -ˌɡræf) *n med* an instrument for recording the movements of breathing > **ˌspiroˈgraphic** *adj*

spirogyra (ˌspaɪrəˈdʒaɪərə) *n* any green freshwater multicellular alga of the genus *Spirogyra*, consisting of minute filaments containing spirally coiled chloroplasts [C20: from New Latin, from SPIRO-² + Greek *guros* a circle]

spirt (spɜːt) *n* a variant spelling of **spurt**

spiry (ˈspaɪərɪ) *adj poetic* of spiral form; helical

spit¹ (spɪt) *vb* **spits**, **spitting**, **spat** or **spit** **1** (*intr*) to expel saliva from the mouth; expectorate **2** (*intr*) *informal* to show disdain or hatred by spitting **3** (of a fire, hot fat, etc) to eject (fragments of coal, sparks, etc) violently and with an explosive sound; splutter **4** (*intr*) to rain very lightly **5** (*tr*; often foll by *out*) to eject or discharge (something) from the mouth: *he spat the food out; to spit blood* **6** (*tr*; often foll by *out*) to utter (short sharp words or syllables), esp in a violent manner **7 spit it out!** *Brit informal* a command given to someone that he should speak forthwith ▷ *n* **8** another name for **spittle** **9** a light or brief fall of rain, snow, etc **10** the act or an instance of spitting **11** *informal, chiefly Brit* another word for **spitting image** [Old English *spittan*; related to *spǣtan* to spit, German dialect *spitzen*] > **ˈspitter** *n*

spit² (spɪt) *n* **1** a pointed rod on which meat is skewered and roasted before or over an open fire **2** Also called: **rotisserie, rotating spit** a similar device rotated by electricity or clockwork, fitted onto a cooker **3** an elongated often hooked strip of sand or shingle projecting from the shore, deposited by longshore drift, and usually above water ▷ *vb* **spits**, **spitting**, **spitted** **4** (*tr*) to impale on or transfix with or as if with a spit [Old English *spitu*; related to Old High German *spiz* spit, Norwegian *spit* tip]

spit and polish *n informal* punctilious attention to neatness, discipline, etc, esp in the armed forces

spite (spaɪt) *n* **1** maliciousness involving the desire to harm another; venomous ill will **2** an instance of such malice; grudge **3** *archaic* something that induces vexation **4 in spite of** (*preposition*) in defiance of; regardless of; notwithstanding ▷ *vb* (*tr*) **5** to annoy in order to vent spite [C13: variant of DESPITE] > **ˈspiteful** *adj*

spitfire (ˈspɪtˌfaɪə) *n* a person given to outbursts of spiteful temper and anger, esp a woman or girl

Spithead (ˌspɪtˈhɛd) *n* an extensive anchorage between the mainland of England and the Isle of Wight, off Portsmouth

Spitsbergen (ˈspɪtsˌbɜːɡən) *n* another name for **Svalbard**

spitting image *n informal* a person who bears a strong physical resemblance to another, esp to a relative. Also called: **spit, spit and image** [C19: modification of *spit and image*, from SPIT¹ (as in the phrase *the very spit of*, the exact likeness of (someone))]

spitting snake *n* another name for the **rinkhals**

spittle (ˈspɪtᵊl) *n* **1** the fluid secreted in the mouth; saliva or spit **2** Also called: **cuckoo spit, frog spit** the frothy substance secreted on plants by the larvae of certain froghoppers [Old English *spǣtl* saliva; see SPIT¹]

spittoon (spɪˈtuːn) *n* a receptacle for spit, usually in a public place [c19: from SPIT¹ + *-oon*: see SALOON, BALLOON, etc]

spitz (spɪts) *n* any of various breeds of dog characterized by very dense hair, a stocky build, a pointed muzzle, erect ears, and a tightly curled tail [c19: from German, from *spitz* pointed]

Spitz (spɪts) *n* **Mark**. born 1950, US swimmer, who won seven gold medals at the 1972 Olympic Games

spiv (spɪv) *n Brit slang* a person who makes a living by underhand dealings or swindling; black marketeer [c20: back formation from dialect *spiving* smart; compare SPIFFY, SPIFFING] > ˈspivvy *adj*

splake (spleɪk) *n* a type of hybrid trout bred by Canadian zoologists [from *sp(eckled)* + *lake* (trout)]

splanchnic (ˈsplæŋknɪk) *adj* of or relating to the viscera; visceral: *a splanchnic nerve* [c17: from New Latin *splanchnicus*, from Greek *splankhnikos* concerning the entrails, from *splankhna* the entrails]

splash (splæʃ) *vb* **1** to scatter (liquid) about in blobs; spatter **2** to descend or cause to descend upon in blobs: *he splashed his jacket* **3** to make (one's way) by or as if by splashing: *he splashed through the puddle* **4** (*tr*) to print (a story or photograph) prominently in a newspaper ⊳ *n* **5** an instance or sound of splashing **6** an amount splashed **7** a patch created by or as if by splashing **8** *informal* an extravagant display, usually for effect (esp in the phrase **make a splash**) **9** a small amount of soda water, water, etc, added to an alcoholic drink [c18: alteration of PLASH¹] > ˈsplashy *adj*

splashdown (ˈsplæʃˌdaʊn) *n* **1** the controlled landing of a spacecraft on water at the end of a space flight **2** the time scheduled for this event ⊳ *vb* **splash down 3** (*intr, adverb*) (of a spacecraft) to make a splashdown

splat¹ (splæt) *n* a wet slapping sound [c19: of imitative origin]

splat² (splæt) *n* a wide flat piece of wood, esp one that is the upright central part of a chair back [c19: perhaps related to Old English *splātan* to SPLIT]

splatter (ˈsplætə) *vb* **1** to splash with small blobs; spatter ⊳ *n* **2** a splash of liquid, mud, etc

splatter movie *n slang* a film in which the main feature is the graphic and gory murder of numerous victims

splay (spleɪ) *adj* **1** spread out; broad and flat **2** turned outwards in an awkward manner ⊳ *vb* **3** to spread out; turn out or expand ⊳ *n* **4** a surface of a wall that forms an oblique angle to the main flat surfaces, esp at a doorway or window opening [c14: short for DISPLAY]

splayfoot (ˈspleɪˌfʊt) *n, pl* **-feet** *pathol* another word for **flatfoot** (sense 1) > ˈsplayˌfooted *adj*

spleen (spliːn) *n* **1** a spongy highly vascular organ situated near the stomach in man. It forms lymphocytes, produces antibodies, aids in destroying worn-out red blood cells, and filters bacteria and foreign particles from the blood **2** the corresponding organ in other animals **3** spitefulness or ill humour; peevishness: *to vent one's spleen* **4** *archaic* the organ in the human body considered to be the seat of the emotions **5** *archaic* another word for **melancholy** [c13: from Old French *esplen*, from Latin *splēn*, from Greek; related to Latin *lien* spleen] > ˈspleenish *or* ˈspleeny *adj*

spleenwort (ˈspliːnˌwɜːt) *n* any of various ferns of the genus *Asplenium*, esp *A. trichomanes*, that often grows on walls, having linear or oblong sori on the undersurface of the fronds

splendent (ˈsplɛndənt) *adj archaic* **1** shining brightly; lustrous: *a splendent sun* **2** famous; illustrious [c15: from Latin *splendēns* brilliant, from *splendēre* to shine]

splendid (ˈsplɛndɪd) *adj* **1** brilliant or fine, esp in appearance **2** characterized by magnificence; imposing **3** glorious or illustrious: *a splendid reputation* **4** brightly gleaming; radiant: *her splendid face; splendid colours* **5** very good or satisfactory: *a splendid time* [c17: from Latin *splendidus*, from *splendēre* to shine] > ˈsplendidly *adv* > ˈsplendidness *n*

splendiferous (splɛnˈdɪfərəs) *adj* facetious grand; splendid: *that was a really splendiferous meal* [c15: from Medieval Latin *splendiferus*, from Latin *splendor*

radiance + *ferre* to bring]

splendour *or US* **splendor** (ˈsplɛndə) *n* **1** the state or quality of being splendid **2** *sun* in splendour *heraldry* a representation of the sun with rays and a human face

splenetic (splɪˈnɛtɪk) *adj* **1** of or relating to the spleen **2** spiteful or irritable; peevish ⊳ *n* **3** a spiteful or irritable person [c16: from Late Latin *splēnēticus*, from Latin *splēn* SPLEEN] > spleˈnetically *adv*

splenic (ˈsplɛnɪk, ˈspliː-) *adj* **1** of, relating to, or in the spleen **2** having a disease or disorder of the spleen

splenius (ˈspliːnɪəs) *n, pl* **-nii** (-nɪˌaɪ) *anatomy* either of two flat muscles situated at the back of the neck that rotate, flex, and extend the head and neck [c18: via New Latin from Greek *splēnion* a plaster] > ˈsplenial *adj*

splenomegaly (ˌsplɪnəʊˈmɛɡəlɪ) *n pathol* abnormal enlargement of the spleen [c20: from Greek *splēno-*, from *splēn* SPLEEN + *megalo-*, from *megas* large + -Y³]

splice (splaɪs) *vb* (*tr*) **1** to join (two ropes) by intertwining the strands **2** to join up the trimmed ends of (two pieces of wire, film, magnetic tape, etc) with solder or an adhesive material **3** to join (timbers) by overlapping and binding or bolting the ends together **4** (*passive*) *informal* to enter into marriage: *the couple got spliced last Saturday* **5 splice the mainbrace** *nautical history* to issue and partake of an extra allocation of alcoholic spirits ⊳ *n* **6** a join made by splicing **7** the place where such a join occurs **8** the wedge-shaped end of a cricket-bat handle or similar instrument that fits into the blade [c16: probably from Middle Dutch *splissen*; related to German *spleissen*, Swedish *splitsa*; see SPLIT] > ˈsplicer *n*

spline (splaɪn) *n* **1** any one of a series of narrow keys (**external splines**) formed longitudinally around the circumference of a shaft that fit into corresponding grooves (**internal splines**) in a mating part: used to prevent movement between two parts, esp in transmitting torque **2** a long narrow strip of wood, metal, etc; slat **3** a thin narrow strip made of wood, metal, or plastic fitted into a groove in the edge of a board, tile, etc, to connect it to another ⊳ *vb* **4** (*tr*) to provide (a shaft, part, etc) with splines [c18: East Anglian dialect; perhaps related to Old English *splin* spindle; see SPLINT]

splint (splɪnt) *n* **1** a rigid support for restricting movement of an injured part, esp a broken bone **2** a thin sliver of wood, esp one that is used to light cigars, a fire, etc **3** a thin strip of wood woven with others to form a chair seat, basket, etc **4** *vet science* inflammation of the small metatarsal or metacarpal bones along the side of the cannon bone of a horse ⊳ *vb* **5** to apply a splint to (a broken arm, etc) [c13: from Middle Low German *splinte*; related to Middle Dutch *splinte* splint, Old High German *spaltan* to split]

splinter (ˈsplɪntə) *n* **1** a very small sharp piece of wood, glass, metal, etc, characteristically long and thin, broken off from a whole **2** a metal fragment, from the container of a shell, bomb, etc, thrown out during an explosion ⊳ *vb* **3** to reduce or be reduced to sharp fragments; shatter **4** to break or be broken off in small sharp fragments [c14: from Middle Dutch *splinter*; see SPLINT] > ˈsplintery (ˈsplɪntərɪ, ˈsplɪntrɪ) *adj*

splinter group *n* a number of members of an organization, political party, etc, who split from the main body and form an independent association, usually as the result of dissension

split (splɪt) *vb* **splits, splitting, split 1** to break or cause to break, lengthwise, by cleaving into separate pieces, often into two roughly equal pieces: *to split a brick* **2** to separate or be separated from a whole: *he split a piece of wood from the block* **3** to separate or be separated into factions, usually through discord **4** (often foll by *up*) to separate or cause to separate through a disagreement **5** (when *tr*, often foll by *up*) to divide or be divided among two or more persons: *split up the pie among the three of us* **6** *slang* to depart; leave: *let's split; we split the scene* **7** (*tr*) to separate (something) into its components by interposing something else: *to split a word with hyphens* **8** (*intr*; usually foll by *on*) *slang* to betray the trust, plans, etc (of); inform: *he split on me to the cops* **9** (*tr*) *US politics* to mark (a ballot) so as to vote for the candidates of more than one party: *he split the ticket* **10** (*tr*) to separate (an animal hide or skin) into layers ▷ *n* **11** the act or process of splitting **12** a breach or schism in a group or the faction resulting from such a breach **13** a dessert of sliced fruit and ice cream, covered with whipped cream, nuts, etc: *banana split* **14** *tenpin bowling* a formation of the pins after the first bowl in which there is a large gap between two pins or groups of pins **15** *informal* an arrangement or process of dividing up loot or money ▷ *adj* **16** having been split; divided: *split logs* **17** having a split or splits: *hair with split ends* ▷ See also **splits, split up,** etc [c16: from Middle Dutch *splitten* to cleave; related to Middle High German *splīzen*; see SPLICE] > 'splitter *n*

Split (Croatian *split*) *n* a port and resort in W Croatia on the Adriatic: remains of the palace of Diocletian (295–305). Pop: 188 000 (2005 est). Italian name: Spalato

split infinitive *n* (in English grammar) an infinitive used with another word between *to* (the infinitive marker) and the verb itself, as in *I want to really finish it this time*

● **USAGE** The traditional rule against placing an adverb
● between *to* and its verb is gradually disappearing.
● Although it is true that a split infinitive may result in
● a clumsy sentence (*he decided to firmly and definitively deal*
● *with the problem*), this is not enough to justify the
● absolute condemnation that this practice has
● attracted. Indeed, very often the most natural
● position of the adverb is between *to* and the verb (*he*
● *decided to really try next time*) and to change it would
● result in an artificial and awkward construction (*he*
● *decided really to try next time*). The current view is
● therefore that the split infinitive is not a grammatical
● error. Nevertheless, many writers prefer to avoid
● splitting infinitives in formal written English, since
● readers with a more traditional point of view are
● likely to interpret them as incorrect

split-level *adj* (of a house, room, etc) having the floor level of one part about half a storey above or below the floor level of an adjoining part

split pea *n* a pea dried and split and used in soups, pease pudding, or as a vegetable

split personality *n* **1** the tendency to change rapidly in mood or temperament **2** a nontechnical term for **multiple personality**

split pin *n* a metal pin made by bending double a wire, often of hemispherical section, so that it can be passed through a hole in a nut, shaft, etc, to secure another part by bending back the ends of the wire

split ring *n* a steel ring having two helical turns, often used as a key ring

split run *n Canadian* a divided print run of a periodical in which a number of copies contain advertisements not included in the rest, esp a Canadian edition of a US magazine which contains Canadian advertisements but no Canadian editorial content

splits (splɪts) *n* (*functioning as singular*) (in gymnastics, etc) the act of sinking to the floor to achieve a sitting position in which both legs are straight, pointing in opposite directions, and at right angles to the body

split-screen technique *n* a cinematic device by which two or more complete images are projected simultaneously onto separate parts of the screen. Also called: **split screen**

split second *n* **1** an extremely small period of time; instant ▷ *adj* **split-second** (*prenominal*) **2** made or arrived at in an infinitely short time: *a split-second decision* **3** depending upon minute precision: *split-second timing*

split shift *n* a work period divided into two parts that are separated by an interval longer than a normal rest period

splitting ('splɪtɪŋ) *adj* **1** (of a headache) intolerably painful; acute **2** (of the head) assailed by an overpowering unbearable pain

split up *vb* (*adverb*) **1** (*tr*) to separate out into parts; divide **2** (*intr*) to become separated or parted through disagreement: *they split up after years of marriage* **3** to break down or be capable of being broken down into constituent parts ▷ *n* **split-up 4** the act or an instance of separating

splodge (splɒdʒ) *n* **1** a large irregular spot or blot ▷ *vb* **2** (*tr*) to mark (something) with such a blot or blots [c19: alteration of earlier SPLOTCH] > 'splodginess *n* > 'splodgy *adj*

splotch (splɒtʃ) *n, vb* the usual US word for **splodge** [c17: perhaps a blend of SPOT + BLOTCH] > 'splotchy *adj*

splurge (splɜːdʒ) *n* **1** an ostentatious display, esp of wealth **2** a bout of unrestrained extravagance ▷ *vb* **3** (often foll by *on*) to spend (money) unrestrainedly or extravagantly [c19: of uncertain origin]

splutter ('splʌtə) *vb* **1** to spit out (saliva, food particles, etc) from the mouth in an explosive manner, as through choking or laughing **2** to utter (words) with spitting sounds, as through rage or choking **3** to eject or be ejected in an explosive manner: *sparks spluttered from the fire.* Also: **sputter 4** (*tr*) to bespatter (a person) with tiny particles explosively ejected ▷ *n* **5** the process or noise of spluttering **6** spluttering incoherent speech, esp in argument **7** anything ejected through spluttering [c17: variant of SPUTTER, influenced by SPLASH] > 'splutterer *n*

Spock (spɒk) *n* **Benjamin**, known as *Dr Spock*. 1903–98, US paediatrician, noted for his influential work *The Common Sense Book of Baby and Child* (1946), which challenged traditional notions of child care, advocating a more permissive approach

spode (spəʊd) *n* china or porcelain manufactured by Josiah Spode, English potter (1754–1827), or his company

spoil (spɔɪl) *vb* **spoils, spoiling, spoilt** or **spoiled 1** (*tr*) to cause damage to (something), in regard to its value, beauty, usefulness, etc **2** (*tr*) to weaken the character of (a child) by complying unrestrainedly with its desires **3** (*intr*) (of perishable substances) to become unfit for consumption or use **4** (*intr*) *sport* to disrupt the play or style of an opponent, as to prevent him from settling into a rhythm **5** *archaic* to strip (a person or place) of (property or goods) by force or violence **6** be spoiling for to have an aggressive desire for (a fight, etc) ▷ *n* **7** waste material thrown up by an excavation **8** any treasure accumulated by a person **9** *obsolete* the act of plundering ▷ See also **spoils** [c13: from Old French *espoillier*, from Latin *spoliāre* to strip, from *spolium* booty]

spoilage ('spɔɪlɪdʒ) *n* **1** the act or an instance of spoiling or the state or condition of being spoilt **2** an amount of material that has been wasted by being spoilt

spoiler ('spɔɪlə) *n* **1** plunderer or robber **2** a person or thing that causes spoilage or corruption **3** a device fitted to an aircraft wing to increase drag and reduce lift It is usually extended into the airflow to assist descent and banking **4** a similar device fitted to a car **5** *sport* a competitor who adopts spoiling tactics, as in boxing **6** a magazine, newspaper, etc produced specifically to coincide with the production of a rival magazine, newspaper, etc in order to divert public interest and reduce its sales

spoils (spɔɪlz) *pl n* **1** (*sometimes singular*) valuables seized by violence, esp in war **2** *chiefly US* the rewards and benefits of public office regarded as plunder for the winning party or candidate. See also **spoils system**

spoilsport ('spɔɪl,spɔːt) *n informal* a person who spoils the pleasure of other people by his actions or attitudes

spoils system *n chiefly US* the practice of filling appointive public offices with friends and supporters of the ruling political party

spoilt (spɔɪlt) *vb* a past tense and past participle of **spoil**

Spokane (spəʊˈkæn) *n* a city in E Washington: commercial centre of an agricultural region. Pop: 196 624 (2003 est)

spoke¹ (spəʊk) *vb* **1** the past tense of **speak 2** *archaic* or *dialect* a past participle of **speak**

spoke² (spəʊk) *n* **1** a radial member of a wheel, joining the hub to the rim **2** a radial projection from the rim of a wheel, as in a ship's wheel **3** a rung of a ladder **4** put a spoke in someone's wheel *Brit* to thwart someone's plans ▷ *vb* **5** (*tr*) to equip with or as if with spokes [Old English *spāca*]

spoken ('spəʊkən) *vb* **1** the past participle of **speak** ▷ *adj* **2** uttered through the medium of speech **3** (*in combination*) having speech as specified: *soft-spoken*

S

4 spoken for engaged, reserved, or allocated

spokeshave ('spəʊkˌʃeɪv) *n* a small plane with two handles, one on each side of its blade, used for shaping or smoothing cylindrical wooden surfaces, such as spokes

spokesman ('spəʊksmən), **spokesperson** ('spəʊksˌpɜːsᵊn) *or feminine* **spokeswoman** ('spəʊksˌwʊmən) *n*, *pl* -men, -persons *or* -people, -women a person authorized to speak on behalf of another person, group of people, or organization

spoliation (ˌspəʊlɪ'eɪʃən) *n* **1** the act or an instance of despoiling or plundering **2** the authorized seizure or plundering of neutral vessels on the seas by a belligerent state in time of war **3** *law* the material alteration of a document so as to render it invalid **4** *English ecclesiastical law* the taking of the fruits of a benefice by a person not entitled to them [c14: from Latin *spoliātiō*, from *spoliāre* to SPOIL] > **'spoliatory** *adj*

spondee ('spɒndiː) *n* *prosody* a metrical foot consisting of two long syllables (– –) [c14: from Old French *spondée*, from Latin *spondēus*, from Greek *spondeios*, from *spondē* a ritual libation; from the use of spondee in the music that characteristically accompanied such ceremonies]

spondylitis (ˌspɒndɪ'laɪtɪs) *n* inflammation of the vertebrae [c19: from New Latin, from Greek *spondulos* vertebra; see -ITIS]

sponge (spʌndʒ) *n* **1** any multicellular typically marine animal of the phylum *Porifera*, usually occurring in complex sessile colonies in which the porous body is supported by a fibrous, calcareous, or siliceous skeletal framework **2** a piece of the light porous highly absorbent elastic skeleton of certain sponges, used in bathing, cleaning, etc **3** any of a number of light porous elastic materials resembling a sponge **4** another word for **sponger** (sense 1) **5** *informal* a person who indulges in heavy drinking **6** leavened dough, esp before kneading **7** See **sponge cake 8** Also called: **sponge pudding** *Brit* a light steamed or baked pudding, spongy in texture, made with various flavourings or fruit **9** porous metal produced by electrolysis or by reducing a metal compound without fusion or sintering and capable of absorbing large quantities of gas: *platinum sponge* **10** a rub with a sponge **11 throw in the sponge** See **throw in** (sense 4) ▷ *vb* **12** (*tr*; often foll by *off or down*) to clean (something) by wiping or rubbing with a damp or wet sponge **13** (*tr*; usually foll by *off, away, out*, etc) to remove (marks, etc) by rubbing with a damp or wet sponge or cloth **14** (when *tr*, often foll by *up*) to absorb (liquids, esp when spilt) in the manner of a sponge **15** (*tr*; often foll by *off*) to get (something) from (someone) by presuming on his generosity **16** (*intr*; often foll by *off or on*) to obtain one's subsistence, welfare, etc, unjustifiably (from): *he sponges off his friends* **17** (*intr*) to go collecting sponges [Old English, from Latin *spongia*, from Greek] > **'sponge,like** *adj* > **'spongy** *adj*

sponge bag *n* a small bag made of plastic, etc, that holds toilet articles, used esp when travelling

sponge bath *n* a washing of the body with a wet sponge or cloth, but without immersion in water

sponge cake *n* a light porous cake, made of eggs, sugar, flour, and flavourings traditionally without any fat

sponger ('spʌndʒə) *n* **1** *informal* a person who lives off other people by continually taking advantage of their generosity; parasite or scrounger **2** a person or ship employed in collecting sponges

spongiform ('spʌndʒɪˌfɔːm) *adj* **1** resembling a sponge in appearance, esp in having many holes **2** denoting diseases characterized by this appearance of affected tissues

sponsion ('spɒnʃən) *n* **1** the act or process of becoming surety; sponsorship **2** (*often plural*) *international law* an unauthorized agreement made by a public officer, esp an admiral or general in time of war, requiring ratification by the government of the state concerned **3** any act or promise, esp one made on behalf of someone else [c17: from Latin *sponsiō*, from *spondēre* to pledge]

sponson ('spɒnsən) *n* **1** *naval* an outboard support for a gun enabling it to shoot fore and aft **2** a semicircular gun turret on the side of a tank **3** a float or flotation

chamber along the gunwale of a boat or ship **4** a structural unit attached to a helicopter fuselage by fixed struts, housing the main landing gear and inflatable flotation bags [c19: perhaps from EXPANSION]

sponsor ('spɒnsə) *n* **1** a person or group that provides funds for an activity, esp **2** *chiefly US & Canadian* a person or business firm that pays the costs of a radio or television programme in return for advertising time **3** a legislator who presents and supports a bill, motion, etc **4** Also called: **godparent a** an authorized witness who makes the required promises on behalf of a person to be baptized and thereafter assumes responsibility for his Christian upbringing **b** a person who presents a candidate for confirmation **5** *chiefly US* a person who undertakes responsibility for the actions, statements, obligations, etc, of another, as during a period of apprenticeship; guarantor ▷ *vb* **6** (*tr*) to act as a sponsor for [c17: from Latin, from *spondēre* to promise solemnly] > **'sponsorial** (spɒn'sɔːrɪəl) *adj* > **'sponsor,ship** *n*

sponsored ('spɒnsəd) *adj* denoting an activity organized to raise money for a charity in which sponsors agree to donate money on completion of the activity, or a specified period or amount of it, by participants

spontaneity (ˌspɒntə'niːɪtɪ, -'neɪ-) *n*, *pl* -ties **1** the state or quality of being spontaneous **2** (*often plural*) the exhibiting of actions, impulses, or behaviour that are stimulated by internal processes

spontaneous (spɒn'teɪnɪəs) *adj* **1** occurring, produced, or performed through natural processes without external influence **2** arising from an unforced personal impulse; voluntary; unpremeditated **3** (of plants) growing naturally; indigenous [c17: from Late Latin *spontāneus*, from Latin *sponte* voluntarily] > **spon'taneously** *adv* > **spon'taneousness** *n*

spontaneous combustion *n* the ignition of a substance or body as a result of internal oxidation processes, without the application of an external source of heat, occurring in finely powdered ores, coal, straw, etc

spontaneous generation *n* a theory, widely held in the 19th century and earlier but now discredited, stating that living organisms could arise directly and rapidly from nonliving material. Also called: **abiogenesis**

spoof (spuːf) *informal* ▷ *n* **1** a mildly satirical mockery or parody; lampoon **2** a good-humoured deception or trick; prank ▷ *vb* **3** to indulge in a spoof of (a person or thing) [c19: coined by A. Roberts (1852–1933), English comedian, to designate a game of his own invention] > **'spoofer** *n*

spook (spuːk) *informal* ▷ *n* **1** a ghost or a person suggestive of this **2** *US & Canadian* a spy ▷ *vb* (*tr*) *US & Canadian* **3** to frighten: *to spook horses; to spook a person* **4** (of a ghost) to haunt [c19: Dutch *spook*, from Middle Low German *spōk* ghost] > **'spooky** *adj informal*

spool (spuːl) *n* **1** a device around which magnetic tape, film, cotton, etc, can be automatically wound, with plates at top and bottom to prevent it from slipping off **2** anything round which other materials, esp thread, are wound ▷ *vb* **3** (sometimes foll by *up*) to wind or be wound onto a spool or reel [c14: of Germanic origin; compare Old High German *spuolo*, Middle Dutch *spoele*]

spoon (spuːn) *n* **1** a metal, wooden, or plastic utensil having a shallow concave part, usually elliptical in shape, attached to a handle, used in eating or serving food, stirring, etc **2** Also called: **spoonbait** an angling lure for spinning or trolling, consisting of a bright piece of metal which swivels on a trace to which are attached a hook or hooks **3** *golf* a former name for a No. 3 wood **4 be born with a silver spoon in one's mouth** to inherit wealth or social standing **5** *rowing* a type of oar blade that is curved at the edges and tip to gain a firm grip on the water ▷ *vb* **6** (*tr*) to scoop up or transfer (food, liquid, etc) from one container to another with or as if with a spoon **7** (*intr*) *slang, old-fashioned* to kiss and cuddle **8** *sport* to hit (a ball) with a weak lifting motion, as in golf, cricket, etc [Old English *spōn* splinter; related to Old Norse *spónn* spoon, chip, Old High German *spān*]

spoonbill ('spuːnˌbɪl) *n* any of several wading birds of warm regions, such as *Platalea leucorodia* (**common spoonbill**) and *Ajaia ajaja* (**roseate spoonbill**), having a long horizontally flattened bill: family *Threskiornithidae*, order *Ciconiiformes*

spoondrift ('spu:n,drɪft) *n* a less common spelling of **spindrift**

spoonerism ('spu:nə,rɪzəm) *n* the transposition of the initial consonants or consonant clusters of a pair of words, often resulting in an amusing ambiguity of meaning, such as *hush my brat for brush my hat* [C20: named after W. A. *Spooner* (1844–1930), English clergyman renowned for slips of this kind]

spoon-feed *vb* **-feeds, -feeding, -fed** (*tr*) **1** to feed with a spoon **2** to overindulge or spoil **3** to provide (a person) with ready-made opinions, judgments, etc, depriving him of original thought or action

spoonful ('spu:n,fʊl) *n, pl* **-fuls 1** the amount that a spoon is able to hold **2** a small quantity

spoony *or* **spooney** ('spu:nɪ) *slang, rare, old-fashioned ▷ adj* **spoonier, spooniest 1** foolishly or stupidly amorous ▷ *n, pl* **spoonies 2** a fool or silly person, esp one in love

spoor (spʊə, spɔ:) *n* **1** the trail of an animal or person, esp as discernible to the human eye ▷ *vb* **2** to track (an animal) by following its trail [C19: from Afrikaans, from Middle Dutch *spor*; related to Old English *spor* track, Old High German *spor*; see SPUR]

Sporades ('spɒrə,di:z) *pl n* two groups of Greek islands in the Aegean: the **Northern Sporades**, lying northeast of Euboea, and the **Southern Sporades**, which include the Dodecanese and lie off the SW coast of Turkey

sporadic (spə'rædɪk) *adj* **1** occurring at irregular points in time; intermittent: *sporadic firing* **2** scattered; isolated: *a sporadic disease* [C17: from Medieval Latin *sporadicus*, from Greek *sporadikos*, from *sporas* scattered; related to Greek *speirein* to sow; see SPORE] **> spo'radically** *adv*

sporangium (spə'rændʒɪəm) *n, pl* **-gia** (-dʒɪə) any organ, esp in fungi, in which asexual spores are produced [C19: from New Latin, from SPORO- + Greek *angeion* receptacle] **> spo'rangial** *adj*

spore (spɔ:) *n* **1** a reproductive body, produced by bacteria, fungi, various plants and some protozoans, that develops into a new individual. A **sexual spore** is formed after the fusion of gametes and an **asexual spore** is the result of asexual reproduction **2** a germ cell, seed, dormant bacterium, or similar body ▷ *vb* **3** (*intr*) to produce, carry, or release spores [C19: from New Latin *spora*, from Greek: a sowing; related to Greek *speirein* to sow]

spore case *n* the nontechnical name for **sporangium**

sporo- *or before a vowel* **spor-** *combining form* (in botany) spore: *sporophyte* [from New Latin *spora*]

sporogenesis (,spɔ:rəʊ'dʒɛnɪsɪs, ,spɒ-) *n* the process of spore formation in plants and animals **> sporogenous** (spɔ:'rɒdʒɪnəs, spɒ-) *adj*

sporogonium (,spɔ:rəʊ'gəʊnɪəm, ,spɒ-) *n, pl* **-nia** (-nɪə) the sporophyte of mosses and liverworts, consisting of a spore-bearing capsule on a short stalk that arises from the parent plant (the gametophyte) **> ,sporo'gonial** *adj*

sporophyll *or* **sporophyl** ('spɔ:rəʊfɪl, 'spɒ-) *n* a leaf in ferns and other spore-bearing plants that bears the sporangia

sporophyte ('spɔ:rəʊ,faɪt, 'spɒ-) *n* the diploid form of plants that have alternation of generations. It develops from a zygote and produces asexual spores. Compare **gametophyte > sporophytic** (,spɔ:rə'fɪtɪk, ,spɒ-) *adj*

-sporous *adj combining form* (in botany) having a specified type or number of spores

sporozoan (,spɔ:rə'zəʊən, ,spɒ-) *n* **1** any parasitic protozoan of the phylum *Apicomplexa* (or *Sporozoa*), characterized by a complex life cycle, part of which is passed in the cells of the host, and the production of asexual spores: includes the malaria parasite ▷ *adj* **2** of or relating to sporozoans

sporran ('spɒrən) *n* a large pouch, usually of fur, worn hanging from a belt in front of the kilt in men's Scottish Highland dress [C19: from Scottish Gaelic *sporan* purse; compare Irish Gaelic *sparán* purse, Late Latin *bursa* bag]

sport (spɔ:t) *n* **1** an individual or group activity pursued for exercise or pleasure, often involving the testing of physical capabilities and taking the form of a competitive game such as football, tennis, etc **2** such activities considered collectively **3** any particular pastime indulged in for pleasure **4** the pleasure derived from a pastime, esp hunting, shooting, or fishing: *we had good sport today* **5** playful or good-humoured joking: *to say a thing in sport* **6** derisive mockery or the object of such mockery: *to make sport of someone* **7** someone or something that is controlled by external influences: *the sport of fate* **8** *informal* (sometimes qualified by *good, bad*, etc) a person who reacts cheerfully in the face of adversity, esp a good loser **9** *informal* a person noted for being scrupulously fair and abiding by the rules of a game **10** *informal* a person who leads a merry existence, esp a gambler: *he's a bit of a sport* **11** *Austral & NZ informal* a form of address used esp between males **12** *biology* **a** an animal or plant that differs conspicuously in one or more aspects from other organisms of the same species, usually because of a mutation **b** an anomalous characteristic of such an organism ▷ *vb* **13** (*tr*) *informal* to wear or display in an ostentatious or proud manner: *she was sporting a new hat* **14** (*intr*) to skip about or frolic happily **15** to amuse (oneself), esp in outdoor physical recreation **16** (*intr; often foll by with*) to dally or trifle (with) **17** (*tr; often foll by away*) *rare* to squander (time or money): *sporting one's life away* **18** (*intr; often foll by with*) *archaic* to make fun (of) **19** (*intr*) *biology* to produce or undergo a mutation ▷ See also **sports** [C15 *sporten*, variant of *disporten* to DISPORT] **> 'sporter** *n* **> 'sportful** *adj* **> 'sportfully** *adv* **> 'sportfulness** *n*

sporting ('spɔ:tɪŋ) *adj* **1** (*prenominal*) of, relating to, or used or engaged in a sport or sports **2** relating or conforming to sportsmanship; fair **3** of, relating to, or characterized by an interest in gambling **4** willing to take a risk **> 'sportingly** *adv*

sportive ('spɔ:tɪv) *adj* **1** playful or joyous **2** done in jest rather than seriously **> 'sportively** *adv* **> 'sportiveness** *n*

sports (spɔ:ts) *n* **1** (*modifier*) relating to, concerned with, or used in sports: *sports equipment* **2** (*modifier*) relating to or similar to a sports car **3** Also called: **sports day** *Brit* a meeting held at a school or college for competitions in various athletic events

sports cap *n* **1** a hat designed for sports or to look sporty **2** a special top for a bottle, designed to aid drinking without spilling

sports car *n* a production car designed for speed, high acceleration, and manoeuvrability, having a low body and usually adequate seating for only two persons

sportscast ('spɔ:ts,kɑ:st) *n* a radio or television broadcast consisting of sports news **> 'sports,caster** *n*

sports jacket *n* a man's informal jacket, made esp of tweed: worn with trousers of different material. Also called (US, Austral and NZ): **sports coat**

sportsman ('spɔ:tsmən) *n, pl* **-men 1** a man who takes part in sports, esp of the outdoor type **2** a person who exhibits qualities highly regarded in sport, such as fairness, generosity, observance of the rules, and good humour when losing **> 'sportsman-,like** *or* **'sportsmanly** *adj* **> 'sportsman,ship** *n*

sports medicine *n* the branch of medicine concerned with injuries sustained through sport

sportswear ('spɔ:ts,wɛə) *n* clothes worn for sport or outdoor leisure wear

sportswoman ('spɔ:ts,wʊmən) *n, pl* **-women** a woman who takes part in sports, esp of the outdoor type

sport utility vehicle *or* **sports utility vehicle** *n* a high-powered car with four-wheel drive, originally designed for off-road use. Abbreviation: **SUV**

sporty ('spɔ:tɪ) *adj* **sportier, sportiest 1** (of a person) fond of sport or outdoor activities **2** (of clothes) having the appearance of sportswear **3** (of a car) having the performance or appearance of a sports car **> 'sportily** *adv* **> 'sportiness** *n*

sporule ('spɒruːl) *n* a spore, esp a very small spore [C19: from New Latin *sporula* a little SPORE]

spot (spɒt) *n* **1** a small mark on a surface, such as a circular patch or stain, differing in colour or texture from its surroundings **2** a geographical area that is restricted in extent: *a beauty spot* **3** a location: *this is the exact spot on which he died* **4** a blemish of the skin, esp a

pimple or one occurring through some disease **5** a
blemish on the character of a person; moral flaw
6 *informal* a place of entertainment **7** *informal, chiefly Brit*
a small quantity or amount: *a spot of lunch* **8** *informal* an
awkward situation: *that puts me in a bit of a spot* **9** a short
period between regular television or radio programmes
that is used for advertising **10** a position or length of
time in a show assigned to a specific performer **11** short
for **spotlight 12** (in billiards) the player using this ball
13 *billiards, snooker* one of several small black dots on a
table that mark where a ball is to be placed **14** (*modifier*)
a denoting or relating to goods, currencies, or securities
available for immediate delivery and payment: *spot
goods*. See also **spot price b** involving immediate cash
payment: *spot sales* **15** change one's spots (*used mainly in
negative constructions*) to reform one's character **16** high
spot an outstanding event: *the high spot of the holiday was
the visit to the winery* **17** knock spots off to outstrip or
outdo with ease **18** on the spot **a** immediately **b** at the
place in question **c** in the best possible position to deal
with a situation **d** in an awkward predicament
e without moving from the place of one's location, etc
f (*as modifier*): *our on-the-spot reporter* **19** soft spot a special
sympathetic affection or weakness for a person or thing
20 tight spot a serious, difficult, or dangerous situation
21 weak spot **a** some aspect of a character or situation
that is susceptible to criticism **b** a flaw in a person's
knowledge: *classics is my weak spot* ▷ *vb* **spots, spotting,
spotted 22** (*tr*) to observe or perceive suddenly, esp under
difficult circumstances; discern **23** to put stains or spots
upon (something) **24** (*intr*) (of some fabrics) to be
susceptible to spotting by or as if by water: *silk spots easily*
25 (*tr*) to place here and there: *they spotted observers along
the border* **26** to look out for and note (trains, talent, etc)
27 (*intr*) to rain slightly; spit **28** (*tr*) *billiards* to place (a
ball) on one of the spots [c12 (in the sense: moral
blemish): of German origin; compare Middle Dutch
spotte, Old Norse *spotti*] ▷ **ˈspotless** *adj* ▷ **ˈspotlessly** *adv*
▷ **ˈspotlessness** *n*

spot check *n* **1** a quick random examination **2** a check
made without prior warning ▷ *vb* **spot-check 3** (*tr*) to
perform a spot check on

spot height *n* a mark on a map indicating the height of
a hill, mountain, etc

spotlight ('spɒtˌlaɪt) *n* **1** a powerful light focused so as to
illuminate a small area, usually mounted so that it can
be directed at will **2** the spotlight the focus of attention
▷ *vb* **-lights, -lighting, -lit** or **-lighted** (*tr*) **3** to direct a
spotlight on **4** to focus attention on

spot-on *adj informal* absolutely correct; very accurate

spot price *n* the price of goods, currencies, or securities
that are offered for immediate delivery and payment

spotted ('spɒtɪd) *adj* **1** characterized by spots or marks,
esp in having a pattern of spots **2** stained or blemished;
soiled or bespattered

spotted dick *n Brit* a steamed or boiled suet pudding
containing dried fruit [c19: perhaps from the man's
name *Dick* (short for *Richard*), or from dialect *dick*
pudding. The dried fruit gives it a speckled appearance]

spotted fever *n* any of various severe febrile diseases
characterized by small irregular spots on the skin, as in
Rocky Mountain spotted fever or tick fever

spotted gum *n* **1** an Australian eucalyptus tree,
Eucalyptus maculata **2** the wood of this tree, used for
shipbuilding, sleepers, etc

spotted mackerel *n* a small mackerel, *Scomberomorus
queenslandicus*, of northern Australian waters

spotter ('spɒtə) *n* **1** a **a** person or thing that watches or
observes **b** (*as modifier*): *a spotter plane* **2** a person who
makes a hobby of watching for and noting numbers or
types of trains, buses, etc: *a train spotter* **3** *military* a
person who orders or advises adjustment of fire on a
target by observations **4** a person, esp one engaged in
civil defence, who watches for enemy aircraft

spottie ('spɒtɪ) *n NZ* a young deer of up to three months
of age

spotty ('spɒtɪ) *adj* **-tier, -tiest 1** abounding in or
characterized by spots or marks, esp on the skin: *a spotty
face* **2** not consistent or uniform; irregular or uneven,

often in quality ▷ **ˈspottily** *adv* ▷ **ˈspottiness** *n*

spot-weld *vb* **1** (*tr*) to join (two pieces of metal, esp in the
form of wire or sheet) by one or more small circular
welds by means of heat, usually electrically generated,
and pressure ▷ *n* **2** a weld so formed ▷ **ˈspot-ˌwelder** *n*

spousal ('spaʊzəl) *n* **1** (*often plural*) **a** the marriage
ceremony **b** a wedding ▷ *adj* **2** of or relating to marriage
▷ **ˈspousally** *adv*

spouse (spaʊs, spaʊz) *n* **1** a person's partner in
marriage. Related adj: **spousal** ▷ *vb* (spaʊz, spaʊs) **2** (*tr*)
obsolete to marry [c12: from Old French *spus* (masculine),
spuse (feminine), from Latin *sponsus, sponsa* betrothed
man or woman, from *spondēre* to promise solemnly]

spout (spaʊt) *vb* **1** to discharge (a liquid) in a continuous
jet or in spurts, esp through a narrow gap or under
pressure, or (of a liquid) to gush thus **2** (of a whale, etc)
to discharge air through the blowhole, so that it forms a
spray at the surface of the water **3** *informal* to utter (a
stream of words) on a subject, often at length ▷ *n* **4** a
tube, pipe, chute, etc, allowing the passage or pouring
of liquids, grain, etc **5** a continuous stream or jet of
liquid **6** short for **waterspout 7** up the spout *slang*
a ruined or lost: *any hope of rescue is right up the spout*
b pregnant [c14: perhaps from Middle Dutch *spouten*,
from Old Norse *spyta* to spit] ▷ **ˈspouter** *n*

spouting ('spaʊtɪŋ) *n NZ* **a** a rainwater downpipe on the
exterior of a building **b** such pipes collectively

SPQR *abbreviation* Senatus Populusque Romanus [Latin:
the Senate and People of Rome.]

sprag (spræg) *n* **1** a chock or steel bar used to prevent a
vehicle from running backwards on an incline **2** a
support or post used in mining [c19: of uncertain origin]

sprain (spreɪn) *vb* **1** (*tr*) to injure (a joint) by a sudden
twisting or wrenching of its ligaments ▷ *n* **2** the
resulting injury to such a joint, characterized by
swelling and temporary disability [c17: of uncertain
origin]

sprang (spræŋ) *vb* the past tense of **spring**

sprat (spræt) *n* **1** a small marine food fish, *Clupea sprattus*,
of the NE Atlantic Ocean and North Sea: family *Clupeidae*
(herrings). See also **brisling 2** any of various small or
young herrings [c16: variant of Old English *sprott*; related
to Middle Low German *sprott*, Norwegian *sprot* small rod]

Spratly Islands ('sprætlɪ) *n* a widely-scattered group of
uninhabited islets and reefs in the S South China Sea,
the subject of territorial claims wholly or in part by six
neighbouring nations

sprawl (sprɔːl) *vb* **1** (*intr*) to sit or lie in an ungainly
manner with one's limbs spread out **2** to fall down or
knock down with the limbs spread out in an ungainly
way **3** to spread out or cause to spread out in a
straggling fashion: *his handwriting sprawled all over the paper*
▷ *n* **4** the act or an instance of sprawling **5** a sprawling
posture or arrangement of items **6** a the urban area
formed by the expansion of a town or city into
surrounding countryside: *the urban sprawl* **b** the process
by which this has happened [Old English *spreawlian*;
related to Old English *spryttan* to sprout, **spurt**, Greek
speirein to scatter] ▷ **ˈsprawly** *adj*

spray¹ (spreɪ) *n* **1** fine particles of a liquid **2 a** a liquid,
such as perfume, paint, etc, designed to be discharged
from an aerosol or atomizer: *hair spray* **b** the aerosol or
atomizer itself **3** a quantity of small objects flying
through the air: *a spray of bullets* ▷ *vb* **4** to scatter (liquid)
in the form of fine particles **5** to discharge (a liquid)
from an aerosol or atomizer **6** (*tr*) to treat or bombard
with a spray: *to spray the lawn* [c17: from Middle Dutch
sprāien; related to Middle High German *spræjen*]
▷ **ˈsprayer** *n*

spray² (spreɪ) *n* **1** a single slender shoot, twig, or branch
that bears buds, leaves, flowers, or berries, either
growing on or detached from a plant [c13: of Germanic
origin; compare Old English *spræc* young shoot, Old
Norse *sprek* brittle wood, Old High German *sprahhula*
splinter]

spray gun *n* a device that sprays a fluid in a finely
divided form by atomizing the fluid in an air jet

spread (sprɛd) *vb* **spreads, spreading, spread 1** to extend
or unfold or be extended or unfolded to the fullest

width: *she spread the map on the table* **2** to extend or cause to extend over a larger expanse of space or time: *the milk spread all over the floor; the political unrest spread over several years* **3** to apply or be applied in a coating: *butter does not spread very well when cold* **4** to distribute or be distributed over an area or region **5** to display or be displayed in its fullest extent: *the landscape spread before us* **6** (*tr*) to prepare (a table) for a meal **7** (*tr*) to lay out (a meal) on a table **8** to send or be sent out in all directions; disseminate or be disseminated: *someone has been spreading rumours; the disease spread quickly* **9** (of rails, wires, etc) to force or be forced apart **10** to increase the breadth of (a part), esp to flatten the head of a rivet by pressing, hammering, or forging **11** (*tr*) *agriculture* **a** to lay out (hay) in a relatively thin layer to dry **b** to scatter (seed, manure, etc) over a relatively wide area **12** (*tr; often foll by around*) *informal* to make (oneself) agreeable to a large number of people, often of the opposite sex **13** *phonetics* to narrow and lengthen the aperture of (the lips) as for the articulation of a front vowel, such as (iː) in English *see* (siː) ▷ *n* **14** the act or process of spreading; diffusion, dispersal, expansion, etc: *the spread of the Christian religion* **15** *informal* the wingspan of an aircraft **16** an extent of space or time; stretch: *a spread of 50 years* **17** *informal, chiefly US & Canadian* a ranch or relatively large tract of land **18** the limit of something fully extended: *the spread of a bird's wings* **19** a covering for a table or bed **20** *informal* a large meal or feast, esp when it is laid out on a table **21** a food which can be spread on bread, etc: *salmon spread* **22** two facing pages in a book or other publication **23** a widening of the hips and waist: *middle-age spread* **24** *stock exchange* **a** the difference between the bid and offer prices quoted by a market maker **b** the excess of the price at which stock is offered for public sale over the price paid for the same stock by an underwriter **c** *chiefly US* a double option [Old English *sprǣdan*; related to Old High German *spreiten* to spread, Old Lithuanian *sprainas* stiff] ▷ **'spreadable** *adj* ▷ **'spreader** *n*

spread betting *n* a form of gambling in which stakes are placed not on the results of contests but on the number of points scored, etc. Winnings and losses are calculated according to the accuracy or inaccuracy of the prediction

spread eagle *n* **1** the representation of an eagle with outstretched wings, used as an emblem of the US **2** an acrobatic skating figure

spread-eagle *adj* Also: **spread-eagled 1** lying or standing with arms and legs outstretched ▷ *vb* **2** to assume or cause to assume the shape of a spread eagle **3** (*intr*) *skating* to execute a spread eagle

spreadsheet ('sprɛd,ʃiːt) *n* a computer program that allows easy entry and manipulation of figures, equations, and text, used esp for financial planning and budgeting

sprechgesang (German 'ʃprɛçɡəzaŋ) *n* *music* a type of vocalization between singing and recitation in which the voice sings the beginning of each note and then falls rapidly from the notated pitch. It was originated by Arnold Schoenberg, who used it in *Pierrot Lunaire* (1912) [C20: from German, literally: speaking-song]

spree (spriː) *n* **1** a session of considerable overindulgence, esp in drinking, squandering money, etc **2** a romp [C19: perhaps changed from Scottish *spreath* plundered cattle, ultimately from Latin *praeda* booty]

sprig (sprɪɡ) *n* **1** a shoot, twig, or sprout of a tree, shrub, etc; spray **2** an ornamental device resembling a spray of leaves or flowers **3** a small wire nail without a head **4** *informal, rare* a youth **5** *informal, rare* a person considered as the descendant of an established family, social class, etc **6** *NZ* another name for **stud¹** (sense 5) ▷ *vb* **sprigs, sprigging, sprigged** (*tr*) **7** to fasten or secure with sprigs **8** to ornament (fabric, wallpaper, etc) with a design of sprigs [C15: probably of Germanic origin; compare Low German *sprick*, Swedish *sprygg*] ▷ **'sprigger** *n* ▷ **'spriggy** *adj*

sprightly ('spraɪtlɪ) *adj* **-lier, -liest 1** full of vitality; lively ▷ *adv* **2** *obsolete* in a lively manner [C16: from *spright*, variant of SPRITE + -LY¹] ▷ **'sprightliness** *n*

spring (sprɪŋ) *vb* **springs, springing, sprang** *or* **sprung, sprung 1** to move or cause to move suddenly upwards or

forwards in a single motion **2** to release or be released from a forced position by elastic force: *the bolt sprang back* **3** (*tr*) to leap or jump over **4** (*intr*) to come, issue, or arise suddenly **5** (*intr*) (of a part of a mechanism, etc) to jump out of place **6** to make (wood, etc) warped or split or (of wood, etc) to become warped or split **7** to happen or cause to happen unexpectedly: *to spring a surprise; the boat sprung a leak* **8** (*intr*) to develop or originate: *the idea sprang from a chance meeting* **9** (*intr; usually foll by from*) to be descended: *he sprang from peasant stock* **10** (*intr; often foll by up*) to come into being or appear suddenly: *factories springing up* **11** (*tr*) (of a gun dog) to rouse (game) from cover **12** (*intr*) (of game or quarry) to start or rise suddenly from cover **13** (*intr*) to appear to have a strong upward movement: *the beam springs away from the pillar* **14** to explode (a mine) or (of a mine) to explode **15** (*tr*) to provide with a spring or springs **16** (*tr*) *informal* to arrange the escape of (someone) from prison **17** (*intr*) *archaic or poetic* (of daylight or dawn) to begin to appear ▷ *n* **18** the act or an instance of springing **19** a leap, jump, or bound **20 a** the quality of resilience; elasticity **b** (*as modifier*): *spring steel* **21** the act or an instance of moving rapidly back from a position of tension **22 a** a natural outflow of ground water, as forming the source of a stream **b** (*as modifier*): *spring water* **23 a** a device, such as a coil or strip of steel, that stores potential energy when it is compressed, stretched, or bent and releases it when the restraining force is removed **b** (*as modifier*): *a spring mattress* **24** a structural defect such as a warp or bend **25 a** (*sometimes capital*) the season of the year between winter and summer, astronomically from the March equinox to the June solstice in the N hemisphere and from the September equinox to the December solstice in the S hemisphere **b** (*as modifier*): *spring showers*. Related adj: **vernal 26** the earliest or freshest time of something **27** a source or origin [Old English *springan*; related to Old Norse *springa*, Old High German *springan*, Sanskrit *sprhayati* he desires, Old Slavonic *pragu* grasshopper] ▷ **'springless** *adj* ▷ **'spring,like** *adj*

spring balance *or esp US* **spring scale** *n* a device in which an object to be weighed is attached to the end of a helical spring, the extension of which indicates the weight of the object on a calibrated scale

springboard ('sprɪŋ,bɔːd) *n* **1** a flexible board, usually projecting low over the water, used for diving **2** a similar board used for gaining height or momentum in gymnastics **3** *Austral & NZ* a board inserted into the trunk of a tree at some height above the ground on which a lumberjack stands to chop down the tree **4** anything that serves as a point of departure or initiation

springbok *or less commonly* **springbuck** ('sprɪŋ,bʌk) *n, pl* **-bok, -boks** *or* **-buck, -bucks** an antelope, *Antidorcas marsupialis*, of semidesert regions of southern Africa, which moves in leaps exposing a patch of white erectile hairs on the rump that are usually covered by a fold of skin [C18: from Afrikaans, from Dutch *springen* to SPRING + *bok* goat, BUCK¹]

Springbok ('sprɪŋ,bʌk, -,bɒk) *n* a person who has represented South Africa at rugby union

spring chicken *n* **1** Also called: **springer** *chiefly US & Canadian* a young chicken, tender for cooking, esp one from two to ten months old **2 she is no spring chicken** *informal* she is no longer young

spring-clean *vb* **1** to clean (a house) thoroughly: traditionally at the end of the winter ▷ *n* **2** an instance of spring-cleaning ▷ **,spring-'cleaning** *n*

springe (sprɪndʒ) *n* **1** a snare set to catch small wild animals or birds and consisting of a loop attached to a bent twig or branch under tension ▷ *vb* **2** (*intr*) to set such a snare **3** (*tr*) to catch (small wild animals or birds) with such a snare [C13: related to Old English *springan* to SPRING]

springer ('sprɪŋə) *n* **1** short for **springer spaniel 2** *architect* **a** the first and lowest stone of an arch **b** the impost of an arch

springer spaniel *n* either of two breeds of large quick-moving spaniels bred to spring game, having a slightly domed head and ears of medium length. The **English**

S

springer spaniel is the larger and can be of various colours; the **Welsh springer spaniel** is always a rich red and white

Springfield ('sprɪŋ,fiːld) n 1 a city in S Massachusetts, on the Connecticut River: the site of the US arsenal and armoury (1794–1968), which developed the Springfield and Garand rifles. Pop: 152 157 (2003 est) 2 a city in SW Missouri. Pop: 150 867 (2003 est) 3 a city in central Illinois, capital of the state: the home and burial place of Abraham Lincoln. Pop: 113 586 (2003 est)

springhaas ('sprɪŋ,haːs) n, pl -haas or -hase (-,haːzə) a S and E African nocturnal rodent, *Pedetes capensis*, resembling a small kangaroo: family *Pedetidae* [from Afrikaans: spring hare]

springing ('sprɪŋɪŋ) n the level where an arch or vault rises from a support

spring lock n a type of lock having a spring-loaded bolt, a key being required only to unlock it

spring onion n an immature form of the onion (*Allium cepa*), widely cultivated for its tiny bulb and long green leaves which are eaten in salads, etc. Also called: **green onion, scallion**

spring roll n a Chinese dish consisting of a savoury mixture of vegetables and meat rolled up in a thin pancake and fried

Springs (sprɪŋz) n a city in E South Africa: developed around a coal mine established in 1885 and later became a major world gold-mining centre, now with uranium extraction. Pop: 80 776 (2001)

Springsteen ('sprɪŋ,stiːn) n **Bruce**. born 1949, US rock singer, songwriter, and guitarist. His albums include *Born to Run* (1975), *Darkness on the Edge of Town* (1978), *Born in the USA.* (1984), *The Ghost of Tom Joad* (1995), *The Rising* (2002), and *Magic* (2007)

springtail ('sprɪŋ,teɪl) n any primitive wingless insect of the order *Collembola*, having a forked springing organ with which it projects itself forward

spring tide n 1 either of the two tides that occur at or just after new moon and full moon when the tide-generating force of the sun acts in the same direction as that of the moon, reinforcing it and causing the greatest rise and fall in tidal level. The highest spring tides (**equinoctial springs**) occur at the equinoxes. See **neap tide** 2 any great rush or flood

springtime ('sprɪŋ,taɪm) n 1 Also called: **springtide** ('sprɪŋ,taɪd) the season of spring 2 the earliest, usually the most attractive, period of the existence of something

springy ('sprɪŋɪ) adj **springier, springiest** 1 possessing or characterized by resilience or bounce 2 (of a place) having many wells or springs of water > 'springily adv > 'springiness n

sprinkle ('sprɪŋkᵊl) vb 1 to scatter (liquid, powder, etc) in tiny particles or droplets over (something) 2 (tr) to distribute over (something): *the field was sprinkled with flowers* 3 (intr) to drizzle slightly ▷ n 4 the act or an instance of sprinkling or a quantity that is sprinkled 5 a slight drizzle [c14: probably from Middle Dutch *sprenkelen*; related to Old English *spearca* SPARK¹] > 'sprinkler n

sprinkler system n a fire-extinguishing system that releases water from overhead pipes through nozzles (**sprinklers**) opened automatically by a rise in temperature

sprinkling ('sprɪŋklɪŋ) n a small quantity or amount: *a sprinkling of commonsense*

sprint (sprɪnt) n 1 *athletics* a short race run at top speed, such as the 100 metres 2 a fast finishing speed at the end of a longer race, as in running or cycling, etc 3 any quick run ▷ vb (intr) 4 to go at top speed, as in running, cycling, etc [c16: from Scandinavian; related to Old English *gesprintan* to emit, Old Norse *spretta* to jump up, Old High German *sprinzan* to jump up, Swedish *sprata* to kick] > 'sprinter n

sprit (sprɪt) n *nautical* a light spar pivoted at the mast and crossing a fore-and-aft quadrilateral sail diagonally to the peak [Old English *spreot*; related to Old High German *spriuzen* to support, Dutch *spriet* sprit, Norwegian *sprýta*]

sprite (spraɪt) n 1 (in folklore) a nimble elflike creature, esp one associated with water 2 a small dainty person [c13: from Old French *esprit*, from Latin *spīritus* SPIRIT¹]

spritsail ('sprɪt,seɪl; *Nautical* 'sprɪtsəl) n *nautical* a rectangular sail mounted on a sprit in some 19th-century small vessels

spritzer ('sprɪtsə) n a drink, usually white wine, with soda water added [from German *spritzen* to splash]

sprocket ('sprɒkɪt) n 1 Also called: **sprocket wheel** a relatively thin wheel having teeth projecting radially from the rim, esp one that drives or is driven by a chain 2 an individual tooth on such a wheel 3 a cylindrical wheel with teeth on one or both rims for pulling film through a camera or projector 4 a small wedge-shaped piece of wood used to extend a roof over the eaves [c16: of unknown origin]

sprog (sprɒg) n *slang* 1 a child; baby 2 (esp in RAF) a recruit

sprout (spraʊt) vb 1 (of a plant, seed, etc) to produce (new leaves, shoots, etc) 2 (intr; often foll by *up*) to begin to grow or develop: *new office blocks are sprouting up all over the city* ▷ n 3 a newly grown shoot or bud 4 something that grows like a sprout 5 See **Brussels sprout** [Old English *sprūtan*; related to Middle High German *sprūzen* to sprout, Lettish *sprausties* to jostle]

spruce¹ (spruːs) n 1 any coniferous tree of the N temperate genus *Picea*, cultivated for timber and for ornament: family *Pinaceae*. They grow in a pyramidal shape and have needle-like leaves and light-coloured wood. See also **Norway spruce** 2 the wood of any of these trees [c17: short for *Spruce fir*, from C14 *Spruce* Prussia, changed from *Pruce*, via Old French from Latin *Prussia*]

spruce² (spruːs) adj neat, smart, and trim [c16: perhaps from *Spruce leather* a fashionable leather imported from Prussia; see SPRUCE¹] > 'sprucely adv > 'spruceness n

spruce beer n an alcoholic drink made of fermented molasses flavoured with spruce twigs and cones

spruce grouse n a game bird, *Dendragapus canadensis*, occurring in Canadian coniferous forests

spruce up vb (adverb) to make (oneself, a person, or thing) smart and neat

sprue¹ (spruː) n 1 a vertical channel in a mould through which plastic or molten metal is introduced or out of which it flows when the mould is filled 2 plastic or metal that solidifies in a sprue [c19: of unknown origin]

sprue² (spruː) n a chronic disease, esp of tropical climates, characterized by flatulence, diarrhoea, frothy foul-smelling stools, and emaciation [c19: from Dutch *spruw*; related to Middle Low German *sprüwe* tumour]

spruik ('spruːɪk) vb (intr) *Austral archaic, slang* to speak in public (used esp of a showman or salesman) [c20: of unknown origin] > 'spruiker n

spruit (spreɪt) n *South African* a small tributary stream or watercourse [Afrikaans *spruit* offshoot, tributary]

sprung (sprʌŋ) vb the past participle and a past tense of **spring**

sprung rhythm n *prosody* a type of poetic rhythm characterized by metrical feet of irregular composition, each having one strongly stressed syllable, often the first, and an indefinite number of unstressed syllables

spry (spraɪ) adj **spryer, spryest** or **sprier, spriest** active and brisk; nimble [c18: perhaps of Scandinavian origin; compare Swedish dialect *spragg* SPRIG] > 'spryly adv > 'spryness n

spud (spʌd) n 1 an informal word for **potato** (sense 1) 2 a narrow-bladed spade for cutting roots, digging up weeds, etc ▷ vb **spuds, spudding, spudded** 3 (intr) to drill the first foot of an oil-well [c15 *spudde* short knife, of unknown origin; applied later to a digging tool, and hence to a potato]

spuddle ('spʌdᵊl) n *Southwest English dialect* a feeble movement

Spud Island n a slang name for **Prince Edward Island**

spue (spjuː) vb **spues, spuing, spued** an archaic spelling of **spew** > 'spuer n

spume (spjuːm) n 1 foam or surf, esp on the sea; froth ▷ vb 2 (intr) to foam or froth [c14: from Old French *espume*, from Latin *spūma*] > 'spumous or 'spumy adj

spun (spʌn) *vb* **1** the past tense and past participle of **spin** ▷ *adj* **2** formed or manufactured by spinning: *spun gold; spun glass*

spunk (spʌŋk) *n* **1** *informal* courage or spirit **2** *Brit* a slang word for **semen** **3** touchwood or tinder, esp originally made from various spongy types of fungus **4** *Austral & NZ informal* a person, esp male, who is attractive to the opposite sex [C16 (in the sense: a spark): from Scottish Gaelic *spong* tinder, sponge, from Latin *spongia* sponge] > 'spunky *adj* > 'spunkily *adv*

spun silk *n* yarn or fabric made from silk waste

spur (spɜː) *n* **1** a pointed device or sharp spiked wheel fixed to the heel of a rider's boot to enable him to urge his horse on **2** anything serving to urge or encourage: *the increase in salary was a spur to their production* **3** a sharp horny projection from the leg just above the claws in male birds, such as the domestic cock **4** a pointed process in any of various animals; calcar **5** a tubular extension at the base of the corolla in flowers such as larkspur **6** a short or stunted branch of a tree **7** a ridge projecting laterally from a mountain or mountain range **8** a wooden prop or a masonry reinforcing pier **9** another name for **groyne** **10** Also called: **spur track** a railway branch line or siding **11** a short side road leading off a main road: *a motorway spur* **12** a sharp cutting instrument attached to the leg of a gamecock **13 on the spur of the moment** on impulse **14 win one's spurs a** *history* to earn knighthood **b** to prove one's ability; gain distinction ▷ *vb* **spurs, spurring, spurred** **15** (*tr*) to goad or urge with or as if with spurs **16** (*intr*) to go or ride quickly; press on **17** (*tr*) to injure or strike with a spur **18** (*tr*) to provide with a spur or spurs [Old English *spura*; related to Old Norse *spori*, Old High German *sporo*]

spurge (spɜːdʒ) *n* any of various euphorbiaceous plants of the genus *Euphorbia* that have milky sap and small flowers typically surrounded by conspicuous bracts. Some species have purgative properties [C14: from Old French *espurge*, from *espurgier* to purge, from Latin *expurgāre* to cleanse, from EX-¹ + *purgāre* to PURGE]

spur gear or **spur wheel** *n* a gear having involuted teeth either straight or helically cut on a cylindrical surface. Two such gears are used to transmit power between parallel shafts

spurious ('spjʊərɪəs) *adj* **1** not genuine or real **2** (of a plant part or organ) having the appearance of another part but differing from it in origin, development, or function; false **3** *rare* illegitimate [C17: from Latin *spurius* of illegitimate birth] > 'spuriously *adv* > 'spuriousness *n*

spurn (spɜːn) *vb* **1** to reject (a person or thing) with contempt **2** (when *intr*, often foll by *against*) *archaic* to kick (at) ▷ *n* **3** an instance of spurning **4** *archaic* a kick or thrust [Old English *spurnan*; related to Old Norse *sporna*, Old High German *spurnan*, Latin *spernere* to despise, Lithuanian *spiriu* to kick] > 'spurner *n*

spurt or **spirt** (spɜːt) *vb* **1** to gush or cause to gush forth in a sudden stream or jet **2** to make a sudden effort ▷ *n* **3** a sudden forceful stream or jet **4** a short burst of activity, speed, or energy [C16: perhaps related to Middle High German *sprützen* to squirt]

Sputnik ('spʊtnɪk, 'spʌt-) *n* any of a series of unmanned Soviet satellites, **Sputnik 1** (launched in 1957) being the first man-made satellite to orbit the earth [C20: from Russian, literally: fellow traveller, from s- with + *put* path + -*nik* suffix indicating agent]

sputter ('spʌtə) *vb* **1** *physics* **a** to undergo or cause to undergo a process in which atoms of a solid are removed from its surface by the impact of high-energy ions, as in a discharge tube **b** to coat (a film of a metal) onto (a solid surface) by using this process ▷ *n* **2** the process or noise of sputtering **3** incoherent stammering speech **4** something that is ejected while sputtering [C16: from Dutch *sputteren*, of imitative origin] > 'sputterer *n*

sputum ('spjuːtəm) *n*, *pl* -**ta** (-tə) saliva ejected from the mouth mixed with mucus or pus exuded from the respiratory passages, as in bronchitis or bronchiectasis [C17: from Latin: spittle, from *spuere* to spit out]

spy (spaɪ) *n*, *pl* **spies** **1** a person employed by a state or institution to obtain secret information from rival countries, organizations, companies, etc **2** a person who keeps secret watch on others **3** *obsolete* a close view ▷ *vb* **spies, spying, spied** **4** (*intr*; usually foll by *on*) to keep a secret or furtive watch (on) **5** (*intr*) to engage in espionage **6** (*tr*) to catch sight of; descry [C13 *spien*, from Old French *espier*, of Germanic origin; related to Old High German *spehōn*, Middle Dutch *spien*]

spyglass ('spaɪˌɡlɑːs) *n* a small telescope

spy out *vb* (*tr, adverb*) **1** to discover by careful observation: *to spy out a route* **2** to make a close scrutiny of: *to spy out the land*

spyware ('spaɪˌwɛə) *n* *computing* software installed via the internet on a computer without the user's knowledge and used to send information about the user to another computer

sq. *abbreviation* **1** sequence **2** square **3** *pl* **sqq** the following one [from Latin *sequens*]

Sq. *abbreviation* **1** Squadron **2** (in place names) Square

SQL *abbreviation* structured query language: a computer programming language used for database management

squab (skwɒb) *n*, *pl* **squabs** or **squab** **1** a young unfledged bird, esp a pigeon **2** a short fat person **3 a** a well-stuffed bolster or cushion **b** a sofa ▷ *adj* **4** (of birds) recently hatched and still unfledged **5** short and fat [C17: probably of Germanic origin; compare Swedish dialect *sqvabb* flabby skin, *sqvabba* fat woman, German *Quabbe* soft mass, Norwegian *kvabb* mud] > 'squabby *adj*

squabble ('skwɒbªl) *vb* **1** (*intr*) to quarrel over a small matter ▷ *n* **2** a petty quarrel [C17: probably of Scandinavian origin; related to Swedish dialect *sqvabbel* to quarrel] > 'squabbler *n*

squad (skwɒd) *n* **1** the smallest military formation, typically comprising a dozen soldiers, used esp as a drill formation **2** any small group of people engaged in a common pursuit **3** *sport* a number of players from which a team is to be selected [C17: from Old French *esquade*, from Old Spanish *escuadra*, from *escuadrar* to SQUARE, from the square formations used]

squaddie or **squaddy** ('skwɒdɪ) *n*, *pl* -**dies** *Brit slang* a private soldier. See **swaddy** [C20: from SQUAD]

squadron ('skwɒdrən) *n* **1 a** a subdivision of a naval fleet detached for a particular task **b** a number of naval units usually of similar type and consisting of two or more divisions **2** a cavalry unit comprising two or more troops, headquarters, and supporting arms **3** the basic tactical and administrative air force unit comprising two or more flights. Abbreviation: **sqn** [C16: from Italian *squadrone* soldiers drawn up in square formation, from *squadro* SQUARE]

squadron leader *n* an officer holding commissioned rank, between flight lieutenant and wing commander in the air forces of Britain and certain other countries

squalene ('skweɪˌliːn) *n* *biochem* a terpene first found in the liver of sharks but also present in the livers of most higher animals: an important precursor of cholesterol [C20: from New Latin *squalus* genus name of the shark]

squalid ('skwɒlɪd) *adj* **1** dirty and repulsive, esp as a result of neglect or poverty **2** sordid [C16: from Latin *squālidus*, from *squālēre* to be stiff with dirt] > squalidity (skwɒ'lɪdɪtɪ) or 'squalidness *n* > 'squalidly *adv*

squall¹ (skwɔːl) *n* **1** a sudden strong wind or brief turbulent storm **2** any sudden commotion or show of temper ▷ *vb* **3** (*intr*) to blow in a squall [C18: perhaps a special use of SQUALL²] > 'squallish *adj* > 'squally *adj*

squall² (skwɔːl) *vb* **1** (*intr*) to cry noisily; yell ▷ *n* **2** a shrill or noisy yell or howl [C17: probably of Scandinavian origin; compare Icelandic *skvala* to shout; see SQUEAL] > 'squaller *n*

squalor ('skwɒlə) *n* the condition or quality of being squalid; disgusting dirt and filth [C17: from Latin]

squama ('skweɪmə) *n*, *pl* -**mae** (-miː) *biology* a scale or scalelike structure [C18: from Latin] > squamate ('skweɪmeɪt) *adj*

squander ('skwɒndə) *vb* (*tr*) **1** to spend wastefully or extravagantly; dissipate **2** an obsolete word for **scatter** [C16: of unknown origin] > 'squanderer *n*

square (skwɛə) *n* **1** a plane geometric figure having four equal sides and four right angles **2** any object, part, or arrangement having this or a similar shape **3** (*capital* *when part of name*) an open area in a town, sometimes including the surrounding buildings, which may form a square **4** *maths* the product of two equal factors; the second power: *9 is the square of 3, written 3²* **5** an instrument having two strips of wood, metal, etc, set in the shape of a T or L, used for constructing or testing right angles **6** *cricket* the closely-cut area in the middle of a ground on which wickets are prepared **7** *informal* a person who is old-fashioned in views, customs, appearance, etc **8** *obsolete* a standard, pattern, or rule **9** back to square one indicating a return to the starting-point of an investigation, experiment, etc, because of failure, lack of progress, etc **10** on the square **a** at right angles **b** on equal terms **c** *informal* honestly and openly **11** out of square **a** not at right angles or not having a right angle **b** not in order or agreement ▷ *adj* **12** being a square in shape **13** having or forming one or more right angles or being at right angles to something **14 a** (*prenominal*) denoting a measure of area of any shape: *a circle of four square feet* **b** (*immediately postpositive*) denoting a square having a specified length on each side: *a board four feet square contains 16 square feet* **15** fair and honest (esp in the phrase **a square deal**) **16** straight, even, or level: *a square surface* **17** *cricket* at right angles to the wicket: *square leg* **18** *sport* in a straight line across the pitch: *a square pass* **19** *nautical* (of the sails of a square-rigger) set at right angles to the keel **20** *informal* old-fashioned in views, customs, appearance, etc **21** stocky or sturdy: *square shoulders* **22** (*postpositive*) having no remaining debts or accounts to be settled **23** (*prenominal*) unequivocal or straightforward: *a square contradiction* **24** (*postpositive*) neat and tidy **25** *maths* (of a matrix) having the same number of rows and columns **26** all square on equal terms; even in score **27** square peg or square peg in a round hole *informal* a person or thing that is a misfit, such as an employee in a job for which he is unsuited ▷ *vb* (*mainly tr*) **28** to make into a square or similar shape **29** *maths* to raise (a number or quantity) to the second power **30** to test or adjust for deviation with respect to a right angle, plane surface, etc **31** (sometimes foll by *off*) to divide into squares **32** to position so as to be rectangular, straight, or level: *square the shoulders* **33** (sometimes foll by *up*) to settle (debts, accounts) etc **34** to level (the score) in a game, etc **35** (*also intr*; often foll by *with*) to agree or cause to agree: *your ideas don't square with mine* **36** to arrange (something), esp by a corrupt method or come to an arrangement with (someone), as by bribery **37** square the circle to attempt the impossible (in reference to the insoluble problem of constructing a square having exactly the same area as a given circle) ▷ *adv* **38** in order to be square **39** at right angles **40** *sport* in a straight line across the pitch: *pass the ball square* **41** *informal* squarely ▷ See also **square away, square off**, etc [c13: from Old French *esquare*, from Vulgar Latin *exquadra* (unattested), from Latin ex-¹ + *quadrāre* to make square; see QUADRANT]

square away *vb* (*adverb*) **1** to set the sails of (a square-rigger) at right angles to the keel **2** (*tr*) *US & Canadian* to make neat and tidy

square-bashing *n* *Brit military slang* drill on a barrack square

square bracket *n* **1** either of a pair of characters [ ], used to enclose a section of writing or printing to separate it from the main text **2** Also called: **bracket** either of these characters used as a sign of aggregation in mathematical or logical expressions indicating that the expression contained in the brackets is to be evaluated first and treated as a unit in the evaluation of the whole

square dance *n* **1** *chiefly US & Canadian* any of various formation dances, such as a quadrille, in which the couples form squares ▷ *vb* **square-dance 2** (*intr*) to perform such a dance > **'square-,dancer** *n*

square go *n* *Scot informal* a fair fight between two individuals

square knot *n* another name for **reef knot**

square leg *n* *cricket* **1** a fielding position on the on side approximately at right angles to the batsman **2** a person who fields in this position

squarely ('skweəlɪ) *adv* **1** in a direct way; straight: *he hit*

me squarely on the nose **2** in an honest, frank, and just manner **3** at right angles

square meal *n* a substantial meal consisting of enough food to satisfy

square measure *n* a unit or system of units for measuring areas

square number *n* an integer, such as 1, 4, 9, or 16, that is the square of an integer

square off *vb* (*intr, adverb*) to assume a posture of offence or defence, as in boxing

square of opposition *n* See **opposition** (sense 9b)

square-rigged *adj* *nautical* rigged with square sails

square root *n* a number or quantity that when multiplied by itself gives a given number or quantity: *2 is a square root of 4, usually written √4 or 4^{1/2}*

square sail *n* *nautical* a rectangular or square sail set on a horizontal yard rigged more or less athwartships

square shooter *n* *informal, chiefly US* an honest or frank person > **square shooting** *n*

square up *vb* (*adverb*) **1** to pay or settle (bills, debts, etc) **2** *informal* to arrange or be arranged satisfactorily **3** (*intr*; foll by *to*) to prepare to be confronted (with), esp courageously **4** (*tr*; foll by *to*) to adopt a position of readiness to fight (an opponent) **5** *Scot* to tidy up

squarrose ('skwærəʊz, 'skwɒ-) *adj* **1** *biology* having a rough surface, caused by the presence of projecting hairs, scales, etc **2** *botany* having or relating to parts that are recurved [c18: from Latin *squarrōsus* scabby]

squash¹ (skwɒʃ) *vb* **1** to press or squeeze or be pressed or squeezed in or down so as to crush, distort, or pulp **2** (*tr*) to suppress or overcome **3** (*tr*) to humiliate or crush (a person), esp with a disconcerting retort **4** (*intr*) to make a sucking, splashing, or squelching sound **5** (often foll by *in* or *into*) to enter or insert in a confined space ▷ *n* **6** *Brit* a still drink made from fruit juice or fruit syrup diluted with water **7** a crush, esp of people in a confined space **8** something that is squashed **9** the act or sound of squashing or the state of being squashed **10** Also called: **squash rackets, squash racquets** a game for two or four players played in an enclosed court with a small rubber ball and light long-handled rackets. The ball may be hit against any of the walls but must hit the facing wall at a point above a horizontal line. See also **rackets 11** Also called: **squash tennis** a similar game played with larger rackets and a larger pneumatic ball [c16: from Old French *esquasser*, from Vulgar Latin *exquassāre* (unattested), from Latin ex-¹ + *quassāre* to shatter] > **'squasher** *n*

squash² (skwɒʃ) *n, pl* **squashes** or **squash** *US & Canadian* **1** any of various marrow-like cucurbitaceous plants of the genus *Cucurbita*, esp *C. pepo* and *C. moschata*, the fruits of which have a hard rind surrounding edible flesh **2** the fruit of any of these plants, eaten as a vegetable [c17: from Narraganset *askutasquash*, literally: green vegetable eaten green]

squashy ('skwɒʃɪ) *adj* **squashier, squashiest 1** easily squashed; pulpy: *a squashy peach* **2** soft and wet; marshy: *squashy ground* > **'squashily** *adv* > **'squashiness** *n*

squat (skwɒt) *vb* **squats, squatting, squatted** (*intr*) **1** to rest in a crouching position with the knees bent and the weight on the feet **2** to crouch down, esp in order to hide **3** *law* (*tr*) to occupy land or property to which the occupant has no legal title ▷ *adj* **4** Also called: **squatty** ('skwɒtɪ) short and broad ▷ *n* **5** a squatting position **6** a house occupied by squatters [c13: from Old French *esquatir*, from *es-* ex-¹ + *catir* to press together, from Vulgar Latin *coactīre* (unattested), from Latin *cōgere* to compress, from co- + *agere* to drive] > **'squatly** *adv* > **'squatness** *n*

squatter ('skwɒtə) *n* **1** a person who occupies property or land to which he has no legal title **2** (in Australia) **a** (formerly) a person who occupied a tract of land, esp pastoral land, as tenant of the Crown **b** a farmer of sheep or cattle on a large scale **3** (in New Zealand) a 19th-century settler who took up large acreage on a Crown lease

squat thrust *n* an exercise in which the hands are kept on the floor with the arms held straight while the legs are straightened out behind and quickly drawn in towards the body again

squattocracy (skwɒˈtɒkrəsɪ) n chiefly Austral squatters collectively, regarded as rich and influential. See **squatter** (sense 2b) [c19: from SQUATTER + -CRACY]

squaw (skwɔː) n **1** offensive a North American Indian woman **2** slang, usually facetious a woman or wife [c17: of Algonquian origin; compare Natick squa female creature]

squawk (skwɔːk) n **1** a loud raucous cry; screech **2** informal a loud complaint or protest ▷ vb **3** to utter a squawk or with a squawk **4** (intr) informal to complain loudly [c19: of imitative origin] > **'squawker** n

squaw man n offensive a White or other non-American-Indian man married to a North American Indian woman

squeak (skwiːk) n **1** a short shrill cry or high-pitched sound **2** informal an escape (esp in the phrases **narrow squeak, near squeak**) ▷ vb **3** to make or cause to make a squeak **4** (intr; usually foll by through or by) to pass with only a narrow margin: to squeak through an examination **5** (intr) informal to confess information about oneself or another **6** (tr) to utter with a squeak [c17: probably of Scandinavian origin; compare Swedish skväka to croak] > **'squeaky** adj > **'squeakily** adv > **'squeakiness** n

squeaky-clean adj **1** (of hair) washed so clean that wet strands squeak when rubbed **2** completely clean **3** informal, derogatory (of a person) cultivating a virtuous and wholesome image

squeal (skwiːl) n **1** a high shrill yelp, as of pain **2** a screaming sound, as of tyres when a car brakes suddenly ▷ vb **3** to utter a squeal or with a squeal **4** (intr) slang to confess information about another **5** (intr) informal, chiefly Brit to complain or protest loudly [c13 squelen, of imitative origin] > **'squealer** n

squeamish ('skwiːmɪʃ) adj **1** easily sickened or nauseated, as by the sight of blood **2** easily shocked; fastidious or prudish **3** easily frightened: squeamish about spiders [c15: from Anglo-French escoymous, of unknown origin] > **'squeamishly** adv > **'squeamishness** n

squeegee ('skwiːdʒiː) or less commonly **squilgee** n **1** an implement with a rubber blade used for wiping away surplus water from a surface, such as a windowpane **2** any of various similar devices used in photography for pressing the water out of wet prints or negatives or for squeezing prints onto a glazing surface ▷ vb **-gees, -geeing, -geed 3** to remove (water or other liquid) from (something) by use of a squeegee [c19: probably of imitative origin, influenced by SQUEEZE]

squeeze (skwiːz) vb (mainly tr) **1** to grip or press firmly, esp so as to crush or distort; compress **2** to crush or press (something) so as to extract (a liquid): to squeeze the juice from an orange; to squeeze an orange **3** to apply gentle pressure to, as in affection or reassurance: he squeezed her hand **4** to push or force in a confined space: to squeeze six lettuces into one box; to squeeze through a crowd **5** to hug closely **6** to oppress with exacting demands, such as excessive taxes **7** to exert pressure on (someone) in order to extort (something): to squeeze money out of a victim by blackmail **8** bridge, whist to lead a card that forces (opponents) to discard potentially winning cards ▷ n **9** the act or an instance of squeezing or of being squeezed **10** a hug or handclasp **11** a crush of people in a confined space **12** chiefly Brit a condition of restricted credit imposed by a government to counteract price inflation **13** an amount extracted by squeezing: add a squeeze of lemon juice **14** commerce any action taken by a trader or traders on a market that forces buyers to make purchases and prices to rise **15** informal pressure brought to bear in order to extort something (esp in the phrase **put the squeeze on**) **16** Also called: **squeeze play** bridge, whist a manoeuvre that forces opponents to discard potentially winning cards [c16: from Middle English queysen to press, from Old English cwȳsan] > **'squeezable** adj > **'squeezer** n

squeezy ('skwiːzɪ) adj **squeezier, squeeziest** (of bottles, tubes, mops, etc) designed to be squeezed, especially in order to extract something

squelch (skwɛltʃ) vb **1** (intr) to walk laboriously through soft wet material or with wet shoes, making a sucking noise **2** (intr) to make such a noise **3** (tr) to crush

completely; squash **4** (tr) informal to silence, as by a crushing retort ▷ n **5** a squelching sound **6** something that has been squelched **7** informal a crushing remark [c17: of imitative origin] > **'squelcher** n > **'squelchy** adj

squib (skwɪb) n **1** a firework, usually having a tube filled with gunpowder, that burns with a hissing noise and culminates in a small explosion **2** a short witty attack; lampoon **3** damp squib something intended but failing to impress ▷ vb **squibs, squibbing, squibbed 4** (intr) to sound, move, or explode like a squib **5** (intr) to let off or shoot a squib **6** to write a squib against (someone) [c16: probably imitative of a quick light explosion]

squid (skwɪd) n, pl **squid** or **squids** any of various fast-moving pelagic cephalopod molluscs of the genera Loligo, Ommastrephes, etc, of most seas, having a torpedo-shaped body ranging from about 10 centimetres to 16.5 metres long and a pair of triangular tail fins: order Decapoda (decapods). See also **cuttlefish** [c17: of unknown origin]

squiffy ('skwɪfɪ) adj **-fier, -fiest** Brit informal slightly drunk. Also called: **squiffed** [c19: of unknown origin]

squiggle ('skwɪgᵊl) n **1** a mark or movement in the form of a wavy line; curlicue **2** an illegible scrawl ▷ vb **3** (intr) to wriggle **4** (intr) to form or draw squiggles **5** (tr) to make into squiggles [c19: perhaps a blend of SQUIRM + WIGGLE] > **'squiggler** n > **'squiggly** adj

squilgee ('skwɪldʒiː) n a variant of **squeegee** [c19: perhaps from SQUEEGEE, influenced by SQUELCH]

squill (skwɪl) n **1** the bulb of the sea squill, formerly used medicinally as an expectorant after being sliced and dried **2** any Old World liliaceous plant of the genus Scilla, such as S. verna (**spring squill**) of Europe, having small blue or purple flowers [c14: from Latin squilla sea onion, from Greek skilla, of obscure origin]

squinch (skwɪntʃ) n a small arch, corbelling, etc, across an internal corner of a tower, used to support a superstructure such as a spire. Also called: **squinch arch** [c15: from obsolete scunch, from Middle English sconcheon, from Old French escoinson, from es- EX-¹ + coin corner]

squint (skwɪnt) vb **1** (usually intr) to cross or partly close (the eyes) **2** (intr) to have a squint **3** (intr) to look or glance sideways or askance ▷ n **4** the nontechnical name for **strabismus 5** the act or an instance of squinting; glimpse **6** Also called: **hagioscope** a narrow oblique opening in a wall or pillar of a church to permit a view of the main altar from a side aisle or transept **7** informal a quick look; glance ▷ adj **8** having a squint **9** informal crooked; askew [c14: short for ASQUINT] > **'squinter** n > **'squinty** adj

squire (skwaɪə) n **1** a country gentleman in England, esp the main landowner in a rural community **2** feudal history a young man of noble birth, who attended upon a knight **3** rare a man who courts or escorts a woman **4** informal, chiefly Brit a term of address used by one man to another, esp, unless ironic, to a member of a higher social class ▷ vb **5** (tr) (of a man) to escort (a woman) [c13: from Old French esquier; see ESQUIRE]

squirearchy or **squirarchy** ('skwaɪəˌrɑːkɪ) n, pl **-chies 1** government by squires **2** squires collectively, esp as a political or social force [c19: from SQUIRE + -ARCHY, on the model of HIERARCHY, MONARCHY, etc] > **squire'archal, squir'archal, squire'archical** or **squir'archical** adj

squireen (skwaɪˈriːn) or **squireling** ('skwaɪəlɪŋ) n rare a petty squire [c19: from SQUIRE + -een, Anglo-Irish diminutive suffix, from Irish Gaelic -ín]

squirm (skwɜːm) vb (intr) **1** to move with a wriggling motion; writhe **2** to feel deep mental discomfort, guilt, embarrassment, etc ▷ n **3** a squirming movement [c17: of imitative origin (perhaps influenced by WORM)] > **'squirmer** n

squirrel ('skwɪrᵊl; US 'skwɜːrᵊl, 'skwʌr-) n, pl **-rels** or **-rel 1** any arboreal sciurine rodent of the genus Sciurus, such as S. vulgaris (**red squirrel**) or S. carolinensis (**grey squirrel**), having a bushy tail and feeding on nuts, seeds, etc **2** any other rodent of the family Sciuridae, such as a ground squirrel or a marmot **3** the fur of such an animal **4** informal a person who hoards things ▷ vb **-rels, -relling, -relled** or esp US **-rels, -reling, -reled 5** (tr; usually foll by away) informal to store for future use; hoard [c14: from Old French esquireul, from Late Latin sciūrus, from Greek

S

skiouros, from *skia* shadow + *oura* tail]

squirrel cage *n* **1** a cage consisting of a cylindrical framework that is made to rotate by a small animal running inside the framework **2** a repetitive purposeless task, way of life, etc **3** Also called: **squirrel-cage motor** *electrical engineering* the rotor of an induction motor with a cylindrical winding having copper bars around the periphery parallel to the axis

squirt (skw3:t) *vb* **1** to force (a liquid) or (of a liquid) to be forced out of a narrow opening **2** (*tr*) to cover or spatter with liquid so ejected ▷ *n* **3** a jet or amount of liquid so ejected **4** the act or an instance of squirting **5** any instrument used for squirting **6** *informal* **a** a person regarded as insignificant or contemptible **b** a short person [c15: of imitative origin] > **'squirter** *n*

squirting cucumber *n* a hairy cucurbitaceous plant, *Ecballium elaterium*, of the Mediterranean region, having a fruit that discharges its seeds explosively when ripe

squish (skwɪʃ) *vb* **1** (*tr*) to crush, esp so as to make a soft splashing noise **2** (*intr*) (of mud, etc) to make a splashing noise ▷ *n* **3** a soft squashing sound [c17: of imitative origin] > **'squishy** *adj*

squit (skwɪt) *n* *Brit slang* **1** an insignificant person **2** nonsense; rubbish [c19: dialectal variant of SQUIRT]

squiz (skwɪz) *n, pl* **squizzes** *Austral & NZ slang* a look or glance, esp an inquisitive one [c20: perhaps a blend of SQUINT and QUIZ]

sr *symbol for* steradian

Sr *abbreviation* **1** (after a name) senior **2** Señor **3** Sir **4** Sister (religious) **5** *the chemical symbol for* strontium

Sra *abbreviation* Señora

SRA *abbreviation* (in Britain) Strategic Rail Authority

Srbija ('sɜ°rbija) *n* a transliteration of the Serbian name for: **Serbia**

Sri Lanka (‚sri: 'læŋkə) *n* a republic in S Asia, occupying the island of Ceylon: settled by the Sinhalese from S India in about 550 BC; became a British colony 1802; gained independence in 1948, becoming a republic within the Commonwealth in 1972. Exports include tea, cocoa, cinnamon, and copra. Official languages: Sinhalese and Tamil; English is also widely spoken. Religion: Hinayana Buddhist majority. Currency: Sri Lanka rupee. Capital: Colombo (administrative), Sri Jayewardenepura Kotte (legislative). Parts of the coast suffered badly in the Indian Ocean tsunami of December 2004. Pop: 19 218 000 (2004 est). Area: 65 610 sq km (25 332 sq miles). Former name (until 1972): **Ceylon** > **Sri Lankan** *adj, n*

Srinagar (sri:'nʌgə) *n* a city in N India, the summer capital of the state of Jammu and Kashmir, at an altitude of 1600 m (5250 ft) on the Jhelum River: seat of the University of Jammu and Kashmir (1948). Pop: 894 940 (2001)

SRN *abbreviation* (formerly, in Britain) State Registered Nurse

SRO *abbreviation* **1** standing room only **2** *Brit* Statutory Rules and Orders **3** self-regulatory organization

Srta *abbreviation* Señorita

SS *abbreviation* **1** a paramilitary organization within the Nazi party that provided Hitler's bodyguard, security forces including the Gestapo, concentration camp guards, and a corp of combat troops (the Waffen-SS) in World War II [German *Schutzstaffel* protection squad] **2** steamship

SSE *symbol for* south-southeast

SSL *abbreviation* Secure Sockets Layer: a way of enabling the secure encrypted transmission of sensitive data via the internet

ssp. *pl* **sspp.** *abbreviation biology* subspecies

SSR *abbreviation* (formerly) Soviet Socialist Republic

SST *abbreviation* supersonic transport

Ssu-ma Ch'ien ('su:ma: 'tʃɪən) *n* a variant transliteration of **Si-ma Qian**

SSW *symbol for* south-southwest

St *abbreviation* **1** Saint (all entries that are usually preceded by *St* are in this dictionary listed alphabetically under **Saint**) **2** statute **3** strait **4** street

st. *abbreviation* **1** stanza **2** statute **3** *cricket* stumped by

-st *suffix* a variant of **-est²**

Sta *abbreviation* (in the names of places or churches) Saint (female) [Italian *Santa*]

stab (stæb) *vb* **stabs**, **stabbing**, **stabbed** **1** (*tr*) to pierce or injure with a sharp pointed instrument **2** (*tr*) (of a sharp pointed instrument) to pierce or wound **3** (when *intr*, often foll by *at*) to make a thrust (at); jab **4** (*tr*) to inflict with a sharp pain **5 stab in the back a** (*verb*) to do damage to the reputation of (a person, esp a friend) in a surreptitious way **b** (*noun*) a treacherous action or remark that causes the downfall of or injury to a person ▷ *n* **6** the act or an instance of stabbing **7** an injury or rift made by stabbing **8** a sudden sensation, esp an unpleasant one: *a stab of pity* **9** *informal* an attempt (esp in the phrase **make a stab at**) [c14: from *stabbe* stab wound; probably related to Middle English *stob* stick] > **'stabber** *n*

Stabat Mater ('sta:bæt 'ma:tə) *n* **1** *RC Church* a Latin hymn, probably of the 13th century, commemorating the sorrows of the Virgin Mary at the crucifixion and used in the Mass and various other services **2** a musical setting of this hymn [from the opening words, literally: the mother was standing]

stabile ('steɪbaɪl) *n* **1** *arts* a stationary abstract construction, usually of wire, metal, wood, etc ▷ *adj* **2** fixed; stable **3** resistant to chemical change [c18: from Latin *stabilis*]

stability (stə'bɪlɪtɪ) *n, pl* **-ties** **1** the quality of being stable **2** the ability of an aircraft to resume its original flight path after inadvertent displacement

stabilize *or* **stabilise** ('steɪbɪ‚laɪz) *vb* **1** to make or become stable or more stable **2** to keep or be kept stable **3** to put or keep (an aircraft, vessel, etc) in equilibrium by one or more special devices, or (of an aircraft, vessel, etc) to become stable > ‚stabili'zation *or* ‚stabili'sation *n*

stabilizer *or* **stabiliser** ('steɪbɪ‚laɪzə) *n* **1** any device for stabilizing an aircraft **2** a substance added to something to maintain it in a stable or unchanging state, such as an additive to food to preserve its texture during distribution and storage **3** *nautical* **a** a system of one or more pairs of fins projecting from the hull of a ship and controllable to counteract roll **b** See **gyrostabilizer** **4** either of a pair of brackets supporting a small wheel that can be fitted to the back wheel of a bicycle to help an inexperienced cyclist to maintain balance **5** *economics* a measure, such as progressive taxation, interest-rate control, or unemployment benefit, used to restrict swings in prices, employment, production, etc, in a free economy **6** a person or thing that stabilizes

stable¹ ('steɪbəl) *n* **1** a building, usually consisting of stalls, for the lodging of horses or other livestock **2** the animals lodged in such a building, collectively **3 a** the racehorses belonging to a particular establishment or owner **b** the establishment itself **c** (*as modifier*): *stable companion* **4** *informal* a source of training, such as a school, theatre, etc: *the two athletes were out of the same stable* **5** a number of people considered as a source of a particular talent: *a stable of writers* **6** (*modifier*) of, relating to, or suitable for a stable: *stable manners* ▷ *vb* **7** to put, keep, or be kept in a stable [c13: from Old French *estable* cowshed, from Latin *stabulum* shed, from *stāre* to stand]

stable² ('steɪbəl) *adj* **1** steady in position or balance; firm **2** lasting or permanent: *a stable relationship* **3** steadfast or firm of purpose **4** (of an elementary particle, atomic nucleus, etc) not undergoing decay; not radioactive **5** (of a chemical compound) not readily partaking in a chemical change [c13: from Old French *estable*, from Latin *stabilis* steady, from *stāre* to stand] > **'stableness** *n* > **'stably** *adv*

stableboy ('steɪb°l‚bɔɪ) *or* **stableman** ('steɪb°l‚mæn, -mən) *n, pl* **-boys** *or* **-men** a boy or man who works in a stable

stable door *n* a door with an upper and lower leaf that may be opened separately. US and Canadian equivalent: **Dutch door**

Stableford ('steɪb°lfəd) *n golf* **a** a scoring system in which points are awarded according to the number of strokes taken at each hole, whereby a hole completed in one stroke over par counts as one point, a hole completed in level par counts as two points, etc **b** (*as* *modifier*): *a Stableford competition* ▷ See **match play, stroke play** [C20: named after its inventor, Dr Frank *Stableford* (1870–1959), English amateur golfer]

stable lad *n* a person who looks after the horses in a racing stable

stabling ('steɪblɪŋ) *n* stable buildings or accommodation

stablish ('stæblɪʃ) *vb* an archaic variant of **establish**

Stabroek (Dutch 'sta:bru:k) *n* the former name (until 1812) of **Georgetown** (sense 1)

staccato (stə'ka:təʊ) *adj* **1** *music* (of notes) short, clipped, and separate **2** characterized by short abrupt sounds, as in speech: *a staccato command* ▷ *adv* **3** (esp used as a musical direction) in a staccato manner [C18: from Italian, from *staccare* to detach, shortened from *distaccare*]

stachys ('steɪkɪs) *n* any plant of the genus *Stachys*, esp *S. lanata* (lamb's ears) and *S. officinalis* (betony) [New Latin, from Greek *stachys* ear of corn, used as a plant name]

stack (stæk) *n* **1** an ordered pile or heap **2** a large orderly pile of hay, straw, etc, for storage in the open air **3** (*often plural*) *library science* compactly spaced bookshelves, used to house collections of books in an area usually prohibited to library users **4** a number of aircraft circling an airport at different altitudes, awaiting their signal to land **5** a large amount **6** *military* a pile of rifles or muskets in the shape of a cone **7** *Brit* a measure of coal or wood equal to 108 cubic feet **8** See **chimney stack**, **smokestack 9** a vertical pipe, such as the funnel of a ship or the soil pipe attached to the side of a building **10** a high column of rock, esp one isolated from the mainland by the erosive action of the sea **11** an area in a computer memory for temporary storage ▷ *vb* (*tr*) **12** to place in a stack; pile **13** to load or fill up with piles of something: *to stack a lorry with bricks* **14** to control (a number of aircraft waiting to land at an airport) so that each flies at a different altitude **15 stack the cards** to prearrange the order of a pack of cards secretly so that the deal will benefit someone [C13: from Old Norse *stakkr* haystack, of Germanic origin; related to Russian *stog*] ▷ 'stackable *adj* ▷ 'stacker *n*

stacked (stækt) *adj slang* a variant of **well-stacked**

stadholder *or* **stadtholder** ('stæd,hɒldə) *n* **1** the chief magistrate of the former Dutch republic or of any of its provinces (from about 1580 to 1802) **2** a viceroy or governor of a province [C16: partial translation of Dutch *stad houder*, from *stad* city (see **STEAD**) + *houder* holder]

stadia¹ ('steɪdɪə) *n* **1 a** a tacheometry that makes use of a telescopic surveying instrument and a graduated staff calibrated to correspond with the distance from the observer **b** (*as modifier*): *stadia surveying* **2** the two parallel cross hairs or **stadia hairs** in the eyepiece of the instrument used **3** the staff used [C19: probably from **STADIA²**]

stadia² ('steɪdɪə) *n* a plural of **stadium**

stadium ('steɪdɪəm) *n, pl* **-diums** *or* **-dia** (-dɪə) **1** a sports arena with tiered seats for spectators **2** (in ancient Greece) a course for races, usually located between two hills providing natural slopes for tiers of seats **3** an ancient Greek measure of length equivalent to about 607 feet or 184 metres [C16: via Latin from Greek *stadion*, changed from *spadion* a racecourse, from *span* to pull; also influenced by Greek *stadios* steady]

Staël (French stal) *n* **Madame de**. full name *Baronne Anne Louise Germaine* (née *Necker*) *de Staël-Holstein*. 1766–1817, French writer, whose works, esp *De l'Allemagne* (1810), anticipated French romanticism

staff¹ (sta:f) *n, pl* **staffs** (for senses 1, 3, 4), **staffs** *or* **staves** (steɪvz) (for senses 5–9) **1** a group of people employed by a company, individual, etc, for executive, clerical, sales work, etc **2** (*modifier*) attached to or provided for the staff of an establishment: *a staff doctor* **3** the body of teachers or lecturers of an educational institution, as distinct from the students **4** the officers appointed to assist a commander, service, or central headquarters organization in establishing policy, plans, etc **5** a stick with some special use, such as a walking stick or an emblem of authority **6** something that sustains or supports: *bread is the staff of life* **7** a pole on which a flag is hung **8** *chiefly Brit* a graduated rod used in surveying, esp for sighting to with a levelling instrument. Usual

US name: **rod 9** Also called: **stave** *music* **a** the system of horizontal lines grouped into sets of five (four in the case of plainsong) upon which music is written. The spaces between them are also used, being employed in conjunction with a clef in order to give a graphic indication of pitch **b** any set of five lines in this system together with its clef: *the treble staff* ▷ *vb* **10** (*tr*) to provide with a staff [Old English *stæf*; related to Old Frisian *stef*, Old Saxon *staf*, German *Stab*, Old Norse *stafr*, Gothic *Stafs*; see **STAVE**]

staff² (sta:f) *n US* a mixture of plaster and hair used to cover the external surface of temporary structures and for decoration [C19: of unknown origin]

Staffa ('stæfə) *n* an island in W Scotland, in the Inner Hebrides west of Mull: site of Fingal's Cave

staff corporal *n* a noncommissioned rank in the British Army above that of staff sergeant and below that of warrant officer

staff nurse *n* (formerly, in Britain) a qualified nurse ranking immediately below a sister

staff officer *n* a commissioned officer serving on the staff of a commander, service, or central headquarters

Stafford¹ ('stæfəd) *n* a market town in central England, administrative centre of Staffordshire. Pop: 63 681 (2001)

Stafford² ('stæfəd) *n* **Sir Edward William**. 1819–1901, New Zealand statesman, born in Scotland: prime minister of New Zealand (1856–61; 1865–69; 1872)

Staffordshire ('stæfəd,ʃɪə, -ʃə) *n* a county of central England: lowlands in the east and south rise to the Pennine uplands in the north; important in the history of industry, coal and iron having been worked at least as early as the 13th century. In 1974 the industrial area in the S passed to the new county of West Midlands; Stoke-on-Trent became an independent unitary authority in 1997. Administrative centre: Stafford. Pop (excluding Stoke-on-Trent): 811 000 (2003 est). Area (excluding Stoke-on-Trent): 2624 sq km (1013 sq miles)

Staffordshire bull terrier *n* a breed of smooth-coated terrier with a stocky frame and generally a pied or brindled coat

staffrider ('sta:f,raɪdə) *n South African* a person who illegally rides on the outside of a suburban train

Staffs (stæfs) *abbreviation* Staffordshire

staff sergeant *n military* **1** *Brit* a noncommissioned officer holding a rank between sergeant and warrant officer and employed on administrative duties **2** *US* **a** (in the Army) a noncommissioned officer who ranks above sergeant and below sergeant first class **b** (in the Air Force) a noncommissioned officer who ranks above airman first class and below technical sergeant **c** (in the Marine Corps) a noncommissioned officer who ranks above sergeant and below gunnery sergeant

stag (stæg) *n* **1** the adult male of a deer, esp a red deer **2** a man unaccompanied by a woman at a social gathering **3** *stock exchange, Brit* a speculator who applies for shares in a new issue in anticipation of a rise in price when trading commences in order to make a quick profit on resale **4** (*modifier*) (of a social gathering) attended by men only ▷ *adv* **5** without a female escort ▷ *vb* (*tr*) **6** *stock exchange* to apply for (shares in a new issue) with the intention of selling them for a quick profit when trading commences [Old English *stagga* (unattested); related to Old Norse *steggr* male bird]

stag beetle *n* any lamellicorn beetle of the family *Lucanidae*, the males of which have large branched mandibles

stage (steɪdʒ) *n* **1** a distinct step or period of development, growth, or progress **2** a raised area or platform **3** the platform in a theatre where actors perform **4 the stage** the theatre as a profession **5** any scene regarded as a setting for an event or action **6** a portion of a journey or a stopping place after such a portion **7** short for **stagecoach 8** *Brit* a division of a bus route for which there is a fixed fare **9** one of the separate propulsion units of a rocket that can be jettisoned when it has burnt out. See also **multistage** (sense 1) **10** a small stratigraphical unit; a subdivision of a rock series or system **11** the platform on a microscope on which the specimen is mounted for examination

12 *electronics* a part of a complex circuit, esp one of a number of transistors with the associated elements required to amplify a signal in an amplifier **13 by easy stages** *or* **in easy stages** not hurriedly: *he learned French by easy stages* ▷ *vb* **14** (*tr*) to perform (a play), esp on a stage: *we are going to stage "Hamlet"* **15** (*tr*) to set the action of (a play) in a particular time or place **16** (*tr*) to plan, organize, and carry out (an event) [c13: from Old French *estage* position, from Vulgar Latin *staticum* (unattested), from Latin *stāre* to stand]

stagecoach ('steɪdʒ,kəʊtʃ) *n* a large four-wheeled horse-drawn vehicle formerly used to carry passengers, mail, etc, on a regular route between towns and cities

stagecraft ('steɪdʒ,krɑːft) *n* skill in or the art of writing or staging plays

stage direction *n* *theatre* an instruction to an actor or director, written into the script of a play

stage door *n* a door at a theatre leading backstage

stage fright *n* nervousness or panic that may beset a person about to appear in front of an audience

stagehand ('steɪdʒ,hænd) *n* a person who sets the stage, moves props, etc, in a theatrical production

stage left *n* the part of the stage to the left of a performer facing the audience

stage-manage *vb* **1** to work as stage manager for (a play, etc) **2** (*tr*) to arrange, present, or supervise from behind the scenes: *to stage-manage a campaign*

stage manager *n* a person who supervises the stage arrangements of a theatrical production

stager ('steɪdʒə) *n* **1** a person of experience; veteran (esp in the phrase **old stager**) **2** an archaic word for **actor**

stage right *n* the part of the stage to the right of a performer facing the audience

stage-struck *adj* infatuated with the glamour of theatrical life, esp with the desire to act

stage whisper *n* **1** a loud whisper from one actor to another onstage intended to be heard by the audience **2** any loud whisper that is intended to be overheard

stagflation (stæg'fleɪʃən) *n* a situation in which inflation is combined with stagnant or falling output and employment [c20: blend of STAGNATION + INFLATION]

stagger ('stægə) *vb* **1** (*usually intr*) to walk or cause to walk unsteadily as if about to fall **2** (*tr*) to astound or overwhelm, as with shock: *I am staggered by his ruthlessness* **3** (*tr*) to place or arrange in alternating or overlapping positions or time periods to prevent confusion or congestion: *a staggered junction; to stagger holidays* **4** (*intr*) to falter or hesitate: *his courage staggered in the face of the battle* ▷ *n* **5** the act or an instance of staggering [c13 dialect *stacker*, from Old Norse *staka* to push] > 'staggerer *n* > 'staggering *adj* > 'staggeringly *adv*

staggered directorships *pl n* *business* a defence against unwelcome takeover bids in which a company resolves that its directors should serve staggered terms of office and that no director can be removed from office without just cause, thus preventing a bidder from controlling the board for some years

staggers ('stægəz) *n* (*functioning as singular or plural*) **1** a form of vertigo associated with decompression sickness **2** Also called: **blind staggers** a disease of horses and some other domestic animals characterized by a swaying unsteady gait, caused by infection, toxins, or lesions of the central nervous system

staghorn fern ('stæg,hɔːn) *n* any of various tropical and subtropical ferns of the genus *Platycerium* with fronds resembling antlers

staging ('steɪdʒɪŋ) *n* any temporary structure used in the process of building, esp the horizontal platforms supported by scaffolding [c14: from STAGE + -ING¹]

staging area *n* a general locality used as a checkpoint or regrouping area for military formations in transit

staging post *n* a place where a journey is usually broken, esp a stopover on a flight

Stagira (stə'dʒaɪrə) *n* an ancient city on the coast of Chalcidice in Macedonia: the birthplace of Aristotle

stagnant ('stægnənt) *adj* **1** (of water, etc) standing still; without flow or current **2** brackish and foul from standing still **3** stale, sluggish, or dull from inaction **4** not growing or developing; static [c17: from Latin

stagnāns, from *stagnāre* to be stagnant, from *stagnum* a pool] > 'stag'nancy *or* 'stagnance *n*

stagnate (stæg'neɪt, 'stæg,neɪt) *vb* (*intr*) to be or to become stagnant > stag'nation *n*

stag night *or* **stag party** *n* a party for men only, esp one held for a man before he is married

stagy *or* US **stagey** ('steɪdʒɪ) *adj* stagier, stagiest excessively theatrical or dramatic > 'stagily *adv* > 'staginess *n*

staid (steɪd) *adj* of a settled, sedate, and steady character [c16: obsolete past participle of STAY¹] > 'staidly *adv* > 'staidness *n*

stain (steɪn) *vb* (*mainly tr*) **1** to mark or discolour with patches of something that dirties **2** to dye with a penetrating dyestuff or pigment **3** to bring disgrace or shame on: *to stain someone's honour* **4** to colour (specimens) for microscopic study by treatment with a dye or similar reagent **5** (*intr*) to produce indelible marks or discoloration: *does ink stain?* ▷ *n* **6** a spot, mark, or discoloration **7** a moral taint; blemish or slur **8** a dye or similar reagent, used to colour specimens for microscopic study **9** a solution or liquid used to penetrate the surface of a material, esp wood, and impart a rich colour without covering up the surface or grain **10** any dye that is made into a solution and used to colour textiles and hides [c14 *steynen* (vb), shortened from *disteynen* to remove colour from, from Old French *desteindre* to discolour, from *des-* DIS-¹ + *teindre*, from Latin *tingere* to TINGE] > 'stainable *adj* > ,staina'bility *n* > 'stainer *n*

stained glass *n* **a** glass that has been coloured in any of various ways, as by fusing with a film of metallic oxide or burning pigment into the surface, used esp for church windows **b** (*as modifier*): *a stained-glass window*

stained glass ceiling *n* a situation in a church organization in which promotion for a female member of the clergy appears to be possible, but discrimination prevents it

Stainer ('steɪnə) *n* Sir John. 1840–1901, British composer and organist, noted for his sacred music, esp the oratorio *The Crucifixion* (1887)

Staines (steɪnz) *n* a town in SE England, in N Surrey on the River Thames. Pop: 50 538 (2001)

stainless ('steɪnlɪs) *adj* **1** resistant to discoloration, esp discoloration resulting from corrosion; rust-resistant: *stainless steel* **2** having no blemish: *a stainless reputation* > 'stainlessly *adv*

stainless steel *n* **a** a type of steel resistant to corrosion as a result of the presence of large amounts of chromium (12–15 per cent). The carbon content depends on the application, being 0.2–0.4 per cent for steel used in cutlery, etc, and about 1 per cent for use in scalpels and razor blades **b** (*as modifier*): *stainless-steel cutlery*

stair (steə) *n* **1** one of a flight of stairs **2** a series of steps: *a narrow stair* ▷ See also **stairs** [Old English *stæger*; related to *stīg* narrow path, *stīgan* to ascend, descend, Old Norse *steigurligr* upright, Middle Dutch *steiger* ladder]

staircase ('steə,keɪs) *n* a flight of stairs, its supporting framework and, usually, a handrail or banisters

stairlift ('steə,lɪft) *n* a mechanical device with a seat for carrying an elderly or infirm person up a flight of stairs

stairs (steəz) *pl n* **1** a flight of steps leading from one storey or level to another, esp indoors **2 below stairs** Brit in the servants' quarters; in domestic service

stairway ('steə,weɪ) *n* a means of access consisting of stairs; staircase or flight of steps

stairwell ('steə,wel) *n* a vertical shaft or opening that contains a staircase

stake¹ (steɪk) *n* **1** a stick or metal bar driven into the ground as a marker, part of a fence, support for a plant, etc **2** one of a number of vertical posts that fit into sockets around a flat truck or railway wagon to hold the load in place **3** a method or the practice of executing a person by binding him to a stake in the centre of a pile of wood that is then set on fire **4 pull up stakes** to leave one's home or temporary resting place and move on ▷ *vb* (*tr*) **5** to tie, fasten, or tether with or to a stake **6** (often foll by *out* or *off*) to fence or surround with stakes **7** (often foll by *out*) to lay (a claim) to land, rights, etc

8 to support with a stake [Old English *staca* pin; related to Old Frisian *staka*, Old High German *stehho*, Old Norse *stjaki*; see STICK¹]

stake² (steɪk) *n* **1** the money or valuables that a player must hazard in order to buy into a gambling game or make a bet **2** an interest, often financial, held in something: *a stake in the company's future* **3** (often plural) the money that a player has available for gambling **4** (often plural) a prize in a race, etc, esp one made up of contributions from contestants or owners **5** (plural) *horse racing* a race in which all owners of competing horses contribute to the prize money **6** *US & Canadian informal* short for **grubstake** (sense 1) **7at stake** at risk: *two lives are at stake* **8**raise the stakes **a** to increase the amount of money or valuables hazarded in a gambling game **b** to increase the costs, risks, or considerations involved in taking an action or reaching a conclusion ▷ *vb* (*tr*) **9** to hazard (money, etc) on a result **10** to invest in or support by supplying with money, etc: *to stake a business enterprise* [C16: of uncertain origin]

Staked Plain *n* another name for the **Llano Estacado**

stakeholder ('steɪkˌhəʊldə) *n* **1** a person or group owning a significant percentage of a company's shares **2** a person or group not owning shares in an enterprise but affected by or having an interest in its operations, such as the employees, customers, local community, etc ▷ *adj* **3** of or relating to policies intended to allow people to participate in and benefit from decisions made by enterprises in which they have a stake: *a stakeholder economy*

stakeholder pension *n* (in Britain) a flexible pension scheme with low charges, in which contributors can stop and restart payments and switch funds to another scheme without paying a penalty

stakeout ('steɪkaʊt) *slang, chiefly US & Canadian* ▷ *n* **1** a police surveillance of an area, house, or criminal suspect **2** an area or house kept under such surveillance ▷ *vb* **stake out** **3** (*tr, adverb*) to keep under surveillance

Stakhanovism (stæˈkænəˌvɪzəm) *n* (in the former Soviet Union) a system designed to raise production by offering incentives to efficient workers [C20: named after A. G. *Stakhanov* (1906–77), Soviet coal miner, the worker first awarded benefits under the system in 1935] >Staˈkhanovˌite *n, adj*

stalactite ('stæləkˌtaɪt) *n* a cylindrical mass of calcium carbonate hanging from the roof of a limestone cave: formed by precipitation from continually dripping water. See **stalagmite** [C17: from New Latin *stalactites*, from Greek *stalaktos* dripping, from *stalassein* to drip] >stalactiform (stəˈlæktɪˌfɔːm) *adj* >stalactitic (ˌstæləkˈtɪtɪk) *or*ˌstalacˈtitical *adj*

stalag ('stælæg; *German* 'ʃtalak) *n* a German prisoner-of-war camp in World War II, esp for noncommissioned officers and other ranks [short for *Stammlager* base camp, from *Stamm* base (related to STEM¹) + *Lager* camp]

stalagmite ('stæləgˌmaɪt) *n* a cylindrical mass of calcium carbonate projecting upwards from the floor of a limestone cave: formed by precipitation from continually dripping water. See **stalactite** [C17: from New Latin *stalagmites*, from Greek *stalagmos* dripping; related to Greek *stalassein* to drip; compare STALACTITE] >stalagmitic (ˌstæləgˈmɪtɪk) *or*ˌstalagˈmitical *adj*

stale¹ (steɪl) *adj* **1** (esp of food) hard, musty, or dry from being kept too long **2** (of beer, etc) flat and tasteless from being kept open too long **3** (of air) stagnant; foul **4** uninteresting from overuse; hackneyed: *stale clichés* **5** no longer new: *stale news* **6** lacking in energy or ideas through overwork or lack of variety **7** *banking* (of a cheque) not negotiable by a bank as a result of not having been presented within six months of being written **8** *law* (of a claim, etc) having lost its effectiveness or force, as by failure to act or by the lapse of time ▷ *vb* **9** to make or become stale [C13 (originally applied to liquor in the sense: well matured): probably via Norman French from Old French *estale* (unattested) motionless, of Frankish origin; related to STALL¹, INSTALL] >**staleness** *n*

stale² (steɪl) *vb* **1** (*intr*) (of livestock) to urinate ▷ *n* **2** the urine of horses or cattle [C15: perhaps from Old French

estaler to stand in one position; see STALL¹; compare Middle Low German *stallen* to urinate, Greek *stalassein* to drip]

stale bull *n* *business* a dealer or speculator who holds unsold commodities after a rise in market prices but who cannot trade because there are no buyers at the new levels and because his financial commitments prevent him from making further purchases

stalemate ('steɪlˌmeɪt) *n* **1** a chess position in which any of a player's possible moves would place his king in check: in this position the game ends in a draw **2** a situation in which two opposing forces find that further action is impossible or futile; deadlock ▷ *vb* **3** (*tr*) to subject to a stalemate [C18: from obsolete *stale*, from Old French *estal* STALL¹ + MATE²]

Stalin¹ ('stɑːlɪn) *n* **1** Also called: **Stalino** a former name (from after the Revolution until 1961) of **Donetsk** **2** the former name (1950–61) of **Braşov** **3** the former name (1949–56) of **Varna**

Stalin² ('stɑːlɪn) *n* **Joseph**. original name *Iosif Vissarionovich Dzhugashvili*. 1879–1953, Soviet leader; general secretary of the Communist Party of the Soviet Union (1922–53). He succeeded Lenin as head of the party and created a totalitarian state, crushing all opposition, esp in the great purges of 1934–37. He instigated rapid industrialization and the collectivization of agriculture and established the Soviet Union as a world power

Stalinabad (*Russian* stəlinaˈbat) *n* the former name (1929–61) of **Dushanbe**

Stalingrad ('stɑːlɪnˌgræd; *Russian* stəlin'grat) *n* the former name (1925–61) of **Volgograd**

Stalinism ('stɑːlɪˌnɪzəm) *n* the theory and form of government associated with the Soviet leader Joseph Stalin (original name *Iosif Vissarionovich Dzhugashvili*; 1879–1953): a variant of Marxism-Leninism characterized by totalitarianism, rigid bureaucracy, and loyalty to the state >'**Stalinist** *n, adj*

Stalinogrod (*Polish* stali'nɔgrɔt) *n* the former name (1953–56) for **Katowice**

Stalin Peak *n* a former name for **Ismoil Somoni**

Stalinsk (*Russian* 'stalinsk) *n* the former name (1932–61) of **Novokuznetsk**

stalk¹ (stɔːk) *n* **1** the main stem of a herbaceous plant **2** any of various subsidiary plant stems, such as a leafstalk (petiole) or flower stalk (peduncle) **3** a slender supporting structure in animals such as crinoids and certain protozoans, coelenterates, and barnacles **4** any long slender supporting shaft or column [C14: probably a diminutive form from Old English *stalu* upright piece of wood; related to Old Frisian *staal* handle] >**stalked** *adj* >'**stalkˌlike** *adj*

stalk² (stɔːk) *vb* **1** to follow or approach (game, prey, etc) stealthily and quietly **2** to pursue persistently and, sometimes, attack (a person with whom one is obsessed, often a celebrity) **3** to spread over (a place) in a menacing or grim manner: *fever stalked the camp* **4** (*intr*) to walk in a haughty, stiff, or threatening way **5** to search or draw (a piece of land) for prey ▷ *n* **6** the act of stalking **7** a stiff or threatening stride [Old English *bestealcian* to walk stealthily; related to Middle Low German *stolkeren*, Danish *stalke*] >'**stalker** *n*

stalking-horse *n* **1** a horse or an imitation one used by a hunter to hide behind while stalking his quarry **2** something serving as a means of concealing plans; pretext **3** a candidate put forward by one group to divide the opposition or mask the candidacy of another person for whom the stalking-horse would then withdraw

stalky ('stɔːkɪ) *adj* **stalkier, stalkiest** **1** like a stalk; slender and tall **2** having or abounding in stalks >'**stalkily** *adv* >'**stalkiness** *n*

stall¹ (stɔːl) *n* **1 a** a compartment in a stable or shed for confining or feeding a single animal **b** another name for **stable¹** (sense 1) **2** a small often temporary stand or booth for the display and sale of goods **3** (in a church) **a** one of a row of seats, usually divided from the others by armrests or a small screen, for the use of the choir or clergy **b** a pen **4** an instance of an engine stalling **5** a condition of an aircraft in flight in which a reduction in speed or an increase in the aircraft's angle of attack causes a sudden loss of lift resulting in a downward plunge **6** any small room or compartment **7** *Brit* **a** a seat in a theatre or cinema that resembles a chair, usually fixed to the floor **b** (*plural*) the area of seats on the ground floor of a theatre or cinema nearest to the stage or screen **8** a tubelike covering for a finger, as in a glove **9** (*plural*) short for **starting stalls** ▷ *vb* **10** to cause (a motor vehicle or its engine) to stop, usually by incorrect use of the clutch or incorrect adjustment of the fuel mixture, or (of an engine or motor vehicle) to stop, usually for these reasons **11** to cause (an aircraft) to go into a stall or (of an aircraft) to go into a stall **12** to stick or cause to stick fast, as in mud or snow **13** (*tr*) to confine (an animal) in a stall [Old English *steall* a place for standing; related to Old High German *stall*, and *stellen* to set]

stall² (stɔːl) *vb* **1** to employ delaying tactics towards (someone); be evasive ▷ *n* **2** an evasive move; pretext [C16: from Anglo-French *estale* bird used as a decoy, influenced by STALL¹]

stall-feed *vb* **-feeds, -feeding, -fed** (*tr*) to keep and feed (an animal) in a stall, esp as an intensive method of fattening it for slaughter

stallholder (ˈstɔːlˌhəʊldə) *n* a person who sells goods at a market stall

stallion (ˈstæljən) *n* an uncastrated male horse, esp one used for breeding [C14: *staloun*, from Old French *estalon* of Germanic origin; related to Old High German *stal* STALL¹]

stalwart (ˈstɔːlwət) *adj* **1** strong and sturdy; robust **2** solid, dependable, and courageous: *stalwart citizens* **3** resolute and firm ▷ *n* **4** a stalwart person, esp a supporter [Old English *stælwirthe* serviceable, from *stæl*, shortened from *stathol* support + *wierthe* WORTH¹] > ˈstalwartly *adv* > ˈstalwartness *n*

Stambul *or* **Stamboul** (stæmˈbuːl) *n* the old part of Istanbul, Turkey, south of the Golden Horn: the site of ancient Byzantium; sometimes used as a name for the whole city

stamen (ˈsteɪmɛn) *n*, *pl* **stamens** *or* **stamina** (ˈstæmɪnə) the male reproductive organ of a flower, consisting of a stalk (filament) bearing an anther in which pollen is produced [C17: from Latin: the warp in an upright loom, from *stāre* to stand] > **staminiferous** (ˌstæmɪˈnɪfərəs) *adj*

Stamford (ˈstæmfəd) *n* a city in SW Connecticut, on Long Island Sound: major chemical research laboratories. Pop: 120 107 (2003 est)

Stamford Bridge *n* a village in N England, east of York: site of a battle (1066) in which King Harold of England defeated his brother Tostig and King Harald Hardrada of Norway, three weeks before the Battle of Hastings

stamina¹ (ˈstæmɪnə) *n* enduring energy, strength, and resilience [C19: identical with STAMINA² from Latin *stāmen* thread, hence the threads of life spun out by the Fates, hence energy, etc]

stamina² (ˈstæmɪnə) *n* a plural of **stamen**

staminate (ˈstæmɪnɪt, -ˌneɪt) *adj* (of plants) having stamens, esp having stamens but no carpels; male [C19: from Latin *stāminātus* consisting of threads. See STAMEN, -ATE¹]

stammer (ˈstæmə) *vb* **1** to speak or say (something) in a hesitant way, esp as a result of a speech disorder or through fear, stress, etc ▷ *n* **2** a speech disorder characterized by involuntary repetitions and hesitations [Old English *stamerian*; related to Old Saxon *stamarōn*, Old High German *stamm*] > ˈstammerer *n* > ˈstammering *n, adj*

stamp (stæmp) *vb* **1** (when *intr*, often foll by *on*) to bring (the foot) down heavily (on the ground, etc) **2** (*intr*) to walk with heavy or noisy footsteps **3** (*intr*; foll by *on*) to repress, extinguish, or eradicate: *he stamped on any criticism* **4** (*tr*) to impress or mark (a particular device or sign) on (something) **5** to mark (something) with an official impress, seal, or device: *to stamp a passport* **6** (*tr*) to fix or impress permanently: *the date was stamped on her memory* **7** (*tr*) to affix a postage stamp to **8** (*tr*) to distinguish or reveal: *that behaviour stamps him as a cheat* **9** to pound or crush (ores, etc) ▷ *n* **10** the act or an instance of stamping **11 a** See **postage stamp b** a mark applied to postage stamps for cancellation purposes **12** a similar

piece of gummed paper used for commercial or trading purposes **13** a block, die, etc, used for imprinting a design or device **14** a design, device, or mark that has been stamped **15** a characteristic feature or trait; hallmark: *the story had the stamp of authenticity* **16** a piece of gummed paper or other mark applied to official documents to indicate payment of a fee, validity, ownership, etc **17** *Brit informal* a national insurance contribution, formerly recorded by means of a stamp on an official card **18** type or class: *we want to employ men of his stamp* **19** an instrument or machine for crushing or pounding ores, etc, or the pestle in such a device ▷ See also **stamp out** [C13: from Old English *stampe*; related to Old High German *stampfōn* to stamp, Old Norse *stappa*] > ˈstamper *n*

stamp duty *or* **stamp tax** *n* a tax on legal documents, publications, etc, the payment of which is certified by the attaching or impressing of official stamps

stampede (stæmˈpiːd) *n* **1** an impulsive headlong rush of startled cattle or horses **2** headlong rush of a crowd **3** any sudden large-scale movement or other action, such as a rush of people to support a candidate **4** *Western US & Canadian* a rodeo event featuring fairground and social elements ▷ *vb* **5** to run away or cause to run away in a stampede [C19: from American Spanish *estampida*, from Spanish: a din, from *estampar* to stamp, of Germanic origin; see STAMP] > stamˈpeder *n*

stamping ground *n* a habitual or favourite meeting or gathering place

stamp mill *n metallurgy* a machine for crushing ore

stamp out *vb* (*tr, adverb*) **1** to put out or extinguish by stamping: *to stamp out a fire* **2** to crush or suppress by force: *to stamp out a rebellion*

stance (stæns, staːns) *n* **1** the manner and position in which a person or animal stands **2** *sport* the posture assumed when about to play the ball, as in golf, cricket, etc **3** general emotional or intellectual attitude: *a leftist stance* **4** *Scot* a place where buses or taxis wait [C16: via French from Italian *stanza* place for standing, from Latin *stāns*, from *stāre* to stand]

stanch (staːntʃ) *or* **staunch** (stɔːntʃ) *vb* **1** to stem the flow of (a liquid, esp blood) or (of a liquid) to stop flowing **2** to prevent the flow of a liquid, esp blood, from (a hole, wound, etc) [C14: from Old French *estanchier*, from Vulgar Latin *stanticāre* (unattested) to cause to stand, from Latin *stāre* to stand, halt] > ˈstanchable *or* ˈstaunchable *adj* > ˈstancher *or* ˈstauncher *n*

stanchion (ˈstaːnʃən) *n* **1** any vertical pole, rod, etc, used as a support ▷ *vb* **2** (*tr*) to provide or support with a stanchion or stanchions [C14: from Old French *estanchon*, from *estance*, from Vulgar Latin *stantia* (unattested) a standing, from Latin *stāre* to stand]

stand (stænd) *vb* **stands, standing, stood** (*mainly intr*) **1** (*also tr*) to be or cause to be in an erect or upright position **2** to rise to, assume, or maintain an upright position **3** (*copula*) to have a specified height when standing: *to stand six feet* **4** to be situated or located: *the house stands in the square* **5** to be or exist in a specified state or condition: *to stand in awe of someone* **6** to adopt or remain in a resolute position or attitude **7** (*may take an infinitive*) to be in a specified position: *I stand to lose money in this venture; he stands high in the president's favour* **8** to remain in force or continue in effect: *whatever the difficulties, my orders stand* **9** to come to a stop or halt, esp temporarily **10** (of water, etc) to collect and remain without flowing **11** (often foll by *at*) (of a score, account, etc) to indicate the specified position of the parties involved: *the score stands at 20 to 1* **12** (*also tr*; when *intr*, foll by *for*) to tolerate or bear: *I won't stand for your nonsense any longer; I can't stand spiders* **13** (*tr*) to resist; survive: *to stand the test of time* **14** (*tr*) to submit to: *to stand trial* **15** (often foll by *for*) *chiefly Brit* to be or become a candidate: *will he stand for Parliament?* **16** to navigate in a specified direction: *we were standing for Madeira when the storm broke* **17** (of a gun dog) to point at game **18** to halt, esp to give action, repel attack, or disrupt an enemy advance when retreating **19** (*tr*) *informal* to bear the cost of; pay for: *to stand someone a drink* **20 stand a chance** to have a hope or likelihood of winning, succeeding, etc **21 stand fast** to maintain one's position firmly **22 stand one's ground** to maintain a stance or position in the face of opposition **23 stand still a** to remain motionless **b** (foll by *for*) *US* to tolerate: *I won't stand still for your threats* **24 stand to someone** *Irish informal* to be useful to someone: *your knowledge of English will stand to you* ▷ *n* **25** the act or an instance of standing **26** an opinion, esp a resolutely held one: *he took a stand on capital punishment* **27** a halt or standstill **28** a place where a person or thing stands **29** *Austral & NZ* **a** a position on the floor of a shearing shed allocated to one shearer **b** the shearing equipment belonging to such a position **30** a structure, usually of wood, on which people can sit or stand **31** a frame or rack on which such articles as coats and hats may be hung **32** a small table or piece of furniture where articles may be placed or stored: *a music stand* **33** a supporting framework, esp for a tool or instrument **34** a stall, booth, or counter from which goods may be sold **35** a halt to give action, etc, esp one taken during a retreat and having some duration or some success **36** *cricket* an extended period at the wicket by two batsmen **37** a growth of plants in a particular area, esp trees in a forest or a crop in a field **38** a stop made by a touring theatrical company, pop group, etc, to give a performance (esp in the phrase **one-night stand**) **39** (of a gun dog) the act of pointing at game ▷ See also **stand by**, **stand down**, etc [Old English *standan*; related to Old Norse *standa*, Old High German *stantan*, Latin *stāre* to stand; see STEAD] >'**stander** *n*

standard ('stændəd) *n* **1** an accepted or approved example of something against which others are judged or measured **2** (*often plural*) a principle of propriety, honesty, and integrity **3** a level of excellence or quality **4** any distinctive flag, device, etc, as of a nation, sovereign, or special cause **5** a flag or emblem formerly used to show the central or rallying point of an army in battle **6** a large tapering flag ending in two points, originally borne by a sovereign or high-ranking noble **7** the commodity or commodities in which is stated the value of a basic monetary unit: *the gold standard* **8** an authorized model of a unit of measure or weight **9** a unit of board measure equal to 1980 board feet **10** (in coinage) the prescribed proportion by weight of precious metal and base metal that each coin must contain **11** an upright pole or beam, esp one used as a support **12 a** a piece of furniture consisting of an upright pole or beam on a base or support **b** (*as modifier*): *a standard lamp* **13 a** a plant, esp a fruit tree, that is trained so that it has an upright stem free of branches **b** (*as modifier*): *a standard cherry* **14** a song or piece of music that has remained popular for many years ▷ *adj* **15** of the usual, regularized, medium, or accepted kind: *a standard size* **16** of recognized authority, competence, or excellence: *the standard work on Greece* **17** denoting or characterized by idiom, vocabulary, etc, that is regarded as correct and acceptable by educated native speakers **18** *Brit* (formerly) (of eggs) of a size that is smaller than *large* and larger than *medium* [C12: from Old French *estandart* gathering place, flag to mark such a place, probably of Germanic origin; compare Old High German *stantan* to stand, Old High German *ort* place]

standard assessment tasks, **standard assessment tests** or**standard attainment tests** *pl n Brit education* the former name for **National Tests**. Abbreviation SATS

standard-bearer *n* **1** an officer or man who carries a standard **2** a leader of a cause or party

standard cell *n* a voltaic cell producing a constant and accurately known electromotive force that can be used to calibrate voltage-measuring instruments

standard cost *n* *accounting* the predetermined budgeted cost of a regular manufacturing process against which actual costs are compared

standard deviation *n* *statistics* a measure of dispersion obtained by extracting the square root of the mean of the squared deviations of the observed values from their mean in a frequency distribution

standard function *n* *computing* a subprogram provided by a translator that carries out a task, for example the computation of a mathematical function, such as sine,

square root, etc

standard gauge *n* **1** a railway track with a distance of 4 ft 8½ in. (1.435 m) between the lines; used on most railways. See also **narrow gauge**, **broad gauge** ▷ *adj* **standard-gauge** or**standard-gauged** **2** of, relating to, or denoting a railway with a standard gauge

standard generalized mark-up language *n* See SGML

Standard Grade *n* (in Scotland) a type of examination designed to test skills and the application of knowledge, replaced O grade

standardize or**standardise** ('stændə,daız) *vb* **1** to make or become standard **2** (*tr*) to test by or compare with a standard >,standardi'zation or,standardi'sation *n* >'standard,izer or'standard,iser *n*

standard model *n* *physics* a theory of fundamental interactions in which the electromagnetic, weak, and strong interactions are described in terms of the exchange of virtual particles

standard of living *n* a level of subsistence or material welfare of a community, class, or person

standard time *n* the official local time of a region or country determined by the distance from Greenwich of a line of longitude passing through the area

stand by *vb* **1** (*intr, adverb*) to be available and ready to act if needed or called upon **2** (*intr, adverb*) to be present as an onlooker or without taking any action: *he stood by at the accident* **3** (*intr, preposition*) to be faithful to: *to stand by one's principles* ▷ *n* **stand-by 4 a** a person or thing that is ready for use or can be relied on in an emergency **b** (*as modifier*): *modifier*): *stand-by provisions* **5** on **stand-by** in a state of readiness for action or use ▷ *adj* **6** (of an airline passenger, fare, or seat) not booked in advance but awaiting or subject to availability

stand down *vb* (*adverb*) **1** (*intr*) to resign or withdraw, esp in favour of another **2** (*intr*) to leave the witness box in a court of law after giving evidence **3** *chiefly Brit* to go or be taken off duty

stand for *vb* (*intr, preposition*) **1** to represent or mean **2** *chiefly Brit* to be or become a candidate for **3** to support or recommend **4** *informal* to tolerate or bear: *he won't stand for any disobedience*

stand in *vb* **1** (*intr, adverb*; usually foll by *for*) to act as a substitute **2 stand someone in good stead** to be of benefit or advantage to someone ▷ *n* **stand-in 3 a** a person or thing that serves as a substitute **b** (*as modifier*): *a stand-in teacher* **4** a person who substitutes for an actor during intervals of waiting or in dangerous stunts

standing ('stændıŋ) *n* **1** social or financial position, status, or reputation: *a man of some standing* **2** length of existence, experience, etc **3** (*modifier*) used to stand in or on: *standing room* ▷ *adj* **4** *athletics* **a** (of the start of a race) begun from a standing position without the use of starting blocks **b** (of a jump, leap, etc) performed from a stationary position without a run-up **5** (*prenominal*) permanent, fixed, or lasting **6** (*prenominal*) still or stagnant: *a standing pond* **7** *printing* (of type) set and stored for future use

standing army *n* a permanent army of paid soldiers maintained by a nation

standing order *n* **1** Also called: **banker's order** an instruction to a bank by a depositor to pay a stated sum at regular intervals. See **direct debit 2** a rule or order governing the procedure, conduct, etc, of a legislative body **3** *military* one of a number of orders which have or are likely to have long-term validity

standing rigging *n* the stays, shrouds, and other more or less fixed, though adjustable, wires and ropes that support the masts of a sailing vessel

standing wave *n* *physics* the periodic disturbance in a medium resulting from the combination of two waves of equal frequency and intensity travelling in opposite directions. There are generally two kinds of displacement, and the maximum value of the amplitude of one of these occurs at the same points as the minimum value of the amplitude of the other. Thus in the case of electromagnetic radiation the amplitude of the oscillations of the electric field has its greatest value at the points at which the magnetic oscillation is zero, and vice versa. Also called: **stationary wave**

S

Standish ('stændɪʃ) *n* **Myles** (or **Miles**). ?1584–1656, English military leader of the Pilgrim Fathers at Plymouth, New England

standoff ('stænd,ɒf) *n* **1** *US & Canadian* the act or an instance of standing off or apart **2** a deadlock or stalemate **3** *rugby* short for **stand-off half** ▷ *vb* **stand off** (*adverb*) **4** (*intr*) to navigate a vessel so as to avoid the shore, an obstruction, etc **5** (*tr*) to keep or cause to keep at a distance **6** (*intr*) to reach a deadlock or stalemate **7** (*tr*) to dismiss (workers), esp temporarily

stand-off half *n* *rugby* **1** a player who acts as a link between his scrum half and three-quarter backs **2** this position in a team ▷ Also called: **fly half**

standoffish (,stænd'ɒfɪʃ) *adj* reserved, haughty, or aloof > ,stand'offishness *n*

stand on *vb* (*intr*) **1** (*adverb*) to continue to navigate a vessel on the same heading **2** (*preposition*) to insist on: *to stand on ceremony*

stand out *vb* (*intr, adverb*) **1** to be distinctive or conspicuous **2** to refuse to agree, consent, or comply: *they stood out for a better price* **3** to protrude or project **4** to navigate a vessel away from a port, harbour, anchorage, etc ▷ *n* **standout 5** *informal* **a** a person or thing that is distinctive or outstanding **b** (*as modifier*): *the standout track from the album*

stand over *vb* **1** (*intr, preposition*) to watch closely; keep tight control over **2** (*intr, preposition*) *Austral & NZ informal* to threaten or intimidate (a person)

standover man ('stænd,əʊvə) *n* *Austral informal* a person who extorts money by intimidation

standpipe ('stænd,paɪp) *n* **1** a vertical pipe, open at the upper end, attached to a pipeline or tank serving to limit the pressure head to that of the height of the pipe **2** a temporary freshwater outlet installed in a street during a period when household water supplies are cut off

standpoint ('stænd,pɔɪnt) *n* a physical or mental position from which things are viewed

standstill ('stænd,stɪl) *n* a complete cessation of movement; stop; halt: *the car came to a standstill*

stand to *vb* **1** (*adverb*) *military* to assume positions or cause to assume positions to resist a possible attack **2** **stand to reason** to conform with the dictates of reason: *it stands to reason that pigs can't fly*

stand up *vb* (*adverb*) **1** (*intr*) to rise to the feet **2** (*intr*) to resist or withstand wear, criticism, etc **3** (*tr*) *informal* to fail to keep an appointment with, esp intentionally **4** **stand up for a** to support, side with, or defend **b** *US* to serve as best man for (the groom) at a wedding **5** **stand up to a** to confront or resist courageously **b** to withstand or endure (wear, criticism, etc) ▷ *adj* **stand-up** (*prenominal*) **6** having or being in an erect position: *a stand-up collar* **7** done, performed, taken, etc, while standing: *a stand-up meal* **8** (of comedy or a comedian) performed or performing solo ▷ *n* **stand-up 9** a stand-up comedian **10** stand-up comedy

Stanford ('stænfəd) *n* Sir **Charles** (**Villiers**). 1852–1924, Anglo-Irish composer and conductor, who as a teacher at the Royal College of Music had much influence on the succeeding generation of composers: noted esp for his church music, oratorios, and cantatas

Stanford-Binet test ('stænfədbɪ'neɪ) *n* *psychol* a revision, esp for US use, of the Binet-Simon scale designed to measure mental ability by comparing the performance of an individual with the average performance for his age group. See also **Binet-Simon scale**, **intelligence test** [C20: named after *Stanford University*, California, and Alfred *Binet* (1857–1911), French psychologist]

stanhope ('stænəp) *n* a light one-seater carriage with two or four wheels [C18: named after Fitzroy *Stanhope* (1787–1864), English clergyman for whom it was first built]

Stanhope ('stænəp) *n* **1 Charles**, 3rd Earl. 1753–1816, British radical politician and scientist. His inventions included two calculating machines, a microscope lens, and a stereotyping machine **2** his grandfather, **James**, 1st Earl. 1673–1721, British soldier and statesman; George I's chief minister (1717–21). He fought under

Marlborough in the War of the Spanish Succession (1701–14) and negotiated the Triple Alliance with France and Holland (1717)

Stanislavsky or **Stanislavski** (,stænɪ'slævskɪ; *Russian* stənɪ'slafskij) *n* **Konstantin** (kənstan'tin). 1863–1938, Russian actor and director, cofounder of the Moscow Art Theatre (1897). He is famous for his theory of acting, known as the Method, which directs the actor to find the truth within himself about the role he is playing

Stanisław (*Polish* 'stanɪswaf) or **Stanislaus** *n* **Saint**. 1030–79, the patron saint of Poland. As Bishop of Cracow (1072–79) he excommunicated King Bolesław II, who arranged his murder. Feast day: May 11

Stanisław II *n* surnamed *Poniatowski*. 1732–98, the last king of Poland (1764–95), during whose reign Poland was repeatedly invaded and partitioned (1772, 1791, 1795) by its neighbours: abdicated

stank (stæŋk) *vb* a past tense of **stink**

Stanley¹ ('stænlɪ) *n* **1** the capital of the Falkland Islands, in NE East Falkland Island: scene of fighting in the Falklands War of 1982. Pop: 1989 (2001) **2** a town in NE England, in N Durham. Pop: 19 072 (2001) **3** **Mount Stanley** a mountain in central Africa, between Uganda and the Democratic Republic of Congo (formerly Zaïre): the highest peak of the Ruwenzori range. Height: 5109 m (16 763 ft) Congolese name **Ngaliema Mountain**

Stanley² ('stænlɪ) *n* Sir **Henry Morton**. 1841–1904, British explorer and journalist, who led an expedition to Africa in search of Livingstone, whom he found on Nov 10, 1871. He led three further expeditions in Africa (1874–77; 1879–84; 1887–89) and was instrumental in securing Belgian sovereignty over the Congo Free State

Stanley Falls *pl n* the former name of **Boyoma Falls**

Stanley knife *n* *trademark* a type of knife used for carpet fitting, etc, consisting of a thick hollow metal handle with a short, very sharp, replaceable blade inserted at one end [C19: named after F.T. *Stanley*, US businessman and founder of the Stanley Rule and Level Company]

Stanley Pool *n* a lake between the Democratic Republic of Congo (formerly Zaïre) and Congo-Brazzaville, formed by a widening of the River Congo. Area: 829 sq km (320 sq miles). Congolese name: **Pool Malebo**

Stanleyville ('stænlɪ,vɪl) *n* the former name (until 1966) of **Kisangani**

stann- *combining form* denoting tin: *stannite* [from Late Latin *stannum* tin]

Stannaries ('stænərɪz) *n* **the Stannaries** a tin-mining district of Devon and Cornwall, formerly under the jurisdiction of special courts

stannary ('stænərɪ) *n*, *pl* **-ries** a place or region where tin is mined or worked [C15: from Medieval Latin *stannāria*, from Late Latin: STANNUM, TIN]

stannic ('stænɪk) *adj* of or containing tin, esp in the tetravalent state [C18: from Late Latin *stannum* tin]

stannite ('stænaɪt) *n* a grey metallic mineral that consists of a sulphide of tin, copper, and iron and is a source of tin. Formula: Cu_2FeSnS_4 [C19: from STANNUM + -ITE¹]

stannous ('stænəs) *adj* of or containing tin, esp in the divalent state

stannum ('stænəm) *n* an obsolete name for **tin** (sense 1) [C18: from Late Latin: tin, from Latin: alloy of silver and lead, perhaps of Celtic origin; compare Welsh *ystaen* tin]

Stanovoi Range or **Stanovoy Range** (*Russian* stəna'vɔj) *n* a mountain range in SE Russia; forms part of the watershed between rivers flowing to the Arctic and the Pacific. Highest peak: Mount Skalisty, 2482 m (8143 ft)

Stans¹ (*German* ʃtans) *n* a town in central Switzerland, capital of Nidwalden demicanton, 11 km (7 miles) southeast of Lucerne: tourist centre. Pop: 6983 (2000)

Stans² (stænz) *pl n* **the Stans** a region in Central Asia that consists of Kazakhstan, Kyrgyzstan, Uzbekistan, and Tajikistan

stanza ('stænzə) *n* **1** *prosody* a fixed number of verse lines arranged in a definite metrical pattern, forming a unit of a poem **2** *US & Austral* a half or a quarter in a football match [C16: from Italian: halting place, from Vulgar Latin *stantia* (unattested) station, from Latin *stāre* to stand] > 'stanzaed *adj* > stanzaic (stæn'zeɪɪk) *adj*

stapelia (stə'piːliə) *n* any fleshy cactus-like leafless African plant of the asclepiadaceous genus *Stapelia*, having thick four-angled stems and large typically fetid mottled flowers [c18: from New Latin, named after J. B. van Stapel, (died 1636), Dutch botanist]

stapes ('steipiːz) *n, pl* **stapes** *or* **stapedes** (stæ'piːdiːz) the stirrup-shaped bone that is the innermost of three small bones in the middle ear of mammals. See **incus**, **malleus** [c17: via New Latin from Medieval Latin, perhaps a variant of *staffa, stapeda* stirrup, influenced in form by Latin *stāre* to stand + *pēs* a foot]

staphylo- *combining form* **1** uvula: *staphyloplasty* **2** resembling a bunch of grapes: *staphylococcus* [from Greek *staphulē* bunch of grapes, uvula]

staphylococcus (ˌstæfɪləʊ'kɒkəs) *n, pl* **-cocci** (-'kɒkaɪ; *US* -'kɒksaɪ) any spherical Gram-positive bacterium of the genus *Staphylococcus*, typically occurring in clusters and including many pathogenic species, causing boils, infection in wounds, and septicaemia: family *Micrococcaceae*. Often shortened to: **staph** [c19: from STAPHYLO- (in the sense: like a bunch of grapes) + COCCUS so called because of their shape] > **staphylococcal** (ˌstæfɪləʊ'kɒkəl) *adj*

staphyloplasty ('stæfɪləʊˌplæstɪ) *n* plastic surgery or surgical repair involving the soft palate or the uvula [c19: from STAPHYLO- + -PLASTY] > ˌstaphylo'plastic *adj*

staple[1] ('steipəl) *n* **1** a short length of thin wire bent into a square U-shape, used to fasten papers, cloth, etc **2** a short length of stiff wire formed into a U-shape with pointed ends, used for holding a hasp to a post, securing electric cables, etc ▷ *vb* **3** (*tr*) to secure (papers, wire, etc) with a staple or staples [Old English *stapol* prop, of Germanic origin; related to Middle Dutch *stapel* step, Old High German *staffal*] > 'stapler *n*

staple[2] ('steipəl) *adj* **1** of prime importance; principal: *staple foods* **2** (of a commodity) forming a predominant element in the product, consumption, or trade of a nation, region, etc ▷ *n* **3** a staple commodity **4** a main constituent; integral part **5** *chiefly US & Canadian* a principal raw material produced or grown in a region **6** the fibre of wool, cotton, etc, graded as to length and fineness ▷ *vb* **7** (*tr*) to arrange or sort (wool, cotton, etc) according to length and fineness [c15: from Middle Dutch *stapel* warehouse; see STAPLE[1]]

staple gun *n* a mechanism that fixes staples to a surface

star (staː) *n* **1** any of a vast number of celestial objects that are visible in the clear night sky as points of light **2 a** a hot gaseous mass, such as the sun, that radiates energy, esp as light and infrared radiation, usually derived from thermonuclear reactions in the interior, and in some cases as ultraviolet, radio waves, and X-rays. The surface temperature can range from about 2100 to 40 000°C **b** (*as modifier*): *a star catalogue*. Related adjs: **astral, sidereal, stellar 3** *astrology* **a** a celestial body, esp a planet, supposed to influence events, personalities, etc **b** (*plural*) another name for **horoscope** (sense 1) **4** an emblem shaped like a conventionalized star, usually with five or more points, often used as a symbol of rank, an award, etc **5** a small white blaze on the forehead of an animal, esp a horse **6 a** a distinguished or glamorous celebrity, often from the entertainment world **b** (*as modifier*): *star quality* **7** another word for **asterisk 8** **see stars** to see or seem to see bright moving pinpoints of light, as from a blow on the head, increased blood pressure, etc ▷ *vb* **stars, starring, starred 9** (*tr*) to mark or decorate with a star or stars **10** to feature or be featured as a star: *"Greed" starred Erich von Stroheim; Olivier starred in "Hamlet"* [Old English *steorra*; related to Old Frisian *stēra*, Old Norse *stjarna*, German *Stern*, Latin *stella*] > 'starless *adj* > 'star,like *adj*

Stara Zagora (*Bulgarian* 'stara za'gɔra) *n* a city in central Bulgaria: ceded to Bulgaria by Turkey in 1877. Pop: 163 000 (2005 est)

starboard ('staːbəd, -ˌbɔːd) *n* **1** the right side of an aeroplane or vessel when facing the nose or bow. See **port**[2] ▷ *adj* **2** relating to or on the starboard ▷ *vb* **3** to turn or be turned towards the starboard [Old English *stēorbord*, literally: steering side, from *stēor* steering paddle + *bord*

side; see STEER[1], board; from the fact that boats were formerly steered by a paddle held over the right-hand side]

starburst ('staːˌbɜːst) *n* **1** a pattern of rays or lines radiating from a light source **2** *photog* a lens attachment which produces a starburst effect

starch (staːtʃ) *n* **1** a polysaccharide composed of glucose units that occurs widely in plant tissues in the form of storage granules, consisting of amylose and amylopectin **2** Also called: **amylum** a starch obtained from potatoes and some grain: it is fine white powder that forms a translucent viscous solution on boiling with water and is used to stiffen fabric and in many industrial processes **3** any food containing a large amount of starch, such as rice and potatoes **4** stiff or pompous formality of manner or conduct ▷ *vb* **5** (*tr*) to stiffen or soak in starch [Old English *stercan* (unattested except by the past participle *sterced*) to stiffen; related to Old Saxon *sterkian*, Old High German *sterken* to strengthen, Dutch *sterken*; see STARK] > 'starcher *n*

Star Chamber *n* **1** *English history* the Privy Council sitting as a court of equity, esp powerful under the Tudor monarchs; abolished 1641 **2** (*sometimes not capitals*) any arbitrary tribunal dispensing summary justice **3** (*sometimes not capitals*) (in Britain, in a Conservative government) a group of senior ministers who make the final decision on the public spending of each government department

starch-reduced *adj* (of food, esp bread) having the starch content reduced, as in proprietary slimming products

starchy ('staːtʃɪ) *adj* **starchier, starchiest 1** of, relating to, or containing starch **2** extremely formal, stiff, or conventional: *a starchy manner* **3** stiffened with starch > 'starchily *adv* > 'starchiness *n*

star connection *n* a connection used in a polyphase electrical device or system of devices in which the windings each have one end connected to a common junction, the **star point**, and the other end to a separate terminal

star-crossed *adj* dogged by ill luck; destined to misfortune [c16: from CROSS (in the sense: thwart): so called because of the astrological belief that the stars affect people's destinies]

stardom ('staːdəm) *n* **1** the fame and prestige of being a star in films, sport, etc **2** the world of celebrities

stardust ('staːˌdʌst) *n* **1** a large number of distant stars appearing to the observer as a cloud of dust **2** a dreamy romantic or sentimental quality or feeling

stare (steə) *vb* **1** (*intr*; often foll by *at*) to look or gaze fixedly, often with hostility or rudeness **2** (*intr*) to stand out as obvious; glare **3 stare one in the face** to be glaringly obvious or imminent ▷ *n* **4** the act or an instance of staring [Old English *starian*; related to Old Norse *stara*, Old High German *starēn* to stare, Greek *stereos* stiff, Latin *consternāre* to confuse] > 'starer *n*

starfish ('staːˌfɪʃ) *n, pl* **-fish** *or* **-fishes** any echinoderm of the class *Asteroidea*, such as *Asterias rubens*, typically having a flattened body covered with a flexible test and five arms radiating from a central disc

star fruit *n* another name for **carambola**

starfucker ('staːˌfʌkə) *offensive, taboo, slang* ▷ *n* **1** a person who seeks to have sexual relations with celebrities; groupie **2** a person who seeks to associate with famous or powerful people > 'star,fucking *n*

stargaze ('staːˌgeɪz) *vb* (*intr*) **1** to observe the stars **2** to daydream > 'star,gazer *n* > 'star,gazing *n, adj*

stark (staːk) *adj* **1** (*usually prenominal*) devoid of any elaboration; blunt: *the stark facts* **2** grim; desolate: *a stark landscape* **3** (*usually prenominal*) utter; absolute: *stark folly* **4** *archaic* severe; violent **5** *archaic or poetic* rigid, as in death (esp in the phrases **stiff and stark, stark dead**) **6** short for **stark-naked** ▷ *adv* **7** completely: *stark mad* [Old English *stearc* stiff; related to Old Norse *sterkr*, Gothic *gastaurknan* to stiffen] > 'starkly *adv* > 'starkness *n*

Stark *n* **1** (staːk) Dame Freya (**Madeline**) ('freɪə). 1893–1993, British traveller and writer, whose many books include *The Southern Gates of Arabia* (1936), *Beyond*

Euphrates (1951), and *The Journey's Echo* (1963) **2** (*German* ʃtark) **Johannes** (joˈhanəs). 1874–1957, German physicist, who discovered the splitting of the lines of a spectrum when the source of light is subjected to a strong electrostatic field (**Stark effect**, 1913): Nobel prize for physics 1919

Starkey (ˈstɑːkɪ) *n* **David**. born 1945, British historian and broadcaster, noted for his books and television series on the Tudor period

stark-naked *adj* completely naked [C13 *stert naket*, literally: tail naked; *stert*, from Old English *steort* tail; related to Old Norse *stertr* tail + NAKED]

starlet (ˈstɑːlɪt) *n* **1** a young and inexperienced actress who is projected as a potential star **2** a small star

starlight (ˈstɑːˌlaɪt) *n* **1** the light emanating from the stars ▷ *adj* Also: **starlighted 2** of or like starlight **3** Also called: **starlit** (ˈstɑːˌlɪt) illuminated by starlight

starling (ˈstɑːlɪŋ) *n* any gregarious passerine songbird of the Old World family *Sturnidae*, esp *Sturnus vulgaris*, which has a blackish plumage and a short tail [Old English *stærlinc*, from *stær* starling (related to Icelandic *stari*) + *-line* -LING[1]]

Starling (ˈstɑːlɪŋ) *n* **Ernest Henry**. 1866–1927, British physiologist, who contributed greatly to the understanding of many bodily functions and with William Bayliss (1860–1924) discovered the hormone secretin (1902)

star-of-Bethlehem *n* **1** Also called: **starflower** a Eurasian liliaceous plant, *Ornithogalum umbellatum*, naturalized in the eastern US, having narrow leaves and starlike white flowers **2** any of several similar and related plants

Star of Bethlehem *n* the star that is supposed to have appeared above Bethlehem at the birth of Christ

Star of David *n* an emblem symbolizing Judaism and consisting of a six-pointed star formed by superimposing one inverted equilateral triangle upon another of equal size

Starr (stɑː) *n* **1** (**Myra**) **Belle**. 1848–89, US outlaw, a famous rustler of horses and cattle **2** **Ringo**, original name *Richard Starkey*. born 1940, British rock musician; drummer (1962–70) with the Beatles

starry (ˈstɑːrɪ) *adj* **-rier, -riest 1** filled, covered with, or illuminated by stars **2** of, like, or relating to a star or stars ▷ˈ**starriness** *n*

starry-eyed *adj* given to naive wishes, judgments, etc; full of unsophisticated optimism; gullible

Stars and Stripes *n* the Stars and Stripes (*functioning as singular*) the national flag of the United States of America, consisting of 50 white stars representing the present states on a blue field and seven red and six white horizontal stripes representing the original states

star sapphire *n* a sapphire showing a starlike figure in reflected light because of its crystalline structure

star sign *n* another name for **sign of the zodiac**

Star-Spangled Banner the Star-Spangled Banner *n* **1** the national anthem of the United States of America **2** another term for the **Stars and Stripes**

star stream *n* one of two main streams of stars that, because of the rotation of the Milky Way, appear to move in opposite directions, one towards Orion, the other towards Ara

star-studded *adj* featuring a large proportion of well-known actors or other performers: *a star-studded cast*

start (stɑːt) *vb* **1** to begin or cause to begin (something or to do something); come or cause to come into being, operation, etc: *he started a quarrel; they started to work* **2** (when *intr*, sometimes foll by *on*) to make or cause to make a beginning of (a process, series of actions, etc): *they started on the project* **3** (sometimes foll by *up*) to set or be set in motion: *he started up the machine* **4** (*intr*) to make a sudden involuntary movement of one's body, from or as if from fright; jump **5** (*intr*; sometimes foll by *up, away*, etc) to spring or jump suddenly from a position or place **6** to establish or be established; set up: *to start a business* **7** (*tr*) to support (someone) in the first part of a venture, career, etc **8** to work or cause to work loose **9** to enter or be entered in a race **10** (*intr*) to flow violently from a source: *wine started from a hole in the cask* **11** (*tr*) to rouse

(game) from a hiding place, lair, etc **12** (*intr*) (esp of eyes) to bulge; pop **13** (*intr*) *Brit informal* to commence quarrelling or causing a disturbance **14** to start with in the first place ▷ *n* **15** the first or first part of a series of actions or operations, a journey, etc **16** the place or time of starting, as of a race or performance **17** a signal to proceed, as in a race **18** a lead or advantage, either in time or distance and usually of specified extent, in a competitive activity: *he had an hour's start on me* **19** a slight involuntary movement of the body, as through fright, surprise, etc: *she gave a start as I entered* **20** an opportunity to enter a career, undertake a project, etc **21** *informal* a surprising incident **22** for a start in the first place ▷ See also **start in, start off**, etc [Old English *styrtan*; related to Old Norse *sterta* to crease, Old High German *sturzen* to rush]

starter (ˈstɑːtə) *n* **1** a device for starting an internal-combustion engine, usually consisting of a powerful electric motor that engages with the flywheel. Formerly called: **self-starter 2** a person who supervises and signals the start of a race **3** a competitor who starts in a race or contest **4** *informal, chiefly Austral & NZ* an acceptable or practicable proposition, plan, idea, etc **5** *chiefly Brit* the first course of a meal **6** (*modifier*) designed to be used by a novice: *a starter kit* **7** for starters *slang* in the first place **8** under starter's orders **a** (of horses in a race) awaiting the start signal **b** (of a person) eager or ready to begin

starter home *n* a compact flat or house marketed by price and size specifications to suit the requirements of first-time home buyers

start in *vb* (*adverb*) to undertake (something or doing something); commence or begin

starting block *n* one of a pair of adjustable devices with pads or blocks against which a sprinter braces his feet in crouch starts

starting gate *n* **1** a movable barrier so placed on the starting line of a racecourse that the raising of it releases all the contestants simultaneously **2** the US name for **starting stalls**

starting grid *n* *motor racing* a marked section of the track at the start where the cars line up according to their times in practice, the fastest occupying the front position

starting price *n* (esp in horse racing) the latest odds offered by bookmakers at the start of a race

starting rate *n* (in Britain) a rate of income tax below the basic rate

starting stalls *pl n* *Brit* a line of stalls in which horses are enclosed at the start of a race and from which they are released by the simultaneous springing open of retaining barriers at the front of each stall

startle (ˈstɑːtᵊl) *vb* to be or cause to be surprised or frightened, esp so as to start involuntarily [Old English *steartlian* to stumble; related to Middle High German *starzen* to strut, Norwegian *sterta* to strain oneself]

startling (ˈstɑːtlɪŋ) *adj* causing surprise or fear; striking; astonishing ▷ˈ**startlingly** *adv*

start off *vb* (*adverb*) **1** (*intr*) to set out on a journey **2** to be or make the first step in an activity; initiate: *he started the show off with a lively song* **3** (*tr*) to cause (a person) to act or do something, such as to laugh, to tell stories, etc

start on *vb* (*intr, preposition*) *Brit informal* to pick a quarrel with (someone)

start out *vb* (*intr, adverb*) **1** to set out on a journey **2** to take the first steps, as in life, one's career, etc: *he started out as a salesman* **3** to take the first actions in an activity in a particular way or specified aim: *they started out wanting a house, but eventually bought a flat*

start up *vb* (*adverb*) **1** to come or cause to come into being for the first time; originate **2** (*intr*) to spring or jump suddenly from a position or place **3** to set in or go into motion, activity, etc: *he started up the engine; the orchestra started up* ▷ *adj* **start-up 4** of or relating to input, usually financial, made to establish a new project or business ▷ *n* **start-up 5** a business enterprise that has been launched recently

starve (stɑːv) *vb* **1** to die or cause to die from lack of food **2** to deprive (a person or animal) or (of a person, etc) to be deprived of food **3** (*intr*) *informal* to be very hungry **4** (foll by *of* or *for*) to deprive or be deprived (of something necessary), esp so as to cause suffering or malfunctioning: *the engine was starved of fuel* **5** (*tr*; foll by *into*) to bring (to) a specified condition by starving: *to starve someone into submission* **6** *archaic* to be or cause to be extremely cold [Old English *steorfan* to die; related to Old Frisian *sterva* to die, Old High German *sterban* to die] > star'vation *n*

starveling ('stɑ:vlɪŋ) *archaic* ▷ *n* **1 a** a starving or poorly fed person, animal, etc **b** (*as modifier*): *a starveling child* ▷ *adj* **2** insufficient; meagre; scant [c16: from STARVE + -LING[1]]

Star Wars *n* (*functioning as singular*) Also called: *formal* **Strategic Defense Initiative** (in the US) a proposed system of artificial satellites armed with lasers to destroy enemy missiles in space. Abbreviation: **SDI** [c20: popularly named after the science fiction film *Star Wars* (1977) by George Lucas]

starwort ('stɑ:,wɜ:t) *n* **1** any of several plants with star-shaped flowers, esp the stitchwort **2** water starwort any of several aquatic plants of the genus *Callitriche*, having a star-shaped rosette of floating leaves: family *Callitrichaceae*

stash (stæʃ) *vb* **1** (*tr*; often foll by *away*) *informal* to put or store (money, valuables, etc) in a secret place, as for safekeeping ▷ *n* **2** *informal* a secret store or the place where this is hidden **3** *slang* drugs kept for personal consumption [c20: origin unknown]

stasis ('steɪsɪs) *n* **1** *pathol* a stagnation in the normal flow of bodily fluids, such as the blood or urine **2** *literature* a state or condition in which there is no action or progress; static situation [c18: via New Latin from Greek: a standing, from *histanai* to cause to stand; related to Latin *stāre* to stand]

-stat *n combining form* indicating a device that causes something to remain stationary or constant: *thermostat* [from Greek *-statēs*, from *histanai* to cause to stand]

state (steɪt) *n* **1** the condition of a person, thing, etc, with regard to main attributes **2** the structure, form, or constitution of something: *a solid state* **3** any mode of existence **4** position in life or society; estate **5** ceremonious style, as befitting wealth or dignity: *to live in state* **6** a sovereign political power or community **7** the territory occupied by such a community **8** the sphere of power in such a community: *affairs of state* **9** (*often capital*) one of a number of areas or communities having their own governments and forming a federation under a sovereign government, as in the US **10** (*often capital*) the body politic of a particular sovereign power, esp as contrasted with a rival authority such as the Church **11** *obsolete* a class or order; estate **12** *informal* a nervous, upset, or excited condition (esp in the phrase **in a state**) **13** lie in state (of a body) to be placed on public view before burial **14** state of affairs a situation; present circumstances or condition ▷ *modifier* **15** controlled or financed by a state: *state university* **16** of, relating to, or concerning the State: *State trial* **17** involving ceremony or concerned with a ceremonious occasion: *state visit* ▷ *vb* (*tr*; may take a clause as object) **18** to articulate in words; utter **19** to declare formally or publicly [c13: from Old French *estat*, from Latin *status* a standing, from *stāre* to stand] > 'statable *or* 'stateable *adj* > 'statehood *n*

state bank *n* (in the US) a commercial bank incorporated under a State charter and not required to be a member of the Federal Reserve System

statecraft ('steɪt,krɑːft) *n* the art of conducting public affairs; statesmanship

State Duma *n* another name for **duma** (sense 3)

state house *n* NZ a house built by the government for renting

Statehouse ('steɪt,haʊs) *n* (in the US) the building which houses a state legislature; State capitol

stateless ('steɪtlɪs) *adj* **1** without nationality: *stateless persons* **2** without a state or states > 'statelessness *n*

stately ('steɪtlɪ) *adj* **-lier, -liest 1** characterized by a graceful, dignified, and imposing appearance or manner ▷ *adv* **2** in a stately manner > 'stateliness *n*

stately home *n* Brit a large mansion, esp one open to the general public

statement ('steɪtmənt) *n* **1** the act of stating **2** something that is stated, esp a formal prepared announcement or reply **3** *law* a declaration of matters of fact, esp in a pleading **4** an account containing a summary of bills or invoices and displaying the total amount due **5** an account prepared by a bank for each of its clients, usually at regular intervals, to show all credits and debits since the last account and the balance at the end of the period **6** a computer instruction written in a source language, such as FORTRAN, which is converted into one or more machine code instructions by a compiler **7** *logic* the content of a sentence that affirms or denies something and may be true or false; what is thereby affirmed or denied abstracted from the act of uttering it. Thus *I am warm* said by me and *you are warm* said to me make the same statement **8** *Brit education* a legally binding account of the needs of a pupil with special educational needs and the provisions that will be made to meet them ▷ *vb* (*tr*; *usually passive*) **9** to assess (a pupil) with regard to his or her special educational needs

statement of claim *n law* (in England) the first pleading made by the claimant in a civil court action showing the facts upon which he or she relies in support of the claim and the relief asked for

Staten Island ('stætᵊn) *n* an island in SE New York State, in New York Harbor: a borough of New York city; heavy industry. Pop: 443 728 (2000). Area: 155 sq km (60 sq miles)

state of the art *n* **1** the level of knowledge and development achieved in a technique, science, etc, esp at present ▷ *adj* state-of-the-art (*prenominal*) **2** the most recent and therefore considered the best; up-to-the-minute: *a state-of-the-art amplifier*

State Registered Nurse *n* (formerly in Britain) a nurse who had extensive training and passed examinations enabling him or her to perform all nursing services. See **Registered General Nurse**

stateroom ('steɪt,ruːm, -,rʊm) *n* **1** a private cabin or room on a ship, train, etc **2** *chiefly Brit* a large room in a palace or other building for use on state occasions

States (steɪts) *n* **the states** (*functioning as singular or plural*) an informal name for the **United States of America**

state school *n* any school maintained by the state, in which education is free

stateside ('steɪt,saɪd) *adj, adv* US of, in, to, or towards the US

statesman ('steɪtsmən) *n*, *pl* **-men 1** a political leader whose wisdom, integrity, etc, win great respect **2** a person active and influential in the formulation of high government policy, such as a cabinet member **3** a politician > 'statesman-,like *or* 'statesmanly *adj* > 'statesmanship *n* > 'states,woman *fem n*

state socialism *n* a variant of socialism in which the power of the state is employed for the purpose of creating an egalitarian society by means of public control of major industries, banks, etc, coupled with economic planning and a social security system > **state socialist** *n*

state trooper *n* US a state policeman

static ('stætɪk) *adj* Also: **statical 1** not active or moving; stationary **2** (of a weight, force, or pressure) acting but causing no movement **3** of or concerned with forces that do not produce movement. See **dynamic** (sense 1) **4** relating to or causing stationary electric charges; electrostatic **5** of or relating to interference in the reception of radio or television transmissions **6** of or concerned with statics **7** *computing* (of a memory) not needing its contents refreshed periodically ▷ *n* **8** random hissing or crackling or a speckled picture caused by the interference of electrical disturbances in the reception of radio or television transmissions **9** electric sparks or crackling produced by friction [c16: from New Latin *staticus*, from Greek *statikos* causing to stand, from *histanai* to stand, put in the scales] > 'statically *adv*

statice ('stætɪsɪ) *n* See **sea lavender** [Latin: thrift, from Greek *statikē*, from *statikos* astringent (from a medicinal use of thrift)]

statics ('stætɪks) n (functioning as singular) the branch of mechanics concerned with the forces that produce a state of equilibrium in a system of bodies

station ('steɪʃən) n 1 the place or position at which a thing or person stands or is supposed to stand 2 a a place along a route or line at which a bus, train, etc, stops for fuel or to pick up or let off passengers or goods, esp one with ancillary buildings and services b (as modifier): a station buffet 3 a the headquarters or local offices of an official organization such as the police or fire services b (as modifier): a station sergeant. See **police station**, **fire station** 4 a building, depot, etc, with special equipment for some particular purpose: power station; petrol station; television station 5 military a place of duty: an action station 6 navy a a location to which a ship or fleet is assigned for duty b an assigned location for a member of a ship's crew 7 a radio or television channel 8 a position or standing, as in a particular society or organization 9 the type of one's occupation; calling 10 (in British India) a place where the British district officials or garrison officers resided 11 biology the type of habitat occupied by a particular animal or plant 12 Austral & NZ a large sheep or cattle farm 13 (often capital) RC Church a one of the Stations of the Cross b any of the churches (**station churches**) in Rome that have been used from ancient times as points of assembly for religious processions and ceremonies on particular days (**station days**) ▷ vb 14 (tr) to place in or assign to a station [C14: via Old French from Latin statiō a standing still, from stāre to stand]

stationary ('steɪʃənərɪ) adj 1 not moving; standing still 2 not able to be moved 3 showing no change: the doctors said his condition was stationary 4 tending to remain in one place [C15: from Latin statiōnārius, from statiō STATION]

stationary orbit n astronautics an orbit lying in, or approximately in, the plane of the equator for which the orbital period is equal to the spin period of the central body

stationary wave n another name for **standing wave**

stationer ('steɪʃənə) n a person who sells stationery or a shop where stationery is sold [C14: from Medieval Latin stationarius a person having a regular station, hence a shopkeeper (esp a bookseller) as distinguished from an itinerant tradesman; see STATION]

stationery ('steɪʃənərɪ) n any writing materials, such as paper, envelopes, pens, ink, rulers, etc

station house n chiefly US a house that is situated by or serves as a station, esp as a police or fire station

stationmaster ('steɪʃən,mɑːstə) n the senior official in charge of a railway station

Stations of the Cross pl n RC Church 1 a series of 14 crosses, often accompanied by 14 pictures or carvings, arranged in order around the walls of a church, to commemorate 14 supposed stages in Christ's journey to Calvary 2 a devotion consisting of 14 prayers relating to each of these stages

station wagon n a US, Canadian, Austral and NZ name for **estate car**

statism ('steɪtɪzəm) n the theory or practice of concentrating economic and political power in the state, resulting in a weak position for the individual or community with respect to the government

statistic (stə'tɪstɪk) n any function of a number of random variables, usually identically distributed, that may be used to estimate a population parameter. See also **sampling statistic**, **estimator** (sense 2),**parameter** (sense 3)

statistical mechanics n (functioning as singular) the study of the properties of physical systems as predicted by the statistical behaviour of their constituent particles

statistics (stə'tɪstɪks) n 1 (functioning as plural) quantitative data on any subject, esp data comparing the distribution of some quantity for different subclasses of the population 2 (functioning as singular) the classification and interpretation of such data in accordance with probability theory and the application of methods such as hypothesis testing to them [C18 (originally "science dealing with facts of a state"): via

German Statistik, from New Latin statisticus concerning state affairs, from Latin status STATE]

Statius ('steɪʃɪəs) n Publius Papinius ('pʌblɪəs pə'pɪnɪəs). ?45–96 AD, Roman poet; author of the collection Silvae and two epics, Thebais and the unfinished Achilleis

stator ('steɪtə) n the stationary part of a rotary machine or device, esp of a motor or generator [C20: from Latin: one who stands (by), from stāre to stand]

statoscope ('stætə,skəʊp) n a very sensitive form of aneroid barometer used to detect and measure small variations in atmospheric pressure, such as one used in an aircraft to indicate small changes in altitude

statuary ('stætjʊərɪ) n 1 statues collectively 2 the art of making statues ▷ adj 3 of, relating to, or suitable for statues [C16: from Latin statuārius]

statue ('stætjuː) n a wooden, stone, metal, plaster, or other kind of sculpture of a human or animal figure, usually life-size or larger [C14: via Old French from Latin statua, from statuere to set up; compare STATUTE]

statuesque (,stætjʊ'ɛsk) adj like a statue, esp in possessing great formal beauty or dignity [C19: from STATUE + -ESQUE, on the model of PICTURESQUE] ▷,statu'esquely adv ▷,statu'esqueness n

statuette (,stætjʊ'ɛt) n a small statue

stature ('stætʃə) n 1 the height of something, esp a person or animal when standing 2 the degree of development of a person: the stature of a champion 3 intellectual or moral greatness: a man of stature [C13: via Old French from Latin statūra, from stāre to stand]

status ('steɪtəs) n, pl-tuses 1 a social or professional position, condition, or standing to which varying degrees of responsibility, privilege, and esteem are attached 2 the relative position or standing of a person or thing 3 a high position or standing; prestige: he has acquired a new status since he has been in that job 4 the legal standing or condition of a person 5 a state of affairs [C17: from Latin: posture, from stāre to stand]

status asthmaticus (æs'mætɪkəs) n a severe attack of asthma in which the patient may die from respiratory failure if not treated with inhaled oxygen or other appropriate measures

status bar n a narrow horizontal area at the foot of a computer screen or window in which details are displayed about the program that is running or the document that is being edited

status epilepticus (,ɛpɪ'lɛptɪkəs) n a condition in which repeated epileptic seizures occur without the patient gaining consciousness between them. If untreated for a prolonged period it can lead to long-term disability or death

status Indian n Canadian a member of a native Canadian people who is registered as an Indian under the federal Indian Act

status quo (kwəʊ) n the status quo the existing state of affairs [literally: the state in which]

status symbol n a possession which is regarded as proof of the owner's social position, wealth, prestige, etc

status zero n the condition of young people who are out of school but not in further education or training, permanently or regularly out of work, and dropping out of the mainstream of society

statute ('stætjuːt) n 1 a an enactment of a legislative body expressed in a formal document b this document 2 a permanent rule made by a body or institution for the government of its internal affairs [C13: from Old French estatut, from Late Latin statūtum, from Latin statuere to set up, decree, ultimately from stāre to stand]

statute book n chiefly Brit a register of enactments passed by the legislative body of a state, usually made up of a series of volumes that form a complete official record: not on the statute book

statute law n 1 a law enacted by a legislative body 2 a particular example of this ▷ See **common law**, **equity**

statute mile n a legal or formal name for **mile** (sense 1)

statute of limitations n a legislative enactment prescribing the period of time within which proceedings must be instituted to enforce a right or bring an action at law

S

statutory ('stætjʊtərɪ, -trɪ) *adj* **1** of, relating to, or having the nature of a statute **2** prescribed or authorized by statute **3** (of an offence) **a** recognized by statute **b** subject to a punishment or penalty prescribed by statute > 'statutorily *adv*

statutory order *n* a statute that applies further legislation to an existing act

Stauffenberg ('ʃtaʊfənˌbɔːɡ) *n* **Claus** (klaʊs), **Graf von**. 1907–44, German army officer, who tried to assassinate Hitler (1944). He and his fellow conspirators were executed

staunch[1] (stɔːntʃ) *adj* **1** loyal, firm, and dependable: *a staunch supporter* **2** solid or substantial in construction **3** *rare* (of a ship, etc) watertight; seaworthy [C15: (originally: watertight): from Old French *estanche*, from *estanchier* to STANCH] > 'staunchly *adv* > 'staunchness *n*

staunch[2] (stɔːntʃ) *vb, n* a variant spelling of **stanch**

Stavanger (Norwegian staˈvaŋər) *n* a port in SW Norway: canning and shipbuilding industries. Pop: 112 405 (2004 est)

stave (steɪv) *n* **1** any one of a number of long strips of wood joined together to form a barrel, bucket, boat hull, etc **2** any of various bars, slats, or rods, usually of wood, such as a rung of a ladder or a crosspiece bracing the legs of a chair **3** any stick, staff, etc **4** a stanza or verse of a poem **5** *music* **a** *Brit* an individual group of five lines and four spaces used in staff notation **b** another word for: **staff**[1] (sense 9) ▷ *vb* **staves, staving, staved** or **stove 6** (often foll by *in*) to break or crush (the staves of a boat, barrel, etc) or (of the staves of a boat) to be broken or crushed **7** (*tr*; usually foll by *in*) to burst or force (a hole in something) **8** (*tr*) to provide (a ladder, chair, etc) with a stave or staves **9** (*tr*) *Scot* to sprain (a finger, toe, etc) [C14: back formation from *staves*, plural of STAFF[1]]

stave off *vb* (*tr, adverb*) to avert or hold off (something undesirable or harmful), esp temporarily: *to stave off hunger*

staves (steɪvz) *n* a plural of **staff**[1] or **stave**

stavesacre ('steɪvzˌeɪkə) *n* **1** a Eurasian ranunculaceous plant, *Delphinium staphisagria*, having purple flowers and poisonous seeds **2** the seeds of this plant, which have strong emetic and cathartic properties [C14 *staphisagre*, from Latin *staphis agria*, from Greek *staphis* raisin + *agria* wild]

Stavropol (Russian 'stavrəpəlj) *n* **1** a city in SW Russia: founded as a fortress in 1777. Pop: 362 000 (2005 est). Former name (1940–44): **Voroshilovsk 2** the former name (until 1964) of **Togliatti**[1]

stay[1] (steɪ) *vb* **1** (*intr*) to continue or remain in a certain place, position, etc: *to stay outside* **2** (*copula*) to continue to be; remain: *to stay awake* **3** (*intr*; often foll by *at*) to reside temporarily, esp as a guest: *to stay at a hotel* **4** (*tr*) to remain for a specified period: *to stay the weekend* **5** (*intr*) *Scot & South African* to reside permanently or habitually; live **6** *archaic* to stop or cause to stop **7** (*intr*) to wait, pause, or tarry **8** (*tr*) to delay or hinder **9** (*tr*) **a** to discontinue or suspend (a judicial proceeding) **b** to hold in abeyance or restrain from enforcing (an order, decree, etc) **10** to endure (something testing or difficult, such as a race): *a horse that stays the course* **11** (*tr*) to hold back or restrain: *to stay one's anger* **12** (*tr*) to satisfy or appease (an appetite, etc) temporarily ▷ *n* **13** the act of staying or sojourning in a place or the period during which one stays **14** the act of stopping or restraining or state of being stopped, etc **15** the suspension of a judicial proceeding, etc: *stay of execution* [C15 *staien*, from Anglo-French *estaier*, to stay, from Old French *ester* to stay, from Latin *stāre* to stand] > 'stayer *n*

stay[2] (steɪ) *n* **1** anything that supports or steadies, such as a prop or buttress **2** a thin strip of metal, plastic, bone, etc, used to stiffen corsets, etc ▷ *vb* (*tr*) *archaic* **3** (often foll by *up*) to prop or hold **4** (often foll by *up*) to comfort or sustain **5** (foll by *on* or *upon*) to cause to rely or depend [C16: from Old French *estaye*, of Germanic origin; compare STAY[3]]

stay[3] (steɪ) *n* a rope, cable, or chain, usually one of a set, used for bracing uprights, such as masts, funnels, flagpoles, chimneys, etc; guy. See also **stays** (senses 2, 3) [Old English *stæg*; related to Old Norse *stag*, Middle Low

German *stach*, Norwegian *stagle* wooden post]

stay-at-home *adj* **1** (of a person) enjoying a quiet, settled, and unadventurous use of leisure ▷ *n* **2** a stay-at-home person

staying power *n* endurance; stamina

stays (steɪz) *pl n* **1** *now rare* corsets with bones in them **2** a position of a sailing vessel relative to the wind so that the sails are luffing or aback **3** **miss stays** or **refuse stays** (of a sailing vessel) to fail to come about

staysail ('steɪˌseɪl, 'steɪsʲl) *nautical* ▷ *n* an auxiliary sail, often triangular, set to catch the wind, as between the masts of a yawl (**mizzen staysail**), aft of a spinnaker (**spinnaker staysail**), etc

STD *abbreviation* **1** *NZ* subscriber toll dialling **2** sexually transmitted disease **3** Doctor of Sacred Theology

STD code *n* *Brit* a code of four or more digits, other than those comprising a subscriber's local telephone number, that determines the routing of a call [C20: s(*ubscriber*) t(*runk*) d(*ialling*)]

Ste *abbreviation* Saint (female) [French *Sainte*]

stead (stɛd) *n* **1** (preceded by *in*) *rare* the place, function, or position that should be taken by another: *to come in someone's stead* **2** **stand someone in good stead** to be useful or of good service to (someone) ▷ *vb* **3** (*tr*) *archaic* to help or benefit [Old English *stede*; related to Old Norse *stathr* place, Old High German *stat* place, Latin *statiō* a standing, *statim* immediately]

Stead (stɛd) *n* **Christina (Ellen)**. 1902–83, Australian novelist. Her works include *Seven Poor Men of Sydney* (1934), *The Man who Loved Children* (1940), and *Cotters' England* (1966)

steadfast or **stedfast** ('stɛdfəst, -ˌfɑːst) *adj* **1** (esp of a person's gaze) fixed in intensity or direction; steady **2** unwavering or determined in purpose, loyalty, etc: *steadfast resolve* > 'steadfastly or 'stedfastly *adv* > 'steadfastness or 'stedfastness *n*

steading ('stɛdɪŋ) *n* *Brit* **1** a farmstead **2** the outbuildings of a farm [C15: from STEAD + -ING[1]]

steady ('stɛdɪ) *adj* **steadier, steadiest 1** not able to be moved or disturbed easily; stable **2** free from fluctuation **3** not easily excited; imperturbable **4** staid; sober **5** regular; habitual: *a steady drinker* **6** continuous: *a steady flow* **7** *nautical* (of a vessel) keeping upright, as in heavy seas ▷ *vb* **steadies, steadying, steadied 8** to make or become steady ▷ *adv* **9** in a steady manner **10** **go steady** *informal* to date one person regularly ▷ *n, pl* **steadies 11** *informal* one's regular boyfriend or girlfriend ▷ *interj* **12** *nautical* an order to the helmsman to stay on a steady course **13** a warning to keep calm, be careful, etc **14** *Brit* a command to get set to start, as in a race: *ready, steady, go!* [C16: from STEAD + -Y[1]; related to Old High German *stātīg*, Middle Dutch *stēdig*] > 'steadily *adv* > 'steadiness *n*

steady state *n* *physics* the condition of a system when some or all of the quantities describing it are independent of time but not necessarily in thermodynamic or chemical equilibrium

steady-state theory *n* a cosmological theory postulating that the universe exists throughout time in a steady state such that the average density of matter does not vary with distance or time. Matter is continuously created in the space left by the receding stars and galaxies of the expanding universe. Compare **big-bang theory**

steak (steɪk) *n* **1** See **beefsteak 2** any of various cuts of beef of varying quality, used for braising, stewing, etc **3** a thick slice of pork, veal, etc, or of a large fish, esp cod or salmon **4** minced meat prepared in the same way as steak: *hamburger steak* [C15: from Old Norse *steik* roast; related to *steikja* to roast on a spit; see STICK[1]]

steak tartare or **steak tartar** *n* raw minced steak, mixed with onion, seasonings, and raw egg. Also called: **tartare steak, tartar steak**

steal (stiːl) *vb* **steals, stealing, stole, stolen 1** to take (something) from someone, etc without permission or unlawfully, esp in a secret manner **2** (*tr*) to obtain surreptitiously **3** (*tr*) to appropriate (ideas, etc) without acknowledgment, as in plagiarism **4** to move or convey stealthily: *they stole along the corridor* **5** (*intr*) to pass unnoticed: *the hours stole by* **6** (*tr*) to win or gain by strategy or luck, as in various sports: *to steal a few yards* ▷ *n informal* **7** the act of stealing **8** something stolen or acquired easily or at little cost [Old English *stelan*; related to Old Frisian, Old Norse *stela* Gothic *stilan*, German *stehlen*] > '**stealer** *n*

stealth (stɛlθ) *n* **1** the act or characteristic of moving with extreme care and quietness, esp so as to avoid detection **2** cunning or underhand procedure or dealing [C13 *stelthe*; see STEAL, -TH¹] > '**stealthy** *adj* > '**stealthily** *adv*

Stealth (stɛlθ) *n* (*modifier*) *informal* denoting or referring to technology that aims to reduce the radar, thermal, and acoustic recognizability of aircraft and missiles

Stealth bomber *or* **Stealth plane** *n* a type of US military aircraft using advanced technology to render it virtually undetectable to sight, radar, or infrared sensors

stealth tax *n Brit informal* an indirect tax, such as that on fuel or pension funds, esp one of which people are unaware or that is felt to be unfair

steam (stiːm) *n* **1** the gas or vapour into which water is changed when boiled **2** the mist formed when such gas or vapour condenses in the atmosphere **3** any vaporous exhalation **4** *informal* power, energy, or speed **5 get up steam a** (of a ship, etc) to work up a sufficient head of steam in a boiler to drive an engine **b** *informal* to go quickly **6 let off steam** *informal* to release pent-up energy or emotions **7 under one's own steam** without the assistance of others **8** (*modifier*) driven, operated, heated, powered, etc, by steam: *a steam radiator* **9** (*modifier*) treated by steam: *steam ironed; steam cleaning* **10** (*modifier*) *humorous* old-fashioned; outmoded: *steam radio* ▷ *vb* **11** to emit or be emitted as steam **12** (*intr*) to generate steam, as a boiler, etc **13** (*intr*) to move or travel by steam power, as a ship, etc **14** (*intr*) *informal* to proceed quickly and sometimes forcefully **15** to cook or be cooked in steam **16** (*tr*) to treat with steam or apply steam to, as in cleaning, pressing clothes, etc ▷ See also **steam up** [Old English; related to Dutch *stoom* steam, perhaps to Old High German *stioban* to raise dust, Gothic *stubjus* dust]

steam bath *n* **1** a room or enclosure that can be filled with steam in which people bathe to induce sweating and refresh or cleanse themselves **2** an act of taking such a bath

steamboat ('stiːmˌbəʊt) *n* a boat powered by a steam engine

steam-boiler *n* a vessel in which water is boiled to generate steam. An industrial boiler usually consists of a system of parallel tubes through which water passes, suspended above a furnace

steam-engine *n* an engine that uses the thermal energy of steam to produce mechanical work, esp one in which steam from a boiler is expanded in a cylinder to drive a reciprocating piston

steamer ('stiːmə) *n* **1** a boat or ship driven by steam engines **2** a vessel used to cook food by steam **3** *Austral slang* a clash of sporting teams characterized by rough play

steaming ('stiːmɪŋ) *adj* **1** very hot **2** *informal* angry **3** *slang* drunk ▷ *n* **4** *informal* robbery, esp of passengers in a railway carriage or bus, by a large gang of armed youths

steam iron *n* an electric iron that emits steam from channels in the iron face to facilitate the pressing and ironing of clothes, etc, the steam being produced from water contained within the iron

steam jacket *n engineering* a jacket containing steam that surrounds and heats a cylinder

steam organ *n* a type of organ powered by steam, once common at fairgrounds, in which the pipes are sounded either by a keyboard or in a sequence determined by a moving punched card. US name: **calliope**

steam point *n* the temperature at which the maximum vapour pressure of water is equal to one atmosphere $(1.01325 \times 10^5 \text{ N/m}^2)$. It has the value of 100° on the Celsius scale

steam reforming *n chem* a process in which methane from natural gas is heated, with steam, usually with a catalyst, to produce a mixture of carbon monoxide and hydrogen used in organic synthesis and as a fuel

steam roller ('stiːmˌrəʊlə) *n* **1 a** a steam-powered vehicle with heavy rollers at the front and rear used for compressing road surfaces during road-making **b** another word for **roadroller 2 a** an overpowering force or a person with such force that overcomes all opposition **b** (*as modifier*): *steamroller tactics* ▷ *vb* **3** (*tr*) to crush (opposition, etc) by overpowering force

steamship ('stiːmˌʃɪp) *n* a ship powered by one or more steam engines

steam-shovel *n* a steam-driven mechanical excavator, esp one having a large bucket or grab on a beam slung from a revolving jib

steam turbine *n* a turbine driven by steam

steam up *vb* (*adverb*) **1** to cover (windows, etc) or (of windows, etc) to become covered with a film of condensed steam **2** (*tr; usually passive*) *slang* to excite or make angry: *he's all steamed up about the delay*

steamy ('stiːmɪ) *adj* steamier, steamiest **1** of, resembling, full of, or covered with steam **2** *informal* lustful or erotic: *steamy nightlife* > '**steaminess** *n*

stearic (stɪˈærɪk) *adj* **1** of or relating to suet or fat **2** of, consisting of, containing, or derived from stearic acid [C19: from French *stéarique*, from Greek *stear* fat, tallow]

stearic acid *n* a colourless odourless insoluble waxy carboxylic acid used for making candles and suppositories; octadecanoic acid. Formula: $CH_3(CH_2)_{16}COOH$

stearin *or* **stearine** ('stɪərɪn) *n* **1** Also called: **tristearin** a colourless crystalline ester of glycerol and stearic acid, present in fats and used in soap and candles; glycerol tristearate; glycerol trioctadecanoate. Formula: $(C_{17}H_{35}COO)_3C_3H_5$ **2** another name for stearic acid, esp a commercial grade containing other fatty acids **3** fat in its solid form [C19: from French *stéarine*, from Greek *stear* fat, tallow + -IN]

steatite ('stɪəˌtaɪt) *n* another name for **soapstone** [C18: from Latin *steatitēs*, from Greek *stear* fat + -ITE¹] > **steatitic** (ˌstɪəˈtɪtɪk) *adj*

steato- *combining form* denoting fat [from Greek *stear*, *steat-* fat, tallow]

steatolysis (ˌstɪəˈtɒlɪsɪs) *n physiol* **1** the digestive process whereby fats are emulsified and then hydrolysed to fatty acids and glycerine **2** the breaking down of fat

steatopygia (ˌstɪətəʊˈpɪdʒɪə, -ˈpaɪ-) *or* **steatopyga** (ˌstɪətəʊˈpaɪɡə) *n* excessive fatness of the buttocks [C19: from New Latin, from STEATO- + Greek *pugē* the buttocks] > **steatopygic** (ˌstɪətəʊˈpɪdʒɪk) *or* **steatopygous** (ˌstɪəˈtɒpɪɡəs) *adj*

Stębark ('stɛmbark) *n* the Polish name for **Tannenberg**

stedfast ('stɛdfəst, -ˌfɑːst) *adj* a less common spelling of **steadfast**

steed (stiːd) *n archaic or literary* a horse, esp one that is spirited or swift [Old English *stēda* stallion; related to German *Stute* female horse; see STUD²]

steel (stiːl) *n* **1 a** any of various alloys based on iron containing carbon (usually 0.1–1.7 per cent) and often small quantities of other elements such as phosphorus, sulphur, manganese, chromium, and nickel. Steels exhibit a variety of properties, such as strength, machinability, malleability, etc, depending on their composition and the way they have been treated **b** (*as modifier*): *steel girders*. See also **stainless steel 2** something that is made of steel **3** a steel stiffener in a corset, etc **4** a ridged steel rod with a handle used for sharpening knives **5** the quality of hardness, esp with regard to a person's character or attitudes **6** *stock exchange* the quotation for steel shares **7** (*modifier*) resembling steel: *steel determination* ▷ *vb* **8** to fit, plate, edge, or point with steel **9** to make hard and unfeeling: *he steeled his heart against her sorrow; he steeled himself for the blow* [Old English *stēli*; related to Old High German *stehli*, Middle Dutch *stael*] > '**steely** *adj* > '**steeliness** *n*

Steel (stiːl) *n* **1 Danielle**, full name *Danielle Fernande Schüelein-Steel*. born 1950, US writer of romantic fiction **2 Baron David** (**Martin Scott**). born 1938, British politician; leader of the Liberal Party (1976–88); Presiding Officer of the Scottish Parliament (1999–2003)

steel band *n music* a type of instrumental band, popular in the Caribbean Islands, consisting mainly of tuned percussion instruments made chiefly from the heads of oil drums, hammered or embossed to obtain different notes

steel blue *n* **a** a dark bluish-grey colour **b** (*as adjective*): *steel-blue eyes*

Steele (stiːl) *n* Sir **Richard**. 1672–1729, British essayist and dramatist, born in Ireland; with Joseph Addison he was the chief contributor to the periodicals *The Tatler* (1709–11) and *The Spectator* (1711–12)

steel engraving *n* **a** a method or art of engraving (letters, etc) on a steel plate **b** a print made from such a plate

steel grey *n* **a** a dark grey colour, usually slightly purple **b** (*as adjective*): *a steel-grey suit*

steelhead (ˈstiːlˌhɛd) *n*, *pl* **-heads** or **-head** a silvery North Pacific variety of the rainbow trout (*Salmo gairdneri*)

steel wool *n* a tangled or woven mass of fine steel fibres, used for cleaning or polishing

steelworks (ˈstiːlˌwɜːks) *n* (*functioning as singular or plural*) a plant in which steel is made from iron ore and rolled or forged into blooms, billets, bars, or sheets
> ˈsteelˌworker *n*

steelyard (ˈstiːlˌjɑːd) *n* a portable balance consisting of a pivoted bar with two unequal arms. The load is suspended from the shorter one and the bar is returned to the horizontal by adding weights to the longer one [C17: from STEEL + YARD¹ (in the archaic sense: a rod or pole)]

Steen (stein) *n* **Jan** (jɑn). 1626–79, Dutch genre painter

steenbok (ˈstiːnˌbɒk) *n*, *pl* **-boks** or **-bok** a small antelope, *Raphicerus campestris*, of central and southern Africa, having a reddish-brown coat and straight smooth horns. Also called: **steinbok** [C18: from Afrikaans, from Dutch *steen* stone + *bok* BUCK¹; Compare STEENBOK]

steenbras (ˈstiːnˌbræs) *n* *South African* a variety of sea bream, *Lithognathos lithognathos*, valued as a food fish in South Africa [C17: from Afrikaans, from Dutch *steen* stone + *brasen* bream]

steep¹ (stiːp) *adj* **1 a** having or being a slope or gradient approaching the perpendicular **b** (*as noun*): *the steep* **2** *informal* (of a fee, price, demand, etc) unduly high; unreasonable (esp in the phrase **that's a bit steep**) **3** *informal* excessively demanding or ambitious: *a steep task* **4** *Brit informal* (of a statement) extreme or far-fetched **5** *obsolete* elevated [Old English *steap*; related to Old Frisian *stāp*, Old High German *stouf* cliff, Old Norse *staup*] > ˈsteeply *adv* > ˈsteepness *n*

steep² (stiːp) *vb* **1** to soak or be soaked in a liquid in order to soften, cleanse, extract an element, etc **2** (*tr*; *usually passive*) to saturate; imbue: *steeped in ideology* ▷ *n* **3** an instance or the process of steeping or the condition of being steeped **4** a liquid or solution used for the purpose of steeping something [Old English *stēpan*; related to *steap* vessel, cup, Old High German *stouf*, Old Norse *staup*, Middle Dutch *stōp*] > ˈsteeper *n*

steepen (ˈstiːpən) *vb* to become or cause to become steep or steeper

steeple (ˈstiːpəl) *n* **1** a tall ornamental tower that forms the superstructure of a church, temple, etc **2** such a tower with the spire above it **3** any spire or pointed structure [Old English *stēpel*; see STEEP¹] > ˈsteepled *adj*

steeplechase (ˈstiːpəlˌtʃeɪs) *n* **1** a horse race over a course equipped with obstacles to be jumped, esp artificial hedges, ditches, water jumps, etc **2** a track race, usually of 3000 metres, in which the runners have to leap hurdles, a water jump, etc **3** *archaic* **a** a horse race across a stretch of open countryside including obstacles to be jumped **b** a rare word for **point-to-point** ▷ *vb* **4** (*intr*) to take part in a steeplechase [C19: so called because it originally took place cross-country, with a church tower serving as a landmark to guide the riders] > ˈsteepleˌchasing *n* > ˈsteepleˌchaser *n*

steeplejack (ˈstiːpəlˌdʒæk) *n* a person trained and skilled in the construction and repair of steeples, chimneys, etc [C19: from STEEPLE + JACK¹ (in the sense: a man or fellow)]

steer¹ (stɪə) *vb* **1** to direct the course of (a vehicle or vessel) with a steering wheel, rudder, etc **2** (*tr*) to guide with tuition: *his teachers steered him through his exams* **3** (*tr*) to direct the movements or course of (a person, conversation, etc) **4** to pursue (a specified course) **5** (*intr*) (of a vessel, vehicle, etc) to admit of being guided in a specified fashion: *this boat does not steer properly* **6 steer clear of** to keep away from; shun ▷ *n* **7** *chiefly US* information; guidance (esp in the phrase **a bum steer**) [Old English *stieran*; related to Old Frisian *stiūra*, Old Norse *stȳra*, German *stevern*; see STARBOARD, STERN²] > ˈsteerable *adj* > ˈsteerer *n*

steer² (stɪə) *n* a castrated male ox or bull; bullock [Old English *stēor*; related to Old Norse *stjōrr*, Gothic *stiur*, Old High German *stior*, Middle Dutch *stēr*]

steerage (ˈstɪərɪdʒ) *n* **1** the cheapest accommodation on a passenger ship, originally the compartments containing the steering apparatus **2** an instance or the practice of steering and the effect of this on a vessel or vehicle

steerageway (ˈstɪərɪdʒˌweɪ) *n* *nautical* enough forward movement to allow a vessel to be steered

steering committee *n* a committee set up to prepare and arrange topics to be discussed, the order of business, etc, for a legislative assembly or other body

steering wheel *n* a wheel turned by the driver of a motor vehicle, ship, etc, when he wishes to change direction. It is connected to the front wheels, rudder, etc

steersman (ˈstɪəzmən) *n*, *pl* **-men** the helmsman of a vessel

Stefan Dušan (ˈstɛfən ˈduːʃæn) *n* 1308–55, king of Serbia (1331–55), who conquered Albania (1343) and large parts of the Byzantine empire, into which he introduced legal and administrative reforms

Stefansson (ˈstɛfənsən) *n* **Vilhjalmur** (ˈvɪlˌhjaʊmɛr). 1879–1962, Canadian explorer, noted for his books on the Inuit

Steffens (ˈstɛfənz) *n* **(Joseph) Lincoln**. 1866–1936, US political analyst, known for his exposure of political corruption

stegosaur (ˈstɛgəˌsɔː) or **stegosaurus** (ˌstɛgəˈsɔːrəs) *n* any quadrupedal herbivorous ornithischian dinosaur of the suborder *Stegosauria*, esp any of the genus *Stegosaurus*, of Jurassic and early Cretaceous times, having an armour of bony plates [C19: from Greek *stegos* roof + -SAUR]

Steiermark (ˈʃtaɪərˌmark) *n* the German name for **Styria**

stein (staɪn) *n* **1** an earthenware beer mug, esp of a German design **2** the quantity contained in such a mug [German, literally: STONE]

Stein *n* **1** (staɪn) **Gertrude**. 1874–1946, US writer, resident in Paris (1903–1946). Her works include *Three Lives* (1908) and *The Autobiography of Alice B. Toklas* (1933) **2** (German ʃtaɪn) **Heinrich Friedrich Carl** (ˈhaɪnrɪç ˈfriːdrɪç karl), **Baron Stein**. 1757–1831, Prussian statesman, who contributed greatly to the modernization of Prussia and played a major role in the European coalition against Napoleon (1813–15) **3** (stiːn) **Jock**, real name **John**. 1922–85, Scottish footballer and manager: managed Celtic (1965–78) and Scotland (1978–85)

Steinbeck (ˈstaɪnbɛk) *n* **John (Ernst)**. 1902–68, US writer, noted for his novels about agricultural workers, esp *The Grapes of Wrath* (1939): Nobel prize for literature 1962

steinbock (ˈstaɪnˌbɒk) *n* another name for **ibex** [C17: from German *Steinbock*; compare STEENBOK]

steinbok (ˈstaɪnˌbɒk) *n*, *pl* **-boks** or **-bok** a variant spelling of **steenbok**

Steiner (ˈstaɪnə; German ˈʃtaɪnər) *n* **Rudolf** (ˈruːdɔlf). 1861–1925, Austrian philosopher, founder of anthroposophy. He was particularly influential in education. See also **anthroposophy**

Steinitz (ˈstaɪnɪts; German ˈʃtaɪnɪts) *n* **Wilhelm** (ˈvɪlhɛlm). 1836–1900, US chess player, born in Prague; world champion (1866–94)

Steinway (ˈstaɪnweɪ) *n* **Henry (Engelhard)**, original name *Heinrich Engelhardt Steinweg*. 1797–1871, US piano maker, born in Germany

stele (ˈstiːlɪ, stiːl) *n*, *pl* **stelae** (ˈstiːliː) or **steles** (ˈstiːlɪz, stiːlz) **1** an upright stone slab or column decorated with figures or inscriptions, common in prehistoric times **2** a prepared vertical surface that has a commemorative inscription or design, esp one on the face of a building **3** the conducting tissue of the stems and roots of plants, which is in the form of a cylinder, principally containing xylem, phloem, and pericycle [C19: from Greek *stēlē*; related to Greek *histanai* to stand, Latin *stāre*] ⊳ **stelar** ('sti:lə) *adj*

stellar ('stɛlə) *adj* **1** of, relating to, involving, or resembling a star or stars **2** of or relating to star entertainers **3** *informal* outstanding or immense: *companies are registering stellar profits* [C17: from Late Latin *stellāris*, from Latin *stella* star]

stellar evolution *n astronomy* the sequence of changes that occurs in a star as it ages

stellate ('stɛlɪt, -eɪt) *or* **stellated** *adj* resembling a star in shape; radiating from the centre: *a stellate arrangement of petals* [C16: from Latin *stellātus* starry, from *stellāre* to stud with stars, from *stella* a star] ⊳ **stellately** *adv*

stellular ('stɛljʊlə) *adj* **1** displaying or abounding in small stars: *a stellular pattern* **2** resembling a little star or little stars [C18: from Late Latin *stellula*, diminutive of Latin *stella* star] ⊳ **stellularly** *adv*

stem¹ (stɛm) *n* **1** the main axis of a plant, which bears the leaves, axillary buds, and flowers and contains a hollow cylinder of vascular tissue **2** any similar subsidiary structure in such plants that bears a flower, fruit, or leaf **3** a corresponding structure in algae and fungi **4** any long slender part, such as the hollow part of a tobacco pipe that lies between the bit and the bowl, or the support between the base and the bowl of a wineglass, goblet, etc **5** a banana stalk with several bunches attached **6** the main line of descent or branch of a family **7** a round pin in some locks on which a socket in the end of a key fits and about which it rotates **8** any projecting feature of a component: a shank or cylindrical pin or rod, such as the pin that carries the winding knob on a watch **9** *linguistics* the form of a word that remains after removal of all inflectional affixes; the root of a word, esp as occurring together with a thematic element. See **root¹** (sense 8) **10** the main, usually vertical, stroke of a letter or of a musical note such as a minim **11** *electronics* the tubular glass section projecting from the base of a light bulb or electronic valve, on which the filament or electrodes are mounted **12 a** the main upright timber or structure at the bow of a vessel **b** the very forward end of a vessel (esp in the phrase **from stem to stern**) ⊳ *vb* **stems, stemming, stemmed 13** (*intr*; usually foll by *from*) to be derived; originate: *the instability stems from the war* **14** (*tr*) to make headway against (a tide, wind, etc) **15** (*tr*) to remove or disengage the stem or stems from **16** (*tr*) to supply (something) with a stem or stems [Old English *stemn*; related to Old Norse *stafn* stem of a ship, German *Stamm* tribe, Gothic *stōma* basis, Latin *stāmen* thread] ⊳ **stem,like** *adj*

stem² (stɛm) *vb* **stems, stemming, stemmed 1** (*tr*) to restrain or stop (the flow of something) by or as if by damming up **2** (*tr*) to pack tightly or stop up **3** *skiing* to manoeuvre (a ski or skis), as in performing a stem ⊳ *n* **4** *skiing* a technique in which the heel of one ski or both skis is forced outwards from the direction of movement in order to slow down or turn [C15 *stemmen*, from Old Norse *stemma*; related to Old Norse *stamr* blocked, stammering, German *stemmen* to prop; see **STAMMER**]

Stem (stɛm) *n* **die Stem** (di) the South African national anthem until 1991, when part of it was incorporated into the current anthem, *Nkosi sikelel' iAfrika* [C19: from Afrikaans, the call]

stem cell *n histology* an undifferentiated cell that gives rise to specialized cells, such as blood cells

stem ginger *n* the choice pieces of the underground stem of the ginger plant, which are crystallized or preserved in syrup and eaten as a sweetmeat

stemma ('stɛmə) *n* a family tree; pedigree [C19: via Latin from Greek *stemma* garland, wreath, from *stephein* to crown, wreathe]

stemmed (stɛmd) *adj* **1 a** having a stem **b** (*in combination*): *a thin-stemmed plant; a long-stemmed glass* **2** having had the stem or stems removed

stem turn *n skiing* a turn in which the heel of one ski is

stemmed and the other ski is brought parallel. Also called: **stem**

stench (stɛntʃ) *n* a strong and extremely offensive odour; stink [Old English *stenc*; related to Old Saxon, Old High German *stank*; see **STINK**]

stencil ('stɛnsəl) *n* **1** a device for applying a design, characters, etc, to a surface, consisting of a thin sheet of plastic, metal, cardboard, etc in which the design or characters have been cut so that ink or paint can be applied through the incisions onto the surface **2** a decoration, design, or characters produced in this way ⊳ *vb* **-cils, -cilling, -cilled** *or US* **-cils, -ciling, -ciled** (*tr*) **3** to mark (a surface) with a stencil **4** to produce (characters or a design) with a stencil [C14 *stanselen* to decorate with bright colours, from Old French *estenceler*, from *estencele* a spark, from Latin *scintilla*]

Stendhal (French stɛ̃dal) *n* original name *Marie Henri Beyle*. 1783–1842, French writer, who anticipated later novelists in his psychological analysis of character. His two chief novels are *Le Rouge et le noir* (1830) and *La Chartreuse de Parme* (1839)

Sten gun (stɛn) *n* a light 9 mm sub-machine-gun formerly used in the British Army and Commonwealth forces, developed during World War II [C20: from *s* and *t* (initials of Shepherd and Turpin, the inventors) + *-en*, as in **BREN GUN**]

steno- *or before a vowel* **sten-** *combining form* indicating narrowness or contraction: *stenography; stenosis* [from Greek *stenos* narrow]

stenograph ('stɛnə,grɑ:f, -,grɑ:f) *n* **1** any of various keyboard machines for writing in shorthand **2** any character used in shorthand ⊳ *vb* **3** (*tr*) to record (speeches, minutes, letters, etc) in shorthand

stenographer (stə'nɒgrəfə) *n Chiefly US & Canadian* a person skilled in the use of shorthand and in typing. Brit equivalent: **shorthand typist**

stenography (stə'nɒgrəfɪ) *n* **1** the act or process of writing in shorthand by hand or machine **2** matter written in shorthand ⊳ **stenographic** (,stɛnə'græfɪk) *adj*

stenosis (stɪ'nəʊsɪs) *n, pl* **-ses** (-si:z) *pathol* an abnormal narrowing of a bodily canal or passage [C19: via New Latin from Greek *stenōsis*, from *stenoun* to constrict, from *stenos* narrow] ⊳ **stenotic** (stɪ'nɒtɪk) *adj*

Stenotype ('stɛnə,taɪp) *n* **1** *trademark* a machine with a keyboard for recording speeches, etc, in a phonetic shorthand **2** any machine resembling this **3** the phonetic symbol typed in one stroke of such a machine

stenotypy ('stɛnə,taɪpɪ) *n* a form of shorthand in which alphabetic combinations are used to represent groups of sounds or short common words [C19: from **STENO-** + **TYPE** + **-Y³**, on the model of **STENOGRAPHY**] ⊳ **'steno,typist** *n*

stent (stɛnt) *n medicine* a tube of plastic or sprung metal mesh placed inside a hollow tube to reopen it or keep it open; uses in surgery include preventing a blood vessel from closing, esp after angioplasty, and assisting healing after an anastomosis [C19: after Charles *Stent* (1807–85), English dentist]

stentor (stɛntɔ:) *n* a person with an unusually loud voice [C19: after **STENTOR**]

Stentor ('stɛntɔ:) *n Greek myth* a Greek herald with a powerful voice who died after he lost a shouting contest with Hermes, herald of the gods

stentorian (stɛn'tɔ:rɪən) *adj* (of the voice, etc) uncommonly loud: *stentorian tones*

step (stɛp) *n* **1** the act of motion brought about by raising the foot and setting it down again in coordination with the transference of the weight of the body **2** the distance or space covered by such a motion **3** the sound made by such a movement **4** the impression made by such movement of the foot; footprint **5** the manner of walking or moving the feet; gait: *he received his prize with a proud step* **6** a sequence of foot movements that make up a particular dance or part of a dance: *I have mastered the steps of the waltz* **7** any of several paces or rhythmic movements in marching, dancing, etc: *the goose step* **8** (*plural*) a course followed by a person in walking or as walking: *they followed in their leader's steps* **9** one of a sequence of separate consecutive stages in the progression towards some goal: *another step* *towards socialism* **10** a rank or grade in a series or scale: *he was always a step behind* **11** an object or device that offers support for the foot when ascending or descending **12** (*plural*) a flight of stairs, esp out of doors **13** (*plural*) another name for **stepladder** **14** a very short easily walked distance: *it is only a step to my place* **15** *music* a melodic interval of a second **16** an offset or change in the level of a surface similar to the step of a stair **17** a strong block or frame bolted onto the keel of a vessel and fitted to receive the base of a mast **18** a ledge cut in mining or quarrying excavations **19 break step** to cease to march in step **20 keep step** to remain walking, marching, dancing, etc, in unison or in a specified rhythm **21 in step a** marching, dancing, etc, in conformity with a specified pace or moving in unison with others **b** *informal* in agreement or harmony **22 out of step a** not moving in conformity with a specified pace or in accordance with others **b** *informal* not in agreement; out of harmony **23 step by step** with care and deliberation; gradually **24 take steps** to undertake measures (to do something) with a view to the attainment of some end **25 watch one's step a** *informal* to conduct oneself with caution and good behaviour **b** to walk or move carefully ▷ *vb* **steps, stepping, stepped 26** (*intr*) to move by raising the foot and then setting it down in a different position, transferring the weight of the body to this foot and repeating the process with the other foot **27** (*intr*; often foll by *in, out,* etc) to move or go on foot, esp for a short distance: *step this way, ladies* **28** (*intr*) *informal, chiefly US* to move, often in an attractive graceful manner, as in dancing: *he can really step around* **29** (*intr*; usually foll by *on* or *upon*) to place or press the foot; tread: *to step on the accelerator* **30** (*intr*; usually foll by *into*) to enter (into a situation) apparently with ease: *she stepped into a life of luxury* **31** (*tr*) to walk or take (a number of paces, etc): *to step ten paces* **32** (*tr*) to perform the steps of: *they step the tango well* **33** (*tr*) to set or place (the foot) **34** (*tr*; usually foll by *off* or *out*) to measure (some distance of ground) by stepping **35** (*tr*) to arrange in or supply with a series of steps so as to avoid coincidence or symmetry **36** (*tr*) to raise (a mast) and fit it into its step ▷ See also **step down, step in,** etc [Old English *stepe, stæpe*; related to Old Frisian *stap, stepe,* Old High German *stapfo* (German *Stapfe* footprint), Old Norse *stapi* high rock] > 'step,like *adj*

Step (stɛp) *n* **a** a set of aerobic exercises designed to improve the cardiovascular system, which consists of stepping on and off a special box of adjustable height **b** (*as modifier*): *Step aerobics*

step- *combining form* indicating relationship through the previous marriage of a spouse or parent rather than by blood: *stepson; stepfather* [Old English *stēop-*; compare *āstŷpan* to bereave]

stepbrother ('stɛp,brʌðə) *n* a son of one's stepmother or stepfather by a union with someone other than one's father or mother respectively

stepchild ('stɛp,tʃaɪld) *n, pl* **-children** a stepson or stepdaughter

stepdaughter ('stɛp,dɔːtə) *n* a daughter of one's husband or wife by a former union

step down *vb* (*adverb*) **1** (*tr*) to reduce gradually **2** (*intr*) *informal* to resign or abdicate (from a position) **3** (*intr*) *informal* to assume an inferior or less senior position ▷ *adj* **step-down** (*prenominal*) **4** (of a transformer) reducing the high voltage applied to the primary winding to a lower voltage on the secondary winding **5** decreasing or falling by stages ▷ *n* **step-down 6** *informal* a decrease in quantity or size

stepfather ('stɛp,fɑːðə) *n* a man who has married one's mother after the death or divorce of one's father

Stepford ('stɛp,fəd) *adj informal, derogatory* **1** blandly conformist and submissive: *a Stepford employee* ▷ *n* **2 Stepford wife** a married woman who submits to her husband's will and is preoccupied with domestic concerns and her own personal appearance [c20: from *The Stepford Wives* (1972), a book by US writer Ira Levin which depicted a neighbourhood in which men turn their wives into placid and obedient robots]

stephanotis (,stɛfə'nəʊtɪs) *n* any climbing

asclepiadaceous shrub of the genus *Stephanotis*, esp *S. floribunda,* of Madagascar and Malaya: cultivated for their fragrant white waxy flowers [c19: via New Latin from Greek: fit for a crown, from *stephanos* a crown]

Stephen ('stiːvᵊn) *n* **1** ?1097–1154, king of England (1135–54); grandson of William the Conqueror. He seized the throne on the death of Henry I, causing civil war with Henry's daughter Matilda. He eventually recognized her son (later Henry II) as his successor **2 Saint.** died ?35 AD, the first Christian martyr. Feast day: Dec 26 or 27 **3 Saint,** Hungarian name *István.* ?975–1038 AD, first king of Hungary as Stephen I (997–1038). Feast day: Aug 16 or 20 **4 Sir Leslie.** 1832–1904, English biographer, critic, and first editor of the *Dictionary of National Biography;* father of the novelist Virginia Woolf

Stephenson ('stiːvᵊnsən) *n* **1 George.** 1781–1848, British inventor of the first successful steam locomotive (1814); constructed the first railway line to carry passengers, the Stockton and Darlington Railway (opened 1825) **2** his son, **Robert.** 1803–59, British engineer, noted for his construction of railway bridges and viaducts, esp the tubular bridge over the Menai Strait

step in *vb* **1** (*intr, adverb*) *informal* to intervene or involve oneself, esp dramatically or at a senior level ▷ *adj* **step-in 2** (*prenominal*) (of garments, etc) put on by being stepped into; without fastenings **3** (of a ski binding) engaging automatically when the boot is positioned on the ski ▷ *n* **step-in 4** (*often plural*) a step-in garment, esp underwear

stepladder ('stɛp,lædə) *n* a folding portable ladder that is made of broad flat steps fixed to a supporting frame hinged at the top to another supporting frame

stepmother ('stɛp,mʌðə) *n* a woman who has married one's father after the death or divorce of one's mother

step on *vb* (*intr, preposition*) **1** to place or press the foot on **2** *informal* to behave harshly or contemptuously towards **3 step on it** *informal* to go more quickly, hurry up

step out *vb* (*intr, adverb*) **1** to go outside or leave a room, building, etc, esp briefly **2** to begin to walk more quickly and take longer strides **3** *US & Canadian informal* to withdraw from involvement; bow out

stepover ('stɛp,əʊvə) *n football* an instance of raising the foot over the ball while in possession in order to wrongfoot an opponent

step-parent ('stɛp,pɛərənt) *n* a stepfather or stepmother > 'step-,parenting *n*

steppe (stɛp) *n* (*often plural*) an extensive grassy plain usually without trees [c17: from Old Russian *step* lowland]

stepper ('stɛpə) *n* a person who or animal that steps, esp a horse or a dancer

Steppes (stɛps) **the Steppes** *pl n* **1** the huge grasslands of Eurasia, chiefly in Ukraine and Russia **2** another name for **Kyrgyz Steppe**

stepping stone *n* **1** one of a series of stones acting as footrests for crossing streams, marshes, etc **2** a circumstance that assists progress towards some goal

stepsister ('stɛp,sɪstə) *n* a daughter of one's stepmother or stepfather by a union with someone other than one's father or mother respectively

stepson ('stɛp,sʌn) *n* a son of one's husband or wife by a former union

step up *vb* (*adverb*) *informal* **1** (*tr*) to increase or raise by stages; accelerate **2** (*intr*) to make progress or effect an advancement; be promoted ▷ *adj* **step-up** (*prenominal*) **3** (of a transformer) increasing a low voltage applied to the primary winding to a higher voltage on the secondary winding **4** *informal* involving a rise by stages ▷ *n* **step-up 5** *informal* an increment in quantity, size, etc

-ster *suffix forming nouns* **1** indicating a person who is engaged in a certain activity: *prankster; songster* **2** indicating a person associated with or being something specified: *mobster; youngster* [Old English *-estre*]

steradian (stə'reɪdɪən) *n* an SI unit of solid angle; the angle that, having its vertex in the centre of a sphere, cuts off an area of the surface of the sphere equal to the square of the length of the radius. Symbol: sr [c19: from STEREO- + RADIAN]

stercoraceous (,stɜːkə'reɪʃəs) *adj* of, relating to, or consisting of dung or excrement [c18: from Latin *stercus* dung + -ACEOUS]

stere (stɪə) *n* a unit used to measure volumes of stacked timber equal to one cubic metre (35.315 cubic feet) [c18: from French *stère*, from Greek *stereos* solid]

stereo ('stɛrɪəʊ, 'stɪər-) *adj* **1** short for **stereophonic, stereoscopic** ▷ *n, pl* stereos **2** stereophonic sound: *to broadcast in stereo* **3** a stereophonic record player, tape recorder, etc **4** *photog* **a** stereoscopic photography **b** a stereoscopic photograph **5** *printing* short for **stereotype** [c20: shortened form]

stereo- *or sometimes before a vowel* **stere-** *combining form* indicating three-dimensional quality or solidity: *stereoscope* [from Greek *stereos* solid]

stereochemistry (,stɛrɪəʊ'kɛmɪstrɪ, ,stɪər-) *n* the study of the spatial arrangement of atoms in molecules and the effect of spatial arrangement on chemical properties

stereograph ('stɛrɪə,grɑːf, -,grɑːf, 'stɪər-) *n* two almost identical pictures, or one special picture, that when viewed through special glasses or a stereoscope form a single three-dimensional image. Also called: stereogram

stereoisomer (,stɛrɪəʊ'aɪsəmə, ,stɪər-) *n chem* one of the isomers of a compound that exhibits stereoisomerism

stereoisomerism (,stɛrɪəʊaɪ'sɒmə,rɪzəm, ,stɪər-) *n chem* isomerism caused by differences in the spatial arrangement of atoms in molecules ▷ stereoisometric (,stɛrɪəʊ,aɪsə'mɛtrɪk, ,stɪər-) *adj*

stereophonic (,stɛrɪə'fɒnɪk, ,stɪər-) *adj* (of a system for recording, reproducing, or broadcasting sound) using two or more separate microphones to feed two or more loudspeakers through separate channels in order to give a spatial effect to the sound. Often shortened to: stereo ▷ ,stereo'phonically *adv* ▷ stereophony (,stɛrɪ'ɒfənɪ, ,stɪər-) *n*

stereoscope ('stɛrɪə,skəʊp, 'stɪər-) *n* an optical instrument for viewing two-dimensional pictures and giving them an illusion of depth and relief. It has a binocular eyepiece through which two slightly different pictures of the same object are viewed, one with each eye ▷ stereoscopic (,stɛrɪə'skɒpɪk, ,stɪər-) *adj*

stereoscopy (,stɛrɪ'ɒskəpɪ, ,stɪər-) *n* **1** the viewing or appearance of objects in or as if in three dimensions **2** the study and use of the stereoscope ▷ ,stere'oscopist *n*

stereospecific (,stɛrɪəʊspɪ'sɪfɪk, ,stɪər-) *adj chem* relating to or having fixed position in space, as in the spatial arrangements of atoms in certain polymers

stereotype ('stɛrɪə,taɪp, 'stɪər-) *n* **1 a** a method of producing cast-metal printing plates from a mould made from a forme of type matter in papier-mâché or some other material **b** the plate so made **2** another word for **stereotypy 3** an idea, trait, convention, etc, that has grown stale through fixed usage **4** *sociol* a set of inaccurate, simplistic generalizations about a group that allows others to categorize them and treat them accordingly ▷ *vb* (*tr*) **5 a** to make a stereotype of **b** to print from a stereotype **6** to impart a fixed usage or convention to ▷ 'stereo,typer *or* 'stereo,typist *n*

stereotyped ('stɛrɪə,taɪpt, 'stɪər-) *adj* **1** lacking originality or individuality; conventional; trite **2** reproduced from or on a stereotype printing plate

stereotypy ('stɛrɪə,taɪpɪ, 'stɪər-) *n* **1** the act or process of making stereotype printing plates **2** a tendency to think or act in rigid, repetitive, and often meaningless patterns

stereovision ('stɛrɪəʊ,vɪʒən, 'stɪər-) *n* the perception or exhibition of three-dimensional objects in three dimensions

steric ('stɛrɪk, 'stɪər-) *or* **sterical** *adj chem* of, concerned with, or caused by the spatial arrangement of atoms in a molecule [c19: from STEREO- + -IC]

sterile ('stɛraɪl) *adj* **1** unable to produce offspring; infertile **2** free from living, esp pathogenic, microorganisms; aseptic **3** (of plants or their parts) not producing or bearing seeds, fruit, spores, stamens, or pistils **4** lacking inspiration or vitality; fruitless [c16: from Latin *sterilis*] ▷ 'sterilely *adv* ▷ sterility (stɛ'rɪlɪtɪ) *n*

sterilize *or* **sterilise** ('stɛrɪ,laɪz) *vb* (*tr*) to render sterile; make infertile or barren ▷ sterilization *or* sterilisation

(,stɛrɪlaɪ'zeɪʃən) *n* ▷ sterilizer *or* steriliser ('stɛrɪ,laɪzə) *n*

sterling ('stɜːlɪŋ) *n* **1 a** British money: *pound sterling* **b** (*as modifier*): *sterling reserves* **2** the official standard of fineness of British coins: for gold 0.91666 and for silver 0.925 **3 a** short for **sterling silver b** (*as modifier*): *a sterling bracelet* **4** an article or articles manufactured from sterling silver ▷ *adj* **5** (*prenominal*) genuine and reliable; first-class: *sterling quality* [c13: probably from Old English *steorra* STAR + -LING¹; referring to a small star on early Norman pennies; related to Old French *esterlin*]

Sterling ('stɜːlɪŋ) *n* **Peter.** born 1960, Australian rugby league player

sterling area *n* a group of countries that use sterling as a medium of international payments and sometimes informally as a currency against which to peg their own currencies. For these purposes they deposit sterling balances and hold gold and dollar reserves in the Bank of England. Also called: sterling bloc, scheduled territories

sterling silver *n* **1** an alloy containing not less than 92.5 per cent of silver, the remainder usually being copper **2** sterling-silver articles collectively

Sterlitamak (*Russian* stjerlitə'mak) *n* an industrial city in W Russia, in the Bashkir Republic. Pop: 268 000 (2005 est)

stern¹ (stɜːn) *adj* **1** showing uncompromising or inflexible resolve; firm, strict, or authoritarian **2** lacking leniency or clemency; harsh or severe **3** relentless; unyielding: *the stern demands of parenthood* **4** having an austere or forbidding appearance or nature [Old English *styrne*; related to Old High German *stornēn* to alarm, Latin *sternāx* stubborn, Greek *stereos* hard] ▷ 'sternly *adv* ▷ 'sternness *n*

stern² (stɜːn) *n* **1** the rear or after part of a vessel, opposite the bow or stem **2** the rear part of any object ▷ *adj* **3** relating to or located at the stern [c13: from Old Norse *stjörn* steering; see STEER¹]

Stern (stɜːn) *n* **Isaac.** 1920–2001, US concert violinist, born in (what is now) Ukraine

Sternberg ('stɜːn,bɜːg, 'ʃtɜːn-) *n* See von Sternberg

Sterne (stɜːn) *n* **Laurence.** 1713–68, English novelist, born in Ireland, author of *The Life and Opinions of Tristram Shandy, Gentleman* (1759–67) and *A Sentimental Journey through France and Italy* (1768)

sternforemost ('stɜːn'fɔː,məʊst) *adv nautical* backwards

sternmost ('stɜːn,məʊst) *adj nautical* **1** farthest to the stern; aftmost **2** nearest the stern

sternpost ('stɜːn,pəʊst) *n nautical* the main upright timber or structure at the stern of a vessel

stern sheets *pl n nautical* the part of an open boat near the stern

sternum ('stɜːnəm) *n, pl* -na (-nə) *or* -nums **1** (in man) a long flat vertical bone, situated in front of the thorax, to which are attached the collarbone and the first seven pairs of ribs. Nontechnical name: breastbone **2** the corresponding part in many other vertebrates [c17: via New Latin from Greek *sternon* breastbone] ▷ 'sternal *adj*

sternutation (,stɜːnjʊ'teɪʃən) *n* a sneeze or the act of sneezing [c16: from Late Latin *sternūtāre* to sneeze, from *sternuere* to sputter (of a light)]

sternutator ('stɜːnjʊ,teɪtə) *n* a substance that causes sneezing, coughing, and tears; used in chemical warfare ▷ sternutatory (stɜː'njuːtətərɪ, -trɪ) *adj*

sternwards ('stɜːnwədz) *or* **sternward** *adv nautical* towards the stern; astern

sternway ('stɜːn,weɪ) *n nautical* movement of a vessel sternforemost

stern-wheeler *n* a vessel, esp a riverboat, propelled by a large paddle wheel at the stern

steroid ('stɪərɔɪd, 'stɛr-) *n biochem* any of a large group of fat-soluble organic compounds containing a characteristic chemical ring system. The majority, including the sterols, bile acids, many hormones, and the D vitamins, have important physiological action [c20: from STEROL + -OID] ▷ ste'roidal *adj*

sterol ('stɛrɒl) *n biochem* any of a group of natural steroid alcohols, such as cholesterol and ergosterol, that are waxy insoluble substances [c20: shortened from CHOLESTEROL, ERGOSTEROL, etc]

stertorous ('stɜːtərəs) *adj* **1** marked or accompanied by heavy snoring **2** breathing in this way > **'stertorously** *adv* > **'stertorousness** *n*

stet (stɛt) *n* **1** a word or mark indicating that certain deleted typeset or written matter is to be retained ▷ *vb* **stets, stetting, stetted 2** (*tr*) to mark (matter to be retained) with a stet [Latin, literally: let it stand]

stethoscope ('stɛθəˌskəʊp) *n med* an instrument for listening to the sounds made within the body, typically consisting of a hollow disc that transmits the sound through hollow tubes to earpieces [C19: from French, from Greek *stēthos* breast + -SCOPE] > **stethoscopic** (ˌstɛθə'skɒpɪk) *adj* > **stethoscopy** (stɛ'θɒskəpɪ) *n*

Stetson ('stɛtsᵊn) *n trademark* a type of felt hat with a broad brim and high crown, worn mainly by cowboys [C20: named after John *Stetson* (1830–1906), American hatmaker who designed it]

Stettin (ʃtɛ'tiːn) *n* the German name for **Szczecin**

stevedore ('stiːvɪˌdɔː) *n* **1** a person employed to load or unload ships ▷ *vb* **2** to load or unload (a ship, ship's cargo, etc) [C18: from Spanish *estibador* a packer, from *estibar* to load (a ship), from Latin *stīpāre* to pack full]

Stevenage ('stiːvənɪdʒ) *n* a town in SE England, in N Hertfordshire on the Great North Road: developed chiefly as the first of the new towns (1946). Pop: 81 482 (2001)

Stevens ('stiːvᵊnz) *n* **1 Thaddeus** ('θædɪəs). 1792–1868, US Radical Republican politician. An opponent of slavery, he supported Reconstruction and entered the resolution calling for the impeachment of President Andrew Johnson **2 Wallace.** 1879–1955, US poet, whose books include the collections *Harmonium* (1923), *The Man with the Blue Guitar* (1937), and *Transport to Summer* (1947)

Stevenson ('stiːvənsən) *n* **1 Adlai Ewing** ('ædleɪ 'juːɪŋ). 1900–68, US statesman: twice defeated as Democratic presidential candidate (1952; 1956); US delegate at the United Nations (1961–65) **2 Robert Louis** (**Balfour**). 1850–94, Scottish writer: his novels include *Treasure Island* (1883), *Kidnapped* (1886), and *The Master of Ballantrae* (1889)

stew¹ (stjuː) *n* **1 a** a dish of meat, fish, or other food, cooked by stewing **b** (*as modifier*): *stew pot* **2** *informal* a difficult or worrying situation or a troubled state (esp in the phrase **in a stew**) **3** a heterogeneous mixture: *a stew of people of every race* **4** (*usually plural*) *archaic* a brothel ▷ *vb* **5** to cook or cause to cook by long slow simmering **6** (*intr*) *informal* to be troubled or agitated **7** (*intr*) *informal* to be oppressed with heat or crowding **8** to cause (tea) to become bitter or (of tea) to become bitter through infusing for too long **9 stew in one's own juice** to suffer unaided the consequences of one's actions [C14: *stuen* to take a very hot bath, from Old French *estuver*, from Vulgar Latin *extūfāre* (unattested), from EX-¹ + (unattested) *tūfus* vapour, from Greek *tuphos*]

stew² (stjuː) *n Brit* **1** a fishpond or fishtank **2** an artificial oyster bed [C14: from Old French *estui*, from *estoier* to shut up, confine, ultimately from Latin *studium* STUDY]

steward ('stjʊəd) *n* **1** a person who administers the property, house, finances, etc, of another **2** a person who manages the eating arrangements, staff, or service at a club, hotel, etc **3** a person who attends to passengers on an aircraft, ship or train **4** a mess attendant in a naval mess afloat or ashore **5** a person who helps to supervise some event or proceedings in an official capacity **6** short for **shop steward** ▷ *vb* **7** to act or serve as a steward (of something) [Old English *stigweard*, from *stig* hall (see STY) + *weard* WARD] > **'steward,ship** *n*

stewardess ('stjʊədɪs, ˌstjʊə'dɛs) *n* a woman who performs a steward's job on an aircraft or ship

Stewart ('stjʊət) *n* **1** the usual spelling for the royal house of Stuart before the reign of Mary Queen of Scots (Mary Stuart) **2 Sir Jackie**, full name *John Young Stewart*. born 1939, Scottish motor-racing driver: world champion 1969, 1971, and 1973 **3 James** (**Maitland**). 1908–97, US film actor, known for his distinctive drawl; appeared in many films including *Destry Rides Again* (1939), *It's a Wonderful Life* (1946), *The Glenn Miller Story* (1953), and *Vertigo* (1958) **4 Rod.** born 1945, British rock singer: vocalist with the Faces (1969–75). His albums include *Gasoline*

Alley (1970), *Every Picture Tells a Story* (1971), and *Atlantic Crossing* (1975)

Stewart Island *n* the third largest island of New Zealand, in the SW Pacific off the S tip of South Island. Pop: 387 (2001). Area: 1735 sq km (670 sq miles)

stewed (stjuːd) *adj* **1** (of meat, fruit, etc) cooked by stewing **2** *Brit* (of tea) having a bitter taste through having been left to infuse for too long **3** a slang word for **drunk** (sense 1)

Steyr *or* **Steier** (*German* 'ʃtaɪər) *n* an industrial city in N central Austria, in Upper Austria. Pop: 39 340 (2001)

stg *abbreviation* sterling

sthenic ('sθɛnɪk) *adj* abounding in energy or bodily strength; active or strong [C18: from New Latin *sthenicus*, from Greek *sthenos* force, on the model of *asthenic*]

Stheno ('sθiːnəʊ, 'sθɛnəʊ) *n Greek myth* one of the three Gorgons

stibine ('stɪbaɪn) *n* **1** a colourless slightly soluble poisonous gas with an offensive odour: made by the action of hydrochloric acid on an alloy of antimony and zinc. Formula: SbH_3 **2** any one of a class of stibine derivatives in which one or more hydrogen atoms have been replaced by organic groups [C19: from Latin STIBIUM + -INE²]

stibium ('stɪbɪəm) *n* an obsolete name for **antimony** [C14: from Latin: antimony (used as a cosmetic in ancient Rome), via Greek from Egyptian *stm*] > **'stibial** *adj*

stibnite ('stɪbnaɪt) *n* a soft greyish mineral consisting of antimony sulphide in orthorhombic crystalline form. It occurs in quartz veins and is the chief ore of antimony. Formula: Sb_2S_3 [C19: from obsolete *stibine* stibnite + -ITE¹]

stich (stɪk) *n* a line of poetry; verse [C18: from Greek *stikhos* row, verse; related to *steikhein* to walk] > **'stichic** *adj* > **'stichically** *adv*

-stichous *adj combining form* having a certain number of rows [from Late Latin -*stichus*, from Greek -*stikhos*, from *stikhos* line, row; see STICH]

stick¹ (stɪk) *n* **1 a** a small thin branch of a tree **2 a** any long thin piece of wood **b** such a piece of wood having a characteristic shape for a special purpose: *a walking stick; a hockey stick* **c** a baton, wand, staff, or rod **3** an object or piece shaped like a stick: *a stick of celery, a stick of dynamite* **4** *informal* the lever used to change gear in a motor vehicle **5** *printing* **6 a** a group of bombs arranged to fall at intervals across a target **b** a number of paratroops jumping in sequence **7** *slang* **a** verbal abuse, criticism: *I got some stick for that blunder* **b** physical power, force (esp in the phrase **give it some stick**) **8** (*usually plural*) a piece of furniture: *these few sticks are all I have* **9** (*plural*) *informal* a rural area considered remote or backward (esp in the phrase **in the sticks**) **10** (*plural*) *hockey* a declaration made by the umpire if a player's stick is above the shoulders **11** (*plural*) goalposts **12** *US obsolete* a cannabis cigarette **13** a means of coercion **14** *informal* a dull boring person **15** (*usually preceded by old*) *informal* a familiar name for a person: *not a bad old stick* **16** **in a cleft stick** in a difficult position **17 wrong end of the stick** a complete misunderstanding of a situation, explanation, etc ▷ *vb* **sticks, sticking, sticked 18** to support (a plant) with sticks; stake [Old English *sticca*; related to Old Norse *stikka*, Old High German *stecca*]

stick² (stɪk) *vb* **sticks, sticking, stuck 1** (*tr*) to pierce or stab with or as if with something pointed **2** to thrust or push (a sharp or pointed object) or (of a sharp or pointed object) to be pushed into or through another object **3** (*tr*) to fasten in position by pushing or forcing a point into something: *to stick a peg in a hole* **4** (*tr*) to fasten in position by or as if by pins, nails, etc: *to stick a picture on the wall* **5** (*tr*) to transfix or impale on a pointed object **6** (*tr*) to cover with objects piercing or set in the surface **7** (when *intr*, foll by *out*, *up*, *through*, etc) to put forward or be put forward; protrude or cause to protrude: *to stick one's head out of the window* **8** (*tr*) *informal* to place or put in a specified position: *stick your coat on this chair* **9** to fasten or be fastened by or as if by an adhesive substance: *stick the pages together; they won't stick* **10** (*tr*) *informal* to cause to become sticky **11** (when *tr*, *usually passive*) to come or cause to come to a standstill: *we were stuck for hours in a traffic jam;*

the wheels stuck **12** (*intr*) to remain for a long time: *the memory sticks in my mind* **13** (*tr*) *slang, chiefly Brit* to tolerate; abide: *I can't stick that man* **14** (*intr*) to be reluctant **15** (*tr; usually passive*) *informal* to cause to be at a loss; baffle, puzzle, or confuse: *I was totally stuck for an answer* **16** (*tr*) *slang* to force or impose something unpleasant on: *they stuck me with the bill for lunch* **17** (*tr*) to kill by piercing or stabbing **18 stick in one's throat** *or* **stick in one's craw** *informal* to be difficult, or against one's conscience, for one to accept, utter, or believe **19 stick one's nose into 20 stick to the ribs** *informal* (of food) to be hearty and satisfying ▷ *n* **21** the state or condition of adhering **22** *informal* a substance causing adhesion **23** *obsolete* something that causes delay or stoppage ▷ See also **stick around, stick by,** etc [Old English *stician*; related to Old High German *stehhan* to sting, Old Norse *steikja* to roast on a spit]

stick around *or* **stick about** *vb* (*intr, adverb*) *informal* to remain in a place, esp awaiting something

stick by *vb* (*intr, preposition*) to remain faithful to; adhere to

sticker ('stɪkə) *n* **1** an adhesive label, poster, or paper **2** a person or thing that sticks **3** a persevering or industrious person **4** something prickly, such as a thorn, that clings to one's clothing, etc **5** *informal* something that perplexes **6** *informal* a knife used for stabbing or piercing

stickhandle ('stɪk,hænd³l) *vb* *ice hockey* to manoeuvre (the puck) deftly

sticking plaster *n* a thin cloth with an adhesive substance on one side, used for covering slight or superficial wounds

stick insect *n* any of various mostly tropical insects of the family *Phasmidae* that have an elongated cylindrical body and long legs and resemble twigs: order *Phasmida*

stick-in-the-mud *n* *informal* a staid or predictably conservative person who lacks initiative or imagination

stickle ('stɪk³l) *vb* (*intr*) **1** to dispute stubbornly, esp about minor points **2** to refuse to agree or concur, esp by making petty stipulations [C16 *stightle* (in the sense: to arbitrate): frequentative of Old English *stihtan* to arrange; related to Old Norse *stētta* to support]

stickleback ('stɪk³l,bæk) *n* any small teleost fish of the family *Gasterosteidae*, such as *Gasterosteus aculeatus* (**three-spined stickleback**) of rivers and coastal regions and *G. pungitius* (**ten-spined stickleback**) confined to rivers. They have a series of spines along the back and occur in cold and temperate northern regions [C15: from Old English *stickel* prick, sting + BACK[1]]

stickler ('stɪklə) *n* **1** (usually foll by *for*) a person who makes insistent demands: *a stickler for accuracy* **2** a problem or puzzle: *the investigation proved to be a stickler*

stick out *vb* (*adverb*) **1** to project or cause to project **2** (*tr*) *informal* to endure (something disagreeable) (esp in the phrase **stick it out**) **3 stick out a mile** *or* **stick out like a sore thumb** *informal* to be extremely obvious **4 stick out for** (*intr*) to insist on (a demand), refusing to yield until it is met

stick shift *n* *US & Canadian* **1 a** a manually operated transmission system in a motor vehicle **b** a motor vehicle having manual transmission **2** a gear lever

stick to *vb* (*preposition, mainly intr*) **1** (*also tr*) to adhere or cause to adhere to **2** to continue constantly at **3** to remain faithful to **4** not to move or digress from: *the speaker stuck closely to his subject* **5 stick to someone's fingers** *informal* to be stolen by someone

stick-up *n* **1** *slang, chiefly US* a robbery at gunpoint; hold-up ▷ *vb* **stick up** (*adverb*) **2** (*tr*) *slang, chiefly US* to rob, esp at gunpoint **3** (*intr; foll by for*) *informal* to support or defend: *stick up for oneself*

sticky ('stɪkɪ) *adj* **stickier, stickiest 1** covered or daubed with an adhesive or viscous substance: *sticky fingers* **2** having the property of sticking to a surface **3** (of weather or atmosphere) warm and humid; muggy **4** *informal* difficult, awkward, or painful: *a sticky business* **5** (of a website) encouraging users to visit repeatedly ▷ *vb* **stickies, stickying, stickied 6** (*tr*) *informal* to make sticky > '**stickily** *adv* > '**stickiness** *n*

stickybeak ('stɪkɪ,biːk) *Austral & NZ informal* ▷ *n* **1** an inquisitive person ▷ *vb* **2** (*intr*) to pry [from STICKY + BEAK[1] (in the slang sense: a human nose)]

sticky end *n* *informal* an unpleasant finish or death (esp in the phrase **come to** *or* **meet a sticky end**)

sticky wicket *n* **1** a cricket pitch that is rapidly being dried by the sun after rain and is particularly conducive to spin **2** *informal* a difficult or awkward situation (esp in the phrase **on a sticky wicket**)

Stieglitz ('stiːglɪts) *n* **Alfred.** 1864–1946, US photographer, whose work helped to develop photography as an art: among his best photographs are those of his wife Georgia O'Keeffe. He was also well known as a promoter of modern art

stiff (stɪf) *adj* **1** not easily bent; rigid; inflexible **2** not working or moving easily or smoothly: *a stiff handle* **3** difficult to accept in its severity or harshness: *a stiff punishment* **4** moving with pain or difficulty; not supple: *a stiff neck* **5** difficult; arduous: *a stiff climb* **6** unrelaxed or awkward; formal **7** firmer than liquid in consistency; thick or viscous **8** powerful; strong: *a stiff breeze; a stiff drink* **9** excessively high: *a stiff price* **10** lacking grace or attractiveness **11** stubborn or stubbornly maintained: *a stiff fight* **12** *obsolete* tightly stretched; taut **13** *slang, chiefly Austral* unlucky **14** *slang* intoxicated **15 stiff with** *informal* amply provided with ▷ *n* **16** *slang* a corpse **17** *slang* anything thought to be a loser or a failure; flop ▷ *adv* **18** completely or utterly: *bored stiff; frozen stiff* ▷ *vb* **19** (*intr*) *slang* to fail: *the film stiffed* **20** (*tr*) *slang, chiefly US* to cheat or swindle [Old English *stīf*; related to Old Norse *stīfla* to dam up, Middle Low German *stīf* stiff, Latin *stīpes* wooden post, *stīpāre* to press] > '**stiffish** *adj* > '**stiffly** *adv* > '**stiffness** *n*

stiffen ('stɪf³n) *vb* **1** to make or become stiff or stiffer **2** (*intr*) to become suddenly tense or unyielding > '**stiffener** *n*

stiff-necked *adj* haughtily stubborn or obstinate

stifle ('staɪf³l) *vb* **1** (*tr*) to smother or suppress: *stifle a cough* **2** to feel or cause to feel discomfort and difficulty in breathing **3** to prevent or be prevented from breathing so as to cause death **4** (*tr*) to crush or stamp out [C14: variant of *stuflen*, probably from Old French *estouffer* to smother]

stigma ('stɪgmə) *n, pl* **stigmas** *or for sense 7* **stigmata** ('stɪgmətə, stɪg'mɑːtə) **1** a distinguishing mark of social disgrace: *the stigma of having been in prison* **2** a small scar or mark such as a birthmark **3** *pathol* any mark on the skin, such as one characteristic of a specific disease **4** *botany* the receptive surface of a carpel, where deposited pollen germinates **5** *zoology* **a** a pigmented eyespot in some protozoans and other invertebrates **b** the spiracle of an insect **6** *archaic* a mark branded on the skin **7** (*plural*) *Christianity* marks resembling the wounds of the crucified Christ, believed to appear on the bodies of certain individuals [C16: via Latin from Greek: brand, from *stizein* to tattoo]

stigmatic *adj* (stɪg'mætɪk) **1** relating to or having a stigma or stigmata **2** another word for **anastigmatic** ▷ *n* Also: **stigmatist** ('stɪgmətɪst) **3** *chiefly RC Church* a person marked with the stigmata

stigmatism ('stɪgmə,tɪzəm) *n* **1** *physics* the state or condition of being anastigmatic **2** *pathol* the condition resulting from or characterized by stigmata

stigmatize *or* **stigmatise** ('stɪgmə,taɪz) *vb* (*tr*) **1** to mark out or describe (as something bad) **2** to mark with a stigma or stigmata > ,**stigmati'zation** *or* ,**stigmati'sation** *n* > '**stigma,tizer** *or* '**stigma,tiser** *n*

stilbene ('stɪlbiːn) *n* a colourless or slightly yellow crystalline water-insoluble unsaturated hydrocarbon used in the manufacture of dyes; *trans*-1,2-diphenylethene. Formula: $C_6H_5CH:CHC_6H_5$ [C19: from Greek *stilbos* glittering + -ENE]

stilbestrol *or* **stilboestrol** (stɪl'biːstrɒl) *n* another name for **diethylstilbestrol** [C20: from STILBENE + OESTRUS + -OL[1]]

stile[1] (staɪl) **1** *n* a set of steps or rungs in a wall or fence to allow people, but not animals, to pass over **2** short for **turnstile** [Old English *stigel*; related to *stīgan* to climb, Old High German *stigilla*; see STAIR]

stile[2] (staɪl) *n* a vertical framing member in a door, window frame, or piece of panelling. See **rail¹** (sense 3) [c17: probably from Dutch *stijl* pillar, ultimately from Latin *stilus* writing instrument; see STYLE]

stiletto (stɪˈlɛtəʊ) *n, pl* **-tos** 1 a small dagger with a slender tapered blade 2 a sharply pointed tool used to make holes in leather, cloth, etc 3 Also called: **spike heel, stiletto heel** a very high heel on a woman's shoe, tapering to a very narrow tip ▷ *vb* **-toes, -toing, -toed** 4 (*tr*) to stab with a stiletto [c17: from Italian, from *stilo* a dagger, from Latin *stilus* a stake, pen; see STYLUS]

Stilicho (ˈstɪlɪkəʊ) *n* **Flavius** (ˈfleɪvɪəs). ?365–408 AD, Roman general and statesman, born a Vandal. As the guardian of Emperor Theodosius' son Honorius, he was effective ruler of the Western Roman Empire (395–408), which he defended against the Visigoths

still¹ (stɪl) *adj* 1 (*usually predicative*) motionless; stationary 2 undisturbed or tranquil; silent and calm 3 not sparkling or effervescent: *a still wine* 4 gentle or quiet; subdued 5 *obsolete* (of a child) dead at birth ▷ *adv* 6 continuing now or in the future as in the past: *do you still love me?* 7 up to this or that time; yet: *I still don't know your name* 8 (*often used with a comparative*) even or yet: *still more insults* 9 quiet or without movement: *sit still* 10 *poetic, dialect* always ▷ *n* 11 *poetic* silence or tranquillity: *the still of the night* 12 a a still photograph, esp of a scene from a motion-picture film b (*as modifier*): *a still camera* ▷ *vb* 13 to make or become still, quiet, or calm 14 (*tr*) to allay or relieve: *her fears were stilled* ▷ *sentence connector* 15 even then; nevertheless: *the child has some new toys and still cries* [Old English *stille*; related to Old Saxon, Old High German *stilli*, Dutch *stollen* to curdle, Sanskrit *sthānús* immobile] > **ˈstillness** *n*

still² (stɪl) *n* an apparatus for carrying out distillation, consisting of a vessel in which a mixture is heated, a condenser to turn the vapour back to liquid, and a receiver to hold the distilled liquid, used esp in the manufacture of spirits [c16: from Old French *stiller* to drip, from Latin *stillāre*, from *stilla* a drip; see DISTIL]

stillage (ˈstɪlɪdʒ) *n* 1 a frame or stand for keeping things off the ground, such as casks in a brewery 2 a container in which goods, machinery, etc, are transported [c16: probably from Dutch *stillagie* frame, scaffold, from *stellen* to stand; see -AGE]

stillborn (ˈstɪlˌbɔːn) *adj* 1 (of a fetus) dead at birth 2 (of an idea, plan, etc) fruitless; abortive; unsuccessful > **ˈstillˌbirth** *n*

still life *n, pl* **still lifes** 1 a a painting or drawing of inanimate objects, such as fruit, flowers, etc b (*as modifier*): *a still-life painting* 2 the genre of such paintings

still room *n Brit* 1 a room in which distilling is carried out 2 a pantry or storeroom, as in a large house

Stillson wrench (ˈstɪlsən) *n trademark* a large wrench having adjustable jaws that tighten as the pressure on the handle is increased

stilly *adv* (ˈstɪlɪ) 1 *archaic or literary* quietly or calmly ▷ *adj* (ˈstɪlɪ) 2 *poetic* still, quiet, or calm

stilt (stɪlt) *n* 1 either of a pair of two long poles with footrests on which a person stands and walks, as used by circus clowns 2 a long post or column that is used with others to support a building above ground level 3 any of several shore birds of the genera *Himantopus* and *Cladorhynchus*, similar to the avocets but having a straight bill ▷ *vb* 4 (*tr*) to raise or place on or as if on stilts [c14 (in the sense: crutch, handle of a plough): related to Low German *stilte* pole, Norwegian *stilta*]

stilted (ˈstɪltɪd) *adj* 1 (of speech, writing, etc) formal, pompous, or bombastic 2 not flowing continuously or naturally: *stilted conversation* 3 *architect* (of an arch) having vertical piers between the impost and the springing > **ˈstiltedly** *adv* > **ˈstiltedness** *n*

Stilton (ˈstɪltən) *n trademark* either of two rich cheeses made from whole milk, blue-veined (**blue Stilton**) or white (**white Stilton**), both very strong in flavour [c18: named after *Stilton*, Cambridgeshire, where it was originally sold]

Stilwell (ˈstɪlwɛl) *n* **Joseph W(arren)**, known as *Vinegar Joe*. 1883–1946, US general, who was (1941–44) Chiang Kai-shek's chief of staff and commander of all US forces in China, Burma (Myanmar), and India

stimulant (ˈstɪmjʊlənt) *n* 1 a drug or similar substance that increases physiological activity, esp of a particular organ 2 any stimulating agent or thing ▷ *adj* 3 increasing physiological activity; stimulating [c18: from Latin *stimulāns* goading, from *stimulāre* to urge on; see STIMULUS]

stimulate (ˈstɪmjʊˌleɪt) *vb* (*tr*) *physiol* to excite (a nerve, organ, etc) with a stimulus [c16: from Latin *stimulāre*; see STIMULANT] > **ˌstimuˈlation** *n* > **ˈstimulative** *adj, n* > **ˈstimuˌlator** or **ˈstimuˌlater** *n* > **ˈstimuˌlating** *adj*

stimulus (ˈstɪmjʊləs) *n, pl* **-li** (-ˌlaɪ, -ˌliː) 1 something that stimulates or acts as an incentive 2 any drug, agent, electrical impulse, or other factor able to cause a response in an organism [c17: from Latin: a cattle goad]

Stine (staɪn) *n* **R(obert) L(awrence)**. born 1943, US writer, noted for his numerous bestselling horror novels for older children, esp those in the *Goosebumps* and *Fear Street* series

sting (stɪŋ) *vb* **stings, stinging, stung** 1 (of certain animals and plants) to inflict a wound on (an organism) by the injection of poison 2 to feel or cause to feel a sharp mental or physical pain 3 (*tr*) to goad or incite (esp in the phrase **sting into action**) 4 (*tr*) *informal* to cheat, esp by overcharging ▷ *n* 5 a skin wound caused by the poison injected by certain insects or plants 6 pain caused by or as if by the sting of a plant or animal 7 a mental pain or pang: *a sting of conscience* 8 a sharp pointed organ, such as the ovipositor of a wasp, by which poison can be injected into the prey 9 the ability to sting: *a sharp sting in his criticism* 10 something as painful or swift of action as a sting: *the sting of death* 11 a sharp stimulus or incitement 12 *slang* a swindle or fraud 13 *slang* a trap set up by the police to entice a person to commit a crime and thereby produce evidence 14 **sting in the tail** an unexpected and unpleasant ending [Old English *stingan*; related to Old Norse *stinga* to pierce, Gothic *usstangan* to pluck out, Greek *stakhus* ear of corn] > **ˈstinging** *adj* > **ˈstinger** *n*

stinging nettle *n* See **nettle** (sense 1)

stingray (ˈstɪŋˌreɪ) *n* any ray of the family *Dasyatidae*, having a whiplike tail bearing a serrated venomous spine capable of inflicting painful weals on man

stingy¹ (ˈstɪndʒɪ) *adj* **-gier, -giest** 1 unwilling to spend or give 2 insufficient or scanty [c17 (perhaps in the sense: ill-tempered): perhaps from *stinge*, dialect variant of STING] > **ˈstingily** *adv* > **ˈstinginess** *n*

stingy² (ˈstɪŋɪ) *adj* **stingier, stingiest** *informal* stinging or capable of stinging

stink (stɪŋk) *n* 1 a strong foul smell; stench 2 *slang* a great deal of trouble (esp in the phrase **to make** or **raise a stink**) 3 **like stink** intensely; furiously ▷ *vb* **stinks, stinking, stank** or **stunk, stunk** (*mainly intr*) 4 to emit a foul smell 5 *slang* to be thoroughly bad or abhorrent: *this town stinks* 6 *informal* to have a very bad reputation: *his name stinks* 7 to be of poor quality 8 (foll by *of* or *with*) *slang* to have or appear to have an excessive amount (of money) 9 (*tr;* usually foll by *up*) *informal* to cause to stink ▷ See also **stink out** [Old English *stincan*; related to Old Saxon *stinkan*, German *stinken*, Old Norse *stökkva* to burst; see STENCH] > **ˈstinky** *adj*

stink bomb *n* a small glass globe, used by practical jokers: it releases a liquid with an offensive smell when broken

stinker (ˈstɪŋkə) *n* 1 a person or thing that stinks 2 *slang* a difficult or very unpleasant person or thing 3 *slang* something of very poor quality 4 *informal* any of several fulmars or related birds that feed on carrion

stinkhorn (ˈstɪŋkˌhɔːn) *n* any of various basidiomycetous saprotrophic fungi of the genus *Phallus*, such as *P. impudicus*, having an offensive odour

stinking (ˈstɪŋkɪŋ) *adj* 1 having a foul smell 2 *informal* unpleasant or disgusting 3 (*postpositive*) *slang* very drunk ▷ *adv* 4 *informal* (intensifier, expressing contempt for the person referred to): *stinking rich* > **ˈstinkingly** *adv* > **ˈstinkingness** *n*

stinko (ˈstɪŋkəʊ) *adj* (*postpositive*) a slang word for **drunk**

stink out *vb* (*tr, adverb*) 1 to drive out or away by a foul smell 2 *Brit* to cause to stink: *the smell of orange peel stinks out the room*

stinkweed ('stɪŋk,wiːd) n 1 Also called: **wall mustard** a plant, *Diplotaxis muralis*, naturalized in Britain and S and central Europe, having pale yellow flowers, cylindrical seed pods, and a disagreeable smell when bruised: family *Brassicaceae* (crucifers) 2 any of various other ill-smelling plants, such as mayweed

stinkwood ('stɪŋk,wʊd) n 1 any of various trees having offensive-smelling wood, esp *Ocotea bullata*, a southern African lauraceous tree yielding a hard wood used for furniture 2 the heavy durable wood of any of these trees

stint[1] (stɪnt) vb 1 to be frugal or miserly towards (someone) with (something) 2 archaic to stop or check (something) ▷ n 3 an allotted or fixed amount of work 4 a limitation or check 5 obsolete a pause or stoppage [Old English *styntan* to blunt; related to Old Norse *stytta* to cut short; see STUNT[1]] > **'stinter** n

stint[2] (stɪnt) n any of various small sandpipers of the chiefly northern genus *Calidris* (or *Erolia*), such as *C. minuta* (**little stint**) [Old English; related to Middle High German *stinz* small salmon, Swedish dialect *stinta* teenager; see STUNT[1]]

stipe (staɪp) n 1 a stalk in plants that bears reproductive structures, esp the stalk bearing the cap of a mushroom 2 the stalk that bears the leaflets of a fern or the thallus of a seaweed 3 zoology any stalklike part; stipes [c18: via French from Latin *stipes* tree trunk; related to Latin *stipāre* to pack closely; see STIFF]

stipel ('staɪpᵊl) n a small paired leaflike structure at the base of certain leaflets; secondary stipule [c19: via New Latin from Latin *stipula*, diminutive of *stipes* a log] > **stipellate** (staɪˈpɛlɪt, -eɪt) adj

stipend ('staɪpɛnd) n a fixed or regular amount of money paid as a salary or allowance, as to a clergyman [c15: from Old French *stipende*, from Latin *stīpendium* tax, from *stips* a contribution + *pendere* to pay out]

stipendiary (staɪˈpɛndɪərɪ) adj 1 receiving or working for regular pay: *a stipendiary magistrate* 2 paid for by a stipend ▷ n, pl **-aries** 3 a person who receives regular payment [c16: from Latin *stīpendiārius* concerning tribute, from *stīpendium* STIPEND]

stipes ('staɪpiːz) n, pl **stipites** ('stɪpɪˌtiːz) zoology 1 the second maxillary segment in insects and crustaceans 2 the eyestalk of a crab or similar crustacean 3 any similar stemlike structure [c18: from Latin; see STIPE] > **stipiform** ('staɪpɪˌfɔːm) or **stipitiform** ('stɪpɪtɪˌfɔːm) adj

stipple ('stɪpᵊl) vb (tr) 1 to draw, engrave, or paint using dots or flecks 2 to apply paint, powder, etc, to (something) with many light dabs ▷ n Also: **stippling** 3 the technique of stippling or a picture produced by or using stippling [c18: from Dutch *stippelen*, from *stippen* to prick, from *stip* point] > **'stippler** n

stipulate ('stɪpjʊ,leɪt) vb 1 (tr; may take a clause as object) to specify, often as a condition of an agreement 2 (intr; foll by for) to insist (on) as a term of an agreement 3 Roman law to make (an oral contract) in the form of question and answer necessary to render it legally valid 4 (tr; may take a clause as object) to guarantee or promise [c17: from Latin *stipulārī*, probably from Old Latin *stipulus* firm, but perhaps from *stipula* a stalk, from the convention of breaking a straw to ratify a promise] > **stipulable** ('stɪpjʊləbᵊl) adj > **,stipu'lation** n > **'stipu,lator** n

stipule ('stɪpjuːl) n a small paired usually leaflike outgrowth occurring at the base of a leaf or its stalk [c18: from Latin; see STIPE, STIPES] > **stipular** ('stɪpjʊlə) adj

stir[1] (stɜː) vb **stirs, stirring, stirred** 1 to move an implement such as a spoon around in (a liquid) so as to mix up the constituents: *she stirred the porridge* 2 to change or cause to change position; disturb or be disturbed: *he stirred in his sleep* 3 (intr; often foll by from) to venture or depart (from one's usual or preferred place): *he won't stir from the fireside* 4 (intr) to be active after a rest; be up and about 5 (tr) to excite or stimulate, esp emotionally 6 to move (oneself) briskly or vigorously; exert (oneself) 7 (tr) to rouse or awaken: *to stir someone from sleep; to stir memories* 8 informal (when tr, foll by up) to cause or incite others to cause (trouble, arguments, etc) 9 **stir one's stumps** informal to move or become active ▷ n **10** the act or an instance of stirring or the state of being stirred **11** a strong reaction, esp of excitement: *his publication caused a*

stir 12 a slight movement **13** NZ informal a noisy party ▷ See also **stir up** [Old English *styrian*; related to Middle High German *stürn* to poke, stir, Norwegian *styrja* to cause a commotion; see STORM, STURGEON]

stir[2] (stɜː) n a slang word for prison in **stir** [c19: perhaps from Romany *stariben* prison]

Stir. abbreviation Stirlingshire

stir-fry ('stɜː'fraɪ) vb **-fries, -frying, -fried** 1 to cook (small pieces of meat, vegetables, etc) rapidly by stirring them in a wok or frying pan over a high heat: used esp for Chinese food ▷ n, pl **-fries** 2 a dish cooked in this way

stirk (stɜːk) n 1 a heifer of 6 to 12 months old 2 a yearling heifer or bullock [Old English *stierc*; related to Middle Low German *sterke*, Old High German *stero* ram, Latin *sterilis* sterile, Greek *steira*; see STEER[2]]

Stirling[1] ('stɜːlɪŋ) n 1 a city in central Scotland, in Stirling council area on the River Forth: its castle was a regular residence of many Scottish monarchs between the 12th century and 1603. Pop: 32 673 (2001) 2 a council area of central Scotland, created from part of Central Region in 1996; includes most of the historical county of Stirlingshire: the Forth valley rises to the Grampian Mountains in the N. Administrative centre: Stirling. Pop: 86 370 (2003 est). Area: 2173 sq km (839 sq miles)

Stirling[2] ('stɜːrlɪŋ) n Sir **James.** 1926–92, British architect; buildings include the Neue Staatsgalerie in Stuttgart (1977–84)

Stirlingshire ('stɜːlɪŋˌʃɪə, -ʃə) n a former county of central Scotland: mostly became part of Central Region in 1975: now covered by the council areas of Stirling, Falkirk, and East Dunbartonshire

stirps (stɜːps) n, pl **stirpes** ('stɜːpiːz) 1 genealogy a line of descendants from an ancestor; stock or strain 2 botany a race or variety, esp one in which the characters are maintained by cultivation [c17: from Latin: root, family origin]

stirrer ('stɜːrə) n 1 a person or thing that stirs 2 informal a person who deliberately causes trouble 3 Austral & NZ informal a political activist or agitator

stirring ('stɜːrɪŋ) adj 1 exciting the emotions; stimulating 2 active, lively, or busy > **'stirringly** adv

stirrup ('stɪrəp) n 1 Also called: **stirrup iron** either of two metal loops on a riding saddle, with a flat footpiece through which a rider puts his foot for support. They are attached to the saddle by **stirrup leathers** 2 a U-shaped support or clamp made of metal, wood, leather, etc 3 nautical one of a set of ropes fastened to a yard at one end and having a thimble at the other through which a footrope is rove for support [Old English *stigrāp*, from *stīg* path, step (related to Old High German *stīgan* to move up) + *rāp* ROPE; related to Old Norse *stigreip*, Old High German *stegareif*]

stirrup cup n a cup containing an alcoholic drink offered to a horseman ready to ride away

stirrup pump n a hand-operated vertical reciprocating pump, such as one used in fire-fighting, etc, in which the base of the cylinder is placed in a bucket of water

stir up vb (tr, adverb) to set in motion; instigate: *he stirred up trouble*

stitch (stɪtʃ) n 1 a link made by drawing a thread through material by means of a needle 2 a loop of yarn formed around an implement used in knitting, crocheting, etc 3 a particular method of stitching or shape of stitch 4 a sharp spasmodic pain in the side resulting from running or exercising 5 (usually used with a negative) informal the least fragment of clothing: *he wasn't wearing a stitch* 6 agriculture the ridge between two furrows 7 **in stitches** informal laughing uncontrollably 8 **drop a stitch** to allow a loop of wool to fall off a knitting needle accidentally while knitting ▷ vb 9 (tr) to sew, fasten, etc, with stitches 10 (tr) to be engaged in sewing 11 (tr) to bind together (the leaves of a book, pamphlet, etc) with wire staples or thread ▷ n, vb 12 an informal word for **suture** (sense 1b)(sense 5) [Old English *stice* sting; related to Old Frisian *steke*, Old High German *stih*, Gothic *stiks*, Old Norse *tikta* sharp] > **'stitcher** n

stitch up vb (tr, adverb) 1 to join or mend by means of stitches or sutures 2 slang **a** to incriminate (someone) on a false charge by manufacturing evidence **b** to betray, cheat, or defraud **3** *slang* to prearrange (something) in a clandestine manner ▷ *n* **stitch-up 4** *slang* a matter that has been prearranged clandestinely

stitchwort ('stɪtʃˌwɜːt) *n* any of several low-growing N temperate herbaceous plants of the caryophyllaceous genus *Stellaria*, having small white star-shaped flowers [C13: so named because it was once thought to be a remedy for stitches in the side]

stiver ('staɪvə) *n* **1** a former Dutch coin worth one twentieth of a guilder **2** a small amount, esp of money [C16: from Dutch *stuiver*; related to Middle Low German *stüver*, Danish *styver*]

stoa ('stəʊə) *n, pl* **stoae** ('stəʊiː) *or* **stoas** a covered walk that has a colonnade on one or both sides, esp as used in ancient Greece [C17: from Greek]

stoat (stəʊt) *n* a small Eurasian musteline mammal, *Mustela erminea*, closely related to the weasels, having a brown coat and a black-tipped tail: in the northern parts of its range it has a white winter coat and is then known as an ermine [C15: of unknown origin]

stochastic (stɒˈkæstɪk) *adj* **1** *statistics* **a** (of a random variable) having a probability distribution, usually with finite variance **b** (of a process) involving a random variable the successive values of which are not independent **c** (of a matrix) square with non-negative elements that add to unity in each row **2** *rare* involving conjecture [C17: from Greek *stokhastikos* capable of guessing, from *stokhazesthai* to aim at, conjecture, from *stokhos* a target]

stock (stɒk) *n* **1 a** (*sometimes plural*) the total goods or raw material kept on the premises of a shop or business **b** (*as modifier*): *a stock clerk; stock book* **2** a supply of something stored for future use: *he keeps a good stock of whisky* **3** *finance* **a** the capital raised by a company through the issue and subscription of shares entitling their holders to dividends, partial ownership, and usually voting rights **b** the proportion of such capital held by an individual shareholder **c** the shares of a specified company or industry **4** standing or status **5 a** farm animals, such as cattle and sheep, bred and kept for their meat, skins, etc **b** (*as modifier*): *stock farming* **6** the trunk or main stem of a tree or other plant **7** *horticulture* **a** a rooted plant into which a scion is inserted during grafting **b** a plant or stem from which cuttings are taken. See also **rootstock 8** the original type from which a particular race, family, group, etc, is derived **9** a race, breed, or variety of animals or plants **10** (*often plural*) a small pen in which a single animal can be confined **11** a line of descent **12** any of the major subdivisions of the human species; race or ethnic group **13** the part of a rifle, sub-machine-gun, etc, into which the barrel and firing mechanism is set: held by the firer against the shoulder **14** the handle of something, such as a whip or fishing rod **15** the main body of a tool, such as the block of a plane **16** short for **diestock, gunstock, rolling stock 17** (*formerly*) the part of a plough to which the irons and handles were attached **18** the main upright part of a supporting structure **19** a liquid or broth in which meat, fish, bones, or vegetables have been simmered for a long time **20** film material before exposure and processing **21** Also called: **gillyflower** any of several plants of the genus *Matthiola*, such as *M. incana* and *M. bicornis* (**evening** or **night-scented stock**), of the Mediterranean region, cultivated for their brightly coloured flowers: Brassicaceae (crucifers) **22 Virginian stock** a similar and related North American plant, *Malcolmia maritima* **23** a long usually white neckcloth wrapped around the neck, worn in the 18th century and as part of modern riding dress **24 a** the repertoire of plays available to a repertory company **b** (*as modifier*): *a stock play* **25** (on some types of anchors) a crosspiece at the top of the shank under the ring **26** the centre of a wheel **27** an exposed igneous intrusion that is smaller in area than a batholith **28** a log or block of wood **29** See **laughing stock 30** an archaic word for **stocking 31 in stock a** stored on the premises or available for sale or use **b** supplied with goods of a specified kind **32 out of stock a** not immediately available for sale or use **b** not having goods of a specified kind immediately available **33 take stock a** to

make an inventory **b** to make a general appraisal, esp of prospects, resources, etc **34 take stock in** to attach importance to **35 lock, stock, and barrel** See **lock¹** (sense 7) ▷ *adj* **36** staple, standard: *stock sizes in clothes* **37** (*prenominal*) being a cliché; hackneyed: *a stock phrase* ▷ *vb* **38** (*tr*) to keep (goods) for sale **39** (*intr*; usually foll by *up* or *up on*) to obtain a store of (something) for future use or sale: *to stock up on beer* **40** (*tr*) to supply with live animals, fish, etc: *to stock a farm* **41** (*intr*) (of a plant) to put forth new shoots **42** (*tr*) *obsolete* to punish by putting in the stocks ▷ See also **stocks** [Old English *stocc* trunk (of a tree), stem, stick (the various senses developed from these meanings, as trunk of a tree, hence line of descent; structures made of timber; a store of timber or other goods for future use, hence an aggregate of goods, animals, etc); related to Old Saxon, Old High German *stock* stick, stump] ▷ '**stocker** *n*

stockade (stɒˈkeɪd) *n* **1** an enclosure or barrier of stakes and timbers ▷ *vb* **2** (*tr*) to surround with a stockade [C17: from Spanish *estacada*, from *estaca* a stake, post, of Germanic origin; see **STAKE¹**]

stockbreeder ('stɒkˌbriːdə) *n* a person who breeds or rears livestock as an occupation ▷ '**stock,breeding** *n*

stockbroker ('stɒkˌbrəʊkə) *n* a person who buys and sells securities on a commission basis for customers ▷ **stockbrokerage** ('stɒkˌbrəʊkərɪdʒ) *or* '**stock,broking** *n*

stockbroker belt *n* Brit informal the area outside a city, esp London, in which rich commuters live

stock car *n* **1** a car, usually a production saloon, strengthened and modified for a form of racing in which the cars often collide **2** US & Canadian a railway wagon designed for carrying livestock

stock dove *n* a European dove, *Columba oenas*, smaller than the wood pigeon and having a uniformly grey plumage [C14: so called because it lives in tree trunks. See STOCK]

stock exchange *n* (*often capitals*) **1** Also called: **stock market a** a highly organized market facilitating the purchase and sale of securities and operated by professional stockbrokers and market makers according to fixed rules **b** a place where securities are regularly traded **c** (*as modifier*): *a stock-exchange operator; stock-exchange prices* **2** the prices or trading activity of a stock exchange: *the stock exchange fell heavily today*

stockfish ('stɒkˌfɪʃ) *n, pl* **-fish** *or* **-fishes** fish, such as cod or haddock, cured by splitting and drying in the air [C13: of uncertain origin. Perhaps from STOCK (in the sense: stem, tree trunk) because it was dried on wooden racks. Compare Middle Dutch *stocvisch*]

Stockhausen (*German* 'ʃtɔkhaʊzən) *n* **Karlheinz** (karl'haints). 1928–2007, German composer, whose avant-garde music exploits advanced serialization, electronic sounds, group improvization, and vocal and instrumental timbres and techniques. Works include *Gruppen* (1959) for three orchestras, *Stimmung* (1968) for six vocalists, and the operas *Donnerstag* (1980) and *Freitag* (1996)

stockholder ('stɒkˌhəʊldə) *n* **1** an owner of corporate capital stock **2** *Austral* a person who keeps livestock ▷ '**stock,holding** *n*

Stockholm ('stɒkhəʊm; *Swedish* 'stɔkhɔlm) *n* the capital of Sweden, a port in the E central part at the outflow of Lake Mälaren into the Baltic: situated partly on the mainland and partly on islands; traditionally founded about 1250; university (1877). Pop: 765 582 (2004 est)

stockhorse ('stɒkˌhɔːs) *n* Austral a horse trained in the handling of stock

stockinet (ˌstɒkɪ'nɛt) *n* a machine-knitted elastic fabric used, esp formerly, for stockings, undergarments, etc [C19: perhaps changed from earlier *stocking-net*]

stocking ('stɒkɪŋ) *n* **1** one of a pair of close-fitting garments made of knitted yarn to cover the foot and part or all of the leg **2** something resembling this in position, function, appearance, etc **3 in one's stocking feet** *or* **in one's stockinged feet** wearing stockings or socks but no shoes [C16: from dialect *stock* stocking + -ING¹] ▷ '**stockinged** *adj*

stocking cap *n* a conical knitted cap, often with a tassel

stocking filler *n* Brit a present, esp a toy, of a size suitable for inclusion in a child's Christmas stocking

stock in trade n 1 goods in stock necessary for carrying on a business 2 anything constantly used by someone as a part of his profession, occupation, or trade: *friendliness is the salesman's stock in trade*

stockist ('stɒkɪst) n *commerce, Brit* a dealer who undertakes to maintain stocks of a specified product at or above a certain minimum in return for favourable buying terms granted by the manufacturer of the product

stockjobber ('stɒk,dʒɒbə) n 1 *Brit* (formerly) a wholesale dealer on a stock exchange who sold securities to brokers without transacting directly with the public. Often shortened to **jobber, market maker** 2 *US disparaging* a stockbroker, esp one dealing in worthless securities > 'stock,jobbery or 'stock,jobbing n

stockman ('stɒkmən, -,mæn) n, pl **-men** 1 a a man engaged in the rearing or care of farm livestock, esp cattle b an owner of cattle or other livestock 2 *US & Canadian* a man employed in a warehouse or stockroom

stock market n 1 another name for **stock exchange** (sense 1) 2 the usual US name for **stock exchange** (sense 2)

stockpile ('stɒk,paɪl) vb 1 to acquire and store a large quantity of (something) ▷ n 2 a large store or supply accumulated for future use > 'stock,piler n

Stockport ('stɒk,pɔːt) n 1 a town in NW England, in Stockport unitary authority, Greater Manchester: an early textile centre and scene of several labour disturbances in the early 19th century; engineering, electronics. Pop: 136 082 (2001) 2 a unitary authority in NW England, in Greater Manchester. Pop: 282 500 (2003 est). Area: 126 sq km (49 sq miles)

stockpot ('stɒk,pɒt) n *chiefly Brit* a pot in which stock for soup, etc, is made or kept

stockroom ('stɒk,ruːm, -,rʊm) n a room in which a stock of goods is kept, as in a shop or factory

stockroute ('stɒk,ruːt) n *Austral & NZ* a route designated for droving sheep or cattle

stocks (stɒks) pl n 1 *history* an instrument of punishment consisting of a heavy wooden frame with holes in which the feet, hands, or head of an offender were locked 2 a frame in which an animal is held while receiving veterinary attention or while being shod 3 a frame used to support a boat while under construction 4 *nautical* a vertical post or shaft at the forward edge of a rudder, extended upwards for attachment to the steering controls 5 **on the stocks** in preparation or under construction

stock-still adv absolutely still; motionless

stocktaking ('stɒk,teɪkɪŋ) n 1 the examination, counting, and valuing of goods on hand in a shop or business 2 a reassessment of one's current situation, progress, prospects, etc

Stockton[1] ('stɒktən) n an inland port in central California, on the San Joaquin River: seat of the University of the Pacific (1851). Pop: 271 466 (2003 est)

Stockton[2] ('stɒktən) n **1st Earl of.** title of (Maurice Harold) **Macmillan**

Stockton-on-Tees n 1 a former port and industrial centre in NE England, in Stockton-on-Tees unitary authority, Co Durham, on the River Tees: famous for the **Stockton-Darlington Railway** (1825), the first passenger-carrying railway in the world; now mainly residential. Pop: 80 060 (2001) 2 a unitary authority in NE England, in Co Durham and North Yorkshire: created in 1996 from part of Cleveland county. Pop: 186 300 (2003 est). Area: 195 sq km (75 sq miles)

stock watering n *business* the creation of more new shares in a company than is justified by its assets

stock whip n a whip with a long lash and a short handle, as used to herd cattle

Stockwood ('stɒkwʊd) n (**Arthur**) **Mervyn**. 1913–95, British Anglican prelate; bishop of Southwark (1959–80)

stocky ('stɒkɪ) adj **stockier, stockiest** (usually of a person) thickset; sturdy > 'stockily adv > 'stockiness n

stockyard ('stɒk,jɑːd) n a large yard with pens or covered buildings where farm animals are assembled, sold, etc

stodge (stɒdʒ) *informal* ▷ n 1 heavy filling starchy food 2 a dull person or subject ▷ vb 3 to stuff (oneself or another) with food [C17: perhaps a blend of STUFF + PODGE]

stodgy ('stɒdʒɪ) adj **stodgier, stodgiest** 1 (of food) heavy or uninteresting 2 excessively formal and conventional [C19: from STODGE] > 'stodgily adv > 'stodginess n

stoep (stʊp) n *South African* a veranda [Afrikaans from Dutch]

stoic ('stəʊɪk) n 1 a person who maintains stoical qualities ▷ adj 2 a variant of **stoical**

Stoic ('stəʊɪk) n 1 a member of the ancient Greek school of philosophy founded by Zeno of Citium, the Greek philosopher (?336–?264 BC), holding that virtue and happiness can be attained only by submission to destiny and the natural law ▷ adj 2 of or relating to the doctrines of the Stoics [C16: via Latin from Greek *stōikos*, from *stoa* the porch in Athens where Zeno taught]

stoical ('stəʊɪkᵊl) adj characterized by impassivity or resignation > 'stoically adv

stoichiometry, stoicheiometry or **stoechiometry** (,stɔɪkɪ'ɒmɪtrɪ) n the branch of chemistry concerned with the proportions in which elements are combined in compounds and the quantitative relationships between reactants and products in chemical reactions [C19: from Greek *stoikheion* element + -METRY] > **stoichiometric, stoicheiometric,** or **stoechiometric** (,stɔɪkɪə'mɛtrɪk) adj [C19: see STOICHIOMETRY]

stoicism ('stəʊɪ,sɪzəm) n 1 indifference to pleasure and pain 2 (*capital*) the philosophy of the Stoics

stoke (stəʊk) vb 1 to feed, stir, and tend (a fire, furnace, etc) 2 (tr) to tend the furnace of; act as a stoker for ▷ See also **stoke up** [C17: back formation from STOKER]

stoked (stəʊkt) adj *NZ informal* very pleased; elated: *really stoked to have got the job*

stokehold ('stəʊk,həʊld) n *nautical* 1 a coal bunker for a ship's furnace 2 the hold for a ship's boilers; fire room

stokehole ('stəʊk,həʊl) n 1 another word for **stokehold** 2 a hole in a furnace through which it is stoked

Stoke-on-Trent n 1 a city in central England, in Stoke-on-Trent unitary authority, Staffordshire on the River Trent: a centre of the pottery industry; university (1992). Pop: 259 252 (2001) 2 a unitary authority in central England, in N Staffordshire. Pop: 238 000 (2003 est). Area: 93 sq km (36 sq miles)

stoker ('stəʊkə) n a person employed to tend a furnace, as on a steamship [C17: from Dutch, from *stoken* to STOKE]

Stoker ('stəʊkə) n **Bram**, original name *Abraham Stoker*. 1847–1912, Irish novelist, author of *Dracula* (1897)

stoke up vb (*adverb*) 1 to feed and tend (a fire, etc) with fuel 2 (*intr*) to fill oneself with food

Stokowski (stə'kɒfskɪ) n **Leopold**. 1887–1977, US conductor, born in Britain. He did much to popularize classical music with orchestral transcriptions and film appearances, esp in *Fantasia* (1940)

stokvel ('stɒk,fɛl) n *South African* an informal savings pool or syndicate, usually among Black people, in which funds are contributed in rotation, allowing participants lump sums for family needs (esp funerals) [C20: of uncertain origin]

STOL (stɒl) n 1 a system in which an aircraft can take off and land in a short distance 2 an aircraft using this system ▷ See VTOL [C20: s(hort) t(ake) o(ff and) l(anding)]

stole[1] (stəʊl) vb the past tense of **steal**

stole[2] (stəʊl) n 1 a long scarf or shawl, worn by women 2 a long narrow scarf worn by various officiating clergymen [Old English *stole*, from Latin *stola*, Greek *stolē* clothing; related to *stellein* to array]

stolen ('stəʊlən) vb the past participle of **steal**

stolen generation n *Austral* Aboriginal children removed from their families and placed in institutions or fostered by White families

stolid ('stɒlɪd) adj showing little or no emotion or interest [C17: from Latin *stolidus* dull; compare Latin *stultus* stupid; see STILL[1]] > **stolidity** (stɒ'lɪdɪtɪ) or 'stolidness n > 'stolidly adv

stolon ('stəʊlən) n 1 a long horizontal stem, as of the currants, that grows along the surface of the soil and propagates by producing roots and shoots at the nodes or tip **2** a branching structure in lower animals, esp the anchoring rootlike part of colonial organisms, such as hydroids, on which the polyps are borne [c17: from Latin *stolō* shoot] > **stoloniferous** (ˌstəʊləˈnɪfərəs) *adj*

Stolypin (ˌstɒlɪˈpjɪn) *n* Petr Arkadievich. 1863–1911, Russian conservative statesman: prime minister (1906–11). He instituted agrarian reforms but was ruthless in suppressing rebellion: assassinated

stoma (ˈstəʊmə) *n*, *pl* **stomata** (ˈstəʊmətə, ˈstɒm-, stəʊˈmɑːtə) **1** *botany* an epidermal pore, present in large numbers in plant leaves, that controls the passage of gases into and out of a plant **2** *zoology, anatomy* a mouth or mouthlike part **3** *surgery* an artificial opening made in a tubular organ, esp the colon or ileum. See **colostomy**, **ileostomy** [c17: via New Latin from Greek: mouth]

stomach (ˈstʌmək) *n* **1** (in vertebrates) the enlarged muscular saclike part of the alimentary canal in which food is stored until it has been partially digested and rendered into chyme. Related adj: **gastric 2** the corresponding digestive organ in invertebrates **3** the abdominal region **4** desire, appetite, or inclination: *I have no stomach for arguments* **5** an archaic word for **temper 6** an obsolete word for **pride** ▷ *vb* (*tr; used mainly in negative constructions*) **7** to tolerate; bear: *I can't stomach his bragging* **8** to eat or digest: *he cannot stomach oysters* [c14: from Old French *stomaque*, from Latin *stomachus* (believed to be the seat of the emotions), from Greek *stomakhos*, from *stoma* mouth]

stomachache (ˈstʌməkˌeɪk) *n* pain in the stomach or abdominal region, as from acute indigestion. Also called: **stomach upset**, **upset stomach**

stomacher (ˈstʌməkə) *n* a decorative V-shaped panel of stiff material worn over the chest and stomach by men and women in the 16th century, later only by women

stomachic (stəˈmækɪk) *adj* Also: **stomachical 1** stimulating gastric activity **2** of or relating to the stomach ▷ *n* **3** a stomachic medicine

stomach pump *n med* a suction device for removing stomach contents by a tube inserted through the mouth

stomata (ˈstəʊmətə, ˈstɒm-, stəʊˈmɑːtə) *n* the plural of **stoma**

stomatitis (ˌstəʊməˈtaɪtɪs, ˌstɒm-) *n* inflammation of the mouth > **stomatitic** (ˌstəʊməˈtɪtɪk, ˌstɒm-) *adj*

stomato- *or before a vowel* **stomat-** *combining form* indicating the mouth or a mouthlike part: *stomatology* [from Greek *stoma, stomat-*]

stomatology (ˌstəʊməˈtɒlədʒɪ) *n* the branch of medicine or dentistry concerned with the structures, functions, and diseases of the mouth > **stomatological** (ˌstəʊmətəˈlɒdʒɪkᵊl) *adj*

-stome *n combining form* indicating a mouth or opening resembling a mouth: *peristome* [from Greek *stoma* mouth, and *stomion* little mouth]

-stomous *adj combining form* having a specified type of mouth

stomp (stɒmp) *vb* (*intr*) **1** *informal* to tread or stamp heavily ▷ *n* **2** a rhythmic stamping jazz dance [variant of STAMP] > **stomper** *n*

stompie (ˈstɒmpɪ) *n South African slang* **1** a cigarette butt **2** a short man [from Afrikaans *stomp* stump]

-stomy *n combining form* indicating a surgical operation performed to make an artificial opening into or for a specified part: *cytostomy* [from Greek *-stomia*, from *stoma* mouth]

stone (stəʊn) *n* **1** the hard compact nonmetallic material of which rocks are made **2** a small lump of rock; pebble **3** *jewellery* short for **gemstone 4 a** a piece of rock designed or shaped for some particular purpose **b** (*in combination*): *gravestone; millstone* **5 a** something that resembles a stone **b** (*in combination*): *hailstone* **6** the woody central part of such fruits as the peach and plum, that contains the seed; endocarp **7** any similar hard part of a fruit, such as the stony seed of a date **8** *pl* **stone** *Brit* a unit of weight, used esp to express human body weight, equal to 14 pounds or 6.350 kilograms **9** Also called: **granite** the rounded heavy mass of granite or iron used in the game of curling **10** *pathol* a nontechnical name for **calculus 11** *printing* a table with a very flat iron or

stone surface upon which hot-metal pages are composed during imposition into formes; imposition table **12** (*modifier*) relating to or made of stone: *a stone house* **13** (*modifier*) made of stoneware: *a stone jar* **14** cast a stone at cast aspersions upon **15** heart of stone an obdurate or unemotional nature **16** leave no stone unturned to do everything possible to achieve an end ▷ *vb* (*tr*) **17** to throw stones at, esp to kill **18** to remove the stones from **19** to furnish or provide with stones [Old English *stān*; related to Old Saxon *stēn*, Old Norse *steinn*, German *Stein*, Gothic *stains*, Greek *stion* pebble] > **'stoneless** *adj* > **'stone,like** *adj* > **'stoner** *n*

Stone (stəʊn) *n* **1** Oliver. born 1946, US film director and screenwriter: his films include *Platoon* (1986), *Born on the Fourth of July* (1989), *JFK* (1991), *Nixon* (1995), and *Alexander* (2004) **2** Sharon. born 1958, US film actress: her films include *Basic Instinct* (1991), *Casino* (1995), and *Cold Creek Manor* (2003)

stone- *prefix* very; completely: *stone-blind; stone-cold* [from STONE in the sense of "like a stone"]

Stone Age *n* **1** a period in human culture identified by the use of stone implements and usually divided into the Palaeolithic, Mesolithic, and Neolithic stages ▷ *modifier* **Stone-Age 2** (*sometimes not capitals*) of or relating to this period: *stone-age man*

stone-blind *adj* completely blind. See **sand-blind**

stonechat (ˈstəʊnˌtʃæt) *n* an Old World songbird, *Saxicola torquata*, having a black plumage with a reddish-brown breast: subfamily *Turdinae* (thrushes) [c18: so called from its cry, which sounds like clattering pebbles]

stone-cold *adj* **1** completely cold ▷ *adv* **2** (intensifier): *stone-cold sober*

stonecrop (ˈstəʊnˌkrɒp) *n* any of various N temperate crassulaceous plants of the genus *Sedum*, having fleshy leaves and typically red, yellow, or white flowers [Old English: so named because it grows on rocks and walls]

stone curlew *n* any of several brownish shore birds of the family *Burhinidae*, esp *Burhinus oedicnemus*, having a large head and eyes: order *Charadriiformes*. Also called: **thick-knee** [c17: so called because it is found in stony habitats and resembles a curlew]

stonecutter (ˈstəʊnˌkʌtə) *n* **1** a person who is skilled in cutting and carving stone **2** a machine used to dress stone > **'stone,cutting** *n*

stoned (stəʊnd) *adj slang* under the influence of drugs or alcohol

stone-deaf *adj* completely deaf

stonefish (ˈstəʊnˌfɪʃ) *n*, *pl* **-fish** *or* **-fishes** a venomous tropical marine scorpaenid fish, *Synanceja verrucosa*, that resembles a piece of rock on the seabed

stonefly (ˈstəʊnˌflaɪ) *n*, *pl* **-flies** any insect of the order *Plecoptera*, in which the larvae are aquatic, living beneath stones, and the adults have long antennae and two pairs of large wings and occur near water [c15: so called because its larvae live under stones in rivers]

stone fruit *n* the nontechnical name for **drupe**

Stonehenge (ˌstəʊnˈhɛndʒ) *n* a prehistoric ruin in S England, in Wiltshire on Salisbury Plain: constructed over the period of roughly 3000–1600 BC; one of the most important megalithic monuments in Europe; believed to have had religious and astronomical purposes

stonemason (ˈstəʊnˌmeɪsᵊn) *n* a person who is skilled in preparing stone for building > **'stone,masonry** *n*

stone pine *n* a Mediterranean pine tree, *Pinus pinea*, having a short bole and radiating branches forming an umbrella shape

Stones (stəʊnz) *pl n* See **Rolling Stones**

Stone sheep *or* **Stone's sheep** *n* a wild sheep found in the Yukon and the northern Rocky Mountains [c19: after the US naturalist Andrew Jackson Stone, who first discovered the breed in 1896]

stone's throw *n* a short distance

stonewall (ˌstəʊnˈwɔːl) *vb* **1** (*intr*) *cricket* (of a batsman) to play defensively **2** to obstruct or hinder (parliamentary business) > **'stone'waller** *n*

stoneware (ˈstəʊnˌwɛə) *n* **1** a hard opaque pottery, fired at a very high temperature ▷ *adj* **2** made of stoneware

stonewashed (ˈstəʊnˌwɒʃt) *adj* (of new clothes or fabric, esp denim jeans) given a worn faded look by being

S

subjected to the abrasive action of many small pieces of pumice

stonework ('stəʊn,wɜːk) n 1 any structure or part of a building made of stone 2 the process of dressing or setting stones > 'stone,worker n

Stoney ('stəʊnɪ) n a member of a Native Canadian people of Alberta [from Siouan]

stonkered ('stɒŋkəd) adj slang completely exhausted or beaten [c20: from stonker to beat, of unknown origin]

stony or **stoney** ('stəʊnɪ) adj stonier, stoniest 1 of or resembling stone 2 abounding in stone or stones 3 unfeeling, heartless, or obdurate 4 short for stony-broke > 'stonily adv > 'stoniness n

stony-broke adj Brit slang completely without money; penniless

stony-hearted adj unfeeling; hardhearted > ,stony'heartedness n

stood (stʊd) vb the past tense and past participle of stand

stooge (stuːdʒ) n 1 an actor who feeds lines to a comedian or acts as his foil or butt 2 slang someone who is taken advantage of by another ▷ vb (intr) 3 slang to act as a stooge [c20: of unknown origin]

stook (stuːk) n 1 a number of sheaves set upright in a field to dry with their heads together ▷ vb 2 (tr) to set up (sheaves) in stooks [c15: variant of stouk, of Germanic origin; compare Middle Low German stūke, Old High German stūhha sleeve] > 'stooker n

stool (stuːl) n 1 a backless seat or footrest consisting of a small flat piece of wood, etc, resting on three or four legs, a pedestal, etc 2 a rootstock or base of a plant, usually a woody plant, from which shoots, etc, are produced 3 a cluster of shoots growing from such a base 4 chiefly US a decoy used in hunting 5 waste matter evacuated from the bowels 6 a lavatory seat 7 (in W Africa, esp Ghana) a chief's throne 8 fall between two stools a to fail through vacillation between two alternatives b to be in an unsatisfactory situation through not belonging to either of two categories or groups ▷ vb (intr) 9 (of a plant) to send up shoots from the base of the stem, rootstock, etc 10 to lure wildfowl with a decoy [Old English stōl; related to Old Norse stōll, Gothic stōls, Old High German stuol chair, Greek stulos pillar]

stool ball n a game resembling cricket, still played by girls and women in Sussex, England

stool pigeon n 1 an informer for the police; nark 2 US slang a person acting as a decoy

stoop¹ (stuːp) vb (mainly intr) 1 (also tr) to bend (the body or the top half of the body) forward and downward 2 to carry oneself with head and shoulders habitually bent forward 3 (often foll by to) to abase or degrade oneself 4 (often foll by to) to condescend; deign 5 (of a bird of prey) to swoop down ▷ n 6 the act, position, or characteristic of stooping 7 a lowering from a position of dignity or superiority 8 a downward swoop, esp of a bird of prey [Old English stūpan; related to Middle Dutch stupen to bow, Old Norse stūpa, Norwegian stupa to fall; see STEEP¹] > 'stooping adj

stoop² (stuːp) n US & Canadian a small platform with steps up to it at the entrance to a building [c18: from Dutch stoep, of Germanic origin; compare Old High German stuofa stair, Old English stōpel footprint; see STEP]

stop (stɒp) vb stops, stopping, stopped 1 to cease from doing or being (something); discontinue: stop talking 2 to cause (something moving) to halt or (of something moving) to come to a halt 3 (tr) to prevent the continuance or completion of 4 (tr; often foll by from) to prevent or restrain: to stop George from fighting 5 (tr) to keep back: to stop supplies to the navy 6 (tr) to intercept or hinder in transit: to stop a letter 7 (tr; often foll by up) to block or plug, esp so as to close: to stop up a pipe 8 (tr; often foll by up) to fill a hole or opening in: to stop up a wall 9 (tr) to staunch or stem: to stop a wound 10 (tr) to instruct a bank not to honour (a cheque) 11 (tr) to deduct (money) from pay 12 (tr) Brit to provide with punctuation 13 (tr) boxing to beat (an opponent) either by a knockout or a technical knockout 14 (tr) informal to receive (a blow, hit, etc)

15 (intr) to stay or rest: we stopped at the Robinsons' for three nights 16 (tr) rare to defeat, beat, or kill 17 (tr) music a to alter the vibrating length of (a string on a violin, guitar, etc) by pressing down on it at some point with the finger b to alter the vibrating length of an air column in a wind instrument by closing (a finger hole, etc) c to produce (a note) in this manner 18 (tr) to place a hand inside (the bell of a French horn) to alter the tone colour and pitch or play (a note) on a French horn in such a manner 19 bridge to have a protecting card or winner in (a suit in which one's opponents are strong) 20 stop at nothing to be prepared to do anything; be unscrupulous or ruthless ▷ n 21 an arrest of movement or progress 22 the act of stopping or the state of being stopped 23 a place where something halts or pauses: a bus stop 24 a stay in or as if in the course of a journey 25 the act or an instance of blocking or obstructing 26 a plug or stopper 27 a block, screw, or other device or object that prevents, limits, or terminates the motion of a mechanism or moving part 28 Brit a punctuation mark, esp a full stop 29 Also called: stop thrust fencing a counterthrust made without a parry in the hope that one's blade will touch before one's opponent's blade 30 music a the act of stopping the string, finger hole, etc, of an instrument b a set of organ pipes or harpsichord strings that may be allowed to sound as a group by muffling or silencing all other such sets c a knob, lever, or handle on an organ, etc, that is operated to allow sets of pipes to sound d an analogous device on a harpsichord or other instrument with variable registers, such as an electrophonic instrument 31 pull out all the stops a to play at full volume b to spare no effort 32 Austral a stud on a football boot 33 the angle between the forehead and muzzle of a dog or cat, regarded as a point in breeding 34 nautical a short length of line or small stuff used as a tie, esp for a furled sail 35 Also called: stop consonant phonetics any of a class of consonants articulated by first making a complete closure at some point of the vocal tract and then releasing it abruptly with audible plosion. Stops include the labials (p, b), the alveolars or dentals (t, d), the velars (k, g). See continuant 36 Also called: f-stop photog a a setting of the aperture of a camera lens, calibrated to the corresponding f-number b another name for diaphragm (sense 4) 37 a block or carving used to complete the end of a moulding 38 Also called: stopper bridge a protecting card or winner in a suit in which one's opponents are strong ▷ See also stop off, stopover, etc [c14: from Old English stoppian (unattested), as in forstoppian to plug the ear, ultimately from Late Latin stuppāre to stop with a tow, from Latin stuppa tow, from Greek stuppē] > 'stoppable adj

stopbank ('stɒp,bæŋk) n NZ an embankment to prevent flooding

stop bath n a weakly acidic solution used in photographic processing to stop the action of a developer on a film, plate, or paper before the material is immersed in fixer

stopcock ('stɒp,kɒk) n a valve used to control or stop the flow of a fluid in a pipe

stope (stəʊp) n 1 a steplike excavation made in a mine to extract ore ▷ vb 2 to mine (ore, etc) by cutting stopes [c18: probably from Low German stope; see STOOP²]

Stopes (stəʊps) n Marie Carmichael. 1880–1958, English pioneer of birth control, who established the first birth-control clinic in Britain (1921)

stopgap ('stɒp,gæp) n a a temporary substitute for something else b (as modifier): a stopgap programme

stop-go adj Brit (of economic policy) characterized by deliberate alternate expansion and contraction of aggregate demand in an effort to curb inflation and eliminate balance of payments deficits, and yet maintain full employment

stoplight ('stɒp,laɪt) n 1 a red light on a traffic signal indicating that vehicles or pedestrians coming towards it should stop 2 another word for brake light

stop-loss adj business of or relating to an order to a broker in a commodity or security market to close an open position at a specified price in order to limit any loss

stop-motion *n* **a** a technique used in animation and photography in which a subject is filmed then adjusted a frame at a time **b** (*as modifier*): *stop-motion animation*

stop off, stop in *or esp US* **stop by** *vb* **1** (*intr, adverb*; often foll by *at*) to halt and call somewhere, as on a visit or errand, esp en route to another place ▷ *n* **stopoff 2 a** a break in a journey **b** (*as modifier*): *stopoff point*

stopover ('stɒp,əʊvə) *n* **1** a stopping place on a journey ▷ *vb* **stop over 2** (*intr, adverb*) to make a stopover

stoppage ('stɒpɪdʒ) *n* **1** the act of stopping or the state of being stopped **2** something that stops or blocks **3** a deduction of money, as from pay **4** an organized cessation of work, as during a strike

stoppage time *n sport* another name for **injury time**

Stoppard ('stɒpɑːd) *n* Sir **Tom**, original name *Thomas Strausser* born 1937, British playwright, born in Czechoslovakia: his works include *Rosencrantz and Guildenstern are Dead* (1967), *Travesties* (1974), *Hapgood* (1988), *The Invention of Love* (1997), and the trilogy *The Coast of Utopia* (2002)

stopped (stɒpt) *adj* (of a pipe or tube, esp an organ pipe) closed at one end and thus sounding an octave lower than an open pipe of the same length

stopper ('stɒpə) *n* **1** Also called: **stopple** ('stɒpᵊl) a plug or bung for closing a bottle, pipe, duct, etc **2** a person or thing that stops or puts an end to something **3** *bridge* another name for **stop** (sense 39) ▷ *vb* **4** Also called: **stopple** (*tr*) to close or fit with a stopper

stopping ('stɒpɪŋ) *n* **1** *Brit informal* a dental filling ▷ *adj* **2** *chiefly Brit* making many stops in a journey: *a stopping train*

stop press *n Brit* **1** news items inserted into a newspaper after the printing has been started **2** the space regularly left blank for this

stopwatch ('stɒp,wɒtʃ) *n* a type of watch used for timing events, such as sporting events, accurately, having a device for stopping the hand or hands instantly

storage ('stɔːrɪdʒ) *n* **1** the act of storing or the state of being stored **2** space or area reserved for storing **3** a charge made for storing **4** *computing* **a** the act or process of storing information in a computer memory or on a magnetic tape, disk, etc **b** (*as modifier*): *a storage device; storage capacity*

storage battery *n* another name (esp US) for **accumulator** (sense 1)

storage capacity *n* the maximum number of bits, bytes, words, or items that can be held in a memory system such as that of a computer or of the brain

storage device *n* a piece of computer equipment, such as a magnetic tape, disk, etc, in or on which data and instructions can be stored, usually in binary form

storage heater *n* an electric device capable of accumulating and radiating heat generated by off-peak electricity

storax ('stɔːræks) *n* **1** any of numerous styracaceous trees or shrubs of the genus *Styrax*, of tropical and subtropical regions, having drooping showy white flowers **2** a vanilla-scented solid resin obtained from one of these trees, *Styrax officinalis* of the Mediterranean region and SW Asia, formerly used as incense and in perfumery and medicine **3** a liquid aromatic balsam obtained from liquidambar trees, esp *Liquidambar orientalis* of SW Asia, and used in perfumery and medicine [c14: via Late Latin from Greek, variant of STYRAX]

store (stɔː) *vb* **1** (*tr*) to keep, set aside, or accumulate for future use **2** (*tr*) to place in a warehouse, depository, etc, for safekeeping **3** (*tr*) to supply, provide, or stock **4** (*intr*) to be put into storage **5** *computing* to enter or retain (information) in a storage device ▷ *n* **6 a** an establishment for the retail sale of goods and services **b** (*in combination*): *storefront* **7** a large supply or stock kept for future use **8** short for **department store 9 a** a storage place such as a warehouse or depository **b** (*in combination*): *storeman* **10** the state of being stored (esp in the phrase **in store**) **11** a large amount or quantity **12** *computing chiefly Brit* another name for **memory** (sense 7) **13 in store** forthcoming or imminent **14 lay store by, put store by** *or* **set store by** to value or reckon as

important ▷ See also **stores** [c13: from Old French *estor*, from *estorer* to restore, from Latin *instaurāre* to refresh; related to Greek *stauros* stake] > **'storable** *adj*

Store Bælt ('sdoːrə 'bɛld) *n* the Danish name for the **Great Belt**

store card *n* another name for **charge card**

storehouse ('stɔː,haʊs) *n* a place where things are stored

storekeeper ('stɔː,kiːpə) *n* a manager, owner, or keeper of a store > **'store,keeping** *n*

store of value *n economics* the function of money that enables goods and services to be paid for a considerable time after they have been acquired

storeroom ('stɔː,ruːm, -,rʊm) *n* **1** a room in which things are stored **2** room for storing

stores (stɔːz) *pl n* a supply or stock of something, esp essentials, for a specific purpose

storey *or US* **story** ('stɔːrɪ) *n, pl* **-reys** *or* **-ries 1** a floor or level of a building **2** a set of rooms on one level [c14: from Anglo-Latin *historia*, picture, from Latin: narrative, probably arising from the pictures on medieval windows]

Storey ('stɔːrɪ) *n* **David** (**Malcolm**). born 1933, British novelist and dramatist. His best-known works include the novels *This Sporting Life* (1960) and *A Serious Man* (1998) and the plays *In Celebration* (1969), *Home* (1970), and *Stages* (1992)

storeyed *or US* **storied** ('stɔːrɪd) *adj* **a** having a storey or storeys **b** (*in combination*): *a two-storeyed house*

storied ('stɔːrɪd) *adj* **1** recorded in history or in a story; fabled **2** decorated with narrative scenes or pictures

stork (stɔːk) *n* any large wading bird of the family *Ciconiidae*, chiefly of warm regions of the Old World, having very long legs and a long stout pointed bill, and typically having a white-and-black plumage: order *Ciconiiformes* [Old English *storc*; related to Old High German *storah*, Old Norse *storkr*, Old English *stearc* stiff; from the stiff appearance of its legs; see STARK]

storksbill ('stɔːks,bɪl) *n* any of various geraniaceous plants of the genus *Erodium*, esp *E. cicutarium* (**common storksbill**), having pink or reddish-purple flowers and fruits with a beaklike process

storm (stɔːm) *n* **1 a** a violent weather condition of strong winds, rain, hail, thunder, lightning, blowing sand, snow, etc **b** (*as modifier*): *storm signal; storm sail* **c** (*in combination*): *stormproof* **2** a strong or violent reaction: *a storm of protest* **3** a direct assault on a stronghold **4** a heavy discharge or rain, as of bullets or missiles **5** short for **storm window** (sense 1) **6 storm in a teacup** *Brit* a violent fuss or disturbance over a trivial matter **7 take by storm a** to capture or overrun by a violent assault **b** to overwhelm and enthral ▷ *vb* **8** to attack or capture (something) suddenly and violently **9** (*intr*) to be vociferously angry **10** (*intr*) to move or rush violently or angrily **11** (*intr; with it* as subject) to rain, hail, or snow hard and be very windy, often with thunder or lightning [Old English, related to Old Norse *stormr*, German *Sturm*; see STIR¹]

stormbound ('stɔːm,baʊnd) *adj* detained or harassed by storms

storm centre *n* **1** the centre of a cyclonic storm, etc, where pressure is lowest **2** the centre of any disturbance or trouble

storm cloud *n* **1** a heavy dark cloud presaging rain or a storm **2** a herald of disturbance, anger, or violence: *the storm clouds of war*

storm-cock *n* another name for **mistle thrush** [c18: so called because it was believed to give forewarning of bad weather]

storm cone *n Brit* a canvas cone hoisted as a warning of high winds

storm door *n* an extra outer door for protection in bad weather

storming ('stɔːmɪŋ) *adj informal* characterized by or displaying dynamism, speed, and energy: *a storming performance*

storm lantern *n* another name for **hurricane lamp**

Stormont ('stɔːmənt) *n* a suburb of Belfast: site of Parliament House (1928–30), formerly the seat of the parliament of Northern Ireland (1922–72) and since 1998 of the Northern Ireland assembly, and Stormont Castle, formerly the residence of the prime minister of Northern Ireland and since 1998 the office of the province's first minister

storm petrel *n* any small petrel, such as the northern *Hydrobates pelagicus*, of the family *Hydrobatidae*, typically having a dark plumage with paler underparts. Also called: **Mother Carey's chicken**, **stormy petrel** [C19: so named because it was thought to be a harbinger of rough weather]

stormstayed ('stɔːmˌsteɪd) *adj Canadian* isolated or unable to travel because of adverse weather conditions, esp a snowstorm

storm trooper *n* **1** a member of the Nazi SA **2** a member of a force of shock troops

storm window *n* **1** an additional window fitted to the outside of an ordinary window to provide insulation against wind, cold, rain, etc **2** a type of dormer window

stormy ('stɔːmɪ) *adj* **stormier, stormiest** **1** characterized by storms **2** subject to, involving, or characterized by violent disturbance or emotional outburst > **'stormily** *adv* > **'storminess** *n*

stormy petrel *n* a person who brings or portends trouble

Stornoway ('stɔːnəˌweɪ) *n* a port in NW Scotland, on the E coast of Lewis in the Outer Hebrides, administrative centre of the Western Isles. Pop: 5602 (2001)

Storting *or* **Storthing** ('stɔːtɪŋ) *n* the parliament of Norway [C19: Norwegian, from *stor* great + *thing* assembly]

story[1] ('stɔːrɪ) *n, pl* **-ries** **1** a narration of a chain of events told or written in prose or verse **2** Also called: **short story** a piece of fiction, briefer and usually less detailed than a novel **3** Also called: **story line** the plot of a book, film, etc **4** an event that could be the subject of a narrative **5** a report or statement on a matter or event **6** the event or material for such a report **7** *informal* a lie, fib, or untruth **8 cut a long story short** *or* **make a long story short** to leave out details in a narration **9 the same old story** *informal* the familiar or regular course of events **10 the story goes** it is commonly said or believed ▷ *vb* **-ries, -rying, -ried** (*tr*) **11** to decorate (a pot, wall, etc) with scenes from history or legends [C13: from Anglo-French *estorie*, from Latin *historia*; see HISTORY]

story[2] ('stɔːrɪ) *n, pl* **-ries** another spelling (esp US) of **storey**

story arc *n* a continuing storyline in a television series that gradually unfolds over several episodes

storyboard ('stɔːrɪˌbɔːd) *n* (in films, television, advertising, etc) a series of sketches or photographs showing the sequence of shots or images planned for a film

storybook ('stɔːrɪˌbʊk) *n* **1** a book containing stories, esp for children ▷ *adj* **2** unreal or fantastic: *a storybook world*

storyteller ('stɔːrɪˌtɛlə) *n* **1** a person who tells stories **2** *informal* a liar > **'story,telling** *n, adj*

Stoss (German ʃtoːs) *n* **Viet** (faɪt). ?1445–1533, German Gothic sculptor and woodcarver. His masterpiece is the high altar in the Church of St Mary, Cracow (1477–89)

stoup *or* **stoop** (stuːp) *n* **1** a small basin for holy water **2** Also called: **stowp** *Scot & northern English dialect* a bucket or drinking vessel [C14 (in the sense: bucket): of Scandinavian origin; compare Old Norse *staup* beaker, Old English *stēap* flagon; see STEEP[1]]

Stour (staʊə) *n* **1** Also called: **Great Stour** a river in S England, in Kent, rising in the Weald and flowing N to the North Sea: separates the Isle of Thanet from the mainland **2** any of several smaller rivers in England

Stourbridge ('staʊəˌbrɪdʒ) *n* an industrial town in W central England, in Dudley unitary authority, West Midlands. Pop: 55 480 (2001)

stoush (staʊʃ) *Austral & NZ slang* ▷ *vb* **1** (*tr*) to hit or punch ▷ *n* **2** fighting, violence, or a fight [C19: of uncertain origin]

stout (staʊt) *adj* **1** solidly built or corpulent **2** (*prenominal*) resolute or valiant: *stout fellow* **3** strong, substantial, and robust **4** a **stout heart** courage; resolution ▷ *n* **5** strong porter highly flavoured with malt [C14: from Old French

estout bold, of Germanic origin; related to Middle High German *stolz* proud, Middle Dutch *stolt* brave] > **'stoutly** *adv* > **'stoutness** *n*

Stout (staʊt) *n* **Sir Robert.** 1844–1930, New Zealand statesman, born in Scotland: prime minister of New Zealand (1884–87)

stouthearted (ˌstaʊt'hɑːtɪd) *adj* valiant; brave > ˌstout'heartedly *adv* > ˌstout'heartedness *n*

stove[1] (stəʊv) *n* **1** another word for **cooker** (sense 1) **2** any heating apparatus, such as a kiln [Old English *stofa* bathroom; related to Old High German *stuba* steam room, Greek *tuphos* smoke]

stove[2] (stəʊv) *vb* a past tense and past participle of **stave**

stove enamel *n* a type of enamel made heatproof by treatment in a stove

stovepipe ('stəʊvˌpaɪp) *n* **1** a pipe that serves as a flue to a stove **2** Also called: **stovepipe hat** a man's tall silk hat

stow (stəʊ) *vb* (*tr*) **1** (often foll by *away*) to pack or store **2** to fill by packing **3** *nautical* to pack or put away (cargo, sails and other gear, etc) **4** to have enough room for **5** (*usually imperative*) *Brit slang* to cease from: *stow your noise!; stow it!* [Old English *stōwian* to keep, hold back, from *stōw* a place; related to Old High German *stouwen* to accuse, Gothic *stōjan* to judge, Old Slavonic *staviti* to place]

Stow (stəʊ) *n* **John.** 1525–1605, English antiquary, noted for his *Survey of London and Westminster* (1598; 1603)

stowage ('stəʊɪdʒ) *n* **1** space, room, or a charge for stowing goods **2** the act or an instance of stowing or the state of being stowed **3** something that is stowed

stowaway ('stəʊəˌweɪ) *n* **1** a person who hides aboard a vehicle, ship, or aircraft in order to gain free passage ▷ *vb* **stow away** **2** (*intr, adverb*) to travel in such a way

Stowe[1] (stəʊ) *n* a mansion near Buckingham in N Buckinghamshire: built and decorated in the 17th and 18th centuries by Vanbrugh, Robert Adam, Grinling Gibbons, and William Kent; formerly the seat of the Dukes of Buckingham; fine landscaped gardens: now occupied by a public school

Stowe (stəʊ) *n* **Harriet Elizabeth Beecher.** 1811–96, US writer, whose bestselling novel *Uncle Tom's Cabin* (1852) contributed to the antislavery cause

STP *abbreviation* **1** *trademark* scientifically treated petroleum: an oil substitute promising renewed power for an internal-combustion engine **2** Also called: **NTP** standard temperature and pressure: standard conditions of 0°C temperature and 101.325 kPa (760 mmHg) pressure **3** Professor of Sacred Theology [from Latin: *Sanctae Theologiae Professor*] ▷ *n* **4** a synthetic hallucinogenic drug related to mescaline [Sense 4 from humorous reference to the extra power resulting from scientifically treated petroleum]

Strabane (strə'bæn) *n* a district of W Northern Ireland, in Co Tyrone. Pop: 38 565 (2003 est.). Area: 862 sq km (333 sq miles)

strabismus (strə'bɪzməs) *n* abnormal alignment of one or both eyes, characterized by a turning inwards or outwards from the nose thus preventing parallel vision: caused by paralysis of an eye muscle, etc. Also called: **squint** [C17: via New Latin from Greek *strabismos*, from *strabizein* to squint, from *strabos* cross-eyed] > stra'bismal, stra'bismic *or* stra'bismical *adj*

Strabo ('streɪbəʊ) *n* ?63 BC–?23 AD, Greek geographer and historian, noted for his *Geographica*

Strachey ('streɪtʃɪ) *n* (**Giles**) **Lytton.** 1880–1932, English biographer and critic, best known for *Eminent Victorians* (1918) and *Queen Victoria* (1921)

straddle ('stræd°l) *vb* **1** (*tr*) to have one leg, part, or support on each side of **2** (*tr*) *US & Canadian informal* to be in favour of both sides of (something) **3** (*intr*) to stand, walk, or sit with the legs apart **4** (*tr*) to spread (the legs) apart **5** *military* to fire a number of shots slightly beyond and slightly short of (a target) to determine the correct range **6** (*intr*) (in poker, of the second player after the dealer) to double the ante before looking at one's cards ▷ *n* **7** the act or position of straddling **8** a noncommittal attitude or stand **9** *business* a contract or option permitting its purchaser to either sell or buy securities or commodities within a specified period of time at

S

specified prices. It is a combination of a put and a call option **10** *athletics* a high-jumping technique in which the body is parallel with the bar and the legs straddle it at the highest point of the jump **11** (in poker) the stake put up after the ante in poker by the second player after the dealer [C16: frequentative formed from obsolete *strad-* (Old English *strode*), past stem of STRIDE] > **'straddler** *n*

Stradivari (ˌstrædɪˈvɑːrɪ) *n* **Antonio** (anˈtɔːnjo). ?1644–1737, Italian violin, viola, and cello maker

Stradivarius (ˌstrædɪˈvɛərɪəs) *n* any of a number of violins manufactured by Antonio Stradivari (?1644–1737), Italian violin, viola, and cello maker, or his family

strafe (streɪf, strɑːf) *vb* (*tr*) **1** to machine-gun (troops, etc) from the air **2** *slang* to punish harshly ▷ *n* **3** an act or instance of strafing [C20: from German *strafen* to punish] > **'strafer** *n*

Strafford (ˈstræfəd) *n* **Thomas Wentworth, Earl of.** 1593–1641, English statesman. As lord deputy of Ireland (1632–39) and a chief adviser to Charles I, he was a leading proponent of the king's absolutist rule. He was impeached by Parliament and executed

straggle (ˈstrægʰl) *vb* (*intr*) **1** to go, come, or spread in a rambling or irregular way; stray **2** to linger behind or wander from a main line or part [C14: of uncertain origin; perhaps related to STRAKE and STRETCH] > **'straggler** *n* > **'straggly** *adj*

straight (streɪt) *adj* **1** not curved or crooked; continuing in the same direction without deviating **2** straightforward, outright, or candid: *a straight rejection* **3** even, level, or upright in shape or position **4** in keeping with the facts; accurate **5** honest, respectable, or reliable **6** accurate or logical: *straight reasoning* **7** continuous; uninterrupted **8** (esp of an alcoholic drink) undiluted; neat **9** not crisp, kinked, or curly: *straight hair* **10** correctly arranged; orderly **11** (of a play, acting style, etc) straightforward or serious **12** *boxing* (of a blow) delivered with an unbent arm: *a straight left* **13** (of the cylinders of an internal-combustion engine) in line, rather than in a V-formation or in some other arrangement: *a straight eight* **14** a slang word for **heterosexual** **15** *informal* no longer owing or being owed something: *if you buy the next round we'll be straight* **16** *slang* conventional in views, customs, appearance, etc **17** *slang* not using narcotics; not addicted ▷ *adv* **18** in a straight line or direct course **19** immediately; at once: *he came straight back* **20** in an even, level, or upright position **21** without cheating, lying, or unreliability: *tell it to me straight* **22** continuously; uninterruptedly **23** (often foll by *out*) frankly; candidly: *he told me straight out* **24** go straight *informal* to reform after having been dishonest or a criminal ▷ *n* **25** the state of being straight **26** a straight line, form, part, or position **27** *Brit* a straight part of a racetrack **28** *poker* **a** five cards that are in sequence irrespective of suit **b** a hand containing such a sequence **c** (*as modifier*): *a straight flush* **29** *slang* a conventional person **30** *slang* a heterosexual person **31** *slang* a cigarette containing only tobacco, without marijuana, etc [C14: from the past participle of Old English *streccan* to STRETCH] > **'straightly** *adv* > **'straightness** *n*

straight and narrow *n informal* the proper, honest, and moral path of behaviour [perhaps an alteration of *strait and narrow*, an allusion to Matthew 7:14: "strait is the gate, and narrow is the way, which leadeth unto life"]

straight angle *n* an angle of 180°

straightaway (ˌstreɪtəˈweɪ) *adv* Also: **straight away 1** at once ▷ *n* **2** the US word for **straight** (sense 27)

straight chair *n* a straight-backed side chair

straightedge (ˈstreɪtˌɛdʒ) *n* a stiff strip of wood or metal that has one edge straight and true and is used for ruling and testing straight lines

straighten (ˈstreɪtʰn) *vb* (sometimes foll by *up* or *out*) **1** to make or become straight **2** (*tr*) to make neat or tidy > **'straightener** *n*

straighten out *vb* (*adverb*) **1** to become or make less complicated or confused **2** *US & Canadian* to reform or become reformed

straight face *n* a serious facial expression, esp one that conceals the impulse to laugh > **straight-'faced** *adj*

straight fight *n* a contest between two candidates only

straight flush *n* (in poker) five consecutive cards of the same suit

straightforward (ˌstreɪtˈfɔːwəd) *adj* **1** (of a person) honest, frank, or simple **2** *chiefly Brit* (of a task, etc) simple; easy ▷ *adv, adj* **3** in a straight course > **ˌstraight'forwardly** *adv* > **ˌstraight'forwardness** *n*

straightjacket (ˈstreɪtˌdʒækɪt) *n* a less common spelling of **straitjacket**

straight-laced *adj* a variant spelling of **strait-laced**

straight man *n* a subsidiary actor who acts as stooge to a comedian

straight-out *adj informal* **1** complete; thoroughgoing **2** frank or honest

straight razor *n* another name for **cut-throat** (sense 2)

straightway (ˈstreɪtˌweɪ) *adv archaic* at once

strain¹ (streɪn) *vb* **1** to draw or be drawn taut; stretch tight **2** to exert, tax, or use (resources) to the utmost extent **3** to injure or damage or be injured or damaged by overexertion: *he strained himself* **4** to deform or be deformed as a result of a stress **5** (*intr*) to make intense or violent efforts; strive **6** to subject or be subjected to mental tension or stress **7** to pour or pass (a substance) or (of a substance) to be poured or passed through a sieve, filter, or strainer **8** (*tr*) to draw off or remove (one part of a substance or mixture from another) by or as if by filtering **9** (*tr*) to clasp tightly; hug **10** (*intr; foll by at*) to push, pull, or work with violent exertion (upon) ▷ *n* **11** the act or an instance of straining **12** the damage resulting from excessive exertion **13** an intense physical or mental effort **14** *music* (*often plural*) a theme, melody, or tune **15** a great demand on the emotions, resources, etc **16** a feeling of tension and tiredness resulting from overwork, worry, etc; stress **17** a particular style or recurring theme in speech or writing **18** *physics* the change in dimension of a body under load expressed as the ratio of the total deflection or change in dimension to the original unloaded dimension. It may be a ratio of lengths, areas, or volumes [C13: from Old French *estreindre* to press together, from Latin *stringere* to bind tightly]

strain² (streɪn) *n* **1** the main body of descendants from one ancestor **2** a group of organisms within a species or variety, distinguished by one or more minor characteristics **3** a variety of bacterium or fungus, esp one used for a culture **4** a streak; trace **5** *archaic* a kind, type, or sort [Old English *strēon*; related to Old High German *gistriuni* gain, Latin *struere* to CONSTRUCT]

strained (streɪnd) *adj* **1** (of an action, performance, etc) not natural or spontaneous **2** (of an atmosphere, relationship, etc) not relaxed; tense

strainer (ˈstreɪnə) *n* **1** a sieve used for straining sauces, vegetables, tea, etc **2** a gauze or simple filter used to strain liquids

strait (streɪt) *n* **1** (*often plural*) a narrow channel of the sea linking two larger areas of sea **2** (*often plural*) a position of acute difficulty (often in the phrase **in dire** or **desperate straits**) **3** *archaic* a narrow place or passage ▷ *adj archaic* **4** (of spaces, etc) affording little room [C13: from Old French *estreit* narrow, from Latin *strictus* constricted, from *stringere* to bind tightly] > **'straitly** *adv* > **'straitness** *n*

straiten (ˈstreɪtʰn) *vb* **1** (*tr; usually passive*) to embarrass or distress, esp financially **2** (*tr*) to limit, confine, or restrict **3** *archaic* to make or become narrow

straitjacket (ˈstreɪtˌdʒækɪt) *n* **1** Also called: **straightjacket** a jacket made of strong canvas material with long sleeves for binding the arms of violent prisoners or mental patients **2** a severe restriction or limitation ▷ *vb* **3** (*tr*) to confine in or as if in a straitjacket

strait-laced *or* **straight-laced** *adj* prudish or puritanical

Straits Settlements (streɪts) *pl n* (formerly) a British crown colony of SE Asia that included Singapore, Penang, Malacca, Labuan, and some smaller islands

strake (streɪk) *n* **1 a** a curved metal plate forming part of the metal rim on a wooden wheel **b** any metal plate let into a rubber tyre **2** Also called: **streak** *nautical* one of a

S

continuous range of planks or plates forming the side of a vessel [C14: related to Old English *streccan* to STRETCH]

Stralsund (*German* ˈʃtraːlzʊnt) *n* a port in NE Germany, in Mecklenburg-West Pomerania on a strait of the Baltic: one of the leading towns of the Hanseatic League. Pop: 59 140 (2003 est)

stramonium (strəˈməʊnɪəm) *n* **1** a preparation of the dried leaves and flowers of the thorn apple, containing hyoscyamine and formerly used as a drug to treat asthma **2** another name for **thorn apple** (sense 1) [C17: from New Latin, of uncertain origin]

strand¹ (strænd) *vb* **1** to leave or drive (ships, fish, etc) aground or ashore or (of ships, fish, etc) to be left or driven ashore **2** (*tr; usually passive*) to leave helpless, as without transport or money, etc ▷ *n chiefly poetic* **3** a shore or beach [Old English; related to Old Norse *strönd* side, Middle High German *strant* beach, Latin *sternere* to spread]

strand² (strænd) *n* **1** a set of or one of the individual fibres or threads of string, wire, etc, that form a rope, cable, etc **2** a single length of string, hair, wool, wire, etc **3** a string of pearls or beads **4** a constituent element in a complex whole ▷ *vb* **5** (*tr*) to form (a rope, cable, etc) by winding strands together [C15: of uncertain origin]

Strand (strænd) *n* **the Strand** a street in W central London, parallel to the Thames: famous for its hotels and theatres

strange (streɪndʒ) *adj* **1** odd, unusual, or extraordinary in appearance, effect, manner, etc; peculiar **2** not known, seen, or experienced before; unfamiliar **3** not easily explained **4** (usually foll by *to*) inexperienced (in) or unaccustomed (to): *strange to a task* **5** not of one's own kind, locality, etc; alien; foreign **6** shy; distant; reserved **7** strange to say it is unusual or surprising that **8** *physics* **a** denoting a particular flavour of quark **b** denoting or relating to a hypothetical form of matter composed of such quarks: *strange matter; a strange star* ▷ *adv* **9** *not standard* in a strange manner [C13: from Old French *estrange*, from Latin *extrāneus* foreign; see EXTRANEOUS] ▷ ˈstrangely *adv*

strangeness (ˈstreɪndʒnɪs) *n* **1** the state or quality of being strange **2** *physics* a property of certain elementary particles, characterized by a quantum number (**strangeness number**) conserved in strong and electromagnetic but not in weak interactions. It is associated with the presence of strange quarks

stranger (ˈstreɪndʒə) *n* **1** any person whom one does not know **2** a person who is new to a particular locality, from another region, town, etc **3** a guest or visitor **4** (foll by *to*) a person who is unfamiliar (with) or new (to) something: *he is no stranger to computers*

strangle (ˈstræŋɡ³l) *vb* **1** (*tr*) to kill by compressing the windpipe; throttle **2** (*tr*) to prevent or inhibit the growth or development of: *to strangle originality* **3** (*tr*) to suppress (an utterance) by or as if by swallowing suddenly: *to strangle a cry* ▷ See also **strangles** [C13: via Old French, ultimately from Greek *strangalē* a halter]

stranglehold (ˈstræŋɡ³lˌhəʊld) *n* **1** a wrestling hold in which a wrestler's arms are pressed against his opponent's windpipe **2** complete power or control over a person or situation

strangler (ˈstræŋɡlə) ˈstrangler *n* **1** a person or thing that strangles **2** a plant, esp a fig in tropical rain forests, that starts as an epiphyte but sends roots to the ground and eventually forms a tree with many aerial roots, usually killing the host

strangles (ˈstræŋɡ³lz) *n* (*functioning as singular*) an acute bacterial disease of horses caused by infection with *Streptococcus equi*, characterized by inflammation of the mucous membranes of the respiratory tract, resulting in abscesses and a nasal discharge. Also called: equine distemper [C18: from STRANGLE]

strangulate (ˈstræŋɡjʊˌleɪt) *vb* (*tr*) **1** to constrict (a hollow organ, vessel, etc) so as to stop the natural flow of air, blood, etc, through it **2** another word for **strangle** [C18: from Latin *strangulāt-*, past participle stem of *strangulāre* to STRANGLE] ▷ ˌstranguˈlation *n*

strangury (ˈstræŋɡjʊrɪ) *n pathol* painful excretion of urine, drop by drop, caused by muscular spasms of the

urinary tract [C14: from Latin *strangūria*, from Greek, from *stranx* a drop squeezed out + *ouron* urine]

Stranraer (strænˈrɑː) *n* a market town in SW Scotland, in W Dumfries and Galloway: fishing port with a ferry service to Northern Ireland. Pop: 10 851 (2001)

strap (stræp) *n* **1** a long strip of leather or similar material, for binding trunks, baggage, or other objects **2** a strip of leather or similar material used for carrying, lifting, or holding **3** a loop of leather, rubber, etc, suspended from the roof in a bus or train for standing passengers to hold on to **4** a razor strop **5** *business* a triple option on a security or commodity consisting of one put option and two call options at the same price and for the same period. See **strap²** (sense 4) **6** *Irish derogatory, slang* a shameless or promiscuous woman **7** the strap a beating with a strap as a punishment **8** short for **shoulder strap 9** hit one's straps *Austral informal* to achieve one's full potential or become fully effective ▷ *vb* **straps, strapping, strapped** (*tr*) **10** to tie or bind with a strap **11** to beat with a strap **12** to sharpen with a strap or strop [C16: variant of STROP]

straphanger (ˈstræpˌhæŋə) *n informal* a passenger in a bus, train, etc, who has to travel standing, esp by holding on to a strap ▷ ˈstrapˌhanging *n*

strapping (ˈstræpɪŋ) *adj* (*prenominal*) tall and sturdy [C17: from STRAP (in the archaic sense: to work vigorously)]

strap work *n architect* decorative work resembling interlacing straps

Strasbourg (*French* strasbur; *English* ˈstræzbɜːɡ) *n* a city in NE France, on the Rhine: the chief French inland port; under German rule (1870–1918); university (1567); seat of the Council of Europe and of the European Parliament. Pop: 264 115 (1999)

strata (ˈstrɑːtə) *n* a plural of **stratum**

● USAGE *Strata* is sometimes wrongly used as a singular

● noun: *this stratum* (not *strata*) *of society is often disregarded*

stratagem (ˈstrætɪdʒəm) *n* a plan or trick, esp one to deceive an enemy [C15: ultimately from Greek *stratēgos* a general, from *stratos* an army + *agein* to lead]

strategic (strəˈtiːdʒɪk) or **strategical** *adj* **1** of, relating to, or characteristic of strategy **2** important to a strategy or to strategy in general **3** (of weapons, attacks, etc) directed against an enemy's homeland rather than used on a battlefield ▷ straˈtegically *adv*

strategics (strəˈtiːdʒɪks) *n* (*functioning as singular*) strategy, esp in a military sense

strategist (ˈstrætɪdʒɪst) *n* a specialist or expert in strategy

strategy (ˈstrætɪdʒɪ) *n, pl* **-gies 1** the art or science of the planning and conduct of a war; generalship **2** a particular long-term plan for success, esp in business or politics **3** a plan or stratagem [C17: from French *stratégie*, from Greek *stratēgia* function of a general; see STRATAGEM]

Stratford-on-Avon or **Stratford-upon-Avon** (ˈstrætfəd) *n* a market town in central England, in SW Warwickshire on the River Avon: the birthplace and burial place of William Shakespeare and home of the Royal Shakespeare Company; tourist centre. Pop: 22 187 (2001)

strath (stræθ) *n Scot* a broad flat river valley [C16: from Scot and Irish Gaelic *srath*, Welsh *ystrad*]

Strathclyde Region (ˌstræθˈklaɪd) *n* a former local government region in W Scotland: formed in 1975 from Glasgow, Renfrewshire, Lanarkshire, Buteshire, Dunbartonshire, and parts of Argyllshire, Ayrshire, and Stirlingshire; replaced in 1996 by the council areas of Glasgow, Renfrewshire, East Renfrewshire, Inverclyde, North Lanarkshire, South Lanarkshire, Argyll and Bute, East Dunbartonshire, West Dunbartonshire, North Ayrshire, South Ayrshire, and East Ayrshire

strathspey (ˌstræθˈspeɪ) *n* **1** a Scottish dance with gliding steps, slower than a reel **2** a piece of music in four-four time composed for this dance [after *Strathspey* valley of the rived Spey]

strati- *combining form* indicating stratum or strata: *stratiform; stratigraphy*

straticulate (strəˈtɪkjʊlɪt, -ˌleɪt) *adj* (of a rock formation) composed of very thin even strata [C19: from New Latin *strāticulum* (unattested), diminutive of Latin *strātum* something strewn; see STRATUS] > stra,ticu'lation *n*

stratification (,strætɪfɪ'keɪʃən) *n* **1** the arrangement of sedimentary rocks in distinct layers (strata), each layer representing the sediment deposited over a specific period **2** the act of stratifying or state of being stratified [C17 (in the obsolete sense: the act of depositing in layers) and C18 (in the current senses): from New Latin *strātificātiōnem*, from *stratificāre* to STRATIFY]

stratify ('strætɪ,faɪ) *vb* **-fies, -fying, -fied 1** to form or be formed in layers or strata **2** *sociol* to divide (a society) into horizontal status groups or (of a society) to develop such groups [C17: from French *stratifier*, from New Latin *strātificāre*, from Latin STRATUM] > 'strati,fied *adj*

stratigraphy (strə'tɪgrəfɪ) *n* **1** the study of the composition, relative positions, etc, of rock strata in order to determine their geological history **2** *archaeol* a vertical section through the earth showing the relative positions of the human artefacts and therefore the chronology of successive levels of occupation > stratigraphic (,strætɪ'græfɪk) or ,strati'graphical *adj*

stratocumulus (,strætəʊ'kjuːmjʊləs, ,streɪtəʊ-) *n, pl* **-li** (-,laɪ) *meteorol* a uniform stretch of cloud containing dark grey globular masses

stratopause ('strætə,pɔːz) *n meteorol* the transitional zone of maximum temperature between the stratosphere and the mesosphere

stratosphere ('strætə,sfɪə) *n* the atmospheric layer lying between the troposphere and the mesosphere, in which temperature generally increases with height > stratospheric (,strætə'sfɛrɪk) or ,strato'spherical *adj*

stratum ('strɑːtəm) *n, pl* **-ta** (-tə) or **-tums 1** (usually plural) any of the distinct layers into which sedimentary rocks are divided **2** *biology* a single layer of tissue or cells **3** a layer of any material, esp one of several parallel layers **4** a layer of ocean or atmosphere either naturally or arbitrarily demarcated **5** a level of a social hierarchy that is distinguished according to such criteria as educational achievement or caste status [C16: via New Latin from Latin: something strewn, from *sternere* to scatter] > 'stratal *adj*

stratus ('streɪtəs) *n, pl* **-ti** (-taɪ) a grey layer cloud [C19: via New Latin from Latin: strewn, from *sternere* to extend]

Straus (straʊs) *n* Oscar (ɔskar). 1870–1954, French composer, born in Austria, noted for such operettas as *Waltz Dream* (1907) and *The Chocolate Soldier* (1908)

Strauss (straʊs; *German* ʃtraus) *n* **1 David Friedrich** ('daːfɪt 'friːdrɪç). 1808–74, German Protestant theologian: in his *Life of Jesus* (1835–36) he treated the supernatural elements of the story as myth **2 Johann** (joʹhan). 1804–49, Austrian composer, noted for his waltzes **3** his son, **Johann**, called the *Waltz King*. 1825–99, Austrian composer, whose works include *The Blue Danube Waltz* (1867) and the operetta *Die Fledermaus* (1874) **4 Richard** ('rɪçart). 1864–1949, German composer, noted esp for his symphonic poems, including *Don Juan* (1889) and *Till Eulenspiegel* (1895), his operas, such as *Elektra* (1909) and *Der Rosenkavalier* (1911), and his *Four Last Songs* (1948)

stravaig (strə'veɪg) *vb* (intr) *Scot & northern English dialect* to wander aimlessly [C19: perhaps a variant of obsolete *extravage*, from Medieval Latin *extrāvagārī*, from *vagārī* to wander]

Stravinsky (*Russian* stra'vinskij) *n* **Igor Fyodorovich** ('ɪgər 'fjɔdərəvɪtʃ). 1882–1971, US composer, born in Russia. He created ballet scores, such as *The Firebird* (1910), *Petrushka* (1911), and *The Rite of Spring* (1913), for Diaghilev. These were followed by neoclassical works, including *Oedipus Rex* (1927) and the *Symphony of Psalms* (1930). The 1950s saw him reconciled to serial techniques, which he employed in such works as the *Canticum Sacrum* (1955), the ballet *Agon* (1957), and *Requiem Canticles* (1966)

straw (strɔː) *n* **1 a** stalks of threshed grain, esp of wheat, rye, oats, or barley, used in plaiting hats, baskets, etc, or as fodder **b** (as modifier): *a straw hat* **2** a single dry or ripened stalk, esp of a grass **3** a long thin hollow paper or plastic tube or stem of a plant, used for sucking up liquids into the mouth **4** (usually used with a negative)

anything of little value or importance: *I wouldn't give a straw for our chances* **5** a measure or remedy that one turns to in desperation (esp in the phrases **clutch** or **grasp at a straw** or **straws**) **6 a** a pale yellow colour **b** (as adjective): *straw hair* **7** the last straw a small incident, setback, etc that, coming after others, proves intolerable **8** straw in the wind a hint or indication [Old English *streaw*; related to Old Norse *strā*, Old Frisian *strē*, Old High German *strō*; see STREW] > 'strawy *adj*

Straw (strɔː) *n* **Jack**, full name *John Whitaker Straw*. born 1946, British Labour politician; Home Secretary (1997–2001); Foreign Secretary (2001–06); Lord Chancellor from 2007

strawberry ('strɔːbərɪ, -brɪ) *n, pl* **-ries 1** any of various low-growing rosaceous plants of the genus *Fragaria*, such as *F. vesca* (**wild strawberry**) and *F. ananassa* (**garden strawberry**), which have white flowers and red edible fruits and spread by runners **2 a** the fruit of any of these plants, consisting of a sweet fleshy receptacle bearing small seedlike parts (the true fruits) **b** (as modifier): *strawberry ice cream* **3 a** a purplish-red colour **b** (as adjective): *strawberry shoes* [Old English *strēawberige*; perhaps from the strawlike appearance of the runners]

strawberry blonde *adj* **1** (of hair) reddish blonde ▷ *n* **2** a woman with such hair

strawberry mark *n* a soft raised swelling on the skin, often red, appearing in the weeks after birth. Most will shrink and disappear without treatment. Also called: **strawberry**

strawberry tomato *n* **1** a tropical solanaceous annual plant, *Physalis peruviana*, having bell-shaped whitish-yellow flowers and small edible round yellow berries **2** the fruit of either of these plants, eaten fresh or made into preserves and pickles ▷ Also called: **Cape gooseberry**

strawberry tree *n* a S European evergreen tree, *Arbutus unedo*, having white or pink flowers and red strawberry-like berries. See also **arbutus**

strawboard ('strɔː,bɔːd) *n* a board made of compressed straw and adhesive, used esp in book covers

strawflower ('strɔː,flaʊə) *n* an Australian plant, *Helichrysum bracteatum*, in which the coloured bracts retain their colour when the plant is dried: family *Asteraceae* (composites). See also **immortelle**

straw man *n chiefly US* **1** a figure of a man made from straw **2** another term for **man of straw**

straw poll or chiefly US, Canadian and NZ **straw vote** *n* an unofficial poll or vote taken to determine the opinion of a group or the public on some issue

Strawson ('strɔːsən) *n* Sir **Peter (Frederick)**. 1919–2006, British philosopher. His early work deals with the relationship between language and logic, his later work with metaphysics. His books include *The Bounds of Sense* (1966) and *Freedom and Resentment* (1974)

strawweight ('strɔː,weɪt) *n* **a** a professional boxer weighing not more than 47.6 kg (105 pounds) **b** (as modifier): *the strawweight title*. Also called: **mini-flyweight**

stray (streɪ) *vb* (intr) **1** to wander away, as from the correct path or from a given area **2** to wander haphazardly **3** to digress from the point, lose concentration, etc **4** to deviate from certain moral standards ▷ *n* **5 a** a domestic animal, fowl, etc, that has wandered away from its place of keeping and is lost **b** (as modifier): *stray dogs* **6** a lost or homeless person, esp a child: *waifs and strays* **7** an isolated or random occurrence, specimen, etc, that is out of place or outside the usual pattern ▷ *adj* **8** scattered, random, or haphazard [C14: from Old French *estraier*, from Vulgar Latin *estragāre* (unattested), from Latin *extrā-* outside + *vagārī* to roam; see ASTRAY, EXTRAVAGANT, STRAVAIG] > 'strayer *n*

Strayhorn ('streɪ,hɔːn) *n* **Billy**, full name *William Strayhorn*. 1915–67, US jazz composer and pianist, noted esp for his association (1939–67) with Duke Ellington

strays (streɪz) *pl n* Also called: **stray capacitance** *electronics* undesired capacitance in equipment, occurring between the wiring, between the wiring and the chassis, or between components and the chassis **2** *telecomm* another word for **static** (sense 8)

streak (striːk) *n* **1** a long thin mark, stripe, or trace of some contrasting colour **2** (of lightning) a sudden flash **3** an element or trace, as of some quality or characteristic **4** a strip, vein, or layer **5** a short stretch or run, esp of good or bad luck **6** *informal* an act or the practice of running naked through a public place ▷ *vb* **7** (*tr*) to mark or daub with a streak or streaks **8** (*intr*) to form streaks or become streaked **9** (*intr*) to move rapidly in a straight line **10** (*intr*) *informal* to run naked through a crowd of people in a public place in order to shock or amuse them [Old English *strica*, related to Old Frisian *strike*, Old High German *strih*, Norwegian, Swedish *strika*] ⊳ **streaked** *adj* ⊳ **'streaker** *n* ⊳ **'streak,like** *adj*

streaky ('striːkɪ) *adj* **streakier, streakiest** **1** marked with streaks **2** occurring in streaks **3** (of bacon) having alternate layers of meat and fat **4** of varying or uneven quality ⊳ **'streakiness** *n*

stream (striːm) *n* **1** a small river; brook **2** any steady flow of water or other fluid **3** something that resembles a stream in moving continuously in a line or particular direction **4** a rapid or unbroken flow of speech, etc: *a stream of abuse* **5** *Brit* any of several parallel classes of schoolchildren, or divisions of children within a class, grouped together because of similar ability **6** **go with the stream** *or* **drift with the stream** to conform to the accepted standards **7** **off stream** (of an industrial plant, manufacturing process, etc) shut down or not in production **8** **on stream** **a** (of an industrial plant, manufacturing process, etc) in or about to go into operation or production **b** available or in existence ▷ *vb* **9** to emit or be emitted in a continuous flow: *his nose streamed blood* **10** (*intr*) to move in unbroken succession, as a crowd of people, vehicles, etc **11** (*intr*) to float freely or with a waving motion: *bunting streamed in the wind* **12** (*tr*) to unfurl (a flag, etc) **13** *Brit education* to group or divide (children) in streams [Old English; related to Old Frisian *strām*, Old Norse *straumr*, Old High German *stroum*, Greek *rheuma*] ⊳ **'streamlet** *n*

streamer ('striːmə) *n* **1** a long narrow flag or part of a flag **2** a long narrow coiled ribbon of coloured paper that becomes unrolled when tossed **3** a stream of light, esp one appearing in some forms of the aurora **4** *journalism* a large heavy headline printed across the width of a page of a newspaper **5** *computing* another word for **tape streamer**

streamline ('striːm,laɪn) *n* **1** a contour on a body that offers the minimum resistance to a gas or liquid flowing around it ▷ *vb* (*tr*) **2** to make streamlined

streamlined ('striːm,laɪnd) *adj* **1** offering or designed to offer the minimum resistance to the flow of a gas or liquid **2** made more efficient, esp by simplifying

stream of consciousness *n* **1** *psychol* the continuous flow of ideas, thoughts, and feelings forming the content of an individual's consciousness. The term was originated by William James **2** a literary technique that reveals the flow of thoughts and feelings of characters through long passages of soliloquy

streamy ('striːmɪ) *adj* **streamier, streamiest** *chiefly poetic* **1** (of an area, land, etc) having many streams **2** flowing or streaming

Streep (striːp) *n* **Meryl**, original name *Mary Louise Streep*. born 1949, US actress. Her films include *The Deerhunter* (1978), *Kramer vs Kramer* (1979), *The French Lieutenant's Woman* (1981), *Sophie's Choice* (1982), *Out of Africa* (1986), *Dancing at Lughnasa* (1999), and *The Hours* (2002)

street (striːt) *n* **1 a** (*capital when part of a name*) a public road that is usually lined with buildings, esp in a town: *Oxford Street* **b** (*as modifier*): *a street directory* **2** the buildings lining a street **3** the part of the road between the pavements, used by vehicles **4** the people living, working, etc, in a particular street **5** (*modifier*) of or relating to the urban counterculture **6** **on the streets** **a** earning a living as a prostitute **b** homeless **7** **up one's street** *or* **right up one's street** *informal* (just) what one knows or likes best **8** **streets ahead of** *informal* superior to, more advanced than, etc **9** **streets apart** *informal* markedly different [Old English *strǣt*, from Latin *via strāta* paved way (*strāta*, from *strātus*, past participle of *sternere* to stretch out); compare Old Frisian *strēte*, Old High German *strāza*; see STRATUS]

street Arab *n literary, old-fashioned* a homeless child, esp one who survives by begging and stealing; urchin

streetcar ('striːt,kɑː) *n US & Canadian* an electrically driven public transport vehicle that runs on rails let into the surface of the road, power usually being taken from an overhead wire. Also called: **trolley car**, (*esp Brit*) **tram, tramcar**

street credibility *n* a convincing command or display of the style, fashions, knowledge, etc, associated with urban counterculture. Often shortened to: **street cred** ⊳ **,street-'credible** *adj*

street cry *n* (*often plural*) the cry of a street hawker

street furniture *n* pieces of equipment, such as streetlights and pillar boxes, placed in the street for the benefit of the public

street value *n* the monetary worth of a commodity, usually an illicit commodity such as a drug, considered as the price it would fetch when sold to the ultimate user

streetwalker ('striːt,wɔːkə) *n* a prostitute who solicits on the streets ⊳ **'street,walking** *n, adj*

streetwear ('striːt,wɛə) *n* fashionable casual clothes

streetwise ('striːt,waɪz) *adj* attuned to and adept at surviving in an urban, poor and often criminal environment

Streicher ('ʃtraɪkə) *n* **Julius.** 1885–1946, German Nazi journalist and politician, who spread anti-Semitic propaganda as editor of *Der Stürmer* (1923–45). He was hanged as a war criminal

Streisand ('straɪsænd) *n* **Barbra.** born 1942, US singer, actress, and film director: the films she has acted in include *Funny Girl* (1968) and *A Star is Born* (1976); her films as actress and director include *Yentl* (1983), *Prince of Tides* (1990), and *The Mirror has Two Faces* (1996)

strelitzia (strɛ'lɪtsɪə) *n* any southern African perennial herbaceous plant of the genus *Strelitzia*, cultivated for its showy flowers: includes the bird-of-paradise flower: family *Strelitziaceae* [c18: named after Charlotte of Mecklenburg-*Strelitz* (1744–1818), queen of George III of Great Britain and Ireland]

strength (strɛŋθ) *n* **1** the state or quality of being physically or mentally strong **2** the ability to withstand or exert great force, stress, or pressure **3** something that is regarded as being beneficial or a source of power: *their chief strength is technology* **4** potency, as of a drink, drug, etc **5** power to convince; cogency: *the strength of an argument* **6** degree of intensity or concentration of colour, light, sound, flavour, etc **7** the full or part of the full complement as specified: *at full strength; below strength* **8** **from strength to strength** with ever-increasing success **9** **in strength** in large numbers **10** **on the strength of** on the basis of or relying upon [Old English *strengthu*; related to Old High German *strengida*; see STRONG]

strengthen ('strɛŋθən) *vb* to make or become stronger ⊳ **'strengthener** *n*

strenuous ('strɛnjʊəs) *adj* **1** requiring or involving the use of great energy or effort **2** characterized by great activity, effort, or endeavour [c16: from Latin *strēnuus* brisk, vigorous] ⊳ **strenuosity** (,strɛnjʊ'ɒsɪtɪ) *or* **'strenuousness** *n* ⊳ **'strenuously** *adv*

strep (strɛp) *n informal* short for **streptococcus**

strepitoso ('strɛpɪ'təʊsəʊ) *adj, adv music* (to be performed) boisterously [Italian, literally; noisily]

strepto- *combining form* **1** indicating a shape resembling a twisted chain: *streptococcus* **2** indicating streptococcus [from Greek *streptos* twisted, from *strephein* to twist]

streptocarpus (,strɛptə'kɑːpəs) *n* any plant of the typically stemless subtropical perennial genus *Streptocarpus*, some species of which are grown as greenhouse plants for their tubular flowers in a range of bright colours: family *Gesneriaceae* [New Latin, from Greek *streptos* twisted + *karpos* fruit (from the shape of the capsule)]

streptococcus (,strɛptəʊ'kɒkəs) *n, pl* **-cocci** (-'kɒkaɪ; *US* -'kɒksaɪ) any Gram-positive spherical bacterium of the genus *Streptococcus*, typically occurring in chains and including many pathogenic species, such as *S. pyogenes*, which causes scarlet fever, sore throat, etc: family

S

Lactobacillaceae. Often shortened to **strep** > **streptococcal** (ˌstrɛptəʊˈkɒkəl) or less commonly **streptococcic** (ˌstrɛptəʊˈkɒkɪk; US -ˈkɒksɪk) adj

streptomycin (ˌstrɛptəʊˈmaɪsɪn) n an antibiotic obtained from the bacterium *Streptomyces griseus*: used in the treatment of tuberculosis and Gram-negative bacterial infections. Formula: $C_{21}H_{39}N_7O_{12}$ [from *Streptomyces*, genus name of bacteria (from STREPTO- + Greek *mukēs* fungus + -IN)]

streptothricin (ˌstrɛptəʊˈθraɪsɪn) n an antibiotic active against bacteria and some fungi, produced by the bacterium *Streptomyces lavendulae* [from *Streptothrix*, genus name of bacteria (from STREPTO- + Greek *thrix* hair + -IN)]

Stresemann (German ˈʃtreːzəman) n **Gustav**. 1878–1929, German statesman; chancellor (1923) and foreign minister (1923–29) of the Weimar Republic. He gained (1926) Germany's admission to the League of Nations and shared the Nobel peace prize (1926) with Aristide Briand

stress (strɛs) n **1** special emphasis or significance attached to something **2** mental, emotional, or physical strain or tension **3** emphasis placed upon a syllable by pronouncing it more loudly than those that surround it **4** such emphasis as part of a regular rhythmic beat in music or poetry **5** a syllable so emphasized **6** physics **a** a force or a system of forces producing deformation or strain **b** the force acting per unit area ▷ vb **7** (tr) to give emphasis or prominence to **8** (tr) to pronounce (a word or syllable) more loudly than those that surround it **9** (tr) to subject to stress or strain [c14: *stresse*, shortened from DISTRESS] > ˈstressful adj

-stress suffix forming nouns indicating a woman who performs or is engaged in a certain activity [from -ST(E)R + -ESS]

stressor (ˈstrɛsə) n an event, experience, etc, that causes stress

stretch (strɛtʃ) vb **1** to draw out or extend or be drawn out or extended in length, area, etc **2** to extend or be extended to an undue degree, esp so as to distort or lengthen permanently **3** to extend (the limbs, body, etc) **4** (tr) to reach or suspend (a rope, etc) from one place to another **5** (tr) to draw tight; tighten **6** (often foll by *out, forward*, etc) to reach or hold (out); extend **7** (intr; usually foll by *over*) to extend in time: *the course stretched over three months* **8** (intr; foll by *for, over*, etc) (of a region, etc) to extend in length or area **9** (intr) (esp of a garment) to be capable of expanding, as to a larger size: *socks that will stretch* **10** (tr) to put a great strain upon or extend to the limit **11** to injure (a muscle, tendon, ligament, etc) by means of a strain or sprain **12** (tr; often foll by *out*) to make do with (limited resources): *to stretch one's budget* **13** (tr) informal to expand or elaborate (a story, etc) beyond what is credible or acceptable **14** (tr; often passive) to extend, as to the limit of one's abilities or talents **15** archaic or slang to hang or be hanged by the neck **16 stretch a point a** to make a concession or exception not usually made **b** to exaggerate ▷ n **17** the act of stretching or state of being stretched **18** a large or continuous expanse or distance: *a stretch of water* **19** extent in time, length, area, etc **20 a** capacity for being stretched, as in some garments **b** (as modifier): *stretch pants* **21** horse racing the section or sections of a racecourse that are straight, esp the final straight section leading to the finishing line **22** slang a term of imprisonment **23 at a stretch** chiefly Brit **a** with some difficulty; by making a special effort **b** if really necessary or in extreme circumstances **c** at one time [Old English *streccan*; related to Old Frisian *strekka*, Old High German *strecken*; see STRAIGHT, STRAKE] > ˈstretchable adj > ˌstretchaˈbility n

stretcher (ˈstrɛtʃə) n **1 a** a device for transporting the ill, wounded, or dead, consisting of a frame covered by canvas or other material **2** a strengthening often decorative member joining the legs of a chair, table, etc **3** the wooden frame on which canvas is stretched and fixed for oil painting **4** a tie beam or brace used in a structural framework **5** a brick or stone laid horizontally with its length parallel to the length of a wall **6** rowing a fixed board across a boat on which an oarsman braces his feet **7** Austral & NZ a camp bed ▷ vb (tr) **8** to transport (a sick or injured person) on a stretcher

stretcher-bearer n a person who helps to carry a stretcher, esp in wartime

stretch limo n informal a limousine that has been lengthened to provide extra seating accommodation and more legroom

stretchmarks (ˈstrɛtʃˌmɑːks) pl n marks that remain visible on the abdomen after its distension, esp in pregnancy

stretchy (ˈstrɛtʃɪ) adj **stretchier**, **stretchiest** characterized by elasticity > ˈstretchiness n

Stretford (ˈstrɛtfəd) n an industrial town in NW England, in Trafford unitary authority, Greater Manchester. Pop: 42 103 (2001)

stretto (ˈstrɛtəʊ) n, pl **-tos** or **-ti** (-tiː) **1** (in a fugue) the close overlapping of two parts or voices, the second one entering before the first has completed its statement of the subject **2** Also called: **stretta** (ˈstrɛtə) a concluding passage in a composition, played at a faster speed than the earlier material [c17: from Italian, from Latin *strictus* tightly bound; see STRICT]

strew (struː) vb **strews, strewing, strewed, strewn** or **strewed** to spread or scatter or be spread or scattered, as over a surface or area [Old English *streowian*; related to Old Norse *strā*, Old High German *streuwen*, Latin *struere* to spread] > ˈstrewer n

strewth (struːθ) interj an expression of surprise or dismay [c19: alteration of *God's truth*]

stria (ˈstraɪə) n, pl **striae** (ˈstraɪiː) (often plural) **1** Also called: **striation** geology any of the parallel scratches or grooves on the surface of a rock caused by abrasion resulting from the passage of a glacier, motion on a fault surface, etc **2** biology, anatomy a narrow band of colour or a ridge, groove, or similar linear mark, usually occurring in a parallel series **3** architect a narrow channel, such as a flute on the shaft of a column [c16: from Latin: a groove]

striate adj (ˈstraɪɪt) Also called: **striated 1** marked with striae; striped ▷ vb (ˈstraɪeɪt) **2** (tr) to mark with striae [c17: from Latin *striāre* to make grooves, from STRIA]

striation (straɪˈeɪʃən) n **1** an arrangement or pattern of striae **2** the condition of being striate **3** another word for **stria** (sense 1)

stricken (ˈstrɪkən) adj **1** laid low, as by disease or sickness **2** deeply affected, as by grief, love, etc **3** archaic wounded or injured [c14: past participle of STRIKE] > ˈstrickenly adv

strict (strɪkt) adj **1** adhering closely to specified rules, ordinances, etc **2** complied with or enforced stringently; rigorous: *a strict code of conduct* **3** severely correct in attention to rules of conduct or morality: *a strict teacher* **4** (of a punishment, etc) harsh; severe **5** (prenominal) complete; absolute: *in strict secrecy* [c16: from Latin *strictus*, from *stringere* to draw tight] > ˈstrictly adv > ˈstrictness n

stricture (ˈstrɪktʃə) n **1** a severe criticism; censure **2** pathol an abnormal constriction of a tubular organ, structure, or part [c14: from Latin *strictūra* contraction; see STRICT] > ˈstrictured adj

stride (straɪd) n **1 a** a long step or pace **2** the space measured by such a step **3** a striding gait **4** an act of forward movement by an animal, completed when the legs have returned to their initial relative positions **5** progress or development (esp in the phrase **make rapid strides**) **6** a regular pace or rate of progress: *to get into one's stride; to be put off one's stride* **7** Also called: **stride piano** jazz a piano style characterized by single bass notes on the first and third beats and chords on the second and fourth **8** (plural) informal, chiefly Austral men's trousers **9 take something in one's stride** to do something without difficulty or effort ▷ vb **strides, striding, strode, stridden 10** (intr) to walk with long regular or measured paces, as in haste **11** (tr) to cover or traverse by striding: *he strode thirty miles* **12** (often foll by *over, across*, etc) to cross (over a space, obstacle, etc) with a stride [Old English *strīdan*; related to Old High German *strītan* to quarrel; see STRADDLE] > ˈstrider n

strident (ˈstraɪdənt) adj **1** (of a shout, voice, etc) having or making a loud or harsh sound **2** urgent, clamorous, or vociferous: *strident demands* [C17: from Latin *strīdēns*, from *strīdēre* to make a grating sound] > **'stridence** or **'stridency** n > **'stridently** adv

stridor ('straɪdɔː) n **1** pathol a high-pitched whistling sound made during respiration, caused by obstruction of the air passages **2** chiefly literary a harsh or shrill sound [C17: from Latin; see STRIDENT]

stridulate ('strɪdjʊˌleɪt) vb (intr) (of insects such as the cricket) to produce sounds by rubbing one part of the body against another [C19: back formation from *stridulation*, from Latin *strīdulus* creaking, hissing, from *strīdēre* to make a harsh noise] > ˌstridu'lation n > 'striduˌlator n

stridulous ('strɪdjʊləs) or **stridulant** adj **1** making a harsh, shrill, or grating noise **2** pathol of, relating to, or characterized by stridor [C17: from Latin *strīdulus*, from *strīdēre* to make a harsh noise. See STRIDENT] > 'stridulousness or 'stridulance n

strife (straɪf) n **1** angry or violent struggle; conflict **2** rivalry or contention, esp of a bitter kind **3** Austral & NZ trouble or discord of any kind **4** archaic striving [C13: from Old French *estrif*, probably from *estriver* to STRIVE]

strigil ('strɪdʒɪl) n a curved blade used by the ancient Romans and Greeks to scrape the body after bathing [C16: from Latin *strigilis*, from *stringere* to graze]

strigose ('straɪgəʊs) adj **1** botany bearing stiff hairs or bristles **2** zoology marked with fine closely set grooves or ridges [C18: via New Latin *strigōsus*, from *striga* a bristle, from Latin: grain cut down]

strike (straɪk) vb strikes, striking, struck **1** to deliver (a blow or stroke) to (a person) **2** to come or cause to come into sudden or violent contact (with) **3** (tr) to make an attack on **4** to produce (fire, sparks, etc) or (of fire, sparks, etc) to be produced by ignition **5** to cause (a match) to light by friction or (of a match) to be lighted **6** to press (the key of a piano, organ, etc) or to sound (a specific note) in this or a similar way **7** to indicate (a specific time) by the sound of a hammer striking a bell or by any other percussive sound **8** (of a venomous snake) to cause injury by biting **9** (tr) to affect or cause to affect deeply, suddenly, or radically, as if by dealing a blow: *her appearance struck him as strange; I was struck on his art* **10** past part struck or stricken (tr; passive; usually foll by *with*) to render incapable or nearly so: *she was stricken with grief* **11** (tr) to enter the mind of: *it struck me that he had become very quiet* **12** past part struck or stricken to render: *I was struck dumb* **13** (tr) to be perceived by; catch: *the glint of metal struck his eye* **14** to arrive at or come upon (something), esp suddenly or unexpectedly: *to strike the path for home; to strike upon a solution* **15** (intr; sometimes foll by *out*) to set (out) or proceed, esp upon a new course: *to strike for the coast* **16** (tr; usually passive) to afflict with a disease, esp unexpectedly: *he was struck with polio when he was six* **17** (tr) to discover or come upon a source of (ore, petroleum, etc) **18** (tr) (of a plant) to produce or send down (a root or roots) **19** (tr) to take apart or pack up; break (esp in the phrase **strike camp**) **20** (tr) to take down or dismantle (a stage set, formwork, etc) **21** (tr) nautical **a** to lower or remove (a specified piece of gear) **b** to haul down or dip (a flag, sail, etc) in salute or in surrender **22** to attack (an objective) with the intention of causing damage to, seizing, or destroying it **23** to impale the hook in the mouth of (a fish) by suddenly tightening or jerking the line after the bait or fly has been taken **24** (tr) to form or impress (a coin, metal, etc) by or as if by stamping **25** to level (a surface) by use of a flat board **26** (tr) to assume or take up (an attitude, posture, etc) **27** (intr) (of workers in a factory, etc) to cease work collectively as a protest against working conditions, low pay, etc **28** (tr) to reach by agreement: *to strike a bargain* **29** (tr) to form (a jury, esp a special jury) by cancelling certain names among those nominated for jury service until only the requisite number remains **30** strike home **a** to deliver an effective blow **b** to achieve the intended effect **31** strike it lucky or strike lucky to have some good luck **32** strike it rich informal **a** to discover an extensive deposit of a mineral, petroleum, etc **b** to have an unexpected financial

success ▷ n **33** an act or instance of striking **34** a cessation of work by workers in a factory, industry, etc, as a protest against working conditions or low pay **35** a military attack, esp an air attack on a surface target: *air strike* **36** baseball a pitched ball judged good but missed or not swung at, three of which cause a batter to be out **37** Also called: ten-strike tenpin bowling **a** the act or an instance of knocking down all the pins with the first bowl of a single frame **b** the score thus made **38** a sound made by striking **39** the mechanism that makes a clock strike **40** the discovery of a source of ore, petroleum, etc **41** the horizontal direction of a fault, rock stratum, etc, which is perpendicular to the direction of the dip **42** angling the act or an instance of striking **43** informal an unexpected or complete success, esp one that brings financial gain **44** take strike cricket (of a batsman) to prepare to play a ball delivered by the bowler ▷ See also **strike down, strike off**, etc [Old English *strīcan*; related to Old Frisian *strīka* to stroke, Old High German *strīhhan* to smooth, Latin *stria* furrow]

strikebound ('straɪkˌbaʊnd) adj (of a factory, etc) closed or made inoperative by a strike

strikebreaker ('straɪkˌbreɪkə) n a person who tries to make a strike ineffectual by working or by taking the place of those on strike > 'strikeˌbreaking n, adj

strike down vb (tr, adverb) to cause to die, esp suddenly: *he was struck down in his prime*

strike off vb (tr) **1** to remove or erase from (a list, record, etc) by or as if by a stroke of the pen **2** (adverb) to cut off or separate by or as if by a blow: *she was struck off from the inheritance*

strike out vb (adverb) **1** (tr) to remove or erase **2** (intr) to start out or begin: *to strike out on one's own* **3** baseball to put out or be put out on strikes **4** (intr) US & Canadian informal to fail utterly

strike pay n money paid to strikers from the funds of a trade union

striker ('straɪkə) n **1** a person who is on strike **2** the hammer in a timepiece that rings a bell or alarm **3** any part in a mechanical device that strikes something, such as the firing pin of a gun **4** soccer informal an attacking player, esp one who generally positions himself near his opponent's goal in the hope of scoring **5** cricket the batsman who is about to play a ball

strike up vb (adverb) **1** (of a band, orchestra, etc) to begin to play or sing **2** (tr) to bring about; cause to begin: *to strike up a friendship*

striking ('straɪkɪŋ) adj **1** attracting attention; fine; impressive: *a striking beauty* **2** conspicuous; noticeable: *a striking difference* > 'strikingly adv > 'strikingness n

striking circle n hockey the semicircular area in front of each goal, which an attacking player must have entered before scoring a goal

Strimmer ('strɪmə) n trademark an electrical tool for trimming the edges of lawns

Strimon ('strɪmɒn) n a transliteration of the Greek name for the **Struma**

Strindberg ('strɪndbɜːɡ; Swedish 'strɪndbærj) n **August** ('aʊɡʊst). 1849–1912, Swedish dramatist and novelist, whose plays include *The Father* (1887), *Miss Julie* (1888), and *The Ghost Sonata* (1907)

Strine (straɪn) n a humorous transliteration of Australian pronunciation, as in *Gloria Soame* for *glorious home* [C20: a jocular rendering, coined by Alastair Morrison, of the Australian pronunciation of *Australian*]

string (strɪŋ) n **1** a thin length of cord, twine, fibre, or similar material used for tying, hanging, binding, etc **2** a group of objects threaded on a single strand: *a string of beads* **3** a series or succession of things, events, acts, utterances, etc: *a string of oaths* **4** a number, chain, or group of similar things, animals, etc, owned by or associated with one person or body: *a string of girlfriends* **5** a tough fibre or cord in a plant **6** music a tightly stretched wire, cord, etc, found on stringed instruments, such as the violin, guitar, and piano **7** short for **bowstring 8** architect short for **string course** or **stringer** (sense 1) **9** physics a one-dimensional entity postulated to be a fundamental component of matter in some theories of particle physics. See also **cosmic string**

10 a group of characters that can be treated as a unit by a computer program **11** the strings (*plural*) **a** violins, violas, cellos, and double basses collectively **b** the section of a symphony orchestra constituted by such instruments **12** (*plural*) complications or conditions (esp in the phrase **no strings attached**) **13** (*modifier*) composed of stringlike strands woven in a large mesh: *a string bag; string vest* **14** pull strings *informal* to exert personal influence, esp secretly or unofficially **15** pull the strings to have real or ultimate control of something ▷ *vb* strings, stringing, strung (strʌŋ) **16** (*tr*) to provide with a string or strings **17** (*tr*) to suspend or stretch from one point to another **18** (*tr*) to thread on a string **19** (*tr*) to form or extend in a line or series **20** (foll by *out*) to space or spread out at intervals **21** (*tr*; usually foll by *up*) *informal* to kill (a person) by hanging **22** (*tr*) to remove the stringy parts from (vegetables, esp beans) **23** (*intr*) (esp of viscous liquids) to become stringy or ropey **24** (*tr*; often foll by *up*) to cause to be tense or nervous [Old English *streng*; related to Old High German *strang*, Old Norse *strengr*; see STRONG] > ˈstringˌlike *adj*

string along *vb* (*adverb*) *informal* **1** (*intr*; often foll by *with*) to agree or appear to be in agreement (with) **2** (*intr*; often foll by *with*) to accompany **3** Also called: **string on** (*tr*) to deceive, fool, or hoax, esp in order to gain time

stringboard (ˈstrɪŋˌbɔːd) *n* a skirting that covers the ends of the steps in a staircase. Also called: **stringer**

string course *n* another name for **cordon** (sense 4)

stringed (strɪŋd) *adj* (of musical instruments) having or provided with strings

stringendo (strɪnˈdʒɛndəʊ) *adj, adv music* to be performed with increasing speed [Italian, from *stringere* to compress, from Latin: to draw tight; see STRINGENT]

stringent (ˈstrɪndʒənt) *adj* **1** requiring strict attention to rules, procedure, detail, etc **2** *finance* characterized by or causing a shortage of credit, loan capital, etc [C17: from Latin *stringere* to bind] > ˈstringency *n* > ˈstringently *adv*

stringer (ˈstrɪŋə) *n* **1** *architect* **a** a long horizontal beam that is used for structural purposes **b** another name for **stringboard** **2** *nautical* a longitudinal structural brace for strengthening the hull of a vessel **3** a journalist retained by a newspaper or news service on a part-time basis to cover a particular town or area

stringhalt (ˈstrɪŋˌhɔːlt) *n vet science* a sudden spasmodic lifting of the hind leg of a horse, resulting from abnormal contraction of the flexor muscles of the hock. Also called: **springhalt** [C16: probably STRING + HALT²]

stringpiece (ˈstrɪŋˌpiːs) *n* a long horizontal timber beam used to strengthen or support a framework

string quartet *n music* **1** an instrumental ensemble consisting of two violins, one viola, and one cello **2** a piece of music written for such a group, usually having the form and commonest features of a sonata

string tie *n* a very narrow tie, usually tied in a bow

stringy (ˈstrɪŋɪ) *adj* stringier, stringiest **1** made of strings or resembling strings **2** (of meat, etc) fibrous **3** (of a person's build) wiry; sinewy **4** (of liquids) forming in strings > ˈstringily *adv* > ˈstringiness *n*

stringy-bark *n Austral* any of several eucalyptus trees having a fibrous bark

strip¹ (strɪp) *vb* strips, stripping, stripped **1** to take or pull (the covering, clothes, etc) off (oneself, another person, or thing) **2** (*intr*) **a** to remove all one's clothes **b** to perform a striptease **3** (*tr*) to denude or empty completely **4** (*tr*) to deprive: *he was stripped of his pride* **5** (*tr*) to rob or plunder **6** (*tr*) to remove (paint, varnish, etc) from (a surface, furniture, etc) by sanding, with a solvent, etc: *stripped pine* **7** Also called: **pluck** (*tr*) to pull out the old coat of hair from (dogs of certain long- and wire-haired breeds) **8 a** to remove the leaves from the stalks of (tobacco, etc) **b** to separate the two sides of a leaf from the stem of (tobacco, etc) **9** (*tr*) *agriculture* to draw the last milk from each of the teats of (a cow) **10** to dismantle (an engine, mechanism, etc) **11** to tear off or break (the thread) from (a screw, bolt, etc) or (the teeth) from (a gear) **12** (often foll by *down*) to remove the accessories from (a motor vehicle): *his car was stripped down* ▷ *n* **13** the act or an instance of undressing or of performing a striptease [Old English *bestriepan* to

plunder; related to Old High German *stroufen* to plunder, strip]

strip² (strɪp) *n* **1** a relatively long, flat, narrow piece of something **2** short for **airstrip 3** the clothes worn by the members of a team, esp a football team **4** *business* a triple option on a security or commodity consisting of one call option and two put options at the same price and for the same period. See **strap** (sense 5) **5** tear someone off a strip *informal* to rebuke (someone) angrily ▷ *vb* strips, stripping, stripped **6** to cut or divide into strips [C15: from Middle Dutch *strīpe* STRIPE¹]

strip cartoon *n* another term for **comic strip**

strip club *n* a small club in which striptease performances take place

stripe¹ (straɪp) *n* **1** a relatively long band of distinctive colour or texture that differs from the surrounding material or background **2** a fabric having such bands **3** a strip, band, or chevron of fabric worn on a military uniform, etc, esp one that indicates rank **4** *chiefly US & Canadian* kind; sort; type: *a man of a certain stripe* ▷ *vb* **5** (*tr*) to mark with a stripe or stripes [C17: probably from Middle Dutch *strīpe*; related to Middle High German *strīfe*, of obscure origin] > **striped** *adj*

stripe² (straɪp) *n* a stroke from a whip, rod, cane, etc [C15: perhaps from Middle Low German *strippe*; related to STRIPE¹]

striped muscle or **striated muscle** *n* a type of contractile tissue that is marked by transverse striations; it is concerned with moving skeletal parts to which it is usually attached. Also called: **skeletal muscle**. See **smooth muscle**

strip lighting *n* electric lighting by means of long glass tubes that are fluorescent lamps or that contain long filaments

stripling (ˈstrɪplɪŋ) *n* a lad [C13: from STRIP² + -LING¹]

strip mining *n* another term (esp US) for **opencast mining**

stripper (ˈstrɪpə) *n* **1** a striptease artist **2** a person or thing that strips **3** a device or substance for removing paint, varnish, etc

strip-search *vb* **1** (*tr*) (of police, customs officials, etc) to strip (a prisoner or suspect) naked to search him or her for contraband, narcotics, etc ▷ *n* **2** a search that involves stripping a person naked > ˈstrip-ˌsearching *n*

striptease (ˈstrɪpˌtiːz) *n* **a** a form of erotic entertainment in which a person gradually undresses to music **b** (*as modifier*): *a striptease club* [from STRIP¹ + TEASE] > ˈstripˌteaser *n*

stripy or **stripey** (ˈstraɪpɪ) *adj* stripier, stripiest marked by or with stripes; striped

strive (straɪv) *vb* strives, striving, strove, striven (ˈstrɪvᵊn) **1** (*may take a clause as object or an infinitive*) to make a great and tenacious effort **2** (*intr*) to fight; contend [C13: from Old French *estriver*, of Germanic origin; related to Middle High German *streben* to strive, Old Norse *strītha* to fight] > ˈstriver *n*

strobe (strəʊb) *n* short for **strobe lighting, stroboscope**

strobe lighting *n* **1** a high-intensity flashing beam of light produced by rapid electrical discharges in a tube or by a perforated disc rotating in front of an intense light source: used in discotheques, etc **2** the use of or the apparatus for producing such light ▷ Sometimes shortened to: **strobe**

strobila (ˈstrəʊbɪlə) *n, pl* -bilae (-bɪliː) the body of a tapeworm, consisting of a string of similar segments (proglottides) [C19: from New Latin, from Greek *strobilē* plug of lint twisted into a cone shape, from *strobilos* a fir cone]

strobilus (ˈstrəʊbɪləs) or **strobile** (ˈstrəʊbaɪl) *n, pl* -biluses, -bili (-bɪlaɪ) or -biles *botany* the technical name for **cone** (sense 3) [C18: via Late Latin from Greek *strobilos* a fir cone; see STROBILA]

stroboscope (ˈstrəʊbəˌskəʊp) *n* **1** an instrument producing a flashing light, the frequency of which can be synchronized with some multiple of the frequency of rotation, vibration, or operation of an object, etc, making it appear stationary. It is used to determine speeds of rotation or vibration, or to adjust objects or parts. Sometimes shortened to: **strobe 2** a similar device synchronized with the opening of the shutter of a camera so that a series of still photographs can be taken of a moving object [C19: from strobo-, from Greek *strobos* a twisting, whirling + -SCOPE] > **stroboscopic** (ˌstrəʊbəˈskɒpɪk) *or* ˌstroboˈscopical *adj* > ˌstroboˈscopically *adv*

strode (strəʊd) *vb* the past tense of **stride**

Stroessner (ˈstrɔʊsnə) *n* **Alfredo**. 1912–2006, Paraguayan soldier and politician; president (1954–89): deposed in a military coup

stroganoff (ˈstrɒɡəˌnɒf) *n* short for **beef stroganoff**

Stroheim (ˈstrəʊˌhaɪm, ˈʃtrəʊ-) *n* See **von Stroheim**

stroke (strəʊk) *n* **1** the act or an instance of striking; a blow, knock, or hit **2** a sudden action, movement, or occurrence: *a stroke of luck* **3** a brilliant or inspired act or feat: *a stroke of genius* **4** *pathol* apoplexy; rupture of a blood vessel in the brain resulting in loss of consciousness, often followed by paralysis, or embolism or thrombosis affecting a cerebral vessel **5 a** the striking of a clock **b** the hour registered by the striking of a clock: *on the stroke of three* **6** a mark, flourish, or line made by a writing implement **7** another name for a solidus, used esp when dictating or reading aloud **8** a light touch or caress, as with the fingers **9** a pulsation, esp of the heart **10** a single complete movement or one of a series of complete movements **11** *sport* the act or manner of striking the ball with a racket, club, bat, etc **12** any one of the repeated movements used by a swimmer to propel himself through the water **13** a manner of swimming, esp one of several named styles such as the crawl or butterfly **14 a** any one of a series of linear movements of a reciprocating part, such as a piston **b** the distance travelled by such a part from one end of its movement to the other **15** a single pull on an oar or oars in rowing **16** manner or style of rowing **17** the oarsman who sits nearest the stern of a shell, facing the cox, and sets the rate of striking for the rest of the crew **18** *a* stroke *or a* stroke of work (*usually used with a negative*) a small amount of work **19** off one's stroke performing or working less well than usual **20** on the stroke of punctually at ⊳ *vb* **21** (*tr*) to touch, brush, or caress lightly or gently **22** (*tr*) to mark a line or a stroke on or through **23** to act as the stroke of (a racing shell) **24** (*tr*) *sport* to strike (a ball) with a smooth swinging blow [Old English *strācian*; related to Middle Low German *strēken*; see STRIKE]

stroke play *n golf* a scoring by counting the number of strokes taken **b** (*as modifier*): *a strokeplay tournament*. Also called: **medal play**. See **match play, Stableford**

stroll (strəʊl) *vb* **1** to walk about in a leisurely manner **2** (*intr*) to wander from place to place ⊳ *n* **3** a leisurely walk [C17: probably from dialect German *strollen*, of obscure origin; compare German *Strolch* tramp]

stroller (ˈstrəʊlə) *n US, Canadian & Austral.* a usually collapsible chair-shaped carriage in which a small child may be wheeled. Also called (in Britain and certain other countries): **buggy, pushchair**

stroma (ˈstrəʊmə) *n, pl* -**mata** (-mətə) *biology* **1** the gel-like matrix of chloroplasts and certain cells **2** the fibrous connective tissue forming the matrix of the mammalian ovary and testis **3** a dense mass of hyphae that is produced by certain fungi and gives rise to spore-producing bodies [C19: via New Latin from Late Latin: a mattress, from Greek; related to Latin *sternere* to strew] > **stromatic** (strəʊˈmætɪk) *or* **stromatous** *adj*

Stromboli (ˈstrɒmbəlɪ) *n* an island in the Tyrrhenian Sea, in the Lipari Islands off the N coast of Sicily: famous for its active volcano, 927 m (3040 ft) high

Strombolian (strɒmˈbəʊlɪən) *adj* relating to or denoting a type of volcanic eruption characterized by repeated fountaining or jetting of fluid lava into the air

strong (strɒŋ) *adj* **stronger** (ˈstrɒŋɡə), **strongest** (ˈstrɒŋɡɪst) **1** involving or possessing physical or mental strength **2** solid or robust in construction; not easily broken or injured **3** having a resolute will or morally firm and incorruptible character **4** intense in quality; not faint or feeble: *a strong voice; a strong smell* **5** easily defensible; incontestable or formidable **6** concentrated; not weak or diluted **7 a** (*postpositive*) containing or having

a specified number: *a navy 40 000 strong* **b** (*in combination*): *a 40 000-strong navy* **8** having an unpleasantly powerful taste or smell **9** having an extreme or drastic effect: *strong discipline* **10** emphatic or immoderate: *strong language* **11** convincing, effective, or cogent **12** (of a colour) having a high degree of saturation or purity; being less saturated than a vivid colour but more so than a moderate colour; produced by a concentrated quantity of colouring agent **13** *grammar* **a** denoting or belonging to a class of verbs, in certain languages including the Germanic languages, whose conjugation shows vowel gradation, as *sing, sang, sung* **b** belonging to any part-of-speech class, in any of various languages, whose inflections follow the less regular of two possible patterns. See **weak** (sense 10) **14** (of a wind, current, etc) moving fast **15** (of a syllable) accented or stressed **16** (of an industry, market, currency, securities, etc) firm in price or characterized by firm or increasing prices **17** (of certain acids and bases) producing high concentrations of hydrogen or hydroxide ions in aqueous solution **18** have a strong stomach not to be prone to nausea ⊳ *adv* **19** *informal* in a strong way; effectively: *going strong* **20** come on strong to make a forceful or exaggerated impression [Old English *strang*; related to Old Norse *strangr*, Middle High German *strange*, Lettish *strans* courageous] > ˈstrongly *adv* > ˈstrongness *n*

strong-arm *informal* ⊳ *n* **1** (*modifier*) relating to or involving physical force or violence: *strong-arm tactics* ⊳ *vb* **2** (*tr*) to show violence towards

strongbox (ˈstrɒŋˌbɒks) *n* a specially designed box or safe in which valuables are locked for safety

strong breeze *n meteorol* a considerable wind of force six on the Beaufort scale, reaching speeds of 25–31 mph

strong drink *n* alcoholic drink

strong-eye dog *n NZ* a dog trained to control sheep by its gaze

strong gale *n meteorol* a strong wind of force nine on the Beaufort scale, reaching speeds of 47–54 mph: capable of causing minor structural damage to buildings

stronghold (ˈstrɒŋˌhəʊld) *n* **1** a defensible place; fortress **2** a major centre or area of predominance [C15: from STRONG + HOLD¹ (in the archaic sense: a fortified place)]

strong interaction *or* **strong force** *n physics* an interaction between elementary particles responsible for the forces between nucleons in the nucleus. It operates at distances less than about 10^{-15} metres, and is about a hundred times more powerful than the electromagnetic interaction. Also called: strong nuclear interaction, strong nuclear force. See **interaction** (sense 2)

strong-minded *adj* having strength of mind; firm, resolute, and determined > ˌstrong-ˈmindedly *adv* > ˌstrong-ˈmindedness *n*

strong point *n* something at which one excels; forte

strongroom (ˈstrɒŋˌruːm, -ˌrʊm) *n* a specially designed room in which valuables are locked for safety

strong-willed *adj* having strength of will

strontian (ˈstrɒntɪən) *n* another name for **strontium** *or* **strontium monoxide** [C18: named after a parish in Argyll, where it was discovered]

strontium (ˈstrɒntɪəm) *n* a soft silvery-white element of the alkaline earth group of metals, occurring chiefly in celestite and strontianite. Its compounds burn with a crimson flame and are used in fireworks. The radioisotope **strontium-90**, with a half-life of 28.1 years, is used in nuclear power sources and is a hazardous nuclear fall-out product. Symbol: Sr; atomic no: 38; atomic wt: 87.62; valency: 2; relative density: 2.54; melting pt: 769°C; boiling pt: 1384°C [C19: from New Latin, from STRONTIAN]

strontium unit *n* a unit expressing the concentration of strontium-90 in an organic medium, such as soil, milk, bone, etc, relative to the concentration of calcium in the same medium

strop (strɒp) *n* **1** a leather strap or an abrasive strip for sharpening razors **2** a rope or metal band around a block or deadeye for support **3** *chiefly Brit informal* a temper tantrum: *he threw a strop and stormed off* ⊳ *vb* **strops**, stropping, stropped 4 (tr) to sharpen (a razor, etc) on a strop [c14 (in nautical use: a strip of rope): via Middle Low German or Middle Dutch strop, ultimately from Latin stroppus, from Greek strophos cord; see STROPHE]

strophanthus (strəʊˈfænθəs) n 1 any small tree or shrub of the apocynaceous genus Strophanthus, of tropical Africa and Asia, having strap-shaped twisted petals. The seeds of certain species yield the drug strophanthin 2 the seeds of any of these plants [c19: New Latin, from Greek strophos twisted cord + anthos flower]

strophe (ˈstrəʊfɪ) n prosody (in ancient Greek drama) a the first of two movements made by a chorus during the performance of a choral ode b the first part of a choral ode sung during this movement ▷ See also antistrophe, epode [c17: from Greek: a verse, literally: a turning, from strephein to twist]

stroppy (ˈstrɒpɪ) adj -pier, -piest Brit informal angry or awkward [c20: changed and shortened from OBSTREPEROUS] > ˈstroppily adv > ˈstroppiness n

strove (strəʊv) vb the past tense of strive

strow (strəʊ) vb strows, strowing, strowed, strown or strowed an archaic variant of strew

struck (strʌk) vb 1 the past tense and past participle of strike ▷ adj 2 chiefly US & Canadian (of an industry, factory, etc) shut down or otherwise affected by a labour strike

structural (ˈstrʌktʃərəl) adj 1 of, relating to, or having structure or a structure 2 of, relating to, or forming part of the structure of a building 3 of or relating to the structure and deformation of rocks and other features of the earth's crust 4 of or relating to the structure of organisms; morphological 5 chem of, concerned with, caused by, or involving the arrangement of atoms in molecules > ˈstructurally adv

structural formula n a chemical formula showing the composition and structure of a molecule. The atoms are represented by symbols and the structure is indicated by showing the relative positions of the atoms in space and the bonds between them

structuralism (ˈstrʌktʃərəˌlɪzəm) n 1 an approach to anthropology and other social sciences and to literature that interprets and analyses its material in terms of oppositions, contrasts, and hierarchical structures, esp as they might reflect universal mental characteristics or organizing principles 2 an approach to linguistics that analyses and describes the structure of language, as distinguished from its comparative and historical aspects > ˈstructuralist n, adj

structural linguistics n (functioning as singular) a descriptive approach to a synchronic or diachronic analysis of language on the basis of its structure as reflected by irreducible units of phonological, morphological, and semantic features

structural unemployment n economics unemployment resulting from changes in the structure of an industry as a result of changes in either technology or taste

structure (ˈstrʌktʃə) n 1 a complex construction or entity 2 the arrangement and interrelationship of parts in a construction, such as a building 3 the manner of construction or organization 4 chem the arrangement of atoms in a molecule of a chemical compound 5 geology the way in which a mineral, rock, rock mass or stratum, etc, is made up of its component parts ▷ vb 6 (tr) to impart a structure to [c15: from Latin structūra, from struere to build]

strudel (ˈstruːdʲl; German ˈʃtruːdəl) n a thin sheet of filled dough rolled up and baked: apple strudel [German, from Middle High German strodel eddy, whirlpool, so called from the way the pastry is rolled]

struggle (ˈstrʌɡʲl) vb 1 (intr; usually foll by for or against; may take an infinitive) to exert strength, energy, and force; work or strive 2 (intr) to move about strenuously so as to escape from something confining 3 (intr) to contend, battle, or fight 4 (intr) to go or progress with difficulty ▷ n 5 a laboured or strenuous exertion or effort 6 a fight or battle 7 the act of struggling 8 the struggle S African the radical and armed opposition to apartheid, especially by the military wings of the ANC and the PAC [c14: of obscure origin] > ˈstruggling adj

strum (strʌm) vb strums, strumming, strummed 1 to

sound (the strings of a guitar, banjo, etc) with a downward or upward sweep of the thumb or of a plectrum 2 to play (chords, a tune, etc) in this way [c18: probably of imitative origin; see THRUM¹] > ˈstrummer n

struma (ˈstruːmə) n, pl -mae (-miː) 1 pathol an abnormal enlargement of the thyroid gland; goitre 2 botany a swelling, esp one at the base of a moss capsule 3 another word for scrofula [c16: from Latin: a scrofulous tumour, from struere to heap up] > ˈstrumatic (struːˈmætɪk) or strumous (ˈstruːməs) or Also called: strumose (ˈstruːməʊs) adj

Struma (ˈstruːmə) n a river in S Europe, rising in SW Bulgaria near Sofia and flowing generally southeast through Greece to the Aegean. Length: 362 km (225 miles). Greek names: Strimon, Strymon

strumpet (ˈstrʌmpɪt) n archaic a prostitute or promiscuous woman [c14: of unknown origin]

strung (strʌŋ) vb 1 a past tense and past participle of string ▷ adj 2 a (of a piano, etc) provided with strings, esp of a specified kind or in a specified manner b (in combination): gut-strung 3 highly strung very nervous or volatile in character

strung up adj (postpositive) informal tense or nervous

strut (strʌt) vb struts, strutting, strutted 1 (intr) to walk in a pompous manner; swagger 2 (tr) to support or provide with struts ▷ n 3 a structural member used mainly in compression, esp as part of a framework 4 an affected, proud, or stiff walk [c14 strouten (in the sense: swell, stand out; c16: to walk stiffly), from Old English strūtian to stand stiffly; related to Low German strutt stiff] > ˈstrutter n > ˈstrutting adj > ˈstruttingly adv

struthious (ˈstruːθɪəs) adj 1 (of birds) related to or resembling the ostrich 2 of, relating to, or designating all flightless (ratite) birds [c18: from Late Latin strūthiō, from Greek strouthiōn, from strouthos an ostrich]

Struve (ˈstruːvə) n Otto. 1897–1963, US astronomer, born in Russia, noted for his work in stellar spectroscopy and his discovery (1937) of interstellar hydrogen

strychnine (ˈstrɪkniːn) n a white crystalline very poisonous alkaloid, obtained from the drug nux vomica: formerly used in small quantities as a stimulant of the central nervous system and the appetite. Formula: $C_{21}H_{22}O_2N_2$ [c19: via French from New Latin Strychnos, from Greek strukhnos nightshade]

Strymon (ˈstraɪmən) n transliteration of the Greek name for the Struma

Stuart (ˈstjʊət) n 1 the royal house that ruled in Scotland from 1371 to 1714 and in England from 1603 to 1714. See also Stewart (sense 1) 2 Charles Edward, called the Young Pretender or Bonnie Prince Charlie. 1720–88, pretender to the British throne. He led the Jacobite Rebellion (1745–46) in an attempt to re-establish the Stuart succession 3 his father, James Francis Edward, called the Old Pretender. 1688–1766, pretender to the British throne; son of James II (James VII of Scotland) and his second wife, Mary of Modena. He made two unsuccessful attempts to realize his claim to the throne (1708; 1715) 4 Mary. See Mary, Queen of Scots

stub (stʌb) n 1 a short piece remaining after something has been cut, removed, etc: a cigar stub 2 the residual piece or section of a receipt, ticket, cheque, etc 3 US & Canadian also called (in Britain): counterfoil 4 any short projection or blunted end 5 the stump of a tree or plant ▷ vb stubs, stubbing, stubbed (tr) 6 to strike (one's toe, foot, etc) painfully against a hard surface 7 (usually foll by out) to put (out a cigarette or cigar) by pressing the end against a surface 8 to clear (land) of stubs 9 to dig up (the roots) of (a tree or bush) [Old English stubb; related to Old Norse stubbi, Middle Dutch stubbe, Greek stupos stem, stump]

stub axle n a short axle that carries one of the front steered wheels of a motor vehicle and is capable of limited angular movement about a kingpin

stubble (ˈstʌbʲl) n 1 a the stubs of stalks left in a field where a crop has been cut and harvested b (as modifier): a stubble field 2 any bristly growth or surface [c13: from Old French estuble, from Latin stupula, variant of stipula stalk, stem, stubble] > ˈstubbly adj > ˈstubbled adj

stubble-jumper n Canadian slang a prairie grain farmer

stubborn ('stʌbˀn) *adj* **1** refusing to comply, agree, or give in; obstinate **2** difficult to handle, treat, or overcome **3** persistent and dogged [C14 *stoborne*, of obscure origin] > **'stubbornness** *n*

Stubbs (stʌbz) *n* **George**. 1724–1806, English painter, noted esp for his pictures of horses

stubby ('stʌbɪ) *adj* -bier, -biest **1** short and broad; stumpy or thickset **2** bristling and stiff ▷ *n* **3** Also called: **stubbie** *Austral slang* a small bottle of beer > **'stubbily** *adv* > **'stubbiness** *n*

stucco ('stʌkəʊ) *n, pl* -coes *or* -cos **1** a weather-resistant mixture of dehydrated lime, powdered marble, and glue, used in decorative mouldings on buildings **2** any of various types of cement or plaster used for coating outside walls **3** Also called: **stuccowork** decorative work moulded in stucco ▷ *vb* -coes *or* -cos, -coing, -coed **4** (*tr*) to apply stucco to [C16: from Italian, of Germanic origin; compare Old High German *stukki* a fragment, crust, Old English *stycce*]

stuck (stʌk) *vb* **1** the past tense and past participle of **stick²** ▷ *adj* **2** *informal* baffled or nonplussed **3** (foll by *on*) *slang* keen (on) or infatuated (with) **4 get stuck in** *or* **get stuck into** *informal* **a** to perform (a task) with determination **b** to attack (a person) verbally or physically

stuck-up *adj informal* conceited, arrogant, or snobbish > **'stuck-'upness** *n*

stud¹ (stʌd) *n* **1** a large-headed nail or other projection protruding from a surface, usually as decoration **2** a type of fastener consisting of two discs at either end of a short shank, used to fasten shirtfronts, collars, etc **3** *building trades* a vertical member made of timber, steel, etc, that is used with others to construct the framework of a wall **4** the crossbar in the centre of a link of a heavy chain **5** one of a number of rounded projections on the sole of a boot or shoe to give better grip, as on a football boot ▷ *vb* studs, studding, studded (*tr*) **6** to provide, ornament, or make with studs **7** to dot or cover (with): *the park was studded with daisies* **8** *building trades* to provide or support (a wall, partition, etc) with studs [Old English *studu*; related to Old Norse *stoth* post, Middle High German *stud* post]

stud² (stʌd) *n* **1** a group of pedigree animals, esp horses, kept for breeding purposes **2** any male animal kept principally for breeding purposes, esp a stallion **3** a farm or stable where a stud is kept **4** the state or condition of being kept for breeding purposes: *at stud; put to stud* **5** (*modifier*) of or relating to such animals or the place where they are kept: *a stud farm; a stud horse* **6** *slang* a virile or sexually active man **7** short for **stud poker** [Old English *stōd*; related to Old Norse *stōth*, Old High German *stuot*]

studbook ('stʌd,bʊk) *n* a written record of the pedigree of a purebred stock, esp of racehorses

studding ('stʌdɪŋ) *n* **1** building studs collectively, esp as used to form a wall or partition **2** material that is used to form studs or serve as studs

studdingsail ('stʌdɪŋ,seɪl; *Nautical* 'stʌns°l) *n nautical* a light auxiliary sail set outboard on spars on either side of a square sail. Also called: **stunsail, stuns'l** [C16: *studding*, perhaps from Middle Low German, Middle Dutch *stōtinge*, from *stōten* to thrust; related to German *stossen*]

student ('stju:d°nt) *n* **1 a** a person following a course of study, as in a school, college, university, etc **b** (*as modifier*): *student teacher* **2** a person who makes a thorough study of a subject [C15: from Latin *studēns* diligent, from *studēre* to be zealous; see STUDY]

Student's t *n* a statistic often used to test the hypothesis that a random sample of normally distributed observations has a given mean, μ; given by *t* = (x̄−μ)·√n/s where x̄ is the mean of the sample, *s* is its standard deviation, and *n* is the size of the sample [after *Student*, the pen name of W. S. Gosset (1876–1937), English statistician and research scientist]

studenty ('stju:dəntɪ) *adj informal, sometimes derogatory* denoting or exhibiting the characteristics believed typical of an undergraduate student

studhorse ('stʌd,hɔːs) *n* another word for **stallion**

studied ('stʌdɪd) *adj* carefully practised, designed, or premeditated: *a studied reply* > **'studiedly** *adv* > **'studiedness** *n*

studio ('stju:dɪ,əʊ) *n, pl* -dios **1** a room in which an artist, photographer, or musician works **2** a room used to record television or radio programmes, make films, etc **3** (*plural*) the premises of a radio, television, or film company [C19: from Italian, literally: study, from Latin *studium* diligence]

studio couch *n* an upholstered couch, usually backless, convertible into a double bed

studio flat *n* a flat with one main room

studious ('stju:dɪəs) *adj* **1** given to study **2** of a serious, thoughtful, and hard-working character **3** showing deliberation, care, or precision [C14: from Latin *studiōsus* devoted to, from *studium* assiduity] > **'studiously** *adv* > **'studiousness** *n*

stud poker *n* a variety of poker in which the first card is dealt face down before each player and the next four are dealt face up (**five-card stud**) or in which the first two cards and the last card are dealt face down and the intervening four cards are dealt face up (**seven-card stud**), with bets made after each round [C19: from STUD² + POKER²]

study ('stʌdɪ) *vb* studies, studying, studied **1** to apply the mind to the learning or understanding of (a subject), esp by reading **2** (*tr*) to investigate or examine, as by observation, research, etc **3** (*tr*) to look at minutely; scrutinize **4** (*tr*) to give much careful or critical thought to **5** to take a course in (a subject), as at a college **6** (*tr*) to try to memorize: *to study a part for a play* **7** (*intr*) to meditate or contemplate; reflect ▷ *n, pl* studies **8 a** the act or process of studying **b** (*as modifier*): *study group* **9** a room used for studying, reading, writing, etc **10** (*often plural*) work relating to a particular discipline: *environmental studies* **11** an investigation and analysis of a subject, situation, etc **12** a product of studying, such as a written paper or book **13** a drawing, sculpture, etc, executed for practice or in preparation for another work **14** a musical composition intended to develop one aspect of performing technique **15 in a brown study** in a reverie or daydream [C13: from Old French *estudie*, from Latin *studium* zeal, inclination, from *studēre* to be diligent]

stuff (stʌf) *vb* (*mainly tr*) **1** to pack or fill completely; cram **2** (*intr*) to eat large quantities **3** to force, shove, or squeeze: *to stuff money into a pocket* **4** to fill (food such as poultry or tomatoes) with a stuffing **5** to fill (an animal's skin) with material so as to restore the shape of the live animal **6** *slang* to have sexual intercourse with (a woman) **7** *US & Canadian* to fill (a ballot box) with a large number of fraudulent votes **8** *slang* to ruin, frustrate, or defeat ▷ *n* **9** the raw material or fabric of something **10** woollen cloth or fabric **11** any general or unspecified substance or accumulation of objects **12** stupid or worthless actions, speech, ideas, etc **13** subject matter, skill, etc: *he knows his stuff* **14** a slang word for **money 15** *slang* a drug, esp cannabis **16 do one's stuff** *informal* to do what is expected of one **17 that's the stuff** that is what is needed **18** *Brit slang* a girl or woman considered sexually (esp in the phrase **bit of stuff**) [C14: from Old French *estoffe*, from *estoffer* to furnish, provide, of Germanic origin; related to Middle High German *stopfen* to cram full] > **'stuffer** *n*

stuffed (stʌft) *adj* **1** filled with something, esp (of poultry and other food) filled with stuffing **2** (foll by *up*) (of the nasal passages) blocked with mucus **3 get stuffed!** *Brit slang* an exclamation of contemptuous anger or annoyance, esp against another person

stuffed shirt *n informal* a pompous or formal person

stuff gown *n Brit* a woollen gown worn by a barrister who has not taken silk

stuffing ('stʌfɪŋ) *n* **1** the material with which something is stuffed **2** a mixture of chopped and seasoned ingredients with which poultry, meat, etc, is stuffed before cooking **3 knock the stuffing out of someone** to upset or dishearten someone completely

stuffing box *n* a small chamber in which an annular packing is compressed around a reciprocating or rotating rod or shaft to form a seal

stuffy ('stʌfɪ) *adj* stuffier, stuffiest **1** lacking fresh air **2** excessively dull, staid, or conventional **3** (of the nasal passages) blocked with mucus > 'stuffily *adv* > 'stuffiness *n*

stultify ('stʌltɪˌfaɪ) *vb* -fies, -fying, -fied (*tr*) **1** to make useless, futile, or ineffectual, esp by routine **2** to cause to appear absurd or inconsistent [c18: from Latin *stultus* stupid + *facere* to make] > ˌstultifiˈcation *n* > 'stultiˌfier *n*

stum (stʌm) (in wine-making) *n* **1** a less common word for **must²** **2** partly fermented wine added to fermented wine as a preservative ⊳ *vb* stums, stumming, stummed **3** to preserve (wine) by adding stum [c17: from Dutch *stom* dumb; related to German *stumm*]

stumble ('stʌmbᵊl) *vb* (*intr*) **1** to trip or fall while walking or running **2** to walk in an awkward, unsteady, or unsure way **3** to make mistakes or hesitate in speech or actions **4** (foll by *across* or *upon*) to come (across) by accident ⊳ *n* **5** a false step, trip, or blunder **6** the act of stumbling [c14: related to Norwegian *stumla*, Danish dialect *stumle*; see STAMMER] > 'stumbler *n* > 'stumbling *adj* > 'stumblingly *adv*

stumbling block *n* any impediment or obstacle

stumer ('stjuːmə) *n* **1** *slang* a forgery or cheat **2** *Irish dialect* a poor bargain **3** *Scot* a stupid person **4** come a stumer *Austral slang* to crash financially [of unknown origin]

stump (stʌmp) *n* **1** the base part of a tree trunk left standing after the tree has been felled or has fallen **2** the part of something, such as a tooth, limb, or blade, that remains after a larger part has been removed **3** *informal, facetious* (*often plural*) a leg **4** *cricket* any of three upright wooden sticks that, with two bails laid across them, form a wicket (the **stumps**) **5** Also called: tortillon a short sharply-pointed stick of cork or rolled paper or leather, used in drawing and shading **6** a heavy tread or the sound of heavy footsteps **7** a platform used by an orator when addressing a meeting ⊳ *vb* **8** (*tr*) to stop, confuse, or puzzle **9** (*intr*) to plod or trudge heavily **10** (*tr*) *cricket* (of a fielder, esp a wicketkeeper) to dismiss (a batsman) by breaking his wicket with the ball or with the ball in the hand while he is out of his crease **11** *chiefly US & Canadian* to campaign or canvass (an area), esp by political speech-making [c14: from Middle Low German *stump*; related to Dutch *stomp*, German *Stumpf*; see STAMP] > 'stumper *n*

stump up *vb* (*adverb*) *Brit informal* to give (the money required)

stumpy ('stʌmpɪ) *adj* stumpier, stumpiest **1** short and thickset like a stump; stubby **2** abounding in or full of stumps > 'stumpiness *n*

stun (stʌn) *vb* stuns, stunning, stunned (*tr*) **1** to render unconscious, as by a heavy blow or fall **2** to shock or overwhelm **3** to surprise or astound ⊳ *n* **4** the state or effect of being stunned [c13 *stunen*, from Old French *estoner* to daze, stupefy, from Vulgar Latin *extonāre* (unattested), from Latin EX-¹ + *tonāre* to thunder]

stung (stʌŋ) *vb* the past tense and past participle of sting

stunk (stʌŋk) *vb* a past tense and past participle of stink

stunner ('stʌnə) *n informal* a person or thing of great beauty, quality, size, etc

stunning ('stʌnɪŋ) *adj informal* very attractive, impressive, astonishing, etc > 'stunningly *adv*

stunsail or **stuns'l** ('stʌnsᵊl) *n* another word for studdingsail

stunt¹ (stʌnt) *vb* **1** (*tr*) to prevent or impede (the growth or development) of (a plant, animal, etc) ⊳ *n* **2** the act or an instance of stunting **3** a person, animal, or plant that has been stunted [c17 (as *vb*: to check the growth of): perhaps from c15 *stont* of short duration, from Old English *stunt* simple, foolish; sense probably influenced by Old Norse *stuttr* short in stature, dwarfed] > 'stunted *adj* > 'stuntedness *n*

stunt² (stʌnt) *n* **1** an acrobatic, dangerous, or spectacular action **2** an acrobatic or dangerous piece of action in a film or television programme **3** anything spectacular or unusual done to gain publicity ⊳ *vb* **4** (*intr*) to perform a stunt or stunts [c19: US student slang, of unknown origin]

stupa ('stuːpə) *n* a domed edifice housing Buddhist or Jain relics [c19: from Sanskrit: dome]

stupe (stjuːp) *n med* a hot damp cloth, usually sprinkled with an irritant, applied to the body to relieve pain by counterirritation [c14: from Latin *stuppa* flax, from Greek *stuppē*]

stupefacient (ˌstjuːpɪˈfeɪʃɪənt) *n* **1** a drug that causes stupor ⊳ *adj* **2** of, relating to, or designating this type of drug [c17: from Latin *stupefacere* to make senseless, from *stupēre* to be stunned + *facere* to make]

stupefaction (ˌstjuːpɪˈfækʃən) *n* **1** astonishment **2** the act of stupefying or the state of being stupefied

stupefy ('stjuːpɪˌfaɪ) *vb* -fies, -fying, -fied (*tr*) **1** to render insensitive or lethargic **2** to confuse or astound [c16: from Old French *stupefier*, from Latin *stupefacere*; see STUPEFACIENT] > 'stupeˌfying *adj*

stupendous (stjuːˈpɛndəs) *adj* astounding, wonderful, huge, etc [c17: from Latin *stupēre* to be amazed] > stuˈpendously *adv* > stuˈpendousness *n*

stupid ('stjuːpɪd) *adj* **1** lacking in common sense, perception, or normal intelligence **2** (*usually postpositive*) stunned, dazed, or stupefied: *stupid from lack of sleep* **3** having dull mental responses; slow-witted **4** trivial, silly, or frivolous ⊳ *n* **5** *informal* a stupid person [c16: from French *stupide*, from Latin *stupidus* silly, from *stupēre* to be amazed] > 'stupidness *n* > stu'pidity *n*

stupor ('stjuːpə) *n* **1** a state of unconsciousness **2** mental dullness; torpor [c17: from Latin, from *stupēre* to be aghast] > 'stuporous *adj*

sturdy ('stɜːdɪ) *adj* -dier, -diest **1** healthy, strong, and vigorous **2** strongly built; stalwart [c13 (in the sense: rash, harsh): from Old French *estordi* dazed, from *estordir* to stun, perhaps ultimately related to Latin *turdus* a thrush (taken as representing drunkenness)] > 'sturdily *adv* > 'sturdiness *n*

sturgeon ('stɜːdʒən) *n* any primitive bony fish of the family *Acipenseridae*, of temperate waters of the N hemisphere, having an elongated snout and rows of spines along the body: valued as a source of caviar and isinglass [c13: from Old French *estourgeon*, of Germanic origin; related to Old English *styria*, Old High German *sturio*]

Sturt (stɜːt) *n* **Charles.** 1795–1869, English explorer, who led three expeditions (1828–29; 1829; 1844–45) into the Australian interior, discovering the Darling River (1828)

Sturt's desert pea *n Austral* the desert pea [named after Charles Sturt (1795–1869), English explorer of the Australian interior]

stutter ('stʌtə) *vb* **1** to speak (a word, phrase, etc) with recurring repetition of consonants, esp initial ones **2** to make (an abrupt sound) repeatedly: *the gun stuttered* ⊳ *n* **3** the act or habit of stuttering **4** a stuttering sound [c16: related to Middle Low German *stötern*, Old High German *stōzan* to push against, Latin *tundere* to beat] > 'stutterer *n* > 'stuttering *n*, *adj* > 'stutteringly *adv*

Stuttgart (*German* 'ʃtʊtɡart) *n* an industrial city in W Germany, capital of Baden-Württemberg state, on the River Neckar: developed around a stud farm (*Stuotgarten*) of the Counts of Württemberg. Pop: 589 161 (2003 est)

Stuyvesant ('staɪvɪsᵊnt) *n* **Peter.** ?1610–72, Dutch colonial administrator of New Netherland (later New York) (1646–64)

sty (staɪ) *n*, *pl* sties **1** a pen in which pigs are housed and fed **2** any filthy or corrupt place ⊳ *vb* sties, stying, stied **3** to enclose or be enclosed in a sty [Old English *stig*; related to Old Norse *stia* pen, fold, Old High German *stīga*, Middle Dutch *stije*]

stye or **sty** (staɪ) *n*, *pl* styes or sties inflammation of a sebaceous gland of the eyelid, usually caused by bacteria [c15 *styanye* (mistakenly taken as *sty on eye*), from Old English *stīgend* rising, hence swelling, stye + *ye* eye]

Stygian ('stɪdʒɪən) *adj* **1** of or relating to the river Styx **2** *chiefly literary* dark, gloomy, or hellish [c16: from Latin *Stygius*, from Greek *Stugios*, from *Stux* STYX; related to *stugein* to hate]

style (staɪl) *n* **1** a form of appearance, design, or production; type or make **2** the way in which something is done: *good or bad style* **3** the manner in which something is expressed or performed, considered as separate from its intrinsic content, meaning, etc **4** a distinctive, formal, or characteristic manner of expression in words, music, painting, etc **5** elegance or refinement of manners, dress, etc **6** prevailing fashion in dress, looks, etc **7** a fashionable or ostentatious mode of existence: *to live in style* **8** the particular mode of orthography, punctuation, design, etc, followed in a book, journal, etc, or in a printing or publishing house **9** *chiefly Brit* the distinguishing title or form of address of a person or firm **10** *botany* the stalk of a carpel, bearing the stigma **11** a method of expressing or calculating dates. See **Old Style, New Style 12** another word for **stylus** (sense 1) **13** the arm of a sundial ▷ *vb* (*mainly tr*) **14** to design, shape, or tailor: *to style hair* **15** to adapt or make suitable (for) **16** to make consistent or correct according to a printing or publishing style **17** to name or call; designate: *to style a man a fool* [c13: from Latin *stylus, stilus* writing implement, hence characteristics of the writing, style] ▷'stylar *adj* ▷'styler *n*

stylebook ('staɪl,bʊk) *n* a book containing rules and examples of punctuation, typography, etc, for the use of writers, editors, and printers

stylet ('staɪlɪt) *n surgery* **a** a wire for insertion into a flexible cannula or catheter to maintain its rigidity or patency during passage **b** a slender probe [c17: from French *stilet*, from Old Italian STILETTO; influenced in spelling by Latin *stylus* STYLE]

styling mousse *n hairdressing* a light foamy substance applied to the hair before styling in order to retain the shape of the style

stylish ('staɪlɪʃ) *adj* having style; smart; fashionable ▷'stylishly *adv* ▷'stylishness *n*

stylist ('staɪlɪst) *n* **1** a person who performs, writes, or acts with attention to style **2** a designer of clothes, décor, etc **3** a hairdresser who styles hair

stylistic (staɪ'lɪstɪk) *adj* of or relating to style, esp artistic or literary style ▷ sty'listically *adv*

stylite ('staɪlaɪt) *n Christianity* one of a class of recluses who in ancient times lived on the top of high pillars [c17: from Late Greek *stulitēs*, from Greek *stulos* a pillar] ▷ stylitic (staɪ'lɪtɪk) *adj*

stylize or **stylise** ('staɪlaɪz) *vb* (*tr*) to give a conventional or established stylistic form to ▷ ,styli'zation or ,styli'sation *n*

stylo- or before a vowel **styl-** *combining form* **1** (in biology) a style **2** indicating a column or point: *stylobate; stylograph* [from Greek *stulos* column]

stylobate ('staɪlə,beɪt) *n* a continuous horizontal course of masonry that supports a colonnade [c17: from Latin *stylobatēs*, from Greek *stulos* pillar + *-batēs*, from *bainein* to tread, walk]

stylograph ('staɪlə,græf, -,grɑːf) *n* a fountain pen having a fine hollow tube as the writing point instead of a nib [c19: from STYL(US) + -GRAPH]

styloid ('staɪlɔɪd) *adj* **1** resembling a stylus **2** *anatomy* of or relating to a projecting process of the temporal bone [c18: from New Latin *styloides*, from Greek *stuloeidēs* like a STYLUS; influenced also by Greek *stulos* pillar]

stylops ('staɪlɒps) *n, pl* **-lopes** (-lə,piːz) any insect of the order *Strepsiptera*, including the genus *Stylops*, living as a parasite in other insects, esp bees and wasps: the females remain in the body of the host but the males move between hosts [c19: New Latin, from Greek, from *stulos* a pillar + *ōps* an eye, from the fact that the male insect has stalked compound eyes]

stylus ('staɪləs) *n, pl* **-li** (-laɪ) or **-luses 1** Also called: **style** a pointed instrument for engraving, drawing, or writing **2** a tool used in ancient times for writing on wax tablets, which was pointed at one end and blunt at the other for erasing mistakes **3** a device attached to the cartridge in the pick-up arm of a record player that rests in the groove in the record, transmitting the vibrations to the sensing device in the cartridge. It consists of or is tipped with a hard material, such as diamond or sapphire [c18: from Latin, variant of *stilus* writing implement; see STYLE]

stymie or **stymy** ('staɪmɪ) *vb* **-mies, -mieing, -mied** or **-mies, -mying, -mied** (*tr; often passive*) **1** to hinder or thwart **2** *golf* to impede with a stymie ▷ *n, pl* **-mies 3** *golf*

(formerly) a situation on the green in which an opponent's ball is blocking the line between the hole and the ball about to be played: an obstructing ball may now be lifted and replaced by a marker **4** a situation of obstruction [c19: of uncertain origin]

stypsis ('stɪpsɪs) *n* the action, application, or use of a styptic [c19: via New Latin from Late Latin: astringency, from Greek *stupsis*, from *stuphein* to contract]

styptic ('stɪptɪk) *adj* **1** contracting the blood vessels or tissues ▷ *n* **2** a styptic drug [c14: via Late Latin, from Greek *stuptikos* capable of contracting; see STYPSIS]

styrax ('staɪræks) *n* any tropical or subtropical tree of the genus *Styrax*, which includes the storaxes [c16: via Latin from Greek *sturax*]

subvene (səb'viːn) *vb* (*intr*) *rare* to happen in such a way as to be of assistance, esp in preventing something [c18: from Latin *subvenīre*, from *venīre* to come]

styrene ('staɪriːn) *n* a colourless oily volatile flammable water-insoluble liquid made from ethylene and benzene. It is an unsaturated compound and readily polymerizes: used in making synthetic plastics and rubbers. Formula: $C_6H_5CH:CH_2$. See also **polystyrene** [c20: from STYR(AX) + -ENE]

Styria ('stɪərɪə) *n* a mountainous state of SE Austria: rich mineral resources. Capital: Graz. Pop: 1 190 574 (2003 est). Area: 16 384 sq km (6326 sq miles). German name: Steiermark

Styrofoam ('staɪrə,fəʊm) *n trademark* (*sometimes not capital*) a light, expanded polystyrene plastic [c20: from POLYSTYRENE + FOAM]

Styx (stɪks) *n Greek myth* a river in Hades across which Charon ferried the souls of the dead [from Greek *Stux*; related to *stugein* to hate]

suable ('sjuːəbᵊl) *adj* liable to be sued in a court [c17: from SUE + -ABLE] ▷ ,sua'bility *n*

Suakin ('suːɑːkɪn) *n* a port in the NE Sudan, on the Red Sea: formerly the chief port of the African Red Sea; now obstructed by a coral reef. Pop: reliable recent estimates are not available

Suárez (*Spanish* 'swareθ) *n* **Francisco de.** 1548–1617, Spanish theologian, considered the leading scholastic philosopher after Aquinas and the principal Jesuit theologian. His works include *Disputationes Metaphysicae* (1597) and *De Legibus* (1612)

suasion ('sweɪʒən) *n* a rare word for **persuasion** [c14: from Latin *suāsiō*, from *suādēre* to PERSUADE] ▷'suasive *adj*

suave (swɑːv) *adj* (*esp of a man*) displaying smoothness and sophistication in manner or attitude; urbane [c16: from Latin *suāvis* sweet] ▷'suavely *adv* ▷ suavity ('swɑːvɪtɪ) or'suaveness *n*

sub (sʌb) *n* **1** short for several words beginning with *sub-*. See **subeditor, submarine, subordinate, subscription, substitute 2** *Brit informal* an advance payment of wages or salary. Formal term: **subsistence allowance** ▷ *vb* **subs, subbing, subbed 3** (*intr*) to serve as a substitute **4** (*intr*) *informal* to act as a substitute (for) **5** *Brit informal* to grant or receive (an advance payment of wages or salary) **6** (*tr*) *informal* short for **subedit**

sub. *abbreviation* **1** subeditor **2** subito (in music) **3** subscription **4** substitute

sub- *prefix* **1** situated under or beneath: *subterranean* **2** secondary in rank; subordinate: *subeditor* **3** falling short of; less than or imperfectly: *subarctic; subhuman* **4** forming a subdivision or subordinate part of a whole: *subcommittee* **5** (in chemistry) **a** indicating that a compound contains a relatively small proportion of a specified element: *suboxide* **b** indicating that a salt is basic salt: *subacetate* [from Latin *sub*]

subacid (sʌb'æsɪd) *adj* (*esp of some fruits*) moderately acid or sour ▷ subacidity (,sʌbə'sɪdɪtɪ) or'sub'acidness *n*

subadar or **subahdar** ('suːbə,dɑː) *n* (formerly) the chief native officer of a company of Indian soldiers in the British service [c17: via Urdu from Persian, from *sūba* province + *-dār* holding]

subalpine (sʌb'ælpaɪn) *adj* **1** situated in or relating to the regions at the foot of mountains **2** (*of plants*) growing below the treeline in mountainous regions

subaltern ('sʌbᵊltən) *n* **1** a commissioned officer below the rank of captain in certain armies, esp the British

2 *logic* the relation of one proposition to another when the first is implied by the second, esp the relation of a particular to a universal proposition ▷ *adj* **3** of inferior position or rank [c16: from Late Latin *subalternus*, from Latin SUB- + *alternus* alternate, from *alter* the other]

subantarctic (ˌsʌbæntˈɑːktɪk) *adj* of or relating to latitudes immediately north of the Antarctic Circle

subaqua (ˌsʌbˈækwə) *adj* of or relating to underwater sport: *subaqua swimming; a subaqua club* [from SUB- + Latin *aqua* water]

subaqueous (sʌbˈeɪkwɪəs, -ˈækwɪ-) *adj* occurring, appearing, formed, or used under water

subarctic (sʌbˈɑːktɪk) *adj* of or relating to latitudes immediately south of the Arctic Circle

subatomic (ˌsʌbəˈtɒmɪk) *adj* **1** of, relating to, or being a particle making up an atom or a process occurring within atoms **2** having dimensions smaller than atomic dimensions

subbasement (ˈsʌbˌbeɪsmənt) *n* an underground storey of a building beneath the main basement

subclass (ˈsʌbˌklɑːs) *n* **1** a principal subdivision of a class **2** *biology* a taxonomic group that is a subdivision of a class **3** *maths* another name for **subset**

subclavian (sʌbˈkleɪvɪən) *adj anatomy* (of an artery, vein, area, etc) situated below the clavicle [c17: from New Latin *subclāvius*, from SUB- + *clavis* key]

subclinical (sʌbˈklɪnɪkᵊl) *adj med* of or relating to the stage in the course of a disease before the symptoms are first noted ▷ **sub'clinically** *adv*

subconscious (sʌbˈkɒnʃəs) *adj* **1** acting or existing without one's awareness ▷ *n* **2** *psychoanal* that part of the mind which is on the fringe of consciousness and contains material of which it is possible to become aware by redirecting attention ▷ **sub'consciously** *adv* ▷ **sub'consciousness** *n*

subcontinent (sʌbˈkɒntɪnənt) *n* a large land mass that is a distinct part of a continent, such as India is of Asia ▷ **subcontinental** (ˌsʌbkɒntɪˈnɛntᵊl) *adj*

subcontract *n* (sʌbˈkɒntrækt) **1** a subordinate contract under which the supply of materials, services, or labour is let out to someone other than a party to the main contract ▷ *vb* (ˌsʌbkənˈtrækt) **2** (*intr*; often foll by *for*) to enter into or make a subcontract **3** (*tr*) to let out (work) on a subcontract ▷ **subcontractor** (ˌsʌbkənˈtræktə) *n*

subcontrary (sʌbˈkɒntrərɪ) *logic* ▷ *adj* **1** (of a pair of propositions) related such that they cannot both be false at once, although they may be true together ▷ *n, pl* -ries **2** a statement that cannot be false when a given statement is false

subcritical (sʌbˈkrɪtɪkᵊl) *adj physics* (of a nuclear reaction, power station, etc) having or involving a chain reaction that is not self-sustaining; not yet critical

subculture (ˈsʌbˌkʌltʃə) *n* a subdivision of a national culture or an enclave within it with a distinct integrated network of behaviour, beliefs, and attitudes ▷ **sub'cultural** *adj*

subcutaneous (ˌsʌbkjuːˈteɪnɪəs) *adj med* situated, used, or introduced beneath the skin [c17: from Late Latin *subcutāneus*, from SUB- + Latin *cutis* skin + -EOUS] ▷ **ˌsubcu'taneously** *adv*

subdeacon (ˌsʌbˈdiːkən) *n chiefly RC Church* **1** a cleric who assists at High Mass **2** (formerly) a person ordained to the lowest of the major orders

subdivide (ˌsʌbdɪˈvaɪd, ˈsʌbdɪˌvaɪd) *vb* to divide (something) resulting from an earlier division ▷ **sub'divider** *n* ▷ **subdivision** (ˈsʌbdɪˌvɪʒən) *n*

subdominant (sʌbˈdɒmɪnənt) *music* ▷ *n* **1** the fourth degree of a major or minor scale **2** a key or chord based on this ▷ *adj* **3** of or relating to the subdominant

subdue (səbˈdjuː) *vb* -dues, -duing, -dued (*tr*) **1** to establish ascendancy over by force **2** to overcome and bring under control, as by intimidation or persuasion **3** to hold in check or repress (feelings, emotions, etc) **4** to render less intense or less conspicuous [c14 *sobdue*, from Old French *soduire* to mislead, from Latin *subdūcere* to remove; English sense influenced by Latin *subdere* to subject] ▷ **sub'duable** *adj* ▷ **sub'dual** *n*

subdued (səbˈdjuːd) *adj* **1** cowed, passive, or shy **2** gentle or quiet: *a subdued whisper* **3** (of colours, etc) not harsh or bright: *a subdued shade of blue*

subdural (sʌbˈdjʊərəl) *adj anatomy* between the dura mater and the arachnoid: *subdural haematoma*

subedit (sʌbˈɛdɪt) *vb* to edit and correct (written or printed material)

subeditor (sʌbˈɛdɪtə) *n* a person who checks and edits copy, esp on a newspaper

subequatorial (sʌbˌɛkwəˈtɔːrɪəl) *adj* situated in or characteristic of regions immediately north or south of equatorial regions

suberose (ˈsjuːbəˌrəʊs), **subereous** (sjuːˈbɛrɪəs) *or* **suberic** (sjuːˈbɛrɪk) *adj botany* relating to, resembling, or consisting of cork; corky

subfamily (ˈsʌbˌfæmɪlɪ) *n, pl* -lies **1** *biology* a taxonomic group that is a subdivision of a family **2** any analogous subdivision, as of a family of languages

subfusc (ˈsʌbfʌsk) *adj* **1** devoid of brightness or appeal; drab, dull, or dark ▷ *n* **2** (at Oxford University) formal academic dress [c18: from Latin *subfuscus* dusky, from *fuscus* dark]

subgenus (sʌbˈdʒiːnəs, -ˈdʒɛn-, ˈsʌbˌdʒiːnəs, -ˌdʒɛn-) *n, pl* -genera (-ˈdʒɛnərə) *or* -genuses *biology* a taxonomic group that is a subdivision of a genus but of higher rank than a species ▷ **subgeneric** (ˌsʌbdʒəˈnɛrɪk) *adj*

subheading (ˈsʌbˌhedɪŋ) *or* **subhead** *n* **1** the heading or title of a subdivision or subsection of a printed work **2** a division subordinate to a main heading or title

subhuman (sʌbˈhjuːmən) *adj* **1** of, relating to, or designating animals that are below man (*Homo sapiens*) in evolutionary development **2** less than human

subindex (sʌbˈɪndɛks) *n, pl* -dices (-dɪˌsiːz) *or* -dexes another word for **subscript** (sense 2)

subitize *or* **subitise** (ˈsʌbɪˌtaɪz) *vb psychol* to perceive the number of (a group of items) at a glance and without counting: *the maximum number of items that can be subitized is about five* [c20: from Latin *subitus* sudden + -IZE]

subito (ˈsuːbɪˌtəʊ) *adv music* (preceding or following a dynamic marking, etc) suddenly; immediately [c18: via Italian from Latin: suddenly, from *subitus* sudden, from *subīre* to approach, from SUB- (indicating stealth) + *īre* to go]

subj. *abbreviation* **1** subject **2** subjective(ly) **3** subjunctive

subjacent (sʌbˈdʒeɪsᵊnt) *adj* **1** forming a foundation; underlying **2** lower than though not directly below [c16: from Latin *subjacēre* to lie close, adjoin, be under, from SUB- + *jacēre* to lie] ▷ **sub'jacency** *n* ▷ **sub'jacently** *adv*

subject *n* (ˈsʌbdʒɪkt) **1** the predominant theme or topic, as of a book, discussion, etc **2** any branch of learning considered as a course of study **3** *grammar, logic* a word, phrase, or formal expression about which something is predicated or stated in a sentence; for example, *the cat* in the sentence *The cat catches mice* **4** a person or thing that undergoes experiment, analysis, treatment, etc **5** a person who lives under the rule of a monarch, government, etc **6** an object, figure, scene, etc, as selected by an artist or photographer for representation **7** *philosophy* **a** that which thinks or feels as opposed to the object of thinking and feeling; the self or the mind **b** a substance as opposed to its attributes **8** Also called: theme *music* a melodic or thematic phrase used as the principal motif of a fugue, the basis from which the musical material is derived in a sonata-form movement, or the recurrent figure in a rondo **9** *logic* the term of a categorial statement of which something is predicated **10** an originating motive **11** change the subject to select a new topic of conversation ▷ *adj* (ˈsʌbdʒɪkt) (*usually postpositive* and foll by *to*) **12** being under the power or sovereignty of a ruler, government, etc: *subject peoples* **13** showing a tendency (towards): *a child subject to indiscipline* **14** exposed or vulnerable: *subject to ribaldry* **15** conditional upon: *the results are subject to correction* ▷ *adv* **16** subject to (*preposition*) under the condition that: *we accept, subject to her agreement* ▷ *vb* (səbˈdʒɛkt) (*tr*) **17** (foll by *to*) to cause to undergo the application (of): *they subjected him to torture* **18** (*often passive*; foll by *to*) to expose or render vulnerable or liable (to some experience): *he was subjected to great danger* **19** (foll by *to*) to bring under the control or authority (of): *to subject a soldier to discipline* **20** *now rare* to subdue or subjugate **21** *rare* to present for consideration;

submit [c14: from Latin *subjectus* brought under, from *subicere* to place under, from sub- + *jacere* to throw] > sub'jectable *adj* > sub,jecta'bility *n*

subjective (səb'dʒɛktɪv) *adj* 1 belonging to, proceeding from, or relating to the mind of the thinking subject and not the nature of the object being considered 2 of, relating to, or emanating from a person's emotions, prejudices, etc 3 relating to the inherent nature of a person or thing; essential 4 existing only as perceived and not as a thing in itself 5 *med* (of a symptom, condition, etc) experienced only by the patient and incapable of being recognized or studied by anyone else 6 *grammar* denoting a case of nouns and pronouns, esp in languages having only two cases, that identifies the subject of a finite verb and (in formal use in English) is selected for predicate complements, as in *It is I* ▷ *n* 7 *grammar* a the subjective case b a subjective word or speech element ▷ See **objective** > sub'jectively *adv* > ,subjec'tivity, sub'jectiveness *n*

subjectivism (səb'dʒɛktɪ,vɪzəm) *n* the meta-ethical doctrine that there are no absolute moral values but that these are variable in the same way as taste is > sub'jectivist *n*

subjoin (sʌb'dʒɔɪn) *vb* (*tr*) to add or attach at the end of something spoken, written, etc [c16: from French *subjoindre*, from Latin *subjungere* to add to, from *sub-* in addition + *jungere* to JOIN] > sub'joinder *n*

sub judice ('dʒuː,dɪsɪ) *adj* (*usually postpositive*) before a court of law or a judge; under judicial consideration [Latin]

subjugate ('sʌbdʒʊ,geɪt) *vb* (*tr*) 1 to bring into subjection 2 to make subservient or submissive [c15: from Late Latin *subjugāre* to subdue, from Latin sub- + *jugum* yoke] > subjugable ('sʌbdʒəgəbəl) *adj* > ,subju'gation *n* > 'subju,gator *n*

subjunctive (səb'dʒʌŋktɪv) *adj* 1 *grammar* denoting a mood of verbs used when the content of the clause is being doubted, supposed, feared true, etc, rather than being asserted. The rules for its use and the range of meanings it may possess vary considerably from language to language. In the following sentence, *were* is in the subjunctive: *I'd think very seriously about that if I were you*. See **indicative** ▷ *n* 2 *grammar* a the subjunctive mood b a verb in this mood [c16: via Late Latin *subjunctīvus*, from Latin *subjungere* to SUBJOIN] > sub'junctively *adv*

sublease *n* ('sʌb,liːs) 1 a lease of property made by a person who is himself a lessee or tenant of that property ▷ *vb* (sʌb'liːs) 2 to grant a sublease of (property); sublet 3 (*tr*) to take, obtain, or hold by sublease > sublessee (,sʌblɛ'siː) *n* > sublessor (,sʌblɛ'sɔː) *n*

sublet (sʌb'lɛt) *vb* -lets, -letting, -let 1 to grant a sublease of (property) 2 to let out (work, etc) under a subcontract

sublieutenant (,sʌblə'tɛnənt) *n* the most junior commissioned officer in the Royal Navy and certain other navies > ,sublieu'tenancy *n*

sublimate ('sʌblɪ,meɪt) *vb* 1 *psychol* to direct the energy of (a primitive impulse, esp a sexual one) into activities that are considered to be socially more acceptable 2 (*tr*) to make purer; refine ▷ *n* 3 *chem* the material obtained when a substance is sublimed [c16: from Latin *sublīmāre* to elevate, from *sublīmis* lofty; see SUBLIME] > ,subli'mation *n*

sublime (sə'blaɪm) *adj* 1 of high moral, aesthetic, intellectual, or spiritual value; noble; exalted 2 inspiring deep veneration, awe, or uplifting emotion because of its beauty, nobility, grandeur, or immensity 3 unparalleled; supreme 4 *poetic* of proud bearing or aspect 5 *archaic* raised up the sublime *n* 6 something that is sublime 7 the ultimate degree or perfect example: *the sublime of folly* ▷ *vb* 8 (*tr*) to make higher or purer 9 to change or cause to change directly from a solid to a vapour or gas without first melting 10 to undergo or cause to undergo this process followed by a reverse change directly from a vapour to a solid: *to sublime iodine onto glass* [c14: from Latin *sublīmis* lofty, perhaps from *sub-* up to + *līmen* lintel] > sub'limely *adv* > sublimity (sə'blɪmɪtɪ) *n*

subliminal (sʌb'lɪmɪnəl) *adj* 1 resulting from processes of which the individual is not aware 2 (of stimuli) less than the minimum intensity or duration required to elicit a response [c19: from Latin sub- below + *līmen* threshold] > sub'liminally *adv*

subliminal advertising *n* a form of advertising on film or television that employs subliminal images to influence the viewer unconsciously

sublingual (sʌb'lɪŋgwəl) *adj* *anatomy* situated beneath the tongue

sublunary (sʌb'luːnərɪ) *adj* 1 situated between the moon and the earth 2 of or relating to the earth or world [c16: via Late Latin, from Latin *sub-* + *lūna* moon]

sub-machine-gun *n* a portable automatic or semiautomatic light gun with a short barrel, firing pistol ammunition: designed to be fired from the hip or shoulder

submarginal (sʌb'mɑːdʒɪnəl) *adj* 1 below the minimum requirements 2 (of land) infertile and unprofitable for cultivation > sub'marginally *adv*

submarine ('sʌbmə,riːn, ,sʌbmə'riːn) *n* 1 a vessel, esp one designed for warfare, capable of operating for protracted periods below the surface of the sea 2 (*modifier*) a of or relating to a submarine: *a submarine captain* b occurring or situated below the surface of the sea: *a submarine cable* > submariner (sʌb'mærɪnə) *n*

submaxillary gland *n* (in mammals) either of a pair of salivary glands situated on each side behind the lower jaw

submediant (sʌb'miːdɪənt) *music* ▷ *n* 1 the sixth degree of a major or minor scale 2 a key or chord based on this ▷ *adj* 3 of or relating to the submediant

submerge (səb'mɜːdʒ) or **submerse** (səb'mɜːs) *vb* 1 to plunge, sink, or dive or cause to plunge, sink, or dive below the surface of water, etc 2 (*tr*) to cover with water or some other liquid 3 (*tr*) to hide; suppress 4 (*tr*) to overwhelm, as with work, difficulties, etc [c17: from Latin *submergere*, from sub- + *mergere* to immerse] > sub'mergence or submersion (səb'mɜːʃən) *n*

submersible (səb'mɜːsəbəl) or **submergible** (səb'mɜːdʒɪbəl) *adj* 1 able to be submerged 2 capable of operating under water, etc ▷ *n* 3 a vessel designed to operate under water for short periods 4 a submarine taking one or more men that is designed and equipped to carry out work in deep water below the levels at which divers can work > sub,mersi'bility or sub,mergi'bility *n*

subminiature (sʌb'mɪnɪətʃə) *adj* smaller than miniature

subminiature camera *n* a pocket-sized camera, usually using 16 millimetre film with a very fine grain so that negatives can produce considerably enlarged prints

submission (səb'mɪʃən) *n* 1 an act or instance of submitting 2 something submitted; a proposal, argument, etc 3 the quality or condition of being submissive to another 4 the act of referring a document, etc, for the consideration of someone else

submissive (səb'mɪsɪv) *adj* of, tending towards, or indicating submission, humility, or servility > sub'missively *adv* > sub'missiveness *n*

submit (səb'mɪt) *vb* -mits, -mitting, -mitted 1 (often foll by *to*) to yield (oneself), as to the will of another person, a superior force, etc 2 (foll by *to*) to subject or be voluntarily subjected (to analysis, treatment, etc) 3 (*tr*; often foll by *to*) to refer (something to someone) for judgment or consideration 4 (*tr*; may take a clause as object) to state, contend, or propose deferentially 5 (*intr*; often foll by *to*) to defer or accede (to the decision, opinion, etc, of another) [c14: from Latin *submittere* to place under, from sub- + *mittere* to send] > sub'mittable or sub'missible *adj* > sub'mittal *n* > sub'mitter *n*

submultiple (sʌb'mʌltɪpəl) *n* 1 a number that can be divided into another number an integral number of times without a remainder ▷ *adj* 2 being a submultiple of a quantity or number

subnormal (sʌb'nɔːməl) *adj* 1 less than the normal 2 having a low intelligence, esp having an IQ of less than 70 ▷ *n* 3 a subnormal person > subnormality (,sʌbnɔː'mælɪtɪ) *n*

subnuclear (sʌb'njuːklɪə) *adj* of or relating to particles within the nucleus of an atom

suborbital (sʌbˈɔːbɪtᵊl) *adj* 1 (of a rocket, missile, etc) having a flight path that is less than one complete orbit of the earth or other celestial body 2 *anatomy* situated beneath the orbit of the eye

suborder (ˈsʌbˌɔːdə) *n* *biology* a taxonomic group that is a subdivision of an order > sub'ordinal *adj*

subordinate *adj* (səˈbɔːdɪnɪt) 1 of lesser order or importance 2 under the authority or control of another: *a subordinate functionary* ▷ *n* (səˈbɔːdɪnɪt) 3 a person or thing that is subordinate ▷ *vb* (səˈbɔːdɪˌneɪt) (*tr*, usually foll by *to*) 4 to put in a lower rank or position (than) 5 to make subservient: *to subordinate mind to heart* [c15: from Medieval Latin *subordināre*, from Latin sub- + *ordō* rank] > sub'ordinately *adv* > sub,ordi'nation *or* sub'ordinateness *n* > sub'ordinative *adj*

subordinate clause *n* *grammar* a clause with an adjectival, adverbial, or nominal function, rather than one that functions as a separate sentence in its own right

subordinating conjunction *n* a conjunction that introduces subordinate clauses, such as *if*, *because*, *although*, and *until*

suborn (səˈbɔːn) *vb* (*tr*) 1 to bribe, incite, or instigate (a person) to commit a wrongful act 2 *criminal law* to induce (a witness) to commit perjury [c16: from Latin *subornāre*, from *sub-* secretly + *ornāre* to furnish] > subornation (ˌsʌbɔːˈneɪʃən) *n* > subornative (sʌˈbɔːnətɪv) *adj* > sub'orner *n*

Subotica (Serbian ˈsubɔtitsa) *n* a town in Serbia, in the NE near the border with Hungary: agricultural and industrial centre. Pop: 107 139 (2002). Hungarian name: Szabadka

suboxide (sʌbˈɒksaɪd) *n* an oxide of an element containing less oxygen than the common oxide formed by the element: *carbon suboxide*, C_2O_3

subplot (ˈsʌbˌplɒt) *n* a subordinate or auxiliary plot in a novel, play, film, etc

subpoena (səbˈpiːnə) *n* 1 a writ issued by a court of justice requiring a person to appear before the court at a specified time ▷ *vb* -nas, -naing, -naed 2 (*tr*) to serve with a subpoena [c15: from Latin: under penalty]

subprime (ˈsʌbˌpraɪm) US ▷ *adj* 1 (of a loan) made to a borrower with a poor credit rating, usually at a high rate of interest ▷ *n* 2 a loan made to a borrower with a poor credit rating

subrogate (ˈsʌbrəˌgeɪt) *vb* (*tr*) *law* to put (one person or thing) in the place of another in respect of a right or claim [c16: from Latin *subrogāre*, from *sub-* in place of + *rogāre* to ask]

subrogation (ˌsʌbrəˈgeɪʃən) *n* *law* the substitution of one person or thing for another, esp the placing of a surety who has paid the debt in the place of the creditor, entitling him to payment from the original debtor

sub rosa (ˈrəʊzə) *adv* in secret [Latin, literally: under the rose; from the rose that, in ancient times, was hung over the council table, as a token of secrecy]

subroutine (ˈsʌbruːˌtiːn) *n* a section of a computer program that is stored only once but can be used when required at several different points in the program, thus saving space. Also called: procedure

sub-Saharan *adj* in, of, or relating to Africa south of the Sahara desert

subscribe (səbˈskraɪb) *vb* 1 (usually foll by *to*) to pay or promise to pay (a sum of money) as a contribution (to a fund or charity, for a magazine, etc), esp at regular intervals 2 to inscribe or sign (one's name, etc) at the end of a contract, will, or other document 3 (*intr*, foll by *to*) to give support or approval: *to subscribe to the theory of transubstantiation* [c15: from Latin *subscrībere* to write underneath, from sub- + *scrībere* to write] > sub'scriber *n*

subscriber trunk dialling *n* *Brit* a service by which telephone subscribers can obtain trunk calls by dialling direct without the aid of an operator. Abbreviation: STD

subscript (ˈsʌbskrɪpt) *adj* 1 *printing* (of a character) written or printed below the line. See **superscript** ▷ *n* 2 Also called: subindex a subscript character

subscription (səbˈskrɪpʃən) *n* 1 a payment or promise of payment for consecutive issues of a magazine, newspaper, book, etc, over a specified period of time

2 a the advance purchase of tickets for a series of concerts, operas, etc b (*as modifier*): *a subscription concert* 3 an amount of money paid or promised, as to a charity, or the fund raised in this way 4 an offer to buy shares or bonds issued by a company 5 the act of signing one's name to a document, etc 6 a signature or other appendage attached to the bottom of a document, etc 7 agreement, consent, or acceptance expressed by or as if by signing one's name 8 a signed document, statement, etc 9 *chiefly Brit* the membership dues or fees paid to a society or club 10 an advance order for a new product 11 a the sale of books, etc, prior to printing b (*as modifier*): *a subscription edition* > sub'scriptive *adj*

subsequence (ˈsʌbsɪkwəns) *n* 1 the fact or state of being subsequent 2 a subsequent incident or occurrence

subsequent (ˈsʌbsɪkwənt) *adj* occurring after; succeeding [c15: from Latin *subsequēns* following on, from *subsequī*, from sub- near + *sequī* to follow] > 'subsequently *adv* > 'subsequentness *n*

subserve (səbˈsɜːv) *vb* (*tr*) to be helpful or useful to [c17: from Latin *subservīre* to be subject to, from sub- + *servīre* to serve]

subservient (səbˈsɜːvɪənt) *adj* 1 obsequious in behaviour or attitude 2 serving as a means to an end 3 a less common word for **subordinate** (sense 2) [c17: from Latin *subserviēns* complying with, from *subservīre* to subserve] > sub'serviently *adv* > sub'servience *or* sub'serviency *n*

subset (ˈsʌbˌsɛt) *n* a set within a larger set

subshrub (ˈsʌbˌʃrʌb) *n* a small bushy plant that is woody except for the tips of the branches

subside (səbˈsaɪd) *vb* (*intr*) 1 to become less loud, excited, violent, etc; abate 2 to sink or fall to a lower level 3 (of the surface of the earth, etc) to cave in; collapse 4 (of sediment, etc) to sink or descend to the bottom; settle [c17: from Latin *subsīdere* to settle down, from sub- down + *sīdere* to settle] > sub'sider *n*

subsidence (səbˈsaɪdᵊns, ˈsʌbsɪdᵊns) *n* 1 the act or process of subsiding or the condition of having subsided 2 *geology* the gradual sinking of landforms to a lower level as a result of earth movements, mining operations, etc

subsidiarity (səbˌsɪdɪˈærɪtɪ) *n* (in political systems) the principle of devolving decisions to the lowest practical level

subsidiary (səbˈsɪdɪərɪ) *adj* 1 serving to aid or supplement; auxiliary 2 of lesser importance; subordinate in function ▷ *n*, *pl* -aries 3 a person who or thing that is subsidiary 4 short for **subsidiary company** [c16: from Latin *subsidiārius* supporting, from *subsidium* SUBSIDY] > sub'sidiarily *adv* > sub'sidiariness *n*

subsidiary company *n* a company with at least half of its capital stock owned by another company

subsidize *or* **subsidise** (ˈsʌbsɪˌdaɪz) *vb* (*tr*) 1 to aid or support with a subsidy 2 to obtain the aid of by means of a subsidy > ˌsubsidi'zation *or* ˌsubsidi'sation *n* > 'subsiˌdizer *or* 'subsiˌdiser *n*

subsidy (ˈsʌbsɪdɪ) *n*, *pl* -dies 1 a financial aid supplied by a government, as to industry, for reasons of public welfare, the balance of payments, etc 2 *English history* a financial grant made originally for special purposes by Parliament to the Crown 3 any monetary contribution, grant, or aid [c14: from Anglo-Norman *subsidie*, from Latin *subsidium* assistance, from *subsidēre* to remain, from sub- down + *sedēre* to sit]

subsist (səbˈsɪst) *vb* (*mainly intr*) 1 (often foll by *on*) to be sustained; manage to live: *to subsist on milk* 2 to continue in existence 3 (foll by *in*) to lie or reside by virtue (of); consist 4 (*tr*) *obsolete* to provide with support [c16: from Latin *subsistere* to stand firm, from sub- up + *sistere* to make a stand] > sub'sistent *adj*

subsistence (səbˈsɪstəns) *n* 1 the means by which one maintains life 2 the act or condition of subsisting

subsistence farming *n* a type of farming in which most of the produce (**subsistence crop**) is consumed by the farmer and his family, leaving little or nothing to be marketed

subsistence level *n* a standard of living barely adequate to support life

subsistence wage *n* the lowest wage upon which a

worker and his family can survive

subsoil ('sʌb,sɔɪl) *n* **1** Also called: **undersoil** the layer of soil beneath the surface soil and overlying the bedrock ▷ *vb* **2** (*tr*) to plough (land) to a depth below the normal ploughing level and so break up the subsoil

subsonic (sʌb'sɒnɪk) *adj* being, having, or travelling at a velocity below that of sound

subspecies ('sʌb,spiːʃiːz) *n*, *pl* **-cies** *biology* a taxonomic group that is a subdivision of a species: usually occurs because of isolation within a species

subst. *abbreviation* **1** substantive **2** substitute

substance ('sʌbstəns) *n* **1** the tangible matter of which a thing consists **2** a specific type of matter, esp a homogeneous material with a definite composition **3** the essence, meaning, etc, of a written or spoken thought **4** solid or meaningful quality **5** material density: *a vacuum has no substance* **6** material possessions or wealth: *a man of substance* **7** *philosophy* the supposed immaterial substratum that can receive modifications and in which attributes and accidents inhere **8** in substance with regard to the salient points [c13: via Old French from Latin *substantia*, from *substāre*, from SUB- + *stāre* to stand]

substandard (sʌb'stændəd) *adj* **1** below an established or required standard **2** another word for **nonstandard**

substantial (səb'stænʃəl) *adj* **1** of a considerable size or value: *substantial funds* **2** worthwhile; important: *a substantial reform* **3** having wealth or importance **4** (of food or a meal) sufficient and nourishing **5** solid or strong in construction, quality, or character: *a substantial door* **6** real; actual; true: *the evidence is substantial* **7** of or relating to the basic or fundamental substance or aspects of a thing

substantialism (səb'stænʃə,lɪzəm) *n* *philosophy* the doctrine that a substantial reality underlies phenomena > sub'stantialist *n*

substantia nigra (səb'stænʃə 'naɪɡrə) *n* a layer of grey matter in the brain that produces dopamine and contains pigmented nerve cells, loss of which has been associated with Parkinson's disease [c20: from Latin, literally: dark material]

substantiate (səb'stænʃɪ,eɪt) *vb* (*tr*) **1** to establish as valid or genuine **2** to give form or real existence to [c17: from New Latin *substantiāre*, from Latin *substantia* SUBSTANCE] > sub,stanti'ation *n*

substantive ('sʌbstəntɪv) *n* **1** *grammar* a noun or pronoun used in place of a noun ▷ *adj* **2** of, relating to, containing, or being the essential element of a thing **3** having independent function, resources, or existence **4** of substantial quantity **5** solid in foundation or basis **6** *grammar* denoting, relating to, or standing in place of a noun **7** (səb'stæntɪv) (of a dye or colour) staining the material directly without use of a mordant [c15: from Late Latin *substantīvus*, from Latin *substāre* to stand beneath; see SUBSTANCE] > substantival (,sʌbstən'taɪvəl) *adj* > ,substan'tivally *adv* > 'substantively *adv*

substantive rank (səb'stæntɪv) *n* a permanent rank in the armed services obtained by length of service, selection, etc

substation ('sʌb,steɪʃən) *n* **1** a subsidiary station **2** an installation at which electricity is received from one or more power stations for conversion from alternating to direct current, reducing the voltage, or switching before distribution by a low-tension network

substituent (sʌb'stɪtjʊənt) *n* **1** *chem* an atom or group that replaces another atom or group in a molecule or can be regarded as replacing an atom in a parent compound ▷ *adj* **2** substituted or substitutable [c19: from Latin *substituere* to SUBSTITUTE]

substitute ('sʌbstɪ,tjuːt) *vb* **1** (often foll by *for*) to serve or cause to serve in place of another person or thing **2** *chem* to replace (an atom or group in a molecule) with (another atom or group) ▷ *n* **3** a person or thing that serves in place of another, such as a player in a game who takes the place of an injured colleague **b** (*as modifier*): *a substitute goalkeeper* [c16: from Latin *substituere*, from *sub-* in place of + *statuere* to set up] > ,substi'tutable *adj* 'substi,tutive *adj*

● USAGE *Substitute* is sometimes wrongly used where ● *replace* is meant: *he replaced* (not *substituted*) *the worn tyre* ● *with a new one*

substitution (,sʌbstɪ'tjuːʃən) *n* **1** the act of substituting or state of being substituted **2** something or someone substituted

substrate ('sʌbstreɪt) *n* **1** *biochem* the substance upon which an enzyme acts **2** another word for **substratum**

substratum (sʌb'strɑːtəm, -'streɪ-) *n*, *pl* **-strata** (-'strɑːtə, -'streɪtə) **1** any layer or stratum lying underneath another **2** a basis or foundation; groundwork [c17: from New Latin, from Latin *substrātus* strewn beneath, from *substernere* to spread under, from SUB- + *sternere* to spread] > sub'strative *or* sub'stratal *adj*

substructure ('sʌb,strʌktʃə) *n* **1** a structure, pattern, etc, that forms the basis of anything **2** a structure forming a foundation or framework for a building or other construction > sub'structural *adj*

subsume (səb'sjuːm) *vb* (*tr*) **1** to incorporate (an idea, proposition, case, etc) under a comprehensive or inclusive classification or heading **2** to consider (an instance of something) as part of a general rule or principle [c16: from New Latin *subsumere*, from Latin SUB- + *sumere* to take] > sub'sumable *adj* > subsumption (səb'sʌmpʃən) *n*

subtemperate (sʌb'tempərɪt) *adj* of or relating to the colder temperate regions

subtenant (sʌb'tenənt) *n* a person who rents or leases property from a tenant > sub'tenancy *n*

subtend (səb'tend) *vb* (*tr*) **1** *geometry* to be opposite to and delimit (an angle or side) **2** (of a bract, stem, etc) to have (a bud or similar part) growing in its axil [c16: from Latin *subtendere* to extend beneath, from SUB- + *tendere* to stretch out]

subterfuge ('sʌbtə,fjuːdʒ) *n* a stratagem employed to conceal something, evade an argument, etc [c16: from Late Latin *subterfugium*, from Latin *subterfugere* to escape by stealth, from *subter* secretly + *fugere* to flee]

subterminal (sʌb'tɜːmɪnəl) *adj* almost at an end

subterranean (,sʌbtə'reɪnɪən) *adj* **1** Also called: **subterraneous**, **subterrestrial** situated, living, or operating below the surface of the earth **2** existing or operating in concealment [c17: from Latin *subterrāneus*, from SUB- + *terra* earth] > ,subter'raneanly *or* ,subter'raneously *adv*

subtext ('sʌb,tekst) *n* **1** an underlying theme in a piece of writing **2** a message which is not stated directly but can be inferred

subtile ('sʌtəl) *adj* a rare spelling of **subtle** > 'subtilely *adv* > subtility (sʌb'tɪlɪtɪ) *or* 'subtileness *n* > 'subtilty *n*

subtilize *or* **subtilise** ('sʌtɪ,laɪz) *vb* **1** (*tr*) to bring to a purer state; refine **2** to debate subtly **3** (*tr*) to make (the mind, etc) keener > ,subtili'zation *or* ,subtili'sation *n*

subtitle ('sʌb,taɪtəl) *n* **1** an additional subordinate title given to a literary or other work **2** Also called: **caption** (*often plural*) *films* **a** a written translation superimposed on a film that has foreign dialogue **b** explanatory text on a silent film ▷ *vb* **3** (*tr; usually passive*) to provide a subtitle for

subtle ('sʌtəl) *adj* **1** not immediately obvious or comprehensible **2** difficult to detect or analyse, often through being delicate or highly refined: *a subtle scent* **3** showing or making or capable of showing or making fine distinctions of meaning **4** marked by or requiring mental acuteness or ingenuity; discriminating **5** delicate or faint: *a subtle shade* **6** cunning or wily: *a subtle rogue* **7** operating or executed in secret: *a subtle intrigue* [c14: from Old French *soutil*, from Latin *subtīlis* finely woven] > 'subtleness *n* > 'subtly *adv*

subtlety ('sʌtəltɪ) *n*, *pl* **-ties** **1** the state or quality of being subtle; delicacy **2** a fine distinction or the ability to make such a distinction **3** something subtle

subtonic (sʌb'tɒnɪk) *n* *music* the seventh degree of a major or minor scale

subtotal (sʌb'təʊtəl, 'sʌb,təʊtəl) *n* **1** the total made up by a column of figures, etc, forming part of the total made up by a larger column or group ▷ *vb* **-tals**, **-talling**, **-talled** *or US* **-tals**, **-taling**, **-taled** **2** to establish or work out a subtotal for (a column, group, etc)

subtract (səb'trækt) *vb* 1 to calculate the difference between (two numbers or quantities) by subtraction 2 to remove (a part of a thing, quantity, etc) from the whole [c16: from Latin *subtractus* withdrawn, from *subtrahere* to draw away from beneath, from SUB- + *trahere* to draw] > sub'tracter *n* > sub'tractive *adj*

subtraction (səb'trækʃən) *n* 1 the act or process of subtracting 2 a mathematical operation in which the difference between two numbers or quantities is calculated. Usually indicated by the symbol (–)

subtrahend ('sʌbtrə,hɛnd) *n* the number to be subtracted from another number (the **minuend**) [c17: from Latin *subtrahendus*, from *subtrahere* to SUBTRACT]

subtropics (sʌb'trɒpɪks) *pl n* the region lying between the tropics and temperate lands > subtropical (sʌb'trɒpɪkᵊl) *adj*

subulate ('su:bjəlɪt, -,leɪt) *adj* (esp of plant parts) tapering to a point; awl-shaped [c18: from New Latin *subulatus* like an awl, from Latin *sūbula* awl]

suburb ('sʌbɜ:b) *n* a residential district situated on the outskirts of a city or town [c14: from Latin *suburbium*, from *sub*- close to + *urbs* a city]

suburban (sə'bɜ:bᵊn) *adj* 1 of, relating to, situated in, or inhabiting a suburb or the suburbs 2 characteristic of or typifying a suburb or the suburbs 3 *mildly derogatory* narrow or unadventurous in outlook > su'burban,ite *n* > suburbanize *or* suburbanise (sʌ'bɜ:bə,naɪz) *vb*

suburbia (sə'bɜ:bɪə) *n* 1 suburbs or the people living in them considered as an identifiable community or class in society 2 the life, customs, etc, of suburbanites

subvene (səb'vi:n) *vb* (*intr*) *rare* to happen in such a way as to be of assistance, esp in preventing something [c18: from Latin *subvenīre*, from *venīre* to come]

subvention (səb'vɛnʃən) *n* 1 a grant, aid, or subsidy, as from a government to an educational institution 2 *sport* a fee paid indirectly to a supposedly amateur athlete for appearing at a meeting [c15: from Late Latin *subventiō* assistance, from *subvenīre* to SUBVENE]

subversion (səb'vɜ:ʃən) *n* 1 the act or an instance of subverting or overthrowing a legally constituted government, institution, etc 2 the state of being subverted; destruction or ruin [c14: from Late Latin *subversiō* destruction, from *subvertere* to SUBVERT]

subversive (səb'vɜ:sɪv) *adj* 1 liable to subvert or overthrow a government, legally constituted institution, etc ▷ *n* 2 a person engaged in subversive activities, etc > sub'versively *adv* > sub'versiveness *n*

subvert (səb'vɜ:t) *vb* (*tr*) 1 to bring about the complete downfall or ruin of (something existing or established by a system of law, etc) 2 to undermine the moral principles of (a person, etc); corrupt [c14: from Latin *subvertere* to overturn, from *sub*- from below + *vertere* to turn] > sub'verter *n*

subway ('sʌb,weɪ) *n* 1 *Brit* an underground passage or tunnel enabling pedestrians to cross a road, railway, etc 2 an underground passage or tunnel for traffic, electric power supplies, etc 3 *chiefly US & Canadian* an underground railway

subwoofer ('sʌb,wu:fə) *n* a loudspeaker for reproducing very low frequencies only

succedaneum (,sʌksɪ'deɪnɪəm) *n, pl* -**nea** (-nɪə) *obsolete* something that is used as a substitute, esp any medical drug or agent that may be taken or prescribed in place of another [c17: from Latin *succēdāneus* following after, from *succēdere* to SUCCEED] > ,succe'daneous *adj*

succeed (sək'si:d) *vb* 1 (*intr*) to accomplish an aim, esp in the manner desired 2 (*intr*) to happen in the manner desired: *the plan succeeded* 3 (*intr*) to acquit oneself satisfactorily or do well, as in a specified field 4 (when *intr*, often foll by *to*) to come next in order (after someone or something, post 5 (when *intr*, often foll by *to*) to take over an office, post, etc (from a person) 6 (*intr*; usually foll by *to*) to come into possession (of property, etc); inherit 7 (*intr*) to have a result according to a specified manner: *the plan succeeded badly* [c15: from Latin *succēdere* to follow after, from *sub*- after + *cēdere* to go] > suc'ceedingly *adv*

success (sək'sɛs) *n* 1 the favourable outcome of something attempted 2 the attainment of wealth,

fame, etc 3 an action, performance, etc, that is characterized by success 4 a person or thing that is successful [c16: from Latin *successus* an outcome, from *succēdere* to SUCCEED]

successful (sək'sɛsfʊl) *adj* 1 having succeeded in one's endeavours 2 marked by a favourable outcome 3 having obtained fame, wealth, etc > suc'cessfully *adv* > suc'cessfulness *n*

succession (sək'sɛʃən) *n* 1 the act or an instance of one person or thing following another 2 a number of people or things following one another in order 3 the act, process, or right by which one person succeeds to the office, etc, of another 4 the order that determines how one person or thing follows another 5 a line of descent to a title, etc 6 **in succession** in a manner such that one thing is followed uninterruptedly by another [c14: from Latin *successio*, from *succēdere* to SUCCEED] > suc'cessional *adj*

successive (sək'sɛsɪv) *adj* 1 following another without interruption 2 of or involving succession: *a successive process* > suc'cessively *adv* > suc'cessiveness *n*

successor (sək'sɛsə) *n* a person or thing that follows, esp a person who succeeds another in an office

succinct (sək'sɪŋkt) *adj* marked by brevity and clarity; concise [c15: from Latin *succinctus* girt about, from *succingere* to gird from below, from *sub*- from below + *cingere* to gird] > suc'cinctly *adv* > suc'cinctness *n*

succinic acid *n* a colourless odourless water-soluble dicarboxylic acid found in plant and animal tissues: used in making lacquers, dyes, perfumes, etc; 1,4-butanedioic acid. Formula: $HOOCCH_2:CH_2COOH$

succotash ('sʌkə,tæʃ) *n US & Canadian* a mixture of cooked sweet corn kernels and lima beans, served as a vegetable [c18: from Narraganset *msiquatash*, literally: broken pieces]

succour *or US* **succor** ('sʌkə) *n* 1 help or assistance, esp in time of difficulty 2 a person or thing that provides help ▷ *vb* 3 (*tr*) to give aid to [c13: from Old French *sucurir*, from Latin *succurrere* to hurry to help, from *sub*- under + *currere* to run]

succubus ('sʌkjʊbəs) *n, pl* -**bi** (-,baɪ) 1 Also called: **succuba** a female demon fabled to have sexual intercourse with sleeping men. See **incubus** 2 any evil demon [c16: from Medieval Latin, from Late Latin *succuba* harlot, from *succubāre* to lie beneath, from SUB- + *cubāre* to lie]

succulent ('sʌkjʊlənt) *adj* 1 abundant in juices; juicy 2 (of plants) having thick fleshy leaves or stems ▷ *n* 3 a plant that is able to exist in arid or salty conditions by using water stored in its fleshy tissues [c17: from Latin *succulentus*, from *sūcus* juice] > 'succulence *or* 'succulency *n* > 'succulently *adv*

succumb (sə'kʌm) *vb* (*intr*; often foll by *to*) 1 to give way in face of the overwhelming force (of) or desire (for) 2 to be fatally overwhelmed (by disease, old age, etc); die (of) [c15: from Latin *succumbere* to be overcome, from SUB- + *-cumbere* from *cubāre* to lie down]

succursal (sʌ'kɜ:sᵊl) *adj* 1 (esp of a religious establishment) subsidiary ▷ *n* 2 a subsidiary establishment [c19: from French, from Medieval Latin *succursus*, from Latin *succurrere* to SUCCOUR]

such (sʌtʃ) (often foll by a corresponding subordinate clause introduced by *that* or *as*) *determiner* 1 **a** of the sort specified or understood: *such books shouldn't be sold here* **b** (*as pronoun*): *such is life; robbers, rapists, and such* 2 so great; so much: *such a help; I've never seen such weeping* 3 **as such a** in the capacity previously specified or understood: *a judge as such hasn't so much power* **b** in itself or themselves: *intelligence as such can't guarantee success* 4 **such and such** specific, but not known or named: *at such and such a time* 5 **such as a** for example: *animals, such as elephants and tigers* **b** of a similar kind; like: *people such as your friend John make me angry* **c** of the (usually small) amount, etc: *the food, such as there was, was excellent* 6 **such that** so that: used to express purpose or result: *power such that it was effortless* ▷ *adv* 7 (*intensifier*): *such nice people; such a nice person that I gave him a present* [Old English *swilc*; related to Old Frisian *sālik*, Old Norse *slīkr*, Gothic *swaleiks*, Old High German *sulih*]

suchlike ('sʌtʃ,laɪk) *adj* **1** (*prenominal*) of such a kind; similar: *John, Ken, and other suchlike idiots* ▷ *n* **2** such or similar persons or things: *hyenas, jackals, and suchlike*

Su-chou (su:'tʃəʊ) *n* a variant transliteration of the Chinese name for **Suzhou**

Süchow ('ʃu:'tʃəʊ) *n* a variant transliteration of the Chinese name for **Xuzhou**

suck (sʌk) *vb* **1** to draw (a liquid or other substance) into the mouth by creating a partial vacuum in the mouth **2** to draw in (fluid, etc) by or as if by a similar action: *plants suck moisture from the soil* **3** to drink milk from (a mother's breast); suckle **4** (*tr*) to extract fluid content from (a solid food): *to suck a lemon* **5** (*tr*) to take into the mouth and moisten, dissolve, or roll around with the tongue: *to suck one's thumb* **6** (*tr*; often foll by *down, in*, etc) to draw by using irresistible force **7** (*intr*) (of a pump) to draw in air because of a low supply level or leaking valves, pipes, etc **8** (*tr*) to assimilate or acquire (knowledge, comfort, etc) **9** (*intr*) *slang* to be contemptible or disgusting ▷ *n* **10** the act or an instance of sucking **11** something that is sucked, esp milk from the mother's breast **12** **give suck** to give to (a baby or young animal) milk from the breast or udder **13** an attracting or sucking force **14** a sound caused by sucking ▷ See also **suck in, sucks**, etc [Old English *sūcan*; related to Old Norse *súga*, Middle Dutch *sūgen*, Latin *sūgere* to suck, exhaust; see **SOAK**]

sucker ('sʌkə) *n* **1** a person or thing that sucks **2** *slang* a person who is easily deceived or swindled **3** *slang* a person who cannot resist the attractions of a particular type of person or thing: *he's a sucker for blondes* **4** a young animal that is not yet weaned, esp a suckling pig **5** *zoology* an organ that is specialized for sucking or adhering **6** a cup-shaped device, generally made of rubber, that may be attached to articles allowing them to adhere to a surface by suction **7** *botany* **a** a strong shoot that arises in a mature plant from a root, rhizome, or the base of the main stem **b** a short branch of a parasitic plant that absorbs nutrients from the host **8** a pipe or tube through which a fluid is drawn by suction **9** any small mainly North American cyprinoid fish of the family *Catostomidae*, having toothless jaws and a large sucking mouth **10** any of certain fishes that have sucking discs, esp the clingfish or sea snail **11** a piston in a suction pump or the valve in such a piston ▷ *vb* **12** (*tr*) to strip off the suckers from (a plant) **13** (*intr*) (of a plant) to produce suckers

suck in *vb* (*adverb*) **1** (*tr*) to attract by using an inexorable force, inducement, etc **2** to draw in (one's breath) sharply

suckle ('sʌkᵊl) *vb* **1** to give (a baby or young animal) milk from the breast or (of a baby, etc) to suck milk from the breast **2** (*tr*) to bring up; nurture [c15: probably back formation from **SUCKLING**] ▷ '**suckler** *n*

suckling ('sʌklɪŋ) *n* **1** an infant or young animal that is still taking milk from the mother **2** a very young child [c15: see **SUCK, -LING**[1]; related to Middle Dutch *sūgeling*, Middle High German *sōgelinc*]

Suckling ('sʌklɪŋ) *n* Sir **John**. 1609–42, English Cavalier poet and dramatist

sucks (sʌks) *interj slang* **1** an expression of disappointment **2** an exclamation of defiance or derision (esp in the phrase **yah boo sucks to you**)

suck up to *vb* (*intr, adverb + preposition*) *informal* to flatter for one's own profit; toady

sucrase ('sju:kreɪz) *n* another name for **invertase** [c19: from French *sucre* sugar + -**ASE**]

sucre (Spanish 'sukre) *n* the former standard monetary unit of Ecuador (until the US dollar was adopted in 2000), divided into 100 centavos [c19: after Antonio José de Sucre (1795–1830), South American liberator]

Sucre[1] (Spanish 'sukre) *n* the legal capital of Bolivia, in the south central part of the country in the E Andes: university (1624). Pop: 231 000 (2005 est). Former name (until 1839): **Chuquisaca**

Sucre[2] (Spanish 'sukre) *n* **Antonio José de** (an'tonjo xo'se de). 1795–1830, South American liberator, born in Venezuela, who assisted Bolívar in the colonial revolt against Spain; first president of Bolivia (1826–28)

sucrose ('sju:krəʊz, -krəʊs) *n* the technical name for **sugar** (sense 1) [c19: from French *sucre* sugar + -**OSE**[2]]

suction ('sʌkʃən) *n* **1** the act or process of sucking **2** the force or condition produced by a pressure difference, as the force holding a suction cap onto a surface **3** the act or process of producing such a force or condition [c17: from Late Latin *suctiō* a sucking, from Latin *sūgere* to suck] ▷ '**suctional** *adj*

suction pump *n* a pump for raising water or other fluid by suction. It usually consists of a cylinder containing a piston fitted with a flap valve

suctorial (sʌk'tɔ:rɪəl) *adj* **1** specialized for sucking or adhering **2** relating to or possessing suckers or suction [c19: from New Latin *suctōrius*, from Latin *sūgere* to suck]

Sudan (su:'dɑ:n, -'dæn) *n* **1** a republic in NE Africa, on the Red Sea: the largest country in Africa; conquered by Mehemet Ali of Egypt (1820–22) and made an Anglo-Egyptian condominium in 1899 after joint forces defeated the Mahdist revolt; became a republic in 1956; civil war has been waged between separatists, in the mainly Christian south, and the government since independence, apart from a period of peace (1972–83). It consists mainly of a plateau, with the Nubian Desert in the north. Official language: Arabic. Official religion: Muslim; there are large Christian and animist minorities. Currency: Sudanese pound or Sudani (replacing the Sudanese dinar in 2007). Capital: Khartoum. Pop: 34 333 000 (2004 est). Area: 2 505 805 sq km (967 491 sq miles). Former name (1899–1956): Anglo-Egyptian Sudan. French name: Soudan **2** the Sudan a region stretching across Africa south of the Sahara and north of the tropical zone: inhabited chiefly by Negroid tribes rather than Arabs ▷ ,**Suda'nese** *adj, n*

sudarium (sjʊ'dɛərɪəm) *n, pl* **-daria** (-'dɛərɪə) another word for **sudatorium** [c17: from Latin, from *sūdāre* to sweat]

sudatorium (,sju:də'tɔ:rɪəm) or **sudatory** *n, pl* **-toria** (-'tɔ:rɪə) or **-tories** a room, esp in a Roman bathhouse, where sweating is induced by heat [c18: from Latin, from *sūdāre* to sweat]

sudatory ('sju:dətərɪ, -trɪ) *adj* **1** relating to or producing sweating; sudorific ▷ *n, pl* **-ries** **2** *med* a sudatory agent **3** another word for **sudatorium**

Sudbury ('sʌdbərɪ, -brɪ) *n* a city in central Canada, in Ontario: a major nickel-mining centre. Pop: 103 879 (2001)

sudd (sʌd) *n* floating masses of reeds and weeds that occur on the White Nile and obstruct navigation [c19: from Arabic, literally: obstruction]

sudden ('sʌdᵊn) *adj* **1** occurring or performed quickly and without warning **2** marked by haste; abrupt **3** *rare* rash; precipitate ▷ *n* **4** *archaic* an abrupt occurrence or the occasion of such an occurrence (in the phrase **on a sudden**) **5** all of a sudden without warning; unexpectedly [c13: via French from Late Latin *subitāneus*, from Latin *subitus* unexpected, from *subīre* to happen unexpectedly, from *sub-* secretly + *īre* to go] ▷ '**suddenness** *n*

sudden adult death syndrome *n* the unexpected death of a young adult, usually due to undetected inherited heart disease. Also called: **sudden death syndrome, sudden cardiac death** Abbreviation: **SADS**

sudden death *n* **1** (in sports, etc) an extra game or contest to decide the winner of a tied competition **2** an unexpected or quick death

sudden infant death syndrome *n* a technical term for **cot death** Abbreviation: **SIDS**

suddenly ('sʌdᵊnlɪ) *adv* quickly and without warning; unexpectedly

Sudetenland (su:'deɪtᵊn,lænd) *n* a mountainous region of the N Czech Republic: part of Czechoslovakia (1919–38; 1945–93); occupied by Germany (1938–45). Also called: the **Sudeten**

Sudetes (su:'di:ti:z) or **Sudeten Mountains** *pl n* a mountain range in E central Europe, along the N border of the Czech Republic, extending into Germany and Poland: rich in minerals, esp coal. Highest peak: Schneekoppe, 1603 m (5259 ft)

sudor ('sju:dɔ:) *n* a technical name for **sweat** [Latin]

> **sudoral** ('sju:dərəl) *adj*

sudoriferous (ˌsju:də'rɪfərəs) *adj* producing or conveying sweat. Also called: **sudatory** ▷ n **2** a sudorific agent [c16: via New Latin from SUDOR + Latin *ferre* to bear]
> ˌsudor'iferousness *n*

sudorific (ˌsju:də'rɪfɪk) *adj* **1** producing or causing sweating; sudatory ▷ n **2** a sudorific agent [c17: from New Latin *sūdōrificus*, from SUDOR + Latin *facere* to make]

suds (sʌdz) *pl n* **1** the bubbles on the surface of water in which soap, detergents, etc, have been dissolved; lather **2** soapy water [c16: probably from Middle Dutch *sudse* marsh; related to Middle Low German *sudde* swamp; see SEETHE] > 'sudsy *adj*

sue (sju:, su:) *vb* **sues, suing, sued 1** to institute legal proceedings (against) **2** to make suppliant requests of (someone for something) [c13: via Anglo-Norman from Old French *sivre*, from Latin *sequī* to follow] > 'suer *n*

Sue (*French* sy) *n* **Eugène** (ø3ɛn). original name *Marie-Joseph Sue.* 1804–57, French novelist, whose works, notably *Les mystères de Paris* (1842–43) and *Le juif errant* (1844–45), were among the first to reflect the impact of the industrial revolution on France

suede (sweɪd) *n* **a** a leather finished with a fine velvet-like nap, usually on the flesh side of the skin or hide, produced by abrasive action **b** (*as modifier*): *a suede coat* [c19: from French *gants de Suède*, literally: gloves from Sweden]

suet ('su:ɪt, 'sju:ɪt) *n* a hard waxy fat around the kidneys and loins in sheep, cattle, etc, used in cooking and making tallow [c14: from Old French *seu*, from Latin *sēbum*] > 'suety *adj*

Suetonius (swi:'təʊnɪəs) *n* full name *Gaius Suetonius Tranquillus.* 75–150 AD, Roman biographer and historian, whose chief works were *Concerning Illustrious Men* and *The Lives of the Caesars* (from Julius Caesar to Domitian)

suet pudding *n Brit* any of a variety of sweet or savoury puddings made with suet and steamed or boiled

Suez ('su:ɪz) *n* **1** a port in NE Egypt, at the head of the Gulf of Suez at the S end of the Suez Canal: an ancient trading site and a major naval station under the Ottoman Empire; port of departure for pilgrims to Mecca; oil-refining centre. It suffered severely in the Arab-Israeli conflicts of 1967 and 1973. Pop: 513 000 (2005 est) **2 Isthmus of Suez** a strip of land in NE Egypt, between the Mediterranean and the Red Sea: links Africa and Asia and is crossed by the Suez Canal **3 Gulf of Suez** the NW arm of the Red Sea: linked with the Mediterranean by the Suez Canal

Suez Canal *n* a sea-level canal in NE Egypt, crossing the Isthmus of Suez and linking the Mediterranean with the Red Sea: built (1854–69) by de Lesseps with French and Egyptian capital; nationalized in 1956 by the Egyptians. Length: 163 km (101 miles)

Suff. *abbreviation* **1** Suffolk **2** Suffragan

suffer ('sʌfə) *vb* **1** to undergo or be subjected to (pain, punishment, etc) **2** (*tr*) to undergo or experience (anything): *to suffer a change of management* **3** (*intr*) to be set at a disadvantage: *this author suffers in translation* **4** (*tr*) *archaic* to permit (someone to do something): *suffer the little children to come unto me* **5 suffer from a** to be ill with, esp recurrently **b** to be given to: *he suffers from a tendency to exaggerate* [c13: from Old French *soffrir*, from Latin *sufferre*, from SUB- + *ferre* to bear] > 'sufferer *n*

sufferable ('sʌfərəbəl, 'sʌfrə-) *adj* able to be tolerated or suffered; endurable

sufferance ('sʌfərəns, 'sʌfrəns) *n* **1** tolerance arising from failure to prohibit; tacit permission **2** capacity to endure pain, injury, etc **3** the state or condition of suffering **4 on sufferance** with reluctance [c13: via Old French from Late Latin *sufferentia* endurance, from Latin *sufferre* to SUFFER]

suffering ('sʌfərɪŋ, 'sʌfrɪŋ) *n* **1** the pain, misery, or loss experienced by a person who suffers **2** the state or an instance of enduring pain, etc

suffice (sə'faɪs) *vb* **1** to be adequate or satisfactory for (something) **2 suffice it to say that** (*takes a clause as object*) let us say no more than that; I shall just say that [c14: from Old French *suffire*, from Latin *sufficere* from *sub*-below + *facere* to make]

sufficiency (sə'fɪʃənsɪ) *n, pl* **-cies 1** the quality or condition of being sufficient **2** an adequate amount or quantity, as of income **3** *archaic* efficiency

sufficient (sə'fɪʃənt) *adj* **1** enough to meet a need or purpose; adequate **2** *logic* (of a condition) assuring the truth of a statement; requiring but not necessarily required by some other state of affairs. See **necessary** (sense 3c) **3** *archaic* competent; capable ▷ n **4** a sufficient quantity [c14: from Latin *sufficiens* supplying the needs of, from *sufficere* to SUFFICE] > suf'ficiently *adv*

suffix ('sʌfɪks) *n* **1** *grammar* an affix that follows the stem to which it is attached, as for example *-s* and *-ness* in *dogs* and *softness.* See **prefix** (sense 1) **2** anything that is added at the end of something else *vb* ('sʌfɪks, sə'fɪks) **3** (*tr*) *grammar* to add (a morpheme) as a suffix to the end of a word **4** (*tr*) to add (something) at the end of a sentence, comment, or piece of writing [c18: from New Latin *suffixum*, from Latin *suffixus* fastened below, from *suffigere*, from SUB- + *figere* to fasten]

suffocate ('sʌfəˌkeɪt) *vb* **1** to kill or be killed by the deprivation of oxygen, as by obstruction of the air passage or inhalation of noxious gases **2** to block the air passages or have the air passages blocked **3** to feel or cause to feel discomfort from heat and lack of air [c16: from Latin *suffocāre*, from SUB- + *faucēs* throat] > 'suffoˌcating *adj*, ˌsuffo'cation *n*

Suffolk ('sʌfək) *n* a county of SE England, on the North Sea: its coast is flat and marshy, indented by broad tidal estuaries. Administrative centre: Ipswich. Pop: 678 100 (2003 est). Area: 3800 sq km (1467 sq miles)

Suffolk punch *n* a breed of draught horse with a chestnut coat and short legs [c18: from dialect *punch* squat, short and thick]

suffragan ('sʌfrəgən) *adj* **1 a** (of any bishop of a diocese) subordinate to and assisting his superior archbishop or metropolitan **b** (of any assistant bishop) having the duty of assisting the bishop of the diocese to which he is appointed but having no ordinary jurisdiction in that diocese ▷ n **2** a suffragan bishop [c14: from Medieval Latin *suffragāneus*, from *suffrāgium* assistance, from Latin: SUFFRAGE] > 'suffraganship *n*

suffrage ('sʌfrɪdʒ) *n* **1** the right to vote, esp in public elections; franchise **2** the exercise of such a right; casting a vote **3** a prayer, esp a short intercessory prayer [c14: from Latin *suffrāgium*]

suffragette (ˌsʌfrə'dʒɛt) *n* a female advocate of the extension of the franchise to women, esp a militant one, as in Britain at the beginning of the 20th century [c20: from SUFFRAG(E) + -ETTE]

suffragist ('sʌfrədʒɪst) *n* an advocate of the extension of the franchise, esp to women > 'suffragism *n*

suffruticose (sə'fru:tɪˌkəʊz) *adj* (of a plant) having a permanent woody base and herbaceous branches [c18: from New Latin *suffruticōsus*, from Latin SUB- + *frutex* a shrub]

suffuse (sə'fju:z) *vb* (*tr; usually passive*) to spread or flood through or over (something) [c16: from Latin *suffūsus* overspread with, from *suffundere*, from SUB- + *fundere* to pour] > suffusion (sə'fju:ʒən) *n* > suf'fusive *adj*

Sufi ('su:fɪ) *n, pl* **-fis** an adherent of any of various Muslim mystical orders or teachings, which emphasize the direct personal experience of God [c17: from Arabic *sūfiy*, literally: (man) of wool, from *sūf* wool; probably from the ascetic's woollen garments] > 'Sufic *adj*

sugar ('ʃʊgə) *n* **1** Also called: sucrose, saccharose a white crystalline sweet carbohydrate, a disaccharide, found in many plants and extracted from sugar cane and sugar beet: it is used esp as a sweetening agent in food and drinks. Formula: $C_{12}H_{22}O_{11}$. Related adj: **saccharine** **2** any of a class of simple water-soluble carbohydrates, such as sucrose, lactose, and fructose **3** *informal, chiefly US & Canadian* a term of affection, esp for one's sweetheart ▷ *vb* **4** (*tr*) to add sugar to; make sweet **5** (*tr*) to cover or sprinkle with sugar **6** (*intr*) to produce sugar **7 sugar the pill** *or* **sugar the medicine** to make something unpleasant more agreeable by adding something pleasant: *the government stopped wage increases but sugared the pill by reducing taxes* [C13 *suker*, from Old French *çucre*, from Medieval Latin *zuccārum*, from Italian *zucchero*, from

Arabic *sukkar*, from Persian *shakar*, from Sanskrit *śarkarā*] > 'sugared *adj*

Sugar ('ʃʊgə) *n* Sir Alan (**Michael**). born 1947, British electronics entrepreneur; chairman of Amstrad from 1968

sugar beet *n* a variety of the plant *Beta vulgaris* that is cultivated for its white roots from which sugar is obtained

sugar candy *n* **1** Also called: **rock candy** large crystals of sugar formed by suspending strings in a strong sugar solution that hardens on the strings, used chiefly for sweetening coffee **2** *chiefly US* confectionery; sweets

sugar cane *n* a coarse perennial grass, *Saccharum officinarum*, of Old World tropical regions, having tall stout canes that yield sugar: widely cultivated in tropical regions

sugar-coat *vb* (*tr*) to coat or cover with sugar

sugar diabetes *n* an informal name for **diabetes mellitus**

sugar glider *n* a common Australian phalanger, *Petaurus breviceps*, that glides from tree to tree feeding on insects and nectar

sugaring off ('ʃʊgərɪŋ) *n Canad* the boiling down of maple sap to produce sugar, traditionally a social event in early spring

sugar loaf *n* **1** a large conical mass of hard refined sugar **2** something resembling this in shape

Sugar Loaf Mountain *n* a mountain in SE Brazil, in Rio de Janeiro on Guanabara Bay. Height: 390 m (1280 ft). Portuguese name: Pão de Açúcar

sugar maple *n* a North American maple tree, *Acer saccharum*, that is grown as a source of sugar, which is extracted from the sap, and for its hard wood

sugar of lead (lɛd) *n* another name for **lead acetate**

sugar pie *n Canadian* an open pie with a brown sugar filling

sugarplum ('ʃʊgə,plʌm) *n* a crystallized plum

sugary ('ʃʊgərɪ) *adj* **1** of, like, or containing sugar **2** containing too much sugar; excessively sweet **3** deceptively pleasant; insincere > 'sugariness *n*

Suger (su:'ʒɛə) *n* 1081–1151, French ecclesiastic and statesman, who acted as adviser to Louis VI and regent (1147–49) to Louis VII. As abbot of Saint-Denis (1122–51) he influenced the development of Gothic architecture

suggest (sə'dʒɛst; *US* səg'dʒɛst) *vb* (*tr; may take a clause as object*) **1** to put forward (a plan, idea, etc) for consideration: *I suggest Smith for the post; a plan suggested itself* **2** to evoke (a person, thing, etc) in the mind of someone by the association of ideas: *that painting suggests home to me* **3** to give an indirect or vague hint of: *his face always suggests his peace of mind* [c16: from Latin *suggerere* to bring up, from SUB- + *gerere* to bring] > sug'gester *n*

suggestible (sə'dʒɛstɪbəl) *adj* **1** easily influenced by ideas provided by other persons **2** characteristic of something that can be suggested > sug'gestibleness *n*

suggestion (sə'dʒɛstʃən) *n* **1** something that is suggested **2** a hint or indication: *a suggestion of the odour of violets* **3** *psychol* the process whereby the mere presentation of an idea to a receptive individual leads to the acceptance of that idea. See also **autosuggestion**

suggestive (sə'dʒɛstɪv) *adj* **1** (*postpositive; foll by of*) conveying a hint (of something) **2** tending to suggest something improper or indecent > sug'gestively *adv* > sug'gestiveness *n*

Suharto (sʊ'hɑːtaʊ) *n* T. N. J. 1921–2008, Indonesian general and statesman; president (1968–98)

suicidal (,su:ɪ'saɪdəl, ,sju:-) *adj* **1** involving, indicating, or tending towards suicide **2** liable to result in suicide: *a suicidal attempt* **3** liable to destroy one's own interests or prospects; dangerously rash > ,sui'cidally *adv*

suicide ('su:ɪ,saɪd, 'sju:-) *n* **1** the act or an instance of killing oneself intentionally **2** the self-inflicted ruin of one's own prospects or interests: *a merger would be financial suicide* **3** a person who kills himself intentionally **4** (*modifier*) reckless; extremely dangerous: *a suicide mission* **5** (*modifier*) (of an action) undertaken or (of a person) undertaking an action in the knowledge that it will result in the death of the person performing it in order that maximum damage may be inflicted on an enemy: *a*

suicide attack; suicide bomber [c17: from New Latin *suīcīdium*, from Latin *suī* of oneself + *-cīdium*, from *caedere* to kill]

suicide bomber *n* a terrorist who carries out a bomb attack, knowing that he or she will be killed in the explosion. Also called: **homicide bomber**

suicide watch *n* a round-the-clock watch by warders on a prisoner considered to be in danger of harming himself or herself

sui generis (,su:aɪ 'dʒɛnərɪs) *adj* unique [Latin, literally: of its own kind]

suint ('su:ɪnt, swɪnt) *n* a water-soluble substance found in the fleece of sheep, consisting of peptides, organic acids, metal ions, and inorganic cations and formed from dried perspiration [c18: from French *suer* to sweat, from Latin *sūdāre*]

Suisse (sɥis) *n* the French name for **Switzerland**

suit (su:t, sju:t) *n* **1** any set of clothes of the same or similar material designed to be worn together, now usually (for men) a jacket with matching trousers or (for women) a jacket with matching or contrasting skirt or trousers **2** (*in combination*) any outfit worn for a specific purpose: *a spacesuit* **3** any set of items, such as the full complement of sails of a vessel or parts of personal armour **4** any of the four sets of 13 cards in a pack of playing cards, being spades, hearts, diamonds, and clubs. The cards in each suit are two to ten, jack, queen, and king in the usual order of ascending value, with ace counting as either the highest or lowest according to the game **5** a civil proceeding; lawsuit **6** the act or process of suing in a court of law **7** a petition or appeal made to a person of superior rank or status or the act of making such a petition **8** *slang* a business executive or white-collar manager **9** a man's courting of a woman **10 follow suit a** to play a card of the same suit as the card played immediately before it **b** to act in the same way as someone else **11 strong suit** *or* **strongest suit** something that one excels in ▷ *vb* **12** to make or be fit or appropriate for **13** to meet the requirements or standards (of) **14** to be agreeable or acceptable to (someone) **15 suit oneself** to pursue one's own intentions without reference to others [c13: from Old French *sieute* set of things, from *sivre* to follow; compare SUE]

suitable ('su:təbəl, 'sju:t-) *adj* appropriate; proper; fit > ,suita'bility *or* 'suitableness *n* > 'suitably *adv*

suitcase ('su:t,keɪs, 'sju:t-) *n* a portable rectangular travelling case, usually stiffened, for carrying clothing, etc

suite (swi:t) *n* **1** a series of items intended to be used together; set **2** a number of connected rooms in a hotel forming one living unit **3** a matching set of furniture, esp of two armchairs and a settee **4** a number of attendants or followers **5** *music* **a** an instrumental composition consisting of several movements in the same key based on or derived from dance rhythms, esp in the baroque period **b** an instrumental composition in several movements less closely connected than a sonata [c17: from French, from Old French *sieute*; see SUIT]

suiting ('su:tɪŋ, 'sju:t-) *n* a fabric used for suits

suitor ('su:tə, 'sju:t-) *n* **1** a man who courts a woman; wooer **2** *law* a person who brings a suit in a court of law; plaintiff **3** *rare* a person who makes a request or appeal for anything [c13: from Anglo-Norman *suter*, from Latin *secūtor* follower, from *sequī* to follow]

Suiyüan (swi:'yɑːn) *n* a former province in N China: now part of the Inner Mongolian Autonomous Region

Sukarnapura (sʊ,kɑːnə'pʊərə) *n* a former name of **Jayapura**

Sukarno *or* **Soekarno** (su:'kɑːnaʊ) *n* Achmed ('ɑːkmɛd). 1901–70, Indonesian statesman; first president of the Republic of Indonesia (1945–67)

Sukarno Peak *n* a former name of (Mount) **Jaya**

Sukarnoputri (su:,kɑːnaʊ'pu:trɪ) *n* Megawati ('mɛgə,wɒtɪ). born 1949, Indonesian politician; president of Indonesia (2001–04): daughter of Achmed Sukarno

Sukhumi (Russian su'xumi) *n* a port and resort in W Georgia, on the Black Sea: site of an ancient Greek colony. Pop: 134 000 (2005 est)

sukiyaki (,su:kɪ'jɑːkɪ) *n* a Japanese dish consisting of very thinly sliced beef or other meat, vegetables, and seasonings cooked together quickly, usually at the table [from Japanese]

Sukkoth or **Succoth** ('sʊkəʊt, -kəʊθ; *Hebrew* suːˈkɔt) *n* an eight-day Jewish harvest festival beginning on Tishri 15, which commemorates the period when the Israelites lived in the wilderness. Also called: **Feast of Tabernacles** [from Hebrew, literally: tabernacles]

Sulawesi (,suːləˈweɪsɪ) *n* an island in E Indonesia: mountainous and forested, with volcanoes and hot springs. Pop: 14 946 488 (2000). Area (including adjacent islands): 229 108 sq km (88 440 sq miles). Also called: **Celebes**

sulcate ('sʌlkeɪt) *adj biology* marked with longitudinal parallel grooves [c18: via Latin *sulcātus* from *sulcāre* to plough, from *sulcus* a furrow]

sulcus ('sʌlkəs) *n*, *pl* -ci (-saɪ) **1** a linear groove, furrow, or slight depression **2** any of the narrow grooves on the surface of the brain that mark the cerebral convolutions [c17: from Latin]

Suleiman I (,suːlɪˈmɑːn, -leɪ-), **Soliman** or **Solyman** *n* called *the Magnificent*. ?1495–1566, sultan of the Ottoman Empire (1520–66), whose reign was noted for its military power and cultural achievements

sulf- *combining form* a US variant of **sulph-**

sulfadiazine (,sʌlfəˈdaɪəˌziːn) *n* an important sulfa drug used chiefly in combination with an antibiotic. Formula: $C_{10}H_{10}N_4O_2S$

sulfur ('sʌlfə) *n* the US preferred spelling of **sulphur**

sulk (sʌlk) *vb* **1** (*intr*) to be silent and resentful because of a wrong done to one, esp in order to gain sympathy; brood sullenly: *the child sulked in a corner after being slapped* ▷ *n* **2** (*often plural*) a state or mood of feeling resentful or sullen: *he's in a sulk because he lost the game; he's got the sulks* **3** Also called: **sulker** a person who sulks [c18: perhaps a back formation from SULKY[1]]

sulky[1] ('sʌlkɪ) *adj* **sulkier, sulkiest 1** sullen, withdrawn, or moody, through or as if through resentment **2** dull or dismal: *sulky weather* [c18: perhaps from obsolete *sulke* sluggish, probably related to Old English *āseolcan* to be lazy] > **'sulkily** *adv* > **'sulkiness** *n*

sulky[2] ('sʌlkɪ) *n*, *pl* **sulkies** a light two-wheeled vehicle for one person, usually drawn by one horse [c18: from SULKY[1], because it can carry only one person]

Sulla ('sʌlə) *n* full name *Lucius Cornelius Sulla Felix*. 138–78 BC, Roman general and dictator (82–79). He introduced reforms to strengthen the power of the Senate

sullage ('sʌlɪdʒ) *n* filth or waste, esp sewage [c16: perhaps from French *souiller* to sully; compare Old English *sol* mud]

sullen ('sʌlən) *adj* **1** unwilling to talk or be sociable; sulky; morose **2** sombre; gloomy ▷ *n* **3** (*plural*) *archaic* a sullen mood [c16: perhaps from Anglo-French *solain* (unattested), ultimately related to Latin *sōlus* alone] > **'sullenly** *adv* > **'sullenness** *n*

Sullivan ('sʌlɪvˀn) *n* **1** Sir Arthur (**Seymour**). 1842–1900, English composer who wrote operettas, such as *H.M.S. Pinafore* (1878) and *The Mikado* (1885), with W. S. Gilbert as librettist **2** Louis (**Henri**). 1856–1924, US pioneer of modern architecture: he coined the slogan "form follows function"

Sullom Voe ('sʌləm vəʊ) *n* a deep coastal inlet in the Shetland Islands, on the N coast of Mainland. It is used for the storage and transshipment of oil

sully ('sʌlɪ) *vb* -lies, -lying, -lied to stain or tarnish (a reputation, etc) or (of a reputation) to become stained or tarnished [c16: probably from French *souiller* to soil]

Sully ('sʌlɪ; *French* sylli) *n* **Maximilien de Béthune** (maksimiljɛ̃ də betyn), Duc de Sully. 1559–1641, French statesman; minister of Henry IV. He helped restore the finances of France after the Wars of Religion

Sully-Prudhomme (*French* sylli prydɔm) *n* **René François Armand** (rəne frɑswa armɑ̃). 1839–1907, French poet: Nobel prize for literature 1901

sulph- or US **sulf-** *combining form* containing sulphur: *sulphate; sulphonic acid*

sulphanilamide (,sʌlfəˈnɪləˌmaɪd) *n* a white odourless crystalline compound formerly used in medicine in the treatment of bacterial infections. Formula: $NH_2C_6H_4SO_2NH_2$

sulphate ('sʌlfeɪt) *n* **1** any salt or ester of sulphuric acid, such as sodium sulphate, Na_2SO_4, sodium hydrogen sulphate, or diethyl sulphate, $(C_2H_5)_2SO_4$ ▷ *vb* **2** (*tr*) to treat with a sulphate or convert into a sulphate **3** to undergo or cause to undergo the formation of a layer of lead sulphate on the plates of an accumulator [c18: from New Latin *sulfātum*; see SULPHUR] > **sul'phation** *n*

sulphide ('sʌlfaɪd) *n* a compound of sulphur with a more electropositive element

sulphite ('sʌlfaɪt) *n* any salt or ester of sulphurous acid, containing the ions SO_3^{2-} or HSO_3^- (**hydrogen sulphite**) or the groups $-SO_3$ or $-HSO_3$. The salts are usually soluble crystalline compounds > **sulphitic** (sʌlˈfɪtɪk) *adj*

sulphonamide (sʌlˈfɒnəˌmaɪd) *n* any of a class of organic compounds that are amides of sulphonic acids containing the group $-SO_2NH_2$ or a group derived from this. An important class of sulphonamides are the sulfa drugs

sulphone ('sʌlfəʊn) *n* any of a class of organic compounds containing the divalent group $-SO_2$ linked to two other organic groups. Certain sulphones are used in the treatment of leprosy and tuberculosis

sulphonic acid (sʌlˈfɒnɪk) *n* any of a large group of strong organic acids that contain the group $-SO_2OH$ and are used in the manufacture of dyes and drugs

sulphonmethane (,sʌlfɒnˈmiːθeɪn) *n* a colourless crystalline compound used medicinally as a hypnotic. Formula: $C_7H_{16}O_4S_2$

sulphur or US **sulfur** ('sʌlfə) *n* **a** an allotropic nonmetallic element, occurring free in volcanic regions and in combined state in gypsum, pyrite, and galena. The stable yellow rhombic form converts on heating to monoclinic needles. It is used in the production of sulphuric acid, in the vulcanization of rubber, and in fungicides. Symbol: S; atomic no: 16; atomic wt: 32.066; valency: 2, 4, or 6; relative density: 2.07 (rhombic), 1.957 (monoclinic); melting pt: 115.22°C (rhombic), 119.0°C (monoclinic); boiling pt: 444.674°C **b** (*as modifier*): *sulphur springs* [c14 soufre, from Old French, from Latin *sulfur*] > **sulphuric** or US **sulfuric** (sʌlˈfjʊərɪk) *adj*

sulphurate ('sʌlfjʊˌreɪt) *vb* (*tr*) to combine or treat with sulphur or a sulphur compound > **sulphu'ration** *n*

sulphur-bottom *n* another name for **blue whale**

sulphur-crested cockatoo *n* a large Australian white parrot, *Kakatoe galerita*, with a yellow erectile crest. Also called: **white cockatoo**

sulphur dioxide *n* a colourless soluble pungent gas produced by burning sulphur. It is both an oxidizing and a reducing agent and is used in the manufacture of sulphuric acid, the preservation of a wide range of foodstuffs (**E220**), bleaching, and disinfecting. Formula: SO_2

sulphureous (sʌlˈfjʊərɪəs) *adj* **1** another word for **sulphurous** (sense 1) **2** of the yellow colour of sulphur

sulphuretted hydrogen *n* another name for **hydrogen sulphide**

sulphuric acid *n* a colourless dense oily corrosive liquid produced by the reaction of sulphur trioxide with water and used in accumulators and in the manufacture of fertilizers, dyes, and explosives. Formula: H_2SO_4

sulphurize or **sulphurise** ('sʌlfjʊˌraɪz) *vb* (*tr*) to combine or treat with sulphur or a sulphur compound > **,sulphuri'zation** or **,sulphuri'sation** *n*

sulphurous ('sʌlfərəs) *adj* **1** Also called: **sulphureous** of, relating to, or resembling sulphur: *a sulphurous colour* **2** of or containing sulphur with an oxidation state of 4: *sulphurous acid* **3** of or relating to hellfire **4** hot-tempered > **'sulphurously** *adv* > **'sulphurousness** *n*

sulphurous acid *n* an unstable acid produced when sulphur dioxide dissolves in water: used as a preservative for food and a bleaching agent. Formula: H_2SO_3

sulphur trioxide *n* a white corrosive substance existing in three crystalline forms of which the stable (*alpha*-) form is usually obtained as silky needles. It is produced by the oxidation of sulphur dioxide, and is used in the sulphonation of organic compounds. Formula: SO_3

sultan ('sʌltən) *n* **1** the sovereign of a Muslim country,

S

esp of the former Ottoman Empire **2** a small domestic fowl with a white crest and heavily feathered legs and feet: originated in Turkey [C16: from Medieval Latin *sultānus*, from Arabic *sultān* rule, from Aramaic *salita* to rule]

sultana ('sʌl'tɑ:nə) *n* **1 a** the dried fruit of a small white seedless grape, originally produced in SW Asia: used in cakes, curries, etc; seedless raisin **b** the grape itself **2** Also called: **sultaness** a wife, concubine, or female relative of a sultan **3** a mistress; concubine [C16: from Italian, feminine of *sultano* SULTAN]

sultanate ('sʌltə,neɪt) *n* **1** the territory or a country ruled by a sultan **2** the office, rank, or jurisdiction of a sultan

sultry ('sʌltrɪ) *adj* -trier, -triest **1** (of weather or climate) oppressively hot and humid **2** characterized by or emitting oppressive heat **3** displaying or suggesting passion; sensual: *sultry eyes* [C16: from obsolete *sulter* to SWELTER + -Y¹] > '**sultrily** *adv* > '**sultriness** *n*

Sulu Archipelago ('su:lu:) *n* a chain of over 500 islands in the SW Philippines, separating the Sulu Sea from the Celebes Sea: formerly a sultanate, ceded to the Philippines in 1940. Capital: Jolo. Pop: 619 668 (2000). Area: 2686 sq km (1037 sq miles)

Sulu Sea *n* part of the W Pacific between Borneo and the central Philippines

sum (sʌm) *n* **1** the result of the addition of numbers, quantities, objects, etc **2** one or more columns or rows of numbers to be added, subtracted, multiplied, or divided **3** *maths* the limit of a series of sums of the first *n* terms of a converging infinite series as *n* tends to infinity **4** a quantity, esp of money: *he borrows enormous sums* **5** the essence or gist of a matter (esp in the phrases **in sum, in sum and substance**) **6** a less common word for **summary 7** (*modifier*) complete or final (esp in the phrase **sum total**) ▷ *vb* sums, summing, summed **8** (often foll by *up*) to add or form a total of (something) **9** (*tr*) to calculate the sum of (the terms in a sequence) ▷ See also **sum up** [C13 *summe*, from Old French, from Latin *summa* the top, sum, from *summus* highest, from *superus* in a higher position; see SUPER]

sumach or *US* **sumac** ('su:mæk, 'ʃu:-) *n* **1** any temperate or subtropical shrub or small tree of the anacardiaceous genus *Rhus*, having compound leaves, clusters of green flowers, and red hairy fruits **2** a preparation of powdered leaves of certain species of *Rhus*, esp *R. coriaria*, used in dyeing and tanning **3** the wood of any of these plants [C14: via Old French from Arabic *summāq*]

Sumatra (sʊ'mɑ:trə) *n* a mountainous island in W Indonesia, in the Greater Sunda Islands, separated from the Malay Peninsula by the Strait of Malacca: Dutch control began in the 16th century; joined Indonesia in 1945. Northern coastal areas, esp Aceh province, suffered devastation as a result of the Indian Ocean tsunami of December 2004. Pop: 42 409 510 (2000). Area: 473 606 sq km (182 821 sq miles) > Su'matran *adj, n*

Sumba ('su:mbə) *n* an island in Indonesia, in the Lesser Sunda Islands, separated from Flores by the **Sumba Strait**: formerly important for sandalwood exports. Pop: 355 073 (1990). Area: 11 153 sq km (4306 sq miles). Former name: Sandalwood Island

Sumbawa (su:m'bɑ:wə) *n* a mountainous island in Indonesia, in the Lesser Sunda Islands, between Lombok and Flores islands. Pop: 1 540 000 (2000). Area: 14 750 sq km (5695 sq miles). Former spelling: Soembawa

Sumer ('su:mə) *n* the S region of Babylonia; seat of a civilization of city-states that reached its height in the 3rd millennium BC

Sumerian (su:'mɪərɪən, -'mɛər-) *n* **1** a member of a people who established a civilization in Sumer during the 4th millennium BC **2** the extinct language of this people, of no known relationship to any other language ▷ *adj* **3** of or relating to ancient Sumer, its inhabitants, or their language or civilization

summa cum laude ('sʊmɑ: kʊm 'laʊdeɪ) *adv, adj chiefly US* with the utmost praise: the highest of three designations for above-average achievement in examinations. In Britain it is sometimes used to designate a first-class honours degree [from Latin]

summarize or **summarise** ('sʌmə,raɪz) *vb* (*tr*) to make or

be a summary of; express concisely > ,summari'zation or ,summari'sation *n* > 'summa,rizer, 'summa,riser or 'summarist *n*

summary ('sʌmərɪ) *n, pl* -maries **1** a brief account giving the main points of something ▷ *adj* (*usually prenominal*) **2** performed arbitrarily and quickly, without formality: *a summary execution* **3** (of legal proceedings) short and free from the complexities and delays of a full trial **4** summary jurisdiction the right a court has to adjudicate immediately upon some matter arising during its proceedings **5** giving the gist or essence [C15: from Latin *summārium*, from *summa* SUM¹] > 'summarily *adv* > 'summariness *n*

summary offence *n* an offence that is triable in a magistrates' court

summation (sʌ'meɪʃən) *n* **1** the act or process of determining a sum; addition **2** the result of such an act or process **3** a summary **4** *US law* the concluding statements made by opposing counsel in a case before a court [C18: from Medieval Latin *summātiō*, from *summāre* to total, from Latin *summa* SUM¹] > sum'mational *adj* > 'summative *adj*

summative assessment ('sʌmətɪv) *n Brit education* general assessment of a pupil's achievements over a range of subjects by means of a combined appraisal of formative assessments

summer ('sʌmə) *n* **1** (*sometimes capital*) **a** the warmest season of the year, between spring and autumn, astronomically from the June solstice to the September equinox in the N hemisphere and at the opposite time of year in the S hemisphere **b** (*as modifier*): *summer flowers; a summer dress*. Related adj: **aestival 2** the period of hot weather associated with the summer **3** a time of blossoming, greatest happiness, etc **4** *chiefly poetic* a year represented by this season: *a child of nine summers* ▷ *vb* **5** (*intr*) to spend the summer (at a place) **6** (*tr*) to keep or feed (farm animals) during the summer: *they summered their cattle on the mountain slopes* [Old English *sumor*; related to Old Frisian *sumur*, Old Norse *sumar*, Old High German *sumar*, Sanskrit *samā* season] > 'summerly *adj, adv* > 'summery *adj*

summerhouse ('sʌmə,haʊs) *n* a small building in a garden or park, used for shade or recreation in the summer

summer pudding *n Brit* a pudding made by filling a bread-lined basin with a purée of fruit, leaving it to soak, and then turning it out

summersault ('sʌmə,sɔ:lt) *n, vb* a variant spelling of **somersault**

summer school *n* a school, academic course, etc, held during the summer

summer solstice *n* **1** the time at which the sun is at its northernmost point in the sky (southernmost point in the S hemisphere), appearing at noon at its highest altitude above the horizon. It occurs about June 21 (December 22 in the S hemisphere) **2** *astronomy* the point on the celestial sphere, opposite the **winter solstice**, at which the ecliptic is furthest north from the celestial equator. Right ascension: 6 hours; declination: 23.5°

summertime ('sʌmə,taɪm) *n* the period or season of summer

summer time *n Brit* any daylight-saving time, esp British Summer Time

summerweight ('sʌmə,weɪt) *adj* (of clothes) suitable in weight for wear in the summer; relatively light

summing-up *n* **1** a review or summary of the main points of an argument, speech, etc **2** a direction regarding the law and a summary of the evidence, given by a judge in his address to the jury before they retire to consider their verdict

summit ('sʌmɪt) *n* **1** the highest point or part, esp of a mountain or line of communication; top **2** the highest possible degree or state; peak or climax: *the summit of ambition* **3** the highest level, importance, or rank: *a meeting at the summit* **4 a** a meeting of chiefs of governments or other high officials **b** (*as modifier*): *a summit conference* [C15: from Old French *somet*, diminutive of *som*, from Latin *summum*; see SUM¹]

summon ('sʌmən) *vb* (*tr*) **1** to order to come; send for, esp to attend court, by issuing a summons **2** to order or instruct (to do something) or call (to something): *the bell summoned them to their work* **3** to call upon to meet or convene **4** (often foll by *up*) to muster or gather (one's strength, courage, etc) [c13: from Latin *summonēre* to give a discreet reminder, from *monēre* to advise]

summons ('sʌmənz) *n, pl* -**monses 1** a call, signal, or order to do something, esp to appear in person or attend at a specified place or time **2 a** an official order requiring a person to attend court, either to answer a charge or to give evidence **b** the writ making such an order **3** a call or command given to the members of an assembly to convene a meeting ▷ *vb* **4** to take out a summons against (a person) [c13: from Old French *somonse*, from *somondre* to SUMMON]

summum bonum *Latin* ('sʊmʊm 'bɒnʊm) *n* the principle of goodness in which all moral values are included or from which they are derived; highest or supreme good

sumo ('suːməʊ) *n* the national style of wrestling of Japan, the object of which is to force one's opponent to touch the ground with any part of his body except the soles of his feet or to step out of the ring [from Japanese *sumō*]

sump (sʌmp) *n* **1** a receptacle, such as the lower part of the crankcase of an internal-combustion engine, into which liquids, esp lubricants, can drain to form a reservoir **2** another name for **cesspool 3** *mining* a depression at the bottom of a shaft where water collects before it is pumped away [c17: from Middle Dutch *somp* marsh; see SWAMP]

sumpter ('sʌmptə) *n archaic* a packhorse, mule, or other beast of burden [c14: from Old French *sometier* driver of a baggage horse, from Vulgar Latin *sagmatārius* (unattested), from Late Latin *sagma* packsaddle]

sumptuary ('sʌmptjʊərɪ) *adj* relating to or controlling expenditure or extravagance [c17: from Latin *sumptuārius* concerning expense, from *sumptus* expense, from *sūmere* to spend]

sumptuous ('sʌmptjʊəs) *adj* **1** expensive or extravagant: *sumptuous costumes* **2** magnificent; splendid: *a sumptuous scene* [c16: from Old French *sumptueux*, from Latin *sumptuōsus* costly, from *sumptus*; see SUMPTUARY]
> '**sumptuously** *adv* > '**sumptuousness** *or* **sumptuosity** (,sʌmptjʊ'ɒsɪtɪ) *n*

Sumter ('sʌmtə) *n* See **Fort Sumter**

sum up *vb* (*adverb*) **1** to summarize (feelings, the main points of an argument, etc): *the judge began to sum up* **2** (*tr*) to form a quick opinion of: *I summed him up in five minutes*

Sumy (*Russian* 'sumi) *n* a city in Ukraine, on the River Pysol: site of early Slav settlements. Pop: 294 000 (2005 est)

sun (sʌn) *n* **1** the star at the centre of our solar system. It is a gaseous body having a highly compressed core, in which energy is generated by thermonuclear reactions (at about 15 million kelvins), surrounded by less dense radiative and convective zones serving to transport the energy to the surface (the **photosphere**). The atmospheric layers (the **chromosphere** and **corona**) are normally invisible except during a total eclipse. Mass and diameter: 333 000 and 109 times that of earth respectively; mean distance from earth: 149.6 million km (1 astronomical unit). Related adj: **solar 2** any star around which a planetary system revolves **3** the sun as it appears at a particular time or place: *the winter sun* **4** the radiant energy, esp heat and light, received from the sun; sunshine **5** a person or thing considered as a source of radiant warmth, glory, etc **6** a pictorial representation of the sun, often depicted with a human face **7** *poetic* a year or a day **8** *poetic* a climate **9** *archaic* sunrise or sunset (esp in the phrase **from sun to sun**) **10** catch the sun to become slightly sunburnt **11** place in the sun a prominent or favourable position **12** shoot the sun *or* take the sun *nautical* to measure the altitude of the sun in order to determine latitude **13** touch of the sun slight sunstroke **14** under the sun on earth; at all: *nobody under the sun eats more than you do* ▷ *vb* **suns, sunning, sunned 15** (*tr*) to expose to the sunshine in order to warm, tan, etc [Old English *sunne*; related to Old High German *sunna*, Old Frisian *senne*,

Gothic *sunno*]

Sun. *abbreviation* Sunday

sunbaked ('sʌn,beɪkt) *adj* **1** (esp of roads, etc) dried or cracked by the sun's heat **2** baked hard by the heat of the sun: *sunbaked bricks*

sun bath *n* the exposure of the body to the rays of the sun or a sun lamp, esp in order to get a suntan

sunbathe ('sʌn,beɪð) *vb* (*intr*) to bask in the sunshine, esp in order to get a suntan > '**sun,bather** *n*

sunbeam ('sʌn,biːm) *n* a beam, ray, or stream of sunlight > '**sun,beamed** *or* '**sun,beamy** *adj*

sunbed ('sʌn,bɛd) *n Brit* **1** a piece of equipment, usu consisting of rows of lights, which surrounds a person with ultraviolet rays in order to induce an artificial suntan **2** a bed or couch for lying on in the sun

Sunbelt ('sʌn,bɛlt) *n* the southern states of the USA

sunbird ('sʌn,bɜːd) *n* any small songbird of the family *Nectariniidae*, of tropical regions of the Old World, esp Africa, having a long slender curved bill and a bright plumage in the males

sun block *n* a chemical, usually in the form of a cream, applied to exposed skin to block out all or almost all of the ultraviolet rays of the sun

sunbonnet ('sʌn,bɒnɪt) *n* a hat that shades the face and neck from the sun, esp one made of cotton with a projecting brim now worn esp by babies

sunburn ('sʌn,bɜːn) *n* **1** inflammation of the skin caused by overexposure to the sun **2** another word for **suntan** > '**sun,burnt** *or* '**sun,burned** *adj*

sunburst ('sʌn,bɜːst) *n* **1** a burst of sunshine, as through a break in the clouds **2** a pattern or design resembling that of the sun **3** a jewelled brooch with this pattern

Sunbury-on-Thames ('sʌnbərɪ, -brɪ) *n* a town in SE England, in N Surrey. Pop: 27 415 (2001)

sun-cured *adj* cured or preserved by exposure to the sun

sundae ('sʌndɪ, -deɪ) *n* ice cream topped with a sweet sauce, nuts, whipped cream, etc [c20: of uncertain origin]

Sunda Islands ('sʌndə) *pl n* a chain of islands in the Malay Archipelago, consisting of the **Greater Sunda Islands** (chiefly Sumatra, Java, Borneo, and Sulawesi) and **Nusa Tenggara** (the Lesser Sunda Islands)

Sunda Strait *n* a strait between Sumatra and Java, linking the Java Sea with the Indian Ocean. Narrowest point: about 26 km (16 miles)

Sunday ('sʌndɪ) *n* the first day of the week and the Christian day of worship [Old English *sunnandæg*, translation of Latin *diēs sōlis* day of the sun, translation of Greek *hēmera hēliou*; related to Old Norse *sunnu dagr*, German *Sonntag*]

Sunday best *n* one's best clothes, esp regarded as those most suitable for churchgoing

Sunday school *n* **1 a** a school for the religious instruction of children on Sundays, usually held in a church hall and formerly also providing secular education **b** (*as modifier*): *a Sunday-school outing* **2** the members of such a school

sunder ('sʌndə) *archaic or literary* ▷ *vb* **1** to break or cause to break apart or in pieces ▷ *n* **2** in sunder into pieces; apart [Old English *sundrian*; related to Old Norse *sundr* asunder, Gothic *sundrō* apart, Old High German *suntar*, Latin *sine* without]

Sunderland ('sʌndələnd) *n* **1** a city and port in NE England, in Sunderland unitary authority, Tyne and Wear at the mouth of the River Wear: formerly known for shipbuilding now has car manufacturing, chemicals; university (1992). Pop: 177 739 (2001) **2** a unitary authority in NE England, in Tyne and Wear. Pop: 283 100 (2003 est). Area: 138 sq km (53 sq miles)

sundew ('sʌn,djuː) *n* any of several bog plants of the genus *Drosera*, having leaves covered with sticky hairs that trap and digest insects: family *Droseraceae* [c16: translation of Latin *ros solis*]

sundial ('sʌn,daɪəl) *n* a device indicating the time during the hours of sunlight by means of a stationary arm (the **gnomon**) that casts a shadow onto a plate or surface marked in hours

sun disc *n* a disc symbolizing the sun, esp one flanked by two serpents and the extended wings of a vulture,

S

used as a religious figure in ancient Egypt

sundog ('sʌnˌdɒg) n another word for **parhelion**

sundown ('sʌnˌdaʊn) n another name for **sunset**

sundowner ('sʌnˌdaʊnə) n **1** Austral & NZ obsolete, slang a tramp, esp one who seeks food and lodging at sundown when it is too late to work **2** informal, chiefly Brit an alcoholic drink taken at sunset

sundress ('sʌnˌdrɛs) n a dress for hot weather that exposes the shoulders, arms, and back, esp one with straps over the shoulders

sun-dried adj dried or preserved by exposure to the sun

sundry ('sʌndrɪ) determiner **1** several or various; miscellaneous ▷ pron **2** all and sundry all the various people, individually and collectively ▷ n **3** (plural) miscellaneous unspecified items [Old English syndrig separate; related to Old High German suntarīg; see SUNDER, -Y¹]

Sundsvall (Swedish 'sʊndsval) n a port in E Sweden, on the Gulf of Bothnia: icebound in winter; cellulose industries. Pop: 93 623 (2004 est)

sunfast ('sʌnˌfaːst) adj chiefly US & Canadian not fading in sunlight

sunfish ('sʌnˌfɪʃ) n, pl -fish or -fishes **1** any large plectognath fish of the family Molidae, of temperate and tropical seas, esp Mola mola, which has a large rounded compressed body, long pointed dorsal and anal fins, and a fringelike tail fin **2** any of various small predatory North American freshwater percoid fishes of the family Centrarchidae, typically having a compressed brightly coloured body

sunflower ('sʌnˌflaʊə) n **1** any of several American plants of the genus Helianthus, esp H. annuus, having very tall thick stems, large flower heads with yellow rays, and seeds used as food, esp for poultry: family Asteraceae (composites). See also **Jerusalem artichoke 2** sunflower seed oil the oil extracted from sunflower seeds, used as a salad oil, in the manufacture of margarine, etc

sung (sʌŋ) vb **1** the past participle of **sing** ▷ adj **2** produced by singing: a sung syllable
◉ USAGE See at **ring²**

Sung or **Song** (sʊŋ) n an imperial dynasty of China (960–1279 AD), notable for its art, literature, and philosophy

Sungari ('sʊŋgərɪ) n another name for the **Songhua**

Sungkiang ('sʊŋ'kjæŋ, -kaɪ'æŋ) n a former province of NE China: now part of the Inner Mongolian Autonomous Region

sunglass ('sʌnˌglaːs) n a convex lens used to focus the sun's rays and thus produce heat or ignition; burning glass

sunglasses ('sʌnˌglaːsɪz) pl n glasses with darkened or polarizing lenses that protect the eyes from the sun's glare

sun-god n **1** the sun considered as a personal deity **2** a deity associated with the sun or controlling its movements

sunk (sʌŋk) vb **1** a past participle of **sink** ▷ adj **2** informal with all hopes dashed; ruined

sunken ('sʌŋkən) vb **1** a past participle of **sink** ▷ adj **2** unhealthily hollow: sunken cheeks **3** situated at a lower level than the surrounding or usual one **4** situated under water; submerged **5** depressed; low: sunken spirits

sunk fence n a ditch, one side of which is made into a retaining wall so as to enclose an area of land while remaining hidden in the total landscape. Also called: ha-ha

Sun King n the an epithet of **Louis XIV**

sun lamp n **1** a lamp that generates ultraviolet rays, used for obtaining an artificial suntan, for muscular therapy, etc **2** a lamp used in film studios, etc, to give an intense beam of light by means of parabolic mirrors

sunless ('sʌnlɪs) adj **1** without sun or sunshine **2** gloomy; depressing ▷ 'sunlessly adv

sunlight ('sʌnlaɪt) n **1** the light emanating from the sun **2** an area or the time characterized by sunshine ▷ 'sunlit adj

sun lounge or US **sun parlor** n a room with large windows positioned to receive as much sunlight as possible

Sunna ('sʌnə) n the body of traditional Islamic law accepted by most orthodox Muslims as based on the words and acts of Mohammed [c18: from Arabic sunnah rule]

Sunni ('sʌnɪ) n **1** one of the two main branches of orthodox Islam (the other being the Shiah), consisting of those who acknowledge the authority of the Sunna **2** pl -nis or -ni another term for **Sunnite**

sunnies ('sʌnɪz) pl n NZ informal a pair of sunglasses

Sunnite ('sʌnaɪt) n Islam an adherent of the Sunni

sunny ('sʌnɪ) adj -nier, -niest **1** full of or exposed to sunlight **2** radiating good humour **3** of or resembling the sun ▷ 'sunnily adv ▷ 'sunniness n

sunrise ('sʌnˌraɪz) n **1** the daily appearance of the sun above the horizon **2** the atmospheric phenomena accompanying this appearance

sunrise industry n any of the high-technology industries, such as electronics, that hold promise of future development

sunroof ('sʌnˌruːf) or **sunshine roof** n a panel, often translucent, that may be opened in the roof of a car

sunscreen ('sʌnˌskriːn) n a cream or lotion applied to exposed skin to protect it from the ultraviolet rays of the sun

sunset ('sʌnˌsɛt) n **1** the daily disappearance of the sun below the horizon **2** the atmospheric phenomena accompanying this disappearance **3** Also called: sundown the time at which the sun sets at a particular locality **4** the final stage or closing period, as of a person's life

sunset clause n chiefly US & Canadian a provision of a law that it will automatically be terminated after a fixed period unless it is extended by law

sunshade ('sʌnˌʃeɪd) n a device, esp a parasol or awning, serving to shade from the sun

sunshine ('sʌnˌʃaɪn) n **1** the light received directly from the sun **2** the warmth from the sun **3** a sunny area **4** a light-hearted or ironic term of address ▷ 'sunˌshiny adj

sun sign n another name for **sign of the zodiac**

sunspot ('sʌnˌspɒt) n **1** any of the dark cool patches, with a diameter of up to several thousand kilometres, that appear on the surface of the sun and last about a week. They occur in approximately 11-year cycles and possess a strong magnetic field **2** informal a sunny holiday resort **3** Austral a small cancerous spot produced by overexposure to the sun

sunstroke ('sʌnˌstrəʊk) n heatstroke caused by prolonged exposure to intensely hot sunlight

sunsuit ('sʌnˌsuːt, -ˌsjuːt) n a child's outfit consisting of a brief top and shorts or a short skirt

suntan ('sʌnˌtæn) n **a** a brownish colouring of the skin caused by the formation of the pigment melanin within the skin on exposure to the ultraviolet rays of the sun or a sunlamp. Often shortened to: tan **b** (as modifier): suntan oil ▷ 'sunˌtanned adj

suntrap ('sʌnˌtræp) n a very sunny sheltered place

sunward ('sʌnwəd) adj directed or moving towards the sun ▷ adv

Sun Yat-sen (sʊn 'jɑːt'sɛn) n 1866–1925, Chinese statesman, who was instrumental in the overthrow of the Manchu dynasty and was the first president of the Republic of China (1911). He reorganized the Kuomintang

Suomi ('sʊɒmi) n the Finnish name for **Finland**

sup¹ (sʌp) vb sups, supping, supped (intr) archaic to have supper [c13: from Old French soper; see SUP²]

sup² (sʌp) vb sups, supping, supped **1** to partake of (liquid) by swallowing a little at a time **2** Scot & northern English dialect to drink ▷ n **3** a sip [Old English sūpan; related to Old High German sūfan, German saufen; see also SUP¹]

sup. abbreviation **1** above [from Latin supra] **2** superior **3** grammar superlative

super ('suːpə) adj **1** informal outstanding; exceptionally fine ▷ n **2** petrol with a high octane rating **3** informal a superintendent or supervisor **4** Austral & NZ informal superannuation benefits **5** Austral & NZ informal superphosphate ▷ interj **6** Brit informal an enthusiastic expression of approval or assent [from Latin: above]

super- *prefix* **1** placed above or over: *superscript* **2** of greater size, extent, quality, etc: *supermarket* **3** surpassing others; outstanding: *superstar* **4** beyond a standard or norm; exceeding or exceedingly: *supersonic* **5** indicating that a chemical compound contains a specified element in a higher proportion than usual: *superoxide* [from Latin *super* above]

superable ('su:pərəbəl, -prəbəl) *adj* able to be surmounted or overcome [c17: from Latin *superābilis*, from *superāre* to overcome] > ,supera'bility *or* 'superableness *n* > 'superably *adv*

superannuate (,su:pər'ænjʊ,eɪt) *vb* (*tr*) **1** to pension off **2** to discard as obsolete or old-fashioned

superannuated (,su:pər'ænjʊ,eɪtɪd) *adj* **1** discharged, esp with a pension, owing to age or illness **2** too old to serve usefully **3** obsolete [c17: from Medieval Latin *superannnātus* aged more than one year, from Latin SUPER- + *annus* a year]

superannuation (,su:pər,ænjʊ'eɪʃən) *n* **1 a** the amount deducted regularly from employees' incomes in a contributory pension scheme **b** the pension finally paid to such employees **2** the act or process of superannuating or the condition of being superannuated

superb (sʊ'pɜ:b, sjʊ-) *adj* **1** surpassingly good; excellent **2** majestic or imposing [c16: from Old French *superbe*, from Latin *superbus* distinguished, from *super* above] > su'perbly *adv* > su'perbness *n*

superbike ('su:pə,baɪk) *n* a high-performance motorcycle

Super Bowl *n American football* the main championship game of the sport, held annually in January between the champions of the American Football Conference and the National Football Conference

superbug ('su:pə,bʌg) *n informal* an infective microorganism that has become resistant to antibiotics

supercalender (,su:pə'kæləndə) *n* **1** a calender with a number of rollers that gives a high gloss to paper ▷ *vb* **2** (*tr*) to produce a glossy finish on (paper) by pressing in a supercalender > ,super'calendered *adj*

supercargo (,su:pə'kɑ:gəʊ) *n*, *pl* -goes an officer on a merchant ship who supervises commercial matters and is in charge of the cargo [c17: changed from Spanish *sobrecargo*, from *sobre* over (from Latin SUPER) + *cargo* CARGO]

supercharge ('su:pə,tʃɑ:dʒ) *vb* (*tr*) **1** to increase the air intake pressure of (an internal-combustion engine) with a supercharger; boost **2** to charge (the atmosphere, a remark, etc) with an excess amount of (tension, emotion, etc) **3** to apply pressure to (a fluid); pressurize

supercharger ('su:pə,tʃɑ:dʒə) *n* a device, usually a fan or compressor driven by the engine, that increases the mass of air drawn into an internal-combustion engine by raising the intake pressure. Also called: blower, booster

superciliary (,su:pə'sɪlɪərɪ) *adj* relating to or situated over the eyebrow or a corresponding region in lower animals [c18: from New Latin *superciliaris*, from Latin *supercilium*, from SUPER- + *cilium* eyelid]

supercilious (,su:pə'sɪlɪəs) *adj* displaying arrogant pride, scorn, or indifference [c16: from Latin *superciliōsus*, from *supercilium* eyebrow; see SUPERCILIARY] > ,super'ciliously *adv* > ,super'ciliousness *n*

superclass ('su:pə,klɑ:s) *n* a taxonomic group that is a subdivision of a subphylum

supercolumnar (,su:pəkə'lʌmnə) *adj architect* **1** having one colonnade above another **2** placed above a colonnade or a column > ,supercol,umni'ation *n*

superconductivity (,su:pə,kɒndʌk'tɪvɪtɪ) *n physics* the property of certain substances that have no electrical resistance. In metals it occurs at very low temperatures, but higher temperature superconductivity occurs in some ceramic materials > superconduction (,su:pəkən'dʌkʃən) *n* > ,supercon'ductive *or* ,supercon'ducting *adj* > ,supercon'ductor *n*

supercontinent ('su:pə,kɒntɪnənt) *n* a great landmass thought to have existed in the geological past and to have split into smaller landmasses, which drifted and formed the present continents

supercool (,su:pə'ku:l) *vb chem* to cool or be cooled without freezing or crystallization to a temperature below that at which freezing or crystallization should occur. Supercooled liquids are not in equilibrium

supercritical (,su:pə'krɪtɪkəl) *adj* **1** *physics* (of a fluid) brought to a temperature and pressure higher than its critical temperature and pressure, so that its physical and chemical properties change **2** *nuclear physics* of or containing more than the critical mass

superdense theory (,su:pə'dɛns) *n astronomy* a former name for the **big-bang theory**

super-duper ('su:pə'du:pə) *adj informal* extremely pleasing, impressive, etc: often used as an exclamation

superego (,su:pər'i:gəʊ, -'ɛgəʊ) *n*, *pl* -gos *psychoanal* that part of the unconscious mind that acts as a conscience for the ego, developing mainly from the relationship between a child and his parents. See also **id¹, ego**

superelevation (,su:pər,ɛlɪ'veɪʃən) *n* **1** another name for **bank²** (sense 7) **2** the difference between the heights of the sides of a road or railway track on a bend

supereminent (,su:pər'ɛmɪnənt) *adj* of distinction, dignity, or rank superior to that of others; pre-eminent > ,super'eminence *n*

supererogate (,su:pər'ɛrə,geɪt) *vb* (*intr*) *obsolete* to do or perform more than is required [c16: from Late Latin *supererogāre* to spend over and above, from Latin SUPER- + *ērogāre* to pay out] > ,super'ero,gator *n*

supererogation (,su:pər,ɛrə'geɪʃən) *n* **1** the performance of work in excess of that required **2** *RC Church* supererogatory prayers, devotions, etc

supererogatory (,su:pərɛ'rɒgətərɪ, -trɪ) *adj* **1** performed to an extent exceeding that required or expected **2** exceeding what is needed; superfluous **3** *RC Church* of, characterizing, or relating to prayers, good works, etc, performed over and above those prescribed as obligatory [c16: from Medieval Latin *supererogātōrius*; see SUPEREROGATE]

superfamily ('su:pə,fæmɪlɪ) *n*, *pl* -lies **1** *biology* a taxonomic group that is a subdivision of a suborder **2** any analogous group, such as a group of related languages

superfecundation (,su:pə,fi:kən'deɪʃən) *n physiol* the fertilization of two or more ova, produced during the same menstrual cycle, by sperm ejaculated during two or more acts of sexual intercourse

superfetation (,su:pəfi'teɪʃən) *n physiol* the presence in the uterus of two fetuses developing from ova fertilized at different times [C17 *superfetate*, from Latin *superfētāre* to fertilize when already pregnant, from SUPER- + *fētāre* to impregnate, from *fētus* offspring]

superficial (,su:pə'fɪʃəl) *adj* **1** of, relating to, being near, or forming the surface: *superficial bruising* **2** displaying a lack of thoroughness or care: *a superficial inspection* **3** only outwardly apparent rather than genuine or actual: *the similarity was merely superficial* **4** of little substance or significance; trivial: *superficial differences* **5** lacking originality or profundity: *the film's plot was quite superficial* **6** (of measurements) involving only the surface area [c14: from Late Latin *superficiālis* of the surface, from Latin SUPERFICIES] > superficiality (,su:pə,fɪʃɪ'ælɪtɪ) *or less commonly* ,super'ficialness *n* > ,super'ficially *adv*

superficies (,su:pə'fɪʃɪ:z) *n*, *pl* -cies *rare* **1** a surface or outer face **2** the outward form of a thing [c16: from Latin: upper side, from super- + *faciēs* face]

superfine (,su:pə'faɪn) *adj* **1** of exceptional fineness or quality **2** excessively refined > ,super'fineness *n*

superfix ('su:pə,fɪks) *n linguistics* a suprasegmental feature distinguishing the meaning or grammatical function of one word or phrase from that of another, as stress does for example between the noun *conduct* and the verb *conduct* [from SUPER- + -*fix*, on the model of PREFIX, SUFFIX]

superfluid (,su:pə'flu:ɪd) *n* **1** *physics* a fluid in a state characterized by a very low viscosity, high thermal conductivity, high capillarity, etc. The only known example is that of liquid helium at temperatures close to absolute zero ▷ *adj* **2** being or relating to a superfluid

superfluity (,su:pə'flu:ɪtɪ) *n* **1** the condition of being superfluous **2** a quantity or thing that is in excess of what is needed **3** a thing that is not needed [c14: from Old French *superfluité*, via Late Latin from Latin *superfluus* SUPERFLUOUS]

superfluous (suːˈpɜːflʊəs) *adj* **1** exceeding what is sufficient or required **2** not necessary or relevant; uncalled-for [c15: from Latin *superfluus* overflowing, from SUPER- + *fluere* to flow] > su'perfluously *adv* > su'perfluousness *n*

Super-G *n skiing* a type of slalom in which the course is shorter than in a standard slalom and the obstacles are farther apart than in a giant slalom [c20: from SUPER- + G(IANT)]

supergiant ('suːpəˌdʒaɪənt) *n* any of a class of extremely large and luminous stars, such as Betelgeuse, which have expanded to a large diameter and are eventually likely to explode as supernovae

superglue ('suːpəˌgluː) *n* any of various impact adhesives that quickly make an exceptionally strong bond

supergrass ('suːpəˌɡrɑːs) *n* an informer whose information implicates a large number of people in terrorist activities or other major crimes

supergravity (ˌsuːpəˈɡrævɪtɪ) *n physics* any of various theories in which supersymmetry is applied to the theory of gravitation

superheat (ˌsuːpəˈhiːt) *vb* (*tr*) **1** to heat (a vapour, esp steam) to a temperature above its saturation point for a given pressure **2** to heat (a liquid) to a temperature above its boiling point without boiling occurring **3** to heat excessively; overheat > ˌsuper'heater *n*

superheavy (ˌsuːpəˈhɛvɪ) *adj physics* denoting or relating to elements of high atomic number (above 109) postulated to exist with special stability as a consequence of the shell model of the nucleus

superheavyweight (ˌsuːpəˈhɛvɪweɪt) *n* an amateur boxer weighing more than 91 kg

superheterodyne receiver (ˌsuːpəˈhɛtərəˌdaɪn) *n* a radio receiver that combines two radio-frequency signals by heterodyne action, to produce a signal above the audible frequency limit. This signal is amplified and demodulated to give the desired audio-frequency signal [c20: from SUPER(SONIC) + HETERODYNE]

superhigh frequency ('suːpəˌhaɪ) *n* a radio-frequency band or radio frequency lying between 30 000 and 3000 megahertz

superhuman (ˌsuːpəˈhjuːmən) *adj* **1** having powers above and beyond those of mankind **2** exceeding normal human ability or experience > ˌsuper'humanly *adv*

superimpose (ˌsuːpərɪmˈpəʊz) *vb* (*tr*) **1** to set or place on or over something else **2** (usually foll by *on* or *upon*) to add (to) > ˌsuperˌimpo'sition *n*

superinduce (ˌsuːpərɪnˈdjuːs) *vb* (*tr*) to introduce as an additional feature, factor, etc > superinduction (ˌsuːpərɪnˈdʌkʃən) *n*

superintend (ˌsuːpərɪnˈtɛnd, ˌsuːprɪn-) *vb* to undertake the direction or management (of); undertake the direction of [c17: from Church Latin *superintendere*, from Latin SUPER- + *intendere* to give attention to] > ˌsuperin'tendence *n*

superintendent (ˌsuːpərɪnˈtɛndənt, ˌsuːprɪn-) *n* **1 a** person who directs and manages an organization, office, etc **2** (in Britain) a senior police officer higher in rank than an inspector but lower than a chief superintendent **3** (in the US) the head of a police department **4** *chiefly US & Canadian* a caretaker, esp of a block of apartments ▷ *adj* **5** of or relating to supervision; superintending [c16: from Church Latin *superintendens* overseeing] > ˌsuperin'tendency *n*

superior (suːˈpɪərɪə) *adj* **1** greater in quality, quantity, etc **2** of high or extraordinary worth, merit, etc **3** higher in rank or status: *a superior tribunal* **4** displaying a conscious sense of being above or better than others; supercilious **5** (*often postpositive*; foll by *to*) not susceptible (to) or influenced (by) **6** placed higher up; situated further from the base **7** *astronomy* (of a planet) having an orbit further from the sun than the orbit of the earth **8** (of a plant ovary) situated above the calyx and other floral parts **9** *printing* (of a character) written or printed above the line; superscript ▷ *n* **10** a person or thing of greater

rank or quality **11** *printing* a character set in a superior position **12** (*often capital*) the head of a community in a religious order [c14: from Latin, from *superus* placed above, from *super* above] > su'periores *fem n* > superiority (suːˌpɪərɪˈɒrɪtɪ) *n*

● USAGE *Superior* should not be used with *than*: *he is a better* (not *a superior*) *poet than his brother*; *his poetry is superior to* (not *superior than*) *his brother's*

Superior (suːˈpɪərɪə, sjuː-) *n* Lake Superior a lake in the N central US and S Canada: one of the largest freshwater lakes in the world and westernmost of the Great Lakes. Area: 82 362 sq km (31 800 sq miles)

superior court *n* **1** (in England) a higher court not subject to control by any other court except by way of appeal. See also **Supreme Court of Judicature 2** *US* (in several states) a court of general jurisdiction ranking above the inferior courts and below courts of last resort

superiority complex *n informal* an inflated estimate of one's own merit, usually manifested in arrogance

superior planet *n* any of the six planets (Mars, Jupiter, Saturn, Uranus, Neptune, and (formerly) Pluto) whose orbit lies outside that of the earth

superjumbo ('suːpəˌdʒʌmbəʊ) *n*, *pl* -jumbos *informal* an extremely large twin-deck jet-propelled airliner that can carry over 500 passengers

superlative (suːˈpɜːlətɪv) *adj* **1** of outstanding quality, degree, etc; supreme **2** *grammar* denoting the form of an adjective or adverb that expresses the highest or a very high degree of quality. In English the superlative degree is usually marked by the suffix -*est* or the word *most*, as in *loudest* or *most loudly* **3** (of language or style) excessive; exaggerated ▷ *n* **4** a thing that excels all others or is of the highest quality **5** *grammar* the superlative form of an adjective **6** the highest degree; peak [c14: from Old French *superlatif*, via Late Latin from Latin *superlātus* extravagant, from *superferre* to carry beyond, from SUPER- + *ferre* to bear] > su'perlatively *adv* > su'perlativeness *n*

superlunar (ˌsuːpəˈluːnə) *adj* situated beyond the moon; celestial > ˌsuper'lunary *adj*

superman ('suːpəˌmæn) *n*, *pl* -men **1** (in the philosophy of Nietzsche) an ideal man who through integrity and creativity would rise above good and evil and who represents the goal of human evolution **2** any man of apparently superhuman powers

supermarket ('suːpəˌmɑːkɪt) *n* a large self-service store retailing food and household supplies

supermassive (ˌsuːpəˈmæsɪv) *adj* (of a black hole or star) having a mass in the range of millions or billions of times that of the sun

supermembrane (ˌsuːpəˈmɛmbreɪn) *n physics* a type of two-dimensional entity postulated in certain theories of elementary particles that involve supersymmetry

supermini ('suːpəˌmɪnɪ) *n pl* -nis a small car, usually a hatchback, that is economical to run but has a high level of performance

supermodel ('suːpəˌmɒdəl) *n* a very successful and well-known photographic or catwalk model

supermoto (ˌsuːpəˈməʊtə) *n* a form of motorcycle racing in which powerful motorbikes are raced over a circuit that is part tarmac and part dirt [c20: from SUPERBIKE + MOTOCROSS]

supermundane (ˌsuːpəˈmʌndeɪn) *adj* of or relating to what is elevated above earthly things

supernal (suːˈpɜːnəl, sjuː-) *adj literary* **1** of or from the world of the divine; celestial **2** of or emanating from above or from the sky [c15: from Medieval Latin *supernālis*, from Latin *supernus* that is on high, from *super* above] > su'pernally *adv*

supernatant (ˌsuːpəˈneɪtənt) *adj* **1** floating on the surface or over something **2** *chem* (of a liquid) lying above a sediment or settled precipitate [c17: from Latin *supernatāre* to float, from SUPER- + *natāre* to swim] > ˌsuperna'tation *n*

supernatural (ˌsuːpəˈnætʃrəl, -ˈnætʃərəl) *adj* **1** of or relating to things that cannot be explained according to natural laws **2** characteristic of or caused by or as if by a god; miraculous **3** of, involving, or ascribed to occult beings **4** exceeding the ordinary; abnormal ▷ *n* **5** the supernatural supernatural forces, occurrences, and beings collectively or their realm > ˌsuper'naturally *adv* > ˌsuper'naturalness *n*

supernaturalism (ˌsuːpə'nætʃrəlɪzəm, -'nætʃərə-) *n* **1** the quality or condition of being supernatural **2** a supernatural agency, the effects of which are felt to be apparent in this world > ˌsuper'naturalist *n, adj* > ˌsuperˌnatural'istic *adj*

supernormal (ˌsuːpə'nɔːməl) *adj* greatly exceeding the normal > supernormality (ˌsuːpənɔː'mælɪtɪ) *n* > ˌsuper'normally *adv*

supernova (ˌsuːpə'nəʊvə) *n, pl* **-vae** (-viː) *or* **-vas** a star that explodes catastrophically owing to either instabilities following the exhaustion of its nuclear fuel or gravitational collapse following the accretion of matter from an orbiting companion star, becoming for a few days up to one hundred million times brighter than the sun. The expanding shell of debris (the **supernova remnant**) creates a nebula that radiates radio waves, X-rays, and light, for hundreds or thousands of years. See **nova**

supernumerary (ˌsuːpə'njuːmərərɪ, -'njuːmrərɪ) *adj* **1** exceeding a regular or proper number; extra **2** functioning as a substitute or assistant with regard to a regular body or staff ▷ *n, pl* **-aries 3** a person or thing that exceeds the normal, required, or regular number **4** a person who functions as a substitute or assistant **5** an actor who has no lines, esp a nonprofessional one [c17: from Late Latin *supernumerārius*, from Latin SUPER- + *numerus* number]

supernurse ('suːpəˌnɜːs) *n* (in Britain) an experienced senior nurse on an elevated salary who is responsible for running clinics and managing nursing teams

superorder ('suːpərˌɔːdə) *n biology* a taxonomic group that is a subdivision of a subclass

superordinate (ˌsuːpər'ɔːdɪnɪt) *adj* **1** of higher status or condition *n* (ˌsuːpər'ɔːdɪnɪt) **2** a person or thing that is superordinate **3** a word the meaning of which includes the meaning of another word or words: *"red"* is a superordinate of *"scarlet", "vermilion", and "crimson"*

superphosphate (ˌsuːpə'fɒsfeɪt) *n* **1** a mixture of the diacid calcium salt of orthophosphoric acid $Ca(H_2PO_4)_2$ with calcium sulphate and small quantities of other phosphates: used as a fertilizer **2** a salt of phosphoric acid formed by incompletely replacing its acidic hydrogen atoms; acid phosphate; hydrogen phosphate

superpose (ˌsuːpə'pəʊz) *vb* (tr) *geometry* to transpose (the coordinates of one geometric figure) to coincide with those of another [c19: from French *superposer*, from Latin *superpōnere*, from SUPER- + *pōnere* to place] > ˌsuper'posable *adj*

superposition (ˌsuːpəpə'zɪʃən) *n* **1** the act of superposing or state of being superposed **2** *geology* the principle that in any sequence of sedimentary rocks which has not been disturbed, the oldest strata lie at the bottom and the youngest at the top

superpower ('suːpəˌpaʊə) *n* **1** an extremely powerful state, such as the US **2** extremely high power, esp electrical or mechanical > 'superˌpowered *adj*

supersaturated (ˌsuːpə'sætʃəˌreɪtɪd) *adj* **1** (of a solution) containing more solute than a saturated solution and therefore not in equilibrium **2** (of a vapour) containing more material than a saturated vapour and therefore not in equilibrium > ˌsuperˌsatu'ration *n*

superscribe (ˌsuːpə'skraɪb) *vb* (tr) to write (an inscription, name, etc) above, on top of, or outside [c16: from Latin *superscrībere*, from SUPER- + *scrībere* to write]

superscript ('suːpəˌskrɪpt) *adj* **1** *printing* (of a character) written or printed above the line; superior. See **subscript** ▷ *n* **2** a superscript or superior character [c16: from Latin *superscriptus*; see SUPERSCRIBE]

supersede (ˌsuːpə'siːd) *vb* (tr) **1** to take the place of (something old-fashioned or less appropriate); supplant **2** to replace in function, office, etc; succeed **3** to discard or set aside or cause to be set aside as obsolete or inferior [c15: via Old French from Latin *supersedēre* to sit above, from SUPER- + *sedēre* to sit] > ˌsuper'sedence *n* > supersedure (ˌsuːpə'siːdʒə) *n* > supersession (ˌsuːpə'sɛʃən) *n*

supersex ('suːpəˌsɛks) *n genetics* a sterile organism in

which the ratio between the sex chromosomes is disturbed

supersonic (ˌsuːpə'sɒnɪk) *adj* being, having, or capable of reaching a speed in excess of the speed of sound > ˌsuper'sonically *adv*

supersonics (ˌsuːpə'sɒnɪks) *n* (functioning as singular) **1** the study of supersonic motion **2** a less common name for **ultrasonics**

superstar ('suːpəˌstɑː) *n* a popular singer, film star, etc, who is idolized by fans and elevated to a position of importance in the entertainment industry > 'superˌstardom *n*

superstition (ˌsuːpə'stɪʃən) *n* **1** irrational belief usually founded on ignorance or fear and characterized by obsessive reverence for omens, charms, etc **2** a notion, act or ritual that derives from such belief **3** any irrational belief, esp with regard to the unknown [c15: from Latin *superstitiō* dread of the supernatural, from *superstāre* to stand still by something (as in amazement)]

superstitious (ˌsuːpə'stɪʃəs) *adj* **1** disposed to believe in superstition **2** of or relating to superstition > ˌsuper'stitiously *adv* > ˌsuper'stitiousness *n*

superstore ('suːpəˌstɔː) *n* a very large supermarket, often selling household goods, clothes, etc, as well as food

superstratum (ˌsuːpə'strɑːtəm, -'streɪ-) *n, pl* **-ta** (-tə) *or* **-tums** *geology* a layer or stratum overlying another layer or similar structure

superstring ('suːpəˌstrɪŋ) *n physics* a type of one-dimensional entity postulated in certain theories of elementary particles that involve supersymmetry

superstructure ('suːpəˌstrʌktʃə) *n* **1** the part of a building above its foundation **2** any structure or concept erected on something else **3** *nautical* any structure above the main deck of a ship with sides flush with the sides of the hull **4** the part of a bridge supported by the piers and abutments > 'superˌstructural *adj*

supersymmetry (ˌsuːpə'sɪmɪtrɪ) *n physics* a symmetry of elementary particles having a higher order than that in the standard model, postulated to encompass the behaviour of both bosons and fermions

supertanker ('suːpəˌtæŋkə) *n* a large fast tanker of more than 275 000 tons capacity

supertax ('suːpəˌtæks) *n* a tax levied in addition to the basic tax, esp a graduated surtax on incomes above a certain level

superteacher ('suːpəˌtiːtʃə) *n Brit education* an informal name for an **advanced skills teacher**

supertonic (ˌsuːpə'tɒnɪk) *n music* **1** the second degree of a major or minor scale **2** a key or chord based on this

Super Twelve *n* an annual international southern hemisphere Rugby Union tournament between teams from South Africa, Australia, and New Zealand

supervene (ˌsuːpə'viːn) *vb* (intr) **1** to follow closely; ensue **2** to occur as an unexpected or extraneous development [c17: from Latin *supervenīre* to come upon, from SUPER- + *venīre* to come] > ˌsuper'venience or supervention (ˌsuːpə'venʃən) *n* > ˌsuper'venient *adj*

supervise ('suːpəˌvaɪz) *vb* (tr) **1** to direct or oversee the performance or operation of **2** to watch over so as to maintain order, etc [c16: from Medieval Latin *supervidēre*, from Latin SUPER- + *vidēre* to see] > supervision (ˌsuːpə'vɪʒən) *n*

supervisor ('suːpəˌvaɪzə) *n* **1** a person who manages or supervises **2** a foreman or forewoman **3** (in some British universities) a tutor supervising the work, esp research work, of a student **4** (in some US schools) an administrator running a department of teachers > 'superˌvisorship *n* > 'superˌvisory *adj*

supinate ('suːpɪˌneɪt, 'sjuː-) *vb* to turn (the hand and forearm) so that the palm faces up or forwards [c19: from Latin *supināre* to lay on the back, from *supīnus* SUPINE] > supi'nation *n*

supine *adj* (suː'paɪn, sjuː-, 'suːpaɪn, 'sjuː-) **1** lying or resting on the back with the face, palm, etc, upwards **2** displaying no interest or animation; lethargic ▷ *n* ('suːpaɪn, 'sjuː-) **3** *grammar* a noun form derived from a verb in Latin, often used to express purpose with verbs of motion [c15: from Latin *supīnus* related to *sub* under,

up; (in grammatical sense) from Latin *verbum supīnum* supine word (the reason for this use is unknown)]
▷ su'pinely *adv* ▷ su'pineness *n*

supper ('sʌpə) *n* **1** an evening meal, esp a light one **2** an evening social event featuring a supper **3** sing for one's supper to obtain something by performing a service [c13: from Old French *soper*; see SUP¹] ▷ 'supperless *adj*

Suppiluliumas I (ˌsʌpɪlʌlɪ'uːməs) *n* king of the Hittites (?1375–?1335 BC); founder of the Hittite empire

supplant (sə'plɑːnt) *vb* (*tr*) to take the place of, often by trickery or force [c13: via Old French from Latin *supplantāre* to trip up, from *sub-* from below + *planta* sole of the foot] ▷ sup'planter *n*

supple ('sʌpᵊl) *adj* **1** bending easily without damage **2** capable of or showing easy or graceful movement; lithe **3** mentally flexible; responding readily **4** disposed to agree, sometimes to the point of servility ▷ *vb* **5** *rare* to make or become supple [c13: from Old French *souple*, from Latin *supplex* bowed] ▷ 'suppleness *n*

supplejack ('sʌpᵊlˌdʒæk) *n* **1** a North American twining rhamnaceous woody vine, *Berchemia scandens*, that has greenish-white flowers and purple fruits **2** a liliaceous plant of New Zealand, *Ripogonum scandens*, having tough climbing vines **3** a tropical American woody sapindaceous vine, *Paullinia curassavica*, having strong supple wood **4** any of various other vines with strong supple stems **5** *US* a walking stick made from the wood of *Paullinia curassavica* [c18: from SUPPLE + JACK¹]

supplement *n* ('sʌplɪmənt) **1** an addition designed to complete, make up for a deficiency, etc **2** a section appended to a publication to supply further information, correct errors, etc **3** a magazine or section inserted into a newspaper or periodical, such as one with colour photographs issued every week **4** *geometry* **a** either of a pair of angles whose sum is 180° **b** an arc of a circle that when added to another arc forms a semicircle ▷ *vb* ('sʌplɪˌmɛnt) **5** (*tr*) to provide a supplement to, esp in order to remedy a deficiency [c14: from Latin *supplēmentum*, from *supplēre* to SUPPLY¹] ▷ ˌsupplemen'tation *n*

supplementary (ˌsʌplɪ'mɛntərɪ, -trɪ) *adj* **1** forming or acting as a supplement ▷ *n*, *pl* **-ries** **2** a person or thing that is a supplement ▷ ˌsupple'mentarily *or less commonly* ˌsupple'mentally *adv*

supplementary angle *n* either of two angles whose sum is 180°. See **complementary angle**

suppliant ('sʌplɪənt) *adj* **1** expressing entreaty or supplication ▷ *n*, *adj* **2** another word for **supplicant** [c15: from French *supplier* to beseech, from Latin *supplicāre* to kneel in entreaty; see SUPPLE] ▷ 'suppliantly *adv*

supplicant ('sʌplɪkənt) *or* **suppliant** *n* **1** a person who supplicates ▷ *adj* **2** entreating humbly; supplicating [c16: from Latin *supplicāns* beseeching; see SUPPLE]

supplicate ('sʌplɪˌkeɪt) *vb* **1** to make a humble request to (someone); plead **2** (*tr*) to ask for or seek humbly [c15: from Latin *supplicāre* to beg on one's knees; see SUPPLE] ▷ 'suppliˌcatory *adj*

supplication (ˌsʌplɪ'keɪʃən) *n* **1** the act of supplicating **2** a humble entreaty or petition; prayer

supply (sə'plaɪ) *vb* **-plies**, **-plying**, **-plied** **1** (*tr*; often foll by *with*) to furnish with something that is required **2** (*tr*; often foll by *to* or *for*) to make available or provide (something that is desired or lacking): *to supply books to the library* **3** (*tr*) to provide for adequately; make good; satisfy: *who will supply their needs?* **4** to serve as a substitute, usually temporary, in (another's position, etc): *there are no clergymen to supply the pulpit* **5** (*tr*) *Brit* to fill (a vacancy, position, etc) ▷ *n*, *pl* **-plies** **6** **a** the act of providing or something that is provided **b** (*as modifier*): *a supply dump* **7** (*often plural*) an amount available for use; stock **8** (*plural*) food, equipment, etc, needed for a campaign or trip **9** *economics* **a** willingness and ability to offer goods and services for sale **b** the amount of a commodity that producers are willing and able to offer for sale at a specified price. See **demand** (sense 9) **10** *military* **a** the management and disposal of food and equipment **b** (*as modifier*): *supply routes* **11** (*often plural*) a grant of money voted by a legislature for government expenses, esp those not covered by other revenues **12** (in

Parliament and similar legislatures) the money voted annually for the expenses of the civil service and armed forces **13 a** a person who acts as a temporary substitute **b** (*as modifier*): *a supply vicar* **14** a source of electrical energy, gas, etc [c14: from Old French *souppleier*, from Latin *supplēre* to complete, from *sub-* up + *plēre* to fill]

support (sə'pɔːt) *vb* (*tr*) **1** to carry the weight of **2** to bear or withstand (pressure, weight, etc) **3** to provide the necessities of life for (a family, person, etc) **4** to tend to establish (a theory, statement, etc) by providing new facts; substantiate **5** to speak in favour of (a motion) **6** to give aid or courage to **7** to give approval to (a cause, principle, etc); subscribe to: *to support a political candidature* **8** to endure with forbearance: *I will no longer support bad behaviour* **9** to give strength to; maintain: *to support a business* **10** (*tr*) (in a concert) to perform earlier than (the main attraction) **11** *films, theatre* **a** to play a subordinate role to **b** to accompany (the feature) in a film programme **12** to act or perform (a role or character) ▷ *n* **13** the act of supporting or the condition of being supported **14** a thing that bears the weight or part of the weight of a construction **15** a person who or thing that furnishes aid **16** the means of maintenance of a family, person, etc **17** a band or entertainer not topping the bill **18** the support an actor or group of actors playing subordinate roles **19** *med* an appliance worn to ease the strain on an injured bodily structure or part **20** the solid material on which a painting is executed, such as canvas **21** See **athletic support** [c14: from Old French *supporter*, from Latin *supportāre* to bring, from *sub-* up + *portāre* to carry] ▷ sup'portable *adj*

supporter (sə'pɔːtə) *n* **1** a person who or thing that acts as a support **2** a person who backs a sports team, politician, etc **3** a garment or device worn to ease the strain on or restrict the movement of a bodily structure or part **4** *heraldry* a figure or beast in a coat of arms depicted as holding up the shield

supporting (sə'pɔːtɪŋ) *adj* **1** (of a role) being a fairly important but not leading part, esp in a play or film **2** (of an actor or actress) playing a supporting role

supportive (sə'pɔːtɪv) *adj* providing support, esp moral or emotional support

suppose (sə'pəʊz) *vb* (*tr*; *may take a clause as object*) **1** to presume (something) to be true without certain knowledge: *I suppose he meant to kill her* **2** to consider as a possible suggestion for the sake of discussion, elucidation, etc; postulate: *suppose that he wins the election* **3** (of theories, propositions, etc) to imply the inference or assumption (of): *your policy supposes full employment* [c14: from Old French *suposer*, from Medieval Latin *suppōnere*, from Latin: to substitute, from *sub-* + *pōnere* to put] ▷ sup'posable *adj* ▷ sup'poser *n*

supposed (sə'pəʊzd, -'pəʊzɪd) *adj* **1** (*prenominal*) presumed to be true without certain knowledge **2** (*prenominal*) believed to be true on slight grounds; highly doubtful **3** (sə'pəʊzd) (*postpositive*; foll by *to*) expected or obliged (to) **4** (*postpositive*; *used in negative*; foll by *to*) expected or obliged not (to): *you're not supposed to walk on the grass* ▷ supposedly (sə'pəʊzɪdlɪ) *adv*

supposition (ˌsʌpə'zɪʃən) *n* **1** the act of supposing **2** a fact, theory, etc, that is supposed ▷ ˌsuppo'sitional *adj* ▷ ˌsuppo'sitionally *adv*

supposititious (ˌsʌpə'zɪʃəs) *adj* deduced from supposition; hypothetical ▷ ˌsuppo'sitiously *adv* ▷ ˌsuppo'sitiousness *n*

supposititious (səˌpɒzɪ'tɪʃəs) *adj* substituted with intent to mislead or deceive ▷ supˌposi'titiously *adv* ▷ supˌposi'titiousness *n*

suppositive (sə'pɒzɪtɪv) *adj* **1** of, involving, or arising out of supposition **2** *grammar* denoting a conjunction introducing a clause expressing a supposition, as for example *if*, *supposing*, or *provided that* ▷ *n* **3** *grammar* a suppositive conjunction ▷ sup'positively *adv*

suppository (sə'pɒzɪtərɪ, -trɪ) *n*, *pl* **-ries** *med* an encapsulated or solid medication for insertion into the vagina, rectum, or urethra, where it melts and releases the active substance [c14: from Medieval Latin *suppositōrium*, from Latin *suppositus* placed beneath, from *suppōnere*; see SUPPOSE]

suppress (sə'prɛs) *vb* (*tr*) **1** to put an end to; prohibit **2** to hold in check; restrain: *I was obliged to suppress a smile* **3** to withhold from circulation or publication: *to suppress seditious pamphlets* **4** to stop the activities of; crush: *to suppress a rebellion* **5** *electronics* **a** to reduce or eliminate (unwanted oscillations) in a circuit **b** to eliminate (a particular frequency or group of frequencies) in a signal **6** *psychiatry* to resist consciously (an idea or a desire entering one's mind) [c14: from Latin *suppressus* held down, from *supprimere* to restrain, from *sub-* down + *premere* to press] > sup'pressible *adj*

suppressant (sə'prɛsənt) *adj* **1** tending to suppress or restrain an action or condition ▷ *n* **2** a suppressant drug or agent: *a cough suppressant*

suppression (sə'prɛʃən) *n* **1** the act or process of suppressing or the condition of being suppressed **2** *psychoanal* the conscious avoidance of unpleasant thoughts

suppressor (sə'prɛsə) *n* **1** a person or thing that suppresses **2** a device fitted to an electrical appliance to suppress unwanted electrical interference to audiovisual signals

suppurate ('sʌpjʊˌreɪt) *vb* (*intr*) *pathol* (of a wound, sore, etc) to discharge pus; fester [c16: from Latin *suppūrāre*, from *sub-* + *pūs* PUS]

supra- *prefix* over, above, beyond, or greater than: *supranational; supramolecular* [from Latin *suprā* above]

supraliminal (ˌsuːprə'lɪmɪn³l, ˌsjuː-) *adj* of or relating to any stimulus that is above the threshold of sensory awareness > ˌsupra'liminally *adv*

supramolecular (ˌsuːprəmə'lɛkjʊlə, ˌsjuː-) *adj* **1** more complex than a molecule **2** consisting of more than one molecule

supranational (ˌsuːprə'næʃn³l, ˌsjuː-) *adj* beyond the authority or jurisdiction of one national government: *the supranational institutions of the EU* > ˌsupra'nationalism *n*

supraorbital (ˌsuːprə'ɔːbɪt³l, ˌsjuː-) *adj* *anatomy* situated above the orbit

suprarenal (ˌsuːprə'riːn³l, ˌsjuː-) *adj* *anatomy* situated above a kidney [c19: from New Latin *suprārēnālis*. See SUPRA-, RENAL]

suprarenal gland *n* another name for **adrenal gland**

supremacist (sʊ'prɛməsɪst, sjʊ-) *n* **1** a person who promotes or advocates the supremacy of any particular group ▷ *adj* **2** characterized by belief in the supremacy of any particular group > su'premacism *or* su'prematism *n*

supremacy (sʊ'prɛməsɪ, sjʊ-) *n* **1** supreme power; authority **2** the quality or condition of being supreme

supreme (sʊ'priːm, sjʊ-) *adj* **1** of highest status or power **2** (*usually prenominal*) of highest quality, importance, etc **3** greatest in degree; extreme **4** (*prenominal*) final or last, esp being last in one's life or progress; ultimate: *the supreme judgment* [c16: from Latin *suprēmus* highest, from *superus* that is above, from *super* above] > su'premely *adv*

Supreme Being *n* the most exalted being; God

Supreme Court *n* (in the US) **1** the highest Federal court, possessing final appellate jurisdiction and exercising supervisory jurisdiction over the lower courts **2** (in many states) the highest state court

Supreme Court of Judicature *n* (in England) a court formed in 1873 by the amalgamation of several superior courts into two divisions, the High Court of Justice and the Court of Appeal

supreme sacrifice *n* the supreme sacrifice the sacrifice of one's life

Supreme Soviet *n* (in the former Soviet Union) **1** the bicameral legislature, comprising the **Soviet of the Union** and the **Soviet of the Nationalities**; officially the highest organ of state power **2** a similar legislature in each former Soviet republic

supremo (sʊ'priːməʊ, sjʊ-) *n, pl* -mos *Brit informal* a person in overall authority [c20: from SUPREME]

Supt *or* **supt** *abbreviation* superintendent

Sur *or* **Sour** (sʊə) *n* transliteration of the Arabic name for Tyre

sur-¹ *prefix* over; above; beyond: *surcharge; surrealism*. See **super-** [from Old French, from Latin SUPER-]

sur-² *prefix* a variant of **sub**: *surrogate*

sura ('sʊərə) *n* any of the 114 chapters of the Koran [c17: from Arabic *sūrah* section]

Surabaya *or* **Surabaja** (ˌsʊərə'baɪə) *n* a port in Indonesia, on E Java on the **Surabaya Strait**: the country's second port and chief naval base; university (1954); fishing and ship-building industries; oil refinery. Pop: 2 599 796 (2000)

surah ('sʊərə) *n* a twill-weave fabric of silk or rayon, used for dresses, blouses, etc [c19: from the French pronunciation of SURAT]

Surakarta (ˌsʊərə'kɑːtə) *n* a town in Indonesia, on central Java: textile manufacturing. Pop: 516 500 (1995 est)

sural ('sjʊərəl) *adj* *anatomy* of or relating to the calf of the leg [c17: via New Latin from Latin *sūra* calf]

Surat (sʊ'ræt, 'sʊərət) *n* a port in W India, in W Gujarat: a major port in the 17th century; textile manufacturing. Pop: 2 433 787 (2001)

surbase ('sɜːˌbeɪs) *n* the uppermost part, such as a moulding, of a pedestal, base, or skirting

surcease (sɜː'siːs) *archaic* ▷ *n* **1** cessation or intermission ▷ *vb* **2** to desist from (some action) **3** to cease or cause to cease [c16: from earlier *sursesen*, from Old French *surseoir*, from Latin *supersedēre*; see SUPERSEDE]

surcharge *n* ('sɜːˌtʃɑːdʒ) **1** a charge in addition to the usual payment, tax, etc **2** an excessive sum charged, esp when unlawful **3** an extra and usually excessive burden or supply **4** an overprint that alters the face value of a postage stamp ▷ *vb* (sɜː'tʃɑːdʒ, 'sɜːˌtʃɑːdʒ) (*tr*) **5** to charge an additional sum, tax, etc **6** to overcharge (a person) for something **7** to put an extra physical burden upon; overload **8** to fill to excess; overwhelm **9** *law* to insert credits for sums that have been omitted in (an account) **10** to overprint a surcharge on (a stamp)

surcingle ('sɜːˌsɪŋg³l) *n* a girth for a horse which goes around the body, used esp with a racing saddle [c14: from Old French *surcengle*, from *sur-* over + *cengle* a belt, from Latin *cingulum*]

surcoat ('sɜːˌkəʊt) *n* **1** a tunic, often embroidered with heraldic arms, worn by a knight over his armour during the Middle Ages **2** an outer coat or other garment

surculose ('sɜːkjʊˌləʊs) *adj* (of a plant) bearing suckers [c19: from Latin *surculōsus* woody, from *surculus* twig, from *sūrus* a branch]

surd (sɜːd) *n* **1** *maths* an expression containing one or more irrational roots of numbers, such as $2\sqrt{3} + 3\sqrt{2} + 6$ ▷ *adj* **2** of or relating to a surd [c16: from Latin *surdus* muffled]

sure (ʃʊə, ʃɔː) *adj* **1** (sometimes foll by *of*) free from hesitancy or uncertainty (with regard to a belief, conviction, etc): *we are sure of the accuracy of the data; I am sure that he is lying* **2** (foll by *of*) having no doubt, as of the occurrence of a future state or event: *sure of success* **3** always effective; unfailing: *a sure remedy* **4** reliable in indication or accuracy: *a sure criterion* **5** (of persons) worthy of trust or confidence: *a sure friend* **6** not open to doubt: *sure proof* **7** admitting of no vacillation or doubt: *he is very sure in his beliefs* **8** bound to be or occur; inevitable: *victory is sure* **9** (*postpositive*) bound inevitably (to be or do something); certain: *she is sure to be there tonight* **10** physically secure or dependable: *a sure footing* **11** be sure (*usually imperative or dependent imperative; takes a clause as object or an infinitive, sometimes with *to* replaced by *and*) to be careful or certain: *be sure and shut the door; I told him to be sure to shut the door* **12** for sure without a doubt; surely **13** make sure **a** (*takes a clause as object*) to make certain; ensure **b** (foll by *of*) to establish or confirm power or possession (over) **14** sure enough *informal* as might have been confidently expected; definitely: often used as a sentence substitute **15** to be sure **a** without doubt; certainly **b** it has to be acknowledged; admittedly ▷ *adv* **16** (*sentence substitute*) *informal* willingly; yes **17** (*sentence modifier*) *informal*, *chiefly US & Canadian* without question; certainly [c14: from Old French *seur*, from Latin *sēcūrus* SECURE] > 'sureness *n*

sure-fire *adj* (*usually prenominal*) *informal* certain to succeed or meet expectations; assured

sure-footed *adj* **1** unlikely to fall, slip, or stumble **2** not likely to err or fail, as in judgment > ˌsure-'footedly *adv* > ˌsure-'footedness *n*

surely ('ʃʊəlɪ, 'ʃɔː-) *adv* **1** without doubt; assuredly

2 without fail; inexorably (esp in the phrase **slowly but surely**) **3** (*sentence modifier*) am I not right in thinking that?; I am sure that: *surely you don't mean it?* **4** *rare* in a sure manner **5** *archaic* safely; securely **6** (*sentence substitute*) *chiefly US & Canadian* willingly; of course; yes

sure thing *informal* *n* something guaranteed to be successful

surety ('ʃʊətɪ, 'ʃʊərɪtɪ) *n, pl* **-ties 1** a person who assumes legal responsibility for the fulfilment of another's debt or obligation and himself becomes liable if the other defaults **2** security given against loss or damage or as a guarantee that an obligation will be met **3** *obsolete* the quality or condition of being sure **4 stand surety** to act as a surety [C14: from Old French *seurte*, from Latin *sēcūritās* SECURITY] > '**surety,ship** *n*

surf (sɜːf) *n* **1** waves breaking on the shore or on a reef **2** foam caused by the breaking of waves ▷ *vb* **3** (*intr*) to take part in surfing **4 a** *computing* (on the internet) to move freely from website to website (esp in the phrase **surf the net**) **b** to move freely between (TV channels or radio stations) **5** *informal* to be carried on top of something [C17: probably variant of SOUGH[1]]

surface ('sɜːfɪs) *n* **1 a** the exterior face of an object or one such face **b** (*as modifier*): *surface gloss* **2** the area or size of such a face **3** material resembling such a face, with length and width but without depth **4 a** the superficial appearance as opposed to the real nature **b** (*as modifier*): *a surface resemblance* **5** *geometry* **a** the complete boundary of a solid figure **b** a continuous two-dimensional configuration **6 a** the uppermost level of the land or sea **b** (*as modifier*): *surface transportation* **7** come to the surface to emerge; become apparent **8** on the surface to all appearances ▷ *vb* **9** to rise or cause to rise to or as if to the surface (of water, etc) **10** (*tr*) to treat the surface of, as by polishing, smoothing, etc **11** (*tr*) to furnish with a surface **12** (*intr*) to become apparent; emerge **13** (*intr*) *informal* **a** to wake up **b** to get up [C17: from French, from *sur* on + *face* FACE, probably on the model of Latin SUPERFICIES] > '**surfacer** *n*

surface-active *adj* (of a substance, esp a detergent) capable of lowering the surface tension of a liquid, usually water. See also **surfactant**

surface mail *n* mail transported by land or sea. See **airmail**

surface structure *n* *generative grammar* a representation of a string of words or morphemes as they occur in a sentence, together with labels and brackets that represent syntactic structure. See **deep structure**

surface tension *n* **1** a property of liquids caused by intermolecular forces near the surface leading to the apparent presence of a surface film and to capillarity, etc **2** a measure of this property expressed as the force acting normal to one side of a line of unit length on the surface: measured in newtons per metre

surface-to-air *adj* of or relating to a missile launched from the surface of the earth against airborne targets

surfactant (sɜː'fæktənt) *n* **1** Also called: **surface-active agent** a substance, such as a detergent, that can reduce the surface tension of a liquid and thus allow it to foam or penetrate solids; a wetting agent ▷ *adj* **2** having the properties of a surfactant [C20: *surf*(*ace*)-*act*(*ive*) *a*(*ge*)*nt*]

surfboard ('sɜːf,bɔːd) *n* a long narrow board used in surfing

surfboat ('sɜːf,bəʊt) *n* a boat with a high bow and stern and flotation chambers, equipped for use in rough surf

surfcasting ('sɜːf,kɑːstɪŋ) *n* fishing from the shore by casting into the surf > '**surf,caster** *n*

surfeit ('sɜːfɪt) *n* **1** (usually foll by *of*) an excessive or immoderate amount **2** overindulgence, esp in eating or drinking **3** disgust, nausea, etc, caused by such overindulgence ▷ *vb* **4** (*tr*) to supply or feed excessively; satiate **5** (*intr*) *archaic* to eat, drink, or be supplied to excess [C13: from French *sourfait*, from *sourfaire* to overdo, from SUR-[1] + *faire*, from Latin *facere* to do]

surfie ('sɜːfɪ) *n* *Austral & NZ slang* a young person whose main interest is in surfing, esp when considered as a cult figure

surfing ('sɜːfɪŋ) *n* the sport of riding towards shore on the crest of a wave by standing or lying on a surfboard

> '**surfer** or '**surf,rider** *n*

surf mat *n* *Austral informal* a small inflatable rubber mattress used to ride on waves

surg. *abbreviation* **1** surgeon **2** surgery **3** surgical

surge (sɜːdʒ) *n* **1** a strong rush or sweep; sudden increase: *a surge of anger* **2** the rolling swell of the sea, esp after the passage of a large wave **3** a heavy rolling motion or sound: *the surge of the trumpets* **4** an undulating rolling surface, as of hills **5** a billowing cloud or volume **6** *nautical* a temporary release or slackening of a rope or cable **7** a large momentary increase in the voltage or current in an electric circuit **8** an upward instability or unevenness in the power output of an engine ▷ *vb* **9** (*intr*) (of waves, the sea, etc) to rise or roll with a heavy swelling motion **10** (*intr*) to move like a heavy sea **11** *nautical* to slacken or temporarily release (a rope or cable) from a capstan or (of a rope, etc) to be slackened or released and slip back **12** (*intr*) (of an electric current or voltage) to undergo a large momentary increase **13** (*tr*) *rare* to cause to move in or as if in a wave or waves [C15: from Latin *surgere* to rise, from *sub-* up + *regere* to lead] > '**surger** *n*

surgeon ('sɜːdʒən) *n* **1** a medical practicioner who specializes in surgery **2** a medical officer in the Royal Navy [C14: from Anglo-Norman *surgien*, from Old French *cirurgien*; see SURGERY]

surgeonfish ('sɜːdʒən,fɪʃ) *n, pl* **-fish** or **-fishes** any tropical marine spiny-finned fish of the family *Acanthuridae*, having a compressed brightly coloured body with one or more knifelike spines at the base of the tail

surgeon general *n, pl* **surgeons general 1** (in the British, US, and certain other armies and navies) the senior officer of the medical service **2** the head of the public health service in the US

surgery ('sɜːdʒərɪ) *n, pl* **-geries 1** the branch of medicine concerned with treating disease, injuries, etc, by means of manual or operative procedures, esp by incision into the body **2** the performance of such procedures by a surgeon **3** *Brit* a place where a doctor, dentist, etc, can be consulted **4** *Brit* an occasion when an MP, lawyer, etc, is available for consultation **5** *US & Canadian* an operating theatre where surgical operations are performed [C14: via Old French from Latin *chirurgia*, from Greek *kheirurgia*, from *kheir* hand + *ergon* work]

surgical ('sɜːdʒɪkəl) *adj* of, relating to, involving, or used in surgery > '**surgically** *adv*

surgical boot *n* a specially designed boot or shoe that compensates for deformities of the foot or leg

surgical spirit *n* methylated spirit containing small amounts of oil of wintergreen and castor oil: used medically for sterilizing

Suribachi (,sʊərɪ'bɑːtʃɪ) *n* Mount Suribachi a volcanic hill in the Volcano Islands, on Iwo Jima: site of a US victory (1945) over the Japanese in World War II

suricate ('sjʊərɪ,keɪt) *n* the slender-tailed meerkat. See **meerkat** [C18: from French *surikate*, probably from a native South African word]

surimi (,suː'riːmɪ) *n* a blended seafood product made from precooked fish, restructured into stick shapes

Surinam (,sʊərɪ'næm) *n* a republic in NE South America, on the Atlantic: became a self-governing part of the Netherlands in 1954 and fully independent in 1975. Official languages: Dutch; English is also widely spoken. Religion: Hindu, Christian, and Muslim. Currency: guilder. Capital: Paramaribo. Pop: 439 000 (2004 est.). Area: 163 820 sq km (63 251 sq miles). Former names: **Dutch Guiana**, **Netherlands Guiana**

surly ('sɜːlɪ) *adj* **-lier, -liest 1** sullenly ill-tempered or rude **2** (of an animal) ill-tempered or refractory [C16: from obsolete *sirly* haughty; see SIR] > '**surlily** *adv* > '**surliness** *n*

surmise *vb* (sɜː'maɪz) **1** (when tr, may take a clause as object) to infer (something) from incomplete or uncertain evidence ▷ *n* (sɜː'maɪz, 'sɜːmaɪz) **2** an idea inferred from inconclusive evidence [C15: from Old French, from *surmettre* to accuse, from Latin *supermittere* to throw over, from SUPER- + *mittere* to send]

surmount (sɜː'maʊnt) *vb* (*tr*) **1** to prevail over; overcome **2** to ascend and cross to the opposite side of **3** to lie on top of or rise above **4** to put something on top of or above [C14: from Old French *surmonter*, from SUR-[1] + *monter* to MOUNT[1]] > sur'mountable *adj*

surname ('sɜː,neɪm) *n* **1** Also called: last name, second name a family name as opposed to a first or Christian name **2** (formerly) a descriptive epithet attached to a person's name to denote a personal characteristic, profession, etc; nickname ▷ *vb* **3** (*tr*) to furnish with or call by a surname [C14: via Anglo-French from Old French *surnom*. See SUR-[1], NAME] > 'sur,namer *n*

surpass (sɜː'pɑːs) *vb* (*tr*) **1** to be greater than in degree, extent, etc **2** to be superior to in achievement or excellence **3** to overstep the limit or range of: *the theory surpasses my comprehension* [C16: from French *surpasser*, from SUR-[1] + *passer* to PASS] > sur'passable *adj*

surpassing (sɜː'pɑːsɪŋ) *adj* **1** exceptional; extraordinary ▷ *adv* **2** *obsolete or poetic* (intensifier): *surpassing fair* > sur'passingly *adv*

surplice ('sɜːplɪs) *n* a loose wide-sleeved liturgical vestment of linen, reaching to the knees, worn over the cassock by clergymen, choristers, and acolytes [C13: via Anglo-French from Old French *sourpelis*, from Medieval Latin *superpellīcium*, from SUPER- + *pellīcium* coat made of skins, from Latin *pellis* a skin]

surplus ('sɜːpləs) *n, pl* **-pluses 1** a quantity or amount in excess of what is required **2** *accounting* **a** an excess of total assets over total liabilities **b** an excess of actual net assets over the nominal value of capital stock **c** an excess of revenues over expenditures during a certain period of time **3** *economics* **a** an excess of government revenues over expenditures during a certain financial year **b** an excess of receipts over payments on the balance of payments ▷ *adj* **4** being in excess; extra [C14: from Old French, from Medieval Latin *superplus*, from Latin SUPER- + *plūs* more]

surprise (sə'praɪz) *vb* (*tr*) **1** to cause to feel amazement or wonder **2** to encounter or discover unexpectedly or suddenly **3** to capture or assault suddenly and without warning **4** to present with something unexpected, such as a gift **5** (foll by *into*) to provoke (someone) to unintended action by a trick, etc **6** (often foll by *from*) to elicit by unexpected behaviour or by a trick: *to surprise information from a prisoner* ▷ *n* **7** the act or an instance of surprising; the act of taking unawares **8** a sudden or unexpected event, gift, etc **9** the feeling or condition of being surprised; astonishment **10** (*modifier*) causing, characterized by, or relying upon surprise: *a surprise move* **11** take by surprise **a** to come upon suddenly and without warning **b** to capture unexpectedly or catch unprepared **c** to astonish; amaze [C15: from Old French, from *surprendre* to overtake, from SUR-[1] + *prendre* from Latin *prehendere* to grasp; see PREHENSILE] > sur'prisal *n* > sur'prised *adj* > surprisedly (sə'praɪzɪdlɪ) *adv*

surprising (sə'praɪzɪŋ) *adj* causing surprise; unexpected or amazing > sur'prisingly *adv*

surra ('sʊərə) *n* a tropical febrile disease of cattle, horses, camels, and dogs, characterized by severe emaciation: caused by the protozoan *Trypanosoma evansi* and transmitted by fleas [from Marathi]

surrealism (sə'rɪə,lɪzəm) *n* (*sometimes capital*) a movement in art and literature in the 1920s, which developed esp from dada, characterized by the evocative juxtaposition of incongruous images in order to include unconscious and dream elements [C20: from French *surréalisme*, from SUR-[1] + *réalisme* REALISM] > sur'realist *n, adj* > sur,real'istic *adj* > sur'real *adj*

surrebutter (,sɜːrɪ'bʌtə) *n law* (in pleading) the claimant's reply to the defendant's rebutter > ,surre'buttal *n*

surrejoinder (,sɜːrɪ'dʒɔɪndə) *n law* (in pleading) the claimant's reply to the defendant's rejoinder

surrender (sə'rɛndə) *vb* **1** (*tr*) to relinquish to the control or possession of another under duress or on demand: *to surrender a city* **2** (*tr*) to relinquish or forego (an office, position, etc), esp as a voluntary concession to another: *he surrendered his place to a lady* **3** to give (oneself) up physically, as or as if to an enemy **4** to allow (oneself) to yield, as to a temptation, influence, etc **5** (*tr*) to give up (hope, etc) **6** (*tr*) *law* to give up or restore (an estate), esp to give up a lease before expiration of the term

7 surrender to bail to present oneself at court at the appointed time after having been on bail ▷ *n* **8** the act or instance of surrendering **9** *insurance* the voluntary discontinuance of a life policy by its holder in return for a consideration (the **surrender value**) **10** *law* **a** the yielding up or restoring of an estate, esp the giving up of a lease before its term has expired **b** the giving up to the appropriate authority of a fugitive from justice **c** the act of surrendering or being surrendered to bail **d** the deed by which a legal surrender is effected [C15: from Old French *surrendre* to yield, from SUR-[1] + *rendre* to RENDER]

surreptitious (,sʌrəp'tɪʃəs) *adj* **1** done, acquired, etc, in secret or by improper means **2** operating by stealth [C15: from Latin *surreptīcius* furtive, from *surripere* to steal, from *sub-* secretly + *rapere* to snatch] > ,surrep'titiously *adv* > ,surrep'titiousness *n*

surrey ('sʌrɪ) *n* a light four-wheeled horse-drawn carriage having two or four seats [C19: shortened from *Surrey cart*, after SURREY, where it was originally made]

Surrey[1] ('sʌrɪ) *n* a county of SE England, on the River Thames: urban in the northeast; crossed from east to west by the North Downs and drained by tributaries of the Thames. Administrative centre: Kingston upon Thames. Pop: 1 064 600 (2003 est). Area: 1679 sq km (648 sq miles)

Surrey[2] ('sʌrɪ) *n* **Earl of,** title of *Henry Howard.* ?1517–47, English courtier and poet; one of the first in England to write sonnets. He was beheaded for high treason

surrogate *n* ('sʌrəgɪt) **1** a person or thing acting as a substitute **2** *chiefly Brit* a deputy, such as a clergyman appointed to deputize for a bishop in granting marriage licences **3** (in some US states) a judge with jurisdiction over the probate of wills, etc **4** (*modifier*) of, relating to, or acting as a surrogate: *a surrogate pleasure* ▷ *vb* ('sʌrə,geɪt) (*tr*) **5** to put in another's position as a deputy, substitute, etc [C17: from Latin *surrogāre* to substitute; see SUBROGATE] > 'surrogateship *n* > ,surro'gation *n*

surrogate mother *n* a woman who bears a child on behalf of a couple unable to have a child, either by artificial insemination from the man or implantation of an embryo from the woman > surrogacy ('sʌrəgəsɪ) *n*

surround (sə'raʊnd) *vb* (*tr*) **1** to encircle or enclose or cause to be encircled or enclosed **2** to deploy forces on all sides of (a place or military formation), so preventing access or retreat **3** to exist around: *I dislike the people who surround her* ▷ *n* **4** *chiefly Brit* a border, esp the area of uncovered floor between the walls of a room and the carpet or around an opening or panel **5** *chiefly US* **a** a method of capturing wild beasts by encircling the area in which they are believed to be **b** the area so encircled [C15 *surrounden* to overflow, from Old French *suronder*, from Late Latin *superundāre*, from Latin SUPER- + *undāre* to abound, from *unda* a wave] > sur'rounding *adj*

surroundings (sə'raʊndɪŋz) *pl n* the conditions, scenery, etc, around a person, place, or thing; environment

sursum corda ('sɜːsəm 'kɔːdə) *n* **1** *RC Church* a Latin versicle meaning *Lift up your hearts,* said by the priest at Mass **2** a cry of exhortation, hope, etc [C16: Latin, literally: up hearts]

surtax ('sɜː,tæks) *n* **1** a tax, usually highly progressive, levied on the amount by which a person's income exceeds a specific level **2** an additional tax on something that has already been taxed ▷ *vb* **3** (*tr*) to assess for liability to surtax; charge with an extra tax

Surtees ('sɜːtiːz) *n* **1 John.** born 1934, British racing motorcyclist and motor-racing driver. He was motorcycling world champion (1956, 1958–60) and world champion motor-racing driver (1964), the only man to have been world champion in both sports **2 Robert Smith.** 1803–64, British journalist and novelist, who satirized the sporting life of the English gentry in such works as *Jorrocks's Jaunts and Jollities* (1838)

surtitles ('sɜː,taɪt*ə*lz) *pl n* brief translations of the text of an opera or play that is being sung or spoken in a foreign language, projected above the stage

surtout (sɜː'tuː:; *French* syrtu) *n* a man's overcoat resembling a frock coat, popular in the late 19th century [C17: from French, from *sur* over + *tout* all]

surveil (sɜː'veɪl) *vb* (*tr*) to observe closely the activities of

S

(a person or group) [c20: back formation from SURVEILLANCE]

surveillance (sɜ:ˈveɪləns) *n* close observation or supervision maintained over a person, group, etc, esp one in custody or under suspicion [c19: from French, from *surveiller* to watch over, from SUR-¹ + *veiller* to keep watch (from Latin *vigilāre*; see VIGIL)] ▷ surˈveillant *adj*, *n*

surveillance society *n* a society where surveillance technology is widely used to monitor people's everyday activities

survey *vb* (sɜ:ˈveɪ, ˈsɜ:veɪ) 1 (*tr*) to view or consider in a comprehensive or general way 2 (*tr*) to examine carefully, as or as if to appraise value 3 to plot a detailed map of (an area of land) by measuring or calculating distances and height 4 *Brit* to inspect a building to determine its condition and value 5 to examine a vessel thoroughly in order to determine its seaworthiness 6 (*tr*) to run a statistical survey on (incomes, opinions, etc) ▷ *n* (ˈsɜ:veɪ) 7 a comprehensive or general view 8 a critical, detailed, and formal inspection 9 *Brit* an inspection of a building to determine its condition and value 10 a report incorporating the results of such an inspection 11 **a** a body of surveyors **b** an area surveyed [c15: from French *surveoir*, from SUR-¹ + *veoir* to see, from Latin *vidēre*]

surveying (sɜ:ˈveɪɪŋ) *n* 1 the study or practice of measuring altitudes, angles, and distances on the land surface so that they can be accurately plotted on a map 2 the setting out on the ground of the positions of proposed construction or engineering works

surveyor (sɜ:ˈveɪə) *n* 1 a person whose occupation is to survey land or buildings. See also **quantity surveyor** 2 *chiefly Brit* a person concerned with the official inspection of something for purposes of measurement and valuation 3 a person who carries out surveys, esp of ships (**marine surveyor**) to determine seaworthiness, etc 4 a customs official 5 *archaic* a supervisor ▷ surˈveyorˌship *n*

surveyor's measure *n* the system of measurement based on the chain (66 feet) as a unit

survival (səˈvaɪvəl) *n* 1 a person or thing that survives, such as a custom 2 **a** the act or fact of surviving or condition of having survived **b** (*as modifier*): survival kit

survival bag *n* a large plastic bag carried by climbers for use in an emergency as protection against exposure

survivalist (səˈvaɪvəlɪst) *n US* a person who believes in ensuring his personal survival of a catastrophic event by arming himself and often by living in the wild **b** (*as modifier*): survivalist weapons ▷ surˈvivalˌism *n*

survival of the fittest *n* a popular term for **natural selection**

survive (səˈvaɪv) *vb* 1 (*tr*) to live after the death of (another) 2 to continue in existence or use after (a passage of time, an adversity, etc) 3 *informal* to endure (something): I don't know how I survive such an awful job [c15: from Old French *sourvivre*, from Latin *supervīvere*, from SUPER- + *vīvere* to live] ▷ surˈvivor *n*

sus (sʌs) *Brit slang* ▷ *n* 1 suspicion ▷ *vb* 2 a variant spelling of **suss** (sense 2) [c20: shortened from SUSPICION]

Susa (ˈsuːsə) *n* an ancient city north of the Persian Gulf: capital of Elam and of the Persian Empire; flourished as a Greek polis under the Seleucids and Parthians. Biblical name: Shushan

Susah or **Susa** (ˈsuːzə) *n* other names for **Sousse**

Susanna (suːˈzænə) *n Apocrypha* 1 the wife of Joachim, who was condemned to death for adultery because of a false accusation, but saved by Daniel's sagacity 2 the book of the Apocrypha containing this story

susceptance (səˈsɛptəns) *n physics* the imaginary component of the admittance [c19: from SUSCEPT(IBILITY) + -ANCE]

susceptibility (səˌsɛptəˈbɪlɪtɪ) *n, pl* -ties 1 the quality or condition of being susceptible 2 the ability or tendency to be impressed by emotional feelings; sensitivity 3 (*plural*) emotional sensibilities; feelings 4 *physics* **a** Also called: electric susceptibility (of a dielectric) the amount by which the relative permittivity differs from unity. Symbol: X **b** Also called: magnetic susceptibility

(of a magnetic medium) the amount by which the relative permeability differs from unity. Symbol: K

susceptible (səˈsɛptəbəl) *adj* 1 (*postpositive; foll by of or to*) yielding readily (to); capable (of): hypotheses susceptible of refutation; susceptible to control 2 (*postpositive; foll by to*) liable to be afflicted (by): susceptible to colds 3 easily impressed emotionally [c17: from Late Latin *susceptibilis*, from Latin *suscipere* to take up, from SUB- + *capere* to take] ▷ susˈceptibly *adv*

sushi (ˈsuːʃɪ) *n* a Japanese dish consisting of small cakes of cold rice with a topping esp of raw fish [from Japanese]

suslik (ˈsʌslɪk) or **souslik** *n* a central Eurasian ground squirrel, *Citellus citellus*, of dry open areas, having large eyes and small ears [from Russian]

suspect *vb* (səˈspɛkt) 1 (*tr*) to believe guilty of a specified offence without proof 2 (*tr*) to think false, questionable, etc: she suspected his sincerity 3 (*tr; may take a clause as object*) to surmise to be the case; think probable: to suspect fraud 4 (*intr*) to have suspicion ▷ *n* (ˈsʌspɛkt) 5 a person who is under suspicion ▷ *adj* (ˈsʌspɛkt) 6 causing or open to suspicion [c14: from Latin *suspicere* to mistrust, from SUB- + *specere* to look]

suspend (səˈspɛnd) *vb* 1 (*tr*) to hang from above so as to permit free movement 2 (*tr; passive*) to cause to remain floating or hanging: a cloud of smoke was suspended over the town 3 (*tr*) to render inoperative or cause to cease, esp temporarily 4 (*tr*) to hold in abeyance; postpone action on 5 (*tr*) to debar temporarily from privilege, office, etc, as a punishment 6 (*tr*) *chem* to cause (particles) to be held in suspension in a fluid 7 (*tr*) *music* to continue (a note) until the next chord is sounded, with which it usually forms a dissonance. See **suspension** (sense 11) 8 (*intr*) to cease payment, as from incapacity to meet financial obligations [c13: from Latin *suspendere* from SUB- + *pendere* to hang] ▷ susˈpendible or susˈpensible *adj* ▷ susˌpendiˈbility *n*

suspended animation *n* a temporary cessation of the vital functions, as by freezing an organism

suspended sentence *n* a sentence of imprisonment that is not served by an offender unless he commits a further offence during its currency

suspender (səˈspɛndə) *n* 1 (*often plural*) *Brit* **a** an elastic strap attached to a belt or corset having a fastener at the end, for holding up women's stockings **b** a similar fastener attached to a garter worn by men in order to support socks 2 (*plural*) *US & Canadian* also called (in Britain and certain other countries): braces 3 a person or thing that suspends, such as one of the vertical cables that carries the deck in a suspension bridge

suspender belt *n* a belt with suspenders hanging from it to hold up women's stockings

suspense (səˈspɛns) *n* 1 the condition of being insecure or uncertain 2 mental uncertainty; anxiety: their father's illness kept them in a state of suspense 3 excitement felt at the approach of the climax: a play of terrifying suspense 4 the condition of being suspended [c15: from Medieval Latin *suspensum* delay, from Latin *suspendere* to hang up; see SUSPEND] ▷ susˈpenseful *adj*

suspense account *n book-keeping* an account in which entries are made until determination of their proper disposition

suspension (səˈspɛnʃən) *n* 1 an interruption or temporary revocation: the suspension of a law 2 a temporary debarment, as from position, privilege, etc 3 a deferment, esp of a decision, judgment, etc 4 *law* a postponement of execution of a sentence or the deferring of a judgment, etc 5 cessation of payment of business debts, esp as a result of insolvency 6 the act of suspending or the state of being suspended 7 a system of springs, shock absorbers, etc, that supports the body of a wheeled or tracked vehicle and insulates it and its occupants from shocks transmitted by the wheels 8 a device or structure, usually a wire or spring, that serves to suspend or support something, such as the pendulum of a clock 9 *chem* a dispersion of fine solid or liquid particles in a fluid, the particles being supported by buoyancy. See also **colloid** 10 the process by which eroded particles of rock are transported in a river 11 *music* one or more notes of a chord that are prolonged until a subsequent chord is sounded, usually to form a dissonance

suspension bridge n a bridge that has a deck suspended by cables or rods from other cables or chains that hang between two towers and are anchored at both ends

suspensive (sə'spɛnsɪv) adj **1** having the power of deferment; effecting suspension **2** causing, characterized by, or relating to suspense > sus'pensively adv > sus'pensiveness n

suspensory (sə'spɛnsərɪ) n, pl -ries **1** Also called: suspensor anatomy a ligament or muscle that holds a structure or part in position **2** med a bandage, sling, etc, for supporting a dependent part ▷ adj **3** suspending or supporting **4** anatomy (of a ligament or muscle) supporting or holding a structure or part in position

suspicion (sə'spɪʃən) n **1** the act or an instance of suspecting; belief without sure proof, esp that something is wrong **2** the feeling of mistrust of a person who suspects **3** the state of being suspected: to be shielded from suspicion **4** a slight trace **5** above suspicion in such a position that no guilt may be thought or implied, esp through having an unblemished reputation **6** on suspicion as a suspect **7** under suspicion regarded with distrust [c14: from Old French sospeçon, from Latin suspīciō distrust, from suspicere to mistrust; see suspect] > sus'picional adj

suspicious (sə'spɪʃəs) adj **1** exciting or liable to excite suspicion; questionable **2** disposed to suspect something wrong **3** indicative or expressive of suspicion > sus'piciously adv > sus'piciousness n

suspire (sə'spaɪə) vb archaic, or poetic **1** to sigh or utter with a sigh; yearn **2** (intr) to breathe; respire [c15: from Latin suspīrāre to take a deep breath, from sub- + spīrāre to breathe] > suspiration (,sʌspɪ'reɪʃən) n

Susquehanna (,sʌskwɪ'hænə) n a river in the eastern US, rising in Otsego Lake and flowing generally south to Chesapeake Bay at Havre de Grace: the longest river in the eastern US Length: 714 km (444 miles)

suss (sʌs) vb (tr) slang **1** (often foll by out) to attempt to work out (a situation, person's character, etc), esp using one's intuition **2** Also called: sus to become aware of; suspect (esp in the phrase **suss it**) ▷ n **3** sharpness of mind; social astuteness [c20: shortened from suspect]

sussed (sʌst) adj Brit informal well-informed; aware

Sussex ('sʌsɪks) n **1** (until 1974) a county of SE England, now divided into the separate counties of East Sussex and West Sussex **2** (in Anglo-Saxon England) the kingdom of the South Saxons, which became a shire of the kingdom of Wessex in the early 9th century AD **3** a breed of red beef cattle originally from Sussex **4** a heavy and long-established breed of domestic fowl used principally as a table bird

sustain (sə'steɪn) vb (tr) **1** to hold up under; withstand: to sustain great provocation **2** to undergo (an injury, loss, etc); suffer: to sustain a broken arm **3** to maintain or prolong: to sustain a discussion **4** to support physically from below **5** to provide for or give support to, esp by supplying necessities: to sustain one's family; to sustain a charity **6** to keep up the vitality or courage of **7** to uphold or affirm the justice or validity of: to sustain a decision **8** to establish the truth of; confirm ▷ n **9** music the prolongation of a note, by playing techniques and electronics [c13: via Old French from Latin sustinēre to hold up, from sub- + tenēre to hold] > sus'tained adj > sustainedly (sə'steɪnɪdlɪ) adv > sus'taining adj > sus'tainment n > sus'tainer n

sustainable (sə'steɪnəbəl) adj **1** capable of being sustained **2** (of economic development, energy sources, etc) capable of being maintained at a steady level without exhausting natural resources or causing severe ecological damage: sustainable development

sustaining pedal n music a foot-operated lever on a piano, usually the right one of two, that keeps the dampers raised from the strings when keys are released, allowing them to continue to vibrate

sustenance ('sʌstənəns) n **1** means of sustaining health or life; nourishment **2** means of maintenance;

livelihood **3** Also called: sustention (sə'stɛnʃən) the act or process of sustaining or the quality of being sustained [c13: from Old French sostenance, from sustenir to sustain]

sustentation (,sʌstɛn'teɪʃən) n a less common word for sustenance [c14: from Latin sustentātiō, from sustentāre, frequentative of sustinēre to sustain]

susurrate ('sju:sə,reɪt) vb (intr) literary to make a soft rustling sound; whisper; murmur [c17: from Latin susurrāre to whisper] > ,susur'ration or 'susurrus n

Sutcliffe ('sʌt,klɪf) n Herbert. 1894–1978, English cricketer, who played for Yorkshire; scorer of 149 centuries and 1000 runs in a season 24 times

Suth. abbreviation Sutherland

Sutherland[1] ('sʌðələnd) n (until 1975) a county of N Scotland, now part of Highland

Sutherland[2] ('sʌðələnd) n **1 Graham.** 1903–80, English artist, noted for his work as an official war artist (1941–44), for his tapestry Christ in Majesty (1962) in Coventry Cathedral, and for his portraits **2 Dame Joan,** known as La Stupenda. born 1926, Australian operatic soprano

Sutherland Falls n a waterfall in New Zealand, on SW South Island. Height: 580 m (1904 ft)

Sutlej ('sʌtlɪdʒ) n a river in S Asia, rising in SW Tibet and flowing west through the Himalayas: crosses Himachal Pradesh and the Punjab (India), enters Pakistan, and joins the Chenab west of Bahawalpur: the longest of the five rivers of the Punjab. Length: 1368 km (850 miles)

sutler ('sʌtlə) n (formerly) a merchant who accompanied an army in order to sell provisions to the soldiers [c16: from obsolete Dutch soeteler, from Middle Low German suteler, from Middle High German sudelen to do dirty work; related to soot, seethe]

sutra ('su:trə) n **1** Hinduism Sanskrit sayings or collections of sayings on Vedic doctrine dating from about 200 AD onwards **2** (modifier) Hinduism **a** of or relating to the last of the Vedic literary periods, from about 500 to 100 BC: the sutra period **b** of or relating to the sutras or compilations of sutras of about 200 AD onwards **3** Buddhism collections of dialogues and discourses of classic Mahayana Buddhism dating from the 2nd to the 6th centuries AD [c19: from Sanskrit: list of rules]

suttee (sʌ'ti:, 'sʌti:) n **1** the former Hindu custom whereby a widow burnt herself to death on her husband's funeral pyre **2** a Hindu widow who immolated herself in this way [c18: from Sanskrit satī virtuous woman, from sat good] > sut'teeism n

Sutton ('sʌtⁿn) n a borough of S Greater London. Pop: 178 500 (2003 est). Area: 43 sq km (17 sq miles)

Sutton Coldfield (-'kəʊld,fi:ld) n a town in central England, in Birmingham unitary authority, West Midlands; a residential suburb of Birmingham. Pop: 105 452 (2001)

Sutton-in-Ashfield (-'æʃ,fi:ld) n a market town in N central England, in W Nottinghamshire. Pop: 41 951 (2001)

suture ('su:tʃə) n **1** surgery **a** catgut, silk thread, or wire used to stitch together two bodily surfaces **b** the surgical seam formed after joining two surfaces, **2** anatomy a type of immovable joint, esp between the bones of the skull (**cranial suture**) **3** a seam or joining, as in sewing **4** zoology a line of junction in a mollusc shell, esp the line between adjacent chambers of a nautiloid shell ▷ vb **5** (tr) surgery to join (the edges of a wound, etc) by means of sutures [c16: from Latin sūtūra, from suere to sew] > 'sutural adj

Suu Kyi n See Aung San Suu Kyi

SUV abbreviation sport (or sports) utility vehicle

Suva ('su:və) n the capital and chief port of Fiji, on the SE coast of Viti Levu; popular tourist resort; University of the South Pacific (1968). Pop: 219 000 (2005 est)

Suvorov (Russian su'vɔrəf) n Aleksandr Vasilyevich (alɪk'sandr va'siljivitʃ). 1729–1800, Russian field marshal, who fought successfully against the Turks (1787–91), the Poles (1794), and the French in Italy (1798–99)

Suwannee (su'wɒnɪ) or **Swanee** n a river in the southeastern US, rising in SE Georgia and flowing across Florida to the Gulf of Mexico at **Suwannee Sound**. Length: about 400 km (250 miles)

suzerain ('suːzəˌreɪn) *n* **1 a** a state or sovereign exercising some degree of dominion over a dependent state, usually controlling its foreign affairs **b** (*as modifier*): *a suzerain power* **2 a** a feudal overlord **b** (*as modifier*): *suzerain lord* [C19: from French, from *sus* above (from Latin *sursum* turned upwards, from *sub-* up + *vertere* to turn) + *-erain*, as in *souverain* SOVEREIGN]

suzerainty ('suːzərəntɪ) *n, pl* **-ties 1** the position, power, or dignity of a suzerain **2** the relationship between suzerain and subject

Suzhou ('suː'dʒəʊ), **Su-chou** *or* **Soochow** *n* a city in E China, on S Jiangsu on the Grand Canal: noted for its gardens; produces chiefly silk. Pop: 1 201 000 (2005 est). Also called: Wuhsien

sv *abbreviation* **1** sailing vessel **2** side valve **3** sub verbo *or* voce [sense 3 from Latin: under the word *or* voice]

Svalbard (*Norwegian* 'svɑːlbɑr) *n* a Norwegian archipelago in the Arctic Ocean, about 650 km (400 miles) north of Norway: consists of the main group (Spitsbergen, North East Land, Edge Island, Barents Island, and Prince Charles Foreland) and a number of outlying islands; sovereignty long disputed but granted to Norway in 1920; coal mining. Administrative centre: Longyearbyen. Area: 62 050 sq km (23 958 sq miles). Also called: Spitsbergen

svelte (svɛlt, sfɛlt) *adj* attractively or gracefully slim; slender [C19: from French, from Italian *svelto*, from *svellere* to pull out, from Latin *ēvellere*, from EX-¹ + *vellere* to pull]

Svengali (svɛn'gɑːlɪ) *n* a person who controls another's mind, usually with sinister intentions [after a character in George Du Maurier's novel *Trilby* (1894)]

Sverdlovsk (*Russian* svɪr'dlɔfsk) *n* the former name (1924–91) of **Yekaterinburg**

Sverige ('sværjə) *n* the Swedish name for **Sweden**

Svevo (*Italian* 'svevo) *n* **Italo** (ɪ'talo), original name *Ettore Schnitz*. 1861–1928, Italian novelist and short-story writer, best known for the novel *Confessions of Zeno* (1923)

SVGA *abbreviation* super video graphics array. See **VGA**

Svizzera ('zvittsera) *n* the Italian name for **Switzerland**

SVQ *abbreviation* Scottish Vocational Qualification

SW *symbol for* **1** southwest(ern) ▷ *abbreviation* **2** short wave

Sw. *abbreviation* **1** Sweden **2** Swedish

swab (swɒb) *n* **1** *med* **a** a small piece of cotton, gauze, etc, for use in applying medication, cleansing a wound, or obtaining a specimen of a secretion, etc **b** the specimen so obtained **2** a mop for cleaning floors, decks, etc **3** a brush used to clean a firearm's bore **4** *slang* an uncouth or worthless fellow ▷ *vb* swabs, swabbing, swabbed **5** (*tr*) to clean or medicate with or as if with a swab **6** (*tr*; foll by *up*) to take up with a swab [C16: probably from Middle Dutch *swabbe* mop; related to Norwegian *svabba* to splash, Dutch *zwabberen* to mop, German *schwappen* to slop over] > 'swabber *n*

Swabia ('sweɪbɪə) *n* a region and former duchy (from the 10th century to 1313) of S Germany, now part of Baden-Württemberg and Bavaria: part of West Germany until 1990. German name: Schwaben ('ʃvaːbᵊn) > 'Swabian *adj, n*

swaddle ('swɒdᵊl) *vb* (*tr*) **1** to wind a bandage round **2** to wrap (a baby) in swaddling clothes **3** to restrain as if by wrapping with bandages; smother ▷ *n* **4** *chiefly US* swaddling clothes [C15: from Old English *swæthel* swaddling clothes; related to *swathian* to SWATHE]

swaddling clothes *pl n* **1** long strips of linen or other cloth formerly wrapped round a newly born baby **2** restrictions or supervision imposed on the immature

swaddy *or* **swaddie** ('swɒdɪ) *n, pl* **-dies** *Brit slang* a private soldier [C19: from dialect *swad* a country bumpkin]

swag (swæg) *n* **1** *slang* property obtained by theft or other illicit means **2** *slang* goods; valuables **3** an ornamental festoon of fruit, flowers, or drapery or a representation of this **4** a swaying movement; lurch **5** swags of *Austral & NZ informal* lots of ▷ *vb* swags, swagging, swagged **6** *chiefly Brit* to lurch or sag or cause to lurch or sag **7** (*tr*) to adorn or arrange with swags [C17: perhaps of Scandinavian origin; compare Norwegian

svagga to SWAY]

swage (sweɪdʒ) *n* **1** a shaped tool or die used in forming cold metal by hammering, pressing, etc ▷ *vb* **2** (*tr*) to form (metal) with a swage [C19: from French *souage*, of unknown origin] > 'swager *n*

swage block *n* an iron block cut with holes, recesses, and grooves to assist in the cold-working of metal

swagger ('swægə) *vb* **1** (*intr*) to walk or behave in an arrogant manner **2** (*intr*; often foll by *about*) to brag loudly ▷ *n* **3** arrogant gait, conduct, or manner ▷ *adj* **4** *Brit informal, rare* elegantly fashionable [C16: probably from SWAG]

swagger stick *or esp Brit* **swagger cane** *n* a short cane or stick carried on occasion mainly by army officers

swaggie ('swægɪ) *n Austral & NZ slang* short for **swagman**

swagman ('swæɡˌmæn, -mən) *n, pl* **-men** *Austral & NZ informal* a labourer who carries his personal possessions in a pack or swag while travelling about in search of work; vagrant worker. Also called: swagger, swaggie

Swahili (swɑː'hiːlɪ) *n* **1** Also called: Kiswahili a language of E Africa that is an official language of Kenya and Tanzania and is widely used as a lingua franca throughout E and central Africa. It is a member of the Bantu group of the Niger-Congo family, originally spoken in Zanzibar, and has a large number of loan words taken from Arabic and other languages **2** *pl* -lis *or* -li, Also called: Mswahili *pl* Waswahili a member of a people speaking this language, living chiefly in Zanzibar ▷ *adj* **3** of or relating to the Swahilis or their language [C19: from Arabic *sawāhil* coasts] > Swa'hilian *adj*

swain (sweɪn) *n archaic, or poetic* **1** a male lover or admirer **2** a country youth [Old English *swān* swineherd; related to Old High German *swein*, Old Norse *sveinn* boy; see SWINE]

swallow¹ ('swɒləʊ) *vb* (*mainly tr*) **1** to pass (food, drink, etc) through the mouth to the stomach by means of the muscular action of the oesophagus **2** (often foll by *up*) to engulf or destroy as if by ingestion **3** *informal* to believe gullibly: *he will never swallow such an excuse* **4** to refrain from uttering or manifesting: *to swallow one's disappointment* **5** to endure without retaliation **6** to enunciate (words, etc) indistinctly; mutter **7** (often foll by *down*) to eat or drink reluctantly **8** (*intr*) to perform or simulate the act of swallowing, as in gulping ▷ *n* **9** the act of swallowing **10** the amount swallowed at any single time; mouthful [Old English *swelgan*; related to Old Norse *svelga*, Old High German *swelgan* to swallow, Swedish *svalg* gullet] > 'swallowable *adj* > 'swallower *n*

swallow² ('swɒləʊ) *n* any passerine songbird of the family Hirundinidae, esp Hirundo rustica (**common** or **barn swallow**), having long pointed wings, a forked tail, short legs, and a rapid flight [Old English *swealwe*; related to Old Frisian *swale*, Old Norse *svala*, Old High German *swalwa*]

swallow dive *n* a type of dive in which the diver arches back while in the air, keeping his legs straight and together and his arms oustretched, finally entering the water headfirst. US and Canadian equivalent: swan dive

swallow hole *n chiefly Brit* another word for **sinkhole** (sense 1)

swallowtail ('swɒləʊˌteɪl) *n* **1** any of various butterflies of the genus Papilio and related genera, esp P. machaon of Europe, having a tail-like extension of each hind wing: family Papilionidae **2** the forked tail of a swallow or similar bird **3** short for **swallow-tailed coat** > swallow-tailed *adj*

swallow-tailed coat *n* another name for **tail coat**

swam (swæm) *vb* the past tense of **swim**

swami ('swɑːmɪ) *n, pl* **-mies** *or* **-mis** (in India) a title of respect for a Hindu saint or religious teacher [C18: from Hindi *svāmī*, from Sanskrit *svāmin* master, from *sva* one's own]

swamp (swɒmp) *n* **1** permanently waterlogged ground that is usually overgrown and sometimes partly forested. Compare **marsh** ▷ *vb* **2** to drench or submerge or be drenched or submerged **3** *nautical* to cause (a boat) to sink or fill with water or (of a boat) to sink or fill with water **4** to overburden or overwhelm or be overburdened or overwhelmed, as by excess work or great numbers **5** (*tr*) to render helpless [C17: probably from Middle Dutch *somp*; compare Middle High German *sumpf*, Old Norse *svöppr* sponge, Greek *somphos* spongy] > **'swampy** *adj*

swamp boat *n* a shallow-draught boat powered by an æroplane engine mounted on a raised structure for use in swamps. Also called: **airboat**

swamp cypress *n* a North American deciduous coniferous tree, *Taxodium distichum*, that grows in swamps and sends up aerial roots from its base. Also called: **bald cypress**

swamp fever *n* **1** Also called: **equine infectious anaemia** a viral disease of horses characterized by recurring fever, staggering gait, and general debility **2** *US* another name for **malaria**

swampland ('swɒmp,lænd) *n* a permanently waterlogged area; marshland

swan (swɒn) *n* **1** any large aquatic bird of the genera *Cygnus* and *Coscoroba*, having a long neck and usually a white plumage: family *Anatidae*, order *Anseriformes* **2** *rare, literary* **a** a poet **b** (*capital when part of a title or epithet*): *the Swan of Avon* (Shakespeare) > *vb* **swans, swanning, swanned 3** (*intr*; usually foll by *around* or *about*) *informal* to wander idly [Old English; related to Old Norse *svanr*, Middle Low German *swōn*] > **'swan,like** *adj*

Swan¹ (swɒn) *n* a river in SW Western Australia, rising as the Avon northeast of Narrogin and flowing northwest and west to the Indian Ocean below Perth. Length: about 240 km (150 miles)

Swan² (swɒn) *n* Sir Joseph Wilson. 1828–1914, English physicist and chemist, who developed the incandescent electric light (1880) independently of Edison

swan dive *n* *US & Canadian* a type of dive in which the diver arches back while in the air, keeping his legs straight and together and his arms outstretched, finally entering the water headfirst. Also called (in Britain and certain other countries): **swallow dive**

Swanee ('swɒnɪ) *n* a variant spelling of **Suwannee**

swank (swæŋk) *informal* > *vb* **1** (*intr*) to show off or swagger > *n* **2** Also called: **swankpot** *Brit* a swaggering or conceited person **3** *chiefly US* elegance or style, esp of a showy kind **4** swagger; ostentation > *adj* **5** another word (esp *US*) for **swanky** [C19: perhaps from Middle High German *swanken* to sway; see SWAG]

swanky ('swæŋkɪ) *adj* **swankier, swankiest** *informal* **1** expensive and showy; stylish: *a swanky hotel* **2** boastful or conceited > **'swankily** *adv* > **'swankiness** *n*

Swanndri or **Swandri** ('swɒn,draɪ) *n, pl* -**dris** *trademark NZ* an all-weather heavy woollen shirt. Also called: **swannie** ('swɒnɪ)

swan neck *n* a tube, rail, etc, curved like a swan's neck

swannery ('swɒnərɪ) *n, pl* -**neries** a place where swans are kept and bred

swan's-down *n* **1** the fine soft down feathers of a swan, used to trim powder puffs, clothes, etc **2** a thick soft fabric of wool with silk, cotton, or rayon, used for infants' clothing, etc **3** a cotton fabric with a heavy nap

Swansea ('swɒnzɪ) *n* **1** a port in S Wales, in Swansea county on an inlet of the Bristol Channel (**Swansea Bay**); a metallurgical and oil-refining centre; university (1920). Pop: 169 880 (2001) **2** a county of S Wales on the Bristol Channel, created in 1996 from part of West Glamorgan: includes the Swansea conurbation and the Gower peninsula. Administrative centre: Swansea. Pop: 224 600 (2003 est). Area: 378 sq km (146 sq miles)

swan song *n* **1** the last act, appearance, publication, or utterance of a person before retirement or death **2** the song that a dying swan is said to sing

swan-upping *n* *Brit* **1** the practice or action of marking nicks in swans' beaks as a sign of ownership **2** the annual swan-upping of royal cygnets on the River Thames [C16: from UP (in the archaic sense: to catch and mark a swan)]

swap or **swop** (swɒp) *vb* **swaps, swapping, swapped** or **swops, swopping, swopped 1** to trade or exchange (something or someone) for another > *n* **2** an exchange **3** something that is exchanged **4** Also called: **swap option, swaption** *finance* a contract in which the parties

to it exchange liabilities on outstanding debts, often exchanging fixed interest-rate for floating-rate debts (**debt swap**), either as a means of managing debt or in trading (**swap trading**) [C14 (in the sense: to shake hands on a bargain, strike): probably of imitative origin] > **'swapper** or **'swopper** *n*

SWAPO or **Swapo** ('swɑːpəʊ) *n acronym for* South-West Africa People's Organization

swaption ('swɒpʃən) *n* another name for **swap** (sense 4)

swaraj (swəˈrɑːdʒ) *n* (in British India) self-government; independence [C20: from Sanskrit *svarāj*, from *sva* self + *rājya* rule] > **swa'rajism** *n* > **swa'rajist** *n, adj*

sward (swɔːd) *n* **1** turf or grass or a stretch of turf or grass > *vb* **2** to cover or become covered with grass [Old English *sweard* skin; related to Old Frisian *swarde* scalp, Middle High German *swart* hide]

swarf (swɔːf, swɑːf) *n* **1** material removed by cutting or grinding tools in the machining of metals, stone, etc **2** radioactive metal waste from a nuclear power station **3** small fragments of disintegrating spacecraft, orbiting the earth [C16: of Scandinavian origin; related to Old Norse *svarf* metallic dust]

swarm¹ (swɔːm) *n* **1** a group of social insects, esp bees led by a queen, that has left the parent hive in order to start a new colony **2** a large mass of small animals, esp insects **3** a throng or mass, esp when moving or in turmoil > *vb* **4** (*intr*) (of small animals, esp bees) to move in or form a swarm **5** (*intr*) to congregate, move about or proceed in large numbers **6** (when *intr*, often foll by *with*) to overrun or be overrun (with): *the house swarmed with rats* **7** (*tr*) to cause to swarm [Old English *swearm*; related to Old Norse *svarmr* uproar, Old High German *swaram* swarm]

swarm² (swɔːm) *vb* (when *intr*, usually foll by *up*) to climb (a ladder, etc) by gripping with the hands and feet: *the boys swarmed up the rigging* [C16: of unknown origin]

swarm intelligence *n* **1** the collective behaviour of a group of animals, esp social insects such as ants, bees, and termites, that are each following very basic rules **2** an artificial-intelligence approach to problem solving using algorithms based on the self-organized collective behaviour of social insects

swart (swɔːt) or **swarth** (swɔːθ) *adj archaic or dialect* swarthy [Old English *sweart*; related to Old Frisian *swart*, Old Norse *svartr*, Old High German *swarz* black, Latin *sordēs* dirt; see SORDID]

swarthy ('swɔːðɪ) *adj* **swarthier, swarthiest** dark-hued or dark-complexioned [C16: from obsolete *swarty*, from SWART + -Y¹] > **'swarthily** *adv* > **'swarthiness** *n*

swash (swɒʃ) *vb* **1** (*intr*) (esp of water or things in water) to wash or move with noisy splashing **2** (*tr*) to dash (a liquid, esp water) against or upon **3** *archaic* to swagger or bluster > *n* **4** Also called: **send** the dashing movement or sound of water, such as that of waves on a beach **5** any other swashing movement or sound **6** Also called: **swash channel** a channel of moving water cutting through or running behind a sandbank **7** *archaic* swagger or bluster [C16: probably of imitative origin]

swashbuckler ('swɒʃ,bʌklə) *n* **1** a swaggering or flamboyant adventurer **2** a film, book, play, etc, depicting excitement and adventure, esp in a historical setting [C16: from SWASH (in the archaic sense: to make the noise of a sword striking a shield) + BUCKLER]

swash letter *n* *printing* a decorative letter, esp an ornamental italic capital [C17 *swash* (n, in the sense: the decorative flourish of an ornamental letter) from *aswash* aslant]

swastika ('swɒstɪkə) *n* **1** a primitive religious symbol or ornament in the shape of a Greek cross, usually having the ends of the arms bent at right angles in either a clockwise or anticlockwise direction **2** this symbol with clockwise arms, officially adopted in 1935 as the emblem of Nazi Germany [C19: from Sanskrit *svastika*, from *svasti* prosperity; from the belief that it brings good luck]

swat (swɒt) *vb* **swats, swatting, swatted** (*tr*) **1** to strike or hit sharply: *to swat a fly* > *n* **2** a sharp or violent blow > Also called: **swot** [C17: northern English dialect and US variant of SQUAT] > **'swatter** *n*

Swat (swɒt) *n* **1** a former princely state of NW India: passed to Pakistan in 1947 **2** a river in Pakistan, rising in the north and flowing south to the Kabul River north of Peshawar. Length: about 640 km (400 miles)

swatch (swɒtʃ) *n* **1** a sample of cloth **2** a number of such samples, usually fastened together in book form [c16: Scottish and northern English, of uncertain origin]

swath (swɔːθ) *or* **swathe** (sweɪð) *n, pl* swaths (swɔːðz) *or* swathes **1** the width of one sweep of a scythe or of the blade of a mowing machine **2** the strip cut by either of these in one course **3** the quantity of cut grass, hay, or similar crop left in one course of such mowing **4** a long narrow strip or belt [Old English *swæth*; related to Old Norse *svath* smooth patch]

swathe (sweɪð) *vb* (*tr*) **1** to bandage (a wound, limb, etc), esp completely **2** to wrap a band, garment, etc, around, esp so as to cover completely; swaddle **3** to envelop ▷ *n* **4** a bandage or wrapping **5** a variant spelling of **swath** [Old English *swathian*; related to *swæthel* swaddling clothes, Old High German *swedil*, Dutch *zwadel*; see SWADDLE]

Swatow ('swɒ'taʊ) *n* a variant transliteration of the Chinese name for **Shantou**

sway (sweɪ) *vb* **1** (*usually intr*) to swing or cause to swing to and fro **2** (*usually intr*) to lean or incline or cause to lean or incline to one side or in different directions in turn **3** (*usually intr*) to vacillate or cause to vacillate between two or more opinions **4** to be influenced or swerve or influence or cause to swerve to or from a purpose or opinion **5** *archaic, or poetic* to rule or wield power (over) ▷ *n* **6** control; power **7** a swinging or leaning movement **8** *archaic* dominion; governing authority **9** hold sway to be master; reign [c16: probably from Old Norse *sveigja* to bend; related to Dutch *zwaaien*, Low German *swãjen*]

sway-back *n* **1** *vet science* an abnormal sagging or concavity of the spine in older horses **2** a paralytic disease of new-born and young lambs caused by demyelination of the central nervous system due to copper deficiency > 'sway-,backed *adj*

Swaziland ('swɑːzɪˌlænd) *n* a kingdom in southern Africa: made a protectorate of the Transvaal by Britain in 1894; gained independence in 1968; a member of the Commonwealth. Official languages: Swazi and English. Religion: Christian majority, traditional beliefs. Currency: lilangeni (plural emalangeni) and South African rand. Capital: Mbabane (administrative), Lobamba (legislative). Pop: 1 083 000 (2004 est). Area: 17 363 sq km (6704 sq miles)

Swazi Territory the former name of **Ka Ngwane**

swear (sweə) *vb* swears, swearing, swore, sworn **1** to declare or affirm (a statement) as true, esp by invoking a deity, etc, as witness **2** (foll by *by*) **a** to invoke (a deity, etc) by name as a witness or guarantee to an oath **b** to trust implicitly; have complete confidence (in) **3** (*intr*; often foll by *at*) to curse, blaspheme, or use swearwords **4** (when *tr*, may take a clause as object or an infinitive) to promise solemnly on oath; vow **5** (*tr*) to assert or affirm with great emphasis or earnestness **6** (*intr*) to give evidence or make any statement or solemn declaration on oath **7** to take an oath in order to add force or solemnity to (a statement or declaration) ▷ *n* **8** a period of swearing [Old English *swerian*; related to Old Norse *sverja*, Gothic *swaran*, Old Frisian *swera*, German *schwören*] > 'swearer *n*

swear in *vb* (*tr, adverb*) to administer an oath to (a person) on his assuming office, entering the witness box to give evidence, etc

swear off *vb* (*intr, preposition*) to promise to abstain from something: *to swear off drink*

swearword ('sweəˌwɜːd) *n* a socially taboo word or phrase of a profane, obscene, or insulting character

sweat (swɛt) *n* **1** the secretion from the sweat glands, esp when profuse and visible, as during strenuous activity, from excessive heat, etc; commonly also called perspiration **2** the act or process of secreting this fluid **3** the act of inducing the exudation of moisture **4** drops of moisture given forth or gathered on the surface of something **5** *informal* a state or condition of worry or eagerness (esp in the phrase **in a sweat**) **6** *slang* drudgery or hard labour: *mowing lawns is a real sweat!* **7** *slang, chiefly Brit* a soldier, esp one who is old and experienced **8** **no sweat!** (*interjection*) *slang* an expression suggesting that something can be done without problems or difficulty ▷ *vb* **sweats, sweating, sweat or sweated 9** to secrete (sweat) through the pores of the skin, esp profusely **10** (*tr*) to make wet or stain with sweat **11** to give forth or cause to give forth (moisture) in droplets: *a sweating cheese; the maple sweats sap* **12** (*intr*) to collect and condense moisture on an outer surface: *a glass of beer sweating in the sun* **13** (*intr*) (of a liquid) to pass through a porous surface in droplets **14** (of tobacco leaves, cut and dried hay, etc) to exude moisture and, sometimes, begin to ferment or to cause (tobacco leaves, etc) to exude moisture **15** (*tr*) to heat (food, esp vegetables) slowly in butter in a tightly closed saucepan **16** (*tr*) to join (pieces of metal) by pressing together and heating **17** (*tr*) to heat (solder) until it melts **18** (*tr*) to heat (a partially fused metal) to extract an easily fusible constituent **19** *informal* to suffer anxiety, impatience, or distress **20** *informal* to overwork or be overworked **21** (*tr*) *informal* to employ at very low wages and under bad conditions **22** (*tr*) *informal* to extort, esp by torture: *to sweat information out of a captive* **23** (*intr*) *informal* to suffer punishment: *you'll sweat for this!* **24** **sweat blood** *informal* **a** to work very hard **b** to be filled with anxiety or impatience ▷ See also **sweat out, sweat off**, etc [Old English *swǣtan* to sweat, from *swāt* sweat; related to Old Saxon *swēt*, Old Norse *sveiti*, Old High German *sweiz*, Latin *sūdor*, Sanskrit *svedas*]

sweatband ('swɛtˌbænd) *n* **1** a band of material set in a hat or cap to protect it from sweat **2** a piece of cloth tied around the forehead to keep sweat out of the eyes or around the wrist to keep the hands dry, as in sports

sweated ('swɛtɪd) *adj* **1** made by exploited labour: *sweated goods* **2** (of workers, etc) forced to work in poor conditions for low pay

sweater ('swɛtə) *n* **1** a garment made of knitted or crocheted material covering the upper part of the body, esp a heavy one worn for warmth **2** a person or thing that sweats **3** an employer who overworks and underpays his employees

sweat gland *n* any of the coiled tubular subcutaneous glands that secrete sweat by means of a duct that opens on to the skin

sweating sickness *n* an acute infectious febrile disease that was widespread in Europe during the late 15th century, characterized by profuse sweating

sweat lodge *n* (among native North American peoples) a structure in which water is poured onto hot stones to make the occupants sweat for religious or medicinal purposes

sweat off *or* **sweat away** *vb* (*tr, adverb*) *informal* to get rid of (weight) by strenuous exercise or sweating

sweat out *vb* (*tr, adverb*) **1** to cure or lessen the effects of (a cold, respiratory infection, etc) by sweating **2** *informal* to endure (hardships) for a time (often in the phrase **sweat it out**) **3** **sweat one's guts out** *informal* to work extremely hard

sweat pants *pl n* loose thick cotton trousers with elasticated cuffs and an elasticated or drawstring waist, worn esp by athletes warming up or training

sweats (swɛts) *pl n* sweatshirts and sweat-suit trousers: *jeans and sweats*

sweatshirt ('swɛtˌʃɜːt) *n* a long-sleeved knitted cotton sweater worn by athletes, etc

sweatshop ('swɛtˌʃɒp) *n* a workshop where employees work long hours under bad conditions for low wages

sweat suit *n* a suit worn by athletes for training comprising knitted cotton trousers fitting closely at the ankle and a light cotton sweater

sweaty ('swɛtɪ) *adj* sweatier, sweatiest **1** covered with sweat; sweating **2** smelling of or like sweat **3** causing sweat > 'sweatily *adv* > 'sweatiness *n*

swede (swiːd) *n* **1** a Eurasian plant, *Brassica napus* (or *B. napobrassica*), cultivated for its bulbous edible root, which is used as a vegetable and as cattle fodder: family *Brassicaceae* (crucifers) **2** the root of this plant [c19: so called after being introduced into Scotland from Sweden in the 18th century]

Swede (swiːd) *n* a native, citizen, or inhabitant of Sweden

Sweden ('swiːdᵊn) *n* a kingdom in NW Europe, occupying the E part of the Scandinavian Peninsula, on the Gulf of Bothnia and the Baltic: first united during the Viking period (8th–11th centuries); a member of the European Union. About 50 per cent of the total area is forest and 9 per cent lakes. Exports include timber, pulp, paper, iron ore, and steel. Official language: Swedish. Official religion: Church of Sweden (Lutheran). Currency: krona. Capital: Stockholm. Pop: 8 886 000 (2004 est). Area: 449 793 sq km (173 665 sq miles). Swedish name: **Sverige**

Swedenborg ('swiːdᵊn,bɔːɡ; *Swedish* 'sveːdənbɔrj) *n* **Emanuel** (e'manuel). original surname *Svedberg*. 1688–1772, Swedish scientist and theologian, whose mystical ideas became the basis of a religious movement

Swedish ('swiːdɪʃ) *adj* **1** of, relating to, or characteristic of Sweden, its people, or their language ▷ *n* **2** the official language of Sweden, belonging to the North Germanic branch of the Indo-European family: one of the two official languages of Finland

Sweelinck (*Dutch* 'sweːlɪŋk) *n* **Jan Pieterszoon** (jan 'piːtərˌzoːn). 1562–1621, Dutch composer and organist, whose organ works are important for being the first to incorporate independent parts for the pedals

sweep (swiːp) *vb* **sweeps, sweeping, swept** **1** to clean or clear (a space, chimney, etc) with a brush, broom, etc **2** (often foll by *up*) to remove or collect (dirt, rubbish, etc) with a brush, broom, etc **3** to move in a smooth or continuous manner, esp quickly or forcibly: *cars swept along the road* **4** to move in a proud or dignified fashion: *she swept past* **5** to spread or pass rapidly across, through, or along (a region, area, etc): *the news swept through the town* **6** (*tr*) to direct (the gaze, line of fire, etc) over; survey **7** (*tr*; foll by *away* or *off*) to overwhelm emotionally: *she was swept away by his charm* **8** (*tr*) to brush or lightly touch (a surface, etc): *the dress swept along the ground* **9** (*tr*; often foll by *away*) to convey, clear, or abolish, esp with strong or continuous movements: *the sea swept the sandcastle away; secondary modern schools were swept away* **10** (*intr*) to extend gracefully or majestically, esp in a wide circle: *the plains sweep down to the sea* **11** to search (a body of water) for mines, etc, by dragging **12** (*tr*) to win overwhelmingly, esp in an election: *Labour swept the country* **13** (*tr*) to propel (a boat) with sweeps **14 sweep the board** **a** (in gambling) to win all the cards or money **b** to win every event or prize in a contest **15 sweep something under the carpet** to conceal (something, esp a problem) in the hope that it will be overlooked by others ▷ *n* **16** the act or an instance of sweeping; removal by or as if by a brush or broom **17** a swift or steady movement, esp in an arc **18** the distance, arc, etc, through which something, such as a pendulum, moves **19** a wide expanse or scope: *the sweep of the plains* **20** any curving line or contour **21** short for **sweepstake 22 a** a long oar used on an open boat **b** *Austral* a person steering a surf boat with such an oar **23** any of the sails of a windmill **24** *electronics* a steady horizontal or circular movement of an electron beam across or around the fluorescent screen of a cathode-ray tube **25** a curving driveway **26** *chiefly Brit* See **chimney sweep 27** another name for **swipe** (sense 6) **28 clean sweep a** an overwhelming victory or success **b** a complete change; purge: *to make a clean sweep* [C13 *swepen*; related to Old English *swāpan*, Old Norse *sveipa*; see **SWIPE**, **SWOOP**] ▷ **'sweepy** *adj*

sweeper ('swiːpə) *n* **1** a person employed to sweep, such as a roadsweeper **2** any device for sweeping: *a carpet sweeper* **3** *informal soccer* a player who supports the main defenders, as by intercepting loose balls, etc

sweep hand *n* *horology* a long hand that registers seconds or fractions of seconds on the perimeter of the dial

sweeping ('swiːpɪŋ) *adj* **1** comprehensive and wide-ranging: *sweeping reforms* **2** indiscriminate or without

reservations: *sweeping statements* **3** decisive or overwhelming: *a sweeping victory* **4** taking in a wide area: *a sweeping glance* **5** driving steadily onwards, esp over a large area: *a sweeping attack* ▷ **'sweepingly** *adv* ▷ **'sweepingness** *n*

sweep-saw *n* a saw with a thin blade that can be used for cutting curved shapes

sweepstake ('swiːpˌsteɪk) *or esp US* **sweepstakes** *n* **1 a** a lottery in which the stakes of the participants constitute the prize **b** the prize itself **2** any event involving a lottery, esp a horse race in which the prize is the competitors' stakes ▷ Often shortened to: **sweep** [C15: originally referring to someone who *sweeps* or takes all the stakes in a game]

sweet (swiːt) *adj* **1** having or denoting a pleasant taste like that of sugar **2** agreeable to the senses or the mind: *sweet music* **3** having pleasant manners; gentle: *a sweet child* **4** (of wine, etc) having a relatively high sugar content; not dry **5** (of foods) not decaying or rancid: *sweet milk* **6** not salty: *sweet water* **7** free from unpleasant odours: *sweet air* **8** containing no corrosive substances: *sweet soil* **9** (of petrol) containing no sulphur compounds **10** sentimental or unrealistic **11** *jazz* performed with a regular beat, with the emphasis on clearly outlined melody and little improvisation **12** *archaic* respected; dear (used in polite forms of address): *sweet sir* **13** smooth and precise; perfectly executed: *a sweet shot* **14 keep someone sweet** to ingratiate oneself in order to ensure cooperation ▷ *adv* **15** *informal* in a sweet manner ▷ *n* **16** a sweet taste or smell; sweetness in general **17** (*often plural*) *Brit* any of numerous kinds of confectionery consisting wholly or partly of sugar, esp of sugar boiled and crystallized (**boiled sweets**) **18** *Brit* a pudding, fruit, or any sweet dish served as a dessert **19** dear; sweetheart (used as a form of address) **20** anything that is sweet **21** (*often plural*) a pleasurable experience, state, etc: *the sweets of success* [Old English *swēte*; related to Old Saxon *swōti*, Old High German *suozi*, Old Norse *sætr*, Latin *suādus* persuasive, *suāvis* sweet, Greek *hēdus*, Sanskrit *svādu*; see **PERSUADE, SUAVE**] ▷ **'sweetish** *adj* ▷ **'sweetly** *adv* ▷ **'sweetness** *n*

Sweet *n* **Henry**. 1845–1912, English philologist; a pioneer of modern phonetics. His books include *A History of English Sounds* (1874)

sweet alyssum *n* a Mediterranean plant, *Lobularia maritima*, having clusters of small fragrant white or violet flowers, that is widely grown in gardens: family Brassicaceae (crucifers). See also **alyssum**

sweet-and-sour *adj* (of food) cooked in a sauce made from sugar and vinegar and other ingredients

sweet bay *n* a small tree, *Magnolia virginiana*, of SE North America, having large fragrant white flowers: family Magnoliaceae (magnolias). Sometimes shortened to: **bay**

sweetbread ('swiːtˌbred) *n* the pancreas (**stomach sweetbread**) or the thymus gland (**neck** or **throat sweetbread**) of an animal, used for food [C16: **SWEET** + **BREAD**, perhaps from Old English *brǣd* meat; related to Old Saxon *brādo* ham, Old High German *brāt*, Old Norse *brāth*]

sweetbrier ('swiːtˌbraɪə) *n* a Eurasian rose, *Rosa rubiginosa*, having a tall bristly stem, fragrant leaves, and single pink flowers. Also called: **eglantine**

sweet cherry *n* either of two types of cherry tree that are cultivated for their red edible sweet fruit, the gean having tender-fleshed fruit, the bigarreau having firm-fleshed fruit

sweet chestnut *n* See **chestnut** (sense 1)

sweet cicely *n* **1** Also called: **myrrh** an aromatic umbelliferous European plant, *Myrrhis odorata*, having compound leaves and clusters of small white flowers **2** the leaves of this plant, formerly used in cookery for their flavour of aniseed **3** any of various plants of the umbelliferous genus *Osmorhiza*, of Asia and America, having aromatic roots and clusters of small white flowers

sweet corn *n* **1** Also called: **sugar corn, green corn** a variety of maize, *Zea mays saccharata*, whose kernels are rich in sugar and eaten as a vegetable when young **2** the unripe ears of maize, esp the sweet kernels removed from the cob, cooked as a vegetable

sweeten ('swi:tᵊn) vb (mainly tr) 1 (also intr) to make or become sweet or sweeter 2 to mollify or soften (a person) 3 to make more agreeable 4 (also intr) chem to free or be freed from unpleasant odours, acidic or corrosive substances, or the like

sweetener ('swi:tᵊnə) n 1 a sweetening agent, esp one that does not contain sugar 2 informal a bribe 3 informal a financial inducement

sweetening ('swi:tᵊnɪŋ) n something that sweetens

sweet flag n an aroid marsh plant, Acorus calamus, having swordlike leaves, small greenish flowers, and aromatic roots. Also called: calamus [C18: see FLAG²]

sweet gale n a shrub, Myrica gale, of northern swamp regions, having yellow catkin-like flowers and aromatic leaves: family Myricaceae. Also called: bog myrtle Often shortened to: gale

sweet gum n 1 a North American liquidambar tree, Liquidambar styraciflua, having prickly spherical fruit clusters and fragrant sap: the wood (called satin walnut) is used to make furniture 2 the sap of this tree ▷ Also called: red gum

sweetheart ('swi:t,hɑ:t) n 1 a person loved by another 2 informal a lovable, generous, or obliging person 3 a term of endearment for a beloved or lovable person

sweetheart agreement n an industrial agreement made at a local level between an employer and employees, often with clauses advantageous to the employer, such as no strikes, but without the recognition of the national union representing the employees

sweetie ('swi:tɪ) n informal 1 sweetheart; darling: used as a term of endearment 2 Brit another word for sweet (sense 17) 3 chiefly Brit an endearing person 4 a large seedless variety of grapefruit which has a green to yellow rind and juicy sweet pulp

sweeting ('swi:tɪŋ) n 1 a variety of sweet apple 2 an archaic word for sweetheart

sweet marjoram n another name for marjoram (sense 1)

sweetmeat ('swi:t,mi:t) n a sweetened delicacy, such as a preserve, sweet, or, formerly, a cake or pastry

sweet pea n a climbing leguminous plant, Lathyrus odoratus, of S Europe, widely cultivated for its butterfly-shaped fragrant flowers of delicate pastel colours

sweet pepper n 1 a pepper plant, Capsicum frutescens grossum, with large bell-shaped fruits that are eaten unripe (green pepper) or ripe (red pepper) 2 the fruit of this plant

sweet potato n 1 a convolvulaceous twining plant, Ipomoea batatas, of tropical America, cultivated in the tropics for its edible fleshy yellow root 2 the root of this plant

sweet shop n chiefly Brit a shop solely or largely selling sweets, esp boiled sweets

sweetsop ('swi:t,sɒp) n 1 a small West Indian tree, Annona squamosa, having yellowish-green fruit: family Annonaceae 2 the fruit of this tree, which has a sweet edible pulp ▷ Also called: custard apple [C19: so called because of the flavour and consistency of its pulp]

sweet spot n sport the centre area of a racquet, golf club, etc, from which the cleanest shots are made

sweet-talk informal ▷ vb 1 to coax, flatter, or cajole (someone) ▷ n sweet talk 2 cajolery; coaxing

sweet tooth n a strong liking for sweet foods

sweetveld ('swi:t,fɛlt) n (in South Africa) a type of grazing characterized by high-quality grass [from Afrikaans soetveld]

sweet william n a widely cultivated Eurasian caryophyllaceous plant, Dianthus barbatus, with flat clusters of white, pink, red, or purple flowers

swell (swɛl) vb swells, swelling, swelled, swollen or swelled 1 to grow or cause to grow in size, esp as a result of internal pressure 2 to expand or cause to expand at a particular point or above the surrounding level; protrude 3 to grow or cause to grow in size, amount, intensity, or degree: the party is swelling with new recruits 4 to puff or be puffed up with pride or another emotion 5 (intr) (of seas or lakes) to rise in waves 6 (intr) to well up

or overflow 7 (tr) to make (a musical phrase) increase gradually in volume and then diminish ▷ n 8 a the undulating movement of the surface of the open sea b a succession of waves or a single large wave 9 a swelling or being swollen; expansion 10 an increase in quantity or degree; inflation 11 a bulge; protuberance 12 a gentle hill 13 informal a person very fashionably dressed 14 informal a man of high social or political standing 15 music a crescendo followed by an immediate diminuendo 16 Also called: swell organ music a a set of pipes on an organ housed in a box (swell box) fitted with a shutter operated by a pedal, which can be opened or closed to control the volume b the manual on an organ controlling this ▷ adj 17 informal stylish or grand 18 slang excellent; first-class [Old English swellan; related to Old Norse svella, Old Frisian swella, German schwellen]

swelled head or **swollen head** n informal an inflated view of one's own worth, often caused by sudden success ▷ swelled-headed or swell-headed or swollen-headed adj

swelling ('swɛlɪŋ) n 1 the act of expansion or inflation 2 the state of being or becoming swollen 3 a swollen or inflated part or area 4 an abnormal enlargement of a bodily structure or part, esp as the result of injury Related adj: tumescent

swelter ('swɛltə) vb 1 (intr) to suffer under oppressive heat, esp to sweat and feel faint 2 (tr) rare to cause to suffer under oppressive heat ▷ n 3 a sweltering condition (esp in the phrase in a swelter) 4 oppressive humid heat [C15 swelten, from Old English sweltan to die; related to Old Norse svelta to starve, Old High German swelzan to burn with passion; see SULTRY]

sweltering ('swɛltərɪŋ) adj oppressively hot and humid: a sweltering day ▷ swelteringly adv

swept (swɛpt) vb the past tense of sweep

sweptback ('swɛpt,bæk) adj (of an aircraft wing) having leading edge and trailing edges inclined backwards towards the rear of the fuselage

sweptwing ('swɛpt,wɪŋ) adj (of an aircraft, winged missile, etc) having wings swept (usually) backwards

swerve (swɜ:v) vb 1 to turn or cause to turn aside, usually sharply or suddenly, from a course ▷ n 2 the act, instance, or degree of swerving [Old English sweorfan to scour; related to Old High German swerban to wipe off, Gothic afswairban to wipe off, Old Norse sverfa to file] ▷ 'swervable adj ▷ 'swerver n

Sweyn (swein) n known as Sweyn Forkbeard. died 1014, king of Denmark (?986–1014). He conquered England, forcing Ethelred II to flee (1013); father of Canute

swift (swɪft) adj 1 moving or able to move quickly; fast 2 occurring or performed quickly or suddenly; instant 3 (postpositive; foll by to) prompt to act or respond: swift to take revenge ▷ adv 4 a swiftly or quickly b (in combination): swift-moving ▷ n 5 any bird of the families Apodidae and Hemiprocnidae, such as Apus apus (common swift) of the Old World: order Apodiformes. They have long narrow wings and spend most of the time on the wing 6 any of certain North American lizards of the genera Sceloporus and Uta that can run very rapidly: family Iguanidae (iguanas) 7 the main cylinder in a carding machine 8 an expanding circular frame used to hold skeins of silk, wool, etc [Old English, from swifan to turn; related to Old Norse svifa to rove, Old Frisian swivia to waver, Old High German sweib a reversal; see SWIVEL] ▷ 'swiftly adv ▷ 'swiftness n

Swift (swɪft) n 1 Graham (Colin). born 1949, British writer: his novels include Waterland (1983), Last Orders (1996), which won the Booker prize, and The Light of Day (2002) 2 Jonathan. 1667–1745, Anglo-Irish satirist and churchman, who became dean of St Patrick's, Dublin, in 1713. His works include A Tale of a Tub (1704) and Gulliver's Travels (1726) ▷ 'Swiftian adj

swiftlet ('swɪftlɪt) n any of various small swifts of the Asian genus Collocalia that often live in caves and use echolocation: the nests, which are made of hardened saliva, are used in oriental cookery to make birds' nest soup

swig (swɪg) informal ▷ n 1 a large swallow or deep drink, esp from a bottle ▷ vb swigs, swigging, swigged 2 to drink (some liquid) deeply, esp from a bottle [c16: of unknown origin] ▷ 'swigger n

swiler ('swaɪlə) n Canadian (in Newfoundland) a seal hunter

swill (swɪl) vb 1 to drink large quantities of (liquid, esp alcoholic drink); guzzle 2 (tr; often foll by out) chiefly Brit to drench or rinse in large amounts of water 3 (tr) to feed swill to (pigs, etc) ▷ n 4 wet feed, esp for pigs, consisting of kitchen waste, skimmed milk, etc 5 garbage or refuse, esp from a kitchen 6 a deep draught of drink, esp beer 7 any liquid mess 8 the act of swilling [Old English swilian to wash out] ▷ 'swiller n

swim (swɪm) vb swims, swimming, swam, swum 1 (intr) to move along in water, etc, by means of movements of the body or parts of the body, esp the arms and legs, or (in the case of fish) tail and fins 2 (tr) to cover (a distance or stretch of water) in this way 3 (tr) to compete in (a race) in this way 4 (intr) to be supported by and on a liquid; float 5 (tr) to use (a particular stroke) in swimming 6 (intr) to move smoothly, usually through air or over a surface 7 (intr) to reel or seem to reel: my head swam; the room swam around me 8 (intr; often foll by in or with) to be covered or flooded with water or other liquid 9 (intr; often foll by in) to be liberally supplied (with): he's swimming in money 10 (tr) to cause to float or swim 11 swim with the tide or swim with the stream to conform to prevailing opinion 12 swim against the tide or swim against the stream to resist prevailing opinion ▷ n 13 the act, an instance, or period of swimming 14 any graceful gliding motion 15 a condition of dizziness; swoon 16 a pool in a river good for fishing 17 in the swim informal fashionable or active in social or political activities [Old English swimman; related to Old Norse svima, German schwimmen, Gothic swumsl pond, Norwegian svamla to paddle] ▷ 'swimmable adj ▷ 'swimmer n ▷ 'swimming n, adj

swim bladder n ichthyol another name for **air bladder** (sense 1)

swimmeret ('swɪmə,rɛt) n any of the small paired appendages on the abdomen of crustaceans, used chiefly in locomotion and reproduction [c19: from SWIM + -ER¹ + -ET]

swimming bath n (often plural) an indoor swimming pool

swimming costume or **bathing costume** n chiefly Brit any apparel worn for swimming or sunbathing, such as a woman's one-piece garment covering most of the torso but not the limbs

swimmingly ('swɪmɪŋlɪ) adv successfully, effortlessly, or well (esp in the phrase **go swimmingly**)

swimming pool n an artificial pool for swimming

swimsuit ('swɪm,suːt, -,sjuːt) n a woman's one-piece swimming garment that leaves the arms and legs bare

Swinburne ('swɪn,bɜːn) n Algernon Charles. 1837–1909, English lyric poet and critic

swindle ('swɪnd³l) vb 1 to cheat (someone) of money, etc; defraud 2 (tr) to obtain (money, etc) by fraud ▷ n 3 a fraudulent scheme or transaction [c18: back formation from German Schwindler, from schwindeln, from Old High German swintilōn, frequentative of swintan to disappear] ▷ 'swindler n

swindle sheet n a slang term for **expense account**

Swindon ('swɪndən) n 1 a town in S England, in NE Wiltshire: railway workshops, high technology. Pop: 155 432 (2001) 2 a unitary authority in S England, in Wiltshire. Pop: 181 200 (2003 est). Area: 230 sq km (89 sq miles)

swine (swaɪn) n 1 pl swines a coarse or contemptible person 2 pl swine another name for a **pig** [Old English swīn; related to Old Norse svīn, Gothic swein, Latin suīnus relating to swine] ▷ 'swinish adj ▷ 'swinishly adv ▷ 'swinishness n

swine fever n an infectious viral disease of pigs, characterized by fever, refusal to eat, weight loss, and diarrhoea

swineherd ('swaɪn,hɜːd) n archaic a person who looks after pigs

swing (swɪŋ) vb swings, swinging, swung 1 to move or cause to move rhythmically to and fro, as a free-

hanging object; sway 2 (intr) to move, walk, etc, with a relaxed and swaying motion 3 to pivot or cause to pivot, as on a hinge 4 to move or cause to move in a curve: the car swung around the bend 5 to move or cause to move by suspending or being suspended 6 to hang or be hung so as to be able to turn freely 7 (intr) slang to be hanged: he'll swing for it 8 to alter or cause to alter habits, a course, etc 9 (tr) informal to influence or manipulate successfully: I hope he can swing the deal 10 (tr; foll by up) to raise or hoist, esp in a sweeping motion 11 (intr; often foll by at) to hit out or strike (at), esp with a sweeping motion 12 (tr) to wave (a weapon, etc) in a sweeping motion; flourish 13 to arrange or play (music) with the rhythmically flexible and compulsive quality associated with jazz 14 (intr) (of popular music, esp jazz, or of the musicians who play it) to have this quality 15 slang to be lively and modern 16 (intr) cricket to bowl (a ball) with swing or (of a ball) to move with a swing 17 swing the lead informal to malinger or make up excuses ▷ n 18 the act or manner of swinging or the distance covered while swinging: a wide swing 19 a sweeping stroke or blow 20 boxing a wide punch from the side similar to but longer than a hook 21 cricket the lateral movement of a bowled ball through the air 22 any free-swaying motion 23 any curving movement; sweep 24 something that swings or is swung, esp a suspended seat on which a person may sit and swing back and forth 25 a kind of popular dance music influenced by jazz, usually played by big bands and originating in the 1930s 26 prosody a steady distinct rhythm or cadence in prose or verse 27 informal the normal round or pace: get into the swing of things 28 a a fluctuation, as in some business activity, voting pattern etc b (as modifier) able to bring about a swing in a voting pattern 29 chiefly US a circular tour 30 go with a swing to go well; be successful 31 in full swing at the height of activity 32 swings and roundabouts equal advantages and disadvantages [Old English swingan; related to Old Frisian swinga, Old High German swingan]

swingboat ('swɪŋ,bəʊt) n a piece of fairground equipment consisting of a boat-shaped carriage for swinging in

swing bridge n Also called: pivot bridge, turn bridge a low bridge that can be rotated about a vertical axis, esp to permit the passage of ships

swing by vb (prep) informal to go somewhere to pay a visit

swinge (swɪndʒ) vb swinges, swingeing or swinging, swinged (tr) archaic to beat, flog, or punish [Old English swengan; related to Old Frisian swenga to drench, Gothic afswaggwjan to cause to sway; see SWING]

swingeing ('swɪndʒɪŋ) adj chiefly Brit punishing; severe

swinger ('swɪŋə) slang n 1 a person regarded as being modern and lively 2 a person who swaps sexual partners in a group, esp habitually

swinging ('swɪŋɪŋ) adj 1 moving rhythmically to and fro 2 slang modern and lively ▷ 'swingingly adv

swingle ('swɪŋg³l) n 1 a flat-bladed wooden instrument used for beating and scraping flax or hemp to remove coarse matter from it ▷ vb 2 (tr) to use a swingle on [Old English swingel stroke; related to Middle High German swüngel, Middle Dutch swinghel]

swingletree ('swɪŋg³l,triː) n a crossbar in a horse's harness to which the ends of the traces are attached. Also called: whippletree [c15: from SWINGLE + TREE (in the sense: a post or bar)]

swing shift n US & Canadian the period worked. Also called (in Britain and certain other countries): **back shift**

swing-wing adj 1 of or relating to a variable-geometry aircraft ▷ n 2 a such an aircraft b either wing of such an aircraft

Swinney ('swɪnɪ) n John (Ramsay). born 1964, Scottish politician; leader of the Scottish National Party (2000–04)

swipe (swaɪp) vb 1 (when intr, usually foll by at) informal to hit hard with a sweeping blow 2 (tr) slang to steal 3 (tr) to pass a machine-readable card, such as a credit card, debit card, etc, through a machine that electronically interprets the information encoded, usu. in a magnetic strip, on the card ▷ n 4 informal a hard blow 5 an unexpected criticism of someone or something while discussing another subject **6** Also called: **sweep** a type of lever for raising and lowering a weight, such as a bucket in a well [c19: perhaps related to SWEEP]

swipe card n a credit card, identity card, etc, with a magnetic strip that holds encoded information that can be electronically interpreted as it is passed through the slot of a machine designed to read it

swirl (swɜːl) vb **1** to turn or cause to turn in a twisting spinning fashion **2** (intr) to be dizzy; swim: *my head was swirling* ▷ n **3** a whirling or spinning motion, esp in water **4** a whorl; curl **5** the act of swirling or stirring **6** dizzy confusion [c15: probably from Dutch *zwirrelen*; related to Norwegian *svirla*, German *schwirren*] > 'swirling adj > 'swirly adj

swish (swɪʃ) vb **1** to move with or make or cause to move with or make a whistling or hissing sound **2** (intr) (of fabrics) to rustle **3** (tr) slang, now rare to whip; flog **4** (tr; foll by off) to cut with a swishing blow ▷ n **5** a hissing or rustling sound or movement **6** a rod for flogging or a blow from such a rod **7** informal, chiefly Brit fashionable; smart [c18: of imitative origin] > 'swishy adj

Swiss (swɪs) adj **1** of, relating to, or characteristic of Switzerland, its inhabitants, or their dialects of German, French, and Italian ▷ n **2** a native, inhabitant, or citizen of Switzerland

Swiss ball n a very large inflatable ball made of strong elastic rubber, used for physical exercise and in physiotherapy

Swiss chard n another name for **chard**

Swiss cheese plant n See **monstera**

Swiss Re Tower (riː) n a bluish cigar-shaped office block, London's first environmental skyscraper, located at 30 St Mary Axe, in the City of London: headquarters of the financial services group Swiss Re. Standing 180 m (585 ft) high and having 40 storeys, the building was completed in 2004

swiss roll n a sponge cake spread with jam, cream, or some other filling, and rolled up

switch (swɪtʃ) n **1** a mechanical, electrical, electronic, or optical device for opening or closing a circuit or for diverting energy from one part of a circuit to another **2** a swift and usually sudden shift or change **3** an exchange or swap **4** a flexible rod or twig, used esp for punishment **5** the sharp movement or blow of such an instrument **6** a tress of false hair used to give added length or bulk to a woman's own hairstyle **7** the tassel-like tip of the tail of cattle and certain other animals **8** any of various card games in which the suit is changed during play **9** US & Canadian a railway siding **10** US & Canadian a railway point **11** Austral informal See **switchboard** ▷ vb **12** to shift, change, turn aside, or change the direction of (something) **13** to exchange (places); replace (something by something else) **14** chiefly US & Canadian to transfer (rolling stock) from one railway track to another **15** (tr) to cause (an electric current) to start or stop flowing or to change its path by operating a switch **16** (tr) to lash or whip with or as if with a switch ▷ See also **switch off, switch on**, etc [c16: perhaps from Middle Dutch *swijch* branch, twig] > 'switcher n

switchback ('swɪtʃˌbæk) n **1** a mountain road, railway, or track which rises and falls sharply many times or a sharp rise and fall on such a road, railway, or track **2** another word (esp Brit) for **big dipper**

switchblade or **switchblade knife** ('swɪtʃˌbleɪd) n US & Canadian a knife with a retractable blade that springs out when a button is pressed. Also called (in Britain and certain other countries): **flick knife**

switchboard ('swɪtʃˌbɔːd) n **1** an installation in a telephone exchange, office, hotel, etc, at which the interconnection of telephone lines is manually controlled **2** an assembly of switchgear for the control of power supplies in an installation or building

switched-on adj informal well-informed or aware of what is up to date

switchgear ('swɪtʃˌɡɪə) n electrical engineering any of several devices used for opening and closing electric circuits, esp those that pass high currents

switchman ('swɪtʃmən) n, pl -men US & Canadian a person who operates railway points. Also called (in Britain and certain other countries): **pointsman**

switch off vb (adverb) **1** to cause (a device) to stop operating by or as if by moving a switch, knob, or lever; turn off **2** informal to cease to interest or be interested; make or become bored, alienated, etc

switch on vb (adverb) **1** to cause (a device) to operate by or as if by moving a switch, knob, or lever; turn on **2** (tr) informal to produce (charm, tears, etc) suddenly or automatically **3** (tr) informal (now slightly dated) to make up-to-date, esp regarding outlook, dress, etc

swither ('swɪðər) Scot ▷ vb (intr) **1** to hesitate; vacillate; be perplexed ▷ n **2** hesitation; perplexity; agitation [c16: of unknown origin]

Swithin or **Swithun** ('swɪðɪn, 'swɪθ-) n Saint. died 862 AD, English ecclesiastic: bishop of Winchester (?852–862). Feast day: July 15

Switz. or **Swit.** abbreviation Switzerland

Switzer ('swɪtsə) n a less common word for **Swiss** [c16: from Middle High German, from *Swīz* Switzerland]

Switzerland ('swɪtsələnd) n a federal republic in W central Europe: the cantons of Schwyz, Uri, and Unterwalden formed a defensive league against the Hapsburgs in 1291, later joined by other cantons; gained independence in 1499; adopted a policy of permanent neutrality from 1516; a leading centre of the Reformation in the 16th century. It lies in the Jura Mountains and the Alps, with a plateau between the two ranges. Official languages: German, French, and Italian; Romansch minority. Religion: mostly Protestant and Roman Catholic. Currency: Swiss franc. Capital: Bern. Pop: 7 163 000 (2004 est). Area: 41 288 sq km (15 941 sq miles). German name: Schweiz. French name: Suisse. Italian name: Svizzera. Italian name: Helvetia (hɛlˈviːʃə)

swivel ('swɪvəl) n **1 a** a coupling device which allows an attached object to turn freely **2** such a device made of two parts which turn independently, such as a compound link of a chain **3 a** a pivot on which is mounted a gun that may be swung from side to side in a horizontal plane **b** Also called: **swivel gun** the gun itself ▷ vb -els, -elling, -elled or US -els, -eling, -eled **4** to turn or swing on or as if on a pivot **5** (tr) to provide with, secure by, or support with a swivel [c14: from Old English *swīfan* to turn; see SWIFT]

swivel chair n a chair, the seat of which is joined to the legs by a swivel and which thus may be spun round

swivel pin n another name for **kingpin** (sense 2)

swiz or **swizz** (swɪz) n Brit informal a swindle or disappointment; swizzle

swizzle ('swɪzəl) n **1** an alcoholic drink containing gin or rum **2** Brit informal a swiz ▷ vb **3** (tr) to stir a swizzle stick in (a drink) **4** Brit informal to swindle; cheat [c19: of unknown origin]

swizzle stick n a small rod used to agitate an effervescent drink to facilitate the escape of carbon dioxide

swob (swɒb) n, vb swobs, swobbing, swobbed a less common word for **swab**

swollen ('swəʊlən) vb **1** a past participle of **swell** ▷ adj **2** tumid or enlarged by or as if by swelling **3** turgid or bombastic > 'swollenness n

swoon (swuːn) vb (intr) **1** a literary word for **faint 2** to become ecstatic ▷ n **3** an instance of fainting [Old English *geswōgen* insensible, past participle of *swōgan* (unattested except in compounds) to suffocate] > 'swooning adj

swoop (swuːp) vb **1** (intr; usually foll by down, on, or upon) to sweep or pounce suddenly **2** (tr; often foll by up, away, or off) to seize or scoop suddenly ▷ n **3** the act of swooping **4** a swift descent [Old English *swāpan* to sweep; related to Old High German *sweifan* to swing around, Old Norse *sveipa* to throw]

swoosh (swʊʃ) vb **1** to install or cause to make a rustling or swirling sound, esp when moving or pouring out ▷ n **2** a swirling or rustling sound or movement [c20: of imitative origin (probably influenced by SWISH and SWOOP)]

swop (swɒp) *n, vb* swops, swopping, swopped a variant spelling of **swap**

sword (sɔːd) *n* 1 a thrusting, striking, or cutting weapon with a long blade having one or two cutting edges, a hilt, and usually a crosspiece or guard 2 such a weapon worn on ceremonial occasions as a symbol of authority 3 something resembling a sword, such as the snout of a swordfish 4 **the sword a** violence or power, esp military power **b** death; destruction: *to put to the sword* [Old English *sweord*; related to Old Saxon *swerd*, Old Norse *sverth*, Old High German *swert*]

swordbearer ('sɔːdˌbɛərə) *n* an official who carries a ceremonial sword

sword dance *n* a dance in which the performers dance nimbly over swords on the ground or brandish them in the air > **sword dancer** *n* > **sword dancing** *n*

swordfish ('sɔːdˌfɪʃ) *n, pl* -fish *or* -fishes a large scombroid fish, *Xiphias gladius*, with a very long upper jaw: valued as a food and game fish: family *Xiphiidae*

sword grass *n* any of various grasses and other plants having sword-shaped sharp leaves

sword knot *n* a loop on the hilt of a sword by which it was attached to the wrist, now purely decorative

sword lily *n* another name for **gladiolus** (sense 1) [c18: so called because of its sword-shaped leaves]

Sword of Damocles *n* a closely impending disaster [see **DAMOCLES**]

swordplay ('sɔːdˌpleɪ) *n* 1 the action or art of fighting with a sword 2 verbal sparring

swordsman ('sɔːdzmən) *n, pl* -men one who uses or is skilled in the use of a sword > **'swordsmanˌship** *n*

swordstick ('sɔːdˌstɪk) *n* a hollow walking stick containing a short sword or dagger

swordtail ('sɔːdˌteɪl) *n* any of several small freshwater cyprinodont fishes of the genus *Xiphophorus*, esp *X. helleri*, of Central America, having a long swordlike tail

swore (swɔː) *vb* the past tense of **swear**

sworn (swɔːn) *vb* 1 the past participle of **swear** ▷ *adj* 2 bound, pledged, or made inveterate, by or as if by an oath: *a sworn statement; he was sworn to God*

swot¹ (swɒt) *Brit informal* ▷ *vb* swots, swotting, swotted 1 (often foll by *up*) to study (a subject) intensively, as for an examination; cram ▷ *n* 2 Also called: **swotter** ('swɒtə) a person who works or studies hard 3 hard work or grind ▷ Also called: **swat** [c19: dialect variant of SWEAT (n)]

swot² (swɒt) *vb* swots, swotting, swotted 1 a variant of **swat¹** ▷ *n* 2 a variant of **swat¹**

SWOT *abbreviation* strengths, weaknesses, opportunities, and threats: an analysis of a product made before it is marketed

swotty ('swɒtɪ) *adj* -tier, -tiest *Brit informal* given to studying hard, esp to the exclusion of other activities

swounds *or* **'swounds** (zwaʊndz, zaʊndz) *interj archaic* less common spellings of **zounds**

swum (swʌm) *vb* the past participle of **swim**

swung (swʌŋ) *vb* the past tense and past participle of **swing**

swy (swaɪ) *n Austral* another name for **two-up** [c20: from German *zwei* two]

Syal (saɪˌæl) *n* **Meera** ('mɪərə). born 1964, British actress and writer of Punjabi origin, who appeared in the TV comedy series *Goodness Gracious Me* (1998) and *The Kumars at No. 42* (2001–06); her screenplays include *Bhaji on the Beach* (1993)

Sybaris ('sɪbərɪs) *n* a Greek colony in S Italy, on the Gulf of Taranto: notorious for its luxurious living, founded about 720 BC and sacked in 510 > **'Sybaˌrite** *n* > **Sybaritic** (ˌsɪbəˈrɪtɪk) *adj*

sybarite ('sɪbəˌraɪt) *n* 1 (*sometimes capital*) a devotee of luxury and the sensual vices ▷ *adj* 2 luxurious; sensuous [c16: from Latin *Sybarīta*, from Greek *Subarītēs* inhabitant of *SYBARIS*] > **sybaritic** (ˌsɪbəˈrɪtɪk) *adj* > ˌsybaˈritically *adv* > **'sybaritism** *n*

sycamore ('sɪkəˌmɔː) *n* 1 a Eurasian maple tree, *Acer pseudoplatanus*, naturalized in Britain and North America, having five-lobed leaves, yellow flowers, and two-winged fruits 2 *US & Canadian* an American plane tree, *Platanus occidentalis*. See **plane tree** 3 Also called:

sycomore a moraceous tree, *Ficus sycomorus*, of N Africa and W Asia, having an edible figlike fruit [c14: from Old French *sicamor*, from Latin *sȳcomorus*, from Greek *sukomoros*, from *sukon* fig + *moron* mulberry]

syconium (saɪˈkəʊnɪəm) *n, pl* -nia (-nɪə) *botany* the fleshy fruit of the fig, consisting of a greatly enlarged receptacle completely surrounding the inflorescence [c19: from New Latin, from Greek *sukon* fig]

sycophant ('sɪkəfənt) *n* a person who uses flattery to win favour from individuals wielding authority; toady [c16: from Latin *sȳcophanta*, from Greek *sukophantēs*, literally: the person showing a fig, apparently referring to the fig sign used in making an accusation, from *sukon* fig + *phainein* to show; sense probably developed from "accuser" to "informer, flatterer"] > **'sycophancy** *n* > ˌsycho'phantic *adj* > ˌsyco'phantically *adv*

sycosis (saɪˈkəʊsɪs) *n* chronic inflammation of the hair follicles, esp those of the beard, caused by a staphylococcal infection [c16: via New Latin from Greek *sukōsis*, from *sukon* fig]

Sydenham's chorea ('sɪdⁿnəmz) *n* a form of chorea affecting children, often associated with rheumatic fever. Nontechnical name: **Saint Vitus's dance** [named after T. *Sydenham* (1624–89), English physician]

Sydney¹ ('sɪdnɪ) *n* 1 a port in SE Australia, capital of New South Wales, on an inlet of the S Pacific: the largest city in Australia and the first British settlement, established as a penal colony in 1788; developed rapidly after 1820 with the discovery of gold in its hinterland; large wool market; three universities. Pop: 3 502 301 (2001) 2 a port in SE Canada, in Nova Scotia on NE Cape Breton Island: capital of Cape Breton Island until 1820, when the island united administratively with Nova Scotia. Pop: 32 286 (2006)

Sydney² ('sɪdnɪ) *n* a variant spelling of (Sir Philip) **Sidney**

Syene (saɪˈiːnɪ) *n* transliteration of the Ancient Greek name for **Aswan**

syenite ('saɪəˌnaɪt) *n* a light-coloured coarse-grained plutonic igneous rock consisting of feldspars with hornblende or biotite [c18: from French *syénite*, from Latin *syēnītēs lapis* stone from *Syene* (Aswan), where it was originally quarried] > **syenitic** (ˌsaɪəˈnɪtɪk) *adj*

Syktyvkar (*Russian* siktif'kar) *n* a city in NW Russia, capital of the Komi Republic: timber industry. Pop: 230 000 (2005 est)

syllabary ('sɪləbərɪ) *n, pl* -baries 1 a table or list of syllables 2 a set of symbols used in certain writing systems, such as one used for Japanese, in which each symbol represents a spoken syllable [c16: from New Latin *syllabārium*, from Latin *syllaba* SYLLABLE]

syllabi ('sɪləˌbaɪ) *n* a plural of **syllabus**

syllabic (sɪˈlæbɪk) *adj* 1 of or relating to syllables or the division of a word into syllables 2 denoting a kind of verse line based on a specific number of syllables rather than being regulated by stresses or quantities 3 (of a consonant) constituting a syllable ▷ *n* 4 a syllabic consonant > **syl'labically** *adv*

syllabify (sɪˈlæbɪˌfaɪ) *or* **syllabicate** *vb* -fies, -fying, -fied *or* -cates, -cating, -cated (*tr*) to divide (a word) into its constituent syllables > ˌsylˌlabifi'cation *or* sylˌlabi'cation *n*

syllable ('sɪləbⁿl) *n* 1 a combination or set of one or more units of sound in a language that must consist of a sonorous element (a sonant or vowel) and may or may not contain less sonorous elements (consonants or semivowels) flanking it on either or both sides: for example "paper" has two syllables 2 (in the writing systems of certain languages, esp ancient ones) a symbol or set of symbols standing for a syllable 3 the least mention in speech or print: *don't breathe a syllable of it* 4 in words of one syllable simply; bluntly ▷ *vb* 5 to pronounce syllables of (a text); articulate 6 (*tr*) to write down in syllables [c14: via Old French from Latin *syllaba*, from Greek *sullabē*, from *sullambanein* to collect together, from *sul-* SYN- + *lambanein* to take]

syllabub *or* **sillabub** ('sɪləˌbʌb) *n* 1 a spiced drink made of milk with rum, port, brandy, or wine, often hot 2 *Brit* a cold dessert made from milk or cream beaten with sugar, wine, and lemon juice [c16: of unknown origin]

S

syllabus ('sɪləbəs) *n, pl* -buses *or* -bi (-ˌbaɪ) **1** an outline of a course of studies, text, etc **2** *Brit* **a** the subjects studied for a particular course **b** a document which lists these subjects and states how the course will be assessed [C17: from Late Latin, erroneously from Latin *sittybus* parchment strip giving title and author, from Greek *sittuba*]

syllepsis (sɪ'lɛpsɪs) *n, pl* -ses (-siːz) **1** (in grammar or rhetoric) the use of a single sentence construction in which a verb, adjective, etc is made to cover two syntactical functions, as the verb form *have* in *she and they have promised to come* **2** another word for **zeugma** [C16: from Late Latin, from Greek *sullēpsis*, from *sul-* SYN- + *lēpsis* a taking, from *lambanein* to take] > **syl'leptic** *adj* > **syl'leptically** *adv*

syllogism ('sɪləˌdʒɪzəm) *n* **1** a deductive inference consisting of two premises and a conclusion, all of which are categorial propositions. The subject of the conclusion is the **minor term** and its predicate the **major term**; the **middle term** occurs in both premises but not the conclusion. There are 256 such arguments but only 24 are valid. *Some men are mortal; some men are angelic; so some mortals are angelic* is invalid, while *some temples are in ruins; all ruins are fascinating; so some temples are fascinating* is valid. Here *fascinating, in ruins,* and *temples* are respectively major, middle, and minor terms **2** a piece of deductive reasoning from the general to the particular [C14: via Latin from Greek *sullogismos*, from *sullogizesthai* to reckon together, from *sul-* SYN- + *logizesthai* to calculate, from *logos* a discourse] > ˌsyllo'gistic *or* syllo'gistical *adj* > **syllogize** *or* **syllogise** ('sɪləˌdʒaɪz) *vb*

sylph (sɪlf) *n* **1** a slender graceful girl or young woman **2** any of a class of imaginary beings assumed to inhabit the air [C17: from New Latin *sylphus,* probably coined from Latin *silva* wood + Greek *numphē* NYMPH] > **'sylph,like** *or less commonly* **'sylphic** *adj*

sylva *or* **silva** ('sɪlvə) *n, pl* -vas *or* -vae (-viː) the trees growing in a particular region [C17: Latin *silva* a wood]

sylvan *or* **silvan** ('sɪlvən) *chiefly poetic* ▷ *adj* **1** of, characteristic of, or consisting of woods or forests **2** living or located in woods or forests **3** idyllically rural or rustic ▷ *n* **4** an inhabitant of the woods, esp a spirit [C16: from Latin *silvānus,* from *silva* forest]

sylvanite ('sɪlvəˌnaɪt) *n* a silver-white mineral consisting of a telluride of gold and silver in the form of elongated striated crystals: a source of gold in Australia and North America. Formula: (Au,Ag)Te$_2$ [C18: from (TRAN)SYLVAN(IA) + -ITE[1], with reference to the region where it was first found]

Sylvanus (sɪl'veɪnəs) *n* a variant spelling of **Silvanus**

Sylvester II (sɪl'vɛstə) *n* original name *Gerbert of Aurillac. c.* 940–1003 AD, French ecclesiastic and scholar; pope (999–1003): noted for his achievements in mathematics and astronomy

sylviculture ('sɪlvɪˌkʌltʃə) *n* a variant spelling of **silviculture**

sym- *prefix* a variant of **syn-** before *b, p,* and *m*

symbiont ('sɪmbɪˌɒnt) *n* an organism living in a state of symbiosis [C19: from Greek *sumbioun* to live together, from *bioun* to live] > ˌsymbi'ontic *adj* > ˌsymbi'ontically *adv*

symbiosis (ˌsɪmbɪ'əʊsɪs, ˌsɪmbaɪ'əʊsɪs) *n* **1** a close and usually obligatory association of two organisms of different species that live together, often to their mutual benefit **2** a similar relationship between interdependent persons or groups [C19: via New Latin from Greek: a living together; see SYMBIONT] > ˌsymbi'otic *or less commonly* ˌsymbi'otical *adj*

symbol ('sɪmbəl) *n* **1** something that represents or stands for something else, usually by convention or association, esp a material object used to represent something abstract **2** an object, person, idea, etc, used in a literary work, film, etc, to stand for or suggest something else with which it is associated either explicitly or in some more subtle way **3** a letter, figure, or sign used in mathematics, science, music, etc to represent a quantity, phenomenon, operation, function, etc ▷ *vb* -bols, -bolling, -bolled *or US* -bols, -boling, -boled **4** (tr) another word for **symbolize** [C15: from Church

Latin *symbolum,* from Greek *sumbolon* sign, from *sumballein* to throw together, from SYN- + *ballein* to throw]

symbolic (sɪm'bɒlɪk) *or* **symbolical** *adj* **1** of or relating to a symbol or symbols **2** serving as a symbol **3** characterized by the use of symbols or symbolism > sym'bolically *adv*

symbolic logic *n* another term for **formal logic**

symbolism ('sɪmbəˌlɪzəm) *n* **1** the representation of something in symbolic form or the attribution of symbolic meaning or character to something **2** a system of symbols or symbolic representation **3** a symbolic significance or quality **4** (*often capital*) a late 19th-century movement in art that sought to express mystical or abstract ideas through the symbolic use of images

symbolist ('sɪmbəlɪst) *n* **1** a person who uses or can interpret symbols, esp as a means to revealing aspects of truth and reality **2** an artist or writer who practises symbolism in his work **3** (*usually capital*) a writer associated with the symbolist movement **4** (*often capital*) an artist associated with the movement of symbolism ▷ *adj* **5** of, relating to, or characterizing symbolism or symbolists > ˌsymbol'istic *adj* > ˌsymbol'istically *adv*

symbolist movement *n* (*usually capital*) a movement beginning in French and Belgian poetry towards the end of the 19th century with the verse of Mallarmé, Valéry, Verlaine, Rimbaud, Maeterlinck, and others, and seeking to express states of mind rather than objective reality by making use of the power of words and images to suggest as well as denote

symbolize *or* **symbolise** ('sɪmbəˌlaɪz) *vb* **1** (tr) to serve as or be a symbol of **2** (tr; usually foll by by) to represent by a symbol or symbols **3** (intr) to use symbols **4** (tr) to treat or regard as symbolic or figurative > ˌsymboli'zation *or* ˌsymboli'sation *n*

symbol retailer *n* any member of a voluntary group of independent retailers, often using a common name or symbol, formed to obtain better prices from wholesalers or manufacturers in competition with supermarket chains. Also called: **voluntary retailer**

symmetrical (sɪ'mɛtrɪkəl) *adj* possessing or displaying symmetry

symmetry ('sɪmɪtrɪ) *n, pl* -tries **1** similarity, correspondence, or balance among systems or parts of a system **2** *maths* an exact correspondence in position or form about a given point, line, or plane **3** beauty or harmony of form based on a proportionate arrangement of parts [C16: from Latin *symmetria,* from Greek *summetria* proportion, from SYN- + *metron* measure]

Symonds ('sɪməndz) *n* **John Addington** ('ædɪŋtən). 1840–93, English writer, noted for his *Renaissance in Italy* (1875–86) and for studies of homosexuality

Symons ('saɪmənz) *n* **Arthur.** 1865–1945, English poet and critic, who helped to introduce the French symbolists to England

sympathectomy (ˌsɪmpə'θɛktəmɪ) *n, pl* -mies the surgical excision or chemical destruction (**chemical sympathectomy**) of one or more parts of the sympathetic nervous system [C20: from SYMPATHETIC + -ECTOMY]

sympathetic (ˌsɪmpə'θɛtɪk) *adj* **1** characterized by, feeling, or showing sympathy; understanding **2** in accord with the subject's personality or mood; congenial: *a sympathetic atmosphere* **3** (when *postpositive,* often foll by *to* or *towards*) showing agreement (with) or favour (towards) **4** *anatomy, physiol* of or relating to the division of the autonomic nervous system that acts in opposition to the parasympathetic system accelerating the heartbeat, dilating the bronchi, inhibiting the smooth muscles of the digestive tract, etc. See **parasympathetic 5** relating to vibrations occurring as a result of similar vibrations in a neighbouring body: *sympathetic strings on a sitar* > ˌsympa'thetically *adv*

sympathetic magic *n* a type of magic in which it is sought to produce a large-scale effect, often at a distance, by performing some small-scale ceremony resembling it, such as the pouring of water on an altar to induce rainfall

sympathize *or* **sympathise** ('sɪmpəˌθaɪz) *vb* (intr; often foll by *with*) **1** to feel or express compassion or sympathy (for); commiserate: *he sympathized with my troubles* **2** to share or understand the sentiments or ideas (of); be in sympathy (with) > 'sympa,thizer *or* 'sympa,thiser *n*

sympatholytic (,sɪmpəθəʊ'lɪtɪk) *med* ▷ *adj* **1 a** inhibiting or antagonistic to nerve impulses of the sympathetic nervous system **b** of or relating to such inhibition ▷ *n* **2** a sympatholytic drug. See **sympathomimetic** [C20: from SYMPATH(ETIC) + -LYTIC]

sympathomimetic (,sɪmpəθəʊmɪ'mɛtɪk) *med* ▷ *adj* **1** causing a physiological effect similar to that produced by stimulation of the sympathetic nervous system ▷ *n* **2** a sympathomimetic drug. See **sympatholytic** [C20: from SYMPATH(ETIC) + MIMETIC]

sympathy ('sɪmpəθɪ) *n, pl* **-thies 1** the sharing of another's emotions, esp of sorrow or anguish; pity; compassion **2** an affinity or harmony, usually of feelings or interests, between persons or things: *to be in sympathy with someone* **3** mutual affection or understanding arising from such a relationship; congeniality **4** the condition of a physical system or body when its behaviour is similar or corresponds to that of a different system that influences it, such as the vibration of sympathetic strings **5** (*sometimes plural*) a feeling of loyalty, support, or accord, as for an idea, cause, etc **6** *physiol* the mutual relationship between two organs or parts whereby a change in one has an effect on the other [C16: from Latin *sympathīa*, from Greek *sumpatheia*, from *sumpathēs*, from SYN- + *pathos* suffering]

sympathy strike *n* a strike organized in support of another section of workers or a cause and not because of direct grievances. Also called: **sympathetic strike**

symphonic poem *n music* an extended orchestral composition, originated by Liszt, based on nonmusical material, such as a work of literature or folk tale. Also called: **tone poem**

symphony ('sɪmfənɪ) *n, pl* **-nies 1** an extended large-scale orchestral composition, usually with several movements, at least one of which is in sonata form. The classical form of the symphony was fixed by Haydn and Mozart, but the innovations of subsequent composers have freed it entirely from classical constraints. It continues to be a vehicle for serious, large-scale orchestral music **2** a piece of instrumental music in up to three very short movements, used as an overture to or interlude in a baroque opera **3** any purely orchestral movement in a vocal work, such as a cantata or oratorio **4** short for **symphony orchestra 5** anything distinguished by a harmonious composition: *the picture was a symphony of green* **6** *archaic* harmony in general; concord [C13: from Old French *symphonie*, from Latin *symphōnia* concord, concert, from Greek *sumphōnia*, from SYN- + *phōnē* sound] > **symphonic** (sɪm'fɒnɪk) *adj* > sym'phonically *adv*

symphony orchestra *n music* an orchestra capable of performing symphonies, esp the large orchestra comprising strings, brass, woodwind, harp and percussion

symphysis ('sɪmfɪsɪs) *n, pl* **-ses** (-,siːz) **1** *anatomy, botany* a growing together of parts or structures, such as two bony surfaces joined by an intermediate layer of fibrous cartilage **2** a line marking this growing together **3** *pathol* an abnormal adhesion of two or more parts or structures [C16: via New Latin from Greek *sumphusis*, from *sumphuein*, from SYN- + *phuein* to grow] > symphysial *or* symphyseal (sɪm'fɪzɪəl) *adj*

sympodium (sɪm'pəʊdɪəm) *n, pl* **-dia** (-dɪə) the main axis of growth in the grapevine and similar plants: a lateral branch that arises from just behind the apex of the main stem, which ceases to grow, and continues growing in the same direction as the main stem [C19: from New Latin, from SYN- + Greek *podion* a little foot, from *pous* foot] > sym'podial *or* sym'podially *adv*

symposium (sɪm'pəʊzɪəm) *n, pl* **-siums** *or* **-sia** (-zɪə) **1** a conference or meeting for the discussion of some subject, esp an academic topic or social problem **2** a collection of scholarly contributions, usually published together, on a given subject **3** (in classical Greece) a drinking party with intellectual conversation, music, etc [C16: via Latin from Greek *sumposion*, from *sumpinein* to

drink together, from *sum-* SYN- + *pinein* to drink]

symptom ('sɪmptəm) *n* **1** *med* any sensation or change in bodily function experienced by a patient that is associated with a particular disease **2** any phenomenon or circumstance accompanying something and regarded as evidence of its existence; indication [C16: from Late Latin *symptōma*, from Greek *sumptōma* chance, from *sumpiptein* to occur, from SYN- + *piptein* to fall]

symptomatic (,sɪmptə'mætɪk) *adj* **1** (often foll by *of*) being a symptom; indicative: *symptomatic of insanity* **2** of or relating to a symptom or symptoms **3** according to symptoms: *a symptomatic analysis of a case* > ,sympto'matically *adv*

symptomatology (,sɪmptəmə'tɒlədʒɪ) *or* **symptomology** *n* the branch of medicine concerned with the study and classification of the symptoms of disease

syn. *abbreviation* synonym(ous)

syn- *prefix* **1** with or together: *synecology* **2** fusion: *syngamy* [from Greek *sun* together, with]

synaeresis (sɪ'nɪərɪsɪs) *n* a variant spelling of **syneresis**

synaesthesia *or US* **synesthesia** (,sɪniːs'θiːzɪə) *n* **1** *physiol* a sensation experienced in a part of the body other than the part stimulated **2** *psychol* the subjective sensation of a sense other than the one being stimulated. For example, a sound may evoke sensations of colour [from New Latin, from SYN- + -*esthesia*, from Greek *aisthēsis* sensation] > synaesthetic *or* synesthetic *US* (,sɪniːs'θɛtɪk) *adj*

synagogue ('sɪnə,gɒg) *n* **1 a** a building for Jewish religious services and usually also for religious instruction **b** (*as modifier*): *synagogue services* **2** a congregation of Jews who assemble for worship or religious study **3** the religion of Judaism as organized in such congregations [C12: from Old French *sinagoge*, from Late Latin *synagōga*, from Greek *sunagōgē* a gathering, from *sunagein* to bring together, from SYN- + *agein* to lead] > synagogical (,sɪnə'gɒdʒɪkᵊl) *or* synagogal ('sɪnə,gɒgᵊl) *adj*

synapse ('saɪnæps) *n* the point at which a nerve impulse is relayed from the terminal portion of an axon to the dendrites of an adjacent neuron

synapsis (sɪ'næpsɪs) *n, pl* **-ses** (-siːz) **1** *cytology* the association in pairs of homologous chromosomes at the start of meiosis **2** another word for **synapse** [C19: from New Latin, from Greek *sunapsis* junction, from *sunaptein* to join together, from SYN- + *haptein* to connect]

synaptic (sɪ'næptɪk) *or* **synaptical** *adj* of or relating to a synapse > syn'aptically *adv*

synarthrosis (,sɪnɑː'θrəʊsɪs) *n, pl* **-ses** (-siːz) *anatomy* any of various joints which lack a synovial cavity and are virtually immovable; a fixed joint [via New Latin from Greek *sunarthrōsis*, from *sunarthrousthai* to be connected by joints, from *sun-* SYN- + *arthron* a joint] > ,synar'throdial *adj*

sync *or* **synch** (sɪŋk) *films, television, computing* ▷ *vb* **1** an informal word for **synchronize** ▷ *n* **2** an informal word for **synchronization**: *in sync; out of sync*

syncarp ('sɪnkɑːp) *n botany* a fleshy multiple fruit, formed from two or more carpels of one flower or the aggregated fruits of several flowers [C19: from New Latin *syncarpium*, from SYN- + Greek *karpos* fruit]

syncarpous (sɪn'kɑːpəs) *adj* **1** (of the ovaries of certain flowering plants) consisting of united carpels **2** of or relating to a syncarp

synchro ('sɪŋkrəʊ) *n, pl* **-chros 1** Also called: **selsyn** any of a number of electrical devices in which the angular position of a rotating part is transformed into a voltage, or vice versa **2** short for **synchronized swimming**

synchro- *combining form* indicating synchronization

synchrocyclotron (,sɪŋkrəʊ'saɪklə,trɒn) *n* a type of cyclotron in which the frequency of the electric field is modulated to allow for relativistic effects at high velocities and thus produce higher energies

synchromesh ('sɪŋkrəʊ,mɛʃ) *adj* **1** (of a gearbox, etc) having a system of clutches that synchronizes the speeds of the driving and driven members before engagement to avoid shock in gear changing and to reduce noise and wear ▷ *n* **2** a gear system having these

S

features [C20: shortened from *synchronized mesh*]

synchronic (sɪn'krɒnɪk) *adj* **1** concerned with the events or phenomena at a particular period without considering historical antecedents: *synchronic linguistics*. See **diachronic 2** synchronous > syn'chronically *adv*

synchronicity (ˌsɪnkrə'nɪsɪtɪ) *n* an apparently meaningful coincidence in time of two or more similar or identical events that are causally unrelated [C20: coined by Carl Jung from SYNCHRONIC + -ITY]

synchronism ('sɪŋkrəˌnɪzəm) *n* **1** the quality or condition of being synchronous **2** a chronological usually tabular list of historical persons and events, arranged to show parallel or synchronous occurrence **3** the representation in a work of art of one or more incidents that occurred at separate times [C16: from Greek *sunkhronismos*; see SYNCHRONOUS, -ISM]

synchronistic (ˌsɪŋkrə'nɪstɪk) *adj* of, relating to, or exhibiting synchronism > ˌsynchro'nistically *adv*

synchronize or **synchronise** ('sɪŋkrəˌnaɪz) *vb* **1** (when *intr*, usually foll by *with*) to occur or recur or cause to occur or recur at the same time or in unison **2** to indicate or cause to indicate the same time: *synchronize your watches* **3** (*tr*) *films* to establish (the picture and soundtrack records) in their correct relative position **4** (*tr*) to designate (events) as simultaneous > ˌsynchroni'zation or ˌsynchroni'sation > 'synchroˌnizer or 'synchroˌniser *n*

synchronized swimming *n* the art or sport of one or more swimmers moving in patterns in the water in time to music. Sometimes shortened to: **synchro**

synchronous ('sɪŋkrənəs) *adj* **1** occurring at the same time; contemporaneous **2** *physics* (of periodic phenomena, such as voltages) having the same frequency and phase **3** occurring or recurring exactly together and at the same rate [C17: from Late Latin *synchronus*, from Greek *sunkhronos*, from SYN- + *khronos* time] > 'synchronously *adv* > 'synchronousness *n*

synchronous machine *n* an electrical machine, whose rotating speed is proportional to the frequency of the alternating-current supply and independent of the load

synchronous motor *n* an alternating-current motor that runs at a speed that is equal to or is a multiple of the frequency of the supply

synchrony ('sɪŋkrənɪ) *n* the state of being synchronous; simultaneity

synchrotron ('sɪŋkrəˌtrɒn) *n* a type of particle accelerator similar to a betatron but having an electric field of fixed frequency with electrons but not with protons as well as a changing magnetic field. It is capable of producing very high energies in the GeV range [C20: from SYNCHRO- + (ELEC)TRON]

syncline ('sɪŋklaɪn) *n* a downward fold of stratified rock in which the strata slope towards a vertical axis [C19: from SYN- + Greek *klīnein* to lean] > syn'clinal *adj*

Syncom ('sɪnˌkɒm) *n* a communications satellite in stationary orbit [C20: from *syn*(chronous) *com*(munication)]

syncopate ('sɪŋkəˌpeɪt) *vb* **1** *music* to modify or treat (a beat, rhythm, note, etc) by syncopation **2** to shorten (a word) by omitting sounds or letters from the middle [C17: from Medieval Latin *syncopāre* to omit a letter or syllable, from Late Latin *syncopa* SYNCOPE] > 'syncoˌpator *n*

syncopation (ˌsɪŋkə'peɪʃən) *n* **1** *music* **a** the displacement of the usual rhythmic accent away from a strong beat onto a weak beat **b** a note, beat, rhythm, etc, produced by syncopation **2** another word for **syncope** (sense 2)

syncope ('sɪŋkəpɪ) *n* **1** *pathol* a technical word for a **faint 2** the omission of one or more sounds or letters from the middle of a word [C16: from Late Latin *syncopa*, from Greek *sunkopē* a cutting off, from SYN- + *koptein* to cut] > syncopic (sɪn'kɒpɪk) or 'syncopal *adj*

syncretism ('sɪŋkrɪˌtɪzəm) *n* **1** the tendency to syncretize **2** the historical tendency of languages to reduce their use of inflection, as in the development of Old English with all its case endings into Modern English [C17: from New Latin *syncrētismus*, from Greek *sunkrētismos* alliance of Cretans, from *sunkrētizein* to join forces (in the manner of the Cretan towns), from SYN- + *Krēs* a Cretan] > syncretic (sɪn'krɛtɪk) or ˌsyncre'tistic *adj* > 'syncretist *n*

syncretize or **syncretise** ('sɪŋkrɪˌtaɪz) *vb* to combine or attempt to combine the characteristic teachings, beliefs, or practices of (differing systems of religion or philosophy) > ˌsyncreti'zation or ˌsyncreti'sation *n*

syndactyl (sɪn'dæktɪl) *adj* **1** (of certain animals) having two or more digits growing fused together ▷ *n* **2** an animal with this arrangement of digits > syn'dactylism *n*

syndesmosis (ˌsɪndɛs'məʊsɪs) *n*, *pl* -ses (-siːz) *anatomy* a type of joint in which the articulating bones are held together by a ligament of connective tissue [New Latin, from Greek *sundein* to bind together; see SYNDESIS] > syndesmotic (ˌsɪndɛs'mɒtɪk) *adj*

syndetic (sɪn'dɛtɪk) *adj* denoting a grammatical construction in which two clauses are connected by a conjunction [C17: from Greek *sundetikos*, from *sundetos* bound together] > syn'detically *adv* > syn'desis *n*

syndeton (sɪn'diːtᵊn) *n* *grammar* a syndetic construction [C20: from Greek *sundeton*, from *sundetos* bound together]

syndic ('sɪndɪk) *n* **1** *Brit* a business agent of some universities or other bodies **2** (in several countries) a government administrator or magistrate with varying powers [C17: via Old French from Late Latin *syndicus*, from Greek *sundikos* defendant's advocate, from SYN- + *dikē* justice] > 'syndical *adj*

syndicalism ('sɪndɪkəˌlɪzəm) *n* **1** a revolutionary movement and theory advocating the seizure of the means of production and distribution by syndicates of workers through direct action, esp a general strike **2** an economic system resulting from such action > 'syndical *adj* > 'syndicalist *adj*, *n* > ˌsyndical'istic *adj*

syndicate *n* ('sɪndɪkɪt) **1** an association of business enterprises or individuals organized to undertake a joint project requiring considerable capital **2** a news agency that sells articles, photographs, etc, to a number of newspapers for simultaneous publication **3** any association formed to carry out an enterprise or enterprises of common interest to its members **4** a board of syndics or the office of syndic ▷ *vb* ('sɪndɪˌkeɪt) **5** (*tr*) to sell (articles, photographs etc) to several newspapers for simultaneous publication **6** (*tr*) *US* to sell (a programme or programmes) to several local commercial television or radio stations **7** to form a syndicate of (people) [C17: from Old French *syndicat* office of a SYNDIC] > ˌsyndi'cation *n*

syndrome ('sɪndrəʊm) *n* **1** *med* any combination of signs and symptoms that are indicative of a particular disease or disorder **2** a symptom, characteristic, or set of symptoms or characteristics indicating the existence of a condition, problem, etc [C16: via New Latin from Greek *sundromē*, literally: a running together, from SYN- + *dramein* to run] > syndromic (sɪn'drɒmɪk) *adj*

syndrome X *n* another name for **IRS** (sense 2)

syne or **syn** (saɪn) *adv*, *prep*, *conj* a Scot word for **since** [C14: probably related to Old English *sīth* since]

synecdoche (sɪ'nɛkdəkɪ) *n* a figure of speech in which a part is substituted for a whole or a whole for a part, as in *50 head of cattle* for *50 cows*, or *the army* for *a soldier* [C14: via Latin from Greek *sunekdokhē*, from SYN- + *ekdokhē* interpretation, from *dekhesthai* to accept] > synecdochic (ˌsɪnɛk'dɒkɪk) or ˌsynec'dochical *adj*

synecious (sɪ'niːʃəs) *adj* a variant spelling of **synoecious**

synecology (ˌsɪnɪ'kɒlədʒɪ) *n* the ecological study of communities of plants and animals > synecologic (sɪnˌɛkə'lɒdʒɪk) or synˌeco'logical *adj* > synˌeco'logically *adv*

syneresis or **synaeresis** (sɪ'nɪərɪsɪs) *n* **1** *chem* the process in which a gel contracts on standing and exudes liquid, as in the separation of whey in cheese-making **2** the contraction of two vowels into a diphthong [C16: via Late Latin from Greek *sunairesis* a shortening, from *sunairein* to draw together, from SYN- + *hairein* to take]

synergism ('sɪnəˌdʒɪzəm, sɪ'nɜː-) *n* **1** Also called: **synergy** the working together of two or more drugs, muscles, etc, to produce an effect greater than the sum of their individual effects **2** another name for **synergy** (sense 1) [C18: from New Latin *synergismus*, from Greek *sunergos*, from SYN- + *ergon* work] > ˌsyner'getic or ˌsyner'gistic *adj* > synergist ('sɪnədʒɪst, sɪ'nɜː-) *n*, *adj*

synergy ('sınədʒı) *n, pl* -gies 1 Also called: synergism the potential ability of individual organizations or groups to be more successful or productive as a result of a merger 2 another name for **synergism** (sense 1) [C19: from New Latin *synergia*, from Greek *sunergos*; see SYNERGISM] > synergic (sı'nɜːdʒık) *adj*

synesis ('sınısıs) *n* a grammatical construction in which the inflection or form of a word is conditioned by the meaning rather than the syntax, as for example the plural form *have* with the singular noun *group* in the sentence *the group have already assembled* [via New Latin from Greek *sunesis* union, from *sunienai* to bring together, from SYN- + *hienai* to send]

synesthesia (,sınıːs'θiːzıə) *n* the usual US spelling of **synaesthesia**

syngamy ('sıŋəmı) *or* **syngenesis** (sın'dʒɛnısıs) *n* other names for **sexual reproduction** > syngamic (sın'gæmık) *or* syngamous ('sıŋgəməs) *adj*

Synge (sıŋ) *n* **John Millington**. 1871–1909, Irish playwright. His plays, marked by vivid colloquial Irish speech, include *Riders to the Sea* (1904) and *The Playboy of the Western World*, produced amidst uproar at the Abbey Theatre, Dublin, in 1907

synod ('sınəd, 'sınɒd) *n* a local or special ecclesiastical council, esp of a diocese, formally convened to discuss ecclesiastical affairs [C14: from Late Latin *synodus*, from Greek *sunodos*, from SYN- + *hodos* a way] > 'synodal *or less commonly* syn'odical *adj*

synodic (sı'nɒdık) *adj* relating to or involving a conjunction or two successive conjunctions of the same star, planet, or satellite

synodic month *n* See **month** (sense 6)

synoecious, synecious (sı'niːʃəs) *or* **synoicous** (sı'nɔıkəs) *adj* (of a bryophyte) having male and female organs together on a branch, usually mixed at the tip [C19: SYN- + -oecious, from Greek *oikion* diminutive of *oikos* house]

synonym ('sınənım) *n* 1 a word that means the same or nearly the same as another word, such as *bucket* and *pail* 2 a word or phrase used as another name for something, such as *Hellene* for a Greek [C16: via Late Latin from Greek *sunōnumon*, from SYN- + *onoma* name] > ,syno'nymic *or* ,syno'nymical *adj* > ,syno'nymity *n*

synonymous (sı'nɒnıməs) *adj* 1 (often foll by *with*) being a synonym (of) 2 (postpositive; foll by *with*) closely associated (with) or suggestive (of): *his name was synonymous with greed* > syn'onymously *adv* > syn'onymousness *n*

synonymy (sı'nɒnımı) *n, pl* -mies 1 the study of synonyms 2 the character of being synonymous; equivalence 3 a list or collection of synonyms, esp one in which their meanings are discriminated 4 *biology* a collection of the synonyms of a species or group

synopsis (sı'nɒpsıs) *n, pl* -ses (-siːz) a condensation or brief review of a subject; summary [C17: via Late Latin from Greek *sunopsis*, from SYN- + *opsis* view]

synopsize *or* **synopsise** (sı'nɒpsaız) *vb* (*tr*) 1 to make a synopsis of 2 US variants of **epitomize**

synoptic (sı'nɒptık) *adj* 1 of or relating to a synopsis 2 (*often capital*) *Bible* **a** (of the Gospels of Matthew, Mark, and Luke) presenting the narrative of Christ's life, ministry, etc from a point of view held in common by all three, and with close similarities in content, order, etc **b** of, relating to, or characterizing these three Gospels 3 *meteorol* showing or concerned with the distribution of meteorological conditions over a wide area at a given time: *a synoptic chart* ▷ *n* 4 (*often capital*) *Bible* **a** any of the three synoptic Gospels **b** any of the authors of these three Gospels [C18: from Greek *sunoptikos*, from SYNOPSIS] > syn'optically *adv* > syn'optist *n*

synovia (saı'nəuvıə, sı-) *n* a transparent viscid lubricating fluid, secreted by the membrane lining joints, tendon sheaths, etc [C17: from New Latin, probably from SYN- + Latin *ōvum* egg]

synovial (saı'nəuvıəl, sı-) *adj* of or relating to the synovia; (of a joint) surrounded by a synovia-secreting membrane

synovitis (,saınəu'vaıtıs, ,sın-) *n* inflammation of the membrane surrounding a joint > synovitic

(,saınəu'vıtık, ,sın-) *adj*

synroc ('sın,rɒk) *n* a titanium-ceramic substance that can incorporate nuclear waste in its crystals [from *syn(thetic)* + *roc(k)*]

syntactics (sın'tæktıks) *n* (*functioning as singular*) the branch of semiotics that deals with the formal properties of symbol systems; proof theory

syntagma (sın'tægmə) *or* **syntagm** ('sın,tæm) *n, pl* -tagmata (-'tægmətə) *or* -tagms 1 a syntactic unit or a word or phrase forming a syntactic unit 2 a systematic collection of statements or propositions [C17: from Late Latin, from Greek, from *suntassein* to put in order; see SYNTAX] > ,syntag'matic *adj*

syntax ('sıntæks) *n* 1 the branch of linguistics that deals with the grammatical arrangement of words and morphemes in the sentences of a language or of languages in general 2 the totality of facts about the grammatical arrangement of words in a language 3 a systematic statement of the rules governing the grammatical arrangement of words and morphemes in a language 4 *logic* a systematic statement of the rules governing the properly formed formulas of a logical system [C17: from Late Latin *syntaxis*, from Greek *suntaxis*, from *suntassein* to put in order, from SYN- + *tassein* to arrange] > syn'tactic *adj* > syn'tactically *adv*

synteny (sın'tɛnı) *n* the presence of two or more genes on the same chromosome [C20: SYN- + Greek TAINIA ribbon] > syn'tenic *adj*

synth (sınθ) *n* short for **synthesizer**

synthesis ('sınθısıs) *n, pl* -ses (-,siːz) 1 the process of combining objects or ideas into a complex whole 2 the combination or whole produced by such a process 3 the process of producing a compound by a chemical reaction or series of reactions, usually from simpler or commonly available starting materials 4 *linguistics* the use of inflections rather than word order and function words to express the syntactic relations in a language [C17: via Latin from Greek *sunthesis*, from *suntithenai* to put together, from SYN- + *tithenai* to place] > 'synthesist *n*

synthesis gas *n chem* 1 a mixture of carbon dioxide, carbon monoxide, and hydrogen formerly made by using water gas and reacting it with steam to enrich the proportion of hydrogen for use in the synthesis of ammonia 2 a similar mixture of gases made by steam reforming natural gas, used for synthesizing organic chemicals and as a fuel

synthesize ('sınθı,saız), **synthetize, synthesise** *or* **synthetise** *vb* 1 to combine or cause to combine into a whole 2 (*tr*) to produce by synthesis > ,synthesi'zation, ,syntheti'zation, ,synthesi'sation *or* ,syntheti'sation *n*

synthesizer ('sınθı,saızə) *n* 1 an electrophonic instrument, usually operated by means of a keyboard and pedals, in which sounds are produced by voltage-controlled oscillators, filters, and amplifiers, with an envelope generator module that controls attack, decay, sustain, and release 2 a person or thing that synthesizes

synthespian (,sın'θɛspıən) *n* a computer-generated image of a film actor, esp used in place of the real actor when shooting special effects or stunts [C20: from SYN(THETIC) + THESPIAN]

synthetic (sın'θɛtık) *adj* Also: synthetical 1 (of a substance or material) made artificially by chemical reaction 2 not genuine; insincere: *synthetic compassion* 3 denoting languages, such as Latin, whose morphology is characterized by synthesis 4 *philosophy* **a** (of a proposition) having a truth-value that is not determined solely by virtue of the meanings of the words, as in *all men are arrogant* **b** contingent ▷ *n* 5 a synthetic substance or material [C17: from New Latin *syntheticus*, from Greek *sunthetikos* expert in putting together, from *suntithenai* to put together; see SYNTHESIS] > syn'thetically *adv*

synthetic phonics *n* (*functioning as singular*) a method of teaching people to read by training them to pronounce sounds associated with particular letters in isolation and then blend them together. See **phonics** (sense 2)

syphilis ('sıfılıs) *n* a venereal disease caused by infection with the microorganism *Treponema pallidum*: characterized by an ulcerating chancre, usually on the genitals and progressing through the lymphatic system to nearly all tissues of the body, producing serious clinical manifestations [c18: from New Latin *Syphilis* (*sive Morbus Gallicus*) "Syphilis (or the French disease)", title of a poem (1530) by G. Fracastoro, Italian physician and poet, in which a shepherd *Syphilus* is portrayed as the first victim of the disease] > **syphilitic** (ˌsɪfɪˈlɪtɪk) *adj* > ˈsyphiˌloid *adj*

syphon (ˈsaɪfᵊn) *n* a variant spelling of **siphon**

Syr. *abbreviation* **1** Syria **2** Syriac **3** Syrian

Syracuse *n* **1** (ˈsaɪrəˌkjuːz) a port in SW Italy, in SE Sicily on the Ionian Sea: founded in 734 BC by Greeks from Corinth and taken by the Romans in 212 BC, after a siege of three years. Pop: 123 657 (2001) **2** (ˈsɪrəˌkjuːs) a city in central New York State, on Lake Onondaga: site of the capital of the Iroquois Indian federation. Pop: 144 001 (2003 est)

Syrah (ˈsaɪrə) *n* **1** a red grape grown in France and Australia, used, often in a blend, for making wine **2** any of various wines made from this grape ▷ Australian name: Shiraz [from SHIRAZ¹, the city in Iran where the wine supposedly originated]

Syr Darya (*Russian* sir darjˈja) *n* a river in central Asia, formed from two headstreams rising in the Tian Shan: flows generally west to the Aral Sea: the longest river in central Asia. Length: (from the source of the Naryn) 2900 km (1800 miles). Ancient name: Jaxartes

Syria (ˈsɪrɪə) *n* **1** a republic in W Asia, on the Mediterranean: ruled by the Ottoman Turks (1516–1918); made a French mandate in 1920; became independent in 1944; joined Egypt in the United Arab Republic (1958–61). Official language: Arabic. Religion: Muslim majority. Currency: Syrian pound. Capital: Damascus. Pop: 18 223 000 (2004 est). Area: 185 180 sq km (71 498 sq miles) **2** (formerly) the region between the Mediterranean, the Euphrates, the Taurus, and the Arabian Desert

Syriac (ˈsɪrɪˌæk) *n* a dialect of Aramaic spoken in Syria until about the 13th century AD and still in use as a liturgical language of certain Eastern churches

Syrian (ˈsɪrɪən) *adj* **1** of, relating to, or characteristic of Syria, its people, or their dialect of Arabic ▷ *n* **2** a native or inhabitant of Syria

syringa (sɪˈrɪŋgə) *n* another name for **mock orange lilac** (sense 1) [c17: from New Latin, from Greek *surinx* tube, alluding to the use of its hollow stems for pipes]

syringe (ˈsɪrɪndʒ, sɪˈrɪndʒ) *n* **1** *med* an instrument, such as a hypodermic syringe or a rubber ball with a slender nozzle, for use in withdrawing or injecting fluids, cleaning wounds, etc **2** any similar device for injecting, spraying, or extracting liquids by means of pressure or suction ▷ *vb* **3** (*tr*) to cleanse, inject, or spray with a syringe [c15: from Late Latin, from Latin: SYRINX]

syringomyelia (səˌrɪŋgəʊmaɪˈiːlɪə) *n* a chronic progressive disease of the spinal cord in which cavities form in the grey matter: characterized by loss of the sense of pain and temperature [c19: *syringo-*, from Greek: SYRINX + *-myelia* from Greek *muelos* marrow] > **syringomyelic** (səˌrɪŋgəʊmaɪˈɛlɪk) *adj*

syrinx (ˈsɪrɪŋks) *n, pl* **syringes** (sɪˈrɪndʒiːz) *or* **syrinxes** **1** the vocal organ of a bird, which is situated in the lower part of the trachea **2** (in classical Greek music) a panpipe or set of panpipes [c17: via Latin from Greek *surinx* pipe] > **syringeal** (sɪˈrɪndʒɪəl) *adj*

Syrinx (ˈsɪrɪŋks) *n Greek myth* a nymph who was changed into a reed to save her from the amorous pursuit of Pan. From this reed Pan then fashioned his musical pipes

syrup (ˈsɪrəp) *n* **1** a solution of sugar dissolved in water and often flavoured with fruit juice: used for sweetening fruit, etc **2** any of various thick sweet liquids prepared for cooking or table use from molasses, sugars, etc **3** a liquid medicine containing a sugar solution for flavouring or preservation **4** *informal* cloying sentimentality ▷ Also called: sirup [c15: from Medieval Latin *syrupus*, from Arabic *sharāb* a drink, from *shariba* to drink; sense 4 from rhyming slang *syrup of fig*] > ˈsyrupy *adj*

sysop *or* **SYSOP** (ˈsɪsˌɒp) *n computing* a person who runs a system or network [c20: SYS(TEM) + OP(ERATOR)]

syssarcosis (ˌsɪsɑːˈkəʊsɪs) *n, pl* **-ses** (-siːz) *anatomy* the union or articulation of bones by muscle [c17: from New Latin, from Greek *sussarkōsis*, from *sussarkousthai*, from *sus-* SYN- + *sarkoun* to become fleshy, from *sarx* flesh] > **syssarcotic** (ˌsɪsɑːˈkɒtɪk) *adj*

systaltic (sɪˈstæltɪk) *adj* (esp of the action of the heart) of, relating to, or characterized by alternate contractions and dilations; pulsating [c17: from Late Latin *systalticus*, from Greek *sustaltikos*, from *sustellein* to contract, from SYN- + *stellein* to place]

system (ˈsɪstəm) *n* **1** a group or combination of interrelated, interdependent, or interacting elements forming a collective entity; a methodical or coordinated assemblage of parts, facts, concepts, etc **2** any scheme of classification or arrangement **3** a network of communications, transportation, or distribution **4** a method or complex of methods: *he has a perfect system at roulette* **5** orderliness; an ordered manner **6** the system (*often capital*) society seen as an environment exploiting, restricting, and repressing individuals **7** an organism considered as a functioning entity **8** any of various bodily parts or structures that are anatomically or physiologically related: *the digestive system* **9** one's physiological or psychological constitution: *get it out of your system* **10** any assembly of electronic, electrical, or mechanical components with interdependent functions, usually forming a self-contained unit: *a brake system* **11** a group of celestial bodies that are associated as a result of natural laws, esp gravitational attraction: *the solar system* **12** a point of view or doctrine used to interpret a branch of knowledge **13** *mineralogy* one of a group of divisions into which crystals may be placed on the basis of the lengths and inclinations of their axes **14** *geology* a stratigraphical unit for the rock strata formed during a period of geological time. It can be subdivided into series [c17: from French *système*, from Late Latin *systēma*, from Greek *sustēma*, from SYN- + *histanai* to cause to stand]

systematic (ˌsɪstɪˈmætɪk) *adj* **1** characterized by the use of order and planning; methodical: *a systematic administrator* **2** comprising or resembling a system: *systematic theology* **3** Also called: **systematical** (sɪstəˈmætɪkᵊl) *biology* of or relating to the taxonomic classification of organisms > ˌsystemˈatically *adv* > ˈsystemaˌtism *n* > ˈsystematist *n*

systematics (ˌsɪstɪˈmætɪks) *n* (*functioning as singular*) the study of systems and the principles of classification and nomenclature

systematize (ˈsɪstɪməˌtaɪz), **systemize, systematise** *or* **systemise** *vb* (*tr*) to arrange in a system > ˌsystematiˈzation *or* ˌsystematiˈsation *n* > ˈsystemaˌtizer, ˈsystemaˌtiser, ˈsystemˌizer *or* ˈsystemˌiser *n*

system building *n* a method of building in which prefabricated components are used to speed the construction of buildings > system built *adj*

Système International d'Unités (*French* sistɛm ēternasjɔnal dynite) *n* the International System of units. See **SI unit**

systemic (sɪˈstɛmɪk, -ˈstiː-) *adj* **1** another word for **systematic** (senses 1, 2) **2** *physiol* (of a poison, disease, etc) affecting the entire body **3** (of a pesticide, fungicide, etc) spreading through all the parts of a plant and making it toxic to pests or parasites without destroying it ▷ *n* **4** a systemic pesticide, fungicide, etc > sysˈtemically *adv*

systems analysis *n* the analysis of the requirements of a task and the expression of those requirements in a form that permits the assembly of computer hardware and software to perform the task > systems analyst *n*

systems engineering *n* the branch of engineering, based on systems analysis and information theory, concerned with the design of integrated systems

systole (ˈsɪstəlɪ) *n* contraction of the heart, during which blood is pumped into the aorta and the arteries that lead to the lungs. See **diastole** [c16: via Late Latin from Greek *sustolē*, from *sustellein* to contract; see SYSTALTIC] > **systolic** (sɪˈstɒlɪk) *adj*

Syzran (*Russian* ˈsizrənj) *n* a port in W central Russia, on the Volga River: oil refining. Pop: 191 000 (2005 est)

syzygy ('sızıdʒı) *n*, *pl* **-gies** 1 either of the two positions (conjunction or opposition) of a celestial body when sun, earth, and the body lie in a straight line: *the moon is at syzygy when full* 2 *rare* any pair, usually of opposites [c17: from Late Latin *syzygia*, from Greek *suzugia*, from *suzugos* yoked together, from SYN- + *zugon* a yoke] > **syzygial** (sı'zıdʒıəl, **syzygetic** (,sızı'dʒɛtık) or **syzygal** ('sızıgᵊl) *adj* > ,**syzy'getically** *adv*

Szabadka ('sɔbɔtkɔ) *n* the Hungarian name for **Subotica**

Szczecin (*Polish* 'ʃtʃɛtsin) *n* a port in NW Poland, on the River Oder, and the busiest Polish port and leading coal exporter; shipbuilding. Pop: 435 000 (2005 est). German name: Stettin

Szechuan or **Szechwan** ('sıtʃwɑːn) *n* a variant transliteration of the Chinese name for **Sichuan**

Szeged (*Hungarian* 'sɛgɛd) *n* an industrial city in S Hungary, on the Tisza River. Pop: 162 860 (2003 est)

Szell (sɛl) *n* **George**. 1897–1970, US conductor, born in Hungary

Szent-Györgyi (sɛnt'dʒɜ:dʒı) *n* **Albert** (**von Nagyrapolt**). 1893–1986, US biochemist, born in Hungary, who isolated ascorbic acid and identified it as vitamin C. Nobel prize for physiology or medicine 1937

Szilard ('sılaːd) *n* **Leo**. 1898–1964, US physicist, born in Hungary, who originated the idea of a self-sustaining nuclear chain reaction (1934). He worked on the atomic bomb during World War II but later pressed for the international control of nuclear weapons

Szombathely (*Hungarian* 'sombɔthɛj) *n* a city in W Hungary: site of the Roman capital of Pannonia. Pop: 81 113 (2003 est)

Szymanowski (*Polish* ʃima'nɔfski) *n* **Karol** ('karɔl) 1882–1937, Polish composer, whose works include the opera *King Roger* (1926), two violin concertos, symphonies, piano music, and songs

Szymborska (*Polish* ʃim'bɔrskə) *n* **Wisława** (vı'swavə) born 1923, Polish poet and writer: Nobel prize for literature 1996

S

Tt

t¹ *or* **T** (tiː) *n*, *pl* **t's**, **T's** *or* **Ts** **1** the 20th letter and 16th consonant of the modern English alphabet **2** a speech sound represented by this letter, usually a voiceless alveolar stop, as in *tame* **3** something shaped like a T **4** **to a T** in every detail; perfectly

t² *symbol for* **1** tonne(s) **2** troy (weight) **3** *statistics* distribution

T *symbol for* **1** absolute temperature **2** tera- **3** *chem* tritium **4** *biochem* thymine **5** tesla **6** surface tension

t. *abbreviation* **1** *commerce* tare **2** teaspoon(ful) **3** temperature **4** *music* tempo [Latin: in the time of] **5** tenor **6** *grammar* tense **7** ton(s) **8** transitive

't *contraction of* it

ta (tɑː) *interj Brit informal* thank you [c18: imitative of baby talk]

Ta *the chemical symbol for* tantalum

TA *abbreviation* (in Britain) Territorial Army (now superseded by **TAVR**)

taal (tɑːl) *n* the taal *South African* language: usually, by implication, Afrikaans [Afrikaans from Dutch]

Taal (tɑːˈɑːl) *n* an active volcano in the Philippines, on S Luzon on an island in the centre of **Lake Taal**. Height: 300 m (984 ft). Area of lake: 243 sq km (94 sq miles)

tab¹ (tæb) *n* **1** a small flap of material, esp one on a garment for decoration or for fastening to a button **2** any similar flap, such as a piece of paper attached to a file for identification **3** *Brit military* the insignia on the collar of a staff officer **4** *chiefly US & Canadian* a bill, esp one for a meal or drinks **5 keep tabs on** *informal* to keep a watchful eye on ▷ *vb* **tabs, tabbing, tabbed** **6** (*tr*) to supply (files, clothing, etc) with a tab or tabs [c17: of unknown origin]

tab² (tæb) *n* short for **tabulator, tablet**

TAB *abbreviation* **1** typhoid-paratyphoid A and B (vaccine) **2** *Austral & NZ* Totalizator Agency Board

tabard (ˈtæbəd) *n* a sleeveless or short-sleeved jacket, esp one worn by a herald, bearing a coat of arms, or by a knight over his armour [c13: from Old French *tabart*, of uncertain origin]

tabaret (ˈtæbərɪt) *n* a hard-wearing fabric of silk or similar cloth with stripes of satin or moire, used esp for upholstery [c19: perhaps from TABBY¹]

Tabari (təˈbɑːrɪ) *n* **Muhammad ibn Jarir al-**. 838–923 AD, Arab scholar, whose works include a history of the world from the Creation to 915 AD and a commentary on the Koran

Tabasco¹ (təˈbæskəʊ) *n* *trademark* a very hot red sauce made from matured capsicums

Tabasco² (*Spanish* taˈβasko) *n* a state in SE Mexico, on the Gulf of Campeche: mostly flat and marshy with extensive jungles; hot and humid climate. Capital: Villahermosa. Pop: 1 889 367 (2000). Area: 24 661 sq km (9520 sq miles)

tabby¹ (ˈtæbɪ) *n* a fabric with a watered pattern, esp silk or taffeta [c17: from Old French *tabis* silk cloth, from Arabic *al-'attabiya*, literally: the quarter of (Prince) 'Attab, the part of Baghdad where the fabric was first made]

tabby² (ˈtæbɪ) *adj* **1** (esp of cats) brindled with dark stripes or wavy markings on a lighter background **2** having a wavy or striped pattern, particularly in colours of grey and brown ▷ *n*, *pl* -bies **3** a tabby cat **4** any female domestic cat [c17: from *Tabby*, pet form of the girl's name *Tabitha*, probably influenced by TABBY¹]

tabernacle (ˈtæbəˌnækəl) *n* **1** (*often capital*) *Old Testament* **a** the portable sanctuary in the form of a tent in which the ancient Israelites carried the Ark of the Covenant (Exodus 25–27) **b** the Jewish Temple regarded as the shrine of the divine presence **2** a meeting place for worship used by Mormons or Nonconformists **3** a small ornamented cupboard or box used for the reserved sacrament of the Eucharist **4** *chiefly RC Church* a canopied niche or recess forming the shrine of a statue **5** *nautical* a strong framework for holding the foot of a mast stepped on deck, allowing it to be swung down horizontally to pass under low bridges, etc [c13: from Latin *tabernāculum* a tent, from *taberna* a hut; see TAVERN] > ˌtaberˈnacular *adj*

tabes (ˈteɪbiːz) *n*, *pl* tabes **1** a wasting of a bodily organ or part **2** short for **tabes dorsalis** [c17: from Latin: a wasting away] > tabetic (təˈbɛtɪk) *adj*

tabescent (təˈbɛsᵊnt) *adj* **1** progressively emaciating; wasting away **2** of, relating to, or having tabes [c19: from Latin *tābēscere*, from TABES] > taˈbescence *n*

tabes dorsalis (dɔːˈsɑːlɪs) *n* a form of late syphilis that attacks the spinal cord causing degeneration of the nerve fibres, pains in the legs, paralysis of the leg muscles, acute abdominal pain, etc [New Latin, literally: tabes of the back; see TABES, DORSAL]

tabla ('tʌblə, 'ta:bla:) n a musical instrument of India consisting of a pair of drums whose pitches can be varied [Hindu, from Arabic *tabla* drum]

tablature ('tæblətʃə) n *music* any of a number of forms of musical notation, esp for playing the lute, consisting of letters and signs indicating rhythm and fingering [c16: from French, ultimately from Latin *tabulātum* wooden floor, from *tabula* a plank]

table ('teɪbʰl) n 1 a flat horizontal slab or board, usually supported by one or more legs, on which objects may be placed 2 such a slab or board on which food is served b (*as modifier*): *table linen* 3 food as served in a particular household or restaurant: *a good table* 4 such a piece of furniture specially designed for any of various purposes: *a backgammon table; bird table* 5 a a company of persons assembled for a meal, game, etc b (*as modifier*): *table talk* 6 any flat or level area, such as a plateau 7 a rectangular panel set below or above the face of a wall 8 an upper horizontal facet of a cut gem 9 *music* the sounding board of a violin, guitar, or similar stringed instrument 10 a an arrangement of words, numbers, or signs, usually in parallel columns, to display data or relations b See **multiplication table** 11 a tablet on which laws were inscribed by the ancient Romans, the Hebrews, etc 12 **turn the tables on someone** to cause a complete reversal of circumstances, esp to defeat or get the better of someone who was previously in a stronger position ▷ vb (tr) 13 to place on a table 14 *Brit* to submit (a bill, etc) for consideration by a legislative body 15 *US* to suspend discussion of (a bill, etc) indefinitely or for some time 16 to enter in or form into a list; tabulate [c12: via Old French from Latin *tabula* a writing tablet]

tableau ('tæbləʊ) n, pl -leaux (-ləʊ, -ləʊz) or -leaus 1 a pause during or at the end of a scene on stage when all the performers briefly freeze in position 2 any dramatic group or scene [c17: from French, from Old French *tablel* a picture, diminutive of TABLE]

tableau vivant *French* (tablo vivã) n, pl *tableaux vivants* (tablo vivã) a representation of a scene, painting, sculpture, etc, by a person or group posed silent and motionless [c19: literally: living picture]

Table Bay n the large bay on which Cape Town is situated, on the SW coast of South Africa

tablecloth ('teɪbʰl,klɒθ) n a cloth for covering the top of a table, esp during meals

table d'hôte ('ta:bʰl 'dəʊt; *French* tablə dot) adj 1 (of a meal) consisting of a set number of courses with limited choice of dishes offered at a fixed price. See **à la carte** ▷ n, pl tables d'hôte ('ta:bʰlz 'dəʊt; *French* tablə dot) 2 a table d'hôte meal or menu [c17: from French, literally: the host's table]

table football n a game based on soccer, played on a table with sets of miniature human figures mounted on rods allowing them to be tilted or spun to strike the ball. US name: foosball

tableland ('teɪbʰl,lænd) n flat elevated land; a plateau

table licence n a licence authorizing the sale of alcoholic drinks with meals only

Table Mountain n a mountain in SW South Africa, overlooking Cape Town and Table Bay: flat-topped and steep-sided. Height: 1087 m (3567 ft)

tablespoon ('teɪbʰl,spu:n) n 1 a spoon, larger than a dessertspoon, used for serving food, etc 2 Also called: tablespoonful the amount contained in such a spoon 3 a unit of capacity used in cooking, medicine, etc, equal to half a fluid ounce or three teaspoons

tablet ('tæblɪt) n 1 a medicinal formulation made of a compressed powdered substance containing an active drug and excipients 2 a flattish cake of some substance, such as soap 3 *Scot* a sweet made of butter, sugar, and condensed milk, usually shaped in a flat oblong block 4 a a thinner rigid sheet, as of bark, ivory, etc, used for similar purposes b (*often plural*) a set or pair of these fastened together, as in a book 5 *chiefly US & Canadian* a pad of writing paper [c14: from Old French *tablete* a little

table, from Latin *tabula* a board]

table tennis n a miniature form of tennis played on a table with small bats and a light hollow ball

table-turning n the movement of a table attributed by spiritualists to the power of spirits working through a group of persons placing their hands or fingers on the table top

tableware ('teɪbʰl,wɛə) n articles such as dishes, plates, knives, forks, etc, used at meals

tabloid ('tæblɔɪd) n 1 a newspaper with pages about 30 cm (12 inches) by 40 cm (16 inches), usually characterized by an emphasis on photographs and a concise and often sensational style 2 (*modifier*) designed to appeal to a mass audience or readership; sensationalist: *the tabloid press; tabloid television* [c20: from earlier *Tabloid*, a trademark for a medicine in tablet form]

taboo or **tabu** (tə'bu:) adj 1 forbidden or disapproved of; placed under a social prohibition or ban: *taboo words* 2 (in Polynesia and other islands of the South Pacific) marked off as simultaneously sacred and forbidden ▷ n, pl -boos or -bus 3 any prohibition resulting from social or other conventions 4 ritual restriction or prohibition, esp of something that is considered holy or unclean ▷ vb 5 (tr) to place under a taboo [c18: from Tongan *tapu*]

tabor or **tabour** ('teɪbə) n *music* a small drum used esp in the Middle Ages, struck with one hand while the other held a three-holed pipe [c13: from Old French *tabour*, perhaps from Persian *tabīr*]

Tabor ('teɪbə) n **Mount Tabor** a mountain in N Israel, near Nazareth: traditionally regarded as the mountain where the Transfiguration took place. Height: 588 m (1929 ft)

taboret or **tabouret** ('tæbərɪt) n 1 a low stool, originally in the shape of a drum 2 a frame, usually round, for stretching out cloth while it is being embroidered 3 Also called: taborin, tabourin ('tæbərɪn) a small tabor [c17: from French *tabouret*, diminutive of TABOR]

Tabriz (tæ'bri:z) n a city in NW Iran: an ancient city, situated in a volcanic region of hot springs; university (1947); carpet manufacturing. Pop: 1 396 000 (2005 est)

tabular ('tæbjʊlə) adj 1 arranged in systematic or table form 2 calculated from or by means of a table 3 like a table in form; flat [c17: from Latin *tabulāris* concerning boards, from *tabula* a board] > **'tabularly** adv

tabula rasa ('tæbjʊlə 'ra:sə) n, pl tabulae rasae ('tæbjʊli: 'ra:si:) 1 (esp in the philosophy of Locke) the mind in its uninformed original state 2 an opportunity for a fresh start; clean slate [Latin: a scraped tablet (one from which the writing has been erased)]

tabulate vb ('tæbjʊ,leɪt) (tr) 1 Also called: tabularize ('tæbjʊlə,raɪz) to set out, arrange, or write in tabular form 2 to form or cut with a flat surface ▷ adj ('tæbjʊlɪt, -,leɪt) 3 having a flat surface [c18: from Latin *tabula* a board] > **'tabulable** adj, **,tabu'lation** n

tabulator ('tæbjʊ,leɪtə) n 1 a device for setting the automatic stops that locate the column margins on a typewriter 2 *computing* a machine that reads data from one medium, such as punched cards, producing lists, tabulations, or totals, usually on a continuous sheet of paper

TAC *abbreviation* (in South Africa) Treatment Action Campaign, a pressure group that campaigns for the medical rights of pregnant women with HIV or AIDS

tacamahac ('tækəmə,hæk) or **tacmahack** n 1 any of several strong-smelling resinous gums obtained from certain trees, used in making ointments, incense, etc 2 any tree yielding this resin, esp the balsam poplar [c16: from Spanish *tacamahaca*, from Nahuatl *tecomahca* aromatic resin]

tacet ('teɪsɛt, 'tæs-) vb (intr) (on a musical score) a direction indicating that a particular instrument or singer does not take part in a movement or part of a movement [c18: from Latin: it is silent, from *tacēre* to be quiet]

tacheometer (,tækɪ'ɒmɪtə) or **tachymeter** n *surveying* a type of theodolite designed for the rapid measurement of distances, elevations, and directions > **,tache'ometry** or **tachymetry** n

tachisme ('ta:ʃɪzəm; *French* taʃism) n a type of action painting evolved in France in which haphazard dabs and blots of colour are treated as a means of instinctive or unconscious expression [C20: French, from *tache* stain]

tachistoscope (tə'kɪstə,skəʊp) *n* an instrument, used mainly in experiments on perception and memory, for displaying visual images for very brief intervals, usually a fraction of a second [C20: from Greek *takhistos* swiftest (see TACHY-) + -SCOPE] > **tachistoscopic** (tə,kɪstə'skɒpɪk) *adj*

tacho- *combining form* speed: *tachograph; tachometer* [from Greek *takhos*]

tachograph ('tækə,grɑːf, -,græf) *n* a tachometer that produces a graphical record (**tachogram**) of its readings, esp a device for recording the speed of and distance covered by a heavy goods vehicle

tachometer (tæ'kɒmɪtə) *n* any device for measuring speed, esp the rate of revolution of a shaft Tachometers (rev counters) are often fitted to cars to indicate the number of revolutions per minute of the engine > **ta'chometry** *n*

tachy- or **tacheo-** *combining form* swift or accelerated: *tachycardia; tachygraphy; tachylyte; tachyon; tachyphylaxis* [from Greek *takhus* swift]

tachycardia (,tækɪ'kɑːdɪə) *n* *pathol* abnormally rapid beating of the heart, esp over 100 beats per minute

tachygraphy (tæ'kɪgrəfɪ) *n* shorthand, esp as used in ancient Rome or Greece

tachymeter (tæ'kɪmɪtə) *n* another name for **tacheometer**

tachyon ('tækɪ,ɒn) *n* *physics* a hypothetical elementary particle capable of travelling faster than the velocity of light [C20: from TACHY- + -ON]

tachyphylaxis (,tækɪfɪ'læksɪs) *n* very rapid development of tolerance or immunity to the effects of a drug [New Latin, from TACHY- + *phylaxis* on the model of *prophylaxis*. See PROPHYLACTIC]

tacit ('tæsɪt) *adj* implied or inferred without direct expression; understood: *a tacit agreement* [C17: from Latin *tacitus*, past participle of *tacēre* to be silent] > **'tacitly** *adv*

taciturn ('tæsɪ,tɜːn) *adj* habitually silent, reserved, or uncommunicative; not inclined to conversation [C18: from Latin *taciturnus*, from *tacitus* silent, from *tacēre* to be silent] > **,taci'turnity** *n* > **'taci,turnly** *adv*

Tacitus ('tæsɪtəs) *n* **Publius Cornelius** ('pʌblɪəs kɔː'niːljəs). ?55–?120 AD, Roman historian and orator, famous as a prose stylist. His works include the *Histories*, dealing with the period 68–96, and the *Annals*, dealing with the period 14–68

tack¹ (tæk) *n* **1** a short sharp-pointed nail, usually with a flat and comparatively large head **2** *Brit* a long loose temporary stitch used in dressmaking, etc **3** See **tailor's-tack 4** a temporary fastening **5** stickiness, as of newly applied paint, varnish, etc **6** *nautical* the heading of a vessel sailing to windward, stated in terms of the side of the sail against which the wind is pressing **7** *nautical* **a** a course sailed by a sailing vessel with the wind blowing from forward of the beam **b** one such course or a zigzag pattern of such courses **8** *nautical* **a** a sheet for controlling the weather clew of a course **b** the weather clew itself **9** *nautical* the forward lower clew of a fore-and-aft sail **10** a course of action differing from some previous course **11** on the wrong tack under a false impression ▷ *vb* **12** (*tr*) to secure by a tack or series of tacks **13** *Brit* to sew (something) with long loose temporary stitches **14** (*tr*) to attach or append **15** *nautical* to change the heading of (a sailing vessel) to the opposite tack **16** *nautical* to steer (a sailing vessel) on alternate tacks **17** (*intr*) *nautical* (of a sailing vessel) to proceed on a different tack or to alternate tacks **18** (*intr*) to follow a zigzag route; keep changing one's course of action [C14 *tak* fastening, nail; related to Middle Low German *tacke* pointed instrument]

tack² (tæk) *n* **a** a riding harness for horses, such as saddles, bridles, etc **b** (*as modifier*): *the tack room* [C20: shortened from TACKLE]

tacker ('tækə) *n* **1** a person or thing that tacks **2** *Austral slang* a young person; child

tack hammer *n* a light hammer for driving tacks

tackies or **takkies** ('tækɪz) *pl n, sing* **tacky** *South African informal* tennis shoes or plimsolls [C20: probably from TACKY¹, with reference to their nonslip rubber soles]

tackle ('tækəl; *Nautical often* 'teɪkəl) *n* **1** any mechanical system for lifting or pulling, esp an arrangement of ropes and pulleys designed to lift heavy weights **2** the equipment required for a particular occupation, etc **3** *nautical* the halyards and other running rigging aboard a vessel **4** *sport* a physical challenge to an opponent, as to prevent his progress with the ball **5** *American football* a defensive lineman ▷ *vb* **6** (*tr*) to undertake (a task, problem, etc) **7** (*tr*) to confront (a person, esp an opponent) with a difficult proposition **8** *sport* (esp in football games) to challenge (an opponent) with a tackle [C13: related to Middle Low German *takel* ship's rigging, Middle Dutch *taken* to TAKE] > **'tackler** *n*

tack rag *n* *building trades* a cotton cloth impregnated with an oil, used to remove dust from a surface prior to painting

tack room *n* a room in a stable building in which bridles, saddles, etc are kept

tacky¹ or **tackey** ('tækɪ) *adj* **tackier, tackiest** slightly sticky or adhesive [C18: from TACK¹ (in the sense: stickiness)] > **'tackiness** *n*

tacky² ('tækɪ) *adj* **tackier, tackiest** *informal* **1** shabby or shoddy **2** ostentatious and vulgar **3** *US* (of a person) dowdy; seedy [C19: from dialect *tacky* an inferior horse, of unknown origin] > **'tackiness** *n*

Tacna-Arica (*Spanish* 'taknaa'rika) *n* a coastal desert region of W South America, long disputed by Chile and Peru: divided in 1929 into the Peruvian department of Tacna and the Chilean department of Arica

tacnode ('tæk,nəʊd) *n* another name for **osculation** (sense 1) [C19: from Latin *tactus* touch (from *tangere* to touch) + NODE]

taco ('tɑːkəʊ) *n, pl* **-cos** *Mexican cookery* a tortilla folded into a roll with a filling and usually fried [from Mexican Spanish, from Spanish: literally, a snack, a bite to eat]

Tacoma (tə'kəʊmə) *n* a port in W Washington, on Puget Sound: industrial centre. Pop: 196 790 (2003 est)

tact (tækt) *n* **1** a sense of what is fitting and considerate in dealing with others, so as to avoid giving offence or to win good will; discretion **2** skill or judgment in handling difficult or delicate situations; diplomacy [C17: from Latin *tactus* a touching, from *tangere* to touch] > **'tactful** *adj* > **'tactfulness** *n* > **'tactless** *adj* > **'tactlessness** *n*

tactic ('tæktɪk) *n* a piece of tactics; tactical move. See also **tactics**

-tactic *adj combining form* having a specified kind of pattern or arrangement or having an orientation determined by a specified force: *syndiotactic; phototactic* [from Greek *taktikos* relating to order or arrangement; see TACTICS]

tactical ('tæktɪkəl) *adj* **1** of, relating to, or employing tactics: *a tactical error* **2** (of weapons, attacks, etc) used in or supporting limited military operations **3** skilful or diplomatic > **'tactically** *adv*

tactical voting *n* (in an election) the practice of casting one's vote not for the party of one's choice but for the second strongest contender in order to defeat the likeliest winner

tactics ('tæktɪks) *pl n* (*functioning as singular*) *military* **1** the art and science of the detailed direction and control of movement or manoeuvre of forces in battle to achieve an aim or task **2** the manoeuvres used or plans followed to achieve a particular short-term aim [C17: from New Latin *tactica*, from Greek *ta taktika* the matters of arrangement, neuter plural of *taktikos* concerning arrangement or order, from *tassein* arranged (for battle), from *tassein* to arrange] > **tac'tician** *n*

tactile ('tæktaɪl) *adj* **1** of, relating to, affecting, or having a sense of touch **2** *now rare* capable of being touched; tangible [C17: from Latin *tactilis*, from *tangere* to touch] > **tactility** (tæk'tɪlɪtɪ) *n*

Tadmor ('tædmɔː) *n* the biblical name for **Palmyra**

tadpole ('tæd,pəʊl) *n* the aquatic larva of frogs, toads, etc, which develops from a limbless tailed form with external gills into a form with internal gills, limbs, and a reduced tail [C15 *taddepol*, from *tadde* TOAD + *pol* head, POLL]

Tadzhik *or* **Tadjik** ('tɑːdʒɪk, tɑːˈdʒiːk) *n, pl* **-dzhik** *or* **-djik** variant spellings of **Tajik**

Tadzhikistan *or* **Tadjikistan** (tɑːˌdʒɪkɪˈstɑːn, -stæn) *n* variant spellings of **Tajikistan**

taedium vitae ('tiːdɪəm 'viːtaɪ, 'vaɪtiː) *n* the feeling that life is boring and dull [Latin, literally: weariness of life]

Taegu (tɛ'guː) *n* a city in SE South Korea: textile and agricultural trading centre. Pop: 2 510 000 (2005 est)

Taejon (tɛ'dʒɒn) *n* a city in W South Korea: market centre of an agricultural region. Pop: 1 464 000 (2005 est)

tae kwon do ('taɪ 'kwɒn 'dəʊ, 'teɪ) *n* a Korean martial art that resembles karate [C20: Korean *tae* kick + *kwon* fist + *do* way, method]

tael (teɪl) *n* **1** a unit of weight, used in the Far East, having various values between one to two and a half ounces **2** (formerly) a Chinese monetary unit equivalent in value to a tael weight of standard silver [C16: from Portuguese, from Malay *tahil* weight, perhaps from Hindi *tolā* weight of a new rupee, from Sanskrit *tulā* weight]

ta'en (teɪn) *vb* a poetic contraction of **taken**

taenia *or US* **tenia** ('tiːnɪə) *n, pl* **-niae** (-nɪˌiː) **1** (in ancient Greece) a narrow fillet or headband for the hair **2** *architect* the fillet between the architrave and frieze of a Doric entablature **3** *anatomy* any bandlike structure or part **4** any tapeworm of the genus *Taenia*, such as *T. soleum*, a parasite of man that uses the pig as its intermediate host [C16: via Latin from Greek *tainia* narrow strip; related to Greek *teinein* to stretch]

taeniasis *or US* **teniasis** (tiːˈnaɪəsɪs) *n pathol* infestation with tapeworms of the genus *Taenia*

taffeta ('tæfɪtə) *n* a crisp lustrous plain-weave silk, rayon, etc, used esp for women's clothes [C14: from Medieval Latin *taffata*, from Persian *tāftah* spun, from *tāftan* to spin]

taffrail ('tæfˌreɪl) *n nautical* a rail at the stern or above the transom of a vessel [C19: changed (through influence of RAIL[1]) from earlier *tafferel*, from Dutch *taffereel* panel (hence applied to the part of a vessel decorated with carved panels), variant of *tafeleel* (unattested), from *tafel* TABLE]

taffy ('tæfɪ) *n, pl* **-fies 1** *US & Canadian* a chewy sweet made of brown sugar or molasses and butter, boiled and then pulled so that it becomes glossy **2** *chiefly US & Canadian* a less common term for **toffee** [C19: perhaps from TAFIA]

Taffy ('tæfɪ) *n, pl* **-fies** a slang word or nickname for a Welshman [C17: from the supposed Welsh pronunciation of *Davy* (from *David*, Welsh *Dafydd*), a common Welsh Christian name]

tafia *or* **taffia** ('tæfɪə) *n* a type of rum, esp from Guyana or the Caribbean [C18: from French, from West Indian Creole, probably from RATAFIA]

Tafilelt (tæˈfiːlɛlt) *or* **Tafilalet** (ˌtæfɪˈlɑːlɛt) *n* an oasis in SE Morocco, the largest in the Sahara. Area: about 1300 sq km (500 sq miles)

Taft (tæft) *n* **William Howard**. 1857–1930, US statesman; 27th president of the US (1909–13)

tag[1] (tæg) *n* **1** a piece or strip of paper, plastic, leather, etc, for attaching to something by one end as a mark or label: *a price tag* **2** Also called: **electronic tag** an electronic device worn, usually on the wrist or ankle, by an offender serving a noncustodial sentence, which monitors the offender's whereabouts by means of a link to a central computer through the telephone system **3** a small piece of material hanging from or loosely attached to a part or piece **4** a point of metal or other hard substance at the end of a cord, lace, etc, to prevent it from fraying and to facilitate threading **5** an epithet or verbal appendage, the refrain of a song, the moral of a fable, etc **6** a brief quotation, esp one in a foreign language **7** an ornamental flourish as at the end of a signature **8** the contrastingly coloured tip to an animal's tail **9** a matted lock of wool or hair **10** *slang* a graffito consisting of a nickname or personal symbol ▷ *vb* **tags, tagging, tagged** (*mainly tr*) **11** to mark with a tag **12** to monitor the whereabouts of (an offender) by means of an electronic tag **13** to add or append as a tag **14** to supply (prose or blank verse) with rhymes **15** (*intr*; usually foll by *on* or *along*) to trail (behind) **16** to name or call (someone something) **17** to cut the tags of wool or hair from (an animal) [C15: of uncertain origin; related to Swedish *tagg* point, perhaps also to TACK[1]]

tag[2] (tæg) *n* **1** Also called: **tig** a children's game in which one player chases the others in an attempt to catch one of them who will then become the chaser **2** the act of tagging one's partner in tag wrestling **3** (*modifier*) denoting or relating to a wrestling contest between two teams of two wrestlers, in which only one from each team may be in the ring at one time. The contestant outside the ring may change places with his team-mate inside the ring after touching his hand ▷ *vb* **tags, tagging, tagged** (*tr*) **4** to catch (another child) in the game of tag **5** (in tag wrestling) to touch the hand of (one's partner) [C18: perhaps from TAG[1]]

Tagalog (tə'gɑːlɒg) *n* **1** *pl* **-logs** *or* **-log** a member of a people of the Philippines, living chiefly in the region around Manila **2** the language of this people, belonging to the Malayo-Polynesian family: the official language of the Philippines ▷ *adj* **3** of or relating to this people or their language

Taganrog (*Russian* təgan'rɔk) *n* a port in SW Russia, on the **Gulf of Taganrog** (an inlet of the Sea of Azov): founded in 1698 as a naval base and fortress by Peter the Great: industrial centre. Pop: 281 000 (2005 est)

tag end *n* **1** the last part of something **2** a loose end of cloth, thread, etc

tagetes (tæˈdʒiːtiːz) *n, pl* **tagetes** See **marigold** (sense 1) [from New Latin, from *Tages*an Etruscan god]

tagliatelle (ˌtæljəˈtɛlɪ) *n* a form of pasta made in narrow strips [Italian, from *tagliare* to cut]

tag line *n* **1** an amusing or memorable phrase designed to catch attention in an advertisement **2** another name for **punch line**

Taglioni (*Italian* taˈʎoni) *n* **Marie**. 1804–84, Italian ballet dancer, whose romantic style greatly influenced ballet in the 19th century

Tagore (tə'gɔː) *n* **Rabindranath** (rə'biːndrəˌnɑːt). 1861–1941, Indian poet and philosopher. His verse collections, written in Bengali and English, include *Gitanjali* (1910; 1912): Nobel prize for literature 1913

Tagus ('teɪgəs) *n* a river in SW Europe, rising in E central Spain and flowing west to the border with Portugal, then southwest to the Atlantic at Lisbon: the longest river of the Iberian Peninsula. Length: 1007 km (626 miles). Portuguese name: **Tejo**. Spanish name: **Tajo**

taha Māori ('tɑːhə) *n NZ* a Māori perspective or dimension of a subject [Māori]

Tahiti (tə'hiːtɪ) *n* an island in the S Pacific, in the Windward group of the Society Islands: the largest and most important island in French Polynesia; became a French protectorate in 1842 and a colony in 1880. Capital: Papeete. Pop: 169 674 (2002). Area: 1005 sq km (388 sq miles) > **Tahitian** (tə'hiːtɪən, tə'hiːʃɪən) *adj, n*

Tahoe ('tɑːhəʊ, 'teɪ-) *n* **Lake Tahoe** a lake between E California and W Nevada, in the Sierra Nevada Mountains at an altitude of 1899 m (6229 ft). Area: about 520 sq km (200 sq miles)

tahr *or* **thar** (tɑː) *n* any of several goatlike bovid mammals of the genus *Hemitragus*, such as *H. jemlahicus* (**Himalayan tahr**), of mountainous regions of S and SW Asia, having a shaggy coat and curved horns [from Nepali *thār*]

tahsil (tə'siːl) *n* an administrative division of a zila in certain states in India [Urdu, from Arabic: collection]

Tai (taɪ) *adj, n* a variant spelling of **Thai**

TAI *abbreviation* International Atomic Time

taiaha ('taɪəˌhɑː) *n NZ* a carved weapon in the form of a staff, now used in Māori ceremonial oratory [Māori]

t'ai chi ch'uan ('taɪ dʒiː 'tʃwɑːn) *n* a Chinese system of callisthenics characterized by coordinated and rhythmic movements. Often shortened to: **t'ai chi** [Chinese, literally: great art of boxing]

Taichung *or* **T'ai-chung** ('taɪ'tʃʊŋ) *n* a city in W Taiwan: commercial centre of an agricultural region. Pop: 1 066 000 (2005 est)

taiga ('taɪgə) *n* the coniferous forests extending across much of subarctic North America and Eurasia, bordered by tundra to the north and steppe to the south [from Russian, of Turkic origin; compare Turkish *dağ* mountain]

taihoa ('taɪhəʊə) *interj NZ* hold on! no hurry! [Māori]

taikonaut ('taɪkəʊ,nɔːt) *n* an astronaut from the People's Republic of China [c20: from Cantonese *taikon(g)* cosmos + -NAUT]

tail¹ (teɪl) *n* **1** the region of the vertebrate body that is posterior to or above the anus and contains an elongation of the vertebral column, esp forming a flexible movable appendage **2** anything resembling such an appendage in form or position; the bottom, lowest, or rear part **3** the last part or parts: *the tail of the storm* **4** the rear part of an aircraft including the fin, tailplane, and control surfaces; empennage **5** *astronomy* the luminous stream of gas and dust particles, up to 200 million kilometres long, driven from the head of a comet, when close to the sun, under the effect of the solar wind and light pressure **6** the rear portion of a bomb, rocket, missile, etc, usually fitted with guiding or stabilizing vanes **7** a line of people or things **8** a long braid or tress of hair: *a ponytail; a pigtail* **9** Also called: tailfly *angling* the lowest fly on a wet-fly cast **10** a final short line in a stanza **11** *informal* a person employed to follow and spy upon another or others **12** *taboo, slang* **a** the female genitals **b** a woman considered sexually (esp in the phrases **piece of tail, bit of tail**) **13** *printing* the margin at the foot of a page **14** the lower end of a pool or part of a stream **15** *informal* the course or track of a fleeing person or animal **16** (*modifier*) coming from or situated in the rear: *a tail wind* **17** turn tail to run away; escape **18** with one's tail between one's legs in a state of utter defeat or confusion ▷ *vb* **19** to form or cause to form the tail **20** to remove the tail of (an animal); dock **21** (*tr*) to remove the stalk of **22** (*tr*) to connect (objects, ideas, etc) together by or as if by the tail **23** (*tr*) *informal* to follow stealthily **24** (*intr*) (of a vessel) to assume a specified position, as when at a mooring **25** to build the end of (a brick, joist, etc) into a wall or (of a brick, etc) to have one end built into a wall ▷ See also **tail off, tail out, tails** [Old English *tægel*; related to Old Norse *tagl* horse's tail, Gothic *tagl* hair, Old High German *zagal* tail] > 'tailless *adj*

tail² (teɪl) *property law* ▷ *n* **1** the limitation of an estate or interest to a person and the heirs of his body ▷ *adj* **2** (*immediately postpositive*) (of an estate or interest) limited in this way [from Old French *taille* a division; see TAILOR, TALLY] > 'tailless *adj*

tailback ('teɪl,bæk) *n* a queue of traffic stretching back from an obstruction

tailboard ('teɪl,bɔːd) *n* a board at the rear of a lorry, wagon, etc, that can be removed or let down on a hinge

tail coat *n* Also called: tails a man's black coat having a horizontal cut over the hips and a tapering tail with a vertical slit up to the waist: worn as part of full evening dress

tail covert *n* any of the covert feathers of a bird covering the bases of the tail feathers

tail end *n* the last, endmost, or final part

tailgate ('teɪl,geɪt) *n* **1** another name for **tailboard 2** a door at the rear of a hatchback vehicle ▷ *vb* **3** to drive very close behind (a vehicle) > 'tail,gater *n*

tail gate *n* a gate that is used to control the flow of water at the lower end of a lock

tailing ('teɪlɪŋ) *n* the part of a beam, rafter, projecting brick or stone, etc, embedded in a wall

tailings ('teɪlɪŋz) *pl n* waste left over after certain processes, such as from an ore-crushing plant or in milling grain

tail-light or **tail lamp** *n* other names for **rear light**

tail off or **tail away** *vb* (*adverb, usually intr*) to decrease or cause to decrease in quantity, degree, etc, esp gradually

tailor ('teɪlə) *n* **1** a person who makes, repairs, or alters outer garments, esp menswear. Related adj: **sartorial 2** a voracious and active marine food fish, *Pomatomus saltator*, of Australia with scissor-like teeth ▷ *vb* **3** to cut or style (material, clothes, etc) to satisfy certain requirements **4** (*tr*) to adapt so as to make suitable for something specific **5** (*intr*) to follow the occupation of a tailor [c13: from Anglo-Norman *taillour*, from Old French *taillier* to cut, from Latin *tālea* a cutting; related to Greek *talis* girl of marriageable age]

tailorbird ('teɪlə,bɜːd) *n* any of several tropical Asian warblers of the genus *Orthotomus*, which build nests by sewing together large leaves using plant fibres

tailor-made *adj* **1** made by a tailor to fit exactly **2** perfectly meeting a particular purpose ▷ *n* **3** a tailor-made garment **4** *slang* a cigarette made in a factory rather than rolled by hand

tailor's chalk *n* pipeclay used by tailors and dressmakers to mark seams, darts, etc, on material

tailor's-tack *n* one of a series of loose looped stitches used to transfer markings for seams, darts, etc, from a paper pattern to material

tail out *vb* (*tr, adverb*) to guide (timber) as it emerges from a power saw

tailpiece ('teɪl,piːs) *n* **1** an extension or appendage that lengthens or completes something **2** *printing* a decorative design at the foot of a page or end of a chapter **3** *music* a piece of wood to which the strings of a violin, etc, are attached at their lower end. It is suspended between the taut strings and the bottom of the violin by a piece of gut or metal **4** Also called: tail beam *architect* a short beam or rafter that has one end embedded in a wall

tailpipe ('teɪl,paɪp) *n* a pipe from which the exhaust gases from an internal-combustion engine are discharged, esp the terminal pipe of the exhaust system of a motor vehicle

tailplane ('teɪl,pleɪn) *n* a small horizontal wing at the tail of an aircraft to provide longitudinal stability

tailrace ('teɪl,reɪs) *n* a channel that carries water away from a water wheel, turbine, etc

tail rotor *n* a small propeller fitted to the rear of a helicopter to counteract the torque reaction of the main rotor and thus prevent the body of the helicopter from rotating in an opposite direction

tails (teɪlz) *pl n* **1** an informal name for **tail coat** ▷ *interj, adv* **2** with the reverse side of a coin uppermost: used as a call before tossing a coin

tailskid ('teɪl,skɪd) *n* **1** a runner under the tail of an aircraft **2** a rear-wheel skid of a motor vehicle

tailspin ('teɪl,spɪn) *n* **1** *aeronautics* another name for **spin** (sense 16) **2** *informal* a state of confusion or panic

tailstock ('teɪl,stɒk) *n* a casting that slides on the bed of a lathe in alignment with the headstock and is locked in position to support the free end of a workpiece

tailwind ('teɪl,wɪnd) *n* a wind blowing in the same direction as the course of an aircraft or ship

Taimyr Peninsula (*Russian* taj'mir) *n* a large peninsula of N central Russia, between the Kara Sea and the Laptev Sea. Also called: Taymyr Peninsula

Tainan or **T'ai-nan** ('taɪ'næn) *n* a city in the SW Taiwan: an early centre of Chinese emigration from the mainland; largest city and capital of the island (1638–1885); Chengkung University. Pop: 754 000 (2005 est)

Taínaron ('tɛnərɒn) *n* a transliteration of the Modern Greek name for (Cape) **Matapan**

Taine (*French* tɛn) *n* **Hippolyte Adolphe** (ipɔlit adɔlf). 1828–93, French literary critic and historian. He applied determinist criteria to the study of literature, art, history, and psychology, regarding them as products of environment and race. His works include *Histoire de la littérature anglaise* (1863–64) and *Les Origines de la France contemporaine* (1875–93)

Taino ('taɪnəʊ) *n* **1** *pl* -nos *or* -no a member of an American Indian people of the Greater Antilles and the Bahamas **2** the language of this people, belonging to the Arawakan family

taint (teɪnt) *vb* **1** to affect or be affected by pollution or contamination **2** to tarnish (someone's reputation, etc) ▷ *n* **3** a defect or flaw **4** a trace of contamination or infection [c14: (influenced by *attaint* infected, from ATTAIN) from Old French *teindre* to dye, from Latin *tingere* to dye] > 'taintless *adj*

taipan ('taɪˌpæn) *n* a large highly venomous elapid snake, *Oxyuranus scutellatus*, of NE Australia [c20: from a native Australian language]

Taipei *or* **T'ai-pei** ('taɪˈpeɪ) *n* the capital of Taiwan (the Republic of China), at the N tip of the island: became capital in 1885; industrial centre; two universities. Pop: 2 473 000 (2005 est)

Taisho (taɪˈʃəʊ) *n* **1** the period of Japanese history and artistic style associated with the reign of Emperor Yoshihito (1912–26) **2** the throne name of Yoshihito (1879–1926), emperor of Japan (1912–26)

Taiwan ('taɪˈwɑːn) *n* an island in SE Asia between the East China Sea and the South China Sea, off the SE coast of the People's Republic of China: the principal territory of the Republic of China; claimed by the People's Republic of China since its political separation from mainland China in the late 1940s. Pop: 22 610 000 (2003 est). Former name: **Formosa** ▷ ˌTaiwan'ese *adj, n*

Taiwan Strait *n* another name for **Formosa Strait**

Taiyuan *or* **T'ai-yüan** ('taɪjuˈɑːn) *n* a city in N China, capital of Shanxi: founded before 450 AD; an industrial centre, surrounded by China's largest reserves of high-grade bituminous coal. Pop: 2 516 000 (2005 est)

Ta'izz (tæˈɪz, teɪˈiːz) *n* a town in SW Yemen, in the former North Yemen until 1990: agricultural trading centre. Pop: 541 000 (2005 est)

taj (tɑːdʒ) *n* a tall conical cap worn as a mark of distinction by Muslims [via Arabic from Persian: crown, crest]

Tajik ('tɑːdʒɪk, tɑːˈdʒiːk) *n, pl* **-jik** a member of a Persian-speaking Muslim people inhabiting Tajikistan and parts of Sinkiang in W China

Tajikistan, Tadzhikistan *or* **Tadjikistan** (tɑːˌdʒɪkɪˈstɑːn, -stæn) *n* a republic in central Asia: under Uzbek rule from the 15th century until taken over by Russia in the 1860s, it became an autonomous Soviet republic in 1929 and gained full independence from the Soviet Union in 1991; it is mainly mountainous. Official language: Tajik or Tajiki. Religion: believers are mainly Muslim. Currency: somoni. Capital: Dushanbe. Pop: 6 297 000 (2004 est). Area: 143 100 sq km (55 240 sq miles)

Taj Mahal ('tɑːdʒ məˈhɑːl) *n* a white marble mausoleum in central India, in Agra on the Jumna River: built (1632–43) by the emperor Shah Jahan in memory of his beloved wife, Mumtaz Mahal; regarded as the finest example of Mogul architecture [Urdu, literally: crown of buildings]

Tajo ('taxo) *n* the Spanish name for **Tagus**

takahe ('tɑːkəˌhiː) *n* a very rare flightless New Zealand rail, *Notornis mantelli* [from Māori, of imitative origin]

Takamatsu (ˌtækəˈmætsuː) *n* a port in SW Japan, on NE Shikoku on the Inland Sea. Pop: 333 387 (2002 est)

Takao (tæˈkaʊ) *n* the Japanese name for **Kaohsiung**

take¹ (teɪk) *vb* **takes, taking, took, taken** (*mainly tr*) **1** (*also intr*) to gain possession of (something) by force or effort **2** to appropriate or steal **3** to receive or accept into a relationship with oneself: *to take a wife* **4** to pay for or buy **5** to rent or lease **6** to receive or obtain by regular payment **7** to obtain by competing for; win **8** to obtain or derive from a source **9** to assume the obligations of: *to take office* **10** to endure, esp with fortitude: *to take punishment* **11** to adopt as a symbol of duty, obligation, etc: *to take the veil* **12** to receive or react to in a specified way: *she took the news very well* **13** to adopt as one's own: *to take someone's part in a quarrel* **14** to receive and make use of: *to take advice* **15** to receive into the body, as by eating, inhaling, etc **16** to eat, drink, etc, esp habitually **17** to have or be engaged in for one's benefit or use: *to take a rest* **18** to work at or study: *to take economics at college* **19** to make, do, or perform (an action) **20** to make use of: *to take an opportunity* **21** to put into effect; adopt: *to take measures* **22** (*also intr*) to make a photograph of or admit of being photographed **23** to act or perform **24** to write down or copy: *to take notes* **25** to experience or feel: *to take pride in one's appearance; to take offence* **26** to consider, believe, or regard: *I take him to be honest* **27** to consider or accept as valid: *I take your point* **28** to hold or maintain in the mind: *his father took a dim view of his career* **29** to deal or contend with **30** to use as a particular case: *take hotels for*

example **31** (*intr*; often foll by *from*) to diminish or detract: *the actor's bad performance took from the effect of the play* **32** to confront successfully: *the horse took the jump at the third attempt* **33** (*intr*) to have or produce the intended effect; succeed: *her vaccination took; the glue is taking well* **34** (*intr*) (of seeds, plants, etc) to start growing successfully **35** to aim or direct: *he took a swipe at his opponent* **36** to deal a blow to in a specified place **37** *archaic* to have sexual intercourse with **38** to carry off or remove from a place **39** to carry along or have in one's possession **40** to convey or transport **41** to use as a means of transport: *I shall take the bus* **42** to conduct or lead **43** to escort or accompany **44** to bring or deliver to a state, position, etc: *his ability took him to the forefront in his field* **45** to go to look for; seek: *to take cover* **46** to ascertain or determine by measuring, computing, etc: *to take a pulse; take a reading from a dial* **47** (*intr*) (of a mechanism) to catch or engage (a part) **48** to put an end to; destroy: *she took her own life* **49** to come upon unexpectedly; discover **50** to contract: *he took a chill* **51** to affect or attack: *the fever took him one night* **52** (*copula*) to become suddenly or be rendered (ill): *he took sick; he was taken sick* **53** (*also intr*) to absorb or become absorbed by something: *to take a polish* **54** (*usually passive*) to charm or captivate: *she was very taken with the puppy* **55** (*intr*) to be or become popular; win favour **56** to require or need: *this job will take a lot of attention; that task will take all your time* **57** to subtract or deduct **58** to hold or contain: *the suitcase won't take all your clothes* **59** to quote or copy **60** to proceed to occupy: *to take a seat* **61** (often foll by *to*) to use or employ: *to take steps to ascertain the answer* **62** to win or capture (a trick, counter, piece, etc) **63** *slang* to cheat, deceive, or victimize **64 take five** *informal, chiefly US & Canadian* to take a break of five minutes **65 take it** **a** to assume; believe **b** *informal* to stand up to or endure criticism, abuse, harsh treatment, etc **66 take one's time** to use as much time as is needed; not rush **67 take someone's name in vain** **a** to use a name, esp of God, disrespectfully or irreverently **b** *jocular* to say (someone's) name **68 take something upon oneself** to assume the right to do or responsibility for (something) ▷ *n* **69** the act of taking **70** the number of quarry killed or captured on one occasion **71** *informal, chiefly US* the amount of anything taken, esp money **72** *films, music* **a** one of a series of recordings from which the best will be selected for release **b** the process of taking one such recording **c** a scene or part of a scene photographed without interruption **73** *informal, chiefly US* a version or interpretation: *Cronenberg's harsh take on the sci-fi story* ▷ See also **take after, take against**, etc [Old English *tacan*, from Old Norse *taka*; related to Gothic *tekan* to touch] ▷ 'takable *or* 'takeable *adj* ▷ 'taker *n*

take² ('tɑːk) *n* NZ a topic or cause [Māori]

take after *vb* (*intr, preposition*) to resemble in appearance, character, behaviour, etc

take against *vb* (*intr, preposition*) to start to dislike, esp without good reason

take apart *vb* (*tr, adverb*) **1** to separate (something) into component parts **2** to criticize or punish severely

take away *vb* (*tr, adverb*) **1** to deduct; subtract: *take away four from nine to leave five* ▷ *prep* **2** minus: *nine take away four is five* ▷ *adj* **takeaway** *Brit, Austral & NZ* **3** sold for consumption away from the premises on which it is prepared: *a takeaway meal* **4** preparing and selling food for consumption away from the premises: *a takeaway Indian restaurant* ▷ *n* **takeaway** *Brit, Austral & NZ* **5** a shop or restaurant that sells such food **6** a meal bought at such a shop or restaurant: *we'll have a Chinese takeaway tonight to save cooking* ▷ Scot word (for senses 3–6): carry-out US & Canadian word (for senses 3–6): takeout

take back *vb* (*adverb, mainly tr*) **1** to retract or withdraw (something said, written, promised, etc) **2** to regain possession of **3** to return for exchange **4** to accept (someone) back (into one's home, affections, etc) **5** to remind one of the past; cause one to reminisce: *that tune really takes me back* **6** (*also intr*) *printing* to move (copy) to the previous line

take down *vb* (*tr, adverb*) **1** to record in writing **2** to dismantle or tear down **3** to lower or reduce in power, arrogance, etc (esp in the phrase **to take down a peg**)

t

▷ *adj* take-down **4** made or intended to be disassembled

take for *vb* (*tr, preposition*) *informal* to consider or suppose to be, esp mistakenly: *the fake coins were taken for genuine; who do you take me for?*

take-home pay *n* the remainder of one's pay after all income tax and other compulsory deductions have been made

take in *vb* (*tr, adverb*) **1** to comprehend or understand **2** to include or comprise **3** to receive into one's house in exchange for payment: *to take in washing; take in lodgers* **4** to make (an article of clothing, etc) smaller by altering seams **5** *informal* to cheat or deceive **6** to go to; visit: *let's take in a movie tonight*

taken ('teɪkən) *vb* **1** the past participle of **take¹** ▷ *adj* **2** (*postpositive; foll by* *with*) enthusiastically impressed (by); infatuated (with)

take off *vb* (*adverb*) **1** (*tr*) to remove or discard (a garment) **2** (*intr*) (of an aircraft) to become airborne **3** *informal* to set out or cause to set out on a journey: *they took off for Spain* **4** (*tr*) (of a disease) to prove fatal to; kill **5** (*tr*) *informal* to mimic or imitate, esp in an amusing or satirical manner **6** (*intr*) *informal* to become successful or popular, esp suddenly ▷ *n* takeoff **7** the act or process of making an aircraft airborne **8** the stage of a country's economic development when rapid and sustained economic growth is first achieved **9** *informal* an act of mimicry; imitation

take on *vb* (*adverb, mainly tr*) **1** to employ or hire **2** to assume or acquire: *his voice took on a plaintive note* **3** to agree to do; undertake **4** (*intr*) *informal* to exhibit great emotion, esp grief

take out *vb* (*tr, adverb*) **1** to extract or remove **2** to obtain or secure (a licence, patent, etc) from an authority **3** to go out with; escort **4** *bridge* to bid a different suit from (one's partner) in order to rescue him from a difficult contract **5** *slang* to kill or destroy **6** *Austral informal* to win, esp in sport **7** take it out of *or* take a lot out of *informal* to sap the energy or vitality of **8** take out on *informal* to vent (anger, frustration, etc) on (esp an innocent person) **9** take someone out of himself *informal* to make someone forget his anxieties, problems, etc ▷ *adj* takeout **10** *bridge* of or designating a conventional informatory bid, asking one's partner to bid another suit **11** *US & Canadian* sold for consumption away from the premises on which it is prepared: *a takeout meal* **12** preparing and selling food for consumption away from the premises: *a takeout Indian restaurant* ▷ *n* takeout *US & Canadian* **13** a shop or restaurant that sells such food **14** a meal bought at such a shop or restaurant

take over *vb* (*adverb*) **1** to assume the control or management of **2** *printing* to move (copy) to the next line ▷ *n* takeover **3** the act of seizing or assuming power, control, etc

take to *vb* (*intr, preposition*) **1** to make for; flee to: *to take to the hills* **2** to form a liking for, esp after a short acquaintance **3** to have recourse to: *to take to the bottle*

take up *vb* (*adverb, mainly tr*) **1** to adopt the study, practice, or activity of: *to take up gardening* **2** *Austral & NZ* to occupy and break in (uncultivated land) **3** to shorten (a garment or part of a garment) **4** to pay off (a note, mortgage, etc) **5** to agree to or accept (an invitation, etc) **6** to pursue further or resume (something): *he took up French where he left off* **7** to absorb (a liquid) **8** to adopt as a protégé; act as a patron to **9** to occupy or fill (space or time) **10** to interrupt, esp in order to contradict or criticize **11** take up on **a** to argue or dispute with (someone): *can I take you up on two points in your talk?* **b** to accept what is offered by (someone): *let me take you up on your invitation* **12** take up with **a** to discuss with (someone); refer to **b** (*intr*) to begin to keep company or associate with ▷ *n* take-up **13 a** the claiming or acceptance of something, esp a state benefit, that is due or available **b** (*as modifier*): *take-up rate*

takin ('tɑːkiːn) *n* a massive bovid mammal, *Budorcas taxicolor*, of mountainous regions of S Asia, having a shaggy coat, short legs, and horns that point backwards and upwards [c19: from Mishmi]

taking ('teɪkɪŋ) *adj* **1** charming, fascinating, or intriguing **2** *informal* infectious; catching ▷ *n*

3 something taken **4** (*plural*) receipts; earnings > 'takingly *adv* > 'takingness *n*

Takoradi (ˌtɑːkəˈrɑːdɪ) *n* the chief port of Ghana, in the southwest on the Gulf of Guinea: modern harbour opened in 1928. Pop (with Sekondi): 335 000 (2005 est)

Talabani (tæləˈbɑːnɪ) *n* **Jalal.** born 1933, Iraqi politician, a Kurd, president of Iraq from 2005

talapoin ('tæləˌpɔɪn) *n* **1** the smallest of the guenon monkeys, *Cercopithecus talapoin*, of swampy central W African forests, having olive-green fur and slightly webbed digits **2** (in Myanmar and Thailand) a Buddhist monk [c16: from French, literally: Buddhist monk, from Portuguese *talapão*, from Mon *tala pôi* our lord; originally jocular, from the appearance of the monkey]

talaq *or* **talak** (tæˈlɑːk) *n* a form of divorce under Islamic law in which the husband repudiates the marriage by saying 'talaq' three times [c21: from Arabic *ṭalaḳ* divorce, from *ṭalaḳas* to repudiate]

talaria (təˈlɛərɪə) *pl n Greek myth* winged sandals, such as those worn by Hermes [c16: from Latin, from *tālāris* belonging to the ankle, from *tālus* ankle]

Talavera de la Reina (*Spanish* talaˈβera ðe la ˈreina) *n* a walled town in central Spain, on the Tagus River: scene of the defeat of the French by British and Spanish forces (1809) during the Peninsular War; agricultural processing centre. Pop: 79 916 (2003 est)

Talbot ('tɔlbət) *n* (**William Henry**) **Fox.** 1800–77, British scientist, a pioneer of photography, who developed the calotype process

talc (tælk) *n* Also: **talcum 1** See **talcum powder 2** a white, grey, brown, or pale green mineral, found in metamorphic rocks. It is used in the manufacture of talcum powder and electrical insulators. Composition: hydrated magnesium silicate. Formula: $Mg_3Si_4O_{10}(OH)_2$. Crystal structure: monoclinic ▷ *vb* talcs, talcking, talcked *or* talcs, talcing, talced **3** (*tr*) to apply talc to [c16: from Medieval Latin *talcum*, from Arabic *ṭalq* mica, from Persian *talk*] > 'talcose *or* 'talcous *adj*

Talca (*Spanish* 'talka) *n* a city in central Chile: scene of the declaration of Chilean independence (1818). Pop: 206 000 (2005 est)

Talcahuano (*Spanish* talkaˈwano) *n* a port in S central Chile, near Concepción on an inlet of the Pacific: oil refinery. Pop: 251 000 (2005 est)

talcum powder ('tælkəm) *n* a powder made of purified talc, usually scented, used for perfuming the body and for absorbing excess moisture. Often shortened to: **talc**

tale (teɪl) *n* **1** a report, narrative, or story **2** one of a group of short stories connected by an overall narrative framework **3 a** a malicious or meddlesome rumour or piece of gossip **b** (*in combination*): *talebearer; taleteller* **4** a fictitious or false statement **5** tell tales **a** to tell fanciful lies **b** to report malicious stories, trivial complaints, etc, esp to someone in authority **6** tell a tale to reveal something important **7** tell its own tale to be self-evident **8** *archaic* a number; amount [Old English *talu* list; related to Old Frisian *tele* talk, Old Saxon, Old Norse *tala* talk, number, Old High German *zala* number]

talent ('tælənt) *n* **1** innate ability, aptitude, or faculty, esp when unspecified; above average ability: *a talent for cooking; a child with talent* **2** a person or persons possessing such ability **3** any of various ancient units of weight and money **4** *informal* members of the opposite sex collectively, esp those living in a particular place: *the local talent* [Old English *talente*, from Latin *talenta*, pl of *talentum* sum of money, from Greek *talanton* unit of money or weight; in Medieval Latin the sense was extended to ability through the influence of the parable of the talents (Matthew 25:14–30)] > 'talented *adj*

talent scout *n* a person whose occupation is the search for talented artists, sportsmen, performers, etc, for engagements as professionals

tales ('teɪliːz) *n law* **1** (*functioning as plural*) a group of persons summoned from among those present in court or from bystanders to fill vacancies on a jury panel **2** (*functioning as singular*) the writ summoning such jurors [c15: from Medieval Latin phrase *tālēs dē circumstantibus* such men from among the bystanders, from Latin *tālis* such] > 'talesman *n*

Taliban, Taleban or **Talibaan** ('tælɪbæn) n (in Afghanistan) a fundamentalist Islamic army: in 1996 it defeated the ruling mujaheddin factions and seized control of the country; overthrown in 2001 by US-led forces, although resistance continues, esp in the south [C20: from Arabic *tāliban* seekers]

Taliesin (,tælɪˈɛsɪn) n 6th century AD, Welsh bard; supposed author of 12 heroic poems in the *Book of Taliesin*

taligrade ('tælɪ,ɡreɪd) adj (of mammals) walking on the outer side of the foot [C20: from New Latin, from Latin *tālus* ankle, heel + -GRADE]

talion ('tælɪən) n the system or legal principle of making the punishment correspond to the crime; retaliation [C15: via Old French from Latin *tāliō*, from *tālis* such]

talipes ('tælɪ,piːz) n 1 a congenital deformity of the foot by which it is twisted in any of various positions 2 a technical name for **club foot** [C19: New Latin, from Latin *tālus* ankle + *pēs* foot]

talipot or **talipot palm** ('tælɪ,pɒt) n a palm tree, *Corypha umbraculifera*, of the East Indies, having large leaves that are used for fans, thatching houses, etc [C17: from Bengali: palm leaf, from Sanskrit *tālī* fan palm + *pattra* leaf]

talisman ('tælɪzmən) n, pl -mans 1 a stone or other small object, usually inscribed or carved, believed to protect the wearer from evil influences 2 anything thought to have magical or protective powers [C17: via French or Spanish from Arabic *tilsam*, from Medieval Greek *telesma* ritual, from Greek: consecration, from *telein* to perform a rite, complete, from *telos* end, result] > talismanic (,tælɪzˈmænɪk) adj

talk (tɔːk) vb 1 (intr; often foll by to or with) to express one's thoughts, feelings, or desires by means of words (to); speak (to) 2 (intr) to communicate or exchange thoughts by other means: *lovers talk with their eyes* 3 (intr; usually foll by about) to exchange ideas, pleasantries, or opinions (about) 4 (intr) to articulate words; verbalize 5 (tr) to give voice to; utter: *to talk rubbish* 6 (tr) to hold a conversation about; discuss: *to talk business* 7 (intr) to reveal information 8 (tr) to know how to communicate in (a language or idiom): *he talks English* 9 (intr) to spread rumours or gossip 10 (intr) to make sounds suggestive of talking 11 (intr) to be effective or persuasive: *money talks* 12 now you're talking *informal* at last you're saying something agreeable 13 talk big to boast or brag 14 talk the talk to speak convincingly on a particular subject, showing apparent mastery of its jargon and themes; often used in combination with the expression *walk the walk*. See also **walk** (sense 13) 15 you can talk *informal* you don't have to worry about doing a particular thing yourself 16 you can't talk *informal* you yourself are guilty of offending in the very matter you are decrying ▷ n 17 a speech or lecture 18 an exchange of ideas or thoughts 19 idle chatter, gossip, or rumour 20 a subject of conversation; theme 21 (often plural) a conference, discussion, or negotiation 22 a specific manner of speaking: *children's talk* ▷ See also **talk about, talk back,** etc [C13 *talken* to talk; related to Old English *talu* TALE, Frisian *talken* to talk] > 'talker n

talk about vb (intr, preposition) 1 to discuss 2 used informally and often ironically to add emphasis to a statement: *all his plays have such ridiculous plots — talk about good drama!*

talkative ('tɔːkətɪv) adj given to talking a great deal > 'talkativeness n

talk back vb (intr, adverb) 1 to answer boldly or impudently 2 NZ to conduct a telephone dialogue for immediate transmission over the air ▷ n talkback 3 *television, radio* a system of telephone links enabling spoken directions to be given during the production of a programme 4 NZ a broadcast telephone dialogue

talk down vb (adverb) 1 (intr; often foll by to) to behave (towards) in a superior or haughty manner 2 (tr) to override (a person or argument) by continuous or loud talking 3 (tr) to give instructions to (an aircraft) by radio to enable it to land

talkie ('tɔːkɪ) n *informal* an early film with a soundtrack. Full name: talking picture

Talking Book n *trademark* a recording of a book, designed to be used by blind people

talking head n (on television) a person, such as a newscaster, who is shown only from the shoulders up, and speaks without the use of any illustrative material

talking-to n *informal* a session of criticism, as of the work or attitude of a subordinate by a person in authority

talk into vb (tr, preposition) to persuade to by talking: *I talked him into buying the house*

talk out vb (adverb) 1 (tr) to resolve or eliminate by talking 2 (tr) *Brit* to block (a bill, etc) in a legislative body by lengthy discussion 3 talk out of to dissuade from by talking

talk round vb 1 Also called: talk over (tr, adverb) 1 to persuade to one's opinion 2 (intr, preposition) to discuss the arguments relating to (a subject), esp without coming to a conclusion

tall (tɔːl) adj 1 of more than average height 2 (postpositive) having a specified height: *a woman five feet tall* 3 *informal* exaggerated or incredible: *a tall story* 4 *informal* difficult to accomplish: *a tall order* [C14 (in the sense: big, comely, valiant); related to Old English *getæl* prompt, Old High German *gizal* quick, Gothic *untals* foolish] > 'tallness n

tallage ('tælɪdʒ) n *English history* a a tax levied by the Norman and early Angevin kings on their Crown lands and royal towns b a toll levied by a lord upon his tenants or by a feudal lord upon his vassals [C13: from Old French *taillage*, from *taillier* to cut; see TAILOR]

Tallahassee (,tæləˈhæsɪ) n a city in N Florida, capital of the state: two universities. Pop: 153 938 (2003 est)

Tall Blacks pl n the Tall Blacks the international basketball team of New Zealand

tallboy ('tɔːl,bɔɪ) n 1 a high chest of drawers made in two sections and placed one on top of the other; chest-on-chest 2 a fitting on the top of a chimney to prevent downdraughts [C18: from TALL + BOY]

Talleyrand-Périgord (,tælɪ,rænd'perɪɡɔː; French talɛrɑ̃periɡɔr) n **Charles Maurice** (ʃarl mɔris). 1754–1838, French statesman; foreign minister (1797–1807; 1814–15). He secretly negotiated with the Allies against Napoleon I from 1808 and was France's representative at the Congress of Vienna (1815)

Tallinn or **Tallin** ('tælɪn) n the capital of Estonia, on the Gulf of Finland: founded by the Danes in 1219; a port and naval base. Pop: 384 000 (2005 est). German name: Reval

tallis ('tɑlɪs) or **tallith** (tɑ'lit) n *Judaism* a fringed shawl worn by Jewish men during morning prayers [from Hebrew, literally: a cover]

Tallis ('tælɪs) n **Thomas**. ?1505–85, English composer and organist; noted for his music for the Anglican liturgy

tallow ('tæləʊ) n 1 a fatty substance consisting of a mixture of glycerides, including stearic, palmitic, and oleic acids and extracted chiefly from the suet of sheep and cattle: used for making soap, candles, food, etc ▷ vb 2 (tr) to cover or smear with tallow [Old English *tælg*, a dye; related to Middle Low German *talch* tallow, Dutch *talk*, Icelandic *tólg*] > 'tallowy adj

tallow wood n *Austral* a tall eucalyptus tree, *Eucalyptus microcorys*, of coastal regions, having soft fibrous bark and conical fruits and yielding a greasy timber

tall poppy n *Austral informal* a person who has a high salary or is otherwise prominent [perhaps from Tarquin's decapitation of the tallest poppies in his garden, to indicate the fate of the most prominent citizens of Gabii]

tall poppy syndrome n *Austral informal* a tendency to disparage any person who has achieved great prominence or wealth

tall ship n any square-rigged sailing ship

tally ('tælɪ) vb -lies, -lying, -lied 1 (intr) to correspond one with the other: *the two stories don't tally* 2 (tr) to supply with an identifying tag 3 (intr) to keep score 4 (tr) *obsolete* to record or mark ▷ n, pl -lies 1 a record of debit, credit, the score in a game, etc 6 a counterpart or duplicate of something, such as the counterfoil of a cheque 7 a stick used (esp formerly) as a record of the amount of a debt according to the notches cut in it 8 a notch or mark cut in or made on such a stick 9 a mark or number of marks used to represent a certain number in counting [c15: from Medieval Latin *tālea*, from Latin: a stick; related to Latin *tālus* heel]

tally clerk *n* a person, esp on a wharf or dock or in an airport, who checks the count of goods being loaded or unloaded

tally-ho (ˌtælɪˈhəʊ) *interj* **1** the cry of a participant at a hunt to encourage the hounds when the quarry is sighted ▷ *n*, *pl* **-hos 2** an instance of crying tally-ho **3** another name for **four-in-hand** (sense 1) ▷ *vb* **-hos, -hoing, -hoed** *or* **-ho'd 4** (*intr*) to make the cry of tally-ho [c18: perhaps from French *taïaut* cry used in hunting]

tallyman (ˈtælɪmən) *n*, *pl* **-men 1** a scorekeeper or recorder **2** *dialect* a travelling salesman for a firm specializing in hire-purchase ▷ ˈtallyˌwoman *fem n*

Talmud (ˈtælmʊd) *n Judaism* the primary source of Jewish religious law, consisting of the Mishnah and the Gemara [c16: from Hebrew *talmūdh*, literally: instruction, from *lāmadh* to learn] ▷ Talˈmudic *or* Talˈmudical *adj* ▷ ˈTalmudism *n* ▷ ˈTalmudist *n*

talon (ˈtælən) *n* **1** a sharply hooked claw, esp of a bird of prey **2** anything resembling a bird's claw **3** the part of a lock that the key presses on when it is turned **4** *cards* the pile of cards left after the deal **5** *architect* another name for **ogee 6** *stock exchange* a printed slip attached to some bearer bonds to enable the holder to apply for a new sheet of coupons [c14: from Old French: heel, from Latin *tālus* heel] ▷ ˈtaloned *adj*

Talos (ˈteɪlɒs) *n Greek myth* the nephew and apprentice of Daedalus, who surpassed his uncle as an inventor and was killed by him out of jealousy

talus¹ (ˈteɪləs) *n*, *pl* **-li** (-laɪ) the bone of the ankle that articulates with the leg bones to form the ankle joint [c18: from Latin: ankle]

talus² (ˈteɪləs) *n*, *pl* **-luses 1** *geology* another name for **scree 2** *fortifications* the sloping side of a wall [c17: from French, from Latin *talūtium* slope, perhaps of Iberian origin]

tam (tæm) *n* short for **tam-o'-shanter**

tamale (təˈmɑːlɪ) *n* a Mexican dish of minced meat mixed with crushed maize and seasonings, wrapped in maize husks and steamed [c19: erroneously for *tamal*, from Mexican Spanish, from Nahuatl *tamalli*]

tamandua (ˌtæmənˈduːə) *or* **tamandu** (ˈtæmənˌduː) *n* a small arboreal edentate mammal, *Tamandua tetradactyla*, of Central and South America, having a prehensile tail and tubular mouth specialized for feeding on termites: family *Myrmecophagidae*. Also called: **lesser anteater** [c17: via Portuguese from Tupi: ant trapper, from *taixi* ant + *mondê* to catch]

tamarack (ˈtæməˌræk) *n* **1** any of several North American larches, esp *Larix laricina*, which has reddish-brown bark, bluish-green needle-like leaves, and shiny oval cones **2** the wood of any of these trees [c19: from Algonquian]

tamari (təˈmɑːrɪ) *n* a Japanese variety of soy sauce [Japanese]

tamarillo (ˌtæməˈrɪləʊ) *n*, *pl* **-los** another name for **tree tomato**

tamarin (ˈtæmərɪn) *n* any of numerous small monkeys of the genera *Saguinus* (or *Leontocebus*) and *Leontideus*, of South and Central American forests; similar to the marmosets: family *Callithricidae* [c18: via French from Galibi]

tamarind (ˈtæmərɪnd) *n* **1** a leguminous tropical evergreen tree, *Tamarindus indica*, having pale yellow red-streaked flowers and brown pulpy pods, each surrounded by a brittle shell **2** the acid fruit of this tree, used as a food and to make beverages and medicines **3** the wood of this tree [c16: from Medieval Latin *tamarindus*, ultimately from Arabic *tamr hindī* Indian date, from *tamr* date + *hindī* Indian, from *Hind* India]

tamarisk (ˈtæmərɪsk) *n* any of various ornamental trees and shrubs of the genus *Tamarix*, of the Mediterranean region and S and SE Asia, having scalelike leaves, slender branches, and feathery clusters of pink or whitish flowers: family *Tamaricaceae* [c15: from Late Latin *tamariscus*, from Latin *tamarix*]

Tamatave (*French* tamatav) *n* the former name (until

1979) of **Toamasina**

Tamaulipas (*Spanish* tamauˈlipas) *n* a state of NE Mexico, on the Gulf of Mexico. Capital: Ciudad Victoria. Pop: 2 747 114 (2000). Area: 79 829 sq km (30 822 sq miles)

Tambo (ˈtæmbəʊ) *n* **Oliver.** 1917–93, South African politician; president (1977–91) of the African National Congress. He was arrested (1956) with Nelson Mandela but released (1957)

Tambora (ˈtæmbəˌrɑː) *n* a volcano in Indonesia, on N Sumbawa: violent eruption of 1815 reduced its height from about 4000 m (13 000 ft) to 2850 m (9400 ft)

tambour (ˈtæmbʊə) *n* **1** *real tennis* the sloping buttress on one side of the receiver's end of the court **2** a small round embroidery frame, consisting of two concentric hoops over which the fabric is stretched while being worked **3** embroidered work done on such a frame **4** a sliding door on desks, cabinets, etc, made of thin strips of wood glued side by side onto a canvas backing **5** *architect* a wall that is circular in plan, esp one that supports a dome or one that is surrounded by a colonnade **6** a drum ▷ *vb* **7** to embroider (fabric or a design) on a tambour [c15: from French, from *tabour* TABOR]

tamboura (tæmˈbʊərə) *n* an instrument with a long neck, four strings, and no frets, used in Indian music to provide a drone [from Persian *tanbūr*, from Arabic *tunbūr*]

tambourin (ˈtæmbʊrɪn) *n* **1** an 18th-century Provençal folk dance **2** a piece of music composed for or in the rhythm of this dance **3** a small drum [c18: from French: a little drum, from TAMBOUR]

tambourine (ˌtæmbəˈriːn) *n music* a percussion instrument consisting of a single drumhead of skin stretched over a circular wooden frame hung with pairs of metal discs that jingle when it is struck or shaken [c16: from Middle Flemish *tamborijn* a little drum, from Old French: TAMBOURIN] ▷ ˌtambouˈrinist *n*

Tambov (*Russian* tamˈbɔf) *n* an industrial city in W Russia: founded in 1636 as a Muscovite fort; a major engineering centre. Pop: 293 000 (2005 est)

Tamburlaine (ˈtæmbəˌleɪn) *n* same as **Tamerlane**

tame (teɪm) *adj* **1** changed by man from a naturally wild state into a tractable, domesticated, or cultivated condition **2** (of animals) not fearful of human contact **3** lacking in spirit or initiative; meek or submissive **4** flat, insipid, or uninspiring ▷ *vb* **5** to make tame; domesticate **6** to break the spirit of, subdue, or curb **7** to tone down, soften, or mitigate [Old English *tam*; related to Old Norse *tamr*, Old High German *zam*] ▷ ˈtamable *or* ˈtameable *adj* ▷ ˈtamely *adv* ▷ ˈtameness *n* ▷ ˈtamer *n*

Tamerlane (ˈtæməˌleɪn) *or* **Tamburlaine** *n* Turkic name *Timur* (tiːˈmʊə). ?1336–1405, Mongol conqueror of the area from Mongolia to the Mediterranean; ruler of Samarkand (1369–1405). He defeated the Turks at Angora (1402) and died while invading China

Tameside (ˈteɪmˌsaɪd) *n* a unitary authority of NW England, in Greater Manchester. Pop: 213 400 (2003 est). Area: 103 sq km (40 sq miles)

Tamiflu (ˈtæmɪˌfluː) *n trademark* an oral antiviral drug that attacks the influenza virus and prevents it spreading inside the body [C19]

Tamil (ˈtæmɪl) *n* **1** *pl* **-ils** *or* **-il** a member of a mixed Dravidian and Caucasoid people of S India and Sri Lanka **2** the language of this people: the state language of Tamil Nadu, also spoken in Sri Lanka and elsewhere, belonging to the Dravidian family of languages ▷ *adj* **3** of or relating to this people or their language

Tamil Nadu (ˈtæmɪl nɑːˈduː) *n* a state of SE India, on the Coromandel Coast: reorganized in 1956 and 1960 and made smaller; consists of a coastal plain backed by hills, including the Nilgiri Hills in the west Capital: Chennai (formerly called Madras). Pop: 62 110 839 (2001). Area: 130 058 sq km (50 216 sq miles). Former name (until 1968): **Madras**

Tammerfors (tamərˈfɔrs) *n* the Swedish name for **Tampere**

tammy (ˈtæmɪ) *n*, *pl* **-mies** another word for **tam-o'-shanter**

tam-o'-shanter (ˌtæməˈʃæntə) *n* a Scottish brimless wool cap with a bobble in the centre, usually worn pulled down at one side [C19: named after the hero of Burns' poem *Tam o' Shanter* (1790)]

tamoxifen (tə'mɒksɪfɛn) *n* a drug that antagonizes the action of oestrogen and is used to treat breast cancer and some types of infertility in women [C20: altered from T(RANS-) + AM(INE) + OXY-² + PHEN(OL)]

tamp (tæmp) *vb* (*tr*) **1** to force or pack down firmly by repeated blows **2** to pack sand, earth, etc into (a drill hole) over an explosive [C17: probably a back formation from *tampin* (obsolete variant of TAMPION), which was taken as being a present participle *tamping*]

Tampa ('tæmpə) *n* a port and resort in W Florida, on **Tampa Bay** (an arm of the Gulf of Mexico): two universities. Pop: 317 647 (2003 est)

tamper¹ ('tæmpə) *vb* (*intr*) **1** (usually foll by *with*) to interfere or meddle **2** to use corrupt practices such as bribery or blackmail **3** (usually foll by *with*) to attempt to influence or corrupt, esp by bribery [C16: alteration of TEMPER (verb)] > 'tamperer *n*

tamper² ('tæmpə) *n* **1** a person or thing that tamps, esp an instrument for packing down tobacco in a pipe **2** a casing around the core of a nuclear weapon to increase its efficiency by reflecting neutrons and delaying the expansion

Tampere (Finnish 'tamperɛ) *n* a city in SW Finland: the second largest town in Finland; textile manufacturing. Pop: 200 966 (2003 est). Swedish name: Tammerfors

Tampico (Spanish tam'piko) *n* a port and resort in E Mexico, in Tamaulipas on the Pánuco River: oil refining. Pop: 702 000 (2005 est)

tampion ('tæmpɪən) *or* **tompion** *n* a plug placed in a gun's muzzle when the gun is not in use to keep out moisture and dust [C15: from French: TAMPON]

tampon ('tæmpɒn) *n* **1** a plug of lint, cotton wool, cotton, etc, inserted into an open wound or body cavity to stop the flow of blood, absorb secretions, etc, esp one inserted into the vagina to absorb menstrual blood ▷ *vb* **2** (*tr*) to plug (a wound, etc) with a tampon [C19: via French from Old French *tapon* a little plug, from *tape* a plug, of Germanic origin] > 'tamponage *n*

tam-tam *n* another name for **gong** (sense 1) [from Hindi: see TOM-TOM]

Tamworth ('tæmwəθ) *n* **1** a market town in W central England, in SE Staffordshire. Pop: 71 650 (2001) **2** a city in SE Australia, in E central New South Wales: industrial centre of an agricultural region. Pop: 32 543 (2001)

tan¹ (tæn) *n* **1** the brown colour produced by the skin after intensive exposure to ultraviolet rays, esp those of the sun **2** a light or moderate yellowish-brown colour **3** short for **tanbark** ▷ *vb* tans, tanning, tanned **4** to go brown or cause to go brown after exposure to ultraviolet rays **5** to convert (a skin or hide) into leather by treating it with a tanning agent, such as vegetable tannins, chromium salts, fish oils, or formaldehyde **6** (*tr*) *slang* to beat or flog ▷ *adj* tanner, tannest **7** of the colour tan [Old English *tannian* (unattested as infinitive, attested as *getanned*, past participle), from Medieval Latin *tannāre*, from *tannum* tanbark, perhaps of Celtic origin; compare Irish *tana* thin] > 'tannable *adj* > 'tannish *adj*

tan² (tæn) *abbreviation* tangent (sense 2)

Tana ('tɑːnə) *n* **1** Lake Tana *Also called*: Lake Tsana a lake in NW Ethiopia, on a plateau 1800 m (6000 ft) high: the largest lake of Ethiopia; source of the Blue Nile. Area: 3673 sq km (1418 sq miles) **2** a river in E Kenya, rising in the Aberdare Range and flowing in a wide curve east to the Indian Ocean: the longest river in Kenya. Length: 708 km (440 miles) **3** a river in NE Norway, flowing generally northeast as part of the border between Norway and Finland to the Arctic Ocean by Tana Fjord. Length: about 320 km (200 miles). Finnish name: Teno

tanager ('tænədʒə) *n* any American songbird of the family *Thraupidae*, having a short thick bill and a brilliantly coloured male plumage [C19: from New Latin *tanagra*, based on Tupi *tangara*]

Tanagra ('tænəgrə) *n* a town in ancient Boeotia, famous for terracotta figurines of the same name, first discovered in its necropolis

Tanana ('tænənɑː) *n* a river in central Alaska, rising in the Wrangell Mountains and flowing northwest to the Yukon River. Length: about 765 km (475 miles)

Tananarive (French tananariv) *n* the former name of **Antananarivo**

tanbark ('tæn,bɑːk) *n* the bark of certain trees, esp the oak and hemlock, used as a source of tannin

Tancred ('tæŋkrɪd) *n* died 1112, Norman hero of the First Crusade, who played a prominent part in the capture of Jerusalem (1099)

tandem ('tændəm) *n* **1** a bicycle with two sets of pedals and two saddles, arranged one behind the other for two riders **2** a two-wheeled carriage drawn by two horses harnessed one behind the other **3** a team of two horses so harnessed **4** any arrangement of two things in which one is placed behind the other **5 in tandem** together or in conjunction ▷ *adj* **6** *Brit* used as, used in, or routed through an intermediate automatic telephone exchange ▷ *adv* **7** one behind the other [C18: whimsical use of Latin *tandem* at length, to indicate a vehicle of elongated appearance]

Tandjungpriok (,tændʒʊŋ'priːɒk) *n* the former spelling of **Tanjungpriok**

tandoori (tæn'dʊərɪ) *n* an Indian method of cooking meat or vegetables on a spit in a clay oven [from Urdu, from *tandoor* an oven]

tang (tæŋ) *n* **1** a strong taste or flavour **2** a pungent or characteristic smell **3** a trace, touch, or hint of something **4** the pointed end of a tool, such as a chisel, file, knife, etc, which is fitted into a handle, shaft, or stock [C14: from Old Norse *tangi* point; related to Danish *tange* point, spit]

Tang (tæŋ) *n* the imperial dynasty of China from 618–907 AD

tanga ('tæŋgə) *n* **1** a triangular loincloth worn by indigenous peoples in tropical America **2** a type of very brief bikini [from Portuguese, ultimately of Banth origin]

Tanga ('tæŋgə) *n* a port in N Tanzania, on the Indian Ocean: Tanzania's second port. Pop: 190 000 (2005 est)

Tanganyika (,tæŋgə'njiːkə) *n* **1** a former state in E Africa: became part of German East Africa in 1884; ceded to Britain as a League of Nations mandate in 1919 and as a UN trust territory in 1946; gained independence in 1961 and united with Zanzibar in 1964 as the United Republic of Tanzania **2 Lake Tanganyika** a lake in central Africa between Tanzania and the Democratic Republic of Congo (formerly Zaïre), bordering also on Burundi and Zambia, in the Great Rift Valley: the longest freshwater lake in the world. Area: 32 893 sq km (12 700 sq miles). Length: 676 km (420 miles) > ,Tanga'nyikan *adj, n*

tangata tiriti ('tɑːŋgɑːtə 'tiːriːti) *n* NZ a Māori term for non-Māori people [Māori, literally: people of the Treaty (of Waitangi)]

tangata whenua ('tɑːŋgɑːtə 'fɛnuːə) *n* NZ the indigenous Māori people of a particular area of New Zealand or of the country as a whole [Māori, literally: people of the land]

Tange ('tæŋgə) *n* Kenzo. 1913–2005, Japanese architect. His buildings include the Kurashiki city hall (1960) and St Mary's Cathedral in Tokyo (1962–64)

tangent ('tændʒənt) *n* **1** a geometric line, curve, plane, or curved surface that touches another curve or surface at one point but does not intersect it **2** (of an angle) a trigonometric function that in a right-angled triangle is the ratio of the length of the opposite side to that of the adjacent side; the ratio of sine to cosine. Abbreviation: tan **3** *music* a part of the action of a clavichord consisting of a small piece of metal that strikes the string to produce a note **4 on a tangent** or **at a tangent** on a completely different or divergent course, esp of thought ▷ *adj* **5 a** of or involving a tangent **b** touching at a single point **6** touching [C16: from Latin phrase *līnea tangēns* the touching line, from *tangere* to touch] > 'tangency *n*

tangent galvanometer *n* a type of galvanometer having a vertical coil of wire with a horizontal magnetic needle at its centre. The current to be measured is passed through the coil and produces a proportional magnetic field which deflects the needle

tangential (tæn'dʒɛnʃəl) *adj* 1 of, being, relating to, or in the direction of a tangent 2 Also called: transverse *astronomy* (of velocity) in a direction perpendicular to the line of sight of a celestial object 3 of superficial relevance only; digressive > tan,genti'ality *n* > tan'gentially *or* tan'gentally *adv*

tangerine (,tændʒə'ri:n) *n* 1 an Asian citrus tree, *Citrus reticulata*, cultivated for its small edible orange-like fruits 2 the fruit of this tree, having a loose rind and sweet spicy flesh 3 a a reddish-orange colour b (*as adjective*): a *tangerine door* [C19: from TANGIER]

tangi ('tʌŋi:) *n*, *pl* -gis NZ 1 a Māori funeral ceremony 2 *informal* a lamentation [Māori]

tangible ('tændʒəbªl) *adj* 1 capable of being touched or felt; having real substance 2 capable of being clearly grasped by the mind; substantial rather than imaginary 3 having a physical existence; corporeal [C16: from Late Latin *tangibilis*, from Latin *tangere* to touch] > ,tangi'bility *or* 'tangibleness *n* > 'tangibly *adv*

Tangier (tæn'dʒɪə) *n* a port in N Morocco, on the Strait of Gibraltar: a Phoenician trading post in the 15th century BC; a neutral international zone (1923–56); made the summer capital of Morocco and a free port in 1962; commercial and financial centre. Pop: 526 000 (2003) > ,Tange'rine *n*, *adj*

tangle ('tæŋgªl) *n* 1 a confused or complicated mass of hairs, lines, fibres, etc, knotted or coiled together 2 a complicated problem, condition, or situation ▷ *vb* 3 to become or cause to become twisted together in a confused mass 4 (*intr*; often foll by *with*) to come into conflict; contend 5 (*tr*) to involve in matters which hinder or confuse 6 (*tr*) to ensnare or trap, as in a net [C14 *tangilen*, variant of *tagilen*, probably of Scandinavian origin; related to Swedish dialect *taggla* to entangle] > 'tangly *adj*

tango ('tæŋgəʊ) *n*, *pl* -gos 1 a Latin American dance in duple time, characterized by long gliding steps and sudden pauses 2 a piece of music composed for or in the rhythm of this dance ▷ *vb* -goes, -going, -goed 3 (*intr*) to perform this dance [C20: from American Spanish, probably of Niger-Congo origin; compare Ibibio *tamgu* to dance]

tangram ('tæŋgræm) *n* a Chinese puzzle in which a square, cut into a parallelogram, a square, and five triangles, is formed into figures [C19: perhaps from Chinese *t'ang* Chinese + -GRAM]

Tangshan ('tæŋ'ʃæn) *n* an industrial city in NE China, in Hebei province: the 1976 earthquake, which killed an estimated 255 000 people, was the most lethal of the 20th century. Pop: 1 773 000 (2005 est)

Tanguy (*French* tãgi) *n* **Yves** (iv). 1900–55, US surrealist painter, born in France

tangy ('tæŋi) *adj* tangier, tangiest having a pungent, fresh, or briny flavour or aroma

tanh (θæn, tænʃ) *n* hyperbolic tangent; a hyperbolic function that is the ratio of sinh to cosh [C20: from TAN(GENT) + H(YPERBOLIC)]

Tanis ('teɪnɪs) *n* an ancient city located in the E part of the Nile delta: abandoned after the 6th century BC; at one time the capital of Egypt. Biblical name: Zoan

taniwha ('tʌni:fɑ:, 'tænəwɑ:) *n* NZ a legendary Māori monster [Māori]

Tanizaki Jun-ichiro (,tɑ:ni:'zɑ:ki: ,dʒu:ni:'tʃi:rɔ:) *n* 1886–1965, Japanese novelist, whose works, such as *Some Prefer Nettles* (1929) and *The Makioka Sisters* (1943–48), reflect the tension between Western values and Japanese traditions

Tanjore (tæn'dʒɔ:) *n* the former name of **Thanjavur**

Tanjungkarang (,tændʒʊŋkæ'ræŋ) *n* a city in in Indonesia, in S Sumatra on the Sunda Strait; merged with Telukbetung to form the city of Bandar Lampung

Tanjungpriok (,tændʒʊŋ'pri:ɒk) *n* a port in Indonesia, on the NW coast of Java adjoining the capital, Jakarta: a major shipping and distributing centre for the whole archipelago. Former spelling: Tandjungpriok

tank (tæŋk) *n* 1 a large container or reservoir for the storage of liquids or gases 2 an armoured combat vehicle moving on tracks and armed with guns, etc,

originally developed in World War I 3 *Brit & US dialect* a reservoir, lake, or pond 4 *slang, chiefly US* a jail 5 Also called: tankful the quantity contained in a tank 6 *Austral* a dam formed by excavation ▷ *vb* 7 (*tr*) to put or keep in a tank 8 *slang* to defeat heavily ▷ See also **tank up** [C17: from Gujarati *tānkh* artificial lake, but influenced also by Portuguese *tanque*, from *estanque* pond, from *estancar* to dam up, from Vulgar Latin *stanticāre* (unattested) to block, STANCH]

tanka ('tɑ:ŋkə) *n*, *pl* -kas *or* -ka a Japanese verse form consisting of five lines, the first and third having five syllables, the others seven [C19: from Japanese, from *tan* short + *ka* verse]

tankage ('tæŋkɪdʒ) *n* 1 the capacity or contents of a tank or tanks 2 the act of storing in a tank or tanks, or a fee charged for such storage 3 *agriculture* a fertilizer consisting of the dried and ground residues of animal carcasses b a protein supplement feed for livestock

tankard ('tæŋkəd) *n* a large one-handled drinking vessel, commonly made of silver, pewter, or glass, sometimes fitted with a hinged lid [C14: related to Middle Dutch *tankaert*, French *tanquart*]

tank engine *or* **tank locomotive** *n* a steam locomotive that carries its water supply in tanks mounted around its boiler

tanker ('tæŋkə) *n* a ship, lorry, or aeroplane designed to carry liquid in bulk, such as oil

tank farming *n* another name for **hydroponics** > tank farmer *n*

tank top *n* a sleeveless upper garment with wide shoulder straps and a low neck, usually worn over a shirt, blouse, or jumper [C20: named after *tank suits*, one-piece bathing costumes of the 1920s worn in tanks or swimming pools]

tank up *vb* (*adverb*) *chiefly Brit* 1 to fill the tank of (a vehicle) with petrol 2 *slang* to imbibe or cause to imbibe a large quantity of alcoholic drink

tank wagon *or esp US and Canadian* **tank car** *n* a form of railway wagon carrying a tank for the transport of liquids

Tannenberg (*German* 'tanənberk) *n* a village in N Poland, formerly in East Prussia: site of a decisive defeat of the Teutonic Knights by the Poles in 1410 and of a decisive German victory over the Russians in 1914. Polish name: Stębark

tanner¹ ('tænə) *n* a person who tans skins and hides

tanner² ('tænə) *n* *Brit* (formerly) an informal word for: **sixpence** [C19: of unknown origin]

tannery ('tænərɪ) *n*, *pl* -neries a place or building where skins and hides are tanned

Tannhäuser ('tæn,hɔɪzə) *n* 13th-century German minnesinger, commonly identified with a legendary knight who sought papal absolution after years spent in revelry with Venus. The legend forms the basis of an opera by Wagner

tannic ('tænɪk) *adj* of, relating to, containing, or produced from tan or tannin

tannie ('tʌnɪ) *n* *South African* a title of respect used to refer to an elderly woman [Afrikaans; literally: aunt]

tannin ('tænɪn) *n* any of a class of yellowish or brownish solid compounds found in many plants and used as tanning agents, mordants, medical astringents, etc Tannins are derivatives of gallic acid with the approximate formula $C_{76}H_{52}O_{46}$. Also called: tannic acid [C19: from French *tanin*, from TAN¹]

Tannoy ('tænɔɪ) *n* *trademark* a sound-amplifying apparatus used as a public-address system esp in a large building, such as a university

Tans (tænz) *pl n* the Tans *Irish informal* short for **Black and Tans**

tansy ('tænzɪ) *n*, *pl* -sies any of numerous plants of the genus *Tanacetum*, esp *T. vulgare*, having yellow flowers in flat-topped clusters and formerly used in medicine and for seasoning; family *Asteraceae* (composites) [C15: from Old French *tanesie*, from Medieval Latin *athanasia* tansy (with reference to its alleged power to prolong life), from Greek: immortality]

Tanta ('tæntə) *n* a city in N Egypt, on the Nile delta: noted for its Muslim festivals. Pop: 413 000 (2005 est)

tantalite ('tæntə,laɪt) n a heavy brownish mineral consisting of a tantalum oxide of iron and manganese in orthorhombic crystalline form: it occurs in coarse granite, often with columbite, and is an ore of tantalum. Formula: $(Fe,Mn)(Ta,N6)_2O_6$ [c19: from TANTALUM + -ITE[1]]

tantalize or **tantalise** ('tæntə,laɪz) vb (tr) to tease or make frustrated, as by tormenting with the sight of something greatly desired but inaccessible [c16: from the punishment of TANTALUS] > ,tantali'zation or ,tantali'sation n > 'tanta,lizing or 'tanta,lising adj > 'tanta,lizingly or 'tanta,lisingly adv

tantalum ('tæntələm) n a hard greyish-white metallic element that occurs with niobium in tantalite and columbite: used in electrical capacitors in most circuit boards and in alloys to increase hardness and chemical resistance, esp in surgical instruments. Symbol: Ta; atomic no: 73; atomic wt: 180.9479; valency: 2, 3, 4, or 5; relative density: 16.654; melting pt: 3020°C; boiling pt: 5458±100°C [c19: named after TANTALUS, with reference to the metal's incapacity to absorb acids]

tantalus ('tæntələs) n Brit a case in which bottles may be locked with their contents tantalizingly visible

Tantalus ('tæntələs) n Greek myth a king, the father of Pelops, punished in Hades for his misdeeds by having to stand in water that recedes when he tries to drink it and under fruit that moves away as he reaches for it

tantamount ('tæntə,maʊnt) adj (postpositive; foll by to) as good (as); equivalent in effect (to) [c17: basically from Anglo-French tant amunter to amount to as much, from tant so much + amunter to AMOUNT]

tantara ('tæntərə, tæn'tɑːrə) n a blast, as on a trumpet or horn [c16: from Latin taratantara, imitative of the sound of the tuba]

tantivy (tæn'tɪvɪ) adv 1 at full speed; rapidly > n 2 pl -tivies a hunting cry, esp at full gallop [c17: perhaps imitative of galloping hooves]

tant mieux French (tã mjø) so much the better

tanto ('tæntəʊ; Italian 'tanto) adv too much [c19: from Italian, from Latin tantum so much]

tant pis French (tã pi) so much the worse

Tantrism ('tæntrɪzəm) n 1 a movement within Hinduism combining magical and mystical elements and with sacred writings of its own 2 a similar movement within Buddhism [c18: from Sanskrit tantra, literally: warp, hence, doctrine] > 'Tantrist n > 'Tantric adj

tantrum ('tæntrəm) n (often plural) a childish fit of rage; outburst of bad temper [c18: of unknown origin]

Tan-tung ('tæn'tʊŋ) n the former spelling of **Dandong**

Tanzania (,tænzə'nɪə) n a republic in E Africa, on the Indian Ocean: formed by the union of the independent states of Tanganyika and Zanzibar in 1964; a member of the Commonwealth. Exports include coffee, tea, sisal, and cotton. Official languages: Swahili and English. Religions: Christian, Muslim, and animist. Currency: Tanzanian shilling. Capital: officially Dodoma (though some functions remain in Dar es Salaam). Pop: 37 671 000 (2004 est). Area: 945 203 sq km (364 943 sq miles) > ,Tanza'nian adj, n

Tao (taʊ) n (in the philosophy of Taoism) 1 that in virtue of which all things happen or exist 2 the rational basis of human conduct 3 the course of life and its relation to eternal truth [Chinese, literally: path, way]

Taoiseach ('tiːʃæx) n the prime minister of the Republic of Ireland [from Irish Gaelic, literally: leader]

Taoism ('taʊɪzəm) n the philosophy of Lao Zi, the Chinese philosopher (?604–?531 BC), that advocates a simple honest life and noninterference with the course of natural events > 'Taoist n, adj > Tao'istic adj

taonga (tɑ'ɒŋgə) n NZ treasure; anything highly prized [Māori]

tap¹ (tæp) vb taps, tapping, tapped 1 to strike (something) lightly and usually repeatedly 2 (tr) to produce by striking in this way: to tap a rhythm 3 (tr) to strike lightly with (something): to tap one's finger on the desk 4 (intr) to walk with a tapping sound 5 (tr) to attach metal or leather reinforcing pieces to (the toe or heel of a shoe) > n 6 a light blow or knock, or the sound made

by it 7 the metal piece attached to the toe or heel of a shoe used for tap-dancing ▷ See also **taps** [c13 tappen, probably from Old French taper, of Germanic origin; related to Middle Low German tappen to pluck, Swedish dialect täpa to tap]

tap² (tæp) n 1 a valve by which a fluid flow from a pipe can be controlled by opening and closing an orifice. US and Canadian name: **faucet** 2 a stopper to plug a cask or barrel and enable the contents to be drawn out in a controlled flow 3 a particular quality of alcoholic drink, esp when contained in casks: an excellent tap 4 Brit short for **taproom** 5 the surgical withdrawal of fluid from a bodily cavity 6 Also called: **screw tap** a tool for cutting female screw threads, consisting of a threaded steel cylinder with longitudinal grooves forming cutting edges 7 electronics chiefly US & Canadian a connection made at some point between the end terminals of an inductor, resistor, or some other component. Usual Brit name: **tapping** 8 stock exchange a an issue of a government security released slowly onto the market when its market price reaches a predetermined level b (as modifier): tap stock; tap issue 9 a concealed listening or recording device connected to a telephone or telegraph wire for the purpose of obtaining information secretly 10 on tap a informal ready for immediate use b (of drinks) on draught ▷ vb taps, tapping, tapped (tr) 11 to furnish with a tap 12 to draw off with or as if with a tap 13 to cut into (a tree) and draw off sap from it 14 Brit informal to ask or beg (someone) for money: he tapped me for a fiver 15 to connect a tap to (a telephone or telegraph wire) 16 to make a connection to (a pipe, drain, etc) 17 to cut a female screw thread in (an object or material) by use of a tap 18 informal (of a sports team or an employer) to make an illicit attempt to recruit (a player or employee bound by an existing contract) [Old English tæppa; related to Old Norse tappi tap, Old High German zapfo] > 'tapper n

tapa ('tɑːpə) n 1 the inner bark of the paper mulberry 2 a paper-like cloth made from this in the Pacific islands [c19: from Marquesan and Tahitian]

Tapajós (Portuguese tapa'ʒɔs) n a river in N Brazil, rising in N central Mato Grosso and flowing northeast to the Amazon. Length: about 800 km (500 miles)

tapas ('tæpəs) pl n a light snacks or appetizers, usually eaten with drinks b (as modifier): a tapas bar [from Spanish tapa cover, lid]

tap dance n 1 a step dance in which the performer wears shoes equipped with taps that make a rhythmic sound on the stage as he dances ▷ vb **tap-dance** (intr) 2 to perform a tap dance > 'tap-,dancer n > 'tap-,dancing n

tape (teɪp) n 1 a long thin strip, made of cotton, linen, etc, used for binding, fastening, etc 2 any long narrow strip of cellulose, paper, metal, etc, having similar uses 3 a string stretched across the track at the end of a race course 4 See **magnetic tape, ticker tape, paper tape, tape recording** ▷ vb (mainly tr) 5 Also called: **tape-record** (also intr) to record (speech, music, etc) 6 to furnish with tapes 7 to bind, measure, secure, or wrap with tape 8 (usually passive) Brit informal to take stock of (a person or situation); sum up [Old English tæppe; related to Old Frisian tapia to pull, Middle Dutch tapen to tear] > 'tape,like adj > 'taper n

tape deck n 1 a tape recording unit in a hi-fi system 2 the platform supporting the spools, cassettes, or cartridges of a tape recorder, incorporating the motor or motors that drive them and the playback, recording, and erasing heads

tape drive n computing a device for reading from or writing to magnetic tape

tape machine n 1 another word for **tape recorder** 2 a telegraphic receiving device that records messages electronically or on ticker tape. US equivalent: **ticker**

tape measure n a tape or length of metal marked off in inches, centimetres, etc, used principally for measuring and fitting garments

tapenade ('tæpənɑːd) n a savoury paste made from capers, olives, and anchovies, with olive oil and lemon juice [c20: French, from Provençal tapéo capers]

t

taper ('teɪpə) *vb* **1** to become or cause to become narrower towards one end **2** (often foll by *off*) to become or cause to become smaller or less significant ▷ *n* **3** a thin candle **4** a thin wooden or waxed strip for transferring a flame; spill **5** a narrowing **6** any feeble source of light [Old English *tapor*, probably from Latin *papῡrus* PAPYRUS (from its use as a wick)] > 'taperer *n* > 'tapering *adj*

tape recorder *n* an electrical device used for recording sounds on magnetic tape and usually also for reproducing them, consisting of a tape deck and one or more amplifiers and loudspeakers

tape recording *n* **1** the act or process of recording on magnetic tape **2** the speech, music, etc, so recorded

taper relief *n* (in Britain) a system of relief from capital gains tax under which the percentage of a chargeable gain considered taxable is reduced for each whole year (from April 1998) that the asset was held by the vendor

tape streamer *n computing* an electromechanical device that enables data to be copied byte by byte from a hard disk onto magnetic tape for security or storage

tapestry ('tæpɪstrɪ) *n, pl* -tries **1** a heavy ornamental fabric, often in the form of a picture, used for wall hangings, furnishings, etc, and made by weaving coloured threads into a fixed warp **2** another word for **needlepoint 3** a colourful and complicated situation: *the rich tapestry of London life* [c15: from Old French *tapisserie* carpeting, from Old French *tapiz* carpet; see TAPIS] > 'tapestried *adj*

tapeworm ('teɪp,wɜːm) *n* any parasitic ribbon-like flatworm of the class *Cestoda*, having a body divided into many egg-producing segments and lacking a mouth and gut. The adults inhabit the intestines of vertebrates

taphole ('tæp,həʊl) *n* a hole in a furnace for running off molten metal or slag

taphouse ('tæp,haʊs) *n now rare* an inn or bar

tapioca (,tæpɪ'əʊkə) *n* a beadlike starch obtained from cassava root, used in cooking as a thickening agent, esp in puddings [c18: via Portuguese from Tupi *tipioca* pressed-out juice, from *tipi* residue + *ok* to squeeze out]

tapir ('teɪpə) *n, pl* -pirs *or* -pir any perissodactyl mammal of the genus *Tapirus*, such as *T. indicus* (**Malayan tapir**), of South and Central America and SE Asia, having an elongated snout, three-toed hind legs, and four-toed forelegs: family *Tapiridae* [c18: from Tupi *tapiira*]

tapis ('tæpiː, 'tæpɪ; *French* tapi) *n, pl* tapis tapestry or carpeting, esp as formerly used to cover a table in a council chamber [c17: from French, from Old French *tapiz*, from Greek *tapētion* rug, from *tapēs* carpet]

tappet ('tæpɪt) *n* a mechanical part that reciprocates to receive or transmit intermittent motion, esp the part of an internal-combustion engine that transmits motion from the camshaft to the push rods or valves [c18: from TAP[1] + -ET]

tapping up *n* Brit informal (esp of a professional soccer club) the illicit practice of attempting to recruit a player while he is still bound by contract to another team

taproom ('tæp,ruːm, -,rʊm) *n* a bar, as in a hotel or pub

taproot ('tæp,ruːt) *n* the large single root of plants such as the dandelion, which grows vertically downwards and bears smaller lateral roots [c17: from TAP[2] + ROOT[1]]

taps (tæps) *n* (functioning as singular) **1** chiefly US **a** (in army camps, etc) a signal given on a bugle, drum, etc, indicating that lights are to be put out **b** any similar signal, as at a military funeral **2** (in the Guide movement) a closing song sung at an evening camp fire or at the end of a meeting [c19: from TAP[1]]

tapster ('tæpstə) *n* **1** rare a barman **2** (in W Africa) a man who taps palm trees to collect and sell palm wine [Old English *tæppestre*, feminine of *tæppere*, from *tappian* to TAP[2]]

tap water *n* water drawn off through taps from pipes in a house, as distinguished from distilled water, mineral water, etc

tar[1] (tɑː) *n* **1** any of various dark viscid substances obtained by the destructive distillation of organic matter such as coal, wood, or peat **2** another name for **coal tar** ▷ *vb* tars, tarring, tarred (tr) **3** to coat with tar **4** tar and feather to punish by smearing tar and

feathers over (someone) **5** tarred with the same brush regarded as having the same faults [Old English *teoru*; related to Old Frisian *tera*, Old Norse *tjara*, Middle Low German *tere* tar, Gothic *triu* tree] > 'tarry *adj* > 'tarriness *n*

tar[2] (tɑː) *n* an informal word for **seaman** [c17: short for TARPAULIN]

Tara ('tæərə, 'tɑːrə) *n* a village in Co Meath near Dublin, by the **Hill of Tara**, the historic seat of the ancient Irish kings

Tarabulus el Gharb (tə'rɑːbələs ɛl 'gɑːb) *n* transliteration of the Arabic name for **Tripoli** (sense 1)

Tarabulus esh Sham (tə'rɑːbələs ɛʃ 'ʃæm) *n* transliteration of the Arabic name for **Tripoli** (sense 2)

taradiddle ('tæərə,dɪdᵊl) *n* another spelling of **tarradiddle**

tarakihi ('tæərə,kiːhiː) *or* **terakihi** *n, pl* -kihis a common edible sea fish of New Zealand waters [Māori]

taramasalata (,tæərəməsə'lɑːtə) *n* a creamy pale pink pâté, made from the roe of grey mullet or smoked cod and served as an hors d'oeuvre [c20: from Modern Greek, from *tarama* cod's roe]

Taranaki (,tæərə'næki:) *n* Mount Taranaki another name for (Mount) **Egmont[1]**

tarantass (,tɑːrən'tæs) *n* a large horse-drawn four-wheeled Russian carriage without springs [c19: from Russian *tarantas*, from Kazan Tatar *taryntas*]

tarantella (,tæərən'tɛlə) *n* **1** a peasant dance from S Italy **2** a piece of music composed for or in the rhythm of this dance, in fast six-eight time [c18: from Italian, from *Taranto* TARANTO; associated with TARANTISM]

Tarantino (,tæərən'tiːnəʊ) *n* Quentin. born 1963, US film director and screenwriter, noted for violent quirky crime dramas including *Reservoir Dogs* (1993), *Pulp Fiction* (1994), *Jackie Brown* (1998), and the two parts of *Kill Bill* (2003, 2004)

tarantism ('tæərən,tɪzəm) *n* a nervous disorder marked by uncontrollable bodily movement, widespread in S Italy during the 15th to 17th centuries: popularly thought to be caused by the bite of a tarantula [c17: from New Latin *tarantismus*, from TARANTO; see TARANTULA]

Taranto (tə'ræntəʊ; *Italian* 'tɑːranto) *n* a port in SE Italy, in Apulia on the **Gulf of Taranto** (an inlet of the Ionian Sea): the chief city of Magna Graecia; taken by the Romans in 272 BC Pop: 202 033 (2001). Latin name: Tarentum

tarantula (tə'ræntjʊlə) *n, pl* -las *or* -lae (-,liː) **1** any of various large hairy mostly tropical spiders of the American family *Theraphosidae* **2** a large hairy spider, *Lycosa tarentula* of S Europe, the bite of which was formerly thought to cause tarantism [c16: from Medieval Latin, from Old Italian *tarantola*, from TARANTO]

Tarawa (tə'rɑːwə) *n* an atoll in Kiribati, occupying a chain of islets surrounding a lagoon in the W central Pacific: the capital of Kiribati, Bairiki, is on this atoll. Pop: 45 989 (2005)

taraxacum (tə'ræksəkəm) *n* **1** any perennial plant of the genus *Taraxacum*, such as the dandelion, having dense heads of small yellow flowers and seeds with a feathery attachment: family *Asteraceae* (composites) **2** the dried root of the dandelion, used as a laxative, diuretic, and tonic [c18: from Medieval Latin, from Arabic *tarakhshaqūn* wild chicory, perhaps of Persian origin]

Tarbes (*French* tarb) *n* a town in SW France: noted for the breeding of Anglo-Arab horses. Pop: 46 275 (1999)

tarboosh, tarbush *or* **tarbouche** (tɑː'buːʃ) *n* a felt or cloth brimless cap resembling the fez, usually red and often with a silk tassel, worn alone or as part of a turban by Muslim men [c18: from Arabic *tarbūsh*]

tar boy *n* Austral & NZ informal a boy who applies tar to the skin of sheep cut during shearing

Tardenoisian (,tɑːdə'nɔɪzɪən) *adj* of or referring to a Mesolithic culture characterized by small flint instruments [c20: after *Tardenois*, France, where implements were found]

tardigrade ('tɑːdɪ,greɪd) *n* any minute aquatic segmented eight-legged invertebrate of the phylum *Tardigrada*, related to the arthropods, occurring in soil, ditches, etc. Popular name: **water bear** [c17: via Latin *tardigradus*, from *tardus* sluggish + *gradī* to walk]

tardy ('tɑːdɪ) *adj* **-dier, -diest 1** occurring later than expected **2** slow in progress, growth, etc [c15: from Old French *tardif*, from Latin *tardus* slow] ▷ '**tardily** *adv* ▷ '**tardiness** *n*

tare¹ (tɛə) *n* **1** any of various vetch plants, such as *Vicia hirsuta* (**hairy tare**) of Eurasia and N Africa **2** the seed of any of these plants **3** *Bible* a troublesome weed, thought to be the darnel [c14: of unknown origin]

tare² (tɛə) *n* **1** the weight of the wrapping or container in which goods are packed **2** a deduction from gross weight to compensate for this **3** the weight of a vehicle without its cargo, passengers, etc ▷ *vb* **4** (*tr*) to weigh (a package, etc) in order to calculate the amount of tare [c15: from Old French: waste, from Medieval Latin *tara*, from Arabic *tarhah* something discarded, from *taraha* to reject]

Tarentum (təˈrɛntəm) *n* the Latin name of **Taranto**

targe (tɑːdʒ) *n* an archaic word for **shield** [c13: from Old French, of Germanic origin; related to Old High German *zarga* rim, frame, Old Norse *targa* shield]

target ('tɑːɡɪt) *n* **1 a** an object or area at which an archer or marksman aims, usually a round flat surface marked with concentric rings **b** (*as modifier*): *target practice* **2** any point or area aimed at; the object of an attack or a takeover bid **b** (*as modifier*): *target area; target company* **3** a fixed goal or objective **4** a person or thing at which an action or remark is directed or the object of a person's feelings **5** a joint of lamb consisting of the breast and neck **6** (formerly) a small round shield **7** *physics, electronics* **a** a substance, object, or system subjected to bombardment by electrons or other particles, or to irradiation **b** an electrode in a television camera tube whose surface, on which image information is stored, is scanned by the electron beam **8** *electronics* an object to be detected by the reflection of a radar or sonar signal, etc ▷ *vb* **-gets, -geting, -geted** (*tr*) **9** to make a target of **10** to direct or aim: *to target benefits at those most in need* [c14: from Old French *targette* a little shield, from Old French TARGE]

targetitis (ˌtɑːɡɪtˈaɪtɪs) *n jocular* the setting of more targets than is strictly necessary for the effective functioning of an organization, esp when it leads to an increase in bureaucracy [c20: TARGET + -ITIS (sense 2)]

Târgu Mureş (Romanian 'tîrgu 'mureʃ) *n* another spelling of **Tîrgu Mureş**

tariff ('tærɪf) *n* **1 a** a tax levied by a government on imports or occasionally exports for purposes of protection, support of the balance of payments, or the raising of revenue **b** a system or list of such taxes **2** any schedule of prices, fees, fares, etc **3** *chiefly Brit* **a** a method of charging for the supply of services, esp public services, such as gas and electricity **b** a schedule of such charges **4** *chiefly Brit* a bill of fare with prices listed; menu ▷ *vb* (*tr*) **5** to set a tariff on **6** to set a price on according to a schedule of tariffs [c16: from Italian *tariffa*, from Arabic *ta'rīfa* to inform]

tariff office *n insurance* a company whose premiums are based on a tariff agreed with other insurance companies

Tarim ('tɑːˈriːm) *n* a river in NW China, in Xinjiang: flows east along the N edge of the Taklimakan Shama desert, dividing repeatedly and forming lakes among the dunes, finally disappearing in the Lop Nor depression; the chief river of Xinjiang; drains the great **Tarim Basin** between the Tian Shan and Kunlun mountain systems of central Asia, an area of about 906 500 sq km (350 000 sq miles). Length: 2190 km (1360 miles)

Tarkington ('tɑːkɪŋtən) *n* (**Newton**) **Booth.** 1869–1946, US novelist. His works include the historical romance *Monsieur Beaucaire* (1900), tales of the Middle West, such as *The Magnificent Ambersons* (1918) and *Alice Adams* (1921), and the series featuring the character Penrod

Tarkovsky (Russian 'takɔfskij) *n* **Andrei** ('andrej). 1932–86, Soviet film director, whose films include *Andrei Rublev* (1966), *Solaris* (1971), *Nostalgia* (1983), and *The Sacrifice* (1986)

tarlatan ('tɑːlətən) *n* an open-weave cotton fabric, used for stiffening garments [c18: from French *tarlatane*, variant of *tarnatane* type of muslin, perhaps of Indian origin]

tarmac ('tɑːmæk) *n* **1** a paving material that consists of crushed stone rolled and bound with a mixture of tar and bitumen, esp as formerly used for a road, airport runway, etc. Full name: tarmacadam. See also **macadam** ▷ *vb* **-macs, -macking, -macked** (*tr*) **2** (*usually not capital*) to apply tarmac to

tarn (tɑːn) *n* a small mountain lake or pool [c14: of Scandinavian origin; related to Old Norse *tjörn* pool]

Tarn (French tarn) *n* **1** a department of S France, in Midi-Pyrénées region. Capital: Albi. Pop: 350 477 (2003 est). Area: 5780 sq km (2254 sq miles) **2** a river in SW France, rising in the Massif Central and flowing generally west to the Garonne River. Length: 375 km (233 miles)

tarnation (tɑːˈneɪʃən) *n* a euphemism for **damnation**

Tarn-et-Garonne (French tarnegarɔn) *n* a department of SW France, in Midi-Pyrénées region. Capital: Montauban. Pop: 214 488 (2003 est). Area: 3731 sq km (1455 sq miles)

tarnish ('tɑːnɪʃ) *vb* **1** to lose or cause to lose the shine, esp by exposure to air or moisture resulting in surface oxidation; discolour **2** to stain or become stained; taint or spoil ▷ *n* **3** a tarnished condition, surface, or film [c16: from Old French *ternir* to make dull, from *terne* lustreless, of Germanic origin; related to Old High German *tarnen* to conceal, Old English *dierne* hidden] ▷ '**tarnishable** *adj*

Tarnopol (tar'nɔpol) *n* the Polish name for **Ternopol**

Tarnów (Polish 'tarnuf) *n* an industrial city in SE Poland. Pop: 119 000 (2005 est)

taro ('tɑːrəʊ) *n, pl* **-ros 1** an aroid plant, *Colocasia esculenta*, cultivated in the tropics for its large edible rootstock **2** the rootstock of this plant ▷ Also called: **eddo** [c18: from Tahitian and Māori]

tarot ('tærəʊ) *n* **1** one of a special pack of cards, now used mainly for fortune-telling, consisting of 78 cards (4 suits of 14 cards each (the minor arcana), and 22 other cards (the major arcana)) **2** a card in a tarot pack with distinctive symbolic design, such as the Wheel of Fortune ▷ *adj* **3** relating to tarot cards [c16: from French, from Old Italian *tarocco*, of unknown origin]

tarpan ('tɑːpæn) *n* a European wild horse, *Equus caballus gomelini*, common in prehistoric times but now extinct [from Kirghiz Tatar]

tarpaulin (tɑːˈpɔːlɪn) *n* **1** a heavy hard-wearing waterproof fabric made of canvas or similar material coated with tar, wax, or paint, for outdoor use as a protective covering against moisture **2** a sheet of this fabric **3** a hat of or covered with this fabric, esp a sailor's hat **4** a rare word for **seaman** [c17: probably from TAR¹ + PALL¹ + -ING¹]

Tarpeia (tɑːˈpiːə) *n* (in Roman legend) a vestal virgin, who betrayed Rome to the Sabines and was killed by them when she requested a reward

Tarpeian Rock (tɑːˈpiːən) *n* (in ancient Rome) a cliff on the Capitoline hill from which traitors were hurled

tarpon ('tɑːpən) *n, pl* **-pons** or **-pon** a large silvery clupeoid game fish, *Tarpon atlanticus*, of warm Atlantic waters, having a compressed body covered with large scales: family *Elopidae* [c17: perhaps from Dutch *tarpoen*, of unknown origin]

Tarquin ('tɑːkwɪn) *n* **1** Latin name *Lucius Tarquinius Priscus*, fifth legendary king of Rome (616–578 BC) **2** Latin name *Lucius Tarquinius Superbus*, seventh and last legendary king of Rome (534–510 BC)

tarradiddle ('tærəˌdɪdᵊl) *n* **1** a trifling lie **2** nonsense; twaddle [of unknown origin]

tarragon ('tærəgən) *n* **1** an aromatic perennial plant, *Artemisia dracunculus*, of the Old World, having whitish flowers and small toothed leaves, which are used as seasoning: family *Asteraceae* (composites) **2** the leaves of this plant [c16: from Old French *targon*, from Medieval Latin *tarcon*, from Arabic *tarkhūn*, perhaps from Greek *drakontion* adderwort]

Tarragona (Spanish tarra'ɣona) *n* a port in NE Spain, on the Mediterranean: one of the richest seaports of the Roman Empire; destroyed by the Moors (714). Pop: 121 076 (2003 est)

Tarrasa (Spanish ta'rrasa) *n* a city in NE Spain: textile centre. Pop: 184 829 (2003 est)

tarry ('tærɪ) *vb* **-ries, -rying, -ried 1** (*intr*) to delay in coming or going; linger **2** (*intr*) to remain temporarily or briefly **3** (*intr*) to wait or stay **4** (*tr*) *archaic or poetic* to await [C14 *tarien*, of uncertain origin] > 'tarrier *n*

tarsal ('taːsᵊl) *adj* **1** of, relating to, or constituting the tarsus or tarsi ▷ *n* **2** a tarsal bone

tarseal ('taːˌsiːl) *n* NZ **1** the bitumen surface of a road **2** the tarseal the main highway

Tarshish ('taːʃɪʃ) *n* Old Testament an ancient port, mentioned in I Kings 10:22, situated in Spain or in one of the Phoenician colonies in Sardinia

tarsia ('taːsɪə) *n* another term for **intarsia** [C17: from Italian, from Arabic *tarsi*; see INTARSIA]

tarsier ('taːsɪə) *n* any of several nocturnal arboreal prosimian primates of the genus *Tarsius*, of Indonesia and the Philippines, having huge eyes, long hind legs, and digits ending in pads to facilitate climbing: family *Tarsiidae* [C18: from French, from *tarse* the flat of the foot; see TARSUS]

tarsus ('taːsəs) *n*, *pl* -si (-saɪ) **1** the bones of the ankle and heel, collectively **2** the corresponding part in other mammals and in amphibians and reptiles **3** the dense connective tissue supporting the free edge of each eyelid **4** the part of an insect's leg that lies distal to the tibia [C17: from New Latin, from Greek *tarsos* flat surface, instep]

Tarsus ('taːsəs) *n* **1** a city in SE Turkey, on the Tarsus River: site of ruins of ancient Tarsus, capital of Cilicia, and birthplace of St Paul. Pop: 231 000 (2005 est) **2** a river in SE Turkey, in Cilicia, rising in the Taurus Mountains and flowing south past Tarsus to the Mediterranean. Length: 153 km (95 miles)

tart¹ (taːt) *n* a pastry case often having no top crust, with a sweet or savour filling [C14: from Old French *tarte*, of uncertain origin; compare Medieval Latin *tarte*]

tart² (taːt) *adj* **1** of a flavour, food, etc) sour, acid, or astringent **2** cutting, sharp, or caustic: *a tart remark* [Old English *teart* rough; related to Dutch *tarten* to defy, Middle High German *traz* defiance] > 'tartly *adv* > 'tartness *n*

tart³ (taːt) *n* informal a promiscuous woman, esp a prostitute: often a term of abuse. See also **tart up** [C19: shortened from SWEETHEART] > 'tarty *adj*

tartan ('taːtᵊn) *n* **1 a** a design of straight lines, crossing at right angles to give a chequered appearance, esp the distinctive design or designs associated with each Scottish clan **b** (*as modifier*): *a tartan kilt* **2** a woollen fabric or garment with this design [C16: perhaps from Old French *tertaine* linsey-woolsey, from Old Spanish *tiritaña* a fine silk fabric, from *tiritar* to rustle] > 'tartaned *adj*

tartar¹ ('taːtə) *n* **1** dentistry a hard crusty deposit on the teeth, consisting of food, cellular debris, and mineral salts **2** Also called: argol a brownish-red substance consisting mainly of potassium hydrogen tartrate, present in grape juice and deposited during the fermentation of wine [C14: from Medieval Latin *tartarum*, from Medieval Greek *tartaron*]

tartar² ('taːtə) *n* (*sometimes capital*) a fearsome or formidable person [C16: special use of TARTAR]

Tartar ('taːtə) *n*, *adj* a variant spelling of **Tatar**

tartare sauce or **tartar sauce** *n* a mayonnaise sauce mixed with hard-boiled egg yolks, chopped herbs, capers, and gherkins [from French *sauce tartare*, from TARTAR]

Tartarean (taːˈtɛərɪən, -'taːrɪ-) *adj* literary of or relating to Tartarus; infernal

tartar emetic *n* another name for **antimony potassium tartrate**

tartaric (taːˈtærɪk) *adj* of, concerned with, containing, or derived from tartar or tartaric acid

tartaric acid *n* a colourless or white odourless crystalline water-soluble dicarboxylic acid existing in four stereoisomeric forms, the commonest being the dextrorotatory (*d*-) compound which is found in many fruits: used as a food additive (E334) in soft drinks, confectionery, and baking powders and in tanning and photography. Formula: $HOOCCH(OH)CH(OH)COOH$

Tartarus ('taːtərəs) *n* Greek myth **1** an abyss under Hades where the Titans were imprisoned **2** a part of Hades reserved for evildoers **3** the underworld; Hades **4** a

primordial god who became the father of the monster Typhon [C16: from Latin, from Greek *Tartaros*, of obscure origin]

Tartary ('taːtərɪ) *n* a variant spelling of **Tatary**

tartine (taːˈtiːn) *n* an open sandwich, esp one with a rich or elaborate topping [C21: from French, diminutive of *tarte* TART¹]

tartlet ('taːtlɪt) *n* Brit an individual pastry case with a filling of fruit or other sweet or savoury mixture

tartrate ('taːtreɪt) *n* any salt or ester of tartaric acid

tartrated ('taːtreɪtɪd) *adj* being in the form of a tartrate

tartrazine ('taːtrəˌziːn, -zɪn) *n* an azo dye that produces a yellow colour: widely used as a food additive (E102) in convenience foods, soft drinks, sweets, etc, and in drugs, and also to dye textiles

Tartu (*Russian* 'tartu) *n* a city in SE Estonia: successively under Polish, Swedish, and Russian rule; university (1632). Pop: 95 000 (2005 est). Former name (11th century until 1918): Yurev. German name: Dorpat

tart up *vb* (*tr, adverb*) Brit informal **1** to dress and make (oneself) up in a provocative way **2** to decorate or improve the appearance of: *to tart up a bar*

tarwhine ('taːˌwaɪn) *n* a bream, *Rhabdosargus sarba*, of E Australia, silver in colour with gold streaks [from a native Australian language]

Tarzan ('taːzən) *n* (*sometimes not capital*) informal, often ironic a man with great physical strength, agility, and virility [C20: after the hero of a series of stories by Edgar Rice Burroughs (1875–1950), US novelist]

Tashkent (*Russian* taʃˈkjɛnt) *n* the capital of Uzbekistan: one of the oldest and largest cities in central Asia; cotton textile manufacturing. Pop: 2 160 000 (2005 est)

tasimeter (təˈsɪmɪtə) *n* a device for measuring small temperature changes. It depends on the changes of pressure resulting from expanding or contracting solids [C19 *tasi-*, from Greek *tasis* tension + -METER] > ta'simetry *n*

task (taːsk) *n* **1** a specific piece of work required to be done as a duty or chore **2** an unpleasant or difficult job or duty **3** any piece of work **4** take to task to criticize or reprove ▷ *vb* (*tr*) **5** to assign a task to **6** to subject to severe strain; tax [C13: from Old French *tasche*, from Medieval Latin *tasca*, from *taxa* tax, from Latin *taxāre* to TAX]

taskbar ('taːskˌbaː) *n* a row of selectable buttons and icons typically running along the bottom of a computer screen, displaying information such as the names of running programs

task force *n* **1** a temporary grouping of military units formed to undertake a specific mission **2** any semipermanent organization set up to carry out a continuing task

taskmaster ('taːskˌmaːstə) *n* a person, discipline, etc, that enforces work, esp hard or continuous work > 'task,mistress *fem n*

taskwork ('taːskˌwɜːk) *n* **1** hard or unpleasant work **2** a rare word for **piecework**

Tasman ('tæzmən) *n* **Abel Janszoon** ('abəl 'jansuːn). 1603–59, Dutch navigator, who discovered Tasmania, New Zealand, and the Tonga and Fiji Islands (1642–43)

Tasmania (tæzˈmeɪnɪə) *n* an island in the S Pacific, south of mainland Australia: forms, with offshore islands, the smallest state of Australia; discovered by the Dutch explorer Tasman in 1642; used as a penal colony by the British (1803–53); mostly forested and mountainous. Capital: Hobart. Pop: 479 958 (2003 est). Area: 68 332 sq km (26 383 sq miles). Former name (1642–1855): Van Diemen's Land > Tas'manian *adj, n*

Tasmanian devil *n* a small ferocious carnivorous marsupial, *Sarcophilus harrisi*, of Tasmania, having black fur with pale markings, strong jaws, and short legs: family *Dasyuridae*

Tasmanian wolf or **Tasmanian tiger** *n* other names for **thylacine**

Tasman Sea *n* the part of the Pacific between SE Australia and NW New Zealand

tass (tæs) or **tassie** ('tæsɪ) *n* Scot & northern English dialect **1** a cup, goblet, or glass **2** the contents of such a vessel; a small alcoholic drink [C15: from Old French *tasse* cup, from Arabic *tassah* basin, from Persian *tast*]

Tass (tæs) *n* (formerly) the principal news agency of the Soviet Union: replaced in 1992 by **Itar Tass** [T(*elegrafnoye*) A(*genstvo*) S(*ovetskovo*) S(*oyuza*) Telegraphic Agency of the Soviet Union]

tassel ('tæsᵊl) *n* 1 a tuft of loose threads secured by a knot or ornamental knob, used to decorate soft furnishings, clothes, etc 2 anything resembling this tuft, esp the tuft of stamens at the tip of a maize inflorescence ▷ *vb* -sels, -selling, -selled *or US* -sels, -seling, -seled 3 (*tr*) to adorn with a tassel or tassels 4 (*intr*) (of maize) to produce stamens in a tuft [c13: from Old French, from Vulgar Latin *tassellus* (unattested), changed from Latin *taxillus* a small die, from *tālus* gaming die]

Tassie *or* **Tassy** ('tæzɪ) *n, pl* -sies *Austral informal* 1 Tasmania 2 a native or inhabitant of Tasmania

Tasso (*Italian* 'tasso) *n* **Torquato** (tor'kwaːto). 1544–95, Italian poet, noted for his pastoral idyll *Aminta* (1573) and for *Jerusalem Delivered* (1581), dealing with the First Crusade

taste (teɪst) *n* 1 the sense by which the qualities and flavour of a substance are distinguished by the taste buds 2 the sensation experienced by means of the taste buds 3 the act of tasting 4 a small amount eaten, drunk, or tried on the tongue 5 a brief experience of something: *a taste of the whip* 6 a preference or liking for something; inclination 7 the ability to make discerning judgments about aesthetic, artistic, and intellectual matters; discrimination 8 judgment of aesthetic or social matters according to a generally accepted standard: *bad taste* 9 discretion; delicacy: *that remark lacks taste* ▷ *vb* 10 to distinguish the taste of (a substance) by means of the taste buds 11 (*usually tr*) to take a small amount of (a food, liquid, etc) into the mouth, esp in order to test the quality 12 (often foll by *of*) to have a specific flavour or taste 13 (when *intr*, usually foll by *of*) to have an experience of (something): *to taste success* 14 (*tr*) an archaic word for **enjoy** [c13: from Old French *taster*, ultimately from Latin *taxāre* to appraise] ▷ '**tastable** *adj*

taste bud *n* any of the elevated oval-shaped sensory end organs on the surface of the tongue, by means of which the sensation of taste is experienced

tasteful ('teɪstfʊl) *adj* indicating good taste: *a tasteful design* ▷ '**tastefully** *adv* ▷ '**tastefulness** *n*

tasteless ('teɪstlɪs) *adj* 1 lacking in flavour; insipid 2 lacking social or aesthetic taste ▷ '**tastelessly** *adv* ▷ '**tastelessness** *n*

taster ('teɪstə) *n* 1 a person who samples food or drink for quality 2 any device used in tasting or sampling 3 a person employed, esp formerly, to taste food and drink prepared for a king, etc, to test for poison 4 a sample or preview of a product, experience, etc, intended to stimulate interest in the product, experience, etc, itself: *the single serves as a taster for the band's new album*

-tastic *adj combining form jocular* denoting excellence in a specified area: *the fun-tastic theme park; their poptastic new single* [c20: from (FAN)TASTIC]

tasty ('teɪstɪ) *adj* **tastier, tastiest** 1 having a pleasant flavour 2 *Brit informal* skilful or impressive: *she was a bit tasty with a cutlass* 3 *NZ* (of cheddar cheese) having a strong flavour ▷ '**tastily** *adv* ▷ '**tastiness** *n*

tat¹ (tæt) *vb* **tats, tatting, tatted** to make (something) by tatting [c19: of unknown origin]

tat² (tæt) *n* 1 a tatty articles or a tatty condition 2 tasteless articles 3 a tangled mass [c20: back formation from TATTY]

tat³ (tæt) *n* See **tit for tat**

ta-ta (tæ'taː) *sentence substitute Brit informal* goodbye; farewell [c19: of unknown origin]

Tatar *or* **Tartar** ('taːtə) *n* 1 a a member of a Mongoloid people who under Genghis Khan established a vast and powerful state in central Asia from the 13th century until conquered by Russia in 1552 b a descendant of this people, now scattered throughout Russia but living chiefly in the Tatar Republic 2 any of the languages spoken by the present-day Tatars, belonging to various branches of the Turkic family of languages, esp Kazan

Tatar [c14: from Old French *Tartare*, from Medieval Latin *Tartarus* (associated with Latin *Tartarus* the underworld), from Persian *Tātār*] ▷ **Tatarian** (taː'tɛərɪən), **Tar'tarian** *or* **Tataric** (taː'tærɪk), **Tar'taric** *adj*

Tatar Republic *n* a constituent republic of W Russia, around the confluence of the Volga and Kama Rivers. Capital: Kazan. Pop: 3 779 800 (2002). Area: 68 000 sq km (26 250 sq miles)

Tatar Strait *n* an arm of the Pacific between the mainland of SE Russia and Sakhalin Island, linking the Sea of Japan with the Sea of Okhotsk. Length: about 560 km (350 miles). Also called: **Gulf of Tatary**

Tatary *or* **Tartary** ('taːtərɪ) *n* 1 a historical region (with indefinite boundaries) in E Europe and Asia, inhabited by Bulgars until overrun by the Tatars in the mid-13th century: extended as far east as the Pacific under Genghis Khan 2 **Gulf of Tatary** another name for **Tatar Strait**

Tate (teɪt) *n* 1 (**John Orley**) **Allen**. 1899–1979, US poet and critic 2 **Sir Henry**. 1819–99, British sugar refiner and philanthropist; founder of the Tate Gallery 3 **Nahum** ('neɪʊm). 1652–1715, British poet, dramatist, and hymn-writer, born in Ireland: poet laureate (1692–1715). He is best known for writing a version of *King Lear* with a happy ending

Tate Galleries *pl n* two art galleries in London, the original Tate Gallery (1897), now **Tate Britain**, and **Tate Modern**, created in the former Bankside power station in 2000

tater ('teɪtə) *n* a dialect word for **potato**

Tati (*French* tati) *n* **Jacques** (ʒak), real name *Jacques Tatischeff*. 1908–82, French film director, pantomimist, and comic actor, creator of the character Monsieur Hulot

tatouay ('tætʊˌeɪ, ˌtaːtuː'aɪ) *n* a large armadillo, *Cabassous tatouay*, of South America [c16: from Spanish *tatuay*, from Guarani *tatu ai*, from *tatu* armadillo + *ai* worthless (because inedible)]

Tatra Mountains ('taːtrə, 'tæt-) *pl n* a mountain range along the border between Slovakia and Poland, extending over 64 km (40 miles): the highest range of the central Carpathians. Highest peak: Gerlachovka, 2663 m (8737 ft). Also called: **High Tatra**

TATT *abbreviation* tired all the time: a term used to describe a set of symptoms often related to doctors by patients

tatter ('tætə) *vb* 1 to make or become ragged or worn to shreds ▷ *n* 2 (*plural*) torn or ragged pieces, esp of material [c14: of Scandinavian origin; compare Icelandic *tӧturr* rag, Old English *tættec*, Old High German *zæter* rag]

tatterdemalion (ˌtætədɪ'meɪljən, -'mæl-) *n rare* a person dressed in ragged clothes [c17: from TATTER + -*demalion*, of uncertain origin]

tattersall ('tætəˌsɔːl) *n* a fabric, sometimes brightly coloured, having stripes or bars in a checked or squared pattern [c19: after TATTERSALL'S; the horse blankets at the market originally had this pattern]

Tattersall's ('tætəˌsɔːlz) *n* 1 *Austral* a large-scale lottery based in Melbourne 2 a name used for sportsmen's clubs in Australia [named after Richard *Tattersall* (died 1795), English horseman, who founded the market]

tatting ('tætɪŋ) *n* 1 an intricate type of lace made by looping a thread of cotton or linen by means of a hand shuttle 2 the act or work of producing this [c19: of unknown origin]

tattle ('tætᵊl) *vb* 1 (*intr*) to gossip about another's personal matters or secrets 2 (*tr*) to reveal by gossiping 3 (*intr*) to talk idly; chat ▷ *n* 4 the act or an instance of tattling 5 a scandalmonger or gossip [c15 (in the sense: to stammer, hesitate): from Middle Dutch *tatelen* to prate, of imitative origin] ▷ '**tattler** *n*

tattletale ('tætᵊlˌteɪl) *n chiefly US & Canadian* 1 a scandalmonger or gossip 2 another word for **telltale** (sense 1)

tattoo¹ (tæ'tuː) *n, pl* -toos 1 (formerly) a signal by drum or bugle ordering the military to return to their quarters 2 a military display or pageant, usually at night 3 any similar beating on a drum, etc [c17: from Dutch *taptoe*, from the command *tap toe!* turn off the taps! from *tap*

tap of a barrel + *toe* to shut]

tattoo² (tæˈtuː) *vb* **-toos, -tooing, -tooed 1** to make (pictures or designs) on (the skin) by pricking and staining with indelible colours ▷ *n, pl* **-toos 2** a design made by this process **3** the practice of tattooing [c18: from Tahitian *tatau*] > **tatˈtooer** or **tatˈtooist** *n*

tatty (ˈtætɪ) *adj* **-tier, -tiest** *chiefly Brit* worn out, shabby, tawdry, or unkempt [c16: of Scottish origin, probably related to Old English *tættec* a tatter] > **ˈtattily** *adv* > **ˈtattiness** *n*

Tatum (ˈteɪtəm) *n* **1 Art**, full name *Arthur Tatum.* 1910–56, US jazz pianist **2** *Edward Lawrie.* 1909–75, US biochemist, who showed how genes regulate biochemical processes in an organism and demonstrated that bacteria reproduce sexually; Nobel prize for physiology or medicine (1958) with Beadle and Lederberg

tau (tɔː, tau) *n* the 19th letter in the Greek alphabet (Τ, τ), a consonant, transliterated as *t* [c13: via Latin from Greek, of Semitic origin; see **TAV**]

tau cross *n* a cross shaped like the Greek letter tau. Also called: **Saint Anthony's cross**

taught (tɔːt) *vb* the past tense and past participle of **teach**

tauiwi (tauˈiːwɪ) *n* *NZ* a Māori term for the non-Māori people of New Zealand [Māori, literally: foreign race]

taunt (tɔːnt) *vb* (*tr*) **1** to provoke or deride with mockery, contempt, or criticism **2** to tease; tantalize ▷ *n* **3** a jeering remark [c16: from French phrase *tant pour tant* like for like, rejoinder] > **ˈtaunting** *adj*

Taunton (ˈtɔːntən) *n* a market town in SW England, administrative centre of Somerset: scene of Judge Jeffreys' "Bloody Assize" (1685) after the Battle of Sedgemoor. Pop: 58 241 (2001)

tauon (ˈtauɒn) *n* *physics* a negatively charged elementary particle of mass 3477.48 × electron mass classed as a lepton, with an associated antiparticle and neutrino [c20: from Greek letter **TAU** + **-ON**]

tau particle *n* *physics* another name for **tauon**

taupe (təʊp) *n* **a** a brownish-grey colour **b** (*as adjective*): *a taupe coat* [c20: from French, literally: mole, from Latin *talpa*]

Taupo (ˈtaupəʊ) *n* **Lake Taupo** a lake in New Zealand, on central North Island: the largest lake of New Zealand. Area: 616 sq km (238 sq miles)

Tauranga (tauˈrænə) *n* a port in New Zealand, on NE North Island on the Bay of Plenty: exports dairy produce, meat, and timber. Pop: 101 300 (2004 est)

taurine (ˈtɔːraɪn) *adj* of, relating to, or resembling a bull [c17: from Latin *taurīnus*, from *taurus* a bull]

tauro- or *before a vowel* **taur-** *combining form* denoting a bull: *tauromachy* [from Latin *taurus* bull, Greek *tauros*]

tauromachy (tɔːˈrɒməkɪ) *n* the art or act of bullfighting [c19: Greek *tauromakhia*, from **TAURO-** + *makhē* fight]

Taurus (ˈtɔːrəs) *n, Latin genitive* **Tauri** (ˈtɔːraɪ) **1** *astronomy* a zodiacal constellation in the N hemisphere lying close to Orion and between Aries and Gemini. It contains the star Aldebaran, the star clusters Hyades and Pleiades, and the Crab Nebula **2** *astrology* Also called: **the Bull** the second sign of the zodiac, symbol ♉, having a fixed earth classification and ruled by the planet Venus. The sun is in this sign between about April 20 and May 20 [c14: from Latin: bull]

Taurus Mountains *pl n* a mountain range in S Turkey, parallel to the Mediterranean coast: crossed by the Cilician Gates; continued in the northeast by the Anti-Taurus range. Highest peak: Kaldi Daǧ, 3734 m (12 251 ft)

taut (tɔːt) *adj* **1** tightly stretched; tense **2** showing nervous strain; stressed **3** *chiefly nautical* in good order; neat [c14: *tought*; probably related to Old English *togian* to **TOW¹**] > **ˈtautly** *adv* > **ˈtautness** *n*

tauten (ˈtɔːt³n) *vb* to make or become taut or tense

tauto- or *before a vowel* **taut-** *combining form* identical or same: *tautology; tautonym* [from Greek *tauto*, from *to auto*]

tautog (tɔːˈtɒg) *n* a large dark-coloured wrasse, *Tautoga onitis*, of the North American coast of the Atlantic Ocean: used as a food fish [c17: from Narraganset *tautauog*, plural of *tautau* sheepshead]

tautology (tɔːˈtɒlədʒɪ) *n, pl* **-gies 1** the use of words that

merely repeat elements of the meaning already conveyed, as in the sentence *Will these supplies be adequate enough?* in place of *Will these supplies be adequate?* **2** *logic* a statement that is always true, esp a truth-functional expression that takes the value true for all combinations of values of its components, as in *either the sun is out or the sun is not out* [c16: from Late Latin *tautologia*, from Greek, from *tautologos*] > **tautological** (ˌtɔːt³ˈlɒdʒɪk³l) or **tauˈtologous** *adj*

tautomer (ˈtɔːtəmə) *n* either of the two forms of a chemical compound that exhibits tautomerism

tautomerism (tɔːˈtɒmə,rɪzəm) *n* the ability of certain chemical compounds to exist as a mixture of two interconvertible isomers in equilibrium [c19: from **TAUTO-** + **ISOMERISM**] > **tautomeric** (ˌtɔːtəˈmɛrɪk) *adj*

tautonym (ˈtɔːtənɪm) *n* *biology* a taxonomic name in which the generic and specific components are the same, as in *Rattus rattus* (black rat) [c20: from Greek *tautonymos.* See **TAUTO-, -ONYM**] > ˌtautoˈnymic or **tautonymous** (tɔːˈtɒnɪməs) *adj* > **tauˈtonymy** *n*

tav or **taw** (taːv, taːf; *Hebrew* tav, taf) *n* the 22nd and last letter in the Hebrew alphabet (ת), transliterated as *t* or when final *th* [from Hebrew: cross, mark]

Tavener (ˈtævənə) *n* **Sir John (Kenneth).** born 1944, British composer, whose works include the cantata *The Whale* (1966), the opera *Thérèse* (1979), and the choral work *The Last Discourse* (1998); many of his later works were inspired by the liturgy of the Russian Orthodox Church

tavern (ˈtævən) *n* **1** a less common word for **pub 2** *US, Eastern Canadian & NZ* a place licensed for the sale and consumption of alcoholic drink [c13: from Old French *taverne*, from Latin *taberna* hut]

taverna (təˈvɜːsnə) *n* **1** (in Greece) a guesthouse that has its own bar **2** a Greek restaurant [c20: Modern Greek, from Latin *taberna*]

Taverner (ˈtævənə) *n* **John.** ?1495–1545, English composer, esp of church music; best known for the mass *Western Wynde*, based on a secular song

TAVR *abbreviation* Territorial and Army Volunteer Reserve

taw¹ (tɔː) *n* **1** the line from which the players shoot in marbles **2** back to taws *Austral informal* back to the beginning **3** a large marble used for shooting **4** a game of marbles [c18: of unknown origin]

taw² (tɔː) *vb* (*tr*) to convert (skins) into white leather by treatment with mineral salts, such as alum and salt, rather than by normal tanning processes [Old English *tawian*; compare Old High German *zouwen* to prepare, Gothic *taujan* to make] > **ˈtawer** *n*

tawa (ˈtaːwə) *n* a tall timber tree, *Beilschmiedia tawa*, of New Zealand, having edible purple berries [Māori]

tawdry (ˈtɔːdrɪ) *adj* **-drier, -driest** cheap, showy, and of poor quality: *tawdry jewellery* [C16 *tawdry lace*, shortened and altered from *Seynt Audries lace*, finery sold at the fair of St *Audrey* (Etheldrida), 7th-century queen of Northumbria and patron saint of Ely, Cambridgeshire] > **ˈtawdrily** *adv* > **ˈtawdriness** *n*

Tawney (ˈtɔːnɪ) *n* **R(ichard) H(enry).** 1880–1962, British economic historian, born in India. His chief works are *The Acquisitive Society* (1920), *Religion and the Rise of Capitalism* (1926), and *Equality* (1931)

tawny or **tawney** (ˈtɔːnɪ) *n* **a** a light brown to brownish-orange colour **b** (*as adjective*): *tawny port* [c14: from Old French *tané*, from *taner* to **TAN¹**] > **ˈtawniness** *n*

tawny owl *n* a European owl, *Strix aluco*, having a reddish-brown or grey plumage, black eyes, and a round head

tawse or **taws** (tɔːz) *n* *chiefly Scot* a leather strap having one end cut into thongs, formerly used as an instrument of punishment by a schoolteacher [c16: probably plural of obsolete *taw* strip of leather; see **TAW²**]

tax (tæks) *n* **1** a compulsory financial contribution imposed by a government to raise revenue, levied on the income or property of persons or organizations, on the production costs or sales prices of goods and services, etc **2** a heavy demand on something; strain: *a tax on our resources* ▷ *vb* (*tr*) **3** to levy a tax on (persons, companies, etc, or their incomes, etc) **4** to make heavy demands on; strain **5** to accuse, charge, or blame **6** to determine (the amount legally chargeable or allowable to a party to a legal action), as by examining the solicitor's bill of costs: *to tax costs* **7** *slang* to steal [c13: from Old French *taxer*, from Latin *taxāre* to appraise, from *tangere* to touch] > 'taxer *n* > 'taxable *adj, n*

taxation (tækˈseɪʃən) *n* **1** the act or principle of levying taxes or the condition of being taxed **2 a** an amount assessed as tax **b** a tax rate **3** revenue from taxes > taxˈational *adj*

tax avoidance *n* reduction or minimization of tax liability by lawful methods

tax credit *n* (in Britain) a social security benefit paid in the form of an additional income tax allowance

tax-deductible *adj* (of an expense, loss, etc) legally deductible from income or wealth before tax assessment

tax disc *n* a paper disc displayed on the windscreen of a motor vehicle showing that the tax due on it has been paid

taxeme (ˈtæksiːm) *n* *linguistics* any element of speech that may differentiate one utterance from another with a different meaning, such as the occurrence of a particular phoneme, the presence of a certain intonation, or a distinctive word order [c20: from Greek *taxis* order, arrangement + -EME] > taxˈemic *adj*

tax evasion *n* reduction or minimization of tax liability by illegal methods

tax exile *n* a person having a high income who chooses to live abroad so as to avoid paying high taxes

tax haven *n* a country or state having a lower rate of taxation than elsewhere

tax holiday *n* a period during which tax concessions are made for some reason; examples include an export incentive or an incentive to start a new business given by some governments, in which a company is excused all or part of its tax liability

taxi (ˈtæksɪ) *n, pl* **taxis** *or* **taxies 1** Also called: **cab**, **taxicab** a car, usually fitted with a taximeter, that may be hired, along with its driver, to carry passengers to any specified destination ▷ *vb* **taxies**, **taxiing** *or* **taxying**, **taxied 2** to cause (an aircraft) to move along the ground under its own power, esp before takeoff and after landing, or (of an aircraft) to move along the ground in this way **3** (*intr*) to travel in a taxi [c20: shortened from *taximeter cab*]

taxidermy (ˈtæksɪˌdɜːmɪ) *n* the art or process of preparing, stuffing, and mounting animal skins so that they have a lifelike appearance [c19: from Greek *taxis* arrangement + -*dermy*, from Greek *derma* skin] > ˌtaxiˈdermal *or* ˌtaxiˈdermic *adj* > ˈtaxiˌdermist *n*

taximeter (ˈtæksɪˌmiːtə) *n* a meter fitted to a taxi to register the fare, based on the length of the journey [c19: from French *taximètre; see* TAX, -METER]

taxing (ˈtæksɪŋ) *adj* demanding, onerous, and wearing

taxi rank *n* a place where taxis wait to be hired

taxis (ˈtæksɪs) *n* **1** the movement of a cell or organism in a particular direction in response to an external stimulus **2** *surgery* the repositioning of a displaced organ or part by manual manipulation only [c18: via New Latin from Greek: arrangement, from *tassein* to place in order]

-taxis *or* **-taxy** *n combining form* **1** indicating movement towards or away from a specified stimulus: *thermotaxis* **2** order or arrangement: *phyllotaxis* [from New Latin, from Greek *taxis* order + -*tactic* or -*taxic adj combining form*

taxiway (ˈtæksɪˌweɪ) *n* a marked path along which aircraft taxi to or from a runway, parking area, etc

tax loss *n* a loss sustained by a company that can be set against future profits for tax purposes

taxman (ˈtæksˌmæn) *n, pl* **-men 1** a collector of taxes **2** *informal* a tax-collecting body personified

taxon (ˈtæksɒn) *n, pl* **taxa** (ˈtæksə) *biology* any taxonomic group or rank [c20: back formation from TAXONOMY]

taxonomy (tækˈsɒnəmɪ) *n* **1** the branch of biology concerned with the classification of organisms into groups based on similarities of structure, origin, etc **2** the science or practice of classification [c19: from French *taxonomie,* from Greek *taxis* order + -NOMY] > taxonomic (ˌtæksəˈnɒmɪk) *or* ˌtaxoˈnomical *adj* > ˌtaxoˈnomically *adv* > taxˈonomist *or* taxˈonomer *n*

taxpayer (ˈtæksˌpeɪə) *n* a person or organization that pays taxes or is liable to taxation

tax relief *n* a reduction in the amount of tax a person or company has to pay

tax return *n* a declaration of personal income made annually to the tax authorities and used as a basis for assessing an individual's liability for taxation

tax shelter *n* *commerce* a form into which business or financial activities may be organized to minimize taxation

-taxy *n combining form* a variant of -**taxis**

Tay (teɪ) *n* **1** Firth of Tay the estuary of the River Tay on the North Sea coast of Scotland. Length: 40 km (25 miles) **2** a river in central Scotland, flowing northeast through Loch Tay, then southeast to the Firth of Tay: the longest river in Scotland; noted for salmon fishing. Length: 193 km (120 miles) **3** Loch Tay a lake in central Scotland, in Stirling council area. Length: 23 km (14 miles)

Taylor (ˈteɪlə) *n* **1** A(lan) J(ohn) P(ercivale). 1906–90, British historian whose many works include *The Origins of the Second World War* (1961) **2** Brook. 1685–1731, English mathematician, who laid the foundations of differential calculus **3** Dame Elizabeth. born 1932, US film actress, born in England: films include *National Velvet* (1944), *Cat on a Hot Tin Roof* (1958), *Suddenly Last Summer* (1959), and *Butterfield 8* (1960) and *Who's Afraid of Virginia Woolf?* (1966), for both of which she won Oscars **4** Frederick Winslow. 1856–1915, US engineer, who pioneered the use of time and motion studies to increase efficiency in industry **5** Jeremy. 1613–67, English cleric, best known for his devotional manuals *Holy Living* (1650) and *Holy Dying* (1651) **6** Zachary. 1784–1850, 12th president of the US (1849–50); hero of the Mexican War

Taylor's Gold *n* a variety of pear from New Zealand

Taymyr Peninsula (taɪˈmɪə) *n* a variant spelling of **Taimyr Peninsula**

Tay-Sachs disease (ˌteɪˈsæks) *n* an inherited disorder, caused by a faulty recessive gene, in which lipids accumulate in the brain, leading to mental retardation and blindness. It occurs mostly in Ashkenazi Jews [c20: named after W. Tay (1843–1927), British physician, and B. Sachs (1858–1944), US neurologist]

Tayside Region (ˈteɪˌsaɪd) *n* a former local government region in E Scotland: formed in 1975 from Angus, Kinross-shire, and most of Perthshire; replaced in 1996 by the council areas of Angus, City of Dundee, and Perth and Kinross

tazza (ˈtætsə) *n* a wine cup with a shallow bowl and a circular foot [c19: from Italian, probably from Arabic *tassah* bowl]

Tb *the chemical symbol for* terbium

TB *abbreviation* **1** torpedo boat **2** Also called: **tb** tuberculosis

tba *or* **TBA** *abbreviation* to be arranged

T-bar *n* **1** a T-shaped wrench for use with a socket **2** a T-shaped bar on a ski tow which skiers hold on to while being pulled up slopes

tbc *or* **TBC** *abbreviation* to be confirmed

Tbilisi (təbɪˈliːsɪ) *n* the capital of Georgia, on the Kura River: founded in 458; taken by the Russians in 1801; university (1918); a major industrial centre. Pop: 1 042 000 (2005 est.) Russian name: **Tiflis**

T-bone steak *n* a large choice steak cut from the sirloin of beef, containing a T-shaped bone

tbs. *or* **tbsp.** *abbreviation* tablespoon(ful)

TBT *abbreviation* tri-*n*-butyl tin: a biocide used in marine paints to prevent fouling

Tc *the chemical symbol for* technetium

T-cell *n* another name for **T-lymphocyte**

Tchad (tʃad) *n* the French name for **Chad**

Tchaikovsky (tʃaɪˈkɒfskɪ; *Russian* tʃijˈkɔfskij) *n* **Pyotr Ilyich** (pjɔtr iljˈjitʃ). 1840–93, Russian composer. His works, which are noted for their expressive melodies, include the *Sixth Symphony* (the *Pathétique*; 1893), ballets, esp *Swan Lake* (1876) and *The Sleeping Beauty* (1889), and operas, including *Eugene Onegin* (1879) and *The Queen of Spades* (1890), both based on works by Pushkin

TCO *abbreviation* total cost of ownership: the real cost of owning and using a piece of equipment such as a computer, taking into account the price of the hardware, software, maintenance, training, and technical support that may be needed

t distribution *n* See **Student's t**

te *or* **ti** (tiː) *n music* (in tonic sol-fa) the syllable used for the seventh note or subtonic of any scale [see GAMUT]

Te *the chemical symbol for* tellurium

tea (tiː) *n* **1** an evergreen shrub or small tree, *Camellia sinensis*, of tropical and subtropical Asia, having toothed leathery leaves and white fragrant flowers: family *Theaceae* **2 a** the dried shredded leaves of this shrub, used to make a beverage by infusion in boiling water **b** such a beverage, served hot or iced **3 a** any of various plants that are similar to *Camellia sinensis* or are used to make a tealike beverage **b** any such beverage **4** *chiefly Brit* **a** Also called: afternoon tea a light meal eaten in mid-afternoon, usually consisting of tea and cakes, biscuits, or sandwiches **b** Also called: high tea afternoon tea that also includes a light cooked dish **5** *Brit, Austral & NZ* the main evening meal **6** *US & Canadian dated, slang* marijuana **7** tea and sympathy *informal* a caring attitude, esp to someone in trouble [C17: from Chinese (Amoy) *t'e*, from Ancient Chinese *d'a*]

tea bag *n* a small bag of paper or cloth containing tea leaves, infused in boiling water to make tea

tea ball *n chiefly US* a perforated metal ball filled with tea leaves and put in boiling water to make tea

tea break *n Brit* a short rest period during working hours during which tea, coffee, etc is drunk

teacake (ˈtiːˌkeɪk) *n Brit* a flat cake made from a yeast dough with raisins in it, usually eaten toasted and buttered

teach (tiːtʃ) *vb* teaches, teaching, taught **1** (*tr; may take a clause as object or an infinitive; often foll by how*) to help to learn; tell or show (how) **2** to give instruction or lessons in (a subject) to (a person or animal) **3** (*tr; may take a clause as object or an infinitive*) to cause to learn or understand: *experience taught him that he could not be a journalist* [Old English *tæcan*; related to *tācen* TOKEN, Old Frisian *tēken*, Old Saxon *tēkan*, Old High German *zeihhan*, Old Norse *teikn* sign] **>** ˈteachable *adj*

Teach (tiːtʃ) *n* Edward, known as Blackbeard. died 1718, English pirate, active in the West Indies and on the Atlantic coast of North America

teacher (ˈtiːtʃə) *n* a person whose occupation is teaching others, esp children

teach-in *n* an informal conference, esp on a topical subject, usually held at a university or college and involving a panel of visiting speakers, lecturers, students, etc

teaching (ˈtiːtʃɪŋ) *n* **1** the art or profession of a teacher **2** (*sometimes plural*) something taught; precept **3** (*modifier*) denoting a person or institution that teaches: *a teaching hospital* **4** (*modifier*) used in teaching: *teaching aids*

teaching machine *n* a machine that presents information and questions to the user, registers the answers, and indicates whether these are correct or acceptable

tea cloth *n* another name for **tea towel**

tea cosy *n* a covering for a teapot to keep the contents hot, often having holes for the handle and spout

teacup (ˈtiːˌkʌp) *n* **1** a cup out of which tea may be drunk, larger than a coffee cup **2** Also called: teacupful the amount a teacup will hold, about four fluid ounces

tea dance *n* a dance held in the afternoon at which tea is served

teahouse (ˈtiːˌhaʊs) *n* a restaurant, esp in Japan or China, where tea and light refreshments are served

teak (tiːk) *n* **1** a large verbenaceous tree, *Tectona grandis*, of the East Indies, having white flowers and yielding a valuable dense wood **2** the hard resinous yellowish-brown wood of this tree, used for furniture making, etc [C17: from Portuguese *teca*, from Malayalam *tēkka*]

teakettle (ˈtiːˌketᵊl) *n* a kettle for boiling water to make tea

teal (tiːl) *n, pl* teals *or* teal **1** any of various small ducks, such as the Eurasian *Anas crecca* (**common teal**) that are

related to the mallard and frequent ponds, lakes, and marshes **2** a greenish-blue colour [C14: related to Middle Low German *tēlink*, Middle Dutch *tēling*]

tea lady *n* a woman employed in a factory, office, etc, to make tea during a tea break

tea leaf *n* **1** the dried leaf of the tea shrub, used to make tea **2** (*usually plural*) shredded parts of these leaves, esp after infusion

tea light *n* a small round candle in a disposable metal container

team (tiːm) *n* (*sometimes functioning as plural*) **1** a group of people organized to work together **2** a group of players forming one of the sides in a sporting contest **3** two or more animals working together to pull a vehicle or agricultural implement **4** such animals and the vehicle **▷** *vb* **5** (when *intr*, often foll by *up*) to make or cause to make a team **6** (*tr*) *US & Canadian* to drag or transport in or by a team **7** (*intr*) *US & Canadian* to drive a team [Old English *team* offspring; related to Old Frisian *tām* bridle, Old Norse *taumr* chain yoking animals together, Old High German *zoum* bridle]

tea-maker *n* a device with perforations used to infuse tea in a cup of boiling water

team-mate *n* a fellow member of a team

team spirit *n* willingness to cooperate as part of a team

teamster (ˈtiːmstə) *n* **1** a driver of a team of horses used for haulage **2** *US & Canadian* the driver of a lorry

team teaching *n* a system whereby two or more teachers pool their skills, knowledge, etc, to teach combined classes

teamwork (ˈtiːmˌwɜːk) *n* **1** the cooperative work done by a team **2** the ability to work efficiently as a team

teapot (ˈtiːˌpɒt) *n* a container with a lid, spout, and handle, in which tea is made and from which it is served

teapoy (ˈtiːpɔɪ) *n* a small table or stand with a tripod base [C19: from Hindi *tipāī*, from Sanskrit *tri* three + *pāda* foot; compare Persian *sipae* three-legged stand]

tear¹ (tɪə) *n* **1** a drop of the secretion of the lacrimal glands. See tears **2** something shaped like a hanging drop: *a tear of amber*. **▷** Also called: teardrop [Old English *tēar*, related to Old Frisian, Old Norse *tār*, Old High German *zahar*, Greek *dakri*] **>** ˈtearless *adj*

tear² (tɛə) *vb* tears, tearing, tore, torn **1** to cause (material, paper, etc) to come apart or (of material, etc) to come apart; rip **2** (*tr*) to make (a hole or split) in (something) **3** (*intr*; often foll by *along*) to hurry or rush **4** (*tr*; usually foll by *away* or *from*) to remove or take by force **5** (when *intr*, often foll by *at*) to cause pain, distress, or anguish (to) **6** tear one's hair *informal* to be angry, frustrated, very worried, etc **▷** *n* **7** a hole, cut, or split **8** the act of tearing **▷** See also **tear away, tear down**, etc [Old English *teran*; related to Old Saxon *terian*, Gothic *gatairan* to destroy, Old High German *zeran* to destroy] **>** ˈtearable *adj* **>** ˈtearer *n*

tear away (tɛə) *vb* **1** (*tr, adverb*) to persuade (oneself or someone else) to leave **▷** *n* tearaway **2** *Brit* a reckless impetuous unruly person

tear down (tɛə) *vb* (*tr, adverb*) to destroy or demolish

tear duct (tɪə) *n* the nontechnical name for **lacrimal duct**

tearful (ˈtɪəfʊl) *adj* **1** about to cry **2** tending to produce tears; sad **>** ˈtearfully *adv* **>** ˈtearfulness *n*

tear gas (tɪə) *n* any one of a number of gases or vapours that make the eyes smart and water, causing temporary blindness; usually dispersed from grenades and used in warfare and to control riots

tearing (ˈtɛərɪŋ) *adj* violent or furious (esp in the phrase **tearing hurry** or **rush**)

tear into (tɛə) *vb* (*intr, preposition*) *informal* to attack vigorously and damagingly

tear-jerker (ˈtɪəˌdʒɜːkə) *n informal* an excessively sentimental film, play, book, etc

tearoom (ˈtiːˌruːm, -ˌrʊm) *n* another name for **teashop**

tea rose *n* any of several varieties of hybrid rose that are derived from *Rosa odorata* and have pink or yellow flowers with a scent resembling that of tea

tears (tɪəz) *pl n* **1** the clear salty solution secreted by the lacrimal glands that lubricates and cleanses the surface of the eyeball and inner surface of the eyelids **2** a state of intense frustration (esp in the phrase **bored to tears**) **3** in tears weeping

tear sheet (tɛə) *n* a page in a newspaper or periodical that is cut or perforated so that it can be easily torn out

teary ('tɪərɪ) *adj* **tearier**, **teariest** **1** characterized by, covered with, or secreting tears **2** given to weeping; tearful > '**tearily** *adv* > '**teariness** *n*

tease (ti:z) *vb* **1** to annoy (someone) by deliberately offering something with the intention of delaying or withdrawing the offer **2** to vex (someone) maliciously or playfully, esp by ridicule **3** (*tr*) to separate the fibres of; comb; card **4** (*tr*) to raise the nap of (a fabric) with a teasel **5** (*tr*) to loosen or pull apart (biological tissues, etc) by delicate agitation or prodding with an instrument ▷ *n* **6** a person or thing that teases **7** the act of teasing ▷ See also **tease out** [Old English *tǣsan*; related to Old High German *zeisan* to pick] > '**teasing** *adj* > '**teasingly** *adv*

teasel, teazel *or* **teazle** ('ti:zəl) *n* **1** any of various stout biennial plants of the genus *Dipsacus*, of Eurasia and N Africa, having prickly leaves and prickly heads of yellow or purple flowers: family *Dipsacaceae* **2 a** the prickly dried flower head of the fuller's teasel, used for teasing **b** any manufactured implement used for the same purpose ▷ *vb* **-sels, -selling, -selled** *or US* **-sels, -seling, -seled** **3** (*tr*) to tease (a fabric) [Old English *tǣsel*; related to Old High German *zeisala* teasel, Norwegian *tīsl* undergrowth, *tīsla* to tear to bits; see TEASE] > '**teaseller** *n*

tease out *vb* (*tr, adverb*) to extract (information) with difficulty

teaser ('ti:zə) *n* **1** a person who teases **2** a preliminary advertisement in a campaign that attracts attention by making people curious to know what product is being advertised **3** a difficult question

tea service *or* **tea set** *n* the china or pottery articles used in serving tea, including a teapot, cups, saucers, etc

teashop ('ti:ʃɒp) *n Brit* a restaurant where tea and light refreshments are served. Also called: **tearoom**

teaspoon ('ti:ˌspu:n) *n* **1** a small spoon used for stirring tea, eating certain desserts, etc **2** Also called: **teaspoonful** ('ti:ˌspu:nfʊl) the amount contained in such a spoon **3** a unit of capacity used in cooking, medicine, etc, equal to about one fluid dram

teat (ti:t) *n* **1 a** the nipple of a mammary gland **b** (in cows, etc) any of the projections from the udder through which milk is discharged **2** something resembling a teat in shape or function, such as the rubber mouthpiece of a feeding bottle [c13: from Old French *tete*, of Germanic origin; compare Old English *titt*, Middle High German *zitze*]

tea towel *or* **tea cloth** *n* a towel for drying dishes and kitchen utensils. US name: **dishtowel**

tea tree *n* any of various myrtaceous trees of the genus *Leptospermum*, of Australia and New Zealand, that yield an oil used as an antiseptic

tea trolley *n chiefly Brit* a trolley from which tea is served

tebi- ('tɛbɪ) *prefix computing* denoting 2⁴⁰: *tebibyte* Symbol: Ti [c20: from TE(RA-) + BI(NARY)]

TEC (tɛk) *n acronym for* (in Britain) Training and Enterprise Council. See **Training Agency**

tech (tɛk) *n informal* short for **technical college**

tech. *abbreviation* **1** technical **2** technology

techie *or* **techy** ('tɛkɪ) *informal* ▷ *n* **1** *pl* **techies** a person who is skilled in the use of technological devices, such as computers ▷ *adj* **2** of, relating to, or skilled in the use of technological devices, such as computers

technetium (tɛk'ni:ʃɪəm) *n* a silvery-grey metallic element, artificially produced by bombardment of molybdenum by deuterons: used to inhibit corrosion in steel. The radioisotope **technetium-99m**, with a half-life of six hours, is used in radiotherapy. Symbol: Tc; atomic no: 43; half-life of most stable isotope, ⁹⁷Tc: 2.6×10^6 years; valency: 0, 2, 4, 5, 6, or 7; relative density: 11.50 (calculated); melting pt: 2204°C; boiling pt: 4265°C [c20: New Latin, from Greek *tekhnētos* manmade, from *tekhnasthai* to devise artificially, from *tekhnē* skill]

technic *n* **1** (tɛk'ni:k) another word for **technique** **2** ('tɛknɪk) another word for **technics** [c17: from Latin *technicus*, from Greek *tekhnikos*, from *tekhnē* art, skill]

technical ('tɛknɪkᵊl) *adj* **1** of, relating to, or specializing in industrial, practical, or mechanical arts and applied sciences **2** skilled in practical and mechanical arts rather than theoretical or abstract thinking **3** relating to or characteristic of a particular field of activity: *the technical jargon of linguistics* **4** existing by virtue of a strict application of the rules or a strict interpretation of the wording: *a technical loophole in the law; a technical victory* **5** of, derived from, or showing technique: *technical brilliance* > '**technically** *adv* > '**technicalness** *n*

technical college *n Brit* an institution for further education that provides courses in technology, art, secretarial skills, agriculture, etc

technical drawing *n* the study and practice, esp as a subject taught in school, of the basic techniques of draughtsmanship, as employed in mechanical drawing, architecture, etc

technicality (ˌtɛknɪ'kælɪtɪ) *n, pl* **-ties** **1** a petty formal point arising from a strict interpretation of rules, etc **2** the state or quality of being technical **3** technical methods and vocabulary

technical knockout *n boxing* a judgment of a knockout given when a boxer is in the referee's opinion too badly beaten to continue without risk of serious injury

technician (tɛk'nɪʃən) *n* **1** a person skilled in mechanical or industrial techniques or in a particular technical field **2** a person employed in a laboratory, technical college, or scientific establishment to do practical work **3** a person having specific artistic or mechanical skill, esp if lacking original flair or genius

Technicolor ('tɛknɪˌkʌlə) *n trademark* the process of producing colour film by means of superimposing synchronized films of the same scene, each of which has a different colour filter, to obtain the desired mix of colour

technics ('tɛknɪks) *n* (*functioning as singular*) the study or theory of industry and industrial arts; technology

technikon ('tɛknɪˌkɒn) *n South African* a technical college

technique *or* **technic** (tɛk'ni:k) *n* **1** a practical method, skill, or art applied to a particular task **2** proficiency in a practical or mechanical skill **3** special facility; knack [c19: from French, from *technique* (adj) TECHNIC]

techno ('tɛknəʊ) *n* a type of very fast dance music, using electronic sounds and fast heavy beats

techno- *combining form* **1** craft or art: *technology; technography* **2** technological or technical: *technocracy* [from Greek *tekhnē* skill]

technocracy (tɛk'nɒkrəsɪ) *n, pl* **-cies** a theory or system of society according to which government is controlled by scientists, engineers, and other experts > **technocrat** ('tɛknəˌkræt) *n* > ˌtechno'cratic *adj*

technology (tɛk'nɒlədʒɪ) *n, pl* **-gies** **1** the application of practical sciences to industry or commerce **2** the methods, theory, and practices governing such application **3** the total knowledge and skills available to any human society for industry, art, science, etc [c17: from Greek *tekhnologia* systematic treatment, from *tekhnē* art, skill] > **technological** (ˌtɛknə'lɒdʒɪkᵊl) *adj* > tech'nologist *n*

technophile ('tɛknəʊˌfaɪl) *n* **1** a person who is enthusiastic about technology ▷ *adj* **2** enthusiastic about technology

technophobe ('tɛknəʊˌfəʊb) *n* **1** someone who fears the effects of technological development on society and the environment **2** someone who is afraid of using technological devices, such as computers > ˌtechno'phobic *adj*

techy¹ ('tɛkɪ) *n, pl* **techies**, *adj informal* a variant spelling of **techie**

techy² ('tɛtʃɪ) *adj* **techier, techiest** a variant spelling of **tetchy** > '**techily** *adv* > '**techiness** *n*

tectonic (tɛk'tɒnɪk) *adj* **1** denoting or relating to construction or building **2** *geology* **a** (of landforms, rock masses, etc) resulting from distortion of the earth's crust due to forces within it **b** (of processes, movements, etc) occurring within the earth's crust and causing structural deformation [c17: from Late Latin *tectonicus*, from Greek *tektonikos* belonging to carpentry, from *tektōn* a builder]

tectonics (tɛkˈtɒnɪks) *n* (*functioning as singular*) **1** the art and science of construction or building **2** the study of the processes by which the earth's crust has attained its present structure

tectrix (ˈtɛktrɪks) *n*, *pl* **tectrices** (ˈtɛktrɪˌsiːz, tɛkˈtraɪsiːz) (*usually plural*) *ornithol* another name for **covert** (sense 5) [c19: New Latin, from Latin *tector* plasterer, from *tegere* to cover] >**tectricial** (tɛkˈtrɪʃəl) *adj*

Tecumseh (tɪˈkʌmsə) *n* ?1768–1813, American Indian chief of the Shawnee tribe. He attempted to unite western Indian tribes against the White people, but was defeated at Tippecanoe (1811). He was killed while fighting for the British in the War of 1812

ted[1] (tɛd) *vb* **teds, tedding, tedded** to shake out and loosen (hay), so as to dry it [c15: from Old Norse *tethja*; related to *tad* dung, Old High German *zetten* to spread]

ted[2] (tɛd) *n* *informal* short for **teddy boy**

tedder (ˈtɛdə) *n* **1** a machine equipped with a series of small rotating forks for tedding hay **2** a person who teds

Tedder (ˈtɛdə) *n* **Arthur William**, 1st Baron Tedder of Glenguin. 1890–1967, British marshal of the Royal Air Force; deputy commander under Eisenhower of the Allied Expeditionary Force (1944–45)

teddy (ˈtɛdɪ) *n*, *pl* **-dies** a woman's one-piece undergarment, incorporating a chemise top and panties

teddy bear *n* a stuffed toy bear made from soft or fluffy material. Often shortened to: **teddy** [c20: from *Teddy*, from *Theodore*, after Theodore Roosevelt (1858–1919), 26th president of the US (1901–09), who was well known as a hunter of bears]

teddy boy *n* **1** (in Britain, esp in the mid-1950s) one of a cult of youths who wore mock Edwardian fashions, such as tight narrow trousers, pointed shoes, and long sideboards **2** any tough or delinquent youth [c20: from *Teddy*, from *Edward*, referring to the Edwardian dress]

Te Deum (ˌtiː ˈdiːəm) *n* **1** an ancient Latin hymn in rhythmic prose, sung or recited at matins in the Roman Catholic Church and in English translation at morning prayer in the Church of England and used by both Churches as an expression of thanksgiving on special occasions **2** a musical setting of this hymn **3** a service of thanksgiving in which the recital of this hymn forms a central part [from the Latin canticle beginning *Tē Deum laudāmus*, literally: Thee, God, we praise]

tedious (ˈtiːdɪəs) *adj* causing fatigue or tedium; monotonous >**ˈtediously** *adv* >**ˈtediousness** *n*

tedium (ˈtiːdɪəm) *n* the state of being bored or the quality of being boring; monotony [c17: from Latin *taedium*, from *taedēre* to weary]

tee[1] (tiː) *n* **1** a pipe fitting in the form of a letter T, used to join three pipes **2** a metal section with a cross section in the form of a letter T, such as a rolled-steel joist

tee[2] (tiː) *golf* ▷ *n* **1** Also called: **teeing ground** an area, often slightly elevated, from which the first stroke of a hole is made **2** a support for a golf ball, usually a small wooden or plastic peg, used when teeing off or in long grass, etc ▷ *vb* **tees, teeing, teed** **3** (when *intr*, often foll by *up*) to position (the ball) ready for striking, on or as if on a tee ▷ See also **tee off** [C17 *teaz*, of unknown origin]

tee[3] (tiː) *n* a mark used as a target in certain games such as curling and quoits [c18: perhaps from T-shaped marks, which may have originally been used in curling]

tee-hee or **te-hee** (ˈtiːˈhiː) *interj* **1** an exclamation of laughter, esp when mocking ▷ *n* **2** a chuckle ▷ *vb* **-hees, -heeing, -heed** **3** (*intr*) to snigger or laugh, esp derisively [c14: of imitative origin]

teem[1] (tiːm) *vb* (*intr*; usually foll by *with*) to be prolific or abundant (in); abound (in) [Old English *tēman* to produce offspring; related to West Saxon *tīeman*; see TEAM]

teem[2] (tiːm) *vb* **1** (*intr*; often foll by *down* or *with rain*) to pour in torrents **2** (*tr*) to pour or empty out [C15 *temen* to empty, from Old Norse *tœma*; related to Old English *tōm*, Old High German *zuomīg* empty]

teen (tiːn) *adj informal* another word for **teenage**

-teen *n combining form* ten: added to modified forms of

the numbers 3 to 9 to form the numbers 13 to 19 [Old English -*tēne*, -*tȳne*] >**-teenth** *adj combining form*

teenage (ˈtiːnˌeɪdʒ) *adj* (*prenominal*) of or relating to the time in a person's life between the ages of 13 and 19 inclusive. Also: **teenaged**

teenager (ˈtiːnˌeɪdʒə) *n* a person between the ages of 13 and 19 inclusive

teens (tiːnz) *pl n* **1** the years of a person's life between the ages of 13 and 19 inclusive **2** all the numbers that end in -*teen*

teeny (ˈtiːnɪ) *adj* **-nier, -niest** *informal* extremely small; tiny. Also called: **teeny-weeny** (ˈtiːnɪˈwiːnɪ) **teensy-weensy** (ˈtiːnzɪˈwiːnzɪ) [c19: variant of TINY]

teenybopper (ˈtiːnɪˌbɒpə) *n* *slang* a young teenager, usually a girl, who avidly follows fashions in clothes and pop music [c20: *teeny*, from TEENAGE + -*bopper* see BOP[1]]

tee off *vb* (*adverb*) **1** *golf* to strike (the ball) from a tee, as when starting a hole **2** *informal* to begin; start

teepee (ˈtiːpiː) *n* a variant spelling of **tepee**

Tees (tiːz) *n* a river in N England, rising in the N Pennines and flowing southeast and east to the North Sea at Middlesbrough. Length: 113 km (70 miles)

tee shirt *n* a variant of **T-shirt**

Teesside (ˈtiːzˌsaɪd) *n* the industrial region around the lower Tees valley and estuary: a county borough, containing Middlesbrough, from 1968 to 1974

teeter (ˈtiːtə) *vb* **1** to move or cause to move unsteadily; wobble ▷ *n*, *vb* **2** another word for **seesaw** [c19: from Middle English *titeren*, related to Old Norse *titra* to tremble, Old High German *zittarōn* to shiver]

teeth (tiːθ) *n* **1** the plural of **tooth** **2** the most violent part: *the teeth of the gale* **3** the power to produce a desired effect: *that law has no teeth* **4** get one's teeth into to become engrossed in **5** in the teeth of in direct opposition to; against **6** show one's teeth to threaten, esp in a defensive manner **7** to the teeth to the greatest possible degree: *armed to the teeth*

teethe (tiːð) *vb* (*intr*) to cut one's baby (deciduous) teeth

teething ring *n* a plastic, hard rubber, or bone ring on which babies may bite while teething

teething troubles *pl n* the difficulties or problems that arise during the initial stages of a project, enterprise, etc

teetotal (tiːˈtəʊtᵊl) *adj* **1** of, relating to, or practising abstinence from alcoholic drink **2** *dialect* complete [c19: allegedly coined in 1833 by Richard Turner, English advocate of total abstinence from alcoholic liquors; probably from TOTAL, with emphatic reduplication] >**teeˈtotaller** *n* >**teeˈtotalism** *n*

teetotum (tiːˈtəʊtəm) *n* *archaic* a spinning top bearing letters of the alphabet on its four sides [c18: from T *totum*, from T inscribed on one of the faces + *totum* the name of the toy, from Latin *tōtum* the whole]

tef or **teff** (tɛf) *n* an annual grass, *Eragrostis abyssinica*, of NE Africa, grown for its grain [c18: from Amharic *ṭēf*]

TEFL (ˈtɛfᵊl) *n acronym* Teaching (of) English as a Foreign Language

Teflon (ˈtɛflɒn) *n* *trademark* polytetrafluoroethylene, when used in nonstick cooking vessels

teg (tɛg) *n* **1** a two-year-old sheep **2** the fleece of a two-year-old sheep [c16: of unknown origin]

tegmen (ˈtɛgmən) *n*, *pl* -**mina** (-mɪnə) **1** either of the leathery forewings of the cockroach and related insects **2** the delicate inner covering of a seed **3** any similar covering or layer [c19: from Latin: a cover, variant of *tegimen*, from *tegere* to cover] >**ˈtegminal** *adj*

Tegucigalpa (Spanish teɣuθiˈɣalpa) *n* the capital of Honduras, in the south on the Choluteca River: founded about 1579; university (1847). Pop: 1 061 000 (2005 est)

tegument (ˈtɛgjʊmənt) *n* a less common word for **integument** [c15: from Latin *tegumentum* a covering, from *tegere* to cover]

te-hee (ˈtiːˈhiː) *interj*, *n*, *vb* a variant spelling of **tee-hee**

Tehran or **Teheran** (teəˈrɑːn, -ˈræn) *n* the capital of Iran, at the foot of the Elburz Mountains: built on the site of the ancient capital Ray, destroyed by Mongols in 1220; became capital in the 1790s; three universities. Pop: 7 352 000 (2005 est)

Tehuantepec (təˈwɑːntə,pɛk) n Isthmus of Tehuantepec the narrowest part of S Mexico, with the Bay of Campeche on the north coast and the **Gulf of Tehuantepec** (an inlet of the Pacific) on the south coast

Teide or **Teyde** (Spanish ˈteiðe) n Pico de Teide (ˈpiko de) a volcanic mountain in the Canary Islands, on Tenerife. Height: 3718 m (12 198 ft)

te igitur (Latin tei ˈigi,tuə; English tei ˈidʒi,tuə) n RC Church the first prayer of the canon of the Mass, which begins *Te igitur clementissime Pater* (Thee, therefore, most merciful Father)

Teilhard de Chardin (French tɛjar də ʃardɛ̃) n **Pierre** (pjɛr). 1881–1955, French Jesuit priest, palaeontologist, and philosopher. *The Phenomenon of Man* (1938–40), uses scientific evolution to prove the existence of God

Tejo (ˈtəʒu) n the Portuguese name for **Tagus**

Te Kanawa (tei ˈkɑːnəwə) n Dame Kiri (ˈkɪri). born 1944, New Zealand operatic soprano

tektite (ˈtɛktaɪt) n a small dark glassy object found in several areas around the world, thought to be a product of meteorite impact [c20: from Greek *tēktos* molten]

tel- combining form a variant of **tele-, telo-**

telaesthesia or US **telesthesia** (,tɛlɪsˈθiːzɪə) n the alleged perception of events that are beyond the normal range of perceptual processes > **telaesthetic** or US **telesthetic** (,tɛlɪsˈθɛtɪk) adj

telamon (ˈtɛləmən) n, pl **telamones** (,tɛləˈməʊniːz) or **-mons** a column in the form of a male figure, used to support an entablature [c18: via Latin from Greek, from *tlēnai* to bear]

Telamon (ˈtɛləmən, -,mɒn) n Greek myth a king of Salamis; brother of Peleus and father of Teucer and Ajax

Telanaipura (,tɛlənaɪˈpʊərə) n another name for **Jambi**

telangiectasis (tɪ,lændʒɪˈɛktəsɪs) or **telangiectasia** (tɪ,lændʒɪɛkˈteɪzɪə) n, pl -ses (-,siːz) pathol an abnormal dilation of the capillaries or terminal arteries producing blotched red spots, esp on the face or thighs [c19: New Latin, from Greek *telos* end + *angeion* vessel + *ektasis* dilation] > **telangiectatic** (tɪ,lændʒɪɛkˈtætɪk) adj

Tel Aviv (ˈtɛl əˈviːv) n a city in W Israel, on the Mediterranean: the largest city and chief financial centre of Israel; incorporated the city of Jaffa in 1950; university (1953): regarded by the international community as the capital of Israel, though most functions of the capital operate from Jerusalem. Pop: 363 400 (2003 est)

tele- or before a vowel **tel-** combining form **1** at or over a distance; distant: *telescope; telegony; telekinesis; telemeter* **2** television: *telecast* **3** by means of or via telephone or television [from Greek *tele* far]

telecast (ˈtɛlɪ,kɑːst) vb -casts, -casting, -cast or -casted **1** to broadcast (a programme) by television ▷ n **2** a television broadcast > **tele,caster** n

telecom (ˈtɛlɪ,kɒm) or **telecoms** (ˈtɛlɪ,kɒmz) n (functioning as singular) short for **telecommunications**

telecommunications (,tɛlɪkə,mjuːnɪˈkeɪʃənz) n (functioning as singular) the science and technology of communications by telephony, radio, television, etc

telecommuting (ˈtɛlɪkə,mjuːtɪŋ) n another name for **teleworking** > **telecom,muter** n

teledu (ˈtɛlɪ,duː) n a badger, *Mydaus javanensis*, of SE Asia and Indonesia, having dark brown hair with a white stripe along the back and producing a fetid secretion from the anal glands when attacked [c19: from Malay]

telegenic (,tɛlɪˈdʒɛnɪk) adj having or showing a pleasant television image [c20: from TELE(VISION) + (PHOTO)GENIC] > **tele'genically** adv

telegnosis (,tɛləˈnəʊsɪs, ,tɛləg-) n knowledge about distant events alleged to have been obtained without the use of any normal sensory mechanism [c20: from TELE- + -gnosis, from Greek *gnōsis* knowledge]

Telegonus (tɪˈlɛgənəs) n Greek myth a son of Odysseus and Circe, who sought his father and mistakenly killed him, later marrying Odysseus' widow Penelope

telegony (tɪˈlɛgənɪ) n genetics the supposed influence of a previous sire on offspring borne by a female to other sires [c19: from TELE- + -GONY. Compare Greek *tēlegonos* "born far from one's homeland"] > **telegonic** (,tɛlɪˈgɒnɪk) or **te'legonous** adj

telegram (ˈtɛlɪ,græm) n a communication transmitted by telegraph

telegraph (ˈtɛlɪ,græf, -,grɑːf) n **1 a** a device, system, or process by which information can be transmitted over a distance, esp using radio signals or coded electrical signals sent along a transmission line connected to a transmitting and a receiving instrument **b** (as modifier): *telegraph pole* ▷ vb **2** to send a telegram to (a person or place); wire **3** (tr) to transmit or send by telegraph **4** (tr) to give advance notice of (anything), esp unintentionally **5** (tr) Canadian informal to cast (votes) illegally by impersonating registered voters > **telegraphist** (tɪˈlɛgrəfɪst) or **te'legrapher** n > ,tele'graphic adj

telegraph plant n a small tropical Asian leguminous shrub, *Desmodium gyrans*, having small leaflets that turn in various directions during the day and droop at night

telegraphy (tɪˈlɛgrəfɪ) n **1** a system of telecommunications involving any process providing reproduction at a distance of written, printed, or pictorial matter **2** the skill or process of operating a telegraph

Telegu (ˈtɛlə,guː) n, adj a variant spelling of **Telugu**

telehealth (ˈtɛlɪ,hɛlθ) n US & Canadian health care based on consultation by telephone and telemedicine

telekinesis (,tɛlɪkɪˈniːsɪs, -kaɪ-) n **1** the movement of a body caused by thought or willpower without the application of a physical force **2** the ability to cause such movement > **telekinetic** (,tɛlɪkɪˈnɛtɪk, -kaɪ-) adj

Telemachus (tɪˈlɛməkəs) n Greek myth the son of Odysseus and Penelope, who helped his father slay his mother's suitors

Telemann (German ˈteːləman) n **Georg Philipp** (ˈgeːɔrk ˈfiːlɪp). 1681–1767, German composer, noted for his prolific output

telemark (ˈtɛlɪ,mɑːk) n skiing a turn in which one ski is placed far forward of the other and turned gradually inwards [c20: named after *Telemark*, county in Norway]

telemarketing (ˈtɛlɪ,mɑːkɪtɪŋ) n another name for **telesales** [c20: short for TELE(PHONE) MARKETING] > ,tele'marketer n

telematics (,tɛlɪˈmætɪks) n (functioning as singular) the branch of science concerned with the use of technological devices to transmit information over long distances [c20: from TELE- + (INFOR)MATICS] > ,tele'matic adj

telemedicine (ˈtɛlɪ,mɛdɪsɪn, -,mɛdsɪn) n the treatment of disease or injury by consultation with a specialist in a distant place, esp by means of a computer or satellite link

Telemessage (ˈtɛlɪ,mɛsɪdʒ) n trademark a message sent by telephone or telex and delivered in printed form; in Britain, it has replaced the telegram

telemeter (tɪˈlɛmɪtə) n **1** any device for recording or measuring a distant event and transmitting the data to a receiver or observer **2** any device or apparatus used to measure a distance without directly comparing it with a measuring rod, etc, esp one that depends on the measurement of angles ▷ vb **3** (tr) to obtain and transmit (data) from a distant source, esp from a spacecraft > **telemetric** (,tɛlɪ'mɛtrɪk) adj

telemetry (tɪˈlɛmɪtrɪ) n **1** the use of radio waves, telephone lines, etc, to transmit the readings of measuring instruments to a device on which the readings can be indicated or recorded **2** the measurement of linear distance using a tellurometer

telencephalon (,tɛlɛnˈsɛfə,lɒn) n the cerebrum together with related parts of the hypothalamus and the third ventricle > **telencephalic** (,tɛlɛnsɪˈfælɪk) adj

teleology (,tɛlɪˈɒlədʒɪ, ,tiːlɪ-) n **1** philosophy **a** the doctrine that there is evidence of purpose or design in the universe, and esp that this provides proof of the existence of a Designer **b** the belief that certain phenomena are best explained in terms of purpose rather than cause **2** biology the belief that natural phenomena have a predetermined purpose and are not determined by mechanical laws [c18: from New Latin *teleologia*, from Greek *telos* end + -LOGY] > **teleological** (,tɛlɪəˈlɒdʒɪkᵊl, ,tiːlɪ-) adj > ,tele'ologist n

teleost ('tɛlɪ,ɒst, 'tiːlɪ-) *n* any bony fish of the subclass *Teleostei*, having rayed fins and a swim bladder: the group contains most of the bony fishes, including the herrings, carps, eels, cod, perches, etc [c19: from New Latin *teleosteī* (pl) creatures having complete skeletons, from Greek *teleos* complete + *osteon* bone]

telepathy (tɪ'lɛpəθɪ) *n psychol* the communication between people of thoughts, feelings, desires, etc, involving mechanisms that cannot be understood in terms of known scientific laws [c19: from TELE- + Greek *patheia* feeling, perception: see -PATHY] > **telepathic** (,tɛlɪ'pæθɪk) *adj* > te'lepathist *n* > telepathize *or* telepathise (tɪ'lɛpə,θaɪz) *vb*

telephone ('tɛlɪ,fəʊn) *n* **1** Also called: **telephone set** an electrical device for transmitting speech, consisting of a microphone and receiver mounted on a handset **2 a** a worldwide system of communications using telephones. The microphone in one telephone converts sound waves into electrical signals that are transmitted along a telephone wire or by radio to one or more distant sets, the receivers of which reconvert the incoming signal into the original sound **b** (*as modifier*): *a telephone exchange; a telephone call* ▷ *vb* **3** to call or talk to (a person) by telephone **4** to transmit (a recorded message, radio or television programme, or other information) by telephone, using special transmitting and receiving equipment > 'tele,phoner *n* > telephonic (,tɛlɪ'fɒnɪk) *adj*

telephone banking *n* a facility enabling customers to make use of banking services, such as oral payment instructions, account movements, raising loans, etc, over the telephone rather than by personal visit

telephone box *n* an enclosure from which a paid telephone call can be made. Also called: **telephone kiosk, telephone booth**

telephone directory *n* a book listing the names, addresses, and telephone numbers of subscribers in a particular area

telephone number *n* **1** a set of figures identifying the telephone of a particular subscriber, and used in making connections to that telephone **2** (*plural*) extremely large numbers, esp in reference to salaries or prices

telephone selling *n* another name for **telesales**

telephonist (tɪ'lɛfənɪst) *n Brit* a person who operates a telephone switchboard

telephony (tɪ'lɛfənɪ) *n* a system of telecommunications for the transmission of speech or other sounds

telephotography (,tɛlɪfə'tɒgrəfɪ) *n* the process or technique of photographing distant objects using a telephoto lens

telephoto lens ('tɛlɪ,fəʊtəʊ) *n* a compound camera lens in which the focal length is greater than that of a simple lens of the same dimensions and thus produces a magnified image of a distant object

telepoint ('tɛlɪ,pɔɪnt) *n* **a** a system providing a place where a cordless telephone can be connected to a telephone network **b** a place where a cordless telephone can be connected to a telephone network

teleprinter ('tɛlɪ,prɪntə) *n* **1** a telegraph apparatus consisting of a keyboard transmitter, which converts a typed message into coded pulses for transmission along a wire or cable, and a printing receiver, which converts incoming signals and prints out the message. US name: **teletypewriter 2** a network of such devices, formerly used for communicating information, etc **3** a similar device used for direct input/output of data into a computer at a distant location

Teleprompter ('tɛlɪ,prɒmptə) *n trademark US & Canadian* an electronic television prompting device whereby a prepared script, unseen by the audience, is enlarged line by line for the speaker

Teleran ('tɛlə,ræn) *n trademark* an electronic navigational aid in which the image of a ground-based radar system is televised to aircraft in flight so that a pilot can see the position of his aircraft in relation to others [c20: from *Tele(vision)* R(*adar*) A(*ir*) N(*avigation*)]

telesales ('tɛlɪ,seɪlz) *n* (*functioning as singular*) the selling or attempted selling of a particular commodity or service by a salesman who makes his initial approach by telephone. Also called: **telemarketing, telephone selling**

telescope ('tɛlɪ,skəʊp) *n* **1** an optical instrument for making distant objects appear larger and brighter by use of a combination of lenses (refracting telescope) or lenses and curved mirrors (reflecting telescope) **2** any instrument, such as a radio telescope, for collecting, focusing, and detecting electromagnetic radiation from space ▷ *vb* **3** to crush together or be crushed together, as in a collision **4** to fit together like a set of cylinders that slide into one another, thus allowing extension and shortening **5** to make or become smaller or shorter [c17: from Italian *telescopio* or New Latin *telescopium*, literally: far-seeing instrument; see TELE-, -SCOPE]

telescopic (,tɛlɪ'skɒpɪk) *adj* **1** of or relating to a telescope **2** seen through or obtained by means of a telescope **3** visible only with the aid of a telescope **4** able to see far **5** having or consisting of parts that telescope > ,tele'scopically *adv*

telescopic sight *n* a telescope mounted on a rifle, etc, used for sighting

telescopy (tɪ'lɛskəpɪ) *n* the branch of astronomy concerned with the use and design of telescopes

teleshopping ('tɛlɪ,ʃɒpɪŋ) *n* the purchase of goods by telephone or via the internet

telespectroscope (,tɛlɪ'spɛktrə,skəʊp) *n* a combination of a telescope and a spectroscope, used for spectroscopic analysis of radiation from stars and other celestial bodies

telestereoscope (,tɛlɪ'stɪərɪə,skəʊp, -'stɛrɪə-) *n* an optical instrument for obtaining stereoscopic images of distant objects

telestich (tɪ'lɛstɪk, 'tɛlɪ,stɪk) *n* a short poem in which the last letters of each successive line form a word [c17: from Greek *telos* end + STICH]

Teletext ('tɛlɪ,tɛkst) *n trademark* (in Britain) the ITV teletext service. See **Ceefax**

telethon ('tɛlə,θɒn) *n* a lengthy television programme to raise charity funds, etc [c20: from TELE- + MARATHON]

Teletype ('tɛlɪ,taɪp) *n* **1** *trademark* a type of teleprinter **2** (*sometimes not capital*) a network of such devices, used for communicating messages, information, etc ▷ *vb* **3** (*sometimes not capital*) to transmit (a message) by Teletype

teletypewriter (,tɛlɪ'taɪp,raɪtə, ,tɛlɪ'taɪp-) *n* a US name for **teleprinter**

televangelist (,tɛlɪ'vændʒəlɪst) *n US* an evangelical preacher who appears regularly on television, preaching the gospel and appealing for donations from viewers [c20: from TELE(VISION + E)VANGELIST]

televise ('tɛlɪ,vaɪz) *vb* **1** to put (a programme) on television **2** (*tr*) to transmit (a programme, signal, etc) by television

television ('tɛlɪ,vɪʒən) *n* **1** the system or process of producing on a distant screen a series of transient visible images, usually with an accompanying sound signal. Electrical signals, converted from optical images by a camera tube, are transmitted by UHF or VHF radio waves or by cable and reconverted into optical images by means of a television tube inside a television set **2** Also called: **television set** a device designed to receive and convert incoming electrical signals into a series of visible images on a screen together with accompanying sound **3** the content, etc, of television programmes **4** the occupation or profession concerned with any aspect of the broadcasting of television programmes **5** (*modifier*) of, relating to, or used in the transmission or reception of video and audio UHF or VHF radio signals: *a television transmitter* ▷ Abbreviation: TV [c20: from TELE- + VISION]

television tube *n* a cathode-ray tube designed for the reproduction of television pictures. Sometimes shortened to: **tube**

televisual (,tɛlɪ'vɪʒʊəl, -zjʊ-) *adj* relating to, shown on, or suitable for production on television > ,tele'visually *adv*

teleworking ('tɛlɪ,wɜːkɪŋ) *n* the use of home computers, telephones, and other communication devices to enable a person to work from home while maintaining contact with colleagues, customers, or a central office. Also called:telecommuting ▷'tele,worker *n*

telex ('tɛlɛks) *n* **1** an international telegraph service in which teleprinters are rented out to subscribers for the purpose of direct communication **2** a teleprinter used in such a service **3** a message transmitted or received by telex ▷ *vb* **4** to transmit (a message) to (a person, office, etc) by telex [c20: from *tel(eprinter) ex(change)*]

Telford¹ ('tɛlfəd) *n* a town in W central England, in Telford and Wrekin unitary authority, Shropshire: designated a new town in 1963. Pop: 138 241 (2001)

Telford² ('tɛlfəd) *n* **Thomas.** 1757–1834, Scottish civil engineer, known esp for his roads and such bridges as the Menai suspension bridge (1825)

Telford and Wrekin *n* a unitary authority in W Central England, in Shropshire. Pop: 160 300 (2003 est). Area: 289 sq km (112 sq miles)

Telidon ('tɛlɪ,dɒn) *n* *trademark* a Canadian interactive viewdata service

Telkom ('tɛl,kɒm) *n* the official telephone service in South Africa

tell¹ (tɛl) *vb* **tells, telling, told 1** (when *tr*, *may take a clause as object*) to let know or notify **2** (*tr*) to order or instruct (someone to do something) **3** (when *intr*, usually foll by *of*) to give an account or narration (of something) **4** (*tr*) to communicate by words; utter: *to tell the truth* **5** (*tr*) to make known; disclose: *to tell fortunes* **6** (*intr*; often foll by *of*) to serve as an indication: *her blush told of her embarrassment* **7** (*tr*; used with *can*, etc; *may take a clause as object*) to comprehend, discover, or discern: *I can tell what is wrong* **8** (*tr*; used with *can*, etc) to distinguish or discriminate: *he couldn't tell chalk from cheese* **9** (*intr*) to have or produce an impact, effect, or strain: *every step told on his bruised feet* **10** (*intr*; sometimes foll by *on*) *informal* to reveal secrets or gossip (about) **11** (*tr*) to assure: *I tell you, I've had enough!* **12** (*tr*) to count (votes) **13** **tell the time** to read the time from a clock **14** **you're telling me** *slang* I know that very well ▷ See also **tell apart, tell off** [Old English *tellan*; related to Old Saxon *tellian*, Old High German *zellen* to tell, count, Old Norse *telja*] ▷'tellable *adj*

tell² (tɛl) *n* a large mound resulting from the accumulation of rubbish on a long-settled site, esp one with mudbrick buildings, particularly in the Middle East [c19: from Arabic *tall*]

Tell (tɛl) *n* **William**, German name *Wilhelm Tell*. a legendary Swiss patriot, who, traditionally, lived in the early 14th century and was compelled by an Austrian governor to shoot an apple from his son's head with one shot of his crossbow. He did so without mishap

tell apart *vb* (*tr, adverb*) to distinguish between; discern

Tell el Amarna ('tɛl ɛl ə'mɑːnə) *n* a group of ruins and rock tombs in Upper Egypt, on the Nile below Asyut: site of the capital of Amenhotep IV, built about 1375 BC; excavated from 1891 onwards

teller ('tɛlə) *n* **1** another name for **cashier¹** (sense 2) **2** a person appointed to count votes in a legislative body, assembly, etc **3** a person who tells; narrator

Teller ('tɛlə) *n* **Edward.** 1908–2003, US nuclear physicist, born in Hungary: a major contributor to the development of the hydrogen bomb (1952)

telling ('tɛlɪŋ) *adj* **1** having a marked effect or impact **2** revealing ▷'tellingly *adv*

tell off *vb* (*tr, adverb*) **1** *informal* to reprimand; scold **2** to count and dismiss

telltale ('tɛl,teɪl) *n* **1** a person who tells tales about others **2** a an outward indication of something concealed **b** (*as modifier*): *a telltale paw mark* **3** any of various indicators or recording devices used to monitor a process, machine, etc

tellurian (tɛ'lʊərɪən) *adj* **1** of or relating to the earth ▷ *n* **2** (esp in science fiction) an inhabitant of the earth [c19: from Latin *tellūs* the earth]

telluric¹ (tɛ'lʊərɪk) *adj* of, relating to, or originating on or in the earth or soil; terrestrial, esp in reference to natural electrical or magnetic fields [c19: from Latin *tellūs* the earth]

telluric² (tɛ'lʊərɪk) *adj* of or containing tellurium, esp in a high valence state [c20: from TELLUR(IUM) + -IC]

tellurion or **tellurian** (tɛ'lʊərɪən) *n* an instrument that shows how day and night and the seasons result from

the tilt of the earth, its rotation on its axis, and its revolution around the sun [c19: from Latin *tellūs* the earth]

tellurium (tɛ'lʊərɪəm) *n* a brittle silvery-white nonmetallic element occurring both uncombined and in combination with metals: used in alloys of lead and copper and as a semiconductor. Symbol: Te; atomic no: 52; atomic wt: 127.60; valency: 2, 4, or 6; relative density: 6.24; melting pt: 449.57±0.3°C; boiling pt: 988°C [c19: New Latin, from Latin *tellūs* the earth, formed by analogy with URANIUM]

tellurometer (,tɛljʊ'rɒmɪtə) *n* *surveying* an electronic instrument for measuring distances of up to about 30 miles that consists of two units, one at each end of the distance to be measured, between which radio waves are transmitted [c20: from Latin *tellūs* the earth + -METER]

Tellus ('tɛləs) *n* the Roman goddess of the earth; protectress of marriage, fertility, and the dead

telly ('tɛlɪ) *n*, *pl* -lies *informal, chiefly Brit* short for **television**

telo- or before a vowel **tel-** *combining form* **1** complete; final; perfect **2** end; at the end [from Greek *telos* end]

telomere ('tɛlə,mɪə) *n* *genetics* either of the ends of a chromosome [c20: from Greek *telos* end + *meros* part]

telpherage or **telferage** ('tɛlfərɪdʒ) *n* an overhead transport system in which an electrically driven truck runs along a single rail or cable, the load being suspended in a separate car beneath. Also called:**telpher**

telson ('tɛlsən) *n* the last segment or an appendage on the last segment of the body of crustaceans and arachnids [c19: from Greek: a boundary; probably related to *telos* end]

Telugu or **Telegu** ('tɛlə,guː) *n* **1** a language of SE India, belonging to the Dravidian family of languages: the state language of Andhra Pradesh **2** *pl* -gus or -gu a member of the people who speak this language ▷ *adj* **3** of or relating to this people or their language

Telukbetung (tə,lʊkbə'tʊŋ) *n* a city in Indonesia, in S Sumatra on the Sunda Strait; merged with Tanjungkarang to form the city of Bandar Lampung.

Tema ('tiːmə) *n* a port in SE Ghana on the Atlantic: oil-refining. Pop: 160 000 (2005 est)

temazepam (tə'mæzə,pæm) *n* a benzodiazepine sedative; the gel-like capsule formulation is properly taken orally but has also been melted and injected by drug users

Témbi ('tɛmbiː) *n* a transliteration of the Modern Greek name for **Tempe**

temblor ('tɛmblə, -blɔː) *n*, *pl* **temblors** or **temblores** (tɛm'blɔːreɪz) *chiefly US* an earthquake or earth tremor [c19: American Spanish, from Spanish *temblar* to shake, tremble]

temerity (tɪ'mɛrɪtɪ) *n* rashness or boldness [c15: from Latin *temeritās* accident, from *temere* at random] ▷**temerarious** (,tɛmə'rɛərɪəs) *adj*

Temesvár ('tɛmɛʃvɑːr) *n* the Hungarian name for **Timişoara**

temp (tɛmp) *informal* ▷ *n* **1** a person, esp a typist or other office worker, employed on a temporary basis ▷ *vb* **2** (*intr*) to work as a temp

temp. *abbreviation* **1** temperature **2** temporary **3** tempore

Tempe ('tɛmpɪ) *n* **Vale of Tempe** a wooded valley in E Greece, in Thessaly between the mountains Olympus and Ossa. Modern Greek name:**Témbi**

temper ('tɛmpə) *n* **1** a frame of mind; mood or humour **2** a sudden outburst of anger; tantrum **3** a tendency to exhibit uncontrolled anger; irritability **4** a mental condition of moderation and calm (esp in the phrases **keep one's temper, lose one's temper, out of temper**) **5** the degree of hardness, elasticity, or a similar property of a metal or metal object ▷ *vb* **6** to make more temperate, acceptable, or suitable by adding something else; moderate: *he tempered his criticism with kindly sympathy* **7** to strengthen or toughen (a metal or metal article) by heat treatment, as by heating and quenching **8** *music* **a** to adjust the frequency differences between the notes of a scale on (a keyboard instrument) in order to allow modulation into other keys **b** to make such an adjustment to the pitches of notes in (a scale) [Old English *temprian* to mingle, (influenced by Old French *temprer*), from Latin *temperāre* to mix, probably from *tempus* time] > 'temperable *adj* > 'temperer *n*

tempera ('tɛmpərə) *n* **1** a painting medium for powdered pigments, consisting usually of egg yolk and water **2 a** any emulsion used as a painting medium, with casein, glue, wax, etc, as a base **b** the paint made from mixing this with pigment **3** the technique of painting with tempera [c19: from Italian phrase *pingere a tempera* painting in tempera, from *temperare* to mingle; see TEMPER]

temperament ('tɛmpərəmənt, -prəmənt) *n* **1** an individual's character, disposition, and tendencies as revealed in his reactions **2** excitability, moodiness, or anger, esp when displayed openly **3** the characteristic way an individual behaves, esp towards other people **4 a** an adjustment made to the frequency differences between notes on a keyboard instrument to allow modulation to other keys **b** any of several systems of such adjustment, such as **just temperament**, a system not practically possible on keyboard instruments, **mean-tone temperament**, a system giving an approximation to natural tuning, and **equal temperament**, the system commonly used in keyboard instruments, giving a scale based on an octave divided into twelve exactly equal semitones **5** *obsolete* the characteristic way an individual behaves, viewed as the result of the influence of the four humours (blood, phlegm, yellow bile, and black bile) [c15: from Latin *temperāmentum* a mixing in proportion, from *temperāre* to TEMPER]

temperamental (,tɛmpərə'mɛnt³l, -prə'mɛnt³l) *adj* **1** easily upset or irritated; excitable; volatile **2** of, relating to, or caused by temperament **3** *informal* working erratically and inconsistently; unreliable > ,tempera'mentally *adv*

temperance ('tɛmpərəns) *n* **1** restraint or moderation, esp in yielding to one's appetites or desires **2** abstinence from alcoholic drink [c14: from Latin *temperantia*, from *temperāre* to regulate]

temperate ('tɛmpərɪt, 'tɛmprɪt) *adj* **1** having a climate intermediate between tropical and polar; moderate or mild in temperature **2** mild in quality or character; exhibiting temperance [c14: from Latin *temperātus*] > 'temperately *adv* > 'temperateness *n*

Temperate Zone *n* those parts of the earth's surface lying between the Arctic Circle and the tropic of Cancer and between the Antarctic Circle and the tropic of Capricorn

temperature ('tɛmprɪtʃə) *n* **1** the degree of hotness of a body, substance, or medium; a physical property related to the average kinetic energy of the atoms or molecules of a substance **2** *informal* a body temperature in excess of the normal [c16 (originally: a mingling): from Latin *temperātūra* proportion, from *temperāre* to TEMPER]

temperature gradient *n* the rate of change in temperature in a given direction, esp in altitude

temperature-humidity index *n* an index of the effect on human comfort of temperature and humidity levels, 65 being the highest comfortable level

tempered ('tɛmpəd) *adj* **1** *music* (of a scale) having the frequency differences between notes adjusted in accordance with the system of equal temperament **2** (*in combination*) having a temper or temperament as specified: *ill-tempered*

tempest ('tɛmpɪst) *n* **1** *chiefly literary* a violent wind or storm **2** a violent commotion, uproar, or disturbance [c13: from Old French *tempeste*, from Latin *tempestās* storm, from *tempus* time]

tempestuous (tɛm'pɛstjʊəs) *adj* **1** of or relating to a tempest **2** violent or stormy > tem'pestuously *adv* > tem'pestuousness *n*

tempi ('tɛmpiː) *n* (in musical senses) the plural of **tempo**

Templar ('tɛmplə) *n* **1** a member of a military religious order (**Knights of the Temple of Solomon**) founded by Crusaders in Jerusalem around 1118 to defend the Holy Sepulchre and Christian pilgrims; suppressed in 1312 **2** (*sometimes not capital*) *Brit* a lawyer, esp a barrister, who

lives or has chambers in the Inner or Middle Temple in London [c13: from Medieval Latin *templārius* of the temple, from Latin *templum* TEMPLE¹; first applied to the knightly order because their house was near the site of the Temple of Solomon]

template *or* **templet** ('tɛmplɪt) *n* **1** a gauge or pattern, cut out in wood or metal, used in woodwork, etc, to help shape something accurately **2** a pattern cut out in card or plastic, used in various crafts to reproduce shapes **3** a short beam, made of metal, wood, or stone, that is used to spread a load, as over a doorway **4** *biochem* the molecular structure of a compound that serves as a pattern for the production of the molecular structure of another specific compound in a reaction [c17 *templet* (later spelling influenced by PLATE), probably from French, diminutive of TEMPLE³]

temple¹ ('tɛmp³l) *n* **1** a building or place dedicated to the worship of a deity or deities **2** a Mormon church **3** *US* another name for **synagogue 4** any Christian church, esp a large or imposing one **5** any place or object regarded as a shrine where God makes himself present, esp the body of a person who has been sanctified or saved by grace **6** a building regarded as the focus of an activity, interest, or practice: *a temple of the arts* [Old English *tempel*, from Latin *templum*; probably related to Latin *tempus* TIME, Greek *temenos* sacred enclosure, literally: a place cut off, from *temnein* to cut]

temple² ('tɛmp³l) *n* the region on each side of the head in front of the ear and above the cheek bone [c14: from Old French *temple*, from Latin *tempora* the temples, from *tempus* temple of the head]

temple³ ('tɛmp³l) *n* the part of a loom that keeps the cloth being woven stretched to the correct width [c15: from French, from Latin *templum* a small timber]

Temple¹ ('tɛmp³l) *n* **1** either of two buildings in London and Paris that belonged to the Templars. The one in London now houses two of the chief law societies **2** any of three buildings or groups of buildings erected by the Jews in ancient Jerusalem for the worship of Jehovah

Temple² ('tɛmp³l) *n* **1 Shirley,** married name *Shirley Temple Black*. born 1928, US film actress and politician. Her films as a child star include *Little Miss Marker* (1934), *Wee Willie Winkie* (1937), and *Heidi* (1937). She was US ambassador to Ghana (1974–76) and to Czechoslovakia (1989–92) **2 Sir William.** 1628–99, English diplomat and essayist. He negotiated the Triple Alliance (1668) and the marriage of William of Orange to Mary II **3 William.** 1881–1944, English prelate and advocate of social reform; archbishop of Canterbury (1942–44)

Temple of Artemis *n* the large temple at Ephesus, on the W coast of Asia Minor: one of the Seven Wonders of the World

tempo ('tɛmpəʊ) *n, pl* **-pos** *or* **-pi** (-piː) **1** the speed at which a piece or passage of music is meant to be played, usually indicated by a musical direction (**tempo marking**) or metronome marking **2** rate or pace [c18: from Italian, from Latin *tempus* time]

temporal¹ ('tɛmpərəl, 'tɛmprəl) *adj* **1** of or relating to time **2** of or relating to secular as opposed to spiritual or religious affairs **3** lasting for a relatively short time **4** *grammar* of or relating to tense or the linguistic expression of time in general [c14: from Latin *temporālis*, from *tempus* time] > 'temporally *adv*

temporal² ('tɛmpərəl, 'tɛmprəl) *adj* *anatomy* of, relating to, or near the temple or temples [c16: from Late Latin *temporālis* belonging to the temples; see TEMPLE²]

temporal bone *n* either of two compound bones forming part of the sides and base of the skull: they surround the organs of hearing

temporality (,tɛmpə'rælɪtɪ) *n, pl* **-ties 1** the state or quality of being temporal **2** something temporal **3** (*often plural*) a secular possession or revenue belonging to a Church, a group within the Church, or the clergy

temporal lobe *n* the laterally protruding portion of each cerebral hemisphere, situated below the parietal lobe and associated with sound perception and interpretation: it is thought to be the centre for memory recall

temporary ('tɛmpərərɪ, 'tɛmprərɪ) *adj* **1** not permanent;

provisional **2** lasting only a short time; transitory ▷ *n, pl* -raries **3** a person, esp a secretary or other office worker, employed on a temporary basis [c16: from Latin *temporārius*, from *tempus* time] > 'temporarily *adv* > 'temporariness *n*

temporize or **temporise** ('tɛmpə,raɪz) *vb* (*intr*) **1** to delay, act evasively, or protract a discussion, negotiation, etc, esp in order to gain time or effect a compromise **2** to adapt oneself to the circumstances or occasion, as by temporary or apparent agreement [c16: from French *temporiser*, from Medieval Latin *temporizāre*, from Latin *tempus* time] > ,tempori'zation or ,tempori'sation *n* > 'tempo,rizer or 'tempo,riser *n*

tempt (tɛmpt) *vb* (*tr*) **1** to attempt to persuade or entice to do something, esp something morally wrong or unwise **2** to allure, invite, or attract **3** to give rise to a desire in (someone) to do something; dispose **4** to risk provoking (esp in the phrase **tempt fate**) [c13: from Old French *tempter*, from Latin *temptāre* to test] > 'temptable *adj* > 'tempter *n* > 'temptress *fem n*

temptation (tɛmp'teɪʃən) *n* **1** the act of tempting or the state of being tempted **2** a person or thing that tempts

tempting ('tɛmptɪŋ) *adj* attractive or inviting: *a tempting meal* > 'temptingly *adv*

tempus fugit (*Latin* 'tɛmpəs 'fjuːdʒɪt, -gɪt) time flies

Temuco (*Spanish* te'muko) *n* a city in S Chile: agricultural trading centre. Pop: 287 000 (2005 est)

ten (tɛn) *n* **1** the cardinal number that is the sum of nine and one. It is the base of the decimal number system and the base of the common logarithm **2** a numeral, 10, X, etc, representing this number **3** something representing, represented by, or consisting of ten units, such as a playing card with ten symbols on it **4** Also called: **ten o'clock** ten hours after noon or midnight ▷ *determiner* **5** amounting to ten ▷ Related adjective: **decimal** [Old English *tēn*; related to Old Saxon *tehan*, Old High German *zehan*, Gothic *taihun*, Latin *decem*, Greek *deka*, Sanskrit *dasa*]

tenable ('tɛnəbəl) *adj* able to be upheld, believed, maintained, or defended [c16: from Old French, from *tenir* to hold, from Latin *tenēre*] > ,tena'bility or 'tenableness *n* > 'tenably *adv*

tenace ('tɛneɪs) *n bridge, whist* a holding of two nonconsecutive high cards of a suit, such as the ace and queen [c17: from French, from Spanish *tenaza* forceps, ultimately from Latin *tenāx* holding fast, from *tenēre* to hold]

tenacious (tɪ'neɪʃəs) *adj* **1** holding or grasping firmly; forceful: *a tenacious grip* **2** retentive: *a tenacious memory* **3** stubborn or persistent **4** holding together firmly; tough or cohesive **5** tending to stick or adhere [c16: from Latin *tenāx*, from *tenēre* to hold] > te'naciously *adv* > te'naciousness or tenacity (tɪ'næsɪtɪ) *n*

tenaculum (tɪ'nækjʊləm) *n, pl* -la (-lə) a surgical or dissecting instrument for grasping and holding parts, consisting of a slender hook mounted in a handle [c17: from Late Latin, from Latin *tenēre* to hold]

tenancy ('tɛnənsɪ) *n, pl* -cies **1** the temporary possession or holding by a tenant of lands or property owned by another **2** the period of holding or occupying such property **3** the period of holding office, a position, etc

tenant ('tɛnənt) *n* **1** a person who holds, occupies, or possesses land or property by any kind of right or title, esp from a landlord under a lease **2** a person who has the use of a house, flat, etc, subject to the payment of rent **3** any holder or occupant ▷ *vb* **4** (*tr*) to hold (land or property) as a tenant [c14: from Old French, literally: (one who is) holding, from *tenir* to hold, from Latin *tenēre*] > 'tenantable *adj* > 'tenantless *adj*

tenant farmer *n* a person who farms land rented from another, the rent usually taking the form of part of the crops grown or livestock reared

tenantry ('tɛnəntrɪ) *n* **1** tenants collectively, esp those with the same landlord **2** the status or condition of being a tenant

tench (tɛntʃ) *n* a European freshwater cyprinid game fish, *Tinca tinca*, having a thickset dark greenish body with a barbel at each side of the mouth [c14: from Old French *tenche*, from Late Latin *tinca*]

Ten Commandments *pl n* the Ten Commandments *Old Testament* the commandments summarizing the basic obligations of man towards God and his fellow men, delivered to Moses on Mount Sinai engraved on two tables of stone (Exodus 20:1–17)

tend[1] (tɛnd) *vb* (when *intr*, usually foll by *to* or *towards*) **1** (when *tr*, *takes an infinitive*) to have a general disposition (to do something); be inclined: *children tend to prefer sweets to meat* **2** (*intr*) to have or be an influence (towards a specific result); be conducive **3** (*intr*) to go or move (in a particular direction): *to tend to the south* [c14: from Old French *tendre*, from Latin *tendere* to stretch]

tend[2] (tɛnd) *vb* **1** (*tr*) to care for **2** (when *intr*, often foll by *to*) to attend (to) **3** (*tr*) to handle or control **4** (*intr*, often foll by *to*) *informal, chiefly US & Canadian* to pay attention [c14: variant of ATTEND]

tendency ('tɛndənsɪ) *n, pl* -cies **1** (often foll by *to*) an inclination, predisposition, propensity, or leaning **2** the general course, purport, or drift of something, esp a written work [c17: from Medieval Latin *tendentia*, from Latin *tendere* to TEND[1]]

tendentious or **tendencious** (tɛn'dɛnʃəs) *adj* having or showing an intentional tendency or bias, esp a controversial one [c20: from TENDENCY] > ten'dentiously or ten'denciously *adv* > ten'dentiousness or ten'denciousness *n*

tender[1] ('tɛndə) *adj* **1** easily broken, cut, or crushed; soft; not tough **2** easily damaged; vulnerable or sensitive: *a tender youth; at a tender age* **3** having or expressing warm and affectionate feelings **4** kind, merciful, or sympathetic: *a tender heart* **5** arousing warm feelings; touching **6** gentle and delicate: *a tender breeze* **7** requiring care in handling; ticklish: *a tender question* **8** painful or sore **9** sensitive to moral or spiritual feelings **10** (*postpositive*; foll by *of*) careful or protective: *tender of one's emotions* [c13: from Old French *tendre*, from Latin *tener* delicate] > 'tenderly *adv* > 'tenderness *n*

tender[2] ('tɛndə) *vb* **1** (*tr*) to give, present, or offer: *to tender one's resignation; tender a bid* **2** (*intr*; foll by *for*) to make a formal offer or estimate for (a job or contract) **3** (*tr*) *law* to offer (money or goods) in settlement of a debt or claim ▷ *n* **4** the act or an instance of tendering; offer **5** *commerce* a formal offer to supply specified goods or services at a stated cost or rate **6** something, esp money, used as an official medium of payment: *legal tender* [c16: from Anglo-French *tendre*, from Latin *tendere* to extend; see TEND[1]] > 'tenderer *n*

tender[3] ('tɛndə) *n* **1** a small boat, such as a dinghy, towed or carried by a yacht or ship **2** a vehicle drawn behind a steam locomotive to carry the fuel and water **3** a person who tends [c15: variant of *attender*]

tenderfoot ('tɛndə,fʊt) *n, pl* -foots or -feet **1** a newcomer, esp to the mines or ranches of the southwestern US **2** (formerly) a beginner in the Scouts or Guides

tenderhearted (,tɛndə'hɑːtɪd) *adj* having a compassionate, kindly, or sensitive disposition

tenderize or **tenderise** ('tɛndə,raɪz) *vb* (*tr*) to make (meat) tender by pounding it to break down the fibres, by steeping it in a marinade, or by treating it with a tenderizer > ,tenderi'zation or ,tenderi'sation *n* > tenderizer or tenderiser ('tɛndə,raɪzə) *n*

tenderloin ('tɛndə,lɔɪn) *n* a tender cut of pork or other meat from between the sirloin and ribs

tendon ('tɛndən) *n* a cord or band of white inelastic collagenous tissue that attaches a muscle to a bone or some other part; sinew [c16: from Medieval Latin *tendō*, from Latin *tendere* to stretch; related to Greek *tenōn* sinew]

tendril ('tɛndrɪl) *n* a specialized threadlike part of a leaf or stem that attaches climbing plants to a support by twining or adhering [c16: perhaps from Old French *tendron* tendril (confused with Old French *tendron* bud), from Medieval Latin *tendō* TENDON]

Tendulkar (tɛn'dʊlkə) *n* **Sachin** ('sætʃɪn) (**Ramesh**). born 1973, Indian cricketer; captain of India (1996–2000)

tenebrism ('tɛnə,brɪzəm) *n* (*sometimes capital*) a school, style, or method of painting, adopted chiefly by 17th-century Spanish and Neapolitan painters, esp Caravaggio, characterized by large areas of dark colours, usually relieved with a shaft of light > 'tenebrist *n, adj*

tenebrous ('tɛnɪbrəs) *or* **tenebrious** (tə'nɛbrɪəs) *adj* gloomy, shadowy, or dark [c15: from Latin *tenebrōsus* from *tenebrae* darkness]

Tenedos ('tɛnɪ,dɒs) *n* an island in the NE Aegean, near the entrance to the Dardanelles: in Greek legend the base of the Greek fleet during the siege of Troy. Modern Turkish name: Bozcaada

tenement ('tɛnəmənt) *n* **1** Also called: **tenement building** (now esp in Scotland) a large building divided into separate flats **2** a dwelling place or residence, esp one intended for rent **3** *chiefly Brit* a room or flat for rent **4** *property law* any form of permanent property, such as land, dwellings, offices, etc [c14: from Medieval Latin *tenementum*, from Latin *tenēre* to hold] > tenemental (,tɛnə'mɛntəl) *adj*

Tenerife (,tɛnə'riːf; *Spanish* teneˈrife) *n* a Spanish island in the Atlantic, off the NW coast of Africa: the largest of the Canary Islands; volcanic and mountainous; tourism and agriculture. Capital: Santa Cruz. Pop: 778 071 (2002 est). Area: 2058 sq km (795 sq miles)

tenesmus (tɪ'nɛzməs, -'nɛs-) *n pathol* an ineffective painful straining to empty the bowels in response to the sensation of a desire to defecate, without producing a significant quantity of faeces [c16: from Medieval Latin, from Latin *tēnesmos*, from Greek *teinesmos*, from *teinein* to strain] > te'nesmic *adj*

tenet ('tɛnɪt, 'tiːnɪt) *n* a belief, opinion, or dogma [c17: from Latin, literally: he (it) holds, from *tenēre* to hold]

tenfold ('tɛn,fəʊld) *adj* **1** equal to or having 10 times as many or as much **2** composed of 10 parts ▷ *adv* **3** by or up to 10 times as many or as much

ten-gallon hat *n* (in the US and Canada) a cowboy's broad-brimmed felt hat with a very high crown [c20: so called because of its large size]

Teng Hsiao-ping ('tɛŋ sjaʊ'pɪŋ) *n* a variant transliteration of the Chinese name for **Deng Xiaoping**

Tengri Khan ('tɛŋgrɪ 'kaːn) *n* a mountain in central Asia, on the border between Kyrgyzstan and the Xinjiang Uygur Autonomous Region of W China. Height: 6995 m (22 951 ft)

Tengri Nor ('tɛŋgrɪ 'nɔː) *n* another name for **Nam Co**

Ten Gurus *pl n* the ten leaders of the Sikh religion from the founder of Sikhism Guru Nanak (1469–1538) to Guru Govind Singh (1666–1708), who ended the line of gurus by calling on Sikhs to rely on the holy text of the Granth to guide them

Teniers ('tɛniəz) *n* **David** ('daːvɪt), called *the Elder*, 1582–1649, and his son **David,** called *the Younger*, 1610–90, Flemish painters

tenner ('tɛnə) *n informal* **1** *Brit* **a** a ten-pound note **b** the sum of ten pounds **2** *US* a ten-dollar bill

Tennessee (,tɛnɪ'siː) *n* **1** a state of the E central US: consists of a plain in the west, rising to the Appalachians and the Cumberland Plateau in the east. Capital: Nashville. Pop: 5 841 748 (2003 est). Area: 109 412 sq km (42 244 sq miles). Abbreviations: Tenn., (with zip code): TN **2** a river in the E central US, flowing southwest from E Tennessee into N Alabama, then west and north to the Ohio River at Paducah: the longest tributary of the Ohio; includes a series of dams and reservoirs under the Tennessee Valley Authority. Length: 1049 km (652 miles) > ,Tennes'sean *n, adj*

Tenniel ('tɛnjəl) *n* Sir **John.** 1820–1914, English caricaturist, noted for his illustrations to Lewis Carroll's *Alice* books and for his political cartoons in *Punch* (1851–1901)

tennis ('tɛnɪs) *n* **a** a racket game played between two players or pairs of players who hit a ball to and fro over a net on a rectangular court of grass, asphalt, clay, etc. See also **lawn tennis**, **real tennis**, **table tennis** **b** (*as modifier*): *tennis court; tennis racket* [c14: probably from Anglo-French *tenetz* hold (imperative), from Old French *tenir* to hold, from Latin *tenēre*]

tennis elbow *n* a painful inflammation of the elbow caused by exertion in playing tennis and similar games

tennis shoe *n* a rubber-soled canvas shoe tied with laces

Tennyson ('tɛnɪsⁿn) *n* **Alfred,** Lord Tennyson. 1809–92, English poet; poet laureate (1850–92). His poems include *The Lady of Shalott* (1832), *Morte d'Arthur* (1842), the collection *In Memoriam* (1850), *Maud* (1855), and *Idylls of the King* (1859) > Tennysonian (,tɛnɪ'səʊnɪən) *adj, n*

Teno ('tɛnə) *n* the Finnish name for **Tana** (sense 3)

teno- *or before a vowel* **ten-** *combining form* tendon: *tenosynovitis* [from Greek *tenōn*]

Tenochtitlán (tɛˌnɔːtʃtiː'tlaːn) *n* an ancient city and capital of the Aztec empire on the present site of Mexico City; razed by Cortés in 1521

tenon ('tɛnən) *n* **1** the projecting end of a piece of wood formed to fit into a corresponding mortise in another piece ▷ *vb* (*tr*) **2** to form a tenon on (a piece of wood) **3** to join with a tenon and mortise [c15: from Old French, from *tenir* to hold, from Latin *tenēre*] > 'tenoner *n*

tenon saw *n* a small fine-toothed saw with a strong back, used esp for cutting tenons

tenor ('tɛnə) *n* **1** *music* **a** the male voice intermediate between alto and baritone, having a range approximately from the B a ninth below middle C to the G a fifth above it **b** a singer with such a voice **c** a saxophone, horn, recorder, etc, intermediate in compass and size between the alto and baritone or bass **2** general drift of thought; purpose **3** a settled course of progress **4** *archaic* general tendency **5** *finance* the time required for a bill of exchange or promissory note to become due for payment **6** *law* **a** the exact words of a deed, etc, as distinct from their effect **b** an exact copy or transcript [c13 (originally: general meaning or sense): from Old French *tenour*, from Latin *tenor* a continuous holding to a course, from *tenēre* to hold; musical sense via Italian *tenore*, referring to the voice part that was continuous, that is, to which the melody was assigned]

tenor clef *n* the clef that establishes middle C as being on the fourth line of the staff, used for the writing of music for the bassoon, cello, or tenor trombone

tenorrhaphy (tɪ'nɒrəfɪ) *n, pl* -phies *surgery* the union of torn or divided tendons by means of sutures [c19: from TENO- + Greek *raphē* a sewing or suture]

tenosynovitis ('tɛnəʊ,saɪnəʊ'vaɪtɪs) *n* painful swelling and inflammation of tendons, usually of the wrist, often the result of repetitive movements such as typing

tenotomy (tə'nɒtəmɪ) *n, pl* -mies surgical division of a tendon > te'notomist *n*

tenpin bowling *n* a bowling game in which heavy bowls are rolled down a long lane to knock over the ten target pins at the other end

tenrec ('tɛnrɛk) *n* any small mammal, such as *Tenrec ecaudatus* (**tailless tenrec**), of the Madagascan family *Tenrecidae*, resembling hedgehogs or shrews: order *Insectivora* (insectivores) [c18: via French from Malagasy *tràndraka*]

TENS (tɛnz) *n acronym for* transcutaneous electrical nerve stimulation: the application of low-voltage electric impulses to the skin to relieve rheumatic pain and provide some pain relief in labour. The pulses are said to stimulate the release of pain-killing endorphins

tense¹ (tɛns) *adj* **1** stretched or stressed tightly; taut or rigid **2** under mental or emotional strain **3** producing mental or emotional strain: *a tense day* **4** (of a speech sound) pronounced with considerable muscular effort and having relatively precise accuracy of articulation and considerable duration: *in English the vowel* (iː) *in "beam" is tense* ▷ *vb* **5** (often foll by *up*) to make or become tense [c17: from Latin *tensus* taut, from *tendere* to stretch] > 'tensely *adv* > 'tenseness *n*

tense² (tɛns) *n grammar* a category of the verb or verbal inflections, such as present, past, and future, that expresses the temporal relations between what is reported in a sentence and the time of its utterance [c14: from Old French *tens* time, from Latin *tempus*] > 'tenseless *adj*

tense logic *n logic* the study of the logical properties of tense operators, and of the logical relations between sentences having tense, by means of consideration of appropriate formal systems

tensile ('tɛnsaɪl) *adj* **1** of or relating to tension **2** sufficiently ductile to be stretched or drawn out [c17: from New Latin *tensilis*, from Latin *tendere* to stretch] > tensility (tɛn'sɪlɪtɪ) *or* 'tensileness *n*

tensile strength *n* a measure of the ability of a material to withstand a longitudinal stress, expressed as the greatest stress that the material can stand without breaking

tensimeter (tɛnˈsɪmɪtə) *n* an instrument used to compare the vapour pressures of two liquids, usually consisting of two sealed bulbs containing the liquids, each being connected to one limb of a manometer [c20: from TENSI(ON) + -METER]

tensiometer (ˌtɛnsɪˈɒmɪtə) *n* **1** an instrument for measuring the tensile strength of a wire, beam, etc **2** a device that measures differences in vapour pressures. It is used to determine transition points by observing changes of vapour pressure with temperature **3** an instrument for measuring the surface tension of a liquid, usually consisting of a sensitive balance for measuring the force needed to pull a wire ring from the surface of the liquid **4** an instrument for measuring the moisture content of soil

tension (ˈtɛnʃən) *n* **1** the act of stretching or the state or degree of being stretched **2** mental or emotional strain; stress **3** a situation or condition of hostility, suspense, or uneasiness **4** *physics* a force that tends to produce an elongation of a body or structure **5** *physics* voltage, electromotive force, or potential difference **6** a device for regulating the tension in a part, string, thread, etc, as in a sewing machine **7** *knitting* the degree of tightness or looseness with which a person knits [c16: from Latin *tensiō*, from *tendere* to strain] > **ˈtensional** *adj* > **ˈtensionless** *adj*

tensor (ˈtɛnsə, -sɔː) *n* **1** *anatomy* any muscle that can cause a part to become firm or tense **2** *maths* a set of components, functions of the coordinates of any point in space, that transform linearly between coordinate systems. For three-dimensional space there are 3^r components, where *r* is the rank. A tensor of zero rank is a scalar, of rank one, a vector [c18: from New Latin, literally: a stretcher] > **tensorial** (tɛnˈsɔːrɪəl) *adj*

tent (tɛnt) *n* **1** a portable shelter of canvas, plastic, or other waterproof material supported on poles and fastened to the ground by pegs and ropes **2** something resembling this in function or shape ▷ *vb* **3** (*intr*) to camp in a tent **4** (*tr*) to cover with or as if with a tent or tents **5** (*tr*) to provide with a tent as shelter [c13: from Old French *tente*, from Latin *tentōrium* something stretched out, from *tendere* to stretch] > **ˈtented** *adj* > **ˈtentage** *n*

tentacle (ˈtɛntəkᵊl) *n* **1** any of various elongated flexible organs that occur near the mouth in many invertebrates and are used for feeding, grasping, etc **2** any of the hairs on the leaf of an insectivorous plant that are used to capture prey **3** something resembling a tentacle, esp in its ability to reach out or grasp [c18: from New Latin *tentāculum*, from Latin *tentāre*, variant of *temptāre* to feel] > **ˈtentacled** *adj* > **tentacular** (tɛnˈtækjʊlə) *adj*

tentation (tɛnˈteɪʃən) *n* a method of achieving the correct adjustment of a mechanical device by a series of trials [c14: from Latin *tentātiō*, variant of *temptātiō* TEMPTATION]

tentative (ˈtɛntətɪv) *adj* **1** provisional or experimental; conjectural **2** hesitant, uncertain, or cautious [c16: from Medieval Latin *tentātīvus*, from Latin *tentāre* to test] > **ˈtentatively** *adv* > **ˈtentativeness** *n*

tenter (ˈtɛntə) *n* **1** a frame on which cloth is stretched during the manufacturing process in order that it may retain its shape while drying **2** a person who stretches cloth on a tenter ▷ *vb* **3** (*tr*) to stretch (cloth) on a tenter [c14: from Medieval Latin *tentōrium*, from Latin *tentus* stretched, from *tendere* to stretch]

tenterhook (ˈtɛntəˌhʊk) *n* **1** one of a series of hooks or bent nails used to hold cloth stretched on a tenter **2 on tenterhooks** in a state of tension or suspense

tenth (tɛnθ) *adj* **1** (*usually prenominal*) **a** coming after the ninth in numbering or counting order, position, time, etc; being the ordinal number of *ten*: often written 10th: *the tenth month of the year* **b** (*as noun*): *see you on the tenth; tenth in line* ▷ *n* **2 a** one of 10 approximately equal parts of something **b** (*as modifier*): *a tenth part* **3** the fraction equal to one divided by ten (1/10) ▷ *adv* **4** Also called: **tenthly** after the ninth person, position, event, etc [C12 *tenthe*, from Old English *tēotha*; see TEN, -TH[2]]

tent stitch *n* another term for **petit point** (sense 1) [c17: of uncertain origin]

tenuis (ˈtɛnjʊɪs) *n*, *pl* **tenues** (ˈtɛnjʊˌiːz) (in the grammar of classical Greek) any of the voiceless stops as represented by kappa, pi, or tau (k, p, t) [c17: from Latin: thin]

tenuous (ˈtɛnjʊəs) *adj* **1** insignificant or flimsy: *a tenuous argument* **2** slim, fine, or delicate: *a tenuous thread* **3** diluted or rarefied in consistency or density: *a tenuous fluid* [c16: from Latin *tenuis*] > **tenuity** (tɛˈnjʊɪtɪ) *or* **ˈtenuousness** *n* > **ˈtenuously** *adv*

tenure (ˈtɛnjʊə, ˈtɛnjə) *n* **1** the possession or holding of an office or position **2** the length of time an office, position, etc, lasts; term **3** *chiefly US & Canadian* the improved security status of a person after having been in the employ of the same company or institution for a specified period **4** the right to permanent employment until retirement, esp for teachers, lecturers, etc **5** *property law* **a** the holding or occupying of property, esp realty, in return for services rendered, etc **b** the duration of such holding or occupation [c15: from Old French, from Medieval Latin *tenitūra*, ultimately from Latin *tenēre* to hold] > **tenˈurial** *adj*

tenuto (tɪˈnjuːtəʊ) *adj*, *adv* *music* (of a note) to be held for or beyond its full time value [from Italian, literally: held, from *tenere* to hold, from Latin *tenēre*]

Tenzing Norgay (ˈtɛnsɪŋ ˈnɔːgeɪ) *n* 1914–86, Nepalese mountaineer. With Sir Edmund Hillary, he was the first to reach the summit of Mount Everest (1953)

teocalli (ˌtiːəʊˈkælɪ) *n*, *pl* **-lis** any of various truncated pyramids built by the Aztecs as bases for their temples [c17: from Nahuatl, from *teotl* god + *calli* house]

tepee *or* **teepee** (ˈtiːpiː) *n* a cone-shaped tent of animal skins used by certain North American Indians [c19: from Siouan *tīpī*, from *ti* to dwell + *pi* used for]

tephra (ˈtɛfrə) *n* *chiefly US* solid matter ejected during a volcanic eruption [c20: Greek, literally: ashes]

Tepic (*Spanish* teˈpik) *n* a city in W central Mexico, capital of Nayarit state: agricultural, trading and processing centre. Pop: 341 000 (2005 est)

tepid (ˈtɛpɪd) *adj* **1** slightly warm; lukewarm **2** relatively unenthusiastic or apathetic [c14: from Latin *tepidus*, from *tepēre* to be lukewarm] > **teˈpidity** *or* **ˈtepidness** *n* > **ˈtepidly** *adv*

teppan-yaki (ˌtɛpænˈjækɪ) *n* a Japanese dish of meat and vegetables stir-fried on, and eaten from, a hot steel plate that forms the centre of a table [c21: Japanese, from *teppan* a steel plate + *yaki* to fry]

tequila (tɪˈkiːlə) *n* **1** a spirit that is distilled in Mexico from an agave plant and forms the basis of many mixed drinks **2** the plant, *Agave tequilana*, from which this drink is made [c19: from Mexican Spanish, from *Tequila*, region of Mexico]

ter- *combining form* three, third, or three times [from Latin *ter* thrice; related to *trēs* THREE]

tera- *prefix* **1** denoting 10^{12}: *terameter* **2** Also called: **tebi-** denoting 2^{40}: *terabyte* ▷ Symbol: T [from Greek *teras* monster]

terabyte (ˈtɛrəˌbaɪt) *n* *computing* 10^{12} or 2^{40} bytes

Terai (təˈraɪ) *n* **1** (in India) a belt of marshy land at the foot of mountains, esp at the foot of the Himalayas in N India **2** a felt hat with a wide brim worn in subtropical regions

terat- *or* **terato-** *combining form* indicating a monster or something abnormal: *teratism; teratoid* [from Greek *terat-*, *teras* monster, prodigy]

teratism (ˈtɛrəˌtɪzəm) *n* a malformed animal or human, esp in the fetal stage; monster

teratogen (ˈtɛrətədʒən, tɪˈrætə-) *n* any substance, organism, or process that causes malformations in a fetus. Teratogens include certain drugs (such as thalidomide), infections (such as German measles), and ionizing radiation > ˌ**teratoˈgenic** *adj*

teratoid (ˈtɛrəˌtɔɪd) *adj* *biology* resembling a monster

teratology (ˌtɛrəˈtɒlədʒɪ) *n* **1** the branch of medical science concerned with the development of physical abnormalities during the fetal or early embryonic stage **2** the branch of biology that is concerned with the

t

structure, development, etc, of monsters **3** a collection of tales about mythical or fantastic creatures, monsters, etc >,tera'tologist n

teratoma (,terə'təʊmə) n, pl-mata (-mətə) or-mas a tumour or group of tumours composed of tissue foreign to the site of growth

Te Rauparaha (teɪ 'rəʊpɑːˌrɑːhɑː) n ?1768–1849, Māori warrior chief, head of the Ngāti Toa tribe and signatory to the **Treaty of Waitangi**; noted for his cunning and his prowess in battle, he is also credited with composing "Ka Mate", the All Blacks' usual pre-match haka

terbium ('tɜːbɪəm) n a soft malleable silvery-grey element of the lanthanide series of metals, occurring in gadolinite and monazite and used in lasers and for doping solid-state devices. Symbol: Tb; atomic no: 65; atomic wt: 158.92534; valency: 3 or 4; relative density: 8.230; melting pt: 1356°C; boiling pt: 3230°C [c19: from New Latin, named after *Ytterby*, Sweden, village where it was discovered] >'terbic adj

terbium metal n chem any of a group of related lanthanides, including terbium, europium, and gadolinium

Ter Borch or**Terborch** (Dutch tɛr 'bɔrx) n Gerard ('xeːrɑrt). 1617–81, Dutch genre and portrait painter

Terbrugghen ('tøbruˌɡən) n Hendrik. 1588–1629, Dutch painter of the Utrecht school, who specialized in religious subjects, for example the *Incredulity of St Thomas* and the *Calling of St Matthew*

terce (tɜːs) or**tierce** n chiefly RC Church the third of the seven canonical hours of the divine office, originally fixed at the third hour of the day, about 9 a.m. [a variant of TIERCE]

Terceira (Portuguese tər'səɪrə) n an island in the N Atlantic, in the Azores: NATO military air base. Pop: 55 833 (2001). Area: 397 sq km (153 sq miles)

tercel ('tɜːsᵊl) or**tiercel** n a male falcon or hawk, esp as used in falconry [c14: from Old French, from Vulgar Latin *tertiolus* (unattested), from Latin *tertius* third, referring to the tradition that only one egg in three hatched a male chick]

tercentenary (,tɜːsɛn'tiːnərɪ) or**tercentennial** adj **1** of or relating to a period of 300 years **2** of or relating to a 300th anniversary or its celebration ▷ n, pl-tenaries or -tennials **3** an anniversary of 300 years or its celebration

tercet ('tɜːsɪt, tɜː'sɛt) n a group of three lines of verse that rhyme together or are connected by rhyme with adjacent groups of three lines [c16: from French, from Italian *terzetto*, diminutive of *terzo* third, from Latin *tertius*]

terebene ('terəˌbiːn) n a mixture of hydrocarbons prepared from oil of turpentine and sulphuric acid, used to make paints and varnishes and medicinally as an expectorant and antiseptic [c19: from TEREB(INTH) + -ENE]

terebinth ('terɪbɪnθ) n a small anacardiaceous tree, *Pistacia terebinthus*, of the Mediterranean region, having winged leafstalks and clusters of small flowers, and yielding a turpentine [c14: from Latin *terebinthus*, from Greek *terebinthos* turpentine tree]

terebinthine (,terɪ'bɪnθaɪn) adj **1** of or relating to terebinth or related plants **2** of, consisting of, or resembling turpentine

teredo (te'riːdəʊ) n, pl-dos or-dines (-dɪˌniːz) any marine bivalve mollusc of the genus *Teredo*. See **shipworm** [c17: via Latin from Greek *terēdōn* wood-boring worm; related to Greek *tetrainein* to pierce]

Terence ('terəns) n Latin name *Publius Terentius Afer*. ?190–159 BC, Roman comic dramatist. His six comedies, *Andria, Hecyra, Heauton Timoroumenos, Eunuchus, Phormio,* and *Adelphoe*, are based on Greek originals by Menander

Terengganu (terɛŋ'ɡɑːnuː) n a variant spelling of **Trengganu**

Teresa or**Theresa** (tə'riːzə; Spanish te'resa) n **1 Saint,** known as *Teresa of Avila*. 1515–82, Spanish nun and mystic. She reformed the Carmelite order and founded 17 convents. Her writings include a spiritual autobiography and *The Way to Perfection*. Feast day: Oct 15 **2 Mother,** original name *Agnes Gonxha Bojaxhiu*. 1910–97, Indian Roman Catholic missionary, born in Skopje, now

in the Former Yugoslav Republic of Macedonia, of Albanian parents: noted for her work among the starving in Calcutta; Nobel peace prize 1979 ▷ See also **Thérèse de Lisieux**

Tereshkova (Russian tɪrɪʃ'kɔvə) n **Valentina Vladimirovna** (vəlɪn'tinə vla'dimirəvnə). born 1937, Soviet cosmonaut; first woman in space (1963)

Teresina (Portuguese tere'zina) n an inland port in NE Brazil, capital of Piauí state, on the Parnaíba River: chief commercial centre of the Parnaíba valley. Pop: 895 000 (2005 est). Former name: Therezina

terete ('terɪt) adj (esp of plant parts) smooth and usually cylindrical and tapering [c17: from Latin *teres* smooth, from *terere* to rub]

Terfel ('tɜːfəl) n **Bryn,** real name *Bryn Terfel Jones*. born 1965, Welsh bass baritone

tergiversate ('tɜːdʒɪvəˌseɪt) vb (intr) **1** to change sides or loyalties; apostatize **2** to be evasive or ambiguous; equivocate [c17: from Latin *tergiversārī* to turn one's back, from *tergum* back + *vertere* to turn] >,tergiver'sation n >'tergiverˌsator or tergiversant ('tɜːdʒɪˌvɜːsᵊnt) n

tergum ('tɜːɡəm) n, pl-ga (-ɡə) a cuticular plate covering the dorsal surface of a body segment of an arthropod [c19: from Latin: the back] >'tergal adj

term (tɜːm) n **1** a name, expression, or word used for some particular thing, esp in a specialized field of knowledge: *a medical term* **2** any word or expression **3** a limited period of time: *his second term of office; a prison term* **4** any of the divisions of the academic year during which a school, college, etc, is in session **5** a point in time determined for an event or for the end of a period **6** Also called: full term the period at which childbirth is imminent **7** law **a** an estate or interest in land limited to run for a specified period **b** the duration of an estate, etc **c** (formerly) a period of time during which sessions of courts of law were held **d** time allowed to a debtor to settle **8** maths either of the expressions the ratio of which is a fraction or proportion, any of the separate elements of a sequence, or any of the individual addends of a polynomial or series **9** logic **a** the word or phrase that forms either the subject or predicate of a proposition **b** a name or variable, as opposed to a predicate **c** any of the three subjects or predicates occurring in a syllogism **10** Also called: terminal, terminus, terminal figure architect a sculptured post, esp one in the form of an armless bust or an animal on the top of a square pillar ▷ vb **11** (tr) to designate; call: *he was termed a thief* ▷ See also **terms** [c13: from Old French *terme*, from Latin *terminus* end] >'termly adv

termagant ('tɜːməɡənt) n a shrewish woman; scold [c13: from earlier *Tervagaunt*, from Old French *Tervagan*, from Italian *Trivigante*; after an arrogant character in medieval mystery plays who was supposed to be a Muslim deity]

-termer n (in combination) a person serving a specified length of time in prison: *a short-termer*

terminable ('tɜːmɪnəbᵊl, 'tɜːmnəbᵊl) adj **1** able to be terminated **2** terminating after a specific period or event >,termina'bility or'terminableness n >'terminably adv

terminal ('tɜːmɪnᵊl) adj **1** of, being, or situated at an end, terminus, or boundary **2** of, relating to, or occurring after or in a term: *terminal leave* **3** (of a disease) terminating in death **4** informal extreme: *terminal boredom* **5** of or relating to the storage or delivery of freight at a warehouse ▷ n **6** a terminating point, part, or place **7 a** a point at which current enters or leaves an electrical device, such as a battery or a circuit **b** a conductor by which current enters or leaves at such a point **8** computing a device having input/output links with a computer but situated at a distance from the computer **9** architect **a** an ornamental carving at the end of a structure **b** another name for **term** (sense 10) **10 a** a point or station usually at the end of the line of a railway, serving as an important access point for passengers or freight **b** a less common name for **terminus 11** a purpose-built reception and departure structure at the terminus of a bus, sea, or air transport route **12** a site where raw material is unloaded, stored, in some cases reprocessed, and reloaded for further transportation, esp an onshore installation designed to receive offshore oil or gas from tankers or a pipeline [c15: from Latin *terminālis*, from *terminus* end] ▷'**terminally** *adv*

terminal market *n* a commodity market in a trading centre rather than at a producing centre

terminal velocity *n* **1** the constant maximum velocity reached by a body falling under gravity through a fluid, esp the atmosphere **2** the velocity of a missile or projectile when it reaches its target **3** the maximum velocity attained by a rocket, missile, or shell flying in a parabolic flight path **4** the maximum velocity that an aircraft can attain, as determined by its total drag

terminate ('tɜːmɪˌneɪt) *vb* (when *intr*, often foll by *in* or *with*) to form, be, or put an end (to); conclude [c16: from Latin *terminātus*, from *termināre* to set boundaries, from *terminus* end] ▷'**terminative** *adj* ▷'**termiˌnator** *n*

termination (ˌtɜːmɪˈneɪʃən) *n* **1** the act of terminating or the state of being terminated **2** something that terminates **3** a final result

terminator seed *n* a seed that produces sterile plants, used in some genetically modified crops so that a new supply of seeds has to be bought every year

terminology (ˌtɜːmɪˈnɒlədʒɪ) *n*, *pl* -gies **1** the body of specialized words relating to a particular subject **2** the study of terms [c19: from Medieval Latin *terminus* term, from Latin: end] ▷**terminological** (ˌtɜːmɪnəˈlɒdʒɪkᵊl) *adj*

term insurance *n* life assurance, usually low in cost and offering no cash value, that provides for the payment of a specified sum of money only if the insured dies within a stipulated period of time

terminus ('tɜːmɪnəs) *n*, *pl* -ni (-naɪ) *or* -nuses **1** the last or final part or point **2** either end of a railway, bus route, etc, or a station or town at such a point **3** a goal aimed for **4** a boundary or boundary marker **5** *architect* another name for **term** (sense 10) [c16: from Latin: end; related to Greek *termōn* boundary]

Terminus ('tɜːmɪnəs) *n* the Roman god of boundaries

terminus ad quem (*Latin* 'tɜːmɪˌnʊs æd 'kwɛm) *n* the aim or terminal point [literally: the end to which]

terminus a quo (*Latin* 'tɜːmɪˌnʊs ɑː 'kwəʊ) *n* the starting point; beginning [literally: the end from which]

termitarium (ˌtɜːmɪˈtɛərɪəm) *n*, *pl* -ia (-ɪə) the nest of a termite colony [c20: from TERMITE + -ARIUM]

termite ('tɜːmaɪt) *n* any whitish ant-like social insect of the order *Isoptera*, of warm and tropical regions. Some species feed on wood, causing damage to furniture, buildings, trees, etc [c18: from New Latin *termitēs* white ants, pl of *termes*, from Latin: a woodworm; related to Greek *tetrainein* to bore through] ▷**termitic** (tɜːˈmɪtɪk) *adj*

termless ('tɜːmlɪs) *adj* **1** without limit or boundary **2** unconditional **3** an archaic word for **indescribable**

termor *or* **termer** ('tɜːmə) *n property law* a person who holds an estate for a term of years or until he dies [c14: from Anglo-French *termer*, from *terme* TERM]

terms (tɜːmz) *pl n* **1** (usually specified predominally) the actual language or mode of presentation used: *he described the project in loose terms* **2** conditions of an agreement **3** a sum of money paid for a service or credit; charges **4** (usually preceded by *on*) mutual relationship or standing: *they are on affectionate terms* **5** in terms of as expressed by; regarding: *in terms of money he was no better off* **6** come to terms to reach acceptance or agreement

terms of trade *pl n economics*, *Brit* the ratio of export prices to import prices. It measures a nation's trading position, which improves when export prices rise faster or fall slower than import prices

tern (tɜːn) *n* any aquatic bird of the subfamily *Sterninae*, having a forked tail, long narrow wings, a pointed bill, and a typically black-and-white plumage: family *Laridae* (gulls, etc), order *Charadriiformes* [c18: from Old Norse *therna*; related to Norwegian *terna*, Swedish *tärna*]

ternary ('tɜːnərɪ) *adj* **1** consisting of three or groups of three **2** *maths* (of a number system) to the base three [c14: from Latin *ternārius*, from *ternī* three each]

ternary form *n* a musical structure consisting of two contrasting sections followed by a repetition of the first; the form *aba*

ternate ('tɜːnɪt, -neɪt) *adj* **1** (esp of a leaf) consisting of three leaflets or other parts **2** (esp of plants) having groups of three members [c18: from New Latin *ternātus*, from Medieval Latin *ternāre* to increase threefold] ▷'**ternately** *adv*

terne (tɜːn) *n* **1** Also called: **terne metal** an alloy of lead containing tin (10–20 per cent) and antimony (1.5–2 per cent) **2** Also called: **terne plate** steel plate coated with this alloy [c16: perhaps from French *terne* dull, from Old French *ternir* to TARNISH]

Terni (*Italian* 'tɛrni) *n* an industrial city in central Italy, in Umbria: site of waterfalls created in Roman times. Pop: 105 018 (2001)

Ternopol (*Russian* tɪr'nɔpəlj) *n* a town in W Ukraine, on the River Siret: formerly under Polish rule. Pop: 235 000 (2005 est). Polish name: **Tarnopol**

terotechnology (ˌtɪərəʊtɛk'nɒlədʒɪ, ˌtɛr-) *n* a branch of technology that utilizes management, financial, and engineering expertise in the installation and efficient operation and maintenance of equipment and machinery [c20: from Greek *tērein* to care for + TECHNOLOGY]

terpene ('tɜːpiːn) *n* any one of a class of unsaturated hydrocarbons, such as the carotenes, that are found in the essential oils of many plants. Their molecules contain isoprene units and have the general formula $(C_5H_8)_n$ [c19: terp- from obsolete *terpentine* TURPENTINE + -ENE]

terpineol (tɜː'pɪnɪˌɒl) *n* a terpene alcohol with an odour of lilac, present in several essential oils. A mixture of the isomers is used as a solvent and in flavourings and perfumes. Formula: $C_{10}H_{17}OH$ [c20: from TERPENE + -INE² + -OL¹]

Terpsichore (tɜːp'sɪkərɪ) *n* the Muse of the dance and of choral song [c18: via Latin from Greek *terpsikhoros* delighting in the dance, from *terpein* to delight + *khoros* dance; see CHORUS]

Terpsichorean (ˌtɜːpsɪkə'rɪən, -'kɔːrɪən) *often used facetiously* ▷ *adj* **1** Also: **Terpsichoreal** of or relating to dancing or the art of dancing ▷ *n* **2** a dancer

terra ('tɛrə) *n* (in legal contexts) earth or land [from Latin]

terra alba ('ælbə) *n* **1** a white finely powdered form of gypsum, used to make paints, paper, etc **2** any of various other white earthy substances, such as kaolin, pipeclay, and magnesia [from Latin, literally: white earth]

terrace ('tɛrəs) *n* **1** a horizontal flat area of ground, often one of a series in a slope **2 a** a row of houses, usually identical and having common dividing walls, or the street onto which they face **b** (*cap when part of a street name*): *Grosvenor Terrace* **3** a paved area alongside a building, serving partly as a garden **4** a balcony or patio **5** the flat roof of a house built in a Spanish or Oriental style **6** a flat area bounded by a short steep slope formed by the down-cutting of a river or by erosion **7** (*usually plural*) unroofed tiers around a football pitch on which the spectators stand ▷ *vb* **8** (*tr*) to make into or provide with a terrace or terraces [c16: from Old French *terrasse*, from Old Provençal *terrassa* pile of earth, from *terra* earth, from Latin]

terraced house *n Brit* a house that is part of a terrace

terracing ('tɛrəsɪŋ) *n* **1** a series of terraces, esp one dividing a slope into a steplike system of flat narrow fields **2** the act of making a terrace or terraces **3** another name for **terrace** (sense 7a)

terracotta (ˌtɛrə'kɒtə) *n* **1** a hard unglazed brownish-red earthenware, or the clay from which it is made **2** something made of terracotta, such as a sculpture **3** a strong reddish-brown to brownish-orange colour [c18: from Italian, literally: baked earth]

terra firma ('fɜːmə) *n* the solid earth; firm ground [c17: from Latin]

terraforming ('tɛrəˌfɔːmɪŋ) *n* planetary engineering designed to enhance the capacity of an extraterrestrial planetary environment to sustain life [c20: from Latin *terra* earth + *forming*]

terrain (tə'reɪn, 'tɛreɪn) *n* ground or a piece of ground, esp with reference to its physical character or military potential: *radio reception can be difficult in mountainous terrain; a rocky terrain* [c18: from French, ultimately from Latin *terrēnum* ground, from *terra* earth]

terra incognita (*Latin* ˈtɛrə ɪnˈkɒɡnɪtə) *n* an unexplored or unknown land, region, or area for study

Terramycin (ˌtɛrəˈmaɪsɪn) *n trademark* a broad-spectrum antibiotic, oxytetracycline, used in treating various infections

terrapin (ˈtɛrəpɪn) *n* any of various web-footed chelonian reptiles that live on land and in fresh water and feed on small aquatic animals: family *Emydidae*. Also called: **water tortoise** [c17: of Algonquian origin; compare Delaware *torope* turtle]

terrarium (tɛˈrɛərɪəm) *n, pl* -rariums *or* -raria (-ˈrɛərɪə) **1** an enclosure for keeping small land animals **2** a glass container, often a globe, in which plants are grown [c19: New Latin, from Latin *terra* earth]

terra sigillata (ˈtɛrə ˌsɪdʒɪˈlɑːtə) *n* **1** *rare* a reddish-brown clayey earth found on the Aegean island of Lemnos: formerly used as an astringent and in the making of earthenware pottery **2** any similar earth resembling this **3** earthenware pottery made from this or a similar earth, esp Samian ware [from Latin: sealed earth]

terrazzo (tɛˈrætsəʊ) *n* a floor or wall finish made by setting marble or other stone chips into a layer of mortar and polishing the surface [c20: from Italian: TERRACE]

terrene (tɛˈriːn) *adj* **1** of or relating to the earth; worldly; mundane **2** *rare* of earth; earthy ▷ *n* **3** a land **4** a rare word for **earth** [c14: from Anglo-Norman, from Latin *terrēnus*, from *terra* earth]

terreplein (ˈtɛəˌpleɪn) *n* the top of a rampart where guns are placed behind the parapet [c16: from French, from Medieval Latin phrase *terrā plēnus* filled with earth]

terrestrial (təˈrɛstrɪəl) *adj* **1** of or relating to the earth **2** of or belonging to the land as opposed to the sea or air **3** (of animals and plants) living or growing on the land **4** earthly, worldly, or mundane **5** (of television signals) sent over the earth's surface from a transmitter on land, rather than by satellite ▷ *n* **6** an inhabitant of the earth [c15: from Latin *terrestris*, from *terra* earth] > ter'restrially *adv* > ter'restrialness *n*

terrestrial telescope *n* a telescope for use on earth rather than for making astronomical observations. Such telescopes contain an additional lens or prism system to produce an erect image

terret (ˈtɛrɪt) *n* **1** either of the two metal rings on a harness saddle through which the reins are passed **2** the ring on a dog's collar for attaching the lead [c15: variant of *toret*, from Old French, diminutive of *tor* loop; see TOUR]

terre-verte (ˈtɛəˌvɜːt) *n* **1** a greyish-green pigment used in paints, consisting of powdered glauconite ▷ *adj* **2** of a greyish-green colour [c17: from French, literally: green earth]

terrible (ˈtɛrəbᵊl) *adj* **1** very serious or extreme **2** *informal* of poor quality; unpleasant or bad **3** causing terror **4** causing awe [c15: from Latin *terribilis*, from *terrēre* to terrify] > 'terribleness *n* > 'terribly *adv*

terricolous (tɛˈrɪkələs) *adj* living on or in the soil [c19: from Latin *terricola*, from *terra* earth + *colere* to inhabit]

terrier[1] (ˈtɛrɪə) *n* any of several usually small, active, and short-bodied breeds of dog, originally trained to hunt animals living underground [c15: from Old French *chien terrier* earth dog, from Medieval Latin *terrārius* belonging to the earth, from Latin *terra* earth]

terrier[2] (ˈtɛrɪə) *n English legal history* a register or survey of land [c15: from Old French, from Medieval Latin *terrārius* of the land, from Latin *terra* land]

terrific (təˈrɪfɪk) *adj* **1** very great or intense **2** *informal* very good; excellent **3** very frightening [c17: from Latin *terrificus*, from *terrēre* to frighten; see -FIC] > ter'rifically *adv*

terrify (ˈtɛrɪˌfaɪ) *vb* -fies, -fying, -fied (*tr*) to inspire fear or dread in; frighten greatly [c16: from Latin *terrificāre*, from *terrēre* to alarm + *facere* to cause]

terrifying (ˈtɛrɪˌfaɪɪŋ) *adj* causing great fear or dread; extremely frightening > 'terri,fyingly *adv*

terrigenous (tɛˈrɪdʒɪnəs) *adj* **1** of or produced by the

earth **2** (of geological deposits) formed in the sea from material derived from the land by erosion [c17: from Latin *terrigenus*, from *terra* earth + *gignere* to beget]

terrine (tɛˈriːn) *n* **1** an oval earthenware cooking dish with a tightly fitting lid used for pâtés, etc **2** the food cooked or served in such a dish, esp pâté **3** another word for **tureen** [c18: earlier form of TUREEN]

territorial (ˌtɛrɪˈtɔːrɪəl) *adj* **1** of or relating to a territory or territories **2** restricted to or owned by a particular territory **3** local or regional **4** pertaining to a territorial army, providing a reserve of trained men for use in emergency > ,terri'torially *adv*

Territorial (ˌtɛrɪˈtɔːrɪəl) *n* a member of a territorial army, esp the British Army's Territorial and Volunteer Reserve

Territorial Army *n* (in Britain) a standing reserve army originally organized between 1907 and 1908

territorial waters *pl n* the waters over which a nation exercises jurisdiction and control

territory (ˈtɛrɪtərɪ, -trɪ) *n, pl* -ries **1** any tract of land; district **2** the geographical domain under the jurisdiction of a political unit, esp of a sovereign state **3** the district for which an agent, etc, is responsible **4** an area inhabited and defended by an individual animal or a breeding group of animals **5** an area of knowledge **6** (in football, hockey, etc) the area defended by a team **7** (*often capital*) a region of a country, esp of a federal state, that enjoys less autonomy and a lower status than most constituent parts of the state **8** (*often capital*) a protectorate or other dependency of a country [c15: from Latin *territōrium* land surrounding a town, from *terra* land]

terror (ˈtɛrə) *n* **1** great fear, panic, or dread **2** a person or thing that inspires great dread **3** *informal* a troublesome person or thing, esp a child **4** terrorism [c14: from Old French *terreur*, from Latin *terror*, from *terrēre* to frighten; related to Greek *trein* to run away in terror] > 'terrorful *adj* > 'terrorless *adj*

terrorism (ˈtɛrəˌrɪzəm) *n* **1** systematic use of violence and intimidation to achieve some goal **2** the act of terrorizing **3** the state of being terrorized

terrorist (ˈtɛrərɪst) *n* **a** a person who employs terror or terrorism, esp as a political weapon **b** (*as modifier*): *terrorist tactics*

terrorize *or* **terrorise** (ˈtɛrəˌraɪz) *vb* (*tr*) **1** to coerce or control by violence, fear, threats, etc **2** to inspire with dread; terrify > ,terrori'zation *or* ,terrori'sation *n* > 'terror,izer *or* 'terror,iser *n*

terror-stricken *or* **terror-struck** *adj* in a state of terror

terry (ˈtɛrɪ) *n, pl* -ries **1** an uncut loop in the pile of towelling or a similar fabric **2** a fabric with such a pile on both sides [c18: perhaps variant of TERRET]

Terry (ˈtɛrɪ) *n* **1** Dame **Ellen**. 1847–1928, British actress, noted for her Shakespearean roles opposite Sir Henry Irving and for her correspondence with George Bernard Shaw **2** (**John**) **Quinlan** (ˈkwɪnlən). born 1937, British architect, noted for his works in neoclassical style, such as the Richmond riverside project (1984)

terse (tɜːs) *adj* **1** neatly brief and concise **2** curt; abrupt [c17: from Latin *tersus* precise, from *tergēre* to polish] > 'tersely *adv* > 'terseness *n*

tertial (ˈtɜːʃəl) *adj, n* another word for **tertiary** (senses 4, 5) [c19: from Latin *tertius* third, from *ter* thrice, from *trēs* three]

tertian (ˈtɜːʃən) *adj* **1** (of a fever or the symptoms of a disease, esp malaria) occurring every other day ▷ *n* **2** a tertian fever or symptoms [c14: from Latin *febris tertiāna* fever occurring every third day, reckoned inclusively, from *tertius* third]

tertiary (ˈtɜːʃərɪ) *adj* **1** third in degree, order, etc **2** (of an industry) involving services as opposed to extraction or manufacture, such as transport, finance, etc **3** *RC Church* of or relating to a Third Order **4** *chem* **a** (of an organic compound) having a functional group attached to a carbon atom that is attached to three other groups **b** (of an amine) having three organic groups attached to a nitrogen atom **c** (of a salt) derived from a tribasic acid by replacement of all its acidic hydrogen atoms with metal atoms or electropositive groups **5** Also called: **tertial** *ornithol rare* of, relating to, or designating any of the small flight feathers attached to the part of the humerus nearest to the body ▷ *n*, *pl*-tiaries **6** Also called: **tertial** *ornithol rare* any of the tertiary feathers **7** *RC Church* a member of a Third Order [C16: from Latin *tertiārius* containing one third, from *tertius* third]

Tertiary ('tɜːʃərɪ) *adj* **1** of, denoting, or formed in the first period of the Cenozoic era, which lasted for 63 million years, during which mammals became dominant ▷ *n* **2** the Tertiary the Tertiary period or rock system, divided into Palaeocene, Eocene, Oligocene, Miocene, and Pliocene epochs or series

tertiary college *n* *Brit* a college system incorporating the secondary school sixth form and vocational courses

tertiary colour *n* a colour formed by mixing two secondary colours

tertium quid ('tɜːtɪəm 'kwɪd) *n* an unknown or indefinite thing related in some way to two known or definite things, but distinct from both [C18: from Late Latin, rendering Greek *triton ti* some third thing]

Tertullian (tɜː'tʌlɪən) *n* Latin name *Quintus Septimius Florens Tertullianus.* ?160–?220 AD, Carthaginian Christian theologian, who wrote in Latin rather than Greek and originated much of Christian terminology

Teruel (*Spanish* te'rwel) *n* a city in E central Spain: 15th-century cathedral; scene of fierce fighting during the Spanish Civil War. Pop: 32 304 (2003 est)

tervalent (tɜː'veɪlənt) *adj* *chem* another word for **trivalent** ▷ **ter'valency** *n*

Terylene ('terɪˌliːn) *n* *trademark* a synthetic polyester fibre or fabric based on terephthalic acid, characterized by lightness and crease resistance and used for clothing, sheets, ropes, sails, etc. US name (trademark): Dacron

terza rima ('tɛətsə 'riːmə) *n*, *pl* terze rime ('tɛətseɪ 'riːmeɪ) a verse form of Italian origin consisting of a series of tercets in which the middle line of one tercet rhymes with the first and third lines of the next [C19: from Italian, literally: third rhyme]

TE score *n* (in Australia) Tertiary Entrance score: a score based on a pupil's performance in secondary school that determines his or her prospects of gaining entrance to tertiary educational institutions

TESL ('tɛsəl) *n* *acronym* Teaching (of) English as a Second Language

tesla ('tɛslə) *n* the derived SI unit of magnetic flux density equal to a flux of 1 weber in an area of 1 square metre. Symbol: T [C20: named after Nikola *Tesla* (1857–1943), Croatian-born US electrical engineer and inventor]

Tesla ('tɛslə) *n* **Nikola** ('nɪkələ). 1857–1943, US electrical engineer and inventor, born in Smiljan, now in Croatia. His inventions include a transformer, generators, and dynamos

tesla coil *n* a step-up transformer with an air core, used for producing high voltages at high frequencies. The secondary circuit is tuned to resonate with the primary winding [C20: named after Nikola *Tesla* (1857–1943), Croatian-born US electrical engineer and inventor]

TESSA ('tɛsə) *n* *acronym for* (in Britain) Tax Exempt Special Savings Account; a former (available 1991–99) tax-free savings scheme

tessellate ('tɛsɪˌleɪt) *vb* **1** (*tr*) to construct, pave, or inlay with a mosaic of small tiles **2** (*intr*) (of identical shapes) to fit together exactly [C18: from Latin *tessellātus* checked, from *tessella* small stone cube, from TESSERA]

tessera ('tɛsərə) *n*, *pl*-serae (-səˌriː) **1** a small square tile of stone, glass, etc, used in mosaics **2** a die, tally, etc, used in classical times, made of bone or wood [C17: from Latin, from Ionic Greek *tesseres* four] ▷ **'tesseral** *adj*

Tessin (tɛ'siːn) *n* the German name for **Ticino**

tessitura (ˌtɛsɪ'tʊərə) *n* *music* the general pitch level of a piece of vocal music [Italian: texture, from Latin *textura*; see TEXTURE]

test¹ (test) *vb* **1** to ascertain (the worth, capability, or endurance) of (a person or thing) by subjection to certain examinations; try **2** (often foll by *for*) to carry out an examination on (a substance, material, or system) by applying some chemical or physical procedure designed to indicate the presence of a substance or the possession of a property: *to test food for arsenic; to test for magnetization*

3 (*intr*) to achieve a specified result in a test: *a quarter of the patients at the clinic tested positive for the AIDS virus* **4** (*tr*) to put under severe strain: *the long delay tested my patience* ▷ *n* **5** a method, practice, or examination designed to test a person or thing **6** a series of questions or problems designed to test a specific skill or knowledge **7** a standard of judgment; criterion **8 a** a chemical reaction or physical procedure for testing a substance, material, etc **b** a chemical reagent used in such a procedure **c** the result of the procedure or the evidence gained from it **9** *sport* See **test match 10** *archaic* a declaration or confirmation of truth, loyalty, etc; oath **11** (*modifier*) performed as a test: *test drive; test flight* (in the sense: vessel used in treating metals): from Latin *testum* earthen vessel] ▷ **'testable** *adj* ▷ ˌtesta'bility *n* ▷ **'testing** *adj*

test² (test) *n* the hard or tough outer covering of certain invertebrates and tunicates [C19: from Latin *testa* shell]

testa ('tɛstə) *n*, *pl*-tae (-tiː) a hard protective outer layer of the seeds of flowering plants; seed coat [C18: from Latin: shell; see TEST²]

testaceous (tɛ'steɪʃəs) *adj* *biology* **1** of, relating to, or possessing a test or testa **2** of the reddish-brown colour of terra cotta [C16: from Latin *testāceus*, from TESTA]

testament ('tɛstəmənt) *n* **1** *law* a will setting out the disposition of personal property (esp in the phrase **last will and testament**) **2** a proof, attestation, or tribute **3 a** a covenant instituted between God and man, esp the covenant of Moses or that instituted by Christ **b** a copy of either the Old or the New Testament, or of the complete Bible [C14: from Latin: a will, from *testāri* to bear witness, from *testis* a witness] ▷ ˌtesta'mental *adj*

Testament ('tɛstəmənt) *n* **1** either of the two main parts of the Bible; the Old Testament or the New Testament **2** the New Testament as distinct from the Old

testate ('tɛsteɪt, 'tɛstɪt) *adj* **1** having left a legally valid will at death ▷ *n* **2** a person who dies testate [C15: from Latin *testārī* to make a will; see TESTAMENT] ▷ **testacy** ('tɛstəsɪ) *n*

testator (tɛ'steɪtə) *or feminine* **testatrix** (tɛ'steɪtrɪks) *n* a person who makes a will, esp one who dies testate [C15: from Anglo-French *testatour*, from Late Latin *testātor*, from Latin *testārī* to make a will; see TESTAMENT]

test ban *n* an agreement among nations to forgo tests of some or all types of nuclear weapons

test-bed *n* *engineering* an area equipped with instruments, etc, used for testing machinery, engines, etc, under working conditions

test card *or* **test pattern** *n* a complex pattern used to test the characteristics of a television transmission system

test case *n* a legal action that serves as a precedent in deciding similar succeeding cases

test-drive *vb* -drives, -driving, -drove, -driven (*tr*) to drive (a car or other motor vehicle) for a limited period in order to assess its capabilities and limitations

tester¹ ('tɛstə) *n* a person or thing that tests or is used for testing

tester² ('tɛstə) *n* (in furniture) a canopy, esp the canopy over a four-poster bed [C14: from Medieval Latin *testerium*, from Late Latin *testa* a skull, from Latin: shell]

testes ('tɛstiːz) *n* the plural of **testis**

testicle ('tɛstɪkəl) *n* either of the two male reproductive glands, in most mammals enclosed within the scrotum, that produce spermatozoa and the hormone testosterone. Also called: **testis** [C15: from Latin *testiculus*, diminutive of *testis* testicle] ▷ **testicular** (tɛ'stɪkjʊlə) *adj*

testiculate (tɛ'stɪkjʊlɪt) *adj* *botany* shaped like testicles: *the testiculate tubers of certain orchids* [C18: from Late Latin *testiculātus*; see TESTICLE]

testify ('tɛstɪˌfaɪ) *vb* -fies, -fying, -fied **1** (when *tr*, *may take a clause as object*) to state (something) formally as a declaration of fact **2** *law* to declare or give (evidence) under oath, esp in court **3** (when *intr*, often foll by *to*) to be evidence (of); serve as witness (to) **4** (*tr*) to declare or acknowledge openly [C14: from Latin *testificārī*, from *testis* witness] ▷ ˌtestifi'cation *n* ▷ **'testiˌfier** *n*

testimonial (ˌtɛstɪ'məʊnɪəl) *n* **1 a** a recommendation of the character, ability, etc, of a person or of the quality of a consumer product or service, esp by a person whose opinion is valued **b** (*as modifier*): *testimonial advertising* **2** a formal statement of truth or fact **3** a tribute given for services or achievements **4** a sports match to raise money for a particular player ▷ *adj* **5** of or relating to a testimony or testimonial

● USAGE *Testimonial* is sometimes wrongly used where
● testimony is meant: *his re-election is a testimony* (not *a*
● *testimonial*) *to his popularity with his constituents*

testimony ('tɛstɪmənɪ) *n, pl* -nies **1** a declaration of truth or fact **2** *law* evidence given by a witness, esp orally in court under oath or affirmation **3** evidence testifying to something **4** *Old Testament* the Ten Commandments, as inscribed on the two stone tables [c15: from Latin *testimōnium*, from *testis* witness]

testis ('tɛstɪs) *n, pl* -tes (-tiːz) another word for **testicle** [c17: from Latin, literally: witness (to masculinity)]

test match *n* (in various sports, esp cricket) an international match, esp one of a series

testosterone (tɛ'stɒstəˌrəʊn) *n* a potent steroid hormone secreted mainly by the testes. It can be extracted from the testes of animals or synthesized and used to treat androgen deficiency or promote anabolism. Formula: $C_{19}H_{28}O_2$ [c20: from TESTIS + STEROL + -ONE]

test paper *n* **1** *chem* paper impregnated with an indicator for use in chemical tests **2** *Brit education* **a** the question sheet of a test **b** the paper completed by a test candidate

test pilot *n* a pilot who flies aircraft of new design to test their performance in the air

test tube *n* **1** a cylindrical round-bottomed glass tube open at one end: used in scientific experiments **2** (*modifier*) made synthetically in, or as if in, a test tube: *a test-tube product*

test-tube baby *n* **1** a fetus that has developed from an ovum fertilized in an artificial womb **2** a baby conceived by artificial insemination

testudinal (tɛ'stjuːdɪn³l) *or* **testudinary** (tɛ'stjuːdɪˌnərɪ) *adj* of, relating to, or resembling a tortoise or turtle or the shell of either of these animals [c19: from Latin TESTUDO]

testudo (tɛ'stjuːdəʊ) *n, pl* -dines (-dɪˌniːz) a form of shelter used by the ancient Roman Army for protection against attack from above, consisting either of a mobile arched structure or of overlapping shields held by the soldiers over their heads [c17: from Latin: a tortoise, from *testa* a shell]

testy ('tɛstɪ) *adj* -tier, -tiest irritable or touchy [c14: from Anglo-Norman *testif* headstrong, from Old French *teste* head, from Late Latin *testa* skull, from Latin: shell]
> 'testily *adv* > 'testiness *n*

tetanus ('tɛtənəs) *n* **1** Also called: lockjaw an acute infectious disease in which sustained muscular spasm, contraction, and convulsion are caused by the release of exotoxins from the bacterium, *Clostridium tetani*: infection usually occurs through a contaminated wound **2** *physiol* any tense contraction of a muscle, esp when produced by electric shocks [c16: via Latin from Greek *tetanos*, from *tetanos* taut, from *teinein* to stretch]
> 'tetanal *adj* > 'teta,noid *adj*

tetany ('tɛtənɪ) *n pathol* an abnormal increase in the excitability of nerves and muscles resulting in spasms of the arms and legs, caused by a deficiency of parathyroid secretion [c19: from French *tétanie*. See TETANUS]

tetchy ('tɛtʃɪ) *adj* tetchier, tetchiest being or inclined to be cross, irritable, or touchy [c16: probably from obsolete *tetch* defect, from Old French *tache* spot, of Germanic origin] > 'tetchily *adv* > 'tetchiness *n*

tête-à-tête (ˌteɪtɑː'teɪt) *n, pl* -têtes *or* -tête **1** a **a** private conversation between two people **b** (*as modifier*): *a tête-à-tête conversation* **2** a small sofa for two people, esp one that is S-shaped in plan so that the sitters are almost face to face ▷ *adv* **3** intimately; in private [c17: from French, literally: head to head]

tête-bêche (tɛt'bɛʃ) *adj philately* (of an unseparated pair of stamps) printed so that one is inverted in relation to the other [c19: from French, from *tête* head + *bêche*, from

obsolete *béchevet* double-headed (originally of a bed)]

tether ('tɛðə) *n* **1** a restricting rope, chain, etc, by which an animal is tied to a particular spot **2** the range of one's endurance, etc **3** at the end of one's tether distressed or exasperated to the limit of one's endurance ▷ *vb* (*tr*) **4** to tie or limit with or as if with a tether [c14: from Old Norse *tjothr*; related to Middle Dutch *tūder* tether, Old High German *zeotar* pole of a wagon]

Tethys¹ ('tiːθɪs, 'tɛθ-) *n Greek myth* a Titaness and sea goddess, wife of Oceanus

Tethys² ('tiːθɪs, 'tɛθ-) *n* the sea that lay between Laurasia and Gondwanaland, the two supercontinents formed by the first split of the larger supercontinent Pangaea. The Tethys Sea can be regarded as the predecessor of today's smaller Mediterranean

Teton Range ('tiːt³n) *n* a mountain range in the N central US, mainly in NW Wyoming. Highest peak: Grand Teton, 4196 m (13 766 ft)

tetra- *or before a vowel* **tetr-** *combining form* four: *tetrameter* [from Greek]

tetrabasic (ˌtɛtrə'beɪsɪk) *adj* (of an acid) containing four replaceable hydrogen atoms > **tetrabasicity** (ˌtɛtrəbeɪ'sɪsɪtɪ)

tetrachloromethane ('tɛtrəklɔːrəˌmiːθeɪn) *n* the systematic name for **carbon tetrachloride**

tetrachord ('tɛtrəˌkɔːd) *n* (in musical theory, esp of classical Greece) any of several groups of four notes in descending order, in which the first and last notes form a perfect fourth [c17: from Greek *tetrakhordos* four-stringed, from TETRA- + *khordē* a string]
> ˌtetra'chordal *adj*

tetracyclic (ˌtɛtrə'saɪklɪk) *adj chem* (of a compound) containing four rings in its molecular structure

tetracycline (ˌtɛtrə'saɪklaɪn, -klɪn) *n* an antibiotic synthesized from chlortetracycline or derived from the bacterium *Streptomyces viridifaciens*: used in treating rickettsial infections and various bacterial infections. Formula: $C_{22}H_{24}N_2O_8$ [c20: from TETRA- + CYCL(IC) + -INE²]

tetrad ('tɛtræd) *n* a group or series of four [c17: from Greek *tetras*, from *tettares* four]

tetraethyl lead (ˌtɛtrə'iːθaɪl lɛd) *n* a colourless oily insoluble liquid used in petrol to prevent knocking. Formula: $Pb(C_2H_5)_4$. Systematic name: lead tetraethyl

tetrafluoroethene ('tɛtrəˌfluərəʊ'eθiːn) *n chem* a dense colourless gas that is polymerized to make polytetrafluoroethene (PTFE). Formula: $F_2C:CF_2$. Also called: tetrafluoroethylene [c20: from TETRA- + FLUORO- + ETHENE]

tetragon ('tɛtrəˌgɒn) *n* a less common name for **quadrilateral** (sense 2) [c17: from Greek *tetragōnon*; see TETRA-, -GON]

tetragonal (tɛ'trægən³l) *adj* **1** Also called: dimetric *crystallog* relating or belonging to the crystal system characterized by three mutually perpendicular axes of which only two are equal **2** of, relating to, or shaped like a quadrilateral > teˈtragonally *adv*

Tetragrammaton (ˌtɛtrə'græmətⁿn) *n Bible* the Hebrew name for God revealed to Moses on Mount Sinai (Exodus 3), consisting of the four consonants Y H V H (or Y H W H) and regarded by Jews as too sacred to be pronounced. It is usually transliterated as *Jehovah* or *Yahweh* [c14: from Greek, from *tetragrammatos* having four letters, from TETRA- + *gramma* letter]

tetrahedron (ˌtɛtrə'hiːdrən) *n, pl* -drons *or* -dra (-drə) a solid figure having four plane faces. A regular **tetrahedron** has faces that are equilateral triangles [c16: from New Latin, from Late Greek *tetraedron*; see TETRA-, -HEDRON] > ˌtetra'hedral *adj*

tetralogy (tɛ'trælədʒɪ) *n, pl* -gies a series of four related works, as in drama or opera [c17: from Greek *tetralogia*; see TETRA-, -LOGY]

tetramerous (tɛ'træmərəs) *adj* (esp of animals or plants) having or consisting of four parts [c19: from New Latin *tetramerus*, from Greek *tetramerēs*]

tetrameter (tɛ'træmɪtə) *n prosody* **1** a line of verse consisting of four metrical feet **2** a verse composed of such lines

tetraplegia (ˌtɛtrə'pliːdʒɪə) *n* another name for **quadriplegia** [from TETRA- + Greek *plegē* a blow, from *plēssein* to strike] > ˌtetraˈplegic *adj*

tetraploid (ˈtetrəˌplɔɪd) *genetics* ▷ *adj* **1** having four times the haploid number of chromosomes in the nucleus ▷ *n* **2** a tetraploid organism, nucleus, or cell

tetrapod (ˈtetrəˌpɒd) *n* **1** any vertebrate that has four limbs **2** Also called: caltrop a device consisting of four arms radiating from a central point, each at about 109° to the others, so that regardless of its position on a surface, three arms form a supporting tripod and the fourth is vertical

tetrapterous (tɛˈtræptərəs) *adj* (of certain insects) having four wings [C19: from New Latin *tetrapterus,* from Greek *tetrapteros,* from TETRA- + *pteron* wing]

tetrarch (ˈtetrɑːk) *n* **1** the ruler of one fourth of a country **2** a subordinate ruler, esp of Syria under the Roman Empire **3** any of four joint rulers [C14: from Greek *tetrarkhēs;* see TETRA-, -ARCH] > **tetrarchate** (tɛˈtrɑːˌkeɪt, -kɪt) *n* > teˈtrarchic *or* teˈtrarchical *adj* > ˈtetrarchy *n*

tetrastich (ˈtetrəˌstɪk) *n* a poem, stanza, or strophe that consists of four lines [C16: via Latin from Greek *tetrastikhon,* from TETRA- + *stikhos* row] > **tetrastichic** (ˌtetrəˈstɪkɪk) *or* **tetrastichal** (tɛˈtræstɪkᵊl) *adj*

tetravalent (ˌtetrəˈveɪlənt) *adj chem* **1** having a valency of four **2** Also called: quadrivalent having four valencies > ˌtetraˈvalency *n*

Tetrazzini (Italian tetratˈtsiːni) *n* **Luisa** (luˈiːza). 1871–1940, Italian coloratura soprano

tetrode (ˈtetrəʊd) *n* an electronic valve having four electrodes, namely a cathode, control grid, screen grid, and anode

tetrodotoxin (ˌtetrəʊdəʊˈtɒksɪn) *n* a highly lethal neurotoxin found in certain puffer fish and in newts of the genus *Taricha.* Formula: $C_{11}H_{17}N_3O_3$ [C20: from New Latin *Tetrodon* (puffer fish genus name, from Greek *tetra-* fourfold + *odont-* tooth) + TOXIN]

tetroxide (tɛˈtrɒksaɪd) *or* **tetroxid** (tɛˈtrɒksɪd) *n* any oxide that contains four oxygen atoms per molecule

tetryl (ˈtetrɪl) *n* a yellow crystalline explosive solid used in detonators; trinitrophenylmethylnitramine. Formula: $(NO_2)_3C_6H_2N(NO_2)CH_3$

Tetuán (tɛˈtwɑːn) *n* a city in N Morocco: capital of Spanish Morocco (1912–56). Pop: 499 000 (2003)

Tetzel *or* **Tezel** (ˈtetsᵊl) *n* **Johann** (joˈhan). ?1465–1519, German Dominican monk. His preaching on papal indulgences provoked Luther's 95 theses at Wittenberg (1517)

Teucer (ˈtjuːsə) *n Greek myth* **1** a Cretan leader, who founded Troy **2** a son of Telamon and Hesione, who distinguished himself by his archery on the side of the Greeks in the Trojan War

Teucrian (ˈtjuːkrɪən) *n, adj* another word for **Trojan**

Teutoburger Wald (German ˈtɔytobʊrgər valt) *n* a low wooded mountain range in N Germany: possible site of the annihilation of three Roman legions by Germans under Arminius in 9 AD

Teuton (ˈtjuːtən) *n* **1** a member of an ancient Germanic people from Jutland who migrated to S Gaul in the 2nd century BC: annihilated by a Roman army in 102 BC **2** a member of any people speaking a Germanic language, esp a German ▷ *adj* **3** Teutonic [C18: from Latin *Teutonī* the Teutons, of Germanic origin]

Teutonic (tjuːˈtɒnɪk) *adj* **1** characteristic of or relating to the German people **2** of or relating to the ancient Teutons **3** (not used in linguistics) of or relating to the Germanic languages

Tevere (ˈteːvere) *n* the Italian name for the **Tiber**

Tevez (ˈtevez) *n* **Carlos** (**Alberto**). born 1984, Argentinian footballer; plays for Argentina and Manchester United (from 2007)

Tewkesbury (ˈtjuːksbəri, -bri) *n* a town in W England, in N Gloucestershire at the confluence of the Rivers Severn and Avon: scene of a decisive battle (1471) in the Wars of the Roses in which the Yorkists defeated the Lancastrians; 12th-century abbey. Pop: 9978 (2001)

Tex. *abbreviation* **1** Texan **2** Texas

Texas (ˈteksəs) *n* a state of the southwestern US, on the Gulf of Mexico: the second largest state; part of Mexico from 1821 to 1836, when it was declared an independent republic; joined the US in 1845; consists chiefly of a plain, with a wide flat coastal belt rising up to the semiarid Sacramento and Davis Mountains of the southwest; a major producer of cotton, rice, and livestock; the chief US producer of oil and gas; a leading world supplier of sulphur. Capital: Austin. Pop: 22 118 509 (2003 est). Area: 678 927 sq km (262 134 sq miles). Abbreviations: Tex., (with zip code) TX

Texas hold 'em *n* a popular variety of poker in which each player can use any or all of five shared cards in combination with either or both of two private cards to form the best possible hand of five cards

Tex-Mex (ˈteksˌmeks) *adj* of, relating to, or denoting the Texan version of something Mexican, such as music, food, or language

text (tekst) *n* **1** the main body of a printed or written work as distinct from commentary, notes, illustrations, etc **2** (often plural) a book prescribed as part of a course of study **3** *computing* the words printed, written, or displayed on a visual display unit **4** the original exact wording of a work, esp the Bible, as distinct from a revision or translation **5** a short passage of the Bible used as a starting point for a sermon or adduced as proof of a doctrine **6** the topic or subject of a discussion or work **7** short for **textbook 8** short for **text message** ▷ *vb* **9** to send a text message from a mobile phone [C14: from Medieval Latin *textus* version, from Latin *textus* texture, from *texere* to compose]

textbook (ˈtekstˌbʊk) *n* a book used as a standard source of information on a particular subject > ˈtextˌbookish *adj*

textile (ˈtekstaɪl) *n* **1** any fabric or cloth, esp woven **2** raw material suitable to be made into cloth; fibre or yarn ▷ *adj* **3** of or relating to fabrics or the making of fabrics [C17: from Latin *textilis* woven, from *texere* to weave]

text message *n* a message sent by means of a mobile phone > text messaging *n*

textual (ˈtekstjʊəl) *adj* **1** of or relating to a text or texts **2** based on or conforming to a text > ˈtextually *adv*

textual criticism *n* **1** the scholarly study of manuscripts, esp of the Bible, in an effort to establish the original text **2** literary criticism emphasizing a close analysis of the text

textualism (ˈtekstjʊəˌlɪzəm) *n* **1** doctrinaire adherence to a text, esp of the Bible **2** textual criticism, esp of the Bible > ˈtextualist *n, adj*

texture (ˈtekstʃə) *n* **1** the surface of a material, esp as perceived by the sense of touch **2** the structure, appearance, and feel of a woven fabric **3** the general structure and disposition of the constituent parts of something: *the texture of a cake* **4** the distinctive character or quality of something: *the texture of life in America* ▷ *vb* **5** (tr) to give a distinctive usually rough or grainy texture to [C15: from Latin *textūra,* from *texere* to weave] > ˈtextural *adj* > ˈtexturally *adv*

Tezel (ˈtetsᵊl) *n* a variant spelling of (Johann) **Tetzel**

TGV (French teʒeve) *abbreviation* (in France) train à grande vitesse: a high-speed passenger train

TGWU *abbreviation* (in Britain) Transport and General Workers' Union

Th *the chemical symbol for* thorium

-th¹ *suffix* forming nouns **1** (from verbs) indicating an action or its consequence: *growth* **2** (from adjectives) indicating a quality: *width* [from Old English -*thu,* -*tho*]

-th² *or* **-eth** *suffix* forming ordinal numbers: *fourth; thousandth* [from Old English -(o)*tha,* -(o)*the*]

Thabana-Ntlenyana (tɑːˈbɑːnəᵊnˈtleɪnjənə) *n* a mountain in Lesotho: the highest peak of the Drakensberg Mountains. Height: 3482 m (11 425 ft). Also called: Thadentsonyane, Thabantshonyana

Thackeray (ˈθækəri) *n* **William Makepeace.** 1811–63, English novelist, born in India. His novels, originally serialized, include *Vanity Fair* (1848), *Pendennis* (1850), *Henry Esmond* (1852), and *The Newcomes* (1855)

Thaddeus *or* **Thadeus** (ˈθædɪəs) *n New Testament* one of the 12 apostles (Matthew 10:3; Mark 3:18), traditionally identified with Jude

Thadentsonyane (ˌtɑːdənˈtsɒnjənə) *n* another name for **Thabana-Ntlenyana**

t

Thai (taɪ) *adj* **1** of, relating to, or characteristic of Thailand, its people, or their language ▷ *n* **2** *pl* **Thais** or **Thai** a native or inhabitant of Thailand **3** the language of Thailand, sometimes classified as belonging to the Sino-Tibetan family

Thailand ('taɪˌlænd) *n* **1** a kingdom in SE Asia, on the Andaman Sea and the Gulf of Thailand: united as a kingdom in 1350 and became a major SE Asian power; consists chiefly of a central plain around the Chao Phraya river system, mountains rising over 2400 m (8000 ft) in the northwest, and rainforest the length of the S peninsula. Parts of the SW coast suffered badly in the Indian Ocean tsunami of December 2004. Official language: Thai. Official religion: (Hinayana) Buddhist. Currency: baht. Capital: Bangkok. Pop: 63 465 000 (2004 est). Area: 513 998 sq km (198 455 sq miles). Former name (until 1939 and 1945–49): Siam **2 Gulf of Thailand** an arm of the South China Sea between the Malay Peninsula and Indochina

Thaïs ('θeɪɪs) *n* 4th-century BC Athenian courtesan; mistress of Alexander the Great

thalamus ('θæləməs) *n, pl* **-mi** (-ˌmaɪ) **1** either of the two contiguous egg-shaped masses of grey matter at the base of the brain **2** both of these masses considered as a functional unit **3** the receptacle or torus of a flower [c18: from Latin, Greek *thalamos* inner room; probably related to Greek *tholos* vault] > **thalamic** (θəˈlæmɪk) *adj*

thalassaemia or *US* **thalassemia** (ˌθælə'siːmɪə) *n* a hereditary disease, common in many parts of the world, resulting from defects in the synthesis of the red blood pigment haemoglobin [New Latin, from Greek *thalassa* sea + -AEMIA, from it being esp prevalent round the eastern Mediterranean Sea]

thalassic (θə'læsɪk) *adj* **1** of or relating to the sea **2** of or relating to small or inland seas, as opposed to open waters [c19: from French *thalassique*, from Greek *thalassa* sea]

thaler or **taler** ('tɑːlə) *n, pl* **-ler** or **-lers** a former German, Austrian, or Swiss silver coin [from German; see DOLLAR]

Thales ('θeɪliːz) *n* ?624–?546 BC, Greek philosopher, mathematician, and astronomer, born in Miletus. He held that water was the origin of all things and he predicted the solar eclipse of May 28, 585 BC

Thalia (θə'laɪə) *n Greek myth* **1** the Muse of comedy and pastoral poetry **2** one of the three Graces [c17: via Latin from Greek, from *thaleia* blooming]

thalidomide (θə'lɪdəˌmaɪd) *n* a synthetic drug formerly used as a sedative and hypnotic but withdrawn from the market when found to cause abnormalities in developing fetuses. Formula: $C_{13}H_{10}N_2O_4$ **b** (*as modifier*): *a thalidomide baby* [c20: from THALLIC + -id- (from IMIDE) + IMIDE]

thallic ('θælɪk) *adj* of or containing thallium, esp in the trivalent state

thallium ('θælɪəm) *n* a soft malleable highly toxic white metallic element used as a rodent and insect poison and in low-melting glass. Its compounds are used as infrared detectors and in photoelectric cells. Symbol: Tl; atomic no: 81; atomic wt: 204.3833; valency: 1 or 3; relative density: 11.85; melting pt: 304°C; boiling pt: 1473±10°C [c20: from New Latin, from Greek *thallos* a green shoot; referring to the green line in its spectrum]

thallus ('θæləs) *n, pl* **thalli** ('θælaɪ) or **thalluses** the undifferentiated vegetative body of algae, fungi, and lichens [c19: from Latin, from Greek *thallos* green shoot, from *thallein* to bloom] > **'thalloid** *adj*

thalweg or **talweg** ('tɑːlvɛg) *n geography rare* **1** the longitudinal outline of a riverbed from source to mouth **2** the line of steepest descent from any point on the land surface [c19: from German, from *Thal* valley + *Weg* way, path]

Thames (tɛmz) *n* **1** (tɛmz) a river in S England, rising in the Cotswolds in several headstreams and flowing generally east through London to the North Sea by a large estuary. Length: 346 km (215 miles) **2** (teɪmz, θeɪmz) a river in SE Canada, in Ontario, flowing south to London, then southwest to Lake St Clair. Length: 217 km (135 miles)

than (ðæn; *unstressed* ðən) *conj, prep* (*coordinating*) **1** used to introduce the second element of a comparison, the first element of which expresses difference: *shorter than you; couldn't do otherwise than love him; he swims faster than I run* **2** used after adverbs such as *rather* or *sooner* to introduce a rejected alternative in an expression of preference: *rather than be imprisoned, I shall die* [Old English *thanne*; related to Old Saxon, Old High German *thanna*; see THEN]
● USAGE In formal English, *than* is usually regarded as a ● conjunction governing an unexpressed verb: *he does it* ● *far better than I* (*do*). The case of any pronoun therefore ● depends on whether it is the subject or object of the ● unexpressed verb: *she likes him more than I* (*like him*); *she* ● *likes him more than* (*she likes*) *me.* However in ordinary ● speech and writing *than* is usually treated as a ● preposition and is followed by the object form of a ● pronoun: *my brother is younger than me*

thanatology (ˌθænə'tɒlədʒɪ) *n* the scientific study of death and the phenomena and practices relating to it [c19: from Greek *thanatos* death + -LOGY]

thanatopsis (ˌθænə'tɒpsɪs) *n* a meditation on death, as in a poem [c19: from Greek *thanatos* death + *opsis* a view]

Thanatos ('θænəˌtɒs) *n* the Greek personification of death: son of Nyx, goddess of night. Thanatos was the name chosen by Freud to represent a universal death instinct. Roman counterpart: **Mors** See **Eros**[1]
> **Thanatotic** (ˌθænə'tɒtɪk) *adj*

thane or commonly **thegn** (θeɪn) *n* **1** (in Anglo-Saxon England) a member of an aristocratic class, ranking below an ealdorman, whose status was hereditary and who held land from the king or from another nobleman in return for certain services **2** (in medieval Scotland) a person of rank, often the chief of a clan, holding land from the king [Old English *thegn*; related to Old Saxon, Old High German *thegan* thane] > **thanage** ('θeɪnɪdʒ) *n*

Thanet ('θænɪt) *n* **Isle of Thanet** an island in SE England, in NE Kent, separated from the mainland by two branches of the River Stour: scene of many Norse invasions. Area: 109 sq km (42 sq miles)

thangka ('θæŋkə) *n* (in Tibetan Buddhism) a religious painting on a scroll [from Tibetan]

Thanjavur (ˌtʌndʒə'vʊə) *n* a city in SE India, in E Tamil Nadu: headquarters of the earliest Protestant missions in India. Pop: 215 725 (2001). Former name: **Tanjore**

thank (θæŋk) *vb* (*tr*) **1** to convey feelings of gratitude to **2** to hold responsible: *he has his creditors to thank for his bankruptcy* [Old English *thancian*; related to Old Frisian *thankia*, Old Norse *thakka*, Old Saxon, Old High German *thancōn*]

thankful ('θæŋkfʊl) *adj* grateful and appreciative > **'thankfulness** *n* > **'thankfully** *adv*

thankless ('θæŋklɪs) *adj* **1** receiving no thanks or appreciation **2** ungrateful > **'thanklessly** *adv* > **'thanklessness** *n*

thanks (θæŋks) *pl n* **1** an expression of appreciation or gratitude or an acknowledgment of services or favours given **2** thanks to because of: *thanks to him we lost the match* ▷ *interj* **3** *informal* an exclamation expressing acknowledgment, gratitude, or appreciation

thanksgiving ('θæŋksˌgɪvɪŋ; *US* θæŋks'gɪvɪŋ) *n* **1** the act of giving thanks **2** an expression of thanks to God

Thanksgiving Day *n* an annual day of holiday celebrated in thanksgiving to God on the fourth Thursday of November in the United States, and on the second Monday of October in Canada

Thant (θænt) *n* **U** (uː). 1909–74, Burmese diplomat; secretary-general of the United Nations (1962–71)

Thapsus ('θæpsəs) *n* an ancient town near Carthage in North Africa: site of Caesar's victory over Pompey in 46 BC

thar (tɑː) *n* a variant spelling of **tahr**

Thar Desert (tɑː) *n* a desert in NW India, mainly in NW Rajasthan state and extending into Pakistan. Area: over 260 000 sq km (100 000 sq miles). Also called: **Indian Desert**, **Great Indian Desert**

Tharp (θɑːp) *n* **Twyla** ('twaɪlə). born 1941, US choreographer, whose work fuses classical ballet with modern dance

Thásos ('θæsɒs) *n* a Greek island in the N Aegean: colonized by Greeks from Paros in the 7th century BC as a gold-mining centre; under Turkish rule (1455–1912).

Pop: 13 761 (2001). Area: 379 sq km (146 sq miles)

that (ðæt; *unstressed* ðət) *determiner* (*used before a singular noun*) **1 a** used preceding a noun that has been mentioned at some time or is understood: *that idea of yours* **b** (*as pronoun*): *don't eat that; that's what I mean* **2 a** used preceding a noun that denotes something more remote or removed: *that dress is cheaper than this one; that building over there is for sale* **b** (*as pronoun*): *that is John and this is his wife; give me that.* See **this 3** used to refer to something that is familiar: *that old chap from across the street* **4** used in the phrase *and all that* informal everything connected with the subject mentioned: *he knows a lot about building and that* **5 at that** (*completive-intensive*) additionally, all things considered, or nevertheless: *he's a pleasant fellow at that; I might decide to go at that* **6** like that **a** with ease; effortlessly: *he gave me the answer just like that* **b** of such a nature, character, etc: *he paid for all our tickets — he's like that* **7** that is **a** to be precise **b** in other words **c** for example **8** that's that there is no more to be done, discussed, etc ▷ *conj* (*subordinating*) **9** used to introduce a noun clause: *I believe that you'll come* **10** Also called: **so that**, in order that used to introduce a clause of purpose: *they fought that others might have peace* **11** used to introduce a clause of result: *he laughed so hard that he cried* **12** used to introduce a clause after an understood sentence expressing desire, indignation, or amazement: *oh, that I had never lived!* ▷ *adv* **13** used with adjectives or adverbs to reinforce the specification of a precise degree already mentioned: *go just that fast and you should be safe* **14** Also called: **all that** (*usually used with a negative*) informal (*intensifier*): *he wasn't that upset at the news* **15** dialect (*intensifier*): *the cat was that weak after the fight* ▷ *pron* **16** used to introduce a restrictive relative clause: *the book that we want* **17** used to introduce a clause with the verb *to be* to emphasize the extent to which the preceding noun is applicable: *genius that she is, she outwitted the computer* [Old English *thæt*; related to Old Frisian *thet*, Old Norse, Old Saxon *that*, Old High German *daz*, Greek *to*, Latin *istud*, Sanskrit *tad*]

● **USAGE** Precise stylists maintain a distinction between
● *that* and *which*: *that* is used as a relative pronoun in
● restrictive clauses and *which* in nonrestrictive clauses.
● In *the book that is on the table is mine*, the clause *that is on*
● *the table* is used to distinguish one particular book (the
● one on the table) from another or others (which may
● be anywhere, but not on the table). In *the book, which is*
● *on the table, is mine*, the *which* clause is merely
● descriptive or incidental. The more formal the level of
● language, the more important it is to preserve the
● distinction between the two relative pronouns; but in
● informal or colloquial usage, the words are often used
● interchangeably

thatch (θætʃ) *n* **1 a** Also called: **thatching** a roofing material that consists of straw, reed, etc **b** a roof made of such a material **2** anything resembling this, such as the hair of the head **3** Also called: **thatch palm** any of various palms with leaves suitable for thatching ▷ *vb* **4** to cover (a roof) with thatch [Old English *theccan* to cover; related to *thæc* roof, Old Saxon *thekkian* to thatch, Old High German *decchen*, Old Norse *thekja*] > **'thatcher** *n*

Thatcher ('θætʃə) *n* **Margaret** (**Hilda**), Baroness (née Roberts). born 1925, British stateswoman; leader of the Conservative Party (1975–90); prime minister (1979–90)

Thatcherism ('θætʃə,rɪzəm) *n* the policies of monetarism, privatization, and self-help promoted by the British Conservative stateswoman and prime minister (1979–90) Margaret, Baroness Thatcher (born Margaret Hilda Roberts, 1925) > **Thatcherite** ('θætʃə,raɪt) *n*, *adj*

thaumato- *or before a vowel* **thaumat-** *combining form* miracle; marvel: *thaumaturge* [from Greek *thauma*, *thaumat-* a marvel]

thaumatology (,θɔːmə'tɒlədʒɪ) *n* the study of or a treatise on miracles

thaumatrope ('θɔːmə,trəʊp) *n* a toy in which partial pictures on the two sides of a card appear to merge when the card is twirled rapidly [c19: from THAUMATO- + -TROPE] > **thaumatropical** (,θɔːmə'trɒpɪk^əl) *adj*

thaumaturge ('θɔːmə,tɜːdʒ) *n* rare a performer of

miracles; magician [c18: from Medieval Latin *thaumaturgus*, from Greek *thaumatourgos* miracle-working, from THAUMATO- + -*ourgos* working, from *ergon* work] > **'thauma,turgy** *n*

thaw (θɔː) *vb* **1** to melt or cause to melt from a solid frozen state: *the snow thawed* **2** to become or cause to become unfrozen; defrost **3** (*intr*) to be the case that the ice or snow is melting: *it's thawing fast* **4** (*intr*) to become more sociable, relaxed, or friendly ▷ *n* **5** the act or process of thawing **6** a spell of relatively warm weather, causing snow or ice to melt **7** an increase in relaxation or friendliness [Old English *thawian*; related to Old High German *douwen* to thaw, Old Norse *theyja* to thaw, Latin *tabēre* to waste away]

THC *abbreviation* tetrahydrocannabidinol: the active ingredient in cannabis, giving it its narcotic and psychoactive effects

ThD *abbreviation* Doctor of Theology

the¹ (*stressed or emphatic* ðiː; *unstressed before a consonant* ðə; *unstressed before a vowel* ðɪ) *determiner* (*article*) **1** used preceding a noun that has been previously specified: *the pain should disappear soon; the man then opened the door.* See **a²** **2** used with a qualifying word or phrase to indicate a particular person, object, etc, as distinct from others: *ask the man standing outside; give me the blue one.* See **a²** **3** used preceding certain nouns associated with one's culture, society, or community: *to go to the doctor; listen to the news; watch the television* **4** used preceding present participles and adjectives when they function as nouns: *the singing is awful; the dead salute you* **5** used preceding titles and certain uniquely specific or proper nouns, such as place names: *the United States; the Honourable Edward Brown; the Chairman; the moon* **6** used preceding a qualifying adjective or noun in certain names or titles: *William the Conqueror; Edward the First* **7** used preceding a noun to make it refer to its class generically: *the white seal is hunted for its fur; this is good for the throat; to play the piano* **8** used instead of *my, your, her,* etc, with parts of the body: *take me by the hand* **9** (*usually stressed*) the best, only, or most remarkable: *Harry's is the club in this town* **10** used with proper nouns when qualified: *written by the young Hardy* **11** another word for per, esp with nouns or noun phrases of cost: *fifty pence the pound* **12** often facetious or derogatory my: *the wife goes out on Thursdays* **13** used preceding a unit of time in phrases or titles indicating an outstanding person, event, etc: *match of the day; player of the year* [Middle English, from Old English *thē*, a demonstrative adjective that later superseded *sē* (masculine singular) and *sēo, sio* (feminine singular); related to Old Frisian *thi, thiu,* Old High German *der, diu*]

the² (ðə, ðɪ) *adv* **1** (often foll by *for*) used before comparative adjectives or adverbs for emphasis: *she looks the happier for her trip* **2** used correlatively before each of two comparative adjectives or adverbs to indicate equality: *the sooner you come, the better; the more I see you, the more I love you* [Old English *thī, thȳ,* instrumental case of THE¹ and THAT; related to Old Norse *thī,* Gothic *thei*]

theanthropism (θiːˈænθrə,pɪzəm) *n* **1** the ascription of human traits or characteristics to a god or gods **2** *Christian theol* the doctrine of the hypostatic union of the divine and human natures in the single person of Christ [c19: from Ecclesiastical Greek *theanthrōpos* (from *theos* god + *anthrōpos* man) + -ISM] > ,**thean'thropic** *adj*

thearchy ('θiːɑːkɪ) *n, pl* -**chies** rule or government by God or gods; theocracy [c17: from Church Greek *thearkhia*; see THEO-, -ARCHY]

theatre *or US* **theater** ('θɪətə) *n* **1** a building designed for the performance of plays, operas, etc **2 a** large room or hall, usually with a raised platform and tiered seats for an audience, used for lectures, film shows, etc **3** Also called: **operating theatre** a room in a hospital or other medical centre equipped for surgical operations **4** plays regarded collectively as a form of art **5** the theatre the world of actors, theatrical companies, etc **6** a setting for dramatic or important events **7** writing that is suitable for dramatic presentation: *a good piece of theatre* **8** US, Austral & NZ the usual word for **cinema** (sense 1) **9** a major area of military activity **10** a circular or semicircular open-air building with tiers of seats [c14:

from Latin *theātrum*, from Greek *theatron* place for viewing, from *theasthai* to look at; related to Greek *thauma* miracle]

theatre-in-the-round *n*, *pl* **theatres-in-the-round** a theatre with seats arranged around a central acting area

theatre of cruelty *n* a type of theatre advocated by Antonin Artaud in *Le Théâtre et son double* that seeks to communicate to its audience a sense of pain, suffering, and evil, using gesture, movement, sound, and symbolism rather than language

theatre of the absurd *n* drama in which normal conventions and dramatic structure are ignored or modified in order to present life as irrational or meaningless

theatrical (θɪˈætrɪkᵊl) *adj* **1** of or relating to the theatre or dramatic performances **2** exaggerated and affected in manner or behaviour; histrionic > the,atri'cality *or* the'atricalness *n* > the'atrically *adv*

theatricals (θɪˈætrɪkᵊlz) *pl n* dramatic performances and entertainments, esp as given by amateurs

theatrics (θɪˈætrɪks) *n* (*functioning as singular*) **1** the art of staging plays **2** exaggerated mannerisms or displays of emotions

Thebaid (ˈθiːbeɪɪd, -bɪ-) *n* the territory around ancient Thebes in Egypt, or sometimes around Thebes in Greece

thebaine (ˈθiːbəˌiːn, θɪˈbeɪiːn, -aɪn) *n* a poisonous white crystalline alkaloid, found in opium but without opioid actions. Formula: $C_{19}H_{21}NO_3$ [C19: from New Latin *thebaia* opium of Thebes (with reference to Egypt as a chief source of opium) + -INE²]

Thebes (θiːbz) *n* **1** (in ancient Greece) the chief city of Boeotia, destroyed by Alexander the Great (336 BC) **2** (in ancient Egypt) a city on the Nile: at various times capital of Upper Egypt or of the entire country

theca (ˈθiːkə) *n*, *pl* -cae (-siː) **1** *botany* an enclosing organ, cell, or spore case, esp the capsule of a moss **2** *zoology* a hard outer covering, such as the cup-shaped container of a coral polyp [C17: from Latin *thēca*, from Greek *thēkē* case; related to Greek *tithenai* to place] > 'thecal *or* 'thecate *adj*

thecodont (ˈθiːkəˌdɒnt) *adj* **1** (of mammals and certain reptiles) having teeth that grow in sockets **2** of or relating to teeth of this type ▷ *n* **3** any extinct reptile of the order *Thecodontia*, of Triassic times, having teeth set in sockets: they gave rise to the dinosaurs, crocodiles, pterodactyls, and birds [C20: from New Latin *Thecodontia*, from Greek *thēkē* case + -ODONT]

thé dansant *French* (te dɑ̃sɑ̃) *n*, *pl* **thés dansant** (te dɑ̃sɑ̃) a dance held while afternoon tea is served, popular in the 1920s and 1930s [literally: dancing tea]

thee (ðiː) *pron* **1** the objective form of **thou**² (*subjective*) *rare* refers to the person addressed: used mainly by members of the Society of Friends [Old English *thē*; see THOU¹]

theft (θɛft) *n* **1** *criminal law* the dishonest taking of property belonging to another person with the intention of depriving the owner permanently of its possession **2** *rare* something stolen [Old English *thēofth*; related to Old Norse *thýfth*, Old Frisian *thiuvethe*, Middle Dutch *düfte*; see THIEF]

thegn (θeɪn) *n* a variant spelling of **thane**

Theiler (ˈtaɪlə) *n* **Max.** 1899–1972, US virologist, born in South Africa, who developed a vaccine against yellow fever. Nobel prize for physiology or medicine 1951

theine (ˈθiːiːn, -ɪn) *n* another name for caffeine, esp when present in tea [C19: from New Latin *thea* tea + -INE²]

their (ðeə) *determiner* **1** of, belonging to, or associated in some way with them: *their finest hour; their own clothes; she tried to combat their mocking her* **2** belonging to or associated in some way with people in general not including the speaker or people addressed: *in many countries they wash their clothes in the river* **3** belonging to or associated in some way with an indefinite antecedent such as *one*, *whoever*, or *anybody*: *everyone should bring their own lunch* [C12: from Old Norse *theira* (genitive plural); see THEY, THEM]
●USAGE See at **they**

theirs (ðeəz) *pron* **1** something or someone belonging to or associated in some way with them: *theirs is difficult*

2 *not standard* something or someone belonging to or associated in some way with an indefinite antecedent such as *one*, *whoever*, or *anybody*: *everyone thinks theirs is best* **3** of theirs belonging to or associated with them

theism (ˈθiːɪzəm) *n* **1** the form of the belief in one God as the transcendent creator and ruler of the universe that does not necessarily entail further belief in divine revelation **2** the belief in the existence of a God or gods [C17: from Greek *theos* god + -ISM] > 'theist *n*, *adj* > the'istic *or* the'istical *adj*

them (ðɛm; *unstressed* ðəm) *pron* **1** (*objective*) refers to things or people other than the speaker or people addressed: *I'll kill them; what happened to them?* ▷ *determiner* **2** a nonstandard word for **those** *three of them oranges* [Old English *thǣm*, influenced by Old Norse *theim*; related to Old Frisian *thām*, Old Saxon, Old High German *thēm*, Old Norse *theimr*, Gothic *thaim*]
●USAGE See at **me¹, they**

thematic apperception test *n* *psychol* a projective test in which drawings of interacting people are shown and the person being tested is asked to make up a story about them

theme (θiːm) *n* **1** an idea or topic expanded in a discourse, discussion, etc **2** (in literature, music, art, etc) a unifying idea, image, or motif, repeated or developed throughout a work **3** *music* a group of notes forming a recognizable melodic unit, often used as the basis of the musical material in a composition **4** a short essay, esp one set as an exercise for a student **5** *grammar* another word for **root¹** (sense 8), **stem¹** (sense 9) **6** (*modifier*) planned or designed round one unifying subject, image, etc: *a theme holiday* ▷ *vb* (*tr*) **7** to design, decorate, arrange, etc, in accordance with a theme [C13: from Latin *thema*, from Greek: deposit, from *tithenai* to lay down] > 'themeless *adj* > thematic (θɪˈmætɪk) *adj*, *n*

theme park *n* an area planned as a leisure attraction, in which all the displays, buildings, activities, etc, are based on or relate to one particular subject

theme song *n* **1** a melody used, esp in a film score, to set a mood, introduce a character, etc **2** another term for **signature tune**

Themis (ˈθiːmɪs) *n* *Greek myth* a goddess of order and justice

Themistocles (θəˈmɪstəˌkliːz) *n* ?527–?460 BC, Athenian statesman, who was responsible for the Athenian victory against the Persians at Salamis (480). He was ostracized in 470

themselves (ðəmˈsɛlvz) *pron* **1 a** the reflexive form of *they* or *them* **b** (*intensifier*): *the team themselves voted on it* **2** (*preceded by a copula*) their normal or usual selves: *they don't seem themselves any more* **3** Also called: **themself** *not standard* a reflexive form of an indefinite antecedent such as *one*, *whoever*, or *anybody*: *everyone has to look after themselves*

then (ðɛn) *adv* **1** at that time; over that period of time **2** (*sentence modifier*) in that case; that being so: *then why don't you ask her?; if he comes, then you'll have to leave; go on then, take it* ▷ *sentence connector* **3** after that; with that: *then John left the room and didn't return* ▷ *n* **4** that time: *before then; from then on* ▷ *adj* **5** (*prenominal*) existing, functioning, etc, at that time: *the then prime minister* [Old English *thenne*; related to Old Saxon, Old High German *thanna*; see THAN]

thenar (ˈθiːnɑː) *n* *anatomy* **1** the palm of the hand **2** the fleshy area of the palm at the base of the thumb [C17: via New Latin from Greek; related to Old High German *tenar* palm of the hand]

thence (ðɛns) *adv* **1** from that place **2** Also called: **thenceforth** (ˈðɛnsˈfɔːθ) from that time or event; thereafter **3** therefore [C13: *thannes*, from *thanne*, from Old English *thanon*; related to Gothic *thanana*, Old Norse *thanan*]

thenceforward (ˈðɛnsˈfɔːwəd) *or* **thenceforwards** *adv* from that time or place on; thence

theo- *or before a vowel* **the-** *combining form* indicating God or gods: *theology* [from Greek *theos* god]

theobromine (ˌθiːəʊˈbrəʊmiːn, -mɪn) *n* a white crystalline slightly water-soluble alkaloid that occurs in many plants, such as tea and cacao: formerly used to treat asthma. Formula: $C_7H_8N_4O_2$ [C18: from New Latin *theobroma* genus of trees, literally: food of the gods, from THEO- + Greek *brōma* food + -INE²]

theocentric (ˌθɪəˈsɛntrɪk) *adj theol* having God as the focal point of attention

theocracy (θɪˈɒkrəsɪ) *n, pl* -cies **1** government by a deity or by a priesthood **2** a community or political unit under such government > ˈtheoˌcrat *n* > ˌtheoˈcratic *or* ˌtheoˈcratical *adj*

theocrasy (θɪˈɒkrəsɪ) *n* **1** a mingling into one of deities or divine attributes previously regarded as distinct **2** the union of the soul with God in mysticism [c19: from Greek *theokrasia*, from THEO- + -*krasia* from *krasis* a blending]

Theocritus (θɪˈɒkrɪtəs) *n* ?310–?250 BC, Greek poet, born in Syracuse. He wrote the first pastoral poems in Greek literature and was closely imitated by Virgil > Theˈocritan *or* Theocritean (θɪˌɒkrɪˈtiːən) *adj, n*

theodicy (θɪˈɒdɪsɪ) *n, pl* -cies the branch of theology concerned with defending the attributes of God against objections resulting from physical and moral evil [c18: coined by Leibnitz in French as *théodicée*, from THEO- + Greek *dikē* justice] > theˌodiˈcean *adj*

theodolite (θɪˈɒdəˌlaɪt) *n* a surveying instrument for measuring horizontal and vertical angles, consisting of a small tripod-mounted telescope that is free to move in both the horizontal and vertical planes. Also called (in the US and Canada): transit [c16: from New Latin *theodolitus*, of uncertain origin] > theodolitic (θɪˌɒdəˈlɪtɪk) *adj*

Theodora (ˌθɪəˈdɔːrə) *n* ?500–548 AD, Byzantine empress; wife and counsellor of Justinian I

Theodorakis (Greek θɛɔðɔˈrakis) *n* **Mikis** (ˈmikis). born 1925, Greek composer, who wrote the music for the film *Zorba the Greek* (1965): imprisoned (1967–70) for his opposition to the Greek military government

Theodore I (ˈθiːədɔː) *n* called *Lascaris*. ?1175–1222, Byzantine ruler, who founded a Byzantine state in exile at Nicaea after Constantinople fell to the Crusaders (1204)

Theodoric *or* **Theoderic** (θɪˈɒdərɪk) *n* called *the Great*. ?454–526 AD, king of the Ostrogoths and founder of the Ostrogothic kingdom in Italy after his murder of Odoacer (493)

Theodosius I (ˌθɪəˈdəʊsɪəs) *n* called *the Great*. ?346–395 AD, Roman emperor of the Eastern Roman Empire (379–95) and of the Western Roman Empire (392–95)

theogony (θɪˈɒɡənɪ) *n, pl* -nies **1** the origin and descent of the gods **2** an account of this, often recited in epic poetry [c17: from Greek *theogonia*; see THEO-, -GONY] > theˈogonic (ˌθɪəˈɡɒnɪk) *adj* > theˈogonist *n*

theol. *abbreviation* **1** theologian **2** theological **3** theology

theologian (ˌθɪəˈləʊdʒɪən) *n* a person versed in or engaged in the study of theology, esp Christian theology

theological (ˌθɪəˈlɒdʒɪkᵊl) *adj* of, relating to, or based on theology > ˌtheoˈlogically *adv*

theological virtues *pl n* (esp among the scholastics) those virtues that are infused into man by a special grace of God, specifically faith, hope, and charity

theologize *or* **theologise** (θɪˈɒləˌdʒaɪz) *vb* **1** (*intr*) to speculate upon theological subjects, engage in theological study or discussion, or formulate theological arguments **2** (*tr*) to render theological or treat from a theological point of view > theˌologiˈzation *or* theˌologiˈsation *n* > theˈoloˌgizer *or* theˈoloˌgiser *n*

theology (θɪˈɒlədʒɪ) *n, pl* -gies **1** the systematic study of the existence and nature of the divine and its relationship to and influence upon other beings **2** a specific branch of this study, undertaken from the perspective of a particular group **3** the systematic study of Christian revelation concerning God's nature and purpose, esp through the teaching of the Church **4** a specific system, form, or branch of this study, esp for those preparing for the ministry or priesthood [c14: from Late Latin *theologia*, from Latin; see THEO-, -LOGY] > theˈologist *n*

theomachy (θɪˈɒməkɪ) *n, pl* -chies a battle among the gods or against them [c16: from Greek *theomakhia*, from THEO- + *makhē* battle]

theomancy (ˈθiːəʊˌmænsɪ) *n* divination or prophecy by an oracle or by people directly inspired by a god [c17: from THEO- + -MANCY]

theomania (ˌθɪəˈmeɪnɪə) *n* religious madness, esp when it takes the form of believing oneself to be a god > ˌtheoˈmaniˌac *n*

theophany (θɪˈɒfənɪ) *n, pl* -nies *theol* a manifestation of a deity to man in a form that, though visible, is not necessarily material [c17: from Late Latin *theophania*, from Late Greek *theophaneia*, from THEO- + *phainein* to show] > theophanic (θɪəˈfænɪk) *or* theˈophanous *adj*

Theophilus (θɪˈɒfɪləs) *n* died 842 AD, Byzantine emperor (829–42); a patron of learning and supporter of iconoclasm

Theophrastus (ˌθɪəˈfræstəs) *n* ?372–?287 BC, Greek Peripatetic philosopher, noted esp for his *Characters*, a collection of sketches of moral types

theophylline (ˌθɪəˈfɪliːn, -ɪn, θɪˈfɪlɪn) *n* a white crystalline slightly water-soluble alkaloid that is an isomer of theobromine: it occurs in plants, such as tea, and is used to treat asthma. Formula: $C_7H_8N_4O_2$ [c19: from THEO(BROMINE) + PHYLLO- + -INE²]

theorem (ˈθɪərəm) *n maths, logic* a statement or formula that can be deduced from the axioms of a formal system by means of its rules of inference [c16: from Late Latin *theōrēma*, from Greek: something to be viewed, from *theōrein* to view] > theorematic (ˌθɪərəˈmætɪk) *or* theoremic (ˌθɪəˈrɛmɪk) *adj* > ˌtheoreˈmatically *adv*

theoretical (ˌθɪəˈrɛtɪkᵊl) *or* **theoretic** (ˌθɪəˈrɛtɪk) *adj* **1** of or based on theory **2** lacking practical application or actual existence; hypothetical **3** using or dealing in theory; impractical > ˌtheoˈretically *adv*

theoretician (ˌθɪərɪˈtɪʃən) *n* a student or user of the theory rather than the practical aspects of a subject

theoretics (ˌθɪəˈrɛtɪks) *n* (*functioning as singular or plural*) the theory of a particular subject

theorize *or* **theorise** (ˈθɪəˌraɪz) *vb* (*intr*) to produce or use theories; speculate > ˌtheoriˈzation *or* ˌtheoriˈsation *n* > ˈtheoˌrizer *or* ˈtheoˌriser *n* > ˈtheorist *n*

theory (ˈθɪərɪ) *n, pl* -ries **1** a system of rules, procedures, and assumptions used to produce a result **2** abstract knowledge or reasoning **3** a speculative or conjectural view or idea: *I have a theory about that* **4** an ideal or hypothetical situation (esp in the phrase **in theory**) **5** a set of hypotheses related by logical or mathematical arguments to explain and predict a wide variety of connected phenomena in general terms: *the theory of relativity* **6** a nontechnical name for **hypothesis** (sense 1) [c16: from Late Latin *theōria*, from Greek: a sight, from *theōrein* to gaze upon]

theory of games *n* another name for **game theory**

theosophy (θɪˈɒsəfɪ) *n* **1** any of various religious or philosophical systems claiming to be based on or to express an intuitive insight into the divine nature **2** the system of beliefs of the Theosophical Society founded in 1875, claiming to be derived from the sacred writings of Brahmanism and Buddhism, but denying the existence of any personal God [c17: from Medieval Latin *theosophia*, from Late Greek; see THEO-, -SOPHY] > theosophical (ˌθɪəˈsɒfɪkᵊl) *adj* > theˈosophist *n*

Thera (ˈθɪərə) *n* a Greek island in the Aegean Sea, in the Cyclades: site of a Minoan settlement and of the volcano that ended Minoan civilization on Crete. Pop: 13 402 (2001). Also called: Santoríni

therapeutic (ˌθɛrəˈpjuːtɪk) *adj* **1** of or relating to the treatment of disease; curative **2** serving or performed to maintain health: *therapeutic abortion* [c17: from New Latin *therapeuticus*, from Greek *therapeutikos*, from *therapeuein* to minister to, from *theraps* an attendant] > ˌheraˈpeutically *adv*

therapeutic cloning *n* the permitted creation of cloned human tissues for surgical transplant

therapeutics (ˌθɛrəˈpjuːtɪks) *n* (*functioning as singular*) the branch of medicine concerned with the treatment of disease

therapy (ˈθɛrəpɪ) *n, pl* -pies **a** the treatment of physical, mental, or social disorders or disease **b** (*in combination*): *physiotherapy*; *electrotherapy* [c19: from New Latin *therapia*, from Greek *therapeia* attendance; see THERAPEUTIC] > ˈtherapist *n*

Theravada (ˌθɛrə'vɑːdə) *n* the southern school of Buddhism, the name preferred by Hinayana Buddhists for their doctrines [from Pali: doctrine of the elders]

there (ðɛə) *adv* **1** in, at, or to that place, point, case, or respect: *we never go there; I'm afraid I disagree with you there* ▷ *pron* **2** used as a grammatical subject with some verbs, esp *be*, when the true subject is an indefinite or mass noun phrase following the verb as complement: *there is a girl in that office; there doesn't seem to be any water left* ▷ *adj* **3** (*postpositive*) who or which is in that place or position: *that boy there did it* **4** all there (*predicative*) having his or her wits about him or her; of normal intelligence **5** so there an exclamation that usually follows a declaration of refusal or defiance **6** there you are **a** an expression used when handing a person something requested or desired **b** an exclamation of triumph: *there you are, I knew that would happen!* ▷ *n* **7** that place: *near there; from there* ▷ *interj* **8** an expression of sympathy, as in consoling a child [Old English *thǣr*; related to Old Frisian *thēr*, Old Saxon, Old High German *thār*, Old Norse, Gothic *thar*]
- ● USAGE In correct usage, the verb should agree with
- ● the number of the subject in such constructions as
- ● *there is a man waiting* and *there are several people waiting.*
- ● However, where the subject is compound, it is
- ● common in speech to use the singular as in *there's a*
- ● *police car and an ambulance outside*

thereabouts (ˈðɛərəˌbaʊts) *or US* **thereabout** *adv* near that place, time, amount, etc

thereafter (ˌðɛər'ɑːftə) *adv* from that time on or after that time

thereat (ˌðɛər'æt) *adv rare* **1** at that point or time **2** for that reason

thereby (ˌðɛə'baɪ, 'ðɛəˌbaɪ) *adv* **1** by that means; because of that **2** *archaic* by or near that place; thereabouts

therefor (ˌðɛə'fɔː) *adv archaic* for this, that, or it

therefore (ˈðɛəˌfɔː) *sentence connector* **1** thus; hence: used to mark an inference on the speaker's part: *those people have their umbrellas up: therefore, it must be raining* **2** consequently; as a result

therefrom (ˌðɛə'frɒm) *adv archaic* from that or there: *the roads that lead therefrom*

therein (ˌðɛər'ɪn) *adv formal* in or into that place, thing, etc

thereinto (ˌðɛər'ɪntuː) *adv formal* into that place, circumstance, etc

thereof (ˌðɛər'ɒv) *adv formal* **1** of or concerning that or it **2** from or because of that

thereon (ˌðɛər'ɒn) *adv* an archaic word for **thereupon**

Theresa (tə'riːzə; *Spanish* te'resa) *n* See **Teresa** (sense 1)

Thérèse de Lisieux (*French* terɛz də lizjø) *n* **Saint**, known as *the Little Flower of Jesus.* 1873–97, French Carmelite nun, noted for her autobiography, *The Story of a Soul* (1897). Feast day: Oct 3

thereto (ˌðɛə'tuː) *adv* **1** *formal* to that or it **2** *obsolete* in addition to that

theretofore (ˌðɛətʊ'fɔː) *adv formal* before that time; previous to that

thereunder (ˌðɛər'ʌndə) *adv formal* **1** (in documents, etc) below that or it; subsequently in that; thereafter **2** under the terms or authority of that

thereupon (ˌðɛərə'pɒn) *adv* **1** immediately after that; at that point **2** *formal* upon that thing, point, subject, etc

therewith (ˌðɛə'wɪθ, -'wɪð) *or* **therewithal** *adv* **1** *formal* with or in addition to that **2** a less common word for **thereupon** (sense 1) **3** *archaic* by means of or on account of that

Therezina (*Portuguese* tere'zina) *n* the former name of Teresina

therianthropic (ˌθɪərɪən'θrɒpɪk) *adj* **1** (of certain mythical creatures or deities) having a partly animal, partly human form **2** of or relating to such creatures or deities [C19: from Greek *thērion* wild animal + *anthrōpos* man] ▷ **therianthropism** (ˌθɪərɪ'ænθrəˌpɪzəm) *n*

theriomorphic (ˌθɪərɪəʊ'mɔːfɪk) *adj* (esp of a deity) possessing or depicted in the form of a beast [C19: from Greek *thēriomorphos*, from *thērion* wild animal + *morphē* shape]

therm (θɜːm) *n Brit* a unit of heat equal to 100 000 British thermal units. One therm is equal to 1.055 056 × 10⁸ joules [C19: from Greek *thermē* heat]

thermae ('θɜːmiː) *pl n* public baths or hot springs, esp in ancient Greece or Rome [C17: from Latin, from Greek *thermai*, pl of *thermē* heat]

thermal ('θɜːməl) *adj* **1** Also called: **thermic** ('θɜːmɪk) of, relating to, caused by, or generating heat or increased temperature **2** hot or warm: *thermal baths; thermal spring* **3** (of garments or fabrics) specially designed so as to have exceptional heat-retaining properties ▷ *n* **4** *meteorol* a column of rising air caused by local unequal heating of the land surface, and used by gliders and birds to gain height **5** (*plural*) thermal garments, esp underclothes ▷ **'thermally** *adv*

thermal barrier *n* an obstacle to flight at very high speeds as a result of the heating effect of air friction. Also called: **heat barrier**

thermal conductivity *n* a measure of the ability of a substance to conduct heat, determined by the rate of heat flow normally through an area in the substance divided by the area and by minus the component of the temperature gradient in the direction of flow: measured in watts per metre per kelvin

thermal efficiency *n* the ratio of the work done by a heat engine to the energy supplied to it

thermal equator *n* an imaginary line round the earth running through the point on each meridian with the highest average temperature. It lies mainly to the north because of the larger landmasses and therefore greater summer heating

thermal imaging *n* the use of heat-sensitive equipment to detect or provide images of people or things

thermalize *or* **thermalise** ('θɜːməˌlaɪz) *vb physics* to undergo or cause to undergo a process in which neutrons lose energy in a moderator and become thermal neutrons ▷ **ˌthermali'zation** *or* **ˌthermali'sation** *n*

thermal neutrons *pl n* slow neutrons that are approximately in thermal equilibrium with a moderator. They have a distribution of speeds similar to that of the molecules of a gas at the temperature of the moderator. Data concerning nuclear interactions are often given for standard thermal neutrons of speed 2200 metres per second, which is approximately the most probable speed at normal laboratory temperatures

thermal reactor *n* a nuclear reactor in which most of the fission is caused by thermal neutrons

thermal shock *n* a fluctuation in temperature causing stress in a material. It often results in fracture, esp in brittle materials such as ceramics

thermion ('θɜːmɪən) *n physics* an electron or ion emitted by a body at high temperature

thermionic (ˌθɜːmɪ'ɒnɪk) *adj* of, relating to, or operated by electrons emitted from materials at high temperatures: *a thermionic valve*

thermionic current *n* an electric current produced between two electrodes as a result of electrons emitted by thermionic emission

thermionic emission *n* the emission of electrons from very hot solids or liquids: used for producing electrons in valves, electron microscopes, X-ray tubes, etc

thermionics (ˌθɜːmɪ'ɒnɪks) *n* (*functioning as singular*) the branch of electronics concerned with the emission of electrons by hot bodies and with devices based on this effect, esp the study and design of thermionic valves

thermionic valve *or esp US and Canadian* **thermionic tube** *n* an electronic valve in which electrons are emitted from a heated rather than a cold cathode

thermistor (θɜː'mɪstə) *n* a semiconductor device having a resistance that decreases rapidly with an increase in temperature. It is used for temperature measurement, to compensate for temperature variations in a circuit, etc [C20: from THERMO- + (RES)ISTOR]

Thermit ('θɜːmɪt) *or* **Thermite** ('θɜːmaɪt) *n trademark* a mixture of aluminium powder and a metal oxide, such as iron oxide, which when ignited reacts with the evolution of heat to yield aluminium oxide and molten metal: used for welding and in some types of incendiary bombs

thermo- *or before a vowel* **therm-** *combining form* related to, caused by, or measuring heat: *thermodynamics; thermophile*

[from Greek *thermos* hot, *thermē* heat]

thermobaric (ˌθɜːməʊˈbærɪk) *adj* (of an explosive device or explosion) detonated by means of an explosive substance reacting spontaneously with air

thermobarograph (ˌθɜːməʊˈbærəˌɡrɑːf, -ˌɡræf) *n* a device that simultaneously records the temperature and pressure of the atmosphere

thermobarometer (ˌθɜːməʊbəˈrɒmɪtə) *n* an apparatus that provides an accurate measurement of pressure by observation of the change in the boiling point of a fluid

thermochemistry (ˌθɜːməʊˈkɛmɪstrɪ) *n* the branch of chemistry concerned with the study and measurement of the heat evolved or absorbed during chemical reactions > ˌthermoˈchemical *adj* > ˌthermoˈchemist *n*

thermochromism (ˌθɜːməʊˈkrəʊmɪzəm) *n* a phenomenon in which certain dyes made from liquid crystals change colour reversibly when their temperature is changed > ˈthermochromy *n* > ˌthermoˈchromic *adj*

thermocline (ˈθɜːməʊˌklaɪn) *n* a temperature gradient in a thermally stratified body of water, such as a lake

thermocouple (ˈθɜːməʊˌkʌpəl) *n* **1** a device for measuring temperature consisting of a pair of wires of different metals or semiconductors joined at both ends. One junction is at the temperature to be measured, the second at a fixed temperature. The electromotive force generated depends upon the temperature difference **2** a similar device with only one junction between two dissimilar metals or semiconductors [C19: from THERMO- + COUPLE]

thermodynamic (ˌθɜːməʊdaɪˈnæmɪk) *or* **thermodynamical** *adj* **1** of or concerned with thermodynamics **2** determined by or obeying the laws of thermodynamics

thermodynamic equilibrium *n* the condition of an isolated system in which the quantities that specify its properties, such as pressure, temperature, etc, all remain unchanged

thermodynamics (ˌθɜːməʊdaɪˈnæmɪks) *n* (*functioning as singular*) the branch of physical science concerned with the interrelationship and interconversion of different forms of energy and the behaviour of macroscopic systems in terms of certain basic quantities, such as pressure, temperature, etc

thermodynamic temperature *n* temperature defined in terms of the laws of thermodynamics and not in terms of the properties of any real material. It is usually expressed on the Kelvin scale

thermoelectric (ˌθɜːməʊɪˈlɛktrɪk) *or* **thermoelectrical** (ˌθɜːməʊɪˈlɛktrɪkəl) *adj* of, relating to, used in, or operated by the generation of an electromotive force by the Seebeck effect or the Thomson effect

thermoelectric effect *n* another name for **Seebeck effect**

thermoelectricity (ˌθɜːməʊɪlɛkˈtrɪsɪtɪ) *n* **1** electricity generated by a thermocouple **2** the study of the relationship between heat and electrical energy

thermoelectron (ˌθɜːməʊɪˈlɛktrɒn) *n* an electron emitted at high temperature, such as one produced in a thermionic valve

thermogenesis (ˌθɜːməʊˈdʒɛnɪsɪs) *n* the production of heat by metabolic processes > thermogenous (θɜːˈmɒdʒɪnəs) *or* ˌthermoˈgenic *adj*

thermogram (ˈθɜːməʊˌɡræm) *n* **1** *med* a picture produced by thermography, using photographic film sensitive to infrared radiation **2** the record produced by a thermograph

thermograph (ˈθɜːməʊˌɡrɑːf, -ˌɡræf) *n* a type of thermometer that produces a continuous record of a fluctuating temperature

thermography (θɜːˈmɒɡrəfɪ) *n* **1** any writing, printing, or recording process involving the use of heat **2** *med* the measurement and recording of heat produced by a part of the body: used in the diagnosis of tumours, esp of the breast (**mammothermography**), which have an increased blood supply and therefore generate more heat than normal tissue. See also **thermogram** > therˈmographer *n* > thermographic (ˌθɜːməʊˈɡræfɪk) *adj*

thermojunction (ˌθɜːməʊˈdʒʌŋkʃən) *n* a point of electrical contact between two dissimilar metals across which a voltage appears, the magnitude of which depends on the temperature of the contact and the nature of the metals

thermolabile (ˌθɜːməʊˈleɪbɪl) *adj* (of certain biochemical and chemical compounds) easily decomposed or subject to a loss of characteristic properties by the action of heat [C20: from THERMO- + LABILE]

thermoluminescence (ˌθɜːməʊˌluːmɪˈnɛsəns) *n* phosphorescence of certain materials or objects as a result of heating. It is caused by pre-irradiation of the material inducing defects which are removed by the heat, the energy released appearing as light: used in archaeological dating

thermolysis (θɜːˈmɒlɪsɪs) *n* **1** *physiol* loss of heat from the body **2** the dissociation of a substance as a result of heating > thermolytic (ˌθɜːməʊˈlɪtɪk) *adj*

thermomagnetic (ˌθɜːməʊmæɡˈnɛtɪk) *adj* of or concerned with the relationship between heat and magnetism, esp the change in temperature of a body when it is magnetized or demagnetized

thermometer (θəˈmɒmɪtə) *n* an instrument used to measure temperature, esp one in which a thin column of liquid, such as mercury, expands and contracts within a graduated sealed tube

thermonuclear (ˌθɜːməʊˈnjuːklɪə) *adj* **1** involving nuclear fusion **2** involving thermonuclear weapons

thermonuclear reaction *n* a nuclear fusion reaction occurring at a very high temperature: responsible for the energy produced in the sun, nuclear weapons, and fusion reactors

thermophile (ˈθɜːməʊˌfaɪl) *or* **thermophil** (ˈθɜːməʊˌfɪl) *n* **1** an organism, esp a bacterium or plant, that thrives under warm conditions ▷ *adj* **2** thriving under warm conditions > ˌthermoˈphilic *or* thermophilous (θɜːˈmɒfɪləs) *adj*

thermopile (ˈθɜːməʊˌpaɪl) *n* an instrument for detecting and measuring heat radiation or for generating a thermoelectric current. It consists of a number of thermocouple junctions, usually joined together in series [C19: from THERMO- + PILE[1] (in the sense: voltaic pile)]

thermoplastic (ˌθɜːməʊˈplæstɪk) *adj* **1** (of a material, esp a synthetic plastic or resin) becoming soft when heated and rehardening on cooling without appreciable change of properties. See **thermosetting** ▷ *n* **2** a synthetic plastic or resin, such as polystyrene, with these properties

Thermopylae (θəˈmɒpəˌliː) *n* (in ancient Greece) a narrow pass between the mountains and the sea linking Locris and Thessaly: a defensible position on a traditional invasion route from N Greece; scene of a famous battle (480 BC) in which a greatly outnumbered Greek army under Leonidas fought to the death to delay the advance of the Persians during their attempted conquest of Greece

Thermos *or* **Thermos flask** (ˈθɜːməs) *n trademark* a type of stoppered vacuum flask used to preserve the temperature of its contents

thermosetting (ˌθɜːməʊˈsɛtɪŋ) *adj* (of a material, esp a synthetic plastic or resin) hardening permanently after one application of heat and pressure. Thermosetting plastics, such as phenol-formaldehyde, cannot be remoulded

thermosiphon (ˌθɜːməʊˈsaɪfən) *n* a system in which a coolant is circulated by convection caused by a difference in density between the hot and cold portions of the liquid

thermosphere (ˈθɜːməˌsfɪə) *n* an atmospheric layer lying between the mesosphere and the exosphere, reaching an altitude of about 400 kilometres where the temperature is over 1000°C

thermostable (ˌθɜːməʊˈsteɪbəl) *adj* (of certain chemical and biochemical compounds) capable of withstanding moderate heat without loss of characteristic properties

thermostat (ˈθɜːməˌstæt) *n* **1** a device that maintains a system at a constant temperature. It often consists of a bimetallic strip that bends as it expands and contracts with temperature, thus breaking and making contact with an electrical power supply **2** a similar device that actuates equipment, such as a sprinkler, when a certain temperature is reached ▷ ,thermo'static *adj* ▷ ,thermo'statically *adv*

thermostatics (,θɜːmə'stætɪks) *n* (*functioning as singular*) the branch of science concerned with thermal equilibrium

thermotaxis (,θɜːməʊ'tæksɪs) *n* the directional movement of an organism in response to the stimulus of a source of heat ▷ ,thermo'taxic *adj*

thermotropism (,θɜːməʊ'trəʊpɪzəm) *n* the directional growth of a plant in response to the stimulus of heat ▷ ,thermo'tropic *adj*

-thermy *n combining form* indicating heat: *diathermy* [from New Latin *-thermia*, from Greek *thermē*] ▷ **-thermic** *or* **-thermal** *adj combining form*

theroid ('θɪərɔɪd) *adj* of, relating to, or resembling a beast [C19: from Greek *thēroeidēs*, from *thēr* wild animal; see **-OID**]

Theron (θə'rɒn) *n* **Charlize** ('ʃɑːliːz) born 1975, South African film actress; her films include *The Cider House Rules* (1999) and *Monster* (2003), which earned her an Oscar

Theroux (θə'ruː) *n* **Paul** (**Edward**). born 1941, US novelist and travel writer. His novels include *Picture Palace* (1978), *The Mosquito Coast* (1981), and *My Other Life* (1996); travel writings include *The Great Railway Bazaar* (1975)

Thersites (θə'saɪtiːz) *n* the ugliest and most evil-tongued fighter on the Greek side in the Trojan War, killed by Achilles when he mocked him

thesaurus (θɪ'sɔːrəs) *n, pl* **-ruses** *or* **-ri** (-raɪ) **1** a book containing systematized lists of synonyms and related words **2** a dictionary of selected words or topics **3** *rare* a treasury [C18: from Latin, Greek: **TREASURE**]

these (ðiːz) *determiner* **a** the form of **this** used before a plural noun: *these men* **b** (*as pronoun*): *I don't much care for these*

Theseus ('θiːsɪəs) *n Greek myth* a hero of Attica, noted for his many great deeds, among them the slaying of the Minotaur, the conquest of the Amazons, whose queen he married, and participation in the Calydonian hunt ▷ **Thesean** (θɪ'siːən) *adj*

Thesiger ('θɛsɪdʒə) *n* **Wilfred** (**Patrick**). 1910–2003, British writer, who explored the Empty Quarter of Arabia (1945–50) and lived with the Iraqi marsh Arabs (1950–58). His books include *Arabian Sands* (1958), *The Marsh Arabs* (1964), and *My Kenya Days* (1994)

thesis ('θiːsɪs) *n, pl* **-ses** (-siːz) **1** a dissertation resulting from original research, esp when submitted by a candidate for a degree or diploma **2** a doctrine maintained or promoted in argument **3** a subject for a discussion or essay **4** an unproved statement, esp one put forward as a premise in an argument [C16: via Late Latin from Greek: a placing, from *tithenai* to place]

thespian ('θɛspɪən) *adj* **1** of or relating to drama and the theatre; dramatic ▷ *n* **2** *often facetious* an actor or actress [C19: from Thespis, the 6th century BC Greek poet, regarded as the founder of tragic drama]

Thespian ('θɛspɪən) *adj* **1** of or relating to Thespis **2** (*usually not capital*) of or relating to drama and the theatre; dramatic ▷ *n* (*usually not capital*) **3** *often facetious* an actor or actress

Thespis ('θɛspɪs) *n* 6th century BC, Greek poet, regarded as the founder of tragic drama

Thess. *Bible abbreviation* Thessalonians

Thessalonian (,θɛsə'ləʊnɪən) *adj* **1** of or relating to ancient Thessalonica (modern Salonika) ▷ *n* **2** an inhabitant of ancient Thessalonica

Thessaloníki (Greek θɛsalɔ'niki) *n* a port in NE Greece, in central Macedonia at the head of the **Gulf of Salonika** (an inlet of the Aegean): capital of the Roman province of Macedonia; university (1926). Pop: 824 000 (2005 est). English name: **Salonika**

Thessaly ('θɛsəlɪ) *n* a region of E Central Greece, on the Aegean: an extensive fertile plain, edged with mountains. Pop: 609 100 (2001). Area: 14 037 sq km (5418 sq miles)

theta ('θiːtə) *n* the eighth letter of the Greek alphabet (H, θ), a consonant, transliterated as *th* [C17: from Greek, of Semitic origin; compare Hebrew *tēth*]

Thetford Mines ('θɛtfəd) *n* a city in SE Canada, in S Quebec: asbestos industry. Pop: 21 651 (2001)

Thetis ('θiːtɪs) *n* one of the Nereids and mother of Achilles by Peleus

theurgy ('θiː,ɜːdʒɪ) *n, pl* **-gies** **1** the intervention of a divine or supernatural agency in the affairs of man **2** beneficent magic as taught and performed by Egyptian Neoplatonists and others [C16: from Late Latin *theūrgia*, from Late Greek *theourgia* the practice of magic, from *theo-* THEO- + *-urgia*, from *ergon* work] ▷ the'urgic *or* the'urgical *adj* ▷ 'theurgist *n*

thew (θjuː) *n* **1** muscle, esp if strong or well-developed **2** (*plural*) muscular strength [Old English *thēaw*; related to Old Saxon, Old High German *thau* discipline, Latin *tuērī* to observe, *tūtus* secure] ▷ 'thewy *adj* ▷ 'thewless *adj*

they (ðeɪ) *pron* (*subjective*) **1** refers to people or things other than the speaker or people addressed: *they fight among themselves* **2** refers to unspecified people or people in general not including the speaker or people addressed: *in Australia they have Christmas in the summer* **3** *not standard* refers to an indefinite antecedent such as *one, whoever,* or *anybody*: *if anyone objects, they can go* [C12: *thei* from Old Norse *their,* masculine nominative plural, equivalent to Old English *thā*]

● **USAGE** It was formerly considered correct to use *he,*
● *him,* or *his* after pronouns such as *everyone, no-one,*
● *anyone,* or *someone* as in *everyone did his best,* but it is now
● more common to use *they, them,* or *their,* and this use
● has become acceptable in all but the most formal
● contexts: *everyone did their best*

they'd (ðeɪd) *contraction of* they would *or* they had

they'll (ðeɪl) *contraction of* they will *or* they shall

they're (ðɛə, ˈðeɪə) *contraction of* they are

they've (ðeɪv) *contraction of* they have

THG *abbreviation* tetrahydrogestrinone

thi- *combining form* a variant of **thio-**

thiamine ('θaɪə,miːn, -mɪn) *or* **thiamin** ('θaɪəmɪn) *n biochem* a soluble white crystalline vitamin that occurs in the outer coat of rice and other grains. It forms part of the vitamin B complex and is essential for carbohydrate metabolism: deficiency leads to nervous disorders and to the disease beriberi. Formula: $C_{12}H_{17}ON_4SCl.H_2O$. Also called: **vitamin B₁**, **aneurin** [C20: THIO- + (VIT)AMIN]

thiazine ('θaɪə,ziːn, -,zaɪn) *n* any of a group of organic compounds containing a ring system composed of four carbon atoms, a sulphur atom, and a nitrogen atom

thiazole ('θaɪə,zəʊl) *n* **1** a colourless liquid with a pungent smell that contains a ring system composed of three carbon atoms, a sulphur atom, and a nitrogen atom. It is used in dyes and fungicides. Formula: C_3H_3NS **2** any of a group of compounds derived from this substance that are used in dyes

thick (θɪk) *adj* **1** of relatively great extent from one surface to the other; fat, broad, or deep: *a thick slice of bread* **2 a** (*postpositive*) of specific fatness: *ten centimetres thick* **b** (*in combination*): *a six-inch-thick wall* **3** having a relatively dense consistency; not transparent: *thick soup* **4** abundantly covered or filled: *a piano thick with dust* **5** impenetrable; dense: *a thick fog* **6** stupid, slow, or insensitive **7** throaty or badly articulated: *a voice thick with emotion* **8** (of accents, etc) pronounced **9** *informal* very friendly (esp in the phrase **thick as thieves**) **10** a bit thick *Brit* unfair or excessive ▷ *adv* **11** in order to produce something thick: *to slice bread thick* **12** profusely; in quick succession (esp in the phrase **thick and fast**) **13** lay it on thick *informal* **a** to exaggerate a story, statement, etc **b** to flatter excessively ▷ *n* **14** a thick piece or part **15** the thick the busiest or most intense part **16** through thick and thin in good times and bad [Old English *thicce*; related to Old Saxon, Old High German *thikki*, Old Norse *thykkr*] ▷ 'thickish *adj* ▷ 'thickly *adv*

thick client *n computing* a computer having its own hard drive, as opposed to one on a network where most functions are carried out on a central server. See **thin client**

thicken ('θɪkən) *vb* **1** to make or become thick or thicker: *thicken the soup by adding flour* **2** (*intr*) to become more involved: *the plot thickened* ▷ 'thickener *n*

thickening ('θɪkənɪŋ) *n* **1** something added to a liquid to thicken it **2** a thickened part or piece

thicket ('θɪkɪt) *n* a dense growth of small trees, shrubs, and similar plants [Old English *thiccet; see* THICK]

thickhead ('θɪk,hɛd) *n* **1** a stupid or ignorant person; fool **2** Also called: **whistler** any of various Australian and SE Asian songbirds of the family *Muscicapidae* (flycatchers, etc) > ,thick'headed *adj*

thickie *or* **thicky** ('θɪkɪ) *n, pl* -ies *Brit slang* a variant of **thicko**

thick-knee *n* another name for **stone curlew** [c19: so called because it has thick knee joints]

thickness ('θɪknɪs) *n* **1** the state or quality of being thick **2** the dimension through an object, as opposed to length or width **3** a layer of something

thicko ('θɪkəʊ) *n, pl* **thickos** *or* **thickoes** *Brit slang* a slow-witted unintelligent person. Also called: **thickie, thicky**

thickset (,θɪk'sɛt) *adj* **1** stocky in build; sturdy **2** densely planted or placed ▷ *n* **3** a rare word for **thicket**

thick-skinned *adj* insensitive to criticism or hints; not easily upset or affected

thick-witted *or* **thick-skulled** *adj* stupid, dull, foolish, or slow to learn > ,thick-'wittedly *adv* > ,thick-'wittedness *n*

thief (θiːf) *n, pl* **thieves** (θiːvz) a person who steals something from another [Old English *thēof;* related to Old Frisian *thiāf,* Old Saxon *thiof,* Old High German *diob,* Old Norse *thjōfr,* Gothic *thiufs*] > 'thievish *adj*

Thiers *(French* tjɛr) *n* **Louis Adolphe** (lwi adɔlf). 1797–1877, French statesman and historian. After the Franco-Prussian war, he suppressed the Paris Commune and became first president of the Third Republic (1871–73). His policies made possible the paying off of the war indemnity exacted by Germany

thieve (θiːv) *vb* to steal (someone's possessions) [Old English *thēofian,* from *thēof* THIEF] > 'thieving *adj*

thigh (θaɪ) *n* **1** the part of the leg between the hip and the knee in man **2** the corresponding part in other vertebrates and insects ▷ Related adjective: **femoral** [Old English *thēh;* related to Old Frisian *thiāch,* Old High German *dioh* thigh, Old Norse *thjō* buttock, Old Slavonic *tyku* fat]

thighbone ('θaɪ,bəʊn) *n* a nontechnical name for **femur**

thill (θɪl) *n archaic* another word for **shaft** (sense 6) [c14: perhaps related to Old English *thille* board, planking, Old High German *dilla* plank, Old Norse *thili*]

thimble ('θɪmbəl) *n* **1** a cap of metal, plastic, etc, used to protect the end of the finger when sewing **2** any small metal cap resembling this **3** *nautical* a loop of metal having a groove at its outer edge for a rope or cable, for lining the inside of an eye [Old English *thȳmel* thumbstall, from *thūma* THUMB]

thimbleful ('θɪmbəl,fʊl) *n* a very small amount, esp of a liquid

thimblerig ('θɪmbəl,rɪg) *n* a game in which the operator rapidly moves about three inverted thimbles, often with sleight of hand, one of which conceals a token, the other player betting on which thimble the token is under [c19: from THIMBLE + rig (in obsolete sense: a trick, scheme)] > 'thimble,rigger *n*

Thimbu ('θɪmbuː) *or* **Thimphu** ('θɪmfuː) *n* the capital of Bhutan, in the west in the foothills of the E Himalayas: became the official capital in 1962. Pop: 40 000 (2005 est)

thin (θɪn) *adj* **thinner, thinnest 1** of relatively small extent from one side or surface to the other; fine or narrow **2** slim or lean **3** sparsely placed; meagre: *thin hair* **4** of relatively low density or viscosity: *a thin liquid* **5** weak; poor; insufficient: *a thin disguise* **6** thin on the ground few in number; scarce ▷ *adv* **7** in order to produce something thin: *to cut bread thin* ▷ *vb* **thins, thinning, thinned 8** to make or become thin or sparse [Old English *thynne;* related to Old Frisian *thenne,* Old Saxon, Old High German *thunni,* Old Norse *thunnr,* Latin *tenuis* thin, Greek *teinein* to stretch] > 'thinly *adv* > 'thinness *n*

thin client *n computing* a computer on a network where most functions are carried out on a central server. See **thick client**

thine (ðaɪn) *determiner archaic* **a** *(preceding a vowel)* of,

belonging to, or associated in some way with you (thou): *thine eyes* **b** *(as pronoun): thine is the greatest burden* [Old English *thīn;* related to Old High German *dīn,* Gothic *theina*]

thin-film *adj* (of an electronic component, device, or circuit) composed of one or more extremely thin layers of metal, semiconductor, etc, deposited on a ceramic or glass substrate

thing (θɪŋ) *n* **1** an object, fact, affair, circumstance, or concept considered as being a separate entity **2** any inanimate object **3** an object or entity that cannot or need not be precisely named **4** *informal* a person or animal regarded as the object of pity, contempt, etc: *you poor thing* **5** an event or act **6** a thought or statement **7** *law* any object or right that may be the subject of property (as distinguished from a person) **8** a device, means, or instrument **9** *(often plural)* a possession, article of clothing, etc **10** *informal* a mental attitude, preoccupation or obsession (esp in the phrase **have a thing about**) **11** an activity or mode of behaviour satisfying to one's personality (esp in the phrase **do one's (own) thing**) **12** the thing the latest fashion **13** make a thing of to make a fuss about; exaggerate the importance of [Old English *thing* assembly; related to Old Norse *thing* assembly, Old High German *ding* assembly]

thing-in-itself *n* (in the philosophy of Kant) an element of the noumenal rather than the phenomenal world, of which the senses give no knowledge but whose bare existence can be inferred from the nature of experience

thingumabob *or* **thingamabob** ('θɪŋəmə,bɒb) *n informal* a person or thing the name of which is unknown, temporarily forgotten, or deliberately overlooked. Also called: **thingumajig, thingamajig** ('θɪŋəmə,dʒɪg), **thingummy** ('θɪŋəmɪ) [c18: from THING, with humorous suffix]

think (θɪŋk) *vb* **thinks, thinking, thought 1** *(tr; may take a clause as object)* to consider, judge, or believe: *he thinks my ideas impractical* **2** *(intr; often foll by about)* to exercise the mind as in order to make a decision; ponder **3** *(intr)* to be capable of conscious thought: *man is the only animal that thinks* **4** to remember; recollect **5** *(intr; foll by of)* to make the mental choice (of): *think of a number* **6** *(may take a clause as object or an infinitive)* **a** to expect; suppose **b** to be considerate or aware enough (to do something): *he did not think to thank them* **7** *(intr)* to focus the attention on being: *think thin; think big* **8** think twice to consider carefully before deciding (about something) ▷ *n* **9** *informal* a careful, open-minded assessment **10** *(modifier) informal* characterized by or involving thinkers, thinking, or thought ▷ See also **think over, think up** [Old English *thencan;* related to Old Frisian *thenza,* Old Saxon *thenkian,* Old High German *denken,* Old Norse *thekkja,* Gothic *thagkjan*] > 'thinker *n*

thinkable ('θɪŋkəbəl) *adj* able to be conceived or considered; possible; feasible

thinking ('θɪŋkɪŋ) *n* **1** opinion or judgment **2** the process of thought ▷ *adj* **3** *(prenominal)* using or capable of using intelligent thought: *thinking people* **4** put on one's thinking cap to ponder a matter or problem

think over *vb* *(tr, adverb)* to ponder or consider

think-tank *n informal* a group of specialists organized by a business enterprise, governmental body, etc, and commissioned to undertake intensive study and research into specified problems

think up *vb* *(tr, adverb)* to invent or devise

thinner ('θɪnə) *n (often plural, functioning as singular)* a solvent, such as turpentine, added to paint or varnish to dilute it, reduce its opacity or viscosity, or increase its penetration into the ground

thin-skinned *adj* sensitive to criticism or hints; easily upset or affected

thio- *or before a vowel* **thi-** *combining form* indicating that a chemical compound contains sulphur, esp denoting that a compound is derived from a specified compound by the replacement of an oxygen atom with a sulphur atom: *thiol; thiosulphate* [from Greek *theion* sulphur]

thiol ('θaɪɒl) *n* any of a class of sulphur-containing organic compounds with the formula RSH, where R is an organic group

thionine (ˈθaɪəʊˌniːn, -ˌnaɪn) *or* **thionin** (ˈθaɪənɪn) *n* **1** a crystalline derivative of thiazine used as a violet dye to stain microscope specimens **2** any of a class of related dyes [C19: by shortening, from *ergothioneine*, a crystalline betaine found in ergot and blood]

thiopental sodium (ˌθaɪəʊˈpɛntæl) *n* a barbiturate drug used in medicine as an intravenous general anaesthetic. Formula: $C_{11}H_{17}NaN_2O_2S$. Also called: **Sodium Pentothal**

thiophen (ˈθaɪəʊˌfɛn) *or* **thiophene** (ˈθaɪəʊˌfiːn) *n* a colourless liquid heterocyclic compound found in the benzene fraction of coal tar and manufactured from butane and sulphur. It has an odour resembling that of benzene and is used as a solvent and in the manufacture of dyes, pharmaceuticals, and resins. Formula: C_4H_4S

thiosulphate (ˌθaɪəʊˈsʌlfeɪt) *n* any salt of thiosulphuric acid

thiosulphuric acid (ˌθaɪəʊsʌlˈfjʊərɪk) *n* an unstable acid known only in solutions and in the form of its salts. Formula: $H_2S_2O_3$

thiouracil (ˌθaɪəʊˈjʊərəsɪl) *n* a white crystalline water-insoluble substance with an intensely bitter taste, used in medicine to treat hyperthyroidism; 2-thio-4-oxypyrimidine. Formula: $C_4H_4N_2OS$ [from THIO- + *uracil* (URO- + AC(ETIC) + -*il* -ILE)]

thiourea (ˌθaɪəʊˈjʊərɪə) *n* a white water-soluble crystalline substance with a bitter taste that forms addition compounds with metal ions and is used in photographic fixing, rubber vulcanization, and the manufacture of synthetic resins. Formula: H_2NCSNH_2

third (θɜːd) *adj* (*usually prenominal*) **1 a** coming after the second and preceding the fourth in numbering or counting order, position, time, etc; being the ordinal number of *three*: often written 3rd **b** (*as noun*): *he arrives on the third; the third got a prize* **2** rated, graded, or ranked below the second level **3** denoting the third from lowest forward ratio of a gearbox in a motor vehicle ▷ *n* **4 a** one of three equal or nearly equal parts of an object, quantity, etc **b** (*as modifier*): *a third part* **5** the fraction equal to one divided by three (1/3) **6** the forward ratio above second of a gearbox in a motor vehicle. In some vehicles it is the top gear **7 a** the interval between one note and another three notes away from it counting inclusively along the diatonic scale **b** one of two notes constituting such an interval in relation to the other **8** *Brit* an honours degree of the third and usually the lowest class. Full term: **third class honours degree** ▷ *adv* **9** Also called: **thirdly** in the third place [Old English *thirda*, variant of *thridda; related to Old Frisian *thredda*, Old Saxon *thriddio*, Old High German *dritto*, Old Norse *thrithi*, Latin *tertius*] > **thirdly** *adv*

Third Age *n* the Third Age old age, esp when viewed as an opportunity for travel, further education, etc

third class *n* **1** the class or grade next in value, quality, etc, to the second ▷ *adj* (**third-class** when prenominal) **2** of the class or grade next in value, quality, etc, to the second ▷ *adv* **3** by third-class mail, transport, etc

third degree *n informal* torture or bullying, esp used to extort confessions or information

third-degree burn *n pathol* See **burn**¹ (sense 15)

third dimension *n* the additional dimension by which a solid object may be distinguished from a two-dimensional drawing or picture of it or from any planar object

third eye *n* the pineal gland, believed by some people to be the source of spiritual insight

third eyelid *n* another name for **nictitating membrane**

Third International *n* another name for **Comintern**

third man *n cricket* **a** a fielding position on the off side near the boundary behind the batsman's wicket **b** a fielder in this position

Third Market *n* a market established by the London Stock Exchange in 1987 to trade in shares in companies required to provide less detailed information than that required by the main market or the unlisted securities market

Third Order *n RC Church* a religious society of laymen affiliated to one of the religious orders and following a mitigated form of religious rule

third party *n* **1** a person who is involved by chance or only incidentally in a legal proceeding, agreement, or other transaction, esp one against whom a defendant claims indemnity ▷ *adj* **2** *insurance* providing protection against liability caused by accidental injury or death of other persons or damage to their property

third person *n* a grammatical category of pronouns and verbs used when referring to objects or individuals other than the speaker or his addressee(s)

third-rate *adj* not of high quality; mediocre or inferior

third reading *n* (in a legislative assembly) **1** *Brit* the process of discussing the committee's report on a bill **2** *US* the final consideration of a bill

Third Way *n* **a** a political ideology that seeks to combine egalitarian and individualist policies, and elements of socialism and capitalism **b** (*as modifier*): *Third Way government*

Third World *n* the less economically advanced countries of Africa, Asia, and Latin America collectively, esp when viewed as underdeveloped and as neutral in the East-West alignment. Also called: **developing world**

Thirlmere (ˈθɜːlmɪə) *n* a lake in NW England, in Cumbria in the Lake District: provides part of Manchester's water supply. Length: 6 km (4 miles)

thirst (θɜːst) *n* **1** a craving to drink, accompanied by a feeling of dryness in the mouth and throat **2** an eager longing, craving, or yearning ▷ *vb* **3** (*intr*) to feel a thirst [Old English *thyrstan*, from *thurst* thirst; related to Old Norse *thyrsta* to thirst, Old High German *dursten* to thirst, Latin *torrēre* to parch]

thirsty (ˈθɜːstɪ) *adj* **thirstier, thirstiest 1** feeling a desire to drink **2** dry; arid **3** (foll by *for*) feeling an eager desire **4** causing thirst > **thirstily** *adv* > **thirstiness** *n*

thirteen (ˈθɜːˈtiːn) *n* **1** the cardinal number that is the sum of ten and three and is a prime number **2** a numeral, 13, XIII, etc, representing this number **3** something represented by, representing, or consisting of 13 units ▷ *determiner* **4 a** amounting to thirteen **b** (*as pronoun*): *thirteen of them fell* [Old English *threotēne; see* THREE, -TEEN] > **thirteenth** *adj, n*

thirteenth chord *n* a chord much used in jazz and pop, consisting of a major or minor triad upon which are superimposed the seventh, ninth, eleventh, and thirteenth above the root. Often shortened to: **thirteenth**

thirty (ˈθɜːtɪ) *n, pl* -**ties 1** the cardinal number that is the product of ten and three. See also **number** (sense 1) **2** a numeral, 30, XXX, etc, representing this number **3** (*plural*) the numbers 30–39, esp the 30th to the 39th year of a person's life or of a century **4** the amount or quantity that is three times as big as ten **5** something representing, represented by, or consisting of 30 units ▷ *determiner* **6 a** amounting to thirty **b** (*as pronoun*): *thirty are broken* [Old English *thrītig; see* THREE, -TY¹] > **thirtieth** *adj, n*

Thirty-nine Articles *pl n* a set of formulas defining the doctrinal position of the Church of England, drawn up in the 16th century, to which the clergy are required to give general consent

thirty-second note *n music, US & Canadian* a note having the time value of one thirty-second of a semibreve. Also called (in Britain and certain other countries): **demisemiquaver**

thirty-twomo (ˌθɜːtɪˈtuːməʊ) *n, pl* -**mos** a book size resulting from folding a sheet of paper into 32 leaves or 64 pages

this (ðɪs) *determiner* (*used before a singular noun*) **1 a** used preceding a noun referring to something or someone that is closer: distinct from **that**: *this dress is cheaper than that one; look at this picture* **b** (*as pronoun*): *this is Mary and that is her boyfriend; take this* **2 a** used preceding a noun that has just been mentioned or is understood: *this plan of yours won't work* **b** (*as pronoun*): *I first saw this on Sunday* **3 a** used to refer to something about to be said, etc: *consider this argument* **b** (*as pronoun*): *listen to this* **4 a** the present or immediate: *this time you'll know better* **b** (*as pronoun*): *before this, I was mistaken* **5** *informal* often used in storytelling, an emphatic form of: **a²**, **the¹** *I saw this big* *brown bear* **6** this and that various unspecified and trivial actions, matters, objects, etc **7** with this *or* at this after this; thereupon ▷ *adv* **8** used with adjectives and adverbs to specify a precise degree that is about to be mentioned: *go just this fast and you'll be safe* [Old English *thēs, thēos, this* (masculine, feminine, neuter singular); related to Old Saxon *thit*, Old High German *diz*, Old Norse *thessi*]

Thisbe ('θɪzbɪ) *n* See **Pyramus and Thisbe**

thistle ('θɪsəl) *n* **1** any of numerous plants of the genera *Cirsium, Carduus*, and related genera, having prickly-edged leaves, pink, purple, yellow, or white dense flower heads, and feathery hairs on the seeds: family *Asteraceae* (composites) **2** a thistle, or a representation of one, as the national emblem of Scotland [Old English *thīstel*, related to Old Saxon, Old High German *thīstil*, Old Norse *thīstill*] > '**thistly** *adj*

thistledown ('θɪsəl,daʊn) *n* the mass of feathery plumed seeds produced by a thistle

thither ('ðɪðə) *or* **thitherward** ('ðɪðəwəd) *adv obsolete or formal* to or towards that place; in that direction [Old English *thider*, variant of *thæder*, influenced by *hider* HITHER; related to Old Norse *thathra* there]

thitherto (,ðɪðə'tuː, 'ðɪðə,tuː) *adv obsolete or formal* until that time

thixotropic (,θɪksə'trɒpɪk) *adj* (of fluids and gels) having a viscosity that decreases when a stress is applied, as when stirred: *thixotropic paints* [C20: from Greek *thixis* the act of touching + -TROPIC] > **thixotropy** (θɪk'sɒtrəpɪ) *n* > **thixotrope** ('θɪksə,trəʊp) *n*

tho' *or* **tho** (ðəʊ) *conj, adv informal* a variant spelling of **though**

thole¹ (θəʊl) *or* **tholepin** ('θəʊl,pɪn) *n* a wooden pin or one of a pair, set upright in the gunwales of a rowing boat to serve as a fulcrum in rowing [Old English *tholl*, related to Middle Low German *dolle*, Norwegian *toll*, Icelandic *thollr*]

thole² (θəʊl) *vb* **1** (*tr*) *Scot & northern English dialect* to put up with; bear **2** an archaic word for **suffer** [Old English *tholian*; related to Old Saxon, Old High German *tholōn*, Old Norse *thola* to endure: compare Latin *tollere* to bear up]

tholos ('θəʊlɒs) *n, pl* **-loi** (-lɔɪ) a dry-stone beehive-shaped tomb associated with the Mycenaean culture of Greece in the 16th to the 12th century BC [C17: from Greek]

Thomas ('tɒməs) *n* **1** Saint. Also called: doubting Thomas. one of the twelve apostles, who refused to believe in Christ's resurrection until he had seen his wounds (John 20:24–29). Feast day: July 3 or Dec 21 or Oct 6 **2** (*French* tɔma) **Ambroise** (ɑ̃brwaz). 1811–96, French composer of light operas, including *Mignon* (1866) **3 Dylan** (**Marlais**) ('dɪlən). 1914–53, Welsh poet and essayist. His works include the prose *Portrait of the Artist as a Young Dog* (1940), the verse collection *Deaths and Entrances* (1946), and his play for voices *Under Milk Wood* (1954) **4** (**Philip**) **Edward**, pen name Edward Eastaway. 1878–1917, British poet and critic: killed in World War I **5 R(onald) S(tuart)**. 1913–2000, Welsh poet and clergyman. His collections include *Song at the Year's Turning* (1955), *Not that He Brought Flowers* (1968), and *Laboratories of the Spirit* (1975)

Thomas à Kempis *n* See **Kempis**

Thomas Becket *n* Saint. See (Saint Thomas) **Becket**

Thomas of Erceldoune ('ɜːsəl,duːn) *n* called *Thomas the Rhymer*. ?1220–?97, Scottish seer and poet; reputed author of a poem on the Tristan legend

Thomas of Woodstock *n* 1355–97, youngest son of Edward III, who led opposition to his nephew Richard II (1386–89); arrested in 1397, he died in prison

Thomism ('təʊmɪzəm) *n* the comprehensive system of philosophy and theology developed by the Italian theologian, scholastic philosopher, and Dominican friar Saint Thomas Aquinas (1225–74), and since taught and maintained by his followers, esp in the Dominican order

Thompson ('tɒmpsən, 'tɒmsən) *n* **1 Benjamin**, Count Rumford. 1753–1814, Anglo-American physicist, noted for his work on the nature of heat **2 Daley**. born 1958,

British athlete: Olympic decathlon champion (1980, 1984) **3 Emma**. born 1959, British actress: her films include *Howards End* (1991), *Sense and Sensibility* (1996; also wrote screenplay), *Primary Colors* (1998), and *Love Actually* (2003) **4 Flora** (**Jane**). 1876–1947, British writer, author of the autobiographical *Lark Rise to Candleford* (1945) **5 Francis**. 1859–1907, British poet, best known for the mystical poem *The Hound of Heaven* (1893)

Thompson sub-machine-gun *n trademark* a .45 calibre sub-machine-gun [C20: after John T. *Thompson* (1860–1940), US Army Officer, its coinventor]

Thomson ('tɒmsən) *n* **1 Sir George Paget**, son of Joseph John Thomson. 1892–1975, British physicist, who discovered (1927) the diffraction of electrons by crystals: shared the Nobel prize for physics 1937 **2 James**. 1700–48, Scottish poet. He anticipated the romantics' feeling for nature in *The Seasons* (1726–30) **3 James**, pen name B.V. 1834–82, British poet, born in Scotland, noted esp for *The City of Dreadful Night* (1874), reflecting man's isolation and despair **4 Sir Joseph John**. 1856–1940, British physicist. He discovered the electron (1897) and his work on the nature of positive rays led to the discovery of isotopes: Nobel prize for physics 1906 **5 Roy**, 1st Baron Thomson of Fleet. 1894–1976, British newspaper proprietor, born in Canada **6 Virgil**. 1896–1989, US composer, music critic, and conductor, whose works include two operas, *Four Saints in Three Acts* (1928) and *The Mother of Us All* (1947), piano sonatas, a cello concerto, songs, and film music **7 Sir William**. See (1st Baron) **Kelvin**

Thomson effect *n physics* the phenomenon in which a temperature gradient along a metallic (or semiconductor) wire or strip causes an electric potential gradient to form along its length [named after Sir William *Thomson*, 1st Baron Kelvin (1824–1907), British physicist]

-thon *suffix forming nouns* indicating a large-scale event or operation of a specified kind: *telethon* [C20: on the pattern of MARATHON]

Thonburi (,tɒnbʊ'riː) *n* a city in central Thailand, part of Bankok Metropolis on the Chao Phraya River; the national capital (1767–82)

thong (θɒŋ) *n* **1** a thin strip of leather or other material, such as one used for lashing things together **2** a whip or whiplash, esp one made of leather **3** *US, Canadian, Austral & NZ* the usual name for **flip-flop** (sense 5) **4 a** a skimpy article of beachwear, worn by men or women, consisting of thin strips of leather or cloth attached to a piece of material that covers the genitals while leaving the buttocks bare **b** a similar item of underwear [Old English *thwang*; related to Old High German *dwang* reins, Old Norse *thvengr* strap]

Thor (θɔː) *n Norse myth* the god of thunder, depicted as wielding a hammer, emblematic of the thunderbolt [Old English *Thōr*, from Old Norse *thōrr* THUNDER]

thoracic (θɔː'ræsɪk) *adj* of, near, or relating to the thorax

thoracic duct *n* the major duct of the lymphatic system, beginning below the diaphragm and ascending in front of the spinal column to the base of the neck

thoraco- *or before a vowel* **thorac-** *combining form* thorax: *thoracotomy*

thoracoplasty ('θɔːrəkəʊ,plæstɪ) *n, pl* **-ties** **1** plastic surgery of the thorax **2** surgical removal of several ribs or a part of them to permit the collapse of a diseased lung, used in cases of pulmonary tuberculosis and bronchiectasis

thorax ('θɔːræks) *n, pl* **thoraxes** *or* **thoraces** ('θɔːrə,siːz, θɔː'reɪsiːz) **1** the part of the human body enclosed by the ribs **2** the corresponding part in other vertebrates **3** the part of an insect's body between the head and abdomen, which bears the wings and legs [C16: via Latin from Greek *thōrax* breastplate, chest]

Thoreau ('θɔːrəʊ, θɔː'rəʊ) *n* **Henry David**. 1817–62, US writer, noted esp for *Walden, or Life in the Woods* (1854), an account of his experiment in living in solitude. A powerful social critic, his essay *Civil Disobedience* (1849) influenced such dissenters as Gandhi

thorium ('θɔːrɪəm) *n* a soft ductile silvery-white metallic element. It is radioactive and occurs in thorite and monazite: used in gas mantles, magnesium alloys, electronic equipment, and as a nuclear power source. Symbol: Th; atomic no: 90; atomic wt: 232.0381; half-life of most stable isotope, ^{232}Th: 1.41×10^{10} years; valency: 4; relative density: 11.72; melting pt: 1755°C; boiling pt: 4788°C [c19: New Latin, from THOR + -IUM] > 'thoric *adj*

thorium dioxide *n* a heavy insoluble white powder used in incandescent mantles. Formula: ThO$_2$. Also called: thoria

thorium series *n* a radioactive series that starts with thorium-232 and ends with lead-208

thorn (θɔːn) *n* **1** a sharp pointed woody extension of a stem or leaf. See **prickle** (sense 1) **2** any of various trees or shrubs having thorns, esp the hawthorn **3** a Germanic character of runic origin Þ used in Old and Modern Icelandic to represent the voiceless dental fricative sound of *th*, as in *thin*, *bath*. Its use in phonetics for the same purpose is now obsolete **4** this same character as used in Old and Middle English as an alternative to *edh*, but indistinguishable from it in function or sound **5** a source of irritation (esp in the phrases **a thorn in one's side** *or* **flesh**) [Old English; related to Old High German *dorn*, Old Norse *thorn*] > 'thornless *adj*

Thorn (tɔːn) *n* the German name for Toruń

thorn apple *n* **1** a poisonous solanaceous plant, *Datura stramonium*, of the N hemisphere, having white funnel-shaped flowers and spiny capsule fruits **2** the fruit of certain types of hawthorn

thornbill ('θɔːn,bɪl) *n* **1** any of various South American hummingbirds of the genera *Chalcostigma*, *Ramphomicron*, etc, having a thornlike bill **2** Also called: **thornbill warbler** any of various Australasian wrens of the genus *Acanthiza* and related genera: family *Muscicapidae* **3** any of various other birds with thornlike bills

Thorndike ('θɔːn,daɪk) *n* **1** Edward Lee. 1874–1949, US psychologist, who worked on animals and proposed that all learnt behaviour is regulated by rewards and punishments (**Thorndike's law** *or* **law of effect**) **2** Dame (Agnes) Sybil. 1882–1976, British actress

Thornhill ('θɔːn,hɪl) *n* Sir James. 1675–1734, English baroque painter. He is best known for decorating the Painted Hall, Greenwich Hospital (1708–27) and the interior of the dome of St Paul's Cathedral (1715–17)

thorny ('θɔːnɪ) *adj* thornier, thorniest **1** bearing or covered with thorns **2** difficult or unpleasant **3** sharp > 'thornily *adv* > 'thorniness *n*

thoron ('θɔːrɒn) *n* a radioisotope of radon that is a decay product of thorium. Symbol: Tn or ^{220}Rn; atomic no: 86; half-life: 54.5s [c20: from THORIUM + -ON]

thorough ('θʌrə) *adj* **1** carried out completely and carefully **2** (*prenominal*) utter: *a thorough bore* **3** painstakingly careful [Old English *thurh*; related to Old Frisian *thruch*, Old Saxon *thuru*, Old High German *duruh*; see THROUGH] > 'thoroughly *adv* > 'thoroughness *n*

thorough bass (beɪs) *n* Also called: **basso continuo**, **continuo** (esp during the baroque period) a bass part underlying a piece of concerted music. It is played on a keyboard instrument, usually supported by a cello, viola da gamba, etc. See also **figured bass**

thoroughbred ('θʌrə,brɛd) *adj* **1** purebred ▷ *n* **2** a pedigree animal; purebred **3** a person regarded as being of good breeding

Thoroughbred ('θʌrə,brɛd) *n* a British breed of horse the ancestry of which can be traced to English mares and Arab sires; most often used as a racehorse

thoroughfare ('θʌrə,fɛə) *n* **1** a road from one place to another, esp a main road **2** way through or access: *no thoroughfare*

thoroughgoing ('θʌrə,gəʊɪŋ) *adj* **1** extremely thorough **2** (*usually prenominal*) absolute; complete: *thoroughgoing incompetence*

thoroughpaced ('θʌrə,peɪst) *adj* **1** (of a horse) showing performing ability in all paces **2** thoroughgoing

thorp *or* **thorpe** (θɔːp) *n* (in place names) a small village [Old English; related to Old Norse *thorp* village, Old High German *dorf*, Gothic *thaurp*]

Thorpe (θɔːp) *n* **1** Ian. born 1982, Australian swimmer; won three gold medals at the 2000 Olympic Games, six gold medals at the 2002 Commonwealth Games, and

two gold medals at the 2004 Olympic Games. **2** James Francis. 1888–1953, American football player and athlete: Olympic pentathlon and decathlon champion (1912) **3** Jeremy. born 1929, British politician; leader of the Liberal party (1967–76)

Thorshavn (*Danish* 'tɔːrshaun) *or* **Tórshavn** *n* the capital of the Faeroes, a port on the northernmost island. Pop: 17 549 (2004 est)

Thorvaldsen (*Danish* 'tɔrvalsən) *n* **Bertel** ('bertəl). 1770–1844, Danish neoclassical sculptor

those (ðəʊz) *determiner* the form of **that** used before a plural noun [Old English *thās*, plural of THIS]

Thoth (θəʊθ, təʊt) *n* (in Egyptian mythology) a moon deity, scribe of the gods and protector of learning and the arts

thou[1] (ðaʊ) *pron* (*subjective*) **1** *archaic*, *dialect* refers to the person addressed: used mainly in familiar address or to a younger person or inferior **2** (*usually capital*) refers to God when addressed in prayer, etc [Old English *thū*; related to Old Saxon *thū*, Old High German *du*, Old Norse *thū*, Latin *tū*, Doric Greek *tu*]

thou[2] (ðaʊ) *n*, *pl* **thous** *or* **thou** **1** one thousandth of an inch. 1 thou is equal to 0.0254 millimetre **2** *informal* short for **thousand**

though (ðəʊ) *conj* (*subordinating*) **1** (sometimes preceded by *even*) despite the fact that: *though he tries hard, he always fails; poor though she is, her life is happy* ▷ *adv* **2** nevertheless; however: *he can't dance: he sings well, though* [Old English *theah*; related to Old Frisian *thāch*, Old Saxon, Old High German *thōh*, Old Norse *thō*]

thought (θɔːt) *vb* **1** the past tense and past participle of **think** ▷ *n* **2** the act or process of thinking; deliberation, meditation, or reflection **3** a concept, opinion, or idea **4** philosophical or intellectual ideas typical of a particular time or place: *German thought in the 19th century* **5** application of mental attention; consideration **6** purpose or intention: *I have no thought of giving up* **7** expectation: *no thought of reward* **8** a small amount; trifle: *you could be a thought more enthusiastic* **9** kindness or regard: *he has no thought for his widowed mother* [Old English *thōht*; related to Old Frisian *thochta*, Old Saxon, Old High German *githācht*]

thoughtful ('θɔːtfʊl) *adj* **1** considerate in the treatment of other people **2** showing careful thought **3** pensive; reflective > 'thoughtfully *adv* > 'thoughtfulness *n*

thoughtless ('θɔːtlɪs) *adj* **1** inconsiderate **2** having or showing lack of thought: *a thoughtless essay* > 'thoughtlessly *adv* > 'thoughtlessness *n*

thought-out *adj* conceived and developed in the manner specified: *a well thought-out scheme*

thought transference *n psychol* another name for **telepathy**

thousand ('θaʊzənd) *n* **1** the cardinal number that is the product of 10 and 100 **2** a numeral, 1000, 10^3, M, etc, representing this number **3** (*often plural*) a very large but unspecified number, amount, or quantity **4** something represented by, representing, or consisting of 1000 units ▷ *determiner* **5 a** amounting to a thousand **b** (*as pronoun*): *a thousand is hardly enough* ▷ Related adjective: **millenary** [Old English *thūsend*; related to Old Saxon *thūsind*, Old High German *thūsunt*, Old Norse *thūsund*] > 'thousandth *adj*, *n*

Thousand Guineas *or usually written* **1000 Guineas** *n* the Thousand Guineas (*functioning as singular*) an annual horse race, restricted to fillies, run at Newmarket since 1814

Thousand Island dressing *n* a salad dressing made from mayonnaise with ketchup, chopped gherkins, etc [probably from the THOUSAND ISLANDS]

Thousand Islands *pl n* a group of about 1500 islands between the US and Canada, in the upper St Lawrence River: administratively divided between the two countries > **Thousand Island** *adj*

Thrace (θreɪs) *n* **1** an ancient country in the E Balkan Peninsula: successively under the Persians, Macedonians, and Romans **2** a region of SE Europe, corresponding to the S part of the ancient country: divided by the Maritsa River into **Western Thrace** (Greece) and **Eastern Thrace** (Turkey)

t

Thracian ('θreɪʃɪən) *n* **1** a member of an ancient Indo-European people who lived in the SE corner of the Balkan Peninsula **2** the ancient language spoken by this people, belonging to the Thraco-Phrygian branch of the Indo-European family: extinct by the early Middle Ages ▷ *adj* **3** of or relating to Thrace, its inhabitants, or the extinct Thracian language

Thrale (θreɪl) *n* **Hester Lynch,** known as *Mrs Thrale* or (later) *Mrs Piozzi* (née *Salusbury*). 1741–1821, English writer of memoirs, noted for her friendship with Dr Johnson. Her works include *Anecdotes of the late Samuel Johnson* (1786) and *Letters to and from the late Samuel Johnson* (1788)

thrall (θrɔːl) *n* **1** Also called: **thraldom,** (*US*) **thralldom** ('θrɔːldəm) the state or condition of being in the power of another person **2** a person who is in such a state **3** a person totally subject to some need, desire, appetite, etc ▷ *vb* **4** (*tr*) to enslave or dominate [Old English *thrǣl* slave, from Old Norse *thrǣll*]

thrash (θræʃ) *vb* **1** (*tr*) to beat soundly, as with a whip or stick **2** (*tr*) to defeat totally; overwhelm **3** (*intr*) to beat or plunge about in a wild manner **4** to sail (a boat) against the wind or tide or (of a boat) to sail in this way **5** another word for **thresh** ▷ *n* **6** the act of thrashing; blow; beating **7** *informal* a party or similar social gathering ▷ See also **thrash out** [Old English *threscan;* related to Old High German *dreskan,* Old Norse *thriskja*]

thrasher[1] ('θræʃə) *n* another name for **thresher** (sense 3)

thrasher[2] ('θræʃə) *n* any of various brown thrushlike American songbirds of the genus *Toxostoma* and related genera, having a long downward-curving bill and long tail: family *Mimidae* (mockingbirds) [c19: perhaps from English dialect *thresher, thrusher* a thrush]

thrashing ('θræʃɪŋ) *n* **1** a physical assault; flogging **2** a convincing defeat

thrash metal *n* a type of very fast, very loud rock music that combines elements of heavy metal and punk rock. Often shortened to: **thrash**

thrash out *vb* (*tr, adverb*) to discuss fully or vehemently, esp in order to come to a solution or agreement

thrasonical (θrəˈsɒnɪkᵊl) *adj rare* bragging; boastful [c16: from Latin *Thrasō* name of boastful soldier in *Eunuchus,* a play by Terence, from Greek *Thrasōn,* from *thrasus* forceful] > **thraˈsonically** *adv*

thrawn (θrɔːn) *adj Scot & northern English dialect* **1** crooked or twisted **2** stubborn; perverse [Northern English dialect, variant of THROWN, from Old English *thrāwan* to twist about, THROW]

thread (θrɛd) *n* **1** a fine strand, filament or fibre of some material **2** a fine cord of twisted filaments, esp of cotton, used in sewing, weaving, etc **3** any of the filaments of which a spider's web is made **4** any fine line, stream, mark, or piece **5** a helical groove in a cylindrical hole (**female thread**), formed by a tap or lathe tool, or a helical ridge on a cylindrical bar, rod, shank, etc (**male thread**), formed by a die or lathe tool **6** a very thin seam of coal or vein of ore **7** something acting as the continuous link or theme of a whole: *the thread of the story* **8** the course of an individual's life believed in Greek mythology to be spun, measured, and cut by the Fates ▷ *vb* **9** (*tr*) to pass (thread, film, magnetic tape, etc) through (something) **10** (*tr*) to string on a thread: *she threaded the beads* **11** to make (one's way) through or over (something) **12** (*tr*) to produce a screw thread by cutting, rolling, tapping, or grinding **13** (*tr*) to pervade: *hysteria threaded his account* **14** (*intr*) (of boiling syrup) to form a fine thread when poured from a spoon ▷ See also **threads** [Old English *thrǣd;* related to Old Frisian *thrēd,* Old High German *drāt,* Old Norse *thrāthr* thread] > **'threader** *n* > **'thread,like** *adj*

threadbare ('θrɛd,bɛə) *adj* **1** (of cloth, clothing, etc) having the nap worn off so that the threads are exposed **2** meagre or poor **3** hackneyed: *a threadbare argument* **4** wearing threadbare clothes; shabby

thread mark *n* a mark put into paper money to prevent counterfeiting, consisting of a pattern of silk fibres

Threadneedle Street (,θrɛdˈniːdᵊl, 'θrɛd,niːdᵊl) *n* a street in the City of London famous for its banks, including the Bank of England, known as **The Old Lady of Threadneedle Street**

threads (θrɛdz) *pl n* a slang word for **clothes**

threadworm ('θrɛd,wɜːm) *n* any of various nematodes, esp the pinworm

thready ('θrɛdɪ) *adj* **threadier, threadiest 1** of, relating to, or resembling a thread or threads **2** *med* (of the pulse) barely perceptible; weak; fine **3** sounding thin, weak, or reedy: *a thready tenor* > **'threadiness** *n*

threat (θrɛt) *n* **1** a declaration of the intention to inflict harm, pain, or misery **2** an indication of imminent harm, danger, or pain **3** a person or thing that is regarded as dangerous or likely to inflict pain or misery [Old English; related to Old Norse *thraut,* Middle Low German *drōt*]

threaten ('θrɛtᵊn) *vb* **1** (*tr*) to be a threat to **2** to be a menacing indication of (something); portend **3** (when *tr, may take a clause as object*) to express a threat to (a person or people) > **'threatening** *adj* > **'threateningly** *adv*

three (θriː) *n* **1** the cardinal number that is the sum of two and one and is a prime number **2** a numeral, 3, III, (iii), representing this number **3** something representing, represented by, or consisting of three units such as a playing card with three symbols on it **4** Also called: **three o'clock** three hours after noon or midnight ▷ *determiner* **5 a** amounting to three **b** (*as pronoun*): *three were killed* ▷ Related adjectives: **ternary, tertiary, treble, triple** [Old English *thrēo;* related to Old Norse *thrīr,* Old High German *drī,* Latin *trēs,* Greek *treis*]

three-card trick *n* a game in which players bet on which of three inverted playing cards is the queen

three-colour *adj* of, relating to, or comprising a colour print or a photomechanical process in which a picture is reproduced by superimposing three prints from half-tone plates in inks corresponding to the three primary colours

three-D *or* **3-D** *n* a three-dimensional effect

three-decker *n* **1 a** anything having three levels or layers **b** (*as modifier*): *a three-decker sandwich* **2** a warship with guns on three decks

three-dimensional, three-D *or* **3-D** *adj* **1** of, having, or relating to three dimensions **2** (of a film, transparency, etc) simulating the effect of depth by presenting slightly different views of a scene to each eye **3** having volume **4** lifelike or real

threefold ('θriː,fəʊld) *adj* **1** equal to or having three times as many or as much; triple **2** composed of three parts ▷ *adv* **3** by or up to three times as many or as much

three-legged race *n* a race in which pairs of competitors run with their adjacent legs tied together

threepenny bit *or* **thrupenny bit** ('θrʌpnɪ, -ənɪ, 'θrɛp-) *n* a twelve-sided British coin of nickel-brass, valued at three old pence, obsolete since 1971

three-phase *adj* (of an electrical system, circuit, or device) having, generating, or using three alternating voltages of the same frequency, displaced in phase by 120°

three-ply *adj* **1** having three layers or thicknesses **2** (of knitting wool, etc) three-stranded

three-point landing *n* an aircraft landing in which the two main wheels and the nose or tail wheel all touch the ground simultaneously

three-point turn *n* a turn reversing the direction of motion of a motor vehicle using forward and reverse gears alternately, and completed after only three movements

three-quarter *adj* **1** being three quarters of something **2** being of three quarters the normal length ▷ *n* **3** *rugby* any of the four players between the fullback and the halfbacks

three-ring circus *n US & Canadian* **1** a circus with three rings in which separate performances are carried on simultaneously **2** a situation of confusion, characterized by a bewildering variety of events or activities

Three Rivers *n* the English name for **Trois-Rivières**

three Rs *pl n* **the three Rs** the three skills regarded as the fundamentals of education; reading, writing, and arithmetic [from the humorous spelling *reading, 'riting, and 'rithmetic*]

threescore ('θriːˈskɔː) *determiner* an archaic or literary

t

word for **sixty**

threesome ('θriːsəm) n 1 a group of three 2 golf a match in which a single player playing his own ball competes against two others playing alternate strokes on the same ball 3 any game, etc, for three people 4 (modifier) performed by three: a threesome game

thremmatology (ˌθrɛmə'tɒlədʒɪ) n the science of breeding domesticated animals and plants [c19: from Greek thremma nursling + -LOGY]

threnody ('θrɛnədɪ, 'θriː-) or **threnode** ('θriːnəʊd, 'θrɛn-) n, pl threnodies or threnodes an ode, song, or speech of lamentation, esp for the dead [c17: from Greek thrēnōidia, from thrēnos dirge + ōidē song] > threnodial (θrɪ'nəʊdɪəl) or threnodic (θrɪ'nɒdɪk) adj > threnodist ('θrɛnədɪst, 'θriː-) n

thresh (θrɛʃ) vb 1 to beat or rub stalks of ripe corn or a similar crop either with a hand implement or a machine to separate the grain from the husks and straw 2 (tr) to beat or strike 3 (intr; often foll by about) to toss and turn; thrash [Old English threscan; related to Gothic thriskan, Old Norse thriskja; see THRASH]

thresher ('θrɛʃə) n 1 a person who threshes 2 short for **threshing machine** 3 Also called: thrasher, thresher shark any of various large sharks of the genus Alopias, esp A. vulpinus, occurring in tropical and temperate seas: family Alopiidae. They have a very long whiplike tail with which they are thought to round up the small fish on which they feed

threshing machine n a machine for threshing crops

threshold ('θrɛʃəʊld, 'θrɛʃˌhəʊld) n 1 Also called: doorsill a sill, esp one made of stone or hardwood, placed at a doorway 2 any doorway or entrance 3 the starting point of an experience, event, or venture 4 psychol the strength at which a stimulus is just perceived: the threshold of consciousness 5 a a level or point at which something would happen, would cease to happen, or would take effect, become true, etc b (as modifier): threshold price; threshold effect 6 the minimum intensity or value of a signal, etc, that will produce a response or specified effect 7 (modifier) designating or relating to a pay agreement, clause, etc, that raises wages to compensate for increases in the cost of living ▷ Related adjective: **liminal** [Old English therscold; related to Old Norse threskoldr, Old High German driscubli, Old Swedish thriskuldi]

threshold agreement n an agreement between an employer and employees or their union to increase wages by a specified sum if inflation exceeds a specified level in a specified time

threw (θruː) vb the past tense of **throw**

thrice (θraɪs) adv 1 three times 2 in threefold degree 3 archaic greatly [Old English thrīwa, thrīga; see THREE]

thrift (θrɪft) n 1 wisdom and caution in the management of money 2 Also called: sea pink any of numerous perennial plumbaginaceous low-growing plants of the genus Armeria, esp A. maritima, of Europe, W Asia, and North America, having narrow leaves and round heads of pink or white flowers [c13: from Old Norse: success; see THRIVE] > 'thriftless adj > 'thriftlessly adv

thrifty ('θrɪftɪ) adj thriftier, thriftiest 1 showing thrift; economical or frugal 2 rare thriving or prospering > 'thriftily adv > 'thriftiness n

thrill (θrɪl) n 1 a sudden sensation of excitement and pleasure 2 a situation producing such a sensation 3 a trembling sensation caused by fear or emotional shock 4 pathol an abnormal slight tremor associated with a heart or vascular murmur, felt on palpation ▷ vb 5 to feel or cause to feel a thrill 6 to tremble or cause to tremble; vibrate or quiver [Old English thȳrlian to pierce, from thyrel hole; see NOSTRIL, THROUGH] > 'thrilling adj

thriller ('θrɪlə) n 1 a book, film, play, etc, depicting crime, mystery, or espionage in an atmosphere of excitement and suspense 2 a person or thing that thrills

thrips (θrɪps) n, pl thrips any of various small slender-bodied insects of the order Thysanoptera, typically having piercing mouthparts and narrow feathery wings and feeding on plant sap. Some species are serious plant pests [c18: via New Latin from Greek: woodworm]

thrive (θraɪv) vb thrives, thriving, thrived or throve, thrived or thriven ('θrɪv³n) 1 to grow strongly and vigorously 2 to do well; prosper [c13: from Old Norse thrífask to grasp for oneself, reflexive of thrífa to grasp, of obscure origin]

thro' or **thro** (θruː) prep, adv informal or poetic variant spellings of **through**

throat (θrəʊt) n 1 a that part of the alimentary and respiratory tracts extending from the back of the mouth (nasopharynx) to just below the larynx b the front part of the neck 2 something resembling a throat, esp in shape or function: the throat of a chimney 3 cut one's throat or cut one's own throat to bring about one's own ruin 4 ram something down someone's throat or force something down someone's throat to insist that someone listen to or accept (something) ▷ Related adjectives: **guttural, laryngeal** [Old English throtu; related to Old High German drozza throat, Old Norse throti swelling]

throaty ('θrəʊtɪ) adj throatier, throatiest 1 indicating a sore throat; hoarse: a throaty cough 2 of, relating to, or produced in or by the throat 3 deep, husky, or guttural > 'throatily adv

throb (θrɒb) vb throbs, throbbing, throbbed (intr) 1 to pulsate or beat repeatedly, esp with increased force 2 (of engines, drums, etc) to have a strong rhythmic vibration or beat ▷ n 3 the act or an instance of throbbing, esp a rapid pulsation as of the heart: a throb of pleasure [c14: perhaps of imitative origin]

Throckmorton ('θrɒkˌmɔːtən) or **Throgmorton** ('θrɒɡˌmɔːtən) n Francis. 1554–84, English conspirator, who with French and Spanish support plotted (1583) to depose Elizabeth I in favour of Mary, Queen of Scots: executed

throes (θrəʊz) pl n 1 a condition of violent pangs, pain, or convulsions: death throes 2 in the throes of struggling with great effort with

thrombin ('θrɒmbɪn) n biochem an enzyme that acts on fibrinogen in blood causing it to clot

thrombocyte ('θrɒmbəˌsaɪt) n another name for **platelet** > thrombocytic (ˌθrɒmbə'sɪtɪk) adj

thromboembolism (ˌθrɒmbəʊ'ɛmbəˌlɪzəm) n pathol the obstruction of a blood vessel by a thrombus that has become detached from its original site

thrombolysis (ˌθrɒm'bɒlɪsɪs) n the breaking up of a blood clot

thrombose ('θrɒmbəʊz) vb to become or affect with a thrombus [c19: back formation from THROMBOSIS]

thrombosis (θrɒm'bəʊsɪs) n, pl -ses (-siːz) 1 the formation or presence of a thrombus 2 informal short for **coronary thrombosis** [c18: from New Latin, from Greek: curdling, from thrombousthai to clot, from thrombos THROMBUS] > thrombotic (θrɒm'bɒtɪk) adj

thrombus ('θrɒmbəs) n, pl -bi (-baɪ) a clot of coagulated blood that forms within a blood vessel or inside the heart and remains at the site of its formation, often impeding the flow of blood [c17: from New Latin, from Greek thrombos lump, of obscure origin]

throne (θrəʊn) n 1 the ceremonial seat occupied by a monarch, bishop, etc, on occasions of state 2 the power, duties, or rank ascribed to a royal person 3 a person holding royal rank 4 (plural; often capital) the third of the nine orders into which the angels are traditionally divided in medieval angelology ▷ vb 5 to place or be placed on a throne [c13: from Old French trone, from Latin thronus, from Greek thronos throne]

throng (θrɒŋ) n 1 a great number of people or things crowded together ▷ vb 2 to gather in or fill (a place) in large numbers; crowd 3 (tr) to hem in (a person); jostle [Old English gethrang; related to Old Norse throng, Old High German drangōd]

thronner ('θrɒnə) n Northern English dialect a person who is good at doing odd jobs

throstle ('θrɒs³l) n 1 a poetic name for the thrush, esp the song thrush 2 a spinning machine for wool or cotton in which the fibres are twisted and wound continuously [Old English; related to Old Saxon throsla, Old Norse thröstr, Middle High German drostel]

throttle ('θrɒt³l) n 1 Also called: throttle valve any

device that controls the quantity of fuel or fuel and air mixture entering an engine **2** an informal or dialect word for **throat** ▷ *vb* (*tr*) **3** to kill or injure by squeezing the throat **4** to suppress: *to throttle the press* **5** to control or restrict (a flow of fluid) by means of a throttle valve [C14: *throtelen*, from *throte* THROAT] > 'throttler *n*

through (θruː) *prep* **1** going in or starting at one side and coming out or stopping at the other side of: *a path through the wood* **2** occupying or visiting several points scattered around in (an area) **3** as a result of; by means of **4** *chiefly US* up to and including: *Monday through Friday* **5** during: *through the night* **6** at the end of; having (esp successfully) completed **7** through with having finished with (esp when dissatisfied with) ▷ *adj* **8** (*postpositive*) having successfully completed some specified activity **9** (on a telephone line) connected **10** (*postpositive*) no longer able to function successfully in some specified capacity: *as a journalist, you're through* **11** (*prenominal*) (of a route, journey, etc) continuous or unbroken: *a through train* ▷ *adv* **12** through some specified thing, place, or period of time **13** thoroughly; completely [Old English *thurh*; related to Old Frisian *thruch*, Old Saxon *thuru*, Old High German *duruh*]

through bridge *n civil engineering* a bridge in which the track is carried by the lower horizontal members

throughout (θruːˈaʊt) *prep* **1** right through; through the whole of (a place or a period of time): *throughout the day* ▷ *adv* **2** through the whole of some specified period or area

throughput ('θruːˌpʊt) *n* the quantity of raw material or information processed or communicated in a given period, esp by a computer

throughway ('θruːˌweɪ) *n US* a thoroughfare, esp a motorway

throve (θrəʊv) *vb* a past tense of **thrive**

throw (θrəʊ) *vb* **throws**, **throwing**, **threw**, **thrown** (*mainly tr*) **1** (*also intr*) to project or cast (something) through the air, esp with a rapid motion of the arm and wrist **2** (foll by *in*, *on*, *onto*, etc) to put or move suddenly, carelessly, or violently **3** to bring to or cause to be in a specified state or condition, esp suddenly or unexpectedly: *the news threw the family into a panic* **4** to direct or cast (a shadow, light, etc) **5** to project (the voice) so as to make it appear to come from other than its source **6** to give or hold (a party) **7** to cause to fall or be upset; dislodge: *the horse soon threw his rider* **8** a to tip (dice) out onto a flat surface **b** to obtain (a specified number) in this way **9** to shape (clay) on a potter's wheel **10** to move (a switch or lever) to engage or disengage a mechanism **11** to be subjected to (a fit) **12** to turn (wood, etc) on a lathe **13** *informal* to baffle or astonish; confuse: *the last question on the test paper threw me* **14** *boxing* to deliver (a punch) **15** *wrestling* to hurl (an opponent) to the ground **16** *informal* to lose (a contest, fight, etc) deliberately, esp in boxing **17 a** to play (a card) **b** to discard (a card) **18** (of a female animal, esp a cow) to give birth to (young) **19** to twist or spin (filaments) into thread **20** throw oneself at to strive actively to attract the attention or affection of **21** throw oneself into to involve oneself enthusiastically in **22** throw oneself on to rely entirely upon ▷ *n* **23** the act or an instance of throwing **24** the distance or extent over which anything may be thrown: *a stone's throw* **25** *informal* a chance, venture, or try **26** an act or result of throwing dice **27 a** the eccentricity of a cam **b** the radial distance between the central axis of a crankshaft and the axis of a crankpin forming part of the shaft **28** a decorative light blanket or cover, as thrown over a chair **29** *geology* the vertical displacement of rock strata at a fault **30** *physics* the deflection of a measuring instrument as a result of a sudden fluctuation ▷ See also **throwaway**, **throwback**, **throw in**, etc [Old English *thrāwan* to turn, torment; related to Old High German *drāen* to twist, Latin *terere* to rub] > 'thrower *n*

throwaway ('θrəʊəˌweɪ) *adj* (*prenominal*) **1** said or done incidentally, esp for rhetorical effect; casual: *a throwaway remark* **2 a** anything designed to be discarded after use rather than reused, refilled, etc; disposable **b** (*as modifier*): *a throwaway carton* ▷ *n* **3** *chiefly US & Canadian* a handbill or advertisement distributed in a public place

▷ *vb* throw away (*tr*, *adverb*) **4** to get rid of; discard **5** to fail to make good use of; waste

throwback ('θrəʊˌbæk) *n* **1 a** a person, animal, or plant that has the characteristics of an earlier or more primitive type **b** a reversion to such an organism ▷ *vb* throw back (*adverb*) **2** (*intr*) to revert to an earlier or more primitive type **3** (*tr*; foll by *on*) to force to depend (on): *the crisis threw her back on her faith in God*

throw in *vb* (*tr*, *adverb*) **1** to add (something extra) at no additional cost **2** to contribute or interpose (a remark, argument, etc), esp in a discussion **3** throw in one's hand to give in and accept defeat; discontinue a venture **4** throw in the towel *or* throw in the sponge to give in and accept defeat; discontinue a venture ▷ *n* throw-in **5** *soccer* the method of putting the ball into play after it has gone into touch by throwing it two-handed from behind the head to a teammate, both feet being kept on the ground

thrown (θrəʊn) *vb* the past participle of **throw**

throw off *vb* (*mainly tr*, *adverb*) **1** to free oneself of; discard **2** to produce or utter in a casual manner **3** to escape from or elude **4** to confuse or disconcert **5** (*intr*, often foll by *at*) *Austral & NZ informal* to deride or ridicule

throw out *vb* (*tr*, *adverb*) **1** to discard or reject **2** to expel or dismiss, esp forcibly **3** to construct (something projecting or prominent, such as a wing of a building) **4** to put forward or offer **5** to utter in a casual or indirect manner **6** to confuse or disconcert **7** to give off or emit **8** *cricket* (of a fielder) to put (the batsman) out by throwing the ball to hit the wicket **9** *baseball* to make a throw to a teammate who in turn puts out (a base runner)

throw over *vb* (*tr*, *adverb*) to forsake or abandon; jilt

throw together *vb* (*tr*, *adverb*) **1** to assemble hurriedly **2** to cause to become casually acquainted

throw up *vb* (*adverb*, *mainly tr*) **1** to give up; abandon, relinquish **2** to build or construct hastily **3** to reveal; produce **4** (*also intr*) *informal* to vomit

thru (θruː) *prep*, *adverb*, *adjective*, *chiefly US* a variant spelling of **through**

thrum[1] (θrʌm) *vb* **thrums**, **thrumming**, **thrummed** **1** to strum rhythmically but without expression on (a musical instrument) **2** (*intr*) to drum incessantly: *rain thrummed on the roof* ▷ *n* **3** a repetitive strumming or recitation [C16: of imitative origin]

thrum[2] (θrʌm) *textiles* ▷ *n* **1 a** any of the unwoven ends of warp thread remaining on the loom when the web has been removed **b** such ends of thread collectively **2** a fringe or tassel of short unwoven threads ▷ *vb* **thrums**, **thrumming**, **thrummed** **3** (*tr*) to trim with thrums [C14: from Old English; related to Old High German *drum* remnant, Dutch *dreum*]

thrush[1] (θrʌʃ) *n* any songbird of the subfamily *Turdinae*, esp those having a brown plumage with a spotted breast, such as the mistle thrush and song thrush: family *Muscicapidae* [Old English *thrȳsce*; related to Old High German *drōsca*; see THROSTLE, THROAT]

thrush[2] (θrʌʃ) *n* **1 a** a fungal disease of the mouth, esp of infants, and the genitals, characterized by the formation of whitish spots and caused by infection with the fungus *Candida albicans* **b** another word for **sprue**[1] **2 a** softening of the frog of a horse's hoof characterized by degeneration and a thick foul discharge [C17: related to Old Danish *törsk*, Danish *troske*]

thrust (θrʌst) *vb* **thrusts**, **thrusting**, **thrust** **1** (*tr*) to push (someone or something) with force or sudden strength: *she thrust him away; she thrust it into the fire* **2** (*tr*) to force or impose upon (someone) or into (some condition or situation): *they thrust extra responsibilities upon her; she was thrust into the limelight* **3** (*tr*; foll by *through*) to pierce; stab **4** (*intr*; usually foll by *through* or *into*) to force a passage or entrance **5** (*tr*; foll by *at*) to make a stab or lunge at (a person or thing) ▷ *n* **6** a forceful drive, push, stab, or lunge **7** a force, esp one that produces motion **8 a** a propulsive force produced by the fluid pressure or the change of momentum of the fluid in a jet engine, rocket engine, etc **b** a similar force produced by a propeller **9** a pressure that is exerted continuously by one part of an object, structure, etc, against another, esp the axial force by or on a shaft **10** force, impetus, or drive **11** the essential or most forceful part: *the thrust of the argument* [c12: from Old Norse *thrysta*; related to Latin *trūdere*; see INTRUDE]

thruster ('θrʌstə) *n* **1** a person or thing that thrusts **2** Also called: **vernier rocket** a small rocket engine, esp one used to correct the altitude or course of a spacecraft

thrust fault *n* a fault in which the rocks on the upper side of an inclined fault plane have been displaced upwards, usually by compression; see reverse fault

thrutch (θrʌtʃ) *n Northern English dialect* a narrow, fast-moving stream

Thucydides (θuːˈsɪdɪˌdiːz) *n* ?460–?395 BC, Greek historian and politician, distinguished for his *History of the Peloponnesian War* ▷ Thu,cydiˈdean *adj*

thud (θʌd) *n* **1** a dull heavy sound **2** a blow or fall that causes such a sound ▷ *vb* **thuds, thudding, thudded 3** to make or cause to make such a sound [Old English *thyddan* to strike; related to *thoddettan* to beat, perhaps of imitative origin]

thug (θʌg) *n* **1** a tough and violent man, esp a criminal **2** (*sometimes capital*) (formerly) a member of an organization of robbers and assassins in India who typically strangled their victims [c19: from Hindi *thag* thief, from Sanskrit *sthaga* scoundrel, from *sthagati* to conceal] ▷ 'thuggery *n* ▷ 'thuggish *adj*

thuja *or* **thuya** ('θuːjə) *n* any of various coniferous trees of the genus *Thuja*, of North America and East Asia, having scalelike leaves, small cones, and an aromatic wood: family *Cupressaceae* [c18: from New Latin, from Medieval Latin *thuia*, ultimately from Greek *thua* name of an African tree]

Thule ('θuːlɪ) *n* **1** Also called: **ultima Thule** a region believed by ancient geographers to be the northernmost land in the inhabited world: sometimes thought to have been Iceland, Norway, or one of the Shetland Islands **2** an Inuit settlement in NW Greenland: a Danish trading post, founded in 1910, and US air force base

thulium ('θjuːlɪəm) *n* a malleable ductile silvery-grey element occurring principally in monazite. The radioisotope **thulium-170** is used as an electron source in portable X-ray units. Symbol: Tm; atomic no: 69; atomic wt: 168.93421; valency: 3; relative density: 9.321; melting pt: 1545°C; boiling pt: 1950°C [c19: New Latin, from THULE + -IUM]

thumb (θʌm) *n* **1** the first and usually shortest and thickest of the digits of the hand, composed of two short bones **2** the corresponding digit in other vertebrates **3** the part of a glove shaped to fit the thumb **4** all thumbs clumsy **5** thumbs down an indication of refusal, disapproval, or negation: *he gave the thumbs down on our proposal* **6** thumbs up an indication of encouragement, approval, or acceptance **7** under someone's thumb at someone's mercy or command ▷ *vb* **8** (*tr*) to touch, mark, or move with the thumb **9** to attempt to obtain (a lift or ride) by signalling with the thumb **10** (when *intr*, often foll by *through*) to flip the pages of (a book, magazine, etc) perfunctorily in order to glance at the contents **11** thumb one's nose at to deride or mock, esp by placing the thumb on the nose with fingers extended [Old English *thūma*; related to Old Saxon *thūma*, Old High German *thūmo*, Old Norse *thumall* thumb of a glove, Latin *tumēre* to swell]

thumb index *n* **1** a series of indentations cut into the fore edge of a book to facilitate quick reference ▷ *vb* **thumb-index 2** (*tr*) to furnish with a thumb index

thumbnail ('θʌmˌneɪl) *n* **1** the nail of the thumb **2** (*modifier*) concise and brief: *a thumbnail sketch* **3** *computing* a small image which can be expanded

thumbnut ('θʌmˌnʌt) *n* a nut with projections enabling it to be turned by the thumb and forefinger; wing nut

thumb piano *n* another name for **mbira**

thumbscrew ('θʌmˌskruː) *n* **1** an instrument of torture that pinches or crushes the thumbs **2** a screw with projections on its head enabling it to be turned by the thumb and forefinger

thumbstall ('θʌmˌstɔːl) *n* a protective sheathlike cover for the thumb

thumbtack ('θʌmˌtæk) *n chiefly US & Canadian* a short

tack with a broad smooth head for fastening papers to a drawing board, etc. Also called (esp in Britain): **drawing pin**

thump (θʌmp) *n* **1** the sound of a heavy solid body hitting or pounding a comparatively soft surface **2** a heavy blow with the hand ▷ *vb* **3** (*tr*) to strike or beat heavily; pound **4** (*intr*) to throb, beat, or pound violently [c16: related to Icelandic, Swedish dialect *dumpa* to thump; see THUD, BUMP] ▷ 'thumper *n*

thumping ('θʌmpɪŋ) *adj* (*prenominal*) *slang* huge or excessive: *a thumping loss*

Thun (*German* tuːn) *n* **1** a town in central Switzerland, in Bern canton on Lake Thun. Pop: 40 377 (2000) **2** a lake in central Switzerland, formed by a widening of the Aar River. Length: about 17 km (11 miles). Width: 3 km (2 miles)

thunbergia (θʊnˈbɜːdʒɪə) *n* any plant of the typically climbing tropical genus *Thunbergia* such as black-eyed Susan: family *Acanthaceae* [named after K. P. *Thunberg* (1743–1822), Swedish traveller and botanist]

thunder ('θʌndə) *n* **1** a loud cracking or deep rumbling noise caused by the rapid expansion of atmospheric gases which are suddenly heated by lightning **2** any loud booming sound **3** *rare* a violent threat or denunciation **4** steal someone's thunder to detract from the attention due to another by forestalling him or her ▷ *vb* **5** to make (a loud sound) or utter (words) in a manner suggesting thunder **6** (*intr*; with *it* as subject) to be the case that thunder is being heard **7** (*intr*) to move fast and heavily: *the bus thundered downhill* **8** (*intr*) to utter vehement threats or denunciation; rail [Old English *thunor*; related to Old Saxon *thunar*, Old High German *donar*, Old Norse *thōrr*; see THOR, THURSDAY] ▷ 'thunderer *n* ▷ 'thundery *adj*

Thunder Bay *n* a port in central Canada, in Ontario on Lake Superior: formed in 1970 by the amalgamation of Fort William and Port Arthur; the head of the St Lawrence Seaway for Canada. Pop: 103 215 (2001)

thunderbolt ('θʌndəˌbəʊlt) *n* **1** a flash of lightning accompanying thunder **2** the imagined agency of destruction produced by a flash of lightning **3** (in mythology) the destructive weapon wielded by several gods, esp the Greek god Zeus **4** something very startling

thunderclap ('θʌndəˌklæp) *n* **1** a loud outburst of thunder **2** something as violent or unexpected as a clap of thunder

thundercloud ('θʌndəˌklaʊd) *n* a towering electrically charged cumulonimbus cloud associated with thunderstorms

thunderhead ('θʌndəˌhɛd) *n chiefly US & Canadian* the anvil-shaped top of a cumulonimbus cloud

thundering ('θʌndərɪŋ) *adj* (*prenominal*) *slang* very great or excessive: *a thundering idiot*

thunderous ('θʌndərəs) *adj* **1** resembling thunder, esp in loudness **2** threatening and extremely angry: *she gave him a thunderous look*

thunderstorm ('θʌndəˌstɔːm) *n* a storm caused by strong rising air currents and characterized by thunder and lightning and usually heavy rain or hail

thunderstruck ('θʌndəˌstrʌk) *or* **thunderstricken** ('θʌndəˌstrɪkən) *adj* **1** completely taken aback; amazed or shocked **2** *rare* struck by lightning

Thurber ('θɜːbə) *n* James (**Grover**). 1894–1961, US humorist and illustrator. He contributed drawings and stories to the *New Yorker* and his books include *Is Sex Necessary?* (1929), written with E. B. White

Thurgau (*German* 'tuːrgaʊ) *n* a canton of NE Switzerland, on Lake Constance: annexed to the confederated Swiss states in 1460. Capital: Frauenfeld. Pop: 229 800 (2002 est). Area: 1007 sq km (389 sq miles)

thurible ('θjʊərɪbəl) *n* another word for **censer** [c15: from Latin *tūribulum* censer, from *tūs* incense]

Thuringia (θjʊˈrɪndʒɪə) *n* a state of central Germany. Pop: 2 373 000 (2003 est) ▷ Thu'ringian *adj, n*

Thuringian Forest *n* a forested mountainous region in E central Germany, rising over 900 m (3000 ft)

Thurrock ('θʌrək) *n* a unitary authority in SE England, in Essex. Pop: 145 300 (2003 est). Area: 163 sq km (63 sq miles)

Thurs. *abbreviation* Thursday

Thursday ('θɜːzdɪ) *n* the fifth day of the week; fourth day of the working week [Old English *Thursdæg*, literally: Thor's day; related to Old High German *Donares tag*; see THOR, THUNDER, DAY]

Thursday Island *n* an island in Torres Strait, between NE Australia and New Guinea: administratively part of Queensland, Australia. Area: 4 sq km (1.5 sq miles)

thus (ðʌs) *adv* **1** in this manner: *do it thus* **2** to such a degree: *thus far and no further* ▷ *sentence connector* **3** therefore: *We have failed. Thus we have to take the consequences* [Old English; related to Old Frisian, Old Saxon *thus*]

Thutmose I (θʊtˈməʊsə, -məʊs) *n* died *c.* 1500 BC, king of Egypt of the 18th dynasty, who extended his territory in Nubia and Syria and enlarged the Temple of Amon at Karnak

Thutmose III *n* died *c.* 1450 BC, king of Egypt of the 18th dynasty, who completed the conquest of Syria and dominated the Middle East. He was also a patron of the arts and a famous athlete

thuya ('θuːjə) *n* a variant spelling of **thuja**

thwack (θwæk) *vb* **1** to beat, hit, or flog, esp with something flat ▷ *n* **2** a blow with something flat **b** the sound made by it [c16: of imitative origin]

thwart (θwɔːt) *vb* **1** to oppose successfully or prevent; frustrate **2** *obsolete* to be or move across ▷ *n* **3** *nautical* a seat lying across a boat and occupied by an oarsman ▷ *adj* **4** passing or being situated across ▷ *prep, adv* **5** *obsolete* across [c13: from Old Norse *thvert*, from *thverr* transverse; related to Old English *thweorh* crooked, Old High German *twerh* transverse]

thy (ðaɪ) *determiner* (*usually preceding a consonant*) *archaic* belonging to or associated in some way with you (thou): *thy goodness and mercy.* See **thine** [c12: variant of THINE]

Thyestes (θaɪˈɛstiːz) *n Greek myth* son of Pelops and brother of Atreus, with whose wife he committed adultery. In revenge, Atreus killed Thyestes' sons and served them to their father at a banquet > **Thyestean** or **Thyestian** (θaɪˈɛstɪən, ˌθaɪɛˈstiːən) *adj*

thylacine ('θaɪləˌsaɪn) *n* an extinct or very rare doglike carnivorous marsupial, *Thylacinus cynocephalus*, of Tasmania, having greyish-brown fur with dark vertical stripes on the back: family *Dasyuridae*. Also called: **Tasmanian tiger, Tasmanian wolf** [c19: from New Latin *thȳlacinus*, from Greek *thulakos* pouch, sack]

thyme (taɪm) *n* any of various small shrubs of the temperate genus *Thymus*, having a strong mintlike odour, small leaves, and white, pink, or red flowers: family *Labiaceae* (labiates) [c14: from Old French *thym*, from Latin *thymum*, from Greek *thumon*, from *thuein* to make a burnt offering] > '**thymy** *adj*

-thymia *n combining form* indicating a certain emotional condition, mood, or state of mind: *cyclothymia* [New Latin, from Greek *thumos* temper]

thymine ('θaɪmiːn) *n* a white crystalline pyrimidine base found in DNA. Formula: $C_5H_6N_2O_2$ [c19: from THYMIC (see THYMUS) + -INE²]

thymol ('θaɪmɒl) *n* a white crystalline substance with an aromatic odour, obtained from the oil of thyme and used as a fungicide, antiseptic, and anthelmintic and in perfumery and embalming; 2-isopropylphenol. Formula: $(CH_3)_2CHC_6H_3(CH_3)OH$ [c19: from THYME + -OL²]

thymus ('θaɪməs) *n, pl* **-muses** *or* **-mi** (-maɪ) a glandular organ of vertebrates, consisting in man of two lobes situated below the thyroid. In early life it produces lymphocytes and is thought to influence certain immunological responses. It atrophies with age and is almost nonexistent in the adult [c17: from New Latin, from Greek *thumos* sweetbread] > '**thymic** *adj*

thyratron ('θaɪrəˌtrɒn) *n electronics* a gas-filled tube that has three electrodes and can be switched between an 'off' state and an 'on' state. It has been superseded, except for application involving high-power switching, by the thyristor [c20: originally a trademark, from Greek *thura* door, valve + -TRON]

thyristor (θaɪˈrɪstə) *n electronics* any of a group of semiconductor devices, such as the silicon-controlled rectifier, that can be switched between two states [c20:

from THYR(ATRON) + (TRANS)ISTOR]

thyro- *or before a vowel* **thyr-** *combining form* thyroid: *thyrotoxicosis; thyrotropin*

thyroid ('θaɪrɔɪd) *adj* **1** of or relating to the thyroid gland **2** of or relating to the largest cartilage of the larynx ▷ *n* **3** See **thyroid gland 4** Also called: **thyroid extract** the powdered preparation made from the thyroid gland of certain animals, used to treat hypothyroidism [c18: from New Latin *thyroïdēs*, from Greek *thureoeidēs*, from *thureos* oblong (literally: door-shaped) shield, from *thura* door]

thyroid gland *n* an endocrine gland of vertebrates, consisting in man of two lobes near the base of the neck. It secretes hormones that control metabolism and body growth

thyrotropin (ˌθaɪrəʊˈtrəʊpɪn) *or* **thyrotrophin** (ˌθaɪrəʊˈtrəʊfɪn) *n* a glycoprotein hormone secreted by the anterior lobe of the pituitary gland: it stimulates the activity of the thyroid gland [c20: from THYRO- + -TROPE + -IN]

thyroxine (θaɪˈrɒksiːn, -sɪn) *or* **thyroxin** (θaɪˈrɒksɪn) *n* the principal hormone produced by the thyroid gland: it increases the metabolic rate of tissues and also controls growth, as in amphibian metamorphosis. It can be synthesized or extracted from the thyroid glands of animals and used to treat hypothyroidism. Chemical name: tetra-iodothyronine; formula: $C_{15}H_{11}I_4NO_4$ [c19: from THYRO- + OXY-² + -INE²]

thyrse (θɜːs) *or* **thyrsus** ('θɜːsəs) *n, pl* **thyrses** *or* **thyrsi** ('θɜːsaɪ) *botany* a type of inflorescence, occurring in the lilac and grape, in which the main branch is racemose and the lateral branches cymose [c17: from French: THYRSUS]

thyrsus ('θɜːsəs) *n, pl* **-si** (-saɪ) **1** *Greek myth* a staff, usually one tipped with a pine cone, borne by Dionysus (Bacchus) and his followers **2** a variant spelling of **thyrse** [c18: from Latin, from Greek *thursos* stalk]

thyself (ðaɪˈsɛlf) *pron archaic* **a** the reflexive form of **thou, thee b** (intensifier): *thou, thyself, wouldst know*

ti (tiː) *n music* a variant spelling of **te**

Ti *the chemical symbol for* titanium

Tianjin ('tjɛnˈdʒɪn), **Tientsin** *or* **T'ien-ching** *n* an industrial city in NE China, capital of Tianjin municipality (traditionally in Hebei province), on the Grand Canal, 51 km (32 miles) from the Yellow Sea: the third largest city in China; seat of Nankai University (1919). Pop: 9 346 000 (2005 est)

Tian Shan *or* **Tien Shan** ('tjɛnˈʃɑːn) *n* a great mountain system of central Asia, in Kyrgyzstan and the Xinjiang Uygur Autonomous Region of W China, extending for about 2500 km (1500 miles). Highest peak: Jengish Chokusu or Tomur Feng (formerly Pobeda Peak), 7439 m (24 406 ft). Russian name: Tyan-Shan

tiara (tɪˈɑːrə) *n* **1** a woman's semicircular jewelled headdress for formal occasions **2** a high headdress worn by Persian kings in ancient times **3** *RC Church* a headdress worn by the pope, consisting of a beehive-shaped diadem surrounded by three coronets [c16: via Latin from Greek, of Oriental origin] > **ti'araed** *adj*

Tiber ('taɪbə) *n* a river in central Italy, rising in the Tuscan Apennines and flowing south through Rome to the Tyrrhenian Sea. Length: 405 km (252 miles). Italian name: Tevere

Tiberias (taɪˈbɪərɪˌæs) *n* **1** a resort in N Israel, on the Sea of Galilee: an important Jewish centre after the destruction of Jerusalem by the Romans. Pop: 40 100 (2003 est) **2** Lake Tiberias another name for (Sea of) **Galilee**

Tiberius (taɪˈbɪərɪəs) *n* full name *Tiberius Claudius Nero Caesar Augustus*. 42 BC–37 AD, Roman emperor (14–37 AD). He succeeded his father-in-law Augustus after a brilliant military career. He became increasingly tyrannical

Tibesti *or* **Tibesti Massif** (tɪˈbɛstɪ) *n* a mountain range of volcanic origin in NW Chad, in the central Sahara extending for about 480 km (300 miles). Highest peak: Emi Koussi, 3415 m (11 204 ft)

Tibet (tɪˈbɛt) *n* an autonomous region of SW China: Europeans strictly excluded in the 19th century; invaded by China in 1950; rebellion (1959) against Chinese rule suppressed and the Dalai Lama fled to India; military rule imposed (1989–90) after continued demands for independence; consists largely of a vast high plateau between the Himalayas and Kunlun Mountains; formerly a theocracy and the centre of Lamaism. Capital: Lhasa. Pop: 2 700 000 (2003 est). Area: 1 221 601 sq km (471 660 sq miles). Chinese names: Xizang Autonomous Region, Sitsang

Tibetan (tɪˈbɛtᵊn) adj **1** of, relating to, or characteristic of Tibet, its people, or their language ▷ n **2** a native or inhabitant of Tibet **3** the language of Tibet, belonging to the Sino-Tibetan family

tibia (ˈtɪbɪə) n, pl tibiae (ˈtɪbɪˌiː) or tibias **1** Also called: shinbone the inner and thicker of the two bones of the human leg between the knee and ankle **2** the corresponding bone in other vertebrates **3** the fourth segment of an insect's leg, lying between the femur and the tarsus [c16: from Latin: leg, pipe] > ˈtibial adj

Tibullus (tɪˈbʌləs) n Albius (ˈælbɪəs). ?54–?19 bc, Roman elegiac poet

Tibur (ˈtaɪbə) n the ancient name for **Tivoli**

tic (tɪk) n pathol spasmodic twitching of a particular group of muscles [c19: from French, of uncertain origin; compare Italian ticche]

tic douloureux (ˈtɪk ˌduːləˈruː) n a condition of momentary stabbing pain along the trigeminal nerve. Also called: trigeminal neuralgia [c19: from French, literally: painful tic]

Ticino (Italian tiˈtʃiːno) n **1** a canton in S Switzerland: predominantly Italian-speaking and Roman Catholic; mountainous. Capital: Bellinzona. Pop: 314 600 (2002 est). Area: 2810 sq km (1085 sq miles). German name: Tessin **2** a river in S central Europe, rising in S central Switzerland and flowing southeast and west to Lake Maggiore, then southeast to the River Po. Length: 248 km (154 miles)

tick¹ (tɪk) n **1** a recurrent metallic tapping or clicking sound, such as that made by a clock or watch **2** Brit informal a moment or instant **3** a mark (√) or dash used to check off or indicate the correctness of something **4** commerce the smallest increment of a price fluctuation in a commodity exchange. Tick size is usually 0.01% of the nominal value of the trading unit ▷ vb **5** to produce a recurrent tapping sound or indicate by such a sound: the clock ticked the minutes away **6** (when tr, often foll by off) to mark or check (something, such as a list) with a tick **7** what makes someone tick informal the basic drive or motivation of a person ▷ See also **tick off, tick over** [c13: from Low German tikk touch; related to Old High German zekōn to pluck, Norwegian tikke to touch]

tick² (tɪk) n any of various small parasitic arachnids of the families Ixodidae (**hard ticks**) and Argasidae, (**soft ticks**), typically living on the skin of warm-blooded animals and feeding on the blood and tissues of their hosts: order Acarina (mites and ticks) [Old English ticca; related to Middle High German zeche tick, Middle Irish dega stag beetle]

tick³ (tɪk) n **1** the strong covering of a pillow, mattress, etc **2** informal short for **ticking** [c15: probably from Middle Dutch tīke; related to Old High German ziecha pillow cover, Latin tēca case, Greek thēkē]

tick⁴ (tɪk) n Brit informal account or credit (esp in the phrase **on tick**) [c17: shortened from TICKET]

tick-bird n another name for oxpecker [c19: so called because it eats insects off animals' backs]

tick box n (on a form, questionnaire, or test) a square in which one places a tick to show agreement with the accompanying statement

ticker (ˈtɪkə) n **1** slang **a** the heart **b** a watch **2** a person or thing that ticks **3** stock exchange the US word for **tape machine** (sense 2)

ticker tape n stock exchange a continuous paper ribbon on which a tape machine automatically prints current stock quotations

ticket (ˈtɪkɪt) n **1 a** a piece of paper, cardboard, etc, showing that the holder is entitled to certain rights, such as travel on a train or bus, entry to a place of public entertainment, etc **b** (modifier) concerned with or relating to the issue, sale, or checking of tickets: a ticket

office; ticket collector **2** a piece of card, cloth, etc, attached to an article showing information such as its price, size, or washing instructions **3** a summons served for a parking offence or violation of traffic regulations **4** informal the certificate of competence issued to a ship's captain or an aircraft pilot **5** chiefly US & NZ the group of candidates nominated by one party in an election; slate **6** chiefly US the declared policy of a political party at an election **7** Brit informal a certificate of discharge from the armed forces **8** informal the right or appropriate thing: that's the ticket **9** have tickets on oneself or have got tickets on oneself Austral informal to be conceited ▷ vb -ets, -eting, -eted (tr) **10** to issue or attach a ticket or tickets to ▷ See also **tickets** [c17: from Old French etiquet, from estiquier to stick on, from Middle Dutch steken to STICK²]

ticket day n (on the London Stock Exchange) the day on which selling brokers receive from buying brokers the names of investors who have made purchases during the previous account

tickets (ˈtɪkɪts) pl n South African informal the end; that was it [of unknown origin]

tick fever n any acute infectious febrile disease caused by the bite of an infected tick

ticking (ˈtɪkɪŋ) n a strong cotton fabric, often striped, used esp for mattress and pillow covers [c17: from TICK³]

ticklace (ˈtɪkəˌlæs) n Canadian (in Newfoundland) a kittiwake [imitative of the bird's cry]

tickle (ˈtɪkᵊl) vb **1** to touch, stroke, or poke (a person, part of the body, etc) so as to produce pleasure, laughter, or a twitching sensation **2** (tr) to excite pleasurably; gratify **3** (tr) to delight or entertain (often in the phrase **tickle one's fancy**) **4** (intr) to itch or tingle **5** (tr) to catch (a fish, esp a trout) by grasping it with the hands and gently moving the fingers into its gills **6** tickle pink or tickle to death informal to please greatly ▷ n **7** a sensation of light stroking or itching **8** the act of tickling **9** Canadian (in the Atlantic Provinces) a narrow strait [c14: related to Old English tinclian, Old High German kizziton, Old Norse kitla, Latin titillāre to TITILLATE]

tickler (ˈtɪklə) n **1** informal, chiefly Brit a difficult or delicate problem **2** Also called: tickler file US a memorandum book or file **3** a person or thing that tickles

ticklish (ˈtɪklɪʃ) adj **1** susceptible and sensitive to being tickled **2** delicate or difficult **3** easily upset or offended > ˈticklishly adv > ˈticklishness n

tick off vb (tr, adverb) **1** to mark with a tick **2** informal, chiefly Brit to scold; reprimand

tick over vb (intr, adverb) **1** Also called: idle Brit (of an engine) to run at low speed with the throttle control closed and the transmission disengaged **2** to run smoothly without any major changes

ticktack (ˈtɪkˌtæk) n **1** Brit a system of sign language, mainly using the hands, by which bookmakers transmit their odds to each other at racecourses **2** US a ticking sound, as made by a clock [from TICK¹]

ticktock (ˈtɪkˌtɒk) n **1** a ticking sound as made by a clock ▷ vb **2** (intr) to make a ticking sound

Ticonderoga (ˌtaɪkɒndəˈrəʊgə) n a village in NE New York State, on Lake George: site of Fort Ticonderoga, scene of battles between the British and French (1758–59) and a strategic point in the War of American Independence

tidal (ˈtaɪdᵊl) adj **1** relating to, characterized by, or affected by tides **2** dependent on the state of the tide: a tidal ferry > ˈtidally adv

tidal bore n another term for bore³

tidal energy n energy obtained by harnessing tidal power

tidal volume n **1** the volume of water associated with a rising tide **2** physiol the amount of air passing into and out of the lungs during normal breathing

tidal wave n **1** a name (not accepted in technical usage) for **tsunami 2** an unusually large incoming wave, often caused by high winds and spring tides **3** a forceful and widespread movement in public opinion, action, etc

tidbit (ˈtɪdˌbɪt) n the usual US spelling of titbit

tiddler (ˈtɪdlə) n Brit informal **1** a very small fish or aquatic creature, esp a stickleback, minnow, or tadpole **2** a small child, esp one undersized for its age [C19: from dialectal *tittlebat*, childish variant of STICKLEBACK, influenced by TIDDLY¹]

tiddly¹ ('tɪdlɪ) *adj* -dlier, -dliest *Brit* small; tiny [C19: childish variant of LITTLE]

tiddly² ('tɪdlɪ) *adj* -dlier, -dliest *slang, chiefly Brit* slightly drunk [C19 (meaning: a drink): of unknown origin]

tiddlywinks ('tɪdlɪ,wɪŋks) *n* (*functioning as singular*) a game in which players try to flick discs of plastic into a cup by pressing them sharply on the side with other larger discs [C19: probably from TIDDLY¹ + dialect *wink*, variant of WINCH]

tide (taɪd) *n* **1** the cyclic rise and fall of sea level caused by the gravitational pull of the sun and moon. There are usually two high tides and two low tides in each lunar day **2** the current, ebb, or flow of water at a specified place resulting from these changes in level **3** See ebb (sense 3), **flood** (sense 3) **4** a widespread tendency or movement **5** a critical point in time; turning point **6** (*in combination*) a season or time: *Christmastide* **7** *archaic* a favourable opportunity ▷ *vb* **8** to carry or be carried with or as if with the tide **9** (*intr*) to ebb and flow like the tide [Old English *tīd* time; related to Old High German *zīt*, Old Norse *tīthr* time] > 'tideless *adj*

tideland ('taɪd,lænd) *n US* land between high-water and low-water marks

tideline ('taɪd,laɪn) *n* the mark or line left by the tide when it retreats from its highest point

tidemark ('taɪd,mɑːk) *n* **1** a mark left by the highest or lowest point of a tide **2** *chiefly Brit* a mark showing a level reached by a liquid: *a tidemark on the bath* **3** *informal, chiefly Brit* a dirty mark on the skin, indicating the extent to which someone has washed

tide over *vb* (*tr*) to help to get through (a period of difficulty, distress, etc)

tide-rip *n* another word for **riptide** (sense 1)

tidewaiter ('taɪd,weɪtə) *n* (formerly) a customs officer who boarded and inspected incoming ships

tidewater ('taɪd,wɔːtə) *n* **1** water that advances and recedes with the tide **2** water that covers land that is dry at low tide **3** *US* coastal land drained by tidal streams

tideway ('taɪd,weɪ) *n* a strong tidal current or its channel, esp the tidal part of a river

tidings ('taɪdɪŋz) *pl n* information or news [Old English *tīdung*; related to Middle Low German *tīdinge* information, Old Norse *tidhendi* events]

tidy ('taɪdɪ) *adj* -dier, -diest **1** characterized by or indicating neatness and order **2** *informal* considerable: *a tidy sum of money* ▷ *vb* -dies, -dying, -died **3** (when *intr*, usually foll by *up*) to put (things) in order; neaten ▷ *n, pl* -dies **4 a** a small container in which odds and ends are kept **b** sink tidy a container with holes in the bottom, kept in the sink to retain rubbish that might clog the plug hole **5** *chiefly US & Canadian* an ornamental protective covering for the back or arms of a chair [C13 (in the sense: timely, seasonable, excellent): from TIDE¹ + -Y¹; related to Dutch *tijdig* timely] > 'tidily *adv* > 'tidiness *n*

tie (taɪ) *vb* ties, tying, tied **1** (when *tr*, often foll by *up*) to fasten or be fastened with string, thread, etc **2** to make (a knot or bow) in (something) **3** (*tr*) to restrict or secure **4** to equal the score of a competitor or fellow candidate **5** (*tr*) *informal* to unite in marriage **6** *music* **a** to execute (two successive notes of the same pitch) as though they formed one note of composite time value **b** to connect (two printed notes) with a tie ▷ *n* **7** a bond, link, or fastening **8** a restriction or restraint **9** a string, wire, ribbon, etc, with which something is tied **10** a long narrow piece of material worn, esp by men, under the collar of a shirt, tied in a knot close to the throat with the ends hanging down the front. US name: necktie **11 a** an equality in score, attainment, etc, in a contest **b** the match or competition in which such a result is attained **12** a structural member carrying tension, such as a tie beam or tie rod **13** *sport, Brit* a match or game in an eliminating competition: *a cup tie* **14** (*usually plural*) a shoe fastened by means of laces **15** the US and Canadian name for **sleeper** (sense 3) **16** *music* a slur connecting

two notes of the same pitch indicating that the sound is to be prolonged for their joint time value ▷ See also **tie in**, **tie up** [Old English *tīgan* to tie; related to Old Norse *teygja* to draw, stretch out, Old English *tēon* to pull; see TUG, TOW¹, TIGHT]

tie beam *n* a horizontal beam that serves to prevent two other structural members from separating, esp one that connects two corresponding rafters in a roof or roof truss

tie-break *or* **tie-breaker** *n* **1** *tennis* a method of deciding quickly the result of a set drawn at six-all, usually involving the playing of one deciding game for the best of twelve points in which the service changes after every two points **2** any contest or game played to decide a winner when contestants have tied scores

Tieck (German tiːk) *n* **Ludwig** ('luːtvɪç). 1773–1853, German romantic writer, noted esp for his fairy tales

tie clasp *n* a clip, often ornamental, which holds a tie in place against a shirt. Also called: **tie clip**

tied (taɪd) *adj Brit* **1** (of a public house, retail shop, etc) obliged to sell only the beer, products, etc, of a particular producer: *a tied house; tied outlet* **2** (of a house or cottage) rented out to the tenant for as long as he or she is employed by the owner **3** (of a loan) made by one nation to another on condition that the money is spent on goods or services provided by the lending nation

tie-dyeing *n* a method of dyeing textiles to produce patterns by tying sections of the cloth together so that they will not absorb the dye. Also called: **tie-and-dye** > 'tie-,dyed *adj*

tie in *vb* (*adverb*) **1** to come or bring into a certain relationship; coordinate ▷ *n* **tie-in 2** a link, relationship, or coordination **3** publicity material, a book, tape, etc, linked to a film or broadcast programme or series **4** *US* **a** a sale or advertisement offering products of which a purchaser must buy one or more in addition to his purchase **b** an item sold or advertised in this way, esp the extra item **c** (*as modifier*): *a tie-in sale*

tie line *n* a telephone line between two private branch exchanges or private exchanges that may or may not pass through a main exchange

Tien Shan ('tjɛn'ʃɑːn) *n* a variant transliteration of the Chinese name for **Tian Shan**

Tientsin ('tjɛn'tsɪn) *n* a variant transliteration of the Chinese name for **Tianjin**

tiepin ('taɪ,pɪn) *n* an ornamental pin of various shapes used to pin the two ends of a tie to a shirt

Tiepolo (Italian 'tjɛːpolo; English tiːˈɛpəˌləʊ) *n* **Giovanni Battista** (dʒoˈvanni batˈtista). 1696–1770, Italian rococo painter, esp of frescoes as in the Residenz at Würzburg

tier¹ (tɪə) *n* **1** one of a set of rows placed one above and behind the other, such as theatre seats **2 a** a layer or level **b** (*in combination*): *a three-tier cake* ▷ *vb* **3** to be or arrange in tiers [C16: from Old French *tire* rank, of Germanic origin; compare Old English *tīr* embellishment]

tier² ('taɪə) *n* a person or thing that ties

tierce (tɪəs) *n* **1** a variant of **terce 2** the third of eight basic positions from which a parry or attack can be made in fencing **3** (tɜːs) *cards* a sequence of three cards in the same suit **4** an obsolete measure of capacity equal to 42 wine gallons [C15: from Old French, feminine of *tiers* third, from Latin *tertius*]

tiercel ('tɪəsᵊl) *n* a variant of **tercel**

Tierra del Fuego (Spanish 'tjɛrra ðɛl 'fweɣo) *n* an archipelago at the S extremity of South America, separated from the mainland by the Strait of Magellan: the west and south belong to Chile, the east to Argentina. Area: 73 643 sq km (28 434 sq miles)

tie up *vb* (*adverb*) **1** (*tr*) to attach or bind securely with or as if with string, rope, etc **2** to moor (a vessel) **3** (*tr; often passive*) to engage the attentions of **4** (*tr; often passive*) to conclude (the organization of something) **5** to come or bring to a complete standstill **6** (*tr*) to invest or commit (funds, etc) and so make unavailable for other uses **7** (*tr*) to subject (property) to conditions that prevent sale, alienation, or other action ▷ *n* **tie-up 8** a link or connection **9** *chiefly US & Canadian* a standstill **10** *chiefly US & Canadian* an informal term for **traffic jam**

t

tiff (tɪf) *n* **1** a petty quarrel **2** a fit of ill humour ▷ *vb* **3** (*intr*) to have or be in a tiff [c18: of unknown origin]

tiffany ('tɪfənɪ) *n*, *pl* **-nies** a sheer fine gauzy fabric [c17: (in the sense: a fine dress worn on Twelfth Night): from Old French *tifanie*, from ecclesiastical Latin *theophania* Epiphany; see THEOPHANY]

Tiffany ('tɪfənɪ) *n* **Louis Comfort**. 1848–1933, US glass-maker and Art-Nouveau craftsman, best known for creating the Favrile style of stained glass

tiffin ('tɪfɪn) *n* (in India) a light meal, esp one taken at midday [c18: probably from obsolete *tiffing*, from *tiff* to sip]

Tiflis (tɪf'liːs) *n* transliteration of the Russian name for **Tbilisi**

tig (tɪg) *n*, *vb* **tigs, tigging, tigged** another name for: **tag¹** (senses 1, 4)

tiger ('taɪgə) *n* **1** a large feline mammal, *Panthera tigris*, of forests in most of Asia, having a tawny yellow coat with black stripes **2** (*not in technical use*) any of various other animals, such as the jaguar, leopard, and thylacine **3** a dynamic, forceful, or cruel person **4 a** a country, esp in E Asia, that is achieving rapid economic growth **b** (*as modifier*): *a tiger economy* [c13: from Old French *tigre*, from Latin *tigris*, from Greek, of Iranian origin] > 'tigerish *or* 'tigrish *adj*

Tiger ('taɪgə) *n* See TIGR

tiger beetle *n* any active predatory beetle of the family *Cicindelidae*, chiefly of warm dry regions, having powerful mandibles and long legs [c19: so called because it has patterned, sometimes striped, wing covers]

tiger cat *n* a medium-sized feline mammal, *Felis tigrina*, of Central and South America, having a dark-striped coat

tiger lily *n* a lily plant, *Lilium tigrinum*, of China and Japan, cultivated for its flowers, which have black-spotted orange reflexed petals

tiger moth *n* any of a group of arctiid moths, mostly boldly marked, often in black, orange, and yellow, of the genera *Arctia, Parasemia, Euplagia*, etc, producing woolly bear larvae and typified by the **garden tiger** (*Arctia caja*)

tiger's-eye ('taɪgəz,aɪ) *or* **tigereye** ('taɪgər,aɪ) *n* a golden brown silicified variety of crocidolite, used as an ornamental stone

tiger shark *n* a voracious omnivorous requiem shark, *Galeocerdo cuvieri*, chiefly of tropical waters, having a striped or spotted body

tiger snake *n* a highly venomous brown-and-yellow elapid snake, *Notechis scutatus*, of Australia

tight (taɪt) *adj* **1** stretched or drawn so as not to be loose; taut **2** fitting or covering in a close manner **3** held, made, fixed, or closed firmly and securely: *a tight knot* **4 a** of close and compact construction or organization, esp so as to be impervious to water, air, etc **b** (*in combination*): *watertight; airtight* **5** unyielding or stringent **6** cramped or constricted: *a tight fit* **7** mean or miserly **8** difficult and problematic: *a tight situation* **9** hardly profitable: *a tight bargain* **10** economics **a** (of a commodity) difficult to obtain; in excess demand **b** (of funds, money, etc) difficult and expensive to borrow because of high demand or restrictive monetary policy **c** (of markets) characterized by excess demand or scarcity with prices tending to rise **11** (of a match or game) very close or even **12** (of a team or group, esp of a pop group) playing well together, in a disciplined coordinated way **13** *informal* drunk **14** *informal* (of a person) showing tension ▷ *adv* **15** in a close, firm, or secure way [c14: probably variant of *thight*, from Old Norse *thēttr* close; related to Middle High German *dīhte* thick] > 'tightly *adv* > 'tightness *n*

tightass ('taɪt,æs) *n* slang, chiefly US an inhibited or excessively self-controlled person > 'tight,assed *adj*

tighten ('taɪt°n) *vb* to make or become tight or tighter

tightfisted (,taɪt'fɪstɪd) *adj* mean; miserly

tight head *n* rugby the prop on the hooker's right in the front row of a scrum. See **loose head**

tightknit (,taɪt'nɪt) *adj* **1** closely integrated: *a tightknit community* **2** organized carefully and concisely

tight-lipped *adj* **1** reticent, secretive, or taciturn **2** with the lips pressed tightly together, as through anger

tightrope ('taɪt,rəʊp) *n* a rope or cable stretched taut above the ground on which acrobats walk or perform balancing feats

tights (taɪts) *pl n* **1 a** a one-piece clinging garment covering the body from the waist to the feet, worn by women in place of stockings. Also called (US, Canadian, Austral., and NZ): pantyhose **b** Also called: leotards US & Canadian a similar, tight-fitting garment worn instead of trousers by either sex **2** a similar garment formerly worn by men, as in the 16th century with a doublet

Tiglath-pileser I ('tɪglæθpɪ'liːzə, -paɪ-) *n* king of Assyria (?1116–?1093 BC), who extended his kingdom to the upper Euphrates and defeated the king of Babylonia

Tiglath-pileser III *n* known as *Pulu*. died ?727 BC, king of Assyria (745–727), who greatly extended his empire, subjugating Syria and Palestine

tiglic acid ('tɪglɪk) *n* a syrupy liquid or crystalline colourless unsaturated carboxylic acid, with the *trans*-configuration, found in croton oil and used in perfumery; *trans*-2-methyl-2-butenoic acid. Formula: $CH_3CH:C(CH_3)COOH$ [C19 *tiglic*, from New Latin phrase *Croton tiglium* (name of the croton plant), of uncertain origin]

tigon ('taɪgən) *or* **tiglon** ('tɪglɒn) *n* the hybrid offspring of a male tiger and a female lion

TIGR *abbreviation* Treasury Investment Growth Receipts: a bond denominated in dollars and linked to US treasury bonds, the yield on which is taxed in the UK as income when it is cashed or redeemed. Also called: **Tiger**

Tigre *or* **Tigray** ('tiːgreɪ) *n* **1** an autonomous region of N Ethiopia, bordering on Eritrea: formerly a separate kingdom. Capital: Mekele. Pop: 4 334 996 (2005 est) **2** a language of NE Ethiopia, belonging to the SE Semitic subfamily of the Afro-Asiatic family

tigress ('taɪgrɪs) *n* **1** a female tiger **2** a fierce, cruel, or wildly passionate woman

tigridia (taɪ'grɪdɪə) *n* any plant of the bulbous genus *Tigridia*, native to subtropical and tropical America, esp *T. pavonia*, the tiger flower or peacock tiger flower, grown for its large strikingly marked red, white, or yellow concave flowers: family *Iridaceae* [New Latin, from Greek *tigris, tigridis* tiger]

Tigris ('taɪgrɪs) *n* a river in SW Asia, rising in E Turkey and flowing southeast through Baghdad to the Euphrates in SE Iraq, forming the delta of the Shatt-al-Arab, which flows into the Persian Gulf: part of a canal and irrigation system as early as 2400 BC, with many ancient cities (including Nineveh) on its banks. Length: 1900 km (1180 miles)

Tihwa *or* **Tihua** ('tiː'hwaː) *n* a former name for **Urumchi**

Tijuana (tiː'waːna; Spanish ti'xwana) *or* **Tia Juana** *n* a city in NW Mexico, in Baja California (Norte). Pop: 1 570 000 (2005 est)

tik (tɪk) *n* South African a slang name for the drug methamphetamine in crystal form

tikanga (tə'kæŋə) *n* NZ Māori ways or customs [Māori]

tike (taɪk) *n* a variant spelling of **tyke**

tiki ('tiːkɪ) *n* an amulet or figurine in the form of a carved representation of an ancestor, worn in some Māori cultures [from Māori]

tiki tour *n* NZ a scenic tour of an area

tikka ('tiːkə) *adj* (*immediately postpositive*) Indian cookery (of meat, esp chicken or lamb) marinated in spices then dry-roasted, usu. in a clay oven

Tikrit (tɪ'kriːt) *n* a town in N central Iraq on the River Tigris; birthplace of Saladin and Saddam Hussein. Pop: 28 900 (2002 est)

tilak ('tɪlək) *n*, *pl* **-ak** *or* **-aks** a coloured spot or mark worn by Hindus, esp on the forehead, often indicating membership of a religious sect, caste, etc, or (in the case of a woman) marital status [from Sanskrit *tilaka*]

Tilak ('tɪlək) *n* **Bal Gangadhar** ('bɐːl 'gæŋədɐː), also called *Lokamanya*. 1856–1920, Indian nationalist leader, educationalist, and scholar, who founded (1914) the Indian Home Rule League

Tilburg ('tɪlbɜːg; Dutch 'tɪlbyrx) *n* a city in the S Netherlands, in North Brabant: textile industries. Pop: 198 000 (2003 est)

tilbury ('tɪlbərɪ, -brɪ) *n*, *pl* **-buries** a light two-wheeled horse-drawn open carriage, seating two people [C19: probably named after the inventor]

Tilbury ('tɪlbərɪ, -brɪ) *n* an area in Essex, on the River Thames: extensive docks; principal container port of the Port of London

tilde ('tɪldə) *n* the diacritical mark (~) placed over a letter to indicate a palatal nasal consonant, as in Spanish *señor*. This symbol is also used in the International Phonetic Alphabet to represent any nasalized vowel [C19: from Spanish, from Latin *titulus* title, superscription]

Tilden ('tɪldən) *n* **Bill**, full name *William Tatem Tilden*, known as *Big Bill*. 1893–1953, US tennis player: won the US singles championship (1920–25, 1929) and the British singles championship (1920–21, 1930)

tile (taɪl) *n* **1 a** a flat thin slab of fired clay, rubber, linoleum, etc, usually square or rectangular and sometimes ornamental, used with others to cover a roof, floor, wall, etc **2** a short pipe made of earthenware, concrete, or plastic, used with others to form a drain **3** tiles collectively **4** a rectangular block used as a playing piece in mah jong and other games **5** on the tiles *informal* on a spree, esp of drinking or debauchery ▷ *vb* **6** (*tr*) to cover with tiles [Old English *tigele*, from Latin *tēgula*; related to German *Ziegel*] > '**tiler** *n*

tiling ('taɪlɪŋ) *n* **1** tiles collectively **2** something made of or surfaced with tiles

till[1] (tɪl) *conj, prep* short for **until** [Old English *til*; related to Old Norse *til* to, Old High German *zil* goal, aim]
- ● USAGE *Till* is a variant of *until* that is acceptable at all
- ● levels of language. *Until* is, however, often preferred at
- ● the beginning of a sentence in formal writing: *until his*
- ● *behaviour improves, he cannot become a member*

till[2] (tɪl) *vb* (*tr*) **1** to cultivate and work (land) for the raising of crops **2** another word for **plough** [Old English *tilian* to try, obtain; related to Old Frisian *tilia* to obtain, Old Saxon *tilōn* to obtain, Old High German *zilōn* to hasten towards] > '**tillable** *adj* > '**tiller** *n*

till[3] (tɪl) *n* a box, case, or drawer into which the money taken from customers is put, now usually part of a cash register [C15 *tylle*, of obscure origin]

till[4] (tɪl) *n* an unstratified glacial deposit consisting of rock fragments of various sizes. The most common is boulder clay [C17: of unknown origin]

tillage ('tɪlɪdʒ) *n* **1** the act, process, or art of tilling **2** tilled land

tiller[1] ('tɪlə) *n* *nautical* a handle fixed to the top of a rudderpost to serve as a lever in steering it [C14: from Anglo-French *teiler* beam of a loom, from Medieval Latin *tēlārium*, from Latin *tēla* web]

tiller[2] ('tɪlə) *n* **1** a shoot that arises from the base of the stem in grasses **2** a less common name for **sapling** ▷ *vb* **3** (*intr*) (of a plant) to produce tillers [Old English *telgor* twig; related to Icelandic *tjalga* branch]

Till Eulenspiegel ('tɪl 'ɔɪlənʃpiːgəl) *n* ?14th century, legendary German peasant, whose pranks became the subject of many tales

Tilley ('tɪlɪ) *n* **Vesta** ('vɛstə), original name *Matilda Alice Powles*. 1864–1952, British music-hall entertainer, best known as a male impersonator

Tillich ('tɪlɪk) *n* **Paul Johannes**. 1886–1965, US Protestant theologian and philosopher, born in Germany. His works include *The Courage to Be* (1952) and *Systematic Theology* (1951–63)

Tilly ('tɪlɪ) *n* **Count Johan Tserclaes von** (joʼhɑn tsɛrʼklas fɔn). 1559–1632, Flemish soldier, who commanded the army of The Catholic League (1618–32) and the imperial forces (1630–32) in the Thirty Years' War

Tilsit ('tɪlzɪt) *n* the former name (until 1945) of **Sovetsk**

tilt (tɪlt) *vb* **1** to incline or cause to incline at an angle **2** (*usually intr*) to attack or overthrow (a person or people) in a tilt or joust **3** (when *intr*, often foll by *at*) to aim or thrust: *to tilt a lance* **4** (*tr*) to work or forge with a tilt hammer ▷ *n* **5** a slope or angle: *at a tilt* **6** the act of tilting **7** (esp in medieval Europe) **a** a jousting contest **b** a thrust with a lance or pole delivered during a tournament **8** an attempt to win a contest **9** See **tilt hammer 10** full tilt or at full tilt at full speed or force [Old English *tealtian*; related to Dutch *touteren* to totter, Norwegian *tylta* to tiptoe, *tylten* unsteady] > '**tilter** *n*

tilth (tɪlθ) *n* **1** the act or process of tilling land **2** the condition of soil or land that has been tilled, esp with respect to suitability for promoting plant growth [Old English *tilthe*; see TILL[2]]

tilt hammer *n* a drop hammer consisting of a heavy head moving at the end of a pivoted arm; used in forging

tiltyard ('tɪlt,jɑːd) *n* (formerly) an enclosed area for tilting

Tim. *Bible abbreviation* Timothy

Timaru ('tɪmə,ruː) *n* a port and resort in S New Zealand, on E South Island. Pop: 43 100 (2004 est)

timbal *or* **tymbal** ('tɪmbəl) *n* *music* a type of kettledrum [C17: from French *timbale*, from Old French *tamballe*, (associated also with *cymbale* cymbal), from Old Spanish *atabal*, from Arabic *at-tabl* the drum]

timbale (tæmʼbɑːl; *French* tɛ̃bal) *n* **1 a** a mixture of meat, fish, etc, in a rich sauce, cooked in a mould lined with potato or pastry **2** a plain straight-sided mould in which such a dish is prepared [C19: from French: kettledrum]

timber ('tɪmbə) *n* **1 a** wood, esp when regarded as a construction material. Usual US and Canadian word: **lumber b** (*as modifier*): *a timber cottage* **2 a** trees collectively **b** *chiefly US* woodland **3** a piece of wood used in a structure **4** *nautical* a frame in a wooden vessel ▷ *vb* **5** (*tr*) to provide with timbers ▷ *interj* **6** a lumberjack's shouted warning when a tree is about to fall [Old English; related to Old High German *zimbar* wood, Old Norse *timbr* timber, Latin *domus* house] > '**timbered** *adj* > '**timbering** *n*

timber hitch *n* a knot used for tying a rope round a spar, log, etc, for haulage

Timberlake ('tɪmbə,leɪk) *n* **Justin**. born 1981, US pop singer; a member of the boy band NSYNC, he later found success with the bestselling solo album *Justified* (2002)

timber limit *n* *Canadian* **1** the area to which rights of cutting timber, granted by government licence, are limited **2** another term for **timberline**

timberline ('tɪmbə,laɪn) *n* the altitudinal or latitudinal limit of normal tree growth. See also **tree line**

timber wolf *n* a variety of the wolf, *Canis lupus*, having a grey brindled coat and occurring in forested northern regions, esp of North America

timberyard ('tɪmbə,jɑːd) *n* *Brit* an establishment where timber and sometimes other building materials are stored or sold. US and Canadian word: **lumberyard**

timbre ('tɪmbə, 'tæmbə; *French* tɛ̃brə) *n* **1** *phonetics* the distinctive tone quality differentiating one vowel or sonant from another **2** *music* tone colour or quality of sound, esp a specific type of tone colour [C19: from French: note of a bell, from Old French: drum, from Medieval Greek *timbanon*, from Greek *tumpanon* drum]

timbrel ('tɪmbrəl) *n* *chiefly biblical* another word for **tambourine** [C16: from Old French; see TIMBRE]

Timbuktu (,tɪmbʌkʼtuː) *n* **1** a town in central Mali, on the River Niger: terminus of a trans-Saharan caravan route; a great Muslim centre (14th–16th centuries). Pop: 31 973 (1998). French name: **Tombouctou 2** any distant or outlandish place: *from here to Timbuktu*

time (taɪm) *n* **1** the continuous passage of existence in which events pass from a state of potentiality in the future, through the present, to a state of finality in the past **2** *physics* a quantity measuring duration, usually with reference to a periodic process such as the rotation of the earth or the vibration of electromagnetic radiation emitted from certain atoms. In classical mechanics, time is absolute in the sense that the time of an event is independent of the observer. According to the theory of relativity it depends on the observer's frame of reference. Time is considered as a fourth coordinate required, along with three spatial coordinates, to specify an event. See **space-time 3** a specific point on this continuum expressed in terms of hours and minutes: *the time is four o'clock* **4** a system of reckoning for expressing time: *Greenwich mean time* **5 a** a definite and measurable portion of this continuum **b** (*as modifier*): *time limit* **6 a** an accepted period such as a day, season, etc **b** (*in combination*): *springtime* **7** an unspecified interval; a while **8** (*often plural*) a period or point marked by specific attributes or events: *the Victorian* times; **time for breakfast** 9 a sufficient interval or period: *have you got time to help me?* 10 an instance or occasion: *I called you three times* 11 an occasion or period of specified quality: *have a good time; a miserable time* 12 the duration of human existence 13 the heyday of human life: *in her time she was a great star* 14 a suitable period or moment: *it's time I told you* 15 the expected interval in which something is done 16 a particularly important moment, esp childbirth or death: *her time had come* 17 (*plural*) indicating a degree or amount calculated by multiplication with the number specified: *ten times three is thirty; he earns four times as much as me* 18 (*often plural*) the fashions, thought, etc, of the present age (esp in the phrases **ahead of one's time, behind the times**) 19 *Brit* (in bars, pubs, etc) short for **closing time** 20 *informal* a term in jail (esp in the phrase **do time**) 21 a a customary or full period of work b the rate of pay for this period 22 Also (*esp US*): **metre** a the system of combining beats or pulses in music into successive groupings by which the rhythm of the music is established b a specific system having a specific number of beats in each grouping or bar: *duple time* 23 *music* short for **time value** 24 **against time** in an effort to complete something in a limited period 25 **ahead of time** before the deadline 26 **at one time** a once; formerly b simultaneously 27 **at the same time** a simultaneously b nevertheless; however 28 **at times** sometimes 29 **beat time** (of a conductor, etc) to indicate the tempo or pulse of a piece of music by waving a baton or a hand, tapping out the beats, etc 30 **for the time being** for the moment; temporarily 31 **from time to time** at intervals; occasionally 32 **have no time for** to have no patience with; not tolerate 33 **in good time** a early b quickly 34 **in no time** very quickly; almost instantaneously 35 **in one's own time** a outside paid working hours b at one's own rate 36 **in time** a early or at the appointed time b eventually c *music* at a correct metrical or rhythmic pulse 37 **keep time** to observe correctly the accent or rhythmic pulse of a piece of music in relation to tempo 38 **make time** a to find an opportunity b (often foll by *with*) *US informal* to succeed in seducing 39 **on time** a at the expected or scheduled time b *US* payable in instalments 40 **pass the time of day** to exchange casual greetings (with an acquaintance) 41 **time and again** frequently 42 **time off** a period when one is absent from work for a holiday, through sickness, etc 43 **time on** *Austral* an additional period played at the end of a match, to compensate for time lost through injury or (in certain circumstances) to allow the teams to achieve a conclusive result 44 **time out of mind** from time immemorial 45 **time of one's life** a memorably enjoyable time 46 (*modifier*) operating automatically at or for a set time, for security or convenience: *time lock; time switch* ▷ *vb* (*tr*) 47 to ascertain or calculate the duration or speed of 48 to set a time for 49 to adjust to keep accurate time 50 to pick a suitable time for 51 *sport* to control the execution or speed of (an action, esp a shot or stroke) so that it has its full effect at the right moment ▷ *interj* 52 the word called out by a publican signalling that it is closing time [Old English *tīma*; related to Old English *tīd* time, Old Norse *tīmi*, Alemannic *zīme*; see TIDE]

time and a half *n* the rate of pay equalling one and a half times the normal rate, often offered for overtime work

time and motion study *n* the analysis of industrial or work procedures to determine the most efficient methods of operation. Also called: **time and motion, time study, motion study**

time bomb *n* a bomb containing a timing mechanism that determines the time at which it will detonate

time capsule *n* a container holding articles, documents, etc, representative of the current age, buried in the earth or in the foundations of a new building for discovery in the future

time charter *n* the hire of a ship or aircraft for a specified period. See **voyage charter**

time clock *n* a clock which records, by punching or stamping cards inserted into it, the time of arrival or departure of people, such as employees in a factory

time-consuming *adj* taking up or involving a great deal of time

time exposure *n* 1 an exposure of a photographic film for a relatively long period, usually a few seconds 2 a photograph produced by such an exposure

time frame *n* the period of time within which certain events are scheduled to occur

time-honoured *adj* having been observed for a long time and sanctioned by custom

time immemorial *n* the distant past beyond memory or record

timekeeper ('taɪmˌkiːpə) *n* 1 a person or thing that keeps or records time 2 an employee who maintains a record of the hours worked by the other employees 3 an employee with respect to his or her record of punctuality ⊳ '**time**ˌ**keeping** *n*

time-lag *n* an interval between two connected events

time-lapse photography *n* the technique of recording a very slow process, such as the withering of a flower, by taking a large number of photographs on a strip of film at regular intervals. The film is then projected at normal speed

timeless ('taɪmlɪs) *adj* 1 unaffected or unchanged by time; ageless 2 eternal ⊳ '**timelessly** *adv* ⊳ '**timelessness** *n*

timeline ('taɪmˌlaɪn) *n* 1 a graphic representation showing the passage of time as a line 2 a time frame during which something is scheduled to happen

timely ('taɪmlɪ) *adj* -lier, -liest at the right or an opportune or appropriate time

time machine *n* (in science fiction) a machine in which people or objects can be transported into the past or the future

time management *n* the analysis of how working hours are spent and the prioritization of tasks in order to maximize personal efficiency in the workplace

time-out *n* 1 *sport* an interruption in play during which players rest, discuss tactics, or make substitutions 2 a break taken during working hours 3 *computing* a condition occurring when the amount of time a computer has been instructed to wait for another device to perform a task has expired, usually indicated by an error message ▷ *vb* **time out** 4 (*intr*) (of a computer) to stop operating because of a time-out

timepiece ('taɪmˌpiːs) *n* any of various devices, such as a clock, watch, or chronometer, which measure and indicate time

timer ('taɪmə) *n* 1 a device for measuring, recording, or indicating time 2 a switch or regulator that causes a mechanism to operate at a specific time or at predetermined intervals 3 a person or thing that times

time-saving ('taɪmˌseɪvɪŋ) *adj* shortening the length of time required for an operation, activity, etc ⊳ '**time**ˌ**saver** *n*

timescale ('taɪmˌskeɪl) *n* the span of time within which certain events occur or are scheduled to occur considered in relation to any broader period of time

time-sensitive *adj* 1 physically changing as time passes 2 only relevant or applicable for a short period of time

time-served *adj* (of a craftsman or tradesman) having completed an apprenticeship; fully trained and competent

timeserver ('taɪmˌsɜːvə) *n* a person who compromises and changes his or her opinions, way of life, etc, to suit the current fashions

time sharing *n* 1 a system of part ownership of a property, such as a flat or villa, for use as a holiday home, whereby each participant buys the right to use the property for the same fixed period annually 2 a system by which users at different terminals of a computer can, because of its high speed, apparently communicate with it at the same time

time signal *n* an announcement of the correct time, esp on radio or television

time signature *n* *music* a sign usually consisting of two figures, one above the other, the upper figure representing the number of beats per bar and the lower one the time value of each beat. This sign is placed after the key signature at the outset of a piece or section of a piece. See also **key signature**

Times Square *n* a square formed by the intersection of Broadway and Seventh Avenue in New York City, extending from 42nd to 45th Street

timetable ('taɪmˌteɪbᵊl) *n* **1** a list or table of events arranged according to the time when they take place; schedule ▷ *vb* **2** (*tr*) to include in or arrange according to a timetable

time value *n music* the duration of a given printed note relative to other notes in a composition or section and considered in relation to the basic tempo

time warp *n* a hypothetical distortion of time in which people and events from one age can be imagined to exist in another age

timeworn ('taɪmˌwɔːn) *adj* **1** showing the adverse effects of overlong use or of old age **2** hackneyed; trite

time zone *n* a region throughout which the same standard time is used. There are 24 time zones in the world, demarcated approximately by meridians at 15° intervals, an hour apart

timid ('tɪmɪd) *adj* **1** easily frightened or upset, esp by human contact; shy **2** indicating shyness or fear [c16: from Latin *timidus*, from *timēre* to fear] > ti'midity *or* 'timidness *n* > 'timidly *adv*

timing ('taɪmɪŋ) *n* the process or art of regulating actions or remarks in relation to others to produce the best effect, as in music, the theatre, sport, etc

Timișoara (*Romanian* timiˈʃwara) *n* a city in W Romania: formerly under Turkish and then Hapsburg rule, being allotted to Romania in 1920; unrest led to the revolution of 1989. Pop: 296 000 (2005 est). Hungarian name: **Temesvár**

timocracy (taɪˈmɒkrəsɪ) *n, pl* **-cies 1** a political unit or system in which possession of property serves as the first requirement for participation in government **2** a political unit or system in which love of honour is deemed the guiding principle of government [c16: from Old French *tymocracie*, ultimately from Greek *timokratia*, from *timē* worth, honour, price + -CRACY]

Timor ('tiːmɔː, ˌtaɪ-) *n* an island in the Malay Archipelago, the largest and easternmost of the Lesser Sunda Islands: the west was a Dutch possession (part of the Dutch East Indies) until 1949, when it became part of Indonesia; the east was held by Portugal until 1975, when it declared independence but was immediately invaded by Indonesia; East Timor finally became an independent state in 2002. Area: 30 775 sq km (11 883 sq miles) > ˌTimoˈrese *adj, n*

Timor-Leste ('tiːmɔːˈlesteɪ) *n* the official name of **East Timor**

timorous ('tɪmərəs) *adj* **1** fearful or timid **2** indicating fear or timidity [c15: from Old French *temoros*, from Medieval Latin *timōrōsus*, from Latin *timor* fear, from *timēre* to be afraid] > 'timorously *adv* > 'timorousness *n*

Timor Sea *n* an arm of the Indian Ocean between Australia and Timor. Width: about 480 km (300 miles)

Timoshenko (ˌtɪməˈʃɛŋkəʊ; *Russian* timaˈʃɛnkə) *n* **Semyon Konstantinovich** (sɪˈmjɔn kənstanˈtinəvitʃ). 1895–1970, Soviet general in World War II

Timothy ('tɪməθɪ) *n New Testament* **1 Saint.** a disciple of Paul, who became leader of the Christian community at Ephesus. Feast day: Jan 26 or 22 **2** either of the two books addressed to him (in full **The First and Second Epistles of Paul the Apostle to Timothy**), containing advice on pastoral matters

timothy grass *or* **timothy** ('tɪməθɪ) *n* a perennial grass, *Phleum pratense*, of temperate regions, having erect stiff stems and cylindrical flower spikes: grown for hay and pasture [c18: apparently named after a *Timothy* Hanson, who brought it to colonial Carolina]

timpani *or* **tympani** ('tɪmpənɪ) *pl n* (*sometimes functioning as singular*) a set of kettledrums, two or more in number [from Italian, pl of *timpano* kettledrum, from Latin: TYMPANUM] > 'timpanist *or* 'tympanist *n*

Timur *or* **Timour** (tiːˈmʊə) *n* See **Tamerlane**

tin (tɪn) *n* **1** a metallic element, occurring in cassiterite, that has several allotropes: the ordinary malleable silvery-white metal slowly changes below 13.2°C to a grey powder. It is used extensively in alloys, esp bronze and pewter, and as a noncorroding coating for steel. Symbol: Sn; atomic no: 50; atomic wt: 118.710; valency: 2 or 4; relative density: 5.75 (grey), 7.31 (white); melting pt: 231.9°C; boiling pt: 2603°C **2** an airtight sealed container of thin sheet metal coated with tin, used for preserving and storing food or drink. Also called (esp US and Canadian): **can 3** any container made of metallic tin **4** Also called: **tinful** the contents of a tin or the amount a tin will hold **5** *Brit, Austral & NZ* corrugated or galvanized iron: *a tin roof* **6** any metal regarded as cheap or flimsy **7** *Brit* a loaf of bread with a rectangular shape, baked in a tin **8** it does exactly what it says on the tin it lives up to expectations ▷ *vb* tins, tinning, tinned (*tr*) **9** to put (food, etc) into a tin or tins; preserve in a tin **10** to plate or coat with tin **11** to prepare (a metal) for soldering or brazing by applying a thin layer of solder to the surface [Old English; related to Old Norse *tin*, Old High German *zin*]

tinamou ('tɪnəˌmuː) *n* any bird of the order *Tinamiformes* of Central and South America, having small wings, a heavy body, and an inconspicuous plumage [c18: via French from Carib (Galibi) *tinamu*]

Tinbergen ('tɪnˌbɜːgən) *n* **1 Jan** (jæn). 1903–94, Dutch economist, noted for his work on econometrics. He shared (1969) the first Nobel prize for economics with Ragnar Frisch **2** his brother, **Nikolaas** ('nɪkəlaːs). 1907–88, British zoologist, born in the Netherlands; studied animal behaviour, esp instincts, and was one of the founders of ethology; Nobel prize for physiology or medicine 1973

tin can *n* a metal food container, esp when empty

tinct (tɪŋkt) *n, vb* **1** an obsolete word for **tint** ▷ *adj* **2** *poetic* tinted or coloured [c15: from Latin *tinctus*, from *tingere* to colour]

tinctorial (tɪŋkˈtɔːrɪəl) *adj* of or relating to colouring, staining, or dyeing [c17: from Latin *tinctōrius*, from *tingere* to tinge]

tincture ('tɪŋktʃə) *n* **1** *pharmacol* a medicinal extract in a solution of alcohol **2** a tint, colour, or tinge **3** a slight flavour, aroma, or trace **4** any one of the colours or either of the metals used on heraldic arms **5** *obsolete* a dye or pigment ▷ *vb* **6** (*tr*) to give a tint or colour to [c14: from Latin *tinctūra* a dyeing, from *tingere* to dye]

Tindal *or* **Tindale** ('tɪndəl) *n* variant spellings of (William) **Tyndale**

tinder ('tɪndə) *n* **1** dry wood or other easily combustible material used for lighting a fire **2** anything inflammatory or dangerous [Old English *tynder*; related to Old Norse *tundr*, Old High German *zuntara*] > 'tindery *adj*

tinderbox ('tɪndəˌbɒks) *n* **1** a box used formerly for holding tinder, esp one fitted with a flint and steel **2** a person or thing that is particularly touchy or explosive

tine (taɪn) *n* **1** a slender prong, esp of a fork **2** any of the sharp terminal branches of a deer's antler [Old English *tind*; related to Old Norse *tindr*, Old High German *zint*] > tined *adj*

tinea ('tɪnɪə) *n* any fungal skin disease, esp ringworm [c17: from Latin: worm] > 'tineal *adj*

tinfoil ('tɪnˌfɔɪl) *n* **1** thin foil made of tin or an alloy of tin and lead **2** thin foil made of aluminium; used for wrapping foodstuffs

ting (tɪŋ) *n* **1** a high metallic sound such as that made by a small bell ▷ *vb* **2** to make or cause to make such a sound [c15: of imitative origin]

Ting (tɪŋ) *n* **Samuel Chao Chung.** born 1936, US physicist, who discovered the J/psi particle independently of Burton Richter, with whom he shared (1976) the Nobel prize for physics

ting-a-ling ('tɪŋə'lɪŋ) *n* the sound of a small bell

tinge (tɪndʒ) *n* **1** a slight tint or colouring **2** any slight addition ▷ *vb* **tinges, tingeing** *or* **tinging, tinged** (*tr*) **3** to colour or tint faintly **4** to impart a slight trace to: *her thoughts were tinged with nostalgia* [c15: from Latin *tingere* to colour]

tingle ('tɪŋgᵊl) *vb* **1** (*usually intr*) to feel or cause to feel a prickling, itching, or stinging sensation of the flesh, as from a cold plunge or electric shock ▷ *n* **2** a sensation of tingling [c14: perhaps a variant of TINKLE] > 'tingler *n*

> ˈtingling *adj* > ˈtingly *adj*

tin god *n* **1** a self-important dictatorial person **2** a person erroneously regarded as holy or venerable

tin hat *n obsolete, informal* a steel helmet worn by military personnel for protection against small metal fragments

tinker (ˈtɪŋkə) *n* **1** (esp formerly) a travelling mender of pots and pans **2** a clumsy worker **3** the act of tinkering **4** *Scot & Irish* another name for **Gypsy** ▷ *vb* **5** (*intr*; foll by *with*) to play, fiddle or meddle with (machinery, etc), esp while under taking repairs **6** to mend (pots and pans) as a tinker [c13 *tinkere*, perhaps from *tink* tinkle, of imitative origin]

tinker's damn *or* **tinker's cuss** *n slang* the slightest heed (esp in the phrase **not give a tinker's damn** *or* **cuss**)

tinkle (ˈtɪŋkᵊl) *vb* **1** to ring or cause to ring with a series of high tinny sounds, like a small bell **2** (*tr*) to announce or summon by such a ringing **3** (*intr*) *Brit informal* to urinate ▷ *n* **4** a high clear ringing sound **5** the act of tinkling **6** *Brit informal* a telephone call [c14: of imitative origin] > ˈtinkly *adj*

tin lizzie (ˈlɪzɪ) *n informal* an old or decrepit car; jalopy [originally a nickname for the Model T Ford]

tinned *adj* **1** plated, coated, or treated with tin **2** *chiefly Brit* preserved or stored in airtight tins **3** coated with a layer of solder

tinnitus (ˈtɪnɪtəs, tɪˈnaɪtəs) *n pathol* a ringing, hissing, or booming sensation in one or both ears, caused by infection of the middle or inner ear, a side effect of certain drugs, etc [c19: from Latin, from *tinnīre* to ring]

tinny (ˈtɪnɪ) *adj* **-nier, -niest 1** of, relating to, or resembling tin **2** cheap, badly made, or shoddy **3** (of a sound) high, thin, and metallic **4** (of food or drink) flavoured with metal, as from a container **5** *Austral informal* lucky ▷ *n, pl* **-nies 6** *Austral slang* a can of beer > ˈtinnily *adv* > ˈtinniness *n*

tin-opener *n* a small tool for opening tins

Tin Pan Alley *n* **1** a district in a city concerned with the production of popular music, originally a small district in New York **2** *derogatory* the strictly commercial side of show business and pop music

tin plate *n* thin steel sheet coated with a layer of tin that protects the steel from corrosion ▷ *vb* **tin-plate 2** (*tr*) to coat (a metal or object) with a layer of tin, usually either by electroplating or by dipping in a bath of molten tin > ˈtin-ˌplater *n*

tinpot (ˈtɪnˌpɒt) *adj* (*prenominal*) *Brit informal* **1** inferior, cheap, or worthless **2** paltry; unimportant

tinsel (ˈtɪnsəl) *n* **1** a decoration consisting of a piece of string with thin strips of metal foil attached along its length **2** a yarn or fabric interwoven with strands of glittering thread **3** anything cheap, showy, and gaudy ▷ *vb* **-sels, -selling, -selled** *or US* **-sels, -seling, -seled** (*tr*) **4** to decorate with or as if with tinsel: *snow tinsels the trees* **5** to give a gaudy appearance to ▷ *adj* **6** made of or decorated with tinsel **7** showily but cheaply attractive; gaudy [c16: from Old French *estincele* a spark, from Latin *scintilla*; compare **STENCIL**] > ˈtinsel-ˌlike *adj* > ˈtinselly *adj*

Tinseltown (ˈtɪnsəlˌtaʊn) *n* an informal name for **Hollywood** [c20: from the insubstantial glitter of the film world]

tinsmith (ˈtɪnˌsmɪθ) *n* a person who works with tin or tin plate

tin soldier *n* a miniature toy soldier, usually made of lead

tinstone (ˈtɪnˌstəʊn) *n* another name for **cassiterite**

tint (tɪnt) *n* **1** a shade of a colour, esp a pale one **2** a colour that is softened or desaturated by the addition of white **3** a tinge **4** a semipermanent dye for the hair **5** a trace or hint **6** *engraving* uniform shading, produced esp by hatching ▷ *vb* **7** (*tr*) to colour or tinge **8** (*intr*) to acquire a tint [c18: from earlier **TINCT**] > ˈtinter *n*

Tintagel Head (tɪnˈtædʒəl) *n* a promontory in SW England, on the W coast of Cornwall: ruins of **Tintagel Castle**, legendary birthplace of King Arthur

tintinnabulation (ˌtɪntɪˌnæbjʊˈleɪʃən) *n* the act or an instance of the ringing or pealing of bells

Tintoretto (ˌtɪntəˈrɛtəʊ; *Italian* tinto'retto) *n* Il (il). original name *Jacopo Robusti*. 1518–94, Italian painter of

the Venetian school. His works include *Susanna bathing* (?1550) and the fresco cycle in the Scuola di San Rocco, Venice (from 1564)

tinware (ˈtɪnˌwɛə) *n* objects made of tin plate

tin whistle *n* another name for **penny whistle**

tinworks (ˈtɪnˌwɜːks) *n* (*functioning as singular or plural*) a place where tin is mined, smelted, or rolled

tiny (ˈtaɪnɪ) *adj* **tinier, tiniest** very small; minute [c16 *tine*, of uncertain origin] > ˈtinily *adv* > ˈtininess *n*

-tion *suffix forming nouns* indicating state, condition, action, process, or result: *election; prohibition* [from Old French, from Latin *-tiō, -tiōn-*]

tip¹ (tɪp) *n* **1** the extreme end of something, esp a narrow or pointed end **2** the top or summit **3** a small piece forming an extremity or end: *a metal tip on a cane* ▷ *vb* **tips, tipping, tipped** (*tr*) **4** to adorn or mark the tip of **5** to cause to form a tip [c15: from Old Norse *typpa*; related to Middle Low German, Middle Dutch *tip*] > ˈtipless *adj*

tip² (tɪp) *vb* **tips, tipping, tipped 1** to tilt or cause to tilt **2** (usually foll by *over* or *up*) to tilt or cause to tilt, so as to overturn or fall **3** *Brit* to dump (rubbish, etc) **4** tip one's hat to take off, raise, or touch one's hat in salutation ▷ *n* **5** the act of tipping or the state of being tipped **6** *Brit* a dump for refuse, etc [c14: of uncertain origin; related to **TOP¹, TOPPLE**]

tip³ (tɪp) *n* **1** a payment given for services in excess of the standard charge; gratuity **2** a helpful hint, warning, or other piece of information **3** a piece of inside information, esp in betting or investing ▷ *vb* **tips, tipping, tipped 4** to give a tip to (a person) [c18: perhaps from **TIP⁴**] > ˈtipper *n*

tip⁴ (tɪp) *vb* **tips, tipping, tipped 1** (*tr*) to hit or strike lightly ▷ *n* **2** a light blow [c13: perhaps from Low German *tippen*]

tip-off *n* **1** a warning or hint, esp given confidentially and based on inside information **2** *basketball* the act or an instance of putting the ball in play by a jump ball ▷ *vb* **tip off 3** (*tr, adverb*) to give a hint or warning to

Tipperary (ˌtɪpəˈrɛərɪ) *n* a county of S Republic of Ireland, in Munster province; divided into the North Riding and South Riding: mountainous. County town: Clonmel; Nenagh serves as administrative capital of the North Riding. Pop: 140 131 (2002). Area: 4255 sq km (1643 sq miles)

tipper truck *or* **tipper lorry** *n* a truck or lorry the rear platform of which can be raised at the front end to enable the load to be discharged by gravity

tippet (ˈtɪpɪt) *n* **1** a woman's fur cape for the shoulders, often consisting of the whole fur of a fox, marten, etc **2** the long stole of Anglican clergy worn during a service **3** a long streamer-like part to a sleeve, hood, etc, esp in the 16th century [c14: perhaps from **TIP¹**]

Tippett (ˈtɪpɪt) *n* Sir **Michael**. 1905–98, English composer, whose works include the oratorio *A Child of Our Time* (1941) and the operas *The Midsummer Marriage* (1952), *King Priam* (1962), *The Knot Garden* (1970), *The Ice Break* (1976), and *New Year* (1989)

tipping point (ˈtɪpɪŋ) *n* the crisis stage in a process, when a significant change takes place

tipple (ˈtɪpᵊl) *vb* **1** to make a habit of taking (alcoholic drink), esp in small quantities ▷ *n* **2** alcoholic drink [c15: back formation from obsolete *tippler* tapster, of unknown origin] > ˈtippler *n*

tipstaff (ˈtɪpˌstɑːf) *n* **1** a court official having miscellaneous duties, mostly concerned with the maintenance of order in court **2** a metal-tipped staff formerly used as a symbol of office [c16 *tipped staff*; see **TIP¹, STAFF¹**]

tipster (ˈtɪpstə) *n* a person who sells tips on horse racing, the stock market, etc

tipsy (ˈtɪpsɪ) *adj* **-sier, -siest 1** slightly drunk **2** slightly tilted or tipped; askew [c16: from **TIP²**] > ˈtipsily *adv* > ˈtipsiness *n*

tipsy cake *n Brit* a kind of trifle made from a sponge cake soaked with white wine or sherry and decorated with almonds and crystallized fruit

tiptoe (ˈtɪpˌtəʊ) *vb* **-toes, -toeing, -toed** (*intr*) **1** to walk with the heels off the ground and the weight supported by the ball of the foot and the toes **2** to walk silently or stealthily ▷ *n* **3** on tiptoe **a** on the tips of the toes or on the ball of the foot and the toes **b** eagerly anticipating something **c** stealthily or silently ▷ *adv* **4** on tiptoe ▷ *adj* **5** walking or standing on tiptoe

tiptop (ˌtɪpˈtɒp) *adj, adv* **1** at the highest point of health, excellence, etc **2** at the topmost point ▷ *n* **3** the best in quality **4** the topmost point

Tiptronic *or* **tiptronic** (tɪpˈtrɒnɪk) *n trademark* a type of gearbox that has both automatic and manual options

tipuna *or* **tupuna** (təˈpuːnə) *n* NZ an ancestor [Māori]

tip-up *adj* (*prenominal*) able to be turned upwards around a hinge or pivot: *a tip-up seat*

Tipu Sahib *or* **Tippoo Sahib** (ˈtɪpuː ˈsɑːɪb) *n* ?1750–99, sultan of Mysore (1782–99): killed fighting the British

TIR *abbreviation* (on continental lorries) Transports Internationaux Routiers [French: International Road Transport]

tirade (taɪˈreɪd) *n* a long angry speech or denunciation [C19: from French, literally: a pulling, from Italian *tirata*, from *tirare* to pull, of uncertain origin]

Tiran (tɪˈrɑːn) *n* **Strait of Tiran** a strait between the Gulf of Aqaba and the Red Sea. Length: 16 km (10 miles). Width: 8 km (5 miles)

Tirana (tɪˈrɑːnə) *or* **Tiranë** (*Albanian* tiˈranə) *n* the capital of Albania, in the central part 32 km (20 miles) from the Adriatic: founded in the early 17th century by Turks; became capital in 1920; the country's largest city and industrial centre. Pop: 390 000 (2005 est)

tire¹ (ˈtaɪə) *vb* **1** (*tr*) to reduce the energy of, esp by exertion; weary **2** (*tr; often passive*) to reduce the tolerance of; bore or irritate: *I'm tired of the children's chatter* **3** (*intr*) to become wearied or bored; flag [Old English *tēorian*, of unknown origin] > ˈtiring *adj*

tire² (ˈtaɪə) *n, vb* the US spelling of **tyre**

tired (ˈtaɪəd) *adj* **1** weary; fatigued **2** hackneyed; stale **3** tired and emotional *euphemistic* slightly drunk > ˈtiredness *n*

Tiree (taɪˈriː) *n* an island off the W coast of Scotland, in the Inner Hebrides. Pop: 770 (2001). Area: 78 sq km (30 sq miles)

tireless (ˈtaɪəlɪs) *adj* unable to be tired; indefatigable > ˈtirelessly *adv* > ˈtirelessness *n*

Tiresias (taɪˈriːsɪˌæs) *n Greek myth* a blind soothsayer of Thebes, who revealed to Oedipus that the latter had murdered his father and married his mother

tiresome (ˈtaɪəsəm) *adj* boring and irritating; irksome > ˈtiresomely *adv* > ˈtiresomeness *n*

tirewoman (ˈtaɪəˌwʊmən) *n, pl* **-women** an absolute term for **lady's maid** [C17: from *tire* (obs) to attire]

Tîrgu Mureş *or* **Târgu Mureş** (*Romanian* ˈtərgu ˈmureʃ) *n* a city in central Romania: manufacturing and cultural centre. Pop: 17 000 (2005 est)

Tirich Mir (ˈtɪərɪtʃ ˈmɪə) *n* a mountain in N Pakistan: highest peak of the Hindu Kush. Height: 7690 m (25 230 ft)

tiring room *n archaic* a dressing room in a theatre

tiro (ˈtaɪrəʊ) *n, pl* **-ros** a variant spelling of **tyro**

Tirol (tɪˈrəʊl, ˈtɪrəʊl; *German* tiˈroːl) *n* a variant spelling of **Tyrol** > ˌTiroˈlean *adj, n* > **Tirolese** (ˌtɪrəˈliːz) *adj, n*

Tirpitz (*German* ˈtɪrpɪts) *n* **Alfred von** (ˈalfreːt fɔn). 1849–1930, German admiral: as secretary of state for the Imperial Navy (1897–1916), he created the modern German navy, which challenged British supremacy at sea

Tirso de Molina (*Spanish* ˈtirso ðe moˈlina) *n* See **de Molina**

Tiruchirapalli (ˌtɪrətʃɪrəˈpʌlɪ, tɪˌruːtʃɪˈrɑːpəlɪ) *or* **Trichinopoly** *n* an industrial city in S India, in central Tamil Nadu on the Cauvery River: dominated by a rock fortress 83 m (273 ft) high. Pop: 746 062 (2001)

Tirunelveli (ˌtɪruːnelˈvelɪ) *n* a city in S India, in Tamil Nadu: site of St Francis Xavier's first preaching in India; textile manufacturing. Pop: 411 298 (2001)

'tis (tɪz) *poetic or dialect* contraction of **it is**

Tisa (ˈtisa) *n* the Slavonic and Romanian name for **Tisza**

tisane (tɪˈzæn) *n* an infusion of dried or fresh leaves or flowers, as camomile [C19: from French, from Latin *ptisana* barley water; see PTISAN]

Tishri (tɪʃˈriː) *n* (in the Jewish calendar) the seventh month of the year according to biblical reckoning and the first month of the civil year, usually falling within September and October [from Hebrew]

Tisiphone (tɪˈsɪfənɪ) *n Greek myth* one of the three Furies; the others are Alecto and Megaera

Tissot (ˈtɪsəʊ) *n* **James Joseph Jacques**. 1836–1902, French painter and etcher, best known for scenes of fashionable Victorian life painted in England

tissue (ˈtɪsjuː, ˈtɪfuː) *n* **1** a part of an organism consisting of a large number of cells having a similar structure and function: *connective tissue; nerve tissue* **2** a thin piece of soft absorbent paper, usually of two or more layers, used as a disposable handkerchief, towel, etc **3** See **tissue paper 4** an interwoven series: *a tissue of lies* **5** a woven cloth, esp of a light gauzy nature, originally interwoven with threads of gold or silver ▷ *vb* **6** (*tr*) to decorate or clothe with tissue or tissue paper [C14: from Old French *tissu* woven cloth, from *tistre* to weave, from Latin *texere*]

tissue culture *n* **1** the growth of small pieces of animal or plant tissue in a sterile controlled medium **2** the tissue produced as a result of this process

tissue paper *n* very thin soft delicate paper used to wrap breakable goods, as decoration, etc

Tisza (*Hungarian* ˈtisɔ) *n* a river in S central Europe, rising in W Ukraine and flowing west, forming part of the border between Ukraine and Romania, then southwest across Hungary into Serbia to join the Danube north of Belgrade. Slavonic and Romanian name: **Tisa**

tit¹ (tɪt) *n* any of numerous small active Old World songbirds of the family *Paridae* (titmice), esp those of the genus *Parus* (bluetit, great tit, etc). They have a short bill and feed on insects and seeds [C16: perhaps of imitative origin, applied to small animate or inanimate objects; compare Icelandic *tittr* pin]

tit² (tɪt) *n* **1** *slang* a female breast **2** a teat or nipple **3** *derogatory* a girl or young woman **4** *slang* a despicable or unpleasant person: often used as a term of address [Old English *titt*; related to Middle Low German *title*, Norwegian *titta*]

Tit. *Bible abbreviation* Titus

titan (ˈtaɪtⁿn) *n* a person of great strength or size [C17: from TITAN]

Titan (ˈtaɪtⁿn) *or feminine* **Titaness** *n Greek myth* **1** any of a family of primordial gods, the sons and daughters of Uranus (sky) and Gaea (earth) **2** any of the offspring of the children of Uranus and Gaea > **Titanesque** (ˌtaɪtəˈnesk) *adj*

Titania (tɪˈtɑːnɪə) *n* **1** (in medieval folklore) the queen of the fairies and wife of Oberon **2** (in classical antiquity) a poetic epithet used variously to characterize Circe, Diana, Latona, or Pyrrha

titanic (taɪˈtænɪk) *adj* possessing or requiring colossal strength: *a titanic battle*

titanium (taɪˈteɪnɪəm) *n* a strong malleable white metallic element, which is very corrosion-resistant and occurs in rutile and ilmenite. It is used in the manufacture of strong lightweight alloys, esp aircraft parts. Symbol: Ti; atomic no: 22; atomic wt: 47.88; valency: 2, 3, or 4; relative density: 4.54; melting pt: 1670±10°C; boiling pt: 3289°C [C18: New Latin; see TITAN, -IUM]

titanium dioxide *n* a white insoluble powder occurring naturally as rutile and used chiefly as a pigment of high covering power and durability. Formula: TiO_2. Also called: **titanium oxide, titanic oxide, titania**

titbit (ˈtɪtˌbɪt) *or esp US* **tidbit** *n* **1** a tasty small piece of food; dainty **2** a pleasing scrap of anything, such as scandal [C17: perhaps from dialect *tid* tender, of obscure origin]

titchy *or* **tichy** (ˈtɪtʃɪ) *adj* **titchier, titchiest** *or* **tichier, tichiest** *Brit slang* very small; tiny [C20: from *tich* or *titch* a small person, from *Little Tich*, the stage name of Harry Relph (1867–1928), English actor noted for his small stature]

titfer (ˈtɪtfə) *n Brit slang* a hat [from rhyming slang *tit for tat* hat]

tit for tat *n* an equivalent given in return or retaliation; blow for blow [C16: from earlier *tip for tap*]

tithe (taɪð) *n* **1** (*often plural*) *Christianity* a tenth part of agricultural or other produce, personal income, or profits, contributed either voluntarily or as a tax for the support of the church or clergy or for charitable purposes **2** any levy, esp of one tenth **3** a tenth or very small part of anything ▷ *vb* **4** (*tr*) **a** to exact or demand a tithe or tithes from (an individual or group) **b** to levy a tithe upon (a crop or amount of produce, etc) **5** (*intr*) to pay a tithe or tithes [Old English *teogoth;* related to Old Frisian *tegotha*, Old Saxon *tegotho*, Old High German *zehando*, Old Norse *tíundi*, Gothic *taihunda*]

tithe barn *n* a large barn where, formerly, the agricultural tithe of a parish was stored

Tithonus (tɪ'θəʊnəs) *n* *Greek myth* the son of Laomedon of Troy who was loved by the goddess Eos. She asked that he be made immortal but forgot to ask that he be made eternally young. When he aged she turned him into a grasshopper

titi ('tiːtiː) *n, pl* **-tis** any of several small omnivorous New World monkeys of the genus *Callicebus*, of South America, having long beautifully coloured fur and a long nonprehensile tail [via Spanish from Aymaran, literally: little cat]

Titian ('tɪʃən) *n* original name *Tiziano Vecellio*. ?1490–1576, Italian painter of the Venetian school, noted for his religious and mythological works, such as *Bacchus and Ariadne* (1523), and his portraits > ,Titian'esque *adj*

Titian red ('tɪʃən) *adj* (*sometimes not capital*) reddish-gold, like the hair colour used in many of the works of Titian (original name *Tiziano Vecellio*), the Italian painter of the Venetian school (?1490–1576)

Titicaca (*Spanish* titi'kaka) *n* Lake Titicaca a lake between S Peru and W Bolivia, in the Andes: the highest large lake in the world; drained by the Desaguadero River flowing into Lake Poopó. Area: 8135 sq km (3141 sq miles). Altitude: 3809 m (12 497 ft). Depth: 370 m (1214 ft)

titillate ('tɪtɪˌleɪt) *vb* (*tr*) **1** to arouse, tease, interest, or excite pleasurably and often superficially **2** to cause a tickling or tingling sensation in, esp by touching [C17: from Latin *tītillāre*] > 'titil,lating *adj* > ,titil'lation *n*

titivate *or* **tittivate** ('tɪtɪˌveɪt) *vb* to smarten up (oneself or another), as by making up, doing the hair, etc [C19: earlier *tidivate*, perhaps based on TIDY and CULTIVATE] > ,titi'vation *or* ,titti'vation *n*

titlark ('tɪtˌlɑːk) *n* another name for the pipit, esp the meadow pipit (*Anthus pratensis*) [C17: from TIT¹ + LARK¹]

title ('taɪtˤl) *n* **1** the distinctive name of a work of art, musical or literary composition, etc **2** a descriptive name, caption, or heading of a section of a book, speech, etc **3** See **title page 4** a name or epithet signifying rank, office, or function **5** a formal designation, such as *Mr, Mrs,* or *Miss* **6** an appellation designating nobility **7** *films* **a** short for **subtitle** (sense 2) **b** written material giving credits in a film or television programme **8** *sport* a championship **9** *property law* **a** the legal right to possession of property, esp real property **b** the basis of such right **c** the documentary evidence of such right: *title deeds* **10 a** any customary or established right **b** a claim based on such a right **11** a definite spiritual charge or office in the church, without appointment to which a candidate for holy orders cannot lawfully be ordained **12** *RC Church* a titular church ▷ *vb* **13** (*tr*) to give a title to [C13: from Old French, from Latin *titulus*]

title deed *n* a deed or document evidencing a person's legal right or title to property, esp real property

titleholder ('taɪtˤlˌhəʊldə) *n* a person who holds a title, esp a sporting championship

title page *n* the page in a book that bears the title, author's name, publisher's imprint, etc

title role *n* the role of the character after whom a play, etc, is named

titmouse ('tɪtˌmaʊs) *n, pl* **-mice** any small active songbird of the family *Paridae*, esp those of the genus *Parus*. See **tit¹** [C14 *titemous*, from *tite* (see TIT¹) + MOUSE]

Tito ('tiːtəʊ) *n* **Marshal.** original name *Josip Broz*. 1892–1980, Yugoslav statesman, who led the communist guerrilla resistance to German occupation during World War II; prime minister of Yugoslavia (1945–53) and president (1953–80)

Titograd (*Serbian* 'titɔgraːd) *n* the former name (1946–92) of **Podgorica**

titrate ('taɪtreɪt) *vb* (*tr*) to measure the volume or concentration of (a solution) by titration [C19: from French *titrer;* see TITRE] > ti'tratable *adj*

titration (taɪ'treɪʃən) *n* an operation, used in volumetric analysis, in which a measured amount of one solution is added to a known quantity of another solution until the reaction between the two is complete. If the concentration of one solution is known, that of the other can be calculated

titre *or US* **titer** ('taɪtə, 'tiː-) *n* the concentration of a solution as determined by titration [C19: from French *titre* proportion of gold or silver in an alloy, from Old French *title* TITLE]

titter ('tɪtə) *vb* **1** (*intr*) to snigger, esp derisively or in a suppressed way ▷ *n* **2** a suppressed laugh, chuckle, or snigger [C17: of imitative origin] > 'titterer *n* > 'tittering *adj*

tittle ('tɪtˤl) *n* **1** a small mark in printing or writing, esp a diacritic **2** a jot; particle [C14: from Medieval Latin *titulus* label, from Latin: TITLE]

tittle-tattle *n* **1** idle chat or gossip ▷ *vb* **2** (*intr*) to chatter or gossip > 'tittle-,tattler *n*

tittup ('tɪtəp) *vb* **-tups, -tupping, -tupped** *or US* **-tups, -tuping, -tuped 1** (*intr*) to prance or frolic ▷ *n* **2** a caper [C18 (in the sense: a horse's gallop): probably imitative]

titubation (,tɪtjʊ'beɪʃən) *n pathol* a disordered gait characterized by stumbling or staggering, often caused by a lesion of the cerebellum [C17: from Latin *titubātiō*, from *titubāre* to reel]

titular ('tɪtjʊlə) *or* **titulary** ('tɪtjʊlərɪ) *adj* **1** of, relating to, or of the nature of a title **2** in name only **3** bearing a title **4** giving a title **5** *RC Church* designating any of certain churches in Rome to whom cardinals or bishops are attached as their nominal incumbents ▷ *n, pl* **-lars** *or* **-laries 6** the bearer of a title **7** the bearer of a nominal office [C18: from French *titulaire*, from Latin *titulus* TITLE]

Titus ('taɪtəs) *n* **1** *New Testament* **a** a Greek disciple and helper of Saint Paul. Feast day: Jan 26 or Aug 25 **b** the book written to him (in full **The Epistle of Paul the Apostle to Titus**), containing advice on pastoral matters **2** full name *Titus Flavius Sabinus Vespasianus*. ?40–81 AD, Roman emperor (78–81 AD)

Tiu ('tiːuː) *n* (in Anglo-Saxon mythology) the god of war and the sky. Norse counterpart: **Tyr**

Tivoli ('tɪvəlɪ; *Italian* 'tiːvoli) *n* a town in central Italy, east of Rome: a summer resort in Roman times; contains the Renaissance Villa d'Este and the remains of Hadrian's Villa. Pop: 49 342 (2001). Ancient name: **Tibur**

Tizard ('tɪzaːd) *n* **Sir Henry (Thomas)**. 1885–1959, British chemist and scientific administrator, who specialized in the military application of science and backed the development of radar

tizzy ('tɪzɪ) *n, pl* **-zies** *informal* a state of confusion, anxiety, or excitement. Also called: **tizz, tiz-woz** ('tɪz,wɒz) [C19: of unknown origin]

Tjirebon ('tʃɪərə,bɒn) *n* a former spelling of **Cirebon**

T-junction *n* a road junction in which one road joins another at right angles but does not cross it

TKO *boxing abbreviation* technical knockout

Tl *the chemical symbol for* thallium

Tlaxcala (*Spanish* tlas'kala) *n* **1** a state of S central Mexico: the smallest Mexican state; formerly an Indian principality, the chief Indian ally of Cortés in the conquest of Mexico. Capital: Tlaxcala. Pop: 961 912 (2000 est). Area: 3914 sq km (1511 sq miles) **2** a city in E central Mexico, on the central plateau, capital of Tlaxcala state: the church of San Francisco (founded 1521 by Cortés) is the oldest in the Americas. Pop: 15 777 (2005)

Tlemcen (*French* tlemsɛn) *n* a city in NW Algeria: capital of an Arab kingdom from the 12th to the late 14th century. Pop: 177 000 (2005 est)

T-lymphocyte *n* a type of lymphocyte that matures in the thymus gland and has an important role in the immune response. There are several subclasses: **killer T-cells** are responsible for killing cells that are infected by a virus; **helper T-cells** induce other cells

(**B-lymphocytes**) to produce antibodies. Also called: T-cell

Tm *the chemical symbol for* thulium

TM *abbreviation* transcendental meditation

tmesis (təˈmiːsɪs, ˈmiːsɪs) *n* interpolation of a word or group of words between the parts of a compound word [c16: via Latin from Greek, literally: a cutting, from *temnein* to cut]

TN *abbreviation* Tennessee

TNT *n* 2,4,6-trinitrotoluene; a yellow solid: used chiefly as a high explosive and is also an intermediate in the manufacture of dyestuffs. Formula: $CH_3C_6H_2(NO_2)_3$

T-number *or* **T number** *n photog* a function of the f-number of a camera lens that takes into account the amount of light actually transmitted by the lens [from T(*otal Light Transmission) Number*]

to (tuː; *unstressed before a vowel* tʊ; *unstressed before a consonant* tə) *prep* **1** used to indicate the destination of the subject or object of an action: *he climbed to the top* **2** used to mark the indirect object of a verb in a sentence: *telling stories to children* **3** used to mark the infinitive of a verb: *he wanted to go* **4** as far as; until: *working from Monday to Friday* **5** used to indicate equality: *16 ounces to the pound* **6** against; upon; onto: *put your ear to the wall* **7** before the hour of: *five minutes to four* **8** accompanied by: *dancing to loud music* **9** as compared with, as against: *the score was eight to three* **10** used to indicate a resulting condition: *he tore her dress to shreds; they starved to death* ▷ *adv* **11** towards a fixed position, esp (of a door) closed [Old English *tō*; related to Old Frisian, Old Saxon *to*, Old High German *zuo*, Latin *do-* as in *dōnec* until]

toad (təʊd) *n* **1** any anuran amphibian of the class *Bufonidae*, such as *Bufo bufo* (**common toad**) of Europe. They are similar to frogs but are more terrestrial, having a drier warty skin **2** a loathsome person [Old English *tādige*, of unknown origin; see TADPOLE] > 'toadish *or* 'toad,like *adj*

toadeater (ˈtəʊdˌiːtə) *n* a rare word for toady (sense 1) [c17: originally a mountebank's assistant who would pretend to eat toads (believed to be poisonous), hence a servile flatterer, toady]

toadfish (ˈtəʊdˌfɪʃ) *n, pl* -fish *or* -fishes any spiny-finned bottom-dwelling marine fish of the family *Batrachoididae*, of tropical and temperate seas, having a flattened tapering body and a wide mouth

toadflax (ˈtəʊdˌflæks) *n* any of various scrophulariaceous plants of the genus *Linaria*, esp *L. vulgaris*, having narrow leaves and spurred two-lipped yellow-orange flowers. Also called: butter-and-eggs

toad-in-the-hole *n Brit & Austral* a dish made of sausages baked in a batter

toadstone (ˈtəʊdˌstəʊn) *n rare* an amygdaloidal basalt occurring in the limestone regions of Derbyshire [c18: perhaps from a supposed resemblance to a toad's spotted skin]

toadstool (ˈtəʊdˌstuːl) *n* (*not in technical use*) any basidiomycetous fungus with a capped spore-producing body that is not edible. See **mushroom** (sense 1a) [c14: from TOAD + STOOL]

toady (ˈtəʊdɪ) *n, pl* toadies **1** a person who flatters and ingratiates himself or herself in a servile way; sycophant ▷ *vb* toadies, toadying, toadied **2** to fawn on and flatter (someone) [c19: shortened from TOADEATER] > 'toadyish *adj* > 'toadyism *n*

Toamasina (tɔ̄umaˈsinə) *n* a port in E Madagascar, on the Indian Ocean: the country's chief commercial centre. Pop: 198 000 (2005 est). Former name (until 1979): Tamatave

to and fro *adj*, **to-and-fro** *adv* **1** back and forth **2** here and there > 'toing and 'froing *n*

toast¹ (təʊst) *n* **1** sliced bread browned by exposure to heat, usually under a grill, over a fire, or in a toaster **2** be *informal* to face certain destruction or defeat ▷ *vb* **3** (*tr*) to brown under a grill or over a fire: *to toast cheese* **4** to warm or be warmed in a similar manner: *to toast one's hands by the fire* [c14: from Old French *toster*, from Latin *tōstus* parched, baked from *torrēre* to dry with heat; see THIRST, TORRID]

toast² (təʊst) *n* **1** a tribute or proposal of health, success, etc, given to a person or thing by a company of people

and marked by raising glasses and drinking together **2** a person or thing honoured by such a tribute or proposal **3** (*esp formerly*) an attractive woman to whom such tributes are frequently made ▷ *vb* **4** (*tr*) to propose or drink a toast to (a person or thing) **5** (*intr*) to add vocal effects to a prerecorded track: a disc-jockey technique. See also **rap¹** (sense 6) [c17 (in the sense: a lady to whom the company is asked to drink): from TOAST¹, from the idea that the name of the lady would flavour the drink like a piece of spiced toast] > 'toaster *n*

toaster (ˈtəʊstə) *n* a device for toasting bread, usually electric, and often equipped with an automatic timer

toastmaster (ˈtəʊstˌmɑːstə) *n* a person who introduces after-dinner speakers, proposes or announces toasts, etc, at public or formal dinners > 'toast,mistress *fem n*

toasty¹ *or* **toastie** (ˈtəʊstɪ) *n, pl* toasties a toasted sandwich

toasty² (ˈtəʊstɪ) *adj* -tier, -tiest tasting or smelling like toast

Tob. *abbreviation* Tobit

tobacco (təˈbækəʊ) *n, pl* -cos *or* -coes **1** any of numerous solanaceous plants of the genus *Nicotiana*, having mildly narcotic properties, tapering hairy leaves, and tubular or funnel-shaped fragrant flowers. The species *N. tabacum* is cultivated as the chief source of commercial tobacco **2** the leaves of certain of these plants dried and prepared for snuff, chewing, or smoking [c16: from Spanish *tabaco*, perhaps from Taino: leaves rolled for smoking, assumed by the Spaniards to be the name of the plant] > to'baccoless *adj*

tobacco mosaic virus *n* the virus that causes mosaic disease in tobacco and related plants: its discovery in 1892 provided the first evidence of the existence of viruses. Abbreviation: TMV

tobacconist (təˈbækənɪst) *n chiefly Brit* a person or shop that sells tobacco, cigarettes, pipes, etc

Tobago (təˈbeɪgəʊ) *n* an island in the SE Caribbean, northeast of Trinidad: ceded to Britain in 1814; joined with Trinidad in 1888 as a British colony; part of the independent republic of Trinidad and Tobago. Pop: 54 084 (2000) > Tobagonian (ˌtəʊbəˈgəʊnɪən) *adj, n*

-to-be *adj* (*in combination*) about to be; future: *a mother-to-be; the bride-to-be*

Tobey (ˈtəʊbɪ) *n* Mark. 1890–1976, US painter. Influenced by Chinese calligraphy, he devised a style of improvisatory abstract painting called "white writing"

Tobit (ˈtəʊbɪt) *n Old Testament* **1** a pious Jew who was released from blindness through the help of the archangel Raphael **2** a book of the Apocrypha relating this story

toboggan (təˈbɒgən) *n* **1** a light wooden frame on runners used for sliding over snow and ice **2** a long narrow sledge made of a thin board curved upwards and backwards at the front ▷ *vb* -gans, -ganing, -ganed **3** (*intr*) to ride on a toboggan [c19: from Canadian French, from Algonquian; related to Abnaki *udābāgan*] > to'bogganer *or* to'bogganist *n*

Tobol (*Russian* taˈbɔl) *n* a river in central Asia, rising in N Kazakhstan and flowing northeast into Russia to join the Irtysh River. Length: about 1300 km (800 miles)

Tobolsk (*Russian* taˈbɔljsk) *n* a town in central Russia, at the confluence of the Irtysh and Tobol Rivers: the chief centre for the early Russian colonization of Siberia. Pop: 100 000 (2005 est)

Tobruk (təˈbruk, təʊ-) *n* a small port in NE Libya, in E Cyrenaica on the Mediterranean coast road: scene of severe fighting in World War II: taken from the Italians by the British in Jan 1941, from the British by the Germans in June 1942, and finally taken by the British in Nov 1942

toby (ˈtəʊbɪ) *n, pl* -bies a water stopcock at the boundary of a street and house section

toby jug *n* a beer mug or jug typically in the form of a stout seated man wearing a three-cornered hat and smoking a pipe. Also called: toby [c19: from the familiar form of the Christian name *Tobias*]

TOC *or* **toc** (tɒk) *n acronym for* train operating company

Tocantins (*Portuguese* tokãˈtĩs) *n* **1** a state of N Brazil, created from the northern part of Goiás state in 1988.

t

Capital: Palmas. Pop: 1 207 014 (2002). Area: 278 421 sq km (107 499 sq miles) **2** a river in E Brazil, rising in S central Goiás state and flowing generally north to the Pará River. Length: about 2700 km (1700 miles)

toccata (tə'kɑːtə) *n* a rapid keyboard composition for organ, harpsichord, etc, dating from the baroque period, usually in a rhythmically free style [c18: from Italian, literally: touched, from *toccare* to play (an instrument), TOUCH]

Toc H ('tɒk 'eɪtʃ) *n* a society formed in England after World War I to fight loneliness and hate and to encourage Christian comradeship [c20: from the obsolete telegraphic code for T.H., initials of *Talbot House*, Poperinge, Belgium, the original headquarters of the society]

Tocharian *or* **Tokharian** (tɒ'kɑːrɪən) *n* **1** a member of an Asian people with a complex material culture, sometimes thought to be of European origin, who lived in the Tarim Basin until overcome by the Uighurs around 800 AD **2** the language of this people, known from records in a N Indian script of the 7th and 8th centuries AD. It belongs to the Indo-European family, is regarded as forming an independent branch, and shows closer affinities with the W or European group than with the E or Indo-Iranian group. The language is recorded in two dialects, known as **Tocharian A** and **Tocharian B** [c20: ultimately from Greek *Tokharoi*, name of uncertain origin]

tocology *or* **tokology** (tɒ'kɒlədʒɪ) *n* the branch of medicine concerned with childbirth; obstetrics [c19: from Greek *tokos* childbirth, from *tiktein* to bear]

tocopherol (tɒ'kɒfə,rɒl) *n* any of a group of fat-soluble alcohols that occur in wheat-germ oil, watercress, lettuce, egg yolk, etc. They are thought to be necessary for healthy human reproduction. Also called: vitamin E [c20: from *toco-*, from Greek *tokos* offspring (see TOCOLOGY) + *-pher-*, from *pherein* to bear + -OL¹]

Tocqueville ('təʊkvɪl, 'tɒk-; *French* tɔkvil) *n* **Alexis Charles Henri Maurice Clérel de** (alɛksi ʃarl ɑ̃ri mɔris klerɛl də). 1805–59, French politician and political writer. His chief works are *De la Démocratie en Amérique* (1835–40) and *L'Ancien régime et la révolution* (1856)

tocsin ('tɒksɪn) *n* **1** an alarm or warning signal, esp one sounded on a bell **2** an alarm bell [c16: from French, from Old French *toquassen*, from Old Provençal *tocasenh*, from *tocar* to TOUCH + *senh* bell, from Latin *signum*]

tod (tɒd) *n* on one's tod *Brit slang* on one's own [c19: rhyming slang *Tod Sloan/alone*, after Tod Sloan, a jockey]

today (tə'deɪ) *n* **1** this day, as distinct from yesterday or tomorrow **2** the present age: *children of today* ▷ *adv* **3** during or on this day **4** nowadays [Old English *tō dæge*, literally: on this day, from TO + *dæge*, dative of *dæg* DAY]

Todd (tɒd) *n* Baron **Alexander Robertus**. 1907–97, Scottish chemist, noted for his research into the structure of nucleic acids: Nobel prize for chemistry 1957

toddle ('tɒdəl) *vb* (*intr*) **1** to walk with short unsteady steps, as a child does when learning to walk **2** (foll by *off*) *jocular* to depart **3** (foll by *round, over*, etc) *jocular* to stroll; amble ▷ *n* **4** the act or an instance of toddling [C16 (Scottish and northern English): of obscure origin]

toddler ('tɒdlə) *n* a young child, usually one between the ages of one and two and a half

toddy ('tɒdɪ) *n, pl* -dies **1** a drink made from spirits, esp whisky, with hot water, sugar, and usually lemon juice **2** the sap of various palm trees (**toddy** or **wine palms**), used as a beverage [c17: from Hindi *tārī* juice of the palmyra palm, from *tār* palmyra palm, from Sanskrit *tāra*, probably of Dravidian origin]

to-do (tə'duː) *n, pl* -dos a commotion, fuss, or quarrel

toe (təʊ) *n* **1** any one of the digits of the foot **2** the corresponding part in other vertebrates **3** the part of a shoe, sock, etc, covering the toe **4** anything resembling a toe in shape or position **5** on one's toes alert **6** tread on someone's toes to offend or insult a person, esp by trespassing on his or her field of responsibility ▷ *vb* toes, toeing, toed **7** (*tr*) to touch, kick, or mark with the toe **8** (*tr*) to drive (a nail, spike, etc) obliquely **9** (*intr*) to walk with the toes pointing in a specified direction: *to toe inwards* **10** toe the line to conform to expected

standards, attitudes, etc [Old English *tā*; related to Old Frisian *tāne*, Old Norse *tā*, Old High German *zēha*, Latin *digitus* finger]

toe and heel *n* a technique used by racing drivers while changing gear on sharp bends, in which the brake is operated by the toe (or heel) of the right foot while the heel (or toe) simultaneously operates the accelerator

toecap ('təʊ,kæp) *n* a reinforced covering for the toe of a boot or shoe

toed (təʊd) *adj* **1** having a part resembling a toe **2** (of a vertical or oblique member of a timber frame) fixed by nails driven in at the foot **3** (*in combination*) having a toe or toes as specified: *five-toed*

toehold ('təʊ,həʊld) *n* **1** a small foothold to facilitate climbing **2** any means of gaining access, support, etc **3** a wrestling hold in which the opponent's toe is held and his leg twisted against the joints

toe-in *n* a slight forward convergence given to the wheels of motor vehicles to improve steering and equalize tyre wear

toenail ('təʊ,neɪl) *n* **1** a thin horny translucent plate covering part of the dorsal surface of the end joint of each toe **2** *carpentry* a nail driven obliquely, as in joining one beam at right angles to another ▷ *vb* **3** (*tr*) *carpentry* to join (beams) by driving nails obliquely

toerag ('təʊ,ræg) *n Brit slang* a contemptible or despicable person [c20: originally, a beggar, tramp: from the pieces of rag they wrapped round their feet]

toe-to-toe *informal* ▷ *adv* **1** in one-to-one combat or in direct competition: *there aren't many fighters willing to go toe-to-toe with him* ▷ *adj* **2** (of battles, confrontations, or contests) involving two people or groups fighting with or competing against each other: *a toe-to-toe battle* ▷ *n* **3** a fight, confrontation, or contest between two people or groups

toey ('təʊɪ) *adj Austral slang* **1** (of a person) nervous or anxious **2** (of a person) eager for sexual activity; aroused **3** *rare* (of a horse) eager to race **4** toey as a Roman sandal very anxious

toff (tɒf) *n Brit slang* a rich, well-dressed, or upper-class person, esp a man [c19: perhaps variant of TUFT, nickname for a titled student at Oxford University, wearing a cap with a gold tassel]

toffee *or* **toffy** ('tɒfɪ) *n, pl* -fees *or* -fies **1** a sweet made from sugar or treacle boiled with butter, nuts, etc **2** for toffee (preceded by *can't*) *informal* to be incompetent at a specified activity: *he can't sing for toffee* [c19: variant of earlier TAFFY]

toffee-apple *n* an apple fixed on a stick and coated with a thin layer of toffee

toffee-nosed *adj slang, chiefly Brit* pretentious or supercilious; used esp of snobbish people [c20: perhaps coined as a pun on *toffy* stylish, grand: see TOFF]

toft (tɒft) *n Brit history* **1** an entire holding, consisting of a homestead and the attached arable land [Old English, from Old Norse *topt*]

tofu ('təʊfuː) *n* unfermented soya-bean curd, a food with a soft cheeselike consistency made from soya-bean milk [from Japanese]

tog¹ (tɒg) *informal* ▷ *vb* togs, togging, togged **1** (often foll by *up* or *out*) to dress oneself, esp in smart clothes ▷ *n* **2** See togs [c18: probably short for obsolete cant *togemans* coat, from Latin *toga* TOGA + *-mans*, of uncertain origin]

tog² (tɒg) *n* **a** a unit of thermal resistance used to measure the power of insulation of a fabric, garment, quilt, etc. The tog-value of an article is equal to ten times the temperature difference between its two faces, in degrees Celsius, when the flow of heat across it is equal to one watt per m² **b** (*as modifier*): *tog-rating* [c20: arbitrary coinage from TOG¹ (noun)]

toga ('təʊgə) *n* **1** a garment worn by citizens of ancient Rome, consisting of a piece of cloth draped around the body **2** the official vestment of certain offices [c16: from Latin, related to *tegere* to cover]

together (tə'gɛðə) *adv* **1** with cooperation and interchange between constituent elements, members, etc: *we worked together* **2** in or into contact or union with each other: *to stick papers together* **3** in or into one place or assembly; with each other: *the people are gathered together*

4 at the same time **5** considered collectively or jointly: *all our wages put together couldn't buy that car* **6** continuously: *working for eight hours together* **7** closely, cohesively, or compactly united or held: *water will hold the dough together* **8** mutually or reciprocally: *to multiply 7 and 8 together* **9** *informal* organized: *to get things together* **10** together with in addition to ▷ *adj* **11** *slang* self-possessed and well-organized; mentally and emotionally stable [Old English *tōgædre*; related to Old Frisian *togadera*, Middle High German *gater*; see GATHER]

● USAGE See at plus

togetherness (təˈɡɛðənɪs) *n* a feeling of closeness or affection from being united with other people

toggery (ˈtɒɡərɪ) *n informal* clothes; togs

toggle (ˈtɒɡ²l) *n* **1** a wooden peg or metal rod fixed crosswise through an eye at the end of a rope, chain, or cable, for fastening temporarily by insertion through an eye in another rope, chain, etc **2** a wooden or plastic bar-shaped button inserted through a loop for fastening **3** *machinery* a toggle joint or a device having such a joint ▷ *vb* **4** (*tr*) to supply or fasten with a toggle or toggles [c18: of unknown origin]

toggle joint *n* a device consisting of two arms pivoted at a common joint and at their outer ends and used to apply pressure by straightening the angle between the two arms

toggle switch *n* **1** an electric switch having a projecting lever that is manipulated in a particular way to open or close a circuit **2** a computer device that is used to turn a feature on or off

Toghril Beg (ˈtɒɡrɪl ˈbɛɡ) *n* ?990–1063 AD, Sultan of Turkey (1055–63), who founded the Seljuq dynasty and conquered Baghdad (1055)

Togliatti[1] (ˌtɒlɪˈætɪ) *n* a city in W central Russia, on the Volga River: automobile industry: renamed in honour of Palmiro Togliatti, an Italian communist. Pop: 718 000 (2005 est). Former name (until 1964): **Stavropol**

Togliatti[2] (*Italian* toˈati) *n* **Palmiro** (palˈmiro). 1893–1964, Italian politician; leader of the Italian Communist Party (1926–64). After Mussolini's fall he became a minister (1944) and vice premier (1945)

Togo[1] (ˈtəʊɡəʊ) *n* a republic in West Africa, on the Gulf of Guinea: became French Togoland (a League of Nations mandate) after the division of German Togoland in 1922; independent since 1960. Official language: French. Religion: animist majority. Currency: franc. Capital: Lomé. Pop: 5 017 000 (2004 est). Area: 56 700 sq km (20 900 sq miles) > **Togolese** (ˌtəʊɡəˈliːz) *adj, n*

Togo[2] (ˈtəʊɡəʊ) *n* Marquis **Heihachiro** (ˌheɪhɑːˈtʃiːrəʊ). 1847–1934, Japanese admiral, who commanded the Japanese fleet in the war with Russia (1904–05)

Togoland (ˈtəʊɡəʊˌlænd) *n* a former German protectorate in West Africa on the Gulf of Guinea: divided in 1922 into the League of Nations mandates of British Togoland (west) and French Togoland (east); the former joined Ghana in 1957; the latter became independent as Togo in 1960 > **Togolander** *n*

togs (tɒɡz) *pl n informal* **1** clothes **2** *Austral, NZ & Irish* a swimming costume [from TOG[1]]

toheroa (ˌtəʊəˈrəʊə) *n* a bivalve mollusc, *Amphidesma* (or *Semele*) *ventricosum*, of New Zealand [from Māori]

tohunga (ˈtɒhʊŋə, tɒˈhʊŋə) *n* NZ a Māori priest, the repository of traditional lore

toil[1] (tɔɪl) *n* **1** hard or exhausting work ▷ *vb* **2** (*intr*) to labour **3** (*intr*) to progress with slow painful movements [c13: from Anglo-French *toiler* to struggle, from Old French *toeillier* to confuse, from Latin *tudiculāre* to stir, from *tudicula* machine for bruising olives, from *tudes* a hammer, from *tundere* to beat] > **toiler** *n*

toil[2] (tɔɪl) *n* **1** (*often plural*) a net or snare **2** *archaic* a trap for wild beasts [c16: from Old French *toile*, from Latin *tēla* loom]

toile (twɑːl) *n* **1** a transparent linen or cotton fabric **2** a garment of exclusive design made up in cheap cloth so that alterations and experiments can be made [c19: from French, from Latin *tēla* a loom]

toilet (ˈtɔɪlɪt) *n* **1** another word for **lavatory 2** *old-fashioned* the act of dressing and preparing oneself **3** *old-fashioned* a dressing table or the articles used when making one's

toilet **4** *rare* costume **5** the cleansing of a wound, etc, after an operation or childbirth [c16: from French *toilette* dress, from TOILE]

toilet paper or **toilet tissue** *n* thin absorbent paper, often wound in a roll round a cardboard cylinder (**toilet roll**), used for cleaning oneself after defecation or urination

toiletry (ˈtɔɪlɪtrɪ) *n, pl* -ries an object or cosmetic used in making up, dressing, etc

toilet set *n* a matching set consisting of a hairbrush, comb, mirror, and clothes brush

toilette (twɑːˈlɛt; *French* twalɛt) *n usually literary* another word for **toilet** (sense 2) [c16: from French; see TOILET]

toilet water *n* a form of liquid perfume lighter than cologne

toilsome (ˈtɔɪlsəm) or **toilful** *adj* laborious > ˈ**toilsomely** or ˈ**toilfully** *adv* > ˈ**toilsomeness** or ˈ**toilfulness** *n*

toitoi (ˈtɔɪtɔɪ) *n, pl* -tois or -toes any of various tall grasses of the genus *Cortaderia* of New Zealand, with feathery fronds [Māori]

Tojo (ˈtəʊdʒəʊ) *n* **Hideki** (ˈhiːdɛˌkiː). 1885–1948, Japanese soldier and statesman; minister of war (1940–41) and premier (1941–44); hanged as a war criminal

tokamak (ˈtɒkəˌmæk) *n physics* a toroidal reactor used in thermonuclear experiments, in which a strong helical magnetic field keeps the plasma from contacting the external walls. The magnetic field is produced partly by current-carrying coils and partly by a large inductively driven current through the plasma [c20: from Russian *to(roidál'naya) kám(era s) ak(siál'nym magnitnym pólem)*, toroidal chamber with magnetic field]

Tokay (təʊˈkeɪ) *n* **1** a fine sweet wine made near Tokaj, Hungary **2** a variety of large sweet grape used to make this wine **3** a similar wine made elsewhere

Tokelau (ˈtəʊkəˌlaʊ) or **Tokelau Islands** *pl n* an island group in the South Pacific composed of three atolls, Nukunono, Atafu, and Fakaofo, dependent territory of New Zealand. Pop: 2000 (2003 est). Area: about 11 sq km (4 sq miles)

token (ˈtəʊkən) *n* **1** an indication, warning, or sign of something **2** a symbol or visible representation of something **3** something that indicates authority, proof, or authenticity **4** a metal or plastic disc, such as a substitute for currency for use in slot machines **5** a memento **6** a gift voucher that can be used as payment for goods of a specified value **7** (*modifier*) as a matter of form only; nominal: *a token increase in salary* ▷ *vb* **8** (*tr*) to act or serve as a warning or symbol of; betoken [Old English *tācen*; related to Old Frisian *tēken*, Old Saxon *tēkan*, Old High German *zeihhan*, Old Norse *teikn*; see TEACH]

tokenism (ˈtəʊkəˌnɪzəm) *n* the practice of making only a token effort or doing no more than the minimum, esp in order to comply with a law > ˌ**token**ˈ**istic** *adj*

token money *n* coins of the regular issue having greater face value than the value of their metal content

token strike *n* a brief strike intended to convey strength of feeling on a disputed issue

token vote *n* a Parliamentary vote of money in which the amount quoted to aid discussion is not intended to be binding

tokoloshe (ˌtɒkɒˈlɒʃ, -ˈlɒʃɪ) or **tokoloshi** *n* (in Bantu folklore) a malevolent mythical manlike animal of short stature. Also called: **tikoloshe** [from Xhosa *uthikoloshe*]

toktokkie (tɒkˈtɒkɪ) *n* a large South African beetle, *Dichtha cubica* [from Afrikaans, from Dutch *tokken* to tap]

Tokugawa Iyeyasu (ˌtəʊkuːˈɡɑːwə ˌiːjeɪˈjɑːsuː) *n* See **Iyeyasu**

Tokyo (ˈtəʊkjəʊ, -kɪˌəʊ) *n* the capital of Japan, a port on SE Honshu on **Tokyo Bay** (an inlet of the Pacific): part of the largest conurbation in the world (the Tokyo-Yokohama metropolitan area) of over 35 million people; major industrial centre and the chief cultural centre of Japan. Pop (city proper): 8 025 538 (2002 est)

tolbooth (ˈtəʊlˌbuːθ, -ˌbuːð, ˈtɒl-) *n chiefly Scot* a town hall **2** a variant spelling of **tollbooth**

tolbutamide (tɒlˈbjuːtəˌmaɪd) *n* a synthetic crystalline compound administered orally in the treatment of diabetes to lower blood glucose concentrations.

Formula: $C_{12}H_{18}N_2O_3S$ [C20: from TOL(UYL) + BUT(YRIC ACID) + AMIDE]

told (təʊld) *vb* **1** the past tense and past participle of **tell**[1] ▷ *adj* **2** See **all told**

tole (təʊl) *n* enamelled or lacquered metal ware, usually gilded, popular in the 18th century [from French *tôle* sheet metal, from French (dialect): table, from Latin *tabula* table]

Toledo *n* **1** (tɒˈleɪdəʊ; *Spanish* toˈleðo) a city in central Spain, on the River Tagus: capital of Visigothic Spain, and of Castile from 1087 to 1560; famous for steel and swords since the first century. Pop: 72 549 (2003 est) **2** (təˈliːdəʊ) an inland port in NW Ohio, on Lake Erie: one of the largest coal-shipping ports in the world; transportation and industrial centre; university (1872). Pop: 308 973 (2003 est) **3** a fine-tapered sword or sword blade

tolerable (ˈtɒlərəbəl) *adj* **1** able to be tolerated; endurable **2** permissible **3** *informal* fairly good > **'tolerableness** or **ˌtolera'bility** *n* > **'tolerably** *adv*

tolerance (ˈtɒlərəns) *n* **1** the state or quality of being tolerant **2** capacity to endure something, esp pain or hardship **3** the permitted variation in some measurement or other characteristic of an object or workpiece **4** *physiol* the capacity of an organism to endure the effects of a poison or other substance, esp after it has been taken over a prolonged period

tolerance zone *n* an designated area where prostitutes can work without being arrested

tolerant (ˈtɒlərənt) *adj* **1** able to tolerate the beliefs, actions, opinions, etc, of others **2** permissive **3** able to withstand extremes, as of heat and cold **4** *med* (of a patient) exhibiting tolerance to a drug > **'tolerantly** *adv*

tolerate (ˈtɒləˌreɪt) *vb* (*tr*) **1** to treat with indulgence, liberality, or forbearance **2** to permit **3** to be able to bear; put up with **4** *med* to have tolerance for (a drug, poison, etc) [c16: from Latin *tolerāre* sustain; related to THOLE[2]]

toleration (ˌtɒləˈreɪʃən) *n* **1** the act or practice of tolerating **2** freedom to hold religious opinions that differ from the established or prescribed religion of a country > **ˌtoler'ationist** *n*

Tolima (*Spanish* toˈlima) *n* a volcano in W Colombia, in the Andes. Height: 5215 m (17 110 ft)

Tolkien (ˈtɒlkiːn) *n* **J(ohn) R(onald) R(euel)**. 1892–1973, British philologist and writer, born in South Africa. He is best known for *The Hobbit* (1937), the trilogy *The Lord of the Rings* (1954–55), and the posthumously published *The Silmarillion* (1977)

Tolkienesque (ˌtɒlkiːnˈɛsk) *adj* referring to or reminiscent of the work of the British novelist and critic J.R.R. Tolkien (1892–1973), who is best known for his fantasy novels *The Hobbit* and *The Lord of the Rings*

toll[1] (təʊl) *vb* **1** to ring or cause to ring slowly and recurrently **2** (*tr*) to summon, warn, or announce by tolling **3** *US & Canadian* to decoy (game, esp ducks) ▷ *n* **4** the act or sound of tolling [c15: perhaps related to Old English *-tyllan*, as in *fortyllan* to attract]

toll[2] (təʊl, tɒl) *n* **1 a** an amount of money levied, esp for the use of certain roads, bridges, etc, to cover the cost of maintenance **b** (*as modifier*): *toll road; toll bridge* **2** loss or damage incurred through an accident, disaster, etc: *the war took its toll of the inhabitants* **3** Also called: **tollage** (formerly) the right to levy a toll [Old English *toln*; related to Old Frisian *tolene*, Old High German *zol* toll, from Late Latin *telōnium* customs house, from Greek *telónion*, ultimately from *telos* tax]

tollbooth or **tolbooth** (ˈtəʊlˌbuːθ, -ˌbuːð, ˈtɒl-) *n* a booth or kiosk at which a toll is collected

Toller (*German* ˈtɔlər) *n* **Ernst** (ɛrnst). 1893–1939, German dramatist and revolutionary, noted particularly for his expressionist plays, esp *Masse Mensch* (1921)

tollgate (ˈtəʊlˌgeɪt, ˈtɒl-) *n* a gate across a toll road or bridge at which travellers must stop and pay

tollhouse (ˈtəʊlˌhaʊs, ˈtɒl-) *n* a small house at a tollgate occupied by a toll collector

tolly or **tollie** (ˈtɒlɪ) *n, pl* **-lies** *South African* a castrated calf [c19: from Xhosa *ithole* calf on which the horns have begun to appear]

Tolstoy (ˈtɒlstɔɪ; *Russian* talˈstɔj) *n* **Leo**, Russian name

Count Lev Nikolayevich Tolstoy. 1828–1910, Russian novelist, short-story writer, and philosopher; author of the two monumental novels *War and Peace* (1865–69) and *Anna Karenina* (1875–77). Following a spiritual crisis in 1879, he adopted a form of Christianity based on a doctrine of nonresistance to evil

Toltec (ˈtɒltɛk) *n, pl* **-tecs** or **-tec 1** a member of a Central American Indian people who dominated the valley of Mexico from their capital Tula from about 950 to 1160 AD, when the valley was overrun by the Aztecs ▷ *adj* **2** Also: **Toltecan** of or relating to this people [c19: from Spanish *tolteca*, of American Indian origin]

tolu (tɒˈluː) *n* an aromatic balsam obtained from a South American tree, *Myroxylon balsamum* [c17: after *Santiago de Tolu*, Colombia, from which it was exported]

Toluca (*Spanish* toˈluka) *n* **1** a city in S central Mexico, capital of Mexico state, at an altitude of 2640 m (8660 ft). Pop: 1 987 000 (2005 est) **2 Nevado de Toluca** (neˈβaðo de) a volcano in central Mexico, in Mexico state near Toluca: crater partly filled by a lake. Height: 4577 m (15 017 ft)

toluene (ˈtɒljʊˌiːn) *n* a colourless volatile flammable liquid with an odour resembling that of benzene, obtained from petroleum and coal tar and used as a solvent and in the manufacture of many organic chemicals. Formula: $C_6H_5CH_3$ [c19: from TOLU + -ENE, since it was previously obtained from tolu]

toluic acid (tɒˈluːɪk) *n* a white crystalline derivative of toluene existing in three isomeric forms; methylbenzoic acid. The *ortho*- and *para*- isomers are used in synthetic resins and the *meta*- isomer is used as an insect repellent. Formula: $C_6H_4CH_3COOH$ [c19: from TOLU(ENE) + -IC]

toluidine (tɒˈljuːɪˌdiːn) *n* an amine derived from toluene existing in three isomeric forms; aminotoluene. The *ortho*- and *meta*- isomers are liquids and the *para*- isomer is a crystalline solid. All three are used in making dyes. Formula: $C_6H_4CH_3NH_2$ [c19: from TOLU(ENE) + -IDE + -INE[2]]

toluyl (ˈtɒljʊɪl) *n* (*modifier*) of, consisting of, or containing any of three isomeric groups $CH_3C_6H_4CO$-, derived from a toluic acid by removal of the hydroxyl group: *toluyl group or radical* [c19: from TOLU(ENE) + -YL]

tom (tɒm) *n* **a** the male of various animals, esp the cat **b** (*as modifier*): *a tom turkey* **c** (*in combination*): *a tomcat* [c16: special use of the shortened form of *Thomas*, applied to any male, often implying a common or ordinary type of person, etc]

tomahawk (ˈtɒməˌhɔːk) *n* a fighting axe, with a stone or later an iron head, used by the North American Indians [c17: from Virginia Algonquian *tamahaac*]

tomato (təˈmɑːtəʊ) *n, pl* **-toes 1** a solanaceous plant, *Lycopersicon* (or *Lycopersicum*) *esculentum*, of South America, widely cultivated for its red fleshy many-seeded edible fruits **2** the fruit of this plant, which has slightly acid-tasting flesh and is eaten in salads, as a vegetable, etc [c17 *tomate*, from Spanish, from Nahuatl *tomatl*]

tomb (tuːm) *n* **1** a place, esp a vault beneath the ground, for the burial of a corpse **2** a stone or other monument to the dead **3 the tomb** a poetic term for **death** [c13: from Old French *tombe*, from Late Latin *tumba* burial mound, from Greek *tumbos*; related to Latin *tumēre* to swell, Middle Irish *tomm* hill]

tombac (ˈtɒmbæk) or **tambac** (ˈtæmbæk) *n* any of various brittle alloys containing copper and zinc and sometimes tin and arsenic: used for making cheap jewellery, etc [c17: from French, from Dutch *tombak*, from Malay *tambâga* copper, apparently from Sanskrit *tāmraka*, from *tāmra* dark coppery red]

Tombaugh (ˈtɒmbəʊ) *n* **Clyde William**. 1906–97, US astronomer, who discovered (1930) the dwarf planet Pluto

tombola (tɒmˈbəʊlə) *n Brit* a type of lottery, esp at a fête, in which tickets are drawn from a revolving drum [c19: from Italian, from *tombolare* to somersault; see TUMBLE]

Tombouctou (tɔ̄buktu) *n* the French name for **Timbuktu**

tomboy (ˈtɒmˌbɔɪ) *n* a girl who acts or dresses in a

boyish way, liking rough outdoor activities
> 'tom,boyish adj > 'tom,boyishly adv

tombstone ('tu:m,stəʊn) n another word for **gravestone**

Tom Collins n a long drink consisting of gin, lime or lemon juice, sugar or syrup, and soda water

Tom, Dick, and Harry or **Tom, Dick, or Harry** n an ordinary, undistinguished, or common person (esp in the phrases **every Tom, Dick, and Harry; any Tom, Dick, or Harry**)

tome (təʊm) n **1** a large weighty book **2** one of the several volumes of a work [c16: from French, from Latin *tomus* section of larger work, from Greek *tomos* a slice, from *temnein* to cut; related to Latin *tondēre* to shear]

-tome n combining form indicating an instrument for cutting: *osteotome* [from Greek *tomē* a cutting, *tomos* a slice, from *temnein* to cut]

tomentum (tə'mɛntəm) n, pl **-ta** (-tə) **1** a feltlike covering of downy hairs on leaves and other plant parts **2** a network of minute blood vessels occurring in the human brain between the pia mater and cerebral cortex [c17: New Latin, from Latin: stuffing for cushions; related to Latin *tumēre* to swell]

tomfool (,tɒm'fu:l) n **a** a fool **b** (as modifier): *tomfool ideas* [c14: from TOM[1] + FOOL[1]] > ,tom'foolishness n

tomfoolery (,tɒm'fu:lərɪ) n, pl **-eries 1** foolish behaviour **2** utter nonsense; rubbish

tommy ('tɒmɪ) n, pl **-mies** (often capital) Brit informal a private in the British Army [c19: originally *Thomas Atkins*, a name representing a typical private in specimen forms; compare TOM[1]]

Tommy gun n an informal name for **Thompson sub-machine-gun**

tommyrot ('tɒmɪ,rɒt) n utter nonsense; tomfoolery

tomography (tə'mɒgrəfɪ) n any of a number of techniques used to obtain an X-ray photograph of a selected plane section of the human body or some other solid object [c20: from Greek *tomē* a cutting + -GRAPHY]

tomorrow (tə'mɒrəʊ) n **1** the day after today **2** the future ▷ adv **3** on the day after today **4** at some time in the future [Old English tō *morgenne*, from TO[1] (at, on) + *morgenne*, dative of *morgen* MORNING; see MORROW]

Tomsk (Russian tɒmsk) n a city in central Russia: formerly an important gold-mining town and administrative centre for a large area of Siberia; university (1888); engineering industries. Pop: 486 000 (2005 est)

Tom Thumb n **1 General**, stage name of *Charles Stratton*. 1838–83, US midget, exhibited in P. T. Barnum's circus **2** a dwarf; midget [after *Tom Thumb*, the tiny hero of several English folk tales]

tomtit ('tɒm,tɪt) n Brit any of various tits, esp the bluetit

tom-tom n a drum associated either with the American Indians or with Eastern cultures, usually beaten with the hands as a signalling instrument [c17: from Hindi *tamtam*, of imitative origin]

-tomy n combining form indicating a surgical cutting of a specified part or tissue: *lobotomy* [from Greek *-tomia*; see -TOME]

ton[1] (tʌn) n **1** Also called: **long ton** Brit a unit of weight equal to 2240 pounds or 1016.046909 kilograms **2** Also called: **short ton, net ton** US a unit of weight equal to 2000 pounds or 907.184 kilograms **3** Also called: **metric ton, tonne** a unit of weight equal to 1000 kilograms **4** Also called: **freight ton** a unit of volume or weight used for charging or measuring freight in shipping. It depends on the type of material being shipped but is often taken as 40 cubic feet, 1 cubic metre, or 1000 kilograms **5** Also called: **measurement ton, shipping ton** a unit of volume used in shipping freight, equal to 40 cubic feet, irrespective of the commodity shipped **6** Also called: **register ton** a unit of internal capacity of ships equal to 100 cubic feet [c14: variant of TUN]

ton[2] (tʌn) n slang, chiefly Brit a score or achievement of a hundred, esp a hundred miles per hour, as on a motorcycle [c20: special use of TON[1] applied to quantities of one hundred]

tonal ('təʊnəl) adj **1** of or relating to tone **2** of, relating to, or utilizing the diatonic system; having an established key **3** (of an answer in a fugue) not having the same

melodic intervals as the subject, so as to remain in the original key > 'tonally adv

tonality (təʊ'nælɪtɪ) n, pl **-ties 1** music **a** the actual or implied presence of a musical key in a composition **b** the system of major and minor keys prevalent in Western music since the decline of modes **2** the overall scheme of colours and tones in a painting

Tonbridge ('tʌn,brɪdʒ) n a market town in SE England, in SW Kent on the River Medway. Pop: 35 833 (2001)

tondo ('tɒndəʊ) n, pl **-di** (-di:) a circular easel painting or relief carving [c19: from Italian: a circle, shortened from *rotondo* round]

tone (təʊn) n **1** sound with reference to quality, pitch, or volume **2** short for **tone colour 3** US & Canadian another word for **note** (sense 10) **4** an interval of a major second; whole tone **5** Also called: **Gregorian tone** any of several plainsong melodies or other chants used in the singing of psalms **6** linguistics any of the pitch levels or pitch contours at which a syllable may be pronounced, such as high tone, falling tone, etc **7** the quality or character of a sound: *a nervous tone of voice* **8** general aspect, quality, or style: *I didn't like the tone of his speech* **9** high quality or style: *to lower the tone of a place* **10** the quality of a given colour, as modified by mixture with white or black; shade; tint: *a tone of red* **11** physiol **a** the normal tension of a muscle at rest **b** the natural firmness of the tissues and normal functioning of bodily organs in health **12** the overall effect of the colour values and gradations of light and dark in a picture **13** photog a colour or shade of colour, including black or grey, of a particular area on a negative or positive that can be distinguished from surrounding lighter or darker areas ▷ vb **14** (intr; often foll by *with*) to be of a matching or similar tone (to) **15** (tr) to give a tone to or correct the tone of **16** (tr) photog (tr) to soften or change the colour of the tones of (a photographic image) by chemical means **17** an archaic word for **intone** ▷ See also **tone down, tone up** [c14: from Latin *tonus*, from Greek *tonos* tension, tone, from *teinein* to stretch] > 'toneless adj > 'tonelessly adv

Tone (təʊn) n **(Theobald)** Wolfe. 1763–98, Irish nationalist, who founded (1791) the Society of United Irishmen and led (1798) French military forces to Ireland. He was captured and sentenced to death but committed suicide

tone colour n the quality of a musical sound that is conditioned or distinguished by the upper partials or overtones present in it

tone-deaf adj unable to distinguish subtle differences in musical pitch > **tone deafness** n

tone down vb (adverb) to moderate or become moderated in tone: *to tone down an argument; to tone down a bright colour*

tone language n a language, such as Chinese or certain African languages, in which differences in tone may make differences in meaning

toneme ('təʊni:m) n linguistics a phoneme that is distinguished from another phoneme only by its tone [c20: from TONE + -EME] > to'nemic adj

tone poem n another term for **symphonic poem**

toner ('təʊnə) n **1** a person or thing that tones or produces tones, esp a concentrated pure organic pigment **2** a cosmetic preparation that is applied to produce a required effect, such as one that softens or alters hair colour or one that reduces the oiliness of the skin **3** photog a chemical solution that softens or alters the colour of the tones of a photographic image **4** a powdered chemical used in photocopying machines and laser printers, which is transferred onto paper to form the printed image

tone row or **tone series** n music a group of notes having a characteristic pattern or order that forms the basis of the musical material in a serial composition, esp one consisting of the twelve notes of the chromatic scale

tone up vb (adverb) to make or become more vigorous, healthy, etc

tong (tɒŋ) n (formerly) a Chinese secret society or association, esp one popularly assumed to engage in criminal activities [c20: from Chinese (Cantonese) *t'ong* meeting place]

tonga ('tɒŋgə) n a light two-wheeled vehicle used in

t

rural areas of India [C19: from Hindi *tāngā*]

Tonga ('tɒŋə, 'tɒŋɡə) *n* a kingdom occupying an archipelago of more than 150 volcanic and coral islands in the SW Pacific, east of Fiji: inhabited by Polynesians; became a British protectorate in 1900 and gained independence in 1970; a member of the Commonwealth. Official languages: Tongan and English. Religion: Christian majority. Currency: pa'anga. Capital: Nuku'alofa. Pop: 104 000 (2004 est). Area: 750 sq km (290 sq miles). Also called: **Friendly Islands** > '**Tongan** *adj, n*

tongs (tɒŋz) *pl n* a tool for grasping or lifting, consisting of a hinged, sprung, or pivoted pair of arms or levers, joined at one end. Also called: **pair of tongs** [plural of Old English *tange*; related to Old Saxon *tanga*, Old High German *zanga*, Old Norse *tong*]

tongue (tʌŋ) *n* 1 a movable mass of muscular tissue attached to the floor of the mouth in most vertebrates. It is the organ of taste and aids the mastication and swallowing of food. In man it plays an important part in the articulation of speech sounds. Related adjs: **glottic**, **lingual** 2 an analogous organ in invertebrates 3 the tongue of certain animals used as food 4 a language, dialect, or idiom: *the English tongue* 5 the ability to speak: *to lose one's tongue* 6 a manner of speaking: *a glib tongue* 7 utterance or voice (esp in the phrase **give tongue**) 8 anything which resembles a tongue in shape or function 9 a promontory or spit of land 10 a flap of leather on a shoe, either for decoration or under the laces or buckles to protect the instep 11 *music* the reed of an oboe or similar instrument 12 the clapper of a bell 13 the harnessing pole of a horse-drawn vehicle 14 a projecting strip along an edge of a board that is made to fit a corresponding groove in the edge of another board 15 **hold one's tongue** to keep quiet 16 **on the tip of one's tongue** about to come to mind: *her name was on the tip of his tongue* 17 **with one's tongue in one's cheek** Also called: **tongue in cheek** with insincere or ironical intent ▷ *vb* **tongues, tonguing, tongued** 18 to articulate (notes played on a wind instrument) by the process of tonguing 19 (*tr*) to lick, feel, or touch with the tongue 20 (*tr*) *carpentry* to provide (a board) with a tongue 21 (*intr*) (of a piece of land) to project into a body of water [Old English *tunge*; related to Old Saxon, Old Norse *tunga*, Old High German *zunga*, Latin *lingua*] > '**tongueless** *adj* > '**tongue,like** *adj*

tongue-and-groove joint *n* a joint made between two boards by means of a tongue along the edge of one board that fits into a groove along the edge of the other board

tongued (tʌŋd) *adj* 1 a having a tongue or tongues b (*in combination*) 2 (*in combination*) having a manner of speech as specified: *sharp-tongued*

tongue-lash *vb* (*tr*) to reprimand severely; scold > '**tongue-,lashing** *n, adj*

tongue-tie *n* a congenital condition in which the tongue has restricted mobility as the result of an abnormally short frenulum

tongue-tied *adj* 1 speechless, esp with embarrassment or shyness 2 having a condition of tongue-tie

tongue twister *n* a sentence or phrase that is difficult to articulate clearly and quickly, such as *Peter Piper picked a peck of pickled pepper*

tonguing ('tʌŋɪŋ) *n* a technique of articulating notes on a wind instrument

tonic ('tɒnɪk) *n* 1 a medicinal preparation intended to improve and strengthen the functioning of the body or increase the feeling of wellbeing 2 anything that enlivens or strengthens 3 Also called: **tonic water** a mineral water, usually carbonated and containing quinine and often mixed with gin or other alcoholic drinks 4 *music* a the first degree of a major or minor scale and the tonal centre of a piece composed in a particular key b a key or chord based on this ▷ *adj* 5 serving to enliven and invigorate: *a tonic wine* 6 of or relating to a tone or tones 7 *music* of or relating to the first degree of a major or minor scale 8 of or denoting the general effect of colour and light and shade in a picture 9 *physiol* of, relating to, characterized by, or affecting normal muscular or bodily tone: *a tonic spasm* [C17: from New Latin *tonicus*, from Greek *tonikos*

concerning tone, from *tonos* TONE] > '**tonically** *adv*

tonic accent *n* 1 emphasis imparted to a note by virtue of its having a higher pitch, rather than greater stress or long duration relative to other notes 2 another term for **pitch accent**

tonicity (təʊ'nɪsɪtɪ) *n* 1 the state, condition, or quality of being tonic 2 *physiol* another name for **tonus**

tonic sol-fa *n* a method of teaching music, esp singing, used mainly in Britain, by which the syllables of a movable system of solmization are used as names for the notes of the major scale in any key. In this system *sol* is usually replaced by *so* as the name of the fifth degree

tonight (tə'naɪt) *n* 1 the night or evening of this present day ▷ *adv* 2 in or during the night or evening of this day 3 *archaic* last night [Old English *tōniht*, from TO¹ (at) + NIGHT]

tonka bean ('tɒŋkə) *n* 1 a tall leguminous tree, *Coumarouna odorata*, of tropical America, having fragrant black almond-shaped seeds 2 the seeds of this tree, used in the manufacture of perfumes, snuff, etc [C18: probably from Tupi *tonka*]

Tonkin ('tɒn'kɪn) *or* **Tongking** ('tɒŋ'kɪŋ) *n* 1 a former state of N French Indochina (1883–1946), on the Gulf of Tonkin: forms the largest part of N Vietnam 2 **Gulf of Tonkin** an arm of the South China Sea, bordered by N Vietnam, the Leizhou Peninsula of SW China, and Hainan Island. Length: about 500 km (300 miles)

Tonle Sap ('tɒnlɪ 'sæp) *n* a lake in W central Cambodia, linked with the Mekong River by the **Tonle Sap River**. Area: (dry season) about 2600 sq km (1000 sq miles); (rainy season) about 10 000 sq km (3860 sq miles)

tonnage *or* **tunnage** ('tʌnɪdʒ) *n* 1 the capacity of a merchant ship expressed in tons, for which purpose a ton is considered as 40 cubic feet of freight or 100 cubic feet of bulk cargo, unless such an amount would weigh more than 2000 pounds in which case the actual weight is used 2 the weight of the cargo of a merchant ship 3 the total amount of shipping of a port or nation, estimated by the capacity of its ships 4 a duty on ships based either on their capacity or their register tonnage [C15: from Old French, from *tonne* barrel]

tonne (tʌn) *n* a unit of mass equal to 1000 kg or 2204.6 pounds. Also called (not in technical use): **metric ton** [from French]

tonneau ('tɒnəʊ) *n, pl* **-neaus** *or* **-neaux** (-nəʊ, -nəʊz) 1 Also called: **tonneau cover** a detachable cover to protect the rear part of an open car when it is not carrying passengers 2 *rare* the part of an open car in which the rear passengers sit [C20: from French: special type of vehicle body, from Old French *tonnel* cask, from *tonne* tun]

tonometer (təʊ'nɒmɪtə) *n* 1 an instrument for measuring the pitch of a sound, esp one consisting of a set of tuning forks 2 any of various types of instrument for measuring pressure or tension, such as the blood pressure, vapour pressure, etc [C18: from Greek *tonos* TONE + -METER] > **tonometric** (,tɒnə'mɛtrɪk, ,təʊ-) *adj*

tons (tʌnz) *informal* ▷ *pl n* 1 a large amount or number: *tons of money, I have tons of shoes* ▷ *adv* 2 (intensifier): I *looked and felt tons better*

tonsil ('tɒnsəl) *n* Also called: **palatine tonsil** either of two small masses of lymphatic tissue situated one on each side of the back of the mouth [C17: from Latin *tōnsillae* (pl) tonsils, of uncertain origin] > '**tonsillar** *or* '**tonsillary** *adj*

tonsillectomy (,tɒnsɪ'lɛktəmɪ) *n, pl* **-mies** surgical removal of the palatine tonsils

tonsillitis (,tɒnsɪ'laɪtɪs) *n* inflammation of the palatine tonsils, causing enlargement, occasionally to the extent that they nearly touch one another > **tonsillitic** (,tɒnsɪ'lɪtɪk) *adj*

tonsorial (tɒn'sɔːrɪəl) *adj* *often facetious* of or relating to barbering or hairdressing [C19: from Latin *tōnsōrius* concerning shaving, from *tondēre* to shave]

tonsure ('tɒnʃə) *n* 1 (in certain religions and monastic orders) a the shaving of the head or the crown of the head only b the part of the head left bare by shaving ▷ *vb* 2 (*tr*) to shave the head of [C14: from Latin *tōnsūra* a clipping, from *tondēre* to shave] > '**tonsured** *adj*

t

tontine ('tɒntiːn, tɒn'tiːn) *n* an annuity scheme by which several subscribers accumulate and invest a common fund out of which they receive an annuity that increases as subscribers die until the last survivor takes the whole [c18: from French, named after Lorenzo *Tonti*, Neapolitan banker who devised the scheme]

ton-up *Brit informal* ▷ *adj* (*prenominal*) **1** (esp of a motorcycle) capable of speeds of a hundred miles per hour or more **2** liking to travel at such speeds: *a ton-up boy* ▷ *n* **3** a person who habitually rides at such speeds

tonus ('təʊnəs) *n physiol* the normal tension of a muscle at rest; tone [c19: from Latin, from Greek *tonos* TONE]

too (tuː) *adv* **1** as well; in addition; also: *can I come too?* **2** in or to an excessive degree; more than a fitting or desirable amount: *I have too many things to do* **3** extremely: *you're too kind* **4** *US & Canadian informal* indeed: used to reinforce a command: *you will too do it!* [Old English *tō*; related to Old Frisian, Old Saxon *to*, Old High German *zou*; see TO¹]

● USAGE See at **very**

took (tʊk) *vb* the past tense of **take¹**

Tooke (tʊk) *n* **John Horne**, original name *John Horne*. 1736–1812, British radical, who founded (1771) the Constitutional Society to press for parliamentary reform: acquitted (1794) of high treason. He also wrote the philological treatise *The Diversions of Purley* (1786)

tool (tuːl) *n* **1 a** an implement, such as a hammer, saw, or spade, that is used by hand **b** a power-driven instrument; machine tool **c** (*in combination*): *a toolkit* **2** the cutting part of such an instrument **3** any of the instruments used by a bookbinder to impress a design on a book cover **4** anything used as a means of performing an operation or achieving an end: *he used his boss's absence as a tool for gaining influence* **5** a person used to perform dishonourable or unpleasant tasks for another **6** a necessary medium for or adjunct to one's profession: *numbers are the tools of the mathematician's trade* ▷ *vb* **7** (*tr*) to work, cut, shape, or form (something) with a tool or tools **8** (*tr*) to decorate (a book cover) with a bookbinder's tool **9** (*tr*; often foll by *up*) to furnish with tools [Old English *tōl*; related to Old Norse *tōl* weapon, Old English *tawian* to prepare; see TAW²] ▷ 'tooler *n*

toolbar ('tuːlˌbɑː) *n* a horizontal row or vertical column of selectable buttons displayed on a computer screen, allowing the user to select a variety of functions

toolie ('tuːlɪ) *n Australian slang, derogatory* (in Australia) an adult who gatecrashes the Schoolies Week celebrations, esp one who makes sexual advances towards students [c21: from *tool*, slang term for PENIS + SCHOOLIE]

tooling ('tuːlɪŋ) *n* **1** any decorative work done with a tool, esp a design stamped onto a book cover, piece of leatherwork, etc **2** the selection, provision, and setting up of tools, esp for a machining operation

toolkit ('tuːlˌkɪt) *n* **1** a set of tools designed to be used together or for a particular purpose **2** software designed to perform a specific function, esp to solve a problem: *your on-line printer toolkit*

tool-maker ('tuːlˌmeɪkə) *n* a person who specializes in the production or reconditioning of precision tools, cutters, etc ▷ 'tool-ˌmaking *n*

tool pusher *n* a foreman who supervises drilling operations on an oil rig

toolroom ('tuːlruːm, -rʊm) *n* a room, as in a machine shop, where tools are made or stored

toolset ('tuːlˌsɛt) *n computing* a set of predefined tools (for opening files, cutting and pasting, etc) that is associated with a particular computer application

toonie *or* **twonie** ('tuːnɪ) *n Canadian informal* a Canadian two-dollar coin

tooshie ('tʊʃɪ) *adj Austral slang* angry; upset [from TUSH buttocks, by analogy with ARSEY]

toot (tuːt) *vb* **1** to give or cause to give (a short blast, hoot, or whistle) ▷ *n* **2** the sound made by or as if by a horn, whistle, etc **3** *slang* any drug for snorting, esp cocaine **4** *US & Canadian slang* a drinking spree **5** (tʊt) *Austral slang* a lavatory [c16: from Middle Low German *tuten*, of imitative origin] ▷ 'tooter *n*

tooth (tuːθ) *n*, *pl* **teeth** (tiːθ) **1** any of various bonelike structures set in the jaws of most vertebrates and modified, according to the species, for biting, tearing, or chewing. Related adj: **dental 2** any of various similar structures in invertebrates, occurring in the mouth or alimentary canal **3** anything resembling a tooth in shape, prominence, or function: *the tooth of a comb* **4** any of the various small indentations occurring on the margin of a leaf, petal, etc **5** any one of a number of uniform projections on a gear, sprocket, rack, etc, by which drive is transmitted **6** taste or appetite (esp in the phrase **sweet tooth**) **7 long in the tooth** old or ageing: used originally of horses, because their gums recede with age **8 tooth and nail** with ferocity and force ▷ *vb* (tuːð, tuːθ) **9** (*tr*) to provide with a tooth or teeth **10** (*intr*) (of two gearwheels) to engage [Old English *tōth*; related to Old Saxon *tand*, Old High German *zand*, Old Norse *tonn*, Gothic *tunthus*, Latin *dens*] ▷ 'toothless *adj* ▷ 'toothˌlike *adj*

toothache ('tuːθˌeɪk) *n* a pain in or about a tooth. Technical name: **odontalgia**

toothbrush ('tuːθˌbrʌʃ) *n* a small brush, usually with a long handle, for cleaning the teeth

toothed (tuːθt) *adj* **a** having a tooth or teeth **b** (*in combination*): *sabre-toothed; six-toothed*

toothpaste ('tuːθˌpeɪst) *n* a paste used for cleaning the teeth, applied with a toothbrush

toothpick ('tuːθˌpɪk) *n* a small sharp sliver of wood, plastic, etc, used for extracting pieces of food from between the teeth

tooth powder *n* a powder used for cleaning the teeth, applied with a toothbrush

tooth shell *n* another name for **tusk shell**

toothsome ('tuːθsəm) *adj* of delicious or appetizing appearance, flavour, or smell

toothwort ('tuːθˌwɜːt) *n* **1** a parasitic European scrophulariaceous plant, *Lathraea squamaria*, having no green parts, scaly cream or pink stems, pinkish flowers, and a rhizome covered with toothlike scales **2** any North American or Eurasian plant of the genus *Dentaria*, having creeping rhizomes covered with toothlike projections: family *Brassicaceae* (crucifers)

toothy ('tuːθɪ) *adj* **toothier, toothiest** having or showing numerous, large, or projecting teeth: *a toothy grin* ▷ 'toothily *adv* ▷ 'toothiness *n*

tootle ('tuːt°l) *vb* **1** to toot or hoot softly or repeatedly: *the flute tootled quietly* ▷ *n* **2** a soft hoot or series of hoots [c19: from TOOT¹] ▷ 'tootler *n*

Toowoomba (tə'wʊmbə) *n* a city in E Australia, in SE Queensland: agricultural and industrial centre. Pop: 89 338 (2001)

top¹ (tɒp) *n* **1** the highest or uppermost part of anything: *the top of a hill* **2** the most important or successful position: *to be at the top of the class; the top of the table* **3** the part of a plant that is above ground: *carrot tops* **4** a thing that forms or covers the uppermost part of anything, esp a lid or cap **5** the highest degree or point: *at the top of his career* **6** the most important person **7** the best or finest part of anything **8** the loudest or highest pitch (esp in the phrase **top of one's voice**) **9** short for **top gear 10** *cards* the highest card of a suit in a player's hand **11** *sport* **a** a stroke that hits the ball above its centre **b** short for **topspin 12** a platform around the head of a lower mast of a sailing vessel, the edges of which serve to extend the topmast shrouds **13** a garment, esp for a woman, that extends from the shoulders to the waist or hips **14 on top of a** in addition to **b** *informal* in complete control of (a difficult situation, job, etc) **15 over the top** over the limit; excessive(ly); lacking restraint or a sense of proportion **16 the top of the morning** a morning greeting regarded as characteristic of Irishmen ▷ *adj* **17** of, relating to, serving as, or situated on the top ▷ *vb* **tops, topping, topped** (*mainly tr*) **18** to form a top on (something) **19** to make (a stroke) by hitting the ball in this way **18** to form a top on (something) **19** to remove the top of or from **20** to reach or pass the top of **21** to be at the top of: *he tops the team* **22** to exceed or surpass **23** *slang* to kill **24** (*also intr*) *sport* **a** to hit (a ball) above the centre **b** to make (a stroke) by hitting the ball in this way **25 top and tail a** to trim off the ends of (fruit or vegetables) before cooking **b** to wash a baby's face and bottom without immersion in a bath ▷ See also **top**

off, top out, tops, top up [Old English *topp*; related to Old High German *zopf* plait, Old Norse *toppr* tuft]

top² (tɒp) *n* **1** a toy that is spun on its pointed base by a flick of the fingers, by pushing a handle at the top up and down, etc **2** sleep like a top to sleep very soundly [Old English, of unknown origin]

topaz ('təʊpæz) *n* **1** a white or colourless mineral often tinted by impurities, found in cavities in igneous rocks and in quartz veins. It is used as a gemstone. Composition: hydrated aluminium silicate. Formula: $Al_2SiO_4(F,OH)_2$. Crystal structure: orthorhombic **2** oriental topaz a yellowish-brown variety of sapphire **3** false topaz another name for **citrine 4 a** a yellowish-brown colour, as in some varieties of topaz **b** (*as adjective*): *topaz eyes* **5** either of two South American hummingbirds, *Topaza pyra* and *T. pella* [c13: from Old French *topaze*, from Latin *topazus*, from Greek *topazos*]

top boot *n* a high boot, often with a decorative or contrasting upper section

top brass *n* (*functioning as plural*) *informal* the most important or high-ranking officials or leaders, as in politics, industry, etc

topcoat ('tɒp,kəʊt) *n* an outdoor coat worn over a suit, etc

top dog *n informal* the leader or chief of a group

top dollar *n informal* the highest level of payment

top drawer *n* people of the highest standing, esp socially (esp in the phrase **out of the top drawer**)

top dressing *n* a surface application of manure or fertilizer to land > top-dress *vb*

tope¹ (təʊp) *vb* to consume (alcoholic drink) as a regular habit, usually in large quantities [c17: from French *toper* to keep an agreement, from Spanish *topar* to take a bet; probably because a wager was generally followed by a drink] > 'toper *n*

tope² (təʊp) *n* a small grey requiem shark, *Galeorhinus galeus*, of European coastal waters [c17: of uncertain origin; compare Norfolk dialect *toper* dogfish]

topee or **topi** ('təʊpiː, -pɪ) *n*, *pl*-pees or-pis another name for **pith helmet** [c19: from Hindi *topī* hat]

Topeka (tə'piːkə) *n* a city in E central Kansas, capital of the state, on the Kansas River: university (1865). Pop: 122 008 (2003 est)

Top End *n* the Top End *Austral* the northern part of the Northern Territory

top-end *adj* of or relating to the best or most expensive products of their kind: *a range of top-end vehicles*

top-flight *adj* of superior or excellent quality; outstanding

topgallant (,tɒp'gælənt; *Nautical* tə'gælənt) *n* **1** Also called: topgallant mast a mast on a square-rigger above a topmast or an extension of a topmast **2** Also called: topgallant sail a sail set on a yard of a topgallant mast **3** (*modifier*) of or relating to a topgallant [c16: from TOP¹ + GALLANT]

top gear *n* the highest gear in a motor vehicle

top hat *n* a man's hat with a tall cylindrical crown and narrow brim, often made of silk, now worn for some formal occasions

top-hat scheme *n informal* a pension scheme for the senior executives of an organization

top-heavy *adj* **1** unstable or unbalanced through being overloaded at the top **2** *finance* (of an enterprise or its capital structure) characterized by or containing too much debt capital in relation to revenue or profit so that too little is left over for dividend distributions; overcapitalized

Tophet or **Topheth** ('təʊfɛt) *n Old Testament* a place in the valley immediately to the southwest of Jerusalem; the Shrine of Moloch, where human sacrifices were offered [from Hebrew *Tōpheth*]

tophus ('təʊfəs) *n*, *pl*-phi (-faɪ) *pathol* a deposit of sodium urate in the helix of the ear or surrounding a joint: a diagnostic of advanced or chronic gout [c16: from Latin, variant of *tōfus* TUFA, TUFF]

topi¹ ('təʊpɪ) *n*, *pl*-pis an antelope, *Damaliscus korrigum*, of grasslands and semideserts of Africa, having angular curved horns and an elongated muzzle [c19: from an African language]

topi² ('təʊpiː, -pɪ) *n*, *pl*-pis another name for **pith helmet** [c19: from Hindi: hat]

topiary ('təʊpɪərɪ) *adj* **1** of, relating to, or characterized by the trimming or training of trees or bushes into artificial decorative animal, geometric, or other shapes ▷ *n* **2** *pl*-aries **a** a topiary garden **b** a topiary work **3** the art of topiary [c16: from French *topiaire*, from Latin *topia* decorative garden work, from Greek *topion* little place, from *topos* place] > 'topiarist *n*

topic ('tɒpɪk) *n* **1** a subject or theme of a speech, essay, book, etc **2** a subject of conversation; item of discussion [c16: from Latin *topica* translating Greek *ta topika*, literally: matters relating to commonplaces, title of a treatise by Aristotle, from *topoi*, pl of *topos* place, commonplace]

topical ('tɒpɪkəl) *adj* **1** of, relating to, or constituting current affairs **2** relating to a particular place; local **3** of or relating to a topic or topics **4** (of a drug, ointment, etc) for application to the body surface; local > topicality (,tɒpɪ'kælɪtɪ) *n* > 'topically *adv*

topknot ('tɒp,nɒt) *n* **1** a crest, tuft, decorative bow, chignon, etc, on the top of the head **2** any of several European flatfishes of the genus *Zeugopterus* and related genera, esp *Z. punctatus*, which has an oval dark brown body marked with darker blotches: family *Bothidae* (turbot, etc)

topless ('tɒplɪs) *adj* **1** having no top **2 a** denoting a costume which has no covering for the breasts **b** wearing such a costume

top-level *n* (*modifier*) of, involving, or by those on the highest level of influence or authority: *top-level talks*

toplofty ('tɒp,lɒftɪ) *adj informal* haughty or pretentious > 'top,loftiness *n*

topmast ('tɒp,mɑːst; *Nautical* 'tɒpməst) *n* the mast next above a lower mast on a sailing vessel

topmost ('tɒp,məʊst) *adj* highest; at or nearest the top

top-notch ('tɒp'nɒtʃ) *adj informal* excellent; superb > 'top-'notcher *n*

topo- or before a vowel **top-** *combining form* indicating place or region: *topography; topology; toponym; topotype* [from Greek *topos* a place, commonplace]

top off *vb* (*tr, adverb*) to finish or complete, esp with some decisive action

topography (tə'pɒgrəfɪ) *n*, *pl*-phies **1** the study or detailed description of the surface features of a region **2** the detailed mapping of the configuration of a region **3** the land forms or surface configuration of a region **4** the surveying of a region's surface features **5** the study or description of the configuration of any object > to'pographer *n* > topographic (,tɒpə'græfɪk) or ,topo'graphical *adj*

topological group *n maths* a group, such as the set of all real numbers, that constitutes a topological space and in which multiplication and inversion are continuous

topological space *n maths* a set *S* with an associated family of subsets τ that is closed under set union and finite intersection. *S* and the empty set are members of τ

topology (tə'pɒlədʒɪ) *n* **1** the branch of mathematics concerned with generalization of the concepts of continuity, limit, etc **2** a branch of geometry describing the properties of a figure that are unaffected by continuous distortion, such as stretching or knotting **3** *maths* a family of subsets of a given set *S*, such that *S* is a topological space **4** the study of the topography of a given place, esp as far as it reflects its history **5** the anatomy of any specific bodily area, structure, or part > topological (,tɒpə'lɒdʒɪk) or ,topo'logical *adj* > ,topo'logically *adv* > to'pologist *n*

Topolski (to'pɒlskɪ) *n* **Feliks** (fiː'lɪks). 1907–89, British painter, born in Poland; best known for his sketches and murals, esp for *Memoir of the Century* (1975–89) painted on viaduct arches on London's South Bank

top out *vb* (*adverb*) to place the highest stone on (a building) or perform a ceremony on this occasion

topper ('tɒpə) *n* **1** an informal name for **top hat 2** a person or thing that tops

topping ('tɒpɪŋ) *n* **1** something that tops something else, esp a sauce or garnish for food ▷ *adj* **2** high or superior in rank, degree, etc **3** *Brit slang* excellent; splendid

topple ('tɒpǝl) *vb* **1** to tip over or cause to tip over, esp from a height **2** (*intr*) to lean precariously or totter **3** (*tr*) to overthrow; oust [c16: frequentative of TOP¹ (verb)]

tops (tɒps) *slang* ▷ *n* **1** a person or thing of top quality ▷ *adj* **2** (*postpositive*) excellent; superb

topsail ('tɒp,seɪl; *Nautical* 'tɒpsǝl) *n* a square sail carried on a yard set on a topmast

topscore ('tɒpskɔː) *vb informal* (*intr*) to be the highest scorer in a sports match or competition

top-secret *adj* containing information whose disclosure would cause exceedingly grave damage to the nation and therefore classified as needing the highest level of secrecy and security

topside ('tɒp,saɪd) *n* **1** the uppermost side of anything **2** *Brit & NZ* a lean cut of beef from the thigh containing no bone **3** (*often plural*) **a** the part of a ship's sides above the waterline **b** the parts of a ship above decks

top slicing *n* the act or process of using a specific part of a sum of money for a special purpose, such as assessing a taxable gain

topsoil ('tɒp,sɔɪl) *n* the surface layer of soil

topspin ('tɒp,spɪn) *n sport* spin imparted to make a ball bounce or travel exceptionally far, high, or quickly, as by hitting it with a sharp forward and upward stroke

topsy-turvy ('tɒpsɪ'tɜːvɪ) *adj* **1** upside down ▷ *adv* **2** in a topsy-turvy manner ▷ *n* **3** a topsy-turvy state [c16: probably from *tops*, plural of TOP¹ + obsolete *tervy* to turn upside down; perhaps related to Old English *tearflian* to roll over]

top up *vb* (*tr, adverb*) *Brit* **1** to raise the level of (a liquid, powder, etc) in (a container), usually bringing it to the brim of the container **2 a** to increase the benefits from (an insurance scheme), esp to increase a pension when a salary rise enables higher premiums to be paid **b** to add money to (a loan, bank account, etc) in order to keep it at a constant or acceptable level ▷ *n* **top-up 3 a** an amount added to something in order to raise it to or maintain it at a desired level **b** (*as modifier*): *a top-up loan; a top-up policy*

top whack *n informal* the maximum price: *paying top whack for your child's education*

toque (tǝʊk) *n* **1** a woman's small round brimless hat, popular esp in Edwardian times **2** a hat with a small brim and a pouched crown, popular in the 16th century **3** a chef's tall white hat [c16: from French, from Old Spanish *toca* headdress, probably from Basque *tauka* hat]

tor (tɔː) *n* a high hill, esp a bare rocky one [Old English *torr*, probably of Celtic origin; compare Scottish Gaelic *torr* pile, Welsh *twr*]

Torah ('tǝʊrǝ; *Hebrew* tɔːˈra) *n* **1 a** the Pentateuch **b** the scroll on which this is written, used in synagogue services **2** the whole body of traditional Jewish teaching, including the Oral Law [c16: from Hebrew: precept, from *yārāh* to instruct]

Torbay ('tɔːˈbeɪ) *n* **1** a unitary authority in SW England, in Devon, consisting of Torquay and two neighbouring coastal resorts. Pop: 131 300 (2003 est). Area: 63 sq km (24 sq miles) **2** Also called: **Tor Bay** an inlet of the English Channel on the coast of SW England, near Torquay

torc (tɔːk) *n* another spelling of **torque** (sense 1)

torch (tɔːtʃ) *n* **1** a small portable electric lamp powered by one or more dry batteries. US and Canadian word: **flashlight 2** a wooden or tow shaft dipped in wax or tallow and set alight **3** anything regarded as a source of enlightenment, guidance, etc **4** any apparatus that burns with a hot flame for welding, brazing, or soldering **5 carry a torch for** to be in love with, esp unrequitedly ▷ *vb* **6** (*tr*) *slang* to set fire to, esp deliberately as an act of arson [c13: from Old French *torche* handful of twisted straw, from Vulgar Latin *torca* (unattested), from Latin *torquēre* to twist]

torchbearer ('tɔːtʃ,bɛǝrǝ) *n* **1** a person or thing that carries a torch **2** a person who leads or inspires

torchère (tɔːˈʃɛǝ) *n* a tall narrow stand for holding a candelabrum [c20: from French, from *torche* TORCH]

torchier *or* **torchiere** (tɔːˈtʃɪǝ) *n* a standing lamp with a bowl for casting light upwards and so giving all-round

indirect illumination [c20: from TORCHÈRE]

torch song *n* a sentimental or romantic popular song, usually sung by a woman [c20: from the phrase *to carry a torch for (someone)*] > **torch singer** *n*

tore (tɔː) *vb* the past tense of **tear¹**

toreador ('tɒrɪǝ,dɔː) *n* a bullfighter [c17: from Spanish, from *torear* to take part in bullfighting, from *toro* a bull, from Latin *taurus*; compare STEER²]

torero (tɒˈrɛǝrǝʊ) *n, pl* -**ros** a bullfighter, esp one who fights on foot [c18: from Spanish, from Late Latin *taurārius*, from Latin *taurus* a bull]

Torfaen ('tɔːˌvæn) *n* a county borough of SE Wales, created in 1996 from part of Gwent. Administrative centre: Pontypool. Pop: 90 700 (2003 est). Area: 290 sq km (112 sq miles)

toric lens *n* a lens used to correct astigmatism, having one of its surfaces shaped like part of a torus so that its focal lengths are different in different meridians

torii ('tɔːrɪ,iː) *n, pl* -**rii** a gateway, esp one at the entrance to a Japanese Shinto temple [c19: from Japanese, literally: a perch for birds]

Torino (tɔːˈriːno) *n* the Italian name for **Turin**

torment *vb* (tɔːˈmɛnt) (*tr*) **1** to afflict with great pain, suffering, or anguish; torture **2** to tease or pester in an annoying way ▷ *n* ('tɔːmɛnt) **3** physical or mental pain **4** a source of pain, worry, annoyance, etc [c13: from Old French, from Latin *tormentum*, from *torquēre*] > **torˈmented** *adj* > **torˈmenting** *adj*, *n* > **torˈmentor** *n*

tormentil ('tɔːmǝntɪl) *n* a rosaceous downy perennial plant, *Potentilla erecta*, of Europe and W Asia, having serrated leaves, four-petalled yellow flowers, and an astringent root used in medicine, tanning, and dyeing [c15: from Old French *tormentille*, from Medieval Latin *tormentilla*, from Latin *tormentum* agony; referring to its use in relieving pain; see TORMENT]

torn (tɔːn) *vb* **1** the past participle of **tear¹** (sense 2) **2 that's torn it** *Brit slang* an unexpected event or circumstance has upset one's plans ▷ *adj* **3** split or cut **4** divided or undecided, as in preference: *he was torn between staying and leaving*

tornado (tɔːˈneɪdǝʊ) *n, pl* -**does** *or* -**dos 1** Also called: **cyclone,** (*US and Canadian informal*) **twister** a violent storm with winds whirling around a small area of extremely low pressure, usually characterized by a dark funnel-shaped cloud causing damage along its path **2** a small but violent squall or whirlwind, such as those occurring on the West African coast **3** any violently active or destructive person or thing [c16: probably alteration of Spanish *tronada* thunderstorm (from *tronar* to thunder, from Latin *tonāre*), through influence of *tornar* to turn, from Latin *tornāre* to turn in a lathe] > **tornadic** (tɔːˈnædɪk) *adj*

toroid ('tɔːrɔɪd) *n* **1** *geometry* a surface generated by rotating a closed plane curve about a coplanar line that does not intersect the curve **2** the solid enclosed by such a surface. See also **torus** > **toˈroidal** *adj*

Toronto (tǝˈrɒntǝʊ) *n* a city in S central Canada, capital of Ontario, on Lake Ontario: the major industrial centre of Canada; two universities. Pop: 2 481 494 (2001) > **Torontonian** (tɒrǝnˈtǝʊnɪǝn) *adj*, *n*

torpedo (tɔːˈpiːdǝʊ) *n, pl* -**does 1** a cylindrical self-propelled weapon carrying explosives that is launched from aircraft, ships, or submarines and follows an underwater path to hit its target **2** *obsolete* a submarine mine **3** *US & Canadian* a firework containing gravel and a percussion cap that explodes when dashed against a hard surface **4** any of various electric rays of the genus *Torpedo* ▷ *vb* -**does, -doing, -doed** (*tr*) **5** to hit (a ship, etc) with one or a number of torpedoes **6** to render ineffective; destroy or wreck: *to torpedo the administration's plan* [c16: from Latin: crampfish (whose electric discharges can cause numbness), from *torpēre* to be inactive; see TORPID] > **torˈpedo-,like** *adj*

torpedo boat *n* (formerly) a small high-speed warship designed to carry out torpedo attacks in coastal waters

torpedo tube *n* the tube from which a torpedo is discharged from submarines or surface ships

torpid ('tɔːpɪd) *adj* **1** apathetic, sluggish, or lethargic **2** (of a hibernating animal) dormant; having greatly reduced metabolic activity **3** unable to move or feel [C17: from Latin *torpidus*, from *torpēre* to be numb, motionless] >**tor'pidity** *n* >**'torpidly** *adv*

torpor ('tɔːpə) *n* a state of torpidity [C17: from Latin: inactivity, from *torpēre* to be motionless]

Torquay (ˌtɔː'kiː) *n* a town and resort in SW England, in Torbay unitary authority, S Devon. Pop: 62 968 (2001)

torque (tɔːk) *n* **1** Also called: **torc** a necklace or armband made of twisted metal, worn esp by the ancient Britons and Gauls **2** any force or system of forces that causes or tends to cause rotation [C19: from Latin *torquēs* necklace, and *torquēre* to twist]

torque converter *n* a hydraulic device for the smooth transmission of power in which an engine-driven impeller transmits its momentum to a fluid held in a sealed container, which in turn drives a rotor. Also called: **hydraulic coupling**

Torquemada (*Spanish* tɔrke'maða) *n* **Tomás de** (to'mas de). 1420–98, Spanish Dominican monk. As first Inquisitor-General of Spain (1483–98), he was responsible for the burning of some 2000 heretics

torques ('tɔːkwiːz) *n* a distinctive band of hair, feathers, skin, or colour around the neck of an animal; a collar [C17: from Latin: necklace, from *torquēre* to twist] >**torquate** ('tɔːkweɪt, -kweɪt) *adj*

torque wrench *n* a type of wrench with a gauge attached to indicate the torque applied to the workpiece

torr (tɔː) *n*, *pl* **torr** a unit of pressure equal to one millimetre of mercury (133.322 newtons per square metre) [C20: named after Evangelista Torricelli (1608–47), Italian physicist and mathematician]

Torrance ('tɒrəns) *n* a city in SW California, southwest of Los Angeles: developed rapidly with the discovery of oil. Pop: 142 621 (2003 est)

Torre del Greco (*Italian* 'torre del 'grɛːko) *n* a city in SW Italy, in Campania near Vesuvius on the Bay of Naples: damaged several times by eruptions. Pop: 90 607 (2001)

torrefy ('tɒrɪˌfaɪ) *vb* **-fies**, **-fying**, **-fied** (*tr*) to dry (drugs, ores, etc) by subjection to intense heat; roast [C17: from French *torréfier*, from Latin *torrefacere*, from *torrēre* to parch + *facere* to make] >**torrefaction** (ˌtɒrɪ'fækʃən) *n*

Torrens ('tɒrənz) *n* **Lake Torrens** a shallow salt lake in E central South Australia, about 8 m (25 ft) below sea level. Area: 5776 sq km (2230 sq miles)

Torrens title *n Austral* legal title to land based on record of registration rather than on title deeds [from Sir Robert Richard Torrens (1814–84), who introduced the system as premier of South Australia in 1857]

torrent ('tɒrənt) *n* **1** a fast, voluminous, or violent stream of water or other liquid **2** an overwhelming flow of thoughts, words, sound, etc [C17: from French, from Latin *torrēns* (noun), from *torrēns* (adjective) burning, from *torrēre* to burn] >**torrential** (tɒ'rɛnʃəl, tə-) *adj*

Torreón (*Spanish* torre'ɔn) *n* an industrial city in N Mexico, in Coahuila state. Pop: 1 057 000 (2005 est)

Torres Strait ('tɒrɪz, 'tɒr-) *n* a strait between NE Australia and S New Guinea, linking the Arafura Sea with the Coral Sea. Width: about 145 km (90 miles)

Torricelli (ˌtɒrɪ'tʃɛlɪ) *n* **Evangelista** (evandʒe'lista). 1608–47, Italian physicist and mathematician, who discovered the principle of the barometer

Torricellian tube (ˌtɒrɪ'sɛlɪən) *n* a vertical glass tube partly evacuated and partly filled with mercury, the height of which is used as a measure of atmospheric pressure [C17: named after Evangelista *Torricelli* (1608–47), Italian physicist and mathematician]

torrid ('tɒrɪd) *adj* **1** so hot and dry as to parch or scorch **2** arid or parched **3** highly charged emotionally: *a torrid love scene* [C16: from Latin *torridus*, from *torrēre* to scorch] >**tor'ridity** *or* **'torridness** *n* >**'torridly** *adv*

Torrid Zone *n rare* that part of the earth's surface lying between the tropics of Cancer and Capricorn

torsion ('tɔːʃən) *n* **1 a** the twisting of a part by application of equal and opposite torques at either end **b** the condition of twist and shear stress produced by a torque on a part or component **2** the act of twisting or the state of being twisted [C15: from Old French, from medical Latin *torsiō* griping pains, from *torquēre* to twist, torture] >**'torsional** *adj* >**'torsionally** *adv*

torsion balance *n* an instrument used to measure small forces, esp electric or magnetic forces, by the torsion they produce in a thin wire, thread, or rod

torsion bar *n* a metal bar acting as a torsional spring, esp as used in the suspensions of some motor vehicles

torsk (tɔːsk) *n*, *pl* **torsks** *or* **torsk** a gadoid food fish, *Brosmius brosme*, of northern coastal waters, having a single long dorsal fin. Usual US and Canadian name: **cusk** [C17: of Scandinavian origin; related to Old Norse *thorskr* codfish, Danish *torsk*]

torso ('tɔːsəʊ) *n*, *pl* **-sos** *or* **-si** (-sɪ) **1** the trunk of the human body **2** a statue of a nude human trunk, esp without the head or limbs [C18: from Italian: stalk, stump, from Latin: THYRSUS]

tort (tɔːt) *n law* a civil wrong arising from an act or failure to act, independently of any contract, for which an action for personal injury or property damages may be brought [C14: from Old French, from Medieval Latin *tortum*, literally: something twisted, from Latin *torquēre* to twist]

torte (tɔːt; *German* 'tɔrtə) *n* a rich cake, originating in Austria, usually decorated or filled with cream, fruit, nuts, and jam [C16: ultimately perhaps from Late Latin *tōrta* a round loaf, of uncertain origin]

Tortelier (*French* tɔrtəlje) *n* **Paul** (pɔl). 1914–90, French cellist and composer

torticollis (ˌtɔːtɪ'kɒlɪs) *n pathol* an abnormal position of the head, usually with the neck bent to one side, caused congenitally by contracture of muscles, muscular spasm, etc [C19: New Latin, from Latin *tortus* twisted (from *torquēre* to twist) + *collum* neck]

tortilla (tɔː'tiːə) *n Mexican cookery* a kind of thin pancake made from corn meal and cooked on a hot griddle until dry [C17: from Spanish: a little cake, from *torta* a round cake, from Late Latin; see TORTE]

tortoise ('tɔːtəs) *n* **1** any herbivorous terrestrial chelonian reptile of the family *Testudinidae*, of most warm regions, having a heavy dome-shaped shell and clawed limbs **2** a slow-moving person **3** another word for **testudo** [C15: probably from Old French *tortue* (influenced by Latin *tortus* twisted), from Medieval Latin *tortūca*, from Late Latin *tartarūcha* coming from Tartarus, from Greek *tartaroukhos*; referring to the belief that the tortoise originated in the underworld]

tortoiseshell ('tɔːtəsˌʃɛl) *n* **1** a horny translucent yellow-and-brown mottled substance obtained from the outer layer of the shell of the hawksbill turtle: used for making ornaments, jewellery, etc **2** a similar synthetic substance, esp plastic or celluloid, now more widely used than the natural product **3** a breed of domestic cat, usually female, having black, cream, and brownish markings **4** any of several nymphalid butterflies of the genus *Nymphalis*, and related genera, having orange-brown wings with black markings **5 a** a yellowish-brown mottled colour **b** (*as adjective*): *a tortoiseshell décor* **6** (*modifier*) made of tortoiseshell

Tortola (tɔː'təʊlə) *n* an island in the NE Caribbean, in the Leeward Islands group: chief island of the British Virgin Islands. Pop: 23 900 (latest est). Area: 62 sq km (24 sq miles)

tortricid ('tɔːtrɪsɪd) *n* any small moth of the chiefly temperate family *Tortricidae*, the larvae of which live concealed in leaves, which they roll or tie together, and are pests of fruit and forest trees: includes the codling moth [C19: from New Latin *Tortrīcidae*, from *tortrix*, feminine of *tortor*, literally: twister, referring to the leaf-rolling of the larvae, from *torquēre* to twist]

Tortuga (tɔː'tuːgə) *n* an island in the Caribbean, off the NW coast of Haiti: haunt of pirates in the 17th century. Area: 180 sq km (70 sq miles)

tortuous ('tɔːtjʊəs) *adj* **1** twisted or winding **2** devious or cunning **3** intricate >**'tortuously** *adv* >**'tortuousness** *n* >**tortuosity** (ˌtɔːtjʊ'ɒsɪtɪ) *n*

torture ('tɔːtʃə) *vb* (*tr*) **1** to cause extreme physical pain to, esp in order to extract information, break resistance, etc: *to torture prisoners* **2** to give mental anguish to **3** to twist into a grotesque form ▷ *n* **4** physical or mental anguish **5** the practice of torturing a person **6** a cause of mental agony or worry [C16: from Late Latin *tortūra* a

twisting, from *torquēre* to twist] >'torturer *n*
>'torturesome *or*'torturous *adj* >'torturously *adv*
● USAGE The adjective *torturous* is sometimes confused
● with *tortuous*. One speaks of a *torturous* experience, i.e.
● one that involves pain or suffering, but of a *tortuous*
● road, i.e. one that winds or twists

Toruń (*Polish* 'tɔrunj) *n* an industrial city in N Poland, on the River Vistula: developed around a castle that was founded by the Teutonic Knights in 1230; under Prussian rule (1793–1919). Pop: 214 000 (2005 est). German name: **Thorn**

torus ('tɔːrəs) *n*, *pl*-ri (-raɪ) **1** Also called: **tore** a large convex moulding approximately semicircular in cross section, esp one used on the base of a classical column **2** *geometry* a ring-shaped surface generated by rotating a circle about a coplanar line that does not intersect the circle. Area: $4\pi^2Rr$; volume: $2\pi^2Rr^2$, where *r* is the radius of the circle and *R* is the distance from the line to the centre of the circle **3** *botany* another name for **receptacle** (sense 2) [c16: from Latin: a swelling, of obscure origin] >'toric ('tɒrɪk) *adj*

Torvill and Dean ('tɔːvɪl) *n* two British ice dancers, **Jayne Torvill,** born 1957, and **Christopher Dean,** born 1958. They won the world championships in 1981–84, the European championships in 1981–82, 1984, and 1994, and the gold medal in the 1984 Olympic Games

Tory ('tɔːrɪ) *n*, *pl*-ries **1** a member or supporter of the Conservative Party in Great Britain or Canada **2** a member of the English political party that opposed the exclusion of James, Duke of York from the royal succession (1679–80). Tory remained the label for subsequent major conservative interests until they gave birth to the Conservative Party in the 1830s **3** an American supporter of the British cause; loyalist. See **Whig 4** (*sometimes not capital*) an ultraconservative or reactionary ▷ *adj* **5** of, characteristic of, or relating to Tories **6** (*sometimes not capital*) ultraconservative or reactionary [c17: from Irish *tōraidhe* outlaw, from Middle Irish *tōir* pursuit] >'Toryish *adj* >'Toryism *n*

tosa ('təʊsə) *n* a large dog, usually red in colour, which is a cross between a mastiff and a Great Dane: originally developed for dog-fighting; it is not recognized as a breed by kennel clubs outside Japan [c20: from the name of a province of the island of Shikoku, Japan]

Toscana (tos'ka:na) *n* the Italian name for **Tuscany**

Toscanini (ˌtɒskə'ni:nɪ) *n* **Arturo** (ar'tu:ro). 1867–1957, Italian conductor; musical director of La Scala, Milan, and of the NBC symphony orchestra (1937–57) in New York

tosh (tɒʃ) *n slang, chiefly Brit* nonsense; rubbish [c19: of unknown origin]

toss (tɒs) *vb* **1** (*tr*) to throw lightly or with a flourish, esp with the palm of the hand upwards **2** to fling or be flung about, esp constantly or regularly in an agitated or violent way: *a ship tosses in a storm* **3** to discuss or put forward for discussion in an informal way **4** (*tr*) (of an animal such as a horse) to throw (its rider) **5** (*tr*) (of an animal) to butt with the head or the horns and throw into the air **6** (*tr*) to shake, agitate, or disturb **7** to toss up a coin with (someone) in order to decide or allot something **8** (*intr*) to move away angrily or impatiently ▷ *n* **9** an abrupt movement **10** a rolling or pitching motion **11** the act or an instance of tossing **12** the act of tossing up a coin **13** a fall from a horse or other animal [c16: of Scandinavian origin; related to Norwegian, Swedish *tossa* to strew]

tosser ('tɒsə) *n Brit slang* a stupid or despicable person [c20: probably from TOSS OFF (to masturbate)]

toss off *vb* (*adverb*) **1** (*tr*) to perform, write, consume, etc, quickly and easily **2** (*tr*) to drink quickly at one draught **3** (*intr*) *Brit slang* to masturbate

toss up *vb* (*adverb*) to spin (a coin) in the air in order to decide between alternatives by guessing which side will fall uppermost ▷ *n* **toss-up 2** an instance of tossing up a coin **3** *informal* an even chance or risk; gamble

Tostig ('tɒstɪg) *n* died 1066, earl of Northumbria (1055–65), brother of King Harold II. He joined the Norwegian forces that invaded England in 1066 and died at Stamford Bridge

tot¹ (tɒt) *n* **1** a young child; toddler **2** *chiefly Brit* a small amount of anything **3** a small measure of spirits [c18: perhaps from *totterer;* see TOTTER]

tot² (tɒt) *vb* tots, totting, totted (*usually foll by up*) *chiefly Brit* to total; add [c17: shortened from TOTAL or from Latin *totum* all]

total ('təʊtªl) *n* **1** the whole, esp regarded as the complete sum of a number of parts ▷ *adj* **2** complete; absolute **3** (*prenominal*) being or related to a total: *the total number of passengers* ▷ *vb* -tals, -talling, -talled *or* US -tals, -taling, -taled **4** (when *intr*, sometimes foll by *to*) to amount: *to total six pounds* **5** (*tr*) to add up [c14: from Old French, from Medieval Latin *tōtālis,* from Latin *tōtus* all] >'totally *adv*

total football *n football* an attacking style of play, popularized by the Dutch national team of the 1970s, in which there are no fixed positions and every outfield player can join in the attack

total internal reflection *n physics* the complete reflection of a light ray at the boundary of two media, when the ray is in the medium with greater refractive index

totalitarian (təʊˌtælɪ'tɛərɪən) *adj* **1** of, denoting, relating to, or characteristic of a dictatorial one-party state that regulates every realm of life ▷ *n* **2** a person who advocates or practises totalitarian policies [from TOTALITY + -ARIAN] >toˌtali'tarianism *n*

totality (təʊ'tælɪtɪ) *n*, *pl*-ties **1** the whole amount **2** the state of being total

totalizator ('təʊtªlaɪˌzeɪtə), **totalizer, totalisator** *or* **totaliser** *n* **1** a system of betting on horse races in which the aggregate stake, less an administration charge and tax, is paid out to winners in proportion to their stake **2** the machine that records bets in this system and works out odds, pays out winnings, etc ▷ *US* and Canadian term: pari-mutuel

total quality management *n* an approach to the management of an organization that integrates the needs of customers with a deep understanding of the technical details, costs, and human-resource relationships of the organization. Abbreviation: TQM

totaquine ('təʊtəˌkwi:n, -kwɪn) *n* a mixture of quinine and other alkaloids derived from cinchona bark, used as a substitute for quinine in treating malaria [c20: from New Latin *tōtaquīna,* from TOTA(L) + Spanish *quina* cinchona bark; see QUININE]

totara ('təʊtərə) *n* a tall coniferous forest tree, *Podocarpus totara,* of New Zealand, having a hard durable wood [Māori]

tote (təʊt) *informal* ▷ *vb* **1** (*tr*) to carry, convey, or drag ▷ *n* **2** the act of or an instance of toting **3** something toted [c17: of obscure origin] >'toter *n*

Tote (təʊt) *n* **the Tote** (*sometimes not capital*) *trademark* short for **totalizator**

tote bag *n* a large roomy handbag or shopping bag

totem ('təʊtəm) *n* **1** (in some societies, esp among North American Indians) an object, species of animal or plant, or natural phenomenon symbolizing a clan, family, etc, often having ritual associations **2** a representation of such an object [c18: from Ojibwa *nintōtēm* mark of my family] >totemic (təʊ'tɛmɪk) *adj* >'totemˌism *n*

totem pole *n* a pole carved or painted with totemic figures set up by certain North American Indians, esp those of the NW Pacific coast, within a village as a tribal symbol or, sometimes, in memory of a dead person

tother *or* **t'other** ('tʌðə) *adj, n archaic or dialect* the other [C13 *the tother,* by mistaken division from *thet other* (thet, from Old English *thæt,* neuter of THE¹)]

totipalmate (ˌtəʊtɪ'pælmɪt, -ˌmeɪt) *adj* (of certain birds) having all four toes webbed [c19: from Latin *tōtus* entire + *palmate,* from Latin *palmātus* shaped like a hand, from *palma* PALM¹]

totter ('tɒtə) *vb* (*intr*) **1** to walk or move in an unsteady manner, as from old age **2** to sway or shake as if about to fall **3** to be failing, unstable, or precarious ▷ *n* **4** the act or an instance of tottering [c12: perhaps from Old English *tealtrian* to waver, and Middle Dutch *touteren* to stagger] >'totterer *n* >'tottering *adj* >'totteringly *adv* >'tottery *adj*

totting ('tɒtɪŋ) *n Brit* the practice of searching through rubbish for usable or saleable items [c19: of unknown origin]

toucan ('tu:kən) *n* any tropical American arboreal fruit-eating bird of the family *Ramphastidae,* having a large brightly coloured bill with serrated edges and a bright plumage [c16: from French, from Portuguese *tucano,* from Tupi *tucana,* probably imitative of its cry]

touch (tʌtʃ) *n* **1** the sense by which the texture and other qualities of objects can be experienced when they come in contact with a part of the body surface, esp the tips of the fingers. Related adjs: **haptic, tactile 2** the quality of an object as perceived by this sense; feel; feeling **3** the act or an instance of something coming into contact with the body **4** a gentle push, tap, or caress **5** a small amount; hint: *a touch of sarcasm* **6** a noticeable effect; influence: *the house needed a woman's touch* **7** any slight stroke or mark: *with a touch of his brush he captured the scene* **8** characteristic manner or style: *the artist had a distinctive touch* **9** a detail of some work, esp a literary or artistic work: *she added a few finishing touches to the book* **10** a slight attack, as of a disease: *a touch of bronchitis* **11** a specific ability or facility: *the champion appeared to have lost his touch* **12** the state of being aware of a situation or in contact with someone: *to get in touch with someone* **13** the state of being in physical contact **14** a trial or test (esp in the phrase **put to the touch) 15** *rugby, soccer* the area outside the touchlines, beyond which the ball is out of play (esp in the phrase **in touch) 16** *archaic* **a** an official stamp on metal indicating standard purity **b** the die stamp used to apply this mark. Now usually called: **hallmark 17** a scoring hit in competitive fencing **18** an estimate of the amount of gold in an alloy as obtained by use of a touchstone **19** the technique of fingering a keyboard instrument **20** the quality of the action of a keyboard instrument with regard to the relative ease with which the keys may be depressed **21** *slang* **a** the act of asking for money as a loan or gift, often by devious means **b** the money received in this way **c** a person asked for money in this way: *he was an easy touch* ▷ *vb* **22** (tr) to cause or permit a part of the body to come into contact with **23** (tr) to tap, feel, or strike, esp with the hand **24** to come or cause (something) to come into contact with (something else): *their hands touched briefly; he touched the match to the fuse* **25** (intr) to be in contact **26** (tr; usually used with a negative) to take hold of (a person or thing), esp in violence: *don't touch the baby!* **27** to be adjacent to (each other): *the two properties touch* **28** (tr) to move or disturb by handling: *someone's touched my desk* **29** (tr) to have an effect on: *the war scarcely touched our town* **30** (tr) to produce an emotional response in: *his sad story touched her* **31** (tr) to affect; concern **32** (tr; usually used with a negative) to partake of, eat, or drink **33** (tr; usually used with a negative) to handle or deal with: *I wouldn't touch that business* **34** (when *intr,* often foll by *on*) to allude (to) briefly or in passing: *the speech touched on several subjects* **35** (tr) to tinge or tint slightly: *brown hair touched with gold* **36** (tr) to spoil or injure slightly: *blackfly touched the flowers* **37** (tr) to mark, as with a brush or pen **38** (tr) to compare to in quality or attainment; equal or match: *there's no-one to touch him* **39** (tr) to reach or attain: *he touched the high point in his career* **40** (intr) to dock or stop briefly: *the ship touches at Tenerife* **41** (tr) *slang* to ask for a loan or gift of money from **42** *rare* **a** to finger (the keys or strings of an instrument) **b** to play (a tune, piece of music, etc) in this way **43 touch base** to make contact ▷ See also **touchdown, touch off, touch up** [c13: from Old French *tochier,* from Vulgar Latin *toccāre* (unattested) to strike, ring (a bell), probably imitative of a tapping sound] > ˈtouchable *adj* > ˈtouchableness *n* > ˈtoucher *n* > ˈtouchless *adj*

touch and go *adj* (**touch-and-go** when prenominal) risky or critical: *a touch-and-go situation*

touchdown ('tʌtʃˌdaʊn) *n* **1** the moment at which a landing aircraft or spacecraft comes into contact with the landing surface **2** *rugby* the act of placing or touching the ball on the ground behind the goal line, as in scoring a try **3** *American football* a scoring play worth six points, achieved by being in possession of the ball in

the opposing team's end zone. See also **field goal** ▷ *vb* **touch down** (intr, adverb) **4** (of a space vehicle, aircraft, etc) to land **5** *rugby* to place the ball behind the goal line, as when scoring a try **6** *informal* to pause during a busy schedule in order to catch up, reorganize, or rest

touché (tu:ˈʃeɪ) *interj* **1** an acknowledgment that a scoring hit has been made in a fencing competition **2** an acknowledgment of the striking home of a remark or the capping of a witticism [from French, literally: touched]

touched (tʌtʃt) *adj* (postpositive) **1** moved to sympathy or emotion; affected **2** showing slight insanity

touchhole ('tʌtʃˌhəʊl) *n* a hole in the breech of early cannon and firearms through which the charge was ignited

touching ('tʌtʃɪŋ) *adj* **1** evoking or eliciting tender feelings: *your sympathy is touching* ▷ *prep* **2** on the subject of; relating to > ˈtouchingly *adv* > ˈtouchingness *n*

touch judge *n* one of the two linesmen in rugby

touchline ('tʌtʃˌlaɪn) *n* either of the lines marking the side of the playing area in certain games, such as rugby

touchmark ('tʌtʃˌmɑːk) *n* a maker's mark stamped on pewter objects

touch-me-not *n* any of several balsaminaceous plants of the genus *Impatiens,* esp *I. noli-me-tangere,* having yellow spurred flowers and seed pods that burst open at a touch when ripe. Also called: **noli-me-tangere**

touch off *vb* (tr, adverb) **1** to cause to explode, as by touching with a match **2** to cause (a disturbance, violence, etc) to begin: *the marchers' action touched off riots*

touchpaper ('tʌtʃˌpeɪpə) *n* **1** paper soaked in saltpetre and used for firing gunpowder **2 light the touchpaper** *or* **light the blue touchpaper** to do something that will cause much anger or excitement

touch rugby *n* a limited-contact version of rugby in which players seek to evade being touched (rather than tackled) while in possession of the ball

touch screen *n* **a** a visual display unit screen that allows the user to give commands to the computer by touching parts of the screen instead of using the keyboard **b** (as modifier): *a touch-screen computer*

touch-sensitive *adj* (of a computer input device) activated by the user touching parts of it, esp a screen

touchstone ('tʌtʃˌstəʊn) *n* **1** a criterion or standard by which judgment is made **2** a hard dark siliceous stone, such as basalt or jasper, that is used to test the quality of gold and silver from the colour of the streak they produce on it

touch-tone *adj* of or relating to a telephone dialling system in which each of the buttons pressed generates a tone of a different pitch, which is transmitted to the exchange

touch-type *vb* (intr) to type without having to look at the keys of the typewriter > ˈtouch-ˌtypist *n*

touch up *vb* (tr, adverb) **1** to put extra or finishing touches to **2** to enhance, renovate, or falsify by putting extra touches to: *to touch up a photograph* **3** to stimulate or rouse as by a tap or light blow **4** *Brit slang* to touch or caress (someone), esp to arouse sexual feelings ▷ *n* **touch-up 5** a renovation or retouching, as of a painting

touchwood ('tʌtʃˌwʊd) *n* something, esp dry wood or fungus material such as amadou, used as tinder [c16: TOUCH (in the sense: to kindle) + WOOD[1]]

touchy ('tʌtʃɪ) *adj* **touchier, touchiest 1** easily upset or irritated; oversensitive **2** extremely risky **3** easily ignited > ˈtouchily *adv* > ˈtouchiness *n*

touchy-feely ('tʌtʃɪˈfiːlɪ) *adj informal, sometimes derogatory* openly displaying one's emotions and affections > ˈtouchy-ˈfeeliness *n*

tough (tʌf) *adj* **1** strong or resilient; durable: *a tough material* **2** not tender: *he could not eat the tough steak* **3** a tough mountaineer **4** rough or pugnacious: *a tough gangster* **5** resolute or intractable: *a tough employer* **6** difficult or troublesome to do or deal with: *a tough problem* **7** *informal* unfortunate or unlucky: *it's tough on him* ▷ *n* **8** a rough, vicious, or pugnacious person ▷ *adv* **9** *informal* violently, aggressively, or intractably: *to treat someone tough* **10 hang tough** *informal* to be or appear to be strong or determined ▷ *vb* **11** (tr) *slang* to stand firm, hold out against (a difficulty or difficult situation) (esp in **tough it out**) [Old English *tōh*; related to Old High German *zāhi* tough, Old Norse *tā* trodden ground in front of a house] > 'toughish *adj* > 'toughly *adv* > 'toughness *n*

toughen ('tʌfən) *vb* to make or become tough or tougher

tough love *n* the practice of taking a stern attitude towards a relative or friend suffering from an addiction, etc, to help the addict overcome the problem

tough-minded *adj* practical, unsentimental, stern or intractable > ,tough-'mindedness *n*

Toul (tu:l) *n* a town in NE France: a leading episcopal see in the Middle Ages. Pop: 16 945 (1999)

Toulon (*French* tulɔ̃) *n* a fortified port and naval base in SE France, on the Mediterranean: naval arsenal developed by Henry IV and Richelieu, later fortified by Vauban. Pop: 160 639 (1999)

Toulouse (tu:'lu:z) *n* a city in S France, on the Garonne River: scene of severe religious strife in the early 13th and mid-16th centuries; university (1229). Pop: 390 350 (1999)

Toulouse-Lautrec (*French* tuluzlotrɛk) *n* **Henri** (**Marie Raymond**) **de** (ɑ̃ri də). 1864–1901, French painter and lithographer, noted for his paintings and posters of the life of Montmartre, Paris

toupee ('tu:peɪ) *n* **1** a wig or hairpiece worn, esp by men, to cover a bald or balding place **2** (formerly) a prominent lock on a periwig, esp in the 18th century [c18: apparently from French *toupet* forelock, from Old French *toup* top, of Germanic origin; see TOP¹]

tour (tʊə) *n* **1** an extended journey, usually taken for pleasure, visiting places of interest along the route **2** *military* a period of service, esp in one place of duty **3** a short trip, as for inspection **4** a trip made by a theatre company, orchestra, etc, to perform in several different places: *a concert tour* **5** an overseas trip made by a cricket or rugby team, etc, to play in several places ▷ *vb* **6** to make a tour of (a place) **7** to perform (a show) or promote (a product) in several different places [c14: from Old French: a turn, from Latin *tornus* a lathe, from Greek *tornos*; compare TURN]

touraco *or* **turaco** ('tʊərə,kəʊ) *n, pl* -cos any brightly coloured crested arboreal African bird of the family *Musophagidae*: order *Cuculiformes* (cuckoos, etc) [c18: of West African origin]

Touraine (*French* turɛn) *n* a former province of NW central France: at its height in the 16th century as an area of royal residences, esp along the Loire. Chief town: Tours

Tourane (tu:'rɑ:n) *n* the former name of **Da Nang**

Tourcoing (*French* turkwɛ̃) *n* a town in NE France: textile manufacturing. Pop: 93 540 (1999)

tour de force *French* (tur də fɔrs; *English* 'tʊə də 'fɔːs) *n, pl* **tours de force** (tur; *English* 'tʊə) a masterly or brilliant stroke, creation, effect, or accomplishment [literally: feat of skill or strength]

Touré ('tʊəreɪ) *n* (**Ahmed**) **Sékou** ('seɪku:). 1922–84, president of the Republic of Guinea (1958–84)

tourer ('tʊərə) *n* a large open car with a folding top, usually seating a driver and four passengers

tourism ('tʊərɪzəm) *n* tourist travel and the services connected with it, esp when regarded as an industry

tourist ('tʊərɪst) *n* **1 a** a person who travels for pleasure, usually sightseeing and staying in hotels **b** (*as modifier*): *tourist attractions* **2** a person on an excursion or sightseeing tour **3** a person travelling abroad as a member of a sports team that is playing a series of usually international matches **4** Also called: **tourist class** the lowest class of accommodation on a passenger ship ▷ *adj* **5** of or relating to tourist accommodation > tour'istic *adj*

touristy ('tʊərɪstɪ) *adj informal, often derogatory* abounding in or designed for tourists

tourmaline ('tʊəmə,li:n) *n* any of a group of hard glassy minerals of variable colour consisting of complex borosilicates of aluminium with quantities of lithium, sodium, calcium, potassium, iron, and magnesium in hexagonal crystalline form: used in optical and electrical equipment and in jewellery [c18: from German *Turmalin*, from Sinhalese *toramalli* carnelian]

Tournai (*French* turnɛ) *n* a city in W Belgium, in Hainaut province on the River Scheldt: under several different European rulers until 1814. Pop: 67 341 (2004 est). Flemish name: Doornik

tournament ('tʊənəmənt, 'tɔ:-, 'tɜ:-) *n* **1** a sporting competition in which contestants play a series of games to determine an overall winner **2** a meeting for athletic or other sporting contestants: *an archery tournament* **3** *medieval history* **a** (originally) a martial sport or contest in which mounted combatants fought for a prize **b** (later) a meeting for knightly sports and exercises [c13: from Old French *torneiement*, from *torneier* to fight on horseback, literally: to turn, from the constant wheeling round of the combatants; see TOURNEY]

tournedos ('tʊənə,dəʊ) *n, pl* -dos (-,dəʊz) a thick round steak of beef cut from the fillet or undercut of sirloin [from French, from *tourner* to TURN + *dos* back]

Tourneur ('tɜ:nə) *n* **Cyril.** ?1575–1626, English dramatist; author of *The Atheist's Tragedy* (1611) and, reputedly, of *The Revenger's Tragedy* (1607)

tourney ('tʊənɪ, 'tɔ:-) *medieval history* ▷ *n* **1** a knightly tournament ▷ *vb* **2** (*intr*) to engage in a tourney [c13: from Old French *torneier*, from Vulgar Latin *tornidiāre* (unattested) to turn constantly, from Latin *tornāre* to TURN (in a lathe); see TOURNAMENT] > 'tourneyer *n*

tourniquet ('tʊənɪ,keɪ, 'tɔ:-) *n med* any instrument or device for temporarily constricting an artery of the arm or leg to control bleeding [c17: from French: device that operates by turning, from *tourner* to TURN]

tour operator *n* a person or company that provides package holidays

Tours (*French* tur) *n* a town in W central France, on the River Loire: nearby is the scene of the defeat of the Arabs in 732, which ended the advance of Islam in W Europe. Pop: 132 820 (1999)

tourtière (,tu:rtɪ'ɛə; *French* turtjɛr) *n Canadian* a type of meat pie [from French]

tousle ('taʊzəl) *vb* (*tr*) **1** to tangle, ruffle, or disarrange **2** to treat roughly ▷ *n* **3** a disorderly, tangled, or rumpled state **4** a dishevelled or disordered mass, esp of hair [c15: from Low German *tūsen* to shake; related to Old High German *zirzūsōn* to tear to pieces]

Toussaint L'Ouverture (*French* tusɛ̃ luvɛrtyr) *n* **Pierre Dominique** (pjɛr dɔminik). ?1743–1803, Haitian revolutionary leader. He was made governor of the island by the French Revolutionary government (1794) and expelled the Spanish and British but when Napoleon I proclaimed the re-establishment of slavery he was arrested. He died in prison in France

tout (taʊt) *vb* **1** to solicit (business, customers, etc) or hawk (merchandise), esp in a brazen way **2** (*intr*) **a** to spy on racehorses being trained in order to obtain information for betting purposes **b** to sell, or attempt to sell, such information or to take bets, esp in public places **3** (*tr*) *informal* to recommend flatteringly or excessively ▷ *n* **4 a** a person who spies on racehorses so as to obtain betting information to sell **b** a person who sells information obtained by such spying **5** a person who solicits business in a brazen way **6** Also called: **ticket tout** a person who sells tickets unofficially for a heavily booked sporting event, concert, etc, at greatly inflated prices **7** *Northern Ireland* a police informer [c14 (in the sense: to peer, look out): related to Old English *tȳtan* to peep out] > 'touter *n*

tout à fait *French* (tut a fɛ) *adv* completely; absolutely

tout de suite *French* (tud sɥit) *adv* at once; immediately

tout le monde *French* (tu lə mɔ̃d) *n* all the world; everyone

tovarisch, tovarich *or* **tovarish** (tə'vɑ:rɪʃ; *Russian* ta'variʃtʃ) *n* comrade: a term of address [from Russian]

tow¹ (təʊ) *vb* **1** (*tr*) to pull or drag (a vehicle, boat, etc), esp by means of a rope or cable ▷ *n* **2** the act or an instance of towing **3** the state of being towed (esp in the phrases **in tow, under tow, on tow**) **4** something towed **5** something used for towing **6** in tow in one's charge or under one's influence **7** *informal* (in motor racing, etc) the act of taking advantage of the slipstream of another car (esp in the phrase **get a tow**) **8** short for **ski tow** [Old English *togian*; related to Old Frisian *togia*, Old Norse *toga*,

Old High German *zogōn*] ▷ 'towable *adj*

tow² (təʊ) *n* 1 the fibres of hemp, flax, jute, etc, in the scutched state 2 synthetic fibres preparatory to spinning [Old English *tōw*; related to Old Saxon *tou*, Old Norse *tō* tuft of wool, Dutch *touwen* to spin] ▷ 'towy *adj*

toward *adj* ('təʊəd) 1 now rare in progress; afoot 2 obsolete about to happen; imminent 3 obsolete promising or favourable ▷ prep (tə'wɔːd, tɔːd) 4 a variant of towards [Old English *tōweard*; see TO, -WARD] ▷ 'towardness *n*

towards (tə'wɔːdz, tɔːdz) prep 1 in the direction or vicinity of: *towards London* 2 with regard to: *her feelings towards me* 3 as a contribution or help to: *money towards a new car* 4 just before: *towards one o'clock*

towbar ('təʊˌbɑː) *n* a rigid metal bar or frame used for towing vehicles

towboat ('təʊˌbəʊt) *n* another word for tug (sense 4)

tow-coloured *adj* pale yellow; flaxen

towel ('taʊəl) *n* 1 a square or rectangular piece of absorbent cloth or paper used for drying the body 2 a similar piece of cloth used for drying plates, cutlery, etc 3 throw in the towel See throw in (sense 4) ▷ *vb* -els, -elling, -elled *or US* -els, -eling, -eled 4 (*tr*) to dry or wipe with a towel 5 (*tr*; often foll by *up*) *Austral slang* to assault or beat (a person) [c13: from Old French *toaille*, of Germanic origin; related to Old High German *dwahal* bath, Old Saxon *twahila* towel, Gothic *thwahan* to wash]

towelling ('taʊəlɪŋ) *n* an absorbent fabric, esp with a nap, used for making towels, bathrobes, etc

tower ('taʊə) *n* 1 a tall, usually square or circular structure, sometimes part of a larger building and usually built for a specific purpose: *a church tower; a control tower* 2 a place of defence or retreat 3 a mobile structure used in medieval warfare to attack a castle, etc 4 tower of strength a person who gives support, comfort, etc ▷ *vb* 5 (*intr*) to be or rise like a tower; loom [c12: from Old French *tur*, from Latin *turris*, from Greek]

Tower Hamlets *n* a borough of E Greater London, on the River Thames: contains the main part of the East End. Pop: 206 600 (2003 est). Area: 20 sq km (8 sq miles)

towering ('taʊərɪŋ) *adj* 1 very tall; lofty 2 outstanding, as in importance or stature 3 (*prenominal*) very intense: *a towering rage*

Tower of London *n* a fortress in the City of London, on the River Thames: begun 1078; later extended and used as a palace, the main state prison, and now as a museum containing the crown jewels

towhead ('təʊˌhed) *n* often disparaging 1 a person with blond or yellowish hair 2 a head of such hair [from TOW² (flax)]

towhee ('taʊhɪ, 'təʊ-) *n* any of various North American brown-coloured sparrows of the genera *Pipilo* and *Chlorura* [c18: imitative of its note]

towie ('təʊɪ) *n Austral informal* a truck used for towing

towline ('təʊˌlaɪn) *n* another name for towrope

town (taʊn) *n* 1 a a densely populated urban area, typically smaller than a city and larger than a village, having some local powers of government and a fixed boundary b (*as modifier*): *town life*. Related adj: urban 2 a city, borough, or other urban area 3 (in the US) a territorial unit of local government that is smaller than a county; township 4 the nearest town or commercial district 5 London or the chief city of an area 6 the inhabitants of a town 7 the permanent residents of a university town as opposed to the university staff and students 8 go to town a to make a supreme or unrestricted effort; go all out b *Austral & NZ informal* to lose one's temper 9 on the town seeking out entertainments and amusements [Old English *tūn* village; related to Old Saxon, Old Norse *tūn*, Old High German *zūn* fence, Old Irish *dūn*] ▷ 'townish *adj*

town clerk *n* 1 (in Britain until 1974) the secretary and chief administrative officer of a town or city 2 (in the US) the official who keeps the records of a town

town crier *n* (formerly) a person employed by a town to make public announcements in the streets

Townes (taʊnz) *n* Charles Hard. born 1915, US physicist, noted for his research in quantum electronics leading to the invention of the maser and the laser; shared the Nobel prize for physics in 1964

town gas *n* coal gas manufactured for domestic and industrial use

town hall *n* the chief building in which municipal business is transacted, often with a hall for public meetings

town house *n* 1 a terraced house in an urban area, esp a fashionable one, often having the main living room on the first floor with an integral garage on the ground floor 2 a person's town residence as distinct from his country residence

townie ('taʊnɪ) *or* townee (taʊ'niː) *n chiefly Brit informal, often disparaging* 1 a permanent resident in a town, esp as distinct from country dwellers or students 2 a young working-class person who dresses in casual sports clothes

townland ('taʊnlænd) *n Irish* a division of land of various sizes

town planning *n* the comprehensive planning of the physical and social development of a town, including the construction of facilities. US term: city planning ▷ town planner *n*

townscape ('taʊnskeɪp) *n* a view of an urban scene

Townshend ('taʊnzend) *n* 1 Charles, 2nd Viscount, nicknamed *Turnip Townshend*. 1674–1738, English politician and agriculturist 2 Pete born 1945, British rock guitarist, singer, and songwriter: member of the Who from 1964 and composer of much of their material

township ('taʊnʃɪp) *n* 1 a small town 2 (in the Scottish Highlands and islands) a small crofting community 3 (in the US and Canada) a territorial area, esp a subdivision of a county: often organized as a unit of local government 4 (formerly, in South Africa) a planned urban settlement of Black Africans or Coloured people. See location (sense 4) 5 *English history* a any of the local districts of a large parish, each division containing a village or small town b the particular manor or parish itself as a territorial division c the inhabitants of a township collectively

townsman ('taʊnzmən) *n, pl* -men 1 an inhabitant of a town 2 a person from the same town as oneself ▷ 'towns,woman *fem n*

townspeople ('taʊnz,piːpʰl) *or* townsfolk ('taʊnz,fəʊkʰl) *n* the inhabitants of a town; citizens

Townsville ('taʊnzvɪl) *n* a port in E Australia, in NE Queensland on the Coral Sea: centre of a vast agricultural and mining hinterland. Pop: 119 504 (2001)

towpath ('təʊˌpɑːθ) *n* a path beside a canal or river, used by people or animals towing boats. Also called: towing path

towrope ('təʊˌrəʊp) *n* a rope or cable used for towing a vehicle or vessel. Also called: towline

tox-, toxic-, *or before a consonant* toxo-, toxico- *combining form*. indicating poison: *toxalbumin* [from Latin *toxicum*]

toxaemia *or US* toxemia (tɒk'siːmɪə) *n* 1 a condition characterized by the presence of bacterial toxins in the blood 2 the condition in pregnancy of pre-eclampsia or eclampsia [c19: from TOX- + -AEMIA] ▷ tox'aemic *or US* tox'emic *adj*

toxic ('tɒksɪk) *adj* 1 of, relating to, or caused by a toxin or poison; poisonous 2 harmful or deadly [c17: from medical Latin *toxicus*, from Latin *toxicum* poison, from Greek *toxikon* (*pharmakon*) (poison) used on arrows, from *toxon* arrow] ▷ 'toxically *adv* ▷ toxicity (tɒk'sɪsɪtɪ) *n*

toxicant ('tɒksɪkənt) *n* 1 a toxic substance; poison 2 a rare word for intoxicant ▷ *adj* 3 poisonous; toxic [c19: from Medieval Latin *toxicāre* to poison; see TOXIC]

toxic effect *n* an adverse effect of a drug produced by an exaggeration of the effect that produces the theraputic response

toxicology (ˌtɒksɪ'kɒlədʒɪ) *n* the branch of science concerned with poisons, their nature, effects, and antidotes ▷ toxicological (ˌtɒksɪkə'lɒdʒɪkʰl) *or* ˌtoxico'logic *adj* ▷ ˌtoxico'logically *adv* ▷ ˌtoxi'cologist *n*

toxic shock syndrome *n* a potentially fatal condition, characterized by fever, stomachache, a painful rash, and a drop in blood pressure, that is caused by staphylococcal blood poisoning. In women it is most commonly caused by a retained tampon during menstruation

toxin ('tɒksɪn) *n* **1** any of various poisonous substances produced by microorganisms that stimulate the production of neutralizing substances (antitoxins) in the body **2** any other poisonous substance of plant or animal origin

toxin-antitoxin *n* a mixture of a specific toxin and antitoxin. The diphtheria toxin-antitoxin was formerly used in the US for active immunization

toxocariasis (ˌtɒksəkəˈraɪəsɪs) *n* the infection of humans with the larvae of a genus of roundworms, *Toxocara*, of dogs and cats. It can cause swelling of the liver and, sometimes, damage to the eyes

toxoid ('tɒksɔɪd) *n* a toxin that has been treated to reduce its toxicity and is used in immunization to stimulate production of antitoxins

toxophilite (tɒkˈsɒfɪˌlaɪt) *formal* ▷ *n* **1** an archer ▷ *adj* **2** of or relating to archery [c18: from *Toxophilus*, the title of a book (1545) by Ascham, designed to mean: a lover of the bow, from Greek *toxon* bow + *philos* loving] > tox'ophily *n*

toxoplasmosis (ˌtɒksəʊplæzˈməʊsɪs) *n* a protozoal disease characterized by jaundice, enlarged liver and spleen, and convulsions, caused by infection with *Toxoplasma gondii* > ˌtoxo'plasmic *adj*

toy (tɔɪ) *n* **1** an object designed to be played with **2 a** something that is a nonfunctioning replica of something else, esp a miniature one **b** (*as modifier*): *a toy guitar* **3** any small thing of little value; trifle **4 a** something small or miniature, esp a miniature variety of a breed of dog **b** (*as modifier*): *a toy poodle* ▷ *vb* **5** (*intr*; usually foll by *with*) to play, fiddle, or flirt [c16 (in the sense: amorous dalliance): of uncertain origin]

Toyama ('tɒjaˌmɑː) *n* a city in central Japan, on W Honshu on **Toyama Bay** (an inlet of the Sea of Japan): chemical and textile centre. Pop: 321 049 (2002 est)

toy boy *n* the much younger male lover of an older woman

Toynbee ('tɔɪnbɪ) *n* **1 Arnold** 1852–83, British economist and social reformer, after whom **Toynbee Hall**, a residential settlement in East London, is named **2** his nephew, **Arnold Joseph**. 1889–1975, British historian. In his chief work, *A Study of History* (1934–61), he attempted to analyse the principles determining the rise and fall of civilizations

toy-toy ('tɔɪˈtɔɪ) *or* **toyi-toyi** ('tɔɪɪ'tɔɪɪ) *South African* ▷ *n* **1** a dance expressing defiance and protest ▷ *vb* **2** (*intr*) to dance in this way [of uncertain origin]

TPI *abbreviation* tax and price index: a measure of the increase in taxable income needed to compensate for an increase in retail prices

TPWS *abbreviation* train protection warning system: a rail safety system fitted to track signals

TQM *abbreviation* total quality management

tr¹ *abbreviation* treasurer

tr² *internet domain name* Turkey

tr. *abbreviation* **1** transitive **2** translated **3** *music* trill

trabeated ('treɪbɪˌeɪtɪd) *or* **trabeate** ('treɪbɪɪt, -eɪt) *adj architect* constructed with horizontal beams as opposed to arches. See **arcuate** [c19: back formation from *trabeation*, from Latin *trabs* a beam] > ˌtrabe'ation *n*

trabecula (trəˈbɛkjʊlə) *n*, *pl* **-lae** (-ˌliː) *anatomy*, *botany* **1** any of various rod-shaped structures that divide organs into separate chambers **2** any of various rod-shaped cells or structures that bridge a cavity, as within the capsule of a moss or across the lumen of a cell [c19: via New Latin from Latin: a little beam, from *trabs* a beam] > tra'becular *or* tra'beculate *adj*

trabs (træbz) *pl n Northern English dialect* training shoes

Trabzon ('trɑːbzɒn) *or* **Trebizond** *n* a port in NE Turkey, on the Black Sea: founded as a Greek colony in the 8th century BC at the terminus of an important trade route from central Europe to Asia. Pop: 246 000 (2005 est)

trace¹ (treɪs) *n* **1** a mark or other sign that something has been in a place; vestige **2** a tiny or scarcely detectable amount or characteristic **3** a footprint or other indication of the passage of an animal or person **4** any line drawn by a recording instrument or a record consisting of a number of such lines **5** something drawn, such as a tracing **6** *chiefly US* a beaten track or path **7** the postulated alteration in the cells of the

nervous system that occurs as the result of any experience or learning **8** *geometry* the intersection of a surface with a coordinate plane **9** *maths* the sum of the diagonal entries of a square matrix **10** *linguistics* a symbol inserted in the constituent structure of a sentence to mark the position from which a constituent has been moved in a generative process **11** *meteorol* an amount of precipitation that is too small to be measured **12** *archaic* a way taken; route ▷ *vb* **13** (*tr*) to follow, discover, or ascertain the course or development of (something): *to trace the history of China* **14** (*tr*) to track down and find, as by following a trail **15** to copy (a design, map, etc) by drawing over the lines visible through a superimposed sheet of transparent paper or other material **16** (*tr*; often foll by *out*) **a** to draw or delineate a plan or diagram of: *she spent hours tracing the models one at a time* **b** to outline or sketch (an idea, policy, etc): *he traced out his scheme for the robbery* **17** (*tr*) to decorate with tracery **18** (*tr*) to imprint (a design) on cloth, etc **19** (usually foll by *back*) to follow or be followed to source; date back: *his ancestors trace back to the 16th century* **20** *archaic* to make one's way over, through, or along (something) [c13: from French *tracier*, from Vulgar Latin *tractiāre* (unattested) to drag, from Latin *tractus*, from *trahere* to drag] > 'traceable *adj* > ˌtracea'bility *or* 'traceableness *n* > 'traceably *adv* > 'traceless *adj* > 'tracelessly *adv*

trace² (treɪs) *n* **1** either of the two side straps that connect a horse's harness to the swingletree **2** *angling* a length of nylon or, formerly, gut attaching a hook or fly to a line **3 kick over the traces** to escape or defy control [c14 *trais*, from Old French *trait*, ultimately from Latin *trahere* to drag]

trace element *n* any of various chemical elements, such as iron, manganese, zinc, copper, and iodine, that occur in very small amounts in organisms and are essential for many physiological and biochemical processes

trace fossil *n* the fossilized remains of a track, trail, footprint, burrow, etc, of an organism

tracer ('treɪsə) *n* **1** a person or thing that traces **2 a** a projectile that can be observed when in flight by the burning of chemical substances in its base **b** ammunition consisting of such projectiles **c** (*as modifier*): *tracer fire* **3** *med* any radioactive isotope introduced into the body to study metabolic processes, absorption, etc, by following its progress through the body with a gamma camera or other detector **4** an investigation to trace missing cargo, mail, etc

tracer bullet *n* a round of small arms ammunition containing a tracer

tracery ('treɪsərɪ) *n*, *pl* **-eries 1** a pattern of interlacing ribs, esp as used in the upper part of a Gothic window, etc **2** any fine pattern resembling this > 'traceried *adj*

trachea (trəˈkiːə) *n*, *pl* **-cheae** (-ˈkiːiː) **1** *anatomy*, *zoology* the membranous tube with cartilaginous rings that conveys inhaled air from the larynx to the bronchi. Nontechnical name: windpipe **2** any of the tubes in insects and related animals that convey air from the spiracles to the tissues **3** *botany* another name for **vessel** (sense 4) [c16: from Medieval Latin, from Greek *trakheia*, shortened from (*artēria*) *trakheia* rough (artery), from *trakhus* rough] > tra'cheal *or* tra'cheate *adj*

tracheitis (ˌtreɪkɪˈaɪtɪs) *n* inflammation of the trachea

tracheo- *or before a vowel* **trache-** *combining form* denoting the trachea: *tracheotomy*

tracheotomy (ˌtrækɪˈɒtəmɪ) *n*, *pl* **-mies** surgical incision into the trachea, usually performed when the upper air passage has been blocked

trachoma (trəˈkəʊmə) *n* a chronic contagious disease of the eye characterized by inflammation of the conjunctiva and cornea and the formation of scar tissue, caused by infection with the virus-like bacterium *Chlamydia trachomatis* [c17: from New Latin, from Greek *trakhōma* roughness, from *trakhus* rough] > trachomatous (trəˈkɒmətəs, -ˈkəʊ-) *adj*

trachyte ('treɪkaɪt, 'træ-) *n* a light-coloured fine-grained volcanic rock of rough texture consisting of feldspars with small amounts of pyroxene or amphibole [c19: from French, from Greek *trakhutēs*, from *trakhus* rough]

>**trachytoid** ('trækɪˌtɔɪd, 'treɪ-) *adj*

tracing ('treɪsɪŋ) *n* **1** a copy made by tracing **2** the act of making a trace **3** a record made by an instrument

track (træk) *n* **1** the mark or trail left by something that has passed by: *the track of an animal* **2** any road or path affording passage, esp a rough one **3** a rail or pair of parallel rails on which a vehicle, such as a locomotive, runs, esp the rails together with the sleepers, ballast, etc, on a railway **4** a course of action, thought, etc: *don't start on that track again!* **5** a line of motion or travel, such as flight **6** an endless jointed metal band driven by the wheels of a vehicle such as a tank or tractor to enable it to move across rough or muddy ground **7** *physics* the path of a particle of ionizing radiation as observed in a cloud chamber, bubble chamber, or photographic emulsion **8 a** a course for running or racing **b** (*as modifier*): *track events* **9** *US & Canadian* **a** sports performed on a track **b** track and field events as a whole **10** a path on a magnetic recording medium, esp magnetic tape, on which information, such as music or speech, from a single input channel is recorded **11** any of a number of separate sections in the recording on a record, CD, or cassette **12** a metal path that makes the interconnections on an integrated circuit **13** the distance between the points of contact with the ground of a pair of wheels, such as the front wheels of a motor vehicle or the paired wheels of an aircraft undercarriage **14** a hypothetical trace made on the surface of the earth by a point directly below an aircraft in flight **15** keep track of to follow the passage, course, or progress of **16** lose track of to fail to follow the passage, course, or progress of **17** off the beaten track See **beaten** (sense 4) **18** off the track away from what is correct or true **19** on the track of on the scent or trail of; pursuing **20** the right track pursuing the correct line of investigation, inquiry, etc **21** the wrong track pursuing the incorrect line of investigation, inquiry, etc ▷ *vb* **22** to follow the trail of (a person, animal, etc) **23** to track the flight path of (a satellite, spacecraft, etc) by picking up radio or radar signals transmitted or reflected by it **24** *US railways* **a** to provide with a track **b** to run on a track of (a certain width) **25** (of a camera or camera operator) to follow (a moving object) in any direction while operating **26** to move (a camera) towards the scene (**track in**) or away from the scene (**track out**) **27** to follow a track through (a place): *to track the jungles* **28** (*intr*) (of the pick-up, stylus, etc, of a record player) to follow the groove of a record: *the pick-up tracks badly* ▷ See also **tracks** [c15: from Old French *trac*, probably of Germanic origin; related to Middle Dutch *tracken* to pull, Middle Low German *trecken*; compare Norwegian *trakke* to trample] >'trackable *adj* >'tracker *n*

track down *vb* (*tr, adverb*) to find by tracking or pursuing

tracker dog *n* a dog specially trained to hunt fugitives or to search for missing people

track event *n* a competition in athletics, such as relay running or sprinting, that takes place on a running track

tracking ('trækɪŋ) *n* **1** the act or process of following something or someone **2** *electrical engineering* a leakage of electric current between two points separated by an insulating material caused by dirt, carbon particles, moisture, etc **3** the way wheels on a vehicle are aligned **4** a function of a video cassette recorder, which adjusts the alignment of the heads in order to achieve the best possible audio and video reproduction from each recording

tracking radar *n* a radar system emitting a narrow beam which oscillates about the target, thus compensating for abrupt changes of direction

tracking shot *n* a camera shot in which the camera follows a specific person or event in the action

tracking station *n* a station that can use a radio or radar beam to determine and follow the path of an object, esp a spacecraft or satellite, in space or in the atmosphere

tracklaying ('trækˌleɪɪŋ) *adj* (of a vehicle) having an endless jointed metal band around the wheels

track record *n informal* the past record of the accomplishments and failures of a person, business, etc

track rod *n* the rod connecting the two front wheels of a motor vehicle ensuring that they turn at the same angle

tracks (træks) *pl n* **1** (*sometimes singular*) marks, such as footprints, tyre impressions, etc, left by someone or something that has passed **2** in one's tracks on the very spot where one is standing (esp in the phrase **stop in one's tracks**) **3** make tracks to leave or depart **4** make tracks for to go or head towards **5** the wrong side of the tracks the unfashionable or poor district or stratum of a community

track shoe *n* either of a pair of light running shoes fitted with steel spikes for better grip. Also called: spike

tracksuit ('trækˌsuːt, -ˌsjuːt) *n* a warm suit worn by athletes, etc, usually over the clothes, esp during training

tract¹ (trækt) *n* **1** an extended area, as of land **2** *anatomy* a system of organs, glands, or other tissues that has a particular function: *the digestive tract* **3** *archaic* an extended period of time [c15: from Latin *tractus* a stretching out, from *trahere* to drag]

tract² (trækt) *n* a treatise or pamphlet, esp a religious or moralistic one [c15: from Latin *tractātus* TRACTATE]

tractable ('træktəbᵊl) *adj* **1** easily controlled or persuaded **2** readily worked; malleable [c16: from Latin *tractābilis*, from *tractāre* to manage, from *trahere* to draw] >ˌtracta'bility *or* 'tractableness *n* >'tractably *adv*

Tractarianism (træk'teərɪəˌnɪzəm) *n* another name for **Oxford Movement** [after the series of tracts, *Tracts for the Times*, published between 1833 and 1841, in which the principles of the movement were presented] >Trac'tarian *n, adj*

tractate ('trækteɪt) *n* a short tract; treatise [c15: from Latin *tractātus*, from *tractāre* to handle; see TRACTABLE]

tractile ('træktaɪl) *adj* capable of being drawn out; ductile [c17: from Latin *trahere* to drag] >tractility (træk'tɪlɪtɪ) *n*

traction ('trækʃən) *n* **1** the act of drawing or pulling, esp by motive power **2** the state of being drawn or pulled **3** *med* the application of a steady pull on a part during healing of a fractured or dislocated bone, using a system of weights and pulleys or splints **4** the adhesive friction between a wheel and a surface, as between a driving wheel of a motor vehicle and the road [c17: from Medieval Latin *tractiō*, from Latin *tractus* dragged; see TRACTILE] >'tractional *adj* >tractive ('træktɪv) *adj*

traction engine *n* a steam-powered locomotive used, esp formerly, for drawing heavy loads along roads or over rough ground. It usually has two large rear wheels and a rope drum for haulage purposes

traction load *n geology* the solid material that is carried along the bed of a river

tractor ('træktə) *n* **1** a motor vehicle used to pull heavy loads, esp farm machinery such as a plough or harvester. It usually has two large rear wheels with deeply treaded tyres **2** a short motor vehicle with a powerful engine and a driver's cab, used to pull a trailer, as in an articulated lorry [c18: from Late Latin: one who pulls, from *trahere* to drag]

Tracy ('treɪsɪ) *n* **Spencer.** 1900–67, US film actor. His films include *The Power and the Glory* (1933), *Captains Courageous* (1937) and *Boys' Town* (1938), for both of which he won Oscars, *Adam's Rib* (1949), and *Bad Day at Black Rock* (1955)

trad (træd) *n* **1** *chiefly Brit* traditional jazz, as revived in the 1950s ▷ *adj* **2** short for **traditional**

trade (treɪd) *n* **1** the act or an instance of buying and selling goods and services either on the domestic (wholesale and retail) markets or on the international (import, export, and entrepôt) markets **2** a personal occupation, esp a craft requiring skill **3** the people and practices of an industry, craft, or business **4** exchange of one thing for something else **5** the regular clientele of a firm or industry **6** amount of custom or commercial dealings; business **7** a specified market or business: *the tailoring trade* **8** an occupation in commerce, as opposed to a profession ▷ *vb* **9** (*tr*) to buy and sell (commercial merchandise) **10** to exchange (one thing) for another **11** (*intr*) to engage in trade **12** (*intr*) to deal or do business (with) ▷ See also **trade down, trade-in, trade on** [C14 (in the sense: track, hence, a regular business): related to Old Saxon *trada*, Old High German *trata* track; see TREAD] > ˈtradable *or* ˈtradeable *adj*

trade agreement *n* a commercial treaty between two or more nations

trade association *n* an association of organizations in the same trade formed to further their collective interests, esp in negotiating with governments, trade unions, etc

trade cycle *n* the recurrent fluctuation between boom and depression in the economic activity of a capitalist country

trade discount *n* a sum or percentage deducted from the list price of a commodity allowed by a manufacturer, distributor, or wholesaler to a retailer or by one enterprise to another in the same trade

traded option *n stock exchange* an option that can itself be bought and sold on a stock exchange. See **traditional option**

trade down *vb* (*intr, adverb*) to sell a large or relatively expensive house, car, etc, and replace it with a smaller or less expensive one

trade gap *n* the amount by which the value of a country's visible imports exceeds that of visible exports; an unfavourable balance of trade

trade-in *n* **1 a** a used article given in part payment for the purchase of a new article **b** a transaction involving such part payment **c** the valuation put on the article traded in ▷ *vb* **trade in 2** (*tr, adverb*) to give (a used article) as part payment for the purchase of a new article

trademark (ˈtreɪdˌmɑːk) *n* **1** the name or other symbol used to identify the goods produced by a particular manufacturer or distributed by a particular dealer and to distinguish them from products associated with competing manufacturers or dealers. A trademark that has been officially registered and is therefore legally protected is known as a Registered Trademark **2** any distinctive sign or mark of the presence of a person or animal ▷ *vb* (*tr*) **3** to label with a trademark **4** to register as a trademark

trade name *n* **1** the name used by a trade to refer to a commodity, service, etc **2** the name under which a commercial enterprise operates in business

trade-off *n* an exchange, esp as a compromise

trade on *vb* (*intr, preposition*) to exploit or take advantage of: *he traded on her endless patience*

trade plate *n* a numberplate attached temporarily to a vehicle by a dealer, etc, before the vehicle has been registered

trader (ˈtreɪdə) *n* **1** a person who engages in trade; dealer; merchant **2** a vessel regularly employed in foreign or coastal trade **3** *stock exchange, US* a member who operates mainly on his or her own account rather than for customers' accounts

trade reference *n* a reference in which one trader gives his opinion as to the creditworthiness of another trader in the same trade, esp to a supplier

Tradescant (ˈtrædɛskaent) *n* **1** **John**. 1570–1638, English botanist and gardener to Charles I. He introduced many plants from overseas into Britain **2** his son, **John**. 1608–62, English naturalist and gardener, who continued his father's work

tradescantia (ˌtrædɛsˈkænʃɪə) *n* any plant of the American genus *Tradescantia*, widely cultivated for their striped variegated leaves: family *Commelinaceae* [C18: New Latin, named after John *Tradescant* (1570–1638), English botanist and gardener]

Trades Council *n* (in Britain) an association of the different trade unions in one town or area

trade secret *n* a secret formula, technique, process, etc, known and used to advantage by only one manufacturer

tradesman (ˈtreɪdzmən) *n, pl* **-men 1** a man engaged in trade, esp a retail dealer **2** a skilled worker > ˈtradesˌwoman *fem n*

tradespeople (ˈtreɪdzˌpiːpəl) *or* **tradesfolk** (ˈtreɪdzˌfəʊk) *pl n chiefly Brit* people engaged in trade, esp shopkeepers

Trades Union Congress *n* the major association of British trade unions, which includes all the larger unions. Abbreviation: TUC

trade union *or* **trades union** *n* an association of employees formed to improve their incomes and working conditions by collective bargaining with the employer or employer organizations > **trade unionism** *or* **trades unionism** *n* > **trade unionist** *or* **trades unionist** *n*

trade up *vb* (*intr, adverb*) to sell a small or relatively inexpensive house, car, etc, and replace it with a larger or more expensive one

trade-weighted *adj* (of exchange rates) weighted according to the volume of trade between the various countries involved

trade wind (wɪnd) *n* a wind blowing obliquely towards the equator either from the northeast in the N hemisphere or the southeast in the S hemisphere, approximately between latitudes 30° N and S, forming part of the planetary wind system [C17: from *to blow trade* to blow steadily in one direction, from TRADE in the obsolete sense: a track]

trading estate *n chiefly Brit* a large area in which a number of commercial or industrial firms are situated. Also called: **industrial estate**

trading floor *n* the area in a bank or stock exchange where securities are traded

trading post *n* a general store established by a trader in an unsettled or thinly populated region

tradition (trəˈdɪʃən) *n* **1** the handing down from generation to generation of the same customs, beliefs, etc, esp by word of mouth **2** the body of customs, thought, practices, etc, belonging to a particular country, people, family, or institution over a relatively long period **3** a specific custom or practice of long standing **4** *Christianity* a doctrine or body of doctrines regarded as having been established by Christ or the apostles though not contained in Scripture **5** (*often capital*) *Judaism* a body of laws regarded as having been handed down from Moses orally and only committed to writing in the 2nd century AD **6** the beliefs and customs of Islam supplementing the Koran, esp as embodied in the Sunna **7** *law chiefly Roman law, Scots law* the act of formally transferring ownership of movable property; delivery [C14: from Latin *trāditiō* a handing down, surrender, from *trādere* to give up, transmit, from TRANS- + *dāre* to give] > traˈditionless *adj*

traditional (trəˈdɪʃənəl) *adj* **1** of, relating to, or being a tradition **2** of or relating to the style of jazz originating in New Orleans, characterized by collective improvisation by a front line of trumpet, trombone, and clarinet accompanied by various rhythm instruments > traˈditionally *adv*

traditionalism (trəˈdɪʃənəˌlɪzəm) *n* **1** the doctrine that all knowledge originates in divine revelation and is perpetuated by tradition **2** adherence to tradition, esp in religion > traˈditionalist *n, adj* > traˌditionalˈistic *adj*

traditional logic *n* the logic of the Late Middle Ages, derived from Aristotelian logic, and concerned esp with the study of syllogism

traditional option *n stock exchange* an option that once purchased cannot be resold. See **traded option**

traditional weapon *n South African* a weapon having ceremonial tribal significance, such as an assegai or knobkerrie

traditor (ˈtrædɪtə) *n, pl* **traditores** (ˌtrædɪˈtɔːriːz) *or* **traditors** *Early Church* a Christian who betrayed his fellow Christians at the time of the Roman persecutions [C15: from Latin: traitor, from *trādere* to hand over]

traduce (trəˈdjuːs) *vb* (*tr*) to speak badly of [C16: from Latin *trādūcere* to lead over, transmit, disgrace, from TRANS- + *dūcere* to lead] > traˈducement *n* > traˈducer *n*

Trafalgar (trəˈfælɡə; *Spanish* trafalˈɣar) *n* **Cape Trafalgar** a cape on the SW coast of Spain, south of Cádiz: scene of the decisive naval battle (1805) in which the French and Spanish fleets were defeated by the British under Nelson, who was mortally wounded

traffic (ˈtræfɪk) *n* **1 a** the vehicles coming and going in a street, town, etc **b** (*as modifier*): *traffic lights* **2** the movement of vehicles, people, etc, in a particular place or for a particular purpose: *sea traffic* **3** (usually foll by *with*) dealings or business **4** trade, esp of an illicit or improper kind: *drug traffic* **5** the aggregate volume of messages transmitted through a communications system in a given period **6** *chiefly US* the number of customers patronizing a commercial establishment in a given time period ▷ *vb* -**fics**, -**ficking**, -**ficked** (*intr*) **7** (often foll by *in*) to carry on trade or business, esp of an illicit kind **8** (usually foll by *with*) to have dealings [c16: from Old French *trafique*, from Old Italian *traffico*, from *trafficare* to engage in trade] > '**trafficker** *n*

trafficator ('træfɪˌkeɪtə) *n* (formerly) an illuminated arm on a motor vehicle that was raised to indicate a left or right turn

traffic calming *n* the use of a series of devices, such as bends and humps in the road, to slow down traffic, esp in residential areas

traffic island *n* a raised area in the middle of a road, designed as a guide for traffic and to provide a stopping place for pedestrians

traffic jam *n* a number of vehicles so obstructed that they can scarcely move

traffic light *or* **traffic signal** *n* one of a set of coloured lights placed at crossroads, junctions, etc, to control the flow of traffic. A red light indicates that traffic must stop and a green light that it may go: usually an amber warning light is added between the red and the green

traffic pattern *n* a pattern of permitted lanes in the air around an airport to which an aircraft is restricted

traffic warden *n Brit* a person who is appointed to supervise road traffic and report traffic offences

Trafford ('træfəd) *n* a unitary authority in NW England, in Greater Manchester. Pop: 211 800 (2003 est). Area: 106 sq km (41 sq miles)

tragacanth ('trægəˌkænθ) *n* **1** any of various spiny leguminous plants of the genus *Astragalus*, esp *A. gummifer*, of Asia, having clusters of white, yellow, or purple flowers, and yielding a substance that is made into a gum **2** the gum obtained from any of these plants, used in the manufacture of pills and lozenges, etc [c16: from French *tragacante*, from Latin *tragacantha* goat's thorn, from Greek *tragakantha*, from *tragos* goat + *akantha* thorn]

tragedian (trə'dʒiːdɪən) *or feminine* **tragedienne** (trəˌdʒiːdɪ'ɛn) *n* **1** an actor who specializes in tragic roles **2** a writer of tragedy

tragedy ('trædʒɪdɪ) *n, pl* -**dies 1** (esp in classical and Renaissance drama) a play in which the protagonist, usually a man of importance and outstanding personal qualities, falls to disaster through the combination of a personal failing and circumstances with which he cannot deal **2** any dramatic or literary composition dealing with serious or sombre themes and ending with disaster **3** the branch of drama dealing with such themes **4** the unfortunate aspect of something **5** a shocking or sad event; disaster [c14: from Old French *tragédie*, from Latin *tragoedia*, from Greek *tragōidia*, from *tragos* goat + *ōidē* song; perhaps a reference to the goat-satyrs of Peloponnesian plays]

tragic ('trædʒɪk) *or less commonly* **tragical** ('trædʒɪkᵊl) *adj* **1** of, relating to, or characteristic of tragedy **2** mournful or pitiable > '**tragically** *adv*

tragic flaw *n* a failing of character in the hero of a tragedy that brings about his downfall

tragic irony *n* the use of dramatic irony in a tragedy (originally, in Greek tragedy), so that the audience is aware that a character's words or actions will bring about a tragic or fatal result, while the character himself is not

tragicomedy (ˌtrædʒɪ'kɒmɪdɪ) *n, pl* -**dies 1** a drama in which aspects of both tragedy and comedy are found **2** an event or incident having both comic and tragic aspects [c16: from French, ultimately from Late Latin *tragicōmoedia*; see TRAGEDY, COMEDY] > ˌtragi'comic *or* ˌtragi'comical *adj*

tragopan ('trægəˌpæn) *n* any pheasant of the genus *Tragopan*, of S and SE Asia, having a brilliant plumage and brightly coloured fleshy processes on the head [c19: via Latin from Greek, from *tragos* goat + PAN]

tragus ('treɪgəs) *n, pl* -**gi** (-dʒaɪ) the cartilaginous fleshy

projection that partially covers the entrance to the external ear [c17: from Late Latin, from Greek *tragos* hairy projection of the ear, literally: goat]

Traherne (trə'hɜːn) *n* **Thomas**. 1637–74, English mystical prose writer and poet. His prose works include *Centuries of Meditations*, which was discovered in manuscript in 1896 and published in 1908

trail (treɪl) *vb* **1** to drag or stream, or permit to drag or stream along a surface, esp the ground **2** to make (a track or path) through (a place) **3** to chase, follow, or hunt (an animal or person) by following marks or tracks **4** (when *intr*, often foll by *behind*) to lag or linger behind (a person or thing) **5** (*intr*) (esp of plants) to extend or droop over or along a surface **6** (*intr*) to be falling behind in a race or competition **7** (*tr*) to carry (a rifle) at the full length of the right arm in a horizontal position, with the muzzle to the fore **8** (*intr*) to move wearily or slowly **9** (*tr*) (on television or radio) to advertise (a future programme) with short extracts ▷ *n* **10** a print, mark, or marks made by a person, animal, or object **11** the act or an instance of trailing **12** a path, track, or road, esp one roughly blazed **13** something that trails behind or trails in loops or strands **14** the part of a towed gun carriage and limber that connects the two when in movement and rests on the ground as a partial support when unlimbered [c14: from Old French *trailler* to draw, tow, from Vulgar Latin *tragulāre* (unattested), from Latin *trāgula* dragnet, from *trahere* to drag; compare Middle Dutch *traghelen* to drag]

trail away *or* **trail off** *vb* (*intr, adverb*) to become fainter, quieter, or weaker

trailblazer ('treɪlˌbleɪzə) *n* **1** a leader or pioneer in a particular field **2** a person who blazes a trail > '**trailˌblazing** *adj, n*

trailer ('treɪlə) *n* **1** a road vehicle, usually two-wheeled, towed by a motor vehicle: used for transporting boats, etc **2** the part of an articulated lorry that is drawn by the cab **3** a series of short extracts from a film, used to advertise it in a cinema or on television **4** a person or thing that trails **5** *US & Canadian* a large enclosed vehicle capable of being pulled by a car or lorry and equipped to be lived in. Also called (in Britain and certain other countries): **caravan**

trailer park *n US* a mobile home site

trailer trash *n disparaging* **a** poor people living in trailer parks in the US **b** (*as modifier*): *trailer-trash culture*

trailing edge *n* the rear edge of a propeller blade or aerofoil. See **leading edge**

train (treɪn) *vb* **1** (*tr*) to guide or teach (to do something), as by subjecting to various exercises or experiences **2** (*tr*) to control or guide towards a specific goal: *to train a plant up a wall* **3** (*intr*) to do exercises and prepare for a specific purpose **4** (*tr*) to improve or curb by subjecting to discipline: *to train the mind* **5** (*tr*) to focus or bring to bear (on something): *to train a telescope on the moon* ▷ *n* **6** a line of coaches or wagons coupled together and drawn by a railway locomotive **7** a sequence or series, as of events, thoughts, etc: *a train of disasters* **8** a procession of people, vehicles, etc, travelling together, such as one carrying supplies of ammunition or equipment in support of a military operation **9** a series of interacting parts through which motion is transmitted: *a train of gears* **10** a fuse or line of gunpowder to an explosive charge, etc **11** something drawn along, such as the long back section of a dress that trails along the floor behind the wearer **12** a retinue or suite [c14: from Old French *trahiner*, from Vulgar Latin *tragināre* (unattested) to draw; related to Latin *trahere* to drag] > '**trainable** *adj*

trainband ('treɪnˌbænd) *n* a company of English militia from the 16th to the 18th century [c17: altered from *trained band*]

trainbearer ('treɪnˌbɛərə) *n* an attendant in a procession who holds up the train of a dignitary's robe

trainee (treɪ'niː) *n* **a** a person undergoing training **b** (*as modifier*): *a trainee journalist*

trainer ('treɪnə) *n* **1** a person who trains athletes in a sport **2** a piece of equipment employed in training, such as a simulated aircraft cockpit **3** *horse racing* a person who schools racehorses and prepares them for racing

4 (*plural*) an informal name for **training shoes**

training ('treɪnɪŋ) *n* **1 a** the process of bringing a person, etc, to an agreed standard of proficiency, etc, by practice and instruction **b** (*as modifier*): *training college* **2** in training **a** undergoing physical training **b** physically fit **3** out of training physically unfit

Training Agency *n* (in Britain) an organization established in 1989 to replace the Training Commission, which itself replaced the Manpower Services Commission; it provides training and retraining for adult workers and operates the Youth Training Scheme, in England and Wales working through the local **Training and Enterprise Councils** (TECs) and in Scotland through the Local Enterprise Companies (LECs) set up in 1990

training shoes *pl n* **1** running shoes for sports training, esp in contrast to studded or spiked shoes worn for the sport itself **2** shoes in the style of those used for sports training ▷ Also called: **trainers**

train oil *n* oil obtained from the blubber of various marine animals, esp the whale [c16: from earlier *train* or *trane*, from Middle Low German *trān* or Middle Dutch *traen* tear, exudation]

train smash *n South African informal* a disaster or serious setback (esp in the phrase **it's not a train smash**)

train spotter *n* **1** a person who collects the numbers of railway locomotives **2** *informal* a person who is obsessed with trivial details, esp of a subject generally considered uninteresting

traipse *or* **trapes** (treɪps) *informal* ▷ *vb* **1** (*intr*) to walk heavily or tiredly ▷ *n* **2** a long or tiring walk; trudge [c16: of unknown origin]

trait (treɪt, treɪ) *n* **1** a characteristic feature or quality distinguishing a particular person or thing **2** *rare* a touch or stroke [c16: from French, from Old French: a pulling, from Latin *tractus*, from *trahere* to drag]

traitor ('treɪtə) *n* a person who is guilty of treason or treachery, in betraying friends, country, a cause or trust, etc [c13: from Old French *traitour*, from Latin TRADITOR] ▷ '**traitorous** *adj* ▷ '**traitress** *fem n*

Trajan ('treɪdʒən) *n* Latin name *Marcus Ulpius Traianus*. ?53–117 AD, Roman emperor (98–117). He extended the empire to the east and built many roads, bridges, canals, and towns

trajectory (trə'dʒɛktəri, -trɪ) *n, pl* -**ries 1** the path described by an object moving in air or space under the influence of such forces as thrust, wind resistance, and gravity, esp the curved path of a projectile **2** *geometry* a curve that cuts a family of curves or surfaces at a constant angle ▷ **trajectile** (trə'dʒɛktaɪl) *adj*

Trakl ('trɑːkəl) *n* **Georg.** 1887–1914, Austrian poet, noted for his expressionist style: died of a drug overdose while serving as a medical officer in World War I

Tralee (trə'liː) *n* a market town in SW Republic of Ireland, county town of Kerry, near **Tralee Bay** (an inlet of the Atlantic). Pop: 21 987 (2002)

tram (træm) *n* **1** Also called: **tramcar** an electrically driven public transport vehicle that runs on rails let into the surface of the road, power usually being taken from an overhead wire. US and Canadian names: **streetcar, trolley car 2** a small vehicle on rails for carrying loads in a mine; tub [C16 (in the sense: shaft of a cart): probably from Low German *traam* beam; compare Old Norse *thrōmr*, Middle Dutch *traem* beam, tooth of a rake] ▷ '**tramless** *adj*

tramline ('træm,laɪn) *n* **1** Also called: **tramway** (*often plural*) the tracks on which a tram runs **2** the route taken by a tram **3** (*often plural*) the outer markings along the sides of a tennis or badminton court

trammel ('træməl) *n* **1** (*often plural*) a hindrance to free action or movement **2** Also called: **trammel net** a fishing net in three sections, the two outer nets having a large mesh and the middle one a fine mesh **3** *rare* a fowling net **4** *US* a fetter or shackle, esp one used in teaching a horse to amble **5** a device for drawing ellipses consisting of a flat sheet of metal, plastic, or wood having a cruciform slot in which run two pegs attached to a beam. The free end of the beam describes an ellipse **6** (*sometimes plural*) another name for **beam**

compass 7 a device set in a fireplace to support cooking pots ▷ *vb* -**els**, -**elling**, -**elled** *or US* -**els**, -**eling**, -**eled** (*tr*) **8** to hinder or restrain **9** to catch or ensnare [c14: from Old French *tramail* three-mesh net, from Late Latin *trēmaculum*, from Latin *trēs* three + *macula* hole, mesh in a net]

tramontane (trə'mɒnteɪn) *adj* **1** Also: **transmontane** being or coming from the far side of the mountains, esp from the other side of the Alps as seen from Italy ▷ *n* **2** an inhabitant of a tramontane country **3** Also called: **tramontana** a cold dry wind blowing south or southwest from the mountains in Italy and the W Mediterranean [c16: from Italian *tramontano*, from Latin *trānsmontānus*, from TRANS- + *montānus*, from *mōns* mountain]

tramp (træmp) *vb* **1** (*intr*) to walk long and far; hike **2** to walk heavily or firmly across or through (a place); march or trudge **3** (*intr*) to wander about as a vagabond or tramp **4** (*tr*) to make (a journey) or traverse (a place) on foot, esp laboriously or wearily **5** (*tr*) to tread or trample ▷ *n* **6** a person who travels about on foot, usually with no permanent home, living by begging or doing casual work **7** a long hard walk; hike **8** a heavy or rhythmic step or tread **9** the sound of heavy treading **10** Also called: **tramp steamer** a merchant ship that does not run between ports on a regular schedule but carries cargo wherever the shippers desire **11** *slang, chiefly US & Canadian* a prostitute or promiscuous girl or woman [c14: probably from Middle Low German *trampen*; compare Gothic *ana-trimpan* to press heavily upon, German *trampen* to hitchhike] ▷ '**trampish** *adj*

tramper ('træmpə) *n* **1** a person who tramps **2** a person who walks long distances, often over rough terrain, for recreation

tramping club *n NZ* an organization of people who walk for recreation, esp in the bush

trample ('træmpᵊl) *vb* (when *intr*, usually foll by *on, upon*, or *over*) **1** to stamp or walk roughly (on) **2** to encroach (upon) so as to violate or hurt ▷ *n* **3** the action or sound of trampling [c14: frequentative of TRAMP; compare Middle High German *trampeln*] ▷ '**trampler** *n*

trampoline ('træmpəlɪn, -,liːn) *n* **1** a tough canvas sheet suspended by springs or elasticated cords from a frame, used by acrobats, gymnasts, etc ▷ *vb* **2** (*intr*) to exercise on a trampoline [c18: via Spanish from Italian *trampolino*, from *trampoli* stilts, of Germanic origin; compare TRAMPLE] ▷ '**trampoliner** *or* '**trampolinist** *n*

trance (trɑːns) *n* **1** a hypnotic state resembling sleep **2** any mental state in which a person is unaware or apparently unaware of the environment, characterized by loss of voluntary movement, rigidity, and lack of sensitivity to external stimuli **3** a dazed or stunned state **4** a state of ecstasy or mystic absorption so intense as to cause a temporary loss of consciousness at the earthly level **5** *spiritualism* a state in which a medium, having temporarily lost consciousness, can supposedly be controlled by an intelligence from without as a means of communication with the dead ▷ *vb* **6** (*tr*) to put into or as into a trance [c14: from Old French *transe*, from *transir* to faint, pass away, from Latin *trānsīre* to go over, from TRANS- + *īre* to go] ▷ '**trance,like** *adj*

tranche (trɑːnʃ) *n* a portion or instalment, esp of a loan or share issue [from French, literally: a slice]

trannie *or* **tranny** ('trænɪ) *n, pl* -**nies 1** a transistor radio **2** a transvestite

tranquil ('træŋkwɪl) *adj* calm, peaceful or quiet [c17: from Latin *tranquillus*] ▷ '**tranquilly** *adv*

tranquillity *or sometimes US* **tranquility** (træŋ'kwɪlɪtɪ) *n* a state of calm or quietude

tranquillize, tranquillise *or US* **tranquilize** ('træŋkwɪ,laɪz) *vb* to make or become calm or calmer ▷ ,**tranquilli'zation**, ,**tranquilli'sation** *or US* ,**tranquili'zation** *n*

tranquillizer, tranquilliser *or US* **tranquilizer** ('træŋkwɪ,laɪzə) *n* **1** a drug that calms a person without affecting clarity of consciousness **2** anything that tranquillizes

trans. *abbreviation* **1** transaction **2** transferred **3** transitive **4** translated **5** translator

trans- *or sometimes before* s- **tran-** *prefix* **1** across, beyond, crossing, on the other side: *transoceanic; trans-Siberian; transatlantic* **2** changing thoroughly: *transliterate* **3** transcending: *transubstantiation* **4** transversely: *transect* **5** (*often in italics*) indicating that a chemical compound has a molecular structure in which two groups or atoms are on opposite sides of a double bond: *trans-butadiene* [from Latin *trāns* across, through, beyond]

transact (trænˈzækt) *vb* to do, conduct, or negotiate (business, a deal, etc) [c16: from Latin *trānsactus*, from *trānsigere*, literally: to drive through, from TRANS- + *agere* to drive] > trans'actor *n*

transactinide (ˌtrænsˈæktɪˌnaɪd) *n* any artificially produced element with an atomic number greater than 103 [c20: from TRANS- + ACTINIDE]

transaction (trænˈzækʃən) *n* **1** something that is transacted, esp a business deal or negotiation **2** (*plural*) the published records of the proceedings of a society, conference, etc > trans'actional *adj*

transalpine (trænzˈælpaɪn) *adj* (*prenominal*) situated in or relating to places beyond the Alps, esp from Italy

Transalpine Gaul *n* (in the ancient world) that part of Gaul northwest of the Alps

transaminase (trænzˈæmɪˌneɪz, -ˌneɪs) *n biochem* an enzyme that catalyses the transfer of an amino group from one molecule, esp an amino acid, to another, esp a keto acid, in the process of transamination

transatlantic (ˌtrænzətˈlæntɪk) *adj* **1** on or from the other side of the Atlantic **2** crossing the Atlantic

transaxle (trænzˈæksəl) *n* a unit in a motor vehicle engine that combines the differential, transmission, and drive axle

Transcaucasia (ˌtrænskɔːˈkeɪzjə) *n* a region in central Asia, south of the Caucasus Mountains between the Black and Caspian Seas in Georgia, Armenia, and Azerbaijan: a constituent republic of the Soviet Union from 1918 until 1936 > ˌTranscau'casian *adj, n*

transceiver (trænˈsiːvə) *n* a device which transmits and receives radio or electronic signals [c20: from TRANS(MITTER) + (RE)CEIVER]

transcend (trænˈsɛnd) *vb* **1** to go above or beyond (a limit, expectation, etc), as in degree or excellence **2** (*tr*) to be superior to [c14: from Latin *trānscendere* to climb over, from TRANS- + *scandere* to climb]

transcendent (trænˈsɛndənt) *adj* **1** exceeding or surpassing in degree or excellence **2** (in the philosophy of Kant) beyond or before experience; a priori **3** *theol* (of God) having continuous existence outside the created world **4** free from the limitations inherent in matter ▷ *n* **5** *philosophy* a transcendent thing > tran'scendence *or* tran'scendency *n* > tran'scendently *adv*

transcendental (ˌtrænsɛnˈdɛntəl) *adj* **1** transcendent, superior, or surpassing **2** (in the philosophy of Kant) **a** (of a judgment or logical deduction) being both synthetic and a priori **b** of or relating to knowledge of the presuppositions of thought **3** *philosophy* beyond our experience of phenomena, although not beyond potential knowledge **4** *theol* surpassing the natural plane of reality or knowledge; supernatural or mystical > ˌtranscen'dentally *adv*

transcendentalism (ˌtrænsɛnˈdɛntəˌlɪzəm) *n* **1 a** any system of philosophy, esp that of Immanuel Kant, the German philosopher (1724–1804), holding that the key to knowledge of the nature of reality lies in the critical examination of the processes of reason on which depends the nature of experience **b** any system of philosophy, esp that of Emerson, that emphasizes intuition as a means to knowledge or the importance of the search for the divine **2** vague philosophical speculation **3** the state of being transcendental **4** something, such as thought or language, that is transcendental > ˌtranscen'dentalist *n, adj*

Transcendental Meditation *n trademark US* a technique, based on Hindu teachings, for relaxing and refreshing the mind and body through the silent repetition of a mantra. Disseminated by an international organization founded by Maharishi Mahesh Yogi (1917–2008), an Indian-born guru. Abbreviation: TM

transcontinental (ˌtrænzkɒntɪˈnɛntəl) *adj* **1** crossing a continent **2** on or from the far side of a continent > ˌtransconti'nentally *adv*

transcranial (trænzˈkreɪnɪəl) *adj* across or through the skull

transcribe (trænˈskraɪb) *vb* (*tr*) **1** to write, type, or print out fully from speech, notes, etc **2** to transliterate or translate **3** to make an electrical recording of (a programme or speech) for a later broadcast **4** *music* to rewrite (a piece of music) for an instrument or medium other than that originally intended; arrange **5** *computing* **a** to transfer (information) from one storage device, such as punched cards, to another, such as magnetic tape **b** to transfer (information) from a computer to an external storage device [c16: from Latin *transcrībere*, from TRANS- + *scrībere* to write] > tran'scribable *adj* > tran'scriber *n*

transcript (ˈtrænskrɪpt) *n* **1** a written, typed, or printed copy or manuscript made by transcribing **2** *education chiefly US & Canadian* an official record of a student's school progress and achievements **3** any reproduction or copy [c13: from Latin *transcriptum*, from *transcrībere* to TRANSCRIBE]

transcriptase (trænˈskrɪpteɪz) *n* See **reverse transcriptase**

transcription (trænˈskrɪpʃən) *n* **1** the act or an instance of transcribing or the state of being transcribed **2** something transcribed **3** a representation in writing of the actual pronunciation of a speech sound, word, or piece of continuous text, using not a conventional orthography but a symbol or set of symbols specially designated as standing for corresponding phonetic values > tran'scriptional *or* tran'scriptive *adj*

transducer (trænzˈdjuːsə) *n* any device, such as a microphone or electric motor, that converts one form of energy into another [c20: from Latin *transducere* to lead across, from TRANS- + *ducere* to lead]

transect *vb* (trænˈsɛkt) (*tr*) **1** to cut or divide crossways ▷ *n* (ˈtrænsɛkt) **2** a sample strip of land used to monitor plant distribution, animal populations, etc, within a given area [c17: from Latin TRANS- + *secāre* to cut] > tran'section *n*

transept (ˈtrænsɛpt) *n* either of the two wings of a cruciform church at right angles to the nave [c16: from Anglo-Latin *transeptum*, from Latin TRANS- + *saeptum* enclosure] > tran'septal *adj*

trans-fatty acid *or* **trans fat** *n* a polyunsaturated fatty acid that has been converted from the cis-form by hydrogenation: used in the manufacture of margarine

transfer *vb* (trænsˈfɜː) -fers, -ferring, -ferred **1** to change or go or cause to change or go from one thing, person, or point to another **2** to change (buses, trains, etc) **3** *law* to make over (property, etc) to another; convey **4** to displace (a drawing, design, etc) from one surface to another **5** (of a football player, esp a professional) to change clubs or (of a club, manager, etc) to sell or release (a player) to another club **6** to leave one school, college, etc, and enrol at another **7** to change (the meaning of a word, etc), esp by metaphorical extension ▷ *n* (ˈtrænsfɜː) **8** the act, process, or system of transferring, or the state of being transferred **9** a person or thing that transfers or is transferred **10** a design or drawing that is transferred from one surface to another, as by ironing a printed design onto cloth **11** *law* the passing of title to property or other right from one person to another by act of the parties or by operation of law; conveyance **12** any document or form effecting or regulating a transfer **13** *chiefly US & Canadian* a ticket that allows a passenger to change routes [c14: from Latin *transferre*, from TRANS- + *ferre* to carry] > trans'ferable *or* trans'ferrable *adj* > transference (ˈtrænsfərəns, -frəns) *n*

transferable vote *n* a vote that is transferred to a second candidate indicated by the voter if the first is eliminated from the ballot

transferee (ˌtrænsfəˈriː) *n* **1** *property law* a person to whom property is transferred **2** a person who is transferred

transfer fee *n* a sum of money paid by one football club to another for a transferred player

transferrin (trænsˈfɜːrɪn) *n biochem* any of a group of blood glycoproteins that transport iron [C20: from TRANS- + FERRO- + -IN]

transfer RNA *n biochem* any of several soluble forms of RNA of low molecular weight, each of which transports a specific amino acid to a ribosome during protein synthesis

transfer station *n* NZ a municipal depot where rubbish is sorted for recycling or relocation to a landfill site

transfiguration (ˌtrænsfɪɡjʊˈreɪʃən) *n* the act or an instance of transfiguring or the state of being transfigured

Transfiguration (ˌtrænsfɪɡjʊˈreɪʃən) *n* **1** *New Testament* the change in the appearance of Christ that took place before three disciples (Matthew 17:1–9) **2** the Church festival held in commemoration of this on Aug 6

transfigure (trænsˈfɪɡə) *vb* (*usually tr*) **1** to change or cause to change in appearance **2** to become or cause to become more exalted [C13: from Latin *transfigūrāre*, from TRANS- + *figūra* appearance] > trans'figurement *n*

transfinite number *n* a cardinal or ordinal number used in the comparison of infinite sets for which several types of infinity can be classified

transfix (trænsˈfɪks) *vb* -fixes, -fixing, -fixed *or* -fixt (*tr*) **1** to render motionless, esp with horror or shock **2** to impale or fix with a sharp weapon or other device [C16: from Latin *transfigere* to pierce through, from TRANS- + *figere* to thrust in] > transfixion (trænsˈfɪkʃən) *n*

transform *vb* (trænsˈfɔːm) **1** to alter or be altered radically in form, function, etc **2** (*tr*) to convert (one form of energy) to another form **3** (*tr*) *maths* to change the form of (an equation, expression, etc) by a mathematical transformation **4** (*tr*) to increase or decrease (an alternating current or voltage) using a transformer ▷ *n* (ˈtrænsˌfɔːm) **5** *maths* the result of a mathematical transformation, esp (of a matrix or an element of a group) another related to the given one by $B = X^{-1} AX$ for some appropriate X [C14: from Latin *transformāre*, from TRANS- + *formāre* to FORM] > trans'formable *adj* > trans'formative *adj*

transformation (ˌtrænsfəˈmeɪʃən) *n* **1** a change or alteration, esp a radical one **2** the act of transforming or the state of being transformed **3** *maths* **a** a change in position or direction of the reference axes in a coordinate system without an alteration in their relative angle **b** an equivalent change in an expression or equation resulting from the substitution of one set of variables by another **4** *physics* a change in an atomic nucleus to a different nuclide as the result of the emission of either an alpha-particle or a beta-particle **5** *linguistics* another word for **transformational rule** **6** an apparently miraculous change in the appearance of a stage set > ˌtransfor'mational *adj*

transformational grammar *n* a grammatical description of a language making essential use of transformational rules. Such grammars are usually but not necessarily generative grammars

transformational rule *n generative grammar* a rule that converts one phrase marker into another. Taken together, these rules, which form the **transformational component** of the grammar, convert the deep structures of sentences into their surface structures

transformer (trænsˈfɔːmə) *n* **1** a device that transfers an alternating current from one circuit to one or more other circuits, usually with an increase (**step-up transformer**) or decrease (**step-down transformer**) of voltage. The input current is fed to a primary winding, the output being taken from a secondary winding or windings inductively linked to the primary **2** a person or thing that transforms

transfuse (trænsˈfjuːz) *vb* (*tr*) **1** to permeate or infuse: *a blush transfused her face* **2 a** to inject (blood, etc) into a blood vessel **b** to give a transfusion to (a patient) [C15: from Latin *transfundere* to pour out, from TRANS- + *fundere* to pour] > trans'fuser *n* > trans'fusible *or* trans'fusable *adj* > trans'fusive *adj*

transfusion (trænsˈfjuːʒən) *n* **1** the act or an instance of transfusing **2** the injection of blood, blood plasma, etc, into the blood vessels of a patient

transgender (ˌtrænzˈdʒɛndə) *adj* of or relating to a person who wants to belong to the opposite sex

transgenic (trænzˈdʒɛnɪk) *adj* (of an animal or plant) containing genetic material artificially transferred from another species

transgenics (ˌtrænzˈdʒɛnɪks) *n* (*functioning as singular*) the branch of biology concerned with the transfer of genetic material from one species to another

transgress (trænzˈɡrɛs) *vb* **1** to break (a law, rule, etc) **2** to go beyond or overstep (a limit) [C16: from Latin *transgredī*, from TRANS- + *gradī* to step] > trans'gressor *n*

transgression (trænzˈɡrɛʃən) *n* **1** a breach of a law, etc; sin or crime **2** the act or an instance of transgressing

transgressive (ˌtrænzˈɡrɛsɪv) *adj* going beyond acceptable boundaries of taste, convention, or the law: *transgressive art; transgressive pursuits*

tranship (trænˈʃɪp) *vb* -ships, -shipping, -shipped a variant spelling of **transship**

transhumance (trænsˈhjuːməns) *n* the seasonal migration of livestock to suitable grazing grounds [C20: from French, from *transhumer* to change one's pastures, from Spanish *trashumar*, from Latin TRANS- + *humus* ground] > trans'humant *adj*

transient (ˈtrænzɪənt) *adj* **1** for a short time only; temporary or transitory ▷ *n* **2** a transient person or thing [C17: from Latin *transiēns* going over, from *transīre* to pass over, from TRANS- + *īre* to go] > 'transiently *adv* > 'transience *or* 'transiency *n*

transistor (trænˈzɪstə) *n* **1** a semiconductor device, having three or more terminals attached to electrode regions, in which current flowing between two electrodes is controlled by a voltage or current applied to one or more specified electrodes. The device is capable of amplification, etc, and has replaced the valve in most circuits since it is much smaller, more robust, and works at a much lower voltage **2** *informal* a transistor radio [C20: originally a trademark, from TRANSFER + RESISTOR, referring to the transfer of electric signals across a resistor]

transistorize *or* **transistorise** (trænˈzɪstəˌraɪz) *vb* **1** to convert (a system, device, industry, etc) to the use or manufacture of or operation by transistors and other solid-state components **2** to equip (a device or circuit) with transistors and other solid-state components

transit (ˈtrænsɪt, ˈtrænz-) *n* **1 a** the passage or conveyance of goods or people **b** (*as modifier*): *a transit visa* **2** a change or transition **3** a route **4** *astronomy* **a** the passage of a celestial body or satellite across the face of a relatively larger body as seen from the earth **b** the apparent passage of a celestial body across the meridian, caused by the earth's diurnal rotation **5 in transit** while being conveyed; during passage ▷ *vb* **6** to make a transit through or over (something) [C15: from Latin *transitus* a going over, from *transīre* to pass over; see TRANSIENT]

transit camp *n* a camp in which refugees, soldiers, etc, live temporarily before moving to another destination

transit instrument *n* an astronomical instrument, mounted on an E-W axis, in which the reticle of a telescope is always in the plane of the meridian. It is used to time the transit of a star, etc, across the meridian

transition (trænˈzɪʃən) *n* **1** change or passage from one state or stage to another **2** the period of time during which something changes from one state or stage to another **3** *music* **a** a movement from one key to another; modulation **b** a linking passage between two divisions in a composition; bridge **4** Also called: **transitional** a style of architecture that was used in western Europe in the late 11th and early 12th century, characterized by late Romanesque forms combined with early Gothic details **5** a sentence, passage, etc, that connects a topic to one that follows or that links sections of a written work [C16: from Latin *transitio*; see TRANSIENT] > tran'sitional *adj* > tran'sitionally *adv*

transition element *or* **transition metal** *n chem* any element belonging to one of three series of elements with atomic numbers between 21 and 30, 39 and 48, and 57 and 80. They have an incomplete penultimate electron shell and tend to exhibit more than one valency and to form complexes

transition temperature *n* the temperature at which a sudden change of physical properties occurs, such as a change of phase or crystalline structure, or at which a substance becomes superconducting

transitive ('trænsɪtɪv) *adj* **1** *grammar* **a** denoting an occurrence of a verb when it requires a direct object or denoting a verb that customarily requires a direct object: *"to find" is a transitive verb* **b** (*as noun*): *these verbs are transitives* **2** *logic, maths* having the property that if one object bears a relationship to a second object that also bears the same relationship to a third object, then the first object bears this relationship to the third object: *mathematical equality is transitive, since if x = y and y = z then x = z* [c16: from Late Latin *transitīvus* from Latin *transitus* a going over; see TRANSIENT] > 'transitively *adv* > ˌtransi'tivity *or* 'transitiveness *n*

transitory ('trænsɪtərɪ, -trɪ) *adj* of short duration; transient or ephemeral [c14: from Church Latin *transitōrius* passing, from Latin *transitus* a crossing over; see TRANSIENT] > 'transitoriness *n*

transit theodolite *n* a theodolite the telescope of which can be rotated completely about its horizontal axis

Trans-Jordan *n* the former name (1922–49) of **Jordan¹** > ˌTrans-Jor'danian *adj, n*

Transkei (træn'skaɪ) *n* (formerly) the largest of the Bantu homelands in South Africa; declared an independent state in 1976 but this was not recognized outside South Africa; abolished in 1993. Capital: Umtata > Trans'keian *adj, n*

translate (træns'leɪt, trænz-) *vb* **1** to express or be capable of being expressed in another language or dialect **2** (*intr*) to act as translator **3** (*tr*) to express or explain in simple or less technical language **4** (*tr*) to interpret or infer the significance of (gestures, symbols, etc) **5** (*tr*) to transform or convert: *to translate hope into reality* **6** (*tr*) **a** to transfer (a cleric) from one ecclesiastical office to another **b** to transfer (a see) from one place to another **7** (*tr*) *theol* to transfer (a person) from one place or plane of existence to another, as from earth to heaven **8** *maths, physics* to move (a figure or body) laterally, without rotation, dilation, or angular displacement [c13: from Latin *translātus* transferred, carried over, from *transferre* to TRANSFER] > trans'latable *adj* > trans'lator *n*

translation (træns'leɪʃən, trænz-) *n* **1** something that is or has been translated, esp a written text **2** the act of translating or the state of being translated **3** *maths* a transformation in which the origin of a coordinate system is moved to another position so that each axis retains the same direction or, equivalently, a figure or curve is moved so that it retains the same orientation to the axes > trans'lational *adj*

transliterate (trænz'lɪtəˌreɪt) *vb* (*tr*) to transcribe (a word, etc, in one alphabet) into corresponding letters of another alphabet [c19: TRANS- + -literate, from Latin *littera* LETTER] > trans'literˌator *n*

translocation (ˌtrænzləʊ'keɪʃən) *n* **1** *genetics* the transfer of one part of a chromosome to another part of the same or a different chromosome, resulting in rearrangement of the genes **2** *botany* the transport of minerals, sugars, etc, in solution within a plant **3** a movement from one position or place to another

translucent (trænz'luːsᵊnt) *adj* allowing light to pass through partially or diffusely; semitransparent [c16: from Latin *translūcēre* to shine through, from TRANS- + *lūcēre* to shine] > trans'lucence *or* trans'lucency *n* > trans'lucently *adv*

translunar (trænz'luːnə) *or* **translunary** (trænz'luːnərɪ) *adj* **1** lying beyond the moon **2** unworldly or ethereal

transmigrate (ˌtrænzmaɪ'greɪt) *vb* (*intr*) **1** to move from one place, state, or stage to another **2** (of souls) to pass from one body into another at death > trans'migratory *adj*

transmission (trænz'mɪʃən) *n* **1** the act or process of transmitting **2** something that is transmitted **3** the extent to which a body or medium transmits light, sound, or some other form of energy **4** the transference of motive force or power **5** a system of shafts, gears, torque converters, etc, that transmits power, esp the arrangement of such parts that transmits the power of the engine to the driving wheels of a motor vehicle **6** the act or process of sending a message, picture, or other information from one location to one or more other locations by means of radio waves, electrical signals, light signals, etc **7** a radio or television broadcast [c17: from Latin *transmissiō* a sending across; see TRANSMIT] > trans'missible *adj* > trans'missive *adj*

transmission density *n* *physics* a measure of the extent to which a substance transmits light or other electromagnetic radiation, equal to the logarithm to base ten of the reciprocal of the transmittance

transmission line *n* a coaxial cable, waveguide, or other system of conductors that transfers electrical signals from one location to another

transmit (trænz'mɪt) *vb* -mits, -mitting, -mitted **1** (*tr*) to pass or cause to go from one place or person to another; transfer **2** (*tr*) to pass on or impart (a disease, infection, etc) **3** (*tr*) to hand down to posterity **4** (*tr; usually passive*) to pass (an inheritable characteristic) from parent to offspring **5** to allow the passage of (particles, energy, etc): *radio waves are transmitted through the atmosphere* **6 a** to send out (signals) by means of radio waves or along a transmission line **b** to broadcast (a radio or television programme) **7** (*tr*) to transfer (a force, motion, power, etc) from one part of a mechanical system to another [c14: from Latin *transmittere* to send across, from TRANS- + *mittere* to send] > trans'mittable *or* trans'mittible *adj* > trans'mittal *n*

transmittance (trænz'mɪtᵊns) *n* **1** the act of transmitting **2** Also called: **transmission factor** *physics* a measure of the ability of anything to transmit radiation, equal to the ratio of the transmitted flux to the incident flux; the reciprocal of the opacity. For a plate of material the ratio of the flux leaving the entry surface to that reaching the exit surface is the internal transmittance

transmitter (trænz'mɪtə) *n* **1** a person or thing that transmits **2** the equipment used for generating and amplifying a radio-frequency carrier, modulating the carrier with information, and feeding it to an aerial for transmission **3** the microphone in a telephone that converts sound waves into audio-frequency electrical signals **4** a device that converts mechanical movements into coded electrical signals transmitted along a telegraph circuit **5** *physiol* short for **neurotransmitter**

transmogrify (trænz'mɒgrɪˌfaɪ) *vb* -fies, -fying, -fied (*tr*) *jocular* to change or transform into a different shape, esp a grotesque or bizarre one [c17: of unknown origin] > transˌmogrifi'cation *n*

transmontane (ˌtrænzmɒn'teɪn) *adj, n* another word for **tramontane**

transmutation (ˌtrænzmjuː'teɪʃən) *n* **1** the act or an instance of transmuting **2** the change of one chemical element into another by a nuclear reaction **3** the attempted conversion, by alchemists, of base metals into gold or silver > ˌtransmu'tational *or* trans'mutative *adj*

transmute (trænz'mjuːt) *vb* (*tr*) **1** to change the form, character, or substance of **2** to alter (an element, metal, etc) by alchemy [c15: via Old French from Latin *transmūtāre* to shift, from TRANS- + *mūtāre* to change] > transˌmuta'bility *n* > trans'mutable *adj*

transnational (trænz'næʃənəl) *adj* extending beyond the boundaries, interests, etc, of a single nation

Transnet ('trænzˌnɛt) *n* South African the official rail and transport service in South Africa

transoceanic (ˌtrænzˌəʊʃɪ'ænɪk) *adj* **1** on or from the other side of an ocean **2** crossing an ocean

transom ('trænsəm) *n* **1 a** a horizontal member that separates a door from a window over it **2** the usual US name for **fanlight** **3** *nautical* **a** a surface forming the stern of a vessel, either vertical or canted either forwards (**reverse transom**) or aft at the upper side **b** any of several transverse beams used for strengthening the stern of a vessel [c14: earlier *traversayn*, from Old French *traversin*, from TRAVERSE] > 'transomed *adj*

transonic (trænˈsɒnɪk) *adj* of or relating to conditions when travelling at or near the speed of sound

transparency (trænsˈpærənsɪ, -ˈpɛər-) *n, pl* **-cies 1** Also called: **transparence** the state of being transparent **2** also called: **slide** a positive photograph on a transparent base, usually mounted in a frame or between glass plates. It can be viewed by means of a slide projector

transparent (trænsˈpærənt, -ˈpɛər-) *adj* **1** permitting the uninterrupted passage of light; clear **2** easy to see through, understand, or recognize; obvious **3** (of a substance or object) permitting the free passage of electromagnetic radiation **4** candid, open, or frank [C15: from Medieval Latin *transpārēre* to show through, from Latin TRANS- + *pārēre* to appear] > **trans'parently** *adv* > **trans'parentness** *n*

transpire (trænˈspaɪə) *vb* **1** (*intr*) to come to light; be known **2** (*intr*) *informal* to happen or occur **3** *physiol* to give off or exhale (water or vapour) through the skin, a mucous membrane, etc **4** (of plants) to lose (water in the form of water vapour), esp through the stomata of the leaves [C16: from Medieval Latin *transpīrāre*, from Latin TRANS- + *spīrāre* to breathe] > **transpiration** (ˌtrænspəˈreɪʃən) *n* > **tran'spiratory** *adj*

● USAGE It is often maintained that *transpire* should not
● be used to mean happen or occur, as in *the event*
● *transpired late in the evening*, and that the word is
● properly used to mean become known, as in *it*
● *transpired later that the thief had been caught*. The word is,
● however, widely used in the former sense, esp in
● spoken English

transplant *vb* (trænsˈplɑːnt) **1** (*tr*) to remove or transfer (esp a plant) from one place to another **2** (*intr*) to be capable of being transplanted **3** *surgery* to transfer (an organ or tissue) from one part of the body to another or from one person or animal to another during a grafting or transplant operation ▷ *n* (ˈtrænsˌplɑːnt) **4** *surgery* **a** the procedure involved in such a transfer **b** the organ or tissue transplanted > **trans'plantable** *adj* > ˌtransplan'tation *n*

transponder *or* **transpondor** (trænˈspɒndə) *n* **1** a type of radio or radar transmitter-receiver that transmits signals automatically when it receives predetermined signals **2** the receiver and transmitter in a communications or broadcast satellite, relaying received signals back to earth [C20: from TRANSMITTER + RESPONDER]

transport *vb* (trænsˈpɔːt) (*tr*) **1** to carry or cause to go from one place to another, esp over some distance **2** to deport or exile to a penal colony **3** (*usually passive*) to have a strong emotional effect on ▷ *n* (ˈtrænsˌpɔːt) **4 a** the business or system of transporting goods or people **b** (*as modifier*): *a modernized transport system* **5** *Brit* freight vehicles generally **6 a** a vehicle used to transport goods or people, esp lorries or ships used to convey troops **b** (*as modifier*): *a transport plane* **7** the act of transporting or the state of being transported **8** ecstasy, rapture, or any powerful emotion **9** a convict sentenced to be transported [C14: from Latin *transportāre*, from TRANS- + *portāre* to carry] > **trans'portable** *adj* > **trans'porter** *n*

transportation (ˌtrænspɔːˈteɪʃən) *n* **1** a means or system of transporting **2** the act of transporting or the state of being transported **3** (esp formerly) deportation to a penal colony

transport café *n Brit* an inexpensive eating place on a main route, used mainly by long-distance lorry drivers

transpose (trænsˈpəʊz) *vb* **1** (*tr*) to alter the positions of; interchange, as words in a sentence; put into a different order **2** *music* **a** to play (notes, music, etc) in a different key from that originally intended **b** to move (a note or series of notes) upwards or downwards in pitch **3** (*tr*) *maths* to move (a term) from one side of an equation to the other with a corresponding reversal in sign [C14: from Old French *transposer*, from Latin *transpōnere* to remove, from TRANS- + *pōnere* to place] > **trans'posable** *adj* > **trans'posal** *n* > **trans'poser** *n* > **transposition** (ˌtrænspəˈzɪʃən) *n*

transposing instrument *n* a musical instrument, esp a horn or clarinet, pitched in a key other than C major,

but whose music is written down as if its basic scale were C major. A piece of music in the key of F intended to be played on a horn pitched in F is therefore written down a fourth lower than an ordinary part in that key and has the same key signature as a part written in C

transposon (trænsˈpəʊzɒn) *n genetics* a genetic element that can move from one site in a chromosome to another site in the same or a different chromosome and thus alter the genetic constitution of the organism [C20: TRANSPOS(E) + -ON]

transputer (trænzˈpjuːtə) *n computing* a type of fast, powerful microchip that is the equivalent of a 32-bit microprocessor with its own RAM facility [C20: from TRANS(ISTOR) + (COM)PUTER]

transsexual *or* **transexual** (trænzˈsɛksjʊəl) *n* **1** a person who permanently acts the part of and completely identifies with the opposite sex **2** a person who has undergone medical and surgical procedures to alter external sexual characteristics to those of the opposite sex

transship (trænsˈʃɪp) *or* **tranship** *vb* **-ships, -shipping, -shipped** to transfer or be transferred from one vessel or vehicle to another > **trans'shipment** *or* **tran'shipment** *n*

transubstantiation (ˌtrænsəbˌstænʃɪˈeɪʃən) *n* **1** (esp in Roman Catholic theology) **a** the doctrine that the whole substance of the bread and wine changes into the substance of the body and blood of Christ when consecrated in the Eucharist **b** the mystical process by which this is believed to take place during consecration. See **consubstantiation 2** a substantial change; transmutation > ˌtransubˌstanti'ationalist *n*

transude (trænˈsjuːd) *vb* (of a fluid) to ooze or pass through interstices, pores, or small holes [C17: from New Latin *transūdāre*, from Latin TRANS- + *sūdāre* to sweat]

transuranic (ˌtrænzjʊˈrænɪk), **transuranian** (ˌtrænzjʊˈreɪnɪən) *or* **transuranium** (trænzjʊˈreɪnɪəm) *adj* **1** (of an element) having an atomic number greater than that of uranium **2** of, relating to, or having the behaviour of transuranic elements [C20: from TRANS- + *uranic*, from URANIUM]

Transvaal (trænzˈvɑːl) *n* former province of NE South Africa: colonized by the Boers after the Great Trek (1836); became a British colony in 1902; joined South Africa in 1910; replaced in 1994 for administrative purposes by a new system of provinces (Eastern Transvaal (later Mpumalanga), Northern Transvaal (later Limpopo), Gauteng, and North West province. Capital: Pretoria > 'Trans,vaaler *n* > Trans'vaalian *adj*

transvaginal (ˌtrænzvəˈdʒaɪnəl, ˌtrænzˈvædʒɪnəl) *adj* through or via the vagina: *transvaginal ultrasound*

transversal (trænzˈvɜːsəl) *n* **1** *geometry* a line intersecting two or more other lines ▷ *adj* **2** a less common word for **transverse** > trans'versally *adv*

transverse (trænzˈvɜːs) *adj* **1** crossing from side to side; athwart; crossways ▷ *n* **2** a transverse piece or object [C16: from Latin *transversus*, from *transvertere* to turn across, from TRANS- + *vertere* to turn] > **trans'versely** *adv*

transverse colon *n anatomy* the part of the large intestine passing transversely in front of the liver and stomach

transverse wave *n* a wave, such as an electromagnetic wave, that is propagated in a direction perpendicular to the direction of displacement of the transmitting field or medium

transvestite (trænzˈvɛstaɪt) *n* a person who seeks sexual pleasure from wearing clothes that are normally associated with the opposite sex [C19: from German *Transvestit*, from TRANS- + Latin *vestītus* clothed, from *vestīre* to clothe] > trans'vestism *or* trans'vestitism *n*

Transylvania (ˌtrænsɪlˈveɪnɪə) *n* a region of central and NW Romania: belonged to Hungary from the 11th century until 1918; restored to Romania in 1947

Transylvanian Alps (ˌtrænsɪlˈveɪnɪən) *pl n* a mountain range in S Romania; a SW extension of the Carpathian Mountains. Highest peak: Mount Negoiu, 2548 m (8360 ft)

trap¹ (træp) *n* **1** a mechanical device or enclosed place or pit in which something, esp an animal, is caught or penned **2** any device or plan for tricking a person or

t

thing into being caught unawares **3** anything resembling a trap or prison **4** a fitting for a pipe in the form of a U-shaped or S-shaped bend that contains standing water to prevent the passage of gases **5** any similar device **6** a device that hurls clay pigeons into the air to be fired at by trapshooters **7** any one of a line of boxlike stalls in which greyhounds are enclosed before the start of a race **8** See **trap door** **9** a light two-wheeled carriage **10** a slang word for **mouth** **11** *golf* an obstacle or hazard, esp a bunker **12** (*plural*) *jazz slang* percussion instruments **13** (*usually plural*) *Austral obsolete, slang* a policeman ▷ *vb* **traps, trapping, trapped** **14** (*tr*) to catch, take, or pen in or as if in a trap; entrap **15** (*tr*) to ensnare by trickery; trick **16** (*tr*) to provide (a pipe) with a trap **17** to set traps in (a place), esp for animals [Old English *træppe*; related to Middle Low German *trappe*, Medieval Latin *trappa*] > 'trap,like *adj*

trap² (træp) *vb* **traps, trapping, trapped** (*tr*; often foll by *out*) to dress or adorn. See also **traps** [c11: probably from Old French *drap* cloth]

trap³ (træp) *or* **traprock** *n* **1** any fine-grained often columnar dark igneous rock, esp basalt **2** any rock in which oil or gas has accumulated [c18: from Swedish *trappa* stair (from its steplike formation); see TRAP¹]

Trapani (*Italian* 'tra:pani) *n* a port in S Italy, in NW Sicily: Carthaginian naval base, ceded to the Romans after the First Punic War. Pop: 68 346 (2001)

trap door *n* a door or flap flush with and covering an opening, esp in a ceiling

trap-door spider *n* any of various spiders of the family *Ctenizidae* that construct a silk-lined hole in the ground closed by a hinged door of earth and silk

trapes (treɪps) *vb, n* a less common spelling of **traipse**

trapeze (trə'pi:z) *n* a free-swinging bar attached to two ropes, used by circus acrobats, etc [c19: from French *trapèze*, from New Latin; see TRAPEZIUM]

trapezium (trə'pi:zɪəm) *n, pl* **-ziums** *or* **-zia** (-zɪə) **1** *chiefly Brit* a quadrilateral having two parallel sides of unequal length. Usual US and Canadian name: **trapezoid 2** *now chiefly US & Canadian* a quadrilateral having neither pair of sides parallel [c16: via Late Latin from Greek *trapezion*, from *trapeza* table] > tra'pezial *adj*

trapezius (trə'pi:zɪəs) *n, pl* **-uses** either of two flat triangular muscles, one covering each side of the back and shoulders, that rotate the shoulder blades [c18: from New Latin *trapezius* (*musculus*) trapezium-shaped (muscle)]

trapezoid ('træpɪ,zɔɪd) *n* **1** a quadrilateral having neither pair of sides parallel **2** Also called: (*Brit, Austral., NZ, and South African*) **trapezium** *US & Canadian* a quadrilateral having two parallel sides of unequal length [c18: from New Latin *trapezoidēs*, from Late Greek *trapezoeidēs*, from *trapeza* table]

trapper ('træpə) *n* a person who traps animals, esp for their furs or skins

trappings ('træpɪŋz) *pl n* **1** the accessories and adornments that characterize or symbolize a condition, office, etc: *the visible trappings of success* **2** ceremonial harness for a horse or other animal, including bridles, saddles, etc [c16: from TRAP²]

Trappist ('træpɪst) *n* **a** a member of a branch of the Cistercian order of Christian monks, the Reformed Cistercians of the Strict Observance which originated at La Trappe in France in 1664. They are noted for their rule of silence **b** (*as modifier*): *a Trappist monk*

traps (træps) *pl n* belongings; luggage [c19: probably shortened from TRAPPINGS]

trapshooting ('træp,ʃu:tɪŋ) *n* the sport of shooting at clay pigeons thrown up by a trap > 'trap,shooter *n*

trash (træʃ) *n* **1** foolish ideas or talk; nonsense **2** *chiefly US & Canadian* useless or unwanted matter or objects **3** a literary or artistic production of poor quality **4** *chiefly US & Canadian* a poor or worthless person or a group of such people **5** bits that are broken or lopped off, esp the trimmings from trees or plants **6** the dry remains of sugar cane after the juice has been extracted ▷ *vb* **7** to remove the outer leaves and branches from (growing plants, esp sugar cane) **8** *slang* to attack or destroy (someone or something) wilfully or maliciously [c16: of

obscure origin; perhaps related to Norwegian *trask*]

trashy ('træʃɪ) *adj* trashier, trashiest cheap, worthless, or badly made > 'trashily *adv* > 'trashiness *n*

Trasimene ('træzɪ,mi:n) *n* Lake Trasimene a lake in central Italy, in Umbria: the largest lake in central Italy; scene of Hannibal's victory over the Romans in 217 BC. Area: 128 sq km (49 sq miles)

trass (træs) *n* a variety of the volcanic rock tuff, used to make a hydraulic cement [from Dutch *tras, tarasse*, from Italian *terrazza* worthless earth; see TERRACE]

trattoria (,trætə'rɪə) *n* an Italian restaurant [c19: from Italian, from *trattore* innkeeper, from French *traiteur*, from Old French *tretier* to TREAT]

trauma ('trɔ:mə) *n, pl* **-mata** (-mətə) *or* **-mas** **1** *psychol* a powerful shock that may have long-lasting effects **2** *pathol* any bodily injury or wound [c18: from Greek: a wound] > **traumatic** (trɔ:'mætɪk) *adj* > trau'matically *adv*

traumatize *or* **traumatise** ('trɔ:mə,taɪz) *vb* **1** (*tr*) to wound or injure (the body) **2** to subject or be subjected to mental trauma > ,traumati'zation *or* ,traumati'sation *n*

travail ('træveɪl) *literary* ▷ *n* **1** painful or excessive labour or exertion **2** the pangs of childbirth; labour ▷ *vb* **3** (*intr*) to suffer or labour painfully, esp in childbirth [c13: from Old French *travaillier*, from Vulgar Latin *tripaliāre* (unattested) to torture, from Late Latin *trepālium* instrument of torture, from Latin *tripālis* having three stakes, from *trēs* three + *pālus* stake]

Travancore (,trævən'kɔ:) *n* a former princely state of S India which joined with Cochin in 1949 to form **Travancore-Cochin**: part of Kerala state since 1956

trave (treɪv) *n* **1** a stout wooden cage in which difficult horses are shod **2** another name for **crossbeam 3** a bay formed by crossbeams [c15: from Old French *trave* beam, from Latin *trabs*]

travel ('træv³l) *vb* **-els, -elling, -elled** *or US* **-els, -eling, -eled** (*mainly intr*) **1** to go, move, or journey from one place to another **2** (*tr*) to go, move, or journey through or across (an area, region, etc) **3** to go, move, or cover a specified or unspecified distance **4** to go from place to place as a salesman **5** (*esp of perishable goods*) to withstand a journey **6** (*of light, sound, etc*) to be transmitted or move **7** to progress or advance **8** *basketball* to take an excessive number of steps while holding the ball **9** (*of part of a mechanism*) to move in a fixed predetermined path **10** *informal* to move rapidly ▷ *n* **11 a** the act of travelling **b** (*as modifier*): *a travel brochure*. Related adj: **itinerant 12** (*usually plural*) a tour or journey **13** the distance moved by a mechanical part, such as the stroke of a piston **14** movement or passage [C14 *travaillen* to make a journey, from Old French *travaillier* to TRAVAIL]

travel agency *or* **travel bureau** *n* an agency that arranges and negotiates flights, holidays, etc, for travellers > **travel agent** *n*

travelled *or US* **traveled** ('træv³ld) *adj* having experienced or undergone much travelling

traveller *or US* **traveler** ('træv³lə, 'trævlə) *n* **1** a person who travels, esp habitually **2** See **travelling salesman 3** a part of a mechanism that moves in a fixed course **4** *Austral* a swagman

traveller's cheque *n* a cheque in any of various denominations sold for use abroad by a bank, etc to the bearer, who signs it on purchase and can cash it by signing it again

traveller's joy *n* a ranunculaceous Old World climbing plant, *Clematis vitalba*, having white flowers and heads of feathery plumed fruits

travelling people *or* **travelling folk** *pl n* (*sometimes capitals*) *Brit* Gypsies or other itinerant people: a term used esp by such people of themselves

travelling salesman *n* a salesman who travels within an assigned territory in order to sell merchandise or to solicit orders for the commercial enterprise he represents by direct personal contact with customers and potential customers

travelling wave *n* **a** a wave carrying energy away from its source **b** (*as modifier*): *a travelling-wave aerial*

travelogue *or sometimes US* **travelog** ('træv³lɒg) *n* a film, lecture, or brochure on travels and travelling [c20: from

TRAVEL + -LOGUE, on the model of MONOLOGUE]

Traven ('trɑːvən) n **B(en)**, original name *Albert Otto Max Feige*. ?1882–1969, US novelist, born in Germany and living in Mexico from 1920, who kept his identity secret. His novels, originally written in German, include *The Treasure of Sierra Madre* (1934)

Travers ('trævɜːz) n **Ben(jamin)**. 1886–1980, British dramatist, best known for such farces as *Rookery Nook* (1926), *Thark* (1927), and *Plunder* (1928)

traverse ('trævɜːs, trəˈvɜːs) vb **1** to pass or go over or back and forth over (something); cross **2** (tr) to go against; oppose; obstruct **3** to move or cause to move sideways or crosswise **4** (tr) to extend or reach across **5** to turn (an artillery gun) laterally on its pivot or mount or (of an artillery gun) to turn laterally **6** (tr) to look over or examine carefully **7** (tr) law to deny (an allegation of fact), as in pleading **8** *mountaineering* to move across (a face) horizontally ▷ n **9** something being or lying across, such as a transom **10** a gallery or loft inside a building that crosses it **11** an obstruction or hindrance **12** *fortifications* a protective bank or other barrier across a trench or rampart **13** a railing, screen, or curtain **14** the act or an instance of traversing or crossing **15** a path or road across **16** *nautical* the zigzag course of a vessel tacking frequently **17** *law* the formal denial of a fact alleged in the opposite party's pleading **18** *surveying* a survey consisting of a series of straight lines, the length of each and the angle between them being measured **19** *mountaineering* a horizontal move across a face ▷ adj **20** being or lying across; transverse [C14: from Old French *traverser*, from Late Latin *trānsversāre*, from Latin *trānsversus* TRANSVERSE] > traˈversal n > ˈtraverser n

travertine or **travertin** ('trævətɪn) n a porous rock consisting of calcium carbonate, used for building [C18: from Italian *travertino* (influenced by *tra-* TRANS-), from Latin *lapis Tīburtīnus* Tiburtine stone, from *Tiburs* the district around Tibur (now Tivoli)]

travesty ('trævɪstɪ) n, pl -ties **1** a farcical or grotesque imitation; mockery; parody ▷ vb -ties, -tying, -tied (tr) **2** to make or be a travesty of [C17: from French *travesti* disguised, from *travestir* to disguise, from Italian *travestire*, from *tra-* TRANS- + *vestire* to clothe]

travois (trəˈvɔɪ) n, pl -vois (-ˈvɔɪz) **1** a sled formerly used by the Plains Indians of North America, consisting of two poles joined by a frame and dragged by an animal **2** *Canadian* a similar sled used for dragging logs [from Canadian French, from French *travail* TRAVE]

trawl (trɔːl) n *sea fishing* **1** Also called: trawl net a large net, usually in the shape of a sock or bag, drawn at deep levels behind special boats (trawlers) **2** Also called: trawl line a long line to which numerous shorter hooked lines are attached, suspended between buoys **3** the act of trawling ▷ vb **4** *sea fishing* to catch or try to catch (fish) with a trawl net or trawl line **5** (intr; foll by for) to seek or gather (something, such as information, or someone, such as a likely appointee) from a wide variety of sources [C17: from Middle Dutch *traghelen* to drag, from Latin *trāgula* dragnet; see TRAIL]

trawler ('trɔːlə) n **1** a vessel used for trawling **2** a person who trawls

tray (treɪ) n **1** a thin flat board or plate of metal, plastic, etc, usually with a raised edge, on which things can be carried **2** a shallow receptacle for papers, etc, sometimes forming a drawer in a cabinet or box [Old English *trieg*; related to Old Swedish *trö* corn measure, Old Norse *treyja* carrier, Greek *driti* tub, German *Trog* TROUGH]

TRC abbreviation (in South Africa) Truth and Reconciliation Commission, a body established in 1996 to investigate political crimes committed under the apartheid system

treacherous ('trɛtʃərəs) adj **1** betraying or likely to betray faith or confidence **2** unstable, unreliable, or dangerous > ˈtreacherously adv > ˈtreacherousness n

treachery ('trɛtʃərɪ) n, pl -eries **1** the act or an instance of wilful betrayal **2** the disposition to betray [C13: from Old French *trecherie*, from *trechier* to cheat; compare TRICK]

treacle ('triːkəl) n **1** Also called: black treacle *Brit* a dark viscous syrup obtained during the refining of sugar **2** *Brit* another name for **golden syrup 3** anything sweet

and cloying [C14: from Old French *triacle*, from Latin *thēriaca* antidote to poison] > ˈtreacly adj

tread (trɛd) vb treads, treading, trod, trodden or trod **1** to walk or trample in, on, over, or across (something) **2** (when intr, foll by on) to crush or squash by or as if by treading **3** (intr; sometimes foll by on) to subdue or repress, as by doing injury (to) **4** (tr) to do by walking or dancing: *to tread a measure* **5** (tr) (of a male bird) to copulate with (a female bird) **6** tread lightly to proceed with delicacy or tact **7** tread water to stay afloat in an upright position by moving the legs in a walking motion ▷ n **8** a manner or style of walking, dancing, etc: *a light tread* **9** the act of treading **10** the top surface of a step in a staircase **11** the outer part of a tyre or wheel that makes contact with the road, esp the grooved surface of a pneumatic tyre **12** the part of a rail that wheels touch **13** the part of a shoe that is generally in contact with the ground [Old English *tredan*; related to Old Norse *trotha* , Old High German *tretan*, Swedish *träda*] > ˈtreader n

treadle ('trɛdᵊl) n **1** a rocking lever operated by the foot to drive a machine ▷ vb **2** to work (a machine) with a treadle [Old English *tredel*, from *trǣde* something firm, from *tredan* to TREAD]

treadmill ('trɛd,mɪl) n **1** Also called: treadwheel (formerly) an apparatus used to produce rotation, in which the weight of men or animals climbing steps on or around the periphery of a cylinder or wheel caused it to turn **2** a dreary round or routine **3** an exercise machine that consists of a continuous moving belt on which to walk or jog

treas. abbreviation **1** treasurer **2** treasury

treason ('triːzᵊn) n **1** violation or betrayal of the allegiance that a person owes his sovereign or his country, esp by attempting to overthrow the government; high treason **2** any treachery or betrayal [C13: from Old French *traïson*, from Latin *trāditiō* a handing over; see TRADITION, TRADITOR] > ˈtreasonable or ˈtreasonous adj > ˈtreasonably adv

treasure ('trɛʒə) n **1** wealth and riches, usually hoarded, esp in the form of money, precious metals, or gems **2** a thing or person that is highly prized or valued ▷ vb (tr) **3** to prize highly as valuable, rare, or costly **4** to store up and save; hoard [C12: from Old French *tresor*, from Latin *thēsaurus* anciently hoarded, from Greek *thēsauros*]

treasure hunt n a game in which players act upon successive clues and are eventually directed to a prize

treasurer ('trɛʒərə) n a person appointed to look after the funds of a society, company, city, or other governing body > ˈtreasurership n

Treasurer ('trɛʒərə) n (in the Commonwealth of Australia and each of the Australian states) the minister of finance

treasure-trove n (in Britain) **1** law valuable articles, such as coins, bullion, etc, found hidden in the earth or elsewhere and of unknown ownership. Such articles become the property of the Crown, which compensates the finder if the treasure is declared. In 1996 treasure was defined as any item over 300 years old and containing more than 5% precious metal **2** anything similarly discovered that is of value [C16: from Anglo-French *tresor trové* treasure found, from Old French *tresor* TREASURE + *trover* to find]

treasury ('trɛʒərɪ) n, pl -uries **1** a storage place for treasure **2** the revenues or funds of a government, private organization, or individual **3** a place where funds are kept and disbursed **4** Also called: treasure house a collection or source of valuable items: *a treasury of information* [C13: from Old French *tresorie*, from *tresor* TREASURE]

Treasury ('trɛʒərɪ) n (in various countries) the government department in charge of finance. In Britain the Treasury is also responsible for economic strategy

Treasury Bench n (in Britain) the front bench to the right of the Speaker in the House of Commons, traditionally reserved for members of the Government

treasury note n a note issued by a government treasury and generally receivable as legal tender for any debt, esp

treat (triːt) n **1** a celebration, entertainment, gift, or

t

feast given for or to someone and paid for by another **2** any delightful surprise or specially pleasant occasion **3** the act of treating ▷ *vb* **4** (*tr*) to deal with or regard in a certain manner: *she treats school as a joke* **5** (*tr*) to apply treatment to: *to treat a patient for malaria* **6** (*tr*) to subject to a process or to the application of a substance: *to treat photographic film with developer* **7** (*tr*; often foll by *to*) to provide (someone) (with) as a treat: *he treated the children to a trip to the zoo* **8** (*intr*; usually foll by *of*) *formal* to deal (with), as in writing or speaking **9** (*intr*) *formal* to discuss settlement; negotiate [c13: from Old French *tretier*, from Latin *tractāre* to manage, from *trahere* to drag] > 'treatable *adj* > 'treater *n*

treatise ('triːtɪz) *n* **1** a formal work on a subject, esp one that deals systematically with its principles and conclusions **2** an obsolete word for **narrative** [c14: from Anglo-French *tretiz*, from Old French *tretier* to **TREAT**]

treatment ('triːtmənt) *n* **1** the application of medicines, surgery, psychotherapy, etc, to a patient or to a disease or symptom **2** the manner of handling or dealing with a person or thing, as in a literary or artistic work **3** the act, practice, or manner of treating **4** *films* an expansion of a script into sequence form, indicating camera angles, dialogue, etc **5** the treatment *slang* the usual manner of dealing with a particular type of person (esp in the phrase **give someone the (full) treatment**)

treaty ('triːtɪ) *n*, *pl* **-ties 1 a** a formal agreement or contract between two or more states, such as an alliance or trade arrangement **b** the document in which such a contract is written **2** any pact or agreement **3** an agreement between two parties concerning the purchase of property at a price privately agreed between them **4** *archaic* negotiation towards an agreement **5** (in Canada) any of the formal agreements between Indian bands and the federal government by which the Indians surrender their land rights in return for various forms of aid [c14: from Old French *traité*, from Medieval Latin *tractātus* treaty, from Latin: discussion, from *tractāre* to manage; see **TREAT**]

treaty port *n* (in China, Japan, and Korea during the second half of the 19th and first half of the 20th century) a city, esp a port, in which foreigners, esp Westerners, were allowed by treaty to conduct trade

Trebizond ('trɛbɪˌzɒnd) *n* a variant of **Trabzon**

treble ('trɛbəl) *adj* **1** threefold; triple **2** of, relating to, or denoting a soprano voice or part or a high-pitched instrument ▷ *n* **3** treble the amount, size, etc **4** a soprano voice or part or a high-pitched instrument **5** the highest register of a musical instrument **6 a** the high-frequency response of an audio amplifier, esp in a record player or tape recorder **b** a control knob on such an instrument by means of which the high-frequency gain can be increased or decreased **7** *bell-ringing* the lightest and highest bell in a ring **8 a** the narrow inner ring on a dartboard **b** a hit on this ring ▷ *vb* **9** to make or become three times as much [c14: from Old French, from Latin *triplus* threefold, **TRIPLE**] > 'trebly *adv*, *adj*

treble chance *n* a method of betting in football pools in which the chances of winning are related to the number of draws and the number of home and away wins forecast by the competitor

treble clef *n* *music* the clef that establishes G a fifth above middle C as being on the second line of the staff. Symbol: 𝄞

trebuchet ('trɛbjuˌʃɛt) *or* **trebucket** ('triːbʌkɪt) *n* a large medieval siege engine for hurling missiles consisting of a sling on a pivoted wooden arm set in motion by the fall of a weight [c13: from Old French, from *trebuchier* to stumble, from *tre-* **TRANS-** + *-buchier*, from *buc* trunk of the body, of Germanic origin; compare Old High German *būh* belly, Old English *buc*]

trecento (treɪ'tʃɛntəʊ) *n* the 14th century, esp with reference to Italian art and literature [c19: shortened from Italian *mille trecento* one thousand three hundred]

tree (triː) *n* **1** any large woody perennial plant with a distinct trunk giving rise to branches or leaves at some distance from the ground. Related adj: **arboreal 2** any plant that resembles this but has a trunk not made of wood, such as a palm tree **3** a wooden post, bar, etc

4 See **family tree, shoetree, saddletree 5** *chem* a treelike crystal growth; dendrite **6 a** a branching diagrammatic representation of something, such as the grammatical structure of a sentence **b** (*as modifier*): *a tree diagram* **7** at the top of the tree in the highest position of a profession, etc **8** up a tree *US & Canadian informal* in a difficult situation; trapped or stumped ▷ *vb* **trees, treeing, treed** (*tr*) **9** to drive or force up a tree **10** to shape or stretch (a shoe) on a shoetree [Old English *trēo*; related to Old Frisian, Old Norse *trē*, Old Saxon *trio*, Gothic *triu*, Greek *doru* wood, *drus* tree] > 'treeless *adj* > 'treelessness *n* > 'tree,like *adj*

Tree (triː) *n* Sir **Herbert Beerbohm**. 1853–1917, English actor and theatre manager; half-brother of Sir Max Beerbohm. He was noted for his lavish productions of Shakespeare

tree creeper *n* any small songbird of the family *Certhiidae* of the N hemisphere, having a brown-and-white plumage and slender downward-curving bill. They creep up trees to feed on insects

tree fern *n* any of numerous large tropical ferns, mainly of the family *Cyatheaceae*, having a trunklike stem bearing fronds at the top

tree frog *n* any arboreal frog of the family *Hylidae*, chiefly of SE Asia, Australia, and America. They are strong jumpers and have long toes ending in adhesive discs, which assist in climbing

treehopper ('triːˌhɒpə) *n* any homopterous insect of the family *Membracidae*, which live among trees and other plants and typically have a large hoodlike thoracic process curving backwards over the body

tree-hugger ('triːˌhʌɡə) *n* *informal, derogatory* an environmental campaigner [c20: from the tactic of embracing trees to prevent their being felled]

tree kangaroo *n* any of several arboreal kangaroos of the genus *Dendrolagus*, of New Guinea and N Australia, having hind and forelegs of a similar length and a long tail

tree line *n* the zone, at high altitudes or high latitudes, beyond which no trees grow. Trees growing between the timberline and the tree line are typically stunted

treen ('triːən) *adj* **1** made of wood; wooden ▷ *n* **2** another name for **treenware** [Old English *trēowen*, from *trēow* **TREE**]

treenail, trenail ('triːneɪl, 'trɛnºl) *or* **trunnel** ('trʌnºl) *n* a dowel used for pinning planks or timbers together

treenware ('triːənˌwɛə) *n* dishes and other household utensils made of wood, as by pioneers in North America [from **TREEN** + **WARE¹**]

tree of heaven *n* another name for **ailanthus**

tree sparrow *n* **1** a small European weaverbird, *Passer montanus*, similar to the house sparrow but having a brown head **2** a small North American finch, *Spizella arborea*, having a reddish-brown head, grey underparts, and brown striped back and wings

tree surgery *n* the treatment of damaged trees by filling cavities, applying braces, etc > **tree surgeon** *n*

tree toad *n* a less common name for **tree frog**

tree tomato *n* **1** an arborescent shrub, *Cyphomandra betacea* or *C. crassifolia*, native to South America but widely cultivated, bearing red egg-shaped edible fruit: family *Solanaceae* **2** the fruit of this plant ▷ Also called: **tamarillo**

tref, treif (treɪf) *or* **treifa** ('treɪfə) *adj* *Judaism* ritually unfit to be eaten; not kosher [Yiddish, from Hebrew *terēphāh*, literally: torn (i.e., animal meat torn by beasts), from *tāraf* to tear]

trefoil ('trɛfɔɪl) *n* **1** any of numerous leguminous plants of the temperate genus *Trifolium*, having leaves divided into three leaflets and dense heads of small white, yellow, red, or purple flowers **2** any of various related plants having leaves divided into three leaflets, such as bird's-foot trefoil **3** a leaf having three leaflets **4** *architect* an ornament in the form of three arcs arranged in a circle [c14: from Anglo-French *trifoil*, from Latin *trifolium* three-leaved herb, from **TRI-** + *folium* leaf] > **trefoiled** *adj*

Treitschke (*German* 'traɪtʃkə) *n* **Heinrich von** ('haɪnrɪç fɔn). 1834–96, German historian, noted for his highly nationalistic views

t

trek (trek) n **1** a long and often difficult journey **2** *South African* a journey or stage of a journey, esp a migration by ox wagon ▷ vb **treks, trekking, trekked 3** (*intr*) to make a trek [C19: from Afrikaans, from Middle Dutch *trekken* to travel; related to Old Frisian *trekka*]

trellis ('trɛlɪs) n **1** a structure or pattern of latticework, esp one used to support climbing plants **2** an arch made of latticework ▷ vb (*tr*) **3** to interweave (strips of wood, etc) to make a trellis **4** to provide or support with a trellis [C14: from Old French *treliz* fabric of open texture, from Late Latin *trilīcius* woven with three threads, from Latin TRI- + *līcium* thread]

trematode ('trɛmə,təʊd, 'triː-) n any parasitic flatworm of the class *Trematoda*, which includes the flukes [C19: from New Latin *Trematoda*, from Greek *trēmatōdēs* full of holes, from *trēma* a hole]

tremble ('trɛmbªl) vb (*intr*) **1** to vibrate with short slight movements; quiver **2** to shake involuntarily, as with cold or fear; shiver **3** to experience fear or anxiety ▷ n **4** the act or an instance of trembling [C14: from Old French *trembler*, from Medieval Latin *tremulāre*, from Latin *tremulus* quivering, from *tremere* to quake] > **'trembling** adj > **'tremblingly** adv > **'trembly** adj

trembler ('trɛmblə) n *electrical engineering* a device that vibrates to make or break an electrical circuit

trembles ('trɛmbªlz) n (*functioning as singular*) **1** Also called: **milk sickness** a disease of cattle and sheep characterized by muscular incoordination and tremor, caused by ingestion of white snakeroot or rayless goldenrod **2** a nontechnical name for **Parkinson's disease**

trembling poplar n another name for **aspen**

tremendous (trɪ'mɛndəs) adj **1** vast; huge **2** *informal* very exciting or unusual **3** *informal* (intensifier): *a tremendous help* **4** *archaic* terrible or dreadful [C17: from Latin *tremendus* terrible, literally: that is to be trembled at, from *tremere* to quake] > **tre'mendously** adv > **tre'mendousness** n

tremolo ('trɛmə,ləʊ) n, pl **-los** *music* **1 a** (in playing the violin, cello, etc) the rapid repetition of a single note produced by a quick back-and-forth movement of the bow **b** the rapid reiteration of two notes usually a third or greater interval apart (**fingered tremolo**). See **trill¹** (sense 1) **2** (in singing) a fluctuation in pitch [C19: from Italian: quavering, from Medieval Latin *tremulāre* to TREMBLE]

tremor ('trɛmə) n **1** an involuntary shudder or vibration, as from illness, fear, shock, etc **2** any trembling or quivering movement **3** a vibrating or trembling effect, as of sound or light **4** Also called: **earth tremor** a minor earthquake ▷ vb (*intr*) **5** to tremble [C14: from Latin: a shaking, from *tremere* to tremble, quake] > **'tremorous** adj

tremulous ('trɛmjʊləs) adj **1** vibrating slightly; quavering; trembling: *a tremulous voice* **2** showing or characterized by fear, anxiety, excitement, etc [C17: from Latin *tremulus* quivering, from *tremere* to shake] > **'tremulously** adv > **'tremulousness** n

trenail ('triː,neɪl, 'trɛnªl) n a variant spelling of **treenail**

trench (trɛntʃ) n **1** a deep ditch or furrow **2** a ditch dug as a fortification, having a parapet of the excavated earth ▷ vb **3** to make a trench in (a place) **4** (*tr*) to fortify with a trench or trenches **5** to slash or be slashed **6** (*intr*; foll by *on* or *upon*) to encroach or verge [C14: from Old French *trenche* something cut, from *trenchier* to cut, from Latin *truncāre* to cut off]

trenchant ('trɛntʃənt) adj **1** keen or incisive: *trenchant criticism* **2** vigorous and effective: *a trenchant foreign policy* **3** distinctly defined: *a trenchant outline* **4** *archaic or poetic* sharp: *a trenchant sword* [C14: from Old French *trenchant* cutting, from *trenchier* to cut; see TRENCH] > **'trenchancy** n > **'trenchantly** adv

Trenchard ('trɛntʃɑːd) n Hugh Montague, 1st Viscount. 1873–1956, British air marshal, who as chief of air staff (1918, 1919–27) and marshal of the RAF (1927–29) established the RAF as a fully independent service. As commissioner of the Metropolitan Police (1931–35) he founded the police college at Hendon

trench coat n a belted double-breasted waterproof coat of gabardine, etc, resembling a military officer's coat

trencher ('trɛntʃə) n **1** (esp formerly) a wooden board on which food was served or cut **2** Also called: **trencher cap** another name for **mortarboard** (sense 1) [C14 *trenchour* knife, plate for carving on, from Old French *trencheoir*, from *trenchier* to cut; see TRENCH]

trencherman ('trɛntʃəmən) n, pl **-men** a person who enjoys food; hearty eater [C16: from TRENCHER + MAN]

trench fever n an acute infectious disease characterized by fever and muscular aches and pains, caused by the microorganism *Rickettsia quintana* and transmitted by the bite of a body louse

trench foot n a form of frostbite affecting the feet of persons standing for long periods in cold water

trench mortar n a portable mortar used in trench warfare to shoot projectiles at a high trajectory over a short range

trench warfare n a type of warfare in which opposing armies face each other in entrenched positions

trend (trɛnd) n **1** general tendency or direction **2** fashion; mode ▷ vb (*intr*) **3** to take a certain trend [Old English *trendan* to turn; related to Middle Low German *trenden*]

trendsetter ('trɛnd,sɛtə) n a person or thing that creates, or may create, a new fashion > **'trend,setting** adj

trendy ('trɛndɪ) *Brit informal, often derogatory* ▷ adj **trendier, trendiest 1** consciously fashionable ▷ n, pl **trendies 2** a trendy person > **'trendily** adv > **'trendiness** n

Trengganu or **Terengganu** (trɛŋ'gɑːnuː, tɛrɛŋ-) n a state of E Peninsular Malaysia, on the South China Sea: under Thai suzerainty until becoming a British protectorate in 1909; joined the Federation of Malaya in 1948; an isolated forested region; mainly agricultural. Capital: Kuala Trengganu. Pop: 898 825 (2000). Area: 12 995 sq km (5002 sq miles)

Trent (trɛnt) n **1** a river in central England, rising in Staffordshire and flowing generally northeast into the Humber: the chief river of the Midlands. Length: 270 km (170 miles) **2** Also called: **Trient** the German name for **Trento**

trente et quarante (French trãt e karãt) n another name for **rouge et noir** [C17: French, literally: thirty and forty; referring to the rule that forty is the maximum number that may be dealt and the winning colour is the one closest to thirty-one]

Trentino-Alto Adige (trɛn'tiːnəʊ'ɑːltəʊ, 'ɑːdɪ,dʒeɪ) n a region of N Italy: consists of the part of the Tyrol south of the Brenner Pass, ceded by Austria after World War I. Pop: 950 495 (2003 est). Area: 13 613 sq km (5256 sq miles). Former name (until 1947): **Venezia Tridentina**

Trento (Italian 'trɛnto) n a city in N Italy, in Trentino-Alto Adige region on the Adige River: Roman military base; seat of the Council of Trent (1545-1563). Pop: 104 946 (2001). Latin name: **Tridentum**. German name: **Trent**

Trenton ('trɛntən) n a city in W New Jersey, capital of the state, on the Delaware River: settled by English Quakers in 1679; scene of the defeat of the British by Washington (1776) during the War of American Independence. Pop: 85 314 (2003 est)

trepan (trɪ'pæn) n **1** *surgery* an instrument resembling a carpenter's brace and bit formerly used to remove circular sections of bone (esp from the skull). See **trephine 2** a tool for cutting out circular blanks or for making grooves around a fixed centre ▷ vb **-pans, -panning, -panned** (*tr*) **3** to cut (a hole or groove) with a trepan **4** *surgery* another word for **trephine** [C14: from Medieval Latin *trepanum* rotary saw, from Greek *trupanon* auger, from *trupan* to bore, from *trupa* a hole] > **trepanation** (,trɛpə'neɪʃən) n

trepang (trɪ'pæŋ) n any of various large sea cucumbers of tropical Oriental seas, the body walls of which are used as food by the Japanese and Chinese. Also called: **bêche-de-mer** [C18: from Malay *těripang*]

trephine (trɪ'fiːn) n **1** a surgical sawlike instrument for removing circular sections of bone, esp from the skull ▷ vb **2** (*tr*) to remove a circular section of bone from (esp the skull) ▷ Also called: **trepan** [C17: from French *tréphine*, from obsolete English *trefine* TREPAN, allegedly from Latin *trēs fīnēs* literally: three ends; influenced also by English *trepane* TREPAN] > **trephination** (,trɛfɪ'neɪʃən) n

t

trepidation (ˌtrɛpɪˈdeɪʃən) *n* **1** a state of fear or anxiety **2** a condition of quaking or palpitation, esp one caused by anxiety [c17: from Latin *trepidātiō*, from *trepidāre* to be in a state of alarm; compare INTREPID]

trespass (ˈtrɛspəs) *vb* (*intr*) **1** (often foll by *on* or *upon*) to go or intrude (on the property, privacy, or preserves of another) with no right or permission **2** *law* to commit trespass, esp to enter wrongfully upon land belonging to another **3** *archaic* (often foll by *against*) to sin or transgress ▷ *n* **4** *law* **a** any unlawful act committed with force or violence, actual or implied, which causes injury to another person, his property, or his rights **b** a wrongful entry upon another's land **c** an action to recover damages for such injury or wrongful entry **5** an intrusion on another's privacy or preserves **6** a sin or offence [c13: from Old French *trespas* a passage, from *trespasser* to pass through, from *tres-* TRANS- + *passer*, ultimately from Latin *passus* a PACE¹] > ˈtrespasser *n*

tress (trɛs) *n* **1** (often plural) a lock of hair, esp a long lock of woman's hair **2** a plait or braid of hair ▷ *vb* (*tr*) **3** to arrange in tresses [c13: from Old French *trece*, of uncertain origin] > ˈtressy *adj*

trestle (ˈtrɛsəl) *n* **1** a framework in the form of a horizontal member supported at each end by a pair of splayed legs, used to carry scaffold boards, a table top, etc **2 a** a braced structural tower-like framework of timber, metal, or reinforced concrete that is used to support a bridge or ropeway **b** a bridge constructed of such frameworks [c14: from Old French *trestel*, ultimately from Latin *trānstrum* TRANSOM]

trestlework (ˈtrɛsəlˌwɜːk) *n* an arrangement of trestles, esp one that supports or makes a bridge

Tretchikoff (ˈtrɛtʃɪkɒf) *n* **Vladimir**. 1913–2006, South African painter, born in Russia, known for his kitsch appeal, especially for his much-reproduced *Chinese Girl* (1950; also known as *The Green Lady*)

trevally (trɪˈvælɪ) *n, pl* **-lies** any of various marine food and game fishes of the genus *Caranx*: family *Carangidae*. Also called: (NZ) araara [c19: probably alteration of *cavally*; see CAVALLA]

Trevelyan (trɪˈveljən, -ˈvɪl-) *n* **1 George Macaulay**. 1876–1962, British historian, noted for his *English Social History* (1944) **2** his father, **Sir George Otto**. 1838–1928, British historian and biographer. His works include a biography of his uncle Lord Macaulay (1876)

Trèves (trɛv) *n* the French name for **Trier**

Trevino (trəˈviːnəʊ) *n* **Lee**, born 1939, US professional golfer: winner of the US Open Championship (1968; 1971) and the British Open Championship (1971; 1972)

Treviso (Italian treˈviːzo) *n* a city in N Italy, in Veneto region: agricultural market centre. Pop: 80 144 (2001)

Trevithick (ˈtrɛvɪθɪk) *n* **Richard**. 1771–1833, British engineer, who built the first steam-driven passenger carriage (1801) and the first locomotive to run on smooth wheels on smooth rails (1804)

Trevor (ˈtrɛvə) *n* **William**, real name William Trevor Cox. born 1928, Irish novelist and short-story writer. His novels include *The Old Boys* (1964), *The Children of Dynmouth* (1977), *Felicia's Journey* (1994), and *The Story of Lucy Gault* (2002)

trews (truːz) *pl n chiefly Brit* close-fitting trousers, esp of tartan cloth and worn by certain Scottish soldiers [c16: from Scottish Gaelic *triubhas*, from Old French *trebus*; see TROUSERS]

trey (treɪ) *n* any card or dice throw with three spots [c14: from Old French *treis* three, from Latin *trēs*]

tri- *prefix* **1** three or thrice: *triaxial; trigon; trisect* **2** occurring every three: *trimonthly* [from Latin *trēs*, Greek *treis*]

triable (ˈtraɪəbəl) *adj* **1 a** liable to be tried judicially **b** subject to examination or determination by a court of law **2** *rare* able to be tested

triacid (traɪˈæsɪd) *adj* (of a base) capable of reacting with three molecules of a monobasic acid

triad (ˈtraɪæd) *n* **1** a group of three; trio **2** *chem* an atom, element, group, or ion that has a valency of three **3** *music* a three-note chord consisting of a note and the third and fifth above it **4** an aphoristic literary form used in medieval Welsh and Irish literature **5** the US strategic nuclear force, consisting of intercontinental ballistic missiles, submarine-launched ballistic missiles, and bombers [c16: from Late Latin *trias*, from Greek; related to Greek *treis* three] > triˈadic *adj* > ˈtriadism *n*

Triad (ˈtraɪæd) *n* any of several Chinese secret societies, esp one involved in criminal activities, such as drug trafficking

triage (ˈtriːɑːʒ, ˌtriːˈɑːʒ, ˈtraɪ-) *n* **1** (in a hospital) the principle or practice of sorting emergency patients into categories of priority for treatment **2** the principle or practice of sorting casualties in battle or disaster into categories of priority for treatment **3** the principle or practice of allocating limited resources, as of food or foreign aid, on a basis of expediency rather than according to moral principles or the needs of the recipients [c18: in the sense: sorting (goods) according to quality): from French; see TRY, -AGE]

trial (ˈtraɪəl, traɪl) *n* **1 a** the act or an instance of trying or proving; test or experiment **b** (*as modifier*): *a trial run* **2** *law* **a** the judicial examination of the issues in a civil or criminal cause by a competent tribunal and the determination of these issues in accordance with the law of the land **b** the determination of an accused person's guilt or innocence after hearing evidence for the prosecution and for the accused and the judicial examination of the issues involved **c** (*as modifier*): *trial proceedings* **3** an effort or attempt to do something: *we had three trials at the climb* **4** trouble or grief **5** an annoying or frustrating person or thing **6** (*often plural*) a competition for individuals: *sheepdog trials* **7** a motorcycling competition in which the skills of the riders are tested over rough ground **8** *ceramics* a piece of sample material used for testing the heat of a kiln and its effects **9** on trial **a** undergoing trial, esp before a court of law **b** being tested, as before a commitment to purchase ▷ *vb* trials, trialling, trialled (*tr*) **10** to test or make experimental use of (something): *the idea has been trialled in several schools* [c16: from Anglo-French, from *trier* to TRY] > ˈtrialling *n*

trial and error *n* a method of discovery, solving problems, etc, based on practical experiment and experience rather than on theory: *he learned to cook by trial and error*

trial balance *n book-keeping* a statement of all the debit and credit balances in the ledger of a double-entry system, drawn up to test their equality

triallist *or* **trialist** (ˈtraɪəlɪst, ˈtraɪlɪst) *n* **1** a person who takes part in a competition, esp a motorcycle trial **2** *sport* a person who takes part in a preliminary match or heat held to determine selection for an event, a team, etc

triangle (ˈtraɪˌæŋɡəl) *n* **1** *geometry* a three-sided polygon that can be classified by angle, as in an acute triangle, or by side, as in an equilateral triangle. Sum of interior angles: 180°; area: ½ base × height **2** any object shaped like a triangle **3** any situation involving three parties or points of view. See also **eternal triangle 4** *music* a percussion instrument consisting of a sonorous metal bar bent into a triangular shape, beaten with a metal stick **5** a group of three [c14: from Latin *triangulum* (noun), from *triangulus* (adjective), from TRI- + *angulus* corner] > ˈtriˌangled *adj* > triangular (traɪˈæŋɡjʊlə) *adj*

triangle of forces *n physics* a triangle whose sides represent the magnitudes and directions of three forces in equilibrium whose resultant is zero and which are therefore in equilibrium

triangulate *vb* (traɪˈæŋɡjʊˌleɪt) (*tr*) **1 a** to survey by the method of triangulation **b** to calculate trigonometrically **2** to divide into triangles **3** to make triangular ▷ *adj* (traɪˈæŋɡjʊlɪt, -ˌleɪt) **4** marked with or composed of triangles > triˈangulately *adv*

triangulation (traɪˌæŋɡjʊˈleɪʃən) *n* **1** a method of surveying in which an area is divided into triangles, one side (the base line) and all angles of which are measured and the lengths of the other lines calculated trigonometrically **2** the network of triangles so formed

triangulation station *n* a point used in triangulation as a basis for making maps. Triangulation stations are marked in a number of ways, such as by a tapering stone pillar on a hilltop

Triassic (traɪˈæsɪk) *adj* **1** of, denoting, or formed in the first period of the Mesozoic era that lasted for 42 million years and during which reptiles flourished ▷ *n* **2 the Triassic** Also called: **Trias** the Triassic period or rock system [c19: from Latin *trias* triad, with reference to the three subdivisions]

triathlon (traɪˈæθlɒn) *n* an athletic contest in which each athlete competes in three different events; swimming, cycling, and running [c20: from TRI- + Greek *athlon* contest] > ˌtriˈathlete *n*

triatomic (ˌtraɪəˈtɒmɪk) *adj chem* having three atoms in the molecule

triazine (ˈtraɪəˌziːn, -zɪn, traɪˈæziːn, -zɪn) *or* **triazin** (ˈtraɪəzɪn, traɪˈæzɪn) *n* **1** any of three azines that contain three nitrogen atoms in their molecules. Formula: $C_3H_3N_3$ **2** any substituted derivative of any of these compounds

tribade (ˈtrɪbəd) *n* a lesbian, esp one who practises tribadism [c17: from Latin *tribas*, from Greek *tribein* to rub]

tribadism (ˈtrɪbəˌdɪzəm) *n* a lesbian practice in which one partner lies on top of the other and simulates the male role in heterosexual intercourse

tribalism (ˈtraɪbəˌlɪzəm) *n* **1** the state of existing as a separate tribe or tribes **2** the customs and beliefs of a tribal society **3** loyalty to a tribe or tribal values > ˈtribalist *n, adj* > ˌtribalˈistic *adj*

tribasic (traɪˈbeɪsɪk) *adj* **1** (of an acid) containing three replaceable hydrogen atoms in the molecule **2** (of a molecule) containing three monovalent basic atoms or groups in the molecule

tribe (traɪb) *n* **1** a social division of a people, esp of a preliterate people, defined in terms of common descent, territory, culture, etc **2** an ethnic or ancestral division of ancient cultures, esp of one of the following **a** any of the three divisions of the ancient Romans, the Latins, Sabines, and Etruscans **b** one of the later political divisions of the Roman people **c** any of the 12 divisions of ancient Israel, each of which was named after and believed to be descended from one of the 12 patriarchs **d** a phyle of ancient Greece **3** *informal, often jocular* **a** a large number of persons, animals, etc **b** a specific class or group of persons **c** a family, esp a large one **4** *biology* a taxonomic group that is a subdivision of a subfamily **5** *stockbreeding* a strain of animals descended from a common related ancestor through the female line [c13: from Latin *tribus*; probably related to Latin *trēs* three] > ˈtribeless *adj* · ˈtribal *adj*

tribesman (ˈtraɪbzmən) *n, pl* -men a member of a tribe

tribo- *combining form* indicating friction: *triboelectricity* [from Greek *tribein* to rub]

triboelectricity (ˌtraɪbəʊɪlekˈtrɪsɪtɪ, -ˌiːlek-) *n* static electricity generated by friction

tribology (traɪˈbɒlədʒɪ) *n* the study of friction, lubrication, and wear between moving surfaces

triboluminescence (ˌtraɪbəʊˌluːmɪˈnɛsəns) *n* luminescence produced by friction, such as the emission of light when certain crystals are crushed > ˌtriboˌlumiˈnescent *adj*

tribrach (ˈtraɪbræk, ˈtrɪb-) *n prosody* a metrical foot of three short syllables (◡◡◡) [c16: from Latin *tribrachys*, from Greek *tribrakhus*, from TRI- + *brakhus* short]

tribromoethanol (traɪˌbrəʊməʊˈɛθəˌnɒl) *n* a soluble white crystalline compound with a slight aromatic odour, used as a general anaesthetic; 2,2,2-tribromoethanol. Formula: CBr_3CH_2OH

tribulation (ˌtrɪbjʊˈleɪʃən) *n* **1** a cause of distress **2** a state of suffering or distress [c13: from Old French, from Church Latin *trībulātiō*, from Latin *trībulāre* to afflict, from *trībulum* a threshing board, from *terere* to rub]

tribunal (traɪˈbjuːnəl, trɪ-) *n* **1** a court of justice or any place where justice is administered **2** (in Britain) a special court, convened by the government to inquire into a specific matter **3** a raised platform containing the seat of a judge or magistrate, originally that in a Roman basilica [c16: from Latin *tribūnus* TRIBUNE¹]

tribune¹ (ˈtrɪbjuːn) *n* **1** (in ancient Rome) **a** an officer elected by the plebs to protect their interests. Originally there were two of these officers but finally there were ten **b** a senior military officer **2** a person or institution that upholds public rights; champion [c14: from Latin *tribunus*, probably from *tribus* TRIBE] > ˈtribunary *adj*

tribune² (ˈtrɪbjuːn) *n* **1 a** the apse of a Christian basilica that contains the bishop's throne **b** the throne itself **2** a gallery or raised area in a church **3** *rare* a raised platform from which a speaker may address an audience; dais [c17: via French from Italian *tribuna*, from Medieval Latin *tribūna*, variant of Latin *tribūnal* TRIBUNAL]

tributary (ˈtrɪbjʊtərɪ, -trɪ) *n, pl* -taries **1** a stream, river, or glacier that feeds another larger one **2** a person, nation, or people that pays tribute ▷ *adj* **3** (of a stream, etc) feeding a larger stream **4** given or owed as a tribute **5** paying tribute > ˈtributarily *adv*

tribute (ˈtrɪbjuːt) *n* **1** a gift or statement made in acknowledgment, gratitude, or admiration **2** a payment by one ruler or state to another, usually as an acknowledgment of submission **3** the obligation to pay tribute [c14: from Latin *tribūtum*, from *tribuere* to grant (originally: to distribute among the tribes), from *tribus* TRIBE]

tribute band *n* a group that plays the songs of a band they admire, often dressing in the style of the original band members

trice¹ (traɪs) *n* moment; instant (esp in the phrase **in a trice**) [c15 (in the phrase *at* or *in a trice*, in the sense: at one tug): apparent substantive use of TRICE²]

trice² (traɪs) *vb* (*tr*; often full by *up*) *nautical* to haul up or secure [c15 from Middle Dutch *tries*, from *trīse* pulley]

tricentenary (ˌtraɪsɛnˈtiːnərɪ) *or* **tricentennial** (ˌtraɪsɛnˈtɛnɪəl) *adj* **1** of or relating to a period of 300 years **2** of or relating to a 300th anniversary or its celebration ▷ *n, pl* -tenaries *or* -tennials **3** an anniversary of 300 years or its celebration

triceps (ˈtraɪsɛps) *n, pl* -cepses (-sɛpsɪz) *or* -ceps any muscle having three heads, esp the one (*triceps brachii*) that extends the forearm [c16: from Latin, from TRI- + *caput* head]

triceratops (traɪˈsɛrəˌtɒps) *n* any rhinoceros-like herbivorous dinosaur of the ornithischian genus *Triceratops*, of Cretaceous times, having a heavily armoured neck and three horns on the skull [c19: from New Latin, from TRI- + Greek *kerat-, keras* horn + *ōps* eye]

trichiasis (trɪˈkaɪəsɪs) *n pathol* an abnormal position of the eyelashes that causes irritation when they rub against the eyeball [c17: via Late Latin from Greek *trikhiasis*, from *thrix* a hair + -IASIS]

trichina (trɪˈkaɪnə) *n, pl* -nae (-niː) a parasitic nematode worm, *Trichinella spiralis*, occurring in the intestines of pigs, rats, and man and producing larvae that form cysts in skeletal muscle [c19: from New Latin, from Greek *trikhinos* relating to hair, from *thrix* a hair] > trichinous (ˈtrɪkɪnəs) *adj*

Trichinopoly (ˌtrɪkɪˈnɒpəlɪ) *n* another name for **Tiruchirapalli**

trichinosis (ˌtrɪkɪˈnəʊsɪs) *n* a disease characterized by nausea, fever, diarrhoea, and swelling of the muscles, caused by ingestion of pork infected with trichina larvae. Also called: **trichiniasis** (ˌtrɪkɪˈnaɪəsɪs) [c19: from New Latin TRICHINA]

trichloride (traɪˈklɔːraɪd) *n* any compound that contains three chlorine atoms per molecule

tricho- *or before a vowel* **trich-** *combining form* indicating hair or a part resembling hair: *trichocyst* [from Greek *thrix* (genitive *trikhos*) hair]

trichology (trɪˈkɒlədʒɪ) *n* the branch of medicine concerned with the hair and its diseases > triˈchologist *n*

trichomonad (ˌtrɪkəʊˈmɒnæd) *n* any parasitic flagellate protozoan of the genus *Trichomonas*, occurring in the digestive and reproductive systems of man and animals > ˌtrichoˈmonadal, Also called: **trichomonal** (ˌtrɪkəʊˈmɒnəl, -ˈməʊ-, trɪˈkɒmənəl) *adj*

trichomoniasis (ˌtrɪkəʊməˈnaɪəsɪs) *n* inflammation of the vagina characterized by a frothy discharge, caused by infection with parasitic protozoa (*Trichomonas vaginalis*) [c19: New Latin; see TRICHOMONAD, -IASIS]

trichopteran (traɪˈkɒptərən) *n* **1** any insect of the order *Trichoptera*, which comprises the caddis flies ▷ *adj* **2** Also called: **trichopterous** (trɪˈkɒptərəs) of, relating to, or belonging to the order *Trichoptera* [c19: from New Latin

Trichoptera, literally: having hairy wings, from Greek *thrix* a hair + *pteron* wing]

trichosis (trɪˈkəʊsɪs) *n* any abnormal condition or disease of the hair [c19: via New Latin from Greek *trikhōsis* growth of hair]

trichotomy (traɪˈkɒtəmɪ) *n, pl* -mies 1 division into three categories 2 *theol* the division of man into body, spirit, and soul [c17: probably from New Latin *trichotomia*, from Greek *trikhotomein* to divide into three, from *trikha* triple + *temnein* to cut] > trichotomic (ˌtrɪkəˈtɒmɪk) *or* triˈchotomous *adj*

trichroism (ˈtraɪkrəʊˌɪzəm) *n* a property of biaxial crystals as a result of which they show a perceptible difference in colour when viewed along three different axes [c19: from Greek *trikhroos* three-coloured, from TRI- + *khrōma* colour]

trichromatic (ˌtraɪkrəʊˈmætɪk) *or* **trichromic** (traɪˈkrəʊmɪk) *adj* 1 *photog, printing* involving the combination of three primary colours in the production of any colour 2 of, relating to, or having normal colour vision 3 having or involving three colours > triˈchromaˌtism *n*

trick (trɪk) *n* 1 a deceitful, cunning, or underhand action or plan 2 a a mischievous, malicious, or humorous action or plan; joke: *the boys are up to their tricks again* b (*as modifier*): *a trick spider* 3 an illusory or magical feat or device 4 a simple feat learned by an animal or person 5 an adroit or ingenious device; knack: *a trick of the trade* 6 a behavioural trait, habit, or mannerism 7 a turn or round of duty or work 8 *cards* a a batch of cards containing one from each player, usually played in turn and won by the player or side that plays the card with the highest value b a card that can potentially win a trick 9 can't take a trick *Austral slang* to be consistently unsuccessful or unlucky 10 do the trick *informal* to produce the right or desired result 11 how's tricks? *slang* how are you? 12 turn a trick *slang* (of a prostitute) to gain a customer ⊳ *vb* 13 to defraud, deceive, or cheat (someone), esp by means of a trick [c15: from Old Northern French *trique*, from *trikier* to deceive, from Old French *trichier*, ultimately from Latin *trīcārī* to play tricks]

trick cyclist *n* a slang term for **psychiatrist**

trickery (ˈtrɪkərɪ) *n, pl* -eries the practice or an instance of using tricks: *he obtained the money by trickery*

trickle (ˈtrɪkˀl) *vb* 1 to run or cause to run in thin or slow streams: *she trickled the sand through her fingers* 2 (*intr*) to move, go, or pass gradually: *the crowd trickled away* ⊳ *n* 3 a thin, irregular, or slow flow of something 4 the act of trickling [c14: perhaps of imitative origin] > ˈtrickling *adj*

trickle charger *n* a small mains-operated battery charger, esp one that delivers less than 5 amperes and is used by car owners

trickle-down *adj* of or concerning the theory that granting concessions such as tax cuts to the rich will benefit all levels of society by stimulating the economy

trick or treat *sentence substitute chiefly US & Canadian* the cry by children at Halloween when they call at houses, indicating that they want a present or money or else they will play a trick on the householder

trick out *or* **trick up** *vb* (*tr, adverb*) to dress up; deck out: *tricked out in frilly dresses*

trickster (ˈtrɪkstə) *n* a person who deceives or plays tricks

tricksy (ˈtrɪksɪ) *adj* -sier, -siest 1 playing tricks habitually; mischievous 2 crafty or difficult to deal with > ˈtricksiness *n*

tricky (ˈtrɪkɪ) *adj* trickier, trickiest 1 involving snags or difficulties: *a tricky job* 2 needing careful and tactful handling: *a tricky situation* 3 characterized by tricks; sly; wily: *a tricky dealer* > ˈtrickily *adv* > ˈtrickiness *n*

triclinic (traɪˈklɪnɪk) *adj* relating to or belonging to the crystal system characterized by three unequal axes, no pair of which are perpendicular. Also called: anorthic

triclinium (traɪˈklɪnɪəm) *n, pl* -ia (-ɪə) (in ancient Rome) 1 an arrangement of three couches around a table for reclining upon while dining 2 a dining room, esp one containing such an arrangement of couches [c17: from Latin, from Greek *triklinion*, from TRI- + *klinē* a couch]

tricolour *or US* **tricolor** (ˈtrɪkələ, ˈtraɪˌkʌl) *adj* 1 Also

called: tricoloured, tricolored (ˈtraɪˌkʌləd) *adj* having or involving three colours ⊳ *n* 2 (*often capital*) the French national flag, having three equal vertical stripes in blue, white, and red 3 any flag, badge, ribbon, etc, with three colours

tricorn (ˈtraɪˌkɔːn) *n* 1 Also: tricorne a cocked hat with opposing brims turned back and caught in three places ⊳ *adj* 2 Also: tricornered having three horns or corners [c18: from Latin *tricornis*, from TRI- + *cornu* HORN]

tricot (ˈtrɪkəʊ, ˈtriː-) *n* 1 a thin rayon or nylon fabric knitted or resembling knitting, used for dresses, etc 2 a type of ribbed dress fabric [c19: from French, from *tricoter* to knit, of unknown origin]

tricuspid (traɪˈkʌspɪd) *anatomy* ⊳ *adj* 1 Also: tricuspidal having three points, cusps, or segments: *a tricuspid tooth; a tricuspid valve* ⊳ *n* 2 a tooth having three cusps

tricycle (ˈtraɪsɪkˀl) *n* a three-wheeled cycle, esp one driven by pedals > ˈtricyclist *n*

trident (ˈtraɪdˀnt) *n* a three-pronged spear, originally from the East [c16: from Latin *tridēns* three-pronged, from TRI- + *dēns* tooth]

Trident (ˈtraɪdˀnt) *n* a type of US submarine-launched ballistic missile with independently targetable warheads

tridentate (traɪˈdɛnteɪt) *or* **tridental** *adj anatomy, botany* having three prongs, teeth, or points

Tridentine (traɪˈdɛntaɪn) *adj* 1 *history* a of or relating to the Council of Trent b in accord with Tridentine doctrine ⊳ *n* 2 an orthodox Roman Catholic [c16: from Medieval Latin *Tridentīnus*, from *Tridentum* TRENT]

Tridentum (traɪˈdɛntəm) *n* the Latin name for **Trento**

tried (traɪd) *vb* the past tense and past participle of **try**

triella (traɪˈɛlə) *n Austral* three nominated horse races in which the punter bets on selecting the three winners

triennial (traɪˈɛnɪəl) *adj* 1 relating to, lasting for, or occurring every three years ⊳ *n* 2 a third anniversary 3 a triennial period, thing, or occurrence [c17: from Latin TRIENNIUM] > triˈennially *adv*

triennium (traɪˈɛnɪəm) *n, pl* -niums *or* -nia (-nɪə) a period or cycle of three years [c19: from Latin, from TRI- + *annus* a year]

Trient (triˈɛnt) *n* the German name for **Trento**. Also called: Trent

trier (ˈtraɪə) *n* a person or thing that tries

Trier (*German* triːr) *n* a city in W Germany, in the Rhineland-Palatinate on the Moselle River: one of the oldest towns of central Europe, ancient capital of a Celto-Germanic tribe (the **Treveri**); an early centre of Christianity, ruled by powerful archbishops until the 18th century; wine trade; important Roman remains. Pop: 100 180 (2003 est). French name: Trèves

Trieste (triːˈɛst; *Italian* triˈɛste) *n* 1 a port in NE Italy, capital of Friuli-Venezia Giulia region, on the **Gulf of Trieste** at the head of the Adriatic Sea: under Austrian rule (1382–1918); capital of the Free Territory of Trieste (1947–54); important transit port for central Europe. Pop: 211 184 (2001). Slovene and Croatian name: Trst 2 Free Territory of Trieste a former territory on the N Adriatic: established by the UN in 1947; most of the N part passed to Italy and the remainder to Yugoslavia in 1954

trifacial (traɪˈfeɪʃəl) *adj* another word for **trigeminal**

trifecta (traɪˈfɛktə) *n* a form of betting in which the punter selects the first three place-winners in a horse race in the correct order [from TRI- + (*per*)*fecta*, a US system of betting]

trifid (ˈtraɪfɪd) *adj* divided or split into three parts or lobes [c18: from Latin *trifidus* from TRI- + *findere* to split]

trifle (ˈtraɪfˀl) *n* 1 a thing of little or no value or significance 2 a small amount; bit: *a trifle more enthusiasm* 3 *Brit* a cold dessert made with sponge cake spread with jam or fruit, soaked in wine or sherry, covered with a custard sauce and cream, and decorated ⊳ *vb* 4 (*intr;* usually foll by *with*) to deal (with) as if worthless; dally: *to trifle with a person's affections* 5 to waste (time) frivolously [c13: from Old French *trufle* mockery, from *trufler* to cheat] > ˈtrifler *n*

trifling (ˈtraɪflɪŋ) *adj* 1 insignificant or petty 2 frivolous or idle > ˈtriflingly *adv*

trifocal *adj* (traɪˈfəʊkˀl) 1 having three focuses 2 having three focal lengths ▷ *n* (traɪˈfəʊkᵊl, ˈtraɪˌfəʊkᵊl) **3** (*plural*) glasses with trifocal lenses

triforium (traɪˈfɔːrɪəm) *n, pl* **-ria** (-rɪə) an arcade above the arches of the nave, choir, or transept of a church [c18: from Anglo-Latin, apparently from Latin TRI- + *foris* a doorway; referring to the fact that each bay characteristically had three openings]

trifurcate (ˈtraɪfɜːkɪt, -ˌkeɪt) *or* **trifurcated** *adj* having three branches or forks [from Latin *trifurcus*, from TRI- + *furca* a fork] > ˌtrifurˈcation *n*

trig (trɪg) *archaic or dialect* ▷ *adj* **1** neat or spruce ▷ *vb* **trigs**, **trigging**, **trigged 2** to make or become trim or spruce [c12 (originally: trusty): of Scandinavian origin; related to Old Norse *tryggr* true] > ˈtrigly *adv* > ˈtrigness *n*

trig. *abbreviation* **1** trigonometrical **2** trigonometry

trigeminal (traɪˈdʒɛmɪnᵊl) *adj anatomy* of or relating to the trigeminal nerve [c19: from Latin *trigeminus* triplet, from TRI- + *geminus* twin]

trigeminal nerve *n* either one of the fifth pair of cranial nerves, having three main branches, which supply the muscles of the mandible and maxilla. Their ophthalmic branches supply the area around the orbit of the eye, the nasal cavity, and the forehead

trigeminal neuralgia *n pathol* another name for **tic douloureux**

trigger (ˈtrɪgə) *n* **1** a small projecting lever that activates the firing mechanism of a firearm **2** *machinery* a device that releases a spring-loaded mechanism or a similar arrangement **3** any event that sets a course of action in motion ▷ *vb* (*tr*) **4** (usually foll by *off*) to give rise (to); set off **5** to fire or set in motion by or as by pulling a trigger [C17 *tricker*, from Dutch *trekker*, from *trekken* to pull; see TREK]

triggerfish (ˈtrɪgəˌfɪʃ) *n, pl* **-fish** *or* **-fishes** any plectognath fish of the family *Balistidae*, of tropical and temperate seas. They have a compressed body with erectile spines in the first dorsal fin

trigger-happy *adj informal* **1** tending to resort to use of firearms or violence irresponsibly **2** tending to act rashly or without due consideration

triglyceride (traɪˈglɪsəˌraɪd) *n* any ester of glycerol and one or more carboxylic acids, in which each glycerol molecule has combined with three carboxylic acid molecules. Most natural fats and oils are triglycerides

triglyph (ˈtraɪˌglɪf) *n architect* a stone block in a Doric frieze, having three vertical channels [c16: via Latin from Greek *trigluphos* three-grooved, from *tri-* TRI- + *gluphē* carving. See GLYPH]

trigonal (ˈtrɪgᵊnᵊl) *adj* Also called: rhombohedral relating or belonging to the crystal system characterized by three equal axes that are equally inclined and not perpendicular to each other

trigonometric function *n* Also called: circular function any of a group of functions of an angle expressed as a ratio of two of the sides of a right-angled triangle containing the angle. The group includes sine, cosine, tangent, secant, cosecant, and cotangent

trigonometry (ˌtrɪgəˈnɒmɪtrɪ) *n* the branch of mathematics concerned with the properties of trigonometric functions and their application to the determination of the angles and sides of triangles. Used in surveying, navigation, etc [c17: from New Latin *trigōnometria* from Greek *trigōnon* triangle] > trigonometric (ˌtrɪgənəˈmɛtrɪk) *or* ˌtrigonoˈmetrical *adj*

trig point *n* an informal name for **triangulation station** [from *trigonometric*]

trigraph (ˈtraɪˌgrɑːf, -ˌgræf) *n* a combination of three letters used to represent a single speech sound or phoneme, such as *eau* in French *beau*

trihedral (traɪˈhiːdrᵊl) *adj* **1** having or formed by three plane faces meeting at a point ▷ *n* **2** a figure formed by the intersection of three lines in different planes [c18: from TRI- + Greek *hedra* base, seat + -AL¹]

trihedron (traɪˈhiːdrən) *n, pl* **-drons** *or* **-dra** (-drə) a figure formed by the intersection of three planes

trike (traɪk) *n* short for **tricycle**

trilateral (traɪˈlætərəl) *adj* having three sides

trilby (ˈtrɪlbɪ) *n, pl* **-bies** *chiefly Brit* a man's soft felt hat with an indented crown [c19: named after *Trilby*, the

heroine of a dramatized novel (1893) of that title by George du Maurier]

trilingual (traɪˈlɪŋgwəl) *adj* **1** able to speak three languages fluently **2** expressed or written in three languages > triˈlingualism *n*

trilithon (traɪˈlɪθɒn, ˈtraɪlɪˌθɒn) *or* **trilith** (ˈtraɪlɪθ) *n* a structure consisting of two upright stones with a third placed across the top, such as those of Stonehenge [c18: from Greek; see TRI-, -LITH] > trilithic (traɪˈlɪθɪk) *adj*

trill (trɪl) *n* **1** *music* a melodic ornament consisting of a rapid alternation between a principal note and the note a whole tone or semitone above it **2** a shrill warbling sound, esp as made by some birds **3** *phonetics* the production of a similar effect using the uvula against the back of the tongue ▷ *vb* **4** to sound, sing, or play (a trill or with a trill) **5** (*tr*) to pronounce (an (r) sound) by the production of a trill [c17: from Italian *trillo*, from *trillare*, apparently from Middle Dutch *trillen* to vibrate]

Trilling (ˈtrɪlɪŋ) *n* **Lionel**. 1905–75, US literary critic, whose works include *The Liberal Imagination* (1950) and *Sincerity and Authenticity* (1974)

trillion (ˈtrɪljən) *n* **1** the number represented as one followed by twelve zeros (10¹²); a million million **2** (formerly, in Britain) the number represented as one followed by eighteen zeros (10¹⁸); a million million million ▷ *determiner* **3** (preceded by *a* or a numeral) amounting to a trillion [c17: from French, on the model of *million*] > ˈtrillionth *n, adj*

trillium (ˈtrɪljəm) *n* any herbaceous plant of the genus *Trillium*, of Asia and North America, having a whorl of three leaves at the top of the stem with a single central white, pink, or purple three-petalled flower: family *Trilliaceae* [c18: from New Latin, modification by Linnaeus of Swedish *trilling* triplet]

trilobate (traɪˈləʊbeɪt, ˈtraɪləˌbeɪt) *adj* (esp of a leaf) consisting of or having three lobes or parts

trilobite (ˈtraɪləˌbaɪt) *n* any extinct marine arthropod of the group *Trilobita*, abundant in Palaeozoic times, having a segmented exoskeleton divided into three parts [c19: from New Latin *Trilobītēs*, from Greek *trilobos* having three lobes; see TRI-, LOBE] > trilobitic (ˌtraɪləˈbɪtɪk) *adj*

trilogy (ˈtrɪlədʒɪ) *n, pl* **-gies 1** a series of three related works, esp in literature, etc **2** (in ancient Greece) a series of three tragedies performed together at the Dionysian festivals [c19: from Greek *trilogia*; see TRI-, -LOGY]

trim (trɪm) *adj* **trimmer**, **trimmest 1** neat and spruce in appearance **2** slim; slender **3** in good condition ▷ *vb* **trims**, **trimming**, **trimmed** (*mainly tr*) **4** to put in good order, esp by cutting or pruning **5** to shape and finish (timber) **6** to adorn or decorate **7** (sometimes foll by *off* or *away*) to cut so as to remove: *to trim off a branch* **8** to cut down to the desired size or shape: *to trim material to a pattern* **9** *nautical* **a** (*also intr*) to adjust the balance of (a vessel) or (of a vessel) to maintain an even balance, by distribution of ballast, cargo, etc **b** (*also intr*) to adjust (a vessel's sails) to take advantage of the wind **c** to stow (cargo) **10** to balance (an aircraft) before flight by adjusting the position of the load or in flight by the use of trim tabs, fuel transfer, etc **11** (*also intr*) to modify (one's opinions, etc) to suit opposing factions or for expediency **12** *informal* to thrash or beat **13** *informal* to rebuke **14** *obsolete* to furnish or equip ▷ *n* **15** a decoration or adornment **16** the upholstery and decorative facings, as on the door panels, of a car's interior **17** proper order or fitness; good shape: *in trim* **18** a haircut that neatens but does not alter the existing hairstyle **19** *nautical* **a** the general set and appearance of a vessel **b** the difference between the draught of a vessel at the bow and at the stern **c** the fitness of a vessel **d** the position of a vessel's sails relative to the wind **e** the relative buoyancy of a submarine **20** dress or equipment **21** *US* window-dressing **22** the attitude of an aircraft in flight when the pilot allows the main control surfaces to take up their own positions **23** *films* a section of shot cut out during editing **24** material that is trimmed off **25** decorative mouldings, such as architraves, picture rails, etc [Old English *trymman* to strengthen; related to *trum* strong, Old Irish *druma* tree, Russian *drom* thicket] > ˈtrimly *adv* > ˈtrimness *n*

Trim (trɪm) *n* the county town of Meath, Republic of Ireland; 12th-century castle, medieval cathedral; textiles and machinery. Pop: 5894 (2002)

trimaran ('traɪməˌræn) *n* a vessel, usually of shallow draught, with two hulls flanking the main hull [C20: from TRI- + (CATA)MARAN]

Trimble ('trɪmbᵊl) *n* (**William**) **David**. born 1944, Northern Irish politician; leader of the Ulster Unionist party (1995–2005), First Minister of Northern Ireland (1998–2001); Nobel peace prize jointly with John Hume in 1998

trimer ('traɪmə) *n* a polymer or a molecule of a polymer consisting of three identical monomers

trimerous ('trɪmərəs) *adj* **1** (of plants) having parts arranged in groups of three **2** consisting of or having three parts

trimester (traɪ'mɛstə) *n* **1** a period of three months **2** (in some US and Canadian universities or schools) any of the three academic sessions [C19: from French *trimestre*, from Latin *trimēstris* of three months, from TRI- + *mēnsis* month] > tri'mestral *or* tri'mestrial *adj*

trimeter ('trɪmɪtə) *prosody* ▷ *n* **1** a verse line consisting of three metrical feet ▷ *adj* **2** designating such a line

trimethadione (ˌtraɪmɛθə'daɪəʊn) *n* a crystalline compound with a bitter taste and camphor-like odour, used in the treatment of epilepsy. Formula: $C_6H_9NO_3$ [from TRI- + METH(YL) + DI-^{1} + -ONE]

trimetric projection *n* a geometric projection, used in mechanical drawing, in which the three axes are at arbitrary angles, often using different linear scales

trimmer ('trɪmə) *n* **1** Also called: **trimmer joist** a beam in a floor or roof structure attached to truncated joists in order to leave an opening for a staircase, chimney, etc **2** a machine for trimming timber **3** Also called: **trimming capacitor** *electronics* a variable capacitor of small capacitance used for making fine adjustments, etc **4** a person who alters his or her opinions on the grounds of expediency **5** a person who fits out motor vehicles

trimming ('trɪmɪŋ) *n* **1** an extra piece used to decorate or complete **2** (*plural*) usual or traditional accompaniments: *roast turkey with all the trimmings* **3** (*plural*) parts that are cut off

trimolecular (ˌtraɪmə'lɛkjʊlə) *adj* *chem* of, concerned with, formed from, or involving three molecules

trimonthly (traɪ'mʌnθlɪ) *adj, adv* every three months

trimorphism (traɪ'mɔːfɪzəm) *n* **1** *biology* the property exhibited by certain species of having or occurring in three different forms **2** the property of certain minerals of existing in three crystalline forms [C19: from Greek *trimorphos* (from TRI- + *morphē* form) + -ISM]

Trinacria (trɪ'neɪkrɪə, traɪ-) *n* the Latin name for **Sicily**

trinary ('traɪnərɪ) *adj* **1** made up of three parts; ternary **2** going in threes [C15: from Late Latin *trīnārius* of three sorts, from Latin *trīnī* three each, from *trēs* three]

Tri-Nations Championship *n* **1** *rugby union* the annual tournament in which the national sides representing Australia, New Zealand, and South Africa compete **2** *rugby league* the annual tournament in which the national sides representing Great Britain, Australia, and New Zealand compete

Trincomalee (ˌtrɪŋkəʊmə'liː) *n* a port in NE Sri Lanka, on the **Bay of Trincomalee** (an inlet of the Bay of Bengal); British naval base until 1957: a centre of conflict in the insurgency by the Tamil Tigers (LTTE). Pop: 44 313 (1981 census); more recent official figures are not available

trine (traɪn) *n* **1** *astrology* an aspect of 120° between two planets, an orb of 8° being allowed **2** anything comprising three parts ▷ *adj* **3** of or relating to a trine **4** threefold; triple [C14: from Old French *trin*, from Latin *trīnus* triple, from *trēs* three] > 'trinal *adj*

Trinidad ('trɪnɪˌdæd) *n* an island in the West Indies, off the NE coast of Venezuela: colonized by the Spanish in the 17th century and ceded to Britain in 1802; joined with Tobago in 1888 as a British colony; now part of the independent republic of Trinidad and Tobago. Pop: 1 208 282 (2000) > ˌTrini'dadian *adj, n*

Trinidad and Tobago *n* an independent republic in the

Caribbean, occupying the two southernmost islands of the Lesser Antilles: became a British colony in 1888 and gained independence in 1962; became a republic in 1976; a member of the Commonwealth. Official language: English. Religion: Christian majority, with a large Hindu minority. Currency: Trinidad and Tobago dollar. Capital: Port of Spain. Pop: 1 307 000 (2004 est). Area: 5128 sq km (1980 sq miles)

Trinitarian (ˌtrɪnɪ'tɛərɪən) *n* **1** a person who believes in the doctrine of the Trinity ▷ *adj* **2** of or relating to the doctrine of the Trinity or those who uphold it > ˌTrini'tarianˌism *n*

trinitroglycerine (traɪˌnaɪtrəʊ'glɪsəˌriːn) *n* the full name for **nitroglycerine**

trinitrotoluene (traɪˌnaɪtrəʊ'tɒljʊˌiːn) *or* **trinitrotoluol** (traɪˌnaɪtrəʊ'tɒljʊˌɒl) *n* the full name for **TNT**

trinity ('trɪnɪtɪ) *n, pl* -ties **1** a group of three **2** the state of being threefold [C13: from Old French *trinite*, from Late Latin *trīnitās*, from Latin *trīnus* triple]

Trinity ('trɪnɪtɪ) *n* Also called: **Holy Trinity, Blessed Trinity** *Christian theol* the union of three persons, the Father, Son, and Holy Spirit, in one Godhead

Trinity Brethren *pl n* the members of Trinity House

Trinity House *n* an association that provides lighthouses, buoys, etc, around the British coast

Trinity Sunday *n* the Sunday after Whit Sunday

Trinity term *n* the summer term at the Inns of Court and some educational establishments

trinket ('trɪŋkɪt) *n* **1** a small or worthless ornament or piece of jewellery **2** a trivial object; trifle [C16: perhaps from earlier *trenket* little knife, via Old Northern French, from Latin *truncāre* to lop]

trinomial (traɪ'nəʊmɪəl) *adj* **1** *maths* consisting of or relating to three terms ▷ *n* **2** *maths* a polynomial consisting of three terms, such as $ax^2 + bx + c$ **3** *biology* the third word in the trinomial name of an organism, which distinguishes between subspecies [C18: TRI- + -*nomial* on the model of *binomial*] > tri'nomially *adv*

trio ('triːəʊ) *n, pl* trios **1** a group of three people or things **2** *music* **a** a group of three singers or instrumentalists or a piece of music composed for such a group **b** a subordinate section in a scherzo, minuet, etc, that is contrastive in style and often in a related key [C18: from Italian, ultimately from Latin *trēs* three; compare DUO]

triode ('traɪəʊd) *n* **1** an electronic valve having three electrodes, a cathode, an anode, and a grid, the potential of the grid controlling the flow of electrons between the cathode and anode. It has been replaced by the transistor **2** any electronic device, such as a thyratron, having three electrodes [C20: TRI- + ELECTRODE]

trioecious *or* **triecious** (traɪ'iːʃəs) *adj* (of a plant species) having male, female, and hermaphrodite flowers in three different plants [C18: from New Latin *trioecia*, from Greek TRI- + *oikos* house]

triolein (traɪ'əʊlɪɪn) *n* a naturally occurring glyceride of oleic acid, found in fats and oils. Formula: $(C_{17}H_{33}COO)_3C_3H_5$

triolet ('triːəʊˌlɛt) *n* a verse form of eight lines, having the first line repeated as the fourth and seventh and the second line as the eighth, rhyming a b a a a b a b [C17: from French: a little TRIO]

trioxide (traɪ'ɒksaɪd) *n* any oxide that contains three oxygen atoms per molecule

trip (trɪp) *n* **1** an outward and return journey, often for a specific purpose **2** any tour, journey, or voyage **3** a false step; stumble **4** any slip or blunder **5** a light step or tread **6** a manoeuvre or device to cause someone to trip **7** Also called: **tripper** any catch on a mechanism that acts as a switch **8** *informal* a hallucinogenic drug experience ▷ *9* *informal* any stimulating, profound, etc, experience ▷ *vb* trips, tripping, tripped **10** (often foll by *up*, or when *intr*, by *on* or *over*) to stumble or cause to stumble **11** to make or cause to make a mistake or blunder **12** (*tr*; often foll by *up*) to trap or catch in a mistake **13** (*intr*) to go on a short tour or journey **14** (*intr*) to move or tread lightly **15** (*intr*) *informal* to experience the effects of LSD or any other hallucinogenic drug **16** (*tr*) to activate (a mechanical trip) [C14: from Old French *triper* to tread, of Germanic origin; related to Low

German *trippen* to stamp, Middle Dutch *trippen* to walk trippingly, *trepelen* to trample]

tripartite (traɪ'pɑːtaɪt) *adj* **1** divided into or composed of three parts **2** involving three participants **3** (esp of leaves) consisting of three parts formed by divisions extending almost to the base ▷ tri'partitely *adv*

tripe (traɪp) *n* **1** the stomach lining of an ox, cow, or other ruminant, prepared for cooking **2** *informal* something silly; rubbish [c13: from Old French, of unknown origin]

triphammer ('trɪp,hæmə) *n* a power hammer that is raised or tilted by a cam and allowed to fall under gravity

triphibious (traɪ'fɪbɪəs) *adj* (esp of military operations) occurring on land, at sea, and in the air [c20: from TRI- + (AM)PHIBIOUS]

triphthong ('trɪfθɒŋ, 'trɪp-) *n* **1** a composite vowel sound during the articulation of which the vocal organs move from one position through a second, ending in a third **2** a trigraph representing a composite vowel sound such as this [c16: via New Latin from Medieval Greek *triphthongos*, from TRI- + *phthongos* sound; compare DIPHTHONG] ▷ triph'thongal *adj*

tripinnate (traɪ'pɪnɪt, -eɪt) *adj* (of a bipinnate leaf) having the pinnules themselves pinnate

triplane ('traɪ,pleɪn) *n* an aeroplane having three wings arranged one above the other

triple ('trɪpəl) *adj* **1** consisting of three parts; threefold **2** (of musical time or rhythm) having three beats in each bar **3** three times as great or as much ▷ *n* **4** a threefold amount **5** a group of three ▷ *vb* **6** to increase or become increased threefold; treble [c16: from Latin *triplus*] ▷ 'triply *adv*

triple A *n military* anti-aircraft artillery. Abbreviation: AAA

triple crown *n* (often capitals) *rugby union* a victory by Scotland, England, Wales, or Ireland in all three games against the others in the annual Six (formerly, Five) Nations Championship

triple jump *n* an athletic event in which the competitor has to perform successively a hop, a step, and a jump in continuous movement

triple play *n* the supply to a customer by one provider of telephone, internet, and television services

triple point *n chem* the temperature and pressure at which the three phases of a substance are in equilibrium. The triple point of water, 273.16 K at a pressure of 611.2 Pa, is the basis of the definition of the kelvin

triplet ('trɪplɪt) *n* **1** a group or set of three similar things **2** one of three offspring born at one birth **3** *music* a group of three notes played in a time value of two, four, etc **4** *chem* a state of a molecule or free radical in which there are two unpaired electrons [c17: from TRIPLE, on the model of *doublet*]

triplex ('trɪpleks) *adj* a less common word for **triple** [c17: from Latin: threefold, from TRI- + *-plex*-FOLD]

Triplex ('trɪpleks) *n trademark Brit* a laminated safety glass, as used in car windows

triplicate *adj* ('trɪplɪkɪt) **1** triple ▷ *vb* ('trɪplɪ,keɪt) **2** to multiply or be multiplied by three ▷ *n* ('trɪplɪkɪt) **3 a** a group of three things **b** one of such a group **4** in triplicate written out three times [c15: from Latin *triplicāre* to triple, from TRIPLEX] ▷ ,tripli'cation *n*

triploid ('trɪplɔɪd) *adj* **1** having or relating to three times the haploid number of chromosomes: *a triploid organism* ▷ *n* **2** a triploid organism [c19: from Greek *tripl(oos)* triple + (HAPL)OID]

tripod ('traɪpɒd) *n* **1** an adjustable and usually collapsible three-legged stand to which a camera, etc, can be attached to hold it steady **2** a stand or table having three legs [c17: via Latin from Greek *tripod-, tripous* three-footed, from TRI- + *pous* foot] ▷ tripodal ('trɪpədəl) *adj*

tripoli ('trɪpəlɪ) *n* a lightweight porous siliceous rock derived by weathering and used in a powdered form as a polish, filter, etc [c17: named after TRIPOLI, in Libya or in Lebanon]

Tripoli ('trɪpəlɪ) *n* **1** the capital and chief port of Libya, in the northwest on the Mediterranean: founded by Phoenicians in about the 7th century BC; the only city that has survived of the three (Oea, Leptis Magna, and Sabratha) that formed the African Tripolis ("three cities"); fishing and manufacturing centre. Pop: 1 223 300 (2002 est). Arabic name: Tarabulus el Gharb **2** a port in N Lebanon, on the Mediterranean: the second largest town in Lebanon; taken by the Crusaders in 1109 after a siege of five years; oil-refining and manufacturing centre. Pop: 212 000 (2005 est). Arabic name: Tarabulus esh Sham

Tripolitania (,trɪpəlɪ'teɪnɪə) *n* the NW part of Libya: established as a Phoenician colony in the 7th century BC; taken by the Turks in 1551 and became one of the Barbary states; under Italian rule from 1912 until World War II

tripos ('traɪpɒs) *n Brit* the final honours degree examinations in all subjects at Cambridge University [c16: from Latin *tripūs*, influenced by Greek noun ending *-os*]

tripper ('trɪpə) *n* **1** *chiefly Brit* a tourist; excursionist **2** another word for **trip** (sense 7) **3** any device that generates a signal causing a trip to operate

trippy ('trɪpɪ) *adj* -pier, -piest *informal* suggestive of or resembling the effect produced by a hallucinogenic drug

triptane ('trɪpteɪn) *n* a colourless highly flammable liquid alkane hydrocarbon, isomeric with heptane, used in aviation fuel; 2,2,3-trimethylbutane. Formula: $CH_3C(CH_3)_2CH(CH_3)CH_3$ [c20: shortened and altered from *trimethylbutane*; see TRI-, METHYL, BUTANE]

Triptolemus (trɪp'tɒlɪməs) *n Greek myth* a favourite of Demeter, sent by her to teach mankind agriculture

triptych ('trɪptɪk) *n* **1** a set of three pictures or panels, usually hinged so that the two wing panels fold over the larger central one: often used as an altarpiece **2** a set of three hinged writing tablets [c18: from Greek *triptukhos*, from TRI- + *ptux* plate; compare DIPTYCH]

triptyque (trɪp'tiːk) *n* a customs permit for the temporary importation of a motor vehicle [from French: TRIPTYCH (referring to its three sections)]

Tripura ('trɪpʊrə) *n* a state of NE India: formerly a princely state, ruled by the Maharajahs for over 1300 years; became a union territory in 1956 and a state in 1972; extensive jungles. Capital: Agartala. Pop: 3 191 168 (2001). Area: 10 486 sq km (4051 sq miles)

tripwire ('trɪp,waɪə) *n* a wire that activates a trap, mine, etc, when tripped over

trireme ('traɪriːm) *n* a galley, developed by the ancient Greeks as a warship, with three banks of oars on each side [c17: from Latin *trirēmis*, from TRI- + *rēmus* oar]

trisect (traɪ'sekt) *vb* (tr) to divide into three parts, esp three equal parts [c17: TRI- + *-sect* from Latin *secāre* to cut] ▷ trisection (traɪ'sekʃən) *n*

trishaw ('traɪʃɔː) *n* another name for **rickshaw** (sense 2) [c20: from TRI- + RICKSHAW]

triskelion (trɪ'skelɪɒn, -ən) *or* **triskele** ('trɪskiːl) *n, pl* triskelia (trɪ'skelɪə) *or* triskeles *or* triskeles a symbol consisting of three bent limbs or lines radiating from a centre [c19: from Greek *triskelēs* three-legged, from TRI- + *skelos* leg]

Trismegistus (,trɪsmɪ'dʒɪstəs) *n* See **Hermes Trismegistus**

trismus ('trɪzməs) *n pathol* the state or condition of being unable to open the mouth because of sustained contractions of the jaw muscles, caused by a form of tetanus. Nontechnical name: lockjaw [c17: from New Latin, from Greek *trismos* a grinding]

Tristan ('trɪstən) *or* **Tristram** ('trɪstrəm) *n* (in medieval romance) the nephew of King Mark of Cornwall who fell in love with his uncle's bride, Iseult, after they mistakenly drank a love potion

Tristan da Cunha (də 'kuːnjə) *n* a group of four small volcanic islands in the S Atlantic, about halfway between South Africa and South America: comprises the main island of Tristan and the uninhabited islands of Gough, Inaccessible, and Nightingale; discovered in 1506 by the Portuguese admiral Tristão da Cunha; annexed to Britain in 1816; now a dependency of Saint Helena; whole population of Tristan evacuated for two years after the volcanic eruption of 1961. Pop: 284 (2003

t

est). Area: about 100 sq km (40 sq miles)

triste (triːst) *or* **tristful** ('trɪstfʊl) *adj* archaic words for **sad** [from French]

trisyllable (traɪˈsɪləbᵊl) *n* a word of three syllables > **trisyllabic** (ˌtraɪsɪˈlæbɪk) *adj*

trite (traɪt) *adj* hackneyed; dull [c16: from Latin *trītus* worn down, from *terere* to rub] > **'tritely** *adv* > **'triteness** *n*

tritheism ('traɪθɪˌɪzəm) *n theol* belief in three gods, esp in the Trinity as consisting of three distinct gods > **'tritheist** *n, adj*

triticum ('trɪtɪkəm) *n* any annual cereal grass of the genus *Triticum*, which includes the wheats [c19: Latin, literally: wheat, probably from *tritum*, supine of *terere* to grind]

tritium ('trɪtɪəm) *n* a radioactive isotope of hydrogen, occurring in trace amounts in natural hydrogen and produced in a nuclear reactor. Tritiated compounds are used as tracers. Symbol: T or ^{3}H; half-life: 12.5 years [c20: New Latin, from Greek *tritos* third]

triton¹ ('traɪtᵊn) *n* any of various chiefly tropical marine gastropod molluscs of the genera *Charonia*, *Cymatium*, etc, having large beautifully-coloured spiral shells [c16: via Latin from Greek *tritōn*]

triton² ('traɪtɒn) *n physics* a nucleus of an atom of tritium, containing two neutrons and one proton [c20: from TRIT(IUM) + -ON]

Triton ('traɪtᵊn) *n Greek myth* a sea god, son of Poseidon and Amphitrite, depicted as having the upper parts of a man with a fish's tail and holding a trumpet made from a conch shell

tritone ('traɪˌtəʊn) *n* a musical interval consisting of three whole tones; augmented fourth

triturate ('trɪtjʊˌreɪt) *vb* **1** (*tr*) to grind or rub into a fine powder or pulp; masticate ▷ *n* **2** the powder or pulp resulting from this grinding [c17: from Late Latin *trītūrāre* to thresh, from Latin *trītūra* a threshing, from *terere* to grind] > **'triturable** *adj* > **'tritu‚rator** *n*

triumph ('traɪəmf) *n* **1** the feeling of exultation and happiness derived from a victory or major achievement **2** the act or condition of being victorious; victory **3** (in ancient Rome) a ritual procession to the Capitoline Hill held in honour of a victorious general ▷ *vb* (*intr*) **4** (often foll by *over*) to win a victory or control: *to triumph over one's weaknesses* **5** to rejoice over a victory **6** to celebrate a Roman triumph [c14: from Old French *triumphe*, from Latin *triumphus*, from Old Latin *triumpus*; probably related to Greek *thriambos* Bacchic hymn] > **'triumpher** *n* > **triumphal** (traɪˈʌmfəl) *adj*

triumphant (traɪˈʌmfənt) *adj* **1** experiencing or displaying triumph **2** exultant through triumph > **tri'umphantly** *adv*

triumvir (traɪˈʌmvə) *n, pl* **-virs** *or* **-viri** (-vɪˌriː) (esp in ancient Rome) a member of a triumvirate [c16: from Latin: one of three administrators, from *triumvirōrum* of three men, from *trēs* three + *vir* man] > **tri'umviral** *adj*

triumvirate (traɪˈʌmvɪrɪt) *n* **1** (in ancient Rome) a board of three officials jointly responsible for some task **2** any joint rule by three men **3** any group of three men associated in some way **4** the office of a triumvir

triune ('traɪjuːn) *adj* constituting three in one, esp the three persons in one God of the Trinity [c17: TRI- + -*une*, from Latin *ūnus* one] > **tri'unity** *n*

trivalent (traɪˈveɪlənt, 'trɪvələnt) *adj chem* **1** having a valency of three **2** having three valencies ▷ Also called: **tervalent** > **tri'valency** *n*

Trivandrum (trɪˈvændrəm) *n* a city in S India, capital of Kerala, on the Malabar Coast: made capital of the kingdom of Travancore in 1745; University of Kerala (1937). Pop: 744 739 (2001)

trivet ('trɪvɪt) *n* **1** a stand, usually three-legged and metal, on which cooking vessels are placed over a fire **2** a short metal stand on which hot dishes are placed on a table **3 as right as a trivet** *old-fashioned* in perfect health [Old English *trefet* (influenced by Old English *thrifēte* having three feet), from Latin *tripēs* having three feet]

trivia ('trɪvɪə) *n* (*functioning as singular or plural*) petty details or considerations; trifles; trivialities [from New Latin, plural of Latin *trivium* junction of three roads; for

meaning, see TRIVIAL]

trivial ('trɪvɪəl) *adj* **1** of little importance; petty or frivolous: *trivial complaints* **2** ordinary or commonplace; trite: *trivial conversation* **3** *biology, chem* denoting the popular name of an organism or substance, as opposed to the scientific one **4** of or relating to the trivium [c15: from Latin *triviālis* belonging to the public streets, common, from *trivium* crossroads, junction of three roads, from TRI- + *via* road] > **'trivially** *adv* > **'trivialness** *n*

triviality (ˌtrɪvɪˈælɪtɪ) *n, pl* **-ties 1** the state or quality of being trivial **2** something, such as a remark, that is trivial

trivialize ('trɪvɪəˌlaɪz) *or* **trivialise** *vb* (*tr*) to cause to seem trivial or more trivial; minimize: *he trivialized his injuries* > ‚triviali'zation *or* ‚triviali'sation *n*

trivium ('trɪvɪəm) *n, pl* **-ia** (-ɪə) (in medieval learning) the lower division of the seven liberal arts, consisting of grammar, rhetoric, and logic. See **quadrivium** [c19: from Medieval Latin, from Latin: crossroads; see TRIVIAL]

-trix *suffix forming nouns* indicating a feminine agent, corresponding to nouns ending in *-tor*: *executrix* [from Latin]

t-RNA *abbreviation* transfer RNA

Troas ('trəʊæs) *n* the region of NW Asia Minor surrounding the ancient city of Troy. Also called: the **Troad** ('trəʊæd)

Trobriand Islands *pl n* a group of coral islands in the Solomon Sea, north of the E part of New Guinea: part of Papua New Guinea. Area: about 440 sq km (170 sq miles)

trocar ('trəʊkaː) *n* a surgical instrument for removing fluid from bodily cavities, consisting of a puncturing device situated inside a tube [c18: from French *trocart* literally: with three sides, from *trois* three + *carre* side]

trochal ('trəʊkᵊl) *adj zoology* shaped like a wheel: *the trochal disc of a rotifer* [c19: from Greek *trokhos* wheel]

trochanter (trəʊˈkæntə) *n* **1** any of several processes on the upper part of the vertebrate femur, to which muscles are attached **2** the third segment of an insect's leg [c17: via French from Greek *trokhantēr*, from *trekhein* to run]

troche (trəʊʃ) *n med* another name for **lozenge** (sense 1) [c16: from French *trochisque*, from Late Latin *trochiscus*, from Greek *trokhiskos* little wheel, from *trokhos* wheel]

trochee ('trəʊkiː) *n prosody* a metrical foot of two syllables, the first long and the second short (‒ ‿). See **iamb** [c16: via Latin from Greek *trokhaios pous*, literally: a running foot, from *trekhein* to run]

trochlea ('trɒklɪə) *n, pl* **-leae** (-lɪˌiː) any bony or cartilaginous part with a grooved surface over which a bone, tendon, etc, may slide or articulate [c17: from Latin, from Greek *trokhileia* a sheaf of pulleys; related to *trokhos* wheel, *trekhein* to run]

trochlear nerve ('trɒklɪə) *n* either one of the fourth pair of cranial nerves, which supply the superior oblique muscle of the eye

trochoid ('trəʊkɔɪd) *n* **1** the curve described by a fixed point on the radius or extended radius of a circle as the circle rolls along a straight line ▷ *adj* Also: **trochoidal** **2** rotating or capable of rotating about a central axis **3** *anatomy* (of a structure or part) resembling or functioning as a pivot or pulley [c18: from Greek *trokhoeidēs* circular, from *trokhos* wheel]

trod (trɒd) *vb* the past tense and a past participle of **tread**

trodden ('trɒdᵊn) *vb* a past participle of **tread**

trode (trəʊd) *vb archaic* a past tense of **tread**

troglodyte ('trɒgləˌdaɪt) *n* **1** a cave dweller, esp one of the prehistoric peoples thought to have lived in caves **2** *informal* a person who lives alone and appears eccentric [c16: via Latin from Greek *trōglodutēs* one who enters caves, from *trōglē* hole + *duein* to enter] > **troglodytic** (ˌtrɒgləˈdɪtɪk) *or* ‚troglo'dytical *adj*

trogon ('trəʊgɒn) *n* any bird of the order *Trogoniformes* of tropical and subtropical regions of America, Africa, and Asia. They have a brilliant plumage, short hooked bill, and long tail. See also **quetzal** [c18: from New Latin, from Greek *trōgōn*, from *trōgein* to gnaw]

troika ('trɔɪkə) *n* **1** a Russian vehicle drawn by three horses abreast **2** three horses harnessed abreast **3** a triumvirate [C19: from Russian, from *troe* three]

Troilus ('trɔɪləs, 'trəʊɪləs) *n Greek myth* the youngest son of King Priam and Queen Hecuba, slain at Troy. In medieval romance he is portrayed as the lover of Cressida

Trois-Rivières (*French* trwa rivjɛr) *n* a port in central Canada, in Quebec on the St Lawrence River: one of the world's largest centres of newsprint production. Pop: 46 264 (2001). English name: **Three Rivers**

Trojan ('trəʊdʒən) *n* **1** a native or inhabitant of ancient Troy **2** a person who is hard-working and determined ▷ *adj* **3** of or relating to ancient Troy or its inhabitants

Trojan Horse *n* **1** Also called: **the Wooden Horse** *Greek myth* the huge wooden hollow figure of a horse left outside Troy by the Greeks when they feigned retreat and dragged inside by the Trojans. The men concealed inside it opened the city to the final Greek assault **2** a trap intended to undermine an enemy **3** *computing* a bug inserted into a program or system designed to be activated after a certain time or a certain number of operations

troll¹ (trəʊl) *vb* **1** *angling* **a** to draw (a baited line, etc) through the water, often from a boat **b** to fish (a stretch of water) by trolling **c** to fish (for) by trolling **2** to roll or cause to roll **3** *archaic* to sing (a refrain, chorus, etc) or (of a refrain, etc) to be sung in a loud hearty voice **4** (*intr*) *Brit informal* to walk or stroll ▷ *n* **5** *angling* a bait or lure used in trolling, such as a spinner [C14: from Old French *troller* to run about; related to Middle High German *trollen* to run with short steps] > **'troller** *n*

troll² (trəʊl) *n* (in Scandinavian folklore) one of a class of supernatural creatures that dwell in caves or mountains and are depicted either as dwarfs or as giants [C19: from Old Norse: demon; related to Danish *trold*]

trolley ('trɒlɪ) *n* **1** *Brit* a small table on casters used for conveying food, drink, etc **2** *Brit* a wheeled cart or stand pushed by hand and used for moving heavy items, such as shopping in a supermarket or luggage at a railway station **3** *Brit* (in a hospital) a bed mounted on casters and used for moving patients who are unconscious, immobilized, etc **4** *Brit* See **trolleybus 5** *US & Canadian* See **trolley car 6** a device that collects the current from an overhead wire (**trolley wire**), third rail, etc, to drive the motor of an electric vehicle **7** a pulley or truck that travels along an overhead wire in order to support a suspended load **8** *chiefly Brit* a low truck running on rails, used in factories, mines, etc, and on railways **9** a truck, cage, or basket suspended from an overhead track or cable for carrying loads in a mine, quarry, etc [C19: probably from TROLL¹]

trolleybus ('trɒlɪˌbʌs) *n* an electrically driven public-transport vehicle that does not run on rails but takes its power from an overhead wire through a trolley

trolley car *n US & Canadian* another word for **streetcar**

trollius ('trɒlɪəs) *n* See **globeflower** [New Latin, from German *Trollblume* globeflower]

trollop ('trɒləp) *n* **1** a promiscuous woman, esp a prostitute **2** an untidy woman; slattern [C17: perhaps from German dialect *Trolle* prostitute; perhaps related to TRULL] > **'trollopy** *adj*

Trollope ('trɒləp) *n* **1** Anthony. 1815–82, English novelist. His most successful novels, such as *The Warden* (1855), *Barchester Towers* (1857), and *Dr Thorne* (1858), are those in the Barsetshire series of studies of English provincial life. The Palliser series of political novels includes *Phineas Redux* (1874) and *The Prime Minister* (1876) **2** Joanna. born 1943, British novelist: her works include *The Choir* (1988), *A Village Affair* (1989), *The Rector's Wife* (1991), *The Best of Friends* (1995), and *The Girl From the South* (2002)

trombone (trɒm'bəʊn) *n* a brass instrument, a low-pitched counterpart of the trumpet, consisting of a tube the effective length of which is varied by means of a U-shaped slide [C18: from Italian, from *tromba* a trumpet, from Old High German *trumba*] > **trom'bonist** *n*

trommel ('trɒməl) *n* a revolving cylindrical sieve used to screen crushed ore [C19: from German: a drum]

Tromp (*Dutch* tromp) *n* **1** Cornelis (Martenszoon) (kɔr'neɪlɪs). 1629–91, Dutch admiral, who fought during

the 2nd and 3rd Anglo-Dutch Wars **2** his father, Maarten (Harpertszoon) ('martən). 1598–1653, Dutch admiral, who fought in the 1st Anglo-Dutch War: killed in action

trompe (trɒmp) *n* an apparatus for supplying the blast of air in a forge, consisting of a thin column down which water falls, drawing in air through side openings [C19: from French, literally: trumpet]

trompe l'oeil (*French* trɔp lœj) *n, pl* **trompe l'oeils** (trɔp lœj) **1** a painting or decoration giving a convincing illusion of reality **2** an effect of this kind [from French, literally: deception of the eye]

Tromsø ('trɒmsəʊ; *Norwegian* 'trumsø) *n* a port in N Norway, on a small island between Kvaløy and the mainland: fishing and sealing centre. Pop: 61 897 (2004 est)

-tron *suffix forming nouns* **1** indicating a vacuum tube: *magnetron* **2** indicating an instrument for accelerating atomic or subatomic particles: *synchrotron* [from Greek, suffix indicating instrument]

tronc (trɒŋk) *n* a pool into which waiters, waitresses, hotel workers, etc, pay their tips and into which some managements pay service charges for later distribution to staff by a **tronc master**, according to agreed percentages [C20: from French: collecting box]

Trondheim ('trɒndˌhaɪm; *Norwegian* 'trɔnheɪm) *n* a port in central Norway, on **Trondheim Fjord** (an inlet of the Norwegian Sea): national capital until 1380; seat of the Technical University of Norway. Pop: 154 351 (2004 est). Former name (until the 16th century and from 1930 to 1931): **Nidaros**

tronk (trɒŋk) *n South African informal* a jail [Afrikaans]

troop (tru:p) *n* **1** a large group or assembly; flock **2** a subdivision of a cavalry squadron or artillery battery of about platoon size **3** (*plural*) armed forces; soldiers **4** a large group of Scouts comprising several patrols ▷ *vb* **5** (*intr*) to gather, move, or march in or as if in a crowd **6** (*tr*) *military chiefly Brit* to parade (the colour or flag) ceremonially [C16: from French *troupe*, from *troupeau* flock, of Germanic origin]

trooper ('tru:pə) *n* **1** a soldier in a cavalry regiment **2** *US & Austral* a mounted policeman **3** *US* a state policeman **4** a cavalry horse **5** *informal, chiefly Brit* a troopship

troopship ('tru:pˌʃɪp) *n* a ship, usually a converted merchant ship, used to transport military personnel

tropaeolum (trəʊ'pi:ələm) *n, pl* **-lums** *or* **-la** (-lə) any garden plant of the genus *Tropaeolum* esp the nasturtium [C18: from New Latin, from Latin *tropaeum* TROPHY; referring to the shield-shaped leaves and helmet-shaped flowers]

trope (trəʊp) *n rhetoric* a word or expression used in a figurative sense [C16: from Latin *tropus* figurative use of a word, from Greek *tropos* style, turn; related to *trepein* to turn]

-trope *n combining form* indicating a turning towards, development in the direction of, or affinity to: *heliotrope* [from Greek *tropos* a turn]

trophic ('trɒfɪk) *adj* of or relating to nutrition: *the trophic levels of a food chain* [C19: from Greek *trophikos*, from *trophē* food, from *trephein* to feed]

tropho- *or before a vowel* **troph-** *combining form* indicating nourishment or nutrition: *trophozoite* [from Greek *trophē* food, from *trephein* to feed]

trophoblast ('trɒfəˌblæst) *n* the outer layer of cells of the embryo of placental mammals, which is attached to the uterus wall and absorbs nourishment from the uterine fluids [C19: from TROPHO- + -BLAST]

trophozoite (ˌtrɒfə'zəʊaɪt) *n* the form of a sporozoan protozoan in the feeding stage. In the malaria parasite this stage occurs in the human red blood cell

trophy ('trəʊfɪ) *n, pl* **-phies 1** an object such as a silver or gold cup that is symbolic of victory in a contest, esp a sporting contest; prize **2** a memento of success, esp one taken in war or hunting **3** (in ancient Greece and Rome) a memorial to a victory, usually consisting of captured arms raised on the battlefield or in a public place **4** an ornamental carving that represents a group of weapons, etc [C16: from French *trophée*, from Latin *tropaeum*, from Greek *tropaion*, from *tropē* a turning, defeat of the enemy;

related to Greek *trepein* to turn]

-trophy *n combining form* indicating a certain type of nourishment or growth: *dystrophy* [from Greek *-trophia*, from *trophē* nourishment] ⊳ **-trophic** *adj combining form*

tropic ('trɒpɪk) *n* **1** (*sometimes capital*) either of the parallel lines of latitude at about 23½°N (**tropic of Cancer**) and 23½°S (**tropic of Capricorn**) of the equator **2** the tropics (*often capital*) that part of the earth's surface between the tropics of Cancer and Capricorn; the Torrid Zone **3** *astronomy* either of the two parallel circles on the celestial sphere having the same latitudes and names as the corresponding lines on the earth ⊳ *adj* **4** a less common word for **tropical** [C14: from Late Latin *tropicus* belonging to a turn, from Greek *tropikos*, from *tropos* a turn; from the ancient belief that the sun turned back at the solstices]

-tropic *adj combining form* turning or developing in response to a certain stimulus: *heliotropic* [from Greek *tropos* a turn; see TROPE]

tropical ('trɒpɪk³l) *adj* **1** situated in, used in, characteristic of, or relating to the tropics **2** (of weather) very hot, esp when humid **3** *rhetoric* of or relating to a trope > ˌtropiˈcality *n* > 'tropically *adv*

tropical depression *n Caribbean* an area of heavy rains and winds, the first stage in the development of a possible hurricane

tropicbird ('trɒpɪkˌbɜːd) *n* any aquatic bird of the tropical family *Phaethontidae*, having long slender tail feathers and a white plumage with black markings: order *Pelecaniformes* (pelicans, cormorants, etc) [C17: so called because it is found in the tropical regions]

tropism ('trəʊpɪzəm) *n* the response of an organism, esp a plant, to an external stimulus by growth in a direction determined by the stimulus [from Greek *tropos* a turn] > ˌtropis'matic *adj* > tropistic (trəʊ'pɪstɪk) *adj*

-tropism or **-tropy** *n combining form* indicating a tendency to turn or develop in response to a certain stimulus: *phototropism* [from Greek *tropos* a turn]

tropo- *combining form* indicating change or a turning: *tropophyte* [from Greek *tropos* a turn]

tropopause ('trɒpəˌpɔːz) *n meteorol* the plane of discontinuity between the troposphere and the stratosphere, characterized by a sharp change in the lapse rate and varying in altitude from about 18 km (11 miles) above the equator to 6 km (4 miles) at the Poles

troposphere ('trɒpəˌsfɪə) *n* the lowest atmospheric layer, about 18 kilometres (11 miles) thick at the equator to about 6 km (4 miles) at the Poles, in which air temperature decreases normally with height at about 6.5°C per km > tropospheric (ˌtrɒpə'sferɪk) *adj*

-tropous *adj combining form* indicating a turning away: *anatropous* [from Greek *-tropos* concerning a turn]

troppo¹ ('trɒpəʊ) *adv music* too much; excessively. See non troppo [Italian]

troppo² ('trɒpəʊ) *adj Austral slang* mentally affected by a tropical climate

Trossachs ('trɒsəks) the Trossachs *n* (*functioning as plural or singular*) **1** a narrow wooded valley in central Scotland, between Loch Achray and Loch Katrine: made famous by Sir Walter Scott's descriptions **2** (*popularly*) the area extending northwards from Loch Ard and Aberfoyle to Lochs Katrine, Achray, and Venachar

trot (trɒt) *vb* trots, trotting, trotted **1** to move or cause to move at a trot **2** *angling* to fish (a fast-moving stream or river) by using a float and weighted line that carries the baited hook just above the bottom ⊳ *n* **3** a gait of a horse or other quadruped, faster than a walk, in which diagonally opposite legs come down together **4** a steady brisk pace **5** (in harness racing) a race for horses that have been trained to trot fast **6** *chiefly Brit* a small child; tot **7** *US slang* a student's crib **8** on the trot *informal* **a** one after the other: *to read two books on the trot* **b** busy, esp on one's feet **9** the trots *informal* **a** diarrhoea **b** NZ trotting races [C13: from Old French *trot*, from *troter* to trot, of Germanic origin; related to Middle High German *trotten* to run]

Trot (trɒt) *n informal* a follower of Trotsky; Trotskyist

troth (trəʊθ) *n archaic* **1** a pledge or oath of fidelity, esp a betrothal **2** truth (esp in the phrase **in troth**) **3** loyalty;

fidelity [Old English *trēowth*; related to Old High German *gitriuwida* loyalty; see TRUTH]

trotline ('trɒtˌlaɪn) *n angling* a long line suspended across a stream, river, etc, to which shorter hooked and baited lines are attached

trot out *vb* (*tr, adverb*) *informal* to bring forward, as for approbation or admiration, esp repeatedly

Trotsky or **Trotski** ('trɒtskɪ) *n* **Leon**, original name *Lev Davidovich Bronstein*. 1879–1940, Russian revolutionary and Communist theorist. He was a leader of the November Revolution (1917) and, as commissar of foreign affairs and war (1917–24), largely created the Red Army. He was ousted by Stalin after Lenin's death and deported from Russia (1929); assassinated by a Stalinist agent

Trotskyism ('trɒtskɪˌɪzəm) *n* the theory of Communism developed by the Russian revolutionary Leon Trotsky (original name *Lev Davidovich Bronstein*; 1879–1940), in which he called for immediate worldwide revolution by the proletariat > 'Trotskyist or 'Trotskyite *n, adj*

trotter ('trɒtə) *n* **1** a person or animal that trots, esp a horse that is specially trained to trot fast **2** (*usually plural*) the foot of certain animals, esp of pigs

troubadour ('truːbəˌdʊə) *n* any of a class of lyric poets who flourished principally in Provence and N Italy from the 11th to the 13th centuries, writing chiefly on courtly love in complex metric form [C18: from French, from Old Provençal *trobador*, from *trobar* to write verses, perhaps ultimately from Latin *tropus* TROPE]

trouble ('trʌb³l) *n* **1** a state or condition of mental distress or anxiety **2** a state or condition of disorder or unrest: *industrial trouble* **3** a condition of disease, pain, or malfunctioning: *she has liver trouble* **4** a cause of distress, disturbance, or pain; problem **5** effort or exertion taken to do something **6** liability to suffer punishment or misfortune (esp in the phrase **be in trouble**): *he's in trouble with the police* **7** a personal quality that is regarded as a weakness, handicap, or cause of annoyance: *his trouble is that he's too soft* **8** (*plural*) the Troubles political violence in Ireland during the 1920s or in Northern Ireland since the late 1960s **9** the condition of an unmarried girl who becomes pregnant (esp in the phrase **in trouble**) ⊳ *vb* **10** (*tr*) to cause trouble to; upset, pain, or worry **11** (*intr; usually with a negative and foll by about*) to put oneself to inconvenience; be concerned: *don't trouble about me* **12** (*intr; usually with a negative*) to take pains; exert oneself: *please don't trouble to write everything down* **13** (*tr*) to cause inconvenience or discomfort to: *does this noise trouble you?* **14** (*tr; usually passive*) to agitate or make rough: *the seas were troubled* **15** (*tr*) *Caribbean* to interfere with: *he wouldn't like anyone to trouble his new bicycle* [C13: from Old French *troubler*, from Vulgar Latin *turbulāre* (unattested), from Late Latin *turbidāre*, from *turbidus* confused, from *turba* commotion] > 'troubler *n*

troublemaker ('trʌb³lˌmeɪkə) *n* a person who makes trouble, esp between people > 'troubleˌmaking *adj, n*

troubleshooter ('trʌb³lˌʃuːtə) *n* a person who locates the cause of trouble and removes or treats it > 'troubleˌshooting *n, adj*

troublesome ('trʌb³lsəm) *adj* **1** causing a great deal of trouble; worrying, upsetting, or annoying **2** characterized by violence; turbulent > 'troublesomeness *n*

troublous ('trʌbləs) *adj archaic or literary* unsettled; agitated > 'troublously *adv*

trough (trɒf) *n* **1** a narrow open container, esp one in which food or water for animals is put **2** a narrow channel, gutter, or gulley **3** a narrow depression either in the land surface, ocean bed, or between two successive waves **4** *meteorol* an elongated area of low pressure, esp an extension of a depression **5** a single or temporary low point; depression **6** *physics* the portion of a wave, such as a light wave, in which the amplitude lies below its average value **7** *economics* the lowest point or most depressed stage of the trade cycle [Old English *trōh*; related to Old Saxon, Old Norse *trog* trough, Dutch *trügge* ladle]

trounce (traʊns) *vb* (*tr*) to beat or defeat utterly; thrash [C16: of unknown origin]

troupe (truːp) *n* **1** a company of actors or other

performers, esp one that travels ▷ *vb* **2** (*intr*) (esp of actors) to move or travel in a group [C19: from French; see TROOP]

trouper ('tru:pə) *n* **1** a member of a troupe **2** an experienced or dependable worker or associate

trouser ('trauzə) *n* **1** (*modifier*) of or relating to trousers: *trouser buttons* ▷ *vb* **2** (*tr*) *slang* to take (something, esp money), sometimes surreptitiously, undeservedly or unlawfully

trousers ('trauzəz) *pl n* a garment shaped to cover the body from the waist to the ankles or knees with separate tube-shaped sections for both legs [C17: from earlier *trouse*, a variant of TREWS, influenced by DRAWERS]

trousseau ('tru:səu) *n, pl* -seaux *or* -seaus (-səuz) the clothes, linen, etc, collected by a bride for her marriage [C19: from Old French, literally: a little bundle, from *trusse* a bundle; see TRUSS]

trout (traut) *n, pl* trout *or* trouts any of various game fishes, esp *Salmo trutta* and related species, mostly of fresh water in northern regions: family *Salmonidae* (salmon). They resemble salmon but are smaller and spotted [Old English *trūht*, from Late Latin *tructa*, from Greek *troktēs* sharp-toothed fish]

trouvère (tru:'vɛə; *French* truvɛr) *n* any of a group of poets of N France during the 12th and 13th centuries who composed chiefly narrative works [C19: from French, from Old French *troveor*, from *trover* to compose; related to TROUBADOUR]

trove (trəuv) *n* See **treasure-trove**

trover ('trəuvə) *n law* (formerly) the act of wrongfully assuming proprietary rights over personal goods or property belonging to another [C16: from Old French, from *trover* to find; see TROUVÈRE, TROUBADOUR]

trow (trəu) *vb archaic* to think, believe, or trust [Old English *treow*; related to Old Frisian *triūwe*, Old Saxon *treuwa*, Old High German *triuwa*; see TROTH, TRUE]

Trowbridge ('trəu,brɪdʒ) *n* a market town in SW England, administrative centre of Wiltshire: woollen manufacturing. Pop: 34 401 (2001)

trowel ('trauəl) *n* **1** any of various small hand tools having a flat metal blade attached to a handle, used for scooping or spreading plaster or similar materials **2** a similar tool with a curved blade used by gardeners for lifting plants, etc ▷ *vb* -els, -elling, -elled *or US* -els, -eling, -eled **3** (*tr*) to use a trowel on (plaster, soil, etc) [C14: from Old French *truele*, from Latin *trulla* a scoop, from *trua* a stirring spoon]

Troy (trɔɪ) *n* any of nine ancient cities in NW Asia Minor, each of which was built on the ruins of its predecessor. The seventh was the site of the Trojan War (mid-13th century BC). Greek name: Ilion Latin name: Ilium Related adj: Trojan

Troyes (*French* trwa) *n* an industrial city in NE France: became prosperous through its great fairs in the early Middle Ages. Pop: 60 958 (1999)

troy weight *or* **troy** (trɔɪ) *n* a system of weights used for precious metals and gemstones, based on the grain, which is identical to the avoirdupois grain. 24 grains = 1 pennyweight; 20 pennyweights = 1 (troy) ounce; 12 ounces = 1 (troy) pound [C14: named after the city of *Troyes*, France, where it was first used]

trs *printing abbreviation* transpose

Trst (trst) *n* the Slovene and Croatian name for **Trieste**

truant ('tru:ənt) *n* **1** a person who is absent without leave, esp from school ▷ *adj* **2** being or relating to a truant ▷ *vb* **3** (*intr*) to play truant [C13: from Old French: vagabond, probably of Celtic origin; compare Welsh *truan* miserable, Old Irish *trōg* wretched] > 'truancy *n*

truce (tru:s) *n* **1** an agreement to stop fighting, esp temporarily **2** temporary cessation of something unpleasant [C13: from the plural of Old English *treow* TROW; see TRUE, TRUST]

Trucial States ('tru:ʃəl) *pl n* a former name (until 1971) of **United Arab Emirates**. Also called: Trucial Sheikhdoms, Trucial Oman, Trucial Coast

truck¹ (trʌk) *n* **1** *Brit* a vehicle for carrying freight on a railway; wagon **2** *US, Canadian & Austral.* a large motor vehivle designed to carry heavy loads, esp one with a flat platform. Also called (esp in Britain): lorry **3** a frame carrying two or more pairs of wheels and usually springs and brakes, attached under an end of a railway coach, etc **4** *nautical* **a** a disc-shaped block fixed to the head of a mast having sheave holes for receiving signal halyards **b** the head of a mast itself **5** any wheeled vehicle used to move goods ▷ *vb* **6** (*tr*) to convey (goods) in a truck **7** (*intr*) *chiefly US & Canadian* to drive a truck [C17: perhaps shortened from TRUCKLE²]

truck² (trʌk) *n* **1** commercial goods **2** dealings (esp in the phrase **have no truck with**) **3** commercial exchange **4** *archaic* payment of wages in kind **5** miscellaneous articles **6** *informal* rubbish **7** *US & Canadian* vegetables grown for market ▷ *vb* **8** *archaic* to exchange (goods); barter **9** (*intr*) to traffic or negotiate [C13: from Old French *troquer* (unattested) to barter, equivalent to Medieval Latin *trocare*, of unknown origin]

trucker ('trʌkə) *n chiefly US & Canadian* **1** a lorry driver **2** a person who arranges for the transport of goods by lorry

truck farm *n US & Canadian* a market garden > truck farmer *n* > truck farming *n*

truckie ('trʌkɪ) *n Austral informal* a truck driver

trucking ('trʌkɪŋ) *n chiefly US & Canadian* the transportation of goods by lorry

truckle ('trʌkᵊl) *vb* (*intr*; usually foll by *to*) to yield weakly; give in [C17: from obsolete *truckle* to sleep in a truckle bed] > 'truckler *n*

truckle bed *n* a low bed on wheels, stored under a larger bed, used esp formerly by a servant

truckstop ('trʌk,stɒp) *n chiefly US & Canadian* a place that supplies fuel, oil, etc, for lorries and trucks, and often provides facilities such as a restaurant for drivers

truck system *n* a system during the early years of the Industrial Revolution of forcing workers to accept payment of wages in kind, usually to the employer's advantage [C19: from TRUCK²]

truculent ('trʌkjʊlənt) *adj* **1** defiantly aggressive, sullen, or obstreperous **2** *archaic* savage, fierce, or harsh [C16: from Latin *truculentus*, from *trux* fierce] > 'truculence *or* 'truculency *n* > 'truculently *adv*

Trudeau (tru:'dəu) *n* Pierre Elliott. 1919–2000, Canadian statesman; Liberal prime minister (1968–79; 1980–84)

Trudeaumania (,tru:dəu'meɪnɪə) *n* the obsessional enthusiasm in Canada for former prime minister Pierre Trudeau (1919–2000)

trudge (trʌdʒ) *vb* **1** (*intr*) to walk or plod heavily or wearily **2** (*tr*) to pass through or over by trudging ▷ *n* **3** a long tiring walk [C16: of obscure origin] > 'trudger *n*

trudgen ('trʌdʒən) *n* a type of swimming stroke that uses overarm action, as in the crawl, and a scissors kick [C19: named after John *Trudgen*, English swimmer, who introduced it]

true (tru:) *adj* truer, truest **1** not false, fictional, or illusory; factual or factually accurate; conforming with reality **2** (*prenominal*) being of real or natural origin; genuine; not synthetic **3** unswervingly faithful and loyal to friends, a cause, etc **4** conforming to a required standard, law, or pattern: *a true aim; a true fit* **5** exactly in tune **6** (of a compass bearing) according to the earth's geographical rather than magnetic poles: *true north* **7** *biology* conforming to the typical structure of a designated type **8** *physics* not apparent or relative; taking into account all complicating factors ▷ *n* **9** correct alignment (esp in the phrases **in true, out of true**) ▷ *adv* **10** truthfully; rightly **11** precisely or unswervingly ▷ *vb* trues, truing, trued **12** (*tr*) to adjust so as to make true [Old English *triewe*; related to Old Frisian *triūwe*, Old Saxon, Old High German *triuwi* loyal, Old Norse *tryggr*; see TROW, TRUST] > 'trueness *n*

true bill *n criminal law* (formerly in Britain; now only US) the endorsement made on a bill of indictment by a grand jury certifying it to be supported by sufficient evidence to warrant committing the accused to trial

true-blue *adj* **1** unwaveringly or staunchly loyal, esp to a person, a cause, etc ▷ *n* **true blue 2** *chiefly Brit* a staunch royalist or Conservative

true-life *adj* directly comparable to reality: *a true-life romance*

truelove ('tru:,lʌv) *n* **1** someone truly loved; sweetheart **2** another name for **herb Paris**

truelove knot or **true-lovers' knot** n a complicated bowknot that is hard to untie, symbolizing ties of love

Trueman ('tru:mən) n **Fred**, full name *Frederick Sewards Trueman*. 1931–2006, English cricketer, a fast bowler for Yorkshire and England

true north n the direction from any point along a meridian towards the North Pole. Also called: geographic north See **magnetic north**

true rib n any of the upper seven pairs of ribs in man

true time n the time shown by a sundial; solar time. When the sun is at the highest point in its daily path, the true time is exactly noon

Truffaut (French tryfo) n **François** (frãswa). 1932–84, French film director of the New Wave. His films include *Les Quatre cents coups* (1959), *Jules et Jim* (1961), *Baisers volés* (1968), and *Le Dernier Métro* (1980)

truffle ('trʌf³l) n 1 Also called: earthnut any of various edible saprotrophic ascomycetous fungi of the European genus *Tuber*. They have a tuberous appearance and are regarded as a delicacy 2 Also called: rum truffle chiefly Brit a sweet resembling this fungus in shape, flavoured with chocolate or rum [c16: from French *truffe*, from Old Provençal *trufa*, ultimately from Latin *tūber*]

trug (trʌg) n Brit a long shallow basket made of curved strips of wood and used for carrying flowers, fruit, etc [c16: perhaps dialect variant of TROUGH]

trugo ('tru:gəʊ) n Austral a game similar to croquet, originally improvised in Victoria from the rubber discs used as buffers on railway carriages [from *true go*, when the wheel is hit between the goalposts]

truism ('tru:ɪzəm) n an obvious truth; platitude [c18: from TRUE + -ISM] ▷ tru'istic adj

Trujillo[1] (Spanish tru'xijo) n a city in NW Peru: founded 1535; university (1824); centre of a district producing rice and sugar cane. Pop: 686 000 (2005 est)

Trujillo[2] (Spanish tru'xijo) n **Rafael** (**Léonidas**) (,rafa'el), original name *Rafael Léonidas Trujillo Molina*. 1891–1961, Dominican dictator, who governed the Dominican Republic (1930–61) with the help of a powerful police force: assassinated

Truk Islands (trʌk) pl n a group of islands in the W Pacific, in the E Caroline Islands: administratively part of the US Trust Territory of the Pacific Islands from 1947; became self-governing in 1979 as part of the Federated States of Micronesia; consists of 11 chief islands; a major Japanese naval base during World War II. Pop: 53 381 (2006). Area: 130 sq km (50 sq miles)

trull (trʌl) n archaic a prostitute; harlot [c16: from German *Trulle*; see TROLLOP]

truly ('tru:lɪ) adv 1 in a true, just, or faithful manner 2 (intensifier): *a truly great man* 3 indeed; really

Truman ('tru:mən) n **Harry S.** 1884–1972, US Democratic statesman; 33rd president of the US (1945–53). He approved the dropping of the two atomic bombs on Japan (1945), advocated the postwar loan to Britain, and involved the US in the Korean War

trumeau (tru'məʊ) n, pl -meaux (-'məʊz) architect a section of a wall or pillar between two openings [from French]

trump[1] (trʌmp) n 1 Also called: trump card **a** any card from the suit chosen as trumps **b** this suit itself; trumps 2 Also called: trump card a decisive or advantageous move, resource, action, etc 3 informal a fine or reliable person ▷ vb 4 to play a trump card on (a suit, or a particular card of a suit, that is not trumps) 5 (tr) to outdo or surpass ▷ See also **trumps, trump up** [c16: variant of TRIUMPH]

trump[2] (trʌmp) n archaic or literary 1 a trumpet or the sound produced by one 2 the last trump the final trumpet call that according to the belief of some will awaken and raise the dead on the Day of Judgment [c13: from Old French *trompe*, from Old High German *trumpa* trumpet; compare TROMBONE]

trumpery ('trʌmpərɪ) n, pl -eries 1 foolish talk or actions 2 a useless or worthless article; trinket ▷ adj 3 useless or worthless [c15: from Old French *tromperie* deceit, from *tromper* to cheat]

trumpet ('trʌmpɪt) n 1 a valved brass instrument of brilliant tone consisting of a narrow tube of cylindrical bore ending in a flared bell, normally pitched in B flat. Range: two and a half octaves upwards from F sharp on the fourth line of the bass staff 2 any instrument consisting of a valveless tube ending in a bell, esp a straight instrument used for fanfares, signals, etc 3 a loud sound such as that of a trumpet, esp when made by an animal 4 an eight-foot reed stop on an organ 5 something resembling a trumpet in shape, esp in having a flared bell 6 short for **ear trumpet** 7 blow one's own trumpet to boast about oneself; brag ▷ vb -pets, -peting, -peted 8 to proclaim or sound loudly [c13: from Old French *trompette* a little TRUMP²]

trumpeter ('trʌmpɪtə) n 1 a person who plays the trumpet, esp one whose duty it is to play fanfares, signals, etc 2 any of three birds of the genus *Psophia* of the forests of South America, having a rounded body, long legs, and a glossy blackish plumage: family *Psophiidae*, order *Gruiformes* (cranes, rails, etc) 3 (sometimes capital) a breed of domestic fancy pigeon with a long ruff

trumpeter swan n a large swan, *Cygnus buccinator*, of W North America, having a white plumage and black bill

trumps (trʌmps) pl n 1 (sometimes singular) cards any one of the four suits, decided by cutting or bidding, that outranks all the other suits for the duration of a deal or game 2 turn up trumps (of a person) to bring about a happy or successful conclusion (to an event, problem, etc), esp unexpectedly

trump up vb (tr, adverb) to concoct or invent (a charge, accusation, etc) so as to deceive or implicate someone

truncate vb (trʌŋ'keɪt, 'trʌŋkeɪt) 1 (tr) to shorten by cutting off a part, end, or top ▷ adj ('trʌŋkeɪt) 2 cut short; truncated 3 biology having a blunt end, as though cut off at the tip [c15: from Latin *truncāre* to lop] ▷ trun'cation n

truncated (trʌŋ'keɪtɪd) adj 1 maths (of a cone, pyramid, prism, etc) having an apex or end removed by a plane intersection that is usually nonparallel to the base 2 shortened by or as if by cutting off; truncate

truncheon ('trʌntʃən) n 1 chiefly Brit a short thick club or cudgel carried by a policeman 2 a baton of office [c16: from Old French *tronchon* stump, from Latin *truncus* trunk; see TRUNCATE]

trundle ('trʌnd³l) vb 1 to move heavily on or as if on wheels: *the bus trundled by* ▷ n 2 the act or an instance of trundling 3 a small wheel or roller [Old English *tryndel*; related to Middle High German *trendel* disc]

trundle bed n a less common word for **truckle bed**

trundler ('trʌndlə) n NZ 1 a golf bag or shopping trolley 2 a child's pushchair

trunk (trʌŋk) n 1 the main stem of a tree, usually thick and upright, covered with bark and having branches at some distance from the ground 2 a large strong case or box used to contain clothes and other personal effects when travelling and for storage 3 anatomy the body excluding the head, neck, and limbs; torso 4 the elongated prehensile nasal part of an elephant; proboscis 5 Also called: (Brit, Austral, NZ, and South African) boot US & Canadian an enclosed compartment of a car for holding luggage, etc, usually at the rear 6 anatomy the main stem of a nerve, blood vessel, etc 7 nautical a watertight boxlike cover within a vessel with its top above the waterline, such as one used to enclose a centreboard 8 an enclosed duct or passageway for ventilation, etc 9 (modifier) of or relating to a main road, railway, etc, in a network: *a trunk line* ▷ See also **trunks** [c15: from Old French *tronc*, from Latin *truncus*, from *truncus* (adj) lopped]

trunk call n chiefly Brit a long-distance telephone call

trunk curl n another name for **sit-up**

trunkfish ('trʌŋk,fɪʃ) n, pl -fish or -fishes any tropical plectognath fish of the family *Ostraciidae*, having the body encased in bony plates with openings for the fins, eyes, mouth, etc

trunk hose n a man's puffed-out breeches reaching to the thighs and worn with tights in the 16th century [c17: of uncertain origin; perhaps from the obsolete *trunk* to truncate]

trunking ('trʌŋkɪŋ) n 1 telecomm the cables that take a

common route through an exchange building linking ranks of selectors **2** plastic housing used to conceal wires, etc; casing **3** the delivery of goods over long distances, esp by road vehicles to local distribution centres, from which deliveries and collections are made

trunk line *n* **1** a direct link between two telephone exchanges or switchboards that are a considerable distance apart **2** the main route or routes on a railway

trunk road *n* *Brit* a main road, esp one that is suitable for heavy vehicles

trunks (trʌŋks) *pl n* *Also called:* swimming trunks a man's garment worn for swimming, either fairly loose and extending from the waist to the thigh or briefer and close-fitting **2** shorts worn for some sports **3** *chiefly Brit* men's underpants with legs that reach midthigh

trunnion ('trʌnjən) *n* one of a pair of coaxial projections attached to opposite sides of a container, cannon, etc, to provide a support about which it can turn in a vertical [c17: from Old French *trognon* trunk]

Truro ('truərəu) *n* a market town in SW England, administrative centre of Cornwall. Pop: 20 920 (2001)

truss (trʌs) *vb* (*tr*) **1** (sometimes foll by *up*) to tie, bind, or bundle **2** to fasten or bind the wings and legs of (a fowl) before cooking to keep them in place **3** to support or stiffen (a roof, bridge, etc) with structural members **4** *med* to supply or support with a truss ▷ *n* **5** a structural framework of wood or metal, esp one arranged in triangles, used to support a roof, bridge, etc **6** *med* a device for holding a hernia in place, typically consisting of a pad held in position by a belt **7** *horticulture* a cluster of flowers or fruit growing at the end of a single stalk **8** *nautical* a metal fitting fixed to a yard at its centre for holding it to a mast while allowing movement **9** *architect* another name for **corbel 10** a bundle or pack **11** *chiefly Brit* a bundle of hay or straw, esp one having a fixed weight of 36, 56, or 60 pounds [c13: from Old French *trousse*, from *trousser*, apparently from Vulgar Latin *torciāre* (unattested), from *torca* (unattested) a bundle, TORCH]

trust (trʌst) *n* **1** reliance on and confidence in the truth, worth, reliability, etc, of a person or thing; faith. Related adj: **fiducial 2** a group of commercial enterprises combined to monopolize and control the market for any commodity: *illegal in the US* **3** the obligation of someone in a responsible position **4** custody, charge, or care **5** a person or thing in which confidence or faith is placed **6** commercial credit **7 a** an arrangement whereby a person to whom the legal title to property is conveyed (the trustee) holds such property for the benefit of those entitled to the beneficial interest **b** property that is the subject of such an arrangement **c** the confidence put in the trustee. Related adj: **fiduciary 8** (in the British National Health Service) a self-governing hospital, group of hospitals, or other body providing health-care services, which operates as an independent commercial unit within the NHS **9** (*modifier*) of or relating to a trust or trusts ▷ *vb* **10** (*tr; may take a clause as object*) to expect, hope, or suppose **11** (when *tr, may take an infinitive;* when *intr,* often foll by *in* or *to*) to place confidence in (someone to do something); have faith (in); rely (upon) **12** (*tr*) to consign for care **13** (*tr*) to allow (someone to do something) with confidence in his or her good sense or honesty **14** (*tr*) to extend business credit to [c13: from Old Norse *traust;* related to Old High German *trost* solace] ▷ 'trustable *adj* ▷ 'truster *n*

trust account *n* **1** *Also called:* trustee account a savings account deposited in the name of a trustee who controls it during his lifetime, after which the balance is payable to a prenominated beneficiary **2** property under the control of a trustee or trustees

trustafarian (ˌtrʌstəˈfɛəriən) *n* (*sometimes capital*) *Brit informal* a young person from a wealthy background whose trust fund enables him or her to eschew conventional attitudes to work, dress, drug taking, etc [c20: from TRUST (FUND) + (RAST)AFARIAN]

trustee (trʌˈstiː) *n* **1** a person to whom the legal title to property is entrusted to hold or use for another's benefit **2** a member of a board that manages the affairs and

administers the funds of an institution or organization

trustee in bankruptcy *n* a person entrusted with the administration of a bankrupt's affairs and with realizing his or her assets for the benefit of the creditors

trustee investment *n* *stock exchange* an investment in which trustees are authorized to invest money belonging to a trust fund

trusteeship (trʌˈstiːʃɪp) *n* **1** the office or function of a trustee **2 a** the administration or government of a territory by a foreign country under the supervision of the **Trusteeship Council** of the United Nations **b** (*often capital*) any such dependent territory; trust territory

trustful ('trʌstful) *or* **trusting** *adj* characterized by a tendency or readiness to trust others ▷ 'trustfully *or* 'trustingly *adv*

trust fund *n* money, securities, etc, held in trust

trust territory *n* (*sometimes capital*) another name for **trusteeship** (sense 2)

trustworthy ('trʌstˌwɜːðɪ) *adj* worthy of being trusted; honest, reliable, or dependable ▷ 'trustˌworthily *adv* ▷ 'trustˌworthiness *n*

trusty ('trʌstɪ) *adj* trustier, trustiest **1** faithful or reliable ▷ *n, pl* trusties **2** someone who is trusted, esp a convict to whom special privileges are granted ▷ 'trustily *adv* ▷ 'trustiness *n*

truth (truːθ) *n* **1** the quality of being true, genuine, actual, or factual **2** something that is true as opposed to false **3** a proven or verified principle or statement; fact: *the truths of astronomy* **4** (*usually plural*) a system of concepts purporting to represent some aspect of the world: *the truths of ancient religions* **5** fidelity to a required standard or law **6** faithful reproduction or portrayal **7** honesty, reliability, or veracity **8** accuracy, as in the setting, adjustment, or position of something, such as a mechanical instrument ▷ Related adjs: **veritable, veracious** [Old English *triewth;* related to Old High German *gitriuwida* fidelity, Old Norse *tryggr* true] ▷ 'truthless *adj*

truth drug *or* **truth serum** *n* *informal* any of various drugs supposed to have the property of making people tell the truth, as by relaxing them

truthful ('truːθful) *adj* **1** telling or expressing the truth; honest or candid **2** realistic: *a truthful portrayal of the king* ▷ 'truthfully *adv* ▷ 'truthfulness *n*

truth-function *n* *logic* a function that determines the truth-value of a complex sentence solely in terms of the truth-values of the component sentences without reference to their meaning

truth set *n* *Also called:* solution set *logic, maths* the set of values that satisfy an open sentence, equation, inequality, etc, having no unique solution

truth table *n* **1** a table, used in logic, indicating the truth-value of a compound statement for every truth-value of its component propositions **2** a similar table, used in transistor technology, to indicate the value of the output signal of a logic circuit for every value of input signal

truth-value *n* *logic* either of the values, true or false, that may be taken by a statement

try (traɪ) *vb* tries, trying, tried **1** (when *tr, may take an infinitive,* sometimes with *to* replaced by *and*) to make an effort or attempt: *he tried to climb a cliff* **2** (*tr;* often foll by *out*) to sample, test, or give experimental use to (something) in order to determine its quality, worth, etc **3** (*tr*) to put strain or stress on: *he tries my patience* **4** (*tr; often passive*) to give pain, affliction, or vexation to: *I have been sorely tried by those children* **5 a** to examine and determine the issues involved in (a cause) in a court of law **b** to hear evidence in order to determine the guilt or innocence of (an accused) **6** (*tr*) to melt (fat, lard, etc) in order to separate out impurities ▷ *n, pl* tries **7** an experiment or trial **8** an attempt or effort **9** *rugby* the act of an attacking player touching the ball down behind the opposing team's goal line, scoring five or, in Rugby League, four points **10** *Also called:* try for a point *American football* an attempt made after a touchdown to score an extra point by kicking a goal or, for two extra points, by running the ball or completing a pass across the opponents' goal line ▷ *See also* **try on, try out** [c13:

from Old French *trier* to sort, sift, of uncertain origin]
● **USAGE** The use of *and* instead of *to* after *try* is very
● common, but should be avoided in formal writing: *we*
● *must try to prevent* (not *try and prevent*) *this happening*

trying ('traɪɪŋ) *adj* upsetting, difficult, or annoying
> 'tryingly *adv*

trying plane *n* a plane with a long body for planing the
edges of long boards. Also called: **try plane**

try line *n* the line behind which the ball must be placed
to score a try in a rugby match

try on *vb* (*tr, adverb*) **1** to put on (an article of clothing) to
find out whether it fits or is suitable **2 try it on** *informal*
to attempt to deceive or fool someone ▷ *n* **try-on 3** *Brit
informal* an action or statement made to test out a
person's gullibility, tolerance, etc

try out *vb* (*adverb*) **1** (*tr*) to test or put to experimental use
2 (when *intr*, usually foll by *for*) *US & Canadian* (of an
athlete, actor, etc) to undergo a test or to submit (an
athlete, actor, etc) to a test to determine suitability for a
place in a team, an acting role, etc ▷ *n* **tryout 3** *chiefly US
& Canadian* a trial or test, as of an athlete or actor

trypanosome (trɪpənə,səʊm) *n* any parasitic flagellate
protozoan of the genus *Trypanosoma*, which lives in the
blood of vertebrates, is transmitted by certain insects,
and causes sleeping sickness and certain other diseases
[c19: from New Latin *Trypanosoma*, from Greek *trupanon*
borer + *sōma* body]

trypanosomiasis (,trɪpənəsə'maɪəsɪs) *n* any infection of
an animal or human with a trypanosome

trypsin ('trɪpsɪn) *n* an enzyme occurring in pancreatic
juice: it catalyses the hydrolysis of proteins to peptides
and is secreted from the pancreas in the form of
trypsinogen [c19 *tryp-*, from Greek *tripsis* a rubbing, from
tribein to rub + *-IN*; referring to the fact that it was
originally produced by rubbing the pancreas with
glycerine] > **tryptic** ('trɪptɪk) *adj*

tryptophan ('trɪptə,fæn) *n* an essential amino acid; a
component of proteins necessary for growth [c20: from
TRYPT(IC) + *-O* + *-phan* variant of *-PHANE*]

trysail ('traɪ,seɪl; *nautical* 'traɪs³l) *n* a small fore-and-aft
sail, triangular or square, set on the mainmast of a
sailing vessel in foul weather to help keep her head to
the wind

try square *n* a device for testing or laying out right
angles, usually consisting of a metal blade fixed at right
angles to a wooden handle

tryst (trɪst, traɪst) *n archaic or literary* **1** an appointment to
meet, esp secretly **2** the place of such a meeting or the
meeting itself [c14: from Old French *triste* lookout post,
apparently of Scandinavian origin; compare Old Norse
traust trust]

Tsana ('tsɑːnə) *n* **Lake Tsana** another name for (Lake)
Tana

tsar *or* **czar** (zɑː, tsɑː) *n* **1** (until 1917) the emperor of
Russia **2** a tyrant; autocrat **3** *informal* a public official
charged with responsibility for dealing with a certain
problem or crisis: *a drugs tsar* [from Russian *tsar*, via
Gothic *kaisar* from Latin: from *Caesar* emperor, from the
cognomen of Gaius Julius Caesar (100–44 BC), Roman
general, statesman, and historian] > **'tsardom** *or*
'czardom *n*

tsarevitch *or* **czarevitch** ('zɑːrəvɪtʃ) *n* a son of a Russian
tsar, esp the eldest son [from Russian *tsarevich*, from TSAR
+ *-evich*, masculine patronymic suffix]

tsarevna *or* **czarevna** (zɑː'rɛvnə) *n* **1** a daughter of a
Russian tsar **2** the wife of a Russian tsarevitch [from
Russian, from TSAR + *-evna*, feminine patronymic suffix]

tsarina, czarina (zɑː'riːnə) *or* **tsaritsa, czaritza**
(zɑː'rɪtsə) *n* the wife of a Russian tsar; Russian empress
[from Italian, Spanish *czarina*, from German *Czarin*]

tsarism *or* **czarism** ('zɑːrɪzəm) *n* a system of
government by a tsar, esp in Russia until 1917 > **'tsarist**
or **'czarist** *n, adj*

Tsaritsyn (*Russian* tsa'ritsɪn) *n* a former name (until
1925) of **Volgograd**

TSE *abbreviation* Toronto Stock Exchange

Tselinograd (*Russian* tsəlɪnɑ'grat) *n* a former name
(1961–94) for **Astana**

tsetse fly *or* **tzetze fly** ('tsɛtsɪ) *n* any of various

bloodsucking African dipterous flies of the genus
Glossina, which transmit the pathogens of various
diseases: family *Muscidae* [c19: via Afrikaans from
Tswana]

T-shirt *or* **tee shirt** *n* a lightweight simple garment for
the upper body, usually short-sleeved [so called because
of its shape]

Tshombe ('tʃɒmbɪ) *n* **Moise** (məʊ'iːz). 1919–69, Congolese
statesman. He led the secession of Katanga (1960) from
the newly independent Congo; forced into exile (1963)
but returned (1964–65) as premier of the Congo; died in
exile

Tshwane ('tʃwɒnɪ) *n* another name for **Pretoria**

Tsimshian ('tʃɪmʃɪən) *n* **1** a member of a Native Canadian
people of northern British Columbia **2** the Penutian
language of this people [c19: from Tsimshian, inside the
Skeena River]

Tsinan ('tsiː'næn) *n* a variant transliteration of the
Chinese name for **Jinan**

Tsinghai ('tsɪŋ'haɪ) *n* **1** a variant transliteration of the
Chinese name for **Qinghai 2** a variant transliteration of
the Chinese name for **Koko Nor**

Tsingtao ('tsɪŋ'taʊ) *n* a variant transliteration of the
Chinese name for **Qingdao**

Tsingyuan ('tsɪŋ'jwɑːn) *or* **Ch'ing-yüan** *n* the former
name of **Baoding**

Tsiolkovski (*Russian* tsʌl'kofskjɪ) *n* **Konstantin
Eduardovich** (kənstʌn'tjin edu'adəvɪtʃ). 1857–1935,
Russian aeronautical engineer, a pioneer of rocket and
space research. His work on liquid-fuelled rockets
anticipated the ideas of Robert Goddard

Tsitsihar ('tsɪtsɪ,hɑː) *n* a variant transliteration of the
Chinese name for **Qiqihar**

TSO *abbreviation* The Stationery Office, formerly His (or
Her) Majesty's Stationery Office

tsotsi ('tsʊtsɪ, 'tsɔ:-) *n, pl* **-tsis** a Black street thug or gang
member; wide boy [c20: perhaps from Nguni *tsotsa* to
dress flashily]

tsp. *abbreviation* teaspoon

T-square *n* a T-shaped ruler used in mechanical
drawing, consisting of a short crosspiece, which slides
along the edge of the drawing board, and a long
horizontal piece: used for drawing horizontal lines and
to support set squares when drawing vertical and
inclined lines

T-stop *n* a setting of the lens aperture on a camera
calibrated photometrically and assigned a T-number

Tsugaru Strait ('tsuga,ru) *n* a channel between N
Honshu and S Hokkaido islands, Japan. Width: about 30
km (20 miles)

tsunami (tsʊ'næmɪ) *n, pl* **-mis** *or* **-mi** a large, often
destructive, sea wave produced by a submarine
earthquake, subsidence, or volcanic eruption.
Sometimes incorrectly called a tidal wave [from
Japanese, from *tsu* port + *nami* wave]

Tsushima ('tsuːʃi,mɑː) *n* a group of five rocky islands
between Japan and South Korea, in the Korea Strait:
administratively part of Japan; scene of a naval defeat
for the Russians (1905) during the Russo-Japanese war.
Pop: 41 230 (2000). Area: 698 sq km (269 sq miles)

tsutsugamushi disease (,tsutsugə'muʃi) *n* one of the
five major groups of acute infectious rickettsial diseases
affecting man, common in Asia and including scrub
typhus. It is caused by the microorganism *Rickettsia
tsutsugamushi*, transmitted by the bite of mites [from
Japanese, from *tsutsuga* disease + *mushi* insect]

Tsvangirai (tsvæn'gɪərɪ) *n* **Morgan**. born 1952,
Zimbabwean trade unionist and politician; leader of the
Movement for Democratic Change, the main opposition
party to President Mugabe's Zanu-PF since 1999

Tsvetaeva (tsfɛtɑ'jeɪvə) *n* **Marina** (**Ivanovna**). 1892–1941,
Russian poet. Opposed to the Revolution, she left Russia
(1922) and lived in Paris: when she returned (1939) her
husband was shot and she committed suicide

Tswana ('tswɑːnə) *n* **1** *pl* **-na** *or* **-nas** a member of a mixed
Negroid and Bushman people of the Sotho group of
southern Africa, living chiefly in Botswana **2** the
language of this people, belonging to the Bantu group of
the Niger-Congo family: the principal language of

Botswana. Also called: Setswana

TT *abbreviation* **1** teetotal **2** teetotaller **3** telegraphic transfer: a method of sending money abroad by cabled transfer between banks **4** Tourist Trophy (annual motorcycle races held in the Isle of Man) **5** tuberculin-tested

TTAn *abbreviation* (in Britain) Teacher Training Agency

TTL *abbreviation* **1** transistor transistor logic: a method of constructing electronic logic circuits **2** through-the-lens: denoting a system of light metering in cameras

TTS *computing abbreviation* text-to-speech: a technology that allows written text to be output as speech

TU *abbreviation* trade union

Tuamotu Archipelago (ˌtuːəˈmoʊtuː) *n* a group of about 80 coral islands in the S Pacific, in French Polynesia. Pop: 15 973 (2002; including the Gambier Islands). Area: 860 sq km (332 sq miles). Also called: Low Archipelago, Paumotu Archipelago

tuan¹ (ˈtuːɑːn) *n* (in Malay-speaking countries) sir; lord: a form of address used as a mark of respect [Malay]

tuan² (ˈtuːən, ˈtjuː-) *n* a flying phalanger, *Phascogale tapoatafa*, of Australia. It is about the size of a rat, bluish grey in colour, brush-tailed, arboreal, and nocturnal. Also called: wambenger, brush-tailed phascogale, phascogale [c19: from a native Australian language]

tuatara (ˌtuːəˈtɑːrə) *n* a greenish-grey lizard-like rhynchocephalian reptile, *Sphenodon punctatus*, occurring only on certain small islands near New Zealand: it is the sole surviving member of a group common in Mesozoic times [c19: from Māori, from *tua* back + *tara* spine]

tub (tʌb) *n* **1** a low wide open container, typically round, originally one made of wood and used esp for washing: now made of wood, plastic, metal, etc, and used in a variety of domestic and industrial situations **2** a small plastic or cardboard container of similar shape for ice cream, margarine, etc **3** Also called: bathtub another word (esp US and Canadian) for **bath¹** (sense 1) **4** Also called: tubful the amount a tub will hold **5** a clumsy slow boat or ship **6** Also called: tram, hutch **a** a small vehicle on rails for carrying loads in a mine **b** a container for lifting coal or ore up a mine shaft; skip ▷ *vb* tubs, tubbing, tubbed **7** *Brit informal* to wash (oneself or another) in a tub **8** (*tr*) to keep or put in a tub [c14: from Middle Dutch *tubbe*] ▷ ˈtubbable *adj* ▷ ˈtubber *n*

tuba (ˈtjuːbə) *n, pl* -bas *or* -bae (-biː) **1** a valved brass instrument of bass pitch, in which the bell points upwards and the mouthpiece projects at right angles. The tube is of conical bore and the mouthpiece cup-shaped **2** a powerful reed stop on an organ [Latin]

tubal (ˈtjuːbᵊl) *adj* **1** of or relating to a tube **2** of, relating to, or developing in a Fallopian tube

Tubal-cain (ˈtjuːbᵊlˌkeɪn) *n Old Testament* a son of Lamech, said in Genesis 4:22 to be the first artificer of metals

tubby (ˈtʌbɪ) *adj* -bier, -biest **1** plump **2** shaped like a tub ▷ ˈtubbiness *n*

tube (tjuːb) *n* **1** a long hollow and typically cylindrical object, used for the passage of fluids or as a container **2** a collapsible cylindrical container of soft metal or plastic closed with a cap, used to hold viscous liquids or pastes **3** *anatomy* a short for **Eustachian tube, Fallopian tube b** any hollow cylindrical structure **4** *botany* any other hollow structure in a plant **5** the tube *Brit* **a** Also called: the underground an underground railway system. US and Canadian equivalent: subway **b** the tunnels through which the railway runs **6** *electronics* **a** another name for **valve** (sense 3) **b** See **electron tube, cathode-ray tube, television tube 7** the tube *slang* a television set **8** *Brit slang* a stupid or despicable person **9** *Austral slang* a bottle or can of beer **10** *surfing* the cylindrical passage formed when a wave breaks and the crest tips forward ▷ *vb* (*tr*) **11** to fit or supply with a tube or tubes **12** to carry or convey in a tube **13** to shape like a tube [c17: from Latin *tubus*] ▷ ˈtubeless *adj*

tube foot *n* any of numerous tubular outgrowths of the body wall of most echinoderms that are used as organs of locomotion and respiration and to aid ingestion of food

tubeless tyre (ˈtjuːblɪs) *n* a pneumatic tyre in which the outer casing makes an airtight seal with the rim of the wheel so that an inner tube is unnecessary

tuber (ˈtjuːbə) *n* **1** a fleshy underground stem (as in the potato) or root (as in the dahlia) that is an organ of vegetative reproduction and food storage **2** *anatomy* a raised area; swelling [c17: from Latin *tūber* hump]

tubercle (ˈtjuːbəkᵊl) *n* **1** any small rounded nodule or elevation, esp on the skin, on a bone, or on a plant **2** any small rounded pathological lesion of the tissues, esp one characteristic of tuberculosis [c16: from Latin *tūberculum* a little swelling, diminutive of TUBER]

tubercle bacillus *n* a rodlike Gram-positive bacterium, *Mycobacterium tuberculosis*, that causes tuberculosis: family *Mycobacteriaceae*

tubercular (tjuːˈbɜːkjʊlə) *adj* **1** of, relating to, or symptomatic of tuberculosis **2** of or relating to a tubercle or tubercles **3** characterized by the presence of tubercles ▷ *n* **4** a person with tuberculosis ▷ tuˈberculosa *adj*

tuberculate (tjuːˈbɜːkjʊlɪt) *adj* covered with tubercles ▷ tuˌbercuˈlation *n*

tuberculin (tjuːˈbɜːkjʊlɪn) *n* a sterile liquid prepared from cultures of attenuated tubercle bacillus and used in the diagnosis of tuberculosis

tuberculin-tested *adj* (of milk) produced by cows that have been certified as free of tuberculosis

tuberculosis (tjuːˌbɜːkjʊˈləʊsɪs) *n* a communicable disease caused by infection with the tubercle bacillus, most frequently affecting the lungs (**pulmonary tuberculosis**) [c19: from New Latin; see TUBERCLE, -OSIS]

tuberose (ˈtjuːbəˌrəʊz) *n* a perennial Mexican agave plant, *Polianthes tuberosa*, having a tuberous root and spikes of white fragrant lily-like flowers [c17: from Latin *tūberōsus* full of lumps; referring to its root]

tuberous (ˈtjuːbərəs) *or* **tuberose** (ˈtjuːbəˌrəʊs) *adj* **1** (of plants or their parts) forming, bearing, or resembling a tuber or tubers **2** *anatomy* of, relating to, or having warty protuberances or tubers [c17: from Latin *tūberōsus* full of knobs; see TUBER]

tube worm *n* any of various polychaete worms that construct and live in a tube made of sand, lime, etc

tubifex (ˈtjuːbɪˌfɛks) *n, pl* -fex *or* -fexes any small reddish freshwater oligochaete worm of the genus *Tubifex*; it characteristically lives in a tube in sand and is used as food for aquarium fish [c19: from New Latin, from Latin *tubus* tube + *facere* to make, do]

tubing (ˈtjuːbɪŋ) *n* **1** tubes collectively **2** a length of tube **3** a system of tubes **4** fabric in the form of a tube, used for pillowcases and some cushions; piping

Tübingen (ˈtjuːbɪŋən) *n* a town in SW Germany, in Baden-Württemberg: university (1477). Pop: 83 137 (2003 est)

Tubman (ˈtʌbmən) *n* **William Vacanarat Shadrach** (vəˈkænəˌræt ˈʃædræk). 1895–1971, Liberian statesman; president of Liberia (1944–71)

tub-thumper *n* a noisy, violent, or ranting public speaker ▷ ˈtub-ˌthumping *adj, n*

Tubuai Islands (ˌtuːbuːˈaɪ) *pl n* a chain of small islands extending about 1400 km (850 miles) in the S Pacific, in French Polynesia; discovered by Captain Cook in 1777; annexed by France in 1880. Pop: 1979 (2002). Area: 173 sq km (67 sq miles). Also called: Austral Islands

tubular (ˈtjuːbjʊlə) *adj* **1** Also called: tubiform (ˈtjuːbɪˌfɔːm) having the form of a tube or tubes **2** of or relating to a tube or tubing

tubular bells *pl n music* an orchestral percussion instrument of 18 chromatically tuned metal tubes suspended vertically and struck near the top

tubule (ˈtjuːbjuːl) *n* any small tubular structure, esp one in an animal, as in the kidney, testis, etc [c17: from Latin *tubulus* a little TUBE]

TUC *abbreviation* (in Britain) Trades Union Congress

tuck (tʌk) *vb* **1** (*tr*) to push or fold into a small confined space or concealed place or between two surfaces **2** (*tr*) to thrust the loose ends or sides of (something) into a confining space, so as to make neat and secure **3** (*tr*) to make a tuck or tucks in (a garment) **4** (*usually tr*) to draw together, contract, or pucker ▷ *n* **5** a tucked object or part **6** a pleat or fold in a part of a garment, usually stitched down so as to make it a better fit or as decoration **7** the part of a vessel where the after ends of the planking or plating meet at the sternpost **8** *Brit* **a** an informal or schoolchild's word for food, esp cakes and sweets **b** (*as modifier*): *a tuck box* **9** a position of the body in certain dives in which the legs are bent with the knees drawn up against the chest and tightly clasped ▷ See also **tuck away, tuck in** [c14: from Old English *tūcian* to torment; related to Middle Dutch *tucken* to tug, Old High German *zucchen* to twitch]

tuck away *vb* (*tr, adverb*) *informal* **1** to eat (a large amount of food) **2** to store, esp in a place difficult to find

tucker[1] ('tʌkə) *n* **1** a person or thing that tucks **2** a detachable yoke of lace, linen, etc, often white, worn over the breast, as of a low-cut dress **3** *Austral & NZ old-fashioned* an informal word for **food**

tucker[2] ('tʌkə) *vb* (*tr; often passive; usually foll by out*) *informal, chiefly US & Canadian* to weary or tire completely

tucker-bag *or* **tuckerbox** ('tʌkə,bɒks) *n* *Austral informal, old-fashioned* a bag or box used for carrying food

tucket ('tʌkɪt) *n* *archaic* a flourish on a trumpet [c16: from Old Northern French *toquer* to sound (on a drum)]

tuck in *vb* (*adverb*) **1** Also called: **tuck into** (*tr*) to put to bed and make snug **2** (*tr*) to thrust the loose ends or sides (of something) into a confining space **3** Also called: **tuck into** (*intr*) *informal* to eat, esp heartily ▷ *n* **tuck-in 4** *Brit informal* a meal, esp a large one

tuck shop *n* *chiefly Brit* a shop, esp one in or near a school, where food such as cakes and sweets are sold

Tucson ('tu:sɒn) *n* a city in SE Arizona, at an altitude of 700m (2400 ft): resort and seat of the University of Arizona (1891). Pop: 507 658 (2003 est)

Tucumán (*Spanish* tuku'man) *n* a city in NW Argentina: scene of the declaration (1816) of Argentinian independence from Spain; university (1914). Pop: 837 000 (2005 est)

-tude *suffix forming nouns* indicating state or condition: *plenitude* [from Latin *-tūdō*]

Tudor ('tju:də) *n* **1** an English royal house descended from a Welsh squire, **Owen Tudor** (died 1461), and ruling from 1485 to 1603. Monarchs of the Tudor line were Henry VII, Henry VIII, Edward VI, Mary I, and Elizabeth I ▷ *adj* **2** denoting a style of architecture of the late perpendicular period and characterized by half-timbered houses

Tues. *abbreviation* Tuesday

Tuesday ('tju:zdɪ) *n* the third day of the week; second day of the working week [Old English *tīwesdæg*, literally: day of Tiw, representing Latin *diēs Martis* day of Mars; compare Old Norse *tȳsdagr*, Old High German *zīostag*; see TIU, DAY]

TUF *abbreviation* (in New Zealand) Trade Union Federation

tufa ('tju:fə) *n* a soft porous rock consisting of calcium carbonate deposited from springs rich in lime [c18: from Italian *tufo*, from Late Latin *tōfus*] > **tufaceous** (tju:'feɪʃəs) *adj*

tuff (tʌf) *n* a rock formed by the fusing together on the ground of small rock fragments (less than 2 mm across) ejected from a volcano [c16: from Old French *tuf*, from Italian *tufo*; see TUFA] > **tuffaceous** (tʌ'feɪʃəs) *adj*

tuffet ('tʌfɪt) *n* a small mound or low seat [c16: alteration of TUFT]

tuft (tʌft) *n* **1** a bunch of feathers, grass, hair, etc, held together at the base **2** a cluster of threads drawn tightly through upholstery, a mattress, a quilt, etc, to secure and strengthen the padding **3** a small clump of trees or bushes **4** (formerly) a gold tassel on the cap worn by titled undergraduates at English universities ▷ *vb* **5** (*tr*) to provide or decorate with a tuft or tufts **6** to form or be formed into tufts **7** to secure and strengthen (a mattress, quilt, etc) with tufts [c14: perhaps from Old French *tufe*, of Germanic origin; compare TOP[1]] > **'tufty** *adj* > **'tufted** *adj*

tufted duck *n* a European lake-dwelling duck, *Aythya fuligula*, the male of which has a black plumage with white underparts and a long black drooping crest

Tu Fu ('du: 'fu:) *n* a variant transliteration of the Chinese name for **Du Fu**

tug (tʌg) *vb* **tugs, tugging, tugged 1** (when *intr*, sometimes foll by *at*) to pull or drag with sharp or powerful movements **2** (*tr*) to tow (a vessel) by means of a tug ▷ *n* **3** a strong pull or jerk **4** Also called: **tugboat, towboat** a boat with a powerful engine, used for towing barges, ships, etc **5** a hard struggle or fight [c13: related to Old English *tēon* to TOW[1]] > **'tugger** *n*

Tugela (tu:'geɪlə) *n* a river in E South Africa, rising in the Drakensberg where it forms the **Tugela Falls**, 856 m (2810 ft) high (highest waterfall in Africa), before flowing east to the Indian Ocean: scene of battles during the Zulu War (1879) and the Boer War (1899–1902). Length: about 500 km (312 miles)

tug-of-love *n* a conflict over custody of a child between divorced parents or between natural parents and foster or adoptive parents

tug-of-war *n* **1** a contest in which two people or teams pull opposite ends of a rope in an attempt to drag the opposition over a central line **2** any hard struggle, esp between two equally matched factions

tui ('tu:ɪ) *n, pl* **tuis** a New Zealand honeyeater, *Prosthemadera novaeseelandiae*, having a glossy bluish-green plumage with white feathers at the throat: it mimics human speech and the songs of other birds [from Māori]

tuition (tju:'ɪʃən) *n* **1** instruction, esp that received in a small group or individually **2** the payment for instruction, esp in colleges or universities [c15: from Old French *tuicion*, from Latin *tuitiō* a guarding, from *tuērī* to watch over] > **tu'itional** *adj*

tuk-tuk ('tʌk,tʌk) *n* (in Thailand) a three-wheeled motor vehicle used as a taxi [c20: of imitative origin]

Tula (*Russian* 'tulə) *n* an industrial city in W central Russia. Pop: 460 000 (2005 est)

tularaemia *or US* **tularemia** (,tu:lə'ri:mɪə) *n* an acute infectious bacterial disease of rodents, transmitted to man by infected ticks or flies or by handling contaminated flesh. It is characterized by fever, chills, and inflammation of the lymph glands [c19/20: from New Latin, from *Tulare*, county in California where it was first observed; see -AEMIA] > **,tula'raemic** *or US* **,tula'remic** *adj*

tulip ('tju:lɪp) *n* **1** any spring-blooming liliaceous plant of the temperate Eurasian genus *Tulipa*, having tapering bulbs, long broad pointed leaves, and single showy bell-shaped flowers **2** the flower or bulb of any of these plants [c17: from New Latin *tulipa*, from Turkish *tülbend* turban, which the opened bloom was thought to resemble]

tulip tree *n* **1** Also called: **tulip poplar, yellow poplar** a North American magnoliaceous forest tree, *Liriodendron tulipifera*, having tulip-shaped greenish-yellow flowers and long conelike fruits **2** a similar and related Chinese tree, *L. chinense* **3** any of various other trees with tulip-shaped flowers, such as the magnolia

tulipwood ('tju:lɪp,wʊd) *n* **1** Also called: **white poplar, yellow poplar** the light soft wood of the tulip tree, used in making furniture and veneer **2** any of several woods having stripes or streaks of colour, esp that of *Dalbergia variabilis*, a tree of tropical South America

Tull (tʌl) *n* **Jethro** ('dʒɛθrəʊ). 1674–1741, English agriculturalist, who invented the seed drill

Tullamore (,tʌlə'mɔ:) *n* the county town of Offaly, Republic of Ireland; food processing and brewing. Pop: 11 098 (2002)

tulle (tju:l) *n* a fine net fabric of silk, rayon, etc, used for evening dresses, as a trimming for hats, etc [c19: from French, from *Tulle*, city in S central France, where it was first manufactured]

tullibee ('tʌlɪ,bi:) *n* a cisco of the Great Lakes of Canada, *Coregonus artedii tullibee* [c19: from French *toulibi*, from Ojibwa]

Tully ('tʌlɪ) *n* the former English name for (Marcus Tullius) Cicero

Tulsa ('tʌlsə) *n* a city in NE Oklahoma, on the Arkansas River: a major oil centre; two universities. Pop: 387 807 (2003 est)

tumble ('tʌmbᵊl) *vb* **1** to fall or cause to fall, esp awkwardly, precipitately, or violently **2** (*intr*; usually foll by *about*) to roll or twist, esp in playing **3** (*intr*) to perform leaps, somersaults, etc **4** to go or move in a heedless or hasty way **5** (*tr*) to polish (gemstones) in a tumbler **6** (*tr*) to disturb, rumple, or toss around ▷ *n* **7** the act or an instance of tumbling **8** a fall or toss **9** an acrobatic feat, esp a somersault **10** a decrease in value, number, etc: *stock markets have taken a tumble* **11** a state of confusion **12** a confused heap or pile ▷ See also **tumble to** [Old English *tumbian*, from Old French *tomber*; related to Old High German *tūmōn* to turn]

tumbledown ('tʌmbⁱl,daʊn) *adj* falling to pieces; dilapidated; crumbling

tumble dryer *or* **tumble drier** *n* a machine that dries wet laundry by rotating it in warmed air inside a metal drum. Also called: **tumbler dryer, tumbler**

tumbler ('tʌmblə) *n* **1 a** a flat-bottomed drinking glass with no handle or stem. Originally, a tumbler had a round or pointed base and so could not stand upright **b** Also called: **tumblerful** the contents or quantity such a glass holds **2** a person, esp a professional entertainer, who performs somersaults and other acrobatic feats **3** another name for **tumble dryer 4** Also called: **tumbling box** a pivoted box or drum rotated so that the contents (usually inferior gemstones) tumble about and become smooth and polished **5** the part of a lock that retains or releases the bolt and is moved by the action of a key **6** a lever in a gunlock that receives the action of the mainspring when the trigger is pressed and thus forces the hammer forwards **7** part that moves a gear in a train of gears into and out of engagement

tumbler switch *n* a switch that is turned over to connect or disconnect an electric current

tumble to *vb* (*intr, preposition*) *informal* to understand; become aware of

tumbleweed ('tʌmbⁱl,wi:d) *n* any densely branched plant that breaks off near the ground on withering and is rolled about by the wind, esp one of several amaranths of the western US and Australia

tumbrel *or* **tumbril** ('tʌmbrəl) *n* **1** a farm cart for carrying dung, esp one that tilts backwards to deposit its load. A cart of this type was used to take condemned prisoners to the guillotine during the French Revolution **2** (formerly) a covered cart that accompanied artillery in order to carry ammunition, tools, etc [C14 *tumberell* ducking stool, from Medieval Latin *tumbrellum* from Old French *tumberel* dump cart, from *tomber* to tumble, of Germanic origin]

tumefacient (,tju:mɪ'feɪʃɪənt) *adj* producing or capable of producing swelling: *a tumefacient drug* [C16: from Latin *tumefacere* to cause to swell, from *tumēre* to swell + *facere* to cause]

tumefy ('tju:mɪ,faɪ) *vb* -fies, -fying, -fied to make or become tumid; swell or puff up [C16: from French *tuméfier*, from Latin *tumefacere*; see TUMEFACIENT]

tumescent (tju:'mɛsənt) *adj* swollen or becoming swollen [C19: from Latin *tumescere* to begin to swell, from *tumēre*] > tu'mescence *n*

tumid ('tju:mɪd) *adj* **1** (of an organ or part) enlarged or swollen **2** bulging or protuberant **3** pompous or fulsome in style [C16: from Latin *tumidus*, from *tumēre* to swell] > tu'midity *or* 'tumidness *n* > 'tumidly *adv*

tummy ('tʌmɪ) *n, pl* -mies an informal or childish word for **stomach**

tummy tuck *n* an informal name for **abdominoplasty**

tumour *or US* **tumor** ('tju:mə) *n pathol* **a** any abnormal swelling **b** a mass of tissue formed by a new growth of cells, normally independent of the surrounding structures [C16: from Latin, from *tumēre* to swell] > 'tumorous *or* 'tumoral *adj*

tumult ('tju:mʌlt) *n* **1** a loud confused noise, as of a crowd; commotion **2** violent agitation or disturbance **3** great emotional or mental agitation [C15: from Latin *tumultus*, from *tumēre* to swell up]

tumultuous (tju:'mʌltjʊəs) *adj* **1** uproarious, riotous, or turbulent **2** greatly agitated, confused, or disturbed **3** making a loud or unruly disturbance > tu'multuously *adv* > tu'multuousness *n*

tumulus ('tju:mjʊləs) *n, pl* -li (-lɪ:) *archaeol* (no longer in technical usage) another word for **barrow²** [C17: from Latin: a hillock, from *tumēre* to swell up]

tun (tʌn) *n* **1** a large beer cask **2** a measure of capacity, usually equal to 252 wine gallons ▷ *vb* **tuns, tunning, tunned 3** (*tr*) to put into or keep in tuns [Old English *tunne*; related to Old High German, Old Norse *tunna*, Medieval Latin *tunna*]

tuna¹ ('tju:nə) *n, pl* -na *or* -nas **1** Also called: **tunny** any of various large marine spiny-finned fishes of the genus *Thunnus*, esp *T. thynnus*, chiefly of warm waters: family *Scombridae*. They have a spindle-shaped body and widely forked tail, and are important food fishes **2** any of various similar and related fishes [C20: from American Spanish, from Spanish *atún*, from Arabic *tūn*, from Latin *thunnus* tunny, from Greek]

tuna² ('tju:nə) *n* any of various tropical American prickly pear cacti, esp *Opuntia tuna*, that are cultivated for their sweet edible fruits [C16: via Spanish from Taino]

tunable *or* **tuneable** ('tju:nəbⁱl) *adj* able to be tuned

Tunbridge Wells ('tʌn,brɪdʒ) *n* a town and resort in SE England, in SW Kent: chalybeate spring discovered in 1606; an important social centre in the 17th and 18th centuries. Pop: 60 095 (2001)

tundra ('tʌndrə) *n* a vast treeless zone lying between the ice cap and the timberline of North America and Eurasia and having a permanently frozen subsoil [C19: from Russian, from Lapp *tundar* hill; related to Finnish *tunturi* treeless hill]

tune (tju:n) *n* **1** a melody, esp one for which harmony is not essential **2** the condition of producing accurately pitched notes, intervals, etc (esp in the phrases **in tune, out of tune**) **3** accurate correspondence of pitch and intonation between instruments (esp in the phrases **in tune, out of tune**) **4** the correct adjustment of a radio, television, or some other electronic circuit with respect to the required frequency (esp in the phrases **in tune, out of tune**) **5** a frame of mind; disposition or mood **6 call the tune** to be in control of the proceedings **7 change one's tune, sing another tune** *or* **sing a different tune** to alter one's attitude or tone of speech **8 to the tune of** *informal* to the amount or extent of ▷ *vb* **9** to adjust (a musical instrument or a changeable part of one) to a certain pitch **10** to adjust (a note, etc) so as to bring it into harmony or concord **11** (*tr*) to adapt or adjust (oneself); attune **12** (*tr*; often foll by *up*) to make fine adjustments to (an engine, machine, etc) to obtain optimum performance **13** *electronics* to adjust (one or more circuits) for resonance at a desired frequency ▷ See also **tune in, tune up** [C14: variant of TONE] > 'tuner *n*

tuneful ('tju:nfʊl) *adj* **1** having a pleasant or catchy tune; melodious **2** producing a melody or music > 'tunefully *adv* > 'tunefulness *n*

tune in *vb* (*adverb*; often foll by *to*) **1** to adjust (a radio or television) to receive (a station or programme) **2** *slang* to make or become more aware, knowledgeable, etc (about)

tuneless ('tju:nlɪs) *adj* having no melody or tune > 'tunelessly *adv* > 'tunelessness *n*

tune up *vb* (*adverb*) **1** to adjust (a musical instrument) to a particular pitch, esp a standard one **2** (esp of an orchestra or other instrumental ensemble) to tune (instruments) to a common pitch **3** (*tr*) to adjust (an engine) in (a car, etc) to improve performance ▷ *n* **tune-up 4** adjustments made to an engine to improve its performance

tung oil (tʌŋ) *n* a fast-drying oil obtained from the seeds of a central Asian euphorbiaceous tree, *Aleurites fordii*, used in paints, varnishes, etc, as a drying agent and to give a water-resistant finish [partial translation of Chinese *yu t'ung* tung tree oil, from *yu* oil + *t'ung* tung tree]

tungsten ('tʌŋstən) *n* a hard malleable ductile greyish-white element. It occurs principally in wolframite and scheelite and is used in lamp filaments, electrical contact points, X-ray targets, and, alloyed with steel, in high-speed cutting tools. Symbol: W; atomic no: 74; atomic wt: 183.85; valency: 2–6; relative density: 19.3; melting pt: 3422±20°C; boiling pt: 5555°C. Also called: **wolfram** [C18: from Swedish *tung* heavy + *sten* STONE]

tungsten lamp *n* a lamp in which light is produced by a tungsten filament heated to incandescence by an electric current. The glass bulb enclosing the filament contains a low pressure of inert gas, usually argon. Sometimes small amounts of a halogen, such as iodine, are added to improve the intensity (**tungsten-halogen lamp**)

tungsten steel *n* any of various hard steels containing tungsten (1–20 per cent) and traces of carbon. They are resistant to wear at high temperatures and are used in tools

Tungting *or* **Tung-t'ing** (ˌtʊŋˈtɪŋ) *n* a variant transliteration of the Chinese name for **Dongting**

Tungusic (tʊŋˈgʊsɪk) *n* a branch or subfamily of the Altaic family of languages, including Tungus and Manchu

Tunguska (*Russian* tunˈguskə) *n* any of three rivers in Russia, in central Siberia, all tributaries of the Yenisei: the **Lower** (Nizhnyaya) **Tunguska** 2690 km (1670 miles) long; the **Stony** (Podkamennaya) **Tunguska** 1550 km (960 miles) long; the **Upper** (Verkhnyaya) **Tunguska** which is the lower course of the Angara

tunic (ˈtjuːnɪk) *n* 1 any of various hip-length or knee-length garments, such as the loose sleeveless garb worn in ancient Greece or Rome, the jacket of some soldiers, or a woman's hip-length garment, worn with a skirt or trousers 2 *anatomy, botany, zoology* a covering, lining, or enveloping membrane of an organ or part [Old English *tunice* (unattested except in the accusative case), from Latin *tunica*]

tunicate (ˈtjuːnɪkɪt, -ˌkeɪt) *n* 1 any minute primitive marine chordate animal of the subphylum *Tunicata* (or *Urochordata, Urochorda*). The adults have a saclike unsegmented body enclosed in a cellulose-like outer covering (tunic) and only the larval forms have a notochord: includes the sea squirts ▷ *adj* 2 Also: **tunicated** (esp of a bulb) having or consisting of concentric layers of tissue [c18: from Latin *tunicātus* clad in a TUNIC]

tuning (ˈtjuːnɪŋ) *n music* 1 a set of pitches to which the open strings of a guitar, violin, etc, are tuned 2 the accurate pitching of notes and intervals by a choir, orchestra, etc; intonation

tuning fork *n* a two-pronged metal fork that when struck produces a pure note of constant specified pitch. It is used to tune musical instruments and in acoustics

Tunis (ˈtjuːnɪs) *n* the capital and chief port of Tunisia, in the northeast on the **Gulf of Tunis** (an inlet of the Mediterranean): dates from Carthaginian times, the ruins of ancient Carthage lying to the northeast; university (1960). Pop: 2 063 000 (2005 est)

Tunisia (tjuːˈnɪzɪə, -ˈnɪsɪə) *n* a republic in N Africa, on the Mediterranean: settled by the Phoenicians in the 12th century BC; made a French protectorate in 1881 and gained independence in 1955. It consists chiefly of the Sahara in the south, a central plateau, and the Atlas Mountains in the north. Exports include textiles, petroleum, and phosphates. Official language: Arabic; French is also widely spoken. Official religion: Muslim. Currency: dinar. Capital: Tunis. Pop: 9 937 000 (2004 est). Area: 164 150 sq km (63 380 sq miles) ▷ Tuˈnisian *adj, n*

tunnage (ˈtʌnɪdʒ) *n* a variant spelling of **tonnage**

tunnel (ˈtʌnᵊl) *n* 1 an underground passageway, esp one for trains or cars that passes under a mountain, river, or a congested urban area 2 any passage or channel through or under something ▷ *vb* -nels, -nelling, -nelled *or US* -nels, -neling, -neled 3 (*tr*) to make or force (a way) through or under (something): *to tunnel a hole in the wall; to tunnel the cliff* 4 (*intr*; foll by *through, under, etc*) to make or force a way (through or under something) [c15: from Old French *tonel* cask, from *tonne* tun, from Medieval Latin *tonna* barrel, of Celtic origin] ▷ ˈtunneller *or US* ˈtunneler *n*

tunnel diode *n* an extremely stable semiconductor diode, having a very narrow highly doped p-n junction, in which electrons travel across the junction by means of the tunnel effect. Also called: **Esaki diode**

tunnel effect *n physics* the phenomenon in which an object, usually an elementary particle, tunnels through a potential barrier even though it does not have

sufficient energy to surmount the barrier. It is explained by wave mechanics and is the cause of alpha decay, field emission, and certain conduction processes in semiconductors

tunnel vision *n* 1 a condition in which peripheral vision is greatly restricted 2 narrowness of viewpoint resulting from concentration on a single idea, opinion, etc, to the exclusion of others

Tunney (ˈtʌnɪ) *n* **Gene**, original name *James Joseph Tunney*. 1897–1978, US boxer; world heavyweight champion (1926–28)

tunny (ˈtʌnɪ) *n, pl* -nies *or* -ny another name for **tuna**[1] [c16: from Old French *thon*, from Old Provençal *ton*, from Latin *thunnus*, from Greek]

tup (tʌp) *n* 1 *chiefly Brit* an uncastrated male sheep; ram 2 the head of a pile-driver or steam hammer ▷ *vb* tups, tupping, tupped (*tr*) 3 to cause (a ram) to mate with a ewe, or (of a ram) to mate with (a ewe) [c14: of unknown origin]

tupelo (ˈtjuːpɪˌləʊ) *n, pl* -los 1 any of several cornaceous trees of the genus *Nyssa*, esp *N. aquatica*, a large tree of deep swamps and rivers of the southern US 2 the light strong wood of any of these trees [c18: from Creek *ito opilwa*, from *ito* tree + *opilwa* swamp]

Tupi (tuːˈpiː) *n* 1 *pl* -pis *or* -pi a member of a South American Indian people of Brazil and Paraguay 2 the language of this people, belonging to the Tupi-Guarani family ▷ Tuˈpian *adj*

tupik *or* **tupek** (ˈtuːpək) *n Canadian* (esp in the Arctic) a tent of animal skins, a traditional type of Inuit summer dwelling [from Inuktitut *tupiq*]

tuple (ˈtjʊpᵊl, ˈtʌpᵊl) *n computing* a row of values in a relational database

Tupolev (*Russian* tuˈpəljif) *n* **Andrei Nikolaievich** (unˈdrjeɪ njɪkəˈlajɪvjɪtʃ). 1888–1972, Soviet aircraft designer, who designed the first supersonic passenger aircraft, the TU-144 (tested 1969). He also designed supersonic bombers and the TU-104, one of the first passenger jet aircraft (1955)

tuppence (ˈtʌpəns) *n Brit* a variant spelling of **twopence** ▷ ˈtuppenny *adj*

Tupperware (ˈtʌpəweə) *n trademark* a range of plastic containers used for storing food [c20: *Tupper*, US manufacturing company + WARE[1]]

tupuna (təˈpuːnə) *n* a variant spelling of **tipuna**

Tupungato (*Spanish* tupuŋˈgato) *n* a mountain on the border between Argentina and Chile, in the Andes. Height: 6550 m (21 484 ft)

tuque (tuːk) *n Canadian* 1 a knitted cap with a long tapering end 2 Also called: **toque** a close-fitting knitted hat often with a tassel or pompom [c19: from Canadian French, from French: TOQUE]

turaco (ˈtʊərəˌkəʊ) *n, pl* -cos a variant spelling of **touraco**

turangawaewae (təˌrʌŋgəˈweɪweɪ) *n NZ* the area that is a person's home [Māori, literally: standing on one's feet]

Turanian (tjʊˈreɪnɪən) *n* 1 a member of any of the peoples inhabiting ancient Turkestan, or their descendants 2 another name for **Ural-Altaic**

turban (ˈtɜːbᵊn) *n* 1 a man's headdress, worn esp by Muslims, Hindus, and Sikhs, made by swathing a length of linen, silk, etc, around the head or around a caplike base 2 a woman's brimless hat resembling this 3 any headdress resembling this [c16: from Turkish *tülbend*, from Persian *dulband*] ▷ ˈturbaned *adj*

turbary (ˈtɜːbərɪ) *n, pl* -ries 1 land where peat or turf is cut or has been cut 2 Also called: **common of turbary** (in England) the legal right to cut peat for fuel on a common [c14: from Old French *turbarie*, from Medieval Latin *turbāria*, from *turba* peat, TURF]

turbellarian (ˌtɜːbɪˈlɛərɪən) *n* 1 any typically aquatic free-living flatworm of the class *Turbellaria*, having a ciliated epidermis and a simple life cycle: includes the planarians ▷ *adj* 2 of, relating to, or belonging to the class *Turbellaria* [c19: from New Latin *Turbellāria*, from Latin *turbellae* (pl) bustle, from *turba* brawl, referring to the swirling motion created in the water]

turbid (ˈtɜːbɪd) *adj* 1 muddy or opaque, as a liquid

clouded with a suspension of particles **2** dense, thick, or cloudy: *turbid fog* **3** in turmoil or confusion [C17: from Latin *turbidus*, from *turbāre* to agitate, from *turba* crowd] > tur'bidity *or* 'turbidness *n* > 'turbidly *adv*

turbinate ('tɜːbɪnɪt, -ˌneɪt) *or* **turbinal** ('tɜːbɪnᵊl) *adj* Also: **turbinated 1** *anatomy* of or relating to any of the thin scroll-shaped bones situated on the walls of the nasal passages **2** shaped like a spiral or scroll **3** (esp of the shells of certain molluscs) shaped like an inverted cone ▷ *n* **4** Also called: **nasal concha** a turbinate bone **5** a turbinate shell [C17: from Latin *turbō* spinning top] > ˌturbi'nation *n*

turbine ('tɜːbɪn, -baɪn) *n* any of various types of machine in which the kinetic energy of a moving fluid is converted into mechanical energy by causing a bladed rotor to rotate. The moving fluid may be water, steam, air, or combustion products of a fuel [C19: from French, from Latin *turbō* whirlwind, from *turbāre* to throw into confusion]

turbine blade *n* any of a number of bladelike vanes assembled around the periphery of a turbine rotor to guide the steam or gas flow

turbit ('tɜːbɪt) *n* a crested breed of domestic pigeon [C17: from Latin *turbō* spinning top, with reference to the bird's shape; compare TURBOT]

turbo- *combining form* of, relating to, or driven by a turbine: *turbofan*

turbocharger ('tɜːbəʊˌtʃɑːdʒə) *n* a centrifugal compressor which boosts the intake pressure of an internal-combustion engine, driven by an exhaust-gas turbine fitted to the engine's exhaust manifold

turbofan ('tɜːbəʊˌfæn) *n* **1** Also called: **high bypass ratio engine** a type of by-pass engine in which a large fan driven by a turbine and housed in a short duct forces air rearwards around the exhaust gases in order to increase the propulsive thrust **2** an aircraft driven by one or more turbofans **3** the ducted fan in such an engine

turbogenerator (ˌtɜːbəʊˈdʒɛnəˌreɪtə) *n* a large electrical generator driven by a steam turbine

turbojet ('tɜːbəʊˌdʒɛt) *n* **1** short for **turbojet engine 2** an aircraft powered by one or more turbojet engines

turbojet engine *n* a gas turbine in which the exhaust gases provide the propulsive thrust to drive an aircraft

turboprop (ˌtɜːbəʊˈprɒp) *n* **1** an aircraft propulsion unit where a propeller is driven by a gas turbine **2** an aircraft powered by turboprops

turbosupercharger (ˌtɜːbəʊˈsuːpəˌtʃɑːdʒə) *n* *obsolete* a supercharging device for an internal-combustion engine, consisting of a turbine driven by the exhaust gases

turbot ('tɜːbət) *n, pl* **-bot** *or* **-bots 1** a European flatfish, *Scophthalmus maximus*, having a pale brown speckled scaleless body covered with tubercles: family *Bothidae*. It is highly valued as a food fish **2** any of various similar or related fishes [C13: from Old French *tourbot*, from Medieval Latin *turbō*, from Latin: spinning top, from a fancied similarity in shape; see TURBIT, TURBINE]

turbulence ('tɜːbjʊləns) *or rarely* **turbulency** ('tɜːbjʊˌlənsɪ) *n* **1** a state or condition of confusion, movement, or agitation; disorder **2** *meteorol* local instability in the atmosphere, oceans, or rivers **3** turbulent flow in a liquid or gas

turbulent ('tɜːbjʊlənt) *adj* **1** being in a state of turbulence **2** wild or insubordinate; unruly [C16: from Latin *turbulentus*, from *turba* confusion] > 'turbulently *adv*

turd (tɜːd) *n slang* **1** a lump of dung; piece of excrement **2** an unpleasant or contemptible person or thing [Old English *tord*; related to Old Norse *tordy fill* dung beetle, Dutch *tort* dung]

turducken ('tɜːdʌkən) *n* a boned turkey stuffed with a boned duck that is stuffed with a small boned chicken, sometimes also containing a breadcrumb or sausagemeat stuffing [C21: from TUR(KEY) + DU(CK) + (CHI)CKEN]

tureen (təˈriːn) *n* a large deep usually rounded dish with a cover, used for serving soups, stews, etc [C18: from French *terrine* earthenware vessel, from *terrin* made of earthenware, from Vulgar Latin *terrīnus* (unattested) earthen, from Latin *terra* earth]

Turenne (*French* tyrɛn) *n* **Vicomte de**, title of *Henri de la Tour d'Auvergne*. 1611–75, French marshal. He commanded armies during the Thirty Years' War and the wars of the Fronde

turf (tɜːf) *n, pl* **turfs** *or* **turves** (tɜːvz) **1** the surface layer of fields and pastures, consisting of earth containing a dense growth of grasses with their roots; sod **2** a piece cut from this layer, used to form lawns, verges, etc **3** the **turf a** a track, usually of grass or dirt, where horse races are run **b** horse racing as a sport or industry **4** an area of knowledge or influence: *he's on home turf when it comes to music* **5** another term for **peat**¹ ▷ *vb* **6** (*tr*) to cover with pieces of turf [Old English; related to Old Norse *torfa*, Old High German *zurba*, Sanskrit *darbha* tuft of grass]

turf accountant *n Brit* a formal name for a **bookmaker**

turfman ('tɜːfmən) *n, pl* **-men** *chiefly US* a person devoted to horse racing

turf out *vb* (*tr, adverb*) *Brit informal* to throw out or dismiss; eject

turf war *n informal* **1** a dispute between criminals or gangs over the right to operate within a particular area **2** any dispute in which one party seeks to obtain increased rights or influence

Turgenev (*Russian* turˈgjenɪf) *n* **Ivan Sergeyevich** (iˈvan sɪrˈgjejɪvitʃ). 1818–83, Russian novelist and dramatist. In *A Sportsman's Sketches* (1852) he pleaded for the abolition of serfdom. His novels, such as *Rudin* (1856) and *Fathers and Sons* (1862), are noted for their portrayal of country life and of the Russian intelligentsia. His plays include *A Month in the Country* (1850)

turgescent (tɜːˈdʒɛsᵊnt) *adj* becoming or being swollen; inflated; tumid > turˈgescence *or* turˈgescency *n*

turgid ('tɜːdʒɪd) *adj* **1** swollen and distended; congested **2** (of style or language) pompous and high-flown; bombastic [C17: from Latin *turgidus*, from *turgēre* to swell] > turˈgidity *or* 'turgidness *n* > 'turgidly *adv*

turgor ('tɜːgə) *n* the normal rigid state of a cell, caused by pressure of the cell contents against the cell wall or membrane [C19: from Late Latin: a swelling, from Latin *turgēre* to swell]

Turgot (*French* tyrgo) *n* **Anne Robert Jacques** (an rɔbɛr ʒak). 1727–81, French economist and statesman. As controller general of finances (1774–76), he attempted to abolish feudal privileges, incurring the hostility of the aristocracy and his final dismissal

Turin (tjʊˈrɪn) *n* a city in NW Italy, capital of Piedmont region, on the River Po: became capital of the Kingdom of Sardinia in 1720; first capital (1861–65) of united Italy; university (1405); a major industrial centre, producing most of Italy's cars. Pop: 865 263 (2001). Italian name: **Torino**

Turing ('tjʊərɪŋ) *n* **Alan Mathison**. 1912–54, English mathematician, who was responsible for formal description of abstract automata, and speculation on computer imitation of humans: a leader of the Allied codebreakers at Bletchley Park during World War II

Turing machine *n* a hypothetical universal computing machine able to modify its original instructions by reading, erasing, or writing a new symbol on a moving tape of fixed length that acts as its program. The concept was instrumental in the early development of computer systems [C20: after Alan *Turing* (1912–54), English mathematician]

turion ('tʊərɪən) *n* a perennating bud produced by many aquatic plants: it detaches from the parent plant and remains dormant until the following spring [C17: from French *turion*, from Latin *turio* shoot]

Turishcheva (*Russian* tuˈrɪʃtʃəvə) *n* **Ludmilla** (lʊdˈmɪlə). born 1952, Soviet gymnast: world champion 1970, 1972 (at the Olympic Games), and 1974

Turk (tɜːk) *n* **1** a native, inhabitant, or citizen of Turkey **2** a native speaker of any Turkic language, such as an inhabitant of Turkmenistan or Kyrgyzstan **3** *obsolete, derogatory* a violent, brutal, or domineering person ▷ See also **Young Turk**

Turk. *abbreviation* **1** Turkey **2** Turkish

Turkana (tɜːˈkɑːnə) *n* **Lake Turkana** a long narrow lake in E Africa, in the Great Rift Valley. Area: 7104 sq km (2743 sq miles). Former name: **Rudolf**

Turkestan *or* **Turkistan** (ˌtɜːkɪˈstɑːn) *n* an extensive region of central Asia between Siberia in the north and Tibet, India, Afghanistan, and Iran in the south: formerly divided into **West** (**Russian**) **Turkestan** (also called Soviet Central Asia), comprising present-day Turkmenistan, Uzbekistan, Tajikistan, and Kyrgyzstan and the S part of Kazakhstan, and **East** (**Chinese**) **Turkestan**, approximating to the Xinjiang Uygur Autonomous Region of China ▷ ˌTurkeˈstani *adj, n*

turkey (ˈtɜːkɪ) *n, pl* -keys *or* -key **1** a large gallinaceous bird, *Meleagris gallopavo*, of North America, having a bare wattled head and neck and a brownish iridescent plumage. The male is brighter and has a fan-shaped tail. A domestic variety is widely bred for its flesh **2** *slang, chiefly US & Canadian* a dramatic production that fails; flop **3** See **cold turkey 4** talk turkey *informal, chiefly US & Canadian* to discuss frankly and practically [c16: shortened from *Turkey cock* (hen), used at first to designate the African guinea fowl (apparently because the bird was brought through Turkish territory), later applied by mistake to the American bird]

Turkey (ˈtɜːkɪ) *n* a republic in W Asia and SE Europe, between the Black Sea, the Mediterranean, and the Aegean: the centre of the Ottoman Empire; became a republic in 1923. The major Asian part, consisting mainly of an arid plateau, is separated from European Turkey by the Bosporus, Sea of Marmara, and Dardanelles. Official languages: Turkish; Kurdish and Arabic minority languages. Religion: Muslim majority. Currency: lira. Capital: Ankara. Pop: 72 320 000 (2004 est). Area: 780 576 sq km (301 380 sq miles)

turkey buzzard *or* **turkey vulture** *n* a New World vulture, *Cathartes aura*, having a dark plumage and naked red head

turkey cock *n* **1** a male turkey **2** an arrogant person

turkey nest *n* *Austral* a small earth dam adjacent to, and higher than, a larger earth dam, to feed water by gravity to a cattle trough, etc

Turkey red *n* **1 a** a moderate or bright red colour **b** (*as adjective*): *a Turkey-red fabric* **2** a cotton fabric of a bright red colour

Turki (ˈtɜːkɪ) *adj* **1** of or relating to the Turkic languages, esp those of central Asia **2** of or relating to speakers of these languages ▷ *n* **3** these languages collectively; esp Eastern Turkic

Turkic (ˈtɜːkɪk) *n* a branch or subfamily of the Altaic family of languages, including Turkish, Turkmen, Kirghiz, Tatar, etc, members of which are found from Turkey to NE China, esp in central Asia

Turkish (ˈtɜːkɪʃ) *adj* **1** of, relating to, or characteristic of Turkey, its people, or their language ▷ *n* **2** the official language of Turkey, belonging to the Turkic branch of the Altaic family ▷ ˈTurkishness *n*

Turkish bath *n* **1** a type of bath in which the bather sweats freely in hot dry air, is then washed, often massaged, and has a cold plunge or shower **2** (*sometimes plural*) an establishment where such a bath is obtainable

Turkish coffee *n* very strong black coffee made with finely ground coffee beans

Turkish delight *n* a jelly-like sweet flavoured with flower essences, usually cut into cubes and covered in icing sugar

Turkish towel *n* a rough loose-piled towel; terry towel

Turkmenistan (ˌtɜːkmɛnɪˈstɑːn) *n* a republic in central Asia: the area has been occupied by a succession of empires; a Turkmen state was established in the 15th century but suffered almost continual civil strife and was gradually conquered by Russia; in 1918 it became a Soviet republic and gained independence from the Soviet Union in 1991: deserts including the Kara Kum cover most of the region; agricultural communities are concentrated around oases; there are rich mineral deposits. Official language: Turkmen. Religion: believers are mainly Muslim. Currency: manat. Capital: Ashkhabad. Pop: 4 940 000 (2004 est). Area: 488 100 sq km (186 400 sq miles)

Turks and Caicos Islands *pl n* a UK Overseas Territory in the Caribbean, southeast of the Bahamas: consists of the eight **Turks Islands**, separated by the Turks Island

Passage from the Caicos group, which has six main islands. Capital: Grand Turk. Pop: 21 000 (2003 est). Area: 430 sq km (166 sq miles)

Turk's-cap lily *n* any of several cultivated lilies, such as *Lilium martagon* and *L. superbum*, that have brightly coloured flowers with reflexed petals [c17: so called because of a resemblance between its flowers and a turban]

Turk's-head *n* an ornamental turban-like knot made by weaving small cord around a larger rope

Turku (*Finnish* ˈturku) *n* a city and port in SW Finland, on the Gulf of Bothnia: capital of Finland until 1812. Pop: 175 059 (2003 est). Swedish name: Åbo

turmeric (ˈtɜːmərɪk) *n* **1** a tropical Asian zingiberaceous plant, *Curcuma longa*, having yellow flowers and an aromatic underground stem **2** the powdered stem of this plant, used as a condiment and as a yellow dye [c16: from Old French *terre merite*, from Medieval Latin *terra merita*, literally: meritorious earth, name applied for obscure reasons to curcuma]

turmeric paper *n chem* paper impregnated with turmeric used as a test for alkalis, which turn it brown, and for boric acid, which turns it reddish brown

turmoil (ˈtɜːmɔɪl) *n* violent or confused movement; agitation; tumult [c16: perhaps from TURN + MOIL]

turn (tɜːn) *vb* **1** to move or cause to move around an axis: *a wheel turning; to turn a knob* **2** (sometimes foll by *round*) to change or cause to change positions by moving through an arc of a circle: *he turned the chair to face the light* **3** to change or cause to change in course, direction, etc **4** to go or pass to the other side of (a corner, etc) **5** to assume or cause to assume a rounded, curved, or folded form: *the road turns here* **6** to reverse or cause to reverse position **7** (*tr*) to perform or do by a rotating movement: *to turn a somersault* **8** (*tr*) to shape or cut a thread in (a workpiece, esp one of metal, wood, or plastic) by rotating it on a lathe against a fixed cutting tool **9** (when *intr*, foll by *into* or *to*) to change or convert or be changed or converted **10** (foll by *into*) to change or cause to change in nature, character, etc: *the frog turned into a prince* **11** (*copula*) to change so as to become: *he turned nasty when he heard the price* **12** to cause (foliage, etc) to change colour or (of foliage, etc) to change colour **13** to cause (milk, etc) to become rancid or sour or (of milk, etc) to become rancid or sour **14** to change or cause to change in subject, trend, etc: *the conversation turned to fishing* **15** to direct or apply or be directed or applied: *he turned his attention to the problem* **16** (*intr*; usually foll by *to*) to appeal or apply (to) for help, advice, etc **17** to reach, pass, or progress beyond in age, time, etc: *she has just turned twenty* **18** (*tr*) to cause or allow to go: *to turn an animal loose* **19** to affect or be affected with nausea **20** to affect or be affected with giddiness: *my head is turning* **21** (*tr*) to affect the mental or emotional stability of (esp in the phrase **turn** (**someone's**) **head**) **22** (*tr*) to release from a container **23** (*tr*) to render into another language **24** (usually foll by *against* or *from*) to transfer or reverse or cause to transfer or reverse (one's loyalties, affections, etc) **25** (*tr*) to cause (an enemy agent) to become a double agent working for one's own side **26** (*tr*) to bring (soil) from lower layers to the surface **27** to blunt (an edge) or (of an edge) to become blunted **28** (*tr*) to give a graceful form to: *to turn a compliment* **29** (*tr*) to reverse (a cuff, collar, etc) in order to hide the outer worn side **30** (*intr*) US to be merchandised as specified: *shirts are turning well this week* **31** *cricket* to spin (the ball) or (of the ball) to spin **32** turn one's hand to to undertake (something, esp something practical) ▷ *n* **33** an act or instance of turning or the state of being turned or the material turned **34** a movement of complete or partial rotation **35** a change or reversal of direction or position **36** direction or drift: *his thoughts took a new turn* **37** a deviation or departure from a course or tendency **38** the place, point, or time at which a deviation or change occurs **39** another word for **turning** (sense 1) **40** the right or opportunity to do something in an agreed order or succession: *we'll take turns to play; now it's George's turn; you must not play out of turn* **41** a change in nature, condition, etc: *his illness took a turn for the worse* **42** a period of action, work, etc **43** a short walk, ride, or excursion **44** natural inclination: *he is of a speculative turn of mind; she has a turn for needlework* **45** distinctive form or style: *a neat turn of phrase* **46** requirement, need, or advantage: *to serve someone's turn* **47** a deed performed that helps or hinders someone **48** a twist, bend, or distortion in shape **49** *music* a melodic ornament that makes a turn around a note, beginning with the note above, in a variety of sequences **50** *theatre chiefly Brit* a short theatrical act, esp in music hall, cabaret, etc **51** *stock exchange Brit* the difference between a market maker's bid and offer prices, representing the market maker's profit **52** *informal* a shock or surprise **53** by turns one after another; alternately **54** the turn *poker slang* the fourth community card to be dealt face-up in a round of Texas holdem **55** turn and turn about one after another; alternately **56** to a turn to the proper amount; perfectly ▷ See also **turn down, turn in**, etc [Old English *tyrnian*, from Old French *torner*, from Latin *tornāre* to turn in a lathe, from *tornus* lathe, from Greek *tornos* dividers] ▷ 'turner *n*

turnabout ('tɜːnəˌbaʊt) *n* **1** the act of turning so as to face a different direction **2** a change or reversal of opinion, attitude, etc

turnaround ('tɜːnəˌraʊnd) *n* **1 a** the act or process in which a ship, aircraft, etc, unloads passengers and freight at the end of a trip and reloads for the next trip **b** the time taken for this **2** the total time taken by a ship, aircraft, or other vehicle in a round trip **3** a complete reversal of a situation or set of circumstances

turnbuckle ('tɜːnˌbʌkᵊl) *n* an open mechanical sleeve usually having a swivel at one end and a thread at the other to enable a threaded wire or rope to be tightened [C19: from TURN + BUCKLE]

turncoat ('tɜːnˌkəʊt) *n* a person who deserts one cause or party for the opposite faction; renegade

turncock ('tɜːnˌkɒk) *n* (formerly) an official employed to turn on the water for the mains supply

turn down *vb* (*tr, adverb*) **1** to reduce (the volume or brightness) of (something) **2** to reject or refuse **3** to fold down (a collar, sheets on a bed, etc) ▷ *adj* **turndown** **4** (*prenominal*) capable of being or designed to be folded or doubled down

Turner ('tɜːnə) *n* **1 Jane**. born 1961, Australian television actress and writer, best known for playing 'Kath' in the comedy series *Kath & Kim* **2 J(oseph) M(allord) W(illiam)**. 1775–1851, British landscape painter; a master of water colours. He sought to convey atmosphere by means of an innovative use of colour and gradations of light **3 Nat**. 1800–31, US rebel slave, who led (1831) Turner's Insurrection, the only major slave revolt in US history: executed **4 Robert Edward III**, known as *Ted*. born 1938, US broadcasting executive and yachtsman; chairman of Turner Broadcasting (1970–96), founder of Cable News Network (1980), and vice-chairman of Time Warner (1996–2003) **5 Tina**, real name *Annie Mae Bullock*. born 1940, US rock singer who performed (1958–75) with her then husband Ike Turner (1931–2007) and later as a solo act. Her recordings include "River Deep, Mountain High" (1966) and "Simply the Best" (1991)

turn in *vb* (*adverb*) *informal* **1** (*intr*) to go to bed for the night **2** (*tr*) to hand in; deliver **3** to give up or conclude (something) **4** (*tr*) to record (a score, etc) **5** turn in on oneself to withdraw or cause to withdraw from contact with others and become preoccupied with one's own problems

turning ('tɜːnɪŋ) *n* **1** Also called: **turn** a road, river, or path that turns off the main way **2** the point where such a way turns off **3** a bend in a straight course **4** an object made on a lathe **5** (*plural*) the waste produced in turning on a lathe

turning circle *n* the smallest circle in which a vehicle can turn

turning point *n* **1** a moment when the course of events is changed **2** a point at which there is a change in direction or motion

turnip ('tɜːnɪp) *n* **1 a** a widely cultivated plant, *Brassica rapa*, of the Mediterranean region, with a large yellow or white edible root: family *Brassicaceae* (crucifers) **2** the root of this plant, which is eaten as a vegetable [C16:

from earlier *turnepe*, perhaps from TURN (indicating its rounded shape) + *nepe*, from Latin *nāpus* turnip; see NEEP]

turnkey ('tɜːnˌkiː) *n* **1** *archaic* a keeper of the keys, esp in a prison; warder or jailer ▷ *adj* **2** denoting a project, as in civil engineering, in which a single contractor has responsibility for the complete job from the start to the time of installation or occupancy

turn off *vb* **1** to leave (a road, pathway, etc) **2** (of a road, pathway, etc) to deviate from (another road, etc) **3** (*tr, adverb*) to cause (something) to cease operating by turning a knob, pushing a button, etc **4** (*tr*) *informal* to cause (a person, etc) to feel dislike or distaste for (something): *this music turns me off* **5** (*tr, adverb*) *Brit informal* to dismiss from employment ▷ *n* **turn-off** **6** a road or other way branching off from the main thoroughfare **7** *informal* a person or thing that elicits dislike or distaste

turn on *vb* **1** (*tr, adverb*) to cause (something) to operate by turning a knob, etc **2** (*intr, preposition*) to depend or hinge on: *the success of the party turns on you* **3** (*preposition*) to change or cause to change one's attitude so as to become hostile or to retaliate: *the dog turned on the children* **4** (*tr, adverb*) *informal* to produce (charm, tears, etc) suddenly or automatically **5** (*tr, adverb*) *slang* to arouse emotionally or sexually **6** (*tr, adverb*) *slang* to take or become intoxicated by drugs **7** (*tr, adverb*) *slang* to introduce (someone) to drugs ▷ *n* **turn-on 8** *slang* a person or thing that causes emotional or sexual arousal

turn out *vb* (*adverb*) **1** (*tr*) to cause (something, esp a light) to cease operating by or as if by turning a knob, etc **2** (*tr*) to produce by an effort or process **3** (*tr*) to dismiss, discharge, or expel **4** (*tr*) to empty the contents of, esp in order to clean, tidy, or rearrange **5** (*copula*) **a** to prove to be **b** to end up; result: *it all turned out well* **6** (*tr*) to fit as with clothes: *that woman turns her children out well* **7** (*intr*) to assemble or gather **8** (of a soldier) to parade or to call (a soldier) to parade **9** (*intr*) *informal* to get out of bed **10** (*intr; foll by for*) *informal* to make an appearance, esp in a sporting competition: *he was asked to turn out for Liverpool* ▷ *n* **turnout 11** the body of people appearing together at a gathering **12** the quantity or amount produced **13** an array of clothing or equipment

turn over *vb* (*adverb*) **1** to change or cause to change position, esp so as to reverse top and bottom **2** to start (an engine), esp with a starting handle, or (of an engine) to start or function correctly **3** to shift or cause to shift position, as by rolling from side to side **4** (*tr*) to deliver; transfer **5** (*tr*) to consider carefully **6** (*tr*) **a** to sell and replenish (stock in trade) **b** to transact business and so generate gross revenue of (a specified sum) **7** (*tr*) to invest and recover (capital) **8** (*tr*) *slang* to rob ▷ *n* **turnover 9 a** the amount of business, usually expressed in terms of gross revenue, transacted during a specified period **b** (*as modifier*): *a turnover tax* **10** the rate at which stock in trade is sold and replenished **11** a change or reversal of position **12** a small semicircular or triangular pastry case filled with fruit, jam, etc **13 a** the number of workers employed by a firm in a given period to replace those who have left **b** the ratio between this number and the average number of employees during the same period **14** *banking* the amount of capital funds loaned on call during a specified period ▷ *adj* **15** (*prenominal*) able or designed to be turned or folded over

turnpike ('tɜːnˌpaɪk) *n* **1** (between the mid-16th and late 19th centuries) **a** gates or some other barrier set across a road to prevent passage until a toll had been paid **b** a road on which a turnpike was operated **2** an obsolete word for **turnstile** (sense 1) **3** *US* a motorway for use of which a toll is charged [C15: from TURN + PIKE²]

turnround ('tɜːnˌraʊnd) *n* another word for **turnaround**

turnspit ('tɜːnˌspɪt) *n* **1** (formerly) a servant or small dog whose job was to turn the spit on which meat, poultry, etc, was roasting **2** a spit that can be so turned

turnstile ('tɜːnˌstaɪl) *n* a mechanical gate or barrier with metal arms that are turned to admit one person at a time, usually in one direction only

turnstone ('tɜːnˌstəʊn) *n* either of two shore birds of the genus *Arenaria*, esp *A. interpres* (**ruddy turnstone**). They are related and similar to plovers and sandpipers [C17: so called because it turns over stones in search of food]

turntable ('tɜːn,teɪbəl) n 1 the circular horizontal platform that rotates a gramophone record while it is being played 2 a flat circular platform that can be rotated about its centre, used for turning locomotives and cars 3 the revolvable platform on a microscope on which specimens are examined

turntable ladder n Brit a power-operated extending ladder mounted on a fire engine. US and Canadian name: aerial ladder

turn to vb (intr, adverb) to set about a task

turn up vb (adverb) 1 (intr) to arrive or appear 2 to find or be found, esp by accident 3 (tr) to increase the flow, volume, etc, of ▷ n **turn-up** 4 (often plural) Brit the turned-up fold at the bottom of some trouser legs.) 5 informal an unexpected or chance occurrence

turpentine ('tɜːpən,taɪn) n 1 Also called: gum turpentine any of various viscous oleoresins obtained from various coniferous trees, esp from the longleaf pine, and used as the main source of commercial turpentine 2 a brownish-yellow sticky viscous oleoresin that exudes from the terebinth tree 3 Also called: oil of turpentine, spirits of turpentine a colourless flammable volatile liquid with a pungent odour, distilled from turpentine oleoresin. It is an essential oil containing a mixture of terpenes and is used as a solvent for paints and in medicine as a rubefacient and expectorant 4 Also called: turpentine substitute, white spirit (not in technical usage) any one of a number of thinners for paints and varnishes, consisting of fractions of petroleum. Related adj: terebinthine ▷ vb (tr) 5 to treat or saturate with turpentine [C14 terebentyne, from Medieval Latin terbentīna, from Latin terebinthīna turpentine, from terebinthus the turpentine tree, TEREBINTH]

turpentine tree n 1 a tropical African leguminous tree, Copaifera mopane, yielding a hard dark wood and a useful resin 2 either of two Australian evergreen myrtaceous trees, Syncarpia laurifolia or S. glomulifera, that have durable wood and are sometimes planted as shade trees

turpeth ('tɜːpɪθ) n 1 a convolvulaceous plant, Operculina turpethum, of the East Indies, having roots with purgative properties 2 the root of this plant or the drug obtained from it [c14: from Medieval Latin turbithum, ultimately from Arabic turbid]

Turpin ('tɜːpɪn) n Dick. 1706–39, English highwayman

turpitude ('tɜːpɪ,tjuːd) n base character or action; depravity [c15: from Latin turpitūdō ugliness, from turpis base]

turps (tɜːps) n (functioning as singular) Brit short for turpentine (sense 3)

turquoise ('tɜːkwɔɪz, -kwɑːz) n 1 a greenish-blue fine-grained secondary mineral consisting of hydrated copper aluminium phosphate. It occurs in igneous rocks rich in aluminium and is used as a gemstone. Formula: $CuAl_6(PO_4)_4(OH)_8.4H_2O$ 2 a the colour of turquoise b (as adjective): a turquoise dress [c14: from Old French turqueise Turkish (stone)]

turret ('tʌrɪt) n 1 a small tower that projects from the wall of a building, esp a medieval castle 2 a a self-contained structure, capable of rotation, in which weapons are mounted, esp in tanks and warships b a similar structure on an aircraft that houses one or more guns and sometimes a gunner 3 (on a machine tool) a turret-like steel structure with tools projecting radially that can be indexed round to select or to bring each tool to bear on the work [c14: from Old French torete, from tor tower, from Latin turris]

turret lathe n another name for capstan lathe

turtle¹ ('tɜːtəl) n 1 any of various aquatic chelonian reptiles, esp those of the marine family Chelonidae, having a flattened shell enclosing the body and flipper-like limbs adapted for swimming 2 turn turtle to capsize [c17: from French tortue TORTOISE (influenced by TURTLE²)]

turtle² ('tɜːtəl) n an archaic name for turtledove [Old English turtla, from Latin turtur, of imitative origin; related to German Turteltaube]

turtleback ('tɜːtəl,bæk) n an arched projection over the upper deck of a ship at the bow and sometimes at the stern for protection in heavy seas

turtledove ('tɜːtəl,dʌv) n 1 any of several Old World doves of the genus Streptopelia, having a brown plumage with speckled wings and a long dark tail 2 a gentle or loving person [see TURTLE²]

turtleneck ('tɜːtəl,nɛk) n a round high close-fitting neck on a sweater or the sweater itself

turves (tɜːvz) n a plural of turf

Tuscan ('tʌskən) adj 1 of or relating to Tuscany, its inhabitants, or their dialect of Italian 2 of, denoting, or relating to one of the five classical orders of architecture: characterized by a column with an unfluted shaft and a capital and base with mouldings but no decoration ▷ n 3 a native or inhabitant of Tuscany 4 any of the dialects of Italian spoken in Tuscany, esp the dialect of Florence: the standard form of Italian

Tuscany ('tʌskənɪ) n a region of central Italy, on the Ligurian and Tyrrhenian Seas: corresponds roughly to ancient Etruria; a region of numerous small states in medieval times; united in the 15th and 16th centuries under Florence; united with the rest of Italy in 1861. Capital: Florence. Pop: 3 516 296 (2003 est). Area: 22 990 sq km (8876 sq miles). Italian name: Toscana

tusche (tʊʃ) n a substance used in lithography for drawing the design and as a resist in silk-screen printing and lithography [from German, from tuschen to touch up with colour or ink, from French toucher to TOUCH]

Tusculum ('tʌskjʊləm) n an ancient city in Latium near Rome

tush (tʌʃ) interj archaic an exclamation of disapproval or contempt [c15: Middle English, of imitative origin]

tusk (tʌsk) n 1 a pointed elongated usually paired tooth in the elephant, walrus, and certain other mammals that is often used for fighting 2 the canine tooth of certain animals, esp horses 3 a sharp pointed projection ▷ vb 4 to stab, tear, or gore with the tusks [Old English tūsc; related to Old Frisian tosk; see TOOTH] > tusked adj

tusker ('tʌskə) n any animal with prominent tusks, esp a wild boar or elephant

tusk shell n any of various burrowing seashore molluscs of the genus Dentalium and related genera that have a long narrow tubular shell open at both ends: class Scaphopoda

Tussaud (French tyso) n Marie (mari). 1760–1850, Swiss modeller in wax, who founded a permanent exhibition in London of historical and contemporary figures

tussis ('tʌsɪs) n the technical name for cough. See pertussis [Latin: cough] > 'tussive adj

tussle ('tʌsəl) vb 1 (intr) to fight or wrestle in a vigorous way; struggle ▷ n 2 a vigorous fight; scuffle; struggle [c15: related to Old High German zūsen; see TOUSLE]

tussock ('tʌsək) n 1 a dense tuft of vegetation, esp of grass 2 Austral & NZ a short for tussock grass b the tussock country where tussock grass grows [c16: perhaps related to TUSK] > 'tussocky adj

tussock grass n Austral & NZ any of several pasture grasses of the genus Poa

tussore (tʊ'sɔː, 'tʌsə), **tusser** ('tʌsə) or chiefly US **tussah** ('tʌsə) n 1 a strong coarse brownish Indian silk obtained from the cocoons of an Oriental saturniid silkworm, Antheraea paphia 2 the silkworm producing this silk [c17: from Hindi tasar shuttle, from Sanskrit tasara a wild silkworm]

tut (pronounced as an alveolar click; spelling pron tʌt) interj, n, vb tuts, tutting, tutted short for tut-tut

Tutankhamen (,tuːtənˈkɑːmɛn, -mən) or **Tutankhamun** (,tuːtənkɑːˈmuːn) n king (1361–1352 BC) of the 18th dynasty of Egypt His tomb near Luxor, discovered in 1922, contained many material objects

tutelage ('tjuːtɪlɪdʒ) n 1 the act or office of a guardian or tutor 2 instruction or guidance, esp by a tutor 3 the condition of being under the supervision of a guardian or tutor [c17: from Latin tūtēla a caring for, from tuērī to watch over; compare TUITION]

tutelary ('tjuːtɪlərɪ) or **tutelar** ('tjuːtɪlə) adj 1 invested with the role of guardian or protector 2 of or relating to a guardian or guardianship ▷ n, pl -laries or -lars 3 a tutelary person, deity, or saint

tutor ('tju:tə) *n* **1** a teacher, usually instructing individual pupils and often engaged privately **2** (at universities, colleges, etc) a member of staff responsible for the teaching and supervision of a certain number of students ▷ *vb* **3** to act as a tutor to (someone); instruct **4** (*tr*) to act as guardian to; have care of [c14: from Latin: a watcher, from *tuērī* to watch over] > 'tutorage *or* 'tutor,ship *n*

tutorial (tju:'tɔ:rɪəl) *n* **1** a period of intensive tuition given by a tutor to an individual student or to a small group of students ▷ *adj* **2** of or relating to a tutor

tutsan ('tʌtsən) *n* a woodland shrub, *Hypericum androsaemum*, of Europe and W Asia, having yellow flowers and reddish-purple fruits: family *Hypericaceae* [c15: from Old French *toute-saine* (unattested), literally: all healthy]

tutti ('tʊtɪ) *adj*, *adv music* to be performed by the whole orchestra, choir, etc [c18: from Italian, pl of *tutto* all, from Latin *tōtus*]

tutti-frutti ('tu:tɪ'fru:tɪ) *n* **1** *pl* -fruttis an ice cream or a confection containing small pieces of candied or fresh fruits **2** a preserve of chopped mixed fruits, often with brandy syrup **3** a flavour like that of many fruits combined [from Italian, literally: all the fruits]

tut-tut (pronounced as alveolar clicks; spelling pron 'tʌt'tʌt) *interj* **1** an exclamation of mild reprimand, disapproval, or surprise ▷ *vb* -tuts, -tutting, -tutted **2** (*intr*) to express disapproval by the exclamation of "tut-tut." ▷ *n* **3** the act of tut-tutting

tutty ('tʌtɪ) *n* finely powdered impure zinc oxide obtained from the flues of zinc-smelting furnaces and used as a polishing powder [c14: from Old French *tutie*, from Arabic *tūtiyā*, probably from Persian, from Sanskrit *tuttha*]

tutu ('tu:tu:) *n* a very short skirt worn by ballerinas, made of projecting layers of stiffened sheer material [from French, changed from the nursery word *cucu* backside, from *cul*, from Latin *cūlus* the buttocks]

Tutu ('tu:tu:) *n* **Desmond**. born 1931, South African clergyman, noted for his opposition to apartheid: Anglican Bishop of Johannesburg (1984–86) and Archbishop of Cape Town (1986–96); in 1995 he became leader of the Truth and Reconciliation Commission, established to investigate human rights violations during the apartheid era. Nobel peace prize 1984

Tutuila (,tu:tu:'i:lə) *n* the largest island of American Samoa, in the SW Pacific. Chief town and port: Pago Pago. Pop: 55 876 (2000). Area: 135 sq km (52 sq miles)

Tutuola ('tu:tu:,əʊlə) *n* **Amos**. 1920–97, Nigerian writer: his books include *The Palm-Wine Drinkard* (1952) and *Pauper, Brawler and Slanderer* (1987)

Tuvalu (,tu:və'lu:) *n* a country in the SW Pacific, comprising a group of nine coral islands: established as a British protectorate in 1892. From 1915 until 1975 the islands formed part of the British colony of the Gilbert and Ellice Islands; achieved full independence in 1978; a member of the Commonwealth (formerly a special member not represented at all meetings, until 2000). Languages: English and Tuvaluan. Religion: Christian majority. Currency: Australian dollar; Tuvalu dollars are also used. Capital: Funafuti. Pop: 11 000 (2003 est). Area: 26 sq km (10 sq miles). Former names: Lagoon Islands, Ellice Islands > ,Tuva'luan *adj*, *n*

Tuva Republic ('tu:və) *n* a constituent republic of S Russia: mountainous. Capital: Kizyl. Pop: 305 500 (2002). Area: 170 500 sq km (65 800 sq miles)

tu-whit tu-whoo (tə'wɪt tə'wu:) *interj* an imitation or representation of the sound made by an owl

tuxedo (tʌk'si:dəʊ) *n*, *pl* -dos the usual US and Canadian name for **dinner jacket** [c19: named after a country club in *Tuxedo Park*, New York]

Tuxtla Gutiérrez (*Spanish* 'tustla gu'tjɛrrɛθ) *n* a city in SE Mexico, capital of Chiapas state: agricultural centre. Pop: 723 000 (2005 est)

tuyère ('twi:ɛə, 'twaɪə; *French* tyjɛr) *or* **twyer** ('twaɪə) *n* a water-cooled nozzle through which air is blown into a cupola, blast furnace, or forge [c18: from French, from *tuyau* pipe, from Old French *tuel*, probably of Germanic origin]

TV *abbreviation* television

TVEI *abbreviation* (in Britain) technical and vocational educational initiative: a national educational scheme in which pupils gain practical experience in technology and industry often through work placement

Tver (*Russian* tvjerj) *n* a city in central Russia, at the confluence of the Volga and Tversta Rivers: chief port of the upper Volga, linked by canal with Moscow. Pop: 402 000 (2005 est). Former name (1932–91): Kalinin

TVM *abbreviation* television movie: a film made specifically for television, and not intended for release in cinemas

TVNZ *abbreviation* Television New Zealand

TVP *abbreviation* textured vegetable protein: a protein obtained from soya beans or other vegetables that have been spun into fibres and flavoured: used esp as a substitute for meat

TVR *abbreviation* television rating: a measurement of the popularity of a television programme based on a survey

TVRO *abbreviation* television receive only: an antenna and associated apparatus for reception from a broadcasting satellite

twaddle ('twɒdəl) *n* **1** silly, trivial, or pretentious talk or writing; nonsense ▷ *vb* **2** to talk or write (something) in a silly or pretentious way [c16 *twattle*, variant of *twittle* or *tittle*; see TITTLE-TATTLE] > 'twaddler *n*

twain (tweɪn) *determiner*, *n* an archaic word for **two** [Old English *twēgen*; related to Old Saxon *twēne*, Old High German *zwēne*, Old Norse *tveir*, Gothic *twai*]

Twain (tweɪn) *n* **1 Mark**, pen name of *Samuel Langhorne Clemens*. 1835–1910, US novelist and humorist, famous for his classics *The Adventures of Tom Sawyer* (1876) and *The Adventures of Huckleberry Finn* (1885) **2 Shania** (ʃə'naɪə), real name *Eilleen Regina Edwards*. born 1965, Canadian country-rock singer; her bestselling recordings include *The Woman In Me* (1995) *Come On Over* (1997), and *UP!* (2002)

twang (twæŋ) *n* **1** a sharp ringing sound produced by or as if by the plucking of a taut string **2** the act of plucking a string to produce such a sound **3** a strongly nasal quality in a person's speech, esp in certain dialects ▷ *vb* **4** to make or cause to make a twang **5** to strum (music, a tune, etc) **6** to speak or utter with a sharp nasal voice **7** (*intr*) to be released or move with a twang: *the arrow twanged away* [c16: of imitative origin] > 'twangy *adj*

'twas (twɒz; *unstressed* twəz) *poetic or dialect contraction of* it was

twat (twæt, twɒt) *n taboo*, *slang* **1** the female genitals **2** a foolish or despicable person [of unknown origin]

twayblade ('tweɪ,bleɪd) *n* **1** any terrestrial orchid of the genus *Listera*, having a basal pair of oval unstalked leaves arranged opposite each other **2** any of various other orchids with paired basal leaves [c16: translation of Medieval Latin *bifolium* having two leaves, from obsolete *tway* TWO + BLADE]

tweak (twi:k) *vb* (*tr*) **1** to twist, jerk, or pinch with a sharp or sudden movement **2** *informal* to make a minor alteration ▷ *n* **3** an instance of tweaking **4** *informal* a minor alteration [Old English *twiccian*; related to Old High German *zwecchōn*; see TWITCH]

twee (twi:) *adj Brit* excessively sentimental, sweet, or pretty [c19: from *tweet*, mincing or affected pronunciation of SWEET] > 'tweely *adv*

tweed (twi:d) *n* **1 a** thick woollen often knobbly cloth produced originally in Scotland **2** (*plural*) clothes made of this cloth, esp a man's or woman's suit **3** (*plural*) *Austral informal* trousers [c19: probably from *tweel*, a Scottish variant of TWILL, influenced by TWEED]

Tweed (twi:d) *n* a river in SE Scotland and NE England, flowing east and forming part of the border between Scotland and England, then crossing into England to enter the North Sea at Berwick. Length: 156 km (97 miles)

Tweeddale ('twi:d,deɪl) *n* another name for **Peeblesshire**

Tweedledum and Tweedledee (,twi:dəl'dʌm, ,twi:dəl'di:) *n* any two persons or things that differ only slightly from each other; two of a kind [c19: from the proverbial names of George Frederick Handel (1685–1759), German composer, and the musician

Buononcini, who were supported by rival factions though it was thought by some that there was nothing to choose between them. The names were popularized by Lewis Carroll's use of them in *Through the Looking Glass* (1872)]

Tweedsmuir ('twiːdzmjʊə) *n* **Baron Tweedsmuir** the title of Scottish novelist John Buchan. See **Buchan**

tweedy ('twiːdɪ) *adj* **tweedier, tweediest** **1** of, made of, or resembling tweed **2** showing a fondness for a hearty outdoor life, usually associated with wearers of tweeds

'tween (twiːn) *poetic or dialect contraction of* between

'tween deck or **'tween decks** *n nautical* a space between two continuous decks of a vessel

tweet (twiːt) *interj* **1** (*often reiterated*) an imitation or representation of the thin chirping sound made by small or young birds ▷ *vb* **2** (*intr*) to make this sound [c19: of imitative origin]

tweeter ('twiːtə) *n* a loudspeaker used in high-fidelity systems for the reproduction of high audio frequencies. It is usually employed in conjunction with a woofer and a crossover network [c20: from TWEET]

tweezers ('twiːzəz) *pl n* a small pincer-like instrument for handling small objects, plucking out hairs, etc. Also called: **pair of tweezers**, (*esp US*) **tweezer** [c17: plural of *tweezer* (on the model of *scissors*, etc), from *tweeze* case of instruments, from French *étuis* cases (of instruments), from Old French *estuier* to preserve, from Vulgar Latin *studiāre* (unattested) to keep, from Latin *studēre* to care about]

Twelfth Day *n* Jan 6, the twelfth day after Christmas and the feast of the Epiphany, formerly observed as the final day of the Christmas celebrations

twelfth man *n* a reserve player in a cricket team

Twelfth Night *n* **a** the evening of Jan 5, the eve of Twelfth Day, formerly observed with various festal celebrations **b** the evening of Twelfth Day itself

twelve (twɛlv) *n* **1** the cardinal number that is the sum of ten and two **2** a numeral, 12, XII, etc, representing this number **3** something represented by, representing, or consisting of 12 units **4** Also called: **twelve o'clock** noon or midnight ▷ *determiner* **5 a** amounting to twelve **b** (*as pronoun*): *twelve have arrived* ▷ Related adj: **duodecimal** [Old English *twelf*; related to Old Frisian *twelif*, Old High German *zwelif*, Old Norse *tolf*, Gothic *twalif*] > **twelfth** (twɛlfθ) *adj, n*

twelve-inch *n* a gramophone record 12 inches in diameter and played at 45 revolutions per minute, usually containing an extended remix of a single

twelvemo ('twɛlvməʊ) *n, pl* **-mos** *bookbinding* another word for **duodecimo**

twelvemonth ('twɛlv,mʌnθ) *n chiefly Brit* an archaic or dialect word for **year**

twelve-tone *adj* of, relating to, or denoting the type of serial music invented and developed by Arnold Schoenberg, which uses as musical material a tone row formed by the 12 semitones of the chromatic scale, together with its inverted and retrograde versions. The technique has been applied in various ways by different composers and usually results in music in which there are few, if any, tonal centres. See **serialism**

twenty ('twɛntɪ) *n, pl* **-ties** **1** the cardinal number that is the product of ten and two; a score **2** a numeral, 20, XX, etc, representing this number **3** something representing, represented by, or consisting of 20 units ▷ *determiner* **4 a** amounting to twenty: *twenty questions* **b** (*as pronoun*): *to order twenty* [Old English *twēntig*; related to Old High German *zweinzug*, German *zwanzig*] > **'twentieth** *adj, n*

twenty-four-seven or **24/7** *adv informal* twenty-four hours a day, seven days a week; constantly; all the time: *consultants would not be available 24/7*

twenty-six counties *pl n* the counties of the Republic of Ireland

twenty-sixer *n Canadian informal* a liquor bottle of around 26 ounces (0.750 litre) capacity

Twenty20 *n* a form of one-day cricket in which each side bats for twenty overs

twenty-twenty *adj med* (of vision) being of normal acuity: usually written 20/20

'twere (twɜː; *unstressed* twə) *poetic or dialect contraction of* it were

twerp or **twirp** (twɜːp) *n informal* a silly, weak-minded, or contemptible person [c20: of unknown origin]

twibill or **twibil** ('twaɪ,bɪl) *n* **1** a mattock with a blade shaped like an adze at one end and like an axe at the other **2** *archaic* a double-bladed battle-axe [Old English, from *twi-* two, double + *bill* sword, BILL³]

twice (twaɪs) *adv* **1** two times; on two occasions or in two cases **2** double in degree or quantity: *twice as long* [Old English *twiwa*; related to Old Norse *tvisvar*, Middle Low German *twiges*]

Twickenham ('twɪkənəm) *n* a former town in SE England, on the River Thames: part of the Greater London borough of Richmond-upon-Thames since 1965; contains the English Rugby Football Union ground

twiddle ('twɪdᵊl) *vb* **1** (*when intr*, often foll *by with*) to twirl or fiddle (with), often in an idle way **2** to do nothing; be unoccupied **3** (*intr*) to turn, twirl, or rotate **4** (*intr*) *rare* to be occupied with trifles ▷ *n* **5** an act or instance of twiddling [c16: probably a blend of TWIRL + FIDDLE] > **'twiddler** *n*

twig¹ (twɪg) *n* **1** any small branch or shoot of a tree or other woody plant **2** something resembling this, esp a minute branch of a blood vessel [Old English *twigge*; related to Old Norse *dvika* consisting of two, Old High German *zwīg* twig, Old Danish *tvige* fork] > **'twiggy** *adj*

twig² (twɪg) *vb* **twigs, twigging, twigged** *Brit informal* **1** to understand (something) **2** to find out or suddenly comprehend (something): *he hasn't twigged yet* [c18: perhaps from Scottish Gaelic *tuig* I understand]

twilight ('twaɪ,laɪt) *n* **1** the soft diffused light occurring when the sun is just below the horizon, esp following sunset **2** the period in which this light occurs **3** any faint light **4** a period in which strength, importance, etc, are waning **5** (*modifier*) **a** of or relating to the period towards the end of the day: *the twilight shift* **b** of or relating to the final phase of a particular era: *the twilight days of the Bush presidency* **c** denoting irregularity and obscurity: *a twilight existence* [c15: literally: half-light (between day and night), from Old English *twi-* half + LIGHT¹] > **'twilit** ('twaɪ,lɪt) *adj*

Twilight of the Gods *n* another term for **Götterdämmerung, Ragnarök**

twilight sleep *n med* a state of partial anaesthesia in which the patient retains a slight degree of consciousness

twilight zone *n* **1** any indefinite or transitional condition or area **2** an area of a city or town, usually surrounding the central business district, where houses have become dilapidated

twill (twɪl) *adj* **1** (in textiles) of or designating a weave in which the weft yarns are worked around two or more warp yarns to produce an effect of parallel diagonal lines or ribs ▷ *n* **2** any fabric so woven ▷ *vb* **3** (*tr*) to weave in this fashion [Old English *twilic* having a double thread; related to Old High German *zwilīth* twill, Latin *bilix* two-threaded]

'twill (twɪl) *poetic or dialect contraction of* it will

twin (twɪn) *n* **1 a** either of two persons or animals conceived at the same time **b** (*as modifier*): *a twin brother*. See also **identical** (sense 3), **fraternal** (sense 3) **2 a** either of two persons or things that are identical or very similar; counterpart **b** (*as modifier*): *twin carburettors* **3** Also called: **macle** a crystal consisting of two parts each of which has a definite orientation to the other ▷ *vb* **twins, twinned 4** to pair or be paired together; couple **5** (*intr*) to bear twins **6** (*intr*) (of a crystal) to form into a twin **7** (*tr*) **a** to create a reciprocal relation between (two towns in different countries); pair (a town) with another in a different country **b** (*intr*) (of a town) to be paired with a town in a different country [Old English *twinn*; related to Old High German *zwiniling* twin, Old Norse *tvinnr* double] > **'twinning** *n*

twin bed *n* one of a pair of matching single beds

twine (twaɪn) *n* **1** string made by twisting together fibres of hemp, cotton, etc **2** the act or an instance of twining **3** something produced or characterized by twining **4** a twist, coil, or convolution **5** a knot, tangle, or snarl ▷ *vb* **6** (*tr*) to twist together; interweave **7** (*tr*) to form by or as if by twining **8** (when *intr*, often foll by *around*) to wind or cause to wind, esp in spirals [Old English *twīn*; related to Old Frisian *twīne*, Dutch *twijn* twine, Lithuanian *dvynu* twins; see TWIN] ▷ **'twiner** *n*

twinge (twɪndʒ) *n* **1** a sudden brief darting or stabbing pain **2** a sharp emotional pang ▷ *vb* **3** to have or cause to have a twinge [Old English *twengan* to pinch; related to Old High German *zwengen*]

twinkle ('twɪŋkəl) *vb* (*mainly intr*) **1** to emit or reflect light in a flickering manner; shine brightly and intermittently; sparkle **2** (of the eyes) to sparkle, esp with amusement or delight **3** *rare* to move about quickly ▷ *n* **4** an intermittent gleam of light; flickering brightness; sparkle or glimmer **5** an instant [Old English *twinclian*; related to Middle High German *zwinken* to blink] ▷ **'twinkler** *n* ▷ **'twinkly** *adj*

twinkling ('twɪŋklɪŋ) *or* **twink** (twɪŋk) *n* a very short time; instant; moment. Also called: **twinkling of an eye**

Twins (twɪnz) *pl n* **the Twins** the constellation Gemini, the third sign of the zodiac

twin-screw *adj* (of a vessel) having two propellers

twinset ('twɪnˌsɛt) *n* Brit a matching jumper and cardigan

twin town *n* Brit a town that has civic associations, such as reciprocal visits and cultural exchanges, with a foreign town, usually of similar size and sometimes with other similarities, as in commercial activities

twin-tub *n* a type of washing machine that has two revolving drums, one for washing and the other for spin-drying

twirl (twɜːl) *vb* **1** to move or cause to move around rapidly and repeatedly in a circle **2** (*tr*) to twist, wind, or twiddle, often idly: *she twirled her hair around her finger* **3** (*intr*; often foll by *around* or *about*) to turn suddenly to face another way ▷ *n* **4** an act of rotating or being rotated; whirl or twist **5** something wound around or twirled; coil **6** a written flourish or squiggle [C16: perhaps a blend of TWIST + WHIRL] ▷ **'twirler** *n*

twirp (twɜːp) *n* a variant spelling of **twerp**

twist (twɪst) *vb* **1** to cause (one end or part) to turn or (of one end or part) to turn in the opposite direction from another; coil or spin **2** to distort or be distorted; change in shape **3** to wind or cause to wind; twine, coil, or intertwine **4** to force or be forced out of the natural form or position **5** (*usually passive*) to change or cause to change for the worse in character, meaning, etc; pervert: *his ideas are twisted; she twisted the statement* **6** to revolve or cause to revolve; rotate **7** (*tr*) to wrench with a turning action **8** (*intr*) to follow a winding course **9** (*intr*) to squirm, as with pain **10** (*intr*) to dance the twist **11** (*tr*) Brit informal to cheat; swindle **12 twist someone's arm** to persuade or coerce someone ▷ *n* **13** the act or an instance of twisting **14** something formed by or as if by twisting **15** a decisive change of direction, aim, meaning, or character **16** (in a novel, play, etc) an unexpected event, revelation, or other development **17** a bend: *a twist in the road* **18** a distortion of the original or natural shape or form **19** a jerky pull, wrench, or turn **20** a strange personal characteristic, esp a bad one **21** a confused mess, tangle, or knot made by twisting **22** a twisted thread used in sewing where extra strength is needed **23 the twist** a modern dance popular in the 1960s, in which couples vigorously twist the hips in time to rhythmic music **24** a bread loaf or roll made of one or more pieces of twisted dough **25** a thin sliver of peel from a lemon, lime, etc, twisted and added to a drink **26 a** a cigar made by twisting three cigars around one another **b** chewing tobacco made in the form of a roll by twisting the leaves together **27** *physics* torsional deformation or shear stress or strain **28** *sport* chiefly US & Canadian spin given to a ball in various games, esp baseball **29** the extent to which the grooves in the bore of a rifled firearm are spiralled **30 round the twist** Brit slang mad; eccentric [Old English; related to German dialect *Zwist* a quarrel, Dutch *twisten* to quarrel] ▷ **'twisty** *adj*

twist drill *n* a drill bit having two helical grooves running from the point along the shank to clear swarf

and cuttings as it turns

twister ('twɪstə) *n* **1** Brit a swindling or dishonest person **2** a person or thing that twists, such as a device used in making ropes **3** US & Canadian an informal name for **tornado 4** a ball moving with a twisting motion

twist grip *n* a handlebar control in the form of a ratchet-controlled rotating grip, used on some bicycles and motorcycles as a gear-change control and on motorcycles as an accelerator

twit¹ (twɪt) *vb* **twits**, **twitting**, **twitted 1** (*tr*) to tease, taunt, or reproach, often in jest ▷ *n* **2** US & Canadian informal a nervous or excitable state **3** *rare* a reproach; taunt [Old English *ætwītan*, from *æt* against + *wītan* to accuse; related to Old High German *wīzan* to punish]

twit² (twɪt) *n* informal, chiefly Brit a foolish or stupid person; idiot [C19: from TWIT¹ (originally in the sense: a person given to twitting)]

twitch (twɪtʃ) *vb* **1** to move or cause to move in a jerky spasmodic way **2** (*tr*) to pull or draw (something) with a quick jerky movement **3** (*intr*) to hurt with a sharp spasmodic pain ▷ *n* **4** a sharp jerking movement **5** a mental or physical twinge **6** a sudden muscular spasm, esp one caused by a nervous condition **7** a loop of cord used to control a horse by drawing it tight about its upper lip [Old English *twiccian* to pluck; related to Old High German *zwecchōn* to pinch, Dutch *twicken*]

twitcher ('twɪtʃə) *n* **1** a person or thing that twitches **2** informal a bird-watcher who tries to spot as many rare varieties as possible

twitch grass *n* another name for **couch grass**. Sometimes shortened to: **twitch** [C16: a variant of QUITCH GRASS]

twite (twaɪt) *n* a N European finch, *Acanthis flavirostris*, with a brown streaked plumage [C16: imitative of its cry]

twitter ('twɪtə) *vb* **1** (*intr*) (esp of a bird) to utter a succession of chirping sounds **2** (*intr*) to talk or move rapidly and tremulously **3** (*intr*) to giggle **4** (*tr*) to utter in a chirping way ▷ *n* **5** a twittering sound, esp of a bird **6** the act of twittering **7** a state of nervous excitement (esp in the phrase **in a twitter**) [C14: of imitative origin] ▷ **'twitterer** *n* ▷ **'twittery** *adj*

'twixt *or* **twixt** (twɪkst) *poetic contraction of* betwixt

two (tuː) *n* **1** the cardinal number that is the sum of one and one. It is a prime number **2** a numeral, 2, II, (ii), etc, representing this number **3** something representing, represented by, or consisting of two units, such as a playing card with two symbols on it **4** Also called: **two o'clock** two hours after noon or midnight **5 in two** in or into two parts **6 put two and two together** to make an inference from available evidence, esp an obvious inference **7 that makes two of us** the same applies to me ▷ *determiner* **8 a** amounting to two: *two nails* **b** (*as pronoun*): *he bought two* Related adjs: **binary**, **double**, **dual** [Old English *twā* (feminine); related to Old High German *zwā*, Old Norse *tvau*, Latin, Greek *duo*]

two-by-four *n* **1** a length of untrimmed timber with a cross section that measures 2 inches by 4 inches **2** a trimmed timber joist with a cross section that measures 1½ inches by 3½ inches

twoccing *or* **twocking** ('twɒkɪŋ) *n* Brit slang the act of breaking into a motor vehicle and driving it away [C20: from T(aking) W(ithout) O(wner's) C(onsent), the legal offence with which car thieves may be charged] ▷ **'twoccer** *or* **'twocker** *n*

two-dimensional *adj* **1** of, having, or relating to two dimensions, usually describable in terms of length and breadth or length and height **2** lying on a plane; having an area but not enclosing any volume **3** lacking in depth, as characters in a literary work

two-edged *adj* **1** having two cutting edges **2** (esp of a remark) having two interpretations, such as *she looks nice when she smiles*

two-faced *adj* deceitful; insincere; hypocritical

twofold ('tuːˌfəʊld) *adj* **1** equal to twice as many or twice as much; double **2** made of two parts; dual ▷ *adv* **3** doubly

two-four *n* Canadian informal a box containing 24 bottles of beer

two-handed *adj* **1** requiring the use of both hands

2 ambidextrous 3 requiring the participation or cooperation of two people

twonie ('tu:nɪ) n variant spelling of **toonie**

two-pack adj (of a paint, filler, etc) supplied as two separate components, for example a base and a catalyst, that are mixed together immediately before use

twopence or **tuppence** ('tʌpəns) n Brit 1 the sum of two pennies 2 (used with a negative) something of little value (in the phrase **not care** or **give twopence**) 3 a former British silver coin, now only coined as Maundy money

twopenny or **tuppenny** ('tʌpənɪ) adj chiefly Brit 1 Also: twopenny-halfpenny cheap or tawdry 2 (intensifier): a twopenny damn 3 worth two pence

two-phase adj (of an electrical circuit, device, etc) generating or using two alternating voltages of the same frequency, displaced in phase by 90°

two-piece adj 1 consisting of two separate parts, usually matching, as of a garment ▷ n 2 such an outfit

two-ply adj 1 made of two thicknesses, layers, or strands ▷ n, pl -plies 2 a two-ply wood, knitting yarn, etc

Two Sicilies pl n the Two Sicilies a former kingdom of S Italy, consisting of the kingdoms of Sicily and Naples (1061–1860)

two-sided adj 1 having two sides or aspects 2 controversial; debatable

two solitudes n Canadian a term for the situation of English and French Canada, considered as socially and culturally isolated from each other [c20: from Two Solitudes, a novel by Canadian writer Hugh MacLennan (1907–90)]

twosome ('tu:səm) n 1 two together, esp two people 2 a match between two people

two-step n 1 an old-time dance in duple time 2 a piece of music composed for or in the rhythm of such a dance

two-stroke adj relating to or designating an internal-combustion engine whose piston makes two strokes for every explosion. US and Canadian word: two-cycle

Two Thousand Guineas or usually written **2000 Guineas** n (functioning as singular) an annual horse race run at Newmarket since 1809

two-time vb informal to deceive (someone, esp a lover) by carrying on a relationship with another ▷ **two-'timer** n

two-tone adj 1 of two colours or two shades of the same colour 2 (esp of sirens, car horns, etc) producing or consisting of two notes

'twould (twʊd) poetic or dialect contraction of it would

two-up n chiefly Austral a gambling game in which two coins are tossed or spun. Bets are made on both coins landing with the same face uppermost

two-way adj 1 moving, permitting movement, or operating in either of two opposite directions 2 involving two participants 3 involving reciprocal obligation or mutual action 4 (of a radio, telephone, etc) allowing communications in two directions using both transmitting and receiving equipment

two-way mirror n a half-silvered sheet of glass that functions as a mirror when viewed from one side but is translucent from the other

two-way street n an arrangement or a situation involving reciprocal obligation or mutual action

TX abbreviation 1 Texas 2 text messaging thanks

TXT text messaging abbreviation text

-ty¹ suffix of numerals denoting a multiple of ten: sixty; seventy [from Old English -tig TEN]

-ty² suffix forming nouns indicating state, condition, or quality: cruelty [from Old French -te, -tet, from Latin -tās, -tāt-; related to Greek -tēs]

Tyan-Shan ('tjan'ʃan) n transliteration of the Russian name for **Tian Shan**

Tyburn ('taɪbɜ:n) n (formerly) a place of execution in London, on the **River Tyburn** (a tributary of the Thames, now entirely below ground)

Tyche ('taɪkɪ) n Greek myth the goddess of fortune. Roman counterpart: Fortuna

tychism ('taɪkɪzəm) n philosophy the theory that chance is an objective reality at work in the universe, esp in evolutionary adaptations [from Greek tukhē chance]

tycoon (taɪ'ku:n) n 1 a business man of great wealth and power 2 an archaic name for **shogun** [c19: from Japanese taikun, from Chinese ta great + chün ruler]

tyke or **tike** (taɪk) n 1 a dog, esp a mongrel 2 informal a small or cheeky child: used esp in affectionate reproof 3 Brit dialect a rough ill-mannered person 4 Also called: Yorkshire tyke Brit slang, often offensive a person from Yorkshire 5 Austral slang, offensive a Roman Catholic [c14: from Old Norse tík bitch]

Tyler ('taɪlə) n 1 **John**. 1790–1862, US statesman; tenth president of the US (1841–45) 2 **Wat** (wɒt). died 1381, English leader of the Peasants' Revolt (1381)

tylopod ('taɪləʊ,pɒd) n any artiodactyl mammal of the suborder Tylopoda, having padded, rather than hoofed, digits: includes the camels and llamas [c19: from New Latin, from Greek tulos knob or tulē cushion + -POD]

Tylor ('taɪlə) n Sir **Edward Burnett**. 1832–1917, British anthropologist; first professor of anthropology at Oxford (1896). His Primitive Culture (1871) became a standard work

tympan ('tɪmpən) n 1 a membrane stretched over a frame or resonating cylinder, bowl, etc 2 printing packing interposed on a hand-operated text between the platen and the paper to be printed in order to provide an even impression 3 architect another name for **tympanum** (sense 3) [Old English timpana, from Latin; see TYMPANUM]

tympani ('tɪmpənɪ) pl n a variant spelling of **timpani**

tympanic bone n the part of the temporal bone in the mammalian skull that surrounds the auditory canal

tympanic membrane n the thin translucent oval membrane separating the external ear from the middle ear. It transmits vibrations produced by sound waves, via the ossicles, to the cochlea. Nontechnical name: eardrum

tympanites (,tɪmpə'naɪti:z) n distension of the abdomen caused by an abnormal accumulation of gas in the intestinal or peritoneal cavity, as in peritonitis. Also called: meteorism, tympany [c14: from Late Latin, from Greek tumpanitēs concerning a drum, from tumpanon drum] > tympanitic (,tɪmpə'nɪtɪk) adj

tympanitis (,tɪmpə'naɪtɪs) n inflammation of the eardrum

tympanum ('tɪmpənəm) n, pl -nums or -na (-nə) 1 a the cavity of the middle ear b another name for **tympanic membrane** 2 any diaphragm resembling that in the middle ear in function 3 Also called: tympan architect a the recessed space bounded by the cornices of a pediment, esp one that is triangular in shape and ornamented b the recessed space bounded by an arch and the lintel of a doorway or window below it 4 music a tympan or drum 5 a scoop wheel for raising water [c17: from Latin, from Greek tumpanon drum; related to Greek tuptein to beat]

Tyndale, Tindal or **Tindale** ('tɪndəl) n **William**. ?1492–1536, English Protestant and humanist, who translated the New Testament (1525), the Pentateuch (1530), and the Book of Jonah (1531) into English. He was burnt at the stake as a heretic

Tyndall ('tɪndəl) n **John**. 1820–93, Irish physicist, noted for his work on the radiation of heat by gases, the transmission of sound through the atmosphere, and the scattering of light

Tyndall effect ('tɪndəl) n the phenomenon in which light is scattered by particles of matter in its path. It enables a beam of light to become visible by illuminating dust particles, etc [c19: named after John Tyndall (1820–93), Irish physicist]

Tyndareus (tɪn'dærɪəs) n Greek myth a Spartan king; the husband of Leda

Tyne (taɪn) n a river in N England, flowing east to the North Sea. Length: 48 km (30 miles)

Tyne and Wear n a metropolitan county of NE England, administered since 1986 by the unitary authorities of Newcastle upon Tyne, North Tyneside, Gateshead, South Tyneside, and Sunderland. Area: 540 sq km (208 sq miles)

Tynemouth ('taɪn,maʊθ) n a port in NE England, in North Tyneside unitary authority, Tyne and Wear, at the mouth of the River Tyne: includes the port and industrial centre of North Shields; fishing, ship-repairing, and marine engineering. Pop: 17 056 (2001)

Tyneside ('taɪnˌsaɪd) n the conurbation on the banks of the Tyne from Newcastle to the coast. Related word: **Geordie**

Tynwald ('tɪnwəld, 'taɪn-) n the Tynwald the Parliament of the Isle of Man, consisting of the crown, lieutenant governor, House of Keys, and legislative council [c15: from Old Norse *thingvollr*, from *thing* assembly + *vollr* field]

typ., typo. or **typog.** abbreviation 1 typographer 2 typographic(al) 3 typography

typal ('taɪpªl) adj a rare word for **typical**

type (taɪp) n 1 a kind, class, or category, the constituents of which share similar characteristics 2 a subdivision of a particular class of things or people; sort: *what type of shampoo do you use?* 3 the general form, plan, or design distinguishing a particular group 4 informal a person who typifies a particular quality: *he's the administrative type* 5 informal a person, esp of a specified kind: *he's a strange type* 6 a a small block of metal or more rarely wood bearing a letter or character in relief for use in printing b such pieces collectively 7 characters printed from type; print 8 biology a the taxonomic group the characteristics of which are used for defining the next highest group, for example *Rattus norvegicus* (brown rat) is the type species of the rat genus *Rattus* b (as modifier): *a type genus; a type species* 9 See **type specimen** 10 the characteristic device on a coin 11 chiefly Christian theol a figure, episode, or symbolic factor resembling some future reality in such a way as to foreshadow or prefigure it ▷ vb 12 to write (copy) on a typewriter 13 (tr) to be a symbol of; typify 14 (tr) to decide the type of; clarify into a type 15 (tr) med to determine the blood group of (a blood sample) 16 (tr) chiefly Christian theol to foreshadow or serve as a symbol of (some future reality) [c15: from Latin *typus* figure, from Greek *tupos* image, from *tuptein* to strike]

-type n, combining form 1 type or form: *archetype* 2 printing type or photographic process: *collotype* [from Latin *-typus*, from Greek *-typos*, from *tupos* TYPE]

typecast ('taɪpˌkɑːst) vb -casts, -casting, -cast (tr) to cast (an actor) in the same kind of role continually, esp because of his physical appearance or previous success in such roles

typeface ('taɪpˌfeɪs) n another name for **face** (sense 16)

type founder n a person who casts metallic printer's type ▷ type foundry n

type metal n printing an alloy of tin, lead, and antimony, from which type is cast

typescript ('taɪpˌskrɪpt) n 1 a typed copy of a document, literary script, etc 2 any typewritten material

typeset ('taɪpˌsɛt) vb -sets, -setting, -set (tr) printing to set (textual matter) in type

typesetter ('taɪpˌsɛtə) n 1 a person who sets type; compositor 2 a typesetting machine

type specimen n biology the original specimen from which a description of a new species is made

typewrite ('taɪpˌraɪt) vb -writes, -writing, -wrote, -written to write by means of a typewriter; type

typewriter ('taɪpˌraɪtə) n a keyboard machine for writing mechanically in characters resembling print. It may be operated entirely by hand (**manual typewriter**) or be powered by electricity (**electric typewriter**)

typewriting ('taɪpˌraɪtɪŋ) n 1 the act or skill of using a typewriter 2 copy produced by a typewriter; typescript

typhlitis (tɪf'laɪtɪs) n 1 inflammation of the caecum 2 an obsolete name for **appendicitis** [c19: from New Latin, from Greek *tuphlon* the caecum, from *tuphlos* blind] ▷ typhlitic (tɪf'lɪtɪk) adj

Typhoeus (taɪ'fiːəs) n Greek myth the son of Gaea and Tartarus who had a hundred dragon heads, which spurted fire, and a bellowing many-tongued voice. He created the whirlwinds and fought with Zeus before the god hurled him beneath Mount Etna ▷ Ty'phoean adj

typhoid ('taɪfɔɪd) pathol 1 ▷ adj Also: typhoidal resembling typhus ▷ n 2 short for **typhoid fever**

typhoid fever n an acute infectious disease characterized by high fever, rose-coloured spots on the chest or abdomen, abdominal pain, and occasionally intestinal bleeding. It is caused by the bacillus *Salmonella*

typhosa ingested with food or water [c19: from TYPHUS + -OID; so called because the symptoms resemble those of typhus]

Typhon ('taɪfɒn) n Greek myth a monster and one of the whirlwinds: later confused with his father Typhoeus

typhoon (taɪ'fuːn) n a violent tropical storm or cyclone, esp in the China seas and W Pacific [c16: from Chinese *tai fung* great wind, from *tai* great + *fung* wind; influenced by Greek *tuphōn* whirlwind] ▷ typhonic (taɪ'fɒnɪk) adj

typhus ('taɪfəs) n any one of a group of acute infectious rickettsial diseases characterized by high fever, skin rash, and severe headache. Also called: typhus fever [c18: from New Latin *tȳphus*, from Greek *tuphos* fever; related to *tuphein* to smoke] ▷ 'typhous adj

typical ('tɪpɪkªl) adj 1 being or serving as a representative example of a particular type; characteristic 2 considered to be an example of some undesirable trait: *that is typical of you!* 3 of or relating to a representative specimen or type 4 conforming to a type 5 biology having most of the characteristics of a particular taxonomic group [c17: from Medieval Latin *typicālis*, from Late Latin *typicus* figurative, from Greek *tupikos*, from *tupos* TYPE] ▷ 'typically adv ▷ 'typicalness or ˌtypi'cality n

typify ('tɪpɪˌfaɪ) vb -fies, -fying, -fied (tr) 1 to be typical of; characterize 2 to symbolize or represent completely, by or as if by a type [c17: from Latin *typus* TYPE + -IFY] ▷ ˌtypifi'cation n

typist ('taɪpɪst) n a person who types, esp for a living

typo ('taɪpəʊ) n, pl -pos informal a typographical error. Also called (Brit): literal

typographer (taɪ'pɒɡrəfə) n 1 a person skilled in typography 2 another name for **compositor**

typography (taɪ'pɒɡrəfɪ) n 1 the art, craft, or process of composing type and printing from it 2 the selection and planning of type for printed publications ▷ typographical (ˌtaɪpə'ɡræfɪkªl) or ˌtypo'graphic adj ▷ ˌtypo'graphically adv

typology (taɪ'pɒlədʒɪ) n chiefly Christian theol the doctrine or study of types or of the correspondence between them and the realities which they typify ▷ typological (ˌtaɪpə'lɒdʒɪkªl) adj ▷ ty'pologist n

Tyr or **Tyrr** (tjʊə, tɪə) n Norse myth the god of war, son of Odin. Anglo-Saxon counterpart: Tiu

tyrannical (tɪ'rænɪkªl) or **tyrannic** (tɪ'rænɪk) adj characteristic of or relating to a tyrant or to tyranny; oppressive ▷ ty'rannically adv

tyrannicide (tɪ'rænɪˌsaɪd) n 1 the killing of a tyrant 2 a person who kills a tyrant

tyrannize or **tyrannise** ('tɪrəˌnaɪz) vb (when intr, often foll by over) to rule or exercise power (over) in a cruel or oppressive manner ▷ 'tyranˌnizer or 'tyranˌniser n

tyrannosaurus (tɪˌrænə'sɔːrəs) or **tyrannosaur** (tɪ'rænəˌsɔː) n any large carnivorous bipedal dinosaur of the genus *Tyrannosaurus*, common in North America in upper Jurassic and Cretaceous times: suborder *Theropoda* (theropods) [c19: from New Latin, from Greek *turannos* TYRANT + *sauros* lizard]

tyranny ('tɪrənɪ) n, pl -nies 1 a government by a tyrant or tyrants; despotism b similarly oppressive and unjust government by more than one person 2 arbitrary, unreasonable, or despotic behaviour or use of authority 3 a tyrannical act [c14: from Old French *tyrannie*, from Medieval Latin *tyrannia*, from Latin *tyrannus* TYRANT] ▷ 'tyrannous adj

tyrant ('taɪrənt) n 1 a person who governs oppressively, unjustly, and arbitrarily; despot 2 any person who exercises authority in a tyrannical manner [c13: from Old French *tyrant*, from Latin *tyrannus*, from Greek *turannos*]

tyre or US **tire** ('taɪə) n 1 a rubber ring placed over the rim of a wheel of a road vehicle to provide traction and reduce road shocks, esp a hollow inflated ring (**pneumatic tyre**) consisting of a reinforced outer casing enclosing an inner tube 2 a metal band or hoop attached to the rim of a wooden cartwheel [c18: variant of c15 *tire*]

Tyre or **Tyr** ('taɪə) n a port in S Lebanon, on the Mediterranean: founded about the 15th century BC; for centuries a major Phoenician seaport, famous for silks and its Tyrian-purple dye; now a small market town. Pop: 141 000 (2005 est). Arabic name: **Sur**

Tyrian purple *n* **1** a deep purple dye obtained from molluscs of the genus *Murex* and highly prized in antiquity **2 a** a vivid purplish-red colour **b** (*as adjective*): *a Tyrian-purple robe*

tyro *or* **tiro** ('taɪrəʊ) *n, pl* **-ros** a novice or beginner [c17: from Latin *tīrō* recruit]

Tyrol *or* **Tirol** (tɪ'rəʊl, 'tɪrəʊl; *German* ti'roːl) *n* a mountainous state of W Austria: passed to the Hapsburgs in 1363; S part transferred to Italy in 1919. Capital: Innsbruck. Pop: 683 317 (2003 est). Area: 12 648 sq km (4883 sq miles) ⊳ **Tyrolese** (,tɪrə'liːz) *or* **Tyrolean** (,tɪrəʊ'lɪən) *adj, n*

Tyrone (tɪ'rəʊn) *n* a historical county of W Northern Ireland, occupying almost a quarter of the total area of Northern Ireland; in 1973 its administrative functions were devolved to several district councils

tyrosinase (,taɪrəʊsɪ'neɪz, ,tɪrəʊ-) *n* an enzyme occurring in many organisms that is a catalyst in the conversion of tyrosine to the pigment melanin; inactivity of this enzyme results in albinism

tyrosine ('taɪrə,siːn, -sɪn, 'tɪrə-) *n* an aromatic nonessential amino acid; a component of proteins. It is a metabolic precursor of thyroxine, the pigment melanin, and other biologically important compounds [c19: from Greek *turos* cheese + -INE²]

tyrothricin (,taɪrəʊ'θraɪsɪn) *n* an antibiotic, obtained from the soil bacterium *Bacillus brevis*, consisting of tyrocidine and gramicidin and active against Gram-positive bacteria such as staphylococci and streptococci: applied locally for the treatment of ulcers and abscesses

[c20: from New Latin *Tyrothrix* (genus name), from Greek *turos* cheese + *thrix* hair]

Tyr (tjʊə, tɪə) *n* a variant spelling of **Tyr**

Tyrrhenian Sea (tɪ'riːnɪən) *n* an arm of the Mediterranean between Italy and the islands of Corsica, Sardinia, and Sicily

Tyson ('taɪsªn) *n* **Mike.** born 1966, US boxer. World heavyweight champion (1986–90, and 1996): jailed for rape (1992–95) and assault (1999); banned from professional boxing (1997–98) after biting off part of his opponent's ear

Tyumen (*Russian* tju'mjenj) *n* a port in S central Russia, on the Tura River: one of the oldest Russian towns in Siberia; industrial centre with nearby oil and natural gas reserves. Pop: 518 000 (2005 est)

tzar (zɑː) *n* a less common spelling of **tsar**

Tzara ('zɑːrə) *n* **Tristan**, original name *Samuel Rosenstock*. 1896–1963, French poet and essayist, born in Romania, best known as the founder of Dada: author of *The Approximate Man* (1931).

tzatziki (tsæt'sɪkɪ) *n* a Greek dip made from yogurt, chopped cucumber, and mint [c20: from Modern Greek]

Tzekung ('tseˈkʊŋ) *or* **Tzu-kung** ('tsuːˈkʊŋ) *n* a variant transliteration of the Chinese name for **Zigong**

tzetze fly ('tsɛtsɪ) *n* a variant spelling of **tsetse fly**

Tzigane (tsɪ'gɑːn, sɪ-) *n* **a** a Gypsy, esp a Hungarian one **b** (*as modifier*): *Tzigane music* [c19: via French from Hungarian *czigány* Gypsy, of uncertain origin]

T-zone *n* the T-shaped area of a person's face that includes the forehead, nose, and chin

Tzu-po ('tsuːˈpəʊ) *or* **Tzepo** ('tsɛˈpəʊ) *n* a variant transliteration of the Chinese name for **Zibo**

t

Uu

u or **U** (juː) *n, pl* **u's, U's** or **Us** **1** the 21st letter and fifth vowel of the modern English alphabet **2** any of several speech sounds represented by this letter, in English as in *mute, cut, hurt, sure, pull,* or *minus* **3 a** something shaped like a U **b** (*in combination*): *a U-bolt; a U-turn*

U *symbol for* **1** united **2** unionist **3** university **4** (in Britain) **a** universal (used to describe a category of film certified as suitable for viewing by anyone) **b** (*as modifier*): *a U film* **5** *chem* uranium **6** *biochem* uracil **7** *text messaging abbreviation* you ▷ *adj* **8** *Brit dated, informal* (esp of language habits) characteristic of or appropriate to the upper class

U. *abbreviation* **1** *maths* union **2** unit **3** united **4** university **5** upper

U2 *text messaging abbreviation* you too

UA (in Britain) *abbreviation* unitary authority

UAE *abbreviation* United Arab Emirates

UAM *abbreviation* underwater-to-air missile

UAR *abbreviation* United Arab Republic

UB40 *n* (in Britain) **1** a registration card issued by the Department of Employment to a person registering as unemployed **2** *informal* a person registered as unemployed

Ubangi (juːˈbæŋɡɪ) *n* a river in central Africa, flowing west and south, forming the border between the Democratic Republic of Congo (formerly Zaïre) and the Central African Republic and Congo-Brazzaville, into the River Congo. Length (with the Uele): 2250 km (1400 miles). French name: **Oubangui**

Ubangi-Shari *n* a former name (until 1958) of the **Central African Republic**

U-bend *n* a U-shaped bend in a pipe or drain that traps water in the lower part of the U and prevents the escape of noxious fumes or vapours; **trap**

uber- or **über-** (ˈuːbə) *combining form* indicating the highest, greatest, or most extreme example of something: *America's ubernerd, Bill Gates; the uber-hip young Bohemians* [C20: from German *über* over, above]

uberrima fides (ˈjuːbəˌriːmə ˈfaɪdiːz, juːˈbɛrɪmə) *n* another name for **utmost good faith** [Latin: utmost good faith]

ubiety (juːˈbaɪɪtɪ) *n* the condition of being in a particular place [C17: from Latin *ubī* where + *-ety*, on the model of *society*]

ubiquitarian (juːˌbɪkwɪˈtɛərɪən) *n* **1** a member of the Lutheran church who holds that Christ is no more present in the elements of the Eucharist than elsewhere, as he is present in all places at all times ▷ *adj* **2** denoting, relating to, or holding this belief [C17: from Latin *ubīque* everywhere; see UBIQUITOUS] > u,biqui'tarian,ism *n*

ubiquitin (juːˈbɪkwɪtɪn) *n biochem* a small polypeptide, found in most eukaryotic cells, that combines with other proteins to make them susceptible to degradation [C20: from UBIQUITOUS + -IN] > u,biqui'nation *n*

ubiquitous (juːˈbɪkwɪtəs) *adj* having or seeming to have the ability to be everywhere at once; omnipresent [C14: from Latin *ubīque* everywhere, from *ubī* where] > u'biquitously *adv* > u'biquity *or* u'biquitousness *n*

U-boat *n* a German submarine, esp in World Wars I and II [from German *U-Boot*, abbreviation for *Unterseeboot*, literally: undersea boat]

UBR *abbreviation* Uniform Business Rate

Ubuntu (uˈbuːntu) *n South African* humanity or fellow feeling; kindness [Nguni]

u.c. *printing abbreviation* upper case

UCAS (ˈjuːkæs) *n acronym for* (in Britain) Universities and Colleges Admissions Service

UCATT (ˈʌkət) *n acronym for* Union of Construction, Allied Trades and Technicians

Ucayali (*Spanish* ukaˈjali) *n* a river in E Peru, flowing north into the Marañón above Iquitos. Length: 1600 km (1000 miles)

Uccello (*Italian* utˈtʃɛllo) *n* **Paolo** (ˈpaːolo). 1397–1475, Florentine painter noted esp for three paintings of *The Battle of San Romano,* 1432 (1456–60)

UDA *abbreviation* Ulster Defence Association

Udaipur (uːˈdaɪpʊə, ˈuːdaɪˌpʊə) *n* **1** Also called: **Mewar** A former state of NW India: became part of Rajasthan in 1947 **2** a city in NW India, in S Rajasthan. Pop: 389 317 (2001)

udal (ˈjuːdªl) *n law* a form of freehold possession of land existing in northern Europe before the introduction of the feudal system and still used in Orkney and Shetland

[c16: Orkney and Shetland dialect, from Old Norse *othal*; related to Old English *ēthel*, *ōethel*, Old High German *wodal*]

Udall ('juː'dəl) *or* **Uvedale** ('juː'dəl, 'juːv,deɪl) *n* Nicholas. ?1505–56, English dramatist, whose comedy *Ralph Roister Doister* (?1553), modelled on Terence and Plautus, is the earliest known English comedy

udder ('ʌdə) *n* the large baglike mammary gland of cows, sheep, etc, having two or more teats [Old English *ūder*; related to Old High German *ūtar*, Old Norse *jūr*, Latin *ūber*, Sanskrit *ūdhar*]

UDI *abbreviation* Unilateral Declaration of Independence

Udine (Italian 'uːdine) *n* a city in NE Italy, in Friuli-Venezia Giulia region: partially damaged in an earthquake in 1976. Pop: 95 030 (2001)

Udmurt Republic ('ʊdmʊət) *n* a constituent republic of W central Russia, in the basin of the middle Kama. Capital: Izhevsk. Pop: 1 570 500 (2002). Area: 42 100 sq km (16 250 sq miles)

udometer (juː'dɒmɪtə) *n* an archaic term for **rain gauge** [c19: from French, from Latin *ūdus* damp]

udon ('uːdɒn) *n* (in Japanese cookery) large noodles made of wheat flour [Japanese]

UDR *abbreviation* Ulster Defence Regiment

U4E *text messaging abbreviation* yours for ever

UEFA (juː'eɪfə) *n acronym for* Union of European Football Associations

Uele ('weɪlə) *n* a river in central Africa, rising near the border between the Democratic Republic of Congo (formerly Zaïre) and Uganda and flowing west to join the Bomu River and form the Ubangi River. Length: about 1100 km (700 miles)

uey ('juːɪ) *n Australian slang* a U-turn

Ufa (Russian u'fa) *n* a city in W central Russia, capital of the Bashkir Republic: university (1957). Pop: 1 035 000 (2005 est)

Uffizi (juː'fiːtsɪ) *n* an art gallery in Florence; built by Giorgio Vasari in the 16th century and opened as a museum in 1765: contains chiefly Italian Renaissance paintings

UFO (*sometimes* 'juːfəʊ) *abbreviation* unidentified flying object

ufology (,juː'fɒlədʒɪ) *n* the study of UFOs ▷ u'**fologist** *n*

Uganda (juː'gændə) *n* a republic in E Africa: British protectorate established in 1894–96; gained independence in 1962 and became a republic in 1963; a member of the Commonwealth. It consists mostly of a savanna plateau with part of Lake Victoria in the southeast and mountains in the southwest, reaching 5109 m (16 763 ft) in the Ruwenzori Range. Official language: English; Swahili, Luganda, and Luo are also widely spoken. Religion: Christian majority. Currency: Ugandan shilling. Capital: Kampala. Pop: 26 699 000 (2004 est). Area: 235 886 sq km (91 076 sq miles) ▷ U'**gandan** *adj, n*

Ugaritic (,uːgə'rɪtɪk) *n* 1 an extinct Semitic language of N Syria ▷ *adj* 2 of or relating to this language [c19: after *Ugarit* (modern name: Ras Shamra), an ancient Syrian city-state]

UGC *abbreviation* (in Britain) University Grants Committee

ugh (ʊx, ʊh, ʌh) *interj* an exclamation of disgust, annoyance, or dislike

UGLI ('ʌglɪ) *n*, *pl* UGLIS *or* UGLIES *trademark* a large juicy yellow-skinned citrus fruit of the Caribbean: a cross between a tangerine, grapefruit, and orange. Also called: UGLI fruit [c20: probably an alteration of UGLY, referring to its wrinkled skin]

uglify ('ʌglɪ,faɪ) *vb* -fies, -fying, -fied to make or become ugly or more ugly ▷ **uglification** ('ʌglɪfɪ'keɪʃən) *n* ▷ 'ugli,fier *n*

ugly ('ʌglɪ) *adj* -lier, -liest 1 of unpleasant or unsightly appearance 2 repulsive, objectionable, or displeasing in any way: *war is ugly*. 3 ominous or menacing: *an ugly situation*. 4 bad-tempered, angry, or sullen: *an ugly mood* [c13: from Old Norse *uggligr* dreadful, from *ugga* fear] ▷ 'uglily *adv* ▷ 'ugliness *n*

ugly duckling *n* a person or thing, initially ugly or unpromising, that changes into something beautiful or admirable [an allusion to *The Ugly Duckling*, a story by Hans Christian Andersen]

Ugrian ('uːgrɪən, 'juː-) *adj* 1 of or relating to a light-haired subdivision of the Turanian people, who include the Samoyeds, Voguls, Ostyaks, and Magyars ▷ *n* 2 a member of this group of peoples 3 another word for **Ugric** [c19: from Old Russian *Ugre* Hungarians]

Ugric ('uːgrɪk, 'juː-) *n* 1 one of the two branches of the Finno-Ugric family of languages, including Hungarian and some languages of NW Siberia. ▷ Compare **Finnic** ▷ *adj* 2 of or relating to this group of languages or their speakers

UHF *radio abbreviation* ultrahigh frequency

uh-huh (ə'hə) *sentence substitute informal* a less emphatic variant of **yes**

uhlan *or* **ulan** ('uːlɑːn, 'juːlən) *n history* a member of a body of lancers first employed in the Polish army and later in W European armies [c18: via German from Polish *ulan*, from Turkish *ōlan* young man]

Uhland (German 'uːlant) *n* Johann Ludwig (jo'han 'luːtvɪç). 1787–1862, German romantic poet, esp of lyrics and ballads

UHT *abbreviation* ultra heat treated

uhuru (uː'huːruː) *n* (esp in E Africa) 1 national independence 2 freedom [c20: from Swahili]

Uigur *or* **Uighur** ('wiːgʊə) *n* 1 (*pl* -gur *or* -gurs) a member of a Mongoloid people of NW China, Uzbekistan, Kyrgyzstan, and Kazakhstan 2 the language of this people, belonging to the Turkic branch of the Altaic family ▷ Ui'gurian, Ui'ghurian, Ui'guric *or* Ui'ghuric *adj*

uillean pipes ('ɪlɪn, 'ɪlən) *pl n* bagpipes developed in Ireland and operated by squeezing bellows under the arm. Also called: Irish pipes, union pipes [c19: Irish *píob uilleann*, from *píob* pipe + *uilleann* genitive sing. of *uille* elbow]

Uinta Mountains (jʊ'ɪntə) *pl n* a mountain range in NE Utah: part of the Rocky Mountains. Highest peak: Kings Peak, 4123 m (13 528 ft)

uitlander ('eɪt,lɑːndə, -,læn-, 'ɔɪt-) *n* (*sometimes capital*) *South African* a foreigner; alien [c19: Afrikaans: outlander]

Ujiji (uː'dʒiːdʒɪ) *n* a town in W Tanzania, on Lake Tanganyika: a former slave and ivory centre; the place where Stanley found Livingstone in 1871. It merged with the neighbouring town of Kigoma to form Kigoma-Ujiji in the 1960s

Ujjain (uː'dʒeɪn) *n* a city in W central India, in Madhya Pradesh: one of the seven sacred cities of the Hindus; a major agricultural trade centre. Pop: 429 933 (2001)

Ujung Pandang ('uːdʒʊŋ pæn'dæŋ) *n* the former name (1971–1999) for **Makassar**

UK *abbreviation* United Kingdom

ukase (juː'keɪz) *n* 1 (in imperial Russia) an edict of the tsar 2 a rare word for **edict** [c18: from Russian *ukaz*, from *ukazat* to command]

UKCC *abbreviation* United Kingdom Central Council for Nursing, Midwifery, and Health Visiting

UKIP ('juː,kɪp) *n acronym* United Kingdom Independence Party: a political party founded in 1993 to seek Britain's withdrawal from the European Union

Ukr. *abbreviation* Ukraine

Ukraine (juː'kreɪn) *n* a republic in SE Europe, on the Black Sea and the Sea of Azov: ruled by the Khazars (7th–9th centuries), by Ruik princes with the Mongol conquest in the 13th century, then by Lithuania, by Poland, and by Russia; one of the four original republics that formed the Soviet Union in 1922; unilaterally declared independence in 1990, which was recognized in 1991. Consists chiefly of lowlands; economy based on rich agriculture and mineral resources and on the major heavy industries of the Donets Basin. Official language: Ukrainian; Russian is also widely spoken. Religion: believers are mainly Christian. Currency: hryvna. Capital: Kiev. Pop: 48 151 000 (2004 est). Area: 603 700 sq km (231 990 sq miles)

Ukrainian (juː'kreɪnɪən) *adj* 1 of or relating to Ukraine, its people, or their language ▷ *n* 2 the official language of Ukraine: an East Slavonic language closely related to Russian 3 a native or inhabitant of Ukraine

u

ukulele or **ukelele** (ˌjuːkəˈleɪlɪ) n a small four-stringed guitar, esp of Hawaii [C19: from Hawaiian, literally: jumping flea, from ‘uku flea + lele jumping]

ulama[1] or **ulema** (ˈuːlɪmə) n 1 a body of Muslim scholars or religious leaders 2 a member of this body [C17: from Arabic ‘ulamā scholars, from ‘alama to know]

ulama[2] (ˌuːˈlɑːmə) n a Meso-American team ball game, with a history dating back to as early as 1500 BC, played with a solid rubber ball on a long narrow court [from Nahuatl Ullamalitztli ball game]

Ulan Bator or **Ulaanbaatar** (ʊˈlɑːn ˈbɑːtɔː) n the capital of Mongolia, in the N central part: developed in the mid-17th century around the Da Khure monastery, residence until 1924 of successive "living Buddhas" (third in rank of Buddhist-Lamaist leaders), and main junction of caravan routes across Mongolia; university (1942); industrial and commercial centre. Pop: 842 000 (2005 est). Former name (until 1924): Urga. Chinese name: Kulun

Ulanova (ʊˈlɑːnəvə) n **Galina** (**Sergeyevna**) (gəˈliːnə) 1910–98, Russian ballet dancer, who performed with the Leningrad Kirov ballet (1928–44) and the Moscow Bolshoi Ballet (1944–62)

Ulan-Ude (ʊˈlɑːnuˈdɛ) n an industrial city in SE Russia, capital of the Buryat Republic: an important rail junction. Pop: 361 000 (2005 est). Former name (until 1934): Verkhne-Udinsk

Ulbricht (German ˈʊlbrɪçt) n **Walter** (ˈvaltər). 1893–1973, East German statesman; largely responsible for the establishment and development of East German communism

ulcer (ˈʌlsə) n 1 a disintegration of the surface of the skin or a mucous membrane resulting in an open sore that heals very slowly. See also **peptic ulcer** 2 a source or element of corruption or evil [C14: from Latin ulcus; related to Greek helkos a sore]

ulcerate (ˈʌlsəˌreɪt) vb to make or become ulcerous > ˌulceˈration n > ˈulcerative adj

ulcerous (ˈʌlsərəs) adj 1 relating to, characteristic of, or characterized by an ulcer or ulcers 2 being or having a corrupting influence > ˈulcerously adv

-ule suffix forming nouns indicating smallness: globule [from Latin -ulus, diminutive suffix]

Uleåborg (ˈuːlɪoˌbɔrjə) n the Swedish name for **Oulu**

ulema (ˈuːlɪmə) n a variant of **ulama**[1]

-ulent suffix forming adjectives abundant or full of: fraudulent [from Latin -ulentus]

Ulfilas (ˈʊlfɪˌlæs), **Ulfila** (ˈʊlfɪlə) or **Wulfila** n ?311–?382 AD, Christian bishop of the Goths who translated the Bible from Greek into Gothic

ullage (ˈʌlɪdʒ) n 1 the volume by which a liquid container falls short of being full 2 a the quantity of liquid lost from a container due to leakage or evaporation b (in customs terminology) the amount of liquid remaining in a container after such loss [C15: from Old French ouillage filling of a cask, from ouiller to fill a cask, from ouil eye, from Latin oculus eye]

Ullswater (ˈʌlzˌwɔːtə) n a lake in NW England, in Cumbria in the Lake District. Length: 12 km (7.5 miles)

Ulm (German ʊlm) n an industrial city in S Germany, in Baden-Württemberg on the Danube: a free imperial city (1155–1802). Pop: 119 807 (2003 est)

ulna (ˈʌlnə) n, pl -nae (-niː) or -nas 1 the inner and longer of the two bones of the human forearm 2 the corresponding bone in other vertebrates [C16: from Latin: elbow, ELL] > ˈulnar adj

ulnar nerve n a nerve situated along the inner side of the arm and passing close to the surface of the skin near the elbow

ulotrichous (juːˈlɒtrɪkəs) adj having woolly or curly hair [C19: from New Latin Ulotrichī (classification applied to humans having this type of hair), from Greek oulothrix, from oulos curly + thrix hair]

Ulpian (ˈʌlpɪən) n Latin name Domitius Ulpianus. died ?228 AD, Roman jurist, born in Phoenicia

ulster (ˈʌlstə) n a man's heavy double-breasted overcoat with a belt or half-belt at the back [C19: so called because it was first produced in Northern Ireland]

Ulster (ˈʌlstə) n 1 a province and former kingdom of N Ireland: passed to the English Crown in 1461; confiscated land given to English and Scottish Protestant settlers in the 17th century, giving rise to serious long-term conflict; partitioned in 1921, six counties forming Northern Ireland and three counties joining the Republic of Ireland. Pop (three Ulster counties of the Republic of Ireland): 46 714 (2002); (six Ulster counties of Northern Ireland): 1 702 628 (2003 est). Area (Republic of Ireland): 8013 sq km (3094 sq miles); (Northern Ireland): 14 121 sq km (5452 sq miles) 2 an informal name for **Northern Ireland**

Ulster Defence Association n (in Northern Ireland) a Loyalist paramilitary organization. Abbreviation: UDA

Ulster Democratic Unionist Party n a Northern Irish political party advocating the maintenance of union with the UK

Ulsterman (ˈʌlstəmən) n, pl -men a native or inhabitant of Ulster > ˈUlsterˌwoman fem n

Ulster Unionist Council n a Northern Irish political party advocating the maintenance of union with the UK

ult. abbreviation 1 ultimate(ly) 2 Also called: ulto ultimo

ulterior (ʌlˈtɪərɪə) adj 1 lying beneath or beyond what is revealed, evident, or supposed: ulterior motives 2 succeeding, subsequent, or later 3 lying beyond a certain line or point [C17: from Latin: further, from ulter beyond] > ulˈteriorly adv

ultima (ˈʌltɪmə) n the final syllable of a word [from Latin: the last, feminine of ultimus last; see ULTIMATE]

ultimate (ˈʌltɪmɪt) adj 1 conclusive in a series or process; last; final: an ultimate question 2 the highest or most significant: the ultimate goal 3 elemental, fundamental, basic, or essential 4 most extreme: genocide is the ultimate abuse of human rights 5 final or total: an ultimate cost of twenty million pounds ▷ n 6 the most significant, highest, furthest, or greatest thing [C17: from Late Latin ultimāre to come to an end, from Latin ultimus last, from ulter distant]

ultimately (ˈʌltɪmɪtlɪ) adv in the end; at last; finally

ultima Thule (ˈθjuːlɪ) n 1 another name for **Thule** 2 any distant or unknown region 3 a remote goal or aim [Latin: the most distant Thule]

ultimatum (ˌʌltɪˈmeɪtəm) n, pl -tums or -ta (-tə) 1 a final communication by a party, esp a government, setting forth conditions on which it insists, as during negotiations on some topic 2 any final or peremptory demand, offer, or proposal [C18: from New Latin, neuter of ultimatus ULTIMATE]

ultimo (ˈʌltɪˌməʊ) adv in or during the previous month (esp abbreviated in formal correspondence): a letter of the 7th ultimo Abbreviation: ult. Compare **instant**, **proximo** [C16: from Latin ultimō on the last]

ultimogeniture (ˌʌltɪməʊˈdʒɛnɪtʃə) n law a principle of inheritance whereby the youngest son succeeds to the estate of his ancestor [C19: ultimo- from Latin ultimus last + Late Latin genitura a birth]

ultra (ˈʌltrə) adj 1 extreme or immoderate, esp in beliefs or opinions ▷ n 2 an extremist [C19: from Latin: beyond, from ulter distant]

ultra- prefix 1 beyond or surpassing a specified extent, range, or limit: ultramicroscopic 2 extreme or extremely: ultramodern [from Latin ultrā beyond; see ULTRA]

ultracentrifuge (ˌʌltrəˈsɛntrɪˌfjuːdʒ) n chem a high-speed centrifuge used to separate colloidal solutions

ultraconservative (ˌʌltrəkənˈsɜːvətɪv) adj 1 highly reactionary ▷ n 2 a reactionary person

ultra-distance n (modifier) athletics covering a distance in excess of 30 miles, often as part of a longer race or competition: an ultra-distance runner

ultrafast (ˈʌltrəˌfaːst) adj extremely fast: an ultrafast internet connection

ultrafiche (ˈʌltrəˌfiːʃ) n a sheet of film, usually the size of a filing card, that is similar to a microfiche but has a much larger number of microcopies [C20: from ULTRA- + French fiche small card. See MICROFICHE]

ultrahigh frequency (ˈʌltrəˌhaɪ) n a radio-frequency band or radio frequency lying between 3000 and 300 megahertz. Abbreviation: UHF

ultraism (ˈʌltrəˌɪzəm) n extreme philosophy, belief, or action > ˈultraist n, adj > ˌultraˈistic adj

ultramarine (ˌʌltrəməˈriːn) *n* **1** a blue pigment consisting of sodium and aluminium silicates and some sodium sulphide, obtained by powdering natural lapis lazuli or made synthetically: used in paints, printing ink, plastics, etc **2** a vivid blue colour ▷ *adj* **3** of the colour ultramarine **4** from across the seas [c17: from Medieval Latin *ultramarinus*, from *ultrā* beyond (see ULTRA-) + *mare* sea; so called because the lapis lazuli from which the pigment was made was imported from Asia]

ultramicroscope (ˌʌltrəˈmaɪkrəˌskəʊp) *n* a microscope used for studying colloids, in which the sample is strongly illuminated from the side and colloidal particles are seen as bright points on a dark background

ultramicroscopic (ˌʌltrəˌmaɪkrəˈskɒpɪk) *adj* **1** too small to be seen with an optical microscope **2** of or relating to an ultramicroscope

ultramodern (ˌʌltrəˈmɒdən) *adj* extremely modern > ˌultraˈmodernism *n* > ˌultraˈmodernist *n* > ˌultraˌmodernˈistic *adj*

ultramontane (ˌʌltrəmɒnˈteɪn) *adj* **1** on the other side of the mountains, esp the Alps, from the speaker or writer **2** of or relating to a movement in the Roman Catholic Church which favours the centralized authority and influence of the pope as opposed to local independence ▷ *n* **3** a resident or native from beyond the mountains, esp the Alps **4** a member of the ultramontane party of the Roman Catholic Church

ultramundane (ˌʌltrəˈmʌndeɪn) *adj* extending beyond the world, this life, or the universe

ultranationalism (ˌʌltrəˈnæʃnəˌlɪzəm) *n* extreme devotion to one's own nation > ˌultraˈnationalist *adj, n* > ˌultraˌnationalˈistic *adj*

ultrashort (ˌʌltrəˈʃɔːt) *adj* (of a radio wave) having a wavelength shorter than 10 metres

ultrasonic (ˌʌltrəˈsɒnɪk) *adj* of, concerned with, or producing waves with the same nature as sound waves but frequencies above audio frequencies. See also **ultrasound** > ˌultraˈsonically *adv*

ultrasonics (ˌʌltrəˈsɒnɪks) *n* (functioning as singular) the branch of physics concerned with ultrasonic waves. Also called: supersonics

ultrasound (ˈʌltrəˌsaʊnd) *n* ultrasonic waves at frequencies above the audible range (above about 20 kHz), used in cleaning metallic parts, echo sounding, medical diagnosis and therapy, etc

ultrasound scanner *n* a device used to examine an internal bodily structure by the use of ultrasonic waves, esp for the diagnosis of abnormality in a fetus

ultrastructure (ˈʌltrəˌstrʌktʃə) *n* the minute structure of a tissue or cell, as revealed by microscopy, esp electron microscopy

ultraviolet (ˌʌltrəˈvaɪəlɪt) *n* **1** the part of the electromagnetic spectrum with wavelengths shorter than light but longer than X-rays; in the range 0.4×10^{-6} and 1×10^{-8} metres ▷ *adj* **2** of, relating to, or consisting of radiation lying in the ultraviolet: *ultraviolet radiation*. Abbreviation: UV

ultraviolet astronomy *n* the study of radiation from celestial sources in the wavelength range 91.2 to 320 nanometres, 12 to 91.2 nanometres being the extreme ultraviolet range

ultra vires (ˈvaɪriːz) *adv, adj* (predicative) law beyond the legal power or authority of a person, corporation, agent, etc [Latin, literally: beyond strength]

ultravirus (ˌʌltrəˈvaɪrəs) *n* a virus small enough to pass through the finest filter

ultrawideband (ˌʌltrəˈwaɪdˌbænd) *n* a transmission technique using a very wide spectrum of frequencies that enables high-speed transfer of data. Abbreviation: UWB

ululate (ˈjuːljʊˌleɪt) *vb* (intr) to howl or wail, as with grief [c17: from Latin *ululāre* to howl, from *ulula* screech owl] > ˈululant *adj* > ˌuluˈlation *n*

Ulundi (ˈjuːlʊndɪ) *n* a town in South Africa: the traditional Zulu capital of KwaZulu-Natal

Uluru (ˌuːləˈruː) *n* a large isolated desert rock, sometimes described as the world's largest monolith, in the Northern Territory of Australia: sacred to local Aboriginal people. Height: 330m (1100 ft). Base

circumference: 9 km (5.6 miles). Former name: Ayers Rock

Ulyanovsk (*Russian* uljˈjanəfsk) *n* the former name (1924–91) of **Simbirsk**

Ulysses (ˈjuːlɪˌsiːz, juːˈlɪsiːz) *n* the Latin name of **Odysseus**

Umar (ˈuːmɑː) *n* a variant transliteration of the Arabic name for **Omar**

Umar Tal (ˈuːmɑː tæl) *n* ?1797–1864, African religious and military leader, who created a Muslim empire in W Africa

Umayyad (uːˈmaɪjæd) *n* a variant spelling of **Omayyad**

umbel (ˈʌmbəl) *n* an inflorescence, characteristic of umbelliferous plants, in which the flowers arise from the same point in the main stem and have stalks of the same length, to give a cluster with the youngest flowers at the centre [c16: from Latin *umbella* a sunshade, from *umbra* shade] > umbellate (ˈʌmbɪlɪt, -ˌleɪt), umbellar (ʌmˈbɛlə) or ˈumbelˌlated *adj* > ˈumbellately *adv*

umbelliferous (ˌʌmbɪˈlɪfərəs) *adj* **1** of, relating to, or belonging to the *Umbelliferae*, a family of herbaceous plants and shrubs, typically having hollow stems, divided or compound leaves, and flowers in umbels: includes fennel, dill, parsley, carrot, celery, and parsnip **2** designating any other plant bearing umbels [c17: from New Latin *umbellifer*, from Latin *umbella* sunshade + *ferre* to bear] > umbellifer (ʌmˈbɛlɪfəʳ) *n*

umber (ˈʌmbə) *n* **1** any of various natural brown earths containing ferric oxide together with lime and oxides of aluminium, manganese, and silicon. See also **burnt umber 2** any of the dark brown to greenish-brown colours produced by this pigment **3** *obsolete* shade or shadow ▷ *adj* **4** of, relating to, or stained with umber [c16: from French (*terre d'*)*ombre* or Italian (*terra di*) *ombra* shadow earth), from Latin *umbra* shade]

Umberto I (*Italian* umˈbɛrto) *n* 1844–1900, king of Italy (1878–1900); son of Victor Emmanuel II: assassinated at Monza

Umberto II *n* 1904–83, the last king of Italy (1946), following the abdication of his father Victor Emmanuel III: abdicated when a referendum supported the abolition of the monarchy

umbilical (ʌmˈbɪlɪkəl, ˌʌmbɪˈlaɪkəl) *adj* **1** of, relating to, or resembling the umbilicus or the umbilical cord **2** in the region of the umbilicus: *an umbilical hernia*

umbilical cord *n* **1** the long flexible tubelike structure connecting a fetus with the placenta: it provides a means of metabolic interchange with the mother **2** any flexible cord, tube, or cable used to transfer information, power, oxygen, etc, as between an astronaut walking in space and his spacecraft or a deep-sea diver and his craft

umbilicate (ʌmˈbɪlɪkɪt, -ˌkeɪt) *adj* **1** having an umbilicus or navel **2** having a central depression: *an umbilicate leaf* **3** shaped like a navel, as some bacterial colonies > umˌbiliˈcation *n*

umbilicus (ʌmˈbɪlɪkəs, ˌʌmbɪˈlaɪkəs) *n, pl* -bilici (-ˈbɪlɪˌsaɪ, -bɪˈlaɪsaɪ) **1** *biology* a hollow or navel-like structure, such as the cavity at the base of a gastropod shell **2** *anatomy* a technical name for the **navel** [c18: from Latin: navel, centre; compare Latin *umbō* shield boss, Greek *omphalos* navel]

umble pie (ˈʌmbəl) *n* See **humble pie** (sense 1)

umbles (ˈʌmbəlz) *pl n* another term for **numbles**

umbo (ˈʌmbəʊ) *n, pl* umbones (ʌmˈbəʊniːz) *or* umbos **1** a small hump projecting from the centre of the cap in certain mushrooms **2** a hooked prominence occurring at the apex of each half of the shell of a bivalve mollusc **3** a large projecting central boss or disk, esp on a Saxon shield [c18: from Latin: boss of a shield, projecting piece] > umbonate (ˈʌmbənɪt, -ˌneɪt) umbonal or umbonic (ʌmˈbɒnɪk) *adj*

umbra (ˈʌmbrə) *n, pl* -brae (-briː) *or* -bras **1** a region of complete shadow resulting from the total obstruction of light by an opaque object, esp the shadow cast by the moon onto the earth during a solar eclipse **2** the darker inner region of a sunspot ▷ Compare **penumbra** [c16: from Latin: shade, shadow] > ˈumbral *adj*

umbrage (ˈʌmbrɪdʒ) *n* **1** displeasure or resentment; offence (in the phrase **give** *or* **take umbrage**) **2** the foliage of trees, considered as providing shade **3** *rare* shadow or shade [C15: from Old French *umbrage*, from Latin *umbrāticus* relating to shade, from *umbra* shade, shadow]

umbrageous (ʌmˈbreɪdʒəs) *adj* shady or shading

umbrella (ʌmˈbrɛlə) *n* **1** a portable device used for protection against rain, snow, etc, and consisting of a light canopy supported on a collapsible metal frame mounted on a central rod **2** the flattened cone-shaped contractile body of a jellyfish or other medusa **3** a protective shield or screen, esp of aircraft or gunfire **4** anything that has the effect of a protective screen or cover [C17: from Italian *ombrella*, diminutive of *ombra* shade; see UMBRA] > um'brella-,like *adj*

umbrella pine *n* another name for **stone pine**

umbrella stand *n* an upright rack or stand for umbrellas

umbrella tree *n* **1** a North American magnolia, *Magnolia tripetala*, having long leaves clustered into an umbrella formation at the ends of the branches and unpleasant-smelling white flowers **2** Also called: **umbrella bush** Any of various other trees or shrubs having leaves shaped like an umbrella or growing in an umbrella-like cluster

Umbria (ˈʌmbrɪə; *Italian* ˈumbrja) *n* a mountainous region of central Italy, in the valley of the Tiber. Pop: 834 210 (2003 est). Area: 8456 sq km (3265 sq miles)

Umbrian (ˈʌmbrɪən) *adj* **1** of or relating to Umbria, its inhabitants, their dialect of Italian, or the ancient language once spoken there **2** of or relating to a Renaissance school of painting that included Raphael ▷ *n* **3** a native or inhabitant of Umbria **4** an extinct language of ancient S Italy, belonging to the Italic branch of the Indo-European family

UMD *n trademark* Universal Media Disc: an optical disc used to store games, films, or music

umfazi (ʊmˈfɑːzɪ) *n South African* an African married woman [Nguni]

umiak or **oomiak** (ˈuːmɪˌæk) *n* a large open boat made of stretched skins, used by Inuit ▷ Compare **kayak** [C18: from Greenland Inuktitut: boat for the use of women]

UML *computing trademark abbreviation* Unified Modeling Language: a standardized language for describing and visualizing the different parts of software systems; used for designing software

umlaut (ˈʊmlaʊt) *n* **1** the mark (¨) placed over a vowel in some languages, such as German, indicating modification in the quality of the vowel. See **diaeresis** **2** (esp in Germanic languages) the change of a vowel within a word brought about by the assimilating influence of a vowel or semivowel in a preceding or following syllable [C19: German, from *um* around (in the sense of changing places) + *Laut* sound]

umlungu (ʊmˈlʊŋɡʊ) *n South African* a white man: used esp as a term of address [Nguni: a white man]

umpie or **umpy** (ˈʌmpɪ) *n, pl* **umpies** *Austral* an informal word for **umpire**

umpire (ˈʌmpaɪə) *n* **1** an official who rules on the playing of a game, as in cricket or baseball **2** a person who rules on or judges disputes between contesting parties ▷ *vb* **3** to act as umpire in (a game, dispute, or controversy) [C15: by mistaken division from *a noumpere*, from Old French *nomper* not one of a pair, from *nom-*, *non-* not + *per* equal, PEER¹]

umpteen (ˌʌmpˈtiːn) *determiner informal* **a** very many: *umpteen things to do* **b** (*as pronoun*): *umpteen of them came* [C20: from *umpty* a great deal (perhaps from *-enty* as in *twenty*) + *-teen* ten] > ,ump'teenth *n, adj*

Umtali (ʊmˈtɑːlɪ) *n* the former name (until 1982) of **Mutare**

Umtata (ʊmˈtɑːtə) *n* a city in South Africa, in Eastern Cape province; the capital of the former Transkei Bantu homeland. Pop: 94 778 (2001)

UN *abbreviation* United Nations

un-¹ *prefix* (*freely used with adjectives, participles, and their derivative adverbs and nouns: less frequently used with certain other nouns*) not; contrary to; opposite of: *uncertain; uncomplaining; unemotionally; untidiness; unbelief; unrest; untruth* [from Old English *on-, un-*; related to Gothic *on-*, German

un-, Latin *in-*]

un-² *prefix forming verbs* **1** denoting reversal of an action or state: *uncover; untangle* **2** denoting removal from, release, or deprivation: *unharness; unman; unthrone* **3** (intensifier): *unloose* [from Old English *un-, on-*; related to Gothic *and-*, German *ent-*, Latin *ante*]

'un or **un** (ən) *pron* a spelling of **one**: *that's a big 'un*
● USAGE This spelling is intended to reflect a dialectal ● or informal pronunciation

unable (ʌnˈeɪbᵊl) *adj* (*postpositive*; *foll by* *to*) lacking the necessary power, ability, or authority (to do something); not able

unaccountable (ˌʌnəˈkaʊntəbᵊl) *adj* **1** allowing of no explanation; inexplicable **2** puzzling; extraordinary: *an unaccountable fear of hamburgers* **3** not accountable or answerable to > ,unac'countableness or ,unac,counta'bility *n* > ,unac'countably *adv*

una corda (ˈuːnə ˈkɔːdə) *adj, adv music* (of the piano) to be played with the soft pedal depressed [Italian, literally: one string; the pedal moves the mechanism so that only one string of the three tuned to each note is struck by the hammer]

unadopted (ˌʌnəˈdɒptɪd) *adj* **1** (of a child) not adopted **2** *Brit* (of a road, etc) not maintained by a local authority

unadvised (ˌʌnədˈvaɪzd) *adj* **1** rash or unwise **2** not having received advice > unadvisedly (ˌʌnədˈvaɪzɪdlɪ) *adv* > ,unad'visedness *n*

unaffected¹ (ˌʌnəˈfɛktɪd) *adj* unpretentious, natural, or sincere > ,unaf'fectedly *adv* > ,unaf'fectedness *n*

unaffected² (ˌʌnəˈfɛktɪd) *adj* not affected

Unalaska Island (ˌʌnəˈlæskə) *n* a large volcanic island in SW Alaska, in the Aleutian Islands. Length: 120 km (75 miles). Greatest width: about 40 km (25 miles)

unalienable (ʌnˈeɪljənəbᵊl) *adj law* a variant of **inalienable**

un-American *adj* **1** not in accordance with the aims, ideals, customs, etc, of the US **2** against the interests of the US > ,un-A'merican,ism *n*

Unamuno (*Spanish* unaˈmuno) *n* **Miguel de** (miˈɣɛl de). 1864–1936, Spanish philosopher and writer

unanimous (juːˈnænɪməs) *adj* **1** in complete or absolute agreement **2** characterized by complete agreement: *a unanimous decision* [C17: from Latin *ūnanimus* from *ūnus* one + *animus* mind] > u'nanimously *adv* > unanimity (ˌjuːnəˈnɪmɪtɪ) or u'nanimousness *n*

unapproachable (ˌʌnəˈprəʊtʃəbᵊl) *adj* **1** discouraging intimacy, friendliness, etc; aloof **2** inaccessible **3** not to be rivalled > ,unap'proachableness *n* > ,unap'proachably *adv*

unappropriated (ˌʌnəˈprəʊprɪˌeɪtɪd) *adj* **1** not set aside for specific use **2** *accounting* designating that portion of the profits of a business enterprise that is retained in the business and not withdrawn by the proprietor **3** (of property) not having been taken into any person's possession or control

unapt (ʌnˈæpt) *adj* **1** (*usually postpositive*; *often foll by* *for*) not suitable or qualified; unfitted **2** mentally slow **3** (*postpositive*; *may take an infinitive*) not disposed or likely (to) > un'aptly *adv* > un'aptness *n*

unarm (ʌnˈɑːm) *vb* a less common word for **disarm**

unarmed (ʌnˈɑːmd) *adj* **1** without weapons **2** (of animals and plants) having no claws, prickles, spines, thorns, or similar structures **3** of or relating to a projectile that does not use a detonator to initiate explosive action

unassailable (ˌʌnəˈseɪləbᵊl) *adj* **1** not able to be attacked **2** undeniable or irrefutable > ,unas'sailableness *n* > ,unas'sailably *adv*

unassuming (ˌʌnəˈsjuːmɪŋ) *adj* modest or unpretentious > ,unas'sumingly *adv* > ,unas'sumingness *n*

unattached (ˌʌnəˈtætʃt) *adj* **1** not connected with any specific thing, body, group, etc; independent **2** not engaged or married **3** (of property) not seized or held as security or in satisfaction of a judgment

unavailing (ˌʌnəˈveɪlɪŋ) *adj* useless or futile > ,una'vailingly *adv*

unavoidable (ˌʌnəˈvɔɪdəbᵊl) *adj* **1** unable to be avoided; inevitable **2** *law* not capable of being declared null and void > ,una,voida'bility or ,una'voidableness *n*

▷ ˌuna'voidably adv

unaware (ˌʌnə'wɛə) adj 1 (postpositive) not aware or conscious (of): unaware of the danger, he ran across the road 2 not fully cognizant of what is going on in the world ▷ adv 3 a variant of **unawares** ▷ ˌuna'warely adv ▷ ˌuna'wareness n

unawares (ˌʌnə'wɛəz) adv 1 without prior warning or plan; unexpectedly: she caught him unawares 2 without being aware of or knowing: he lost it unawares

unbacked (ʌn'bækt) adj 1 (of a book, chair, etc) not having a back 2 bereft of support, esp on a financial basis 3 (of a horse) not supported by bets

unbalance (ʌn'bæləns) vb (tr) 1 to upset the equilibrium or balance of 2 to disturb the mental stability of (a person or his mind) ▷ n 3 imbalance or instability

unbalanced (ʌn'bælənst) adj 1 lacking balance 2 irrational or unsound; erratic 3 mentally disordered or deranged 4 biased; one-sided: unbalanced reporting 5 (in double-entry book-keeping) not having total debit balances equal to total credit balances

unbar (ʌn'bɑː) vb -bars, -barring, -barred (tr) 1 to take away a bar or bars from 2 to unfasten bars, locks, etc, from (a door); open

unbearable (ʌn'bɛərəbəl) adj not able to be borne or endured ▷ un'bearableness n ▷ un'bearably adv

unbeatable (ʌn'biːtəbəl) adj unable to be defeated or outclassed; surpassingly excellent

unbeaten (ʌn'biːtən) adj 1 having suffered no defeat 2 not worn down; untrodden 3 not mixed or stirred by beating: unbeaten eggs

unbecoming (ˌʌnbɪ'kʌmɪŋ) adj 1 unsuitable or inappropriate, esp through being unattractive: an unbecoming hat 2 (when postpositive, usually foll by of or an object) not proper or seemly (for): manners unbecoming a lady ▷ ˌunbe'comingly adv ▷ ˌunbe'comingness n

unbeknown (ˌʌnbɪ'nəʊn) adv (sentence modifier; foll by to) without the knowledge (of a person): unbeknown to him she had left the country [c17: from the archaic beknown known; see BE-, KNOW]

unbelief (ˌʌnbɪ'liːf) n disbelief or rejection of belief

unbelievable (ˌʌnbɪ'liːvəbəl) adj unable to be believed; incredible or astonishing ▷ ˌunbeˌlieva'bility or ˌunbe'lievableness n

unbeliever (ˌʌnbɪ'liːvə) n a person who does not believe or withholds belief, esp in religious matters

unbelieving (ˌʌnbɪ'liːvɪŋ) adj 1 not believing; sceptical 2 proceeding from or characterized by scepticism ▷ ˌunbe'lievingly adv

unbend (ʌn'bɛnd) vb -bends, -bending, -bent 1 to release or be released from the restraints of formality and ceremony 2 informal to relax (the mind) or (of the mind) to become relaxed 3 to become or be made straightened out from an originally bent shape or position 4 (tr) nautical a to remove (a sail) from a stay, mast, yard, etc b to untie (a rope, etc) or cast (a cable) loose

unbending (ʌn'bɛndɪŋ) adj 1 rigid or inflexible 2 characterized by sternness or severity: an unbending rule ▷ un'bendingly adv ▷ un'bendingness n

unbent (ʌn'bɛnt) vb 1 the past tense and past participle of unbend ▷ adj 2 not bent or bowed 3 not compelled to yield or give way by force

unbidden (ʌn'bɪdən) adj 1 not ordered or commanded; voluntary or spontaneous 2 not invited or asked

unbind (ʌn'baɪnd) vb -binds, -binding, -bound (tr) 1 to set free from restraining bonds or chains; release 2 to unfasten or make loose (a bond, tie, etc)

unblessed (ʌn'blɛst) adj 1 deprived of blessing 2 unhallowed, cursed, or evil 3 unhappy or wretched ▷ unblessedness or un'blesidnis) n

unblushing (ʌn'blʌʃɪŋ) adj immodest or shameless ▷ un'blushingly adv

unbolt (ʌn'bəʊlt) vb (tr) 1 to unfasten a bolt of (a door) 2 to undo (the nut) on a bolt

unbolted (ʌn'bəʊltɪd) adj (of grain, meal, or flour) not sifted

unborn (ʌn'bɔːn) adj 1 not yet born or brought to birth 2 still to come in the future: the unborn world

unbosom (ʌn'bʊzəm) vb (tr) to relieve (oneself) of (secrets, etc) by telling someone [c16: from UN-² + BOSOM

(in the sense: seat of the emotions); compare Dutch ontboezemen]

unbounded (ʌn'baʊndɪd) adj having no boundaries or limits ▷ un'boundedly adv ▷ un'boundedness n

unbowed (ʌn'baʊd) adj 1 not bowed or bent 2 free or unconquered

unbridled (ʌn'braɪdəld) adj 1 with all restraints removed 2 (of a horse, etc) wearing no bridle ▷ un'bridledly adv ▷ un'bridledness n

unbroken (ʌn'brəʊkən) adj 1 complete or whole 2 continuous or incessant 3 undaunted in spirit 4 (of animals, esp horses) not tamed; wild 5 not disturbed or upset: the unbroken silence of the afternoon 6 (of a record, esp at sport) not improved upon ▷ un'brokenly adv ▷ un'brokenness n

unbundling (ʌn'bʌndlɪŋ) n commerce the takeover of a large conglomerate with a view to retaining the core business and selling off some of the subsidiaries to help finance the takeover

unburden (ʌn'bɜːdən) vb (tr) 1 to remove a load or burden from 2 to relieve or make free (one's mind, oneself, etc) of a worry, trouble, etc, by revelation or confession

unbutton (ʌn'bʌtən) vb to undo by unfastening (the buttons) of (a garment)

unbuttoned (ʌn'bʌtənd) adj 1 with buttons not fastened 2 informal uninhibited; unrestrained: hours of unbuttoned self-revelation

uncalled-for (ˌʌn'kɔːldfɔː) adj unnecessary or unwarranted

uncanny (ʌn'kænɪ) adj 1 characterized by apparently supernatural wonder, horror, etc 2 beyond what is normal or expected: an uncanny accuracy ▷ un'cannily adv ▷ un'canniness n

uncap (ʌn'kæp) vb -caps, -capping, -capped 1 (tr) to remove a cap or top from (a container): to uncap a bottle 2 to remove a cap from (the head)

uncared-for (ˌʌn'kɛədfɔː) adj not cared for; neglected

unceremonious (ˌʌnsɛrɪ'məʊnɪəs) adj without ceremony; informal, abrupt, rude, or undignified ▷ ˌuncere'moniously adv ▷ ˌuncere'moniousness n

uncertain (ʌn'sɜːtən) adj 1 not able to be accurately known or predicted: the issue is uncertain 2 (when postpositive, often foll by of) not sure or confident (about): a man of uncertain opinion 3 not precisely determined, established, or decided: uncertain plans 4 not to be depended upon; unreliable: an uncertain vote 5 liable to variation; changeable: the weather is uncertain 6 in no uncertain terms a unambiguously b forcefully ▷ un'certainly adv

uncertainty (ʌn'sɜːtənti) n, pl -ties 1 Also called: uncertainness the state or condition of being uncertain 2 an uncertain matter, contingency, etc

uncertainty principle n the principle that energy and time or position and momentum of a quantum mechanical system, cannot both be accurately measured simultaneously. The product of their uncertainties is always greater than or of the order of h, where h is the Planck constant

uncharted (ʌn'tʃɑːtɪd) adj (of a physical or nonphysical region or area) not yet mapped, surveyed, or investigated: uncharted waters; the uncharted depths of the mind

unchartered (ʌn'tʃɑːtəd) adj 1 not authorized by charter; unregulated 2 unauthorized, lawless, or irregular

unchristian (ʌn'krɪstʃən) adj 1 not in accordance with the principles or ethics of Christianity 2 non-Christian or pagan ▷ un'christianly adv

unchurch (ʌn'tʃɜːtʃ) vb (tr) 1 to excommunicate 2 to remove church status from (a building)

uncial ('ʌnsɪəl) adj 1 of, relating to, or written in majuscule letters, as used in Greek and Latin manuscripts of the third to ninth centuries, that resemble modern capitals, but are characterized by much greater curvature and inclination and general inequality of height ▷ n 2 an uncial letter or manuscript [c17: from Late Latin unciālēs litterae letters an inch long, from Latin unciālis, from uncia one twelfth, inch, OUNCE¹] ▷ 'uncially adv

uncinate (ˈʌnsɪnɪt, -ˌneɪt) *adj biology* **1** shaped like a hook: *the uncinate process of the ribs of vertebrates* **2** of, relating to, or possessing uncini [c18: from Latin *uncīnātus*, from *uncīnus* a hook, from *uncus*]

uncircumcised (ʌnˈsɜːkəmˌsaɪzd) *adj* **1** not circumcised **2** not Jewish; gentile

uncivil (ʌnˈsɪvəl) *adj* **1** lacking civility or good manners **2** an obsolete word for **uncivilized** ▷ **uncivility** (ˌʌnsɪˈvɪlɪtɪ) *or* un'civilness *n* ▷ un'civilly *adv*

uncivilized *or* **uncivilised** (ʌnˈsɪvɪˌlaɪzd) *adj* **1** (of a tribe or people) not yet civilized, esp preliterate **2** lacking culture or sophistication ▷ **uncivilizedly** *or* **uncivilisedly** (ʌnˈsɪvɪˌlaɪzɪdlɪ) *adv* ▷ un'civiˌlizedness *or* un'civiˌlisedness *n*

unclad (ʌnˈklæd) *adj* having no clothes on; naked

unclasp (ʌnˈklɑːsp) *vb* **1** (*tr*) to unfasten the clasp of (something) **2** to release one's grip (upon an object)

uncle (ˈʌŋkəl) *n* **1 a** brother of one's father or mother **2** the husband of one's aunt **3** a term of address sometimes used by children for a male friend of their parents **4** *slang* a pawnbroker Related adj: **avuncular** [c13: from Old French *oncle*, from Latin *avunculus*; related to Latin *avus* grandfather]

unclean (ʌnˈkliːn) *adj* lacking moral, spiritual, ritual, or physical cleanliness ▷ un'cleanness *n*

uncleanly[1] (ʌnˈkliːnlɪ) *adv* in an unclean manner

uncleanly[2] (ʌnˈklɛnlɪ) *adj* characterized by an absence of cleanliness; unclean ▷ un'cleanliness *n*

Uncle Sam *n* a personification of the government of the United States [c19: apparently a humorous interpretation of the letters stamped on army supply boxes during the War of 1812; US]

Uncle Tom *n* *informal*, *derogatory* a Black person whose behaviour towards White people is regarded as obsequious and servile [c20: after the slave who is the main character of H.B. Stowe's novel *Uncle Tom's Cabin* (1852)] ▷ ˌUncle 'Tomˌism *n*

unclose (ʌnˈkləʊz) *vb* **1** to open or cause to open **2** to come or bring to light; reveal or be revealed

unclothe (ʌnˈkləʊð) *vb* **-clothes, -clothing, -clothed** *or* **-clad** (*tr*) **1** to take off garments from; strip **2** to uncover or lay bare

unco (ˈʌŋkəʊ) *Scot* ▷ *adj* uncoer, uncoest **1** unfamiliar, strange, or odd **2** remarkable or striking ▷ *adv* **3** very; extremely **4** the unco guid narrow-minded, excessively religious, or self-righteous people ▷ *n*, *pl* uncos *or* uncoes **5** a novel or remarkable person or thing **6** *obsolete* a stranger **7** (*plural*) news [c15: variant of UNCOUTH]

uncoil (ʌnˈkɔɪl) *vb* to unwind or become unwound; untwist

uncomfortable (ʌnˈkʌmftəbəl) *adj* **1** not comfortable **2** feeling or causing discomfort or unease; disquieting ▷ un'comfortableness *n* ▷ un'comfortably *adv*

uncommitted (ˌʌnkəˈmɪtɪd) *adj* not bound or pledged to a specific opinion, course of action, or cause

uncommon (ʌnˈkɒmən) *adj* **1** outside or beyond normal experience, conditions, etc; unusual **2** in excess of what is normal: *an uncommon liking for honey* ▷ *adv* **3** an archaic word for **uncommonly** (sense 2) ▷ un'commonness *n*

uncommonly (ʌnˈkɒmənlɪ) *adv* **1** in an uncommon or unusual manner or degree; rarely **2** (intensifier): *you're uncommonly friendly*

uncommunicative (ˌʌnkəˈmjuːnɪkətɪv) *adj* disinclined to talk or give information or opinions ▷ ˌuncom'municatively *adv* ▷ ˌuncom'municativeness *n*

uncompromising (ʌnˈkɒmprəˌmaɪzɪŋ) *adj* not prepared to give ground or to compromise ▷ un'comproˌmisingly *adv*

unconcern (ˌʌnkənˈsɜːn) *n* apathy or indifference

unconcerned (ˌʌnkənˈsɜːnd) *adj* **1** lacking in concern or involvement **2** not worried; untroubled ▷ **unconcernedly** (ˌʌnkənˈsɜːnɪdlɪ) *adv*

unconditional (ˌʌnkənˈdɪʃənəl) *adj* without conditions or limitations; total: *unconditional surrender* ▷ ˌuncon'ditionally *adv*

unconditioned (ˌʌnkənˈdɪʃənd) *adj* **1** *psychol* characterizing an innate reflex and the stimulus and response that form parts of it **2** *metaphysics* unrestricted by conditions; infinite; absolute **3** without limitations;

unconditional ▷ ˌuncon'ditionedness *n*

unconformable (ˌʌnkənˈfɔːməbəl) *adj* not conformable or conforming

unconscionable (ʌnˈkɒnʃənəbəl) *adj* **1** unscrupulous or unprincipled: *an unconscionable liar* **2** immoderate or excessive: *unconscionable demands* ▷ un'conscionably *adv*

unconscious (ʌnˈkɒnʃəs) *adj* **1** lacking normal sensory awareness of the environment; insensible **2** not aware of one's actions, behaviour, etc: *unconscious of his bad manners* **3** characterized by lack of awareness or intention: *an unconscious blunder* **4** coming from or produced by the unconscious: *unconscious resentment* ▷ *n* **5** *psychoanal* the part of the mind containing instincts, impulses, images, and ideas that are not available for direct examination ▷ un'consciously *adv*

unconstitutional (ˌʌnkɒnstɪˈtjuːʃənəl) *adj* at variance with or not permitted by a constitution ▷ unconstitutionality (ˌʌnkɒnstɪˌtjuːʃəˈnælɪtɪ) *n*

unconventional (ˌʌnkənˈvɛnʃənəl) *adj* not conforming to accepted rules or standards ▷ unconventionality (ˌʌnkənˌvɛnʃəˈnælɪtɪ) *n* ▷ ˌuncon'ventionally *adv*

uncool (ʌnˈkuːl) *adj* *slang* **1** unsophisticated; unfashionable **2** excitable; tense; not cool

uncork (ʌnˈkɔːk) *vb* (*tr*) **1** to draw the cork from (a bottle, etc) **2** to release or unleash (emotions, etc)

uncountable (ʌnˈkaʊntəbəl) *adj* **1** too many to be counted; innumerable **2** *linguistics* denoting a noun that does not refer to an isolable object. See **mass noun**

uncounted (ʌnˈkaʊntɪd) *adj* **1** unable to be counted; innumerable **2** not counted

uncouple (ʌnˈkʌpəl) *vb* **1** to disconnect or unfasten or become disconnected or unfastened **2** (*tr*) to set loose; release

uncouth (ʌnˈkuːθ) *adj* lacking in good manners, refinement, or grace [Old English *uncūth*, from UN-[1] + *cūth* familiar; related to Old High German *kund* known, Old Norse *kunnr*] ▷ un'couthly *adv* ▷ un'couthness *n*

uncover (ʌnˈkʌvə) *vb* **1** (*tr*) to remove the cover, cap, top, etc, from **2** (*tr*) to reveal or disclose: *to uncover a plot* **3** to take off (one's head covering), esp as a mark of respect

uncovered (ʌnˈkʌvəd) *adj* **1** not covered; revealed or bare **2** not protected by insurance, security, etc **3** with head removed as a mark of respect

UNCTAD *abbreviation* United Nations Conference on Trade and Development

unction (ˈʌŋkʃən) *n* **1** *chiefly RC*, *Eastern Churches* the act of anointing with oil in sacramental ceremonies, in the conferring of holy orders **2** excessive suavity or affected charm **3** an ointment or unguent **4** anything soothing or comforting [c14: from Latin *unctiō* an anointing, from *ungere* to anoint; see UNGUENT] ▷ 'unctionless *adj*

unctuous (ˈʌŋktjʊəs) *adj* **1** slippery or greasy **2** affecting an oily charm [c14: from Medieval Latin *unctuōsus*, from Latin *unctum* ointment, from *ungere* to anoint] ▷ **unctuosity** (ˌʌŋktjʊˈɒsɪtɪ) *or* 'unctuousness *n* ▷ 'unctuously *adv*

uncut (ʌnˈkʌt) *adj* **1** (of a book) not having the edges of its pages trimmed or slit **2** (of a gemstone) not cut and faceted **3** not abridged or shortened

undamped (ʌnˈdæmpt) *adj* **1** (of an oscillating system) having unrestricted motion; not damped **2** not repressed, discouraged, or subdued; undiminished

undaunted (ʌnˈdɔːntɪd) *adj* not put off, discouraged, or beaten ▷ un'dauntedly *adv* ▷ un'dauntedness *n*

undead (ʌnˈdɛd) *adj* **a** (of a fictional being, such as a vampire) technically dead but reanimated **b** (*as collective noun; preceded by the*): *the undead*

undecagon (ʌnˈdɛkəˌɡɒn) *n* a polygon having eleven sides [c18: from Latin *undecim* eleven (from *unus* one + *decem* ten) + -GON]

undeceive (ˌʌndɪˈsiːv) *vb* (*tr*) to reveal the truth to (someone previously misled or deceived); enlighten ▷ ˌunde'ceivable *adj* ▷ ˌunde'ceiver *n*

undecided (ˌʌndɪˈsaɪdɪd) *adj* **1** not having made up one's mind **2** (of an issue, problem, etc) not agreed or decided upon ▷ ˌunde'cidedly *adv* ▷ ˌunde'cidedness *n*

undeniable (ˌʌndɪˈnaɪəbəl) *adj* **1** unquestionably or obviously true **2** of unquestionable excellence: *a man of undeniable character* **3** unable to be resisted or denied

> ˌunde'niableness *n* > ˌunde'niably *adv*

under ('ʌndə) *prep* **1** directly below; on, to, or beneath the underside or base of: *under one's feet* **2** less than: *under forty years* **3** lower in rank than: *under a corporal* **4** subject to the supervision, jurisdiction, control, or influence of **5** subject to (conditions); in (certain circumstances) **6** within a classification of: *a book under theology* **7** known by: *under an assumed name* **8** planted with: *a field under corn* **9** powered by: *under sail* **10** *astrology* during the period that the sun is in (a sign of the zodiac): *born under Aries* ▷ *adv* **11** below; to a position underneath something [Old English; related to Old Saxon, Gothic *undar*, Old High German *untar*, Old Norse *undir*, Latin *infra*]

under- *prefix* **1** below or beneath: *underarm; underground* **2** of lesser importance or lower rank: *undersecretary* **3** to a lesser degree than is proper; insufficient or insufficiently: *undercharge; underemployed* **4** indicating secrecy or deception: *underhand*

underachieve (ˌʌndərə'tʃiːv) *vb* (*intr*) to fail to achieve a performance appropriate to one's age or talents > ˌundera'chiever *n* > ˌunderа'chievement *n*

underact (ˌʌndər'ækt) *vb theatre* to play (a role) without adequate emphasis

underage (ˌʌndər'eɪdʒ) *adj* below the required or standard age, esp below the legal age for voting or drinking

underarm ('ʌndərˌɑːm) *adj* **1** (of a measurement) extending along the arm from wrist to armpit **2** *sport* of or denoting a style of throwing, bowling, or serving in which the hand is swung below shoulder level **3** below the arm ▷ *adv* **4** in an underarm style

underbelly ('ʌndəˌbɛlɪ) *n, pl* -lies **1** the part of an animal's belly nearest to the ground **2** a vulnerable or unprotected part, aspect, or region

underbid (ˌʌndə'bɪd) *vb* -bids, -bidding, -bid (*tr*) **1** to submit a bid lower than that of (others): *Irena underbid the other dealers* **2** to submit an excessively low bid for **3** *bridge* to make a bid that will win fewer tricks than is justified by the strength of the hand: *he underbid his hand* > 'underˌbidder *n*

underbody ('ʌndəˌbɒdɪ) *n, pl* -bodies the underpart of a body, as of an animal or motor vehicle

underbred (ˌʌndə'brɛd) *adj* of impure stock; not thoroughbred > ˌunder'breeding *n*

underbuy (ˌʌndə'baɪ) *vb* -buys, -buying, -bought **1** to buy (stock in trade) in amounts lower than required **2** (*tr*) to buy at a price below that paid by (others) **3** (*tr*) to pay a price less than the true value for

undercapitalize *or* **undercapitalise** (ˌʌndə'kæpɪtəˌlaɪz) *vb* to provide or issue capital for (a commercial enterprise) in an amount insufficient for efficient operation

undercarriage ('ʌndəˌkærɪdʒ) *n* **1** Also called: **landing gear** the assembly of wheels, shock absorbers, struts, etc, that supports an aircraft on the ground and enables it to take off and land **2** the framework that supports the body of a vehicle, carriage, etc

undercharge (ˌʌndə'tʃɑːdʒ) *vb* **1** to charge too little (for) **2** (*tr*) to load (a gun, cannon, etc,) with an inadequate charge

underclass ('ʌndəˌklɑːs) *n* a class beneath the usual social scale consisting of the most disadvantaged people, such as the unemployed in inner cities

underclothes ('ʌndəˌkləʊðz) *pl n* a variant of **underwear**. Also called: **underclothing**

undercoat ('ʌndəˌkəʊt) *n* **1** a coat of paint or other substance applied before the top coat **2** a coat worn under an overcoat **3** *zoology* another name for **underfur** **4** the US name for **underseal** ▷ *vb* **5** (*tr*) to apply an undercoat to (a surface)

undercover (ˌʌndə'kʌvə) *adj* done or acting in secret: *undercover operations*

undercroft ('ʌndəˌkrɒft) *n* an underground chamber, such as a church crypt, often with a vaulted ceiling [c14: from *crypt* a vault, cavern, from earlier *crofte*, ultimately from Latin *crypta* CRYPT]

undercurrent ('ʌndəˌkʌrənt) *n* **1** a current that is not apparent at the surface or lies beneath another current **2** an opinion, emotion, etc, lying beneath apparent feeling or meaning ▷ Also called: **underflow**

undercut *vb* (ˌʌndə'kʌt, 'ʌndəˌkʌt) -cuts, -cutting, -cut **1** to charge less than (a competitor) in order to obtain trade **2** to cut away the under part of (something) **3** *sport* to hit (a ball) in such a way as to impart backspin ▷ *n* ('ʌndəˌkʌt) **4** the act or an instance of cutting underneath **5** a part that is cut away underneath **6** a tenderloin of beef, including the fillet **7** *forestry, chiefly US & Canadian* a notch cut in a tree trunk, to ensure a clean break in felling **8** *sport* a stroke that imparts backspin to the ball

underdaks ('ʌndəˌdæks) *pl n Austral* an informal word for **underpants**

underdevelop (ˌʌndədɪ'vɛləp) *vb* (*tr*) *photog* to process (a film, plate, or paper) in developer for less than the required time, or at too low a temperature, or in an exhausted solution

underdeveloped (ˌʌndədɪ'vɛləpt) *adj* **1** immature or undersized **2** relating to societies in which both the surplus capital and the social organization necessary to advance are lacking **3** *photog* (of a film, plate, or print) processed in developer for less than the required time, thus lacking in contrast

underdog ('ʌndəˌdɒg) *n* **1** the competitor least likely to win a fight or contest **2** a person in adversity or in a position of inferiority

underdone (ˌʌndə'dʌn) *adj* insufficiently or lightly cooked

underdressed (ˌʌndə'drɛst) *adj* wearing clothes that are not elaborate or formal enough for a particular occasion

underemployed (ˌʌndərɪm'plɔɪd) *adj* not fully or adequately employed

underestimate *vb* (*tr*) (ˌʌndər'ɛstɪˌmeɪt) **1** to make too low an estimate of: *he underestimated the cost* **2** to think insufficiently highly of: *to underestimate a person* ▷ *n* (ˌʌndər'ɛstɪmɪt) **3** too low an estimate > ˌunderˌesti'mation *n*

● USAGE *Underestimate* is sometimes wrongly used where
● *overestimate* is meant: *the importance of his work cannot be*
● *overestimated* (not *cannot be underestimated*)

underexpose (ˌʌndərɪk'spəʊz) *vb* (*tr*) **1** *photog* to expose (a film, plate, or paper) for too short a period or with insufficient light so as not to produce the required effect **2** (*often passive*) to fail to subject to appropriate or expected publicity

underfeed (ˌʌndə'fiːd) *vb* -feeds, -feeding, -fed (*tr*) **1** to give too little food to **2** to supply (a furnace, engine, etc) with fuel from beneath

underfelt ('ʌndəˌfɛlt) *n* thick felt laid between floorboards and carpet to increase insulation and resilience

underfloor ('ʌndəˌflɔː) *adj* situated beneath the floor: *underfloor heating*

underfoot (ˌʌndə'fʊt) *adv* **1** underneath the feet; on the ground **2** in a position of subjugation or subservience **3** in the way

underfur ('ʌndəˌfɜː) *n* the layer of dense soft fur occurring beneath the outer coarser fur in certain mammals, such as the otter and seal. Also called: **undercoat**

undergarment ('ʌndəˌgɑːmənt) *n* any garment worn under the visible outer clothes, usually next to the skin

undergird (ˌʌndə'gɜːd) *vb* -girds, -girding, -girded *or* -girt (*tr*) to strengthen or reinforce by passing a rope, cable, or chain around the underside of (an object, load, etc) [c16: from UNDER- + GIRD¹]

underglaze ('ʌndəˌgleɪz) *adj* **1** *ceramics* applied to pottery or porcelain before the application of glaze ▷ *n* **2** a pigment, etc, applied in this way

undergo (ˌʌndə'gəʊ) *vb* -goes, -going, -went, -gone (*tr*) to experience, endure, or sustain: *to undergo a dramatic change of feelings* [Old English: earlier meanings were more closely linked with the senses of *under* and *go*] > 'underˌgoer *n*

undergraduate (ˌʌndə'grædjʊɪt) *n* a person studying in a university for a first degree

underground *adj* ('ʌndəˌgraʊnd) **1** occurring, situated, or used below ground level: *an underground tunnel; an underground explosion* **2** secret; hidden: *underground activities*

▷ *adv* (ˌʌndə'graʊnd) **3** going below ground level: *the tunnel led underground* **4** into hiding or secrecy: *the group was driven underground* ▷ *n* (ˌʌndəˌgraʊnd) **5** a space or region below ground level **6 a** a movement dedicated to overthrowing a government or occupation forces, as in the European countries occupied by the German army in World War II **b** (*as modifier*): *an underground group* **7** the underground an electric passenger railway operated in underground tunnels. US and Canadian equivalent: subway **8** (*usually preceded by the*) **a** any avant-garde, experimental, or subversive movement in popular art, films, music, etc **b** (*as modifier*): *the underground press; underground music*

underground railroad *n* (*often capitals*) (in the pre-Civil War US) the system established by abolitionists to aid escaping slaves

undergrowth ('ʌndəˌgrəʊθ) *n* small trees, bushes, ferns, etc, growing beneath taller trees in a wood or forest

underhand ('ʌndəˌhænd) *adj also* underhanded **1** clandestine, deceptive, or secretive **2** *sport* another word for **underarm** ▷ *adv* **3** in an underhand manner or style

underhanded (ˌʌndə'hændɪd) *adj* another word for **underhand** or **short-handed**

underhung (ˌʌndə'hʌŋ) *adj* **1** (of the lower jaw) projecting beyond the upper jaw; undershot **2** (of a sliding door, etc) supported at its lower edge by a track or rail

underlay *vb* (ˌʌndə'leɪ) -lays, -laying, -laid (*tr*) **1** to place (something) under or beneath **2** to support by something laid beneath **3** to achieve the correct printing pressure all over (a forme block) or to bring (a block) up to type height by adding material, such as paper, to the appropriate areas beneath it ▷ *n* ('ʌndəˌleɪ) **4** a layer, lining, support, etc, laid underneath something else **5** *printing* material, such as paper, used to underlay a forme or block **6** felt, rubber, etc, laid beneath a carpet to increase insulation and resilience

underlie (ˌʌndə'laɪ) *vb* -lies, -lying, -lay, -lain (*tr*) **1** to lie or be placed under or beneath **2** to be the foundation, cause, or basis of: *careful planning underlies all our decisions* **3** *finance* to take priority over (another claim, liability, mortgage, etc) **4** to be the root or stem from which (a word) is derived: *"happy" underlies "happiest"* > 'under,lier *n*

underline (ˌʌndə'laɪn) *vb* (*tr*) **1** to put a line under **2** to state forcibly; emphasize or reinforce

underlinen ('ʌndəˌlɪnən) *n* underclothes, esp when made of linen

underling ('ʌndəlɪŋ) *n* a subordinate or lackey

underlying (ˌʌndə'laɪɪŋ) *adj* **1** concealed but detectable: *underlying guilt* **2** fundamental; basic **3** lying under **4** *finance* (of a claim, liability, etc) taking precedence; prior

undermentioned (ˌʌndəˌmɛnʃənd) *adj* mentioned below or subsequently

undermine (ˌʌndə'maɪn) *vb* (*tr*) **1** (of the sea, wind, etc) to wear away the bottom or base of (land, cliffs, etc) **2** to weaken gradually or insidiously: *their insults undermined her confidence* **3** to tunnel or dig beneath > ˌunder'miner *n*

undermost (ˌʌndəˌməʊst) *adj* **1** being the furthest under; lowest ▷ *adv* **2** in the lowest place

underneath (ˌʌndə'ni:θ) *prep, adv* **1** under; beneath ▷ *adj* **2** lower ▷ *n* **3** a lower part, surface, etc [Old English *undernēothan*, from UNDER + *nēothan* below; related to Old Danish *underneden*; see BENEATH]

undernourish (ˌʌndə'nʌrɪʃ) *vb* (*tr; usually passive*) to deprive of or fail to provide with nutrients essential for health and growth > ˌunder'nourishment *n*

underpants (ˌʌndəˌpænts) *pl n* a man's undergarment covering the body from the waist or hips to the top of the thighs or knees. Often shortened to **pants**

underpass ('ʌndəˌpɑ:s) *n* **1** a section of a road that passes under another road, railway line, etc **2** another word for **subway** (sense 1)

underpay (ˌʌndə'peɪ) *vb* -pays, -paying, -paid to pay (someone) insufficiently > ˌunder'payment *n*

underpin (ˌʌndə'pɪn) *vb* -pins, -pinning, -pinned (*tr*) **1** to support from beneath, esp by a prop, while avoiding damaging or weakening the superstructure: *to underpin a*

wall **2** to give corroboration, strength, or support to

underpinning ('ʌndəˌpɪnɪŋ) *n* a structure of masonry, concrete, etc, placed beneath a wall to provide support

underplay (ˌʌndə'pleɪ) *vb* **1** to play (a role) with restraint or subtlety **2** to achieve (an effect) by deliberate lack of emphasis **3** (*intr*) *cards* to lead or follow suit with a lower card when holding a higher one

underprivileged (ˌʌndə'prɪvɪlɪdʒd) *adj* lacking the rights and advantages of other members of society; deprived

underproduction (ˌʌndəprə'dʌkʃən) *n commerce* production below full capacity or below demand

underproof (ˌʌndə'pru:f) *adj* (of a spirit) containing less than 57.1 per cent alcohol by volume

underquote (ˌʌndə'kwəʊt) *vb* **1** to offer for sale (securities, goods, or services) at a price lower than the market price **2** (*tr*) to quote a price lower than that quoted by (another)

underrate (ˌʌndə'reɪt) *vb* (*tr*) to underestimate

underscore (ˌʌndə'skɔ:) *vb* (*tr*) **1** to draw or score a line or mark under **2** to stress or reinforce

undersea ('ʌndəˌsi:) *adj, adv also* underseas (ˌʌndə'si:z) below the surface of the sea

underseal ('ʌndəˌsi:l) *Brit* ▷ *n* **1** a coating of a tar or rubber-based material applied to the underside of a motor vehicle to retard corrosion ▷ *vb* **2** (*tr*) to apply a coating of underseal to (a motor vehicle)

undersecretary (ˌʌndə'sɛkrətrɪ) *n, pl* -taries **1** (in Britain) **a** any of various senior civil servants in certain government departments **b** short for **undersecretary of state**: any of various high officials subordinate only to the minister in charge of a department **2** (in the US) a high government official subordinate only to the secretary in charge of a department

undersell (ˌʌndə'sɛl) *vb* -sells, -selling, -sold **1** to sell for less than the usual or expected price **2** (*tr*) to sell at a price lower than that of (another seller) **3** (*tr*) to advertise (merchandise) with moderation or restraint > ˌunder'seller *n*

undersexed (ˌʌndə'sɛkst) *adj* having weaker sex urges or responses than is considered normal

undershirt ('ʌndəˌʃɜ:t) *n chiefly US & Canadian* an undergarment worn under a blouse or shirt. Brit name: vest

undershoot (ˌʌndə'ʃu:t) *vb* -shoots, -shooting, -shot **1** (of a pilot) to cause (an aircraft) to land short of (a runway) or (of an aircraft) to land in this way **2** to shoot a projectile so that it falls short of (a target)

undershorts ('ʌndəˌʃɔ:ts) *pl n* another word for **shorts** (sense 2)

undershot ('ʌndəˌʃɒt) *adj* **1** (of the lower jaw) projecting beyond the upper jaw; underhung **2** (of a water wheel) driven by a flow of water that passes under the wheel rather than over it

underside ('ʌndəˌsaɪd) *n* the bottom or lower surface

undersigned ('ʌndəˌsaɪnd) *n* **1** the undersigned the person or persons who have signed at the foot of a document, statement, etc ▷ *adj* **2** having signed one's name at the foot of a document, statement, etc

undersized (ˌʌndə'saɪzd) *adj* of less than usual size

underskirt ('ʌndəˌskɜ:t) *n* any skirtlike garment worn under a skirt

underslung (ˌʌndə'slʌŋ) *adj* suspended below a supporting member, esp (of a motor vehicle chassis) suspended below the axles

understand (ˌʌndə'stænd) *vb* -stands, -standing, -stood **1** (*may take a clause as object*) to know and comprehend the nature or meaning of: *I understand you; I understand what you mean* **2** (*may take a clause as object*) to realize or grasp (something): *he understands your position* **3** (*tr; may take a clause as object*) to assume, infer, or believe: *I understand you are thinking of marrying* **4** (*tr*) to know how to translate or read: *can you understand Spanish?* **5** (*tr; may take a clause as object; often passive*) to accept as a condition or proviso: *it is understood that children must be kept quiet* **6** (*tr*) to be sympathetic to or compatible with: *we understand each other* [Old English *understandan*; related to Old Frisian *understonda*, Middle High German *understān* step under; see UNDER, STAND] > ˌunder'standable *adj* > ˌunder'standably *adv*

u

understanding (ˌʌndəˈstændɪŋ) n 1 the ability to learn, judge, make decisions, etc; intelligence or sense 2 personal opinion or interpretation of a subject: *my understanding of your predicament* 3 a mutual agreement or compact, esp an informal or private one 4 *chiefly Brit* an unofficial engagement to be married 5 *philosophy archaic* the mind, esp the faculty of reason 6 **on the understanding that** with the condition that; providing ▷ *adj* 7 sympathetic, tolerant, or wise towards people 8 possessing judgment and intelligence > ˌunderˈstandingly *adv*

understate (ˌʌndəˈsteɪt) vb 1 to state (something) in restrained terms, often to obtain an ironic effect 2 to state that (something, such as a number) is less than it is > ˈunderˌstatement n

understeer (ˈʌndəˌstɪə) vb (*intr*) (of a vehicle) to turn less sharply, for a particular movement of the steering wheel, than anticipated

understood (ˌʌndəˈstʊd) vb 1 the past tense and past participle of **understand** ▷ *adj* 2 implied or inferred 3 taken for granted; assumed

understudy (ˈʌndəˌstʌdɪ) vb -studies, -studying, -studied 1 (*tr*) to study (a role or part) so as to be able to replace the usual actor or actress if necessary 2 to act as understudy to (an actor or actress) ▷ n, *pl* -studies 3 an actor or actress who studies a part so as to be able to replace the usual actor or actress if necessary 4 anyone who is trained to take the place of another in case of need

undertake (ˌʌndəˈteɪk) vb -takes, -taking, -took, -taken 1 (*tr*) to contract to or commit oneself to (something) or (to do something): *to undertake a job; to undertake to deliver the goods* 2 (*tr*) to attempt to; agree to start 3 (*tr*) to take (someone) in charge 4 (*intr; foll by for*) *archaic* to make oneself responsible (for) 5 (*tr*) to promise

undertaker (ˈʌndəˌteɪkə) n a person whose profession is the preparation of the dead for burial or cremation and the management of funerals; funeral director

undertaking (ˈʌndəˌteɪkɪŋ) n 1 something undertaken; task, venture, or enterprise 2 an agreement to do something 3 the business of an undertaker

underthings (ˈʌndəˌθɪŋz) pl n girls' or women's underwear

underthrust (ˈʌndəˌθrʌst) n *geology* a reverse fault in which the rocks on the lower surface of a fault plane have moved under the relatively static rocks on the upper surface

undertone (ˈʌndəˌtəʊn) n 1 a quiet or hushed tone of voice 2 an underlying tone or suggestion in words or actions: *his offer has undertones of dishonesty*

undertow (ˈʌndəˌtəʊ) n 1 the seaward undercurrent following the breaking of a wave on the beach 2 any strong undercurrent flowing in a different direction from the surface current

undertrick (ˈʌndəˌtrɪk) n *bridge* a trick by which a declarer falls short of making his contract

undervalue (ˌʌndəˈvæljuː) vb -values, -valuing, -valued (*tr*) to value at too low a level or price > ˌunderˌvaluˈation n > ˌunderˈvaluer n

undervest (ˈʌndəˌvɛst) n *Brit* another name for **vest** (sense 1)

underwater (ˌʌndəˈwɔːtə) adj 1 being, occurring, or going under the surface of the water, esp the sea: *underwater exploration* 2 *nautical* below the water line of a vessel ▷ *adv* 3 beneath the surface of the water

under way adj (*postpositive*) 1 in progress; in operation: *the show was under way* 2 *nautical* in motion

underwear (ˈʌndəˌwɛə) n clothing worn under the outer garments, usually next to the skin

underweight (ˌʌndəˈweɪt) adj 1 weighing less than is average, expected, or healthy 2 *finance* a having a lower proportion of one's investments in a particular sector of the market than the size of that sector relative to the total market would suggest b (of a fund etc) disproportionately invested in this way: *pension funds have become underweight of equities*

underwent (ˌʌndəˈwɛnt) vb the past tense of **undergo**

underwhelm (ˌʌndəˈwɛlm) vb (*tr*) to make no positive impact or impression on; disappoint [c20: originally a humorous coinage based on *overwhelm*]

underwhelming (ˌʌndəˈwɛlmɪŋ) adj failing to make a positive impact or impression; disappointing

underwing (ˈʌndəˌwɪŋ) n 1 the hind wing of an insect, esp when covered by the forewing 2 See **red underwing**, **yellow underwing**

underwood (ˈʌndəˌwʊd) n a less common word for **undergrowth**

Underwood (ˈʌndəˌwʊd) n **Rory.** born 1963, British Rugby Union football player; played for England (1984–99), becoming Britain's most capped player

underworld (ˈʌndəˌwɜːld) n 1 a criminals and their associates considered collectively b (*as modifier*): *underworld connections* 2 *Greek and Roman myth* the regions below the earth's surface regarded as the abode of the dead; Hades

underwrite (ˈʊndəˌraɪt, ˌʌndəˈraɪt) vb -writes, -writing, -wrote, -written (*tr*) 1 *finance* to undertake to purchase at an agreed price any unsold portion of (a public issue of shares, etc) 2 to accept financial responsibility for (a commercial project or enterprise) 3 *insurance* a to sign and issue (an insurance policy) thus accepting liability if specified losses occur b to insure (a property or risk) c to accept liability up to (a specified amount) in an insurance policy 4 to write (words, a signature, etc) beneath (other written matter); subscribe

underwriter (ˈʌndəˌraɪtə) n 1 a person or enterprise that underwrites public issues of shares, bonds, etc 2 a a person or enterprise that underwrites insurance policies b an employee or agent of an insurance company who assesses risks and determines the premiums payable

undesirable (ˌʌndɪˈzaɪərəbᵊl) adj 1 not desirable or pleasant; objectionable ▷ n 2 a person or thing that is considered undesirable > ˌundeˌsiraˈbility or ˌundeˈsirableness n > ˌundeˈsirably *adv*

undetermined (ˌʌndɪˈtɜːmɪnd) adj 1 not yet resolved; undecided 2 not known or discovered

undies (ˈʌndɪz) pl n *informal* women's underwear

undine (ˈʌndiːn) n any of various female water spirits [c17: from New Latin *undina*, from Latin *unda* a wave]

undisputed world champion n *boxing* a boxer who holds the World Boxing Association, the World Boxing Council, the World Boxing Organization, and the International Boxing Federation world championship titles simultaneously

undistributed (ˌʌndɪsˈtrɪbjʊtɪd) adj 1 *logic* (of a term) referring only to some members of the class designated by the term, as *doctors* in *some doctors are overworked* 2 *business* (of a profit) not paid in dividends to the shareholders of a company but retained to help finance its trading

undo (ʌnˈduː) vb -does, -doing, -did, -done (*mainly tr*) 1 (*also intr*) to untie, unwrap, or open or become untied, unwrapped, etc 2 to reverse the effects of 3 to cause the downfall of

undoing (ʌnˈduːɪŋ) n 1 ruin; downfall 2 the cause of downfall: *drink was his undoing*

undone¹ (ʌnˈdʌn) adj not done or completed; unfinished

undone² (ʌnˈdʌn) adj 1 ruined; destroyed 2 unfastened; untied

undoubted (ʌnˈdaʊtɪd) adj beyond doubt; certain or indisputable > unˈdoubtedly *adv*

undreamed (ʌnˈdriːmd) *or* **undreamt** (ʌnˈdrɛmt) adj (often foll by *of*) not thought of, conceived, or imagined

undress (ʌnˈdrɛs) vb 1 to take off clothes from (oneself or another) 2 (*tr*) to strip of ornamentation 3 (*tr*) to remove the dressing from (a wound) ▷ n 4 partial or complete nakedness 5 informal or normal working clothes or uniform

undressed (ʌnˈdrɛst) adj 1 partially or completely naked 2 (of an animal hide) not fully processed 3 (of food, esp salad) not prepared with sauce or dressing

Undset (*Norwegian* ˈʊnsɛt) n **Sigrid** (ˈsigri). 1882–1949, Norwegian novelist, best known for her trilogy *Kristin Lavransdatter* (1920–22): Nobel prize for literature 1928

undue (ʌnˈdjuː) adj 1 excessive or unwarranted 2 unjust, improper, or illegal 3 (of a debt, bond, etc) not yet payable

undulant (ˈʌndjʊlənt) adj *rare* resembling waves;

undulating ▷ 'undulance n

undulant fever n another name for **brucellosis** [c19: so called because the fever symptoms are intermittent]

undulate vb (ˈʌndjʊˌleɪt) **1** to move or cause to move in waves or as if in waves **2** to have or provide with a wavy form or appearance ▷ adj (ˈʌndjʊlɪt, -ˌleɪt) Also: **undulated 3** having a wavy or rippled appearance, margin, or form: an undulate leaf [c17: from Latin undulātus, from unda a wave] ▷ 'unduˌlator n ▷ 'undulatory adj

undulation (ˌʌndjʊˈleɪʃən) n **1** the act or an instance of undulating **2** any wave or wavelike form, line, etc

unduly (ʌnˈdjuːlɪ) adv immoderately; excessively

undying (ʌnˈdaɪɪŋ) adj unending; eternal ▷ un'dyingly adv

unearned (ʌnˈɜːnd) adj **1** not deserved **2** not yet earned

unearned income n income from property, investment, etc, comprising rent, interest, and dividends

unearth (ʌnˈɜːθ) vb (tr) **1** to dig up out of the earth **2** to reveal or discover, esp by exhaustive searching

unearthly (ʌnˈɜːθlɪ) adj **1** ghostly; eerie; weird: unearthly screams **2** heavenly; sublime: unearthly music **3** ridiculous or unreasonable (esp in the phrase **unearthly hour**) ▷ un'earthliness n

uneasy (ʌnˈiːzɪ) adj **1** (of a person) anxious; apprehensive **2** (of a condition) precarious; uncomfortable: an uneasy truce **3** (of a thought, etc) disturbing; disquieting ▷ un'ease n ▷ un'easily adv ▷ un'easiness n

uneatable (ʌnˈiːtəbəl) adj not pleasant or safe enough to be eaten

uneconomic (ˌʌniːkəˈnɒmɪk, ˌʌnɛkə-) adj not economic; not profitable

uneconomical (ˌʌniːkəˈnɒmɪkəl, ˌʌnɛkə-) adj not economical; wasteful

unemployable (ˌʌnɪmˈplɔɪəbəl) adj unable or unfit to keep a job ▷ ˌunemˌploya'bility n

unemployed (ˌʌnɪmˈplɔɪd) adj **1 a** without remunerative employment; out of work **b** (as collective noun; preceded by the): the unemployed **2** not being used; idle

unemployment (ˌʌnɪmˈplɔɪmənt) n **1** the condition of being unemployed **2** the number of unemployed workers, often as a percentage of the total labour force

unemployment benefit n (in Britain, formerly) a regular payment to a person who is out of work: replaced by jobseeker's allowance in 1996. Informal term: **dole**

unequal (ʌnˈiːkwəl) adj **1** not equal in quantity, size, rank, value, etc **2** (foll by to) inadequate; insufficient **3** not evenly balanced **4** (of character, quality, etc) irregular; varying; inconsistent **5** (of a contest, etc) having competitors of different ability

unequalled or US **unequaled** (ʌnˈiːkwəld) adj not equalled; unparalleled or unrivalled; supreme

unequivocal (ˌʌnɪˈkwɪvəkˤl) adj not ambiguous; plain ▷ ˌune'quivocally adv ▷ ˌune'quivocalness n

unerring (ʌnˈɜːrɪŋ) adj **1** not missing the mark or target **2** consistently accurate; certain ▷ un'erringness n

UNESCO (juːˈnɛskəʊ) n acronym for United Nations Educational, Scientific, and Cultural Organization: an agency of the United Nations that sponsors programmes to promote education, communication, the arts, etc

uneven (ʌnˈiːvən) adj **1** (of a surface, etc) not level or flat **2** spasmodic or variable **3** not parallel, straight, or horizontal **4** not fairly matched: an uneven race **5** archaic not equal ▷ un'evenly adv ▷ un'evenness n

uneventful (ˌʌnɪˈvɛntfʊl) adj ordinary, routine, or quiet ▷ ˌune'ventfully adv ▷ ˌune'ventfulness n

unexampled (ˌʌnɪɡˈzɑːmpˤld) adj without precedent or parallel

unexceptionable (ˌʌnɪkˈsɛpʃənəbˤl) adj beyond criticism or objection ▷ ˌunex'ceptionably adv

unexceptional (ˌʌnɪkˈsɛpʃənˤl) adj **1** usual, ordinary, or normal **2** subject to or allowing no exceptions **3** not standard another word for **unexceptionable** ▷ ˌunex'ceptionally adv

unexcited (ˌʌnɪkˈsaɪtɪd) adj **1** not aroused to pleasure, interest, agitation, etc **2** (of an atom, molecule, etc) remaining in its ground state

unexpected (ˌʌnɪkˈspɛktɪd) adj surprising or unforeseen

▷ ˌunex'pectedly adv ▷ ˌunex'pectedness n

unfailing (ʌnˈfeɪlɪŋ) adj **1** not failing; unflagging **2** continuous or unceasing **3** sure; certain ▷ un'failingly adv ▷ un'failingness n

unfair (ʌnˈfɛə) adj **1** characterized by inequality or injustice **2** dishonest or unethical ▷ un'fairly adv ▷ un'fairness n

unfaithful (ʌnˈfeɪθfʊl) adj **1** not true to a promise, vow, etc **2** not true to a wife, husband, lover, etc, esp in having sexual intercourse with someone else **3** inaccurate; inexact; unreliable; untrustworthy: unfaithful copy **4** obsolete not having religious faith; infidel ▷ un'faithfully adv ▷ un'faithfulness n

unfamiliar (ˌʌnfəˈmɪljə) adj **1** not known or experienced; strange **2** (postpositive; foll by with) not familiar ▷ unfamiliarity (ˌʌnfəˌmɪlɪˈærɪtɪ) n ▷ ˌunfa'miliarly adv

unfasten (ʌnˈfɑːsən) vb to undo, untie, or open or become unfastened, untied, or opened

unfathered (ʌnˈfɑːðəd) adj **1** having no known father **2** of unknown or uncertain origin

unfathomable (ʌnˈfæðəməbˤl) adj **1** incapable of being fathomed; immeasurable **2** incomprehensible ▷ un'fathomableness n ▷ un'fathomably adv

unfavourable or US **unfavorable** (ʌnˈfeɪvərəbˤl, -ˈfeɪvrə-) adj not favourable; adverse or inauspicious ▷ un'favourably or US un'favorably adv

unfazed (ʌnˈfeɪzd) adj informal not disconcerted; unperturbed

Unfederated Malay States (ʌnˈfɛdəˌreɪtɪd) pl n a former group of native states in the Malay Peninsula that became British protectorates between 1885 and 1909. All except Brunei joined the Malayan Union (later Federation of Malaya) in 1946. Brunei joined the Federation of Malaysia in 1963 but later became an independent nation

unfeeling (ʌnˈfiːlɪŋ) adj **1** without sympathy; callous **2** without physical feeling or sensation ▷ un'feelingly adv ▷ un'feelingness n

unfinished (ʌnˈfɪnɪʃt) adj **1** incomplete or imperfect **2** (of paint, polish, varnish, etc) without an applied finish; rough **3** (of fabric) unbleached or not processed

unfit (ʌnˈfɪt) adj **1** (postpositive; often foll by for) unqualified, incapable, or incompetent: unfit for military service **2** (postpositive; often foll by for) unsuitable or inappropriate: the ground was unfit for football **3** in poor physical condition ▷ un'fitness n

unfix (ʌnˈfɪks) vb (tr) **1** to unfasten, detach, or loosen **2** to unsettle or disturb

unflappable (ʌnˈflæpəbˤl) adj informal hard to upset; imperturbable; calm; composed ▷ unˌflappa'bility or un'flappableness n ▷ un'flappably adv

unfledged (ʌnˈflɛdʒd) adj **1** (of a young bird) not having developed adult feathers **2** immature and undeveloped

unflinching (ʌnˈflɪntʃɪŋ) adj not shrinking from danger, difficulty, etc ▷ un'flinchingly adv

unfold (ʌnˈfəʊld) vb **1** to open or spread out or be opened or spread out from a folded state **2** to reveal or be revealed: the truth unfolds **3** to develop or expand or be developed or expanded ▷ un'folder n

unfortunate (ʌnˈfɔːtʃənɪt) adj **1** causing or attended by misfortune **2** unlucky, unsuccessful, or unhappy: an unfortunate character **3** regrettable or unsuitable: an unfortunate speech ▷ n **4** an unlucky person

unfortunately (ʌnˈfɔːtʃənɪtlɪ) adv (sentence modifier) it is regrettable that; unluckily

unfounded (ʌnˈfaʊndɪd) adj **1** (of ideas, allegations, etc) baseless; groundless **2** not yet founded or established ▷ un'foundedly adv ▷ un'foundedness n

unfranked income n any income from an investment that does not qualify as franked investment income

unfreeze (ʌnˈfriːz) vb -freezes, -freezing, -froze, -frozen **1** to thaw or cause to thaw **2** (tr) to relax governmental restrictions on (wages, prices, credit, etc) or on the manufacture or sale of (goods, etc)

unfriended (ʌnˈfrɛndɪd) adj now rare without a friend or friends; friendless

unfriendly (ʌnˈfrɛndlɪ) adj -lier, -liest **1** not friendly; hostile **2** unfavourable or disagreeable ▷ adv **3** rare in an unfriendly manner > un'friendliness *n*

unfrock (ʌnˈfrɒk) *vb* (*tr*) to deprive (a person in holy orders) of ecclesiastical status

unfunded debt (ʌnˈfʌndɪd) *n* a short-term floating debt not represented by bonds

unfurl (ʌnˈfɜːl) *vb* to unroll, unfold, or spread out or be unrolled, unfolded, or spread out from a furled state

ungainly (ʌnˈgeɪnlɪ) *adj* -lier, -liest 1 lacking grace when moving 2 difficult to move or use; unwieldy [c17: from UN-¹ + obsolete or dialect GAINLY graceful] > un'gainliness *n*

Ungaretti (*Italian* uŋgaˈretti) *n* **Giuseppe** (dʒuˈzɛppe). 1888–1970, Italian poet, best known for his collection of war poems *Allegria di naufragi* (1919)

Ungava (ʊŋˈgeɪvə, -ˈgɑː-) *n* a sparsely inhabited region of NE Canada, in N Quebec east of Hudson Bay, part of the Labrador peninsula: rich mineral resources. Area: 911 110 sq km (351 780 sq miles)

ungodly (ʌnˈgɒdlɪ) *adj* -lier, -liest 1 a wicked; sinful b (*as collective noun; preceded by the*): *the ungodly* 2 *informal* unseemly; outrageous (esp in the phrase **an ungodly hour**) > un'godliness *n*

ungovernable (ʌnˈgʌvənəb³l) *adj* not able to be disciplined, restrained, etc: *an ungovernable temper* > un'governableness *n* > un'governably *adv*

ungual (ˈʌŋgwəl) *adj* 1 of, relating to, or affecting the fingernails or toenails 2 of or relating to an unguis [c19: from Latin *unguis* nail, claw]

unguarded (ʌnˈgɑːdɪd) *adj* 1 unprotected; vulnerable 2 guileless; open; frank 3 incautious or careless > un'guardedly *adv* > un'guardedness *n*

unguent (ˈʌŋgwənt) *n* a less common name for an **ointment** [c15: from Latin *unguentum*, from *unguere* to anoint]

unguiculate (ʌŋˈgwɪkjʊlɪt, -ˌleɪt) *adj* 1 (of mammals) having claws or nails 2 (of petals) having a clawlike base ▷ *n* 3 an unguiculate mammal [c19: from New Latin *unguiculātus*, from Latin *unguiculus*, diminutive of *unguis* nail, claw]

unguis (ˈʌŋgwɪs) *n*, *pl* **-gues** (-gwiːz) 1 a nail, claw, or hoof, or the part of the digit giving rise to it 2 the clawlike base of certain petals [c18: from Latin]

ungula (ˈʌŋgjʊlə) *n*, *pl* **-lae** (-ˌliː) 1 *maths* a truncated cone, cylinder, etc 2 a rare word for **hoof** [c18: from Latin: hoof, from *unguis* nail] > 'ungular *adj*

ungulate (ˈʌŋgjʊlɪt, -ˌleɪt) *n* any of a large group of mammals all of which have hooves: divided into odd-toed ungulates (perissodactyls) and even-toed ungulates (artiodactyls) [c19: from Late Latin *ungulātus* having hooves, from UNGULA]

unhallowed (ʌnˈhæləʊd) *adj* 1 not consecrated or holy: *unhallowed ground* 2 sinful or profane

unhand (ʌnˈhænd) *vb* (*tr*) *archaic or literary* to release from the grasp

unhappy (ʌnˈhæpɪ) *adj* -pier, -piest 1 not joyful; sad or depressed 2 unfortunate or wretched: *an unhappy fellow* 3 tactless or inappropriate: *an unhappy remark* > un'happily *adv* > un'happiness *n*

UNHCR *abbreviation* United Nations High Commissioner for Refugees

unhealthy (ʌnˈhɛlθɪ) *adj* -healthier, -healthiest 1 characterized by ill-health; sick; unwell 2 characteristic of, conducive to, or resulting from ill-health: *an unhealthy complexion; an unhealthy atmosphere* 3 morbid or unwholesome 4 *informal* dangerous; risky > un'healthily *adv* > un'healthiness *n*

unheard (ʌnˈhɜːd) *adj* 1 not heard; not perceived by the ear 2 not listened to or granted a hearing: *his warning went unheard* 3 *archaic* unheard-of

unheard-of *adj* 1 previously unknown: *an unheard-of actress* 2 without precedent: *an unheard-of treatment* 3 highly offensive: *unheard-of behaviour*

unhinge (ʌnˈhɪndʒ) *vb* (*tr*) 1 to remove (a door, gate, etc) from its hinges 2 to derange or unbalance (a person, his mind, etc) 3 to disrupt or unsettle (a process or state of affairs) 4 (usually foll by *from*) to detach or dislodge

unhip (ʌnˈhɪp) *adj* unhipper, unhippest *slang* not at all fashionable or up to date: *my terminally unhip parents*

unholy (ʌnˈhəʊlɪ) *adj* -lier, -liest 1 not holy or sacred

2 immoral or depraved 3 *informal* outrageous or unnatural: *an unholy alliance* > un'holiness *n*

unhook (ʌnˈhʊk) *vb* 1 (*tr*) to remove (something) from a hook 2 (*tr*) to unfasten the hook of (a dress, etc) 3 (*intr*) to become unfastened or be capable of unfastening: *the dress wouldn't unhook*

unhorse (ʌnˈhɔːs) *vb* (*tr*) 1 (*usually passive*) to knock or throw from a horse 2 to overthrow or dislodge, as from a powerful position

unhouseled (ʌnˈhaʊzəld) *adj archaic* not having received the Eucharist [c16: from *un-* + obsolete *housel* to administer the sacrament, from Old English *hūsl* (n), *hūslian* (vb), of unknown origin]

uni (ˈjuːnɪ) *n informal* short for **university**

uni- *combining form* consisting of, relating to, or having only one: *unilateral; unisexual* [from Latin *ūnus* one]

Uniat (ˈjuːnɪˌæt) *or* **Uniate** (ˈjuːnɪɪt, -ˌeɪt) *adj* 1 designating any of the Eastern Churches that retain their own liturgy but submit to papal authority ▷ *n* 2 a member of one of these Churches [c19: from Russian *uniyat*, from Polish *unja* union, from Late Latin *ūniō*; see UNION] > 'Uniˌatism *n*

uniaxial (ˌjuːnɪˈæksɪəl) *adj* 1 (esp of plants) having an unbranched main axis 2 (of a crystal) having only one direction along which double refraction of light does not occur

unibrow (ˈjuːnɪˌbraʊ) *n informal* a single eyebrow created when the two eyebrows meet in the middle above the bridge of the nose

unicameral (ˌjuːnɪˈkæmərəl) *adj* of or characterized by a single legislative chamber > ˌuni'cameralist *n* > ˌuni'camerally *adv*

UNICEF (ˈjuːnɪˌsɛf) *n acronym for* United Nations Children's Fund (formerly, United Nations International Children's Emergency Fund): an agency of the United Nations that administers programmes to aid education and child and maternal health in developing countries

unicellular (ˌjuːnɪˈsɛljʊlə) *adj* (of organisms, such as protozoans and certain algae) consisting of a single cell > ˌuniˌcellu'larity *n*

Unicode (ˈjuːnɪˌkəʊd) *n computing* a character set for all languages

unicorn (ˈjuːnɪˌkɔːn) *n* 1 an imaginary creature usually depicted as a white horse with one long spiralled horn growing from its forehead 2 *Old Testament* a two-horned animal, thought to be either the rhinoceros or the aurochs (Deuteronomy 33:17): mistranslation in the Authorized Version of the original Hebrew [c13: from Old French *unicorne*, from Latin *ūnicornis* one-horned, from *ūnus* one + *cornu* a horn]

unicycle (ˈjuːnɪˌsaɪk³l) *n* a one-wheeled vehicle driven by pedals, esp one used in a circus, etc. Also called: monocycle [from UNI- + CYCLE, on the model of TRICYCLE] > 'uniˌcyclist *n*

unidirectional (ˌjuːnɪdɪˈrɛkʃən³l, -daɪ-) *adj* having, moving in, or operating in only one direction

UNIDO (juːˈniːdəʊ) *n acronym for* United Nations Industrial Development Organization

Unification Church *n* a religious sect founded in 1954 by Sun Myung Moon (born 1920), S Korean industrialist and religious leader

unified field theory *n* any theory capable of describing in one set of equations the properties of gravitational fields, electromagnetic fields, and strong and weak nuclear interactions. No satisfactory theory has yet been found

Unified Modeling Language *n trademark* See **UML**

uniform (ˈjuːnɪˌfɔːm) *n* 1 a prescribed identifying set of clothes for the members of an organization, such as soldiers or schoolchildren 2 a single set of such clothes 3 a characteristic feature or fashion of some class or group 4 *informal* a police officer who wears a uniform ▷ *adj* 5 unchanging in form, quality, quantity, etc; regular: *a uniform surface* 6 identical; alike or like: *a line of uniform toys* ▷ *vb* (*tr*) 7 to fit out (a body of soldiers, etc) with uniforms 8 to make uniform [c16: from Latin *ūniformis*, from *ūnus* one + *forma* shape] > 'uniˌformly *adv* > 'uniˌformness *n*

Uniform Business Rate *n* a local tax in the UK paid by

businesses, based on a local valuation of their premises and a rate fixed by central government that applies throughout the country. Abbreviation: **UBR**

uniformitarianism (ˌjuːnɪˌfɔːmɪˈtɛərɪəˌnɪzəm) *n* the concept that the earth's surface was shaped in the past by gradual processes, such as erosion, and by small sudden changes, such as earthquakes, of the type acting today rather than by the sudden divine acts, such as the flood survived by Noah (Genesis 6–8), demanded by the doctrine of catastrophism > ˌuniˌformiˈtarian *adj, n*

uniformity (ˌjuːnɪˈfɔːmɪtɪ) *n, pl* **-ties 1** a state or condition in which everything is regular, homogeneous, or unvarying **2** lack of diversity or variation, esp to the point of boredom or monotony; sameness

unify (ˈjuːnɪˌfaɪ) *vb* **-fies, -fying, -fied** to make or become one; unite [c16: from Medieval Latin *ūnificāre*, from Latin *ūnus* one + *facere* to make] > ˈuniˌfiable *adj* > ˈuniˌfier *n* > **unification** (ˌjuːnɪfɪˈkeɪʃən) *n*

unilateral (ˌjuːnɪˈlætərəl) *adj* **1** of, having, affecting, or occurring on only one side **2** involving or performed by only one party of several: *unilateral disarmament* **3** *law* (of contracts, obligations, etc) made by, affecting, or binding one party only and not involving the other party in reciprocal obligations **4** *botany* having or designating parts situated or turned to one side of an axis > ˌuniˈlateralism *or* ˌuniˌlaterˈality *n* > ˌuniˈlaterally *adv*

Unilateral Declaration of Independence *n* a declaration of independence made by a dependent state without the assent of the protecting state. Abbreviation: **UDI**

unilingual (ˌjuːnɪˈlɪŋgwəl) *adj* **1** of or relating to only one language **2** *chiefly Canadian* knowing only one language ▷ *n* **3** *chiefly Canadian* a person who knows only one language

Unimak Island (ˈjuːnɪˌmæk) *n* an island in SW Alaska, in the Aleutian Islands. Length: 113 km (70 miles)

unimpeachable (ˌʌnɪmˈpiːtʃəbᵊl) *adj* unquestionable as to honesty, truth, etc > ˌunimˈpeachably *adv*

unimproved (ˌʌnɪmˈpruːvd) *adj* **1** not improved or made better **2** (of land) not cleared, drained, cultivated, etc **3** neglected; unused: *unimproved resources*

unincorporated business (ˌʌnɪnˈkɔːpəˌreɪtɪd) *n* a privately owned business, often owned by one person who has unlimited liability as the business is not legally registered as a company

uninstall (ˈʌnɪnˌstɔːl) *vb* (*tr*) *computing* to remove (a program)

uninterested (ʌnˈɪntrɪstɪd, -tərɪs-) *adj* indifferent; unconcerned > un'interestedly *adv* > un'interestedness *n* ● USAGE See at disinterested

union (ˈjuːnjən) *n* **1** the condition of being united, the act of uniting, or a conjunction formed by such an act **2** an association, alliance, or confederation of individuals or groups for a common purpose, esp political **3** agreement or harmony **4** short for **trade union 5** the act or state of marriage or sexual intercourse **6** a device on a flag representing union, such as another flag depicted in the top left corner **7** a device for coupling or linking parts, such as pipes **8** (*often capital*) **a** an association of students at a university or college formed to look after the students' interests, provide facilities for recreation, etc **b** the building or buildings housing the facilities of such an organization **9** Also called: **join** *maths* a set containing all members of two given sets. Symbol: ∪, as in A∪B **10** (in 19th-century England) a number of parishes united for the administration of poor relief **11** *textiles* a piece of cloth or fabric consisting of two different kinds of yarn **12** (*modifier*) of or related to a union, esp a trade union [c15: from Church Latin *ūniō* oneness, from Latin *ūnus* one]

Union (ˈjuːnjən) *n* **the Union 1** *Brit* **a** the union of England and Wales from 1543 **b** the union of the English and Scottish crowns (1603–1707) **c** the union of England and Scotland from 1707 **d** the political union of Great Britain and Ireland (1801–1920) **e** the union of Great Britain and Northern Ireland from 1920 **2** *US* **a** the United States of America **b** the northern states of the US

during the Civil War **c** (*as modifier*): *Union supporters*

union catalogue *n* a catalogue listing every publication held at cooperating libraries

Union flag *n* the national flag of the United Kingdom, being a composite design composed of St George's Cross (England), Saint Andrew's Cross (Scotland), and Saint Patrick's Cross (Ireland). Often called: **Union Jack**

unionism (ˈjuːnjəˌnɪzəm) *n* **1** the principles of trade unions **2** adherence to the principles of trade unions **3** the principle or theory of any union > 'unionist *n, adj*

Unionist (ˈjuːnjənɪst) *n* **1** (*sometimes not capital*) **a** (before 1920) a supporter of the union of all Ireland and Great Britain **b** (since 1920) a supporter of union between Britain and Northern Ireland **2** a supporter of the US federal Union, esp during the Civil War ▷ *adj* **3** of, resembling, or relating to Unionists > 'Unionˌism *n*

Unionist Party *n* (formerly, in Northern Ireland) the major Protestant political party, closely identified with union with Britain. It formed the Northern Ireland Government from 1920 to 1972. See also **Ulster Democratic Unionist Party, Ulster Unionist Council**

unionize *or* **unionise** (ˈjuːnjəˌnaɪz) *vb* **1** to organize (workers) into a trade union **2** to join or cause to join a trade union **3** (*tr*) to subject to the rules or codes of a trade union > ˌunioniˈzation *or* ˌunioniˈsation *n*

Union Jack *n* a common name for **Union flag**

Union of South Africa *n* the former name (1910–61) of (the Republic of) **South Africa**

Union of Soviet Socialist Republics *n* the official name of the former **Soviet Union**

union pipes *pl n* another name for **uillean pipes**

unipolar (ˌjuːnɪˈpəʊlə) *adj* **1** of, concerned with, or having a single magnetic or electric pole **2** (of a nerve cell) having a single process **3** (of a transistor) utilizing charge carriers of one polarity only, as in a field-effect transistor > **unipolarity** (ˌjuːnɪpəʊˈlærɪtɪ) *n*

unique (juːˈniːk) *adj* **1** being the only one of a particular type; single; sole **2** without equal or like; unparalleled **3** *informal* very remarkable or unusual **4** *maths* **a** leading to only one result: *the sum of two integers is unique* **b** having precisely one value: *the unique positive square root of 4 is 2* [c17: via French from Latin *ūnicus* unparalleled, from *ūnus* one] > u'niquely *adv* > u'niqueness *n*

● USAGE *Unique* is normally taken to describe an
● absolute state, i.e. one that cannot be qualified. Thus
● something is either *unique* or *not unique*; it cannot be
● *rather unique* or *very unique*. However, *unique* is sometimes
● used informally to mean very remarkable or unusual
● and this makes it possible to use comparatives or
● intensifiers with it, although many people object to
● this use

unisex (ˈjuːnɪˌsɛks) *adj* of or relating to clothing, a hairstyle, etc, that can be worn by either sex [c20: from UNI- + SEX]

unisexual (ˌjuːnɪˈsɛksjʊəl) *adj* **1** of or relating to one sex only **2** (of some organisms) having either male or female reproductive organs but not both > **unisexuality** *n* > ˌuniˈsexually (ˌjuːnɪˌsɛksjʊˈælɪtɪ) *adv*

unison (ˈjuːnɪsᵊn, -zᵊn) *n* **1** *music* **a** the interval between two sounds of identical pitch **b** (*modifier*) played or sung at the same pitch: *unison singing* **2** complete agreement; harmony (esp in the phrase **in unison**) [c16: from Late Latin *ūnisonus*, from UNI- + *sonus* sound] > u'nisonous, u'nisonal *or* u'nisonant *adj*

UNISON (ˈjuːnɪsᵊn) *n* (in Britain) a trade union representing local government, health care, and other workers: formed in 1993 by the amalgamation of COHSE, NALGO, and NUPE

unit (ˈjuːnɪt) *n* **1** a single undivided entity or whole **2** any group or individual, esp when regarded as a basic element of a larger whole **3** a mechanical part or integrated assembly of parts that performs a subsidiary function: *a filter unit* **4** a complete system, apparatus, or establishment that performs a specific function: *a production unit* **5** a subdivision of a larger military formation **6** Also called: **unit of measurement** A standard amount of a physical quantity, such as length, mass, energy, etc, specified multiples of which are used to express magnitudes of that physical quantity: *the* *second is a unit of time* **7** the amount of a drug, vaccine, etc, needed to produce a particular effect **8** a standard measure used in calculating alcohol intake and its effect **9** *maths (modifier)* having a value defined as one for the system: *unit vector* **10** Also called: **unit set** *maths, logic* a set having a single member **11** short for **home unit 12** NZ a self-propelled railcar [C16: back formation from UNITY, perhaps on the model of *digit*]

unitarian (ˌjuːnɪˈtɛərɪən) *n* **1** a supporter of unity or centralization ▷ *adj* **2** of or relating to unity or centralization

Unitarian (ˌjuːnɪˈtɛərɪən) *n* **1** *theol* a person who believes that God is one being and rejects the doctrine of the Trinity **2** *ecclesiast* an upholder of Unitarianism, esp a member of the Church (**Unitarian Church**) that embodies this system of belief ▷ *adj* **3** of or relating to Unitarians or Unitarianism > ˌUniˈtariaˌnism *n*

unitary (ˈjuːnɪtərɪ, -trɪ) *adj* **1** of a unit or units **2** based on or characterized by unity **3** individual; whole

unitary authority *n* (in the United Kingdom) a district administered by a single tier of local government, esp those districts of England that became administratively independent of the county councils in 1996–98

unit character *n* *genetics* a character inherited as a single unit and depended on a single gene

unit cost *n* the actual cost of producing one article

unite[1] (juːˈnaɪt) *vb* **1** to make or become an integrated whole or a unity; combine **2** to join, unify or be unified in purpose, action, beliefs, etc **3** to enter or cause to enter into an association or alliance **4** to adhere or cause to adhere; fuse **5** (*tr*) to possess or display (qualities) in combination or at the same time: *he united charm with severity* [C15: from Late Latin *ūnīre*, from *ūnus* one]

unite[2] (ˈjuːnaɪt, juːˈnaɪt) *n* an English gold coin minted in the Stuart period, originally worth 20 shillings [C17: from obsolete *unite* joined, alluding to the union of England and Scotland (1603)]

united (juːˈnaɪtɪd) *adj* **1** produced by two or more persons or things in combination or from their union or amalgamation: *a united effort* **2** in agreement **3** in association or alliance > uˈnitedly *adv* > uˈnitedness *n*

United Arab Emirates *pl n* a group of seven emirates in SW Asia, on the Persian Gulf: consists of Abu Dhabi, Dubai, Sharjah, Ajman, Umm al Qaiwain, Ras el Khaimah, and Fujairah; a former British protectorate; became fully independent in 1971; consists mostly of flat desert, with mountains in the east; rich petroleum resources. Official language: Arabic. Official religion: Muslim. Currency: dirham. Capital: Abu Dhabi. Pop: 3 051 000 (2004 est). Area: 83 600 sq km (32 300 sq miles). Former name (until 1971): **Trucial States.** Abbreviation: **UAE**

United Arab Republic *n* the official name (1958–71) of Egypt

United Arab States *pl n* a federation (1958–61) between the United Arab Republic and Yemen

United Church of Canada *n* the largest Protestant denomination in Canada, formed in the 1920s by incorporating some Presbyterians and most Methodists

United Empire Loyalist *n* *Canadian history* any of the American colonists who settled in Canada during or after the War of American Independence because of loyalty to the British Crown

United Kingdom *n* a kingdom of NW Europe, consisting chiefly of the island of Great Britain together with Northern Ireland: became the world's leading colonial power in the 18th century; the first country to undergo the Industrial Revolution. It became the **United Kingdom of Great Britain and Northern Ireland** in 1921, after the rest of Ireland became autonomous as the Irish Free State. Primarily it is a trading nation, the chief exports being manufactured goods; joined the Common Market (now the European Union) in January 1973. Official language: English; Gaelic, Welsh, and other minority languages. Religion: Christian majority. Currency: pound sterling. Capital: London. Pop: 59 428 000 (2004 est). Area: 244 110 sq km (94 251 sq miles). Abbreviation: **UK.** See also **Great Britain**

United Nations *n* (*functioning as singular or plural*) an international organization of independent states, with its headquarters in New York City, that was formed in 1945 to promote peace and international cooperation and security. Abbreviation: **UN**

United Provinces *pl n* **1** a Dutch republic (1581–1795) formed by the union of the seven northern provinces of the Netherlands, which were in revolt against their suzerain, Philip II of Spain **2** short for **United Provinces of Agra and Oudh**: the former name of **Uttar Pradesh**

United States of America *n* (*functioning as singular or plural*) a federal republic mainly in North America consisting of 50 states and the District of Columbia: colonized principally by the English and French in the 17th century, the native Indians being gradually defeated and displaced; 13 colonies under British rule made the Declaration of Independence in 1776 and became the United States after the War of American Independence. The northern states defeated the South in the Civil War (1861–65). It is the world's most productive industrial nation and also exports agricultural products. It consists generally of the Rocky Mountains in the west, the Great Plains in the centre, the Appalachians in the east, deserts in the southwest, and coastal lowlands and swamps in the southeast. Language: predominantly English; Spanish is also widely spoken. Religion: Christian majority. Currency: dollar. Capital: Washington, DC. Pop: 297 043 000 (2004 est). Area: 9 518 323 sq km (3 675 031 sq miles). Often shortened to: **United States.** Abbreviations: **US, USA**

unitive (ˈjuːnɪtɪv) *adj* **1** tending to unite or capable of uniting **2** characterized by unity

unitize *or* **unitise** (ˈjuːnɪˌtaɪz) *vb* (*tr*) *finance* to convert (an investment trust) into a unit trust > ˌunitiˈzation *or* ˌunitiˈsation *n*

unit-linked policy *n* a life-assurance policy, the investment benefits of which are directly in proportion to the number of units in a unit trust purchased on the policyholder's behalf

unit of account *n* **1** *economics* the function of money that enables the user to keep accounts, value transactions, etc **2** a monetary denomination used for accounting purposes, etc, but not necessarily corresponding to any real currency: *the ECU is the unit of account of the European Monetary Fund* **3** the unit of currency of a country

unit price *n* a price for foodstuffs, etc, stated or shown as the cost per unit, as per pound, per kilogram, per dozen, etc

unit pricing *n* a system of pricing foodstuffs, etc, in which the cost of a single unit is shown to enable shoppers to see the advantage of buying multipacks

unit trust *n* *Brit* an investment trust that issues units for public sale, the holders of which are creditors and not shareholders with their interests represented by a trust company independent of the issuing agency

unity (ˈjuːnɪtɪ) *n, pl* **-ties 1** the state or quality of being one; oneness **2** the act, state, or quality of forming a whole from separate parts **3** something whole or complete that is composed of separate parts **4** mutual agreement; harmony or concord: *the participants were no longer in unity* **5** uniformity or constancy: *unity of purpose* **6** *maths* **a** the number or numeral one **b** a quantity assuming the value of one: *the area of the triangle was regarded as unity* **c** the element of a set producing no change in a number following multiplication **7** any one of the three principles of dramatic structure deriving from Aristotle's *Poetics* by which the action of a play should be limited to a single plot (unity of action), a single location (unity of place), and the events of a single day (unity of time) [C13: from Old French *unité*, from Latin *ūnitās*, from *ūnus* one]

Univ. *abbreviation* University

univalent (ˌjuːnɪˈveɪlənt, juːˈnɪvələnt) *adj* **1** (of a chromosome during meiosis) not paired with its homologue **2** *chem* another word for **monovalent** > ˌuniˈvalency *n*

univalve (ˈjuːnɪˌvælv) *zoology* ▷ *adj* **1** relating to, designating, or possessing a mollusc shell that consists of a single piece ▷ *n* **2** a gastropod mollusc or its shell

u

universal (ˌjuːnɪˈvɜːsʰl) *adj* **1** of, relating to, or typical of the whole of mankind or of nature **2** common to, involving, or proceeding from all in a particular group **3** applicable to or affecting many individuals, conditions, or cases; general **4** existing or prevailing everywhere **5** applicable or occurring throughout or relating to the universe; cosmic: *a universal constant* **6** (esp of a language) capable of being used and understood by all **7** embracing or versed in many fields of knowledge, activity, interest, etc **8** machinery designed or adapted for a range of sizes, fittings, or uses **9** *linguistics* (of a constraint in a formal grammar) common to the grammatical description of all human languages, actual or possible **10** *logic* (of a statement or proposition) affirming or denying something about every member of a class, as in *all men are wicked* ▷ Compare **particular** (sense 6) ▷ *n* **11** *philosophy* **a** a general term or concept or the type such a term signifies **b** a metaphysical entity taken to be the reference of a general term, as distinct from the class of individuals it describes **12** *logic* **a** a universal proposition, statement, or formula **b** a universal quantifier **13** a characteristic common to every member of a particular culture or to every human being > ˌuniˈversalness *n*

● **USAGE** The use of *more universal* as in *his writings have long*
● *been admired by fellow scientists, but his latest book should have*
● *more universal appeal* is acceptable in modern English
● usage

universal class *or* **universal set** *n* (in Boolean algebra) the class containing all points and including all other classes

universal gas constant *n* another name for **gas constant**

universalism (ˌjuːnɪˈvɜːsəˌlɪzəm) *n* **1** a universal feature or characteristic **2** another word for **universality**

Universalism (ˌjuːnɪˈvɜːsəˌlɪzəm) *n* a system of religious beliefs maintaining that all men are predestined for salvation > ˌUniˈversalist *n, adj*

universality (ˌjuːnɪvɜːˈsælɪtɪ) *n* the state or quality of being universal

universalize *or* **universalise** (ˌjuːnɪˈvɜːsəˌlaɪz) *vb* (*tr*) to make universal > ˌuniˌversaliˈzation *or* ˌuniˌversaliˈsation *n*

universal joint *or* **universal coupling** *n* a form of coupling between two rotating shafts allowing freedom of angular movement in all directions

universally (ˌjuːnɪˈvɜːsəlɪ) *adv* everywhere or in every case; without exception: *this principle applies universally*

universal motor *n* an electric motor capable of working on either direct current or single-phase alternating current at approximately the same speed and output

universal time *n* **1** (from 1928) name adopted internationally for Greenwich Mean Time (measured from Greenwich midnight), now split into several slightly different scales, one of which (UT1) is used by astronomers. Abbreviation: UT **2** Also called: **universal coordinated time** An internationally agreed system for civil timekeeping introduced in 1960 and redefined in 1972 as an atomic timescale. Available from broadcast signals, it has a second equal to the International Atomic Time (TAI) second, the difference between UTC and TAI being an integral number of seconds with leap seconds inserted when necessary to keep it within 0.9 seconds of UT1. Abbreviation: UTC

universe (ˈjuːnɪˌvɜːs) *n* **1** *astronomy* the aggregate of all existing matter, energy, and space **2** human beings collectively **3** a province or sphere of thought or activity [c16: from French *univers*, from Latin *ūniversum* the whole world, from *ūniversus* all together, from UNI- + *vertere* to turn]

universe of discourse *n* *logic* the complete range of objects, events, attributes, relations, ideas, etc, that are expressed, assumed, or implied in a discussion

university (ˌjuːnɪˈvɜːsɪtɪ) *n, pl* -ties **1** an institution of higher education having authority to award bachelors' and higher degrees, usually having research facilities **2** the buildings, members, staff, or campus of a university [c14: from Old French *universite,* from Medieval Latin *universitās* group of scholars, from Late Latin: guild,

society, body of men, from Latin: whole, totality, universe]

UNIX (ˈjuːnɪks) *n trademark* a multi-user multitasking operating system found on many types of computer

unjust (ʌnˈdʒʌst) *adj* not in accordance with accepted standards of fairness or justice; unfair > unˈjustly *adv* > unˈjustness *n*

unkempt (ʌnˈkɛmpt) *adj* **1** (of the hair) uncombed; dishevelled **2** ungroomed; slovenly: *unkempt appearance* [Old English *uncemban*; from UN-¹ + *cembed*, past participle of *cemban* to COMB; related to Old Saxon *kembian*, Old High German *kemben* to comb] > unˈkemptly *adv* > unˈkemptness *n*

unkind (ʌnˈkaɪnd) *adj* lacking kindness; unsympathetic or cruel > unˈkindly *adv* > unˈkindness *n*

unknowing (ʌnˈnəʊɪŋ) *adj* **1** not knowing; ignorant **2** (*postpositive*; often foll by *of*) without knowledge or unaware (of) > unˈknowingly *adv*

unknown (ʌnˈnəʊn) *adj* **1** not known, understood, or recognized **2** not established, identified, or discovered: *an unknown island* **3** not famous; undistinguished: *some unknown artist* **4** unknown quantity a person or thing whose action, effect, etc, is unknown or unpredictable ▷ *n* **5** an unknown person, quantity, or thing **6** *maths* a variable, or the quantity it represents, the value of which is to be discovered by solving an equation; a variable in a conditional equation > unˈknownness *n*

Unknown Soldier *or* **Warrior** *n* (in various countries) an unidentified soldier who has died in battle and for whom a tomb is established as a memorial to other unidentified dead of the nation's armed forces

unlace (ʌnˈleɪs) *vb* (*tr*) **1** to loosen or undo the lacing of (shoes, garments, etc) **2** to unfasten or remove garments of (oneself or another) by or as if by undoing lacing

unlawful assembly (ʌnˈlɔːfʊl) *n law* a meeting of three or more people with the intent of carrying out any unlawful purpose

unlay (ʌnˈleɪ) *vb* -lays, -laying, -laid (*tr*) to untwist (a rope or cable) to separate its strands

unleaded (ʌnˈlɛdɪd) *adj* **1** (of petrol) containing a reduced amount of tetraethyl lead, in order to reduce environmental pollution ▷ *n* **2** petrol containing a reduced amount of tetraethyl lead

unlearn (ʌnˈlɜːn) *vb* -learns, -learning, -learned (-ˈlɜːnd) *or* -learnt to try to forget (something learnt) or to discard (accumulated knowledge)

unlearned (ʌnˈlɜːnɪd) *adj* ignorant or untaught > unˈlearnedly *adv*

unlearnt (ʌnˈlɜːnt) *or* **unlearned** (ʌnˈlɜːnd) *adj* **1** denoting knowledge or skills innately present and therefore not learnt **2** not learnt or taken notice of: *unlearnt lessons*

unleash (ʌnˈliːʃ) *vb* (*tr*) **1** to release from or as if from a leash **2** to free from restraint or control

unleavened (ʌnˈlɛvənd) *adj* (of bread, biscuits, etc) made from a dough containing no yeast or leavening

unless (ʌnˈlɛs) *conj* (*subordinating*) except under the circumstances that; except on the condition that: *they'll sell it unless he hears otherwise* [c14: *onlesse*, from *on* ON + *lesse* LESS; compare French *à moins que*, literally: at less than]

unlettered (ʌnˈlɛtəd) *adj* uneducated; illiterate

unlike (ʌnˈlaɪk) *adj* **1** not alike; dissimilar or unequal; different ▷ *prep* **2** not like; not typical of: *unlike his father, he lacks intelligence* > unˈlikeness *n*

unlikely (ʌnˈlaɪklɪ) *adj* not likely; improbable > unˈlikeliness *or* unˈlikelihood *n*

unlimber (ʌnˈlɪmbə) *vb* **1** (*tr*) to disengage (a gun) from its limber **2** to prepare (something) for use

unlimited (ʌnˈlɪmɪtɪd) *adj* **1** without limits or bounds: *unlimited knowledge* **2** not restricted, limited, or qualified: *unlimited power* > unˈlimitedly *adv* > unˈlimitedness *n*

unlisted (ʌnˈlɪstɪd) *adj* **1** not entered on a list **2** *US & Canadian* (of a telephone number or telephone subscriber) not listed in a telephone directory. Brit term: ex-directory

unload (ʌnˈləʊd) *vb* **1** to remove a load or cargo from (a ship, lorry, etc) **2** to discharge (cargo, freight, etc) **3** (*tr*) to relieve of a burden or troubles **4** (*tr*) to give vent to

u

(anxiety, troubles, etc) **5** (*tr*) to get rid of or dispose of (esp surplus goods) **6** (*tr*) to remove the charge of ammunition from (a firearm) > un'loader *n*

unlock (ʌnˈlɒk) *vb* **1** (*tr*) to unfasten (a lock, door, etc) **2** (*tr*) to open, release, or let loose **3** (*tr*) to disclose or provide the key to: *unlock a puzzle* **4** (*intr*) to become unlocked > un'lockable *adj*

unlooked-for (ˌʌnˈlʊktfɔː) *adj* unexpected; unforeseen

unloose (ʌnˈluːs) *vb* (*tr*) **1** to set free; release **2** to loosen or relax (a hold, grip, etc) **3** to unfasten or untie

unlovely (ʌnˈlʌvlɪ) *adj* unpleasant in appearance > un'loveliness *n*

unlucky (ʌnˈlʌkɪ) *adj* **1** characterized by misfortune or failure: *an unlucky person; an unlucky chance* **2** ill-omened; inauspicious: *an unlucky date* **3** regrettable; disappointing > un'luckily *adv* > un'luckiness *n*

unmake (ʌnˈmeɪk) *vb* **-makes**, **-making**, **-made** (*tr*) **1** to undo or destroy **2** to depose from office, rank, or authority **3** to alter the nature of

unman (ʌnˈmæn) *vb* **-mans**, **-manning**, **-manned** (*tr*) **1** to cause to lose courage or nerve **2** to make effeminate **3** to remove the men from

unmanly (ʌnˈmænlɪ) *adj* **1** not masculine or virile **2** ignoble, cowardly, or dishonourable > un'manliness *n*

unmanned (ʌnˈmænd) *adj* **1** lacking personnel or crew: *an unmanned ship* **2** (of aircraft, spacecraft, etc) operated by automatic or remote control **3** uninhabited

unmannered (ʌnˈmænəd) *adj* **1** without good manners; coarse; rude **2** not affected; without mannerisms

unmannerly (ʌnˈmænəlɪ) *adj* **1** lacking manners; discourteous ▷ *adv* **2** *archaic* rudely; discourteously > un'mannerliness *n*

unmask (ʌnˈmɑːsk) *vb* **1** to remove (the mask or disguise) from (someone or oneself) **2** to appear or cause to appear in true character > un'masker *n*

unmeaning (ʌnˈmiːnɪŋ) *adj* **1** having no meaning **2** showing no intelligence; vacant: *an unmeaning face* > un'meaningly *adv* > un'meaningness *n*

unmeet (ʌnˈmiːt) *adj literary or archaic* not meet; unsuitable > un'meetly *adv* > un'meetness *n*

unmentionable (ʌnˈmɛnʃənəbəl) *adj* **a** unsuitable or forbidden as a topic of conversation **b** (*as noun*): *the unmentionable* > un'mentionableness *n* > un'mentionably *adv*

unmentionables (ʌnˈmɛnʃənəbəlz) *pl n chiefly humorous* underwear

unmerciful (ʌnˈmɜːsɪfʊl) *adj* **1** showing no mercy; relentless **2** extreme or excessive > un'mercifully *adv* > un'mercifulness *n*

unmindful (ʌnˈmaɪndfʊl) *adj* (*usually postpositive* and foll by *of*) careless, heedless, or forgetful > un'mindfully *adv* > un'mindfulness *n*

unmissable (ʌnˈmɪsəbəl) *adj* (of a film, television programme, etc) so good that it should not be missed

unmistakable *or* **unmistakeable** (ˌʌnmɪsˈteɪkəbəl) *adj* not mistakable; clear, obvious, or unambiguous > ˌunmis'takably *or* ˌunmis'takeably *adv*

unmitigated (ʌnˈmɪtɪˌɡeɪtɪd) *adj* **1** not diminished in intensity, severity, etc **2** (*prenominal*) (intensifier): *an unmitigated disaster* > un'mitigatedly *adv*

unmoderated (ʌnˈmɒdəˌreɪtɪd) *adj* (of an online chatroom, newsgroup, etc) not monitored for inappropriate content, time wasting, or bad language

unmoral (ʌnˈmɒrəl) *adj* outside morality; amoral > unmorality (ˌʌnmɒˈrælɪtɪ) *n* > un'morally *adv*

unmurmuring (ʌnˈmɜːmərɪŋ) *adj* not complaining

unmuzzle (ʌnˈmʌzəl) *vb* (*tr*) **1** to take the muzzle off (a dog, etc) **2** to free from control or censorship

unnatural (ʌnˈnætʃərəl, -ˈnætʃrəl) *adj* **1** contrary to nature; abnormal **2** not in accordance with accepted standards of behaviour or right and wrong: *unnatural love* **3** uncanny; supernatural: *unnatural phenomena* **4** affected or forced **5** inhuman or monstrous; wicked: *an unnatural crime* > un'naturally *adv* > un'naturalness *n*

unnecessary (ʌnˈnɛsɪsərɪ, -ɪsrɪ) *adj* not necessary > un'necessarily *adv* > un'necessariness *n*

unnerve (ʌnˈnɜːv) *vb* (*tr*) to cause to lose courage, strength, confidence, self-control, etc

unnumbered (ʌnˈnʌmbəd) *adj* **1** countless; innumerable **2** not counted or assigned a number

UNO *abbreviation* United Nations Organization

unoccupied (ʌnˈɒkjʊˌpaɪd) *adj* **1** (of a building) without occupants **2** unemployed or idle **3** (of an area or country) not overrun by foreign troops

unofficial (ˌʌnəˈfɪʃəl) *adj* **1** not official or formal: *an unofficial engagement* **2** not confirmed officially: *an unofficial report* **3** (of a strike) not approved by the strikers' trade union **4** (of a medicinal drug) not listed in a pharmacopoeia > ˌunof'ficially *adv*

unorganized *or* **unorganised** (ʌnˈɔːɡəˌnaɪzd) *adj* **1** not arranged into an organized system, structure, or unity **2** (of workers) not unionized **3** nonliving; inorganic

unpack (ʌnˈpæk) *vb* **1** to remove the packed contents of (a case, trunk, etc) **2** (*tr*) to take (something) out of a packed container **3** (*tr*) to remove a pack from; unload: *to unpack a mule* > un'packer *n*

unpaged (ʌnˈpeɪdʒd) *adj* (of a book) having no page numbers

unparalleled (ʌnˈpærəˌlɛld) *adj* unmatched; unequalled

unparliamentary (ˌʌnpɑːləˈmɛntərɪ, -trɪ) *adj* not consistent with parliamentary procedure or practice > ˌunparlia'mentarily *adv* > ˌunparlia'mentariness *n*

unpeg (ʌnˈpɛɡ) *vb* **-pegs**, **-pegging**, **-pegged** (*tr*) **1** to remove the peg or pegs from, esp to unfasten **2** to allow (prices, wages, etc) to rise and fall freely

unpeople (ʌnˈpiːpəl) *vb* (*tr*) to empty of people

unperson (ˈʌnpɜːsən) *n* a person whose existence is officially denied or ignored

unpick (ʌnˈpɪk) *vb* (*tr*) **1** to undo (the stitches) of (a piece of sewing) **2** to unravel or undo (a garment, etc)

unpin (ʌnˈpɪn) *vb* **-pins**, **-pinning**, **-pinned** (*tr*) **1** to remove a pin or pins from **2** to unfasten by removing pins

unpleasant (ʌnˈplɛzənt) *adj* not pleasant or agreeable > un'pleasantly *adv* > un'pleasantness *n*

unplugged (ʌnˈplʌɡd) *adj* (of a performer or performance of popular music) using acoustic rather than electric instruments: *Eric Clapton unplugged; an unplugged version of the song*

unplumbed (ʌnˈplʌmd) *adj* **1** unfathomed; unsounded **2** not understood in depth **3** (of a building) having no plumbing

unpolled (ʌnˈpəʊld) *adj* **1** not included in an opinion poll **2** not having voted

unpopular (ʌnˈpɒpjʊlə) *adj* not popular with an individual or group of people > unpopularity (ˌʌnpɒpjʊˈlærɪtɪ) *n* > un'popularly *adv*

unpractical (ʌnˈpræktɪkəl) *adj* another word for **impractical** > ˌunpracti'cality *or* un'practicalness *n* > un'practically *adv*

unpractised *or US* **unpracticed** (ʌnˈpræktɪst) *adj* **1** without skill, training, or experience **2** not used or done often or repeatedly **3** not yet tested

unprecedented (ʌnˈprɛsɪˌdɛntɪd) *adj* having no precedent; unparalleled > un'prece,dentedly *adv*

unprejudiced (ʌnˈprɛdʒʊdɪst) *adj* not prejudiced or biased; impartial > un'prejudicedly *adv*

unprincipled (ʌnˈprɪnsɪpəld) *adj* lacking moral principles; unscrupulous > un'principledness *n*

unprintable (ʌnˈprɪntəbəl) *adj* unsuitable for printing for reasons of obscenity, libel, bad taste, etc > un'printableness *n* > un'printably *adv*

unprofessional (ˌʌnprəˈfɛʃənəl) *adj* **1** contrary to the accepted code of conduct of a profession **2** amateur **3** not belonging to or having the required qualifications for a profession > ˌunpro'fessionally *adv*

unprompted (ʌnˈprɒmptɪd) *adj* without prompting; spontaneous

unprotected sex (ˌʌnprəˈtɛktɪd) *n* an act of sexual intercourse or sodomy performed without the use of a condom, thus involving the risk of sexually transmitted diseases

unputdownable (ˌʌnpʊtˈdaʊnəbəl) *adj* (of a book, esp a novel) so gripping as to be read right through at one sitting

unqualified (ʌnˈkwɒlɪˌfaɪd) *adj* **1** lacking the necessary qualifications **2** not restricted or modified: *an unqualified criticism* **3** (*usually prenominal*) (intensifier): *an unqualified* *success* > un'quali,fiable *adj*

unquestionable (ʌn'kwɛstʃənəbəl) *adj* **1** indubitable or indisputable **2** not admitting of exception or qualification: *an unquestionable decision* > un,questiona'bility *or* un'questionableness *n* > un'questionably *adv*

unquestioned (ʌn'kwɛstʃənd) *adj* **1** accepted without question **2** not admitting of doubt or question: *unquestioned power* **3** not questioned or interrogated

unquiet (ʌn'kwaɪət) *chiefly literary* ▷ *adj* **1** characterized by disorder, unrest, or tumult: *unquiet times* **2** anxious; uneasy ▷ *n* **3** a state of unrest > un'quietly *adv* > un'quietness *n*

unquote (ʌn'kwəʊt) *interj* **1** an expression used parenthetically to indicate that the preceding quotation is finished ▷ *vb* **2** to close (a quotation), esp in printing

unravel (ʌn'rævəl) *vb* -els, -elling, -elled *or US* -els, -eling, -eled **1** (*tr*) to reduce (something knitted or woven) to separate strands **2** (*tr*) to explain or solve: *the mystery was unravelled* **3** (*intr*) to become unravelled

unreactive (,ʌnrɪ'æktɪv) *adj* (of a substance) not readily partaking in chemical reactions

unread (ʌn'rɛd) *adj* **1** (of a book, newspaper, etc) not yet read **2** (of a person) having read little

unreadable (ʌn'riːdəbəl) *adj* illegible; undecipherable **2** difficult or tedious to read > un,reada'bility *or* un'readableness *n*

unready (ʌn'rɛdɪ) *adj* **1** not ready or prepared **2** slow or hesitant to see or act > un'readily *adv* > un'readiness *n*

unreal (ʌn'rɪəl) *adj* **1** imaginary or fanciful or seemingly so: *an unreal situation* **2** having no actual existence or substance **3** insincere or artificial > un'really *adv* > unreality (,ʌnrɪ'ælɪtɪ) *n*

unreason (ʌn'riːzən) *n* **1** irrationality or madness **2** something that lacks or is contrary to reason **3** lack of order; chaos

unreasonable (ʌn'riːznəbəl) *adj* **1** immoderate; excessive: *unreasonable demands* **2** refusing to listen to reason **3** lacking reason or judgment > un'reasonableness *n* > un'reasonably *adv*

unreasoning (ʌn'riːzənɪŋ) *adj* not controlled by reason; irrational > un'reasoningly *adv*

unregenerate (,ʌnrɪ'dʒɛnərɪt) *adj also* unregenerated **1** unrepentant; unreformed **2** obstinately adhering to one's own views ▷ *n* **3** an unregenerate person > ,unre'generacy *n* > ,unre'generately *adv*

unrelenting (,ʌnrɪ'lɛntɪŋ) *adj* **1** refusing to relent or take pity; relentless; merciless **2** not diminishing in determination, speed, effort, force, etc > ,unre'lentingly *adv* > ,unre'lentingness *n*

unreligious (,ʌnrɪ'lɪdʒəs) *adj* **1** another word for **irreligious 2** secular > ,unre'ligiously *adv*

unremitting (,ʌnrɪ'mɪtɪŋ) *adj* never slackening or stopping; unceasing; constant > ,unre'mittingly *adv* > ,unre'mittingness *n*

unreserved (,ʌnrɪ'zɜːvd) *adj* **1** without reserve; having an open manner **2** without reservation **3** not booked or bookable > unreservedly (,ʌnrɪ'zɜːvɪdlɪ) *adv* > ,unre'servedness *n*

unrest (ʌn'rɛst) *n* **1** a troubled or rebellious state of discontent **2** an uneasy or troubled state

unriddle (ʌn'rɪdəl) *vb* (*tr*) to solve or puzzle out [c16: from UN-² + RIDDLE¹] > un'riddler *n*

unrig (ʌn'rɪg) *vb* -rigs, -rigging, -rigged **1** (*tr*) to strip (a vessel) of standing and running rigging **2** *archaic or dialect* to undress (someone or oneself)

unrighteous (ʌn'raɪtʃəs) *adj* **1 a** sinful; wicked **b** (*as collective noun; preceded by the*): *the unrighteous* **2** not fair or right; unjust > un'righteously *adv* > un'righteousness *n*

unrip (ʌn'rɪp) *vb* -rips, -ripping, -ripped (*tr*) **1** to rip open **2** *obsolete* to reveal; disclose

unripe (ʌn'raɪp) *or* **unripened** *adj* **1** not fully matured **2** not fully prepared or developed; not ready > un'ripeness *n*

unrivalled *or US* **unrivaled** (ʌn'raɪvəld) *adj* having no equal; matchless

unroll (ʌn'rəʊl) *vb* **1** to open out or unwind (something rolled, folded, or coiled) or (of something rolled, etc) to become opened out or unwound **2** to make or become

visible or apparent, esp gradually; unfold

unruffled (ʌn'rʌfəld) *adj* **1** unmoved; calm **2** still: *the unruffled seas* > un'ruffledness *n*

unruly (ʌn'ruːlɪ) *adj* -lier, -liest disposed to disobedience or indiscipline > un'ruliness *n*

UNRWA ('ʌnrə) *n acronym for* United Nations Relief and Works Agency

unsaddle (ʌn'sædəl) *vb* **1** to remove the saddle from (a horse, mule, etc) **2** (*tr*) to unhorse

unsaddling enclosure *n* the area at a racecourse where horses are unsaddled after a race and often where awards are given to owners, trainers, and jockeys

unsafe (ʌn'seɪf) *adj* **1** not safe; perilous **2** (of a criminal conviction) based on inadequate or false evidence

unsaid (ʌn'sɛd) *adj* not said or expressed; unspoken

unsaturated (ʌn'sætʃə,reɪtɪd) *adj* **1** not saturated **2** (of a chemical compound, esp an organic compound) containing one or more double or triple bonds and thus capable of undergoing addition reactions **3** (of a fat, esp a vegetable fat) containing a high proportion of fatty acids having double bonds **4** (of a solution) containing less solute than a saturated solution > ,unsatu'ration *n*

unsavoury *or US* **unsavory** (ʌn'seɪvərɪ) *adj* **1** objectionable or distasteful: *an unsavoury character* **2** disagreeable in odour or taste > un'savourily *or US* un'savorily *adv* > un'savouriness *or US* un'savoriness *n*

unsay (ʌn'seɪ) *vb* -says, -saying, -said (*tr*) to retract or withdraw (something said or written)

unsayable (ʌn'seɪəbəl) *adj* **1** too insulting, indecent, etc, to be said ▷ *n* **2** say the unsayable to express an opinion thought to be too controversial to mention

unscathed (ʌn'skeɪðd) *adj* not harmed or injured

unscramble (ʌn'skræmbəl) *vb* (*tr*) **1** to resolve from confusion or disorderliness **2** to restore (a scrambled message) to an intelligible form > un'scrambler *n*

unscrew (ʌn'skruː) *vb* **1** (*tr*) to draw or remove a screw from (an object) **2** (*tr*) to loosen (a screw, lid, etc) by rotating continuously, usually in an anticlockwise direction **3** (*intr*) (esp of an engaged threaded part) to become loosened or separated

unscripted (ʌn'skrɪptɪd) *adj* (of a speech, play, etc) not using or based on a script

unscrupulous (ʌn'skruːpjʊləs) *adj* without scruples; unprincipled > un'scrupulously *adv* > un'scrupulousness *or* unscrupulosity (ʌn,skruːpjʊ'lɒsɪtɪ) *n*

unseal (ʌn'siːl) *vb* (*tr*) **1** to remove or break the seal of **2** to reveal or free (something concealed or closed as if sealed): *to unseal one's lips*

unsealed (ʌn'siːld) *adj* **1** not sealed **2** *Austral & NZ* (of a road) surfaced with road metal not bound by bitumen or other sealant

unseam (ʌn'siːm) *vb* (*tr*) to open or undo the seam of

unseasonable (ʌn'siːzənəbəl) *adj* **1** (esp of the weather) inappropriate for the season **2** untimely; inopportune > un'seasonableness *n* > un'seasonably *adv*

unseat (ʌn'siːt) *vb* (*tr*) **1** to throw or displace from a seat, saddle, etc **2** to depose from office or position

unseeded (ʌn'siːdɪd) *adj* (of players in various sports) not assigned to a preferential position in the preliminary rounds of a tournament

unseemly (ʌn'siːmlɪ) *adj* **1** not in good style or taste; unbecoming **2** *obsolete* unattractive ▷ *adv* **3** *rare* in an unseemly manner > un'seemliness *n*

unseen (ʌn'siːn) *adj* **1** not observed or perceived; invisible **2** (of passages of writing) not previously seen or prepared ▷ *n* **3** *chiefly Brit* a passage, not previously seen, that is presented to students for translation

unselfish (ʌn'sɛlfɪʃ) *adj* not selfish or greedy; generous > un'selfishly *adv* > un'selfishness *n*

unsettle (ʌn'sɛtəl) *vb* **1** (*usually tr*) to change or become changed from a fixed or settled condition **2** (*tr*) to confuse or agitate (emotions, the mind, etc) > un'settlement *n*

unsettled (ʌn'sɛtəld) *adj* **1** lacking order or stability: *an unsettled era* **2** unpredictable; uncertain: *an unsettled climate* **3** constantly changing or moving from place to place: *an unsettled life* **4** (of controversy, etc) not brought to an agreed conclusion **5** (of debts, law cases, etc) not disposed of > un'settledness *n*

u

unsex (ʌnˈsɛks) vb (tr) chiefly literary to deprive (a person) of the attributes of his or her sex, esp to make a woman more callous

unshapen (ʌnˈʃeɪpən) adj 1 having no definite shape; shapeless 2 deformed; misshapen

unsheathe (ʌnˈʃiːð) vb (tr) to draw or pull out (something, esp a weapon) from a sheath or other covering

unship (ʌnˈʃɪp) vb -ships, -shipping, -shipped 1 to be or cause to be unloaded, discharged, or disembarked from a ship 2 (tr) nautical to remove from a regular place: to unship oars

unsighted (ʌnˈsaɪtɪd) adj 1 not sighted 2 not having a clear view 3 (of a gun) not equipped with a sight > un'sightedly adv

unsightly (ʌnˈsaɪtlɪ) adj unpleasant or unattractive to look at; ugly > un'sightliness n

unskilful or US **unskillful** (ʌnˈskɪlfʊl) adj lacking dexterity or proficiency > un'skilfully or US un'skillfully adv > un'skilfulness or US un'skillfulness n

unskilled (ʌnˈskɪld) adj 1 not having or requiring any special skill or training: unskilled workers; an unskilled job 2 having or displaying no skill; inexpert

unsling (ʌnˈslɪŋ) vb -slings, -slinging, -slung (tr) 1 to remove or release from a slung position 2 to remove slings from

unsnap (ʌnˈsnæp) vb -snaps, -snapping, -snapped (tr) to unfasten (the snap or catch) of (something)

unsnarl (ʌnˈsnɑːl) vb (tr) to free from a snarl or tangle

unsociable (ʌnˈsəʊʃəbªl) adj 1 (of a person) disinclined to associate or fraternize with others 2 unconducive to social intercourse: an unsociable neighbourhood > un,socia'bility or un'sociableness n

unsocial (ʌnˈsəʊʃəl) adj 1 not social; antisocial 2 (of the hours of work of certain jobs) falling outside the normal working day

unsophisticated (ˌʌnsəˈfɪstɪˌkeɪtɪd) adj 1 lacking experience or worldly wisdom 2 marked by a lack of refinement or complexity: an unsophisticated machine 3 unadulterated or genuine > ,unso'phisti,catedly adv > ,unso'phisti,catedness or ,unso,phisti'cation n

unsound (ʌnˈsaʊnd) adj 1 diseased, weak, or unstable: of unsound mind 2 unreliable or fallacious: unsound advice 3 lacking solidity, strength, or firmness: unsound foundations 4 of doubtful financial or commercial viability: an unsound enterprise > un'soundly adv > un'soundness n

unsparing (ʌnˈspɛərɪŋ) adj 1 not sparing or frugal; lavish; profuse 2 showing harshness or severity; unmerciful > un'sparingly adv > un'sparingness n

unspeakable (ʌnˈspiːkəbªl) adj 1 incapable of expression in words: unspeakable ecstasy 2 indescribably bad or evil 3 not to be uttered: unspeakable thoughts > un'speakably adv

unstable (ʌnˈsteɪbªl) adj 1 lacking stability, fixity, or firmness 2 disposed to temperamental, emotional, or psychological variability 3 (of a chemical compound) readily decomposing 4 physics a (of an elementary particle) having a very short lifetime b spontaneously decomposing by nuclear decay; radioactive: an unstable nuclide 5 electronics (of an electrical circuit, mechanical body, etc) having a tendency to self-oscillation > un'stableness n > un'stably adv

unsteady (ʌnˈstɛdɪ) adj 1 not securely fixed: an unsteady foothold 2 (of behaviour, etc) lacking constancy; erratic 3 without regularity: an unsteady rhythm 4 (of a manner of walking, etc) precarious, staggering, as from intoxication > un'steadily adv > un'steadiness n

unstep (ʌnˈstɛp) vb -steps, -stepping, -stepped (tr) nautical to remove (a mast) from its step

unstick (ʌnˈstɪk) vb -sticks, -sticking, -stuck (tr) to free or loosen (something stuck)

unstop (ʌnˈstɒp) vb -stops, -stopping, -stopped (tr) 1 to remove the stop or stopper from 2 to free from any stoppage or obstruction; open 3 to draw out the stops on (an organ)

unstoppable (ʌnˈstɒpəbªl) adj not capable of being stopped; extremely forceful > un'stoppably adv

unstopped (ʌnˈstɒpt) adj 1 not obstructed or stopped up

2 phonetics denoting a speech sound for whose articulation the closure is not complete, as in the pronunciation of a vowel, fricative, or continuant 3 prosody (of verse) having the sense of the line carried over into the next 4 (of an organ pipe or a string on a musical instrument) not stopped

unstriated (ʌnˈstraɪˌeɪtɪd) adj (of muscle) composed of elongated cells that do not have striations; smooth

unstring (ʌnˈstrɪŋ) vb -strings, -stringing, -strung (tr) 1 to remove the strings of 2 (of beads, pearls, etc) to remove or take from a string 3 to weaken or enfeeble emotionally (a person or his nerves)

unstriped (ʌnˈstraɪpt) adj (esp of smooth muscle) not having stripes; unstriated

unstructured (ʌnˈstrʌktʃəd) adj 1 without formal structure or systematic organization 2 without a preformed shape; (esp of clothes) loose; untailored

unstrung (ʌnˈstrʌŋ) adj 1 emotionally distressed; unnerved 2 (of a stringed instrument) with the strings detached

unstuck (ʌnˈstʌk) adj 1 freed from being stuck, glued, fastened, etc 2 come unstuck to suffer failure or disaster

unstudied (ʌnˈstʌdɪd) adj 1 natural; unaffected 2 (foll by in) without knowledge or training

unsubscribe (ˌʌnsəbˈskraɪb) vb (intr) to cancel a subscription, for example to an emailing service: you can unsubscribe at the following URL

unsubstantial (ˌʌnsəbˈstænʃəl) adj 1 lacking weight, strength, or firmness 2 (esp of an argument) of doubtful validity 3 of no material existence or substance; unreal > ,unsub'stantially adv

unsung (ʌnˈsʌŋ) adj 1 not acclaimed or honoured: unsung deeds 2 not yet sung

unsuspected (ˌʌnsəˈspɛktɪd) adj 1 not under suspicion 2 not known to exist > ,unsus'pectedly adv > ,unsus'pectedness n

unswerving (ʌnˈswɜːvɪŋ) adj not turning aside; constant

untangle (ʌnˈtæŋgªl) vb (tr) 1 to free from a tangled condition 2 to free from perplexity or confusion

untaught (ʌnˈtɔːt) adj 1 without training or education 2 attained or achieved without instruction

untenable (ʌnˈtɛnəbªl) adj 1 (of theories, propositions, etc) incapable of being maintained, defended, or vindicated 2 unable to be maintained against attack > un,tena'bility or un'tenableness n > un'tenably adv

Unter den Linden (German ˈʊntər deːn ˈlɪndən) n the main street of Berlin, extending to the Brandenburg Gate

Unterwalden (German ˈʊntərˌvaldən) n a canton of central Switzerland, on Lake Lucerne: consists of the demicantons of **Nidwalden** (east) and **Obwalden** (west). Capitals: (Nidwalden) Stans; (Obwalden) Sarnen. Pop: (Nidwalden) 38 900 (2002 est); (Obwalden) 33 000 (2002 est). Areas: (Nidwalden) 274 sq km (107 sq miles); (Obwalden) 492 sq km (192 sq miles)

unthinkable (ʌnˈθɪŋkəbªl) adj 1 not to be contemplated; out of the question 2 unimaginable; inconceivable 3 unreasonable; improbable > un'thinkably adv

unthinking (ʌnˈθɪŋkɪŋ) adj 1 lacking thoughtfulness; inconsiderate 2 heedless; inadvertent 3 not thinking or able to think > un'thinkingly adv > un'thinkingness n

unthread (ʌnˈθrɛd) vb (tr) 1 to draw out the thread or threads from (a needle, etc) 2 to disentangle

unthrone (ʌnˈθrəʊn) vb (tr) a less common word for **dethrone**

untidy (ʌnˈtaɪdɪ) adj -dier, -diest 1 not neat; slovenly ▷ vb -dies, -dying, -died 2 (tr) to make untidy > un'tidily adv > un'tidiness n

untie (ʌnˈtaɪ) vb -ties, -tying, -tied 1 to unfasten or free (a knot or something that is tied) or (of a knot or something that is tied) to become unfastened 2 (tr) to free from constraint or restriction

until (ʌnˈtɪl) conj (subordinating) 1 up to (a time) that: he laughed until he cried 2 (used with a negative) before (a time or event): until you change, you can't go out ▷ prep 3 (often preceded by up) in or throughout the period before: he waited until six 4 (used with a negative) earlier than; before:

he won't come until tomorrow [c13 *untill*; related to Old High German *unt* unto, until, Old Norse *und*; see TILL¹]

● USAGE The use of *until such time as* (as in *industrial action will continue until such time as our demands are met*) is unnecessary and should be avoided: *industrial action will continue until our demands are met*

untimely (ʌnˈtaɪmlɪ) *adj* **1** occurring before the expected, normal, or proper time: *an untimely death* **2** inappropriate to the occasion, time, or season: *his joking at the funeral was most untimely* ▷ *adv* **3** prematurely or inopportunely > un'timeliness *n*

unto (ˈʌntuː) *prep* an archaic word for **to¹** [c13: of Scandinavian origin; see UNTIL]

untogether (ˌʌntəˈɡɛðə) *adj slang* incompetent or badly organized; mentally or emotionally unstable

untold (ʌnˈtəʊld) *adj* **1** incapable of description or expression: *untold suffering* **2** incalculably great in number or quantity: *untold thousands* **3** not told

untouchable (ʌnˈtʌtʃəbəl) *adj* **1** lying beyond reach **2** above reproach, suspicion, or impeachment **3** unable to be touched ▷ *n* **4** *highly offensive* a former name for **Dalit** > un,touchaˈbility *n*

untoward (ˌʌntəˈwɔːd, ʌnˈtəʊəd) *adj* **1** characterized by misfortune, disaster, or annoyance **2** not auspicious; adverse; unfavourable **3** unseemly or improper **4** out of the ordinary; out of the way **5** *archaic* refractory; perverse **6** *obsolete* awkward, ungainly, or uncouth > ,unto'wardly *adv* > ,unto'wardness *n*

untrue (ʌnˈtruː) *adj* **1** incorrect or false **2** disloyal **3** diverging from a rule, standard, or measure; inaccurate > un'truly *adv*

untruss (ʌnˈtrʌs) *vb* **1** (*tr*) to release from or as if from a truss; unfasten **2** *obsolete* to undress

untruth (ʌnˈtruːθ) *n* **1** the state or quality of being untrue **2** a statement, fact, etc, that is not true

untruthful (ʌnˈtruːθfʊl) *adj* **1** (of a person) given to lying **2** diverging from the truth; untrue > un'truthfulness *n*

untuck (ʌnˈtʌk) *vb* to become or cause to become loose or not tucked in: *to untuck the blankets*

untutored (ʌnˈtjuːtəd) *adj* **1** without formal instruction or education **2** lacking sophistication or refinement

unused *adj* **1** (ʌnˈjuːzd) not being or never having been made use of **2** (ʌnˈjuːst) (*postpositive*; foll by *to*) not accustomed or used (to something)

unusual (ʌnˈjuːʒʊəl) *adj* out of the ordinary; uncommon; extraordinary: *an unusual design* > un'usually *adv*

unutterable (ʌnˈʌtərəbəl) *adj* incapable of being expressed in words > un'utterableness *n* > un'utterably *adv*

unvarnished (ʌnˈvɑːnɪʃt) *adj* not elaborated upon or glossed; plain and direct: *the unvarnished truth*

unveil (ʌnˈveɪl) *vb* **1** (*tr*) to remove the cover or shroud from, esp in the ceremonial unveiling of a monument, etc **2** to remove the veil from (one's own or another person's face) **3** (*tr*) to make (something secret or concealed) known or public; divulge; reveal

unveiling (ʌnˈveɪlɪŋ) *n* **1** a ceremony involving the removal of a veil at the formal presentation of a statue, monument, etc, for the first time **2** the presentation of something, esp for the first time

unvoice (ʌnˈvɔɪs) *vb* (*tr*) **1** to pronounce without vibration of the vocal cords **2** another word for **devoice**

unvoiced (ʌnˈvɔɪst) *adj* **1** not expressed or spoken **2** articulated without vibration of the vocal cords; voiceless

unwaged (ʌnˈweɪdʒd) *adj* of, relating to, or denoting a person who is not receiving pay because of either being unemployed or working in the home

unwarrantable (ʌnˈwɒrəntəbəl) *adj* incapable of vindication or justification > un'warrantableness *n* > un'warrantably *adv*

unwarranted (ʌnˈwɒrəntɪd) *adj* **1** lacking justification or authorization **2** another word for **unwarrantable**

unwary (ʌnˈwɛərɪ) *adj* lacking caution or prudence; not vigilant or careful > un'warily *adv* > un'wariness *n*

unwearied (ʌnˈwɪərɪd) *adj* **1** not abating or tiring **2** not fatigued; fresh > un'weariedly *adv* > un'weariedness *n*

unweighed (ʌnˈweɪd) *adj* **1** (of quantities purchased, etc)

not measured for weight **2** (of statements, etc) not carefully considered

unwell (ʌnˈwɛl) *adj* (*postpositive*) not well; ill

unwept (ʌnˈwɛpt) *adj* **1** not wept for or lamented **2** *rare* (of tears) not shed

unwholesome (ʌnˈhəʊlsəm) *adj* **1** detrimental to physical or mental health: *an unwholesome climate* **2** morally harmful or depraved: *unwholesome practices* **3** indicative of illness, esp in appearance **4** (esp of food) of inferior quality > un'wholesomeness *n*

unwieldy (ʌnˈwiːldɪ) *or* **unwieldly** *adj* **1** too heavy, large, or awkwardly shaped to be easily handled **2** ungainly; clumsy > un'wieldily *or* un'wieldlily *adv* > un'wieldiness *or* un'wieldliness *n*

unwilled (ʌnˈwɪld) *adj* not intentional; involuntary

unwilling (ʌnˈwɪlɪŋ) *adj* **1** unfavourably inclined; reluctant **2** performed, given, or said with reluctance > un'willingly *adv* > un'willingness *n*

unwind (ʌnˈwaɪnd) *vb* **-winds, -winding, -wound 1** to slacken, undo, or unravel or cause to slacken, undo, or unravel **2** (*tr*) to disentangle **3** to make or become relaxed: *he finds it hard to unwind after a busy day at work* > un'windable *adj*

unwise (ʌnˈwaɪz) *adj* lacking wisdom or prudence; foolish > un'wisely *adv* > un'wiseness *n*

unwish (ʌnˈwɪʃ) *vb* (*tr*) **1** to retract or revoke (a wish) **2** to desire (something) not to be or take place

unwitting (ʌnˈwɪtɪŋ) *adj* (*usually prenominal*) **1** not knowing or conscious **2** not intentional; inadvertent [Old English *unwitende*, from UN-¹ + *witting*, present participle of *witan* to know; related to Old High German *wizzan* to know, Old Norse *vita*] > un'wittingly *adv* > un'wittingness *n*

unwonted (ʌnˈwəʊntɪd) *adj* **1** out of the ordinary; unusual **2** (*usually foll by to*) *archaic* unaccustomed; unused > un'wontedly *adv*

unworldly (ʌnˈwɜːldlɪ) *adj* **1** not concerned with material values or pursuits **2** lacking sophistication; naive **3** not of this earth or world > un'worldliness *n*

unworthy (ʌnˈwɜːðɪ) *adj* **1** (often foll by *of*) not deserving or worthy **2** (often foll by *of*) beneath the level considered befitting (to): *that remark is unworthy of you* **3** lacking merit or value **4** (of treatment) not warranted or deserved > un'worthily *adv* > un'worthiness *n*

unwound (ʌnˈwaʊnd) *vb* the past tense and past participle of **unwind**

unwrap (ʌnˈræp) *vb* **-wraps, -wrapping, -wrapped** to remove the covering or wrapping from (something) or (of something wrapped) to have the covering come off

unwritten (ʌnˈrɪtən) *adj* **1** not printed or in writing **2** effective only through custom; traditional

unwritten law *n* the law based upon custom, usage, and judicial decisions, as distinguished from the enactments of a legislature, orders or decrees in writing, etc

unyoke (ʌnˈjəʊk) *vb* **1** to release (an animal, etc) from a yoke **2** (*tr*) to set free; liberate **3** (*tr*) to disconnect or separate

unzip (ʌnˈzɪp) *vb* **-zips, -zipping, -zipped 1** to unfasten the zip of (a garment) or (of a zip or garment with a zip) to become unfastened: *her skirt unzipped as she sat down* **2** (*tr*) *computing* to decompress (a file) that had previously been zipped

up (ʌp) *prep* **1** indicating movement from a lower to a higher position: *climbing up a mountain* **2** at a higher or further level or position in or on: *soot up the chimney; a shop up the road* ▷ *adv* **3** (*often particle*) to an upward, higher, or erect position, esp indicating readiness for an activity: *looking up at the stars; up and doing something* **4** (*particle*) indicating intensity or completion of an action: *he tore up the cheque; drink up now!* **5** to the place referred to or where the speaker is: *the man came up and asked the way* **6 a** to a more important place: *up to London* **b** to a more northerly place: *up to Scotland* **c** (of a member of some British universities) to or at university **d** in a particular part of the country: *up north* **7** above the horizon: *the sun is up* **8** appearing for trial: *up before the magistrate* **9** having gained: *ten pounds up on the deal* **10** higher in price: *coffee is up again* **11** raised (for discussion, etc): *the plan was up for* consideration **12** taught: *well up in physics* **13** (*functioning as imperative*) get, stand, etc, up: *up with you!* **14 all up with** *informal* finished **b** doomed to die **15 up with** (*functioning as imperative*) wanting the beginning or continuation of: *up with the monarchy!* **16 something's up** *informal* something strange is happening **17 up against a** touching **b** having to cope with: *look what we're up against now* **18 up for** as a candidate or applicant for: *he's up for re-election again* **19 up for it** *informal* keen or willing to try something out or make a good effort: *it's a big challenge and I'm up for it* **20 up to a** devising or scheming; occupied with: *she's up to no good* **b** dependent or incumbent upon: *the decision is up to you* **c** equal to (a challenge, etc) or capable of (doing, etc): *are you up to playing in the final?* **d** aware of **e** as far as: *up to his waist in mud* **f** as many as: *up to two years' waiting time* **g** comparable with: *not up to your normal standard* **21 up top** *informal* in the head or mind **22 up yours** *slang* a vulgar expression of contempt or refusal **23 what's up?** *informal* **a** what is the matter? **b** what is happening? ▷ *adj* **24** (*predicative*) of a high or higher position **25** (*predicative*) out of bed; awake: *the children aren't up yet* **26** (*prenominal*) of or relating to a train or trains to a more important place or one regarded as higher: *the up platform* **27** (*predicative*) over or completed: *the examiner announced that their time was up* **28** (*predicative*) beating one's opponent by a specified amount: *three goals up by half-time* ▷ *vb* **ups, upping, upped 29** (*tr*) to increase or raise **30** (*intr*; foll by *and* with a verb) *informal* to do (something) suddenly, unexpectedly, etc: *she upped and married someone else* ▷ *n* **31** high point; good or pleasant period (esp in the phrase **ups and downs**) **32** *slang* another word (esp US) for **upper** (sense 8) **33 on the up and up a** trustworthy or honest **b** *Brit* on the upward trend or movement: *our firm's on the up and up* [Old English *upp*; related to Old Saxon, Old Norse *up*, Old High German *ūf*, Gothic *iup*]

● **USAGE** The use of *up* before *until* is redundant and
● should be avoided: *the talks will continue until* (not *up*
● *until*) *23rd March*

UP *abbreviation* **1** United Press **2** Uttar Pradesh
up- *prefix* up, upper, or upwards: *uproot; upmost; upthrust; upgrade; uplift*
up-anchor *vb* (*intr*) *nautical* to weigh anchor
up-and-comer *n informal* someone who shows promise in a particular field and appears likely to be successful
up-and-coming *adj* promising continued or future success; enterprising
up-and-down *adj* **1** moving, executed, or formed alternately upwards and downwards ▷ *adv, prep* **up and down 2** backwards and forwards (along)
up-and-over *adj* (of a door, etc) opened by being lifted and moved into a horizontal position
up-and-under *n rugby league* a high kick forwards followed by a charge to the place where the ball lands
Upanishad (uːˈpʌnɪʃəd, -ˌʃæd, juː-) *n Hinduism* any of a class of the Sanskrit sacred books probably composed between 400 and 200 BC and embodying the mystical and esoteric doctrines of ancient Hindu philosophy [C19: from Sanskrit *upanisad* a sitting down near something, from *upa* near to + *ni* down + *sīdati* he sits] > U,pani'shadic *adj*
upas (ˈjuːpəs) *n* **1** a large moraceous tree of Java, *Antiaria toxicaria*, having whitish bark and poisonous milky sap **2** the sap of this tree, used as an arrow poison ▷ Also called: **antiar** [C19: from Malay: poison]
upbeat (ˈʌpˌbiːt) *n* **1** *music* **a** a usually unaccented beat, esp the last in a bar **b** the upward gesture of a conductor's baton indicating this ▷ *adj* **2** *informal* marked by cheerfulness or optimism
upbraid (ʌpˈbreɪd) *vb* (*tr*) **1** to reprove or reproach angrily **2** to find fault with [Old English *upbregdan*; related to Danish *bebreide*; see UP, BRAID] > **up'braider** *n* > **up'braiding** *n*
upbringing (ˈʌpˌbrɪŋɪŋ) *n* the education of a person during his formative years
UPC *abbreviation* Universal Product Code: another name for **bar code**
upcast (ˈʌpˌkɑːst) *n* **1** material cast or thrown up **2** a ventilation shaft through which air leaves a mine

3 *geology* (in a fault) the section of strata that has been displaced upwards ▷ *adj* **4** directed or thrown upwards ▷ *vb* **-casts, -casting, -cast 5** (*tr*) to throw or cast up
up close and personal *adv* **1** intimately: *he got to know the prime minister up close and personal* ▷ *adj* (**up-close-and-personal** when prenominal) **2** intimate: *up-close-and-personal interaction*
upcountry (ʌpˈkʌntrɪ) *adj* **1** of or coming from the interior of a country or region ▷ *n* **2** the interior part of a region or country ▷ *adv* **3** towards, in, or into the interior part of a country or region
update *vb* (ʌpˈdeɪt) (*tr*) **1** to bring up to date ▷ *n* (ˈʌpˌdeɪt) **2** the act of updating or something that is updated > **up'dateable** *adj* > **up'dater** *n*
Updike (ˈʌpˌdaɪk) *n* **John** (**Hoyer**). born 1932, US writer. His novels include *Rabbit, Run* (1960), *Couples* (1968), *The Coup* (1979), *Brazil* (1993), *Seek My Face* (2003), and *Rabbit is Rich* (1982) and *Rabbit at Rest* (1990), both of which won Pulitzer prizes
updraught (ˈʌpˌdrɑːft) *n* an upward movement of air or other gas
upend (ʌpˈɛnd) *vb* **1** to turn or set or become turned or set on end **2** (*tr*) to affect or upset drastically
upfront (ˈʌpˈfrʌnt) *adj* **1** *informal* open, frank, honest ▷ *adv, adj* **2** (of money) paid out at the beginning of a business arrangement
upgrade *vb* (ʌpˈgreɪd) (*tr*) **1** to assign or promote (a person or job) to a higher professional rank or position **2** to raise in value, importance, esteem, etc **3** to improve (a breed of livestock) by crossing with a better strain ▷ *n* (ˈʌpˌgreɪd) **4** *US & Canadian* an upward slope **5 on the upgrade** improving or progressing, as in importance, status, health, etc > **up'grader** *n*
Upham (ˈʌpəm) *n* **Charles** (**Hazlitt**). 1908–94, New Zealand soldier; hero of World War II and one of only three people to have been awarded the Victoria Cross twice
upheaval (ʌpˈhiːvᵊl) *n* **1** a strong, sudden, or violent disturbance, as in politics, social conditions, etc **2** *geology* another word for **uplift** (sense 7)
upheave (ʌpˈhiːv) *vb* **-heaves, -heaving, -heaved** *or* **-hove 1** to heave or rise upwards **2** *geology* to thrust (land) upwards or (of land) to be thrust upwards **3** (*tr*) to disturb violently; throw into disorder
upheld (ʌpˈhɛld) *vb* the past tense and past participle of **uphold**
uphill (ˈʌpˈhɪl) *adj* **1** inclining, sloping, or leading upwards **2** requiring arduous and protracted effort: *an uphill task* ▷ *adv* **3** up an incline or slope; upwards **4** against difficulties ▷ *n* **5** a rising incline; ascent
uphold (ʌpˈhəʊld) *vb* **-holds, -holding, -held** (*tr*) **1** to maintain, affirm, or defend against opposition or challenge **2** to give moral support or inspiration to **3** *rare* to support physically **4** to lift up > **up'holder** *n*
upholster (ʌpˈhəʊlstə) *vb* (*tr*) to fit (chairs, sofas, etc) with padding, springs, webbing, and covering
upholsterer (ʌpˈhəʊlstərə) *n* a person who upholsters furniture as a profession [C17: from *upholster* small furniture dealer; see UPHOLD, -STER, -ER¹]
upholstery (ʌpˈhəʊlstərɪ) *n, pl* **-steries 1** the padding, covering, etc, of a piece of furniture **2** the business, work, or craft of upholstering
upkeep (ˈʌpˌkiːp) *n* **1** the act or process of keeping something in good repair, esp over a long period; maintenance **2** the cost of maintenance
upland (ˈʌplənd) *n* **1** an area of high or relatively high ground ▷ *adj* **2** relating to or situated in an upland
uplift *vb* (ʌpˈlɪft) (*tr*) **1** to raise; elevate; lift up **2** to raise morally, spiritually, culturally, etc **3** *Scot & NZ* to collect (a passenger, parcel, etc); pick up ▷ *n* (ˈʌpˌlɪft) **4** the act, process, or result of lifting up **5** the act or process of bettering moral, social or cultural conditions, etc **6 a** a brassiere for lifting and supporting the breasts **b** (*as modifier*): *an uplift bra* **7** the process or result of land being raised to a higher level, as during a period of mountain building > **up'lifter** *n* > **up'lifting** *adj*
uplighter (ˈʌpˌlaɪtə) *n* a lamp or wall light designed or positioned to cast its light upwards
upload (ʌpˈləʊd) *vb* (*tr*) to copy or transfer (data or a

program) from one's own computer into the memory of another computer. Compare **download** (sense 1)

up-market *adj* relating to commercial products, services, etc, that are relatively expensive and of superior quality

upmost ('ʌp,məʊst) *adj* another word for **uppermost**

Upolu (uː'pəʊluː) *n* an island in the SW central Pacific, in Samoa. Chief town: Apia. Pop: 134 400 (2001). Area: 1114 sq km (430 sq miles)

upon (ə'pɒn) *prep* 1 another word for **on** 2 indicating a position reached by going up: *climb upon my knee* 3 imminent for: *the weekend was upon us again* [c13: from UP + ON]

upper ('ʌpə) *adj* 1 higher or highest in relation to physical position, wealth, rank, status, etc 2 (*capital when part of a name*) lying farther upstream, inland, or farther north: *the upper valley of the Loire* 3 (*capital when part of a name*) *geology, archaeol* denoting the late part or division of a period, system, formation, etc: *Upper Palaeolithic* 4 *maths* (of a limit or bound) greater than or equal to one or more numbers or variables ▷ *n* 5 the higher of two objects, people, etc 6 the part of a shoe above the sole, covering the upper surface of the foot 7 on one's uppers extremely poor; destitute 8 *slang* any of various drugs having a stimulant or euphoric effect

upper atmosphere *n meteorol* that part of the atmosphere above the troposphere

Upper Austria *n* a state of N Austria: first divided from Lower Austria in 1251. Capital: Linz. Pop: 1 387 086 (2003 est). Area: 11 978 sq km (4625 sq miles). German name: **Oberösterreich**

Upper Canada *n* 1 *history* (1791–1841) the official name of the region of Canada lying southwest of the Ottawa River and north of the lower Great Lakes. Compare **Lower Canada** 2 (esp in E Canada) another name for **Ontario**

upper case *printing* ▷ *n* 1 the top half of a compositor's type case in which capital letters, reference marks, and accents are kept ▷ *adj* (**upper-case** *when prenominal*) 2 of or relating to capital letters kept in this case and used in the setting or production of printed or typed matter

upper chamber *n* another name for **upper house**

upper class *n* 1 the class occupying the highest position in the social hierarchy, esp the wealthy or the aristocracy ▷ *adj* (**upper-class** *when prenominal*) 2 of or relating to the upper class

upper crust *n informal* the upper class

uppercut ('ʌpə,kʌt) *n* 1 a short swinging upward blow with the fist delivered at an opponent's chin ▷ *vb* -cuts, -cutting, -cut 2 to hit (an opponent) with an uppercut

Upper Egypt *n* one of the four main traditional administrative districts of Egypt: extends south from Cairo to the Sudan

upper hand *n* the upper hand the position of control; advantage (esp in the phrases **have** or **get the upper hand**)

upper house *n* (*often capitals*) one of the two houses of a bicameral legislature

uppermost ('ʌpə,məʊst) *adj also* upmost 1 highest in position, power, importance, etc ▷ *adv* 2 in or into the highest position, etc

Upper Palatinate *n* See **Palatinate**

Upper Peninsula *n* a peninsula in the northern US between Lakes Superior and Michigan, constituting the N part of the state of Michigan

upper regions *pl n* the upper regions *chiefly literary* the sky; heavens

Upper Silesia *n* a region of SW Poland, formerly ruled by Germany: coal mining and other heavy industry

Upper Tunguska *n* See **Tunguska**

Upper Volta ('vɒltə) *n* the former name (until 1984) of **Burkina Faso**

upper works *pl n nautical* the parts of a vessel above the waterline when fully laden

uppish ('ʌpɪʃ) *adj Brit informal* snobbish, arrogant, or presumptuous [c18: from UP + -ISH] > 'uppishly *adv* > 'uppishness *n*

uppity ('ʌpɪtɪ) *adj informal* not yielding easily to persuasion or control [from UP + fanciful ending,

perhaps influenced by -ITY]

Uppsala *or* **Upsala** ('ʌpsɑːlə) *n* a city in E central Sweden: the royal headquarters in the 13th century; Gothic cathedral (the largest in Sweden) and Sweden's oldest university (1477). Pop: 182 124 (2004 est)

upraise (ʌp'reɪz) *vb* (*tr*) *chiefly literary* to lift up; elevate > up'raiser *n*

uprear (ʌp'rɪə) *vb* (*tr*) to lift up; raise

upright ('ʌp,raɪt) *adj* 1 vertical or erect 2 honest, honourable, or just ▷ *n* 3 a vertical support, such as a stake or post 4 short for **upright piano** 5 the state of being vertical > 'up,rightly *adv* > 'up,rightness *n*

upright piano *n* a piano which has a rectangular vertical case

uprise *vb* (ʌp'raɪz) -rises, -rising, -rose, -risen 1 (*tr*) to rise up ▷ *n* ('ʌp,raɪz) 2 another word for **rise** (sense 23) > up'riser *n*

uprising ('ʌp,raɪzɪŋ, ʌp'raɪzɪŋ) *n* 1 a revolt or rebellion 2 *archaic* an ascent

uproar ('ʌp,rɔː) *n* a commotion or disturbance characterized by loud noise and confusion; turmoil

uproarious (ʌp'rɔːrɪəs) *adj* 1 causing or characterized by an uproar; tumultuous 2 extremely funny; hilarious 3 (of laughter) loud and boisterous > up'roariously *adv* > up'roariousness *n*

uproot (ʌp'ruːt) *vb* (*tr*) 1 to pull up by or as if by the roots 2 to displace (a person or persons) from native or habitual surroundings 3 to remove or destroy utterly > up'rooter *n*

uprush ('ʌp,rʌʃ) *n* an upward rush, as of consciousness

upsadaisy ('ʌpsə'deɪzɪ) *interj* a variant of **upsy-daisy**

ups and downs *pl n* alternating periods of good and bad fortune, high and low spirits, etc

upscale ('ʌp'skeɪl) *adj informal* of or for the upper end of an economic or social scale; up-market

up-sell *vb* to attempt to sell a customer (additional or more expensive goods or services) > 'up-,selling *n*

upset *vb* (ʌp'sɛt) -sets, -setting, -set (*mainly tr*) 1 (*also intr*) to tip or be tipped over; overturn, capsize, or spill 2 to disturb the normal state, course, or stability of: *to upset the balance of nature* 3 to disturb mentally or emotionally 4 to defeat or overthrow, usually unexpectedly 5 to make physically ill: *seafood always upsets my stomach* 6 to thicken or spread (the end of a bar, rivet, etc) by forging, hammering, or swagging ▷ *n* ('ʌp,sɛt) 7 an unexpected defeat or reversal, as in a contest or plans 8 a disturbance or disorder of the emotions, body, etc ▷ *adj* (ʌp'sɛt) 9 overturned or capsized 10 emotionally or physically disturbed or distressed 11 disordered; confused 12 defeated or overthrown [c14 (in the sense: to set up, erect; c19 in the sense: to overthrow); related to Middle High German *ûfsetzen* to put on, Middle Dutch *opzetten*] > up'setter *n* > up'setting *adj* > up'settingly *adv*

upset price ('ʌp,sɛt) *n* another name (esp Scot, US, and Canadian) for **reserve price**

upshot ('ʌp,ʃɒt) *n* 1 the final result; conclusion; outcome 2 *archery* the final shot in a match [c16: from UP + SHOT¹]

upside ('ʌp,saɪd) *n* the upper surface or part

upside down *adj* 1 (*usually postpositive*; **upside-down** *when prenominal*) turned over completely; inverted 2 (**upside-down** *when prenominal*) *informal* confused; muddled; topsy-turvy: *an upside-down world* ▷ *adv* 3 in an inverted fashion 4 in a chaotic or crazy manner [c16: variant, by folk etymology, of earlier *upsodown*]

upside-down cake *n* a sponge cake baked with sliced fruit at the bottom, then inverted before serving

upsides ('ʌp,saɪdz) *adv informal, chiefly Brit* (foll by *with*) equal or level (with), as through revenge or retaliation

upsilon ('ʌpsɪ,lɒn, juː'psaɪlən) *n* the 20th letter in the Greek alphabet (Υ, υ), a vowel, transliterated as *y* or *u* [c17: from Medieval Greek *u psilon* simple *u*, name adopted for graphic *u* to avoid confusion with graphic *oi*, since pronunciation was the same for both in Late Greek]

upsize ('ʌp,saɪz) *vb* -sizes, -sizing, -sized (*tr*) 1 to increase the operating costs of (a company) by increasing the number of people it employs 2 to increase the size of or produce a larger version of (something) [c20: modelled on DOWNSIZE]

u

upskill (ˈʌpˌskɪl) *vb* (*tr*) to improve the aptitude for work of (a person) by additional training

upstage (ˈʌpˈsteɪdʒ) *adv* **1** on, at, or to the rear of the stage ⊳ *adj* **2** of or relating to the back half of the stage **3** *informal* haughty; supercilious; aloof ⊳ *vb* (*tr*) **4** to move upstage of (another actor), thus forcing him to turn away from the audience **5** *informal* to draw attention to oneself from (someone else); steal the show from (someone) **6** *informal* to treat haughtily

upstairs (ˈʌpˈstɛəz) *adv* **1** up the stairs; to or on an upper floor or level **2** *informal* to or into a higher rank or office ⊳ *n* (*functioning as singular or plural*) **3 a** an upper floor or level **b** (*as modifier*): *an upstairs room* **4** *Brit informal old-fashioned* the masters and mistresses of a household collectively, esp of a large house

upstanding (ʌpˈstændɪŋ) *adj* **1** of good character **2** upright and vigorous in build **3** be upstanding **a** (in a court of law) a direction to all persons present to rise to their feet before the judge enters or leaves the court **b** (at a formal dinner) a direction to all persons present to rise to their feet for a toast

upstart (ˈʌpˌstɑːt) *n* **1 a** a person, group, etc, that has risen suddenly to a position of power or wealth **b** (*as modifier*): *an upstart tyrant; an upstart family* **2 a** an arrogant or presumptuous person **b** (*as modifier*): *his upstart ambition*

upstate (ˈʌpˈsteɪt) *US* ⊳ *adj, adv* **1** towards, in, from, or relating to the outlying or northern sections of a state, esp of New York State ⊳ *n* **2** the outlying, esp northern, sections of a state **>** ˈupˈstater *n*

upstream (ˈʌpˈstriːm) *adv, adj* **1** in or towards the higher part of a stream; against the current **2** (in the oil industry) of or for any of the stages prior to oil production, such as exploration or research

upstretched (ʌpˈstrɛtʃt) *adj* (esp of the arms) stretched or raised up

upstroke (ˈʌpˌstrəʊk) *n* **1 a** an upward stroke or movement, as of a pen or brush **b** the mark produced by such a stroke **2** the upward movement of a piston in a reciprocating engine

up-sum *n* a summing-up

upsurge *vb* (ʌpˈsɜːdʒ) **1** (*intr*) *chiefly literary* to surge up ⊳ *n* (ˈʌpˌsɜːdʒ) **2** a rapid rise or swell

upsweep *n* (ˈʌpˌswiːp) **1** a curve or sweep upwards ⊳ *vb* (ʌpˈswiːp) -sweeps, -sweeping, -swept **2** to sweep, curve, or brush or be swept, curved, or brushed upwards

upswing (ˈʌpˌswɪŋ) *n* **1** *economics* a recovery period in the trade cycle **2** an upward swing or movement or any increase or improvement

upsy-daisy (ˈʌpsɪˈdeɪzɪ) *or* **upsadaisy** *interj* an expression, usually of reassurance, uttered as when someone, esp a child, stumbles or is being lifted up [c18 *up-a-daisy*, irregularly formed from UP (adv)]

uptake (ˈʌpˌteɪk) *n* **1** a pipe, shaft, etc, that is used to convey smoke or gases, esp one that connects a furnace to a chimney **2** taking up or lifting up **3** the act of accepting or taking up something on offer or available **4** quick on the uptake *informal* quick to understand or learn **5** slow on the uptake *informal* slow to understand or learn

upthrow (ˈʌpˌθrəʊ) *n* *geology* the upward movement of rocks on one side of a fault plane relative to rocks on the other side

upthrust (ˈʌpˌθrʌst) *n* **1** an upward push or thrust **2** *geology* a violent upheaval of the earth's surface

uptight (ʌpˈtaɪt) *adj informal* **1** displaying tense repressed nervousness, irritability, or anger **2** unable to give expression to one's feelings, personality, etc

uptime (ˈʌpˌtaɪm) *n* *commerce* time during which a machine, such as a computer, actually operates

up-to-date *adj* **a** modern, current, or fashionable: *an up-to-date magazine* **b** (*predicative*): *the magazine is up to date* **>** ˈup-to-ˈdateness *n*

uptown (ˈʌpˈtaʊn) *US & Canadian* ⊳ *adj, adv* **1** towards, in, or relating to some part of a town that is away from the centre ⊳ *n* **2** such a part of a town, esp a residential part **>** ˈupˈtowner *n*

upturn *vb* (ʌpˈtɜːn) **1** to turn or cause to turn up, over, or upside down **2** (*tr*) to create disorder **3** (*tr*) to direct upwards ⊳ *n* (ˈʌpˌtɜːn) **4** an upward turn, trend, or improvement **5** an upheaval or commotion

UPVC *abbreviation* unplasticized polyvinyl chloride. See also **PVC**

upward (ˈʌpwəd) *adj* **1** directed or moving towards a higher point or level ⊳ *adv* **2** a variant of **upwards** **>** ˈupwardly *adv* **>** ˈupwardness *n*

upwardly mobile *adj* (of a person or social group) moving or aspiring to move to a higher social class or to a position of increased status or power

upward mobility *n* *sociol* the movement of an individual, social group, or class to a position of increased status or power

upwards (ˈʌpwədz) *or* **upward** *adv* **1** from a lower to a higher place, level, condition, etc **2** towards a higher level, standing, etc

upwind (ˈʌpˈwɪnd) *adv* **1** into or against the wind **2** towards or on the side where the wind is blowing; windward ⊳ *adj* **3** going against the wind: *the upwind leg of the course* **4** on the windward side

Ur (ɜː) *n* an ancient city of Sumer located on a former channel of the Euphrates

UR *text messaging abbreviation* **1** you are **2** your

uracil (ˈjʊərəˌsɪl) *n* *biochem* a pyrimidine present in all living cells, usually in a combined form, as in RNA. Formula: $C_4H_4N_2O_2$ [c20: from URO-¹ + ACETIC + -ILE]

uraemia *or US* **uremia** (jʊˈriːmɪə) *n* *pathol* the accumulation of waste products, normally excreted in the urine, in the blood: causes severe headaches, vomiting, etc. Also called: **azotaemia** [c19: from New Latin, from Greek *ouron* urine + *haima* blood] **>** uˈraemic *or US* uˈremic *adj*

uraeus (jʊˈriːəs) *n, pl* **-uses** the sacred serpent represented on the headdresses of ancient Egyptian kings and gods [c19: from New Latin, from Greek *ouraios*, from Egyptian *uro* asp]

Ural (ˈjʊərəl; *Russian* uˈral) *n* a river in central Russia, rising in the S Ural Mountains and flowing south to the Caspian Sea. Length: 2534 km (1575 miles)

Ural-Altaic *n* **1** a postulated group of related languages consisting of the Uralic and Altaic families of languages ⊳ *adj* **2** of or relating to this group of languages, characterized by agglutination and vowel harmony

Uralic (jʊˈrælɪk) *or* **Uralian** (jʊˈreɪlɪən) *n* **1** a superfamily of languages consisting of the Finno-Ugric family together with Samoyed. See also **Ural-Altaic** ⊳ *adj* **2** of or relating to these languages

Ural Mountains *or* **Urals** *pl n* a mountain system in W central Russia, extending over 2000 km (1250 miles) from the Arctic Ocean towards the Aral Sea: forms part of the geographical boundary between Europe and Asia; one of the richest mineral areas in the world, with many associated major industrial centres. Highest peak: Mount Narodnaya, 1894 m (6214 ft)

uranalysis (ˌjʊərəˈnælɪsɪs) *n, pl* **-ses** (-ˌsiːz) *med* a variant spelling of **urinalysis**

Uranian (jʊˈreɪnɪən) *n* **1** a hypothetical inhabitant of the planet Uranus ⊳ *adj* **2** of, occurring on, or relating to the planet Uranus **3** of the heavens; celestial **4** relating to astronomy; astronomical **5** (as an epithet of Aphrodite) heavenly; spiritual **6** of or relating to the Muse Urania

uranide (ˈjʊərəˌnaɪd) *n* any element having an atomic number greater than that of protactinium

uranism (ˈjʊərænɪzəm) *n* a rare word for (esp male) **homosexuality** [c20: from German *Uranismus*, from Greek *ouranios* heavenly, i.e. spiritual; compare URANIAN (sense 5)]

uranium (jʊˈreɪnɪəm) *n* a radioactive silvery-white metallic element of the actinide series. It occurs in several minerals including pitchblende, carnotite, and autunite and is used chiefly as a source of nuclear energy by fission of the radioisotope **uranium-235**. Symbol: U; atomic no: 92; atomic wt: 238.0289; half-life of most stable isotope, ²³⁸U: 451×10^9 years; valency: 2-6; relative density: 18.95 (approx.); melting pt: 1135°C; boiling pt: 4134°C [c18: from New Latin, from URANUS²; from the fact that the element was discovered soon after the planet]

uranium hexafluoride (ˌhɛksəˈflʊəˌraɪd) *n* a compound used in the process of uranium enrichment that

u

produces fissile material for nuclear reactors and nuclear weapons. Formula: UF_6

uranium series *n physics* a radioactive series that starts with uranium-238 and proceeds by radioactive decay to lead-206

urano- *combining form* denoting the heavens: *uranography* [from Greek *ouranos*]

uranography (ˌjʊərəˈnɒɡrəfɪ) *n obsolete* the branch of astronomy concerned with the description and mapping of the stars, galaxies, etc > ˌuraˈnographer or ˌuraˈnographist *n* > uranographic (ˌjʊərənəˈɡræfɪk) *adj*

Uranus[1] (jʊˈreɪnəs, ˈjʊərənəs) *n Greek myth* the personification of the sky, who, as a god, ruled the universe and fathered the Titans and Cyclopes on his wife and mother Gaea (earth). He was overthrown by his son Cronus

Uranus[2] (jʊˈreɪnəs, ˈjʊərənəs) *n* one of the giant planets, the seventh planet from the sun, sometimes visible to the naked eye. It has about 15 satellites, a ring system, and an axis of rotation almost lying in the plane of the orbit. Mean distance from sun: 2870 million km; period of revolution around sun: 84 years; period of axial rotation: 17.23 hours; diameter and mass: 4 and 14.5 times that of earth respectively [c19: from Latin *Ūranus*, from Greek *Ouranos* heaven]

urate (ˈjʊəreɪt) *n* any salt or ester of uric acid > **uratic** (jʊˈrætɪk) *adj*

urban (ˈɜːbᵊn) *adj* **1** of, relating to, or constituting a city or town **2** living in a city or town **3** (of music) emerging and developing in densely populated areas of large cities, esp those populated by people of African or Caribbean origin. Compare **rural** [c17: from Latin *urbānus*, from *urbs* city]

urban area *n* (in population censuses) a city area considered as the inner city plus built-up environs, irrespective of local body administrative boundaries

urban district *n* **1** (in England and Wales from 1888 to 1974 and Northern Ireland from 1898 to 1973) an urban division of an administrative county with an elected council in charge of housing and environmental services: usually made up of one or more thickly populated areas but lacking a borough charter **2** (in the Republic of Ireland) any of 49 medium-sized towns with their own elected councils

urbane (ɜːˈbeɪn) *adj* characterized by elegance or sophistication [c16: from Latin *urbānus* belonging to the town; see URBAN] > **urˈbanely** *adv* > **urˈbaneness** *n*

urban golf *n* a game played on a large outdoor course in a non-residential area of a city, the object of which is to hit a tennis ball using clubs, with as few strokes as possible, into each of usually 18 holes

urban guerrilla *n* a guerrilla who operates in a town or city, engaging in terrorism, kidnapping, etc

Urban II (ˈɜːbᵊn) *n* original name *Odo* or *Udo*. ?1042–99, French ecclesiastic; pope (1088–99). He inaugurated the First Crusade at the Council of Clermont (1095)

urbanism (ˈɜːbəˌnɪzəm) *n chiefly US* **a** the character of city life **b** the study of this

urbanite (ˈɜːbəˌnaɪt) *n* a resident of an urban community; city dweller

urbanity (ɜːˈbænɪtɪ) *n, pl* **-ties 1** the quality of being urbane **2** (*usually plural*) civilities or courtesies

urbanize or **urbanise** (ˈɜːbəˌnaɪz) *vb* (*tr*) (*usually passive*) **a** to make (esp a predominantly rural area or country) more industrialized and urban **b** to cause the migration of an increasing proportion of (rural dwellers) into cities > ˌurbaniˈzation or ˌurbaniˈsation *n*

urban myth *n* a story, esp one with a shocking or amusing ending, related as having actually happened, usu. to someone vaguely connected with the teller

urban renewal *n* the process of redeveloping dilapidated or no longer functional urban areas

Urban VI *n* original name *Bartolomeo Prignano* ?1318–89, Italian ecclesiastic; pope (1378–89). His policies led to the election of an antipope by the French cardinals, thus beginning the Great Schism in the West

Urban VIII *n* original name *Maffeo Barberini*. 1568–1644, Italian ecclesiastic; pope (1623–44) during the Thirty Years' War, in which he supported Cardinal Richelieu against the Hapsburgs

urbi et orbi *Latin* (ˈɜːbɪ ɛt ˈɔːbɪ) *adv RC Church* to the city and the world: a phrase qualifying the solemn papal blessing

urceolate (ˈɜːsɪəlɪt, -ˌleɪt) *adj biology* shaped like an urn or pitcher: *an urceolate corolla* [c18: via New Latin *urceolātus*, from Latin *urceolus* diminutive of *urceus* a pitcher]

urchin (ˈɜːtʃɪn) *n* **1** a mischievous roguish child, esp one who is young, small, or raggedly dressed **2** See **sea urchin 3** an archaic or dialect name for a **hedgehog 4** *obsolete* an elf or sprite [c13: *urchon*, from Old French *heriçon*, from Latin *ēricius* hedgehog, from *ēr*, related to Greek *khēr* hedgehog]

Urdu (ˈʊəduː, ˈɜː-) *n* an official language of Pakistan, also spoken in India. The script derives primarily from Persia. It belongs to the Indic branch of the Indo-European family of languages, being closely related to Hindi but containing many Arabic and Persian loan words [c18: from Hindustani (*zabāni*) *urdū* (language of the) camp, from Persian *urdū* camp, from Turkish *ordū*]

-ure *suffix forming nouns* **1** indicating act, process, or result: *seizure* **2** indicating function or office: *legislature; prefecture* [from French, from Latin *-ūra*]

urea (ˈjʊərɪə) *n* a white water-soluble crystalline compound with a saline taste and often an odour of ammonia, produced by protein metabolism and excreted in urine. A synthetic form is used as a fertilizer, animal feed, and in the manufacture of synthetic resins. Formula: $CO(NH_2)_2$ [c19: from New Latin, from French *urée*, from Greek *ouron* URINE] > **uˈreal** or **uˈreic** *adj*

urea-formaldehyde resin *n* any one of a class of rigid odourless synthetic materials that are made from urea and formaldehyde and are used in electrical fittings, adhesives, laminates, and finishes for textiles

ureide (ˈjʊərɪˌaɪd) *n chem* **1** any of a class of organic compounds derived from urea by replacing one or more of its hydrogen atoms by organic groups **2** any of a class of derivatives of urea and carboxylic acids, in which one or more of the hydrogen atoms have been replaced by acyl groups: includes the cyclic ureides, such as alloxan

-uret *suffix* formerly used to form the names of binary chemical compounds [from New Latin *-uretum*]

ureter (jʊˈriːtə) *n* the tube that conveys urine from the kidney to the urinary bladder or cloaca [c16: via New Latin from Greek *ourētēr*, from *ourein* to URINATE] > **uˈreteral** or **ureteric** (ˌjʊərɪˈtɛrɪk) *adj*

urethane (ˈjʊərɪˌθeɪn) or **urethan** (ˈjʊərɪˌθæn) *n* short for **polyurethane** [c19: from URO-[1] + ETHYL + -ANE]

urethra (jʊˈriːθrə) *n, pl* **-thrae** (-θriː) or **-thras** the canal that in most mammals conveys urine from the bladder out of the body. In human males it also conveys semen [c17: via Late Latin from Greek *ourēthra*, from *ourein* to URINATE] > **uˈrethral** *adj*

urethritis (ˌjʊərɪˈθraɪtɪs) *n* inflammation of the urethra [c19: from New Latin, from Late Latin URETHRA] > **urethritic** (ˌjʊərɪˈθrɪtɪk) *adj*

urethroscope (jʊˈriːθrəˌskəʊp) *n* a medical instrument for examining the urethra [c20: see URETHRA, -SCOPE] > **urethroscopic** (jʊˌriːθrəˈskɒpɪk) *adj* > **urethroscopy** (ˌjʊərɪˈθrɒskəpɪ) *n*

uretic (jʊˈrɛtɪk) *adj* of or relating to the urine [c19: via Late Latin from Greek *ourētikos*, from *ouron* URINE]

Urey (ˈjʊərɪ) *n* **Harold Clayton**. 1893–1981, US chemist, who discovered the heavy isotope of hydrogen, deuterium (1932), and worked on methods of separating uranium isotopes: Nobel prize for chemistry 1934

Urfa (ˈɜːfə) *n* a city in SE Turkey: market centre. Pop: 451 000 (2005 est). Ancient name: Edessa

Urfé (*French* urfe) *n* **Honoré d'** (ɔnɔre d). 1568–1625, French writer, whose pastoral *L'Astrée* (1607–27) is considered the first French novel

Urga (ˈɜːɡə) *n* the former name (until 1924) of **Ulan Bator**

urge (ɜːdʒ) *vb* **1** (*tr*) to plead, press, or move (someone to do something): *we urged him to surrender* **2** (*tr; may take a clause as object*) to advocate or recommend earnestly and persistently; plead or insist on: *to urge the need for safety* **3** (*tr*) to impel, drive, or hasten onwards: *he urged the horses on* ▷ *n* **4** a strong impulse, inner drive, or yearning [c16: from Latin *urgēre*]

u

urgent ('ɜːdʒənt) *adj* 1 requiring or compelling speedy action or attention: *the matter is urgent; an urgent message* 2 earnest and persistent [c15: via French from Latin *urgent-, urgens*, present participle of *urgēre* to URGE] > **urgency** ('ɜːdʒənsɪ) *n* > **'urgently** *adv*

-urgy *n combining form* indicating technology concerned with a specified material: *metallurgy* [from Greek *-urgia*, from *ergon* WORK]

Uri (*German* 'uːri) *n* one of the original three cantons of Switzerland, in the centre of the country: mainly German-speaking and Roman Catholic. Capital: Altdorf. Pop: 35 200 (2002 est). Area: 1075 sq km (415 sq miles)

-uria *n combining form* indicating a diseased or abnormal condition of the urine: *dysuria; pyuria* [from Greek *-ouria*, from *ouron* urine] > **-uric** *adj combining form*

Uriah (jʊˈraɪə) *n Old Testament* a Hittite officer, who was killed in battle on instructions from David so that he could marry Uriah's wife Bathsheba (II Samuel 11)

uric ('jʊərɪk) *adj* of, concerning, or derived from urine [c18: from URO-¹ + -IC]

uric acid *n* a white odourless tasteless crystalline product of protein metabolism, present in the blood and urine; 2,6,8-trihydroxypurine. Formula: $C_5H_4N_4O_3$

uridine ('jʊərɪˌdiːn) *n biochem* a nucleoside present in all living cells in a combined form, esp in RNA [c20: from URO-¹ + -IDE + -INE²]

urinal (jʊˈraɪnᵊl, 'jʊərɪ-) *n* 1 a sanitary fitting, esp one fixed to a wall, used by men for urination 2 a room containing urinals 3 any vessel for holding urine prior to its disposal

urinalysis (ˌjʊərɪˈnælɪsɪs) *or* **uranalysis** *n, pl* -ses (-ˌsiːz) *med* analysis of the urine to test for the presence of disease by the presence of protein, glucose, ketones, cells, etc

urinary ('jʊərɪnərɪ) *adj* 1 *anatomy* of or relating to urine or to the organs and structures that secrete and pass urine ▷ *n, pl* -naries 2 a reservoir for urine

urinary bladder *n* a distensible muscular sac in which the urine excreted from the kidneys is stored

urinate ('jʊərɪˌneɪt) *vb* (*intr*) to excrete or void urine; micturate > ˌuri'nation *n* > 'urinative *adj*

urine ('jʊərɪn) *n* the pale yellow slightly acid fluid excreted by the kidneys, containing waste products removed from the blood. It is stored in the urinary bladder and discharged through the urethra [c14: via Old French from Latin *ūrina*; related to Greek *ouron*, Latin *ūrīnāre* to plunge under water]

urinogenital (ˌjʊərɪnəʊˈdʒɛnɪtᵊl) *adj* another word for **urogenital**

URL *abbreviation* uniform resource locator; a standardized address of a location on the internet, esp on the World Wide Web

Urmia ('ɜːmɪə) *or* **Orumiyeh** (*Persian* ɒˈruːmiːjə) *n* Lake Urmia a shallow lake in NW Iran, at an altitude of 1300 m (4250 ft): the largest lake in Iran, varying in area from 4000–6000 sq km (1500–2300 sq miles) between autumn and spring

Urmston ('ɜːmstən) *n* a town in NW England, in Trafford unitary authority, Greater Manchester. Pop: 40 964 (2001)

urn (ɜːn) *n* 1 a vaselike receptacle or vessel, esp a large bulbous one with a foot 2 a vase used as a receptacle for the ashes of the dead 3 a large vessel, usually of metal, with a tap, used for making and holding tea, coffee, etc [c14: from Latin *ūrna*; related to Latin *ūrere* to burn, *urceus* pitcher, Greek *hurkhē* jar] > 'urn,like *adj*

urnfield ('ɜːnˌfiːld) *n* 1 a cemetery full of individual cremation urns ▷ *adj* 2 (of a number of Bronze Age cultures) characterized by cremation in urns, which began in E Europe about the second millennium BC and by the seventh century BC had covered almost all of mainland Europe

uro- *or before a vowel* **ur-** *combining form* indicating urine or the urinary tract: *urochrome; urogenital; urolith; urology* [from Greek *ouron* urine]

urogenital (ˌjʊərəʊˈdʒɛnɪtᵊl) *or* **urinogenital** *adj* of or relating to the urinary and genital organs and their functions. Also called: **genitourinary**

urogenital system *or* **urogenital tract** *n anatomy* the urinary tract and reproductive organs

urolith ('jʊərəʊlɪθ) *n pathol* a calculus in the urinary tract [from URO-¹ + Greek *lithos* stone] > ˌuro'lithic *adj*

urology (jʊˈrɒlədʒɪ) *n* the branch of medicine concerned with the study and treatment of diseases of the urogenital tract > **urologic** (ˌjʊərəˈlɒdʒɪk) *or* ˌuro'logical *adj* > u'rologist *n*

uropygial gland *n* a gland, situated at the base of the tail in most birds, that secretes oil used in preening

uropygium (ˌjʊərəˈpɪdʒɪəm) *n* the hindmost part of a bird's body, from which the tail feathers grow [c19: via New Latin from Greek *ouropugion*, from *oura* tail + *pugē* rump] > ˌuro'pygial *adj*

uroscopy (jʊˈrɒskəpɪ) *n med* examination of the urine. See also **urinalysis** > **uroscopic** (ˌjʊərəˈskɒpɪk) *adj* > u'roscopist *n*

Urquhart ('ɜːkət) *n* **Sir Thomas.** 1611–60, Scottish author and translator of Rabelais' *Gargantua and Pantagruel* (1653; 1693)

Ursa Major (ˈɜːsə ˈmeɪdʒə) *n, Latin genitive* **Ursae Majoris** ('ɜːsiː məˈdʒɔːrɪs) an extensive conspicuous constellation in the N hemisphere, visible north of latitude 40°. The seven brightest stars form the Plough. A line through the two brightest stars points to the Pole Star lying in Ursa Minor. Also called: **the Great Bear, the Bear** [Latin: greater bear]

Ursa Minor ('ɜːsə 'maɪnə) *n, Latin genitive* **Ursae Minoris** ('ɜːsiː mɪˈnɔːrɪs) a small faint constellation, the brightest star of which is the Pole Star, lying 1° from the true celestial pole. Also called: **the Little Bear, the Bear,** (*US and Canadian*) **the Little Dipper** [Latin: lesser bear]

ursine ('ɜːsaɪn) *adj* of, relating to, or resembling a bear or bears [c16: from Latin *ursus* a bear]

Ursprache *German* ('uːrʃprɑːxə) *n* any hypothetical extinct and unrecorded language reconstructed from groups of related recorded languages. For example, Germanic is an *Ursprache* reconstructed by comparison of English, Dutch, German, the Scandinavian languages, and Gothic; Indo-European is an *Ursprache* reconstructed by comparison of the Germanic group, Latin, Sanskrit, etc [from *ur-* primeval, original + *Sprache* language]

Ursula ('ɜːsjʊlə) *n* **Saint.** a legendary British princess of the fourth or fifth century AD, said to have been martyred together with 11 000 virgins by the Huns at Cologne. Feast day: Oct 21

Ursuline ('ɜːsjʊˌlaɪn) *n* 1 a member of an order of nuns devoted to teaching in the Roman Catholic Church: founded in 1537 at Brescia ▷ *adj* 2 of or relating to this order [c16: named after St Ursula, legendary British princess and martyr of the fourth or fifth century AD, patron saint of St Angela Merici, who founded the order]

Urtext *German* ('uːrtɛkst) *n* 1 the earliest form of a text as established by linguistic scholars as a basis for variants in later texts still in existence 2 an edition of a musical score showing the composer's intentions without later editorial interpolation [from *ur-* original + TEXT]

urticaceous (ˌɜːtɪˈkeɪʃəs) *adj* of, relating to, or belonging to the *Urticaceae*, a family of plants, having small flowers and, in many species, stinging hairs: includes the nettles and pellitory [c18: via New Latin from Latin *urtīca* nettle, from *ūrere* to burn]

urticaria (ˌɜːtɪˈkɛərɪə) *n* a skin condition characterized by the formation of itchy red or whitish raised patches, usually caused by an allergy. Nontechnical names: **hives, nettle rash** [c18: from New Latin, from Latin *urtīca* nettle]

urtication (ˌɜːtɪˈkeɪʃən) *n* 1 a burning or itching sensation 2 another name for **urticaria**

Uru. *abbreviation* Uruguay

Uruapan (*Spanish* uˈrwapan) *n* a city in SW Mexico, in Michoacán state: agricultural trading centre. Pop: 282 000 (2005 est)

Uruguay ('jʊərəˌgwaɪ) *n* a republic in South America, on the Atlantic: Spanish colonization began in 1624, followed by Portuguese settlement in 1680; revolted against Spanish rule in 1820 but was annexed by the Portuguese to Brazil; gained independence in 1825. It consists mainly of rolling grassy plains, low hills, and plateaus. Official language: Spanish. Religion: Roman

u

Catholic majority. Currency: peso. Capital: Montevideo. Pop: 3 439 000 (2004 est). Area: 176 215 sq km (68 037 sq miles) > ˌUruˈguayan *adj, n*

Urumchi (uːˈruːmtʃɪ), **Ürümqi** *or* **Wu-lu-mu-ch'i** *n* a city in NW China, capital of Xinjiang Uygur Autonomous Region: trading centre on a N route between China and central Asia. Pop: 1 562 000 (2005 est). Former name: Tihwa

Urundi (ʊˈrʊndɪ) *n* the former name (until 1962) of **Burundi**

urus (ˈjʊərəs) *n, pl* **uruses** another name for the **aurochs** [c17: from *ūrus*, of Germanic origin; compare Old High German *ūr*, Old Norse *urr*, Greek *ouros* aurochs]

urushiol (uːˈrʊʃɪˌɒl, uːˈruː-) *n* a poisonous pale yellow liquid occurring in poison ivy and the lacquer tree [from Japanese *urushi* lacquer + -OL²]

us¹ (ʌs) *pron* (*objective*) **1** refers to the speaker or writer and another person or other people: *don't hurt us; to decide among us* **2** refers to all people or people in general: *this table shows us the tides* **3** an informal word for **me¹**: *give us a kiss!* **4** when used by editors, monarchs, etc, a formal word for **me¹** [Old English *ūs*; related to Old High German *uns*, Old Norse *oss*, Latin *nōs*, Sanskrit *nas* we]
● USAGE See at **me¹**

us² *internet domain name* United States

US *or* **U.S.** *abbreviation* United States

USA 1 *abbreviation* United States Army **2** *international car registration* United States of America

U.S.A. *or* **USA** *abbreviation* United States of America

usable *or* **useable** (ˈjuːzəbəl) *adj* able to be used > ˌusaˈbility *or* ˌuseaˈbility *n*

USAF *abbreviation* United States Air Force

usage (ˈjuːsɪdʒ, -zɪdʒ) *n* **1** the act or a manner of using; use; employment **2** constant use, custom, or habit **3** something permitted or established by custom or practice **4** what is actually said in a language, esp as contrasted with what is prescribed [c14: via Old French, from Latin *ūsus* USE (n)]

usance (ˈjuːzəns) *n commerce* the period of time permitted by commercial usage for the redemption of foreign bills of exchange [c14: from Old French, from Medieval Latin *ūsantia*, from *ūsāre* to USE]

USB *abbreviation* Universal Serial Bus: a standard for connection sockets on computers and other electronic equipment

USB drive *n computing* another name for **flash drive**

USB key *n computing* another name for **pocket drive**

USB port *n computing* a type of serial port for connecting peripheral devices in a system

USDAW (ˈʌzˌdɔː) (in Britain) *n acronym for* Union of Shop, Distributive, and Allied Workers

use *vb* (juːz) (*tr*) **1** to put into service or action; employ for a given purpose: *to use a spoon to stir with* **2** to make a practice or habit of employing; exercise: *he uses his brain* **3** to behave towards **4** to behave towards in a particular way for one's own ends: *he uses people* **5** to consume, expend, or exhaust: *the engine uses very little oil* **6** *chiefly US & Canadian* to partake of (alcoholic drink, drugs, etc) or smoke (tobacco, marijuana, etc) ▷ *n* (juːs) **7** the act of using or the state of being used: *the carpet wore out through constant use* **8** the ability, right, or permission to use **9** the occasion to use; need: *I have no use for this paper* **10** an instance or manner of using **11** usefulness; advantage: *it is of no use to complain* **12** custom; practice; habit: *long use has inured him to it* **13** the purpose for which something is used; end **14** *Christianity* a distinctive form of liturgical or ritual observance, esp one that is traditional in a Church or group of Churches **15** the enjoyment of property, land, etc, by occupation or by deriving revenue or other benefit from it **16** *law* the beneficial enjoyment of property the legal title to which is held by another person as trustee **17** have no use for **a** to have no need of **b** to have a contemptuous dislike for **18** make use of **a** to employ; use **b** to exploit (a person) ▷ See also **use up** [c13: from Old French *user* to use, from Latin *ūsus* having used, from *ūtī* to use]

use-by date *n* **1** the date by which perishable goods should be used **2** *NZ* another word for **sell-by date**

used (juːzd) *adj* bought or sold second-hand: *used cars*

used to (juːst) *adj* **1** made familiar with; accustomed to: *I am used to hitchhiking* ▷ *vb* (*tr*) **2** (*takes an infinitive or implied infinitive*) used as an auxiliary to express habitual or accustomed actions, states, etc, taking place in the past but not continuing into the present: *I don't drink these days, but I used to; I used to fish here every day*
● USAGE The most common negative form of *used to* is
● *didn't used to* (or *didn't use to*), but in formal contexts *used*
● *not to* is preferred

useful (ˈjuːsfʊl) *adj* **1** able to be used advantageously, beneficially, or for several purposes; helpful or serviceable **2** *informal* commendable or capable: *a useful term's work* > ˈusefully *adv* > ˈusefulness *n*

useless (ˈjuːslɪs) *adj* **1** having no practical use or advantage **2** *informal* ineffectual, weak, or stupid: *he's useless at history* > ˈuselessly *adv* > ˈuselessness *n*

Usenet (ˈjuːzˌnɛt) *n computing* a vast collection of newsgroups that follow agreed naming, maintaining, and distribution practices

user (ˈjuːzə) *n* **1** *law* **a** the continued exercise, use, or enjoyment of a right, esp in property **b** a presumptive right based on long-continued use: *right of user* **2** (*often in combination*) a person or thing that uses: *a road-user* **3** *informal* a drug addict

user-friendly *adj* easy to use or understand > user-friendliness *n*

username (ˈjuːzəˌneɪm) *n computing* a name that someone uses for identification purposes when logging onto a computer, using chatrooms, or as part of his or her e-mail address

use up *vb* (*tr, adverb*) **1** to finish (a supply); consume completely **2** to exhaust; wear out

Ushant (ˈʌʃənt) *n* an island off the NW coast of France, at the tip of Brittany: scene of naval battles in 1778 and 1794 between France and Britain. Area: about 16 sq km (6 sq miles). French name: Ouessant

Ushas (ˈuːʃəs) *n* the Hindu goddess of the dawn

usher (ˈʌʃə) *n* **1** an official who shows people to their seats, as in a church or theatre **2** a person who acts as doorkeeper, esp in a court of law **3** (in England) a minor official charged with maintaining order in a court of law **4** an officer responsible for preceding persons of rank in a procession or introducing strangers at formal functions **5** *Brit obsolete* a teacher ▷ *vb* (*tr*) **6** to conduct or escort, esp in a courteous or obsequious way **7** (usually foll by in) to be a precursor or herald (of) [c14: from Old French *huissier* doorkeeper, from Vulgar Latin *ustiārius* (unattested), from Latin *ostium* door]

Usher (ˈʌʃə) *n* a variant spelling of (James) **Ussher**

usherette (ˌʌʃəˈrɛt) *n* a woman assistant in a cinema, theatre, etc, who shows people to their seats

Usk (ʌsk) *n* a river in SE Wales, flowing southeast and south to the Bristol Channel. Length: 113 km (70 miles)

Üsküb (ˈʊskuːb) *n* the Turkish name (1392–1913) for **Skopje**

Üsküdar (ˌuːskuːˈdɑː) *n* a town in NW Turkey, across the Bosporus from Istanbul: formerly a terminus of caravan routes from Syria and Asia; base of the British army in the Crimean War. Pop: 495 118 (2000). Former name: Scutari

USM *abbreviation stock exchange* Unlisted Securities Market

Usman dan Fodio (ˈuːsmɑːn dæn ˈfəʊdɪˌəʊ) *n* 1754–1817, African mystic and revolutionary leader, who created a Muslim state in Nigeria

USN *abbreviation* United States Navy

Usnach *or* **Usnech** (ˈʊʃnəx) *n* (in Irish legend) the father of Naoise

USP *abbreviation* unique selling proposition *or* unique selling point: a characteristic of a product that can be used in advertising to differentiate it from its competitors

Uspallata Pass (ˌuːspəˈlɑːtə; *Spanish* uspaˈʎata) *n* a pass over the Andes in S South America, between Mendoza (Argentina) and Santiago (Chile). Height: 3840 m (12 600 ft). Also called: La Cumbre

usquebaugh (ˈʌskwɪˌbɔː) *n* **1** *Irish* the former name for **whiskey 2** *Scot* the former name for **whisky** [c16: from Irish Gaelic *uisce beathadh* or Scot Gaelic *uisge beatha* water of life]

u

USS *abbreviation* **1** United States Senate **2** United States Ship

Ussher *or* **Usher** (ˈʌʃə) *n* **James.** 1581–1656, Irish prelate and scholar. His system of biblical chronology, which dated the creation at 4004 BC, was for long accepted

USSR (formerly) *abbreviation* Union of Soviet Socialist Republics

Ussuri (*Russian* ussuˈri) *n* a river in E central Asia, flowing north, forming part of the Chinese border with Russia, to the Amur River. Length: about 800 km (500 miles)

Ústí nad Labem (*Czech* ˈuːstji nad ˈlabɛm) *n* a port in the Czech Republic, on the Elbe River: textile and chemical industries. Pop: 95 000 (2005 est)

Ustinov (ˈjuːstɪnɒf) *n* **Sir Peter (Alexander).** 1921–2004, British stage and film actor, director, and raconteur

Ust-Kamenogorsk (*Russian* ustjkəmɪnaˈɡɔrsk) *n* a city in E Kazakhstan: centre of a zinc-, lead-, and copper-mining area. Pop: 307 000 (2005 est)

Ustyurt *or* **Ust Urt** (*Russian* usˈtjurt) *n* an arid plateau in central Asia, between the Caspian and Aral seas in Kazakhstan and Uzbekistan. Area: about 238 000 sq km (92 000 sq miles)

usual (ˈjuːʒʊəl) *adj* **1** of the most normal, frequent, or regular type; customary: *that's the usual sort of application to send* ▷ *n* **2** ordinary or commonplace events (esp in the phrase **out of the usual**) **3** the usual *informal* the habitual or usual drink, meal, etc [C14: from Late Latin *ūsuālis* ordinary, from Latin *ūsus* USE]

usually (ˈjuːʒʊəlɪ) *adv* customarily; at most times; in the ordinary course of events

usufruct (ˈjuːsjʊˌfrʌkt) *n* the right to use and derive profit from a piece of property belonging to another, provided the property itself remains undiminished and uninjured in any way [C17: from Late Latin *ūsūfrūctus*, from Latin *ūsus* use + *frūctus* enjoyment] ▷ ˌusuˈfructuary *n, adj*

Usumbura (ˌuːzəmˈbʊərə) *n* the former name of **Bujumbura**

usurer (ˈjuːʒərə) *n* a person who lends funds at an exorbitant rate of interest

usurp (juːˈzɜːp) *vb* to seize, take over, or appropriate (land, a throne, etc) without authority [C14: from Old French *usurper*, from Latin *ūsūrpāre* to take into use, probably from *ūsus* use + *rapere* to seize] ▷ ˌusurˈpation *n* ▷ uˈsurper *n*

usury (ˈjuːʒərɪ) *n, pl* -ries **1** the act or practice of loaning money at an exorbitant rate of interest **2** an exorbitant or unlawfully high amount or rate of interest **3** *obsolete* moneylending [C14: from Medieval Latin *ūsūria*, from Latin *ūsūra* usage, from *ūsus* USE] ▷ **usurious** (juːˈʒʊərɪəs) *adj*

USW *radio abbreviation* ultrashort wave

ut (ʌt, uːt) *n music* the syllable used in the fixed system of solmization for the note C [C14: from Latin *ut*; see GAMUT]

UT *abbreviation* **1** universal time **2** Utah

Utagawa Kuniyoshi (ˌuːtəˈɡɑːwə ˌkuːnɪˈjəʊʃɪ) *n* original name *Igusa Magosabwo.* 1797–1861, Japanese painter and printmaker of the ukiyo-e school, best known for his prints of warriors and landscapes

Utah (ˈjuːtɔː, ˈjuːtɑː) *n* a state of the western US: settled by Mormons in 1847; situated in the Great Basin and the Rockies, with the Great Salt Lake in the northwest; mainly arid and mountainous. Capital: Salt Lake City. Pop: 2 351 467 (2003 est). Area: 212 628 sq km (82 096 sq miles). Abbreviations: Ut, (with zip code) UT ▷ Uˈtahan *adj, n*

Utamaro (ˌuːtəˈmɑːrəʊ) *n* **Kitagawa** (ˌkiːtəˈɡɑːwə), original name *Kitagawa Nebsuyoshi.* 1753–1806, Japanese master of wood-block prints, of the ukiyo-e school; noted esp for his portraits of women

UTC *abbreviation* universal time coordinated. See **universal time**

ute (juːt) *n Austral & NZ informal* short for **utility** (sense 5)

utensil (juːˈtɛnsəl) *n* an implement, tool, or container for practical use: *writing utensils* [C14 *utensele*, via Old French from Latin *ūtēnsilia* necessaries, from *ūtēnsilis* available for use, from *ūtī* to use]

uterine (ˈjuːtəˌraɪn) *adj* **1** of, relating to, or affecting the uterus **2** (of offspring) born of the same mother but not the same father

uterus (ˈjuːtərəs) *n, pl* uteri (ˈjuːtəˌraɪ) **1** *anatomy* a hollow muscular organ lying within the pelvic cavity of female mammals. It houses the developing fetus and by contractions aids in its expulsion at parturition. Nontechnical name: **womb 2** the corresponding organ in other animals [C17: from Latin; compare Greek *hustera* womb, *hoderos* belly, Sanskrit *udara* belly]

Utgard (ˈʊtɡɑːd, ˈuːt-) *n Norse myth* one of the divisions of Jotunheim, land of the giants, ruled by Utgard-Loki

Utgard-Loki *n Norse myth* the giant king of Utgard

U Thant (ˈuː ˈθænt) *n* See **Thant**

Uther (ˈjuːθə) *or* **Uther Pendragon** *n* (in Arthurian legend) a king of Britain and father of Arthur

Uthman (ˈuːθmɑːn) *n* died 656 AD, third caliph of Islam, who established an authoritative version of the Koran

Utica (ˈjuːtɪkə) *n* an ancient city on the N coast of Africa, northwest of Carthage

utilidor (juːˈtɪlɪˌdɔː) *n Canadian* an enclosed and insulated conduit for sewage and other utilities placed above the level of permafrost

utilitarian (juːˌtɪlɪˈtɛərɪən) *adj* **1** of or relating to utilitarianism **2** designed for use rather than beauty ▷ *n* **3** a person who believes in utilitarianism

utilitarianism (juːˌtɪlɪˈtɛərɪəˌnɪzəm) *n ethics* **1** the doctrine that the morally correct course of action consists in the greatest good for the greatest number, that is, in maximizing the total benefit resulting, without regard to the distribution of benefits and burdens **2** the theory that the criterion of virtue is utility

utility (juːˈtɪlɪtɪ) *n, pl* -ties **1 a** the quality of practical use; usefulness; serviceability **b** (*as modifier*): *a utility fabric* **2** something useful **3 a** a public service, such as the bus system; public utility **b** (*as modifier*): *utility vehicle* **4** *economics* **a** the ability of a commodity to satisfy human wants **b** See **disutility 5** Also called: **utility truck**, (*informal*) **ute** *Austral & NZ* a small truck with an open body and low sides, often with a removable tarpaulin cover; pick-up **6** a piece of computer software designed for a routine task, such as examining or copying files [C14: from Old French *utelite*, from Latin *ūtilitās* usefulness, from *ūtī* to use]

utility function *n economics* a function relating specific goods and services in an economy to individual preferences

utility player *n sport* a player who is capable of playing competently in any of several positions

utility room *n* a room with equipment for domestic work like washing and ironing

utility truck *n* another name for **utility** (sense 5)

utilize *or* **utilise** (ˈjuːtɪˌlaɪz) *vb* (*tr*) to make practical or worthwhile use of ▷ ˈutiˌlizable *or* ˈutiˌlisable *adj* ▷ ˌutiliˈzation *or* ˌutiliˈsation *n* ▷ ˈutiˌlizer *or* ˈutiˌliser *n*

utmost (ˈʌtˌməʊst) *or* **uttermost** *adj* (*prenominal*) **1** of the greatest possible degree or amount: *the utmost degree* **2** at the furthest limit: *the utmost town on the peninsula* ▷ *n* **3** the greatest possible degree, extent, or amount: *he tried his utmost* [Old English *ūtemest*, from *ūte* out + *-mest* MOST]

utmost good faith *n* a principle used in insurance contracts, legally obliging all parties to reveal to the others any information that might influence the others' decision to enter into the contract. Also called: **uberrima fides**

Utopia (juːˈtəʊpɪə) *n* (*sometimes not capital*) any real or imaginary society, place, state, etc, considered to be perfect or ideal [C16: from New Latin *Utopia* (coined by Sir Thomas More in 1516 as the title of his book that described an imaginary island representing the perfect society), literally: no place, from Greek *ou* not + *topos* a place]

Utopian (juːˈtəʊpɪən) *(sometimes not capital) adj* **1** of or relating to a perfect or ideal existence ▷ *n* **2** an idealistic social reformer ▷ Uˈtopianˌism *n*

Utrecht (*Dutch* ˈyːtrɛxt; *English* ˈjuːtrɛkt) *n* **1** a province of the W central Netherlands. Capital: Utrecht. Pop: 1 152 000 (2003 est). Area: 1362 sq km (526 sq miles) **2** a city in the central Netherlands, capital of Utrecht province: scene of the signing (1579) of the **Union of Utrecht** (the foundation of the later kingdom of the Netherlands) and of the **Treaty of Utrecht** (1713), ending the War of the Spanish Succession. Pop: 265 000 (2003 est)

utricle ('juːtrɪkªl) *or* **utriculus** (juːˈtrɪkjʊləs) *n, pl* utricles *or* utriculi (juːˈtrɪkjʊˌlaɪ) **1** *anatomy* the larger of the two parts of the membranous labyrinth of the internal ear ▷ Compare **saccule 2** *botany* the bladder-like one-seeded indehiscent fruit of certain plants, esp sedges [C18: from Latin *ūtriculus* diminutive of *ūter* bag] > u'tricular *or* u'triculate *adj*

utriculitis (juːˌtrɪkjʊˈlaɪtɪs) *n* inflammation of the inner ear

Utrillo (*French* ytrijo) *n* **Maurice** (mɔris). 1883–1955, French painter, noted for his Parisian street scenes

Uttarakhand (ˌʊtəˈrækɑːnd) *n* a state of N India, created in 2000 from the N part of Uttar Pradesh: in the Himalayas, it rose to over 7500 m (25 000 ft); rice, tea, and timber. Capital: Dehra Dun. Pop: 8 479 562 (2001). Area: 51 125 sq km (19 739 sq miles)

Uttar Pradesh ('ʊtə 'prɑːdeʃ) *n* a state of N India: the most populous state; originated in 1877 with the merging of Agra and Oudh as the United Provinces; augmented by the states of Rampur, Benares, and Tehri-Garhwal in 1949; the N Himalayan region passed to the new state of Uttaranchal (now Uttarakhand) in 2000; now consists mostly of the Upper Ganges plain; agricultural. Capital: Lucknow. Pop: 166 052 859 (2001). Area: 243 350 sq km (93 933 sq miles)

utter¹ ('ʌtə) *vb* **1** to give audible expression to (something): *to utter a growl* **2** *criminal law* to put into circulation (counterfeit coin, forged banknotes, etc) **3** (*tr*) to make publicly known; publish: *to utter slander* [C14: probably originally a commercial term, from Middle Dutch *ūteren* (modern Dutch *uiteren*) to make known; related to Middle Low German *ūtern* to sell, show] > 'utterable *adj* > 'utterableness *n* > 'utterer *n*

utter² ('ʌtə) *adj* (*prenominal*) (intensifier): *an utter fool; utter bliss; the utter limit* [C15: from Old English *utera* outer, comparative of *ūte* OUT (adv); related to Old High German *ūzaro*, Old Norse *ūtri*] > 'utterly *adv*

utterance ('ʌtərəns) *n* **1** something uttered, such as a statement **2** the act or power of uttering or the ability to utter

utter barrister *n law* the full title of a barrister who is not a Queen's Counsel

uttermost ('ʌtəˌməʊst) *adj, n* a variant of **utmost**

utu ('uːtuː) *n NZ* **1** compensation or reward **2** revenge or retribution **3** payment, price, or money [Māori]

U-turn *n* **1** a turn made by a vehicle in the shape of a U, resulting in a reversal of direction **2** a complete change in direction of political or other policy

Utzon ('utsɔn) *n* **Jørn** (jœrn). born 1918, Danish architect

known primarily for his unique design for the Sydney Opera House (1966)

UV *abbreviation* ultraviolet

UV-A *or* **UVA** *abbreviation* ultraviolet radiation with a range of 315–380 nanometres

uvarovite (uːˈvɑːrəˌvaɪt) *n* an emerald-green garnet found in chromium deposits: consists of calcium chromium silicate. Formula: $Ca_3Cr_2(SiO_4)_3$ [C19: from German *Uvarovit*; named after Count Sergei S. *Uvarov* (1785–1855), Russian author and statesman]

UV-B *or* **UVB** *abbreviation* ultraviolet radiation with a range of 280–315 nanometres

uvea ('juːvɪə) *n* the part of the eyeball consisting of the iris, ciliary body, and choroid [C16: from Medieval Latin *ūvea*, from Latin *ūva* grape] > 'uveal *or* 'uveous *adj*

Uvedale ('juːdªl, 'juːvˌdeɪl) *n* a variant of (Nicholas) **Udall**

UVF *abbreviation* Ulster Volunteer Force

uvula ('juːvjʊlə) *n, pl* **-las** *or* **-lae** (-ˌliː) a small fleshy finger-like flap of tissue that hangs in the back of the throat and is an extension of the soft palate [C14: from Medieval Latin, literally: a little grape, from Latin *ūva* a grape]

uvular ('juːvjʊlə) *adj* **1** of or relating to the uvula **2** *phonetics* articulated with the uvula and the back of the tongue, such as the (r) sound of Parisian French ▷ *n* **3** a uvular consonant

UWB *abbreviation* ultrawideband

Uxbridge ('ʌksˌbrɪdʒ) *n* a town in SE England, part of the Greater London borough of Hillingdon since 1965; chiefly residential; seat of Brunel University (1966)

Uxmal (*Spanish* uzˈmal) *n* an ancient ruined city in SE Mexico, in Yucatán: capital of the later Maya empire

uxorial (ʌkˈsɔːrɪəl) *adj* of or relating to a wife: *her strong uxorial influence* [C19: from Latin *uxor* wife] > ux'orially *adv*

uxoricide (ʌkˈsɔːrɪˌsaɪd) *n* **1** the act of killing one's wife **2** a man who kills his wife [C19: from Latin *uxor* wife + -CIDE] > ux,ori'cidal *adj*

uxorious (ʌkˈsɔːrɪəs) *adj* excessively attached to or dependent on one's wife [C16: from Latin *uxōrius* concerning a wife, from *uxor* wife]

Uys (eɪs) *n* **Pieter-Dirk**. born 1945, South African comedian and satirist, noted for creating the female character Evita Bezuidenhout

Uzbek ('ʊzbɛk, 'ʌz-) *n* **1** (*pl* **-beks** *or* **-bek**) a member of a Mongoloid people of Uzbekistan **2** the language of this people, belonging to the Turkic branch of the Altaic family

Uzbekistan (ˌʌzbekɪˈstɑːn) *n* a republic in central Asia: annexed by Russia in the 19th century, it became a separate Soviet Socialist republic in 1924 and gained independence in 1991. Official language: Uzbek. Religion: believers are mainly Muslim. Currency: sum. Capital: Tashkent. Pop: 26 479 000 (2004 est). Area: 449 600 sq km (173 546 sq miles)

u

Vv

v¹ *or* **V** (viː) *n, pl* **v's, V's** *or* **Vs** **1** the 22nd letter and 17th consonant of the modern English alphabet **2** a speech sound represented by this letter, in English usually a voiced labio-dental fricative, as in *vote* **3** a something shaped like a V **b** (*in combination*): *a V neck*

v² *symbol for* **1** *physics* velocity **2** specific volume (of a gas)

V *symbol for* **1** (in transformational grammar) verb **2** volume (capacity) **3** volt **4** *chem* vanadium **5** luminous efficiency **6** victory **7** the Roman numeral for five

v. *abbreviation* **1** verb **2** verse **3** version **4** verso **5** (*usually italic*) versus **6** very **7** vide [Latin: see] **8** vocative **9** volume **10** von

V. *abbreviation* **1** Venerable **2** (in titles) Very **3** (in titles) Vice **4** Viscount

V-1 *n* a robot bomb invented by the Germans in World War II: used esp to bombard London. It was propelled by a pulsejet. Also called: **doodlebug, buzz bomb, flying bomb** [from German *Vergeltungswaffe* revenge weapon]

V-2 *n* a rocket-powered ballistic missile invented by the Germans in World War II: used esp to bombard London. It used ethanol as fuel and liquid oxygen as the oxidizer [see V-1]

V6 *n* a car or internal-combustion engine having six cylinders arranged in the form of a V

V8 *n* a car or internal-combustion engine having eight cylinders arranged in the form of a V

VA *abbreviation* **1** (in the US) Veterans' Administration **2** Vicar Apostolic **3** Vice Admiral **4** (Order of) Victoria and Albert **5** Virginia **6** volt-ampere

Va. *abbreviation* Virginia

Vaal (vɑːl) *n* a river in South Africa, rising in the Drakensberg and flowing west to join the Orange River. Length: 1160 km (720 miles)

Vaasa (*Finnish* ˈvɑːsɑ) *n* a port in W Finland, on the Gulf of Bothnia: the provisional capital of Finland (1918); textile industries. Pop: 56 953 (2003 est). Former name: Nikolainkaupunki

vac (væk) *n* *Brit informal* short for **vacation**

vacancy (ˈveɪkənsɪ) *n, pl* **-cies** **1** the state or condition of being vacant or unoccupied; emptiness **2** an unoccupied post or office: *we have a vacancy in the accounts department* **3** an unoccupied room in a boarding house, hotel, etc:

put the "No Vacancies" sign in the window **4** lack of thought or intelligent awareness; inanity **5** *physics* a defect in a crystalline solid caused by the absence of an atom, ion, or molecule from its position in the crystal lattice **6** *obsolete* idleness or a period spent in idleness

vacant (ˈveɪkənt) *adj* **1** without any contents; empty **2** (*postpositive; foll by of*) devoid (of something specified) **3** having no incumbent; unoccupied: *a vacant post* **4** having no tenant or occupant: *a vacant house* **5** characterized by or resulting from lack of thought or intelligent awareness: *a vacant stare* **6** (of time, etc) not allocated to any activity: *a vacant hour in one's day* **7** spent in idleness or inactivity: *a vacant life* **8** *law* (of an estate, etc) having no heir or claimant [c13: from Latin *vacāre* to be empty] > **ˈvacantly** *adv*

vacant possession *n* ownership of an unoccupied house or property, any previous owner or tenant having departed

vacate (vəˈkeɪt) *vb* (*mainly tr*) **1** to cause (something) to be empty, esp by departing from or abandoning it: *to vacate a room* **2** (*also intr*) to give up the tenure, possession, or occupancy of (a place, post, etc); leave or quit **3** *law* **a** to cancel or rescind **b** to make void or of no effect; annul > **vaˈcatable** *adj*

vacation (vəˈkeɪʃən) *n* **1** *chiefly Brit* a period of the year when the law courts or universities are closed **2** *chiefly US & Canadian* a period in which a break is taken from work or studies for rest, travel, or recreation. Also called (in Britain and certain other countries): **holiday 3** the act of departing from or abandoning property, etc ▷ *vb* **4** (*intr*) *US & Canadian* to take a vacation; holiday [c14: from Latin *vacātiō* freedom, from *vacāre* to be empty] > **vaˈcationer** *or* **vaˈcationist** *n*

vaccinate (ˈvæksɪˌneɪt) *vb* to inoculate (a person) with a vaccine so as to produce immunity against a specific disease > **ˈvacciˌnator** *n*

vaccination (ˌvæksɪˈneɪʃən) *n* **1** the act of vaccinating **2** the scar left following inoculation with a vaccine

vaccine (ˈvæksiːn) *n* **1** *med* a suspension of dead, attenuated, or otherwise modified microorganisms (viruses, bacteria, or rickettsiae) for inoculation to produce immunity to a disease by stimulating the production of antibodies **2** *med* (originally) a preparation of the virus of cowpox taken from infected cows and inoculated in humans to produce immunity to smallpox **3** (*modifier*) *med* of or relating to vaccination or vaccinia **4** *computing* a piece of software designed to detect and remove computer viruses from a system [c18: from New Latin *variolae vaccīnae* cowpox, title of medical treatise (1798) by Edward Jenner, from Latin *vacca* a cow]

vaccinia (væk'sɪnɪə) *n* a technical name for **cowpox** [c19: New Latin, from Latin *vaccīnus* of cows]

Vacherin (French vaʃrɛ̃) *n* **1** a soft French or Swiss cheese made from cows' milk **2** a dessert consisting of a meringue shell filled with whipped cream, ice cream, fruit, etc [from French *vache* cow, from Latin *vacca*]

vacillate ('væsɪˌleɪt) *vb* (*intr*) **1** to fluctuate in one's opinions; be indecisive **2** to sway from side to side physically; totter or waver [c16: from Latin *vacillāre* to sway, of obscure origin] > ˌvacil'lation *n* > 'vacilˌlator *n*

vacua ('vækjʊə) *n* a plural of **vacuum**

vacuity (væ'kjuːɪtɪ) *n*, *pl* -ties **1** the state or quality of being vacuous; emptiness **2** an empty space or void; vacuum **3** a lack or absence of something specified: *a vacuity of wind* **4** lack of normal intelligence or awareness; vacancy **5** something, such as a statement, saying, etc, that is inane or pointless **6** (in customs terminology) the difference in volume between the actual contents of a container and its full capacity [c16: from Latin *vacuitās* empty space, from *vacuus* empty]

vacuole ('vækjʊˌəʊl) *n* *biology* a fluid-filled cavity in the cytoplasm of a cell [c19: from French, literally: little vacuum, from Latin VACUUM] > ˌvacu'olar *adj*

vacuous ('vækjʊəs) *adj* **1** containing nothing; empty **2** bereft of ideas or intelligence; mindless **3** characterized by or resulting from vacancy of mind: *a vacuous gaze* **4** indulging in no useful mental or physical activity; idle **5** *logic*, *maths* (of an operator or expression) having no import; idle: in (*x*) (*John is tall*) the quantifier (*x*) is vacuous [c17: from Latin *vacuus* empty, from *vacāre* to be empty] > 'vacuously *adv*

vacuum ('vækjʊəm) *n*, *pl* vacuums or vacua ('vækjʊə) **1** a region containing no matter; free space **2** a region in which gas is present at a low pressure **3** the degree of exhaustion of gas within an enclosed space: *a high vacuum; a perfect vacuum* **4** a sense or feeling of emptiness: *his death left a vacuum in her life* **5** short for **vacuum cleaner 6** (*modifier*) of, containing, measuring, producing, or operated by a low gas pressure: *a vacuum tube; a vacuum brake* ▷ *vb* **7** to clean (something) with a vacuum cleaner: *to vacuum a carpet* [c16: from Latin: an empty space, from *vacuus* empty]

vacuum cleaner *n* an electrical household appliance used for cleaning floors, carpets, furniture, etc, by suction > vacuum cleaning *n*

vacuum distillation *n* distillation in which the liquid distilled is enclosed at a low pressure in order to reduce its boiling point

vacuum flask *n* an insulating flask that has double walls, usually of silvered glass, with an evacuated space between them. It is used for maintaining substances at high or low temperatures

vacuum gauge *n* any of a number of instruments for measuring pressures below atmospheric pressure

vacuum-packed *adj* packed in an airtight container or packet under low pressure in order to maintain freshness, prevent corrosion, etc

vacuum pump *n* a pump for producing a low gas pressure

vacuum tube or **vacuum valve** *n* another name for **valve** (sense 3)

VAD *abbreviation* **1** Voluntary Aid Detachment ▷ *n* **2** a nurse serving in the Voluntary Aid Detachment

vade mecum ('vɑːdɪ 'meɪkʊm) *n* a handbook or other aid carried on the person for immediate use when needed [c17: from Latin, literally: go with me]

Vadodara (wə'dəʊdərə) *n* a city in W India, in SE Gujarat: textile manufacturing. Pop: 1 306 035 (2001). Former name (until 1976): Baroda

vadose ('veɪdəʊs) *adj* of, relating to, designating, or derived from water occurring above the water table:

vadose water; vadose deposits [c19: from Latin *vadōsus* full of shallows, from *vadum* a ford]

Vaduz (German fa'duts) *n* the capital of Liechtenstein, in the Rhine valley: an old market town, dominated by a medieval castle, residence of the prince of Liechtenstein. Pop: 5005 (2003 est)

vagabond ('vægəˌbɒnd) *n* **1** a person with no fixed home **2** an idle wandering beggar or thief **3** (*modifier*) of or like a vagabond; shiftless or idle [c15: from Latin *vagābundus* wandering, from *vagārī* to roam, from *vagus* VAGUE] > 'vagaˌbondage *n*

vagal ('veɪɡ°l) *adj* *anatomy* of, relating to, or affecting the vagus nerve: *vagal inhibition*

vagary ('veɪɡərɪ, və'ɡɛərɪ) *n*, *pl* -garies an erratic or outlandish notion or action; whim [c16: probably from Latin *vagārī* to wander; compare Latin *vagus* VAGUE]

vagina (və'dʒaɪnə) *n*, *pl* -nas or -nae (-niː) **1** the moist canal in most female mammals, including humans, that extends from the cervix of the uterus to an external opening between the labia minora **2** *anatomy*, *biology* any sheath or sheathlike structure, such as a leaf base that encloses a stem [c17: from Latin: sheath] > vag'inal *adj*

vaginate ('vædʒɪnɪt, -ˌneɪt) *adj* (esp of plant parts) having a sheath; sheathed: *a vaginate leaf*

vaginectomy (ˌvædʒɪ'nɛktəmɪ) *n*, *pl* -mies **1** surgical removal of all or part of the vagina **2** surgical removal of part of the serous sheath surrounding the testis and epididymis

vaginismus (ˌvædʒɪ'nɪzməs, -'nɪsməs) *n* painful spasm of the vagina [c19: from New Latin, from VAGINA + -*ismus*; see -ISM]

vaginitis (ˌvædʒɪ'naɪtɪs) *n* inflammation of the vagina

vagotomy (væ'ɡɒtəmɪ) *n*, *pl* -mies surgical division of the vagus nerve, performed to limit gastric secretion in patients with severe peptic ulcers [c19: from VAG(US) + -TOMY]

vagotonia (ˌveɪɡə'təʊnɪə) *n* pathological overactivity of the vagus nerve, affecting various bodily functions controlled by this nerve [c19: from VAG(US) + -*tonia*, from Latin *tonus* tension, TONE]

vagrancy ('veɪɡrənsɪ) *n*, *pl* -cies **1** the state or condition of being a vagrant **2** the conduct or mode of living of a vagrant

vagrant ('veɪɡrənt) *n* **1** a person of no settled abode, income, or job; tramp **2** a migratory animal that is off course ▷ *adj* **3** wandering about; nomadic **4** of, relating to, or characteristic of a vagrant or vagabond **5** moving in an erratic fashion, without aim or purpose; wayward **6** (of plants) showing uncontrolled or straggling growth [c15: probably from Old French *waucrant* (from *wancrer* to roam, of Germanic origin), but also influenced by Old French *vagant* vagabond, from Latin *vagārī* to wander] > 'vagrantly *adv*

vague (veɪɡ) *adj* **1** (of statements, meaning, etc) not explicit; imprecise: *vague promises* **2** not clearly perceptible or discernible; indistinct: *a vague idea; a vague shape* **3** not clearly or definitely established or known: *a vague rumour* **4** (of a person or his expression) demonstrating lack of precision or clear thinking; absent-minded [c16: via French from Latin *vagus* wandering, of obscure origin] > 'vaguely *adv* > 'vagueness *n*

vagus or **vagus nerve** ('veɪɡəs) *n*, *pl* -gi (-dʒaɪ) the tenth cranial nerve, which supplies the heart, lungs, and viscera [c19: from Latin *vagus* wandering]

vail (veɪl) *vb* (*tr*) *obsolete* **1** to lower (something, such as a weapon), esp as a sign of deference or submission **2** to remove (the hat, cap, etc) as a mark of respect or meekness [c14 *valen*, from obsolete *avalen*, from Old French *avaler* to let fall, from Latin *ad vallem*, literally: to the valley, that is, down, from *ad* to + *vallis* VALLEY]

vain (veɪn) *adj* **1** inordinately proud of one's appearance, possessions, or achievements **2** given to ostentatious display, esp of one's beauty **3** worthless **4** senseless or futile ▷ *n* **5** in vain to no avail; fruitlessly **6** take someone's name in vain *jocular* to mention someone's name [c13: via Old French from Latin *vānus*] > 'vainly *adv* > 'vainness *n*

vainglory (ˌveɪn'ɡlɔːrɪ) *n* **1** boastfulness or vanity

2 ostentation ▷ ˌvainˈglorious *adj*

vair (veə) *n* **1** a fur, probably Russian squirrel, used to trim robes in the Middle Ages **2** one of the two principal furs used on heraldic shields, conventionally represented by white and blue skins in alternate lines [c13: from Old French: of more than one colour, from Latin *varius* variegated, VARIOUS]

Vaisya (ˈvaɪsjə, ˈvaɪʃjə) *n* the third of the four main Hindu castes, the traders [c18: from Sanskrit, literally: settler, from *viś* settlement]

Vajpayee (ˌvædʒpaɪˈjiː) *n* **A**(**tal**) **B**(**ihari**). born 1926, Indian politician; prime minister of India (1996, 1998–2004)

Valais (*French* valɛ) *n* a canton of S Switzerland: includes the entire valley of the upper Rhône and the highest peaks in Switzerland; produces a quarter of Switzerland's hydroelectricity. Capital: Sion. Pop: 281 000 (2002 est). Area: 5231 sq km (2020 sq miles). German name: Wallis

valance (ˈvæləns) *n* a short piece of drapery hung along a shelf, canopy, or bed, or across a window, to hide structural detail [c15: perhaps named after VALENCE, France, town noted for its textiles] ▷ ˈvalanced *adj*

Valdai Hills (vɑːlˈdaɪ) *pl n* a region of hills and plateaus in NW Russia, between Moscow and St Petersburg. Greatest height: 346 m (1135 ft)

Valdemar I (*Danish* ˈvaldəmar) *n* a variant spelling of **Waldemar I**

Valdemar II *n* See **Waldemar II**

Valdemar IV *n* See **Waldemar IV**

Val-de-Marne (*French* valdəmarn) *n* a department of N France, in Île-de-France region. Capital: Créteil. Pop: 1 239 352 (2003 est). Area: 244 sq km (95 sq miles)

Valdivia¹ (*Spanish* balˈdiβja) *n* a port in S Chile, on the **Valdivia River** about 19 km (12 miles) from the Pacific: developed chiefly by German settlers in the 1850s; university (1954). Pop: 136 000 (2005 est)

Valdivia² (*Spanish* balˈdiβja) *n* **Pedro de** (ˈpeðro de). ?1500–54, Spanish soldier; conqueror of Chile

Val-d'Oise (*French* valdwaz) *n* a department of N France, in Île-de-France region. Capital: Pontoise. Pop: 1 121 614 (2003 est). Area: 1249 sq km (487 sq miles)

vale¹ (veɪl) *n* a literary word for **valley** [c13: from Old French *val*, from Latin *vallis* valley]

vale² *Latin* (ˈvɑːleɪ) *sentence substitute* farewell; goodbye

valediction (ˌvælɪˈdɪkʃən) *n* **1** the act or an instance of saying goodbye **2** any valedictory statement, speech, etc [c17: from Latin *valedīcere*, from *valē* farewell + *dīcere* to say]

valedictory (ˌvælɪˈdɪktərɪ, -trɪ) *n, pl* -ries **1** a farewell address or speech **2** *US & Canadian* a farewell speech delivered at a graduation ceremony, usually by the most outstanding graduate

valence (ˈveɪləns) *n chem* **1** another name (esp US and Canadian) for **valency 2** the phenomenon of forming chemical bonds

Valence (*French* valɑ̃s) *n* a town in SE France, on the River Rhône. Pop: 64 260 (1999)

Valencia (*Spanish* baˈlenθja) *n* **1** a port in E Spain, capital of Valencia province, on the Mediterranean: the third largest city in Spain; capital of the Moorish kingdom of Valencia (1021–1238); university (1501). Pop: 780 653 (2003 est) **2** a region and former kingdom of E Spain, on the Mediterranean **3** a city in N Venezuela: one of the two main industrial centres in Venezuela. Pop: 2 330 000 (2005 est)

Valenciennes¹ (ˌvælənsɪˈɛn) *n* a flat bobbin lace typically having scroll and floral designs and originally made of linen, now often cotton [named after VALENCIENNES², where it was originally made]

Valenciennes² (*French* valɑ̃sjɛn) *n* a town in N France, on the River Escaut: a coal-mining and heavy industrial centre. Pop: 41 278 (1999)

valency (ˈveɪlənsɪ) *or esp US and Canadian* **valence** *n, pl* -cies *or* -ces **1** *chem* a property of atoms or groups, equal to the number of atoms of hydrogen that the atom or group could combine with or displace in forming compounds **2** *linguistics* the number of satellite noun phrases with which a verb combines [c19: from Latin

valentia strength, from *valēre* to be strong]

valency electron *n chem* an electron in the outer shell of an atom, responsible for forming chemical bonds

Valens (ˈveɪlɛnz) *n* ?328–378 AD, emperor of the Eastern Roman Empire (364–378); appointed by his elder brother Valentinian I, emperor of the Western Empire

valentine (ˈvælənˌtaɪn) *n* **1** a card or gift expressing love or affection, sent, often anonymously, to one's sweetheart or satirically to a friend, on Saint Valentine's Day **2** a sweetheart selected for such a greeting

Valentine (ˈvælənˌtaɪn) *n* **Saint.** 3rd century AD, Christian martyr, associated by historical accident with the custom of sending valentines; bishop of Terni. Feast day: Feb 14

Valentinian I (ˌvælənˈtɪnɪən) *or* **Valentinianus I** (ˌvælənˌtɪnɪˈeɪnəs) *n* 321–375 AD, emperor of the Western Roman Empire (364–375); appointed his brother Valens to rule the Eastern Empire

Valentinian II *or* **Valentinianus II** *n* 371–392 AD, emperor of the Western Roman Empire (375–392), reigning jointly with his half brother Gratian until 383

Valentinian III *or* **Valentinianus III** *n* ?419–455 AD, emperor of the Western Roman Empire (425–455). His government lost Africa to the Vandals. With Pope Leo I he issued (444) an edict giving the bishop of Rome supremacy over the provincial churches

Valentino (ˌvælənˈtiːnəʊ) *n* **Rudolph**, original name *Rodolpho Guglielmi di Valentina d'Antonguolla*. 1895–1926, US silent-film actor, born in Italy. He is famous for his romantic roles in such films as *The Sheik* (1921)

Vale of Glamorgan (ɡləˈmɔːɡən) *n* a county borough of S Wales, created in 1996 from parts of South Glamorgan and Mid Glamorgan. Administrative centre: Barry. Pop: 121 200 (2003 est). Area: 295 sq km (114 sq miles)

Valera (vəˈlɛərə, -ˈlɪərə) *n* See **de Valera**

valerian (vəˈlɛərɪən) *n* **1** Also called: **allheal** any of various Eurasian valerianaceous plants of the genus *Valeriana*, esp *V. officinalis*, having small white or pinkish flowers and a medicinal root **2** a sedative drug made from the dried roots of *V. officinalis* [c14: via Old French from Medieval Latin *valeriana* (*herba*) (herb) of *Valerius*, unexplained Latin personal name]

Valerian (vəˈlɛərɪən) *n* Latin name *Publius Licinius Valerianus*. died 260 AD, Roman emperor (253–260): renewed persecution of the Christians; defeated by the Persians

valeric (vəˈlɛrɪk, -ˈlɪərɪk) *adj* of, relating to, or derived from valerian

valeric acid *n* another name for **pentanoic acid**

Valéry (*French* valeri) *n* **Paul** (pɔl). 1871–1945, French poet and essayist, influenced by the symbolists, esp Mallarmé. He wrote lyric poetry, rich in imagery, as in *La Jeune Parque* (1917) and *Album de vers anciens 1890–1900* (1920)

valet (ˈvælɪt, ˈvæleɪ) *n* **1** a manservant who acts as personal attendant to his employer, looking after his clothing, serving his meals, etc **2** a manservant who attends to the requirements of patrons in a hotel, passengers on board ship, etc; steward ▷ *vb* -ets, -eting, -eted **3** to act as a valet for (a person) **4** (*tr*) to clean the bodywork and interior of (a car) as a professional service [c16: from Old French *vaslet* page, from Medieval Latin *vassus* servant; see VASSAL]

valeta *or* **veleta** (vəˈliːtə) *n* a ballroom dance in triple time [from Spanish *veleta* weather vane]

valet de chambre *French* (valɛ də ʃɑ̃brə) *n, pl* **valets de chambre** (valɛ də ʃɑ̃brə) the full French term for **valet** (sense 1)

valet parking *n* a system at hotels, airports, etc, in which patrons' cars are parked by a steward

valetudinarian (ˌvælɪˌtjuːdɪˈnɛərɪən) *or* **valetudinary** (ˌvælɪˈtjuːdɪnərɪ) *n, pl* -narians *or* -naries **1** a person who is or believes himself to be chronically sick; invalid **2** a person excessively worried about the state of his health; hypochondriac ▷ *adj* **3** relating to, marked by, or resulting from poor health **4** being a valetudinarian **5** trying to return to a healthy state [c18: from Latin *valētūdō* state of health, from *valēre* to be well] ▷ ˌvaleˌtudiˈnarianˌism *n*

valgus ('vælgəs) *adj pathol* denoting a deformity in which the distal part of a limb is displaced or twisted away from the midline of the body [c19: from Latin: knock-kneed]

Valhalla (væl'hælə), **Walhalla, Valhall** (væl'hæl, 'vælhæl) *or* **Walhall** *n Norse myth* the great hall of Odin where warriors who die as heroes in battle dwell eternally [c18: from Old Norse, from *valr* slain warriors + *höll* HALL]

valiant ('væljənt) *adj* **1** courageous, intrepid, or stout-hearted; brave **2** marked by bravery or courage: *a valiant deed* [c14: from Old French *vaillant*, from *valoir* to be of value, from Latin *valēre* to be strong] > **'valiantly** *adv*

valid ('vælɪd) *adj* **1** having some foundation; based on truth **2** legally acceptable: *a valid licence* **3 a** having legal force; effective **b** having legal authority; binding **4** having some force or cogency: *a valid point in a debate* **5** *logic* (of an inference or argument) having premises and conclusion so related that whenever the former are true the latter must also be true, esp (**formally valid**) when the inference is justified by the form of the premises and conclusion alone. Thus *Tom is a bachelor; therefore Tom is unmarried* is valid but not formally so, while *today is hot and dry; therefore today is hot* is formally valid. Compare **invalid²** (sense 2) **6** *archaic* healthy or strong [c16: from Latin *validus* robust, from *valēre* to be strong] > **'validly** *adv* > **validity** (və'lɪdɪtɪ) *or* **'validness** *n*

validate ('vælɪ,deɪt) *vb* (*tr*) **1** to confirm or corroborate **2** to give legal force or official confirmation to; declare legally valid > **,vali'dation** *n*

valine ('veɪliːn, 'væl-) *n* an essential amino acid; a component of proteins [c19: from VAL(ERIC ACID) + -INE²]

valise (və'liːz) *n* a small overnight travelling case [c17: via French from Italian *valigia*, of unknown origin]

Valium ('vælɪəm) *n trademark* a brand of diazepam used as a tranquillizer

Valkyrie, Walkyrie (væl'kɪərɪ, 'vælkɪərɪ) *or* **Valkyr** ('vælkɪə) *n Norse myth* any of the beautiful maidens who serve Odin and ride over battlefields to claim the dead heroes and take them to Valhalla [c18: from Old Norse *Valkyrja*, from *valr* slain warriors + *köri* to CHOOSE] > **Val'kyrian** *adj*

Valla (Italian 'valla) *n* **Lorenzo** (lo'rɛntso). 1405–57, Italian humanist cholar. His writings include *De voluptate* (1431), a philosophical dialogue on pleasure

Valladolid (Spanish baʎaðo'lið) *n* **1** a city in NW Spain: residence of the Spanish court in the 16th century; university (1346). Pop: 321 143 (2003 est) **2** the former name (until 1828) of **Morelia**

vallation (və'leɪʃən) *n* **1** the act or process of building fortifications **2** a wall or rampart [c17: from Late Latin *vallātiō*, from *vallum* rampart]

vallecula (və'lɛkjʊlə) *n, pl* **-lae** (-,liː) **1** *anatomy* any of various natural depressions or crevices, such as certain fissures of the brain **2** *botany* a small groove or furrow in a plant stem or fruit [c19: from Late Latin: little valley, from Latin *vallis* valley]

Valle d'Aosta (Italian 'valle da'ɔsta) *n* an autonomous region of NW Italy: under many different rulers until passing to the house of Savoy in the 11th century; established as an autonomous region in 1944. Capital: Aosta. Pop: 120 909 (2003 est). Area: 3263 sq km (1260 sq miles)

Valle-Inclán (Spanish 'baʎeiŋ'klan) *n* **Rámon María del**. 1866–1936, Spanish novelist and dramatist. His works include the novel *Tirano Banderas* (1926) and the satirical play *Don Friolera's Horns* (1925)

Vallejo (və'leɪəʊ, -'leɪhəʊ; Spanish ba'ʎɛxo) *n* **César** (Abraham) ('sesar). 1892–1938, Peruvian poet, living in France and Spain from 1923: noted for his experimental style in such works as *Trilce* (1922)

Valletta *or* **Valetta** (və'lɛtə) *n* the capital of Malta, on the NE coast: founded by the Knights Hospitallers, after the victory over the Turks in 1565; became a major naval base after Malta's annexation by Britain (1814). Pop: 84 000 (2005 est)

valley ('vælɪ) *n* **1** a long depression in the land surface, usually containing a river, formed by erosion or by movements in the earth's crust **2** the broad area drained by a single river system: *the Thames valley* **3** any elongated depression resembling a valley **4** the junction of a roof slope with another or with a wall **5** (*modifier*) relating to or proceeding by way of a valley [c13: from Old French *valee*, from Latin *vallis*]

Valley Forge *n* an area in SE Pennsylvania, northwest of Philadelphia: winter camp (1777–78) of Washington and the American Revolutionary Army

Valley of Ten Thousand Smokes *n* a volcanic region of SW Alaska, formed by the massive eruption of Mount Katmai in 1912; jets of steam issue from vents up to 45 m (150 ft) across

Vallombrosa (Italian vallom'bro:sa) *n* a village and resort in central Italy, in Tuscany region: 11th-century Benedictine monastery

vallum ('væləm) *n archaeol* a Roman rampart or earthwork

Valois¹ (French valwa) *n* a royal house of France, ruling from 1328 to 1589

Valois² (French valwa) *n* a historic region and former duchy of N France

Valois³ ('vælwa:) *n* See **de Valois**

Valona (və'ləʊnə) *n* another name for **Vlorë**

valonia (və'əʊnɪə) *n* the acorn cups and unripe acorns of the Eurasian oak *Quercus aegilops*, used in tanning, dyeing, and making ink [c18: from Italian *vallonia*, ultimately from Greek *balanos* acorn]

valorize *or* **valorise** ('vælə,raɪz) *vb* (*tr*) to fix and maintain an artificial price for (a commodity) by governmental action [c20: back formation from *valorization*; see VALOUR] > **,valori'zation** *or* **,valori'sation** *n*

valour *or* **US valor** ('vælə) *n* courage or bravery, esp in battle [c15: from Late Latin *valor*, from *valēre* to be strong] > **'valorous** *adj*

Valparaíso (Spanish balpara'iso) *n* a port in central Chile, on a wide bay of the Pacific: the third largest city and chief port of Chile; two universities. Pop: 275 000 (2005 est)

valse French (vals) *n* another word, esp used in the titles of some pieces of music, for **waltz**

valuable ('væljʊəbᵊl) *adj* **1** having considerable monetary worth **2** of considerable importance or quality: *a valuable friend; valuable information* **3** able to be valued ▷ *n* **4** (*usually plural*) a valuable article of personal property, esp jewellery > **'valuably** *adv*

valuate ('væljʊ,eɪt) *vb* US another word for **value** (senses 10, 12) *or* **evaluate** > **'valu,ator** *n*

valuation (,væljʊ'eɪʃən) *n* **1** the act of valuing, esp a formal assessment of the worth of property, jewellery, etc **2** the price arrived at by the process of valuing: *the valuation of this property is considerable; I set a high valuation on technical ability* > **,valu'ational** *adj*

value ('væljuː) *n* **1** the desirability of a thing, often in respect of some property such as usefulness or exchangeability; worth, merit, or importance **2** an amount, esp a material or monetary one, considered to be a fair exchange in return for a thing; assigned valuation: *the value of the picture is £10 000* **3** reasonable or equivalent return; satisfaction: *value for money* **4** precise meaning or significance **5** (*plural*) the moral principles and beliefs or accepted standards of a person or social group: *a person with old-fashioned values* **6** *maths* **a** a particular magnitude, number, or amount: *the value of the variable was 7* **b** the particular quantity that is the result of applying a function or operation for some given argument: *the value of the function for x=3 was 9* **7** *music* short for **time value 8** (in painting, drawing, etc) **a** a gradation of tone from light to dark or of colour luminosity **b** the relation of one of these elements to another or to the whole picture **9** *phonetics* the quality or tone of the speech sound associated with a written character representing it: *'g' has the value* (dʒ) *in English 'gem'* ▷ *vb* **-ues, -uing, -ued** (*tr*) **10** to assess or estimate the worth, merit, or desirability of; appraise **11** to have a high regard for, esp in respect of worth, usefulness, merit, etc; esteem or prize: *to value freedom* **12** (foll by *at*) to fix the financial or material worth of (a unit of currency, work of art, etc): *jewels valued at £40 000* [c14: from Old French, from *valoir*, from Latin *valēre* to be worth, be strong] > **'valuer** *n* > **'valueless** *adj*

value added *n* the difference between the total revenues of a firm, industry, etc, and its total purchases from other firms, industries, etc. The aggregate of values added throughout an economy (**gross value added**) represents that economy's gross domestic product

value-added tax *n* (in Britain) the full name for **VAT**

valued policy *n* an insurance policy in which the amount payable in the event of a valid claim is agreed upon between the company and policyholder when the policy is issued and is not related to the actual value of a loss

value judgment *n* a subjective assessment based on one's own code of values or that of one's class

Valuer General *n Austral* a state official who values properties for rating purposes

valuta (və'lu:tə) *n rare* the value of one currency in terms of its exchange rate with another [C20: from Italian, literally: VALUE]

valvate ('vælveɪt) *adj* 1 furnished with a valve or valves 2 functioning as or resembling a valve 3 *botany* a having or taking place by means of valves: *valvate dehiscence* b (of petals or sepals in the bud) having the margins touching but not overlapping

valve (vælv) *n* 1 any device that shuts off, starts, regulates, or controls the flow of a fluid 2 *anatomy* a flaplike structure in a hollow organ, such as the heart, that controls the one-way passage of fluid through that organ 3 Also called: **tube, vacuum tube** an evacuated electron tube containing a cathode, anode, and, usually, one or more additional control electrodes. When a positive potential is applied to the anode, electrons emitted from the cathode are attracted to the anode, constituting a flow of current which can be controlled by a voltage applied to the grid to produce amplification, oscillation, etc 4 *zoology* any of the separable pieces that make up the shell of a mollusc 5 *music* a device on some brass instruments by which the effective length of the tube may be varied to enable a chromatic scale to be produced 6 *botany* any of the several parts that make up a dry dehiscent fruit, esp a capsule 7 *archaic* a leaf of a double door or of a folding door [C14: from Latin *valva* a folding door] > **'valveless** *adj* > **'valve,like** *adj*

valve-in-head engine *n* the US name for **overhead-valve engine**

valvular ('vælvjʊlə) *adj* 1 of, relating to, operated by, or having a valve or valves 2 having the shape or function of a valve

valvule ('vælvju:l) *or* **valvelet** ('vælvlɪt) *n* a small valve or a part resembling one [C18: from New Latin *valvula*, diminutive of VALVE]

valvulitis (,vælvjʊ'laɪtɪs) *n* inflammation of a bodily valve, esp a heart valve [C19: from VALVULE + -ITIS]

vamoose (və'mu:s) *vb* (*intr*) *slang, chiefly US* to leave a place hurriedly; decamp [C19: from Spanish *vamos* let us go, from Latin *vādere* to go, walk rapidly]

vamp¹ (væmp) *informal* ▷ *n* 1 a seductive woman who exploits men by use of her sexual charms ▷ *vb* 2 to exploit (a man) in the fashion of a vamp [C20: short for VAMPIRE]

vamp² (væmp) *n* 1 something patched up to make it look new 2 the reworking of a theme, story, etc 3 an improvised accompaniment, consisting largely of chords 4 the front part of the upper of a shoe ▷ *vb* 5 (*tr*; often foll by *up*) to give a vamp to; make a renovation of 6 to improvise (an accompaniment) to (a tune) [C13: from Old French *avantpié* the front part of a shoe (hence, something patched), from *avant-* fore- + *pié* foot, from Latin *pēs*]

vampire ('væmpaɪə) *n* 1 (in European folklore) a corpse that rises nightly from its grave to drink the blood of the living 2 See **vampire bat** 3 a person who preys mercilessly upon others, such as a blackmailer [C18: from French, from German *Vampir*, from Magyar; perhaps related to Turkish *uber* witch, Russian *upyr* vampire] > **vampiric** (væm'pɪrɪk) *or* **'vampirish** *adj* > **'vampir,ism** *n*

vampire bat *n* any bat, esp *Desmodus rotundus*, of the family *Desmodontidae* of tropical regions of Central and South America, having sharp incisor and canine teeth and feeding on the blood of birds and mammals

van¹ (væn) *n* 1 short for **caravan** (sense 1) 2 a covered motor vehicle for transporting goods, etc, by road 3 *Brit* a closed railway wagon in which the guard travels, for transporting goods, mail, etc

van² (væn) *n* short for **vanguard**

van³ (væn) *n tennis, chiefly Brit* short for **advantage** (sense 3). Usual US and Canadian word: **ad**

van⁴ (væn) *n* 1 any device for winnowing corn 2 an archaic or poetic word for **wing** [C17: variant of FAN¹]

Van (vɑːn) *n* 1 a city in E Turkey, on Lake Van. Pop: 377 000 (2005 est) 2 **Lake Van** a salt lake in E Turkey, at an altitude of 1650 m (5400 ft): fed by melting snow and glaciers. Area: 3737 sq km (1433 sq miles)

vanadium (və'neɪdɪəm) *n* a toxic silvery-white metallic element occurring chiefly in carnotite and vanadinite and used in steel alloys, high-speed tools, and as a catalyst. Symbol: V; atomic no: 23; atomic wt: 50.9415; valency: 2–5; relative density: 6.11; melting pt: 1910±10°C; boiling pt: 3409°C [C19: New Latin, from Old Norse *Vanadis*, epithet of the goddess Freya + -IUM]

Van Allen (væn 'ælən) *n* **James Alfred**. 1914–2006, US physicist, noted for his use of satellites to investigate cosmic radiation in the upper atmosphere

Van Allen belt (væn 'ælən) *n* either of two regions of charged particles above the earth, the inner one extending from 2400 to 5600 kilometres above the earth and the outer one from 13 000 to 19 000 kilometres. The charged particles result from cosmic rays and are trapped by the earth's magnetic field [C20: after its discoverer, J. A. VAN ALLEN]

Vanbrugh ('vænbrə) *n* **Sir John**. 1664–1726, English dramatist and baroque architect. His best-known plays are the Restoration comedies *The Relapse* (1697) and *The Provok'd Wife* (1697). As an architect, he is noted esp for Blenheim Palace

Van Buren (væn 'bjʊərən) *n* **Martin**. 1782–1862, US Democratic statesman; 8th president of the US (1837–41)

Vancouver¹ (væn'ku:və) *n* 1 **Vancouver Island** an island of SW Canada, off the SW coast of British Columbia: separated from the Canadian mainland by the Strait of Georgia and Queen Charlotte Sound, and from the US mainland by Juan de Fuca Strait; the largest island off the W coast of North America. Chief town: Victoria. Pop: 706 243 (2001). Area: 32 137 sq km (12 408 sq miles) 2 a city in SW Canada, in SW British Columbia: Canada's chief Pacific port, named after Captain George Vancouver: university (1908). Pop: 545 671 (2001) 3 **Mount Vancouver** a mountain on the border between Canada and Alaska, in the St Elias Mountains. Height: 4785 m (15 700 ft)

Vancouver² (væn'ku:və) *n* **Captain George**. 1757–98, English navigator, noted for his exploration of the Pacific coast of North America (1792–94)

V and A *abbreviation* (in Britain) Victoria and Albert Museum

vandal ('vændəl) *n* a a person who deliberately causes damage or destruction to personal or public property b (*as modifier*): *vandal instincts* [C17: from VANDAL, from Latin *Vandallus*, of Germanic origin]

Vandal ('vændəl) *n* a member of a Germanic people that raided Roman provinces in the 3rd and 4th centuries AD before devastating Gaul (406–409), conquering Spain and N Africa, and sacking Rome (455): crushed by Belisarius at Carthage (533) > **Vandalic** (væn'dælɪk) *adj*

vandalism ('vændə,lɪzəm) *n* the wanton or deliberate destruction caused by a vandal or an instance of such destruction > **,vandal'istic** *or* **'vandalish** *adj*

vandalize *or* **vandalise** ('vændə,laɪz) *vb* (*tr*) to destroy or damage (something) by an act of vandalism

Van de Graaff generator ('væn də ,grɑːf) *n* a device for producing high electrostatic potentials (up to 15 million volts), consisting of a hollow metal sphere on which a charge is accumulated from a continuous moving belt of insulating material: used in particle accelerators [C20: named after R. J. *Van de Graaff* (1901–67), US physicist]

Vanderbilt ('vændəbɪlt) *n* **Cornelius**, known as

Commodore Vanderbilt. 1794–1877, US steamship and railway magnate and philanthropist

Van der Post ('væn də ˌpəʊst) *n* Sir **Laurens** (**Jan**). 1906–96, South African writer and traveller. His works include the travel books *Venture to the Interior* (1952), *The Lost World of the Kalahari* (1958), and *Testament to the Bushmen* (1984) and the novels *The Hunter and the Whale* (1967) and *The Admiral's Baby* (1996)

van der Waals (*Dutch* væn dər 'wɑːls) *n* **Johannes Diderik** (joːˈhɑnəs ˈdiːdərɪk). 1837–1923, Dutch physicist, noted for his research on the equations of state of gases and liquids: Nobel prize for physics in 1910

van der Weyden (*Dutch* væn də 'wɛjdə) *n* **Rogier** (roˈxiːr). ?1400–64, Flemish painter, esp of religious works and portraits

van de Velde (ˌvæn də 'vɛldə) *n* **1 Adriaen**. 1636–72, Dutch painter of landscapes with animals and figures **2** his uncle, **Esaias**. ?1591–1630, Dutch landscape and genre painter, noted for such works as *The Winter Scene* (1623) **3 Henry**. 1863–1957, Belgian architect and designer, who introduced the British Arts and Crafts movement to the Continent and helped to develop the Art Nouveau style **4 Willem**, known as *the Elder:* father of Adriaen van de Velde. 1611–93, Dutch marine painter, working in England as court painter to Charles II **5** his son, **Willem**, known as *the Younger*. 1633–1707, Dutch marine painter, working in England as court painter to Charles II

Van Diemen Gulf (væn 'diːmən) *n* an inlet of the Timor Sea in N Australia, in the Northern Territory

Van Diemen's Land (væn 'diːmənz) *n* the former name (1642–1855) of **Tasmania**

Van Dyck or **Vandyke** (væn 'daɪk) *n* Sir **Anthony**. 1599–1641, Flemish painter; court painter to Charles I of England (1632–41). He is best known for his portraits of the aristocracy

Vandyke beard ('vændaɪk) *n* a short pointed beard
Vandyke collar or **cape** *n* a large white collar with several very deep points

vane (veɪn) *n* **1** Also called: **weather vane**, **wind vane** a flat plate or blade of metal mounted on a vertical axis in an exposed position to indicate wind direction **2** any one of the flat blades or sails forming part of the wheel of a windmill **3** any flat or shaped plate used to direct fluid flow, esp a stator blade in a turbine, etc **4** a fin or plate fitted to a projectile or missile to provide stabilization or guidance **5** *ornithol* the flat part of a feather, consisting of two rows of barbs on either side of the shaft **6** *surveying* **a** a sight on a quadrant or compass **b** the movable marker on a levelling staff [Old English *fana*; related to Old Saxon, Old High German *fano*, Old Norse *fani*, Latin *pannus* cloth] > **vaned** *adj*

Vane (veɪn) *n* Sir **Henry**, known as *Sir Harry Vane*. 1613–62, English Puritan statesman and colonial administrator; governor of Massachusetts (1636–37). He was executed for high treason after the Restoration

Vänern (*Swedish* 'veːnərn) *n* Lake Vänern a lake in SW Sweden: the largest lake in Sweden and W Europe; drains into the Kattegat. Area: 5585 sq km (2156 sq miles)

van Eyck (væn 'aɪk) *n* **Jan** (jɑn). died 1441, Flemish painter; founder of the Flemish school of painting. His most famous work is the altarpiece *The Adoration of the Lamb*, in Ghent, in which he may have been assisted by his brother **Hubert** ('hyːbərt), died ?1426

Van Gogh (væn 'ɡɒx; *Dutch* væn 'xɔx) *n* **Vincent** (vɪnˈsɛnt). 1853–90, Dutch postimpressionist painter, noted for his landscapes and portraits, in which colour is used essentially for its expressive and emotive value

vanguard ('vænˌɡɑːd) *n* **1** the leading division or units of a military force **2** the leading position in any movement or field, or the people who occupy such a position: *the vanguard of modern literature* [c15: from Old French *avant-garde*, from *avant-* fore- + *garde* GUARD]

vanilla (vəˈnɪlə) *n* **1** any tropical climbing orchid of the genus *Vanilla*, esp *V. plonifolia*, having spikes of large fragrant greenish-yellow flowers and long fleshy pods containing the seeds (**beans**) **2** the pod or bean of certain of these plants, used to flavour food, etc **3** a flavouring extract prepared from vanilla beans and used in cooking ⊳ *adj* **4** flavoured with or as if with vanilla:

vanilla ice cream 5 *slang* ordinary or conventional: *a vanilla kind of guy* [c17: from New Latin, from Spanish *vainilla* pod, from *vaina* a sheath, from Latin *vāgīna* sheath] > **vaˈnillic** *adj*

vanillin ('vænɪlɪn, vəˈnɪlɪn) *n* a white crystalline aldehyde found in vanilla and many natural balsams and resins; 3-methoxy-4-hydroxybenzaldehyde. It is a by-product of paper manufacture and is used as a flavouring and in perfumes and pharmaceuticals. Formula: $(CH_3O)(OH)C_6H_3CHO$

Vanir ('vɑːnɪə) *n* *Norse myth* a race of ancient gods often locked in struggle with the Aesir. The most notable of them are Njord and his children Frey and Freya [from Old Norse *Vanr*, a fertility god]

vanish ('vænɪʃ) *vb* (*intr*) **1** to disappear, esp suddenly or mysteriously **2** to cease to exist; fade away **3** *maths* to become zero ⊳ *n* **4** *phonetics rare* the second and weaker of the two vowels in a falling diphthong [c14 *vanissen*, from Old French *esvanir*, from Latin *ēvānēscere* to evaporate, from *ē-* EX-[1] + *vānēscere* to pass away, from *vānus* empty] > **ˈvanisher** *n*

vanishing cream *n* a cosmetic cream that is colourless once applied, used as a foundation for powder or as a cleansing or moisturizing cream

vanishing point *n* **1** the point to which parallel lines appear to converge in the rendering of perspective, usually on the horizon **2** a point in space or time at or beyond which something disappears or ceases to exist

vanity ('vænɪtɪ) *n*, *pl* **-ties** **1** the state or quality of being vain; excessive pride or conceit **2** ostentation occasioned by ambition or pride **3** an instance of being vain or something about which one is vain **4** the state or quality of being valueless, futile, or unreal **5** something that is worthless or useless [c13: from Old French *vanité*, from Latin *vānitās* emptiness, from *vānus* empty]

vanity bag, **case** or **box** *n* a woman's small bag or hand case used to carry cosmetics, etc

vanity plates *pl n* *informal* personalized car numberplates

vanity unit *n* a hand basin built into a wooden Formica-covered or tiled top, usually with a built-in cupboard below it

vanquish ('væŋkwɪʃ) *vb* (*tr*) **1** to defeat or overcome in a battle, contest, etc; conquer **2** to defeat or overcome in argument or debate **3** to conquer (an emotion) [c14 *vanquisshen*, from Old French *venquis* vanquished, from *veintre* to overcome, from Latin *vincere*] > **ˈvanquishable** *adj* > **ˈvanquisher** *n*

Vansittart (væn'sɪtət) *n* **Robert Gilbert**, **1st Baron Vansittart** of Denham. 1881–1957, British diplomat and writer; a fierce opponent of Nazi Germany and of Communism

vantage ('vɑːntɪdʒ) *n* **1** a state, position, or opportunity affording superiority or advantage **2** superiority or benefit accruing from such a position, state, etc **3** *tennis* short for **advantage** [c13: from Old French *avantage* ADVANTAGE]

vantage point *n* a position or place that allows one a wide or favourable overall view of a scene or situation

van't Hoff (*Dutch* vant 'hɔf) *n* **Jacobus Hendricus** (jaːˈkoːbys hɛnˈdriːkœs). 1852–1911, Dutch physical chemist: founded stereochemistry with his theory of the asymmetric carbon atom; the first to apply thermodynamics to chemical reactions: Nobel prize for chemistry 1901

Vanua Levu (vɑːˈnuːə ˈlɛvuː) *n* the second largest island of Fiji: mountainous. Area: 5535 sq km (2137 sq miles)

Vanuatu ('vænuːˌætuː) *n* a republic comprising a group of islands in the W Pacific, W of Fiji: a condominium under Anglo-French joint rule from 1906; attained partial autonomy in 1978 and full independence in 1980 as a member of the Commonwealth. Its economy is based chiefly on copra. Official languages: Bislama; French; English. Religion: Christian majority. Currency: vatu. Capital: Vila (on Efate). Pop: 217 000 (2004 est). Area: about 14 760 sq km (5700 sq miles). Former name (until 1980): **New Hebrides**

vanward ('vænwəd) *adj*, *adv* in or towards the front
Vanzetti (væn'zɛtɪ) *n* **Bartolomeo** (bartoloˈmɛːo).

1888–1927, US radical agitator, born in Italy: executed with Sacco in a case that had worldwide political repercussions

vapid ('væpɪd) *adj* **1** bereft of strength, sharpness, flavour, etc; flat **2** boring or dull; lifeless [C17: from Latin *vapidus*; related to *vappa* tasteless or flat wine, and perhaps to *vapor* warmth] > va'pidity *n* > 'vapidly *adv*

vapor ('veɪpə) *n* the US spelling of **vapour**

vaporescence (,veɪpə'resəns) *n* the production or formation of vapour > ,vapor'escent *adj*

vaporetto (,veɪpə'retəʊ; *Italian* vapo'retto) *n*, *pl* -ti (-tɪ; *Italian* -ti) *or* -tos a steam-powered passenger boat, as used on the canals in Venice [Italian, from *vapore* a steamboat]

vaporific (,veɪpə'rɪfɪk) *adj* **1** producing, causing, or tending to produce vapour **2** of, concerned with, or having the nature of vapour **3** tending to become vapour; volatile. Also: vaporous [C18: from New Latin *vaporificus*, from Latin *vapor* steam + *facere* to make]

vaporimeter (,veɪpə'rɪmɪtə) *n* an instrument for measuring vapour pressure, used to determine the volatility of oils or the amount of alcohol in alcoholic liquids

vaporize *or* **vaporise** ('veɪpə,raɪz) *vb* **1** to change or cause to change into vapour or into the gaseous state **2** to evaporate or disappear or cause to evaporate or disappear, esp suddenly **3** to destroy or be destroyed by being turned into a gas as a result of extreme heat (for example, generated by a nuclear explosion) > ,vapori'zation *or* ,vapori'sation *n*

vaporizer *or* **vaporiser** ('veɪpə,raɪzə) *n* **1** a substance that vaporizes or a device that causes vaporization **2** *med* a device that produces steam or atomizes medication for inhalation

vaporous ('veɪpərəs) *adj* **1** resembling or full of vapour **2** lacking permanence or substance; ephemeral or fanciful **3** given to foolish imaginings > 'vaporously *adv* > 'vaporousness *or* vaporosity (,veɪpə'rɒsɪtɪ) *n*

vapour *or US* **vapor** ('veɪpə) *n* **1** particles of moisture or other substance suspended in air and visible as clouds, smoke, etc **2** a gaseous substance at a temperature below its critical temperature **3** a substance that is in a gaseous state at a temperature below its boiling point **4** the vapours *archaic* a depressed mental condition believed originally to be the result of vaporous exhalations from the stomach ▷ *vb* **5** to evaporate or cause to evaporate; vaporize **6** (*intr*) to make vain empty boasts; brag [C14: from Latin *vapor*] > 'vapourer *or US* 'vaporer *n* > 'vapourish *or US* 'vaporish > 'vapour-,like *or* 'vapor-,like *adj* > 'vapoury *or US* 'vapory *adj*

vapour density *n* the ratio of the density of a gas or vapour to that of hydrogen at the same temperature and pressure

vapour lock *n* a stoppage in a pipe carrying a liquid caused by a bubble of gas, esp such a stoppage caused by vaporization of the petrol in the pipe feeding the carburettor of an internal-combustion engine

vapour pressure *n physics* the pressure exerted by a vapour. The saturated vapour pressure is that exerted by a vapour in equilibrium with its solid or liquid phase at a particular temperature

vapour trail *n* a visible trail left by an aircraft flying at high altitude or through supercold air, caused by the deposition of water vapour in the engine exhaust as minute ice crystals

Var (*French* var) *n* **1** a department of SE France, in Provence-Alpes-Côte-d'Azur region. Capital: Toulon. Pop: 946 305 (2003 est). Area: 6023 sq km (2349 sq miles) **2** a river in SE France, flowing southeast and south to the Mediterranean near Nice. Length: about 130 km (80 miles)

var. *abbreviation* **1** variable **2** variant **3** variation **4** variety **5** various

varactor ('veə,ræktə) *n* a semiconductor diode that acts as a voltage-dependent capacitor, being operated with a reverse bias [C20: probably a blend of *variable reactor*]

Varah ('værə) *n* (**Edward**) **Chad**. 1911–2007, British Anglican clergyman, who founded (1953) the Samaritans counselling service

Varanasi (və'rɑːnəsɪ) *n* a city in NE India, in SE Uttar Pradesh on the River Ganges: probably dates from the 13th century BC; an early centre of Aryan philosophy and religion; a major place of pilgrimage for Hindus, Jains, Sikhs, and Buddhists, with many ghats along the Ganges; seat of the Banaras Hindu University (1916), India's leading university, and the Sanskrit University (1957). Pop: 1 100 748 (2001). Former names: Benares, Banaras

Vardar (*Serbian* 'vardar) *n* a river in S Europe, rising in W Macedonia and flowing northeast, then south past Skopje into Greece, where it is called the Axios and enters the Aegean at Thessaloníki. Length: about 320 km (200 miles)

Vardhamana (,vɑːdə'mɑːnə) *n* See **Mahavira**

Vardon ('vɑːdᵊn) *n* **Harry**. 1870–1937, British golfer

varec ('værek) *n* **1** another name for **kelp** **2** the ash obtained from kelp [C17: from French, from Old Norse *wrek* (unattested); see WRECK]

Varese (*Italian* va're:se) *n* a historic city in N Italy, in Lombardy near Lake Varese: manufacturing centre, esp for leather goods. Pop: 80 511 (2001)

Varèse (væ'rez) *n* **Edgar(d)** (ɛdgar). 1883–1965, US composer, born in France. His works, which combine extreme dissonance with complex rhythms and the use of electronic techniques, include *Ionisation* (1931) and *Poème électronique* (1958)

Vargas (*Portuguese* 'varɡas) *n* **Getúlio Dornelles** (ʒe'tulju dur'nɛləʃ). 1883–1954, Brazilian statesman; president (1930–45; 1951–54)

Vargas Llosa (*Spanish* 'barɣas 'ʎosa) *n* (**Jorge**) **Mario** (**Pedro**) born 1936, Peruvian novelist, writer, and political figure. His novels include *The City and the Dogs* (1963), *Conversation in the Cathedral* (1969), *The Storyteller* (1990), and *The Notebok of Don Rigoberto* (1998). In 1990 he stood unsuccessfully for the presidency of Peru

variable ('veərɪəbᵊl) *adj* **1** liable to or capable of change: *variable weather* **2** (of behaviour, opinions, emotions, etc) lacking constancy; fickle **3** *maths* having a range of possible values **4** (of a species, characteristic, etc) liable to deviate from the established type **5** (of a wind) varying its direction and intensity **6** (of an electrical component or device) designed so that a characteristic property, such as resistance, can be varied ▷ *n* **7** something that is subject to variation **8** *maths* **a** an expression that can be assigned any of a set of values **b** a symbol, esp *x*, *y*, or *z*, representing an unspecified member of a class of objects, numbers, etc **9** *logic* a symbol, esp *x*, *y*, *z*, representing any member of a class of entities **10** *computing* a named unit of storage that can be changed to any of a set of specified values during execution of a program **11** *astronomy* See **variable star** **12** a variable wind **13** (*plural*) a region where variable winds occur [C14: from Latin *variābilis* changeable, from *variāre* to diversify] > ,varia'bility *or* 'variableness *n* > 'variably *adv*

variable cost *n* a cost that varies directly with output

variable-geometry *or* **variable-sweep** *adj* denoting an aircraft in which the wings are hinged to give the variable aspect ratio colloquially known as a swing-wing

variable star *n* any star that varies considerably in brightness, either irregularly or in regular periods. **Intrinsic variables**, in which the variation is a result of internal changes, include novae, supernovae, and pulsating stars

variance ('veərɪəns) *n* **1** the act of varying or the quality, state, or degree of being divergent; discrepancy **2** an instance of diverging; dissension **3** at variance **a** (often foll by *with*) (of facts, etc) not in accord; conflicting **b** (of persons) in a state of dissension **4** *statistics* a measure of dispersion obtained by taking the mean of the squared deviations of the observed values from their mean in a frequency distribution **5** a difference or discrepancy between two steps in a legal proceeding, esp between a statement in a pleading and the evidence given to support it **6** *chem* the number of degrees of freedom of a system, used in the phase rule

variant ('veərɪənt) *adj* **1** liable to or displaying variation

2 differing from a standard or type: *a variant spelling* ▷ *n* **3** something that differs from a standard or type **4** *statistics* another word for **variate** (sense 1) [c14: via Old French from Latin *variāns*, from *variāre* to diversify, from *varius* VARIOUS]

variant Creutzfeld-Jakob disease *n* another name for **new-variant Creutzfeld-Jakob disease**

variate ('vɛərɪɪt) *n statistics* a random variable or a numerical value taken by it [c16: from Latin *variāre* to VARY]

variation (ˌvɛərɪ'eɪʃən) *n* **1** the act, process, condition, or result of changing or varying; diversity **2** an instance of varying or the amount, rate, or degree of such change **3** something that differs from a standard or convention **4** *music* **a** a repetition of a musical theme in which the rhythm, harmony, or melody is altered or embellished **b** (*as modifier*): *variation form* **5** *biology* a marked deviation from the typical form or function **6** *astronomy* any change in or deviation from the mean motion or orbit of a planet, satellite, etc, esp a perturbation of the moon **7** another word for **magnetic declination 8** *ballet* a solo dance > ˌvari'ational *adj*

varicella (ˌværɪ'sɛlə) *n* the technical name for **chickenpox** [c18: New Latin, irregular diminutive of VARIOLA] > ˌvari'cellar *adj*

varices ('værɪˌsiːz) *n* the plural of **varix**

varico- *or before a vowel* **varic-** *combining form* indicating a varix or varicose veins: *varicotomy* [from Latin *varix, varic-* distended vein]

varicoloured *or US* **varicolored** ('vɛərɪˌkʌləd) *adj* having many colours; variegated; motley

varicose ('værɪˌkəʊs) *adj* of or resulting from varicose veins: *a varicose ulcer* [c18: from Latin *varicōsus*, from VARIX]

varicose veins *pl n* a condition in which the superficial veins, esp of the legs, become tortuous, knotted, and swollen: caused by a defect in the venous valves or in the venous pump that normally moves the blood out of the legs when standing for long periods

varicosis (ˌværɪ'kəʊsɪs) *n pathol* any condition characterized by distension of the veins [c18: from New Latin, from Latin: VARIX]

varicosity (ˌværɪ'kɒsɪtɪ) *n, pl* **-ties** *pathol* **1** the state, condition, or quality of being varicose **2** an abnormally distended vein

varicotomy (ˌværɪ'kɒtəmɪ) *n, pl* **-mies** surgical excision of a varicose vein

varied ('vɛərɪd) *adj* **1** displaying or characterized by variety; diverse **2** modified or altered: *the amount may be varied without notice* **3** varicoloured; variegated > 'variedly *adv*

variegate ('vɛərɪˌɡeɪt) *vb* (*tr*) to alter the appearance of, esp by adding different colours > ˌvarie'gation *n*

variegated ('vɛərɪˌɡeɪtɪd) *adj* **1** displaying differently coloured spots, patches, streaks, etc **2** (of foliage or flowers) having pale patches, usually as a result of mutation, infection, etc

varietal (və'raɪɪt°l) *adj* **1** of, relating to, characteristic of, designating, or forming a variety, esp a biological variety ▷ *n* **2** a wine labelled with the name of the grape from which it is pressed > va'rietally *adv*

variety (və'raɪɪtɪ) *n, pl* **-ties 1** the quality or condition of being diversified or various **2** a collection of unlike things, esp of the same general group; assortment **3** a different form or kind within a general category; sort: *varieties of behaviour* **4** a *taxonomy* a race whose distinct characters are insufficient to justify classification as a separate species; a subspecies **b** *horticulture, stockbreeding* a strain of animal or plant produced by artificial breeding **5** a entertainment consisting of a series of short unrelated performances or acts, such as comedy turns, songs, dances, sketches, etc **b** (*as modifier*): *a variety show* [c16: from Latin *varietās*, from VARIOUS]

varifocal ('vɛərɪˌfəʊk°l) *adj* **1** *optics* having a focus that can vary **2** relating to a lens that is graduated to permit any length of vision between near and distant

varifocals ('vɛərɪˌfəʊk°lz) *pl n* a pair of spectacles with varifocal lenses

variform ('vɛərɪˌfɔːm) *adj* varying in form or shape > 'variˌformly *adv*

variola (və'raɪələ) *n* the technical name for **smallpox** [c18: from Medieval Latin: disease marked by little spots, from Latin *varius* spotted] > va'riolar *adj*

variole ('vɛərɪˌəʊl) *n* any of the rounded masses that make up the rock variolite [c19: from French, from Medieval Latin; see VARIOLA]

variolite ('vɛərɪəˌlaɪt) *n* any basic igneous rock containing rounded bodies (varioles) consisting of radiating crystal fibres [c18: from VARIOLA, referring to the pockmarked appearance of the rock] > variolitic (ˌvɛərɪə'lɪtɪk) *adj*

variometer (ˌvɛərɪ'ɒmɪtə) *n* **1** an instrument for measuring variations in a magnetic field, used esp for studying the magnetic field of the earth **2** *electronics* a variable inductor consisting of a movable coil mounted inside and connected in series with a fixed coil

variorum (ˌvɛərɪ'ɔːrəm) *adj* **1** containing notes by various scholars or critics or various versions of the text ▷ *n* **2** an edition or text of this kind [c18: from Latin phrase *ēditiō cum notīs variōrum* edition with the notes of various commentators]

various ('vɛərɪəs) *determiner* **1** several different: *he is an authority on various subjects* ▷ *adj* **2** of different kinds, though often within the same general category; diverse **3** (*prenominal*) relating to a collection of separate persons or things: *the various members of the club* **4** displaying variety; many-sided: *his various achievements are most impressive* [c16: from Latin *varius* changing; perhaps related to Latin *vārus* crooked] > 'variously *adv* > 'variousness *n*

● USAGE The use of *different* after *various* should be ● avoided: *the disease exists in various forms* (not *in various* ● *different forms*)

varistor (və'rɪstə) *n* a two-electrode semiconductor device having a voltage-dependent nonlinear resistance. Compare **varactor** [c20: a blend of *variable resistor*]

varix ('vɛərɪks) *n, pl* **varices** ('værɪˌsiːz) *pathol* **a** a tortuous dilated vein. See **varicose veins b** Also called: **arterial varix, varix lymphaticus** a similar condition affecting an artery or lymphatic vessel [c15: from Latin]

varlet ('vɑːlɪt) *n archaic* **1** a menial servant **2** a knight's page **3** a rascal [c15: from Old French, variant of *vallet* VALET] > 'varletry *n*

varmint ('vɑːmɪnt) *n informal* an irritating or obnoxious person or animal [c16: dialect variant of *varmin* VERMIN]

varna ('vɑːnə) *n* any of the four Hindu castes; Brahman, Kshatriya, Vaisya, or Sudra [from Sanskrit: class]

Varna (*Bulgarian* 'varna) *n* a port in NE Bulgaria, on the Black Sea: founded by Greeks in the 6th century BC; under the Ottoman Turks (1391–1878). Pop: 340 000 (2005 est). Former name (1949–56): Stalin

varnish ('vɑːnɪʃ) *n* **1** Also called: **oil varnish** a preparation consisting of a solvent, a drying oil, and usually resin, rubber, bitumen, etc, for application to a surface where it polymerizes to yield a hard glossy, usually transparent, coating **2** a similar preparation consisting of a substance, such as shellac or cellulose ester, dissolved in a volatile solvent, such as alcohol. It hardens to a film on evaporation of the solvent **3** Also called: **natural varnish** the sap of certain trees used to produce such a coating **4** a smooth surface, coated with or as with varnish **5** an artificial, superficial, or deceptively pleasing manner, covering, etc; veneer **6** *chiefly Brit* another word for **nail polish** ▷ *vb* (*tr*) **7** to cover with varnish **8** to give a smooth surface to, as if by painting with varnish **9** to impart a more attractive appearance to [c14: from Old French *vernis*, from Medieval Latin *veronix* sandarac, resin, from Medieval Greek *berenikē*, perhaps from Greek *Berenikē*, city in Cyrenaica, Libya where varnishes were used] > 'varnisher *n*

varnish tree *n* any of various trees, such as the lacquer tree, yielding substances used to make varnish or lacquer

Varro ('værəʊ) *n* **Marcus Terentius** ('mɑːkəs tə'rɛntɪəs). 116–27 BC, Roman scholar and satirist

varsity ('vɑːsɪtɪ) *n, pl* **-ties** *Brit, NZ & South African informal* university, formerly used esp at the universities of Oxford and Cambridge

Varuna ('værʊnə, 'vʌ-) n Hinduism the ancient sky god, later the god of the waters and rain-giver. In earlier traditions he was also the all-seeing divine judge

varus ('veərəs) adj pathol denoting a deformity in which the distal part of a limb is turned inwards towards the midline of the body [c19: from Latin: bow-legged]

varve (vɑːv) n geology a typically thin band of sediment deposited annually in glacial lakes, consisting of a light layer and a dark layer deposited at different seasons [c20: from Swedish varv layer, from varva, from Old Norse hverfa to turn]

vary ('veərɪ) vb varies, varying, varied 1 to undergo or cause to undergo change, alteration, or modification in appearance, character, form, attribute, etc 2 to be different or cause to be different; be subject to change 3 (tr) to give variety to 4 (intr; foll by from) to differ, as from a convention, standard, etc 5 (intr) to change in accordance with another variable [c14: from Latin variāre, from varius VARIOUS] > 'varying adj

vas (væs) n, pl vasa ('veɪsə) anatomy, zoology a vessel, duct, or tube that carries a fluid [c17: from Latin: vessel]

Vasarely (,væsər'elɪ) n Victor. 1908–97, French painter, born in Hungary; a leading exponent of op art

Vasari (və'sɑːrɪ; Italian va'zaːri) n Giorgio ('dʒɔrdʒo). 1511–74, Italian architect, painter, and art historian, noted for his Lives of the Most Excellent Italian Architects, Painters, and Sculptors (1550; 1568), a principal source for the history of Italian Renaissance art

Vasco da Gama ('væskəʊ də 'gɑːmə) n See **Gama**

vascular ('væskjʊlə) adj biology, anatomy of, relating to, or having vessels that conduct and circulate liquids [c17: from New Latin vāsculāris, from Latin VASCULUM] > vascularity (,væskjʊ'lærɪtɪ) n > 'vascularly adv

vascular bundle n a longitudinal strand of vascular tissue in the stems and leaves of higher plants

vascular tissue n tissue of higher plants consisting mainly of xylem and phloem and occurring as a continuous system throughout the plant: it conducts water, mineral salts, and synthesized food substances and provides mechanical support. Also called: conducting tissue

vasculum ('væskjʊləm) n, pl -la (-lə) or -lums a metal box used by botanists in the field for carrying botanical specimens [c19: from Latin: little vessel, from VAS]

vas deferens ('væs 'defə,renz) n, pl vasa deferentia ('veɪsə ,defə'renʃɪə) anatomy the duct that conveys spermatozoa from the epididymis to the urethra [c16: from New Latin, from Latin vās vessel + deferēns, present participle of deferre to bear away]

vase (vɑːz) n a vessel used as an ornament or for holding cut flowers [c17: via French from Latin vās vessel]

vasectomy (væ'sektəmɪ) n, pl -mies surgical removal of all or part of the vas deferens, esp as a method of contraception

Vaseline ('væsɪ,liːn) n a trademark for **petrolatum**

Vashti ('væʃtaɪ) n Old Testament the wife of the Persian king Ahasuerus: deposed for refusing to display her beauty before his guests (Esther 1–2)

vaso- or before a vowel **vas-** combining form 1 indicating a blood vessel: vasodilator 2 indicating the vas deferens: vasectomy [from Latin vās vessel]

vasoactive (,veɪzəʊ'æktɪv) adj affecting the diameter of blood vessels: vasoactive peptides

vasoconstrictor (,veɪzəʊkən'strɪktə) n a drug, agent, or nerve that causes narrowing (**vasoconstriction**) of the walls of blood vessels

vasodilator (,veɪzəʊdaɪ'leɪtə) n a drug, agent, or nerve that can cause dilatation (**vasodilatation**) of the walls of blood vessels

vasoinhibitor (,veɪzəʊɪn'hɪbɪtə) n any of a group of drugs that reduce or inhibit the action of the vasomotor nerves

vasomotor (,veɪzəʊ'məʊtə) adj (of a drug, agent, nerve, etc) relating to or affecting the diameter of blood vessels

vasopressin (,veɪzəʊ'presɪn) n a polypeptide hormone secreted by the posterior lobe of the pituitary gland. It increases the reabsorption of water by the kidney tubules and increases blood pressure by constricting the arteries. Also called: antidiuretic hormone [from Vasopressin, a trademark]

vasopressor (,veɪzəʊ'presə) med ▷ adj 1 causing an increase in blood pressure by constricting the arteries ▷ n 2 a substance that has such an effect

vassal ('væsᵊl) n 1 (in feudal society) a man who entered into a personal relationship with a lord to whom he paid homage and fealty in return for protection and often a fief. A **great vassal** was in vassalage to a king and a **rear vassal** to a great vassal 2 a a person, nation, etc, in a subordinate, suppliant, or dependent position relative to another b (as modifier): vassal status ▷ adj 3 of or relating to a vassal [c14: via Old French from Medieval Latin vassallus, from vassus servant, of Celtic origin; compare Welsh gwas boy, Old Irish foss servant] > 'vassalage n

vast (vɑːst) adj 1 unusually large in size, extent, degree, or number; immense 2 (prenominal) (intensifier): in vast haste ▷ n 3 the vast chiefly poetic immense or boundless space [c16: from Latin vastus deserted] > 'vastly adv > 'vastness n

Västerås (Swedish vɛstər'oːs) n a city in central Sweden, on Lake Mälaren: Sweden's largest inland port; site of several national parliaments in the 16th century. Pop: 130 960 (2004 est)

vasty ('vɑːstɪ) adj vastier, vastiest an archaic or poetic word for **vast**

vat (væt) n 1 a large container for holding or storing liquids 2 chem a preparation of reduced vat dye ▷ vb vats, vatting, vatted 3 (tr) to place, store, or treat in a vat [Old English fæt; related to Old Frisian fet, Old Saxon, Old Norse fat, Old High German faz]

VAT (sometimes væt) abbreviation (in Britain) value-added tax: a tax levied on the difference between the cost of materials and the selling price of a commodity or service

vat dye n a dye, such as indigo, that is applied by first reducing it to its leuco base, which is soluble in alkali, and then regenerating the insoluble dye by oxidation in the fibres of the material > 'vat-,dyed adj

vatic ('vætɪk) adj rare of, relating to, or characteristic of a prophet; oracular [c16: from Latin vātēs prophet]

Vatican ('vætɪkən) n 1 a the palace of the popes in Rome and their principal residence there since 1377, which includes administrative offices, a library, museum, etc, and is attached to the basilica of St Peter's b (as modifier): the Vatican Council 2 a the authority of the Pope and the papal curia b (as modifier): a Vatican edict [c16: from Latin Vāticānus mons Vatican hill, on the western bank of the Tiber, of Etruscan origin]

Vatican City n an independent state forming an enclave in Rome, with extraterritoriality over 12 churches and palaces in Rome: the only remaining Papal State; independence recognized by the Italian government in 1929; contains St Peter's Basilica and Square and the Vatican; the spiritual and administrative centre of the Roman Catholic Church. Languages: Italian and Latin. Currency: euro. Pop: 1000 (2003 est). Area: 44 hectares (109 acres). Italian name: Città del Vaticano Also called: the Holy See

Vättern (Swedish 'vetərn) n Lake Vättern a lake in S central Sweden: the second largest lake in Sweden; linked to Lake Vänern by the Göta Canal; drains into the Baltic. Area: 1912 sq km (738 sq miles)

Vauban (French vobɑ̃) n Sébastien Le Prestre de (sebastjɛ̃ lə prɛtrə də). 1633–1707, French military engineer and marshal, who greatly developed the science of fortification and devised novel siege tactics using a series of parallel trenches

Vaucluse (French voklyz) n a department of SE France, in Provence-Alpes-Côte-d'Azur region. Capital: Avignon. Pop: 517 810 (2003 est). Area: 3578 sq km (1395 sq miles)

Vaud (French vo) n a canton of SW Switzerland: mountainous in the southeast; chief Swiss producer of wine. Capital: Lausanne. Pop: 632 000 (2002 est). Area: 3209 sq km (1240 sq miles) German name: Waadt

vaudeville ('vəʊdəvɪl, 'vɔː-) n 1 chiefly US & Canadian variety entertainment consisting of short acts such as acrobatic turns, song-and-dance routines, animal acts, etc, popular esp in the early 20th century. Brit name: music hall **2** a light or comic theatrical piece interspersed with songs and dances [c18: from French, from *vaudevire* satirical folk song, shortened from *chanson du vau de Vire* song of the valley of Vire, a district in Normandy where this type of song flourished] > ˌvaudeˈvillian *n*, *adj*

Vaudois ('vəʊdwɑː) *pl n, sing* -**dois 1** another name for the **Waldenses 2** the inhabitants of Vaud

Vaughan (vɔːn) *n* **1** Henry. 1622–95, Welsh mystic poet, best known for his *Silex Scintillans* (1650; 1655) **2** Dame **Janet (Maria)**. 1899–1993, British physician and university official: helped set up Britain's first National Blood Transfusion Service (1939): after World War II, became Britain's expert on the effects of radiation on humans; Principal of Somerville College, Oxford (1945–67) **3** Sarah (**Lois**). 1924–90, US vocalist and pianist, noted esp for her skill in vocal improvisation

Vaughan Williams ('wɪljəmz) *n* **Ralph**. 1872–1958, English composer, inspired by British folk songs and music of the Tudor period. He wrote operas, symphonies, hymns, and choral music

vault¹ (vɔːlt) *n* **1** an arched structure that forms a roof or ceiling **2** a room, esp a cellar, having an arched roof down to floor level **3** a burial chamber, esp when underground **4** a strongroom for the safe-deposit and storage of valuables **5** an underground room or part of such a room, used for the storage of wine, food, etc **6** *anatomy* any arched or domed bodily cavity or space: *the cranial vault* **7** something suggestive of an arched structure, as the sky ▷ *vb* **8** (*tr*) to furnish with or as if with an arched roof **9** (*tr*) to construct in the shape of a vault **10** (*intr*) to curve, arch, or bend in the shape of a vault [c14 *vaute*, from Old French, from Vulgar Latin *volvita* (unattested) a turn, probably from Latin *volvere* to roll]

vault² (vɔːlt) *vb* **1** to spring over (an object), esp with the aid of a long pole or with the hands resting on the object **2** (*intr*) to do, achieve, or attain something as if by a leap: *he vaulted to fame on the strength of his discovery* ▷ *n* **3** the act of vaulting > ˈvaulter *n*

vaulting¹ ('vɔːltɪŋ) *n* one or more vaults in a building or such structures considered collectively

vaulting² ('vɔːltɪŋ) *adj* (*prenominal*) **1** excessively confident; overreaching; exaggerated: *vaulting arrogance* **2** used to vault: *a vaulting pole*

vaunt (vɔːnt) *vb* **1** (*tr*) to describe, praise, or display (one's success, possessions, etc) boastfully **2** (*intr*) *rare or literary* to use boastful language; brag ▷ *n* **3** a boast [c14: from Old French *vanter*, from Late Latin *vānitāre* to brag, from Latin *vānus* VAIN] > ˈvaunter *n*

Vauxhall ('vɒksˌhɔːl) *n* **1** a district in London, on the south bank of the Thames **2** Also called: **Vauxhall Gardens** a public garden at Vauxhall, laid out in 1661; a fashionable meeting place and site of lavish entertainments. Closed in 1859

vavasour ('vævəˌsɔː) *or* **vavassor** ('vævəˌsʊə) *n* (in feudal society) the noble or knightly vassal of a baron or great lord who also has vassals himself [c13: from Old French *vavasour*, perhaps contraction of Medieval Latin *vassus vassōrum* vassal of vassals; see VASSAL]

Vavilov ('vævɪˌlɒf) *n* **Nikolai Ivanovich**. 1887–?1943, Soviet plant geneticist, noted for his research into the origins of cultivated plants. His findings were regarded as contrary to official ideology and he was arrested (1940), dying in a labour camp

vb *abbreviation* verb

VC *abbreviation* **1** Vice-chairman **2** Vice Chancellor **3** Vice Consul **4** Victoria Cross

VCD *abbreviation* video compact disc: an optical disc used to store audio, video, or computer data, esp feature films for home viewing

V-chip *n* a device within a television set that allows the set to be programmed not to receive transmissions that have been classified as containing sex, violence, or obscene language

vCJD *abbreviation* variant Creutzfeldt-Jakob disease

VCR *abbreviation* video cassette recorder

VD *abbreviation* venereal disease

V-Day *n* a day nominated to celebrate victory, as in V-E Day or V-J Day in World War II

VDQS *abbreviation* vins délimités de qualité supérieure: on a bottle of French wine, indicates that it contains high-quality wine from an approved regional vineyard; the second highest French wine classification. See **AC**, **vin de pays**

VDU *computing abbreviation* visual display unit

've *contraction of* have: *I've; you've*

veal *n* the flesh of the calf used as food [c14: from Old French *veel*, from Latin *vitellus* a little calf]

vealer ('viːlə) *n* NZ a young bovine animal of up to 14 months old grown for veal

Veblen ('vɛblən) *n* **Thorstein** ('θɔːstɪn). 1857–1929, US economist and social scientist, noted for his analysis of social and economic institutions. His works include *The Theory of the Leisure Class* (1899) and *The Theory of Business Enterprise* (1904)

vector ('vɛktə) *n* **1** Also called: **polar vector** *maths* a variable quantity, such as force, that has magnitude and direction and can be resolved into components that are odd functions of the coordinates. It is represented in print by a bold italic symbol: **F** or **F̃ 2** *maths* an element of a vector space **3** Also called: **carrier** *pathol* an organism, esp an insect, that carries a disease-producing microorganism from one host to another, either within or on the surface of its body **4** Also called: **cloning vector** *genetics* an agent, such as a bacteriophage or a plasmid, by means of which a fragment of foreign DNA is inserted into a host cell to produce a gene clone in genetic engineering **5** the course or compass direction of an aircraft ▷ *vb* **6** to direct or guide (a pilot, aircraft, etc) by directions transmitted by radio **7** to alter the direction of (the thrust of a jet engine) as a means of steering an aircraft [c18: from Latin: carrier, from *vehere* to convey] > **vectorial** (vɛkˈtɔːrɪəl) *adj*

vector field *n* a region of space under the influence of some vector quantity, such as magnetic field strength, in which the quantity takes a unique vector value at every point of the region

vector font *n* *computing* another name for **outline font**

vector product *n* the product of two vectors that is a pseudovector, whose magnitude is the product of the magnitudes of the given vectors and the sine of the angle between them. Its axis is perpendicular to the plane of the given vectors. Written: $A \times B$ or $A \wedge B$

vector sum *n* a vector whose length and direction are represented by the diagonal of a parallelogram whose sides represent the given vectors

Veda ('veɪdə) *n* any or all of the most ancient sacred writings of Hinduism, esp the Rig-Veda, Yajur-Veda, Sama-Veda, and Atharva-Veda [c18: from Sanskrit: knowledge; related to *veda* I know]

vedalia (vɪˈdeɪlɪə) *n* an Australian ladybird, *Rodolia cardinalis*, introduced elsewhere to control the scale insect *Icerya purchasi*, which is a pest of citrus fruits [c20: from New Latin]

Vedanta (vɪˈdɑːntə, -ˈdæn-) *n* one of the six main philosophical schools of Hinduism, expounding the monism regarded as implicit in the Veda in accordance with the doctrines of the Upanishads. It teaches that only Brahman has reality, while the whole phenomenal world is the outcome of illusion (maya) [c19: from Sanskrit, from VEDA + *ánta* end] > Veˈdantic *adj* > Veˈdantist *n*

V-E Day *n* the day marking the Allied victory in Europe in World War II (May 8, 1945)

vedette (vɪˈdɛt) *n* **1** Also called: **vedette boat** *naval* a small patrol vessel **2** Also called: **vidette** *military* a mounted sentry posted forward of a formation's position [c17: from French, from Italian *vedetta* (influenced by *vedere* to see), from earlier *veletta*, perhaps from Spanish *vela* watch, from *velar* to keep vigil, from Latin *vigilāre*]

Vedic ('veɪdɪk) *adj* **1** of or relating to the Vedas or the ancient form of Sanskrit in which they are written ▷ *n* **2** the classical form of Sanskrit; the language of the Vedas

veer (vɪə) vb **1** to alter direction (of); swing around **2** (intr) to change from one position, opinion, etc, to another **3** (intr) (of the wind) to change direction clockwise in the northern hemisphere and anticlockwise in the southern ▷ n **4** a change of course or direction [c16: from Old French *virer*, probably of Celtic origin; compare Welsh *gwyro* to diverge]

veg (vɛdʒ) n informal a vegetable or vegetables

Vega[1] ('viːɡə) n the brightest star in the constellation Lyra and one of the most conspicuous in the N hemisphere. It is part of an optical double star having a faint companion. Distance: 25.3 light years; spectral type: AoV [c17: from Medieval Latin, from Arabic (*al nasr*) *al wāqi*, literally: the falling (vulture), that is, the constellation Lyra]

Vega[2] ('veɪɡə; Spanish 'beɣa) n See Lope de Vega

vegan ('viːɡən) n a person who refrains from using any animal product whatever for food, clothing, or any other purpose

vegeburger or **veggieburger** ('vɛdʒɪˌbɜːɡə) n a flat cake of chopped seasoned vegetables and pulses that is grilled or fried and often served in a bread roll

Vegemite ('vɛdʒɪˌmaɪt) n Austral trademark a vegetable extract used as a spread, flavouring, etc

vegetable ('vɛdʒtəbᵊl) n **1** any of various herbaceous plants having parts that are used as food, such as peas, beans, cabbage, potatoes, cauliflower, and onions **2** informal a person who has lost control of his mental faculties, limbs, etc, as from an injury, mental disease, etc **3 a** a dull inactive person **b** (as modifier): *a vegetable life* **4** (modifier) consisting of or made from edible vegetables: *a vegetable diet* **5** (modifier) of, relating to, characteristic of, derived from, or consisting of plants or plant material: *vegetable oils* **6** rare any member of the plant kingdom [c14 (adj): from Late Latin *vegetābilis* animating, from *vegetāre* to enliven, from Latin *vegēre* to excite]

vegetable butter n any of a group of vegetable fats having the consistency of butter

vegetable ivory n the hard whitish material obtained from the endosperm of the ivory nut: used to make buttons, ornaments, etc

vegetable marrow n a cucurbitaceous plant, *Cucurbita pepo*, probably native to America but widely cultivated for its oblong green striped fruit, which is eaten as a vegetable. Often shortened to: marrow

vegetable oil n any of a group of oils that are esters of fatty acids and glycerol and are obtained from plants

vegetable oyster n another name for **salsify** (sense 1)

vegetable silk n any of various silky fibres obtained from the seed pods of certain plants

vegetable wax n any of various waxes that occur on parts of certain plants, esp the trunks of certain palms, and prevent loss of water from the plant

vegetal ('vɛdʒɪtᵊl) adj **1** of, relating to, or characteristic of vegetables or plant life **2** of or relating to processes in plants and animals that do not involve sexual reproduction; vegetative [c15: from Late Latin *vegetāre* to quicken; see VEGETABLE]

vegetarian (ˌvɛdʒɪˈtɛərɪən) n **1** a person who advocates or practises vegetarianism ▷ adj **2** relating to, advocating, or practising vegetarianism **3** cookery strictly, consisting of vegetables and fruit only, but usually including milk, cheese, eggs, etc > ˌvegeˈtarianˌism n

vegetate ('vɛdʒɪˌteɪt) vb (intr) **1** to grow like a plant; sprout **2** to lead a life characterized by monotony, passivity, or mental inactivity **3** pathol (of a wart, polyp, etc) to develop fleshy outgrowths [c17: from Late Latin *vegetāre* to invigorate]

vegetation (ˌvɛdʒɪˈteɪʃən) n **1** plant life as a whole, esp the plant life of a particular region **2** the process of vegetating **3** pathol any abnormal growth, excrescence, etc **4** a vegetative existence > ˌvegeˈtational adj > ˌvegeˈtatious adj

vegetative ('vɛdʒɪtətɪv) adj **1** of, relating to, or denoting the nonreproductive parts of a plant, i.e. the stems, leaves, and roots, or growth that does not involve the reproductive parts **2** (of reproduction) characterized by asexual processes **3** of or relating to functions such as digestion, growth, and circulation rather than sexual

reproduction **4** (of a style of living) dull, stagnant, unthinking, or passive > 'vegetatively adv > 'vegetativeness n

veggie ('vɛdʒɪ) n, adj an informal word for **vegetarian**

vegie ('vɛdʒɪ) adj Austral informal (of school subjects) considered to be trivial; not academically taxing

vego ('vɛdʒəʊ) Austral informal ▷ adj **1** vegetarian ▷ n, pl vegos **2** a vegetarian

veg out vb vegges, vegging, vegged (intr, adv) slang, chiefly US to relax in an inert passive way; vegetate: *vegging out in front of the television set*

vehement ('viːɪmənt) adj **1** marked by intensity of feeling or conviction; emphatic **2** (of actions, gestures, etc) characterized by great energy, vigour, or force; furious [c15: from Latin *vehemēns* ardent; related to *vehere* to carry] > 'vehemence n > 'vehemently adv

vehicle ('viːɪkᵊl) n **1** any conveyance in or by which people or objects are transported, esp one fitted with wheels **2** a medium for the expression, communication, or achievement of ideas, information, power, etc **3** pharmacol a therapeutically inactive substance mixed with the active ingredient to give bulk to a medicine **4** Also called: base a painting medium, such as oil, in which pigments are suspended **5** (in the performing arts) a play, musical composition, etc, that enables a particular performer to display his talents **6** a rocket excluding its payload [c17: from Latin *vehiculum*, from *vehere* to carry] > vehicular (vɪ'hɪkjʊlə) adj

Veii ('viːjaɪ) n an ancient Etruscan city, northwest of Rome: destroyed by the Romans in 396 BC

veil (veɪl) n **1** a piece of more or less transparent material, usually attached to a hat or headdress, used to conceal or protect a woman's face and head **2** part of a nun's headdress falling round the face onto the shoulders **3** something that covers, conceals, or separates; mask: *a veil of reticence* **4** the veil the life of a nun in a religious order and the obligations entailed by it **5** take the veil to become a nun **6** Also called: velum botany a membranous structure, esp the thin layer of cells connecting the edge of a young mushroom cap with the stipe **7** anatomy another word for **caul** ▷ vb **8** (tr) to cover, conceal, or separate with or as if with a veil **9** (intr) to wear or put on a veil [c13: from Norman French *veile*, from Latin *vēla* sails, pl of *vēlum* a covering] > 'veiler n > 'veil-ˌlike adj

Veil (French vaɪl) n Simone (Annie) (simɔn). born 1927, French stateswoman; president of the European Parliament (1979–82): a survivor of Nazi concentration camps

veiled (veɪld) adj **1** disguised: *a veiled insult* **2** (of sound, tone, the voice, etc) not distinct; muffled > veiledly ('veɪlɪdlɪ) adv

veiling ('veɪlɪŋ) n a veil or the fabric used for veils

vein (veɪn) n **1** any of the tubular vessels that convey oxygen-depleted blood to the heart. See **pulmonary vein**, **artery** Related adj: **venous** **2** any of the hollow branching tubes that form the supporting framework of an insect's wing **3** any of the vascular strands of a leaf **4** a clearly defined mass of ore, mineral, etc, filling a fault or fracture, often with a tabular or sheetlike shape **5** an irregular streak of colour or alien substance in marble, wood, or other material **6** a natural underground watercourse **7** a crack or fissure **8** a distinctive trait or quality in speech, writing, character, etc; strain: *a vein of humour* **9** a temporary disposition, attitude, or temper; mood: *the debate entered a frivolous vein* **10** Irish a parting in hair ▷ vb (tr) **11** to diffuse over or cause to diffuse over in streaked patterns **12** to fill, furnish, or mark with or as if with veins [c13: from Old French *veine*, from Latin *vēna*] > 'veinless adj > 'vein,like adj > 'veiny adj

veining ('veɪnɪŋ) n a pattern or network of veins or streaks

veinlet ('veɪnlɪt) n any small vein or venule

velamen (və'leɪmən) n, pl -lamina (-'læmɪnə) **1** the thick layer of dead cells that covers the aerial roots of certain orchids and aroids and absorbs moisture from the surroundings **2** anatomy another word for **velum** [c19: from Latin: a veil, from *vēlāre* to cover]

velar ('viːlə) *adj* **1** of, relating to, or attached to a velum: *velar tentacles* **2** *phonetics* articulated with the soft palate and the back of the tongue, as in the sounds (k), (g), or (ŋ) [c18: from Latin *vēlāris*, from *vēlum* VEIL]

Velázquez (*Spanish* beˈlaθkeθ) *or* **Velásquez** (*Spanish* beˈlaskeθ) *n* **Diego Rodríguez de Silva y** ('djeɣo rɔ'ðriɣeθ de 'silβa i). 1599–1660, Spanish painter, remarkable for the realism of his portraits, esp those of Philip IV of Spain and the royal household

Velcro ('vɛlkrəʊ) *n trademark* a fastening consisting of two strips of nylon fabric, one having tiny hooked threads and the other a coarse surface, that form a strong bond when pressed together

veld *or* **veldt** (fɛlt, vɛlt) *n* elevated open grassland in Southern Africa. See also **bushveld**, **highveld** [c19: from Afrikaans, from earlier Dutch *veldt* FIELD]

Velde ('vɛldə) *n* See **van de Velde**

veldskoen ('fɛlt,skʊn, 'vɛlt-) *n* an ankle-length boot of soft but strong rawhide [c19: from Afrikaans, from *vel* skin + *skoen* shoes]

veleta (və'liːtə) *n* a variant spelling of **valeta**

veliger ('vɛlɪdʒə) *n* the free-swimming larva of many molluscs, having a rudimentary shell and a ciliated velum used for feeding and locomotion [c19: from New Latin, from VELUM + -GER(OUS)]

Vellore (və'lɔː) *n* a town in SE India, in NE Tamil Nadu: medical centre. Pop: 177 413 (2001)

vellum ('vɛləm) *n* **1** a fine parchment prepared from the skin of a calf, kid, or lamb **2** a work printed or written on vellum **3** a creamy coloured heavy paper resembling vellum ▷ *adj* **4** made of or resembling vellum **5** (of a book) bound in vellum [c15: from Old French *velin*, from *velin* of a calf, from *veel* VEAL]

veloce (vɪ'ləʊtʃɪ) *adj, adv music* to be played rapidly [from Italian, from Latin *vēlōx* quick]

velocipede (vɪ'lɒsɪ,piːd) *n* **1** an early form of bicycle propelled by pushing along the ground with the feet **2** any early form of bicycle or tricycle [c19: from French *vélocipède*, from Latin *vēlōx* swift + *pēs* foot] ▷ ve'loci,pedist *n*

velocity (vɪ'lɒsɪtɪ) *n, pl* -ties **1** speed of motion, action, or operation; rapidity; swiftness **2** *physics* a measure of the rate of motion of a body expressed as the rate of change of its position in a particular direction with time. It is measured in metres per second, miles per hour, etc. Symbol: *u, v, w* **3** *physics* (not in technical usage) another word for **speed** (sense 3) [c16: from Latin *vēlōcitās*, from *vēlōx* swift; related to *volāre* to fly]

velocity of circulation *n economics* the average number of times a unit of money is used in a given time, esp calculated as the ratio of the total money spent in that time to the total amount of money in circulation

velodrome ('viːlə,drəʊm, 'vɛl-) *n* an arena with a banked track for cycle racing [c20: from French *vélodrome*, from *vélo-* (from Latin *vēlōx* swift) + -DROME]

velour *or* **velours** (vɛ'lʊə) *n* any of various fabrics with a velvet-like finish, used for upholstery, coats, hats, etc [c18: from Old French *velous*, from Old Provençal *velos* velvet, from Latin *villosus* shaggy, from *villus* shaggy hair; compare Latin *vellus* a fleece]

velouté (və'luːteɪ) *n* a rich white sauce or soup made from stock, egg yolks, and cream [from French, literally: velvety, from French *velous*; see VELOUR]

Velsen (*Dutch* 'vɛlsə) *n* a port in the W Netherlands, in North Holland at the mouth of the canal connecting Amsterdam with the North Sea: fishing and heavy industrial centre. Pop: 68 000 (2003 est)

velum ('viːləm) *n, pl* -la (-lə) **1** *zoology* any of various membranous structures, such as the ciliated oral membrane of certain mollusc larvae or the veil-like membrane running around the rim of a jellyfish **2** *anatomy* any of various veil-like bodily structures, esp the soft palate **3** *botany* another word for **veil** (sense 6) [c18: from Latin: veil]

velure (vɛ'lʊə) *n* **1** velvet or a similar fabric **2** a hatter's pad, used for smoothing silk hats [c16: from Old French *velour*, from Old French *velous*; see VELOUR]

velutinous (və'luːtɪnəs) *adj* covered with short dense soft hairs: *a plant with velutinous leaves* [c19: from New Latin *velūtīnus* like velvet]

velvet ('vɛlvɪt) *n* **1 a** a fabric of silk, cotton, nylon, etc, with a thick close soft usually lustrous pile **b** (*as modifier*): *velvet curtains* **2** anything with a smooth soft surface **3 a** smoothness; softness **b** (*as modifier*): *velvet skin; a velvet night* **4** the furry covering of the newly formed antlers of a deer **5** *slang, chiefly US* **a** gambling or speculative winnings **b** a gain, esp when unexpectedly high **6** velvet glove gentleness or caution, often concealing strength or determination (esp in the phrase **an iron fist** *or* **hand in a velvet glove**) [c14 *veluet*, from Old French *veluotte*, from *velu* hairy, from Vulgar Latin *villutus* (unattested), from Latin *villus* shaggy hair] ▷ 'velvet-,like *adj* ▷ 'velvety *adj*

velveteen (,vɛlvɪ'tiːn) *n* **1 a** a cotton fabric resembling velvet with a short thick pile, used for clothing, etc **b** (*as modifier*): *velveteen trousers* **2** (*plural*) trousers made of velveteen ▷ ,velvet'eened *adj*

Ven. *abbreviation* Venerable

vena ('viːnə) *n, pl* -nae (-niː) *anatomy* a technical word for vein [c15: from Latin *vēna* VEIN]

vena cava ('keɪvə) *n, pl* venae cavae ('keɪviː) either one of the two large veins that convey oxygen-depleted blood to the heart [Latin: hollow vein]

venal ('viːnəl) *adj* **1** easily bribed or corrupted; mercenary: *a venal magistrate* **2** characterized by corruption [c17: from Latin *vēnālis*, from *vēnum* sale] ▷ venality (viː'nælɪtɪ) *n* ▷ 'venally *adv*

venation (viː'neɪʃən) *n* **1** the arrangement of the veins in a leaf or in the wing of an insect **2** such veins collectively ▷ ve'national *adj*

vend (vɛnd) *vb* **1** to sell or be sold **2** to sell (goods) for a living [c17: from Latin *vendere*, contraction of *vēnum dare* to offer for sale]

vendace ('vɛndeɪs) *n, pl* -daces *or* -dace either of two small whitefish, *Coregonus vandesius* (**Lochmaben vendace**) *or* C. *gracilior* (**Cumberland vendace**), occurring in lakes in Scotland and NW England respectively [c18: from New Latin *vandēsius*, from Old French *vandoise*, probably of Celtic origin]

vendee (vɛn'diː) *n chiefly law* a person to whom something, esp real property, is sold; buyer

Vendée (*French* vɑ̃de) *n* a department of W France, in Pays-de-la-Loire region: scene of the **Wars of the Vendée**, a series of peasant-royalist insurrections (1793–95) against the Revolutionary government. Capital: La Roche-sur-Yon. Pop: 565 230 (2003 est). Area: 7016 sq km (2709 sq miles)

vendetta (vɛn'dɛtə) *n* **1** a private feud, originally between Corsican or Sicilian families, in which the relatives of a murdered person seek vengeance by killing the murderer or some member of his family **2** any prolonged feud, quarrel, etc [c19: from Italian, from Latin *vindicta*, from *vindicāre* to avenge; see VINDICATE] ▷ ven'dettist *n*

vendible ('vɛndəbəl) *adj* **1** saleable or marketable ▷ *n* **2** (*usually plural*) *rare* a saleable object ▷ ,vendi'bility *or* 'vendibleness *n*

vending machine *n* a machine that automatically dispenses consumer goods such as cigarettes, food, or petrol, when money is inserted

Vendôme (*French* vɑ̃dom) *n* **Louis Joseph de** (lwi ʒozɛf də). 1654–1712, French marshal, noted for his command during the War of the Spanish Succession (1701–14)

vendor ('vɛndɔː) *or* **vender** ('vɛndə) *n* **1** *chiefly law* a person who sells something, esp real property **2** another name for **vending machine**

vendor placing *n finance* a method of financing the purchase of one company by another in which the purchasing company pays for the target company in its own shares, on condition that the vendor places these shares with investors for cash payment

veneer (vɪ'nɪə) *n* **1 a** a thin layer of wood, plastic, etc, with a decorative or fine finish that is bonded to the surface of a less expensive material, usually wood **2 a** superficial appearance, esp one that is pleasing: *a veneer of gentility* **3** any facing material that is applied to a different backing material **4** any one of the layers of wood that is used to form plywood ▷ *vb* (*tr*) **5** to cover (a surface) with a veneer **6** to bond together (thin layers of wood) to make plywood **7** to conceal (something) under a superficially pleasant surface [c17: from German *furnieren* to veneer, from Old French *fournir* to FURNISH] > ve'neerer *n*

veneering (vɪ'nɪərɪŋ) *n* **1** material used as veneer or a veneered surface **2** *rare* a superficial show

venepuncture ('vɛnɪˌpʌŋktʃə) *n* a variant spelling of **venipuncture**

venerable ('vɛnərəbªl) *adj* **1** (esp of a person) worthy of reverence on account of great age, religious associations, character, position, etc **2** (of inanimate objects) hallowed or impressive on account of historical or religious association **3** ancient **4** *RC Church* a title bestowed on a deceased person when the first stage of his canonization has been accomplished and his holiness has been recognized in a decree of the official Church **5** *Church of England* a title given to an archdeacon [c15: from Latin *venerābilis*, from *venerārī* to venerate] > ˌvenera'bility *or* 'venerableness *n* > 'venerably *adv*

venerate ('vɛnəˌreɪt) *vb* (*tr*) **1** to hold in deep respect; revere **2** to honour in recognition of qualities of holiness, excellence, wisdom, etc [c17: from Latin *venerārī*, from *venus* love] > 'venerˌator *n*

veneration (ˌvɛnə'reɪʃən) *n* **1** a feeling or expression of awe or reverence **2** the act of venerating or the state of being venerated

venereal (vɪ'nɪərɪəl) *adj* **1** of, relating to, or infected with venereal disease **2** (of a disease) transmitted by sexual intercourse **3** of, relating to, or involving the genitals **4** of or relating to sexual intercourse or erotic desire; aphrodisiac [c15: from Latin *venereus* concerning sexual love, from *venus* sexual love, from VENUS[1]]

venereal disease *n* any of various diseases, such as syphilis or gonorrhoea, transmitted by sexual intercourse. Abbreviation: **VD**

venereology (vɪˌnɪərɪ'ɒlədʒɪ) *n* the branch of medicine concerned with the study and treatment of venereal disease > veˌnere'ologist *n*

venery[1] ('vɛnərɪ, 'viː-) *n* *archaic* the pursuit of sexual gratification [c15: from Medieval Latin *veneria*, from Latin *venus* love, VENUS[1]]

venery[2] ('vɛnərɪ, 'viː-) *n* the art, sport, lore, or practice of hunting, esp with hounds; the chase [c14: from Old French *venerie*, from *vener* to hunt, from Latin *vēnārī*]

venesection ('vɛnɪˌsɛkʃən) *n* surgical incision into a vein [c17: from New Latin *vēnae sectiō*; see VEIN, SECTION]

Venetia (vɪ'niːʃə) *n* **1** the area of ancient Italy between the lower Po valley and the Alps: later a Roman province **2** the territorial possessions of the medieval Venetian republic that were at the head of the Adriatic and correspond to the present-day region of Veneto and a large part of Friuli-Venezia Giulia

Venetian (vɪ'niːʃən) *adj* **1** of, relating to, or characteristic of Venice or its inhabitants ▷ *n* **2** a native or inhabitant of Venice **3** See **Venetian blind 4** (*sometimes not capital*) one of the tapes that join the slats of a Venetian blind

Venetian blind *n* a window blind consisting of a number of horizontal slats whose angle may be altered to let in more or less light

Venetian red *n* **1** natural or synthetic ferric oxide used as a red pigment **2 a** a moderate to strong reddish-brown colour **b** (*as adjective*): *a Venetian-red coat*

Veneto (*Italian* 've:neto) *n* a region of NE Italy, on the Adriatic: mountainous in the north with a fertile plain in the south, crossed by the Rivers Po, Adige, and Piave. Capital: Venice. Pop: 4 577 408 (2003 est). Area: 18 377 sq km (7095 sq miles). Also called: **Venezia-Euganea** (ve'nɛttsja eʊ'ga:nea)

Venez. *abbreviation* Venezuela

Venezia (ve'nɛttsja) *n* the Italian name for **Venice**

Venezia Giulia (*Italian* 'dʒuːlja) *n* a former region of NE Italy at the N end of the Adriatic: divided between Yugoslavia and Italy after World War II; now divided between Italy and Slovenia

Venezia Tridentina (*Italian* triden'tiːna) *n* the former name (until 1947) of **Trentino-Alto Adige**

Venezuela (ˌvɛnɪ'zweɪlə) *n* **1** a republic in South America, on the Caribbean: colonized by the Spanish in the 16th century; independence from Spain declared in 1811 and won in 1819 after a war led by Simón Bolívar. It contains Lake Maracaibo and the northernmost chains of the Andes in the northwest, the Orinoco basin in the central part, and the Guiana Highlands in the south. Exports: petroleum, iron ore, and coffee. Official language: Spanish. Religion: Roman Catholic majority. Currency: bolívar. Capital: Caracas. Pop: 26 170 000 (2004 est). Area: 912 050 sq km (352 142 sq miles) **2** Gulf of Venezuela an inlet of the Caribbean in NW Venezuela: continues south as Lake Maracaibo > ˌVene'zuelan *adj, n*

vengeance ('vɛndʒəns) *n* **1** the act of or desire for taking revenge; retributive punishment **2** with a vengeance (intensifier): *the 70's have returned with a vengeance* [c13: from Old French, from *venger* to avenge, from Latin *vindicāre* to punish; see VINDICATE]

vengeful ('vɛndʒfʊl) *adj* **1** desiring revenge; vindictive **2** characterized by or indicating a desire for revenge: *a vengeful glance* **3** inflicting or taking revenge: *with vengeful blows* > 'vengefully *adv*

venial ('viːnɪəl) *adj* easily excused or forgiven: *a venial error* [c13: via Old French from Late Latin *veniālis*, from Latin *venia* forgiveness; related to Latin *venus* love] > veniality (ˌviːnɪ'ælɪtɪ) *n* > 'venially *adv*

venial sin *n* *Christianity* a sin regarded as involving only a partial loss of grace

Venice ('vɛnɪs) *n* a port in NE Italy, capital of Veneto region, built on over 100 islands and mud flats in the **Lagoon of Venice** (an inlet of the **Gulf of Venice** at the head of the Adriatic): united under the first doge in 697 AD; became an independent republic and a great commercial and maritime power, defeating Genoa, the greatest rival, in 1380; contains the Grand Canal and about 170 smaller canals, providing waterways for city transport. Pop: 271 073 (2001). Italian name: Venezia. Related adj: **Venetian**

venin ('vɛnɪn, 'viː-) *n* any of the poisonous constituents of animal venoms [c20: from French *ven(in)* poison + -IN]

venipuncture *or* **venepuncture** ('vɛnɪˌpʌŋktʃə) *n* *med* the puncturing of a vein, esp to take a sample of venous blood or inject a drug

venison ('vɛnɪzªn, -sªn) *n* **1** the flesh of a deer, used as food **2** *archaic* the flesh of any game animal used for food [c13: from Old French *venaison*, from Latin *vēnātiō* hunting, from *vēnārī* to hunt]

Venite (vɪ'naɪtɪ) *n* **1** *ecclesiast* the opening word of the 95th psalm, an invitatory prayer at matins **2** a musical setting of this [Latin: come ye]

Venizélos (*Greek* veni'zɛlɔs) *n* **Eleuthérios** (ɛˌlɛfθe'riɔs). 1864–1936, Greek statesman, who greatly extended Greek territory: prime minister (1910–15; 1917–20; 1924; 1928–32; 1933)

Venlo *or* **Venloo** (*Dutch* 'vɛnloː) *n* a city in the SE Netherlands, in Limburg on the Maas River. Pop: 92 000 (2003 est)

Venn diagram (vɛn) *n* *maths, logic* a diagram in which mathematical sets or terms of a categorial statement are represented by overlapping circles within a boundary representing the universal set, so that all possible combinations of the relevant properties are represented by the various distinct areas in the diagram [c19: named after John Venn (1834–1923), English logician]

venom ('vɛnəm) *n* **1** a poisonous fluid secreted by such animals as certain snakes and scorpions and usually transmitted by a bite or sting **2** malice; spite [c13: from Old French *venim*, from Latin *venēnum* poison, love potion; related to *venus* sexual love] > 'venomous *adj* > 'venomously *adv* > 'venomousness *n*

venose ('viːnəʊs) *adj* **1** having veins; venous **2** (of a plant) covered with veins or similar ridges [c17: via Latin *vēnōsus*, from *vēna* a VEIN]

venosity (vɪ'nɒsɪtɪ) *n* **1** an excessive quantity of blood in the venous system or in an organ or part **2** an unusually large number of blood vessels in an organ or part

venous ('viːnəs) *adj* **1** *physiol* of or relating to the blood circulating in the veins **2** of or relating to the veins [c17: see VENOSE]

vent[1] (vɛnt) *n* **1** a small opening for the passage or escape of fumes, liquids, etc **2** the shaft of a volcano or an aperture in the earth's crust through which lava and gases erupt **3** the external opening of the urinary or genital systems of lower vertebrates **4** a small aperture at the breech of old guns through which the charge was ignited **5** an exit, escape, or passage **6** give vent to to release (an emotion, passion, idea, etc) in an utterance or outburst ▷ *vb* (*mainly tr*) **7** to release or give expression or utterance to (an emotion, idea, etc): *he vents his anger on his wife* **8** to provide a vent for or make vents in **9** to let out (steam, liquid, etc) through a vent [C14: from Old French *esventer* to blow out, from EX-[1] + *venter*, from Vulgar Latin *ventāre* (unattested) to be windy, from Latin *ventus* wind]

vent² (vɛnt) *n* **1** a vertical slit at the back or both sides of a jacket ▷ *vb* **2** (*tr*) to make a vent or vents in (a jacket) [C15: from Old French *fente* slit, from *fendre* to split, from Latin *findere* to cleave]

venter (ˈvɛntə) *n* **1** *anatomy, zoology* **a** the belly or abdomen of vertebrates **b** a protuberant structure or part, such as the belly of a muscle **2** *botany* the swollen basal region of an archegonium, containing the developing ovum **3** *law* the womb [C16: from Latin]

Venter (ˈvɛntə) *n* (**John**) **Craig**. born 1946, US biologist: founder of the Institute for Genomic Research (1992) whose work contributed greatly to the mapping of the human genome

ventilate (ˈvɛntɪˌleɪt) *vb* (*tr*) **1** to drive foul air out of (an enclosed area) **2** to provide with a means of airing **3** to expose (a question, grievance, etc) to public examination or discussion **4** *physiol* to oxygenate (the blood) in the capillaries of the lungs **5** to winnow (grain) [C15: from Latin *ventilāre* to fan, from *ventulus* diminutive of *ventus* wind] ▷ **ˈventilable** *adj*

ventilation (ˌvɛntɪˈleɪʃən) *n* **1** the act or process of ventilating or the state of being ventilated **2** an installation in a building that provides a supply of fresh air

ventilator (ˈvɛntɪˌleɪtə) *n* **1** an opening or device, such as a fan, used to ventilate a room, building, etc **2** *med* a machine that maintains a flow of air into and out of the lungs of a patient who is unable to breathe normally

ventral (ˈvɛntrəl) *adj* **1** relating to the front part of the body; towards the belly. Compare **dorsal** **2** of, relating to, or situated on the upper or inner side of a plant organ, esp a leaf, that is facing the axis [C18: from Latin *ventrālis*, from *venter* abdomen] ▷ **ˈventrally** *adv*

ventral fin *n* **1** another name for **pelvic fin** **2** any unpaired median fin situated on the undersurface of fishes and some other aquatic vertebrates

ventricle (ˈvɛntrɪkᵊl) *n* *anatomy* **1** a chamber of the heart, having thick muscular walls, that receives blood from the atrium and pumps it to the arteries **2** any one of the four main cavities of the vertebrate brain, which contain cerebrospinal fluid **3** any of various other small cavities in the body [C14: from Latin *ventriculus*, diminutive of *venter* belly] ▷ **ven'tricular** *adj*

ventricose (ˈvɛntrɪˌkəʊs) *adj* **1** *botany, zoology, anatomy* having a swelling on one side; unequally inflated: *the ventricose corolla of many labiate plants* **2** another word for **corpulent** [C18: from New Latin *ventricōsus*, from Latin *venter* belly]

ventriculus (vɛnˈtrɪkjʊləs) *n*, *pl* **-li** (-ˌlaɪ) **1** *zoology* **a** the midgut of an insect, where digestion takes place **b** the gizzard of a bird **2** another word for **ventricle** [C18: from Latin, diminutive of *venter* belly]

ventriloquism (vɛnˈtrɪləˌkwɪzəm) *or* **ventriloquy** *n* the art of producing vocal sounds that appear to come from another source [C18: from Latin *venter* belly + *loquī* to speak] ▷ **ventriloquial** (ˌvɛntrɪˈləʊkwɪəl) *adj* ▷ ˌventri'loquially *adv* ▷ ven'triloquist *n*

ventriloquize *or* **ventriloquise** (vɛnˈtrɪləˌkwaɪz) *vb* to produce (sounds) in the manner of a ventriloquist

Ventris (ˈvɛntrɪs) *n* **Michael George Francis**. 1922–56, English architect and scholar, who deciphered the Linear B script, identifying it as an early form of Mycenaean Greek

venture (ˈvɛntʃə) *vb* **1** (*tr*) to expose to danger; hazard: *he ventured his life* **2** (*tr*) to brave the dangers of (something): *I'll venture the seas* **3** (*tr*) to dare (to do something): *does he*

venture to object? **4** (*tr; may take a clause as object*) to express in spite of possible refutation or criticism: *I venture that he is not that honest* **5** (*intr; often foll by out, forth*, etc) to embark on a possibly hazardous journey, undertaking, etc: *to venture forth upon the high seas* ▷ *n* **6** an undertaking that is risky or of uncertain outcome **7** a commercial undertaking characterized by risk of loss as well as opportunity for profit **8** something hazarded or risked in an adventure; stake **9** *archaic* chance or fortune **10** at a venture at random; by chance [C15: variant of *aventure* ADVENTURE] ▷ **ˈventurer** *n*

venture capital *n* another name for **risk capital**

venture capitalist *n* a person or company that provides capital for new commercial enterprises

Venture Scout *or* **Venturer** *n* *Brit* a young man or woman, aged 16–20, who is a member of the senior branch of the Scouts

venturesome (ˈvɛntʃəsəm) *or* **venturous** (ˈvɛntʃərəs) *adj* **1** willing to take risks; daring **2** hazardous

Venturi (vɛnˈtjʊərɪ) *n* **Robert**. born 1925, US architect, a pioneer of the postmodernist style. His writings include *Complexity and Contradiction in Architecture* (1966)

Venturi tube *n* **1** *physics* a device for measuring fluid flow, consisting of a tube so constricted that the pressure differential produced by fluid flowing through the constriction gives a measure of the rate of flow **2** Also called: **venturi** a tube with a constriction used to reduce or control fluid flow, as one in the air inlet of a carburettor [C19: named after G. B. *Venturi* (1746–1822), Italian physicist]

venue (ˈvɛnjuː) *n* **1** *law* **a** the place in which a cause of action arises **b** the place fixed for the trial of a cause **c** the locality from which the jurors must be summoned to try a particular cause **2** a meeting place **3** any place where an organized gathering, such as a rock concert or public meeting, is held **4** *chiefly US* a position in an argument [C14: from Old French, from *venir* to come, from Latin *venīre*]

venule (ˈvɛnjuːl) *n* **1** *anatomy* any of the small branches of a vein that receives oxygen-depleted blood from the capillaries and returns it to the heart via the venous system **2** any of the branches of a vein in an insect's wing [C19: from Latin *vēnula* diminutive of *vēna* VEIN] ▷ **venular** (ˈvɛnjʊlə) *adj*

Venus¹ (ˈviːnəs) *n* the Roman goddess of love. Greek counterpart: Aphrodite

Venus² (ˈviːnəs) *n* **1** one of the inferior planets and the second nearest to the sun, visible as a bright morning or evening star. Its surface is extremely hot (over 400°C) and is completely shrouded by dense cloud. The atmosphere is principally carbon dioxide. Mean distance from sun: 108 million km; period of revolution around sun: 225 days; period of axial rotation: 244.3 days (retrograde motion); diameter and mass: 96.5 and 81.5 per cent that of earth respectively **2** the alchemical name for **copper¹** ▷ Venusian (vɪˈnjuːzɪən) *adj, n*

Venusberg (ˈviːnəsˌbɜːɡ; *German* ˈveːnʊsbɛrk) *n* a mountain in central Germany: contains caverns that, according to medieval legend, housed the palace of the goddess Venus

Venus's-flytrap *or* **Venus flytrap** *n* an insectivorous plant, *Dionaea muscipula*, of Carolina, having hinged two-lobed leaves that snap closed when the sensitive hairs on the surface are touched: family *Droseraceae*

Venus's looking glass *n* a purple-flowered campanulaceous plant, *Legousia hybrida*, of Europe, W Asia, and N Africa

veracious (vɛˈreɪʃəs) *adj* **1** habitually truthful or honest **2** accurate; precise [C17: from Latin *vērax*, from *vērus* true] ▷ **ve'raciously** *adv* ▷ **ve'raciousness** *n*

veracity (vɛˈræsɪtɪ) *n*, *pl* **-ties** **1** truthfulness or honesty, esp when consistent or habitual **2** precision; accuracy **3** something true; a truth [C17: from Medieval Latin *vērācitās*, from Latin *vērax*; see VERACIOUS]

Veracruz (ˌvɛrəˈkruːz; *Spanish* beraˈkruθ) *n* **1** a state of E Mexico, on the Gulf of Mexico: consists of a hot humid coastal strip with lagoons, rising rapidly inland to the central plateau and Sierra Madre Oriental. Capital: Jalapa. Pop: 630 000 (2005 est). Area: 72 815 sq km (28 114 sq miles) **2** the chief port of Mexico, in Veracruz state on the Gulf of Mexico. Pop: 410 000 (2000 est)

veranda or **verandah** (vəˈrændə) n **1** a porch or portico, sometimes partly enclosed, along the outside of a building **2** NZ a canopy sheltering pedestrians in a shopping street [c18: from Portuguese *varanda* railing; related to Hindi *varandā* railing]

veratrine (ˈvɛrəˌtriːn) or **veratrin** (ˈvɛrətrɪn) n a white poisonous mixture obtained from the seeds of sabadilla, consisting of veratridine and several other alkaloids: formerly used in medicine as a counterirritant [c19: from Latin *vērātrum* hellebore + -INE²]

verb (vɜːb) n **1** (in traditional grammar) any of a large class of words in a language that serve to indicate the occurrence or performance of an action, the existence of a state or condition, etc In English, such words as *run*, *make*, *do*, and the like are verbs **2** (in modern descriptive linguistic analysis) **a** a word or group of words that functions as the predicate of a sentence or introduces the predicate **b** (*as modifier*): *a verb phrase* ▷ Abbreviation: vb, v [c14: from Latin *verbum* a word]

verbal (ˈvɜːbᵊl) adj **1** of, relating to, or using words, esp as opposed to ideas, etc: *merely verbal concessions* **2** oral rather than written: *a verbal agreement* **3** verbatim; literal: *an almost verbal copy* **4** grammar of or relating to verbs or a verb ▷ n **5** (*plural*) slang abuse or invective ▷ vb -bals, -balling, -balled (*tr*) **6** slang (of the police) to implicate (someone) in a crime by quoting alleged admission of guilt in court > 'verbally adv

verbalism (ˈvɜːbəˌlɪzəm) n **1** a verbal expression; phrase or word **2** an exaggerated emphasis on the importance of words by the uncritical acceptance of assertions in place of explanations, the use of rhetorical style, etc **3** a statement lacking real content, esp a cliché

verbalist (ˈvɜːbəlɪst) n **1** a person who deals with words alone, rather than facts, ideas, feeling, etc **2** a person skilled in the use of words

verbalize or **verbalise** (ˈvɜːbəˌlaɪz) vb **1** to express (an idea, feeling, etc) in words **2** to change (any word that is not a verb) into a verb or derive a verb from (any word that is not a verb) **3** (*intr*) to be verbose > ˌverbaliˈzation or ˌverbaliˈsation n

verbal noun n a noun derived from a verb, such as *smoking* in the sentence *smoking is bad for you*. See also **gerund**

verbascum (vɜːˈbæskəm) n See **mullein** [Latin: mullein]

verbatim (vɜːˈbeɪtɪm) adv, adj using exactly the same words; word for word [c15: from Medieval Latin: word by word, from Latin *verbum* word]

verbena (vɜːˈbiːnə) n **1** any plant of the verbenaceous genus *Verbena*, chiefly of tropical and temperate America, having red, white, or purple fragrant flowers: much cultivated as garden plants. See also **vervain** **2** any of various similar or related plants, esp the lemon verbena [c16: via Medieval Latin, from Latin: sacred bough used by the priest in religious acts, VERVAIN]

verbiage (ˈvɜːbɪɪdʒ) n **1** the excessive and often meaningless use of words; verbosity **2** *rare* diction; wording [c18: from French, from Old French *verbier* to chatter, from *verbe* word, from Latin *verbum*]

verbose (vɜːˈbəʊs) adj using or containing an excess of words, so as to be pedantic or boring; prolix [c17: from Latin *verbōsus* from *verbum* word] > verˈbosely adv > verbosity (vɜːˈbɒsɪtɪ) n

verboten German (fɛrˈboːtən) adj forbidden; prohibited

verb phrase n grammar a constituent of a sentence that contains the verb and any direct and indirect objects but not the subject. It is a controversial question in grammatical theory whether or not this constituent is to be identified with the predicate of the sentence

Vercelli (*Italian* vɛrˈtʃɛlli) n a city in NW Italy, in Piedmont: an ancient Ligurian and later Roman city; has an outstanding library of manuscripts (notably the *Codex Vercellensis*, dating from the 10th century). Pop: 45 132 (2001)

Vercingetorix (ˌvɜːsɪnˈdʒɛtərɪks) n died ?45 BC, Gallic chieftain and hero, executed for leading a revolt against the Romans under Julius Caesar (52 BC)

verdant (ˈvɜːdᵊnt) adj **1** covered with green vegetation

2 (of plants, etc) green in colour **3** immature or unsophisticated; green [c16: from Old French *verdoyant*, from *verdoyer* to become green, from Old French *verd* green, from Latin *viridis*, from *virēre* to be green] > 'verdancy n > 'verdantly adv

verd antique (vɜːd) n **1** a dark green mottled impure variety of serpentine marble **2** any of various similar marbles or stones **3** another name for **verdigris** [c18: from French, from Italian *verde antico* ancient green]

Verdelho (vəˈdɛljəʊ) n, pl -delhos **1** a white grape grown in Portugal, used for making wine **2** a white wine made from this grape

Verdi (ˈvɛədɪ; *Italian* 'verdi) n **Giuseppe** (dʒuˈzɛppe). 1813–1901, Italian composer of operas, esp *Rigoletto* (1851), *Il Trovatore* (1853), *La Traviata* (1853), and *Aïda* (1871)

verdict (ˈvɜːdɪkt) n **1** the findings of a jury on the issues of fact submitted to it for examination and trial; judgment **2** any decision, judgment, or conclusion [c13: from Medieval Latin *vērdictum*, from Latin *vērē dictum* truly spoken, from *vērus* true + *dīcere* to say]

verdigris (ˈvɜːdɪɡrɪs) n **1** a green or bluish patina formed on copper, brass, or bronze and consisting of a basic salt of copper containing both copper oxide and a copper salt **2** a green or blue crystalline substance obtained by the action of acetic acid on copper and used as a fungicide and pigment; basic copper acetate [c14: from Old French *vert de Grice* green of Greece]

Verdun (*French* vɛrdœ̃; *English* ˈvɜːdʌn) n **1** a fortified town in NE France, on the Meuse: scene of the longest and most severe battle (1916) of World War I, in which the French repelled a powerful German offensive. Pop: 19 624 (1999) **2 Treaty of Verdun** an agreement reached in 843 AD by three grandsons of Charlemagne, dividing his empire into an E kingdom (later Germany), a W kingdom (later France), and a middle kingdom (containing what became the Low Countries, Lorraine, Burgundy, and N Italy)

verdure (ˈvɜːdʒə) n **1** flourishing green vegetation or its colour **2** a condition of freshness or healthy growth [c14: from Old French *verd* green, from Latin *viridis*] > 'verdured adj

Vereeniging (fəˈriːnɪhɪŋ, və-) n a city in E South Africa: scene of the signing (1902) of the treaty ending the Boer War. Pop: 79 630 (2001)

verge¹ (vɜːdʒ) n **1** an edge or rim; margin **2** a limit beyond which something occurs; brink: *on the verge of ecstasy* **3** *Brit* a grass border along a road **4** *architect* the edge of the roof tiles projecting over a gable **5** *English legal history* **a** the area encompassing the royal court that is subject to the jurisdiction of the Lord High Steward **b** a rod or wand carried as a symbol of office or emblem of authority, as in the Church ▷ vb **6** (*intr;* foll by *on*) to be near (to): *to verge on chaos* **7** (when *intr,* sometimes foll by *on*) to serve as the edge of (something): *this narrow strip verges the road* [c15: from Old French, from Latin *virga* rod]

verge² (vɜːdʒ) vb (*intr;* foll by *to* or *towards*) to move or incline in a certain direction [c17: from Latin *vergere*]

verger (ˈvɜːdʒə) n *chiefly Church of England* **1** a church official who acts as caretaker and attendant, looking after the interior of a church and often the vestments and church furnishings **2** an official who carries the verge or rod of office before a bishop, dean, or other dignitary in ceremonies and processions [c15: from Old French, from *verge,* from Latin *virga* rod, twig]

Vergil (ˈvɜːdʒɪl) n a variant spelling of **Virgil**

verglas (ˈvɛəɡlɑː) n, pl -glases (-ɡlɑː, -ɡlɑːz) a thin film of ice on rock [from Old French *verre-glaz* glass-ice, from *verre* glass (from Latin *vitrum*) + *glaz* ice (from Late Latin *glacia,* from Latin *glaciēs*)]

Verhaeren (vɜːˈhɑːrən) n **Émile.** 1855–1916, Belgian poet, writing in French. His works include the collections *Les Flamandes* (1883), *Les Soirs* (1887), and *Les Visages de la Vie* (1899)

veridical (vɪˈrɪdɪkᵊl) adj **1** truthful **2** *psychol* of or relating to revelations in dreams, hallucinations, etc, that appear to be confirmed by subsequent events [c17: from Latin *vēridicus,* from *vērus* true + *dīcere* to say] > veridicality (vɪˌrɪdɪˈkælɪtɪ) n > veˈridically adv

veriest (ˈvɛrɪɪst) adj archaic (intensifier): *the veriest coward*

v

verification (ˌvɛrɪfɪˈkeɪʃən) *n* **1** establishment of the correctness of a theory, fact, etc **2** evidence that provides proof of an assertion, theory, etc ▷ ˈverifiˌcative or ˈverifiˌcatory *adj*

verify (ˈvɛrɪˌfaɪ) *vb* -fies, -fying, -fied (*tr*) **1** to prove to be true; confirm; substantiate **2** to check or determine the correctness or truth of by investigation, reference, etc **3** *law* to add a verification to (a pleading); substantiate or confirm (an oath) [c14: from Old French *verifier*, from Medieval Latin *vērificāre*, from Latin *vērus* true + *facere* to make] ▷ ˈveriˌfiable *adj* ▷ ˈveriˌfiably *adv* ▷ ˈveriˌfier *n*

verily (ˈvɛrɪlɪ) *adv* (*sentence modifier*) *archaic* in truth; truly: *verily, thou art a man of God* [c13: from VERY + -LY²]

verisimilar (ˌvɛrɪˈsɪmɪlə) *adj* appearing to be true; probable; likely [c17: from Latin *vērisimilis*, from *vērus* true + *similis* like]

verisimilitude (ˌvɛrɪsɪˈmɪlɪˌtjuːd) *n* **1** the appearance or semblance of truth or reality; quality of seeming true **2** something that merely seems to be true or real, such as a doubtful statement [c17: from Latin *vērisimilitūdō*, from *vērus* true + *similitūdō* SIMILITUDE]

verism (ˈvɪərɪzəm) *n* extreme naturalism in art or literature [c19: from Italian *verismo*, from *vero* true, from Latin *vērus*] ▷ ˈverist *n, adj* ▷ veˈristic *adj*

verismo (veˈrɪzməʊ; *Italian* veˈrismo) *n* *music* a school of composition that originated in Italian opera towards the end of the 19th century, drawing its themes from real life and emphasizing naturalistic elements. Its chief exponent was Giacomo Puccini (1858–1924) [c19: from Italian; see VERISM]

veritable (ˈvɛrɪtəbᵊl) *adj* (*prenominal*) (*intensifier*; usually qualifying a word used metaphorically): *he's a veritable swine!* [c15: from Old French, from *vérité* truth; see VERITY] ▷ ˈveritableness *n* ▷ ˈveritably *adv*

vérité (ˈveɪrɪˌteɪ; *French* verite) *adj* involving a high degree of realism or naturalism: *a vérité look at David Bowie*. See also **cinéma vérité** [French, literally: truth]

verity (ˈvɛrɪtɪ) *n, pl* -ties **1** the quality or state of being true, real, or correct **2** a true principle, statement, idea, etc; a truth or fact [c14: from Old French *vérité*, from Latin *vēritās*, from *vērus* true]

verjuice (ˈvɜːˌdʒuːs) *n* **1** the acid juice of unripe grapes, apples, or crab apples, formerly much used in making sauces, etc **2** *rare* sourness or sharpness of temper, looks, etc [c14: from Old French *vert jus* green (unripe) juice, from Old French *vert* green (from Latin *viridis*) + *jus* juice (from Latin *jūs*)]

Verkhne-Udinsk (*Russian* ˈvjerxnɪuˈdjinsk) *n* the former name (until 1934) of **Ulan-Ude**

verkrampte (fəˈkramtə) *n* (in South Africa) **a** (during apartheid) an Afrikaner Nationalist who opposed any changes toward liberal trends in government policy, esp relating to racial questions **b** (*as modifier*): *verkrampte politics* [c20: from Afrikaans (adj), literally: restricted]

Verlaine (*French* verlɛn) *n* **Paul** (pɔl). 1844–96, French poet. His verse includes *Poèmes saturniens* (1866), *Fêtes galantes* (1869) and *Romances sans paroles* (1874). He was closely associated with Rimbaud and was a precursor of the symbolists

verligte (fəˈləxtə) *n* (in South Africa) **a** (during apartheid) a person of any of the White political parties who supported liberal trends in government policy **b** (*as modifier*): *verligte politics* [c20: from Afrikaans (adj), literally: enlightened]

Vermeer (veəˈmɪə; *Dutch* vərˈmeːr) *n* **Jan** (jɑn). full name *Jan van der Meer van Delft* 1632–75, Dutch genre painter, noted esp for his masterly treatment of light

vermeil (ˈvɜːmeɪl) *n* **1** gilded silver, bronze, or other metal, used esp in the 19th century **2 a** vermilion **b** (*as adjective*): *vermeil shoes* [c15: from Old French, from Late Latin *vermiculus* insect (of the genus *Kermes*) or the red dye prepared from it, from Latin: little worm]

vermi- *combining form* worm: *vermicide; vermiform; vermifuge* [from Latin *vermis* worm]

vermicelli (ˌvɜːmɪˈsɛlɪ; *Italian* vermiˈtʃɛlli) *n* **1** very fine strands of pasta, used in soups **2** tiny chocolate strands used to coat cakes, etc [c17: from Italian: little worms, from *verme* a worm, from Latin *vermis*]

vermicide (ˈvɜːmɪˌsaɪd) *n* any substance used to kill worms ▷ ˌvermiˈcidal *adj*

vermicular (vɜːˈmɪkjʊlə) *adj* **1** resembling the form, markings, motion, or tracks of worms **2** of or relating to worms or wormlike animals [c17: from Medieval Latin *vermiculāris*, from Latin *vermiculus*, diminutive of *vermis* worm]

vermiculate (vɜːˈmɪkjʊˌleɪt) *vb* **1** (*tr*) to decorate with wavy or wormlike tracery or markings ▷ *adj* (vɜːˈmɪkjʊlɪt, -ˌleɪt) **2** vermicular; sinuous [c17: from Latin *vermiculātus* in the form of worms, from *vermis* worm]

vermiculite (vɜːˈmɪkjʊˌlaɪt) *n* any of a group of micaceous minerals consisting mainly of hydrated silicate of magnesium, aluminium, and iron: on heating they expand and exfoliate and in this form are used in heat and sound insulation, fireproofing, and as a bedding medium for young plants [c19: from VERMICUL(AR) + -ITE¹]

vermiform (ˈvɜːmɪˌfɔːm) *adj* resembling a worm

vermiform appendix or **vermiform process** *n* a wormlike pouch extending from the lower end of the caecum in some mammals. In man it is vestigial. Also called: **appendix**

vermifuge (ˈvɜːmɪˌfjuːdʒ) *n* any drug or agent able to destroy or expel intestinal worms; an anthelmintic ▷ vermifugal (ˌvɜːmɪˈfjuːgᵊl) *adj*

vermilion or **vermillion** (vəˈmɪljən) *n* **1 a** a bright red to reddish-orange colour **b** (*as adjective*): *a vermilion car* **2** mercuric sulphide, esp when used as a bright red pigment; cinnabar [c13: from Old French *vermeillon*, from VERMEIL]

vermin (ˈvɜːmɪn) *n* **1** (*functioning as plural*) small animals collectively, esp insects and rodents, that are troublesome to man, domestic animals, etc **2** (*pl* -min) an unpleasant, obnoxious, or dangerous person [c13: from Old French *vermine*, from Latin *vermis* a worm] ▷ ˈverminous *adj*

vermis (ˈvɜːmɪs) *n, pl* -mes (-miːz) *anatomy* the middle lobe connecting the two halves of the cerebellum [c19: via New Latin from Latin: worm]

Vermont (vɜːˈmɒnt) *n* a state in the northeastern US: crossed from north to south by the Green Mountains; bounded on the east by the Connecticut River and by Lake Champlain in the northwest Capital: Montpelier. Pop: 619 107 (2003 est). Area: 24 887 sq km (9609 sq miles). Abbreviations: Vt (with zip code) VT ▷ Verˈmonter *n*

vermouth (ˈvɜːməθ, vəˈmuːθ) *n* any of several wines containing aromatic herbs and some other flavourings [c19: from French, from German *Wermut* WORMWOOD (absinthe)]

vernacular (vəˈnækjʊlə) *n* **1** the vernacular the commonly spoken language or dialect of a particular people or place **2** a local style of architecture, in which ordinary houses are built: *this architect has re-created a true English vernacular* ▷ *adj* **3** relating to, using, or in the vernacular **4** designating or relating to the common name of an animal or plant **5** built in the local style of ordinary houses, rather than a grand architectural style [c17: from Latin *vernāculus* belonging to a household slave, from *verna* household slave] ▷ verˈnacularly *adv*

vernal (ˈvɜːnᵊl) *adj* **1** of or occurring in spring **2** *poetic* of or characteristic of youth; fresh [c16: from Latin *vernālis*, from *vēr* spring] ▷ ˈvernally *adv*

vernal equinox *n* the time at which the sun crosses the plane of the equator towards the relevant hemisphere, making day and night of equal length. It occurs about March 21 in the N hemisphere (Sept 23 in the S hemisphere)

vernal grass *n* any of various Eurasian grasses of the genus *Anthoxanthum*, such as *A. odoratum* (**sweet vernal grass**), having the fragrant scent of coumarin

vernalize or **vernalise** (ˈvɜːnəˌlaɪz) *vb* to subject ungerminated or germinating seeds to low temperatures, which is essential for many (plants) of temperate environments to ensure germination in some and flowering in others ▷ ˌvernaliˈzation or ˌvernaliˈsation *n*

vernation (vɜːˈneɪʃən) *n* the way in which leaves are

arranged in the bud [c18: from New Latin *vernātiō*, from Latin *vernāre* to be springlike, from *vēr* spring]

Verne (vɜːn; *French* vɛrn) *n* **Jules** (ʒyl). 1828–1905, French writer, esp of science fiction, such as *Twenty Thousand Leagues under the Sea* (1870) and *Around the World in Eighty Days* (1873)

vernier ('vɜːnɪə) *n* **1** a small movable scale running parallel to the main graduated scale in certain measuring instruments, such as theodolites, used to obtain a fractional reading of one of the divisions on the main scale **2** (*modifier*) relating to or fitted with a vernier: *a vernier scale; a vernier barometer* [c18: named after Paul Vernier (1580–1637), French mathematician, who described the scale]

vernissage (,vɜːnɪ'sɑːʒ) *n* a preview or the opening or first day of an exhibition of paintings [French, from *vernis* VARNISH]

Vernoleninsk (*Russian* vɪrnəlɪ'njiːnsk) *n* the former name of **Nikolayev**

Verny (*Russian* 'vjɛrnɪj) *n* a former name (until 1927) of **Almaty**

Verona (və'rəʊnə; *Italian* ve'roːna) *n* a city in N Italy, in Veneto on the Adige River: strategically situated at the junction of major routes between Italy and N Europe; became a Roman colony (89 BC); under Austrian rule (1797–1866); many Roman remains. Pop: 253 208 (2001) > Veronese (,vɛrə'niːz) *adj, n*

Veronese (*Italian* vero'neːse) *n* **Paolo** ('paːolo), original name Paolo Cagliari or Caliari. 1528–88, Italian painter of the Venetian school. His works include *The Marriage at Cana* (1563) and *The Feast of the Levi* (1573)

veronica¹ (və'rɒnɪkə) *n* any scrophulariaceous plant of the genus *Veronica*, esp the speedwells, of temperate and cold regions, having small blue, pink, or white flowers and flattened notched fruits [c16: from Medieval Latin, perhaps from the name *Veronica*]

veronica² (və'rɒnɪkə) *n* *bullfighting* a pass in which the matador slowly swings the cape away from the charging bull [from Spanish, from the name *Veronica*]

Verrazano or **Verrazzano** (*Italian* verra'tsaːno) *n* **Giovanni da** (dʒo'vanni da). ?1485–?1528, Florentine navigator; the first European to sight what was to become New York (1524)

Verrocchio (və'rəʊkɪ,əʊ; *Italian* ver'rɔkkjo) *n* **Andrea del** (an'drɛːa del). 1435–88, Italian sculptor, painter, and goldsmith of the Florentine school: noted esp for the equestrian statue of Bartolommeo Colleoni in Venice

verruca (və'ruːkə) *n, pl* **-cae** (-siː) or **-cas** **1** *pathol* a wart, esp one growing on the hand or foot **2** *biology* a wartlike outgrowth, as in certain plants or on the skin of some animals [c16: from Latin: wart]

verrucose ('vɛrʊ,kəʊs) or **verrucous** ('vɛrʊkəs, və'ruːkəs) *adj* *botany* covered with warty processes [c17: from Latin *verrūcōsus* full of warts, from *verrūca* a wart] > verrucosity (,vɛrʊ'kɒsɪtɪ) *n*

Versace (*Italian* ver'satʃe) *n* **1 Donatella** (dona'tɛlla). born 1955, Italian fashion designer and businesswoman; creative director of the Versace group from 1997 **2** her brother, **Gianni** ('dʒanni). 1946–97, Italian fashion designer

Versailles (vɛə'saɪ, -'seɪlz; *French* vɛrsaj) *n* **1** a city in N central France, near Paris: site of an elaborate royal residence built for Louis XIV; seat of the French kings (1682–1789). Pop: 85 726 (1999) **2 Treaty of Versailles** the treaty of 1919 imposed upon Germany by the Allies (except for the US and the Soviet Union): the most important of the five peace treaties that concluded World War I

versant ('vɜːsᵊnt) *n* **1** *rare* the side or slope of a mountain or mountain range **2** the slope of a region [c19: from French, from *verser* to turn, from Latin *versāre*]

versatile ('vɜːsə,taɪl) *adj* **1** capable of or adapted for many different uses, skills, etc **2** variable or changeable **3** *botany* (of an anther) attached to the filament by a small area so that it moves freely in the wind **4** *zoology* able to turn forwards and backwards [c17: from Latin *versātilis* moving around, from *versāre* to turn] > 'versa,tilely *adv* > versatility (,vɜːsə'tɪlɪtɪ) *n*

verse (vɜːs) *n* **1** (not in technical usage) a stanza or other short subdivision of a poem **2** poetry as distinct from prose **3 a** a series of metrical feet forming a rhythmic unit of one line **b** (as modifier): *verse line* **4** a specified type of metre or metrical structure: *iambic verse* **5** one of the series of short subsections into which most of the writings in the Bible are divided **6** a metrical composition; poem ▷ *vb* **7** a rare word for **versify** [Old English *vers*, from Latin *versus* a furrow, literally: a turning (of the plough), from *vertere* to turn]

versed (vɜːst) *adj* (*postpositive*; foll by *in*) thoroughly knowledgeable (about), acquainted (with), or skilled (in)

versed sine *n* a trigonometric function equal to one minus the cosine of the specified angle [c16: from New Latin *sinus versus*, from SINE¹ + *versus* turned, from *vertere* to turn]

versicle ('vɜːsɪkᵊl) *n* **1** a short verse **2** a short sentence recited or sung by the minister at a liturgical ceremony and responded to by the choir or congregation [c14: from Latin *versiculus* a little line, from *versus* VERSE]

versicolour or US **versicolor** ('vɜːsɪ,kʌlə) *adj* of variable or various colours [c18: from Latin *versicolor*, from *versāre* to turn + *color* COLOUR]

versification (,vɜːsɪfɪ'keɪʃən) *n* **1** the technique or art of versifying **2** the form or metrical composition of a poem **3** a metrical version of a prose text

versify ('vɜːsɪ,faɪ) *vb* **-fies, -fying, -fied 1** (*tr*) to render (something) into metrical form or verse **2** (*intr*) to write in verse [c14: from Old French *versifier*, from Latin *versificāre*, from *versus* VERSE + *facere* to make] > 'versi,fier *n*

version ('vɜːʃən, -ʒən) *n* **1** an account of a matter from a certain point of view, as contrasted with others: *his version of the accident is different from the policeman's* **2** a translation, esp of the Bible, from one language into another **3** a variant form of something; type **4** an adaptation, as of a book or play into a film **5** *med* manual turning of a fetus to correct an irregular position within the uterus [c16: from Medieval Latin *versiō* a turning, from Latin *vertere* to turn] > 'versional *adj*

vers libre *French* (vɛr librə) *n* (in French poetry) another term for **free verse**

verso ('vɜːsəʊ) *n, pl* **-sos 1 a** the back of a sheet of printed paper **b** Also called: **reverso** the left-hand pages of a book, bearing the even numbers. See **recto 2** the side of a coin opposite to the obverse; reverse [c19: from the New Latin phrase *versō foliō* the leaf having been turned, from Latin *vertere* to turn + *folium* a leaf]

verst (vɛəst, vɜːst) *n* a unit of length, used in Russia, equal to 1.067 kilometres (0.6629 miles) [c16: from French *verste* or German *Werst*, from Russian *versta* line]

versus ('vɜːsəs) *prep* **1** (esp in a competition or lawsuit) against; in opposition to. Abbreviation: **v**, (esp US) **vs 2** as opposed to; in contrast with [c15: from Latin: turned (in the direction of), opposite, from *vertere* to turn]

vertebra ('vɜːtɪbrə) *n, pl* **-brae** (-briː) or **-bras** one of the bony segments of the spinal column [c17: from Latin: joint of the spine, from *vertere* to turn] > 'vertebral *adj* > 'vertebrally *adv*

vertebral column *n* another name for **spinal column**

vertebrate ('vɜːtɪ,breɪt, -brɪt) *n* **1** any chordate animal of the subphylum *Vertebrata*, characterized by a bony or cartilaginous skeleton and a well-developed brain: the group contains fishes, amphibians, reptiles, birds, and mammals ▷ *adj* **2** of, relating to, or belonging to the subphylum *Vertebrata*

vertebration (,vɜːtɪ'breɪʃən) *n* the formation of vertebrae or segmentation resembling vertebrae

vertex ('vɜːtɛks) *n, pl* **-texes** or **-tices** (-tɪ,siːz) **1** the highest point **2** *maths* **a** the point opposite to the base of a figure **b** the point of intersection of two sides of a plane figure or angle **c** the point of intersection of a pencil of lines or three or more planes of a solid figure **3** *anatomy* the crown of the head [c16: from Latin: highest point, from *vertere* to turn]

vertical ('vɜːtɪkᵊl) *adj* **1** at right angles to the horizon; perpendicular; upright: *a vertical wall* **2** extending in a perpendicular direction **3** at or in the vertex or zenith; directly overhead **4** *economics* of or relating to associated or consecutive, though not identical, stages of industrial activity: *vertical integration; vertical amalgamation*

5 of or relating to the vertex **6** *anatomy* of, relating to, or situated at the top of the head (vertex) ▷ *n* **7** a vertical plane, position, or line **8** a vertical post, pillar, or other structural member [c16: from Late Latin *verticâlis*, from Latin VERTEX] > verticality (ˌvɜːtɪˈkælɪtɪ) *n*
> 'vertically *adv*

vertical angles *pl n* *geometry* the pair of equal angles between a pair of intersecting lines; opposite angles

vertical mobility *n* *sociol* the movement of individuals or groups to positions in society that involve a change in class, status, and power

vertices ('vɜːtɪˌsiːz) *n* (in technical and scientific senses only) a plural of **vertex**

verticil ('vɜːtɪˌsɪl) *n* *biology* a circular arrangement of parts about an axis, esp leaves around a stem [c18: from Latin *verticillus* whorl (of a spindle), from VERTEX]
> ver'ticillate *adj*

vertiginous (vɜːˈtɪdʒɪnəs) *adj* **1** of, relating to, or having vertigo **2** producing dizziness **3** whirling **4** changeable; unstable [c17: from Latin *vertîginôsus*, from VERTIGO]
> ver'tiginously *adv*

vertigo ('vɜːtɪˌɡəʊ) *n*, *pl* vertigoes *or* vertigines (vɜːˈtɪdʒɪˌniːz) *pathol* a sensation of dizziness or abnormal motion resulting from a disorder of the sense of balance [c16: from Latin: a whirling round, from *vertere* to turn]

vertu (vɜːˈtuː) *n* a variant spelling of **virtu**

Vertumnus (vɜːˈtʌmnəs) *or* **Vortumnus** *n* a Roman god of gardens, orchards, and seasonal change [from Latin, from *vertere* to turn, change]

Verulamium (ˌvɛrʊˈleɪmɪəm) *n* the Latin name of **Saint Albans**

vervain ('vɜːveɪn) *n* any of several verbenaceous plants of the genus *Verbena*, having square stems and long slender spikes of purple, blue, or white flowers [c14: from Old French *verveine*, from Latin *verbêna* sacred bough; see VERBENA]

verve (vɜːv) *n* great vitality, enthusiasm, and liveliness; sparkle [c17: from Old French: garrulity, from Latin *verba* words, chatter]

vervet ('vɜːvɪt) *n* a variety of a South African guenon monkey, *Cercopithecus aethiops*, having dark hair on the hands and feet and a reddish patch beneath the tail [c19: from French, from *vert* green, but influenced by GRIVET]

Verwoerd (fəˈvʊt, fɛəˈvʊət) *n* **Hendrik Frensch** ('hɛndrɪk frɛns). 1901–66, South African statesman, born in the Netherlands: prime minister of South Africa (1958–66) and the principal architect of the apartheid system: assassinated

very ('vɛrɪ) *adv* **1** (intensifier) used to add emphasis to adjectives that are able to be graded: *very good; very tall* ▷ *adj* (prenominal) **2** (intensifier) used with nouns preceded by a definite article or possessive determiner, in order to give emphasis to the significance, appropriateness or relevance of a noun in a particular context, or to give exaggerated intensity to certain nouns: *the very man I want to see; his very name struck terror; the very back of the room* **3** (intensifier) used in metaphors to emphasize the applicability of the image to the situation described: *he was a very lion in the fight* **4** *archaic* real or true; genuine: *the very living God* [c13: from Old French *verai* true, from Latin *vêrax* true, from *vêrus* true]
- USAGE In strict usage adverbs of degree such as *very*,
- *too*, *quite*, *really*, and *extremely* are used only to qualify
- adjectives: *he is very happy; she is too sad*. By this rule,
- these words should not be used to qualify past
- participles that follow the verb *to be*, since they would
- then be technically qualifying verbs. With the
- exception of certain participles, such as *tired* or
- *disappointed*, that have come to be regarded as
- adjectives, all other past participles are qualified by
- adverbs such as *much*, *greatly*, *seriously*, or *excessively: he*
- *has been much* (not *very*) *inconvenienced; she has been*
- *excessively* (not *too*) *criticized*

very high frequency *n* a radio-frequency band or radio frequency lying between 30 and 300 megahertz. Abbreviation: VHF

Very light ('vɛrɪ) *n* a coloured flare fired from a special pistol (**Very pistol**) for signalling at night, esp at sea [c19: named after Edward W. Very (1852–1910), US naval ordnance officer]

very low frequency *n* a radio-frequency band or radio frequency lying between 3 and 30 kilohertz. Abbreviation: VLF

Vesalius (vɪˈseɪlɪəs) *n* **Andreas** (anˈdreːas). 1514–64, Flemish anatomist, whose *De Humani Corporis fabrica* (1543) formed the basis of modern anatomical research and medicine

vesica ('vɛsɪkə) *n*, *pl* -cae (-ˌsiː) *anatomy* a technical name for **bladder** (sense 1) [c17: from Latin: bladder, sac, blister] > vesical *adj* > vesiculate (vɛˈsɪkjʊˌleɪt, lɪt) *vb*, *adj*

vesicant ('vɛsɪkənt) *or* **vesicatory** ('vɛsɪˌkeɪtərɪ) *n*, *pl* -cants *or* -catories **1** any substance that causes blisters, used in medicine and in chemical warfare ▷ *adj* **2** acting as a vesicant [c19: see VESICA]

vesicate ('vɛsɪˌkeɪt) *vb* to blister [c17: from New Latin *vêsîcâre* to blister; see VESICA] > ˌvesi'cation *n*

vesicle ('vɛsɪkᵊl) *n* **1** *pathol* **a** any small sac or cavity, esp one containing serous fluid **b** a blister **2** *geology* a rounded cavity within a rock formed during solidification by expansion of the gases present in the magma **3** *botany* a small bladder-like cavity occurring in certain seaweeds and aquatic plants **4** any small cavity or cell [c16: from Latin *vêsîcula*, diminutive of VESICA] > vesicular (vɛˈsɪkjʊlə) *adj*

Vespasian (vɛsˈpeɪʒɪən) *n* Latin name *Titus Flavius Sabinus Vespasianus*. 9–79 AD, Roman emperor (69–79), who consolidated Roman rule, esp in Britain and Germany. He began the building of the Colosseum

vesper ('vɛspə) *n* **1** an evening prayer, service, or hymn **2** an archaic word for **evening** **3** (modifier) of or relating to vespers ▷ See also **vespers** [c14: from Latin: evening, the evening star; compare Greek *hesperos* evening; see WEST]

vespers ('vɛspəz) *n* (functioning as singular or plural) **1** chiefly RC Church the sixth of the seven canonical hours of the divine office, originally fixed for the early evening and now often made a public service on Sundays and major feast days **2** another word for **evensong** (sense 1)

vespertine ('vɛspəˌtaɪn) *adj* **1** *botany*, *zoology* appearing, opening, or active in the evening: *vespertine flowers* **2** occurring in the evening or (esp of stars) appearing or setting in the evening

vespiary ('vɛspɪərɪ) *n*, *pl* -aries a nest or colony of social wasps or hornets [c19: from Latin *vespa* a wasp, on the model of *apiary*]

vespid ('vɛspɪd) *n* **1** any hymenopterous insect of the family *Vespidae*, including the common wasps and hornets ▷ *adj* **2** of, relating to, or belonging to the family *Vespidae* [c19: from New Latin *Vespidae*, from Latin *vespa* a wasp] [c19: from Latin *vespa* a wasp] > vespine ('vɛspaɪn) *adj*

Vespucci (vɛˈspuːtʃɪ) *n* **Amerigo** (ameˈriːɡo), Latin name *Americus Vespucius*. ?1454–1512, Florentine navigator in the New World (1499–1500; 1501–02), after whom the continent of America was named

vessel ('vɛsᵊl) *n* **1** any object used as a container, esp for a liquid **2** a passenger or freight-carrying ship, boat, etc **3** *anatomy* a tubular structure that transports such body fluids as blood and lymph **4** *botany* a tubular element of xylem tissue consisting of a row of cells in which the connecting cell walls have broken down **5** *rare* a person regarded as an agent or vehicle for some purpose or quality [c13: from Old French *vaissel*, from Late Latin *vascellum* urn, from Latin *vâs* vessel]

vest (vɛst) *n* **1** an undergarment covering the body from the shoulders to the hips, made of cotton, nylon, etc. US and Canadian equivalent: undershirt. Austral. equivalent: **singlet 2** a similar sleeveless garment worn as outerwear. Austral. equivalent: **singlet 3** US, Canadian & Austral. a man's sleeveless waistlength garment worn under a suit jacket, usually buttoning up the front. Also called (in Britain and certain other countries): waistcoat **4** *obsolete* any form of dress, esp a long robe ▷ *vb* **5** (*tr*; foll by *in*) to place or settle (power, rights, etc, in): *power was vested in the committee* **6** (*tr*; foll by *with*) to bestow or confer (on): *the company was vested with authority* **7** (usually foll by *in*) to confer (a right, title, property, etc, upon) or (of a right, title, etc) to pass (to) or devolve (upon) **8** (tr) to clothe or array **9** (intr) to put on clothes, ecclesiastical vestments, etc [c15: from Old French *vestir* to clothe, from Latin *vestīre*, from *vestis* clothing]

vesta ('vɛstə) *n* a short friction match, usually of wood [c19: named after the goddess; see VESTA]

Vesta ('vɛstə) *n* the Roman goddess of the hearth and its fire. In her temple a perpetual flame was tended by the vestal virgins. Greek counterpart: Hestia

vestal ('vɛstᵊl) *adj* **1** chaste or pure; virginal **2** of or relating to the Roman goddess Vesta ▷ *n* **3** a chaste woman; virgin **4** a rare word for **nun¹** (sense 1)

vestal virgin *n* (in ancient Rome) one of the four, later six, virgin priestesses whose lives were dedicated to Vesta and to maintaining the sacred fire in her temple

vested ('vɛstɪd) *adj property law* having a present right to the immediate or future possession and enjoyment of property

vested interest *n* **1** *property law* an existing and disposable right to the immediate or future possession and enjoyment of property **2** a strong personal concern in a state of affairs, system, etc, usually resulting in private gain **3** a person or group that has such an interest

vestiary ('vɛstɪərɪ) *n, pl* -**aries** *obsolete* a room for storing clothes or dressing in, such as a vestry [c17: from Late Latin *vestiārius*, from *vestis* clothing]

vestibule ('vɛstɪ,bjuːl) *n* **1** a small entrance hall or anteroom; lobby **2** any small bodily cavity or space at the entrance to a passage or canal [c17: from Latin *vestibulum*]

vestige ('vɛstɪdʒ) *n* **1** a small trace, mark, or amount; hint: *a vestige of truth; no vestige of the meal* **2** *biology* an organ or part of an organism that is a small nonfunctioning remnant of a functional organ in an ancestor [c17: via French from Latin *vestīgium* track] ▷ ve'stigial *adj*

Vestmannaeyjar (,vɛstmæn'eɪjɑː) *n* a group of islands off the S coast of Iceland: they include the island of Surtsey (emerged 1963) and the volcano Helgafell (erupted 1974). Pop: 4027 (2007)

vestment ('vɛstmənt) *n* **1** a garment or robe, esp one denoting office, authority, or rank **2** any of various ceremonial garments worn by the clergy at religious services [c13: from Old French *vestiment*, from Latin *vestīmentum* clothing, from *vestīre* to clothe] ▷ vest'mental *adj*

vest-pocket *n* (*modifier*) *chiefly US* small enough to fit into a waistcoat pocket

vestry ('vɛstrɪ) *n, pl* -**tries** **1** a room in or attached to a church in which vestments, sacred vessels, etc, are kept **2** a room in or attached to some churches, used for Sunday school, meetings, etc **3** *Church of England* **a** a meeting of all the members of a parish or their representatives, to transact the official business of the parish **b** the body of members meeting for this; the parish council [c14: probably from Old French *vestiarie*; see VEST] ▷ 'vestral *adj*

vestryman ('vɛstrɪmən) *n, pl* -**men** a member of a church vestry

vesture ('vɛstʃə) *n* **1** *archaic* a garment or something that seems like a garment: *a vesture of cloud* ▷ *vb* **2** (tr) *archaic* to clothe [c14: from Old French, from *vestir*, from Latin *vestīre*, from *vestis* clothing] ▷ 'vestural *adj*

Vesuvius (vɪ'suːvɪəs) *n* a volcano in SW Italy, on the Bay of Naples: first recorded eruption in 79 AD, which destroyed Pompeii, Herculaneum, and Stabiae; numerous eruptions since then. Average height: 1220 m (4003 ft)

vet¹ (vɛt) *n* **1** short for **veterinary surgeon** ▷ *vb* vets, vetting, vetted **2** (tr) *chiefly Brit* to make a prior examination and critical appraisal of (a person, document, scheme, etc): *the candidates were well vetted* **3** to examine, treat, or cure (an animal)

vet² (vɛt) *n* *US & Canadian* short for **veteran** (senses 2, 3)

vet. *abbreviation* **1** veteran **2** veterinarian **3** veterinary

vetch (vɛtʃ) *n* **1** any of various climbing leguminous plants of the temperate genus *Vicia*, esp *V. sativa*, having pinnate leaves, typically blue or purple flowers, and

tendrils on the stems **2** any of various similar and related plants, such as *Lathyrus sativus*, cultivated in parts of Europe, and the kidney vetch **3** the beanlike fruit of any of these plants [c14 *fecche*, from Old French *veche*, from Latin *vicia*]

vetchling ('vɛtʃlɪŋ) *n* any of various leguminous tendril-climbing plants of the genus *Lathyrus*, esp *L. pratensis* (**meadow vetchling**), mainly of N temperate regions, having winged or angled stems and showy flowers. See also **sweet pea**

veteran ('vɛtərən, 'vɛtrən) *n* **1 a** a person or thing that has given long service in some capacity **b** (*as modifier*): *veteran firemen* **2** a soldier who has seen considerable active service **3** *US & Canadian* a person who has served in the military forces [c16: from Latin *veterānus*, from *vetus* old]

veteran car *n* *Brit* a car constructed before 1919, esp one constructed before 1905. See **classic car**, **vintage car**

veterinary ('vɛtərɪnərɪ, 'vɛtrɪnrɪ) *adj* of or relating to veterinary medicine [c18: from Latin *veterīnārius* concerning draught animals, from *veterīnae* draught animals; related to *vetus* mature (hence able to bear a burden)]

veterinary medicine *or* **science** *n* the branch of medicine concerned with the health of animals and the treatment of injuries or diseases that affect them

veterinary surgeon *n* *Brit* a person suitably qualified and registered to practise veterinary medicine

veto ('viːtəʊ) *n, pl* -**toes** **1** the power to prevent legislation or action proposed by others; prohibition: *the presidential veto* **2** the exercise of this power ▷ *vb* -**toes**, -**toing**, -**toed** (tr) **3** to refuse consent to (a proposal, esp a government bill) **4** to prohibit, ban, or forbid: *her parents vetoed her trip* [c17: from Latin: I forbid, from *vetāre* to forbid] ▷ 'vetoer *n*

vex (vɛks) *vb* (tr) **1** to anger or annoy **2** to confuse; worry **3** *archaic* to agitate [c15: from Old French *vexer*, from Latin *vexāre* to jolt (in carrying), from *vehere* to convey] ▷ 'vexer *n* ▷ 'vexing *adj*

vexation (vɛk'seɪʃən) *n* **1** the act of vexing or the state of being vexed **2** something that vexes

vexatious (vɛk'seɪʃəs) *adj* **1** vexing or tending to vex **2** vexed **3** *law* (of a legal action or proceeding) instituted without sufficient grounds, esp so as to cause annoyance or embarrassment to the defendant ▷ vex'atiously *adv*

vexed (vɛkst) *adj* **1** annoyed, confused, or agitated **2** much debated and discussed (esp in the phrase **a vexed question**) ▷ vexedly ('vɛksɪdlɪ) *adv*

vexillology (,vɛksɪ'lɒlədʒɪ) *n* the study and collection of information about flags [c20: from Latin *vexillum* flag + -LOGY] ▷ ,vexil'lologist *n*

vexillum (vɛk'sɪləm) *n, pl* -**la** (-lə) **1** *ornithol* the vane of a feather **2** Also called: **standard** *botany* the largest petal of a papilionaceous flower [c18: from Latin: banner, perhaps from *vēlum* sail] ▷ 'vexillate *adj*

VF *abbreviation* video frequency

vg *abbreviation* very good

VG *abbreviation* Vicar General

VGA *abbreviation* video graphics array; a computing standard that has a resolution of 640 × 480 pixels with 16 colours or of 320 × 200 pixels with 256 colours. **SVGA** (**super VGA**) is a later version with higher spatial and colour resolution, esp 800 × 600 pixels with 256 colours

VHF *or* **vhf** *radio abbreviation* very high frequency

VHS *trademark abbreviation* video home system: a video cassette recording system using ½″ magnetic tape

vi *abbreviation* vide infra

VI *abbreviation* Virgin Islands

via ('vaɪə) *prep* by way of; by means of; through: *to London via Paris* [c18: from Latin *viā*, from *via* way]

viable ('vaɪəbᵊl) *adj* **1** capable of becoming actual, useful, etc; practicable: *a viable proposition* **2** (of seeds, eggs, etc) capable of normal growth and development **3** (of a fetus) having reached a stage of development at which further development can occur independently of the mother [c19: from French, from *vie* life, from Latin *vīta*] ▷ ,via'bility *n*

Via Dolorosa ('viːə ,dɒlə'rəʊsə) *n* the route followed by

Christ from the place of his condemnation to Calvary for his crucifixion [Latin, literally: sorrowful road]

viaduct ('vaɪəˌdʌkt) n a bridge, esp for carrying a road or railway across a valley, etc, consisting of a set of arches supported by a row of piers or towers [c19: from Latin *via* way + *dūcere* to bring, on the model of *aqueduct*]

Viagra (vaɪ'ægrə, viː-) n *trademark* a drug, sildenafil, that allows increased blood flow into the penis; used to treat erectile dysfunction in men

vial ('vaɪəl, vaɪl) n a less common variant of **phial** [c14 *fiole*, from Old French, from Old Provençal *fiola*, from Latin *phiala*, from Greek *phialē*; see PHIAL]

via media Latin ('vaɪə 'miːdɪə) n a compromise between two extremes; middle course

viand ('viːənd, 'vaɪ-) n 1 a type of food, esp a delicacy 2 (*plural*) provisions [c14: from Old French *viande*, ultimately from Latin *vīvenda* things to be lived on, from *vīvere* to live]

Viareggio (Italian via'reddʒo) n a town and resort in W Italy, in Tuscany on the Ligurian Sea. Pop: 61 103 (2001)

viatical (vaɪ'ætɪkᵊl) adj 1 of or denoting a road or a journey 2 *botany* (of a plant) growing by the side of a road [c19: from Latin *viāticus* belonging to a journey + -AL¹]

viatical settlement n the purchase by a charity of a life assurance policy owned by a person with only a short time to live, to enable that person to use the proceeds during his or her lifetime. See also **death futures**

viaticum (vaɪ'ætɪkəm) n, pl -ca (-kə) or -cums 1 *Christianity* Holy Communion as administered to a person dying or in danger of death 2 *rare* provisions or a travel allowance for a journey [c16: from Latin, from *viāticus* belonging to a journey, from *viāre* to travel, from *via* way]

vibes (vaɪbz) pl n 1 *informal* (esp in jazz) short for **vibraphone** 2 *slang* short for **vibrations**

Viborg n 1 ('viːbɔːj) the Swedish name for **Vyborg** 2 (Danish 'vibɔr) a town in N central Denmark, in Jutland: formerly a royal town and capital of Jutland. Pop: 33 192 (2004 est)

vibraculum (vaɪ'brækjʊləm) n, pl -la (-lə) *zoology* any of the specialized bristle-like polyps in certain bryozoans, the actions of which prevent parasites from settling on the colony [c19: from New Latin, from Latin *vibrāre* to brandish]

vibrant ('vaɪbrənt) adj 1 characterized by or exhibiting vibration; pulsating or trembling 2 giving an impression of vigour and activity 3 caused by vibration; resonant 4 (of colour) strong and vivid [c16: from Latin *vibrāre* to agitate] > '**vibrancy** n > '**vibrantly** adv

vibraphone ('vaɪbrəˌfəʊn) or esp US **vibraharp** ('vaɪbrəˌhɑːp) n a percussion instrument, used esp in jazz, consisting of a set of metal bars placed over tubular metal resonators, which are made to vibrate electronically > '**vibraˌphonist** n

vibrate (vaɪ'breɪt) vb 1 to move or cause to move back and forth rapidly; shake, quiver, or throb 2 (*intr*) to oscillate to send out (a sound) by vibration; resonate or cause to resonate 4 (*intr*) to waver 5 *physics* to undergo or cause to undergo an oscillatory or periodic process, as of an alternating current; oscillate 6 (*intr*) *rare* to respond emotionally; thrill [c17: from Latin *vibrāre*] > **vibratile** ('vaɪbrəˌtaɪl) adj > vi'**brating** adj > '**vibratory** adj

vibration (vaɪ'breɪʃən) n 1 the act or an instance of vibrating 2 *physics* **a** a periodic motion about an equilibrium position, such as the regular displacement of air in the propagation of sound **b** a single cycle of such a motion 3 the process or state of vibrating or being vibrated > vi'**brational** adj

vibrations (vaɪ'breɪʃənz) pl n *slang* 1 instinctive feelings supposedly influencing human communication 2 a characteristic atmosphere felt to be emanating from places or objects

vibration white finger n a condition affecting workers using vibrating machinery, which causes damage to the blood vessels and nerves of the fingers and leads to a permanent loss of feeling

vibrato (vɪ'brɑːtəʊ) n, pl -tos *music* 1 a slight, rapid, and regular fluctuation in the pitch of a note produced on a

stringed instrument by a shaking movement of the hand stopping the strings 2 an oscillatory effect produced in singing by fluctuation in breath pressure or pitch [c19: from Italian, from Latin *vibrāre* to VIBRATE]

vibrator (vaɪ'breɪtə) n **a** a device for producing a vibratory motion, such as one used in massage or in the distribution of wet concrete in moulds **b** such a device with a vibrating part or tip, used as a dildo

vibrissa (vaɪ'brɪsə) n, pl -sae (-siː) (*usually plural*) 1 any of the bristle-like sensitive hairs on the face of many mammals; a whisker 2 any of the specialized bristle-like feathers around the beak in certain insectivorous birds [c17: from Latin, probably from *vibrāre* to shake] > vi'**brissal** adj

viburnum (vaɪ'bɜːnəm) n 1 any of various temperate and subtropical caprifoliaceous shrubs or trees of the genus *Viburnum*, such as the wayfaring tree, having small white flowers and berry-like red or black fruits 2 the dried bark of several species of this tree, sometimes used in medicine [c18: from Latin: wayfaring tree]

vicar ('vɪkə) n 1 *Church of England* **a** (in Britain) a clergyman appointed to act as priest of a parish from which, formerly, he did not receive tithes but a stipend **b** a clergyman who acts as assistant to or substitute for the rector of a parish at Communion 2 *RC Church* a bishop or priest representing the pope or the ordinary of a diocese and exercising a limited jurisdiction 3 Also called: lay vicar, vicar choral *Church of England* a member of a cathedral choir appointed to sing certain parts of the services [c13: from Old French *vicaire*, from Latin *vicārius* (n) a deputy, from *vicārius* (adj) VICARIOUS] > '**vicarly** adj > **vicarial** (vɪ'kɛərɪəl, vaɪ-) adj > vi'**cariate** n

vicarage ('vɪkərɪdʒ) n the residence or benefice of a vicar

vicar apostolic n *RC Church* a titular bishop having jurisdiction in non-Catholic or missionary countries where the normal hierarchy has not yet been established

vicar general n, pl vicars general an official, usually a layman, appointed to assist the bishop of a diocese in discharging his administrative or judicial duties

vicarious (vɪ'kɛərɪəs, vaɪ-) adj 1 obtained or undergone at second hand through sympathetic participation in another's experiences 2 suffered, undergone, or done as the substitute for another: *vicarious punishment* 3 delegated: *vicarious authority* 4 taking the place of another [c17: from Latin *vicārius* substituted, from *vicis* interchange; see VICE³, VICISSITUDE]

Vicar of Bray (breɪ) n a vicar (Simon Aleyn) appointed to the parish of Bray in Berkshire during Henry VIII's reign who changed his faith to Catholic when Mary I was on the throne and back to Protestant when Elizabeth I succeeded and so retained his living

Vicar of Christ n *RC Church* the Pope when regarded as Christ's earthly representative

vice¹ (vaɪs) n 1 an immoral, wicked, or evil habit, action, or trait 2 habitual or frequent indulgence in pernicious, immoral, or degrading practices 3 a specific form of pernicious conduct, esp prostitution or sexual perversion 4 a failing or imperfection in character, conduct, etc: *smoking is his only vice* 5 a bad trick or disposition, as of horses, dogs, etc [c13: via Old French from Latin *vitium* a defect]

vice² or US (often) **vise** (vaɪs) n 1 an appliance for holding an object while work is done upon it, usually having a pair of jaws ▷ vb 2 (*tr*) to grip (something) with or as if with a vice [c15: from Old French *vis* a screw, from Latin *vītis* vine, plant with spiralling tendrils (hence the later meaning)]

vice³ (vaɪs) adj 1 **a** (*prenominal*) serving in the place of or as a deputy for **b** (*in combination*): *viceroy* ▷ n 2 *informal* a person who serves as a deputy to another [c18: from Latin *vice*, from *vicis* interchange]

vice⁴ ('vaɪsɪ) prep instead of; as a substitute for [c16: from Latin, ablative of *vicis* change]

vice admiral n a commissioned officer of flag rank in certain navies, junior to an admiral and senior to a rear admiral

vice-chairman n, pl -men a person who deputizes for a chairman and serves in his place during his absence or indisposition > ˌvice-ˈchairmanship n

vice chancellor n 1 the chief executive or administrator at some British universities 2 (in the US) a judge in courts of equity subordinate to the chancellor 3 (formerly in England) a senior judge of the court of Chancery who acted as assistant to the Lord Chancellor 4 a person serving as the deputy of a chancellor > ˌvice-ˈchancellorˌship n

vicegerent (ˌvaɪsˈdʒɛrənt) n 1 a person appointed to exercise all or some of the authority of another, esp the administrative powers of a ruler; deputy 2 RC Church the Pope or any other representative of God or Christ on earth, such as a bishop ▷ adj 3 invested with or characterized by delegated authority [c16: from New Latin vicegerēns, from VICE³ + Latin gerere to manage] > ˌvice'gerency n

vicennial (vɪˈsɛnɪəl) adj 1 occurring every 20 years 2 relating to or lasting for a period of 20 years [c18: from Late Latin vīcennium period of twenty years, from Latin vicies twenty times + -ennium, from annus year]

Vicente (Portuguese viˈsetə) n Gil. ?1465–?1536, Portuguese dramatist, noted for his court entertainments, religious dramas, and comedies

Vicenza (Italian viˈtʃɛntsa) n a city in NE Italy, in Veneto: home of the 16th-century architect Andrea Palladio and site of some of his finest works. Pop: 107 223 (2001)

vice president n an officer ranking immediately below a president and serving as his deputy. A vice president takes the president's place during his absence or incapacity, after his death, and in certain other circumstances. Abbreviation: VP > ˌvice-ˈpresidency n

viceregal (ˌvaɪsˈriːgəl) adj 1 of or relating to a viceroy or his viceroyalty 2 chiefly Austral & NZ of or relating to a governor or governor general > ˌvice'regally adv

vicereine (ˌvaɪsˈreɪn) n 1 the wife of a viceroy 2 a female viceroy [c19: from French, from VICE³ + reine queen, from Latin rēgīna]

viceroy (ˈvaɪsrɔɪ) n a governor of a colony, country, or province who acts for and rules in the name of his sovereign or government Related adj: viceregal [c16: from French, from VICE³ + roy king, from Latin rex] > ˈviceroyˌship n > ˌvice'royalty n

vice squad n a police division to which is assigned the enforcement of gaming and prostitution laws

vice versa (ˈvaɪsɪ ˈvɜːsə) adv with the order reversed; the other way around [c17: from Latin: relations being reversed, from vicis change + vertere to turn]

Vichy (French viʃi; English ˈviːʃiː) n a town and spa in central France, on the River Allier: seat of the collaborationist government under Marshal Pétain (1940–44); mineral waters bottled for export. Pop: 26 528 (1999)

vichyssoise (French viʃiswaz) n a thick soup made from leeks, potatoes, chicken stock, and cream, usually served chilled [French, from (crème) Vichyssoise (glacée) (ice-cold cream) from Vichy]

vichy water n 1 (sometimes capital) a natural mineral water from springs at Vichy in France, reputed to be beneficial to the health 2 any sparkling mineral water resembling this

vicinage (ˈvɪsənɪdʒ) n now rare 1 the residents of a particular neighbourhood 2 a less common word for vicinity [c14: from Old French vicenage, from vicin neighbouring, from Latin vīcīnus; see VICINITY]

vicinal (ˈvɪsɪnəl) adj 1 neighbouring 2 (esp of roads) of or relating to a locality or neighbourhood [c17: from Latin vīcīnālis nearby, from vīcīnus, from vīcus a neighbourhood]

vicinity (vɪˈsɪnɪtɪ) n, pl -ties 1 a surrounding, adjacent, or nearby area; neighbourhood 2 the fact or condition of being close in space or relationship [c16: from Latin vīcīnitās, from vīcīnus neighbouring, from vīcus village]

vicious (ˈvɪʃəs) adj 1 wicked or cruel; villainous: a vicious thug 2 characterized by violence or ferocity: a vicious blow 3 informal unpleasantly severe; harsh: a vicious wind 4 characterized by malice: vicious lies 5 (esp of dogs, horses, etc) ferocious or hostile; dangerous 6 characterized by or leading to vice 7 invalidated by defects; unsound: a vicious inference [c14: from Old French vicieus, from Latin vitiōsus full of faults, from vitium a

defect] > ˈviciously adv > ˈviciousness n

vicious circle n 1 Also called: vicious cycle a situation in which an attempt to resolve one problem creates new problems that lead back to the original situation 2 logic a a form of reasoning in which a conclusion is inferred from premises the truth of which cannot be established independently of that conclusion b an explanation given in terms that cannot be understood independently of that which was to be explained

vicissitude (vɪˈsɪsɪˌtjuːd) n 1 variation or mutability in nature or life, esp successive alternation from one condition or thing to another 2 a variation in circumstance, fortune, character, etc [c16: from Latin vicissitūdō, from vicis change, alternation] > viˌcissiˈtudinary or viˌcissiˈtudinous adj

Vicksburg (ˈvɪksˌbɜːg) n a city in W Mississippi, on the Mississippi River: site of one of the most decisive campaigns (1863) of the American Civil War, in which the Confederates were besieged for nearly seven weeks before capitulating. Pop: 26 005 (2003 est)

Vicky (ˈvɪkɪ) n professional name of Victor Weisz. 1913–66, British left-wing political cartoonist, born in Germany

Vico (ˈviːkəʊ; Italian ˈviːko) n Giovanni Battista (dʒoˈvanni batˈtista). 1668–1744, Italian philosopher. In Scienza Nuova (1721) he postulated that civilizations rise and fall in evolutionary cycles, making use of myths, poetry, and linguistics as historical evidence

victim (ˈvɪktɪm) n 1 a person or thing that suffers harm, death, etc, from another or from some adverse act, circumstance, etc: victims of tyranny 2 a person who is tricked or swindled; dupe 3 a living person or animal sacrificed in a religious rite [c15: from Latin victima]

victimize or **victimise** (ˈvɪktɪˌmaɪz) vb (tr) 1 to punish or discriminate against selectively or unfairly 2 to make a victim of > ˌvictimiˈzation or ˌvictimiˈsation n > ˈvictimˌizer or ˈvictimˌiser n

victimology (ˌvɪktɪˈmɒlədʒɪ) n the study of the psychological effects experienced by the victims of crime > ˌvictiˈmologist n

victor (ˈvɪktə) n 1 a a person, nation, etc, that has defeated an adversary in war, etc b (as modifier): the victor army 2 the winner of any contest, conflict, or struggle [c14: from Latin, from vincere to conquer]

Victor Emmanuel II n 1820–78, king of Sardinia-Piedmont (1849–78) and first king of Italy from 1861

Victor Emmanuel III n 1869–1947, last king of Italy (1900–46): dominated after 1922 by Mussolini, whom he appointed as premier; abdicated

victoria (vɪkˈtɔːrɪə) n 1 a light four-wheeled horse-drawn carriage with a folding hood, two passenger seats, and a seat in front for the driver 2 Also called: victoria plum Brit a large sweet variety of plum, red and yellow in colour [c19: both after Queen Victoria]

Victoria¹ (vɪkˈtɔːrɪə) n 1 a state of SE Australia: part of New South Wales colony until 1851; semiarid in the northwest, with the Great Dividing Range in the centre and east and the Murray River along the N border. Capital: Melbourne. Pop: 4 947 985 (2003 est). Area: 227 620 sq km (87 884 sq miles) 2 Lake Victoria Also called: Victoria Nyanza a lake in East Africa, in Tanzania, Uganda, and Kenya, at an altitude of 1134 m (3720 ft): the largest lake in Africa and second largest in the world; drained by the Victoria Nile. Area: 69 485 sq km (26 828 sq miles) 3 a port in SW Canada, capital of British Columbia, on Vancouver Island: founded in 1843 by the Hudson's Bay Company; made capital of British Columbia in 1868; university (1963). Pop: 288 346 (2001) 4 the capital of the Seychelles, a port on NE Mahé. Pop: 25 500 (2004 est) 5 an urban area in S China, part of Hong Kong, on N Hong Kong Island: financial and administrative district; university (1911); the name tends not to be used officially since reunification of Hong Kong with China in 1997 6 Mount Victoria a mountain in SE Papua New Guinea: the highest peak of the Owen Stanley Range. Height: 4073 m (13 363 ft)

Victoria² n 1 (vɪkˈtɔːrɪə) 1819–1901, queen of the United Kingdom (1837–1901) and empress of India (1876–1901). She married Prince Albert of Saxe-Coburg-Gotha (1840). Her sense of vocation did much to restore the prestige of the British monarchy **2** (*Spanish* bik'torja) **Tomás Luis de.** ?1548–1611, Spanish composer of motets and masses in the polyphonic style

Victoria³ (vɪkˈtɔːrɪə) *n* the Roman goddess of victory. Greek counterpart: Nike

Victoria and Albert Museum *n* a museum of the fine and applied arts in London, originating from 1856 and given its present name and site in 1899. Abbreviation: V and A

Victoria Cross *n* the highest decoration for gallantry in the face of the enemy awarded to the British and Commonwealth armed forces: instituted in 1856 by Queen Victoria

Victoria Day *n* the Monday preceding May 24: observed in Canada as a national holiday in commemoration of the birthday of Queen Victoria

Victoria Desert *n* See **Great Victoria Desert**

Victoria Falls *pl n* a major waterfall on the border between Zimbabwe and Zambia, on the Zambezi River. Height: about 108 m (355 ft). Width: about 1400 m (4500 ft)

Victoria Island *n* a large island in the Canadian Arctic, in Nunavut and the Northwest Territories. Area: about 212 000 sq km (82 000 sq miles)

Victoria Land *n* a section of Antarctica, largely in the Ross Dependency on the Ross Sea

Victorian (vɪkˈtɔːrɪən) *adj* **1** of, relating to, or characteristic of Queen Victoria or the period of her reign **2** exhibiting the characteristics popularly attributed to the Victorians, esp prudery, bigotry, or hypocrisy. See **Victorian values 3** denoting, relating to, or having the style of architecture used in Britain during the reign of Queen Victoria, characterized by massive construction and elaborate ornamentation **4** of or relating to Victoria (the state or any of the cities) ▷ *n* **5** a person who lived during the reign of Queen Victoria **6** an inhabitant of Victoria (the state or any of the cities) > Vicˈtorianˌism *n*

Victoriana (vɪkˌtɔːrɪˈɑːnə) *pl n* objects, ornaments, etc, of the Victorian period

Victoria Nile *n* See **Nile**

Victorian values *pl n* qualities considered to characterize the Victorian period, including enterprise and initiative and the importance of the family. See **Victorian** (sense 2)

victorious (vɪkˈtɔːrɪəs) *adj* **1** having defeated an adversary: *the victorious nations* **2** relating to, indicative of, or characterized by victory: *a victorious conclusion* > vicˈtoriously *adv*

victory (ˈvɪktərɪ) *n*, *pl* -ries **1** final and complete superiority in a war **2** a successful military engagement **3** a success attained in a contest or struggle or over an opponent, obstacle, or problem **4** the act of triumphing or state of having triumphed [c14: from Old French *victorie*, from Latin *victōria*, from *vincere* to subdue]

Victory (ˈvɪktərɪ) *n* another name (in English) for the Roman goddess **Victoria** or the Greek **Nike**

victory roll *n* a roll of an aircraft made by a pilot to announce or celebrate the shooting down of an enemy plane or other cause for celebration

victual (ˈvɪtˀl) *vb* -uals, -ualling, -ualled *or US* -uals, -ualing, -ualed to supply with or obtain victuals. See also **victuals** [c14: from Old French *vitaille*, from Late Latin *victuālia* provisions, from Latin *victuālis* concerning food, from *victus* sustenance, from *vīvere* to live] > ˈvictual-less *adj*

victualler (ˈvɪtələ, ˈvɪtlə) *n* **1** a supplier of victuals, as to an army; sutler **2** *Brit* a licensed purveyor of spirits; innkeeper **3** a supply ship, esp one carrying foodstuffs

victuals (ˈvɪtˀlz) *pl n* (*sometimes singular*) food or provisions

vicuña (vɪˈkuːnjə) *or* **vicuna** (vɪˈkjuːnə) *n* **1** a tawny-coloured cud-chewing Andean artiodactyl mammal, *Vicugna vicugna*, similar to the llama: family *Camelidae* **2** the fine light cloth made from the wool obtained from this animal [c17: from Spanish *vicuña*, from Quechuan *wikúña*]

vid (vɪd) *n informal* short for **video** (sense 4)

Vidal (viːˈdæl) *n* **Gore.** born 1925, US novelist and essayist. His novels include *Julian* (1964), *Myra Breckinridge*

(1968), *Burr* (1974), *Lincoln* (1984), and *The Season of Conflict* (1996)

vide (ˈvaɪdɪ) (used to direct a reader to a specified place in a text, another book, etc) refer to, see (often in the phrases **vide ante** (see before), **vide infra** (see below), **vide post** (see after), **vide supra** (see above), **vide ut supra** (see as above), etc). Abbreviation: v, vid. [c16: from Latin]

videlicet (vɪˈdiːlɪˌset) *adv* namely: used to specify items, examples, etc. Abbreviation: viz. [c15: from Latin]

video (ˈvɪdɪˌəʊ) *adj* **1** relating to or employed in the transmission or reception of a televised image **2** of, concerned with, or operating at video frequencies ▷ *n*, *pl* -os **3** the visual elements of a television broadcast **4** a film recorded on a video cassette **5** short for **video cassette, video cassette recorder 6** *US* an informal name for **television** ▷ *vb* videos, videoing, videoed **7** to record (a television programme, etc) on a video cassette recorder ▷ See **audio** [c20: from Latin *vidēre* to see, on the model of AUDIO]

video call *n* a call made via a mobile phone with a camera and a screen, allowing the participants to see each other as they talk

video cassette *n* a cassette containing video tape

video cassette recorder *n* a tape recorder for vision and sound signals using magnetic tape in closed plastic cassettes: used for recording and playing back television programmes and films

videodisk (ˈvɪdɪəʊˌdɪsk) *n* another name for **optical disc**

videofit (ˈvɪdɪəʊˌfɪt) *n* a computer-generated picture of a person sought by the police, created by combining facial characteristics on the basis of witnesses' descriptions [c20: from VIDEO + (PHOTO)FIT]

video frequency *n* the frequency of a signal conveying the image and synchronizing pulses in a television broadcasting system. It lies in the range from about 50 hertz to 8 megahertz

video game *n* any of various games that can be played by using an electronic control to move points of light or graphical symbols on the screen of a visual display unit

video jockey *n* a person who introduces and plays videos, esp of pop songs, on a television programme

video memory *n computing* computer memory used for the processing and displaying of images

video nasty *n*, *pl* nasties a film, usually specially made for video, that is explicitly horrific, brutal, and pornographic

videophone (ˈvɪdɪəˌfəʊn) *n* a telephonic device in which there is both verbal and visual communication between parties

video tape *n* **1** magnetic tape used mainly for recording the vision and sound signals of a television programme or film for subsequent transmission ▷ *vb* video-tape **2** to record (a programme, film, etc) on video tape

video tape recorder *n* a tape recorder for vision signals and sometimes accompanying sound, using magnetic tape on open spools: used in television broadcasting

Videotex (ˈvɪdɪəʊˌteks) *n trademark* an information system that displays information from a distant computer on a television screen. See also **Teletext, Viewdata**

videotext (ˈvɪdɪəʊˌtekst) *n* a means of providing a written or graphical representation of computerized information on a television screen

vidicon (ˈvɪdɪˌkɒn) *n* a small television camera tube, used in closed-circuit television and outside broadcasts, in which incident light forms an electric charge pattern on a photoconductive surface. Scanning by a low-velocity electron beam discharges the surface, producing a current in an adjacent conducting layer [c20: from VID(EO) + ICON(OSCOPE)]

vie (vaɪ) *vb* vies, vying, vied (*intr*; foll by *with* or *for*) to contend for superiority or victory (with) or strive in competition (for) [c15: probably from Old French *envier* to challenge, from Latin *invītāre* to INVITE] > ˈvier *n* > ˈvying *adj*, *n*

Vienna (vɪˈenə) *n* the capital and the smallest state of Austria, in the northeast on the River Danube: seat of the Hapsburgs (1278–1918); residence of the Holy Roman Emperor (1558–1806); withstood sieges by Turks in 1529 and 1683; political and cultural centre in the 18th and 19th centuries, having associations with many composers; university (1365). Pop: 1 590 242 (2003 est). Area: 1075 sq km (415 sq miles). German name: **Wien** > **Viennese** (ˌviəˈniːz) *adj, n*

Vienne (French vjɛn) *n* **1** a department of W central France, in Poitou-Charentes region. Capital: Poitiers. Pop: 402 555 (2003 est). Area: 7044 sq km (2747 sq miles) **2** a town in SE France, on the River Rhône: extensive Roman remains. Ancient name: **Vienna 3** a river in SW central France, flowing west and north to the Loire below Chinon. Length: over 350 km (200 miles)

Vientiane (ˌvjɛntɪˈɑːn) *n* the administrative capital of Laos, in the south near the border with Thailand: capital of the kingdom of Vientiane from 1707 until taken by the Thais in 1827. Pop: 776 000 (2005 est)

Vierwaldstättersee (fiːrˈvaltʃtɛtərˌzeː) *n* the German name for (Lake) **Lucerne**

vies (fiːs) *adj South African slang* angry, furious, or disgusted [Afrikaans]

Vietnam (ˌvjɛtˈnæm) or **Viet Nam** *n* a republic in SE Asia: an ancient empire, conquered by France in the 19th century; occupied by Japan (1940–45) when the Communist-led Vietminh began resistance operations that were continued against restored French rule after 1945. In 1954 the country was divided along the 17th parallel, establishing North Vietnam (under the Vietminh) and South Vietnam (under French control), the latter becoming the independent **Republic of Vietnam** in 1955. From 1959 the country was dominated by war between the Communist Vietcong, supported by North Vietnam, and the South Vietnamese government; increasing numbers of US forces were brought to the aid of the South Vietnamese army until a peace agreement (1973) led to the withdrawal of US troops; further fighting led to the eventual defeat of the South Vietnamese government in March 1975 and in 1976 an elected National Assembly proclaimed the reunification of the country. Official language: Vietnamese. Religion: Buddhist majority. Currency: dong. Capital: Hanoi. Pop: 82 481 000 (2004 est). Area: 331 041 sq km (127 816 sq miles) > ˌVietnaˈmese *adj, n*

vieux jeu French (vjø ʒø) *adj* old-fashioned [literally: old game]

view (vjuː) *n* **1** the act of seeing or observing; an inspection **2** vision or sight, esp range of vision: *the church is out of view* **3** a scene, esp of a fine tract of countryside: *the view from the top was superb* **4** a pictorial representation of a scene, such as a photograph **5** (*sometimes plural*) opinion; thought: *my own view on the matter differs from yours* **6** (foll by *to*) a desired end or intention: *he has a view to securing further qualifications* **7** a general survey of a topic, subject, etc **8** visual aspect or appearance: *they look the same in outward view* **9** a sight of a hunted animal before or during the chase **10** in view of taking into consideration **11** on view exhibited to the public gaze **12** take a dim or poor view of to regard (something) with disfavour or disapproval **13** with a view to **a** with the intention of **b** in anticipation or hope of ⊳ *vb* **14** (*tr*) to look at **15** (*tr*) to consider in a specified manner: *they view the growth of Communism with horror* **16** (*tr*) to examine or inspect carefully: *to view the accounts* **17** (*tr*) to watch (television) **18** (*tr*) to sight (a hunted animal) before or during the chase [c15: from Old French *veue*, from *veoir* to see, from Latin *vidēre*] > ˈviewable *adj*

Viewdata (ˈvjuːˌdeɪtə) *n trademark* an interactive form of Videotex that sends information from a distant computer along telephone lines, enabling shopping, booking theatre and airline tickets, and banking transactions to be conducted from the home

viewer (ˈvjuːə) *n* **1** a person who views something, esp television **2** any optical device by means of which something is viewed, esp one used for viewing photographic transparencies

viewfinder (ˈvjuːˌfaɪndə) *n* a device on a camera, consisting of a lens system and sometimes a ground-glass screen, enabling the user to see what will be included in his photograph

view halloo *interj* a huntsman's cry uttered when the

quarry is seen breaking cover or shortly afterwards

viewing (ˈvjuːɪŋ) *n* **1** the act of watching television **2** television programmes collectively: *late-night viewing*

viewless (ˈvjuːlɪs) *adj* **1** (of windows, etc) not affording a view **2** having no opinions **3** *poetic* invisible

viewpoint (ˈvjuːˌpɔɪnt) *n* **1** the mental attitude that determines a person's opinions or judgments; point of view **2** a place from which something can be viewed

Vigée-Lebrun (French viʒeləbrœ̃) *n* (**Marie Louise**) **Élisabeth**. 1755–1842, French painter, noted for her portraits of women

vigesimal (vaɪˈdʒɛsɪməl) *adj* **1** relating to or based on the number 20 **2** taking place or proceeding in intervals of 20 **3** twentieth [c17: from Latin *vīgēsimus*, variant (influenced by *vigintī* twenty) of *vīcēsimus* twentieth]

vigia (ˈvɪdʒɪə) *n nautical* a navigational hazard marked on a chart although its existence and nature has not been confirmed [c19: from Spanish *vigía* reef, from Latin *vigilāre* to keep watch]

vigil (ˈvɪdʒɪl) *n* **1** a purposeful watch maintained, esp at night, to guard, observe, pray, etc **2** the period of such a watch **3** *RC Church, Church of England* the eve of certain major festivals, formerly observed as a night spent in prayer: often marked by fasting and abstinence and a special Mass and divine office [c13: from Old French *vigile*, from Medieval Latin *vigilia* watch preceding a religious festival, from Latin: vigilance, from *vigil* alert, from *vigēre* to be lively]

vigilance (ˈvɪdʒɪləns) *n* **1** the fact, quality, or condition of being vigilant **2** the abnormal state or condition of being unable to sleep

vigilance committee *n* (in the US) a self-appointed body of citizens organized to maintain order, punish crime, etc, where an efficient system of courts does not exist

vigilant (ˈvɪdʒɪlənt) *adj* keenly alert to or heedful of trouble or danger, as while others are sleeping or unsuspicious [c15: from Latin *vigilāns* keeping awake, from *vigilāre* to be watchful; see VIGIL] > ˈvigilantly *adv*

vigilante (ˌvɪdʒɪˈlæntɪ) *n US* a member of a vigilance committee. Also called: **vigilance man** [c19: from Spanish, from Latin *vigilāre* to keep watch]

vigilantism (ˌvɪdʒɪˈlænˌtɪzəm) *n US* the methods, conduct, attitudes, etc, associated with vigilantes, esp militancy, bigotry, or suspiciousness

Vigil Mass *n RC Church* a Mass held on Saturday evening, attendance at which fulfils one's obligation to attend Mass on Sunday

vigneron (ˈviːnjərɒn; French viɲrɔ̃) *n* a person who grows grapes for winemaking [French, from *vigne* vine]

vignette (vɪˈnjɛt) *n* **1** a small illustration placed at the beginning or end of a book or chapter **2** a short graceful literary essay or sketch **3** a photograph, drawing, etc, with edges that are shaded off **4** any small endearing scene, view, picture, etc ⊳ *vb* **5** to finish (a photograph, picture, etc) with a fading border in the form of a vignette **6** to portray in or as in a vignette [c18: from French, literally: little vine, from *vigne* VINE; with reference to the vine motif frequently used in embellishments to a text] > viˈgnettist *n*

Vignola (Italian viɲˈɲɔːla) *n* **Giacomo Barozzi da** (ˈdʒaːkomo baˈrɔttsi da). 1507–73, Italian architect, whose cruciform design for Il Gesù, Rome, greatly influenced later Church architecture

Vigny (French viɲi) *n* **Alfred Victor de** (alfrɛd viktɔr də). 1797–1863, French romantic poet, novelist, and dramatist, noted for his pessimistic lyric verse *Poèmes antiques et modernes* (1826) and *Les Destinées* (1864), the novel *Cinq-Mars* (1826), and the play *Chatterton* (1835)

Vigo (ˈviːɡəʊ; Spanish ˈbiɡo) *n* a port in NW Spain, in Galicia on **Vigo Bay** (an inlet of the Atlantic): site of a British and Dutch naval victory (1702) over the French and Spanish. Pop: 292 566 (2003 est)

vigoro (ˈvɪɡəˌrəʊ) *n Austral sport* a women's game similar to cricket with paddle-shaped bats, introduced into Australia in 1919 by its British inventor J. J. Grant [c20: from VIGOUR]

vigorous (ˈvɪɡərəs) *adj* **1** endowed with bodily or mental strength or vitality; robust **2** displaying, involving, characterized by, or performed with vigour: *vigorous growth* > **'vigorously** *adv*

vigour *or US* **vigor** ('vɪɡə) *n* **1** exuberant and resilient strength of body or mind; vitality **2** substantial effective energy or force: *the vigour of the tempest* **3** forcefulness; intensity: *the vigour of her complaints* **4** the capacity for survival or strong healthy growth in a plant or animal **5** the most active period or stage of life, manhood, etc; prime [c14: from Old French *vigeur*, from Latin *vigor* activity, from *vigēre* to be lively]

Viipuri ('vi:puri) *n* the Finnish name for **Vyborg**

Vijayawada (ˌviːdʒaɪəˈwɑːdə) *n* a town in SE India, in E central Andra Pradesh on the Krishna River: Hindu pilgrimage centre. Pop: 825 436 (2001). Former name: Bezwada

Viking ('vaɪkɪŋ) *n* (*sometimes not capital*) **1** Also called: **Norseman, Northman** any of the Danes, Norwegians, and Swedes who raided by sea most of N and W Europe from the 8th to the 11th centuries, later often settling, as in parts of Britain **2** (*modifier*) of, relating to, or characteristic of a Viking or Vikings: *a Viking ship* [c19: from Old Norse *vīkingr*, probably from *vīk* creek, sea inlet + -*ingr* (see -ING³); perhaps related to Old English *wīc* camp]

vile (vaɪl) *adj* **1** abominably wicked; shameful or evil **2** morally despicable; ignoble: *vile accusations* **3** disgusting to the senses or emotions; foul: *a vile smell; vile epithets* **4** tending to humiliate or degrade: *only slaves would perform such vile tasks* **5** unpleasant or bad: *vile weather* [c13: from Old French *vil*, from Latin *vīlis* cheap] > **'vilely** *adv* > **'vileness** *n*

vilify ('vɪlɪˌfaɪ) *vb* -**fies**, -**fying**, -**fied** (*tr*) to revile with abusive or defamatory language; malign [c15: from Late Latin *vīlificāre*, from Latin *vīlis* worthless + *facere* to make] > **vilification** (ˌvɪlɪfɪˈkeɪʃən) *n* > **'vili,fier** *n*

vilipend ('vɪlɪˌpɛnd) *vb* (*tr*) *rare* **1** to treat or regard with contempt **2** to speak slanderously or slightingly of [c15: from Late Latin *vīlipendere*, from Latin *vīlis* worthless + *pendere* to esteem] > **'vili,pender** *n*

villa ('vɪlə) *n* **1** (in ancient Rome) a country house, usually consisting of farm buildings and residential quarters around a courtyard **2** a large and usually luxurious country residence **3** *Brit* a detached or semidetached suburban house [c17: via Italian from Latin; related to Latin *vīcus* a village]

Villa ('viːə; *Spanish* 'biʎa) *n* **Francisco** (franˈsisko), called *Pancho Villa*, original name *Doroteo Arango*. ?1877–1923, Mexican revolutionary leader

Villach (*German* 'fɪlax) *n* a city in S central Austria, on the Drava River: nearby hot mineral springs. Pop: 57 497 (2002)

village ('vɪlɪdʒ) *n* **1** a small group of houses in a country area, larger than a hamlet **2** the inhabitants of such a community collectively **3** an incorporated municipality smaller than a town in various parts of the US and Canada **4** (*modifier*) of, relating to, or characteristic of a village: *a village green* [c15: from Old French, from *ville* farm, from Latin: VILLA] > **'villager** *n*

Villahermosa (*Spanish* biʎaɛrˈmosa) *n* a town in E Mexico, capital of Tabasco state: university (1959). Pop: 583 000 (2005 est). Former name: San Juan Bautista

villain ('vɪlən) *n* **1** a wicked or malevolent person **2** (in a novel, play, film, etc) the main evil character and antagonist to the hero **3** *obsolete* an uncouth person; boor [c14: from Old French *vilein* serf, from Late Latin *vīllānus* worker on a country estate, from Latin: VILLA] > **'villainess** *fem n*

villainous ('vɪlənəs) *adj* **1** of, like, or appropriate to a villain **2** very bad or disagreeable: *a villainous climate* > **'villainously** *adv* > **'villainousness** *n*

villainy ('vɪlənɪ) *n, pl* -**lainies** **1** conduct befitting a villain; vicious behaviour or action **2** an evil, abhorrent, or criminal act or deed **3** the fact or condition of being villainous

Villa-Lobos (*Portuguese* vilaˈlobus) *n* **Heitor** (ejˈtor). 1887–1959, Brazilian composer, much of whose work is based on Brazilian folk tunes

villanella (ˌvɪləˈnɛlə) *n, pl* -**las** a type of part song originating in Naples during the 16th century [c16: from Italian, from *villano* rustic, from Late Latin *vīllānus*; see VILLAIN]

villanelle (ˌvɪləˈnɛl) *n* a verse form of French origin consisting of 19 lines arranged in five tercets and a quatrain. The first and third lines of the first tercet recur alternately at the end of each subsequent tercet and both together at the end of the quatrain [c16: from French, from Italian VILLANELLA]

Villars (*French* vilar) *n* **Claude Louis Hector de** (klod lwi ɛktɔr də). 1653–1734, French marshal, distinguished for his command in the War of the Spanish Succession (1701–14)

-**ville** *n and adj combining form slang, chiefly US* (denoting) a place, condition, or quality with a character as specified: *dragsville; squaresville*

villein *or* **villain** ('vɪlən) *n* (in medieval Europe) a peasant personally bound to his lord, to whom he paid dues and services, sometimes commuted to rents, in return for his land [c14: from Old French *vilein* serf; see VILLAIN]

Villeneuve (*French* vilnœv) *n* **Pierre Charles Jean Baptiste Silvestre de** (pjɛr ʃarl ʒɑ̃ batist silvɛstrə də). 1763–1806, French admiral, defeated by Nelson at the Battle of Trafalgar (1805)

Villeurbanne (*French* vijœrban) *n* a town in E France: an industrial suburb of E Lyon. Pop: 124 215 (1999)

Villiers ('vɪləz, 'vɪljəz) *n* **George**. See (Dukes of) **Buckingham¹**

Villiers de l'Isle Adam (*French* vilje də lil adã) *n* **August, Comte de** (ogyst, kɔ̃t də). 1838–89, French poet and dramatist; pioneer of the symbolist movement. His works include *Contes cruels* (1883) and the play *Axel* (1885)

villiform ('vɪlɪˌfɔːm) *adj* having the form of a villus or a series of villi [c19: from New Latin *villiformis*, from Latin *villus* shaggy hair + -FORM]

Villon (*French* vijɔ̃) *n* **1 François** (frãswa). born 1431, French poet. His poems, such as those in *Le Petit testament* (?1456) and *Le Grand testament* (1461), are mostly ballades and rondeaux, verse forms that he revitalized. He was banished in 1463, after which nothing more was heard of him **2 Jacques** (ʒak), real name *Gaston Duchamp*. 1875–1963, French cubist painter and engraver

villus ('vɪləs) *n, pl* **villi** ('vɪlaɪ) (*usually plural*) **1** *zoology, anatomy* any of the numerous finger-like projections of the mucous membrane lining the small intestine of many vertebrates **2** any similar membranous process, such as any of those in the mammalian placenta **3** *botany* any of various hairlike outgrowths, as from the stem of a moss [c18: from Latin: shaggy hair]

Vilnius *or* **Vilnyus** ('vɪlnɪʊs) *n* the capital of Lithuania: passed to Russia in 1795; under Polish rule (1920–39); university (1578); an industrial and commercial centre. Pop: 544 000 (2005 est). Polish name: Wilno

vim (vɪm) *n slang* exuberant vigour and energy [c19: from Latin, from *vis*; related to Greek *is* strength]

Viminal ('vɪmɪnəl) *n* one of the seven hills on which ancient Rome was built [from Latin *Vīminālis Collis* the Viminal Hill, from *vīminālis* of osiers, from *vīmen* an osier, referring to the willow grove on the hill]

vimineous (vɪˈmɪnɪəs) *adj botany, now rare* having, producing, or resembling long flexible shoots [c17: from Latin *vīmineus* made of osiers, from *vīmen* flexible shoot]

vina ('viːnə) *n* a stringed musical instrument, esp of India, related to the sitar [c18: from Hindi *bīnā*, from Sanskrit *vīnā*]

vinaceous (vaɪˈneɪʃəs) *adj* **1** of, relating to, or containing wine **2** having a colour suggestive of red wine [c17: from Late Latin *vīnāceus*, from Latin *vīnum* wine]

Viña del Mar (*Spanish* 'biɲa ðɛl 'mar) *n* a city and resort in central Chile, just north of Valparaíso on the Pacific: the second largest city of Chile. Pop: 323 000 (2005 est)

vinaigrette (ˌvɪneɪˈɡrɛt) *n* **1** Also called: **vinegarette** a small decorative bottle or box with a perforated top, used for holding smelling salts, etc **2** Also called: **vinaigrette sauce** a salad dressing made from oil and vinegar with seasonings; French dressing [c17: from French, from *vinaigre* VINEGAR]

vinca ('vɪŋkə) *n* See **periwinkle²** [New Latin, from Latin *pervinca* periwinkle]

Vincennes (*French* vēsɛn; *English* vɪn'sɛnz) *n* a suburb of E Paris: 14th-century castle. Pop: 43 595 (1999)

Vincent de Paul ('vɪnsənt də 'pɔːl; *French* vēsɑ̃ də pɔl) *n* Saint. ?1581–1660, French Roman Catholic priest, who founded two charitable orders, the Lazarists (1625) and the Sisters of Charity (1634). Feast day: Sept 27

Vincent's angina *or* **disease** ('vɪnsənts) *n* an ulcerative bacterial infection of the mouth, esp involving the throat and tonsils [c20: named after J. H. *Vincent* (died 1950), French bacteriologist]

Vinci ('vɪntʃɪ) *n* See **Leonardo da Vinci**

vincible ('vɪnsɪbəl) *adj rare* capable of being defeated or overcome [c16: from Latin *vincibilis*, from *vincere* to conquer] > ˌvinci'bility *or* 'vincibleness *n*

vincristine (vɪn'krɪstiːn) *n* a cytotoxic drug used in the treatment of leukaemia, derived as an alkaloid from the tropical shrub Madagascar periwinkle (*Vinca rosea*) [c20: from New Latin VINCA + Latin *crista* crest + -INE[2]]

vinculum ('vɪŋkjʊləm) *n*, *pl* -la (-lə) **1** a horizontal line drawn above a group of mathematical terms, used as an alternative to parentheses in mathematical expressions, as in $x + \overline{y - z}$ which is equivalent to $x + (y - z)$ **2** anatomy any bandlike structure, esp one uniting two or more parts [c17: from Latin: bond, from *vincīre* to bind]

vindaloo (ˌvɪndə'luː) *n*, *pl* -loos a type of very hot Indian curry [c20: perhaps from Portuguese *vin d'alho* wine and garlic sauce]

vin de pays *French* (vē də pei) *n*, *pl* **vins de pays** (vē də pei) the third highest French wine classification: indicates that the wine meets certain requirements concerning area of production, strength, etc. Abbreviation: VDP. Also called: *vin du pays* See **AC, VDQS** [literally: local wine]

Vindhya Pradesh ('vɪndjə) *n* a former state of central India: merged with the reorganized Madhya Pradesh in 1956

Vindhya Range *or* **Vindhya Mountains** *n* a mountain range in central India: separates the Ganges basin from the Deccan, marking the limits of northern and peninsular India. Greatest height: 1113 m (3651 ft)

vindicable ('vɪndɪkəbəl) *adj* capable of being vindicated; justifiable > ˌvindica'bility *n*

vindicate ('vɪndɪˌkeɪt) *vb* (*tr*) **1** to clear from guilt, accusation, blame, etc, as by evidence or argument **2** to provide justification for: *his promotion vindicated his unconventional attitude* **3** to uphold, maintain, or defend (a cause, etc): *to vindicate a claim* [c17: from Latin *vindicāre*, from *vindex* claimant] > 'vindiˌcator *n* > 'vindiˌcatory *adj*

vindication (ˌvɪndɪ'keɪʃən) *n* **1** the act of vindicating or the condition of being vindicated **2** a fact, evidence, circumstance, etc, that serves to vindicate a theory or claim

vindictive (vɪn'dɪktɪv) *adj* **1** disposed to seek vengeance **2** characterized by spite or rancour **3** *English law* (of damages) in excess of the compensation due to the plaintiff and imposed in punishment of the defendant [c17: from Latin *vindicta* revenge, from *vindicāre* to VINDICATE] > vin'dictively *adv* > vin'dictiveness *n*

vin du pays *French* (vē du pei) *n*, *pl* **vins du pays** a variant spelling of **vin de pays**

vine (vaɪn) *n* **1** any of various plants, esp the grapevine, having long flexible stems that creep along the ground or climb by clinging to a support by means of tendrils, leafstalks, etc **2** the stem of such a plant [c13: from Old French *vine*, from Latin *vīnea* vineyard, from *vīneus* belonging to wine, from *vīnum* wine] > 'viny *adj*

Vine (vaɪn) *n* **Barbara. See (Ruth) Rendell**

vinedresser ('vaɪnˌdrɛsə) *n* a person who prunes, tends, or cultivates grapevines

vinegar ('vɪnɪgə) *n* **1** a sour-tasting liquid consisting of impure dilute acetic acid, made by oxidation of the ethyl alcohol in beer, wine, or cider. It is used as a condiment or preservative **2** sourness or peevishness of temper, countenance, speech, etc [c13: from Old French *vinaigre*, from *vin* WINE + *aigre* sour, from Latin *acer* sharp] > 'vinegarish *adj* > 'vinegary *adj*

vinery ('vaɪnərɪ) *n*, *pl* -eries **1** a hothouse for growing grapes **2** another name for a **vineyard 3** vines collectively

vineyard ('vɪnjəd) *n* a plantation of grapevines, esp where wine grapes are produced [Old English *wīngeard*; see VINE, YARD[2]; related to Old High German *wīngart*, Old Norse *vingarthr*]

vingt-et-un *French* (vēteœ̃) *n* another name for **pontoon[2]** [literally: twenty-one]

Vinho Verde (ˌviːnjəʊ 'vɜːdɪ) *n* any of a variety of light, slightly sharp-tasting wines made from early-picked grapes in the Minho region of NW Portugal [Portuguese, literally: green (or young) wine]

vini- *or before a vowel* **vin-** *combining form* indicating wine: *viniculture* [from Latin *vīnum*]

viniculture ('vɪnɪˌkʌltʃə) *n* the process or business of growing grapes and making wine > ˌvini'cultural *adj* > ˌvini'culturist *n*

viniferous (vɪ'nɪfərəs) *adj* wine-producing

Vinland ('vɪnlənd) *or* **Vineland** ('vaɪnlənd) *n* the stretch of the E coast of North America visited by Leif Ericson and other Vikings from about 1000

Vinnitsa (*Russian* 'vinnitsə) *n* a city in central Ukraine: passed from Polish to Russian rule in 1793. Pop: 353 000 (2005 est)

vino ('viːnəʊ) *n*, *pl* -nos an informal word for **wine** [jocular use of Italian or Spanish *vino*]

vin ordinaire *French* (vēn ɔrdinɛr) *n*, *pl* **vins ordinaires** (vēz ɔrdinɛr) cheap table wine, esp French

vinosity (vɪ'nɒsɪtɪ) *n* the distinctive and essential quality and flavour of wine [c17: from Late Latin *vīnōsitas*, from Latin *vīnōsus* VINOUS]

vinous ('vaɪnəs) *adj* **1** of, relating to, or characteristic of wine **2** indulging in or indicative of indulgence in wine [c17: from Latin *vīnōsus*, from *vīnum* WINE]

vintage ('vɪntɪdʒ) *n* **1** the wine obtained from a harvest of grapes, esp in an outstandingly good year, referred to by the year involved, the district, or the vineyard **2** the harvest from which such a wine is obtained **3 a** the harvesting of wine grapes **b** the season of harvesting these grapes or for making wine **4** a time of origin: *a car of Edwardian vintage* **5** *informal* a group of people or objects of the same period: *a fashion of last season's vintage* ▷ *adj* **6** (of wine) of an outstandingly good year **7** representative of the best and most typical: *vintage Shakespeare* **8** of lasting interest and importance; venerable; classic: *vintage films* **9** old-fashioned; dated [c15: from Old French *vendage* (influenced by *vintener* VINTNER), from Latin *vindēmia*, from *vīnum* wine, grape + *dēmere* to take away (from *dē-* away + *emere* to take)]

vintage car *n chiefly Brit* an old car, esp one constructed between 1919 and 1930. See **classic car, veteran car**

vintager ('vɪntɪdʒə) *n* a grape harvester

vintner ('vɪntnə) *n* a wine merchant [c15: from Old French *vinetier*, from Medieval Latin *vīnētārius*, from Latin *vīnētum* vineyard, from *vīnum* WINE]

vinyl ('vaɪnɪl) *n* **1** (*modifier*) of, consisting of, or containing the monovalent group of atoms CH₂CH-: *a vinyl polymer; vinyl chloride* **2** (*modifier*) of, consisting of, or made of a vinyl resin: *a vinyl raincoat* **3** any vinyl polymer, resin, or plastic, esp PVC **4** (collectively) conventional records made of vinyl as opposed to compact discs [c19: from VINI- + -YL]

vinyl acetate *n* a colourless volatile liquid unsaturated ester that polymerizes readily in light and is used for making polyvinyl acetate. Formula: $CH_2{:}CHOOCCH_3$

vinyl chloride *n* a colourless flammable gaseous unsaturated compound made by the chlorination of ethylene and used as a refrigerant and in the manufacture of PVC; chloroethylene; chloroethene. Formula: $CH{:}CHCl$

vinyl resin *or* **polymer** *n* any one of a class of thermoplastic materials, esp PVC and polyvinyl acetate, made by polymerizing vinyl compounds

viol ('vaɪəl) *n* any of a family of stringed musical instruments that preceded the violin family, consisting of a fretted fingerboard, a body rather like that of a violin but having a flat back and six strings, played with a curved bow. They are held between the knees when played and have a quiet yet penetrating tone; they were much played, esp in consorts, in the 16th and 17th centuries [c15: from Old French *viole*, from Old Provençal *viola;* see VIOLA¹]

viola¹ (vɪˈəʊlə) *n* **1** a bowed stringed instrument, the alto of the violin family; held beneath the chin when played. It is pitched and tuned an octave above the cello **2** any of various instruments of the viol family, such as the viola da gamba [c18: from Italian *viola*, probably from Old Provençal *viola*, of uncertain origin; perhaps related to Latin *vītulāri* to rejoice]

viola² ('vaɪələ, vaɪˈəʊ-) *n* any temperate perennial herbaceous plant of the violaceous genus *Viola*, the flowers of which have showy irregular petals, white, yellow, blue, or mauve in colour [c15: from Latin: violet]

viola clef (vɪˈəʊlə) *n* another term for **alto clef**

viola da gamba (vɪˈəʊlə də ˈɡæmbə) *n* the second largest and lowest member of the viol family [c18: from Italian, literally: viol for the leg]

viola d'amore (vɪˈəʊlə dæˈmɔːrɪ) *n* an instrument of the viol family having no frets, seven strings, and a set of sympathetic strings. It was held under the chin when played [c18: from Italian, literally: viol of love]

violate ('vaɪəˌleɪt) *vb* (*tr*) **1** to break, disregard, or infringe (a law, agreement, etc) **2** to rape or otherwise sexually assault **3** to disturb rudely or improperly; break in upon **4** to treat irreverently or disrespectfully; outrage: *he violated a sanctuary* [c15: from Latin *violāre* to do violence to, from *vīs* strength] > **'violable** *adj* > **vio'lation** *n* > **'vio,lator** or **'vio,later** *n*

violence ('vaɪələns) *n* **1** the exercise or an instance of physical force, usually effecting or intended to effect injuries, destruction, etc **2** powerful, untamed, or devastating force: *the violence of the sea* **3** great strength of feeling, as in language, etc; fervour **4** an unjust, unwarranted, or unlawful display of force, esp such as tends to overawe or intimidate **5** do violence to **a** to inflict harm upon; damage or violate: *they did violence to the prisoners* **b** to distort or twist the sense or intention of: *the reporters did violence to my speech* [c13: via Old French from Latin *violentia* impetuosity, from *violentus* VIOLENT]

violent ('vaɪələnt) *adj* **1** marked or caused by great physical force or violence: *a violent stab* **2** (of a person) tending to the use of violence, esp in order to injure or intimidate others **3** marked by intensity of any kind: *a violent clash of colours* **4** characterized by an undue use of force; severe; harsh **5** caused by or displaying strong or undue mental or emotional force [c14: from Latin *violentus*, probably from *vīs* strength] > **'violently** *adv*

violent storm *n* a wind of force 11 on the Beaufort scale, reaching speeds of 64–72 mph

violet ('vaɪəlɪt) *n* **1** any of various temperate perennial herbaceous plants of the violaceous genus *Viola*, such as *V. odorata* (**sweet** (or **garden**) **violet**), typically having mauve or bluish flowers with irregular showy petals **2** any other plant of the genus *Viola*, such as the wild pansy **3** any of various similar but unrelated plants, such as the African violet **4 a** any of a group of colours that vary in saturation but have the same purplish-blue hue. They lie at one end of the visible spectrum, next to blue; approximate wavelength range 445–390 nanometres **b** (*as adjective*): *a violet dress* **5** a dye or pigment of or producing these colours **6** violet clothing: *dressed in violet* [c14: from Old French *violete* a little violet, from *viole*, from Latin *viola* violet]

violin (ˌvaɪəˈlɪn) *n* a bowed stringed instrument, the highest member of the violin family, consisting of a fingerboard, a hollow wooden body with waisted sides, and a sounding board connected to the back by means of a soundpost that also supports the bridge. It has two f-shaped sound holes cut in the belly. The instrument, noted for its fine and flexible tone, is the most important of the stringed instruments. It is held under the chin when played. Range: roughly three and a half octaves upwards from G below middle C [c16: from Italian *violino* a little viola, from VIOLA¹]

violinist (ˌvaɪəˈlɪnɪst) *n* a person who plays the violin

violist¹ (vɪˈəʊlɪst) *n US* a person who plays the viola

violist² ('vaɪəlɪst) *n* a person who plays the viol

Viollet-le-Duc (*French* vjɔlɛlədyk) *n* **Eugène Emmanuel** (øʒɛn emanɥɛl). 1814–79, French architect and leader of the Gothic Revival in France, noted for his dictionary of

French architecture (1854–68) and for his restoration of medieval buildings

violoncello (ˌvaɪələnˈtʃɛləʊ) *n*, *pl* **-los** the full name for **cello** [c18: from Italian, from VIOLONE + *-cello*, diminutive suffix] > ˌviolon'cellist *n*

violone (ˌvaɪəˈləʊn) *n* the double-bass member of the viol family lying an octave below the viola da gamba. It corresponds to the double bass in the violin family [c18: from Italian, from VIOLA¹ + *-one*, augmentative suffix]

VIP *abbreviation* **1** very important person **2** visually impaired person

viper ('vaɪpə) *n* **1** any venomous Old World snake of the family Viperidae, esp any of the genus *Vipera* (the adder and related forms), having hollow fangs in the upper jaw that are used to inject venom **2** any of various other snakes, such as the horned viper **3** a malicious or treacherous person [c16: from Latin *vīpera*, perhaps from *vīvus* living + *parere* to bear, referring to a tradition that the viper was viviparous]

viperous ('vaɪpərəs) or **viperish** *adj* **1** Also: **viperine** ('vaɪpəˌraɪn) of, relating to, or resembling a viper **2** malicious

viper's bugloss *n* a Eurasian boraginaceous weed, *Echium vulgare*, having blue flowers and pink buds. See **Paterson's curse**

virago (vɪˈrɑːɡəʊ) *n*, *pl* **-goes** or **-gos 1** a loud, violent, and ill-tempered woman; scold; shrew **2** *archaic* a strong, brave, or warlike woman; amazon [Old English, from Latin: a manlike maiden, from *vir* a man] > vi'rago-ˌlike *adj*

viral ('vaɪrəl) *adj* of, relating to, or caused by a virus

viral marketing *n* **1** a direct marketing technique in which a company persuades internet users to forward its publicity material in e-mails (usually by including jokes, games, video clips, etc) **2** a marketing strategy in which conventional media are eschewed in favour of various techniques designed to generate word-of-mouth publicity, in the hope of creating a fad or craze

Virchow (*German* ˈfɪrçɔf) *n* **Rudolf Ludwig Karl** ('ruːdɔlf 'luːtvɪç karl). 1821–1902, German pathologist, who is considered the founder of modern (cellular) pathology

virelay ('vɪrɪˌleɪ) *n* an old French verse form, rarely used in English, consisting of short lines arranged in stanzas having only two rhymes, and two opening lines recurring at intervals [c14: from Old French *virelai*, probably from *vireli* (associated with *lai* LAY⁴), meaningless word used as a refrain]

Viren ('vɪərən) *n* **Lasse** ('læsɪ). born 1949, Finnish distance runner: winner of the 5000 metres and the 10 000 metres in the 1972 and 1976 Olympic Games

vireo ('vɪrɪəʊ) *n*, *pl* **vireos** any insectivorous American songbird of the family Vireonidae, esp those of the genus *Vireo*, having an olive-grey back with pale underparts [c19: from Latin: a bird, probably a greenfinch; compare *virēre* to be green]

vires *Latin* ('vaɪriːz) *n* the plural of: **vis** *Foreign*

virescent (vɪˈrɛsᵊnt) *adj* greenish or becoming green [c19: from Latin *virescere* to grow green, from *virēre* to be green]

virgate¹ ('vɜːɡɪt, -ɡeɪt) *adj* long, straight, and thin; rod-shaped: *virgate stems* [c19: from Latin *virgātus* made of twigs, from *virga* a rod]

virgate² ('vɜːɡɪt, -ɡeɪt) *n Brit* an obsolete measure of land area, usually taken as equivalent to 30 acres [c17: from Medieval Latin *virgāta* (*terrae*) a rod's measurement (of land), from Latin *virga* rod; the phrase is a translation of Old English *gierd landes* a yard of land]

Virgil or **Vergil** ('vɜːdʒɪl) *n* Latin name *Publius Vergilius Maro*. 70–19 BC, Roman poet, patronized by Maecenas. The *Eclogues* (42–37), ten pastoral poems, and the *Georgics* (37–30), four books on the art of farming, established Virgil as the foremost poet of his age. His masterpiece is the *Aeneid* (30–19) > Vir'gilian or Ver'gilian *adj*

virgin ('vɜːdʒɪn) *n* **1** a person, esp a woman, who has never had sexual intercourse **2** an unmarried woman who has taken a religious vow of chastity in order to dedicate herself totally to God **3** any female animal that has never mated **4** a female insect that produces offspring by parthenogenesis ▷ *adj* (*usually prenominal*)

V

5 of, relating to, resembling, suitable for, or characteristic of a virgin or virgins; chaste **6** pure and natural, uncorrupted, unsullied, or untouched: *virgin purity* **7** not yet cultivated, explored, exploited, etc, by man: *virgin territories* **8** being the first or happening for the first time **9** (of a metal) made from an ore rather than from scrap **10** occurring naturally in a pure and uncombined form: *virgin silver* [C13: from Old French *virgine*, from Latin *virgō* virgin]

Virgin[1] ('vɜːdʒɪn) *n* **1** the Virgin See **Virgin Mary 2** a statue or other artistic representation of the Virgin Mary

Virgin[2] ('vɜːdʒɪn) *n* the Virgin the constellation Virgo, the sixth sign of the zodiac

virginal[1] ('vɜːdʒɪnᵊl) *adj* **1** of, relating to, characterized by, proper to, or maintaining a state of virginity; chaste **2** extremely pure or fresh; untouched; undefiled [C15: from Latin *virginālis* maidenly, from *virgō* virgin] > '**virginally** *adv*

virginal[2] ('vɜːdʒɪnᵊl) *n* (*often plural*) a smaller version of the harpsichord, but oblong in shape, having one manual and no pedals [C16: probably from Latin *virginālis* VIRGINAL[1], perhaps because it was played largely by young ladies] > '**virginalist** *n*

Virgin Birth *n* the doctrine that Jesus Christ had no human father but was conceived solely by the direct intervention of the Holy Spirit so that Mary remained miraculously a virgin during and after his birth

virgin forest *n* a forest in its natural state, before it has been explored or exploited by man

Virginia (vəˈdʒɪnɪə) *n* a state of the eastern US, on the Atlantic: site of the first permanent English settlement in North America; consists of a low-lying deeply indented coast rising inland to the Piedmont plateau and the Blue Ridge Mountains. Capital: Richmond. Pop: 7 386 330 (2003 est). Area: 103 030 sq km (39 780 sq miles). Abbreviations: Va, (with zip code) VA > Vir'ginian *adj, n*

Virginia Beach *n* a city and resort in SE Virginia, on the Atlantic. Pop: 439 467 (2003 est)

Virginia creeper *n* a vitaceous woody vine, *Parthenocissus quinquefolia*, of North America, having tendrils with adhesive tips, bluish-black berry-like fruits, and compound leaves that turn red in autumn: widely planted for ornament

Virginia stock *n* a Mediterranean plant, *Malcolmia maritima*, cultivated for its white and pink flowers: family *Brassicaceae* (crucifers)

Virgin Islands *pl n* a group of about 100 small islands (14 inhabited) in the Caribbean, east of Puerto Rico: discovered by Columbus (1493); consists of the British Virgin Islands in the east and the Virgin Islands of the United States in the west and south. Pop: 132 000 (2004 est). Area: 497 sq km (192 sq miles)

Virgin Islands of the United States *pl n* a territory of the US in the Caribbean, consisting of islands west and south of the British Virgin Islands: purchased from Denmark in 1917 for their strategic importance. Capital: Charlotte Amalie. Pop: 111 000 (2004 est). Area: 344 sq km (133 sq miles). Former name: **Danish West Indies**

virginity (vəˈdʒɪnɪtɪ) *n* **1** the condition or fact of being a virgin; maidenhood; chastity **2** the condition of being untouched, unsullied, etc

virginium (vəˈdʒɪnɪəm) *n chem* a former name for francium

Virgin Mary *n* Mary, the mother of Christ. Also called: **the Virgin**

Virgin Queen *n* the Virgin Queen another name for Queen Elizabeth I of England. See **Elizabeth I**

virgin's-bower *n* any of several American clematis plants, esp *Clematis virginiana*, of E North America, which has clusters of small white flowers

virgin soil *n* **1** soil that has not been cultivated before **2** a person or thing that is as yet undeveloped

virgin wool *n* wool that is being processed or woven for the first time

Virgo ('vɜːgəʊ) *n, Latin genitive* Virginis ('vɜːdʒɪnɪs) **1** *astronomy* a large zodiacal constellation on the celestial equator, lying between Leo and Libra. It contains the star Spica and a cluster of several thousand galaxies, the

Virgo cluster, lying 50 million light years away and itself containing the intense radio source Virgo A, which is the closest active galaxy **2** *astrology* Also called: **the Virgin** the sixth sign of the zodiac, symbol ♍, having a mutable earth classification and ruled by the planet Mercury. The sun is in this sign between about Aug 23 and Sept 22 [C14: from Latin]

virgo intacta ('vɜːgəʊ ɪnˈtæktə) *n* a girl or woman whose hymen has not been broken [Latin, literally: untouched virgin]

virgule ('vɜːgjuːl) *n printing* another name for **solidus** [C19: from French: comma, from Latin *virgula* a little rod, from *virga* rod]

viridescent (ˌvɪrɪˈdɛsᵊnt) *adj* greenish or tending to become green [C19: from Late Latin *viridescere* to grow green, from Latin *viridis* green] > ˌviri'descence *n*

viridian (vɪˈrɪdɪən) *n* a green pigment consisting of a hydrated form of chromic oxide [C19: from Latin *viridis* green]

viridity (vɪˈrɪdɪtɪ) *n* **1** the quality or state of being green; greenness; verdancy **2** innocence, youth, or freshness [C15: from Latin *viriditās*, from *viridis* green]

virile ('vɪraɪl) *adj* **1** of, relating to, or having the characteristics of an adult male **2** (of a male) possessing high sexual drive and capacity for sexual intercourse **3** of or capable of copulation or procreation **4** strong, forceful, or vigorous [C15: from Latin *virīlis* manly, from *vir* a man; related to Old English *wer* man and probably to Latin *vis* strength] > virility (vɪˈrɪlɪtɪ) *n*

virilism ('vɪrɪˌlɪzəm) *n med* the abnormal development in a woman of male secondary sex characteristics

virology (vaɪˈrɒlədʒɪ) *n* the branch of medicine concerned with the study of viruses and the diseases they cause > virological (ˌvaɪrəˈlɒdʒɪkᵊl) *adj*

virtu *or* **vertu** (vɜːˈtuː) *n* **1** a taste or love for curios or works of fine art; connoisseurship **2** such objects collectively **3** the quality of being rare, beautiful, or otherwise appealing to a connoisseur (esp in the phrases **articles of virtu; objects of virtu**) [C18: from Italian *virtù*; see VIRTUE]

virtual ('vɜːtʃʊəl) *adj* **1** having the essence or effect but not the appearance or form of: *a virtual revolution* **2** *physics* being, relating to, or involving a virtual image: *a virtual focus* **3** *computing* of or relating to virtual storage: *virtual memory* **4** of or relating to a computer technique by which a person, wearing a headset or mask, has the experience of being in an environment created by the computer, and of interacting with and causing changes in it [C14: from Medieval Latin *virtuālis* effective, from Latin *virtūs* VIRTUE]

virtual human *n* a computer-generated moving image of a human being, used esp in films as an extra in large crowd scenes

virtual image *n* an optical image formed by the apparent divergence of rays from a point, rather than their actual divergence from a point

virtuality (ˌvɜːtʃʊˈælɪtɪ) *n* virtual reality

virtually ('vɜːtʃʊəlɪ) *adv* in effect though not in fact; practically; nearly

virtual reality *n* a computer-generated environment that, to the person experiencing it, closely resembles reality. Abbreviation: **VR** See also **virtual** (sense 4)

virtual storage *or* **memory** *n* a computer system in which the size of the memory is effectively increased by automatically transferring sections of a program from a large capacity backing store, such as a disk, into the smaller core memory as they are required

virtue ('vɜːtjuː, -tʃuː) *n* **1** the quality or practice of moral excellence or righteousness **2** a particular moral excellence: *the virtue of tolerance* **3** any of the cardinal virtues (prudence, justice, fortitude, and temperance) or theological virtues (faith, hope, and charity) **4** any admirable quality, feature, or trait **5** chastity, esp in women **6** *archaic* an effective, active, or inherent power or force **7** *by or* in virtue of on account of or by reason of **8** make a virtue of necessity to acquiesce in doing something unpleasant with a show of grace because one must do it in any case [C13 *vertu*, from Old French, from Latin *virtūs* manliness, courage, from *vir* man]

virtuoso (ˌvɜːtjʊˈəʊzəʊ, -səʊ) *n, pl* -sos *or* -si (-siː) **1** a consummate master of musical technique and artistry **2** a person who has a masterly or dazzling skill or technique in any field of activity **3** a connoisseur, dilettante, or collector of art objects **4** (*modifier*) showing masterly skill or brilliance: *a virtuoso performance* [c17: from Italian: skilled, from Late Latin *virtuōsus* good, virtuous; see VIRTUE] ▷ ˌvirtuˈosity *n*

virtuous ('vɜːtʃʊəs) *adj* **1** characterized by or possessing virtue or moral excellence; righteous; upright **2** (of women) chaste or virginal ▷ ˈvirtuously *adv*

virulence ('vɪrʊləns) *or* **virulency** *n* **1** the quality of being virulent **2** the capacity of a microorganism for causing disease

virulent ('vɪrʊlənt) *adj* **1 a** (of a microorganism) extremely infective **b** (of a disease) having a rapid course and violent effect **2** extremely poisonous, injurious, etc **3** extremely bitter, hostile, etc [c14: from Latin *vīrulentus* full of poison, from *vīrus* poison; see VIRUS] ▷ ˈvirulently *adv*

virus ('vaɪrəs) *n, pl* -ruses **1** any of a group of submicroscopic entities consisting of a single nucleic acid chain surrounded by a protein coat and capable of replication only within the cells of living organisms: many are pathogenic **2** *informal* a disease caused by a virus **3** any corrupting or infecting influence **4** *computing* an unauthorized program that inserts itself into a computer system and then propagates itself to other computers via networks or disks; when activated it interferes with the operation of the computer [c16: from Latin: slime, poisonous liquid; related to Old English *wāse* marsh, Greek *ios* poison]

vis *Latin* (vɪs) *n, pl* **vires** ('vaɪriːz) power, force, or strength

visa ('viːzə) *n, pl* -sas **1** an endorsement in a passport or similar document, signifying that the document is in order and permitting its bearer to travel into or through the country of the government issuing it ▷ *vb* -sas, -saing, -saed (*tr*) **2** to enter a visa into (a passport) [c19: via French from Latin *vīsa* things seen, from *vīsus*, past participle of *vidēre* to see]

visage ('vɪzɪdʒ) *n chiefly literary* **1** face or countenance **2** appearance; aspect [c13: from Old French: aspect, from *vis* face, from Latin *vīsus* appearance, from *vidēre* to see]

-visaged *adj* (*in combination*) having a visage as specified: *flat-visaged*

Visakhapatnam (vɪˌsɑːkəˈpʌtnəm) *n* a variant spelling of **Vishakhapatnam**

vis-à-vis (ˌviːzɑːˈviː) *prep* **1** in relation to; regarding **2** face to face with; opposite ▷ *adv, adj* **3** face to face; opposite ▷ *n, pl* vis-à-vis **4** a person or thing that is situated opposite to another **5** a person who corresponds to another in office, capacity, etc; counterpart [c18: French, from *vis* face]

Visayan Islands (vɪˈsɑːjən) *pl n* a group of seven large and several hundred small islands in the central Philippines. Chief islands: Negros and Panay. Pop: 15 528 346 (2000). Area: about 61 000 sq km (23 535 sq miles). Spanish name: **Bisayas**

Visby (*Swedish* 'viːsbyː) *n* a port in SE Sweden, on NW Gotland Island in the Baltic: an early member of the Hanseatic League and major N European commercial centre in the Middle Ages. Pop: 22 017 (2000 est)

Visc. *abbreviation* Viscount *or* Viscountess

viscacha *or* **vizcacha** (vɪsˈkætʃə) *n* a gregarious burrowing hystricomorph rodent, *Lagostomus maximus*, of southern South America, similar to but larger than the chinchillas: family Chinchillidae [c17: from Spanish, from Quechuan *wiskácha*]

viscera ('vɪsərə) *pl n, sing* **viscus** ('vɪskəs) **1** *anatomy* the large internal organs of the body collectively, esp those in the abdominal cavity **2** (less formally) the intestines; guts [c17: from Latin: entrails, pl of *viscus* internal organ]

visceral ('vɪsərəl) *adj* **1** of, relating to, or affecting the viscera **2** characterized by intuition or instinct rather than intellect ▷ ˈviscerally *adv*

viscid ('vɪsɪd) *adj* **1** cohesive and sticky; glutinous; viscous **2** (esp of a leaf) covered with a sticky substance [c17: from Late Latin *viscidus* sticky, from Latin *viscum* mistletoe or birdlime]

Visconti (*Italian* visˈkonti) *n* **1** the ruling family of Milan from 1277 to 1447 **2 Luchino,** real name *Luchino Visconti de Modrone.* 1906–76, Italian stage and film director, whose neorealist films include *Ossessione* (1942). His other films include *The Leopard* (1963), *Death in Venice* (1970), and *The Innocents* (1976)

viscose ('vɪskəʊs) *n* **1 a** a viscous orange-brown solution obtained by dissolving cellulose in sodium hydroxide and carbon disulphide. It can be converted back to cellulose by an acid, as in the manufacture of rayon and cellophane **b** (*as modifier*): *viscose rayon* **2** rayon made from this material [c19: from Late Latin *viscōsus* full of birdlime, sticky, from *viscum* birdlime; see VISCID]

viscosity (vɪsˈkɒsɪtɪ) *n, pl* -ties **1** the state or property of being viscous **2** *physics* **a** the extent to which a fluid resists a tendency to flow **b** Also called: **absolute viscosity** a measure of this resistance, equal to the tangential stress on a liquid undergoing streamline flow divided by its velocity gradient. It is measured in newton seconds per metre squared

viscount ('vaɪkaʊnt) *n* **1** (in the British Isles) a nobleman ranking below an earl and above a baron **2** (in various countries) a son or younger brother of a count **3** (in medieval Europe) the deputy of a count [c14: from Old French *visconte*, from Medieval Latin *vicecomes*, from Late Latin *vice-* VICE³ + *comes* COUNT²]

viscountess ('vaɪkaʊntɪs) *n* **1** the wife or widow of a viscount **2** a woman who holds the rank of viscount in her own right

viscous ('vɪskəs) *or* **viscose** *adj* **1** (of liquids) thick and sticky; viscid **2** having or involving viscosity [c14: from Late Latin *viscōsus*; see VISCOSE] ▷ ˈviscously *adv*

viscus ('vɪskəs) *n* the singular of **viscera**

vise (vaɪs) *n, vb US* a variant spelling of **vice²**

Viseu (*Portuguese* viˈzeu) *n* a city in N central Portugal: 12th-century cathedral. Pop: 93 502 (2001)

Vishakhapatnam (vɪˌʃɑːkəˈpʌtnəm), **Visakhapatnam** *or* **Vizagapatam** *n* a port in E India, in NE Andhra Pradesh on the Bay of Bengal: shipbuilding and oil-refining industries. Pop: 969 608 (2001)

Vishinsky (*Russian* viˈʃinskij) *n* a variant spelling of (Andrei Yanuaryevich) **Vyshinsky**

Vishnu ('vɪʃnuː) *n Hinduism* the Pervader or Sustainer: originally a solar deity occupying a secondary place in the Hindu pantheon; later one of the three chief gods, the second member of the Trimurti; and, later still, the saviour appearing in many incarnations [c17: from Sanskrit *Viṣṇu*, literally: the one who works everywhere] ▷ ˈVishnuˌism *n*

visibility (ˌvɪzɪˈbɪlɪtɪ) *n* **1** the condition or fact of being visible **2** clarity of vision or relative possibility of seeing **3** the range of vision: *visibility is 500 yards*

visible ('vɪzɪbəl) *adj* **1** capable of being perceived by the eye **2** capable of being perceived by the mind; evident: *no visible dangers* **3** available: *the visible resources* **4** of or relating to the balance of trade: *visible transactions* [c14: from Latin *visibilis*, from *vidēre* to see] ▷ ˈvisibly *adv*

visible balance *n* another name for **balance of trade**

visible radiation *n* electromagnetic radiation that causes the sensation of sight; light. It has wavelengths between about 380 and 780 nanometres

vision ('vɪʒən) *n* **1** the act, faculty, or manner of perceiving with the eye; sight **2 a** the image on a television screen **b** (*as modifier*): *vision control* **3** the ability or an instance of great perception, esp of future developments: *a man of vision* **4** a mystical or religious experience of seeing some supernatural event, person, etc: *the vision of St John of the Cross* **5** that which is seen, esp in such a mystical experience **6** (*sometimes plural*) a vivid mental image produced by the imagination: *he had visions of becoming famous* **7** a person or thing of extraordinary beauty [c13: from Latin *vīsiō* sight, from *vidēre* to see]

visionary ('vɪʒənərɪ) *adj* **1** marked by vision or foresight: *a visionary leader* **2** incapable of being realized or effected; unrealistic **3** (of people) characterized by idealistic or radical ideas, esp impractical ones **4** given to having visions **5** of, of the nature of, or seen in visions ▷ *n, pl* -aries **6** a visionary person

vision mixer *n television* **1** the person who selects and manipulates the television signals from cameras, film, and other sources, to make the composite programme **2** the equipment used for vision mixing

visit ('vɪzɪt) vb **-its, -iting, -ited 1** to go or come to see (a person, place, etc) **2** to stay with (someone) as a guest **3** to go or come to (an institution, place, etc) for the purpose of inspecting or examining **4** (tr) (of a disease, disaster, etc) to assail; afflict **5** (tr; foll by upon or on) to inflict (punishment, etc) **6** (tr; usually foll by with) archaic to afflict or plague (with punishment, etc) **7** (often foll by with) US & Canadian informal to chat or converse (with someone) ▷ n **8** the act or an instance of visiting **9** a stay as a guest **10** a professional or official call **11** a formal call for the purpose of inspection or examination **12** international law the right of an officer of a belligerent state to stop and search neutral ships in war to verify their nationality and ascertain whether they carry contraband [C13: from Latin vīsitāre to go to see, from vīsere to examine, from vidēre to see] > 'visitable adj

visitant ('vɪzɪtənt) n **1** a supernatural being; ghost; apparition **2** a visitor or guest, usually from far away **3** Also called: **visitor** a migratory bird that is present in a particular region only at certain times: a summer visitant [C16: from Latin vīsitāns going to see, from vīsitāre; see VISIT]

visitation (,vɪzɪ'teɪʃən) n **1** an official call or visit for the purpose of inspecting or examining an institution, esp such a visit made by a bishop to his diocese **2** a visiting of punishment or reward from heaven **3** any disaster or catastrophe: a visitation of the plague **4** an appearance or arrival of a supernatural being **5** informal an unduly prolonged social call

Visitation (,vɪzɪ'teɪʃən) n **1 a** the visit made by the Virgin Mary to her cousin Elizabeth (Luke 1:39–56) **b** the Church festival commemorating this, held on July 2 **2** a religious order of nuns, the **Order of the Visitation,** founded in 1610 by St Francis of Sales and dedicated to contemplation and the cultivation of humility, gentleness, and sisterly love

visiting card n another term for **calling card**

visiting fireman n US informal a visitor whose presence is noticed because he is an important figure, a lavish spender, etc

visitor ('vɪzɪtə) n **1** a person who pays a visit; caller, guest, tourist, etc **2** another name for **visitant** (sense 3)

visitor centre n another term for **interpretive centre**

visitor's passport n (formerly, in Britain) a passport, valid for one year and for certain countries only, that could be purchased from post offices. Also called: **British Visitor's Passport**

Vislinsky Zaliv (Russian vis'linski 'zaːlɪf) n a transliteration of the Russian name for **Vistula** (sense 2)

visor or **vizor** ('vaɪzə) n **1** a transparent flap on a helmet that can be pulled down to protect the face **2** a piece of armour fixed or hinged to the helmet to protect the face and with slits for the eyes **3** another name for **peak** (sense 6) **4** a small movable screen used as protection against glare from the sun, esp one attached above the windscreen of a motor vehicle **5** archaic or literary a mask or any other means of disguise or concealment [C14: from Anglo-French viser, from Old French visiere, from vis face; see VISAGE] > 'visored or 'vizored adj

vista ('vɪstə) n **1** a view, esp through a long narrow avenue of trees, buildings, etc, or such a passage or avenue itself; prospect **2** a comprehensive mental view of a distant time or a lengthy series of events [C17: from Italian: a view, from vedere to see, from Latin vidēre]

Vistula ('vɪstjʊlə) n **1** a river in central and N Poland, rising in the Carpathian Mountains and flowing generally north and northwest past Warsaw and Torun, then northeast to enter the Baltic via an extensive delta region. Length: 1090 km (677 miles). German name: **Weichsel 2 Vistula Lagoon** a shallow lagoon on the SW coast of the Baltic Sea, between Danzig and Kaliningrad, crossed by the border between Poland and Russia. German name: **Frisches Haff.** Polish name: **Wislany Zaiew.** Russian name: **Vislinsky Zaliv**

visual ('vɪʒʊəl, -zjʊ-) adj **1** of, relating to, done by, or used in seeing: visual powers; visual steering **2** another word for

optical 3 capable of being seen; visible **4** of, occurring as, or induced by a mental image ▷ n **5** a sketch to show the proposed layout of an advertisement, as in a newspaper **6** (often plural) a photograph, film, or other display material [C15: from Late Latin vīsuālis, from Latin vīsus sight, from vidēre to see] > 'visually adv

visual aids pl n devices, such as films, slides, models, and blackboards, that display in visual form material to be understood or remembered

visual display unit n computing a device with a screen that displays characters or graphics representing data in a computer memory. It usually has a keyboard or light pen for the input of information or inquiries. Abbreviation: **VDU**

visual field n the whole extent of the image falling on the retina when the eye is fixating a given point in space

visualization or **visualisation** (,vɪʒʊəlaɪ'zeɪʃən, -zjʊ-) n **1** the act or an instance of visualizing **2** a technique involving focusing on positive mental images in order to achieve a particular goal

visualize or **visualise** ('vɪʒʊə,laɪz, -zjʊ-) vb to form a mental image of (something incapable of being viewed or not at that moment visible)

visual magnitude n astronomy the magnitude of a star as determined by visual observation

visual purple n another name for **rhodopsin**

visual violet n another name for **iodopsin**

vital ('vaɪtᵊl) adj **1** essential to maintain life: the lungs perform a vital function **2** forceful, energetic, or lively: a vital person **3** of, relating to, having, or displaying life: a vital organism **4** indispensable or essential: books vital to this study **5** of great importance; decisive: a vital game ▷ n **6** (plural) the bodily organs, such as the brain, liver, heart, lungs, etc, that are necessary to maintain life **7** (plural) the essential elements of anything [C14: via Old French from Latin vītālis belonging to life, from vīta life] > 'vitally adv

vital capacity n physiol the volume of air that can be exhaled from the lungs after the deepest possible breath has been taken: a measure of lung function

vital force n (esp in early biological theory) a hypothetical force, independent of physical and chemical forces, regarded as being the causative factor of the evolution and development of living organisms

vitalism ('vaɪtə,lɪzəm) n the philosophical doctrine that the phenomena of life cannot be explained in purely mechanical terms because there is something immaterial which distinguishes living from inanimate matter > 'vitalist n, adj > ,vital'istic adj

vitality (vaɪ'tælɪtɪ) n, pl **-ties 1** physical or mental vigour, energy, etc **2** the power or ability to continue in existence, live, or grow: the vitality of a movement

vitalize or **vitalise** ('vaɪtə,laɪz) vb (tr) to make vital, living, or alive; endow with life or vigour > ,vitali'zation or ,vitali'sation n

vital staining n the technique of treating living cells and tissues with dyes that do not immediately kill them, facilitating observation with a microscope

vital statistics pl n **1** quantitative data concerning human life or the conditions and aspects affecting it, such as the death rate **2** informal the measurements of a woman's bust, waist, and hips

vitamin ('vɪtəmɪn, 'vaɪ-) n any of a group of substances that are essential, in small quantities, for the normal functioning of metabolism in the body. They cannot usually be synthesized in the body but they occur naturally in certain foods: insufficient supply of any particular vitamin results in a deficiency disease [C20 vit- from Latin vīta life + -amin from AMINE; so named by Casimir Funk (1884–1967), US biochemist who believed the substances to be amines] > ,vita'minic adj

vitamin A n a fat-soluble yellow unsaturated alcohol occurring in green and yellow vegetables (esp carrots), butter, egg yolk, and fish-liver oil (esp halibut oil). It is essential for the prevention of night blindness and the protection of epithelial tissue. Formula: $C_{20}H_{30}O$. Also called: **vitamin A₁, retinol**

vitamin A₂ n a vitamin that occurs in the tissues of

freshwater fish and has a function similar to that of vitamin A. Formula: $C_{20}H_{28}O$. Also called: **dehydroretinol**

vitamin B *n, pl* **B vitamins** any of the vitamins in the vitamin B complex

vitamin B complex *n* a large group of water-soluble vitamins occurring esp in liver and yeast: includes thiamine, riboflavin, nicotinic acid, pyridoxine, pantothenic acid, biotin, choline, folic acid, and cyanocobalamin. Sometimes shortened to: **B complex**

vitamin C *n* another name for **ascorbic acid**

vitamin D *n, pl* **D vitamins** any of the fat-soluble vitamins, including calciferol and cholecalciferol, occurring in fish-liver oils (esp cod-liver oil), milk, butter, and eggs: used in the treatment of rickets and osteomalacia

vitamin E *n* another name for **tocopherol**

vitamin G *n* a former name (esp US and Canadian) for riboflavin

vitamin H *n* another name (esp US and Canadian) for biotin

vitamin K *n, pl* **K vitamins** any of the fat-soluble vitamins, including phylloquinone and the menaquinones, which are essential for the normal clotting of blood

vitamin P *n, pl* **P vitamins** any of a group of water-soluble crystalline substances occurring mainly in citrus fruits, blackcurrants, and rosehips: they regulate the permeability of the blood capillaries

Vitebsk (*Russian* 'vitipsk) *n* a city in E Belarus, a port on the Dvina river: taken by Russia in 1772. Pop: 344 000 (2005 est)

vitellin (vɪ'tɛlɪn) *n biochem* a phosphoprotein that is the major protein in egg yolk [C19: from VITELLUS + -IN]

vitelline membrane (vɪ'tɛlɪn, -aɪn) *n zoology* a membrane that surrounds a fertilized ovum and prevents the entry of other spermatozoa

vitellus (vɪ'tɛləs) *n, pl* -luses *or* -li (-laɪ) *zoology rare* the yolk of an egg [C18: from Latin, literally: little calf, later: yolk of an egg, from *vitulus* calf]

vitiate ('vɪʃɪˌeɪt) *vb* (*tr*) **1** to make faulty or imperfect **2** to debase, pervert, or corrupt **3** to destroy the force or legal effect of (a deed, etc) [C16: from Latin *vitiāre* to injure, from *vitium* a fault] > ˌviti'ation *n* > 'viti,ator *n*

viticulture ('vɪtɪ,kʌltʃə) *n* **1** the science, art, or process of cultivating grapevines **2** the study of grapes and the growing of grapes [C19: viti-, from Latin *vītis* vine] > ˌviti'culturer *or* ˌviti'culturist *n*

Viti Levu ('viːtɪ 'levuː) *n* the largest island of Fiji: mountainous. Chief town (and capital of the state): Suva. Pop: 580 000 (latest est). Area: 10 386 sq km (4010 sq miles)

Vitoria[1] (*Spanish* bi'torja) *n* a city in NE Spain: scene of Wellington's decisive victory (1813) over Napoleon's forces in the Peninsular War. Pop: 223 257 (2003 est)

Vitoria[2] (*Spanish* bi'torja) *n* **Francisco de**. ?1486–1546, Spanish theologian, sometimes considered the father of international law. He criticized Spanish colonial policy in the New World and argued that war was only defensible in certain strictly defined circumstances

Vitória (vɪ'tɔːrɪə; *Portuguese* vi'tɔrja) *n* a port in E Brazil, capital of Espírito Santo state, on an island in the Bay of Espírito Santo. Pop: 1 602 000 (2005 est)

vitreous ('vɪtrɪəs) *adj* **1** of, relating to, or resembling glass **2** made of, derived from, or containing glass **3** of or relating to the vitreous humour or vitreous body [C17: from Latin *vitreus* made of glass, from *vitrum* glass; probably related to *vidēre* to see] > 'vitreously *adv*

vitreous body *n* a transparent gelatinous substance, permeated by fine fibrils, that fills the interior of the eyeball between the lens and the retina

vitrescence (vɪ'trɛsəns) *n* **1** the quality or condition of being or becoming vitreous **2** the process of producing a glass or turning a crystalline material into glass > vi'trescent *adj*

vitrification (,vɪtrɪfɪ'keɪʃən) *n* **1** the process or act of vitrifying or the state of being vitrified **2** something that is or has been vitrified

vitrify ('vɪtrɪ,faɪ) *vb* -fies, -fying, -fied to convert or be converted into glass or a glassy substance [C16: from

French *vitrifier,* from Latin *vitrum* glass] > 'vitri,fiable *adj*

vitrine ('vɪtriːn) *n* a glass display case or cabinet for works of art, curios, etc [C19: from French, from *vitre* pane of glass, from Latin *vitrum* glass]

vitriol ('vɪtrɪ,ɒl) *n* **1** another name for **sulphuric acid** **2** any one of a number of sulphate salts, such as ferrous sulphate (**green vitriol**), copper sulphate (**blue vitriol**), or zinc sulphate (**white vitriol**) **3** speech, writing, etc, displaying rancour, vituperation, or bitterness [C14: from Medieval Latin *vitriolum,* from Late Latin *vitriolus* glassy, from Latin *vitrum* glass, referring to the glossy appearance of the sulphates]

vitriolic (,vɪtrɪ'ɒlɪk) *adj* **1** (of a substance, esp a strong acid) highly corrosive **2** severely bitter or caustic; virulent

vitriolize *or* **vitriolise** ('vɪtrɪə,laɪz) *vb* (*tr*) **1** to convert into or treat with vitriol **2** to burn or injure with vitriol > ,vitrioli'zation *or* ,vitrioli'sation *n*

Vitruvius Pollio (vɪ'truːvɪəs 'pɒlɪ,əʊ) *n* **Marcus** ('mɑːkəs). 1st century BC, Roman architect, noted for his treatise *De architectura,* the only surviving Roman work on architectural theory and a major influence on Renaissance architects > Vi'truvian *adj*

vittle ('vɪtᵊl) *n, vb* an obsolete or dialect spelling of **victual**

vituperate (vɪ'tjuːpə,reɪt) *vb* to berate or rail (against) abusively; revile [C16: from Latin *vituperāre* to blame, from *vitium* a defect + *parāre* to make] > vi'tuper,ator *n*

vituperation (vɪ,tjuːpə'reɪʃən) *n* **1** abusive language or venomous censure **2** the act of vituperating > vituperative (vɪ'tjuːpərətɪv, -prətɪv) *adj*

viva[1] ('viːvə) *interj* long live; up with (a specified person or thing) [C17: from Italian, literally: may (he) live! from *vivere* to live, from Latin *vīvere*]

viva[2] ('vaɪvə) *Brit* ▷ *n* **1** an oral examination ▷ *vb* -vas, -vaing, -vaed (*tr*) **2** to examine orally [shortened from VIVA VOCE]

vivace (vɪ'vɑːtʃɪ) *adj, adv music* to be performed in a brisk lively manner [C17: from Italian, from Latin *vīvax* long-lived, vigorous, from *vīvere* to live]

vivacious (vɪ'veɪʃəs) *adj* full of high spirits and animation; lively or vital [C17: from Latin *vīvax* lively; see VIVACE] > vi'vaciously *adv* > vi'vaciousness *n*

vivacity (vɪ'væsɪtɪ) *n, pl* -ties the quality or condition of being vivacious

Vivaldi (vɪ'vældɪ) *n* **Antonio** (an'tɔːnjo). ?1675–1741, Italian composer and violinist, noted esp for his development of the solo concerto. His best-known work is *The Four Seasons* (1725)

vivarium (vaɪ'vɛərɪəm) *n, pl* -iums *or* -ia (-ɪə) a place where live animals are kept under natural conditions for study, research, etc [C16: from Latin: enclosure where live fish or game are kept, from *vīvus* alive]

viva voce ('vaɪvə 'vəʊtʃɪ) *adv, adj* **1** by word of mouth ▷ *n, vb* **2** the full form of **viva**[2] [C16: from Medieval Latin, literally: with living voice]

vive (viːv) *interj* long live; up with (a specified person or thing) [from French]

Vivekananda (,vi:vɪkə'nʌndə) *n* original name *Narendranath Datta.* 1862–1902, Indian Hindu religious teacher. A disciple of Ramakrishna, he introduced Vedantism to the West

Vivian ('vɪvɪən) *n* (in Arthurian legend) the mistress of Merlin, sometimes identified with the Lady of the Lake

vivid ('vɪvɪd) *adj* **1** (of a colour) very bright; having a very high saturation or purity; produced by a pure or almost pure colouring agent **2** brilliantly coloured: *vivid plumage* **3** conveying to the mind striking realism, freshness, or trueness to life; graphic: *a vivid account* **4** (of a recollection, memory, etc) remaining distinct in the mind **5** (of the imagination, etc) prolific in the formation of lifelike images **6** uttered, operating, or acting with vigour **7** full of life or vitality: *a vivid personality* [C17: from Latin *vīvidus* animated, from *vīvere* to live] > 'vividly *adv* > 'vividness *n*

vivify ('vɪvɪ,faɪ) *vb* -fies, -fying, -fied (*tr*) **1** to bring to life; animate **2** to make more vivid or striking [C16: from Late Latin *vīvificāre,* from Latin *vīvus* alive + *facere* to make] > vivification (,vɪvɪfɪ'keɪʃən) *n*

V

viviparous (vɪˈvɪpərəs) *adj* **1** (of animals) producing offspring that as embryos develop within and derive nourishment from the body of the female parent **2** (of plants) producing bulbils or young plants instead of flowers **3** (of seeds) germinating before separating from the parent plant [c17: from Latin *vīviparus*, from *vīvus* alive + *parere* to bring forth] ▷ viviparity (ˌvɪvɪˈpærɪtɪ) *or* vi'viparousness *n* ▷ vi'viparously *adv*

vivisect (ˌvɪvɪˈsɛkt, ˈvɪvɪˌsɛkt) *vb* to subject (an animal) to vivisection [c19: back formation from VIVISECTION] ▷ 'vivi,sector *n*

vivisection (ˌvɪvɪˈsɛkʃən) *n* the act or practice of performing experiments on living animals, involving cutting into or dissecting the body [c18: from vivi-, from Latin *vīvus* living + SECTION, as in DISSECTION] ▷ ˌvivi'sectional *adj*

vivisectionist (ˌvɪvɪˈsɛkʃənɪst) *n* a person who advocates the practice of vivisection as being useful or necessary to science

vivo ('viːvəʊ) *adj, adv music* (*in combination*) with life and vigour: *allegro vivo* [Italian: lively]

vixen ('vɪksən) *n* **1** a female fox **2** a quarrelsome or spiteful woman [c15 *fixen*; related to Old English *fyxe*, feminine of FOX; compare Old High German *fuhsin*] ▷ 'vixenish *adj* ▷ 'vixenly *adv, adj*

Viyella (vaɪˈɛlə) *n* *trademark* a soft fabric made of wool and cotton, used esp for blouses and shirts

viz *abbreviation* videlicet

Vizagapatam (vɪˌzæɡəˈtʌpəm) *n* a variant spelling of Vishakapatnam

vizard ('vɪzəd) *n* *archaic or literary* a means of disguise; mask; visor [c16: variant of VISOR] ▷ 'vizarded *adj*

vizier (vɪˈzɪə) *n* a high official in certain Muslim countries, esp in the former Ottoman Empire. Viziers served in various capacities, such as that of provincial governor or chief minister to the sultan [c16: from Turkish *vezīr*, from Arabic *wazīr* porter, from *wazara* to bear a burden] ▷ vi'zierial *or* vi'zirial *adj* ▷ vi'ziership *n* ▷ vi'zierate *n*

vizor ('vaɪzə) *n, vb* a variant spelling of **visor**

vizsla ('vɪʒlə) *n* a breed of Hungarian hunting dog with a smooth rusty-gold coat [c20: named after *Vizsla*, Hungary]

VJ *abbreviation* video jockey

V-J Day *n* the day marking the Allied victory over Japan in World War II (Aug 15, 1945)

VL *abbreviation* Vulgar Latin

Vlaardingen (*Dutch* 'vlaːrdɪŋə) *n* a port in the W Netherlands, in South Holland west of Rotterdam: the third largest port in the Netherlands. Pop: 74 000 (2003 est)

Vladikavkaz (*Russian* vlədikafˈkas) *n* a city in S Russia, capital of the North Ossetian Republic on the N slopes of the Caucasus. Pop: 318 000 (2005 est). Former names: Dzaudzhikau (1944–54), Ordzhonikidze (1954–91)

Vladimir[1] (*Russian* vlaˈdimir) *n* a city in W central Russia: capital of the principality of Vladimir until the court transferred to Moscow in 1328. Pop: 310 000 (2005 est)

Vladimir[2] ('vlædɪˌmɪə; *Russian* vlaˈdimir) *n* **Saint,** called *the Great.* ?956–1015, grand prince of Kiev (980–1015); first Christian ruler of Russia. Feast day: July 15

Vladivostok (ˌvlædɪˈvɒstɒk; *Russian* vlədivasˈtɔk) *n* a port in SE Russia, on the Sea of Japan: terminus of the Trans-Siberian Railway; the main Russian Pacific naval base since 1872 and chief commercial and civilian Russian port in the Far East; university (1956). Pop: 584 000 (2005 est)

Vlaminck (*French* vlamɛ̃k) *n* **Maurice de** (mɔris də). 1876–1958, French painter of the Fauve school

vlei (fleɪ, vleɪ) *n* *South African* an area of low marshy ground, esp one that feeds a stream [c19: from Afrikaans]

VLF *or* **vlf** *radio abbreviation* very low frequency

Vlissingen ('vlɪsɪŋə) *n* the Dutch name for **Flushing**

vlog ('vlɒɡ) *n* a video journal uploaded to the internet [c21: from VIDEO + BLOG]

Vlorë (*Albanian* 'vlorə) *or* **Vlonë** (*Albanian* 'vlonə) *n* a port in SW Albania, on the **Bay of Vlorë**: under Turkish rule from 1462 until Albanian independence was declared

here in 1912. Pop: 124 000 (2006 est). Ancient name: Avlona. Also called: Valona

Vltava (*Czech* 'vltava) *n* a river in the Czech Republic, rising in the Bohemian Forest and flowing generally southeast and then north to the River Elbe near Melnik. Length: 434 km (270 miles). German name: Moldau

v-mail ('viːmeɪl) *n* **1** a video message sent by e-mail **2** a computerized communication system designed to send virtual reality messages **3** electronic mail designed to spread a computer virus

V neck *n* a neck on a garment that comes down to a point on the throat or chest, resembling the shape of the letter "V" ▷ 'V-,neck *or* 'V-,necked *adj*

VOC *abbreviation* volatile organic compound: one of a number of chemicals, including benzene and acetone, that evaporate or vaporize readily and are harmful to human health and the environment

voc. *or* **vocat.** *abbreviation* vocative

vocab ('vəʊkæb) *n* short for **vocabulary**

vocable ('vəʊkəbəl) *n* any word, either written or spoken, regarded simply as a sequence of letters or spoken sounds, irrespective of its meaning [c16: from Latin *vocābulum* a designation, from *vocāre* to call] ▷ 'vocably *adv*

vocabulary (vəˈkæbjʊlərɪ) *n, pl* -laries **1** a listing, either selective or exhaustive, containing the words and phrases of a language, with meanings or translations into another language; glossary **2** the aggregate of words in the use or comprehension of a specified person, class, profession, etc **3** all the words contained in a language **4** a range or system of symbols, qualities, or techniques constituting a means of communication or expression, as any of the arts or crafts: *a wide vocabulary of textures and colours* [c16: from Medieval Latin *vocābulārium*, from *vocābulārius* concerning words, from Latin *vocābulum* VOCABLE]

vocal ('vəʊkəl) *adj* **1** of, relating to, or designed for the voice: *vocal music* **2** produced or delivered by the voice: *vocal noises* **3** connected with an attribute or the production of the voice: *vocal organs* **4** frequently disposed to outspoken speech, criticism, etc: *a vocal minority* **5** full of sound or voices: *a vocal assembly* **6** endowed with a voice **7** *phonetics* **a** of or relating to a speech sound **b** of or relating to a voiced speech sound, esp a vowel ▷ **8** a piece of jazz or pop music that is sung **9** a performance of such a piece of music [c14: from Latin *vōcālis* possessed of a voice, from *vōx* voice] ▷ vocality (vəʊˈkælɪtɪ) *n* ▷ 'vocally *adv*

vocal cords *pl n* either of two pairs of mucomembranous folds in the larynx. The upper pair (**false vocal cords**) are not concerned with vocal production; the lower pair (**true vocal cords** or **vocal folds**) can be made to vibrate and produce sound when air from the lungs is forced over them

vocalic (vəʊˈkælɪk) *adj phonetics* of, relating to, or containing a vowel or vowels

vocalise (ˌvəʊkəˈliːz) *n* a musical passage sung upon one vowel as an exercise to develop flexibility and control of pitch and tone; solfeggio

vocalism ('vəʊkəˌlɪzəm) *n* **1** the exercise of the voice, as in singing or speaking **2** *phonetics* **a** a voiced speech sound, esp a vowel **b** a system of vowels as used in a language

vocalist ('vəʊkəlɪst) *n* a singer, esp one who regularly appears with a jazz band or pop group

vocalize *or* **vocalise** ('vəʊkəˌlaɪz) *vb* **1** to express with or use the voice; articulate (a speech, song, etc) **2** (*tr*) to make vocal or articulate **3** (*tr*) *phonetics* to articulate (a speech sound) with voice **4** another word for **vowelize** **5** (*intr*) to sing a melody on a vowel, etc ▷ ˌvocali'zation *or* ˌvocali'sation *n* ▷ 'vocal,izer *or* 'vocal,iser *n*

vocal score *n* a musical score that shows voice parts in full and orchestral parts in the form of a piano transcription

vocation (vəʊˈkeɪʃən) *n* **1** a specified occupation, profession, or trade **2** **a** a special urge, inclination, or predisposition to a particular calling or career, esp a religious one **b** such a calling or career [c15: from Latin *vocātiō* a calling, from *vocāre* to call]

vocational (vəʊˈkeɪʃənᵊl) *adj* **1** of or relating to a vocation or vocations **2** of or relating to applied educational courses concerned with skills needed for an occupation, trade, or profession

vocational guidance *n* a guidance service based on psychological tests and interviews to find out what career or occupation may best suit a person

vocative (ˈvɒkətɪv) *grammar* ▷ *adj* **1** denoting a case of nouns, in some inflected languages, used when the referent of the noun is being addressed ▷ *n* **2 a** the vocative case **b** a vocative noun or speech element [c15: from Latin phrase *vocātīvus cāsus* the calling case, from *vocāre* to call]

voces (ˈvəʊsiːz) *n* the plural of **vox**

vociferate (vəʊˈsɪfəˌreɪt) *vb* to exclaim or cry out about (something) clamorously, vehemently, or insistently [c17: from Latin *vōciferārī* to clamour, from *vōx* voice + *ferre* to bear] > voˌciferˈation *n*

vociferous (vəʊˈsɪfərəs) *adj* **1** characterized by vehemence, clamour, or noisiness: *vociferous protests* **2** making an outcry or loud noises; clamorous: *a vociferous mob* > voˈciferously *adv* > voˈciferousness *n*

vocoder (ˈvəʊˌkəʊdə) *n music* a type of synthesizer that uses the human voice as an oscillator

VOD *abbreviation* video on demand: an interactive TV system that allows the viewer to select content and view it at a time of his or her own choosing

vodka (ˈvɒdkə) *n* an alcoholic drink originating in Russia, made from grain, potatoes, etc, usually consisting only of rectified spirit and water [c19: from Russian, diminutive of *voda* water; related to Sanskrit *udan* water, Greek *hudōr*]

voe (vəʊ; *Scot* vo) *n* (in Orkney and Shetland) a small bay or narrow creek [c17: from Old Norse *vagr*]

voetsek, voetsak (ˈfʊtsak, ˈvʊt-) **or voertsek, voertsak** (ˈfʊrtsak, ˈvʊrt-) *interj South African offensive, informal* an expression of dismissal or rejection [c19: Afrikaans, from Dutch *voort se ek* forward, I say, commonly applied to animals]

voetstoots or voetstoets (ˈfʊtstʊts, ˈvʊt-) *South African* ▷ *adj*, **1** denoting a sale in which the vendor is freed from all responsibility for the condition of the goods being sold ▷ *adv* **2** without responsibility for the condition of the goods sold [from Afrikaans *voetstoots* as it is]

Vogel (ˈvəʊgᵊl) *n* Sir *Julius*. 1835–99, New Zealand statesman; prime minister of New Zealand (1873–75; 1876)

Vogelweide (*German* ˈfoːgəlvaɪdə) *n* See **Walther von der Vogelweide**

Vogts (*German* vokts) *n* Hans-Hubert, known as *Berti*. born 1946, German footballer and coach; played for Germany (1967–79); coach of Germany (1990–98) and Scotland (2002–04)

vogue (vəʊg) *n* **1** the popular style at a specified time (esp in the phrase **in vogue**) **2** a period of general or popular usage or favour: *the vogue for such dances is now over* ▷ *adj* **3** (*usually prenominal*) popular or fashionable: *a vogue word* [c16: from French: a rowing, fashion, from Old Italian *voga*, from *vogare* to row, of unknown origin] > ˈvoguish *adj*

voice (vɔɪs) *n* **1** the sound made by the vibration of the vocal cords, esp when modified by the resonant effect of the tongue and mouth **2** the natural and distinctive tone of the speech sounds characteristic of a particular person **3** the condition, quality, effectiveness, or tone of such sounds: *a hysterical voice* **4** the musical sound of a singing voice, with respect to its quality or range: *she has a lovely voice* **5** the ability to speak, sing, etc: *he has lost his voice* **6** a sound resembling or suggestive of vocal utterance: *the voice of the sea; the voice of hard experience* **7** written or spoken expression, as of feeling, opinion, etc (esp in the phrase **give voice to**) **8** a stated choice, wish, or opinion or the power or right to have an opinion heard and considered: *to give someone a voice in a decision* **9** an agency through which is communicated another's purpose, policy, etc: *such groups are the voice of our enemies* **10** *music* **a** musical notes produced by vibrations of the vocal cords at various frequencies and in certain registers: *a tenor voice* **b** (in harmony) an independent melodic line or part: *a fugue in five voices* **11** *phonetics* the sound characterizing the articulation of several speech sounds, including all vowels or sonants, that is produced when the vocal cords make loose contact with each other and are set in vibration by the breath as it forces its way through the glottis **12** *grammar* a category of the verb or verbal inflections that expresses whether the relation between the subject and the verb is that of agent and action, action and recipient, or some other relation **13** in voice in a condition to sing or speak well **14** with one voice unanimously ▷ *vb* (*tr*) **15** to utter in words; give expression to: *to voice a complaint* **16** to articulate (a speech sound) with voice **17** *music* to adjust (a wind instrument or organ pipe) so that it conforms to the correct standards of tone colour, pitch, etc [c13: from Old French *voiz*, from Latin *vōx*] > ˈvoicer *n*

voice box *n* another word for the **larynx**

voiced (vɔɪst) *adj* **1** declared or expressed by the voice **2** (*in combination*) having a voice as specified: *loud-voiced* **3** *phonetics* articulated with accompanying vibration of the vocal cords: *in English* (b) *is a voiced consonant*

voice input *n* the control and operation of computer systems by spoken commands

voiceless (ˈvɔɪslɪs) *adj* **1** without a voice; mute **2** not articulated: *voiceless misery* **3** silent **4** *phonetics* articulated without accompanying vibration of the vocal cords: *in English* (p) *is a voiceless consonant* > ˈvoicelessly *adv*

voice mail *n* an electronic system for the transfer and storage of telephone messages, which can then be dealt with by the user at his or her convenience

voice-over *n* the voice of an unseen commentator heard during a film, television programme, etc

voice over broadband *n* a transmission technique that enables a user to make and receive telephone calls over a broadband connection

voiceprint (ˈvɔɪsˌprɪnt) *n* a graphic representation of a person's voice recorded electronically, usually having time plotted along the horizontal axis and the frequency of the speech on the vertical axis

void (vɔɪd) *adj* **1** without contents; empty **2** not legally binding: *null and void* **3** (of an office, house, position, etc) without an incumbent; unoccupied **4** (*postpositive; foll by of*) destitute or devoid: *void of resources* **5** having no effect; useless: *all his efforts were rendered void* **6** (of a card suit or player) having no cards in a particular suit: *his spades were void* ▷ *n* **7** an empty space or area: *the huge desert voids of Asia* **8** a feeling or condition of loneliness or deprivation **9** a lack of any cards in one suit: *to have a void in spades* ▷ *vb* (*mainly tr*) **10** to make ineffective or invalid **11** to empty (contents, etc) or make empty of contents **12** (*also intr*) to discharge the contents of (the bowels or urinary bladder) [c13: from Old French *vuide*, from Vulgar Latin *vocītus* (unattested), from Latin *vacuus* empty, from *vacāre* to be empty] > ˈvoider *n* > ˈvoidable *adj*

voidance (ˈvɔɪdᵊns) *n* **1** an annulment, as of a contract **2** the condition of being vacant, as an office, benefice, etc **3** the act of voiding, ejecting, or evacuating [c14: variant of AVOIDANCE]

voile (vɔɪl; *French* vwal) *n* a light semitransparent fabric of silk, rayon, cotton, etc, used for dresses, scarves, shirts, etc [c19: from French: VEIL]

Voiotia (*Greek* vjoˈtiːa) *n* a department of E central Greece: corresponds to ancient Boeotia and part of ancient Phocis. Pop: 123 913 (2001). Area: 3173 sq km (1225 sq miles)

voip (vɔɪp) *n informal* voice-over internet protocol: a system for converting analogue signals to digital so that telephone calls may be made over the internet

Vojvodina or Voivodina (*Serbian* ˈvɔjvɔdina) *n* an autonomous region of Serbia, in the N. Capital: Novi Sad. Pop: 2 024 487 (2002). Area: 22 489 sq km (8683 sq miles)

vol. *abbreviation* **1** volcano **2** volume **3** volunteer

volant (ˈvəʊlənt) *adj* **1** (*usually postpositive*) *heraldry* in a flying position **2** *rare* flying or capable of flight [c16: from French: flying, from *voler* to fly, from Latin *volāre*]

volar (ˈvəʊlə) *adj anatomy* of or relating to the palm of the hand or the sole of the foot [c19: from Latin *vola* hollow of the hand, palm, sole of the foot]

volatile ('vɒlə,taɪl) *adj* 1 (of a substance) capable of readily changing from a solid or liquid form to a vapour; having a high vapour pressure and a low boiling point 2 (of persons) disposed to caprice or inconstancy; fickle; mercurial 3 (of circumstances) liable to sudden, unpredictable, or explosive change 4 lasting only a short time: *volatile business interests* 5 *computing* (of a memory) not retaining stored information when the power supply is cut off ▷ *n* 6 a volatile substance [c17: from Latin *volātilis* flying, from *volāre* to fly] > 'volatileness *or* volatility (,vɒlə'tɪlɪtɪ) *n*

volatilize *or* **volatilise** (vɒ'lætɪ,laɪz) *vb* to change or cause to change from a solid or liquid to a vapour > vo'lati,lizable *or* vo'lati,lisable *adj* > vo,latiliz'ation *or* vo,latilis'ation *n*

vol-au-vent (*French* vɔlovɑ̃) *n* a very light puff pastry case filled either with a savoury mixture in a richly flavoured sauce or sometimes with fruit [c19: from French, literally: flight in the wind]

volcanic (vɒl'kænɪk) *adj* 1 of, relating to, produced by, or characterized by the presence of volcanoes: *a volcanic region* 2 suggestive of or resembling an erupting volcano: *a volcanic era* > vol'canically *adv* > volcanicity (,vɒlkə'nɪsɪtɪ) *n*

volcanic glass *n* any of several glassy volcanic igneous rocks, such as obsidian and pitchstone

volcanism ('vɒlkə,nɪzəm) *or* **vulcanism** *n* those processes collectively that result in the formation of volcanoes and their products

volcano (vɒl'keɪnəʊ) *n, pl* -noes *or* -nos 1 an opening in the earth's crust from which molten lava, rock fragments, ashes, dust, and gases are ejected from below the earth's surface 2 a mountain formed from volcanic material ejected from a vent in a central crater [c17: from Italian, from Latin *Volcānus* VULCAN, whose forges were believed to be responsible for volcanic rumblings]

Volcano Islands *pl n* a group of three volcanic islands in the W Pacific, about 1100 km (700 miles) south of Japan: the largest is Iwo Jima, taken by US forces in 1945 and returned to Japan in 1968. Area: about 28 sq km (11 sq miles). Japanese name: Kazan Retto

volcanology (,vɒlkə'nɒlədʒɪ) *or* **vulcanology** *n* the study of volcanoes and volcanic phenomena > volcanological (,vɒlkənə'lɒdʒɪkᵊl) *or* ,vulcano'logical *adj*

vole (vəʊl) *n* any of numerous small rodents of the genus *Microtus* and related genera, mostly of Eurasia and North America and having a stocky body, short tail, and inconspicuous ears: family *Cricetidae* [c19: short for *volemouse*, from Old Norse *vollr* field + *mus* MOUSE; related to Icelandic *vollarmus*]

Volga ('vɒlgə) *n* a river in W Russia, rising in the Valdai Range and flowing through a chain of small lakes to the Rybinsk Reservoir and south to the Caspian Sea through Volgograd: the longest river in Europe. Length: 3690 km (2293 miles)

Volgograd (*Russian* vəlga'grat; *English* 'vɒlgə,græd) *n* a port in SW Russia, on the River Volga: scene of a major engagement (1918) during the civil war and again in World War II (1942–43), in which the German forces were defeated; major industrial centre. Pop: 1 016 000 (2005 est). Former names: Tsaritsyn (until 1925), Stalingrad (1925–61)

volitant ('vɒlɪtənt) *adj* 1 flying or moving about rapidly 2 capable of flying [c19: from Latin *volitāre* to flit, from *volāre* to fly]

volition (və'lɪʃən) *n* 1 the act of exercising the will: *of one's own volition* 2 the faculty or capability of conscious choice, decision, and intention; the will 3 the resulting choice or resolution [c17: from Medieval Latin *volitiō*, from Latin *vol-* as in *volō* I will, present stem of *velle* to wish] > vo'litional *or* vo'litionary *adj*

volitive ('vɒlɪtɪv) *adj* of, relating to, or emanating from the will

volk (fɒlk) *n* *South African* the people or nation, esp the nation of Afrikaners [Afrikaans]

Volksraad ('fɔlks,rɑ:t) *n* *South African* the legislative assembly of the Boer republics in South Africa during the latter half of the 19th century [Afrikaans *volk* people

+ *raad* council]

volley ('vɒlɪ) *n* 1 the simultaneous discharge of several weapons, esp firearms 2 the projectiles or missiles so discharged 3 a burst of oaths, protests, etc, occurring simultaneously or in rapid succession 4 *sport* a stroke, shot, or kick at a moving ball before it hits the ground 5 *cricket* the flight of such a ball or the ball itself ▷ *vb* 6 to discharge (weapons, etc) in or as if in a volley or (of weapons, etc) to be discharged 7 (*tr*) to utter vehemently or sound loudly and continuously 8 (*tr*) *sport* to strike or kick (a moving ball) before it hits the ground [c16: from French *volée* a flight, from *voler* to fly, from Latin *volāre*] > 'volleyer *n*

volleyball ('vɒlɪ,bɔ:l) *n* 1 a game in which two teams hit a large ball back and forth over a high net with their hands 2 the ball used in this game

Vologda (*Russian* 'vɔləgdə) *n* an industrial city in W central Russia. Pop: 295 000 (2005 est)

Vólos (*Greek* 'vɔlɔs) *n* a port in E Greece, in Thessaly on the Gulf of Volos (an inlet of the Aegean): the third largest port in Greece. Pop: 129 000 (2005 est)

vols. *abbreviation* volumes

Volsung ('vɒlsʊŋ) *n* 1 a great hero of Norse and Germanic legend and poetry who gave his name to a race of warriors; father of Sigmund and Signy 2 any member of his family

volt[1] (vəʊlt) *n* the derived SI unit of electric potential; the potential difference between two points on a conductor carrying a current of 1 ampere, when the power dissipated between these points is 1 watt. Symbol: V [c19: named after Count Alessandro VOLTA]

volt[2] *or* **volte** (vɒlt) *n* 1 a small circle of determined size executed in dressage 2 a leap made in fencing to avoid an opponent's thrust [c17: from French *volte*, from Italian *volta* a turn, ultimately from Latin *volvere* to turn]

volta ('vɒltə; *Italian* 'vɔlta) *n, pl* -te (*Italian* -te) 1 a quick-moving Italian dance popular during the 16th and 17th centuries 2 a piece of music written for or in the rhythm of this dance, in triple time [c17: from Italian: turn; see VOLT[2]]

Volta[1] ('vɒltə) *n* 1 a river in W Africa, formed by the confluence of the **Black Volta** and the **White Volta** in N central Ghana: flows south to the Bight of Benin: the chief river of Ghana. Length: 480 km (300 miles); (including the Black Volta) 1600 km (1000 miles) 2 Lake Volta an artificial lake in Ghana, extending 408 km (250 miles) upstream from the **Volta River Dam** on the Volta River: completed in 1966. Area: 8482 sq km (3275 sq miles)

Volta[2] ('vəʊltə; *Italian* 'vɔlta) *n* Count **Alessandro** (ales'sandro). 1745–1827, Italian physicist after whom the volt is named. He made important contributions to the theory of current electricity and invented the voltaic pile (1800), the electrophorus (1775), and an electroscope

voltage ('vəʊltɪdʒ) *n* an electromotive force or potential difference expressed in volts

voltaic (vɒl'teɪɪk) *adj* another word for **galvanic** (sense 1)

voltaic cell *n* another name for **primary cell**

voltaic couple *n* *physics* a pair of dissimilar metals in an electrolyte with a potential difference between the metals resulting from chemical action

voltaic pile *n* an early form of battery consisting of a pile of paired plates of dissimilar metals, such as zinc and copper, each pair being separated from the next by a pad moistened with an electrolyte

Voltaire (vɒl'teə, vəʊl-; *French* vɔltɛr) *n* pseudonym of François Marie Arouet. 1694–1778, French writer, whose outspoken belief in religious, political, and social liberty made him the embodiment of the 18th-century Enlightenment. His major works include *Lettres philosophiques* (1734) and the satire *Candide* (1759). He also wrote plays, such as *Zaïre* (1732), poems, and scientific studies. He suffered several periods of banishment for his radical views > Vol'tairean *or* Vol'tairian *adj, n*

voltameter (vɒl'tæmɪtə) *n* another name for **coulometer** > voltametric (,vɒltə'mɛtrɪk) *adj*

voltmeter (,vəʊlt'æm,mi:tə) *n* a dual-purpose instrument that can measure both potential difference and electric current, usually in volts and amperes respectively

volt-ampere ('vəʊlt'æmpɛə) n the product of the potential in volts across an electrical circuit and the resultant current in amperes

Volta Redonda (Portuguese 'vɔltə rə'dõdə) n a city in SE Brazil, in Rio de Janeiro state on the Paraíba River: founded in 1941; site of South America's largest steelworks. Pop: 419 000 (2005 est)

volte-face ('vɔlt'fɑːs) n, pl volte-face 1 a reversal, as in opinion or policy 2 a change of position so as to look, lie, etc, in the opposite direction [C19: from French, from Italian volta-faccia, from volta a turn + faccia face]

voltmeter ('vəʊlt,miːtə) n an instrument for measuring potential difference or electromotive force

Volturno (Italian vol'turno) n a river in S central Italy, flowing southeast and southwest to the Tyrrhenian Sea: scene of a battle (1860) during the wars for Italian unity, in which Garibaldi defeated the Neapolitans; German line of defence during World War II. Length: 175 km (109 miles)

voluble ('vɒljʊbᵊl) adj 1 talking easily, readily, and at length; fluent 2 archaic easily turning or rotating, as on an axis 3 rare (of a plant) twining or twisting [C16: from Latin volūbilis turning readily, fluent, from volvere to turn] > ,volu'bility or 'volubleness n > 'volubly adv

volume ('vɒljuːm) n 1 the magnitude of the three-dimensional space enclosed within or occupied by an object, geometric solid, etc 2 a large mass or quantity: the volume of protest 3 an amount or total: the volume of exports 4 fullness or intensity of tone or sound 5 the control on a radio, etc, for adjusting the intensity of sound 6 a bound collection of printed or written pages; book 7 any of several books either bound in an identical format or part of a series 8 the complete set of issues of a periodical over a specified period, esp one year 9 history a roll or scroll of parchment, papyrus, etc 10 speak volumes to convey much significant information [C14: from Old French volum, from Latin volūmen a roll, book, from volvere to roll up]

volumetric (,vɒljʊ'mɛtrɪk) adj of, concerning, or using measurement by volume: volumetric analysis > ,volu'metrically adv

volumetric analysis n chem quantitative analysis of liquids or solutions by comparing the volumes that react with known volumes of standard reagents, usually by titration

voluminous (və'luːmɪnəs) adj 1 of great size, quantity, volume, or extent 2 (of writing) consisting of or sufficient to fill volumes [C17: from Late Latin volūminōsus full of windings, from volūmen VOLUME] > voluminosity (və,luːmɪ'nɒsɪtɪ) n > vo'luminously adv

Völund ('vœlʊnd) n the Scandinavian name of **Wayland**

voluntarism ('vɒləntə,rɪzəm) n 1 philosophy the theory that the will rather than the intellect is the ultimate principle of reality 2 a doctrine or system based on voluntary participation in a course of action 3 another name for **voluntaryism** > 'voluntarist n, adj

voluntary ('vɒləntərɪ, -trɪ) adj 1 performed, undertaken, or brought about by free choice, willingly, or without being asked: a voluntary donation 2 (of persons) serving or acting in a specified function of one's own accord and without compulsion or promise of remuneration: a voluntary social worker 3 done by, composed of, or functioning with the aid of volunteers: a voluntary association 4 endowed with, exercising, or having the faculty of willing: a voluntary agent 5 arising from natural impulse; spontaneous: voluntary laughter 6 law a acting or done without legal obligation, compulsion, or persuasion b made without payment or recompense in any form: a voluntary conveyance 7 (of the muscles of the limbs, neck, etc) having their action controlled by the will 8 maintained or provided by the voluntary actions or contributions of individuals and not by the state: voluntary schools; the voluntary system ▷ n, pl -taries 9 music a composition or improvisation, usually for organ, played at the beginning or end of a church service [C14: from Latin voluntārius, from voluntās will, from velle to wish] > volun'tarily adv

voluntary arrangement n law a procedure enabling an insolvent company to come to an arrangement with its creditors and resolve its financial problems, often in compliance with a court order

voluntaryism ('vɒləntərɪ,ɪzəm, -trɪ-) or **voluntarism** n the principle of supporting churches, schools, and various other institutions by voluntary contributions rather than with state funds > 'voluntaryist or 'voluntarist n

voluntary retailer n another name for **symbol retailer**

volunteer (,vɒlən'tɪə) n 1 a a person who performs or offers to perform voluntary service b (as modifier): a volunteer system; volunteer advice 2 a person who freely undertakes military service, esp temporary or special service 3 a a plant that grows from seed that has not been deliberately sown b (as modifier): a volunteer plant ▷ vb 4 to offer (oneself or one's services) for an undertaking by choice and without request or obligation 5 (tr) to perform, give, or communicate voluntarily: to volunteer help; to volunteer a speech 6 (intr) to enlist voluntarily for military service [C17: from French volontaire, from Latin voluntārius willing; see VOLUNTARY]

voluptuary (və'lʌptjʊərɪ) n, pl -aries 1 a person devoted or addicted to luxury and sensual pleasures ▷ adj 2 of, relating to, characterized by, or furthering sensual gratification or luxury [C17: from Late Latin voluptuārius delightful, from Latin voluptās pleasure]

voluptuous (və'lʌptjʊəs) adj 1 relating to, characterized by, or consisting of pleasures of the body or senses; sensual 2 disposed, devoted, or addicted to sensual indulgence or luxurious pleasures 3 provocative and sexually alluring, esp through shapeliness or fullness: a voluptuous woman [C14: from Latin voluptuōsus full of gratification, from voluptās pleasure] > vo'luptuously adv > vo'luptuousness n

volute ('vɒljuːt, və'luːt) n 1 a spiral or twisting turn, form, or object; spiral; whorl 2 Also called: helix a carved ornament, esp as used on an Ionic capital, that has the form of a spiral scroll 3 any of the whorls of the spirally coiled shell of a snail or similar gastropod mollusc 4 any tropical marine gastropod mollusc of the family Volutidae, typically having a spiral shell with beautiful markings ▷ adj also voluted (və'luːtɪd) 5 having the form of a volute; spiral [C17: from Latin volūta a spiral decoration, from volūtus rolled, from volvere to roll up] > vo'lution n

vomer ('vəʊmə) n the thin flat bone forming part of the separation between the nasal passages in mammals [C18: from Latin: ploughshare]

vomit ('vɒmɪt) vb -its, -iting, -ited 1 to eject (the contents of the stomach) through the mouth as the result of involuntary muscular spasms of the stomach and oesophagus 2 to eject or be ejected forcefully; spew forth ▷ n 3 the matter ejected in vomiting 4 the act of vomiting 5 a drug or agent that induces vomiting; emetic [C14: from Latin vomitāre to vomit repeatedly, from vomere to vomit] > 'vomiter n

vomit comet n informal an aircraft that dives suddenly in altitude, simulating freefall, in order to allow astronauts to experience the nausea that can affect people in a gravity-free environment

vomitory ('vɒmɪtərɪ, -trɪ) adj 1 Also: vomitive ('vɒmɪtɪv) causing vomiting; emetic ▷ n, pl -ries 2 Also called: vomitive a vomitory agent 3 Also called: vomitorium (,vɒmɪ'tɔːrɪəm) a passageway in an ancient Roman amphitheatre that connects an outside entrance to a tier of seats

von Braun (vɒn 'braʊn, fɒn) n **Wernher** ('vɛrnər). 1912–77, US rocket engineer, born in Germany, where he designed the V-2 missile used in World War II. In the US he worked on the Apollo project

Vondel (Dutch 'vɒndəl) n **Joost van den** ('joːst van dən). 1587–1679, Dutch poet and dramatist, author of the Biblical plays Lucifer (1654), Adam in Exile (1664), and Noah (1667)

von Euler (German fɒn 'ɔɪlər) n See Euler (sense 2)

von Laue (German fɒn 'laʊə) n See Laue

Vonnegut ('vɒnɪgʌt) n **Kurt**. 1922–2007, US novelist. His works include Cat's Cradle (1963), Slaughterhouse Five (1969), Galapagos (1985), Hocus Pocus (1990), and Timequake (1997)

von Neumann (vɒn 'njuːmən, fɒn) n **John**. 1903–57, US

mathematician, born in Hungary. He formulated game theory and contributed to the development of the atomic bomb and to the development of the stored-program computer (**von Neumann machine**)

von Rundstedt (German fɔn 'rʊntʃtɛt) n See **Rundstedt**

von Sternberg (vɒn 'stɜːn̩bɜːɡ; German fɔn 'ʃtɛrnbɛrk) n **Joseph** ('joːzɛf), real name *Jonas Sternberg*. 1894–1969, US film director, born in Austria, whose films include *The Blue Angel* (1930), *Blonde Venus* (1932), *The Scarlet Empress* (1934), and the unfinished *I, Claudius* (1937)

von Stroheim (vɒn 'strəʊˌhaɪm, 'ʃtrəʊ-, fɒn) n **Erich** ('eːrɪç), real name *Hans Erich Maria Stroheim von Nordenwall*. 1885–1957, US film director and actor, born in Austria, whose films include *Foolish Wives* (1921), *Greed* (1923), and *The Merry Widow* (1925)

voodoo ('vuːduː) n, pl **-doos** 1 Also called: **voodooism** a religious cult involving witchcraft and communication by trance with ancestors and animistic deities, common in Haiti and other Caribbean islands 2 a person who practises voodoo 3 a charm, spell, or fetish involved in voodoo worship and ritual ▷ adj 4 relating to or associated with voodoo ▷ vb **-doos, -dooing, -dooed** 5 (tr) to affect by or as if by the power of voodoo [c19: from Louisiana French *voudou*, ultimately of West African origin; compare Ewe *vodu* guardian spirit] > **'voodooist** n

voorkamer ('fʊəˌkɑːmə) n South African the front room, esp of a Cape Dutch house or farmhouse [from Afrikaans *voor* front + *kamer* room]

voorskot ('fʊəˌskɒt) n South African advance payment made to a farmer for crops. See **agterskot** [c20: Afrikaans, from *voor* before + *skot* shot, payment]

Voortrekker ('fʊəˌtrɛkə, 'vʊə-) n (in South Africa) 1 one of the original Afrikaner settlers of the Transvaal and the Orange Free State who migrated from the Cape Colony in the 1830s 2 a member of the Afrikaner youth movement founded in 1931 [c19: from Dutch, from *voor*-FORE- + *trekken* to TREK]

voracious (vɒ'reɪʃəs) adj 1 devouring or craving food in great quantities 2 very eager or unremitting in some activity: *voracious reading* [c17: from Latin *vorāx* swallowing greedily, from *vorāre* to devour] > **voracity** (vɒ'ræsɪtɪ) or **vo'raciousness** n

Vorarlberg (German 'foːrarlbɛrk) n a mountainous state of W Austria. Capital: Bregenz. Pop: 356 590 (2003 est). Area: 2601 sq km (1004 sq miles)

Voronezh (Russian va'rɔnɪʃ) n a city in W Russia: engineering, chemical, and food-processing industries; university (1918). Pop: 842 000 (2005 est)

Voroshilov (Russian vərə'ʃiləf) n **Kliment Yefremovich** ('klimɪnt jɪ'frjɛməvitʃ). 1881–1969, Soviet military leader; president of the Soviet Union (1953– 60)

Voroshilovgrad (Russian vərə'ʃiləfˌgrat) n the former name (1935–91) of **Lugansk**

Voroshilovsk (Russian vərə'ʃiləfsk) n the former name (1940–44) of **Stavropol**

-vorous adj combining form feeding on or devouring: *carnivorous* [from Latin *-vorus*; related to *vorāre* to swallow up, DEVOUR] > **-vore** n combining form

Vorster ('fɔːstə, 'vɔː-) n **Balthazar Johannes**, known as *John*. 1915–83, South African statesman; Nationalist prime minister (1966–78); president (1978)

vortex ('vɔːtɛks) n, pl **-texes** or **-tices** (-tɪˌsiːz) 1 a whirling mass or rotary motion in a liquid, gas, flame, etc, such as the spiralling movement of water around a whirlpool 2 any activity, situation, or way of life regarded as irresistibly engulfing [c17: from Latin: a whirlpool; variant of VERTEX] > **'vortical** adj

vorticella (ˌvɔːtɪ'sɛlə) n, pl **-lae** (-liː) any protozoan of the genus *Vorticella*, consisting of a goblet-shaped ciliated cell attached to the substratum by a long contractile stalk [c18: from New Latin, literally: a little eddy, from VORTEX]

vorticism ('vɔːtɪˌsɪzəm) n an art movement in England initiated in 1913 by Wyndham Lewis, the British painter, novelist, and critic (1884–1957), combining the techniques of cubism with the concern for the problems of the machine age evinced in futurism [c20: referring to the "vortices" of modern life on which the movement was based] > **'vorticist** n

Vortumnus (vɔː'tʌmnəs) n a variant spelling of **Vertumnus**

Vosges (French voʒ) n 1 a mountain range in E France, west of the Rhine valley. Highest peak: 1423 m (4672 ft) 2 a department of NE France, in Lorraine region. Capital: Épinal. Pop: 381 277 (2003 est). Area: 5903 sq km (2302 sq miles)

vostro account ('vɒstrəʊ) n a bank account held by a foreign bank with a British bank, usually in sterling. See **nostro account**

votary ('vəʊtərɪ) n, pl **-ries** also **votarist** 1 RC Church, Eastern Churches a person, such as a monk or nun, who has dedicated himself or herself to religion by taking vows 2 a devoted adherent of a religion, cause, leader, pursuit, etc ▷ adj 3 ardently devoted to the services or worship of God, a deity, or a saint [c16: from Latin *vōtum* a vow, from *vovēre* to vow] > **'votaress** or **'votress** fem n

vote (vəʊt) n 1 an indication of choice, opinion, or will on a question, such as the choosing of a candidate, by or as if by some recognized means, such as a ballot: *10 votes for Jones* 2 the opinion of a group of persons as determined by voting: *it was put to the vote; do not take a vote; it came to a vote* 3 a body of votes or voters collectively: *the Jewish vote* 4 the total number of votes cast 5 the ticket, ballot, etc, by which a vote is expressed 6 a the right to vote; franchise; suffrage b a person regarded as the embodiment of this right 7 a means of voting, such as a ballot 8 chiefly Brit a grant or other proposition to be voted upon ▷ vb 9 (when tr, takes a clause as object or an infinitive) to express or signify (one's preference, opinion, or will) (for or against some question, etc): *to vote by ballot; we voted that it was time to adjourn; vote for me!* 10 (intr) to declare oneself as being (something or in favour of something) by exercising one's vote: *to vote socialist* 11 (tr; foll by *into* or *out of*, etc) to appoint or elect (a person to or from a particular post): *they voted him into the presidency; he was voted out of office* 12 (tr) to determine the condition of in a specified way by voting: *the court voted itself out of existence* 13 (tr) to authorize, confer, or allow by voting: *vote us a rise* 14 (tr) informal to declare by common opinion: *the party was voted a failure* [c15: from Latin *vōtum* a solemn promise, from *vovēre* to vow] > **'votable** or **'voteable** adj

vote down vb (tr, adverb) to decide against or defeat in a vote: *the bill was voted down*

vote of no confidence n parliament a vote on a motion put by the Opposition censuring an aspect of the Government's policy; if the motion is carried the Government is obliged to resign. Also called: **vote of censure**

voter ('vəʊtə) n a person who can or does vote

voting machine n (esp in the US) a machine at a polling station that voters operate to register their votes and that mechanically or electronically counts all votes cast

votive ('vəʊtɪv) adj 1 offered, given, undertaken, performed or dedicated in fulfilment of or in accordance with a vow 2 RC Church optional; not prescribed; having the nature of a voluntary offering: *a votive Mass; a votive candle* [c16: from Latin *vōtīvus* promised by a vow, from *vōtum* a vow]

vouch (vaʊtʃ) vb 1 (intr; usually foll by *for*) to give personal assurance; guarantee: *I'll vouch for his safety* 2 (when tr, usually takes a clause as object; when intr, usually foll by *for*) to furnish supporting evidence (for) or function as proof (of) 3 (tr) archaic to cite (authors, principles, etc) in support of something [c14: from Old French *vocher* to summon, ultimately from Latin *vocāre* to call]

voucher ('vaʊtʃə) n 1 a document serving as evidence for some claimed transaction, as the receipt or expenditure of money 2 Brit a ticket or card serving as a substitute for cash: *a gift voucher* 3 a person or thing that vouches for the truth of some statement, etc [c16: from Anglo-French, noun use of Old French *voucher* to summon; see VOUCH]

vouchsafe (ˌvaʊtʃ'seɪf) vb (tr) 1 to give or grant or condescend to give or grant: *she vouchsafed no reply; he vouchsafed me no encouragement* 2 (may take a clause as object or an infinitive) to agree, promise, or permit, often graciously or condescendingly: *he vouchsafed to come yesterday* [C14 *vouchen sauf*; see VOUCH, SAFE]

voussoir (vuːˈswɑː) *n* a wedge-shaped stone or brick that is used with others to construct an arch or vault [c18: from French, from Vulgar Latin *volsōrium* (unattested), ultimately from Latin *volvere* to turn, roll]

vow (vaʊ) *n* **1** a solemn or earnest pledge or promise binding the person making it to perform a specified act or behave in a certain way **2** a solemn promise made to a deity or saint, by which the promiser pledges himself to some future act, course of action, or way of life **3** take vows to enter a religious order and commit oneself to its rule of life by the vows of poverty, chastity, and obedience, which may be taken for a limited period as **simple vows** or as a perpetual and still more solemn commitment as **solemn vows** ▷ *vb* **4** (*tr; may take a clause as object or an infinitive*) to pledge, promise, or undertake solemnly: *he vowed that he would continue; he vowed to return* **5** (*tr*) to dedicate or consecrate to God, a deity, or a saint **6** (*tr; usually takes a clause as object*) to assert or swear emphatically **7** (*intr*) *archaic* to declare solemnly [c13: from Old French *vou*, from Latin *vōtum* a solemn promise, from *vovēre* to vow] > 'vower *n*

vowel ('vaʊəl) *n* **1** *phonetics* a voiced speech sound whose articulation is characterized by the absence of friction-causing obstruction in the vocal tract, allowing the breath stream free passage. The timbre of a vowel is chiefly determined by the position of the tongue and the lips **2** a letter or character representing a vowel [c14: from Old French *vouel*, from Latin *vocālis littera* a vowel, from *vocālis* sonorous, from *vox* a voice] > 'vowel-like *adj*

vowel gradation *n* another name for **ablaut**. See **gradation** (sense 5)

vowelize *or* **vowelise** ('vaʊəˌlaɪz) *vb* (*tr*) to mark the vowel points in (a Hebrew word or text) > ˌvoweli'zation *or* ˌvoweli'sation *n*

vowel mutation *n* another name for **umlaut**

vowel point *n* any of several marks or points placed above or below consonants, esp those evolved for Hebrew or Arabic, in order to indicate vowel sounds

vox (vɒks) *n, pl* **voces** ('vəʊsiːz) a voice or sound [Latin: voice]

vox pop *n* interviews with members of the public on a radio or television programme [c20: shortened from vox POPULI]

vox populi ('pɒpjʊˌlaɪ) *n* the voice of the people; popular or public opinion [Latin]

voyage ('vɔɪɪdʒ) *n* **1** a journey, travel, or passage, esp one to a distant land or by sea or air ▷ *vb* **2** to travel over or traverse (something): *we will voyage to Africa* [c13: from Old French *veiage*, from Latin *viāticum* provision for travelling, from *viāticus* concerning a journey, from *via* a way] > 'voyager *n*

voyage charter *n* the hire of a ship or aircraft for a specified number of voyages. See **time charter**

voyageur (ˌvɔɪəˈdʒɜː) *n Canadian* a woodsman, guide, trapper, boatman, or explorer, esp in the North [c19: from French: traveller, from *voyager* to VOYAGE]

voyeur (vwaːˈɜː; *French* vwajœr) *n* a person who obtains sexual pleasure or excitement from the observation of someone undressing, having intercourse, etc [c20: French, literally: one who sees, from *voir* to see, from Latin *vidēre*] > vo'yeurism *n* > ˌvoyeur'istic *adj*

Voysey ('vɔɪzɪ) *n* **Charles (Francis Annesley)**. 1857–1941, British architect and designer of furniture, fittings, and decor

Voznesensky (*Russian* vəznɪˈsjɛnskij) *n* **Andrei (Andreievich)** (anˈdrjej). born 1933, Russian poet, noted for his experimental style

VP *abbreviation* **1** Vice President **2** verb phrase

VPL *jocular abbreviation* visible panty line

VPN *abbreviation* virtual private network: a network that uses the internet to transfer information using secure methods

VR *abbreviation* **1** variant reading **2** Victoria Regina [Latin: Queen Victoria] **3** virtual reality

V. Rev. *abbreviation* Very Reverend

Vries (vriːs) *n* See **De Vries**

vrou (frəʊ) *n South African* a woman or wife [Afrikaans]

vrystater ('freɪˌstɑːtə) *n South African* a native inhabitant of the Free State, or one who is White [from Afrikaans, from Dutch *vrij* free + *staat* state]

vs *abbreviation* versus

VS *abbreviation* Veterinary Surgeon

v.s. *abbreviation* vide supra. See **vide**

V-sign *n* **1** (in Britain) an offensive gesture made by sticking up the index and middle fingers with the palm of the hand inwards as an indication of contempt, defiance, etc **2** a similar gesture with the palm outwards meaning victory or peace

VSO *abbreviation* **1** very superior old: used to indicate that a brandy, port, etc, is between 12 and 17 years old **2** (in Britain) Voluntary Service Overseas: an organization that sends young volunteers to use and teach their skills in developing countries

VSOP *abbreviation* very special (or superior) old pale: used to indicate that a brandy, port, etc, is between 20 and 25 years old

Vt. *or* **VT** *abbreviation* Vermont

VTOL ('viːtɒl) *n* **1** vertical takeoff and landing; a system in which an aircraft can take off and land vertically **2** an aircraft that uses this system. Compare **STOL**

VTR *abbreviation* video tape recorder

V-type engine *n* a type of internal-combustion engine having two cylinder blocks attached to a single crankcase, the angle between the two blocks forming a V

Vuelta Abajo (*Spanish* 'bwelta aˈβaxo) *n* a region of W Cuba: famous for its tobacco

vug, vugg *or* **vugh** (vʌɡ) *n mining* a small cavity in a rock or vein, usually lined with crystals [c19: from Cornish *vooga* cave] > 'vuggy *or* 'vughy *adj*

Vuillard (*French* vɥijar) *n* **Jean Édouard** (ʒɑ̃ edwar). 1868–1940, French painter and lithographer

Vulcan ('vʌlkən) *n* the Roman god of fire and metalworking. Greek counterpart: **Hephaestus** > Vulcanian (vʌlˈkeɪnɪən) *adj*

vulcanian (vʌlˈkeɪnɪən) *adj geology* of or relating to a volcanic eruption characterized by the explosive discharge of fine ash and large irregular fragments of solidified or viscous lava [C17 after VULCAN]

vulcanism ('vʌlkəˌnɪzəm) *n* a variant of **volcanism**

vulcanite ('vʌlkəˌnaɪt) *n* a hard usually black rubber produced by vulcanizing natural rubber with large amounts of sulphur. It is resistant to chemical attack: used for chemical containers, electrical insulators, etc. Also called: **ebonite**

vulcanize *or* **vulcanise** ('vʌlkəˌnaɪz) *vb* (*tr*) **1** to treat (rubber) with sulphur or sulphur compounds under heat and pressure to improve elasticity and strength or to produce a hard substance such as vulcanite **2** to treat (substances other than rubber) by a similar process in order to improve their properties > ˌvulcani'zation *or* ˌvulcani'sation *n*

vulcanology (ˌvʌlkəˈnɒlədʒɪ) *n* a variant of **volcanology**

Vulg. *abbreviation* Vulgate

vulgar ('vʌlɡə) *adj* **1** marked by lack of taste, culture, delicacy, manners, etc: *vulgar behaviour; vulgar language* **2** (*often capital; usually prenominal*) denoting a form of a language, esp of Latin, current among common people, esp at a period when the formal language is archaic and not in general spoken use **3** *archaic* of, relating to, or current among the great mass of common people, in contrast to the educated, cultured, or privileged; ordinary [c14: from Latin *vulgāris* belonging to the multitude, from *vulgus* the common people] > 'vulgarly *adv*

vulgar fraction *n* another name for **simple fraction**

vulgarian (vʌlˈɡɛərɪən) *n* a vulgar person, esp one who is rich or has pretensions to good taste

vulgarism ('vʌlɡəˌrɪzəm) *n* **1** a coarse, crude, or obscene expression **2** a word or phrase found only in the vulgar form of a language

vulgarity (vʌlˈɡærɪtɪ) *n, pl* -ties **1** the condition of being vulgar; lack of good manners **2** a vulgar action, phrase, etc

vulgarize *or* **vulgarise** ('vʌlɡəˌraɪz) *vb* (*tr*) **1** to make commonplace or vulgar; debase **2** to make (something little known or difficult to understand) widely known or popular among the public; popularize > ˌvulgari'zation or ˌvulgari'sation n

Vulgar Latin n any of the dialects of Latin spoken in the Roman Empire other than classical Latin. The Romance languages developed from them

vulgate ('vʌlgeɪt, -ɡɪt) rare n 1 a commonly recognized text or version 2 everyday or informal speech; the vernacular

Vulgate ('vʌlgeɪt, -ɡɪt) n (from the 13th century onwards) the fourth-century version of the Bible produced by Jerome, partly by translating the original languages, and partly by revising the earlier Latin text based on the Greek versions **b** (as modifier): the Vulgate version [c17: from Medieval Latin Vulgāta, from Late Latin vulgāta editiō popular version (of the Bible), from Latin vulgāre to make common, from vulgus the common people]

vulnerable ('vʌlnərəb³l) adj 1 capable of being physically or emotionally wounded or hurt 2 open to temptation, persuasion, censure, etc 3 military liable or exposed to attack 4 bridge (of a side who have won one game towards rubber) subject to increased bonuses or penalties [c17: from Late Latin vulnerābilis, from Latin vulnerāre to wound, from vulnus a wound] > ˌvulnera'bility or 'vulnerableness n > 'vulnerably adv

vulnerary ('vʌlnərərɪ) med ▷ adj 1 of, relating to, or used to heal a wound ▷ n, pl -aries 2 a vulnerary drug or agent [c16: from Latin vulnerārius belonging to wounds, from vulnus a wound]

vulpine ('vʌlpaɪn) adj 1 Also: vulpecular (vʌl'pɛkjʊlə) of, relating to, or resembling a fox 2 possessing the characteristics often attributed to foxes; crafty, clever,

etc [c17: from Latin vulpīnus foxlike, from vulpēs a fox]

vulture ('vʌltʃə) n 1 any of various very large diurnal birds of prey of the genera Neophron, Gyps, Gypaetus, etc, of Africa, Asia, and warm parts of Europe, typically having broad wings and soaring flight and feeding on carrion: family Accipitridae (hawks) 2 any similar bird of the family Cathartidae of North, Central, and South America 3 a person or thing that preys greedily and ruthlessly on others, esp the helpless [c14: from Old French voltour, from Latin vultur; perhaps related to Latin vellere to pluck, tear] > vulturine ('vʌltʃəˌraɪn) adj

vulva ('vʌlvə) n, pl -vae (-viː) or -vas the external genitals of human females, including the labia, mons veneris, clitoris, and the vaginal orifice [c16: from Latin: covering, womb, matrix] > 'vulval or 'vulvar adj

vulvitis (vʌl'vaɪtɪs) n inflammation of the vulva

vuvuzela (ˌvuːvuːˈzɛlə) n South African an elongated plastic instrument that football fans blow to make a loud noise similar to the trumpeting of an elephant [c20: from Zulu]

vv abbreviation vice versa

Vyatka (Russian 'vjatkə) n the former name (1780–1934) of **Kirov¹**

Vyborg (Russian 'vibərk) n a port in NW Russia, at the head of **Vyborg Bay** (an inlet of the Gulf of Finland): belonged to Finland (1918–40). Pop: 79 224 (2002). Finnish name: Viipuri. Swedish name: Viborg

Vyshinsky or **Vishinsky** (Russian viˈʃɪnskɪj) n **Andrei Yanuaryevich** (anˈdrej jənuˈarjɪvɪtʃ). 1883–1954, Soviet jurist, statesman, and diplomat; foreign minister (1949–53). He was public prosecutor (1935–38) at the trials held to purge Stalin's rivals and was the Soviet representative at the United Nations (1945–49; 1953–54)

Ww

w or **W** ('dʌbªl,juː) *n, pl* **w's, W's** or **Ws** **1** the 23rd letter and 18th consonant of the modern English alphabet **2** a speech sound represented by this letter, in English usually a bilabial semivowel, as in *web*

W *symbol for* **1** watt **2** West **3** *physics* work **4** *chem* tungsten [from New Latin *wolframium,* from German *Wolfram*] **5** women's (size)

w. *abbreviation* **1** week **2** weight **3** width **4** wife **5** with **6** *cricket* **a** wide **b** wicket

W. *abbreviation* **1** Wales **2** Welsh

W8 *abbreviation text messaging* wait

WA *abbreviation* **1** Washington (state) **2** Western Australia

WAAAF *abbreviation* (formerly) Women's Auxiliary Australian Air Force

WAAC (wæk) *n acronym* (formerly) **1** Women's Army Auxiliary Corps **2** Also called: **waac** a member of this corps

Waadt (vat) *n* the German name for **Vaud**

WAAF (wæf) *n acronym* (formerly) **1** Women's Auxiliary Air Force **2** Also called: **Waaf** a member of either of these forces

Waal (*Dutch* waːl) *n* a river in the central Netherlands: the S branch of the Lower Rhine. Length: 84 km (52 miles)

Wabash ('wɔːbæʃ) *n* a river in the E central US, rising in W Ohio and flowing west and southwest to join the Ohio River in Indiana. Length: 764 km (475 miles)

wabble ('wɒbªl) *vb, n* a variant spelling of **wobble**

Wace (weɪs) *n* Robert. born ?1100, Anglo-Norman poet; author of the *Roman de Brut* and *Roman de Rou*

wacke ('wækə) *n obsolete* any of various soft earthy rocks that resemble or are derived from basaltic rocks [c18: from German: rock, gravel, basalt]

wacko ('wækəʊ) *informal* ▷ *adj* **1** mad or eccentric ▷ *n, pl* **wackos 2** a mad or eccentric person [c20: back formation from WACKY]

wacky ('wækɪ) *adj* **wackier, wackiest** *slang* eccentric, erratic, or unpredictable [c19 (in dialect sense: a fool, an eccentric): from WHACK (hence, a *whacky,* a person who behaves as if he had been whacked on the head)] ▷ **'wackily** *adv* ▷ **'wackiness** *n*

wad (wɒd) *n* **1** a small mass or ball of fibrous or soft material, such as cotton wool, used esp for packing or stuffing **2 a** a plug of paper, cloth, leather, etc, pressed against a charge to hold it in place in a muzzle-loading cannon **b** a disc of paper, felt, pasteboard, etc, used to hold in place the powder and shot in a shotgun cartridge **3** a roll or bundle of something, esp of banknotes ▷ *vb* **wads, wadding, wadded 4** to form (something) into a wad **5** (*tr*) to roll into a wad or bundle **6** (*tr*) **a** to hold (a charge) in place with a wad **b** to insert a wad into (a gun) **7** (*tr*) to pack or stuff with wadding; pad [c14: from Late Latin *wadda;* related to German *Watte* cotton wool]

WADA *abbreviation* World Anti-Doping Agency: an independent agency working towards eradicating the improper use of drugs in sport

Wadai (waː'daɪ) *n* a former independent sultanate of NE central Africa: now the E part of Chad

Waddenzee (*Dutch* 'wɑdənzeː) *n* the part of the North Sea between the Dutch mainland and the West Frisian Islands

wadding ('wɒdɪŋ) *n* **1 a** any fibrous or soft substance used as padding, stuffing, etc, esp sheets of carded cotton prepared for the purpose **b** a piece of this **2** material for wads used in cartridges or guns

Waddington ('wɒdɪŋtən) *n* C(onrad) H(all). 1905–75, British embryologist and geneticist: author of *Principles of Embryology* (1956) and *The Ethical Animal* (1960)

waddle ('wɒdªl) *vb* (*intr*) **1** to walk with short steps, rocking slightly from side to side ▷ *n* **2** a swaying gait or motion [c16: probably frequentative of WADE] ▷ **'waddler** *n* ▷ **'waddling** *adj*

waddy ('wɒdɪ) *n, pl* **-dies 1** a heavy wooden club used as a weapon by native Australians ▷ *vb* **-dies, -dying, -died 2** (*tr*) to hit with a waddy [c19: from a native Australian language, perhaps based on English WOOD¹]

wade (weɪd) *vb* **1** to walk with the feet immersed in (water, a stream, etc) **2** (*intr;* often foll by *through*) to proceed with difficulty: *to wade through a book* **3** (*intr;* foll by *in* or *into*) to attack energetically ▷ *n* **4** the act or an instance of wading [Old English *wadan;* related to Old Frisian *wada,* Old High German *watan,* Old Norse *vatha,* Latin *vadum* FORD] ▷ **'wadable** or **'wadeable** *adj*

W

Wade (weɪd) n (**Sarah**) **Virginia**. born 1945, British tennis player: Wimbledon champion 1977

wader ('weɪdə) n **1** a person or thing that wades **2** Also called: **wading bird** any of various long-legged birds, esp those of the order Ciconiiformes (herons, storks, etc), that live near water and feed on fish, etc **3** a Brit name for **shore bird**

waders ('weɪdəz) pl n long waterproof boots, sometimes extending to the chest like trousers, worn by anglers

wadi or **wady** ('wɒdɪ) n, pl **-dies** a watercourse in N Africa and Arabia, dry except in the rainy season [C19: from Arabic]

Wadi Halfa ('wɒdɪ 'hælfə) n a town in the N Sudan that was partly submerged by Lake Nasser: an important archaeological site

Wad Medani (wɑːd mɪ'dɑːniː) n a town in the E Sudan, on the Blue Nile: headquarters of the Gezira irrigation scheme; agricultural research centre. Pop: 332 000 (2005 est)

wafer ('weɪfə) n **1** a thin crisp sweetened biscuit with different flavourings, served with ice cream, etc **2** Christianity a thin disc of unleavened bread used in the Eucharist as celebrated by the Western Church **3** pharmacol an envelope of rice paper enclosing a medicament **4** electronics a large single crystal of semiconductor material, such as silicon, on which numerous integrated circuits are manufactured and then separated **5** a small thin disc of adhesive material used to seal letters, documents, etc ▷ vb **6** (tr) to seal, fasten, or attach with a wafer [C14: from Old Northern French waufre, from Middle Low German wāfel; related to WAFFLE¹] > 'wafer-like or 'wafery adj

waff (wæf, wɑːf) n Scot & northern English dialect **1** a gust or puff of air **2** a glance; glimpse ▷ vb **3** to flutter or cause to flutter [C16: Scottish and northern English variant of WAVE]

waffle¹ ('wɒfəl) n **a** a crisp golden-brown pancake with deep indentations on both sides **b** (as modifier): waffle iron [C19: from Dutch wafel (earlier wæfel), of Germanic origin; related to Old High German wabo honeycomb]

waffle² ('wɒfəl) informal, chiefly Brit ▷ vb **1** (intr; often foll by on) to speak or write in a vague and wordy manner ▷ n **2** vague and wordy speech or writing [C19: of unknown origin] > 'waffling adj, n

waft (wɑːft, wɒft) vb **1** to carry or be carried gently on or as if on the air or water ▷ n **2** the act or an instance of wafting **3** something, such as a scent, carried on the air **4** Also called: **waif** nautical (formerly) a signal flag hoisted furled to signify various messages depending on where it was flown [C16 (in obsolete sense: to convey by ship): back formation from C15 wafter a convoy vessel, from Middle Dutch wachter guard, from wachten to guard; influenced by WAFF]

wag¹ (wæg) vb **wags**, **wagging**, **wagged 1** to move or cause to move rapidly and repeatedly from side to side or up and down **2** to move (the tongue) or (of the tongue) to be moved rapidly in talking, esp in idle gossip **3** to move (the finger) or (of the finger) to be moved from side to side, in or as in admonition **4** slang to play truant (esp in the phrase **wag it**) ▷ n **5** the act or an instance of wagging [C13: from Old English wagian to shake; compare Old Norse vagga cradle]

wag² (wæg) n a humorous or jocular person; wit [C16: of uncertain origin] > 'waggish adj

Wag (wæg) n informal the wife or girlfriend of a famous sportsman [C21: a back formation from an acronym for w(ives) a(nd) g(irlfriends)]

wage (weɪdʒ) n **1** (often plural) payment in return for work or services, esp that made to workmen on a daily, hourly, weekly, or piece-work basis. See **salary 2** (plural) economics the portion of the national income accruing to labour as earned income, as contrasted with the unearned income accruing to capital in the form of rent, interest, and dividends **3** (often plural) recompense, return, or yield ▷ vb (tr) **4** to engage in [C14: from Old Northern French wagier to pledge, from wage, of Germanic origin; compare Old English weddian to pledge, WED] > 'wageless adj

wage differential n the difference in wages between workers with different skills in the same industry or between those with comparable skills in different industries or localities

wage earner or US **wage worker** n **1** a person who works for wages, esp as distinguished from one paid a salary **2** the person who earns money to support a household by working

wager ('weɪdʒə) n **1** an agreement or pledge to pay an amount of money as a result of the outcome of an unsettled matter **2** an amount staked on the outcome of such a matter or event **3 wager of battle** (in medieval Britain) a pledge to do battle for a cause, esp to decide guilt or innocence by single combat **4 wager of law** English legal history a form of trial in which the accused offered to make oath of his innocence, supported by the oaths of 11 of his neighbours declaring their belief in his statements ▷ vb **5** (when tr, may take a clause as object) to risk or bet (something) on the outcome of an unsettled matter **6** (tr) history to pledge oneself to (battle) [C14: from Anglo-French wageure a pledge, from Old Northern French wagier to pledge; see WAGE] > 'wagerer n

wage slave n ironic a person dependent on a wage or salary

wagga ('wɒgə) n Austral a blanket or bed covering made out of sacks stitched together [C19: named after WAGGA WAGGA]

Wagga Wagga ('wɒgə 'wɒgə) n a city in SE Australia, in New South Wales on the Murrumbidgee River: agricultural trading centre. Pop: 44 451 (2001)

waggle ('wægəl) vb **1** to move or cause to move with a rapid shaking or wobbling motion ▷ n **2** a rapid shaking or wobbling motion [C16: frequentative of WAG¹] > 'waggly adj

waggon ('wægən) n, vb a variant spelling (esp Brit) of **wagon**

Wagner ('vɑːgnə) n **1 Otto**. 1841–1918, Austrian architect, whose emphasis on function and structure in such buildings as the Post Office Savings Bank, Vienna (1904–06), influenced the development of modern architecture **2** (**Wilhelm**) **Richard** ('rɪçart). 1813–83, German romantic composer noted chiefly for his invention of the music drama. His cycle of four such dramas The Ring of the Nibelung was produced at his own theatre in Bayreuth in 1876. His other operas include Tannhäuser (1845; revised 1861), Tristan and Isolde (1865), and Parsifal (1882)

Wagnerian (vɑːgˈnɪərɪən) adj **1** of or suggestive of the dramatic musical compositions of Richard Wagner, the German romantic composer (1813–83), their massive scale, dramatic and emotional intensity, etc ▷ n Also: **Wagnerite 2** a follower or disciple of the music or theories of Richard Wagner

Wagner-Jauregg (German 'vɑːgnərˈjaʊrɛk) n **Julius**. 1857–1940, Austrian psychiatrist and neurologist; a pioneer of the use of fever therapy in the treatment of mental disorders. Nobel prize for physiology or medicine 1927

wagon or **waggon** ('wægən) n **1** any of various types of wheeled vehicles, ranging from carts to lorries, esp a vehicle with four wheels drawn by a horse, tractor, etc, and used for carrying crops, heavy loads, etc **2** Brit a railway freight truck, esp an open one **3** US & Canadian a child's four-wheeled cart **4** an obsolete word for **chariot 5 off the wagon** informal no longer abstaining from alcoholic drinks **6 on the wagon** informal abstaining from alcoholic drinks [C16: from Dutch wagen WAIN] > 'wagonless or 'waggonless adj

wagoner or **waggoner** ('wægənə) n a person who drives a wagon

wagonette or **waggonette** (ˌwægəˈnɛt) n a light four-wheeled horse-drawn vehicle with two lengthwise seats facing each other behind a crosswise driver's seat

wagon-lit (French vagɔ̃li) n, pl **wagons-lits** (vagɔ̃li) **1** a sleeping car on a European railway **2** a compartment on such a car [C19: from French, from wagon railway coach + lit bed]

wagonload or **waggonload** ('wægənˌləʊd) n the load that is or can be carried by a wagon

wagon train n a supply train of horses and wagons, esp

W

one going over rough terrain

wagon vault *n* another name for **barrel vault**

Wagram (*German* 'vaːɡram) *n* a village in NE Austria: scene of the defeat of the Austrians by Napoleon in 1809

wagtail ('wæɡˌteɪl) *n* any of various passerine songbirds of the genera *Motacilla* and *Dendronanthus*, of Eurasia and Africa, having a very long tail that wags when the bird walks: family *Motacillidae*

Wagyu ('wæɡjuː) *n* any of several Japanese breeds of beef cattle, raised to produce Kobe beef [Japanese]

Wahhabi or **Wahabi** (wə'hɑːbɪ) *n*, *pl* **-bis** a member of a strictly conservative Muslim sect founded in the 18th century with the aim of eliminating all innovations later than the 3rd century of Islam > **Wah'habism** or **Wa'habism** *n*

wahine (wɑː'hiːnɪ) *n* (esp in the Pacific islands) a Polynesian or Māori woman, esp a girlfriend or wife [c19: from Māori and Hawaiian]

wahoo (wɑː'huː, 'wɑːhuː) *n*, *pl* **-hoos** a large fast-moving food and game fish, *Acanthocybium solandri*, of tropical seas: family *Scombridae* (mackerels and tunnies) [of unknown origin]

wah-wah ('wɑːˌwɑː) *n* 1 the sound made by a trumpet, cornet, etc, when the bell is alternately covered and uncovered: much used in jazz 2 an electronic attachment for an electric guitar, etc, that simulates this effect [c20: of imitative origin]

waif (weɪf) *n* 1 a person, esp a child, who is homeless, friendless, or neglected 2 anything found and not claimed, the owner being unknown 3 *nautical* another name for **waft** (sense 4) 4 *law obsolete* a stolen article thrown away by a thief in his flight and forfeited to the Crown or to the lord of the manor [c14: from Anglo-Norman, variant of Old Northern French *gaif*, of Scandinavian origin; related to Old Norse *veif* a flapping thing] > **'waifˌlike** *adj*

Waikaremoana (waɪˈkɒrəməʊˌɑːnə) *n* Lake Waikaremoana a lake in the North Island of New Zealand in a dense bush setting. Area: about 55 sq km (21 sq miles)

Waikato ('waɪˌkɑːtəʊ) *n* the longest river in New Zealand, flowing northwest across North Island to the Tasman Sea. Length: 350 km (220 miles)

Waikiki ('waɪkɪˌkiː, ˌwaɪkɪ'kiː) *n* a resort area in Hawaii, on SE Oahu: a suburb of Honolulu

wail (weɪl) *vb* 1 (*intr*) to utter a prolonged high-pitched cry, as of grief or misery 2 (*intr*) to make a sound resembling such a cry: *the wind wailed in the trees* 3 (*tr*) to lament, esp with mournful sounds ▷ *n* 4 a prolonged high-pitched mournful cry or sound [c14: of Scandinavian origin; related to Old Norse *vǣla* to wail, Old English *wā* WOE] > **'wailer** *n*

Wailing Wall *n* another name for **Western Wall**

wain (weɪn) *n* *chiefly poetic* a farm wagon or cart [Old English *wægn*; related to Old Frisian *wein*, Old Norse *vagn*]

Wain (weɪn) *n* **John** (**Barrington**). 1925–94, British novelist, poet, and critic. His novels include *Hurry on Down* (1953), *Strike the Father Dead* (1962), and *Young Shoulders* (1982)

wainscot ('weɪnskət) *n* 1 Also called: **wainscoting**, **wainscotting** a lining applied to the walls of a room, esp one of wood panelling 2 the lower part of the walls of a room, esp when finished in a material different from the upper part 3 fine quality oak used as wainscot ▷ *vb* 4 (*tr*) to line (a wall of a room) with a wainscot [c14: from Middle Low German *wagenschot*, perhaps from *wagen* WAGON + *schot* planking, related to German *Scheit* piece of wood]

wainwright ('weɪnˌraɪt) *n* a person who makes wagons

Wainwright ('weɪnˌraɪt) *n* 1 **Loudon**. born 1946, US rock singer and songwriter. His albums include *Loudon Wainwright III* (1970), *Fame and Wealth* (1983), *Grown Man* (1995) and *Strange Weirdos* (2007) 2 his daughter, **Martha**. born 1976, US rock singer and songwriter. Her recordings include the album *Martha Wainwright* (2005) 3 his son, **Rufus**. born 1973, US rock singer and songwriter. His albums include *Want One* (2003), *Want Two* (2004) and *Release the Stars* (2007)

waist (weɪst) *n* 1 *anatomy* the constricted part of the

trunk between the ribs and hips 2 the part of a garment covering the waist 3 the middle part of an object that resembles the waist in narrowness or position 4 the middle part of a ship 5 Also called: **centre section** the middle section of an aircraft fuselage 6 the constriction between the thorax and abdomen in wasps and similar insects [c14: origin uncertain; related to Old English *wæstm* WAX²] > **'waistless** *adj*

waistband ('weɪstˌbænd) *n* an encircling band of material to finish and strengthen a skirt or trousers at the waist

waistcoat ('weɪsˌkəʊt) *n* a sleeveless waist-length garment with buttons at the front, often worn under a suit jacket. US, Canadian, and Austral. name: **vest** > **'waistˌcoated** *adj*

waistline ('weɪstˌlaɪn) *n* 1 a line or indentation around the body at the narrowest part of the waist 2 the intersection of the bodice and the skirt of a dress, etc, or the level of this

wait (weɪt) *vb* 1 (when *intr*, often foll by *for*, *until*, or *to*) to stay in one place or remain inactive in expectation (of something); hold oneself in readiness (for something) 2 to delay temporarily or be temporarily delayed: *that work can wait* 3 (when *intr*, usually foll by *for*) (of things) to be in store (for a person) 4 (*intr*) to act as a waiter or waitress ▷ *n* 5 the act or an instance of waiting 6 a period of waiting 7 (*plural*) *rare* a band of musicians who go around the streets, esp at Christmas, singing and playing carols 8 **lie in wait** to prepare an ambush (for someone) ▷ See also **wait on**, **wait up** [c12: from Old French *waitier*; related to Old High German *wahtēn* to WAKE¹]

wait-a-bit *n* any of various plants having sharp hooked thorns or similar appendages, esp the greenbrier and the grapple plant

Waitangi Day (waɪ'tʌŋiː) *n* the national day of New Zealand (Feb 6), commemorating the signing of the **Treaty of Waitangi** (1840) by Māori chiefs and a representative of the British Government. The treaty provided the basis for the British annexation of New Zealand

Waite (weɪt) *n* **Terry**, full name *Terence Hardy Waite*. born 1939, British special envoy to the Archbishop of Canterbury, who negotiated the release of Western hostages held in the Middle East before being taken hostage himself (1987–91) in Lebanon

waiter ('weɪtə) *n* 1 a man whose occupation is to serve at table, as in a restaurant 2 an attendant at the London Stock Exchange or Lloyd's who carries messages: the modern equivalent of waiters who performed these duties in the 17th-century London coffee houses in which these institutions originated 3 a person who waits 4 a tray or salver on which dishes, etc, are carried

waiting game *n* the postponement of action or decision in order to gain the advantage

waiting list *n* a list of people waiting to obtain some object, treatment, status, etc

waiting room *n* a room in which people may wait, as at a railway station, doctor's or dentist's office, etc

wait on (*intr*, *preposition*) 1 to serve at the table of 2 to act as an attendant or servant to

waitress ('weɪtrɪs) *n* 1 a woman who serves at table, as in a restaurant ▷ *vb* 2 (*intr*) to act as a waitress

wait up *vb* (*intr*, *adverb*) to delay going to bed in order to await some event

Waitz (vaɪts) *n* **Greta**. born 1953, Norwegian long-distance runner and former marathon world champion

waive (weɪv) *vb* (*tr*) 1 to set aside or relinquish: *to waive one's right to something* 2 to refrain from enforcing (a claim) or applying (a law, penalty, etc) 3 to defer [c13: from Old Northern French *weyver*, from *waif* abandoned; see WAIF]

waiver ('weɪvə) *n* 1 the voluntary relinquishment, expressly or by implication, of some claim or right 2 the act or an instance of relinquishing a claim or right 3 a formal statement in writing of such relinquishment [c17: from Old Northern French *weyver* to relinquish, WAIVE]

Wajda (*Polish* 'vajda) *n* **Andrei** or **Andrzej** ('andʒɛj). born

W

1926, Polish film director. His films include *Ashes and Diamonds* (1958), *The Wedding* (1972), *Man of Iron* (1980), *Danton* (1982), and *Miss Nobody* (1997)

Wakayama (ˌwækəˈjɑːmə) *n* an industrial city in S Japan, on S Honshu. Pop: 391 008 (2002 est)

wake¹ (weɪk) *vb* wakes, waking, woke, woken 1 (often foll by *up*) to rouse or become roused from sleep 2 (often foll by *up*) to rouse or become roused from inactivity 3 (*intr*; often foll by *to* or *up to*) to become conscious or aware: *at last he woke to the situation* 4 (*intr*) to be or remain awake 5 (*tr*) to arouse (feelings etc) ▷ *n* 6 a watch or vigil held over the body of a dead person during the night before burial 7 (in Ireland) festivities held after a funeral 8 the patronal or dedication festival of English parish churches 9 a solemn or ceremonial vigil 10 (*usually plural*) an annual holiday in any of various towns in northern England, when the local factory or factories close, usually for a week or two weeks [Old English *wacian*; related to Old Frisian *wakia*, Old High German *wahtēn*] > 'waker *n*

● USAGE Where there is an object and the sense is the
● literal one *wake* (*up*) and *waken* are the commonest
● forms: *I wakened him*; *I woke him* (*up*). Both verbs are also
● commonly used without an object: *I woke up. Awake*
● and *awaken* are preferred to other forms of *wake* where
● the sense is a figurative one: *he awoke to the danger*

wake² (weɪk) *n* 1 the waves or track left by a vessel or other object moving through water 2 the track or path left by anything that has passed: *wrecked houses in the wake of the hurricane* [c16: of Scandinavian origin; compare Old Norse *vaka*, *vǫk* hole cut in ice, Swedish *vak*, Danish *vaage*; perhaps related to Old Norse *vǫkr*, Middle Dutch *wak* wet]

wakeboarding (ˈweɪkˌbɔːdɪŋ) *n* the sport of riding over water on a short surfboard and performing stunts while holding a rope towed by a speedboat

Wakefield (ˈweɪkˌfiːld) *n* 1 a city in N England, in Wakefield unitary authority, West Yorkshire: important since medieval times as an agricultural and textile centre. Pop: 76 886 (2001) 2 a unitary authority in N England, in West Yorkshire. Pop: 318 300 (2003 est). Area: 333 sq km (129 sq miles)

wakeful (ˈweɪkfʊl) *adj* 1 unable or unwilling to sleep 2 sleepless 3 alert > 'wakefully *adv* > 'wakefulness *n*

Wake Island *n* an atoll in the N central Pacific: claimed by the US in 1899; developed as a civil and naval air station in the late 1930s. Area: 8 sq km (3 sq miles)

wakeless (ˈweɪklɪs) *adj* (of sleep) deep or unbroken

waken (ˈweɪkən) *vb* to rouse or be roused from sleep or some other inactive state

wake-robin *n* 1 any of various North American herbaceous plants of the genus *Trillium*, such as *T. grandiflorum*, having a whorl of three leaves and three-petalled solitary flowers: family *Trilliaceae* 2 US any of various aroid plants, esp the cuckoopint

wake-up *n Austral informal* 1 an alert or intelligent person 2 be a wake-up to to be fully alert to (a person, thing, action, etc)

wake-up call *n* 1 a telephone call that wakes a person from sleep 2 an event that alerts people to a danger or difficulty

Waksman (ˈwæksmən) *n* **Selman Abraham.** 1888–1973, US microbiologist, born in Russia. He discovered streptomycin: Nobel prize for physiology or medicine 1952

Walachia *or* **Wallachia** (wɒˈleɪkɪə) *n* a former principality of SE Europe: a vassal state of the Ottoman Empire from the 15th century until its union with Moldavia in 1859, subsequently forming present-day Romania > Wa'lachian *or* Wal'lachian *adj, n*

Wałbrzych (*Polish* ˈvaʊbʒix) *n* an industrial city in SW Poland. Pop: 176 000 (2005 est). German name: Waldenburg

Walcheren (*Dutch* ˈwɑlxərə) *n* an island in the SW Netherlands, in the Scheldt estuary: administratively part of Zeeland province; suffered severely in World War II, when the dykes were breached, and again in the floods of 1953. Area: 212 sq km (82 sq miles)

Walcott (ˈwɔːlkət) *n* 1 **Derek (Alton)**. born 1930, St Lucian poet and playwright, whose works include the poetry

collections *In a Green Night* (1962) and *The Bounty* (1997), the play *The Dream on Monkey Mountain* (1967), and the long poem *Omeros* (1990): Nobel prize for literature 1992 2 **Jersey Joe**, real name *Arnold Raymond Cream*. 1914–94, US boxer: world heavyweight champion 1951–52

Waldemar I *or* **Valdemar I** (ˈvældɪˌmɑː) *n* known as *Waldemar the Great.* 1131–82, king of Denmark (1157–82). He conquered the Wends (1169), increased the territory of Denmark, and established the hereditary rule of his line

Waldemar II *or* **Valdemar II** *n* known as *Waldemar the Victorious.* 1170–1241, king of Denmark (1202–41); son of Waldemar I. He extended the Danish empire, conquering much of Estonia (1219)

Waldemar IV *or* **Valdemar IV** *n* surnamed *Atterdag*. ?1320–75, king of Denmark (1340–75), who reunited the Danish territories but was defeated (1368) by a coalition of his Baltic neighbours

Waldenburg (ˈvaldənbʊrk) *n* the German name for **Wałbrzych**

Waldenses (wɒlˈdɛnsiːz) *pl n* the members of a small sect founded as a reform movement within the Roman Catholic Church by Peter Waldo, a merchant of Lyons in the late 12th century, which in the 16th century joined the Reformation movement. Also called: Vaudois > Waldensian (wɒlˈdɛnsɪən) *n, adj*

Waldheim (*German* ˈvalthaim) *n* **Kurt** (kʊrt). 1918–2007, Austrian diplomat; secretary- general of the United Nations (1972–81); president of Austria (1986–92)

waldo (ˈwɔːldəʊ) *n, pl* **-dos** *or* **-does** a gadget for manipulating objects by remote control [c20: named after *Waldo F. Jones*, inventor in a science-fiction story by Robert Heinlein]

Waldorf salad (ˈwɔːldɔːf) *n* a salad of diced apples, celery, and walnuts mixed with mayonnaise [c20: named after the *Waldorf-Astoria Hotel* in New York City]

Waldstein (*German* ˈvaltʃtain) *n* a variant of (Albrecht Wenzel Eusebius von) **Wallenstein**

waldsterben (ˈwɔːldˌstɜːbən) *n ecology* the symptoms of tree decline in central Europe from the 1970s, considered to be caused by atmospheric pollution [c20: from German *Wald* forest + *sterben* to die]

wale (weɪl) *n* 1 the raised mark left on the skin after the stroke of a rod or whip 2 the weave or texture of a fabric, such as the ribs in corduroy 3 *nautical* a ridge of planking along the rail of a ship ▷ *vb* (*tr*) 4 to raise a wale or wales on by striking 5 to weave with a wale [Old English *walu* WEAL¹; related to Old Norse *vala* knuckle, Dutch *wäle*]

Wales (weɪlz) *n* a principality that is part of the United Kingdom, in the west of Great Britain; conquered by the English in 1282; parliamentary union with England took place in 1536: a separate Welsh Assembly with limited powers was established in 1999. Wales consists mainly of moorlands and mountains and has an economy that is chiefly agricultural, with an industrial and former coal-mining area in the south. Capital: Cardiff. Pop: 2 938 000 (2003 est). Area: 20 768 sq km (8017 sq miles). Welsh name: Cymru. Medieval Latin name: Cambria

Wałęsa (væˈwɛnsə) *n* **Lech** (lɛç). born 1943, Polish statesman: president of Poland (1990–95); leader of the independent trade union Solidarity 1980–90; Nobel peace prize 1983

Waley (ˈweɪlɪ) *n* **Arthur**. real name *Arthur Schloss*. 1889–1966, English orientalist, best known for his translations of Chinese poetry

Walhalla (wælˈhælə, væl-) *or* **Walhall** (wælˈhæl, væl-) *n* variants of **Valhalla**

walk (wɔːk) *vb* 1 (*intr*) to move along or travel on foot at a moderate rate; advance in such a manner that at least one foot is always on the ground 2 (*tr*) to pass through, on, or over on foot 3 (*tr*) to move on foot, esp habitually 4 (*tr*) to escort or conduct by walking: *to walk someone home* 5 (*intr*) (of ghosts, spirits, etc) to appear or move about in visible form 6 (*intr*) to follow a certain course or way of life: *to walk in misery* 7 (*tr*) to bring into a certain condition by walking: *I walked my shoes to shreds* 8 to disappear or be stolen: *where's my pencil? It seems to have walked* 9 walk it to win easily 10 walk on air to be delighted or exhilarated **11 walk tall** *informal* to have self-respect or pride **12 walk the streets** to be a prostitute **b** to wander round a town or city, esp when looking for work or having nowhere to stay **13 walk the walk or walk the talk** *informal* to put theory into practice: *you can talk the talk but can you walk the walk?*. See also **talk** (sense 14) ▷ *n* **14** the act or an instance of walking **15** the distance or extent walked **16** a manner of walking; gait **17** a place set aside for walking; promenade **18** a chosen profession or sphere of activity (esp in the phrase **walk of life**) **19 a** an arrangement of trees or shrubs in widely separated rows **b** the space between such rows **20** an enclosed ground for the exercise or feeding of domestic animals, esp horses **21** *chiefly Brit* the route covered in the course of work, as by a tradesman or postman **22** a procession; march: *Orange walk* **23** *obsolete* the section of a forest controlled by a keeper ▷ See also **walk away, walk into** [Old English *wealcan*; related to Old High German *walchan*, Sanskrit *valgati* he moves] > **'walkable** *adj*

walkabout ('wɔːkə,baʊt) *n* **1** a periodic nomadic excursion into the Australian bush made by a native Australian **2** an occasion when celebrities, royalty, etc, walk among and meet the public **3 go walkabout** *Austral* **a** to wander through the bush **b** *informal* to be lost or misplaced **c** *informal* to lose one's concentration

walk away *vb* (*intr, adverb*) **1** to leave, esp callously and disregarding someone else's distress **2 walk away with** to achieve or win easily

walker ('wɔːkə) *n* **1** a person who walks **2** Also called: **baby walker** a tubular frame on wheels or castors to support a baby learning to walk **3** a similar support for walking, often with rubber feet, for use by disabled or infirm people **4** a woman's escort at a social event

Walker ('wɔːkə) *n* **1 Alice (Malsenior).** born 1944, US writer: her works include *In Love and Trouble: Stories of Black Women* (1973) and the novels *Meridian* (1976), *The Color Purple* (1982), and *Possessing the Secret of Joy* (1992) **2 John.** born 1952, New Zealand middle-distance runner, the first athlete to run one hundred sub-four-minute miles

walkie-talkie *or* **walky-talky** (,wɔːkɪ'tɔːkɪ) *n, pl* **-talkies** a small combined radio transmitter and receiver, usually operating on shortwave, that can be carried around by one person: widely used by the police, medical services, etc

walk-in *adj* **1** (of a cupboard) large enough to allow a person to enter and move about in **2** (of a flat or house) in a suitable condition for immediate occupation

walking papers *pl n* *slang, chiefly US & Canadian* notice of dismissal

walking stick *n* **1** a stick or cane carried in the hand to assist walking **2** the usual US name for **stick insect**

walk into *vb* (*intr, preposition*) to meet with unwittingly: *to walk into a trap*

Walkman ('wɔːkmən) *n* *trademark* a small portable cassette player with light headphones

walk off *vb* **1** (*intr*) to depart suddenly **2** (*tr, adverb*) to get rid of by walking: *to walk off an attack of depression* **3 walk a person off his feet** to make someone walk so fast or far that he or she is exhausted **4 walk off with a** to steal **b** to win, esp easily

walk-on *n* **a** a small part in a play or theatrical entertainment, esp one without any lines **b** (*as modifier*): *a walk-on part*

walk out *vb* (*intr, adverb*) **1** to leave without explanation, esp in anger **2** to go on strike **3 walk out on** *informal* to abandon or desert **4 walk out with** *Brit obsolete or dialect* to court or be courted by ▷ *n* **walkout 5** a strike by workers **6** the act of leaving a meeting, conference, etc, as a protest

walkover ('wɔːk,əʊvə) *n* **1** *informal* an easy or unopposed victory **2** *horse racing* **a** the running or walking over the course by the only contestant entered in a race at the time of starting **b** a race won in this way ▷ *vb* **walk over** (*intr, mainly preposition*) **3** (*also adverb*) to win a race by a walkover **4** *informal* to beat (an opponent) conclusively or easily

walk socks *pl n* *NZ* men's knee-length stockings

walk through *theatre* ▷ *vb* **1** (*tr*) to act or recite (a part) in

a perfunctory manner, as at a first rehearsal ▷ *n* **walk-through 2** a rehearsal of a part

walkway ('wɔːk,weɪ) *n* **1** a path designed, and sometimes landscaped, for pedestrian use **2** a passage or path connecting buildings

Walkyrie (væl'kɪərɪ, 'vælkɪərɪ) *n* a variant spelling of **Valkyrie**

wall (wɔːl) *n* **1 a** a vertical construction made of stone, brick, wood, etc, with a length and height much greater than its thickness, used to enclose, divide, or support **b** (*as modifier*): *wall hangings*. Related adj: **mural 2** (*often plural*) a structure or rampart built to protect and surround a position or place for defensive purposes **3** *anatomy* any lining, membrane, or investing part that encloses or bounds a bodily cavity or structure: *abdominal wall*. Related adj: **parietal 4** *mountaineering* a vertical or almost vertical smooth rock face **5** anything that suggests a wall in function or effect: *a wall of fire; a wall of prejudice* **6 bang one's head against a brick wall** to try to achieve something impossible **7 drive to the wall** or **push to the wall** to force into an awkward situation **8 go to the wall** to be ruined; collapse financially **9 drive up the wall** *slang* to cause to become crazy or furious **10 go up the wall** *slang* to become crazy or furious **11 have one's back to the wall** to be in a very difficult situation ▷ *vb* (*tr*) **12** to protect, provide, or confine in or as if with a wall (often foll by *up*) to block (an opening) with a wall **14** (often foll by *in* or *up*) to seal by or within a wall or walls [Old English *weall*, from Latin *vallum* palisade, from *vallus* stake] > **walled** *adj* > **'wall-less** *adj*

wallaby ('wɒləbɪ) *n, pl* **-bies** *or* **-by** any of various herbivorous marsupials of the genera *Lagorchestes* (**hare wallabies**), *Petrogale* (**rock wallabies**), *Protemnodon*, etc, of Australia and New Guinea, similar to but smaller than kangaroos: family *Macropodidae* [C19: from native Australian *wolabā*]

Wallaby ('wɒləbɪ) *n, pl* **-bies** a member of the international Rugby Union football team of Australia

Wallace ('wɒlɪs) *n* **1 Alfred Russel.** 1823–1913, British naturalist, whose work on the theory of natural selection influenced Charles Darwin **2 Edgar.** 1875–1932, English crime novelist **3 Sir Richard.** 1818–90, English art collector and philanthropist. His bequest to the nation forms the Wallace Collection, London **4 Sir William.** ?1272–1305, Scottish patriot, who defeated the army of Edward I of England at Stirling (1297) but was routed at Falkirk (1298) and later executed

Wallace's line *n* the hypothetical boundary between the Oriental and Australasian zoogeographical regions, which runs between the Indonesian islands of Bali and Lombok, through the Macassar Strait, and SE of the Philippines [C20: named after Alfred Russel *Wallace* (1823–1913), British naturalist]

Wallachia (wɒ'leɪkɪə) *n* a variant spelling of **Walachia**

wallah *or* **walla** ('wɒlə) *n* (*usually in combination*) *informal* a person involved with or in charge of (a specified thing): *the book wallah* [C18: from Hindi *-wālā* from Sanskrit *pāla* protector]

wallaroo (,wɒlə'ruː) *n, pl* **-roos** *or* **-roo** a large stocky Australian kangaroo, *Macropus* (or *Osphranter*) *robustus*, of rocky regions [C19: from native Australian *wolarū*]

Wallasey ('wɒləsɪ) *n* a town in NW England, in Wirral unitary authority, Merseyside; near the mouth of the River Mersey, opposite Liverpool. Pop: 58 710 (2001)

wall bars *pl n* a series of horizontal bars attached to a wall and used in gymnastics

wallboard ('wɔːl,bɔːd) *n* a thin board made of materials, such as compressed wood fibres or gypsum plaster, between stiff paper, and used to cover walls, partitions, etc

wall creeper *n* a pink-and-grey woodpecker-like songbird, *Tichodroma muraria*, of Eurasian mountain regions: family *Sittidae* (nuthatches)

walled plain *n* any of the largest of the lunar craters, having diameters between 50 and 300 kilometres

Wallenberg ('vɑːlənbɜːg) *n* **Raoul** (raʊl). 1912–?, Swedish diplomat, who helped (1944–45) thousands of Hungarian Jews to escape from the Nazis. After his arrest (1945) by the Soviets nothing is certainly known of him: despite claims that he is still alive he is presumed to have died in prison

Wallenstein (*German* ˈvalənʃtain) *or* **Waldstein** *n* Albrecht Wenzel Eusebius von (ˈalbrɛçt ˈvɛntsəl ɔyˈzeːbiʊs fɔn), duke of Friedland and Mecklenburg, prince of Sagan. 1583–1634, German general and statesman, born in Bohemia. As leader of the Hapsburg forces in the Thirty Years' War he won many successes until his defeat at Lützen (1632) by Gustavus Adolphus

Waller (ˈwɒlə) *n* **1** Edmund. 1606–87, English poet and politician, famous for his poem "Go, Lovely Rose" **2 Fats**, real name *Thomas Waller.* 1904–43, US jazz pianist and singer

wallet (ˈwɒlɪt) *n* **1** a small folding case, usually of leather, for holding paper money, documents, etc **2** *archaic, chiefly Brit* a rucksack or knapsack [c14: of Germanic origin; compare Old English *weallian*, Old High German *wallōn* to roam, German *wallen* to go on a pilgrimage]

walleye (ˈwɔːlˌai) *n, pl* **-eyes** *or* **-eye** **1** a divergent squint **2** opacity of the cornea **3** an eye having a white or light-coloured iris **4** (in some collies) an eye that is particoloured white and blue **5** Also called: **walleyed pike** a North American pikeperch, *Stizostedion vitreum,* valued as a food and game fish **6** any of various other fishes having large staring eyes [back formation from earlier *walleyed*, from Old Norse *vagleygr*, from *vage*, perhaps: a film over the eye (compare Swedish *vagel* sty in the eye) + *-eygr* -eyed, from *auga* eye; modern form influenced by WALL] > **ˈwallˌeyed** *adj*

wallflower (ˈwɔːlˌflaʊə) *n* **1** Also called: **gillyflower** a plant, *Cheiranthus cheiri,* of S Europe, grown for its clusters of yellow, orange, brown, red, or purple fragrant flowers and naturalized on old walls, cliffs, etc: family *Brassicaceae* (crucifers) **2** any of numerous other crucifers of the genera *Cheiranthus* and *Erysimum*, having orange or yellow flowers **3** *informal* a person who stays on the fringes of a dance or party on account of lacking a partner or being shy

Wallis¹ (ˈvalɪs) *n* the German name for **Valais**

Wallis² (ˈwɒlɪs) *n* Sir **Barnes** (**Neville**). 1887–1979, English aeronautical engineer. He designed the airship R100, the Wellesley and Wellington bombers, and the bouncing bomb (1943), which was used to destroy the Ruhr dams during World War II

Wallis and Futuna Islands (ˈwɒlɪs, fuːˈtjuːnə) *pl n* a French overseas territory in the SW Pacific, west of Samoa. Capital: Mata-Utu. Pop: 15 000 (2003 est). Area: 367 sq km (143 sq miles)

wall of death *n* (at a fairground) a giant cylinder round the inside walls of which a motorcyclist rides

Walloon (wɒˈluːn) *n* **1** a member of a French-speaking people living chiefly in S Belgium and adjacent parts of France **2** the French dialect of Belgium ▷ *adj* **3** of, relating to, or characteristic of the Walloons or their dialect [c16: from Old French *Wallon*, from Medieval Latin: foreigner, of Germanic origin; compare Old English *wealh* foreign, WELSH]

Walloon Brabant *n* a province of central Belgium, formed in 1995 from the S part of Brabant province: densely populated and intensively farmed, with large industrial centres. Pop: 360 717 (2004 est). Area: 1091 sq km (421 sq miles)

wallop (ˈwɒləp) *vb* **-lops, -loping, -loped** **1** (*tr*) *informal* to beat soundly; strike hard **2** (*tr*) *informal* to defeat utterly **3** (*intr*) *dialect* to move in a clumsy manner **4** (*intr*) (of liquids) to boil violently ▷ *n* **5** *informal* a hard blow **6** *informal* the ability to hit powerfully, as of a boxer **7** *informal* a forceful impression **8** *Brit* a slang word for beer [c14: from Old Northern French *waloper* to gallop, from Old French *galoper*, of unknown origin]

walloper (ˈwɒləpə) *n* **1** a person or thing that wallops **2** *Austral slang* a policeman

walloping (ˈwɒləpɪŋ) *informal* ▷ *n* **1** a thrashing ▷ *adj* **2** (intensifier): *a walloping drop in sales*

wallow (ˈwɒləʊ) *vb* (*intr*) **1** (*esp* of certain animals) to roll about in mud, water, etc, for pleasure **2** to move about with difficulty **3** to indulge oneself in possessions,

emotion, etc: *to wallow in self-pity* ▷ *n* **4** the act or an instance of wallowing **5** a muddy place or depression where animals wallow [Old English *wealwian* to roll (in mud); related to Latin *volvere* to turn, Greek *oulos* curly, Russian *valun* round pebble] > **ˈwallower** *n*

wallpaper (ˈwɔːlˌpeipə) *n* **1** paper usually printed or embossed with designs for pasting onto walls and ceilings **2** *computing* a graphics file that can be displayed in certain applications behind or around the main dialogue boxes, working display areas, etc, for decoration ▷ *vb* **3** to cover (a surface) with wallpaper

wall pepper *n* a small Eurasian crassulaceous plant, *Sedum acre,* having creeping stems, yellow flowers, and acrid-tasting leaves

wall plate *n* a horizontal timber member placed along the top of a wall to support the ends of joists, rafters, etc, and distribute the load

wallposter (ˈwɔːlˌpəʊstə) *n* (in China) a bulletin or political message painted in large characters on walls

wall rocket *n* any of several yellow-flowered European plants of the genus *Diplotaxis,* such as *D. muralis,* that grow on old walls and in waste places: family *Brassicaceae* (crucifers)

wall rue *n* a delicate fern, *Asplenium ruta-muraria,* that grows in rocky crevices and walls in North America and Eurasia

Wallsend (ˈwɔːlzˌɛnd) *n* a town in NE England, in North Tyneside unitary authority, Tyne and Wear: situated on the River Tyne at the E end of Hadrian's Wall. Pop: 42 842 (2001)

Wall Street *n* a street in lower Manhattan, New York, where the Stock Exchange and major banks are situated, regarded as the embodiment of American finance

wall-to-wall *adj* **1** (of carpeting) completely covering a floor **2** *informal* as far as the eye can see; widespread: *wall-to-wall sales in the high street shops*

wally (ˈwɒlɪ) *n, pl* **-lies** *slang* a stupid person [c20: shortened form of the given name *Walter*]

walnut (ˈwɔːlˌnʌt) *n* **1** any juglandaceous deciduous tree of the genus *Juglans,* of America, SE Europe, and Asia, esp *J. regia,* which is native to W Asia but introduced elsewhere. They have aromatic leaves and flowers in catkins and are grown for their edible nuts and for their wood **2** the nut of any of these trees, having a wrinkled two-lobed seed and a hard wrinkled shell **3** the wood of any of these trees, used in making furniture, panelling, etc **4** a light yellowish-brown colour ▷ *adj* **5** made from the wood of a walnut tree: *a walnut table* **6** of the colour walnut [Old English *walh-hnutu,* literally: foreign nut; compare Old French *noux gauge* walnut, probably translation of Vulgar Latin phrase *nux gallica* (unattested) Gaulish (hence, foreign) nut]

Walpole (ˈwɔːlˌpəʊl) *n* **1 Horace**, 4th Earl of Orford. 1717–97, British writer, noted for his letters and for his delight in the Gothic, as seen in his house Strawberry Hill and his novel *The Castle of Otranto* (1764) **2** Sir **Hugh** (**Seymour**). 1884–1941, British novelist, born in New Zealand: best known for *The Herries Chronicle* (1930–33), a sequence of historical novels set in the Lake District **3** Sir **Robert**, 1st Earl of Orford, father of Horace Walpole. 1676–1745, English Whig statesman. As first lord of the Treasury and Chancellor of the Exchequer (1721–42) he was effectively Britain's first prime minister

Walpurgis Night (vælˈpʊəɡɪs) *n* the eve of May 1, believed in German folklore to be the night of a witches' sabbath on the Brocken, in the Harz Mountains [c19: translation of German *Walpurgisnacht,* the eve of the feast day of St Walpurga, 8th-century abbess in Germany]

walrus (ˈwɔːlrəs, ˈwɒl-) *n, pl* **-ruses** *or* **-rus** a pinniped mammal, *Odobenus rosmarus,* of northern seas, having a tough thick skin, upper canine teeth enlarged as tusks, and coarse whiskers and feeding mainly on shellfish: family *Odobenidae* [c17: probably from Dutch, from Scandinavian; compare Old Norse *hrosshvalr* (literally: horse whale) and Old English *horschwæl*; see HORSE, WHALE]

walrus moustache *n* a long thick moustache drooping at the ends

W

Walsall ('wɔːlsɔːl) n 1 an industrial town in central England, in Walsall unitary authority, West Midlands: engineering, electronics. Pop: 170 994 (2001) 2 a unitary authority in central England, in the West Midlands. Pop: 252 400 (2003 est). Area: 106 sq km (41 sq miles)

Walsh (wɒlʃ) n **Courtney** (**Andrew**). born 1962, Jamaican cricketer; a fast bowler, he became the highest wicket-taker in test match history (2000–04)

Walsingham[1] ('wɔːlsɪŋəm) n a village in E England, in Norfolk: remains of a medieval priory; site of the shrine of Our Lady of Walsingham

Walsingham[2] ('wɔːlsɪŋəm) n Sir **Francis**. ?1530–90, English statesman. As secretary of state (1573–90) to Elizabeth I he developed a system of domestic and foreign espionage and uncovered several plots against the Queen

Walter n 1 (German 'valtər) **Bruno** ('bruːno), real name Bruno Walter Schlesinger. 1876–1962, US conductor, born in Germany: famous for his performances of Haydn, Mozart, and Mahler 2 ('wɔːltə) **John**. 1739–1812, English publisher; founded The Daily Universal Register (1785), which in 1788 became The Times

Waltham Forest ('wɔːlθəm) n a borough of NE Greater London. Pop: 221 600 (2003 est). Area: 40 sq km (15 sq miles)

Walther von der Vogelweide (German 'valtər fɔn der 'foːgəlvaidə) n ?1170–?1230, German minnesinger, noted for his lyric verse on political and moral themes

Walton ('wɔːltən) n 1 **Ernest Thomas Sinton**. 1903–95, Irish physicist. He succeeded in producing the first artificial transmutation of an atomic nucleus (1932) with Sir John Cockcroft, with whom he shared the Nobel prize for physics 1951 2 **Izaak** ('aɪzək). 1593–1683, English writer, best known for The Compleat Angler (1653; enlarged 1676) 3 Sir **William** (**Turner**). 1902–83, English composer. His works include Façade (1923), a setting of satirical verses by Edith Sitwell, the Viola Concerto (1929), and the oratorio Belshazzar's Feast (1931)

waltz (wɔːls) n 1 a ballroom dance in triple time in which couples spin around as they progress round the room 2 a piece of music composed for or in the rhythm of this dance ▷ vb 3 to dance or lead (someone) in or as in a waltz: he waltzed her off her feet 4 (intr) to move in a sprightly and self-assured manner 5 (intr) informal to succeed easily [c18: from German Walzer, from Middle High German walzen to roll; compare WELTER]

waltzer ('wɔːlsə) n 1 a person who waltzes 2 a fairground roundabout on which people are spun round and moved up and down as it revolves about a central axis

waltz Matilda vb Austral See **Matilda**[1]

Walvis Bay ('wɔːlvɪs) or **Walfish Bay** n a port in Namibia, on the Atlantic: formed an exclave of South Africa, covering an area of 1124 sq km (434 sq miles) with its hinterland, but has been administered by Namibia since 1992; formally returned to Namibia in 1994; chief port of Namibia and rich fishing centre. Pop: 40 849 (2001)

wampum ('wɒmpəm) n (formerly) money used by North American Indians, made of cylindrical shells strung or woven together, esp white shells rather than the more valuable black or purple ones [c17: short for wampumpeag, from Narraganset wampompeag, from wampan light + api string + -ag plural suffix]

wan (wɒn) adj wanner, wannest 1 unnaturally pale esp from sickness, grief, etc 2 characteristic or suggestive of ill health, unhappiness, etc 3 (of light, stars, etc) faint or dim [Old English wann dark; related to wanian to WANE] > 'wanly adv > 'wanness n

Wanchüan or **Wan-ch'uan** (ˌwæntʃuˈaːn) n a former name of Zhangjiakou

wand (wɒnd) n 1 a slender supple stick or twig 2 a thin rod carried as a symbol of authority 3 a rod used by a magician, water diviner, etc 4 informal a conductor's baton 5 archery a marker used to show the distance at which the archer stands from the target 6 a hand-held electronic device, such as a light pen or bar-code reader, which is pointed at or passed over an item to read the data stored there [c12: from Old Norse vöndr; related to

Gothic wandus and English WEND]

wander ('wɒndə) vb (mainly intr) 1 (also tr) to move or travel about, in, or through (a place) without any definite purpose or destination 2 to proceed in an irregular course; meander 3 to go astray, as from a path or course 4 (of the mind, thoughts, etc) to lose concentration or direction 5 to think or speak incoherently or illogically ▷ n 6 the act or an instance of wandering [Old English wandrian; related to Old Frisian wandria, Middle Dutch, Middle High German wanderen] > 'wanderer n > 'wandering adj, n

wandering albatross n a large albatross, Diomedea exulans, having a very wide wingspan and a white plumage with black wings

Wandering Jew n (in medieval legend) a character condemned to roam the world eternally because he mocked Christ on the day of the Crucifixion

wanderlust ('wɒndəˌlʌst) n a great desire to travel and rove about [German, literally: wander desire]

wanderoo (ˌwɒndəˈruː) n, pl -deroos a macaque monkey, Macaca silenus, of India and Sri Lanka, having black fur with a ruff of long greyish fur on each side of the face [c17: from Sinhalese vanduru monkeys, literally: forest-dwellers, from Sanskrit vānara monkey, from vana forest]

wandoo ('wɒnduː) n a eucalyptus tree, Eucalyptus wandoo, of W Australia, having white bark and durable wood [from a native Australian language]

Wandsworth ('wɒnzwəθ) n a borough of S Greater London, on the River Thames. Pop: 274 100 (2003 est). Area: 35 sq km (13 sq miles)

wane (weɪn) vb (intr) 1 (of the moon) to show a gradually decreasing portion of illuminated surface, between full moon and new moon. See **wax**[2] (sense 2) 2 to decrease gradually in size, strength, power, etc 3 to draw to a close ▷ n 4 a decrease, as in size, strength, power, etc 5 the period during which the moon wanes 6 the act or an instance of drawing to a close 7 a rounded surface or defective edge of a plank, where the bark was 8 on the wane in a state of decline [Old English wanian (vb); related to wan-, prefix indicating privation, wana defect, Old Norse vana] > 'waney or 'wany adj

Wang An Shi or **Wang An-shih** (wæŋ aːn ʃi) n 1021–86, Chinese statesman and writer: remembered for his economic reforms, known as the New Policies (1069–76)

Wanganui (ˌwɒŋəˈnuːɪ) n a port in New Zealand, on SW North Island: centre for a dairy-farming and sheep-rearing district. Pop: 43 600 (2004 est)

Wang Jing Wei or **Wang Ching-wei** ('wæn dʒɪŋ 'weɪ) n 1883–1944, Chinese politician. A leading Kuomintang politician, he struggled (1927–32) with Chiang Kai-shek for control of the Kuomintang. During World War II he was head of a Japanese puppet government in Nanjing

wangle ('wæŋgəl) informal ▷ vb 1 (tr) to use devious or illicit methods to get or achieve (something) for (oneself or another): he wangled himself a salary increase 2 to manipulate or falsify (a situation, action, etc) ▷ n 3 the act or an instance of wangling [c19: originally printers' slang, perhaps a blend of WAGGLE and dialect wankle wavering, from Old English wancol; compare Old High German wankōn to waver] > 'wangler n

Wanhsien or **Wan-Hsien** (wænˈʃjɛn) n a variant transliteration of the Chinese name for **Wanxian**

wanigan or **wannigan** ('wɒnɪgən) n Canadian 1 a lumberjack's chest or box 2 a cabin, caboose or houseboat [c19: from Algonquian]

wank (wæŋk) slang ▷ vb 1 (intr) to masturbate ▷ n 2 an instance of wanking [of uncertain origin]

Wankel engine ('wæŋkəl) n a type of four-stroke internal-combustion engine without reciprocating parts. It consists of one or more approximately elliptical combustion chambers within which a curved triangular-shaped piston rotates, by the explosion of compressed gas, dividing the combustion chamber into three gastight sections [c20: named after Felix Wankel (1902–88), German engineer who invented it]

wanker ('wæŋkə) n slang 1 a person who wanks; masturbator 2 a worthless fellow

Wankie ('wɑːŋkɪ) n the former name (until 1982) of Hwange

W

wannabe or **wannabee** ('wɒnəˌbiː) n informal **a** a person who desires to be, or be like, someone or something else **b** (as modifier): a wannabe film star [c20: phonetic shortening of want to be]

Wanne-Eickel (German 'vanəˈaikəl) n an industrial town in W Germany, in North Rhine-Westphalia on the Rhine-Herne Canal: formed in 1926 by the merging of two townships

want (wɒnt) vb **1** (tr) to feel a need or longing for: I want a new hat **2** (when tr, may take a clause as object or an infinitive) to wish, need, or desire (something or to do something): he wants to go home **3** (intr; usually used with a negative and often foll by for) to be lacking or deficient (in something necessary or desirable): the child wants for nothing **4** (tr) to feel the absence of: lying on the ground makes me want my bed **5** (tr) to fall short by (a specified amount) **6** (tr) chiefly Brit to have need of or require (doing or being something): your shoes want cleaning **7** (intr) to be destitute **8** (tr; often passive) to seek or request the presence of: you're wanted upstairs **9** (intr) to be absent **10** (tr; takes an infinitive) informal should or ought (to do something): you don't want to go out so late ▷ n **11** the act or an instance of wanting **12** anything that is needed, desired, or lacked **13** the state of being in need; destitution: the state should help those in want **14** a sense of lack; craving [C12 (vb, in the sense: it is lacking), C13 (n): from Old Norse vanta to be deficient; related to Old English wanian to WANE]
> 'wanter n

want ad n informal a classified advertisement in a newspaper, magazine, etc, for something wanted, such as property or employment

wantaway ('wɒntəˌweɪ) informal ▷ n **1 a** a footballer who wants a transfer to another club **b** (as modifier): a wantaway player ▷ vb **want away 2** (intr, adverb) (of a footballer) to want a transfer to another club

wanting ('wɒntɪŋ) adj (postpositive) **1** lacking or absent; missing **2** not meeting requirements or expectations: you have been found wanting

wanton ('wɒntən) adj **1** dissolute, licentious, or immoral **2** without motive, provocation, or justification: wanton destruction **3** maliciously and unnecessarily cruel or destructive **4** unrestrained: wanton spending **5** archaic or poetic playful or capricious **6** archaic (of vegetation, etc) luxuriant or superabundant ▷ n **7** a licentious person, esp a woman ▷ vb **8** (intr) to behave in a wanton manner [C13 wantowen (in the obsolete sense: unmanageable, unruly): from wan- (prefix equivalent to UN-¹; related to Old English wanian to WANE) + -towen, from Old English togen brought up, from tēon to bring up] > 'wantonly adv
> 'wantonness n

Wanxian, Wanhsien or **Wan-Hsien** ('wæn'ʃjɛn) n an inland port in central China, in E Sichuan province, on the Yangtze River. Pop: 1 963 000 (2005 est)

WAP (wæp) n acronym for Wireless Application Protocol: a global application that enables mobile phone users to access the internet and other information services

wapentake ('wɒpənˌteɪk, 'wæp-) n English legal history a subdivision of certain shires or counties, esp in the Midlands and North of England, corresponding to the hundred in other shires [Old English wǣpen(ge)tæc, from Old Norse vápnatak, from vápn WEAPON + tak TAKE]

wapiti ('wɒpɪtɪ) n, pl -tis a large deer, Cervus canadensis, with large much-branched antlers, native to North America and now also common in the South Island of New Zealand. Also called: American elk [c19: from Shawnee, literally: white deer, from wap (unattested) white; from the animal's white tail and rump]

war (wɔː) n **1** open armed conflict between two or more parties, nations, or states. Related adjs: **belligerent**, **martial 2** a particular armed conflict **3** the techniques of armed conflict as a study, science, or profession **4** any conflict or contest: a war of wits; the war against crime **5** (modifier) of, relating to, resulting from, or characteristic of war: a war hero; war damage; a war story **6** in the wars informal (esp of a child) hurt or knocked about, esp as a result of quarrelling and fighting ▷ vb wars, warring, warred **7** (intr) to conduct a war [C12: from Old Northern French werre (variant of Old French guerre), of Germanic origin; related to Old High German werra]

War. abbreviation Warwickshire

Warangal ('wʌrəngəl) n a city in S central India, in N Andhra Pradesh: capital of a 12th-century Hindu kingdom. Pop: 528 570 (2001)

waratah (ˌwɒrəˈtɑː, 'wɒrətɑː) n Austral a proteaceous shrub, Telopea speciosissima, the floral emblem of New South Wales, having dark green leaves and large clusters of crimson flowers [from a native Australian language]

Warbeck ('wɔːbɛk) n Perkin ('pɜːkɪn). ?1474–99, Flemish impostor, pretender to the English throne. Professing to be Richard, Duke of York, he led an unsuccessful rising against Henry VII (1497) and was later executed

warble¹ ('wɔːbəl) vb **1** to sing (words, songs, etc) with trills, runs, and other embellishments **2** (tr) to utter in a song ▷ n **3** the act or an instance of warbling [C14: via Old French werbler from Germanic; compare Frankish hwirbilōn (unattested), Old High German wirbil whirlwind; see WHIRL]

warble² ('wɔːbəl) n vet science **1** a small lumpy abscess under the skin of cattle caused by infestation with larvae of the warble fly **2 a** a hard tumorous lump of tissue on a horse's back, caused by prolonged friction of a saddle [c16: of uncertain origin]

warble fly n any of various hairy beelike dipterous flies of the genus Hypoderma and related genera, the larvae of which produce warbles in cattle: family Oestridae

warbler ('wɔːblə) n **1** a person or thing that warbles **2** any small active passerine songbird of the Old World subfamily Sylviinae: family Muscicapidae. They have a cryptic plumage and slender bill and are arboreal insectivores **3** Also called: wood warbler any small bird of the American family Parulidae, similar to the Old World forms but often brightly coloured

Warburg (German 'varburk) n Otto (Heinrich) ('oto). 1883–1970, German biochemist and physiologist: Nobel prize for physiology or medicine (1931) for his work on respiratory enzymes

warchalking ('wɔːtʃɔːkɪŋ) n the practice of marking chalk symbols on walls and pavements at places where local wireless internet connections may be obtained for free via a computer, usually without permission
> 'warchalker n [c21: from w(ireless) a(ccess) r(evolution) + gerund of CHALK]

war correspondent n a journalist who reports on a war from the scene of action

war crime n a crime committed in wartime in violation of the accepted rules and customs of war, such as genocide, ill-treatment of prisoners of war, etc > war criminal n

war cry n **1** a rallying cry used by combatants in battle **2** a cry, slogan, etc, used to rally support for a cause

ward (wɔːd) n **1** (in many countries) a district into which a city, town, parish, or other area is divided for administration, election of representatives, etc **2** a room in a hospital, esp one for patients requiring similar kinds of care: a maternity ward **3** one of the divisions of a prison **4** an open space enclosed within the walls of a castle **5** law Also called: ward of court a person, esp a minor or one legally incapable of managing his own affairs, placed under the control or protection of a guardian or of a court **b** guardianship, as of a minor or legally incompetent person **6** the state of being under guard or in custody **7 a** a means of protection **8 a** an internal ridge or bar in a lock that prevents an incorrectly cut key from turning **b** a corresponding groove cut in a key **9** a less common word for warden¹ ▷ vb **10** (tr) archaic to guard or protect ▷ See also ward off [Old English weard protector; related to Old High German wart, Old Saxon ward, Old Norse vorthr. See GUARD] > 'wardless adj

Ward (wɔːd) n **1** Dame Barbara (Mary), Baroness Jackson. 1914–81, British economist, environmentalist, and writer. Her books include Spaceship Earth (1966) **2** Mrs Humphry, married name of Mary Augusta Arnold. 1851–1920, English novelist. Her novels include Robert Elsmere (1888) and The Case of Richard Meynell (1911) **3** Sir Joseph George. 1856–1930, New Zealand statesman; prime minister of New Zealand (1906–12; 1928–30)

w

-ward *suffix* **1** (*forming adjectives*) indicating direction towards: *a backward step; heavenward progress* **2** (*forming adverbs*) a variant and the usual US and Canadian form of **-wards** [Old English *-weard* towards]

war dance *n* a ceremonial dance performed before going to battle or after victory, esp by certain North American Indian peoples

warden ('wɔːdᵊn) *n* **1** a person who has the charge or care of something, esp a building, or someone **2** any of various public officials, esp one responsible for the enforcement of certain regulations **3** a person employed to patrol a national park or safari park **4** *chiefly US & Canadian* the chief officer in charge of a prison **5** *Brit* the principal or president of any of various universities or colleges **6** See **churchwarden** (sense 1) [c13: from Old Northern French *wardein*, from *warder* to guard, of Germanic origin; see GUARD]

warder ('wɔːdə) *or feminine* **wardress** *n* **1** *chiefly Brit* an officer in charge of prisoners in a jail **2** a person who guards or has charge of something [c14: from Anglo-French *wardere*, from Old French *warder* to GUARD, of Germanic origin]

ward heeler *n* US politics disparaging a party worker who canvasses votes and performs chores for a political boss. Also called: **heeler**

ward off *vb* (*tr, adverb*) to turn aside or repel; avert

Wardour Street ('wɔːdə) *n* **1** a street in Soho where many film companies have their London offices; formerly noted for shops selling antiques and mock antiques **2 Wardour Street English** affectedly archaic speech or writing

wardrobe ('wɔːdrəʊb) *n* **1** a tall closet or cupboard, with a rail or hooks on which to hang clothes **2** the total collection of articles of clothing belonging to one person **3** the collection of costumes belonging to a theatre or theatrical company [c14: from Old Northern French *warderobe*, from *warder* to GUARD + *robe* ROBE]

wardrobe mistress *n* a person responsible for maintaining and sometimes making the costumes in a theatre

wardrobe trunk *n* a large upright rectangular travelling case, usually opening longitudinally, with one side having a hanging rail, the other having drawers or compartments

wardroom ('wɔːd,ruːm, -,rʊm) *n* **1** the quarters assigned to the officers (except the captain) of a warship **2** the officers of a warship collectively, excepting the captain

-wards *or* **-ward** *suffix forming adverbs* indicating direction towards: *a step backwards; to sail shorewards*. See **-ward** [Old English *-weardes* towards]

wardship ('wɔːdʃɪp) *n* the state of being a ward

ware[1] (wɛə) *n* (*often in combination*) **1** (*functioning as singular*) articles of the same kind or material: *glassware; silverware* **2** porcelain or pottery of a specified type: *agateware; jasper ware* ▷ See also **wares** [Old English *waru*; related to Old Frisian *were*, Old Norse *vara*, Middle Dutch *Ware*]

ware[2] (wɛə) *archaic vb* another word for **beware** [Old English *wær*; related to Old Saxon, Old High German *giwar*, Old Norse *varr*, Gothic *war*, Latin *vereor*. See AWARE, BEWARE]

warehou (wɑːrəhuː) *n, pl* **warehou** any of several edible saltwater New Zealand fish of the genus *Seriolella* [Māori]

warehouse *n* ('wɛə,haʊs) **1** a place where goods are stored prior to their use, distribution, or sale **2** See **bonded warehouse 3** *chiefly Brit* a large commercial, esp wholesale, establishment ▷ *vb* ('wɛə,haʊz, -,haʊs) **4** (*tr*) to store or place in a warehouse, esp a bonded warehouse > 'ware,houseman *n*

warehousing ('wɛə,haʊzɪŋ) *n stock exchange* an attempt to maintain the price of a company's shares or to gain a significant stake in a company without revealing the true identity of the purchaser. Shares are purchased through an insurance company, a unit trust, or nominees

wares (wɛəz) *pl n* **1** articles of manufacture considered as being for sale **2** any talent or asset regarded as a commercial or saleable commodity

warez (wɛəz, 'wɛrɛz) *n informal* illegally copied computer software which has had its protection codes

de-activated [c20: possibly from (SOFT)WARE and influenced by the anglicized pronunciation of *Juarez*, a Mexican city known for smuggling]

warfare ('wɔː,fɛə) *n* **1** the act, process, or an instance of waging war **2** conflict, struggle, or strife

warfarin ('wɔːfərɪn) *n* a crystalline insoluble optically active compound, used as a rodenticide and, in the form of its sodium salt, as a medical anticoagulant. Formula: $C_{19}H_{16}O_4$ [c20: from the patent owners W(*isconsin*) A(*lumni*) R(*esearch*) F(*oundation*) + (COUM)ARIN]

war game *n* **1** a notional tactical exercise for training military commanders, in which no military units are actually deployed **2** a game in which model soldiers are used to create battles, esp past battles, in order to study tactics ▷ *vb* **war-game 3** (*intr*) to prepare for battle by considering possible tactics and enemy responses

warhead ('wɔː,hɛd) *n* the part of the fore end of a missile or projectile that contains explosives

Warhol ('wɔː,həʊl) *n* Andy, real name *Andrew Warhola*. ?1926–87, US artist and film maker; one of the foremost exponents of pop art

warhorse ('wɔː,hɔːs) *n* **1** a horse used in battle **2** *informal* a veteran soldier, politician, or elderly person, esp one who is aggressive

Warks *abbreviation* Warwickshire

Warley ('wɔːlɪ) *n* an industrial town in W central England, in Sandwell unitary authority, West Midlands: formed in 1966 by the amalgamation of Smethwick, Oldbury, and Rowley Regis. Pop: 189 854 (2001)

warlike ('wɔː,laɪk) *adj* **1** of, relating to, or used in war **2** hostile or belligerent **3** fit or ready for war

warlock ('wɔː,lɒk) *n* **1** a man who practises black magic; sorcerer **2** a fortune-teller, conjuror, or magician [Old English *wærloga* oath breaker, from *wær* oath + *-loga* liar, from *lēogan* to LIE[1]]

Warlock ('wɔː,lɒk) *n* Peter, real name *Philip Arnold Heseltine*. 1894–1930, British composer and scholar of early English music. His works include song cycles, such as *The Curlew* (1920–22), and the *Capriol Suite* (1926) for strings

warlord ('wɔː,lɔːd) *n* a military leader of a nation or part of a nation, esp one who is accountable to nobody when the central government is weak: *the Chinese warlords*

Warlpiri ('walpri) *n* an Aboriginal language of central Australia

warm (wɔːm) *adj* **1** characterized by or having a moderate degree of heat; moderately hot **2** maintaining or imparting heat: *a warm coat* **3** having or showing ready affection, kindliness, etc: *a warm personality* **4** lively, vigorous, or passionate: *a warm debate* **5** cordial or enthusiastic; ardent: *warm support* **6** quickly or easily aroused: *a warm temper* **7** (of colours) predominantly red or yellow in tone **8** (of a scent, trail, etc) recently made; strong **9** near to finding a hidden object or discovering or guessing facts, as in children's games **10** *informal* uncomfortable or disagreeable, esp because of the proximity of danger ▷ *vb* **11** (sometimes foll by *up*) to raise or be raised in temperature; make or become warm or warmer **12** (when *intr*, often foll by *to*) to make or become excited, enthusiastic, etc (about): *he warmed to the idea of buying a new car* **13** (*intr*; often foll by *to*) to feel affection, kindness, etc (for someone): *I warmed to her mother from the start* ▷ *n* **14** *informal* a warm place or area: *come into the warm* **15** *informal* the act or an instance of warming or being warmed ▷ See also **warm up** [Old English *wearm*; related to Old Frisian, Old Saxon *warm*, Old Norse *varmr*] > 'warmer *n* > 'warmish *adj* > 'warmly *adv* > 'warmness *n*

warm-blooded *adj* **1** ardent, impetuous, or passionate **2** (of birds and mammals) having a constant body temperature, usually higher than the temperature of the surroundings. Technical name: **homoiothermic** > ,warm-'bloodedness *n*

warm-down *n* light exercises performed to aid recovery from strenuous physical activity

war memorial *n* a monument, usually an obelisk or cross, to those who die in a war, esp those from a particular locality

warm front *n meteorol* the boundary between a warm

air mass and the cold air above which it is rising, at a less steep angle than at the cold front

warm-hearted *adj* kindly, generous, forgiving, or readily sympathetic > ˌwarm-'heartedly *adv* > ˌwarm-'heartedness *n*

warming pan *n* a pan, often of copper and having a long handle, filled with hot coals or hot water and formerly drawn over the sheets to warm a bed

warmonger ('wɔːˌmʌŋɡə) *n* a person who fosters warlike ideas or advocates war > 'warˌmongering *n*

warmth (wɔːmθ) *n* 1 the state, quality, or sensation of being warm 2 intensity of emotion: *he denied the accusation with some warmth* 3 affection or cordiality

warm up *vb* (*adverb*) 1 to make or become warm or warmer 2 (*intr*) to exercise in preparation for and immediately before a game, contest, or more vigorous exercise 3 to get ready for something important; prepare 4 to run or operate (an engine, etc) until the normal working temperature or condition is attained, or (of an engine, etc) to undergo this process 5 to make or become more animated or enthusiastic: *the party warmed up when Tom came* 6 to reheat (already cooked food) or (of such food) to be reheated ▷ *n* **warm-up** 7 the act or an instance of warming up 8 a preparatory exercise routine

warn (wɔːn) *vb* 1 to notify or make (someone) aware of danger, harm, etc 2 (*tr; often takes a negative and an infinitive*) to advise or admonish (someone) as to action, conduct, etc: *I warn you not to do that again* 3 (*takes a clause as object or an infinitive*) to inform (someone) in advance: *he warned them that he would arrive late* 4 (*tr; usually foll by away, off*, etc) to give notice to go away, be off, etc [Old English *wearnian*; related to Old High German *warnēn*, Old Norse *varna* to refuse] > 'warner *n*

Warne (wɔːn) *n* **Shane** (**Keith**). born 1969, Australian cricketer; played for Australia (1991–2007), taking 708 test wickets

warning ('wɔːnɪŋ) *n* 1 a hint, intimation, threat, etc, of harm or danger 2 advice to beware or desist 3 an archaic word for **notice** (sense 6) ▷ *adj* 4 (*prenominal*) intended or serving to warn: *a warning look* > 'warningly *adv*

War of American Independence *n* the conflict following the revolt of the North American colonies against British rule, particularly on the issue of taxation. Hostilities began in 1775 when British and American forces clashed at Lexington and Concord. Articles of Confederation agreed in the Continental Congress in 1777 provided for a confederacy to be known as the United States of America. The war was effectively ended with the surrender of the British at Yorktown in 1781 and peace was signed at Paris in Sept 1783. Also called: **American Revolution, Revolutionary War**

warp (wɔːp) *vb* 1 to twist or cause to twist out of shape, as from heat, damp, etc 2 to turn or cause to turn from a true, correct, or proper course 3 to pervert or be perverted 4 *nautical* to move (a vessel) by hauling on a rope fixed to a stationary object ashore or (of a vessel) to be moved thus 5 (*tr*) to flood (land) with water from which alluvial matter is deposited ▷ *n* 6 the state or condition of being twisted out of shape 7 a twist, distortion, or bias 8 a mental or moral deviation 9 the yarns arranged lengthways on a loom, forming the threads through which the weft yarns are woven 10 *nautical* a rope used for warping a vessel 11 alluvial sediment deposited by water [Old English *wearp* a throw; related to Old High German *warf*, Old Norse *varp* throw of a dragging net, Old English *weorpan* to throw] > 'warpage *n* > warped *adj* > 'warper *n*

war paint *n* 1 painted decoration of the face and body applied by certain North American Indians before battle 2 *informal* finery or regalia 3 *informal* cosmetics

warpath ('wɔːˌpɑːθ) *n* 1 the route taken by North American Indians on a warlike expedition 2 on the warpath **a** preparing to engage in battle **b** *informal* in a state of anger

warplane ('wɔːˌpleɪn) *n* any aircraft designed for and used in warfare

warrant ('wɒrənt) *n* 1 anything that gives authority for

an action or decision; authorization; sanction 2 a document that certifies or guarantees, such as a receipt for goods stored in a warehouse, a licence, or a commission 3 *law* an authorization issued by a magistrate or other official allowing a constable or other officer to search or seize property, arrest a person, or perform some other specified act 4 (in certain armed services) the official authority for the appointment of warrant officers 5 a security that functions as a stock option by giving the owner the right to buy ordinary shares in a company at a specified date, often at a specified price ▷ *vb* (*tr*) 6 to guarantee the quality, condition, etc, of (something) 7 to give authority or power to 8 to attest to or assure the character, worthiness, etc, of 9 to guarantee (a purchaser of merchandise) against loss of, damage to, or misrepresentation concerning the merchandise 10 *law* to guarantee (the title to an estate or other property) 11 to declare boldly and confidently [C13: from Anglo-French *warrant*, variant of Old French *guarant*, from *guarantir* to guarantee, of Germanic origin; compare GUARANTY] > 'warrantable *adj* > ˌwarranta'bility *n* > 'warrantably *adv* > 'warranter *n*

warrantee (ˌwɒrən'tiː) *n* a person to whom a warranty is given

warrant officer *n* an officer in certain armed services who holds a rank between those of commissioned and noncommissioned officers. In the British army, the rank has two classes. See **company sergeant major**

Warrant of Fitness *n* NZ a six-monthly certificate required for motor vehicles certifying mechanical soundness

warrantor ('wɒrənˌtɔː) *n* an individual or company that provides a warranty

warrant sale *n* *Scots law* a sale of someone's personal belongings or household effects that have been seized to meet unpaid debts

warranty ('wɒrəntɪ) *n, pl* -ties 1 *property law* a covenant, express or implied, by which the vendor of real property vouches for the security of the title conveyed 2 *contract law* an express or implied term in a contract, such as an undertaking that goods contracted to be sold shall meet specified requirements as to quality, etc 3 *insurance law* an undertaking by the party insured that the facts given regarding the risk are as stated [C14: from Anglo-French *warantie*, from *warantir* to warrant, variant of Old French *guarantir*; see WARRANT]

warren ('wɒrən) *n* 1 a series of interconnected underground tunnels in which rabbits live 2 a colony of rabbits 3 an overcrowded area or dwelling 4 *chiefly Brit* an enclosed place where small game animals or birds are kept, esp for breeding, or a part of a river or lake enclosed by nets in which fish are kept (esp in the phrase **beasts** or **fowls of warren**) [C14: from Anglo-French *warenne*, of Germanic origin; compare Old High German *werien* to preserve]

Warren[1] ('wɒrən) *n* a city in the US, in SE Michigan, northeast of Detroit. Pop: 136 016 (2003 est)

Warren[2] ('wɒrən) *n* **Earl**. 1891–1974, US lawyer; chief justice of the US (1953– 69). He chaired the commission that investigated the murder of President Kennedy

warrigal ('wɒrɪɡæl) *Austral* ▷ *n* 1 a dingo ▷ *adj* 2 untamed or wild [C19: from a native Australian language]

Warrington ('wɒrɪŋtən) *n* 1 an industrial town in NW England, in Warrington unitary authority, Cheshire on the River Mersey: dates from Roman times. Pop: 80 661 (2001) 2 a unitary authority in NW England, in N Cheshire. Pop: 193 200 (2003 est). Area: 176 sq km (68 sq miles)

warrior ('wɒrɪə) *n* **a** a person engaged in, experienced in, or devoted to war **b** (*as modifier*): *a warrior nation* [C13: from Old Northern French *werreieor*, from WAR]

Warsaw ('wɔːsɔː) *n* the capital of Poland, in the E central part on the River Vistula: became capital at the end of the 16th century; almost completely destroyed in World War II as the main centre of the Polish resistance movement; rebuilt within about six years; university (1818); situated at the junction of important trans-European routes. Pop: 2 204 000 (2005 est)

Warsaw Pact *n* a military treaty and association of E European countries, formed in 1955 by the Soviet Union, Bulgaria, Czechoslovakia, East Germany, Hungary, Poland, and Romania: East Germany left in 1990; the remaining members dissolved the Pact in 1991

warship ('wɔːʃɪp) *n* a vessel armed, armoured, and otherwise equipped for naval warfare

Wars of the Roses *pl n* the conflicts in England (1455–85) centred on the struggle for the throne between the houses of York (symbolized by the white rose) and Lancaster (of which one badge was the red rose)

wart (wɔːt) *n* **1** Also called: **verruca** *pathol* any firm abnormal elevation of the skin caused by a virus **2** *botany* a small rounded outgrowth **3** warts and all with all blemishes evident [Old English *weart(e)*; related to Old High German *warza*, Old Norse *varta*] > **'warty** *adj*

Warta (*Polish* 'varta) *n* a river in Poland, flowing generally north and west across the whole W Polish Plain to the River Oder. Length: 808 km (502 miles)

Wartburg (*German* 'vartbʊrk) *n* a medieval castle in central Germany, in Thuringia southwest of Eisenach: residence of Luther (1521–22) when he began his German translation of the New Testament

warthog ('wɔːthɒg) *n* a wild pig, *Phacochoerus aethiopicus*, of southern and E Africa, having heavy tusks, wartlike protuberances on the face, and a mane of coarse hair

wartime ('wɔːˌtaɪm) *n* **a** a period or time of war **b** (*as modifier*) *wartime conditions*

Warton ('wɔːtᵊn) *n* **1 Joseph.** 1722–1800, British poet and critic, noted for his poem *The Enthusiast* (1744) and his *Essay on the Writings and Genius of Pope* (1756) **2** his brother **Thomas.** 1728–90, poet laureate (1785–90); author of the poem *The Pleasures of Melancholy* (1747) and the first *History of English Poetry* (1774–81)

war whoop *n* the yell or howl uttered, esp by North American Indians, while making an attack

Warwick¹ ('wɒrɪk) *n* a town in central England, administrative centre of Warwickshire, on the River Avon: 14th-century castle, with collections of armour and waxworks: the university of Warwick (1965) is in Coventry. Pop: 23 350 (2001)

Warwick² ('wɒrɪk) *n* **Earl of**, title of *Richard Neville*, known as *the Kingmaker*. 1428–71, English statesman. During the Wars of the Roses, he fought first for the Yorkists, securing the throne (1461) for Edward IV, and then for the Lancastrians, restoring Henry VI (1470). He was killed at Barnet by Edward IV

Warwickshire ('wɒrɪkˌʃɪə, -ʃə) *n* a county of central England: until 1974, when the West Midlands metropolitan county was created, it contained one of the most highly industrialized regions in the world, centred on Birmingham. Administrative centre: Warwick. Pop: 519 300 (2003 est). Area: 1981 sq km (765 sq miles)

wary ('wεərɪ) *adj* **warier, wariest 1** watchful, cautious, or alert **2** characterized by caution or watchfulness [c16: from WARE² + -Y¹] > **'warily** *adv* > **'wariness** *n*

was (wɒz; *unstressed* wəz) *vb* (used with I, he, she, it, and with singular nouns) **1** the past tense (indicative mood) of **be¹** *not standard* a form of the subjunctive mood used in place of *were*, esp in conditional sentences: *if the film was to be with you, would you be able to process it?* [Old English *wæs*, from *wesan* to be; related to Old Frisian, Old High German *was*, Old Norse *var*]

wasabi (wə'sɑːbɪ) *n* **1** a Japanese cruciferous plant, *Eutrema Wasabi*, cultivated for its thick green pungent root **2** the root of this plant, esp in paste or powder form, used as a condiment in Japanese cookery [Japanese]

Wasatch Range ('wɔːsætʃ) *n* a mountain range in the W central US, in N Utah and SE Idaho. Highest peak: Mount Timpanogos, 3581 m (11 750 ft)

wash (wɒʃ) *vb* **1** to apply water or other liquid, usually with soap, to (oneself, clothes, etc) in order to cleanse **2** (*tr*; often foll by *away, from, off,* etc) to remove by the application of water or other liquid and usually soap: *she washed the dirt from her clothes* **3** (*intr*) to be capable of being washed without damage or loss of colour **4** (of an animal such as a cat) to cleanse (itself or another

animal) by licking **5** (*tr*) to cleanse from pollution or defilement **6** (*tr*) to make wet or moist **7** (often foll by *away*, etc) to move or be moved by water: *the flood washed away the bridge* **8** (esp of waves) to flow or sweep against or over (a surface or object), often with a lapping sound **9** to form by erosion or be eroded: *the stream washed a ravine in the hill* **10** (*tr*) to apply a thin coating of paint, metal, etc, to **11** (*tr*) to separate (ore, precious stones, etc) from (gravel, earth, or sand) by immersion in water **12** (*intr; usually used with a negative) informal, chiefly Brit* to admit of testing or proof: *your excuses won't wash with me this time* ▷ *n* **13** the act or process of washing; ablution **14** a quantity of articles washed together **15** a preparation or thin liquid used as a coating or in washing: *a thin wash of paint; a hair wash* **16** *med* **a** any medicinal or soothing lotion for application to a part of the body **b** (*in combination*): *an eyewash* **17 a** the technique of making wash drawings **b** See **wash drawing 18** the erosion of soil by the action of flowing water **19** a mass of alluvial material transported and deposited by flowing water **20** land that is habitually washed by tidal or river waters **21** the disturbance in the air or water produced at the rear of an aircraft, boat, or other moving object **22** gravel, earth, etc, from which valuable minerals may be washed **23** waste liquid matter or liquid refuse, esp as fed to pigs; swill **24** an alcoholic liquid resembling strong beer, resulting from the fermentation of wort in the production of whisky **25 come out in the wash** *informal* to become known or apparent in the course of time ▷ See also **wash down, wash out, wash up** [Old English *wæscan, waxan*; related to Old High German *wascan; see* WATER]

Wash (wɒʃ) *n* **the Wash** a shallow inlet of the North Sea on the E coast of England, between Lincolnshire and Norfolk

Wash. *abbreviation* Washington

washable ('wɒʃəbᵊl) *adj* (esp of fabrics or clothes) capable of being washed without deteriorating > ˌwasha'bility *n*

wash-and-wear *adj* (of fabrics, garments, etc) requiring only light washing, short drying time, and little or no ironing

washbasin ('wɒʃˌbeɪsᵊn) *n* **1** Also called: **washbowl** a basin or bowl for washing the face and hands **2** Also called: **wash-hand basin** a bathroom fixture with taps, used for washing the face and hands

washboard ('wɒʃˌbɔːd) *n* **1** a board having a surface, usually of corrugated metal, on which esp formerly, clothes were scrubbed **2** such a board used as a rhythm instrument played with the fingers in skiffle, Country and Western music, etc **3** *nautical* a vertical planklike shield fastened to the gunwales of a boat to prevent water from splashing over the side

washcloth ('wɒʃˌklɒθ) *n* **1** another name for **dishcloth 2** *US & Canadian* a small piece of cloth used to wash the face and hands. Also called (in Britain and certain other countries): **face cloth**

washday ('wɒʃˌdeɪ) *n* a day on which clothes and linen are washed, often the same day each week

wash down *vb* (*tr, adverb*) **1** to wash completely, esp from top to bottom **2** to take drink with or after (food or another drink)

wash drawing *n* a pen-and-ink drawing that has been lightly brushed over with water to soften the lines

washed out *adj* (**washed-out** *when prenominal*) **1** faded or colourless **2** exhausted, esp when being pale in appearance

washed up *adj* (**washed-up** *when prenominal) informal, chiefly US, Canadian & NZ* **1** no longer useful, successful, hopeful, etc **2** exhausted

washer ('wɒʃə) *n* **1** a person or thing that washes **2** a flat ring or drilled disc of metal used under the head of a bolt or nut to spread the load when tightened **3** any flat ring of rubber, felt, metal, etc, used to provide a seal under a nut or in a tap or valve seat **4** See **washing machine 5** *Austral* a face cloth; flannel

washerwoman ('wɒʃəˌwʊmən), **washwoman** or *masculine* **washerman** *n, pl* **-women** *or* **-men** a person who washes clothes for a living

W

washery ('wɒʃərɪ) *n, pl* -ries a plant at a mine where water or other liquid is used to remove dirt from a mineral, esp coal

wash-hand basin *n* another name for **washbasin** (sense 2)

wash house *n* (formerly) a building or outbuilding in which laundry was done

washing ('wɒʃɪŋ) *n* **1** articles that have been or are to be washed together on a single occasion **2** something, such as gold dust or metal ore, that has been obtained by washing **3** a thin coat of something applied in liquid form

washing machine *n* a mechanical apparatus, usually powered by electricity, for washing clothing, linens, etc

washing powder *n* powdered detergent for washing fabrics

washing soda *n* the crystalline decahydrate of sodium carbonate, esp when used as a cleansing agent

Washington[1] ('wɒʃɪŋtən) *n* **1** a state of the northwestern US, on the Pacific: consists of the Coast Range and the Olympic Mountains in the west and the Columbia Plateau in the east. Capital: Olympia. Pop: 6 131 445 (2003 est). Area: 172 416 sq km (66 570 sq miles) **2** Also called: Washington, DC the capital of the US, coextensive with the District of Columbia and situated near the E coast on the Potomac River: site chosen by President Washington in 1790; contains the White House and the Capitol; a major educational and administrative centre. Pop: 563 384 (2003 est) **3** a town in Tyne and Wear: designated a new town in 1964. Pop: 53 388 (2001) **4** Mount Washington a mountain in N New Hampshire, in the White Mountains: the highest peak in the northeast US; noted for extreme weather conditions. Height: 1917 m (6288 ft) **5** Lake Washington a lake in W Washington, forming the E boundary of the city of Seattle: linked by canal with Puget Sound. Length: about 32 km (20 miles). Width: 6 km (4 miles) > Washingtonian (ˌwɒʃɪŋ'təʊnɪən) *adj, n*

Washington[2] ('wɒʃɪŋtən) *n* **1** Booker T(aliaferro). 1856–1915, US Black educationalist and writer **2** Denzil ('dɛnzəl). US film actor; his films include *Glory* (1990), *Malcolm X* (1992), *The Hurricane* (1999), and *John Q.* (2002) **3** George. 1732–99, US general and statesman; first president of the US (1789–97). He was appointed commander in chief of the Continental Army (1775) at the outbreak of the War of American Independence, which ended with his defeat of Cornwallis at Yorktown (1781). He presided over the convention at Philadelphia (1787) that formulated the constitution of the US and elected him president

washing-up *n Brit* **1** the washing of dishes, cutlery, etc, after a meal **2** dishes and cutlery waiting to be washed up **3** (*as modifier*): *a washing-up machine*

wash out *vb* (*adverb*) **1** (*tr*) to wash (the inside of something) so as to remove (dirt) **2** Also called: wash off to remove or be removed by washing: *grass stains don't wash out easily* ▷ *n* washout **3** *geology* **a** erosion of the earth's surface by the action of running water **b** a narrow channel produced by this erosion **4** *informal* **a** a total failure or disaster **b** an incompetent person

wash over *vb* (*tr, prep*) **1** (of an emotion) to affect (a person) suddenly and profoundly **2** (of an event) to have little effect on (a person)

washroom ('wɒʃˌruːm, -ˌrʊm) *n US & Canadian* a euphemism for **lavatory**

washstand ('wɒʃˌstænd) *n* a piece of furniture designed to hold a basin, etc, for washing the face and hands

washtub ('wɒʃˌtʌb) *n* a tub or large container used for washing anything, esp clothes

wash up *vb* (*adverb*) **1** *chiefly Brit* to wash (dishes, cutlery, etc) after a meal **2** (*intr*) *US* to wash one's face and hands ▷ *n* washup **3** *Austral* the end, outcome of a process: *in the washup, three candidates were elected*

washy ('wɒʃɪ) *adj* washier, washiest **1** overdiluted, watery, or weak **2** lacking intensity or strength > 'washiness *n*

Wasim Akram ('wæzɪm 'ækræm) *n* **Chaudhry**. born 1966, Pakistani cricketer; captain of Pakistan 1993–94, 1995–2000

wasn't ('wɒzᵊnt) *vb contraction of* was not

wasp (wɒsp) *n* **1** any social hymenopterous insect of the family *Vespidae*, esp *Vespula vulgaris* (**common wasp**), typically having a black-and-yellow body and an ovipositor specialized for stinging **2** any of various solitary hymenopterans, such as the digger wasp and gall wasp [Old English *wæsp*; related to Old Saxon *waspa*, Old High German *wefsa*, Latin *vespa*] > 'waspily *adv* > 'waspiness *n*

Wasp *or* **WASP** (wɒsp) *n acronym for* (in the US) White Anglo-Saxon Protestant: a person descended from N European, usually Protestant stock, forming a group often considered the most dominant, privileged, and influential in American society

waspish ('wɒspɪʃ) *adj* **1** relating to or suggestive of a wasp **2** easily annoyed or angered > 'waspishly *adv* > 'waspishness *n*

wasp waist *n* a very slender waist, esp one that is tightly corseted > 'wasp-ˌwaisted *adj*

wassail ('wɒseɪl) *n* **1** (formerly) a toast or salutation made to a person at festivities **2** a festivity when much drinking takes place **3** alcoholic drink drunk at such a festivity, esp spiced beer or mulled wine ▷ *vb* **4** to drink the health of (a person) at a wassail **5** (*intr*) to go from house to house singing carols at Christmas [c13: from Old Norse *ves heill* be in good health; related to Old English *wes hāl*; see HALE[1]] > 'wassailer *n*

Wassermann test *or* **Wassermann reaction** ('wæsəmən; German 'vasərman) *n med* a diagnostic test for syphilis [c20: named after August von *Wassermann* (1866–1925), German bacteriologist]

wast (wɒst; *unstressed* wəst) *vb archaic or dialect* (used with the pronoun *thou* or its relative equivalent) a singular form of the past tense (indicative mood) of **be**[1]

wastage ('weɪstɪdʒ) *n* **1** anything lost by wear or waste **2** the process of wasting **3** reduction in size of a workforce by retirement, voluntary resignation, etc (esp in the phrase **natural wastage**)

● **USAGE** *Waste* and *wastage* are to some extent interchangeable, but many people think that *wastage* should not be used to refer to loss resulting from human carelessness, inefficiency, etc: *a waste* (not *a wastage*) *of time/money/effort* etc

waste (weɪst) *vb* **1** (*tr*) to use, consume, or expend thoughtlessly, carelessly, or to no avail **2** (*tr*) to fail to take advantage of: *to waste an opportunity* **3** (when *intr*, often foll by *away*) to lose or cause to lose bodily strength, health, etc **4** to exhaust or become exhausted **5** (*tr*) to ravage **6** (*tr*) *informal* to murder or kill ▷ *n* **7** the act of wasting or state of being wasted **8** a failure to take advantage of something **9** anything unused or not used to full advantage **10** anything or anyone rejected as useless, worthless, or in excess of what is required **11** garbage, rubbish, or trash **12** a land or region that is devastated or ruined **13** a land or region that is wild or uncultivated **14** *physiol* **a** the useless products of metabolism **b** indigestible food residue **15** *law* reduction in the value of an estate caused by act or neglect, esp by a life-tenant ▷ *adj* **16** rejected as useless, unwanted, or worthless **17** produced in excess of what is required **18** not cultivated, inhabited, or productive: *waste land* **19** **a** of or denoting the useless products of metabolism **b** of or denoting indigestible food residue **20** lay waste to devastate or destroy [c13: from Anglo-French *waster*, from Latin *vāstāre* to lay waste, from *vastus* empty]

wastebasket ('weɪstˌbɑːskɪt) *n* an open receptacle for paper and other dry litter. Also called (esp in Britain): wastepaper basket

wasted ('weɪstɪd) *adj* **1** not exploited or taken advantage of: *a wasted opportunity* **2** useless or unprofitable: *wasted effort* **3** physically enfeebled and emaciated: *a thin wasted figure* **4** *slang* showing signs of habitual drug abuse

wasteful ('weɪstfʊl) *adj* **1** tending to waste or squander; extravagant **2** causing waste, destruction, or devastation > 'wastefully *adv* > 'wastefulness *n*

wasteland ('weɪstˌlænd) *n* **1** a barren or desolate area of land, not or no longer used for cultivation or building **2** a region, period in history, etc, that is considered spiritually, intellectually, or aesthetically barren or desolate

wastepaper ('weɪst,peɪpə) n paper discarded after use

wastepaper basket or **wastepaper bin** n chiefly Brit another word for **wastebasket**

waste pipe n a pipe to take excess or used water away, as from a sink to a drain

waster ('weɪstə) n 1 a person or thing that wastes 2 a ne'er-do-well; wastrel

wasting ('weɪstɪŋ) adj (prenominal) reducing the vitality, strength, or robustness of the body: a wasting disease > 'wastingly adv

wasting asset n an unreplaceable business asset of limited life, such as a coal mine or an oil well

wastrel ('weɪstrəl) n 1 a wasteful person; spendthrift; prodigal 2 an idler or vagabond

Wast Water or **Wastwater** (wɒst) n a lake in NW England, in Cumbria in the Lake District. Length: 5 km (3 miles)

wat (wɑːt) n a Thai Buddhist monastery or temple [Thai, from Sanskrit vāta enclosure]

watap (wæˈtɑːp, woˈ-) n a stringy thread made by North American Indians from the roots of various conifers and used for weaving and sewing [c18: from Canadian French, from Cree watapiy]

watch (wɒtʃ) vb 1 to look at or observe closely or attentively 2 (intr; foll by for) to wait attentively or expectantly 3 to guard or tend (something) closely or carefully 4 (intr) to keep vigil 5 (tr) to maintain an interest in: to watch the progress of a child at school 6 watch it! be careful! look out! ▷ n 7 a a small portable timepiece, usually worn strapped to the wrist (a **wristwatch**) or in a waistcoat pocket b (as modifier): a watch spring 8 a period of vigil, esp during the night 9 (formerly) one of a set of periods of any of various lengths into which the night was divided 10 nautical a any of the usually four-hour periods beginning at midnight and again at noon during which part of a ship's crew are on duty b those officers and crew on duty during a specified watch 11 the period during which a guard is on duty 12 (formerly) a watchman or band of watchmen 13 on the watch on the lookout; alert ▷ See also **watch out** [Old English wæccan (vb), wæcce (n); related to WAKE¹] > 'watcher n

-watch suffix of nouns indicating a regular television programme or newspaper feature on the topic specified: Crimewatch

watchable ('wɒtʃəbəl) adj 1 capable of being watched 2 interesting, enjoyable, or entertaining: a watchable television documentary

watchcase ('wɒtʃ,keɪs) n a protective case for a watch, generally of metal such as gold, silver, brass, or gunmetal

watch chain n a chain used for fastening a pocket watch to the clothing. See also **fob¹**

Watch Committee n Brit history a local government committee composed of magistrates and representatives of the county borough council responsible for the efficiency of the local police force

watchdog ('wɒtʃ,dɒg) n 1 a dog kept to guard property 2 a a person or group of persons that acts as a protector or guardian against inefficiency, illegal practices, etc b (as modifier): a watchdog committee

watch fire n a fire kept burning at night as a signal or for warmth and light by a person keeping watch

watchful ('wɒtʃfʊl) adj 1 vigilant or alert 2 archaic not sleeping > 'watchfully adv > 'watchfulness n

watch-glass n 1 a curved glass disc that covers the dial of a watch 2 a similarly shaped piece of glass used in laboratories for evaporating small samples of a solution, etc

watchlist ('wɒtʃ,lɪst) n 1 a list of things to be monitored, esp in order to prevent loss, damage, etc 2 a list of people or organizations to be kept under surveillance, esp because they are suspected of wrongdoing: terrorist watchlist

watchmaker ('wɒtʃ,meɪkə) n a person who makes or mends watches > 'watch,making n

watchman ('wɒtʃmən) n, pl -men 1 a person employed to guard buildings or property 2 (formerly) a man employed to patrol or guard the streets at night

watch night n (in Protestant churches) 1 a the night of December 24, during which a service is held to mark the arrival of Christmas Day b the night of December 31, during which a service is held to mark the passing of the old year and the beginning of the new 2 the service held on either of these nights

watch out vb (intr, adverb) to be careful or on one's guard

watchstrap ('wɒtʃ,stræp) n a strap of leather, cloth, etc, attached to a watch for fastening it around the wrist. Also called (US, Canadian and Austral): watchband

watchtower ('wɒtʃ,tauə) n a tower on which a sentry keeps watch

watchword ('wɒtʃ,wɜːd) n another word for **password**

water ('wɔːtə) n 1 a clear colourless tasteless odourless liquid that is essential for plant and animal life and constitutes, in impure form, rain, oceans, rivers, lakes, etc It is a neutral substance, an effective solvent for many compounds, and is used as a standard for many physical properties. Formula: H_2O. Related adj: **aqueous** 2 a any body or area of this liquid, such as a sea, lake, river, etc b (as modifier): water sports; water transport; a water plant. Related adj: **aquatic** 3 the surface of such a body or area: fish swam below the water 4 any form or variety of this liquid, such as rain 5 See **high water**, **low water** 6 any of various solutions of chemical substances in water: lithia water; ammonia water 7 physiol a any fluid secreted from the body, such as sweat, urine, or tears b (usually plural) the amniotic fluid surrounding a fetus in the womb 8 a wavy lustrous finish on some fabrics, esp silk 9 archaic the degree of brilliance in a diamond. See also **first water** 10 excellence, quality, or degree (in the phrase **of the first water**) 11 finance capital stock issued without a corresponding increase in paid-up capital, so that the book value of the company's capital is not fully represented by assets or earning power 12 (modifier) astrology of or relating to the three signs of the zodiac Cancer, Scorpio, and Pisces 13 hold water to prove credible, logical, or consistent: the alibi did not hold water 14 make water a to urinate b (of a boat, hull, etc) to let in water 15 pass water to urinate 16 water under the bridge events that are past and done with ▷ vb 17 (tr) to sprinkle, moisten, or soak with water 18 (tr; often foll by down) to weaken by the addition of water 19 (intr) (of the eyes) to fill with tears 20 (intr) (of the mouth) to salivate, esp in anticipation of food (esp in the phrase **make one's mouth water**) 21 (tr) to irrigate or provide with water: to water the land; he watered the cattle 22 (intr) to drink water 23 (intr) (of a ship, etc) to take in a supply of water 24 (tr) finance to raise the par value of (issued capital stock) without a corresponding increase in the real value of assets 25 (tr) to produce a wavy lustrous finish on (fabrics, esp silk) ▷ See also **water down** [Old English wæter, of Germanic origin; compare Old Saxon watar, Old High German wazzar, Gothic watō, Old Slavonic voda; related to Greek hudor] > 'waterer n > 'waterless adj

water bag n a bag, sometimes made of skin, leather, etc, but in Australia usually canvas, for holding, carrying, and keeping water cool

water bailiff n an official responsible for enforcing laws on river management and fishing

water bear n another name for a **tardigrade**

water bed n a waterproof mattress filled with water

water beetle n any of various beetles of the families Dysticidae, Hydrophilidae, etc, that live most of the time in freshwater ponds, rivers, etc

water bird n any aquatic bird, including the wading and swimming birds

water biscuit n a thin crisp plain biscuit, usually served with butter or cheese

water blister n a blister containing watery or serous fluid, without any blood or pus

water boatman n any of various aquatic bugs of the families Notonectidae and Corixidae, having a flattened body and oarlike hind legs, adapted for swimming

waterborne ('wɔːtə,bɔːn) adj 1 floating or travelling on water 2 (of a disease, etc) transported or transmitted by water

W

waterbuck (ˈwɔːtəˌbʌk) *n* any of various antelopes of the genus *Kobus*, esp *K. ellipsiprymnus*, of swampy areas of Africa, having long curved ridged horns

water buffalo *or* **water ox** *n* a member of the cattle tribe, *Bubalus bubalis*, of swampy regions of S Asia, having widely spreading back-curving horns. Domesticated forms are used as draught animals

water bug *n* any of various heteropterous insects adapted to living in the water or on its surface, esp any of the family *Belostomatidae* (**giant water bugs**), of North America, India, and southern Africa, which have flattened hairy legs

water butt *n* a barrel for collecting rainwater, esp from a drainpipe

water cannon *n* an apparatus for pumping water through a nozzle at high pressure, used in quelling riots

water carrier *n informal* a football player who is regarded as hard-working and competent but is not a star player

Water Carrier *or* **Water Bearer** *n* the Water Carrier the constellation Aquarius, the 11th sign of the zodiac

water chestnut *n* **1** Also called: **water caltrop** a floating aquatic onagraceous plant, *Trapa natans*, of Asia, having four-pronged edible nutlike fruits **2** Chinese water chestnut a Chinese cyperaceous plant, *Eleocharis tuberosa*, with an edible succulent corm **3** the corm of the Chinese water chestnut, used in Oriental cookery

water clock *or* **water glass** *n* any of various devices for measuring time that use the escape of water as the motive force

water closet *n* **1** a lavatory flushed by water **2** a small room that has a lavatory ▷ Usually abbreviated to: **WC**

watercolour *or* US **watercolor** (ˈwɔːtəˌkʌlə) *n* **1** **a** a painting done in watercolours **b** (*as modifier*): *a watercolour masterpiece* **2** the art or technique of painting with such pigments > ˈwaterˌcolourist *or* US ˈwaterˌcolorist *n*

water-cool *vb* (*tr*) to cool (an engine, etc) by a flow of water circulating in an enclosed jacket > ˈwater-ˌcooled *adj*

water cooler *n* **1** a device for cooling and dispensing drinking water ▷ *modifier* **water-cooler 2** *informal* indicating the kind of informal conversation among office staff that takes place at such a dispenser

watercourse (ˈwɔːtəˌkɔːs) *n* **1** a stream, river, or canal **2** the channel, bed, or route along which this flows

watercraft (ˈwɔːtəˌkrɑːft) *n* **1** a boat or ship or such vessels collectively **2** skill in handling boats or in water sports

watercress (ˈwɔːtəˌkrɛs) *n* an Old World plant, *Nasturtium officinale*, of clear ponds and streams, having pungent leaves that are used in salads and as a garnish: family *Brassicaceae* (crucifers)

water cure *n med* a nontechnical name for **hydropathy, hydrotherapy**

water cycle *n* the circulation of the earth's water, in which water evaporates from the sea into the atmosphere, where it condenses and falls as rain or snow, returning to the sea by rivers or returning to the atmosphere by evapotranspiration

water diviner *n Brit* a person able to locate the presence of water, esp underground, with a divining rod

water down *vb* (*tr, adverb*) **1** to dilute or weaken with water **2** to modify or adulterate, esp so as to omit anything harsh, unpleasant, or offensive: *to water down the truth* > ˌwatered-ˈdown *adj*

waterfall (ˈwɔːtəˌfɔːl) *n* a cascade of falling water where there is a vertical or almost vertical step in a river

water flea *n* any of numerous minute freshwater branchiopod crustaceans of the order *Cladocera*, which swim by means of hairy branched antennae. See also **daphnia**

Waterford (ˈwɔːtəfəd) *n* **1** a county of S Republic of Ireland, in Munster province on the Atlantic: mountainous in the centre and in the northwest County town: Waterford. Pop: 101 546 (2002). Area: 1838 sq km (710 sq miles) **2** a port in S Republic of Ireland, county town of Co Waterford: famous glass industry; fishing. Pop: 44 594 (2002)

waterfowl (ˈwɔːtəˌfaʊl) *n* **1** any aquatic freshwater bird, esp any species of the family *Anatidae* (ducks, geese, and swans) **2** such birds collectively

waterfront (ˈwɔːtəˌfrʌnt) *n* the area of a town or city alongside a body of water, such as a harbour or dockyard

water gap *n* a deep valley in a ridge, containing a stream

water gas *n* a mixture of hydrogen and carbon monoxide produced by passing steam over hot carbon, used as a fuel and raw material

water gate *n* **1** a gate in a canal, leat, etc that can be opened or closed to control the flow of water **2** a gate through which access may be gained to a body of water

Watergate (ˈwɔːtəˌgeɪt) *n* **1** an incident during the 1972 US presidential campaign, when a group of agents employed by the re-election organization of President Richard Nixon were caught breaking into the Democratic Party headquarters in the Watergate building, Washington, DC. The consequent political scandal was exacerbated by attempts to conceal the fact that senior White House officials had approved the burglary, and eventually forced the resignation of President Nixon **2** any similar public scandal, esp involving politicians or a possible cover-up

water gauge *n* an instrument that indicates the presence or the quantity of water in a tank, reservoir, or boiler feed. Also called: **water glass**

water glass *n* **1** a viscous syrupy solution of sodium silicate in water: used as a protective coating for cement and a preservative, esp for eggs **2** another name for **water clock, water gauge**

water gum *n* any of several gum trees, esp *Nyssa biflora* (or *tupelo*), of swampy areas of North America: family *Nyssaceae*

water hammer *n* a sharp concussion produced when the flow of water in a pipe is suddenly blocked

water hen *n* another name for **gallinule**

water hole *n* **1** a depression, such as a pond or pool, containing water, esp one used by animals as a drinking place **2** a source of drinking water in a desert

Waterhouse (ˈwɔːtəˌhaʊs) *n* **1** Alfred. 1830–1905, British architect; a leader of the Gothic Revival. His buildings include Manchester Town Hall (1868) and the Natural History Museum, London (1881) **2** George Marsden. 1824–1906, New Zealand statesman, born in England: prime minister of New Zealand (1872–73) **3** Keith (Spencer). born 1929, British novelist, dramatist, and journalist: best known for the novel *Billy Liar* (1959) and his collaborations with the dramatist Willis Hall (1929–2005)

water hyacinth *n* a floating aquatic plant, *Eichhornia crassipes*, of tropical America, having showy bluish-purple flowers and swollen leafstalks: family *Pontederiaceae*. It forms dense masses in rivers, ponds, etc, and is a serious problem in the southern US, Australia, and parts of Africa

water ice *n* an ice cream made from a frozen sugar syrup flavoured with fruit juice or purée; sorbet

watering can *n* a container with a handle and a spout with a perforated nozzle used to sprinkle water over plants

watering hole *n* **1** a pool where animals drink; water hole **2** *facetious, slang* a pub

watering place *n* **1** a place where drinking water for men or animals may be obtained **2** *Brit* a spa **3** *Brit* a seaside resort

water jacket *n* a water-filled envelope or container surrounding a machine, engine, or part for cooling purposes, esp the casing around the cylinder block of a pump or internal-combustion engine

water jump *n* a ditch, brook, or pond over which athletes or horses must jump in a steeplechase or similar contest

water level *n* **1** the level reached by the surface of a body of water **2** the water line of a boat or ship

water lily *n* any of various aquatic plants of the genus *Nymphaea* and related genera, of temperate and tropical regions, having large leaves and showy flowers that float on the surface of the water: family *Nymphaeaceae*

water line *n* **1** a line marked at the level around a vessel's hull to which the vessel will be immersed when afloat **2** a line marking the level reached by a body of water

waterlogged ('wɔːtəˌlɒgd) *adj* **1** saturated with water **2** (of a vessel still afloat) having taken in so much water as to be unmanageable

Waterloo (ˌwɔːtəˈluː) *n* **1** a small town in central Belgium, in Walloon Brabant province south of Brussels: battle (1815) fought nearby in which British and Prussian forces under the Duke of Wellington and Blücher routed the French under Napoleon. Pop: 29 003 (2004 est) **2** a total or crushing defeat (esp in **meet one's Waterloo**)

water main *n* a principal supply pipe in an arrangement of pipes for distributing water

waterman ('wɔːtəmən) *n, pl* -men a skilled boatman > 'waterman,ship *n*

watermark ('wɔːtəˌmɑːk) *n* **1** a distinguishing mark impressed on paper during manufacture, visible when the paper is held up to the light **2** another word for **water line** (senses 1, 2) ▷ *vb* (*tr*) **3** to mark (paper) with a watermark

water meadow *n* a meadow that remains fertile by being periodically flooded by a stream

watermelon ('wɔːtəˌmɛlən) *n* **1** an African melon, *Citrullus vulgaris*, widely cultivated for its large edible fruit **2** the fruit of this plant, which has a hard green rind and sweet watery reddish flesh

water meter *n* a device for measuring the quantity or rate of water flowing through a pipe

water milfoil *n* any of various pond plants of the genus *Myriophyllum*, having feathery underwater leaves and small inconspicuous flowers: family *Haloragidaceae*

water mill *n* a mill operated by a water wheel

water moccasin *n* a large dark grey venomous snake, *Agkistrodon piscivorus*, of swamps in the southern US: family *Crotalidae* (pit vipers). Also called: cottonmouth

water nymph *n* any fabled nymph of the water, such as the Naiad, Nereid, or Oceanid of Greek mythology

water of crystallization *n* water present in the crystals of certain compounds. It is chemically combined in stoichiometric amounts, usually by coordinate or hydrogen bonds, but can often be easily expelled

water ouzel *n* another name for **dipper** (sense 2)

water paint *n* any water-based paint, such as an emulsion or an acrylic paint

water pipe *n* **1** a pipe for water **2** another name for **hookah**

water pistol *n* a toy pistol that squirts a stream of water or other liquid

water plantain *n* any of several marsh plants of the genus *Alisma*, esp *A. plantago-aquatica*, of N temperate regions and Australia, having clusters of small white or pinkish flowers and broad pointed leaves: family *Alismataceae*

water polo *n* a game played in water by two teams of seven swimmers in which each side tries to throw or propel an inflated ball into the opponents' goal

water power *n* **1** the power latent in a dynamic or static head of water as used to drive machinery, esp for generating electricity **2** a source of such power, such as a drop in the level of a river, etc

waterproof ('wɔːtəˌpruːf) *adj* **1** not penetrable by water. See **water-repellent, water-resistant** ▷ *n* **2** *chiefly Brit* a waterproof garment, esp a raincoat ▷ *vb* (*tr*) **3** to make (a fabric, item of clothing, etc) waterproof

water purslane *n* an onagraceous marsh plant, *Ludwigia palustris*, of temperate and warm regions, having reddish stems and small greenish flowers

water rail *n* a large Eurasian rail, *Rallus aquaticus*, of swamps, ponds, etc, having a long red bill

water rat *n* **1** any of several small amphibious rodents, esp the water vole or the muskrat **2** any of various amphibious rats of the subfamily *Hydromyinae*, of New Guinea, the Philippines, and Australia

water rate *n* a charge made for the public supply of water

water-repellent *adj* (of fabrics, garments, etc) having a finish that resists the absorption of water

water-resistant *adj* (esp of fabrics) designed to resist but not entirely prevent the penetration of water

Waters ('wɔːtəz) *n* **Muddy,** real name *McKinley Morganfield*. 1915–83, US blues guitarist, singer, and songwriter. His songs include "Rollin' Stone" (1948) and "Got my Mojo Working" (1954)

water scorpion *n* any of various long-legged aquatic insects of the heteropterous family *Nepidae*, which breathe by means of a long spinelike tube that projects from the rear of the body and penetrates the surface of the water

watershed ('wɔːtəˌʃɛd) *n* **1** the dividing line between two adjacent river systems, such as a ridge **2** an important period or factor that serves as a dividing line

waterside ('wɔːtəˌsaɪd) *n* **a** the area of land beside a body of water **b** (*as modifier*): *waterside houses*

watersider ('wɔːtəˌsaɪdə) *n* *Austral & NZ* a wharf labourer

water-ski *n* Also: water ski **1** a type of ski used for planing or gliding over water ▷ *vb* -skis, -skiing, -skied or -ski'd **2** (*intr*) to ride over water on a water-ski or water-skis while holding a rope towed by a speedboat > 'water-ˌskier *n* > 'water-ˌskiing *n*

water snake *n* any of various colubrid snakes that live in or near water, esp any of numerous harmless North American snakes of the genus *Natrix*, such as *N. sipedon*

water softener *n* **1** any substance that lessens the hardness of water, usually by precipitating or absorbing calcium and magnesium ions **2** a tank, apparatus, or chemical plant that is used to filter or treat water to remove chemicals that cause hardness

water spaniel *n* either of two large curly-coated breeds of spaniel (the Irish and the American), which are used for hunting waterfowl

water splash *n* a place where a stream runs over a road

water sports *pl n* various sports, such as swimming, water-skiing, or windsurfing, that take place in or on water

waterspout ('wɔːtəˌspaʊt) *n* **1** *meteorol* **a** a tornado occurring over water that forms a column of water and mist extending between the surface and the clouds above **b** a sudden downpour of heavy rain **2** a pipe or channel through which water is discharged, esp one used for drainage from the gutters of a roof

water table *n* **1** the surface of the water-saturated part of the ground, usually following approximately the contours of the overlying land surface **2** an offset or string course that has a moulding designed to throw rainwater clear of the wall below

water thrush *n* either of two North American warblers, *Seiurus motacilla* or *S. noveboracensis*, having a brownish back and striped underparts and tending to occur near water

watertight ('wɔːtəˌtaɪt) *adj* **1** not permitting the passage of water either in or out: *a watertight boat* **2** without loopholes: *a watertight argument* **3** kept separate from other subjects or influences

water tower *n* a reservoir or storage tank mounted on a tower-like structure at the summit of an area of high ground in a place where the water pressure would otherwise be inadequate for distribution at a uniform pressure

water vapour *n* water in the gaseous state, esp when due to evaporation at a temperature below the boiling point

water vole *n* a large amphibious vole, *Arvicola terrestris*, of Eurasian river banks: family *Cricetidae*. Also called: water rat

water wagtail *n* another name for **pied wagtail**

waterway ('wɔːtəˌweɪ) *n* a river, canal, or other navigable channel used as a means of travel or transport

waterweed ('wɔːtəˌwiːd) *n* any of various weedy aquatic plants

water wheel *n* **1** a simple water-driven turbine consisting of a wheel having vanes set axially across its rim, used to drive machinery **2** a wheel with buckets attached to its rim for raising water from a stream, pond, etc

water wings *pl n* an inflatable rubber device shaped like a pair of wings, which is placed round the front of the

W

body and under the arms of a person learning to swim

waterworks ('wɔːtə,wɜːks) n 1 (functioning as singular) an establishment for storing, purifying, and distributing water for community supply 2 (functioning as plural) a display of water in movement, as in fountains 3 (functioning as plural) Brit informal, euphemistic the urinary system, esp with reference to its normal functioning 4 (functioning as plural) informal crying; tears

waterworn ('wɔːtə,wɔːn) adj worn smooth by the action or passage of water

watery ('wɔːtərɪ) adj 1 relating to, consisting of, containing, or resembling water 2 discharging or secreting water or a water-like fluid 3 tearful; weepy 4 insipid, thin, or weak

Watford ('wɒtfəd) n a town in SE England, in SW Hertfordshire: light industries, services. Pop: 120 960 (2001)

Watling Island ('wɒtlɪŋ) n another name for **San Salvador Island**

Watson ('wɒtsən) n 1 **James Dewey**. born 1928, US biologist, whose contribution to the discovery of the helical structure of DNA won him a Nobel prize for physiology or medicine shared with Francis Crick and Maurice Wilkins in 1962 2 **John B**(roadus). 1878–1958, US psychologist; a leading exponent of behaviourism 3 **John Christian**. 1867–1941, Australian statesman, born in Chile: prime minister of Australia (1904) 4 **Russell**. born 1973, British tenor, maker of the bestselling albums The Voice (2001) and Encore (2002) 5 **Tom**, full name Thomas Sturges Watson. born 1949, US golfer: won the US Open Championship (1982), the British Open Championship (1975, 1977, 1980, 1982, 1983), and the World Series (1975, 1977, 1980)

Watson-Watt ('wɒtsən'wɒt) n Sir **Robert Alexander**. 1892–1973, Scottish physicist, who played a leading role in the development of radar

watt (wɒt) n the derived SI unit of power, equal to 1 joule per second; the power dissipated by a current of 1 ampere flowing across a potential difference of 1 volt. 1 watt is equivalent to 1.341×10^{-3} horsepower. Symbol: W [C19: named after James Watt (1736–1819), Scottish engineer and inventor]

Watt (wɒt) n **James**. 1736–1819, Scottish engineer and inventor. His fundamental improvements to the steam engine led to the widespread use of steam power in industry

wattage ('wɒtɪdʒ) n 1 power, esp electric power, measured in watts 2 the power rating, measured in watts, of an electrical appliance

Watteau ('wɒtəʊ; French vato) n **Jean-Antoine** (ʒɑ̃ ɑ̃twan). 1684–1721, French painter, esp of fêtes champêtres

Wattenscheid (German 'vatənʃait) n an industrial town in NW Germany, in North Rhine-Westphalia east of Essen

watt-hour n a unit of energy equal to a power of one watt operating for one hour. 1 watt-hour equals 3600 joules

wattle ('wɒtᵊl) n 1 a frame of rods or stakes interwoven with twigs, branches, etc, esp when used to make fences 2 the material used in such a construction 3 a loose fold of skin, often brightly coloured, hanging from the neck or throat of certain birds, lizards, etc 4 any of various chiefly Australian acacia trees having spikes of small brightly coloured flowers and flexible branches, which were used by early settlers for making fences ▷ vb (tr) 5 to construct from wattle 6 to bind or frame with wattle 7 to weave or twist (branches, twigs, etc) into a frame ▷ adj 8 made of, formed by, or covered with wattle [Old English watol; related to wethel wrap, Old High German wadal, German Wedel] > 'wattled adj

wattle and daub n a form of wall construction consisting of interwoven twigs plastered with a mixture of clay, lime, water, and sometimes dung and chopped straw

wattmeter ('wɒt,miːtə) n a meter for measuring electric power in watts

Watts (wɒts) n 1 **George Frederick**. 1817–1904, English painter and sculptor, noted esp for his painting Hope (1886) and his sculpture Physical Energy (1904) in

Kensington Gardens, London 2 **Isaac**. 1674–1748, English hymn-writer

Waugh (wɔː) n 1 **Evelyn** (**Arthur St John**) ('iːvlɪn). 1903–66, English novelist. His early satirical novels include Decline and Fall (1928), Vile Bodies (1930), A Handful of Dust (1934), and Scoop (1938). His later novels include the more sombre Brideshead Revisited (1945) and the trilogy of World War II Men at Arms (1952), Officers and Gentlemen (1955), and Unconditional Surrender (1961) 2 **Mark** (**Edward**). born 1965, Australian cricketer 3 his twin brother **Steve**, full name Stephen Roger Waugh. born 1965, Australian cricketer; captain of the Australian team that won the 1999 one-day World Cup

waul or **wawl** (wɔːl) vb (intr) to cry or wail plaintively like a cat [C16: of imitative origin]

wave (weɪv) vb 1 to move or cause to move freely to and fro: the banner waved in the wind 2 (intr) to move the hand to and fro as a greeting 3 to signal or signify by or as if by waving something 4 (tr) to direct to move by or as if by waving something: he waved me on 5 to form or be formed into curves, undulations, etc 6 (tr) to set waves in (the hair) ▷ n 7 one of a sequence of ridges or undulations that moves across the surface of a body of a liquid, esp the sea: created by the wind or a moving object and gravity 8 any undulation on or at the edge of a surface reminiscent of such a wave: a wave across the field of corn 9 the waves the sea 10 anything that suggests the movement of a wave, as by a sudden rise: a crime wave 11 a widespread movement that advances in a body: a wave of settlers swept into the country 12 the act or an instance of waving 13 physics an oscillation propagated through a medium or space such that energy is periodically interchanged between two kinds of disturbance. For example, an oscillating electric field generates a magnetic oscillation and vice versa, hence an electromagnetic wave is produced. Similarly a wave on a liquid comprises vertical and horizontal displacements 14 physics a graphical representation of a wave obtained by plotting the magnitude of the disturbance against time at a particular point in the medium or space; waveform 15 a prolonged spell of some weather condition: a heat wave 16 an undulating curve or series of curves or loose curls in the hair 17 make waves to cause trouble; disturb the status quo [Old English wafian (vb); related to Old High German weban to WEAVE, Old Norse vafra; see WAVER; C16 (n) changed from earlier wāwe, probably from Old English wǣg motion; compare WAG¹] > 'waveless adj > 'wave,like adj

waveband ('weɪv,bænd) n a range of wavelengths or frequencies used for a particular type of radio transmission

wave-cut platform n a flat surface at the base of a cliff formed by erosion by waves

wave down vb (tr, adverb) to signal with a wave to (a driver or vehicle) to stop

wave energy n energy obtained by harnessing wave power

wave equation n physics a partial differential equation describing wave motion. It has the form $\nabla^2\varphi = (1/c^2) \times (\partial^2\varphi/\partial t^2)$, where ∇^2 is the Laplace operator, t the time, c the speed of propagation, and φ is a function characterizing the displacement of the wave

waveform ('weɪv,fɔːm) n physics the shape of the graph of a wave or oscillation obtained by plotting the value of some changing quantity against time

wavefront ('weɪv,frʌnt) n physics a surface associated with a propagating wave and passing through all points in the wave that have the same phase. It is usually perpendicular to the direction of propagation

wave function n physics a mathematical function of position and generally time, used in wave mechanics to describe the state of a physical system. Symbol: ψ

waveguide ('weɪv,gaɪd) n electronics a solid rod of dielectric or a hollow metal tube, usually of rectangular cross section, used as a path to guide microwaves

wavelength ('weɪv,lɛŋθ) n 1 the distance, measured in the direction of propagation, between two points of the same phase in consecutive cycles of a wave. Symbol: λ

W

2 the wavelength of the carrier wave used by a particular broadcasting station **3 on someone's wavelength** *or* **on the same wavelength** *informal* having similar views, feelings, or thoughts (as someone else)

wavelet ('weɪvlɪt) *n* a small wave

Wavell ('weɪvəl) *n* **Archibald** (**Percival**), 1st Earl. 1883–1950, British field marshal. During World War II he was commander in chief in the Middle East (1939–41), defeating the Italians in N Africa. He was commander in chief in India (1941–43) and viceroy of India (1943–47)

wave mechanics *n* (*functioning as singular*) *physics* the formulation of quantum mechanics in which the behaviour of systems, such as atoms, is described in terms of their wave functions

wave number *n physics* the reciprocal of the wavelength of a wave

waver ('weɪvə) *vb* (*intr*) **1** to be irresolute; hesitate between two possibilities **2** to become unsteady **3** to fluctuate or vary **4** to move back and forth or one way and another **5** (of light) to flicker or flash ▷ *n* **6** the act or an instance of wavering [c14: from Old Norse *vafra* to flicker; related to German *wabern* to move about] > 'waverer *n* > 'wavering *adj* > 'waveringly *adv*

wave theory *n* **1** the theory proposed by Huygens that light is transmitted by waves **2** any theory that light or other radiation is transmitted as waves ▷ Compare **corpuscular theory**

wavey ('weɪvɪ) *n Canadian* a snow goose or other wild goose. Also called: **wawa** [via Canadian French from Algonquian (Cree *wehwew*)]

wavy ('weɪvɪ) *adj* **wavier, waviest** **1** abounding in or full of waves **2** moving or proceeding in waves or undulations **3** (of hair) set in or having waves and curls > 'wavily *adv* > 'waviness *n*

wax¹ (wæks) *n* **1** any of various viscous or solid materials of natural origin: characteristically lustrous, insoluble in water, and having a low softening temperature, they consist largely of esters of fatty acids **2** any of various similar substances, such as paraffin wax or ozocerite, that have a mineral origin and consist largely of hydrocarbons **3** short for **beeswax, sealing wax** **4** *physiol* another name for **cerumen** **5** a resinous preparation used by shoemakers to rub on thread **6** any substance or object that is pliable or easily moulded: *he was wax in the hands of the political bosses* **7** (*modifier*) made of or resembling wax: *a wax figure* ▷ *vb* **8** (*tr*) to coat, polish, etc, with wax [Old English *weax*, related to Old Saxon, Old High German *wahs*, Old Norse *vax*] > 'waxer *n*

wax² (wæks) *vb* (*intr*) **1** to become larger, more powerful, etc **2** (of the moon) to show a gradually increasing portion of illuminated surface, between new moon and full moon **3** *archaic* to become as specified [Old English *weaxan*; related to Old Frisian *waxa*, Old Saxon, Old High German *wahsan*, Gothic *wahsjan*]

wax³ (wæks) *n Brit informal, old-fashioned* a fit of rage or temper: *he's in a wax today* [of obscure origin; perhaps from the phrase *to wax angry*]

waxberry ('wæksbərɪ, -brɪ) *n, pl* **-ries** the waxy fruit of the wax myrtle or the snowberry

waxbill ('wæks,bɪl) *n* any of various chiefly African finchlike weaverbirds of the genus *Estrilda* and related genera, having a brightly coloured bill and plumage

waxcloth ('wæks,klɒθ) *n* **1** another name for **oilcloth** **2** another name for **linoleum**

waxen ('wæksən) *adj* **1** made of, treated with, or covered with wax **2** resembling wax in colour or texture

waxeye ('wæks,aɪ) *n Austral & NZ* another name for **white-eye**

wax flower *n Austral* any of several rutaceous shrubs of the genus *Eriostemon*, having waxy pink-white five-petalled flowers

wax light *n* a candle or taper of wax

wax myrtle *n* a shrub, *Myrica cerifera*, of SE North America, having evergreen leaves and a small berry-like fruit with a waxy coating: family *Myricaceae*. Also called: bayberry, candleberry, waxberry

wax palm *n* **1** a tall Andean palm tree, *Ceroxylon andicola*, having pinnate leaves that yield a resinous wax used in making candles **2** another name for **carnauba** (sense 1)

wax paper *n* paper treated or coated with wax or paraffin to make it waterproof

waxplant ('wæks,plɑːnt) *n* a climbing asclepiadaceous shrub, *Hoya carnosa*, of E Asia and Australia, having fleshy leaves and clusters of small waxy white pink-centred flowers

waxwing ('wæks,wɪŋ) *n* any of several gregarious passerine songbirds of the genus *Bombycilla*, esp *B. garrulus*, having red waxy wing tips and crested heads: family *Bombycillidae*

waxwork ('wæks,wɜːk) *n* **1** an object reproduced in wax, esp as an ornament **2** a life-size lifelike figure, esp of a famous person, reproduced in wax **3** (*plural; functioning as singular or plural*) a museum or exhibition of wax figures or objects

waxy¹ ('wæksɪ) *adj* **waxier, waxiest** **1** resembling wax in colour, appearance, or texture **2** made of, covered with, or abounding in wax > 'waxily *adv* > 'waxiness *n*

waxy² ('wæksɪ) *adj* **waxier, waxiest** *Brit informal, old-fashioned* bad-tempered or irritable; angry

way (weɪ) *n* **1** a manner, method, or means: *a way of life; a way of knowing* **2** a route or direction: *the way home* **3 a** a means or line of passage, such as a path or track **b** (*in combination*): *waterway* **4** space or room for movement or activity (esp in the phrases **make way, in the way, out of the way**) **5** distance, usually distance in general: *you've come a long way* **6** a passage or journey: *on the way* **7** characteristic style or manner: *I did it in my own way* **8** (*often plural*) habits; idiosyncrasies: *he has some offensive ways* **9** an aspect of something; particular: *in many ways he was right* **10 a** a part in or leading out of a town **b** (*capital when part of a street name*): *Icknield Way* **11** something that one wants in a determined manner (esp in the phrases **get** *or* **have one's (own) way**) **12** the experience or sphere in which one comes into contact with things (esp in the phrase **come one's way**) **13** *informal* a state or condition, usually financial or concerning health (esp in the phrases **in a good** (*or* **bad**) **way**) **14** *informal* the area or direction of one's home: *drop in if you're ever over my way* **15** movement of a ship or other vessel **16** a guide along which something can be moved, such as the surface of a lathe along which the tailstock slides **17** (*plural*) the wooden or metal tracks down which a ship slides to be launched **18** a course of life including experiences, conduct, etc: *the way of sin* **19 by the way** (*sentence modifier*) in passing or incidentally **20 by way of a** via **b** serving as: *by way of introduction* **c** in the state or condition of: *by way of being an artist* **21 each way** (of a bet) laid on a horse, dog, etc, to win or gain a place **22 give way a** to collapse or break down **b** to withdraw or yield **23 give way to a** to step aside for or stop for **b** to give full rein to (emotions, etc) **24 go out of one's way** to take considerable trouble or inconvenience oneself **25 have a way with** to have such a manner or skill as to handle successfully **26 have it both ways** to enjoy two things that would normally contradict each other or be mutually exclusive **27 in a way** in some respects **28 in no way** not at all **29 lead the way a** to go first **b** to set an example or precedent **30 make one's way a** to proceed or advance **b** to achieve success in life **31 on the way out** *informal* **a** becoming unfashionable, obsolete, etc **b** dying **32 out of the way a** removed or dealt with so as to be no longer a hindrance **b** remote **c** unusual and sometimes improper **33 pay one's way** See **pay¹** (sense 9) **34 see one's way** *or* **see one's way clear** to find it possible and be willing (to do something) **35 under way** having started moving or making progress ▷ *adv* **36** *informal* at a considerable distance or extent: *way over yonder* **b** very far: *they're way up the mountain* **37** *informal* by far; considerably: *way better* [Old English *weg*; related to Old Frisian *wei*, Old Norse *vegr*, Gothic *wigs*]

waybill ('weɪ,bɪl) *n* a document attached to goods in transit specifying their nature, point of origin, and destination as well as the route to be taken and the rate to be charged

wayfarer ('weɪ,fɛərə) *n* a person who goes on a journey > 'way,faring *n, adj*

wayfaring tree *n* a caprifoliaceous shrub, *Viburnum lantana*, of Europe and W Asia, having white flowers and

W

berries that turn from red to black

Wayland or **Wayland Smith** ('weɪlənd) n a smith, artificer, and king of the elves in European folklore. Scandinavian name: Völund. German name: Wieland

waylay (weɪ'leɪ) vb -lays, -laying, -laid (tr) 1 to lie in wait for and attack 2 to await and intercept unexpectedly [c16: from WAY + LAY¹] > way'layer n

wayleave ('weɪ,liːv) n access to property granted by a landowner for payment, for example to allow a contractor access to a building site

waymark ('weɪ,mɑːk) n a symbol or signpost marking the route of a footpath > 'way,marked adj

Wayne (weɪn) n **John**, real name Marion Michael Morrison. 1907–79, US film actor, noted esp for his many Westerns, which include Stagecoach (1939), The Alamo (1960), and True Grit (1969), for which he won an Oscar

way-out adj informal 1 extremely unconventional or experimental; avant-garde 2 excellent or amazing

waypoint ('weɪ,pɔɪnt) n the co-ordinates of a specific location as defined by a GPS

-ways suffix forming adverbs indicating direction or manner: sideways [Old English weges, literally: of the way, from weg WAY]

ways and means pl n 1 the revenues and methods of raising the revenues needed for the functioning of a state or other political unit 2 the methods and resources for accomplishing some purpose

wayside ('weɪ,saɪd) n 1 a the side or edge of a road b (modifier) situated by the wayside: a wayside inn 2 fall by the wayside to cease or fail to continue doing something: of the nine starters, three fell by the wayside

wayward ('weɪwəd) adj 1 wanting to have one's own way regardless of the wishes or good of others 2 capricious, erratic, or unpredictable [c14: changed from awayward turned or turning away] > 'waywardly adv > 'waywardness n

wayworn ('weɪ,wɔːn) adj rare worn or tired by travel

Waziristan (wə,zɪərɪ'stɑːn) n a mountainous region of N Pakistan, on the border with Afghanistan

wazzock ('wæzək) n English dialect a foolish or annoying person [c20: of unknown origin]

wb abbreviation 1 water ballast 2 Also called: W/B, WB waybill 3 westbound

Wb physics symbol for weber

WBA abbreviation World Boxing Association

WBC abbreviation World Boxing Council

WBO abbreviation World Boxing Organization

WBU abbreviation World Boxing Union

WC abbreviation 1 water closet 2 (in London postal code) West Central

WD abbreviation 1 War Department 2 Works Department

we (wiː) pron (subjective) 1 refers to the speaker or writer and another person or other people: we should go now 2 refers to all people or people in general: the planet on which we live 3 when used by editors or other writers, and formerly by monarchs, a formal word for: I¹ 4 informal used instead of you with a tone of persuasiveness, condescension, or sarcasm: how are we today? [Old English wē, related to Old Saxon wī, Old High German wir, Old Norse vēr, Danish, Swedish vi, Sanskrit vayam]

WEA abbreviation (in Britain) Workers' Educational Association

weak (wiːk) adj 1 lacking in physical or mental strength or force; frail or feeble 2 liable to yield, break, or give way: a weak link in a chain 3 lacking in resolution or firmness of character 4 lacking strength, power, or intensity: a weak voice 5 lacking strength in a particular part: a team weak in defence 6 a not functioning as well as normal: weak eyes b easily upset: a weak stomach 7 lacking in conviction, persuasiveness, etc: a weak argument 8 lacking in political or strategic strength: a weak state 9 lacking the usual, full, or desirable strength of flavour: weak tea 10 grammar a denoting or belonging to a class of verbs, in certain languages including the Germanic languages, whose conjugation relies on inflectional endings rather than internal vowel gradation, as look, looks, looking, looked b belonging to any part-of-speech class, in any of various languages, whose inflections

follow the more regular of two possible patterns. See strong (sense 13) 11 (of a syllable) not accented or stressed 12 (of an industry, market, currency, securities, etc) falling in price or characterized by falling prices [Old English wāc soft, miserable; related to Old Saxon wēk, Old High German weih, Old Norse veikr] > 'weakish adj

weaken ('wiːkən) vb to become or cause to become weak or weaker > 'weakener n

weak interaction or **weak force** n physics an interaction between elementary particles that is responsible for certain decay processes, operates at distances less than about 10^{-15} metres, and is 10^{12} times weaker than the strong interaction. The weak interaction and electromagnetic interactions are now described by the unifying electroweak theory. Also called: weak nuclear interaction, weak nuclear force

weak-kneed adj informal yielding readily to force, persuasion, intimidation, etc > ,weak-'kneedly adv

weakling ('wiːklɪŋ) n a person or animal that is lacking in strength or weak in constitution or character

weakly ('wiːklɪ) adj -lier, -liest 1 sickly; feeble ▷ adv 2 in a weak or feeble manner

weak-minded adj 1 lacking in stability of mind or character 2 another word for feeble-minded > ,weak-'mindedly adv > ,weak-'mindedness n

weakness ('wiːknɪs) n 1 the state or quality of being weak 2 a deficiency or failing, as in a person's character 3 a self-indulgent fondness or liking: a weakness for chocolates

weal¹ (wiːl) n a raised mark on the surface of the body produced by a blow. Also called: welt [c19: variant of WALE, influenced in form by WHEAL]

weal² (wiːl) n archaic prosperity or wellbeing (now esp in the phrases **the public weal, the common weal**) [Old English wela; related to Old Saxon welo, Old High German wolo]

weald (wiːld) n Brit archaic open or forested country [Old English; related to Old Saxon, Old High German wald, Old Norse vollr, probably related to WILD]

Weald (wiːld) n **the Weald** a region of SE England, in Kent, Surrey, and East and West Sussex between the North Downs and the South Downs: formerly forested

wealth (wɛlθ) n 1 a large amount of money and valuable material possessions 2 the state of being rich 3 a great profusion: a wealth of gifts 4 economics all goods and services with monetary, exchangeable, or productive value [c13 welthe, from WEAL²; related to WELL¹]

wealth tax n a tax on personal property; capital levy

wealthy ('wɛlθɪ) adj wealthier, wealthiest 1 possessing wealth; affluent; rich 2 of, characterized by, or relating to wealth 3 abounding: wealthy in friends > 'wealthily adv > 'wealthiness n

wean¹ (wiːn) vb (tr) 1 to cause (a child or young mammal) to replace mother's milk by other nourishment 2 (usually foll by from) to cause to desert former habits, pursuits, etc [Old English wenian to accustom; related to German gewöhnen to get used to]

wean² (weɪn, wiːn) n Scot & northern English dialect a child; infant [a contraction of wee ane or perhaps a shortened form of WEANLING]

weaner ('wiːnə) n 1 a person or thing that weans 2 a pig that has just been weaned and weighs less than 40 kg 3 Austral & NZ a lamb, pig, or calf in the year in which it is weaned

weanling ('wiːnlɪŋ) n a child or young animal recently weaned [c16: from WEAN¹ + -LING¹]

weapon ('wɛpən) n 1 an object or instrument used in fighting 2 anything that serves to outwit or get the better of an opponent: his power of speech was his best weapon 3 any part of an animal that is used to defend itself, to attack prey, etc, such as claws, teeth, horns, or a sting [Old English wǣpen; related to Old Norse vápn, Old Frisian wēpen, Old High German wāffan] > 'weaponed adj > 'weaponless adj

weaponize or **weaponise** ('wɛpə,naɪz) vb (tr) to adapt (a chemical, bacillus, etc) in such a way that it can be used as a weapon

weaponry ('wɛpənrɪ) n weapons regarded collectively

w

weapons of mass destruction *pl n* nuclear, chemical, or biological weapons that can cause indiscriminate death or injury on a large scale. Abbreviation: **WMD**

wear¹ (wɛə) *vb* **wears, wearing, wore, worn** **1** (*tr*) to carry or have (a garment, etc) on one's person as clothing, ornament, etc **2** (*tr*) to carry or have on one's person habitually: *she wears a lot of red* **3** (*tr*) to have in one's aspect: *to wear a smile* **4** (*tr*) to display, show, or fly: *a ship wears its colours* **5** to deteriorate or cause to deteriorate by constant use or action **6** to produce or be produced by constant rubbing, scraping, etc: *to wear a hole in one's trousers* **7** to bring or be brought to a specified condition by constant use or action: *to wear a tyre to shreds* **8** (*intr*) to submit to constant use or action in a specified way: *his suit wears well* **9** (*tr*) to harass or weaken **10** (when *intr*, often foll by *on*) (of time) to pass or be passed slowly **11** (*tr*) *Brit slang* to accept: *Larry won't wear that argument* ▷ *n* **12** the act of wearing or state of being worn **13 a** anything designed to be worn: *leisure wear* **b** (*in combination*): *nightwear* **14** deterioration from constant or normal use or action **15** the quality of resisting the effects of constant use ▷ See also **wear down, wear off, wear out** [Old English *werian*; related to Old High German *werien*, Old Norse *verja*, Gothic *vasjan*] ▷ **'wearer** *n*

wear² (wɛə) *vb* **wears, wearing, wore, worn** *nautical* to tack by gybing instead of by going through stays [C17: from earlier *weare*, of unknown origin]

Wear (wɪə) *n* a river in NE England, rising in NW Durham and flowing southeast then northeast to the North Sea at Sunderland. Length: 105 km (65 miles)

wearable ('wɛərəbᵊl) *adj* suitable for wear or able to be worn ▷ ,**weara'bility** *n*

wear and tear *n* damage, depreciation, or loss resulting from ordinary use

wear down *vb* (*adverb*) **1** to consume or be consumed by long or constant wearing, rubbing, etc **2** to overcome or be overcome gradually by persistent effort

wearing ('wɛərɪŋ) *adj* causing fatigue or exhaustion; tiring ▷ **'wearingly** *adv*

wearisome ('wɪərɪsəm) *adj* causing fatigue or annoyance; tedious ▷ **'wearisomely** *or* **'wearifully** *adv*

wear off *vb* (*adverb*) **1** (*intr*) to decrease in intensity gradually: *the pain will wear off in an hour* **2** to disappear or cause to disappear gradually through exposure, use, etc: *the pattern on the ring had been worn off*

wear out *vb* (*adverb*) **1** to make or become unfit or useless through wear **2** (*tr*) to exhaust or tire

weary ('wɪərɪ) *adj* **-rier, -riest** **1** tired or exhausted **2** causing fatigue or exhaustion **3** caused by or suggestive of weariness: *a weary laugh* **4** (*postpositive*; often foll by *of* or *with*) discontented or bored, esp by the long continuance of something ▷ *vb* **-ries, -rying, -ried** **5** to make or become weary **6** to make or become discontented or impatient, esp by the long continuance of something [Old English *wērig*; related to Old Saxon *wōrig*, Old High German *wuorag* drunk, Greek *hōrakian* to faint] ▷ **'wearily** *adv* ▷ **'weariness** *n* ▷ **'wearying** *adj* ▷ **'wearyingly** *adv*

weasand ('wiːzənd) *n* a former name for the **trachea** [Old English *wǣsend, wāsend*; related to Old Frisian *wāsenda*, Old High German *weisont* vein, Danish *vissen*]

weasel ('wiːzᵊl) *n, pl* **-sels** *or* **-sel** **1** any of various small predatory musteline mammals of the genus *Mustela* and related genera, esp *M. nivalis* (**European weasel**), having reddish-brown fur, an elongated body and neck, and short legs **2** *informal* a sly or treacherous person [Old English *weosule, wesle*; related to Old Norse *visla*, Old High German *wisula*, Middle Dutch *wesel*] ▷ **'weaselly** *adj*

weasel out *vb* **-sels, -selling, -selled,** *or US* **-sels, -seling, -seled** (*intr, adverb*) *informal* **1** to go back on a commitment **2** to evade a responsibility, esp in a despicable manner

weasel words *pl n informal* intentionally evasive or misleading speech; equivocation [C20: alluding to the weasel's supposed ability to suck an egg out of its shell without seeming to break the shell]

weather ('wɛðə) *n* **1 a** the day-to-day meteorological conditions, esp temperature, cloudiness, and rainfall, affecting a specific place **b** (*modifier*) relating to the forecasting of weather: *a weather ship* **2 make heavy**

weather **a** (of a vessel) to roll and pitch in heavy seas **b** (foll by *of*) to carry out with great difficulty or unnecessarily great effort **3 under the weather** *informal* not in good health ▷ *adj* **4** (*prenominal*) on or at the side or part towards the wind; windward: *the weather anchor*. See **lee** (sense 2) ▷ *vb* **5** to expose or be exposed to the action of the weather **6** to undergo or cause to undergo changes, such as discoloration, due to the action of the weather **7** (*intr*) to withstand the action of the weather **8** (when *intr*, foll by *through*) to endure (a crisis, danger, etc) **9** (*tr*) to slope (a surface, such as a roof, sill, etc) so as to throw rainwater clear **10** (*tr*) to sail to the windward of: *to weather a point* [Old English *weder*; related to Old Saxon *wedar*, Old High German *wetar*, Old Norse *vethr*] ▷ **'weatherer** *n*

weather-beaten *adj* **1** showing signs of exposure to the weather **2** tanned or hardened by exposure to the weather

weatherboard ('wɛðə,bɔːd) *n* a timber board, with a groove (rabbet) along the front of its top edge and along the back of its lower edge, that is fixed horizontally with others to form an exterior cladding on a wall or roof ▷ **'weather,boarding** *n*

weather-bound *adj* (of a vessel, aircraft, etc) delayed by bad weather

weathercock ('wɛðə,kɒk) *n* **1** a weather vane in the form of a cock **2** a person who is fickle or changeable

weathered ('wɛðəd) *adj* **1** affected by or exposure to the action of the weather **2** (of rocks and rock formations) eroded, decomposed, or otherwise altered by the action of water, wind, frost, heat, etc **3** (of a sill, roof, etc) having a sloped surface so as to allow rainwater to run off

weather eye *n* **1** the vision of a person trained to observe changes in the weather **2** *informal* an alert or observant gaze **3 keep one's weather eye open** to stay on the alert

weatherglass ('wɛðə,glɑːs) *n* (*not in technical use*) any of various instruments, esp a barometer, that measure atmospheric conditions

weather house *n* a model house with two human figures, one that comes out to foretell bad weather and the other to foretell good weather

weathering ('wɛðərɪŋ) *n* the mechanical and chemical breakdown of rocks by the action of rain, snow, cold, etc

weatherly ('wɛðəlɪ) *adj* (of a sailing vessel) making very little leeway when close-hauled, even in a stiff breeze ▷ **'weatherliness** *n*

weatherman ('wɛðə,mæn) *n, pl* **-men** a person who forecasts the weather, esp one who works in a meteorological office

weather map *or* **weather chart** *n* a synoptic chart showing weather conditions, compiled from simultaneous observations taken at various weather stations

weatherproof ('wɛðə,pruːf) *adj* **1** designed or able to withstand exposure to weather without deterioration ▷ *vb* **2** (*tr*) to render (something) weatherproof

weather station *n* one of a network of meteorological observation posts where weather data is recorded

weather strip *n* a thin strip of compressible material, such as spring metal, felt, etc, that is fitted between the frame of a door or window and the opening part to exclude wind and rain. Also called: **weatherstripping**

weather vane *n* a vane designed to indicate the direction in which the wind is blowing

weather window *n* a limited interval when weather conditions can be expected to be suitable for a particular project, such as laying offshore pipelines, reaching a high mountain summit, launching a satellite, etc

weather-wise *adj* **1** skilful or experienced in predicting weather conditions **2** skilful or experienced in predicting trends in public opinion, reactions, etc

weatherworn ('wɛðə,wɔːn) *adj* another word for **weather-beaten**

weave (wiːv) *vb* **weaves, weaving, wove** *or* **weaved, woven** *or* **weaved** **1** to form (a fabric) by interlacing (yarn, etc), esp on a loom **2** (*tr*) to make or construct by such a process: *to weave a shawl* **3** (*tr*) to make or construct

W

(an artefact, such as a basket) by interlacing (a pliable material, such as cane) **4** (of a spider) to make (a web) **5** (tr) to construct by combining separate elements into a whole **6** (tr; often foll by *in, into, through*, etc) to introduce: *to weave factual details into a fiction* **7** to create (a way, etc) by moving from side to side: *to weave through a crowd* **8** get weaving *informal* to hurry; start to do something ▷ *n* **9** the method or pattern of weaving or the structure of a woven fabric [Old English *wefan*; related to Old High German *weban*, Old Norse *vefa*, Greek *hyphos*, Sanskrit *vābhis*; compare WEB, WEEVIL, WASP]

weaver ('wiːvə) *n* **1** a person who weaves, esp as a means of livelihood **2** short for **weaverbird**

weaverbird ('wiːvəˌbɜːd) *or* **weaver** *n* any small Old World passerine songbird of the chiefly African family *Ploceidae*, having a short thick bill and a dull plumage and building covered nests: includes the house sparrow and whydahs

web (wɛb) *n* **1** any structure, construction, fabric, etc, formed by or as if by weaving or interweaving **2** a mesh of fine tough scleroprotein threads built by a spider from a liquid secreted from its spinnerets and used to trap insects **3** a similar network of threads spun by certain insect larvae, such as the silkworm **4** a fabric, esp one in the process of being woven **5** a membrane connecting the toes of some aquatic birds or the digits of such aquatic mammals as the otter **6** the vane of a bird's feather **7** the central section of an I-beam or H-beam that joins the two flanges of the beam **8 a** a continuous strip of paper as formed on a paper machine or fed from a reel into some printing presses **b** (*as modifier*): *web offset; a web press* **9 a** the web (*often capital*) short for **World Wide Web b** (*as modifier*): *a web site; web pages* **10** any structure, construction, etc, that is intricately formed or complex: *a web of intrigue* ▷ *vb* **webs**, **webbing**, **webbed 11** (tr) to cover with or as if with a web **12** (tr) to entangle or ensnare **13** (intr) to construct a web [Old English *webb*; related to Old Saxon, Old High German *webbi*, Old Norse *vefr*] > **webless** *adj*

Web 2.0 *n* the internet viewed as a medium in which interactive experience, in the form of blogs, wikis, forums, etc, plays a more important role than simply accessing information

web address *n* computing another name for URL

Webb (wɛb) *n* **1** Sir **Aston**. 1849–1930, British architect. His work includes the Victoria and Albert Museum (1909), the Victoria Memorial (1911), and Admiralty Arch (1911) **2 Mary** (**Gladys**). 1881–1927, British novelist, remembered for her novels of rustic life, notably *Precious Bane* (1924) **3 Sidney** (**James**), Baron Passfield. 1859–1947, British economist, social historian, and Fabian socialist. He and his wife (**Martha**) **Beatrice** (née *Potter*), 1858–1943, British writer on social and economic problems, collaborated in *The History of Trade Unionism* (1894) and *English Local Government* (1906–29), helped found the London School of Economics (1895), and started the *New Statesman* (1913)

webbed (wɛbd) *adj* **1** (of the feet of certain animals) having the digits connected by a thin fold of skin; palmate **2** having, consisting of, or resembling a web

webbing ('wɛbɪŋ) *n* **1** a strong fabric of hemp, cotton, jute, etc, woven in strips and used under springs in upholstery or for straps, etc **2** the skin that unites the digits of a webbed foot

WebBoard ('wɛbˌbɔːd) *n* computing an internet site where users can post messages, tutorials, information, and topics for discussion

webby ('wɛbɪ) *adj* **-bier**, **-biest** of, relating to, resembling, or consisting of a web

webcam ('wɛbˌkæm) *n* a camera that transmits still or moving images over the internet

webcast ('wɛbˌkɑːst) *n* a broadcast of an event over the World Wide Web

web design *n* computing the planning and creation of websites

web directory *n* computing a database of selected websites, ordered in such a way as to facilitate browsing

weber ('veɪbə) *n* the derived SI unit of magnetic flux; the flux that, when linking a circuit of one turn,

produces in it an emf of 1 volt as it is reduced to zero at a uniform rate in one second. 1 weber is equivalent to 10^8 maxwells. Symbol: Wb [C20: named after Wilhelm Eduard *Weber* (1804–91), German physicist]

Weber (*German* 'veːbər) *n* **1** Baron **Carl Maria Friedrich Ernst von** (karl maˈriːa ˈfriːdrɪç ɛrnst fɔn). 1786–1826, German composer and conductor. His three romantic operas are *Der Freischütz* (1821), *Euryanthe* (1823), and *Oberon* (1826) **2 Ernst Heinrich** (ɛrnst ˈhainrɪç). 1795–1878, German physiologist and anatomist. He introduced the psychological concept of the just noticeable difference between stimuli **3 Max** (maks). 1864–1920, German economist and sociologist, best known for *The Protestant Ethic and the Spirit of Capitalism* (1904–05) **4 Wilhelm Eduard** ('vɪlhɛlm 'eːduart), brother of Ernst Heinrich Weber. 1804–91, German physicist, who conducted research into electricity and magnetism

Webern (*German* 'veːbərn) *n* **Anton von** ('antoːn fɔn). 1883–1945, Austrian composer; pupil of Schoenberg, whose twelve-tone technique he adopted. His works include those for chamber ensemble, such as *Five Pieces for Orchestra* (1911–13)

web farm *n* computing a large website that uses two or more servers to handle user requests. Also called: web server farm

webfoot ('wɛbˌfʊt) *n* **1** zoology a foot having the toes connected by folds of skin **2** anatomy a foot having an abnormal membrane connecting adjacent toes

web-footed *or* **web-toed** *adj* (of certain animals) having webbed feet that facilitate swimming

weblish ('wɛblɪʃ) *n* informal the shorthand form of English that is used in text messaging, chat rooms, etc [C20: WEB (sense 14) + (ENG)LISH]

weblog ('wɛbˌlɒg) *n* the full name for **blog** > 'web,logger *n*

webmail ('wɛbˌmeɪl) *n* computing a system of electronic mail that allows account holders to access their mail via an internet site rather than downloading it onto their computer

webmaster ('wɛbˌmɑːstə) *n* a person responsible for the administration of a website on the World Wide Web

web pal *n* informal a person one meets and corresponds with over the internet

website ('wɛbˌsaɪt) *n* a group of connected pages on the World Wide Web containing information on a particular subject

Webster ('wɛbstə) *n* **1 Daniel**. 1782–1852, US politician and orator **2 John**. ?1580–?1625, English dramatist, noted for his revenge tragedies *The White Devil* (?1612) and *The Duchess of Malfi* (?1613) **3 Noah**. 1758–1843, US lexicographer, famous for his *American Dictionary of the English Language* (1828)

webwheel ('wɛbˌwiːl) *n* **1** a wheel containing a plate or web instead of spokes **2** a wheel of which the rim, spokes, and centre are in one piece

wed (wɛd) *vb* **weds**, **wedding**, **wedded** *or* **wed 1** to take (a person of the opposite sex) as a husband or wife; marry **2** (tr) to join (two people) in matrimony **3** (tr) to unite closely [Old English *weddian*; related to Old Frisian *weddia*, Old Norse *vethja*, Gothic *wadi* pledge]

we'd (wiːd; *unstressed* wɪd) *contraction of* we had *or* we would

Wed. *abbreviation* Wednesday

Weddell Sea ('wɛdᵊl) *n* an arm of the S Atlantic in Antarctica

wedding ('wɛdɪŋ) *n* **1 a** the act of marrying or the celebration of a marriage **b** (*as modifier*): *wedding day* **2** the anniversary of a marriage (in such combinations as **silver wedding** or **diamond wedding**)

wedding breakfast *n* the meal usually served after a wedding ceremony or just before the bride and bridegroom leave for their honeymoon

wedding cake *n* a rich fruit cake, with one, two, or more tiers, covered with almond paste and decorated with royal icing, which is served at a wedding reception

wedding ring *n* a band ring with parallel sides, typically of precious metal, worn to indicate married status

Wedekind (*German* 'veːdəkɪnt) *n* **Frank**. 1864–1918,

W

German dramatist, whose plays, such as *The Awakening of Spring* (1891) and *Pandora's Box* (1904), bitterly satirize the sexual repressiveness of society

wedge (wɛdʒ) *n* **1** a block of solid material, esp wood or metal, that is shaped like a narrow V in cross section and can be pushed or driven between two objects or parts of an object in order to split or secure them **2** any formation, structure, or substance in the shape of a wedge **3** something such as an idea, action, etc, that tends to cause division **4** a shoe with a wedge heel **5** *golf* a club with a face angle of more than 50°, used for bunker shots (**sand wedge**) or pitch shots (**pitching wedge**) **6** (formerly) a body of troops formed in a V-shape **7** thin end of the wedge anything unimportant in itself that implies the start of something much larger ▷ *vb* **8** (*tr*) to secure with or as if with a wedge **9** to squeeze or be squeezed like a wedge into a narrow space **10** (*tr*) to force apart or divide with or as if with a wedge [Old English *wecg*; related to Old Saxon *weggi*, Old High German *wecki*, Old Norse *veggr* wall] ▷ 'wedge,like *adj* ▷ 'wedgy *adj*

wedge heel *n* a raised shoe heel with the heel and sole forming a solid block

wedge-tailed eagle *n* a large brown Australian eagle, *Aquila audax*, having a wedge-shaped tail and a wingspan of 3 m. Also called: eaglehawk

wedgie ('wɛdʒɪ) *n informal* the state of having one's underpants or shorts caught between one's buttocks (esp in the phrase **give someone a wedgie**) [C20: from WEDGE]

Wedgwood[1] ('wɛdʒwʊd) *n* **1** *trademark* **a** pottery produced, esp during the late 18th and early 19th centuries, at the Wedgwood factories **b** such pottery having applied classical decoration in white on a blue or other coloured ground ▷ *adj* **2** relating to or characteristic of such pottery: *Wedgwood blue*

Wedgwood[2] ('wɛdʒwʊd) *n* **Josiah**. 1730–95, British potter and industrialist, who founded several pottery works near Stoke-on-Trent in Staffordshire

wedlock ('wɛdlɒk) *n* **1** the state of being married **2** born out of wedlock born when one's parents are not legally married [Old English *wedlāc*, from *wedd* pledge + *-lāc*, suffix denoting activity, perhaps from *lāc* game, battle (related to Gothic *laiks* dance, Old Norse *leikr*)]

Wednesday ('wɛnzdɪ) *n* the fourth day of the week; third day of the working week [Old English *Wōdnes dæg* Woden's day, translation of Latin *mercurii dies* Mercury's day; related to Old Frisian *wōnsdei*, Middle Dutch *wōdensdach* (Dutch *woensdag*)]

wee[1] (wiː) *adj* very small; tiny; minute [C13: from Old English *wǣg* WEIGHT]

wee[2] (wiː) *Brit, Austral & NZ informal* ▷ *n* **1 a** the act or an instance of urinating **b** urine ▷ *vb* **2** (*intr*) to urinate ▷ Also called: wee-wee [of unknown origin]

weed (wiːd) *n* **1** any plant that grows wild and profusely, esp one that grows among cultivated plants, depriving them of space, food, etc **2** *slang* **a** the weed tobacco **b** marijuana **3** *informal* a thin or unprepossessing person **4** an inferior horse, esp one showing signs of weakness of constitution ▷ *vb* **5** to remove (useless or troublesome plants) from (a garden, etc) [Old English *wēod*; related to Old Saxon *wiod*, Old High German *wiota* fern] ▷ 'weeder *n* ▷ 'weedless *adj*

weedkiller ('wiːd,kɪlə) *n* a substance, usually a chemical or hormone, used for killing weeds

weed out *vb* (*tr, adverb*) to separate out, remove, or eliminate (anything unwanted): *to weed out troublesome students*

weeds (wiːdz) *pl n* Also called: widow's weeds a widow's black mourning clothes [C16: pl of Old English *wǣd, wēd* a band worn in mourning]

weedy ('wiːdɪ) *adj* weedier, weediest **1** full of or containing weeds: *weedy land* **2** (of a plant) resembling a weed in rapid or straggling growth **3** *informal* thin or weakly in appearance

week (wiːk) *n* **1** a period of seven consecutive days, esp, one beginning with Sunday. Related adj: **hebdomadal** **2** a period of seven consecutive days beginning from or including a specified day: *Easter week; a week from*

Wednesday **3** the period of time within a week devoted to work ▷ *adv* **4** *chiefly Brit* seven days before or after a specified day: *I'll visit you Wednesday week* [Old English *wice, wicu, wucu*; related to Old Norse *vika*, Gothic *wikō* order]

weekday ('wiːk,deɪ) *n* any day of the week other than Sunday and, often, Saturday

weekend *n* (,wiːk'ɛnd) **1 a** the end of the week, esp the period from Friday night until the end of Sunday **b** (*as modifier*): *a weekend party* ▷ *vb* ('wiːk,ɛnd) **2** (*intr*) *informal* to spend or pass a weekend

weekends (,wiːk'ɛndz) *adv informal* at the weekend, esp regularly or during every weekend

weekly ('wiːklɪ) *adj* **1** happening or taking place once a week or every week **2** determined or calculated by the week ▷ *adv* **3** once a week or every week ▷ *n, pl* -lies **4** a newspaper or magazine issued every week

weeknight ('wiːk,naɪt) *n* the evening or night of a weekday

Weelkes (wiːlks) *n* **Thomas**. ?1575–1623, English composer of madrigals

ween (wiːn) *vb archaic* to think or imagine (something) [Old English *wēnan*; related to Old Saxon *wānian*, Gothic *wēnjan*, German *wähnen* to assume wrongly]

weeny ('wiːnɪ) *or* **weensy** ('wiːnzɪ) *adj* -nier, -niest or -sier, -siest *informal* very small; tiny [C18: from WEE[1] with the ending -ny as in TINY]

weeny-bopper *n informal* a child of 8 to 12 years, esp a girl, who is a keen follower of pop music [C20: formed on the model of TEENYBOPPER, from *weeny*, as in *teeny-weeny* very small]

weep (wiːp) *vb* weeps, weeping, wept **1** to shed (tears) as an expression of grief or unhappiness **2** (*tr*; foll by *out*) to utter, shedding tears **3** (when *intr*, foll by *for*) to mourn or lament (for something) **4** to exude (drops of liquid) **5** (*intr*) (of a wound, etc) to exude a watery or serous fluid ▷ *n* **6** a spell of weeping [Old English *wēpan*; related to Gothic *wōpjan*, Old High German *wuofan*, Old Slavonic *vabiti* to call]

weeper ('wiːpə) *n* **1** a person who weeps, esp a hired mourner **2** something worn as a sign of mourning

weeping ('wiːpɪŋ) *adj* (of plants) having slender hanging branches ▷ 'weepingly *adv*

weeping willow *n* a hybrid willow tree, *Salix alba × S. babylonica*, known as *S. alba* var. *tristis*, having long hanging branches: widely planted for ornament

weepy ('wiːpɪ) *informal* ▷ *adj* weepier, weepiest **1** liable or tending to weep ▷ *n, pl* weepies **2** a romantic and sentimental film or book ▷ 'weepily *adv* ▷ 'weepiness *n*

weever ('wiːvə) *n* any small marine percoid fish of the family *Trachinidae*, such as *Trachinus vipera* of European waters, having venomous spines around the gills and the dorsal fin [C17: from Old Northern French *wivre* viper, ultimately from Latin *vīpera* VIPER]

weevil ('wiːvɪl) *n* Also called: snout beetle any beetle of the family *Curculionidae*, having an elongated snout (rostrum): they are pests, feeding on plants and plant products [Old English *wifel*; related to Old High German *wibil*; compare Old Norse *tordȳfill* dungbeetle] ▷ 'weevily *adj*

wee-wee *n, vb* a variant of **wee**[2]

w.e.f. *abbreviation* with effect from

weft (wɛft) *n* the yarn woven across the width of the fabric through the lengthwise warp yarn. Also called: filling, woof [Old English, related to Old Norse *veptr*; see WEAVE]

Wegener (German 've:gənər) *n* **Alfred** ('alfre:t). 1880–1930, German meteorologist: regarded as the originator of the theory of continental drift

Weichsel ('vaiksəl) *n* the German name for the **Vistula** (sense 1)

weigela (waɪ'giːlə, -'dʒiː-, 'waɪgɪlə) *n* any caprifoliaceous shrub of the Asian genus *Weigela*, having clusters of pink, purple, red, or white showy bell-shaped flowers [C19: from New Latin, named after C. E. *Weigel* (1748–1831), German physician]

weigh[1] (weɪ) *vb* **1** (*tr*) to measure the weight of **2** (*intr*) to have weight or be heavy: *she weighs more than her sister* **3** (*tr*; often foll by *out*) to apportion according to weight **4** (*tr*) to consider carefully: *to weigh the facts of a case* **5** (*intr*) to be influential: *his words weighed little with the jury* **6** (*intr*; often foll by *on*) to be oppressive or burdensome (to) **7 weigh anchor** to raise a vessel's anchor or (of a vessel) to have its anchor raised preparatory to departure ▷ See also **weigh down, weigh in, weigh up** [Old English *wegan*; related to Old Frisian *wega*, Old Norse *vega*, Gothic *gawigan*, German *wiegen*] > 'weighable *adj* > 'weigher *n*

weigh² (weɪ) *n* **under weigh** a variant spelling of **under way** [c18: variation due to the influence of phrases such as *to weigh anchor*]

weighbridge ('weɪˌbrɪdʒ) *n* a machine for weighing vehicles, etc, by means of a metal plate set into a road

weigh down *vb* (*adverb*) to press (a person) down by or as if by weight: *his troubles weighed him down*

weigh in *vb* (*intr, adverb*) **1 a** (of a boxer or wrestler) to be weighed before a bout **b** (of a jockey) to be weighed after, or sometimes before, a race **2** *informal* to contribute, as in a discussion, etc: *he weighed in with a few sharp comments* ▷ *n* **weigh-in 3** the act of checking a competitor's weight, as in boxing, horse racing, etc

weight (weɪt) *n* **1** a measure of the heaviness of an object; the amount anything weighs **2** *physics* the vertical force experienced by a mass as a result of gravitation. It equals the mass of the body multiplied by the acceleration of free fall. Its units are units of force (such as newtons or poundals) but is often given as a mass unit (kilogram or pound) **3** a system of units used to express the weight of a substance: *troy weight* **4** a unit used to measure weight: *the kilogram is the weight used in the metric system* **5** any mass or heavy object used to exert pressure or weigh down **6** an oppressive force: *the weight of cares* **7** any heavy load: *the bag was such a weight* **8** the main or greatest force: preponderance: *the weight of evidence* **9** importance, influence, or consequence: *his opinion carries weight* **10** *statistics* one of a set of coefficients assigned to items of a frequency distribution that are analysed in order to represent the relative importance of the different items **11** *printing* the apparent blackness of a printed typeface **12 pull one's weight** *informal* to do one's full or proper share of a task **13 throw one's weight around** *informal* to act in an overauthoritarian or aggressive manner ▷ *vb* (*tr*) **14** to add weight to **15** to burden or oppress **16** to add importance, value, etc, to one side rather than another; bias; favour **17** *statistics* to attach a weight or weights to [Old English *wiht*; related to Old Frisian, Middle Dutch *wicht*, Old Norse *větt*, German *Gewicht*] > 'weighter *n*

weighted average *n* an average calculated by taking into account not only the frequencies of the values of a variable but also some other factor such as their variance. The weighted average of observed data is the result of dividing the sum of the products of each observed value, the number of times it occurs, and this other factor by the total number of observations

weighting ('weɪtɪŋ) *n* **1** a factor by which some quantity is multiplied in order to make it comparable with others **2** an increase in some quantity, esp an additional allowance paid to compensate for higher living costs: *a London weighting*

weightless ('weɪtləs) *adj* **1** (of a body) having no actual weight; a state in which an object has no actual weight (because it is in space and unaffected by gravitational attraction) or no apparent weight (because the gravitational attraction equals the centripetal force and the object is in free fall) **2** *business* **a** (of economic activity) based on the supply of information and ideas rather than trade in physical goods: *the weightless economy* **b** (of a company) having very few physical assets: *weightless dot.coms* > 'weightlessness *n*

weightlifting ('weɪtˌlɪftɪŋ) *n* the sport of lifting barbells of specified weights in a prescribed manner for competition or exercise > 'weightˌlifter *n*

weight training *n* physical exercise involving lifting weights to improve muscle performance

weight watcher *n* a person who tries to lose weight, esp by dieting

weighty ('weɪtɪ) *adj* **weightier, weightiest 1** having great weight **2** important or momentous **3** causing anxiety or worry > 'weightily *adv* > 'weightiness *n*

weigh up *vb* (*tr, adverb*) to make an assessment of (a person, situation, etc); judge

Weihai *or* **Wei-hai** ('weɪ'haɪ) *n* a port in NE China, in NE Shandong on the Yellow Sea: leased to Britain as a naval base (1898–1930). Pop: 966 000 (2005 est). Also called: Weihaiwei (ˌweɪ'haɪˌweɪ)

Weil (French vail) *n* **Simone** (simɔn). 1909–43, French philosopher and mystic, whose works include *Waiting for God* (1951), *The Need for Roots* (1952), and *Notebooks* (1956)

Weill (vail) *n* **Kurt** (kʊrt). 1900–50, German composer, in the US from 1935. He wrote the music for Brecht's *The Rise and Fall of the City of Mahagonny* (1927) and *The Threepenny Opera* (1928)

Weil's disease (vailz) *n* another name for **leptospirosis** [named after Adolf *Weil* (1848–1916), German physician]

Weimar (German 'vaimar) *n* a city in E central Germany, in Thuringia: a cultural centre in the 18th and early 19th century; scene of the adoption (1919) of the constitution of the Weimar Republic. Pop: 64 409 (2003 est)

Weimaraner ('vaimaˌrɑːnə, 'waimaˌrɑː-) *n* a breed of hunting dog, having a very short sleek grey coat and short tail [c20: named after WEIMAR, where the breed was developed]

Weinberg ('wainbɜːg) *n* **Steven**. born 1933, US physicist, who shared the Nobel prize for physics (1979) with Sheldon Glashow and Abdus Salam for his role in formulating the electroweak theory

weir (wɪə) *n* **1 a** a low dam that is built across a river to raise the water level, divert the water, or control its flow **2** a series of traps or enclosures placed in a stream to catch fish [Old English *wer*; related to Old Norse *ver*, Old Frisian *were*, German *Wehr*]

Weir (wɪə) *n* **1 Judith**. born 1954, Scottish composer, noted esp for her opera *A Night at the Chinese Opera* (1987) **2 Peter**. born 1944, Australian film director; his films include *Dead Poets Society* (1989), *The Truman Show* (1998), and *Master and Commander* (2003)

weird (wɪəd) *adj* **1** suggestive of or relating to the supernatural; eerie **2** strange or bizarre **3** *archaic* of or relating to fate or the Fates ▷ *n* **4** *archaic, chiefly Scot* **a** fate or destiny **b** one of the Fates [Old English (*ge*)*wyrd* destiny; related to *weorthan* to become, Old Norse *urthr* bane, Old Saxon *wurd*] > 'weirdly *adv* > 'weirdness *n*

weirdo ('wɪədəʊ) *or* **weirdie** ('wɪədɪ) *n, pl* -dos *or* -dies *informal* a person who behaves in a bizarre or eccentric manner

Weismannism ('vaismənˌɪzəm) *n* the doctrine of the continuity of the germ plasm. This theory of heredity states that all inheritable characteristics are transmitted by the reproductive cells and that characteristics acquired during the lifetime of the organism are not inherited [c19: named after August *Weismann* (1834–1914), German biologist]

Weisshorn ('vais,hɔːn) *n* a mountain in S Switzerland, in the Pennine Alps. Height: 4505 m (14 781 ft)

Weissmuller ('vais,mʌlə) *n* **John Peter**, known as *Johnny*. 1904–84, US swimmer and film actor, who won Olympic gold medals in 1924 and 1928 and played the title role in the early Tarzan films

Weizmann ('waitsmən, 'waiz-) *n* **Chaim** ('xaiim). 1874–1952, Israeli statesman, born in Russia. As a leading Zionist, he was largely responsible for securing the Balfour Declaration (1917); first president of Israel (1949–52)

weka ('weɪkə, 'wiːkə) *n* any flightless New Zealand rail of the genus *Gallirallus*, having a mottled brown plumage and rudimentary wings. Also called: Māori hen, wood hen [c19: from Māori, of imitative origin]

welch (wɛlʃ) *vb* a variant spelling of **welsh**

Welch (wɛlʃ) *adj* an archaic spelling of **Welsh¹**

welcome ('wɛlkəm) *adj* **1** gladly and cordially received or admitted: *a welcome guest* **2** bringing pleasure or gratitude: *a welcome gift* **3** freely permitted or invited: *you are welcome to call* **4** under no obligation (only in such phrases as **you're welcome** or **he's welcome**, as conventional responses to thanks) ▷ *sentence substitute* **5** an expression of cordial greeting, esp to a person whose arrival is desired or pleasing ▷ *n* **6** the act of greeting or receiving a person or thing; reception: *the* *new theory had a cool welcome* **7** wear out one's welcome to come more often or stay longer than is acceptable or pleasing ▷ *vb* (*tr*) **8** to greet the arrival of (visitors, guests, etc) cordially or gladly **9** to receive or accept, esp gladly [C12: changed (through influence of WELL¹) from Old English *wilcuma* (agent noun referring to a welcome guest), *wilcume* (a greeting of welcome), from *wil* WILL² + *cuman* to COME] ▷ ˈwelcomely *adv* ▷ ˈwelcomer *n*

weld¹ (wɛld) *vb* **1** (*tr*) to unite (pieces of metal or plastic) together, as by softening with heat and hammering or by fusion **2** to bring or admit of being brought into close association or union ▷ *n* **3** a joint formed by welding [C16: variant probably based on past participle of WELL² in obsolete sense to boil, heat] ▷ ˈweldable *adj* ▷ ˌweldaˈbility *n* ▷ ˈwelder *or* ˈweldor *n*

weld² (wɛld), **wold** *or* **woald** (wəʊld) *n* a yellow dye obtained from the plant dyer's rocket [C14: from Low German; compare Middle Low German *walde*, *waude*, Dutch *wouw*]

Weld (wɛld) *n* Sir **Frederick Aloysius**. 1823–91, New Zealand statesman, born in England: prime minister of New Zealand (1864–65)

Weldon (ˈwɛldən) *n* **Fay**. born 1931, British novelist and writer. Her novels include *Praxis* (1978), *Life and Loves of a She-Devil* (1984), *Big Women* (1998), and *Rhode Island Blues* (2003)

welfare (ˈwɛlˌfɛə) *n* **1** health, happiness, prosperity, and well-being in general **2 a** financial and other assistance given to people in need **b** (*as modifier*): *welfare services* **3** Also called: **welfare work** plans or work to better the social or economic conditions of various underprivileged groups **4** on welfare *chiefly US & Canadian* in receipt of financial aid from a government agency or other source [C14: from the phrase *wel fare*; related to Old Norse *velferth*, German *Wohlfahrt*; see WELL¹, FARE]

welfare economics *n* (*functioning as singular*) the aspects of economic theory concerned with the welfare of society and priorities to be observed in the allocation of resources

welfare state *n* a system in which the government undertakes the chief responsibility for providing for the social and economic security of its population, usually through unemployment insurance, old-age pensions, and other social-security measures

welkin (ˈwɛlkɪn) *n* archaic the sky, heavens, or upper air [Old English *wolcen*, *welcen*; related to Old Frisian *wolken*, Old Saxon, Old High German *wolcan*]

Welkom (ˈwɛlkəm, ˈvɛl-) *n* a town in central South Africa; developed rapidly following the discovery of gold. Pop: 34 157 (2001)

well¹ (wɛl) *adv* **better**, **best** **1** (*often used in combination*) in a satisfactory manner: *the party went very well* **2** (*often used in combination*) in a good, skilful, or pleasing manner: *she plays the violin well* **3** in a correct or careful manner: *listen well to my words* **4** in a comfortable or prosperous manner: *to live well* **5** (*usually used with auxiliaries*) suitably; fittingly: *you can't very well say that* **6** intimately: *I knew him well* **7** in a kind or favourable manner: *she speaks well of you* **8** to a great or considerable extent; fully: *to be well informed* **9** by a considerable margin: *let me know well in advance* **10** (preceded by *could*, *might*, *or may*) indeed: *you may well have to do it yourself* **11** informal (intensifier): *well safe* **12** all very well used ironically to express discontent, dissent, etc **13** as well **a** in addition; too **b** (preceded by *may or might*) with equal effect: *you might as well come* **c** just as well preferable or advisable: *it would be just as well if you paid me now* **14** as well as in addition to **15** just leave well alone *or* just leave well enough alone to refrain from interfering with something that is satisfactory **16** well and good used to indicate calm acceptance, as of a decision **17** well up in well acquainted with (a particular subject); knowledgeable about ▷ *adj* (*usually postpositive*) **18** (when *prenominal*, *usually used with a negative*) in good health: *I'm very well, thank you; he's not a well man* **19** satisfactory, agreeable, or pleasing **20** prudent; advisable: *it would be well to make no comment* **21** prosperous or comfortable **22** fortunate or happy: *it is well that you agreed to go* ▷ *interj* **23 a** an expression of surprise, indignation, or reproof **b** an expression of anticipation

in waiting for an answer or remark ▷ *sentence connector* **24** an expression used to preface a remark, gain time, etc: *well, I don't think I will come* [Old English *wel*; related to Old High German *wala*, *wola* (German *wohl*), Old Norse *val*, Gothic *waila*]

well² (wɛl) *n* **1** a hole or shaft that is excavated, drilled, bored, or cut into the earth so as to tap a supply of water, oil, gas, etc **2** a natural pool where ground water comes to the surface **3 a** a cavity, space, or vessel used to contain a liquid **b** (*in combination*): *an inkwell* **4** an open shaft through the floors of a building, such as one used for a staircase **5** a deep enclosed space in a building or between buildings that is open to the sky to permit light and air to enter **6** a bulkheaded compartment built around a ship's pumps for protection and ease of access **7** (in England) the open space in the centre of a law court **8** a source, esp one that provides a continuous supply: *he is a well of knowledge* ▷ *vb* **9** to flow or cause to flow upwards or outwards: *tears welled from her eyes* [Old English *wella*; related to Old High German *wella* (German *Welle* wave), Old Norse *vella* boiling heat]

we'll (wiːl) *contraction of* we will *or* we shall

well-advised *adj* (**well advised** *when postpositive*) **1** acting with deliberation or reason **2** well thought out; considered: *a well-advised plan*

well-affected *adj* (**well affected** *when postpositive*) favourably disposed (towards); steadfast or loyal

Welland Canal (ˈwɛlənd) *n* a canal in S Canada, in Ontario, linking Lake Erie to Lake Ontario: part of the St Lawrence Seaway, with eight locks. Length: 44 km (28 miles). Also called: **Welland Ship Canal**

well-appointed *adj* (**well appointed** *when postpositive*) well equipped or furnished; properly supplied

wellaway (ˈwɛləˈweɪ) *interj archaic* woe! alas! [Old English, from *wei lā wei*, variant of *wā lā wā*, literally: woe! lo woe]

well-balanced *adj* (**well balanced** *when postpositive*) **1** having good balance or proportions **2** of balanced mind; sane or sensible

wellbeing (ˈwɛlˈbiːɪŋ) *n* the condition of being contented, healthy, or successful; welfare

well-bred *adj* (**well bred** *when postpositive*) **1** Also called: **well-born** of respected or noble lineage **2** indicating good breeding: *well-bred manners* **3** of good thoroughbred stock: *a well-bred spaniel*

well-chosen *adj* (**well chosen** *when postpositive*) carefully selected to produce a desired effect; apt: *a few well-chosen words may be more effective than a long speech*

well-connected *adj* (**well connected** *when postpositive*) having influential or important relatives or friends

well-disposed *adj* (**well disposed** *when postpositive*) inclined to be sympathetic, kindly, or friendly

well-done *adj* (**well done** *when postpositive*) **1** (of food, esp meat) cooked thoroughly **2** made or accomplished satisfactorily

well dressing *n* the decoration of wells with flowers, etc: a traditional annual ceremony of great antiquity in some parts of Britain, originally associated with the cult of water deities

Welles (wɛlz) *n* (**George**) **Orson** (ˈɔːsᵊn) 1915–85, US film director, actor, producer, and screenwriter. His *Citizen Kane* (1941) and *The Magnificent Ambersons* (1942) are regarded as film classics

Wellesley (ˈwɛlzlɪ) *n* **1 Arthur**. See (1st Duke of) **Wellington²** **2** his brother, **Richard Colley**, Marquis Wellesley. 1760–1842, British administrator. As governor general of Bengal (1797–1805) he consolidated British power in India

Wellesz (*German* ˈvɛlɛs) *n* **Egon** (ˈeːɡɔn). 1885–1974, British composer, born in Austria

well-favoured *adj* (**well favoured** *when postpositive*) having good features; good-looking

well-formed *adj logic*, *linguistics* (of a formula, expression, etc) constructed in accordance with the syntactic rules of a particular system; grammatically correct

well-found *adj* (**well found** *when postpositive*) furnished or supplied with all or most necessary things

well-founded *adj* (**well founded** *when postpositive*) having

W

good grounds: *well-founded rumours*

well-groomed *adj* (**well groomed** *when postpositive*) (of a person) having a tidy pleasing appearance

well-grounded *adj* (**well grounded** *when postpositive*) 1 well instructed in the basic elements of a subject 2 another term for **well-founded**

wellhead ('wel,hed) *n* 1 the source of a well or stream 2 a source, fountainhead, or origin

well-heeled *adj* (**well heeled** *when postpositive*) *informal* rich; prosperous; wealthy

wellies ('weliz) *pl n Brit informal* Wellington boots

well-informed *adj* (**well informed** *when postpositive*) 1 having knowledge about a great variety of subjects: *he seems to be a well-informed person* 2 possessing reliable information on a particular subject

Wellingborough ('welɪŋbərə, -brə) *n* a town in central England, in Northamptonshire. Pop: 46 959 (2001)

Wellington[1] ('welɪŋtən) *n* 1 an administrative district, formerly a province, of New Zealand, on SW North Island: major livestock producer in New Zealand. Capital: Wellington. Pop: 456 900 (2004 est). Area: 28 153 sq km (10 870 sq miles) 2 the capital city of New Zealand. Its port, historically Port Nicholson, on **Wellington Harbour** has a car and rail ferry link between the North and South Islands; university (1899). Pop: 182 600 (2004 est)

Wellington[2] ('welɪŋtən) *n* **1st Duke of,** title of *Arthur Wellesley.* 1769–1852, British soldier and statesman; prime minister (1828–30). He was given command of the British forces against the French in the Peninsular War (1808–14) and routed Napoleon at Waterloo (1815)

Wellington boots *pl n* 1 Also called: **gumboots, wellingtons** *Brit* knee-length or calf-length rubber or rubberized boots, worn esp in wet conditions. Often shortened to **wellies** 2 military leather boots covering the front of the knee but cut away at the back to allow easier bending of the knee [C19: named after the 1st Duke of *Wellington*]

wellingtonia (,welɪŋ'təʊnɪə) *n* another name for **big tree** [C19: named after the 1st Duke of *Wellington*]

well-intentioned *adj* (**well intentioned** *when postpositive*) having or indicating benevolent intentions, usually with unfortunate results

well-knit *adj* (**well knit** *when postpositive*) strong, firm, or sturdy

well-known *adj* (**well known** *when postpositive*) 1 widely known; famous; celebrated 2 known fully or clearly

well-mannered *adj* (**well mannered** *when postpositive*) having good manners; courteous; polite

well-meaning *adj* (**well meaning** *when postpositive*) having or indicating good or benevolent intentions, usually with unfortunate results

well-nigh *adv* nearly; almost: *it's well-nigh three o'clock*

well-off *adj* (**well off** *when postpositive*) 1 in a comfortable or favourable position or state 2 financially well provided for; moderately rich

well-oiled *adj* (**well oiled** *when postpositive*) *informal* drunk

well-preserved *adj* (**well preserved** *when postpositive*) 1 kept in a good condition 2 continuing to appear youthful: *she was a well-preserved old lady*

well-read ('wel'red) *adj* (**well read** *when postpositive*) having read widely and intelligently; erudite

well-rounded *adj* (**well rounded** *when postpositive*) 1 rounded in shape or well developed: *a well-rounded figure* 2 full, varied, and satisfying: *a well-rounded life*

Wells[1] (welz) *n* a city in SW England, in Somerset: 12th-century cathedral. Pop: 10 406 (2001)

Wells[2] (welz) *n* 1 **Henry.** 1805–78, US businessman, who founded (1852) with William Fargo the express mail service Wells, Fargo and Company 2 **H(erbert) G(eorge).** 1866–1946, British writer. His science-fiction stories include *The Time Machine* (1895), *War of the Worlds* (1898), and *The Shape of Things to Come* (1933). His novels on contemporary social questions, such as *Kipps* (1905), *Tono-Bungay* (1909), and *Ann Veronica* (1909), affected the opinions of his day. His nonfiction works include *The Outline of History* (1920)

well-spoken *adj* (**well spoken** *when postpositive*) 1 having a clear, articulate, and socially acceptable accent and way

of speaking 2 spoken satisfactorily or pleasingly

wellspring ('wel,sprɪŋ) *n* 1 the source of a spring or stream; fountainhead 2 a source of continual or abundant supply [Old English welspryng, wylspring; see WELL[2], SPRING]

well-stacked *adj* (**well stacked** *when postpositive*) *Brit slang* (of a woman) of voluptuous proportions

well sweep *n* a device for raising buckets from and lowering them into a well, consisting of a long pivoted pole, the bucket being attached to one end by a long rope

well-tempered *adj* (**well tempered** *when postpositive*) (of a musical scale or instrument) conforming to the system of equal temperament. See **temperament** (sense 4)

well-thought-of *adj* (**well thought of** *when postpositive*) having a good reputation; respected

well-thumbed *adj* (**well thumbed** *when postpositive*) (of a copy of a book) having the pages marked from frequent turning

well-to-do *adj* moderately wealthy

well-turned *adj* (**well turned** *when postpositive*) 1 (of a phrase, speech, etc) apt and pleasingly sonorous 2 having a pleasing shape: *a well-turned leg*

well-upholstered *adj* (**well upholstered** *when postpositive*) *informal* (of a person) fat

well-wisher *n* a person who shows benevolence or sympathy towards a person, cause, etc ⊳ **'well-,wishing** *adj, n*

well-woman *n, pl* -**women** *social welfare* **a** a woman who, although not ill, attends a health-service clinic for preventive monitoring, health education, and advice **b** (*as modifier*): *well-woman clinic*

well-worn *adj* (**well worn** *when postpositive*) 1 so much used as to be affected by wear: *a well-worn coat* 2 used too often; hackneyed: *a well-worn phrase*

welly ('welɪ) *n* 1 *pl* -**lies** *informal* Also called: **welly boot** a Wellington boot 2 *slang* energy, concentration, or commitment (esp in the phrase **give it some welly**)

Wels (German vels) *n* an industrial city in N central Austria, in Upper Austria. Pop: 56 478 (2002)

welsh *or* **welch** (welʃ) *vb* (*intr*; often foll by *on*) *slang* 1 to fail to pay a gambling debt 2 to fail to fulfil an obligation [C19: of unknown origin] ⊳ **'welsher** *or* **'welcher** *n*

Welsh (welʃ) *adj* 1 of, relating to, or characteristic of Wales, its people, their Celtic language, or their dialect of English ⊳ *n* 2 a language of Wales, belonging to the S Celtic branch of the Indo-European family. Welsh shows considerable diversity between dialects 3 the Welsh (*functioning as plural*) the natives or inhabitants of Wales collectively [Old English Wēlisc, Wǣlisc; related to wealh foreigner, Old High German walahisc (German welsch), Old Norse valskr, Latin Volcae]

Welsh corgi *n* another name for **corgi**

Welsh dresser *n* a sideboard with drawers and cupboards below and open shelves above

Welsh harp *n* a type of harp in which the strings are arranged in three rows, used esp for the accompaniment of singing, improvisation on folk tunes, etc

Welshman ('welʃmən) *or feminine* **Welshwoman** *n, pl* -**men** *or* -**women** a native or inhabitant of Wales

Welsh poppy *n* a perennial W European papaveraceous plant, *Meconopsis cambrica,* with large yellow flowers

Welsh rabbit *n* a savoury dish consisting of melted cheese sometimes mixed with milk, seasonings, etc, on hot buttered toast. Also called: **Welsh rarebit, rarebit** [C18: a fanciful coinage; *rarebit* is a later folk-etymological variant]

Welsh terrier *n* a wire-haired breed of terrier with a black-and-tan coat

welt (welt) *n* 1 a raised or strengthened seam or edge, sewn in or on a knitted garment 2 another word for **weal**[1] 3 (in shoemaking) a strip of leather, etc, put in between the outer sole and the inner sole and upper ⊳ *vb* (*tr*) 4 to put a welt in (a garment, etc) 5 to beat or flog soundly [C15: origin unknown]

welter ('weltə) *vb* (*intr*) 1 to roll about, writhe, or wallow 2 (esp of the sea) to surge, heave, or toss 3 to lie drenched in a liquid, esp blood ▷ *n* **4** a confused mass; jumble [c13: from Middle Low German, Middle Dutch *weltern*; related to Old High German *walzan, welzen* to roll]

welterweight ('wɛltə,weɪt) *n* **a** a professional boxer weighing 140–147 pounds (63.5–66.5 kg) **b** an amateur boxer weighing 63.5–67 kg (140–148 pounds)

Welty ('wɛltɪ) *n* **Eudora.** 1909–2001, US novelist and short-story writer, noted for her depiction of life in the Mississippi delta. Her novels include *Delta Wedding* (1946) and *The Optimist's Daughter* (1972)

Welwyn Garden City ('wɛlɪn) *n* a town in SE England, in Hertfordshire: established (1920) as a planned industrial and residential community. Pop: 43 512 (2001)

Wembley ('wɛmblɪ) *n* part of the Greater London borough of Brent: site of the English national soccer stadium, replaced by the larger multi-purpose Wembley Stadium in 2007

wen[1] (wɛn) *n* **1** *pathol* a sebaceous cyst, esp one occurring on the scalp **2** a large overcrowded city (esp London in the phrase **the great wen**) [Old English *wenn*; related to Danish dialect *van, væne*, Dutch *wenn*]

wen[2] (wɛn) *n* a rune having the sound of Modern English *w* [Old English *wen, wyn*]

Wenceslaus *or* **Wenceslas** ('wɛnsɪsləs) *n* **1** 1361–1419, Holy Roman Emperor (1378–1400) and, as **Wenceslaus IV,** king of Bohemia (1378–1419) **2 Saint,** known as *Good King Wenceslaus.* ?907–929, duke of Bohemia (?925–29); patron saint of Bohemia. Feast day: Sept 28

wench (wɛntʃ) *n* **1** a girl or young woman, esp a buxom or lively one: now used facetiously **2** *archaic* a female servant **3** *archaic* a prostitute ▷ *vb* (*intr*) **4** *archaic* to frequent the company of prostitutes [Old English *wencel* child, from *wancol* weak; related to Old High German *wanchal, wankōn*] > '**wencher** *n*

wend (wɛnd) *vb* to direct (one's course or way); travel: *wend one's way home* [Old English *wendan*; related to Old High German *wenten*, Gothic *wandjan*; see WIND[2]]

Wend (wɛnd) *n* (esp in medieval European history) a Sorb; a member of the Slavonic people who inhabited the area between the Rivers Saale and Oder in the early Middle Ages and were conquered by Germanic invaders by the 12th century

wendigo ('wɛndɪ,gəʊ) *n, Canadian* **1** *pl* -gos (among Algonquian Indians) an evil spirit or cannibal **2** *pl* -go *or* -gos another name for **splake** [from Algonquian: evil spirit or cannibal]

Wendy house ('wɛndɪ) *n* a small model house that children can enter and play in [c20: named after the house built for *Wendy*, the girl in J. M. Barrie's play *Peter Pan* (1904)]

wensleydale ('wɛnzlɪ,deɪl) *n* **1** a type of white cheese with a flaky texture **2** a breed of sheep with long woolly fleece [named after *Wensleydale*, North Yorkshire]

went (wɛnt) *vb* the past tense of **go**[1]

wentletrap ('wɛntᵊl,træp) *n* any marine gastropod mollusc of the family *Epitoniidae*, having a long pointed pale-coloured longitudinally ridged shell [c18: from Dutch *winteltrap* spiral shell, from *wintel*, earlier *windel*, from *wenden* to wind + *trap* a step, stairs]

Wentworth ('wɛntwəθ) *n* **1 Thomas.** See (Earl of): Strafford **2 William Charles.** 1790–1872, Australian explorer and statesman who was a member of the exploring party that first crossed the Blue Mountains in 1813 and was later a leader in the movement for self-government in New South Wales

Wenzhou, Wen-chou *or* **Wenchow** ('wɛn'tʃuː) *n* a port in SE China, in Zhejiang province: noted for its historic buildings. Pop: 1 475 000 (2005 est)

wept (wɛpt) *vb* the past tense and past participle of **weep**

were (wɜː; *unstressed* wə) *vb* the plural form of the past tense (indicative mood) of **be** and the singular form used with *you*. It is also used as a subjunctive, esp in conditional sentences [Old English *wērun, wæron* past tense plural of *wesan* to be; related to Old Norse *vera*, Old Frisian *weria*, Old High German *werōn* to last]

● USAGE *Were,* as a remnant of the past subjunctive in ● English, is used in formal contexts in clauses ● expressing hypotheses (*if he were to die, she would inherit* ● *everything*), suppositions contrary to fact (*if I were you, I* ● *would be careful*), and desire (*I wish he were there now*). In ● informal speech, however, *was* is often used instead

we're (wɪə) *contraction of* we are

weren't (wɜːnt) *contraction of* were not

werewolf ('wɪə,wʊlf, 'wɛə-) *n, pl* **-wolves** a person fabled in folklore and superstition to have been changed into a wolf by being bewitched or said to be able to assume wolf form at will [Old English *werewulf*, from *wer* man + *wulf* WOLF; related to Old High German *werwolf*, Middle Dutch *weerwolf*]

Werfel (*German* 'vɛrfəl) *n* **Franz** (frants). 1890–1945, Austro-Hungarian poet, novelist, and dramatist of the German expressionist movement. His novels include *The Forty Days of Musa Dagh* (1933) and *The Song of Bernadette* (1941)

Wergeland (*Norwegian* 'værgəlan) *n* **Henrik Arnold.** 1808–45, Norwegian poet and nationalist, remembered for his lyric and narrative verse

wergild, weregild ('wɜː,gɪld, 'wɛə-) *or* **wergeld** ('wɜː,gɛld, 'wɛə-) *n* the price set on a man's life in successive Anglo-Saxon and Germanic law codes, to be paid as compensation by his slayer [Old English *wergeld*, from *wer* man (related to Old Norse *ver*, Latin *vir*) + *gield* tribute (related to Gothic *gild*, Old High German *gelt* payment); see YIELD]

Werner (*German* 'vɛrnər) *n* **1 Abraham Gottlieb** ('aːbrəham 'gɔtliːp). 1749–1817, German geologist. He emphasized the importance of field and laboratory observation for understanding the earth **2 Alfred** ('alfreːt). 1866–1919, Swiss chemist, born in Germany. He developed a coordination theory of the valency of inorganic complexes: Nobel prize for chemistry 1913

wero ('wɜːrəʊ) *n* NZ the challenge made by an armed Māori warrior to a visitor to a marae [Māori]

wert (wɜːt; *unstressed* wət) *vb archaic or dialect* (used with the pronoun *thou* or its relative equivalent) a singular form of the past tense (indicative mood) of **be**[1]

Weser (*German* 'veːzər) *n* a river in NW Germany: flows northwest to the North Sea at Bremerhaven and is linked by the Mittelland Canal to the Ems, Rhine, and Elbe waterways. Length: 477 km (196 miles)

Wesermünde (*German* veːzər'myndə) *n* the former name (until 1947) of **Bremerhaven**

Wesker ('wɛskə) *n* **Arnold.** born 1932, British dramatist, whose plays include *Roots* (1959), *Chips With Everything* (1962), *The Merchant* (1976), *Caritas* (1981), and *Break My Heart* (1997)

weskit ('wɛskɪt) *n* an informal word for **waistcoat**

Wesley ('wɛzlɪ) *n* **1 Charles.** 1707–88, English Methodist preacher and writer of hymns **2** his brother, **John.** 1703–91, English preacher, who founded Methodism **3 Mary,** pseudonym of *Mary Aline Siepmann*. 1912–2003, British writer: her novels include *The Camomile Lawn* (1984) and *An Imaginative Experience* (1994)

Wesleyan ('wɛzlɪən) *adj* **1** of, relating to, or deriving from John Wesley, the English preacher and founder of Methodism (1703–91) **2** of, relating to, or characterizing Methodism, esp in its original form or as upheld by the branch of the Methodist Church known as the **Wesleyan Methodists** ▷ *n* **3** a follower of John Wesley **4** a member of the Methodist Church or (formerly) of the Wesleyan Methodists > '**Wesleyanism** *n*

Wessex[1] ('wɛsɪks) *n* **1** an Anglo-Saxon kingdom in S and SW England that became the most powerful English kingdom by the 10th century AD **2 a** (in Thomas Hardy's works) the southwestern counties of England, esp Dorset **b** (*as modifier*): *Wessex Poems*

Wessex[2] *n* Earl of Wessex See **Edward**[2] (sense 2)

west (wɛst) *n* **1** the direction along a parallel towards the sunset, at 270° clockwise from north **2** the west (*often capital*) any area lying in or towards the west. Related adjs: **Hesperian, Occidental 3** *cards* (*usually capital*) the player or position at the table corresponding to west on the compass ▷ *adj* **4** situated in, moving towards, or facing the west **5** (esp of the wind) from the west ▷ *adv* **6** in, to, or towards the west **7** go west *informal* **a** to be lost or destroyed irrevocably **b** to die [Old English; related to Old Norse *vestr*, Sanskrit *avástāt*, Latin *vesper* evening, Greek *hésperos*]

West¹ (wɛst) the West *n* **1** the western part of the world contrasted historically and culturally with the East or Orient; the Occident **2** (formerly) the non-Communist countries of Europe and America contrasted with the Communist states of the East. See **East** (sense 2) **3** (in the US) that part of the US lying approximately to the west of the Mississippi **4** (in the ancient and medieval world) the Western Roman Empire and, later, the Holy Roman Empire *adj* **5** of or denoting the western part of a specified country, area, etc

West² (wɛst) *n* **1 Benjamin.** 1738–1820, US painter, in England from 1763 **2 Kanye,** born 1977, US rap singer and producer; his albums include *The College Dropout* (2004) and *Graduation* (2007) **3 Mae.** 1892–1980, US film actress **4 Nathanael,** real name *Nathan Weinstein.* 1903–40, US novelist: author of *Miss Lonely-Hearts* (1933) and *The Day of the Locust* (1939) **5** Dame **Rebecca,** real name *Cicily Isabel Andrews* (née *Fairfield*). 1892–1983, British journalist, novelist, and critic

West Atlantic *n* **1** the W part of the Atlantic Ocean, esp the N Atlantic around North America **2** a branch of the Niger-Congo family of African languages, spoken in Senegal and in scattered areas eastwards, including Fulani and Wolof ▷ *adj* **3** relating to or belonging to this group of languages

West Bank *n* the West Bank a semi-autonomous Palestinian region in the Middle East on the W bank of the River Jordan, comprising the hills of Judaea and Samaria and part of Jerusalem: formerly part of Palestine (the entity created by the League of Nations in 1922 and operating until 1948): became part of Jordan after the ceasefire of 1949: occupied by Israel since the 1967 Arab-Israeli War. In 1993 a peace treaty between Israel and the Palestine Liberation Organization provided for the West Bank to become a self-governing Palestinian area; a new Palestinian National Authority assumed control of parts of the territory in 1994–95, but subsequent talks broke down and Israel reoccupied much of this in 2001–02 and continues to maintain most existing Israeli settlements. Pop: 2 421 491 (2004 est). Area: 5879 sq km (2270 sq miles)

West Bengal *n* a state of E India, on the Bay of Bengal: formed in 1947 from the Hindu area of Bengal; additional territories added in 1950 (Cooch Behar), 1954 (Chandernagor), and 1956 (part of Bihar); mostly low-lying and crossed by the Hooghly River. Capital: Kolkata (Calcutta). Pop: 80 221 171 (2001). Area: 88 752 sq km (34 260 sq miles)

West Berkshire *n* a unitary authority in S England, in Berkshire. Pop: 144 200 (2003 est). Area: 705 sq km (272 sq miles)

West Berlin *n* (formerly) the part of Berlin under US, British, and French control > West Berliner *n*

westbound ('wɛst,baʊnd) *adj* going or leading west

West Bromwich ('brɒmɪdʒ, -ɪtʃ) *n* a town in central England, in Sandwell unitary authority, West Midlands: industrial centre. Pop: 136 940 (2001)

west by north *n* one point on the compass north of west, 281° 15′ clockwise from north

west by south *n* one point on the compass south of west, 258° 45′ clockwise from north

West Country *n* the West Country the southwest of England, esp Cornwall, Devon, and Somerset

West Dunbartonshire *n* a council area of W central Scotland, on Loch Lomond and the Clyde estuary: corresponds to part of the historical county of Dunbartonshire; part of Strathclyde Region from 1975 to 1996: engineering industries. Administrative centre: Dumbarton. Pop: 92 320 (2003 est). Area: 162 sq km (63 sq miles)

West End *n* the West End a part of W central London containing the main shopping and entertainment areas

Westenra ('wɛstɪnrə) *n* **Hayley** (**Dee**). born 1987, New Zealand singer, known for the purity of her voice in many musical genres

westering ('wɛstərɪŋ) *adj poetic* moving towards the west: *the westering star*

Westerlies ('wɛstəlɪz) *pl n meteorol* the prevailing winds blowing from the west on the poleward sides of the horse latitudes, often bringing depressions and anticyclones

westerly ('wɛstəlɪ) *adj* **1** of, relating to, or situated in the west ▷ *adv, adj* **2** towards or in the direction of the west **3** (esp of the wind) from the west ▷ *n, pl* -lies **4** a wind blowing from the west > **westerliness** *n*

western ('wɛstən) *adj* **1** situated in or towards or facing the west **2** going or directed to or towards the west **3** (of a wind, etc) coming or originating from the west **4** native to, inhabiting, or growing in the west **5** *music* See **country and western** > 'western,most *adj*

Western ('wɛstən) *adj* **1** of, relating to, or characteristic of the West as opposed to the Orient **2** (formerly) of, relating to, or characteristic of the Americas and the parts of Europe not under Communist rule **3** of, relating to, or characteristic of the western states of the US ▷ *n* **4** a film, book, etc, concerned with life in the western states of the US, esp during the era of exploration and early development

Western Australia *n* a state of W Australia: mostly an arid undulating plateau, with the Great Sandy Desert, Gibson Desert, and Great Victoria Desert in the interior; settlement concentrated in the southwest; rich mineral resources. Capital: Perth. Pop: 1 969 046 (2003 est). Area: 2 527 636 sq km (975 920 sq miles)

Western Cape *n* a province of W South Africa, created in 1994 from the SW part of Cape Province: agriculture (esp fruit), wine making, fishing, various industries in Cape Town. Capital: Cape Town. Pop: 4 570 696 (2004 est). Area: 129 370 sq km (49 950 sq miles)

Western Church *n* **1** the part of Christendom that derives its liturgy, discipline, and traditions principally from the patriarchate of Rome, as contrasted with the part that derives these from the other ancient patriarchates, esp that of Constantinople **2** the Roman Catholic Church, sometimes together with the Anglican Communion of Churches

westerner ('wɛstənə) *n* (*sometimes capital*) a native or inhabitant of the west of any specific region, esp of the western states of the US or of the western hemisphere

Western Ghats *pl n* a mountain range in W peninsular India, parallel to the Malabar coast of the Arabian Sea. Highest peak: Anai Mudi, 2695 m (8841 ft)

western hemisphere *n* (*often capitals*) **1** that half of the globe containing the Americas, lying to the west of the Greenwich or another meridian **2** the lands contained in this, esp the Americas

Western Isles *n* (*functioning as singular or plural*) **1** an island authority in W Scotland, consisting of the Outer Hebrides; created in 1975. Administrative centre: Stornoway. Pop: 26 100 (2003 est). Area: 2900 sq km (1120 sq miles) **2** Also called: Western Islands another name for **Hebrides**

westernize or **westernise** ('wɛstə,naɪz) *vb* (*tr*) to influence or make familiar with the customs, practices, etc, of the West > ,westerni'zation or ,westerni'sation *n*

Western Ocean *n* (formerly) another name for the Atlantic Ocean

Western Roman Empire *n* the westernmost of the two empires created by the division of the later Roman Empire, esp after its final severance from the Eastern Roman Empire (395 AD). Also called: Western Empire

Western Sahara *n* a disputed region of NW Africa, on the Atlantic: mainly desert; rich phosphate deposits; a Spanish overseas province from 1958 to 1975; partitioned in 1976 between Morocco and Mauritania who faced growing resistance from the Polisario Front, an organization aiming for the independence of the region as the Democratic Saharan Arab Republic. Mauritania renounced its claim in 1979 and it was taken over by Morocco. Polisario agreed to a UN-brokered cease-fire in 1991 but attempts to settle the status of the region have failed. Pop: 316 000 (2004 est). Area: 266 000 sq km (102 680 sq miles). Former name (until 1975): Spanish Sahara

W

Western Samoa *n* See **Samoa** (sense 1)

Western Wall *n* *Judaism* a wall in Jerusalem, the last extant part of the Temple of Herod, held sacred by Jews as a place of prayer and pilgrimage. Also called: Wailing Wall

Westfalen (vɛstˈfɑːlən) *n* the German name for Westphalia

West Flanders *n* a province of W Belgium: the country's chief agricultural province. Capital: Bruges. Pop: 1 135 802 (2004 est). Area: 3132 sq km (1209 sq miles)

West Germany *n* a former republic in N central Europe, on the North Sea: established in 1949 from the zones of Germany occupied by the British, Americans, and French after the defeat of Nazi Germany; a member of the European Community; reunited with East Germany in 1990. Official name: Federal Republic of Germany. See also **Germany** > West German *adj, n*

West Glamorgan *n* a former county in S Wales, formed in 1974 from part of Glamorgan and the county borough of Swansea: replaced in 1996 by the county of Swansea and the county borough of Neath Port Talbot

westie (ˈwɛstɪ) *n* *informal, derogatory* **1** *Austral* a young working-class person from the western suburbs of Sydney **2** *NZ* a young working-class person from the western suburbs of Auckland

West Indies (ˈɪndɪz) *n* (*functioning as singular or plural*) an archipelago off Central America, extending over 2400 km (1500 miles) in an arc from the peninsula of Florida to Venezuela, separating the Caribbean Sea from the Atlantic Ocean: consists of the Greater Antilles, the Lesser Antilles, and the Bahamas; largest island is Cuba. Area: over 235 000 sq km (91 000 sq miles). Also called: the Caribbean > West Indian *adj, n*

westing (ˈwɛstɪŋ) *n* *navigation* movement, deviation, or distance covered in a westerly direction, esp as expressed in the resulting difference in longitude

West Irian *n* a former English name for **Papua** (sense 2)

West Lothian *n* a council area and historical county of central Scotland, on the Firth of Forth: became part of Lothian region in 1975: reinstated as an independent authority (with revised boundaries) in 1996: agriculture, oil-refining. Administrative centre: Livingston. Pop: 161 020 (2003 est). Area: 425 sq km (164 sq miles)

West Lothian question *n* *Brit* the apparent inconsistency that members of parliament who represent Scottish constituencies are eligible to vote at Westminster on matters that relate only to England, whereas members of parliament from English constituencies are not eligible to vote on Scottish matters [C20: because the issue was first raised by the Scottish politician Tam *Dalyell* (born 1932) at the time when he was MP for *West Lothian*]

Westm. *abbreviation* Westminster

Westmeath (ˌwɛstˈmiːð) *n* a county of N central Republic of Ireland, in Leinster province: mostly low-lying, with many lakes and bogs. County town: Mullingar. Pop: 71 858 (2002). Area: 1764 sq km (681 sq miles)

West Midlands *n* (*functioning as singular or plural*) a metropolitan county of central England, administered since 1986 by the unitary authorities of Wolverhampton, Walsall, Dudley, Sandwell, Birmingham, Solihull, and Coventry. Area: 899 sq km (347 sq miles)

Westminster (ˈwɛstˌmɪnstə) *n* **1** Also called: City of Westminster a borough of Greater London, on the River Thames: contains the Houses of Parliament, Westminster Abbey, and Buckingham Palace. Pop: 222 000 (2003 est). Area: 22 sq km (8 sq miles) **2** the Houses of Parliament at Westminster

Westminster Abbey *n* a Gothic church in London: site of a Benedictine monastery (1050–65); scene of the coronations of almost all English monarchs since William I

Westmorland (ˈwɛstmələnd, ˈwɛsmə-) *n* (until 1974) a county of NW England, now part of Cumbria

west-northwest *n* **1** the point on the compass or the direction midway between west and northwest, 292° 30′ clockwise from north ▷ *adj,* **2** in, from, or towards this direction

Weston standard cell (ˈwɛstən) *n* a primary cell used as a standard of emf, producing 1.018636 volts: consists of a mercury anode and a cadmium amalgam cathode in an electrolyte of saturated cadmium sulphate. Former name: cadmium cell [C20: from a trademark]

Weston-super-Mare (ˈwɛstənˌsuːpəˈmɛə, -ˌsjuː-) *n* a town and resort in SW England, in North Somerset unitary authority, Somerset, on the Bristol Channel. Pop: 78 044 (2001)

West Pakistan *n* the former name (until the end of 1971) of **Pakistan**

Westphalia (wɛstˈfeɪlɪə) *n* a historic region of NW Germany, now mostly in the state of North Rhine-Westphalia. German name: Westfalen > West'phalian *adj, n*

West Prussia *n* a former province of NE Prussia, on the Baltic: assigned to Poland in 1945

West Riding *n* (until 1974) an administrative division of Yorkshire, now part of West Yorkshire, North Yorkshire, Cumbria, and Lancashire

west-southwest *n* **1** the point on the compass or the direction midway between southwest and west, 247° 30′ clockwise from north ▷ *adj, adv* **2** in, from, or towards this direction

West Sussex *n* a county of SE England, comprising part of the former county of Sussex: mainly low-lying, with the South Downs in the S. Administrative centre: Chichester. Pop: 758 600 (2003 est). Area: 1989 sq km (768 sq miles)

West Virginia *n* a state of the eastern US: part of Virginia until the outbreak of the American Civil War (1861); consists chiefly of the Allegheny Plateau; bounded on the west by the Ohio River; coal-mining. Capital: Charleston. Pop: 1 810 354 (2003 est). Area: 62 341 sq km (24 070 sq miles). Abbreviation: W. Va., (with zip code) WV > West Virginian *adj, n*

westward (ˈwɛstwəd) *adj* **1** moving, facing, or situated in the west ▷ *adv* **2** Also called: **westwards** towards the west ▷ *n* **3** the westward part, direction, etc; the west > 'westwardly *adj, adv*

Westwood (ˈwɛstˌwʊd) *n* Vivienne (Isabel). born 1941, British fashion designer: noted for her punk designs of the late 1970s

West Yorkshire *n* a metropolitan county of N England, administered since 1986 by the unitary authorities of Bradford, Leeds, Calderdale, Kirklees, and Wakefield. Area: 2039 sq km (787 sq miles)

wet (wɛt) *adj* wetter, wettest **1** moistened, covered, saturated, etc, with water or some other liquid **2** not yet dry or solid: *wet varnish* **3** rainy, foggy, misty, or humid: *wet weather* **4** employing a liquid, usually water: *a wet method of chemical analysis* **5** *chiefly US & Canadian* characterized by or permitting the free sale of alcoholic beverages: *a wet state* **6** *Brit informal* feeble or foolish **7** wet behind the ears *informal* immature or inexperienced; naive ▷ *n* **8** wetness or moisture **9** damp or rainy weather **10** *Brit informal* a Conservative politician who is considered not to be a hard-liner **11** *Brit informal* a feeble or foolish person **12** *chiefly US & Canadian* a person who advocates free sale of alcoholic beverages **13** the wet *Austral* (in northern and central Australia) the rainy season ▷ *vb* wets, wetting, wet *or* wetted **14** to make or become wet **15** to urinate on (something) **16** (*tr*) *dialect* to prepare (tea) by boiling or infusing [Old English *wǣt*; related to Old Frisian *wēt*, Old Norse *vātr*, Old Slavonic *vedro* bucket] > 'wetly *adv* > 'wetness *n* > 'wettable *adj* > 'wetter *n* > 'wettish *adj*

wet-and-dry-bulb thermometer *n* another name for **psychrometer**

wet blanket *n* *informal* a person whose low spirits or lack of enthusiasm have a depressing effect on other people

wet cell *n* a primary cell in which the electrolyte is a liquid

wet dream *n* an erotic dream accompanied by an emission of semen during or just after sleep

wet fly *n* *angling* an artificial fly designed to float or ride below the water surface

wether (ˈwɛðə) *n* a male sheep, esp a castrated one [Old

English *hwæther*; related to Old Frisian *hweder*, Old High German *hwedar*, Old Norse *hvatharr*]

wetland ('wɛtlənd) *n* (*sometimes plural*) **a** an area of swampy or marshy land, esp considered as part of an ecological system **b** (*as modifier*): *wetland species*

wet look *n* a shiny finish given to certain clothing and footwear materials, esp plastic and leather

wet nurse *n* **1** a woman hired to suckle the child of another ▷ *vb* **wet-nurse** (*tr*) **2** to act as a wet nurse to (a child) **3** *informal* to attend with great devotion

wet pack *n med* a hot or cold damp sheet or blanket for wrapping around a patient

wet room *n* a type of water-proofed room with a drain in the floor often serving as an open-plan shower

wet rot *n* **1** a state of decay in timber caused by various fungi, esp *Coniophora puteana*. The hyphal strands of the fungus are seldom visible and affected timber turns dark brown **2** any of the fungi causing this decay

wet suit *n* a close-fitting rubber suit used by skin divers, yachtsmen, etc, to retain body heat when they are immersed in water or sailing in cold weather

Wetterhorn (German 'vɛtərˌhɔrn) *n* a mountain in S Switzerland, in the Bernese Alps. Height: 3701 m (12 143 ft)

wetting agent *n chem* any substance added to a liquid to lower its surface tension and thus increase its ability to spread across or penetrate into a solid

wetware ('wɛtˌwɛə) *n* **1** *computing* the nervous system of the brain, as opposed to computer hardware or software **2** *computing* the programmers, operators, and administrators who operate a computer system, as opposed to the system's hardware or software

we've (wiːv) *contraction of* we have

Wexford ('wɛksfəd) *n* **1** a county of SE Republic of Ireland, in Leinster province on the Irish Sea: the first Irish county to be colonized from England; mostly low-lying and fertile. County town: Wexford. Pop: 116 596 (2002). Area: 2352 sq km (908 sq miles) **2** a port in SE Republic of Ireland, county town of Co Wexford: sacked by Oliver Cromwell in 1649. Pop: 17 235 (2002)

Weygand (French vɛgɑ̃) *n* **Maxime** (maksim). 1867–1965, French general; as commander in chief of the Allied armies in France (1940) he advised the French Government to surrender to Germany

Weyl (vaɪl) *n* **Hermann**. 1885–1955, US mathematician, born in Germany; noted for his work on group theory and the mathematics of relativity

Weymouth ('weɪməθ) *n* a port and resort in S England, in Dorset on the English Channel: formerly part of the borough of **Weymouth and Melcombe Regis**. Pop (with Melcombe Regis): 48 279 (2001)

wf *abbreviation* wrong fount

WFF *abbreviation logic* well-formed formula

WFTU *abbreviation* World Federation of Trade Unions

whack (wæk) *vb* (*tr*) **1** to strike with a sharp resounding blow **2** (*usually passive*) *Brit informal* to exhaust completely ▷ *n* **3** (*tr*) *US slang* to murder: *if you were out of line you got whacked* **4** a sharp resounding blow or the noise made by such a blow **5** *informal* a share or portion **6** *informal* a try or attempt (esp in the phrase **have a whack at**) **7** out of whack *informal* out of order; unbalanced: *the whole system is out of whack* [c18: perhaps a variant of THWACK, ultimately of imitative origin] > 'whacker *n*

whacking ('wækɪŋ) *informal, chiefly Brit* ▷ *adj* **1** enormous ▷ *adv* **2** (*intensifier*): *a whacking big lie*

whacky ('wækɪ) *adj* **whackier, whackiest** *US slang* a variant spelling of **wacky**

whale[1] (weɪl) *n, pl* **whales** *or* **whale 1** any of the larger cetacean mammals, excluding dolphins, porpoises, and narwhals. They have flippers, a streamlined body, and a horizontally flattened tail and breathe through a blowhole on the top of the head **2 a whale of a** *informal* an exceptionally large, fine, etc, example of a (person or thing) [Old English *hwæl*; related to Old Saxon, Old High German *hwal*, Old Norse *hvalr*, Latin *squalus* seapig]

whale[2] (weɪl) *vb* (*tr*) [c18: variant of WALE]

whaleboat ('weɪlˌbəʊt) *n* a narrow boat from 20 to 30 feet long having a sharp prow and stern, formerly used in whaling. Also called: **whaler**

whalebone ('weɪlˌbəʊn) *n* **1** Also called: **baleen** a horny elastic material forming a series of numerous thin plates that hang from the upper jaw on either side of the palate in the toothless (whalebone) whales and strain plankton from water entering the mouth **2** a thin strip of this substance, used in stiffening corsets, bodices, etc

whalebone whale *n* any whale belonging to the cetacean suborder *Mysticeti*, having a double blowhole and strips of whalebone between the jaws instead of teeth: includes the rorquals, right whales, and the blue whale

whale oil *n* oil obtained either from the blubber of whales (train oil) or the head of the sperm whale (sperm oil)

whaler ('weɪlə) *n* **1** a person employed in whaling **2** a vessel engaged in whaling **3** *Austral* a nomad surviving in the bush without working **4** *Austral* short for **whaler shark**

whaler shark *n Austral* a large voracious shark, *Galeolamna macrurus*, of E. Australian waters

whale shark *n* a large spotted whalelike shark, *Rhincodon typus*, of warm seas, that feeds on plankton and small animals: family *Rhincodontidae*

whaling ('weɪlɪŋ) *n* the work or industry of hunting and processing whales for food, oil, etc

wham (wæm) *n* **1** a forceful blow or impact or the sound produced by such a blow or impact ▷ *vb* **whams, whamming, whammed 2** to strike or cause to strike with great force [c20: of imitative origin]

whammy ('wæmɪ) *n, pl* **-mies 1** something which has great, often negative, impact: *the double whammy of high interest rates and low wage increases* **2** an evil spell or curse [c20: WHAM + -Y[2]]

whanau ('fɑːnaʊ) *n NZ* (in Māori societies) a family, esp an extended family [Māori]

whang (wæŋ) *vb* **1** to strike or be struck so as to cause a resounding noise ▷ *n* **2** the resounding noise produced by a heavy blow **3** a heavy blow [c19: of imitative origin]

Whangarei (ˌwɑːŋɑˈreɪ) *n* a port in New Zealand, the northernmost city of North Island: oil refinery. Pop: 72 200 (2004 est)

whangee (wæŋˈiː) *n* **1** any tall woody grass of the S and SE Asian genus *Phyllostachys*, grown for its stems, which are used for bamboo canes and as a source of paper pulp **2** a cane or walking stick made from the stem of any of these plants [c19: probably from Chinese (Mandarin) *huangli*, from *huang* yellow + *li* bamboo cane]

whare ('wɔːrɪ; Māori 'fɔrɛ) *n NZ* a Māori hut or dwelling place **2** any simple dwelling place, esp at a beach or in the bush [from Māori]

wharepuni ('fɔrɛˌpʊnɪ) *n NZ* another name for **meeting house** (sense 2) [Māori WHARE + *puni* company]

whare wanaga ('fɔrɛ wəˈnɑːgə) *n NZ* a university [Māori]

wharf (wɔːf) *n, pl* **wharves** (wɔːvz) *or* **wharfs 1** a platform of timber, stone, concrete, etc, built parallel to the waterfront at a harbour or navigable river for the docking, loading, and unloading of ships ▷ *vb* (*tr*) **2** to moor or dock at a wharf **3** to store or unload on a wharf [Old English *hwearf* heap; related to Old Saxon *hwarf*, Old High German *hwarb* a turn, Old Norse *hvarf* circle]

wharfage ('wɔːfɪdʒ) *n* **1** accommodation for ships at wharves **2** a charge for use of a wharf **3** wharves collectively

wharfie ('wɔːfɪ) *n Austral & NZ* a wharf labourer; docker

wharfinger ('wɔːfɪndʒə) *n* an owner or manager of a wharf [c16: probably alteration of *wharfager* (see WHARFAGE, -ER[1]); compare HARBINGER]

Wharton ('wɔːt³n) *n* **Edith** (**Newbold**). 1862–1937, US novelist; author of *The House of Mirth* (1905) and *Ethan Frome* (1911)

wharve (wɔːv) *n* a wooden disc or wheel on a shaft serving as a flywheel or pulley [Old English *hweorfa*, from *hweorfan* to revolve; related to Old Saxon *hwervo* axis, Old High German *hwerbo* a turn]

what (wɒt; *unstressed* wət) *determiner* **1 a** used with a noun in requesting further information about the identity or categorization of something: *what job does he do?* **b** (*as pronoun*): *what is her address?* **c** (*used in indirect questions*): *does he know what man did this?*; *tell me what he said* **2 a** the (person, thing, persons, or things) that: *we photographed what animals we could see* **b** (*as pronoun*): *bring me what you've written; come what may* **3** (*intensifier; used in exclamations*): *what a good book!* ▷ *adv* **4** in what respect? to what degree?: *what do you care?* ▷ *pron* **5** what about what do you think, know, feel, etc, concerning? **6** what for **a** for what purpose? why? **b** *informal* a punishment or reprimand (esp in the phrase **give (a person) what for**) **7** what have you someone, something, or somewhere unknown or unspecified: *cars, motorcycles, or what have you* **8** what if **a** what would happen if? **b** what difference would it make if? **9** what matter what does it matter? **10** what's what *informal* the true or real state of affairs [Old English *hwæt*; related to Old Frisian *whet*, Old High German *hwaz* (German *was*), Old Norse *hvatr*]

whatever (wɒtˈɛvə, wət-) *pron* **1** everything or anything that: *do whatever he asks you to* **2** no matter what: *whatever he does, he is forgiven* **3** *informal* an unknown or unspecified thing or things: *take a hammer, chisel, or whatever* **4** an intensive form of *what*, used in questions: *whatever can he have said to upset her so much?* ▷ *determiner* **5** an intensive form of *what*: *use whatever tools you can get hold of* ▷ *adj* **6** (*postpositive*) absolutely; whatsoever: *I saw no point whatever in continuing*

whatnot (ˈwɒtˌnɒt) *n* **1** Also called: what-d'you-call-it *informal* a person or thing the name of which is unknown, temporarily forgotten, or deliberately overlooked **2** *informal* unspecified assorted material **3** a portable stand with shelves, used for displaying ornaments, etc

whatsit (ˈwɒtsɪt), **whatsitsname**, *masculine* **whatshisname** *or feminine* **whatshername** *n informal* a person or thing the name of which is unknown, temporarily forgotten, or deliberately overlooked

whatsoever (ˌwɒtsəʊˈɛvə) *adj* **1** (*postpositive*) at all: used as an intensifier with indefinite pronouns and determiners such as *none, any, no one, anybody,* etc ▷ *pron* **2** an archaic word for **whatever**

whaup (wɔːp; *Scot* hwɔːp) *n chiefly Scot* a popular name for the **curlew** [c16: related to Old English *huilpe*, ultimately imitative of the bird's cry; compare Low German *regenwilp* sandpiper]

wheal (wiːl) *n* a variant spelling of **weal¹**

wheat (wiːt) *n* **1** any annual or biennial grass of the genus *Triticum*, native to the Mediterranean region and W Asia but widely cultivated, having erect flower spikes and light brown grains **2** the grain of any of these grasses, used in making flour, pasta, etc ▷ See also **durum** [Old English *hwǣte*, related to Old Frisian, Old Saxon *hwēti*, Old High German *hweizi*, Old Norse *hveiti*; see WHITE]

wheatear (ˈwiːtˌɪə) *n* any small northern songbird of the genus *Oenanthe*, esp *O. oenanthe*, a species having a pale grey back, black wings and tail, white rump, and pale brown underparts: subfamily *Turdinae* (thrushes) [c16: back formation from *wheatears* (wrongly taken as plural), probably from WHITE + ARSE; compare Dutch *witstaart*, French *culblanc* white tail]

wheaten (ˈwiːtᵊn) *adj* **1** made of the grain or flour of wheat **2** of a pale yellow colour

wheat germ *n* the vitamin-rich embryo of the wheat kernel, which is largely removed before milling and is used in cereals, as a food supplement, etc

wheatmeal (ˈwiːtˌmiːl) *n* **a** a brown flour intermediate between white flour and wholemeal flour **b** (*as modifier*): *a wheatmeal loaf*

wheat pool *n* (in Western Canada) a cereal farmers' cooperative

Wheatstone bridge (ˈwiːtstən) *n* a device for determining the value of an unknown resistance by comparison with a known standard resistance [c19: named after Sir Charles *Wheatstone* (1802–75), British physicist and inventor]

whee (wiː) *interj* an exclamation of joy, thrill, etc

wheedle (ˈwiːdᵊl) *vb* **1** to persuade or try to persuade (someone) by coaxing words, flattery, etc **2** (*tr*) to obtain by coaxing and flattery: *she wheedled some money out of her father* [c17: perhaps from German *wedeln* to wag one's tail, from Old High German *wedil, wadil* tail] > ˈwheedler *n* > ˈwheedling *adj* > ˈwheedlingly *adv*

wheel (wiːl) *n* **1** a solid disc, or a circular rim joined to a hub by radial or tangential spokes, that is mounted on a shaft about which it can turn, as in vehicles and machines **2** anything like a wheel in shape or function **3** a device consisting of or resembling a wheel or having a wheel as its principal component: *a steering wheel; a water wheel* **4** the wheel a medieval torture consisting of a wheel to which the victim was tied and then had his limbs struck and broken by an iron bar **5** short for **wheel of fortune, potter's wheel** **6** the act of turning **7** a pivoting movement of troops, ships, etc **8** a type of firework coiled to make it rotate when let off **9** a set of short rhyming lines, usually four or five in number, forming the concluding part of a stanza **10** *US & Canadian* an informal word for **bicycle** **11** *informal, chiefly US & Canadian* a person of great influence (esp in the phrase **big wheel**) **12** at the wheel **a** driving or steering a vehicle or vessel **b** in charge ▷ *vb* **13** (when *intr* sometimes foll by *about* or *round*) to turn or cause to turn on or as if on an axis **14** to move or cause to move on or as if on wheels; roll **15** (*tr*) to perform with or in a circular movement **16** (*tr*) to provide with a wheel or wheels **17** (*intr; often foll by about*) to change one's mind or opinion **18** wheel and deal *informal* to be a free agent, esp to advance one's own interests ▷ See also **wheels** [Old English *hweol, hweowol*; related to Old Norse *hvēl*, Greek *kuklos*, Middle Low German *wēl*, Dutch *wiel*]

wheel and axle *n* a simple machine for raising weights in which a rope unwinding from a wheel is wound onto a cylindrical drum or shaft coaxial with or joined to the wheel to provide mechanical advantage

wheel animalcule *n* another name for **rotifer**

wheelbarrow (ˈwiːlˌbærəʊ) *n* a simple vehicle for carrying small loads, typically being an open container supported by a wheel at the front and two legs and two handles behind

wheelbase (ˈwiːlˌbeɪs) *n* the distance between the front and back axles of a motor vehicle

wheelchair (ˈwiːlˌtʃɛə) *n med* a special chair mounted on large wheels, for use by invalids or others for whom walking is impossible or temporarily inadvisable

wheel clamp *n* a device fixed onto one wheel of an illegally parked car in order to immobilize it. The driver has to pay to have it removed

wheeled (wiːld) *adj* **a** having or equipped with a wheel or wheels **b** (*in combination*): *four-wheeled*

wheeler (ˈwiːlə) *n* **1** Also called: wheel horse a horse or other draught animal nearest the wheel **2** (*in combination*) something equipped with a specified sort or number of wheels: *a three-wheeler* **3** a person or thing that wheels

Wheeler (ˈwiːlə) *n* **1 John Archibald.** born 1911, US physicist, noted for his work on nuclear fission and the development (1949–51) of the hydrogen bomb, also for his work on unified field theory **2** Sir (**Robert Eric**) **Mortimer.** 1890–1976, Scottish archaeologist, who did much to popularize public interest in archaeology. He is noted esp for his excavations at Mohenjo-Daro and Harappa in the Indus Valley and at Maiden Castle in Dorset

wheeler-dealer *n informal* a person who wheels and deals

wheel horse *n* **1** another word for **wheeler** (sense 1) **2** *US & Canadian* a person who works steadily or hard

wheelhouse (ˈwiːlˌhaʊs) *n* another term for **pilot house**

wheelie (ˈwiːlɪ) *n, pl* -ies a manoeuvre on a bicycle or motorbike in which the front wheel is raised off the ground

wheelie bin *or* **wheely bin** *n* a large container for rubbish, esp one used by a household, mounted on wheels so that it can be moved more easily

wheel lock *n* **1** a gunlock formerly in use in which the firing mechanism was activated by sparks produced by friction between a small steel wheel and a flint **2** a gun having such a lock

W

wheel of fortune *n* (in mythology and literature) a revolving device spun by a deity of fate selecting random changes in the affairs of man

wheels (wi:lz) *pl n* **1** the main directing force behind an organization, movement, etc: *the wheels of government* **2** an informal word for **car** **3** wheels within wheels a series of intricately connected events, plots, etc

wheel trim *n* metallic decorative trim over or around the wheels of a motor vehicle

wheel window *n* another name for **rose window**

wheel wobble *n* an oscillation of the front wheels of a vehicle caused by a defect in the steering gear, unbalanced wheels, etc

wheelwright ('wi:l‚raɪt) *n* a person who makes or mends wheels as a trade

wheeze (wi:z) *vb* **1** to breathe or utter (something) with a rasping or whistling sound **2** (*intr*) to make or move with a noise suggestive of wheezy breathing ▷ *n* **3** a husky, rasping, or whistling sound or breathing **4** *Brit slang* a trick, idea, or plan (esp in the phrase **good wheeze**) **5** *informal* a hackneyed joke or anecdote [c15: probably from Old Norse *hvǣsa* to hiss] > 'wheezer *n* > 'wheezy *adj* > 'wheezily *adv* > 'wheeziness *n*

whelk¹ (wɛlk) *n* any carnivorous marine gastropod mollusc of the family *Buccinidae*, of coastal waters and intertidal regions, having a strong snail-like shell [Old English *weoloc*; related to Middle Dutch *willok*, Old Norse *vil* entrails]

whelk² (wɛlk) *n* a raised lesion on the skin; wheal [Old English *hwylca*, of obscure origin] > 'whelky *adj*

whelm (wɛlm) *vb* (*tr*) *archaic* **1** to engulf entirely with or as if with water **2** another word for **overwhelm** [c13: *whelmen* to turn over, of uncertain origin]

whelp (wɛlp) *n* **1** a young offspring of certain animals, esp of a wolf or dog **2** *disparaging* a young man or youth **3** *jocular* a young child **4** *nautical* any of the ridges, parallel to the axis, on the drum of a capstan to keep a rope, cable, or chain from slipping ▷ *vb* **5** (of an animal or, disparagingly, a woman) to give birth to (young) [Old English *hwelp(a)*; related to Old High German *hwelf*, Old Norse *hvelpr*, Danish *hvalp*]

when (wɛn) *adv* **1 a** at what time? over what period?: *when is he due?* **b** (*used in indirect questions*): *ask him when he's due* **2** say when to state when an action is to be stopped or begun, as when someone is pouring a drink **3** (*subordinating*) at the time at which; the time at which; just as; after: *I found it easily when I started to look seriously* **4** although: *he drives when he might walk* **5** considering the fact that: *how did you pass the exam when you'd not worked for it?* **6** at which (time); over which (period): *an age when men were men* ▷ *n* **7** (*usually plural*) a question as to the time of some occurrence [Old English *hwanne, hwænne*; related to Old High German *hwanne, hwenne*, Latin *cum*]
  ● **USAGE** *When* should not be used loosely as a substitute
  ● for *in which* after a noun which does not refer to a
  ● period of time: *paralysis is a condition in which* (not *when*)
  ● parts of the body cannot be moved

whenas (wɛn'æz) *conj* **1** *archaic* **a** when; whenever **b** inasmuch as; while **2** *obsolete* whereas; although

whence (wɛns) *archaic or formal adv* **1** from what place, cause, or origin? ▷ *pron* **2** (*subordinating*) from what place, cause, or origin [c13 *whannes*, adverbial genitive of Old English *hwanon*; related to Old Frisian *hwana*, Old High German *hwanan*]
  ● **USAGE** The expression *from whence* should be avoided,
  ● since *whence* already means from which place: *the*
  ● *tradition whence* (not *from whence*) *such ideas flowed*

whencesoever (‚wɛnssəʊ'ɛvə) *conj, adv* (*subordinating*) *archaic* out of whatsoever place, cause, or origin

whenever (wɛn'ɛvə) *conj* **1** (*subordinating*) at every or any time that; when: *I laugh whenever I see that* ▷ *adv* Also: **when ever 2** no matter when: *it'll be here, whenever you decide to come for it* **3** *informal* at an unknown or unspecified time: *I'll take it if it comes today, tomorrow, or whenever* **4** an intensive form of *when*, used in questions: *whenever did he escape?*

whensoever (‚wɛnsəʊ'ɛvə) *conj, adv rare* an intensive form of **whenever**

whenua (fɛn'uə) *n* NZ land [Māori]

whenwe ('wɛnwi:) *n South African informal* a White immigrant from Zimbabwe, caricatured as being tiresomely over-reminiscent of happier times [c20: from WHEN + WE]

where (wɛə) *adv* **1 a** in, at, or to what place, point, or position?: *where are you going?* **b** (*used in indirect questions*): *I don't know where they are* **2** in, at, or to which (place): *the hotel where we spent our honeymoon* **3** (*subordinating*) in the place at which: *where we live it's always raining* ▷ *n* **4** (*usually plural*) a question as to the position, direction, or destination of something [Old English *hwēr, hwār(a)*; related to Old Frisian *hwēr*, Old Saxon, Old High German *hwār*, Old Norse, Gothic *hvar*]
  ● **USAGE** It was formerly considered incorrect to use
  ● *where* as a substitute for *in which* after a noun which
  ● did not refer to a place or position, but this use has
  ● now become acceptable: *we now have a situation where/in*
  ● *which no further action is needed*

whereabouts ('wɛərə‚baʊts) *adv* **1** Also called: **whereabout** at what approximate location or place; where: *whereabouts are you?* ▷ *n* **2** (*functioning as singular or plural*) the place, esp the approximate place, where a person or thing is

whereas (wɛər'æz) *conj* **1** (*coordinating*) but on the other hand: *I like to go swimming whereas Sheila likes to sail* ▷ *sentence connector* **2** (in formal documents to begin sentences) it being the case that; since

whereat (wɛər'æt) *archaic* ▷ *adv* **1** at or to which place ▷ *sentence connector* **2** upon which occasion

whereby (wɛə'baɪ) *pron* by or because of which: *the means whereby he took his life*

wherefore ('wɛə‚fɔ:) *n* **1** (*usually plural*) an explanation or reason (esp in the phrase **the whys and wherefores**) ▷ *adv* **2** *archaic* for what reason? why? ▷ *sentence connector* **3** *archaic or formal* for which reason: used as an introductory word in legal preambles

wherefrom (wɛə'frɒm) *archaic* ▷ *adv* **1** from what or where? whence? ▷ *pron* **2** from which place; whence

wherein (wɛər'ɪn) *archaic or formal* ▷ *adv* **1** in what place or respect? ▷ *pron* **2** in which place, thing, etc

whereof (wɛər'ɒv) *archaic or formal* ▷ *adv* **1** of what or which person or thing? ▷ *pron* **2** of which (person or thing): *the man whereof I speak is no longer alive*

whereon (wɛər'ɒn) *archaic* ▷ *adv* **1** on what thing or place? ▷ *pron* **2** on which thing, place, etc

wheresoever (‚wɛərsəʊ'ɛvə) *conj, pron, adv* (*subordinating*) *rare* an intensive form of **wherever**

whereto (wɛə'tu:) *archaic or formal* ▷ *adv* **1** towards what (place, end, etc)? ▷ *pron* **2** to which ▷ Also (archaic): **whereunto**

whereupon (‚wɛərə'pɒn) *sentence connector* at which; at which point; upon which

wherever (wɛər'ɛvə) *pron* **1** at, in, or to every place or point which; where: *wherever she went, he would be there* **2** (*subordinating*) in, to, or at whatever place: *wherever we go the weather is always bad* ▷ *adv* Also: **where ever 3** no matter where: *I'll find you, wherever you are* **4** *informal* at, in, or to an unknown or unspecified place: *I'll go anywhere to escape: London, Paris, or wherever* **5** an intensive form of *where*, used in questions: *wherever can they be?*

wherewith (wɛə'wɪθ, -'wɪð) *archaic or formal* ▷ *pron* **1** (*often foll by an infinitive*) with or by which: *the pen wherewith I am wont to write* **2** something with which: *I have not wherewith to buy my bread* ▷ *adv* **3** with what? ▷ *sentence connector* **4** with or after that; whereupon

wherewithal *n* ('wɛəwɪð‚ɔ:l) **1** the wherewithal necessary funds, resources, or equipment (for something or to do something): *these people lack the wherewithal for a decent existence* ▷ *pron* (‚wɛəwɪð'ɔ:l) **2** a less common word for **wherewith** (sense 1)

wherrit ('wɛrɪt) *vb* **1** to worry or cause to worry **2** (*intr*) to complain or moan [perhaps from *thwert*, obsolete variant of THWART; compare WORRIT]

wherry ('wɛrɪ) *n, pl* -ries **1** any of certain kinds of half-decked commercial boats, such as barges, used in Britain **2** a light rowing boat used in inland waters and harbours [c15: origin unknown] > 'wherryman *n*

whet (wɛt) *vb* whets, whetting, whetted (*tr*) **1** to sharpen, as by grinding or friction **2** to increase or enhance (the appetite, desire, etc); stimulate ▷ *n* **3** the act of whetting **4** a person or thing that whets [Old English *hwettan*; related to *hvæt* sharp, Old High German *hwezzen*, Old Norse *hvetja*, Gothic *hvatjan*] ⟩ 'whetter *n*

whether ('wɛðə) *conj* **1** (*subordinating*) used to introduce an indirect question or a clause after a verb expressing or implying doubt or choice in order to indicate two or more alternatives, the second or last of which is introduced by *or* or *or whether*: *he doesn't know whether she's in Britain or whether she's gone to France* **2** (*coordinating*) another word for **either** (sense 3) *any man, whether liberal or conservative, would agree with me* **3** whether or no **a** used as a conjunction as a variant of: **whether** (sense 1) **b** under any circumstances: *he will be here tomorrow, whether or no* **4** whether...or or whether...or whether if on the one hand...or on the other hand: *you'll eat that, whether you like it or not* [Old English *hwæther, hwether*; related to Old Frisian *hweder, hoder*, Old High German *hwedar*, Old Norse *hvatharr, hvarr*, Gothic *hwathar*]

whetstone ('wɛt,stəʊn) *n* **1** a stone used for sharpening edged tools, knives, etc **2** something that sharpens

whew (hwjuː) *interj* an exclamation or sharply exhaled breath expressing relief, surprise, delight, etc

whey (weɪ) *n* the watery liquid that separates from the curd when the milk is clotted, as in making cheese [Old English *hwæg*; related to Middle Low German *wei, heie*, Dutch *hui*] ⟩ 'wheyey or 'wheyish

wheyface ('weɪ,feɪs) *n* **1** a pale bloodless face **2** a person with such a face ⟩ 'whey,faced *adj*

which (wɪtʃ) *determiner* **1 a** used with a noun in requesting that its referent be further specified, identified, or distinguished from the other members of a class: *which house did you want to buy?* **b** (*as pronoun*): *which did you find?* **c** (*used in indirect questions*): *I wondered which apples were cheaper* **2 a** whatever of a class; whichever: *bring which car you want* **b** (*as pronoun*): *choose which of the cars suit you* **3** used in relative clauses with inanimate antecedents: *the house, which is old, is in poor repair* **4** as; and that: used in relative clauses with verb phrases or sentences as their antecedents: *he died of cancer, which is what I predicted* **5** the which *archaic* a longer form of which, often used as a sentence connector [Old English *hwelc, hwilc*; related to Old High German *hwelīh* (German *welch*), Old Norse *hvelīkr*, Gothic *hvileiks*, Latin *quis, quid*]
● USAGE See at **that**

whichever (wɪtʃ'ɛvə) *determiner* **1 a** any (one, two, etc, out of several): *take whichever car you like* **b** (*as pronoun*): *choose whichever appeals to you* **2 a** no matter which (one or ones): *whichever card you pick you'll still be making a mistake* **b** (*as pronoun*): *it won't make any difference, whichever comes first*

whichsoever (ˌwɪtʃsəʊ'ɛvə) *pron* an archaic or formal word for **whichever**

whicker ('wɪkə) *vb* (*intr*) (of a horse) to whinny or neigh; nicker [c17: of imitative origin]

whidah ('wɪdə) *n* a variant spelling of **whydah**

whiff (wɪf) *n* **1 a** a passing odour **2** a brief gentle gust of air **3** a single inhalation or exhalation from the mouth or nose ▷ *vb* **4** (*tr*) to sniff or smell [c16: of imitative origin]

whiffle ('wɪfəl) *vb* **1** (*intr*) to think or behave in an erratic or unpredictable way **2** to blow or be blown fitfully or in gusts **3** (*intr*) to whistle softly [c16: frequentative of WHIFF]

whiffletree ('wɪfəl,triː) *n* another name (esp US) for **swingletree** [c19: variant of WHIPPLETREE]

Whig (wɪg) *n* **1 a** a member of the English political party or grouping that in 1679–80 opposed the succession to the throne of James, Duke of York (1633–1701; king of England and Ireland as James II, and of Scotland as James VII, 1685–88), on the grounds that he was a Catholic. Standing for a limited monarchy, the Whigs represented the great aristocracy and the moneyed middle class for the next 80 years. In the late 18th and early 19th centuries the Whigs represented the desires of industrialists and Dissenters for political and social reform. The Whigs provided the core of the Liberal Party **2** (in the US) a supporter of the War of American Independence. See **Tory 3** a member of the American political party that opposed the Democrats from about

1834 to 1855 and represented propertied and professional interests **4** *history* a 17th-century Scottish Presbyterian, esp one in rebellion against the Crown ▷ *adj* **5** of, characteristic of, or relating to Whigs [c17: probably shortened from *whiggamore*, one of a group of 17th-century Scottish rebels who joined in an attack on Edinburgh known as the *whiggamore raid*; probably from Scottish *whig* to drive (of obscure origin) + *more, mer, maire* horse, MARE] ⟩ 'Whiggery or 'Whiggism *n* ⟩ 'Whiggish *adj*

while (waɪl) *conj* Also: **whilst** (waɪlst) **1** (*subordinating*) at the same time that: *please light the fire while I'm cooking* **2** (*subordinating*) all the time that: *I stay inside while it's raining* **3** (*subordinating*) in spite of the fact that: *while I agree about his brilliance I still think he's rude* **4** (*coordinating*) whereas; and in contrast: *flats are expensive, while houses are cheap* **5** (*subordinating; used with a gerund*) during the activity of: *while walking I often whistle prep, conj* **6** *Scot & northern English dialect* another word for **until** *you'll have to wait while Monday for these sheets; you'll never make any progress while you listen to me* ▷ *n* **7** (*usually used in adverbial phrases*) a period or interval of time: *once in a long while* **8** trouble or time (esp in the phrase **worth one's while**): *it's hardly worth your while to begin work today* **9** the while at that time: *he was working the while* ▷ See also **whiles** [Old English *hwīl*; related to Old High German *hwīla* (German *Weile*), Gothic *hveila*, Latin *quiēs* peace, *tranquīlus* TRANQUIL]
● USAGE It was formerly considered incorrect to use
● *while* to mean *in spite of the fact that* or *whereas*, but these
● uses have now become acceptable

while away *vb* (*tr, adverb*) to pass (time) idly and usually pleasantly

whiles (waɪlz; *Scot* hwaɪlz) *archaic or dialect* ▷ *adv* **1** at times; occasionally ▷ *conj* **2** while; whilst

whilom ('waɪləm) *archaic* ▷ *adv* **1** formerly; once ▷ *adj* **2** (*prenominal*) one-time; former [Old English *hwīlum*, dative plural of *hwīl* WHILE; related to Old High German *hwīlōm*, German *weiland* of old]

whilst (waɪlst) *conj chiefly Brit* another word for **while** (sense 1–5) [c13: from WHILES + -*t* as in *amidst*]

whim (wɪm) *n* **1 a** a sudden, passing, and often fanciful idea; impulsive or irrational thought **2** a horse-drawn winch formerly used in mining to lift ore or water [c17: from WHIM-WHAM]

whimbrel ('wɪmbrəl) *n* a small European curlew, *Numenius phaeopus*, with a striped head [c16: from dialect *whimp* or from WHIMPER, alluding to its cry]

whimper ('wɪmpə) *vb* **1** (*intr*) to cry, sob, or whine softly or intermittently **2** to complain or say (something) in a whining plaintive way ▷ *n* **3** a soft plaintive whine [c16: from dialect *whimp*, of imitative origin] ⟩ 'whimperer *n* ⟩ 'whimpering *adv*

whimsical ('wɪmzɪkəl) *adj* **1** spontaneously fanciful or playful **2** given to whims; capricious **3** quaint, unusual, or fantastic ⟩ whimsicality (ˌwɪmzɪ'kælɪtɪ) *n* ⟩ 'whimsically *adv*

whimsy or **whimsey** ('wɪmzɪ) *n, pl* -sies or -seys **1** a capricious idea or notion **2** light or fanciful humour **3** something quaint or unusual ▷ *adj* -sier, -siest **4** quaint, comical, or unusual, often in a tasteless way [c17: from WHIM; compare FLIMSY]

whim-wham *n archaic* something fanciful; a trifle [c16: of unknown origin; compare FLIMFLAM]

whin (wɪn) *n* another name for **gorse** [c11: from Scandinavian; compare Old Danish *hvine* (*græs*), Norwegian *hvine*, Swedish *hven*]

whine (waɪn) *n* **1** a long high-pitched plaintive cry or moan **2** a continuous high-pitched sound **3** a peevish complaint, esp one repeated ▷ *vb* **4** to make a whine or utter in a whine [Old English *hwīnan*; related to Old Norse *hvīna*, Swedish *hvija* to scream] ⟩ 'whiner *n* ⟩ 'whining *adj* ⟩ 'whiningly *adv*

whinge (wɪndʒ) *informal* ▷ *vb* whinges, whingeing, whinged (*intr*) **1** to cry in a fretful way **2** to complain ▷ *n* **3** a complaint [from a Northern variant of Old English *hwinsian* to whine; related to Old High German *winsan, winisan*, whence Middle High German *winsen*] ⟩ 'whingeing *n, adj* ⟩ 'whinger *n*

whinny ('wɪnɪ) *vb* -nies, -nying, -nied (*intr*) **1** (of a horse)

W

to neigh softly or gently **2** to make a sound resembling a neigh, such as a laugh ▷ *n, pl* **-nies 3** a gentle or low-pitched neigh [c16: of imitative origin]

whip ('wɪp) *vb* **whips, whipping, whipped 1** to strike (a person or thing) with several strokes of a strap, rod, etc **2** (*tr*) to punish by striking in this manner **3** (*tr*; foll by *out, away*, etc) to pull, remove, etc, with sudden rapid motion: *to whip out a gun* **4** (*intr*; foll by *down, into, out of*, etc) *informal* to come, go, etc, in a rapid sudden manner: *they whipped into the bar for a drink* **5** to strike or be struck as if by whipping: *the tempest whipped the surface of the sea* **6** (*tr*) to criticize virulently **7** (*tr*) to bring, train, etc, forcefully into a desired condition (esp in the phrases **whip into line** and **whip into shape**) **8** (*tr*) *informal* to overcome or outdo: *I know when I've been whipped* **9** (*tr*; often foll by *on, out, off*) to drive, urge, compel, etc, by or as if by whipping **10** (*tr*) to wrap or wind (a cord, thread, etc) around (a rope, cable, etc) to prevent chafing or fraying **11** (*tr*) *nautical* to hoist by means of a rope through a single pulley **12** (*tr*) (in fly-fishing) to cast the fly repeatedly onto (the water) in a whipping motion **13** (*tr*) (in sewing) to join, finish, or gather with whipstitch **14** to beat (eggs, cream, etc) with a whisk or similar utensil to incorporate air and produce expansion **15** (*tr*) to spin (a top) **16** (*tr*) *informal* to steal: *he whipped her purse* ▷ *n* **17** a device consisting of a lash or flexible rod attached at one end to a stiff handle and used for driving animals, inflicting corporal punishment, etc **18** a whipping stroke or motion **19** a person adept at handling a whip, as a coachman, etc **20** (in a legislative body) **a** a member of a party chosen to organize and discipline the members of his faction, esp in voting and to assist in the arrangement of the business **b** a call issued to members of a party, insisting with varying degrees of urgency upon their presence or loyal voting behaviour **c** (in the British Parliament) a schedule of business sent to members of a party each week. Each item on it is underlined to indicate its importance: one line means that no division is expected, two lines means that the item is fairly important, and three lines means that the item is very important and every member must attend and vote according to the party line **21** an apparatus for hoisting, consisting of a rope, pulley, and snatch block **22** any of a variety of desserts made from egg whites or cream beaten stiff, sweetened, and flavoured with fruit, fruit juice, etc **23** See **whipper-in 24** a windmill vane **25** transient elastic movement of a structure or part when subjected to sudden release of load or dynamic excitation **26** a percussion instrument consisting of two strips of wood, joined forming the shape of a V, and clapped loudly together **27** flexibility, as in the shaft of a golf club, etc **28** a ride in a funfair involving bumper cars that move with sudden jerks **29** a wrestling throw in which a wrestler seizes his opponent's arm and spins him to the floor **30 a fair crack of the whip** *informal* a fair chance or opportunity ▷ See also **whip-round, whips, whip up** [c13: perhaps from Middle Dutch *wippen* to swing; related to Middle Dutch *wipfen* to dance, German *Wipfel* tree top]

▷ 'whip,like *adj* ▷ 'whipper *n*

whipbird ('wɪp,bɜːd) *n Austral* **1** any of several birds of the genus *Psophodes*, esp *P. olivaceus* (**eastern whipbird**) and *P. nigrogularis* (**black-throated whipbird**), having a whistle ending in a whipcrack note **2** any of various other birds, such as *Pachycephala pectoralis* and *P. rufiventris* (**mock whipbird**)

whipcord ('wɪp,kɔːd) *n* **1** a strong worsted or cotton fabric with a diagonally ribbed surface **2** a closely twisted hard cord used for the lashes of whips, etc

whip graft *n horticulture* a graft made by inserting a tongue cut on the sloping base of the scion into a slit in the sloping top of the stock

whip hand the whip hand *n* **1** (in driving horses) the hand holding the whip **2** advantage or dominating position

whiplash ('wɪp,læʃ) *n* a quick lash or stroke of a whip or like that of a whip

whiplash injury *n med informal* any injury to the neck resulting from a sudden thrusting forwards and

snapping back of the unsupported head

whipper-in *n, pl* **whippers-in** a person employed to assist the huntsman managing the hounds in a hunt

whippersnapper ('wɪpə,snæpə) *n* an insignificant but pretentious or cheeky person, often a young one. Also called: **whipster** [c17: probably from *whipsnapper* a person who snaps whips, influenced by earlier *snippersnapper*, of obscure origin]

whippet ('wɪpɪt) *n* a small slender breed of dog similar to a greyhound in appearance [c16: of uncertain origin; perhaps based on the phrase *whip it!* move quickly!]

whipping ('wɪpɪŋ) *n* **1** a thrashing or beating with a whip or similar implement **2** cord or twine used for binding or lashing

whipping boy *n* a person of little importance who is blamed for the errors, incompetence, etc, of others, esp his superiors; scapegoat [c17: originally referring to a boy who was educated with a prince and who received punishment for any faults committed by the prince]

whippletree ('wɪpəl,triː) *n* another name for swingletree [c18: apparently from WHIP]

whippoorwill ('wɪpʊ,wɪl) *n* a nightjar, *Caprimulgus vociferus*, of North and Central America, having a dark plumage with white patches on the tail [c18: imitative of its cry]

whip-round *informal, chiefly Brit* ▷ *n* **1** an impromptu collection of money ▷ *vb* **whip round 2** (*intr, adverb*) to make such a collection of money

whips (wɪps) *pl n* (often foll by *of*) *Austral informal* a large quantity: *I've got whips of cash at the moment*

whipsaw ('wɪp,sɔː) *n* **1** any saw with a flexible blade, such as a bandsaw ▷ *vb* **-saws, -sawing, -sawed, -sawed** or **-sawn** (*tr*) **2** to saw with a whipsaw **3** *US* to defeat in two ways at once

whip scorpion *n* any nonvenomous arachnid of the order *Uropygi* (or *Pedipalpi*), typically resembling a scorpion but lacking a sting

whip snake *n* any of several long slender fast-moving nonvenomous snakes of the colubrid genus *Coluber*, such as *C. hippocrepis* (**horseshoe whipsnake**) of Eurasia

whipstitch ('wɪp,stɪtʃ) *n* **1** a sewing stitch passing over an edge **2** *US slang* an instant; moment ▷ *vb* **3** (*tr*) to sew (an edge) using whipstitch; overcast

whipstock ('wɪp,stɒk) *n* a whip handle

whip up *vb* (*tr, adverb*) **1** to excite; arouse: *to whip up a mob; to whip up discontent* **2** *informal* to prepare quickly: *to whip up a meal*

whir or **whirr** (wɜː) *n* **1** a prolonged soft swish or buzz, as of a motor working or wings flapping **2** a bustle or rush ▷ *vb* **whirs** or **whirrs, whirring, whirred 3** to make or cause to make a whir [c14: probably from Scandinavian; compare Norwegian *kvirra*, Danish *hvirre*; see WHIRL]

whirl (wɜːl) *vb* **1** to spin, turn, or revolve or cause to spin, turn, or revolve **2** (*intr*) to turn around or away rapidly **3** (*intr*) to have a spinning sensation, as from dizziness, etc **4** to move or drive or be moved or driven at high speed ▷ *n* **5** the act or an instance of whirling; swift rotation or a rapid whirling movement **6** a condition of confusion or giddiness: *her accident left me in a whirl* **7** a swift round, as of events, meetings, etc **8** a tumult; stir **9** *informal* a brief trip, dance, etc **10 give something a whirl** *informal* to attempt or give a trial to something [c13: from Old Norse *hvirfla* to turn about; related to Old High German *wirbil* whirlwind] ▷ 'whirler *n* ▷ 'whirling *adj* ▷ 'whirlingly *adv*

whirligig ('wɜːlɪ,gɪg) *n* **1** any spinning toy, such as a top **2** another name for merry-go-round **3** anything that whirls about, spins, or moves in a circular or giddy way: *the whirligig of social life* **4** another name for **windmill** (sense 3) [c15: *whirlegigge*, from WHIRL + GIG¹]

whirlpool ('wɜːl,puːl) *n* **1** a powerful circular current or vortex of water, usually produced by conflicting tidal currents or by eddying at the foot of a waterfall **2** something resembling a whirlpool in motion or the power to attract into its vortex

whirlwind ('wɜːl,wɪnd) *n* **1** a column of air whirling around and towards a more or less vertical axis of low pressure, which moves along the land or ocean surface **2 a** a motion or course resembling this, esp in rapidity

b (as modifier): a whirlwind romance **3** an impetuously active person

whish (wɪʃ) n, vb a less common word for **swish**

whisht (hwɪʃt) or **whist** (hwɪst) Scot interj **1** hush! be quiet! ▷ vb **2** to make or become silent [c14: compare HIST; also obsolete v. whist to become silent]

whisk (wɪsk) vb **1** (tr; often foll by away or off) to brush, sweep, or wipe off lightly **2** (tr) to move, carry, etc, with a light or rapid sweeping motion: the taxi whisked us to the airport **3** (intr) to move, go, etc, quickly and nimbly: to whisk downstairs for a drink **4** (tr) to whip (eggs, cream, etc) to a froth ▷ n **5** the act of whisking **6** a light rapid sweeping movement or stroke **7** a utensil, often incorporating a coil of wires, for whipping eggs, etc **8** a small brush or broom **9** a small bunch or bundle, as of grass, straw, etc [c14: from Old Norse visk wisp; related to Middle Dutch wisch, Old High German wisc]

whisker ('wɪskə) n **1** any of the stiff sensory hairs growing on the face of a cat, rat, or other mammal. Technical name: **vibrissa 2** any of the hairs growing on a person's face, esp on the cheeks or chin **3** (plural) a beard or that part of it growing on the sides of the face **4** (plural) informal a moustache **5** Also called: whisker boom, whisker pole any light spar used for extending the clews of a sail, esp in light airs **6** chem a very fine filamentary crystal having greater strength than the bulk material since it is a single crystal. Such crystals often show unusual electrical properties **7** a person or thing that whisks **8** a narrow margin; a small distance: he escaped death by a whisker

whiskered ('wɪskəd) adj having whiskers

whiskery ('wɪskərɪ) adj -skerier, -skeriest **1** having whiskers **2** old; unkempt

whiskey ('wɪskɪ) n the usual Irish and US spelling of **whisky**

whiskey sour n US a mixed drink of whisky and lime or lemon juice, sometimes sweetened

whisky ('wɪskɪ) n, pl -kies a spirit made by distilling fermented cereals, which is matured and often blended [c18: shortened from whiskybae, from Scottish Gaelic uisge beatha, literally: water of life; see USQUEBAUGH]

whisky-jack n Canadian another name for **Canada jay**

whisky mac n Brit a drink consisting of whisky and ginger wine

whisper ('wɪspə) vb **1** to speak or utter (something) in a soft hushed tone, esp without vibration of the vocal cords **2** (intr) to speak secretly or furtively, as in promoting intrigue, gossip, etc **3** (intr) (of leaves, trees, etc) to make a low soft rustling sound **4** (tr) to utter or suggest secretly or privately: to whisper treason ▷ n **5** a low soft voice: to speak in a whisper **6** something uttered in such a voice **7** a low soft rustling sound **8** a trace or suspicion **9** informal a rumour or secret [Old English hwisprian; related to Old Norse hvīskra, Old High German hwispalōn, Dutch wispern] > 'whisperer n

whispering campaign n the organized diffusion by word of mouth of defamatory rumours designed to discredit a person, group, etc

whispering gallery n a gallery or dome with acoustic characteristics such that a sound made at one point is audible at distant points

whist¹ (wɪst) n a card game for four in which the two sides try to win the balance of the 13 tricks: forerunner of bridge [c17: perhaps changed from WHISK, referring to the sweeping up or whisking up of the tricks]

whist² (hwist) interj, adj, vb a variant of **whisht**

whist drive n a social gathering where whist is played; the winners of each hand move to different tables to play the losers of the previous hand

whistle ('wɪsºl) vb **1** to produce (shrill or flutelike musical sounds), as by passing breath through a narrow constriction most easily formed by the pursed lips: he whistled a melody **2** (tr) to signal, summon, or command by whistling or blowing a whistle: the referee whistled the end of the game **3** (of a kettle, train, etc) to produce (a shrill sound) caused by the emission of steam through a small aperture **4** (intr) to move with a whistling sound caused by rapid passage through the air **5** (of animals, esp birds) to emit (a shrill sound) resembling human

whistling **6 whistle in the dark** to try to keep up one's confidence in spite of fear ▷ n **7** a device for making a shrill high-pitched sound by means of air or steam under pressure **8** a shrill sound effected by whistling **9** a whistling sound, as of a bird, bullet, the wind, etc **10** a signal, warning, command, etc, transmitted by or as if by a whistle **11** the act of whistling **12** music any pipe that is blown down its end and produces sounds on the principle of a flue pipe, usually having as a mouthpiece a fipple cut in the side **13** wet one's whistle informal to take an alcoholic drink **14 blow the whistle** (usually foll by on) informal **a** to inform (on) **b** to bring a stop (to) ▷ See also **whistle for**, **whistle up** [Old English hwistlian; related to Old Norse hvīsla]

whistle-blower n informal a person who informs on someone or puts a stop to something

whistle for vb (intr, preposition) informal to seek or expect in vain

whistler ('wɪslə) n **1** a person or thing that whistles **2** radio an atmospheric disturbance picked up by radio receivers, characterized by a whistling sound of decreasing pitch. It is caused by the electromagnetic radiation produced by lightning **3** any of various birds having a whistling call, such as certain Australian flycatchers and the goldeneye. See also **thickhead** (sense 2) **4** any of various North American marmots of the genus Marmota, esp M. caligata (**hoary marmot**) **5** vet science a horse affected with an abnormal respiratory noise, resembling whistling **6** informal a referee

Whistler ('wɪslə) n **James Abbott McNeill.** 1834–1903, US painter and etcher, living in Europe. He is best known for his sequence of nocturnes and his portraits

whistle stop n **1** US & Canadian **a** a minor railway station where trains stop only on signal **b** a small town having such a station **2 a** a brief appearance in a town, esp by a political candidate to make a speech, shake hands, etc **b** (as modifier): a whistle-stop tour ▷ vb whistle-stop -stops, -stopping, -stopped **3** (intr) to campaign for office by visiting many small towns to give short speeches

whistle up vb (tr, adverb) to call or summon (a person or animal) by whistling

whit (wɪt) n (usually used with a negative) the smallest particle; iota; jot: he has changed not a whit [c15: probably variant of WIGHT¹]

Whit (wɪt) n **1** See **Whitsuntide** ▷ adj **2** of or relating to Whitsuntide

Whitaker ('wɪtəkə) n **1** Sir **Frederick.** 1812–91, New Zealand statesman, born in England: prime minister of New Zealand (1863–64; 1882–83) **2 Forrest (Steven),** born 1961, US actor and film director; his films include (as actor) Ghost Dog (1999) and The Last King of Scotland (2006); (as director) Waiting to Exhale (1995)

Whitbread ('wɪt,bred) n **Fatima.** born 1961, British javelin thrower

Whitby ('wɪtbɪ) n a fishing port and resort in NE England, in E North Yorkshire at the mouth of the River Esk: an important ecclesiastical centre in Anglo-Saxon times; site of an abbey founded in 656. Pop: 13 594 (2001)

white (waɪt) adj **1** having no hue due to the reflection of all or almost all incident light. See **black** (sense 1) **2** (of light, such as sunlight) consisting of all the colours of the spectrum or produced by certain mixtures of three additive primary colours, such as red, green, and blue **3** comparatively white or whitish-grey in colour or having parts of this colour: white clover **4** (of an animal) having pale-coloured or white skin, fur, or feathers **5** bloodless or pale, as from pain, emotion, etc **6** (of hair, a beard, etc) silvery or grey, usually from age **7** benevolent or without malicious intent: white magic **8** colourless or transparent: white glass **9** capped with or accompanied by snow: a white Christmas **10** (sometimes capital) counterrevolutionary, very conservative, or royalist. See **Red** (sense 2) **11** blank, as an unprinted area of a page **12** (of wine) made from pale grapes or from black grapes separated from their skins **13 a** (of coffee or tea) with milk or cream **b** (of bread) made with white flour **14** physics having or characterized by a continuous distribution of energy, wavelength, or frequency: white noise **15** informal honourable or generous **16** (of armour) made completely of iron or steel (esp in the phrase **white harness**) **17** *rare* morally unblemished **18** *rare* (of times, seasons, etc) auspicious; favourable **19** *poetic or archaic* having a fair complexion; blond **20 bleed white** to deprive slowly of resources **21 whiter than white a** extremely clean and white **b** *informal* very pure, honest, and moral ▷ *n* **22** a white colour **23** the condition or quality of being white; whiteness **24** the white or lightly coloured part or area of something **25** the white the viscous fluid that surrounds the yolk of a bird's egg, esp a hen's egg; albumen **26** *anatomy* the white part (sclera) of the eyeball **27** any of various butterflies of the family *Pieridae*. See **cabbage white 28** *chess, draughts* **a** a white or light-coloured piece or square **b** (*usually capital*) the player playing with such pieces **29** anything that has or is characterized by a white colour, such as a white paint or pigment, a white cloth, a white ball in billiards **30** an unprinted area of a page **31** *archery* **a** the outer ring of the target, having the lowest score **b** a shot or arrow hitting this ring **32** *poetic* fairness of complexion **33** the white (of wood or furniture) left unpainted or unvarnished ▷ *vb* **34** (usually foll by *out*) to create or leave white spaces in (printed or other matter) **35** *obsolete* to make or become white ▷ See also **white out, whites** [Old English *hwīt*; related to Old Frisian *hwīt*, Old Saxon *hwīt*, Old Norse *hvītr*, Gothic *hveits*, Old High German *hwīz* (German *weiss*)] > 'whitely *adv* > 'whiteness *n* > 'whitish *adj*

White¹ (waɪt) *n* **1** a person, esp one of European ancestry, from a human population having light pigmentation of the skin ▷ *adj* **2** denoting or relating to a White person or White people

White² (waɪt) *n* **1 Gilbert**. 1720–93, English clergyman and naturalist, noted for his *Natural History and Antiquities of Selborne* (1789) **2 Jimmy**. born 1962, British snooker player **3 Marco Pierre**. born 1961, British chef and restaurateur **4 Patrick** (**Victor Martindale**). 1912–90, Australian novelist: his works include *Voss* (1957), *The Eye of the Storm* (1973), and *A Fringe of Leaves* (1976): Nobel prize for literature 1973 **5 T**(**erence**) **H**(**anbury**). 1906–64, British novelist: author of the Arthurian sequence *The Once and Future King* (1939–58) **6 Willard** (**Wentworth**) (ˈwɪlɑːd). born 1946, British operatic bass, born in Jamaica

white admiral *n* a nymphalid butterfly, *Limenitis camilla*, of Eurasia, having brown wings with white markings. See also **red admiral**

white ant *n* another name for **termite**

whitebait (ˈwaɪtˌbeɪt) *n* **1** the young of herrings, sprats, etc, cooked and eaten whole as a delicacy **2** any of various small silvery fishes, such as *Galaxias attenuatus* of Australia and New Zealand and *Allosmerus elongatus* of North American coastal regions of the Pacific [c18: from its formerly having been used as bait]

whitebeam (ˈwaɪtˌbiːm) *n* **1** a N temperate rosaceous tree, *Sorbus aria*, having leaves with dense white hairs on the undersurface and hard timber **2** any of several similar and closely related trees

white blood cell *n* a nontechnical name for **leucocyte**

whiteboard (ˈwaɪtˌbɔːd) *n* **1** a shiny white surface that can be wiped clean after being used for writing or drawing on, used esp in teaching **2** a large screen used to project computer images to a group of people

whitecap (ˈwaɪtˌkæp) *n* a wave with a white broken crest

white cedar *n* a coniferous tree, *Chamaecyparis thyoides*, of swampy regions in North America, having scalelike leaves and boxlike cones: family *Cupressaceae*

white clover *n* a Eurasian clover plant, *Trifolium repens*, with rounded white flower heads: cultivated as a forage plant

white coal *n* water, esp when flowing and providing a potential source of usable power

white-coat hypertension *or* **syndrome** *n* the phenomenon of having elevated blood pressure only during a medical consultation

white-collar *adj* of, relating to, or designating nonmanual and usually salaried workers employed in professional and clerical occupations: *white-collar union*

white currant *n* a cultivated N temperate shrub, *Ribes sativum*, having small rounded white edible berries: family *Grossulariaceae*

whitedamp (ˈwaɪtˌdæmp) *n* a mixture of poisonous gases, mainly carbon monoxide, occurring in coal mines. See also **afterdamp**

whited sepulchre (ˈwaɪtɪd) *n* a hypocrite [from Matthew 23:27]

white dwarf *n* one of a large class of small faint stars of enormous density (on average 10^8 kg/m³) with diameters only about 1 per cent that of the sun, and masses less than the Chandrasekhar limit (about 1.4 solar masses). It is thought to mark the final stage in the evolution of a sun-like star

white elephant *n* **1** a rare albino or pale grey variety of the Indian elephant, regarded as sacred in parts of S Asia **2** a possession that is unwanted by its owner **3** an elaborate venture, construction, etc, that proves useless **4** a rare or valuable possession the upkeep of which is very expensive

White Ensign *n* the ensign of the Royal Navy and the Royal Yacht Squadron, having a red cross on a white background with the Union Jack at the upper corner of the vertical edge alongside the hoist. See **Red Ensign**

white-eye *n* any songbird of the family *Zosteropidae* of Africa, Australia, New Zealand, and Asia, having a greenish plumage with a white ring around each eye

white feather *n* **1** a symbol or mark of cowardice **2 show the white feather** to act in a cowardly manner [from the belief that a white feather in a gamecock's tail was a sign of a poor fighter]

Whitefield (ˈwɪtˌfiːld) *n* **George**. 1714–70, English Methodist preacher, who separated from the Wesleys (?1741) because of his Calvinistic views

whitefish (ˈwaɪtˌfɪʃ) *n*, *pl* -**fish** *or* -**fishes** any herring-like salmonoid food fish of the genus *Coregonus* and family *Coregonidae*, typically of deep cold lakes of the N hemisphere, having large silvery scales and a small head

white fish *n* (in the British fishing industry) any edible marine fish or invertebrate in which the main reserves of fat are in the liver, excluding herring, trout, sprat, mackerel, salmon, and shellfish

white flag *n* a white flag or a piece of white cloth hoisted to signify surrender or request a truce

white flour *n* flour that consists substantially of the starchy endosperm of wheat, most of the bran and the germ having been removed by the milling process

whitefly (ˈwaɪtˌflaɪ) *n*, *pl* -**flies** any hemipterous insect of the family *Aleyrodidae*, typically having a body covered with powdery wax. Many are pests of greenhouse crops

white friar *n* a Carmelite friar, so called because of the white cloak that forms part of the habit of this order

white gold *n* any of various white lustrous hard-wearing alloys containing gold together with platinum and palladium and sometimes smaller amounts of silver, nickel, or copper: used in jewellery

white goods *pl n* **1** *marketing* large household appliances, such as refrigerators, cookers **2** household linen such as sheets, towels, tablecloths, etc

Whitehall (ˌwaɪtˈhɔːl) *n* **1** a street in London stretching from Trafalgar Square to the Houses of Parliament: site of the main government offices **2** the British Government or its central administration

white hat *n* *informal* **a** a computer hacker who is hired by an organization to undertake nonmalicious hacking work in order to discover computer-security flaws **b** (*as modifier*): *a white-hat hacker*

Whitehead (ˈwaɪtˌhɛd) *n* **Alfred North**. 1861–1947, English mathematician and philosopher, who collaborated with Bertrand Russell in writing *Principia Mathematica* (1910–13), and developed a finite philosophy of science, chiefly in *Process and Reality* (1929)

white heat *n* **1** intense heat or a very high temperature, characterized by emission of white light **2** *informal* a state of intense excitement or activity

white hope *n* *informal* a person who is expected to bring honour or glory to his group, team, etc

white horse *n* **1** the outline of a horse carved into the side of a chalk hill, usually dating to the Neolithic, Bronze, or Iron Ages, such as that at Uffington, Berkshire **2** (*usually plural*) a wave with a white broken crest

Whitehorse ('waɪt,hɔːs) *n* a town in NW Canada: capital of the Yukon Territory. Pop: 16 843 (2001)

white-hot *adj* **1** at such a high temperature that white light is emitted **2** *informal* in a state of intense emotion

White House the White House *n* **1** the official Washington residence of the president of the US **2** the US presidency

white knight *n* a champion or rescuer, esp a person or organization that rescues a company from financial difficulties, an unwelcome takeover bid, etc

white-knuckle *adj* causing or experiencing fear or anxiety: *a white-knuckle ride*

Whitelaw ('waɪt,lɔː) *n* **William** (**Stephen Ian**), 1st Viscount Whitelaw of Penrith. 1918–99, British Conservative politician; Home Secretary (1979– 83); leader of the House of Lords (1983–88)

white lead (lɛd) *n* **1** Also called: **ceruse** a white solid usually regarded as a mixture of lead carbonate and lead hydroxide; basic lead carbonate: used in paint and in making putty and ointments for the treatment of burns. Formula: $2PbCO_3.Pb(OH)_2$ **2** either of two similar white pigments based on lead sulphate or lead silicate

white leg *n* another name for **milk leg**

Whiteley ('waɪtlɪ) *n* **Brett**. 1939–1992, Australian artist, who travelled widely in Europe and Asia; his works include landscapes, nudes, and portraits

white lie *n* a minor or unimportant lie, esp one uttered in the interests of tact or politeness

white light *n* light that contains all the wavelengths of visible light at approximately equal intensities, as in sunlight or the light from white-hot solids

white list *n* **1** a list of countries considered to pose an insignificant threat to human rights, from which applications for political asylum are presumed to be unfounded **2** *computing* a list of websites considered to have inoffensive and acceptable content

white-livered *adj* **1** lacking in spirit or courage **2** pallid and unhealthy in appearance

White man's burden *n* the supposed duty of the White race to bring education and Western culture to the non-White inhabitants of their colonies

white matter *n* the whitish tissue of the brain and spinal cord, consisting mainly of myelinated nerve fibres

white meat *n* any meat that is light in colour, such as veal or the breast of turkey

white metal *n* any of various alloys, such as Babbitt metal, used for bearings

white meter *n* *Brit obsolete* an electricity meter used to record the consumption of off-peak electricity

White Mountains *pl n* **1** a mountain range in the US, chiefly in N New Hampshire: part of the Appalachians. Highest peak: Mount Washington, 1917 m (6288 ft) **2** a mountain range in the US, in E California and SW Nevada. Highest peak: White Mountain, 4342 m (14 246 ft)

whiten ('waɪt³n) *vb* to make or become white or whiter; bleach > 'whitening *n*

whitener ('waɪt³nə) *n* a powdered substitute for milk or cream, used in coffee or tea

White Nile *n* See **Nile**

white noise *n* **a** sound or electrical noise that has a relatively wide continuous range of frequencies of uniform intensity **b** noise containing all frequencies rising in level by six decibels every octave

white oak *n* a large oak tree, *Quercus alba*, of E North America, having pale bark, leaves with rounded lobes, and heavy light-coloured wood

white out *vb* (*adverb*) **1** (*intr*) to lose or lack daylight visibility owing to snow or fog **2** (*tr*) to create or leave white spaces in (printed or other matter) **3** (*tr*) to delete (typewritten words or characters) with a white correcting fluid ▷ *n* **whiteout 4** an atmospheric condition consisting of loss of visibility and sense of distance and direction due to a uniform whiteness of a

heavy cloud cover and snow-covered ground, which reflects almost all the light it receives

white paper *n* (*often capitals*) an official government report in any of a number of countries, including Britain, Australia, New Zealand, and Canada, which sets out the government's policy on a matter that is or will come before Parliament

white pepper *n* a condiment, less pungent than black pepper, made from the husked dried beans of the pepper plant *Piper nigrum*, used either whole or ground

white pine *n* a North American coniferous tree, *Pinus strobus*, having blue-green needle-like leaves, hanging brown cones, and rough bark: family *Pinaceae*

white poplar *n* **1** Also called: **abele** a Eurasian salicaceous tree, *Populus alba*, having leaves covered with dense silvery-white hairs **2** another name for **tulipwood** (sense 1)

white rose *n* *English history* a widely used emblem or badge of the House of York. See also **Wars of the Roses, red rose**

White Russia *n* another name for **Belarus** > White Russian *adj, n*

whites (waɪts) *pl n* **1** household linen or cotton goods, such as sheets **2** white or off-white clothing, such as that worn for playing cricket

white sale *n* a sale of household linens at reduced prices

white sauce *n* a thick sauce made from flour, butter, seasonings, and milk or stock

White Sea *n* an almost landlocked inlet of the Barents Sea on the coast of NW Russia. Area: 90 000 sq km (34 700 sq miles)

white settler *n* a well-off incomer to a district who takes advantage of what it has to offer without regard to the local inhabitants [c20: from earlier colonial sense]

white slave *n* a girl or woman forced or sold into prostitution > white slavery *n*

white spirit *n* a colourless liquid obtained from petroleum and used as a substitute for turpentine

white spruce *n* a N North American spruce tree, *Picea glauca*, having grey bark, pale brown oblong cones, and bluish-green needle-like leaves

white squall *n* a violent highly localized weather disturbance at sea, in which the surface of the water is whipped to a white spray by the winds

whitethorn ('waɪt,θɔːn) *n* another name for **hawthorn**

whitethroat ('waɪt,θrəʊt) *n* either of two Old World warblers, *Sylvia communis* or *S. curruca* (**lesser whitethroat**), having a greyish-brown plumage with a white throat and underparts

white tie *n* **1** a white bow tie worn as part of a man's formal evening dress **2 a** a formal evening dress for men **b** (*as modifier*): *a white-tie occasion*

white toast *n* *Canadian* toasted white bread

white trash *n* *disparaging* **a** poor White people living in the US, esp the South **b** (*as modifier*): *white-trash culture*

White Van Man *n* *informal, derogatory* a male van driver, often of a white van, whose driving is selfish and aggressive

White Volta *n* a river in W Africa, rising in N Burkina Faso flowing southwest and south to join the Black Volta in central Ghana and form the Volta River. Length: about 885 km (550 miles)

whitewall ('waɪt,wɔːl) *n* a pneumatic tyre having white sidewalls

whitewash ('waɪt,wɒʃ) *n* **1** a substance used for whitening walls and other surfaces, consisting of a suspension of lime or whiting in water, often with other substances, such as size, added **2** *informal* deceptive or specious words or actions intended to conceal defects, gloss over failings, etc **3** *informal* a defeat in a sporting contest in which the loser is beaten in every match, game, etc in a series: *they face the prospect of a whitewash in the five-test series* ▷ *vb* (*tr*) **4** to cover or whiten with whitewash **5** *informal* to conceal, gloss over, or suppress **6** *informal* to defeat (an opponent or opposing team) by winning every match in a series

white water *n* **1** a stretch of water with a broken foamy surface, as in rapids **2** light-coloured sea water, esp over shoals or shallows

W

whitewater rafting *n* the sport of rafting down fast-flowing rivers, esp over rapids

white whale *n* a small white toothed whale, *Delphinapterus leucas*, of northern waters: family Monodontidae. Also called: **beluga**

whitewood ('waɪt,wʊd) *n* **1** any of various trees with light-coloured wood, such as the tulip tree, basswood, and cottonwood **2** the wood of any of these trees **3** Also called: **whiteywood**

whitey *or* **whity** ('waɪtɪ) *n chiefly US* (used contemptuously by Black people) a White man

Whitgift ('wɪt,gɪft) *n* **John.** ?1530–1604, English churchman; as archbishop of Canterbury (1583–1604) he tried to curb the influence of Puritanism

whither ('wɪðə) *archaic or poetic ▷ adv* **1** to what place? **2** to what end or purpose? ▷ *conj* **3** to whatever place, purpose, etc [Old English *hwider, hwæder*; related to Gothic *hvadrē*; modern English form influenced by HITHER]

whithersoever (,wɪðəsəʊˈɛvə) *adv, conj archaic or poetic* to whichever place

whiting¹ ('waɪtɪŋ) *n* **1** an important gadoid food fish, *Merlangius* (or *Gadus*) *merlangus*, of European seas, having a dark back with silvery sides and underparts **2** any of various similar fishes, such as *Merluccius bilinearis*, a hake of American Atlantic waters, and any of several Atlantic sciaenid fishes of the genus *Menticirrhus* **3** *Austral* any of several marine food fishes of the genus *Sillago* **4** whiting pout another name for **bib** (sense 3) [C15: perhaps from Old English *hwītling*; related to Middle Dutch *wijting*. See WHITE, -ING³]

whiting² ('waɪtɪŋ) *n* white chalk that has been ground and washed, used in making whitewash, metal polish, etc. Also called: **whitening**

Whitlam ('wɪtləm) *n* (**Edward**) **Gough** (gɒf). born 1916, Australian Labor statesman: prime minister (1972–75)

Whitley Bay ('wɪtlɪ) *n* a resort in NE England, in North Tyneside unitary authority, Tyne and Wear, on the North Sea. Pop: 36 544 (2001)

whitlow ('wɪtləʊ) *n* any pussy inflammation of the end of a finger or toe [C14: changed from *whitflaw*, from WHITE + FLAW¹]

Whitman ('wɪtmən) *n* **Walt(er)**. 1819–92, US poet, whose life's work is collected in *Leaves of Grass* (1855 and subsequent enlarged editions). His poems celebrate existence and the multiple elements that make up a democratic society

Whitney¹ ('wɪtnɪ) *n* **Mount Whitney** a mountain in E California: the highest peak in the Sierra Nevada Mountains and in continental US (excluding Alaska). Height: 4418 m (14 495 ft)

Whitney² ('wɪtnɪ) *n* **1 Eli.** 1765–1825, US inventor of a mechanical cotton gin (1793) and pioneer manufacturer of interchangeable parts **2 William Dwight.** 1827–94, US philologist, noted esp for his *Sanskrit Grammar* (1879)

Whitsun ('wɪtsʰn) *n* **1** short for **Whitsuntide** ▷ *adj* **2** of or relating to Whit Sunday or Whitsuntide

Whitsunday (,hwɪtˈsʌndɪ, ,wɪt-) *n* (in Scotland) May 15, one of the four quarter days

Whit Sunday *n* the seventh Sunday after Easter, observed as a feast in commemoration of the descent of the Holy Spirit on the apostles 50 days after Easter. Also called: **Pentecost** [Old English *hwīta sunnandæg* white Sunday, probably named after the ancient custom of wearing white robes at or after baptism]

Whitsuntide ('wɪtsʰn,taɪd) *n* the week that begins with Whit Sunday, esp the first three days

Whittier ('wɪtɪə) *n* **John Greenleaf.** 1807–92, US poet and humanitarian: a leading campaigner in the antislavery movement. His poems include *Moll Pitcher* (1832) and *Snow-Bound* (1866)

Whittington ('wɪtɪŋtən) *n* **Richard,** known as **Dick.** died 1423, English merchant, three times mayor of London. According to legend, he walked to London at the age of 13 with his cat and was prevented from leaving again only by the call of the church bells

whittle ('wɪtʰl) *vb* **1** to cut or shave strips or pieces from (wood, a stick, etc), esp with a knife **2** (*tr*) to make or shape by paring or shaving **3** (*tr*; often foll by *away, down, off*, etc) to reduce, destroy, or wear away gradually **4** *Northern English dialect* (*intr*) to complain or worry about something continually ▷ *n* **5** *Brit dialect* a knife, esp a large one [C16: variant of C15 *thwittle* large knife, from Old English *thwitel*, from *thwītan* to cut; related to Old Norse *thveitr* cut, *thveita* to beat] > 'whittler *n*

Whittle ('wɪtʰl) *n* **Sir Frank.** 1907–96, English engineer, who invented the jet engine for aircraft; flew first British jet aircraft (1941)

whity ('waɪtɪ) *n, pl* **whities 1** *informal* a variant spelling of **whitey** ▷ *adj* **2 a** whitish in colour **b** (*in combination*): *whity-brown*

whizz *or* **whiz** (wɪz) *vb* **whizzes, whizzing, whizzed 1** to make or cause to make a loud humming or buzzing sound **2** to move or cause to move with such a sound **3** (*intr*) *informal* to move or go rapidly ▷ *n* **4** a loud humming or buzzing sound **5** *informal* a person who is extremely skilful at some activity **6** a slang word for **amphetamine 7** take a whizz *US informal* to urinate [C16: of imitative origin]

whizz-bang *or* **whiz-bang** *n* **1** a small-calibre World War I shell that, when discharged, travelled at such a high velocity that the sound of its flight was heard only an instant, if at all, before the sound of its explosion **2** a type of firework that jumps around emitting a whizzing sound and occasional bangs ▷ *adj* **3** *informal* excellent or first-rate

whizz kid, whiz kid *or* **wiz kid** *n informal* a person who is outstandingly successful for his or her age [C20: from WHIZZ, perhaps influenced by WIZARD]

whizzy ('wɪzɪ) *adj* **-zier, -ziest** *informal* using sophisticated technology to produce vivid effects: *a whizzy new computer game*

who (hu:) *pron* **1** which person? what person? used in direct and indirect questions: *he can't remember who did it; who met you?* **2** used to introduce relative clauses with antecedents referring to human beings: *the people who lived here have left* **3** the one or ones who; whoever: *bring who you want* [Old English *hwā*; related to Old Saxon *hwē*, Old High German *hwer*, Gothic *hvas*, Lithuanian *kàs*, Danish *hvo*]

● USAGE See at **whom**

WHO *abbreviation* World Health Organization

whoa (wəʊ) *interj* a command used esp to horses to stop or slow down [C19: variant of HO¹]

who-does-what *adj* (of a dispute, strike, etc) relating to the separation of kinds of work performed by different trade unions

whodunnit *or* **whodunit** (hu:ˈdʌnɪt) *n informal* a novel, play, etc, concerned with a crime, usually murder

whoever (hu:ˈɛvə) *pron* **1** any person who; anyone that: *whoever wants it can have it* **2** no matter who: *I'll come round tomorrow, whoever may be here* **3** an intensive form of *who*, used in questions: *whoever could have thought that?* **4** *informal* an unknown or unspecified person: *give those to John, or Cathy, or whoever*

whole (həʊl) *adj* **1** containing all the component parts necessary to form a total; complete: *a whole apple* **2** constituting the full quantity, extent, etc **3** uninjured or undamaged **4** healthy **5** having no fractional or decimal part; integral: *a whole number* **6** of, relating to, or designating a relationship established by descent from the same parents; full: *whole brothers* **7** out of whole cloth *US & Canadian informal* entirely without a factual basis ▷ *adv* **8** in an undivided or unbroken piece: *to swallow a plum whole* ▷ *n* **9** all the parts, elements, etc, of a thing **10** an assemblage of parts viewed together as a unit **11** a thing complete in itself **12** as a whole considered altogether; completely **13** on the whole **a** taking all things into consideration **b** in general [Old English *hāl, hǣl*; related to Old Frisian *hāl, hēl*, Old High German *heil*, Gothic *hails*; compare HALE¹] > 'wholeness *n*

whole blood *n* blood obtained from a donor for transfusion from which none of the elements has been removed

wholefood ('həʊl,fu:d) *n* (*sometimes plural*) **a** food that has been refined or processed as little as possible and is eaten in its natural state, such as brown rice, wholemeal flour, etc **b** (*as modifier*): *a wholefood restaurant*

wholehearted (,həʊlˈhɑːtɪd) *adj* done, acted, given, etc, with total sincerity, enthusiasm, or commitment > ˌwhole'heartedly *adv* > ˌwhole'heartedness *n*

whole hog *n slang* the whole or total extent (esp in the phrase **go the whole hog**)

wholemeal ('həʊlˌmiːl) *adj Brit* (of flour, bread, etc) made from the entire wheat kernel. US and Canadian term: **whole-wheat**

whole milk *n* milk from which no constituent has been removed. See **skimmed milk**

whole note *n US & Canadian* a note, now the longest in common use, having a time value that may be divided by any power of 2 to give all other notes. Also called (in Britain and certain other countries): **semibreve**

whole number *n* 1 an integer 2 a natural number

wholesale ('həʊlˌseɪl) *n* 1 the business of selling goods to retailers in larger quantities than they are sold to final consumers but in smaller quantities than they are purchased from manufacturers. See **retail** (sense 1) 2 at wholesale **a** in large quantities **b** at wholesale prices ▷ *adj* 3 of, relating to, or engaged in such business 4 made, done, etc, on a large scale or without discrimination ▷ *adv* 5 on a large scale or without discrimination ▷ *vb* 6 to sell (goods) at wholesale > 'wholeˌsaler *n*

wholesale price index *n* an indicator of price changes in the wholesale market

wholesome ('həʊlsəm) *adj* 1 conducive to health or physical wellbeing 2 conducive to moral wellbeing 3 characteristic or suggestive of health or wellbeing, esp in appearance [c12: from WHOLE (healthy) + -SOME¹; related to German *heilsam* healing] > 'wholesomely *adv* > 'wholesomeness *n*

whole tone *or US and Canadian* **whole step** *n* an interval of two semitones; a frequency difference of 200 cents in the system of equal temperament. Often shortened to **tone**

whole-tone scale *n* either of two scales produced by commencing on one of any two notes a chromatic semitone apart and proceeding upwards or downwards in whole tones for an octave. Such a scale, consisting of six degrees to the octave, is used by Debussy and subsequent composers

whole-wheat *adj* (of flour, bread, etc) made from the entire wheat kernel. Also called (esp in Britain and certain other countries): **wholemeal**

who'll (huːl) *contraction of* who will *or* who shall

wholly ('həʊllɪ) *adv* 1 completely, totally, or entirely 2 without exception; exclusively

whom (huːm) *pron* the objective form of *who*, used when *who* is not the subject of its own clause: *whom did you say you had seen?*; *he can't remember whom he saw* [Old English *hwām*, dative of *hwā* WHO]

● **USAGE** It was formerly considered correct to use *whom*
● whenever the objective form of *who* was required. This
● is no longer thought to be necessary and the objective
● form *who* is now commonly used, even in formal
● writing: *there were several people there who he had met before.*
● *Who* cannot be used directly after a preposition – the
● preposition is usually displaced, as in *the man (who) he*
● *sold his car to.* In formal writing *whom* is preferred in
● sentences like these: *the man to whom he sold his car.*
● There are some types of sentence in which *who* cannot
● be used: *the refugees, many of whom were old and ill, were*
● *allowed across the border*

whomever (huːm'ɛvə) *pron* the objective form of *whoever*: *I'll hire whomever I can find*

whomsoever (ˌhuːmsəʊ'ɛvə) *pron archaic or formal* the objective form of *whosoever*: *to whomsoever it may concern*

whoop (wuːp) *vb* 1 to utter (speech) with loud cries, as of enthusiasm or excitement 2 *med* to cough convulsively with a crowing sound made at each inspiration 3 (of certain birds) to utter (a hooting cry) 4 (*tr*) to urge on or call with or as if with whoops 5 whoop it up (wʊp, wuːp) *informal* **a** to indulge in a noisy celebration **b** *US* to arouse enthusiasm ▷ *n* 6 a loud cry, esp one expressing enthusiasm or excitement 7 *med* the convulsive crowing sound made during a paroxysm of whooping cough 8 not worth a whoop *informal* worthless ▷ See also **whoops** [c14: of imitative origin]

whoopee *informal* ▷ *interj* (wʊ'piː) 1 an exclamation of joy, excitement, etc ▷ *n* ('wʊpiː) 2 make whoopee **a** to engage in noisy merrymaking **b** to make love

whoopee cushion *n* a joke cushion that emits a sound like the breaking of wind when someone sits on it

whooper *or* **whooper swan** ('wuːpə) *n* a large white Old World swan, *Cygnus cygnus*, having a black bill with a yellow base and a noisy whooping cry

whooping cough ('huːpɪŋ) *n* an acute infectious disease characterized by coughing spasms that end with a shrill crowing sound on inspiration: caused by infection with the bacillus *Bordetella pertussis*. Technical name: **pertussis**

whoops (wʊps) *interj* an exclamation of surprise, as when a person falls over, or of apology

whoosh *or* **woosh** (wʊʃ) *n* 1 a hissing or rushing sound ▷ *vb* 2 (*intr*) to make or move with a hissing or rushing sound

whop, wop *or less commonly* **whap** (wɒp) *informal* ▷ *vb* whops, whopping, whopped 1 (*tr*) to strike, beat, or thrash 2 (*tr*) to defeat utterly 3 (*intr*) to drop or fall ▷ *n* 4 a heavy blow or the sound made by such a blow [c14: variant of *wap*, perhaps of imitative origin]

whopper ('wɒpə) *n informal* 1 anything uncommonly large of its kind 2 a big lie [c18: from WHOP]

whopping ('wɒpɪŋ) *adj informal* uncommonly large

whore (hɔː) *n* 1 a prostitute or promiscuous woman: often a term of abuse ▷ *vb* (*intr*) 2 to be or act as a prostitute 3 (of a man) to have promiscuous sexual relations, esp with prostitutes 4 (often foll by *after*) to seek that which is immoral, idolatrous, etc [Old English *hōre*; related to Old Norse *hōra*, Old High German *hvora*, Latin *carus* dear] > 'whorish *adj* > 'whoredom *n*

whorehouse ('hɔːˌhaʊs) *n* another word for **brothel**

whoremonger ('hɔːˌmʌŋgə) *n* a person who consorts with whores; lecher

whoreson ('hɔːsən) *archaic* ▷ *n* 1 a bastard 2 a scoundrel; wretch ▷ *adj* 3 vile or hateful

Whorf (wɔːf) *n* **Benjamin Lee.** 1897–1943, US linguist, who argued that human language determines perception

whorl (wɜːl) *n* 1 *botany* a radial arrangement of three or more petals, stamens, leaves, etc, around a stem 2 *zoology* a single turn in a spiral shell 3 anything shaped like a coil [c15: probably variant of *wherville* WHIRL, influenced by Dutch *worvel*] > whorled *adj*

whortleberry ('wɜːtəlˌbɛrɪ) *n, pl* -ries 1 Also called: huckleberry, (*dialect*) hurt, whort a small Eurasian ericaceous shrub, *Vaccinium myrtillus*, greenish-pink flowers and edible sweet blackish berries 2 the fruit of this shrub 3 bog whortleberry a related plant, *V. uliginosum*, of mountain regions, having pink flowers and black fruits [c16: southwestern English dialect form of *hurtleberry*; of unknown origin]

who's (huːz) *contraction of* who is

whose (huːz) *determiner* 1 **a** of whom? belonging to whom? used in direct and indirect questions: *I told him whose fault it was; whose car is this?* **b** (*as pronoun*): *whose is that?* 2 of whom; belonging to whom; of which; belonging to which: used as a relative pronoun: *a house whose windows are broken* [Old English *hwæs*, genitive of *hwā* WHO and *hwæt* WHAT]

whoso ('huːsəʊ) *pron* an archaic word for **whoever**

whosoever (ˌhuːsəʊ'ɛvə) *pron* an archaic or formal word for **whoever**

who's who *n* a book or list containing the names and short biographies of famous people

why (waɪ) *adv* 1 **a** for what reason, purpose, or cause?: *why are you here?* **b** (*used in indirect questions*): *tell me why you're here* ▷ *pron* 2 for or because of which: *there is no reason why he shouldn't come* ▷ *n, pl* whys 3 (*usually plural*) the reason, purpose, or cause of something (esp in the phrase **the whys and wherefores**) ▷ *interj* 4 an introductory expression of surprise, disagreement, indignation, etc: *why, don't be silly!* [Old English *hwī*; related to Old Norse *hví*, Gothic *hveileiks* what kind of, Latin *quī*]

Whyalla (waɪ'ælə) *n* a port in S South Australia, on Spencer Gulf: iron and steel and shipbuilding industries. Pop: 21 271 (2001)

w

whydah *or* **whidah** ('wɪdə) *n* any of various predominantly black African weaverbirds of the genus *Vidua* and related genera, the males of which grow very long tail feathers in the breeding season. Also called: whydah bird, whidah bird, widow bird [C18: after the name of a town in Benin]

whydunnit *or* **whydunit** ('waɪ,dʌnɪt) *n* informal a novel, film, etc, concerned with the motives of the criminal rather than his or her identity

WI *abbreviation* **1** West Indian **2** West Indies **3** Wisconsin **4** (in Britain) Women's Institute

Wicca ('wɪkə) *n* (*sometimes not capital*) the cult or practice of witchcraft [C20: revival of Old English *wicca* witch] > 'Wiccan *n*, *adj*

Wichita ('wɪtʃɪ,tɔː) *n* a city in S Kansas, on the Arkansas River: the largest city in the state; two universities. Pop: 354 617 (2003 est)

wick¹ (wɪk) *n* **1 a** a cord or band of loosely twisted or woven fibres, as in a candle, cigarette lighter, etc, that supplies fuel to a flame by capillary action **2** get on someone's wick *Brit slang* to cause irritation to a person [Old English *weoce*; related to Old High German *wioh*, Middle Dutch *wēke* (Dutch *wiek*)]

wick² (wɪk) *n* archaic a village or hamlet [Old English *wīc*; related to -*wich* in place names, Latin *vīcus*, Greek *oîkos*]

Wick (wɪk) *n* a town in N Scotland, in Highland, at the head of **Wick Bay** (an inlet of the North Sea). Pop: 7333 (2001)

wicked ('wɪkɪd) *adj* **1 a** morally bad in principle or practice **b** (*as collective noun; preceded by the*): *the wicked* **2** mischievous or roguish, esp in a playful way: *a wicked grin* **3** causing injury or harm **4** troublesome, unpleasant, or offensive **5** *slang* very good [C13: from dialect *wick*, from Old English *wicca* sorcerer, *wicce* WITCH¹] > 'wickedly *adv* > 'wickedness *n*

wicker ('wɪkə) *n* **1** a slender flexible twig or shoot, esp of willow **2** short for **wickerwork** ▷ *adj* **3** made, consisting of, or constructed from wicker [C14: from Scandinavian; compare Swedish *viker*, Danish *viger* willow, Swedish *vika* to bend]

wickerwork ('wɪkə,wɜːk) *n* **a** a material consisting of wicker **b** (*as modifier*): *a wickerwork chair*

wicket ('wɪkɪt) *n* **1** a small door or gate, esp one that is near to or part of a larger one **2** *US* a small window or opening in a door, esp one fitted with a grating or glass pane, used as a means of communication in a ticket office, bank, etc **3** a small sluicegate, esp one in a canal lock gate or by a water wheel **4 a** *cricket* either of two constructions, placed 22 yards apart, consisting of three pointed stumps stuck parallel in the ground with two wooden bails resting on top, at which the batsman stands **b** the strip of ground between these **c** a batsman's turn at batting or the period during which two batsmen bat **d** the act or instance of a batsman being got out: *the bowler took six wickets* **5** keep wicket to act as a wicketkeeper [C18: from Old Northern French *wiket*; related to Old Norse *vikja* to move]

wicketkeeper ('wɪkɪt,kiːpə) *n* cricket the player on the fielding side positioned directly behind the wicket

wicking ('wɪkɪŋ) *adj* acting to move moisture by capillary action from the inside to the surface: *wicking fabric*

wickiup, wikiup *or* **wickyup** ('wɪkɪ,ʌp) *n* US & Canadian a crude shelter made of brushwood, mats, or grass and having an oval frame, esp of a kind used by nomadic Indians from Oklahoma and neighbouring states of the US [C19: from Sac, Fox, and Kickapoo *wikiyap*; compare WIGWAM]

Wickliffe *or* **Wiclif** ('wɪklɪf) *n* variant spellings of (John) **Wycliffe**

Wicklow ('wɪkləʊ) *n* **1** a county of E Republic of Ireland, in Leinster province on the Irish Sea: consists of a coastal strip rising inland to the **Wicklow Mountains**; mainly agricultural, with several resorts. County town: Wicklow. Pop: 114 676 (2002). Area: 2025 sq km (782 sq miles) **2** a port in E Republic of Ireland, county town of Co Wicklow. Pop: 9355 (2002)

widdershins ('wɪdə,ʃɪnz; *Scot* 'wɪdər-) *adv* chiefly Scot a variant spelling of **withershins**

wide (waɪd) *adj* **1** having a great extent from side to side **2** of vast size or scope; spacious or extensive **3 a** (*postpositive*) having a specified extent, esp from side to side: *two yards wide* **b** (*in combination*) covering or extending throughout: *nationwide* **4** distant or remote from the desired point, mark, etc: *your guess is wide of the mark* **5** (of eyes) opened fully **6** loose, full, or roomy: *wide trousers* **7** exhibiting a considerable spread, as between certain limits: *a wide variation* **8** phonetics another word for **lax** (sense 4) or **open** (sense 29) ▷ *adv* **9** over an extensive area: *to travel far and wide* **10** to the full extent: *he opened the door wide* **11** far from the desired point, mark, etc ▷ *n* **12** (in cricket) a bowled ball that is outside the batsman's reach and scores a run for the batting side **13** archaic or poetic a wide space or extent **14** to the wide completely [Old English *wīd*; related to Old Norse *vīthr*, Old High German *wīt*] > 'widely *adv* > 'wideness *n* > 'widish *adj*

wide-angle lens *n* a lens system on a camera that can cover an angle of view of 60° or more and therefore has a fairly small focal length. See also **fisheye lens**

wide-awake *adj* (**wide awake** *when postpositive*) **1** fully awake **2** keen, alert, or observant ▷ *n* **3** Also called: wide-awake hat a hat with a low crown and very wide brim

wide-body *adj* (of an aircraft) having a wide fuselage, esp wide enough to contain three rows of seats abreast

wide boy *n* Brit slang a man who is prepared to use unscrupulous methods to progress or make money

wide-eyed *adj* innocent or credulous

widen ('waɪdᵊn) *vb* to make or become wide or wider

wide-open *adj* (**wide open** *when postpositive*) **1** open to the full extent **2** (*postpositive*) exposed to attack; vulnerable **3** uncertain as to outcome **4** US informal (of a town or city) lax in the enforcement of certain laws, esp those relating to the sale and consumption of alcohol, gambling, the control of vice, etc

wide receiver *n* American football a player whose function is to catch long passes from the quarterback

widespread ('waɪd,spred) *adj* **1** extending over a wide area **2** accepted by or occurring among many people

widgeon ('wɪdʒən) *n* a variant spelling of **wigeon**

widget ('wɪdʒɪt) *n* informal any small mechanism or device, the name of which is unknown or temporarily forgotten [C20: changed from GADGET]

Widnes ('wɪdnɪs) *n* a town in NW England, in Halton unitary authority, N Cheshire, on the River Mersey: chemical industry. Pop: 55 686 (2001)

widow ('wɪdəʊ) *n* **1** a woman who has survived her husband, esp one who has not remarried **2** (*usually with a modifier*) informal a woman whose husband frequently leaves her alone while he indulges in a sport, etc: *a golf widow* **3** printing a short line at the end of a paragraph, esp one that occurs as the top line of a page or column **4** (in some card games) an additional hand or set of cards exposed on the table ▷ *vb* (*tr; usually passive*) **5** to cause to become a widow **6** to deprive of something valued or desirable [Old English *widuwe*; related to German *Witwe*, Latin *vidua* (feminine of *viduus* deprived), Sanskrit *vidhavā*] > 'widowhood *n*

widow bird *n* another name for **whydah**

widower ('wɪdəʊə) *n* a man whose wife has died and who has not remarried

widow's cruse *n* an endless or unfailing source of supply [allusion to I Kings 17:16]

widow's mite *n* a small contribution given by a person who has very little [allusion to Mark 12:43]

widow's peak *n* a V-shaped point in the hairline in the middle of the forehead [from the belief that it presaged early widowhood]

width (wɪdθ) *n* **1** the linear extent or measurement of something from side to side, usually being the shortest dimension or (for something fixed) the shortest horizontal dimension **2** the state or fact of being wide **3** a piece or section of something at its full extent from side to side: *a width of cloth* **4** the distance across a rectangular swimming bath, as opposed to its length [C17: from WIDE + -TH¹, analogous to BREADTH]

Wieland¹ ('viːlant) *n* the German name for **Wayland**

Wieland² (*German* 'viːlant) *n* **Christoph Martin** ('krɪstɔf 'martiːn). 1733–1813, German writer, noted esp for his verse epic *Oberon* (1780)

wield (wiːld) *vb* (*tr*) **1** to handle or use (a weapon, tool, etc) **2** to exert or maintain (power or authority) **3** *obsolete* to rule [Old English *wieldan, wealdan;* related to Old Norse *valda,* Old Saxon *waldan,* German *walten,* Latin *valēre* to be strong] > **wieldable** *adj* > **wielder** *n*

wieldy ('wiːldɪ) *adj* **wieldier, wieldiest** easily handled, used, or managed

Wien¹ (viːn) *n* the German name for **Vienna**

Wien² (*German* viːn) *n* **Wilhelm** ('vɪlhɛlm). 1864–1928, German physicist, who studied black-body radiation: Nobel prize for physics 1911

wiener ('wiːnə) *or* **wienerwurst** ('wiːnə,wɜːst) *n US & Canadian* a kind of smoked beef or pork sausage, similar to a frankfurter. Also called: **weenie** ('wiːnɪ) [c20: shortened from German *Wiener Wurst* Viennese sausage]

Wiener ('wiːnə) *n* **Norbert** ('nɔːbət). 1894–1964, US mathematician, who developed the concept of cybernetics

Wiener Neustadt (*German* 'viːnər 'nɔyʃtat) *n* a city in E Austria, in Lower Austria. Pop: 37 627 (2002)

Wiener schnitzel ('viːnə 'ʃnɪtsəl) *n* a large thin escalope of veal, coated in egg and crumbs, fried, and traditionally served with a garnish [German: Viennese cutlet]

Wiesbaden (*German* 'viːsbaːdən) *n* a city in W Germany, capital of Hesse state: a spa resort since Roman times. Pop: 271 995 (2003 est)

Wiesel ('viːzəl) *n* **Elie**. born 1928, US human rights campaigner: noted esp for his documentaries of wartime atrocities against the Jews; Nobel peace prize 1986

Wiesenthal ('viːzən,taːl) *n* **Simon**. 1908–2005, Austrian investigator of Nazi war crimes. A survivor of the concentration camps, he has been active since 1945 in documenting Nazi crimes against the Jews, tracking down their perpetrators, and assisting surviving victims

wife (waɪf) *n, pl* **wives** (waɪvz) **1** a man's partner in marriage; a married woman. Related adj: **uxorial 2** an archaic or dialect word for **woman 3** take to wife to marry (a woman) [Old English *wīf;* related to Old Norse *vīf* (perhaps from *vīfathr* veiled), Old High German *wīb* (German *Weib*)] > **wifehood** *n* > **wifely** *adj*

wifey (waɪfɪ) *n* an informal word for **wife**

Wi-Fi ('waɪ,faɪ) *n computing* a system of accessing the internet from remote machines such as laptop computers that have wireless connections [c20: from *wi(reless)* fi(delity)]

wig (wɪg) *n* **1** an artificial head of hair, either human or synthetic, worn to disguise baldness, as part of a theatrical or ceremonial dress, as a disguise, or for adornment ▷ *vb* **wigs, wigging, wigged** (*tr*) **2** *Brit slang* to berate severely [c17: shortened from PERIWIG] > **wigged** *adj* > **wigless** *adj*

Wig. *abbreviation* Wigtownshire

Wigan ('wɪgən) *n* **1** an industrial town in NW England, in Wigan unitary authority, Greater Manchester: former coal-mining centre. Pop: 81 203 (2001) **2** a unitary authority in NW England, in Greater Manchester. Pop: 303 800 (2003 est). Area: 199 sq km (77 sq miles)

wigeon *or* **widgeon** ('wɪdʒən) *n* **1** a Eurasian duck, *Anas penelope,* of marshes, swamps, etc, the male of which has a reddish-brown head and chest and grey and white back and wings **2** American wigeon Also called: **baldpate** a similar bird, *Anas americana,* of North America, the male of which has a white crown [c16: of uncertain origin]

wigging ('wɪgɪŋ) *n Brit slang* a rebuke or reprimand

wiggle ('wɪgªl) *vb* **1** to move or cause to move with jerky movements, esp from side to side ▷ *n* **2** the act or an instance of wiggling [c13: from Middle Low German, Middle Dutch *wiggelen*] > **wiggler** *n* > **wiggly** *adj*

wight (waɪt) *n archaic* a human being [Old English *wiht;* related to Old Frisian *āwet* something, Old Norse *vættr* being, Gothic *waihts* thing, German *Wicht* small person]

Wight (waɪt) *n* Isle of Wight an island and county of S England in the English Channel. Administrative centre: Newport. Pop: 136 300 (2003 est). Area: 380 sq km (147 sq miles)

Wigner ('wɪgnə) *n* **Eugene Paul**. 1902–95, US physicist, born in Hungary. He is noted for his contributions to nuclear physics: shared the Nobel prize for physics 1963

Wigtownshire ('wɪgtən,ʃɪə, -,ʃə) *n* (until 1975) a county of SW Scotland, now part of Dumfries and Galloway

wigwag ('wɪg,wæg) *vb* **-wags, -wagging, -wagged 1** to move (something) back and forth ▷ *n* **3 a** a system of communication by flag semaphore **b** the message signalled [c16: from obsolete *wig,* probably short for WIGGLE + WAG¹] > **wig,wagger** *n*

wigwam ('wɪg,wæm) *n* **1** any dwelling of the North American Indians, esp one made of bark, rushes, or skins spread over or enclosed by a set of arched poles lashed together **2** a similar structure for children [from Abnaki and Massachuset *wīkwām,* literally: their abode]

wiki ('wɪkɪ) *n* **a** a web application that allows anyone visiting a website to edit content on it **b** (*as modifier*): *wiki technology* [c20: from Hawaiian *wiki-wiki* quick, coined by Ward Cunningham (born 1949), US computer programmer who invented the concept]

Wilberforce ('wɪlbə,fɔːs) *n* **1** **Samuel**. 1805–73, British Anglican churchman; bishop of Oxford (1845–69) and Winchester (1869–73) **2** his father, **William**. 1759–1833, British politician and philanthropist, whose efforts secured the abolition of the slave trade (1807) and of slavery (1833) in the British Empire

wilco ('wɪl,kəʊ) *interj* an expression in signalling, telecommunications, etc, indicating that a message just received will be complied with [c20: abbreviation for *I will comply*]

wild (waɪld) *adj* **1** (of animals) living independently of man; not domesticated or tame **2** (of plants) growing in a natural state; not cultivated **3** uninhabited or uncultivated; desolate: *a wild stretch of land* **4** living in a savage or uncivilized way: *wild tribes* **5** lacking restraint: *wild merriment* **6** of great violence or intensity: *a wild storm* **7** disorderly or chaotic: *wild thoughts; wild talk* **8** dishevelled; untidy: *wild hair* **9** in a state of extreme emotional intensity: *wild with anger* **10** reckless: *wild speculations* **11** not calculated; random: *a wild guess* **12** unconventional; fantastic; crazy: *wild friends* **13** (*postpositive;* foll by *about*) *informal* intensely enthusiastic or excited **14** (of a card, such as a joker or deuce in some games) able to be given any value the holder pleases **15** wild and woolly **a** rough; untamed; barbarous **b** (of theories, plans, etc) not fully thought out ▷ *adv* **16** in a wild manner **17** run wild **a** to grow without cultivation or care **b** to behave without restraint ▷ *n* **18** (*often plural*) a desolate, uncultivated, or uninhabited region **19** the wild **a** a free natural state of living **b** the wilderness [Old English *wilde;* related to Old Saxon, Old High German *wildi,* Old Norse *villr,* Gothic *wiltheis*] > **wildish** *adj* > **wildly** *adv* > **wildness** *n*

Wild (waɪld) *n* **Jonathan**. ?1682–1725, British criminal, who organized a network of thieves, highwaymen, etc, while also working as an informer: said to have sent over a hundred men to the gallows before being hanged himself

wild boar *n* a wild pig, *Sus scrofa,* of parts of Europe and central Asia, having a pale grey to black coat, thin legs, a narrow body, and prominent tusks

wild brier *n* another name for **wild rose**

wild card *n* **1** See **wild** (sense 14) **2** *sport* a player or team that has not qualified for a competition but is allowed to take part, at the organizers' discretion, after all the regular places have been taken **3** an unpredictable element in a situation **4** *computing* a symbol that can represent any character or group of characters, as in a filename

wild carrot *n* an umbelliferous plant, *Daucus carota,* of temperate regions, having clusters of white flowers and hooked fruits

wildcat ('waɪld,kæt) *n, pl* **-cats** *or* **-cat 1** a wild European cat, *Felis silvestris,* that resembles the domestic tabby but is larger and has a bushy tail **2** any of various other

W

felines, esp of the genus *Lynx*, such as the lynx and the caracal **3** US & Canadian another name for **bobcat** **4** *informal* a savage or aggressive person **5** an exploratory drilling for petroleum or natural gas **6** (*modifier*) US & Canadian **a** of or relating to an unsound business enterprise: *wildcat stock* **b** financially or commercially unsound: *a wildcat project* ▷ *vb* -cats, -catting, -catted **7** (*intr*) to drill for petroleum or natural gas in an area having no known reserves ▷ 'wild,catting *n, adj* ▷ 'wild,catter *n*

wildcat strike *n* a strike begun by workers spontaneously or without union approval

wild cherry *n* another name for **gean** (sense 1)

wild dog *n* another name for **dingo**

Wilde (waɪld) *n* **Oscar** (Fingal O'Flahertie Wills). 1854–1900, Irish writer and wit, famous for such plays as *Lady Windermere's Fan* (1892) and *The Importance of being Earnest* (1895). *The Picture of Dorian Gray* (1891) is a macabre novel about a hedonist and *The Ballad of Reading Gaol* (1898) relates to his experiences in prison while serving a two- year sentence for homosexuality

wildebeest ('wɪldɪ,biːst, 'vɪl-) *n, pl* -beests *or* -beest another name for **gnu** [c19: from Afrikaans, literally: wild beast]

wilder ('waɪldə) *vb archaic* **1** to lead or be led astray **2** to bewilder or become bewildered [c17: of uncertain origin]

Wilder ('waɪldə) *n* **1 Billy**, real name *Samuel Wilder*. 1906–2002, US film director and screenwriter, born in Austria. His films include *Double Indemnity* (1944), *The Lost Weekend* (1945), *Sunset Boulevard* (1950), *The Seven Year Itch* (1955), *Some Like it Hot* (1959), *The Apartment* (1960), and *Buddy Buddy* (1981) **2 Thornton**. 1897–1975 US novelist and dramatist. His works include the novel *The Bridge of San Luis Rey* (1927) and the play *The Skin of Our Teeth* (1942)

wilderness ('wɪldənɪs) *n* **1 a** wild, uninhabited, and uncultivated region **2** any desolate tract or area **3** a confused mass or collection **4** a voice in the wilderness or a voice crying in the wilderness a person, group, etc, making a suggestion or plea that is ignored [Old English *wildēornes*, from *wildēor* wild beast (from WILD + *dēor* beast, DEER) + -NESS; related to Middle Dutch *wildernisse*, German *Wildernis*]

Wilderness ('wɪldənɪs) *n* the Wilderness the barren regions to the south and east of Palestine, esp those in which the Israelites wandered before entering the Promised Land and in which Christ fasted for 40 days and nights

wild-eyed *adj* **1** glaring in an angry, distracted, or wild manner **2** ill-conceived or totally impracticable

wildfire ('waɪld,faɪə) *n* **1 a** a highly flammable material, such as Greek fire, formerly used in warfare **2 a** a raging and uncontrollable fire **b** anything that is disseminated quickly (esp in the phrase **spread like wildfire**) **3** another name for **will-o'-the-wisp**

wild flower *n* **1** Also called: wildflower any flowering plant that grows in an uncultivated state **2** the flower of such a plant

wildfowl ('waɪld,faʊl) *n* **1** any bird that is hunted by man, esp any duck or similar aquatic bird **2** such birds collectively ▷ 'wild,fowler *n* ▷ 'wild,fowling *adj, n*

wild-goose chase *n* an absurd or hopeless pursuit, as of something unattainable

wilding ('waɪldɪŋ) *n* **1** an uncultivated plant, esp the crab apple, or a cultivated plant that has become wild **2** a wild animal ▷ Also called: wildling

Wilding ('waɪldɪŋ) *n* (**Frederick**) **Anthony**. 1883–1915, New Zealand tennis player; Wimbledon singles champion (1910–1913) and doubles champion (1907–08, 1910, 1913)

wildlands ('waɪld,lændz) *pl n chiefly US* wild, uncultivated, and uninhabited areas

wildlife ('waɪld,laɪf) *n* wild animals and plants collectively

wild pansy *n* Also called: heartsease, love-in-idleness, (*in the US*) Johnny-jump-up a Eurasian violaceous plant, *Viola tricolor*, having purple, yellow, and pale mauve spurred flowers

wild parsley *n* any of various uncultivated umbelliferous plants that resemble parsley

wild rice *n* another name for **Indian rice**

wild rose *n* any of numerous roses, such as the dogrose and sweetbrier, that grow wild and have flowers with only one whorl of petals

wild rubber *n* rubber obtained from uncultivated rubber trees

wild silk *n* **1** silk produced by wild silkworms **2** a fabric made from this, or from short fibres of silk designed to imitate it

wild type *n biology* the typical form of a species of organism resulting from breeding under natural conditions

Wild West *n* the western US during its settlement, esp with reference to its frontier lawlessness

wildwood ('waɪld,wʊd) *n archaic* a wood or forest growing in a natural uncultivated state

wile (waɪl) *n* **1** trickery, cunning, or craftiness **2** (*usually plural*) an artful or seductive trick or ploy ▷ *vb* **3** (*tr*) to lure, beguile, or entice [c12: from Old Norse *vel* craft; probably related to Old French *wile*, Old English *wigle* magic. See GUILE]

Wilfrid ('wɪlfrɪd) *n* **Saint**. 634–709 AD, English churchman; bishop of York (?663–?703). At the Synod of Whitby (664) he argued successfully that Celtic practices should be replaced by Roman ones in the English Church. Feast day: Oct 12

wilful *or US* **willful** ('wɪlfʊl) *adj* **1** intent on having one's own way **2** intentional: *wilful murder* ▷ 'wilfully *or US* 'willfully *adv* ▷ 'wilfulness *or US* 'willfulness *n*

Wilhelm I ('vɪlhɛlm) *n* the German name of **William I** (sense 5)

Wilhelm II *n* the German name of **William II** (sense 4)

Wilhelmina I (,wɪlə'miːnə; *Dutch* wɪlhɛl'miːnaː) *n* 1880–1962, queen of the Netherlands from 1890 until her abdication (1948) in favour of her daughter Juliana

Wilhelmshaven (*German* 'vɪlhɛlms'haːfən) *n* a port and resort in NW Germany, in Lower Saxony: founded in 1853; was the chief German North Sea naval base until 1945; a major oil port. Pop: 84 586 (2003 est)

Wilhelmstrasse (*German* 'vɪlhɛlmʃtraːsə) *n* **1** a street in the centre of Berlin, where the German foreign office and other government buildings were situated until 1945 **2** Germany's ministry of foreign affairs until 1945

Wilkes (wɪlks) *n* **1 Charles**. 1798–1877, US explorer of Antarctica **2 John**. 1727–97, English politician, who was expelled from the House of Commons and outlawed for writing scurrilous articles about the government. He became a champion of parliamentary reform

Wilkes Land *n* a region in Antarctica south of Australia, on the Indian Ocean

Wilkins ('wɪlkɪnz) *n* **1 Sir George Hubert**. 1888–1958, Australian polar explorer and aviator **2 Maurice Hugh Frederick**. 1916–2004, British biochemist, born in New Zealand. With Crick and Watson, he shared the Nobel prize 1962 for his work on the structure of DNA

Wilkinson ('wɪlkɪnsən) *n* **Jonny**. born 1979, English Rugby Union player; he scored the last-minute drop goal that won England victory in the final of the 2003 World Cup

will[1] (wɪl) *vb, past* would (takes an infinitive without *to* or an implied infinitive) **1** (esp with *you, he, she, it, they*, or a noun as subject) used as an auxiliary to make the future tense. See **shall** (sense 1) **2** used as an auxiliary to express resolution on the part of the speaker: *I will buy that ring if it's the last thing I do* **3** used as an auxiliary to indicate willingness or desire: *will you help me with this problem?* **4** used as an auxiliary to express compulsion, as in commands: *you will report your findings to me tomorrow* **5** used as an auxiliary to express capacity or ability: *this rope will support a load* **6** used as an auxiliary to express probability or expectation on the part of the speaker: *that will be Jim telephoning* **7** used as an auxiliary to express customary practice or inevitability: *boys will be boys* **8** (*with the infinitive always implied*) used as an auxiliary to express desire: usually in polite requests: *stay if you will* **9** what you will whatever you like, etc *informal* a declaration of willingness to do what is requested [Old English *willan*; related to Old Saxon *willian*, Old Norse *vilja*, Old High German *wollen*, Latin *velle* to wish, will]

● USAGE See at **shall**

will² (wɪl) n **1** the faculty of conscious and deliberate choice of action; volition. Related adjs: **voluntary, volitive 2** the act or an instance of asserting a choice **3 a** the declaration of a person's wishes regarding the disposal of his or her property after death. Related adj: **testamentary b** a revocable instrument by which such wishes are expressed **4** anything decided upon or chosen, esp by a person in authority; desire; wish **5** determined intention: *where there's a will there's a way* **6** disposition or attitude towards others: *he bears you no ill will* **7** at will at one's own desire, inclination, or choice **8** with a will heartily; energetically **9** with the best will in the world even with the best of intentions ▷ *vb* (mainly tr; often takes a clause as object or an infinitive) **10** (also intr) to exercise the faculty of volition in an attempt to accomplish (something): *he willed his wife's recovery from her illness* **11** to give (property) by will to a person, society, etc: *he willed his art collection to the nation* **12** (also intr) to order or decree: *the king wills that you shall die* **13** to choose or prefer: *wander where you will* **14** to yearn for or desire: *to will that one's friends be happy* [Old English *willa*; related to Old Norse *vili*, Old High German *willeo* (German *Wille*), Gothic *wilja*, Old Slavonic *volja*] ▷ **'willer** n

willed (wɪld) *adj* (*in combination*) having a will as specified: *weak-willed*

Willemstad (*Dutch* 'wɪləmstɑt) n the capital of the Netherlands Antilles, a port on the SW coast of Curaçao: important for refining Venezuelan oil. Pop: 137 000 (2005 est)

willet ('wɪlɪt) n a large American shore bird, *Catoptrophorus semipalmatus*, having a long stout bill, long legs, and a grey plumage with black-and-white wings: family *Scolopacidae* (sandpipers, etc), order *Charadriiformes* [short for *pill-will-willet* imitation of its cry]

willful ('wɪlfʊl) *adj* the US spelling of **wilful**

William ('wɪljəm) n **1** known as *William the Lion*. ?1143–1214, king of Scotland (1165– 1214) **2 Prince.** born 1982, first son of Prince Charles and Diana, Princess of Wales

William I n **1** known as *William the Conqueror*. ?1027–1087, duke of Normandy (1035–87) and king of England (1066–87). He claimed to have been promised the English crown by Edward the Confessor, after whose death he disputed the succession of Harold II, invading England in 1066 and defeating Harold at Hastings. The conquest of England resulted in the introduction to England of many Norman customs, esp feudalism. In 1085 he ordered the Domesday Book to be compiled **2** known as *William the Bad*. 1120–66, Norman king of Sicily (1154–66) **3** known as *William the Silent*. 1533–84, prince of Orange and count of Nassau: led the revolt of the Netherlands against Spain (1568–76) and became first stadholder of the United Provinces of the Netherlands (1579–84); assassinated **4** 1772–1843, king of the Netherlands (1815–40): abdicated in favour of his son William II **5** German name *Wilhelm I*. 1797–1888, king of Prussia (1861–88) and first emperor of Germany (1871–88)

William II n **1** known as *William Rufus*. ?1056–1100, king of England (1087–1100); the son of William the Conqueror. He was killed by an arrow while hunting in the New Forest **2** known as *William the Good*. 1154–89, last Norman king of Sicily (1166–89) **3** 1792–1849, king of the Netherlands (1840–49); son of William I **4** German name *Kaiser Wilhelm*. 1859–1941, German emperor and king of Prussia (1888–1918): asserted Germany's claim to world leadership. He was forced to abdicate at the end of World War I

William III n known as *William of Orange*. 1650–1702, stadholder of the Netherlands (1672–1702) and king of Great Britain and Ireland (1689–1702). He was invited by opponents of James II to accept the British throne (1688) and ruled jointly with his wife Mary II (James' daughter) until her death in 1694

William IV n known as the *Sailor King*. 1765–1837, king of the United Kingdom and of Hanover (1830–37), succeeding his brother George IV; the third son of George III

William of Malmesbury ('mɑːmzbəri, -bri) n ?1090–?1143, English monk and chronicler, whose *Gesta*

regum Anglorum and *Historia novella* are valuable sources for English history to 1142

Williams ('wɪljəmz) n **1 Hank,** real name *Hiram Williams*. 1923–53, US country singer and songwriter. His songs (all 1948–52) include "Jambalaya", "Your Cheatin' Heart", and "Why Don't you Love me (like you Used to Do?)" **2 John.** born 1941, Australian classical guitarist, living in Britain **3 John (Towner).** born 1932, US composer of film music; his scores include those for *Jaws* (1975), *Star Wars* (1977), *E.T.* (1982), *Schindler's List* (1993), and *Harry Potter and the Philosopher's Stone* (2001) **4 Ralph Vaughan.** See (Ralph) **Vaughan Williams 5 Raymond (Henry).** 1921–88, British literary critic and novelist, noted esp for such works as *Culture and Society* (1958) and *The Long Revolution* (1961), which offer a socialist analysis of the relationship between society and culture **6 Robbie,** full name *Robert Peter Williams*. born 1974, British pop singer and songwriter. A member of Take That (1990–95), he later found success with "Angels" (1997) and the albums *Life Thru a Lens* (1997), *Swing When You're Winning* (2001), and *Escapology* (2002) **7 Robin (McLaurim).** born 1951, US film actor and comedian; films include *Good Morning, Vietnam* (1987), *Dead Poets' Society* (1989), *Mrs Doubtfire* (1993), and *Insomnia* (2002) **8 Rowan (Douglas).** born 1950, Archbishop of Canterbury from 2002; formerly Archbishop of Wales (2000–02) **9 Serena.** born 1981, US tennis player: Wimbledon champion 2002–03; US champion 1999, 2002 **10 Tennessee,** real name *Thomas Lanier Williams*. 1911–83, US dramatist. His plays include *The Glass Menagerie* (1944), *A Streetcar Named Desire* (1947), *Cat on a Hot Tin Roof* (1955), and *Night of the Iguana* (1961) **11 Venus.** born 1980, US tennis player, sister of Serena Williams: Wimbledon champion 2000, 2001, 2005, 2007; US champion 2000–01 **12 William Carlos** ('kɑːləs). 1883–1963, US poet, who formulated the poetic concept "no ideas but in things". His works include *Paterson* (1946–58), which explores the daily life of a man living in a modern city, and the prose work *In the American Grain* (1925)

Williamsburg ('wɪljəmz,bɜːg) n a city in SE Virginia: the capital of Virginia (1693–1779); the restoration of large sections of the colonial city was begun in 1926. Pop: 11 605 (2003 est)

Williamson ('wɪljəmsən) n **1 David.** born 1942, Australian dramatist. His plays include *Don's Party* (1971), *Emerald City* (1987) and *Brilliant Lies* (1993) **2 Henry.** 1895–1977, British novelist, best known for *Tarka the Otter* (1927) and other animal stories **3 Malcolm.** 1931–2003, Australian composer, living in Britain: Master of the Queen's Music since 1975. His works include operas and music for children

Williams syndrome n *pathol* an abnormality in the genes involved in calcium metabolism, resulting in mental retardation [C20: after J.C.P. *Williams* (born 1900), New Zealand cardiologist]

William the Conqueror n See **William I** (sense 1)

willies ('wɪlɪz) pl n the *slang* nervousness, jitters, or fright (esp in the phrase **give** (or **get**) **the willies**) [C20: of unknown origin]

willing ('wɪlɪŋ) *adj* **1** favourably disposed or inclined; ready **2** cheerfully or eagerly compliant **3** done, given, accepted, etc, freely or voluntarily ▷ **'willingly** *adv* ▷ **'willingness** n

Willis ('wɪlɪs) n **1 Norman (David).** born 1933, British trade union leader; general secretary of the Trades Union Congress (1984–93) **2 Ted.** Baron Willis of Chislehurst. 1918–92, British author. His works include the play *Hot Summer Night* (1959) and the novel *Death May Surprise Us* (1974)

williwaw ('wɪlɪ,wɔː) n *US & Canadian* **1** a sudden strong gust of cold wind blowing offshore from a mountainous coast, as in the Strait of Magellan **2** a state of great turmoil [C19: of unknown origin]

will-o'-the-wisp (,wɪləðə'wɪsp) n **1** Also called: friar's lantern, ignis fatuus, jack-o'-lantern a pale flame or phosphorescence sometimes seen over marshy ground at night. It is believed to be due to the spontaneous combustion of methane or other hydrocarbons originating from decomposing organic matter **2** a person or thing that is elusive or allures and misleads [c17: originally *Will with the wisp*, from *Will* short for *William* and *wisp* in former sense of a twist of hay or straw burning as a torch] > ,will-o'-the-'wispish *or* ,will-o'-the-'wispy

willow ('wɪləʊ) *n* **1** the whitish wood of certain of these trees **2** something made of willow wood, such as a cricket or baseball bat **3** a machine having a system of revolving spikes for opening and cleaning raw textile fibres [Old English *welig*; related to *wilige* wicker basket, Old Saxon *wilgia*, Middle High German *wilge*, Greek *helikē* willow, *helix* twisted]

willowherb ('wɪləʊ,hɜːb) *n* **1** any of various temperate and arctic onagraceous plants of the genus *Epilobium*, having narrow leaves, terminal clusters of pink, purplish, or white flowers, and willow-like feathery seeds **2** rosebay willowherb See **rosebay**

willow pattern *n* **a** a pattern incorporating a willow tree, river, bridge, and figures, typically in blue on a white ground, used on pottery and porcelain **b** (*as modifier*): *a willow-pattern plate*

Willow *n* a small town in S Alaska, about 113 km (70 miles) northwest of Anchorage: chosen as the site of the projected new state capital in 1976, a plan which never came to fruition. Pop: 1658 (2000)

willow warbler *n* an Old World warbler, *Phylloscopus trochilis*, of Eurasian woodlands

willowy ('wɪləʊɪ) *adj* **1** slender and graceful **2** flexible or pliant **3** covered or shaded with willows

willpower ('wɪl,paʊə) *n* **1** the ability to control oneself and determine one's actions **2** firmness of will

Wills (wɪlz) *n* **1 Helen Newington**, married name *Helen Wills Moody Roark*. 1905–98, US tennis player. She was Wimbledon singles champion eight times between 1927 and 1938. She also won the US title seven times and the French title four times **2 William John**. 1834–61, English explorer: Robert Burke's deputy in an expedition on which both men died after crossing Australia from north to south for the first time

willy ('wɪlɪ) *n Brit informal* a childish or jocular term for **penis**

willy-nilly (,wɪlɪ'nɪlɪ) *adv* **1** whether desired or not ▷ *adj* **2** occurring or taking place whether desired or not **3** occurring haphazardly [Old English *wile hē*, *nyle hē*, literally: will he or will he not; *nyle*, from *ne* not + *willan* to **WILL¹**]

willy wagtail *n Austral* a black-and-white flycatcher, *Rhipidura leucophrys*, having white feathers over the brows

willy-willy ('wɪlɪ'wɪlɪ) *n Austral obsolete* a tropical cyclone [from a native Australian language]

Wilmington ('wɪlmɪŋtən) *n* a port in N Delaware, on the Delaware River: industrial centre. Pop: 72 051 (2003 est)

Wilno ('viːlnɔ) *n* the Polish name for **Vilnius**

Wilson ('wɪlsən) *n* **1 Alexander**. 1766–1813, Scottish ornithologist in the US **2** Sir **Angus** (**Frank Johnstone**). 1913–91, British writer, whose works include the collection of short stories *The Wrong Set* (1949) and the novels *Anglo-Saxon Attitudes* (1956) and *No Laughing Matter* (1967) **3 Charles Thomson Rees**. 1869–1959, Scottish physicist, who invented the cloud chamber: shared the Nobel prize for physics 1927 **4 Edmund**. 1895–1972, US critic, noted esp for *Axel's Castle* (1931), a study of the symbolist movement **5** (**James**) **Harold**, Baron Wilson of Rievaulx. 1916–95, British Labour statesman; prime minister (1964–70; 1974–76) **6 Jacqueline**. born 1945, British writer for older girls; her best-selling books include *The Story of Tracey Beaker* (1991), *The Illustrated Mum* (1998), and *Girls in Tears* (2002). **7 Richard**. 1714–82, Welsh landscape painter **8** (**Thomas**) **Woodrow** ('wʊdrəʊ). 1856–1924, US Democratic statesman; 28th president of the US (1913–21). He led the US into World War I in 1917 and proposed the Fourteen Points (1918) as a basis for peace. Although he secured the formation of the League of Nations, the US Senate refused to support it: Nobel peace prize 1919 > **Wilsonian** (wɪl'səʊnɪən) *adj*

wilt¹ (wɪlt) *vb* **1** to become or cause to become limp, flaccid, or drooping: *insufficient water makes plants wilt* **2** to lose or cause to lose courage, strength, etc **3** (*tr*) to cook (a leafy vegetable) very briefly until it begins to collapse

▷ *n* **4** the act of wilting or state of becoming wilted **5** any of various plant diseases characterized by permanent wilting, usually caused by fungal parasites attacking the roots [c17: perhaps variant of *wilk* to wither, from Middle Dutch *welken*]

wilt² (wɪlt) *vb archaic or dialect* (used with the pronoun *thou* or its relative equivalent) a singular form of the present tense (indicative mood) of **will¹**

Wilton ('wɪltən) *n* a kind of carpet with a close velvet pile of cut loops [c18: named after *Wilton*, Wiltshire, noted for carpet manufacture]

Wilts (wɪlts) *abbreviation* Wiltshire

Wiltshire ('wɪltʃə, -ʃɪə) *n* a county of S England, consisting mainly of chalk uplands, with Salisbury Plain in the south and the Marlborough Downs in the north; prehistoric remains (at Stonehenge and Avebury): the geographical and ceremonial county includes Swindon unitary authority (established in 1997). Administrative centre: Trowbridge. Pop (excluding Swindon): 440 800 (2003 est). Area (excluding Swindon): 3481 sq km (1344 sq miles)

wily ('waɪlɪ) *adj* wilier, wiliest characterized by or proceeding from wiles; sly or crafty > **'wiliness** *n*

wimble ('wɪmbəl) *n* **1** any of a number of hand tools, such as a brace and bit or a gimlet, used for boring holes ▷ *vb* **2** to bore (a hole) with or as if with a wimble [c13: from Middle Dutch *wimmel* auger]

Wimbledon ('wɪmbəldən) *n* part of the Greater London borough of Merton: headquarters of the All England Lawn Tennis Club since 1877 and the site of the annual international tennis championships

wimp (wɪmp) *n informal* a feeble ineffective person [c20: of unknown origin] > **'wimpish** *or* **'wimpy** *adj*

WIMP (wɪmp) *acronym for* **1** windows, icons, menus (*or* mice), pointers: denoting a type of user-friendly screen display used on small computers **2** *physics* weakly interacting massive particle

wimple ('wɪmpəl) *n* **1** a piece of cloth draped around the head to frame the face, worn by women in the Middle Ages and still a part of the habit of some nuns ▷ *vb* **2** *rare* to ripple or cause to ripple or undulate **3** (*tr*) *archaic* to cover with or put a wimple on **4** *archaic* (esp of a veil) to lie or cause to lie in folds or pleats [Old English *wimpel*; related to Old Saxon *wimpal*, Middle Dutch *wumpel*, Middle High German *bewimpfen* to veil]

wimp out *vb* (*intr, adverb*) *informal* to fail to do or complete something through fear or lack of conviction

win (wɪn) *vb* wins, winning, won **1** (*intr*) to achieve first place in a competition **2** (*tr*) to gain or receive (a prize, first place, etc) in a competition **3** (*tr*) to succeed in or gain (something) with an effort: *we won recognition* **4** to gain victory or triumph in (a battle, argument, etc) **5** (*tr*) to earn or procure (a living, etc) by work **6** (when *intr*, foll by *out, through*, etc) to reach with difficulty (a desired condition or position) or become free, loose, etc, with effort: *the boat won the shore; the boat won through to the shore* **7** (*tr*) to gain (the sympathy, loyalty, etc) of someone **8** (*tr*) to obtain (a woman, etc) in marriage **9** (*tr*) **a** to extract (ore, coal, etc) from a mine **b** to extract (metal or other minerals) from ore **c** to discover and make (a mineral deposit) accessible for mining **10 you can't win** *informal* an expression of resignation after an unsuccessful attempt to overcome difficulties ▷ *n* **11** *informal* a success, victory, or triumph **12** profit; winnings **13** the act or fact of reaching the finishing line or post first [Old English *winnan*; related to Old Norse *vinna*, German *gewinnen*] > **'winnable** *adj*

wince¹ (wɪns) *vb* **1** (*intr*) to start slightly, as with sudden pain; flinch ▷ *n* **2** the act of wincing [c13 (earlier: c13 meaning: to kick): via Old French *wencier, guenchir* to avoid, from Germanic; compare Old Saxon *wenkian*, Old High German *wenken*] > **'wincer** *n*

wince² (wɪns) *n* a roller for transferring pieces of cloth between dyeing vats [c17: variant of **WINCH**]

winceyette (,wɪnsɪ'ɛt) *n Brit* a plain-weave cotton fabric with slightly raised two-sided nap

winch¹ (wɪntʃ) *n* **1** a windlass driven by a hand- or power-operated crank **2** a hand- or power-operated crank by which a machine is driven ▷ *vb* **3** (*tr*; often foll by *up* or *in*) to pull (in a rope) or lift (a weight) using a winch [Old English *wince* pulley; related to WINK]

winch² (wɪntʃ) *vb* (intr) an obsolete word for **wince¹**

Winchester (ˈwɪntʃɪstə) *n* a city in S England, administrative centre of Hampshire: a Romano-British town; Saxon capital of Wessex; 11th-century cathedral; site of **Winchester College** (1382), English public school. Pop: 41 420 (2001)

Winchester rifle *n* *trademark* a breech-loading lever-action repeating rifle with a tubular magazine under the barrel. Often shortened to **Winchester** [C19: named after O. F. *Winchester* (1810–80), US manufacturer]

Winckelmann (German ˈvɪŋkəlman) *n* **Johann Joachim** (joˈhan ˈjoːaxɪm). 1717–68, German archaeologist and art historian; one of the founders of neoclassicism

wind¹ (wɪnd) *n* **1** a current of air, sometimes of considerable force, moving generally horizontally from areas of high pressure to areas of low pressure **2** *chiefly poetic* the direction from which a wind blows, usually a cardinal point of the compass **3** air artificially moved, as by a fan, pump, etc **4** a trend, tendency, or force: *the winds of revolution* **5** *informal* a hint; suggestion: *we got wind that you were coming* **6** something deemed insubstantial: *his talk was all wind* **7** breath, as used in respiration or talk: *you're just wasting wind* **8** (often used in sports) the power to breathe normally: *his wind is weak.* See also **second wind** **9** *music* **a** a wind instrument or wind instruments considered collectively **b** (*often plural*) the musicians who play wind instruments in an orchestra **c** (*modifier*) of, relating to, or composed of wind instruments: *a wind ensemble* **10** an informal name for **flatus** **11** the air on which the scent of an animal is carried to hounds or on which the scent of a hunter is carried to his quarry **12** between wind and water **a** the part of a vessel's hull below the water line that is exposed by rolling or by wave action **b** any point particularly susceptible to attack or injury **13** break wind to release intestinal gas through the anus **14** get the wind up *or* have the wind up *informal* to become frightened **15** have in the wind to be in the act of following (quarry) by scent **16** how the wind blows, how the wind lies, which way the wind blows *or* which way the wind lies what appears probable **17** in the wind about to happen **18** three sheets in the wind *informal* intoxicated; drunk **19** in the teeth of the wind *or* in the eye of the wind directly into the wind **20** into the wind against the wind *or* upwind **21** off the wind *nautical* away from the direction from which the wind is blowing **22** on the wind *nautical* as near as possible to the direction from which the wind is blowing **23** put the wind up *informal* to frighten or alarm **24** raise the wind *Brit informal* to obtain the necessary funds **25** sail close to the wind *or* sail near to the wind **a** to come near the limits of danger or indecency **b** to live frugally or manage one's affairs economically **26** take the wind out of someone's sails to destroy someone's advantage; disconcert or deflate ▷ *vb* (tr) **27** to cause (someone) to be short of breath: *the blow winded him* **28** to **a** to detect the scent **b** to pursue (quarry) by following its scent **29** to cause (a baby) to bring up wind after feeding by patting or rubbing on the back **30** to expose to air, as in drying, ventilating, etc [Old English *wind;* related to Old High German *wint,* Old Norse *vindr,* Gothic *winds,* Latin *ventus*] ▷ ˈwindless *adj* ▷ ˈwindlessly *adv* ▷ ˈwindlessness *n*

wind² (waɪnd) *vb* winds, winding, wound **1** (often foll by *around, about,* or *upon*) to turn or coil (string, cotton, etc) around some object or point *or* (of string, etc) to be turned etc, around some object or point: *he wound a scarf around his head* **2** (tr) to twine, cover, or wreathe by or as if by coiling, wrapping, etc; encircle: *we wound the body in a shroud* **3** (tr; often foll by *up*) to tighten the spring of (a clockwork mechanism) **4** (tr; foll by *off*) to remove by uncoiling or unwinding **5** (usually intr) to move or cause to move in a sinuous, spiral, or circular course: *the river winds through the hills* **6** (tr) to introduce indirectly or deviously: *he is winding his own opinions into the report* **7** (tr) to cause to twist or revolve: *he wound the handle* **8** (tr; usually foll by *up* or *down*) to move by cranking: *please wind up the*

window ▷ *n* **9** a single turn, bend, etc: *a wind in the river* **10** Also called: **winding** a twist in a board or plank ▷ See also **wind down, wind up** [Old English *windan;* related to Old Norse *vinda,* Old High German *wintan* (German *winden*)] ▷ ˈwindable *adj*

wind³ (waɪnd) *vb* winds, winding, winded *or* wound (tr) *poetic* to blow (a note or signal) on (a horn, bugle, etc) [C16: special use of WIND¹]

windage (ˈwɪndɪdʒ) *n* **1 a** a deflection of a projectile as a result of the effect of the wind **b** the degree of such deflection **c** the extent to which it is necessary to adjust the wind gauge of a gun sight in order to compensate for such deflection **2** the difference between a firearm's bore and the diameter of its projectile **3** *nautical* the exposed part of the hull of a vessel responsible for wind resistance **4** the retarding force upon a rotating machine resulting from the drag of the air

windbag (ˈwɪndˌbæg) *n* **1** *slang* a voluble person who has little of interest to communicate **2** the bag in a set of bagpipes, which provides a continuous flow of air to the pipes

windblown (ˈwɪndˌbləʊn) *adj* **1** blown by the wind **2** (of a woman's hair style) cut short and combed to look as though it has been dishevelled by the wind **3** (of trees, shrubs, etc) growing in a shape determined by the prevailing winds

wind-borne *adj* (esp of plant seeds or pollen) transported by wind

windbound (ˈwɪndˌbaʊnd) *adj* (of a sailing vessel) prevented from sailing by an unfavourable wind

windbreak (ˈwɪndˌbreɪk) *n* a fence, line of trees, etc, serving as a protection from the wind by breaking its force

windburn (ˈwɪndˌbɜːn) *n* irritation and redness of the skin caused by prolonged exposure to winds of high velocity

windcheater (ˈwɪndˌtʃiːtə) *n* a warm jacket, usually with a close-fitting knitted neck, cuffs, and waistband

wind chest (wɪnd) *n* a box in an organ in which air from the bellows is stored under pressure before being supplied to the pipes or reeds

wind-chill (wɪnd-) *n* **a** the serious chilling effect of wind and low temperature: it is measured on a scale that runs from hot to fatal to life and allows for varying combinations of air temperature and wind speed **b** (as *modifier*): *wind-chill factor*

wind cone (wɪnd) *n* another name for **windsock**

wind down (waɪnd) *vb* (*adverb*) **1** (tr) to lower or move down by cranking **2** (intr) (of a clock spring) to become slack **3** (intr) to diminish gradually in force or power; relax

winded (ˈwɪndɪd) *adj* **1** out of breath, as from strenuous exercise **2** (in combination) having breath or wind as specified: *broken-winded; short-winded*

winder (ˈwaɪndə) *n* **1** a person or device that winds, as an engine for hoisting the cages in a mine shaft or a device for winding the yarn in textile manufacture **2** an object, such as a bobbin, around which something is wound **3** a knob or key used to wind up a clock, watch, or similar mechanism **4** any plant that twists itself around a support **5** a step of a spiral staircase

Windermere (ˈwɪndəˌmɪə) *n* a lake in NW England, in Cumbria in the SE part of the Lake District: the largest lake in England. Length: 17 km (10.5 miles)

windfall (ˈwɪndˌfɔːl) *n* **1** a piece of unexpected good fortune, esp financial gain **2** something blown down by the wind, esp a piece of fruit

windfall tax *n* a tax levied on an organization considered to have made excessive profits, esp a privatized utility company that has exploited a monopoly

wind farm *n* a large group of wind-driven generators for electricity supply

windflower (ˈwɪndˌflaʊə) *n* any of various anemone plants, such as the wood anemone

wind gauge (wɪnd) *n* **1** a scale on a gun sight indicating the amount of deflection necessary to allow for windage **2** *music* a device for measuring the wind pressure in the bellows of an organ

W

wind harp (wɪnd) *n* a less common name for **aeolian harp**

Windhoek ('vɪnt,hʊk, 'vɪnt-) *n* the capital of Namibia, in the centre, at an altitude of 1654 m (5428 ft). Pop: 252 000 (2005 est)

windhover ('wɪnd,hɒvə) *n* Brit a dialect name for a **kestrel**

windigo ('wɪndɪ,gəʊ) *n* a variant of **wendigo**

winding ('waɪndɪŋ) *n* 1 a curving or sinuous course or movement 2 anything that has been wound or wrapped around something 3 a particular manner or style in which something has been wound 4 a curve, bend, or complete turn in wound material, a road, etc 5 (often plural) devious thoughts or behaviour: *the tortuous windings of political argumentation* 6 one or more turns of wire forming a continuous coil through which an electric current can pass, as used in transformers, generators, etc 7 another name for **wind²** (sense 10) 8 a coil of tubing in certain brass instruments, esp the French horn ▷ *adj* 9 curving; sinuous: *a winding road* ▷ '**windingly** *adv*

winding sheet *n* a sheet in which a corpse is wrapped for burial; shroud

winding-up *n* the process of finishing or closing something, esp the process of closing down a business

wind instrument (wɪnd) *n* any musical instrument sounded by the breath, such as the woodwinds and brass instruments of an orchestra

windjammer ('wɪnd,dʒæmə) *n* a large merchant sailing ship

windlass ('wɪndləs) *n* 1 a machine for raising weights by winding a rope or chain upon a barrel or drum driven by a crank, motor, etc ▷ *vb* 2 (*tr*) to raise or haul (a weight, etc) by means of a windlass [c14: from Old Norse *vindáss*, from *vinda* to **WIND²** + *ass* pole; related to Old French *guindas*, Middle Low German, Dutch *windas*]

windlestraw ('wɪndᵊl,strɔː) *n* Irish, Scot & English dialect the dried stalk of any of various grasses [Old English *windelstrēaw*, from *windel* basket, from *windan* to **WIND²** + *strēaw* **STRAW¹**]

wind machine (wɪnd) *n* a machine used, esp in the theatre, to produce wind or the sound of wind

windmill ('wɪnd,mɪl, 'wɪn,mɪl) *n* 1 a machine for grinding or pumping driven by a set of adjustable vanes or sails that are caused to turn by the force of the wind 2 the set of vanes or sails that drives such a mill 3 Also called: **whirligig** Brit a toy consisting of plastic or paper vanes attached to a stick in such a manner that they revolve like the sails of a windmill 4 an imaginary opponent or evil (esp in the phrase **tilt at** or **fight windmills**) ▷ *vb* 5 to move or cause to move like the arms of a windmill

window ('wɪndəʊ) *n* 1 a light framework, made of timber, metal, or plastic, that contains glass or glazed opening frames and is placed in a wall or roof to let in light or air or to see through. Related adj: **fenestral** 2 an opening in the wall or roof of a building that is provided to let in light or air or to see through 3 See **windowpane** 4 the display space in and directly behind a shop window: *the dress in the window* 5 any opening or structure resembling a window in function or appearance, such as the transparent area of an envelope revealing an address within 6 an opportunity to see or understand something usually unseen: *a window on the workings of Parliament* 7 a period of unbooked time in a diary, schedule, etc 8 short for **launch window, weather window** 9 physics a region of the spectrum in which a medium transmits electromagnetic radiation 10 computing an area of a VDU display that may be manipulated separately from the rest of the display area; typically different files can be displayed simultaneously in different overlapping windows 11 (modifier) of or relating to a window or windows: *a window ledge* 12 out of the window informal dispensed with; disregarded ▷ *vb* 13 (*tr*) to furnish with or as if with windows [c13: from Old Norse *vindauga*, from *vindr* **WIND¹** + *auga* **EYE¹**]

window box *n* a long narrow box, placed on or outside a windowsill, in which plants are grown

window-dresser *n* a person employed to design and build up a display in a shop window

window-dressing *n* 1 the ornamentation of shop windows, designed to attract customers 2 the pleasant, showy, or false aspect of an idea, policy, etc, which is stressed to conceal the real or unpleasant nature; façade

windowpane ('wɪndəʊ,peɪn) *n* a sheet of glass in a window

window sash *n* a glazed window frame, esp one that opens

window seat *n* 1 a seat below a window, esp in a bay window 2 a seat beside a window in a bus, train, etc

window-shop *vb* -shops, -shopping, -shopped (*intr*) to look at goods in shop windows without buying them ▷ '**window-,shopper** *n* ▷ '**window-,shopping** *n*

windowsill ('wɪndəʊ,sɪl) *n* a sill below a window

windpipe ('wɪnd,paɪp) *n* a nontechnical name for **trachea** (sense 1) Related adj: **tracheal**

Wind River Range (wɪnd) *n* a mountain range in W Wyoming: one of the highest ranges of the central Rockies. Highest peak: Gannet Peak, 4202 m (13 785 ft)

wind rose (wɪnd) *n* a diagram with radiating lines showing the frequency and strength of winds from each direction affecting a specific place

windrow ('wɪnd,rəʊ, 'wɪn,rəʊ) *n* 1 a long low ridge or line of hay or a similar crop, designed to achieve the best conditions for drying or curing 2 a line of leaves, snow, dust, etc, swept together by the wind

Windscale ('wɪnd,skeɪl) *n* the former name of **Sellafield**

windscreen ('wɪnd,skriːn) *n* Brit, Austral., NZ & South African the sheet of flat or curved glass that forms a window of a motor vehicle, esp the front window. US and Canadian name: **windshield**

windscreen wiper *n* Brit an electrically operated blade with a rubber edge that wipes a windscreen clear of rain, snow, etc. US and Canadian name: **windscreen wiper**

windshield ('wɪnd,ʃiːld) *n* US & Canadian the sheet of flat or curved glass that forms a window of a motor vehicle, esp the front window. Also called (in Britain and certain other countries): **windscreen**

windsock ('wɪnd,sɒk) *n* a truncated cone of textile mounted on a mast so that it is free to rotate about a vertical axis: used, esp at airports, to indicate the local wind direction. Also called: **air sock, drogue, wind sleeve, wind cone**

Windsor¹ ('wɪnzə) *n* 1 a town in S England, in Windsor and Maidenhead unitary authority, Berkshire, on the River Thames, linked by bridge with Eton: site of **Windsor Castle**, residence of English monarchs since its founding by William the Conqueror; **Old Windsor**, royal residence in the time of Edward the Confessor, is 3 km (2 miles) southeast. Pop: 26 747 (2001 est) 2 a city in SE Canada, in S Ontario on the Detroit River opposite Detroit: motor-vehicle manufacturing; university (1963). Pop: 208 402 (2001)

Windsor² ('wɪnzə) *n* 1 the official name of the British royal family since 1917 2 Duke of Windsor the title, from 1937, of **Edward VIII**

Windsor and Maidenhead *n* a unitary authority in S England, in Berkshire. Pop: 135 300 (2003 est). Area: 197 sq km (76 sq miles)

Windsor chair *n* a simple wooden chair, popular in England and America from the 18th century, usually having a shaped seat, splayed legs, and a back of many spindles

Windsor knot *n* a wide triangular knot, produced by making extra turns in tying a tie

windstorm ('wɪnd,stɔːm) *n* a storm consisting of violent winds

wind-sucking *n* a harmful habit of horses in which the animal arches its neck and swallows a gulp of air

windsurfing ('wɪnd,sɜːfɪŋ) *n* the sport of sailing standing up on a sailboard that is equipped with a mast, sail, and wishbone boom

windswept ('wɪnd,swɛpt) *adj* open to or swept by the wind

wind tunnel (wɪnd) *n* a chamber for testing the aerodynamic properties of aircraft, aerofoils, etc, in which a current of air can be maintained at a constant velocity

wind up (waɪnd) vb (adverb) **1** to bring to or reach a conclusion: he wound up the proceedings **2** (tr) to tighten the spring of (a clockwork mechanism) **3** (tr; usually passive) informal to make nervous, tense, etc; excite: he was all wound up before the big fight **4** (tr) to roll (thread, etc) into a ball **5** an informal word for **liquidate** (sense 2) **6** (intr) informal to end up (in a specified state): you'll wind up without any teeth **7** (tr; usually passive) to involve; entangle: they were wound up in three different scandals **8** (tr) to hoist or haul up **9** (tr) Brit slang to tease (someone) ▷ n **wind-up 10** the act of concluding **11** the finish; end **12** Brit slang an act or instance of teasing: she just thinks it's a big wind-up

windward ('wɪndwəd) chiefly nautical ▷ adj **1** of, in, or moving to the quarter from which the wind blows ▷ n **2** the windward point **3** the side towards the wind ▷ adv **4** towards the wind ▷ Compare **leeward**

Windward Islands pl n **1** a group of islands in the SE Caribbean, in the Lesser Antilles: consists of the French Overseas Department of Martinique and the independent states of Grenada, St Lucia, and St Vincent and the Grenadines **2** a group of islands in the S Pacific, in French Polynesia in the W Society Archipelago: Moorea, Maio (Tubuai Manu), and Mehetia and Tetiaroa. Pop: 184 222 (2002)

Windward Passage n a strait in the Caribbean, between E Cuba and NW Haiti. Width: 80 km (50 miles)

windy ('wɪndɪ) adj windier, windiest **1** of, characterized by, resembling, or relating to wind; stormy **2** swept by or open to powerful winds **3** marked by or given to empty, prolonged, and often boastful speech; bombastic: windy orations **4** void of substance **5** an informal word for **flatulent 6** slang afraid; frightened; nervous > 'windily adv > 'windiness n

wine (waɪn) n **1 a** an alcoholic drink produced by the fermenting of grapes with water and sugar **b** an alcoholic drink produced in this way from other fruits, flowers, etc: elderberry wine **2 a** a dark red colour, sometimes with a purplish tinge **b** (as adjective): wine-coloured **3** anything resembling wine in its intoxicating or invigorating effect **4** new wine in old bottles something new added to or imposed upon an old or established order ▷ vb **5** (intr) to drink wine **6** wine and dine to entertain or be entertained with wine and fine food [Old English wīn, from Latin vīnum; related to Greek oinos, of obscure origin] > 'wineless adj

wine bar n a bar in a restaurant, etc, or an establishment that specializes in serving wine and usually food

winebibber ('waɪnˌbɪbə) n a person who drinks a great deal of wine > 'wineˌbibbing n

wine box n wine sold in a cubic carton, usually of three-litre capacity, having a plastic lining and a tap for dispensing

wine cellar n **1** a place, such as a dark cool cellar, where wine is stored **2** the stock of wines stored there

wine cooler n **1** a bucket-like vessel containing ice in which a bottle of wine is placed to be cooled **2** the full name for **cooler** (sense 2)

wine gallon n Brit a former unit of capacity equal to 231 cubic inches

wineglass ('waɪnˌɡlɑːs) n **1** a glass drinking vessel, typically having a small bowl on a stem, with a flared foot **2** Also called: wineglassful the amount that such a glass will hold

wine grower n a person engaged in cultivating vines in order to make wine > wine growing n

Winehouse (waɪnˌhaʊs) n **Amy (Jade)**. born 1983, English rock singer and songwriter; her albums include Frank (2003) and Back to Black (2006)

wine palm n any of various palm trees, the sap of which is used, esp when fermented, as a drink. Also called: toddy palm

winepress ('waɪnˌprɛs) n any equipment used for squeezing the juice from grapes in order to make wine

winery ('waɪnərɪ) n, pl -eries chiefly US & Canadian a place where wine is made

wineskin ('waɪnˌskɪn) n the skin of a sheep or goat sewn

up and used as a holder for wine

winey or **winy** ('waɪnɪ) adj winier, winiest having the taste or qualities of wine

wing (wɪŋ) n **1** either of the modified forelimbs of a bird that are covered with large feathers and specialized for flight in most species **2** one of the organs of flight of an insect, consisting of a membranous outgrowth from the thorax containing a network of veins **3** either of the organs of flight in certain other animals, esp the forelimb of a bat **4 a** a half of the main supporting surface on an aircraft, confined to one side of it **b** the full span of the main supporting surface on both sides of an aircraft **c** an aircraft designed as one complete wing **d** a position in flight formation, just to the rear and to one side of an aircraft **5** an organ or apparatus resembling a wing **6** anything suggesting a wing in form, function, or position, such as a sail of a windmill or a ship **7** botany **a** either of the lateral petals of a sweetpea or related flower **b** any of various outgrowths of a plant part, esp the process on a wind-dispersed fruit or seed **8** a means or cause of flight or rapid motion; flight: fear gave wings to his feet **9** Brit the part of a car body that surrounds the wheels. US and Canadian name: **fender 10** sport **a** either of the two sides of the pitch near the touchline **b** a player stationed in such a position; **winger 11** a faction or group within a political party or other organization. See also **left wing, right wing 12** a part of a building that is subordinate to the main part **13** (plural) the space offstage to the right or left of the acting area in a theatre **14** in the wings ready to step in when needed **15** either of the two pieces that project forwards from the sides of some chairbacks **16** (plural) an insignia in the form of stylized wings worn by a qualified aircraft pilot **17** a tactical formation in some air forces, consisting of two or more squadrons **18** any of various flattened organs or extensions in lower animals, esp when used in locomotion **19** on a wing and a prayer with only the slightest hope of succeeding **20** on the wing **a** flying **b** travelling **21** take wing **a** to lift off or fly away **b** to depart in haste **c** to become joyful **22** under one's wing in one's care or tutelage **23** clip someone's wings **a** to restrict someone's freedom **b** to thwart someone's ambition ▷ vb (mainly tr) **24** (also intr) to make (one's way) swiftly on or as if on wings **25** to shoot or wound (a bird, person, etc) superficially, in the wing or arm, etc **26** to cause to fly or move swiftly: to wing an arrow **27** to provide with wings [c12: from Scandinavian; compare Old Norse vængir (plural), Norwegian veng] > 'wing‚like adj > winged adj > 'wingless adj

Wingate ('wɪnˌɡeɪt) n **Orde (Charles)** (ɔːd). 1903-44, British soldier. During World War II he organized the Chindits in Burma (Myanmar) to disrupt Japanese communications. He died in an air crash

wing beat n a complete cycle of moving the wing by a bird when flying

wing-case n the nontechnical name for **elytron**

wing chair n an easy chair having wings on each side of the back

wing collar n a stiff turned-up shirt collar worn with the points turned down over the tie

wing commander n an officer holding commissioned rank in certain air forces, such as the Royal Air Force: junior to a group captain and senior to a squadron leader

wing covert n any of the covert feathers of the wing of a bird, occurring in distinct rows

wingding ('wɪŋˌdɪŋ) n slang, chiefly US & Canadian **1** a noisy lively party or festivity **2** a real or pretended fit or seizure [c20: of unknown origin]

winge (wɪndʒ) vb, n Austral a variant spelling of **whinge**

winger ('wɪŋə) n sport a player stationed on the wing

wing loading n the total weight of an aircraft divided by its wing area

wingman ('wɪŋˌmæn) n, pl -men a player in the wing position in Australian Rules

wing nut n a threaded nut tightened by hand by means of two flat lugs or wings projecting from the central body. Also called: butterfly nut

wingspan ('wɪŋ,spæn) *or* **wingspread** ('wɪŋ,sprɛd) *n* the distance between the wing tips of an aircraft, bird, etc

wing tip *n* the outermost edge of a wing

wink (wɪŋk) *vb* **1** (*intr*) to close and open one eye quickly, deliberately, or in an exaggerated fashion to convey friendliness, etc **2** to close and open (an eye or the eyes) momentarily **3** (*tr*; foll by *away*, *back*, etc) to force away (tears, etc) by winking **4** (*tr*) to signal with a wink **5** (*intr*) (of a light) to gleam or flash intermittently ▷ *n* **6** a winking movement, esp one conveying a signal, etc, or such a signal **7** an interrupted flashing of light **8** a brief moment of time; instant **9** *informal* the smallest amount, esp of sleep. See also **forty winks 10** tip the wink *Brit informal* to give a hint [Old English *wincian*; related to Old Saxon *wincon*, Old High German *winchan*, German *winken* to wave. See WENCH, WINCH]

wink at *vb* (*intr*, *preposition*) to connive at; disregard: *the authorities winked at corruption*

Winkelried (German 'vɪŋkəlriːt) *n* Arnold von ('arnɔlt fɔn). died ?1386, Swiss hero of the battle of Sempach (1386) against the Austrians

winker ('wɪŋkə) *n* **1** a person or thing that winks **2** *US & Canadian slang*, *English dialect* an eye, eyelash, or eyelid **3** another name for **blinker** (sense 1)

winkle ('wɪŋk⁹l) *n* **1** See **periwinkle¹** ▷ *vb* **2** (*tr*; usually foll by *out*, *out of*, etc) *informal*, *chiefly Brit* to extract or prise out [C16: shortened from PERIWINKLE¹]

winkle-pickers *pl n* shoes or boots with very pointed narrow toes, popular in the mid-20th century

Winnebago (,wɪnɪ'beɪɡəʊ) *n* **1** Lake Winnebago a lake in E Wisconsin, fed and drained by the Fox river: the largest lake in the state. Area: 557 sq km (215 sq miles) **2** *pl* -gos *or* -go a member of a North American Indian people living in Wisconsin and Nebraska **3** the language of this people, belonging to the Siouan family

winner ('wɪnə) *n* **1** a person or thing that wins **2** *informal* a person or thing that seems sure to win or succeed

winning ('wɪnɪŋ) *adj* **1** (of a person, character, etc) charming, engaging, or attractive: *winning ways*; *a winning smile* **2** gaining victory: *the winning stroke* ▷ *n* **3** (*plural*) money, prizes, or valuables won, esp in gambling ▷ 'winningly *adv* ▷ 'winningness *n*

winning gallery *n* real tennis the gallery farthest from the net on either side of the court, into which any shot played wins a point

winning opening *n* real tennis the grille, dedans, or winning gallery, into which any shot played wins a point

winning post *n* the post marking the finishing line on a racecourse

Winnipeg ('wɪnɪ,pɛɡ) *n* **1** a city in S Canada, capital of Manitoba at the confluence of the Assiniboine and Red Rivers: University of Manitoba (1877) and University of Winnipeg (1871). Pop: 626 685 (2001) **2** Lake Winnipeg a lake in S Canada, in Manitoba: drains through the Nelson River into Hudson Bay. Area: 23 553 sq km (9094 sq miles)

Winnipeg couch *n* *Canadian* a couch with no arms or back, opening out into a double bed

Winnipegosis (,wɪnɪpə'ɡəʊsɪs) *n* Lake Winnipegosis a lake in S Canada, in W Manitoba. Area: 5400 sq km (2086 sq miles)

winnow ('wɪnəʊ) *vb* **1** to separate (grain) from (chaff) by means of a wind or current of air **2** (*tr*) to examine in order to select the desirable elements **3** (*tr*) *rare* to blow upon; fan ▷ *n* **4 a** a device for winnowing **b** the act or process of winnowing [Old English *windwian*; related to Old High German *wintōn*, Gothic *diswinthjan*, Latin *ventilāre*. See WIND¹]

win over *vb* (*tr*, *adverb*) to gain the support or consent of (someone). Also called: **win round**

wino ('waɪnəʊ) *n*, *pl* -os *informal* a person who habitually drinks wine as a means of getting drunk

Winslet ('wɪnzlət) *n* Kate. born 1975, British film actress; her films include *Sense and Sensibility* (1995), *Titanic* (1997), *Iris* (2001), and *Little Children* (2006)

winsome ('wɪnsəm) *adj* charming; winning; engaging: *a winsome smile* [Old English *wynsum*, from *wynn* joy

(related to Old High German *wunnia*, German *Wonne*) + -*sum* -SOME¹] ▷ 'winsomely *adv*

Winstanley ('wɪnstənlɪ, wɪn'stænlɪ) *n* Gerrard. ?1609–60, English radical; leader of the Diggers (1649–50) and author of the pamphlet *The Law of Freedom in a Platform* (1652)

Winston ('wɪnstən) *n* Robert (Maurice Lipson, Baron. born 1940, British obstetrician and gynaecologist, noted for his work on human infertility treatment; also a well-known broadcaster

Winston-Salem ('wɪnstən'seɪləm) *n* a city in N central North Carolina: formed in 1913 by the uniting of Salem and Winston; a major tobacco manufacturing centre. Pop: 190 299 (2003 est)

winter ('wɪntə) *n* **1 a** (*sometimes capital*) the coldest season of the year, between autumn and spring, astronomically from the December solstice to the March equinox in the N hemisphere and at the opposite time of year in the S hemisphere **b** (*as modifier*): *winter pasture* **2** the period of cold weather associated with the winter **3** a time of decline, decay, etc **4** *chiefly poetic* a year represented by this season: *a man of 72 winters*. Related adjs: **hibernal** ▷ *vb* **5** (*intr*) to spend the winter in a specified place **6** to keep or feed (farm animals, etc) during the winter or (of farm animals) to be kept or fed during the winter [Old English; related to Old Saxon, Old High German *wintar*, Old Norse *vetr*, Gothic *wintrus*] ▷ 'winterer *n* ▷ 'winterish *or* 'winter-,like *adj* ▷ 'winterless *adj*

winter aconite *n* a small Old World ranunculaceous herbaceous plant, *Eranthis hyemalis*, cultivated for its yellow flowers, which appear early in spring

winter cherry *n* **1** a Eurasian solanaceous plant, *Physalis alkekengi*, cultivated for its ornamental inflated papery orange-red calyx **2** the calyx of this plant. ▷ See also **Chinese lantern**

winter garden *n* **1** a garden of evergreen plants and plants that flower in winter **2** a conservatory in which flowers are grown in winter

wintergreen ('wɪntə,griːn) *n* **1** Also called: **boxberry, checkerberry, teaberry, spiceberry, partridgeberry** any of several evergreen ericaceous shrubs of the genus *Gaultheria*, esp *G. procumbens*, of E North America, which has white bell-shaped flowers and edible red berries **2** oil of wintergreen an aromatic compound, formerly made from this and various other plants but now synthesized: used medicinally and for flavouring **3** any of various plants of the genus *Pyrola*, such as *P. minor* (**common wintergreen**), of temperate and arctic regions, having rounded leaves and small pink globose flowers: family *Pyrolaceae* **4** any of several plants of the genera *Orthilia* and *Moneses*: family *Pyrolaceae* **5** chickweed wintergreen a primulaceous plant, *Trientalis europaea*, of N Europe and N Asia, having white flowers and leaves arranged in a whorl [C16: from Dutch *wintergroen* or German *Wintergrün*; see WINTER, GREEN]

winterize *or* **winterise** ('wɪntə,raɪz) *vb* (*tr*) *US & Canadian* to prepare (a house, car, etc) to withstand winter conditions ▷ ,winteri'zation *or* ,winteri'sation *n*

winter jasmine *n* a jasmine shrub, *Jasminum nudiflorum*, widely cultivated for its winter-blooming yellow flowers

winter solstice *n* the time at which the sun is at its southernmost point in the sky (northernmost point in the S hemisphere) appearing at noon at its lowest altitude above the horizon. It occurs about December 22 (June 21 in the S hemisphere)

winter sports *pl n* sports held in the open air on snow or ice, esp skiing

Winterthur (German 'vɪntərtuːr) *n* an industrial town in NE central Switzerland, in Zürich canton: has the largest technical college in the country. Pop: 90 483 (2000)

wintertime ('wɪntə,taɪm) *n* the winter season. Also (*archaic*): wintertide

winterweight ('wɪntə,weɪt) *adj* (of clothes) suitable in weight for wear in the winter; relatively heavy

winter wheat *n* a type of wheat that is planted in the autumn and is harvested the following summer

Winthrop ('wɪnθrɒp) *n* **1** John. 1588–1649, English lawyer and colonist, first governor of the Massachusetts

w

Bay colony: the leading figure among the Puritan settlers of New England **2** his son, **John.** 1606–76, English lawyer and colonist; a founder of Agawan (now Ipswich), Massachusetts; governor of Connecticut

Winton ('wɪntən) *n* Tim, full name *Timothy John Winton.* born 1960. Australian writer. His novels include *Cloudstreet* (1992), *The Riders* (1995) and *Dirt Music* (2002)

wintry ('wɪntrɪ) *or* **wintery** ('wɪntərɪ, -trɪ) *adj* -**trier**, -**triest 1** (esp of weather) of or characteristic of winter **2** lacking cheer or warmth; bleak > 'wintrily *adv* > 'wintriness, 'winteriness *or less commonly* 'winterliness *n*

win-win *adj* guaranteeing a favourable outcome for everyone involved: *a win-win situation for NATO* [C20: modelled on NO-WIN]

winy ('waɪnɪ) *adj* winier, winiest a variant spelling of **winey**

wipe (waɪp) *vb* (*tr*) **1** to rub (a surface or object) lightly, esp with (a cloth, hand, etc), as in removing dust, water, grime, etc **2** (usually foll by *off, away, from, up,* etc) to remove by or as if by rubbing lightly: *he wiped the dirt from his hands* **3** to eradicate or cancel (a thought, memory, etc) **4** to erase a recording from (an audio or video tape) **5** *Austral informal* to abandon or reject (a person) **6** to apply (oil, grease, etc) by wiping **7** to form (a joint between two lead pipes) with solder or soft lead **8** wipe the floor with someone *informal* to defeat someone decisively > *n* **9** the act or an instance of wiping **10** *dialect* a sweeping blow or stroke **11** *Brit dialect* a gibe or jeer [Old English *wīpian*, related to Middle Low German *wipen*, *wīp* bundle (of cloth), Old High German *wiffa*, *wīfan* to wind, Gothic *weipan* to wreathe]

wipe out *vb* (*adverb*) **1** (*tr*) to destroy completely; eradicate **2** (*tr*) *informal* to murder or kill **3** (*intr*) to fall or jump off a surfboard or skateboard > *n* **wipeout 4** an act or instance of wiping out **5** the interference of one radio signal by another so that reception is impossible

wiper ('waɪpə) *n* **1** any piece of cloth, such as a handkerchief, towel, etc, used for wiping **2** a cam rotated to ease a part and allow it to fall under its own weight, as used in stamping machines, etc **3** See **windscreen wiper 4** *electrical engineering* a movable conducting arm, esp one in a switching or selecting device, that makes contact with a row or ring of contacts

WIPO *or* **Wipo** ('waɪpəʊ) *n acronym for* World Intellectual Property Organization

wire (waɪə) *n* **1** a slender flexible strand or rod of metal **2** a cable consisting of several metal strands twisted together **3** a flexible metallic conductor, esp one made of copper, usually insulated, and used to carry electric current in a circuit **4** (*modifier*) of, relating to, or made of wire **5** anything made of wire, such as wire netting, a barbed wire fence, etc **6** a long continuous wire or cable connecting points in a telephone or telegraph system **7** *old-fashioned* **a** an informal name for **telegram**, **telegraph b** the wire an informal name for **telephone 8** a metallic string on a guitar, piano, etc **9** *horse racing chiefly US & Canadian* the finishing line on a racecourse **10** a wire-gauze screen upon which pulp is spread to form paper during the manufacturing process **11** anything resembling a wire, such as a hair **12** a snare made of wire for rabbits and similar animals **13** to the wire *or* down to the wire *informal* right up to the last moment **14** get in under the wire *informal, chiefly US & Canadian* to accomplish something with little time to spare **15** get one's wires crossed *informal* to misunderstand **16** pull wires *chiefly US & Canadian* to exert influence behind the scenes, esp through personal connections; pull strings **17** take it to the wire to compete to the bitter end to win a competition or title > *vb* (*mainly tr*) **18** (*also intr*) to send a telegram to (a person or place) **19** to send (news, a message, etc) by telegraph **20** to equip (an electrical system, circuit, or component) with wires **21** to fasten or furnish with wire **22** (often foll by *up*) to provide (an area) with fibre optic cabling to receive cable television **23** to snare with wire **24** wire in *informal* to set about (something, esp food) with enthusiasm [Old English *wīr*; related to Old High German *wiara*, Old Norse *vīra*, Latin *viriae* bracelet]

wire brush *n* a brush having wire bristles, used for cleaning metal, esp for removing rust, or for brushing against a cymbal

wire cloth *n* a mesh or netting woven from fine wire, used in window screens, strainers, etc

wired (waɪəd) *adj informal* **1** edgy from stimulant intake **2** excited, nervous, or tense **3** using computers to send and receive information, esp via the internet

wiredraw ('waɪə,drɔː) *vb* -**draws**, -**drawing**, -**drew**, -**drawn** to convert (metal) into wire by drawing through successively smaller dies

wireframe ('waɪə,freɪm) *n* a visual representation of the structure of a web page

wire-gauge *n* **1** a flat plate with slots in which standard wire sizes can be measured **2** a standard system of sizes for measuring the diameters of wires

wire gauze *n* a stiff meshed fabric woven of fine wires

wire grass *n* any of various grasses, such as Bermuda grass, that have tough wiry roots or rhizomes

wire-guided *adj* (of a missile) controlled by signals transmitted through fine wires uncoiled during the missile's flight

wire-haired *adj* (of an animal) having a rough wiry coat

wireless ('waɪəlɪs) *adj* **1** communicating without connecting wires or other material contacts: *wireless networks; wireless internet connection* > *n* **2** *chiefly Brit old-fashioned* another word for **radio**

wireless application protocol *n* a global application that enables mobile phone users to access the internet and other information services. Usually abbreviated to: WAP

wireless telegraphy *n* another name for **radiotelegraphy**

wireless telephone *n* another name for **radiotelephone** > **wireless telephony** *n*

wire netting *n* a net made of wire, often galvanized, that is used for fencing, as a light reinforcement, etc

wirepuller ('waɪə,pʊlə) *n chiefly US & Canadian* a person who uses private or secret influence for his own ends > 'wire,pulling *n*

wire recorder *n* an early type of magnetic recorder in which sounds were recorded on a thin steel wire magnetized by an electromagnet > wire recording *n*

wire service *n chiefly US & Canadian* an agency supplying news, etc, to newspapers, radio and television stations, etc

wiretap ('waɪə,tæp) *vb* -**taps**, -**tapping**, -**tapped** to make a connection to a telegraph or telephone wire in order to obtain information secretly > 'wire,tapper *n* > 'wire,tapping *n*

wire wheel *n* a wheel in which the rim is held to the hub by wire spokes, esp one used on a sports car

wire wool *n* a mass of fine wire used for cleaning and scouring

wirework ('waɪə,wɜːk) *n* **1** functional or decorative work made of wire **2** objects made of wire, esp netting

wireworks ('waɪə,wɜːks) *n* (*functioning as singular or plural*) a factory where wire or articles of wire are made

wireworm ('waɪə,wɜːm) *n* the wormlike larva of various elaterid beetles, which feeds on the roots of many crop plants and is a serious agricultural pest

wiring ('waɪərɪŋ) *n* **1** the network of wires used in an electrical system, device, or circuit > *adj* **2** used in wiring

Wirral ('wɪrəl) *n* **1** the Wirral a peninsula in NW England between the estuaries of the Rivers Mersey and Dee **2** a unitary authority in NW England, in Merseyside. Pop: 313 800 (2003 est). Area: 158 sq km (61 sq miles)

wiry ('waɪərɪ) *adj* wirier, wiriest **1** (of people or animals) slender but strong in constitution **2** made of or resembling wire, esp in stiffness: *wiry hair* **3** (of a sound) produced by or as if by a vibrating wire > 'wirily *adv* > 'wiriness *n*

wis (wɪs) *vb archaic* to know or suppose (something) [C17: a form derived from IWIS, mistakenly interpreted as *I wis* I know, as if from Old English *witan* to know]

Wis. *abbreviation* Wisconsin

Wisbech ('wɪzbiːtʃ) *n* a town in E England, in N Cambridgeshire: market-gardening. Pop: 26 536 (2001)

Wisconsin (wɪsˈkɒnsɪn) *n* **1** a state of the N central US, on Lake Superior and Lake Michigan: consists of an undulating plain, with uplands in the north and west; over 168 m (550 ft) above sea level along the shore of Lake Michigan. Capital: Madison. Pop: 5 472 299 (2003 est). Area: 141 061 sq km (54 464 sq miles). Abbreviation: Wis., (with zip code) WI **2** a river in central and SW Wisconsin, flowing south and west to the Mississippi. Length: 692 km (430 miles) > Wis'consin,ite *n*

Wisden (ˈwɪzdən) *n* **John.** 1826–84, English cricketer; publisher of *Wisden Cricketers' Almanack*, which first appeared in 1864

wisdom (ˈwɪzdəm) *n* **1** the ability or result of an ability to think and act utilizing knowledge, experience, understanding, common sense, and insight **2** accumulated knowledge, erudition, or enlightenment **3** *archaic* a wise saying or wise sayings or teachings ▷ Related adjective: **sagacious** [Old English *wīsdōm*; see WISE¹, -DOM]

wisdom tooth *n* **1** any of the four molar teeth, one at the back of each side of the jaw, that are the last of the permanent teeth to erupt **2** cut one's wisdom teeth to arrive at the age of discretion

wise¹ (waɪz) *adj* **1** possessing, showing, or prompted by wisdom or discernment **2** prudent; sensible **3** shrewd; crafty: *a wise plan* **4** well-informed; erudite **5** aware, informed, or knowing (esp in the phrase **none the wiser**) **6** *slang* (*postpositive*; often foll by *to*) in the know, esp possessing inside information (about) **7** *archaic* possessing powers of magic **8** be wise *or* get wise (often foll by *to*) *informal* to be or become aware or informed (of something) or to face up (to facts) **9** put wise (often foll by *to*) *slang* to inform or warn (of) ▷ *vb* **10** See **wise up** [Old English *wīs*; related to Old Norse *vīss*, Gothic *weis*, German *weise*] > 'wisely *adv* > 'wiseness *n*

wise² (waɪz) *n archaic* way, manner, fashion, or respect (esp in the phrases **any wise, in no wise**) [Old English *wīse* manner; related to Old Saxon *wīsa*, German *Weise*, Old Norse *vīsa* verse, Latin *vīsus* face]

-wise *adv combining form* **1** Also called: -ways indicating direction or manner: *clockwise; likewise* **2** with reference to: *profitwise; businesswise* [Old English *-wisan*; see WISE²]

wiseacre (ˈwaɪzˌeɪkə) *n* **1** a person who wishes to seem wise **2** a wise person: often used facetiously or contemptuously [c16: from Middle Dutch *wijsseggher* soothsayer; related to Old High German *wīssaga*, German *Weissager*. See WISE¹, SAY]

wisecrack (ˈwaɪzˌkræk) *informal* ▷ *n* **1** a flippant gibe or sardonic remark ▷ *vb* **2** to make a wisecrack > 'wise,cracker *n*

wise guy *n* **1** *informal* a person who is given to making conceited, sardonic, or insolent comments **2** *US* a member of the Mafia

Wiseman (ˈwaɪzmən) *n* **Nicholas Patrick Stephen.** 1802–65, British cardinal; first Roman Catholic archbishop of Westminster (1850–65)

wisent (ˈwiːzənt) *n* the European bison. See **bison** (sense 2) [German, from Old High German *wisunt* BISON]

wise up *vb* (*adverb*) *slang* (often foll by *to*) to become or cause to become aware or informed (of)

wish (wɪʃ) *vb* **1** (when tr, takes a clause as object or an infinitive; when intr, often foll by *for*) to want or desire (something, often that which cannot be or is not the case): *I wish I lived in Italy; to wish for peace* **2** (*tr*) to feel or express a desire or hope concerning the future or fortune of: *I wish you well* **3** (*tr*) to desire or prefer to be as specified **4** (*tr*) to greet as specified; bid: *he wished us good afternoon* ▷ *n* **5** the act of wishing; the expression of some desire or mental inclination **6** something desired or wished for: *he got his wish* **7** (*usually plural*) expressed hopes or desire, esp for someone's welfare, health, etc **8** (*often plural*) *formal* a polite order or request ▷ See also **wish on** [Old English *wȳscan*; related to Old Norse *öskja*, German *wünschen*, Dutch *wenschen*] > 'wisher *n*

wishbone (ˈwɪʃˌbəʊn) *n* the V-shaped bone above the breastbone in most birds consisting of the fused clavicles; furcula [c17: from the custom of two people breaking apart the bone after eating: the person with the longer part makes a wish]

wishful (ˈwɪʃfʊl) *adj* having wishes or characterized by wishing > 'wishfully *adv* > 'wishfulness *n*

wish fulfilment *n* (in Freudian psychology) any successful attempt to fulfil a wish stemming from the unconscious mind, whether in fact, in fantasy, or by such disguised means as sublimation

wishful thinking *n* the erroneous belief that one's wishes are in accordance with reality > **wishful thinker** *n*

wish list *n* a list of things desired by a person or organization: *the Polish government's wish list*

wish on *vb* (*tr, preposition*) to hope that (someone or something) should be imposed (on someone); foist: *I wouldn't wish my cold on anyone*

wishy-washy (ˈwɪʃɪˌwɒʃɪ) *adj informal* **1** lacking in substance, force, colour, etc **2** watery; thin

Wisła (ˈviswa) *n* the Polish name for **Vistula** (sense 1)

Wislany Zalew (*Polish* viʃˈlaːni ˈzaːlɛf) *n* the Polish name for the **Vistula** (sense 2)

Wismar (*German* ˈvɪsmar) *n* a port in NE Germany, on an inlet of the Baltic, in Mecklenburg-West Pomerania: shipbuilding industries. Pop: 45 714 (2003 est)

wisp (wɪsp) *n* **1** a thin, light, delicate, or fibrous piece or strand, such as a streak of smoke or a lock of hair **2** a small bundle, as of hay or straw **3** anything slender and delicate: *a wisp of a girl* **4** a mere suggestion or hint **5** a flock of birds, esp snipe [c14: variant of *wips*, of obscure origin; compare WIPE] > 'wisp,like *adj* > 'wispy *adj*

wist (wɪst) *vb archaic* the past tense and past participle of **wit²**

wisteria (wɪˈstɪərɪə) *n* any twining leguminous woody climbing plant of the genus *Wisteria*, of E Asia and North America, having blue, purple, or white flowers in large drooping clusters [c19: from New Latin, named after Caspar *Wistar* (1761–1818), American anatomist]

wistful (ˈwɪstfʊl) *adj* sadly pensive, esp about something yearned for > 'wistfully *adv* > 'wistfulness *n*

wit¹ (wɪt) *n* **1** the talent or quality of using unexpected associations between contrasting or disparate words or ideas to make a clever humorous effect **2** speech or writing showing this quality **3** a person possessing, showing, or noted for such an ability, esp in repartee **4** practical intelligence (esp in the phrase **have the wit to**) **5** *archaic* mental capacity or a person possessing it ▷ See also **wits** [Old English *witt*; related to Old Saxon *giwitt*, Old High German *wizzi* (German *Witz*), Old Norse *vit*, Gothic *witi*. See WIT²]

wit² (wɪt) *vb* **1** *archaic* to be or become aware of (something) ▷ *adv* **2** to wit that is to say; namely (used to introduce statements, as in legal documents) [Old English *witan*; related to Old High German *wizzan* (German *wissen*), Old Norse *vita*, Latin *vidēre* to see]

witan (ˈwɪtən) *n* (in Anglo-Saxon England) **1** an assembly of higher ecclesiastics and important laymen, including king's thegns, that met to counsel the king on matters such as judicial problems **2** the members of this assembly ▷ Also called: witenagemot [Old English *witan*, plural of *wita* wise man; see WIT², WITNESS]

witblits (ˈvɪtˌblɪts) *n South African* an extremely potent illegally distilled spirit [from Afrikaans *wit* white + *blits* lightning]

witch¹ (wɪtʃ) *n* **1** a person, usually female, who practises or professes to practise magic or sorcery, esp black magic, or is believed to have dealings with the devil **2** an ugly or wicked old woman **3** a fascinating or enchanting woman ▷ *vb* **4** a less common word for **bewitch** [Old English *wicca*; related to Middle Low German *wicken* to conjure, Swedish *vicka* to move to and fro] > 'witch,like *adj*

witch² (wɪtʃ) *n* a flatfish, *Pleuronectes* (or *Glyptocephalus*) *cynoglossus*, of N Atlantic coastal waters, having a narrow greyish-brown body marked with tiny black spots: family *Pleuronectidae* (plaice, flounders, etc) [c19: perhaps from WITCH¹, alluding to the appearance of the fish]

witchcraft (ˈwɪtʃˌkrɑːft) *n* **1** the art or power of bringing magical or preternatural power to bear or the act or practice of attempting to do so **2** the influence of magic or sorcery **3** fascinating or bewitching influence or charm

witch doctor *n* Also called: shaman, medicine man a

man in certain societies, esp preliterate ones, who appears to possess magical powers, used esp to cure sickness but also to harm people

witch-elm n a variant spelling of **wych-elm**

witchery ('wɪtʃərɪ) n, pl -eries **1** the practice of witchcraft **2** magical or bewitching influence or charm

witches'-broom, witchbroom ('wɪtʃˌbruːm) or **witches'-besom** n a dense abnormal growth of shoots on a tree or other woody plant, usually caused by parasitic fungi of the genus *Taphrina*

witchetty grub ('wɪtʃɪtɪ) n the wood-boring edible larva of certain Australian moths and beetles [c19: *witchetty*, from a native Australian language]

witch hazel or **wych-hazel** n **1** any of several trees and shrubs of the genus *Hamamelis*, esp *H. virginiana*, of North America, having ornamental yellow flowers and medicinal properties: family *Hamamelidaceae* **2** an astringent medicinal solution containing an extract of the bark and leaves of *H. virginiana*, applied to treat bruises, inflammation, etc

witch-hunt n a rigorous campaign to round up or expose dissenters on the pretext of safeguarding the welfare of the public > 'witch-ˌhunting n, adj

witching ('wɪtʃɪŋ) adj **1** relating to or appropriate for witchcraft **2** now rare bewitching ▷ n **3** witchcraft; magic > 'witchingly adv

witching hour n the witching hour the hour at which witches are supposed to appear, usually midnight

witenagemot (ˌwɪtɪnəgɪ'məʊt) n another word for **witan** [Old English *witena*, genitive plural of *wita* councillor + *gemōt* meeting, MOOT]

with (wɪð, wɪθ) prep **1** using; by means of: *he killed her with an axe* **2** accompanying; in the company of: *the lady you were with* **3** possessing; having: *a man with a red moustache* **4** concerning or regarding: *be patient with her* **5** in spite of: *with all his talents, he was still humble* **6** used to indicate a time or distance by which something is away from something else: *with three miles to go, he collapsed* **7** in a manner characterized by: *writing with abandon* **8** caused or prompted by: *shaking with rage* **9** often used with a verb indicating a reciprocal action or relation between the subject and the preposition's object: *agreeing with me; chatting with the troops* **10** not with you *informal* not able to grasp or follow what you are saying **11** with it *informal* **a** fashionable; in style **b** comprehending what is happening or being said **12** with that after that; having said or done that [Old English; related to Old Norse *vith*, Gothic *withra*, Latin *vitricus* stepfather, Sanskrit *vitarám* wider]

withal (wɪ'ðɔːl) adv **1** literary as well; likewise **2** archaic therewith ▷ prep **3** (postpositive) an archaic word for **with** [c12: from WITH + ALL]

withdraw (wɪð'drɔː) vb -draws, -drawing, -drew, -drawn **1** (tr) to take or draw back or away; remove **2** (tr) to remove from deposit or investment in a bank, building society, etc **3** (tr) to retract or recall (a statement, promise, etc) **4** (intr) to retire or retreat: *the troops withdrew* **5** (intr) to detach oneself socially, emotionally, or mentally [c13: from WITH (in the sense: away from) + DRAW] > with'drawable adj > with'drawer n

withdrawal (wɪð'drɔːəl) n **1** an act or process of withdrawing; retreat, removal, or detachment **2** the period a drug addict goes through following abrupt termination in the use of narcotics, usually characterized by physical and mental symptoms (**withdrawal symptoms**)

withdrawing room n an archaic term for **drawing room**

withdrawn (wɪð'drɔːn) vb **1** the past participle of **withdraw** ▷ adj **2** unusually reserved, introverted, or shy **3** secluded or remote

withe (wɪθ, wɪð, waɪð) n **1** a strong flexible twig, esp of willow, suitable for binding things together; withy **2** a band or rope of twisted twigs or stems ▷ vb **3** (tr) to bind with withes [Old English *withthe*; related to Old Norse *vithja*, Old High German *witta*, *widi*, Gothic *wida*]

wither ('wɪðə) vb **1** (intr) (esp of a plant) to droop, wilt, or shrivel up **2** (intr; often foll by *away*) to fade or waste: *all hope withered away* **3** (intr) to decay, decline, or disintegrate **4** (tr) to cause to wilt, fade, or lose vitality **5** (tr) to abash,

esp with a scornful look **6** (tr) to harm or damage [c14: perhaps variant of WEATHER (vb); related to German *verwittern* to decay] > 'witherer n > 'withering adj > 'witheringly adv

withers ('wɪðəz) pl n the highest part of the back of a horse, behind the neck between the shoulders [c16: short for *widersones*, from *wider* WITH + -*sones*, perhaps variant of SINEW; related to German *Widerrist*, Old English *withre* resistance]

withershins ('wɪðəˌʃɪnz; *Scot* 'wɪðər-) or **widdershins** adv chiefly Scot **1** in the direction contrary to the apparent course of the sun; anticlockwise **2** in a direction contrary to the usual; in the wrong direction [c16: from Middle Low German *weddersinnes*, from Middle High German *widersinnes*, literally: opposite course, from *wider* against + *sinnes*, genitive of *sin* course]

withhold (wɪð'həʊld) vb -holds, -holding, -held **1** (tr) to keep back; refrain from giving **2** (tr) to hold back; restrain **3** (intr; usually foll by *from*) to refrain or forbear > with'holder n

within (wɪ'ðɪn) prep **1** in; inside; enclosed or encased by **2** before (a period of time) has elapsed: *within a week* **3** not beyond the limits of; not differing by more than (a specified amount) from: *live within your means; within seconds of the world record* ▷ adv **4** formal inside; internally

without (wɪ'ðaʊt) prep **1** not having: *a traveller without much money* **2** not accompanied by: *he came without his wife* **3** not making use of: *it is not easy to undo screws without a screwdriver* **4** (foll by a verbal noun or noun phrase) not, while not, or after not: *she can sing for two minutes without drawing breath* **5** archaic on the outside of ▷ adv **6** formal outside; outwardly

withstand (wɪð'stænd) vb -stands, -standing, -stood **1** (tr) to stand up to forcefully; resist **2** (intr) to remain firm in endurance or opposition > with'stander n

withy ('wɪðɪ) n, pl withies **1** a variant spelling of **withe** (senses 1, 2) **2** a willow tree, esp an osier [Old English *wīdig(e)*; related to Old Norse *vīthir*, Old High German *wīda*, Latin *vītis* vine, Sanskrit *vītika* fetter. See WITHE, WIRE]

witless ('wɪtlɪs) adj lacking wit, intelligence, or sense; stupid > 'witlessly adv > 'witlessness n

witling ('wɪtlɪŋ) n archaic a person who thinks himself witty

witness ('wɪtnɪs) n **1** a person who has seen or can give first-hand evidence of some event **2** a person or thing giving or serving as evidence **3** a person who testifies, esp in a court of law, to events or facts within his own knowledge **4** a person who attests to the genuineness of a document, signature, etc, by adding his own signature **5** bear witness **a** to give written or oral testimony **b** to be evidence or proof of. Related adjective: **testimonial** ▷ vb **6** (tr) to see, be present at, or know at first hand **7** to give or serve as evidence (of) **8** (tr) to be the scene or setting of: *this field has witnessed a battle* **9** (intr) to testify, esp in a court of law, to events within a person's own knowledge **10** (tr) to attest to the genuineness of (a document, signature, etc) by adding one's own signature [Old English *witnes* (meaning both *testimony* and *witness*), from *witan* to know, WIT² + -NESS; related to Old Norse *vitni*] > 'witnessable adj > 'witnesser n

witness box or esp US **witness stand** n the place in a court of law in which witnesses stand to give evidence

wits (wɪts) pl n **1** (sometimes singular) the ability to reason and act, esp quickly (esp in the phrase **have one's wits about one**) **2** (sometimes singular) right mind, sanity (esp in the phrase **out of one's wits**) **3** at one's wits' end at a loss to know how to proceed **4** five wits obsolete the five senses or mental faculties **5** live by one's wits to gain a livelihood by craftiness and cunning rather than by hard work

Wits (wɪts) n South African informal University of the Witwatersrand

Witt (wɪt) n See **de Witt**

Witte ('vɪtə; *Russian* 'vjitjə) n **Sergei Yulievich** (sjɪr'gjej ju'ljevitʃ). 1849–1915, Russian statesman; prime minister (1905–06). As minister of finance (1892–1903) he tried to modernize the Russian economy

-witted adj (in combination) having wits or intelligence as specified: *slow-witted; dim-witted*

Wittenberg (*German* 'vɪtənbɛrk; *English* 'wɪtˀn,bɜːɡ) *n* a city in E Germany, on the River Elbe, in Brandenburg: Martin Luther, as a philosophy teacher at Wittenberg university, began the Reformation here in 1517 by nailing his 95 theses to the doors of a church. Pop: 46 295 (2003 est)

witter ('wɪtə) *informal* ▷ *vb* **1** (*intr*, often foll by *on*) to chatter or babble pointlessly or at unnecessary length ▷ *n* **2** pointless chat; chatter [c20: from dialect; compare TWITTER]

Wittgenstein ('vɪtɡənˌʃtaɪn, -,staɪn) *n* **Ludwig Josef Johann** ('luːtvɪç 'joːzɛf joˈhan). 1889– 1951, British philosopher, born in Austria. After studying with Bertrand Russell, he wrote the *Tractatus Logico-Philosophicus* (1921), which explores the relationship of language to the world. He was a major influence on logical positivism but later repudiated this, and in *Philosophical Investigations* (1953) he argues that philosophical problems arise from insufficient attention to the variety of natural language use

Wittgensteinian ('vɪtɡənˌʃtaɪnɪən, -,staɪnɪən) *adj* (of a philosophical position or argument) derived from or related to the work of Ludwig Wittgenstein, the Austrian-born British philosopher (1889–1951), and esp the later work in which he attacks essentialism and stresses the open texture and variety of use of ordinary language

witticism ('wɪtɪ,sɪzəm) *n* a clever or witty remark [c17: from WITTY; coined by Dryden (1677) by analogy with *criticism*]

witting ('wɪtɪŋ) *adj rare* **1** deliberate; intentional: *a witting insult* **2** aware; knowing > 'wittingly *adv*

witty ('wɪtɪ) *adj* **-tier, -tiest** **1** characterized by clever humour or wit **2** *archaic or dialect* intelligent or sensible > 'wittily *adv* > 'wittiness *n*

Witwatersrand (wɪt'wɔːtəz,rænd; *Afrikaans* vət'vɑːtərs'rant) *n* a rocky ridge in NE South Africa: contains the richest gold deposits in the world, also coal and manganese; chief industrial centre is Johannesburg. Height: 1500–1800 m (5000–6000 ft). Also called: the Rand, the Reef

wive (waɪv) *vb archaic* **1** to marry (a woman) **2** (*tr*) to supply with a wife [Old English *gewīfian*, from *wīf* WIFE]

wivern ('waɪvən) *n* a less common spelling of **wyvern**

wives (waɪvz) *n* the plural of **wife**

wiz (wɪz) *n informal* a variant spelling of **whizz** (sense 6)

wizard ('wɪzəd) *n* **1** a male witch or a man who practises or professes to practise magic or sorcery **2** a person who is outstandingly clever in some specified field; expert **3** *obsolete* a wise man **4** *computing* a computer program that guides a user through a complex task ▷ *adj* **5** *informal, chiefly Brit* superb; outstanding **6** of or relating to a wizard or wizardry [c15: variant of *wissard*, from WISE + -ARD] > 'wizardly *adj*

wizardry ('wɪzədrɪ) *n* the art, skills, and practices of a wizard, sorcerer, or magician

wizen¹ ('wɪzˀn) *vb* **1** to make or become shrivelled ▷ *adj* **2** a variant of **wizened** [Old English *wisnian*; related to Old Norse *visna*, Old High German *wesanēn*]

wizen² ('wiːzˀn) *n* an archaic word for **weasand**

wizened ('wɪzˀnd) *or* **wizen** *adj* shrivelled, wrinkled, or dried up, esp with age

wk *abbreviation* **1** *pl* **wks** week **2** work **3** weak

WK *abbreviation text messaging* week

wkly *abbreviation* weekly

WKND *abbreviation text messaging* weekend

Władysław II ('vlædɪslæf) *n* original name *Jogaila*. ?1351–1434, grand duke of Lithuania (1377–1401) and king of Poland (1386–1434). He united Lithuania and Poland and founded the Jagiellon dynasty

Władysław IV *n* 1595–1648, king of Poland (1632–48)

WMD *abbreviation* weapon(s) of mass destruction

WMO *abbreviation* World Meteorological Organization

WNW *symbol for* west-northwest

wo (wəʊ) *n*, *pl* **wos** an archaic spelling of **woe**

WO *abbreviation* **1** War Office **2** Warrant Officer **3** wireless operator

woad (wəʊd) *n* **1** a European plant, *Isatis tinctoria*, formerly cultivated for its leaves, which yield a blue dye: family *Brassicaceae* (crucifers) **2** the dye obtained from this plant, used esp by the ancient Britons, as a body dye [Old English *wād*; related to Old High German *weit*; Middle Dutch *wēd*, Latin *vitrum*]

wobbegong ('wɒbɪ,ɡɒŋ) *n* an Australian carpet shark, *Orectolobus maculatus*, with brown-and-white skin [from a native Australian language]

wobble ('wɒbˀl) *vb* **1** (*intr*) to move, rock, or sway unsteadily **2** (*intr*) to tremble or shake: *her voice wobbled with emotion* **3** (*intr*) to vacillate with indecision **4** (*tr*) to cause to wobble ▷ *n* **5** a wobbling movement, motion, or sound ▷ Also called: **wabble** [c17: variant of *wabble*, from Low German *wabbeln*; related to Middle High German *wabelen* to WAVER] > 'wobbler *n*

wobble board *n Austral* a piece of fibreboard used as a musical instrument, producing a characteristic sound when flexed

wobbly ('wɒblɪ) *adj* **-blier, -bliest** **1** unsteady ▷ *n* **2** throw a wobbly *slang* to become suddenly very agitated or angry > 'wobbliness *n*

Wodehouse ('wʊd,haʊs) *n* **Sir P(elham) G(renville)**. 1881–1975, US author, born in England. His humorous novels of upper-class life in England include the *Psmith* and *Jeeves* series > Wode'housian *adj*

Woden *or* **Wodan** ('wəʊdˀn) *n* the foremost Anglo-Saxon god. Norse counterpart: **Odin** [Old English *Wōden*; related to Old Norse *Ōthinn*, Old High German *Wuotan*, German *Wotan*; see WEDNESDAY]

wodge (wɒdʒ) *n Brit informal* a thick lump or chunk cut or broken off something [c20: alteration of WEDGE]

woe (wəʊ) *n* **1** *literary* intense grief or misery **2** (*often plural*) affliction or misfortune **3** woe betide someone misfortune will befall someone: *woe betide you if you arrive late* ▷ *interj* **4** Also called: woe is me *archaic* an exclamation of sorrow or distress [Old English *wā, wē*; related to Old Saxon, Old High German *wē*, Old Norse *vei*, Gothic *wai*, Latin *vae*, Sanskrit *uvē*; see WAIL]

woebegone ('wəʊbɪ,ɡɒn) *adj* sorrowful or sad in appearance [c14: from a phrase such as *me is wo begon* woe has beset me]

woeful ('wəʊfˀl) *adj* **1** expressing or characterized by sorrow **2** bringing or causing woe **3** pitiful; miserable: *a woeful standard of work* > 'woefully *adv* > 'woefulness *n*

WOF *abbreviation* (in New Zealand) Warrant of Fitness

Woffington ('wɒfɪŋtən) *n* **Peg**, full name *Margaret Woffington*. ?1714–60, Irish actress

wog¹ (wɒɡ) *n Brit slang, derogatory* a foreigner, esp one who is not White [probably from GOLLIWOG]

wog² (wɒɡ) *n slang, chiefly Austral* influenza or any similar illness [c20: of unknown origin]

woggle ('wɒɡˀl) *n* the ring of leather through which a Scout neckerchief is threaded [c20: of unknown origin]

Wöhler (*German* 'vøːlər) *n* **Friedrich** ('friːdrɪç). 1800–82, German chemist, who proved that organic compounds could be synthesized from inorganic compounds

wok (wɒk) *n* a large metal Chinese cooking pot having a curved base like a bowl and traditionally with a wooden handle [from Chinese (Cantonese)]

woke (wəʊk) *vb* a past tense of **wake¹**

woken ('wəʊkən) *vb* a past participle of **wake¹**

Woking ('wəʊkɪŋ) *n* a town in SE England, in central Surrey: mainly residential. Pop: 101 127 (2001)

Wokingham *n* a unitary authority in SE England, in Berkshire. Pop: 151 200 (2003 est). Area: 179 sq km (69 sq miles)

wokka board ('wɒkə) *n Austral* another name for **wobble board**

wold¹ (wəʊld) *n chiefly literary* a tract of open rolling country, esp upland [Old English *weald* bush; related to Old Saxon *wald*, German *Wald* forest, Old Norse *vollr* ground; see WILD]

wold² (wəʊld) *n* another name for **weld²**

Wolds (wəʊldz) *pl n* the Wolds a range of chalk hills in NE England: consists of the **Yorkshire Wolds** to the north, separated from the **Lincolnshire Wolds** by the Humber estuary

wolf (wʊlf) *n*, *pl* **wolves** (wʊlvz) **1** a predatory canine mammal, *Canis lupus*, which hunts in packs and was formerly widespread in North America and Eurasia but is now less common. Related adj: **lupine 2** any of several similar and related canines, such as the red wolf and the coyote (**prairie wolf**) **3** the fur of any such animal **4** a voracious, grabbing, or fiercely cruel person or thing **5** *informal* a man who habitually tries to seduce women **6** Also called: **wolf note** *music* **a** an unpleasant sound produced in some notes played on the violin, cello, etc, owing to resonant vibrations of the belly **b** an out-of-tune effect produced on keyboard instruments accommodated esp to the system of mean-tone temperament **7** cry wolf to give a false alarm **8** keep the wolf from the door to ward off starvation or privation **9** lone wolf a person or animal who prefers to be alone **10** wolf in sheep's clothing a malicious person in a harmless or benevolent disguise ▷ *vb* **11** (*tr*; often foll by *down*) to gulp (down) **12** (*intr*) to hunt wolves [Old English *wulf*; related to Old High German *wolf*, Old Norse *ulfr*, Gothic *wulfs*, Latin *lupus* and *vulpēs* fox] ▷ 'wolfish *adj* ▷ 'wolf,like *adj*

Wolf (*German* vɔlf) *n* **1 Friedrich August** ('friːdrɪç 'auɡʊst). 1759–1824, German classical scholar, who suggested that the Homeric poems, esp the *Iliad*, are products of an oral tradition **2 Hugo** ('huːɡo). 1860–1903, Austrian composer, esp of songs, including the *Italienisches Liederbuch* and the *Spanisches Liederbuch* **3** (wʊlf) **Howlin'**. See **Howlin' Wolf**

wolfberry ('wʊlf,bɛrɪ) *n* Also called: goji the berry of either of two plants of the genus *Lycium*, valued for its nutritional qualities

Wolf Cub *n Brit* the former name for **Cub Scout**

Wolfe (wʊlf) *n* **1 James.** 1727–59, English soldier, who commanded the British capture of Quebec, in which he was killed **2 Thomas** (**Clayton**). 1900–38, US novelist, noted for his autobiographical fiction, esp *Look Homeward, Angel* (1929) **3 Tom**, full name *Thomas Kennerly Wolfe*. born 1931, US author and journalist; his books include *The Right Stuff* (1979) and the novels *Bonfire of the Vanities* (1987), and *A Man in Full* (1998)

Wolfensohn ('wʊlfən,sɔʊn) *n* **James D.**, known as **Jim.** born 1933, US businessman and international official, born in Australia; president of the International Bank for Reconstruction and Development (the World Bank) (1995–2005)

Wolf-Ferrari (*Italian* 'vɔlffer'raːri) *n* **Ermanno** (er'manno). 1876–1948, Italian composer born of a German father, in Germany from 1909. His works, mainly in a lyrical style, include operas, such as *The Jewels of the Madonna* (1911) and *Susanna's Secret* (1909)

wolffish ('wʊlf,fɪʃ) *n, pl* -fish or -fishes any large northern deep-sea blennioid fish of the family *Anarhichadidae*, such as *Anarhichas lupus*. They have large sharp teeth and no pelvic fins and are used as food fishes. Also called: catfish

wolfhound ('wʊlf,haʊnd) *n* the largest breed of dog, used formerly to hunt wolves

Wolfit ('wʊlfɪt) *n* **Sir Donald.** 1902–68, English stage actor and manager

wolfram ('wʊlfrəm) *n* another name for **tungsten** [c18: from German, originally perhaps from the proper name, *Wolfram*, used pejoratively of tungsten because it was thought inferior to tin]

wolframite ('wʊlfrə,maɪt) *n* a black to reddish-brown mineral consisting of tungstates of iron and manganese in monoclinic crystalline form: it occurs mainly in quartz veins and is the chief ore of tungsten. Formula: (Fe,Mn)WO$_4$

Wolfram von Eschenbach (*German* 'vɔlfram fɔn 'ɛʃənbax) *n* died ?1220, German poet: author of the epic *Parzival*, incorporating the story of the Grail

wolfsbane or **wolf's-bane** ('wʊlfs,beɪn) *n* any of several poisonous N temperate plants of the ranunculaceous genus *Aconitum*, esp *A. lycoctonum*, which has yellow hoodlike flowers

Wolfsburg (*German* 'vɔlfsbʊrk) *n* a city in N central Germany, in Lower Saxony: founded in 1938; motor-vehicle industry. Pop: 122 724 (2003 est)

wolf spider *n* any spider of the family *Lycosidae*, which chase their prey to catch it. Also called: hunting spider

wolf whistle *n* **1** a whistle made by a man to express admiration of a woman's appearance ▷ *vb* wolf-whistle **2** (when *intr*, sometimes foll by *at*) to make such a whistle (at someone)

Wollongong ('wʊlən,ɡɒŋ) *n* a city in E Australia, in E New South Wales on the Pacific: an early centre of dairy farming; now a coal-mining and heavy industrial centre. Pop: 228 846 (2001)

Wollstonecraft ('wʊlstən,krɑːft) *n* **Mary.** 1759–97, British feminist and writer, author of *A Vindication of the Rights of Women* (1792); wife of William Godwin and mother of Mary Shelley

Wolof ('wɒlɒf) *n* **1** *pl* -of *or* -ofs a member of a Negroid people of W Africa living chiefly in Senegal **2** the language of this people, belonging to the West Atlantic branch of the Niger-Congo family

Wolseley ('wʊlzlɪ) *n* **Garnet Joseph**, 1st Viscount. 1833–1913, British field marshal, noted for his army reforms

Wolsey ('wʊlzɪ) *n* **Thomas.** ?1475–1530, English cardinal and statesman; archbishop of York (1514–30); lord chancellor (1515–29). He dominated Henry VIII's foreign and domestic policies but his failure to obtain papal consent for the annulment of the king's marriage to Catherine of Aragon led to his arrest for high treason (1530); he died on the journey to face trial

Wolverhampton (,wʊlvə'hæmptən) *n* **1** a city in W central England, in Wolverhampton unitary authority, West Midlands: iron and steel foundries; university (1992). Pop: 251 462 (2001) **2** a unitary authority in W central England, in the West Midlands. Pop: 238 900 (2003 est). Area: 69 sq km (27 sq miles)

wolverine ('wʊlvə,riːn) *n* a large musteline mammal, *Gulo gulo*, of northern forests of Eurasia and North America having dark very thick water-resistant fur. Also called: glutton [c16 *wolvering*, from WOLF + -ING³ (later altered to -*ine*)]

wolves (wʊlvz) *n* the plural of **wolf**

woman ('wʊmən) *n, pl* women ('wɪmɪn) **1** an adult female human being **2** (*modifier*) female or feminine: *a woman politician; woman talk* **3** women collectively; womankind **4** the woman feminine nature or feelings: *babies bring out the woman in her* **5** a female servant or domestic help **6** a man considered as having supposed female characteristics, such as meekness or timidity **7** *informal* a wife, mistress, or girlfriend **8** the little woman *informal* one's wife **9** woman of the streets a prostitute ▷ *vb* (*tr*) **10** *obsolete* to make effeminate [Old English *wīfmann, wimman*; from WIFE + MAN (human being)] ▷ 'womanless *adj* ▷ 'woman-,like *adj*

womanhood ('wʊmən,hʊd) *n* **1** the state or quality of being a woman or being womanly **2** women collectively

womanish ('wʊmənɪʃ) *adj* **1** having qualities or characteristics regarded as unsuitable to a strong character of either sex, esp a man **2** characteristic of or suitable for a woman ▷ 'womanishly *adv* ▷ 'womanishness *n*

womanize or **womanise** ('wʊmə,naɪz) *vb* **1** (*intr*) (of a man) to indulge in many casual affairs with women; philander **2** (*tr*) to make effeminate ▷ 'woman,izer or 'woman,iser *n* ▷ 'woman,izing or 'woman,ising *n, adj*

womankind ('wʊmən,kaɪnd) *n* the female members of the human race; women collectively

womanly ('wʊmənlɪ) *adj* **1** possessing qualities, such as warmth, attractiveness, etc, generally regarded as typical of a woman, esp a mature woman **2** characteristic of or belonging to a woman

womb (wuːm) *n* **1** the nontechnical name for **uterus 2** a hollow space enclosing something, esp when dark, warm, or sheltering **3** a place where something is conceived: *the Near East is the womb of western civilization* **4** *obsolete* the belly [Old English *wamb*; related to Old Norse *vomb*, Gothic *wamba*, Middle Low German *wamme*, Swedish *våmm*] ▷ wombed *adj* ▷ 'womblike *adj*

wombat ('wɒmbæt) *n* any of various burrowing herbivorous Australian marsupials, esp *Vombatus ursinus*, constituting the family *Vombatidae* and having short limbs, a heavy body, and coarse dense fur [c18: from a native Australian language]

women ('wɪmɪn) *n* the plural of **woman**

womenfolk ('wɪmɪn,fəʊk) *pl n* **1** women collectively **2** a group of women, esp the female members of one's family

Women's Institute *n* (in Britain and Commonwealth countries) a society for women interested in the problems of the home and in engaging in social activities

Women's Liberation *n* a movement directed towards the removal of attitudes and practices that preserve inequalities based upon the assumption that men are superior to women. Also called: **women's lib**

Women's Movement *n* a grass-roots movement of women concerned with women's liberation. See **Women's Liberation**

won (wʌn) *vb* the past tense of **win**[1]

wonder ('wʌndə) *n* **1** the feeling excited by something strange; a mixture of surprise, curiosity, and sometimes awe **2** something that causes such a feeling, such as a miracle **3** (*modifier*) exciting wonder by virtue of spectacular results achieved, feats performed, etc: *a wonder drug; a wonder horse* **4** do wonders or work wonders to achieve spectacularly fine results **5** for a wonder surprisingly or amazingly **6** nine days' wonder a subject that arouses general surprise or public interest for a short time **7** no wonder (*sentence connector*) (I am) not surprised at all (that): *no wonder he couldn't come* **8** small wonder (*sentence connector*) (I am) hardly surprised (that): *small wonder he couldn't make it tonight* ▷ *vb* (when *tr*, may take a clause as object) **9** (when *intr*, often foll by *about*) to indulge in speculative inquiry, often accompanied by an element of doubt (concerning something): *I wondered about what she said; I wonder what happened* **10** (when *intr*, often foll by *at*) to be amazed (at something): *I wonder at your impudence* [Old English *wundor*; related to Old Saxon *wundar*, Old Norse *undr*, German *Wunder*] ▷ 'wonderer *n*

Wonder ('wʌndə) *n* **Stevie**. real name *Steveland Judkins Morris*. born 1950, US Motown singer, songwriter, and multi-instrumentalist. His recordings include *Up-Tight* (1966), "Superstition" (1972), *Innervisions* (1973), *Songs in the Key of Life* (1976), and "I Just Called to Say I Love You" (1985)

wonderful ('wʌndəfʊl) *adj* **1** exciting a feeling of wonder; marvellous or strange **2** extremely fine; excellent ▷ 'wonderfully *adv*

wonderkid ('wʌndə,kɪd) *n informal* a young person whose excellence in his or her discipline is appropriate to someone older and more experienced

wonderland ('wʌndə,lænd) *n* **1** an imaginary land of marvels or wonders **2** an actual place or scene of great or strange beauty or wonder

wonderment ('wʌndəmənt) *n* **1** rapt surprise; awe **2** puzzled interest **3** something that excites wonder

wonderwork ('wʌndə,wɜːk) *n* something done or made that excites wonder; miracle or wonder ▷ 'wonder-,worker *n* ▷ 'wonder-,working *n, adj*

wondrous ('wʌndrəs) *archaic or literary* ▷ *adj* **1** exciting wonder; marvellous ▷ *adv* **2** (*intensifier*): *it is wondrous cold* ▷ 'wondrously *adv* ▷ 'wondrousness *n*

wonky ('wɒŋkɪ) *adj* -kier, -kiest *Brit informal* **1** shaky or unsteady **2** not in correct alignment; askew **3** liable to break down or develop a fault [C20: variant of dialect *wanky*, from Old English *wancol*]

Wŏnsan (wɒn'sæn) *n* a port in SE North Korea, on the Sea of Japan (East Sea): oil refineries. Pop: 319 000 (2005 est)

wont (wəʊnt) *adj* **1** (*postpositive*) accustomed (to doing something): *he was wont to come early* ▷ *n* **2** a manner or action habitually employed by or associated with someone (often in the phrases **as is my wont, as is his wont**, etc) ▷ *vb* **3** (when *tr*, usually passive) to become or cause to become accustomed [Old English *gewunod*, past participle of *wunian* to be accustomed to; related to Old High German *wunēn* (German *wohnen*), Old Norse *una* to be satisfied; see WEAN[1], WISH, WINSOME]

won't (wəʊnt) *vb* contraction of will not

wonted ('wəʊntɪd) *adj* **1** (*postpositive*) accustomed or habituated (to doing something) **2** (*prenominal*) customary; usual: *she is in her wonted place*

woo (wuː) *vb* woos, wooing, wooed **1** to seek the affection, favour, or love of (a woman) with a view to marriage **2** (*tr*) to seek after zealously or hopefully: *to woo fame* **3** (*tr*) to bring upon oneself (good or evil results) by one's own action **4** (*tr*) to beg or importune (someone) [Old English *wōgian*, of obscure origin] ▷ 'wooer *n* ▷ 'wooing *n*

wood (wʊd) *n* **1** the hard fibrous substance consisting of xylem tissue that occurs beneath the bark in trees, shrubs, and similar plants **2** the trunks of trees that have been cut and prepared for use as a building material **3** a collection of trees, shrubs, herbs, grasses, etc, usually dominated by one or a few species of tree: usually smaller than a forest: *an oak wood*. Related adj: **sylvan 4** fuel; firewood **5** *golf* **a** a long-shafted club with a broad wooden or metal head, used for driving: numbered from 1 to 7 according to size, angle of face, etc **b** (*as modifier*): *a wood shot* **6** *tennis, squash, badminton* the frame of a racket: *he hit a winning shot off the wood* **7** one of the biased wooden bowls used in the game of bowls **8** *music* short for **woodwind** See also **woods** (sense 3) **9** out of the wood *or* out of the woods clear of or safe from dangers or doubts: *we're not out of the wood yet* **10** see the wood for the trees (used with a negative) to obtain a general view of a situation, problem, etc, without allowing details to cloud one's analysis: *he can't see the wood for the trees* **11** (*modifier*) made of, used for, employing, or handling wood: *a wood fire* **12** (*modifier*) dwelling in, concerning, or situated in a wood: *a wood nymph* ▷ *vb* **13** (*tr*) to plant a wood upon **14** to supply or be supplied with fuel or firewood ▷ See also **woods** [Old English *widu, wudu*; related to Old High German *witu*, Old Norse *vithr*]

Wood (wʊd) *n* **1** Mrs **Henry**, married name of *Ellen Price*. 1814–87, British novelist, noted esp for the melodramatic novel *East Lynne* (1861) **2** Sir **Henry (Joseph)**. 1869–1944, English conductor, who founded the Promenade Concerts in London **3 John**, known as *the Elder*. 1707–54, British architect and town planner, working mainly in Bath, where he designed the North and South Parades (1728) and the Circus (1754) **4** his son, **John**, known as *the Younger*. 1727–82, British architect: designed the Royal Crescent (1767–71) and the Assembly Rooms (1769–71), Bath **5 Ralph**. 1715–72, British potter, working in Staffordshire, who made the first toby jug (1762)

wood alcohol *n* another name for **methanol**

wood anemone *n* any of several woodland anemone plants, esp *Anemone quinquefolia* of E North America and *A. nemorosa* of Europe, having finely divided leaves and solitary white flowers. Also called: **windflower**

wood avens *n* another name for **herb bennet**

woodbine ('wʊd,baɪn) *n* **1 a** a honeysuckle, *Lonicera periclymenum*, of Europe, SW Asia, and N Africa, having fragrant creamy flowers **2** *US* another name for **Virginia creeper** (sense 1) **3** *Austral obsolete, slang* an Englishman [sense 3 from the English brand of cigarettes so named]

wood block *n* a small rectangular flat block of wood that is laid with others as a floor surface

woodcarving ('wʊd,kɑːvɪŋ) *n* **1** the act of carving wood, esp as an art form **2** a work of art produced by carving wood ▷ 'wood,carver *n*

woodchuck ('wʊd,tʃʌk) *n* a North American marmot, *Marmota monax*, having coarse reddish-brown fur. Also called: **groundhog** [C17: by folk etymology from Cree *otcheck* fisher, marten]

woodcock ('wʊd,kɒk) *n* an Old World game bird, *Scolopax rusticola*, resembling the snipe but larger and having shorter legs and neck: family *Scolopacidae* (sandpipers, etc), order *Charadriiformes*

woodcraft ('wʊd,krɑːft) *n chiefly US & Canadian* **1** ability and experience in matters concerned with living in a wood or forest **2** ability or skill at woodwork, carving, etc

woodcut ('wʊd,kʌt) *n* **1** a block of wood cut along the grain and with a design, illustration, etc, incised with a knife, from which prints are made **2** a print from a woodcut

woodcutter ('wʊd,kʌtə) *n* **1** a person who fells trees or

chops wood 2 a person who makes woodcuts
> 'wood,cutting n

wooded ('wʊdɪd) adj 1 covered with or abounding in woods or trees 2 (in combination) having wood of a specified character: a soft-wooded tree

wooden ('wʊdⁿn) adj 1 made from or consisting of wood 2 awkward or clumsy 3 bereft of spirit or animation: a wooden expression 4 obstinately unyielding: a wooden attitude 5 mentally slow or dull 6 not highly resonant: a wooden thud > 'woodenly adv

wood engraving n 1 the art of engraving pictures or designs on wood for printing by incising them with a burin on a block of wood cut across the grain 2 a block of wood so engraved or a print taken from it > wood engraver n

woodenhead ('wʊdⁿn,hɛd) n informal a dull, foolish, or unintelligent person > ,wooden'headed adj > ,wooden'headedness n

Wooden Horse n another name for the Trojan Horse (sense 1)

wooden spoon n a booby prize, esp in sporting contests

woodgrouse ('wʊd,graʊs) n another name for capercaillie

woodland ('wʊdlənd) n a land that is mostly covered with woods or dense growths of trees and shrubs b (as modifier): woodland fauna > 'woodlander n

woodlark ('wʊd,lɑːk) n an Old World lark, Lullula arborea, similar to but slightly smaller than the skylark

woodlouse ('wʊd,laʊs) n, pl -lice (-,laɪs) any of various small terrestrial isopod crustaceans of the genera Oniscus, Porcellio, etc, which have a flattened segmented body and occur in damp habitats

woodman ('wʊdmən) n, pl -men 1 a person who looks after and fells trees used for timber 2 another word for woodsman

woodnote ('wʊd,nəʊt) n a natural musical note or song, like that of a wild bird

wood nymph n one of a class of nymphs fabled to inhabit the woods, such as a dryad

woodpecker ('wʊd,pɛkə) n any climbing bird of the family Picidae, typically having a brightly coloured plumage and strong chisel-like bill with which they bore into trees for insects: order Piciformes

wood pigeon n a large Eurasian pigeon, Columba palumbus, having white patches on the wings and neck. Also called: ringdove, cushat

woodpile ('wʊd,paɪl) n a pile or heap of firewood

wood preservative n a coating applied to timber as a protection against decay, insects, weather, etc

wood pulp n 1 wood that has been ground to a fine pulp for use in making newsprint and other cheap forms of paper, and in the production of hardboard 2 finely pulped wood that has been digested by a chemical, such as caustic soda, and sometimes bleached: used in making paper

woodruff ('wʊdrʌf) n any of several rubiaceous plants of the genus Galium, esp G. odoratum (sweet woodruff), of Eurasia, which has small sweet-scented white flowers and whorls of narrow fragrant leaves used to flavour wine and liqueurs and in perfumery [Old English wudurofe, from WOOD¹ + rōfe, related to Old High German ruoba, Middle Low German rōve (beet)root, Latin rēpere to creep]

woods (wʊdz) pl n 1 closely packed trees forming a forest or wood, esp a specific one 2 another word for backwoods (sense 2) 3 the woodwind instruments in an orchestra

Woods¹ n Lake of the Woods See Lake of the Woods

Woods² n Tiger, real name Eldrick Woods. born 1975, US golfer: youngest US Masters champion and first Black golfer to win a major championship; winner of the US Masters (1997, 2001–02, 2005), US Open (2000, 2002), British Open Championship (2000, 2005–06), and the PGA Championship (1999, 2000, 2006-07); in 2001 he became the only player to hold all four major titles at once

woodscrew ('wʊd,skruː) n a metal screw that tapers to a point so that it can be driven into wood by a screwdriver

woodshed ('wʊd,ʃɛd) n a small outbuilding where

firewood, garden tools, etc, are stored

woodsman ('wʊdzmən) n, pl -men a person who lives in a wood or who is skilled in woodcraft. Also called: woodman

wood sorrel n a Eurasian plant, Oxalis acetosella, having trifoliate leaves, an underground creeping stem, and white purple-veined flowers: family Oxalidaceae

wood spirit n chem another name for methanol

Woodstock ('wʊdstɒk) n a town in New York State, the site of a large rock festival in August 1969. Pop: 6253 (2003 est)

wood tar n any tar produced by the destructive distillation of wood: used in producing tarred cord and rope and formerly in medicine as disinfectants and antiseptics

Woodville ('wʊdvɪl) n Elizabeth. ?1437–92, wife of Edward IV of England and mother of Edward V

wood warbler n 1 a European woodland warbler, Phylloscopus sibilatrix, with a dull yellow plumage 2 another name for the American warbler. See warbler (sense 3)

Woodward ('wʊdwəd) n 1 Sir Clive. born 1956, English Rugby Union player and subsequently (1997–2004) coach of the England team that won the Rugby World Cup in 2003. 2 R(obert) B(urns). 1917–79, US chemist. For his work on the synthesis of quinine, strychnine, cholesterol, and other organic compounds he won the Nobel prize for chemistry 1965

woodwind ('wʊd,wɪnd) music ▷ adj 1 of, relating to, or denoting a type of wind instrument, excluding the brass instruments, formerly made of wood but now often made of metal, such as the flute or clarinet ▷ n 2 (functioning as plural) woodwind instruments collectively

woodwork ('wʊd,wɜːk) n 1 the art, craft, or skill of making things in wood; carpentry 2 components made of wood, such as doors, staircases, etc

woodworking ('wʊd,wɜːkɪŋ) n 1 the process of working wood ▷ adj 2 of, relating to, or used in woodworking > 'wood,worker n

woodworm ('wʊd,wɜːm) n 1 any of various insect larvae that bore into wooden furniture, beams, etc, esp the larvae of the furniture beetle, Anobium punctatum, and the deathwatch beetle 2 the condition caused in wood by any of these larvae

woody ('wʊdɪ) adj woodier, woodiest 1 abounding in or covered with forest or woods 2 connected with, belonging to, or situated in a wood 3 consisting of or containing wood or lignin: woody tissue; woody stems 4 resembling wood in hardness or texture > 'woodiness n

woodyard ('wʊd,jɑːd) n a place where timber is cut and stored

woody nightshade n a scrambling woody Eurasian solanaceous plant, Solanum dulcamara, having purple flowers with recurved petals and a protruding cone of yellow anthers and producing poisonous red berry-like fruits. Also called: bittersweet

woof¹ (wuːf) n 1 the crosswise yarns that fill the warp yarns in weaving; weft 2 a woven fabric or its texture [Old English ōwef, from ō-, perhaps from ON, + wef WEB (see WEAVE); modern form influenced by WARP]

woof² (wʊf) interj 1 an imitation of the bark or growl of a dog ▷ vb 2 (intr) (of dogs) to bark or growl

woofer ('wuːfə) n a loudspeaker used in high-fidelity systems for the reproduction of low audio frequencies

woofter ('wʊftə, 'wuːftə) n derogatory, slang a male homosexual [C20: altered from POOFTER]

Wookey Hole ('wʊkɪ həʊl) n a village in SW England, in Somerset, near Wells: noted for the nearby limestone cave in which prehistoric remains have been found

wool (wʊl) n 1 the outer coat of sheep, yaks, etc, which consists of short curly hairs 2 yarn spun from the coat of sheep, etc, used in weaving, knitting, etc 3 a cloth or a garment made from this yarn b (as modifier): a wool dress 4 any of certain fibrous materials: glass wool; steel wool 5 informal short thick curly hair 6 a tangled mass of soft fine hairs that occurs in certain plants 7 pull the wool over someone's eyes to deceive or delude someone [Old English wull; related to Old Frisian, Middle Dutch wulle,

W

Old High German *wolla* (German *Wolle*), Old Norse *ull*, Latin *lāna* and *vellus* fleece]

wool clip *n* the total amount of wool shorn from a particular flock, or from flocks in a particular region or country, in one year

Woolf (wʊlf) *n* **1 Leonard Sidney**. 1880–1969, English publisher and political writer **2** his wife, **Virginia**. 1882–1941, English novelist and critic. Her novels, which include *Mrs Dalloway* (1925), *To the Lighthouse* (1927), and *Between the Acts* (1941), employ such techniques as the interior monologue and stream of consciousness

wool fat *or* **wool grease** *n* another name for **lanolin**

woolfell ('wʊlˌfɛl) *n obsolete* the skin of a sheep or similar animal with the fleece still attached

woolgathering ('wʊlˌgæðərɪŋ) *n* idle or absent-minded indulgence in fantasy; daydreaming

woolgrower ('wʊlˌɡrəʊə) *n* a person who keeps sheep for their wool > 'wool,growing *n*, *adj*

Woollcott ('wʊlkɒt) *n* **Alexander**. 1887–1943, US writer and critic. His collected essays include *Shouts and Murmurs* (1922)

woolled (wʊld) *adj* **1** (of animals) having wool **2** having wool as specified: *coarse-woolled*

woollen *or US* **woolen** ('wʊlən) *adj* **1** relating to or consisting partly or wholly of wool ▷ *n* **2** (*often plural*) a garment or piece of cloth made wholly or partly of wool, esp a knitted one

Woolley ('wʊlɪ) *n* Sir (**Charles**) **Leonard**. 1880–1960, British archaeologist, noted for his excavations at Ur in Mesopotamia (1922–34)

woolly *or sometimes US* **wooly** ('wʊlɪ) *adj* **woollier**, **woolliest** *or sometimes US* **woolier**, **wooliest 1** consisting of, resembling, or having the nature of wool **2** covered or clothed in wool or something resembling it **3** lacking clarity or substance: *woolly thinking* **4** *botany* covered with long soft whitish hairs: *woolly stems* ▷ *n*, *pl* **woollies** *or* **woolies 5** (*often plural*) a garment, such as a sweater, made of wool or something similar > 'woollily *adv* > 'woolliness *n*

woolly bear *n* the caterpillar of any of various tiger moths, esp *Arctia caja* of Europe and *Isia isabella* of North America, having a dense covering of soft hairs

woolpack ('wʊlˌpæk) *n* **1** the cloth or canvas wrapping used to pack a bale of wool **2** a bale of wool

woolsack ('wʊlˌsæk) *n* **1** a sack containing or intended to contain wool **2** (in Britain) the seat of the Lord Chancellor in the House of Lords, formerly made of a large square sack of wool

woolshed ('wʊlˌʃɛd) *n Austral & NZ* a shearing shed

wool stapler *n* a person who sorts wool into different grades or classifications

Woolworth ('wʊlwəθ) *n* **Frank Winfield** (ˈwɪnˌfiːld). 1852–1919, US merchant; founder of an international chain of department stores selling inexpensive goods

woomera *or* **womera** ('wʊmərə) *n Austral* a type of notched stick used by native Australians to increase leverage and propulsion in the throwing of a spear [from a native Australian language]

Woomera ('wʊmərə) *n* a town in South Australia: site of the Long Range Weapons Establishment. Pop: 602 (2001)

Woop Woop ('wuːp ˌwuːp) *n Austral slang* a jocular name for any backward or remote town or district

Wootton ('wʊtᵊn) *n* **Barbara** (**Frances**), Baroness of Abinger. 1897–1988, English economist, educationalist, social scientist, and criminologist

woozy ('wuːzɪ) *adj* **woozier**, **wooziest** *informal* **1** dazed or confused **2** experiencing dizziness, nausea, etc [C19: perhaps from a blend of *woolly* + *muzzy* or *dizzy*] > 'woozily *adv* > 'wooziness *n*

wop (wɒp) *n slang*, *derogatory* a member of a Latin people, esp an Italian [C20: probably from southern Italian dialect *guappo* dandy, braggart, from Spanish *guapo*]

wop-wops ('wɒpˌwɒps) *n* (*functioning as plural or singular*) **the wop-wops** *NZ informal* the backblocks; the back of beyond

Worcester ('wʊstə) *n* **1** a cathedral city in W central England, the administrative centre of Worcestershire on the River Severn: scene of the battle (1651) in which Charles II was defeated by Cromwell. Pop: 94 029 (2001)

2 an industrial city in the US, in central Massachusetts: Clark University (1887). Pop: 175 706 (2003 est) **3** a town in S South Africa; centre of a fruit-growing region. Pop: 66 349 (2001)

Worcester sauce *or* **Worcestershire sauce** *n* a commercially prepared piquant sauce, made from a basis of soy sauce, with vinegar, spices, etc

Worcestershire ('wʊstəˌʃɪə, -ʃə) *n* a county of W central England, formerly (1974–98) part of Hereford and Worcester. Administrative centre: Worcester. Pop: 549 300 (2003 est). Area: 1742 sq km (674 sq miles)

Worcs *abbreviation* Worcestershire

word (wɜːd) *n* **1** one of the units of speech or writing that native speakers of a language usually regard as the smallest isolable meaningful element of the language, although linguists would analyse these further into morphemes **2** an instance of vocal intercourse; chat, talk, or discussion: *to have a word with someone* **3** an utterance or expression, esp a brief one: *a word of greeting* **4** news or information: *he sent word that he would be late* **5** a verbal signal for action; command: *when I give the word, fire!* **6** an undertaking or promise: *I give you my word; he kept his word* **7** an autocratic decree or utterance; order: *his word must be obeyed* **8** a watchword or slogan, as of a political party: *the word now is "freedom"* **9** *computing* a set of bits used to store, transmit, or operate upon an item of information in a computer, such as a program instruction **10 as good as one's word** doing what one has undertaken or promised to do **11 at a word** at once **12 by word of mouth** orally rather than by written means **13 in a word** briefly or in short **14 my word! a** an exclamation of surprise, annoyance, etc **b** *Austral* an exclamation of agreement **15 of one's word** given to or noted for keeping one's promises: *I am a man of my word* **16 put in a word for** *or* **put in a good word for** to make favourable mention of (someone); recommend **17 take someone at his word** *or* **take someone at her word** to assume that someone means, or will do, what he or she says: *when he told her to go, she took him at his word and left* **18 take someone's word for it** to accept or believe what someone says **19 the last word a** the latest or most fashionable design, make, or model: *the last word in bikinis* **b** the finest example (of some quality, condition, etc): *the last word in luxury* **20 the word** the proper or most fitting expression: *cold is not the word for it, it's freezing!* **21 upon my word! a** *archaic* on my honour **b** an exclamation of surprise, annoyance, etc **22 word for word** (of a report, transcription, etc) using exactly the same words as those employed in the situation being reported; verbatim **23 word of honour** a promise; oath **24** (*modifier*) of, relating to, or consisting of words ▷ *vb* **25** (*tr*) to state in words, esp specially selected ones; phrase **26** (*tr*; often foll by *up*) *Austral informal* to inform or advise (a person) ▷ See also **words** [Old English *word*; related to Old High German *wort*, Old Norse *orth*, Gothic *waurd*, Latin *verbum*, Sanskrit *vratá* command] > 'wordless *adj* > 'wordlessly *adv*

Word (wɜːd) *n* **the Word 1** *Christianity* the 2nd person of the Trinity **2** Scripture, the Bible, or the Gospels as embodying or representing divine revelation [translation of Greek *logos*, as in John 1:1]

-word *n combining form* (*preceded by* **the** *and an initial letter*) a euphemistic way of referring to a word by its first letter because it is considered to be in some way unmentionable by the user: *the C-word, meaning cancer*

wordage ('wɜːdɪdʒ) *n* words considered collectively, esp a quantity of words

word association *n* an early method of psychoanalysis in which the patient thinks of the first word that comes into consciousness on hearing a given word. In this way it was claimed that aspects of the unconscious could be revealed before defence mechanisms intervene

word blindness *n* the nontechnical name for **alexia**, **dyslexia** > 'word-ˌblind *adj*

wordbook ('wɜːdˌbʊk) *n* a book containing words, usually with their meanings

word deafness *n* loss of ability to understand spoken words, esp as the result of a cerebral lesion. Also called: auditory aphasia

word game n any game involving the formation, discovery, or alteration of a word or words

wording ('wɜːdɪŋ) n 1 the way in which words are used to express a statement, report, etc, esp a written one 2 the words themselves, as used in a written statement or a sign

word order n the arrangement of words in a phrase, clause, or sentence. In many languages, including English, word order plays an important part in determining meanings expressed in other languages by inflections

word-perfect or US **letter-perfect** adj 1 correct in every detail 2 (of a speaker, actor, etc) knowing one's speech, role, etc, perfectly

wordplay ('wɜːd,pleɪ) n verbal wit based on the meanings and ambiguities of words; puns, clever repartee, etc

word processing n the composition of documents using a computer system to input, edit, store, and print them

word processor n **a** a computer program that performs word processing **b** a computer system designed for word processing

words (wɜːdz) pl n 1 the text of a part of an actor, etc 2 the text or lyrics of a song, as opposed to the music 3 angry speech (esp in the phrase **have words with someone**) 4 **eat one's words** to retract a statement 5 **for words** (preceded by too and an adjective or adverb) indescribably; extremely: the play was too funny for words 6 **have no words for** to be incapable of describing 7 **in other words** expressing the same idea but differently 8 **in so many words** explicitly or precisely 9 **of few words** not talkative 10 **of many words** talkative 11 **put into words** to express in speech or writing as well as thought 12 **say a few words** to give a brief speech 13 **take the words out of someone's mouth** to say exactly what someone else was about to say 14 **words fail me** I am too happy, sad, amazed, etc, to express my thoughts

wordsearch ('wɜːd,sɜːtʃ) n a puzzle made up of letters arranged in a grid which contains a number of hidden words running in various directions

word square n a puzzle in which the player must fill a square grid with words that read the same across as down

Wordsworth ('wɜːdz,wəθ) n 1 **Dorothy**. 1771–1855, English writer, whose Journals are noted esp for their descriptions of nature 2 her brother, **William**. 1770–1850, English poet, whose work, celebrating nature, was greatly inspired by the Lake District, in which he spent most of his life. Lyrical Ballads (1798), to which Coleridge contributed, is often taken as the first landmark of English romantic poetry and includes his Lines Written above Tintern Abbey. Among his other works are The Prelude (completed in 1805; revised thereafter and published posthumously) and Poems in Two Volumes (1807), which includes The Solitary Reaper and Intimations of Immortality > Wordsworthian (,wɜːdz'wɜːðɪən) adj, n

word wrapping n computing the automatic shifting of a word at the end of a line to a new line in order to keep within preset margins

wordy ('wɜːdɪ) adj wordier, wordiest using, inclined to use, or containing an excess of words > **wordily** adv > **wordiness** n

wore (wɔː) vb the past tense of **wear**[1]

work (wɜːk) n 1 physical or mental effort directed towards doing or making something 2 paid employment at a job or a trade, occupation, or profession 3 a duty, task, or undertaking 4 something done, made, etc, as a result of effort or exertion: a work of art 5 another word for **workmanship** (sense 3) 6 the place, office, etc, where a person is employed 7 **a** decoration or ornamentation, esp of a specified kind **b** (in combination): wirework; woolwork 8 an engineering structure such as a bridge, building, etc 9 physics the transfer of energy expressed as the product of a force and the distance through which its point of application moves in the direction of the force 10 a structure, wall, etc, built or used as part of a fortification system 11 **at work a** at one's job or place of employment **b** in action; operating 12 **make short work of** informal to handle or dispose of very quickly 13 (modifier) of, relating to, or used for work: work clothes; a work permit ▷ vb 14 (intr) to exert effort in order to do, make, or perform something 15 (intr) to be employed 16 (tr) to carry on operations, activity, etc, in (a place or area): that salesman works the southern region 17 (tr) to cause to labour or toil: he works his men hard 18 to operate or cause to operate, esp properly or effectively: to work a lathe; that clock doesn't work 19 (tr) to till or cultivate (land) 20 to handle or manipulate or be handled or manipulated: to work dough 21 to shape, form, or process or be shaped, formed, or processed: to work copper 22 to reach or cause to reach a specific condition, esp gradually: the rope worked loose 23 (intr) to move in agitation: his face worked with anger 24 (tr; often foll by up) to provoke or arouse: to work someone into a frenzy 25 (tr) to effect or accomplish: to work one's revenge 26 to make (one's way) with effort: he worked his way through the crowd 27 (tr) to make or decorate by hand in embroidery, tapestry, etc 28 (intr) (of liquids) to ferment, as in brewing 29 (tr) informal to manipulate or exploit to one's own advantage ▷ See also **work in**, **work off** [Old English weorc (n), wircan, wyrcan (vb); related to Old High German wurchen, German wirken, Old Norse yrkja, Gothic waurkjan] > **workless** adj

workable ('wɜːkəbəl) adj 1 practicable or feasible 2 able to be worked > **,worka'bility** or **'workableness** n

workaday ('wɜːkə,deɪ) adj (usually prenominal) 1 being a part of general human experience; ordinary 2 suitable for working days; everyday or practical

workaholic (,wɜːkə'hɒlɪk) n **a** a person obsessively addicted to work **b** (as modifier): workaholic behaviour [C20: from WORK + -HOLIC, coined in 1971 by Wayne Oates, US author]

workaround ('wɜːkə,raʊnd) n a method of circumventing or overcoming a problem in a computer program or system

workbag ('wɜːk,bæg) n a container for implements, tools, or materials, esp sewing equipment. Also called: **work basket**, **workbox**

workbench ('wɜːk,bentʃ) n a heavy table at which work is done by a carpenter, mechanic, toolmaker, etc

workbook ('wɜːk,bʊk) n 1 an exercise book or textbook used for study, esp a textbook with spaces for answers 2 a book of instructions for some process 3 a book in which is recorded all work done or planned

work camp n a camp set up for young people who voluntarily do manual work on a worthwhile project

workday ('wɜːk,deɪ) n 1 the usual US term for **working day** ▷ adj 2 another word for **workaday**

worked (wɜːkt) adj made or decorated with evidence of workmanship; wrought, as with embroidery or tracery

worked up adj agitated or excited

worker ('wɜːkə) n 1 a person or thing that works, usually at a specific job: a good worker; a research worker 2 an employee in an organization, as opposed to an employer or manager 3 a manual labourer or other employee working in a manufacturing or other industry 4 any other member of the working class 5 a sterile female member of a colony of bees, ants, or wasps that forages for food, cares for the larvae, etc

worker director n a worker elected to the governing board of a business concern to represent the interests of the employees in decision making

worker-priest n a Roman Catholic priest who has full-time or part-time employment in a secular job to be more closely in touch with the problems of the laity

work ethic n a belief in the moral value of work (often in the phrase **Protestant work ethic**)

workfare ('wɜːk,feə) n a scheme under which the government of a country requires unemployed people to do community work or undergo job training in return for social-security payments [C20: from WORK + (WEL)FARE]

workforce ('wɜːk,fɔːs) n 1 the total number of workers employed by a company on a specific job, project, etc 2 the total number of people who could be employed: the country's workforce is growing rapidly

w

work function *n physics* the minimum energy required to transfer an electron from a point within a solid to a point just outside its surface. Symbol: φ or Φ

work-harden *vb* (*tr*) to increase the strength or hardness of (a metal) by a mechanical process, such as tension, compression, or torsion

workhorse ('wɜːkˌhɔːs) *n* **1** a horse used for nonrecreational activities **2** *informal* a person who takes on the greatest amount of work in a project or job

workhouse ('wɜːkˌhaʊs) *n* **1** (formerly in England) an institution maintained at public expense where able-bodied paupers did unpaid work in return for food and accommodation **2** (in the US) a prison for petty offenders serving short sentences at manual labour

work in *vb* (*adverb*) **1** to insert or become inserted: *she worked the patch in carefully* **2** (*tr*) to find space for: *I'll work this job in during the day* ▷ *n* **work-in 3** a form of industrial action in which a factory that is to be closed down is occupied and run by its workers

working ('wɜːkɪŋ) *n* **1** the operation or mode of operation of something **2** the act or process of moulding something pliable **3** a convulsive or jerking motion, as from excitement **4** (*often plural*) a part of a mine or quarry that is being or has been worked **5** a record of the steps by which the result of a calculation or the solution of a problem is obtained: *all working is to be submitted to the examiners* ▷ *adj* (*prenominal*) **6** relating to or concerned with a person or thing that works: *a working man* **7** concerned with, used in, or suitable for work: *working clothes* **8** (of a meal or occasion) during which business discussions are carried on: *working lunch; working breakfast* **9** capable of being operated or used: *a working model* **10** sufficiently large or accurate to be useful or to accomplish a desired end: *a working majority; a working knowledge of German* **11** (of a theory, etc) providing a basis, usually a temporary one, on which operations or procedures may be carried out

working bee *n NZ* a voluntary group doing a job for charity

working capital *n* **1** *accounting* current assets minus current liabilities **2** current or liquid assets **3** that part of the capital of a business enterprise available for operations

working class *n* **1** Also called: proletariat the social stratum, usually of low status, that consists of those who earn wages, esp as manual workers ▷ *adj* **working-class 2** of, relating to, or characteristic of the working class

working day *or esp US* **workday** *n* **1** a day on which work is done, esp for an agreed or stipulated number of hours in return for a salary or wage **2** the part of the day allocated to work **3** (*often plural*) *commerce* any day of the week except Sunday, public holidays, and, in some cases, Saturday

working drawing *n* a scale drawing of a part or assembly that provides a guide for manufacture

Working Families Tax Credit *n* (in Britain) a means-tested allowance paid to single parents or families who have at least one dependent child, who work at least 16 hours per week, and whose earnings are low. It replaced family credit

working girl *n* **1** a girl or woman who works, esp one who supports herself **2** *informal* a prostitute

working memory *n psychol* the current contents of a person's consciousness

working party *n* **1** a committee established to investigate a problem, question, etc **2** a group of soldiers or prisoners assigned to perform some manual task or duty

working week *or esp US and Canadian* **workweek** ('wɜːkˌwiːk) *n* the number of hours or days in a week actually or officially allocated to work

work-in-progress *n book-keeping* the value of work begun but not completed, as shown in a profit-and-loss account

workload ('wɜːkˌləʊd) *n* the amount of work to be done, esp in a specified period by a person, machine, etc

workman ('wɜːkmən) *n, pl* **-men 1** a man who is employed in manual labour or who works an industrial

machine **2** a craftsman of skill as specified: *a bad workman*

workmanlike ('wɜːkmənˌlaɪk) *or less commonly* **workmanly** ('wɜːkmənlɪ) *adj* appropriate to or befitting a good workman

workmanship ('wɜːkmənʃɪp) *n* **1** the art or skill of a workman **2** the art or skill with which something is made or executed **3** the degree of art or skill exhibited in the finished product **4** the piece of work so produced

workmate ('wɜːkˌmeɪt) *n* a person who works with another; fellow worker

work of art *n* **1** a piece of fine art, such as a painting or sculpture **2** something that may be likened to a piece of fine art, esp in beauty, intricacy, etc

work off *vb* (*tr, adverb*) **1** to get rid of or dissipate, as by effort: *he worked off some of his energy by digging the garden* **2** to discharge (a debt) by labour rather than payment

work on *vb* (*intr, preposition*) to persuade or influence or attempt to persuade or influence

work out *vb* (*adverb*) **1** (*tr*) to achieve or accomplish by effort **2** (*tr*) to solve or find out by reasoning or calculation: *to work out an answer; to work out a sum* **3** (*tr*) to devise or formulate: *to work out a plan* **4** (*intr*) to happen as specified: *it all worked out well* **5** (*intr*) to take part in physical exercise, as in training **6** (*tr*) to remove all the mineral in (a mine, body of ore, etc) that can be profitably exploited **7** (*intr; often foll by to or at*) to reach a total: *your bill works out at a pound* ▷ *n* **work-out 8** a session of physical exercise, esp for training or practice

work over *vb* **1** (*tr, adverb*) to do again; repeat **2** (*intr, preposition*) to examine closely and thoroughly **3** (*tr, adverb*) *slang* to assault or thrash

workpeople ('wɜːkˌpiːpᵊl) *pl n* the working members of a population, esp those employed in manual tasks

workroom ('wɜːkˌruːm, -ˌrʊm) *n* **1** a room in which work, usually manual labour, is done **2** a room in a house set aside for a hobby, such as sewing

works (wɜːks) *pl n* **1** (*often functioning as singular*) a place where a number of people are employed, such as a factory **2** the sum total of a writer's or artist's achievements, esp when considered together: *the works of Shakespeare* **3** the deeds of a person, esp virtuous or moral deeds performed as religious acts: *works of charity* **4** the interior parts of the mechanism of a machine, etc: *the works of a clock* **5** in the works *informal* in preparation **6** the works *slang* **a** full or extreme treatment **b** a very violent physical beating: *to give someone the works*

works council *n chiefly Brit* **1** a council composed of both employer and employees convened to discuss matters of common interest concerning a factory, plant, business policy, etc, not covered by regular trade union agreements **2** a body representing the workers of a plant, factory, etc, elected to negotiate with the management about working conditions, wages, etc ▷ Also called: works committee

worksheet ('wɜːkˌʃiːt) *n* **1** a sheet of paper used for the preliminary or rough draft of a problem, design, etc **2** a piece of paper recording work being planned or already in progress

workshop ('wɜːkˌʃɒp) *n* **1** a room or building in which manufacturing or other forms of manual work are carried on **2** a room in a private dwelling, school, etc, set aside for crafts **3** a group of people engaged in study and work on a creative project or subject: *a music workshop*

workshy ('wɜːkˌʃaɪ) *adj* not inclined to work

Worksop ('wɜːksɒp) *n* a town in N central England, in N Nottinghamshire. Pop: 39 072 (2001)

work station *n* **1** an area in an office where one person works **2** *computing* a device or component of an electronic office system consisting of a display screen and keyboard used to handle electronic office work

workstream ('wɜːkˌstriːm) *n commerce* any one of the areas of activity into which a company's business may be divided

work-study *n* an examination of ways of finding the most efficient method of doing a job, esp in terms of time and effort

worktable ('wɜːkˌteɪbᵊl) *n* **a** any table at which writing, sewing, or other work may be done **b** (in English

w

cabinetwork) a small elegant table fitted with sewing accessories

worktop ('wɜːk,tɒp) *n* a surface in a kitchen, often of heat-resistant laminated plastic, that is used for food preparation

work-to-rule *n* **1** a form of industrial action in which employees adhere strictly to all the working rules laid down by their employers, with the deliberate intention of reducing the rate of working ▷ *vb* **work to rule** **2** (*intr*) to decrease the rate of working by this means

work up *vb* (*tr, mainly adverb*) **1** to arouse the feelings of; excite **2** to cause to grow or develop: *to work up a hunger* **3** (*also preposition*) to move or cause to move gradually upwards **4** to manipulate or mix into a specified object or shape **5** to gain knowledge of or skill at (a subject)

world (wɜːld) *n* **1** the earth as a planet, esp including its inhabitants **2** mankind; the human race **3** people generally; the public: *in the eyes of the world* **4** social or public life: *to go out into the world* **5** the universe or cosmos; everything in existence **6** a complex united whole regarded as resembling the universe **7** any star or planet, esp one that might be inhabited **8** (*often capital*) a division or section of the earth, its history, or its inhabitants: *the Western World; the Ancient World; the Third World* **9** an area, sphere, or realm considered as a complete environment: *the animal world* **10** any field of human activity or way of life or those involved in it: *the world of television* **11** a period or state of existence: *the next world* **12** the total circumstances and experience of an individual that make up his life, esp that part of it relating to happiness: *you have shattered my world* **13** a large amount, number, or distance: *worlds apart* **14** worldly or secular life, ways, or people **15** bring into the world **a** (of a midwife, doctor, etc) to deliver (a baby) **b** to give birth to **16** come into the world to be born **17** for all the world in every way; exactly **18** give to the world to publish **19** in the world (*usually used with a negative*) (*intensifier*): *no-one in the world can change things* **20** man of the world or woman of the world a man or woman experienced in social or public life **21** not long for this world nearing death **22** on top of the world *informal* exultant, elated, or very happy **23** *informal* wonderful; excellent **24** set the world on fire to be exceptionally or sensationally successful **25** the best of both worlds the benefits from two different or opposed ways of life, philosophies, etc **26** think the world of to be extremely fond of or hold in very high esteem **27** world of one's own a state of mental detachment from other people **28** world without end for ever **29** (*modifier*) of or concerning most or all countries; worldwide: *world politics; a world record* **30** (*in combination*) throughout the world: *world-famous* [Old English *w(e)orold*, from *wer* man + *ald* age, life; related to Old Frisian *warld, wrald*, Old Norse *verold*, Old High German *wealt* (German *Welt*)]

World Bank *n* an international cooperative organization established in 1945 under the Bretton Woods Agreement to assist economic development, esp of backward nations, by the advance of loans guaranteed by member governments. Officially called: **International Bank for Reconstruction and Development**

world-beater *n* a person or thing that surpasses all others in its category; champion

world-class *adj* of or denoting someone with a skill or attribute that puts him or her in the highest class in the world: *a world-class swimmer*

World Court *n* another name for **International Court of Justice**

World Cup *n* an international competition held between national teams in various sports, most notably association football

worldling ('wɜːldlɪŋ) *n* a person who is primarily concerned with worldly matters or material things

worldly ('wɜːldlɪ) *adj* -lier, -liest **1** not spiritual; mundane or temporal **2** Also called: **worldly-minded** absorbed in or concerned with material things or matters that are immediately relevant **3** Also called: **worldly-wise** versed in the ways of the world; sophisticated ▷ '**worldliness** *n*

world music *n* popular music of various ethnic origins

and styles outside the tradition of Western pop and rock music

world power *n* a state that possesses sufficient power to influence events throughout the world

world-shaking *adj* of enormous significance

World Trade Organization *n* an international body concerned with promoting and regulating trade between its member states; established in 1995 as a successor to GATT

World War I *n* the war (1914–18), fought mainly in Europe and the Middle East, in which the Allies (principally France, Russia, Britain, Italy after 1915, and the US after 1917) defeated the Central Powers (principally Germany, Austria-Hungary, and Turkey). The war was precipitated by the assassination of Austria's crown prince (Archduke Franz Ferdinand) at Sarajevo on June 28, 1914 and swiftly developed its major front in E France, where millions died in static trench warfare. After the October Revolution (1917) the Bolsheviks ended Russian participation in the war (Dec 15, 1917). The exhausted Central Powers agreed to an armistice on Nov 11, 1918 and quickly succumbed to internal revolution, before being forced to sign the Treaty of Versailles (June 28, 1919) and other treaties. Also called: **First World War, Great War**

World War II *n* the war (1939–45) in which the Allies (principally Britain, the Soviet Union, and the US) defeated the Axis powers (principally Germany, Italy, and Japan). Britain and France declared war on Germany (Sept 3, 1939) as a result of the German invasion of Poland (Sept 1, 1939). Italy entered the war on June 10, 1940 shortly before the collapse of France (armistice signed June 22, 1940). On June 22, 1941 Germany attacked the Soviet Union and on Dec 7, 1941 the Japanese attacked the US at Pearl Harbor. On Sept 8, 1943 Italy surrendered, the war in Europe ending on May 7, 1945 with the unconditional surrender of the Germans. The Japanese capitulated on Aug 14, 1945 as a direct result of the atomic bombs dropped by the Americans on Hiroshima and Nagasaki. Also called: **Second World War**

world-weary *adj* no longer finding pleasure in living; tired of the world > '**world-,weariness** *n*

worldwide ('wɜːld'waɪd) *adj* applying or extending throughout the world; universal

World Wide Web *n computing* a vast network of linked hypertext files, stored on computers throughout the world, that can provide a computer user with information on a huge variety of subjects. Abbreviation: **WWW**

worm (wɜːm) *n* **1** any of various invertebrates, esp the annelids (earthworms, etc), nematodes (roundworms), and flatworms, having a slender elongated body **2** any of various insect larvae having an elongated body, such as the silkworm and wireworm **3** any of various unrelated animals that resemble annelids, nematodes, etc, such as the glow-worm and shipworm **4** a gnawing or insinuating force or agent that torments or slowly eats away **5** a wretched or spineless person **6** anything that resembles a worm in appearance or movement **7** a shaft on which a helical groove has been cut, as in a gear arrangement in which such a shaft meshes with a toothed wheel **8** a spiral pipe cooled by air or flowing water, used as a condenser in a still **9** *computing* a program that duplicates itself many times in a network and prevents its destruction. It often carries a logic bomb or virus ▷ *vb* **10** to move, act, or cause to move or act with the slow sinuous movement of a worm **11** (foll by *in, into, out of,* etc) to make (one's way) slowly and stealthily; insinuate (oneself) **12** (*tr;* often foll by *out of* or *from*) to extract (information, a secret, etc) from by persistent questioning **13** (*tr*) to free from or purge of worms ▷ See also **worms** [Old English *wyrm*; related to Old Frisian *wirm*, Old High German *wurm*, Old Norse *ormr*, Gothic *waurms*, Latin *vermis*, Greek *romos* woodworm] > '**wormer** *n* > '**worm,like** *or* '**wormish** *adj*

WORM (wɜːm) *n acronym computing* write once read many times: an optical disk that enables users to store data but not change it

wormcast ('wɜːm,kɑːst) *n* a coil of earth or sand that has been egested by a burrowing earthworm or lugworm

worm-eaten *adj* 1 eaten into by worms: *a worm-eaten table* 2 decayed; rotten 3 old-fashioned; antiquated

worm gear *n* 1 a device consisting of a threaded shaft (**worm**) that mates with a gearwheel (**worm wheel**) so that rotary motion can be transferred between two shafts at right angles to each other 2 Also called: **worm wheel** a gearwheel driven by a threaded shaft or worm

wormhole ('wɜːm,həʊl) *n* a hole made by a worm in timber, plants, etc ▷ 'worm,holed *adj*

worms (wɜːmz) *n* (*functioning as singular*) any disease or disorder, usually of the intestine, characterized by infestation with parasitic worms

Worms (wɜːmz; *German* vɔrms) *n* a city in SW Germany, in Rhineland-Palatinate on the Rhine: famous as the seat of imperial diets, notably that of 1521, before which Luther defended his doctrines in the presence of Charles V; river port and manufacturing centre with a large wine trade. Pop: 81 100 (2003 est)

worm's eye view *n* a view seen from below or from a more lowly or humble point

wormwood ('wɜːm,wʊd) *n* 1 Also called: **absinthe** any of various plants of the chiefly N temperate genus *Artemisia*, esp *A. absinthium*, a European plant yielding a bitter extract used in making absinthe: family *Asteraceae* (composites) 2 something that embitters, such as a painful experience [C15: changed (through influence of WORM and WOOD) from Old English *wormōd*, *wermōd*; related to Old High German *werrnuata*, German *Wermut*; see VERMOUTH]

wormy ('wɜːmɪ) *adj* **wormier, wormiest** 1 worm-infested or worm-eaten 2 resembling a worm in appearance, ways, or condition 3 (of wood) having irregular small tunnels bored into it and tracked over its surface, made either by worms or artificially 4 low or grovelling ▷ 'worminess *n*

worn (wɔːn) *vb* 1 the past participle of WEAR¹ ▷ *adj* 2 affected, esp adversely, by long use or action: *a worn suit* 3 haggard; drawn 4 exhausted; spent ▷ 'wornness *n*

worn-out *adj* (**worn out** *when postpositive*) 1 worn or used until threadbare, valueless, or useless 2 exhausted; very weary

worried ('wʌrɪd) *adj* feeling uneasy about a situation or thing; anxious ▷ 'worriedly *adv*

worried well *n* the worried well *informal* the people who do not need medical treatment, but who visit the doctor to be reassured, or with emotional problems

worriment ('wʌrɪmənt) *n* *informal, chiefly US & Canadian* anxiety or the trouble that causes it; worry

worrisome ('wʌrɪsəm) *adj* 1 causing worry; vexing 2 tending to worry ▷ 'worrisomely *adv*

worrit ('wʌrɪt) *vb* (*tr*) *dialect* to tease or worry [probably variant of WORRY, but compare WHERRIT]

worry ('wʌrɪ) *vb* **-ries, -rying, -ried** 1 to be or cause to be anxious or uneasy, esp about something uncertain or potentially dangerous 2 (*tr*) to disturb the peace of mind of; bother: *don't worry me with trivialities* 3 (*intr*; often foll by *along* or *through*) to proceed despite difficulties 4 (*intr*; often foll by *away*) to struggle or work: *to worry away at a problem* 5 (*tr*) (of a dog, wolf, etc) to lacerate or kill by biting, shaking, etc 6 (when *intr*, foll by *at*) to bite, tear, or gnaw (at) with the teeth: *a dog worrying a bone* 7 (*tr*) to touch or poke repeatedly and idly 8 not to worry *informal* you need not worry ▷ *n*, *pl* **-ries** 9 a state or feeling of anxiety 10 a person or thing that causes anxiety 11 an act of worrying 12 no worries *informal* an expression used to express agreement or to convey that something is proceeding or has proceeded satisfactorily; no problem [Old English *wyrgan*; related to Old Frisian *wergia* to kill, Old High German *wurgen* (German (*er*)*würgen* to strangle), Old Norse *virgill*, *urga* rope] ▷ 'worrying *adj* ▷ 'worryingly *adv*

worry beads *pl n* a string of beads that when fingered or played with supposedly relieves nervous tension

worryguts ('wʌrɪ,gʌts) *or* **worrywart** ('wʌrɪ,wɔːt) *n* *informal* a person who tends to worry, esp about insignificant matters

worse (wɜːs) *adj* 1 the comparative of BAD¹ 2 none the worse for not harmed by (adverse events or circumstances) 3 the worse for wear a shabby or worn b a slang term for drunk 4 worse luck! *informal* unhappily; unfortunately 5 worse off (*postpositive*) in a worse, esp a worse financial, condition ▷ *n* 6 something that is worse 7 for the worse into a less desirable or inferior state or condition: *a change for the worse* ▷ *adv* 8 in a more severe or unpleasant manner 9 in a less effective or successful manner [Old English *wiersa*; related to Old Frisian *werra*, Old High German *wirsiro*, Old Norse *verri*, Gothic *wairsiza*]

worsen ('wɜːsən) *vb* to grow or cause to grow worse

worship ('wɜːʃɪp) *vb* **-ships, -shipping, -shipped** *or US* **-ships, -shiping, -shiped** 1 (*tr*) to show profound religious devotion and respect to; adore or venerate (God or any person or thing considered divine) 2 (*tr*) to be devoted to and full of admiration for 3 (*intr*) to have or express feelings of profound adoration 4 (*intr*) to attend services for worship ▷ *n* 5 religious adoration or devotion 6 the formal expression of religious adoration; rites, prayers, etc 7 admiring love or devotion [Old English *weorthscipe*, from WORTH + -SHIP] ▷ 'worshipper *n*

Worship ('wɜːʃɪp) *n* *chiefly Brit* (preceded by *Your, His,* or *Her*) a title used to address or refer to a mayor, magistrate, or a person of similar high rank

worshipful ('wɜːʃɪpfʊl) *adj* 1 feeling or showing reverence or adoration 2 (*often capital*) *chiefly Brit* a title used to address or refer to various people or bodies of distinguished rank, such as mayors and certain ancient companies of the City of London ▷ 'worshipfully *adv* ▷ 'worshipfulness *n*

worst (wɜːst) *adj* 1 the superlative of BAD¹ ▷ *adv* 2 in the most extreme or bad manner or degree 3 least well, suitably, or acceptably 4 (*in combination*) in or to the smallest degree or extent; least: *worst-loved* ▷ *n* 5 the worst the least good or most inferior person, thing, or part in a group, narrative, etc 6 (*often preceded by at*) the most poor, unpleasant, or unskilled quality or condition: *television is at its worst these days* 7 the greatest amount of damage or wickedness of which a person or group is capable: *the invaders came and did their worst* 8 the weakest effort or poorest achievement that a person or group is capable of making: *the applicant did his worst at the test because he did not want the job* 9 the worst a in the least favourable interpretation or view b under the least favourable conditions 10 if the worst comes to the worst if all the more desirable alternatives become impossible or if the worst possible thing happens 11 come off worst *or* get the worst of it to enjoy the least benefit from an issue or be defeated in it ▷ *vb* 12 (*tr*) to get the advantage over; defeat or beat [Old English *wierrest*; related to Old Frisian *wersta*, Old Saxon, Old High German *wirsisto*, Old Norse *verstr*]

worsted ('wʊstɪd) *n* 1 a closely twisted yarn or thread made from combed long-staple wool 2 a fabric made from this, with a hard smooth close-textured surface and no nap 3 (*modifier*) made of this yarn or fabric: *a worsted suit* [C13: named after *Worstead*, a district in Norfolk]

wort (wɜːt) *n* 1 (*in combination*) any of various unrelated plants, esp ones formerly used to cure diseases: *liverwort; spleenwort* 2 the sweet liquid obtained from the soaked mixture of warm water and ground malt, used to make a malt liquor [Old English *wyrt* root, related to Old High German *warz*, Gothic *waurts* root]

worth (wɜːθ) *adj* (governing a noun with prepositional force) 1 worthy of; meriting or justifying: *it's not worth discussing; an idea worth some thought* 2 having a value of: *the book is worth 30 pounds* 3 for all one is worth to the utmost; to the full extent of one's powers or ability 4 worth one's weight in gold extremely helpful, kind, etc ▷ *n* 5 high quality; excellence 6 value, price 7 the amount or quantity of something of a specified value: *five pounds worth of petrol* [Old English *weorth*; related to Old Saxon, Old High German *werth* (German *Wert*), Old Norse *verthr*, Gothic *wairths*]

Worth (wɜːθ; *French* vɔrt) *n* **Charles Frederick.** 1825–95, English couturier, who founded Parisian *haute couture*

w

worthless ('wɜːθlɪs) *adj* **1** without practical value or usefulness **2** without merit; good-for-nothing > 'worthlessly *adv* > 'worthlessness *n*

worthwhile (,wɜːθ'waɪl) *adj* sufficiently important, rewarding, or valuable to justify time or effort spent

worthy ('wɜːðɪ) *adj* **-thier, -thiest 1** (*postpositive*; often foll by *of* or an infinitive) having sufficient merit or value (for something or someone specified); deserving **2** having worth, value, or merit ▷ *n, pl* **-thies 3** *often facetious* a person of distinguished character, merit, or importance > 'worthily *adv* > 'worthiness *n*

wot (wɒt) *vb archaic or dialect* (used with I, *she, he, it*, or a singular noun) a form of the present tense (indicative mood) of **wit²**

Wotan ('vəʊtɑːn, 'vɔː-) *n* the supreme god in Germanic mythology. Norse counterpart: Odin

Wotton ('wɒtən, 'wʊtən) *n* Sir **Henry.** 1568–1639, English poet and diplomat

would (wʊd; *unstressed* wəd) *vb* (takes an infinitive without *to* or an implied infinitive) **1** used as an auxiliary to form the past tense or subjunctive mood of **will¹ 2** (with *you, he, she, it, they*, or a noun as subject) used as an auxiliary to indicate willingness or desire in a polite manner: *would you help me, please?* **3** used as an auxiliary to describe a past action as being accustomed or habitual: *every day we would go for walks* **4** I wish: *would that he were here*

⬤ USAGE See at **should**

would-be *adj* (*prenominal*) **1** *usually derogatory* wanting or professing to be: *a would-be politician* **2** intended to be

wouldn't ('wʊdənt) *vb contraction of* would not

wouldst (wʊdst) *vb archaic or dialect* (used with the pronoun *thou* or its relative equivalent) a singular form of the past tense of **will¹**

Woulfe bottle (wʊlf) *n chem* a bottle with more than one neck, used for passing gases through liquids [c18: named after Peter *Woulfe* (?1727–1803), English chemist]

wound¹ (wuːnd) *n* **1** any break in the skin or an organ or part as the result of violence or a surgical incision **2** an injury to plant tissue **3** any injury or slight to the feelings or reputation ▷ *vb* **4** to inflict a wound or wounds upon (someone or something) [Old English *wund*; related to Old Frisian *wunde*, Old High German *wunta* (German *Wunde*), Old Norse *und*, Gothic *wunds*] > 'woundable *adj* > 'wounder *n* > 'wounding *adj* > 'woundingly *adv* > 'woundless *adj*

wound² (waʊnd) *vb* the past tense and past participle of **wind²**

wounded ('wuːndɪd) *adj* **1 a** suffering from wounds; injured, esp in a battle or fight **b** (*as collective noun; preceded by the*): *the wounded* **2** (of feelings) damaged or hurt

woundwort ('wuːnd,wɜːt) *n* **1** any of various plants of the genus *Stachys*, such as *S. arvensis* (**field woundwort**), having purple, scarlet, yellow, or white flowers and formerly used for dressing wounds: family *Lamiaceae* (labiates) **2** any of various other plants used in this way

wove (wəʊv) *vb* a past tense of **weave**

woven ('wəʊvən) *vb* a past participle of **weave**

wove paper *n* paper with a very faint mesh impressed on it by the dandy roller on the paper-making machine

wow¹ (waʊ) *interj* **1** an exclamation of admiration, amazement, etc ▷ *n* **2** *slang* a person or thing that is amazingly successful, attractive, etc ▷ *vb* **3** (*tr*) *slang* to arouse great enthusiasm in [c16: originally Scottish, expressive of surprise, amazement, etc]

wow² (waʊ, wəʊ) *n* a slow variation or distortion in pitch that occurs at very low audio frequencies in sound-reproducing systems, such as a record player, usually due to variation in speed of the turntable, etc. See also **flutter** (sense 12) [c20: of imitative origin]

wow factor *n informal* a striking or impressive feature

wowser ('waʊzə) *n* **1** *Austral & NZ slang* a fanatically puritanical person **2** a teetotaller [c20: from English dialect *wow* to whine, complain]

Wozniak ('wɒznɪæk) *n* full name *Stephan Gary Wozniak*. born 1950, US computer scientist and executive: co-founder (with Steve Jobs, 1976) of Apple Inc

WP *abbreviation* **1** weather permitting **2** word processing

3 word processor

WPB *or* **wpb** *abbreviation* waste paper basket

WPC *abbreviation* (in Britain) woman police constable

wpm *abbreviation* words per minute

Wraac (ræk) *n* a member of the Women's Royal Australian Army Corps

WRAAC *abbreviation* Women's Royal Australian Army Corps

WRAAF *abbreviation* Women's Royal Australian Air Force

WRAC *abbreviation* (in Britain) Women's Royal Army Corps

wrack¹ *or* **rack** (ræk) *n* **1** collapse or destruction (esp in the phrase **wrack and ruin**) **2** something destroyed or a remnant of such ▷ *vb* **3** a variant spelling of **rack¹** [Old English *wræc* persecution, misery; related to Gothic *wraka*, Old Norse *rāk*. Compare WRECK, WRETCH]

⬤ USAGE The use of the spelling *wrack* rather than *rack* in
⬤ sentences such as *she was wracked by grief* or *the country*
⬤ *was wracked by civil war* is very common but is thought
⬤ by many people to be incorrect

wrack² (ræk) *n* **1** seaweed or other marine vegetation that is floating in the sea or has been cast ashore **2** any of various seaweeds of the genus *Fucus*, such as *F. serratus* (**serrated wrack**) **3** *literary or dialect* **a** a wreck or piece of wreckage **b** a remnant or fragment of something destroyed [c14 (in the sense: a wrecked ship, wreckage, hence later applied to marine vegetation washed ashore): perhaps from Middle Dutch *wrak* wreckage; the term corresponds to Old English *wræc* WRACK¹]

WRAF *abbreviation* (in Britain) Women's Royal Air Force

wraith (reɪθ) *n* **1** the apparition of a person living or thought to be alive, supposed to appear around the time of his death **2** a ghost or any apparition **3** an insubstantial copy of something [c16: Scottish, of unknown origin] > 'wraith,like *adj*

Wran (ræn) *n* a member of the Women's Royal Australian Naval Service

Wrangel Island ('ræŋɡəl) *n* an island in the Arctic Ocean, off the coast of the extreme NE of Russia: administratively part of Russia; mountainous and mostly tundra. Area: about 7300 sq km (2800 sq miles)

Wrangell ('ræŋɡəl) *n* Mount Wrangell a mountain in S Alaska, in the W Wrangell Mountains. Height: 4269 m (14 005 ft)

Wrangell Mountains *pl n* a mountain range in SE Alaska, extending into the Yukon, Canada. Highest peak: Mount Blackburn, 5037 m (16 523 ft)

wrangle ('ræŋɡəl) *vb* **1** (*intr*) to argue, esp noisily or angrily **2** (*tr*) to encourage, persuade, or obtain by argument **3** (*tr*) *Western US & Canadian* to herd (cattle or horses) ▷ *n* **4** a noisy or angry argument [c14: from Low German *wrangeln*; related to Norwegian *vrangla*]

wrangler ('ræŋɡlə) *n* **1** one who wrangles **2** *Western US & Canadian* a herder; cowboy **3** a person who handles or controls animals involved in the making of a film or television programme: *a snake wrangler* **4** *Brit* (at Cambridge University) a candidate who has obtained first-class honours in Part II of the mathematics tripos. The wrangler with the highest marks is called the **senior wrangler**

WRANS *abbreviation* Women's Royal Australian Naval Service

wrap (ræp) *vb* **wraps, wrapping, wrapped** (*mainly tr*) **1** to fold or wind (paper, cloth, etc) around (a person or thing) so as to cover **2** (often foll by *up*) to fold paper, etc, around to fasten securely **3** to surround or conceal by surrounding **4** to enclose, immerse, or absorb: *wrapped in sorrow* **5** to fold, wind, or roll up **6** (*intr*; often foll by *about, around*, etc) to be or become wound or extended **7** to complete the filming of (a motion picture or television programme) **8** Also called: **rap** (often foll by *up*) *Austral informal* to praise (someone) ▷ *n* **9** a garment worn wrapped around the body, esp the shoulders, such as a shawl or cloak **10** short for **wraparound** (sense 5) **11** a type of sandwich consisting of a tortilla wrapped round a filling **12** *chiefly US* wrapping or a wrapper **13** *Brit slang* a small package of an illegal drug in powder form: *a wrap of heroin* **14** Also called: **rap** *Austral informal* a commendation **15 a** the end of a working day during the filming of a motion picture or television programme **b** the completion of filming of a motion picture or television programme **16** keep under wraps to keep secret **17** take the wraps off to reveal [c14: origin unknown]

wrapover ('ræp,əʊvə) or **wrapround** adj **1** (of a garment, esp a skirt) not sewn up at one side, but worn wrapped round the body and fastened so that the open edges overlap ▷ n **2** such a garment

wrap party n a party held for cast and crew to celebrate the completion of filming of a motion picture or television programme

wrapped (ræpt) vb **1** the past tense and past participle of **wrap** ▷ adj **2** Austral & NZ informal a variant spelling of **rapt²** **3** wrapped up informal **a** completely absorbed or engrossed in **b** implicated or involved in

wrapper ('ræpə) n **1** the cover, usually of paper or cellophane, in which something is wrapped **2** a dust jacket of a book **3** the ripe firm tobacco leaf forming the outermost portion of a cigar and wound around its body **4** a loose negligee or dressing gown, esp in the 19th century

wrapping ('ræpɪŋ) n the material used to wrap something

wraparound ('ræp,raʊnd) or **wraparound** ('ræpə,raʊnd) adj **1** made so as to be wrapped round something: a wraparound skirt **2** surrounding, curving round, or overlapping **3** curving round in one continuous piece: a wraparound windscreen ▷ n **4** printing a flexible plate of plastic, metal, or rubber that is made flat but used wrapped round the plate cylinder of a rotary press **5** Also called: outsert printing a separately printed sheet folded around a section for binding. Sometimes shortened to: wrap **6** a slip of paper folded round the dust jacket of a book to announce a price reduction, special offer, etc **7** another name for **wrapover**

wrap up vb (adverb) **1** (tr) to fold paper around **2** to put warm clothes on **3** (usually imperative) slang to be silent **4** (tr) informal **a** to settle the final details of **b** to make a summary of

wrasse (ræs) n any marine percoid fish of the family Labridae, of tropical and temperate seas, having thick lips, strong teeth, and usually a bright coloration: many are used as food fishes [c17: from Cornish wrach; related to Welsh gwrach old woman]

wrath (rɒθ) n **1** angry, violent, or stern indignation **2** divine vengeance or retribution **3** archaic a fit of anger or an act resulting from anger ▷ adj **4** obsolete incensed; angry [Old English wrǣththu; see WROTH] ▷ 'wrathless adj

Wrath (rɒθ, rɔːθ) n Cape Wrath a promontory at the NW extremity of the Scottish mainland

wrathful ('rɒθfʊl) adj **1** full of wrath; raging or furious **2** resulting from or expressing wrath ▷ 'wrathfully adv ▷ 'wrathfulness n

wreak (riːk) vb (tr) **1** to inflict (vengeance, etc) or to cause (chaos, etc) **2** to express, or gratify (anger, hatred, etc) **3** archaic to take vengeance for [Old English wrecan; related to Old Frisian wreka, Old High German rehhan (German rächen), Old Norse reka, Latin urgēre to push] ▷ 'wreaker n

● USAGE See at **wrought**

wreath (riːθ) n, pl wreaths (riːðz, riːθs) **1** a band of flowers or foliage intertwined into a ring, usually placed on a grave as a memorial or worn on the head as a garland or a mark of honour **2** any circular or spiral band or formation **3** a spiral or circular defect appearing in porcelain and glassware [Old English wrǣth, wrǣd; related to Middle Low German wrēden to twist. See WRITHE] ▷ 'wreathless adj ▷ 'wreath,like adj

wreathe (riːð) vb **1** to form into or take the form of a wreath by intertwining or twisting together **2** (tr) to decorate, crown, or encircle with wreaths **3** to move or cause to move in a twisting way: smoke wreathed up to the ceiling [c16: perhaps back formation from wrēthen, from Old English writhen, past participle of wrīthan to WRITHE; see WREATH]

wreck (rɛk) vb **1** to involve in or suffer disaster or destruction **2** (tr) to cause the wreck of (a ship) ▷ n **3 a** the accidental destruction of a ship at sea **b** the ship

so destroyed **4** maritime law goods cast ashore from a wrecked vessel **5** a person or thing that has suffered ruin or dilapidation **6** the remains of something that has been destroyed **7** old-fashioned the act of wrecking or the state of being wrecked; ruin or destruction [c13: from Scandinavian; compare Icelandic rek. See WRACK², WREAK]

wreckage ('rɛkɪdʒ) n **1** same as **wreck** (sense 6) **2** the act of wrecking or the state of being wrecked; ruin or destruction

wrecked (rɛkt) adj slang in a state of intoxication, stupor, or euphoria, induced by drugs or alcohol

wrecker ('rɛkə) n **1** a person or thing that ruins or destroys **2** chiefly US & Canadian a person whose job is to demolish buildings or dismantle cars **3** (formerly) a person who lures ships to destruction to plunder the wreckage **4** US & Canadian a breakdown van

wrecking bar n a short crowbar, forked at one end and slightly angled at the other to make a fulcrum

Wrekin ('riːkɪn) n **1** the Wrekin an isolated hill in the English Midlands in Telford and Wrekin unitary authority, Shropshire. Height: 400 m (1335 ft) **2** round the Wrekin or all round the Wrekin Midland English dialect the long way round: he went all round the Wrekin instead of explaining clearly

wren (rɛn) n **1** any small brown passerine songbird of the chiefly American family Troglodytidae, esp Troglodytes troglodytes (**wren** in Britain, **winter wren** in the US and Canada). They have a slender bill and feed on insects **2** any of various similar birds of the families Muscicapidae (Australian warblers), Xenicidae (New Zealand wrens), etc [Old English wrenna, werna; related to Old High German wrendo, rentilo, Old Norse rindill]

Wren¹ (rɛn) n history informal (in Britain and certain other nations) a member of the former Women's Royal Naval Service [c20: from the abbreviation WRNS]

Wren² (rɛn) n Sir **Christopher**. 1632–1723, English architect. He designed St Paul's Cathedral and over 50 other London churches after the Great Fire as well as many secular buildings

wrench (rɛntʃ) vb **1** to give (something) a sudden or violent twist or pull esp so as to remove (something) from that to which it is attached: to wrench a door off its hinges **2** (tr) to twist suddenly so as to sprain (a limb): to wrench one's ankle **3** (tr) to give pain to **4** (tr) to twist from the original meaning or purpose **5** (intr) to make a sudden twisting motion ▷ n **6** a forceful twist or pull **7** an injury to a limb, caused by twisting **8** sudden pain caused esp by parting **9** a parting that is difficult or painful to make **10** a distorting of the original meaning or purpose **11** a spanner, esp one with adjustable jaws. See also **torque wrench** [Old English wrencan; related to Old High German renken, Lithuanian rangyti to twist. See WRINKLE¹]

wrest (rɛst) vb (tr) **1** to take or force away by violent pulling or twisting **2** to seize forcibly by violent or unlawful means **3** to obtain by laborious effort **4** to distort in meaning, purpose, etc ▷ n **5** the act or an instance of wresting **6** archaic a small key used to tune a piano or harp [Old English wrǣstan; related to Old Norse reista. See WRITHE] ▷ 'wrester n

wrestle ('rɛsəl) vb **1** to fight (another person) by holding, throwing, etc, without punching with the closed fist **2** (intr) to participate in wrestling **3** (when intr, foll by with or against) to fight with (a person, problem, or thing): wrestle with one's conscience **4** (tr) to move laboriously, as with wrestling movements **5** (tr) US & Canadian to throw (an animal) for branding ▷ n **6** the act of wrestling **7** a struggle or tussle [Old English wrǣstlian; related to Middle Dutch wrastelen (Dutch worstelen), Old Norse rost current, race] ▷ 'wrestler n

wrestling ('rɛslɪŋ) n any of certain sports in which the contestants fight each other according to various rules governing holds and usually forbidding blows with the closed fist. The principal object is to overcome the opponent either by throwing or pinning him to the ground or by causing him to submit

wrest pin n (on a piano, harp, etc) a pin around which one end of a string is wound: it may be turned by means of a tuning key to alter the tension of the string. In a piano the wrest pin is embedded in the **wrest plank**

wretch (rɛtʃ) *n* **1** a despicable person **2** a person pitied for his misfortune [Old English *wrecca*; related to Old Saxon *wrekkeo*, Old High German *reccheo* (German *Recke* warrior), Old Norse *rek(n)ingr*]

wretched ('rɛtʃɪd) *adj* **1** in poor or pitiful circumstances **2** characterized by or causing misery **3** despicable; base **4** poor, inferior, or paltry **5** (*prenominal*) (intensifier qualifying something undesirable): *a wretched nuisance* > 'wretchedly *adv* > 'wretchedness *n*

Wrexham ('rɛksəm) *n* **1** a town in N Wales, in Wrexham county borough: seat of the Roman Catholic bishopric of Wales (except the former Glamorganshire); formerly noted for coal-mining. Pop: 42 576 (2001) **2** a county borough in NE Wales, created in 1996 from part of Clwyd. Pop: 129 700 (2003 est.). Area: 500 sq km (193 sq miles)

wrick (rɪk) *vb* a variant spelling (chiefly Brit) of **rick²** [C19: earlier *rick*; perhaps from Middle Low German *wricken* to move jerkily, sprain]

wrier *or* **wryer** ('raɪə) *adj* the comparative of **wry**

wriest *or* **wryest** ('raɪɪst) *adj* the superlative of **wry**

wriggle ('rɪgəl) *vb* **1** to make or cause to make twisting movements **2** (*intr*) to progress by twisting and turning **3** (*intr*; foll by *into* or *out of*) to manoeuvre oneself by clever or devious means: *wriggle out of an embarrassing situation* ▷ *n* **4** a wriggling movement or action **5** a sinuous marking or course [C15: from Middle Low German; compare Dutch *wriggelen*] > 'wriggler *n* > 'wriggly *adj*

wright (raɪt) *n* (*now chiefly in combination*) a person who creates, builds, or repairs something specified: *a playwright; a shipwright* [Old English *wryhta, wyrhta*; related to Old Frisian *wrichta*, Old Saxon, Old High German *wurhtio*. See **work**]

Wright (raɪt) *n* **1** Frank Lloyd. 1869–1959, US architect, whose designs include the Imperial Hotel, Tokyo (1916), the Guggenheim Museum, New York (1943), and many private houses. His "organic architecture" sought a close relationship between buildings and their natural surroundings **2** Joseph, known as *Wright of Derby*. 1734–97, British painter, noted for his paintings of industrial and scientific subjects, esp *The Orrery* (?1765) and *The Air Pump* (1768) **3** Joseph. 1855–1930, British philologist; editor of *The English Dialect Dictionary* (1898–1905) **4** Judith (Arundel). 1915–2000, Australian poet, critic, and conservationist. Her collections of poetry include *The Moving Image* (1946), *Woman to Man* (1949), and *A Human Pattern* (1990) **5** Richard. 1908–60, US Black novelist and short-story writer, best known for the novel *Native Son* (1940) **6** Wilbur (1867–1912) and his brother, Orville (1871–1948), US aviation pioneers, who designed and flew the first powered aircraft (1903) **7** William, known as Billy. 1924–94, English footballer: winner of 105 caps

wring (rɪŋ) *vb* wrings, wringing, wrung **1** (often foll by *out*) to twist and compress to squeeze (a liquid) from (cloth, etc) **2** (*tr*) to twist forcibly: *wring its neck* **3** (*tr*) to clasp and twist (one's hands), esp in anguish **4** (*tr*) to distress: *wring one's heart* **5** (*tr*) to grip (someone's hand) vigorously in greeting **6** (*tr*) to obtain by or as if by forceful means: *wring information out of* **7** (*intr*) to writhe with or as if with pain **8** wringing wet soaking; drenched ▷ *n* **9** an act or the process of wringing [Old English *wringan*; related to Old High German *ringan* (German *wringen*), Gothic *wrungō* snare. See **wrangle**, **wrong**]

wringer ('rɪŋə) *n* another name for **mangle²** (sense 1)

wrinkle¹ ('rɪŋkəl) *n* **1** a slight ridge in the smoothness of a surface, such as a crease in the skin as a result of age ▷ *vb* **2** to make or become wrinkled, as by crumpling, creasing, or puckering [C15: back formation from *wrinkled*, from Old English *gewrinclod*, past participle of *wrinclian* to wind around; related to Swedish *vrinka* to sprain, Lithuanian *reñgti* to twist. See **wrench**] > 'wrinkleless *adj* > 'wrinkly *adj*

wrinkle² ('rɪŋkəl) *n* informal a clever or useful trick, hint, or dodge [Old English *wrenc* trick; related to Middle Low German *wrank* struggle, Middle High German *ranc* sudden turn. See **wrench**]

wrinklies ('rɪŋklɪz) *pl n* informal, derogatory old people

wrist (rɪst) *n* **1** anatomy the joint between the forearm and the hand. Technical name: **carpus 2** the part of a sleeve or glove that covers the wrist **3** machinery **a** See **wrist pin b** a joint in which a wrist pin forms the pivot [Old English; related to Old High German, Old Norse *rist*. See **wriggle, wry**]

wristband ('rɪst,bænd) *n* **1** a band around the wrist, esp one attached to a watch or forming part of a long sleeve **2** a sweatband around the wrist

wristlet ('rɪstlɪt) *n* a band or bracelet worn around the wrist

wrist pin *n* a cylindrical boss or pin attached to the side of a wheel parallel with the axis, esp one forming a bearing for a crank

wristwatch ('rɪst,wɒtʃ) *n* a watch worn strapped around the wrist

wristy ('rɪstɪ) *adj* (of a player's style of hitting the ball in cricket, tennis, etc) characterized by considerable movement of the wrist

writ (rɪt) *n* **1** law (formerly) a document under seal, issued in the name of the Crown or a court, commanding the person to whom it is addressed to do or refrain from doing some specified act. Official name: claim **2** archaic a piece or body of writing: *Holy Writ* [Old English; related to Old Norse *rit*, Gothic *writs* stroke, Old High German *riz* (German *Riss* a tear). See **write**]

write (raɪt) *vb* writes, writing, wrote, written **1** to draw or mark (symbols, words, etc) on a surface, usually paper, with a pen, pencil, or other instrument **2** to describe or record (ideas, experiences, etc) in writing **3** to compose (a letter) or correspond regularly with (a person, organization, etc) **4** (*tr; may take a clause as object*) to say or communicate by letter: *he wrote that he was on his way* **5** (*tr*) informal, chiefly US & Canadian to send a letter to (a person, etc) **6** to write (words) in cursive as opposed to printed style **7** (*tr*) to be sufficiently familiar with (a specified style, language, etc) to use it in writing **8** to be the author or composer of (books, music, etc) **9** (*tr*) to fill in the details for (a document, form, etc) **10** (*tr*) to draw up or draft **11** (*tr*) to produce by writing: *he wrote ten pages* **12** (*tr*) to show clearly: *envy was written all over his face* **13** (*tr*) to spell, inscribe, or entitle **14** (*tr*) to ordain or prophesy: *it is written* **15** (*tr*) to sit (an examination) **16** (*intr*) to produce writing as specified **17** computing to record (data) in a location in a storage device. See **read¹** (sense 15) **18** (*tr*) See **underwrite** (sense 3a) ▷ See also **write down, write in, write off, write out, write up** [Old English *wrītan* (originally: to scratch runes into bark); related to Old Frisian *rīta*, Old Norse *rīta*, Old High German *rīzan* (German *reissen* to tear)] > 'writable *adj*

write down *vb* (*adverb*) **1** (*tr*) to set down in writing **2** (*tr*) to harm or belittle by writing about (a person) in derogatory terms **3** (*intr*; foll by *to* or *for*) to write in a simplified way (to a supposedly less cultured readership) **4** (*tr*) accounting to decrease the book value of (an asset) ▷ n **write-down 5** accounting a reduction made in the book value of an asset

write in *vb* (*tr*) **1** to insert in (a document, form, etc) in writing **2** (*adverb*) to write a letter to a company, institution, etc **3** (*adverb*) US to vote for (a person not on a ballot) by writing in his name

write off *vb* (*tr, adverb*) **1** accounting **a** to cancel (a bad debt or obsolete asset) from the accounts **b** to consider (a transaction, etc) as a loss or set off (a loss) against revenues **c** to depreciate (an asset) by periodic charges **d** to charge (a specified amount) against gross profits as depreciation of an asset **2** to cause or acknowledge the complete loss of **3** to send a written order for (something): *she wrote off for a brochure* **4** informal to damage (something, esp a car) beyond repair ▷ n **write-off 5** accounting **a** the act of cancelling a bad debt or obsolete asset from the accounts **b** the bad debt or obsolete asset cancelled **c** the amount cancelled against gross profits, corresponding to the book value of the bad debt or obsolete asset **6** informal something damaged beyond repair, esp a car

write out *vb* (*tr, adverb*) **1** to put into writing or reproduce in full form in writing **2** to exhaust (oneself or one's creativity) by excessive writing **3** to remove (a character) from a television or radio series

writer ('raɪtə) *n* **1** a person who writes books, articles, etc, esp as an occupation **2** the person who has written something specified **3** a person who is able to write or write well **4** a scribe or clerk **5** a composer of music **6** *Scot* a legal practitioner, such as a notary or solicitor **7** Writer to the Signet (in Scotland) a member of an ancient society of solicitors, now having the exclusive privilege of preparing crown writs

writer's cramp *n* a muscular spasm or temporary paralysis of the muscles of the thumb and first two fingers caused by prolonged writing

write up *vb* (*tr, adverb*) **1** to describe fully, complete, or bring up to date in writing: *write up a diary* **2** to praise or bring to public notice in writing **3** *accounting, US* **a** to place an excessively high value on (an asset) **b** to increase the book value of (an asset) in order to reflect more accurately its current worth in the market ▷ *n* write-up **4** a published account of something, such as a review in a newspaper or magazine

writhe (raɪð) *vb* **1** to twist or squirm in or as if in pain **2** (*intr*) to move with such motions **3** (*intr*) to suffer acutely from embarrassment, revulsion, etc ▷ *n* **4** the act or an instance of writhing [Old English *wrīthan*; related to Old High German *rīdan*, Old Norse *rītha*. See WRATH, WREATH, WRIST, WROTH] > 'writher *n*

writing ('raɪtɪŋ) *n* **1** a group of letters or symbols written or marked on a surface as a means of communicating ideas by making each symbol stand for an idea, concept, or thing, by using each symbol to represent a set of sounds grouped into syllables (**syllabic writing**), or by regarding each symbol as corresponding roughly or exactly to each of the sounds in the language (**alphabetic writing**). See also **ideogram 2** short for **handwriting 3** anything expressed in letters, esp a literary composition **4** the work of a writer **5** literary style, art, or practice **6** written form: *give it to me in writing* **7** (*modifier*) related to or used in writing: *writing ink* **8** writing on the wall a sign or signs of approaching disaster [sense 8: allusion to Daniel 5:5]

writing desk *n* a piece of furniture with a writing surface and drawers and compartments for papers, writing materials, etc

writing paper *n* paper sized to take writing ink and used for letters and other manuscripts

writ of execution *n law* a writ ordering that a judgment be enforced

written ('rɪt°n) *vb* **1** the past participle of **write** ▷ *adj* **2** taken down in writing; transcribed: *written evidence; the written word*. See **spoken** (sense 2)

WRNS *abbreviation history* Women's Royal Naval Service. See also **Wren¹**

Wrocław (Polish 'vrɔtswaf) *n* an industrial city in SW Poland, on the River Oder: passed to Austria (1527) and to Prussia (1741); returned to Poland in 1945. Pop: 647 000 (2005 est). German name: Breslau

wrong (rɒŋ) *adj* **1** not correct or truthful: *the wrong answer* **2** acting or judging in error: *you are wrong to think that* **3** (*postpositive*) immoral; bad: *it is wrong to cheat* **4** deviating from or unacceptable to correct or conventional laws, usage, etc **5** not intended or wanted: *the wrong road* **6** (*postpositive*) not working properly; amiss: *something is wrong with the engine* **7** (of a side, esp of a fabric) intended to face the inside so as not to be seen **8** get on the wrong side of *or US* get in wrong with *informal* to come into disfavour with **9** go down the wrong way (of food) to pass into the windpipe instead of the gullet ▷ *adv* **10** in the wrong direction or manner **a** to turn out other than intended **b** to make a mistake **c** (of a machine, etc) to cease to function properly **d** to go astray morally **12** get wrong **a** to fail to understand properly **b** to fail to provide the correct answer to ▷ *n* **13** a bad, immoral, or unjust thing or action **14** *law* **a** an infringement of another person's rights, rendering the offender liable to a civil action, as for breach of contract or tort: *a private wrong* **b** a violation of public rights and duties, affecting the community as a whole and actionable at the instance of the Crown **15** in the wrong

mistaken or guilty ▷ *vb* (*tr*) **16** to treat unjustly **17** to discredit, malign, or misrepresent **18** to seduce or violate [Old English *wrang* injustice, from Old Norse *vrang*; related to WRING] > 'wronger *n* > 'wrongly *adv* > 'wrongness *n*

wrongdoer ('rɒŋ,duːə) *n* a person who acts immorally or illegally

wrongdoing ('rɒŋ,duːɪŋ) *n* the act or an instance of doing something immoral or illegal

wrong-foot *vb* (*tr*) **1** *sport* to play a shot in such a way as to cause (one's opponent) to be off balance **2** to take by surprise so as to place in an embarrassing or disadvantageous situation

wrongful ('rɒŋfʊl) *adj* immoral, unjust, or illegal > 'wrongfully *adv* > 'wrongfulness *n*

wrong-headed *adj* **1** constantly wrong in judgment **2** foolishly stubborn; obstinate > ,wrong-'headedly *adv* > ,wrong-'headedness *n*

wrong number *n* a telephone number wrongly connected or dialled in error or the person so contacted

wrong 'un *n informal* **1** a dishonest or unscrupulous person **2** *cricket chiefly Austral* another term for **googly**

wrote (rəʊt) *vb* the past tense of **write**

wroth (rəʊθ, rɒθ) *adj archaic or literary* angry; irate [Old English *wrāth*; related to Old Saxon *wrēth*, Old Norse *reithr*, Old High German *reid* curly haired]

wrought (rɔːt) *vb* **1** *archaic* a past tense and past participle of **work** ▷ *adj* **2** *metallurgy* shaped by hammering or beating **3** (*often in combination*) formed, fashioned, or worked as specified: *well-wrought* **4** decorated or made with delicate care [c16: variant of *worht*, from Old English *geworht*, past participle of (*ge*)*wyrcan* to WORK]

● USAGE *Wrought* is sometimes used as if it were the past ● tense and past participle of *wreak* as in *the hurricane* ● *wrought havoc in coastal areas*. Many people think this ● use is incorrect

wrought iron *n* **a** a pure form of iron having a low carbon content and a fibrous microstructure. It is made by various processes and is often used for decorative work **b** (*as modifier*): *wrought-iron gates*

wrought-up *adj* agitated or excited

wrung (rʌŋ) *vb* the past tense and past participle of **wring**

WRVS *abbreviation* Women's Royal Voluntary Service

wry (raɪ) *adj* wrier, wriest *or* wryer, wryest **1** twisted, contorted, or askew **2** (of a facial expression) produced or characterized by contorting of the features, usually indicating dislike **3** drily humorous; sardonic **4** warped, misdirected, or perverse **5** (of words, thoughts, etc) unsuitable or wrong ▷ *vb* wries, wrying, wried **1** (*tr*) to twist or contort [c16: from dialect *wry* to twist, from Old English *wrīgian* to turn; related to Old Frisian *wrīgia* to bend, Old Norse *riga* to move, Middle Low German *wrīch* bent, stubborn] > 'wryly *adv* > 'wryness *n*

wrybill ('raɪ,bɪl) *n* a New Zealand plover, *Anarhynchus frontalis*, having its bill deflected to one side enabling it to search for food beneath stones

wryneck ('raɪ,nɛk) *n* **1** either of two cryptically coloured Old World woodpeckers, *Jynx torquilla* or *J. ruficollis*, which do not drum on trees **2** another name for **torticollis** **3** *informal* a person who has a twisted neck

WST *abbreviation* (in Australia) Western Standard Time

WSW *symbol for* west-southwest

wt. *abbreviation* weight

WTO *abbreviation* World Trade Organization

Wu (wuː) *n* **Harry**, real name Wu Hongda. born 1937, Chinese dissident and human-rights campaigner, a US citizen from 1994: held in labour camps (1960–79); exiled to the US in 1985 but returned secretly to document forced labour in Chinese prisons

Wuchang *or* **Wu-ch'ang** ('wuː'tʃæŋ) *n* a former city of E central China: now a part of Wuhan

Wu Di ('wuː 'diː) *or* **Wu Ti** *n* 156 BC–86 BC, Chinese emperor (140–86) of the Han dynasty, who greatly extended the Chinese empire and made Confucianism the state religion

Wuhan ('wuː'hæn) *n* a city in SE China, in Hubei province, at the confluence of the Han and Yangtze

w

Rivers: formed in 1950 by the union of the cities of Hanyang, Hankou, and Wuchang (the Han Cities); river port and industrial centre; university (1913). Pop: 6 003 000 (2005 est)

Wu Hou ('wuː 'haʊ) n 625–705 AD Chinese empress (655–705) of the Tang dynasty

Wuhsien ('wuː'ʃjen) n another name for **Suzhou**

Wuhu ('wuː'huː) n a port in E China, in E Anhui province on the Yangtze River. Pop: 701 000 (2005 est)

wukkas ('wʌkəz) pl n no wukkas Austral taboo, slang an expression used to express agreement or to convey that something is proceeding or has proceeded satisfactorily; no problem [c20: short for no wukking furries, a euphemism for no fucking worries]

Wulfila ('wʊlfɪlə) n same as **Ulfilas**

Wu-lu-mu-ch'i ('wuː'luː'muː'tʃiː) n a variant of **Urumchi**

wunderkind ('wʌndə,kɪnd; German 'vʊndər,kɪnt) n, pl -kinds or -kinder (German -kɪndər) 1 a child prodigy 2 a person who is exceptionally successful in his field while still young [c20: German, literally: wonder child]

Wundt (German vʊnt) n **Wilhelm Max** ('vɪlhɛlm maks). 1832–1920, German experimental psychologist

Wuppertal (German 'vʊpərtaːl) n a city in W Germany, in North Rhine-Westphalia state on the **Wupper River** (a Rhine tributary): formed in 1929 from the amalgamation of the towns of Barmen and Elberfeld and other smaller towns; textile centre. Pop: 362 137 (2003 est)

wurst (wɜːst, wʊəst, vʊəst) n a large sausage, esp of a type made in Germany, Austria, etc [from German, literally: something rolled; related to Latin vertere to turn]

Württemberg ('vɜːtəm,bɜːɡ; German 'vyrtəmberk) n a historic region and former state of S Germany; since 1952 part of the state of Baden-Württemberg

Würzburg ('vɜːts,bɜːɡ; German 'vyrtsbʊrk) n a city in S central Germany, in NW Bavaria on the River Main: university (1582). Pop: 132 687 (2003 est)

wushu ('wuː'ʃuː) n a general term for Chinese martial arts [from Chinese wǔ military + shù art]

wuss, woose (wʊs) or **wussy** ('wʊsɪ) n, pl wusses or wussies slang, chiefly US a feeble or effeminate person [c20: perhaps from PUSSY¹ (cat)]

wuthering ('wʌðərɪŋ) adj Northern English dialect 1 (of a wind) blowing strongly with a roaring sound 2 (of a place) characterized by such a sound [variant of whitherin, from whither blow, from Old Norse hvithra; related to hvitha squall of wind, Old English hweothu wind]

Wu Ti ('wuː 'tiː) n See **Wu Di**

Wutsin ('wuː'tsɪn) n a former name (until 1949) of **Changzhou**

Wuxi, Wusih or **Wu-hsi** ('wuː'ʃiː, -'siː) n a city in E China, in S Jiangsu province on the Grand Canal: textile industry. Pop: 1 192 000 (2005 est)

WV abbreviation West Virginia

W. Va. abbreviation West Virginia

WWI abbreviation World War One

WWII abbreviation World War Two

WWF abbreviation Worldwide Fund for Nature

WWW abbreviation World Wide Web

WY or **Wy.** abbreviation Wyoming

Wyatt ('waɪət) n 1 **James**. 1746–1813, British architect; a pioneer of the Gothic Revival 2 **Sir Thomas**. ?1503–42, English poet at the court of Henry VIII

wych-elm or **witch-elm** ('wɪtʃ,ɛlm) n 1 Eurasian elm tree, Ulmus glabra, having a rounded shape, longish pointed leaves, clusters of small flowers, and winged fruits 2 the wood of this tree [c17: from Old English wice wych-elm]

Wycherley ('wɪtʃəlɪ) n **William**. ?1640–1716, English dramatist. His Restoration comedies include The Country Wife (1675) and The Plain Dealer (1676)

Wycliffe or **Wyclif** ('wɪklɪf) n **John**. ?1330–84, English religious reformer. A precursor of the Reformation, whose writings were condemned as heretical, he attacked the doctrines and abuses of the Church. He instigated the first complete translation of the Bible into English. His followers were called Lollards. Also called: 'Wiclif or 'Wickliffe > 'Wycliffism or 'Wyclifism n > 'Wycli,ffite or 'Wycli,fite n

Wye (waɪ) n a river in E Wales and W England, rising in Powys and flowing southeast into Herefordshire, then south to the Severn estuary. Length: 210 km (130 miles)

Wykeham ('wɪkəm) n **William of**. 1324–1404, English prelate and statesman, who founded New College, Oxford, and Winchester College: chancellor of England (1367–71; 1389–91); bishop of Winchester (1367–1404)

wynd (waɪnd) n Scot a narrow lane or alley [c15: from the stem of WIND²]

Wyndham ('wɪndəm) n **John**, pseudonym of John Wyndham Parkes Lucas Beynon Harris. 1903–69, British writer of science fiction novels and stories. His works include The Day of the Triffids (1951), The Kraken Wakes (1953), and The Midwich Cuckoos (1957)

Wynette (wɪ'nɛt) n **Tammy**, original name Virginia Wynette Pugh. 1942–98, US country singer; her bestselling records include "Your Good Girl's Gonna Go Bad" (1967) and "Stand By Your Man" (1969)

Wyn Jones (wɪn dʒəʊnz) n **Ieuan** ('jʊən). born 1949, Welsh politician; leader of Plaid Cymru from 2000

Wyo. abbreviation Wyoming

Wyoming (waɪ'əʊmɪŋ) n a state of the western US: consists largely of ranges of the Rockies in the west and north, with part of the Great Plains in the east and several regions of hot springs. Capital: Cheyenne. Pop: 501 242 (2003 est). Area: 253 597 sq km (97 914 sq miles). Abbreviation: Wyo., (with zip code) WY

WYSIWYG ('wɪzɪ,wɪɡ) n, adj computing acronym what you see is what you get: referring to what is displayed on the screen being the same as what will be printed out

wyvern or less commonly **wivern** ('waɪvən) n a heraldic beast having a serpent's tail and a dragon's head and a body with wings and two legs [c17: variant of earlier wyver, from Old French, from Latin vīpera VIPER]

W

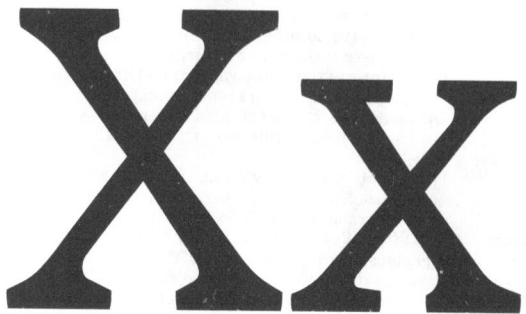

x¹ *or* **X** (ɛks) *n, pl* **x's, X's** *or* **Xs** **1** the 24th letter and 19th consonant of the modern English alphabet **2** a speech sound sequence represented by this letter, in English pronounced as *ks* or *gz* or, in initial position, *z*, as in *xylophone*

x² *symbol for* **1** *commerce, banking, finance ex* **2** *maths* the *x*-axis or a coordinate measured along the *x*-axis in a Cartesian coordinate system **3** an algebraic variable

X *symbol for* **1** (formerly, in Britain) **a** indicating a film that may not be publicly shown to anyone under 18. Since 1982 replaced by symbol 18 **b** (*as modifier*): *an X film* **2** denoting any unknown, unspecified, or variable factor, number, person, or thing **3** (on letters, cards, etc) denoting a kiss **4** (on ballot papers, etc) indicating choice **5** (on examination papers, etc) indicating error **6** Christ; Christian [from the form of the Greek letter khi (X), first letter of *Khristos* Christ] **7** *the Roman numeral for* ten. See **Roman numerals**

xanthein (ˈzænθiːɪn) *n* the soluble part of the yellow pigment that is found in the cell sap of some flowers

xanthene (ˈzænθiːn) *n* a yellowish crystalline heterocyclic compound used as a fungicide; benzo-1,4-pyran. Its molecular structural unit is found in many dyes, such as rhodamine and fluorescein. Formula: $CH_2(C_6H_4)_2O$

xanthic (ˈzænθɪk) *adj* **1** of, containing, or derived from xanthic acid **2** *botany rare* having a yellow colour

xanthic acid *n* any of a class of organic sulphur-containing acids with the general formula $ROC(S)SH$, where R is an organic group.

xanthine (ˈzænθiːn, -θaɪn) *n* **1** a crystalline compound related in structure to uric acid and found in urine, blood, certain plants, and certain animal tissues. Formula: $C_5H_4N_4O_2$ **2** any substituted derivative of xanthine, esp one of the three pharmacologically active methylated xanthines, caffeine, theophylline, or theobromine, which act as stimulants and diuretics

Xanthippe (zænˈθɪpɪ) *or* **Xantippe** (zænˈtɪpɪ) *n* **1** the wife of Socrates, proverbial as a scolding and quarrelsome woman **2** any nagging, peevish, or irritable woman

xantho- *or before a vowel* **xanth-** *combining form* indicating yellow: *xanthophyll* [from Greek *xanthos*]

xanthochroism (zænˈθɒkrəʊˌɪzəm) *n* a condition in certain animals, esp aquarium goldfish, in which all skin pigments other than yellow and orange disappear [C19: from Greek *xanthokhro(os)* yellow-skinned (from *xanthos* yellow + *khroia* skin) + -ISM]

xanthoma (zænˈθəʊmə) *n pathol* the presence in the skin of fatty yellow or brownish plaques or nodules, esp on the eyelids, caused by a disorder of lipid metabolism

xanthophyll *or esp US* **xanthophyl** (ˈzænθəʊfɪl) *n* any of a group of yellow carotenoid pigments occurring in plant and animal tissue > ˌxanthoˈphyllous *adj*

xanthous (ˈzænθəs) *adj* of, relating to, or designating races with yellowish hair and a light complexion

Xanthus (ˈzænθəs) *n* the chief city of ancient Lycia in SW Asia Minor: source of some important antiquities

Xavier (ˈzeɪvɪə, ˈzæv-; *Spanish* xaˈβjɛr) *n* **Saint Francis,** known as the *Apostle of the Indies.* 1506– 52, Spanish missionary, who was a founding member of the Jesuit society (1534) and later preached in Goa, Ceylon, the East Indies, and Japan. Feast day: Dec 3

***x*-axis** *n* a reference axis, usually horizontal, of a graph or two- or three-dimensional Cartesian coordinate system along which the *x*-coordinate is measured

X-chromosome *n* the sex chromosome that occurs in pairs in the diploid cells of the females of many animals, including humans, and as one of a pair with the Y-chromosome in those of males. See **Y-chromosome**

Xda *or* **xda** *n trademark* a combined computer and mobile phone

Xe *the chemical symbol for* xenon

xebec, zebec *or* **zebeck** (ˈziːbɛk) *n* a small three-masted Mediterranean vessel with both square and lateen sails, formerly used by Algerian pirates and later used for commerce [C18: earlier *chebec* from French, ultimately from Arabic *shabbāk*; present spelling influenced by Catalan *xabec*, Spanish *xabeque* (now *jabeque*)]

Xenakis (zɛˈnɑːkɪs; *Greek* ksɛˈnakis) *n* **Yannis** (ˈjanis). 1922–2001, Greek composer and musical theorist, born in Romania: later a French citizen. He was noted for his use of computers in composition: his works include *ST/10-1, 080262* (1962) and *Dox-orkh* (1991)

Xenical ('zɛnɪkʰl) *n trademark* a drug that reduces the ability to absorb fats; used in the medical treatment of obesity

xeno- *or before a vowel* **xen-** *combining form* indicating something strange, different, or foreign: *xenogamy* [from Greek *xenos* strange]

Xenocrates (zɛ'nɒkrə,tiːz) *n* ?396–314 BC, Greek Platonic philosopher ▷ **Xenocratic** (,zɛnə'krætɪk) *adj*

xenogamy (zɛ'nɒgəmɪ) *n botany* another name for **cross-fertilization** ▷ xe'nogamous *adj*

xenogeneic (,zɛnəʊdʒɪ'neɪɪk) *adj med* derived from an individual of a different species: *a xenogeneic tissue graft*

xenoglossia (,zɛnə'glɒsɪə) *or* **xenoglossy** ('zɛnə,glɒsɪ) *n* an ability claimed by some mediums, clairvoyants, etc, to speak a language with which they are unfamiliar [C20: from Greek, from XENO- + Attic Greek *glossa* tongue, language]

xenolith ('zɛnəlɪθ) *n* a fragment of rock differing in origin, composition, structure, etc, from the igneous rock enclosing it ▷ ,xeno'lithic *adj*

xenon ('zɛnɒn) *n* a colourless odourless gaseous element occurring in trace amounts in air; formerly considered inert it is now known to form compounds and is used in radio valves, stroboscopic and bactericidal lamps, and bubble chambers. Symbol: Xe; atomic no: 54; atomic wt: 131.29; valency: 0; density: 5.887 kg/m³; melting pt: –111.76°C; boiling pt: –108.0°C [C19: from Greek: something strange]

Xenophanes (zɛ'nɒfə,niːz) *n* ?570–?480 BC, Greek philosopher and poet, noted for his monotheism and regarded as a founder of the Eleatic school

xenophile ('zɛnə,faɪl) *n* a person who likes foreigners or things foreign [C19: from Greek, from XENO- + -PHILE]

xenophobia (,zɛnə'fəʊbɪə) *n* hatred or fear of foreigners or strangers or of their politics or culture ▷ ,xeno'phobic *adj* ▷ 'xeno,phobe *n* [C20: from Greek, from XENO- + -PHOBE]

Xenophon ('zɛnəfən) *n* 431–?355 BC, Greek general and historian; a disciple of Socrates. He accompanied Cyrus the Younger against Artaxerxes II and, after Cyrus' death at Cunaxa (401), he led his army of 10 000 Greek soldiers to the Black Sea, an expedition described in his *Anabasis*. His other works include *Hellenica*, a history of Greece, and the *Memorabilia*, *Apology*, and *Symposium*, which contain recollections of Socrates

Xeres (*Spanish* 'xɛrɛθ) *n* the former name of **Jerez**

xeric ('zɪərɪk) *adj ecology* of, relating to, or growing in dry conditions ▷ 'xerically *adv*

xero- *or before a vowel* **xer-** *combining form* indicating dryness: *xeroderma* [from Greek *xēros* dry]

xeroderma (,zɪərəʊ'dɜːmə) *or* **xerodermia** (,zɪərəʊ'dɜːmɪə) *n pathol* **1** any abnormal dryness of the skin as the result of diminished secretions from the sweat or sebaceous glands **2** another name for **ichthyosis** ▷ xerodermatic (,zɪərəʊdə'mætɪk) *or* ,xero'dermatous *adj*

xerography (zɪ'rɒgrəfɪ) *n* a photocopying process in which an electrostatic image is formed on a selenium plate or cylinder. The plate or cylinder is dusted with a resinous powder, which adheres to the charged regions, and the image is then transferred to a sheet of paper on which it is fixed by heating ▷ xe'rographer *n* ▷ xerographic (,zɪərə'græfɪk) *adj* ▷ ,xero'graphically *adv*

xerophilous (zɪ'rɒfɪləs) *adj* (of plants or animals) adapted for growing or living in dry surroundings ▷ xerophile ('zɪərəʊ,faɪl) *n* ▷ xe'rophily *n*

xerophthalmia (,zɪərɒf'θælmɪə) *n pathol* excessive dryness of the cornea and conjunctiva, caused by a deficiency of vitamin A. Also called: **xeroma** (zɪ'rəʊmə) ▷ ,xeroph'thalmic *adj*

xerophyte ('zɪərə,faɪt) *n* a xerophilous plant, such as a cactus ▷ xerophytic (,zɪərə'fɪtɪk) *adj* ▷ ,xero'phytically *adv* ▷ 'xero,phytism *n*

Xerox ('zɪərɒks) *n* **1** *trademark* **a** a xerographic copying process **b** a machine employing this process **c** a copy produced by this process ▷ *vb* **2** to produce a copy of (a document, illustration, etc) by this process

Xerxes I ('zɜːksiːz) *n* ?519–465 BC, king of Persia (485–465), who led a vast army against Greece. His forces

were victorious at Thermopylae but his fleet was defeated at Salamis (480) and his army at Plataea (479)

Xhosa ('kɔːsə) *n* **1** *pl* **-sa** *or* **-sas** a member of a cattle-rearing Negroid people of southern Africa, living chiefly in South Africa **2** the language of this people, belonging to the Bantu group of the Niger-Congo family: one of the Nguni languages, closely related to Swazi and Zulu and characterized by several clicks in its sound system ▷ 'Xhosan *adj*

xi (zaɪ, saɪ, ksaɪ, ksiː) *n*, *pl* **xis** the 14th letter in the Greek alphabet (Ξ, ξ), a composite consonant, transliterated as *x*

Xi, Hsi *or* **Si** (ʃiː) *n* a river in S China, rising in Yunnan province and flowing east to the Canton delta on the South China Sea: the main river system of S China. Length: about 1900 km (1200 miles)

Xia Gui (ʃjɑː 'kweɪ) *or* **Hsia Kuei** *n* ?1180–1230, Chinese landscape painter of the Sung dynasty; noted for his misty mountain landscapes in ink monochrome

Xiamen ('ʃjɑː'mɛn) *n* a variant transliteration of the Chinese name for **Amoy**

Xi'an, Hsian *or* **Sian** (ʃjɑːn) *n* an industrial city in central China, capital of Shaanxi province: capital of China for 970 years at various times between the 3rd century BC and the 10th century AD; seat of the Northwestern University (1937); famous for Qin dynasty emperor Qinshihuang's tomb (207 BC) with 8000-strong terracotta army. Pop: 3 256 000 (2005 est). Former name: **Siking**

Xiang, Hsiang *or* **Siang** (ʃjɑːŋ) *n* **1** a river in SE central China, rising in NE Guangxi and flowing northeast and north to Dongting Lake. Length: about 1150 km (715 miles) **2** a river in S China, rising in SE Yunnan and flowing generally east to the Hongxiu (the upper course of the Xi River). Length: about 800 km (500 miles)

Xiangtan *or* **Siangtan** ('ʃjɑːŋ'tɑːn) *n* a city in S central China, in NE Hunan on the Xiang River: centre of a region noted for tea production. Pop: 592 000 (2005 est)

Ximenes *or* **Ximenez** (*Spanish* xi'menes; *English* 'zɪmɪ,niːz) *n* See **Jiménez de Cisneros**

Xingú (*Portuguese* ʃiŋ'gu) *n* a river in central Brazil, rising on the Mato Grosso plateau and flowing north to the Amazon delta, with over 650 km (400 miles) of rapids in its middle course. Length: 1932 km (1200 miles)

Xining, Hsining *or* **Sining** ('ʃiː'nɪŋ) *n* a city in W China, capital of Qinghai province, at an altitude of 2300 m (7500 ft). Pop: 689 000 (2005 est)

Xinjiang Uygur Autonomous Region ('ʃɪn'dʒjæŋ 'wiːgʊə) *or* **Sinkiang-Uighur Autonomous Region** ('sɪn'kjæŋ) *n* an administrative division of NW China: established in 1955 for the Uygur ethnic minority, with autonomous subdivisions for other small minorities; produces over half China's wool and contains valuable mineral resources. Capital: Ürümqi. Pop: 19 340 000 (2003 est). Area: 1 646 799 sq km (635 829 sq miles)

xiphisternum (,zɪfɪ'stɜːnəm) *n*, *pl* **-na** (-nə) *anatomy*, *zoology* the cartilaginous process forming the lowermost part of the breastbone (sternum). Also called: **xiphoid**, **xiphoid process**

xiphoid ('zɪfɔɪd) *adj* **1** *biology* shaped like a sword **2** of or relating to the xiphisternum ▷ *n* **3** Also called: **xiphoid process** another name for **xiphisternum** [C18: from New Latin, from Greek, from *xiphos* sword + *eidos* form]

Xizang Autonomous Region ('ʃiː'zæŋ) *n* the Pinyin transliteration of the Chinese name for **Tibet**

Xmas ('ɛksməs, 'krɪsməs) *n informal* short for **Christmas** [C16: from symbol X for Christ + -MAS]

XML *abbreviation* extensible markup language: a computer language used in text formatting

Xochimilco (,kɒtʃɪ'mɪlkəʊ) *n* a town in central Mexico, on Lake Xochimilco: noted for its floating gardens. Pop: 364 647 (2000)

XP¹ *n* the Christian monogram made up of the Greek letters *khi* and *rho*, the first two letters of *Khristos*, the Greek form of Christ's name

XP² *abbreviation* extreme programming

X-rated *adj* **1** (formerly, in Britain) (of a film) considered suitable for viewing by adults only **2** *informal* involving bad language, violence, or sex: *an X-rated conversation*

X

X-ray *or* **x-ray** *n* **1 a** electromagnetic radiation emitted when matter is bombarded with fast electrons. X-rays have wavelengths shorter than that of ultraviolet radiation, that is less than about 1×10^{-8} metres. They extend to indefinitely short wavelengths, but below about 1×10^{-11} metres they are often called gamma radiation **b** (*as modifier*): *X-ray astronomy* **2** a picture produced by exposing photographic film to X-rays: used in medicine as a diagnostic aid as parts of the body, such as bones, absorb X-rays and so appear as opaque areas on the picture **3** (*usually capital*) *communications* a code word for the letter *x* ▷ *vb* (*tr*) **4** to photograph (part of the body, etc) using X-rays **5** to treat or examine by means of X-rays [c19: partial translation of German *X-Strahlen* (from *Strahl* ray), coined in 1895 by W. K. Röntgen (1845–1923), German physicist]

X-ray astronomy *n* the branch of astronomy concerned with the detection and measurement of X-rays emitted by certain celestial bodies. As X-rays are absorbed by the atmosphere, satellites and rockets are used

X-ray binary *n* a binary star that is an intense source of X-rays and is composed of a normal star in close orbit with a white dwarf, neutron star, or black hole

X-ray crystallography *n* the study and practice of determining the structure of a crystal by passing a beam of X-rays through it and observing and analysing the diffraction pattern produced

X-ray tube *n* an evacuated tube containing a metal target onto which is directed a beam of electrons at high energy for the generation of X-rays

Xuan-tong (ˈʃwɑːnˈtʊŋ) *n* the Pinyin transliteration of the title as emperor of China of (Henry) **Pu-yi**

Xuan Zang (ˈʃwɑːn ˈtsæn) *or* **Hsüan-tsang** *n* 602–664 AD, Chinese Buddhist monk, who travelled to India to study the Buddhist scriptures, many of which he translated into Chinese

Xuan Zong (ˈʃwɑːn ˈtsʊŋ) *or* **Hsüan-tsung** *n* 685–762 AD, Chinese emperor (712–56) of the Tang dynasty

Xun Zi (ˈtʃʊn ˈdʒiː) *or* **Hsün-tzu** *n* original name *Hsun Kuang*. c. 300 BC–c. 230 BC, Chinese philosopher, who systematized Confucian teaching

Xuthus (ˈzuːθəs) *n* *Greek myth* a son of Hellen, regarded as an ancestor of the Ionian Greeks through his son Ion

Xuzhou (ˈʃuːˈdʒəʊ), **Hsü-chou** *or* **Süchow** *n* a city in N central China, in NW Jiangsu province: scene of a decisive battle (1949) in which the Communists defeated the Nationalists. Pop: 1 662 000 (2005 est)

xylem (ˈzaɪləm, -lɛm) *n* a plant tissue that conducts water and mineral salts from the roots to all other parts, provides mechanical support, and forms the wood of trees and shrubs. It is of two types (protoxylem and metaxylem), both of which are made up mainly of vessels and tracheids [c19: from Greek *xulon* wood]

xylene (ˈzaɪliːn) *n* an aromatic hydrocarbon existing in three isomeric forms, all three being colourless flammable volatile liquids used as solvents and in the manufacture of synthetic resins, dyes, and insecticides; dimethylbenzene. Formula: $C_6H_4(CH_3)_2$. Also called: xylol

xylitol (ˈzaɪlɪˌtɒl) *n* *chem* an artificial sweetener produced from xylose and used esp in chewing gum. Formula: $CH_2HOH(CHOH)_3CH_2OH$ [c19: from XYL(OSE) + -ITE² + -OL¹]

xylo- *or before a vowel* **xyl-** *combining form* **1** indicating wood: *xylophone* **2** indicating xylene: *xylidine* [from Greek *xulon* wood]

xylocarp (ˈzaɪləˌkɑːp) *n* *botany* a fruit, such as a coconut, having a hard woody pericarp ▷ ˌxyloˈcarpous *adj*

xylograph (ˈzaɪləˌgrɑːf, -ˌɡræf) *n* **1** an engraving in wood **2** a print taken from a wood block ▷ *vb* **3** (*tr*) to print (a design, illustration, etc) from a wood engraving

xylophagous (zaɪˈlɒfəɡəs) *adj* (of certain insects, crustaceans, etc) feeding on or living within wood

xylophone (ˈzaɪləˌfəʊn) *n* *music* a percussion instrument consisting of a set of wooden bars of graduated length. It is played with hard-headed hammers [c19: from XYLO- + -PHONE] ▷ xylophonic (ˌzaɪləˈfɒnɪk) *adj* ▷ xylophonist (zaɪˈlɒfənɪst) *n*

xylose (ˈzaɪləʊz, -ləʊs) *n* a white crystalline dextrorotatory sugar found in wood and straw. It is extracted by hydrolysis with acids and used in dyeing, tanning, and in foods for diabetics. Formula: $C_5H_{10}O_5$

xyster (ˈzɪstə) *n* a surgical instrument for scraping bone; surgical rasp or file [c17: via New Latin from Greek: tool for scraping, from *xuein* to scrape, make smooth]

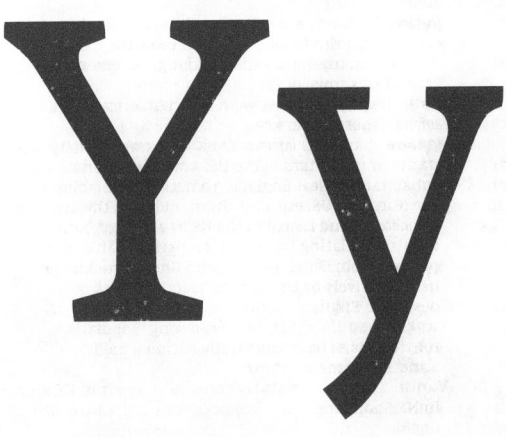

y¹ or **Y** (waɪ) *n, pl* **y's, Y's** or **Ys 1** the 25th letter of the modern English alphabet **2** a speech sound represented by this letter, in English usually a semivowel, as in *yawn*, or a vowel, as in *symbol* or *shy* **3** something shaped like a Y

y² *maths symbol for* **1** the y-axis or a coordinate measured along the y-axis in a Cartesian coordinate system **2** an algebraic variable

Y *symbol for* **1** any unknown, unspecified, or variable factor, number, person, or thing **2** *chem* yttrium

y. *abbreviation* year

-y¹ or **-ey** *suffix forming adjectives* **1** (*from nouns*) characterized by; consisting of; filled with; relating to; resembling: *sunny; sandy; smoky; classy* **2** (*from verbs*) tending to; acting or existing as specified: *leaky; shiny* [from Old English *-ig*, *-æg*]

-y², **-ie** or **-ey** *suffix of nouns informal* **1** denoting smallness and expressing affection and familiarity: *a doggy; a granny; Jamie* **2** a person or thing concerned with or characterized by being: *a groupie; a fatty* [c14: from Scottish *-ie*, *-y*, familiar suffix occurring originally in names, as in *Jamie* (*James*)]

-y³ *suffix forming nouns* **1** (*from verbs*) indicating the act of doing what is indicated by the verbal element: *inquiry* **2** (*esp with combining forms of Greek, Latin, or French origin*) indicating state, condition, or quality: *geography; jealousy* [from Old French *-ie*, from Latin *-ia*]

yabba ('jæbə) *n slang* a form of methamphetamine [c20: of unknown origin]

yabby or **yabbie** ('jæbɪ) *Austral* ▷ *n, pl* **-bies 1** a small freshwater crayfish of the genus *Cherax*, esp *C. destructor* **2** Also called: **nipper** a marine prawn used as bait ▷ *vb* **-bies, -bying, -bied 3** (*intr*) to go out to catch yabbies [from a native Australian language]

Yablonovy Mountains (*Russian* ˈjablənəvij) *pl n* a mountain range in Siberia. Highest peak: 1680 m (5512 ft). Also called: **Yablonoi Mountains** (ˈjɑːblənɔɪ)

yacca or **yacka** ('jækə) *n Austral* another word for **grass tree** (sense 1) [from a native Australian language]

yacht (jɒt) *n* **1** a vessel propelled by sail or power, used esp for pleasure cruising, racing, etc ▷ *vb* **2** (*intr*) to sail or cruise in a yacht [c16: from obsolete Dutch *jaghte*, short for *jahtschip*, from *jagen* to chase + *schip* SHIP] ▷ **ˈyachting** *n*

yachtie ('jɒtɪ) *n Austral & NZ informal* a yachtsman; sailing enthusiast

yachtsman ('jɒtsmən) or *feminine* **yachtswoman** *n, pl* **-men** or **-women** a person who sails a yacht or yachts ▷ **ˈyachtsˌship** *n*

yack (jæk) *n* a variant spelling of **yak²**

yackety-yak (ˌjækɪtɪˈjæk) *n slang* noisy, continuous, and trivial talk or conversation [of imitative origin]

yaffle ('jæfᵊl) *n* another name for green woodpecker [c18: imitative of its cry]

Yafo ('jɑːfɔ:) *n* transliteration of the Hebrew name for **Jaffa** (sense 1)

Yagi aerial ('jɑːgɪ, 'jægɪ) *n* a highly directional aerial, used esp in television and radio astronomy, consisting of three or more elements lying parallel to each other, the principal direction of radiation being along the line of the centres [c20: named after Hidetsugu *Yagi* (1886–1976), Japanese engineer]

yaffle ('jæfᵊl) *n* another name for **green woodpecker** [c18: imitative of its cry]

yah (jɑː, jɛə) *sentence substitute* **1** an informal word for yes, often used to indicate derision or contempt ▷ *interj* **2** an exclamation of derision or disgust

yahoo (jə'huː) *n, pl* **-hoos** a crude, brutish, or obscenely coarse person [c18: from the name of a race of brutish creatures resembling men in Jonathan Swift's *Gulliver's Travels* (1726)] ▷ ya'hooism *n*

Yahweh, Jahweh ('jɑːweɪ) or **Yahveh, Jahveh** ('jɑːveɪ) *n Old Testament* a vocalization of the Tetragrammaton, used esp by Christian theologians [from Hebrew, from YHVH, with conjectural vowels; perhaps related to *hāwāh* to be; see also Jehovah]

Yahwism, Jahwism ('jɑːwɪzəm) or **Yahvism, Jahvism** ('jɑːvɪzəm) *n* the use of the name Yahweh, esp in parts of the Old Testament, as the personal name of God

Yahwist, Jahwist ('jɑːwɪst) or **Yahvist, Jahvist** ('jɑːvɪst) *n* the Yahwist *Bible* the conjectured author or authors of the earliest of four main sources or strands of tradition of which the Pentateuch is composed and in which God is called *Yahweh* throughout ▷ Yah'wistic or Jah'wistic *adj*

yak¹ (jæk) *n* a wild and domesticated type of cattle, *Bos* *grunniens*, of Tibet, having long horns and long shaggy hair [C19: from Tibetan *gyag*]

yak² (jæk) *slang* ▷ *n* **1** Also: **yakety-yak** noisy, continuous, and trivial talk or conversation ▷ *vb* yaks, yakking, yakked **2** (*intr*) to chatter or talk in this way; jabber [C20: of imitative origin]

yakka, yakker *or* **yacker** ('jækə) *n Austral & NZ informal* work [C19: from a native Australian language]

Yakutsk (*Russian* jɪ'kutsk) *n* a port in E Russia, capital of the Sakha Republic (Yakutia), on the Lena River. Pop: 214 000 (2005 est)

Yale lock (jeɪl) *n trademark* a type of cylinder lock using a flat serrated key [C19: after L *Yale* (1821–68), US inventor]

Yalta (*Russian* 'jaltə) *n* a port and resort in S Ukraine, in the Crimea on the Black Sea: scene of a conference (1945) between Churchill, Roosevelt, and Stalin, who met to plan the final defeat and occupation of Nazi Germany. Pop: 80 552 (2005 est)

Yalu ('jɑː‚luː) *n* a river in E Asia, rising in N North Korea and flowing southwest to Korea Bay, forming a large part of the border between North Korea and NE China. Length: 806 km (501 miles)

yam (jæm) *n* **1** any of various twining plants of the genus *Dioscorea*, of tropical and subtropical regions, cultivated for their edible tubers: family *Dioscoreaceae* **2** the starchy tuber of any of these plants, which is eaten as a vegetable **3** *Southern US* any of certain large varieties of sweet potato [C17: from Portuguese *inhame*, ultimately of West African origin; compare Senegal *nyami* to eat]

Yamagata (‚jæmɪ'gɑːtə) *n* Prince **Aritomo** (‚ærɪ'təʊməʊ). 1838–1922, Japanese soldier and politician. As war minister (1873) and chief of staff (1878), he modernized Japan's military system. He was premier of Japan (1889–93; 1898)

Yamani (jə'mɑːnɪ) *n* Sheikh **Ahmed Zaki** ('ɑːmɛd 'zɑːkɪ). born 1930, Saudi Arabian politician; minister of petroleum and mineral resources (1962–86)

Yamasaki (‚jæmə'sɑːkɪ) *n* **Minoru**. 1912–86, US architect. His buildings include St Louis Airport, Missouri (1953–55) and the World Trade Center, New York (1970–77)

Yamashita (‚jʊməʊ'ʃiːtə) *n* **Tomoyuki** (‚təʊməʊ'juːkɪ). 1885–1946, Japanese general. He commanded Japanese forces in the Malayan campaign in World War II and took Singapore (1942); captured (1945) and hanged

yammer ('jæmə) *informal* ▷ *vb* **1** to utter or whine in a complaining or peevish manner **2** to make (a complaint) loudly or persistently ▷ *n* **3** a yammering sound, wail, or utterance **4** nonsense; jabber [Old English *gēomrian* to grumble, complain; related to Old High German *iâmar* misery, lamentation, Old Norse *amra* to howl] > '**yammerer** *n*

Yamoussoukro (‚jæmʊ'suːkrəʊ) *n* the capital of Côte d'Ivoire, situated in the S centre of the country. It replaced Abidjan as capital in 1983. Pop: 468 000 (2005 est)

Yanan ('jæn'æn) *or* **Yenan** *n* a city in NE China, in N Shaanxi province: political and military capital of the Chinese Communists (1935–49). Pop: 343 000 (2005 est). Also called: **Fushih**

Yang¹ (jæŋ) *n* See **Yin and Yang**

Yang² (jæŋ) *n* **Chen Ning** ('tʃɛn 'nɪŋ). born 1922, US physicist, born in China: with Tsung-Dao Lee, he disproved the physical principle known as the conservation of parity and shared the Nobel prize for physics (1957)

Yangon (jæŋ'gɒn) *n* the largest city and chief port of Myanmar (Burma): officially superseded as capital in 2006 by Nay Pyi Taw (Naypyidaw), though still retaining some of the functions of government; an industrial city and transport centre; dominated by the gold-covered Shwe Dagon pagoda, 112 m (368 ft) high. Pop: 4 082 000 (2005 est). Former name (official until 1989, still widely used in English): **Rangoon**

Yangtze ('jæŋtsɪ, ‚jæŋktsɪ) *n* the longest river in China, rising in SE Qinghai province and flowing east to the East China Sea near Shanghai: a major commercial waterway in one of the most densely populated areas of the world. The **Three Gorges dam** near Yichang, the world's biggest hydroelectric and flood-control project,

was begun in 1994 and the dam was completed in 2003, with filling taking several years thereafter. Length: 5528 km (3434 miles). Also called: **Yangtze Kiang, Chang Jiang, Chang**

Yanina ('jɑːnɪnə) *n* a variant spelling of **Ioánnina**

yank (jæŋk) *vb* **1** to pull, jerk, or move with a sharp movement; tug ▷ *n* **2** a sharp jerking movement; tug [C19: of unknown origin]

Yank (jæŋk) *n* **1** a slang word for an American **2** *US informal* short for **Yankee**

Yankee ('jæŋkɪ) *or informal* **Yank** *n* **1** *often disparaging* a native or inhabitant of the US; American **2** a native or inhabitant of New England **3** a native or inhabitant of the Northern US, esp a Northern soldier in the Civil War **4** *finance* a bond issued in the US by a foreign borrower ▷ *adj* **5** of, relating to, or characteristic of Yankees [C18: perhaps from Dutch *Jan Kees* John Cheese, nickname used derisively by English settlers in New York to designate English colonists in Connecticut]

Yankee Doodle *n* **1** an American song, popularly regarded as a characteristically national melody **2** another name for **Yankee**

Yantai ('jæn'taɪ), **Yentai** *or* **Yen-t'ai** *n* a port in E China, in NE Shandong. Pop: 1 707 000 (2005 est). Also called: **Chefoo**

Yaoundé *or* **Yaunde** (*French* jaunde) *n* the capital of Cameroon, in the southwest: University of Cameroon (1962). Pop: 1 727 000 (2005 est)

yap (jæp) *vb* yaps, yapping, yapped (*intr*) **1** (of a dog) to bark in quick sharp bursts; yelp **2** *informal* to talk at length in an annoying or stupid way; jabber ▷ *n* **3** a high-pitched or sharp bark; yelp **4** *slang* annoying or stupid speech; jabber **5** *slang* a derogatory word for **mouth** [C17: of imitative origin] > '**yapper** *n* > '**yappy** *adj*

Yap (jɑːp, jæp) *n* a group of four main islands in the W Pacific, in the W Caroline Islands: administratively a district of the US Trust Territory of the Pacific Islands from 1947; became self-governing in 1979 as part of the Federated States of Micronesia; important Japanese naval base in World War II. Pop: 11 647 (2006 est). Area: 101 sq km (39 sq miles)

Yapurá (japu'ra) *n* the Spanish name for **Japurá**

Yaqui (*Spanish* 'jaki) *n* a river in NW Mexico, rising near the border with the US and flowing south to the Gulf of California. Length: about 676 km (420 miles)

yarborough ('jɑːbərə, -brə) *n bridge, whist* a hand of 13 cards in which no card is higher than nine [C19: supposed to be named after the second Earl of *Yarborough* (1809–62), who is said to have bet a thousand to one against the occurrence of such a hand]

yard¹ (jɑːd) *n* **1** a unit of length equal to 3 feet and defined in 1963 as exactly 0.9144 metre **2** a cylindrical wooden or hollow metal spar, tapered at the ends, slung from a mast of a square-rigged or lateen-rigged vessel and used for suspending a sail **3** the whole nine yards *informal* everything that is required; the whole thing [Old English *gierd* rod, twig; related to Old Frisian *jerde*, Old Saxon *gerdia*, Old High German *gertia*, Old Norse *gaddr*]

yard² (jɑːd) *n* **1** a piece of enclosed ground, usually either paved or laid with concrete and often adjoining or surrounded by a building or buildings **2 a** an enclosed or open area used for some commercial activity, for storage, etc **b** (*in combination*): *a brickyard; a shipyard* **3** a US and Canadian word for **garden** (sense 1) **4** an area having a network of railway tracks and sidings, used for storing rolling stock, making up trains, etc **5** *US & Canadian* the winter pasture of deer, moose, and similar animals **6** *NZ* short for **stockyard** [Old English *geard*; related to Old Saxon *gard*, Old High German *gart*, Old Norse *garthr* yard, Gothic *gards* house, Old Slavonic *gradu* town, castle, Albanian *garth* hedge]

Yard *n* **the Yard** *Brit informal* short for **Scotland Yard**

yardage¹ ('jɑːdɪdʒ) *n* a length measured in yards

yardage² ('jɑːdɪdʒ) *n* **1** the use of a railway yard in the transportation of cattle **2** the charge for this

yardarm ('jɑːd‚ɑːm) *n nautical* the two tapering outer ends of a ship's yard

yard grass *n* an Old World perennial grass, *Eleusine*

indica, with prostrate leaves, growing as a troublesome weed on open ground, yards, etc

Yardie (ˈjɑːdɪ) *n* a member of a Black criminal syndicate originally based in Jamaica [C20: from Jamaican dialect *yard* home or (by expatriate Jamaicans) Jamaica]

yard of ale *n* **1** the beer or ale contained in a narrow horn-shaped drinking glass, usually about one yard long and holding between two and three pints **2** such a drinking glass itself

yardstick (ˈjɑːdˌstɪk) *n* **1** a measure or standard used for comparison **2** a graduated stick, one yard long, used for measurement

Yarkand (ˌjɑːˈkænd) *n* another name for **Shache**

Yarmouth (ˈjɑːməθ) *n* short for **Great Yarmouth**

yarmulke (ˈjɑːməlkə) *n Judaism* a skullcap worn by orthodox male Jews at all times, and by others during prayer [from Yiddish, from Ukrainian and Polish *yarmulka* cap, probably from Turkish *yağmurluk* raincoat, from *yağmur* rain]

yarn (jɑːn) *n* **1** a continuous twisted strand of natural or synthetic fibres, used in weaving, knitting, etc **2** *informal* a long and often involved story or account, usually telling of incredible or fantastic events **3** **spin a yarn** *informal* **a** to tell such a story **b** to make up or relate a series of excuses ▷ *vb* **4** (*intr*) to tell such a story or stories [Old English *gearn*; related to Old High German *garn* yarn, Old Norse *görn* gut, Greek *khordē* string, gut]

yarn-dyed *adj* (of fabric) dyed while still in yarn form, before being woven

Yaroslavl (*Russian* jɪrɑˈslavlj) *n* a city in W Russia, on the River Volga: a major trading centre since early times and one of the first industrial centres in Russia; textile industries were established in the 18th century. Pop: 609 000 (2005 est)

yarran (ˈjærən) *n* a small hardy tree, *Acacia homalophylla*, of inland Australia: useful as fodder and for firewood [from a native Australian language]

Yarra River (ˈjærə) *n* a river in SE Australia, rising in the Great Dividing Range and flowing west and southwest through Melbourne to Port Phillip Bay. Length: 250 km (155 miles)

yarrow (ˈjærəʊ) *n* any of several plants of the genus *Achillea*, esp *A. millefolium*, of Eurasia, having finely dissected leaves and flat clusters of white flower heads: family *Asteraceae* (composites). Also called: **milfoil** [Old English *gearwe*; related to Old High German *garwa*, Dutch *gerwe*]

yashmak *or* **yashmac** (ˈjæʃmæk) *n* the face veil worn by Muslim women when in public [C19: from Arabic]

yataghan (ˈjætəɡən) *or* **ataghan** *n* a Turkish sword with a curved single-edged blade [C19: from Turkish *yatağan*]

Yathrib (ˈjæθrɪb) *n* the ancient Arabic name for **Medina**

Yaunde (*French* jaʊndɛ) *n* a variant spelling of **Yaoundé**

yaup (jɔːp) *vb, n* a variant spelling of **yawp** ▷ **ˈyauper** *n*

Yavarí (jaβaˈri) *n* the Spanish name for **Javari**

yaw (jɔː) *vb* **1** (*intr*) (of an aircraft, missile, etc) to turn about its vertical axis **2** (*intr*) (of a ship, etc) to deviate temporarily from a straight course **3** (*tr*) to cause (an aircraft, ship, etc) to yaw ▷ *n* **4** the angular movement of an aircraft, missile, etc, about its vertical axis **5** the deviation of a vessel from a straight course [C16: of unknown origin]

yawl (jɔːl) *n* **1** a two-masted sailing vessel, rigged fore-and-aft, with a large mainmast and a small mizzenmast stepped aft of the rudderpost **2** a ship's small boat, usually rowed by four or six oars [C17: from Dutch *jol* or Middle Low German *jolle*, of unknown origin]

yawn (jɔːn) *vb* **1** (*intr*) to open the mouth wide and take in air deeply, often as in involuntary reaction to tiredness, sleepiness, or boredom **2** (*tr*) to express or utter while yawning **3** (*intr*) to be open wide as if threatening to engulf (someone or something): *the mine shaft yawned below* ▷ *n* **4** the act or an instance of yawning [Old English *gionian*; related to Old Saxon *ginōn*, Old High German *ginēn* to yawn, Old Norse *gjā* gap] ▷ **ˈyawner** *n* ▷ **ˈyawning** *adj* ▷ **ˈyawningly** *adv*

yawp (jɔːp) *vb* (*intr*) **1** to gape or yawn, esp audibly **2** to shout, cry, or talk noisily; bawl **3** to bark, yelp, or yowl

▷ *n* **4** a shout, bark, yelp, or cry **5** *US & Canadian* a noisy, foolish, or raucous utterance [C15 *yolpen*, probably of imitative origin; see YAP, YELP] ▷ **ˈyawper** *n*

yaws (jɔːz) *n* (*usually functioning as singular*) an infectious nonvenereal disease of tropical climates with early symptoms resembling syphilis, characterized by red skin eruptions and, later, pain in the joints: it is caused by the spiral bacterium *Treponema pertenue* [C17: of Carib origin]

y-axis *n* a reference axis, usually vertical, of a graph or two- or three-dimensional Cartesian coordinate system along which the *y*-coordinate is measured

Yazd (jɑːzd) *or* **Yezd** *n* a city in central Iran: a major centre of silk weaving. Pop: 436 000 (2005 est)

Yb *the chemical symbol for* ytterbium

YC *abbreviation* (in Britain) Young Conservative

Y-chromosome *n* the sex chromosome that occurs as one of a pair with the X-chromosome in the diploid cells of the males of many animals, including humans. See **X-chromosome**

yclept (ɪˈklɛpt) *adj obsolete* having the name of; called [Old English *gecleopod*, past participle of *cleopian* to call]

Y connection *n electrical engineering* a three-phase star connection

yd *or* **yd.** *abbreviation* yard (measure)

ye¹ (jiː; *unstressed* jɪ) *pron* **1** *archaic or dialect* refers to more than one person including the person addressed but not including the speaker **2** Also called: **ye** (ɪ:) *dialect* refers to one person addressed: *I tell ye* [Old English *gē*; related to Dutch *gij*, Old Norse *ēr*, Gothic *jus*]

ye² (ðiː; *spelling pron* jiː) *determiner* a form of the, used in conjunction with other putative archaic spellings: *ye olde oake* [from a misinterpretation of *the* as written in some Middle English texts. The runic letter thorn (Þ, representing *th*) was incorrectly transcribed as *y* because of a resemblance in their shapes]

yea (jeɪ) *sentence substitute* **1** a less common word for **aye¹** (sense 1) ▷ *adv* **2** (*sentence modifier*) *archaic or literary* indeed; truly: *yea, though my enemies spurn me, I shall prevail* [Old English *gēa*; related to Old Frisian *jē*, Old Saxon, Old Norse, Old High German *jā*, Gothic *jai*]

yeah (jɛə) *sentence substitute* an informal word for **yes**

yean (jiːn) *vb* (of a sheep or goat) to give birth to (offspring) [Old English *geēanian*; related to Dutch *oonen* to bring forth young, Latin *agnus* lamb; see EWE]

yeanling (ˈjiːnlɪŋ) *n* the young of a goat or sheep

year (jɪə) *n* **1** Also called: **civil year** the period of time, the **calendar year**, containing 365 days or in a **leap year** 366 days. It is based on the Gregorian calendar, being divided into 12 calendar months, and is reckoned from January 1 to December 31 **2** a period of twelve months from any specified date, such as one based on the four seasons **3** a specific period of time, usually occupying a definite part or parts of a twelve-month period, used for some particular activity: *a school year* **4** Also called: **astronomical year**, **tropical year** the period of time, the **solar year**, during which the earth makes one revolution around the sun, measured between two successive vernal equinoxes: equal to 365.242 19 days **5** the period of time, the **sidereal year**, during which the earth makes one revolution around the sun, measured between two successive conjunctions of a particular distant star: equal to 365.256 36 days **6** the period of time, the **lunar year**, containing 12 lunar months and equal to 354.3671 days **7** the period of time taken by a specified planet to complete one revolution around the sun **8** (*plural*) age, esp old age: *a man of his years should be more careful* **9** (*plural*) time: *in years to come* **10** a group of pupils or students, who are taught or study together, divided into classes at school **11** **the year dot** *informal* as long ago as can be remembered **12** **year in, year out** regularly or monotonously, over a long period Related adjective: **annual** [Old English *gear*; related to Gothic *jēr*, Old Saxon, Old High German *jār*, Old Norse *ār* year, Polish *jar* springtime, Latin *hōrnus* of this year]

● USAGE In writing spans of years, it is important to
● choose a style that avoids ambiguity. The practice
● adopted in this dictionary is, in four-figure dates, to
● specify the last two digits of the second date if it falls

● within the same century as the first: *1801–08; 1850–51;*
● *1899–1901.* In writing three-figure BC dates, it is
● advisable to give both dates in full: *159–156* BC, not
● *159–56* BC unless of course the span referred to consists
● of 103 years rather than three years. It is also
● advisable to specify BC or AD in years under 1000
● unless the context makes this self-evident

yearbook ('jɪəˌbʊk) *n* an almanac or reference book published annually and containing details of events of the previous year

yearling ('jɪəlɪŋ) *n* **1** the young of any of various animals, including the antelope and buffalo, between one and two years of age **2** a thoroughbred racehorse counted for racing purposes as being one year old until the second Jan 1 following its birth **3 a** a bond that is intended to mature after one year **b** (*as modifier*): *yearling bonds* ▷ *adj* **4** being a year old

yearlong ('jɪə'lɒŋ) *adj* throughout a whole year

yearly ('jɪəlɪ) *adj* **1** occurring, done, appearing, etc, once a year or every year; annual **2** lasting or valid for a year; annual: *a yearly subscription* ▷ *adv* **3** once a year; annually

yearn (jɜːn) *vb* (*intr*) **1** (usually foll by *for* or *after* or an infinitive) to have an intense desire or longing (for); pine (for) **2** to feel tenderness or affection [Old English *giernan*; related to Old Saxon *girnian*, Old Norse *girna*, Gothic *gairnjan*, Old High German *gerōn* to long for, Sanskrit *haryati* he likes] > 'yearner *n* > 'yearning *n* > 'yearningly *adv*

year of grace *n* any year of the Christian era, as dated from the presumed date of Christ's birth

year-round *adj* open, in use, operating, etc, throughout the year

year zero *n* **1** the beginning (1975) of the period during which Cambodia was under the control of the Khmer Rouge **2** the beginning of revolutionary change **3** the beginning of any new system or regime [C20: by analogy with *Year One* of the French Revolutionary calendar]

yeast (jiːst) *n* **1** any of various single-celled ascomycetous fungi of the genus *Saccharomyces* and related genera, which reproduce by budding and are able to ferment sugars: a rich source of vitamins of the B complex **2** any yeastlike fungus, esp of the genus *Candida*, which can cause thrush in areas infected with it **3** a commercial preparation containing yeast cells and inert material such as meal, used in raising dough for bread or for fermenting beer, whisky, etc **4** a preparation containing yeast cells, used to treat diseases caused by vitamin B deficiency **5** froth or foam, esp on beer ▷ *vb* **6** (*intr*) to froth or foam [Old English *giest*; related to Old Norse *jostr*, Old High German *jesan*, Swedish *esa*, Norwegian *asa*, Sanskrit *yasati*] > 'yeastless *adj* > 'yeast,like *adj*

yeasty ('jiːstɪ) *adj* yeastier, yeastiest **1** of, resembling, or containing yeast **2** fermenting or causing fermentation **3** tasting of or like yeast **4** insubstantial or frivolous **5** restless, agitated, or unsettled **6** covered with or containing froth or foam > 'yeastily *adv* > 'yeastiness *n*

Yeats (jeɪts) *n* **1** Jack Butler. 1871–1957, Irish painter and his brother **W**(**illiam**) **B**(**utler**). 1865–1939, Irish poet and dramatist. His collections of verse include *Responsibilities* (1914), *The Tower* (1928), and *The Winding Stair* (1929). Among his plays are *The Countess Cathleen* (1892; 1912) and *Cathleen ni Houlihan* (1902); he was a founder of the Irish National Theatre Company at the Abbey Theatre in Dublin. He was awarded the Nobel prize for literature 1923

yebo ('jebaʊ) *sentence substitute South African informal* an expression of affirmation [Zulu *yebo* yes, I agree]

yegg (jɛg) *n slang, chiefly US* a burglar or safe-breaker [C20: perhaps from the surname of a burglar]

Yeisk, Yeysk *or* **Eisk** (*Russian* jejsk) *n* a port and resort in SW Russia, on the Sea of Azov. Pop: 86 349 (2002)

Yekaterinburg *or* **Ekaterinburg** (*Russian* jɪkətɪrimˈburk) *n* a city in NW Russia, in the Ural Mountains: scene of the execution (1918) of Nicholas II and his family; university (1920); one of the largest centres of heavy engineering in Russia. Pop: 1 281 000 (2005 est). Former name (1924–91): Sverdlovsk

Yekaterinodar *or* **Ekaterinodar** (*Russian* jɪkətɪrina'dar) *n* the former name (until 1920) of **Krasnodar**

Yekaterinoslav *or* **Ekaterinoslav** (*Russian* jɪkətɪrina'slaf) *n* the former name (1787–96, 1802–1926) of **Dnepropetrovsk**

Yelisavetgrad *or* **Elisavetgrad** (*Russian* jɪliza'vjɛtgrət) *n* the former name (until 1924) of **Kirovograd**

Yelisavetpol *or* **Elisavetpol** (*Russian* jɪliza'vjɛtpəlj) *n* the former name (until 1920) of **Gandzha**

Yelizaveta Petrovna (*Russian* jɪliza'vjɛtə pɪ'trɔvnə) *n* See **Elizabeth²** (sense 3)

yell (jɛl) *vb* **1** to shout, scream, cheer, or utter in a loud or piercing way ▷ *n* **2** a loud piercing inarticulate cry, as of pain, anger, or fear **3** *US & Canadian* a rhythmic cry of words or syllables, used in cheering in unison [Old English *giellan*; related to Old Saxon *gellon*, Old High German *gellan*, Old Norse *gjalla*; see NIGHTINGALE] > 'yeller *n*

yellow ('jɛləʊ) *n* **1** any of a group of colours that vary in saturation but have the same hue. They lie in the approximate wavelength range 585–575 nanometres. Yellow is the complementary colour of blue and with cyan and magenta forms a set of primary colours. Related adj: **xanthous 2** a pigment or dye of or producing these colours **3** yellow cloth or clothing: *dressed in yellow* **4** the yolk of an egg **5** a yellow ball in snooker, etc ▷ *adj* **6** of the colour yellow **7** yellowish in colour or having parts or marks that are yellowish **8** having a yellowish skin; Mongoloid **9** *informal* cowardly or afraid **10** offensively sensational, as a cheap newspaper (esp in the phrase **yellow press**) ▷ *vb* **11** to make or become yellow ▷ See also **yellows** [Old English *geolu*; related to Old Saxon, Old High German *gelo*, Old Norse *gulr*, Latin *helvus*] > 'yellowish *adj* > 'yellowly *adv* > 'yellowness *n* > 'yellowy *adj*

yellow-belly *n, pl* -lies **1** a slang word for **coward 2** *Austral* another name for **callop** > 'yellow-,bellied *adj*

yellow bile *n archaic* one of the four bodily humours, choler

yellow card *n sport* a card of a yellow colour displayed by a referee to indicate that a player has been officially cautioned for some offence

yellow fever *n* an acute infectious disease of tropical and subtropical climates, characterized by fever, haemorrhages, vomiting of blood, and jaundice: caused by a virus transmitted by the bite of a female mosquito of the species *Aedes aegypti*. Also called: yellow jack

yellowfin tuna ('jɛləʊˌfɪn) *n* a large marine food fish, *Scomber albacares*, of tropical and subtropical waters, having yellow dorsal and anal fins: family *Scombridae*

yellowhammer ('jɛləʊˌhæmə) *n* a European bunting, *Emberiza citrinella*, having a yellowish head and body and brown streaked wings and tail [C16: of uncertain origin]

yellow jack *n* **1** *pathol* another name for **yellow fever 2** another name for **quarantine flag 3** any of certain large yellowish carangid food fishes, esp *Caranx bartholomaei*, of warm and tropical Atlantic waters

yellow jacket *n US & Canadian* any of several social wasps of the genus *Vespa*, having yellow markings on the body

yellow jersey *n* (in the Tour de France) a yellow jersey worn by the overall leader of the race

yellow journalism *n* the type of journalism that relies on sensationalism and lurid exaggeration to attract readers [C19: perhaps shortened from the phrase *Yellow Kid journalism*, referring to the *Yellow Kid*, a cartoon (1895) in the *New York World*, a newspaper having a reputation for sensationalism]

Yellowknife ('jɛləʊˌnaɪf) *n* a city in N Canada, capital of the Northwest Territories on Great Slave Lake. Pop: 16 055 (2001)

yellow line *n Brit* a yellow line painted along the edge of a road indicating waiting restrictions

yellow metal *n* **1** a type of brass having about 60 per cent copper and 40 per cent zinc **2** another name for **gold**

Yellow Pages *pl n trademark* a classified telephone directory, often printed on yellow paper, that lists subscribers by the business or service provided

yellow peril *n* the power or alleged power of Asiatic peoples, esp the Chinese, to threaten or destroy the supremacy of White or Western civilization

Yellow River n the second longest river in China, rising in SE Qinghai and flowing east, south, and east again to the Gulf of Bohai south of Tianjin; it has changed its course several times in recorded history. Length: about 4350 km (2700 miles). Chinese name: Hwang Ho

yellows ('jɛləʊz) n (functioning as singular) **1** any of various fungal or viral diseases of plants, characterized by yellowish discoloration and stunting **2** vet science another name for **jaundice**

Yellow Sea n a shallow arm of the Pacific between Korea and NE China. Area: about 466 200 sq km (180 000 sq miles). Chinese name: Hwang Hai

yellow spot n anatomy another name for **macula lutea**

Yellowstone ('jɛləʊˌstəʊn) n a river rising in N Wyoming and flowing north through Yellowstone National Park, then east to the Missouri. Length: 1080 km (671 miles)

Yellowstone Falls pl n a waterfall in NW Wyoming, in Yellowstone National Park on the Yellowstone River

Yellowstone National Park n a national park in the NW central US, mostly in NW Wyoming: the oldest and largest national park in the US, containing unusual geological formations and geysers. Area: 8956 sq km (3458 sq miles)

yellow streak n informal a cowardly or weak trait, characteristic, or flaw in a person's nature

yellowtail kingfish n a large carangid game fish, *Seriola grandis*, of S Australian waters. Also called: **yellowtail**

yellow underwing n any of several species of noctuid moths (*Noctua* and *Anarta* species), the hind wings of which are yellow with a black bar

yellowwood ('jɛləʊˌwʊd) n **1** any of several leguminous trees of the genus *Cladrastis*, esp *C. lutea*, of the southeastern US, having clusters of white flowers and yellow wood yielding a yellow dye **2** Also called: **West Indian satinwood** a rutaceous tree, *Zanthoxylum flavum*, of the Caribbean, with smooth hard wood **3** any of several other trees with yellow wood, esp *Podocarpus falcatus*, a conifer of southern Africa: family *Podocarpaceae* **4** the wood of any of these trees

yelp (jɛlp) vb (intr) **1** (esp of a dog) to utter a sharp or high-pitched cry or bark, often indicating pain ▷ n **2** a sharp or high-pitched cry or bark [Old English *gielpan* to boast; related to Low German *galpen* to croak, Danish *gylpe* to croak] > **'yelper** n

Yeltsin ('jɛltsɪn; *Russian* jeltsin) n **Boris (Nicolayevich)**. 1931–2007, Russian politician: president of the Russian Soviet Federative Socialist Republic (1990–91); president of Russia (1991–99)

Yemen ('jɛmən) n a republic in SW Arabia, on the Red Sea and the Gulf of Aden: formed in 1990 from the union of North Yemen and South Yemen: consists of arid coastal lowlands, rising to fertile upland valleys and mountains in the west and to the Hadhramaut plateau in the SE: the north and east contains part of the Great Sandy Desert. Official language: Arabic. Official religion: Muslim. Currency: riyal. Capital: San'a. Pop: 20 732 000 (2004 est). Area (including territory claimed by Yemen along the undemarcated eastern border with Saudi Arabia): 472 099 sq km (182 278 sq miles). See also **North Yemen, South Yemen** > **'Yemeni** adj, n

yen¹ (jɛn) n, pl yen the standard monetary unit of Japan, (notionally) divided into 100 sen [c19: from Japanese *en*, from Chinese *yüan* circular object, dollar]

yen² (jɛn) informal ▷ n **1** a passionate, ardent, or intense longing or desire ▷ vb **yens, yenning, yenned 2** (intr) to yearn [perhaps from Chinese (Cantonese) *yǎn* a craving, addiction]

Yenan ('jɛn'æn) n a variant transliteration of the Chinese name for **Yanan**

Yenisei or **Yenisey** (ˌjɛnɪ'seɪ; *Russian* jɪni'sjej) n a river in central Russia, in central Siberia, formed by the confluence of two headstreams in the Tuva Republic: flows west and north to the Arctic Ocean; the largest river in volume in Russia. Length: 4129 km (2566 miles)

Yentai or **Yen-t'ai** ('jɛn'taɪ) n a variant transliteration of the Chinese name for **Yantai**

yeoman ('jəʊmən) n, pl -men **1** history **a** a member of a class of small freeholders of common birth who cultivated their own land **b** an attendant or lesser official in a royal or noble household **2** (in Britain) another name for **yeoman of the guard 3** (modifier) characteristic of or relating to a yeoman **4** a petty officer or noncommissioned officer in the Royal Navy or Marines in charge of signals [c15: perhaps from *yongman* young man]

yeomanly ('jəʊmənlɪ) adj **1** of, relating to, or like a yeoman **2** having the virtues attributed to yeomen, such as staunchness, loyalty, and courage ▷ adv **3** in a yeomanly manner, as in being brave, staunch, or loyal

yeoman of the guard n a member of the bodyguard (Yeomen of the Guard) of the English monarch. This unit was founded in 1485 and now retains ceremonial functions only

yeomanry ('jəʊmənrɪ) n **1** yeomen collectively **2** (in Britain) a volunteer cavalry force, organized in 1761 for home defence: merged into the Territorial Army in 1907

yep (jɛp) sentence substitute an informal word for **yes**

yerba or **yerba maté** ('jɛəbə, 'jɜːbə) n another name for **maté** [from Spanish *yerba maté* herb maté]

Yerevan (*Russian* jɪrɪ'van) n the capital of Armenia: founded in the 8th century BC; an industrial city and a main focus of trade routes since ancient times; university. Pop: 1 066 000 (2005 est). Also called: Erevan, Erivan

Yerwa-Maiduguri ('jɜːwəˌmaɪdʊ'guːrɪ) n another name for **Maiduguri**

yes (jɛs) sentence substitute **1** used to express acknowledgment, affirmation, consent, agreement, or approval or to answer when one is addressed **2** used, often with interrogative intonation, to signal someone to speak or keep speaking, enter a room, or do something ▷ n **3** an answer or vote of yes **4** (often plural) a person who votes in the affirmative [Old English *gēse*, from *iā sīe* may it be; see YEA]

Yesenin (jɛ'sɛnɪn) n **Sergey Aleksandrovich**. See (Sergey Aleksandrovich) **Esenin**

yeshiva (jə'ʃiːvə; *Hebrew* jə'ʃiːva) n, pl -vahs or -voth (*Hebrew* -vɔt) **1** a traditional Jewish school devoted chiefly to the study of rabbinic literature and the Talmud **2** a school run by Orthodox Jews for children of primary school age, providing both religious and secular instruction [from Hebrew *yěshībhāh* a sitting, seat, hence, an academy]

Yeşil Irmak (jɛ'ʃiːl ɪə'mɑːk) n a river in N Turkey, flowing northwest to the Black Sea. Length: 418 km (260 miles). Ancient name: Iris

Yeşilköy (jɛ'ʃilˌkœi) n the Turkish name for **San Stefano**

yes man n a servile, submissive, or acquiescent subordinate, assistant, or associate; sycophant

yester ('jɛstə) adj archaic of or relating to yesterday: *yester sun* [Old English *geostror*; related to Old High German *gestaron*, Gothic *gistra*, Old Norse *ī gǣr*]

yester- prefix indicating a period of time before the present one: *yesteryear* [Old English *geostran*; compare German *gestern*, Latin *hesternus* of yesterday]

yesterday ('jɛstədɪ, -ˌdeɪ) n **1** the day immediately preceding today **2** (often plural) the recent past ▷ adv **3** on or during the day before today **4** in the recent past

yesteryear ('jɛstəˌjɪə) formal or literary ▷ n **1** last year or the past in general ▷ adv **2** during last year or the past in general

yestreen (jɛ'striːn) adv Scot yesterday evening [c14: from YEST(E)R- + E(V)EN²]

yet (jɛt) sentence connector **1** nevertheless; still; in spite of that: *I want to and yet I haven't the courage; she is strange yet kind* ▷ adv **2** (usually used with a negative or interrogative) so far; up until then or now: *they're not home yet; is it teatime yet?* **3** (often preceded by *just*; usually used with a negative) now (as contrasted with later): *we can't stop yet* **4** (often used with a comparative) even; still: *yet more potatoes for sale; yet another problem family* **5** eventually, in spite of everything: *we'll convince him yet* **6** as yet so far; up until then or now [Old English *gēta*; related to Old Frisian *jēta*]

yeti ('jɛtɪ) n another term for **abominable snowman** [c20: from Tibetan]

yettie ('jɛtɪ) n acronym for young, entrepreneurial, and technology-based (person)

Yevtushenko (ˌjɛvtuː'ʃɛnkəʊ; *Russian* jɪftu'ʃɛnkə) *n* **Yevgeny Aleksandrovich** (jɪv'gjenij alɪk'sandrəvitʃ). born 1933, Russian poet. His often outspoken poetry includes *Babi Yar* (1962), *Bratsk Station* (1966), and *Farewell to Red Banner* (1992)

yew (juː) *n* **1** any coniferous tree of the genus *Taxus*, of the Old World and North America, esp *T. baccata*, having flattened needle-like leaves, fine-grained elastic wood, and solitary seeds with a red waxy aril resembling berries: family *Taxaceae* **2** the wood of any of these trees, used to make bows for archery **3** *archery* a bow made of yew [Old English *īw*; related to Old High German *īwa*, Old Norse *ȳr* yew, Latin *ūva* grape, Russian *iva* willow]

Yezd (jɛzd) *n* a variant of **Yazd**

Y-fronts *pl n trademark* boys' or men's underpants having a front opening within an inverted Y shape

Yggdrasil, Ygdrasil or **Igdrasil** ('ɪgdrəsɪl) *n Norse myth* the ash tree that was thought to overshadow the whole world, binding together earth, heaven, and hell with its roots and branches [Old Norse (probably meaning: Uggr's horse), from *Uggr* a name of Odin, from *yggr, uggr* frightful + *drasill* horse, of obscure origin]

YHA *abbreviation* Youth Hostels Association

YHVH, YHWH, JHVH or **JHWH** *n Old Testament* the letters of the **Tetragrammaton**

Yibin ('jiːˈbɪn) or **I-pin** *n* a port in S central China, in Sichuan province: a commercial centre. Pop: 784 000 (2005 est)

Yichang ('jiːˈtʃæŋ), **Ichang** or **I-ch'ang** *n* a port in S central China, in Hubei province on the Yangtze River 1600 km (1000 miles) from the East China Sea: the Three Gorges dam, the world's biggest hydroelectric and flood-control project, is nearby. Pop: 724 000 (2005 est)

yid (jɪd) *n slang* a derogatory word for a Jew [c20: probably from *Yiddish*, from Middle High German *Jude* JEW]

Yiddish ('jɪdɪʃ) *n* **1** a language spoken as a vernacular by Jews in Europe and elsewhere by Jewish emigrants, usually written in the Hebrew alphabet. Historically, it is a dialect of High German with an admixture of words of Hebrew, Romance, and Slavonic origin, developed in central and E Europe during the Middle Ages ▷ *adj* **2** in or relating to this language [c19: from German *jüdisch*, from *Jude* JEW]

Yiddisher ('jɪdɪʃə) *adj* **1** in or relating to Yiddish **2** Jewish ▷ *n* **3** a speaker of Yiddish; Jew

yield (jiːld) *vb* **1** to give forth or supply (a product, result, etc), esp by cultivation, labour, etc; produce or bear **2** (*tr*) to furnish as a return: *the shares yielded three per cent* **3** (*tr*; often foll by *up*) to surrender or relinquish, esp as a result of force, persuasion, etc **4** (*intr*; sometimes foll by *to*) to give way, submit, or surrender, as through force or persuasion: *she yielded to his superior knowledge* **5** (*intr*; often foll by *to*) to agree; comply; assent: *he eventually yielded to their request for money* **6** (*tr*) to grant or allow; concede: *to yield right of way* ▷ *n* **7** the result, product, or amount yielded **8** the profit or return, as from an investment or tax **9** the annual income provided by an investment, usually expressed as a percentage of its cost or of its current value **10** the energy released by the explosion of a nuclear weapon expressed in terms of the amount of TNT necessary to produce the same energy **11** *chem* the quantity of a specified product obtained in a reaction or series of reactions, usually expressed as a percentage of the quantity that is theoretically obtainable [Old English *gieldan*; related to Old Frisian *jelda*, Old High German *geltan*, Old Norse *gjalda*, Gothic *gildan*] ▷ 'yieldable *adj* ▷ 'yielder *n*

yielding ('jiːldɪŋ) *adj* **1** compliant, submissive, or flexible **2** pliable or soft: *a yielding material*

yield point *n* the stress at which an elastic material under increasing stress ceases to behave elastically; under conditions of tensile strength the elongation is no longer proportional to the increase in stress

Yin and Yang (jɪn) *n* two complementary principles of Chinese philosophy: Yin is negative, dark, and feminine, Yang positive, bright, and masculine. Their interaction is thought to maintain the harmony of the universe and to influence everything within it [from Chinese (Peking) *yin* dark + *yang* bright]

Yinchuan, Yin-ch'uan or **Yinchwan** ('jɪn'tʃwaːn) *n* a city in N central China, capital of Ningxia, on the Yellow River. Pop: 642 000 (2005 est)

Yingkou or **Yingkow** ('jɪn'kaʊ) *n* a port in NE China, in SW Liaoning province: a major shipping centre for Manchuria. Pop: 723 000 (2005 est)

yippee (jɪ'piː) *interj* an exclamation of joy, pleasure, anticipation, etc

yips (jɪps) *pl n* the yips *informal* (in sport, originally esp golf) nervous twitching or tension that destroys concentration and spoils performance [c20: of unknown origin]

Y2K *n informal* another name for the year 2000 AD (esp referring to the millennium bug) [c20: Y(EAR) + 2 + K (in the sense: thousand)]

-yl *suffix of nouns* (in chemistry) indicating a group or radical: *methyl; carbonyl* [from Greek *hulē* wood, matter]

ylang-ylang or **ilang-ilang** (ˌiːlæŋ'iːlæŋ) *n* **1** an aromatic Asian tree, *Cananga odorata* (or *Canangium odoratum*), with fragrant greenish-yellow flowers yielding a volatile oil: family *Annonaceae* **2** the oil obtained from this tree, used in perfumery [c19: from Tagalog *ilang-ilang*]

ylem ('aɪləm) *n* the original matter from which the basic elements are said to have been formed following the explosion postulated in the big bang theory of cosmology [Middle English, from Old French *ilem*, from Latin *hȳlē* stuff, matter, from Greek *hulē* wood, matter]

YMCA *abbreviation* Young Men's Christian Association

Ymir ('iːmɪə) or **Ymer** ('iːmə) *n Norse myth* the first being and forefather of the giants. He was slain by Odin and his brothers, who made the earth from his flesh, the water from his blood, and the sky from his skull

-yne *suffix forming nouns* denoting an organic chemical containing a triple bond: *alkyne* [alteration of -INE²]

yo (jəʊ) *sentence substitute* an expression used as a greeting, to attract someone's attention, etc [c20: of unknown origin]

yob (jɒb) or **yobbo** ('jɒbəʊ) *n, pl* yobs or yobbos *Brit slang* an aggressive and surly youth, esp a teenager [c19: perhaps back slang for BOY] ▷ 'yobbish *adj*

yodel ('jəʊdˀl) *n* **1** an effect produced in singing by an abrupt change of register from the chest voice to falsetto, esp in popular folk songs of the Swiss Alps ▷ *vb* -dels, -delling, -delled or US -dels, -deling, -deled **2** to sing (a song) in which a yodel is used [c19: from German *jodeln*, of imitative origin] ▷ 'yodeller *n*

yoga ('jəʊgə) *n* (*often capital*) **1** a Hindu system of philosophy aiming at the mystical union of the self with the Supreme Being in a state of complete awareness and tranquillity through certain physical and mental exercises **2** any method by which such awareness and tranquillity are attained, esp a course of related exercises and postures designed to promote physical and spiritual wellbeing [c19: from Sanskrit: a yoking, union, from *yunakti* he yokes] ▷ yogic ('jəʊgɪk) *adj*

yogh (jɒg) *n* **1** a character (ȝ) used in Old and Middle English to represent a palatal fricative very close to the semivowel sound of Modern English *y*, as in Old English ȝ*eong* (young) **2** this same character as used in Middle English for both the voiced and voiceless palatal fricatives; when final or in a closed syllable in medial position the sound approached that of German *ch* in *ich*, as in *knyȝt* (knight). After the 14th century this symbol became the modern consonantal (semivocalic) *y* when initial or commencing a syllable, and though no longer pronounced in medial position it is preserved in many words by a modern *gh*, as in *thought* [c14: perhaps from *yok* YOKE, referring to the letter's shape]

yogi ('jəʊgɪ) *n, pl* -gis or -gin (-gɪn) a person who is a master of yoga

yogurt or **yoghurt** ('jəʊgət, 'jɒg-) *n* a thick custard-like food prepared from milk that has been curdled by bacteria, often sweetened and flavoured with fruit, chocolate, etc [c19: from Turkish *yoğurt*]

Yogyakarta (ˌjəʊgjaːˈkaːtaː, ˌjɒg-) *n* a city in S Indonesia, in central Java: seat of government of

Indonesia (1946–49); university (1949). Pop: 396 711 (2000). Former spellings: Jogjakarta, Jokjakarta

yo-heave-ho (ˌjəʊhiːˈhəʊ) *interj* a cry formerly used by sailors while pulling or lifting together in rhythm

yohimbine (jəʊˈhɪmbiːn) *n* an alkaloid found in the bark of the tree *Corynanthe yohimbe*. It is used in medicine as an adrenergic blocking agent. Formula: $C_{21}H_{26}N_2O_3$ [C19: from Bantu *yohimbé* a tropical African tree + -INE[1]]

yo-ho-ho *interj* **1** an exclamation to call attention **2** another word for **yo-heave-ho**

yoicks (haɪk; *spelling pron* jɔɪks) *interj* a cry used by huntsmen to urge on the hounds to the fox

yoke (jəʊk) *n, pl* **yokes** *or* **yoke 1** a wooden frame, usually consisting of a bar with an oxbow or similar collar-like piece at either end, for attaching to the necks of a pair of draught animals, esp oxen, so that they can be worked as a team **2** something resembling a yoke in form or function, such as a frame fitting over a person's shoulders for carrying buckets suspended at either end **3** a fitted part of a garment, esp around the neck, shoulders, and chest or around the hips, to which a gathered, pleated, flared, or unfitted part is attached **4** an immense oppressive force or burden: *under the yoke of a tyrant* **5** a pair of oxen or other draught animals joined together by a yoke **6** a part, esp one of relatively thick cross section, that secures two or more components so that they move together **7** (in the ancient world) a symbolic reconstruction of a yoke, consisting of two upright spears with a third lashed across them, under which conquered enemies were compelled to march, esp in Rome **8** a mark, token, or symbol of slavery, subjection, or suffering **9** *now rare* a link, tie, or bond: *the yoke of love* ▷ *vb* **10** (*tr*) to secure or harness (a draught animal) to (a plough, vehicle, etc) by means of a yoke **11** to join or be joined by means of a yoke; couple, unite, or link [Old English *geoc*; related to Old High German *ioh*, Old Norse *ok*, Gothic *juk*, Latin *iugum*, Sanskrit *yugam*]

yokel (ˈjəʊkəl) *n disparaging* (used chiefly by townspeople) a person who lives in the country, esp one who appears to be simple and old-fashioned [C19: perhaps from dialect *yokel* green woodpecker, yellowhammer]

Yokohama (ˌjəʊkəʊˈhɑːmə) *n* a port in central Japan, on SE Honshu on Tokyo Bay: a major port and the country's second largest city situated in the largest and most populous industrial region of Japan. Pop: 3 433 612 (2002 est)

Yokosuka (ˌjəʊkəʊˈsuːkə) *n* a port in Japan, in SE Honshu: a major naval base with shipbuilding industries. Pop: 434 613 (2002 est)

yolk (jəʊk) *n* **1** the substance in an animal ovum consisting of protein and fat that nourishes the developing embryo **2** a greasy substance secreted by the skin of a sheep and present in the fleece [Old English *geoloca*, from *geolu* YELLOW] ▷ ˈ**yolky** *adj*

yolk sac *n zoology* the membranous sac that is attached to the ventral surface of the embryos of birds, reptiles, and some fishes and contains yolk

Yom Kippur (jɒm ˈkɪpə; *Hebrew* jɔm kiˈpur) *n* an annual Jewish holiday celebrated on Tishri 10 as a day of fasting, on which prayers of penitence are recited in the synagogue throughout the day. Also called: **Day of Atonement** [from Hebrew, from *yōm* day + *kippūr* atonement]

yomp (jɒmp) *vb* (*intr*) to walk or trek laboriously, esp heavily laden and over difficult terrain [C20: military slang, of uncertain origin]

yon (jɒn) *or* **yond** (jɒnd) *determiner* **1** chiefly Scot & northern English **a** an archaic or dialect word for **that**: *yon man* **b** (*as pronoun*): *yon's a fool* **2** variants of **yonder** [Old English *geon*; related to Old Frisian *jen*, Old High German *jenēr*, Old Norse *enn*, Gothic *jains*]

yonder (ˈjɒndə) *adv* **1** at, in, or to that relatively distant place; over there ▷ *determiner* **2** being at a distance, either within view or as if within view: *yonder valleys* [C13: from Old English *geond* yond; related to Old Saxon *jendra*, Old High German *jenēr*, Gothic *jaind*]

Yonge (jʌŋ) *n* **Charlotte M(ary)**. 1823–1901, British novelist, whose works reflect the religious ideals of the Oxford Movement. Her best-known book is *The Heir of Redclyffe* (1853)

Yong Lo (ˈjɒŋ ˈləʊ) *or* **Yung-Lo** *n* 1360–1424, Chinese emperor (1404–24) of the Ming dynasty. He moved the capital from Nanjing to Peking (now Beijing), which he rebuilt. Also called: **Ch'eng Tsu**

yoni (ˈjəʊnɪ) *n Hinduism* **1** the female genitalia, regarded as a divine symbol of sexual pleasure and matrix of generation and the visible form of Sakti **2** an image of these as an object of worship [C18: from Sanskrit, literally: vulva, womb]

Yonkers (ˈjɒŋkəz) *n* a city in SE New York State, near New York City on the Hudson River. Pop: 197 388 (2003 est)

yonks (jɒŋks) *pl n informal* a very long time; ages: *I haven't seen him for yonks* [C20: of unknown origin]

Yonne (*French* jɔn) *n* **1** a department of N central France, in Burgundy region. Capital: Auxerre. Pop: 335 917 (2003 est). Area: 7461 sq km (2910 sq miles) **2** a river in N France, flowing generally northwest to the Seine at Montereau. Length: 290 km (180 miles)

yoo-hoo (ˈjuːˌhuː) *interj* a call to attract a person's attention

yore (jɔː) *n* **1** time long past (now only in the phrase **of yore**) ▷ *adv* **2** *obsolete* in the past; long ago [Old English *geāra*, genitive plural of *gēar* YEAR; see HOUR]

york (jɔːk) *vb* (*tr*) *cricket* to bowl or try to bowl (a batsman) by pitching the ball under or just beyond the bat [C19: back formation from YORKER]

York[1] (jɔːk) *n* **1** a historic city in NE England, in York unitary authority, North Yorkshire, on the River Ouse: the military capital of Roman Britain; capital of the N archiepiscopal province of Britain since 625, with a cathedral (the Minster) begun in 1154; noted for its cycle of medieval mystery plays; unusually intact medieval walls; university (1963). Pop: 137 505 (2001). Latin name: **Eboracum 2** a unitary authority in NE England, in North Yorkshire. Pop: 183 100 (2003 est). Area: 272 sq km (105 sq miles) **3 Cape York** a cape in NE Australia, in Queensland at the N tip of the Cape York Peninsula, extending into the Torres Strait: the northernmost point of Australia

York[2] (jɔːk) *n* **1** the English royal house that reigned from 1461 to 1485 and was descended from Richard Plantagenet, **Duke of York** (1411–60), whose claim to the throne precipitated the Wars of the Roses. His sons reigned as Edward IV and Richard III **2 Alvin C(ullum)**. 1887–1964, US soldier and hero of World War I **3 Duke of,** full name *Prince Frederick Augustus, Duke of York and Albany*. 1763–1827, second son of George III of Great Britain and Ireland. An undistinguished commander-in-chief of the British army (1798–1809), he is the "grand old Duke of York" of the nursery rhyme **4 Prince Andrew, Duke of.** born 1960, second son of Elizabeth II of Great Britain and Northern Ireland. He married (1986) Miss Sarah Ferguson; they divorced in 1996; their first daughter, Princess Beatrice of York, was born in 1988 and their second, Princess Eugenie of York, in 1990

Yorke Peninsula (jɔːk) *n* a peninsula in South Australia, between Spencer Gulf and St Vincent Gulf: mainly agricultural with several coastal resorts

yorker[1] (jɔːkə) *n cricket* a ball bowled so as to pitch just under or just beyond the bat [C19: probably named after the *Yorkshire* County Cricket Club]

yorkie (ˈjɔːkɪ) *n* another name for **Yorkshire terrier**

Yorkist (ˈjɔːkɪst) *English history* ▷ *n* **1** a member or adherent of the royal house of York, esp during the Wars of the Roses ▷ *adj* **2** of, belonging to, or relating to the supporters or members of the house of York

Yorks. (jɔːks) *abbreviation* Yorkshire

Yorkshire (ˈjɔːkˌfɪə, -fə) *n* a historic county of N England: the largest English county, formerly divided administratively into East, West, and North Ridings. In 1974 it was much reduced in size and divided into the new counties of North, West, and South Yorkshire: in 1996 the East Riding of Yorkshire was reinstated as a unitary authority and parts of the NE were returned to North Yorkshire for geographical and ceremonial purposes

Yorkshire Dales *pl n* the valleys of the rivers flowing from the Pennines in W Yorkshire: chiefly Ribblesdale, Swaledale, Nidderdale, Wharfedale, and Wensleydale; tourist area. Also called: **the Dales**

Yorkshire pudding *n chiefly Brit* a light puffy baked pudding made from a batter of flour, eggs, and milk, traditionally served with roast beef

Yorkshire terrier *n* a very small breed of terrier with a long straight glossy coat of steel-blue and tan. Also called: **yorkie**

Yorktown ('jɔːk̩taʊn) *n* a village in SE Virginia: scene of the surrender (1781) of the British under Cornwallis to the Americans under Washington at the end of the War of American Independence

Yoruba ('jɒrʊbə) *n* 1 *pl* **-bas** *or* **-ba** a member of a Negroid people of W Africa, living chiefly in the coastal regions of SW Nigeria: noted for their former city states and complex material culture, particularly as evidenced in their music, art, and sculpture 2 the language of this people, belonging to the Kwa branch of the Niger-Congo family ▷ 'Yoruban *adj*

Yosemite Falls (jəʊˈsɛmɪtɪ) *pl n* a series of waterfalls in central California, in the Yosemite National Park, with a total drop of 770 m (2525 ft): includes the **Upper Yosemite Falls,** 436 m (1430 ft) high, and the **Lower Yosemite Falls,** 98 m (320 ft) high

Yosemite National Park *n* a national park in central California, in the Sierra Nevada Mountains: contains the **Yosemite Valley,** at an altitude of about 1200 m (4000 ft), with sheer walls rising about another 1200 m (4000 ft). Area: 3061 sq km (1182 sq miles)

Yoshihito (ˌjɒʃiˈhiːtəʊ) *n* See **Taisho²**

Yoshkar-Ola (*Russian* jaʃˈkarɑˈlɑ) *n* a city in Russia, capital of the Mari El Republic. Pop: 260 000 (2005 est)

you (juː; *unstressed* jʊ) *pron* (*subjective or objective*) 1 refers to the person addressed or to more than one person including the person or persons addressed but not including the speaker: *you know better; the culprit is among you* 2 Also called: **one** refers to an unspecified person or people in general: *you can't tell the boys from the girls* ▷ *n* 3 *informal* the personality of the person being addressed or something that expresses it: *that hat isn't really you* 4 *you know what or* **you know who** a thing or person that the speaker cannot or does not want to specify [Old English *ēow,* dative and accusative of *gē* YE¹; related to Old Saxon *eu,* Old High German *iu,* Gothic *izwis*]

◉ USAGE See at **me¹**

you'd (juːd; *unstressed* jʊd) *contraction of* you had *or* you would

you'll (juːl; *unstressed* jʊl) *contraction of* you will *or* you shall

young (jʌŋ) *adj* **younger** ('jʌŋgə), **youngest** ('jʌŋgɪst) 1 a having lived, existed, or been made or known for a relatively short time: *a young man; a young movement; a young country* b (*as collective noun; preceded by the*): *the young* 2 youthful or having qualities associated with youth; vigorous or lively 3 of or relating to youth: *in my young days* 4 having been established or introduced for a relatively short time: *a young member* 5 in an early stage of progress or development; not far advanced: *the day was young* 6 (*often capital*) of or relating to a rejuvenated group or movement or one claiming to represent the younger members of the population, esp one adhering to a political ideology: *Young England; Young Socialists* ▷ *n* 7 (*functioning as plural*) offspring, esp young animals: *a rabbit with her young* 8 **with young** (*of animals*) pregnant [Old English *geong*; related to Old Saxon, Old High German *iung,* Old Norse *ungr,* Latin *iuvenis,* Sanskrit *yuvan*] ▷ 'youngish *adj*

Young (jʌŋ) *n* 1 **Brigham** ('brɪɡəm). 1801–77, US Mormon leader, who led the Mormon migration to Utah and founded Salt Lake City (1847) 2 **Edward.** 1683–1765, English poet and dramatist, noted for his *Night Thoughts on Life, Death, and Immortality* (1742–45) 3 **Lester.** 1909–59, US saxophonist and clarinetist. He was a leading early exponent of the tenor saxophone in jazz 4 **Neil (Percival).** born 1945, Canadian rock guitarist, singer, and songwriter. His albums include *Harvest* (1972), *Rust Never Sleeps* (1979), and *Prairie Wind*

(2005) 5 **Thomas.** 1773–1829, English physicist, physician, and Egyptologist. He helped to establish the wave theory of light by his experiments on optical interference and assisted in the decipherment of the Rosetta Stone

young blood *n* young, fresh, or vigorous new people, ideas, attitudes, etc

Young Fogey *n* a young or fairly young person who adopts the conservative values of an older generation

young gun *n* an up-and-coming young man, esp one considered as being assertive and confident

Younghusband ('jʌn̩hʌsbənd) *n* Sir **Francis Edward.** 1863–1942, British explorer, mainly of N India and Tibet. He used military force to compel the Dalai Lama to sign (1904) a trade agreement with Britain

young lady *n* a girlfriend; sweetheart

youngling ('jʌŋlɪŋ) *n literary* a a young person, animal, or plant b (*as modifier*): *a youngling brood* [Old English *geongling*]

young man *n* a boyfriend; sweetheart

young offender institution *n* (in Britain) a place where offenders aged 15 to 21 may be detained and given training, instruction, and work. Former name: **borstal**

Young Pretender *n* See (**Charles Edward**) **Stuart**

Young's modulus *n* a modulus of elasticity, applicable to the stretching of a wire etc, equal to the ratio of the applied load per unit area of cross section to the increase in length per unit length [c19: named after Thomas Young (1773–1829), English physicist, physician, and Egyptologist]

youngster ('jʌŋstə) *n* 1 a young person; child or youth 2 a young animal, esp a horse

Youngstown ('jʌŋz̩taʊn) *n* a city in NE Ohio: a major centre of steel production; university (1908). Pop: 79 271 (2003 est)

Young Turk *n* 1 a progressive, revolutionary, or rebellious member of an organization, political party, etc, esp one agitating for radical reform 2 a member of an abortive reform movement in the Ottoman Empire, originally made up of exiles in W Europe who advocated liberal reforms. The movement fell under the domination of young Turkish army officers of a nationalist bent, who wielded great influence in the government between 1908 and 1918

younker ('jʌŋkə) *n* 1 *archaic or literary* a young man; lad 2 *obsolete* a young gentleman or knight [c16: from Dutch *jonker,* from Middle Dutch *jonc* YOUNG]

your (jɔː; *unstressed* jə) *determiner* 1 of, belonging to, or associated with you: *your nose; your house; your first taste of freedom* 2 belonging to or associated with an unspecified person or people in general: *the path is on your left heading north; this lotion is for your head only* 3 *informal* used to indicate all things or people of a certain type: *your part-time worker is a problem* [Old English *eower,* genitive of *gē* YE¹; related to Old Frisian *jūwe,* Old Saxon *euwa,* Old High German *iuwēr*]

Yourcenar ('jʊkənɑː) *n* **Marguerite,** original name *Marguerite de Crayencour.* 1903– 87, French novelist and writer, in the US from 1939; noted for her historical novels, esp *Mémoires d'Hadrien* (1952)

you're (jʊə, jɔː; *unstressed* jə) *contraction of* you are

yours (jɔːz, jʊəz) *pron* 1 something or someone belonging to or associated in some way with you 2 your family: *greetings to you and yours* 3 used in conventional closing phrases at the end of a letter: *yours sincerely; yours faithfully* 4 of yours belonging to or associated with you

yourself (jɔːˈsɛlf, jʊə-) *pron, pl* **-selves** 1 a the reflexive form of *you* b (*intensifier*): *you yourself control your destiny* 2 (*preceded by a copula*) your normal or usual self: *you're not yourself these days*

yours truly *pron* an informal term for *I, myself,* or *me* [from the conventional closing phrase used at the end of letters]

youth (juːθ) *n, pl* **youths** (juːðz) 1 the quality or condition of being young, immature, or inexperienced: *his youth told against him in the contest* 2 the period between childhood and maturity, esp adolescence and early adulthood 3 the freshness, vigour, or vitality characteristic of young people 4 any period of early development **5** a young person, esp a young man or boy **6** young people collectively: *youth everywhere is rising in revolt* [Old English *geogoth*; related to Old Frisian *jogethe*, Old High German *iugund*, Gothic *junda*, Latin *juventus*]

Youth (ju:θ) *n* **Isle of Youth** an island in the NW Caribbean, south of Cuba: administratively part of Cuba from 1925. Chief town: Nueva Gerona. Pop: 80 600 (2002 est). Area: 3061 sq km (1182 sq miles). Former name: **Isle of Pines**

youth club *n* a centre providing leisure activities for young people, often associated with a church or community centre

youth court *n* a court that deals with juvenile offenders and children beyond parental control or in need of care

youthful ('ju:θful) *adj* **1** of, relating to, possessing, or characteristic of youth **2** fresh, vigorous, or active: *he's surprisingly youthful for his age* **3** in an early stage of development: *a youthful culture* **4** Also called: **young** (of a river, valley, or land surface) in the early stage of the cycle of erosion, characterized by steep slopes, lack of flood plains, and V-shaped valleys > '**youthfully** *adv* > '**youthfulness** *n*

youth hostel *n* one of a chain of inexpensive lodging places for young people travelling cheaply. Often shortened to: **hostel**

you've (ju:v; *unstressed* juv) *contraction of* you have

yowie ('jauɪ) *n* a large legendary manlike or apelike creature, alleged to inhabit the Australian outback [C21: from an Aboriginal word *yuwi*]

yowl (jaul) *vb* **1** to express with or produce a loud mournful wail or cry; howl ▷ *n* **2** a loud mournful cry; wail or howl [C13: from Old Norse *gaula*] > '**yowler** *n*

yo-yo ('jəujəu) *n, pl -yos* **1** a toy consisting of a spool attached to a string, the end of which is held while it is repeatedly spun out and reeled in **2** *US & Canadian slang* a stupid person, esp one who is easily manipulated ▷ *vb* yo-yos, yo-yoing, yo-yoed (*intr*) **3** informal to change repeatedly from one position to another; fluctuate [from Filipino *yo yo*, come come, a weapon consisting of a spindle attached to a thong]

Ypres (French iprə) *n* a town in W Belgium, in W Flanders province near the border with France: scene of many sieges and battles, esp in World War I, when it was completely destroyed. Pop: 35 021 (2004 est). Flemish name: **Ieper**

Ypsilanti (ˌɪpsɪˈlæntɪ), **Hypsilantis** or **Hypsilantes** *n* **1 Alexander** (ˌalekˈsander). 1792–1828, Greek patriot, who led an unsuccessful revolt against the Turks (1821) **2** his brother, **Demetrios** (ðimitriˈɔs). 1793–1832, Greek revolutionary leader; commander in chief of Greek forces (1828–30) during the war of independence

yr *abbreviation* **1** *pl* yrs year **2** younger **3** your

yrs *abbreviation* **1** years **2** yours

Yser (French izɛr) *n* a river in NW central Europe, rising in N France and flowing through SW Belgium to the North Sea: scene of battles in World War I. Length: 77 km (48 miles)

Yseult (ɪˈsuːlt) *n* a variant spelling of **Iseult**

YT *abbreviation* (esp in postal addresses) Yukon Territory

YTS *abbreviation* (in Britain) (the former) Youth Training Scheme

ytterbia (ɪˈtɜːbɪə) *n* another name for **ytterbium oxide** [C19: New Latin, named after *Ytterby*, Swedish quarry where it was discovered]

ytterbium (ɪˈtɜːbɪəm) *n* a soft malleable silvery element of the lanthanide series of metals that occurs in monazite and is used to improve the mechanical properties of steel. Symbol: Yb; atomic no: 70; atomic wt: 173.04; valency: 2 or 3; relative density: 6.903 (alpha), 6.966 (beta); melting pt: 819°C; boiling pt: 1196°C [C19: New Latin; see YTTERBIA]

ytterbium oxide *n* a colourless weakly basic hygroscopic substance used in certain alloys and ceramics. Formula: Yb_2O_3

yttria ('ɪtrɪə) *n* another name for **yttrium oxide** [C19: New Latin, named after *Ytterby*; see YTTERBIA]

yttrium ('ɪtrɪəm) *n* a silvery metallic element occurring in monazite and gadolinite and used in various alloys, in lasers, and as a catalyst. Symbol: Y; atomic no: 39;

atomic wt: 88.90585; valency: 3; relative density: 4.469; melting pt: 1522°C; boiling pt: 3338°C [C19: New Latin; see YTTERBIA]

yttrium metal *n* *chem* any one of a group of elements including yttrium and the related lanthanides, holmium, erbium, thulium, ytterbium, and lutetium

yttrium oxide *n* a colourless or white insoluble solid used mainly in incandescent mantles. Formula: Y_2O_3

yuan ('juːˈæn) *n, pl -an* the standard monetary unit of China, divided into 10 jiao and 100 fen [from Chinese *yüan* round object; see YEN¹]

Yüan¹ ('juːˈæn) *n* **1** the imperial dynasty of China from 1279 to 1368 ▷ *adj* **2** of or relating to the Chinese porcelain produced during the Yüan dynasty, characterized by the appearance of under-glaze blue-and-white ware

Yüan² ('juːˈæn) *or* **Yüen** ('juːˈɛn) *n* a river in SE central China, rising in central Guizhou province and flowing northeast to Lake Tungting. Length: about 800 km (500 miles)

Yuan Shi Kai ('juːˈæn 'ʃiː 'kaɪ) *n* 1859–1916, Chinese general and statesman: first president (1912–16) of the Chinese republic

Yuan Tan ('juːˈæn 'tæn) *n* an annual Chinese festival marking the Chinese New Year. It can last over three days and includes the exchange of gifts, firework displays, and dancing

Yucatán (ˌjuːkəˈtɑːn; *Spanish* jukaˈtan) *n* **1** a state of SE Mexico, occupying the N part of the Yucatán peninsula. Capital: Mérida. Pop: 1 655 707 (2000). Area: 39 340 sq km (15 186 sq miles) **2** a peninsula of Central America between the Gulf of Mexico and the Caribbean, including the Mexican states of Campeche, Yucatán, and Quintana Roo, and part of Belize: a centre of Mayan civilization from about 100 BC to the 18th century. Area: about 181 300 sq km (70 000 sq miles)

Yucatán Channel *n* a channel between W Cuba and the Yucatán peninsula

yucca ('jʌkə) *n* any of several plants of the genus *Yucca*, of tropical and subtropical America, having stiff lancelike leaves and spikes of white flowers: family *Agaraceae* [C16: from American Spanish *yuca*, ultimately from an American Indian word]

yuck or **yuk** (jʌk) *interj* *slang* an exclamation indicating contempt, dislike, or disgust

yucko ('jʌkəu) *Austral slang* ▷ *adj* **1** disgusting; unpleasant ▷ *interj* **2** an exclamation of disgust

yucky or **yukky** ('jʌkɪ) *adj* **yuckier, yuckiest** or **yukkier, yukkiest** *slang* disgusting; sickening; nasty

Yugo. *abbreviation* (the former) Yugoslavia

Yugoslav or **Jugoslav** ('juːgəuˌslɑːv) *n* **1** (formerly) a native, inhabitant, or citizen of Yugoslavia (sense 1 or 2) **2** (not in technical use) another name for **Serbo-Croat** (sense 1) ▷ *adj* **3** (formerly) of, relating to, or characteristic of Yugoslavia (sense 1 or 2) or its people

Yugoslavia or **Jugoslavia** (ˌjuːgəuˈslɑːvɪə) *n* **1** Federal Republic of Yugoslavia a former country in SE Europe, comprising Serbia and Montenegro, that was formed in 1991 but not widely internationally recognized until 2000; it was replaced by the Union of Serbia and Montenegro in 2003 (dissolved 2006) **2** a former country in SE Europe, on the Adriatic: established in 1918 from the independent states of Serbia and Montenegro, and regions that until World War I had belonged to Austria-Hungary (Croatia, Slovenia, and Bosnia-Herzegovina); the name was changed from Kingdom of Serbs, Croats, and Slovenes to Yugoslavia in 1929; German invasion of 1941–44 was resisted chiefly by a Communist group led by Tito, who declared a people's republic in 1945; it became the Socialist Federal Republic of Yugoslavia in 1963; in 1991 Slovenia, Croatia, and Bosnia-Herzegovina declared independence, followed by Macedonia in 1992; Serbia and Montenegro formed the Federal Republic of Yugoslavia, subsequently (2003) replaced by the Union of Serbia and Montenegro (dissolved 2006)
> **Yugo'slavian** or **Jugo'slavian** *adj, n*

Yukawa (juːˈkɑːwə) *n* **Hideki** ('hiːdɛki). 1907–81, Japanese nuclear physicist, who predicted (1935) the existence of mesons: Nobel prize for physics 1949

Yukon ('juːkɒn) *n* **the Yukon** a territory of NW Canada,

y

on the Beaufort Sea, between the Northwest Territories and Alaska: arctic and mountainous, reaching 5959 m (19 550 ft) at Mount Logan, Canada's highest peak; mineral resources. Capital: Whitehorse. Pop: 31 209 (2004 est). Area: 536 327 sq km (207 076 sq miles). Abbreviation: YT ⊳ 'Yukoner *n*

Yukon Gold *n* a variety of yellow-fleshed potato developed in Canada

Yukon River *n* a river in NW North America, rising in NW Canada on the border between the Yukon Territory and British Columbia: flows northwest into Alaska, US, and then southwest to the Bering Sea; navigable for about 2850 km (1775 miles) to Whitehorse. Length: 3185 km (1979 miles)

yulan ('ju:læn) *n* a Chinese magnolia, *Magnolia denudata*, that is often cultivated for its showy white flowers [C19: from Chinese, from *yu* a gem + *lan* plant]

yule (ju:l) *n* (*sometimes capital*) *literary, archaic, or dialect* **a** Christmas, the Christmas season, or Christmas festivities **b** (*in combination*): *yuletide* [Old English *geōla*, originally a name of a pagan feast lasting 12 days; related to Old Norse *jōl*, Swedish *jul*, Gothic *jiuleis*]

yule log *n* a large log of wood traditionally used as the foundation of a fire in the hearth at Christmas

yummo ('jʌməʊ) *Austral slang* ⊳ *adj* **1** tasty; delicious ⊳ *interj* **2** an exclamation of delight or approval

yummy ('jʌmɪ) *slang* ⊳ *interj* **1** Also called: **yum-yum** an exclamation indicating pleasure or delight, as in anticipation of delicious food ⊳ *adj* **-mier, -miest** **2** delicious, delightful, or attractive [C20: from *yum-yum*, of imitative origin]

Yung-lo ('jʊŋ'ləʊ) *n* a variant transliteration of the Chinese name for **Yong Lo**

Yunnan *or* **Yünnan** (ju:'næn) *n* a province of SW China:

consists mainly of a plateau broken in the southeast by the Red and Black Rivers, with mountains in the west, rising over 5500 m (18 000 ft); large deposits of tin, lead, zinc, and coal. Capital: Kunming. Pop: 43 760 000 (2003 est). Area: 436 200 sq km (168 400 sq miles)

yuppie *or* **yuppy** ('jʌpɪ) (*sometimes capital*) *n* **1** an affluent young professional person ⊳ *adj* **2** typical of or reflecting the values characteristic of yuppies [C20: from *y(oung)* *u(rban)* or *up(wardly mobile)* *p(rofessional)* + -IE] ⊳ 'yuppiedom *n*

yuppie disease *or* **yuppie flu** *n* *informal, sometimes considered offensive* any of a number of debilitating long-lasting viral disorders associated with stress, such as chronic fatigue syndrome, whose symptoms include muscle weakness, chronic tiredness, and depression

yuppify ('jʌpɪ,faɪ) *vb* **-fies, -fying, -fied** (*tr*) to make yuppie in nature ⊳ ,yuppifi'cation *n*

Yurev (*Russian* 'jurjɪf) *n* the former name (11th century until 1918) of **Tartu**

yurt (jʊət) *n* a circular tent consisting of a framework of poles covered with felt or skins, used by Mongolian and Turkic nomads of E and central Asia [from Russian *yurta*, of Turkic origin; compare Turkish *yurt* abode, home]

Yuzovka (*Russian* 'juzəfkə) *n* a former name (1872 until after the Revolution) of **Donetsk**

yuzu ('ju:zu:) *n* a citrus fruit about the size of a golf ball, a hybrid of a primitive citrus called *Ichang papeda* and a mandarin, which grows on tall trees in Japan and has a strong sour flavour. Its rind and juice are a popular ingredient in Japanese cookery [C21: Japanese]

Yvelines (*French* ivlin) *n* a department of N France, in Île de France region. Capital: Versailles. Pop: 1 370 443 (2003 est). Area: 2271 sq km (886 sq miles)

YWCA *abbreviation* Young Women's Christian Association

Zz

z¹ or **Z** (zɛd; US ziː) n, pl **z's**, **Z's** or **Zs 1** the 26th and last letter and the 20th consonant of the modern English alphabet **2** a speech sound represented by this letter, in English usually a voiced alveolar fricative, as in *zip* **3 a** something shaped like a Z **b** (*in combination*): *a Z-bend in a road*

z² *maths symbol for* **1** the z-axis or a coordinate measured along the z-axis in a Cartesian or cylindrical coordinate system **2** an algebraic variable

Z *symbol for* **1** any unknown, variable, or unspecified factor, number, person, or thing **2** *chem* atomic number **3** *physics* impedance **4** zone

Zaandam (*Dutch* zaːnˈdɑm) n a former town in the W Netherlands, in North Holland: an important shipbuilding centre in the 17th century. It became part of Zaanstad in 1974

Zaanstad (*Dutch* zaːnˈʃtat) n a port in the W Netherlands, in North Holland: formed (1974) from Zaandam, Koog a/d Zaan, Zaandijk, Wormerveer, Krommenie, Westzaan, and Assendelft; food and machinery industries. Pop: 189 656 (2007 est)

zabaglione (ˌzæbəˈljəʊnɪ) n a light foamy dessert made of egg yolks, sugar, and marsala, whipped together and served warm in a glass [Italian; probably related to Late Latin *sabaia* Illyrian drink made from grain]

Zabrze (*Polish* ˈzabʒɛ) n a city in SW Poland: a Prussian and German town from 1742 until 1945, when it passed to Poland; industrial centre in a coal-mining region. Pop: 189 656 (2007 est). German name: Hindenburg

Zacatecas (*Spanish* θakaˈtekas) n **1** a state of N central Mexico, on the central plateau: rich mineral resources. Capital: Zacatecas. Pop: 1 351 207 (2000). Area: 75 040 sq km (28 973 sq miles) **2** a city in N central Mexico, capital of Zacatecas state: silver mines. Pop: 241 000 (2005 est)

Zacharias (ˌzækəˈraɪəs), **Zachariah** (ˌzækəˈraɪə) or **Zachary** (ˈzækərɪ) n *New Testament* John the Baptist's father, who underwent a temporary period of dumbness for his lack of faith (Luke 1)

Zacynthus (zəˈsɪnθəs, -ˈkɪn-) n the Latin name for **Zante**

zaffer or **zaffre** (ˈzæfə) n impure cobalt oxide, used to impart a blue colour to enamels [c17: from Italian *zaffera*; perhaps related to Latin *sapphīrus* SAPPHIRE]

Zagazig (ˈzægəˌzɪɡ) or **Zaqaziq** n a city in NE Egypt, in the Nile Delta: major cotton market. Pop: 291 000 (2005 est)

Zaghlul (ˈzaːɡluːl) n **Saad** (saːd). 1857–1927, Egyptian nationalist politician; prime minister (1924)

Zagreb (ˈzaːɡrɛb) n the capital of Croatia, on the River Sava; gothic cathedral; university (1874); industrial centre. Pop: 685 000 (2005 est). German name: Agram

Zagreus (ˈzæɡrɪəs) n *Greek myth* a young god whose cult came from Crete to Greece, where he was identified with Dionysus. The son of Zeus by either Demeter or Persephone, he was killed by the Titans at the behest of Hera

Zagros Mountains (ˈzæɡrɒs) pl n a mountain range in S Iran: has Iran's main oilfields in its W central foothills. Highest peak: Zard Kuh, 4548 m (14 920 ft)

Zahir-ud-din Muhammad n the original name of **Baber**

zaibatsu (ˈzaɪbætˈsuː) n (*functioning as singular or plural*) the group or combine comprising a few wealthy families that controls industry, business, and finance in Japan [from Japanese, from *zai* wealth, from Chinese *ts'ai* + *batsu* family, person of influence, from Chinese *fa*]

Zaïre (zaːˈɪə) n **1** the former name (1971–97) of the **Democratic Republic of Congo** (sense 1) **2** (formerly) the Zaïrian name (1971–97) for the (River) **Congo** > Zaˈïrian or Zaˈïrean adj, n

Zákinthos (ˈzakinˌθɒs) n a transliteration of the Modern Greek name for **Zante**

zakuski or **zakouski** (zæˈkʊskɪ) pl n, sing **-ka** (-kə) *Russian cookery* hors d'oeuvres, consisting of tiny open sandwiches spread with caviar, smoked sausage, etc, or a cold dish such as radishes in sour cream, all usually served with vodka [Russian, from *zakusit'* to have a snack]

Zama (ˈzaːmə) n the name of several ancient cities in N Africa, including the one near the site of Scipio's decisive defeat of Hannibal (202 BC)

Zambezi or **Zambese** (zæmˈbiːzɪ) n a river in S central and E Africa, rising in NW Zambia and flowing across E Angola back into Zambia, continuing south to the Caprivi Strip of Namibia, then east forming the Zambia–Zimbabwe border, and finally crossing

Z

Mozambique to the Indian Ocean: the fourth longest river in Africa. Length: 2740 km (1700 miles) > Zam'bezian *adj*

Zambia ('zæmbɪə) *n* a republic in southern Africa: an early site of human settlement; controlled by the British South Africa Company by 1900 and unified as Northern Rhodesia in 1911; made a British protectorate in 1924; part of the Federation of Rhodesia and Nyasaland (1953–63), gaining independence as a member of the Commonwealth in 1964; important mineral exports, esp copper. Official language: English. Religion: Christian majority, animist minority. Currency: kwacha. Capital: Lusaka. Pop: 10 924 000 (2004 est). Area: 752 617 sq km (290 587 sq miles). Former name (until 1964): Northern Rhodesia > 'Zambian *adj, n*

Zamboanga (,zæmbəʊ'æŋgə) *n* a port in the Philippines, on SW Mindanao on Basilan Strait: founded by the Spanish in 1635; tourist centre, with fisheries. Pop: 716 000 (2005 est)

zambuck ('zæmbʌk) *n* Austral & NZ informal a St John ambulance attendant, esp at a sports meeting [c20: from Zam-Buck, the trade name of an ointment which comes in a black-and-white container, black and white being the colours of the St John uniform]

Zamenhof (Polish 'zamɛnxɔf) *n* **Lazarus Ludwig** (la'zarus 'ludvik). 1859–1917, Polish oculist; invented Esperanto

Zamora (Spanish θa'mora) *n* a city in NW central Spain, on the Douro River. Pop: 65 639 (2003 est)

Zamyatin (Russian za'mjatjin) *n* **Yevgenii Ivanovich** (jɪv'gjenij ɪ'vanəvitʃ). 1884–1937, Russian novelist and writer, in Paris from 1931, whose works include satirical studies of provincial life in Russia and England, where he worked during World War I, and the dystopian novel We (1924)

Zante ('zæntɪ) *n* an island in the Ionian Sea, off the W coast of Greece: southernmost of the Ionian Islands; traditionally belonged to Ulysses, king of Ithaca. Pop: 38 957 (2001). Area: 402 sq km (155 sq miles). Latin name: Zacynthus. Modern Greek name: Zákinthos

Zanu PF (,zænu: ,piː'ɛf) *n acronym for* Zimbabwe African National Union Patriotic Front

zany ('zeɪnɪ) *adj* -nier, -niest 1 comical in an endearing way; imaginatively funny or comical, esp in behaviour ▷ *n, pl* -nies 2 a clown or buffoon, esp one in old comedies who imitated other performers with ludicrous effect 3 a ludicrous or foolish person [c16: from Italian zanni, from dialect (Venice and Lombardy) Zanni, nickname for Giovanni John; one of the traditional names for a clown] > 'zanily *adv* > 'zaniness *n*

Zanzibar (,zænzɪ'bɑː) *n* an island in the Indian Ocean, off the E coast of Africa: settled by Persians and Arabs from the 7th century onwards; became a flourishing trading centre for slaves, ivory, and cloves; made a British protectorate in 1890, becoming independent within the Commonwealth in 1963 and a republic in 1964; joined with Tanganyika in 1964 to form the United Republic of Tanzania. Pop: 622 459 (2002) > ,Zanzi'bari *adj, n*

zap (zæp) slang ▷ *vb* zaps, zapping, zapped 1 (tr) to attack, kill, or destroy, as with a sudden bombardment 2 (intr) to move quickly; rush 3 (tr) computing a to clear from the screen b to erase 4 (intr) television to change channels rapidly by remote control ▷ *n* 5 energy, vigour, or pep ▷ *interj* 6 an exclamation used to express sudden or swift action [c20: of imitative origin]

Zapata (zə'pɑːtə; Spanish θa'pata) *n* **Emiliano** (emi'ljano). ?1877–1919, Mexican guerrilla leader

zapateado Spanish (θapate'aðo) *n, pl* -dos (-ðos) a Spanish dance with stamping and very fast footwork [from zapatear to tap with the shoe, from zapato shoe]

Zaporozhye (Russian zəpɐ'rɔʒjɛ) *n* a city in E Ukraine on the Dnieper River: developed as a major industrial centre after the construction (1932) of the Dnieper hydroelectric station. Pop: 798 000 (2005 est). Former name (until 1921): Aleksandrovsk

Zappa ('zæpə) *n* **Frank**. 1940–93, US rock musician, songwriter, and experimental composer: founder and only permanent member of the Mothers of Invention. His recordings include Freak Out (1966), Hot Rats (1969),

200 Motels (1971), and Sheik Yerbouti (1979)

zappy ('zæpɪ) *adj* zappier, zappiest slang full of energy; snappy; zippy

ZAPU ('zæpuː) *n acronym for* Zimbabwe African People's Union

Zaqaziq ('zækə,zɪk) *n* a variant of **Zagazig**

Zaragoza (Spanish θara'γoθa) *n* a city in NE Spain, on the River Ebro: Roman colony established 25 BC; under Moorish rule (714–1118); capital of Aragon (12th–15th centuries); twice besieged by the French during the Peninsular War and captured (1809); university (1474). Pop: 626 081 (2003 est). Pre-Roman name: Salduba. Latin name: Caesaraugusta. English name: Saragossa

Zarathustra (,zærə'θuːstrə) *n* the Avestan name of **Zoroaster** > ,Zara'thustrian or ,Zara'thustric *adj, n*

zareba or **zareeba** (zə'riːbə) *n* (in northern E Africa, esp formerly) 1 a stockade or enclosure of thorn bushes around a village or campsite 2 the area so protected or enclosed [c19: from Arabic zarībah cattlepen, from zarb sheepfold]

zarf (zɑːf) *n* (esp in the Middle East) a holder, usually ornamental, for a hot coffee cup [from Arabic: container, sheath]

Zaria ('zɑːrɪə) *n* a city in N central Nigeria: former capital of a Hausa state; agricultural trading centre; university (1962). Pop: 822 000 (2005 est)

Zarqa ('zɑːkə) *n* the second largest town in Jordan, northeast of Amman. Pop: 494 000 (2005 est)

zarzuela (zɑː'zweɪlə) *n* 1 a type of Spanish vaudeville or operetta, usually satirical in nature 2 a seafood stew [from Spanish, from La Zarzuela, name of the palace near Madrid where such vaudeville was first performed (1629)]

Zatlers ('zætləz) *n* **Valdis**. born 1955, Latvian politician, president of Latvia from 2007

Zátopek (Czech 'za:topɛk) *n* **Emil** ('emil). 1922–2000, Czech runner; winner of the 5000 and 10 000 metres and the marathon at the 1952 Olympic Games in Helsinki

z-axis *n* a reference axis of a three-dimensional Cartesian coordinate system along which the z-coordinate is measured

ZB station *n* (in New Zealand) a radio station of a commercial network

Z chart *n* statistics a chart often used in industry and constructed by plotting on it three series: monthly, weekly, or daily data, the moving annual total, and the cumulative total dating from the beginning of the current year

Zea ('tseːa) *n* the Italian name for **Keos**

zeal (ziːl) *n* fervent or enthusiastic devotion, often extreme or fanatical in nature, as to a religious movement, political cause, ideal, or aspiration [c14: from Late Latin zēlus, from Greek zēlos]

Zealand ('ziːlənd) *n* the largest island of Denmark, separated from the island of Funen by the Great Belt and from S Sweden by the Sound (both now spanned by road bridges). Chief town: Copenhagen. Pop: 2 096 449 (2003 est). Area: 7016 sq km (2709 sq miles). Danish name: Sjælland. German name: Seeland

zealot ('zɛlət) *n* an immoderate, fanatical, or extremely zealous adherent to a cause, esp a religious one [c16: from Late Latin zēlōtēs, from Greek, from zēloun to be zealous, from zēlos ZEAL] > 'zealotry *n*

Zealot ('zɛlət) *n* any of the members of an extreme Jewish sect or political party that resisted all aspects of Roman rule in Palestine in the 1st century AD

zealous ('zɛləs) *adj* filled with or inspired by intense enthusiasm or zeal; ardent; fervent > 'zealously *adv* > 'zealousness *n*

Zeami or **Seami** (siː'ɑːmɪ) *n* **Motokiyo** (,məʊtəʊ'kiː∂ʊ). 1363–1443, Japanese dramatist, regarded as the greatest figure in the history of No drama

zebec or **zebeck** ('ziːbɛk) *n* variant spellings of **xebec**

Zebedee ('zɛbɪ,diː) *n* New Testament the father of the apostles James and John (Matthew 4:21)

zebra ('ziːbrə, 'zɛbrə) *n, pl* -ras or -ra any of several mammals of the horse family (Equidae), such as Equus burchelli (the **common zebra**), of southern and eastern

Africa, having distinctive black-and-white striped hides [c16: via Italian from Old Spanish: wild ass, probably from Vulgar Latin *eciferus* (unattested) wild horse, from Latin *equiferus*, from *equus* horse + *ferus* wild] > **zebrine** ('zi:braɪn, 'zɛb-) *or* 'zebroid *adj*

Zebra ('zi:brə, 'zɛbrə) *n finance* a noninterest-paying bond in which the accrued income is taxed annually rather than on redemption. See **zero** (sense 10) [c20: from *zero-coupon bond*]

zebra crossing *n Brit* a pedestrian crossing marked on a road by broad alternate black and white stripes. Once on the crossing the pedestrian has right of way

zebra finch *n* any of various Australasian songbirds with zebra-like markings, such as the grassfinch *Poephila castanotis*

zebra mussel *n Canadian* a small striped variety of mussel

zebrawood ('zɛbrə,wʊd, 'zi:-) *n* 1 a tree, *Connarus guianensis*, of tropical America, Asia, and Africa, yielding striped hardwood used in cabinetwork: family *Connaraceae* 2 any of various other trees or shrubs having striped wood 3 the wood of any of these trees

zebu ('zi:bu:) *n* a domesticated ox, *Bos indicus*, having a humped back, long horns, and a large dewlap: used in India and E Asia as a draught animal [c18: from French *zébu*, perhaps of Tibetan origin]

Zebulun ('zɛbjʊlən, zə'bju:-) *n Old Testament* 1 the sixth son whom Leah bore to Jacob: one of the 12 patriarchs of Israel (Genesis 30:20) 2 the tribe descended from him 3 the territory of this tribe, lying in lower Galilee to the north of Mount Carmel and to the east of the coastal plain

Zech. *Bible abbreviation* Zechariah

Zechariah (,zɛkə'raɪə) *n* 1 *Old Testament* a a Hebrew prophet of the late 6th century BC b the book containing his oracles, which are chiefly concerned with the renewal of Israel after the exile as a national, religious, and messianic community with the restored Temple and rebuilt Jerusalem as its centre. Douay spelling: Zacharias 2 See **Zacharias**

zed (zɛd) *n* the British spoken form of the letter z [c15: from Old French *zede*, via Late Latin from Greek *zēta*]

Zedekiah (,zɛdə'kaɪə) *n Old Testament* the last king of Judah, who died in captivity at Babylon

zedoary ('zɛdəʊərɪ) *n* the dried rhizome of the tropical Asian plant *Curcuma zedoaria*, used as a stimulant and a condiment: family *Zingiberaceae* [c15: from Medieval Latin *zedoaria*, from Arabic *zadwār*, of Persian origin]

zee (zi:) *n* the US word for **zed**

Zeebrugge (*Flemish* 'ze:bryxə; *English* 'zi:,brʊgə) *n* a port in NW Belgium, in W Flanders on the North Sea: linked by canal with Bruges; German submarine base in World War I

Zeeland (*Dutch* 'ze:lɑnt; *English* 'zi:lənd) *n* a province of the SW Netherlands: consists of a small area on the mainland together with a number of islands in the Scheldt estuary; mostly below sea level. Capital: Middelburg. Pop: 378 000 (2003 est). Area: 1787 sq km (690 sq miles) > 'Zeelander *n*

Zeeman effect ('zi:mən) *n* the splitting of a spectral line of a substance into several closely spaced lines when the substance is placed in a magnetic field [c20: named after Pieter *Zeeman* (1865–1943), Dutch physicist]

Zeffirelli (*Italian* dzeffi'rɛlli) *n* Franco ('fraŋko). born 1923, Italian stage and film director and designer, noted esp for his work in opera

zein ('zi:ɪn) *n* a protein of the prolamine group occurring in maize and used in the manufacture of plastics, paper coatings, adhesives, etc [c19: from New Latin *zēa* maize, from Latin: a kind of grain, from Greek *zeia* barley]

Zeist (zaɪst; *Dutch* zɛjst) *n* a city in the central Netherlands, near Utrecht. Pop: 60 000 (2003 est)

Zeitgeist *German* ('tsaɪtgaɪst) *n* the spirit, attitude, or general outlook of a specific time or period, esp as it is reflected in literature, philosophy, etc [German, literally: time spirit; see TIDE¹, GHOST]

Zellweger ('zɛl,weɪgə) *n* Renée (**Kathleen**). born 1969, US film actress, best known for her performances in *Nurse Betty* (2000), *Bridget Jones's Diary* (2001) and its sequel *Bridget Jones and the Edge of Reason* (2004), and *Chicago* (2002)

Zemlinsky (zɛm'lɪnski) *n* Alexander. 1871–1942, Austrian composer, living in the US from 1938. His works include the operas *Es war einmal* (1900) and *Eine florentische Tragödie* (1917) and the *Lyric Symphony* (1923)

Zen (zɛn) *Buddhism n* 1 a Japanese school, of 12th-century Chinese origin, teaching that contemplation of one's essential nature to the exclusion of all else is the only way of achieving pure enlightenment 2 (*modifier*) of or relating to this school: *Zen Buddhism* [from Japanese, from Chinese *ch'an* religious meditation, from Pali *jhāna*, from Sanskrit *dhyāna*] > 'Zenic *adj* > 'Zenist *n*

zenana (zɛ'nɑ:nə) *n* (in the East, esp in Muslim and Hindu homes) part of a house reserved for the women and girls of a household [c18: from Hindi *zanāna*, from Persian, from *zan* woman]

Zend (zɛnd) *n* 1 a former name for **Avestan** 2 short for **Zend-Avesta** 3 an exposition of the Avesta in the Middle Persian language (Pahlavi) [c18: from Persian *zand* commentary, exposition; used specifically of the Middle Persian commentary on the Avesta, hence of the language of the Avesta itself] > 'Zendic *adj*

Zend-Avesta (,zɛndə'vɛstə) *n* the Avesta together with the traditional interpretative commentary known as the Zend, esp as preserved in the Avestan language among the Parsees [from Avestan, representing *Avesta'-va-zend* Avesta with interpretation]

Zener diode ('zi:nə) *n* a semiconductor diode that exhibits a sharp increase in reverse current at a well-defined reverse voltage: used as a voltage regulator [c20: named after C. M. *Zener* (1905–93), US physicist]

zenith ('zɛnɪθ; *US* 'zi:nɪθ) *n* 1 *astronomy* the point on the celestial sphere vertically above an observer 2 the highest point; peak; acme: *the zenith of someone's achievements* [c17: from French *cenith*, from Medieval Latin, from Old Spanish *zenit*, based on Arabic *samt*, as in *samt arrās* path over one's head, from *samt* way, path + *al* the + *rās* head] > 'zenithal *adj*

zenithal projection *n* a type of map projection in which part of the earth's surface is projected onto a plane tangential to it, either at one of the poles (**polar zenithal**), at the equator (**equatorial zenithal**), or between (**oblique zenithal**)

Zenobia (zɪ'nəʊbɪə) *n* 3rd century AD, queen of Palmyra (?267–272), who was captured by the Roman emperor Aurelian

Zeno of Citium ('zi:nəʊ əv 'sɪtɪəm) *n* ?336–?264 BC, Greek philosopher, who founded the Stoic school in Athens

Zeno of Elea *n* ?490–?430 BC, Greek Eleatic philosopher; disciple of Parmenides. He defended the belief that motion and change are illusions in a series of paradoxical arguments, of which the best known is that of Achilles and the tortoise

zeolite ('zi:ə,laɪt) *n* 1 any of a large group of glassy secondary minerals consisting of hydrated aluminium silicates of calcium, sodium, or potassium: formed in cavities in lava flows and plutonic rocks 2 any of a class of similar synthetic materials used in ion exchange and as selective absorbents [c18: *zeo-*, from Greek *zein* to boil + *-LITE*; from the swelling up that occurs under the blowpipe] > zeolitic (,zi:ə'lɪtɪk) *adj*

Zeph. *Bible abbreviation* Zephaniah

Zephaniah¹ (,zɛfə'naɪə) *n Old Testament* 1 a Hebrew prophet of the late 7th century BC 2 the book containing his oracles, which are chiefly concerned with the approaching judgment by God upon the sinners of Judah

Zephaniah² (,zɛfə'naɪə) *n* Benjamin. born 1958, British poet, writer, and activist, born in Jamaica. His poetry collections include *The Dread Affair* (1985) and *Too Black, Too Strong* (2001)

zephyr ('zɛfə) *n* 1 a soft or gentle breeze 2 any of several delicate soft yarns, fabrics, or garments, usually of wool [c16: from Latin *zephyrus*, from Greek *zephuros* the west wind; probably related to Greek *zophos* darkness, west]

Zephyrus ('zɛfərəs) *n Greek myth* the god of the west wind

zeppelin ('zɛpəlɪn) *n* (*sometimes capital*) a large cylindrical rigid airship built from 1900 to carry passengers, and

Z

used in World War I for bombing and reconnaissance [c20: named after Count Ferdinand von *Zeppelin* (1838–1917), German aeronautical pioneer, designer and manufacturer of airships]

Zeppelin (*German* 'tsɛpəli:n) *n* Count **Ferdinand von** ('fɛrdinant fɔn). 1838–1917, German aeronautical pioneer, who designed and manufactured airships (zeppelins)

Zermatt (tsɛr'mat) *n* a village and resort in S Switzerland, in Valais canton at the foot of the Matterhorn: cars are not allowed in the area. Pop: 5988 (2000)

zero ('zɪərəʊ) *n, pl* -**ros** *or* -**roes** **1** the symbol 0, indicating an absence of quantity or magnitude; nought. Former name: **cipher 2** the integer denoted by the symbol 0; nought **3** the cardinal number between +1 and –1 **4** nothing; nil **5** a person or thing of no significance; nonentity **6** the lowest point or degree: *his prospects were put at zero* **7** the line or point on a scale of measurement from which the graduations commence **8 a** the temperature, pressure, etc, that registers a reading of zero on a scale **b** the value of a variable, such as temperature, obtained under specified conditions **9** *maths* **a** the cardinal number of a set with no members **b** the identity element of addition **10** Also called: **zero-coupon bond** *finance* a bond that pays no interest, the equivalent being paid in its redemption value. See **Zebra** ▷ *adj* **11** having no measurable quantity, magnitude, etc **12** *meteorol* **a** (of a cloud ceiling) limiting visibility to 15 metres (50 feet) or less **b** (of horizontal visibility) limited to 50 metres (165 feet) or less ▷ *vb* -**roes,** -**roing,** -**roed 13** (*tr*) to adjust (an instrument, apparatus, etc) so as to read zero or a position taken as zero ▷ *determiner* **14** *informal, chiefly US* no (thing) at all: *this job has zero interest* ▷ See also **zero in** [c17: from Italian, from Medieval Latin *zephirum,* from Arabic *sifr* empty, **CIPHER**]

zero gravity *n* the state or condition of weightlessness

zero hour *n* **1** *military* the time set for the start of an attack or the initial stage of an operation **2** *informal* a critical time, esp at the commencement of an action

zero in *vb* (*adverb*) **1** (often foll by *on*) to bring (a weapon) to bear (on a target), as while firing repeatedly **2** (*intr;* foll by *on*) *informal* to bring one's attention to bear (on a problem, etc) **3** (*intr;* foll by *on*) *informal* to converge (upon)

zero option *n* (in international nuclear arms negotiations) an offer to remove all shorter-range nuclear missiles or, in the case of the **zero-zero option** all intermediate-range nuclear missiles, if the other side will do the same

zero-rated *adj* (**zero rated** *when postpositive*) denoting goods on which the buyer pays no value-added tax although the seller can claim back any tax he has paid

zero stage *n* a solid-propellant rocket attached to a liquid-propellant rocket to provide greater thrust at liftoff

zeroth ('zɪərəʊθ) *adj* denoting a term in a series that precedes the term otherwise regarded as the first term [c20: from **ZERO** + -**TH²**]

zero tolerance *n* **a** the policy of applying laws or penalties to even minor infringements of a code in order to reinforce its overall importance **b** (*as modifier*): *a zero-tolerance policy on drugs*

zest (zɛst) *n* **1** invigorating or keen excitement or enjoyment: *a zest for living* **2** added interest, flavour, or charm; piquancy: *her presence gave zest to the occasion* **3** something added to give flavour or relish **4** the peel or skin of an orange or lemon, used as flavouring in drinks, etc ▷ *vb* **5** (*tr*) to give flavour, interest, or piquancy to [c17: from French *zeste* peel of citrus fruits used as flavouring, of unknown origin] > '**zestful** *adj* > '**zestfully** *adv* > '**zestfulness** *n* > '**zesty** *adj*

zester ('zɛstə) *n* a kitchen utensil used to scrape fine shreds of peel from citrus fruits

zeta ('zi:tə) *n* the sixth letter in the Greek alphabet (Z, ζ), a consonant, transliterated as *z* [from Greek, of Semitic origin; compare Hebrew *sādhē*]

ZETA ('zi:tə) *n* a torus-shaped apparatus used for research in the 1950s and early 1960s on controlled thermonuclear reactions and plasma physics [c20: from *z*(ero-)*e*(nergy) *t*(hermonuclear) *a*(pparatus)]

Zeta-Jones (,zi:tə'dʒəʊnz) *n* **Catherine,** original name *Catherine Jones.* born 1969, Welsh actress, who made her name in the TV series *The Darling Buds of May* (1991) before starring in the films *Traffic* (2000), *Chicago* (2002), and *Smoke and Mirrors* (2004). She is married to the US actor Michael Douglas

Zetland ('zɛtlənd) *n* the official name (until 1974) of **Shetland**

zeugma ('zju:gmə) *n* a figure of speech in which a word is used to modify or govern two or more words although appropriate to only one of them or making a different sense with each, as in the sentence *Mr. Pickwick took his hat and his leave* (Charles Dickens) [c16: via Latin from Greek: a yoking, from *zeugnunai* to yoke] > **zeugmatic** (zju:g'mætɪk) *adj*

Zeus (zju:s) *n* the supreme god of the ancient Greeks, who became ruler of gods and men after he dethroned his father Cronus and defeated the Titans. He was the husband of his sister Hera and father by her and others of many gods, demigods, and mortals. He wielded thunderbolts and ruled the heavens, while his brothers Poseidon and Hades ruled the sea and underworld respectively. Roman counterpart: **Jupiter**

Zeuxis ('zju:ksɪs) *n* late 5th century BC, Greek painter, noted for the verisimilitude of his works

Zhangjiakou ('dʒæŋ'dʒjækəʊ), **Changchiakow** *or* **Changchiak'ou** *n* a city in NE China, in NW Hebei province: a military centre, controlling the route to Mongolia, under the Ming and Manchu dynasties. Pop: 973 000 (2005 est). Former names: Wanchüan, Kalgan

Zhangzhou ('dʒæŋ'dʒəʊ), **Changchow** *or* **Ch'ang-chou** *n* a city in SE China, in S Fujian province on the Saikoe River. Pop 410 000 (2005 est). Former name: Lungki

Zhdanov (*Russian* 'ʒdanəf) *n* the former name (1948–91) of **Mariupol**

Zhejiang ('dʒɛ'dʒjæn) *or* **Chekiang** *n* a province of E China: mountainous and densely populated; a cultural centre since the 12th century. Capital: Hangzhou. Pop: 46 800 000 (2003 est). Area: 102 000 sq km (39 780 sq miles)

Zhengzhou ('dʒʌŋ'dʒəʊ), **Chengchow** *or* **Cheng-chou** *n* a city in E central China, capital of Henan province; an administrative centre. Pop: 2 250 000 (2005 est)

Zhenjiang ('dʒʌn'dʒjæn) *or* **Chinkiang** *n* a port in E China, in S Jiangsu at the confluence of the Yangtze River and the Grand Canal. Pop: 620 000 (2005 est)

Zhitomir (*Russian* ʒi'tɔmir) *n* a city in central Ukraine; centre of an agricultural region. Pop: 282 000 (2005 est)

Zhivkov (*Bulgarian* 'ʒifkɔf) *n* **Todor** ('tɔdɔr). 1911–98, Bulgarian statesman and party leader; prime minister (1962–71); president (1971–89)

zho (zəʊ) *n, pl* **zhos** *or* **zho** a variant spelling of **zo**

Zhou (dʒəʊ) *n* the Pinyin transliteration of the Chinese name for **Chou**

Zhou En Lai (ɛn laɪ) *n* the Pinyin transliteration of the Chinese name for **Chou En-lai**

Zhuangzi ('ʒwæŋ'zi:) *or* **Chuang-tzu** *n* ?369–286 BC, Chinese philosopher, who greatly influenced Chinese religion through the book of Taoist philosophy that bears his name

Zhu De ('dʒu: 'deɪ) *n* the Pinyin transliteration of the Chinese name for **Chu Teh**

Zhu Jiang ('dʒu: 'dʒjæn), **Chu Chiang** *or* **Chu Kiang** *n* a river in SE China, in S Guangdong province, flowing southeast from Canton to the South China Sea. Length: about 177 km (110 miles). Also called: **Canton River, Pearl River**

Zhukov (*Russian* 'ʒukəf) *n* **Georgi Konstantinovich** (gɪ'ɔrgij kənstan'tinəvitʃ). 1896–1974, Soviet marshal. In World War II, he led the offensives that broke the sieges of Stalingrad and Leningrad (1942–43) and later captured Warsaw and Berlin; minister of defence (1955–57)

Zia ul Haq ('zɪə ʊl 'hak) *n* **Mohammed** (məʊ'hæmɪd). 1924–88, Pakistani general: president of Pakistan (1978–88), following the overthrow (1977) of Z. A. Bhutto by a military coup. He was killed in an air crash, possibly through sabotage

zibeline ('zɪbə,laɪn, -lɪn) *n* **1** a sable or the fur of this animal **2** a thick cloth made of wool or other animal hair, having a long nap and a dull sheen ▷ *adj* **3** of, relating to, or resembling a sable [c16: from French, from Old Italian *zibellino*, ultimately of Slavonic origin; compare SABLE]

zibet ('zɪbɪt) *n* a large civet, *Viverra zibetha*, of S and SE Asia, having tawny fur marked with black spots and stripes [c16: from Medieval Latin *zibethum*, from Arabic *zabād* CIVET]

Zibo ('dzɪ,bɔ:), **Tzu-po** *or* **Tzepo** *n* a city in NE China, in Shandong province. Pop: 2 775 000 (2005 est)

Zidane (*French* zidan) *n* **Zinedine** (zinedin). born 1972, French football player, known as Zizou; scored two goals in the 1998 World Cup final

zidovudine (zaɪ'dɒvju,di:n) *n* a drug that is used to treat AIDS. Also called: AZT

Ziegfeld ('zi:g,fɛld) *n* **Florenz** ('flɒrənz). 1869–1932, US theatrical producer, noted for his series of extravagant revues (1907–31), known as the Ziegfeld Follies

ziff (zɪf) *n Austral informal* a beard [c20: of unknown origin]

ziggurat ('zɪgʊ,ræt) *or* **zikkurat** *or* **zikurat** ('zɪkuˌræt) *n* a type of rectangular temple tower or tiered mound erected by the Sumerians, Akkadians, and Babylonians in Mesopotamia. The tower of Babel is thought to be one of these [c19: from Assyrian *ziqqurati* summit, height]

Zigong ('dzɪgʊŋ), **Tzekung** *or* **Tzu-kung** *n* an industrial city in W central China, in Sichuan. Pop: 1 123 000 (2005 est)

zigzag ('zɪg,zæg) *n* **1** a line or course characterized by sharp turns in alternating directions **2** one of the series of such turns **3** something having the form of a zigzag ▷ *adj* **4** (*usually prenominal*) formed in or proceeding in a zigzag **5** (of sewing machine stitches) produced in a zigzag by a swing needle used for joining stretch fabrics, neatening raw edges, etc ▷ *adv* **6** in a zigzag manner ▷ *vb* -zags, -zagging, -zagged **7** to proceed or cause to proceed in a zigzag **8** (*tr*) to form into a zigzag [c18: from French, from German *zickzack*, from *Zacke* point, jagged projection; see TACK¹] ▷ 'zig,zagger *n*

zilch (zɪltʃ) *n slang* **1** nothing **2** *US & Canadian sport* nil [c20: of uncertain origin]

Zille ('zɪlə) *n* **Helen**. born 1951, South African politician and journalist; mayor of Cape Town from 2006 and leader of the Democratic Alliance party from 2007

zillion ('zɪljən) *informal* ▷ *n, pl* -lions *or* -lion **1** (*often plural*) an extremely large but unspecified number, quantity, or amount: *zillions of flies in this camp* ▷ *determiner* **2** amounting to a zillion: *a zillion different problems* [c20: on the model of *million*]

Zilpah ('zɪlpə) *n Old Testament* Leah's maidservant, who bore Gad and Asher to Jacob (Genesis 30:10–13)

Zimbabwe (zɪm'bɑ:bwɪ, -weɪ) *n* **1** a country in SE Africa, formerly a self-governing British colony founded in 1890 by the British South Africa Company, which administered the country until a self-governing colony was established in 1923; joined with Northern Rhodesia (now Zambia) and Nyasaland (now Malawi) as the Federation of Rhodesia and Nyasaland from 1953 to 1963; made a unilateral declaration of independence (UDI) under the leadership of Ian Smith in 1965 on the basis of White minority rule; proclaimed a republic in 1970; in 1976 the principle of Black majority rule was accepted and in 1978 a transitional government was set up; gained independence under Robert Mugabe in 1980; effectively a one-party state since 1987; a member of the Commonwealth until 2003, when it withdrew as a result of conflict with other members. Official language: English. Religion: Christian majority. Currency: Zimbabwe dollar. Capital: Harare. Pop: 12 932 000 (2004 est). Area: 390 624 sq km (150 820 sq miles). Former names: **Southern Rhodesia, Rhodesia 2** Also called: **Great Zimbabwe** a ruined fortified settlement in Zimbabwe, which at its height, in the 15th century, was probably the capital of an empire covering SE Africa ▷ Zim'babwean *adj, n*

Zimmer ('zɪmə) *n trademark* another name for **walker** (sense 3)

zinc (zɪŋk) *n* **1** a brittle bluish-white metallic element

that becomes coated with a corrosion-resistant layer in moist air and occurs chiefly in sphalerite and smithsonite. It is a constituent of several alloys, esp brass and nickel-silver, and is used in die-casting, galvanizing metals, and in battery electrodes. Symbol: Zn; atomic no: 30; atomic wt: 65.39; valency: 2; relative density: 7.133; melting pt: 419.58°C; boiling pt: 907°C **2** *informal* corrugated galvanized iron [c17: from German *Zink*, perhaps from *Zinke* prong, from its jagged appearance in the furnace] ▷ 'zincic, 'zincous *or* 'zincoid *adj* ▷ 'zincky, 'zincy *or* 'zinky *adj*

zinc blende *n* another name for **sphalerite**

zinc chloride *n* a white odourless soluble poisonous granular solid used in manufacturing parchment paper and vulcanized fibre and in preserving wood. It is also a soldering flux, embalming agent, and a medical astringent and antiseptic. Formula: ZnCl₂

zincite ('zɪŋkaɪt) *n* a red or yellow mineral consisting of zinc oxide in hexagonal crystalline form. It occurs in metamorphosed limestone. Formula: ZnO

zincography (zɪŋ'kɒgrəfɪ) *n* the art or process of etching on zinc to form a printing plate ▷ zin'cographer *n* ▷ 'zinco,graph *n*

zinc ointment *n* a medicinal ointment consisting of zinc oxide, petrolatum, and paraffin, used to treat certain skin diseases

zinc oxide *n* a white insoluble powder used as a pigment in paints (**zinc white** *or* **Chinese white**), cosmetics, glass, and printing inks. It is an antiseptic and astringent and is used in making zinc ointment. Formula: ZnO. Also called: **flowers of zinc**

zinc sulphate *n* a colourless soluble crystalline substance usually existing as the heptahydrate or monohydrate: used as a mordant, in preserving wood and skins, and in the electrodeposition of zinc. Formula: ZnSO₄. Also called: **zinc vitriol**

zine (zi:n) *n informal* a magazine or fanzine

zing (zɪŋ) *informal* ▷ *n* **1** a short high-pitched buzzing sound, as of a bullet or vibrating string **2** vitality; zest ▷ *vb* **3** (*intr*) to make or move with or as if with a high-pitched buzzing sound [c20: of imitative origin] ▷ 'zingy *adj*

zinjanthropus (zɪn'dʒænθrəpəs) *n* a type of australopithecine, *Australopithecus boisei* (formerly *Zinjanthropus boisei*), remains of which were discovered in the Olduvai Gorge in Tanzania in 1959 [c20: New Latin, from Arabic *Zinj* East Africa + Greek *anthrōpos* man]

zinnia ('zɪnɪə) *n* any annual or perennial plant of the genus *Zinnia*, of tropical and subtropical America, having solitary heads of brightly coloured flowers: family *Asteraceae* (composites) [c18: named after J. G. Zinn (died 1759), German botanist]

Zinoviev (zɪ'nəʊvɪəf; *Russian* zi'nɔvjɪf) *n* **Grigori Yevseevich**, original name *Ovsel Gershon Aronov Radomyslsky*. 1883–1936, Soviet politician; chairman of the Comintern (1919–26) executed for supposed complicity in the murder of Kirov. He was the supposed author of the forged 'Zinoviev letter' urging British Communists to revolt, publication of which helped to defeat (1924) the first Labour Government

Zinovievsk (*Russian* zi'nɔvjɪfsk) *n* a former name (1924–36) for **Kirovograd**

Zinzendorf (*German* 'tsɪntsəndɔrf) *n* **Count Nikolaus Ludwig von** ('ni:klaus 'lu:tvɪç fɔn). 1700–60, German religious reformer, who organized the Moravian Church

Zion ('zaɪən) *or* **Sion** *n* **1** the hill on which the city of Jerusalem stands **2** *Judaism* **a** the ancient Israelites of the Bible **b** the modern Jewish nation **c** Israel as the national home of the Jewish people **3** *Christianity* heaven regarded as the city of God and the final abode of his elect

Zionism ('zaɪə,nɪzəm) *n* **1** a political movement for the establishment and support of a national homeland for Jews in Palestine, now concerned chiefly with the development of the modern state of Israel **2** a policy or movement for Jews to return to Palestine from the Diaspora ▷ 'Zionist *n, adj* ▷ ,Zion'istic *adj*

zip (zɪp) *n* **1 a** Also called: **zip fastener** a fastening device operating by means of two parallel rows of metal or plastic teeth on either side of a closure that are interlocked by a sliding tab. US and Canadian term: **zipper b** (*modifier*) having or equipped with such a device: *a zip bag* **2** a short sharp whizzing sound, as of a passing bullet **3** *informal* energy; vigour; vitality **4** *US slang* nothing **5** *sport, US & Canadian slang* nil ▷ *vb* **zips, zipping, zipped 6** (*tr*; often foll by *up*) to fasten (clothing, a bag, etc) with a zip **7** (*intr*) to move with a zip: *the bullet zipped past* **8** (*intr*; often foll by *along, through*, etc) to hurry; rush **9** (*tr*) *computing* to compress (a file) in order to reduce the amount of memory required to store it or to make sending it electronically quicker [c19: of imitative origin]

zip code *n* the US equivalent of **postcode** [c20: from *z(one) i(mprovement) p(lan)*]

zip gun *n US & Canadian slang* a crude homemade pistol, esp one powered by a spring or rubber band

zipper ('zɪpə) *n* Also called (in Britain and certain other countries): **zip**

zippy ('zɪpɪ) *adj* **-pier, -piest** *informal* full of energy; lively

zircalloy (zɜːˈkælɔɪ) *n* an alloy of zirconium containing small amounts of tin, chromium, and nickel. It is used in pressurized-water reactors

zircon ('zɜːkɒn) *n* a reddish-brown, grey, green, blue, or colourless hard mineral consisting of zirconium silicate in tetragonal crystalline form with hafnium and some rare earths as impurities. It occurs principally in igneous rocks and is an important source of zirconium, zirconia, and hafnia: it is used as a gemstone and a refractory. Formula: $ZrSiO_4$ [c18: from German *Zirkon*, from French *jargon*, via Italian and Arabic, from Persian *zargūn* golden]

zirconium (zɜːˈkəʊnɪəm) *n* a greyish-white metallic element, occurring chiefly in zircon, that is exceptionally corrosion-resistant and has low neutron absorption. It is used as a coating in nuclear and chemical plants, as a deoxidizer in steel, and alloyed with niobium in superconductive magnets. Symbol: Zr; atomic no: 40; atomic wt: 91.224; valency: 2, 3, or 4; relative density: 6.506; melting pt: 1855±2°C; boiling pt: 4409°C [c19: from New Latin; see ZIRCON] > **zirconic** (zɜːˈkɒnɪk) *adj*

zirconium oxide *n* a white amorphous powder that is insoluble in water and highly refractory, used as a pigment for paints, a catalyst, and an abrasive. Formula: ZrO_2

Ziska ('zɪskə) or **Žižka** (*Czech* 'ʒɪʃka) *n* **Jan** (jan). ?1370–1424, Bohemian soldier, who successfully led the Hussite rebellion (1420–24) against emperor Sigismund

zit (zɪt) *n slang* a pimple [of unknown origin]

zither ('zɪðə) *n* a plucked musical instrument consisting of numerous strings stretched over a resonating box, a few of which may be stopped on a fretted fingerboard [c19: from German, from Latin *cithara*, from Greek *kithara*] > **'zitherist** *n*

Zi Xi ('tsi: 'ʃi:) or **Tz'u-hsi** *n* 1835–1908, Chinese empress dowager, who as regent for her son Tong Zhi and her nephew Guang Xu dominated Chinese politics from 1861 to 1908. Her reactionary policies were instrumental in the fall of imperial China

Zlatoust (*Russian* zlətaˈust) *n* a town in W Russia, on the Ay river: one of the chief metallurgical centres of the Urals since the 18th century. Pop: 192 000 (2005 est)

złoty ('zlɒtɪ) *n, pl* **-tys, -ty** the standard monetary unit of Poland, divided into 100 groszy [from Polish: golden, from *zlyoto* gold; related to Russian *zoloto* gold]

Zn *the chemical symbol for* zinc

zo, zho or **dzo** (zəʊ) *n, pl* **zos, zhos, dzos** or **zo, zho, dzo** a Tibetan breed of cattle, developed by crossing the yak with common cattle [c20: from Tibetan]

zo- *combining form* a variant of **zoo-** before a vowel

-zoa *suffix forming plural proper nouns* indicating groups of animal organisms: *Metazoa* [from New Latin, from Greek *zōia*, plural of *zōion* animal, living being]

Zoan ('zəʊæn) *n* the Biblical name for **Tanis**

zodiac ('zəʊdɪˌæk) *n* **1** an imaginary belt extending 8° either side of the ecliptic, which contains the 12 zodiacal constellations and within which the moon and planets appear to move. It is divided into 12 equal areas, called signs of the zodiac, each named after the constellation which once lay in it. See **zodiacal constellation 2** *astrology* a diagram, usually circular, representing this belt and showing the symbols, illustrations, etc, associated with each of the 12 signs of the zodiac, used to predict the future [c14: from Old French *zodiaque*, from Latin *zōdiacus*, from Greek *zōidiakos* (kuklos) (circle) of signs, from *zōidion* animal sign, carved figure, from *zōion* animal] > **zodiacal** (zəʊˈdaɪəkəl) *adj*

zodiacal constellation *n* any of the 12 constellations after which the signs of the zodiac are named: Aries, Taurus, Gemini, Cancer, Leo, Virgo, Libra, Scorpio, Sagittarius, Capricorn, Aquarius, or Pisces

zodiacal light *n* a very faint cone of light in the sky, visible in the east just before sunrise and in the west just after sunset. It is probably due to the reflection of sunlight from cosmic dust in the plane of the ecliptic

Zoffany ('zɒfənɪ) *n* **John** or **Johann** ?1733–1810, British painter, esp of portraits; born in Germany

Zog I (zɒg) *n* 1895–1961, king of Albania (1928–39), formerly prime minister (1922–24) and president (1925–28). He allowed Albania to become dominated by Fascist Italy and fled into exile when Mussolini invaded (1939)

zoic ('zəʊɪk) *adj* **1** relating to or having animal life **2** *geology* (of rocks, strata, etc) containing fossilized animals [c19: from New Latin, from Greek *zōion* animal]

-zoic *adj combining form, n combining form* indicating a geological era: *Palaeozoic* [from Greek *zōē* life + -IC]

Zola ('zəʊlə; *French* zɔla) *n* **Émile** (emil). 1840–1902, French novelist and critic; chief exponent of naturalism. In *Les Rougon-Macquart* (1871–93), a cycle of 20 novels, he explains the behaviour of his characters in terms of their heredity: it includes *L'Assommoir* (1877), *Nana* (1880), *Germinal* (1885), and *La Terre* (1887). He is also noted for his defence of Dreyfus in his pamphlet *J'accuse* (1898)

Zollverein *German* ('tsɔlfɛrˌaɪn) *n* the customs union of German states organized in the early 1830s under Prussian auspices [c19: from *Zoll* tax, TOLL² + *Verein* union]

Zomba ('zɒmbə) *n* a city in S Malawi: the capital of Malawi until 1971. Pop: 101 423 (2005)

zombie or **zombi** ('zɒmbɪ) *n, pl* **-bies** or **-bis 1** a person who is or appears to be lifeless, apathetic, or totally lacking in independent judgment; automaton **2** a supernatural spirit that reanimates a dead body **3** a corpse brought to life in this manner [from Kongo *zumbi* good-luck fetish]

zonation (zəʊˈneɪʃən) *n* arrangement in zones

zone (zəʊn) *n* **1** a region, area, or section characterized by some distinctive feature or quality **2** an area subject to a particular political, military, or government function, use, or jurisdiction: *a demilitarized zone* **3** (*often capital*) *geography* one of the divisions of the earth's surface, esp divided into latitudinal belts according to temperature. See **Torrid Zone, Frigid Zone, Temperate Zone 4** *geology* a distinctive layer or region of rock, characterized by particular fossils (zone fossils), metamorphism, structural deformity, etc **5** *ecology* an area, esp a belt of land, having a particular flora and fauna determined by the prevailing environmental conditions **6** *maths* a portion of a sphere between two parallel planes intersecting the sphere **7** *sport* **a** a mental state that enables a competitor to perform to the best of his or her ability: *Hingis is in the zone at the moment* **b** (*modifier*) of or relating to competitive performance that depends on the mood or state of mind of the participant: *a zone player* **8** *archaic* or *literary* a girdle or belt **9** NZ a section on a transport route; fare stage **10** NZ a catchment area for pupils for a specific school **11** in the zone See **zone** (sense 7) ▷ *vb* (*tr*) **12** to divide into zones, as for different use, jurisdiction, activities, etc **13** to designate as a zone **14** to mark with or divide into zones [c15: from Latin *zōna* girdle, climatic zone, from Greek *zōnē*] > **'zoning** *n* > **'zonal** *adj* > **'zonally** *adv*

zone refining *n* a technique for producing solids of extreme purity, esp for use in semiconductors. The material, in the form of a bar, is melted in one small region that is passed along the solid. Impurities concentrate in the melt and are moved to the end of the bar

zonetime ('zəʊn,taɪm) n the standard time of the time zone in which a ship is located at sea, each zone extending 7½° to each side of a meridian

zonked (zɒŋkt) adj slang **1** highly intoxicated from drugs or alcohol **2** utterly exhausted [c20: of imitative origin]

zonk out vb (intr, adverb) slang to fall asleep, esp from physical exhaustion or the effects of alcohol or drugs

zoo (zu:) n, pl zoos a place where live animals are kept, studied, bred, and exhibited to the public. Formal term: zoological garden [c19: shortened from zoological gardens (originally applied to those in London)]

zoo- or before a vowel **zo-** combining form indicating animals: zooplankton [from Greek zōion animal]

zoogeography (,zəʊədʒɪ'ɒɡrəfɪ) n the branch of zoology concerned with the geographical distribution of animals > ,zooge'ographer n > zoogeographic (,zəʊə,dʒɪə'ɡræfɪk) or ,zoo,geo'graphical adj > ,zoo,geo'graphically adv

zoography (zəʊ'ɒɡrəfɪ) n the branch of zoology concerned with the description of animals > zo'ographer n > zoographic (,zəʊə'ɡræfɪk) or ,zoo'graphical adj

zooid ('zəʊɔɪd) n **1** any independent animal body, such as an individual of a coelenterate colony **2** a motile cell or body, such as a gamete, produced by an organism > zo'oidal adj

zool. abbreviation **1** zoological **2** zoology

zoolatry (zəʊ'ɒlətrɪ) n **1** (esp in ancient or primitive religions) the worship of animals as the incarnations of certain deities, symbols of particular qualities or natural forces, etc **2** extreme or excessive devotion to animals, particularly domestic pets > zo'olatrous adj

zoological garden n the formal term for **zoo**

zoology (zəʊ'ɒlədʒɪ, zu:-) n, pl -gies **1** the study of animals, including their classification, structure, physiology, and history **2** the biological characteristics of a particular animal or animal group **3** the fauna characteristic of a particular region > zoological (,zəʊə'lɒdʒɪkəl, ,zu:ə-) adj > zo'ologist n

zoom (zu:m) vb **1** to make or cause to make a continuous buzzing or humming sound **2** to move or cause to move with such a sound **3** (intr) to move very rapidly; rush: we zoomed through town **4** to cause (an aircraft) to climb briefly at an unusually steep angle, or (of an aircraft) to climb in this way **5** (intr) (of prices) to rise rapidly ▷ n **6** the sound or act of zooming **7** See **zoom lens** [c20: of imitative origin]

zoom in vb (intr, adverb) photog, films, television to increase rapidly the magnification of the image of a distant object by means of a zoom lens

zoom lens n a lens system that allows the focal length of a camera lens to be varied continuously without altering the sharpness of the image

zoomorphism (,zəʊə'mɔ:fɪzəm) n **1** the conception or representation of deities in the form of animals **2** the use of animal forms or symbols in art, literature, etc > ,zoo'morphic adj

-zoon n combining form indicating an individual animal or an independently moving entity derived from an animal: spermatozoon [from Greek zōion animal]

zoophilism (zəʊ'ɒfɪ,lɪzəm) n the tendency to be emotionally attached to animals > zoophile ('zəʊə,faɪl) n

zoophobia (,zəʊə'fəʊbɪə) n an unusual or morbid dread of animals > zoophobous (zəʊ'ɒfəbəs) adj

zoophyte ('zəʊə,faɪt) n any animal resembling a plant, such as a sea anemone > zoophytic (,zəʊə'fɪtɪk) or ,zoo'phytical adj

zooplankton (,zəʊə'plæŋktən) n the animal constituent of plankton, which consists mainly of small crustaceans and fish larvae

zoospore (,zəʊə,spɔ:) n an asexual spore of some algae and fungi that moves by means of flagella > ,zoo'sporic or zoosporous (zəʊ'ɒspərəs, ,zəʊə'spɔ:rəs) adj

zoosterol (zəʊ'ɒstə,rɒl) n any of a group of animal sterols, such as cholesterol

zootechnics (,zəʊə'tɛknɪks) n (functioning as singular) the science concerned with the domestication and breeding

of animals

zootomy (zəʊ'ɒtəmɪ) n the branch of zoology concerned with the dissection and anatomy of animals > zootomic (,zəʊə'tɒmɪk) or ,zoo'tomical adj > ,zoo'tomically adv > zo'otomist n

zootoxin (,zəʊə'tɒksɪn) n a toxin, such as snake venom, that is produced by an animal

zoot suit (zu:t) n slang a man's suit consisting of baggy trousers with very tapered bottoms and a long jacket with wide padded shoulders, popular esp in the US in the 1940s [c20: of uncertain origin; perhaps an arbitrary rhyme on suit]

zorbing ('zɔ:bɪŋ) n informal the activity of travelling downhill inside a large air-cushioned hollow ball [c20: z + ORB (sphere) + -ING¹]

zorbonaut ('zɔ:bə,nɔ:t) n jocular a person who engages in the activity of zorbing [c20: from ZORB(ING) + -NAUT]

Zorn (Swedish sɔːrn) n **Anders Leonhard** ('andərs 'leːɔnard). 1860–1920, Swedish painter and etcher, esp of impressionist portraits and landscapes

Zoroaster (,zɒrəʊ'æstə) n ?628–?551 BC, Persian prophet; founder of Zoroastrianism. Avestan name: Zarathustra

Zoroastrian (,zɒrəʊ'æstrɪən) adj **1** of or relating to Zoroastrianism or Zoroaster ▷ n **2** a follower of Zoroaster or adherent of Zoroastrianism: in modern times a Gabar or a Parsee

Zoroastrianism (,zɒrəʊ'æstrɪən,ɪzəm) or **Zoroastrism** n the dualistic religion founded by the Persian prophet Zoroaster in the late 7th or early 6th centuries BC and set forth in the sacred writings of the Zend-Avesta. It is based on the concept of a continuous struggle between Ormazd (or Ahura Mazda), the god of creation, light, and goodness, and his arch enemy, Ahriman, the spirit of evil and darkness, and it includes a highly developed ethical code

Zorrilla y Moral (Spanish θɔ'rriʎa i mo'ral) n José (xo'se). 1817–93, Spanish poet and dramatist, noted for his romantic plays based on national legends, esp Don Juan Tenorio (1844)

zoster ('zɒstə) n pathol short for **herpes zoster** [c18: from Latin: shingles, from Greek zōstēr girdle]

Zouave (zu:'a:v, zwa:v) n **1** (formerly) a member of a body of French infantry composed of Algerian recruits noted for their dash, hardiness, and colourful uniforms **2** a member of any body of soldiers wearing a similar uniform or otherwise modelled on the French Zouaves, esp a volunteer in such a unit of the Union Army in the American Civil War [c19: from French, from Zwāwa, tribal name in Algeria]

Zoug n the French name for **Zug**

zouk (zu:k) n a style of dance music that combines African and Latin American rhythms and uses electronic instruments and modern studio technology [c20: from West Indian Creole zouk to have a good time]

zounds (zaʊndz) or **swounds** (zwaʊndz, zaʊndz) interj archaic a mild oath indicating surprise, indignation, etc [c16: euphemistic shortening of God's wounds]

Zr the chemical symbol for zirconium

Zsigmondy (German 'ʃɪɡmɔndɪ) n **Richard Adolf** ('rɪçart 'a:dɔlf). 1865–1929, German chemist, born in Austria, noted for his work on colloidal particles and, with H. Siedentopf, his introduction (1903) of the ultramicroscope: Nobel prize for chemistry 1925

zucchetto (tsu:'kɛtəʊ, su:-, zu:-) n, pl -tos RC Church a small round skullcap worn by certain ecclesiastics and varying in colour according to the rank of the wearer, the Pope wearing white, cardinals red, bishops violet, and others black [c19: from Italian, from zucca a gourd, head, from Late Latin cucutia gourd, probably from Latin cucurbita]

zucchini (tsu:'ki:nɪ, zu:-) n, pl -ni or -nis a small variety of vegetable marrow, cooked and eaten as a vegetable. Also called (esp in Britain): courgette [Italian, pl of zucchino, literally: a little gourd, from zucca gourd; see ZUCCHETTO]

Zuckerman ('zʊkəmən) n **Solly** ('sɒlɪ), Baron. 1904–93, British zoologist, born in South Africa; chief scientific adviser (1964–71) to the British Government. His books include The Social Life of Monkeys (1932) and the autobiography From Apes to Warlords (1978)

z

Zug (*German* tsu:k) *n* **1** a canton of N central Switzerland: the smallest Swiss canton; mainly German-speaking and Roman Catholic; joined the Swiss Confederation in 1352. Capital: Zug. Pop: 102 200 (2004 est). Area: 239 sq km (92 sq miles) **2** a town in N central Switzerland, the capital of Zug canton, on Lake Zug. Pop: 22 973 (2000) **3** Lake Zug a lake in N central Switzerland, in Zug and Schwyz cantons. Area: 39 sq km (15 sq miles) ▷ French name: Zoug

Zugspitze ('tsʊgˌʃpɪtsə) *n* a mountain peak in S Germany in the Bavarian Alps, on the Austrian border: the highest peak in Germany. Height: 2963 m (9721 ft)

zugzwang (*German* 'tsu:ktsvaŋ) *chess* ▷ *n* **1** a position in which one player can move only with loss or severe disadvantage ▷ *vb* **2** (*tr*) to manoeuvre (one's opponent) into a zugzwang [from German, from *Zug* a pull, tug + *Zwang* force, compulsion]

Zuider Zee *or* **Zuyder Zee** ('zaɪdə 'zi:; *Dutch* 'zœɪdər 'ze:) *n* a former inlet of the North Sea in the N coast of the Netherlands sealed off from the sea by a dam in 1932, dividing it into the Waddenzee and the freshwater IJsselmeer, with several large reclaimed areas

Zuidholland (zœɪt'hɔlɑnt) *n* the Dutch name for **South Holland**

Zukerman ('zʊkəmən) *n* **Pinchas**. born 1948, Israeli violinist

Zulu ('zu:lu, -lu:) *n pl* **-lus** *or* **-lu** a member of a tall Negroid people of SE Africa, living chiefly in South Africa, who became dominant during the 19th century due to a warrior-clan system organized by the powerful leader, Shaka **2** the language of this people, belonging to the Bantu group of the Niger-Congo family, closely related to Swazi and Xhosa [from Zulu *amaZulu* people of the sky]

Zululand ('zu:luˌlænd, 'zu:lu:-) *n* a region of E South Africa, on the Indian Ocean; partly corresponds to KwaZulu-Natal. Chief town: Eshowe

Zuma ('zu:mə) *n* **Jacob** (**Gidleyihlekisa**). born 1942; Black South African statesman: Deputy President of South Africa (1999–2005), President of the African National Congress from 2007

Zungaria (zʊŋ'gɛərɪə) *n* another name for **Junggar Pendi**

Zuñi ('zu:nji:, 'su:-) *n* **1** *pl* **-ñis** *or* **-ñi** a member of a North American Indian people of W New Mexico **2** the language of this people, a member of the Penutian phylum of languages > 'Zuñian *adj*, *n*

Zurbarán (*Spanish* θurβa'ran) *n* **Francisco de** (fran'θisko de). 1598–1664, Spanish Baroque painter, esp of religious subjects

Zürich ('zjʊərɪk; *German* 'tsy:rɪç) *n* **1** a canton of NE Switzerland: mainly Protestant and German-speaking. Capital: Zürich. Pop: 342 500 (2002 est). Area: 1729 sq km (668 sq miles) **2** a city in NE Switzerland, the capital of Zürich canton, on Lake Zürich: the largest city and industrial centre in Switzerland; centre of the Swiss Reformation; financial centre. Pop: 336 821 (1999 est) **3** Lake Zürich a lake in N Switzerland, mostly in Zürich canton. Area: 89 sq km (34 sq miles)

Zuyder Zee ('zaɪdə 'zi:; *Dutch* 'zœɪdər 'ze:) *n* a variant spelling of **Zuider Zee**

Zweig (*German* tsvaik) *n* **1** **Arnold** ('arnɔlt). 1887–1968, German novelist, famous for his realistic war novel *The Case of Sergeant Grischa* (1927) **2** **Stefan** ('ʃtɛfan). 1881–1942, Austrian novelist, dramatist, essayist, and poet

Zwickau (*German* 'tsvɪkaʊ) *n* a city in E Germany, in Saxony: Anabaptist movement founded 1520; coal-mining and industrial centre. Pop: 99 846 (2003 est)

Zwicky ('tsvɪki) *n* **Fritz**. 1898–1974, Swiss astronomer and physicist, working in the US from 1925; noted for his study of supernovae

zwieback ('zwaɪˌbæk, 'zwi:-; *German* 'tsvi:bak) *n* a small type of rusk, which has been baked first as a loaf, then sliced and toasted [German: twice-baked]

Zwingli (*German* 'tsvɪŋli) *n* **Ulrich** ('ʊlrɪç) *or* **Huldreich** ('hʊltraiç). 1484–1531, Swiss leader of the Reformation, based in Zurich. He denied the Eucharistic presence, holding that the Communion was merely a commemoration of Christ's death

Zwinglian ('zwɪŋlɪən, 'swɪŋ-, 'tsvɪŋ-) *n* **1** an upholder of the religious doctrines or movement of the Swiss Reformation leader Ulrich Zwingli (1484–1531), who denied the Eucharistic presence, holding that the Communion was merely a commemoration of Christ's death ▷ *adj* **2** of or relating to Zwingli, his religious movement, or his doctrines, esp his interpretation of the Eucharist

zwitterion ('tsvɪtərˌaɪən) *n* *chem* an ion that carries both a positive and a negative charge [c20: from German *Zwitter* hermaphrodite + **ION**]

Zwolle (*Dutch* 'zwɔlə) *n* a town in the central Netherlands, capital of Overijssel province. Pop: 104 431 (1999 est)

Zworykin ('zwɔ:rɪkɪn) *n* **Vladimir Kosma** ('vlædɪmɪə 'kɒsmə). 1889–1982, US physicist and television pioneer, born in Russia. He developed the first practical television camera

Zyban ('zaɪˌbæn) *n* *trademark* a drug that acts on the brain; used to help people give up smoking

zygapophysis (ˌzɪgə'pɒfɪsɪs, ˌzaɪgə-) *n*, *pl* **-ses** (-ˌsi:z) *anatomy*, *zoology* one of several processes on a vertebra that articulates with the corresponding process on an adjacent vertebra [c19: from **ZYGO-** + **APOPHYSIS**]

zygo- *or before a vowel* **zyg-** *combining form* indicating a pair or a union: *zygodactyl*; *zygospore* [from Greek *zugon* yoke]

zygodactyl (ˌzaɪgəʊ'dæktɪl, ˌzɪgə-) *adj* Also: **zygodactylous 1** (of the feet of certain birds) having the first and fourth toes directed backwards and the second and third forwards ▷ *n* **2** a zygodactyl bird

zygoma (zaɪ'gəʊmə, zɪ-) *n*, *pl* **-mata** (-mətə) another name for **zygomatic arch** [c17: via New Latin from Greek, from *zugon* yoke]

zygomatic (ˌzaɪgəʊ'mætɪk, ˌzɪg-) *adj* of or relating to the zygoma

zygomatic arch *n* the slender arch of bone forming a bridge between the cheekbone and the temporal bone on each side of the skull of mammals. Also called: zygoma

zygomatic bone *n* either of two bones, one on each side of the skull, that form part of the side wall of the eye socket and part of the zygomatic arch; cheekbone

zygomorphic (ˌzaɪgəʊ'mɔːfɪk, ˌzɪg-) *or* **zygomorphous** *adj* (of a flower) capable of being cut in only one plane so that the two halves are mirror images

zygomycete (ˌzaɪgəʊ'maɪsiːt) *n* any filamentous fungus of the phylum *Zygomycota* (or *Zygomycetes*), which reproduces sexually by means of zygospores: includes the bread mould > ˌzygomy'cetous *adj*

zygophyte ('zaɪgəʊˌfaɪt, 'zɪg-) *n* a plant, such as an alga, that reproduces by means of zygospores

zygospore ('zaɪgəʊˌspɔː, 'zɪg-) *n* a thick-walled sexual spore formed from the zygote of some fungi and algae > ˌzygo'sporic *adj*

zygote ('zaɪgəʊt, 'zɪg-) *n* **1** the cell resulting from the union of an ovum and a spermatozoon **2** the organism that develops from such a cell [c19: from Greek *zugōtos* yoked, from *zugoun* to yoke] > zygotic (zaɪ'gɒtɪk, zɪ-) *adj* > zy'gotically *adv*

zymase ('zaɪmeɪs) *n* a mixture of enzymes that is obtained as an extract from yeast and causes fermentation in sugars

zymo- *or before a vowel* **zym-** *combining form* indicating fermentation: *zymology* [from Greek *zumē* leaven]

zymogen ('zaɪməʊˌdʒɛn) *n* *biochem* any of a group of compounds that are inactive precursors of enzymes and are activated by a kinase

zymology (zaɪ'mɒlədʒɪ) *n* the chemistry of fermentation > zymologic (ˌzaɪməʊ'lɒdʒɪk) *or* ˌzymo'logical *adj* > zy'mologist *n*

zymolysis (zaɪ'mɒlɪsɪs) *n* the process of fermentation. Also called: zymosis

zymosis (zaɪ'məʊsɪs) *n*, *pl* **-ses** (-siːz) **1** *med* **a** any infectious disease **b** the development process or spread of such a disease **2** another name for **zymolysis**

zymotic (zaɪ'mɒtɪk) *adj* **1** of, relating to, or causing fermentation **2** relating to or caused by infection; denoting or relating to an infectious disease > zy'motically *adv*

zymurgy ('zaɪmɜːdʒɪ) *n* the branch of chemistry concerned with fermentation processes in brewing, etc

Z

Defining the Moment

Collins Dictionaries give you the clearest possible picture of English as it is used today. To achieve this we have positioned ourselves at the forefront of language monitoring. In addition to an extensive reading and viewing programme, our editors keep a constant watch on Collins corpus, our unparalleled 2.5-billion-word database of lexical data. A constant flow of text is fed into it from sources around the globe – newspapers, books, websites, and even transcripts of radio and TV shows. Every month the Collins corpus grows by 30 million words, making it the biggest such resource in the world. And it's in the discovery of new words and phrases that Collins corpus comes into its own – our 'monitor corpus' automatically alerts us to new coinages at the moment of their acceptance, however fleeting, into the language.

New words mirror their times. Even a quick look at the developments of the last decade bears this out. It's hard to imagine life without the terms *blog*, *texting* and *podcast*, yet they have all achieved their prominence within the last 10 years. The following is a selection of the more interesting neologisms that our various programmes have unearthed recently. Many will undoubtedly sink back into obscurity, being bound up with today's ephemera, but others will take root and establish themselves firmly in the ever-evolving lexicon of English.

above-the-fold *adj* **1** of or relating to the top part of the front page of a newspaper, which is visible when the newspaper is folded breadthways and is usually reserved for the most important news and features **2** of or relating to the top part of a website page, which is visible without the need for scrolling and is usually reserved for the most important features
> Not only did it get the kind of attention from cable news channels that is normally reserved for teenaged white girls gone missing, it got daily above-the-fold treatment in even the stodgiest of Old Media (The Guardian)

anaerobic digester *n* a biological system which brings about the breaking down by microorganisms of organic material, such as sewage, in the absence of oxygen. The resultant methane can then be used as a fuel
> Listeners claim that the current storyline about whether Home Farm should have a machine which converts waste into electricity is an endorsement of Labour's green credentials and is out of place in a BBC drama. Others say that the level of detail required to explain the purpose of an "anaerobic digester" is getting in the way of a good radio soap (The Daily Telegraph)

bagvertising ('bægvəˌtaɪzɪŋ) *n informal* advertising on the outside of handbags or backpacks [c21: from BAG + (AD)VERTISING]
> Likewise, manufacturers have caught on to the value of buying advertising space on shopping bags and creating specialized bags to promote their own products. As expected, a good deal of creative effort now goes into trying to make such advertisements as eye-catchingly memorable as possible, a process colloquially dubbed "bagvertising" (allbusiness.com)

Bollyline ('bɒlɪˌlaɪn) *n informal* the controversy surrounding India's cricket tour of Australia in 2007/08, which was marred by ill-feeling between the sides and allegations of racism [c21: from BOLLY(WOOD) + (body)line, a reference to a similarly controversial cricket series between Australia and England in 1932/33]
> The International Cricket Council tried to take firmer control of the Bollyline affair yesterday when Malcolm Speed, the chief executive, suggested that India had a duty to accept the findings of the appeal into Harbhajan Singh's three-Test ban for an alleged racist jibe against the Australia all-rounder Andrew Symonds (The Guardian)

Chuppy ('tʃʌpɪ) *n, pl* **-ies** *informal* a wealthy young professional person living in the People's Republic of China [c21: from CH(INA) + (Y)UPPY]
> "Chuppies" are China's young well-off generation. With money in their pockets and different consumer habits from their parents, China's new "Supershoppers" are spending up on brand name cosmetics and clothes according to a report in The US News & World Report (China Daily)

churnalism ('tʃɜːnəˌlɪzəm) *n informal, derogatory* low-grade journalism in which press releases from PR firms, advertisers, etc are quickly and uncritically rewritten as copy [c21: CHURN (as in 'to churn out') + (JOURN)ALISM]
> It is an unloveliness located, according to him, in the quick turnover, ultra-competitive world of "churnalism", in which fewer and fewer journalists file more and more stories, engaging in what he describes as "the rapid repackaging of largely unchecked second-hand material" (The Times)

digital dirt *n informal* personal information, images, and opinions left by someone on the internet, which may be found and then used against him or her

> *Digital dirt is the information about you – your hobbies, your photos, your rants and raves – that's available on the Internet through personal websites, profiles on popular social-networking sites, and comments on blogs* (ABC News)

eco-village *n* a small community designed so as to cause minimal damage to the environment

> *A successful developer, he is building what he believes will be Britain's first eco-village. It will put into practice all he knows about sustainability. So strong is his belief in the £7million project, he intends to be one of the first occupants of the self-sufficient community in upmarket Ilkley, West Yorkshire* (The Daily Telegraph)

euromyth ('jʊərəʊ,mɪə) *n* an overstated or fabricated report that creates an impression of the European Union as being governed by excessive or pedantic bureaucracy

> *Few things make European Union bosses so cross as "euromyths": those invented or exaggerated tales of barmy Brussels bureaucrats trying to outlaw a cherished feature of everyday life, be it pints of British milk or low-cut blouses on Bavarian barmaids* (The Economist)

facadism (fə'sɑːdɪzəm) *n* the practice of property developers preserving the facade of an old building while demolishing the rest of it

> *For facadism holds out a great temptation – it seems, on the surface, to give both sides what they want. The small, older buildings valued by preservationists appear to be saved, while the large new ones developers seek can still be built* (The New York Times)

glamping ('glæmpɪŋ) *n informal* an upmarket form of camping in which the privations normally associated with holidaying in a tent are exchanged for luxury and comfort [C21: from GLAM(OROUS) + (CAM)PING] > **'glamper** *n*

> *Glamping is a heady mix of glamour and the great outdoors, in which the freedom and challenge of going back to nature are tempered by home-making skills and the pleasures of domesticity. Glampers donate their roll mats to the boy scouts. For them, sheepskin rugs, leather pouffes, chilled champagne boxes, silk- and muslin-strewn gazebos, Egyptian-cotton sheets, blow-up sofas, double duvets – even tea-light chandeliers – are all part of the alfresco setup* (The Times)

goat (gəʊt) *n informal* a senior policy adviser to the British government under the premiership of Gordon Brown [C21: an acronym of 'government of all the talents', a phrase used by Brown]

Malloch Brown is one of the most colourful 'goats', the name given to the four outsiders recruited by Brown to his 'government of all the talents' in the summer (The Observer)

google-stalking *n informal* the practice of finding out personal information about someone by keying their name into an internet search engine [C21: from GOOGLE] > **'google-,stalk** *vb* > **'google-,stalker** *n*

> *The term google-stalking first came to my notice when a guy called Phil asked me on a date, and I was curious about him so googled his name. From this, I found out that the band he'd bragged about being in was not a good one, and that he'd been a political activist at university* (Cosmopolitan)

gravanity (græ'vænɪtɪ) *n informal* the practice of consumers customizing and personalizing mass-produced goods and displaying them in public [from GRA(FFITI) + VANITY)

> *Tapping into consumers' gravanity, KLM (Royal Dutch Airlines) is inviting customers to create their own baggage labels using a favourite holiday snapshot, company logo or creative design* (seedsofgrowth.com)

laughter boss *n Austral* a person appointed to provide regular doses of humour to the members of a workforce or community

> *The 'laughter boss' program is based on the concept that laughter in the aged care facility meets quality of life and psychosocial issues. Staff are trained in laughter therapy with the aim of the program being to create bonds, be nourishing, help improve coping, be supportive, give cognitive control, provide positive diversion and increase the 'smile-age factor'* (accreditation.org.au)

locavore ('ləʊkə,vɔː) *n* a person who eats or aims to eat only food that has been locally produced [C21: from LOCA(L) + -VORE]

> *The bestselling American novelist Barbara Kingsolver has just spent a year as a "locavore", relying almost entirely on her garden cum smallholding in Virginia for produce* (The Times)

mankini (mæn'kiːnɪ) *n informal* a revealing one-piece swimsuit for men, consisting of a thong held in place by shoulder straps [C21: from MAN + (BI)KINI]

> *Rugby may be a man's game, but there is no place for the luminous 'mankini' at the stadium, New Zealand police said on Tuesday, provoking howls of protest from fans of the skimpy swimsuit* (Reuters)

misery memoir *n informal* a book in which the author recounts unpleasant experiences from his or her own life

Now we have what Bookseller *magazine refers to as "mis lit", or "misery memoirs", in which the author tells of his or her triumph over personal trauma. Referred to by publishing houses as "inspirational lit" - or "inspi-lit" - many, though by no means all, of the harrowing memoirs tell of being sexually abused as a child* (bbc.co.uk)

nonebrity (nɒn'ɛbrɪtɪ) *n informal, disparaging* a minor celebrity [c21: from NON(ENTITY) + (CEL)EBRITY]

So, four desperate nonebrities, none of whom have any connection to or special interest in the 1972 tragedy, get to walk the route taken by Nando Parrado and Roberto Canessa, the two who made the 10-day trek out of the mountains to get help. To make it more realistic they will be given no food (The Guardian)

password fatigue *n informal* the frustration experienced by those who are unable to remember the various passwords, codes, and PIN numbers they are required to use on the internet, at banks, etc

The internet continues to be increasingly valuable, and yet also faces significant challenges. Online identity theft, fraud, and privacy concerns are rising. Users must track a growing number of accounts and passwords. This burden results in "password fatigue," and that results in insecure practices, such as reusing the same account names and passwords at many sites (microsoft.com)

pay-as-you-throw *adj* denoting a system of refuse collection in which householders are charged according to the amount of waste they throw out

Nearly two-thirds of householders in England say they are in favour of a "pay-as-you-throw" system of collecting their rubbish, the Local Government Association claimed yesterday. Local council chiefs said their survey of 1,028 adults found 64% would support a variable charging system which would reward individuals who actively recycled their domestic waste by offering them a council tax rebate (The Guardian)

phantom vibrations *pl n* imaginary vibrations, similar to those indicating that a message has arrived, experienced by the owner of a hand-held computer even when it is not switched on or is not on the owner's person, suggesting that the owner is in some way psychologically dependent on the device

Some users speak of "phantom vibrations", sensing an alert even when they're apart from their BlackBerry - even, for heaven's sake, when they're in the shower (The Guardian)

semi-somnia *n* persistent low-level exhaustion caused by lack of sleep [c21: from SEMI- + (IN)SOMNIA]

Many people use the clocks going back to gain an extra hour in bed – but a sleep expert says the change can actually leave people tired. Even such small changes, said Dr Neil Stanley, can disrupt sleep routines and cause semi-somnia – low grade exhaustion caused by inadequate rest (bbc.co.uk)

showroom tax *n Brit informal* a higher rate of vehicle excise duty, payable on new cars with high carbon emissions

Motorists will be spared any increase in fuel duty for six months, but gas-guzzling vehicles will incur a new "showroom tax" of up to £950 (The Times)

social shopping *n* retailing that takes advantage of social networking websites to reach potential customers and encourage purchasing

Sites like ThisNext and a handful of services like Kaboodle.com, Wists.com and StyleHive.com are spearheading a new category of e-commerce called "social shopping," that tries to combine two favourite online activities: shopping and social networking. These sites are hoping to ride the MySpace wave by gathering people in one place to swap shopping ideas (The New York Times)

tag hag *n informal, derogatory* a woman who has an excessive interest in designer clothes

That last possibility would get a snort of derision from a fair whack of the green movement, who are only too keen to dismiss the happy shoppers of Britain as a bunch of corporate pups, all brands and no balls; a ragbag of tag hags who only ever read the label, stuck fast in the most superficial semiotics (forumforthefuture.org.uk)

Wii elbow (wiː) *n informal* painful inflammation of the elbow caused by exertion in playing with a computer games system which uses motion-sensitive technology that requires players to act out their on-screen character's movements [c21: from the Wii computer games system produced by Nintendo, and influenced by TENNIS ELBOW]

But as players spend more time with the Wii, some are noticing that hours waving the game's controller around can add up to fairly intense exertion – resulting in aches and pains common in more familiar forms of exercise. They're reporting aching backs, sore shoulders – even something some have dubbed "Wii elbow" (The Wall Street Journal)

Supplement

Reports and Presentations

Contents

Writing reports

A report is a document that presents information about an investigation or a body of research. It should have a clear structure. This structure should enable specific pieces of information to be located easily by the reader. Reports are used in many areas of business, including accounting, finance, management, and marketing, as well as in scientific research work.

Initial planning

Before starting to write any report, there are a number of questions you need to be able to answer. The answers to these questions will largely define the approach you take when putting together the report.

▷ *what is the purpose of the report?*
Ideally, you should be able to summarize the purpose in one sentence
▷ *is there an outline or remit for the report?*
If there is, the purpose of the report should be clear
▷ *who will read the report?*
Reports can be written for internal and external office use, for professionals in a particular field, or for members of the public, for instance shareholders in a large corporation
▷ *will the report be formal or informal?*
This largely depends on who the report is written for
▷ *is there a timescale for completion of the report?*
▷ *is there a word limit for the report?*
▷ *are you the sole author of the report?*
▷ *how will you undertake research for the report?*
Research can take a number of forms: consulting reference sources, previous reports on the subject, and the internet; interviewing professionals in the area of research; asking colleagues for information; or undertaking new market research
▷ *how will the report be presented?*
The report could be for internal use only, or widely distributed inside and outside the work environment. The prospective readership will affect the design, approach, and style of the whole report.

When you have answered these questions, you will be in a position to organize the subject matter for your report into sections.

Organizing the report into sections

The organization or layout of the report must make it as easy as possible for readers to get to the information they need. By subdividing the report into sections, you should be able to accommodate all the information in a clear, straightforward fashion.

The following list covers all the section headings for a major report, but smaller or less important reports may not require all of them.

Title page

This page includes the report title, the author's name, and the date of completion or release. If the report has more than one author, consider putting the authors' names in alphabetical order. Alternatively, it may be more appropriate to place the main or most prestigious author first. Remember that, unless alphabetical, the order of names sends out messages about seniority or the level of contribution of each person.

Abstract

A short summary of the report, including aims, methods, conclusions, and any recommendations. Scientific research abstracts generally appear in library files or journals of abstracts. As they don't appear with the main report in these instances, they need to be comprehensible in isolation.

Contents

A list of the sections within the report, along with their corresponding page numbers.

Introduction

This explains the purpose of the report and the methods used in its or background compilation. The introduction should be concise and explain:

▷ what the subject of the report is
▷ who commissioned the report
▷ what the background to the commissioning of the report is
▷ what the method of working in compiling the report was
▷ what the main sources are

Main body of the report

This contains the information you have collected for the report in a number of clearly headed sections. Ensure that each section is treated in a similar way and that the most important information always comes first within a section. See **Presentation** below for more details.

Conclusions

A brief, easy-to-understand section giving an overview of the results gained from the information given in the main body of the report.

Recommendations

A section detailing possible action points and strategies for improvement in the light of the conclusions.

Appendices

These contain additional information or samples omitted from the main body of the text but which are relevant to the report as a whole.

Notes

These give details that would be too cumbersome to include in the main text. Clear cross-reference superscript numbers should appear within the text, immediately after the information to which the note refers. The notes should appear in numerical order in the Notes section.

Bibliography

This is an alphabetical listing, normally by author, of all the sources used in the report. For example:

Stirling, E.Q., 2004. *Bovine Anatomy Revisited*. 2nd ed. Jersey: Hursto Press

Wilson, J., 2002. Better milking practices. *Farm and Field*, 24 (3), 36–38.

As you can see, each source should have the following information, though the order can be varied slightly but consistently, depending on the system used:

▷ the author's name
▷ the date of publication
▷ the title of the book, newspaper, or journal, or the website address
▷ the title of the newspaper or journal article, if appropriate
▷ any edition number, other than the first edition of a book
▷ the name of the publisher of the journal or magazine

Presentation

All reports need to be as clear as possible. If they are not, readers will lose interest in their contents. Ways of making information easily accessible include:

▷ Organizing information into different sections (see **Organizing the report into sections**), giving each one a clear heading.
▷ Breaking up larger sections into manageable subsections, each with its own subheading. Bear in mind that the longer a section is, the less likely it is that it will be fully read. Sections and subsections should be numbered as follows:

1. [section heading]
1.1 [subsection heading]
1.2 [subsection heading] etc
2. [section heading]
2.1 [subsection heading] etc

▷ Maintaining consistency in the presentation of similar information.
▷ Paying attention to the numbering of sections and appendices.
▷ If appropriate, adding simple graphs, tables, and illustrations. These break up the text and often provide a quick, easy-to-understand

overview of the information.

▷ Putting large and unwieldy amounts of data into appendices, so as not to interrupt the flow of the text.

▷ Using a clear typeface for all of the text in the report. The reader wants to take in the essential points of the report as quickly as possible.

SUMMARY

▷ **Know the subject and purpose of the report**
▷ **Know who is going to read the report**
▷ **Set out the report in clearly defined sections**
▷ **Make the essential points and conclusions as clear as possible**

Giving presentations

As with writing reports, one of the keys to giving a good presentation is organizing your material. Your subject should be clearly stated, logically thought through, and explained interestingly enough to hold your audience's attention.

Notes

▷ don't learn your presentation by heart or write it down word for word. Such strategies usually result in boring delivery. Instead, make notes to refer to during the presentation so that you have something to prompt you

▷ write the notes on numbered index cards. You can then move each card to the bottom of the pile when you have used it and will always keep your place

Content

▷ try to start with something exciting but relevant to make your audience sit up and take notice. A short, telling anecdote can be useful for this

▷ give an introductory outline of your presentation, and make sure you keep to this. Avoid introducing a completely new subject without warning halfway through, or changing the tone of your presentation

▷ use links to lead logically from one section to the next: *while we're on the subject of; in view of; as for; before moving on to; in spite of*

▷ provide specific examples. These give the audience something to think about, and can be a source for a later question-and-answer session
▷ if you are presenting an argument, build from the weakest point to the strongest
▷ include a few light jokes or puns, but always ensure that they are appropriate to the presentation subject and to the audience
▷ don't be afraid to express your opinions. When you are expressing opinion rather than stating facts, remember to make this clear by using expressions such as *I believe that*; *in my opinion*; *to my mind*. You can show how strong your beliefs are by slightly amending some of these expressions: *I firmly believe that*; *I strongly believe that*; *we are absolutely certain that*; *we are pretty sure that*
▷ consider including some aspect of audience participation. Some degree of interaction tends to make a presentation more interesting
▷ end the presentation with a brief recap of the main points and a strong, persuasive conclusion

Visual aids

▷ use visual aids to illustrate your presentation, but ensure that they are simple, useful and clearly visible from the back of the room. Well-explained, well-chosen and simple visual aids are more effective than under-explained, complicated visual aids. Avoid having too many visual aids since constant changes can be distracting. Be careful not to stand in front of any visuals
▷ if you have access to a computer, you might consider using a presentation program such as PowerPoint®. Keep the number of slides to a minimum, with no more than a few concise bullet points to each slide
▷ if you are providing handouts, ensure you have made enough copies for everyone beforehand. Remember too that you must allow some time for the handouts to be received and viewed before you continue your presentation

Practice and timing

▷ try recording your presentation beforehand. This will help you get your timing and pacing right. It will also allow you to check that you sound clear and confident, that you are not mumbling or talking too fast
▷ if you can enlist the help of a supportive friend or family member, try out your presentation in front of them and ask for comments on any distracting habits you may have, such as fiddling with your hair or endlessly repeating a particular expression
▷ before the event, make sure you run through your presentation exactly as you intend to do it on the day, complete with any visuals and handouts. Time how long it takes and tailor it as necessary to fit the time allotted for it. It is very important to ensure that it does not overrun

Venue
▷ if you are using a computer or overhead projector for your presentation, ensure that you have time to find out how to work it before the presentation
▷ make sure that there are enough seats for your audience
▷ familiarize yourself with the venue and its acoustics, to ensure that you feel comfortable speaking in it and that you are able to project your voice across the whole room

You, your body and your voice
▷ if you feel nervous before giving your presentation, practise deep breathing and rehearse your opening sentences
▷ if you are very nervous, standing behind a lectern may help you feel less vulnerable, as well as giving you something to lean on and somewhere to place your notes
▷ as you give your presentation, stand straight and keep you chin up as you speak. A strong, positive posture will both improve your confidence and convince the audience that you have something interesting to say
▷ look round all the faces in the audience with sweeping glances. Look members of the audience very briefly in the eye when you can, avoiding looking at any one individual for too long
▷ speak sincerely and with warmth
▷ subtly vary your tone of voice to add interest, but make sure that you do not overdo this
▷ vary your pace, but never talk too quickly as you may well lose your audience if you do
▷ pause slightly between points to show the audience when you are about to move on to a different subject. Allow pauses for audience reaction
▷ smile from time to time where appropriate. It will help you feel more relaxed and it will encourage a bond with your audience
▷ do not be put off if you make a mistake during the presentation. Apologize quickly and move on

SUMMARY

Three helpful steps to remember when planning your presentation:
▷ **Say what you are going to say.**
▷ **Say it.**
▷ **Say what you've said.**